THE OXFORD
MODERN ENGLISH
DICTIONARY

Oxford Modern English Dictionary

PROJECT TEAM

EXECUTIVE EDITOR:	Julia Swannell
MANAGING EDITOR:	Sara Tulloch
ASSISTANT EDITORS:	Christine Cowley
	Louise Jones
	Christopher King

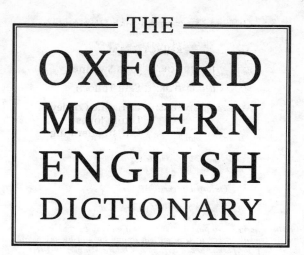

THE OXFORD MODERN ENGLISH DICTIONARY

EDITED BY

Julia Swannell

CLARENDON PRESS · OXFORD

Oxford University Press, Walton Street, Oxford OX2 6DP

Oxford New York
Athens Auckland Bangkok Bombay
Calcutta Cape Town Dar es Salaam Delhi
Florence Hong Kong Istanbul Karachi
Kuala Lumpur Madras Madrid Melbourne
Mexico City Nairobi Paris Singapore
Taipei Tokyo Toronto
and associated companies in
Berlin Ibadan

Oxford is a trade mark of Oxford University Press

Published in the United States by
Oxford University Press Inc., New York

British Library Cataloguing in Publication Data
Data available

Library of Congress Cataloging in Publication Data
Data available

ISBN 0-19-861267-2

Printed in Great Britain by
Clays Ltd., St. Ives plc, Bungay, Suffolk

Contents

Preface

The *Oxford Modern English Dictionary* has been compiled with the purpose of providing accessible, up-to-date information about a broad range of modern English vocabulary in a conveniently-sized book. The emphasis has been placed on the language of every day but also including the essential vocabulary of science and technology, especially computers and matters environmental, as well as idiomatic colloquial English and the vocabulary of the extensive English-speaking world beyond the shores of Britain. The definitions are written in clear, continuous prose; special conventions have been kept to a minimum. Information about spelling and the formation of routine derivatives such as those in *-ly*, *-ness*, *-able* is consistently provided, and explanations of grammatical constructions and inflections are both clear and comprehensive. In common with many of the Oxford family of dictionaries, the *Oxford Modern English Dictionary* uses the International Phonetic Alphabet to provide guidance on pronunciation that is precise, consistent, and internationally valid. The origin and source of words is explained concisely but in a straightforward and readable way, and authoritative notes have been included on points of grammar and usage of particular concern to many people.

Julia Swannell, February 1992

Guide to Use of the Dictionary

USE OF CONVENTIONS

In this edition, a great deal of the information given in the dictionary entries is self-explanatory, and the use of special conventions has been kept to a minimum. The following pages are meant to explain the editorial approach and to assist the user by explaining the principles involved in assembling the information.

HEADWORD

The **headword** is printed in bold roman type, or in bold italic type if the word is not naturalized in English and is usually found in italics in printed matter:

> **garble** /ˈgɑːb(ə)l/ *v.tr.* **1** unintentionally distort or confuse (facts, messages, etc.). **2** make (usu. unfair or malicious) selections from (facts, statements, etc.). □ **garbler** *n.* [It. *garbellare* f. Arab. *ġarbala* sift, perh. f. LL *cribellare* to sieve f. L *cribrum* sieve]

Variant spellings are given before the definition; in all such cases the form given as the headword is the preferred form:

> **ginkgo** /ˈgɪŋkgəʊ/ *n.* (also **gingko** /ˈgɪŋkəʊ/) (*pl.* **-os** or **-oes**) an orig. Chinese and Japanese tree, *Ginkgo biloba*, with fan-shaped leaves and yellow flowers. [Jap. *ginkyo* f. Chin. *yinxing* silver apricot]

When variants apply only to certain functions or senses of a word, these are given in brackets at the relevant point in the entry.

Variant American spellings are indicated by the designation *US*. These variants are often found in American use in addition to the main forms given:

> **garrotte** /gəˈrɒt/ *v.* & *n.* (also **garotte**; *US* **garrote**) —*v.tr.* execute or kill by strangulation, esp. with an iron or wire collar etc. —*n.* **1** a Spanish method of execution by garrotting. **2** the apparatus used for this. [F *garrotter* or Sp. *garrotear* f. *garrote* a cudgel, of unkn. orig.]

Words that are normally spelt with a **capital initial** are given in this form as the headword; when they are in some senses spelt with a small initial and in others with a capital initial this is indicated by repetition of the full word in the appropriate form within the entry.

Words that are different but spelt the same way (**homographs**) are distinguished by superior numerals:

> **bat**[1] /bæt/ *n.* & *v.* —*n.* **1** an implement with a handle, usu. of wood and with a flat or curved surface, used for hitting balls in games. **2** a turn at using this. **3** a batsman, esp. in cricket, usu. described in some way (*an excellent bat*). **4** (usu. in *pl.*) an object like a table-tennis bat used to guide aircraft when taxiing. —*v.* (**batted**, **batting**) **1** *tr.* hit with or as with a bat. **2** *intr.* take a turn at batting. □ **off one's own bat** unprompted, unaided. **right off the bat** *US*

immediately. [ME f. OE *batt* club, perh. partly f. OF *batte* club f. *battre* strike]

bat² /bæt/ *n.* any mouselike nocturnal mammal of the order Chiroptera, capable of flight by means of membranous wings extending from its forelimbs. □ **have bats in the belfry** be eccentric or crazy. **like a bat out of hell** very fast. [16th c., alt. of ME *bakke* f. Scand.]

bat³ /bæt/ *v.tr.* (**batted**, **batting**) wink (one's eyelid) (now usu. in phr.). □ **not** (or **never**) **bat an eyelid** *colloq.* show no reaction or emotion. [var. of obs. *bate* flutter]

PRONUNCIATION

Guidance on pronunciation follows the system of the International Phonetic Alphabet (IPA), and is based on the pronunciation associated especially with southern England (sometimes called 'Received Pronunciation'). For a key to the symbols used, see p. xxi.

PART OF SPEECH

The **grammatical identity** of words as *noun*, *verb*, *adjective*, and so on, is given for all headwords and derivatives, and for compounds and phrases when necessary to aid clarity. The same part-of-speech label is used of groups of more than one word when the group has the function of that part of speech, e.g. **ad hoc**, **Parthian shot**.

When a headword has **more than one part of speech**, a list is given at the beginning of the entry, and the treatment of the successive parts of speech (in the same order as the list) is introduced by a bold dash in each case:

game¹ *n., adj., & v.* —*n.* **1** a form or spell of play or sport, esp. a competitive one played according to rules and decided by skill, strength, or luck. **2** a single portion of play forming a scoring unit in some contests, e.g. bridge or tennis. **3** (in *pl.*) **a** athletics or sports as organized in a school etc. **b** a meeting for athletic etc. contests (*Olympic Games*). **4** a winning score in a game; the state of the score in a game (*the game is two all*). **5** the equipment for a game. **6** one's level of achievement in a game, as specified (*played a good game*). **7 a** a piece of fun; a jest. **b** (in *pl.*) dodges, tricks (*none of your games!*). **8** a scheme or undertaking etc. regarded as a game (*so that's your game*). **9** a policy or line of action. **10** (*collect.*) **a** wild animals or birds hunted for sport or food. **b** the flesh of these. **11** a hunted animal; a quarry or object of pursuit or attack. —*adj.* **1** spirited; eager and willing. **2** (foll. by *for*, or *to* + infin.) having the spirit or energy; eagerly prepared. —*v.intr.* play at games of chance for money; gamble.

The standard part-of-speech names are used, and the following additional explanations should be noted:

Nouns used attributively are designated *attrib.* when their function is not fully adjectival (e.g. **model** in *a model student*; *the student is very model* is not acceptable usage).

Adjectives are labelled *attrib.* (= attributive) when they are placed before the word they modify (as in *a blue car*), and *predic.* (= predicative) when they occur (usually after a verb) in the predicate of a sentence (as in *the car is blue*).

Some adjectives are restricted in such use: for example **aware** is normally used predicatively and **undue** is normally used attributively.

The designation *absol.* (= absolute) refers to uses of transitive verbs with an object implied but not stated (as in *smoking kills* and *let me explain*).

The designation 'in *comb.*' (= in combination), or 'also in *comb.*', refers to uses of words (especially adjectives) as an element joined by a hyphen with another word, as with **crested**, which often appears in forms such as *red-crested*, *large-crested*, and so on.

INFLECTION

Inflection of words (i.e. plurals, past tenses, etc.) is given after the part of speech concerned:

> **garibaldi** /ˌgærɪˈbɔːldɪ/ *n.* (*pl.* **garibaldis**) 1 a kind of woman's or child's loose blouse, orig. of bright red material. 2 *Brit.* a biscuit containing a layer of currants. [G. *Garibaldi*, It. patriot d. 1882]
>
> **gambol** /ˈgæmb(ə)l/ *v.* & *n.* —*v.intr.* (**gambolled**, **gambolling**; *US* **gamboled**, **gamboling**) skip or frolic playfully. —*n.* a playful frolic. [f. It. & Sp. *gamba* leg]

In general, the inflection of nouns, verbs, adjectives, and adverbs is given when it is irregular (as described further below) or when, though regular, it causes difficulty (as with forms such as **budgeted**, **coos**, and **taxis**).

Plurals of nouns: nouns that form their plural regularly by adding *-s* (or *-es* when they end in *-s*, *-x*, *-z*, *-sh*, or soft *-ch*) receive no comment. Other plural forms are given, notably:

nouns ending in *-i* or *-o*.
nouns ending in *-y*.
nouns ending in Latinate forms such as *-a* and *-um*.
nouns with more than one plural form, e.g. **fish** and **aquarium**.
nouns with plurals involving a change in the stem, e.g. **foot**, **feet**.
nouns with a plural form identical to the singular form, e.g. **sheep**.
nouns in *-ful*, e.g. **handful**.

Forms of verbs:

The following forms are regarded as regular:

third person singular present forms adding *-s* to the stem (or *-es* to stems ending in *-s*, *-x*, *-z*, *-sh*, or soft *-ch*).
past tenses and past participles adding *-ed* to the stem, dropping a final silent *e* (e.g. **changed**, **danced**).
present participles adding *-ing* to the stem, dropping a final silent *e* (e.g. **changing**, **dancing**).

Other forms are given, notably:

doubling of a final consonant, e.g. **bat**, **batted**, **batting**.
strong and irregular forms involving a change in the stem, e.g. **come**, **came**, **come**, and **go**, **went**, **gone**.

Comparative and Superlative of Adjectives and Adverbs:

Words of one syllable adding *-er* or *-est*, those ending in silent *e* dropping the *e* (e.g. **braver**, **bravest**) are regarded as regular. Most one-syllable words have these forms, but participial adjectives (e.g. **pleased**) do not.
Those that double a final consonant (e.g. **hot**, **hotter**, **hottest**) are given, as are two-syllable words that have comparative and superlative forms in *-er* and *-est* (of which very many are forms ending in *-y*, e.g. **happy**, **happier**, **happiest**), and their negative forms (e.g. **unhappier**, **unhappiest**).

It should be noted that specification of these forms indicates only that they are available; it is usually also possible to form comparatives with *more* and superlatives with *most* (as in *more happy, most unhappy*), which is the standard way of proceeding with adjectives and adverbs that do not admit of inflection.

Adjectives in -able *formed from Transitive Verbs*:

These are given as derivatives when there is sufficient evidence of their currency; in general they are formed as follows:

Verbs drop silent final -*e* except after *c* and *g* (e.g. **movable** but **changeable**).

Verbs of more than one syllable ending in -*y* (preceded by a consonant or *qu*) change *y* to *i* (e.g. **enviable, undeniable**).

A final consonant is often doubled as in normal inflection (e.g. **conferrable, regrettable**).

DEFINITION

Definitions are listed in a numbered sequence in order of comparative familiarity and importance, with the most current and important senses first:

> **gamble** /ˈgæmb(ə)l/ *v. & n.* —*v.* **1** *intr.* play games of chance for money, esp. for high stakes. **2** *tr.* **a** bet (a sum of money) in gambling. **b** (often foll. by *away*) lose (assets) by gambling. **3** *intr.* take great risks in the hope of substantial gain. **4** *intr.* (foll. by *on*) act in the hope or expectation of (*gambled on fine weather*). —*n.* **1** a risky undertaking or attempt. **2** a spell of gambling. □ **gambler** *n.* [obs. *gamel* to sport, *gamene* GAME[1]]

They are subdivided into lettered senses (**a**, **b**, etc.) when these are closely related or call for collective treatment.

ILLUSTRATIVE EXAMPLES

Many examples of words in use are given to support, and in some cases supplement, the definitions. These appear in italics in brackets. They are meant to amplify meaning and (especially when following a grammatical point) illustrate how the word is used in context, as in the following sense of **saint**:

> a very virtuous person; a person of great real or affected holiness (*would try the patience of a saint*).

GRAMMATICAL INFORMATION

Definitions are often accompanied by explanations in brackets of how the word or phrase in question is used in context. Often, the comment refers to words that usually follow (foll. by) or precede (prec. by) the word being explained. For example, at **sack**[1]:

> **sack**[1] /sæk/ *n. & v.* —*n.* **1 a** a large strong bag, usu. made of hessian, paper, or plastic, for storing or conveying goods. **b** (usu. foll. by *of*) this with its contents (*a sack of potatoes*). **c** a quantity contained in a sack. **2** (prec. by *the*) *colloq.* dismissal from employment. **3** (prec. by *the*) *US sl.* bed. **4** a woman's short loose dress with a sacklike appearance. **5** a man's or woman's loose-hanging coat not shaped to the back. —*v.tr* **1** put into a sack or sacks. **2** *colloq.* dismiss from employment. □ **sack race** a race between competitors in sacks up to the waist or neck. □ **sackful** *n.* (*pl.* **-fuls**).

sacklike *adj.* [OE *sacc* f. L *saccus* f. Gk *sakkos*, of Semitic orig.]

sense 1b usually appears as *a sack of* (something), as the example further shows; and senses 2 and 3 always appear as *the sack*.

With verbs, the fact that a sense is transitive or intransitive can affect the construction. In the examples given below, **prevail** is intransitive (and the construction is *prevail on a person*) and **urge** is transitive (and the construction is *urge a person on*).

prevail /prɪˈveɪl/ *v.intr.* **1** (often foll. by *against, over*) be victorious or gain mastery. **2** be the more usual or predominant. **3** exist or occur in general use or experience; be current. **4** (foll. by *on, upon*) persuade.

urge /ɜːdʒ/ *v. & n.* —*v.tr.* **1** (often foll. by *on*) drive forcibly; impel; hasten (*urged them on; urged the horses forward*). **2** (often foll. by *to* + infin. or *that* + clause) encourage or entreat earnestly or persistently (*urged them to go; urged them to action; urged that they should go*).

The formula (foll. by *to* + infin.) means that the word is followed by a normal infinitive with *to*, as in *want to leave* and *eager to learn*.

The formula (foll. by *that* + clause) indicates the routine addition of a clause with *that*, as in *said that it was late*. (For the omission of *that*, as in *said it was late*, see the usage note in the entry for **that**.)

'pres. part.' and 'verbal noun' denote verbal forms in *-ing* that function as adjectives and nouns respectively, as in *set him laughing* and *tired of asking*.

USAGE

If the use of a word is restricted in any way, this is indicated by any of various labels printed in italics, as follows:

Geographical

Brit. indicates that the use is found chiefly in British English (and often also in Australian and New Zealand English, and in other parts of the Commonwealth) but not in American English.

US indicates that the use is found chiefly in American English (often including Canada and also in Australian and New Zealand English) but not in British English except as a conscious Americanism.

Other geographical designations (e.g. *Austral., NZ, S.Afr.*) restrict uses to the areas named. These usage labels should be distinguished from comments of the type '(in the UK)' or '(in the US)' preceding definitions, which denote that the thing defined is associated with the country named. For example, **Pentagon** is a US institution, but the term is not restricted to American English.

Register

Levels of usage, or *registers*, are indicated as follows:

formal indicates uses that are normally restricted to formal (esp. written) English, e.g. **commence**.

colloq. (= colloquial) indicates a use that is normally restricted to informal (esp. spoken) English.

sl. (= slang) indicates a use of the most informal kind, unsuited to written English and often restricted to a particular social group.

archaic indicates a word that is restricted to special contexts such as legal or religious use, or is used for special effect.

literary indicates a word or use that is found chiefly in literature.

poet. (= poetic) indicates uses confined to poetry or other contexts with romantic connotations.

joc. (= jocular) indicates uses that are intended to be humorous or playful.

derog. (= derogatory) denotes uses that are intentionally disparaging.

offens. (= offensive) denotes uses that cause offence, whether intentionally or not.

disp. (= disputed) indicates a use that is disputed or controversial. Often this is enough to alert the user to a danger or difficulty; when further explanation is needed a usage note (see below) is used as well or instead.

hist. (= historical) denotes a word or use that is confined to historical reference, normally because the thing referred to no longer exists.

propr. (= proprietary) denotes a term that has the status of a trade mark (see the Note on Proprietary Status, p. xx).

Subject

The many subject labels, e.g. *Law*, *Math.*, *Naut.*, show that a word or sense is current only in a particular field of activity, and is not in general use.

Usage Notes

These are added to give extra information not central to the definition, and to explain points of grammar and usage. They always occur at the end of the entry and are introduced by a horizontal rule and ■ **Usage**. The purpose of these notes is not to prescribe usage but to alert the user to a difficulty or controversy attached to particular uses.

PHRASES AND IDIOMS

These are listed (together with compounds) in alphabetical order after the treatment of the main senses, introduced by the symbol □. The words *a*, *the*, *one*, and *person* do not count for purposes of alphabetical order:

> □ **the game is up** the scheme is revealed or foiled. **game** (or **games**) **theory** the mathematical analysis of conflict in war, economics, games of skill, etc. **gaming-house** a place frequented for gambling; a casino. **gaming-table** a table used for gambling. **make game** (or **a game**) **of** mock, taunt. **off** (or **on**) **one's game** playing badly (or well). **on the game** *Brit. sl.* involved in prostitution or thieving. **play the game** behave fairly or according to the rules.

They are normally defined under the earliest important word in the phrase, except when a later word is more clearly the key word or is the common word in a phrase with variants.

COMPOUNDS

Compound terms forming one word (e.g. **bathroom**, **newspaper**) are listed as main entries; those consisting of two or more words (e.g. **chain reaction**) or joined by a hyphen (e.g. **chain-gang**) are given under the first element or occasionally as main entries.

DERIVATIVES

Words formed by adding a suffix to another word are in many cases listed at the end of the entry for the main word, introduced by the symbol □. In this position they are not defined since they can be understood from the sense of the main word and that given at the suffix concerned:

> □ **saintdom** *n.* **sainthood** *n.* **saintlike** *adj.*
> **saintling** *n.* **saintship** *n.*

When further definition is called for they are given main entries in their own right (e.g. **changeable**).

For derivative words used in combination (e.g. **-crested** in *red-crested*), see 'Part of speech' above.

ETYMOLOGY

A brief account of the etymology, or origin, of words is given in square brackets at the end of entries. It is not given for compound words of obvious formation (such as **bathroom** and **jellyfish**), for routinely formed derivatives (such as **changeable**, **muddy**, and **seller**), or for words consisting of clearly identified elements already explained (such as **Anglo-Saxon**, **overrun**, and many words in *in-*, *re-*, *un-*, etc.). It is also not always given for every word of a set sharing the same basic origin (such as the group from **proprietary** to **propriety**). Noteworthy features, such as an origin in Old English, are however always given.

More detailed information can be found in the *Oxford Dictionary of English Etymology* (ed. C. T. Onions *et al.*, 1966) and the *Concise Oxford Dictionary of English Etymology* (ed. T. F. Hoad, 1986).

When the origin of a word cannot be reliably established, the forms 'orig. unkn.' (= origin unknown) and 'orig. uncert.' (= origin uncertain) are used, even if frequently canvassed speculative derivations exist (as with **gremlin** and **pommy**). In these cases the century of the first recorded occurrence of the word in English is given.

An equals sign (=) precedes words in other languages that are parallel formations from a common source (cognates) rather than sources of the English word.

CROSS-REFERENCES

These are introduced by any of a number of reference types, as follows:

'=' denotes that the meaning of the item at which the cross-reference occurs is the same as that of the item referred to.
'see' indicates that information will be found at the point referred to, and is widely used for encyclopedic matter and in the idiom sections of entries to deal with items that can be located at any of a number of words included in the idiom (see *Phrases and Idioms* above).
'see also' indicates that further information can be found at the point referred to.
'cf.' denotes an item related or relevant to the one being consulted, and the reference often completes or clarifies the exact meaning of the item being treated.

'opp.' refers to a word or sense that is opposite to the one being treated, and again often completes or clarifies the sense.

References of the kind '*pl.* of' (= plural of), '*past* of' (= past tense of), etc., are given at entries for inflections and other related forms.

Cross-references preceded by any of these reference types appear in small capitals if the reference is to a main headword, and in italics if the reference is to a compound or idiom within an entry.

References in italics to compounds and defined phrases are to the entry for the first word unless another is specified.

Abbreviations used in the Dictionary

Some abbreviations (especially of language-names) occur only in etymologies. Others may appear in italics. Abbreviations in general use (such as etc., i.e., and those for books of the Bible) are explained in the dictionary itself.

abbr.	abbreviation
ablat.	ablative
absol.	absolute(ly)
acc.	according
accus.	accusative
adj.	adjective
adv.	adverb
Aeron.	Aeronautics
AF	Anglo-French
Afr.	Africa, African
Afrik.	Afrikaans
Akkad.	Akkadian
AL	Anglo-Latin
alt.	alteration
Amer.	America, American
Anat.	Anatomy
anc.	ancient
Anglo-Ind.	Anglo-Indian
Anthropol.	Anthropology
Antiq.	Antiquities, Antiquity
app.	apparently
Arab.	Arabic
Aram.	Aramaic
arbitr.	arbitrary, arbitrarily
Archaeol.	Archaeology
Archit.	Architecture
Arith.	Arithmetic
assim.	assimilated
assoc.	associated, association
Assyr.	Assyrian
Astrol.	Astrology
Astron.	Astronomy
Astronaut.	Astronautics
attrib.	attributive(ly)
attrib.adj.	attributive adjective
augment.	augmentative
Austral.	Australia, Australian
aux.	auxiliary
back-form.	back-formation
Bibl.	Biblical
Bibliog.	Bibliography
Biochem.	Biochemistry
Biol.	Biology
Bot.	Botany
Braz.	Brazil, Brazilian
Bret.	Breton

Brit.	British, in British use
Bulg.	Bulgarian
Burm.	Burmese
Byz.	Byzantine
c.	century
c.	*circa*
Can.	Canada, Canadian
Cat.	Catalan
Celt.	Celtic
Ch.	Church
Chem.	Chemistry
Chin.	Chinese
Cinematog.	Cinematography
class.	classical
coarse sl.	coarse slang
cogn.	cognate
collect.	collective(ly)
colloq.	colloquial(ly)
comb.	combination; combining
compar.	comparative
compl.	complement
Conchol.	Conchology
conj.	conjunction
conn.	connected
constr.	construction
contr.	contraction
Corn.	Cornish
corresp.	corresponding
corrupt.	corruption
Criminol.	Criminology
Crystallog.	Crystallography
Da.	Danish
decl.	declension
def.	definite
Demog.	Demography
demons.	demonstrative
demons.adj.	demonstrative adjective
demons.pron.	demonstrative pronoun
deriv.	derivative
derog.	derogatory
dial.	dialect
different.	differentiated
dimin.	diminutive
disp.	disputed (use)
dissim.	dissimilated

distrib.	distributive	hist.	with historical reference
Du.	Dutch	Horol.	Horology
		Hort.	Horticulture
E	English	Hung.	Hungarian
Eccl.	Ecclesiastical		
Ecol.	Ecology	Icel.	Icelandic
Econ.	Economics	IE	Indo-European
EFris.	East Frisian	illit.	illiterate
Egypt.	Egyptian	imit.	imitative
E.Ind.	East Indian, of the East	immed.	immediate(ly)
	Indies	imper.	imperative
Electr.	Electricity	impers.	impersonal
elem.	elementary	incept.	inceptive
ellipt.	elliptical(ly)	incl.	including; inclusive
emphat.	emphatic(ally)	Ind.	of the subcontinent
Engin.	Engineering		comprising India,
Engl.	England; English		Pakistan, and Bangladesh
Entomol.	Entomology	ind.	indirect
erron.	erroneous(ly)	indecl.	indeclinable
esp.	especial(ly)	indef.	indefinite
est.	estimated	infin.	infinitive
etym.	etymology	infl.	influence(d)
euphem.	euphemism	instr.	instrumental (case)
Eur.	Europe, European	int.	interjection
ex.	example	interrog.	interrogative(ly)
exc.	except	interrog.adj.	interrogative adjective
exclam.	exclamation	interrog.pron.	interrogative pronoun
		intr.	intransitive
F	French	Ir.	Irish (language or usage)
f.	from	iron.	ironical(ly)
fam.	familiar	irreg.	irregular(ly)
fem.	feminine	It.	Italian
fig.	figurative(ly)		
Finn.	Finnish	Jap.	Japan, Japanese
Flem.	Flemish	Jav.	Javanese
foll.	followed, following	joc.	jocular(ly)
form.	formation		
Fr.	French	L	Latin
Frank.	Frankish	lang.	language
frequent.	frequentative(ly)	LG	Low German
		LHeb.	Late Hebrew
		lit.	literal(ly)
G	German	LL	Late Latin
Gael.	Gaelic		
Gallo-Rom.	Gallo-Roman	M	Middle (with languages)
gen.	general	masc.	masculine
genit.	genitive	Math.	Mathematics
Geog.	Geography	MDa.	Middle Danish
Geol.	Geology	MDu.	Middle Dutch
Geom.	Geometry	ME	Middle English
Ger.	German	Mech.	Mechanics
Gk	Greek	Med.	Medicine
Gk Hist.	Greek History	med.	medieval
Gmc	Germanic	med.L	medieval Latin
Goth.	Gothic	metaph.	metaphorical
Gram.	Grammar	metath.	metathesis
		Meteorol.	Meteorology
		Mex.	Mexican
Heb.	Hebrew	MFlem.	Middle Flemish
Hind.	Hindustani	MHG	Middle High German
Hist.	History		

Mil.	Military	OSlav.	Old Slavonic
Mineral.	Mineralogy	OSp.	Old Spanish
mistransl.	mistranslation	OSw.	Old Swedish
MLG	Middle Low German		
mod.	modern	Palaeog.	Palaeography
mod.L	modern Latin	Parl.	Parliament;
MSw.	Middle Swedish		Parliamentary
Mus.	Music	part.	participle
Mythol.	Mythology	past part.	past participle
		Pathol.	Pathology
n.	noun	pejor.	pejorative
N.Amer.	North America, North	perf.	perfect (tense)
	American	perh.	perhaps
Nat.	National	Pers.	Persian
Naut.	Nautical	pers.	person(al)
neg.	negative(ly)	Peruv.	Peruvian
N.Engl.	North of England	Pharm.	Pharmacy; Pharmacology
neut.	neuter	Philol.	Philology
Norm.	Norman	Philos.	Philosophy
north.	northern	Phoen.	Phoenician
Norw.	Norwegian	Phonet.	Phonetics
n.pl.	noun plural	Photog.	Photography
num.	numeral	phr.	phrase
NZ	New Zealand	Phrenol.	Phrenology
		Physiol.	Physiology
O	Old (with languages)	pl.	plural
obj.	object; objective	poet.	poetical
OBret.	Old Breton	Pol.	Polish
OBrit.	Old British	Polit.	Politics
obs.	obsolete	pop.	popular, not technical
Obstet.	Obstetrics	pop.L	popular Latin, informal
OBulg.	Old Bulgarian		spoken Latin
occas.	occasional(ly)	Port.	Portuguese
OCelt.	Old Celtic	poss.	possessive
ODa.	Old Danish	poss.pron.	possessive pronoun
ODu.	Old Dutch	prec.	preceded, preceding
OE	Old English	predic.	predicate; predicative(ly)
OF	Old French	predic.adj.	predicative adjective
offens.	offensive	prep.	preposition
OFrank.	Old Frankish	pres.part.	present participle
OFris.	Old Frisian	prob.	probable, probably
OGael.	Old Gaelic	pron.	pronoun
OHG	Old High German	pronunc.	pronunciation
OIcel.	Old Icelandic	propr.	proprietary term
OIr.	Old Irish	Prov.	Provençal
OIt.	Old Italian	Psychol.	Psychology
OL	Old Latin		
OLG	Old Low German		
ON	Old Norse	RC Ch.	Roman Catholic Church
ONF	Old Northern French	redupl.	reduplicated
ONorw.	Old Norwegian	ref.	reference
OPers.	Old Persian	refl.	reflexive(ly)
OPort.	Old Portuguese	rel.	related; relative
opp.	(as) opposed (to);	rel.adj.	relative adjective
	opposite (of)	Relig.	Religion
OProv.	Old Provençal	rel.pron.	relative pronoun
orig.	origin; original(ly)	repr.	representing
Ornithol.	Ornithology	Rhet.	Rhetoric
OS	Old Saxon	rhet.	rhetorical(ly)
OScand.	Old Scandinavian	Rmc	Romanic

Rom.	Roman	Theol.	Theology
Rom.Hist.	Roman History	tr.	transitive
Russ.	Russian	transf.	in transferred sense
		transl.	translation
S.Afr.	South Africa, South	Turk.	Turkish
	African	Typog.	Typography
S.Amer.	South America, South		
	American	ult.	ultimate(ly)
Sc.	Scottish	uncert.	uncertain
Scand.	Scandinavia,	unexpl.	unexplained
	Scandinavian	univ.	university
Sci.	Science	unkn.	unknown
Shakesp.	Shakespeare	US	American, in American
sing.	singular		use
Sinh.	Sinhalese	usu.	usual(ly)
Skr.	Sanskrit		
sl.	slang	v.	verb
Slav.	Slavonic	var.	variant(s)
Sociol.	Sociology	v.aux.	auxiliary verb
Sp.	Spanish	Vet.	Veterinary
spec.	special(ly)	v.intr.	intransitive verb
Stock Exch.	Stock Exchange	voc.	vocative
subj.	subject; subjunctive	v.refl.	reflexive verb
superl.	superlative	v.tr.	transitive verb
Sw.	Swedish		
syll.	syllable	WFris.	West Frisian
symb.	symbol	WG	West Germanic
syn.	synonym	W.Ind.	West Indian, of the West
			Indies
techn.	technical(ly)	WS	West Saxon
Telev.	Television	WSlav.	West Slavonic
Teut.	Teutonic		
Theatr.	Theatre, Theatrical	Zool.	Zoology

Note on Proprietary Status

This dictionary includes some words which are, or are asserted to be, proprietary names or trade marks. Their inclusion does not imply that they have acquired for legal purposes a non-proprietary or general significance, nor is any other judgement implied concerning their legal status. In cases where the editor has some evidence that a word is used as a proprietary name or trade mark this is indicated by the designation *propr.*, but no judgement concerning the legal status of such words is made or implied thereby.

Key to the Pronunciation

The symbols used, with their values, are as follows:

Consonants:

b, d, f, h, k, l, m, n, p, r, s, t, v, w, and z have their usual English values. Other symbols are used as follows:

g	(*get*)	ŋ	(*ring*)	ʃ	(*she*)
tʃ	(*chip*)	θ	(*thin*)	ʒ	(*decision*)
dʒ	(*jar*)	ð	(*this*)	j	(*yes*)
x	(*loch*)				

Vowels:

short vowels		long vowels		diphthongs	
æ	(*cat*)	ɑː	(*arm*)	eɪ	(*day*)
e	(*bed*)	iː	(*see*)	aɪ	(*my*)
ə	(*ago*)	ɔː	(*saw*)	ɔɪ	(*boy*)
ɪ	(*sit*)	ɜː	(*her*)	əʊ	(*no*)
ɒ	(*hot*)	uː	(*too*)	aʊ	(*how*)
ʌ	(*run*)			ɪə	(*near*)
ʊ	(*put*)			eə	(*hair*)
				ʊə	(*poor*)
				aɪə	(*fire*)
				aʊə	(*sour*)

(ə) signifies the indeterminate sound as in gard*e*n, carn*a*l, and rhyth*m*.
(r) at the end of a word indicates an r that is sounded when a word beginning with a vowel follows, as in *clutter up* and *an acre of land*.
The mark ˜ indicates a nasalized sound, as in the following sounds that are not natural in English:

æ̃	(*timbre*)
ɑ̃	(*élan*)
ɔ̃	(*garçon*)

The main or primary stress of a word is shown by ˈ preceding the relevant syllable; any secondary stress in words of three or more syllables is shown by ˌ preceding the relevant syllable.

Aa

A¹ /eɪ/ n. (also **a**) (pl. **As** or **A's**) **1** the first letter of the alphabet. **2** Mus. the sixth note of the diatonic scale of C major. **3** the first hypothetical person or example. **4** the highest class or category (of roads, academic marks, etc.). **5** (usu. **a**) Algebra the first known quantity. **6** a human blood type. □ **A1** /eɪ ˈwʌn/ **1** Naut. **a** a first-class vessel in Lloyd's Register of Shipping. **b** first-class. **2** colloq. excellent. **A1, A2**, etc. the standard paper sizes, each half the previous one.

A² /eɪ/ abbr. (also **A.**) **1** = A LEVEL. **2** ampere(s). **3** answer. **4** Associate of. **5** atomic (energy etc.).

a¹ /ə, eɪ/ adj. (also **an** before a vowel) (called the indefinite article) **1** (as an unemphatic substitute) one, some, any. **2** one like (a Judas). **3** one single (not a thing in sight). **4** the same (all of a size). **5** in, to, or for each (twice a year; £20 a man; seven a side). [weakening of OE ān one; sense 5 orig. = A²]

a² /ə/ prep. **1** to, towards (ashore; aside). **2** (with verb in pres. part. or infin.) in the process of; in a specified state (a-hunting; a-wandering; abuzz; aflutter). **3** on (afire; afoot). **4** in (nowadays). [weakening of OE prep. an, on (see ON)]

Å abbr. ångström(s).

a-¹ /eɪ, æ/ prefix not, without (amoral; agnostic). [Gk a-, or L f. Gk, or F f. L f. Gk]

a-² /ə/ prefix implying motion onward or away, adding intensity to verbs of motion (arise; awake). [OE a-, orig. ar-]

a-³ /ə/ prefix to, at, or into a state (agree; amass). [ME a- (= OF prefix a-), (f. F) f. L ad- to, at]

a-⁴ /ə/ prefix **1** from, away (abridge). **2** of (akin; anew). **3** out, utterly (abash; affray). **4** in, on, engaged in, etc. (see A²). [sense 1 f. ME a-, OF a-, f. L ab; sense 2 f. ME a- f. OE of prep.; sense 3 f. ME, AF a- = OF e-, es- f. L ex]

-a¹ /ə/ suffix forming nouns from Greek, Latin, and Romanic feminine singular, esp.: **1** ancient or Latinized modern names of animals and plants (amoeba; campanula). **2** oxides (alumina). **3** geographical names (Africa). **4** ancient or Latinized modern feminine names (Lydia; Hilda).

-a² /ə/ suffix forming plural nouns from Greek and Latin neuter plural, esp. names (often from modern Latin) of zoological groups (phenomena; Carnivora).

aardvark /ˈɑːdvɑːk/ n. a nocturnal mammal of southern Africa, Orycteropus afer, that feeds on termites. [Afrik. f. aarde earth + vark pig]

Aaron's rod /ˈeərənz/ n. any of several tall plants, esp. the great mullein (Verbascum thapsus). [ref. to Num. 17:8]

AB /eɪˈbiː/ n. a human blood type.

ab- /əb, æb/ prefix off, away, from (abduct; abnormal; abuse). [F or L]

aback /əˈbæk/ adv. archaic backwards, behind. □ **take aback** surprise, disconcert (your request took me aback; I was greatly taken aback by the news). [OE on bæc (as A², BACK)]

abacus /ˈæbəkəs/ n. (pl. **abacuses**) **1** an oblong frame with rows of wires or grooves along which beads are slid, used for calculating. **2** Archit. the flat slab on top of a capital, supporting the architrave. [L f. Gk abax abakos slab, drawing-board, f. Heb. 'ābāk dust]

abaft /əˈbɑːft/ adv. & prep. Naut. —adv. in the stern half of a ship. —prep. nearer the stern than; aft of. [A² + -baft f. OE beæftan f. be BY + æftan behind]

abalone /ˌæbəˈləʊnɪ/ n. any mollusc of the genus Haliotis, with a shallow ear-shaped shell and lined with mother-of-pearl. [Amer. Sp. abulón]

abandon /əˈbænd(ə)n/ v. & n. —v.tr. **1** give up completely or before completion (abandoned hope; abandoned the game). **2 a** forsake or desert (a person or a post of responsibility). **b** leave or desert (a motor vehicle or ship). **3 a** give up to another's control or mercy. **b** refl. yield oneself completely to a passion or impulse. —n. lack of inhibition or restraint; reckless freedom of manner. □ **abandoner** n. **abandonment** n. [ME f. OF abandoner f. à bandon under control ult. f. LL bannus, -um BAN]

abandoned /əˈbænd(ə)nd/ adj. **1 a** (of a person) deserted, forsaken (an abandoned child). **b** (of a building, vehicle, etc.) left empty or unused (an abandoned cottage; an abandoned ship). **2** (of a person or behaviour) unrestrained, profligate.

abase /əˈbeɪs/ v.tr. & refl. humiliate or degrade (another person or oneself). □ **abasement** n. [ME f. OF abaissier (as A-³, baissier to lower ult. f. LL bassus short of stature): infl. by BASE²]

abash /əˈbæʃ/ v.tr. (usu. as **abashed** adj.) embarrass, disconcert. □ **abashment** n. [ME f. OF esbair (es- = A-⁴ 3, bair astound or baer yawn)]

abate /əˈbeɪt/ v. **1** tr. & intr. make or become less strong, severe, etc. **2** tr. Law **a** quash (a writ or action). **b** put an end to (a nuisance). □ **abatement** n. [ME f. OF abatre f. Rmc (as A-³, L batt(u)ere beat)]

abattoir /ˈæbətwɑː(r)/ n. a slaughterhouse. [F f. abatre fell: see ABATE and -ORY¹]

abbacy /ˈæbəsɪ/ n. (pl. **-ies**) the office, jurisdiction, or period of office of an abbot or abbess. [ME f. eccl.L abbacia f. abbat- ABBOT]

abbatial /əˈbeɪʃ(ə)l/ adj. of an abbey, abbot, or abbess. [F abbatial or med.L abbatialis (as ABBOT)]

abbé /ˈæbeɪ/ n. (in France) an abbot; a male entitled to wear ecclesiastical dress. [F f. eccl.L abbas abbatis ABBOT]

abbess /ˈæbɪs/ n. a woman who is the head of certain communities of nuns. [ME f. OF abbesse f. eccl.L abbatissa (as ABBOT)]

abbey /ˈæbɪ/ n. (pl. **-eys**) **1** the building(s) occupied by a community of monks or nuns. **2** the community itself. **3** a church or house that was once an abbey. [ME f. OF abbeie etc. f. med.L abbatia ABBACY]

abbot /ˈæbət/ n. a man who is the head of an abbey of monks. □ **abbotship** n. [OE *abbod* f. eccl.L *abbas -atis* f. Gk *abbas* father f. Aram. *'abbā*]

abbreviate /əˈbriːvɪˌeɪt/ v.tr. shorten, esp. represent (a word etc.) by a part of it. [ME f. LL *abbreviare* shorten f. *brevis* short: cf. ABRIDGE]

abbreviation /əˌbriːvɪˈeɪʃ(ə)n/ n. **1** an abbreviated form, esp. a shortened form of a word or phrase. **2** the process of abbreviating.

ABC /ˌeɪbiːˈsiː/ n. **1** the alphabet. **2** the rudiments of any subject. **3** an alphabetical guide.

abdicate /ˈæbdɪˌkeɪt/ v.tr. **1** (usu. *absol.*) give up or renounce (the throne). **2** renounce (a responsibility, duty, etc.). □ **abdication** /ˌæbdɪˈkeɪʃ(ə)n/ n. **abdicator** n. [L *abdicare abdicat-* (as AB-, *dicare* declare)]

abdomen /ˈæbdəmən/ n. **1** the part of the body containing the stomach, bowels, reproductive organs, etc. **2** *Zool.* the hinder part of an insect, crustacean, spider, etc. □ **abdominal** /æbˈdɒmɪn(ə)l/ adj. **abdominally** /æbˈdɒmɪnəlɪ/ adv. [L]

abduct /əbˈdʌkt/ v.tr. carry off or kidnap (a person) illegally by force or deception. □ **abduction** n. **abductor** n. [L *abducere abduct-* (as AB-, *ducere* draw)]

abeam /əˈbiːm/ adv. **1** on a line at right angles to a ship's or an aircraft's length. **2** (foll. by *of*) opposite the middle of (a ship etc.). [A² + BEAM]

abed /əˈbed/ adv. archaic in bed. [OE (as A², BED)]

abele /əˈbiːl, ˈeɪb(ə)l/ n. the white poplar, *Populus alba*. [Du. *abeel* f. OF *abel, aubel* ult. f. L *albus* white]

Aberdeen Angus /ˌæbədiːn ˈæŋgəs/ n. **1** an animal of a breed of hornless black beef cattle. **2** this breed. [*Aberdeen* in Scotland, *Angus* Scottish county]

Aberdonian /ˌæbəˈdəʊnɪən/ adj. & n. —adj. of Aberdeen. —n. a native or citizen of Aberdeen. [med.L *Aberdonia*]

aberrant /əˈberənt/ adj. **1** esp. *Biol.* diverging from the normal type. **2** departing from an accepted standard. □ **aberrance** n. **aberrancy** n. [L *aberrare aberrant-* (as AB-, *errare* stray)]

aberration /ˌæbəˈreɪʃ(ə)n/ n. **1** a departure from what is normal or accepted or regarded as right. **2** a moral or mental lapse. [L *aberratio* (as ABERRANT)]

abet /əˈbet/ v.tr. (**abetted, abetting**) (usu. in **aid and abet**) encourage or assist (an offender or offence). □ **abetment** n. **abetter** n. **abettor** n. [ME f. OF *abeter* f. *à* to + *beter* BAIT]

abeyance /əˈbeɪəns/ n. (usu. prec. by *in, into*) a state of temporary disuse or suspension. □ **abeyant** adj. [AF *abeiance* f. OF *abeer* f. *à* to + *beer* f. med.L *batare* gape]

abhor /əbˈhɔː(r)/ v.tr. (**abhorred, abhorring**) detest; regard with disgust and hatred. [ME f. F *abhorrer* or f. L *abhorrēre* (as AB-, *horrēre* shudder)]

abhorrence /əbˈhɒrəns/ n. **1** disgust; detestation. **2** a detested thing.

abhorrent /əbˈhɒrənt/ adj. **1** (often foll. by *to*) (of conduct etc.) inspiring disgust, detestable. **2** (foll. by *to*) not in accordance with; strongly conflicting with (*abhorrent to the spirit of the law*). **3** (foll. by *from*) inconsistent with. □ **abhorrer** n.

abide /əˈbaɪd/ v. (*past* **abided** or rarely **abode** /əˈbəʊd/) **1** tr. (usu. in *neg.* or *interrog.*) tolerate, endure (*can't abide him*). **2** intr. (foll. by *by*) **a** act in accordance with. **b** remain faithful to (a promise). **3** intr. archaic **a** remain, continue. **b** dwell. □ **abidance** n. [OE *ābīdan* (as A-², *bidan* BIDE)]

abiding /əˈbaɪdɪŋ/ adj. enduring, permanent (*an abiding sense of loss*). □ **abidingly** adv.

ability /əˈbɪlɪtɪ/ n. (*pl.* **-ies**) **1** (often foll. by *to* + infin.) capacity or power (*has the ability to write songs*). **2** cleverness, talent; mental power (*a person of great ability; has many abilities*). [ME f. OF *ablete* f. L *habilitas -tatis* f. *habilis* able]

-ability /əˈbɪlɪtɪ/ suffix forming nouns of quality from, or corresponding to, adjectives in *-able* (*capability; vulnerability*). [F *-abilité* or L *-abilitas*: cf. -ITY]

abject /ˈæbdʒekt/ adj. **1** miserable, wretched. **2** degraded, self-abasing, humble. **3** despicable. □ **abjectly** adv. **abjectness** n. [ME f. L *abjectus* past part. of *abicere* (as AB-, *jacere* throw)]

abjection /əbˈdʒekʃ(ə)n/ n. a state of misery or degradation. [ME f. OF *abjection* or L *abjectio* (as ABJECT)]

abjure /əbˈdʒʊə(r)/ v.tr. **1** renounce on oath (an opinion, cause, claim, etc.). **2** swear perpetual absence from (one's country etc.). □ **abjuration** /ˌæbdʒʊˈreɪʃ(ə)n/ n. [L *abjurare* (as AB-, *jurare* swear)]

ablative /ˈæblətɪv/ n. & adj. *Gram.* —n. the case (esp. in Latin) of nouns and pronouns (and words in grammatical agreement with them) indicating an agent, instrument, or location. —adj. of or in the ablative. [ME f. OF *ablatif -ive* or L *ablativus*, f. L *ablat-* (as AB-, *lat-* past part. stem of *ferre* carry)]

ablaut /ˈæblaʊt/ n. a change of vowel in related words or forms, e.g. in *sing, sang, sung*. [G]

ablaze /əˈbleɪz/ predic.adj. & adv. **1** on fire (*set it ablaze; the house was ablaze*). **2** (often foll. by *with*) glittering, glowing.

able /ˈeɪb(ə)l/ adj. (**abler, ablest**) **1** (often foll. by *to* + infin.; used esp. in *is able, will be able, was able,* etc., replacing tenses of *can*) having the capacity or power (*was not able to come*). **2** having great abil- ity; clever, skilful. □ **able-bodied** fit, healthy. **able-bodied rating** (or **seaman**) *Naut.* one able to perform all duties. [ME f. OF *hable, able* f. L *habilis* handy f. *habēre* to hold]

-able /əb(ə)l/ suffix forming adjectives meaning: **1** that may or must be (*eatable; forgiveable; payable*). **2** that can be made the subject of (*dutiable; objectionable*). **3** that is relevant to or in accordance with (*fashionable; seasonable*). **4** (with active sense, in earlier word-formations) that may (*comfortable; suitable*). [F *-able* or L *-abilis* forming verbal adjectives f. verbs of first conjugation]

ablution /əˈbluːʃ(ə)n/ n. (usu. in *pl.*) **1** the ceremonial washing of parts of the body or sacred vessels etc. **2** *colloq.* the ordinary washing of the body. **3** a building containing washing-places etc. in a camp, ship, etc. □ **ablutionary** adj. [ME f. OF *ablution* or L *ablutio* (as AB-, *lutio* f. *luere lut-* wash)]

ably /ˈeɪblɪ/ adv. capably, cleverly, competently.

-ably /əblɪ/ suffix forming adverbs corresponding to adjectives in *-able*.

abnegate /ˈæbnɪˌgeɪt/ v.tr. **1** give up or deny oneself (a pleasure etc.). **2** renounce or reject (a right or belief). □ **abnegator** n. [L *abnegare abnegat-* (as AB-, *negare* deny)]

abnegation /ˌæbnɪˈɡeɪʃ(ə)n/ n. **1** denial; the rejection or renunciation of a doctrine. **2** = SELF-ABNEGATION. [OF *abnegation* or LL *abnegatio* (as ABNEGATE)]

abnormal /æbˈnɔːm(ə)l/ adj. **1** deviating from what is normal or usual; exceptional. **2** relating to or dealing with what is abnormal (*abnormal psychology*). □ **abnormally** adv. [earlier and F *anormal, anomal* f. Gk *anōmalos* ANOMALOUS, assoc. with L *abnormis*: see ABNORMITY]

abnormality /ˌæbnɔːˈmælɪtɪ/ n. (pl. **-ies**) **1 a** an abnormal quality, occurrence, etc. **b** the state of being abnormal. **2** a physical irregularity.

abnormity /æbˈnɔːmɪtɪ/ n. (pl. **-ies**) **1** an abnormality or irregularity. **2** a monstrosity. [L *abnormis* (as ABNORMAL) var. *normis* f. *norma* rule)]

Abo /ˈæbəʊ/ n. & adj. (also **abo**) *Austral. sl.* usu. *offens.* —n. (pl. **Abos**) an Aboriginal. —adj. Aboriginal. [abbr.]

aboard /əˈbɔːd/ adv. & prep. **1** on or into (a ship, aircraft, train, etc.). **2** alongside. [ME f. A² + BOARD & F *à bord*]

abode¹ /əˈbəʊd/ n. a dwelling-place; one's home. [verbal noun of ABIDE: cf. *ride, rode, road*]

abode² past of ABIDE.

abolish /əˈbɒlɪʃ/ v.tr. put an end to the existence or practice of. □ **abolishable** adj. **abolisher** n. **abolishment** n. [ME f. F *abolir* f. L *abolēre* destroy]

abolition /ˌæbəˈlɪʃ(ə)n/ n. **1** the act or process of abolishing or being abolished. **2** an instance of this. [F *abolition* or L *abolitio* (as ABOLISH)]

abolitionist /ˌæbəˈlɪʃənɪst/ n. one who favours the abolition of a practice or institution. □ **abolitionism** n.

abomasum /ˌæbəˈmeɪs(ə)m/ n. (pl. **abomasa** /-sə/) the fourth stomach of a ruminant. [mod.L f. AB- + L *omasum* bullock's tripe]

A-bomb /ˈeɪbɒm/ n. = atomic bomb. [A (for ATOMIC) + BOMB]

abominable /əˈbɒmɪnəb(ə)l/ adj. **1** detestable; loathsome; morally reprehensible. **2** *colloq.* very bad or unpleasant (*abominable weather*). □ **Abominable Snowman** an unidentified manlike or bearlike animal said to exist in the Himalayas; a yeti. □ **abominably** adv. [ME f. OF f. L *abominabilis* f. *abominari* deprecate (as AB-, *ominari* f. OMEN)]

abominate /əˈbɒmɪneɪt/ v.tr. detest, loathe. □ **abominator** n. [L *abominari* (as ABOMINABLE)]

abomination /əˌbɒmɪˈneɪʃ(ə)n/ n. **1** loathing. **2** an odious or degrading habit or act. **3** (often foll. by *to*) an object of disgust. [ME f. OF (as ABOMINATE)]

aboriginal /ˌæbəˈrɪdʒɪn(ə)l/ adj. & n. —adj. **1** (of races and natural phenomena) inhabiting or existing in a land from the earliest times or from before the arrival of colonists. **2** (usu. **Aboriginal**) of the Australian Aboriginals. —n. **1** an aboriginal inhabitant. **2** (usu. **Aboriginal**) an aboriginal inhabitant of Australia. □ **aboriginally** adv. [as ABORIGINE + -AL]

aborigine /ˌæbəˈrɪdʒɪnɪ/ n. (usu. in *pl.*) **1** an aboriginal inhabitant. **2** (usu. **Aborigine**) an aboriginal inhabitant of Australia. **3** an aboriginal plant or animal. [back-form. f. pl. *aborigines* f. L, prob. f. phr. *ab origine* from the beginning]

■ **Usage** When referring to the people, *Aborigine* is preferred to *Aboriginal*.

abort /əˈbɔːt/ v. **1** *intr.* **a** (of a woman) undergo abortion; miscarry. **b** (of a foetus) suffer abortion. **2** *tr.* **a** effect the abortion of (a foetus). **b** effect abortion in (a mother). **3 a** *tr.* cause to end fruitlessly or prematurely; stop in the early stages. **b** *intr.* end unsuccessfully or prematurely. **4 a** *tr.* abandon or terminate (a space flight or other technical project) before its completion, usu. because of a fault. **b** *intr.* terminate or fail to complete such an undertaking. [L *aboriri* miscarry (as AB-, *oriri ort-* be born)]

abortifacient /əˌbɔːtɪˈfeɪʃ(ə)nt/ adj. & n. —adj. effecting abortion. —n. a drug or other agent that effects abortion.

abortion /əˈbɔːʃ(ə)n/ n. **1** the expulsion of a foetus (naturally or esp. by medical induction) from the womb before it is able to survive independently, esp. in the first 28 weeks of a human pregnancy. **2** a stunted or deformed creature or thing. **3** the failure of a project or an action. [L *abortio* (as ABORT)]

abortionist /əˈbɔːʃənɪst/ n. a person who carries out abortions.

abortive /əˈbɔːtɪv/ adj. **1** fruitless, unfinished. **2** resulting in abortion. □ **abortively** adv. [ME f. OF *abortif -ive* f. L *abortivus* (as ABORT)]

abound /əˈbaʊnd/ v.intr. **1** be plentiful. **2** (foll. by *in, with*) be rich; teem or be infested. [ME f. OF *abunder* etc. f. L *abundare* overflow (as AB-, *undare* f. *unda* wave)]

about /əˈbaʊt/ prep. & adv. —prep. **1 a** on the subject of; in connection with (*a book about birds; what are you talking about?; argued about money*). **b** relating to (*something funny about this*). **c** in relation to (*symmetry about a plane*). **d** so as to affect (*can do nothing about it; what are you going to do about it?*). **2** at a time near to (*come about four*). **3 a** in, round, surrounding (*wandered about the town; a scarf about her neck*). **b** all round from a centre (*look about you*). **4** here and there in; at points throughout (*toys lying about the house*). **5** at a point or points near to (*fighting going on about us*). **6** carried with (*have no money about me*). —adv. **1 a** approximately (*costs about a pound; is about right*). **b** *colloq.* used to indicate understatement (*it's about time they came*). **2** here and there; at points nearby (*I've seen him about recently*). **3** all round; in every direction (*look about*). **4** on the move; in action (*out and about*). **5** in partial rotation or alteration from a given position (*the wrong way about*). **6** in rotation or succession (*turn and turn about*). **7** *Naut.* on or to the opposite tack (*go about; put about*). □ **be about to** be on the point of (doing something) (*was about to laugh*). [OE *onbūtan* (on = A², *būtan* BUT)]

about-face /əbaʊtˈfeɪs/ n., v., & int. —n. & v.intr. = ABOUT-TURN. & v. —int. = ABOUT TURN int.

about-turn /əbaʊtˈtɜːn/ n., v., & int. —n. **1** a turn made so as to face the opposite direction. **2** a change of opinion or policy etc. —v.intr. make an about-turn. —int. (**about turn**) *Mil.* a command to make an about-turn. [orig. as int.]

above /əˈbʌv/ prep., adv., adj., & n. —prep. **1** over; on the top of; higher (vertically, up a slope or stream etc.) than; over the surface of (*head above water; above the din*). **2** more than (*above twenty people; above average*). **3** higher in rank, position, importance, etc., than (*above all*). **4 a** too great or good for (*is not above cheating at cards*). **b** beyond the reach of; not affected by (*above my understanding*). —adv. **1** at or to a higher point; overhead (*the floor above*). **2 a** upstairs. **b**

upstream. **3** (of a text reference) further back on a page or in a book (*as noted above*). **4** on the upper side (*looks similar above and below*). **5** in addition (*over and above*). **6** *rhet.* in heaven (*Lord above!*). —*adj.* mentioned earlier; preceding (*the above argument*). —*n.* (prec. by *the*) what is mentioned above (*the above shows*). □ **above-board** *adj.* & *adv.* without concealment; fair or fairly; open or openly. **above ground** alive. **above oneself** conceited, arrogant. [A² + OE *bufan* f. *be* = BY + *ufan* above]

abracadabra /ˌæbrəkə'dæbrə/ *int.* a supposedly magic word used by conjurors in performing a trick. [a mystical word engraved and used as a charm: L f. Gk]

abrade /ə'breɪd/ *v.tr.* scrape or wear away (skin, rock, etc.) by rubbing. □ **abrader** *n.* [L f. *radere ras-* scrape]

abrasion /ə'breɪʒ(ə)n/ *n.* **1** the scraping or wearing away (of skin, rock, etc.). **2** a damaged area resulting from this. [L *abrasio* (as ABRADE)]

abrasive /ə'breɪsɪv/ *adj.* & *n.* —*adj.* **1 a** tending to rub or graze. **b** capable of polishing by rubbing or grinding. **2** harsh or hurtful in manner. —*n.* an abrasive substance. [as ABRADE + -IVE]

abreaction /ˌæbrɪ'ækʃ(ə)n/ *n. Psychol.* the free expression and consequent release of a previously repressed emotion. □ **abreact** *v.tr.* **abreactive** *adj.* [AB- + REACTION after G *Abreagierung*]

abreast /ə'brest/ *adv.* **1** side by side and facing the same way. **2 a** (often foll. by *with*) up to date. **b** (foll. by *of*) well-informed (*abreast of all the changes*). [ME f. A² + BREAST]

abridge /ə'brɪdʒ/ *v.tr.* **1** shorten (a book, film, etc.). **2** curtail (liberty). □ **abridgable** *adj.* **abridger** *n.* [ME f. OF *abreg(i)er* f. LL *abbreviare* ABBREVIATE]

abridgement /ə'brɪdʒmənt/ *n.* (also **abridgment**) **1 a** a shortened version, esp. of a book; an abstract. **b** the process of producing this. **2** a curtailment (of rights). □ [F *abrégement* (as ABRIDGE)]

abroad /ə'brɔːd/ *adv.* **1** in or to a foreign country or countries. **2** over a wide area; in different directions; everywhere (*scatter abroad*). **3** at large; freely moving about; in circulation (*there is a rumour abroad*). [ME f. A² + BROAD]

abrogate /'æbrəgeɪt/ *v.tr.* repeal, annul, abolish (a law or custom). □ **abrogation** /ˌæbrə'geɪʃ(ə)n/ *n.* **abrogator** *n.* [L *abrogare* (as AB-, *rogare* propose a law)]

abrupt /ə'brʌpt/ *adj.* **1** sudden and unexpected; hasty (*his abrupt departure*). **2** (of speech, manner, etc.) uneven; lacking continuity; curt. **3** steep, precipitous. □ **abruptly** *adv.* **abruptness** *n.* [L *abruptus* past part. of *abrumpere* (as AB-, *rumpere* break)]

abscess /'æbsɪs/ *n.* a swollen area accumulating pus within a body tissue. □ **abscessed** *adj.* [L *abscessus* a going away (as AB-, *cedere cess-* go)]

abscissa /əb'sɪsə/ *n.* (pl. **abscissae** /-siː/ or **abscissas**) *Math.* (in a system of coordinates) the shortest distance from a point to the vertical axis. [mod.L *abscissa* (*linea*) fem. past part. of *abscindere absciss-* (as AB-, *scindere* cut)]

abscission /əb'sɪʒ(ə)n/ *n.* the act or an instance of cutting off. [L *abscissio* (as ABSCISSA)]

abscond /əb'skɒnd/ *v.intr.* depart hurriedly and furtively, esp. unlawfully or to avoid arrest. □ **absconder** *n.* [L *abscondere* (as AB-, *condere* stow)]

abseil /'æbseɪl, -ziːl/ *v.* & *n. Mountaineering* —*v.intr.* descend a steep rock-face by using a doubled rope coiled round the body and fixed at a higher point. —*n.* a descent made by abseiling. [G *abseilen* f. *ab* down + *Seil* rope]

absence /'æbs(ə)ns/ *n.* **1** the state of being away from a place or person. **2** the time or duration of being away. **3** (foll. by *of*) the non-existence or lack of. □ **absence of mind** inattentiveness. [ME f. OF f. L *absentia* (as ABSENT)]

absent *adj.* & *v.* —*adj.* /'æbs(ə)nt/ **1 a** not present. **b** (foll. by *from*) not present at or in. **2** not existing. **3** inattentive to the matter in hand. —*v.refl.* /əb'sent/ **1** stay away. **2** withdraw. □ **absently** *adv.* (in sense 3 of *adj.*). [ME ult. f. L *absent-* pres. part. of *abesse* be absent]

absentee /ˌæbsən'tiː/ *n.* a person not present, esp. one who is absent from work or school. □ **absentee landlord** a landlord who lets a property while living elsewhere.

absenteeism /ˌæbsən'tiːɪz(ə)m/ *n.* the practice of absenting oneself from work or school etc., esp. frequently or illicitly.

absent-minded /ˌæbs(ə)nt'maɪndɪd/ *adj.* inattentive; with one's mind on other things. □ **absent-mindedly** *adv.* **absent-mindedness** *n.*

absinth /'æbsɪnθ/ *n.* **1** a shrubby plant, *Artemisia absinthium*, or its essence. **2** (usu. **absinthe**) a green aniseed-flavoured liqueur based on wormwood. [F *absinthe* f. L *absinthium* f. Gk *apsinthion*]

absolute /'æbsəˌluːt, -ˌljuːt/ *adj.* & *n.* —*adj.* **1** complete, utter, perfect (*an absolute fool; absolute bliss*). **2** unconditional, unlimited (*absolute authority*). **3** despotic; ruling with unrestricted power (*an absolute monarch*). **4** (of a standard or other concept) universally valid; not relative or comparative. **5** *Gram.* **a** (of a construction) syntactically independent of the rest of the sentence. **b** (of an adjective or transitive verb) used or usable without an expressed noun or object. **6** (of a legal decree etc.) final. —*n. Philos.* **1** a value, standard, etc., which is objective and universally valid, not subjective or relative. **2** (prec. by *the*) **a** *Philos.* that which can exist without being related to anything else. **b** *Theol.* ultimate reality; God. □ **absolute majority 1** a majority over all others combined. **2** more than half. **absolute pitch** *Mus.* **1** the ability to recognize the pitch of a note or produce any given note. **2** a fixed standard of pitch defined by the rate of vibration. **absolute temperature** one measured from absolute zero. **absolute zero** a theoretical lowest possible temperature, calculated as −273.15 °C. □ **absoluteness** *n.* [ME f. L *absolutus* past part.: see ABSOLVE]

absolutely /'æbsəˌluːtlɪ, -ˌljuːtlɪ/ *adv.* **1** completely, utterly, perfectly (*absolutely marvellous*). **2** independently; in an absolute sense (*God exists absolutely*). **3** (foll. by *neg.*) (no or none) at all (*absolutely no chance of winning*). **4** *Gram.* in an absolute way, esp. (of a verb) without a stated object. **5** /-ˈluːtlɪ, -ˈljuːtlɪ/ *colloq.* (used in reply) quite so; yes.

absolution /ˌæbsə'luːʃ(ə)n, -'ljuːʃ(ə)n/ *n.* **1** a formal release from guilt, obligation, or punishment. **2** forgiveness. [ME f. OF f. L *absolutio -onis* (as ABSOLVE)]

absolutism /ˈæbsəluːˌtɪz(ə)m, -ljuːˌtɪz(ə)m/ *n.* the belief in absolute principles in political or philosophical matters. □ **absolutist** *n.* & *adj.*

absolve /əbˈzɒlv/ *v.tr.* **1** (often foll. by *from*, *of*) **a** set or pronounce free from blame or obligation etc. **b** acquit; pronounce not guilty. **2** pardon or give absolution for (a sin etc.). □ **absolver** *n.* [L *absolvere* (as AB-, *solvere solut-* loosen)]

absorb /əbˈsɔːb, -ˈzɔːb/ *v.tr.* **1** include or incorporate as part of itself or oneself (*the country successfully absorbed its immigrants*). **2** take in; suck up (liquid, heat, knowledge, etc.). **3** reduce the effect or intensity of; deal easily with. **4** consume (*his debts absorbed half his income*). **5** engross the attention of. □ **absorbable** *adj.* **absorbability** /-ˈbɪlɪtɪ/ *n.* **absorber** *n.* [ME f. F *absorber* or L *absorbēre absorpt-* (as AB-, *sorbēre* suck in)]

absorbed /əbˈsɔːbd, -ˈzɔːbd/ *adj.* intensely engaged or interested. □ **absorbedly** /-bɪdlɪ/ *adv.*

absorbent /əbˈsɔːbənt, -ˈzɔːbənt/ *adj.* & *n.* —*adj.* having a tendency to absorb (esp. liquids). —*n.* an absorbent substance. □ **absorbency** *n.* [L *absorbent-* f. *absorbēre* ABSORB]

absorbing /əbˈsɔːbɪŋ, -ˈzɔːbɪŋ/ *adj.* engrossing; intensely interesting. □ **absorbingly** *adv.*

absorption /əbˈsɔːpʃ(ə)n, -ˈzɔːpʃ(ə)n/ *n.* **1** the process or action of absorbing or being absorbed. **2** disappearance through incorporation into something else. **3** mental engrossment. □ **absorptive** *adj.* [L *absorptio* (as ABSORB)]

abstain /əbˈsteɪn/ *v.intr.* **1 a** (usu. foll. by *from*) restrain oneself; refrain from indulging in (*abstained from cakes and sweets.* **b** refrain from drinking alcohol. **2** formally decline to use one's vote. □ **abstainer** *n.* [ME f. AF *astener* f. OF *abstenir* f. L *abstinēre abstent-* (as AB-, *tenēre* hold)]

abstemious /æbˈstiːmɪəs/ *adj.* (of a person, habit, etc.) moderate, not self-indulgent, esp. in eating and drinking. □ **abstemiously** *adv.* **abstemiousness** *n.* [L *abstemius* (as AB-, *temetum* strong drink)]

abstention /əbˈstenʃ(ə)n/ *n.* the act or an instance of abstaining, esp. from voting. [F *abstention* or LL *abstentio -onis* (as ABSTAIN)]

abstinence /ˈæbstɪnəns/ *n.* **1** the act of abstaining, esp. from food or alcohol. **2** the habit of abstaining from pleasure, food, etc. [ME f. OF f. L *abstinentia* (as ABSTINENT)]

abstinent /ˈæbstɪnənt/ *adj.* practising abstinence. □ **abstinently** *adv.* [ME f. OF f. L (as ABSTAIN)]

abstract *adj.*, *v.*, & *n.* —*adj.* /ˈæbstrækt/ **1 a** to do with or existing in thought rather than matter, or in theory rather than practice (*abstract questions rarely concerned him*). **b** (of a word, esp. a noun) denoting a quality or condition rather than a concrete object. **2** (of art) achieving its effect by grouping shapes and colours in satisfying patterns rather than by the recognizable representation of physical reality. —*v.* /əbˈstrækt/ **1** *tr.* (often foll. by *from*) take out of; extract; remove. **2** *tr.* summarize (an article, book, etc.). **3** *tr.* & *refl.* (often foll. by *from*) distract. **4** *tr.* (foll. by *from*) consider abstractly or separately from something else. —*n.* /ˈæbstrækt/ **1** a summary or statement of the contents of a book etc. **2** an abstract work of art. **3** an abstraction or abstract term. □ **in the abstract** in theory rather than in practice.

□ **abstractly** /ˈæbstræktlɪ/ *adv.* **abstractor** /əbˈstræktə(r)/ *n.* (in sense 2 of *v.*). [ME f. OF *abstract* or L *abstractus* past part. of *abstrahere* (as AB-, *trahere* draw)]

abstracted /əbˈstræktɪd/ *adj.* inattentive to the matter in hand; preoccupied. □ **abstractedly** *adv.*

abstraction /əbˈstrækʃ(ə)n/ *n.* **1** the act or an instance of abstracting or taking away. **2 a** an abstract or visionary idea. **b** the formation of abstract ideas. **3** abstract qualities (esp. in art). **4** absent-mindedness. [F *abstraction* or L *abstractio* (as ABSTRACT)]

abstruse /əbˈstruːs/ *adj.* hard to understand; obscure; profound. □ **abstrusely** *adv.* **abstruseness** *n.* [F *abstruse* or L *abstrusus* (as AB-, *trusus* past part. of *trudere* push)]

absurd /əbˈsɜːd/ *adj.* **1** (of an idea, suggestion, etc.) wildly unreasonable, illogical, or inappropriate. **2** (of a person) unreasonable or ridiculous in manner. **3** (of a thing) ludicrous, incongruous. □ **absurdly** *adv.* **absurdness** *n.* [F *absurde* or L *absurdus* (as AB-, *surdus* deaf, dull)]

absurdity /əbˈsɜːdɪtɪ/ *n.* (*pl.* **-ies**) **1** absurdness. **2** an absurd statement or act. [F *absurdité* or LL *absurditas* (as ABSURD)]

abundance /əˈbʌnd(ə)ns/ *n.* **1** a very great quantity, more than enough. **2** wealth, affluence. [ME f. OF *abundance* f. L *abundantia* (as ABUNDANT)]

abundant /əˈbʌnd(ə)nt/ *adj.* **1** existing or available in large quantities; plentiful. **2** (foll. by *in*) having an abundance of (*a country abundant in fruit*). □ **abundantly** *adv.* [ME f. L (as ABOUND)]

abuse *v.* & *n.* —*v.tr.* /əˈbjuːz/ **1** use to bad effect or for a bad purpose; misuse. **2** insult verbally. **3** maltreat. —*n.* /əˈbjuːs/ **1 a** incorrect or improper use. **b** an instance of this. **2** insulting language (*a torrent of abuse*). **3** unjust or corrupt practice. **4** maltreatment of a person (*child abuse*). □ **abuser** *n.* [ME f. OF *abus* (n.), *abuser* (v.) f. L *abusus*, *abuti* (as AB-, *uti us-* USE)]

abusive /əˈbjuːsɪv/ *adj.* **1** using or containing insulting language. **2** (of language) insulting. □ **abusively** *adv.* **abusiveness** *n.*

abut /əˈbʌt/ *v.* (**abutted**, **abutting**) **1** *intr.* (foll. by *on*) (of estates, countries, etc.) adjoin (another). **2** *intr.* (foll. by *on*, *against*) (of part of a building) touch or lean upon (another) with a projecting end or point (*the shed abutted on the side of the house*). **3** *tr.* abut on. [OF *abouter* (BUTT¹) and AL *abuttare* f. OF *but* end]

abutment /əˈbʌtmənt/ *n.* the lateral supporting structure of a bridge, arch, etc.

abysmal /əˈbɪzm(ə)l/ *adj.* **1** *colloq.* extremely bad (*abysmal weather; the standard is abysmal*). **2** profound, utter (*abysmal ignorance*). □ **abysmally** *adv.* [archaic or poet. *abysm* = ABYSS, f. OF *abi(s)me* f. med.L *abysmus*]

abyss /əˈbɪs/ *n.* **1** a seemingly bottomless chasm. **2 a** an immeasurable depth (*abyss of despair*). **b** a catastrophic situation as contemplated or feared (*a step nearer the abyss*). [ME f. LL *abyssus* f. Gk *abussos* bottomless (as A-¹, *bussos* depth)]

abyssal /əˈbɪs(ə)l/ *adj.* **1** at or of the ocean depths or floor. **2** *Geol.* plutonic.

AC *abbr.* **1** (also **ac**) alternating current. **2** *Brit.* aircraftman.

Ac *symb. Chem.* the element actinium.

a/c *abbr.* account. [*account current*: see ACCOUNT *n.* 2, 3]

-ac /æk/ *suffix* forming adjectives which are often also (or only) used as nouns (*cardiac*; *maniac*). [F *-aque* or L *-acus* or Gk *-akos* adj. suffix]

acacia /əˈkeɪʃə/ *n.* 1 any tree of the genus *Acacia*, with yellow or white flowers, esp. *A. senegal* yielding gum arabic. 2 (also **false acacia**) the locust tree, *Robinia pseudoacacia*. [L f. Gk *akakia*]

academe /ˈækəˌdiːm/ *n.* 1 the world of learning. 2 universities collectively. [Gk *Akadēmos* (see ACADEMY)]

academia /ˌækəˈdiːmɪə/ *n.* the academic world; scholastic life. [mod.L: see ACADEMY]

academic /ˌækəˈdemɪk/ *adj.* & *n.* —*adj.* 1 a scholarly; to do with learning. b of or relating to a scholarly institution (*academic dress*). 2 abstract; theoretical; not of practical relevance. —*n.* a teacher or scholar in a university or institute of higher education. □ **academic year** a period of nearly a year reckoned from the beginning of the autumn term to the end of the summer term. □ **academically** *adv.* [F *académique* or L *academicus* (as ACADEMY)]

academician /əˌkædəˈmɪʃ(ə)n/ *n.* a member of an Academy. [F *académicien* (as ACADEMIC)]

academicism /ˌækəˈdemɪˌsɪz(ə)m/ *n.* (also **academism** /əˈkædəˌmɪz(ə)m/) academic principles or their application in art.

academy /əˈkædəmɪ/ *n.* (*pl.* **-ies**) 1 a place of study or training in a special field (*military academy*; *academy of dance*). 2 (usu. **Academy**) a society or institution of distinguished scholars, artists, scientists, etc. (*Royal Academy*). 3 *Sc.* a secondary school. [F *académie* or L *academia* f. Gk *akadēmeia* f. *Akadēmos* the hero after whom the garden where Plato taught was named]

-acal /ək(ə)l/ *suffix* forming adjectives, often used to distinguish them from nouns in *-ac* (*heliacal*; *maniacal*).

acanthus /əˈkænθəs/ *n.* 1 any herbaceous plant or shrub of the genus *Acanthus*, with spiny leaves. 2 *Archit.* a conventionalized representation of an acanthus leaf. [L f. Gk *akanthos* f. *akantha* thorn perh. f. *akē* sharp point]

a cappella /ˌɑː kəˈpelə, ˌæ kəˈpelə/ *adj.* & *adv.* (also **alla cappella** /ˌælə/) *Mus.* (of choral music) unaccompanied. [It., = in church style]

acarid /ˈækərɪd/ *n.* any small arachnid of the order Acarina, including mites and ticks. [mod.L *acarida* f. *acarus* f. Gk *akari* mite]

ACAS /ˈeɪkæs/ *abbr.* (in the UK) Advisory, Conciliation, and Arbitration Service.

accede /ækˈsiːd/ *v.intr.* (often foll. by *to*) 1 take office, esp. become monarch. 2 assent or agree (*acceded to the proposal*). 3 (foll. by *to*) formally subscribe to a treaty or other agreement. [ME f. L *accedere* (as AD-, *cedere* cess- go)]

accelerate /əkˈseləˌreɪt/ *v.* 1 *intr.* a (of a moving body) move or begin to move more quickly; increase speed. b (of a process) happen or reach completion more quickly. 2 *tr.* cause to accelerate. [L *accelerare* (as AD-, *celerare* f. *celer* swift)]

acceleration /əkˌseləˈreɪʃ(ə)n/ *n.* 1 the process or act of accelerating or being accelerated. 2 an instance of this. 3 (of a vehicle etc.) the capacity to gain speed (*the car has good acceleration*). [F *accélération* or L *acceleratio* (as ACCELERATE)]

accelerative /əkˈselərətɪv/ *adj.* tending to increase speed; quickening.

accelerator /əkˈseləˌreɪtə(r)/ *n.* 1 a device for increasing speed, esp. the pedal that controls the speed of a vehicle's engine. 2 *Physics* an apparatus for imparting high speeds to charged particles. 3 *Chem.* a substance that speeds up a chemical reaction.

accent *n.* & *v.* —*n.* /ˈæks(ə)nt, -sent/ 1 a particular mode of pronunciation, esp. one associated with a particular region or group. 2 prominence given to a syllable by stress or pitch. 3 a mark on a letter or word to indicate pitch, stress, or the quality of a vowel. 4 a distinctive feature or emphasis (*an accent on comfort*). 5 *Mus.* emphasis on a particular note or chord. —*v.tr.* /ækˈsent/ 1 pronounce with an accent; emphasize (a word or syllable). 2 write or print accents on (words etc.). 3 accentuate. 4 *Mus.* play (a note etc.) with an accent. □ **accentual** /əkˈsentjʊəl/ *adj.* [L *accentus* (as AD-, *cantus* song) repr. Gk *prosōidia* (PROSODY), or through F *accent*, *accenter*]

accentuate /ækˈsentjʊˌeɪt/ *v.tr.* emphasize; make prominent. □ **accentuation** /ækˌsentjʊˈeɪʃ(ə)n/ *n.* [med.L *accentuare accentuat-* (as ACCENT)]

accept /əkˈsept/ *v.tr.* 1 (also *absol.*) consent to receive (a thing offered). 2 (also *absol.*) give an affirmative answer to (an offer or proposal). 3 regard favourably; treat as welcome. 4 a believe, receive (an opinion, explanation, etc.) as adequate or valid. b be prepared to subscribe to (a belief, philosophy, etc.). 5 receive as suitable (*the hotel accepts cheques*). 6 a tolerate; submit to (*accepted the umpire's decision*). b (often foll. by *that* + clause) be willing to believe (*we accept that you meant well*). 7 undertake (an office or responsibility). □ **accepted opinion** one generally held to be correct. □ **accepter** *n.* [ME f. OF *accepter* or L *acceptare* f. *accipere* (as AD-, *capere* take)]

acceptable /əkˈseptəb(ə)l/ *adj.* 1 a worthy of being accepted. b pleasing, welcome. 2 adequate, satisfactory. 3 tolerable (*an acceptable risk*). □ **acceptability** /əkˌseptəˈbɪlɪtɪ/ *n.* **acceptableness** *n.* **acceptably** *adv.* [ME f. OF f. LL *acceptabilis* (as ACCEPT)]

acceptance /əkˈsept(ə)ns/ *n.* 1 willingness to receive or accept. 2 an affirmative answer to an invitation or proposal. 3 a approval, belief (*found wide acceptance*). b willingness or ability to tolerate. [F *accepter* (as ACCEPT)]

acceptor /əkˈseptə(r)/ *n.* 1 *Physics* an atom or molecule able to receive an extra electron. 2 *Chem.* a molecule or ion etc. to which electrons are donated in the formation of a bond. 3 *Electr.* a circuit able to accept a given frequency.

access /ˈækses/ *n.* & *v.* —*n.* 1 a way of approaching or reaching or entering (*a building with rear access*). 2 a (often foll. by *to*) the right or opportunity to reach or use or visit; admittance (*has access to secret files*). b accessibility. 3 (often foll. by *of*) an attack or outburst (*an access of anger*). 4 (*attrib.*) *Brit.* (of broadcasting) allowed to minority or special-interest groups to undertake (*access television*). —*v.tr.* *Computing* gain access to (data, a file, etc.). 2 accession. [ME f. OF *acces* or L *accessus* f. *accedere* (as AD-, *cedere* cess- go)]

accessible /əkˈsesɪb(ə)l/ *adj.* (often foll. by *to*) 1 that can readily be reached, entered, or used. 2 (of a person) readily available (esp. to subordinates). 3 (in a form) easy to understand. □ **accessibility** /əkˌsesɪˈbɪlɪtɪ/ *n.* **accessibly** *adv.* [F *accessible* or LL *accessibilis* (as ACCEDE)]

accession /əkˈseʃ(ə)n/ n. & v. —n. 1 entering upon an office (esp. the throne) or a condition (as manhood). 2 (often foll. by *to*) a thing added (e.g. a book to a library); increase, addition. 3 assent; the formal acceptance of a treaty etc. —v.tr. record the addition of (a new item) to a library or museum. [F *accession* or L *accessio -onis* (as ACCEDE)]

accessorize /əkˈsesəˌraɪz/ v.tr. provide (a costume etc.) with accessories.

accessory /əkˈsesərɪ/ n. & adj. (also **accessary**) —n. (pl. **-ies**) 1 an additional or extra thing. 2 (usu. in *pl.*) **a** a small attachment or fitting. **b** a small item of (esp. a woman's) dress (e.g. gloves, handbag). 3 (often foll. by *to*) a person who helps in or knows the details of an (esp. illegal) act, without taking part in it. —adj. additional; contributing or aiding in a minor way; dispensable. □ **accessorial** /ˌækseˈsɔːrɪəl/ adj. [med.L *accessorius* (as ACCEDE)]

accidence /ˈæksɪd(ə)ns/ n. the part of grammar that deals with the variable parts or inflections of words. [med.L sense of L *accidentia* (transl. Gk *parepomena*) neut. pl. of *accidens* (as ACCIDENT)]

accident /ˈæksɪd(ə)nt/ n. 1 an event that is without apparent cause, or is unexpected. 2 an unfortunate event, esp. one causing physical harm or damage, brought about unintentionally. 3 occurrence of things by chance; the working of fortune (*accident accounts for much in life*). □ **accident-prone** (of a person) subject to frequent accidents. **by accident** unintentionally. [ME f. OF f. LL *accidens* f. L *accidere* (as AD-, *cadere* fall)]

accidental /ˌæksɪˈdent(ə)l/ adj. & n. —adj. 1 happening by chance, unintentionally, or unexpectedly. 2 not essential to a conception; subsidiary. —n. 1 Mus. a sign indicating a momentary departure from the key signature by raising or lowering a note. 2 something not essential to a conception. □ **accidentally** adv. [ME f. LL *accidentalis* (as ACCIDENT)]

acclaim /əˈkleɪm/ v. & n. —v.tr. 1 welcome or applaud enthusiastically; praise publicly. 2 (foll. by *compl.*) hail as (*acclaimed him king*). —n. 1 applause; welcome; public praise. 2 a shout of acclaim. □ **acclaimer** n. [ME f. L *acclamare* (as AD-, *clamare* shout: spelling assim. to *claim*)]

acclamation /ˌækləˈmeɪʃ(ə)n/ n. 1 loud and eager assent to a proposal. 2 (usu. in *pl.*) shouting in a person's honour. 3 the act or process of acclaiming. □ **by acclamation** US Polit. (elected) unanimously and without ballot. [L *acclamatio* (as ACCLAIM)]

acclimate /ˈæklɪˌmeɪt, əˈklaɪ-/ v.tr. US acclimatize. [F *acclimater* f. à to + *climat* CLIMATE]

acclimation /ˌæklaɪˈmeɪʃ(ə)n/ n. acclimatization. [irreg. f. ACCLIMATE]

acclimatize /əˈklaɪməˌtaɪz/ v. (also **-ise**) 1 tr. accustom to a new climate or to new conditions. 2 intr. become acclimatized. □ **acclimatization** /-ˈzeɪʃ(ə)n/ n. [F *acclimater*: see ACCLIMATE]

acclivity /əˈklɪvɪtɪ/ n. (pl. **-ies**) an upward slope. □ **acclivitous** adj. [L *acclivitas* f. *acclivis* (as AD-, *clivis* f. *clivus* slope)]

accolade /ˈækəˌleɪd, -ˈleɪd/ n. 1 an acknowledgement of merit. 2 a touch made with a sword at the bestowing of a knighthood. [F f. Prov. *acolada* (as AD-, L *collum* neck)]

accommodate /əˈkɒməˌdeɪt/ v.tr. 1 provide lodging or room for. 2 adapt, harmonize, reconcile (*must accommodate ourselves to new surroundings*). 3 do service or favour to; oblige (a person). [L *accommodare* (as AD-, *commodus* fitting)]

accommodating /əˈkɒməˌdeɪtɪŋ/ adj. obliging, compliant. □ **accommodatingly** adv.

accommodation /əˌkɒməˈdeɪʃ(ə)n/ n. 1 (in sing. or US in pl.) lodgings; a place to live. 2 an adaptation to suit a special purpose. 3 a convenient arrangement; a compromise. 4 (in pl.) US a seat in a vehicle etc. □ **accommodation address** an address used on letters to a person who is unable or unwilling to give a permanent address. [F *accommodation* or L *accommodatio -onis* (as ACCOMMODATE)]

accompaniment /əˈkʌmpənɪmənt/ n. 1 Mus. an instrumental or orchestral part supporting a solo instrument, voice, or group. 2 an accompanying thing. [F *accompagnement* (as ACCOMPANY)]

accompanist /əˈkʌmpənɪst/ n. (also **accompanyist** /-nɪɪst/) a person who provides a musical accompaniment.

accompany /əˈkʌmpənɪ/ v.tr. (**-ies**, **-ied**) 1 go with; escort, attend. 2 (usu. in *passive*; foll. by *with*, *by*) **a** be done or found with; supplement (*speech accompanied with gestures*). **b** have as a result (*pills accompanied by side effects*). 3 Mus. support or partner with accompaniment. [ME f. F *accompagner* f. à to + OF *compaing* COMPANION[1]: assim. to COMPANY]

accomplice /əˈkʌmplɪs, -ˈkɒm-/ n. a partner in a crime or wrongdoing. [ME and F *complice* (prob. by assoc. with ACCOMPANY), f. LL *complex complicis* confederate: cf. COMPLICATE]

accomplish /əˈkʌmplɪʃ, əˈkɒm-/ v.tr. perform; complete; succeed in doing. [ME f. OF *acomplir* f. L *complēre* COMPLETE]

accomplished /əˈkʌmplɪʃd, əˈkɒm-/ adj. clever, skilled; well trained or educated.

accomplishment /əˈkʌmplɪʃmənt, əˈkɒm-/ n. 1 the fulfilment or completion (of a task etc.). 2 an acquired skill, esp. a social one. 3 a thing done or achieved.

accord /əˈkɔːd/ v. & n. —v. 1 intr. (often foll. by *with*) (esp. of a thing) be in harmony; be consistent. 2 tr. **a** grant (permission, a request, etc.). **b** give (a welcome etc.). —n. 1 agreement, consent. 2 harmonious correspondence in pitch, tone, colour, etc. □ **of one's own accord** on one's own initiative; voluntarily. **with one accord** unanimously; in a united way. [ME f. OF *acord, acorder* f. L *cor cordis* heart]

accordance /əˈkɔːd(ə)ns/ n. harmony, agreement. [ME f. OF *acordance* (as ACCORD)]

accordant /əˈkɔːd(ə)nt/ adj. (often foll. by *with*) in tune; agreeing. □ **accordantly** adv. [ME f. OF *acordant* (as ACCORD)]

according /əˈkɔːdɪŋ/ adv. 1 (foll. by *to*) **a** as stated by or in (*according to their statement*). **b** in a manner corresponding to (*he lives according to his principles*). 2 (foll. by *as* + clause) in a manner or to a degree that varies as (*he pays according as he is able*).

accordingly /əˈkɔːdɪŋlɪ/ adv. 1 as suggested or required by the circumstances. 2 consequently, therefore.

accordion /əˈkɔːdɪən/ n. a portable musical instrument with reeds blown by bellows and played by means of keys and buttons. □ **accordionist** n. [G *Akkordion* f. It. *accordare* to tune]

accost /əˈkɒst/ v.tr. approach and address (a person), esp. boldly. [F *accoster* f. It. *accostare* ult. f. L *costa* rib: see COAST]

account /əˈkaʊnt/ n. & v. —n. **1** a narration or description. **2 a** an arrangement or facility at a bank etc. for commercial or financial transactions, esp. for depositing and withdrawing money. **b** the assets credited by such an arrangement (*has a large account; paid the money into her account*). **c** an arrangement at a shop for buying goods on credit. **3 a** (often in *pl.*) a record or statement of money, goods, or services received or expended, with the balance. **b** (in *pl.*) the practice of accounting or reckoning (*is good at accounts*). **4** a statement of the administration of money in trust (*demand an account*). **5** counting, reckoning. —v.tr. (foll. by *to be* or compl.) consider, regard as (*account him wise; account him to be guilty*). □ **account for 1** serve as or provide an explanation or reason for. **2 a** give a reckoning of or answer for (money etc. entrusted). **b** answer for (one's conduct). **3** succeed in killing, destroying, disposing of, or defeating. **4** supply or make up a specified amount or proportion of (*rent accounts for 50% of expenditure*). **by all accounts** in everyone's opinion. **call to account** require an explanation from (a person). **give a good** (or **bad**) **account of oneself** make a favourable (or unfavourable) impression; be successful (or un- successful). **keep account of** keep a record of; follow closely. **leave out of account** fail or decline to consider. **of no account** unimportant. **of some account** important. **on account 1** (of goods) to be paid for later. **2** (of money) in part payment. **on account of** because of. **on no account** under no circumstances; certainly not. **on one's own account** for one's own purposes; at one's own risk. **take account of** (or **take into account**) consider along with other factors (*took their age into account*). **turn to account** (or **good account**) turn to one's advantage. [ME f. OF *acont, aconter* (as AD-, *conter* COUNT¹)]

accountable /əˈkaʊntəb(ə)l/ adj. **1** responsible; required to account for one's conduct (*accountable for one's actions*). **2** explicable, understandable. □ **accountability** /-ˈbɪlɪtɪ/ n. **accountably** adv.

accountancy /əˈkaʊntənsɪ/ n. the profession or duties of an accountant.

accountant /əˈkaʊnt(ə)nt/ n. a professional keeper or inspector of accounts. [legal F f. pres. part. of OF *aconter* ACCOUNT]

accounting /əˈkaʊntɪŋ/ n. **1** the process of or skill in keeping and verifying accounts. **2** in senses of ACCOUNT v.

accoutrement /əˈkuːtrəmənt, -təmənt/ n. (US **accouterment** /-təmənt/) (usu. in pl.) **1** equipment, trappings. **2** Mil. a soldier's outfit other than weapons and garments. [F *accoutrer* f. OF *acoustrer* as A-³, *cousture* sewing: cf. SUTURE)]

accredit /əˈkrɛdɪt/ v.tr. (**accredited, accrediting**) **1** (foll. by *to*) attribute (a saying etc.) to (a person). **2** (foll. by *with*) credit (a person) with (a saying etc.). **3** (usu. foll. by *to* or *at*) send (an ambassador etc.) with credentials (*was accredited to the sovereign*). **4** gain belief for, make credible (an adviser, a statement, etc.). □ **accreditation** /-ˈteɪʃ(ə)n/ n. [F *accréditer* (as AD-, *crédit* CREDIT)]

accredited /əˈkrɛdɪtd/ adj. **1** officially recognized. **2** (of a belief) generally accepted; orthodox.

accrete /əˈkriːt/ v. **1** intr. grow together or into one. **2** intr. (often foll. by *to*) form round or on, as round a nucleus. **3** tr. attract (such additions). [L *accrescere* (as AD-, *crescere cret-* grow)]

accretion /əˈkriːʃ(ə)n/ n. **1** growth by organic enlargement. **2 a** the growing of separate things into one. **b** the product of such growing. **3 a** extraneous matter added to anything. **b** the adhesion of this. □ **accretive** adj. [L *accretio* (as ACCRETE)]

accrue /əˈkruː/ v.intr. (**accrues, accrued, accruing**) come as an increase or advantage, esp. financial. □ **accrual** n. **accrued** adj. [ME f. AF *acru(e)*, past part. of *acreistre* increase f. L *accrescere* ACCRETE]

acculturate /əˈkʌltʃəˌreɪt/ v. **1** intr. adapt to a different culture. **2** tr. cause to do this. □ **acculturation** /-ˈreɪʃ(ə)n/ n. **acculturative** /-rətɪv/ adj.

accumulate /əˈkjuːmjʊˌleɪt/ v. **1** tr. **a** acquire an increasing number or quantity of; heap up. **b** produce or acquire (a resulting whole) in this way. **2** intr. grow numerous or considerable; form an increasing quantity. [L *accumulare* (as AD-, *cumulus* heap)]

accumulation /əˌkjuːmjʊˈleɪʃ(ə)n/ n. **1** the act or process of accumulating or being accumulated. **2** an accumulated mass. [L *accumulatio* (as ACCUMULATE)]

accumulative /əˈkjuːmjʊlətɪv/ adj. **1** arising from accumulation (*accumulative evidence*). **2** arranged so as to accumulate. □ **accumulatively** adv.

accumulator /əˈkjuːmjʊˌleɪtə(r)/ n. **1** Brit. a rechargeable electric cell. **2** a bet placed on a sequence of events, the winnings and stake from each being placed on the next. **3** a register in a computer used to contain the results of an operation. **4** a person who accumulates things.

accuracy /ˈækjʊrəsɪ/ n. exactness or precision.

accurate /ˈækjʊrət/ adj. **1** careful, precise; lacking errors. **2** conforming exactly with a given standard. □ **accurately** adv. [L *accuratus* done carefully, past part. of *accurare* (as AD-, *cura* care)]

accursed /əˈkɜːsɪd, əˈkɜːst/ adj. **1** lying under a curse; ill-fated. **2** colloq. detestable, annoying. [past part. of *accurse*, f. A-² + CURSE]

accusation /ˌækjuːˈzeɪʃ(ə)n/ n. **1** the act or process of accusing or being accused. **2** a statement charging a person with an offence or crime. [ME f. OF f. L *accusatio -onis* (as ACCUSE)]

accusative /əˈkjuːzətɪv/ n. & adj. Gram. —n. the case of nouns, pronouns, and adjectives, expressing the object of an action or the goal of motion. —adj. of or in this case. □ **accusatival** /-ˈtaɪv(ə)l/ adj. **accusatively** adv. [ME f. OF *accusatif -ive* or L (*casus*) *accusativus*, transl. Gk (*ptōsis*) *aitiatikē*]

accusatorial /əˌkjuːzəˈtɔːrɪəl/ adj. Law (of proceedings) involving accusation by a prosecutor and a verdict reached by an impartial judge or jury (opp. INQUISITORIAL). [L *accusatorius* (as ACCUSE)]

accusatory /əˈkjuːzətərɪ/ adj. (of language, manner, etc.) of or implying accusation.

accuse /əˈkjuːz/ v.tr. **1** (foll. by *of*) charge (a person etc.) with a fault or crime; indict (*accused them of murder*). **2** lay the blame on. □ **accuser** n.

accusingly *adv.* [ME *acuse* f. OF *ac(c)user* f. L *accusare* (as AD-, CAUSE)]

accustom /əˈkʌstəm/ *v.tr.* & *refl.* (foll. by *to*) make (a person or thing or oneself) used to. [ME f. OF *acostumer* (as AD-, *costume* CUSTOM)]

accustomed /əˈkʌstəmd/ *adj.* **1** (usu. foll. by *to*) used to (*accustomed to hard work*). **2** customary, usual.

ace *n.* & *adj.* —*n.* **1 a** a playing-card, domino, etc., with a single spot and generally having the value 'one' or in card-games the highest value in each suit. **b** a single spot on a playing-card etc. **2 a** a person who excels in some activity. **b** *Aeron.* a pilot who has shot down many enemy aircraft. **3** (in lawn tennis) a stroke (esp. a service) too good for the opponent to return. —*adj. sl.* excellent. **within an ace of** on the verge of. [ME f. OF f. L *as* unity]

-acea /ˈeɪʃə/ *suffix* forming the plural names of orders and classes of animals (*Crustacea*) (cf. -ACEAN). [neut. pl. of L adj. suffix -*aceus* of the nature of]

-aceae /ˈeɪsiiː/ *suffix* forming the plural names of families of plants (*Rosaceae*). [fem. pl. of L adj. suffix -*aceus* of the nature of]

-acean /ˈeɪʃ(ə)n/ *suffix* **1** forming adjectives, = -ACEOUS. **2** forming nouns as the sing. of names in -acea (*crustacean*). [L -*aceus*: see -ACEA]

acellular /eɪˈseljʊlə(r)/ *adj. Biol.* **1** having no cells; not consisting of cells. **2** (esp. of protozoa) consisting of one cell only; unicellular.

-aceous /ˈeɪʃəs/ *suffix* forming adjectives, esp. from nouns in -acea, -aceae (*herbaceous*; *rosaceous*). [L -*aceus*: see -ACEA]

acephalous /əˈsefələs, əˈke-/ *adj.* **1** headless. **2** having no chief. **3** *Zool.* having no part of the body specially organized as a head. **4** *Bot.* with a head aborted or cut off. [med.L *acephalus* f. Gk *akephalos* headless (as A-¹, *kephalē* head)]

acerbic /əˈsɜːbɪk/ *adj.* **1** astringently sour. **2** bitter in speech, manner, or temper. □ **acerbically** *adv.* **acerbity** *n.* (pl. -**ies**). [L *acerbus* sour-tasting]

acetaldehyde /ˌæsɪˈtældɪˌhaɪd/ *n.* a colourless volatile liquid aldehyde. [ACETIC + ALDEHYDE]

acetate /ˈæsɪˌteɪt/ *n.* **1** a salt or ester of acetic acid, esp. the cellulose ester used to make textiles, gramophone records, etc. **2** a fabric made from cellulose acetate. [ACETIC + -ATE¹ ²]

acetic /əˈsiːtɪk/ *adj.* of or like vinegar. □ **acetic acid** the clear liquid acid that gives vinegar its characteristic taste. [F *acétique* f. L *acetum* vinegar]

aceto- /ˈæsɪtəʊ/ *comb. form Chem.* acetic, acetyl.

acetone /ˈæsɪˌtəʊn/ *n.* a colourless volatile liquid ketone valuable as a solvent of organic compounds esp. paints, varnishes, etc. [ACETO- + -ONE]

acetous /ˈæsɪtəs/ *adj.* **1** having the qualities of vinegar. **2** producing vinegar. **3** sour. [LL *acetosus* sour (as ACETIC)]

acetyl /ˈæsɪtɪl, -ˌtaɪl/ *n. Chem.* the univalent radical of acetic acid. [ACETIC + -YL]

acetylene /əˈsetɪˌliːn/ *n.* a colourless hydrocarbon gas, burning with a bright flame, used esp. in welding. [ACETIC + -YL + -ENE]

acetylide /əˈsetɪˌlaɪd/ *n.* any of a class of salts formed from acetylene and a metal.

acetylsalicylic acid /ˌæsɪtaɪlˌsælɪˈsɪlɪk/ *n.* = ASPIRIN. [ACETYL + SALICYLIC ACID]

Achaean /əˈkiːən/ *adj.* & *n.* —*adj.* **1** of or relating to Achaea in ancient Greece. **2** *literary* (esp. in Homeric contexts) Greek. —*n.* **1** an inhabitant of Achaea. **2** *literary* (usu. in *pl.*) a Greek. [L *Achaeus* f. Gk *Akhaios*]

ache /eɪk/ *n.* & *v.* —*n.* **1** a continuous or prolonged dull pain. **2** mental distress. —*v.intr.* **1** suffer from or be the source of an ache (*I ached all over*; *my left leg ached*). **2** (foll. by *to* + infin.) desire greatly. □ **achingly** *adv.* [ME f. OE *æce*, *acan*]

achieve /əˈtʃiːv/ *v.tr.* **1 a** reach or attain by effort (*achieved victory*). **b** acquire, gain, earn (*achieved notoriety*). **2** accomplish or carry out (a feat or task). **3** *absol.* be successful; attain a desired level of performance. □ **achievable** *adj.* **achiever** *n.* [ME f. OF *achever* f. *a chief* to a head]

achievement /əˈtʃiːvmənt/ *n.* **1** something achieved. **2 a** the act of achieving. **b** an instance of this. **3** *Psychol.* performance in a standardized test.

Achilles' heel /əˈkɪliːz/ *n.* a person's weak or vulnerable point. [L *Achilles* f. Gk *Akhilleus*, a hero in the *Iliad*, invulnerable except in the heel]

Achilles' tendon /əˈkɪliːz/ *n.* the tendon connecting the heel with the calf muscles.

achromatic /ˌækrəʊˈmætɪk/ *adj. Optics* **1** that transmits light without separating it into constitu- ent colours (*achromatic lens*). **2** without colour (*achromatic fringe*). □ **achromatically** *adv.* **achromaticity** /əˌkrəʊməˈtɪsɪtɪ/ *n.* **achromatism** /əˈkrəʊməˌtɪz(ə)m/ *n.* [F *achromatique* f. Gk *akhro- matos* (as A-¹, CHROMATIC)]

achy /ˈeɪkɪ/ *adj.* (**achier**, **achiest**) full of or suffering from aches.

acid /ˈæsɪd/ *n.* & *adj.* —*n.* **1** *Chem.* any of a class of substances that liberate hydrogen ions in water, are usu. sour and corrosive, turn litmus red, and have a pH of less than 7. **2** (in general use) any sour substance. **3** *sl.* the drug LSD. —*adj.* **1** sharp-tasting, sour. **2** biting, sharp (*an acid wit*). **3** *Chem.* having the essential properties of an acid. **4** *Geol.* containing much silica. **5** (of a colour) intense, bright. □ **acid drop** *Brit.* a kind of sweet with a sharp taste. **acid house** a kind of synthesized music with a simple repetitive beat. **acid rain** acid formed in the atmosphere esp. from industrial waste gases and falling with rain. **acid test** a severe or conclusive test. **2** a test in which acid is used to test for gold etc. **put the acid on** *Austral. sl.* seek to extract a loan or favour etc. from. □ **acidic** /əˈsɪdɪk/ *adj.* **acidimeter** /ˌæsɪˈdɪmɪtə(r)/ *n.* **acidimetry** /ˌæsɪˈdɪmɪtrɪ/ *n.* **acidly** *adv.* **acidness** *n.* [F *acide* or L *acidus* f. *acēre* be sour]

acidify /əˈsɪdɪˌfaɪ/ *v.tr.* & *intr.* (-**ies**, -**ied**) make or become acid. □ **acidification** /-fɪˈkeɪʃ(ə)n/ *n.*

acidity /əˈsɪdɪtɪ/ *n.* (pl. -**ies**) an acid quality or state, esp. an excessively acid condition of the stomach.

acidosis /ˌæsɪˈdəʊsɪs/ *n.* an over-acid condition of the body fluids or tissues. □ **acidotic** /-ˈdɒtɪk/ *adj.*

acidulate /əˈsɪdjʊˌleɪt/ *v.tr.* make somewhat acid. □ **acidulation** /-ˈleɪʃ(ə)n/ *n.* [L *acidulus* dimin. of *acidus* sour]

acidulous /əˈsɪdjʊləs/ *adj.* somewhat acid.

-acious /ˈeɪʃəs/ *suffix* forming adjectives meaning 'inclined to, full of' (*vivacious*; *pugnacious*;

voracious; *capacious*). [L *-ax -acis*, added chiefly to verbal stems to form adjectives + -OUS]

-acity /ˈæsɪtɪ/ *suffix* forming nouns of quality or state corresponding to adjectives in *-acious*. [F *-acité* or L *-acitas -tatis*]

ack-ack /ˈækæk/ *adj.* & *n. colloq.* —*adj.* anti-aircraft. —*n.* an anti-aircraft gun etc. [formerly signallers' name for the letters *AA*]

ackee /ˈækiː/ *n.* (also **akee**) **1** a tropical tree, *Blighia sapida.* **2** its fruit, edible when cooked. [Kru *ākee*]

ack emma /æk ˈemə/ *adv.* & *n. Brit. colloq.* = A.M. [formerly signallers' name for the letters *AM*]

acknowledge /əkˈnɒlɪdʒ/ *v.tr.* **1 a** recognize; accept; admit the truth of. **b** (often foll. by *to be* + compl.) recognize as. **c** (often foll. by *that* + clause or *to* + infin.) admit that something is so. **2** confirm the receipt of. **3 a** show that one has noticed. **b** express appreciation of (a service etc.). **4** own; recognize the validity of (*the acknowledged king*). □ **acknowledgeable** *adj.* [obs. KNOWLEDGE *v.* after obs. *acknow* (as A-⁴, KNOW), or f. obs. noun *acknowledge*]

acknowledgement /əkˈnɒlɪdʒmənt/ *n.* (also **acknowledgment**) **1** the act or an instance of acknowledging. **2 a** a thing given or done in return for a service etc. **b** a letter confirming receipt of something. **3** (usu. in *pl.*) an author's statement of indebtedness to others.

acme /ˈækmɪ/ *n.* the highest point or period (of achievement, success, etc.); the peak of perfection. [Gk, = highest point]

acne /ˈæknɪ/ *n.* a skin condition, usu. of the face, characterized by red pimples. □ **acned** *adj.* [mod.L f. erron. Gk *aknas* for *akmas* accus. pl. of *akmē* facial eruption: cf. ACME]

acolyte /ˈækəlaɪt/ *n.* **1** a person assisting a priest in a service or procession. **2** an assistant; a beginner. [ME f. OF *acolyt* or eccl.L *acolytus* f. Gk *akolouthos* follower]

aconite /ˈækənaɪt/ *n.* **1 a** any poisonous plant of the genus *Aconitum*, esp. monkshood or wolfsbane. **b** aconitine. **2** (in full **winter aconite**) any ranunculaceous plant of the genus *Eranthis*, with yellow flowers. □ **aconitic** /ˌækəˈnɪtɪk/ *adj. Chem.* [F *aconit* or L *aconitum* f. Gk *akoniton*]

aconitine /əˈkɒnɪˌtiːn/ *n. Pharm.* a poisonous alkaloid obtained from the aconite plant.

acorn /ˈeɪkɔːn/ *n.* the fruit of the oak, with a smooth nut in a rough cuplike base. [OE *æcern*, rel. to *æcer* ACRE, later assoc. with OAK and CORN¹]

acotyledon /əˌkɒtɪˈliːd(ə)n/ *n.* a plant with no distinct seed-leaves. □ **acotyledonous** *adj.* [mod.L *acotyledones* pl. (as A-¹, COTYLEDON)]

acoustic /əˈkuːstɪk/ *adj.* & *n.* —*adj.* **1** relating to sound or the sense of hearing. **2** (of a musical instrument, gramophone, or recording) not having electrical amplification. **3** (of building materials) used for soundproofing or modifying sound. —*n.* **1** (usu. in *pl.*) the properties or qualities (esp. of a room or hall etc.) in transmitting sound (*good acoustics*; *a poor acoustic*). **2** (in *pl.*; usu. treated as *sing.*) the science of sound. □ **acoustic coupler** *Computing* a modem which converts digital signals into audible signals and vice versa, so that the former can be transmitted and received over telephone lines. □ **acoustical**

adj. **acoustically** *adv.* [Gk *akoustikos* f. *akouō* hear]

acoustician /ˌækuːˈstɪʃ(ə)n/ *n.* an expert in acoustics.

acquaint /əˈkweɪnt/ *v.tr.* & *refl.* (usu. foll. by *with*) make (a person or oneself) aware of or familiar with (*acquaint me with the facts*). □ **be acquainted with** have personal knowledge of (a person or thing). [ME f. OF *acointier* f. LL *accognitare* (as AD-, *cognoscere cognit-* come to know)]

acquaintance /əˈkweɪnt(ə)ns/ *n.* **1** (usu. foll. by *with*) slight knowledge (of a person or thing). **2** the fact or process of being acquainted. **3** a person one knows slightly. □ **make a person's acquaintance** first meet or introduce oneself to another person. **make the acquaintance of** come to know. □ **acquaintanceship** *n.* [ME f. OF *acointance* (as ACQUAINT)]

acquiesce /ˌækwɪˈes/ *v.intr.* **1** agree, esp. tacitly. **2** raise no objection. **3** (foll. by *in*) accept (an arrangement etc.). □ **acquiescence** *n.* **acquiescent** *adj.* [L *acquiescere* (as AD-, *quiescere* rest)]

acquire /əˈkwaɪə(r)/ *v.tr.* **1** gain by and for oneself; obtain. **2** come into possession of. □ **acquired characteristic** *Biol.* a characteristic caused by the environment, not inherited. □ **acquirable** *adj.* [ME f. OF *aquerre* ult. f. L *acquirere* (as AD-, *quaerere* seek)]

acquirement /əˈkwaɪəmənt/ *n.* **1** something acquired, esp. a mental attainment. **2** the act or an instance of acquiring.

acquisition /ˌækwɪˈzɪʃ(ə)n/ *n.* **1** something acquired, esp. if regarded as useful. **2** the act or an instance of acquiring. [L *acquisitio* (as ACQUIRE)]

acquisitive /əˈkwɪzɪtɪv/ *adj.* keen to acquire things; materialistic. □ **acquisitively** *adv.* **acquisitiveness** *n.* [F *acquisitive* or LL *acquisitivus* (as ACQUIRE)]

acquit /əˈkwɪt/ *v.* (**acquitted, acquitting**) **1** *tr.* (often foll. by *of*) declare (a person) not guilty (*were acquitted of the offence*). **2** *refl.* **a** conduct oneself or perform in a specified way (*we acquitted ourselves well*). **b** (foll. by *of*) discharge (a duty or responsibility). [ME f. OF *aquiter* f. med.L *acquitare* pay a debt (as AD-, QUIT)]

acquittal /əˈkwɪt(ə)l/ *n.* **1** the process of freeing or being freed from a charge, esp. by a judgement of not guilty. **2** performance of a duty.

acquittance /əˈkwɪt(ə)ns/ *n.* **1** payment of or release from a debt. **2** a written receipt attesting settlement of a debt. [ME f. OF *aquitance* (as ACQUIT)]

acre /ˈeɪkə(r)/ *n.* **1** a measure of land, 4,840 sq. yds., 0.405 ha. **2** a piece of land; a field. **3** (in *pl.*) a large area. □ **acred** *adj.* (also in *comb.*). [OE *æcer* f. Gmc]

acreage /ˈeɪkərɪdʒ/ *n.* **1** a number of acres. **2** an extent of land.

acrid /ˈækrɪd/ *adj.* (**acrider, acridest**) **1** bitterly pungent; irritating; corrosive. **2** bitter in temper or manner. □ **acridity** /əˈkrɪdɪtɪ/ *n.* **acridly** *adv.* [irreg. f. L *acer acris* keen + -ID¹, prob. after *acid*]

acrimonious /ˌækrɪˈməʊnɪəs/ *adj.* bitter in manner or temper. □ **acrimoniously** *adv.* [F *acrimonieux, -euse* f. med.L *acrimoniosus* f. L *acrimonia* ACRIMONY]

acrimony /ˈækrɪmənɪ/ *n.* (*pl.* **-ies**) bitterness of temper or manner; ill feeling. [F *acrimonie* or L *acrimonia* pungency (as ACRID)]

acrobat /ˈækrəˌbæt/ n. **1** a performer of spectacular gymnastic feats. **2** a person noted for constant change of mind, allegiance, etc. □ **acrobatic** /ˌækrəˈbætɪk/ adj. **acrobatically** /ˌækrəˈbætɪkəlɪ/ adv. [F acrobate f. Gk akrobatēs f. akron summit + bainō walk]

acrobatics /ˌækrəˈbætɪks/ n.pl. **1** acrobatic feats. **2** (as sing.) the art of performing these. **3** a skill requiring ingenuity (mental acrobatics).

acromegaly /ˌækrəˈmegəlɪ/ n. Med. the abnormal growth of the hands, feet, and face, caused by excessive activity of the pituitary gland. □ **acromegalic** /-mɪˈgælɪk/ adj. [F acromégalie f. Gk akron extremity + megas megal- great]

acronym /ˈækrənɪm/ n. a word, usu. pronounced as such, formed from the initial letters of other words (e.g. Ernie, laser, Nato). [Gk akron end + -onum- = onoma name]

acrophobia /ˌækrəˈfəʊbɪə/ n. Psychol. an abnormal dread of heights. □ **acrophobic** adj. [Gk akron peak + -PHOBIA]

acropolis /əˈkrɒpəlɪs/ n. **1** a citadel or upper fortified part of an ancient Greek city. **2** (**Acropolis**) the ancient citadel at Athens. [Gk akropolis f. akron summit + polis city]

across /əˈkrɒs/ prep. & adv. —prep. **1** to or on the other side of (walked across the road; lives across the river). **2** from one side to another side of (a bridge across the river). **3** at or forming an angle (esp. a right angle) with (deep cuts across his legs). —adv. **1** to or on the other side (ran across; shall soon be across). **2** from one side to another (a blanket stretched across). **3** forming a cross (with cuts across). □ **across the board** general; generally; applying to all. [ME f. OF a croix, en croix, later regarded as f. A² + CROSS]

acrostic /əˈkrɒstɪk/ n. **1** a poem or other composition in which certain letters in each line (usu. first or last) form a word or words. **2** a word-puzzle constructed in this way. [F acrostiche or Gk akrostikhis f. akron end + stikhos row, line of verse, assim. to -IC]

acrylic /əˈkrɪlɪk/ adj. & n. —adj. **1** of material made with a synthetic polymer derived from acrylic acid. **2** Chem. of or derived from acrylic acid. —n. an acrylic fibre. □ **acrylic acid** a pungent liquid organic acid. [acrolein f. L acer acris pungent + olēre to smell + -IN + -YL + -IC]

act n. & v. —n. **1** something done; a deed; an action. **2** the process of doing something (caught in the act). **3 a** a piece of entertainment, usu. one of a series in a programme. **b** the performer(s) of this. **4** a pretence; behaviour intended to deceive or impress (it was all an act). **5** a main division of a play or opera. **6 a** a written ordinance of a parliament or other legislative body. **b** a document attesting a legal transaction. **7** (often in pl.) the recorded decisions or proceedings of a committee, an academic body, etc. **8** (**Acts**) (in full **Acts of the Apostles**) the New Testament book relating the growth of the early Church. —v. **1** intr. behave. **2** intr. perform actions or functions; operate effectively; take action (act as referee; the brakes failed to act. **3** intr. (also foll. by on) exert energy or influence (alcohol acts on the brain). **4** intr. **a** perform a part in a play, film, etc. **b** pretend. **5** tr. **a** perform the part of (acted Othello; acts the fool). **b** perform (a play etc.). **c** portray (an incident) by actions. **d** feign (we acted indifference). □ **act for** be the

(esp. legal) representative of. **act of God** the operation of uncontrollable natural forces. **act on** (or **upon**) perform or carry out; put into operation (acted on my advice). **act out 1** translate (ideas etc.) into action. **2** Psychol. represent (one's subconscious desires etc.) in action. **act up** colloq. misbehave; give trouble (my car is acting up again). □ **actable** adj. (in sense 5 of v.). **actability** /-ˈbɪlɪtɪ/ n. (in sense 5 of v.). [ME ult. f. L agere act- do]

acting /ˈæktɪŋ/ n. & attrib. adj. —n. **1** the art or occupation of performing parts in plays, films, etc. **2** in senses of ACT v. —attrib.adj. serving temporarily or on behalf of another or others (acting manager).

actinide /ˈæktɪˌnaɪd/ n. (also **actinoid** /ˈæktɪˌnɔɪd/) Chem. any of the series of 15 radioactive elements having increasing atomic numbers from actinium to lawrencium. □ **actinide series** this series of elements. [ACTINIUM + -IDE as in lanthanide]

actinism /ˈæktɪˌnɪz(ə)m/ n. the property of short-wave radiation that produces chemical changes, as in photography. □ **actinic** /ækˈtɪnɪk/ adj. [Gk aktis -inos ray]

actinium /ækˈtɪnɪəm/ n. Chem. a radioactive metallic element of the actinide series, occurring naturally in pitchblende.

action /ˈækʃ(ə)n/ n. & v. —n. **1** the fact or process of doing or acting (demanded action; put ideas into action). **2** forcefulness or energy as a characteristic (a woman of action). **3** the exertion of energy or influence (the action of acid on metal). **4** something done; a deed or act. **5 a** a series of events represented in a story, play, etc. **b** sl. exciting activity (arrived late and missed the action). **6 a** armed conflict; fighting (killed in action). **b** an occurrence of this, esp. a minor military engagement. **7 a** the way in which a machine, instrument, etc. works (explain the action of a pump). **b** the mechanism that makes a machine, instrument, etc. work. **c** the mode or style of movement of an animal or human (a runner with good action). **8** a legal process; a lawsuit (bring an action). **9** (in imper.) a word of command to begin, esp. used by a film director etc. —v.tr. bring a legal action against. □ **action painting** an aspect of abstract expressionism with paint applied by the artist's random or spontaneous gestures. **action replay** a playback of part of a television broadcast, esp. a sporting event, often in slow motion. **action stations** positions taken up by troops etc. ready for battle. **go into action** start work. **take action** begin to act (esp. energetically in protest). [ME f. OF f. L actio -onis (as ACT)]

actionable /ˈækʃənəb(ə)l/ adj. giving cause for legal action. □ **actionably** adv.

activate /ˈæktɪˌveɪt/ v.tr. **1** make active; bring into action. **2** Chem. cause reaction in; excite (a substance, molecules, etc.). **3** Physics make radioactive. □ **activated carbon** carbon, esp. charcoal, treated to increase its adsorptive power. **activated sludge** aerated sewage containing aerobic bacteria. □ **activation** /-ˈveɪʃ(ə)n/ n. **activator** n.

active /ˈæktɪv/ adj. & n. —adj. **1 a** consisting in or marked by action; energetic; diligent (leads an active life; an active helper). **b** able to move about or accomplish practical tasks. **2** working, operative (an active volcano). **3** originating action;

not merely passive or inert (*active ingredients*). **4** radioactive. **5** *Gram.* designating the voice that attributes the action of a verb to the person or thing from which it logically proceeds (e.g. of the verbs in *guns kill; we saw him*). —*n. Gram.* the active form or voice of a verb. □ **active carbon** = activated carbon. **active citizen** a person who takes an active role in the community through crime prevention etc. **active service** full-time service in the armed forces. □ **actively** *adv.* **activeness** *n.* [ME f. OF *actif -ive* or L *activus* (as ACT *v.*)]

activism /ˈæktɪˌvɪz(ə)n/ *n.* a policy of vigorous action in a cause, esp. in politics. □ **activist** *n.*

activity /ækˈtɪvɪtɪ/ *n.* (*pl.* **-ies**) **1 a** the condition of being active or moving about. **b** the exertion of energy; vigorous action. **2** (often in *pl.*) a particular occupation or pursuit (*outdoor activities*). **3** = RADIOACTIVITY. [F *activité* or LL *activitas* (as ACTIVE)]

actor /ˈæktə(r)/ *n.* **1** the performer of a part in a play, film, etc. **2** a person whose profession is performing such parts. [L, = doer, actor (as ACT, -OR¹)]

actress /ˈæktrɪs/ *n.* a female actor.

actual /ˈæktʃʊəl, ˈæktjʊəl/ *adj.* (usu. *attrib.*) **1** existing in fact; real (often as distinct from ideal). **2** existing now; current. □ **actualize** *v.tr.* (also **-ise**). **actualization** /-ˈzeɪʃ(ə)n/ *n.* [ME f. OF *actuel* f. LL *actualis* f. *agere* ACT]

actuality /ˌæktʃʊˈælɪtɪ, ˌæktjʊ-/ *n.* (*pl.* **-ies**) **1** reality; what is the case. **2** (in *pl.*) existing conditions. [ME f. OF *actualité* entity or med.L *actualitas* (as ACTUAL)]

actually /ˈæktʃʊəlɪ/ *adv.* **1** as a fact, really (*I asked for ten, but actually got nine*). **2** as a matter of fact, even (strange as it may seem) (*he actually refused!*).

actuary /ˈæktʃʊərɪ/ *n.* (*pl.* **-ies**) an expert in statistics, esp. one who calculates insurance risks and premiums. □ **actuarial** /-ˈeərɪəl/ *adj.* **actuarially** /-ˈeərɪəlɪ/ *adv.* [L *actuarius* book-keeper f. *actus* past part. of *agere* ACT]

actuate /ˈæktʃʊˌeɪt/ *v.tr.* **1** communicate motion to (a machine etc.). **2** cause the operation of (an electrical device etc.). **3** cause (a person) to act. □ **actuation** /-ˈeɪʃ(ə)n/ *n.* **actuator** *n.* [med.L *actuare* f. L *actus*: see ACTUAL]

acuity /əˈkjuːɪtɪ/ *n.* sharpness, acuteness (of a needle, senses, understanding). [F *acuité* or med.L *acuitas* f. *acuere* sharpen: see ACUTE]

acumen /ˈækjʊmən, əˈkjuːmən/ *n.* keen insight or discernment, penetration. [L *acumen -minis* anything sharp f. *acuere* sharpen: see ACUTE]

acupressure /ˈækjʊˌpreʃə(r)/ *n.* a form of therapy in which symptoms are relieved by applying pressure with the thumbs or fingers to specific points on the body. [alt. of ACUPUNCTURE]

acupuncture /ˈækjuːˌpʌŋktʃə(r)/ *n.* a method (orig. Chinese) of treating various conditions by pricking the skin or tissues with needles. □ **acupuncturist** *n.* [L *acu* with a needle + PUNCTURE]

acushla /əˈkʊʃlə/ *n.* *Ir.* darling. [Ir. *a cuisle* O pulse (of my heart)!]

acute /əˈkjuːt/ *adj.* & *n.* —*adj.* (**acuter, acutest**) **1** (of sensation or senses) keen, penetrating. **2** shrewd, perceptive (*an acute critic*). **3** (of a disease) coming sharply to a crisis; severe, not chronic. **4** (of a difficulty or controversy) critical, serious. **5 a** (of an angle) less than 90°. **b** sharp, pointed.

6 (of a sound) high, shrill. —*n.* = acute accent. □ **acute accent** a mark (´) placed over letters in some languages to show quality, vowel length, pronunciation (e.g. *maté*), etc. □ **acutely** *adv.* **acuteness** *n.* [L *acutus* past part. of *acuere* sharpen f. *acus* needle]

-acy /əsɪ/ *suffix* forming nouns of state or quality (*accuracy; piracy; supremacy*), or an instance of it (*conspiracy; fallacy*) (see also -CRACY). [a branch of the suffix -CY from or after F *-acie* or L *-acia* or *-atia* or Gk *-ateia*]

AD *abbr.* (of a date) of the Christian era. [*Anno Domini* 'in the year of the Lord']

ad *n.* *colloq.* an advertisement. [abbr.]

ad- /əd, æd/ *prefix* (also **a-** before *sc, sp, st,* **ac-** before *c, k, q,* **af-** before *f,* **ag-** before *g,* **al-** before *l,* **an-** before *n,* **ap-** before *p,* **ar-** before *r,* **as-** before *s,* **at-** before *t*) **1** with the sense of motion or direction to, reduction or change into, addition, adherence, increase, or intensification. **2** formed by assimilation of other prefixes (*accurse; admiral; advance; affray*). [(sense 1) (through OF *a-*) f. L *ad* to: (sense 2) *a-* repr. various prefixes other than *ad-*]

-ad¹ /əd, æd/ *suffix* forming nouns: **1** in collective numerals (*myriad; triad*). **2** in fem. patronymics (*Dryad*). **3** in names of poems and similar compositions (*Iliad; Dunciad; jeremiad*). [Gk *-as -ada*]

-ad² /əd/ *suffix* forming nouns (*ballad; salad*) (cf. -ADE¹). [F *-ade*]

adage /ˈædɪdʒ/ *n.* a traditional maxim, a proverb. [F f. L *adagium* (as AD-, root of *aio* say)]

adagio /əˈdɑːʒɪəʊ/ *adv., adj.,* & *n. Mus.* —*adv.* & *adj.* in slow time. —*n.* (*pl.* **-os**) an adagio movement or passage. [It.]

Adam /ˈædəm/ *n.* the first man, in the Biblical and Koranic traditions. □ **Adam's ale** water. **Adam's apple** a projection of the thyroid cartilage of the larynx. [Heb. *'ādām* man]

adamant /ˈædəmənt/ *adj.* & *n.* —*adj.* stubbornly resolute; resistant to persuasion. —*n.* archaic diamond or other hard substance. □ **adamance** *n.* **adamantine** /-ˈmæntaɪn/ *adj.* **adamantly** *adv.* [OF *adamaunt* f. L *adamas adamant-* untameable f. Gk (as A-¹, root of *aio* say)]

adapt /əˈdæpt/ *v.* **1** *tr.* **a** (foll. by *to*) fit, adjust (one thing to another). **b** (foll. by *to, for*) make suitable for a purpose. **c** alter or modify (esp. a text). **d** arrange for broadcasting etc. **2** *intr.* & *refl.* (usu. foll. by *to*) become adjusted to new conditions. □ **adaptive** *adj.* **adaptively** *adv.* [F *adapter* f. L *adaptare* (as AD-, *aptare* f. *aptus* fit)]

adaptable /əˈdæptəb(ə)l/ *adj.* **1** able to adapt oneself to new conditions. **2** that can be adapted. □ **adaptability** /-ˈbɪlɪtɪ/ *n.* **adaptably** *adv.*

adaptation /ˌædæpˈteɪʃ(ə)n/ *n.* **1** the act or process of adapting or being adapted. **2** a thing that has been adapted. [F f. LL *adaptatio -onis* (as ADAPT)]

adaptor /əˈdæptə(r)/ *n.* (also **adapter**) **1** a device for making equipment compatible. **2** a device for connecting several electrical plugs to one socket. **3** a person who adapts.

add *v.tr.* **1** join (one thing to another) as an increase or supplement (*add insult to injury*). **2** put together (two or more numbers) to find a number denoting their combined value. **3** say in addition (*added that I was wrong*). □ **add up 1** find the total of. **2** (foll. by *to*) amount to; constitute (*adds up to a disaster*). **3** *colloq.* make sense; be understandable. □ **added** *adj.* [ME f. L *addere* (as AD-, *dare* put)]

addendum /ə'dendəm/ *n.* (*pl.* **addenda** /-də/) **1** a thing (usu. something omitted) to be added, esp. (in *pl.*) as additional matter at the end of a book. **2** an appendix; an addition. [L, gerundive of *addere* ADD]

adder /'ædə(r)/ *n.* any of various small venomous snakes, esp. the common viper, *Vipera berus*. [OE *nædre*: *n* lost in ME by wrong division of *a naddre*: cf. APRON, AUGER, UMPIRE]

addict *v.* & *n.* —*v.tr.* & *refl.* /ə'dɪkt/ (usu. foll. by *to*) devote or apply habitually or compulsively; make addicted. —*n.* /'ædɪkt/ **1** a person addicted to a habit, esp. one dependent on a (specified) drug (*drug addict; heroin addict*). **2** *colloq.* an enthusiastic devotee of a sport or pastime (*film addict*). [L *addicere* assign (as AD-, *dicere dict*- say)]

addicted /ə'dɪktɪd/ *adj.* (foll. by *to*) **1** dependent on as a habit; unable to do without (*addicted to heroin; addicted to smoking*). **2** devoted (*addicted to football*).

addiction /ə'dɪkʃ(ə)n/ *n.* the fact or process of being addicted, esp. the condition of taking a drug habitually and being unable to give it up without incurring adverse effects. [L *addictio*: see ADDICT]

addictive /ə'dɪktɪv/ *adj.* (of a drug, habit, etc.) causing addiction or dependence.

addition /ə'dɪʃ(ə)n/ *n.* **1** the act or process of adding or being added. **2** a person or thing added (*a useful addition to the team*). □ **in addition** (often foll. by *to*) as something added. [ME f. OF *addition* or f. L *additio* (as ADD)]

additional /ə'dɪʃən(ə)l/ *adj.* added, extra, supplementary. □ **additionally** *adv.*

additive /'ædɪtɪv/ *n.* & *adj.* —*n.* a thing added, esp. a substance added to another so as to give it specific qualities. —*adj.* characterized by addition (*additive process*). [LL *additivus* (as ADD)]

addle /'æd(ə)l/ *v.* & *adj.* —*v.* **1** *tr.* muddle, confuse. **2** *intr.* (of an egg) become addled. —*adj.* muddled, unsound (*addle-brained; addle-head*). [OE *adela* filth, used as adj., then as verb]

addled /'æd(ə)ld/ *adj.* **1** (of an egg) rotten, producing no chick. **2** muddled. [ADDLE *adj.*, assim. to past part. form]

address /ə'dres/ *n.* & *v.* —*n.* **1 a** the place where a person lives or an organization is situated. **b** particulars of this, esp. for postal purposes. **c** *Computing* the location of an item of stored information. **2** a discourse delivered to an audience. **3** skill, dexterity. **4** (in *pl.*) a courteous approach, courtship (*pay one's addresses to*). —*v.tr.* **1** write directions for delivery (esp. the name and address of the intended recipient) on (an envelope, packet, etc.). **2** direct in speech or writing (remarks, a protest, etc.). **3** speak or write to, esp. formally (*addressed the audience; asked me how to address a duke*). **4** direct one's attention to. **5** *Golf* take aim at or prepare to hit (the ball). □ **address oneself to 1** speak or write to. **2** attend to. □ **addresser** *n.* [ME f. OF *adresser* ult. f. L (as AD-, *directus* DIRECT): (n.) perh. f. F *adresse*]

addressee /ˌædre'siː/ *n.* the person to whom something (esp. a letter) is addressed.

adduce /ə'djuːs/ *v.tr.* cite as an instance or as proof or evidence. □ **adducible** *adj.* [L *adducere adduct*- (as AD-, *ducere* lead)]

-ade[1] /eɪd/ *suffix* forming nouns: **1** an action done (*blockade; tirade*). **2** the body concerned in an action or process (*cavalcade*). **3** the product or result of a material or action (*arcade; lemonade; masquerade*). [from or after F -*ade* f. Prov., Sp., or Port. -*ada* or It. -*ata* f. L -*ata* fem. sing. past part. of verbs in -*are*]

-ade[2] /eɪd/ *suffix* forming nouns (*decade*) (cf. -AD[1]). [F -*ade* f. Gk -*as* -*ada*]

-ade[3] /eɪd/ *suffix* forming nouns: **1** = -ADE[1] (*brocade*). **2** a person concerned (*renegade*). [Sp. or Port. -*ado*, masc. form of -*ada*: see -ADE[1]]

adenine /'ædəˌniːn/ *n.* a purine derivative found in all living tissue as a component base of DNA or RNA. [G *Adenin* formed as ADENOIDS: see -INE[4]]

adenoids /'ædɪˌnɔɪdz/ *n.pl. Med.* a mass of enlarged lymphatic tissue between the back of the nose and the throat, often hindering speaking and breathing in the young. □ **adenoidal** /-'nɔɪd(ə)l/ *adj.* **adenoidally** /-'nɔɪdəlɪ/ *adv.* [Gk *adēn -enos* gland + -OID]

adept /'ædept, ə'dept/ *adj.* & *n.* —*adj.* (foll. by *at, in*) thoroughly proficient. —*n.* a skilled performer; an expert. □ **adeptly** *adv.* **adeptness** *n.* [L *adeptus* past part. of *adipisci* attain]

adequate /'ædɪkwət/ *adj.* **1** sufficient, satisfactory. **2** (foll. by *to*) proportionate. **3** barely sufficient. □ **adequacy** *n.* **adequately** *adv.* [L *adaequatus* past part. of *adaequare* make equal (as AD-, *aequus* equal)]

adhere /əd'hɪə(r)/ *v.intr.* **1** (usu. foll. by *to*) (of a substance) stick fast to a surface, another substance, etc. **2** (foll. by *to*) behave according to; follow in detail (*adhered to our plan*). **3** (foll. by *to*) give support or allegiance. [F *adhérer* or L *adhaerēre* (as AD-, *haerēre haes*- stick)]

adherent /əd'hɪərənt/ *n.* & *adj.* —*n.* **1** a supporter of a party, person, etc. **2** a devotee of an activity —*adj.* **1** (foll. by *to*) faithfully observing a rule etc. **2** (often foll. by *to*) (of a substance) sticking fast. □ **adherence** *n.* [F *adhérent* (as ADHERE)]

adhesion /əd'hiːʒ(ə)n/ *n.* **1** the act or process of adhering. **2** the capacity of a substance to stick fast. **3** *Med.* a union of surfaces due to inflammation. **4** the maintenance of contact between the wheels of a vehicle and the road. **5** the giving of support or allegiance. [F *adhésion* or L *adhaesio* (as ADHERE)]

adhesive /əd'hiːsɪv/ *adj.* & *n.* —*adj.* sticky, enabling surfaces or substances to adhere to one another. —*n.* an adhesive substance, esp. one used to stick other substances together. □ **adhesively** *adv.* **adhesiveness** *n.* [F *adhésif -ive* (as ADHERE)]

ad hoc /æd 'hɒk/ *adv.* & *adj.* for a particular (usu. exclusive) purpose (*an ad hoc appointment*). [L, = to this]

ad hominem /æd 'hɒmɪˌnem/ *adv.* & *adj.* **1** relating to or associated with a particular person. **2** (of an argument) appealing to the emotions and not to reason. [L, = to the person]

adiabatic /ˌeɪdɪə'bætɪk/ *adj.* & *n. Physics* —*adj.* **1** impassable to heat. **2** occurring without heat entering or leaving the system. —*n.* a curve or formula for adiabatic phenomena. □ **adiabatically** *adv.* [Gk *adiabatos* impassable (as A-[1], *diabainō* pass)]

adiantum /ˌædɪ'æntəm/ *n.* **1** any fern of the genus *Adiantum*, e.g. maidenhair. **2** (in general use) a spleenwort. [L f. Gk *adianton* maidenhair (as A-¹, *diantos* wettable)]

adieu /əˈdjuː/ *int.* & *n.* —*int.* goodbye. —*n.* (*pl.* **adieus** or **adieux** /əˈdjuːz/) a goodbye. [ME f. OF f. *à* to + *Dieu* God)]

ad infinitum /ˌæd ˌɪnfɪˈnaɪtəm/ *adv.* without limit; for ever. [L]

adipose /ˈædɪpəʊz/ *adj.* of or characterized by fat; fatty. □ **adipose tissue** fatty connective tissue in animals. □ **adiposity** /-ˈpɒsɪtɪ/ *n.* [mod.L *adiposus* f. *adeps adipis* fat]

adit /ˈædɪt/ *n.* **1** a horizontal entrance or passage in a mine. **2** a means of approach. [L *aditus* (as AD-, *itus* f. *ire it-* go)]

adjacent /əˈdʒeɪs(ə)nt/ *adj.* (often foll. by *to*) lying near or adjoining. □ **adjacency** *n.* [ME f. L *adjacēre* (as AD-, *jacēre* lie)]

adjective /ˈædʒɪktɪv/ *n.* a word or phrase naming an attribute, added to or grammatically related to a noun to modify it or describe it. □ **adjectival** /ˌædʒɪkˈtaɪv(ə)l/ *adj.* **adjectivally** /ˌædʒɪkˈtaɪvəlɪ/ *adv.* [ME f. OF *adjectif -ive* ult. f. L *adjicere adject-* (as AD-, *jacere* throw)]

adjoin /əˈdʒɔɪn/ *v.tr.* be next to and joined with. [ME f. OF *ajoindre*, *ajoign-* f. L *adjungere adjunct-* (as AD-, *jungere* join)]

adjourn /əˈdʒɜːn/ *v.* **1** *tr.* **a** put off; postpone. **b** break off (a meeting, discussion, etc.) with the intention of resuming later. **2** *intr.* of persons at a meeting: **a** break off proceedings and disperse. **b** (foll. by *to*) transfer the meeting to another place. [ME f. OF *ajorner* (as AD-, *jorn* day ult. f. L *diurnus* DIURNAL): cf. JOURNAL, JOURNEY]

adjournment /əˈdʒɜːnmənt/ *n.* adjourning or being adjourned.

adjudge /əˈdʒʌdʒ/ *v.tr.* **1** adjudicate (a matter). **2** (often foll. by *that* + clause, or *to* + infin.) pronounce judicially. **3** (foll. by *to*) award judicially. □ **adjudgement** *n.* (also **adjudgment**). [ME f. OF *ajuger* f. L *adjudicare*: see ADJUDICATE]

adjudicate /əˈdʒuːdɪˌkeɪt/ *v.* **1** *intr.* act as judge in a competition, court, tribunal, etc. **2** *tr.* **a** decide judicially regarding (a claim etc.). **b** (foll. by *to be* + compl.) pronounce (*was adjudicated to be bankrupt*). □ **adjudication** /-ˈkeɪʃ(ə)n/ *n.* **adjudicative** *adj.* **adjudicator** *n.* [L *adjudicare* (as AD-, *judicare* f. *judex -icis* judge)]

adjunct /ˈædʒʌŋkt/ *n.* **1** (foll. by *to*, *of*) a subordinate or incidental thing. **2** an assistant; a subordinate person, esp. one with temporary appointment only. □ **adjunctive** /əˈdʒʌŋktɪv/ *adj.* **adjunctively** /əˈdʒʌŋktɪvlɪ/ *adv.* [L *adjunctus*: see ADJOIN]

adjure /əˈdʒʊə(r)/ *v.tr.* (usu. foll. by *to* + infin.) charge or request (a person) solemnly or earnestly, esp. under oath. □ **adjuration** /ˌædʒʊəˈreɪʃ(ə)n/ *n.* **adjuratory** /-rətərɪ/ *adj.* [ME f. L *adjurare* (as AD-, *jurare* swear) in LL sense 'put a person to an oath']

adjust /əˈdʒʌst/ *v.* **1** *tr.* **a** arrange; put in the correct order or position. **b** regulate, esp. by a small amount. **2** *tr.* (usu. foll. by *to*) make suitable. **3** *tr.* harmonize (discrepancies). **4** *tr.* assess (loss or damages). **5** *intr.* (usu. foll. by *to*) make oneself suited to (*adjust to one's surroundings*). □ **adjustable** *adj.* **adjustability** /-ˈbɪlɪtɪ/ *n.* **adjuster** *n.* **adjustment** *n.* [F *adjuster* f. OF *ajoster* ult. f. L *juxta* near]

adjutant /ˈædʒʊt(ə)nt/ *n.* **1 a** Mil. an officer who assists superior officers by communicating orders, conducting correspondence, etc. **b** an

assistant. **2** (in full **adjutant bird**) a giant Indian stork. □ **Adjutant-General** a high-ranking Army administrative officer. □ **adjutancy** *n.* [L *adjutare* frequent. of *adjuvare* (as AD-, *juvare jut-* help)]

ad lib /æd ˈlɪb/ *v.*, *adj.*, *adv.*, & *n.* —*v.intr.* (**ad libbed**, **ad libbing**) speak or perform without formal preparation; improvise. —*adj.* improvised. —*adv.* as one pleases, to any desired extent. —*n.* something spoken or played extempore. [abbr. of L *ad libitum* according to pleasure]

adman /ˈædmæn/ *n.* (*pl.* **admen**) *colloq.* a person who produces advertisements commercially.

admass /ˈædmæs/ *n.* esp. *Brit.* the section of the community that is regarded as readily influenced by advertising and mass communication.

admeasure /ədˈmeʒə(r)/ *v.tr.* apportion; assign in due shares. □ **admeasurement** *n.* [ME f. OF *amesurer* f. med.L *admensurare* (as AD-, MEASURE)]

admin /ˈædmɪn/ *n.* *colloq.* administration. [abbr.]

administer /ədˈmɪnɪstə(r)/ *v.* **1** *tr.* attend to the running of (business affairs etc.); manage. **2** *tr.* **a** be responsible for the implementation of (the law, justice, punishment, etc.). **b** *Eccl.* give out, or perform the rites of (a sacrament). **c** (usu. foll. by *to*) direct the taking of (an oath). **3** *tr.* **a** provide, apply (a remedy). **b** give, deliver (a rebuke). **4** *intr.* act as administrator. □ **administrable** *adj.* [ME f. OF *aministrer* f. L *administrare* (as AD-, MINISTER)]

administrate /ədˈmɪnɪˌstreɪt/ *v.tr.* & *intr.* administer (esp. business affairs); act as an administrator. [L *administrare* (as ADMINISTER)]

administration /ədˌmɪnɪˈstreɪʃ(ə)n/ *n.* **1** management of a business. **2** the management of public affairs; government. **3** the government in power; the ministry. **4** *US* a President's period of office. **5** *Law* the management of another person's estate. **6** (foll. by *of*) **a** the administering of justice, an oath, etc. **b** application of remedies. [ME f. OF *administration* or L *administratio* (as ADMINISTRATE)]

administrative /ədˈmɪnɪstrətɪv/ *adj.* concerning or relating to the management of affairs. □ **administratively** *adv.* [F *administratif -ive* or L *administrativus* (as ADMINISTRATION)]

administrator /ədˈmɪnɪˌstreɪtə(r)/ *n.* **1** a person who administers a business or public affairs. **2** a person capable of organizing. **3** *Law* a person appointed to manage the estate of a person who has died intestate. □ **administratorship** *n.* **administratrix** *n.* [L (as ADMINISTER)]

admirable /ˈædmərəb(ə)l/ *adj.* **1** deserving admiration. **2** excellent. □ **admirably** *adv.* [F f. L *admirabilis* (as ADMIRE)]

admiral /ˈædmər(ə)l/ *n.* **1 a** the commander-in-chief of a country's navy. **b** a naval officer of high rank, the commander of a fleet or squadron. **c** (**Admiral**) an admiral of the second grade. **2** any of various butterflies (*red admiral*; *white admiral*). □ **Admiral of the Fleet** an admiral of the first grade. **Fleet Admiral** *US* = *Admiral of the Fleet.* □ **admiralship** *n.* [ME f. OF *a(d)mira(i)l* etc. f. med.L *a(d)miralis* etc., f. Arab. *ʼamīr* commander (cf. AMIR), assoc. with ADMIRABLE]

Admiralty /ˈædmərəltɪ/ *n.* (*pl.* **-ies**) **1** (*hist.* except in titles) (in the UK) the department administering the Royal Navy. **2** (**admiralty**) *Law* trial and decision of maritime questions and offences. [ME f. OF *admiral(i)té* (as ADMIRAL)]

admiration /ˌædmɪˈreɪʃ(ə)n/ *n.* **1** pleased contemplation. **2** respect, warm approval. **3** an object of this (*was the admiration of the whole town*). [F *admiration* or L *admiratio* (as ADMIRE)]

admire /ədˈmaɪə(r)/ *v.tr.* **1** regard with approval, respect, or satisfaction. **2** express admiration of. [F *admirer* or L *admirari* (as AD-, *mirari* wonder at)]

admirer /ədˈmaɪərə(r)/ *n.* **1** a woman's suitor. **2** a person who admires, esp. a devotee of an able or famous person.

admiring /ədˈmaɪərɪŋ/ *adj.* showing or feeling admiration (*an admiring follower; admiring glances*). □ **admiringly** *adv.*

admissible /ədˈmɪsɪb(ə)l/ *adj.* **1** (of an idea or plan) worth accepting or considering. **2** *Law* allowable as evidence. **3** (foll. by *to*) capable of being admitted. □ **admissibility** /-ˈbɪlɪtɪ/ *n.* [F *admissible* or med.L *admissibilis* (as ADMIT)]

admission /ədˈmɪʃ(ə)n/ *n.* **1** an acknowledgement. **2 a** the process or right of entering. **b** a charge for this (*admission is £5*). **3** a person admitted to a hospital. [ME f. L *admissio* (as ADMIT)]

admit /ədˈmɪt/ *v.* (**admitted, admitting**) **1** *tr.* (often foll. by *to be, to that* + clause) acknowledge; recognize as true. **b** accept as valid or true. **2** *intr.* (foll. by *to*) acknowledge responsibility for a deed, fault, etc. **3** *tr.* **a** allow (a person) entrance or access. **b** allow (a person) to be a member of (a class, group, etc.) or to share in (a privilege etc.). **c** (of a hospital etc.) bring in (a person) for residential treatment. **4** *tr.* (of an enclosed space) have room for; accommodate. **5** *intr.* (foll. by *of*) allow as possible. [ME f. L *admittere admiss-* (as AD-, *mittere* send)]

admittance /ədˈmɪt(ə)ns/ *n.* the right or process of admitting or being admitted, usu. to a place (*no admittance except on business*).

admittedly /ədˈmɪtɪdlɪ/ *adv.* as an acknowledged fact (*admittedly there are problems*).

admix /ædˈmɪks/ *v.* **1** *tr.* & *intr.* (foll. by *with*) mingle. **2** *tr.* add as an ingredient.

admixture /ædˈmɪkstʃə(r)/ *n.* **1** a thing added, esp. a minor ingredient. **2** the act of adding this. [L *admixtus* past part. of *admiscēre* (as AD-, *miscēre* mix)]

admonish /ədˈmɒnɪʃ/ *v.tr.* **1** reprove. **2** (foll. by *to* + infin., or *that* + clause) urge. **3** give advice to. **4** (foll. by *of*) warn. □ **admonishment** *n.* **admonition** /ˌædmə'nɪʃ(ə)n/ *n.* **admonitory** *adj.* [ME f. OF *amonester* ult. f. L *admonēre* (as AD-, *monēre monit-* warn)]

ad nauseam /æd ˈnɔːzɪˌæm, ˈnɔːsɪˌæm/ *adv.* to an excessive or disgusting degree. [L, = to sickness]

ado /əˈduː/ *n.* (*pl.* **ados**) fuss, busy activity; trouble, difficulty. [orig. in *much ado* = much to do, f. north. ME *at do* (= to do) f. ON *at* AT as sign of infin. + DO¹]

adobe /əˈdəʊbɪ, əˈdəʊb/ *n.* **1** an unburnt sun-dried brick. **2** the clay used for making such bricks. [Sp. f. Arab.]

adolescent /ˌædəˈles(ə)nt/ *adj.* & *n.* —*adj.* between childhood and adulthood. —*n.* an adolescent person. □ **adolescence** *n.* [ME OF f. L *adolescere* grow up]

adopt /əˈdɒpt/ *v.tr.* **1** take (a person) into a relationship, esp. another's child as one's own. **2** choose to follow (a course of action etc.). **3** take over (an idea etc.) from another person. **4** choose as a candidate for office. **5** *Brit.* (of a local authority) accept responsibility for the maintenance of (a road etc.). **6** accept; formally approve (a report, accounts, etc.). □ **adoption** *n.* [F *adopter* or L *adoptare* (as AD-, *optare* choose)]

adoptive /əˈdɒptɪv/ *adj.* due to adoption (*adoptive son; adoptive father*). □ **adoptively** *adv.* [ME f. OF *adoptif -ive* f. L *adoptivus* (as ADOPT)]

adorable /əˈdɔːrəb(ə)l/ *adj.* **1** deserving adoration. **2** *colloq.* delightful, charming. □ **adorably** *adv.* [F f. L *adorabilis* (as ADORE)]

adore /əˈdɔː(r)/ *v.tr.* **1** regard with honour and deep affection. **2** worship as divine. **3** *colloq.* like very much. □ **adoration** /ˌædəˈreɪʃ(ə)n/ *n.* **adoring** *adj.* **adoringly** *adv.* [ME f. OF *aourer* f. L *adorare* worship (as AD-, *orare* speak, pray)]

adorer /əˈdɔːrə(r)/ *n.* **1** a worshipper. **2** an ardent admirer.

adorn /əˈdɔːn/ *v.tr.* **1** add beauty or lustre to; be an ornament to. **2** furnish with ornaments; decorate. □ **adornment** *n.* [ME f. OF *ao(u)rner* f. L *adornare* (as AD-, *ornare* furnish, deck)]

adrenal /əˈdriːn(ə)l/ *adj.* & *n.* —*adj.* **1** at or near the kidneys. **2** of the adrenal glands. —*n.* (in full **adrenal gland**) either of two ductless glands above the kidneys, secreting adrenalin. [AD- + RENAL]

adrenalin /əˈdrenəlɪn/ *n.* (also **adrenaline**) **1** a hormone secreted by the adrenal glands, affecting circulation and muscular action, and causing excitement and stimulation. **2** the same substance obtained from animals or by synthesis, used as a stimulant.

adrift /əˈdrɪft/ *adv.* & *predic.adj.* **1** drifting. **2** at the mercy of circumstances. **3** *colloq.* **a** unfastened. **b** out of touch. **c** absent without leave. **d** (often foll. by *of*) failing to reach a target. **e** out of order. **f** ill-informed. [A² + DRIFT]

adroit /əˈdrɔɪt/ *adj.* dextrous, skilful. □ **adroitly** *adv.* **adroitness** *n.* [F f. *à droit* according to right]

adsorb /ədˈsɔːb/ *v.tr.* (usu. of a solid) hold (molecules of a gas or liquid or solute) to its surface, causing a thin film to form. □ **adsorbable** *adj.* **adsorbent** *adj.* & *n.* **adsorption** *n.* (also **adsorbtion**). [AD-, after ABSORB]

adsuki var. of ADZUKI.

adulate /ˈædjʊˌleɪt/ *v.tr.* flatter obsequiously. □ **adulation** /-ˈleɪʃ(ə)n/ *n.* **adulator** *n.* **adulatory** *adj.* [L *adulari adulat-* fawn on]

adult /ˈædʌlt, əˈdʌlt/ *adj.* & *n.* —*adj.* **1** mature, grown-up. **2 a** of or for adults (*adult education*). **b** *euphem.* sexually explicit; indecent (*adult films*). —*n.* **1** an adult person. **2** *Law* a person who has reached the age of majority. □ **adulthood** *n.* **adultly** *adv.* [L *adultus* past part. of *adolescere* grow up: cf. ADOLESCENT]

adulterant /əˈdʌltərənt/ *adj.* & *n.* —*adj.* used in adulterating. —*n.* an adulterant substance.

adulterate *v.* & *adj.* —*v.tr.* /əˈdʌltəˌreɪt/ debase (esp. foods) by adding other or inferior substances. —*adj.* /əˈdʌltərət/ spurious, debased, counterfeit. □ **adulteration** /-ˈreɪʃ(ə)n/ *n.* **adulterator** *n.* [L *adulterare adulterat-* corrupt]

adulterer /əˈdʌltərə(r)/ *n.* (*fem.* **adulteress** /-ərɪs/) a person who commits adultery. [obs. *adulter* (v.) f. OF *avoutrer* f. L *adulterare*: see ADULTERATE]

adulterous /ə'dʌltərəs/ adj. of or involved in adultery. □ **adulterously** adv. [ME f. adulter: see ADULTERER]

adultery /ə'dʌltəri/ n. voluntary sexual intercourse between a married person and a person (married or not) other than his or her spouse. [ME f. OF avoutrie etc. f. avoutre adulterer f. L adulter, assim. to L adulterium]

adumbrate /'ædʌm,breit/ v.tr. 1 indicate faintly. 2 represent in outline. 3 foreshadow, typify. 4 overshadow. □ **adumbration** /-'breiʃ(ə)n/ n. **adumbrative** /ə'dʌmbrətiv/ adj. [L adumbrare (as AD-, umbrare f. umbra shade)]

advance /əd'vɑːns/ v., n., & adj. —v. 1 tr. & intr. move or put forward. 2 intr. make progress. 3 tr. **a** pay (money) before it is due. **b** lend (money). 4 tr. give active support to; promote (a person, cause, or plan). 5 tr. put forward (a claim or suggestion). 6 tr. cause (an event) to occur at an earlier date (advanced the meeting three hours). 7 tr. raise (a price). 8 intr. rise (in price). 9 tr. as **advanced** adj. **a** far on in progress (the work is well advanced). **b** ahead of the times (advanced ideas). —n. 1 an act of going forward. 2 progress. 3 a payment made before the due time. 4 a loan. 5 (esp. in pl.; often foll. by to) an amorous or friendly approach. 6 a rise in price. —attrib.adj. done or supplied beforehand (advance warning; advance copy). □ **advanced** (or **advanced supplementary) level** (in the UK) a GCE examination of a standard higher than ordinary level and GCSE. **advance guard** a body of soldiers preceding the main body of an army. **advance on** approach threateningly. **in advance** ahead in place or time. □ **advancer** n. [ME f. OF avancer f. LL abante in front f. L ab away + ante before: (n.) partly through F avance]

advancement /əd'vɑːnsmənt/ n. the promotion of a person, cause, or plan. [ME f. F avancement f. avancer (as ADVANCE)]

advantage /əd'vɑːntɪdʒ/ n. & v. —n. 1 a beneficial feature; a favourable circumstance. 2 benefit, profit (is not to your advantage). 3 (often foll. by over) a better position; superiority in a particular respect. 4 (in lawn tennis) the next point won after deuce. —v.tr. 1 be beneficial or favourable to. 2 further, promote. □ **take advantage of 1** make good use of (a favourable circumstance). 2 exploit or outwit (a person), esp. unfairly. 3 euphem. seduce. □ **advantageous** /,ædvən'teɪdʒəs/ adj. **advantageously** /,ædvən'teɪdʒəsli/ adv. [ME f. OF avantage, avantager f. avant in front f. LL abante: see ADVANCE]

Advent /'ædvent/ n. 1 the season before Christmas, including the four preceding Sundays. 2 the coming or second coming of Christ. 3 (**advent**) the arrival of esp. an important person or thing. □ **Advent calendar** Brit. a calendar for Advent, usu. of card with flaps to open each day revealing a picture or scene. **Advent Sunday** the first Sunday in Advent. [OE f. OF advent, auvent f. L adventus arrival f. advenire (as AD-, venire vent- come)]

Adventist /'ædventɪst/ n. a member of a Christian sect that believes in the imminent second coming of Christ. □ **Adventism** n.

adventitious /,ædven'tɪʃəs/ adj. 1 accidental, casual. 2 added from outside. 3 Biol. formed accidentally or under unusual conditions. □ **adventitiously** adv. [L adventicius (as ADVENT)]

adventure /əd'ventʃə(r)/ n. & v.—n. 1 an unusual and exciting experience. 2 a daring enterprise; a hazardous activity. 3 enterprise (the spirit of adventure). 4 a commercial speculation. —v.intr. 1 (often foll. by into, upon) dare to go or come. 2 (foll. by on, upon) dare to undertake. 3 incur risk; engage in adventure. □ **adventure playground** a playground where children are provided with functional materials for climbing on, building with, etc. □ **adventuresome** adj. [ME f. OF aventure, aventurer f. L adventurus about to happen (as ADVENT)]

adventurer /əd'ventʃərə(r)/ n. (fem. **adventuress** /-ərɪs/) 1 a person who seeks adventure, esp. for personal gain or enjoyment. 2 a financial speculator. [F aventurier (as ADVENTURE)]

adventurism /əd'ventʃə,rɪz(ə)m/ n. a tendency to take risks, esp. in foreign policy. □ **adventurist** n.

adventurous /əd'ventʃərəs/ adj. 1 rash, venturesome; enterprising. 2 characterized by adventures. □ **adventurously** adv. **adventurousness** n. [ME f. OF aventuros (as ADVENTURE)]

adverb /'ædvɜːb/ n. a word or phrase that modifies or qualifies another word (esp. an adjective, verb, or other adverb) or a word-group, expressing a relation of place, time, circumstance, manner, cause, degree, etc. □ **adverbial** /əd'vɜːbɪəl/ adj. [F adverbe or L adverbium (as AD-, VERB)]

adversarial /,ædvə'seərɪəl/ adj. 1 involving conflict or opposition. 2 opposed, hostile. [ADVERSARY + -IAL]

adversary /'ædvəsərɪ/ n. (pl. -ies) 1 an enemy. 2 an opponent in a sport or game; an antagonist. [ME f. OF adversarie f. L adversarius f. adversus: see ADVERSE]

adverse /'ædvɜːs/ adj. (often foll. by to) 1 contrary, hostile. 2 hurtful, injurious. □ **adversely** adv. **adverseness** n. [ME f. OF advers f. L adversus past part. of advertere (as AD-, vertere vers- turn)]

adversity /əd'vɜːsɪtɪ/ n. (pl. -ies) 1 the condition of adverse fortune. 2 a misfortune. [ME f. OF adversité f. L adversitas -tatis (as ADVERSE)]

advert[1] /'ædvɜːt/ n. Brit. colloq. an advertisement. [abbr.]

advert[2] /əd'vɜːt/ v.intr. (foll. by to) literary refer in speaking or writing. [ME f. OF avertir f. L advertere: see ADVERSE]

advertise /'ædvə,taɪz/ v. 1 tr. draw attention to or describe favourably (goods or services) in a public medium to promote sales. 2 tr. make generally or publicly known. 3 intr. (foll. by for) seek by public notice, esp. in a newspaper. 4 tr. (usu. foll. by of, or that + clause) notify. □ **advertiser** n. [ME f. OF avertir (stem advertiss-): see ADVERT[2]]

advertisement /əd'vɜːtɪsmənt, -tɪzmənt/ n. 1 a public notice or announcement, esp. one advertising goods or services in newspapers, on posters, or in broadcasts. 2 the act or process of advertising. [earlier avert- f. F avertissement (as ADVERTISE)]

advice /əd'vaɪs/ n. 1 words given or offered as an opinion or recommendation about future action or behaviour. 2 information given; news. 3 formal notice of a transaction. [ME f. OF avis f. L ad to + visum past part. of vidēre see]

advisable /əd'vaɪzəb(ə)l/ adj. 1 (of a course of action etc.) to be recommended. 2 expedient. □ **advisability** /-'bɪlɪtɪ/ n. **advisably** adv.

advise /əd'vaɪz/ v. **1** tr. (also *absol.*) give advice to. **2** tr. recommend; offer as advice (*advised me to rest*). **3** tr. (usu. foll. by *of*, or *that* + clause) inform, notify. **4** intr. (foll. by *with*) *US* consult. [ME f. OF *aviser* f. L *ad* to + *visare* frequent. of *vidēre* see]

advised /əd'vaɪzd/ adj. **1** judicious (*well-advised*). **2** deliberate, considered. □ **advisedly** /-zɪdlɪ/ adv.

adviser /əd'vaɪzə(r)/ n. (also *disp.* **advisor**) **1** a person who advises, esp. one appointed to do so and regularly consulted. **2** *US* a person who advises students on education, careers, etc.

■ **Usage** The variant *advisor* is fairly common, but is considered incorrect by many people.

advisory /əd'vaɪzərɪ/ adj. **1** giving advice; constituted to give advice (*an advisory body*). **2** consisting in giving advice.

advocaat /ˌædvə'kɑːt/ n. a liqueur of eggs, sugar, and brandy. [Du., = ADVOCATE (being orig. an advocate's drink)]

advocacy /'ædvəkəsɪ/ n. **1** (usu. foll. by *of*) verbal support or argument for a cause, policy, etc. **2** the function of an advocate. [ME f. OF *a(d)vocacie* f. med.L *advocatia* (as ADVOCATE)]

advocate n. & v. —n. /'ædvəkət/ **1** (foll. by *of*) a person who supports or speaks in favour. **2** a person who pleads for another. **3** a a professional pleader in a court of justice. **b** *Sc.* a barrister. —v.tr. /'ædvə,keɪt/ **1** support by argument (a cause, policy, etc.). **2** plead for, defend. □ **advocateship** n. **advocatory** /'ædvə,keɪtərɪ/ adj. [ME f. OF *avocat* f. L *advocatus* past part. of *advocare* (as AD-, *vocare* call)]

adze /ædz/ n. & v. (*US* **adz**) —n. a tool for cutting away the surface of wood, like an axe with an arched blade at right angles to the handle. —v.tr. dress or cut with an adze. [OE *adesa*]

adzuki /əd'zuːkɪ/ n. (also **adsuki**, **azuki**) **1** a leguminous plant, *Vigna angularis*, native to China and Japan. **2** the red edible bean of this plant. [Jap. *azuki*]

aegis /'iːdʒɪs/ n. a protection; an impregnable defence. □ **under the aegis of** under the auspices of. [L f. Gk *aigis* mythical shield of Zeus or Athene]

aegrotat /'iːgrəʊ,tæt/ n. *Brit.* **1** a certificate that a university student is too ill to attend an examination. **2** an examination pass awarded in such circumstances. [L, = is sick f. *aeger* sick]

aeolian /iː'əʊlɪən/ adj. (*US* **eolian**) wind-borne. □ **aeolian harp** a stringed instrument or toy that produces musical sounds when the wind passes through it. [L *Aeolius* f. *Aeolus* god of the winds f. Gk *Aiolos*]

aeon /'iːɒn/ n. (also **eon**) **1** a very long or indefinite period. **2** an age of the universe. **3** *Astron.* a thousand million years. [eccl.L f. Gk *aiōn* age]

aerate /'eəreɪt/ v.tr. **1** charge (a liquid) with a gas, esp. carbon dioxide, e.g. to produce effervescence. **2** expose to the mechanical or chemical action of the air. □ **aeration** /-'reɪʃ(ə)n/ n. **aerator** n. [L *aer* AIR + -ATE³, after F *aérer*]

aerial /'eərɪəl/ n. & adj. —n. a metal rod, wire, or other structure by which signals are transmitted or received as part of a radio transmission or receiving system. —adj. **1** by or from or involving aircraft (*aerial navigation*; *aerial photography*). **2** a existing, moving, or happening in the air. **b** of or in the atmosphere, atmospheric. □ **aeriality** /-'ælɪtɪ/ n. **aerially** adv. [L *aerius* f. Gk *aerios* f. *aēr* air]

aerialist /'eərɪəlɪst/ n. a high-wire or trapeze artist.

aerie var. of EYRIE.

aero- /'eərəʊ/ comb. form **1** air. **2** aircraft. [Gk *aero-* f. *aēr* air]

aerobatics /ˌeərə'bætɪks/ n.pl. **1** feats of expert and usu. spectacular flying and manoeuvring of aircraft. **2** (as *sing.*) a performance of these. [AERO- + ACROBATICS]

aerobe /'eərəʊb/ n. a micro-organism usu. growing in the presence of air, or needing air for growth. [F *aérobie* (as AERO-, Gk *bios* life)]

aerobic /eə'rəʊbɪk, eə'rɒb-/ adj. **1** of or relating to aerobics. **2** of or relating to aerobes.

aerobics /eə'rəʊbɪks/ n.pl. vigorous exercises designed to increase the body's oxygen intake.

aerodrome /'eərə,drəʊm/ n. *Brit.* a small airport or airfield.

aerodynamics /ˌeərəʊdaɪ'næmɪks/ n.pl. (usu. treated as *sing.*) the study of the interaction between the air and solid bodies moving through it. □ **aerodynamic** adj. **aerodynamically** adv. **aerodynamicist** n.

aerofoil /'eərə,fɔɪl/ n. *Brit.* a structure with curved surfaces (e.g. a wing, fin, or tailplane) designed to give lift in flight.

aeronautics /ˌeərəʊ'nɔːtɪks/ n.pl. (usu. treated as *sing.*) the science or practice of motion or travel in the air. □ **aeronautic** adj. **aeronautical** adj. [mod.L *aeronautica* (as AERO-, NAUTICAL)]

aeroplane /'eərə,pleɪn/ n. esp. *Brit.* a powered heavier-than-air flying vehicle with fixed wings. [F *aéroplane* (as AERO-, PLANE¹)]

aerosol /'eərə,sɒl/ n. **1** a a container used to hold a substance packed under pressure with a device for releasing it as a fine spray. **b** the releasing device. **c** the substance contained in an aerosol. **2** a system of colloidal particles dispersed in a gas (e.g. fog or smoke). [AERO- + SOL²]

aerospace /'eərəʊ,speɪs/ n. **1** the earth's atmosphere and outer space. **2** the technology of aviation in this region.

aeruginous /ɪə'ruːdʒɪnəs/ adj. of the nature or colour of verdigris. [L *aeruginosus* f. *aerugo -inis* verdigris f. *aes aeris* bronze]

aesthete /'iːsθiːt/ n. (*US* **esthete**) a person who has or professes to have a special appreciation of beauty. [Gk *aisthētēs* one who perceives, or f. AESTHETIC]

aesthetic /iːs'θetɪk/ adj. & n. (*US* **esthetic**) —adj. **1** concerned with beauty or the appreciation of beauty. **2** having such appreciation; sensitive to beauty. **3** in accordance with the principles of good taste. —n. **1** (in *pl.*) the philosophy of the beautiful, esp. in art. **2** a set of principles of good taste and the appreciation of beauty. □ **aesthetically** adv. **aestheticism** /-,sɪz(ə)m/ n. [Gk *aisthētikos* f. *aisthanomai* perceive]

aestival /'estɪv(ə)l, e'staɪv(ə)l, iː'staɪv(ə)l/ adj. (*US* **estival**) *formal* belonging to or appearing in summer. [ME f. OF *estival* f. L *aestivalis* f. *aestivus* f. *aestus* heat]

aestivate /'estɪ,veɪt, 'iːs-/ v.intr. (*US* **estivate**) **1** *Zool.* spend the summer or dry season in a state of torpor. **2** *formal* pass the summer. **aestivation** n. [L *aestivare aestivat-*]

aether var. of ETHER 2, 3.

aetiology /ˌiːtɪˈɒlədʒɪ/ n. (US etiology) 1 the assignment of a cause or reason. 2 the philosophy of causation. 3 Med. the science of the causes of disease. □ **aetiologic** /-əˈlɒdʒɪk/ adj. **aetiological** /-əˈlɒdʒɪk(ə)l/ adj. **aetiologically** /-əˈlɒdʒɪkəlɪ/ adv. [LL aetiologia f. Gk aitiologia f. aitia cause]

AF abbr. audio frequency.

afar /əˈfɑː(r)/ adv. at or to a distance. □ **from afar** from a distance. [ME f. A-², A-⁴ + FAR]

affable /ˈæfəb(ə)l/ adj. 1 (of a person) approachable and friendly. 2 kind and courteous, esp. to inferiors. □ **affability** /-ˈbɪlɪtɪ/ n. **affably** adv. [F f. L affabilis f. affari (as AD-, fari speak)]

affair /əˈfeə(r)/ n. 1 a concern; a business; a matter to be attended to (that is my affair). 2 a celebrated or notorious happening or sequence of events. 3 = love affair. 4 (in pl.) a ordinary pursuits of life. b business dealings. c public matters (current affairs). [ME f. AF afere f. OF afaire f. à faire to do: cf. ADO]

affect¹ /əˈfekt/ v.tr. 1 a produce an effect on. b (of a disease etc.) attack (his liver is affected). 2 move; touch the feelings of (affected me deeply). □ **affecting** adj. **affectingly** adv. [F affecter or L afficere affect- influence (as AD-, facere do)]

■ **Usage** This word should not be confused with effect, meaning 'to bring about'. Note also that effect is used as a noun as well as a verb.

affect² /əˈfekt/ v.tr. 1 pretend to have or feel (affected indifference). 2 (foll. by to + infin.) pretend. 3 assume the character or manner of; pose as (affect the freethinker). 4 make a show of liking or using (she affects fancy hats). [F affecter or L affectare aim at, frequent. of afficere (as AFFECT¹)]

affectation /ˌæfekˈteɪʃ(ə)n/ n. 1 an assumed or contrived manner of behaviour, esp. in order to impress. 2 (foll. by of) a studied display. 3 pretence. [F affectation or L affectatio (as AFFECT²)]

affected /əˈfektɪd/ adj. 1 in senses of AFFECT¹, AFFECT². 2 artificially assumed or displayed; pretended (an affected air of innocence). 3 (of a person) full of affectation; artificial. □ **affectedly** adv.

affection /əˈfekʃ(ə)n/ n. 1 (often foll. by for, towards) goodwill; fond or kindly feeling. 2 a disease; a diseased condition. 3 a mental state; an emotion. 4 a mental disposition. 5 the act or process of affecting or being affected. □ **affectional** adj. (in sense 3). **affectionally** adv. [ME f. OF f. L affectio -onis (as AFFECT¹)]

affectionate /əˈfekʃənət/ adj. loving, fond; showing love or tenderness. □ **affectionately** adv. [F affectionné or med.L affectionatus (as AFFECTION)]

affective /əˈfektɪv/ adj. concerning the affections; emotional. □ **affectivity** /ˌæfekˈtɪvɪtɪ/ n. [F affectif -ive f. LL affectivus (as AFFECT¹)]

afferent /ˈæfərənt/ adj. Physiol. conducting inwards or towards (afferent nerves; afferent vessels). [L afferre (as AD-, ferre bring)]

affiance /əˈfaɪəns/ v.tr. (usu. in passive) literary promise solemnly to give (a person) in marriage. [ME f. OF afiancer f. med.L affidare (as AD-, fidus trusty)]

affidavit /ˌæfɪˈdeɪvɪt/ n. a written statement confirmed by oath, for use as evidence in court. [med.L, = has stated on oath, f. affidare: see AFFIANCE]

affiliate v. & n. —v. /əˈfɪlɪˌeɪt/ 1 tr. (usu. in passive; foll. by to, with) attach or connect (a person or society) with a larger organization. 2 tr. (of an institution) adopt (persons as members, societies as branches). 3 intr. a (foll. by to) associate oneself with a society. b (foll. by with) associate oneself with a political party. —n. /əˈfɪlɪˌeɪt, -lɪɪt/ an affiliated person or organization. [med.L affiliare adopt (as AD-, filius son]

affiliation /əˌfɪlɪˈeɪʃ(ə)n/ n. the act or process of affiliating or being affiliated. □ **affiliation order** Brit. a legal order that the man judged to be the father of an illegitimate child must help to support it. [F f. med.L affiliatio f. affiliare: see AFFILIATE]

affinity /əˈfɪnɪtɪ/ n. (pl. -ies) 1 (often foll. by between, or disp. to, for) a spontaneous or natural liking for or attraction to a person or thing. 2 relationship, esp. by marriage. 3 resemblance in structure between animals, plants, or languages. 4 a similarity of characters suggesting a relationship. 5 Chem. the tendency of certain substances to combine with others. [ME f. OF afinité f. L affinitas -tatis f. affinis related, lit. bordering on (as AD- + finis border)]

affirm /əˈfɜːm/ v. 1 tr. assert strongly; state as a fact. 2 intr. a Law make an affirmation. b make a formal declaration. □ **affirmatory** adj. **affirmer** n. [ME f. OF afermer f. L affirmare (as AD-, firmus strong)]

affirmation /ˌæfəˈmeɪʃ(ə)n/ n. 1 the act or process of affirming or being affirmed. 2 Law a declaration by a person who conscientiously declines to take an oath. [F affirmation or L affirmatio (as AFFIRM)]

affirmative /əˈfɜːmətɪv/ adj. & n. —adj. 1 affirming; asserting that a thing is so. 2 (of a vote) expressing approval. —n. 1 an affirmative statement, reply, or word. 2 (prec. by the) a positive or affirming position. □ **affirmative action** esp. US action favouring those who often suffer from discrimination. □ **affirmatively** adv. [ME f. OF affirmatif -ive f. LL affirmativus (as AFFIRM)]

affix v. & n. —v.tr. /əˈfɪks/ 1 (usu. foll. by to, on) attach, fasten. 2 add in writing (a signature or postscript). 3 impress (a seal or stamp). —n. /ˈæfɪks/ 1 an appendage; an addition. 2 Gram. an addition or element placed at the beginning (prefix) or end (suffix) of a root, stem, or word, or in the body of a word (infix), to modify its meaning. □ **affixture** /əˈfɪkstʃə(r)/ n. [F affixer, affixe or med.L affixare frequent. of L affigere (as AD-, figere fix- fix)]

afflict /əˈflɪkt/ v.tr. inflict bodily or mental suffering on. □ **afflicted with** suffering from. □ **afflictive** adj. [ME f. L afflictare, or afflict- past part. stem of affligere (as AD-, fligere flict- dash)]

affliction /əˈflɪkʃ(ə)n/ n. 1 physical or mental distress, esp. pain or illness. 2 a cause of this. [ME f. OF f. L afflictio -onis (as AFFLICT)]

affluence /ˈæfluəns/ n. an abundant supply of money, commodities, etc.; wealth. [ME f. F f. L affluentia f. affluere: see AFFLUENT]

affluent /ˈæfluənt/ adj. & n. —adj. 1 wealthy, rich. 2 abundant. 3 flowing freely or copiously. —n. a tributary stream. □ **affluently** adv. [ME OF f. L affluere (as AD-, fluere flux- flow)]

afford /əˈfɔːd/ v.tr. 1 (prec. by can or be able to; often foll. by to + infin.) a have enough money, means, time, etc., for; be able to spare (can afford

£50; can we afford to buy a television?). **b** be in a position to do something (*can't afford to let him think so*). **2** provide (*affords a view of the sea*). □

affordable *adj.* **affordability** /-'bɪlɪtɪ/ *n.* [ME f. OE *geforthian* promote (as Y-, FORTH), assim. to words in *af-* (see AD-)]

afforest /ə'fɒrɪst, æ-/ *v.tr.* **1** convert into forest. **2** plant with trees. □ **afforestation** /-'steɪʃ(ə)n/ *n.* [med.L *afforestare* (as AD-, *foresta* FOREST)]

affray /ə'freɪ/ *n.* a breach of the peace by fighting or rioting in public. [ME f. AF *afrayer* (v.) f. OF *esfreer* f. Rmc]

affront /ə'frʌnt/ *n.* & *v.* —*n.* an open insult. —*v.tr.* **1** insult openly. **2** offend the modesty or self-respect of. [ME f. OF *afronter* slap in the face, insult, ult. f. L *frons frontis* face]

Afghan /'æfgæn/ *n.* & *adj.* —*n.* **1 a** a native or national of Afghanistan. **b** a person of Afghan descent. **2** the official language of Afghanistan. **3** (**afghan**) a knitted and sewn woollen blanket or shawl. **4** (in full **Afghan coat**) a kind of sheepskin coat with the skin outside and usu. with a shaggy border. —*adj.* of or relating to Afghanistan or its people or language. □ **Afghan hound** a tall hunting dog with long silky hair. [Pashto *afghānī*]

aficionado /ə,fɪsjə'nɑːdəʊ/ *n.* (*pl.* **-os**) a devotee of a sport or pastime (orig. of bullfighting). [Sp.]

afield /ə'fiːld/ *adv.* away from home; to or at a distance (esp. *far afield*). [OE (as A², FIELD)]

afire /ə'faɪə(r)/ *adv.* & *predic.adj.* **1** on fire. **2** intensely roused or excited.

aflame /ə'fleɪm/ *adv.* & *predic.adj.* **1** in flames. **2** = AFIRE 2.

afloat /ə'fləʊt/ *adv.* & *predic.adj.* **1** floating in water or air. **2** at sea; on board ship. **3** out of debt or difficulty. **4** in general circulation; current. **5** full of or covered with a liquid. **6** in full swing. [OE (as A², FLOAT)]

afoot /ə'fʊt/ *adv.* & *predic.adj.* **1** in operation; progressing. **2** astir; on the move.

afore /ə'fɔː(r)/ *prep.* & *adv.* archaic before; previously; in front (of). [OE *onforan* (as A², FORE)]

afore- /ə'fɔː(r)/ *comb. form* before, previously (*aforementioned*); *aforesaid*).

aforethought /ə'fɔːθɔːt/ *adj.* premeditated (following a noun: *malice aforethought*).

a fortiori /eɪ fɔːtɪ'ɔːraɪ/ *adv.* & *adj.* with a yet stronger reason (than a conclusion already accepted); more conclusively. [L]

afraid /ə'freɪd/ *predic.adj.* **1** (often foll. by *of*, or *that* or *lest* + clause) alarmed, frightened. **2** (foll. by *to* + infin.) unwilling or reluctant for fear of the consequences (*was afraid to go in*). □ **be afraid** (foll. by *that* + clause) *colloq.* admit or declare with regret (*I'm afraid there's none left*). [ME, past part. of obs. *affray* (v.) f. AF *afrayer* f. OF *esfreer*]

afresh /ə'freʃ/ *adv.* anew; with a fresh beginning. [A-² + FRESH]

African /'æfrɪkən/ *n.* & *adj.* —*n.* **1** a native of Africa (esp. a dark-skinned person). **2** a person of African descent. —*adj.* of or relating to Africa. □ **African violet** a saintpaulia, *Saintpaulia ionantha*, with velvety leaves and blue, purple, or pink flowers. [L *Africanus*]

Afrikaans /,æfrɪ'kɑːns/ *n.* the language of the Afrikaner people developed from Cape Dutch, an official language of the Republic of South Africa. [Du., = African]

Afrikaner /,æfrɪ'kɑːnə(r)/ *n.* an Afrikaans-speaking White person in S. Africa, esp. one of Dutch descent. [Afrik. f. Du. *Afrikaner*]

Afro /'æfrəʊ/ *adj.* & *n.* —*adj.* (of a hairstyle) long and bushy, as naturally grown by some Blacks. —*n.* (*pl.* **-os**) an Afro hairstyle. [AFRO-, or abbr. of AFRICAN]

Afro- /'æfrəʊ/ *comb. form* African (*Afro-Asian*). [L *Afer Afr-* African]

afrormosia /,æfrɔː'məʊzɪə/ *n.* **1** an African tree, *Pericopsis* (formerly *Afrormosia*) *elata*, yielding a hard wood resembling teak and used for furniture. **2** this wood. [mod.L f. AFRO- + *Ormosia* genus of trees]

aft /ɑːft/ *adv.* *Naut.* & *Aeron.* at or towards the stern or tail. [prob. f. ME *baft*: see ABAFT]

after /'ɑːftə(r)/ *prep.*, *conj.*, *adv.*, & *adj.* —*prep.* **1 a** following in time; later than (*after six months*; *after midnight*; *day after day*). **b** *US* in specifying time (*a quarter after eight*). **2** (with causal force) in view of (something that happened shortly before) (*after your behaviour tonight what do you expect?*). **3** (with concessive force) in spite of (*after all my efforts I'm no better off*). **4** behind (*shut the door after you*). **5** in pursuit or quest of (*run after them*; *inquire after him*; *hanker after it*; *is after a job*). **6** about, concerning (*asked after her*; *asked after her health*). **7** in allusion to (*named him William after the prince*). **8** in imitation of (*a painting after Rubens*). **9** next in importance to (*the best book on the subject after mine*). **10** according to (*after a fashion*). —*conj.* in or at a time later than that when (*left after they arrived*). —*adv.* **1** later in time (*soon after*; *a week after*). **2** behind in place (*followed on after*; *look before and after*). —*adj.* **1** later, following (*in after years*). **2** *Naut.* nearer the stern (*after cabins*; *after mast*). □ **after all 1** in spite of all that has happened or has been said etc. (*after all, what does it matter?*). **2** in spite of one's exertions, expectations, etc. (*they tried for an hour and failed after all*; *so you have come after all!*).

after-care care of a patient after a stay in hospital or of a person on release from prison.

after-effect an effect that follows after an interval or after the primary action of something. **after-image** an image retained by a sense-organ, esp. the eye, and producing a sensation after the cessation of the stimulus. **after-taste** a taste remaining or recurring after eating or drinking. [OE *æfter* f. Gmc]

afterbirth /'ɑːftəbɜːθ/ *n.* *Med.* the placenta and foetal membranes discharged from the womb after childbirth.

afterburner /'ɑːftəbɜːnə(r)/ *n.* an auxiliary burner in a jet engine to increase thrust.

afterglow /'ɑːftəgləʊ/ *n.* a light or radiance remaining after its source has disappeared or been removed.

afterlife /'ɑːftəlaɪf/ *n.* **1** *Relig.* life after death. **2** life at a later time.

aftermath /'ɑːftəmæθ, -,mɑːθ/ *n.* **1** consequences; after-effects (*the aftermath of war*). **2** new grass growing after mowing or after a harvest. [AFTER *adj.* + *math* mowing f. OE *mæth* f. Gmc]

aftermost /'ɑːftəməʊst/ *adj.* **1** last. **2** *Naut.* furthest aft. [AFTER *adj.* + -MOST]

afternoon /,ɑːftə'nuːn, *attrib.* 'ɑːft-/ *n.* & *int.* —*n.* **1** the time from noon or lunch-time to evening (*this afternoon*; *during the afternoon*). **2** this time spent in a particular way (*had a lazy afternoon*). —*int.* = *good afternoon* (see GOOD *adj.* 14).

afters /ˈɑːftəz/ *n.pl. Brit. colloq.* the course following the main course of a meal.

aftershave /ˈɑːftəˌʃeɪv/ *n.* an astringent lotion for use after shaving.

afterthought /ˈɑːftəˌθɔːt/ *n.* an item or thing that is thought of or added later.

afterwards /ˈɑːftəwədz/ *adv.* (US **afterward**) later, subsequently. [OE *æftanwearde adj.* f. *æftan* AFT + -WARD]

afterword /ˈɑːftəˌwɜːd/ *n.* concluding remarks in a book, esp. by a person other than its author.

Ag *symb. Chem.* the element silver. [L *argentum*]

aga /ˈɑːgə/ *n.* (in Muslim countries, esp. under the Ottoman Empire) a commander, a chief. □ **Aga Khan** the spiritual leader of the Ismaili Muslims. [Turk. *ağa* master]

again /əˈgeɪn, əˈgen/ *adv.* **1** another time; once more. **2** as in a previous position or condition (*back again*; *quite well again*). **3** in addition (*half as many again*). **4** further, besides (*again, what about the children?*). **5** on the other hand (*I might, and again I might not*). [orig. a northern form of ME *ayen* etc., f. OE *ongēan, ongægn*, etc., f. Gmc]

against /əˈgeɪnst, əˈgenst/ *prep.* **1** in opposition to (*fight against the invaders*; *arson is against the law*). **2** into collision or in contact with (*ran against a rock*; *lean against the wall*). **3** to the disadvantage of (*his age is against him*). **4** in contrast to (*against a dark background*; *99 as against 102 yesterday*). **5** in anticipation of or preparation for (*against his coming*; *protected against the cold*). **6** as a compensating factor to (*income against expenditure*). **7** in return for (*issued against payment of the fee*). [ME *ayenes* etc. f. *ayen* AGAIN + -*t* as in *amongst*: see AMONG]

agapanthus /ˌægəˈpænθəs/ *n.* any African plant of the genus *Agapanthus*, esp. the ornamental African lily. [mod.L f. Gk *agapē* love + *anthos* flower]

agape[1] /əˈgeɪp/ *adv. & predic.adj.* gaping, open-mouthed, esp. with wonder or expectation.

agape[2] /ˈægəˌpeɪ/ *n.* **1** a Christian feast in token of fellowship, esp. one held by early Christians in commemoration of the Last Supper. **2** *Theol.* Christian fellowship, esp. as distinct from erotic love. [Gk, = brotherly love]

agar /ˈeɪgɑː(r)/ *n.* (also **agar-agar** /ˌeɪgɑːˈeɪgɑː(r)/) a gelatinous substance obtained from any of various kinds of red seaweed and used in food, micro- biological media, etc. [Malay]

agaric /ˈægərɪk/ *n.* any fungus of the family Agaricaceae, with cap and stalk, including the common edible mushroom. [L *agaricum* f. Gk *agarikon*]

agate /ˈægət/ *n.* any of several varieties of hard usu. streaked chalcedony. [F *agate, -the*, f. L *achates* f. Gk *akhatēs*]

agave /əˈgeɪvɪ/ *n.* any plant of the genus *Agave*, with rosettes of narrow spiny leaves, and tall inflorescences, e.g. the American aloe. [L f. Gk *Agauē*, proper name in myth f. *agauos* illustrious]

age *n. & v.* —*n.* **1 a** the length of time that a person or thing has existed or is likely to exist. **b** a particular point in or part of one's life, often as a qualification (*old age*; *voting age*). **2 a** *colloq.* (often in *pl.*) a long time (*took an age to answer*; *have been waiting for ages*). **b** a distinct period of the past (*golden age*; *Middle Ages*). **c** *Geol.* a period of time. **d** a generation. **3** the

latter part of life; old age (*the peevishness of age*). —*v.* (*pres. part.* **ageing, aging**) **1** *intr.* show signs of advancing age (*has aged a lot recently*). **2** *intr.* grow old. **3** *intr.* mature. **4** *tr.* cause or allow to age. □ **age-long** lasting for a very long time. **come of age** reach adult status (esp. in Law at 18, formerly 21). [ME f. OF ult. f. L *aetas -atis* age]

-age /ɪdʒ/ *suffix* forming nouns denoting: **1** an action (*breakage*; *spillage*). **2** a condition or function (*bondage*; *a peerage*). **3** an aggregate or number of (*coverage*; *the peerage*; *acreage*). **4** fees payable for; the cost of using (*postage*). **5** the product of an action (*dosage*; *wreckage*). **6** a place; an abode (*anchorage*; *orphanage*; *parsonage*). [OF ult. f. L *-aticum* neut. of *adj.* suffix *-aticus -ATIC*]

aged *adj.* **1** /eɪdʒd/ **a** of the age of (*aged ten*). **b** that has been subjected to ageing. **2** /ˈeɪdʒɪd/ having lived long; old.

ageing /ˈeɪdʒɪŋ/ *n.* (also **aging**) **1** growing old. **2** giving the appearance of advancing age.

ageism /ˈeɪdʒɪz(ə)m/ *n.* (also **agism**) prejudice or discrimination on the grounds of age. □ **ageist** *adj. & n.* (also **agist**).

ageless /ˈeɪdʒlɪs/ *adj.* **1** never growing or appearing old or outmoded. **2** eternal, timeless.

agency /ˈeɪdʒənsɪ/ *n.* (*pl.* -**ies**) **1 a** the business or establishment of an agent (*employment agency*). **b** the function of an agent. **2 a** active operation; action. **b** intervening action (*fertilized by the agency of insects*). **c** action personified (*an invisible agency*). **3** a specialized department of the United Nations. [med.L *agentia* f. L *agere* do]

agenda /əˈdʒendə/ *n.* **1** (*pl.* **agendas**) **a** a list of items of business to be considered at a meeting. **b** a series of things to be done. **2** (as *pl.*) **a** items to be considered. **b** things to be done. [L, neut. pl. of gerundive of *agere* do]

agent /ˈeɪdʒ(ə)nt/ *n.* **1 a** a person who acts for another in business, politics, etc. (*estate agent*; *insurance agent*). **b** a spy. **2** a person or thing that exerts power or produces an effect. □ **agential** /əˈdʒenʃ(ə)l/ *adj.* [L *agent-* part. stem of *agere* do]

agent provocateur /ˌɑːʒ̃ prəˌvɒkəˈtɜː(r)/ *n.* (*pl.* ***agents provocateurs*** *pronunc.* same) a person employed to detect suspected offenders by tempting them to overt self-incriminating action. [F, = provocative agent]

agglomerate *v., n., & adj.* —*v.tr. & intr.* /əˈglɒməˌreɪt/ collect into a mass. **2** accumulate in a disorderly way. —*n.* /əˈglɒmərət/ **1** a mass or collection of things. —*adj.* /əˈglɒmərət/ collected into a mass. □ **agglomeration** /-ˈreɪʃ(ə)n/ *n.* **agglomerative** /əˈglɒmərətɪv/ *adj.* [L *agglomerare* (as AD-, *glomerare* f. *glomus -meris* ball)]

agglutinate /əˈgluːtɪˌneɪt/ *v.* **1** *tr.* unite as with glue. **2** *tr. & intr. Biol.* cause or undergo adhesion. □ **agglutination** /-ˈneɪʃ(ə)n/ *n.* **agglutinative** /əˈgluːtɪnətɪv/ *adj.* [L *agglutinare* (as AD-, *glutinare* f. *gluten -tinis* glue)]

aggrandize /əˈgrændaɪz/ *v.tr.* (also **-ise**) **1** increase the power, rank, or wealth of (a person or State). **2** cause to appear greater than is the case. □ **aggrandizement** /-dɪzmənt/ *n.* **aggrandizer** *n.* [F *agrandir* (stem *agrandiss-*), prob. f. It. *aggrandire* f. L *grandis* large: assim. to verbs in -IZE]

aggravate /ˈægrəˌveɪt/ *v.tr.* **1** increase the gravity of (an illness, offence, etc.). **2** *disp.* annoy, exasperate (a person). □ **aggravation** /-ˈveɪʃ(ə)n/

n. [L *aggravare aggravat-* make heavy f. *gravis* heavy]

■ **Usage** Sense 2 is regarded by some people as incorrect but is common in informal use.

aggregate *n., adj.,* & *v.* —*n.* /ˈægrɪgət/ **1** a collection of, or the total of, disparate elements. **2** pieces of crushed stone, gravel, etc. used in making concrete. **3 a** *Geol.* a mass of minerals formed into solid rock. **b** a mass of particles. —*adj.* /ˈægrɪgət/ **1** (of disparate elements) collected into one mass. **2** constituted by the collection of many units into one body. —*v.* /ˈægrɪˌgeɪt/ **1** *tr.* & *intr.* collect together; combine into one mass. **2** *tr. colloq.* amount to (a specified total). □ **in the aggregate** as a whole. □ **aggregation** /-ˈgeɪʃ(ə)n/ *n.* **aggregative** /ˈægrɪˌgeɪtɪv/ *adj.* [L *aggregare aggregat-* herd together (as AD-, *grex gregis* flock)]

aggression /əˈgreʃ(ə)n/ *n.* **1** the act or practice of attacking without provocation. **2** an unprovoked attack. **3** self-assertiveness; forcefulness. **4** *Psychol.* hostile or destructive tendency or behaviour. [F *agression* or L *aggressio* attack f. *aggredi aggress-* (as AD-, *gradi* walk)]

aggressive /əˈgresɪv/ *adj.* **1** of a person: **a** given to aggression; openly hostile. **b** forceful; self-assertive. **2** (of an act) offensive, hostile. **3** of aggression. □ **aggressively** *adv.* **aggressiveness** *n.*

aggressor /əˈgresə(r)/ *n.* a person who attacks without provocation. [L (as AGGRESSION)]

aggrieved /əˈgriːvd/ *adj.* having a grievance. □ **aggrievedly** /-vɪdlɪ/ *adv.* [ME, past part. of *aggrieve* f. OF *agrever* make heavier (as AD-, GRIEVE)]

aggro /ˈægrəʊ/ *n. sl.* **1** aggressive troublemaking. **2** trouble, difficulty. [abbr. of AGGRAVATION (see AGGRAVATE) or AGGRESSION]

aghast /əˈgɑːst/ *adj.* (usu. *predic.*; often foll. by *at*) filled with dismay or consternation. [ME, past part. of obs. *agast, gast* frighten: see GHASTLY]

agile /ˈædʒaɪl/ *adj.* quick-moving, nimble, active. □ **agilely** *adv.* **agility** /əˈdʒɪlɪtɪ/ *n.* [F f. L *agilis* f. *agere* do]

agitate /ˈædʒɪˌteɪt/ *v.* **1** *tr.* disturb or excite (a person or feelings). **2** *intr.* (often foll. by *for*, *against*) stir up interest or concern, esp. publicly (*agitated for tax reform*). **3** *tr.* shake or move, esp. briskly. □ **agitatedly** *adv.* [L *agitare agitat-* frequent. of *agere* drive]

agitation /ˌædʒɪˈteɪʃ(ə)n/ *n.* **1** the act or process of agitating or being agitated. **2** mental anxiety or concern. [F *agitation* or L *agitatio* (as AGITATE)]

agitator /ˈædʒɪˌteɪtə(r)/ *n.* **1** a person who agitates, esp. publicly for a cause etc. **2** an apparatus for shaking or mixing liquid etc. [L (as AGITATE)]

agitprop /ˈædʒɪtˌprɒp, ˈæg-/ *n.* the dissemination of Communist political propaganda, esp. in plays, films, books, etc. [Russ. (as AGITATION, PROPAGANDA)]

agley /əˈgleɪ, -ˈliː/ *adv. Sc.* askew, awry. [A² + Sc. *gley* squint]

AGM *abbr.* annual general meeting.

agnail /ˈægneɪl/ *n.* **1** a piece of torn skin at the root of a fingernail. **2** the soreness resulting from this. [OE *angnægl* f. *nægl* NAIL *n.* 2a: cf. HANGNAIL]

agnate /ˈægneɪt/ *adj.* & *n.* —*adj.* **1** descended esp. by male line from the same male ancestor. **2** of the same clan or nation. **3** of the same

nature; akin. —*n.* one who is descended esp. by male line from the same male ancestor. □ **agnatic** /-ˈnætɪk/ *adj.* **agnation** /-ˈneɪʃ(ə)n/ *n.* [L *agnatus* f. *ad* to + *gnasci* be born f. stem *gen-beget*]

agnostic /ægˈnɒstɪk/ *n.* & *adj.* —*n.* a person who believes that nothing is known, or can be known, of the existence or nature of God or of anything beyond material phenomena. —*adj.* of or relating to agnostics. □ **agnosticism** *n.* [A-¹ + GNOSTIC]

ago /əˈgəʊ/ *adv.* earlier, before the present (*ten years ago; long ago*). [ME (*ago, agone*), past part. of obs. *ago* (v.) (as A-², GO¹)]

agog /əˈgɒg/ *adv.* & *adj.* —*adv.* eagerly, expectantly. —*predic.adj.* eager, expectant. [F *en gogues* f. *en* in + pl. of *gogue* fun]

agonistic /ˌægəˈnɪstɪk/ *adj.* polemical, combative. □ **agonistically** *adv.* [LL *agonisticus* f. Gk *agōnistikos* f. *agōnistēs* contestant f. *agōn* contest]

agonize /ˈægəˌnaɪz/ *v.* (also **-ise**) **1** *intr.* (often foll. by *over*) undergo (esp. mental) anguish; suffer agony. **2** *tr.* cause agony to. **3** *tr.* (as **agonized** *adj.*) expressing agony (*an agonized look*). □ **agonizingly** *adv.* [F *agoniser* or LL *agonizare* f. Gk *agōnizomai* contend f. *agōn* contest]

agony /ˈægənɪ/ *n.* (pl. **-ies**) **1** extreme mental or physical suffering. **2** a severe struggle. □ **agony aunt** *colloq.* a person (esp. a woman) who answers letters in an agony column. **agony column** *colloq.* **1** a column in a newspaper or magazine offering personal advice to readers who write in. **2** = *personal column.* [ME f. OF *agonie* or LL f. Gk *agōnia* f. *agōn* contest]

agoraphobia /ˌægərəˈfəʊbɪə/ *n. Psychol.* an abnormal fear of open spaces or public places. □ **agoraphobe** *n.* **agoraphobic** *adj.* & *n.* [mod.L f. Gk *agora* place of assembly, market-place + -PHOBIA]

agrarian /əˈgreərɪən/ *adj.* **1** of or relating to the land or its cultivation. **2** relating to landed property. [L *agrarius* f. *ager agri* field]

agree /əˈgriː/ *v.* (**agrees, agreed, agreeing**) **1** *intr.* hold a similar opinion (*I agree with you about that; they agreed that it would rain*). **2** *intr.* (often foll. by *to*, or *to* + infin.) consent (*agreed to the arrangement; agreed to go*). **3** *intr.* (often foll. by *with*) **a** become or be in harmony. **b** suit; be good for (*caviar didn't agree with him*). **c** *Gram.* have the same number, gender, case, or person as. **4** *tr.* reach agreement about (*agreed a price*). **5** *tr.* consent to or approve of (terms, a proposal, etc.). **6** *tr.* bring (things, esp. accounts) into harmony. **7** *intr.* (foll. by *on*) decide by mutual consent (*agreed on a compromise*). □ **be agreed** have reached the same opinion. [ME f. OF *agreer* ult. f. L *gratus* pleasing]

agreeable /əˈgriːəb(ə)l/ *adj.* **1** (often foll. by *to*) pleasing. **2** (often foll. by *to*) (of a person) willing to agree (*was agreeable to going*). **3** (foll. by *to*) conformable. □ **agreeableness** *n.* **agreeably** *adv.* [ME f. OF *agreable* f. *agreer* AGREE]

agreement /əˈgriːmənt/ *n.* **1** the act of agreeing; the holding of the same opinion (*reached agreement*). **2** mutual understanding. **3** an arrangement between parties as to a course of action etc. **4** *Gram.* having the same number, gender, case, or person. **5** a state of being harmonious. [ME f. OF (as AGREE)]

agribusiness /ˈægrɪˌbɪznɪs/ n. agriculture conducted on strictly commercial principles, esp. using advanced technology. □ **agri-businessman** /-ˈbɪznɪsmən/ n. (pl. **-men**). [AGRICULTURE + BUSINESS]

agriculture /ˈægrɪˌkʌltʃə(r)/ n. the science or practice of cultivating the soil and rearing animals. □ **agricultural** /-ˈkʌltʃər(ə)l/ adj. **agriculturalist** /-ˈkʌltʃərəlɪst/ n. **agriculturally** /-ˈkʌltʃərəlɪ/ adv. **agriculturist** /-ˈkʌltʃərɪst/ n. [F agriculture or L agricultura f. ager agri field + cultura CULTURE]

agrimony /ˈægrɪmənɪ/ n. (pl. **-ies**) any perennial plant of the genus Agrimonia, esp. A. eupatoria with small yellow flowers. [ME f. OF aigremoine f. L agrimonia alt. of argemonia f. Gk argemōnē poppy]

agro- /ˈægrəʊ/ comb. form agricultural (agro-climatic; agro-ecological). [Gk agros field]

agrochemical /ˌægrəʊˈkemɪk(ə)l/ n. a chemical used in agriculture.

agronomy /əˈgrɒnəmɪ/ n. the science of soil man- agement and crop production. □ **agronomic** /ˌægrəˈnɒmɪk/ adj. **agronomical** /ˌægrəˈnɒmɪk(ə)l/ adj. **agronomically** /ˌægrəˈnɒmɪkəlɪ/ adv. **agronomist** n. [F agronomie f. agronome agriculturist f. Gk agros field + -nomos f. nemō arrange]

aground /əˈgraʊnd/ predic.adj. & adv. (of a ship) on or on to the bottom of shallow water (be aground; run aground). [ME f. A² + GROUND¹]

ague /ˈeɪgjuː/ n. 1 hist. a malarial fever, with cold, hot, and sweating stages. 2 a shivering fit. □ **agued** adj. **aguish** adj. [ME f. OF f. med.L acuta (febris) acute (fever)]

AH abbr. in the year of the Hegira (AD 622); of the Muslim era. [L anno Hegirae]

ah int. expressing surprise, pleasure, sudden realization, resignation, etc. [ME f. OF a]

aha /ɑːˈhɑː, əˈhɑː/ int. expressing surprise, triumph, mockery, irony, etc. [ME f. AH + HA]

ahead /əˈhed/ adv. 1 further forward in space or time. 2 in the lead; further advanced (ahead on points). 3 in the line of one's forward motion (roadworks ahead). 4 straight forwards. [orig. Naut., f. A² + HEAD]

ahem /əˈhəm, əˈhem/ (not usu. clearly articulated) int. used to attract attention, gain time, or express disapproval. [lengthened form of HEM²]

ahoy /əˈhɔɪ/ int. Naut. a call used in hailing. [AH + HOY]

AI abbr. 1 artificial intelligence. 2 artificial insemination.

AID abbr. artificial insemination by donor.

aid n. & v. —n. 1 help. 2 financial or material help, esp. given by one country to another. 3 a person or thing that helps. —v.tr. 1 (often foll. by to + infin.) help. 2 promote or encourage (sleep will aid recovery). □ **in aid of** in support of. [ME f. OF aide, aidier, ult. f. L adjuvare (as AD-, juvare jut- help)]

aide /eɪd/ n. 1 an aide-de-camp. 2 esp. US an assistant. 3 an unqualified assistant to a social worker. [abbr.]

aide-de-camp /ˌeɪd də ˈkɑ̃/ n. (pl. **aides-de-camp** pronunc. same) an officer acting as a confidential assistant to a senior officer. [F]

aide-mémoire /ˌeɪdmeɪˈmwɑː(r)/ n. (pl. **aides-mémoire** pronunc. same) an aid to the memory. [F f. aider to help + mémoire memory]

Aids /eɪdz/ n. (also **AIDS**) acquired immune deficiency syndrome, an often fatal syndrome caused by a virus transmitted in the blood, marked by severe loss of resistance to infection. □ **Aids-related complex** the symptoms of a person affected with the Aids virus without necessarily developing the disease. [abbr.]

aigrette /ˈeɪgret, eɪˈgret/ n. 1 an egret. 2 its white plume. 3 a tuft of feathers or hair. 4 a spray of gems or similar ornament. [F]

aikido /ˈaɪkɪˌdəʊ/ n. a Japanese form of self-defence making use of the attacker's own movements without causing injury. [Jap. f. ai mutual + ki mind + dō way]

ail v. 1 tr. archaic (only in 3rd person interrog. or indefinite constructions) trouble or afflict in mind or body (what ails him?). 2 intr. (usu. be ailing) be ill. [OE egl(i)an f. egle troublesome]

aileron /ˈeɪləˌrɒn/ n. a hinged surface in the trailing edge of an aeroplane wing, used to control lateral balance. [F, dimin. of aile wing f. L ala]

ailing /ˈeɪlɪŋ/ adj. 1 ill, esp. chronically. 2 in poor condition.

ailment /ˈeɪlmənt/ n. an illness, esp. a minor one.

aim v. & n. —v. 1 intr. (foll. by at + verbal noun, or to + infin.) intend or try (aim at winning; aim to win). 2 tr. (usu. foll. by at) direct or point (a weapon, remark, etc.). 3 intr. take aim. 4 intr. (foll. by at, for) seek to attain or achieve. —n. 1 a purpose, a design, an object aimed at. 2 the directing of a weapon, missile, etc., at an object. □ **take aim** direct a weapon etc. at an object. [ME f. OF ult. f. L aestimare reckon]

aimless /ˈeɪmlɪs/ adj. without aim or purpose. □ **aimlessly** adv. **aimlessness** n.

ain't /eɪnt/ contr. colloq. 1 am not; are not; is not (you ain't doing it right; she ain't nice). 2 has not; have not (we ain't seen him). [contr. of are not]

■ **Usage** This word is usually regarded as unacceptable in spoken and written English.

air n. & v. —n. 1 an invisible gaseous substance surrounding the earth, a mixture mainly of oxygen and nitrogen. 2 **a** the earth's atmosphere. **b** the free or unconfined space in the atmosphere (birds of the air; in the open air). **c** the atmosphere as a place where aircraft operate. 3 **a** a distinctive impression or characteristic (an air of absurdity). **b** one's manner or bearing, esp. a confident one (with a triumphant air; does things with an air). **c** (esp. in pl.) an affected manner; pretentiousness (gave himself airs; airs and graces). 4 Mus. a tune or melody; a melodious composition. 5 a breeze or light wind. —v.tr. 1 warm (washed laundry) to remove damp, esp. at a fire or in a heated cupboard. 2 expose (a room etc.) to the open air; ventilate. 3 express publicly (an opinion, grievance, etc.). 4 parade; show ostentatiously (esp. qualities). 5 refl. go out in the fresh air. □ **air-bed** an inflatable mattress. **air brake 1** a brake worked by air pressure. **2** a movable flap or other device on an aircraft to reduce its speed. **air-brick** a brick perforated with small holes for ventilation. **Air Chief Marshal** an RAF officer of high rank, below Marshal of the RAF and above Air Marshal. **Air Commodore** an RAF officer next above Group Captain. **air-conditioned** (of a room, building, etc.) equipped with air-conditioning. **air-conditioner** an air-conditioning apparatus. **air-conditioning 1** a system for regulating the humidity, ventilation, and temperature in a building. **2** the apparatus for this. **air-cushion 1** an inflatable cushion. **2** the layer of air supporting a hovercraft or similar vehicle. **air force** a branch of the armed forces concerned with fighting or defence in the air. **air hostess** a stewardess in a passenger aircraft. **air lane** a path or course regularly used by aircraft (cf. LANE 4). **air letter** a sheet of light paper forming a letter for sending by airmail. **air line** a pipe supplying air, esp. to a diver. **Air Marshal** an RAF officer of high rank, below Air Chief Marshal and above Air Vice-Marshal. **Air Officer** any RAF officer above the rank of Group Captain. **air raid** an attack by aircraft. **air rifle** a rifle using compressed air to propel pellets. **air speed** the speed of an aircraft relative to the air through which it is moving. **air terminal** a building in a city or town to which passengers report and which serves as a base for transport to and from an airport. **air traffic controller** an airport official who controls air traffic by giving radio instructions to pilots concerning route, altitude, take-off, and landing. **Air Vice-Marshal** an RAF officer of high rank, just below Air Marshal. **air waves** *colloq.* radio waves used in broadcasting. **by air** by aircraft; in an aircraft. **in the air 1** (of opinions or feelings) prevalent; gaining currency. **2** (of projects etc.) uncertain, not decided. **on** (or **off**) **the air** in (or not in) the process of broadcasting. [ME f. F and L f. Gk *aēr*]

airbase /ˈeəbeɪs/ n. a base for the operation of military aircraft.

airborne /ˈeəbɔːn/ adj. **1** transported by air. **2** (of aircraft) in the air after taking off.

airbrush /ˈeəbrʌʃ/ n. & v. —n. an artist's device for spraying paint by means of compressed air. —v.tr. paint with an airbrush.

aircraft /ˈeəkrɑːft/ n. (pl. **aircraft**) a machine capable of flight, esp. an aeroplane or helicopter. □ **aircraft-carrier** a warship that carries and serves as a base for aeroplanes.

aircraftman /ˈeəˌkrɑːftmən/ n. (pl. **-men**) the lowest rank in the RAF.

aircraftwoman /ˈeəkrɑːftˌwʊmən/ n. (pl. **-women**) the lowest rank in the WRAF.

aircrew /ˈeəkruː/ n. **1** the crew manning an aircraft. **2** (pl. **aircrew**) a member of such a crew.

Airedale /ˈeədeɪl/ n. **1** a large terrier of a rough-coated breed. **2** this breed. [*Airedale* in Yorkshire]

airer /ˈeərə(r)/ n. a frame or stand for airing or drying clothes etc.

airfield /ˈeəfiːld/ n. an area of land where aircraft take off and land, are maintained, etc.

airgun /ˈeəgʌn/ n. a gun using compressed air to propel pellets.

airhead /ˈeəhed/ n. **1** *Mil.* a forward base for aircraft in enemy territory. **2** esp. *US sl.* a silly or foolish person.

airing /ˈeərɪŋ/ n. **1** exposure to fresh air, esp. for exercise or an excursion. **2** exposure (of laundry etc.) to warm air. **3** public expression of an opinion etc. (*the idea will get an airing at tomorrow's meeting*).

airless /ˈeəlɪs/ adj. **1** stuffy; not ventilated. **2** without wind or breeze; still. □ **airlessness** n.

airlift /ˈeəlɪft/ n. & v. —n. the transport of troops and supplies by air, esp. in a blockade or other emergency. —v.tr. transport in this way.

airline /ˈeəlaɪn/ n. an organization providing a regular public service of air transport on one or more routes.

airliner /ˈeəˌlaɪnə(r)/ n. a large passenger aircraft.

airlock /ˈeəlɒk/ n. **1** a stoppage of the flow in a pump or pipe, caused by an air bubble. **2** a compartment with controlled pressure and parallel sets of doors, to permit movement between areas at different pressures.

airmail /ˈeəmeɪl/ n. & v. —n. **1** a system of transporting mail by air. **2** mail carried by air. —v.tr. send by airmail.

airman /ˈeəmən/ n. (pl. **-men**) **1** a pilot or member of the crew of an aircraft, esp. in an air force. **2** a member of the RAF below commissioned rank.

airmiss /ˈeəmɪs/ n. a circumstance in which two or more aircraft in flight on different routes are less than a prescribed distance apart.

airplane /ˈeəpleɪn/ n. US = AEROPLANE.

airplay /ˈeəpleɪ/ n. broadcasting (of recorded music).

airport /ˈeəpɔːt/ n. a complex of runways and buildings for the take-off, landing, and maintenance of civil aircraft, with facilities for passengers.

airship /ˈeəʃɪp/ n. a power-driven aircraft that is lighter than air.

airsick /ˈeəsɪk/ adj. affected with nausea due to travel in an aircraft. □ **airsickness** n.

airspace /ˈeəspeɪs/ n. the air available to aircraft to fly in, esp. the part subject to the jurisdiction of a particular country.

airstrip /ˈeəstrɪp/ n. a strip of ground suitable for the take-off and landing of aircraft.

airtight /ˈeətaɪt/ adj. not allowing air to pass through.

airway /ˈeəweɪ/ n. **1** a recognized route followed by aircraft. **2** (often in pl.) = AIRLINE.

airwoman /ˈeəˌwʊmən/ n. (pl. **-women**) **1** a woman pilot or member of the crew of an aircraft, esp. in an air force. **2** a member of the WRAF below commissioned rank.

airworthy /ˈeəˌwɜːðɪ/ adj. (of an aircraft) fit to fly.

airy /ˈeərɪ/ adj. (**airier**, **airiest**) **1** well-ventilated, breezy. **2** flippant, superficial. **3 a** light as air. **b** graceful, delicate. **4** insubstantial, ethereal, immaterial. □ **airy-fairy** *colloq.* unrealistic, impractical, foolishly idealistic. □ **airily** adv. **airiness** n.

aisle /aɪl/ n. **1** part of a church, esp. one parallel to and divided by pillars from the nave, choir, or transept. **2** a passage between rows of pews, seats, etc. □ **aisled** adj. [ME *ele*, *ile* f. OF *ele* f. L *ala* wing: confused with *island* and F *aile* wing]

aitch /eɪtʃ/ n. the name of the letter H. □ **drop one's aitches** fail to pronounce the initial *h* in words. [ME f. OF *ache*]

aitchbone /ˈeɪtʃbəʊn/ n. **1** the buttock or rump bone. **2** a cut of beef lying over this. [ME *nage-*, *nache-bone* buttock, ult. f. L *natis*, *-es* buttock(s): for loss of *n* cf. ADDER, APRON]

ajar /əˈdʒɑː(r)/ adv. & predic.adj. (of a door) slightly open. [A² + obs. char f. OE cerr a turn]

a.k.a. abbr. also known as.

akee var. of ACKEE.

akela /ɑːˈkeɪlə/ n. the adult leader of a group of Cub Scouts. [name of the leader of a wolf-pack in Kipling's Jungle Book]

akimbo /əˈkɪmbəʊ/ adv. (of the arms) with hands on the hips and elbows turned outwards. [ME in kenebowe, prob. f. ON]

akin /əˈkɪn/ predic.adj. 1 related by blood. 2 of similar or kindred character. [A-⁴ + KIN]

akvavit var. of AQUAVIT.

Al symb. Chem. the element aluminium.

-al suffix 1 forming adjectives meaning 'relating to, of the kind of': a from Latin or Greek words (central; regimental; colossal; tropical) (cf. -IAL, -ICAL). b from English nouns (tidal). 2 forming nouns, esp. of verbal action (animal; rival; arrival; proposal; trial). [sense 1 f. F -el or L -alis adj. suffix rel. to -ous; sense 2 f. F -aille or f. (or after) L -alis etc. used as noun]

à la /ɑː lɑː/ prep. after the manner of (à la russe). [F, f. À LA MODE]

alabaster /ˈæləˌbɑːstə(r), -ˌbæstə(r), ˌæləˈb-/ n. & adj. —n. a translucent usu. white form of gypsum, often carved into ornaments. —adj. 1 of alabaster. 2 like alabaster in whiteness or smoothness. □ **alabastrine** /-ˈbɑːstrɪn, -ˈbæstrɪn, -aɪn/ adj. [ME f. OF alabastre f. L alabaster, -trum, f. Gk alabast(r)os]

à la carte /ˌɑː lɑː ˈkɑːt/ adv. & adj. ordered as separately priced item(s) from a menu, not as part of a set meal. [F]

alack /əˈlæk/ int. (also **alack-a-day** /əˈlækəˌdeɪ/) archaic an expression of regret or surprise. [prob. f. AH + LACK]

alacrity /əˈlækrɪtɪ/ n. briskness or cheerful readiness. [L alacritas f. alacer brisk]

à la mode /ˌɑː lɑː ˈməʊd/ adv. & adj. 1 in fashion; fashionable. 2 a (of beef) braised in wine. b US served with ice-cream. [F, = in the fashion]

alarm /əˈlɑːm/ n. & v. —n. 1 a warning of danger etc. (gave the alarm). 2 a a warning sound or device (burglar alarm). b = alarm clock. 3 frightened expectation of danger or difficulty (were filled with alarm). —v.tr. 1 frighten or disturb. 2 arouse to a sense of danger. □ **alarm clock** a clock with a device that can be made to sound at the time set in advance. [ME f. OF alarme f. It. allarme f. all'arme! to arms]

alarming /əˈlɑːmɪŋ/ adj. disturbing, frightening. □ **alarmingly** adv.

alarmist /əˈlɑːmɪst/ n. & adj. —n. a person given to spreading needless alarm. —adj. creating needless alarm. □ **alarmism** n.

alas /əˈlæs, əˈlɑːs/ int. an expression of grief, pity, or concern. [ME f. OF a las(se) f. a ah + las(se) f. L lassus weary]

Alaska /əˈlæskə/ n. □ **baked Alaska** sponge cake and ice-cream in a meringue covering. [name of a State of the US]

alb n. a white vestment reaching to the feet, worn by some Christian priests at church ceremonies. [OE albe f. eccl.L alba fem. of L albus white]

albacore /ˈælbəˌkɔː(r)/ n. 1 a long-finned tunny, Thunnus alalunga. 2 any of various other related fish. [Port. albacor, -cora, f. Arab. al the + bakr young camel or bakūr premature, precocious]

albatross /ˈælbəˌtrɒs/ n. 1 any long-winged stout-bodied bird of the family Diomedeidae, inhabiting the Pacific and Southern Oceans. 2 an encumbrance. [alt. (after L albus white) of 17th-c. alcatras, applied to various sea-birds, f. Sp. and Port. alcatraz, var. of Port. alcatruz f. Arab. alḵādūs the pitcher]

albeit /ɔːlˈbiːɪt/ conj. literary though (he tried, albeit without success).

albino /ælˈbiːnəʊ/ n. (pl. **-os**) 1 a person or animal having a congenital absence of pigment in the skin and hair (which are white), and the eyes (which are usu. blue). 2 a plant lacking normal colouring. □ **albinism** /ˈælbɪˌnɪz(ə)m/ n. **albinotic** /ˌælbɪˈnɒtɪk/ adj. [Sp. & Port. (orig. of White Negroes) f. albo L f. albus white + -ino = -INE¹]

Albion /ˈælbɪən/ n. (also **perfidious Albion**) Britain or England. [OE f. L f. Celt. Albio (unrecorded): F la perfide Albion with ref. to alleged treachery to other nations]

album /ˈælbəm/ n. 1 a blank book for the insertion of photographs, stamps, etc. 2 a a long-playing gramophone record. b a set of these. [L, = blank tablet, neut. of albus white]

albumen /ˈælbjʊmɪn/ n. 1 egg-white. 2 Bot. the substance found between the skin and germ of many seeds, usu. the edible part; = ENDOSPERM. [L albumen -minis white of egg f. albus white]

albumin /ˈælbjʊmɪn/ n. any of a class of water-soluble proteins found in egg-white, milk, blood, etc. □ **albuminous** /ælˈbjuːmɪnəs/ adj. [F albumine f. L albumin-: see ALBUMEN]

alcalde /ɑːlˈkɑːldeɪ/ n. a magistrate or mayor in a Spanish, Portuguese, or Latin American town. [Sp. f. Arab. al-ḵāḍī the judge: see CADI]

alchemy /ˈælkəmɪ/ n. (pl. **-ies**) 1 the medieval forerunner of chemistry, esp. seeking to turn base metals into gold or silver. 2 a miraculous transformation or the means of achieving this. □ **alchemic** /ælˈkemɪk/ adj. **alchemical** /ælˈkemɪk(ə)l/ adj. **alchemist** n. **alchemize** v.tr. (also **-ise**). [ME f. OF alkemie, alkamie f. med.L alchimia, -emia, f. Arab. al-kīmiyā' f. al the + kīmiyā' f. Gk khēmia, -meia art of transmuting metals]

alcheringa /ˌæltʃəˈrɪŋɡə/ n. (in the mythology of some Australian Aboriginals) the 'golden age' when the first ancestors were created. [Aboriginal, = dream-time]

alcohol /ˈælkəˌhɒl/ n. 1 (in full **ethyl alcohol**) a colourless volatile inflammable liquid forming the intoxicating element in wine, beer, spirits, etc., and also used as a solvent, as fuel, etc. 2 any liquor containing this. 3 Chem. any of a large class of organic compounds that contain one or more hydroxyl groups attached to carbon atoms. [F or med.L f. Arab. al-kuḥl f. al the + KOHL]

alcoholic /ˌælkəˈhɒlɪk/ adj. & n. —adj. of, relating to, containing, or caused by alcohol. —n. a person suffering from alcoholism.

alcoholism /ˈælkəhɒˌlɪz(ə)m/ n. 1 an addiction to the consumption of alcoholic liquor. 2 the diseased condition resulting from this. [mod.L alcoholismus (as ALCOHOL)]

alcove /ˈælkəʊv/ n. a recess, esp. in the wall of a room or of a garden. [F f. Sp. alcoba f. Arab. al-ḵubba f. al the + ḵubba vault]

aldehyde /ˈældɪˌhaɪd/ n. Chem. any of a class of compounds formed by the oxidation of alcohols. □ **aldehydic** /ˌældɪˈhɪdɪk/ adj. [abbr. of mod.L alcohol dehydrogenatum alcohol deprived of hydrogen]

al dente /æl ˈdenti/ *adj.* (of pasta etc.) cooked so as to be still firm when bitten. [It., lit. 'to the tooth']

alder /ˈɔːldə(r)/ *n.* any tree of the genus *Alnus*, related to the birch, with catkins and toothed leaves. [OE *alor, aler*, rel. to L *alnus*, with euphonic *d*]

alderman /ˈɔːldəmən/ *n.* (*pl.* **-men**) **1** *esp. hist.* a co-opted member of an English county or borough council, next in dignity to the Mayor. **2** *US & Austral.* the elected governor of a city. □ **aldermanic** /-ˈmænɪk/ *adj.* **aldermanship** *n.* [OE *aldor* patriarch f. *ald* old + MAN]

aldrin /ˈældrɪn/ *n.* a white crystalline chlorinated hydrocarbon used as an insecticide. [K. *Alder*, Ger. chemist d. 1958 + -IN]

ale *n.* beer (usu. as a trade word). [OE *alu*, = ON *ǫl*]

aleatoric /ˌeɪlɪəˈtɒrɪk/ *adj.* depending on the throw of a die or on chance. [L *aleatorius aleator* dice-player f. *alea* die]

aleatory /ˈeɪlɪətərɪ/ *adj.* = ALEATORIC. [as ALEATORIC]

alembic /əˈlembɪk/ *n.* **1** *hist.* an apparatus formerly used in distilling. **2** a means of refining or extracting. [ME f. OF f. med.L *alembicus* f. Arab. *al-'anbīq* f. *al* the + *'anbīq* still f. Gk *ambix, -ikos* cup, cap of a still]

alert /əˈlɜːt/ *adj., n.,* & *v.* —*adj.* **1** watchful or vigilant; ready to take action. **2** nimble (esp. of mental faculties); attentive. —*n.* a warning call or alarm. —*v.tr.* (often foll. by *to*) make alert; warn (*were alerted to the danger*). □ **on the alert** on the lookout against danger or attack. □ **alertly** *adv.* **alertness** *n.* [F *alerte* f. It. *all' erta* to the watch-tower]

A level /eɪ/ *n.* Brit. = *advanced level* (see ADVANCE).

alexandrine /ˌælɪgˈzændraɪn/ *adj.* & *n.* —*adj.* (of a line of verse) having six iambic feet. —*n.* an alexandrine line. [F *alexandrin* f. Alexandre Alexander (the Great), the subject of an Old French poem in this metre]

alexandrite /ˌælɪgˈzɑːndraɪt/ *n.* Mineral. a green variety of chrysoberyl. [Tsar *Alexander* I of Russia + -ITE[1]]

alexia /əˈleksɪə/ *n.* the inability to see words or to read, caused by a condition of the brain. [mod.L, A-[1] + Gk *lexis* speech f. *legein* to speak, confused with L *legere* to read]

alfalfa /ælˈfælfə/ *n.* a leguminous plant, *Medicago sativa*, with clover-like leaves and flowers used for fodder. [Sp. f. Arab. *al-faṣfaṣa*, a green fodder]

alfresco /ælˈfreskəʊ/ *adv.* & *adj.* in the open air (*we lunched alfresco; an alfresco lunch*). [It. *al fresco* in the fresh (air)]

alga /ˈælgə/ *n.* (*pl.* **algae** /ˈældʒiː, ˈælgiː/) (usu. in *pl.*) a non-flowering stemless water-plant, esp. seaweed and phytoplankton. □ **algal** *adj.* **algoid** *adj.* [L]

algebra /ˈældʒɪbrə/ *n.* the branch of mathematics that uses letters and other general symbols to represent numbers and quantities in formulae and equations. □ **algebraic** /ˌældʒɪˈbreɪɪk/ *adj.* **algebraical** /ˌældʒɪˈbreɪɪk(ə)l/ *adj.* **algebraically** /ˌældʒɪˈbreɪɪkəlɪ/ *adv.* **algebraist** /ˌældʒɪˈbreɪɪst/ *n.* [It. & Sp. & med.L, f. Arab. *al-jabr* f. *al* the + *jabr* reunion of broken parts f. *jabara* reunite]

-algia /ˈældʒə/ *comb. form* Med. denoting pain in a part specified by the first element (*neuralgia*). □ **-algic** *comb. form* forming adjectives. [Gk f. *algos* pain]

algicide /ˈælgɪˌsaɪd/ *n.* a preparation for destroying algae.

alginate /ˈældʒɪˌneɪt/ *n.* a salt or ester of alginic acid. [ALGA + -IN + -ATE[1]]

alginic acid /ælˈdʒɪnɪk/ *n.* an insoluble carbohydrate found (chiefly as salts) in many brown seaweeds. [ALGA + -IN + -IC]

algoid see ALGA.

Algol /ˈælgɒl/ *n.* a high-level computer programming language. [ALGORITHMIC (see ALGORITHM) + LANGUAGE]

algorithm /ˈælgəˌrɪð(ə)m/ *n.* (also **algorism** /ˈælgəˌrɪz(ə)m/) Math. a process or set of rules used for calculation or problem-solving, esp. with a computer. □ **algorithmic** /ˌælgəˈrɪðmɪk/ *adj.* [*algorism* ME ult. f. Pers. *al-Kuwārizmī* 9th-c. mathematician: *algorithm* infl. by Gk *arithmos* number (cf. F *algorithme*)]

alias /ˈeɪlɪəs/ *adv.* & *n.* —*adv.* also named or known as. —*n.* a false or assumed name. [L, = at another time, otherwise]

alibi /ˈælɪˌbaɪ/ *n.* & *v.* —*n.* **1** a claim, or the evidence supporting it, that when an alleged act took place one was elsewhere. **2** an excuse of any kind; a pretext or justification. —*v.* (**alibis, alibied, alibiing**) colloq. **1** *tr.* provide an alibi or offer an excuse for (a person). **2** *intr.* provide an alibi. [L, = elsewhere]

■ **Usage** The use of this noun in sense 2 is considered incorrect by some people.

alien /ˈeɪlɪən/ *adj.* & *n.* —*adj.* **1 a** (often foll. by *to*) unfamiliar; unfriendly; unacceptable or repugnant (*discipline was alien to him; struck an alien note*). **b** (often foll. by *from*) different or separated. **2** foreign; from a foreign country. **3** of or relating to beings supposedly from other worlds. **4** *Bot.* (of a plant) introduced from elsewhere. —*n.* **1** a foreigner, esp. one who is not a naturalized citizen of the country where he or she is living. **2** a being from another world. **3** *Bot.* an alien plant. □ **alienness** *n.* [ME f. OF f. L *alienus* belonging to another (*alius*)]

alienable /ˈeɪlɪənəb(ə)l/ *adj.* Law able to be transferred to new ownership. □ **alienability** /-ˈbɪlɪtɪ/ *n.*

alienate /ˈeɪlɪəˌneɪt/ *v.tr.* **1 a** cause (a person) to become unfriendly or hostile. **b** (often foll. by *from*) cause (a person) to feel isolated or estranged from (friends, society, etc.). **2** transfer ownership of (property) to another person etc. □ **alienation** *n.* **alienator** *n.* [ME f. L *alienare alienat-* (as ALIEN)]

alienist /ˈeɪlɪənɪst/ *n.* US a psychiatrist, esp. a legal adviser on psychiatric problems. [F *aliéniste* (as ALIEN)]

alight[1] /əˈlaɪt/ *v.intr.* **1 a** (often foll. by *from*) descend from a vehicle. **b** dismount from a horse. **2** come to earth from the air. **3** (foll. by *on*) find by chance; notice. [OE *ālīhtan* (as A-[2], *līhtan* LIGHT[2] *v.*)]

alight[2] /əˈlaɪt/ *predic.adj.* **1** on fire; burning (*they set the old shed alight; is the fire still alight?*). **2** lighted up; excited (*eyes alight with expectation*). [ME, prob. f. phr. *on a light* (= lighted) *fire*]

align /əˈlaɪn/ *v.tr.* **1** put in a straight line or bring into line (*three books were neatly aligned on the shelf*). **2** esp. *Polit.* (usu. foll. by *with*) bring (oneself etc.) into agreement or alliance with (a cause, policy, political party, etc.). □ **alignment** *n.* [F *aligner* f. phr. *à ligne* into line: see LINE[1]]

alike /ə'laɪk/ *adj.* & *adv.* —*adj.* (usu. *predic.*) similar, like one another; indistinguishable. —*adv.* in a similar way or manner (*all were treated alike*). [ME f. OE *gelīc* and ON *glíkr* (LIKE¹)]

alimentary /ˌælɪ'mentərɪ/ *adj.* of, relating to, or providing nourishment or sustenance. □ **alimentary canal** *Anat.* the passage along which food is passed from the mouth to the anus during digestion. [L *alimentarius* f. *alimentum* f. *alere* nourish]

alimentation /ˌælɪmen'teɪʃ(ə)n/ *n.* **1** nourishment; feeding. **2** maintenance, support. [F *alimentation* or med.L *alimentatio* f. *alimentare* (as ALIMENTARY)]

alimony /'ælɪmənɪ/ *n.* the money payable by a man to his wife or former wife or by a woman to her husband or former husband after they are separated or divorced. [L *alimonia* nutriment f. *alere* nourish]

■ **Usage** In UK usage this term has been replaced by *maintenance*.

A-line /'eɪlaɪn/ *adj.* (of a garment) having a narrow waist or shoulders and somewhat flared skirt.

aliphatic /ˌælɪ'fætɪk/ *adj. Chem.* of, denoting, or relating to organic compounds in which carbon atoms form open chains, not aromatic rings. [Gk *aleiphar -atos* fat]

aliquot /'ælɪˌkwɒt/ *adj.* & *n.* —*adj.* (of a part or portion) contained by the whole an integral or whole number of times (*4 is an aliquot part of 12*). —*n.* **1** an aliquot part; an integral factor. **2** (in general use) any known fraction of a whole; a sample. [F *aliquote* f. L *aliquot* some, so many]

alive /ə'laɪv/ *adj.* (usu. *predic.*) **1** (of a person, animal, plant, etc.) living, not dead. **2 a** (of a thing) existing; continuing; in operation or action (*kept his interest alive*). **b** under discussion; provoking interest (*the topic is still very much alive today*). **3** (of a person or animal) lively, active. **4** charged with an electric current; connected to a source of electricity. **5** (foll. by *to*) aware of; alert or responsive to. **6** (foll. by *with*) **a** swarming or teeming with. **b** full of. □ **aliveness** *n.* [OE *on līfe* (as A², LIFE)]

alkali /'ælkəˌlaɪ/ *n.* (pl. **alkalis**). **1 a** any of a class of substances that liberate hydroxide ions in water, usu. form caustic or corrosive solutions, turn litmus blue, and have a pH of more than 7, e.g. caustic soda. **b** any other substance with similar but weaker properties, e.g. sodium carbonate. **2** *Chem.* any substance that reacts with or neutralizes hydrogen ions. □ **alkalimeter** /ˌælkə'lɪmɪtə(r)/ *n.* **alkalimetry** /ˌælkə'lɪmɪtrɪ/ *n.* [ME f. med.L, f. Arab. *al-ḳalī* calcined ashes f. ḳala fry]

alkaline /'ælkəˌlaɪn/ *adj.* of, relating to, or having the nature of an alkali; rich in alkali. □ **alkalinity** /ˌælkə'lɪnɪtɪ/ *n.*

alkaloid /'ælkəˌlɔɪd/ *n.* any of a series of nitrogenous organic compounds of plant origin, many of which are used as drugs. [G (as ALKALI)]

alkalosis /ˌælkə'ləʊsɪs/ *n. Med.* an excessive alkaline condition of the body fluids or tissues.

alkane /'ælkeɪn/ *n. Chem.* any of a series of saturated aliphatic hydrocarbons, including methane, ethane, and propane. [ALKYL + -ANE²]

alkene /'ælkiːn/ *n. Chem.* any of a series of unsaturated aliphatic hydrocarbons containing a double bond, including ethylene. [ALKYL + -ENE]

alkyd /'ælkɪd/ *n.* any of the group of synthetic resins derived from various alcohols and acids. [ALKYL + ACID]

alkyl /'ælkaɪl, 'ælkɪl/ *n.* (in full **alkyl radical**) *Chem.* any radical derived from an alkane by the removal of a hydrogen atom. [G *Alkohol* ALCOHOL + -YL]

alkylate /'ælkɪˌleɪt/ *v.tr. Chem.* introduce an alkyl radical into (a compound).

alkyne /'ælkaɪn/ *n. Chem.* any of a series of unsaturated aliphatic hydrocarbons containing a triple bond, including acetylene. [ALKYL + suffix *-yne* denoting compounds with a triple bond]

all /ɔːl/ *adj., n.,* & *adv.* —*adj.* **1 a** the whole amount, quantity, or extent of (*waited all day; we all know why; take it all*). **b** (with *pl.*) the entire number of (*all the others left; all ten men; the children are all boys; film stars all*). **2** any whatever (*beyond all doubt*). **3** greatest possible (*with all speed*). —*n.* **1 a** all the persons or things concerned (*all were present; all were thrown away*). **b** everything (*all is lost; that is all*). **2** (foll. by *of*) **a** the whole of (*take all of it*). **b** every one of (*all of us*). **3** one's whole strength or resources (prec. by *my, your,* etc.). **4** (in games) on both sides (*two goals all*). —*adv.* **1 a** entirely, quite (*dressed all in black; all round the room; the all-important thing*). **b** as an intensifier (*a book all about ships; stop all this grumbling*). **2** (foll. by *the* + compar.) **a** by so much; to that extent (*if they go, all the better*). **b** in the full degree to be expected (*that makes it all the worse*). □ **all along** all the time (*he was joking all along*). **all-American 1** representing the whole of (or only) America or the US. **2** truly American (*all-American boy*). **all and sundry** everyone. **all-around** US = *all-round*. **all but** very nearly (*it was all but impossible; he was all but drowned*). **all-clear** a signal that danger or difficulty is over. **All Fools' Day** 1 April. **all for** *colloq.* strongly in favour of. **all in** *colloq.* exhausted. **all-in** (*attrib.*) inclusive of all. **all in all** everything considered. **all-in wrestling** wrestling with few or no restrictions. **all one** (or **the same**) (usu. foll. by *to*) a matter of indifference (*it's all one to me*). **all out** involving all one's strength; at full speed (also with hyphen) *attrib.*: *an all-out effort*). **all over 1** completely finished. **2** in or on all parts of (esp. the body) (*went hot and cold all over; mud all over the carpet*). **3** *colloq.* typically (*that is you all over*). **4** *sl.* effusively attentive to (a person). **all right** (*predic.*) **1** satisfactory; safe and sound; in good condition. **2** satisfactorily, as desired (*it worked out all right*). **3 a** an interjection expressing consent or assent to a proposal or order. **b** as an intensifier (*that's the one all right*). **all-right** *attrib.adj. colloq.* fine, acceptable (*an all-right guy*). **all round 1** in all respects (*a good performance all round*). **2** for each person (*he bought drinks all round*). **all-round** (*attrib.*) (of a person) versatile. **all-rounder** *Brit.* a versatile person. **All Saints' Day** 1 Nov. **all the same** nevertheless, in spite of this (*he was innocent but was punished all the same*). **all set** *colloq.* ready to start. **All Souls' Day** 2 Nov. **all there** *colloq.* mentally alert. **all-time** (of a record etc.) hitherto unsurpassed. **all together** all at once; all in one place or in a group (*they came all together*) (cf. ALTOGETHER). **all told** in all. **at all** (with *neg.* or *interrog.*) in any way; to any extent (*did not swim at all; did you like it at all?*). **in all** in total number; altogether (*there were 10 people in* *all*). **one and all** everyone. [OE *all*, *eall*, prob. f. Gmc]

■ **Usage** Note the differences in meaning between *all together* and *altogether*: see note at *altogether*.

---

alla cappella var. of A CAPPELLA.

Allah /ˈælə/ n. the name of God among Arabs and Muslims. [Arab. *'allāh* contr. of *al-'ilāh* f. *al* the + *ilāh* god]

allay /əˈleɪ/ v.tr. **1** diminish (fear, suspicion, etc.). **2** relieve or alleviate (pain, hunger, etc.). [OE *ālecgan* (as A-², LAY¹)]

allegation /ˌælɪˈgeɪʃ(ə)n/ n. **1** an assertion, esp. an unproved one. **2** the act or an instance of alleging. [ME f. F *allégation* or L *allegatio* f. *allegare* allege]

allege /əˈledʒ/ v.tr. **1** (often foll. by *that* + clause, or *to* + infin.) declare to be the case, esp. without proof. **2** advance as an argument or excuse. □ **alleged** adj. [ME f. AF *alegier*, OF *esligier* clear at law; confused in sense with L *allegare*: see ALLEGATION]

allegedly /əˈledʒɪdlɪ/ adv. as is alleged or said to be the case.

allegiance /əˈliːdʒ(ə)ns/ n. **1** loyalty (to a person or cause etc.). **2** the duty of a subject to his or her sovereign or government. [ME f. AF f. OF *ligeance* (as LIEGE): perh. assoc. with ALLIANCE]

allegorical /ˌælɪˈgɒrɪk(ə)l/ adj. (also **allegoric** /-rɪk/) consisting of or relating to allegory; by means of allegory. □ **allegorically** adv.

allegorize /ˈælɪgəˌraɪz/ v.tr. (also **-ise**) treat as or by means of an allegory. □ **allegorization** /-ˈzeɪʃ(ə)n/ n.

allegory /ˈælɪgərɪ/ n. (pl. **-ies**) **1** a story, play, poem, picture, etc., in which the meaning or message is represented symbolically. **2** the use of such symbols. **3** a symbol. □ **allegorist** n. [ME f. OF *allegorie* f. L *allegoria* f. Gk *allēgoria* f. *allos* other + *-agoria* speaking]

allegro /əˈleɪgrəʊ, əˈleg-/ adv., adj., & n. *Mus.* —adv. & adj. in a brisk tempo. —n. (pl. **-os**) an allegro passage or movement. [It., = lively, gay]

allele /ˈæliːl/ n. (also **allel** /ˈælel/) one of the (usu. two) alternative forms of a gene. □ **allelic** /əˈliːlɪk/ adj. [G *Allel*, abbr. of *allelomorph* (f. Gk *allēl-* one another + *morphē* form)]

alleluia /ˌælɪˈluːjə/ int. & n. (also **alleluya**, **hallelujah** /hæl-/) —int. God be praised. —n. **1** praise to God. **2** a song of praise to God. [ME f. eccl.L f. (Septuagint) Gk *allēlouia* f. Heb. *hallʼlūyāh* praise ye the Lord]

Allen key /ˈælən/ n. *propr.* a spanner designed to fit into and turn an Allen screw. [*Allen*, name of the US manufacturer]

Allen screw /ˈælən/ n. *propr.* a screw with a hexagonal socket in the head.

allergen /ˈælədʒ(ə)n/ n. any substance that causes an allergic reaction. □ **allergenic** /ˌælədʒˈdʒenɪk/ adj. [ALLERGY + -GEN]

allergic /əˈlɜːdʒɪk/ adj. **1** (foll. by *to*) **a** having an allergy to. **b** *colloq.* having a strong dislike for (a person or thing). **2** caused by or relating to an allergy.

allergy /ˈælədʒɪ/ n. (pl. **-ies**) **1** *Med.* a condition of reacting adversely to certain substances, esp. particular foods, pollen, fur, or dust. **2** *colloq.* an antipathy. □ **allergist** n. [G *Allergie*, after *Energie* ENERGY, f. Gk *allos* other]

alleviate /əˈliːvɪˌeɪt/ v.tr. lessen or make less severe (pain, suffering, etc.). □ **alleviation** /-ˈeɪʃ(ə)n/ n. **alleviative** /əˈliːvɪətɪv/ adj. **alleviator** n. **alleviatory** /əˈliːvɪətərɪ/ adj. [LL *alleviare* lighten f. L *allevare* (as AD-, *levare* raise)]

alley /ˈælɪ/ n. (pl. **-eys**) **1** (also **alley-way**) **a** a narrow street. **b** a narrow passageway, esp. between or behind buildings. **2** a path or walk in a park or garden. **3** an enclosure for skittles, bowling, etc. [ME f. OF *alee* walking, passage f. *aler* go f. L *ambulare* walk]

alliaceous /ˌælɪˈeɪʃəs/ adj. **1** of or relating to the genus *Allium*. **2** tasting or smelling like onion or garlic. [mod.L *alliaceus* f. L *allium* garlic]

alliance /əˈlaɪəns/ n. **1 a** a union or agreement to cooperate, esp. of States by treaty or families by marriage. **b** the parties involved. **2** a relationship resulting from an affinity in nature or qualities etc. (*the old alliance between logic and metaphysics*). [ME f. OF *aliance* (as ALLY)]

allied /ˈælaɪd/ adj. **1 a** united or associated in an alliance. **b** (**Allied**) of or relating to Britain and her allies in the wars of 1914–18 or 1939–45. **2** connected or related (*studied medicine and allied subjects*).

alligator /ˈælɪˌgeɪtə(r)/ n. **1** a large reptile of the crocodile family native to S. America and China. **2** (in general use) any of several large members of the crocodile family. **3** the skin of such an animal or material resembling it. □ **alligator clip** a clip with teeth for gripping. [Sp. *el lagarto* the lizard f. L *lacerta*]

alliterate /əˈlɪtəˌreɪt/ v. **1** *intr.* **a** contain alliteration. **b** use alliteration in speech or writing. **2** *tr.* **a** construct (a phrase etc.) with alliteration. **b** speak or pronounce with alliteration. □ **alliterative** /əˈlɪtərətɪv/ adj. [back-form. f. ALLITERATION]

alliteration /əˌlɪtəˈreɪʃ(ə)n/ n. the occurrence of the same letter or sound at the beginning of adjacent or closely connected words (e.g. *cool, calm, and collected*). [mod.L *alliteratio* (as AD-, *littera* letter)]

allium /ˈælɪəm/ n. any plant of the genus *Allium*, usu. bulbous and strong smelling, e.g. onion and garlic. [L, = garlic]

allo- /ˈæləʊ, əˈlɒ/ *comb. form* other (*allophone*; *allogamy*). [Gk *allos* other]

allocate /ˈæləˌkeɪt/ v.tr. (usu. foll. by *to*) assign or devote to (a purpose, person, or place). □ **allocable** /ˈæləkəb(ə)l/ adj. **allocation** /ˌæləˈkeɪʃ(ə)n/ n. **allocator** n. [med.L *allocare* f. *locus* place]

allopath /ˈæləˌpæθ/ n. one who practises allopathy. [F *allopathe* back-form. f. *allopathie* = ALLOPATHY]

allopathy /əˈlɒpəθɪ/ n. the treatment of disease by conventional means, i.e. with drugs having opposite effects to the symptoms. □ **allopathic** /ˌæləˈpæθɪk/ adj. **allopathist** n. [G *Allopathie* (as ALLO-, -PATHY)]

allot /əˈlɒt/ v.tr. (**allotted**, **allotting**) **1** give or apportion to (a person) as a share or task; distribute officially to (*they allotted us each a pair of boots*; *the men were allotted duties*). **2** (foll. by *to*) give or distribute officially to (*a sum was allotted to each charity*). [OF *aloter* f. *a* to + LOT]

allotment /əˈlɒtmənt/ n. **1** a small piece of land rented (usu. from a local authority) for cultivation. **2** a share allotted. **3** the action of allotting.

allotrope /ˈælətrəʊp/ n. any of two or more different physical forms in which an element can exist (*graphite, charcoal, and diamond are all allotropes of carbon*). [back-form. f. ALLOTROPY]

allotropy /əˈlɒtrəpɪ/ n. the existence of two or more different physical forms of a chemical element. □ **allotropic** /ˌælə'trɒpɪk/ adj. **allotropical** /ˌælə'trɒpɪk(ə)l/ adj. [Gk allotropos of another form f. allos different + tropos manner f. trepō to turn]

allottee /əlɒ'tiː/ n. a person to whom something is allotted.

allow /əˈlaʊ/ v. 1 tr. permit (a practice, a person to do something, a thing to happen, etc.) (*smoking is not allowed; we allowed them to speak*). 2 tr. give or provide; permit (a person) to have a (limited quantity or sum) (*we were allowed £500 a year*). 3 tr. provide or set aside for a purpose; add or deduct in consideration of something (*allow 10% for inflation*). 4 tr. a admit, agree, concede (*he allowed that it was so*). b US state; be of the opinion. 5 refl. permit oneself, indulge oneself in (conduct) (*allowed herself to be persuaded*). 6 intr. (foll. by of) admit of. 7 intr. (foll. by for) take into consideration or account; make addition or deduction corresponding to (*allowing for wastage*). □ **allowable** adj. **allowably** adv. [ME, orig. = 'praise', f. OF alouer f. L allaudare to praise, and med.L allocare to place]

allowance /əˈlaʊəns/ n. & v. —n. 1 an amount or sum allowed to a person, esp. regularly. 2 an amount allowed in reckoning. 3 a deduction or discount (*an allowance on your old cooker*). 4 (foll. by of) tolerance of. —v.tr. make an allowance to (a person). □ **make allowances** (often foll. by for) 1 take into consideration (mitigating circumstances) (*made allowances for his demented state*). 2 look with tolerance upon, make excuses for (a person, bad behaviour, etc.). [ME f. OF alouance (as ALLOW)]

alloy /ˈælɔɪ, əˈlɔɪ/ n. & v. —n. 1 a mixture of two or more metals. 2 an inferior metal mixed esp. with gold or silver. —v.tr. 1 mix (metals). 2 debase (a pure substance) by admixture. [F aloi (n.), aloyer (v.) f. OF aloier, aleier combine f. L alligare bind]

allspice /ˈɔːlspaɪs/ n. 1 the aromatic spice obtained from the ground berry of the pimento plant, Pimenta dioica. 2 the berry of this plant.

allude /əˈluːd, əˈljuːd/ v.intr. (foll. by to) refer, esp. indirectly, covertly, or briefly to. [L alludere (as AD-, ludere lus- play)]

allure /əˈljʊə(r)/ v. & n. —v.tr. attract, charm, or fascinate. —n. attractiveness, personal charm, fascination. □ **allurement** n. [ME f. OF alurer attract (as AD-, luere LURE v. 1)]

allusion /əˈluːʒ(ə)n, əˈljuː-/ n. (often foll. by to) a reference, esp. a covert, passing, or indirect one. [F allusion or LL allusio (as ALLUDE)]

allusive /əˈluːsɪv, əˈljuː-/ adj. 1 (often foll. by to) containing an allusion. 2 containing many allusions. □ **allusively** adv. **allusiveness** n.

alluvial /əˈluːvɪəl/ adj. & n. —adj. of or relating to alluvium. —n. alluvium, esp. containing a precious metal.

alluvium /əˈluːvɪəm/ n. (pl. **alluvia** /-vɪə/ or **alluviums**) a deposit of usu. fine fertile soil left during a time of flood, esp. in a river valley or delta. [L neut. of alluvius adj. f. luere wash]

ally /ˈælaɪ/ n. & v. —n. (pl. **-ies**) 1 a State formally cooperating or united with another for a purpose,

esp. by a treaty. 2 a person or organization that cooperates with another. —v.tr. /also əˈlaɪ/ (**-ies**, **-ied**) (often foll. by with) combine or unite in alliance. [ME f. OF al(e)ier f. L alligare bind: cf. ALLOY]

-ally /əlɪ/ suffix forming adverbs from adjectives in -al (cf. -AL, -LY², -ICALLY).

Alma Mater /ˌælmə ˈmɑːtə(r), ˈmeɪtə(r)/ n. the university, school, or college one attends or attended. [L. = bounteous mother]

almanac /ˈɔːlmə,næk, ˈɒl-/ n. (also **almanack**) an annual calendar of months and days, usu. with astronomical data and other information. [ME f. med.L almanac(h) f. Gk almenikhiaka]

almighty /ɔːlˈmaɪtɪ/ adj. & adv. —adj. 1 having complete power; omnipotent. 2 (**the Almighty**) God. 3 sl. very great (*an almighty crash*). —adv. sl. extremely; very much. [OE ælmihtig (as ALL, MIGHTY)]

almond /ˈɑːmənd/ n. 1 the oval nutlike seed (kernel) of the stone-fruit from the tree Prunus dulcis. 2 the tree itself, allied to the peach and plum. □ **almond paste** = MARZIPAN. [ME f. OF alemande etc. f. med.L amandula f. L amygdala f. Gk amugdalē: assoc. with words in al- (see AD-)]

almoner /ˈɑːmənə(r)/ n. Brit. a social worker attached to a hospital and seeing to the after-care of patients. [ME f. AF aumoner, OF aumonier, ult. f. med.L eleēmosynarius (as ALMS)]

■ **Usage** The usual term now is *medical social worker*.

almost /ˈɔːlməʊst/ adv. all but; very nearly. [OE ælmæst for the most part (as ALL, MOST)]

alms /ɑːmz/ n.pl. hist. the charitable donation of money or food to the poor. [OE ælmysse, -messe, f. Gmc ult. f. Gk eleēmosunē compassionateness f. eleēmōn (adj.) f. eleos compassion]

almshouse /ˈɑːmzhaʊs/ n. hist. a house founded by charity for the poor.

almucantar /ˌælmə'kæntə(r)/ n. (also **almacantar**) Astron. a line of constant altitude above the horizon. [ME f. med.L almucantarath or F almucantara etc., f. Arab. almukanṭarāt sundial f. kanṭara arch]

aloe /ˈæləʊ/ n. 1 any plant of the genus Aloe, usu. having toothed fleshy leaves. 2 (in pl.) (in full **bitter aloes**) a strong laxative obtained from the bitter juice of various species of aloe. 3 (also **American aloe**) an agave native to Central America. [OE al(e)we f. L aloē f. Gk]

aloft /əˈlɒft/ predic.adj. & adv. 1 high up; overhead. 2 upwards. [ME f. ON á lopt(i) f. á in, on, to + lopt air: cf. LIFT, LOFT]

alogical /eɪ'lɒdʒɪk(ə)l/ adj. 1 not logical. 2 opposed to logic.

alone /əˈləʊn/ adj. & adv. —predic.adj. 1 a without others present (*they wanted to be alone; the tree stood alone*). b without others' help. c lonely. 2 (often foll. by in) standing by oneself in an opinion etc. (*was alone in thinking this*). —adv. only, exclusively (*you alone can help me*). □ **aloneness** n. [ME f. ALL + ONE]

along /əˈlɒŋ/ prep. & adv. —prep. 1 from one end to the other end of (*a handkerchief with lace along the edge*). 2 on or through any part of the length of (*was walking along the road*). 3 beside or through the length of (*shelves stood along the wall*). —adv. 1 onward; into a more advanced state (*come along; getting along nicely*). 2 at or to a particular place; arriving (*I'll be along soon*). 3 in company with a person, esp. oneself (*bring a book along*). **4** beside or through part or the whole length of a thing. □ **along with** in addition to; together with. [OE *andlang* f. WG, rel. to LONG¹]

alongshore /əlɒŋˈʃɔː(r)/ *adv.* along or by the shore.

alongside /əlɒŋˈsaɪd/ *adv.* & *prep.* —*adv.* at or to the side (of a ship, pier, etc.). —*prep.* close to the side of; next to. □ **alongside of** side by side with; together or simultaneously with.

aloof /əˈluːf/ *adj.* & *adv.* distant, unsympathetic. —*adv.* away, apart. □ **aloofly** *adv.* **aloofness** *n.* [orig. Naut., f. A² + LUFF]

alopecia /ˌæləˈpiːʃə/ *n. Med.* the absence of hair from areas of the body where it normally grows; baldness. [L f. Gk *alōpekia* fox-mange f. *alōpēx* fox]

aloud /əˈlaʊd/ *adv.* **1** audibly; not silently or in a whisper. **2** *archaic* loudly. [A² + LOUD]

alp /ælp/ *n.* **1 a** a high mountain. **b** (**the Alps**) the high range of mountains in Switzerland and adjoining countries. **2** (in Switzerland) pastureland on a mountainside. [orig. pl., f. F f. L *Alpes* f. Gk *Alpeis*]

alpaca /ælˈpækə/ *n.* **1** a S. American mammal, *Lama pacos*, related to the llama, with long shaggy hair. **2** the wool from the animal. **3** fabric made from the wool. [Sp. f. Aymará or Quechua]

alpenstock /ˈælpənstɒk/ *n.* a long iron-tipped staff used in hillwalking. [G, = Alp-stick]

alpha /ˈælfə/ *n.* the first letter of the Greek alphabet (A, α). □ **alpha and omega** the beginning and the end; the most important features. **alpha particle** (or **ray**) a helium nucleus emitted by a radioactive substance. [ME f. L f. Gk]

alphabet /ˈælfəbet/ *n.* **1** the set of letters used in writing a language. **2** a set of symbols or signs representing letters. [LL *alphabetum* f. Gk *alpha*, *bēta*, the first two letters of the alphabet]

alphabetical /ˌælfəˈbetɪk(ə)l/ *adj.* (also **alphabetic** /-ˈbetɪk/) **1** of or relating to an alphabet. **2** in the order of the letters of the alphabet. □ **alphabetically** *adv.*

alphabetize /ˈælfəbətaɪz/ *v.tr.* (also **-ise**) arrange in alphabetical order. □ **alphabetization** /-ˈzeɪʃ(ə)n/ *n.*

alphanumeric /ˌælfənjuːˈmerɪk/ *adj.* (also **alphameric** /ˌælfəˈmerɪk/, **alphanumerical**) containing both alphabetical and numerical symbols. [ALPHABETIC (see ALPHABETICAL) + NUMERICAL]

alpine /ˈælpaɪn/ *adj.* & *n.* —*adj.* **1 a** of or relating to high mountains. **b** growing or found on high mountains. **2** (**Alpine**) of or relating to the Alps. —*n.* a plant native or suited to mountain districts. [L *Alpinus*: see ALP]

Alpinist /ˈælpɪnɪst/ *n.* (also **alpinist**) a climber of high mountains, esp. the Alps. [F *alpiniste* (as ALPINE; see -IST)]

already /ɔːlˈredɪ/ *adv.* **1** before the time in question (*I knew that already*). **2** as early or as soon as this (*already at the age of six*). [ALL *adv.* + READY]

alright /ɔːlˈraɪt/ *adv. disp.* = all right.

■ **Usage** Although widely used, *alright* is still non-standard and is considered incorrect by many people.

Alsatian /ælˈseɪʃ(ə)n/ *n.* **1 a** a large dog of a breed of wolfhound. **b** this breed. **2** a native of Alsace, a region of E. France. [*Alsatia* (= Alsace) + -AN]

also /ˈɔːlsəʊ/ *adv.* in addition; likewise; besides. □ **also-ran 1** a horse or dog etc. not among the

winners in a race. **2** an undistinguished person. [OE *alswā* (as ALL *adv.*, SO¹)]

altar /ˈɔːltə(r), ˈɒl-/ *n.* **1** a table or flat-topped block, often of stone, for sacrifice or offering to a deity. **2** a Communion-table. [OE *altar* -er, Gmc adoption of LL *altar*, *altarium* f. L *altaria* (pl.) burnt offerings, altar, prob. rel. to *adolēre* burn in sacrifice]

altarpiece /ˈɔːltəpiːs, ˈɒl-/ *n.* a piece of art, esp. a painting, set above or behind an altar.

alter /ˈɔːltə(r), ˈɒl-/ *v.* **1** *tr.* & *intr.* make or become different; change. **2** *tr.* US & *Austral.* castrate or spay. □ **alterable** *adj.* **alteration** /-ˈreɪʃ(ə)n/ *n.* [ME f. OF *alterer* f. LL *alterare* f. L *alter* other]

alterative /ˈɔːltərətɪv, ˈɒl-/ *adj.* tending to alter. [ME f. med.L *alterativus* (as ALTER)]

altercate /ˈɔːltəkeɪt, ˈɒl-/ *v.intr.* (often foll. by *with*) dispute hotly; wrangle. □ **altercation** /-ˈkeɪʃ(ə)n/ *n.* [L *altercari* altercat-]

alter ego /ˌæltər ˈiːgəʊ, ˈegəʊ/ *n.* (pl. ***alter egos***) **1** an intimate and trusted friend. **2** a person's secondary or alternative personality. [L, = other self]

alternate *v.*, *adj.*, & *n.* —*v.* /ˈɔːltəneɪt, ˈɒl-/ **1** *intr.* (often foll. by *with*) (of two things) succeed each other by turns (*elation alternated with depression*). **2** *intr.* (foll. by *between*) change repeatedly (between two conditions). **3** *tr.* (often foll. by *with*) cause (two things) to succeed each other by turns (*the band alternated fast and slow tunes*; *we alternated criticism with reassurance*). —*adj.* /ɔːlˈtɜːnət, ɒl-/ **1** (with noun in *pl.*) every other (*comes on alternate days*). **2** (of things of two kinds) each following and succeeded by one of the other kind (*alternate joy and misery*). **3** (of a sequence etc.) consisting of alternate things. **4** = ALTERNATIVE. —*n.* /ɔːlˈtɜː-nət, ɒl-/ esp. *US* a deputy or substitute. □ **alternate angles** two angles, not adjoining one another, that are formed on opposite sides of a line that intersects two other lines. **alternating current** an electric current that reverses its direction at regular intervals. □ **alternately** /ɔːlˈtɜːnətlɪ, ɒl-/ *adv.* [L *alternatus* past part. of *alternare* do things by turns f. *alternus* every other f. *alter* other]

■ **Usage** See note at *alternative*.

alternation /ˌɔːltəˈneɪʃ(ə)n, ˌɒl-/ *n.* the action or result of alternating.

alternative /ɔːlˈtɜːnətɪv, ɒl-/ *adj.* & *n.* —*adj.* **1** (of one or more things) available or usable instead of another (*an alternative route*). **2** (of two things) mutually exclusive. **3** of or relating to practices that offer a substitute for the conventional ones (*alternative medicine*). —*n.* **1** any of two or more possibilities. **2** the freedom or opportunity to choose between two or more things (*I had no alternative but to go*). □ **alternatively** *adv.* [F *alternatif -ive* or med.L *alternativus* (as ALTERNATE)]

■ **Usage** The adjective *alternative* should not be confused with *alternate*, as in 'there will be a dance on alternate Saturdays'.

alternator /ˈɔːltəneɪtə(r), ˈɒl-/ *n.* a dynamo that generates an alternating current.

although /ɔːlˈðəʊ/ *conj.* = THOUGH *conj.* 1–3. [ME f. ALL *adv.* + THOUGH]

altimeter /ˈæltɪmiːtə(r)/ *n.* an instrument for showing height above sea or ground level, esp. one fitted to an aircraft. [L *altus* high + -METER]

altitude /ˈæltɪtjuːd/ *n.* **1** the height of an object in relation to a given point, esp. sea level or the horizon. **2** a high or exalted position (*a social altitude*). □ **altitude sickness** a sickness experienced at high altitudes. □ **altitudinal** /ˌæltɪˈtjuːdɪn(ə)l/ *adj.* [ME f. L *altitudo* f. *altus* high]

alto /ˈæltəʊ/ *n.* (*pl.* **-os**) **1** = CONTRALTO. **2 a** the highest adult male singing-voice, above tenor. **b** a singer with this voice. **c** a part written for it. **3 a** (*attrib.*) denoting the member of a family of instruments pitched second- or third-highest. **b** an alto instrument, esp. an alto saxophone. [It. *alto (canto)* high (singing)]

altocumulus /ˌæltəʊˈkjuːmjʊləs/ *n.* (*pl.* **altocumuli** /-ˌlaɪ/) *Meteorol.* a cloud formation at medium altitude consisting of rounded masses with a level base. [mod.L f. L *altus* high + CUMULUS]

altogether /ˌɔːltəˈgeðə(r)/ *adv.* **1** totally, completely (*you are altogether wrong*). **2** on the whole (*altogether it had been a good day*). **3** in total (*there are six bedrooms altogether*). □ **in the altogether** *colloq.* naked. [ME f. ALL + TOGETHER]

■ **Usage** Note that *altogether* means 'in total', whereas *all together* means 'all at once' or 'all in one place'. The phrases *six rooms altogether* (in total) and *six rooms all together* (in one place) illustrate the difference.

altostratus /ˌæltəʊˈstreɪtəs, -ˈstrɑːtəs/ *n.* (*pl.* **altostrati** /-tɪ/) a continuous and uniformly flat cloud formation at medium altitude. [mod.L f. L *altus* high + STRATUS]

altruism /ˈæltruːˌɪz(ə)m/ *n.* **1** regard for others as a principle of action. **2** unselfishness; concern for other people. □ **altruist** *n.* **altruistic** /ˌæltruːˈɪstɪk/ *adj.* **altruistically** /ˌæltruːˈɪstɪkəlɪ/ *adv.* [F *altruisme* f. It. *altrui* somebody else (infl. by L *alter* other)]

alum /ˈæləm/ *n.* a double sulphate of aluminium and potassium. [ME f. OF f. L *alumen aluminis*]

alumina /əˈluːmɪnə/ *n.* the compound aluminium oxide occurring naturally as corundum and emery. [L *alumen* alum, after *soda* etc.]

aluminium /ˌæljʊˈmɪnɪəm/ *n.* (US **aluminum** /əˈluːmɪnəm/) a silvery light and malleable metallic element resistant to tarnishing by air. [*aluminium*, alt. (after *sodium* etc.) f. *aluminum*, earlier *alumium* f. ALUM + -IUM]

aluminize /əˈluːmɪˌnaɪz/ *v.tr.* (also **-ise**) coat with aluminium. □ **aluminization** /-ˈzeɪʃ(ə)n/ *n.*

alumnus /əˈlʌmnəs/ *n.* (*pl.* **alumni** /-nɪ/; *fem.* **alumna**, *pl.* **alumnae** /-nɪ/) a former pupil or student. [L = nursling, pupil f. *alere* nourish]

alveolus /ælˈvɪələs, ˌælvɪˈəʊləs/ *n.* (*pl.* **alveoli** /-laɪ, -lɪ/) **1** a small cavity, pit, or hollow. **2** any of the many tiny air sacs of the lungs which allow for rapid gaseous exchange. **3** the bony socket for the root of a tooth. **4** the cell of a honeycomb. □ **alveolar** *adj.* **alveolate** *adj.* [L dimin. of *alveus* cavity]

always /ˈɔːlweɪz/ *adv.* **1** at all times; on all occasions (*they are always late*). **2** whatever the circumstances (*I can always sleep on the floor*). **3** repeatedly; often (*they are always complaining*). [ME, prob. distrib. genit. f. ALL + WAY + -'S¹]

alyssum /ˈælɪsəm/ *n.* any plant of the genus *Alyssum*, usu. having yellow or white flowers. [L f. Gk *alusson*]

Alzheimer's disease /ˈælts̩haɪməz/ *n.* a serious disorder of the brain manifesting itself in premature senility. [A. *Alzheimer*, Ger. neurologist d. 1915]

AM *abbr.* amplitude modulation.

Am *symb. Chem.* the element americium.

am 1st person sing. present of BE.

a.m. *abbr.* before noon. [L *ante meridiem*]

amalgam /əˈmælgəm/ *n.* **1** a mixture or blend. **2** an alloy of mercury with one or more other metals, used esp. in dentistry. [ME f. F *amalgame* or med.L *amalgama* f. Gk *malagma* an emollient]

amalgamate /əˈmælgəˌmeɪt/ *v.* **1** tr. & intr. combine or unite to form one structure, organization, etc. **2** *intr.* (of metals) alloy with mercury. □ **amalgamation** /-ˈmeɪʃ(ə)n/ *n.* [med.L *amalgamare amalgamat-* (as AMALGAM)]

amanuensis /əˌmænjʊˈensɪs/ *n.* (*pl.* **amanuenses** /-siːz/) **1** a person who writes from dictation or copies manuscripts. **2** a literary assistant. [L f. (*servus*) *a manu* secretary + *-ensis* belonging to]

amaranth /ˈæməˌrænθ/ *n.* **1** any plant of the genus *Amaranthus*, usu. having small green, red, or purple tinted foliage. **2** an imaginary flower that never fades. **3** a purple colour. □ **amaranthine** /ˌæməˈrænθaɪn/ *adj.* [F *amarante* or mod.L *amaranthus* f. L f. Gk *amarantos* everlasting f. *a-* not + *marainō* wither, alt. after *polyanthus* etc.]

amaryllis /ˌæməˈrɪlɪs/ *n.* **1** a plant genus with a single species, *Amaryllis belladonna*, a bulbous lily-like plant native to S. Africa with white or rose-pink flowers. [L f. Gk *Amarullis*, name of a country girl]

amass /əˈmæs/ *v.tr.* **1** gather or heap together. **2** accumulate (esp. riches). □ **amasser** *n.* [F *amasser* or med.L *amassare* ult. f. L *massa* MASS¹]

amateur /ˈæmətə(r)/ *n.* **1** a person who engages in a pursuit (e.g. an art or sport) as a pastime rather than a profession. **2** (*attrib.*) for or done by amateurs (*amateur athletics*). **3** (foll. by *of*) a person who is fond of a thing. □ **amateurism** *n.* [F f. It. *amatore* f. L *amator* *-oris* lover f. *amare* love]

amateurish /ˈæmətərɪʃ/ *adj.* characteristic of an amateur, esp. unskilful or inexperienced. □ **amateurishly** *adv.* **amateurishness** *n.*

amatory /ˈæmətərɪ/ *adj.* of or relating to sexual love or desire. [L *amatorius* f. *amare* love]

amaze /əˈmeɪz/ *v.tr.* (often foll. by *at*, or *that* + clause, or *to* + infin.) surprise greatly; overwhelm with wonder. □ **amazement** *n.* **amazing** *adj.* **amazingly** *adv.* **amazingness** *n.* [ME f. OE *āmasod* past part. of *āmasian*, of uncert. orig.]

Amazon /ˈæməz(ə)n/ *n.* **1** a member of a mythical race of female warriors in Scythia and elsewhere. **2** (**amazon**) a very tall, strong, or athletic woman. □ **Amazonian** /ˌæməˈzəʊnɪən/ *adj.* [ME f. L f. Gk: expl. by the Greeks as 'breastless' (as if A-¹ + *mazos* breast), but prob. of foreign orig.]

ambassador /æmˈbæsədə(r)/ *n.* **1** an accredited diplomat sent by a State on a mission to, or as its permanent representative in, a foreign country. **2** a representative or promoter of a specified thing (*an ambassador of peace*). □ **ambassadorial** /ˌæmbæsəˈdɔːrɪəl/ *adj.* **ambassadorship** *n.* [ME f. F *ambassadeur* f. It. *ambasciator*, ult. f. L *ambactus* servant]

ambassadress /æmˈbæsədrɪs/ *n.* **1** a female ambassador. **2** an ambassador's wife.

amber /ˈæmbə(r)/ *n.* & *adj.* —*n.* **1 a** a yellowish translucent fossilized resin deriving from extinct (esp. coniferous) trees and used in jewellery. **b** the honey-yellow colour of this. **2** a yellow traffic-light meaning caution, showing between red for 'stop' and green for 'go'. —*adj.* made of or coloured like amber. [ME f. OF *ambre* f. Arab. *'anbar* ambergris, amber]

ambergris /ˈæmbəgrɪs, -ˌgriːs/ *n.* a strong-smelling waxlike secretion of the intestine of the sperm whale, found floating in tropical seas and used in perfume manufacture. [ME f. OF *ambre gris* grey AMBER]

ambidextrous /ˌæmbɪˈdekstrəs/ *adj.* (also **ambidexterous**) able to use the right and left hands equally well. □ **ambidexterity** /-ˈsterɪtɪ/ *n.* **ambidextrously** *adv.* **ambidextrousness** *n.* [LL *ambidexter* f. *ambi-* on both sides + *dexter* right-handed]

ambience /ˈæmbɪəns/ *n.* (also **ambiance**) the surroundings or atmosphere of a place. [AMBIENT + -ENCE or F *ambiance*]

ambient /ˈæmbɪənt/ *adj.* surrounding. [F *ambiant* or L *ambiens -entis* pres. part. of *ambire* go round]

ambiguity /ˌæmbɪˈgjuːɪtɪ/ *n.* (*pl.* **-ies**) **1 a** a double meaning which is either deliberate or caused by inexactness of expression. **b** an example of this. **2** an expression able to be interpreted in more than one way. [ME f. OF *ambiguité* or L *ambiguitas* (as AMBIGUOUS)]

ambiguous /æmˈbɪgjʊəs/ *adj.* **1** having an obscure or double meaning. **2** difficult to classify. □ **ambiguously** *adv.* **ambiguousness** *n.* [L *ambiguus* doubtful f. *ambigere* f. *ambi-* both ways + *agere* drive]

ambit /ˈæmbɪt/ *n.* **1** the scope, extent, or bounds of something. **2** precincts or environs. [ME f. L *ambitus* circuit f. *ambire*: see AMBIENT]

ambition /æmˈbɪʃ(ə)n/ *n.* **1** (often foll. by *to* + infin.) the determination to achieve success or distinction, usu. in a chosen field. **2** the object of this determination. [ME f. OF f. L *ambitio -onis* f. *ambire ambit-* canvass for votes: see AMBIENT]

ambitious /æmˈbɪʃəs/ *adj.* **1 a** full of ambition. **b** showing ambition (*an ambitious attempt*). **2** (foll. by *of*, or *to* + infin.) strongly determined. □ **ambitiously** *adv.* **ambitiousness** *n.* [ME f. OF *ambitieux* f. L *ambitiosus* (as AMBITION)]

ambivalence /æmˈbɪvələns/ *n.* (also **ambivalency** /-ənsɪ/) the coexistence in one person's mind of opposing feelings, in a single context. □ **ambivalent** *adj.* **ambivalently** *adv.* [G *Ambivalenz* f. L *ambo* both, after *equivalence*, *-ency*]

amble /ˈæmb(ə)l/ *v.* & *n.* —*v.intr.* **1** move at an easy pace. **2** (of a horse etc.) move by lifting the two feet on one side together. **3** ride an ambling horse; ride at an easy pace. —*n.* an easy pace; the gait of an ambling horse. [ME f. OF *ambler* f. L *ambulare* walk]

amboyna /æmˈbɔɪnə/ *n.* the decorative wood of the SE Asian tree *Pterocarpus indicus*. [*Amboyna* Island in Indonesia]

ambrosia /æmˈbrəʊzɪə, -ʒjə/ *n.* **1** (in Greek and Roman mythology) the food of the gods; the elixir of life. **2** anything very pleasing to taste or smell. □ **ambrosial** *adj.* **ambrosian** *adj.* [L f. Gk, = elixir of life f. *ambrotos* immortal]

ambulance /ˈæmbjʊləns/ *n.* **1** a vehicle specially equipped for conveying the sick or injured to and from hospital, esp. in emergencies. **2** a mobile hospital following an army. [F (as AMBULANT)]

ambulant /ˈæmbjʊlənt/ *adj. Med.* **1** (of a patient) able to walk about; not confined to bed. **2** (of treatment) not confining a patient to bed. [L *ambulare ambulant-* walk]

ambulatory /ˈæmbjʊlətərɪ/ *adj.* & *n.* —*adj.* **1** = AMBULANT. **2** of or adapted for walking. **3** movable. —*n.* (*pl.* **-ies**) a place for walking, esp. an aisle or cloister in a church or monastery. [L *ambulatorius* f. *ambulare* walk]

ambuscade /ˌæmbəˈskeɪd/ *n.* & *v.* —*n.* an ambush. —*v.* **1** *tr.* attack by means of an ambush. **2** *intr.* lie in ambush. **3** *tr.* conceal in an ambush. [F *embuscade* f. It. *imboscata* or Sp. *emboscada* f. L *imboscare*: see AMBUSH, -ADE[1]]

ambush /ˈæmbʊʃ/ *n.* & *v.* —*n.* **1** a surprise attack by persons in a concealed position. **2 a** the concealment of troops etc. to make such an attack. **b** the place where they are concealed. **c** the troops etc. concealed. —*v.tr.* **1** attack by means of an ambush. **2** lie in wait for. [ME f. OF *embusche, embuschier,* f. a Rmc form = 'put in a wood': rel. to BUSH[1]]

ameba US var. of AMOEBA.

ameer var. of AMIR.

ameliorate /əˈmiːlɪəˌreɪt/ *v.tr.* & *intr. formal* make or become better; improve. □ **amelioration** /əˌmiːlɪəˈreɪʃ(ə)n/ *n.* **ameliorative** *adj.* **ameliorator** *n.* [alt. of MELIORATE after F *améliorer*]

amen /ɑːˈmen, eɪ-/ *int.* & *n.* —*int.* **1** uttered at the end of a prayer or hymn etc., meaning 'so be it'. **2** (foll. by *to*) expressing agreement or assent (*amen to that*). —*n.* an utterance of 'amen' (sense 1). [ME f. eccl.L f. Gk f. Heb. *'āmēn* certainly]

amenable /əˈmiːnəb(ə)l/ *adj.* **1** responsive, tractable. **2** (often foll. by *to*) (of a person) responsible to law. **3** (foll. by *to*) (of a thing) subject or liable. □ **amenability** /-ˈbɪlɪtɪ/ *n.* **amenableness** *n.* **amenably** *adv.* [AF (Law) f. F *amener* bring to f. *a-* to + *mener* bring f. LL *minare* drive animals f. L *minari* threaten]

amend /əˈmend/ *v.tr.* **1** make minor improvements in (a text or a written proposal). **2** correct an error or errors in (a document). **3** make better; improve. □ **amendable** *adj.* **amender** *n.* [ME f. OF *amender* ult. f. L *emendare* EMEND]

■ **Usage** This word is often confused with *emend,* a more technical word used in the context of textual correction.

amendment /əˈmendmənt/ *n.* **1** a minor improvement in a document (esp. a legal or statutory one). **2** an article added to the US Constitution. [AMEND + -MENT]

amends /əˈmendz/ *n.* □ **make amends** (often foll. by *for*) compensate or make up (for). [ME f. OF *amendes* penalties, fine, pl. of *amende* reparation f. *amender* AMEND]

amenity /əˈmiːnɪtɪ, əˈmenɪtɪ/ *n.* (*pl.* **-ies**) **1** (usu. in *pl.*) a pleasant or useful feature. **2** pleasantness (of a place, person, etc.). [ME f. OF *amenité* or L *amoenitas* f. *amoenus* pleasant]

amenorrhoea /eɪˌmenəˈrɪə/ *n.* (US **amenorrhea**) *Med.* an abnormal absence of menstruation. [A-[1] + MENO- + Gk *-rrhoia* f. *rheō* flow]

amentia /əˈmenʃə/ *n. Med.* severe congenital mental deficiency. [L f. *amens ament-* mad (as A-[1], *mens* mind)]

American /əˈmerɪkən/ *adj.* & *n.* —*adj.* **1** of, relating to, or characteristic of the United States or its inhabitants. **2** (usu. in *comb.*) of or relating to the continents of America (*Latin-American*). —*n.* **1** a native or citizen of the United States. **2** (usu. in *comb.*) a native or inhabitant of the continents of America (*North Americans*). **3** the English language as it is used in the United

States. □ **American football** a kind of football played with an oval ball, evolved from Rugby football. [mod.L *Americanus* f. *America* f. Latinized name of *Amerigo* Vespucci, It. navigator d. 1512]

Americanism /ə'merɪkə,nɪz(ə)m/ *n.* **1 a** a word, sense, or phrase peculiar to or originating from the United States. **b** a thing or feature characteristic of or peculiar to the United States. **2** attachment to or sympathy for the United States.

Americanize /ə'merɪkə,naɪz/ *v.* (also **-ise**) **1** *tr.* **a** make American in character. **b** naturalize as an American. **2** *intr.* become American in character. □ **Americanization** /-'zeɪʃ(ə)n/ *n.*

americium /ˌæmə'rɪsɪəm, -ʃɪəm/ *n. Chem.* an artificially made transuranic radioactive metallic element. [*America* (where first made) + -IUM]

Amerind /'æmərɪnd/ *adj. & n.* (also **Amerindian** /ˌæmə'rɪndɪən/) = *American Indian* □ **Amerindic** /-'rɪndɪk/ *adj.* [portmanteau word]

amethyst /'æmɪθɪst/ *n.* a precious stone of a violet or purple variety of quartz. □ **amethystine** /-'θɪstɪːn/ *adj.* [ME f. OF *ametiste* f. L *amethystus* f. Gk *amethustos* not drunken, the stone being supposed to prevent intoxication]

Amharic /æm'hærɪk/ *adj. & n.* —*n.* the official and commercial language of Ethiopia. —*adj.* of this language. [*Amhara*, Ethiopian province + -IC]

amiable /'eɪmɪəb(ə)l/ *adj.* friendly and pleasant in temperament; likeable. □ **amiability** /ˌeɪmɪə'bɪlɪtɪ/ *n.* **amiableness** *n.* **amiably** *adv.* [ME f. OF f. LL *amicabilis* amicable: confused with F *aimable* lovable]

amicable /'æmɪkəb(ə)l/ *adj.* showing or done in a friendly spirit (*an amicable meeting*). □ **amicability** /ˌæmɪkə'bɪlɪtɪ/ *n.* **amicableness** *n.* **amicably** *adv.* [LL *amicabilis* f. *amicus* friend]

amice[1] /'æmɪs/ *n.* a white linen cloth worn on the neck and shoulders by a priest celebrating the Eucharist. [ME f. med.L *amicia*, *-sia* (earlier *amit* f. OF), f. L *amictus* outer garment]

amice[2] /'æmɪs/ *n.* a cap, hood, or cape worn by members of certain religious orders. [ME f. OF *aumusse* f. med.L *almucia* etc., of unkn. orig.]

amid /ə'mɪd/ *prep.* (also **amidst** /ə'mɪdst/) **1** in the middle of. **2** in the course of. [ME *amidde(s)* f. OE *on* ON + MID[1]]

amide /'eɪmaɪd, 'æm-/ *n. Chem.* a compound formed from ammonia by replacement of one (or sometimes more than one) hydrogen atom by a metal or an acyl radical. [AMMONIA + -IDE]

amidships /ə'mɪdʃɪps/ *adv.* (US **amidship**) in or into the middle of a ship. [MIDSHIP after AMID]

amine /'eɪmɪːn, 'æm-/ *n. Chem.* a compound formed from ammonia by replacement of one or more hydrogen atoms by an organic radical or radicals. [AMMONIA + -INE[4]]

amino acid /ə'miːnəʊ/ *n. Biochem.* any of a group of organic compounds occurring naturally in plant and animal tissues and forming the basic constituents of proteins. [AMINE + ACID]

amir /ə'mɪə(r)/ *n.* (also **ameer**) the title of some Arab rulers. [Arab. *'amīr* commander f. *amara* command: cf. EMIR]

Amish /'ɑːmɪʃ, 'eɪ-/ *adj.* belonging to a strict US Mennonite sect. [prob. f. G *Amisch* f. J. *Amen* 17th-c. Swiss preacher]

amiss /ə'mɪs/ *predic.adj. & adv.* —*predic.adj.* wrong; out of order; faulty (*knew something was amiss*).

—*adv.* wrong; wrongly; inappropriately (*everything went amiss*). □ **take amiss** be offended by (*took my words amiss*). [ME prob. f. ON *à mis* so as to miss f. *à* on + *mis* rel. to MISS[1]]

amity /'æmɪtɪ/ *n.* friendship; friendly relations. [ME f. OF *amitié* ult. f. L *amicus* friend]

ammeter /'æmɪtə(r)/ *n.* an instrument for measuring electric current in amperes. [AMPERE + -METER]

ammo /'æməʊ/ *n. colloq.* ammunition. [abbr.]

ammonia /ə'məʊnɪə/ *n.* **1** a colourless strongly alkaline gas with a characteristic pungent smell. **2** (in full **ammonia water**) a solution of ammonia gas in water. [mod.L f. SAL AMMONIAC]

ammoniacal /ˌæmə'naɪək(ə)l/ *adj.* of, relating to, or containing ammonia or sal ammoniac. [ME *ammoniac* f. OF (*arm-*, *amm-*) f. L f. Gk *ammōniakos* of Ammon (cf. SAL AMMONIAC) + -AL]

ammoniated /ə'məʊnɪ,eɪtɪd/ *adj.* combined or treated with ammonia.

ammonite /'æmə,naɪt/ *n.* any extinct cephalopod mollusc of the order Ammonoidea, with a flat coiled spiral shell found as a fossil. [mod.L *ammonites*, after med.L *cornu Ammonis*, = L *Ammonis cornu* (Pliny), horn of (Jupiter) Ammon]

ammunition /ˌæmjʊ'nɪʃ(ə)n/ *n.* **1** a supply of projectiles (esp. bullets, shells, and grenades). **2** points used or usable to advantage in an argument. [obs. F *amunition*, corrupt. of (*la) munition* (the) MUNITION]

amnesia /æm'niːzɪə/ *n.* a partial or total loss of memory. □ **amnesiac** /-zɪ,æk/ *n.* **amnesic** *adj. & n.* [mod.L f. Gk, = forgetfulness]

amnesty /'æmnɪstɪ/ *n. & v.* —*n.* (*pl.* **-ies**) a general pardon. —*v.tr.* (**-ies**, **-ied**) grant an amnesty to. [F *amnestie* or L f. Gk *amnēstia* oblivion]

amniocentesis /ˌæmnɪəʊsen'tiːsɪs/ *n.* (*pl.* **amniocenteses** /-siːz/) *Med.* the sampling of amniotic fluid to determine the condition of an embryo. [AMNION + Gk *kentēsis* pricking f. *kentō* to prick]

amnion /'æmnɪən/ *n.* (*pl.* **amnia**) *Zool. & Physiol.* the innermost membrane that encloses the embryo of a reptile, bird, or mammal. □ **amniotic** /ˌæmnɪ'ɒtɪk/ *adj.* [Gk, = caul (dimin. of *amnos* lamb)]

amoeba /ə'miːbə/ *n.* (US **ameba**) (*pl.* **amoebas** or **amoebae** /-biː/) any usu. aquatic protozoan of the genus *Amoeba*, esp. *A. proteus*, capable of changing shape. □ **amoebic** *adj.* **amoeboid** *adj.* [mod.L f. Gk *amoibē* change]

amok /ə'mɒk/ *adv.* (also **amuck** /ə'mʌk/) □ **run amok** run about wildly in an uncontrollable violent rage. [Malay *amok* rushing in a frenzy]

among /ə'mʌŋ/ *prep.* (also **amongst** /ə'mʌŋst/) **1** surrounded by; in the company of (*lived among the trees*; *be among friends*). **2** in the number of (*among us were those who disagreed*). **3** an example of; in the class or category of (*is among the richest men alive*). **4 a** between; within the limits of (collectively or distributively); shared by (*divide it among you*). **b** by the joint action or from the joint resources of (*among us we can manage it*). **5** with one another; by the reciprocal action of (*was decided among the participants*). **6** as distinguished from; preeminent in the category of (*she is one among many*). [OE *ongemang* f. *on* ON + *gemang* assemblage (cf. MINGLE): *-st* = adverbial genitive *-s* + *-t* as in AGAINST]

amoral /eɪ'mɒr(ə)l/ *adj.* **1** outside the scope of morality. **2** having no moral principles. □

amoralism n. **amoralist** n. **amorality** /-ˈrælɪtɪ/ n.

amorous /ˈæmərəs/ adj. **1** showing, feeling, or inclined to sexual love. **2** of or relating to sexual love. □ **amorously** adv. **amorousness** n. [ME f. OF f. med.L amorosus f. L amor love]

amorphous /əˈmɔːfəs/ adj. **1** shapeless. **2** vague, ill-organized. **3** Mineral. & Chem. non-crystalline; having neither definite form nor structure. □ **amorphously** adv. **amorphousness** n. [med.L amorphus f. Gk amorphos shapeless f. a- not + morphē form]

amortize /əˈmɔːtaɪz/ v.tr. (also **-ise**) Commerce **1** gradually extinguish (a debt) by money regularly put aside. **2** gradually write off the initial cost of (assets). □ **amortization** /-ˈzeɪʃ(ə)n/ n. [ME f. OF amortir (stem amortiss-) ult. f. L ad to + mors mortdeath]

amount /əˈmaʊnt/ n. & v. —n. **1** a quantity, esp. the total of a thing or things in number, size, value, extent, etc. (a large amount of money). **2** the full effect or significance. —v.intr. (foll. by to) be equivalent to in number, size, significance, etc. (amounted to £100; amounted to a disaster). [ME f. OF amunter f. amont upward, lit. uphill, f. L ad montem]

amour /əˈmʊə(r)/ n. a love affair, esp. a secret one. [F, = love, f. L amor amoris]

amour propre /æˌmʊə ˈprɒpr/ n. self-respect. [F]

amp[1] n. Electr. an ampere. [abbr.]

amp[2] n. colloq. an amplifier. [abbr.]

ampelopsis /ˌæmpɪˈlɒpsɪs/ n. any plant of the genus Ampelopsis or Parthenocissus, usu. a climber supporting itself by twining tendrils, e.g. Virginia creeper. [mod.L f. Gk ampelos vine + opsis appearance]

amperage /ˈæmpərɪdʒ/ n. Electr. the strength of an electric current in amperes.

ampere /ˈæmpeə(r)/ n. Electr. the SI base unit of electric current. [A. M. Ampère, Fr. physicist d. 1836]

ampersand /ˈæmpəˌsænd/ n. the sign & (= and). [corrupt. of and per se and ('&' by itself is 'and')]

amphetamine /æmˈfetəmɪn, -ˌmiːn/ n. a synthetic drug used esp. as a stimulant. [abbr. of chemical name alpha-methyl phenethylamine]

amphi- /ˈæmfɪ/ comb. form **1** both. **2** of both kinds. **3** on both sides. **4** around. [Gk]

amphibian /æmˈfɪbɪən/ adj. & n. —adj. **1** living both on land and in water. **2** Zool. of or relating to the class Amphibia. **3** (of a vehicle) able to operate on land and water. —n. **1** Zool. any vertebrate of the class Amphibia, including frogs, toads and newts. **2** (in general use) a creature living both on land and in water. **3** an amphibian vehicle.

amphibious /æmˈfɪbɪəs/ adj. **1** living both on land and in water. **2** of or relating to both land and water. **3** Mil. **a** (of a military operation) involving forces landed from the sea. **b** (of forces) trained for such operations. □ **amphibiously** adv.

amphitheatre /ˈæmfɪˌθɪətə(r)/ n. (US **amphitheater**) **1** a round, usu. unroofed building with tiers of seats surrounding a central space. **2** a semicircular gallery in a theatre. [L amphitheatrum f. Gk amphitheatron (as AMPHI-, THEATRE)]

amphora /ˈæmfərə/ n. (pl. **amphorae** /-ˌriː/ or **amphoras**) a Greek or Roman vessel with two handles and a narrow neck. [L f. Gk amphoreus]

amphoteric /ˌæmfəˈterɪk/ adj. Chem. able to react as a base and an acid. [Gk amphoteros compar. of amphō both]

ample /ˈæmp(ə)l/ adj. (**ampler**, **amplest**) **1 a** plentiful, abundant, extensive. **b** euphem. (esp. of a person) large, stout. **2** enough or more than enough. □ **ampleness** n. **amply** adv. [F f. L amplus]

amplifier /ˈæmplɪˌfaɪə(r)/ n. an electronic device for increasing the strength of electrical signals, esp. for conversion into sound in radio etc. equipment.

amplify /ˈæmplɪˌfaɪ/ v. (**-ies**, **-ied**) **1** tr. increase the volume or strength of (sound, electrical signals, etc.). **2** tr. enlarge upon or add detail to (a story etc.). **3** intr. expand what is said or written. □ **amplification** /-fɪˈkeɪʃ(ə)n/ n. [ME f. OF amplifier f. L amplificare (as AMPLE, -FY)]

amplitude /ˈæmplɪˌtjuːd/ n. **1 a** Physics the maximum extent of a vibration or oscillation from the position of equilibrium. **b** Electr. the maximum departure of the value of an alternating current or wave from the average value. **2 a** spaciousness, breadth; wide range. **b** abundance. □ **amplitude modulation** Electr. **1** the modulation of a wave by variation of its amplitude. **2** the system using such modulation. [F amplitude or L amplitudo (as AMPLE)]

ampoule /ˈæmpuːl/ n. a small capsule in which measured quantities of liquids or solids, esp. for injecting, are sealed ready for use. [F f. L AMPULLA]

ampulla /æmˈpʊlə/ n. (pl. **ampullae** /-liː/) **1** a Roman globular flask with two handles. **2** a vessel for sacred uses. [L]

amputate /ˈæmpjʊˌteɪt/ v.tr. cut off by surgical operation (a part of the body, esp. a limb), usu. because of injury or disease. □ **amputation** /-ˈteɪʃ(ə)n/ n. **amputator** n. [L amputare f. ambabout + putare prune]

amputee /ˌæmpjʊˈtiː/ n. a person who has lost a limb etc. by amputation.

amtrac /ˈæmtræk/ n. (also **amtrak**) US an amphibious tracked vehicle used for landing assault troops on a shore. [amphibious + tractor]

amuck var. of AMOK.

amulet /ˈæmjʊlɪt/ n. **1** an ornament or small piece of jewellery worn as a charm against evil. **2** something which is thought to give such protection. [L amuletum, of unkn. orig.]

amuse /əˈmjuːz/ v. **1** tr. cause (a person) to laugh or smile. **2** tr. & refl. (often foll. by with, by) interest or occupy; keep (a person) entertained. □ **amusing** adj. **amusingly** adv. [ME f. OF amuser cause to muse (see MUSE[2]) f. causal a to + muser stare]

amusement /əˈmjuːzmənt/ n. **1** something that amuses, esp. a pleasant diversion, game, or pastime. **2 a** the state of being amused. **b** the act of amusing. **3** a mechanical device (e.g. a roundabout) for entertainment at a fairground etc. □ **amusement arcade** Brit. an indoor area for entertainment with automatic game-machines. [F f. amuser: see AMUSE, -MENT]

amylase /ˈæmɪˌleɪz/ n. Biochem. any of several enzymes that convert starch and glycogen into simple sugars. [L amylum starch: see DIASTASE]

an /æn, ən/ adj. the form of the indefinite article (see A[1]) used before words beginning with a vowel sound (an egg; an hour; an MP).

an- /ən, æn/ prefix not, without (anarchy) (cf. A-[1]). [Gk an-]

-an /ən/ *suffix* (also **-ean, -ian**) forming adjectives and nouns, esp. from names of places, systems, zoological classes or orders, and founders (*Mexican*; *Anglican*; *crustacean*; *European*; *Lutheran*; *Georgian*; *theologian*). [ult. f. L adj. endings -(*i*)*anus*, *-aeus*: cf. Gk *-aios, -eios*]

ana- /ˈænə/ *prefix* (usu. **an-** before a vowel) **1** up (*anadromous*). **2** back (*anamnesis*). **3** again (*anabaptism*). [Gk *ana* up]

-ana /ˈɑːnə/ *suffix* forming plural nouns meaning 'things associated with' (*Victoriana*; *Americana*). [neut. pl. of L adj. ending *-anus*]

Anabaptism /ˌænəˈbæptɪz(ə)m/ *n.* the doctrine that baptism should only be administered to believing adults. □ **Anabaptist** *n.* [eccl.L *anabaptismus* f. Gk *anabaptismos* (as ANA-, BAPTISM)]

anabolic /ˌænəˈbɒlɪk/ *adj. Biochem.* of or relating to anabolism. □ **anabolic steroid** any of a group of synthetic steroid hormones used to increase muscle size.

anabolism /əˈnæbəˌlɪz(ə)m/ *n. Biochem.* the synthesis of complex molecules in living organisms from simpler ones together with the storage of energy; constructive metabolism. [Gk *anabolē* ascent (as ANA-, *ballō* throw)]

anachronism /əˈnækrəˌnɪz(ə)m/ *n.* **1 a** the attribution of a custom, event, etc., to a period to which it does not belong. **b** a thing attributed in this way. **2 a** anything out of harmony with its period. **b** an old-fashioned or out-of-date person or thing. □ **anachronistic** /-ˈnɪstɪk/ *adj.* **anachronistically** /-ˈnɪstɪkəlɪ/ *adv.* [F *anachronisme* or Gk *anakhronismos* (as ANA-, *khronos* time)]

anaconda /ˌænəˈkɒndə/ *n.* a large non-poisonous snake that kills its prey by constriction. [alt. of *anacondaia* f. Sinh. *henakandayā* whip-snake f. *hena* lightning + *kanda* stem: orig. of a snake in Sri Lanka]

anaemia /əˈniːmɪə/ *n.* (US **anemia**) a deficiency in the blood, usu. of red cells or their haemoglobin, resulting in pallor and weariness. □ **pernicious anaemia** a defective formation of red blood cells through a lack of vitamin B_{12} or folic acid. [mod.L f. Gk *anaimia* f. AN-, *haima* blood]

anaemic /əˈniːmɪk/ *adj.* (US **anemic**) **1** relating to or suffering from anaemia. **2** pale; lacking in vitality.

anaerobe /ˈænəˌrəʊb, əˈneərəʊb/ *n.* an organism that grows without air, or requires oxygen-free conditions to live. □ **anaerobic** /ˌæneəˈrəʊbɪk/ *adj.* [F *anaérobie* formed as AN- + AEROBE]

anaesthesia /ˌænɪsˈθiːzɪə/ *n.* (US **anesthesia**) the absence of sensation, esp. artificially induced insensitivity to pain. □ **anaesthesiology** /-ˈɒlədʒɪ/ *n.* [mod.L f. Gk *anaisthēsia* (as AN-, *aisthēsis* sensation)]

anaesthetic /ˌænɪsˈθetɪk/ *adj. & n.* (US **anesthetic**) —*n.* a substance that produces insensibility to pain etc. —*adj.* producing partial or complete insensibility to pain etc. □ **general anaesthetic** an anaesthetic that affects the whole body, usu. with loss of consciousness. **local anaesthetic** an anaesthetic that affects a restricted area of the body. [Gk *anaisthētos* insensible (as ANAESTHESIA)]

anaesthetist /əˈniːsθətɪst/ *n.* a specialist in the administration of anaesthetics.

anaesthetize /əˈniːsθəˌtaɪz/ *v.tr.* (also **-ise,** US **anesthetize**) **1** administer an anaesthetic to. **2** deprive of physical or mental sensation. □ **anaesthetization** /-ˈzeɪʃ(ə)n/ *n.*

anaglypta /ˌænəˈglɪptə/ *n.* a type of thick embossed wallpaper, usu. for painting over. [L *anaglypta* work in bas-relief]

anagram /ˈænəˌgræm/ *n.* a word or phrase formed by transposing the letters of another word or phrase. □ **anagrammatic** /-grəˈmætɪk/ *adj.* **anagrammatical** /-grəˈmætɪk(ə)l/ *adj.* **anagrammatize** /-ˈgræməˌtaɪz/ *v.tr.* (also **-ise**). [F *anagramme* or mod.L *anagramma* f. Gk ANA- + *gramma -atos* letter: cf. -GRAM]

anal /ˈeɪn(ə)l/ *adj.* relating to or situated near the anus. □ **anal retentive** (of a person) excessively orderly and fussy (supposedly owing to aspects of toilet-training in infancy). □ **anally** *adv.* [mod.L *analis* (as ANUS)]

analgesia /ˌænælˈdʒiːzɪə, -sɪə/ *n.* the absence or relief of pain. [mod.L f. Gk, = painlessness]

analgesic /ˌænælˈdʒiːsɪk, -zɪk/ *adj. & n.* —*adj.* relieving pain. —*n.* an analgesic drug.

analogize /əˈnæləˌdʒaɪz/ *v.* (also **-ise**) **1** *tr.* represent or explain by analogy. **2** *intr.* use analogy.

analogous /əˈnæləgəs/ *adj.* (usu. foll. by *to*) partially similar or parallel; showing analogy. □ **analogously** *adv.* [L *analogus* f. Gk *analogos* proportionate]

analogue /ˈænəˌlɒg/ *n.* (US **analog**) **1** an analogous or parallel thing. **2** (*attrib.*) (usu. **analog**) (of a computer or electronic process) using physical variables, e.g. voltage, weight, or length, to represent numbers. [F f. Gk *analogon* neut. adj.: see ANALOGOUS]

analogy /əˈnælədʒɪ/ *n.* (pl. **-ies**) **1** (usu. foll. by *to, with, between*) correspondence or partial similarity. **2** *Logic* a process of arguing from similarity in known respects to similarity in other respects. **3** *Philol.* the imitation of existing words in forming inflections or constructions of others. **4** *Biol.* the resemblance of function between organs essentially different. □ **analogical** /ˌænəˈlɒdʒɪk(ə)l/ *adj.* **analogically** /ˌænəˈlɒdʒɪkəlɪ/ *adv.* [F *analogie* or L *analogia* proportion f. Gk (as ANALOGOUS)]

analyse /ˈænəˌlaɪz/ *v.tr.* (US **analyze**) **1** examine in detail the constitution or structure of. **2** *Chem.* ascertain the constituents of (a sample of a mixture or compound). **3** find or show the essence or structure of (a book, music, etc.). **4** psychoanalyse. □ **analysable** *adj.* **analyser** *n.* [obs. *analyse* (n.) or F *analyser* f. *analyse* (n.) f. med.L ANALYSIS]

analysis /əˈnælɪsɪs/ *n.* (pl. **analyses** /-ˌsiːz/) **1 a** a detailed examination of the elements or structure of a substance etc. **b** a statement of the result of this. **2** *Chem.* the determination of the constituent parts of a mixture or compound. **3** psychoanalysis. [med.L f. Gk *analusis* (as ANA-, *luō* set free)]

analyst /ˈænəlɪst/ *n.* **1** a person skilled in (esp. chemical) analysis. **2** a psychoanalyst. [F *analyste*]

analytic /ˌænəˈlɪtɪk/ *adj.* of or relating to analysis. [LL f. Gk *analutikos* (as ANALYSIS)]

analytical /ˌænəˈlɪtɪk(ə)l/ *adj.* using analytic methods. □ **analytical geometry** geometry using coordinates. □ **analytically** *adv.*

anamnesis /ˌænəmˈniːsɪs/ *n.* (pl. **anamneses** /-siːz/) recollection (esp. of a supposed previous existence). [Gk, = remembrance]

anapaest /ˈænəˌpiːst/ *n.* (US **anapest**) *Prosody* a foot consisting of two short or unstressed syllables followed by one long or stressed syllable. □ **anapaestic** /-ˈpiːstɪk/ *adj.* [L *anapaestus* f. Gk

anapaistos reversed (because the reverse of a dactyl)]

anaphora /əˈnæfərə/ *n.* **1** *Rhet.* the repetition of a word or phrase at the beginning of successive clauses. **2** *Gram.* the use of a word referring to or replacing a word used earlier in a sentence, to avoid repetition (e.g. *do* in *I like it and so do they*). □ **anaphoric** /ænəˈfɒrɪk/ *adj.* [L f. Gk, = repetition (as ANA-, *pherō* to bear)]

anaphrodisiac /ænˌæfrəˈdɪzɪˌæk/ *adj.* & *n.* —*adj.* tending to reduce sexual desire. —*n.* an anaphrodisiac drug.

anarchism /ˈænəˌkɪz(ə)m/ *n.* the doctrine that all government should be abolished. [F *anarchisme* (as ANARCHY)]

anarchist /ˈænəkɪst/ *n.* an advocate of anarchism or of political disorder. □ **anarchistic** /-ˈkɪstɪk/ *adj.* [F *anarchiste* (as ANARCHY)]

anarchy /ˈænəkɪ/ *n.* **1** disorder, esp. political or social. **2** lack of government in a society. □ **anarchic** /əˈnɑːkɪk/ *adj.* **anarchical** /əˈnɑːkɪk(ə)l/ *adj.* **anarchically** /əˈnɑːkɪkəlɪ/ *adv.* [med.L f. Gk *anarkhia* (as AN-, *arkhē* rule)]

anastigmat /əˈnæstɪɡˌmæt/ *n.* a lens or lens-system made free from astigmatism by correction. [G f. *anastigmatisch* ANASTIGMATIC]

anastigmatic /ˌænəstɪɡˈmætɪk/ *adj.* free from astigmatism.

anathema /əˈnæθəmə/ *n.* (*pl.* **anathemas**) **1** a detested thing or person (*is anathema to me*). **2 a** a curse of the Church, excommunicating a person or denouncing a doctrine. **b** a cursed thing or person. **c** a strong curse. [eccl.L, = excommunicated person, excommunication, f. Gk *anathema* thing devoted, (later) accursed thing, f. *anatithēmi* set up]

anathematize /əˈnæθəməˌtaɪz/ *v.tr.* & *intr.* (also **-ise**) curse. [F *anathématiser* f. L *anathematīzāre* f. Gk *anathematizo* (as ANATHEMA)]

anatomical /ˌænəˈtɒmɪk(ə)l/ *adj.* **1** of or relating to anatomy. **2** structural. □ **anatomically** *adv.* [F *anatomique* or LL *anatomicus* (as ANATOMY)]

anatomist /əˈnætəmɪst/ *n.* a person skilled in anatomy. [F *anatomiste* or med.L *anatomista* (as ANATOMIZE)]

anatomize /əˈnætəˌmaɪz/ *v.tr.* (also **-ise**) **1** examine in detail. **2** dissect. [F *anatomiser* or med.L *anatomizare* f. *anatomia* (as ANATOMY)]

anatomy /əˈnætəmɪ/ *n.* (*pl.* **-ies**) **1** the science of the bodily structure of animals and plants. **2** this structure. **3** *colloq.* a human body. **4** analysis. [F *anatomie* or LL *anatomia* f. Gk (as ANA-, -TOMY)]

anatta (also **anatto**) var. of ANNATTO.

-ance /əns/ *suffix* forming nouns expressing: **1** a quality or state or an instance of one (*arrogance*; *protuberance*; *relevance*; *resemblance*). **2** an action (*assistance*; *furtherance*; *penance*). [from or after F *-ance* f. L *-antia*, *-entia* (cf. -ENCE) f. pres. part. stem *-ant-*, *-ent-*]

ancestor /ˈænsestə(r)/ *n.* (*fem.* **ancestress** /-strɪs/) **1** any (esp. remote) person from whom one is descended. **2** an early type of animal or plant from which others have evolved. **3** an early prototype or forerunner (*ancestor of the computer*). [ME f. OF *ancestre* f. L *antecessor* *-oris* f. *antecedere* (as ANTE-, *cedere cess-* go)]

ancestral /ænˈsestr(ə)l/ *adj.* belonging to or inherited from one's ancestors. [F *ancestrel* (as ANCESTOR)]

ancestry /ˈænsestrɪ/ *n.* (*pl.* **-ies**) **1** one's (esp. remote) family descent. **2** one's ancestors collectively. [ME alt. of OF *ancesserie* (as ANCESTOR)]

anchor /ˈæŋkə(r)/ *n.* & *v.* —*n.* **1** a heavy metal weight used to moor a ship to the sea-bottom or a balloon to the ground. **2** a thing affording stability. **3** a source of confidence. —*v.* **1** *tr.* secure (a ship or balloon) by means of an anchor. **2** *tr.* fix firmly. **3** *intr.* cast anchor. **4** *intr.* be moored by means of an anchor. □ **anchor-plate** a heavy piece of timber or metal, e.g. as support for suspension-bridge cables. **cast** (or **come to**) **anchor** let the anchor down. **weigh anchor** take the anchor up. [OE *ancor* f. L *anchora* f. Gk *agkura*]

anchorage /ˈæŋkərɪdʒ/ *n.* **1** a place where a ship may be anchored. **2** the act of anchoring or lying at anchor. **3** anything dependable.

anchorite /ˈæŋkəˌraɪt/ *n.* (also **anchoret** /-rɪt/) (*fem.* **anchoress** /-rɪs/) **1** a hermit; a religious recluse. **2** a person of secluded habits. □ **anchoretic** /-ˈretɪk/ *adj.* **anchoritic** /-ˈrɪtɪk/ *adj.* [ME f. med.L *anc(h)orita*, eccl.L *anchoreta* f. eccl.Gk *anakhōrētēs* f. *anakhōreō* retire]

anchorman /ˈæŋkəmən/ *n.* (*pl.* **-men**) **1** a person who coordinates activities, esp. as compère in a broadcast. **2** a person who plays a crucial part, esp. at the back of a tug-of-war team or as the last runner in a relay race.

anchovy /ˈæntʃəvɪ, ænˈtʃəʊvɪ/ *n.* (*pl.* **-ies**) any of various small silvery fish of the herring family usu. preserved in salt and oil and having a strong taste. [Sp. & Port. *ancho(v)a*, of uncert. orig.]

anchusa /ænˈkjuːzə, ænˈtʃuːzə/ *n.* any plant of the genus *Anchusa*, akin to borage. [L f. Gk *agkhousa*]

anchylose var. of ANKYLOSE.

anchylosis var. of ANKYLOSIS.

ancien régime /ɑ̃sjæ̃ reˈʒiːm/ *n.* (*pl.* **anciens régimes** *pronunc.* same) **1** the political and social system in France before the Revolution of 1789. **2** any superseded regime. [F, = old rule]

ancient /ˈeɪnʃ(ə)nt/ *adj.* & *n.* —*adj.* **1** of long ago. **2** having lived or existed long. —*n.* *archaic* an old man. □ **ancient history 1** the history of the ancient civilizations of the Mediterranean area and the Near East before the fall of the Western Roman Empire in 476. **2** something already long familiar. **ancient lights** a window that a neighbour may not deprive of light by building. **ancient monument** *Brit.* an old building etc. preserved usu. under Government control. □ **ancientness** *n.* [ME f. AF *auncien* f. OF *ancien*, ult. f. L *ante* before]

anciently /ˈeɪnʃəntlɪ/ *adv.* long ago.

ancillary /ænˈsɪlərɪ/ *adj.* & *n.* —*adj.* **1** (of a person, activity, or service) providing essential support to a central service or industry, esp. the medical service. **2** (often foll. by *to*) subordinate, subservient. —*n.* (*pl.* **-ies**) **1** an ancillary worker. **2** something which is ancillary; an auxiliary or accessory. [L *ancillaris* f. *ancilla* maidservant]

-ancy /ənsɪ/ *suffix* forming nouns denoting a quality (*constancy*; *relevancy*) or state (*expectancy*; *infancy*) (cf. -ANCE). [from or after L *-antia*: cf. -ENCY]

and /ænd, ənd/ *conj.* **1 a** connecting words, clauses, or sentences, that are to be taken jointly (*cakes and buns*; *white and brown bread*; *buy and sell*; *two hundred and forty*). **b** implying progression (*better and better*). **c** implying causation (*do that and I'll* hit you; *she hit him and he cried*). **d** implying great duration (*he cried and cried*). **e** implying a great number (*miles and miles*). **f** implying addition (*two and two are four*). **g** implying variety (*there are books and books*). **h** implying succession (*walking two and two*). **2** *colloq.* to (*try and open it*). **3** in relation to (*Britain and the EC*). [OE *and*]

-and /ænd/ *suffix* forming nouns meaning 'a person or thing to be treated in a specified way' (*ordinand*). [L gerundive ending -*andus*]

andante /æn'dænti/ *adv., adj., & n. Mus.* —*adv. & adj.* in a moderately slow tempo. —*n.* an andante passage or movement. [It., part. of *andare* go]

andiron /'ænd,aɪən/ *n.* a metal stand (usu. one of a pair) for supporting burning wood in a fire-place; a firedog. [ME f. OF *andier*, of unkn. orig.: assim. to IRON]

androgen /'ændrədʒ(ə)n/ *n.* a male sex hormone or other substance capable of developing and maintaining certain male sexual characteristics. □ **androgenic** /-'dʒenɪk/ *adj.* [Gk *andro-* male + -GEN]

androgyne /'ændrə,dʒaɪn/ *adj. & n.* —*adj.* hermaphrodite. —*n.* a hermaphrodite person. [OF *androgyne* or L *androgynus* f. Gk *androgunos* (*anēr andros* male, *gunē* woman)]

androgynous /æn'drɒdʒɪnəs/ *adj.* **1** hermaphrodite. **2** *Bot.* with stamens and pistils in the same flower or inflorescence.

androgyny /æn'drɒdʒɪnɪ/ *n.* hermaphroditism.

android /'ændrɔɪd/ *n.* a robot with a human appearance. [Gk *andro-* male, man + -OID]

-androus /'ændrəs/ *comb. form Bot.* forming adjectives meaning 'having specified male organs or stamens' (*monandrous*). [mod.L f. Gk -*andros* f. *anēr andros* male + -OUS]

-ane¹ *suffix* var. of -AN; usu. with distinction of sense (*germane; humane; urbane*) but sometimes with no corresponding form in -*an* (*mundane*).

-ane² *suffix Chem.* forming names of paraffins and other saturated hydrocarbons (*methane; propane*). [after -*ene*, -*ine*, etc.]

anecdote /'ænɪk,dəʊt/ *n.* a short account (or painting etc.) of an entertaining or interesting incident. □ **anecdotal** /-'dəʊt(ə)l/ *adj.* **anecdotalist** /-'dəʊtəlɪst/ *n.* **anecdotic** /-'dɒtɪk/ *adj.* **anecdotist** *n.* [F *anecdote* or mod.L f. Gk *anekdota* things unpublished (as AN-, *ekdotos* f. *ekdidōmi* publish)]

anechoic /,ænɪ'kəʊɪk/ *adj.* free from echo.

anemia *US* var. of ANAEMIA.

anemic *US* var. of ANAEMIC.

anemometer /,ænɪ'mɒmɪtə(r)/ *n.* an instrument for measuring the force of the wind. [Gk *anemos* wind + -METER]

anemone /ə'nemənɪ/ *n.* **1** any plant of the genus *Anemone*, akin to the buttercup, with flowers of various vivid colours. **2** = PASQUE-FLOWER. [L f. Gk *anemōnē* wind-flower f. *anemos* wind]

-aneous /'eɪnɪəs/ *suffix* forming adjectives (*cutaneous; miscellaneous*). [L -*aneus* + -OUS]

aneroid /'ænə,rɔɪd/ *adj. & n.* —*adj.* (of a barometer) that measures air-pressure by its action on the elastic lid of an evacuated box, not by the height of a column of fluid. —*n.* an aneroid barometer. [F *anéroïde* f. Gk *a-* not + *nēros* water]

anesthesia etc. *US* var. of ANAESTHESIA etc.

aneurysm /'ænjʊ,rɪz(ə)m/ *n.* (also **aneurism**) an excessive localized enlargement of an artery. □ **aneurysmal** /-'rɪzm(ə)l/ *adj.* (also **aneurismal**).

[Gk *aneurusma* f. *aneurunō* widen out f. *eurus* wide]

anew /ə'nju:/ *adv.* **1** again. **2** in a different way. [ME, f. A-⁴ + NEW]

angel /'eɪndʒ(ə)l/ *n.* **1 a** an attendant or messenger of God. **b** a conventional representation of this in human form with wings. **c** an attendant spirit (*evil angel; guardian angel*). **2 a** a very virtuous person. **b** an obliging person (*be an angel and answer the door*). **3** *sl.* a financial backer of an enterprise, esp. in the theatre. **4** an unexplained radar echo. □ **angel cake** a very light sponge cake. **angel-fish** any of various fish, esp. *Pterophyllum scalare*, with large fins. [ME f. OF *angele* f. eccl.L *angelus* f. Gk *aggelos* messenger]

angelic /æn'dʒelɪk/ *adj.* **1** like or relating to angels. **2** having characteristics attributed to angels, esp. sublime beauty or innocence. □ **angelical** *adj.* **angelically** *adv.* [ME f. F *angélique* or LL *angelicus* f. Gk *aggelikos* (as ANGEL)]

angelica /æn'dʒelɪkə/ *n.* **1** an aromatic umbel-liferous plant, *Angelica archangelica*, used in cooking and medicine. **2** its candied stalks. [med.L (*herba*) *angelica* angelic herb]

angelus /'ændʒɪləs/ *n.* **1** a Roman Catholic devotion commemorating the Incarnation, said at morning, noon, and sunset. **2** a bell rung to announce this. [opening words *Angelus domini* (L, = the angel of the Lord)]

anger /'æŋgə(r)/ *n. & v.* —*n.* extreme or passionate displeasure. —*v.tr.* make angry; enrage. [ME f. ON *angr* grief, *angra* vex]

angina /æn'dʒaɪnə/ *n.* **1** an attack of intense constricting pain often causing suffocation. **2** (in full **angina pectoris** /'pektərɪs/) pain in the chest brought on by exertion, owing to an inadequate blood supply to the heart. [L, = spasm of the chest f. *angina* quinsy f. Gk *agkhonē* strangling]

angiosperm /'ændʒɪə,spɜ:m/ *n.* any plant producing flowers and reproducing by seeds enclosed within a carpel, including herbaceous plants, herbs, shrubs, grasses and most trees. □ **angiospermous** /,ændʒɪə'spɜ:məs/ *adj.* [Gk *aggeion* vessel + *sperma* seed]

Angle /'æŋg(ə)l/ *n.* (usu. in *pl.*) a member of a tribe from Schleswig that settled in Eastern Britain in the 5th c. □ **Anglian** *adj.* [L *Anglus* f. Gmc (OE *Engle*: cf. ENGLISH) f. *Angul* a district of Schleswig (now in N. Germany) (as ANGLE²)]

angle¹ /'æŋg(ə)l/ *n. & v.* —*n.* **1 a** the space between two meeting lines or surfaces. **b** the inclination of two lines or surfaces to each other. **2 a** a corner. **b** a sharp projection. **3 a** the direction from which a photograph etc. is taken. **b** the aspect from which a matter is considered. —*v.* **1** *tr.* move or place obliquely. **2** *tr.* present (information) from a particular point of view (*was angled in favour of the victim*). [ME f. OF *angle* or f. L *angulus*]

angle² /'æŋg(ə)l/ *v.intr.* **1** (often foll. by *for*) fish with hook and line. **2** (foll. by *for*) seek an objective by calculated means (*angled for a pay rise*). [OE *angul*]

angled /'æŋg(ə)ld/ *adj.* **1** placed at an angle to something else. **2** presented to suit a particular point of view. **3** having an angle.

angler /'æŋglə(r)/ *n.* **1** a person who fishes with a hook and line. **2** = *angler-fish*. □ **angler-fish** any of various fishes that prey upon small fish, attracting them by filaments arising from the dorsal fin.

Anglican /ˈæŋɡlɪkən/ adj. & n. —adj. of or relating to the Church of England or any Church in communion with it. —n. a member of an Anglican Church. □ **Anglicanism** n. [med.L Anglicanus (Magna Carta) f. Anglicus (Bede) f. Anglus ANGLE]

Anglicism /ˈæŋɡlɪˌsɪz(ə)m/ n. 1 a peculiarly English word or custom. 2 Englishness. 3 preference for what is English. [L Anglicus (see ANGLICAN) + -ISM]

Anglicize /ˈæŋɡlɪˌsaɪz/ v.tr. (also -ise) make English in form or character.

Anglo /ˈæŋɡləʊ/ n. (pl. -os) US a person of British or northern-European origin. [abbr. of ANGLO-SAXON]

Anglo- /ˈæŋɡləʊ/ comb. form 1 English (Anglo-Catholic). 2 of English origin (an Anglo-American). 3 English or British and (an Anglo-American agreement). [f. mod.L f. L Anglus English]

Anglo-Catholic /ˌæŋɡləʊˈkæθəlɪk/ adj. & n. —adj. of a High Church Anglican group which emphasizes its Catholic tradition. —n. a member of this group.

Anglocentric /ˌæŋɡləʊˈsentrɪk/ adj. centred on or considered in terms of England.

Anglo-French /ˌæŋɡləʊˈfrentʃ/ adj. & n. —adj. 1 English (or British) and French. 2 of Anglo-French. —n. the French language as retained and separately developed in England after the Norman Conquest.

Anglo-Indian /ˌæŋɡləʊˈɪndɪən/ adj. & n. —adj. 1 of or relating to England and India. 2 a of British descent or birth but living or having lived long in India. b of mixed British and Indian parentage. 3 (of a word) adopted into English from an Indian language. —n. an Anglo-Indian person.

Anglo-Norman /ˌæŋɡləʊˈnɔːmən/ adj. & n. —adj. 1 English and Norman. 2 of the Normans in England after the Norman Conquest. 3 of the dialect of French used by them. —n. the Anglo-Norman dialect.

Anglophile /ˈæŋɡləʊˌfaɪl/ n. & adj. (also **Anglophil** /-fɪl/) —n. a person who is fond of or greatly admires England or the English. —adj. being or characteristic of an Anglophile.

Anglophobe /ˈæŋɡləʊˌfəʊb/ n. & adj. —n. a person who greatly hates or fears England or the English. —adj. being or characteristic of an Anglophobe.

Anglophobia /ˌæŋɡləʊˈfəʊbɪə/ n. intense hatred or fear of England or the English.

anglophone /ˈæŋɡləʊˌfəʊn/ adj. & n. —adj. English-speaking. —n. an English-speaking person. [ANGLO-, after FRANCOPHONE]

Anglo-Saxon /ˌæŋɡləʊˈsæks(ə)n/ adj. & n. —adj. 1 of the English Saxons (as distinct from the Old Saxons of the continent, and from the Angles) before the Norman Conquest. 2 of the Old English people as a whole before the Norman Conquest. 3 of English descent. —n. 1 an Anglo-Saxon person. 2 the Old English language. 3 a colloq. plain (esp. crude) English. b US the modern English language. [mod.L Anglo-Saxones, med.L Angli Saxones after OE Angulseaxe, -an]

angora /æŋˈɡɔːrə/ n. 1 a fabric made from the hair of the angora goat or rabbit. 2 a long-haired variety of cat, goat, or rabbit. □ **angora wool** a mixture of sheep's wool and angora rabbit hair. [Angora (Ankara) in Turkey]

angostura /ˌæŋɡəˈstjʊərə/ n. (in full **angostura bark**) an aromatic bitter bark used as a flavouring, and formerly used as a tonic and to reduce fever. [Angostura, a town in Venezuela on the Orinoco, now Ciudad Bolívar]

angry /ˈæŋɡrɪ/ adj. (**angrier, angriest**) 1 feeling or showing anger; extremely displeased or resentful. 2 (of a wound, sore, etc.) inflamed, painful. 3 suggesting or seeming to show anger (an angry sky). □ **angrily** adv. [ME, f. ANGER + -Y¹]

angst /æŋst/ n. 1 anxiety. 2 a feeling of guilt or remorse. [G]

angstrom /ˈæŋstrəm/ n. (also **ångström** /ˈɒn strɜːm/) a unit of length equal to 10^{-10} metre. [A. J. Ångström, Swedish physicist d. 1874]

anguish /ˈæŋɡwɪʃ/ n. severe misery or mental suffering. [ME f. OF anguisse choking f. L angustia tightness f. angustus narrow]

anguished /ˈæŋɡwɪʃt/ adj. suffering or expressing anguish. [past part. of anguish (v.) f. OF anguissier f. eccl.L angustiare to distress, formed as ANGUISH]

angular /ˈæŋɡjʊlə(r)/ adj. 1 a having angles or sharp corners. b (of a person) having sharp features; lean and bony. c awkward in manner. 2 forming an angle. 3 measured by angle (angular distance). □ **angularity** /-ˈlærɪtɪ/ n. **angularly** adv. [L angularis f. angulus ANGLE¹]

anhydrous /ænˈhaɪdrəs/ adj. Chem. without water, esp. water of crystallization. [Gk anudros (as AN-, hudōr water)]

aniline /ˈænɪˌliːn, -lɪn, -ˌlaɪn/ n. a colourless oily liquid, used in the manufacture of dyes, drugs, and plastics. □ **aniline dye 1** any of numerous dyes made from aniline. **2** any synthetic dye. [G Anilin f. Anil indigo (from which it was orig. obtained), ult. f. Arab. an-nīl]

anima /ˈænɪmə/ n. Psychol. 1 the inner personality. 2 Jung's term for the feminine part of a man's personality. [L, = mind, soul]

animadvert /ˌænɪmædˈvɜːt/ v.intr. (foll. by on) criticize, censure (conduct, a fault, etc.). □ **animadversion** n. [L animadvertere f. animus mind + advertere (as AD-, vertere vers- turn)]

animal /ˈænɪm(ə)l/ n. & adj. —n. 1 a living organism which feeds on organic matter, usu. one with specialized sense-organs and nervous system, and able to respond rapidly to stimuli. 2 such an organism other than man. 3 a brutish or uncivilized person. 4 colloq. a person or thing of any kind (there is no such animal). —adj. 1 characteristic of animals. 2 of animals as distinct from vegetables (animal charcoal). 3 characteristic of the physical needs of animals; carnal, sensual. □ **animal husbandry** the science of breeding and caring for farm animals. **animal rights** (a movement upholding) the natural right of animals to live free from human exploitation. [L f. animale neut. of animalis having breath f. anima breath]

animalism /ˈænɪməˌlɪz(ə)m/ n. 1 the nature and activity of animals. 2 the belief that humans are not superior to other animals. 3 concern with physical matters; sensuality.

animality /ˌænɪˈmælɪtɪ/ n. 1 the animal world. 2 the nature or behaviour of animals. [F animalité f. animal (adj.)]

animalize /ˈænɪməˌlaɪz/ v.tr. (also -ise) 1 make (a person) bestial; sensualize. 2 convert to animal substance. □ **animalization** /-ˈzeɪʃ(ə)n/ n.

animate adj. & v. —adj. /ˈænɪmət/ 1 having life. 2 lively. —v.tr. /ˈænɪˌmeɪt/ 1 enliven, make lively.

2 give life to. **3** inspire, actuate. **4** encourage. [L *animatus* past part. of *animare* give life to f. *anima* life, soul]

animated /ˈænɪˌmeɪtɪd/ *adj.* **1** lively, vigorous. **2** having life. **3** (of a film etc.) using techniques of animation. □ **animatedly** *adv.* **animator** *n.* (in sense 3).

animation /ˌænɪˈmeɪʃ(ə)n/ *n.* **1** vivacity, ardour. **2** the state of being alive. **3** *Cinematog.* the technique of filming successive drawings or positions of puppets to create an illusion of movement when the film is shown as a sequence.

animism /ˈænɪˌmɪz(ə)m/ *n.* the attribution of a living soul to plants, inanimate objects, and natural phenomena. □ **animist** *n.* **animistic** /-ˈmɪstɪk/ *adj.* [L *anima* life, soul + -ISM]

animosity /ˌænɪˈmɒsɪtɪ/ *n.* (pl. **-ies**) a spirit or feeling of strong hostility. [ME f. OF *animosité* or LL *animositas* f. *animosus* spirited, formed as ANIMUS]

animus /ˈænɪməs/ *n.* **1** a display of animosity. **2** ill feeling. **3** a motivating spirit or feeling. **4** *Psychol.* Jung's term for the masculine part of a woman's personality. [L, = spirit, mind]

anion /ˈænˌaɪən/ *n.* a negatively charged ion; an ion that is attracted to the anode in electrolysis. [ANA- + ION]

anionic /ˌænaɪˈɒnɪk/ *adj.* **1** of an anion or anions. **2** having an active anion.

anise /ˈænɪs/ *n.* an umbelliferous plant, *Pimpinella anisum*, having aromatic seeds. [ME f. OF *anis* f. L f. Gk *anison* anise, dill]

aniseed /ˈænɪˌsiːd/ *n.* the seed of the anise, used to flavour liqueurs and sweets. [ME f. ANISE + SEED]

anisette /ˌænɪˈzet/ *n.* a liqueur flavoured with aniseed. [F, dimin. of *anis* ANISE]

ankh /æŋk/ *n.* a device consisting of a looped bar with a shorter crossbar, used in ancient Egypt as a symbol of life. [Egypt, = life, soul]

ankle /ˈæŋk(ə)l/ *n.* & *v.* —*n.* **1** the joint connecting the foot with the leg. **2** the part of the leg between this and the calf. —*v.intr. sl.* walk. [ME f. ON *ankul-* (unrecorded) f. Gmc: rel. to ANGLE¹]

anklet /ˈæŋklɪt/ *n.* an ornament or fetter worn round the ankle. [ANKLE + -LET, after BRACELET]

ankylose /ˈæŋkɪˌləʊz/ *v.tr.* & *intr.* (also **anchylose**) (of bones or a joint) stiffen or unite by ankylosis. [back-form. f. ANKYLOSIS after *anastomose* etc.]

ankylosis /ˌæŋkɪˈləʊsɪs/ *n.* (also **anchylosis**) **1** the abnormal stiffening and immobility of a joint by fusion of the bones. **2** such fusion. □ **ankylotic** *adj.* [mod.L f. Gk *agkulōsis* f. *agkuloō* crook]

anna /ˈænə/ *n.* a former monetary unit of India and Pakistan, one-sixteenth of a rupee. [Hind. *ānā*]

annal /ˈæn(ə)l/ *n.* **1** the annals of one year. **2** a record of one item in a chronicle. [back-form. f. ANNALS]

annalist /ˈænəlɪst/ *n.* a writer of annals. □ **annalistic** /-ˈlɪstɪk/ *adj.* **annalistically** /-ˈlɪstɪkəlɪ/ *adv.*

annals /ˈæn(ə)lz/ *n.pl.* **1** a narrative of events year by year. **2** historical records. [F *annales* or L *annales* (*libri*) yearly (books) f. *annus* year]

annatto /əˈnætəʊ/ *n.* (also **anatta** /-tə/, **anatto**) an orange-red dye from the pulp of a tropical fruit, used for colouring foods. [Carib name of the fruit-tree]

anneal /əˈniːl/ *v.* & *n.* —*v.tr.* **1** heat (metal or glass) and allow it to cool slowly, esp. to toughen it. **2** toughen. —*n.* treatment by annealing. □ **annealer** *n.* [OE *onǣlan* f. *on* + *ǣlan* burn, bake f. *āl* fire]

annelid /ˈænəlɪd/ *n.* any segmented worm of the phylum Annelida, e.g. earthworms, lugworms, etc. □ **annelidan** *adj.* [F *annélide* or mod.L *annelida* (pl.) f. F *annelés* ringed animals f. OF *anel* ring f. L *anellus* dimin. of *anulus* ring]

annex /æˈneks, əˈn-/ *v.tr.* **1 a** add as a subordinate part. **b** (often foll. by *to*) append to a book etc. **2** incorporate (territory of another) into one's own. **3** add as a condition or consequence. **4** *colloq.* take without right. □ **annexation** /-ˈseɪʃ(ə)n/ *n.* [ME f. OF *annexer* f. L *anneetere* (as AD-, *nectere nex-* bind)]

annexe /ˈæneks/ *n.* (also **annex**) **1** a separate or added building, esp. for extra accommodation. **2** an addition to a document. [F *annexe* f. L *annexum* past part. of *annectere* bind: see ANNEX]

annihilate /əˈnaɪəˌleɪt, əˈnaɪɪl-/ *v.tr.* **1** completely destroy. **2** defeat utterly; make insignificant or powerless. □ **annihilation** *n.* **annihilator** *n.* [LL *annihilare* (as AD-, *nihil* nothing)]

anniversary /ˌænɪˈvɜːsərɪ/ *n.* (pl. **-ies**) **1** the date on which an event took place in a previous year. **2** the celebration of this. [ME f. L *anniversarius* f. *annus* year + *versus* turned]

Anno Domini /ˌænəʊ ˈdɒmɪˌnaɪ/ *adv.* & *n.* —*adv.* in the year of our Lord, in the year of the Christian era. —*n. colloq.* advancing age (*suffering from Anno Domini*). [L, = in the year of the Lord]

annotate /ˈænəʊˌteɪt, ˈænəˌteɪt/ *v.tr.* add explanatory notes to (a book, document, etc.). □ **annotatable** *adj.* **annotation** /-ˈteɪʃ(ə)n/ *n.* **annotative** *adj.* **annotator** *n.* [L *annotare* (as AD-, *nota* mark)]

announce /əˈnaʊns/ *v.tr.* **1** (often foll. by *that*) make publicly known. **2** make known the arrival or imminence of (a guest, dinner, etc.). **3** make known (without words) to the senses or the mind; be a sign of. □ **announcement** *n.* [ME f. OF *annoncer* f. L *annuntiare* (as AD-, *nuntius* messenger)]

announcer /əˈnaʊnsə(r)/ *n.* a person who announces, esp. introducing programmes in broadcasting.

annoy /əˈnɔɪ/ *v.tr.* **1** cause slight anger or mental distress to. **2** (in *passive*) be somewhat angry (*am annoyed with you*; *was annoyed at my remarks*). **3** molest; harass repeatedly. □ **annoyance** *n.* **annoyer** *n.* [ME f. OF *anuier*, *anui*, *anoi*, etc., ult. f. L *in odio* hateful]

annual /ˈænjʊəl/ *adj.* & *n.* —*adj.* **1** reckoned by the year. **2** occurring every year. **3** living or lasting for one year. —*n.* **1** a book etc. published once a year; a yearbook. **2** a plant that lives only for a year or less. □ **annual general meeting** a yearly meeting of members or shareholders, esp. for holding elections and reporting on the year's events. **annual ring** a ring in the cross-section of a plant, esp. a tree, produced by one year's growth. □ **annually** *adv.* [ME f. OF *annuel* f. LL *annualis* f. L *annalis* f. *annus* year]

annualized /ˈænjʊəˌlaɪzd/ *adj.* (of rates of interest, inflation, etc.) calculated on an annual basis, as a projection from figures obtained for a shorter period.

annuitant /əˈnjuːɪt(ə)nt/ *n.* a person who holds or receives an annuity. [ANNUITY + -ANT, by assim. to *accountant* etc.]

annuity /əˈnjuːɪtɪ/ n. (pl. **-ies**) **1** a yearly grant or allowance. **2** an investment of money entitling the investor to a series of equal annual sums. [ME f. F *annuité* f. med.L *annuitas -tatis* f. L *annuus* yearly (as ANNUAL)]

annul /əˈnʌl/ v.tr. (**annulled, annulling**) **1** declare (a marriage etc.) invalid. **2** cancel, abolish. □ **annulment** n. [ME f. OF *anuller* f. LL *annullare* (as AD-, *nullus* none)]

annular /ˈænjʊlə(r)/ adj. ring-shaped; forming a ring. □ **annularly** adv. [F *annulaire* or L *annularis* f. *an(n)ulus* ring]

annulate /ˈænjʊlət/ adj. having rings; marked with or formed of rings. □ **annulation** /-ˈleɪʃ(ə)n/ n. [L *annulatus* (as ANNULUS)]

annulus /ˈænjʊləs/ n. (pl. **annuli** /-laɪ/) esp. *Math.* & *Biol.* a ring. [L *an(n)ulus*]

annunciate /əˈnʌnʃɪeɪt/ v.tr. **1** proclaim. **2** indicate as coming or ready. [LL *annunciare* f. L *annuntiare annuntiat-* announce]

annunciation /əˌnʌnsɪˈeɪʃ(ə)n/ n. **1** (**Annunciation**) **a** the announcing of the Incarnation, made by the angel Gabriel to Mary. **b** the festival commemorating this on 25 March. **2 a** the act or process of announcing. **b** an announcement. [ME f. OF *annonciation* f. LL *annuntiatio -onis* (as ANNUNCIATE)]

annunciator /əˈnʌnʃɪˌeɪtə(r)/ n. **1** a device giving an audible or visible indication of which of several electrical circuits has been activated, of the position of a train, etc. **2** an announcer. [LL *annuntiator* (as ANNUNCIATE)]

anode /ˈænəʊd/ n. *Electr.* **1** the positive electrode in an electrolytic cell or electronic valve or tube. **2** the negative terminal of a primary cell such as a battery. □ **anodal** adj. **anodic** /əˈnɒdɪk/ adj. [Gk *anodos* way up f. *ana* up + *hodos* way]

anodize /ˈænəˌdaɪz/ v.tr. (also **-ise**) coat (a metal, esp. aluminium) with a protective oxide layer by electrolysis. □ **anodizer** n. [ANODE + -IZE]

anodyne /ˈænəˌdaɪn/ adj. & n. —adj. **1** able to relieve pain. **2** mentally soothing. —n. an anodyne drug or medicine. [L *anodynus* f. Gk *anōdunos* painless (as AN-, *odunē* pain)]

anoint /əˈnɔɪnt/ v.tr. **1** apply oil or ointment to, esp. as a religious ceremony (e.g. at baptism, or the consecration of a priest or king, or in ministering to the sick). **2** (usu. foll. by *with*) smear, rub. □ **anointer** n. [ME f. AF *anoint* (adj.) f. OF *enoint* past part. of *enoindre* f. L *inungere* (as IN-², *ungere unct-* smear with oil)]

anomalous /əˈnɒmələs/ adj. having an irregular or deviant feature; abnormal. □ **anomalously** adv. **anomalousness** n. [LL *anomalus* f. Gk *anōmalos* (as AN-, *homalos* even)]

anomaly /əˈnɒməlɪ/ n. (pl. **-ies**) **1** an anomalous circumstance or thing; an irregularity. **2** irregularity of motion, behaviour, etc. [L f. Gk *anōmalia* f. *anōmalos* ANOMALOUS]

anomy /ˈænəmɪ/ n. (also **anomie**) lack of the usual social or ethical standards in an individual or group. □ **anomic** /əˈnɒmɪk/ adj. [Gk *anomia* f. *anomos* lawless: -ie f. F]

anon /əˈnɒn/ adv. archaic or literary soon, shortly (*will say more of this anon*). [OE *on ān* into one, *on āne* in one]

anon. /əˈnɒn/ abbr. anonymous; an anonymous author.

anonymous /əˈnɒnɪməs/ adj. **1** of unknown name. **2** of unknown or undeclared source or authorship. **3** without character; featureless,

impersonal. □ **anonymity** /ˌænəˈnɪmɪtɪ/ n. **anonymously** adv. [LL *anonymus* f. Gk *anōnumos* nameless (as AN-, *onoma* name)]

anopheles /əˈnɒfɪˌliːz/ n. any of various mosquitoes of the genus *Anopheles*, many of which are carriers of the malarial parasite. [mod.L f. Gk *anōphelēs* unprofitable]

anorak /ˈænəˌræk/ n. a waterproof jacket of cloth or plastic, usu. with a hood, of a kind orig. used in polar regions. [Greenland Eskimo *anoraq*]

anorectic /ˌænəˈrektɪk/ adj. & n. (also **anorexic** /-ˈreksɪk/) —adj. involving, producing, or characterized by a lack of appetite, esp. in anorexia nervosa. —n. **1** an anorectic agent. **2** a person with anorexia. [Gk *anorektos* without appetite (as ANOREXIA): *anorexic* f. F *anoréxique*]

anorexia /ˌænəˈreksɪə/ n. **1** a lack or loss of appetite for food. **2** (in full **anorexia nervosa** /nɜːˈvəʊsə/) a psychological illness, characterized by an obsessive desire to lose weight by refusing to eat. [LL f. Gk f. *an-* not + *orexis* appetite]

another /əˈnʌðə(r)/ adj. & pron. —adj. **1** an additional; one more (*have another cake*; *after another six months*). **2** a person like or comparable to (*another Callas*). **3** a different (*quite another matter*). **4** some or any other (*will not do another man's work*). —pron. **1** an additional one (*have another*). **2** a different one (*take this book away and bring me another*). **3** some or any other one (*I love another*). **4** *Brit.* an unnamed additional party to a legal action (*X versus Y and another*). □ **another place** *Brit.* the other House of Parliament (used in the Commons to refer to the Lords, and vice versa). **such another** another of the same sort. [ME f. AN + OTHER]

anovulant /æˈnɒvjʊlənt/ n. & adj. *Pharm.* —n. a drug preventing ovulation. —adj. preventing ovulation. [AN- + *ovulation* (see OVULATE) + -ANT]

anserine /ˈænsəˌraɪn/ adj. **1** of or like a goose. **2** silly. [L *anserinus* f. *anser* goose]

answer /ˈɑːnsə(r)/ n. & v. —n. **1** something said or done to deal with or in reaction to a question, statement, or circumstance. **2** the solution to a problem. —v. **1** tr. make an answer to (*answer me*; *answer my question*). **2** intr. (often foll. by *to*) make an answer. **3** tr. respond to the summons or signal of (*answer the door*; *answer the telephone*). **4** tr. be satisfactory for (a purpose or need). **5** intr. (foll. by *for*, *to*) be responsible (*you will answer to me for your conduct*). **6** intr. (foll. by *to*) correspond, esp. to a description. **7** intr. be satisfactory or successful. □ **answering machine** a tape recorder which supplies a recorded answer to a telephone call. **answering service** a business that receives and answers telephone calls for its clients. [OE *andswaru, andswarian* f. Gmc, = swear against (charge)]

answerable /ˈɑːnsərəb(ə)l/ adj. **1** (usu. foll. by *to*, *for*) responsible (*answerable to them for any accident*). **2** that can be answered.

answerphone /ˈɑːnsəˌfəʊn/ n. a telephone answering machine.

ant n. any small insect of a widely distributed hymenopterous family, living in complex social colonies, and proverbial for industry. □ **white ant** = TERMITE. [OE *ǣmet(t)e, ēmete* f. WG]

-ant /ənt/ suffix **1** forming adjectives denoting attribution of an action (*pendant*; *repentant*) or state (*arrogant*; *expectant*). **2** forming nouns denoting an agent (*assistant*; *celebrant*; *deodorant*). [F -*ant* or L -*ant*-, -*ent*-, pres. part. stem of verbs: cf. -ENT]

antacid /ænt'æsɪd/ *n.* & *adj.* —*n.* a substance that prevents or corrects acidity esp. in the stomach. —*adj.* having these properties.

antagonism /æn'tægəˌnɪz(ə)m/ *n.* active opposition or hostility. [F *antagonisme* (as ANTAGONIST)]

antagonist /æn'tægənɪst/ *n.* **1** an opponent or adversary. **2** *Biol.* a substance or organ that partially or completely opposes the action of another. □ **antagonistic** /-'nɪstɪk/ *adj.* **antagonistically** /-'nɪstɪkəlɪ/ *adv.* [F *antagoniste* or LL *antagonista* f. Gk *antagōnistēs* (as ANTAGONIZE)]

antagonize /æn'tægəˌnaɪz/ *v.tr.* (also -**ise**) **1** evoke hostility or opposition or enmity in. **2** (of one force etc.) counteract or tend to neutralize (another). □ **antagonization** /-'zeɪʃ(ə)n/ *n.* [Gk *antagōnizomai* (as ANTI-, *agōnizomai* f. *agōn* contest)]

Antarctic /ænt'ɑːktɪk/ *adj.* & *n.* —*adj.* of the south polar regions. —*n.* this region. □ **Antarctic Circle** the parallel of latitude 66° 32′ S., forming an imaginary line round this region. [ME f. OF *antartique* or L *antarcticus* f. Gk *antarktikos* (as ANTI-, *arktikos* ARCTIC)]

ante /'æntɪ/ *n.* & *v.* —*n.* **1** a stake put up by a player in poker etc. before receiving cards. **2** an amount to be paid in advance. —*v.tr.* (**antes**, **anted**) **1** put up as an ante. **2** *US* a bet, stake. **b** (foll. by *up*) pay. [L = before]

ante- /'æntɪ/ *prefix* forming nouns and adjectives meaning 'before, preceding' (*ante-room*; *antenatal*; *ante-post*). [L *ante* (prep. & adv.), = before]

anteater /'æntˌiːtə(r)/ *n.* any of various mammals feeding on ants and termites, e.g. a tamandua.

antecedent /ˌæntɪ'siːd(ə)nt/ *n.* & *adj.* —*n.* **1** a preceding thing or circumstance. **2** *Gram.* a word, phrase, clause, or sentence, to which another word (esp. a relative pronoun, usu. following) refers. **3** (in *pl.*) past history, esp. of a person. **4** *Logic* the statement contained in the 'if' clause of a conditional proposition. —*adj.* **1** (often foll. by *to*) previous. **2** presumptive, a priori. □ **antecedence** *n.* **antecedently** *adv.* [ME f. F *antecedent* or L *antecedere* (as ANTE-, *cedere* go)]

antechamber /'æntɪˌtʃeɪmbə(r)/ *n.* a small room leading to a main one. [earlier *anti*-, f. F *antichambre* f. It. *anticamera* (as ANTE-, CHAMBER)]

antedate *v.tr.* /ˌæntɪ'deɪt/ **1** exist or occur at a date earlier than. **2** assign an earlier date to (a document, event, etc.), esp. one earlier than its actual date.

antediluvian /ˌæntɪdɪ'luːvɪən, -'ljuːvɪən/ *adj.* **1** of or belonging to the time before the Biblical Flood. **2** *colloq.* very old or out of date. [ANTE- + L *diluvium* DELUGE + -AN]

antelope /'æntɪˌləʊp/ *n.* (*pl.* same or **antelopes**) **1** any of various deerlike ruminants of the family Bovidae, esp. abundant in Africa, e.g. gazelles, gnus, kudus, and impala. **2** leather made from the skin of any of these. [ME f. OF *antelop* or f. med.L *ant(h)alopus* f. late Gk *antholops*, of unkn. orig.]

antenatal /ˌæntɪ'neɪt(ə)l/ *adj.* **1** existing or occurring before birth. **2** relating to the period of pregnancy.

antenna /æn'tenə/ *n.* (*pl.* **antennae** /-niː/) **1** *Zool.* one of a pair of mobile appendages on the heads of insects, crustaceans, etc., sensitive to touch and taste; a feeler. **2** (*pl.* **antennas**) = AERIAL *n.*

□ **antennal** *adj.* (in sense 1). **antennary** *adj.* (in sense 1). [L = sail-yard]

antenuptial /ˌæntɪ'nʌpʃ(ə)l/ *adj.* existing or occurring before marriage. □ **antenuptial contract** *S.Afr.* a contract between two persons intending to marry each other, setting out the terms and conditions of their marriage. [LL *antenuptialis* (as ANTE-, NUPTIAL)]

antepenultimate /ˌæntɪpɪ'nʌltɪmət/ *adj.* & *n.* —*adj.* last but two. —*n.* anything that is last but two.

ante-post /ˌæntɪ'pəʊst/ *adj.* *Brit.* (of betting) done at odds determined at the time of betting, in advance of the event concerned. [ANTE- + POST¹]

anterior /æn'tɪərɪə(r)/ *adj.* **1** nearer the front. **2** (often foll. by *to*) earlier, prior. □ **anteriority** /-rɪ'ɒrɪtɪ/ *n.* **anteriorly** *adv.* [F *antérieur* or L *anterior* f. *ante* before]

ante-room /'æntɪˌruːm, -ˌrʊm/ *n.* **1** a small room leading to a main one. **2** *Mil.* a sitting-room in an officers' mess.

antheap /'ænthiːp/ *n.* = ANTHILL.

anthelmintic /ˌænθel'mɪntɪk/ (also **anthelminthic** /-θɪk/) *n.* & *adj.* —*n.* any drug or agent used to destroy parasitic, esp. intestinal, worms, e.g. tapeworms, roundworms, and flukes. —*adj.* having the power to eliminate or destroy parasitic worms. [ANTI- + Gk *helmins helminthos* worm]

anthem /'ænθəm/ *n.* **1** an elaborate choral composition usu. based on a passage of scripture for (esp. Anglican) church use. **2** a solemn hymn of praise etc., esp. = *national anthem.* **3** a composition sung antiphonally. [OE *antefn*, *antifne* f. LL *antiphona* ANTIPHON]

anther /'ænθə(r)/ *n.* *Bot.* the apical portion of a stamen containing pollen. □ **antheral** *adj.* [F *anthère* or mod.L *anthera*, in L 'medicine extracted from flowers' f. Gk *anthēra* flowery, fem. adj. f. *anthos* flower]

anthill /'ænthɪl/ *n.* **1** a moundlike nest built by ants or termites. **2** a community teeming with people.

anthologize /æn'θɒləˌdʒaɪz/ *v.tr.* & *intr.* (also -**ise**) compile or include in an anthology.

anthology /æn'θɒlədʒɪ/ *n.* (*pl.* -**ies**) a published collection of passages from literature (esp. poems), songs, reproductions of paintings, etc. □ **anthologist** *n.* [F *anthologie* or med.L f. Gk *anthologia* f. *anthos* flower + -*logia* collection f. *legō* gather]

anthracite /'ænθrəˌsaɪt/ *n.* coal of a hard variety burning with little flame and smoke. □ **anthracitic** /-'sɪtɪk/ *adj.* [Gk *anthrakitis* a kind of coal f. *anthrax* -*akos* coal]

anthrax /'ænθræks/ *n.* a disease of sheep and cattle transmissible to humans. [LL f. Gk, = carbuncle]

anthropo- /'ænθrəpəʊ/ *comb. form* human, mankind. [Gk *anthrōpos* human being]

anthropocentric /ˌænθrəpəʊ'sentrɪk/ *adj.* regarding mankind as the centre of existence. □ **anthropocentrically** *adv.* **anthropocentrism** *n.*

anthropoid /'ænθrəˌpɔɪd/ *adj.* & *n.* —*adj.* **1** resembling a human being in form. **2** *colloq.* (of a person) apelike. —*n.* a being that is human in form only, esp. an anthropoid ape. [Gk *anthrōpoeidēs* (as ANTHROPO-, -OID)]

anthropology /ˌænθrə'pɒlədʒɪ/ *n.* **1** the study of mankind, esp. of its societies and customs. **2** the study of the structure and evolution of man as an animal. □ **anthropological** /-pə'lɒdʒɪk(ə)l/ *adj.* **anthropologist** *n.*

anthropomorphic /ˌænθrəpə'mɔːfɪk/ *adj.* of or characterized by anthropomorphism. □ **anthropomorphically** *adv.* [as ANTHROPOMORPHOUS + -IC]

anthropomorphism /ˌænθrəpə'mɔːfɪz(ə)m/ *n.* the attribution of a human form or personality to a god, animal, or thing. □ **anthropomorphize** *v.tr.*

anthropomorphous /ˌænθrəpə'mɔːfəs/ *adj.* human in form. [Gk *anthrōpomorphos* (as ANTHROPO-, *morphē* form)]

anthropophagy /ˌænθrə'pɒfədʒɪ/ *n.* cannibalism. □ **anthropophagous** *adj.* [Gk *anthrōpophagia* (as ANTHROPO-, *phagō* eat)]

anti /'æntɪ/ *prep.* & *n.* —*prep.* (also *absol.*) opposed to (*is anti everything; seems to be rather anti*). —*n.* (*pl.* **antis**) a person opposed to a particular policy etc. [ANTI-]

anti- /'æntɪ/ *prefix* (also **ant-** before a vowel or *h*) forming nouns and adjectives meaning: **1** opposed to; against (*antivivisectionism*). **2** preventing (*antiscorbutic*). **3** the opposite of (*anticlimax*). **4** rival (*antipope*). **5** unlike the conventional form (*anti-hero; anti-novel*). **6** *Physics* the antiparticle of a specified particle (*antineutrino; antiproton*). [from or after Gk *anti-* against]

anti-abortion /ˌæntɪə'bɔːʃ(ə)n/ *adj.* opposing abortion. □ **anti-abortionist** *n.*

anti-aircraft /ˌæntɪ'eəkrɑːft/ *adj.* (of a gun, missile, etc.) used to attack enemy aircraft.

antibiotic /ˌæntɪbaɪ'ɒtɪk/ *n.* & *adj.* *Pharm.* —*n.* any of various substances (e.g. penicillin) produced by micro-organisms or made synthetically, that can inhibit or destroy susceptible micro-organisms. —*adj.* functioning as an antibiotic. [F *antibiotique* (as ANTI-, Gk *biōtikos* fit for life f. *bios* life)]

antibody /'æntɪˌbɒdɪ/ *n.* (*pl.* **-ies**) any of various blood proteins produced in response to and then counteracting antigens. [transl. of G *Antikörper* (as ANTI-, *Körper* body)]

antic /'æntɪk/ *n.* **1** (usu. in *pl.*) absurd or foolish behaviour. **2** an absurd or silly action. [It. *antico* ANTIQUE, used as = grotesque]

anticathode /ˌæntɪ'kæθəʊd/ *n.* the target (or anode) of an X-ray tube on which the electrons from the cathode impinge and from which X-rays are emitted.

Antichrist /'æntɪˌkraɪst/ *n.* **1** an arch-enemy of Christ. **2** a postulated personal opponent of Christ expected by the early Church to appear before the end of the world. [ME f. OF *antecrist* f. eccl.L *antichristus* f. Gk *antikhristos* (as ANTI-, *Khristos* CHRIST)]

anticipate /æn'tɪsɪˌpeɪt/ *v.tr.* **1** deal with or use before the proper time. **2** *disp.* expect, foresee; regard as probable (*did not anticipate any difficulty*). **3** forestall (a person or thing). **4** look forward to. □ **anticipation** *n.* **anticipative** *adj.* **anticipation** *n.* **anticipatory** *adj.* [L *anticipare* f. *anti-* for ANTE- + -*cipare* f. *capere* take]

■ **Usage** The use of this word in sense 2 is well-established in informal use but is regarded as incorrect by some people.

anticlerical /ˌæntɪ'klerɪk(ə)l/ *adj.* & *n.* —*adj.* opposed to the influence of the clergy, esp. in

politics. —*n.* an anticlerical person. □ **anticlericalism** *n.*

anticlimax /ˌæntɪ'klaɪmæks/ *n.* a trivial conclusion to something significant or impressive, esp. where a climax was expected. □ **anticlimactic** /-'mæktɪk/ *adj.* **anticlimactically** /-'mæktɪkəlɪ/ *adv.*

anticline /'æntɪˌklaɪn/ *n.* *Geol.* a ridge or fold of stratified rock in which the strata slope down from the crest. □ **anticlinal** /-'klaɪn(ə)l/ *adj.* [ANTI- + Gk *klinō* lean, after INCLINE]

anticlockwise /ˌæntɪ'klɒkwaɪz/ *adv.* & *adj.* —*adv.* in a curve opposite in direction to the movement of the hands of a clock. —*adj.* moving anticlockwise.

anticoagulant /ˌæntɪkəʊ'ægjʊlənt/ *n.* & *adj.* —*n.* any drug or agent that retards or inhibits coagulation, esp. of the blood. —*adj.* retarding or inhibiting coagulation.

anticonvulsant /ˌæntɪkən'vʌls(ə)nt/ *n.* & *adj.* —*n.* any drug or agent that prevents or reduces the severity of convulsions, esp. epileptic fits. —*adj.* preventing or reducing convulsions.

anticyclone /ˌæntɪ'saɪkləʊn/ *n.* a system of winds rotating outwards from an area of high barometric pressure, producing fine weather. □ **anticyclonic** /-'klɒnɪk/ *adj.*

antidepressant /ˌæntɪdɪ'pres(ə)nt/ *n.* & *adj.* —*n.* any drug or agent that alleviates depression. —*adj.* alleviating depression.

antidote /'æntɪˌdəʊt/ *n.* **1** a medicine etc. taken or given to counteract poison. **2** anything that counteracts something unpleasant or evil. □ **antidotal** *adj.* [F *antidote* or L *antidotum* f. Gk *antidoton* neut. of *antidotos* given against (as ANTI- + stem of *didonai* give)]

antifreeze /'æntɪˌfriːz/ *n.* a substance (usu. ethylene glycol) added to water to lower its freezing-point, esp. in the radiator of a motor vehicle.

antigen /'æntɪdʒ(ə)n/ *n.* a foreign substance (e.g. toxin) which causes the body to produce antibodies. □ **antigenic** /-'dʒenɪk/ *adj.* [G (as ANTIBODY, -GEN)]

anti-hero /'æntɪˌhɪərəʊ/ *n.* (*pl.* **-oes**) a central character in a story or drama who noticeably lacks conventional heroic attributes.

antihistamine /ˌæntɪ'hɪstəmɪn, -ˌmiːn/ *n.* a substance that counteracts the effects of histamine, used esp. in the treatment of allergies.

antiknock /'æntɪˌnɒk/ *n.* a substance added to motor fuel to prevent premature combustion.

anti-lock /'æntɪˌlɒk/ *n.* & *attrib. adj.* (of brakes) set up so as to prevent locking and skidding when applied suddenly.

antilogarithm /ˌæntɪ'lɒgəˌrɪð(ə)m/ *n.* the number to which a logarithm belongs.

antimacassar /ˌæntɪmə'kæsə(r)/ *n.* a covering put over furniture, esp. over the back of a chair, as a protection from grease in the hair or as an ornament. [ANTI- + MACASSAR]

antimatter /'æntɪˌmætə(r)/ *n.* *Physics* matter composed solely of antiparticles.

antimony /'æntɪmənɪ/ *n.* *Chem.* a brittle silvery-white metallic element used esp. in alloys. □ **antimonial** /-'məʊnɪəl/ *adj.* **antimonic** /-'məʊnɪk/ *adj.* **antimonious** /-'məʊnɪəs/ *adj.* [ME f. med.L *antimonium* (11th c.), of unkn. orig.]

antinode /'æntɪˌnəʊd/ *n.* *Physics* the position of maximum displacement in a standing wave system.

antinomian /ˌæntɪˈnəʊmɪən/ adj. & n. —adj. of or relating to the view that Christians are released from the obligation of observing the moral law. —n. (**Antinomian**) hist. a person who holds this view. □ **antinomianism** n. [med.L Antinomi, name of a sect in Germany (1535) alleged to hold this view (as ANTI-, Gk nomos law)]

antinomy /ænˈtɪnəmɪ/ n. (pl. **-ies**) **1** a contradiction between two beliefs or conclusions that are in themselves reasonable; a paradox. **2** a conflict between two laws or authorities. [L antinomia f. Gk (as ANTI-, nomos law)]

anti-nuclear /ˌæntɪˈnjuːklɪə(r)/ adj. opposed to the development of nuclear weapons or nuclear power.

antioxidant /ˌæntɪˈɒksɪd(ə)nt/ n. an agent that inhibits oxidation, esp. used to reduce deterioration of products stored in air.

antiparticle /ˈæntɪˌpɑːtɪk(ə)l/ n. Physics an elementary particle having the same mass as a given particle but opposite electric or magnetic properties.

antipasto /ˌæntɪˈpɑːstəʊ, -ˈpæstəʊ/ n. (pl. **-os** or **antipasti** /-tɪ/) an hors d'œuvre, esp. in an Italian meal. [It.]

antipathetic /ˌæntɪpəˈθetɪk/ adj. (usu. foll. by to) having a strong aversion or natural opposition. □ **antipathetical** adj. **antipathetically** adv. [as ANTIPATHY after PATHETIC]

antipathy /ænˈtɪpəθɪ/ n. (pl. **-ies**) (often foll. by to, for, between) a strong or deep-seated aversion or dislike. [F antipathie or L antipathia f. Gk antipatheia f. antipathēs opposed in feeling (as ANTI-, pathos -eos feeling)]

anti-personnel /ˌæntɪˌpɜːsəˈnel/ adj. (of a bomb, mine, etc.) designed to kill or injure people rather than to damage buildings or equipment.

antiperspirant /ˌæntɪˈpɜːspɪrənt/ n. & adj. —n. a substance applied to the skin to prevent or reduce perspiration. —adj. that acts as an antiperspirant.

antiphlogistic /ˌæntɪfləˈdʒɪstɪk/ n. & adj. —n. any drug or agent that alleviates or reduces inflammation. —adj. alleviating or reducing inflammation.

antiphon /ˈæntɪf(ə)n/ n. **1** a hymn or psalm, the parts of which are sung or recited alternately by two groups. **2** a versicle or phrase from this. [eccl.L antiphona f. Gk (as ANTI-, phōnē sound)]

antiphonal /ænˈtɪfən(ə)l/ adj. **1** sung or recited alternately by two groups. **2** responsive, answering. □ **antiphonally** adv.

antiphony /ænˈtɪfənɪ/ n. (pl. **-ies**) **1** antiphonal singing or chanting. **2** a response or echo.

antipodes /ænˈtɪpədiːz/ n.pl. **1 a** (also **Antipodes**) a place diametrically opposite to another, esp. Australasia as the region on the opposite side of the earth to Europe. **b** places diametrically opposite to each other. **2** (usu. foll. by of, to) the exact opposite. □ **antipodal** adj. **antipodean** /-ˈdiːən/ adj. & n. [F or LL f. Gk antipodes having the feet opposite (as ANTI-, pous podos foot)]

antipole /ˈæntɪˌpəʊl/ n. **1** the direct opposite. **2** the opposite pole.

antipope /ˈæntɪˌpəʊp/ n. a person set up as pope in opposition to one (held by others to be) canonically chosen. [F antipape f. med.L antipapa, assim. to POPE]

antiproton /ˌæntɪˈprəʊtɒn/ n. Physics the negatively charged antiparticle of a proton.

antipyretic /ˌæntɪpaɪˈretɪk/ adj. & n. —adj. preventing or reducing fever. —n. an antipyretic drug or agent.

antiquarian /ˌæntɪˈkweərɪən/ adj. & n. —adj. **1** of or dealing in antiques or rare books. **2** of the study of antiquities. —n. an antiquary. □ **antiquarianism** n. [see ANTIQUARY]

antiquary /ˈæntɪkwərɪ/ n. (pl. **-ies**) a student or collector of antiques or antiquities. [L antiquarius f. antiquus ancient]

antiquated /ˈæntɪˌkweɪtɪd/ adj. old-fashioned; out of date. [eccl.L antiquare antiquat- make old]

antique /ænˈtiːk/ n., adj., & v. —n. an object of considerable age, esp. an item of furniture or the decorative arts having a high value. —adj. **1** of or existing from an early date. **2** old-fashioned, archaic. **3** of ancient times. —v.tr. (**antiques, antiqued, antiquing**) give an antique appearance to (furniture etc.) by artificial means. [F antique or L antiquus, anticus former, ancient f. ante before]

antiquity /ænˈtɪkwɪtɪ/ n. (pl. **-ies**) **1** ancient times, esp. the period before the Middle Ages. **2** great age (a city of great antiquity). **3** (usu. in pl.) physical remains or relics from ancient times, esp. buildings and works of art. **4** (in pl.) customs, events, etc., of ancient times. [ME f. OF antiquité f. L antiquitas -tatis f. antiquus: see ANTIQUE]

antirrhinum /ˌæntɪˈraɪnəm/ n. any plant of the genus Antirrhinum, esp. the snapdragon. [L f. Gk antirrhinon f. anti counterfeiting + rhis rhinos nose, from the resemblance of the flower to an animal's snout)]

antiscorbutic /ˌæntɪskɔːˈbjuːtɪk/ adj. & n. —adj. preventing or curing scurvy. —n. an antiscorbutic agent or drug.

anti-Semite /ˌæntɪˈsiːmaɪt, -ˈsemaɪt/ n. a person hostile to or prejudiced against Jews. □ **anti-Semitic** /-sɪˈmɪtɪk/ adj. **anti-Semitism** /-ˈsemɪˌtɪz(ə)m/ n.

antisepsis /ˌæntɪˈsepsɪs/ n. the process of using antiseptics to eliminate undesirable micro-organisms such as bacteria, viruses, and fungi that cause disease. [mod.L (as ANTI-, SEPSIS)]

antiseptic /ˌæntɪˈseptɪk/ adj. & n. —adj. **1** counteracting sepsis esp. by preventing the growth of disease-causing micro-organisms. **2** sterile or free from contamination. **3** lacking character. —n. an antiseptic agent. □ **antiseptically** adv.

antiserum /ˈæntɪˌsɪərəm/ n. (pl. **antisera** /-rə/) a blood serum containing antibodies against specific antigens, injected to treat or protect against specific diseases.

antisocial /ˌæntɪˈsəʊʃ(ə)l/ adj. **1** opposed to or contrary to normal social instincts or practices. **2** not sociable. **3** opposed or harmful to the existing social order.

antistatic /ˌæntɪˈstætɪk/ adj. that counteracts the effects of static electricity.

antithesis /ænˈtɪθɪsɪs/ n. (pl. **antitheses** /-ˌsiːz/) **1** (foll. by of, to) the direct opposite. **2** (usu. foll. by of, between) contrast or opposition between two things. **3** a contrast of ideas expressed by parallelism of strongly contrasted words. [LL f. Gk antitithēmi set against (as ANTI-, tithēmi place)]

antithetical /ˌæntɪˈθetɪk(ə)l/ adj. (also **antithetic**) **1** contrasted, opposite. **2** connected with, containing, or using antithesis. □ **antithetically** adv. [Gk antithetikos (as ANTITHESIS)]

antitoxin /ˌæntɪˈtɒksɪn/ n. an antibody that counteracts a toxin. □ **antitoxic** adj.

antitrades /ˌæntɪˈtreɪdz, ˈæntɪ-/ *n.pl.* winds that blow in the opposite direction to (and usu. above) a trade wind.

antiviral /ˌæntɪˈvaɪər(ə)l/ *adj.* effective against viruses.

antivivisectionism /ˌæntɪˌvɪvɪˈsekʃ(ə)nɪz(ə)m/ *n.* opposition to vivisection. □ **antivivisectionist** *n.*

antler /ˈæntlə(r)/ *n.* **1** each of the branched horns of a stag or other (usu. male) deer. **2** a branch of this. □ **antlered** *adj.* [ME f. AF, var. of OF *antoillier*, of unkn. orig.]

antonym /ˈæntənɪm/ *n.* a word opposite in meaning to another in the same language (e.g. *bad* and *good*). □ **antonymous** /ænˈtɒnɪməs/ *adj.* [F *antonyme* (as ANTI-, SYNONYM)]

antrum /ˈæntrəm/ *n.* (pl. **antra** /-trə/) *Anat.* a natural chamber or cavity in the body, esp. in a bone. □ **antral** *adj.* [L f. Gk *antron* cave]

anus /ˈeɪnəs/ *n. Anat.* the excretory opening at the end of the alimentary canal. [L]

anvil /ˈænvɪl/ *n.* a block (usu. of iron) with a flat top, concave sides, and often a pointed end, on which metals are worked in forging. [OE *anfilte* etc.]

anxiety /æŋˈzaɪətɪ/ *n.* (pl. **-ies**) **1** the state of being anxious. **2** concern about an imminent danger, difficulty, etc. **3** (foll. by *for*, or *to* + infin.) anxious desire. **4** a thing that causes anxiety (*my greatest anxiety is that I shall fall ill*). **5** *Psychol.* a nervous disorder characterized by a state of excessive uneasiness. [F *anxiété* or L *anxietas -tatis* (as ANXIOUS)]

anxious /ˈæŋkʃəs/ *adj.* **1** troubled; uneasy in the mind. **2** causing or marked by anxiety (*an anxious moment*). **3** (foll. by *for*, or *to* + infin.) earnestly or uneasily wanting or trying (*anxious to please*; *anxious for you to succeed*). □ **anxiously** *adv.* **anxiousness** *n.* [L *anxius* f. *angere* choke]

any /ˈenɪ/ *adj., pron., & adv. —adj.* **1** (with *interrog.*, *neg.*, or conditional expressed or implied) **a** one, no matter which, of several (*cannot find any answer*). **b** some, no matter how much or many or of what sort (*if any books arrive*; *have you any sugar?*). **2** a minimal amount of (*hardly any difference*). **3** whichever is chosen (*any fool knows that*). **4 a** an appreciable or significant (*did not stay for any length of time*). **b** a very large (*has any amount of money*). —*pron.* **1** any one (*did not know any of them*). **2** any number (*are any of them yours?*). **3** any amount (*is there any left?*). —*adv.* (usu. with *neg.* or *interrog.*) at all, in some degree (*is that any good?*; *do not make it any larger*; *without being any the wiser*). □ **any more** to any further extent (*don't like you any more*). [OE *ænig* f. Gmc (as ONE, -Y¹)]

anybody /ˈenɪˌbɒdɪ/ *n. & pron.* **1 a** a person, no matter who. **b** a person of any kind. **c** whatever person is chosen. **2** a person of importance (*are you anybody?*).

anyhow /ˈenɪˌhaʊ/ *adv.* **1** anyway. **2** in a disorderly manner or state (*does his work anyhow*; *things are all anyhow*).

anyone /ˈenɪˌwʌn/ *pron.* anybody.

■ **Usage** *Anyone* is written as two words to emphasize a numerical sense, as in *any one of us can do it.*

anyplace /ˈenɪˌpleɪs/ *adv. US* anywhere.

anything /ˈenɪθɪŋ/ *pron.* **1** a thing, no matter which. **2** a thing of any kind. **3** whatever thing is chosen. □ **anything but** not at all (*was anything but honest*).

anyway /ˈenɪˌweɪ/ *adv.* **1** in any way or manner. **2** at any rate. **3** in any case. **4** to resume (*anyway, as I was saying*).

anywhere /ˈenɪˌweə(r)/ *adv. & pron.* —*adv.* in or to any place. —*pron.* any place (*anywhere will do*).

Anzac /ˈænzæk/ *n.* **1** a soldier in the Australian and New Zealand Army Corps (1914–18). **2** any person, esp. a member of the armed services, from Australia or New Zealand. □ **Anzac Day** 25 April. [acronym]

Anzus /ˈænzəs/ *n.* (also **ANZUS**) Australia, New Zealand, and the US, as an alliance for the Pacific area.

AOB *abbr.* any other business.

A-OK *abbr. US colloq.* excellent; in good order. [all systems *OK*]

aorist /ˈeɔrɪst/ *n. & adj. Gram.* —*n.* an unqualified past tense of a verb (esp. in Greek), without reference to duration or completion. —*adj.* of or designating this tense. □ **aoristic** /eəˈrɪstɪk/ *adj.* [Gk *aoristos* indefinite f. *a-* not + *horizō* define, limit]

aorta /eɪˈɔːtə/ *n.* (pl. **aortas**) the main artery, giving rise to the arterial network through which oxygenated blood is supplied to the body from the heart. □ **aortic** *adj.* [Gk *aortē* f. *a(e)irō* raise]

apace /əˈpeɪs/ *adv. literary* swiftly, quickly. [OF *à pas* at (a considerable) pace]

apart /əˈpɑːt/ *adv.* **1** separately; not together (*keep your feet apart*). **2** into pieces (*came apart in my hands*). **3 a** to or on one side. **b** out of consideration (placed after noun: *joking apart*). **4** to or at a distance. □ **apart from 1** excepting; not considering. **2** in addition to (*apart from roses we grow irises*). [ME f. OF f. *à* to + *part* side]

apartheid /əˈpɑːteɪt/ *n.* **1** (esp. in S. Africa) a policy or system of segregation or discrimination on grounds of race. **2** segregation in other contexts. [Afrik. (as APART, -HOOD)]

apartment /əˈpɑːtmənt/ *n.* **1** (in *pl.*) a suite of rooms, usu. furnished and rented. **2** a single room in a house. **3** *US* a flat. □ **apartment house** *US* a block of flats. [F *appartement* f. It. *appartamento* f. *appartare* to separate f. *a parte* apart]

apathetic /ˌæpəˈθetɪk/ *adj.* having or showing no emotion or interest. □ **apathetically** *adv.* [APATHY, after PATHETIC]

apathy /ˈæpəθɪ/ *n.* (often foll. by *towards*) lack of interest or feeling; indifference. [F *apathie* f. L *apathia* f. Gk *apatheia* f. *apathēs* without feeling f. *a-* not + *pathos* suffering]

ape *n. & v.* —*n.* **1** any of the various primates of the family Pongidae characterized by the absence of a tail, e.g. the gorilla or chimpanzee. **2** (in general use) any monkey. **3 a** an imitator. **b** an apelike person. —*v.tr.* imitate, mimic. □ **ape-man** (pl. **-men**) any of various apelike primates held to be forerunners of present-day man. **go ape** *sl.* become crazy. **naked ape** present-day man. [OE *apa* f. Gmc]

aperient /əˈpɪərɪənt/ *adj. & n.* —*adj.* laxative. —*n.* a laxative medicine. [L *aperire aperient-* to open]

aperiodic /ˌeɪpɪərɪˈɒdɪk/ *adj.* not periodic; irregular. □ **aperiodicity** /-rɪəˈdɪsɪtɪ/ *n.*

aperitif /əˌperɪˈtiːf, əˈpe-/ *n.* an alcoholic drink taken before a meal to stimulate the appetite. [F *apéritif* f. med.L *aperitivus* f. L *aperire* to open]

aperture /ˈæpəˌtjʊə(r)/ n. **1** an opening; a gap. **2** a space through which light passes in an optical or photographic instrument, esp. a variable space in a camera. [L apertura (as APERITIF)]

Apex /ˈeɪpeks/ n. (also **APEX**) (often attrib.) a system of reduced fares for scheduled airline flights when paid for before a certain period in advance of departure. [Advance Purchase Excursion]

apex /ˈeɪpeks/ n. (pl. **apexes** or **apices** /ˈeɪpɪˌsiː/) **1** the highest point. **2** a climax; a high point of achievement etc. **3** the vertex of a triangle or cone. **4** a tip or pointed end. [L, = peak, tip]

aphasia /əˈfeɪzɪə/ n. Med. the loss of ability to understand or express speech, owing to brain damage. □ **aphasic** adj. & n. [mod.L f. Gk f. aphatos speechless f. a- not + pha- speak]

aphelion /æpˈhiːlɪən, əˈfiːlɪən/ (pl. **aphelia** /-lɪə/) the point in a body's orbit where it is furthest from the sun. [Graecized f. mod.L aphelium f. Gk aph' hēliou from the sun]

aphid /ˈeɪfɪd/ n. any small homopterous insect which feeds by sucking sap from leaves, stems, or roots of plants; a plant-louse. [back-form. f. aphides: see APHIS]

aphis /ˈeɪfɪs/ n. (pl. **aphides** /-ˌdiːz/) an aphid, esp. of the genus Aphis including the greenfly. [mod.L (Linnaeus) f. Gk (1523), perh. a misreading of koris bug]

aphorism /ˈæfəˌrɪz(ə)m/ n. **1** a short pithy maxim. **2** a brief statement of a principle. □ **aphorist** n. **aphoristic** /-ˈrɪstɪk/ adj. **aphoristically** /-ˈrɪstɪkəlɪ/ adv. **aphorize** v.intr. (also **-ise**). [F aphorisme or LL f. Gk aphorismos definition f. aphorizō (as APO-, horos boundary)]

aphrodisiac /ˌæfrəˈdɪzɪˌæk/ adj. & n. —adj. that arouses sexual desire. —n. an aphrodisiac drug. [Gk aphrodisiakos f. aphrodisios f. Aphroditē Gk goddess of love]

apian /ˈeɪpɪən/ adj. of or relating to bees. [L apianus f. apis bee]

apiary /ˈeɪpɪərɪ/ n. (pl. **-ies**) a place where bees are kept. □ **apiarist** n. [L apiarium f. apis bee]

apical /ˈeɪpɪk(ə)l, ˈæp-/ adj. of, at, or forming an apex. □ **apically** adv. [L apex apicis: see APEX]

apices pl. of APEX.

apiculture /ˈeɪpɪˌkʌltʃə(r)/ n. bee-keeping. □ **apicultural** /-ˈkʌltʃər(ə)l/ adj. **apiculturist** /-ˈkʌltʃərɪst/ n. [L apis bee, after AGRICULTURE]

apiece /əˈpiːs/ adv. for each one; severally (had five pounds apiece). [A² + PIECE]

apish /ˈeɪpɪʃ/ adj. **1** of or like an ape. **2** silly; affected. □ **apishly** adv. **apishness** n.

aplenty /əˈplentɪ/ adv. in plenty.

aplomb /əˈplɒm/ n. assurance; self-confidence. [F, = perpendicularity, f. à plomb according to a plummet]

apnoea /æpˈniːə/ n. (US **apnea**) Med. a temporary cessation of breathing. [mod.L f. Gk apnoia f. apnous breathless]

apo- /ˈæpə/ prefix **1** away from (apogee). **2** separate (apocarpous). [Gk apo from, away, un-, quite]

apocalypse /əˈpɒkəlɪps/ n. **1** (**the Apocalypse**) Revelation, the last book of the New Testament, recounting a divine revelation to St John. **2** a revelation, esp. of the end of the world. **3** a grand or violent event resembling those described in the Apocalypse. [ME f. OF ult. f. Gk apokalupsis f. apokaluptō uncover, reveal]

apocalyptic /əˌpɒkəˈlɪptɪk/ adj. **1** of or resembling the Apocalypse. **2** revelatory; prophetic. □ **apocalyptically** adv. [Gk apokaluptikos (as APOCALYPSE)]

Apocrypha /əˈpɒkrɪfə/ n.pl. **1** the books included in the Septuagint and Vulgate versions of the Old Testament but not in the Hebrew Bible. **2** (**apocrypha**) writings or reports not considered genuine. [ME f. eccl.L apocrypha (scripta) hidden writings f. Gk apokruphos f. apokruptō hide away]

apocryphal /əˈpɒkrɪf(ə)l/ adj. **1** of doubtful authenticity (orig. of some early Christian texts resembling those of the New Testament). **2** invented, mythical (an apocryphal story). **3** of or belonging to the Apocrypha.

apodosis /əˈpɒdəsɪs/ n. (pl. **apodoses** /-ˌsiːz/) the main (consequent) clause of a conditional sentence (e.g. I would agree in if you asked me I would agree). [LL f. Gk f. apodidōmi give back (as APO-, didōmi give)]

apogee /ˈæpəˌdʒiː/ n. **1** the point in a celestial body's orbit where it is furthest from the earth. **2** the most distant or highest point. □ **apogean** /ˌæpəˈdʒiːən/ adj. [F apogée or mod.L apogaeum f. Gk apogeion away from earth (as APO-, gē earth)]

apolitical /ˌeɪpəˈlɪtɪk(ə)l/ adj. not interested in or concerned with politics.

apologetic /əˌpɒləˈdʒetɪk/ adj. & n. —adj. **1** regretfully acknowledging or excusing an offence or failure. **2** diffident. **3** of reasoned defence or vindication. —n. (usu. in pl.) a reasoned defence, esp. of Christianity. □ **apologetically** adv. [F apologétique f. LL apologeticus f. Gk apologētikos f. apologeomai speak in defence]

apologia /ˌæpəˈləʊdʒɪə/ n. a formal defence of one's opinions or conduct. [L: see APOLOGY]

apologist /əˈpɒlədʒɪst/ n. a person who defends something by argument. [F apologiste f. Gk apologizomai render account f. apologos account]

apologize /əˈpɒləˌdʒaɪz/ v.intr. (also **-ise**) make an apology; express regret. [Gk apologizomai: see APOLOGIST]

apologue /ˈæpəˌlɒg/ n. a moral fable. [F apologue or L apologus f. Gk apologos story (as APO-, logos discourse)]

apology /əˈpɒlədʒɪ/ n. (pl. **-ies**) **1** a regretful acknowledgement of an offence or failure. **2** an assurance that no offence was intended. **3** an explanation or defence. **4** (foll. by for) a poor or scanty specimen of (this apology for a letter). [F apologie or LL apologia f. Gk (as APOLOGETIC)]

apolune /ˈæpəˌluːn, -ˌljuːn/ n. the point in a body's lunar orbit where it is furthest from the moon's centre (opp. PERILUNE). [APO- + L luna moon, after apogee]

apophthegm /ˈæpəˌθem, ˈæpəfˌθem/ n. (US **apothegm**) a terse saying or maxim, an aphorism. □ **apophthegmatic** /-θegˈmætɪk/ adj. [F apophthegme or mod.L apothegma f. Gk apophthegma -matos f. apophtheggomai speak out]

apoplectic /ˌæpəˈplektɪk/ adj. **1** of, causing, suffering, or liable to apoplexy. **2** colloq. enraged. □ **apoplectically** adv. [F apoplectique or LL apoplecticus f. Gk apoplēktikos f. apoplēssō strike completely (as APO-, plēssō strike)]

apoplexy /ˈæpəˌpleksɪ/ n. a sudden loss of consciousness, voluntary movement, and sensation caused by blockage or rupture of a brain artery; a stroke. [ME f. OF apoplexie f. LL apoplexia f. Gk apoplēxia (as APOPLECTIC)]

apostasy /ə¹pɒstəsɪ/ n. (pl. **-ies**) **1** renunciation of a belief or faith, esp. religious. **2** abandonment of principles or of a party. **3** an instance of apostasy. [ME f. eccl.L f. NT Gk *apostasia* f. *apostasis* defection (as APO-, *stat-* stand)]

apostate /ə¹pɒsteɪt/ n. & adj. —n. a person who renounces a former belief, adherence, etc. —adj. engaged in apostasy. □ **apostatical** /ˌæpə¹stætɪk(ə)l/ adj. [ME f. OF *apostate* or eccl.L *apostata* f. Gk *apostatēs* deserter (as APOSTASY)]

apostatize /ə¹pɒstə₁taɪz/ v.intr. (also **-ise**) renounce a former belief, adherence, etc. [med.L *apostatizare* f. *apostata*: see APOSTATE]

a posteriori /ˌeɪ pɒ₁sterɪ¹ɔːraɪ/ adj. & adv. —adj. (of reasoning) inductive, empirical; proceeding from effects to causes. —adv. inductively, empirically; from effects to causes. [L, = from what comes after]

apostle /ə¹pɒs(ə)l/ n. **1** (**Apostle**) **a** any of the chosen twelve sent out to preach the Christian Gospel. **b** the first successful Christian missionary in a country or to a people. **2** a leader or outstanding figure, esp. of a reform movement (*apostle of temperance*). **3** a messenger or representative. □ **apostleship** n. [OE *apostol* f. eccl.L *apostolus* f. Gk *apostolos* messenger (as APO-, *stellō* send forth)]

apostolate /ə¹pɒstələt/ n. **1** the position or authority of an Apostle. **2** leadership in reform. [eccl.L *apostolatus* (as APOSTLE)]

apostolic /ˌæpə¹stɒlɪk/ adj. **1** of or relating to the Apostles. **2** of the Pope regarded as the successor of St Peter. **3** of the character of an Apostle. **apostolic succession** the uninterrupted transmission of spiritual authority from the Apostles through successive popes and bishops. [F *apostolique* or eccl.L *apostolicus* f. Gk *apostolikos* (as APOSTLE)]

apostrophe[1] /ə¹pɒstrəfɪ/ n. a punctuation mark used to indicate: **1** the omission of letters or numbers (e.g. *can't; he's; 1 Jan. '92*). **2** the possessive case (e.g. *Harry's book; boys' coats*). [F *apostrophe* or LL *apostrophus* f. Gk *apostrophos* accent of elision f. *apostrephō* turn away (as APO-, *strephō* turn)]

apostrophe[2] /ə¹pɒstrəfɪ/ n. an exclamatory passage in a speech or poem, addressed to a person (often dead or absent) or thing (often personified). □ **apostrophize** v.tr. & intr. (also **-ise**). [L f. Gk, lit. 'turning away' (as APOSTROPHE[1])]

apothecary /ə¹pɒθəkərɪ/ n. (pl. **-ies**) *archaic* a chemist licensed to dispense medicines and drugs. □ **apothecaries' measure** (or **weight**) *Brit.* units of weight and liquid volume formerly used in pharmacy. [ME f. OF *apotecaire* f. LL *apothecarius* f. L *apotheca* f. Gk *apothēkē* storehouse]

apotheosis /ə₁pɒθɪ¹əʊsɪs/ n. (pl. **apotheoses** /-siːz/) **1** elevation to divine status; deification. **2** a glorification of a thing; a sublime example (*apotheosis of the dance*). **3** a deified ideal. [eccl.L f. Gk *apotheoō* make a god of (as APO-, *theos* god)]

apotheosize /ə₁pɒθɪə₁saɪz/ v.tr. (also **-ise**) **1** make divine; deify. **2** idealize, glorify.

apotropaic /ˌæpətrə¹peɪɪk/ adj. supposedly having the power to avert an evil influence or bad luck. [Gk *apotropaios* (as APO-, *trepō* turn)]

appal /ə¹pɔːl/ v.tr. (US **appall**) (**appalled, appalling**) **1** greatly dismay or horrify. **2** (as **appalling** adj.) *colloq.* shocking, unpleasant; bad. □ **appallingly** adv. [ME f. OF *apalir* grow pale]

apparat /ˌæpə¹rɑːt/ n. *hist.* the administrative system of a Communist party, esp. in a Communist country. [Russ. f. G, = apparatus]

apparatchik /ˌæpə¹rɑːtʃɪk/ n. (pl. **apparatchiks** or **apparatchiki** /-₁kiː/) *hist.* **1 a** a member of a Communist *apparat*. **b** a Communist agent or spy. **2 a** a member of a political party in any country who executes policy; a jealous functionary. **b** an official of a public or private organization. [Russ.: see APPARAT]

apparatus /ˌæpə¹reɪtəs, ¹æp-/ n. **1** the equipment needed for a particular purpose or function, esp. scientific or technical. **2** a political or other complex organization. [L f. *apparare apparat-* make ready for]

apparel /ə¹pær(ə)l/ n. & v. —n. *formal* clothing, dress. —v.tr. (**apparelled, apparelling**; US **appareled, appareling**) *archaic* clothe. [ME *aparailen* (v.) f. OF *apareillier* f. Rmc *appariculare* (unrecorded) make equal or fit, ult. f. L *par* equal]

apparent /ə¹pærənt/ adj. **1** readily visible or perceivable. **2** seeming. □ **apparently** adv. [ME f. OF *aparant* f. L (as APPEAR)]

apparition /ˌæpə¹rɪʃ(ə)n/ n. a sudden or dramatic appearance, esp. of a ghost or phantom; a visible ghost. [ME f. F *apparition* or f. L *apparitio* attendance (as APPEAR)]

appeal /ə¹piːl/ v. & n. —v. **1** intr. make an earnest or formal request; plead (*appealed for calm; appealed to us not to leave*). **2** intr. (usu. foll. by *to*) be attractive or of interest; be pleasing. **3** intr. (foll. by *to*) resort to or cite for support. **4** *Law* intr. (often foll. by *to*) apply (to a higher court) for a reconsideration of the decision of a lower court. **b** tr. refer to a higher court to review (a case). **c** intr. (foll. by *against*) apply to a higher court to reconsider (a verdict or sentence). **5** intr. *Cricket* call on the umpire for a decision on whether a batsman is out. —n. **1** the act or an instance of appealing. **2** a formal or urgent request for public support, esp. financial, for a cause. **3** *Law* the referral of a case to a higher court. **4** attractiveness; appealing quality. □ **appealer** n. [ME f. OF *apel, apeler* f. L *appellare* to address]

appealable /ə¹piːləb(ə)l/ adj. *Law* (of a case) that can be referred to a higher court for review.

appealing /ə¹piːlɪŋ/ adj. attractive, likeable. □ **appealingly** adv.

appear /ə¹pɪə(r)/ v.intr. **1** become or be visible. **2** be evident (*a new problem then appeared*). **3** seem; have the appearance of being (*appeared unwell; you appear to be right*). **4** present oneself publicly or formally. **5** be published (*it appeared in the papers; a new edition will appear*). [ME f. OF *apareir* f. L *apparēre apparit-* come in sight]

appearance /ə¹pɪərəns/ n. **1** the act or an instance of appearing. **2** an outward form as perceived (whether correctly or not), esp. visually (*has an appearance of prosperity*). **3** a semblance. □ **keep up appearances** maintain an impression or pretence of virtue, affluence, etc. **make** (or **put in**) **an appearance** be present, esp. briefly. **to all appearances** as far as can be seen; apparently. [ME f. OF *aparance, -ence* f. LL *apparentia* (as APPEAR, -ENCE)]

appease /ə¹piːz/ v.tr. **1** make calm or quiet, esp. conciliate (a potential aggressor) by making concessions. **2** satisfy (an appetite, scruples). □ **appeasement** n. **appeaser** n. [ME f. AF *apeser*, OF *apaisier* f. *à* to + *pais* PEACE]

appellant /əˈpelənt/ n. Law a person who appeals to a higher court. [ME f. F (as APPEAL, -ANT)]

appellate /əˈpelət/ adj. Law (esp. of a court) concerned with or dealing with appeals. [L appellatus (as APPEAL, -ATE²)]

appellation /ˌæpəˈleɪʃ(ə)n/ n. formal a name or title; nomenclature. [ME f. OF f. L appellatio -onis (as APPEAL, -ATION)]

appellative /əˈpelətɪv/ adj. 1 naming. 2 Gram. (of a noun) that designates a class; common. [LL appellativus (as APPEAL, -ATIVE)]

append /əˈpend/ v.tr. (usu. foll. by to) attach, affix, add, esp. to a written document etc. [L appendere hang]

appendage /əˈpendɪdʒ/ n. 1 something attached; an addition. 2 Zool. a leg or other projecting part of an arthropod.

appendectomy /ˌæpenˈdektəmɪ/ n. (also **appendicectomy** /-dɪˈsektəmɪ/) (pl. **-ies**) the surgical removal of the appendix. [APPENDIX + -ECTOMY]

appendicitis /əˌpendɪˈsaɪtɪs/ n. inflammation of the appendix. [APPENDIX + -ITIS]

appendix /əˈpendɪks/ n. (pl. **appendices** /-ˌsiːz/; **appendixes**) 1 (in full **vermiform appendix**) Anat. a small outgrowth of tissue forming a tube-shaped sac attached to the lower end of the large intestine. 2 subsidiary matter at the end of a book or document. [L appendix -icis f. appendere APPEND]

appertain /ˌæpəˈteɪn/ v.intr. (foll. by to) 1 relate. 2 belong as a possession or right. 3 be appropriate. [ME f. OF apertenir f. LL appertinēre f. pertinēre PERTAIN]

appetence /ˈæpɪt(ə)ns/ n. (also **appetency** /-sɪ/) (foll. by for) longing or desire. [F appétence or L appetentia f. appetere seek after]

appetite /ˈæpɪˌtaɪt/ n. 1 a natural desire to satisfy bodily needs. 2 (usu. foll. by for) an inclination or desire. □ **appetitive** /əˈpetɪtɪv/ adj. [ME f. OF apetit f. L appetitus f. appetere seek after]

appetizer /ˈæpɪˌtaɪzə(r)/ n. (also **-iser**) a small amount, esp. of food or drink, to stimulate an appetite. [appetize (back-form. f. APPETIZING)]

appetizing /ˈæpɪˌtaɪzɪŋ/ adj. (also **-ising**) stimulating an appetite, esp. for food. □ **appetizingly** adv. [F appétissant irreg. f. appétit, formed as APPETITE]

applaud /əˈplɔːd/ v. 1 intr. express strong approval or praise, esp. by clapping. 2 tr. express approval of (a person or action). [L applaudere applaus- clap hands]

applause /əˈplɔːz/ n. 1 an expression of approbation, esp. from an audience etc. by clapping. 2 emphatic approval. [med.L applausus (as APPLAUD)]

apple /ˈæp(ə)l/ n. 1 the fruit of a tree of the genus Malus, rounded in form and with a crisp flesh. 2 the tree bearing this. □ **apple of one's eye** a cherished person or thing. **apple-pie bed** a bed made (as a joke) with the sheets folded short, so that the legs cannot be accommodated. **apple-pie order** perfect order; extreme neatness. **upset the apple-cart** spoil careful plans. [OE æppel f. Gmc]

applejack /ˈæp(ə)lˌdʒæk/ n. US a spirit distilled from fermented apple juice. [APPLE + JACK]

appliance /əˈplaɪəns/ n. a device or piece of equipment used for a specific task. [APPLY + -ANCE]

applicable /ˈæplɪkəb(ə)l, əˈplɪkəb(ə)l/ adj. (often foll. by to) 1 that may be applied. 2 having reference; appropriate. □ **applicability** /-ˈbɪlɪtɪ/ n. **applicably** adv. [OF applicable or med.L applicabilis (as APPLY, -ABLE)]

applicant /ˈæplɪkənt/ n. a person who applies for something, esp. a post. [APPLICATION + -ANT]

application /ˌæplɪˈkeɪʃ(ə)n/ n. 1 the act of applying, esp. medicinal ointment to the skin. 2 a formal request, usu. in writing, for employment, membership, etc. 3 a relevance. b the use to which something can or should be put. 4 sustained or concentrated effort; diligence. [ME f. F f. L applicatio -onis (as APPLY, -ATION)]

applicator /ˈæplɪˌkeɪtə(r)/ n. a device for applying a substance to a surface, esp. the skin. [APPLICATION + -OR¹]

applied /əˈplaɪd/ adj. (of a subject of study) put to practical use as opposed to being theoretical.

appliqué /æˈpliːkeɪ/ n., adj., & v. —n. ornamental work in which fabric is cut out and attached, usu. sewn, to the surface of another fabric to form pictures or patterns. —adj. executed in appliqué. —v.tr. (**appliqués, appliquéd, appliquéing**) decorate with appliqué; make using appliqué technique. [F, past part. of appliquer apply f. L applicare: see APPLY]

apply /əˈplaɪ/ v. (**-ies, -ied**) 1 intr. (often foll. by for, to, or to + infin.) make a formal request for something to be done, given, etc. (apply for a job; apply for help to the governors; applied to be sent overseas). 2 intr. have relevance (does not apply in this case). 3 tr. a make use of as relevant or suitable; employ (apply the rules). b operate (apply the handbrake). 4 tr. (often foll. by to) a put or spread on (applied the ointment to the cut). b administer (applied common sense to the problem). 5 refl. (often foll. by to) devote oneself (applied myself to the task). □ **applier** n. [ME f. OF aplier f. L applicare fold, fasten to]

appoint /əˈpɔɪnt/ v.tr. 1 assign a post or office to (appoint him governor; appoint him to govern; appointed to the post). 2 (often foll. by for) fix, decide on (a time, place, etc.) (Wednesday was appointed for the meeting). 3 (as **appointed** adj.) equipped, furnished (a well appointed hotel). □ **appointee** /-ˈtiː/ n. **appointer** n. **appointive** adj. US [ME f. OF apointer f. à point to a point]

appointment /əˈpɔɪntmənt/ n. 1 an arrangement to meet at a specific time and place. 2 a a post or office available for applicants, or recently filled (took up the appointment on Monday). b a person appointed. 3 (usu. in pl.) a furniture, fittings. b equipment. [ME f. OF apointement (as APPOINT, -MENT)]

apportion /əˈpɔːʃ(ə)n/ v.tr. (often foll. by to) share out; assign as a share. □ **apportionable** adj. **apportionment** n. [F apportionner or f. med.L apportionare (as AD-, PORTION)]

apposite /ˈæpəzɪt/ adj. (often foll. by to) 1 apt; well chosen. 2 well expressed. □ **appositely** adv. **appositeness** n. [L appositus past part. of apponere (as AD-, ponere put)]

apposition /ˌæpəˈzɪʃ(ə)n/ n. 1 placing side by side; juxtaposition. 2 Gram. the placing of a word next to another, esp. the addition of one noun to another, in order to qualify or explain the first (e.g. William the Conqueror; my friend Sue). □ **appositional** adj. [ME f. F apposition or f. LL appositio (as APPOSITE, -ITION)]

appraisal /əˈpreɪz(ə)l/ n. the act or an instance of appraising.

appraise /əˈpreɪz/ v.tr. **1** estimate the value or quality of (*appraised her skills*). **2** set a price on; value. □ **appraisable** adj. **appraiser** n. **appraisive** adj. [APPRIZE by assim. to PRAISE]

appreciable /əˈpriːʃəb(ə)l/ adj. large enough to be noticed; significant; considerable. □ **appreciably** adv. [F f. *apprécier* (as APPRECIATE)]

appreciate /əˈpriːʃɪeɪt, -sɪeɪt/ v. **1** tr. **a** esteem highly; value. **b** be grateful for (*we appreciate your sympathy*). **c** be sensitive to (*appreciate the nuances*). **2** tr. (often foll. by *that* + clause) understand; recognize. **3 a** intr. (of property etc.) rise in value. **b** tr. raise in value. □ **appreciatively** /-ʃətɪvlɪ/ adj. **appreciatively** /-ʃətɪvlɪ/ adv. **appreciativeness** /-ʃətɪvnɪs/ n. **appreciator** n. **appreciatory** /-ʃətərɪ/ adj. [LL *appretiare* appraise (as AD-, *pretium* price)]

appreciation /əˌpriːʃɪˈeɪʃ(ə)n, əˌpriːs-/ n. **1** favourable or grateful recognition. **2** an estimation or judgement; a sensitive understanding or reaction (*a quick appreciation of the problem*). **3** an increase in value. [F f. LL *appretiatio -onis* (as APPRECIATE, -ATION)]

apprehend /ˌæprɪˈhend/ v.tr. **1** understand, perceive (*apprehend your meaning*). **2** seize, arrest (*apprehended the criminal*). **3** anticipate with uneasiness (*apprehending the results*). [F *appréhender* or L *apprehendere* (as AD-, *prehendere prehens-* lay hold of)]

apprehensible /ˌæprɪˈhensɪb(ə)l/ adj. capable of being apprehended by the senses or the intellect. □ **apprehensibility** /-ˈbɪlɪtɪ/ n. [LL *apprehensibilis* (as APPREHEND, -IBLE)]

apprehension /ˌæprɪˈhenʃ(ə)n/ n. **1** uneasiness; dread. **2** understanding, grasp. **3** arrest, capture (*apprehension of the suspect*). **4** an idea; a conception. [F *appréhension* or LL *apprehensio* (as APPREHEND, -ION)]

apprehensive /ˌæprɪˈhensɪv/ adj. (often foll. by *of*, *for*) uneasily fearful; dreading. □ **apprehensively** adv. **apprehensiveness** n. [F *appréhensif* or med.L *apprehensivus* (as APPREHEND, -IVE)]

apprentice /əˈprentɪs/ n. & v. —n. **1** a person who is learning a trade by being employed in it for an agreed period at low wages. **2** a beginner; a novice. —v.tr. (usu. foll. by *to*) engage or bind as an apprentice (*was apprenticed to a builder*). □ **apprenticeship** n. [ME f. OF *aprentis* f. *apprendre* learn (as APPREHEND), after words in *-tis*, *-tif*, f. L *-tivus*: see -IVE]

apprise /əˈpraɪz/ v.tr. inform. □ **be apprised of** be aware of. [F *appris -ise* past part. of *apprendre* learn, teach (as APPREHEND)]

apprize /əˈpraɪz/ v.tr. archaic **1** esteem highly. **2** appraise. [ME f. OF *aprisier* f. *à* to + *pris* PRICE]

appro /ˈæprəʊ/ n. Brit. colloq. □ **on appro** = *on approval* (see APPROVAL). [abbr. of *approval* or *approbation*]

approach /əˈprəʊtʃ/ v. & n. —v. **1** tr. come near or nearer to (a place or time). **2** intr. come near or nearer in space or time (*the hour approaches*). **3** tr. make a tentative proposal or suggestion to (*approached me about a loan*). **4** tr. **a** be similar in character, quality, etc., to (*doesn't approach her for artistic skill*). **b** approximate to (*a population approaching 5 million*). **5** tr. attempt to influence or bribe. **6** tr. set about (a task etc.) **7** intr. Golf play an approach shot. —n. **1** an act or means of approaching (*made an approach; an approach lined*

with trees). **2** an approximation (*an approach to an apology*). **3** a way of dealing with a person or thing (*needs a new approach*). **4** (usu. in pl.) a sexual advance. **5** Golf a stroke from the fairway to the green. **6** Aeron. the final part of a flight before landing. □ **approach road** Brit. a road by which traffic enters a motorway. [ME f. OF *aproch(i)er* f. eccl.L *appropiare* draw near (as AD-, *propius* compar. of *prope* near)]

approachable /əˈprəʊtʃəb(ə)l/ adj. **1** friendly; easy to talk to. **2** able to be approached. □ **approachability** /-ˈbɪlɪtɪ/ n.

approbation /ˌæprəˈbeɪʃ(ə)n/ n. approval, consent. □ **approbative** /ˈæprəˌbeɪtɪv/ adj. **approbatory** /-ˈbeɪt-/ adj. [ME f. OF f. L *approbatio -onis* f. *approbare* (as AD-, *probare* test f. *probus* good)]

appropriate adj. & v. —adj. /əˈprəʊprɪət/ **1** suitable or proper. **2** formal belonging or particular. —v.tr. /əˈprəʊprɪeɪt/ **1** take possession of, esp. without authority. **2** devote (money etc.) to special purposes. □ **appropriately** adv. **appropriateness** n. **appropriation** /əˌprəʊprɪˈeɪʃ(ə)n/ n. **appropriator** /-ˌeɪtə(r)/ n. [LL *appropriatus* past part. of *appropriare* (as AD-, *proprius* own)]

approval /əˈpruːv(ə)l/ n. **1** the act of approving. **2** an instance of this; consent; a favourable opinion (*looked at him with approval*). □ **on approval** (of goods supplied) to be returned if not satisfactory.

approve /əˈpruːv/ v. **1** tr. confirm; sanction. **2** intr. give or have a favourable opinion. **3** tr. commend (*approved the new hat*). □ **approve of 1** pronounce or consider good or satisfactory; commend. **2** agree to. □ **approvingly** adv. [ME f. OF *aprover* f. L *approbare* (as APPROBATION)]

approximate adj. & v. —adj. /əˈprɒksɪmət/ fairly correct or accurate; near to the actual (*the approximate time of arrival*). —v.tr. & intr. /əˈprɒksɪˌmeɪt/ (often foll. by *to*) bring or come near (esp. in quality, number, etc.), but not exactly (*approximates to the truth; approximates the amount required*). □ **approximately** /-mətlɪ/ adv. **approximation** /-ˈmeɪʃ(ə)n/ n. [LL *approximatus* past part. of *approximare* (as AD-, *proximus* very near)]

appurtenance /əˈpɜːtɪnəns/ n. (usu. in pl.) a belonging; an appendage; an accessory. [ME f. AF *apurtenaunce*, OF *apertenance* (as APPERTAIN, -ANCE)]

appurtenant /əˈpɜːtɪnənt/ adj. (often foll. by *to*) belonging or appertaining; pertinent. [ME f. OF *apartenant* pres. part. (as APPERTAIN)]

APR abbr. annual or annualized percentage rate (esp. of interest on loans or credit).

Apr. abbr. April.

apricot /ˈeɪprɪˌkɒt/ n. & adj. —n. **1 a** a juicy soft fruit, of an orange-yellow colour. **b** the tree, *Prunus armeniaca*, bearing it. **2** the ripe fruit's orange-yellow colour. —adj. orange-yellow (*apricot dress*). [Port. *albricoque* or Sp. *albaricoque* f. Arab., ultimately f. L *praecox* early-ripe]

April /ˈeɪprɪl, ˈeɪprɪ(ə)l/ n. the fourth month of the year. □ **April Fool** a person successfully tricked on 1 April. **April Fool's** (or **Fools'**) **Day** 1 April. [ME f. L *Aprilis*]

a priori /ˌeɪ praɪˈɔːraɪ/ adj. & adv. —adj. **1** (of reasoning) deductive; proceeding from causes to effects. **2** (of concepts, knowledge, etc.) logically independent of experience; not derived from experience. **3** not submitted to critical investigation (*an a priori conjecture*). —adv. **1** in an a priori manner. **2** as far as one knows; presumptively. □ **apriorism** /eɪˈpraɪəˌrɪz(ə)m/ *n*. [L, = from what is before]

apron /ˈeɪprən/ *n*. **1 a** a garment covering and protecting the front of a person's clothes and tied at the back. **b** anything resembling an apron in shape or function. **2** *Theatr.* the part of a stage in front of the curtain. **3** the hard-surfaced area on an airfield used for manoeuvring or loading aircraft. **4** an endless conveyor belt. □ **aproned** *adj.* **apronful** *n*. (*pl.* **-fuls**). [ME *naperon* etc. f. OF dimin. of *nape* table-cloth f. L *mappa*: for loss of *n* cf. ADDER]

apropos /ˈæprəˌpəʊ, -ˈpəʊ/ *adj.* & *adv.* —*adj.* **1** to the point or purpose; appropriate (*his comment was apropos*). **2** *colloq.* (often foll. by *of*) in respect of; concerning (*apropos the meeting; apropos of the talk*). —*adv.* **1** appropriately. **2** (*absol.*) by the way; incidentally (*apropos, she's not going*). [F *à propos* f. *à* to + *propos* PURPOSE]

apse /æps/ *n*. **1** a large semicircular or polygonal recess, arched or with a domed roof, esp. at the eastern end of a church. **2** = APSIS. □ **apsidal** /ˈæpsɪd(ə)l/ *adj.* [L APSIS]

apsis /ˈæpsɪs/ *n*. (*pl.* **apsides** /-ˌdiːz/) either of two points on the orbit of a planet or satellite that are nearest to or furthest from the body round which it moves. □ **apsidal** *adj.* [L f. Gk (h)*apsis*, -*idos* arch, vault]

apt *adj.* **1** appropriate, suitable. **2** (foll. by *to* + infin.) having a tendency (*apt to lose his temper*). **3** clever; quick to learn (*an apt pupil; apt at the work*). □ **aptly** *adv.* **aptness** *n*. [ME f. L *aptus* fitted, past part. of *apere* fasten]

apteryx /ˈæptərɪks/ *n*. = KIWI. [mod.L f. Gk *a-* not + *pterux* wing]

aptitude /ˈæptɪˌtjuːd/ *n*. **1** a natural propensity or talent (*shows an aptitude for drawing*). **2** ability or fitness, esp. to acquire a particular skill. [F f. LL *aptitudo* -*inis* (as APT, -TUDE)]

aqua /ˈækwə/ *n*. the colour aquamarine. [abbr.]

aqualung /ˈækwəˌlʌŋ/ *n*. & *v*. —*n*. a portable breathing-apparatus for divers, consisting of cylinders of compressed air strapped on the back, feeding air automatically through a mask or mouthpiece. —*v.intr.* use an aqualung. [L *aqua* water + LUNG]

aquamarine /ˌækwəməˈriːn/ *n*. **1** a light bluish-green beryl. **2** its colour. [L *aqua marina* sea water]

aquaplane /ˈækwəˌpleɪn/ *n*. & *v*. —*n*. a board for riding on the water, pulled by a speedboat. —*v.intr.* **1** ride on an aquaplane. **2** (of a vehicle) glide uncontrollably on the wet surface of a road. [L *aqua* water + PLANE¹]

aquarelle /ˌækwəˈrel/ *n*. a painting in thin, usu. transparent water-colours. [F f. It. *acquarella* water-colour, dimin. of *acqua* f. L *aqua* water]

aquarium /əˈkweərɪəm/ *n*. (*pl.* **aquariums** or **aquaria** /-rɪə/) an artificial environment designed for keeping live aquatic plants and animals, esp. a tank of water with transparent sides. [neut. of L *aquarius* of water (*aqua*) after *vivarium*]

Aquarius /əˈkweərɪəs/ *n*. **1** a constellation, traditionally regarded as contained in the figure of a water-carrier. **2 a** the eleventh sign of the zodiac (the Water-carrier). **b** a person born when the sun is in this sign. □ **Aquarian** *adj.* & *n*. [ME f. L (as AQUARIUM)]

aquatic /əˈkwætɪk/ *adj.* & *n*. —*adj.* **1** growing or living in or near water. **2** (of a sport) played in or on water. —*n*. **1** an aquatic plant or animal. **2** (in *pl.*) aquatic sports. [ME f. F *aquatique* or L *aquaticus* f. *aqua* water]

aquatint /ˈækwətɪnt/ *n*. **1** a print resembling a water-colour, produced from a copper plate etched with nitric acid. **2** the process of producing this. [F *aquatinte* f. It. *acqua tinta* coloured water]

aquavit /ˈækwəvɪt, -ˌviːt/ (also **akvavit** /ˈækvə-/) *n*. an alcoholic spirit made from potatoes etc. [Scand.]

aqua vitae /ˌækwə ˈviːtaɪ/ *n*. a strong alcoholic spirit, esp. brandy. [L = water of life]

aqueduct /ˈækwɪˌdʌkt/ *n*. an artificial channel for conveying water, esp. in the form of a bridge supported by tall columns across a valley. [L *aquae ductus* conduit f. *aqua* water + *ducere* duct- to lead]

aqueous /ˈeɪkwɪəs/ *adj.* **1** of, containing, or like water. **2** *Geol.* produced by water (*aqueous rocks*). □ **aqueous humour** *Anat.* the clear fluid in the eye between the lens and the cornea. [med.L *aqueus* f. L *aqua* water]

aquifer /ˈækwɪfə(r)/ *n*. *Geol.* a layer of rock or soil able to hold or transmit much water. [L *aqui-* f. *aqua* water + *-fer* bearing f. *ferre* bear]

aquilegia /ˌækwɪˈliːdʒə/ *n*. any (often blue-flowered) plant of the genus *Aquilegia*. [mod. use of a med.L word: orig. unkn.]

aquiline /ˈækwɪˌlaɪn/ *adj.* **1** of or like an eagle. **2** (of a nose) curved like an eagle's beak. [L *aquilinus* f. *aquila* eagle]

Ar *symb.* *Chem.* the element argon.

-ar¹ /ə(r)/ *suffix* **1** forming adjectives (*angular; linear; nuclear; titular*). **2** forming nouns (*scholar*). [OF *-aire* or *-ier* or L *-aris*]

-ar² /ə(r)/ *suffix* forming nouns (*pillar*). [F *-er* or L *-ar, -are*, neut. of *-aris*]

-ar³ /ə(r)/ *suffix* forming nouns (*bursar; exemplar; mortar; vicar*). [OF *-aire* or *-ier* or L *-arius, -arium*]

-ar⁴ /ə(r)/ *suffix* assim. form of -ER¹, -OR¹ (*liar; pedlar*).

Arab /ˈærəb/ *n*. & *adj.* —*n*. **1** a member of a Semitic people inhabiting originally Saudi Arabia and the neighbouring countries, now the Middle East generally. **2** a horse of a breed orig. native to Arabia. —*adj.* of Arabia or the Arabs (esp. with ethnic reference). [F *Arabe* f. L *Arabs Arabis* f. Gk *Araps -abos* f. Arab. *ʾarab*]

arabesque /ˌærəˈbesk/ *n*. **1** *Ballet* a posture with one leg extended horizontally backwards, torso extended forwards, and arms outstretched. **2** a design of intertwined leaves, scrolls, etc. **3** *Mus.* a florid melodic section or composition. [F f. It. *arabesco* f. *arabo* Arab]

Arabian /əˈreɪbɪən/ *adj.* & *n*. —*adj.* of or relating to Arabia (esp. with geographical reference) (*the Arabian desert*). —*n*. a native of Arabia. [ME f. OF *arabi* prob. f. Arab. *ʾarabī*, or f. L *Arabus, Arabius* f. Gk *Arabios*]

■ **Usage** In the sense 'native of Arabia', the usual term is now *Arab*.

Arabic /ˈærəbɪk/ *n*. & *adj.* —*n*. the Semitic language of the Arabs, now spoken in much of N. Africa and the Middle East. —*adj.* of or relating to Arabia (esp. with reference to language or literature). □ **arabic numerals** the numerals 0, 1, 2, 3, 4, etc. [ME f. OF *arabic* f. L *arabicus* f. Gk *arabikos*]

arable /ˈærəb(ə)l/ *adj.* & *n*. —*adj.* **1** (of land) suitable for ploughing and crop production. **2**

(of crops) that can be grown on arable land.
—n. arable land or crops. [F *arable* or L *arabilis* f.
arare to plough]

arachnid /əˈræknɪd/ n. any arthropod of the
class Arachnida, having four pairs of walking
legs and characterized by simple eyes, e.g.
scorpions, spiders, mites, and ticks. □ **arach-
nidan** *adj.* & n. [F *arachnide* or mod.L *arachnida*
f. Gk *arakhnē* spider]

arachnophobia /əˌræknəˈfəʊbɪə/ n. an abnormal fear of spiders. □ **arachnophobe**
/əˈræknəˌfəʊb/ n. [mod. L. f. Gk *arakhne* spider +
-PHOBIA]

arak var. of ARRACK.

Aramaic /ˌærəˈmeɪɪk/ n. & adj. —n. a branch
of the Semitic family of languages, esp. the
language of Syria used as a lingua franca in the
Near East from the sixth century BC. —adj. of
or in Aramaic. [L *Aramaeus* f. Gk *Aramaios* of
Aram (bibl. name of Syria)]

araucaria /ˌærɔːˈkeərɪə/ n. any evergreen conifer
of the genus *Araucaria*, e.g. the monkey-puzzle
tree. [mod.L f. *Arauco*, name of a province in
Chile]

arb /ɑːb/ n. *colloq.* = ARBITRAGEUR.

arbiter /ˈɑːbɪtə(r)/ n. (*fem.* **arbitress** /-trɪs/) **1 a**
an arbitrator in a dispute. **b** a judge; an authority
(*arbiter of taste*). **2** (often foll. by *of*) a person who
has entire control of something. [L]

arbitrage /ˈɑːbɪˌtrɑːʒ, -trɪdʒ/ n. the buying and
selling of stocks or bills of exchange to take
advantage of varying prices in different markets.
[F f. *arbitrer* (as ARBITRATE)]

arbitrageur /ˌɑːbɪtrɑːˈʒɜː(r)/ n. (also **arbitrager**
/ˈɑːbɪtrɪdʒə(r)/) a person who engages in arbitrage. [F]

arbitral /ˈɑːbɪtr(ə)l/ *adj.* concerning arbitration.
[F *arbitral* or LL *arbitralis*: see ARBITER]

arbitrary /ˈɑːbɪtrərɪ/ *adj.* **1** based on or derived
from uninformed opinion or random choice;
capricious. **2** despotic. □ **arbitrarily** *adv.* **arbit-
rariness** n. [L *arbitrarius* or F *arbitraire* (as
ARBITER, -ARY[1])]

arbitrate /ˈɑːbɪˌtreɪt/ *v.tr.* & *intr.* decide by
arbitration. [L *arbitrari* judge]

arbitration /ˌɑːbɪˈtreɪʃ(ə)n/ n. the settlement of
a dispute by an arbitrator. [ME f. OF f. L *arbitratio
-onis* (as ARBITER, -ATION)]

arbitrator /ˈɑːbɪˌtreɪtə(r)/ n. a person appointed
to settle a dispute; an arbiter. □ **arbitratorship**
n. [ME f. LL (as ARBITRATION, -OR[1])]

arbor[1] /ˈɑːbə(r)/ n. **1** an axle or spindle on which
something revolves. **2** US a device holding a tool
in a lathe etc. [F *arbre* tree, axis, f. L *arbor*:
refashioned on L]

arbor[2] US var. of ARBOUR.

arboraceous /ˌɑːbəˈreɪʃəs/ *adj.* **1** treelike. **2**
wooded. [L *arbor* tree + -ACEOUS]

Arbor Day /ˈɑːbə/ n. a day dedicated annually
to public tree-planting in the US, Australia, and
other countries. [L *arbor* tree]

arboreal /ɑːˈbɔːrɪəl/ *adj.* of, living in, or connected with trees. [L *arboreus* f. *arbor* tree]

arborescent /ˌɑːbəˈres(ə)nt/ *adj.* treelike in
growth or general appearance. □ **arborescence**
n. [L *arborescere* grow into a tree (*arbor*)]

arboretum /ˌɑːbəˈriːtəm/ n. (pl. **arboretums** or
arboreta /-tə/) a botanical garden devoted to
trees. [L f. *arbor* tree]

arboriculture /ˈɑːbərɪˌkʌltʃə(r)/ n. the cultivation of trees and shrubs. □ **arboricultural**
/-ˈkʌltʃər(ə)l/ *adj.* **arboriculturist** /-ˈkʌltʃərɪst/ n.
[L *arbor -oris* tree, after *agriculture*]

arbor vitae /ˌɑːbə ˈviːtaɪ, ˈvaɪtɪ/ n. any of the
evergreen conifers of the genus *Thuja*, with
flattened shoots bearing scale leaves. [L, = tree
of life]

arbour /ˈɑːbə(r)/ n. (US **arbor**) a shady garden
alcove with the sides and roof formed by trees
or climbing plants; a bower. □ **arboured** *adj.*
[ME f. AF *erber* f. OF *erbier* f. *erbe* herb f. L *herba*:
phonetic change to *ar*- assisted by assoc. with L
arbor tree]

arbutus /ɑːˈbjuːtəs/ n. any evergreen ericaceous
tree or shrub of the genus *Arbutus*, having white
or pink clusters of flowers and strawberry-like
berries. [L]

arc /ɑːk/ n. & v. —n. **1** part of the circumference
of a circle or any other curve. **2** *Electr.* a luminous
discharge between two electrodes. —*v.intr.*
(**arced** /ɑːkt/; **arcing** /ˈɑːkɪŋ/) form an arc. □ **arc
lamp** (or **light**) a light source using an electric
arc. **arc welding** a method of using an electric
arc to melt metals to be welded. [ME f. OF f. L
arcus bow, curve]

arcade /ɑːˈkeɪd/ n. **1** a passage with an arched
roof. **2** any covered walk, esp. with shops along
one or both sides. **3** *Archit.* a series of arches
supporting or set along a wall. □ **arcaded** *adj.*
[F f. Prov. *arcada* or It. *arcata* f. Rmc: rel. to
ARCH[1]]

Arcadian /ɑːˈkeɪdɪən/ n. & adj. —n. an idealized
peasant or country dweller, esp. in poetry. —
adj. simple and poetically rural. □ **Arcadianism**
n. [L *Arcadius* f. Gk *Arkadia* mountain district in
Peloponnese]

arcane /ɑːˈkeɪn/ *adj.* mysterious, secret; understood by few. □ **arcanely** *adv.* [F *arcane* or L
arcanus f. *arcēre* shut up f. *arca* chest]

arch[1] /ɑːtʃ/ n. & v. —n. **1 a** a curved structure as
an opening or a support for a bridge, roof, floor,
etc. **b** an arch used in building as an ornament.
2 any arch-shaped curve, e.g. as on the inner
side of the foot, the eyebrows, etc. —v. **1** tr.
provide with or form into an arch. **2** tr. span
like an arch. **3** intr. form an arch. [ME f. OF *arche*
ult. f. L *arcus* arc]

arch[2] /ɑːtʃ/ *adj.* self-consciously or affectedly
playful or teasing. □ **archly** *adv.* **archness** n.
[ARCH-, orig. in *arch rogue* etc.]

arch- /ɑːtʃ/ *comb. form* **1** chief, superior (*archbishop; archdiocese; archduke*). **2** pre-eminent of its
kind (esp. in unfavourable senses) (*arch-enemy*).
[OE *arce-* or OF *arche-*, ult. f. Gk *arkhos* chief]

Archaean /ɑːˈkiːən/ *adj.* & n. (US **Archean**)
—*adj.* of or relating to the earlier part of the
Precambrian era. —n. this time. [Gk *arkhaios*
ancient f. *arkhē* beginning]

archaeology /ˌɑːkɪˈɒlədʒɪ/ n. (US **archeology**)
the study of human history and prehistory
through the excavation of sites and the analysis
of physical remains. □ **archaeologic** /-ˈlɒdʒɪk/
adj. **archaeological** /-ˈlɒdʒɪk(ə)l/ *adj.* **archaeologist** n. **archaeologize** *v.intr.* (also **-ise**).
[mod.L *archaeologia* f. Gk *arkhaiologia* ancient
history (as ARCHAEAN, -LOGY[2])]

archaic /ɑːˈkeɪɪk/ *adj.* **1 a** antiquated. **b** (of a
word etc.) no longer in ordinary use, though
retained for special purposes. **2** primitive. **3** of

an early period of art or culture. □ **archaically** *adv.* [F *archaïque* f. Gk *arkhaïkos* (as ARCHAEAN)]

archaism /ˈɑːkeɪˌɪz(ə)m/ *n.* **1** the retention or imitation of the old or obsolete, esp. in language or art. **2** an archaic word or expression. □ **archaist** *n.* **archaistic** /-ˈɪstɪk/ *adj.* [mod.L f. Gk *arkhaïsmos* f. *arkhaïzō* (as ARCHAIZE, -ISM)]

archaize /ˈɑːkeɪˌaɪz/ *v.* (also **-ise**) **1** *intr.* imitate the archaic. **2** *tr.* make (a work of art, literature, etc.) imitate the archaic. [Gk *arkhaïzō* be old-fashioned f. *arkhaios* ancient]

archangel /ˈɑːkˌeɪndʒ(ə)l/ *n.* **1** an angel of the highest rank. **2** a member of the eighth order of the nine ranks of heavenly beings. □ **archangelic** /-ænˈdʒelɪk/ *adj.* [OE f. AF *archangele* f. eccl.L *archangelus* f. eccl.Gk *arkhaggelos* (as ARCH-, ANGEL)]

archbishop /ɑːtʃˈbɪʃəp/ *n.* the chief bishop of a province. [OE (as ARCH-, BISHOP)]

archbishopric /ɑːtʃˈbɪʃəprɪk/ *n.* the office or diocese of an archbishop. [OE (as ARCH-, BISHOPRIC)]

archdeacon /ɑːtʃˈdiːkən/ *n.* **1** an Anglican cleric ranking below a bishop. **2** a member of the clergy of similar rank in other Churches. □ **archdeaconry** *n.* (*pl.* **-ies**). **archdeaconship** *n.* [OE *arce-*, *ercediacon*, f. eccl.L *archidiaconus* f. eccl.Gk *arkhidiakonos* (as ARCH-, DEACON)]

archdiocese /ɑːtʃˈdaɪəsɪs/ *n.* the diocese of an archbishop. □ **archdiocesan** /ˌɑːtʃdaɪˈɒsɪs(ə)n/ *adj.*

archduke /ɑːtʃˈdjuːk/ *n.* (*fem.* **archduchess** /-ˈdʌtʃɪs/) *hist.* the chief duke (esp. as the title of a son of the Emperor of Austria). □ **archducal** *adj.* **archduchy** /-ˈdʌtʃɪ/ *n.* (*pl.* **-ies**). [OF *archeduc* f. med.L *archidux -ducis* (as ARCH-, DUKE)]

archer /ˈɑːtʃə(r)/ *n.* **1** a person who shoots with a bow and arrows. **2** (**the Archer**) the zodiacal sign or constellation Sagittarius. [AF f. OF *archier* ult. f. L *arcus* bow]

archery /ˈɑːtʃərɪ/ *n.* shooting with a bow and arrows, esp. as a sport. [OF *archerie* f. *archier* (as ARCHER, -ERY)]

archetype /ˈɑːkɪˌtaɪp/ *n.* **1 a** an original model; a prototype. **b** a typical specimen. **2** a recurrent symbol or motif in literature, art, etc. □ **archetypal** /-ˈtaɪp(ə)l/ *adj.* **archetypical** /-ˈtɪpɪk(ə)l/ *adj.* [L *archetypum* f. Gk *arkhetupon* (as ARCH-, *tupos* stamp)]

archidiaconal /ˌɑːkɪdaɪˈækən(ə)l/ *adj.* of or relating to an archdeacon. □ **archidiaconate** /-nət, -ˌneɪt/ *n.* [med.L *archidiaconalis* (as ARCH-, DIACONAL)]

archiepiscopal /ˌɑːkɪɪˈpɪskəp(ə)l/ *adj.* of or relating to an archbishop. □ **archiepiscopate** /-pət, -ˌpeɪt/ *n.* [eccl.L *archiepiscopus* f. Gk *arkhiepiskopos* archbishop]

archimandrite /ˌɑːkɪˈmændraɪt/ *n.* **1** the superior of a large monastery or group of monasteries in the Orthodox Church. **2** an honorary title given to a monastic priest. [F *archimandrite* or eccl.L *archimandrita* f. eccl. Gk *arkhimandrites* (as ARCH-, *mandra* monastery)]

archipelago /ˌɑːkɪˈpeləˌɡəʊ/ *n.* (*pl.* **-os** or **-oes**) **1** a group of islands. **2** a sea with many islands. [It. *arcipelago* f. Gk *arkhi-* chief + *pelagos* sea (orig. = the Aegean Sea)]

architect /ˈɑːkɪˌtekt/ *n.* **1** a designer who prepares plans for buildings, ships, etc., and supervises their construction. **2** (foll. by *of*) a person who brings about a specified thing (*the architect*

of his own fortune). [F *architecte* f. It. *architetto*, or L *architectus* f. Gk *arkhitektōn* (as ARCH-, *tektōn* builder)]

architectonic /ˌɑːkɪtekˈtɒnɪk/ *adj.* & *n.* —*adj.* **1** of or relating to architecture or architects. **2** of or relating to the systematization of knowledge. —*n.* (in *pl.*; usu. treated as *sing.*) **1** the scientific study of architecture. **2** the study of the systematization of knowledge. [L *architectonicus* f. Gk *arkhitektonikos* (as ARCHITECT)]

architecture /ˈɑːkɪˌtektʃə(r)/ *n.* **1** the art or science of designing and constructing buildings. **2** the style of a building as regards design and construction. **3** buildings or other structures collectively. □ **architectural** /-ˈtektʃər(ə)l/ *adj.* **architecturally** /-ˈtektʃərəlɪ/ *adv.* [F *architecture* or L *architectura* f. *architectus* ARCHITECT]

architrave /ˈɑːkɪˌtreɪv/ *n.* **1** (in classical architecture) a main beam resting across the tops of columns. **2** the moulded frame around a doorway or window. **3** a moulding round the exterior of an arch. [F f. It. (as ARCH-, *trave* f. L *trabs trabis* beam)]

archive /ˈɑːkaɪv/ *n.* & *v.* —*n.* (usu. in *pl.*) **1** a collection of esp. public or corporate documents or records. **2** the place where these are kept. —*v.tr.* **1** place or store in an archive. **2** *Computing* transfer (data) to a less frequently used file, e.g. from disc to tape. □ **archival** /ɑːˈkaɪv(ə)l/ *adj.* [F *archives* (pl.) f. L *archi*(*v*)*a* f. Gk *arkheia* public records f. *arkhē* government]

archivist /ˈɑːkɪvɪst/ *n.* a person who maintains and is in charge of archives.

archway /ˈɑːtʃweɪ/ *n.* **1** a vaulted passage. **2** an arched entrance.

Arctic /ˈɑːktɪk/ *adj.* & *n.* —*adj.* **1** of the north polar regions. **2** (**arctic**) *colloq.* (esp. of weather) very cold. —*n.* **1** the Arctic regions. **2** (**arctic**) *US* a thick waterproof overshoe. □ **Arctic Circle** the parallel of latitude 66° 33′ N, forming an imaginary line round this region. [ME f. OF *artique* f. L *ar(c)ticus* f. Gk *arktikos* f. *arktos* bear, Ursa Major]

arcuate /ˈɑːkjʊət/ *adj.* shaped like a bow; curved. [L *arcuatus* past part. of *arcuare* curve f. *arcus* bow, curve]

-ard /əd/ *suffix* **1** forming nouns in depreciatory senses (*drunkard*; *sluggard*). **2** forming nouns in other senses (*bollard*; *Spaniard*; *wizard*). [ME & OF f. G *-hard* hardy (in proper names)]

ardent /ˈɑːd(ə)nt/ *adj.* **1** eager, zealous; (of persons or feelings) fervent, passionate. **2** burning. □ **ardency** *n.* **ardently** *adv.* [ME f. OF *ardant* f. L *ardens -entis* f. *ardēre* burn]

ardour /ˈɑːdə(r)/ *n.* (*US* **ardor**) zeal, burning enthusiasm, passion. [ME f. OF f. L *ardor -oris* f. *ardēre* burn]

arduous /ˈɑːdjʊəs/ *adj.* **1** hard to achieve or overcome; laborious, strenuous. **2** steep, difficult (*an arduous path*). □ **arduously** *adv.* **arduousness** *n.* [L *arduus* steep, difficult]

are[1] *2nd sing. present* & *1st, 2nd, 3rd pl. present of* BE.

are[2] /ɑː(r)/ *n.* a metric unit of measure, equal to 100 square metres. [F f. L AREA]

area /ˈeərɪə/ *n.* **1** the extent or measure of a surface (*over a large area*; *the area of a triangle*). **2** a region or tract (*the southern area*). **3** a space allocated for a specific purpose (*dining area*). **4** the scope or range of an activity or study. **5** *US* a space below ground level in front of the basement of a building. □ **areal** *adj.* [L, = vacant piece of level ground]

areca /ˈærɪkə, əˈriːkə/ *n.* any tropical palm of the genus *Areca*, native to Asia. □ **areca nut** the astringent seed of a species of areca, *A. catechu*. [Port. f. Malayalam *áḍekka*]

arena /əˈriːnə/ *n.* **1** the central part of an amphitheatre etc., where contests take place. **2** a scene of conflict; a sphere of action or discussion. [L (*h*)*arena* sand, sand-strewn place of combat]

arenaceous /ˌærɪˈneɪʃəs/ *adj.* **1** (of rocks) containing sand; having a sandy texture. **2** sandlike. **3** (of plants) growing in sand. [L *arenaceus* (as ARENA, -ACEOUS)]

aren't /ɑːnt/ *contr.* **1** are not. **2** (in interrog.) am not (*aren't I coming too?*).

areola /æˈrɪələ/ *n.* (*pl.* **areolae** /-liː/) *Anat.* a circular pigmented area, esp. that surrounding a nipple. □ **areolar** *adj.* [L, dimin. of *area* AREA]

arête /æˈret/ *n.* a sharp mountain ridge. [F f. L *arista* ear of corn, fishbone, spine]

argent /ˈɑːdʒ(ə)nt/ *n. & adj. Heraldry* silver; silvery white. [F f. L *argentum*]

argentiferous /ˌɑːdʒənˈtɪfərəs/ *adj.* containing natural deposits of silver. [L *argentum* + -FEROUS]

Argentine /ˈɑːdʒəntaɪn, -ˌtiːn/ *adj. & n.* (also **Argentinian** /-ˈtɪnɪən/) —*adj.* of or relating to Argentina in S. America. —*n.* **1** a native or national of Argentina. **2** a person of Argentine descent. □ **the Argentine** Argentina. [Sp. *Argentina*: cf. F *argentin* f. *argent* silver]

argil /ˈɑːdʒɪl/ *n.* clay, esp. that used in pottery. □ **argillaceous** *adj.* [F *argille* f. L *argilla* f. Gk *argillos* f. *argos* white]

argon /ˈɑːgɒn/ *n. Chem.* an inert gaseous element, of the noble gas group. [Gk, neut. of *argos* idle f. *a-* not + *ergon* work]

argosy /ˈɑːgəsɪ/ *n.* (*pl.* **-ies**) *poet.* a large merchant ship, orig. esp. from Ragusa (now Dubrovnik) or Venice. [prob. It. *Ragusea* (*nave*) Ragusan (vessel)]

argot /ˈɑːgəʊ/ *n.* the jargon of a group or class, formerly esp. of criminals. [F: orig. unkn.]

arguable /ˈɑːgjʊəb(ə)l/ *adj.* **1** that may be argued or reasonably proposed. **2** reasonable; supported by argument. □ **arguably** *adv.*

argue /ˈɑːgjuː/ *v.* (**argues, argued, arguing**) **1** *intr.* (often foll. by *with, about,* etc.) exchange views or opinions, especially heatedly or contentiously (with a person). **2** *tr. & intr.* (often foll. by *that* + clause) indicate; maintain by reasoning. **3** *intr.* (foll. by *for, against*) reason (*argued against joining*). **4** *tr.* treat by reasoning (*argue the point*). **5** *tr.* (foll. by *into, out of*) persuade (*argued me into going*). □ **argue the toss** *colloq.* dispute a decision or choice already made. □ **arguer** *n.* [ME f. OF *arguer* f. L *argutari* prattle, frequent. of *arguere* make clear, prove, accuse]

argument /ˈɑːgjʊmənt/ *n.* **1** an exchange of views, esp. a contentious or prolonged one. **2** (often foll. by *for, against*) a reason advanced; a reasoning process (*an argument for abolition*). **3** a summary of the subject-matter or line of reasoning of a book. **4** *Math.* an independent variable determining the value of a function. [ME f. OF f. L *argumentum* f. *arguere* (as ARGUE, -MENT)]

argumentation /ˌɑːgjʊmenˈteɪʃ(ə)n/ *n.* **1** methodical reasoning. **2** debate or argument. [F f. L *argumentatio* f. *argumentari* (as ARGUMENT, -ATION)]

argumentative /ˌɑːgjʊˈmentətɪv/ *adj.* **1** fond of arguing; quarrelsome. **2** using methodical reasoning. □ **argumentatively** *adv.* **argumentativeness** *n.* [F *argumentatif* -*ive* or LL *argumentativus* (as ARGUMENT, -ATIVE)]

Argus /ˈɑːgəs/ *n.* a watchful guardian. □ **Argus-eyed** vigilant. [ME f. L f. Gk *Argos* mythical person with a hundred eyes]

argy-bargy /ˌɑːdʒɪˈbɑːdʒɪ/ *n. & v. joc.* —*n.* (*pl.* **-ies**) a dispute or wrangle. —*v.intr.* (**-ies, -ied**) quarrel, esp. loudly. [orig. Sc.]

aria /ˈɑːrɪə/ *n. Mus.* a long accompanied song for solo voice in an opera, oratorio, etc. [It.]

-arian /ˈeərɪən/ *suffix* forming adjectives and nouns meaning '(one) concerned with or believing in' (*agrarian; antiquarian; humanitarian; vegetarian*). [L *-arius* (see -ARY¹)]

arid /ˈærɪd/ *adj.* **1 a** (of ground, climate, etc.) dry, parched. **b** too dry to support vegetation; barren. **2** uninteresting. □ **aridity** /əˈrɪdɪtɪ/ *n.* **aridly** *adv.* **aridness** *n.* [F *aride* or L *aridus* f. *arēre* be dry]

Aries /ˈeəriːz/ *n.* (*pl.* same) **1** a constellation, traditionally regarded as contained in the figure of a ram. **2 a** the first sign of the zodiac (the Ram). **b** a person born when the sun is in this sign. □ **Arian** /-rɪən/ *adj. & n.* [ME f. L = ram]

aright /əˈraɪt/ *adv.* rightly. [OE (as A², RIGHT)]

-arious /ˈeərɪəs/ *suffix* forming adjectives (*gregarious; vicarious*). [L *-arius* (see -ARY¹) + -OUS]

arise /əˈraɪz/ *v.intr.* (*past* **arose** /əˈrəʊz/; *past part.* **arisen** /əˈrɪz(ə)n/) **1** begin to exist; originate. **2** (usu. foll. by *from, out of*) result (*accidents can arise from carelessness*). **3** come to one's notice; emerge (*the question of payment arose*). **4** rise, esp. from the dead. [OE *ārīsan* (as A-², RISE)]

aristocracy /ˌærɪˈstɒkrəsɪ/ *n.* (*pl.* **-ies**) **1 a** the highest class in society; the nobility. **b** the nobility as a ruling class. **2 a** a government by the nobility or a privileged group. **b** a State governed in this way. **3** (often foll. by *of*) the best representatives or upper echelons (*aristocracy of intellect; aristocracy of labour*). [F *aristocratie* f. Gk *aristokratia* f. *aristos* best + *kratia* (as -CRACY)]

aristocrat /ˈærɪstəˌkræt/ *n.* a member of the nobility. [F *aristocrate* (as ARISTOCRATIC)]

aristocratic /ˌærɪstəˈkrætɪk/ *adj.* **1** of or relating to the aristocracy. **2 a** distinguished in manners or bearing. **b** grand; stylish. □ **aristocratically** *adv.* [F *aristocratique* f. Gk *aristokratikos* (as ARISTOCRACY)]

Aristotelian /ˌærɪstəˈtiːlɪən/ *n. & adj.* —*n.* a disciple or student of the Greek philosopher Aristotle (d. 322 BC). —*adj.* of or concerning Aristotle or his ideas.

arithmetic *n. & adj.* —*n.* /əˈrɪθmətɪk/ **1 a** the science of numbers. **b** one's knowledge of this (*have improved my arithmetic*). **2** the use of numbers; computation (*a problem involving arithmetic*). —*adj.* /ˌærɪθˈmetɪk/ (also **arithmetical** /-ˈmetɪk(ə)l/) of or concerning arithmetic. □ **arithmetic mean** the central number in an arithmetic progression. **arithmetic progression 1** an increase or decrease by a constant quantity (e.g. 1, 2, 3, 4, etc., 9, 7, 5, 3, etc.). **2 a** sequence of numbers showing this. □ **arithmetician** /əˌrɪθməˈtɪʃ(ə)n/ *n.* [ME f. OF *arismetique*

f. L *arithmetica* f. Gk *arithmētikē* (*tekhnē*) art of counting f. *arithmos* number]

-arium /ˈeərɪəm/ *suffix* forming nouns usu. denoting a place (*aquarium*; *planetarium*). [L, neut. of adjs. in -*arius*: see -ARY¹]

ark *n.* **1** = NOAH'S ARK 1. **2** *archaic* a chest or box. □ **Ark of the Covenant** (or **Testimony**) a chest or cupboard containing the scrolls or tables of Jewish Law. [OE *ærc* f. L *arca* chest]

arm¹ *n.* **1** each of the two upper limbs of the human body from the shoulder to the hand. **2 a** the forelimb of an animal. **b** the flexible limb of an invertebrate animal (e.g. an octopus). **3 a** the sleeve of a garment. **b** the side part of a chair etc., used to support a sitter's arm. **c** a thing resembling an arm in branching from a main stem (*an arm of the sea*). **4** a control; a means of reaching (*arm of the law*). □ **arm in arm** (of two or more persons) with arms linked. **arm-wrestling** a trial of strength in which each party tries to force the other's arm down on to a table on which their elbows rest. **at arm's length 1** as far as an arm can reach. **2** far enough to avoid undue familiarity. **in arms** (of a baby) too young to walk. **on one's arm** supported by one's arm. **under one's arm** between the arm and the body. □ **armful** *n.* (*pl.* **-fuls**). **armless** *adj.* [OE f. Gmc]

arm² *n.* & *v.* —*n.* **1** (usu. in *pl.*) **a** a weapon. **b** = FIREARM. **2** (in *pl.*) the military profession. **3** a branch of the military (e.g. infantry, cavalry, artillery, etc.). **4** (in *pl.*) heraldic devices (*coat of arms*). —*v.tr.* & *refl.* **1** (also *absol.*) supply with weapons. **2** supply with tools or other requisites or advantages (*armed with the truth*). **3** make (a bomb etc.) able to explode. □ **in arms** armed. **lay down one's arms** cease fighting. **take up arms** begin fighting. **under arms** ready for war or battle. **up in arms** (usu. foll. by *against*, *about*) actively rebelling. □ **armless** *adj.* [ME f. OF *armes* (pl.), *armer*, f. L *arma* arms, fittings]

armada /ɑːˈmɑːdə/ *n.* a fleet of warships, esp. that sent by Spain against England in 1588. [Sp. f. Rmc *armata* army]

armadillo /ˌɑːməˈdɪləʊ/ *n.* (*pl.* **-os**) any nocturnal insect-eating mammal of the family Dasypodidae, with a body covered in bony plates. [Sp. dimin. of *armado* armed man f. L *armatus* past part. of *armare* ARM²]

Armageddon /ˌɑːməˈged(ə)n/ *n.* **1 a** (in the New Testament) the last battle between good and evil before the Day of Judgement. **b** the place where this will be fought. **2** a bloody battle or struggle on a huge scale. [Gk f. Heb. *har megiddōn* hill of Megiddo: see Rev. 16:16]

armament /ˈɑːməmənt/ *n.* **1** (often in *pl.*) military weapons and equipment, esp. guns on a warship. **2** the process of equipping for war. **3** a force equipped for war. [L *armamentum* (as ARM², -MENT)]

armature /ˈɑːməˌtjʊə(r)/ *n.* **1 a** the rotating coil or coils of a dynamo or electric motor. **b** any moving part of an electrical machine in which a voltage is induced by a magnetic field. **2** a piece of soft iron placed in contact with the poles of a horseshoe magnet to preserve its power. **3** *Biol.* the protective covering of an animal or plant. **4** a metal framework on which a sculpture is moulded. [F f. L *armatura* armour (as ARM², -URE)]

armband /ˈɑːmbænd/ *n.* a band worn around the upper arm to hold up a shirtsleeve or as a form of identification etc.

armchair /ɑːmˈtʃeə(r), ˈɑːm-/ *n.* **1** a comfortable, usu. upholstered, chair with side supports for the arms. **2** (*attrib.*) theoretical rather than active or practical (*an armchair critic*).

armhole /ˈɑːmhəʊl/ *n.* each of two holes in a garment through which the arms are put, usu. into a sleeve.

armillary /ɑːˈmɪlərɪ/ *adj.* relating to bracelets. □ **armillary sphere** *hist.* a representation of the celestial globe constructed from metal rings and showing the equator, the tropics, etc. [mod.L *armillaris* f. L *armilla* bracelet]

armistice /ˈɑːmɪstɪs/ *n.* a stopping of hostilities by common agreement of the opposing sides; a truce. □ **Armistice Day** the anniversary of the armistice of 11 Nov. 1918. [F *armistice* or mod.L *armistitium*, f. *arma* arms (ARM²) + -*stitium* stoppage]

armlet /ˈɑːmlɪt/ *n.* **1** a band worn round the arm. **2** a small inlet of the sea, or branch of a river.

armory /ˈɑːmərɪ/ *n.* (*pl.* **-ies**) heraldry. □ **armorial** /ɑːˈmɔːrɪəl/ *adj.* [OF *armoierie*: see ARMOURY]

armour /ˈɑːmə(r)/ *n.* & *v.* (US **armor**) —*n.* **1** a defensive covering, usu. of metal, formerly worn to protect the body in fighting. **2 a** (in full **armour-plate**) a protective metal covering for an armed vehicle, ship, etc. **b** armoured fighting vehicles collectively. **3** a protective covering or shell on certain animals and plants. **4** heraldic devices. —*v.tr.* (usu. as **armoured** *adj.*) provide with a protective covering, and often with guns (*armoured car*). [ME f. OF *armure* f. L *armatura*: see ARMATURE]

armourer /ˈɑːmərə(r)/ *n.* (US **armorer**) **1** a maker or repairer of arms or armour. **2** an official in charge of a ship's or a regiment's arms. [AF *armurer*, OF -*urier* (as ARMOUR, -ER⁵)]

armoury /ˈɑːmərɪ/ *n.* (US **armory**) (*pl.* **-ies**) **1** a place where arms are kept; an arsenal. **2** an array of weapons, defensive resources, usable material, etc. **3** US a place where arms are manufactured. [ME f. OF *armoirie*, *armoierie* f. *armoier* to blazon f. *arme* ARM²: assim. to ARMOUR]

armpit /ˈɑːmpɪt/ *n.* the hollow under the arm at the shoulder.

armrest /ˈɑːmrest/ *n.* = ARM¹ 3b.

army /ˈɑːmɪ/ *n.* (*pl.* **-ies**) **1** an organized force armed for fighting on land. **2** (prec. by *the*) the military profession. **3** (often foll. by *of*) a very large number (*an army of helpers*). **4** an organized body regarded as fighting for a particular cause (*Salvation Army*). □ **Army List** *Brit.* an official list of commissioned officers. [ME f. OF *armee* f. Rmc *armata* fem. past part. of *armare* arm]

arnica /ˈɑːnɪkə/ *n.* **1** any composite plant of the genus *Arnica*, having yellow daisy-like flower heads, e.g. mountain tobacco. **2** a medicine prepared from this, used for bruises etc. [mod.L: orig. unkn.]

aroma /əˈrəʊmə/ *n.* **1** a fragrance; a distinctive and pleasing smell, often of food. **2** a subtle pervasive quality. [L f. Gk *arōma* -*atos* spice]

aromatherapy /əˌrəʊməˈθerəpɪ/ *n.* the use of plant extracts and essential oils in massage. □ **aromatherapeutic** /-ˈpjuːtɪk/ *adj.* **aromatherapist** *n.*

aromatic /ˌærəˈmætɪk/ *adj.* & *n.* —*adj.* **1** fragrant, spicy; (of a smell) pleasantly pungent. **2** *Chem.* of organic compounds having an unsaturated ring, esp. containing a benzene ring. —*n.* an aromatic substance. □ **aromatically** *adv.* **aromaticity** /ˌærəməˈtɪsɪtɪ/ *n.* [ME f. OF *aromatique* f. LL *aromaticus* f. Gk *arōmatikos* (as AROMA, -IC)]

arose *past of* ARISE.

around /əˈraʊnd/ *adv.* & *prep.* —*adv.* **1** on every side; all round; round about. **2** in various places; here and there; at random (*fool around*; *shop around*). **3** *colloq.* **a** in existence; available (*has been around for weeks*). **b** near at hand (*it's good to have you around*). —*prep.* **1** on or along the circuit of. **2** on every side of; enveloping. **3** here and there in or near (*chairs around the room*). **4** *US* (and increasingly *Brit.*) **a** round (*the church around the corner*). **b** approximately at; at a time near to (*come around four o'clock*; *happened around June*). [A² + ROUND]

arouse /əˈraʊz/ *v.tr.* **1** induce; call into existence (esp. a feeling, emotion, etc.). **2** awake from sleep. **3** stir into activity. **4** stimulate sexually. □ **arousable** *adj.* **arousal** *n.* **arouser** *n.* [A-² + ROUSE]

arpeggio /ɑːˈpedʒɪəʊ/ *n.* (*pl.* -os) *Mus.* the notes of a chord played in succession. [It. f. *arpeggiare* play the harp f. *arpa* harp]

arrack /ˈærək/ *n.* (also **arak** /əˈræk/) an alcoholic spirit, esp. distilled from coco sap or rice. [Arab. ʻaraḵ sweat, alcoholic spirit from grapes or dates]

arraign /əˈreɪn/ *v.tr.* **1** indict before a tribunal; accuse. **2** find fault with; call into question (an action or statement). □ **arraignment** *n.* [ME f. AF *arainer* f. OF *araisnier* (ult. as AD-, L *ratio -onis* reason, discourse)]

arrange /əˈreɪndʒ/ *v.* **1** *tr.* put into the required order; classify. **2** *tr.* plan or provide for; cause to occur (*arranged a meeting*). **3** *tr.* settle beforehand the order or manner of. **4** *intr.* take measures; form plans; give instructions (*arrange to be there at eight*; *arranged for a taxi to come*). **5** *intr.* come to an agreement (*arranged with her to meet later*). **6** *tr.* *Mus.* adapt (a composition) for performance with instruments or voices other than those originally specified. □ **arrangeable** *adj.* **arranger** *n.* (esp. in sense 6). [ME f. OF *arangier* f. *à* to + *rangier* RANGE]

arrangement /əˈreɪndʒmənt/ *n.* **1** the act or process of arranging or being arranged. **2** the condition of being arranged; the manner in which a thing is arranged. **3** something arranged. **4** (in *pl.*) plans, measures (*make your own arrangements*). **5** *Mus.* a composition arranged for performance by different instruments or voices. [F (as ARRANGE, -MENT)]

arrant /ˈærənt/ *adj.* downright, utter, notorious (*arrant liar*; *arrant nonsense*). □ **arrantly** *adv.* [ME, var. of ERRANT, orig. in phrases like *arrant* (= outlawed, roving) *thief*]

arras /ˈærəs/ *n.* *hist.* a rich tapestry, often hung on the wall. [*Arras*, a town in NE France famous for the fabric]

array /əˈreɪ/ *n.* & *v.* —*n.* **1** an imposing or well-ordered series or display. **2** an ordered arrangement, esp. of troops (*battle array*). **3** *poet.* an outfit or dress (*in fine array*). **4 a** *Math.* an arrangement of quantities or symbols in rows and columns; a matrix. **b** *Computing* an ordered set of related elements. —*v.tr.* **1** deck, adorn. **2** set in order; marshal (forces). [ME f. AF *araier*, OF *areer* ult. f. a Gmc root, = prepare]

arrears /əˈrɪəz/ *n.pl.* an amount still outstanding or uncompleted. □ **in arrears** (or **arrear**) behindhand, esp. in payment. □ **arrearage** *n.* [ME (orig. as adv.) f. OF *arere* f. med.L *adretro* (as AD-, *retro* backwards): first used in phr. *in arrear*]

arrest /əˈrest/ *v.* & *n.* —*v.tr.* **1 a** seize (a person) and take into custody, esp. by legal authority. **b** seize (a ship) by legal authority. **2** stop or check (esp. a process or moving thing). **3 a** attract (a person's attention). **b** attract the attention of (a person). —*n.* **1** the act of arresting or being arrested, esp. the legal seizure of a person. **2** a stoppage or check (*cardiac arrest*). □ **arrestingly** *adv.* [ME f. OF *arester* ult. f. L *restare* remain, stop]

arrestable /əˈrestəb(ə)l/ *adj.* **1** susceptible of arrest. **2** *Law* (esp. of an offence) such that the offender may be arrested without a warrant.

arrester /əˈrestə(r)/ *n.* (also **arrestor**) a device for slowing an aircraft after landing.

arrival /əˈraɪv(ə)l/ *n.* **1 a** the act of arriving. **b** an appearance on the scene. **2** a person or thing that has arrived. □ **new arrival** *colloq.* a new-born child. [ME f. AF *arrivaille* (as ARRIVE, -AL)]

arrive /əˈraɪv/ *v.intr.* (often foll. by *at*, *in*) **1** reach a destination; come to the end of a journey or a specified part of a journey (*arrived in Tibet*; *arrived late*). **2** (foll. by *at*) reach (a conclusion, decision, etc.). **3** *colloq.* establish one's reputation or position. **4** *colloq.* (of a child) be born. **5** (of a thing) be brought (*the flowers have arrived*). **6** (of a time) come (*her birthday arrived at last*). [ME f. OF *ariver*, ult. as AD- + L *ripa* shore]

arriviste /ˌæriːˈviːst/ *n.* an ambitious or ruthlessly self-seeking person. [F f. *arriver* f. OF (as ARRIVE, -IST)]

arrogant /ˈærəgənt/ *adj.* (of a person, attitude, etc.) aggressively assertive or presumptuous; over-bearing. □ **arrogance** *n.* **arrogantly** *adv.* [ME f. OF (as ARROGATE, -ANT)]

arrogate /ˈærəˌgeɪt/ *v.tr.* **1** (often foll. by *to* oneself) claim (power, responsibility, etc.) without justification. **2** (often foll. by *to*) attribute unjustly (to a person). □ **arrogation** /-ˈgeɪʃ(ə)n/ *n.* [L *arrogare arrogat-* (as AD-, *rogare* ask)]

arrow /ˈærəʊ/ *n.* **1** a sharp pointed wooden or metal stick shot from a bow as a weapon. **2** a drawn or printed etc. representation of an arrow indicating a direction; a pointer. □ **arrowy** *adj.* [OE *ar(e)we* f. ON *ör* f. Gmc]

arrowhead /ˈærəʊˌhed/ *n.* **1** the pointed end of an arrow. **2** a decorative device resembling an arrowhead.

arrowroot /ˈærəʊˌruːt/ *n.* a plant of the family Marantaceae from which a starch is prepared and used for nutritional and medicinal purposes.

arse /ɑːs/ *n.* & *v.* (*US* **ass** /æs/) *coarse sl.* —*n.* the buttocks. —*v.intr.* (usu. foll. by *about*, *around*) play the fool. □ **arse-hole 1** the anus. **2** *offens.* a term of contempt for a person. **arse-licking** obsequiousness for the purpose of gaining favour; toadying. [OE *ærs*]

arsenal /ˈɑːsən(ə)l/ *n.* **1** a store of weapons. **2** a government establishment for the storage and manufacture of weapons and ammunition. **3** resources of anything compared with weapons (e.g. abuse), regarded collectively. [obs. F *arsenal*

or It. *arzanale* f. Arab. *dāršinā'a* f. *dār* house +
sinā'a art, industry f. *ṣana'a* fabricate]

arsenic *n. & adj.* —*n.* /ˈɑːsənɪk/ **1** a non-scientific
name for arsenic trioxide, a highly poisonous
white powdery substance used in weed-killers,
rat poison, etc. **2** *Chem.* a brittle semi-metallic
element, used in semiconductors and alloys.
—*adj.* /ɑːˈsenɪk/ **1** of or concerning arsenic. **2**
Chem. containing arsenic with a valency of five. □
arsenious /ɑːˈsiːnɪəs/ *adj.* [ME f. OF f. L *arsenicum*
f. Gk *arsenikon* yellow orpiment, identified with
arsenikos male, but in fact f. Arab. *al-zarnīk* f. *al*
the + *zarnīk* orpiment f. Pers. f. *zar* gold]

arsenical /ɑːˈsenɪk(ə)l/ *adj. & n.* —*adj.* of or
containing arsenic. —*n.* a drug containing
arsenic.

arson /ˈɑːs(ə)n/ *n.* the act of maliciously setting
fire to property. □ **arsonist** *n.* [legal AF, OF, f.
med.L *arsio -onis* f. L *ardēre arx-* burn]

art *n.* **1 a** human creative skill or its application.
b work exhibiting this. **2 a** (in *pl.*; prec. by *the*)
the various branches of creative activity e.g.
painting, music, writing, considered collectively.
b any one of these branches. **3** creative activity,
esp. painting and drawing, resulting in visual
representation (*interested in music but not art*). **4**
human skill or workmanship as opposed to the
work of nature. **5** (often foll. by *of*) a skill,
aptitude, or knack (*the art of writing clearly*). **6** (in
pl.; usu. prec. by *the*) those branches of learning
(esp. languages, literature, and history) associated with creative skill as opposed to scientific,
technical, or vocational skills. □ **arts and crafts**
decorative design and handicraft. [ME f. OF f. L
ars artis]

artefact /ˈɑːtɪˌfækt/ *n.* (also **artifact**) **1** a product
of human art and workmanship. **2** *Archaeol.* a
product of prehistoric workmanship as distinguished from a similar object naturally produced. □ **artefactual** *adj.* (in senses 1 and 2). [L
arte (ablat. of *ars* art) + *factum* (neut. past part.
of *facere* make)]

arterial /ɑːˈtɪərɪəl/ *adj.* **1** of or relating to an
artery (*arterial blood*). **2** (esp. of a road) main,
important, esp. linking large cities or towns. [F
artériel f. *artère* artery]

arteriosclerosis /ɑːˌtɪərɪəʊsklɪəˈrəʊsɪs/ *n.* the
loss of elasticity and thickening of the walls of
the arteries, esp. in old age; hardening of the
arteries. □ **arteriosclerotic** /-ˈrɒtɪk/ *adj.* [ARTERY
+ SCLEROSIS]

artery /ˈɑːtərɪ/ *n.* (*pl.* **-ies**) **1** any of the muscular-
walled tubes forming part of the blood cir-
culation system of the body, carrying
oxygen-enriched blood from the heart. **2** a main
road or railway line. □ **arteritis** /-ˈraɪtɪs/ *n.* [ME
f. L *arteria* f. Gk *artēria* prob. f. *airō* raise]

artesian well /ɑːˈtiːzɪən, -ʒ(ə)n/ *n.* a well bored
perpendicularly, so that natural pressure produces a constant supply of water. [F. *artésien* f.
Artois, an old French province]

artful /ˈɑːtfʊl/ *adj.* (of a person or action) crafty,
deceitful. □ **artfully** *adv.* **artfulness** *n.*

arthritis /ɑːˈθraɪtɪs/ *n.* inflammation of a joint
or joints. □ **arthritic** /-ˈθrɪtɪk/ *adj. & n.* [L f. Gk
f. *arthron* joint]

arthropod /ˈɑːθrəˌpɒd/ *n.* *Zool.* any invertebrate
animal of the phylum Arthropoda, with a
segmented body, jointed limbs, and an external
skeleton, e.g. an insect, spider, or crustacean.
[Gk *arthron* joint + *pous podos* foot]

Arthurian /ɑːˈθjʊərɪən/ *adj.* relating to or associated with King Arthur, the legendary British
ruler, or his court.

artichoke /ˈɑːtɪˌtʃəʊk/ *n.* **1** a European plant,
Cynara scolymus, allied to the thistle. **2** (in
full **globe artichoke**) the flower-head of the
artichoke, the bracts of which have edible bases
(see also JERUSALEM ARTICHOKE). [It. *articiocco* f.
Arab. *al-karšūfa*]

article /ˈɑːtɪk(ə)l/ *n. & v.* —*n.* **1** (often in *pl.*) an
item or commodity, usu. not further dis-
tinguished (*a collection of odd articles*). **2** a non-
fictional essay, esp. one included with others in
a newspaper, magazine, journal, etc. **3 a** a
particular part (*an article of faith*). **b** a separate
clause or portion of any document (*articles of
apprenticeship*). **4** *Gram.* the definite or indefinite
article. —*v.tr.* bind by articles of apprenticeship.
□ **definite article** *Gram.* the word (*the* in
English) preceding a noun and implying a
specific or known instance (as in *the book on the
table*; *the art of government*; *the famous public school
in Berkshire*). **indefinite article** *Gram.* the word
(e.g. *a*, *an*, *some* in English) preceding a noun
and implying lack of specificity (as in *bought me
a book*; *government is an art*). [ME f. OF f. L *articulus*
dimin. of *artus* joint]

articular /ɑːˈtɪkjʊlə(r)/ *adj.* of or relating to the
joints. [ME f. L *articularis* (as ARTICLE, -AR¹)]

articulate *adj. & v.* —*adj.* /ɑːˈtɪkjʊlət/ **1** able to
speak fluently and coherently. **2** (of sound or
speech) having clearly distinguishable parts. **3**
having joints. —*v.* /ɑːˈtɪkjʊˌleɪt/ **1** *tr.* **a** pronounce
(words, syllables, etc.) clearly and distinctly. **b**
express (an idea etc.) coherently. **2** *intr.* speak
distinctly (*was quite unable to articulate*). **3** *tr.* (usu.
in *passive*) connect by joints. **4** *intr.* (often foll. by
with) form a joint. □ **articulated lorry** *Brit.*
a lorry consisting of two or more sections
connected by a flexible joint. □ **articulacy** *n.*
articulately *adv.* **articulateness** *n.* **artic-
ulator** *n.* [L *articulatus* (as ARTICLE, -ATE²)]

articulation /ɑːˌtɪkjʊˈleɪʃ(ə)n/ *n.* **1 a** the act of
speaking. **b** articulate utterance; speech. **2 a** the
act or a mode of jointing. **b** a joint. [F *articulation*
or L *articulatio* f. *articulare* joint (as ARTICLE,
-ATION)]

artifice /ˈɑːtɪfɪs/ *n.* **1** a clever device; a contrivance. **2 a** cunning. **b** an instance of this. **3** skill,
dexterity. [F f. L *artificium* f. *ars artis* art, *-ficium*
making f. *facere* make]

artificer /ɑːˈtɪfɪsə(r)/ *n.* **1** an inventor. **2** a
craftsman. **3** a skilled mechanic in the armed
forces. [ME f. AF, prob. alt. of OF *artificien*]

artificial /ˌɑːtɪˈfɪʃ(ə)l/ *adj.* **1** produced by human
art or effort rather than originating naturally
(*an artificial lake*). **2** formed in imitation of
something natural (*artificial flowers*). **3** affected,
insincere (*an artificial smile*). □ **artificial insemination** the injection of semen into the vagina
or uterus other than by sexual intercourse.
artificial intelligence the application of computers to areas normally regarded as requiring
human intelligence. **artificial respiration** the
restoration or initiation of breathing by manual
or mechanical or mouth-to-mouth methods. □
artificiality /-ʃɪˈælɪtɪ/ *n.* **artificially** *adv.* [ME f.
OF *artificiel* or L *artificialis* (as ARTIFICE, -AL)]

artillery /ɑːˈtɪlərɪ/ *n.* (*pl.* **-ies**) **1** large-calibre
guns used in warfare on land. **2** a branch of the
armed forces that uses these. □ **artillerist** *n.*

[ME f. OF *artillerie* f. *artiller* alt. of *atillier, atirier* equip, arm]

artilleryman /ɑːˈtɪlərɪˌmæn/ *n.* (*pl.* **-men**) a member of the artillery.

artisan /ˌɑːtɪˈzæn, ˈɑː-/ *n.* **1** a skilled (esp. manual) worker. **2** a mechanic. [F f. It. *artigiano*, ult. f. L *artitus* past part. of *artire* instruct in the arts]

artist /ˈɑːtɪst/ *n.* **1** a painter. **2** a person who practises any of the arts. **3** an artiste. **4** a person who works with the dedication and attributes associated with an artist (*an artist in crime*). □ **artistry** *n.* [F *artiste* f. It. *artista* (as ART, -IST)]

artiste /ɑːˈtiːst/ *n.* a professional performer, esp. a singer or dancer. [F: see ARTIST]

artistic /ɑːˈtɪstɪk/ *adj.* **1** having natural skill in art. **2** made or done with art. **3** of art or artists. □ **artistically** *adv.*

artless /ˈɑːtlɪs/ *adj.* **1** guileless, ingenuous. **2** not resulting from or displaying art. **3** clumsy. □ **artlessly** *adv.*

artwork /ˈɑːtwɜːk/ *n.* the illustrations in a printed work.

arty /ˈɑːtɪ/ *adj.* (**artier, artiest**) *colloq.* pretentiously or affectedly artistic. □ **artiness** *n.*

arum /ˈeərəm/ *n.* any plant of the genus *Arum*, e.g. lords and ladies. □ **arum lily** a tall lily-like plant, *Zantedeschia aethiopica*, with white spathe and spadix. [L f. Gk *aron*]

arvo /ˈɑːvəʊ/ *n.* Austral. *sl.* afternoon. [abbr.]

-ary[1] /ərɪ/ *suffix* **1** forming adjectives (*budgetary; contrary; primary; unitary*). **2** forming nouns (*dictionary; fritillary; granary; January*). [F *-aire* or L *-arius* 'connected with']

-ary[2] /ərɪ/ *suffix* forming adjectives (*military*). [F *-aire* or f. L *-aris* 'belonging to']

Aryan /ˈeərɪən/ *n. & adj.* —*n.* **1** a member of the peoples speaking any of the languages of the Indo-European family. **2** the parent language of this family. **3** *improperly* (in Nazi ideology) a Caucasian not of Jewish descent. —*adj.* of or relating to Aryan or the Aryans. [Skr. *āryas* noble]

As *symb. Chem.* the element arsenic.

as /æz, unstressed əz/ *adv., conj., & pron.* —*adv. & conj.* (*adv.* as antecedent in main sentence; *conj.* in relative clause expressed or implied) ... to the extent to which ... is or does etc. (*I am as tall as he; am as tall as he is;* (*colloq.*) *am as tall as him; as many as six; it is not as easy as you think*). —*conj.* (with relative clause expressed or implied) **1** (with antecedent *so*) expressing result or purpose (*came early so as to meet us; so good as to exceed all hopes*). **2** (with antecedent adverb omitted) having concessive force (*good as it is =* although it is good; *try as he might =* although he might try). **3** (without antecedent adverb) **a** in the manner in which (*do as you like; was regarded as a mistake*). **b** in the capacity or form of (*I speak as your friend; as a matter of fact*). **c** during or at the time that (*came up as I was speaking; fell just as I reached the door*). **d** for the reason that; seeing that (*as you are here, we can talk*). **e** for instance (*cathedral cities, as York*). —*rel.pron.* (with verb of relative clause expressed or implied) **1** that, who, which (*I had the same trouble as you; he is a writer, as is his wife; such money as you have; such countries as France*). **2** (with sentence as antecedent) a fact that (*he lost, as you know*). □ **as for** with regard to (*as for you, I think you are wrong*). **as from** on and after (a specified date). **as if** (or **though**) as would be

the case if (*acts as if he were in charge; looks as though we've won*). **as it is** (or **as is**) in the existing circumstances or state. **as it were** in a way; to a certain extent (*he is, as it were, infatuated*). **as of 1** = *as from.* **2** as at (a specified time). **as though** see *as if.* **as to** with respect to; concerning (*said nothing as to money; as to you, I think you are wrong*). **as was** in the previously existing circumstances or state. **as yet** until now or a particular time in the past (usu. with neg. and with implied reserve about the future: *have received no news as yet*). [reduced form of OE *alswá* ALSO]

asafoetida /ˌæsəˈfiːtɪdə, -ˈfetɪdə/ *n.* (US **asafetida**) a resinous plant gum with a fetid ammoniac smell. [ME f. med.L f. *asa* f. Pers. *azā* mastic + *fetida* (as FETID)]

a.s.a.p. *abbr.* as soon as possible.

asbestos /æzˈbestɒs, æs-/ *n.* **1** a fibrous silicate mineral that is incombustible. **2** this used as a heat-resistant or insulating material. □ **asbestine** /-tɪn/ *adj.* [ME f. OF *albeston*, ult. f. Gk *asbestos* unquenchable f. *a-* not + *sbestos* f. *sbennumi* quench]

asbestosis /ˌæzbeˈstəʊsɪs, ˌæs-/ *n.* a lung disease resulting from the inhalation of asbestos particles.

ascend /əˈsend/ *v.* **1** *intr.* move upwards; rise. **2** *intr.* **a** slope upwards. **b** lie along an ascending slope. **3** *tr.* climb; go up. **4** *intr.* rise in rank or status. **5** *tr.* mount upon. **6** *intr.* (of sound) rise in pitch. □ **ascend the throne** become king or queen. [ME f. L *ascendere* (as AD-, *scandere* climb)]

ascendancy /əˈsendənsɪ/ *n.* (also **ascendency**) (often foll. by *over*) a superior or dominant condition or position.

ascendant /əˈsendənt/ *adj. & n.* —*adj.* **1** rising. **2** *Astron.* rising towards the zenith. **3** *Astrol.* just above the eastern horizon. **4** predominant. —*n. Astrol.* the point of the sun's apparent path that is ascendant at a given time (*Aries in the ascendant*). □ **in the ascendant 1** supreme or dominating. **2** gaining power or authority. [ME f. OF f. L (as ASCEND, -ANT)]

ascension /əˈsenʃ(ə)n/ *n.* **1** the act or an instance of ascending. **2** (**Ascension**) the ascent of Christ into heaven on the fortieth day after the Resurrection. □ **Ascension Day** the Thursday on which this is celebrated annually. □ **ascensional** *adj.* [ME f. OF f. L *ascensio -onis* (as ASCEND, -ION)]

ascent /əˈsent/ *n.* **1** the act or an instance of ascending. **2 a** an upward movement or rise. **b** advancement or progress (*the ascent of man*). **3** an upward slope. [ASCEND, after *descent*]

ascertain /ˌæsəˈteɪn/ *v.tr.* **1** find out as a definite fact. **2** get to know. □ **ascertainable** *adj.* **ascertainment** *n.* [ME f. OF *acertener*, stem *acertain-* f. *à* to + CERTAIN]

ascetic /əˈsetɪk/ *n. & adj.* —*n.* a person who practises severe self-discipline and abstains from all forms of pleasure, esp. for religious or spiritual reasons. —*adj.* relating to or characteristic of ascetics or asceticism; abstaining from pleasure. □ **ascetically** *adv.* **asceticism** /-tɪˌsɪz(ə)m/ *n.* [med.L *asceticus* or Gk *askētikos* f. *askētēs* monk f. *askeō* exercise]

ASCII /ˈæskɪ/ *abbr. Computing* American Standard Code for Information Interchange.

ascorbic acid /ə'skɔːbɪk/ n. a vitamin found in citrus fruits and green vegetables, a deficiency of which results in scurvy.

ascribe /ə'skraɪb/ v.tr. (usu. foll. by to) **1** attribute or impute (ascribes his well-being to a sound constitution). **2** regard as belonging. □ **ascribable** adj. **ascription** n. [ME f. L ascribere (as AD-, scribere script- write)]

asdic /'æzdɪk/ n. an early form of echo-sounder. [initials of Allied Submarine Detection Investigation Committee]

asepsis /eɪ'sepsɪs, ə-/ n. **1** the absence of harmful bacteria, viruses, or other micro-organisms. **2** a method of achieving asepsis in surgery.

aseptic /eɪ'septɪk/ adj. **1** free from contamination caused by harmful bacteria, viruses, or other micro-organisms. **2** (of a wound, instrument, or dressing) surgically sterile or sterilized. **3** (of a surgical method etc.) aiming at the elimination of harmful micro-organisms, rather than counteraction.

asexual /eɪ'seksjʊəl, æ-/ adj. Biol. **1** without sex or sexual organs. **2** (of reproduction) not involving the fusion of gametes. **3** without sexuality. □ **asexuality** /-'ælɪtɪ/ n. **asexually** adv.

ash[1] n. **1** (often in pl.) the powdery residue left after the burning of any substance. **2** (pl.) the remains of the human body after cremation or disintegration. **3** (**the Ashes**) Cricket a trophy competed for regularly by Australia and England. **4** ashlike material thrown out by a volcano. □ **ash blonde 1** a very pale blonde colour. **2** a person with hair of this colour. **Ash Wednesday** the first day of Lent. [OE æsce]

ash[2] n. **1** any forest-tree of the genus Fraxinus, with silver-grey bark, compound leaves, and hard, tough, pale wood. **2** its wood. [OE æsc f. Gmc]

ashamed /ə'ʃeɪmd/ adj. (usu. predic.) **1** (often foll. by of (= with regard to), for (= on account of), or to + infin.) embarrassed or disconcerted by shame (ashamed of his aunt; ashamed of having lied; ashamed to be seen with him). **2** (foll. by to + infin.) hesitant, reluctant (am ashamed to admit that I was wrong). □ **ashamedly** /-mɪdlɪ/ adv. [OE āscamod past part. of āscamian feel shame (as A-[2], SHAME)]

ashbin /'æʃbɪn/ n. a receptacle for the disposal of ashes.

ashcan /'æʃkæn/ n. US a dustbin.

ashen /'æʃ(ə)n/ adj. **1** of or resembling ashes. **2** ash-coloured; grey or pale.

ashet /'æʃɪt/ n. Sc. & NZ a large plate or dish. [F assiette]

Ashkenazi /ˌæʃkə'nɑːzɪ/ n. (pl. **Ashkenazim** /-zɪm/) a Jew of East European ancestry. □ **Ashkenazic** adj. [mod.Heb., f. Ashkenaz (Gen. 10:3)]

ashlar /'æʃlə(r)/ n. **1** a large square-cut stone used in building. **2** masonry made of ashlars. **3** such masonry used as a facing on a rough rubble or brick wall. [ME f. OF aisselier f. L axilla dimin. of axis board]

ashore /ə'ʃɔː(r)/ adv. towards or on the shore or land (sailed ashore; stayed ashore).

ashram /'æʃrəm/ n. Ind. a place of religious retreat for Hindus; a hermitage. [Skr. āshrama hermitage]

ashtray /'æʃtreɪ/ n. a small receptacle for cigarette ash, stubs, etc.

ashy /'æʃɪ/ adj. (**ashier, ashiest**) **1** = ASHEN. **2** covered with ashes.

Asian /'eɪʃ(ə)n, -ʒ(ə)n/ n. & adj. —n. **1** a native of Asia. **2** a person of Asian descent. —adj. of or relating to Asia or its people, customs, or languages. [L Asianus f. Gk Asianos f. Asia]

Asiatic /ˌeɪʃɪ'ætɪk, ˌeɪz-/ n. & adj. —n. offens. an Asian. —adj. Asian. [L Asiaticus f. Gk Asiatikos]

aside /ə'saɪd/ adv. & n. —adv. **1** to or on one side; away. **2** out of consideration (placed after noun: joking aside). —n. **1** words spoken in a play for the audience to hear, but supposed not to be heard by the other characters. **2** an incidental remark. □ **aside from** US apart from. [orig. on side: see A[2]]

A-side /'eɪsaɪd/ n. the side of a gramophone record regarded as the main one.

asinine /'æsɪˌnaɪn/ adj. **1** stupid. **2** of or concerning asses; like an ass. □ **asininity** /-'nɪnɪtɪ/ n. [L asininus f. asinus ass]

ask /ɑːsk/ v. **1** tr. call for an answer to or about (ask her about it; ask him his name; ask a question of him). **2** tr. seek to obtain from another person (ask a favour of; ask to be allowed). **3** tr. (usu. foll. by out or over, or to (a function etc.)) invite; request the company of (must ask them over; asked her to dinner). **4** intr. (foll. by for) seek to obtain, meet, or be directed to (ask for a donation; ask for the post office). **5** tr. archaic require (a thing). □ **asking price** the price of an object set by the seller. □ **asker** n. [OE āscian etc. f. WG]

askance /ə'skæns, -'skɑːns/ adv. (also **askant** /-'skænt, -'skɑːnt/) sideways or squinting. □ **look askance at** regard with suspicion or disapproval. [16th c.: orig. unkn.]

askew /ə'skjuː/ adv. & predic.adj. —adv. obliquely; awry. —predic.adj. oblique; awry. [A[2] + SKEW]

aslant /ə'slɑːnt/ adv. & prep. —adv. obliquely or at a slant. —prep. obliquely across (lay aslant the path).

asleep /ə'sliːp/ predic.adj. & adv. **1 a** in or into a state of sleep (he fell asleep). **b** inactive, inattentive (the nation is asleep). **2** (of a limb etc.) numb. **3** euphem. dead.

asocial /eɪ'səʊʃ(ə)l/ adj. **1** not social; antisocial. **2** colloq. inconsiderate of or hostile to others.

asp /æsp/ n. **1** a small viper, Vipera aspis, native to Southern Europe. **2** a small venomous snake, Naja haje, native to North Africa and Arabia. [ME f. OF aspe or L aspis f. Gk]

asparagus /ə'spærəgəs/ n. **1** any plant of the genus Asparagus. **2** one species of this, A. officinalis, with edible young shoots and leaves; this as food. [L f. Gk asparagos]

aspartame /ə'spɑːteɪm/ n. a low-calorie substance used as a sweetener. [contr. of the chem. name 1-methyl N-L-aspartyl-L-phenylalanine, f. aspartic acid (invented name)]

aspect /'æspekt/ n. **1 a** a particular component or feature of a matter (only one aspect of the problem). **b** a particular way in which a matter may be considered. **2 a** a facial expression; a look (a cheerful aspect). **b** the appearance of a person or thing, esp. as presented to the mind of the viewer. **3** the side of a building or location facing a particular direction (southern aspect). **4** Astrol. the relative position of planets etc. measured by angular distance. □ **aspectual** /æ'spektjʊəl/ adj. (in sense 4). [ME f. L aspectus f. adspicere adspect- look at (as AD-, specere look)]

aspen /ˈæspən/ n. a poplar tree, *Populus tremula*, with especially tremulous leaves. [earlier name *asp* f. OE *æspe* + -EN² forming adj. taken as noun]

asperity /əˈsperɪtɪ/ n. (pl. **-ies**) **1** harshness or sharpness of temper or tone. **2** roughness. [ME f. OF *asperité* or L *asperitas* f. *asper* rough]

asperse /əˈspɜːs/ v.tr. (often foll. by *with*) attack the reputation of; calumniate. [ME, = besprinkle, f. L *aspergere aspers-* (as AD-, *spargere* sprinkle)]

aspersion /əˈspɜːʃ(ə)n/ n. □ **cast aspersions on** attack the reputation or integrity of. [L *aspersio* (as ASPERSE, -ION)]

asphalt /ˈæsfælt/ n. & v. —n. **1** a dark bituminous pitch occurring naturally or made from petroleum. **2** a mixture of this with sand, gravel, etc., for surfacing roads etc. —v.tr. surface with asphalt. □ **asphalter** n. **asphaltic** /-ˈfæltɪk/ adj. [ME, ult. f. LL *asphalton, -um*, f. Gk *asphalton*]

asphodel /ˈæsfəˌdel/ n. **1** any plant of the genus *Asphodelus*, of the lily family. **2** *poet.* an immortal flower growing in Elysium. [L *asphodelus* f. Gk *asphodelos*: cf. DAFFODIL]

asphyxia /æsˈfɪksɪə/ n. a lack of oxygen in the blood, causing unconsciousness or death; suffocation. □ **asphyxial** adj. **asphyxiant** adj. & n. [mod.L f. Gk *asphuxia* f. *a-* not + *sphuxis* pulse]

asphyxiate /æsˈfɪksɪˌeɪt/ v.tr. cause (a person) to have asphyxia; suffocate. □ **asphyxiation** /-ˈeɪʃ(ə)n/ n. **asphyxiator** n.

aspic /ˈæspɪk/ n. a meat jelly used as a garnish or to contain game, eggs, etc. [F, = ASP, from the colours of the jelly (compared to those of the asp)]

aspidistra /ˌæspɪˈdɪstrə/ n. a foliage plant of the genus *Aspidistra*, with broad tapering leaves. [mod.L f. Gk *aspis -idos* shield (from the shape of the leaves)]

aspirant /ˈæspɪrənt, əˈspaɪərənt/ adj. & n. (usu. foll. by *to, after, for*) —adj. aspiring. —n. a person who aspires. [F *aspirant* or f. L *aspirant-* (as ASPIRE, -ANT)]

aspirate /ˈæspərət/ adj., n., & v. *Phonet.* —adj. **1** pronounced with an exhalation of breath. **2** blended with the sound of *h*. —n. **1** a consonant pronounced in this way. **2** the sound of *h*. —v. /-ˌreɪt/ **1 a** tr. pronounce with a breath. **b** intr. make the sound of *h*. **2** tr. draw (fluid) by suction from a vessel or cavity. [L *aspiratus* past part. of *aspirare*: see ASPIRE]

aspiration /ˌæspɪˈreɪʃ(ə)n/ n. **1** a strong desire to achieve an end; an ambition. **2** the act or process of drawing breath. **3** the action of aspirating. [ME f. OF *aspiration* or L *aspiratio* (as ASPIRATE, -ATION)]

aspirator /ˈæspɪˌreɪtə(r)/ n. an apparatus for aspirating fluid. [L *aspirare* (as ASPIRATE, -OR¹)]

aspire /əˈspaɪə(r)/ v.intr. (usu. foll. by *to* or *after*, or *to* + infin.) **1** have ambition or strong desire. **2** *poet.* rise high. [ME f. F *aspirer* or L *aspirare* f. *ad* to + *spirare* breathe]

aspirin /ˈæsprɪn/ n. (pl. same or **aspirins**) **1** a white powder, acetylsalicylic acid, used to relieve pain and reduce fever. **2** a tablet of this. [G, formed as ACETYL + *spiraeic* (= salicylic) *acid* + -IN]

ass¹ /æs/ n. & v. —n. **1 a** either of two kinds of four-legged long-eared mammal of the horse genus *Equus*, *E. africana* of Africa and *E. hemionus* of Asia. **b** (in general use) a donkey. **2** a stupid person. —v.intr. *sl.* (foll. by *about, around*) act the fool. [OE *assa* through OCelt. f. L *asinus*]

ass² *US* var. of ARSE.

assail /əˈseɪl/ v.tr. **1** make a strong or concerted attack on. **2** make a resolute start on (a task). **3** make a strong or constant verbal attack on (*was assailed with angry questions*). □ **assailable** adj. [ME f. OF *asaill-* stressed stem of *asalir* f. med.L *assalire* f. L *assilire* (as AD-, *salire salt-* leap)]

assailant /əˈseɪlənt/ n. a person who attacks another physically or verbally. [F (as ASSAIL)]

assassin /əˈsæsɪn/ n. a killer, esp. of a political or religious leader. [F *assassin* or f. med.L *assassinus* f. Arab. *ḥaššāš* hashish-eater]

assassinate /əˈsæsɪˌneɪt/ v.tr. kill (esp. a political or religious leader) for political or religious motives. □ **assassination** /-ˈneɪʃ(ə)n/ n. **assassinator** n. [med.L *assassinare* f. *assassinus*: see ASSASSIN]

assault /əˈsɔːlt, əˈsɒlt/ n. & v. —n. **1** a violent physical or verbal attack. **2 a** *Law* an act that threatens physical harm to a person (whether or not actual harm is done). **b** *euphem.* an act of rape. **3** (*attrib.*) relating to or used in an assault (*assault troops*). **4** a vigorous start made to a lengthy or difficult task. **5** a final rush on a fortified place. —v.tr. **1** make an assault on. **2** *euphem.* rape. □ **assault and battery** *Law* a threatening act that results in physical harm done to a person. **assault course** an obstacle course used in training soldiers etc. □ **assaulter** n. **assaultive** adj. [ME f. OF *asaut, assauter* ult. f. L (*salire salt-* leap)]

assay /əˈseɪ, ˈæseɪ/ n. & v. —n. the testing of a metal or ore to determine its ingredients and quality. —v. **1** tr. make an assay of (a metal or ore). **2** tr. *archaic* attempt. □ **Assay Office** an establishment which awards hallmarks. □ **assayer** n. [ME f. OF *assaier, assai*, var. of *essayer, essai*: see ESSAY]

assegai /ˈæsɪˌgaɪ/ n. (also **assagai** /ˈæsəˌgaɪ/) a slender iron-tipped spear of hard wood, esp. as used by S. African peoples. [obs. F *azagaie* or Port. *azagaia* f. Arab. *az-zaḡāyah* f. *al* the + *zaḡāyah* spear]

assemblage /əˈsemblɪdʒ/ n. **1** the act or an instance of bringing or coming together. **2** a collection of things or gathering of people.

assemble /əˈsemb(ə)l/ v. **1** tr. & intr. gather together; collect. **2** tr. arrange in order. **3** tr. esp. *Mech.* fit together the parts of. [ME f. OF *asembler* ult. f. L *ad* to + *simul* together]

assembler /əˈsemblə(r)/ n. **1** a person who assembles a machine or its parts. **2** *Computing* **a** a program for converting instructions written in low-level symbolic code into machine code. **b** the low-level symbolic code itself; an assembly language.

assembly /əˈsemblɪ/ n. (pl. **-ies**) **1** the act or an instance of assembling or gathering together. **2 a** a group of persons gathered together, esp. as a deliberative body or a legislative council. **b** a gathering of the entire members of a school. **3** the assembling of a machine or structure or its parts. □ **assembly language** *Computing* the low-level symbolic code converted by an assembler. **assembly line** machinery arranged in stages by which a product is progressively assembled. [ME f. OF *asemblee* fem. past part. of *asembler*: see ASSEMBLE]

assent /əˈsent/ v. & n. —v.intr. (usu. foll. by to) **1** express agreement (assented to my view). **2** consent (assented to my request). —n. **1** mental or inward acceptance or agreement (a nod of assent). **2** consent or sanction, esp. official. □ **royal assent** assent of the sovereign to a bill passed by Parliament. □ **assenter** n. (also **assentor**). [ME f. OF asenter, as(s)ente ult. f. L assentari (ad to, sentire think)]

assert /əˈsɜːt/ v. **1** tr. declare; state clearly (assert one's beliefs; assert that it is so). **2** refl. insist on one's rights or opinions; demand recognition. **3** tr. vindicate a claim to (assert one's rights). □ **assertor** n. [L asserere (as AD-, serere sert- join)]

assertion /əˈsɜːʃ(ə)n/ n. **1** a declaration; a forthright statement. **2** the act or an instance of asserting. **3** (also **self-assertion**) insistence on the recognition of one's rights or claims. [ME f. F assertion or L assertio (as ASSERT, -ION)]

assertive /əˈsɜːtɪv/ adj. **1** tending to assert oneself; forthright, positive. **2** dogmatic. □ **assertively** adv. **assertiveness** n.

assess /əˈses/ v.tr. **1 a** estimate the size or quality of. **b** estimate the value of (a property) for taxation. **2 a** (usu. foll. by on) fix the amount of (a tax etc.) and impose it on a person or community. **b** (usu. foll. by in, at) fine or tax (a person, community, etc.) in or at a specific amount (assessed them at £100). □ **assessable** adj. **assessment** n. [ME f. F assesser f. L assidēre (as AD-, sedēre sit)]

assessor /əˈsesə(r)/ n. **1** a person who assesses taxes or estimates the value of property for taxation or insurance purposes. **2** a person called upon to advise a judge, committee of inquiry, etc., on technical questions. □ **assessorial** /ˌæseˈsɔːrɪəl/ adj. [ME f. OF assessour f. L assessor -oris assistant-judge (as ASSESS, -OR¹): sense 1 f. med.L]

asset /ˈæset/ n. **1 a** a useful or valuable quality. **b** a person or thing possessing such a quality or qualities (is an asset to the firm). **2** (usu. in pl.) property and possessions, esp. regarded as having value in meeting debts, commitments, etc. **b** any possession having value. □ **asset-stripping** Commerce the practice of taking over a company and selling off its assets to make a profit. [assets (taken as pl.), f. AF asetz f. OF asez enough, ult. f. L ad to + satis enough]

asseverate /əˈsevəˌreɪt/ v.tr. declare solemnly. □ **asseveration** /-ˈreɪʃ(ə)n/ n. [L asseverare (as AD-, severus serious)]

assiduity /ˌæsɪˈdjuːɪtɪ/ n. (pl. **-ies**) constant or close attention to what one is doing. [L assiduitas (as ASSIDUOUS, -ITY)]

assiduous /əˈsɪdjʊəs/ adj. **1** persevering, hardworking. **2** attending closely. □ **assiduously** adv. **assiduousness** n. [L assiduus (as ASSESS)]

assign /əˈsaɪn/ v. & n. —v.tr. **1** (usu. foll. by to) **a** allot as a share or responsibility. **b** appoint to a position, task, etc. **2** fix (a time, place, etc.) for a specific purpose. **3** (foll. by to) ascribe or refer to (a reason, date, etc.) (assigned the manuscript to 1832). **4** (foll. by to) transfer formally (esp. personal property) to (another). —n. a person to whom property or rights are legally transferred. □ **assignable** adj. **assigner** n. **assignor** n. (in sense 4 of v.). [ME f. OF asi(g)ner f. L assignare mark out to (as AD-, signum sign)]

assignation /ˌæsɪɡˈneɪʃ(ə)n/ n. **1 a** an appointment to meet. **b** a secret appointment, esp.

between illicit lovers. **2** the act or an instance of assigning or being assigned. [ME f. OF f. L assignatio -onis (as ASSIGN, -ATION)]

assignee /ˌæsaɪˈniː/ n. **1** a person appointed to act for another. **2** an assign. [ME f. OF assigné past part. of assigner ASSIGN]

assignment /əˈsaɪnmənt/ n. **1** something assigned, esp. a task allotted to a person. **2** the act or an instance of assigning or being assigned. **3 a** a legal transfer. **b** the document effecting this. [ME f. OF assignement f. med.L assignamentum (as ASSIGN, -MENT)]

assimilate /əˈsɪmɪˌleɪt/ v. **1** tr. **a** absorb and digest (food etc.) into the body. **b** absorb (information etc.) into the mind. **c** absorb (people) into a larger group. **2** tr. (usu. foll. by to, with) make like; cause to resemble. **3** intr. be absorbed into the body, mind, or a larger group. □ **assimilable** adj. **assimilation** /-ˈleɪʃ(ə)n/ n. **assimilative** adj. **assimilator** n. **assimilatory** /-lətərɪ/ adj. [ME f. L assimilare (as AD-, similis like)]

assist /əˈsɪst/ v. **1** tr. (often foll. by in + verbal noun) help (a person, process, etc.) (assisted them in running the playgroup). **2** intr. (often foll. by in, at) take part or be present (assisted in the ceremony). □ **assistance** n. **assister** n. [ME f. F assister f. L assistere take one's stand by (as AD-, sistere take one's stand)]

assistant /əˈsɪst(ə)nt/ n. **1** a helper. **2** (often attrib.) a person who assists, esp. as a subordinate in a particular job or role. [ME assistent f. med.L assistens assistent- present (as ASSIST, -ANT, -ENT)]

assize /əˈsaɪz/ n. (usu. in pl.) hist. a court sitting at intervals in each county of England and Wales to administer the civil and criminal law. [ME f. OF as(s)ise, fem. past part. of aseeir sit at, f. L assidēre: cf. ASSESS]

■ **Usage** In 1972 the civil jurisdiction of the assizes was transferred to the High Court and the criminal jurisdiction to the Crown Court.

associate v., n., & adj. —v. /əˈsəʊʃɪˌeɪt, -sɪˌeɪt/ **1** tr. connect in the mind (associate holly with Christmas). **2** tr. join or combine. **3** refl. make oneself a partner; declare oneself in agreement (associate myself in your endeavour). **4** intr. combine for a common purpose. **5** intr. (usu. foll. by with) meet frequently or have dealings. —n. /əˈsəʊʃɪət, -sɪət/ **1** a business partner or colleague. **2** a friend or companion. **3** a subordinate member of a body, institute, etc. **4** a thing connected with another. —adj. /əˈsəʊʃɪət, -sɪət/ **1** joined in companionship, function, or dignity. **2** allied; in the same category. **3** of less than full status (associate member). □ **associateship** /əˈsəʊʃɪətʃɪp, əˈsəʊs-/ n. **associator** /əˈsəʊʃɪˌeɪtə(r), əˈsəʊs-/ n. **associatory** /əˈsəʊʃɪətərɪ, əˈsəʊs-/ adj. [E f. L associatus past part. of associare (as AD-, socius sharing, allied)]

association /əˌsəʊsɪˈeɪʃ(ə)n/ n. **1** a group of people organized for a joint purpose; a society. **2** the act or an instance of associating. **3** fellowship or companionship. **4** a mental connection between ideas. □ **Association Football** Brit. football played by sides of 11 with a round ball which may not be handled during play except by the goalkeepers. □ **associational** adj. [F association or med.L associatio (as ASSOCIATE, -ATION)]

associative /əˈsəʊʃɪətɪv, əˈsəʊs-/ adj. of or involving association.

assonance /ˈæsənəns/ n. the resemblance of sound between two syllables in nearby words, arising from the rhyming of two or more accented vowels, but not consonants, or the use of identical consonants with different vowels, e.g. *sonnet, porridge,* and *killed, cold, culled.* □ **assonant** *adj.* **assonate** /-ˌneɪt/ *v.intr.* [F f. L *assonare* respond to (as AD-, *sonus* sound)]

assort /əˈsɔːt/ v. 1 *tr.* (usu. foll. by *with*) classify or arrange in groups. 2 *intr.* suit; fit into; harmonize with (usu. *assort ill* or *well with*). [OF *assorter* f. à to + *sorte* SORT]

assorted /əˈsɔːtɪd/ *adj.* 1 of various sorts put together; miscellaneous. 2 sorted into groups. 3 matched (*ill-assorted; poorly assorted*).

assortment /əˈsɔːtmənt/ n. a set of various sorts of things or people put together; a mixed collection.

assuage /əˈsweɪdʒ/ *v.tr.* 1 calm or soothe (a person, pain, etc.). 2 appease or relieve (an appetite or desire). □ **assuagement** n. **assuager** n. [ME f. OF *as(s)ouagier* ult. f. L *suavis* sweet]

assume /əˈsjuːm/ *v.tr.* 1 (usu. foll. by *that* + clause) take or accept as being true, without proof, for the purpose of argument or action. 2 simulate or pretend (ignorance etc.). 3 undertake (an office or duty). 4 take or put on oneself or itself (an aspect, attribute, etc.) (*the problem assumed immense proportions*). 5 (usu. foll. by *to*) arrogate, usurp, or seize (credit, power, etc.) (*assumed to himself the right of veto*). □ **assumable** *adj.* **assumedly** /-mɪdlɪ/ *adv.* [ME f. L *assumere* (as AD-, *sumere sumpt-* take)]

assuming /əˈsjuːmɪŋ/ *adj.* (of a person) taking too much for granted; arrogant, presumptuous.

assumption /əˈsʌmpʃ(ə)n/ n. 1 the act or an instance of assuming. 2 a the act or an instance of accepting without proof. b a thing assumed in this way. 3 arrogance. 4 (**Assumption**) the reception of the Virgin Mary bodily into heaven. [ME f. OF *asompsion* or L *assumptio* (as ASSUME, -ION)]

assumptive /əˈsʌmptɪv/ *adj.* 1 taken for granted. 2 arrogant. [L *assumptivus* (as ASSUME, -IVE)]

assurance /əˈʃʊərəns/ n. 1 a positive declaration that a thing is true. 2 a solemn promise or guarantee. 3 insurance, esp. life insurance. 4 certainty. 5 a self-confidence. b impudence. [ME f. OF *aseürance* f. *aseürer* (as ASSURE, -ANCE)]

assure /əˈʃʊə(r)/ *v.tr.* 1 (often foll. by *of*) a make (a person) sure; convince (*assured him of my sincerity*). b tell (a person) confidently (*assured him the bus went to Westminster*). 2 a make certain of; ensure the happening etc. of (*will assure her success*). b make safe (against overthrow etc.). 3 insure (esp. a life). 4 (as **assured** *adj.*) a guaranteed. b self-confident. □ **assurable** *adj.* **assurer** n. [ME f. OF *aseürer* ult. f. L *securus* safe, SECURE]

assuredly /əˈʃʊərɪdlɪ/ *adv.* certainly.

astatic /eɪˈstætɪk, ə-/ *adj.* 1 not static; unstable or unsteady. 2 *Physics* not tending to keep one position or direction. [Gk *astatos* unstable f. *a*-not + *sta*- stand]

astatine /ˈæstəˌtiːn/ n. *Chem.* a radioactive element which occurs naturally and can be artificially made. [formed as ASTATIC + -INE⁴]

aster /ˈæstə(r)/ n. any composite plant of the genus *Aster*, with bright daisy-like flowers, e.g. the Michaelmas daisy. [L f. Gk *astēr* star]

-aster /ˈæstə(r)/ *suffix* 1 forming nouns denoting poor quality (*criticaster; poetaster*). 2 *Bot.* denoting incomplete resemblance (*oleaster; pinaster*). [L]

asterisk /ˈæstərɪsk/ n. & v. —n. a symbol (*) used in printing and writing to mark words etc. for reference, to stand for omitted matter, etc. —v.tr. mark with an asterisk. [ME f. LL *asteriscus* f. Gk *asteriskos* dimin. (as ASTER)]

astern /əˈstɜːn/ *adv. Naut. & Aeron.* (often foll. by *of*) 1 aft; away to the rear. 2 backwards. [A² + STERN²]

asteroid /ˈæstəˌrɔɪd/ n. 1 any of the minor planets revolving round the sun, mainly between the orbits of Mars and Jupiter. 2 *Zool.* a starfish. □ **asteroidal** /ˌæstəˈrɔɪd(ə)l/ *adj.* [Gk *asteroeidēs* (as ASTER, -OID)]

asthma /ˈæsmə/ n. a usu. allergic respiratory disease, often with paroxysms of difficult breathing. [ME f. Gk *asthma -matos* f. *azō* breathe hard]

asthmatic /æsˈmætɪk/ *adj.* & n. —*adj.* relating to or suffering from asthma. —n. a person suffering from asthma. □ **asthmatically** *adv.* [L *asthmaticus* f. Gk *asthmatikos* (as ASTHMA, -IC)]

astigmatism /əˈstɪgməˌtɪz(ə)m/ n. a defect in the eye or in a lens resulting in distorted images, as light rays are prevented from meeting at a common focus. □ **astigmatic** /ˌæstɪgˈmætɪk/ *adj.* [A-¹ + Gk *stigma -matos* point]

astir /əˈstɜː(r)/ *predic.adj.* & *adv.* 1 in motion. 2 awake and out of bed (*astir early; already astir*). 3 excited. [A² + STIR¹ n.]

astonish /əˈstɒnɪʃ/ *v.tr.* amaze; surprise greatly. □ **astonishing** *adj.* **astonishingly** *adv.* **astonishment** n. [obs. *astone* f. OF *estoner* f. Gallo-Roman: see -ISH²]

astound /əˈstaʊnd/ *v.tr.* shock with alarm or surprise; amaze. □ **astounding** *adj.* **astoundingly** *adv.* [obs. *astound* (adj.) = *astoned* past part. of obs. *astone*: see ASTONISH]

astraddle /əˈstræd(ə)l/ *adv.* & *predic.adj.* in a straddling position.

astrakhan /ˌæstrəˈkæn/ n. 1 the dark curly fleece of young lambs from Astrakhan. 2 a cloth imitating astrakhan. [*Astrakhan* in Russia]

astral /ˈæstr(ə)l/ *adj.* 1 of or connected with the stars. 2 consisting of stars; starry. [LL *astralis* f. *astrum* star]

astray /əˈstreɪ/ *adv.* & *predic.adj.* 1 in or into error or sin (esp. *lead astray*). 2 out of the right way. □ **go astray** be lost or mislaid. [ME f. OF *estraié* past part. of *estraier* ult. f. L *extra* out of bounds + *vagari* wander]

astride /əˈstraɪd/ *adv.* & *prep.* —*adv.* 1 (often foll. by *of*) with a leg on each side. 2 with legs apart. —*prep.* with a leg on each side of; extending across.

astringent /əˈstrɪndʒ(ə)nt/ *adj.* & n. —*adj.* 1 causing the contraction of body tissues. 2 checking bleeding. 3 severe, austere. —n. an astringent substance or drug. □ **astringency** n. **astringently** *adv.* [F f. L *astringere* (as AD-, *stringere* bind)]

astro- /ˈæstrəʊ/ *comb. form* 1 relating to the stars or celestial bodies. 2 relating to outer space. [Gk f. *astron* star]

astrolabe /ˈæstrəˌleɪb/ n. an instrument formerly used to make astronomical measurements and as an aid in navigation. [ME f. OF *astrelabe* f. med.L *astrolabium* f. Gk *astrolabon*, neut. of *astrolabos* star-taking]

astrology /ə'strɒlədʒɪ/ n. the study of the movements and relative positions of celestial bodies interpreted as an influence on human affairs. □ **astrologer** n. **astrological** /ˌæstrə'lɒdʒɪk(ə)l/ adj. **astrologist** n. [ME f. OF astrologie f. L astrologia f. Gk (as ASTRO-, -LOGY)]

astronaut /'æstrənɔːt/ n. a person who is trained to travel in a spacecraft. □ **astronautical** /ˌæstrə'nɔːtɪk(ə)l/ adj. [ASTRO-, after aeronaut]

astronautics /ˌæstrə'nɔːtɪks/ n. the science of space travel.

astronomical /ˌæstrə'nɒmɪk(ə)l/ adj. (also **astronomic**) 1 of or relating to astronomy. 2 extremely large; too large to contemplate. □ **astronomically** adv. [L astronomicus f. Gk astronomikos]

astronomy /ə'strɒnəmɪ/ n. the scientific study of celestial bodies. □ **astronomer** n. [ME f. OF astronomie f. L f. Gk astronomia f. astronomos (adj.) star-arranging f. nemō arrange]

astrophysics /ˌæstrəʊ'fɪzɪks/ n. a branch of astronomy concerned with the physics and chemistry of celestial bodies. □ **astrophysical** adj. **astrophysicist** /-sɪst/ n.

astute /ə'stjuːt/ adj. 1 shrewd; sagacious. 2 crafty. □ **astutely** adv. **astuteness** n. [obs. F astut or L astutus f. astus craft]

asunder /ə'sʌndə(r)/ adv. literary apart. [OE on sundran into pieces: cf. SUNDER]

asylum /ə'saɪləm/ n. 1 sanctuary; protection, esp. for those pursued by the law (seek asylum). 2 hist. any of various kinds of institution offering shelter and support to distressed or destitute individuals, esp. the mentally ill. □ **political asylum** protection given by a State to a political refugee from another country. [ME f. L f. Gk asulon refuge f. a- not + sulon right of seizure]

asymmetry /eɪ'sɪmɪtrɪ, æ'sɪmɪtrɪ/ n. lack of sym- metry. □ **asymmetric** /-'metrɪk/ adj. **asymmetrical** /-'metrɪk(ə)l/ adj. **asymmetrically** /-'metrɪkəlɪ/ adv. [Gk asummetria (as A-¹, SYMMETRY)]

asymptomatic /eɪˌsɪmptə'mætɪk/ adj. producing or showing no symptoms.

At symb. Chem. the element astatine.

at /æt, unstressed ət/ prep. 1 expressing position, exact or approximate (wait at the corner; at the top of the hill; met at Bath; is at school; at a distance). 2 expressing a point in time (see you at three; went at dawn). 3 expressing a point in a scale or range (at boiling-point; at his best). 4 expressing engagement or concern in a state or activity (at war; at work; at odds). 5 expressing a value or rate (sell at £10 each). 6 a with or with reference to; in terms of (at a disadvantage; annoyed at losing; good at cricket; play at fighting; sick at heart; came at a run; at short notice; work at it). b by means of (starts at a touch; drank it at a gulp). 7 expressing: a motion towards (arrived at the station; went at them). b aim towards or pursuit of (physically or conceptually) (aim at the target; work at a solution; guess at the truth; laughed at us; has been at the milk again). □ **at that** moreover (found one, and a good one at that). [OE æt, rel. to L ad to]

atavism /'ætəvɪz(ə)m/ n. 1 a resemblance to remote ancestors rather than to parents in plants or animals. 2 reversion to an earlier type. □ **atavistic** /-'vɪstɪk/ adj. **atavistically** /-'vɪstɪkəlɪ/ adv. [F atavisme f. L atavus great-grandfather's grandfather]

ate past of EAT.

-ate¹ /ət, eɪt/ suffix 1 forming nouns denoting: **a** status or office (doctorate; episcopate). **b** state or function (curate; magistrate; mandate). 2 Chem. forming nouns denoting the salt of an acid with a corresponding name ending in -ic (chlorate; nitrate). 3 forming nouns denoting a group (electorate). 4 Chem. forming nouns denoting a product (condensate; filtrate). [from or after OF -at or é(e) or f. L -atus noun or past part.: cf. -ATE²]

-ate² /ət, eɪt/ suffix 1 forming adjectives and nouns (associate; delegate; duplicate; separate). 2 forming adjectives from Latin or English nouns and adjectives (cordate; insensate; Italianate). [from or after (F -é f.) L -atus past part. of verbs in -are]

-ate³ /eɪt/ suffix forming verbs (associate; duplicate; fascinate; hyphenate; separate). [from or after (F -er f.) L -are (past part. -atus): cf. -ATE²]

atelier /ə'telɪˌeɪ, 'ætəˌljeɪ/ n. a workshop or studio, esp. of an artist or designer. [F]

a tempo /ɑ: 'tempəʊ/ adv. Mus. in the previous tempo. [It., lit. 'in time']

atheism /'eɪθɪˌɪz(ə)m/ n. the theory or belief that God does not exist. □ **atheist** n. **atheistic** /-'ɪstɪk/ adj. **atheistical** /-'ɪstɪk(ə)l/ adj. [F athéisme f. Gk atheos without God f. a- not + theos god]

atherosclerosis /ˌæθərəʊskliə'rəʊsɪs/ n. a form of arteriosclerosis characterized by the degeneration of the arteries because of the build-up of fatty deposits. □ **atherosclerotic** /-'rɒtɪk/ adj. [G Atherosklerose f. Gk athērē groats + SCLEROSIS]

athirst /ə'θɜːst/ predic.adj. poet. 1 (usu. foll. by for) eager (athirst for knowledge). 2 thirsty. [OE ofthyrst for ofthyrsted past part. of ofthyrstan be thirsty]

athlete /'æθliːt/ n. 1 a skilled performer in physical exercises, esp. in track and field events. 2 a healthy person with natural athletic ability. □ **athlete's foot** a fungal foot condition affecting esp. the skin between the toes. [L athleta f. Gk athlētēs f. athleō contend for a prize (athlon)]

athletic /æθ'letɪk/ adj. 1 of or relating to athletes or athletics (an athletic competition). 2 muscular or physically powerful. □ **athletically** adv. **athleticism** /-'letɪˌsɪz(ə)m/ n. [F athlétique or L athleticus f. Gk athlētikos (as ATHLETE, -IC)]

athletics /æθ'letɪks/ n.pl. (usu. treated as sing.) 1 **a** physical exercises, esp. track and field events. **b** the practice of these. 2 US physical sports and games of any kind.

athwart /ə'θwɔːt/ adv. & prep. —adv. 1 across from side to side (usu. obliquely). 2 perversely or in opposition. —prep. 1 from side to side of. 2 in opposition to. [A² + THWART]

-atic /'ætɪk/ suffix forming adjectives and nouns (aquatic; fanatic; idiomatic). [F -atique or L -aticus, often ult. f. Gk -atikos]

-ation /'eɪʃ(ə)n/ suffix 1 forming nouns denoting an action or an instance of it (alteration; flirtation; hesitation). 2 forming nouns denoting a result or product of action (plantation; starvation; vexation) (see also -FICATION). [from or after F -ation or L -atio -ationis f. verbs in -are: see -ION]

-ative /ətɪv, eɪtɪv/ suffix forming adjectives denoting a characteristic or propensity (authoritative; imitative; pejorative; qualitative; talkative). [from or after F -atif -ative or f. L -ativus f. past part. stem -at- of verbs in -are + -ivus (see -IVE): cf. -ATIC]

Atlantic /ət'læntɪk/ n. & adj. —n. the ocean between Europe and Africa to the east, and America to the west. —adj. of or adjoining the Atlantic. [ME f. L Atlanticus f. Gk Atlantikos (as

ATLAS, -IC): orig. of the Atlas Mountains, then of the sea near the W. African coast]

atlas /ˈætləs/ n. a book of maps or charts. [L f. Gk Atlas -antos a Titan who held up the pillars of the universe, whose picture appeared at the beginning of early atlases]

atmosphere /ˈætməsˌfɪə(r)/ n. **1 a** the envelope of gases surrounding the earth, any other planet, or any substance. **b** the air in any particular place, esp. if unpleasant. **2** the pervading tone or mood of a place or situation, esp. with reference to the feelings or emotions evoked. **3** Physics a unit of pressure equal to mean atmospheric pressure at sea level. □ **atmospheric** /-ˈferɪk/ adj. **atmospherical** /-ˈferɪk(ə)l/ adj. **atmospherically** /-ˈferɪkəlɪ/ adv. [mod.L atmosphaera f. Gk atmos vapour]

atmospherics /ˌætməsˈferɪks/ n.pl. **1** electrical disturbance in the atmosphere. **2** interference with telecommunications caused by this.

atoll /ˈætɒl/ n. a ring-shaped coral reef enclosing a lagoon. [Maldive atolu]

atom /ˈætəm/ n. **1 a** the smallest particle of a chemical element that can take part in a chemical reaction. **b** this particle as a source of nuclear energy. **2** (usu. with neg.) the least portion of a thing or quality (not an atom of pity). □ **atom bomb** a bomb involving the release of energy by nuclear fission. [ME f. OF atome f. L atomus f. Gk atomos indivisible]

atomic /əˈtɒmɪk/ adj. **1** concerned with or using atomic energy or atomic bombs. **2** of or relating to an atom or atoms. □ **atomic bomb** = atom bomb. **atomic energy** nuclear energy. **atomic mass** the mass of an atom measured in atomic mass units. **atomic mass unit** a unit of mass used to express atomic and molecular weights. **atomic particle** any one of the particles of which an atom is constituted. **atomic physics** the branch of physics concerned with the structure of the atom and the characteristics of the elementary particles of which it is composed. **atomic pile** a nuclear reactor. **atomic power** nuclear power. **atomic theory 1** the concept of an atom as being composed of elementary particles. **2** the theory that all matter is made up of small indivisible particles called atoms, and that the atoms of any one element are identical in all respects but differ from those of other elements and only unite to form compounds in fixed proportions. **atomic weight** the ratio of the average mass of one atom of an element to $\frac{1}{12}$ of the mass of an atom of carbon 12. □ **atomically** adv. [mod.L atomicus (as ATOM, -IC)]

atomize /ˈætəˈmaɪz/ v.tr. (also **-ise**) reduce to atoms or fine particles. □ **atomization** /-ˈzeɪʃ(ə)n/ n.

atomizer /ˈætəˌmaɪzə(r)/ n. (also **-iser**) an instrument for emitting liquids as a fine spray.

atonal /eɪˈtəʊn(ə)l, ə-/ adj. Mus. not written in any key or mode. □ **atonality** /-ˈnælɪtɪ/ n.

atone /əˈtəʊn/ v.intr. (usu. foll. by for) make amends; expiate (for a wrong). [back-form. f. ATONEMENT]

atonement /əˈtəʊnmənt/ n. **1** expiation; reparation for a wrong or injury. **2** the reconciliation of God and man. □ **the Atonement** the expiation by Christ of mankind's sin. **Day of Atonement** the most solemn religious fast of the Jewish year, eight days after the Jewish New

Year. [at one + -MENT, after med.L adunamentum and earlier onement f. obs. one (v.) unite]

atonic /əˈtɒnɪk/ adj. **1** without accent or stress. **2** Med. lacking bodily tone. □ **atony** /ˈætənɪ/ n.

atop /əˈtɒp/ adv. & prep. —adv. (often foll. by of) on the top. —prep. on the top of.

-ator /ˈeɪtə(r)/ suffix forming agent nouns, usu. from Latin words (sometimes via French) (agitator; creator; equator; escalator). See also -OR[1]. [L -ator]

-atory /ˈətərɪ/ suffix forming adjectives meaning 'relating to or involving (a verbal action)' (amatory; explanatory; predatory). See also -ORY[2]. [L -atorius]

atrium /ˈeɪtrɪəm/ n. (pl. **atriums** or **atria** /-trɪə/) **1 a** the central court of an ancient Roman house. **b** a usu. skylit central court rising through several storeys with galleries and rooms opening off at each level. **c** US (in a modern house) a central hall or glazed court with rooms opening off it. **2** Anat. a cavity in the body, esp. one of the two upper cavities of the heart, receiving blood from the veins. □ **atrial** adj. [L]

atrocious /əˈtrəʊʃəs/ adj. **1** very bad or unpleasant (atrocious weather; their manners were atrocious). **2** extremely savage or wicked (atrocious cruelty). □ **atrociously** adv. **atrociousness** n. [L atrox -ocis cruel]

atrocity /əˈtrɒsɪtɪ/ n. (pl. **-ies**) **1** an extremely wicked or cruel act, esp. one involving physical violence or injury. **2** extreme wickedness. [F atrocité or L atrocitas (as ATROCIOUS, -ITY)]

atrophy /ˈætrəfɪ/ v. & n. —v. (**-ies**, **-ied**) **1** intr. waste away through undernourishment, ageing, or lack of use; become emaciated. **2** tr. cause to atrophy. —n. the process of atrophying; emaciation. [F atrophie or LL atrophia f. Gk f. a- not + trophē food]

atropine /ˈætrəˌpiːn, -pɪn/ n. a poisonous alkaloid found in deadly nightshade, used in medicine. [mod.L Atropa belladonna deadly nightshade f. Gk Atropos inflexible, the name of one of the Fates]

attach /əˈtætʃ/ v. **1** tr. fasten, affix, join. **2** tr. (in passive; foll. by to) be very fond of or devoted to (am deeply attached to her). **3** tr. attribute, assign (some function, quality, or characteristic) (attaches great importance to it). **4 a** tr. accompany; form part of (no conditions are attached). **b** intr. (foll. by to) be an attribute or characteristic (great prestige attaches to the job). **5** refl. (usu. foll. by to) take part in; join (attached themselves to the expedition). **6** tr. appoint for special or temporary duties. **7** tr. Law seize (a person or property) by legal authority. □ **attachable** adj. **attacher** n. [ME f. OF estachier fasten f. Gmc: in Law sense through OF atachier]

attaché /əˈtæʃeɪ/ n. a person appointed to an ambassador's staff, usu. with a special sphere of activity (military attaché; press attaché). □ **attaché case** a small flat rectangular case for carrying documents etc. [F, past part. of attacher: see ATTACH]

attachment /əˈtætʃmənt/ n. **1** a thing attached or to be attached, esp. to a machine, device, etc., for a special function. **2** affection, devotion. **3** a means of attaching. **4** the act of attaching or the state of being attached. **5** legal seizure. **6** a temporary position in, or secondment to, an organization. [ME f. F *attachement* f. *attacher* (as ATTACH, -MENT)]

attack /əˈtæk/ v. & n. —v. **1** tr. act against with (esp. armed) force. **2** tr. seek to hurt or defeat. **3** tr. criticize adversely. **4** tr. act harmfully upon (*a virus attacking the nervous system*). **5** tr. vigorously apply oneself to; begin work on (*attacked his meal with gusto*). **6** intr. make an attack. **7** intr. be in a mode of attack. —n. **1** the act or process of attacking. **2** an offensive operation or mode of behaviour. **3** Mus. the action or manner of beginning a piece, passage, etc. **4** gusto, vigour. **5** a sudden occurrence of an illness. **6** a player or players seeking to score goals etc. □ **attacker** n. [F *attaque*, *attaquer* f. It. *attacco* attack, *attaccare* ATTACH]

attain /əˈteɪn/ v. **1** tr. arrive at; reach (a goal etc.). **2** tr. gain, accomplish (an aim, distinction, etc.). **3** intr. (foll. by *to*) arrive at by conscious development or effort. □ **attainable** adj. **attainability** /-ˈbɪlɪtɪ/ n. **attainableness** n. [ME f. AF *atain-*, *atein-*, OF *ataign-* stem of *ataindre* f. L *attingere* (as AD-, *tangere* touch)]

attainment /əˈteɪnmənt/ n. **1** (often in pl.) something attained or achieved; an accomplishment. **2** the act or an instance of attaining.

attar /ˈætɑː(r)/ n. (also **otto** /ˈɒtəʊ/) a fragrant essential oil, esp. made from rose-petals. [Pers. ˈatar f. Arab. f. ˈiṭr perfume]

attempt /əˈtempt/ v. & n. —v.tr. **1** (often foll. by *to* + infin.) seek to achieve or complete (a task or action) (*attempted the exercise; attempted to explain*). **2** seek to climb or master (a mountain etc.). —n. (often foll. by *at, on,* or *to* + infin.) an act of attempting; an endeavour (*made an attempt at winning; an attempt to succeed; an attempt on his life*). □ **attemptable** adj. [OF *attempter* f. L *attemptare* (as AD-, *temptare* TEMPT)]

attend /əˈtend/ v. **1** tr. **a** be present at (*attended the meeting*). **b** go regularly to (*attends the local school*). **2** intr. **a** be present (*many members failed to attend*). **b** be present in a serving capacity; wait. **3 a** tr. escort, accompany (*the king was attended by soldiers*). **b** intr. (foll. by *on*) wait on; serve. **4** intr. **a** (usu. foll. by *to*) turn or apply one's mind; focus one's attention (*attend to what I am saying; was not attending*). **b** (foll. by *to*) deal with (*shall attend to the matter myself*). **5** tr. (usu. in passive) follow as a result from (*the error was attended by serious consequences*). □ **attender** n. [ME f. OF *atendre* f. L *attendere* (as AD-, *tendere* tent- stretch)]

attendance /əˈtend(ə)ns/ n. **1** the act of attending or being present. **2** the number of people present (*a high attendance*). □ **attendance allowance** (in the UK) a State benefit paid to disabled people in need of constant care at home. **attendance centre** Brit. a place where young offenders report by order of a court as a minor penalty. [ME f. OF *atendance* (as ATTEND, -ANCE)]

attendant /əˈtend(ə)nt/ n. & adj. —n. a person employed to wait on others or provide a service (*cloakroom attendant; museum attendant*). —adj. **1** accompanying (*attendant circumstances*). **2** waiting on; serving (*ladies attendant on the queen*). [ME f. OF (as ATTEND, -ANT)]

attention /əˈtenʃ(ə)n/ n. & int. —n. **1** the act or faculty of applying one's mind (*attract his attention*). **2 a** consideration (*give attention to the problem*). **b** care (*give special attention to your handwriting*). **3** (in pl.) **a** ceremonious politeness (*he paid his attentions to her*). **b** wooing, courting (*she was the subject of his attentions*). **4** Mil. an erect attitude of readiness (*stand at attention*). —int. (in full **stand at attention!**) an order to assume an attitude of attention. [ME f. L *attentio* (as ATTEND, -ION)]

attentive /əˈtentɪv/ adj. **1** concentrating; paying attention. **2** assiduously polite. **3** heedful. □ **attentively** adv. **attentiveness** n. [ME f. F *attentif -ive* f. *attente*, OF *atente*, fem. past part. of *atendre* ATTEND]

attenuate v. & adj. —v.tr. /əˈtenjʊˌeɪt/ **1** make thin. **2** reduce in force, value, or virulence. —adj. /əˈtenjʊət/ **1** slender. **2** tapering gradually. **3** rarefied. □ **attenuated** adj. **attenuation** /-ˈeɪʃ(ə)n/ n. **attenuator** n. [L *attenuare* (as AD-, *tenuis* thin)]

attest /əˈtest/ v. **1** tr. certify the validity of. **2** intr. (foll. by *to*) bear witness to. □ **attestable** adj. **attestor** n. [F *attester* f. L *attestari* (as AD-, *testis* witness)]

attestation /ˌæteˈsteɪʃ(ə)n/ n. **1** the act of attesting. **2** a testimony. [F *attestation* or LL *attestatio* (as ATTEST, -ATION)]

Attic /ˈætɪk/ adj. of ancient Athens or Attica, or the form of Greek spoken there. [L *Atticus* f. Gk *Attikos*]

attic /ˈætɪk/ n. **1** the uppermost storey in a house, usu. under the roof. **2** a room in the attic area. [F *attique*, as ATTIC: orig. (Archit.) a small order above a taller one]

attire /əˈtaɪə(r)/ v. & n. formal —v.tr. dress, esp. in fine clothes or formal wear. —n. clothes, esp. fine or formal. [ME f. OF *atir(i)er* equip f. *à tire* in order, of unkn. orig.]

attitude /ˈætɪˌtjuːd/ n. **1 a** a settled opinion or way of thinking. **b** behaviour reflecting this (*I don't like his attitude*). **2 a** a bodily posture. **b** a pose adopted in a painting or a play, esp. for dramatic effect (*strike an attitude*). □ **attitudinal** /ˌætɪˈtjuːdɪn(ə)l/ adj. [F f. It. *attitudine* fitness, posture, f. LL *aptitudo -dinis* f. *aptus* fit]

attitudinize /ˌætɪˈtjuːdɪˌnaɪz/ v.intr. (also **-ise**) **1** practise or adopt attitudes, esp. for effect. **2** speak, write, or behave affectedly. [It. *attitudine* f. LL (as ATTITUDE) + -IZE]

attorney /əˈtɜːnɪ/ n. (pl. **-eys**) **1** a person, esp. a lawyer, appointed to act for another in business or legal matters. **2** US a qualified lawyer, esp. one representing a client in a lawcourt. □ **Attorney-General** the chief legal officer in England, the US, and other countries. **power of attorney** the authority to act for another person in legal or financial matters. □ **attorneyship** n. [ME f. OF *atorné* past part. of *atorner* assign f. *à* to + *torner* turn]

attract /əˈtrækt/ v.tr. **1** (also absol.) draw or bring to oneself or itself (*attracts attention*). **2** be attractive to; fascinate. **3** (of a magnet, gravity, etc.) exert a pull on (an object). □ **attractable** adj. **attractor** n. [L *attrahere* (as AD-, *trahere* tract- draw)]

attractant /əˈtrækt(ə)nt/ n. & adj. —n. a substance which attracts (esp. insects). —adj. attracting.

attraction /əˈtrækʃ(ə)n/ n. **1 a** the act or power of attracting (*the attraction of foreign travel*). **b** a person or thing that attracts by arousing interest (*the fair is a big attraction*). **2** Physics the force by which bodies attract or approach each other. [F *attraction* or L *attractio* (as ATTRACT, -ION)]

attractive /əˈtræktɪv/ *adj.* **1** attracting or capable of attracting; interesting (*an attractive proposition*). **2** aesthetically pleasing or appealing. □ **attractively** *adv.* **attractiveness** *n.* [F *attractif* *-ive* f. LL *attractivus* (as ATTRACT, -IVE)]

attribute *v. & n.* —*v.tr.* /əˈtrɪbjuːt/ (usu. foll. by *to*) **1** regard as belonging or appropriate to (*a poem attributed to Shakespeare*). **2** ascribe to; regard as the effect of a stated cause (*the delays were attributed to the heavy traffic*). —*n.* /ˈætrɪˌbjuːt/ **1 a** a quality ascribed to a person or thing. **b** a characteristic quality. **2** a material object recognized as appropriate to a person, office, or status (*a large car is an attribute of seniority*). **3** *Gram.* an attributive adjective or noun. □ **attributable** /əˈtrɪbjʊtəb(ə)l/ *adj.* **attribution** /ˌætrɪˈbjuːʃ(ə)n/ *n.* [ME f. L *attribuere attribut-* (as AD-, *tribuere* assign): (n.) f. OF *attribut* or L *attributum*]

attributive /əˈtrɪbjʊtɪv/ *adj.* *Gram.* (of an adjective or noun) preceding the word described and expressing an attribute, as *old* in *the old dog* (but not in *the dog is old*) and *expiry* in *expiry date*. □ **attributively** *adv.* [F *attributif -ive* (as ATTRIBUTE, -IVE)]

attrit /əˈtrɪt/ *v.tr.* *US colloq.* wear (an enemy or opponent) down by attrition. [back-form. f. ATTRITION]

attrition /əˈtrɪʃ(ə)n/ *n.* **1** the act or process of gradually wearing out, esp. by friction. **2** abrasion. □ **war of attrition** a war in which one side wins by gradually wearing the other down with repeated attacks etc. □ **attritional** *adj.* [ME f. LL *attritio* f. *atterere attrit-* rub]

attune /əˈtjuːn/ *v.tr.* **1** (usu. foll. by *to*) adjust (a person or thing) to a situation. **2** bring (an orchestra, instrument, etc.) into musical accord. [AD- + TUNE]

atypical /eɪˈtɪpɪk(ə)l/ *adj.* not typical; not conforming to a type. □ **atypically** *adv.*

Au *symb. Chem.* the element gold. [L *aurum*]

aubergine /ˈəʊbəˌʒiːn/ *n.* **1** a tropical plant, *Solanum melongena*, having erect or spreading branches bearing white or purple egg-shaped fruit. **2** this fruit eaten as a vegetable. **3** the dark purple colour of this fruit. [F f. Cat. *alberginia* f. Arab. *al-bādinjān* f. Pers. *bādingān* f. Skr. *vātiṃgaṇa*]

aubrietia /ɔːˈbriːʃə/ *n.* (also **aubretia**) any dwarf perennial rock-plant of the genus *Aubrieta*, having purple or pink flowers in spring. [mod.L f. Claude *Aubriet*, Fr. botanist d. 1743]

auburn /ˈɔːbən/ *adj.* reddish brown (usu. of a person's hair). [ME, orig. yellowish white, f. OF *auborne*, *alborne*, f. L *alburnus* whitish f. *albus* white]

auction /ˈɔːkʃ(ə)n/ *n. & v.* —*n.* a sale of goods in which articles are sold to the highest bidder. —*v.tr.* sell by auction. □ **auction bridge** a form of bridge in which players bid for the right to name trumps. **Dutch auction** a sale of goods in which the price is reduced by the auctioneer until a buyer is found. [L *auctio* increase, auction f. *augēre auct-* increase]

auctioneer /ˌɔːkʃəˈnɪə(r)/ *n.* a person who conducts auctions professionally, by calling for bids and declaring goods sold. □ **auctioneering** *n.*

audacious /ɔːˈdeɪʃəs/ *adj.* **1** daring, bold. **2** impudent. □ **audaciously** *adv.* **audaciousness** *n.* **audacity** /ɔːˈdæsɪtɪ/ *n.* [L *audax -acis* bold f. *audēre* dare]

audible /ˈɔːdɪb(ə)l/ *adj.* capable of being heard. □ **audibility** /-ˈbɪlɪtɪ/ *n.* **audibleness** *n.* **audibly** *adv.* [LL *audibilis* f. *audire* hear]

audience /ˈɔːdɪəns/ *n.* **1 a** the assembled listeners or spectators at an event, esp. a stage performance, concert, etc. **b** the people addressed by a film, book, play, etc. **2** a formal interview with a person in authority. **3** *archaic* a hearing (*give audience to my plea*). [ME f. OF f. L *audientia* f. *audire* hear]

audio /ˈɔːdɪəʊ/ *n.* (usu. *attrib.*) sound or the reproduction of sound. □ **audio frequency** a frequency capable of being perceived by the human ear. **audio typist** a person who types direct from a recording. [AUDIO-]

audio- /ˈɔːdɪəʊ/ *comb. form* hearing or sound. [L *audire* hear + -O-]

audiology /ˌɔːdɪˈɒlədʒɪ/ *n.* the science of hearing. □ **audiologist** *n.*

audiotape /ˈɔːdɪəʊˌteɪp/ *n. & v.* —*n.* **1** magnetic tape on which sound can be recorded. **2** a sound recording on tape. —*v.tr.* record (sound) on tape.

audiovisual /ˌɔːdɪəʊˈvɪʒʊəl/ *adj.* (esp. of teaching methods) using both sight and sound.

audit /ˈɔːdɪt/ *n. & v.* —*n.* an official examination of accounts. —*v.tr.* (**audited, auditing**) **1** conduct an audit of. **2** *US* attend (a class) informally, without working for credits. [ME f. L *auditus* hearing f. *audire audit-* hear]

audition /ɔːˈdɪʃ(ə)n/ *n. & v.* —*n.* an interview for a role as a singer, actor, dancer, etc., consisting of a practical demonstration of suitability. —*v.* **1** *tr.* interview (a candidate at an audition). **2** *intr.* be interviewed at an audition. [F *audition* or L *auditio* f. *audire audit-* hear]

auditor /ˈɔːdɪtə(r)/ *n.* **1** a person who audits accounts. **2** a listener. □ **auditorial** /-ˈtɔːrɪəl/ *adj.* [ME f. AF *auditour* f. L *auditor -oris* hearer]

auditorium /ˌɔːdɪˈtɔːrɪəm/ *n.* (pl. **auditoriums** or **auditoria** /-rɪə/) the part of a theatre etc. in which the audience sits. [L neut. of *auditorius* (adj.): see AUDITORY, -ORIUM]

auditory /ˈɔːdɪtərɪ/ *adj.* **1** concerned with hearing. **2** received by the ear. [L *auditorius* (as AUDITOR, -ORY²)]

au fait /əʊ ˈfeɪ/ *predic.adj.* (usu. foll. by *with*) having current knowledge; conversant (*fully au fait with the arrangements*). [F]

Aug. *abbr.* August.

Augean /ɔːˈdʒiːən/ *adj.* filthy; extremely dirty. [L *Augeas* f. Gk *Augeias* (in Gk mythology, the owner of stables cleaned by Hercules by diverting a river through them)]

auger /ˈɔːgə(r)/ *n.* **1** a tool resembling a large corkscrew, for boring holes in wood. **2** a similar larger tool for boring holes in the ground. [OE *nafogār* f. *nafu* NAVE², + *gār* pierce: for loss of *n* cf. ADDER]

aught /ɔːt/ *n.* (also **ought**) *archaic* (usu. implying *neg.*) anything at all. [OE *āwiht* f. Gmc]

augment —*v.tr. & intr.* /ɔːgˈment/ make or become greater; increase. □ **augmentation** *n.* **augmenter** *n.* [ME f. OF *augment* (n.), F *augmenter* (v.), or LL *augmentum*, *augmentare* f. L *augēre* increase]

augmentative /ɔːgˈmentətɪv/ *adj.* having the property of increasing. [F *augmentatif -ive* or med.L *augmentativus* (as AUGMENT)]

au gratin /ˌəʊ ˈgrætæ̃/ *adj.* *Cookery* cooked with a crisp brown crust usu. of breadcrumbs or melted cheese. [F f. *gratter*, = by grating, f. GRATE¹]

augur /ˈɔːgə(r)/ v. & n. —v. **1** intr. **a** (of an event, circumstance, etc.) suggest a specified outcome (usu. *augur well* or *ill*). **b** portend, bode (*all augured well for our success*). **2** tr. **a** foresee, predict. **b** portend. —n. a Roman religious official who observed natural signs, esp. the behaviour of birds, interpreting these as an indication of divine approval or disapproval of a proposed action. □ **augural** adj. [L]

augury /ˈɔːgjərɪ/ n. (pl. -ies) **1** an omen; a portent. **2** the work of an augur; the interpretation of omens. [ME f. OF *augurie* or L *augurium* f. AUGUR]

August /ˈɔːgəst/ n. the eighth month of the year. [OE f. L *Augustus* Caesar, the first Roman emperor]

august /ɔːˈgʌst/ adj. inspiring reverence and admiration; venerable, impressive. □ **augustly** adv. **augustness** n. [F *auguste* or L *augustus* consecrated, venerable]

Augustan /ɔːˈgʌst(ə)n/ adj. & n. —adj. **1** connected with or occurring during the reign of the Roman emperor Augustus, esp. as an outstanding period of Latin literature. **2** (of a nation's literature) refined and classical in style (in England of the literature of the 17th–18th c.). —n. a writer of the Augustan age of any literature. [L *Augustanus* f. *Augustus*]

Augustinian /ˌɔːgəˈstɪnɪən/ adj. & n. —adj. belonging to a religious order observing a rule derived from St Augustine's writings. —n. one of the order of Augustinian friars. [L *Augustinus* Augustine]

auk /ɔːk/ n. any sea diving-bird of the family Alcidae, with heavy body, short wings, and black and white plumage, e.g. the puffin. [ON *álka*]

auld /ɔːld/ adj. Sc. old. [OE *ald*, Anglian form of OLD]

auld lang syne /ˌɔːld læŋ ˈsaɪn/ n. times long past. [Sc., = old long since: also as the title and refrain of a song]

aunt /ɑːnt/ n. **1** the sister of one's father or mother. **2** an uncle's wife. **3** colloq. an unrelated woman friend of a child or children. □ **Aunt Sally 1** a game in which players throw sticks or balls at a wooden dummy. **2** the object of an unreasonable attack. [ME f. AF *aunte*, OF *ante*, f. L *amita*]

auntie /ˈɑːntɪ/ n. (also **aunty**) (pl. -ies) colloq. **1** = AUNT. **2** (Auntie) an institution considered to be conservative or cautious, esp. the BBC.

au pair /əʊ ˈpeə(r)/ n. a young foreign person, esp. a woman, helping with housework etc. in exchange for room, board, and pocket money. [F]

aura /ˈɔːrə/ n. (pl. **aurae** /-riː/ or **auras**) **1** the distinctive atmosphere diffused by or attending a person, place, etc. **2** (in mystic or spiritualistic use) a supposed subtle emanation, visible as a sphere of white or coloured light, surrounding the body of a living creature. **3** a subtle emanation or aroma from flowers etc. □ **aural** adj. **auric** adj. [ME f. L f. Gk, = breeze, breath]

aural /ˈɔːr(ə)l/ adj. of or relating to or received by the ear. □ **aurally** adv. [L *auris* ear]

aureate /ˈɔːrɪət/ adj. **1** golden, gold-coloured. **2** resplendent. [ME f. LL *aureatus* f. L *aureus* golden f. *aurum* gold]

aureole /ˈɔːrɪˌəʊl/ n. (also **aureola** /ɔːˈrɪələ/) **1** a halo or circle of light, esp. round the head or body of a portrayed religious figure. **2** a corona round the sun or moon. [ME f. L *aureola* (corona), = golden (crown), fem. of *aureolus* f. *aureus* f. *aurum* gold: *aureole* f. OF f. L *aureola*]

au revoir /əʊ rəˈvwɑː(r)/ int. & n. goodbye (until we meet again). [F]

auricle /ˈɔːrɪk(ə)l/ n. Anat. **1 a** a small muscular pouch on the surface of each atrium of the heart. **b** the atrium itself. **2** the external ear of animals. [AURICULA]

auricula /ɔːˈrɪkjʊlə/ n. a primula, *Primula auricula*, with leaves shaped like bears' ears. [L, dimin. of *auris* ear]

auricular /ɔːˈrɪkjʊlə(r)/ adj. **1** of or relating to the ear or hearing. **2** of or relating to the auricle of the heart. □ **auricularly** adv. [LL *auricularis* (as AURICULA)]

auriferous /ɔːˈrɪfərəs/ adj. naturally bearing gold. [L *aurifer* f. *aurum* gold]

aurochs /ˈɔːrɒks, ˈaʊrɒks/ n. (pl. same) an extinct wild ox, *Bos primigenius*, ancestor of domestic cattle. [G f. OHG *ūrohso* f. *ūr*- urus + *ohso* ox]

aurora /ɔːˈrɔːrə/ n. (pl. **auroras** or **aurorae** /-riː/) **1** a luminous electrical atmospheric phenomenon, usu. of streamers of light in the sky above the northern or southern magnetic pole. **2** poet. the dawn. □ **aurora australis** /ɔːˈstreɪlɪs/ a southern occurrence of aurora. **aurora borealis** /ˌbɒrɪˈeɪlɪs/ a northern occurrence of aurora. □ **auroral** adj. [L, = dawn, goddess of dawn]

auscultation /ˌɔːskəlˈteɪʃ(ə)n/ n. the act of listening, esp. to sounds from the heart, lungs, etc., as a part of medical diagnosis. □ **auscultatory** /-ˈkʌltətərɪ/ adj. [L *auscultatio* f. *auscultare* listen to]

auspice /ˈɔːspɪs/ n. **1** (in pl.) patronage (esp. *under the auspices of*). **2** a forecast. [orig. 'observation of bird-flight in divination': F *auspice* or L *auspicium* f. *auspex* observer of birds f. *avis* bird]

auspicious /ɔːˈspɪʃəs/ adj. **1** of good omen; favourable. **2** prosperous. □ **auspiciously** adv. **auspiciousness** n. [AUSPICE + -OUS]

Aussie /ˈɒzɪ, ˈɒsɪ/ n. & adj. (also **Ossie**, **Ozzie**) colloq. —n. **1** an Australian. **2** Australia. —adj. Australian. [abbr.]

austere /ɒˈstɪə(r), ɔːˈstɪə(r)/ adj. (**austerer**, **austerest**) **1** severely simple. **2** morally strict. **3** harsh, stern. □ **austerely** adv. [ME f. OF f. L *austerus* f. Gk *austēros* severe]

austerity /ɒˈstɛrɪtɪ, ɔːˈstɛrɪtɪ/ n. (pl. -ies) **1** sternness; moral severity. **2** severe simplicity, e.g. of nationwide economies. **3** (esp. in pl.) an austere practice (*the austerities of a monk's life*).

austral /ˈɔːstr(ə)l, ˈɒstr(ə)l/ adj. **1** southern. **2** (Austral) of Australia or Australasia. [ME f. L *australis* f. *Auster* south wind]

Australasian /ˌɒstrəˈleɪʒ(ə)n, -ʃ(ə)n/ adj. of or relating to Australasia, a region consisting of Australia and islands of the SW Pacific. [*Australasia* f. F *Australasie*, formed as *Australia* + *Asia*]

Australian /ɒˈstreɪlɪən/ n. & adj. —n. **1** a native or national of Australia. **2** a person of Australian descent. —adj. of or relating to Australia. □ **Australian bear** a koala bear. **Australian Rules** a form of football played with a Rugby ball by teams of 18. □ **Australianism** n. [F *australien* f. L (as AUSTRAL)]

Austro- /ˈɒstrəʊ/ comb. form Austrian; Austrian and (*Austro-Hungarian*).

autarchy /ˈɔːtɑːkɪ/ n. (pl. **-ies**) **1** absolute sovereignty. **2** despotism. **3** an autarchic country or society. □ **autarchic** /ɔːˈtɑːkɪk/ adj. **autarchical** /ɔːˈtɑːkɪk(ə)l/ adj. [mod.L autarchia (as AUTO-, Gk -arkhia f. arkhō rule)]

autarky /ˈɔːtɑːkɪ/ n. (pl. **-ies**) **1** self-sufficiency, esp. as an economic system. **2** a state etc. run according to such a system. □ **autarkic** /ɔːˈtɑːkɪk/ adj. **autarkical** /ɔːˈtɑːkɪk(ə)l/ adj. **autarkist** n. [Gk autarkeia (as AUTO-, arkeō suffice)]

authentic /ɔːˈθentɪk/ adj. **1** of undisputed origin; genuine. **2** reliable or trustworthy. □ **authentically** adv. **authenticity** /ɔːθenˈtɪsɪtɪ/ n. [ME f. OF autentique f. LL authenticus f. Gk authentikos principal, genuine]

authenticate /ɔːˈθentɪˌkeɪt/ v.tr. **1** establish the truth or genuineness of. **2** validate. □ **authentication** /-ˈkeɪʃ(ə)n/ n. **authenticator** n. [med.L authenticare f. LL authenticus: see AUTHENTIC]

author /ˈɔːθə(r)/ n. (fem. **authoress** /ˈɔːθrɪs, ˌɔːθəˈres/) **1** a writer, esp. of books. **2** the originator of an event, a condition, etc. (the author of all my woes). □ **authorial** /ɔːˈθɔːrɪəl/ adj. [ME f. AF autour, OF f. L auctor f. L augēre auct- increase, originate, promote]

authoritarian /ɔːˌθɒrɪˈteərɪən/ adj. & n. —adj. **1** favouring or enforcing strict obedience to authority. **2** tyrannical or domineering. —n. a person favouring absolute obedience to a constituted authority. □ **authoritarianism** n.

authoritative /ɔːˈθɒrɪtətɪv/ adj. **1** being recognized as true or dependable. **2** (of a person, behaviour, etc.) commanding or self-confident. **3** official; supported by authority (an authoritative document). □ **authoritatively** adv. **authoritativeness** n.

authority /ɔːˈθɒrɪtɪ/ n. (pl. **-ies**) **1** a the power or right to enforce obedience. **b** (often foll. by for, or to + infin.) delegated power. **2** (esp. in pl.) a person or body having authority, esp. political or administrative. **3** a an influence exerted on opinion because of recognized knowledge or expertise. **b** such an influence expressed in a book, quotation, etc. **c** an expert in a subject. [ME f. OF autorité f. L auctoritas f. auctor: see AUTHOR]

authorize /ˈɔːθəˌraɪz/ v.tr. (also **-ise**) **1** sanction. **2** (foll. by to + infin.) a give authority. **b** commission (a person or body). □ **Authorized Version** an English translation of the Bible made in 1611. □ **authorization** /ˌɔːθəraɪˈzeɪʃ(ə)n/ n. [ME f. OF autoriser f. med.L auctorizare f. auctor: see AUTHOR]

authorship /ˈɔːθəʃɪp/ n. **1** the origin of a book or other written work (of unknown authorship). **2** the occupation of writing.

autism /ˈɔːtɪz(ə)m/ n. Psychol. a mental condition characterized by complete self-absorption and a reduced ability to respond to or communicate with the outside world. □ **autistic** /ɔːˈtɪstɪk/ adj. [mod.L autismus (as AUTO-, -ISM)]

auto /ˈɔːtəʊ/ n. (pl. **-os**) US colloq. a motor car. [abbr. of AUTOMOBILE]

auto- /ˈɔːtəʊ/ comb. form (usu. **aut-** before a vowel) **1** self (autism). **2** one's own (autobiography). **3** by oneself or spontaneous (auto-suggestion). **4** by itself or automatic (automobile). [from or after Gk auto- f. autos self]

autobiography /ˌɔːtəbaɪˈɒɡrəfɪ/ n. (pl. **-ies**) **1** a personal account of one's own life, esp. for publication. **2** this as a process or literary form. □ **autobiographer** n. **autobiographic** /ˌɔːtəˌbaɪəˈɡræfɪk/ adj. **autobiographical** /-ˈɡræfɪk(ə)l/ adj.

autochthon /ɔːˈtɒkθ(ə)n/ n. (pl. **autochthons** or **autochthones** /-θəˌniːz/) (in pl.) the original or earliest known inhabitants of a country; aboriginals. □ **autochthonal** adj. **autochthonic** /-ˈθɒnɪk/ adj. **autochthonous** adj. [Gk, = sprung from the earth (as AUTO-, khthōn, -onos earth)]

autoclave /ˈɔːtəˌkleɪv/ n. **1** a strong vessel used for chemical reactions at high pressures and temperatures. **2** a sterilizer using high-pressure steam. [AUTO- + L clavus nail or clavis key]

autocracy /ɔːˈtɒkrəsɪ/ n. (pl. **-ies**) **1** absolute government by one person. **2** the power exercised by such a person. **3** an autocratic country or society. [Gk autokrateia (as AUTOCRAT)]

autocrat /ˈɔːtəˌkræt/ n. **1** an absolute ruler. **2** a dictatorial person. □ **autocratic** /-ˈkrætɪk/ adj. **autocratically** /-ˈkrætɪkəlɪ/ adv. [F autocrate f. Gk autokratēs (as AUTO-, kratos power)]

autocross /ˈɔːtəʊˌkrɒs/ n. motor-racing across country or on unmade roads. [AUTOMOBILE + CROSS-1]

Autocue /ˈɔːtəʊˌkjuː/ n. propr. a device, unseen by the audience, displaying a television script to a speaker or performer as an aid to memory.

auto-da-fé /ˌɔːtəʊdɑːˈfeɪ/ n. (pl. **autos-da-fé** /ˌɔːtəʊz-/) **1** a sentence of punishment by the Spanish Inquisition. **2** the execution of such a sentence, esp. the burning of a heretic. [Port., = act of the faith]

autodidact /ˈɔːtəʊˌdaɪdækt/ n. a self-taught person. □ **autodidactic** /-ˈdæktɪk/ adj. [AUTO- + didact as DIDACTIC]

auto-erotism /ˌɔːtəʊˈerəˌtɪz(ə)m/ n. (also **auto-eroticism** /-ɪˈrɒtɪˌsɪz(ə)m/) Psychol. sexual excitement generated by stimulating one's own body; masturbation. □ **auto-erotic** /-ɪˈrɒtɪk/ adj.

autofocus /ˈɔːtəʊˌfəʊkəs/ n. a device for focusing a camera etc. automatically.

autograph /ˈɔːtəˌɡrɑːf/ n. & v. —n. **1** a a signature, esp. that of a celebrity. **b** handwriting. **2** a manuscript in an author's own handwriting. **3** a document signed by its author. —v.tr. **1** sign (a photograph, autograph album, etc.). **2** write (a letter etc.) by hand. [F autographe or LL autographum f. Gk autographon neut. of autographos (as AUTO-, -GRAPH)]

autoharp /ˈɔːtəˌhɑːp/ n. a kind of zither with a mechanical device to allow the playing of chords.

autoimmune /ˌɔːtəʊɪˈmjuːn/ adj. Med. (of a disease) caused by antibodies produced against substances naturally present in the body. □ **autoimmunity** n.

automat /ˈɔːtəˌmæt/ n. US **1** a slot-machine that dispenses goods. **2** a cafeteria containing slot-machines dispensing food and drink. [G f. automate, formed as AUTOMATION]

automate /ˈɔːtəˌmeɪt/ v.tr. convert to or operate by automation (the ticket office has been automated). [back-form. f. AUTOMATION]

automatic /ˌɔːtəˈmætɪk/ adj. & n. —adj. **1** (of a machine etc., or its function) working by itself, without direct human intervention. **2** a done spontaneously, without conscious intention (an automatic reaction). **b** necessary and inevitable (an automatic penalty). **3** Psychol. performed unconsciously or subconsciously. **4** (of a firearm) that continues firing until the ammunition is exhausted or the pressure on the trigger is released. **5** (of a motor vehicle or its transmission) using gears that change automatically according to speed and acceleration. —*n.* **1** an automatic device, esp. a gun or transmission. **2** *colloq.* a vehicle with automatic transmission. □ **automatic pilot** a device for keeping an aircraft on a set course. □ **automatically** *adv.* **automaticity** /ˌɔːtəməˈtɪsɪtɪ/ *n.* [formed as AUTOMATON + -IC]

automation /ˌɔːtəˈmeɪʃ(ə)n/ *n.* **1** the use of automatic equipment to save mental and manual labour. **2** the automatic control of the manufacture of a product. [irreg. f. AUTOMATIC + -ATION]

automatism /ɔːˈtɒməˌtɪz(ə)m/ *n.* **1** *Psychol.* the performance of actions unconsciously or subconsciously. **2** involuntary action. **3** unthinking routine. [F *automatisme* f. *automate* AUTOMATON]

automaton /ɔːˈtɒmət(ə)n/ *n.* (*pl.* **automata** /-tə/ or **automatons**) **1** a piece of mechanism with concealed motive power. **2** a person who behaves mechanically. [L f. Gk, neut. of *automatos* acting of itself: see AUTO-]

automobile /ˈɔːtəməbiːl/ *n.* US a motor car. [F (as AUTO-, MOBILE)]

automotive /ˌɔːtəˈməʊtɪv/ *adj.* concerned with motor vehicles.

autonomic /ˌɔːtəˈnɒmɪk/ *adj.* esp. *Physiol.* functioning involuntarily. □ **autonomic nervous system** the part of the nervous system responsible for control of the bodily functions not consciously directed, e.g. heartbeat. [AUTONOMY + -IC]

autonomous /ɔːˈtɒnəməs/ *adj.* **1** having self-government. **2** acting independently or having the freedom to do so. □ **autonomously** *adv.* [Gk *autonomos* (as AUTONOMY)]

autonomy /ɔːˈtɒnəmɪ/ *n.* (*pl.* **-ies**) **1** the right of self-government. **2** personal freedom. **3** freedom of the will. **4** a self-governing community. □ **autonomist** *n.* [Gk *autonomia* f. *autos* self + *nomos* law]

autopilot /ˈɔːtəʊˌpaɪlət/ *n.* an automatic pilot. [abbr.]

autopsy /ˈɔːtɒpsɪ, ɔːˈtɒpsɪ/ *n.* (*pl.* **-ies**) **1** a post-mortem examination. **2** any critical analysis. **3** a personal inspection. [F *autopsie* or mod.L *autopsia* f. Gk f. *autoptēs* eye-witness]

auto-suggestion /ˌɔːtəʊsəˈdʒestʃ(ə)n/ *n.* a hypnotic or subconscious suggestion made by a person to himself or herself and affecting behaviour.

autumn /ˈɔːtəm/ *n.* **1** the third season of the year, when crops and fruits are gathered, and leaves fall. **2** *Astron.* the period from the autumnal equinox to the winter solstice. **3** a time of maturity or incipient decay. [ME f. OF *autompne* f. L *autumnus*]

autumnal /ɔːˈtʌmn(ə)l/ *adj.* **1** of, characteristic of, or appropriate to autumn (*autumnal colours*). **2** occurring in autumn (*autumnal equinox*). [L *autumnalis* (as AUTUMN, -AL)]

auxiliary /ɔːgˈzɪljərɪ/ *adj. & n.* —*adj.* **1** (of a person or thing) that gives help. **2** (of services or equipment) subsidiary, additional. —*n.* (*pl.* **-ies**) **1** an auxiliary person or thing. **2** (in *pl.*) *Mil.* auxiliary troops. **3** *Gram.* an auxiliary verb. □ **auxiliary troops** *Mil.* foreign or allied troops in a belligerent nation's service. **auxiliary verb** *Gram.* one used in forming tenses, moods, and voices of other verbs. [L *auxiliarius* f. *auxilium* help]

avail /əˈveɪl/ *v. & n.* —*v.* **1** *tr.* help, benefit. **2** *refl.* (foll. by *of*) take advantage of. **3** *intr.* **a** provide help. **b** be of use or profit. —*n.* (usu. in *neg.* or *interrog.* phrases) use, profit (*of no avail*; *of what avail?*). [ME f. obs. *vail* (v.) f. OF *valoir* be worth f. L *valēre*]

available /əˈveɪləb(ə)l/ *adj.* (often foll. by *to, for*) **1** capable of being used; at one's disposal. **2** within one's reach. □ **availability** /-ˈbɪlɪtɪ/ *n.* **availableness** *n.* **availably** *adv.* [ME f. AVAIL + -ABLE]

avalanche /ˈævəlɑːnʃ/ *n.* **1** a mass of snow and ice, tumbling rapidly down a mountain. **2** a sudden appearance or arrival of anything in large quantities (*faced with an avalanche of work*). [F, alt. of dial. *lavanche* after *avaler* descend]

avant-garde /ˌævãˈgɑːd/ *n. & adj.* —*n.* pioneers or innovators esp. in art and literature. —*adj.* (of ideas etc.) new, progressive. □ **avant-gardism** *n.* **avant-gardist** *n.* [F, = vanguard]

avarice /ˈævərɪs/ *n.* extreme greed for money or gain; cupidity. □ **avaricious** /ˌævəˈrɪʃəs/ *adj.* **avariciously** /-ˈrɪʃəslɪ/ *adv.* **avariciousness** /-ˈrɪʃəsnɪs/ *n.* [ME f. OF f. L *avaritia* f. *avarus* greedy]

avatar /ˈævətɑː(r)/ *n.* **1** (in Hindu mythology) the descent of a deity or released soul to earth in bodily form. **2** incarnation; manifestation. [Skr. *avatāra* descent f. *áva* down + *tṛ-* pass over]

ave /ˈɑːveɪ, ˈɑːvɪ/ *int. & n.* —*int.* **1** welcome. **2** farewell. —*n.* (in full **Ave Maria**) a prayer to the Virgin Mary, the opening line from Luke 1:28. [ME f. L, 2nd sing. imper. of *avēre* fare well]

avenge /əˈvendʒ/ *v.tr.* **1** inflict retribution on behalf of (a person, a violated right, etc.). **2** take vengeance for (an injury). □ **be avenged** avenge oneself. □ **avenger** *n.* [ME f. OF *avengier* f. *à* to + *vengier* f. L *vindicare* vindicate]

avenue /ˈævənjuː/ *n.* **1 a** a broad road or street, often with trees at regular intervals along its sides. **b** a tree-lined approach to a country house. **2** a way of approaching or dealing with something (*explored every avenue to find an answer*). [F, fem. past part. of *avenir* f. L *advenire* come to]

aver /əˈvɜː(r)/ *v.tr.* (**averred**, **averring**) assert, affirm. **averment** *n.* [ME f. OF *averer* (as AD-, *verus* true)]

average /ˈævərɪdʒ/ *n., adj., & v.* —*n.* **1 a** the usual amount, extent, or rate. **b** the ordinary standard. **2** an amount obtained by dividing the total of given amounts by the number of amounts in the set. **3** *Law* the distribution of loss resulting from damage to a ship or cargo. —*adj.* **1** usual, ordinary. **2** estimated or calculated by average. —*v.tr.* **1** amount on average to (*the sale of the product averaged one hundred a day*). **2** do on average (*averages six hours' work a day*). **3 a** estimate the average of. **b** estimate the general standard of. □ **average out** result in an average. **batting average 1** *Cricket* a batsman's runs scored per completed innings. **2** *Baseball* a batter's safe hits per time at bat. **bowling average** *Cricket* a bowler's conceded runs per wicket taken. **law of averages** the principle that if one of two extremes occurs the other will also tend to. **on** (or **on an**) **average** as an average rate or estimate. □ **averagely** *adv.* [F *avarie* damage to ship or cargo (see sense 3), f.

It. *avaria* f. Arab. ʿ*awārīya* damaged goods f. ʿ*awār* damage at sea, loss: -*age* after *damage*]

averse /əˈvɜːs/ *predic.adj.* opposed, disinclined (*was not averse to helping me*). [L *aversus* (as AVERT)]

aversion /əˈvɜːʃ(ə)n/ *n.* **1** a dislike or unwillingness (*has an aversion to hard work*). **2** an object of dislike (*my pet aversion*). □ **aversion therapy** therapy designed to make a subject averse to an existing habit. [F *aversion* or L *aversio* (as AVERT, -ION)]

avert /əˈvɜːt/ *v.tr.* (often foll. by *from*) **1** turn away (one's eyes or thoughts). **2** prevent or ward off (an undesirable occurrence). □ **avertable** *adj.* **avertible** *adj.* [ME f. L *avertere* (as AB-, *vertere* vers- turn): partly f. OF *avertir* f. Rmc]

Avesta /əˈvestə/ *n.* (usu. prec. by *the*) the sacred writings of Zoroastrianism. [Pers.]

Avestan /əˈvest(ə)n/ *adj.* & *n.* —*adj.* of or relating to the Avesta. —*n.* the ancient Iranian language of the Avesta.

avian /ˈeɪvɪən/ *adj.* of or relating to birds. [L *avis* bird]

aviary /ˈeɪvɪərɪ/ *n.* (*pl.* -**ies**) a large enclosure or building for keeping birds. [L *aviarium* (as AVIAN, -ARY¹)]

aviate /ˈeɪvɪeɪt/ *v.* **1** *intr.* fly in an aeroplane. **2** *tr.* pilot (an aeroplane). [back-form. f. AVIATION]

aviation /ˌeɪvɪˈeɪʃ(ə)n/ *n.* **1** the skill or practice of operating aircraft. **2** aircraft manufacture. [F f. L *avis* bird]

aviator /ˈeɪvɪˌeɪtə(r)/ *n.* (*fem.* **aviatrix** /ˈeɪvɪətrɪks/) an airman or airwoman. [F *aviateur* f. L *avis* bird]

aviculture /ˈeɪvɪˌkʌltʃə(r)/ *n.* the rearing and keeping of birds. □ **aviculturist** /-ˈkʌltʃərɪst/ *n.* [L *avis* bird, after AGRICULTURE]

avid /ˈævɪd/ *adj.* (usu. foll. by *of*, *for*) eager, greedy. □ **avidity** /əˈvɪdɪtɪ/ *n.* **avidly** *adv.* [F *avide* or L *avidus* f. *avēre* crave]

avionics /ˌeɪvɪˈɒnɪks/ *n.* electronics as applied to aviation.

avocado /ˌævəˈkɑːdəʊ/ *n.* (*pl.* -**os**) **1** (in full **avocado pear**) a pear-shaped fruit with smooth oily edible flesh and a large stone. **2** the tropical evergreen tree, *Persea americana*, bearing this fruit. **3** the light green colour of the flesh of this fruit. [Sp., = advocate (substituted for Aztec *ahuacatl*)]

avocation /ˌævəˈkeɪʃ(ə)n/ *n.* **1** a minor occupation. **2** *colloq.* a vocation or calling. [L *avocatio* f. *avocare* call away]

avocet /ˈævəˌset/ *n.* any wading bird of the genus *Recurvirostra* with long legs and a long slender upward-curved bill. [F *avocette* f. It. *avosetta*]

avoid /əˈvɔɪd/ *v.tr.* **1** keep away or refrain from (a thing, person, or action). **2** escape; evade. **3** *Law* **a** nullify (a decree or contract). **b** quash (a sentence). □ **avoidable** *adj.* **avoidably** *adv.* **avoidance** *n.* **avoider** *n.* [AF *avoider*, OF *evuider* clear out, get quit of, f. *vuide* empty, VOID]

avoirdupois /ˌævədəˈpɔɪz/ *n.* (in full **avoir-dupois weight**) a system of weights based on a pound of 16 ounces or 7,000 grains. [ME f. OF *aveir de peis* goods of weight f. *aveir* f. L *habēre* have + *peis* (see POISE)]

avouch /əˈvaʊtʃ/ *v.tr.* & *intr.* archaic or *rhet.* guarantee, affirm, confess. □ **avouchment** *n.* [ME f. OF *avochier* f. L *advocare* (as AD-, *vocare* call)]

avow /əˈvaʊ/ *v.tr.* **1** admit, confess. **2 a** *refl.* admit that one is (*avowed himself the author*). **b** (as **avowed** *adj.*) admitted (*the avowed author*). □ **avowal** *n.* **avowedly** /əˈvaʊɪdlɪ/ *adv.* [ME f. OF *avouer* acknowledge f. L *advocare* (as AD-, *vocare* call)]

avuncular /əˈvʌŋkjʊlə(r)/ *adj.* like or of an uncle; kind and friendly, esp. towards a younger person. [L *avunculus* maternal uncle, dimin. of *avus* grandfather]

AWACS /ˈeɪwæks/ *n.* a long-range radar system for detecting enemy aircraft. [abbr. of airborne warning and control system]

await /əˈweɪt/ *v.tr.* **1** wait for. **2** (of an event or thing) be in store for (*a surprise awaits you*). [ME f. AF *awaitier*, OF *aguaitier* (as AD-, *waitier* WAIT)]

awake /əˈweɪk/ *v.* & *adj.* —*v.* (*past* **awoke** /əˈwəʊk/; *past part.* **awoken** /əˈwəʊkən/) **1** *intr.* **a** cease to sleep. **b** become active. **2** *intr.* (foll. by *to*) become aware of. **3** *tr.* rouse from sleep. —*predic.adj.* **1 a** not asleep. **b** vigilant. **2** (foll. by *to*) aware of. [OE *āwæcnan*, *āwacian* (as A-², WAKE¹)]

awaken /əˈweɪkən/ *v.tr.* & *intr.* **1** = AWAKE *v.* **2** *tr.* (often foll. by *to*) make aware. [OE *onwæcnan* etc. (as A-², WAKEN)]

award /əˈwɔːd/ *v.* & *n.* —*v.tr.* **1** give or order to be given as a payment, penalty, or prize (*awarded him a knighthood; was awarded damages*). **2** grant, assign. —*n.* **1** a payment, penalty, or prize awarded. **2** a judicial decision. □ **awarder** *n.* [ME f. AF *awarder*, ult. f. Gmc: see WARD]

aware /əˈweə(r)/ *predic.adj.* **1** (often foll. by *of*, or *that* + clause) conscious; not ignorant; having knowledge. **2** well-informed. □ **awareness** *n.* [OE *gewær*]

■ **Usage** This word is also found in *attrib.* use in sense 2, as in *a very aware person*, but this should be avoided in formal contexts.

awash /əˈwɒʃ/ *predic.adj.* **1** level with the surface of water, so that it just washes over. **2** flooded.

away /əˈweɪ/ *adv.* & *adj.* —*adv.* **1** to or at a distance from the place, person, or thing in question (*go away; give away; look away; they are away; 5 miles away*). **2** towards or into non-existence (*sounds die away; idled their time away*). **3** constantly, persistently, continuously (*work away; laugh away*). **4** without delay (*ask away*). —*adj. Sport* played on an opponent's ground etc. (*away match; away win*). [OE *onweg*, *aweg* on one's way f. A² + WAY]

awe /ɔː/ *n.* & *v.* —*n.* reverential fear or wonder (*stand in awe of*). —*v.tr.* inspire with awe. □ **awe-inspiring** causing awe or wonder; amazing, magnificent. [ME *age* f. ON *agi* f. Gmc]

aweigh /əˈweɪ/ *predic.adj. Naut.* (of an anchor) clear of the sea or river bed; hanging. [A² + WEIGH]

awesome /ˈɔːsəm/ *adj.* **1** inspiring awe; dreaded. **2** *colloq.* outstanding, marvellous, excellent. □ **awesomely** *adv.* **awesomeness** *n.* [AWE + -SOME¹]

awestricken /ˈɔːˌstrɪkən/ *adj.* (also **awestruck** /-strʌk/) struck or afflicted with awe.

awful /ˈɔːfʊl/ *adj.* **1** *colloq.* **a** unpleasant or horrible (*awful weather*). **b** poor in quality; very bad (*has awful writing*). **c** (*attrib.*) excessive; large (*an awful lot of money*). **2** *poet.* inspiring awe. □ **awfulness** *n.* [AWE + -FUL]

awfully /'ɔːfəlɪ, -flɪ/ *adv.* **1** *colloq.* in an unpleasant, bad, or horrible way (*he played awfully*). **2** *colloq.* very (*she's awfully pleased*; *thanks awfully*).

awhile /ə'waɪl/ *adv.* for a short time. [OE *āne hwīle* a while]

awkward /'ɔːkwəd/ *adj.* **1** ill-adapted for use; causing difficulty in use. **2** clumsy or bungling. **3 a** embarrassed (*felt awkward about it*). **b** embarrassing (*an awkward situation*). **4** difficult to deal with (*an awkward customer*). □ **awkwardly** *adv.* **awkwardness** *n.* [obs. *awk* backhanded, untoward (ME f. ON *afugr* turned the wrong way) + -WARD]

awl *n.* a small pointed tool used for piercing holes, esp. in leather. [OE *æl*]

awn *n.* a stiff bristle growing from the grain-sheath of grasses, or terminating a leaf etc. □ **awned** *adj.* [ME f. ON *ögn*]

awning /'ɔːnɪŋ/ *n.* a sheet of canvas or similar material stretched on a frame and used to shade a shop window, doorway, ship's deck, or other area from the sun or rain. [17th c. (Naut.): orig. uncert.]

awoke *past* of AWAKE.

awoken *past part.* of AWAKE.

AWOL /'eɪwɒl/ *abbr. colloq.* absent without leave.

awry /ə'raɪ/ *adv.* & *adj.* —*adv.* **1** crookedly or askew. **2** improperly or amiss. —*predic.adj.* crooked; deviant or unsound (*his theory is awry*). □ **go awry** go or do wrong. [ME f. A² + WRY]

axe /æks/ *n.* & *v.* (US **ax**) —*n.* **1** a chopping-tool, usu. of iron with a steel edge and wooden handle. **2** the drastic cutting of expenditure, staff, etc. —*v.tr.* (**axing**) **1** cut (esp. costs or services) drastically. **2** remove or dismiss. □ **an axe to grind** private ends to serve. [OE *æx* f. Gmc]

axial /'æksɪəl/ *adj.* **1** forming or belonging to an axis. **2** round an axis (*axial rotation*; *axial symmetry*). □ **axiality** (/ˌæksɪ'ælɪtɪ/) *n.* **axially** *adv.*

axil /'æksɪl/ *n.* the upper angle between a leaf and the stem it springs from, or between a branch and the trunk. [L *axilla*: see AXILLA]

axilla /æk'sɪlə/ *n.* (pl. **axillae** /-liː/) **1** *Anat.* the armpit. **2** an axil. [L, = armpit, dimin. of *ala* wing]

axillary /æk'sɪlərɪ/ *adj.* **1** *Anat.* of or relating to the armpit. **2** *Bot.* in or growing from the axil.

axiom /'æksɪəm/ *n.* **1** an established or widely accepted principle. **2** a self-evident truth. [F *axiome* or L *axioma* f. Gk *axiōma axiōmat-* f. *axios* worthy]

axiomatic /ˌæksɪə'mætɪk/ *adj.* **1** self-evident. **2** relating to or containing axioms. □ **axiomatically** *adv.* [Gk *axiōmatikos* (as AXIOM)]

axis /'æksɪs/ *n.* (pl. **axes** /-siːz/) **1 a** an imaginary line about which a body rotates or about which a plane figure is conceived as generating a solid. **b** a line which divides a regular figure symmetrically. **2** *Math.* a fixed reference line for the measurement of coordinates etc. **3** *Bot.* the central column of an inflorescence or other growth. **4** (**the Axis**) the alliance of Germany and Italy formed before and during the war of 1939–45, later extended to include Japan. [L, = axle, pivot]

axle /'æks(ə)l/ *n.* a rod or spindle (either fixed or rotating) on which a wheel or group of wheels is fixed. [orig. *axle-tree* f. ME *axel-tre* f. ON *öxull-tré*]

axolotl /'æksəlɒt(ə)l/ *n.* an aquatic newtlike salamander, *Ambystoma mexicanum*, from Mexico. [Nahuatl f. *atl* water + *xolotl* servant]

ayatollah /ˌaɪə'tɒlə/ *n.* a Shiite religious leader in Iran. [Pers. f. Arab., = token of God]

aye¹ /aɪ/ *adv.* & *n.* (also **ay**) —*adv.* **1** *archaic* or *dial.* yes. **2** (in voting) I assent. **3** (as aye aye) *Naut.* a response accepting an order. —*n.* an affirmative answer or assent, esp. in voting. [16th c.: prob. f. first pers. personal pron. expressing assent]

aye² /eɪ/ *adv.* *archaic* ever, always. □ **for aye** for ever. [ME f. ON *ei, ey* f. Gmc]

Aylesbury /'eɪlzbərɪ/ *n.* (pl. **Aylesburys**) **1** a bird of a breed of large white domestic ducks. **2** this breed. [*Aylesbury* in S. England]

Ayrshire /'eəʃə(r)/ *n.* **1** an animal of a mainly white breed of dairy cattle. **2** this breed. [name of a former Scottish county]

azalea /ə'zeɪlɪə/ *n.* any of various flowering deciduous shrubs of the genus *Rhododendron*, with large pink, purple, white, or yellow flowers. [mod.L f. Gk, fem. of *azaleos* dry (from the dry soil in which it was believed to flourish)]

azimuth /'æzɪməθ/ *n.* **1** the angular distance from a north or south point of the horizon to the intersection with the horizon of a vertical circle passing through a given celestial body. **2** the horizontal angle or direction of a compass bearing. □ **azimuthal** /-'mjuː:θ(ə)l/ *adj.* [ME f. OF *azimut* f. Arab. *as-sumūt* f. *al* the + *sumūt* pl. of *samt* way, direction]

Aztec /'æztek/ *n.* & *adj.* —*n.* **1** a member of the native people dominant in Mexico before the Spanish conquest of the 16th century. **2** the language of the Aztecs. —*adj.* of the Aztecs or their language. [F *Aztèque* or Sp. *Azteca* f. Nahuatl *aztecatl* men of the north]

azuki var. of ADZUKI.

azure /'æʒə(r), -zjə(r), 'eɪ-/ *n.* & *adj.* —*n.* **1 a** a deep sky-blue colour. **b** *Heraldry* blue. **2** *poet.* the clear sky. —*adj.* of the colour azure. [ME f. OF *asur, azur,* f. med.L *azzurum, azolum* f. Arab. *al* the + *lāzaward* f. Pers. *lāžward* lapis lazuli]

B[1] /biː/ *n.* (also **b**) (*pl.* **Bs** or **B's**) **1** the second letter of the alphabet. **2** *Mus.* the seventh note of the diatonic scale of C major. **3** the second hypothetical person or example. **4** the second highest class or category (of roads, academic marks, etc.). **5** *Algebra* (usu. **b**) the second known quantity. **6** a human blood type.

B[2] *symb. Chem.* the element boron.

B[3] *abbr.* (also **B.**) **1** Bachelor. **2** black (pencil-lead).

b. *abbr.* **1** born. **2** *Cricket* **a** bowled by. **b** bye.

BA *abbr.* Bachelor of Arts.

Ba *symb. Chem.* the element barium.

baa /bɑː/ *v. & n.* —*v.intr.* (**baas, baaed** or **baa'd**) (esp. of a sheep) bleat. —*n.* (*pl.* **baas**) the cry of a sheep or lamb. [imit.]

baba /ˈbɑːbɑː/ *n.* (in full **rum baba**) a small rich sponge cake, usu. soaked in rum-flavoured syrup. [F f. Pol.]

babble /ˈbæb(ə)l/ *v. & n.* —*v.* **1** *intr.* **a** talk in an inarticulate or incoherent manner. **b** chatter excessively or irrelevantly. **c** (of a stream etc.) murmur, trickle. **2** *tr.* repeat foolishly; divulge through chatter. —*n.* **1 a** incoherent speech. **b** idle, or childish talk. **2** the murmur of voices, water, etc. □ **babblement** *n.* [ME f. MLG *babbelen*, or imit.]

babbler /ˈbæbl(ə)r/ *n.* **1** a chatterer. **2** a person who reveals secrets.

babe /beɪb/ *n.* **1** *literary* a baby. **2** an innocent or helpless person (*babes and sucklings; babes in the wood*). **3** *US sl.* a young woman (often as a form of address). [ME: imit. of child's *ba, ba*]

babel /ˈbeɪb(ə)l/ *n.* **1** a confused noise, esp. of voices. **2** a noisy assembly. **3** a scene of confusion. [ME f. Heb. *Bābel* Babylon f. Akkad. *bab ili* gate of god (with ref. to the biblical account of the tower that was built to reach heaven but ended in chaos when Jehovah confused the builders' speech: see Gen. 11)]

baboon /bəˈbuːn/ *n.* any of various large Old World monkeys of the genus *Papio*, having a long doglike snout and naked callosities on the buttocks. [ME f. OF *babuin* or med.L *babewynus*, of unkn. orig.]

babu /ˈbɑːbuː/ *n.* (also **baboo**) *Ind.* **1** a title of respect, esp. to Hindus. **2** *derog.* formerly, an English-writing Indian clerk. [Hindi *bābū*]

babushka /bəˈbuːʃkə/ *n.* a headscarf tied under the chin. [Russ., = grandmother]

baby /ˈbeɪbɪ/ *n. & v.* —*n.* (*pl.* **-ies**) **1** a very young child or infant, esp. one not yet able to walk. **2** an unduly childish person (*is a baby about injections*). **3** the youngest member of a family, team, etc. **4** (often *attrib.*) **a** a young or newly born animal. **b** a thing that is small of its kind (*baby car; baby rose*). **5** *sl.* a young woman; a sweetheart (often as a form of address). **6** one's own responsibility, invention, concern, achievement, etc., regarded in a personal way. —*v.tr.* (**-ies, -ied**) **1** treat like a baby. **2** pamper. □ **baby boom** *colloq.* a temporary marked increase in the birthrate. **baby boomer** a person born during a baby boom, esp. after the war of 1939–45. **Baby Buggy** (*pl.* **-ies**) *Brit. propr.* a kind of child's collapsible pushchair. **baby grand** the smallest size of grand piano. **baby-snatcher** *colloq.* **1** a person who kidnaps babies. **2** *sl.* a person amorously attached to a much younger person. **baby-talk** childish talk used by or to young children. **baby-walker** a wheeled frame in which a baby learns to walk. **carry** (or **hold**) **the baby** bear unwelcome responsibility. □ **babyhood** *n.* [ME, formed as BABE, -Y[2]]

babyish /ˈbeɪbɪɪʃ/ *adj.* **1** childish, simple. **2** immature. □ **babyishly** *adv.* **babyishness** *n.*

babysit /ˈbeɪbɪsɪt/ *v.intr.* (**-sitting**; *past* and *past part.* **-sat**) look after a child or children while the parents are out. □ **babysitter** *n.*

baccalaureate /ˌbækəˈlɔːrɪət/ *n.* **1** the university degree of bachelor. **2** an examination intended to qualify successful candidates for higher education. [F *baccalauréat* or med.L *baccalaureatus* f. *baccalaureus* bachelor]

baccarat /ˈbækərɑː/ *n.* a gambling card-game played by punters in turn against the banker. [F]

bacchanal /ˈbækən(ə)l/ *n. & adj.* —*n.* **1** a wild and drunken revelry. **2** a drunken reveller. —*adj.* **1** of or like Bacchus, the Greek or Roman god of wine, or his rites. **2** riotous, roistering. [L *bacchanalis* f. *Bacchus* god of wine f. Gk *Bakkhos*]

Bacchanalia /ˌbækəˈneɪlɪə/ *n.pl.* **1** the Roman festival of Bacchus. **2** (**bacchanalia**) a drunken revelry. □ **Bacchanalian** *adj. & n.* [L, neut. pl. of *bacchanalis*: see BACCHANAL]

bacchant /ˈbækənt/ *n. & adj.* —*n.* (*pl.* **bacchants** or **bacchantes** /bəˈkæntiːz/; *fem.* **bacchante** /bəˈkæntɪ/) **1** a priest, worshipper, or follower of Bacchus. **2** a drunken reveller. —*adj.* **1** of or like Bacchus or his rites. **2** riotous, roistering. □ **bacchantic** /bəˈkæntɪk/ *adj.* [F *bacchante* f. L *bacchari* celebrate Bacchanal rites]

Bacchic /ˈbækɪk/ *adj.* = BACCHANAL *adj.* [L *bacchicus* f. Gk *bakkhikos* of Bacchus]

baccy /ˈbækɪ/ *n.* (*pl.* **-ies**) *Brit. colloq.* tobacco. [abbr.]

bachelor /ˈbætʃələ(r)/ *n.* **1** an unmarried man. **2** a man or woman who has taken the degree of Bachelor of Arts or Science etc. □ **bachelorhood** *n.* **bachelorship** *n.* [ME & OF *bacheler* aspirant to knighthood, of uncert. orig.]

bacillary /bəˈsɪlərɪ/ *adj.* relating to or caused by bacilli.

bacillus /bəˈsɪləs/ *n.* (*pl.* **bacilli** /-laɪ/) **1** any rod-shaped bacterium. **2** (usu. in *pl.*) any pathogenic bacterium. [LL, dimin. of L *baculus* stick]

back *n., adv., v., & adj.* —*n.* **1 a** the rear surface of the human body from the shoulders to the hips. **b** the corresponding upper surface of an animal's body. **c** the spine (*fell and broke his back*). **2 a** any surface regarded as corresponding to the human back, e.g. of the head or hand, or of a chair. **b** the part of a garment that covers the back. **3 a** the less active or visible or important part of something functional, e.g. of a knife or a piece of paper. **b** the side or part normally away from the spectator or the direction of motion or attention, e.g. of a car, house, or room (*stood at the back*). **4 a** a defensive player in field games. **b** this position. —*adv.* **1** to the rear; away from what is considered to be the front (*go back a bit; ran off without looking back*). **2 a** in or into an earlier or normal position or condition (*came back late; went back home; put it back on the shelf*). **b** in return (*pay back*). **3** in or into the past (*back in June; three years back*). **4** at a distance (*stand back from the road*). **5** in check (*hold him back*). **6** (foll. by *of*) US behind (*was back of the house*). —*v.* **1** *tr.* **a** help with moral or financial support. **b** bet on the success of (a horse etc.). **2** *tr.* & *intr.* move, or cause (a vehicle etc.) to move, backwards. **3** *tr.* **a** put or serve as a back, background, or support to. **b** *Mus.* accompany. **4** *tr.* lie at the back of (*a beach backed by steep cliffs*). **5** *intr.* (of the wind) move round in an anticlockwise direction. —*adj.* **1** situated behind, esp. as remote or subsidiary (*backstreet; back teeth*). **2** of or relating to the past; not current (*back pay; back issue*). **3** reversed (*back flow*). □ **at the back of one's mind** remembered but not consciously thought of. **back and forth** to and fro. **back bench** a back-bencher's seat in the House of Commons. **back-bencher** a member of Parliament not holding a senior office. **back-boiler** *Brit.* a boiler behind and integral with a domestic fire. **back country** esp. *Austral.* & *NZ* an area away from settled districts. **back door** a secret or ingenious means of gaining an objective. **back-door** *adj.* (of an activity) clandestine, underhand (*a back-door deal*). **back down** withdraw one's claim or point of view etc.; concede defeat in an argument etc. **back-fill** refill an excavated hole with the material dug out of it. **back-formation 1** the formation of a word from its seeming derivative (e.g. *laze* from *lazy*). **2** a word formed in this way. **back number 1** an issue of a periodical earlier than the current one. **2** *sl.* an out-of-date person or thing. **the back of beyond** a very remote or inaccessible place. **back off 1** draw back, retreat. **2** abandon one's intention, stand, etc. **back on** to have its back adjacent to (*the house backs on to a field*). **back out** (often foll. by *of*) withdraw from a commitment. **back passage** *colloq.* the rectum. **back-pedal** (-**pedalled**, -**pedalling**; US -**pedaled**, -**pedaling**) **1** pedal backwards on a bicycle etc. **2** reverse one's previous action or opinion. **back-projection** the projection of a picture from behind a translucent screen for viewing or filming. **back room** (often with hyphen *attrib.*) a place where secret work is done. **back seat** an inferior position or status. **back-seat driver** a person who is eager to advise without responsibility (orig. of a passenger in a car etc.). **back slang** slang using words spelt backwards (e.g. *yob*). **back-stop** = LONGSTOP. **back talk** US = BACKCHAT. **back to front 1** with the back at the front and the front at the back. **2** in disorder. **back up 1** give (esp. moral) support to. **2** *Computing* make a spare copy of (data, a disk, etc.). **3** (of running water) accumulate behind an obstruction. **4** reverse (a vehicle) into a desired position. **5** US form a queue of vehicles etc., esp. in congested traffic. **get** (or **put**) **a person's back up** annoy or anger a person. **get off a person's back** stop troubling a person. **go back on** fail to honour (a promise or commitment). **put one's back into** approach (a task etc.) with vigour. **turn one's back on 1** abandon. **2** ignore. **with one's back to** (or **up against**) **the wall** in a desperate situation; hard-pressed. □ **backer** *n.* (in sense 1 of *v.*). **backless** *adj.* [OE *bæc* f. Gmc]

backache /ˈbækeɪk/ *n.* a (usu. prolonged) pain in one's back.

backbite /ˈbækbaɪt/ *v.tr.* slander; speak badly of. □ **backbiter** *n.*

backblocks /ˈbækblɒks/ *n.pl. Austral.* & *NZ* land in the remote and sparsely inhabited interior.

backbone /ˈbækbəʊn/ *n.* **1** the spine. **2** the main support of a structure. **3** firmness of character.

backchat /ˈbæktʃæt/ *n. Brit. colloq.* the practice of replying rudely or impudently.

backcloth /ˈbækklɒθ/ *n. Brit. Theatr.* a painted cloth at the back of the stage as a main part of the scenery.

backcomb /ˈbækkəʊm/ *v.tr.* comb (the hair) towards the scalp to make it look thicker.

backdate /bækˈdeɪt/ *v.tr.* **1** put an earlier date to (an agreement etc.) than the actual one. **2** make retrospectively valid.

backdrop /ˈbækdrɒp/ *n.* = BACKCLOTH.

backfire *v.* & *n.* —*v.intr.* /bækˈfaɪə(r)/ **1** undergo a mistimed explosion in the cylinder or exhaust of an internal-combustion engine. **2** (of a plan etc.) rebound adversely on the originator; have the opposite effect to what was intended. —*n.* /ˈbækfaɪə(r)/ an instance of backfiring.

backgammon /ˈbækˌgæmən, bækˈgæmən/ *n.* a game for two played on a board with pieces moved according to throws of the dice. [BACK + ME *gamen* GAME¹]

background /ˈbækgraʊnd/ *n.* **1** part of a scene, picture, or description, that serves as a setting to the chief figures or objects and foreground. **2** an inconspicuous or obscure position (*kept in the background*). **3** a person's education, knowledge, or social circumstances. **4** explanatory or contributory information or circumstances.

backhand /ˈbækhænd/ *n. Tennis* etc. **1** a stroke played with the back of the hand turned towards the opponent. **2** (*attrib.*) of or made with a backhand (*backhand volley*).

backhanded /bækˈhændɪd/ *adj.* **1** (of a blow etc.) delivered with the back of the hand, or in a direction opposite to the usual one. **2** indirect; ambiguous (*a backhanded compliment*). **3** = BACKHAND *adj.*

backhander /ˈbækˌhændə(r)/ *n.* **1 a** a backhand stroke. **b** a backhanded blow. **2** *colloq.* an indirect attack. **3** *Brit. sl.* a bribe.

backing /ˈbækɪŋ/ *n.* **1 a** support. **b** a body of supporters. **c** material used to form a back or support. **2** musical accompaniment, esp. to a singer.

backlash /ˈbæklæʃ/ *n.* **1** an excessive or marked adverse reaction. **2 a** a sudden recoil or reaction between parts of a mechanism. **b** excessive play between such parts.

backlit /ˈbæklɪt/ *adj.* (esp. in photography) illuminated from behind.

backlog /ˈbæklɒg/ *n.* **1** arrears of uncompleted work etc. **2** a reserve; reserves (*a backlog of goodwill*).

backmost /ˈbækməʊst/ adj. furthest back.

backpack /ˈbækpæk/ n. & v. —n. a rucksack. —v.intr. travel or hike with a backpack. □ **backpacker** n.

backrest /ˈbækrest/ n. a support for the back.

backsheesh var. of BAKSHEESH.

backside /bækˈsaɪd, ˈbæk-/ n. colloq. the buttocks.

backsight /ˈbæksaɪt/ n. the sight of a rifle etc. that is nearer the stock.

backslash /ˈbækslæʃ/ n. a backward-sloping diagonal line; a reverse solidus (\).

backslide /ˈbækslaɪd/ v.intr. (past **-slid**; past part. **-slid** or **-slidden**) relapse into bad ways or error. □ **backslider** n.

backspace /ˈbækspeɪs/ v.intr. move a typewriter carriage etc. back one or more spaces.

backspin /ˈbækspɪn/ n. a backward spin imparted to a ball causing it to fly off at an angle on hitting a surface.

backstage /bækˈsteɪdʒ/ adv. & adj. —adv. **1** Theatr. out of view of the audience, esp. in the wings or dressing-rooms. **2** not known to the public. —adj. /also ˈbæk-/ that is backstage; concealed.

backstairs /ˈbæksteəz/ n.pl. **1** stairs at the back or side of a building. **2** (also **backstair**) (attrib.) denoting underhand or clandestine activity.

backstreet /ˈbækstriːt/ n. **1** a street in a quiet part of a town, away from the main streets. **2** (attrib.) denoting illicit or illegal activity (a backstreet abortion).

backstroke /ˈbækstrəʊk/ n. a swimming stroke performed on the back.

backtrack /ˈbæktræk/ v.intr. **1** retrace one's steps. **2** reverse one's previous action or opinion.

backup /ˈbækʌp/ n. **1** moral or technical support (called for extra backup). **2** a reserve. **3** Computing (often attrib.) **a** the procedure for making security copies of data (backup facilities). **b** the copy itself. **4** US a queue of vehicles etc., esp. in congested traffic. □ **backup light** US a reversing light.

backveld /ˈbækvelt/ n. S.Afr. remote country districts. □ **backvelder** n.

backward /ˈbækwəd/ adv. & adj. —adv. = BACKWARDS. —adj. **1** directed to the rear or starting-point (a backward look). **2** reversed. **3** mentally retarded or slow. **4** reluctant, shy, unassertive. □ **backwardness** n. [earlier abackward, assoc. with BACK]

backwards /ˈbækwədz/ adv. **1** away from one's front (lean backwards; look backwards). **2 a** with the back foremost (walk backwards). **b** in reverse of the usual way (count backwards). **3 a** into a worse state (new policies are taking us backwards). **b** into the past (looked backwards over the years). **c** (of a thing's motion) back towards the starting-point (rolled backwards). □ **bend** (or **fall** or **lean**) **over backwards** (often foll. by to + infin.) colloq. make every effort, esp. to be fair or helpful.

backwash /ˈbækwɒʃ/ n. **1 a** receding waves created by the motion of a ship etc. **b** a backward current of air created by a moving aircraft. **2** repercussions.

backwater /ˈbækwɔːtə(r)/ n. **1** a place or condition remote from the centre of activity or thought. **2** stagnant water fed from a stream.

backwoods /ˈbækwʊdz/ n.pl. **1** remote uncleared forest land. **2** any remote or sparsely inhabited region.

backwoodsman /ˈbækˌwʊdzmən/ n. (pl. **-men**) **1** an inhabitant of backwoods. **2** an uncouth person.

backyard /bækˈjɑːd/ n. a yard at the back of a house etc. □ **in one's own backyard** colloq. near at hand.

baclava var. of BAKLAVA.

bacon /ˈbeɪkən/ n. cured meat from the back or sides of a pig. □ **bring home the bacon** colloq. **1** succeed in one's undertaking. **2** supply material provision or support. [ME f. OF f. Frank. bako = OHG bahho ham, flitch]

bactericide /bækˈtɪərɪˌsaɪd/ n. a substance capable of destroying bacteria. □ **bactericidal** /-ˈsaɪd(ə)l/ adj.

bacteriology /ˌbæktɪərɪˈɒlədʒɪ/ n. the study of bacteria. □ **bacteriological** /-əˈlɒdʒɪk(ə)l/ adj. **bacteriologically** /-əˈlɒdʒɪkəlɪ/ adv. **bacteriologist** n.

bacterium /bækˈtɪərɪəm/ n. (pl. **bacteria** /-rɪə/) a member of a large group of unicellular micro-organisms lacking an organized nucleus, some of which can cause disease. □ **bacterial** adj. [mod.L f. Gk baktērion dimin. of baktron stick]

■ **Usage** A common mistake is the use of plural form bacteria as the singular. This should be avoided.

Bactrian camel /ˈbæktrɪən/ n. a camel, Camelus bactrianus, native to central Asia, with two humps. [L Bactrianus f. Gk Baktrianos]

bad adj., n., & adv. —adj. (**worse** /wɜːs/; **worst** /wɜːst/) **1** inferior, inadequate, defective (bad work; a bad driver; bad light). **2 a** unpleasant, unwelcome (bad weather; bad news). **b** unsatisfactory, unfortunate (a bad business). **3** harmful (is bad for you). **4** (of food) decayed, putrid. **5** colloq. ill, injured (am feeling bad today; a bad leg). **6** colloq. regretful, guilty, ashamed (feels bad about it). **7** (of an unwelcome thing) serious, severe (a bad headache; a bad mistake). **8 a** morally wicked or offensive (a bad man; bad language). **b** naughty, badly behaved (a bad child). **9** worthless; not valid (a bad cheque). **10** (**badder**, **baddest**) esp. US sl. good, excellent. —n. **1 a** ill fortune (take the bad with the good). **b** ruin; a degenerate condition (go to the bad). **2** the debit side of an account (£500 to the bad). **3** (as pl.; prec. by the) bad or wicked people. —adv. US colloq. badly (took it bad). □ **bad blood** ill feeling. **bad breath** unpleasant-smelling breath. **bad debt** a debt that is not recoverable. **a bad job** colloq. an unfortunate state of affairs. **bad mouth** US malicious gossip or criticism. **bad-mouth** v.tr. US subject to malicious gossip or criticism. **in a bad way** ill; in trouble (looked in a bad way). □ **baddish** adj. **badness** n. [ME, perh. f. OE bæddel hermaphrodite, womanish man: for loss of l cf. MUCH, WENCH]

baddy /ˈbædɪ/ n. (pl. **-ies**) colloq. a villain or criminal, esp. in a story, film, etc.

bade see BID.

badge n. **1** a distinctive emblem worn as a mark of office, membership, etc. **2** any feature or sign which reveals a characteristic condition or quality. [ME: orig. unkn.]

badger /ˈbædʒə(r)/ n. & v. —n. an omnivorous grey-coated nocturnal mammal of the family Mustelidae with a white stripe flanked by black stripes on its head, which lives in sets. —v.tr.

pester, harass, tease. [16th C.: perh. f. BADGE, with ref. to its white forehead mark]

badinage /ˈbædɪˌnɑːʒ/ *n.* humorous or playful ridicule. [F f. *badiner* to joke]

badlands /ˈbædlændz/ *n.* extensive uncultivable eroded tracts in arid areas. [transl. F *mauvaises terres*]

badly /ˈbædlɪ/ *adv.* (**worse** /wɜːs/; **worst** /wɜːst/) **1** in a bad manner (*works badly*). **2** *colloq.* very much (*wants it badly*). **3** severely (*was badly defeated*).

badminton /ˈbædmɪnt(ə)n/ *n.* a game with rackets in which a shuttlecock is played back and forth across a net. [*Badminton* in S. England]

bad-tempered /bædˈtempəd/ *adj.* having a bad temper; irritable; easily annoyed. □ **bad-temperedly** *adv.*

baffle /ˈbæf(ə)l/ *v.* & *n.* —*v.tr.* **1** confuse or perplex (a person, one's faculties, etc.). **2 a** frustrate or hinder (plans etc.). **b** restrain or regulate the progress (of fluids, sounds, etc.). —*n.* (also **baffle-plate**) a device used to restrain the flow of fluid, gas, etc., through an opening, often found in microphones etc. to regulate the emission of sound. □ **bafflement** *n.* **baffling** *adj.* **bafflingly** *adv.* [perh. rel. to F *bafouer* ridicule, OF *beffer* mock]

bag *n.* & *v.* —*n.* **1** a receptacle of flexible material with an opening at the top. **2 a** (usu. in *pl.*) a piece of luggage (*put the bags in the boot*). **b** a woman's handbag. **3** (in *pl.*; usu. foll. by *of*) *colloq.* a large amount; plenty (*bags of time*). **4** *sl. derog.* a woman, esp. regarded as unattractive or unpleasant. **5** an amount of game shot by a sportsman. **6** (usu. in *pl.*) baggy folds of skin under the eyes. —*v.* (**bagged, bagging**) **1** *tr.* put in a bag. **2** *tr. colloq.* **a** secure; get hold of (*bagged the best seat*). **b** *colloq.* steal. **c** shoot (game). **d** (often in phr. **bags I**) *Brit. colloq.* claim on grounds of being the first to do so (*bagged first go; bags I go first*). **3 a** *intr.* hang loosely; bulge; swell. **b** *tr.* cause to do this. □ **bag lady** *US* a homeless woman who carries her possessions around in shopping bags. **in the bag** *colloq.* achieved; as good as secured. □ **bagful** *n.* (*pl.* **-fuls**). [ME, perh. f. ON *baggi*]

bagatelle /ˌbægəˈtel/ *n.* **1** a game in which small balls are struck into numbered holes on a board, with pins as obstructions. **2** a mere trifle; a negligible amount. **3** *Mus.* a short piece of music, esp. for the piano. [F f. It. *bagatella* dimin., perh. f. *baga* BAGGAGE]

bagel /ˈbeɪg(ə)l/ *n.* (also **beigel**) *US* a hard bread roll in the shape of a ring. [Yiddish *beygel*]

baggage /ˈbægɪdʒ/ *n.* **1** everyday belongings packed up in suitcases etc. for travelling; luggage. **2** the portable equipment of an army. **3** *joc.* or *derog.* a girl or woman. □ **baggage check** *US* a luggage ticket. [ME f. OF *bagage* f. *baguer* tie up or *bagues* bundles: perh. rel. to BAG]

baggy /ˈbægɪ/ *adj.* (**baggier, baggiest**) **1** hanging in loose folds. **2** puffed out. □ **baggily** *adv.* **bagginess** *n.*

bagpipe /ˈbægpaɪp/ *n.* (usu. in *pl.*) a musical instrument consisting of a windbag connected to two kinds of reeded pipes: drone pipes which produce single sustained notes and a fingered melody pipe or 'chanter'. □ **bagpiper** *n.*

baguette /bæˈget/ *n.* a long narrow French loaf. [F f. It. *bacchetto* dimin. of *bacchio* f. L *baculum* staff]

bah *int.* an expression of contempt or disbelief. [prob. F]

bail[1] *n.* & *v.* —*n.* **1** money etc. required as security against the temporary release of a prisoner pending trial. **2** a person or persons giving such security. —*v.tr.* (usu. foll. by *out*) **1** release or secure the release of (a prisoner) on payment of bail. **2** (also **bale** by assoc. with *bale out* 1: see BALE[1]) release from a difficulty; come to the rescue of (a person). □ **forfeit** (*colloq.* **jump**) **bail** fail to appear for trial after being released on bail. **go** (or **stand**) **bail** (often foll. by *for*) act as surety (for an accused person). □ **bailable** *adj.* [ME f. OF *bail* custody, *bailler* take charge of, f. L *bajulare* bear a burden]

bail[2] *n.* & *v.* —*n.* **1** *Cricket* either of the two crosspieces bridging the stumps. **2** the bar on a typewriter holding the paper against the platen. **3** a bar separating horses in an open stable. **4** *Austral.* & *NZ* a framework for securing the head of a cow during milking. —*v. Austral.* & *NZ* (usu. foll. by *up*) **1** *tr.* secure (a cow) during milking. **2 a** *tr.* make (a person) hold up his or her arms to be robbed. **b** *intr.* surrender by throwing up one's arms. **c** *tr.* buttonhole (a person). [ME f. OF *bail(e)*, perh. f. *bailler* enclose]

bail[3] *v.tr.* (also **bale**) **1** (usu. foll. by *out*) scoop water out of (a boat etc.). **2** scoop (water etc.) out. □ **bail out** var. of *bale out* 1 (see BALE[1]). □ **bailer** *n.* [obs. *bail* (n.) bucket f. F *baille* ult. f. L *bajulus* carrier]

bailey /ˈbeɪlɪ/ *n.* (*pl.* **-eys**) **1** the outer wall of a castle. **2** a court enclosed by it. [ME, var. of BAIL[2]]

Bailey bridge /ˈbeɪlɪ/ *n.* a temporary bridge of lattice steel designed for rapid assembly from prefabricated standard parts, used esp. in military operations. [Sir D. *Bailey* (d. 1985), its designer]

bailie /ˈbeɪlɪ/ *n.* esp. *hist.* a municipal officer and magistrate in Scotland. [ME, f. OF *bailli(s)* BAILIFF]

bailiff /ˈbeɪlɪf/ *n.* **1** a sheriff's officer who executes writs and processes and carries out distraints and arrests. **2** *Brit.* the agent or steward of a landlord. **3** *US* an official in a court of law who keeps order, looks after prisoners, etc. [ME f. OF *baillif* ult. f. L *bajulus* carrier, manager]

bailiwick /ˈbeɪlɪwɪk/ *n.* **1** *Law* the district or jurisdiction of a bailie or bailiff. **2** *joc.* a person's particular area of interest. [BAILIE + OE *wīc* town]

bailsman /ˈbeɪlzmən/ *n.* (*pl.* **-men**) a person who stands bail for another. [BAIL[1] + MAN]

bain-marie /ˌbæmæˈriː/ *n.* (*pl.* **bains-marie** *pronunc.* same) a cooking utensil consisting of a vessel of hot water in which a receptacle containing a sauce etc. can be gently heated. [F, transl. med.L *balneum Mariae* bath of Maria (an alleged Jewish alchemist)]

Bairam /baɪˈræm, ˈbaɪræm/ *n.* either of two annual Muslim festivals. □ **Greater Bairam** at the end of the Islamic year. **Lesser Bairam** at the end of Ramadan. [Turk. & Pers.]

bairn /beən/ *n. Sc.* & *N.Engl.* a child. [OE *bearn*]

bait *n.* & *v.* —*n.* **1** food used to entice a prey, esp. a fish or an animal. **2** an allurement; something intended to tempt or entice. —*v.* **1** *tr.* **a** harass or annoy (a person). **b** torment (a chained animal). **2** *tr.* put bait on (a hook, trap, etc.) to entice a prey. [ME f. ON *beita* hunt or chase]

baize *n.* a coarse usu. green woollen material resembling felt used as a covering or lining. [F *baies* (pl.) fem. of *bai* chestnut-coloured (BAY⁴), treated as sing.: cf. BODICE]

bake *v. & n.* —*v.* **1** *tr.* cook (food) by dry heat in an oven or on a hot surface, without direct exposure to a flame. **b** *intr.* undergo the process of being baked. **2** *intr. colloq.* **a** (usu. as **be baking**) (of weather etc.) be very hot. **b** (of a person) become hot. **3 a** *tr.* harden (clay etc.) by heat. **b** *intr.* (of clay etc.) be hardened by heat. —*n.* **1** the act or an instance of baking. **2** a batch of baking. **3** *US* a social gathering at which baked food is eaten. □ **baked beans** baked haricot beans, usu. tinned in tomato sauce. **baking-powder** a mixture of sodium bicarbonate, cream of tartar, etc., used instead of yeast in baking. **baking-soda** sodium bicarbonate. [OE *bacan*]

bakehouse /ˈbeɪkhaʊs/ *n.* = BAKERY.

Bakelite /ˈbeɪkəˌlaɪt/ *n. propr.* any of various thermosetting resins or plastics made from formaldehyde and phenol. [G *Bakelit* f. L.H. Baekeland its Belgian-born inventor d. 1944]

baker[1] /ˈbeɪkə(r)/ *n.* a person who bakes and sells bread, cakes, etc., esp. professionally. □ **baker's dozen** thirteen (so called from the former custom of adding an extra loaf to a dozen sold. [OE *bæcere*]

Baker[2] /ˈbeɪkə(r)/ *n.* □ **Baker day** *colloq.* a day set aside for in-service training of teachers. [*Kenneth Baker*, the name of the Education Secretary responsible for introducing them]

bakery /ˈbeɪkərɪ/ *n.* (*pl.* **-ies**) a place where bread and cakes are made or sold.

baklava /ˈbækləvə, ˌbækləˈvɑː/ *n.* (also **baclava**) a rich sweetmeat of flaky pastry, honey, and nuts. [Turk.]

baksheesh /ˈbækʃiːʃ/ *n.* (also **backsheesh**) (in some oriental countries) a small sum of money given as a gratuity or as alms. [ult. f. Pers. *bakšīš* f. *bakšīdan* give]

Balaclava /ˌbæləˈklɑːvə/ *n.* (in full **Balaclava helmet**) a tight woollen garment covering the whole head and neck except for parts of the face. [*Balaclava* in the Crimea, the site of a battle in 1854]

balalaika /ˌbæləˈlaɪkə/ *n.* a guitar-like musical instrument having a triangular body and 2–4 strings, popular in Russia and other Slav countries. [Russ.]

balance /ˈbæləns/ *n. & v.* —*n.* **1** an apparatus for weighing, esp. one with a central pivot, beam, and two scales. **2 a** a counteracting weight or force. **b** (in full **balance-wheel**) the regulating device in a clock etc. **3 a** an even distribution of weight or amount. **b** stability of body or mind (*regained his balance*). **4** a preponderating weight or amount (*the balance of opinion*). **5 a** an agreement between or the difference between credits and debits in an account. **b** the difference between an amount due and an amount paid (*will pay the balance next week*). **c** an amount left over; the rest. **6 a** *Art* harmony of design and proportion. **b** *Mus.* the relative volume of various sources of sound. **7** (**the Balance**) the zodiacal sign or constellation Libra. —*v.* **1** *tr.* (foll. by *with*, *against*) offset or compare (one thing) with another (*must*

balance the advantages with the disadvantages). **2** *tr.* counteract, equal, or neutralize the weight or importance of. **3 a** *tr.* bring into or keep in equilibrium (*balanced a book on her head*). **b** *intr.* be in equilibrium (*balanced on one leg*). **4** *tr.* (usu. as **balanced** *adj.*) establish equal or appropriate proportions of elements in (*a balanced diet*; *balanced opinion*). **5** *tr.* weigh (arguments etc.) against each other. **6 a** *tr.* compare and esp. equalize debits and credits of (an account). **b** *intr.* (of an account) have credits and debits equal. □ **balance of payments** the difference in value between payments into and out of a country. **balance of power 1** a situation in which the chief States of the world have roughly equal power. **2** the power held by a small group when larger groups are of equal strength. **balance of trade** the difference in value between imports and exports. **balance sheet** a statement giving the balance of an account. **in the balance** uncertain; at a critical stage. **on balance** all things considered. **strike a balance** choose a moderate course or compromise. □ **balanceable** *adj.* **balancer** *n.* [ME f. OF, ult. f. LL (*libra*) *bilanx bilancis* two-scaled (balance)]

balcony /ˈbælkənɪ/ *n.* (*pl.* **-ies**) **1** a usu. balustraded platform on the outside of a building, with access from an upper-floor window or door. **2 a** the tier of seats in a theatre above the dress circle. **b** the upstairs seats in a cinema etc. **c** *US* the dress circle in a theatre. □ **balconied** *adj.* [It. *balcone*]

bald /bɔːld/ *adj.* **1** (of a person) with the scalp wholly or partly lacking hair. **2** (of an animal, plant, etc.) not covered by the usual hair, feathers, leaves, etc. **3** *colloq.* with the surface worn away (*a bald tyre*). **4** blunt, unelaborated (*a bald statement*). **b** undisguised (*the bald effrontery*). □ **balding** *adj.* (in senses 1–3). **baldish** *adj.* **baldly** *adv.* (in sense 4). **baldness** *n.* [ME *ballede*, orig. 'having a white blaze', prob. f. an OE root *ball-* 'white patch']

baldachin /ˈbɔːldəkɪn/ *n.* (also **baldaquin**) a canopy over an altar, throne, etc. [It. *baldacchino* f. *Baldacco* Baghdad, its place of origin]

balderdash /ˈbɔːldədæʃ/ *n.* senseless talk or writing; nonsense. [earlier = 'mixture of drinks': orig. unkn.]

baldric /ˈbɔːldrɪk/ *n. hist.* a belt for a sword, bugle, etc., hung from the shoulder across the body to the opposite hip. [ME *baudry* f. OF *baudrei*: cf. MHG *balderich*, of unkn. orig.]

bale[1] *n. & v.* —*n.* **1** a bundle of merchandise or hay etc. tightly wrapped and bound with cords or hoops. **2** the quantity in a bale as a measure, esp. *US* 500 lb. of cotton. —*v.tr.* make up into bales. □ **bale** (or **bail**) **out 1** (of an airman) make an emergency parachute descent from an aircraft (cf. BAIL³). **2** = BAIL¹ *v.* 2. [ME prob. f. MDu., ult. identical with BALL¹]

bale[2] var. of BAIL³.

baleful /ˈbeɪlfʊl/ *adj.* **1** (esp. of a manner, look, etc.) gloomy, menacing. **2** harmful, malignant, destructive. □ **balefully** *adv.* **balefulness** *n.* [OE *b(e)alu* + -FUL]

baler /ˈbeɪlə(r)/ *n.* a machine for making bales of hay, straw, metal, etc.

balk var. of BAULK.

Balkan /ˈbɔːlkən/ *adj. & n.* —*adj.* **1** of or relating to the region of SE Europe bounded by the Adriatic, the Aegean, and the Black Sea. **2** of or relating to its peoples or countries. —*n.* (**the Balkans**) the Balkan countries. [Turk.]

ball¹ /bɔːl/ *n.* & *v.* —*n.* **1** a solid or hollow sphere, esp. for use in a game. **2 a** a ball-shaped object; material forming the shape of a ball (*ball of snow*; *ball of wool*; *rolled himself into a ball*). **b** a rounded part of the body (*ball of the foot*). **3** a solid non-explosive missile for a cannon etc. **4** a single delivery of a ball in cricket, baseball, etc., or passing of a ball in football. **5** (in *pl.*) *coarse sl.* **a** the testicles. **b** (usu. as an exclam. of contempt) nonsense, rubbish. **c** courage, 'guts'. —*v.* **1** *tr.* squeeze or wind into a ball. **2** *intr.* form or gather into a ball or balls. □ **ball-bearing 1** a bearing in which the two halves are separated by a ring of small metal balls which reduce friction. **2** one of these balls. **ball game 1 a** any game played with a ball. **b** *US* a game of baseball. **2** esp. *US colloq.* a particular affair or concern (*a whole new ball game*). **ball-point** (**pen**) a pen with a tiny ball as its writing point. **balls** (or **ball**) **up** *coarse sl.* bungle; make a mess of. **balls-up** *n. coarse sl.* a mess; a confused or bungled situation. **keep the ball rolling** maintain the momentum of an activity. **on the ball** *colloq.* alert. **play ball** *colloq.* cooperate. **start** etc. **the ball rolling** set an activity in motion; make a start. [ME f. ON *bǫllr* f. Gmc]

ball² /bɔːl/ *n.* **1** a formal social gathering for dancing. **2** *sl.* an enjoyable time (esp. *have a ball*). [F *bal* f. LL *ballare* to dance]

ballad /ˈbæləd/ *n.* **1** a poem or song narrating a popular story. **2** a slow sentimental or romantic song. [ME f. OF *balade* f. Prov. *balada* dancing-song f. *balar* to dance]

ballade /bæˈlɑːd/ *n.* **1** a poem of one or more triplets of stanzas with a repeated refrain and an envoy. **2** *Mus.* a short lyrical piece, esp. for piano. [earlier spelling and pronunc. of BALLAD]

balladry /ˈbælədrɪ/ *n.* ballad poetry.

ballast /ˈbæləst/ *n.* & *v.* —*n.* **1** any heavy material placed in a ship etc. to secure stability. **2** coarse stone etc. used to form the bed of a railway track or road. **3** anything that affords stability or permanence. —*v.tr.* **1** provide with ballast. **2** afford stability or weight to. [16th c.: f. LG or Scand., of uncert. orig.]

ballboy /ˈbɔːlbɔɪ/ *n.* (*fem.* **ballgirl** /-ɡɜːl/) (in lawn tennis) a boy or girl who retrieves balls that go out of play during a game.

ballcock /ˈbɔːlkɒk/ *n.* a floating ball on a hinged arm, whose movement up and down controls the water level in a cistern.

ballerina /ˌbæləˈriːnə/ *n.* a female ballet-dancer. [It., fem. of *ballerino* dancing-master f. *ballare* dance f. LL: see BALL²]

ballet /ˈbæleɪ/ *n.* **1 a** a dramatic or representational style of dancing and mime, usu. accompanied by music. **b** a particular piece or performance of ballet. **c** the music for this. **2** a company performing ballet. □ **balletic** /bəˈletɪk/ *adj.* [F f. It. *balletto* dimin. of *ballo* BALL²]

balletomane /ˈbælɪtəʊˌmeɪn/ *n.* a devotee of ballet. □ **balletomania** /-ˈmeɪnɪə/ *n.*

ballista /bəˈlɪstə/ *n.* (*pl.* **ballistae** /-stiː/) a catapult used in ancient warfare for hurling large stones etc. [L f. Gk *ballō* throw]

ballistic /bəˈlɪstɪk/ *adj.* **1** of or relating to projectiles. **2** moving under the force of gravity only. □ **ballistic missile** a missile which is initially powered and guided but falls under gravity on its target. □ **ballistically** *adv.* [BALLISTA + -IC]

ballistics /bəˈlɪstɪks/ *n.pl.* (usu. treated as *sing.*) the science of projectiles and firearms.

ballocks var. of BOLLOCKS.

balloon /bəˈluːn/ *n.* & *v.* —*n.* **1** a small inflatable rubber pouch with a neck, used as a child's toy or as decoration. **2** a large usu. round bag inflatable with hot air or gas to make it rise in the air, often carrying a basket for passengers. **3** *colloq.* a balloon shape enclosing the words or thoughts of characters in a cartoon. **4** a large globular drinking glass, usu. for brandy. —*v.* **1** *intr.* & *tr.* swell out or cause to swell out like a balloon. **2** *intr.* travel by balloon. □ **balloonist** *n.* [F *ballon* or It. *ballone* large ball]

ballot /ˈbælət/ *n.* & *v.* —*n.* **1** a process of voting, in writing and usu. secret. **2** the total of votes recorded in a ballot. **3** the drawing of lots. **4** a paper or ticket etc. used in voting. —*v.* (**balloted**, **balloting**) **1** *intr.* (usu. foll. by *for*) **a** hold a ballot; give a vote. **b** draw lots for precedence etc. **2** *tr.* take a ballot of (*the union balloted its members*). □ **ballot-box** a sealed box into which voters put completed ballot-papers. **ballot-paper** a slip of paper used to register a vote. [It. *ballotta* dimin. of *balla* BALL¹]

ballpark /ˈbɔːlpɑːk/ *n. US* **1** a baseball ground. **2** (*attrib.*) *colloq.* approximate, rough (*a ballpark figure*).

ballroom /ˈbɔːlruːm, -rʊm/ *n.* a large room or hall for dancing. □ **ballroom dancing** formal social dancing as a recreation.

bally /ˈbælɪ/ *adj.* & *adv. Brit. sl.* a mild form of *bloody* (see BLOODY *adj.* 3) (*took the bally lot*). [alt. of BLOODY]

ballyhoo /ˌbælɪˈhuː/ *n.* **1** a loud noise or fuss; a confused state or commotion. **2** extravagant or sensational publicity. [19th or 20th c., orig. US (in sense 2): orig. unkn.]

balm /bɑːm/ *n.* **1** an aromatic ointment for anointing, soothing, or healing. **2** a fragrant and medicinal exudation from certain trees and plants. **3** a healing or soothing influence. **4** any aromatic herb, esp. one of the genus *Melissa*. **5** a pleasant perfume or fragrance. [ME f. OF *ba(s)me* f. L *balsamum* BALSAM]

balmy /ˈbɑːmɪ/ *adj.* (**balmier**, **balmiest**) **1** mild and fragrant; soothing. **2** yielding balm. **3** *sl.* = BARMY. □ **balmily** *adv.* **balminess** *n.*

baloney var. of BOLONEY.

balsa /ˈbɒlsə, ˈbɔːl-/ *n.* **1** (in full **balsa-wood**) a type of tough lightweight wood used for making models etc. **2** the tropical American tree, *Ochroma lagopus*, from which it comes. [Sp., = raft]

balsam /ˈbɒlsəm, ˈbɔːl-/ *n.* **1** any of several aromatic resinous exudations, such as balm, obtained from various trees and shrubs and used as a base for fragrances and medical preparations. **2** an ointment, esp. one composed of a substance dissolved in oil or turpentine. **3** any of various trees or shrubs which yield balsam. **4** any of several flowering plants of the genus *Impatiens*. **5** a healing or soothing agency. □ **balsamic** /-ˈsæmɪk/ *adj.* [OE f. L *balsamum*]

Baltic /ˈbɔːltɪk, ˈbɒl-/ *n.* & *adj.* —*n.* **1** (**the Baltic**) an almost land-locked sea of NE Europe. **2** the States bordering this sea. —*adj.* of or relating to the Baltic. [med.L *Balticus* f. LL *Balthae* dwellers near the Baltic Sea]

baluster /ˈbæləstə(r)/ n. each of a series of often ornamental short posts or pillars supporting a rail or coping etc. [F *balustre* f. It. *balaustro* f. L f. Gk *balaustion* wild-pomegranate flower]

■ **Usage** This word is often confused with *banister*. A baluster is usually part of a balustrade whereas a banister supports a stair handrail.

balustrade /ˌbæləˈstreɪd/ n. a railing supported by balusters, esp. forming an ornamental parapet to a balcony, bridge, or terrace. [F (as BALUSTER)]

bamboo /bæmˈbuː/ n. **1** a mainly tropical giant woody grass of the subfamily Bambusidae. **2** its hollow jointed stem, used as a stick or to make furniture etc. [Du. *bamboes* f. Port. *mambu* f. Malay]

bamboozle /bæmˈbuːz(ə)l/ v.tr. colloq. cheat, hoax, mystify. □ **bamboozlement** n. **bamboozler** n. [c.1700: prob. of cant orig.]

ban /bæn/ v. & n. —v.tr. (**banned, banning**) forbid, prohibit, esp. formally. —n. a formal or authoritative prohibition (*a ban on smoking*). [OE *bannan* summon f. Gmc]

banal /bəˈnɑːl/ adj. trite, feeble, commonplace. □ **banality** /-ˈnælɪtɪ/ n. (pl. **-ies**). **banally** adv. [orig. in sense 'compulsory', hence 'common to all', f. F f. *ban* (as BAN)]

banana /bəˈnɑːnə/ n. **1** a long curved fruit with soft pulpy flesh and yellow skin when ripe, growing in clusters. **2** (in full **banana-tree**) the tropical and subtropical treelike plant, *Musa sapientum*, bearing this. □ **banana republic** derog. a small State, esp. in Central America, dependent on the influx of foreign capital. **banana skin 1** the skin of a banana. **2** a cause of upset or humiliation; a blunder. **go bananas** sl. become crazy or angry. [Port. or Sp., f. a name in Guinea]

band[1] n. & v. —n. **1** a flat, thin strip or loop put round something esp. to hold it together or decorate it (*headband*). **2 a** a strip of material forming part of a garment (*hatband; waistband*). **b** a stripe of a different colour or material on an object. **3 a** a range of frequencies or wavelengths in a spectrum (esp. of radio frequencies). **b** a range of values within a series. **4** Mech. a belt connecting wheels or pulleys. **5** (in pl.) a collar having two hanging strips, worn by some lawyers, ministers, and academics in formal dress. —v.tr. **1** put a band on. **2 a** mark with stripes. **b** (as **banded** adj.) Bot. & Zool. marked with coloured bands or stripes. □ **band-saw** a mechanical saw with a blade formed by an endless toothed band. [ME f. OF *bande, bende* f. Gmc]

band[2] n. & v. —n. **1** an organized group of people having a common object, esp. of a criminal nature (*band of cutthroats*). **2 a** a group of musicians, esp. playing wind instruments (*brass band; military band*). **b** a group of musicians playing jazz, pop, or dance music. **c** colloq. an orchestra. —v.tr. & intr. form into a group for a purpose (*band together for mutual protection*). [ME f. OF *bande, bander*, med.L *banda*, prob. of Gmc orig.]

bandage /ˈbændɪdʒ/ n. & v. —n. a strip of material for binding up a wound etc. —v.tr. bind (a wound etc.) with a bandage. [F f. *bande* (as BAND[1])]

bandanna /bænˈdænə/ n. a large coloured handkerchief or neckerchief, usu. of silk or cotton, and often having white spots. [prob. Port. f. Hindi]

b. & b. abbr. bed and breakfast.

bandbox /ˈbændbɒks/ n. a usu. circular cardboard box for carrying hats. □ **out of a bandbox** extremely neat. [BAND[1] + BOX[1]]

bandeau /ˈbændəʊ, -ˈdəʊ/ n. (pl. **bandeaux** /-dəʊz/) a narrow band worn round the head. [F]

banderole /ˌbændəˈrəʊl/ n. (also **banderol**) **1** a long narrow flag with a cleft end. **2** a ribbon-like scroll, bearing an inscription. [F *banderole* f. It. *banderuola* dimin. of *bandiera* BANNER]

bandicoot /ˈbændɪˌkuːt/ n. **1** any of the insect- and plant-eating marsupials of the family *Peramelidae*. **2** (in full **bandicoot rat**) Ind. a destructive rat, *Bandicota benegalensis*. [Telugu *pandikokku* pig-rat]

bandit /ˈbændɪt/ n. (pl. **bandits** or **banditti** /-ˈdɪtɪ/) **1** a robber or murderer, esp. a member of a gang; a gangster. **2** an outlaw. □ **banditry** n. [It. *bandito* (pl. *-iti*), past part. of *bandire* ban, = med.L *bannire* proclaim: see BANISH]

bandmaster /ˈbændˌmɑːstə(r)/ n. the conductor of a (esp. military or brass) band. [BAND[2] + MASTER]

bandolier /ˌbændəˈlɪə(r)/ n. (also **bandoleer**) a shoulder belt with loops or pockets for cartridges. [Du. *bandelier* or F *bandoulière*, prob. formed as BANDEROLE]

bandsman /ˈbændzmən/ n. (pl. **-men**) a player in a (esp. military or brass) band.

bandstand /ˈbændstænd/ n. a covered outdoor platform for a band to play on, usu. in a park.

bandwagon /ˈbændˌwægən/ n. US a wagon used for carrying a band in a parade etc. □ **climb** (or **jump**) **on the bandwagon** join a party, cause, or group that seems likely to succeed.

bandwidth /ˈbændwɪtθ, -wɪdθ/ n. the range of frequencies within a given band (see BAND[1] n. 3a).

bandy[1] /ˈbændɪ/ adj. (**bandier, bandiest**) **1** (of the legs) curved so as to be wide apart at the knees. **2** (also **bandy-legged**) (of a person) having bandy legs. [perh. f. obs. *bandy* curved stick]

bandy[2] /ˈbændɪ/ v.tr. (**-ies, -ied**) **1** (often foll. by *about*) **a** pass (a story, rumour, etc.) to and fro. **b** throw or pass (a ball etc.) to and fro. **2** (often foll. by *about*) discuss disparagingly (*bandied her name about*). **3** (often foll. by *with*) exchange (blows, insults, etc.) (*don't bandy words with me*). [perh. f. F *bander* take sides f. *bande* BAND[2]]

bane n. **1** the cause of ruin or trouble; the curse (esp. *the bane of one's life*). **2** poet. ruin; woe. **3** archaic (except in comb.) poison (*ratsbane*). □ **baneful** adj. **banefully** adv. [OE *bana* f. Gmc]

bang n., v., & adv. —n. **1 a** a loud short sound. **b** an explosion. **c** the report of a gun. **2 a** a sharp blow. **b** the sound of this. **3** esp. US a fringe of hair cut straight across the forehead. —v. **1** tr. & intr. strike or shut noisily (*banged the door shut; banged on the table*). **2** tr. & intr. make or cause to make the sound of a blow or an explosion. **3** tr. esp. US cut (hair) in a bang. —adv. **1** with a bang or sudden impact. **2** colloq. exactly (*bang in the middle*). □ **bang on** Brit. colloq. exactly right. **bang-up** US sl. first-class, excellent (esp. *bang-up job*). **go bang 1** (of a door etc.) shut noisily. **2** explode. **3** colloq. be suddenly

banger /ˈbæŋə(r)/ n. Brit. **1** sl. a sausage. **2** sl. an old car, esp. a noisy one. **3** a loud firework.

bangle /ˈbæŋg(ə)l/ n. a rigid ornamental band worn round the arm or occas. the ankle. [Hindi *bangri* glass bracelet]

banian var. of BANYAN.

banish /ˈbænɪʃ/ v.tr. **1** formally expel (a person), esp. from a country. **2** dismiss from one's presence or mind. □ **banishment** n. [ME f. OE *banir* ult. f. Gmc]

banister /ˈbænɪstə(r)/ n. (also **bannister**) **1** (in pl.) the uprights and handrail at the side of a staircase. **2** (usu. in pl.) an upright supporting a handrail. [earlier *barrister*, corrupt. of BALUSTER]

■ **Usage** See note at *baluster*.

banjo /ˈbændʒəʊ/ n. (pl. **-os** or **-oes**) a stringed musical instrument with a neck and head like a guitar and an open-backed body consisting of parchment stretched over a metal hoop. □ **banjoist** n. [US southern corrupt. of earlier *bandore* ult. f. Gk *pandoura* three-stringed lute]

bank¹ n. & v. —n. **1 a** the sloping edge of land by a river. **b** the area of ground alongside a river (*had a picnic on the bank*). **2** a raised shelf of ground; a slope. **3** an elevation in the sea or a river bed. **4** the artificial slope of a road etc., enabling vehicles to maintain speed round a curve. **5** a mass of cloud, fog, snow, etc. —v. **1** tr. & intr. (often foll. by *up*) heap or rise into banks. **2** tr. heap up (a fire) tightly so that it burns slowly. **3 a** intr. (of a vehicle or aircraft or its occupant) travel with one side higher than the other in rounding a curve. **b** tr. cause (a vehicle or aircraft) to do this. **4** tr. build (a road etc.) higher at the outer edge of a bend to enable fast cornering. [ME f. Gmc f. ON *banki* (unrecorded: cf. OIcel. *bakki*): rel. to BENCH]

bank² n. & v. —n. **1 a** a financial establishment which uses money deposited by customers for investment, pays it out when required, makes loans at interest, exchanges currency, etc. **b** a building in which this business takes place. **2** = *piggy bank*. **3 a** the money or tokens held by the banker in some gambling games. **b** the banker in such games. **4** a place for storing anything for future use (*blood bank*; *data bank*). —v. **1** tr. deposit (money or valuables) in a bank. **2** intr. engage in business as a banker. **3** intr. (often foll. by *at*, *with*) keep money (at a bank). □ **bank card** = *cheque card*. **bank holiday** a day on which banks are officially closed, (in the UK) usu. kept as a public holiday. **the Bank of England** the central bank of England and Wales, issuing banknotes and having the Government as its main customer. **bank on** rely on (*I'm banking on your help*). **bank statement** a printed statement of transactions and balance issued periodically to the holder of a bank account. [F *banque* or It. *banca* f. med.L *banca*, *bancus*, f. Gmc: rel. to BANK¹]

bank³ n. **1** a row of similar objects, esp. of keys, lights, or switches. **2** a tier of oars. [ME f. OF *banc* f. Gmc: rel. to BANK¹, BENCH]

bankable /ˈbæŋkəb(ə)l/ adj. **1** certain to bring profit; good for the box office (*Hollywood's most bankable stars*). **2** acceptable at a bank. **3** reliable (*a bankable reputation*).

banker /ˈbæŋkə(r)/ n. **1** a person who manages or owns a bank or group of banks. **2** a keeper of the bank or dealer in some gambling games. □ **banker's card** = *cheque card*. **banker's order** an instruction to a bank to pay money or deliver property, signed by the owner or the owner's agent. [F *banquier* f. *banque* BANK²]

banking /ˈbæŋkɪŋ/ n. the business transactions of a bank.

banknote /ˈbæŋknəʊt/ n. a banker's promissory note, esp. from a central bank, payable to the bearer on demand, and serving as money.

bankroll /ˈbæŋkrəʊl/ n. & v. US —n. **1** a roll of banknotes. **2** funds. —v.tr. colloq. support financially.

bankrupt /ˈbæŋkrʌpt/ adj., n., & v. —adj. **1 a** insolvent; declared in law unable to pay debts. **b** undergoing the legal process resulting from this. **2** (often foll. by *of*) exhausted or drained (of some quality etc.); deficient, lacking. —n. **1** an insolvent person whose estate is administered and disposed of for the benefit of the creditors. **2** an insolvent debtor. —v.tr. make bankrupt. □ **bankruptcy** /-ˌrʌptsɪ/ n. (pl. **-ies**). [16th c.: f. It *banca rotta* broken bench (as BANK², L *rumpere rupt-* break), assim. to L]

banksia /ˈbæŋksɪə/ n. any evergreen flowering shrub of the genus *Banksia*, native to Australia. [Sir J. *Banks*, Engl. naturalist d. 1820]

banner /ˈbænə(r)/ n. **1 a** a large sign bearing a slogan or design and carried in a demonstration or procession. **b** a long strip of cloth etc. hung across a street or along the front of a building etc. and bearing a slogan. **2** a slogan or phrase used to represent a belief or principle. **3** a flag on a pole used as the standard of a king, knight, etc., esp. in battle. □ **banner headline** a large newspaper headline, esp. one across the top of the front page. □ **bannered** adj. [ME f. AF *banere*, OF *baniere* f. Rmc ult. f. Gmc]

bannock /ˈbænək/ n. Sc. & N.Engl. a round flat loaf, usu. unleavened. [OE *bannuc*, perh. f. Celt.]

banns /bænz/ n.pl. a notice read out on three successive Sundays in a parish church, announcing an intended marriage. [pl. of BAN]

banquet /ˈbæŋkwɪt/ n. & v. —n. **1** an elaborate usu. extensive feast. **2** a dinner for many people followed by speeches. —v. (**banqueted**, **banqueting**) intr. hold a banquet; feast. □ **banqueter** n. [F, dimin. of *banc* bench, BANK²]

banquette /bæŋˈket/ n. an upholstered bench along a wall, esp. in a restaurant or bar. [F f. It. *banchetta* dimin. of *banca* bench, BANK²]

banshee /ˈbænʃiː, -ˈʃiː/ n. Ir. & Sc. a female spirit whose wailing warns of a death in a house. [Ir. *bean sídhe* f. OIr. *ben síde* woman of the fairies]

bantam /ˈbæntəm/ n. **1** any of several small breeds of domestic fowl, of which the cock is very aggressive. **2** a small but aggressive person. [app. f. *Bāntān* in Java, although the fowl is not native there]

bantamweight /ˈbæntəmˌweɪt/ n. **1** a weight in certain sports intermediate between flyweight and featherweight. **2** a sportsman of this weight.

banter /ˈbæntə(r)/ n. & v. —n. good-humoured teasing. —v. **1** tr. ridicule in a good-humoured way. **2** intr. talk humorously or teasingly. □ **banterer** n. [17th c.: orig. unkn.]

Bantu /bænˈtuː/ n. & adj. —n. (pl. same or **Bantus**) **1** often offens. **a** a large group of Negroid peoples of central and southern Africa.

b a member of any of these peoples. **2** the group of languages spoken by them. —*adj*. of or relating to these peoples or languages. [Bantu, = people]

Bantustan /ˌbæntuːˈstɑːn/ *n. S.Afr. often offens.* any of several partially self-governing areas reserved for Black South Africans. [BANTU + *-stan* as in *Hindustan*]

banyan /ˈbænɪən, -jən/ *n.* (also **banian**) an Indian fig tree, *Ficus benghalensis*, the branches of which hang down and root themselves. [Port. *banian* f. Gujarati *vāṇiyo* man of trading caste, f. Skr.: applied orig. to one such tree under which banyans had built a pagoda]

banzai /baːnˈzʌɪ/ *int.* **1** a Japanese battle cry. **2** a form of greeting used to the Japanese emperor. [Jap., = ten thousand years (of life to you)]

baobab /ˈbeɪəʊˌbæb/ *n.* an African tree, *Adansonia digitata*, with an enormously thick trunk and large edible fruit. [L (1592), prob. f. an Afr. lang.]

bap *n. Brit.* a soft flattish bread roll. [16th c.: orig. unkn.]

baptism /ˈbæptɪz(ə)m/ *n.* **1 a** the religious rite, symbolizing admission to the Christian Church, of sprinkling the forehead with water, or (usu. only with adults) by immersion, generally accompanied by name-giving. **b** the act of baptizing or being baptized. **2** an initiation, e.g. into battle. □ **baptism of fire** initiation into battle. □ **baptismal** /-ˈtɪzm(ə)l/ *adj.* [ME f. OF *ba(p)te(s)me* f. eccl.L *baptismus* f. eccl.Gk *baptismos* f. *baptizō* BAPTIZE]

baptist /ˈbæptɪst/ *n.* **1** a person who baptizes, esp. John the Baptist. **2** (**Baptist**) a Christian advocating baptism by total immersion. [ME f. OF *baptiste* f. eccl.L *baptista* f. eccl.Gk *baptistēs* f. *baptizō* BAPTIZE]

baptistery /ˈbæptɪstərɪ/ *n.* (also **baptistry** /-trɪ/) (*pl.* **-ies**) **1 a** the part of a church used for baptism. **b** *hist.* a building next to a church, used for baptism. **2** (in a Baptist chapel) a sunken receptacle used for total immersion. [ME f. OF *baptisterie* f. eccl.L *baptisterium* f. eccl.Gk *baptistērion* bathing-place f. *baptizō* BAPTIZE]

baptize /bæpˈtaɪz/ *v.tr.* (also **-ise**) **1** (also *absol.*) administer baptism to. **2** give a name or nickname to; christen. [ME f. OF *baptiser* f. eccl.L *baptizare* f. Gk *baptizō* immerse, baptize]

bar¹ *n., v., & prep.* —*n.* **1** a long rod or piece of rigid wood, metal, etc., esp. used as an obstruction, confinement, fastening, weapon, etc. **2 a** something resembling a bar in being (thought of as) straight, narrow, and rigid (*bar of soap; bar of chocolate*). **b** the heating element of an electric fire. **c** = CROSSBAR. **d** *Brit.* a metal strip below the clasp of a medal, awarded as an extra distinction. **e** a sandbank or shoal at the mouth of a harbour or an estuary. **f** *Brit.* a rail marking the end of each chamber in the Houses of Parliament. **3 a** a barrier of any shape. **b** a restriction (*colour bar; a bar to promotion*). **4 a** a counter in a public house, restaurant, or café across which alcohol or refreshments are served. **b** a room in a public house in which customers may sit and drink. **c** *US* a public house. **d** a small shop or stall serving refreshments (*snack bar*). **e** a specialized department in a large store (*heel bar*). **5 a** an enclosure in which a prisoner stands in a lawcourt. **b** a particular court of law. **6** *Mus.* **a** any of the sections of usu. equal time-value into which a musical

composition is divided by vertical lines across the staff. **b** = *bar-line*. **7** (**the Bar**) *Law* **a** barristers collectively. **b** the profession of barrister. —*v.tr.* (**barred, barring**) **1 a** fasten (a door, window, etc.) with a bar or bars. **b** (usu. foll. by *in, out*) shut or keep in or out (*barred him in*). **2** obstruct, prevent (*bar his progress*). **3 a** (usu. foll. by *from*) prohibit, exclude (*bar them from attending*). **b** exclude from consideration (cf. BARRING). **4** mark with stripes. —*prep.* **1** except (*all were there bar a few*). **2** *Racing* except (the horses indicated: used in stating the odds, indicating the number of horses excluded) (*33–1 bar three*). □ **bar chart** a chart using bars to represent quantity. **bar-code** a machine-readable code in the form of a pattern of stripes printed on and identifying a commodity, used esp. for stock-control. **bar-line** *Mus.* a vertical line used to mark divisions between bars. **bar none** with no exceptions. **bar person** a barmaid or barman. [ME f. OF *barre, barrer*, f. Rmc]

bar² *n.* esp. *Meteorol.* a unit of pressure, 10^5 newton per square metre, approx. one atmosphere. [Gk *baros* weight]

barathea /ˌbærəˈθɪə/ *n.* a fine woollen cloth, sometimes mixed with silk or cotton, used esp. for coats, suits, etc. [19th c.: orig. unkn.]

barb *n. & v.* —*n.* **1** a secondary backward-facing projection from an arrow, fish-hook, etc., angled to make extraction difficult. **2** a deliberately hurtful remark. **3** a beardlike filament at the mouth of some fish, e.g. barbel and catfish. —*v.tr.* **1** provide (an arrow, a fish-hook, etc.) with a barb or barbs. **2** (as **barbed** *adj.*) of a remark etc.) deliberately hurtful. □ **barbed wire** wire bearing sharp pointed spikes close together and used in fencing, or in warfare as an obstruction. [ME f. OF *barbe* f. L *barba* beard]

barbarian /baːˈbeərɪən/ *n. & adj.* —*n.* **1** an uncultured or brutish person; a lout. **2** a member of a primitive community or tribe. —*adj.* **1** rough and uncultured. **2** uncivilized. [orig. of any foreigner with a different language or customs: F *barbarien* f. *barbare* (as BARBAROUS)]

barbaric /baːˈbærɪk/ *adj.* **1** brutal; cruel. **2** rough and uncultured; unrestrained. **3** of or like barbarians and their art or taste; primitive. □ **barbarically** *adv.* [ME f. OF *barbarique* or L *barbaricus* f. Gk *barbarikos* f. *barbaros* foreign]

barbarism /ˈbaːbəˌrɪz(ə)m/ *n.* **1 a** the absence of culture and civilized standards; ignorance and rudeness. **b** an example of this. **2** a word or expression not considered correct; a solecism. **3** anything considered to be in bad taste. [F *barbarisme* f. L *barbarismus* f. Gk *barbarismos* f. *barbarizō* speak like a foreigner f. *barbaros* foreign]

barbarity /baːˈbærɪtɪ/ *n.* (*pl.* **-ies**) **1** savage cruelty. **2** an example of this.

barbarize /ˈbaːbəˌrʌɪz/ *v.tr. & intr.* (also **-ise**) make or become barbarous. □ **barbarization** /-ˈzeɪʃ(ə)n/ *n.*

barbarous /ˈbaːbərəs/ *adj.* **1** uncivilized. **2** cruel. **3** coarse and unrefined. □ **barbarously** *adv.* **barbarousness** *n.* [orig. of any foreign language or people: f. L f. Gk *barbaros* foreign]

barbecue /ˈbaːbɪˌkjuː/ *n. & v.* —*n.* **1 a** a meal cooked on an open fire out of doors, esp. meat grilled on a metal appliance. **b** a party at which such a meal is cooked and eaten. **2 a** the metal appliance used for the preparation of a barbecue. **b** a fireplace, usu. of brick, containing such an appliance. —*v.tr.* (**barbecues, barbecued, barbecuing**) cook (esp. meat) on a barbecue. [Sp. *barbacòa* f. Haitian *barbaca* wooden frame on posts]

barbel /ˈbɑːb(ə)l/ *n.* **1** any large European freshwater fish of the genus *Barbus*, with fleshy filaments hanging from its mouth. **2** such a filament growing from the mouth of any fish. [ME f. OF f. LL *barbellus* dimin. of *barbus* barbel f. *barba* beard]

barbell /ˈbɑːbel/ *n.* an iron bar with a series of graded discs at each end, used for weightlifting exercises. [BAR¹ + BELL¹]

barber /ˈbɑːbə(r)/ *n. & v.* —*n.* a person who cuts men's hair and shaves or trims beards as an occupation. —*v.tr.* cut the hair, shave or trim the beard of. □ **barber-shop** (or **barber-shop quartet**) *US colloq.* a popular style of close harmony singing for four male voices. **barber's pole** a spirally painted striped red and white pole hung outside barbers' shops as a business sign. [ME & AF f. OF *barbeor* f. med.L *barbator -oris* f. *barba* beard]

barberry /ˈbɑːbərɪ/ *n.* (*pl.* **-ies**) **1** any shrub of the genus *Berberis*, with spiny shoots, yellow flowers, and red berries. **2** its berry. [ME f. OF *berberis*, of unkn. orig.: assim. to BERRY]

barbican /ˈbɑːbɪkən/ *n.* the outer defence of a city, castle, etc., esp. a double tower above a gate or drawbridge. [ME f. OF *barbacane*, of unkn. orig.]

barbitone /ˈbɑːbɪˌtəʊn/ *n.* a sedative drug. [as BARBITURIC ACID + -ONE]

barbiturate /bɑːˈbɪtjʊrət, -ˌreɪt/ *n.* any derivative of barbituric acid used in the preparation of sedative and sleep-inducing drugs. [as BARBITURIC ACID + -ATE¹]

barbituric acid /ˌbɑːbɪˈtjʊərɪk/ *n. Chem.* an organic acid from which various sedatives and sleep-inducing drugs are derived. [F *barbiturique* f. G *Barbitursäure* (*Säure* acid) f. the name *Barbara*]

barcarole /ˈbɑːkəˌrəʊl/ *n.* (also **barcarolle** /-ˌrɒl/) **1** a song sung by Venetian gondoliers. **2** music in imitation of this. [F *barcarolle* f. Venetian It. *barcarola* boatman's song f. *barca* boat]

bard *n.* **1 a** *hist.* a Celtic minstrel. **b** the winner of a prize for Welsh verse at an Eisteddfod. **2** *poet.* a poet, esp. one treating heroic themes. □ **bardic** *adj.* [Gael. & Ir. *bárd*, Welsh *bardd*, f. OCelt.]

bare /beə(r)/ *adj. & v.* —*adj.* **1** (esp. of part of the body) unclothed or uncovered (*with bare head*). **2** without appropriate covering or contents: **a** (of a tree) leafless. **b** unfurnished; empty (*bare rooms*; *the cupboard was bare*). **c** (of a floor) uncarpeted. **3** (*attrib.*) **a** scanty (*a bare majority*). **b** mere (*bare necessities*). —*v.tr.* **1** uncover, unsheathe (*bared his teeth*). **2** reveal (*bared his soul*). □ **bare of** without. **with one's bare hands** without using tools or weapons. □ **bareness** *n.* [OE *bær, barian* f. Gmc]

bareback /ˈbeəbæk/ *adj. & adv.* on an unsaddled horse, donkey, etc.

barefaced /ˈbeəfeɪst/ *adj.* undisguised; impudent (*barefaced cheek*). □ **barefacedly** /-ˈfeɪsɪdlɪ/ *adv.* **barefacedness** *n.*

barefoot /ˈbeəfʊt/ *adj. & adv.* (also **barefooted** /-ˈfʊtɪd/) with nothing on the feet.

bareheaded /beəˈhedɪd/ *adj. & adv.* without a covering for the head.

barely /ˈbeəlɪ/ *adv.* **1** only just; scarcely (*barely escaped*). **2** scantily (*barely furnished*).

barfly /ˈbɑːflaɪ/ *n.* (*pl.* **-flies**) *colloq.* a person who frequents bars.

bargain /ˈbɑːgɪn/ *n. & v.* —*n.* **1 a** an agreement on the terms of a transaction or sale. **b** this seen from the buyer's viewpoint (*a bad bargain*). **2** something acquired or offered cheaply. —*v.intr.* (often foll. by *with, for*) discuss the terms of a transaction. □ **bargain for** (or *colloq.* **on**) (usu. with *neg.* actual or implied) be prepared for; expect (*more than I bargained for*). **bargain on** rely on. **drive a hard bargain** pursue one's own profit in a transaction keenly. **into** (*US* **in**) **the bargain** moreover; in addition to what was expected. □ **bargainer** *n.* [ME f. OF *bargaine, bargaignier*, prob. f. Gmc]

barge /bɑːdʒ/ *n. & v.* —*n.* **1** a long flat-bottomed boat for carrying freight on canals, rivers, etc. **2** a long ornamental boat used for pleasure or ceremony. **3** a boat used by the chief officers of a man-of-war. —*v.intr.* **1** (often foll. by *around*) lurch or rush clumsily about. **2** (foll. by *in, into*) **a** intrude or interrupt rudely or awkwardly (*barged in while we were kissing*). **b** collide with (*barged into her*). [ME f. OF perh. f. med.L *barica* f. Gk *baris* Egyptian boat]

bargeboard /ˈbɑːdʒbɔːd/ *n.* a board fixed to the gable-end of a roof to hide the ends of the roof timbers. [perh. f. med.L *bargus* gallows]

bargee /bɑːˈdʒiː/ *n. Brit.* a person in charge of or working on a barge.

bargepole /ˈbɑːdʒpəʊl/ *n.* a long pole used for punting barges etc. and for fending off obstacles. □ **would not touch with a bargepole** refuse to be associated or concerned with (a person or thing).

baritone /ˈbærɪˌtəʊn/ *n. & adj.* —*n.* **1 a** the second-lowest adult male singing voice. **b** a singer with this voice. **c** a part written for it. **2 a** an instrument that is second-lowest in pitch in its family. **b** its player. —*adj.* of the second-lowest range. [It. *baritono* f. Gk *barutonos* f. *barus* heavy + *tonos* TONE]

barium /ˈbeərɪəm/ *n. Chem.* a white reactive soft metallic element of the alkaline earth group. □ **barium meal** a mixture of barium sulphate and water, which is opaque to X-rays, and is given to patients requiring radiological examination of the stomach and intestines. [Gk *barus* heavy + -IUM]

bark¹ *n. & v.* —*n.* **1** the sharp explosive cry of a dog, fox, etc. **2** a sound resembling this cry. —*v.* **1** *intr.* (of a dog, fox, etc.) give a bark. **2** *tr. & intr.* speak or utter sharply or brusquely. [OE *beorcan*]

bark² *n. & v.* —*n.* the tough protective outer sheath of the trunks, branches, and twigs of trees or woody shrubs. —*v.tr.* **1** graze or scrape (one's shin etc.). **2** strip bark from (a tree etc.). [ME f. OIcel. *börkr bark-*: perh. rel. to BIRCH]

barkeeper /ˈbɑːˌkiːpə(r)/ *n.* (also **barkeep**) *US* a person serving drinks in a bar.

barker /ˈbɑːkə(r)/ *n.* a tout at an auction, sideshow, etc., who calls out for custom to passers-by. [BARK¹ + -ER¹]

barley /ˈbɑːlɪ/ *n.* **1** any of various hardy awned cereals of the genus *Hordeum*, used as food and in malt liquors and spirits such as whisky. **2** the grain produced from this. □ **barley sugar** an amber-coloured sweet made of boiled sugar. **barley water** a drink made from water and a boiled barley mixture. [OE *bærlic* (adj.) f. *bære*, *bere* barley]

barleycorn /ˈbɑːliˌkɔːn/ *n*. the grain of barley.

barm *n*. **1** the froth on fermenting malt liquor. **2** *archaic or dial.* yeast or leaven. [OE *beorma*]

barmaid /ˈbɑːmeɪd/ *n*. a woman serving behind the bar of a public house, hotel, etc.

barman /ˈbɑːmən/ *n*. (*pl.* **-men**) a man serving behind the bar of a public house, hotel, etc.

bar mitzvah /bɑː ˈmɪtzvə/ *n*. **1** the religious initiation ceremony of a Jewish boy who has reached the age of 13. **2** the boy undergoing this ceremony. [Heb., = 'son of the commandment']

barmy /ˈbɑːmɪ/ *adj.* (**barmier**, **barmiest**) esp. *Brit. sl.* crazy, stupid. □ **barmily** *adv.* **barminess** *n*. [earlier = frothy, f. BARM]

barn *n*. **1** a large farm building for storing grain etc. **2** *derog.* a large plain or unattractive building. **3** *US* a large shed for storing road or railway vehicles. □ **barn dance** an informal social gathering for country dancing, orig. in a barn. **barn-owl** a kind of owl, *Tyto alba*, frequenting barns. [OE *bern*, *beren* f. *bere* barley + *ern*, *ærn* house]

barnacle /ˈbɑːnək(ə)l/ *n*. any of various species of small marine crustaceans of the class Cirripedia which cling to rocks, ships' bottoms, etc. □ **barnacle goose** an Arctic goose, *Branta leucopsis*, which visits Britain in winter. □ **barnacled** *adj.* [ME *bernak* (= med.L *bernaca*), of unkn. orig.]

barney /ˈbɑːnɪ/ *n*. (*pl.* **-eys**) *Brit. colloq.* a noisy quarrel. [perh. dial.]

barnstorm /ˈbɑːnstɔːm/ *v.intr.* **1** tour rural districts giving theatrical performances (formerly often in barns). **2** *US* make a rapid tour holding political meetings. □ **barnstormer** *n*.

barnyard /ˈbɑːnjɑːd/ *n*. the area around a barn; a farmyard.

barograph /ˈbærəˌɡrɑːf/ *n*. a barometer equipped to record its readings. [Gk *baros* weight + -GRAPH]

barometer /bəˈrɒmɪtə(r)/ *n*. **1** an instrument measuring atmospheric pressure, esp. in forecasting the weather and determining altitude. **2** anything which reflects changes in circumstances, opinions, etc. □ **barometric** /ˌbærəʊˈmetrɪk/ *adj.* **barometrical** /ˌbærəʊˈmetrɪk(ə)l/ *adj.* **barometry** *n*.

baron /ˈbærən/ *n*. **1 a** a member of the lowest order of the British nobility. **b** a similar member of a foreign nobility. **2** an important businessman or other powerful or influential person (*sugar baron*; *newspaper baron*). **3** *hist.* a person who held lands or property from the sovereign or a powerful overlord. □ **baron of beef** an undivided double sirloin. [ME f. AF *barun*, OF *baron* f. med.L *baro*, *-onis* man, of unkn. orig.]

baroness /ˈbærənɪs/ *n*. a woman holding the rank of baron either as a life peerage or as a hereditary rank. **2** the wife or widow of a baron. [ME f. OF *baronesse* (as BARON)]

baronet /ˈbærənɪt/ *n*. a member of the lowest hereditary titled British order. [ME f. AL *baronettus* (as BARON)]

baronetcy /ˈbærənɪtsɪ/ *n*. (*pl.* **-ies**) the domain, rank, or tenure of a baronet.

baronial /bəˈrəʊnɪəl/ *adj.* of, relating to, or befitting barons.

barony /ˈbærənɪ/ *n*. (*pl.* **-ies**) the domain, rank, or tenure of a baron. [ME f. OF *baronie* (as BARON)]

baroque /bəˈrɒk/ *adj.* & *n*. —*adj.* **1** highly ornate and extravagant in style, esp. of European art, architecture, and music of the 17th and 18th c. **2** of or relating to this period. —*n.* **1** the baroque style. **2** baroque art collectively. [F (orig. = 'irregular pearl') f. Port. *barroco*, of unkn. orig.]

barque /bɑːk/ *n*. **1** a type of sailing-ship. **2** *poet.* any boat. [ME f. F prob. f. Prov. *barca* f. L *barca* ship's boat]

barrack[1] /ˈbærək/ *n*. (usu. in *pl.*, often treated as *sing.*) **1** a building or building complex used to house soldiers. **2** any building used to accommodate large numbers of people. **3** a large building of a bleak or plain appearance. □ **barrack-room lawyer** a pompously argumentative person. [F *baraque* f. It. *baracca* or Sp. *barraca* soldier's tent, of unkn. orig.]

barrack[2] /ˈbærək/ *v. Brit.* **1** *tr.* shout or jeer at (players in a game, a performer, speaker, etc.). **2** *intr.* shout or jeer. [app. f. BORAK]

barracouta /ˌbærəˈkuːtə/ *n*. (*pl.* same or **barracoutas**) **1** a long slender fish, *Thyrsites atun*, usu. found in southern oceans. **2** *NZ* a small narrow loaf of bread. [var. of BARRACUDA]

barracuda /ˌbærəˈkuːdə/ *n*. (*pl.* same or **barracudas**) a large and voracious tropical marine fish of the family Sphyraenidae. [Amer. Sp. *barracuda*]

barrage /ˈbærɑːʒ/ *n*. **1** a concentrated artillery bombardment over a wide area. **2** a rapid succession of questions or criticisms. **3** an artificial barrier, esp. in a river. □ **barrage balloon** a large anchored balloon, used (usu. as one of a series) as a defence against low-flying aircraft. [F f. *barrer* (as BAR[1])]

barratry /ˈbærətrɪ/ *n*. fraud or gross negligence of a ship's master or crew at the expense of its owners or users. □ **barratrous** *adj.* [ME f. OF *baraterie* f. *barateor* trickster, f. *barat* deceit]

barre /bɑː(r)/ *n*. a horizontal bar at waist level used in dance exercises. [F]

barrel /ˈbær(ə)l/ *n*. & *v*. —*n.* **1** a cylindrical container usu. bulging out in the middle, traditionally made of wooden staves with metal hoops round them. **2** the contents of this. **3** a measure of capacity, usu. varying from 30 to 40 gallons. **4** a cylindrical tube forming part of an object such as a gun or a pen. —*v.* (**barrelled**, **barrelling**; *US* **barreled**, **barreling**) **1** *tr.* put into a barrel or barrels. **2** *intr. US sl.* drive fast. □ **barrel-chested** having a large rounded chest. **barrel-organ** a mechanical musical instrument in which a rotating pin-studded cylinder acts on a series of pipe-valves, strings, or metal tongues. **over a barrel** *colloq.* in a helpless position; at a person's mercy. [ME f. OF *baril* perh. f. Rmc.: rel to BAR[1]]

barren /ˈbærən/ *adj.* (**barrener**, **barrenest**) **1 a** unable to bear young. **b** unable to produce fruit or vegetation. **2** meagre, unprofitable. **3** dull, unstimulating. **4** (foll. by *of*) lacking in (*barren of wit*). □ **barrenly** *adv.* **barrenness** *n*. [ME f. AF *barai(g)ne*, OF *barhaine* etc., of unkn. orig.]

barricade /ˌbærɪˈkeɪd/ *n*. & *v*. —*n.* a barrier, esp. one improvised across a street etc. —*v.tr.* block or defend with a barricade. [F f. *barrique* cask f. Sp. *barrica*, rel. to BARREL]

barrier /ˈbærɪə(r)/ *n*. **1** a fence or other obstacle that bars advance or access. **2** an obstacle or circumstance that keeps people or things apart, or prevents communication (*class barriers*; *a* *language barrier*). **3** anything that prevents progress or success. □ **barrier cream** a cream used to protect the skin from damage or infection. **barrier reef** a coral reef separated from the shore by a broad deep channel. [ME f. AF *barrere*, OF *barriere*]

barring /ˈbɑːrɪŋ/ *prep.* except, not including. [BAR¹ + -ING²]

barrio /ˈbɑːrɪəʊ/ *n.* (*pl.* **-os**) (in the US) the Spanish-speaking quarter of a town or city. [Sp., = district of a town]

barrister /ˈbærɪstə(r)/ *n.* (in full **barrister-at-law**) **1** *Brit.* a person called to the bar and entitled to practise as an advocate in the higher courts. **2** *US* a lawyer. [16th c.: f. BAR¹, perh. after *minister*]

barrow¹ /ˈbærəʊ/ *n.* **1** *Brit.* a two-wheeled handcart used esp. by street vendors. **2** = WHEELBARROW. □ **barrow boy** *Brit.* a boy who sells wares from a barrow. [OE *bearwe* f. Gmc]

barrow² /ˈbærəʊ/ *n.* *Archaeol.* an ancient gravemound or tumulus. [OE *beorg* f. Gmc]

bartender /ˈbɑːˌtendə(r)/ *n.* a person serving behind the bar of a public house.

barter /ˈbɑːtə(r)/ *v.* & *n.* —*v.* **1** *tr.* exchange (goods or services) without using money. **2** *intr.* make such an exchange. —*n.* trade by exchange of goods. □ **barterer** *n.* [prob. OF *barater*: see BARRATRY]

baryon /ˈbærɪɒn/ *n.* *Physics* an elementary particle that is of equal mass to or greater mass than a proton (i.e. is a nucleon or a hyperon). □ **baryonic** /-ˈɒnɪk/ *adj.* [Gk *barus* heavy + -ON]

barysphere /ˈbærɪˌsfɪə(r)/ *n.* the dense interior of the earth, including the mantle and core, enclosed by the lithosphere. [Gk *barus* heavy + *sphaira* sphere]

basal /ˈbeɪs(ə)l/ *adj.* **1** of, at, or forming a base. **2** fundamental. □ **basal metabolism** the chemical processes occurring in an organism at complete rest. [BASE¹ + -AL]

basalt /ˈbæsɔːlt/ *n.* **1** a dark basic volcanic rock whose strata sometimes form columns. **2** a kind of black stoneware resembling basalt. □ **basaltic** /bəˈsɔːltɪk/ *adj.* [L *basaltes* var. of *basanites* f. Gk f. *basanos* touchstone]

base¹ /beɪs/ *n.* & *v.* —*n.* **1 a** a part that supports from beneath or serves as a foundation for an object or structure. **b** a notional structure or entity on which something draws or depends (*power base*). **2** a principle or starting-point; a basis. **3** esp. *Mil.* a place from which an operation or activity is directed. **4 a** a main or important ingredient of a mixture. **b** a substance, e.g. water, in combination with which pigment forms paint etc. **5** a substance used as a foundation for make-up. **6** *Chem.* a substance capable of combining with an acid to form a salt and water and usu. producing hydroxide ions when dissolved in water. **7** *Math.* a number in terms of which other numbers or logarithms are expressed (see RADIX). **8** *Geom.* a line or surface on which a figure is regarded as standing. **9** *Baseball* etc. one of the four stations that must be reached in turn when scoring a run. —*v.tr.* **1** (usu. foll. by *on*, *upon*) found or establish (*a theory based on speculation; his opinion was soundly based*). **2** (foll. by *at*, *in*, etc.) station (*troops were based in Malta*). □ **base rate** *Brit.* the interest rate set by the Bank of England, used as the basis for other banks' rates. **base unit** a

unit that is defined arbitrarily and not by combinations of other units. [F *base* or L *basis* stepping f. Gk]

base² /beɪs/ *adj.* **1** lacking moral worth; cowardly, despicable. **2** menial. **3** not pure; alloyed (*base coin*). **4** (of a metal) low in value. □ **basely** *adv.* **baseness** *n.* [ME in sense 'of small height', f. F *bas* f. med.L *bassus* short (in L as a cognomen)]

baseball /ˈbeɪsbɔːl/ *n.* **1** a game played esp. in the US with teams of nine, a bat and ball, and a circuit of four bases which the batsman must complete. **2** the ball used in this game.

baseless /ˈbeɪslɪs/ *adj.* unfounded, groundless. □ **baselessly** *adv.* **baselessness** *n.*

baseline /ˈbeɪslaɪn/ *n.* **1** a line used as a base or starting-point. **2** (in lawn tennis) the line marking each end of a court.

baseman /ˈbeɪsmən/ *n.* (*pl.* **-men**) *Baseball* a fielder stationed near a base.

basement /ˈbeɪsmənt/ *n.* the lowest floor of a building, usu. at least partly below ground level. [prob. Du., perh. f. It. *basamento* column-base]

bases pl. of BASE¹, BASIS.

bash /bæʃ/ *v.* & *n.* —*v.* **1** *tr.* **a** strike bluntly or heavily. **b** (often foll. by *up*) *colloq.* attack violently. **c** (often foll. by *down*, *in*, etc.) damage or break by striking forcibly. **2** *intr.* (foll. by *into*) collide with. —*n.* **1** a heavy blow. **2** *sl.* an attempt (*had a bash at painting*). **3** *sl.* a party or social event. [imit., perh. f. *bang*, *smash*, *dash*, etc.]

bashful /ˈbæʃfʊl/ *adj.* **1** shy, diffident, self-conscious. **2** sheepish. □ **bashfully** *adv.* **bashfulness** *n.* [obs. *bash* (v.), = ABASH]

BASIC /ˈbeɪsɪk/ *n.* a computer programming language using familiar English words, designed for beginners and widely used on microcomputers. [Beginner's All-purpose Symbolic Instruction Code]

basic /ˈbeɪsɪk/ *adj.* & *n.* —*adj.* **1** forming or serving as a base. **2** fundamental. **3 a** simplest or lowest in level (*basic pay; basic requirements*). **b** vulgar (*basic humour*). **4** *Chem.* having the properties of or containing a base. —*n.* (usu. in pl.) the fundamental facts or principles. □ **basic industry** an industry of fundamental economic importance. **basic slag** fertilizer containing phosphates formed as a by-product during steel manufacture. **basic wage** *Austral.* & *NZ* the minimum living wage, fixed by industrial tribunal. □ **basically** *adv.* [BASE¹ + -IC]

basil /ˈbæz(ə)l/ *n.* an aromatic herb of the genus *Ocimum*, esp. *O. basilicum* (in full **sweet basil**), whose leaves are used in cooking. [ME f. OF *basile* f. med.L *basilicus* f. Gk *basilikos* royal]

basilica /bəˈzɪlɪkə/ *n.* **1** an ancient Roman public hall with an apse and colonnades, used as a lawcourt and place of assembly. **2** a similar building used as a Christian church. □ **basilican** *adj.* [L. f. Gk *basilikē* (*oikia*, *stoa*) royal (house, portico) f. *basileus* king]

basilisk /ˈbæzɪlɪsk/ *n.* **1** a mythical reptile with a lethal breath and look. **2** any small American lizard of the genus *Basiliscus*. [ME f. L *basiliscus* f. Gk *basiliskos* kinglet, serpent]

basin /ˈbeɪs(ə)n/ *n.* **1** a wide shallow open container, esp. a fixed one for holding water. **2** a hollow rounded depression. **3** any sheltered area of water where boats can moor safely. **4** a round valley. **5** an area drained by rivers and tributaries. □ **basinful** *n.* (*pl.* **-fuls**). [ME f. OF *bacin* f. med.L *ba(s)cinus*, perh. f. Gaulish]

basis /ˈbeɪsɪs/ n. (pl. **bases** /-siːz/) **1** the foundation or support of something, esp. an idea or argument. **2** the main or determining principle or ingredient (*on a purely friendly basis*). **3** the starting-point for a discussion etc. [L f. Gk, = BASE¹]

bask /bɑːsk/ v.intr. **1** sit or lie back lazily in warmth and light (*basking in the sun*). **2** (foll. by *in*) derive great pleasure (from) (*basking in glory*). □ **basking shark** a very large shark, *Cetorhinus maximus*, which often lies near the surface. [ME, app. f. ON: rel. to BATHE]

basket /ˈbɑːskɪt/ n. **1** a container made of interwoven cane etc. **2** a container resembling this. **3** the amount held by a basket. **4** the goal in basketball, or a goal scored. **5** *Econ.* a group or range (of currencies). □ **basketful** n. (pl. **-fuls**). [AF & OF *basket*, AL *baskettum*, of unkn. orig.]

basketball /ˈbɑːskɪtbɔːl/ n. **1** a game between two teams of five or six, in which goals are scored by making the ball drop through hooped nets fixed high up at each end of the court. **2** the ball used in this game.

basketry /ˈbɑːskɪtrɪ/ n. **1** the art of making baskets. **2** baskets collectively.

basketwork /ˈbɑːskɪtwɜːk/ n. **1** material woven in the style of a basket. **2** the art of making this.

basmati /bæzˈmɑːtɪ/ n. (in full **basmati rice**) a superior kind of Indian rice. [Hindi, = fragrant]

Basque /bæsk, bɑːsk/ n. & adj. —n. **1** a member of a people of the Western Pyrenees. **2** the language of this people. —adj. of or relating to the Basques or their language. [F f. L *Vasco -onis*]

basque /bæsk/ n. a close-fitting bodice extending from the shoulders to the waist and often with a short continuation below waist level. [BASQUE]

bas-relief /ˈbæsrɪˌliːf/ n. sculpture or carving in which the figures project slightly from the background. [earlier *basse relieve* f. It. *basso rilievo* low relief: later altered to F form]

bass¹ /beɪs/ n. & adj. —n. **1 a** the lowest adult male singing voice. **b** a singer with this voice. **c** a part written for it. **2** the lowest part in harmonized music. **3 a** an instrument that is the lowest in pitch in its family. **b** its player. **4** *colloq.* **a** a bass guitar or double-bass. **b** its player. **5** the low-frequency output of a radio, record-player, etc., corresponding to the bass in music. —adj. **1** lowest in musical pitch. **2** deep-sounding. □ **bass clef** a clef placing F below middle C on the second highest line of the staff. □ **bassist** n. (in sense 4). [alt. of BASE² after It. *basso*]

bass² /bæs/ n. (pl. same or **basses**) **1** the common perch. **2** a marine fish of the family Serranidae, with spiny fins. [earlier *barse* f. OE *bærs*]

bass³ /bæs/ n. = BAST. [alt. f. BAST]

basset /ˈbæsɪt/ n. (in full **basset-hound**) **1** a sturdy hunting-dog of a breed with a long body, short legs, and big ears. **2** this breed. [F, dimin. of *bas basse* low: see BASE²]

basset-horn /ˈbæsɪtˌhɔːn/ n. an alto clarinet in F, with a dark tone. [G, transl. of F *cor de bassette* f. It. *corno di bassetto* f. *corno* horn + *bassetto* dimin. of *basso* BASE²]

bassinet /ˌbæsɪˈnet/ n. a child's wicker cradle, usu. with a hood. [F, dimin. of *bassin* BASIN]

basso /ˈbæsəʊ/ n. (pl. **-os** or **bassi** /-sɪ/) a singer with a bass voice. □ **basso profondo** a bass

singer with an exceptionally low range. [It., = BASS¹; *profondo* deep]

bassoon /bəˈsuːn/ n. **1** a bass instrument of the oboe family, with a double reed. **2** its player. □ **bassoonist** n. (in sense 1). [F *basson* f. *bas* BASS¹]

bast /bæst/ n. the inner bark of lime, or other flexible fibrous bark, used as fibre in matting etc. [OE *bæst* f. Gmc]

bastard /ˈbɑːstəd, ˈbæ-/ n. & adj. —n. **1** a person born of parents not married to each other. **2** *sl.* **a** an unpleasant or despicable person. **b** a person of a specified kind (*rotten bastard*; *lucky bastard*). **3** *sl.* a difficult or awkward thing, undertaking, etc. —adj. **1** born of parents not married to each other; illegitimate. **2** (of things): **a** unauthorized, counterfeit. **b** hybrid. □ **bastardy** n. (in sense 1 of n.). [ME f. OF f. med.L *bastardus*, perh. f. *bastum* pack-saddle]

bastardize /ˈbɑːstəˌdaɪz/ v.tr. (also **-ise**) **1** declare (a person) illegitimate. **2** corrupt, debase. □ **bastardization** /-ˈzeɪʃ(ə)n/ n.

baste¹ /beɪst/ v.tr. moisten (meat) with gravy or melted fat during cooking. [16th c.: orig. unkn.]

baste² /beɪst/ v.tr. stitch loosely together in preparation for sewing; tack. [ME f. OF *bastir* sew lightly, ult. f. Gmc]

baste³ /beɪst/ v.tr. beat soundly; thrash. [perh. figurative use of BASTE¹]

bastinado /ˌbæstɪˈneɪdəʊ/ n. & v. —n. punishment by beating with a stick on the soles of the feet. —v.tr. (**-oes**, **-oed**) punish (a person) in this way. [Sp. *bastonada* f. *baston* BATON]

bastion /ˈbæstɪən/ n. **1** a projecting part of a fortification built at an angle of, or against the line of, a wall. **2** a thing regarded as protecting (*bastion of freedom*). [F f. It. *bastione* f. *bastire* build]

basuco /bəˈzuːkəʊ/ n. a cheap impure form of cocaine smoked for its stimulating effect. [Colombian Sp.]

bat¹ n. & v. —n. **1** an implement with a handle, usu. of wood and with a flat or curved surface, used for hitting balls in games. **2** a turn at using this. **3** a batsman, esp. in cricket, usu. described in some way (*an excellent bat*). **4** (usu. in *pl.*) an object like a table-tennis bat used to guide aircraft when taxiing. —v. (**batted**, **batting**) **1** *tr.* hit with or as with a bat. **2** *intr.* take a turn at batting. □ **off one's own bat** unprompted, unaided. **right off the bat** *US* immediately. [ME f. OE *batt* club, perh. partly f. OF *batte* club f. *battre* strike]

bat² n. any mouselike nocturnal mammal of the order Chiroptera, capable of flight by means of membranous wings extending from its fore-limbs. □ **have bats in the belfry** be eccentric or crazy. **like a bat out of hell** very fast. [16th c., alt. of ME *bakke* f. Scand.]

bat³ v.tr. (**batted**, **batting**) wink (one's eyelid) (now usu. in phr.). □ **not** (or **never**) **bat an eyelid** *colloq.* show no reaction or emotion. [var. of obs. *bate* flutter]

batch n. & v. —n. **1** a number of things or persons forming a group or dealt with together. **2** an instalment (*have sent off the latest batch*). **3** the loaves produced at one baking. **4** (*attrib.*) using or dealt with in batches, not as a continuous flow (*batch production*). **5** *Computing* a group of records processed as a single unit. —v.tr. arrange or deal with in batches. [ME f. OE *bæcce* f. *bacan* BAKE]

bated /ˈbeɪtɪd/ *adj.* □ **with bated breath** very anxiously. [past part. of obs. *bate* (v.) restrain, f. ABATE]

bath /bɑːθ/ *n. & v.* —*n.* (*pl.* **baths** /bɑːðz/) **1 a** (in full **bath-tub**) a container for liquid, usu. water, used for immersing and washing the body. **b** this with its contents (*your bath is ready*). **2** the act or process of immersing the body for washing or therapy (*have a bath; take a bath*). **3 a** a vessel containing liquid in which something is immersed, e.g. a film for developing, for controlling temperature, etc. **b** this with its contents. **4** (usu. in *pl.*) a building with baths or a swimming pool, usu. open to the public. —*v. Brit.* **1** *tr.* wash (esp. a person) in a bath. **2** *intr.* take a bath. □ **bath cube** a cube of compacted bath salts. **bath salts** soluble salts used for softening or scenting bath-water. [OE *bæth* f. Gmc]

Bath bun /bɑːθ/ *n. Brit.* a round spiced kind of bun with currants, often iced. [*Bath* in S. England, named from its hot springs]

Bath chair /bɑːθ/ *n.* a wheelchair for invalids.

bathe /beɪð/ *v. & n.* —*v.* **1** *intr.* immerse oneself in water, esp. to swim or esp. *US* wash oneself. **2** *tr.* immerse in or wash or treat with liquid esp. for cleansing or medicinal purposes. **3** *tr.* (of sunlight etc.) envelop. —*n. Brit.* immersion in liquid, esp. to swim. □ **bathing-costume** (or **-suit**) a garment worn for swimming. [OE *bathian* f. Gmc]

bather /ˈbeɪðə(r)/ *n.* **1** a person who bathes. **2** (in *pl.*) *Austral.* a bathing-suit.

bathhouse /ˈbɑːθhaʊs/ *n.* a building with baths for public use.

bathos /ˈbeɪθɒs/ *n.* an unintentional lapse in mood from the sublime to the absurd or trivial; a commonplace or ridiculous feature offsetting an otherwise sublime situation; an anticlimax. □ **bathetic** /bəˈθetɪk/ *adj.* **bathotic** /bəˈθɒtɪk/ *adj.* [Gk, = depth]

bathrobe /ˈbɑːθrəʊb/ *n. US* a loose coat usu. of towelling worn before and after taking a bath.

bathroom /ˈbɑːθruːm, -rʊm/ *n.* **1** a room containing a bath and usu. other washing facilities. **2** esp. *US* a room containing a lavatory.

bathyscaphe /ˈbæθɪˌskæf/ *n.* a manned vessel for deep-sea diving. [Gk *bathus* deep + *skaphos* ship]

bathysphere /ˈbæθɪˌsfɪə(r)/ *n.* a spherical vessel for deep-sea observation. [Gk *bathus* deep + SPHERE]

batik /bəˈtiːk, ˈbætɪk/ *n.* a method (orig. used in Java) of producing coloured designs on textiles by applying wax to the parts to be left uncoloured; a piece of cloth treated in this way. [Jav., = painted]

batiste /bæˈtiːst/ *n. & adj.* —*n.* a fine linen or cotton cloth. —*adj.* made of batiste. [F (earlier *batiche*), perh. rel. to *battre* BATTER¹]

batman /ˈbætmən/ *n.* (*pl.* **-men**) *Mil.* an attendant serving an officer. [OF *bat, bast* f. med.L *bastum* pack-saddle + MAN]

baton /ˈbæt(ə)n/ *n.* **1** a thin stick used by a conductor to direct an orchestra, choir, etc. **2** *Athletics* a short stick or tube carried and passed on by the runners in a relay race. **3** a long stick carried and twirled by a drum major. **4** a staff of office or authority, esp. a Field Marshal's. **5** a

policeman's truncheon. □ **baton round** a rubber or plastic bullet. [F *bâton, baston* ult. f. LL *bastum* stick]

batrachian /bəˈtreɪkɪən/ *n. & adj.* —*n.* any of the amphibians that discard gills and tails, esp. the frog and toad. —*adj.* of or relating to the batrachians. [Gk *batrakhos* frog]

bats *predic.adj. sl.* crazy. [f. phr. (*have*) *bats in the belfry*: see BAT²]

batsman /ˈbætsmən/ *n.* (*pl.* **-men**) **1** a person who bats or is batting, esp. in cricket. **2** a signaller using bats to guide aircraft on the ground. □ **batsmanship** *n.* (in sense 1).

battalion /bəˈtælɪən/ *n.* **1** a large body of men ready for battle, esp. an infantry unit forming part of a brigade. **2** a large group of people pursuing a common aim. [F *battaillon* f. It. *battaglione* f. *battaglia* BATTLE]

batten¹ /ˈbæt(ə)n/ *n. & v.* —*n.* **1** a long flat strip of squared timber or metal, esp. used to hold something in place or as a fastening against a wall etc. **2** *Naut.* a strip of wood or metal for securing a tarpaulin over a ship's hatchway. —*v.tr.* strengthen or fasten with battens. □ **batten down the hatches 1** *Naut.* secure a ship's tarpaulins. **2** prepare for a difficulty or crisis. [OF *batant* part. of *batre* beat f. L *battuere*]

batten² /ˈbæt(ə)n/ *v.intr.* (foll. by *on*) thrive or prosper at another's expense. [ON *batna* get better f. *bati* advantage]

batter¹ /ˈbætə(r)/ *v.* **1 a** *tr.* strike repeatedly with hard blows, esp. so as to cause visible damage. **b** *intr.* (often foll. by *against, at*, etc.) strike repeated blows; pound heavily and insistently (*batter at the door*). **2** *tr.* (often in *passive*) handle roughly, esp. over a long period. □ **battered baby** an infant that has suffered repeated violence from adults. **battered wife** a wife subjected to repeated violence by her husband. **battering-ram** *hist.* a heavy beam, orig. with an end in the form of a carved ram's head, used in breaching fortifications. □ **batterer** *n.* [ME f. AF *baterer* f. OF *batre* beat f. L *battuere*]

batter² /ˈbætə(r)/ *n.* a fluid mixture of flour, egg, and milk or water, used in cooking, esp. for pancakes and for coating food before frying. [ME f. AF *batour* f. OF *bateüre* f. *batre*: see BATTER¹]

batter³ /ˈbætə(r)/ *n. Sport* a player batting, esp. in baseball.

battered /ˈbætəd/ *adj.* (esp. of fish) coated in batter and deep-fried.

battery /ˈbætərɪ/ *n.* (*pl.* **-ies**) **1** a usu. portable container of a cell or cells carrying an electric charge, as a source of current. **2** (often *attrib.*) esp. *Brit.* a series of cages for the intensive breeding and rearing of poultry or cattle. **3** a set of similar units of equipment, esp. connected. **4 a** a fortified emplacement for heavy guns. **b** an artillery unit of guns, men, and vehicles. **5** *Law* an act inflicting unlawful personal violence on another (see ASSAULT). [F *batterie* f. *batre, battre* strike f. L *battuere*]

batting /ˈbætɪŋ/ *n.* the action of hitting with a bat. □ **batting order** the order in which people act or take their turn, esp. of batsmen in cricket.

battle /ˈbæt(ə)l/ *n. & v.* —*n.* **1** a prolonged fight between large organized armed forces. **2** a contest; a prolonged or difficult struggle. —*v.* **1** *intr.* struggle; fight persistently (*battled against the elements; battled for women's rights*). **2** *tr.* fight (one's way etc.). □ **battle-cruiser** *hist.* a heavy-gunned ship faster and more lightly armoured than a battleship. **battle-cry** a cry or slogan of participants in a battle or contest. **battle royal 1** a battle in which several combatants or all available forces engage; a free fight. **2** a heated argument. □ **battler** n. [ME f. OF *bataille* ult. f. LL *battualia* gladiatorial exercises f. L *battuere* beat]

battleaxe /ˈbæt(ə)lˌæks/ n. **1** a large axe used in ancient warfare. **2** colloq. a formidable or domineering older woman.

battledore /ˈbæt(ə)lˌdɔː(r)/ n. hist. **1** (in full **battledore and shuttlecock**) a game played with a shuttlecock and rackets. **2** the racket used in this. [15th c., perh. f. Prov. *batedor* beater f. *batre* beat]

battledress /ˈbæt(ə)lˌdres/ n. the everyday uniform of a soldier.

battlefield /ˈbæt(ə)lˌfiːld/ n. (also **battleground** /-ˌgraʊnd/) the piece of ground on which a battle is or was fought.

battlement /ˈbæt(ə)lmənt/ n. (usu. in pl.) **1** a parapet with recesses along the top of a wall, as part of a fortification. **2** a section of roof enclosed by this (*walking on the battlements*). □ **battlemented** adj. [OF *bataillier* furnish with ramparts + -MENT]

battleship /ˈbæt(ə)lˌʃɪp/ n. a warship with the heaviest armour and the largest guns.

batty /ˈbætɪ/ adj. (**battier, battiest**) sl. crazy. □ **battily** adv. **battiness** n. [BAT² + -Y¹]

batwing /ˈbætwɪŋ/ adj. (esp. of a sleeve or a flame) shaped like the wing of a bat.

batwoman /ˈbætˌwʊmən/ n. (pl. **-women**) a female attendant serving an officer in the women's services. [as BATMAN + WOMAN]

bauble /ˈbɔːb(ə)l/ n. a showy trinket or toy of little value. [ME f. OF *ba(u)bel* child's toy, of unkn. orig.]

baud /bɔːd, bɔːd/ n. (pl. same or **bauds**) Computing etc. **1** a unit used to express the speed of electronic code signals, corresponding to one information unit per second. **2** (loosely) a unit of data-transmission speed of one bit per second. [J. M. E. *Baudot*, Fr. engineer d. 1903]

baulk /bɔːlk, bɔːk/ v. & n. (also **balk**) —v. **1** intr. **a** refuse to go on. **b** (often foll. by *at*) hesitate. **2** tr. **a** thwart, hinder. **b** disappoint. **3** tr. **a** miss, let slip (a chance etc.). **b** ignore, shirk. —n. **1** a hindrance; a stumbling-block. **2** a roughly-squared timber beam. **3** *Billiards* etc. the area on a billiard-table from which a player begins a game. **4** *Baseball* an illegal action made by a pitcher. □ **baulker** n. [OE *balc* f. ON *bálkr* f. Gmc]

bauxite /ˈbɔːksaɪt/ n. a claylike mineral containing varying proportions of alumina, the chief source of aluminium. □ **bauxitic** /-ˈsɪtɪk/ adj. [F f. *Les Baux* near Arles in S. France + -ITE¹]

bawd n. a woman who runs a brothel. [ME *bawdstrot* f. OF *baudetrot, baudestroyt* procuress]

bawdy /ˈbɔːdɪ/ adj. & n. —adj. (**bawdier, bawdiest**) humorously indecent. —n. bawdy talk or writing. □ **bawdy-house** a brothel. □ **bawdily** adv. **bawdiness** n. [BAWD + -Y¹]

bawl /bɔːl/ v. **1** tr. speak or call out noisily. **2** intr. weep loudly. □ **bawl out** colloq. reprimand angrily. □ **bawler** n. [imit.: cf. med.L *baulare* bark, Icel. *baula* (Sw. *böla*) to low]

bay¹ n. **1** a broad inlet of the sea where the land curves inwards. **2** a recess in a mountain range. [ME f. OF *baie* f. OSp. *bahia*]

bay² n. **1** (in full **bay laurel**) a laurel, *Laurus nobilis*, having deep green leaves and purple berries. **2** (in pl.) a wreath made of bay-leaves, for a victor or poet. □ **bay-leaf** the aromatic (usu. dried) leaf of the bay-tree, used in cooking. **bay rum** a perfume, esp. for the hair, distilled orig. from bayberry leaves in rum. [OF *baie* f. L *baca* berry]

bay³ n. **1** a space created by a window-line projecting outwards from a wall. **2** a recess; a section of wall between buttresses or columns, esp. in the nave of a church etc. **3** a compartment (*bomb bay*). **4** an area specially allocated or marked off (*sick bay; loading bay*). □ **bay window** a window built into a bay. [ME f. OF *baie* f. ba(y)er gape f. med.L *batare*]

bay⁴ adj. & n. —adj. (esp. of a horse) dark reddish-brown. —n. a bay horse with a black mane and tail. [OF *bai* f. L *badius*]

bay⁵ v. & n. —v. **1** intr. (esp. of a large dog) bark or howl loudly and plaintively. **2** tr. bay at. —n. the sound of baying, esp. in chorus from hounds in close pursuit. □ **at bay 1** cornered, apparently unable to escape. **2** in a desperate situation. **hold** (or **keep**) **at bay** hold off (a pursuer). [ME f. OF *bai, baiier* bark f. It. *baiare*, of imit. orig.]

bayberry /ˈbeɪbərɪ/ n. (pl. **-ies**) any of various N. American plants of the genus *Myrica*, having aromatic leaves. [BAY² + BERRY]

bayonet /ˈbeɪəˌnet/ n. & v. —n. **1** a stabbing blade attachable to the muzzle of a rifle. **2** an electrical or other fitting engaged by being pushed into a socket and twisted. —v.tr. (**bayoneted, bayoneting**) stab with a bayonet. [F *baïonnette*, perh. f. *Bayonne* in SW France, where they were first made]

bayou /ˈbaɪuː/ n. a marshy offshoot of a river etc. in the southern US. [Amer. F: cf. Choctaw *bayuk*]

bazaar /bəˈzɑː(r)/ n. **1** a market in an oriental country. **2** a fund-raising sale of goods, esp. for charity. **3** a large shop selling fancy goods etc. [Pers. *bāzār*, prob. through Turk. and It.]

bazooka /bəˈzuːkə/ n. a tubular short-range rocket-launcher used against tanks. [app. f. *bazoo* mouth, of unkn. orig.]

BB abbr. double-black (pencil-lead).

BBC abbr. British Broadcasting Corporation.

BC abbr. (of a date) before Christ.

BCE abbr. before the Common Era.

BD abbr. Bachelor of Divinity.

bdellium /ˈdelɪəm/ n. **1** any of various trees, esp. of the genus *Commiphora*, yielding resin. **2** this fragrant resin used in perfumes. [L f. Gk *bdellion* f. Heb. *bʹdhōlaḥ*]

BDS abbr. Bachelor of Dental Surgery.

BE abbr. **1** Bachelor of Education. **2** Bachelor of Engineering.

Be symb. Chem. the element beryllium.

be /biː, bɪ/ v. & v.aux. (sing. present **am** /æm, əm/; **are** /ɑː(r), ə(r)/; **is** /ɪz/; pl. present **are**; 1st and 3rd sing. past **was** /wɒz, wəz/; 2nd sing. past and pl. past **were** /wɜː(r), wə(r)/; present subj. **be**; past subj. **were**; pres. part. **being**; past part. **been** /biːn, bɪn/. —v.intr. **1** (often prec. by *there*) exist, live (*I think, therefore I am; there is a house on the corner; there is no God*). **2 a** occur; take place (*dinner is at* *eight*). **b** occupy a position in space (*he is in the garden; she is from abroad; have you been to Paris?*). **3** remain, continue (*let it be*). **4** linking subject and predicate, expressing: **a** identity (*she is the person; today is Thursday*). **b** condition (*he is ill today*). **c** state or quality (*he is very kind; they are my friends*). **d** opinion (*I am against hanging*). **e** total (*two and two are four*). **f** cost or significance (*it is £5 to enter; it is nothing to me*). —*v.aux.* **1** with a past participle to form the passive mood (*it was done; it is said; we shall be helped*). **2** with a present participle to form continuous tenses (*we are coming; it is being cleaned*). **3** with an infinitive to express duty or commitment, intention, possibility, destiny, or hypothesis (*I am to tell you; he is to come at four; they were never to meet again; if I were to die*). **4** *archaic* with the past participle of intransitive verbs to form perfect tenses (*Babylon is fallen*). □ **be about** occupy oneself with (*is about his business*). **be-all and end-all** *colloq.* (often foll. by *of*) the whole being or essence. **be at** occupy oneself with (*what is he at?; mice have been at the food*). **be off** *colloq.* go away; leave. **-to-be** of the future (in *comb.*: *bride-to-be*). [OE *beo(m)*, *(e)am*, *is*, *(e)aron*; past f. OE *wæs* f. *wesan* to be; there are numerous Gmc cognates]

be- /bɪ/ *prefix* forming verbs: **1** (from transitive verbs) **a** all over; all round (*beset; besmear*). **b** thoroughly, excessively (*begrudge; belabour*). **2** (from intransitive verbs) expressing transitive action (*bemoan; bestride*). **3** (from adjectives and nouns) expressing transitive action (*befool; befoul*). **4** (from nouns) **a** affect with (*befog*). **b** treat as (*befriend*). **c** (forming adjectives in *-ed*) having; covered with (*bejewelled; bespectacled*). [OE *be-*, weak form of *bī* BY as in *bygone, byword*, etc.]

beach *n. & v.* —*n.* a pebbly or sandy shore esp. of the sea between high- and low-water marks. —*v.tr.* run or haul up (a boat etc.) on to a beach. □ **beach buggy** a low wide-wheeled motor vehicle for recreational driving on sand. [16th c.: orig. unkn.]

beachcomber /ˈbiːtʃˌkəʊmə(r)/ *n.* a vagrant who lives by searching beaches for articles of value.

beachhead /ˈbiːtʃhed/ *n. Mil.* a fortified position established on a beach by landing forces. [after *bridgehead*]

beacon /ˈbiːkən/ *n.* **1 a** a fire or light set up in a high or prominent position as a warning etc. **b** *Brit.* a hill suitable for this. **2** a visible warning or guiding point or device (e.g. a lighthouse, navigation buoy, etc.). **3** a radio transmitter whose signal helps fix the position of a ship or aircraft. **4** *Brit.* = BELISHA BEACON. [OE *bēacn* f. WG]

bead *n. & v.* —*n.* **1 a** a small usu. rounded and perforated piece of glass, stone, etc., for threading with others to make jewellery, or sewing on to fabric, etc. **b** (in *pl.*) a string of beads; a rosary. **2** a drop of liquid; a bubble. **3 a** small knob in the foresight of a gun. **4** the inner edge of a pneumatic tyre that grips the rim of the wheel. —*v.* **1** *tr.* furnish or decorate with beads. **2** *tr.* string together. **3** *intr.* form or grow into beads. □ **draw a bead on** take aim at. □ **beaded** *adj.* [orig. = 'prayer' (for which the earliest use of beads arose): OE *gebed* f. Gmc, rel. to BID]

beading /ˈbiːdɪŋ/ *n.* **1** decoration in the form of or resembling a row of beads, esp. looped edging. **2** the bead of a tyre.

beadle /ˈbiːd(ə)l/ *n.* **1** *Brit.* a ceremonial officer of a church, college, etc. **2** *Sc.* a church officer attending on the minister. **3** *Brit. hist.* a minor parish officer dealing with petty offenders etc. □ **beadleship** *n.* [ME f. OF *bedel* ult. f. Gmc]

beady /ˈbiːdɪ/ *adj.* (**beadier, beadiest**) **1** (of the eyes) small, round, and bright. **2** covered with beads or drops. □ **beady-eyed** with beady eyes. □ **beadily** *adv.* **beadiness** *n.*

beagle /ˈbiːg(ə)l/ *n. & v.* —*n.* **1** a small hound of a breed with a short coat, used for hunting hares. **2** this breed. —*v.intr.* (often as **beagling** *n.*) hunt with beagles. □ **beagler** *n.* [ME f. OF *beegueule* noisy person, prob. f. *beer* open wide + *gueule* throat]

beak¹ *n.* **1 a** a bird's horny projecting jaws; a bill. **b** the similar projecting jaw of other animals, e.g. a turtle. **2** *Naut. hist.* the projection at the prow of a warship. **3** a spout. □ **beaked** *adj.* **beaky** *adj.* [ME f. OF *bec* f. L *beccus*, of Celt. orig.]

beak² *n. Brit. sl.* **1** a magistrate. **2** a schoolmaster. [19th c.: prob. f. thieves' cant]

beaker /ˈbiːkə(r)/ *n.* **1** a tall drinking-vessel, usu. of plastic and tumbler-shaped. **2** a lipped cylindrical glass vessel for scientific experiments. **3** *archaic* or *literary* a large drinking-vessel with a wide mouth. [ME f. ON *bikarr*, perh. f. Gk *bikos* drinking-bowl]

beam *n. & v.* —*n.* **1** a long sturdy piece of squared timber or metal spanning an opening or room, usu. to support the structure above. **2 a** a ray or shaft of light. **b** a directional flow of particles or radiation. **3** a bright look or smile. **4 a** a series of radio or radar signals as a guide to a ship or aircraft. **b** the course indicated by this (*off beam*). **5** the crossbar of a balance. **6 a** a ship's breadth at its widest point. **b** the width of a person's hips (esp. *broad in the beam*). **7** (in *pl.*) the horizontal cross-timbers of a ship supporting the deck and joining the sides. **8** the side of a ship (*land on the port beam*). **9** the chief timber of a plough. —*v.* **1** *tr.* emit or direct (light, radio waves, etc.). **2** *intr.* **a** shine. **b** look or smile radiantly. □ **off beam** *colloq.* mistaken. **on the beam** *colloq.* on the right track. **on the beam-ends** (of a ship) on its side; almost capsizing. **on one's beam-ends** near the end of one's resources. [OE *bēam* tree f. WG]

bean *n. & v.* —*n.* **1 a** any kind of leguminous plant with edible usu. kidney-shaped seeds in long pods. **b** one of these seeds. **2** a similar seed of coffee and other plants. **3** (in *pl.*) *sl.* the head. —*v.tr. US sl.* hit on the head. □ **bean curd** jelly or paste made from beans, used esp. in Asian cookery. **bean sprout** a sprout of a bean seed, esp. of the mung bean, used as food. **full of beans** *colloq.* lively; in high spirits. **not a bean** *Brit. sl.* no money. [OE *bēan* f. Gmc]

beanbag /ˈbiːnbæg/ *n.* **1** a small bag filled with dried beans and used esp. in children's games. **2** a large cushion filled usu. with polystyrene beads and used as a seat.

beanfeast /ˈbiːnfiːst/ *n.* **1** *Brit. colloq.* a celebration; a merry time. **2** an employer's annual dinner given to employees. [BEAN + FEAST, beans and bacon being regarded as an indispensable dish]

beanie /ˈbiːnɪ/ n. a small close-fitting hat worn on the back of the head. [perh. f. BEAN 'head' + -IE]

beano /ˈbiːnəʊ/ n. (pl. **-os**) Brit. sl. a celebration; a party. [abbr. of BEANFEAST]

beanpole /ˈbiːnpəʊl/ n. **1** a stick for supporting bean plants. **2** colloq. a tall thin person.

beanstalk /ˈbiːnstɔːk/ n. the stem of a bean plant.

bear[1] /beə(r)/ v. (past **bore** /bɔː(r)/; past part. **borne, born** /bɔːn/) ¶ In the passive born is used with reference to birth (e.g. was born in July), except for borne by foll. by the name of the mother (e.g. was borne by Sarah). **1** tr. carry, bring, or take (bear gifts). **2** tr. show; be marked by; have as an attribute or characteristic (bear marks of violence; bears no relation to the case; bore no name). **3** tr. **a** produce, yield (fruit etc.). **b** give birth to (has borne a son; was born last week). **4** tr. **a** sustain (a weight, responsibility, cost, etc.). **b** stand, endure (an ordeal, difficulty, etc.). **5** tr. (usu. with neg. or interrog.) **a** tolerate; put up with (can't bear him; how can you bear it?). **b** admit of; be fit for (does not bear thinking about). **6** tr. carry in thought or memory (bear a grudge). **7** intr. veer in a given direction (bear left). □ **bear arms 1** carry weapons; serve as a soldier. **2** wear or display heraldic devices. **bear down** exert downward pressure. **bear down on** approach rapidly or purposefully. **bear hard on** oppress. **bear in mind** take into account having remembered. **bear on** (or **upon**) be relevant to. **bear out** support or confirm (an account or the person giving it). **bear up** raise one's spirits; not despair. **bear with** treat forbearingly; tolerate patiently. **bear witness** testify. [OE beran f. Gmc]

bear[2] /beə(r)/ n. **1** any large heavy mammal of the family Ursidae, having thick fur and walking on its soles. **2** a rough, unmannerly, or uncouth person. **3** Stock Exch. a person who sells shares hoping to buy them back later at a lower price. **4** = TEDDY. □ **bear-hug** a tight embrace. **the Great Bear, the Little Bear** two constellations near the North Pole. [OE bera f. WG]

bearable /ˈbeərəb(ə)l/ adj. that may be endured or tolerated. □ **bearability** /-ˈbɪlɪtɪ/ n. **bearableness** n. **bearably** adv.

beard /bɪəd/ n. & v. —n. **1** hair growing on the chin and lower cheeks of the face. **2** a similar tuft or part on an animal (esp. a goat). **3** the awn of a grass, sheath of barley, etc. —v.tr. oppose openly; defy. □ **bearded** adj. **beardless** adj. [OE f. WG]

bearer /ˈbeərə(r)/ n. **1** a person or thing that bears, carries, or brings. **2** a carrier of equipment on an expedition etc. **3** a person who presents a cheque or other order to pay money.

beargarden /ˈbeəˌɡɑːd(ə)n/ n. a rowdy or noisy scene.

bearing /ˈbeərɪŋ/ n. **1** a person's bodily attitude or outward behaviour. **2** (foll. by on, upon) relation or relevance to (his comments have no bearing on the subject). **3** endurability (beyond bearing). **4** a part of a machine that supports a rotating or other moving part. **5** direction or position relative to a fixed point, measured esp. in degrees. **6** (in pl.) **a** one's position relative to one's surroundings. **b** awareness of this; a sense of one's orientation (get one's bearings; lose one's bearings). **7** Heraldry a device or charge.

bearskin /ˈbeəskɪn/ n. **1** the skin of a bear. **2** a tall furry hat worn ceremonially by some regiments.

beast /biːst/ n. **1** an animal other than a human being, esp. a wild quadruped. **2 a** a brutal person. **b** colloq. an objectionable or unpleasant person or thing. **3** (prec. by the) a human being's brutish or uncivilized characteristics (saw the beast in him). □ **beast of burden** an animal, e.g. an ox, used for carrying loads. [ME f. OF beste f. Rmc besta f. L bestia]

beastly /ˈbiːstlɪ/ adj. & adv. —adj. (**beastlier, beastliest**) **1** colloq. objectionable, unpleasant. **2** like a beast; brutal. —adv. colloq. very, extremely. □ **beastliness** n.

beat v., n., & adj. —v. (past **beat**; past part. **beaten** /ˈbiːt(ə)n/) **1** tr. **a** strike (a person or animal) persistently or repeatedly, esp. to harm or punish. **b** strike (a thing) repeatedly, e.g. to remove dust from (a carpet etc.), to sound (a drum etc.). **2** intr. (foll. by against, at, on, etc.) pound or knock repeatedly (waves beat against the shore; beat at the door). **3** tr. **a** overcome; surpass; win a victory over. **b** complete an activity before (another person etc.). **c** be too hard for; perplex. **4** tr. (often foll. by up) stir (eggs etc.) vigorously into a frothy mixture. **5** tr. (often foll. by out) fashion or shape (metal etc.) by blows. **6** intr. (of the heart, a drum, etc.) pulsate rhythmically. **7** tr. (often foll. by out) **a** indicate (a tempo or rhythm) by gestures, tapping, etc. **b** sound (a signal etc.) by striking a drum or other means (beat a tattoo). **8 a** intr. (of a bird's wings) move up and down. **b** tr. cause (wings) to move in this way. **9** tr. make (a path etc.) by trampling. **10** tr. strike (bushes etc.) to rouse game. —n. **1 a** a main accent or rhythmic unit in music or verse (three beats to the bar; missed a beat and came in early). **b** the indication of rhythm by a conductor's movements (watch the beat). **c** (in popular music) a strong rhythm. **d** (attrib.) characterized by a strong rhythm (beat music). **2 a** a stroke or blow (e.g. on a drum). **b** a measured sequence of strokes (the beat of the waves on the rocks). **c** a throbbing movement or sound (the beat of his heart). **3 a** a route or area allocated to a police officer etc. **b** a person's habitual round. —adj. (predic.) sl. exhausted; tired out. □ **beat about** (often foll. by for) search (for an excuse etc.). **beat about the bush** discuss a matter without coming to the point. **beat one's breast** strike one's chest in anguish or sorrow. **beat the clock** complete a task within a stated time. **beat down 1** bargain with (a seller) to lower the price. **b** cause a seller to lower (the price). **2** strike (a resisting object) until it falls (beat the door down). **3** (of the sun, rain, etc.) radiate heat or fall continuously and vigorously. **beat in** crush. **beat it** sl. go away. **beat off** drive back (an attack etc.). **beat a retreat** withdraw; abandon an undertaking. **beat time** indicate or follow a musical tempo with a baton or other means. **beat a person to it** arrive or achieve something before another person. **beat up** give a beating to, esp. with punches and kicks. **beat-up** adj. colloq. dilapidated; in a state of disrepair. □ **beatable** adj. [OE bēatan f. Gmc]

beaten /ˈbiːt(ə)n/ adj. **1** outwitted; defeated. **2** exhausted; dejected. **3** (of gold or any other metal) shaped by a hammer. **4** (of a path etc.)

well-trodden, much-used. □ **off the beaten track 1** in or into an isolated place. **2** unusual. [past part. of BEAT]

beater /ˈbiːtə(r)/ n. **1** a person employed to rouse game for shooting. **2** an implement used for beating (esp. a carpet or eggs). **3** a person who beats metal.

beatific /ˌbiːəˈtɪfɪk/ adj. **1** colloq. blissful (a beatific smile). **2 a** of or relating to blessedness. **b** making blessed. □ **beatifically** adv. [F béatifique or L beatificus f. beatus blessed]

beatification /bɪˌætɪfɪˈkeɪʃ(ə)n/ n. **1** RC Ch. the act of formally declaring a dead person 'blessed'. **2** making or being blessed. [F béatification or eccl.L beatificatio (as BEATIFY)]

beatify /biːˈætɪˌfaɪ/ v.tr. (**-ies, -ied**) **1** RC Ch. announce the beatification of. **2** make happy. [F béatifier or eccl.L beatificare f. L beatus blessed]

beating /ˈbiːtɪŋ/ n. **1** a physical punishment or assault. **2** a defeat.

beatitude /biːˈætɪˌtjuːd/ n. **1** blessedness. **2** (in pl.) the declarations of blessedness in Matt. 5:3–11. [F béatitude or L beatitudo f. beatus blessed]

beatnik /ˈbiːtnɪk/ n. a member of a movement of young people esp. in the 1950s who rejected conventional society. [BEAT + -nik after sputnik, perh. infl. by US use of Yiddish -nik agent-suffix]

beau /bəʊ/ n. (pl. **beaux** or **beaus** /bəʊz, bəʊ/) **1** esp. US an admirer; a boyfriend. **2** a fop; a dandy. [F, = handsome, f. L bellus]

Beaufort scale /ˈbəʊfət/ n. a scale of wind speed ranging from 0 (calm) to 12 (hurricane). [Sir F. Beaufort, Engl. admiral d. 1857]

Beaujolais /ˈbəʊʒəˌleɪ/ n. a red or white burgundy wine from the Beaujolais district of France. □ **Beaujolais nouveau** Beaujolais wine sold in the first year of a vintage.

beaut /bjuːt/ n. & adj. Austral. & NZ sl. —n. an excellent or beautiful person or thing. —adj. excellent; beautiful. [abbr. of BEAUTY]

beauteous /ˈbjuːtɪəs/ adj. poet. beautiful. [ME f. BEAUTY + -OUS, after bounteous, plenteous]

beautician /bjuːˈtɪʃ(ə)n/ n. **1** a person who gives beauty treatment. **2** a person who runs or owns a beauty salon.

beautiful /ˈbjuːtɪˌfʊl/ adj. **1** delighting the aesthetic senses (a beautiful voice). **2** pleasant, enjoyable (had a beautiful time). **3** excellent (a beautiful specimen). □ **beautifully** adv.

beautify /ˈbjuːtɪˌfaɪ/ v.tr. (**-ies, -ied**) make beautiful; adorn. □ **beautification** /-fɪˈkeɪʃ(ə)n/ n. **beautifier** /-ˌfaɪə(r)/ n.

beauty /ˈbjuːtɪ/ n. (pl. **-ies**) **1 a** a combination of qualities such as shape, colour, etc., that pleases the aesthetic senses, esp. the sight. **b** a combination of qualities that pleases the intellect or moral sense (the beauty of the argument). **2** colloq. **a** an excellent specimen (what a beauty!). **b** an attractive feature; an advantage (that's the beauty of it!). **3** a beautiful woman. □ **beauty parlour** (or **salon**) an establishment in which hairdressing, make-up, etc., are offered to women. **beauty queen** the woman judged most beautiful in a competition. **beauty sleep** sleep before midnight, supposed to be health-giving. **beauty spot 1** a place known for its beauty. **2** a small natural or artificial mark such as a mole on the face, considered to enhance another feature. [ME f. AF beuté, OF bealté, beauté, ult. f. L (as BEAU)]

beaux pl. of BEAU.

beaver¹ /ˈbiːvə(r)/ n. & v. —n. (pl. same or **beavers**) **1 a** any large amphibious broad-tailed rodent of the genus Castor, native to N. America, Europe, and Asia, and able to cut down trees and build dams. **b** its soft light-brown fur. **c** a hat of this. **2** (**Beaver**) a boy aged six or seven who is an affiliate member of the Scout Association. —v.intr. colloq. (usu. foll. by away) work hard. □ **eager beaver** colloq. an over-zealous person. [OE be(o)for f. Gmc]

beaver² /ˈbiːvə(r)/ n. hist. the lower face-guard of a helmet. [OF baviere bib f. baver slaver f. beve saliva f. Rmc]

bebop /ˈbiːbɒp/ n. a type of jazz originating in the 1940s and characterized by complex rhythms. □ **bebopper** n. [imit. of the typical rhythm]

becalm /bɪˈkɑːm/ v.tr. (usu. in passive) deprive (a ship) of wind.

became past of BECOME.

because /bɪˈkɒz/ conj. for the reason that; since. □ **because of** on account of; by reason of. [ME f. BY prep. + CAUSE, after OF par cause de by reason of]

béchamel /ˈbeʃəˌmel/ n. a kind of thick white sauce. [invented by the Marquis de Béchamel, Fr. courtier d. 1703]

beck¹ n. N.Engl. a brook; a mountain stream. [ME f. ON bekkr f. Gmc]

beck² n. poet. a gesture requesting attention, e.g. a nod, wave, etc. □ **at a person's beck and call** having constantly to obey a person's orders. [beck (v.) f. BECKON]

beckon /ˈbekən/ v. **1** tr. attract the attention of; summon by gesture. **2** intr. (usu. foll. by to) make a signal to attract a person's attention; summon a person by doing this. [OE bīecnan, bēcnan ult. f. WG baukna BEACON]

become /bɪˈkʌm/ v. (past **became** /bɪˈkeɪm/; past part. **become**) **1** intr. (foll. by compl.) begin to be (became president; will become famous). **2** tr. **a** look well on; suit (blue becomes him). **b** befit (it ill becomes you to complain). **3** intr. (as **becoming** adj.) **a** flattering the appearance. **b** suitable; decorous. □ **become of** happen to (what will become of me?). □ **becomingly** adv. **becomingness** n. [OE becuman f. Gmc: cf. BE-, COME]

becquerel /ˈbekəˌrel/ n. Physics the SI unit of radioactivity, corresponding to one disintegration per second. [A. H. Becquerel, Fr. physicist d. 1908]

bed n. & v. —n. **1 a** a piece of furniture used for sleeping on. **b** a mattress, with or without coverings. **2** any place used by a person or animal for sleep or rest; a litter. **3 a** a garden plot, esp. one used for planting flowers. **b** a place where other things may be grown (osier bed). **4** the use of a bed: **a** colloq. for sexual intercourse (only thinks of bed). **b** for rest (needs his bed). **5** something flat, forming a support or base as in: **a** the bottom of the sea or a river. **b** the foundations of a road or railway. **6** a stratum. —v. (**bedded, bedding**) **1** tr. & intr. (usu. foll. by down) put or go to bed. **2** tr. colloq. have sexual intercourse with. **3** tr. (usu. foll. by out) plant in a garden bed. **4** tr. cover up or fix firmly in something. **5 a** tr. arrange as a layer. **b** intr. be or form a layer. □ **bed and breakfast 1** one night's lodging and breakfast in a hotel etc. **2** an establishment that provides this. **brought to bed** (often foll. by of) delivered of a child. **go**

to bed 1 retire for the night. **2** have sexual intercourse. **3** (of a newspaper) go to press. **make the bed** tidy and arrange the bed for use. **put to bed 1** cause to go to bed. **2** make (a newspaper) ready for press. **take to one's bed** stay in bed because of illness. [OE *bed*(d), *beddian* f. Gmc]

B.Ed. *abbr.* Bachelor of Education.

bedabble /bɪˈdæb(ə)l/ *v.tr.* stain or splash with dirty liquid, blood, etc.

bedaub /bɪˈdɔːb/ *v.tr.* smear or daub with paint etc.; decorate gaudily.

bedazzle /bɪˈdæz(ə)l/ *v.tr.* **1** dazzle. **2** confuse (a person). □ **bedazzlement** *n.*

bedbug /ˈbedbʌg/ *n.* either of two flat, wingless, evil-smelling insects of the genus *Cimex* infesting beds and unclean houses and sucking blood.

bedchamber /ˈbedˌtʃeɪmbə(r)/ *n.* **1** *archaic* a bedroom. **2** (**Bedchamber**) part of the title of some of the sovereign's attendants (*Lady of the Bedchamber*).

bedclothes /ˈbedkləʊðz/ *n.pl.* coverings for a bed, such as sheets, blankets, etc.

beddable /ˈbedəb(ə)l/ *adj. colloq.* sexually attractive. [BED + -ABLE]

bedding /ˈbedɪŋ/ *n.* **1** a mattress and bedclothes. **2** a litter for cattle, horses, etc. **3** a bottom layer. **4** *Geol.* the stratification of rocks, esp. when clearly visible. □ **bedding plant** a plant suitable for a garden bed.

bedeck /bɪˈdek/ *v.tr.* adorn.

bedevil /bɪˈdev(ə)l/ *v.tr.* (**bedevilled, bedevilling**; *US* **bedeviled, bedeviling**) **1** plague; afflict. **2** confound; confuse. **3** possess as if with a devil; bewitch. **4** treat with diabolical violence or abuse. □ **bedevilment** *n.*

bedew /bɪˈdjuː/ *v.tr.* **1** cover or sprinkle with dew or drops of water. **2** *poet.* sprinkle with tears.

bedfellow /ˈbedˌfeləʊ/ *n.* **1** a person who shares a bed. **2** an associate.

bedim /bɪˈdɪm/ *v.tr.* (**bedimmed, bedimming**) *poet.* make (the eyes, mind, etc.) dim.

bedizen /bɪˈdaɪz(ə)n, -ˈdɪz(ə)n/ *v.tr. poet.* deck out gaudily. [BE- + obs. *dizen* deck out]

bedjacket /ˈbedˌdʒækɪt/ *n.* a jacket worn when sitting up in bed.

bedlam /ˈbedləm/ *n.* **1** a scene of uproar and confusion (*the traffic was bedlam*). **2** *archaic* a madhouse; an asylum. [hospital of St Mary of *Bethlehem* in London]

bedlinen /ˈbedˌlɪnɪn/ *n.* sheets and pillowcases.

Bedouin /ˈbeduɪn/ *n. & adj.* (also **Beduin**) (*pl.* same) —*n.* **1** a nomadic Arab of the desert. **2** a wanderer; a nomad. —*adj.* **1** of or relating to the Bedouin. **2** wandering; nomadic. [ME f. OF *beduin* ult. f. Arab. *badwiyyīn* (oblique case) dwellers in the desert f. *badw* desert]

bedpan /ˈbedpæn/ *n.* a receptacle used by a bedridden patient for urine and faeces.

bedpost /ˈbedpəʊst/ *n.* any of the four upright supports of a bedstead.

bedraggle /bɪˈdræg(ə)l/ *v.tr.* **1** wet (a dress etc.) by trailing it, or so that it hangs limp. **2** (as **bedraggled** *adj.*) untidy; dishevelled. [BE- + DRAGGLE]

bedrest /ˈbedrest/ *n.* confinement of an invalid to bed.

bedridden /ˈbedˌrɪd(ə)n/ *adj.* **1** confined to bed by infirmity. **2** decrepit. [OE *bedreda* f. *ridan* ride]

bedrock /ˈbedrɒk/ *n.* **1** solid rock underlying alluvial deposits etc. **2** the underlying principles or facts of a theory, character, etc.

bedroll /ˈbedrəʊl/ *n.* esp. *US* portable bedding rolled into a bundle, esp. a sleeping-bag.

bedroom /ˈbedruːm, -rʊm/ *n.* **1** a room for sleeping in. **2** (*attrib.*) of or referring to sexual relations (*bedroom comedy*).

bedside /ˈbedsaɪd/ *n.* **1** the space beside esp. a patient's bed. **2** (*attrib.*) of or relating to the side of a bed (*bedside lamp*). □ **bedside manner** (of a doctor) an approach or attitude to a patient.

bedsitter /bedˈsɪtə(r)/ *n.* (also **bedsit**) *colloq.* = BEDSITTING ROOM. [contr.]

bedsitting room /bedˈsɪtɪŋ/ *n.* *Brit.* a one-roomed unit of accommodation usu. consisting of combined bedroom and sitting-room with cooking facilities.

bedsore /ˈbedsɔː(r)/ *n.* a sore developed by an invalid because of pressure caused by lying in bed.

bedspread /ˈbedspred/ *n.* an often decorative cloth used to cover a bed when not in use.

bedstead /ˈbedsted/ *n.* the framework of a bed.

bedtime /ˈbedtaɪm/ *n.* **1** the usual time for going to bed. **2** (*attrib.*) of or relating to bedtime (*bedtime drink*).

bedwetting /ˈbedˌwetɪŋ/ *n.* involuntary urination during the night.

bee /biː/ *n.* **1** any four-winged insect of the superfamily Apoidea which collects nectar and pollen, produces wax and honey, and lives in large communities. **2** any insect of a similar type. **3** (usu. **busy bee**) a busy person. **4** esp. *US* a meeting for communal work or amusement. □ **a bee in one's bonnet** an obsession. **bee-keeper** a keeper of bees. **bee-keeping** the occupation of keeping bees. **the bee's knees** *sl.* something outstandingly good (*thinks he's the bee's knees*). [OE *bēo* f. Gmc]

Beeb /biːb/ *n.* (prec. by *the*) *Brit. colloq.* the BBC. [abbr.]

beech /biːtʃ/ *n.* **1** any large forest tree of the genus *Fagus*, having smooth grey bark and glossy leaves. **2** (also **beechwood**) its wood. **3** *Austral.* any of various similar trees in Australia. □ **beechy** *adj.* [OE *bēce* f. Gmc]

beechmast /ˈbiːtʃmɑːst/ *n.* (*pl.* same) the small rough-skinned fruit of the beech tree. [BEECH + MAST²]

beef *n. & v.* —*n.* **1** the flesh of the ox, bull, or esp. the cow, for eating. **2** (*pl.* **beeves** /biːvz/ or *US* **beefs**) a cow, bull, or ox fattened for beef; its carcass. **3** (*pl.* **beefs**) *sl.* a complaint; a protest. —*v.intr. sl.* complain. □ **beef tea** stewed extract of beef, given to invalids. **beef up** *sl.* strengthen, reinforce, augment. [ME f. AF, OF *boef* f. L *bos bovis* ox]

beefburger /ˈbiːfˌbɜːgə(r)/ *n.* = HAMBURGER.

beefcake /ˈbiːfkeɪk/ *n.* esp. *US sl.* well-developed male muscles, esp. when displayed for admiration.

beefeater /ˈbiːfˌiːtə(r)/ *n.* a warder in the Tower of London; a Yeoman of the Guard. [f. obs. sense 'well-fed menial']

beefsteak /biːfˈsteɪk, ˈbiːf-/ *n.* a thick slice of lean beef, esp. from the rump, usu. for grilling or frying.

beefy /ˈbiːfɪ/ *adj.* (**beefier, beefiest**) **1** like beef. **2** solid; muscular. □ **beefily** *adv.* **beefiness** *n.*

beehive /ˈbiːhaɪv/ n. **1** an artificial habitation for bees. **2** a busy place. **3** anything resembling a wicker beehive in being domed.

beeline /ˈbiːlaɪn/ n. a straight line between two places. □ **make a beeline for** hurry directly to.

been past part. of BE.

beep n. & v. —n. **1** the sound of a motor-car horn. **2** any similar high-pitched noise. —v.intr. emit a beep. □ **beeper** n. [imit.]

beer n. **1 a** an alcoholic drink made from yeast-fermented malt etc., flavoured with hops. **b** a glass of this, esp. a pint or half-pint. **2** any of several other fermented drinks, e.g. ginger beer. □ **beer-engine** Brit. a machine that draws up beer from a barrel in a cellar. **beer-mat** a small table-mat for a beer-glass. **beer pump** US = beer-engine. [OE bēor f. LL biber drink f. L bibere]

beery /ˈbɪərɪ/ adj. (**beerier, beeriest**) **1** showing the influence of drink in one's appearance or behaviour. **2** smelling or tasting of beer. □ **beerily** adv. **beeriness** n.

beeswax /ˈbiːzwæks/ n. & v. —n. **1** the wax secreted by bees to make honeycombs. **2** this wax refined and used to polish wood. —v.tr. polish (furniture etc.) with beeswax.

beeswing /ˈbiːzwɪŋ/ n. a filmy second crust on old port.

beet /biːt/ n. any plant of the genus Beta with an edible root (see BEETROOT, sugar beet). [OE bēte f. L beta, perh. of Celt. orig.]

beetle¹ /ˈbiːt(ə)l/ n. & v. —n. **1** any insect of the order Coleoptera, with modified front wings forming hard protective cases closing over the back wings. **2** colloq. any similar, usu. black, insect. —v.intr. colloq. (foll. by about, away, etc.) Brit. hurry, scurry. [OE bitula biter f. bītan BITE]

beetle² /ˈbiːt(ə)l/ n. & v. —n. a tool with a heavy head and a handle, used for ramming, crushing, driving wedges, etc. —v.tr ram, crush, drive, etc., with a beetle. [OE bētel f. Gmc]

beetle³ /ˈbiːt(ə)l/ adj. & v. —adj. (esp. of the eyebrows) projecting, shaggy, scowling. —v.intr. (usu. as **beetling** adj.) (of brows, cliffs, etc.) projecting; overhanging threateningly. □ **beetle-browed** with shaggy, projecting, or scowling eyebrows. [ME: orig. unkn.]

beetroot /ˈbiːtruːt/ n. esp. Brit. **1** a beet, Beta vulgaris, with an edible spherical dark red root. **2** this root used as a vegetable.

befall /bɪˈfɔːl/ v. (past **befell** /bɪˈfel/; past part. **befallen** /bɪˈfɔːlən/) poet. **1** intr. happen (so it befell). **2** tr. happen to (a person etc.) (what has befallen her?). [OE befeallan (as BE-, feallan FALL)]

befit /bɪˈfɪt/ v.tr. (**befitted, befitting**) **1** be fitted or appropriate for; suit. **2** be incumbent on. □ **befitting** adj. **befittingly** adv.

befog /bɪˈfɒg/ v.tr. (**befogged, befogging**) **1** confuse; obscure. **2** envelop in fog.

befool /bɪˈfuːl/ v.tr. make a fool of; delude.

before /bɪˈfɔː(r)/ conj., prep., & adv. —conj. **1** earlier than the time when (crawled before he walked). **2** rather than that (would starve before he stole). —prep. **1 a** in front of. **b** ahead of (crossed the line before him). **c** under the impulse of (recoil before the attack). **d** awaiting (the future before them). **2** earlier than; preceding (Lent comes before Easter). **3** rather than (death before dishonour). **4 a** in the presence of (appear before the judge). **b** for the attention of (a plan put before the committee). —adv. **1 a** earlier than the time in question;

already (heard it before). **b** in the past (happened long before). **2** ahead (go before). **3** on the front (hit before and behind). □ **Before Christ** (of a date) reckoned backwards from the birth of Christ. [OE beforan f. Gmc]

beforehand /bɪˈfɔːhænd/ adv. in anticipation; in advance (had prepared the meal beforehand). [ME f. BEFORE + HAND: cf. AF avant main]

befoul /bɪˈfaʊl/ v.tr. poet. **1** make foul or dirty. **2** degrade; defile (befouled her name).

befriend /bɪˈfrend/ v.tr. act as a friend to; help.

befuddle /bɪˈfʌd(ə)l/ v.tr. **1** make drunk. **2** confuse. □ **befuddlement** n.

beg v. (**begged, begging**) **1 a** intr. (usu. foll. by for) ask for (esp. food, money, etc.) (begged for alms). **b** tr. ask for (food, money, etc.) as a gift. **c** intr. live by begging. **2** tr. & intr. (usu. foll. by for, or to + infin.) ask earnestly or humbly. **3** tr. ask formally for (beg leave). **4** intr. (of a dog etc.) sit up with the front paws raised. **5** tr. take or ask leave (to do something) (I beg to differ; beg to enclose). □ **beg off 1** decline to take part in or attend. **2** get (a person) excused a penalty etc. **beg the question** assume the truth of an argument or proposition to be proved, without arguing it. **go begging** (or **a-begging**) (of a chance or a thing) not be taken; be unwanted. [ME prob. f. OE bedecian f. Gmc: rel. to BID]

■ **Usage** The expression beg the question is often used incorrectly to mean (1) to avoid giving a straight answer, or (2) to invite the obvious question (that . . .). These uses should be avoided.

began past of BEGIN.

beget /bɪˈget/ v.tr. (**begetting**; past **begot** /bɪˈgɒt/; archaic **begat** /bɪˈgæt/; past part. **begotten** /bɪˈgɒt(ə)n/) literary **1** (usu. of a father, sometimes of a father and mother) procreate. **2** give rise to; cause (beget strife). □ **begetter** n. [OE begietan, formed as BE- + GET = procreate]

beggar /ˈbegə(r)/ n. & v. —n. **1** a person who begs, esp. one who lives by begging. **2** a poor person. **3** colloq. a person (poor beggar). —v.tr. **1** reduce to poverty. **2** outshine. **3** exhaust the resources of (beggar description). [ME f. BEG + -AR³]

beggarly /ˈbegəlɪ/ adj. **1** poverty-stricken; needy. **2** intellectually poor. **3** mean; sordid. **4** ungenerous. □ **beggarliness** n.

beggary /ˈbegərɪ/ n. extreme poverty.

begin /bɪˈgɪn/ v. (**beginning**; past **began** /bɪˈgæn/; past part. **begun** /bɪˈgʌn/) **1** tr. perform the first part of; start (begin work; begin crying). **2** intr. come into being; arise: **a** in time (war began in 1939). **b** in space (Wales begins beyond the river). **3** tr. (usu. foll. by to + infin.) start at a certain time (then began to feel ill). **4** intr. be begun (the meeting will begin at 7). **5** intr. **a** start speaking. **b** take the first step; be the first to do something (who wants to begin?). **6** intr. colloq. (usu. with neg.) show any attempt or likelihood (can't begin to compete). [OE beginnan f. Gmc]

beginner /bɪˈgɪnə(r)/ n. a person just beginning to learn a skill etc.

beginning /bɪˈgɪnɪŋ/ n. **1** the time or place at which anything begins. **2** a source or origin. **3** the first part.

begone /bɪˈgɒn/ int. poet. go away at once!

begonia /bɪˈgəʊnjə/ n. any plant of the genus Begonia with brightly coloured sepals and no petals. [M. Bégon, Fr. patron of science d. 1710] ·

begot past of BEGET.

begotten past part. of BEGET.

begrudge /bɪˈgrʌdʒ/ v.tr. **1** resent; be dissatisfied at. **2** envy (a person) the possession of. □ **begrudgingly** adv.

beguile /bɪˈgaɪl/ v.tr. **1** charm; amuse. **2** divert attention pleasantly from (toil etc.). **3** (usu. foll. by of, out of, or into + verbal noun) delude; cheat (beguiled him into paying). □ **beguilement** n. **beguiler** n. **beguiling** adj. **beguilingly** adv. [BE- + obs. guile to deceive]

beguine /bɪˈgiːn/ n. **1** a popular dance of W. Indian origin. **2** its rhythm. [Amer. F f. F béguin infatuation]

begum /ˈbeɪgəm/ n. in the Indian subcontinent: **1** a Muslim lady of high rank. **2** (**Begum**) the title of a married Muslim woman, equivalent to Mrs. [Urdu begam f. E.Turk. bīgam princess, fem. of big prince]

begun past part. of BEGIN.

behalf /bɪˈhɑːf/ n. □ **on** (US **in**) **behalf of** (or **on a person's behalf**) **1** in the interests of (a person, principle, etc.). **2** as representative of (acting on behalf of my client). [mixture of earlier phrases on his halve and bihalve him, both = on his side: see BY, HALF]

behave /bɪˈheɪv/ v. **1** intr. **a** act or react (in a specified way) (behaved well). **b** (esp. to or of a child) conduct oneself properly. **2** refl. (esp. of or to a child) show good manners (behaved herself). □ **ill-behaved** having bad manners or conduct. **well-behaved** having good manners or conduct. [BE- + HAVE]

behaviour /bɪˈheɪvjə(r)/ n. (US **behavior**) **1 a** the way one conducts oneself; manners. **b** the treatment of others; moral conduct. **2** the way in which a machine, chemical substance, etc., acts or works. [BEHAVE after demeanour and obs. haviour f. have]

behavioural /bɪˈheɪvjər(ə)l/ adj. (US **behavioral**) of or relating to behaviour. □ **behavioural science** the scientific study of human behaviour. □ **behaviouralist** n.

behaviourism /bɪˈheɪvjəˌrɪz(ə)m/ n. (US **behaviorism**) Psychol. **1** the theory that human behaviour is determined by conditioning rather than by thoughts or feelings, and that psychological disorders are best treated by altering behaviour patterns. **2** such study and treatment in practice. □ **behaviourist** n. **behaviouristic** /-ˈrɪstɪk/ adj.

behead /bɪˈhed/ v.tr. **1** cut off the head of (a person), esp. as a form of execution. **2** kill by beheading. [OE behēafdian (as BE-, hēafod HEAD)]

beheld past and past part. of BEHOLD.

behemoth /bɪˈhiːmɒθ/ n. an enormous creature or thing. [ME f. Heb. bʰhēmôt intensive pl. of bʰhēmāh beast, perh. f. Egyptian p-ehe-mau water-ox]

behest /bɪˈhest/ n. literary a command; an entreaty (went at his behest). [OE behǣs f. Gmc]

behind /bɪˈhaɪnd/ prep., adv., & n. —prep. **1 a** in, towards, or to the rear of. **b** on the further side of (behind the bush). **c** hidden by (something behind that remark). **2 a** in the past in relation to (trouble is behind me now). **b** late in relation to (behind schedule). **3** inferior to; weaker than (rather behind the others in his maths). **4 a** in support of (she's right behind us). **b** responsible for; giving rise to (the man behind the project; the reasons behind his resignation). **5** in the tracks of; following. —adv.

1 a in or to or towards the rear; further back (the street behind; glance behind). **b** on the further side (a high wall with a field behind). **2** remaining after departure (leave behind; stay behind). **3** (usu. foll. by with) **a** in arrears (behind with the rent). **b** late in accomplishing a task etc. (working too slowly and getting behind). **4** in a weak position; backward (behind in Latin). **5** following (his dog running behind). —n. colloq. the buttocks. □ **behind time** late. **behind the times** antiquated. **come from behind** win after lagging. **fall** (or **lag**) **behind** not keep up. [OE behindan, bihindan f. bi BY + hindan from behind, hinder below]

behindhand /bɪˈhaɪndhænd/ adv. & predic.adj. **1** (usu. foll. by with, in) late (in discharging a duty, paying a debt, etc.). **2** out of date; behind time. [BEHIND + HAND: cf. BEFOREHAND]

behold /bɪˈhəʊld/ v.tr. (past & past part. **beheld** /bɪˈheld/) literary (esp. in imper.) see, observe. □ **beholder** n. [OE bihaldan (as BE-, haldan hold)]

beholden /bɪˈhəʊld(ə)n/ predic.adj. (usu. foll. by to) under obligation. [past part. (obs. except in this use) of BEHOLD, = bound]

behove /bɪˈhəʊv/ v.tr. (US **behoove** /-ˈhuːv/) formal (prec. by it as subject; foll. by to + infin.) **1** be incumbent on. **2** (usu. with neg.) befit (ill behoves him to protest). [OE behōfian f. behōf benefit]

beige /beɪʒ/ n. & adj. —n. a pale sandy fawn colour. —adj. of this colour. [F: orig. unkn.]

beigel var. of BAGEL.

being /ˈbiːɪŋ/ n. **1** existence. **2** the nature or essence (of a person etc.) (his whole being revolted). **3** a human being. **4** anything that exists or is imagined.

bejewelled /bɪˈdʒuːəld/ adj. (US **bejeweled**) adorned with jewels.

bel /bel/ n. a unit used in the comparison of power levels in electrical communication or intensities of sound, corresponding to an intensity ratio of 10 to 1 (cf. DECIBEL). [A. G. Bell, Amer. inventor of telephone d. 1922]

belabour /bɪˈleɪbə(r)/ v.tr. (US **belabor**) **1 a** thrash; beat. **b** attack verbally. **2** argue or elaborate (a subject) in excessive detail. [BE- + LABOUR = exert one's strength]

belated /bɪˈleɪtɪd/ adj. **1** coming late or too late. **2** overtaken by darkness. □ **belatedly** adv. **belatedness** n. [past part. of obs. belate delay (as BE-, LATE)]

belay /bɪˈleɪ/ v. & n. —v. **1** tr. fix (a running rope) round a cleat, pin, rock, etc., to secure it. **2** tr. & intr. (usu. in imper.) Naut. sl. stop; enough! (esp. belay there!). —n. **1** an act of belaying. **2** a spike of rock etc. used for belaying. [Du. beleggen]

bel canto /bel ˈkæntəʊ/ n. **1** a lyrical style of operatic singing using a full rich broad tone. **2** (attrib.) (of a type of aria or voice) characterized by this type of singing. [It., = fine song]

belch /beltʃ/ v. & n. —v. **1** intr. emit wind noisily from the stomach through the mouth. **2** tr. (of a chimney, volcano, gun, etc.) send (smoke etc.) out or up. —n. an act of belching. [OE belcettan]

beleaguer /bɪˈliːgə(r)/ v.tr. **1** besiege. **2** vex; harass. [Du. belegeren camp round (as BE-, leger a camp)]

belfry /ˈbelfrɪ/ n. (pl. **-ies**) **1** a tower or steeple housing bells, esp. forming part of a church. **2** a space for hanging bells in a church tower. [ME f. OF berfrei f. Frank.: altered by assoc. with bell]

belie /bɪˈlaɪ/ v.tr. (**belying**) **1** give a false notion of; fail to corroborate (*its appearance belies its age*). **2 a** fail to fulfil (a promise etc.). **b** fail to justify (a hope etc.). [OE *beléogan* (as BE-, *léogan* LIE²)]

belief /bɪˈliːf/ n. **1 a** a person's religion; religious conviction (*has no belief*). **b** a firm opinion (*my belief is that he did it*). **c** an acceptance (of a thing, fact, statement, etc.) (*belief in the afterlife*). **2** (usu. foll. by *in*) trust or confidence. [ME f. OE *geléafa* (as BELIEVE)]

believe /bɪˈliːv/ v. **1** tr. accept as true or as conveying the truth (*I believe it*; *don't believe him*; *believes what he is told*). **2** tr. think, suppose (*I believe it's raining*; *Mr Smith, I believe?*). **3** intr. (foll. by *in*) **a** have faith in the existence of (*believes in God*). **b** have confidence in (a remedy, a person, etc.) (*believes in alternative medicine*). **c** have trust in the advisability of (*believes in telling the truth*). **4** intr. have (esp. religious) faith. □ **make believe** (often foll. by *that* + clause, or *to* + infin.) pretend (*let's make believe that we're young again*). □ **believable** adj. **believability** /-ˌliːvəˈbɪlɪtɪ/ n. [OE *belīefan*, *belēfan*, with change of prefix f. *gelēfan* f. Gmc: rel. to LIEF]

believer /bɪˈliːvə(r)/ n. **1** an adherent of a specified religion. **2** a person who believes, esp. in the efficacy of something (*a great believer in exercise*).

Belisha beacon /bəˈliːʃə/ n. Brit. a flashing orange ball surmounted on a striped post, marking some pedestrian crossings. [L. Hore-Belisha d. 1957, Minister of Transport 1934]

belittle /bɪˈlɪt(ə)l/ v.tr. **1** depreciate. **2** make small; dwarf. □ **belittlement** n. **belittler** n. **belittlingly** adv.

bell¹ n. & v. —n. **1** a hollow usu. metal object in the shape of a deep upturned cup usu. widening at the lip, made to sound a clear musical note when struck. **2 a** a sound or stroke of a bell, esp. as a signal. **b** (prec. by a numeral) *Naut.* the time as indicated every half-hour of a watch by the striking of the ship's bell one to eight times. **3** anything that sounds like or functions as a bell, esp. an electronic device that rings etc. as a signal. **4 a** any bell-shaped object or part, e.g. of a musical instrument. **b** the corolla of a flower when bell-shaped. **5** (in pl.) *Mus.* a set of cylindrical metal tubes of different lengths, suspended in a frame and played by being struck with a hammer. —v.tr. **1** provide with a bell or bells; attach a bell to. **2** (foll. by *out*) form into the shape of the lip of a bell. □ **bell-bottom 1** a marked flare below the knee (of a trouser-leg). **2** (in pl.) trousers with bell-bottoms. **bell-glass** a bell-shaped glass cover for plants. **bell-jar** a bell-shaped glass cover or container for use in a laboratory. **bell-metal** an alloy of copper and tin for making bells. **bell-pull** a cord or handle which rings a bell when pulled. **bell-push** a button that operates an electric bell when pushed. **bell-tent** a cone-shaped tent supported by a central pole. **bell-wether 1** the leading sheep of a flock, with a bell on its neck. **2** a ringleader. **give a person a bell** colloq. telephone a person. **ring a bell** colloq. revive a distant recollection; sound familiar. [OE *belle*: perh. rel. to BELL²]

bell² n. & v. —n. the cry of a stag or buck at rutting-time. —v.intr. make this cry. [OE *bellan* bark, bellow]

belladonna /ˌbeləˈdɒnə/ n. **1** *Bot.* a poisonous plant, *Atropa belladonna*, with purple flowers and purple-black berries. **2** *Med.* a drug prepared from this. [mod.L f. It., = fair lady, perh. from its use as a cosmetic]

bellboy /ˈbelbɔɪ/ n. esp. *US* a page in a hotel or club.

belle /bel/ n. **1** a beautiful woman. **2** a woman recognized as the most beautiful (*the belle of the ball*). [F f. L *bella* fem. of *bellus* beautiful]

belles-lettres /bel ˈletr/ n.pl. (also treated as sing.) writings or studies of a literary nature, esp. essays and criticisms. □ **belletrism** /beˈletrɪz(ə)m/ n. **belletrist** /beˈletrɪst/ n. **belletristic** /ˌbeləˈtrɪstɪk/ adj. [F, = fine letters]

bellicose /ˈbelɪkəʊz/ adj. eager to fight; warlike. □ **bellicosity** /-ˈkɒsɪtɪ/ n. [ME f. L *bellicosus* f. *bellum* war]

belligerence /bɪˈlɪdʒərəns/ n. (also **belligerency** /-rənsɪ/) **1** aggressive or warlike behaviour. **2** the status of a belligerent.

belligerent /bɪˈlɪdʒərənt/ adj. & n. —adj. **1** engaged in war or conflict. **2** given to constant fighting; pugnacious. —n. a nation or person engaged in war or conflict. □ **belligerently** adv. [L *belligerare* wage war f. *bellum* war + *gerere* wage]

bellow /ˈbeləʊ/ v. & n. —v. **1** intr. **a** emit a deep loud roar. **b** cry or shout with pain. **2** tr. utter loudly and usu. angrily. —n. a bellowing sound. [ME: perh. rel. to BELL²]

bellows /ˈbeləʊz/ n.pl. (also treated as sing.) **1** a device with an air bag that emits a stream of air when squeezed, esp. (in full **pair of bellows**) a kind with two handles used for blowing air on to a fire. **2** an expandable component, e.g. joining the lens to the body of a camera. [ME prob. f. OE *belga* pl. of *belig* belly]

belly /ˈbelɪ/ n. & v. —n. (pl. **-ies**) **1** the part of the human body below the chest, containing the stomach and bowels. **2** the stomach, esp. representing the body's need for food. **3** the front of the body from the waist to the groin. **4** the underside of a four-legged animal. **5 a** a cavity or bulging part of anything. **b** the surface of an instrument of the violin family, across which the strings are placed. —v.tr. & intr. (**-ies**, **-ied**) (often foll. by *out*) swell or cause to swell; bulge. □ **belly button** colloq. the navel. **belly-dance** an oriental dance performed by a woman, involving voluptuous movements of the belly. **belly-laugh** a loud unrestrained laugh. [OE *belig* (orig. = bag) f. Gmc]

bellyache /ˈbelɪeɪk/ n. & v. —n. colloq. a stomach pain. —v.intr. sl. complain noisily or persistently. □ **bellyacher** n.

bellyflop /ˈbelɪflɒp/ n. & v. colloq. —n. a dive into water in which the body lands with the belly flat on the water. —v.intr. (**-flopped**, **-flopping**) perform this dive.

bellyful /ˈbelɪfʊl/ n. (pl. **-fuls**) **1** enough to eat. **2** colloq. enough or more than enough of anything (esp. unwelcome).

belong /bɪˈlɒŋ/ v.intr. **1** (foll. by *to*) **a** be the property of. **b** be rightly assigned to as a duty, right, part, member, characteristic, etc. **c** be a member of (a club, family, group, etc.). **2** have the right personal or social qualities to be a member of a particular group (*he's nice but just doesn't belong*). **3** (foll. by *in*, *under*): **a** be rightly placed or classified. **b** fit a particular environment. □ **belongingness** n. [ME f. intensive BE- + *longen* belong f. OE *langian* (*gelang* at hand)]

belongings /bɪˈlɒŋɪŋz/ n.pl. one's movable possessions or luggage.

beloved /bɪˈlʌvɪd, *predic.* also -lʌvd/ adj. & n. —adj. much loved. —n. a much loved person. [obs. *belove* (v.)]

below /bɪˈləʊ/ prep. & adv. —prep. **1** lower in position (vertically, down a slope or stream, etc.) than. **2** beneath the surface of; at or to a greater depth than (*head below water; below 500 feet*). **3** lower or less than in amount or degree (*below freezing-point; temperature is 20 below*). **4** lower in rank, position, or importance than. **5** unworthy of. —adv. **1** at or to a lower point or level. **2 a** downstairs (*lives below*). **b** downstream. **3** (of a text reference) further forward on a page or in a book (*as noted below*). **4** on the lower side (*looks similar above and below*). □ **below stairs** in the basement of a house esp. as the part occupied by servants. [BE- + LOW¹]

belt n. & v. —n. **1** a strip of leather or other material worn round the waist or across the chest, esp. to retain or support clothes or to carry weapons or as a safety-belt. **2** a belt worn as a sign of rank or achievement. **3 a** a circular band of material used as a driving medium in machinery. **b** a conveyor belt. **c** a flexible strip carrying machine-gun cartridges. **4** a strip of colour or texture etc. differing from that on each side. **5** a distinct region or extent (*cotton belt; commuter belt; a belt of rain*). **6** sl. a heavy blow. —v. **1** tr. put a belt round. **2** tr. (often foll. by *on*) fasten with a belt. **3** tr. **a** beat with a belt. **b** sl. hit hard. **4** intr. sl. rush, hurry (usu. with compl.: *belted along; belted home*). □ **below the belt** unfair or unfairly; disregarding the rules. **belt out** sl. sing or utter loudly and forcibly. **belt up** Brit. **1** sl. be quiet. **2** colloq. put on a seat belt. **tighten one's belt** live more frugally. **under one's belt 1** (of food) eaten. **2** securely acquired (*has a degree under her belt*). □ **belter** n. (esp. in sense of *belt out*). [OE f. Gmc f. L *balteus*]

beluga /bəˈluːgə/ n. **1 a** a large kind of sturgeon, *Huso huso*. **b** caviare obtained from it. **2** a white whale. [Russ. *beluga* f. *belyi* white]

belvedere /ˈbɛlvɪˌdɪə(r)/ n. a summer-house or open-sided gallery usu. at rooftop level. [It. f. *bel* beautiful + *vedere* see]

belying *pres. part.* of BELIE.

BEM abbr. British Empire Medal.

bemoan /bɪˈməʊn/ v.tr. **1** express regret or sorrow over; lament. **2** complain about. [BE- + MOAN]

bemuse /bɪˈmjuːz/ v.tr. stupefy or bewilder (a person). □ **bemusedly** /-zɪdlɪ/ adv. **bemusement** n. [BE- + MUSE²]

bench n. **1** a long seat of wood or stone for seating several people. **2** a working-table, e.g. for a carpenter, mechanic, or scientist. **3** (prec. by *the*) **a** the office of judge or magistrate. **b** a judge's seat in a lawcourt. **c** a lawcourt. **d** judges and magistrates collectively. **4** (often in *pl.*) *Sport* an area to the side of a pitch, with seating where coaches and players not taking part can watch the game. **5** Brit. Parl. a seat appropriated as specified (*front bench*). □ **King's** (or **Queen's**) **Bench** (in the UK) a division of the High Court

of Justice. **on the bench** appointed a judge or magistrate.

bencher /ˈbɛntʃə(r)/ n. Brit. **1** Law a senior member of any of the Inns of Court. **2** (in comb.) Parl. an occupant of a specified bench (*backbencher*).

benchmark /ˈbɛntʃmɑːk/ n. **1** a surveyor's mark cut in a wall, pillar, building, etc., used as a reference point in measuring altitudes. **2** a standard or point of reference.

bend¹ v. & n. —v. (*past* bent; *past part.* bent exc. in *bended knee*) **1 a** tr. force or adapt (something straight) into a curve or angle. **b** intr. (of an object) be altered in this way. **2** intr. move or stretch in a curved course (*the road bends to the left*). **3** intr. & tr. (often foll. by *down, over, etc.*) incline or cause to incline from the vertical (*bent down to pick it up*). **4** tr. interpret or modify (a rule) to suit oneself. **5** tr. & refl. (foll. by *to, on*) direct or devote (oneself or one's attention, energies, etc.). **6** tr. turn (one's steps or eyes) in a new direction. **7** tr. (in *passive*; foll. by *on*) have firmly decided; be determined (*was bent on selling*). **8 a** intr. stoop or submit (*bent before his master*). **b** tr. force to submit. —n. **1** a curve in a road or other course. **2** a departure from a straight course. **3** a bent part of anything. **4** (in *pl.*; prec. by *the*) colloq. sickness due to too rapid decompression underwater. □ **round the bend** colloq. crazy, insane. □ **bendable** adj. [OE *bendan* f. Gmc]

bend² n. **1** Naut. any of various knots for tying ropes (*fisherman's bend*). **2** Heraldry **a** a diagonal stripe from top right to bottom left of a shield. **b** (**bend sinister**) a diagonal stripe from top left to bottom right, as a sign of bastardy. [OE *bend* band, bond f. Gmc]

bender /ˈbɛndə(r)/ n. sl. a wild drinking-spree. [BEND¹ + -ER¹]

bendy /ˈbɛndɪ/ adj. (**bendier, bendiest**) colloq. capable of bending; soft and flexible. □ **bendiness** n.

beneath /bɪˈniːθ/ prep. & adv. —prep. **1** not worthy of; too demeaning for (*it was beneath him to reply*). **2** below, under. —adv. below, underneath. [OE *binithan, bineothan* f. *bi* BY + *nithan* etc. below f. Gmc]

Benedictine /ˌbɛnɪˈdɪktɪn, (in sense 2) -ˌtiːn/ n. & adj. —n. **1** a monk or nun of an order following the rule of St Benedict. **2** propr. a liqueur based on brandy, orig. made by Benedictines in France. —adj. of St Benedict or the Benedictines. [F *bénédictine* or mod.L *benedictinus* f. *Benedictus* Benedict]

benediction /ˌbɛnɪˈdɪkʃ(ə)n/ n. **1** the utterance of a blessing, esp. at the end of a religious service or as a special Roman Catholic service. **2** the state of being blessed. [ME f. OF f. L *benedictio -onis* f. *benedicere -dict-* bless]

benefaction /ˌbɛnɪˈfækʃ(ə)n/ n. **1** a donation or gift. **2** an act of giving or doing good. [LL *benefactio* (as BENEFIT)]

benefactor /ˈbɛnɪˌfæktə(r)/ n. (fem. **benefactress** /-trɪs/) a person who gives support (esp. financial) to a person or cause. [ME f. LL (as BENEFIT)]

benefice /ˈbɛnɪfɪs/ n. **1** a living from a church office. **2** the property attached to a church office, esp. that bestowed on a rector or vicar. □ **beneficed** adj. [ME f. OF f. L *beneficium* favour f. *bene* well + *facere* do]

beneficent /bɪˈnefɪs(ə)nt/ adj. doing good; generous, actively kind. □ **beneficence** n. **beneficently** adv. [L beneficent- (as BENEFICE)]

beneficial /ˌbenɪˈfɪʃ(ə)l/ adj. advantageous; having benefits. □ **beneficially** adv. [ME f. F bénéficial or LL beneficialis (as BENEFICE)]

beneficiary /ˌbenɪˈfɪʃərɪ/ n. (pl. **-ies**) **1** a person who receives benefits, esp. under a person's will. **2** a holder of a church living. [L beneficiarius (as BENEFICE)]

benefit /ˈbenɪfɪt/ n. & v. —n. **1** a favourable or helpful factor or circumstance; advantage, profit. **2** (often in pl.) payment made under insurance or social security (sickness benefit). **3** a public performance or game of which the proceeds go to a particular player or company or charitable cause. —v. (**benefited, benefiting**; US **benefitted, benefitting**) **1** tr. do good to; bring advantage to. **2** intr. (often foll. by from, by) receive an advantage or gain. □ **the benefit of the doubt** a concession that a person is innocent, correct, etc., although doubt exists. **benefit society** a society for mutual insurance against illness or the effects of old age. [ME f. AF benfet, OF bienfet, f. L benefactum f. bene facere do well]

benevolent /bɪˈnevələnt/ adj. **1** wishing to do good; actively friendly and helpful. **2** charitable (benevolent fund; benevolent society). □ **benevolence** n. **benevolently** adv. [ME f. OF benivolent f. L bene volens -entis well wishing f. velle wish]

Bengali /beŋˈɡɔːlɪ/ n. & adj. —n. **1** a native of Bengal, a former Indian province now consisting of Bangladesh and the Indian State of W. Bengal. **2** the language of this people. —adj. of or relating to Bengal or its people or language.

benighted /bɪˈnaɪtɪd/ adj. **1** intellectually or morally ignorant. **2** overtaken by darkness. □ **benightedness** n. [obs. benight (v.)]

benign /bɪˈnaɪn/ adj. **1** gentle, mild, kindly. **2** fortunate, salutary. **3** (of the climate, soil, etc.) mild, favourable. **4** Med. (of a disease, tumour, etc.) not malignant. □ **benignly** adv. [ME f. OF benigne f. L benignus f. bene well + -genus born]

benignant /bɪˈnɪɡnənt/ adj. **1** kindly, esp. to inferiors. **2** salutary, beneficial. **3** Med. = BENIGN. □ **benignancy** n. **benignantly** adv. [f. BENIGN or L benignus, after malignant]

benignity /bɪˈnɪɡnɪtɪ/ n. (pl. **-ies**) **1** kindliness. **2** an act of kindness. [ME f. OF benignité or L benignitas (as BENIGN)]

bent[1] past and past part. of BEND[1] v. —adj. **1** curved or having an angle. **2** sl. dishonest, illicit. **3** sl. sexually deviant. **4** (foll. by on) determined to do or have. —n. **1** an inclination or bias. **2** (foll. by for) a talent for something specified (a bent for mimicry).

bent[2] n. **1 a** any stiff grass of the genus Agrostis. **b** any of various grasslike reeds, rushes, or sedges. **2** a stiff stalk of a plant. [ME repr. OE beonet- (in place-names), f. Gmc]

benthos /ˈbenθɒs/ n. the flora and fauna found at the bottom of a sea or lake. □ **benthic** adj. [Gk, = depth of the sea]

bentwood /ˈbentwʊd/ n. wood that is artificially shaped for use in making furniture.

benumb /bɪˈnʌm/ v.tr. **1** make numb; deaden. **2** paralyse (the mind or feelings). [orig. = deprived, as past part. of ME benimen f. OE beniman (as BE-, niman take)]

Benzedrine /ˈbenzɪˌdriːn/ n. propr. amphetamine. [BENZOIN + EPHEDRINE]

benzene /ˈbenziːn/ n. a colourless carcinogenic volatile liquid found in coal tar, petroleum, etc., and used as a solvent and in the manufacture of plastics etc. □ **benzene ring** the hexagonal unsaturated ring of six carbon atoms in the benzene molecule. □ **benzenoid** adj. [BENZOIN + -ENE]

benzine /ˈbenziːn/ n. (also **benzin** /-zɪn/) a mixture of liquid hydrocarbons obtained from petroleum. [BENZOIN + -INE[4]]

benzoin /ˈbenzəʊɪn/ n. a fragrant gum resin obtained from various E. Asian trees of the genus Styrax, and used in the manufacture of perfumes and incense. [earlier benjoin ult. f. Arab. lubān jāwī incense of Java]

benzol /ˈbenzɒl/ n. (also **benzole** /-zəʊl/) benzene, esp. unrefined and used as a fuel.

bequeath /bɪˈkwiːð/ v.tr. **1** leave (a personal estate) to a person by a will. **2** hand down to posterity. □ **bequeathal** n. **bequeather** n. [OE becwethan (as BE-, cwethan say: cf. QUOTH)]

bequest /bɪˈkwest/ n. **1** the act or an instance of bequeathing. **2** a thing bequeathed. [ME f. BE- + obs. quiste f. OE -cwiss, cwide saying]

berate /bɪˈreɪt/ v.tr. scold, rebuke. [BE- + RATE[2]]

berberis /ˈbɜːbərɪs/ n. = BARBERRY. [med.L & OF, of unkn. orig.]

bereave /bɪˈriːv/ v.tr. (esp. as **bereaved** adj.) (foll. by of) deprive of a relation, friend, etc., esp. by death. □ **bereavement** n. [OE berēafian (as BE-, REAVE)]

bereft /bɪˈreft/ adj. (foll. by of) deprived (esp. of a non-material asset) (bereft of hope). [past part. of BEREAVE]

beret /ˈbereɪ/ n. a round flattish cap of felt or cloth. [F béret Basque cap f. Prov. berret]

berg[1] n. = ICEBERG. [abbr.]

berg[2] n. S.Afr. a mountain or hill. □ **berg wind** a hot dry northerly wind blowing from the interior to coastal districts. [Afrik. f. Du.]

bergamot[1] /ˈbɜːɡəˌmɒt/ n. **1** an aromatic herb, esp. Mentha citrata. **2** an oily perfume extracted from the rind of the fruit of the citrus tree Citrus bergamia, a dwarf variety of the Seville orange tree. **3** the tree itself. [Bergamo in N. Italy]

bergamot[2] /ˈbɜːɡəˌmɒt/ n. a variety of fine pear. [F bergamotte f. It. bergamotta f. Turk. begarmūdi prince's pear f. beg prince + armudi pear]

beriberi /ˌberɪˈberɪ/ n. a disease causing inflammation of the nerves due to a deficiency of vitamin B_1. [Sinh., f. beri weakness]

berk n. (also **burk**) Brit. sl. a fool; a stupid person. [abbr. of Berkeley or Berkshire Hunt, rhyming sl. for cunt]

berkelium /bɜːˈkiːlɪəm, ˈbɜːklɪəm/ n. Chem. a transuranic radioactive metallic element produced by bombardment of americium. [mod.L f. Berkeley in California (where first made) + -IUM]

berm n. a narrow path or grass strip beside a road, canal, etc. [F berme f. Du. berm]

Bermuda shorts /bəˈmjuːdə/ n.pl. (also **Bermudas**) close-fitting shorts reaching the knees. [Bermuda in the W. Atlantic]

berry /ˈberɪ/ n. (pl. **-ies**) **1** any small roundish juicy fruit without a stone. **2** Bot. a fruit with its seeds enclosed in a pulp (e.g. a banana, tomato, etc.). **3** any of various kernels or seeds (e.g.

coffee bean etc.). □ **berried** adj. (also in comb.). [OE berie f. Gmc]

berserk /bəˈsɜːk, -ˈzɜːk/ adj. (esp. in **go berserk**) wild, frenzied; in a violent rage. [Icel. berserkr (n.) prob. f. bern- BEAR² + serkr coat]

berth /bɜːθ/ n. & v. —n. **1** a fixed bunk on a ship, train, etc., for sleeping in. **2** a ship's place at a wharf. **3** room for a ship to swing at anchor. **4** adequate sea room. **5** colloq. a situation or appointment. **6** the proper place for anything. —v. **1** tr. moor (a ship) in its berth. **2** tr. provide a sleeping place for. **3** intr. (of a ship) come to its mooring-place. □ **give a wide berth to** stay away from. [prob. f. naut. use of BEAR¹ + -TH²]

beryl /ˈberɪl/ n. **1** a kind of transparent precious stone, esp. pale green, blue, or yellow. **2** a mineral species which includes this, emerald, and aquamarine. [ME f. OF f. L beryllus f. Gk bērullos]

beryllium /bəˈrɪlɪəm/ n. Chem. a hard white metallic element used in the manufacture of light corrosion-resistant alloys. [BERYL + -IUM]

beseech /bɪˈsiːtʃ/ v.tr. (past and past part. **besought** /-ˈsɔːt/ or **beseeched**) **1** (foll. by for, or to + infin.) entreat. **2** ask earnestly for. □ **beseeching** adj. [ME f. BE- + secan SEEK]

beset /bɪˈset/ v.tr. (**besetting**; past and past part. **beset**) **1** attack or harass persistently (beset by worries). **2** surround or hem in (a person etc.). □ **besetment** n. [OE besettan f. Gmc]

beside /bɪˈsaɪd/ prep. **1** at the side of; near. **2** compared with. **3** irrelevant to (beside the point). □ **beside oneself** overcome with worry, anger, etc. [OE be sīdan (as BY, SIDE)]

besides /bɪˈsaɪdz/ prep. & adv. —prep. in addition to; apart from. —adv. also; as well; moreover.

besiege /bɪˈsiːdʒ/ v.tr. **1** lay siege to. **2** crowd round vigorously. **3** harass with requests. □ **besieger** n. [ME f. assiege by substitution of BE-, f. OF asegier f. Rmc]

besmirch /bɪˈsmɜːtʃ/ v.tr. **1** soil, discolour. **2** dishonour; sully the reputation or name of. [BE- + SMIRCH]

besom /ˈbiːz(ə)m/ n. a broom made of twigs tied round a stick. [OE besema]

besotted /bɪˈsɒtɪd/ adj. **1** infatuated. **2** foolish, confused. **3** stupefied. [besot (v.) (as BE-, SOT)]

besought past and past part. of BESEECH.

bespangle /bɪˈspæŋɡ(ə)l/ v.tr. adorn with spangles.

bespatter /bɪˈspætə(r)/ v.tr. **1** spatter (an object) all over. **2** spatter (liquid etc.) about. **3** overwhelm with abuse etc.

bespeak /bɪˈspiːk/ v.tr. (past **bespoke** /-ˈspəʊk/; past part. **bespoken** /-ˈspəʊkən/ or as adj. **bespoke**) **1** engage in advance. **2** order (goods). **3** be evidence of (his gift bespeaks a kind heart). [OE bisprecan (as BE-, SPEAK)]

bespectacled /bɪˈspektək(ə)ld/ adj. wearing spectacles.

bespoke past and past part. of BESPEAK. —adj. **1** (of goods, esp. clothing) made to order. **2** (of a tradesman) making goods to order.

besprinkle /bɪˈsprɪŋk(ə)l/ v.tr. **1** sprinkle or strew all over with liquid etc. **2** sprinkle (liquid etc.) over. [ME f. BE- + sprengen in the same sense]

best /best/ adj., adv., n., & v. —adj. (superl. of GOOD) of the most excellent or outstanding or desirable kind (my best work; the best thing to do would be to confess). —adv. (superl. of WELL¹). **1** in

the best manner (does it best). **2** to the greatest degree (like it best). **3** most usefully (is best ignored). —n. **1** that which is best (the best is yet to come). **2** the chief merit or advantage (brings out the best in him). **3** (foll. by of) a winning majority of (a certain number of games etc. played) (the best of five). —v.tr. colloq. defeat, outwit, outbid, etc. □ **as best one can** (or **may**) as effectively as possible under the circumstances. **at best** on the most optimistic view. **at one's best** in peak condition etc. **be for** (or **all for**) **the best** be desirable in the end. **best end of neck** the rib end of a neck of lamb etc. for cooking. **best man** the bridegroom's chief attendant at a wedding. **the best part of** most of. **do one's best** do all one can. **get the best of** defeat, outwit. **had best** would find it wisest to. **make the best of** derive what limited advantage one can from (something unsatisfactory or unwelcome); put up with. **to the best of one's ability, knowledge**, etc. as far as one can do, know, etc. [OE betest (adj.), bet(o)st (adv.), f. Gmc]

bestial /ˈbestɪəl/ adj. **1** brutish, cruel, savage. **2** sexually depraved; lustful. **3** of or like a beast. □ **bestialize** v.tr. (also **-ise**). **bestially** adv. [ME f. OF f. LL bestialis f. bestia beast]

bestiality /ˌbestɪˈælɪtɪ/ n. (pl. **-ies**) **1** bestial behaviour or an instance of this. **2** sexual intercourse between a person and an animal. [F bestialité (as BESTIAL)]

bestiary /ˈbestɪərɪ/ n. (pl. **-ies**) a moralizing medieval treatise on real and imaginary beasts. [med.L bestiarium f. L bestia beast]

bestir /bɪˈstɜː(r)/ v.refl. (**bestirred, bestirring**) exert or rouse (oneself).

bestow /bɪˈstəʊ/ v.tr. **1** (foll. by on, upon) confer (a gift, right, etc.). **2** deposit. □ **bestowal** n. [ME f. BE- + OE stow a place]

bestrew /bɪˈstruː/ v.tr. (past part. **bestrewed** or **bestrewn** /-ˈstruːn/) **1** (foll. by with) cover or partly cover (a surface). **2** scatter (things) about. **3** lie scattered over. [OE bestrēowian (as BE-, STREW)]

bestride /bɪˈstraɪd/ v.tr. (past **bestrode** /-ˈstrəʊd/; past part. **bestridden** /-ˈstrɪd(ə)n/) **1** sit astride on. **2** stand astride over. [OE bestrīdan]

bet /bet/ v. & n. —v. (**betting**; past and past part. **bet** or **betted**) **1** intr. (foll. by on or against with ref. to the outcome) risk a sum of money etc. against another's on the basis of the outcome of an unpredictable event. **2** tr. risk (an amount) on such an outcome or result (bet £10 on a horse). **3** tr. risk a sum of money against (a person). **4** tr. colloq. feel sure (bet they've forgotten it). —n. **1** the act of betting (make a bet). **2** the money etc. staked (put a bet on). **3** colloq. an opinion, esp. a quickly formed or spontaneous one (my bet is that he won't come). □ **you bet** you may be sure. [16th c.: perh. a shortened form of ABET]

beta /ˈbiːtə/ n. **1** the second letter of the Greek alphabet (B, β). **2** the second member of a series. □ **beta-blocker** Pharm. a drug that prevents the stimulation of increased cardiac action, used to treat angina and reduce high blood pressure. **beta particle** (or **ray**) a fast-moving electron emitted by radioactive decay of substances. [ME f. L f. Gk]

betake /bɪˈteɪk/ v.refl. (past **betook** /bɪˈtʊk/; past part. **betaken** /bɪˈteɪkən/) (foll. by to) go to (a place or person).

betatron /ˈbiːtəˌtrɒn/ n. Physics an apparatus for accelerating electrons in a circular path by magnetic induction. [BETA + -TRON]

betel /ˈbiːt(ə)l/ n. the leaf of the Asian evergreen climbing plant *Piper betle*, chewed in the East with parings of the areca nut. □ **betel-nut** the areca nut. [Port. f. Malayalam *veṭṭila*]

bête noire /beɪt ˈnwɑː(r)/ n. (pl. **bêtes noires** *pronunc.* same) a person or thing one particularly dislikes or fears. [F. = black beast]

bethink /bɪˈθɪŋk/ v.refl. (past and past part. **bethought** /-ˈθɔːt/) (foll. by *of*, *how*, or *that* + clause) formal **1** reflect; stop to think. **2** be reminded by reflection. [OE *bithencan* f. Gmc (as BE-, THINK)]

betide /bɪˈtaɪd/ v. (only in infin. and 3rd sing. subj.) **1** tr. happen to (*woe betide him*). **2** intr. happen. [ME f. obs. *tide* befall f. OE *tīdan*]

betimes /bɪˈtaɪmz/ adv. literary early; in good time. [ME f. obs. *betime* (as BY, TIME)]

betoken /bɪˈtəʊkən/ v.tr. **1** be a sign of; indicate. **2** augur. [OE (as BE-, *tācnian* signify: see TOKEN)]

betray /bɪˈtreɪ/ v.tr. **1** place (a person, one's country, etc.) in the hands or power of an enemy. **2** be disloyal to (another person, a person's trust, etc.). **3** reveal involuntarily or treacherously; be evidence of (*his shaking hand betrayed his fear*). **4** lead astray or into error. □ **betrayal** n. **betrayer** n. [ME f. obs. *tray*, ult. f. L *tradere* hand over]

betroth /bɪˈtrəʊð/ v.tr. (usu. as **betrothed** adj.) bind with a promise to marry. □ **betrothal** n. [ME f. BE- + *trouthe*, *treuthe* TRUTH, later assim. to TROTH]

better[1] /ˈbetə(r)/ adj., adv., n., & v. —adj. (compar. of GOOD). **1** of a more excellent or outstanding or desirable kind (*a better product*; *it would be better to go home*). **2** partly or fully recovered from illness (*feeling better*). —adv. (compar. of WELL[1]). **1** in a better manner. **2** to a greater degree (*like it better*). **3** more usefully or advantageously (*is better forgotten*). —n. **1** that which is better (*the better of the two*). **2** (usu. in pl.; prec. by *my* etc.) one's superior in ability or rank. —v. **1** tr. improve on; surpass. **2** tr. make better; improve. **3** refl. improve one's position etc. □ **better half** colloq. one's wife or husband. **the better part of** most of. **get the better of** defeat, outwit; win an advantage over. **had better** would find it wiser to. [OE *betera* f. Gmc]

better[2] /ˈbetə(r)/ n. (also **bettor**) a person who bets.

betterment /ˈbetəmənt/ n. making better; improvement.

betting /ˈbetɪŋ/ n. **1** gambling by risking money on an unpredictable outcome. **2** the odds offered in this. □ **betting-shop** Brit. a bookmaker's shop or office.

between /bɪˈtwiːn/ prep. & adv. —prep. **1 a** at or to a point in the area or interval bounded by two or more other points in space, time, etc. (*broke down between London and Dover*; *we must meet between now and Friday*). **b** along the extent of such an area or interval (*there are five shops between here and the main road*; *works best between five and six*; *the numbers between 10 and 20*). **2** separating, physically or conceptually (*the distance between here and Leeds*; *the difference between right and wrong*). **3 a** by combining the resources of (*great potential between them*; *between us we could afford it*). **b** shared by; as the joint resources of

(*£5 between them*). **c** by joint or reciprocal action (*an agreement between us*; *sorted it out between themselves*). **4** to and from (*runs between London and Sheffield*). **5** taking one and rejecting the other of (*decide between eating here and going out*). —adv. (also **in between**) at a point or in the area bounded by two or more other points in space, time, sequence, etc. □ **between times** (or **whiles**) in the intervals between other actions; occasionally. [OE *betwēonum* f. Gmc (as BY, TWO)]

betwixt /bɪˈtwɪkst/ prep. & adv. archaic between. □ **betwixt and between** colloq. neither one thing nor the other. [ME f. OE *betwēox* f. Gmc: cf. AGAINST]

bevel /ˈbev(ə)l/ n. & v. —n. **1** a slope from the horizontal or vertical in carpentry and stonework; a sloping surface or edge. **2** (in full **bevel square**) a tool for marking angles in carpentry and stonework. —v. (**bevelled, bevelling**; US **beveled, beveling**) **1** tr. reduce (a square edge) to a sloping edge. **2** intr. slope at an angle; slant. □ **bevel gear** a gear working another gear at an angle to it by means of bevel wheels. **bevel wheel** a toothed wheel whose working face is oblique to the axis. [OF *bevel* (unrecorded) f. *baif* f. *baer* gape]

beverage /ˈbevərɪdʒ/ n. formal a drink (*hot beverage*; *alcoholic beverage*). [ME f. OF *be(u)vrage*, ult. f. L *bibere* drink]

bevy /ˈbevɪ/ n. (pl. **-ies**) **1** a flock of quails or larks. **2** a company or group (orig. of women). [15th c.: orig. unkn.]

bewail /bɪˈweɪl/ v.tr. **1** greatly regret or lament. **2** wail over; mourn for. □ **bewailer** n.

beware /bɪˈweə(r)/ v. (only in imper. or infin.) **1** intr. (often foll. by *of*, or *that*, *lest*, etc. + clause) be cautious, take heed (*beware of the dog*; *told us to beware*; *beware that you don't fall*). **2** tr. be cautious of (*beware the Ides of March*). [BE + OE *wær*: see AWARE]

bewilder /bɪˈwɪldə(r)/ v.tr. utterly perplex or confuse. □ **bewilderedly** adv. **bewildering** adj. **bewilderingly** adv. **bewilderment** n. [BE- + obs. *wilder* lose one's way]

bewitch /bɪˈwɪtʃ/ v.tr. **1** enchant; greatly delight. **2** cast a spell on. □ **bewitching** adj. **bewitchingly** adv. [ME f. BE- + OE *wiccian* enchant f. *wicca* WITCH]

beyond /bɪˈjɒnd/ prep., adv., & n. —prep. **1** at or to the further side of (*beyond the river*). **2** outside the scope, range, or understanding of (*beyond repair*; *beyond a joke*; *it is beyond me*). **3** more than. —adv. **1** at or to the further side. **2** further on. —n. (prec. by *the*) the unknown after death. [OE *beg(e)ondan* (as BY, YON, YONDER)]

bezel /ˈbez(ə)l/ n. **1** the sloped edge of a chisel. **2** the oblique faces of a cut gem. **3** a groove holding a watch-glass or gem. [OF *besel* (unrecorded: cf. F *béseau*, *bizeau*) of unkn. orig.]

bezique /bɪˈziːk/ n. a card-game for two with a double pack of 64 cards, including the ace to seven only in each suit. [F *bésigue*, perh. f. Pers. *bāzīgar* juggler]

bhang /bæŋ/ n. the leaves and flower-tops of Indian hemp used as a narcotic. [Port. *bangue*, Pers. *bang*, & Urdu etc. *bhāng* f. Skr. *bhaṅgā*]

bhangra /ˈbɑːŋgrə, ˈbæŋgrə/ n. a kind of rock music that combines Punjabi folk traditions with Western popular music. [Punjabi *bhāngrā*, a traditional folk-dance]

Bi *symb. Chem.* the element bismuth.

bi- /baɪ/ *comb. form* (often **bin-** before a vowel) forming nouns and adjectives meaning: **1** having two; a thing having two (*bilateral; binaural; biplane*). **2 a** occurring twice in every one or once in every two (*bi-weekly*). **b** lasting for two (*biennial*). **3** doubly; in two ways (*biconcave*). **4** *Chem.* a substance having a double proportion of the acid etc. indicated by the simple word (*bicarbonate*). **5** *Bot.* & *Zool.* (of division and subdivision) twice over (*bipinnate*). [L]

biannual /baɪˈænjʊəl/ *adj.* occurring, appearing, etc., twice a year. □ **biannually** *adv.*

bias /ˈbaɪəs/ *n.* & *v.* —*n.* **1** a predisposition or prejudice. **2** *Statistics* a systematic distortion of a statistical result due to a factor not allowed for in its derivation. **3** an edge cut obliquely across the weave of a fabric. **4** *Sport* **a** the irregular shape given to a bowl. **b** the oblique course this causes it to run. **5** *Electr.* a steady voltage, magnetic field, etc., applied to an electronic system or device. —*v.tr.* (**biased, biasing; biassed, biassing**) **1** (esp. as **biased** *adj.*) influence (usu. unfairly); prejudice. **2** give a bias to. □ **bias binding** a strip of fabric cut obliquely and used to bind edges. **on the bias** obliquely, diagonally. [F *biais*, of unkn. orig.]

bib *n.* **1** a piece of cloth or plastic fastened round a child's neck to keep the clothes clean while eating. **2** the top front part of an apron, dungarees, etc. [perh. ult. f. L *bibere* drink]

bibelot /ˈbiːbləʊ/ *n.* a small curio or artistic trinket. [F]

Bible /ˈbaɪb(ə)l/ *n.* **1 a** the Christian scriptures consisting of the Old and New Testaments. **b** the Jewish scriptures. **c** (**bible**) any copy of these (*three bibles on the table*). **d** a particular edition of the Bible (*New English Bible*). **2** *colloq.* any authoritative book (*Wisden is his Bible*). **3** the scriptures of any non-Christian religion. □ **Bible belt** esp. *US* the reputedly puritanical area of the southern and central US. [ME f. OF f. eccl.L *biblia* f. Gk *biblia* books (pl. of *biblion*), orig. dimin. of *biblos, bublos* papyrus]

biblical /ˈbɪblɪk(ə)l/ *adj.* **1** of, concerning, or contained in the Bible. **2** resembling the language of the Authorized Version of the Bible. □ **biblically** *adv.*

biblio- /ˈbɪblɪəʊ/ *comb. form* denoting a book or books. [Gk f. *biblion* book]

bibliography /ˌbɪblɪˈɒgrəfɪ/ *n.* (pl. **-ies**) **1 a** a list of the books referred to in a scholarly work, usu. printed as an appendix. **b** a list of the books of a specific author or publisher, or on a specific subject, etc. **2 a** the history or description of books, including authors, editions, etc. **b** any book containing such information. □ **bibliographer** *n.* **bibliographic** /-əˈgræfɪk/ *adj.* **bibliographical** /-əˈgræfɪk(ə)l/ *adj.* **bibliographically** /-əˈgræfɪkəlɪ/ *adv.* **bibliographize** *v.tr.* (also **-ise**). [F *bibliographie* f. mod.L *bibliographia* f. Gk (as BIBLE, -GRAPHY)]

bibliomania /ˌbɪblɪəʊˈmeɪnɪə/ *n.* an extreme enthusiasm for collecting and possessing books. □ **bibliomaniac** /-nɪˌæk/ *n.* & *adj.*

bibliophile /ˈbɪblɪəʊˌfaɪl/ *n.* (also **bibliophil** /-fɪl/) a person who collects or is fond of books. □ **bibliophilic** /-ˈfɪlɪk/ *adj.* **bibliophily** /-ˈɒfɪlɪ/ *n.* [F *bibliophile* (as BIBLIO-, -PHILE)]

bibulous /ˈbɪbjʊləs/ *adj.* given to drinking alcoholic liquor. □ **bibulously** *adv.* **bibulousness** *n.* [L *bibulus* freely drinking f. *bibere* drink]

bicameral /baɪˈkæmər(ə)l/ *adj.* (of a parliament or legislative body) having two chambers. □ **bicameralism** *n.* [BI- + L *camera* chamber]

bicarbonate /baɪˈkɑːbənɪt/ *n.* **1** *Chem.* any acid salt of carbonic acid. **2** (in full **bicarbonate of soda**) sodium bicarbonate used as an antacid or in baking powder.

bicentenary /ˌbaɪsenˈtiːnərɪ/ *n.* & *adj.* —*n.* (pl. **-ies**) **1** a two-hundredth anniversary. **2** a celebration of this. —*adj.* of or concerning a bicentenary.

bicentennial /ˌbaɪsenˈtenɪəl/ *n.* & *adj.* esp. *US* —*n.* a bicentenary. —*adj.* **1** lasting two hundred years or occurring every two hundred years. **2** of or concerning a bicentenary.

bicephalous /baɪˈsefələs/ *adj.* having two heads.

biceps /ˈbaɪseps/ *n.* a muscle having two heads or attachments, esp. the one which bends the elbow. [L, = two-headed, formed as BI- + -*ceps* f. *caput* head]

bicker /ˈbɪkə(r)/ *v.intr.* **1** quarrel pettily; wrangle. **2** *poet.* **a** (of a stream, rain, etc.) patter (over stones etc.). **b** (of a flame, light, etc.) flash, flicker. □ **bickerer** *n.* [ME *biker, beker*, of unkn. orig.]

biconcave /baɪˈkɒnkeɪv/ *adj.* (esp. of a lens) concave on both sides.

biconvex /baɪˈkɒnveks/ *adj.* (esp. of a lens) convex on both sides.

bicultural /baɪˈkʌltʃər(ə)l/ *adj.* having or combining two cultures.

bicuspid /baɪˈkʌspɪd/ *adj.* & *n.* —*adj.* having two cusps or points. —*n.* **1** the premolar tooth in humans. **2** a tooth with two cusps. □ **bicuspidate** *adj.* [BI- + L *cuspis -idis* sharp point]

bicycle /ˈbaɪsɪk(ə)l/ *n.* & *v.* —*n.* a vehicle of two wheels held in a frame one behind the other, propelled by pedals and steered with handlebars attached to the front wheel. —*v.intr.* ride a bicycle. □ **bicycler** *n.* **bicyclist** /-klɪst/ *n.* [F f. BI- + Gk *kuklos* wheel]

bid *v.* & *n.* —*v.* (**bidding;** *past* **bid,** *archaic* **bade** /beɪd, bæd/; *past part.* **bid,** *archaic* **bidden** /ˈbɪd(ə)n/) **1** *tr.* (*past* and *past part.* **bid**) (often foll. by *for, against*) **a** (esp. at an auction) offer (a certain price) (*did not bid for the vase; bid against the dealer, bid £20*). **b** offer to do work etc. for a stated price. **2** *tr. archaic* or *literary* **a** command; order (*bid the soldiers shoot*). **b** invite (*bade her start*). **3** *tr. archaic* or *literary* utter (greeting or farewell) to (*I bade him welcome*). **4** (*past* and *past part.* **bid**) *Cards* **a** *intr.* state before play how many tricks one intends to make. **b** *tr.* state (one's intended number of tricks). —*n.* **1 a** (esp. at an auction) an offer (of a price) (*a bid of £5*). **b** an offer (to do work, supply goods, etc.) at a stated price; a tender. **2** *Cards* a statement of the number of tricks a player proposes to make. **3** *colloq.* an attempt; an effort (*a bid for power*). □ **bid fair to** seem likely to. **make a bid for** try to gain (*made a bid for freedom*). □ **bidder** *n.* [OE *biddan* ask f. Gmc, & OE *bēodan* offer, command]

biddable /ˈbɪdəb(ə)l/ *adj.* obedient. □ **biddability** /-ˈbɪlɪtɪ/ *n.*

bidding /ˈbɪdɪŋ/ *n.* **1** the offers at an auction. **2** *Cards* the act of making a bid or bids. **3** a command, request, or invitation.

biddy /ˈbɪdɪ/ n. (pl. **-ies**) sl. derog. a woman (esp. old biddy). [pet-form of the name Bridget]

bide /baɪd/ v.intr. archaic or dial. remain; stay. □ **bide one's time** await one's best opportunity. [OE bīdan f. Gmc]

bidet /ˈbiːdeɪ/ n. a low oval basin used esp. for washing the genital area. [F, = pony]

biennial /baɪˈenɪəl/ adj. & n. —adj. **1** lasting two years. **2** recurring every two years. —n. **1** Bot. a plant that takes two years to grow from seed to fruition and die. **2** an event celebrated or taking place every two years. □ **biennially** adv. [L biennis (as BI-, annus year)]

biennium /baɪˈenɪəm/ n. (pl. **bienniums** or **biennia** /-nɪə/) a period of two years. [L (as BIENNIAL)]

bier /bɪə(r)/ n. a movable frame on which a coffin or a corpse is placed. [OE bēr f. Gmc]

biff n. & v. sl. —n. a sharp blow. —v.tr. strike (a person). [imit.]

bifid /ˈbaɪfɪd/ adj. divided by a deep cleft into two parts. [L bifidus (as BI-, fidus f. stem of findere cleave)]

bifocal /baɪˈfəʊk(ə)l/ adj. & n. —adj. having two focuses, esp. of a lens with a part for distant vision and a part for near vision. —n. (in pl.) bifocal spectacles.

bifurcate /ˈbaɪfəˌkeɪt/ v. & adj. —v.tr. & intr. divide into two branches; fork. —adj. forked; branched. □ **bifurcation** n. [med.L bifurcare f. L bifurcus two-forked (as BI-, furca fork)]

big adj. & adv. —adj. (**bigger, biggest**) **1 a** of considerable size, amount, intensity, etc. (a big mistake; a big helping). **b** of a large or the largest size (big toe; big drum). **2** important; significant; outstanding (my big chance). **3 a** grown up (a big boy now). **b** elder (big sister). **4** colloq. **a** boastful (big words). **b** often iron. generous (big of him). **c** ambitious (big ideas). **5** (usu. foll. by with) advanced in pregnancy; fecund (big with consequences). —adv. colloq. in a big manner, esp.: **1** effectively (went over big). **2** boastfully (talk big). **3** ambitiously (think big). □ **Big Apple** US sl. New York City. **big business** large-scale financial dealings, esp. when sinister or exploitative. **big deal!** sl. iron. I am not impressed. **big dipper 1** a fairground switchback. **2** US = the Great Bear (see BEAR²). **big end** (in a motor vehicle) the end of the connecting-rod that encircles the crankpin. **big game** large animals hunted for sport. **big-head** colloq. a conceited person. **big-headed** colloq. conceited. **big-hearted** generous. **big money** large amounts; high profit; high pay. **big name** a famous person. **big noise** (or **pot** or **shot**) colloq. = BIGWIG. **big stick** a display of force. **the big time** sl. success in a profession, esp. show business. **big top** the main tent in a circus. **big tree** US a giant evergreen conifer, Sequoiadendron giganteum. **big wheel 1** a Ferris wheel. **2** US sl. = BIGWIG. **in a big way 1** on a large scale. **2** colloq. with great enthusiasm, display, etc. **look** (or **talk**) **big** boast. □ **biggish** adj. **bigness** n. [ME: orig. unkn.]

bigamy /ˈbɪgəmɪ/ n. (pl. **-ies**) the crime of marrying when one is lawfully married to another person. □ **bigamist** n. **bigamous** adj. [ME f. OF bigamie f. bigame bigamous f. LL bigamus (as BI-, Gk gamos marriage)]

bight /baɪt/ n. **1** a curve or recess in a coastline, river, etc. **2** a loop of rope. [OE byht, MLG bucht f. Gmc: see BOW²]

bigot /ˈbɪgət/ n. an obstinate and intolerant believer in a religion, political theory, etc. □ **bigotry** n. [16th c. f. F: orig. unkn.]

bigoted /ˈbɪgətɪd/ adj. unreasonably prejudiced and intolerant.

bigwig /ˈbɪgwɪg/ n. colloq. an important person.

bijou /ˈbiːʒuː/ n. & adj. —n. (pl. **bijoux** pronunc. same) a jewel; a trinket. —attrib.adj. (**bijou**) small and elegant. [F]

bike n. & v. colloq. —n. a bicycle or motor cycle. —v.intr. ride a bicycle or motor cycle. [abbr.]

biker /ˈbaɪkə(r)/ n. a cyclist, esp. a motor cyclist.

bikini /bɪˈkiːnɪ/ n. a two-piece swimsuit for women. [Bikini, an atoll in the Marshall Islands in the Pacific where an atomic bomb was exploded in 1946, from the supposed 'explosive' effect]

bilateral /baɪˈlætər(ə)l/ adj. **1** of, on, or with two sides. **2** affecting or between two parties, countries, etc. (bilateral negotiations). □ **bilateral symmetry** symmetry about a plane. □ **bilaterally** adv.

bilberry /ˈbɪlbərɪ/ n. (pl. **-ies**) **1** a hardy dwarf shrub, Vaccinium myrtillus, of N. Europe, growing on heaths and mountains, and having dark blue berries. **2** the small blue edible berry of this species. [orig. uncert.: cf. Da. bøllebær]

bile n. **1** a bitter greenish-brown alkaline fluid which aids digestion and is secreted by the liver. **2** bad temper; peevish anger. [F f. L bilis]

bilge n. & v. —n. **1 a** the almost flat part of a ship's bottom, inside or out. **b** (in full **bilge-water**) filthy water that collects inside the bilge. **2** sl. nonsense. —v. **1** tr. stave in the bilge of (a ship). **2** intr. spring a leak in the bilge. **3** intr. swell out; bulge. [prob. var. of BULGE]

bilharzia /bɪlˈhɑːtsɪə/ n. **1** a tropical flatworm of the genus Schistosoma (formerly Bilharzia) which is parasitic in blood vessels in the human pelvic region. **2** the chronic tropical disease produced by its presence. [mod.L f. T. Bilharz, Ger. physician d. 1862]

bilharziasis /ˌbɪlhɑːˈtsaɪəsɪs/ n. the disease of bilharzia.

biliary /ˈbɪlɪərɪ/ adj. of the bile. [F biliaire: see BILE, -ARY²]

bilingual /baɪˈlɪŋgw(ə)l/ adj. & n. —adj. **1** able to speak two languages, esp. fluently. **2** spoken or written in two languages. —n. a bilingual person. □ **bilingualism** n. [L bilinguis (as BI-, lingua tongue)]

bilious /ˈbɪlɪəs/ adj. **1** affected by a disorder of the bile. **2** bad-tempered. □ **biliously** adv. **biliousness** n. [L biliosus f. bilis bile]

bilk v.tr. sl. **1** cheat. **2** give the slip to. **3** avoid paying (a creditor or debt). □ **bilker** n. [orig. uncert., perh. = earliest use (17th c.) in cribbage; = spoil one's opponent's score]

bill¹ n. & v. —n. **1 a** a printed or written statement of charges for goods supplied or services rendered. **b** the amount owed (ran up a bill of £300). **2** a draft of a proposed law. **3 a** a poster; a placard. **b** = HANDBILL. **4 a** a printed list, esp. a theatre programme. **b** the entertainment itself (top of the bill). **5** US a banknote (ten dollar bill). —v.tr. **1** put in the programme; announce. **2** (foll. by as) advertise. **3** send a note of charges to (*billed him for the books*). □ **bill of exchange** *Econ.* a written order to pay a sum of money on a given date to the drawer or to a named payee. **bill of fare** 1 a menu. **2** a programme (for a theatrical event). **bill of health 1** *Naut.* a certificate regarding infectious disease on a ship or in a port at the time of sailing. **2** (**clean bill of health**) **a** such a certificate stating that there is no disease. **b** a declaration that a person or thing examined has been found to be free of illness or in good condition. **bill of lading** *Naut.* 1 a shipmaster's detailed list of the ship's cargo. **2** *US* a list of passengers or parcels on a vehicle. **Bill of Rights** a statement of the rights of a class of people. □ **billable** *adj.* [ME f. AF *bille*, AL *billa*, prob. alt. of med.L *bulla* seal, sealed documents]

bill² *n. & v.* —*n.* **1** the beak of a bird, esp. when it is slender, flattened, or weak, or belongs to a web-footed bird or a bird of the pigeon family. **2** the muzzle of a platypus. **3** a narrow promontory. —*v.intr.* (of doves etc.) stroke a bill with a bill. □ **bill and coo** exchange caresses. □ **billed** *adj.* (usu. in *comb.*). [OE *bile*, of unkn. orig.]

bill³ *n.* **1** *hist.* a weapon like a halberd with a hook instead of a blade. **2** = BILLHOOK. [OE *bil*, ult. f. Gmc]

billabong /ˈbɪləˌbɒŋ/ *n. Austral.* a branch of a river forming a backwater or a stagnant pool. [Aboriginal *Billibang* Bell River f. *billa* water]

billboard /ˈbɪlbɔːd/ *n.* esp. *US* a large outdoor board for advertisements etc.

billet¹ /ˈbɪlɪt/ *n. & v.* —*n.* **1 a** a place where troops etc. are lodged, usu. with civilians. **b** a written order requiring a householder to lodge the bearer, usu. a soldier. **2** *colloq.* a situation; a job. —*v.tr.* (**billeted, billeting**) **1** (usu. foll. by *on*, *in*, *at*) quarter (soldiers etc.). **2** (of a householder) provide (a soldier etc.) with board and lodging. □ **billetee** /-ˈtiː/ *n.* **billeter** *n.* [ME f. AF *billette*, AL *billetta*, dimin. of *billa* BILL¹]

billet² /ˈbɪlɪt/ *n.* **1** a thick piece of firewood. **2** a small metal bar. [ME f. F *billette* small log, ult. prob. of Celtic orig.]

billet-doux /ˌbɪlɪˈduː/ *n.* (*pl.* **billets-doux** /-ˈduːz/) often *joc.* a love-letter. [F, = sweet note]

billfold /ˈbɪlfəʊld/ *n. US* a wallet for keeping banknotes.

billhook /ˈbɪlhʊk/ *n.* a sickle-shaped tool with a sharp inner edge, used for pruning, lopping, etc.

billiards /ˈbɪljədz/ *n.* **1** a game played on an oblong cloth-covered table, with three balls struck with cues into pockets round the edge of the table. **2** (**billiard**) (in *comb.*) used in billiards (*billiard-ball; billiard-table*). [orig. pl., f. F *billard* billiards, cue, dimin. of *bille* log: see BILLET²]

billion /ˈbɪljən/ *n. & adj.* —*n.* (*pl.* same or (in sense 3) **billions**) (in *sing.* prec. by *a* or *one*) **1** a thousand million (1,000,000,000 or 10⁹). **2** (now less often, esp. *Brit.*) a million million (1,000,000,000,000 or 10¹²). **3** (in *pl.*) *colloq.* a very large number (*billions of years*). —*adj.* that amount to a billion. □ **billionth** *adj. & n.* [F (as BI-, MILLION)]

billionaire /ˌbɪljəˈneə(r)/ *n.* a person possessing over a billion pounds, dollars, etc. [after MILLIONAIRE]

billow /ˈbɪləʊ/ *n. & v.* —*n.* **1** a wave. **2** a soft upward-curving flow. **3** any large soft mass.

—*v.intr.* move or build up in billows. □ **billowy** *adj.* [ON *bylgja* f. Gmc]

billposter /ˈbɪlˌpəʊstə(r)/ *n.* (also **billsticker** /-ˌstɪkə(r)/) a person who pastes up advertisements on hoardings. □ **billposting** *n.*

billy¹ /ˈbɪlɪ/ *n.* (*pl.* **-ies**) (in full **billycan**) (orig. *Austral.*) a cooking-pot with a lid and wire handle, for use out of doors. [perh. f. Aboriginal *billa* water]

billy² /ˈbɪlɪ/ *n.* (*pl.* **-ies**) = BILLY-GOAT.

billy-goat /ˈbɪlɪˌɡəʊt/ *n.* a male goat. [*Billy*, pet-form of the name *William*]

biltong /ˈbɪltɒŋ/ *n. S.Afr.* boneless meat salted and dried in strips. [Afrik., of uncert. orig.]

bimbo /ˈbɪmbəʊ/ *n.* (*pl.* **-os** or **-oes**) *sl.* usu. *derog.* **1** a person. **2** a woman, esp. a young empty-headed one. [It., = little child]

bimetallic /ˌbaɪmɪˈtælɪk/ *adj.* made of two metals. [F *bimétallique* (as BI-, METALLIC)]

bimonthly /baɪˈmʌnθlɪ/ *adj., adv., & n.* —*adj.* occurring twice a month or every two months. —*adv.* twice a month or every two months. —*n.* (*pl.* **-ies**) a periodical produced bimonthly.

bin *n. & v.* —*n.* a large receptacle for storage or for depositing rubbish. —*v.tr. colloq.* (**binned, binning**) store or put in a bin. □ **bin end** one of the last bottles from a bin of wine, usu. sold at a reduced price. **bin-liner** a bag (usu. of plastic) for lining a rubbish bin. [OE *bin(n)*, *binne*]

binary /ˈbaɪnərɪ/ *adj. & n.* —*adj.* **1 a** dual. **b** of or involving pairs. **2** of the arithmetical system using 2 as a base. —*n.* (*pl.* **-ies**) **1** something having two parts. **2** a binary number. **3** a binary star. □ **binary code** *Computing* a coding system using the binary digits 0 and 1. **binary compound** *Chem.* a compound having two elements or radicals. **binary number** (or **digit**) one of two digits (usu. 0 or 1) in a binary system of notation. **binary star** a system of two stars orbiting each other. **binary system** a system in which information can be expressed by combinations of the digits 0 and 1 (corresponding to 'off' and 'on' in computing). [LL *binarius* f. *bini* two together]

binaural /baɪˈnɔːr(ə)l/ *adj.* **1** of or used with both ears. **2** (of sound) recorded using two microphones and usu. transmitted separately to the two ears.

bind /baɪnd/ *v. & n.* —*v.* (*past* and *past part.* **bound** /baʊnd/) (see also BOUNDEN). **1** *tr.* (often foll. by *to*, *on*, *together*) tie or fasten tightly. **2** *tr.* **a** restrain; put in bonds. **b** (as **-bound** *adj.*) constricted, obstructed (*snowbound*). **3** *tr.* esp. *Cookery* cause (ingredients) to cohere using another ingredient. **4** *tr.* fasten or hold together as a single mass. **5** *tr.* compel; impose an obligation or duty on. **6** *tr.* **a** edge (fabric etc.) with braid etc. **b** fix together and fasten (the pages of a book) in a cover. **7** *tr.* constipate. **8** *tr.* (in *passive*) be required by an obligation or duty (*am bound to answer*). **9** *tr.* (often foll. by *up*) **a** put a bandage or other covering round. **b** fix together with something put round (*bound her hair*). **10** *tr.* indenture as an apprentice. —*n.* **1** *colloq.* a nuisance; a restriction. **2** = BINE. □ **be bound up with** be closely associated with. **bind over** *Law* order (a person) to do something, esp. keep the peace. **I'll be bound** a statement of assurance, or guaranteeing the truth of something. [OE *bindan*]

binder /ˈbaɪndə(r)/ n. **1** a cover for sheets of paper, for a book, etc. **2** a substance that acts cohesively. **3** a reaping-machine that binds grain into sheaves. **4** a bookbinder.

bindery /ˈbaɪndərɪ/ n. (pl. **-ies**) a workshop or factory for binding books.

binding /ˈbaɪndɪŋ/ n. & adj. —n. something that binds, esp. the covers, glue, etc., of a book. —adj. (often foll. by on) obligatory.

bindweed /ˈbaɪndwiːd/ n. **1** convolvulus. **2** any of various species of climbing plants such as honeysuckle.

bine /baɪn/ n. **1** the twisting stem of a climbing plant, esp. the hop. **2** a flexible shoot. [orig. a dial. form of BIND]

binge /bɪndʒ/ n. & v. sl. —n. a spree; a period of uncontrolled eating, drinking, etc. —v.intr. go on a spree; indulge in uncontrolled eating, drinking, etc. [prob. orig. dial., = soak]

bingo /ˈbɪŋɡəʊ/ n. & int. —n. a game for any number of players, each having a card of squares with numbers, which are marked off as numbers are randomly drawn by a caller. —int. expressing sudden surprise, satisfaction, etc., as in winning at bingo. [prob. imit.: cf. dial. *bing* 'with a bang']

binman /ˈbɪnmæn/ n. (pl. **-men**) colloq. a dustman.

binnacle /ˈbɪnək(ə)l/ n. a built-in housing for a ship's compass. [earlier *bittacle*, ult. f. L *habitaculum* habitation f. *habitare* inhabit]

binocular /baɪˈnɒkjʊlə(r)/ adj. adapted for or using both eyes. [BI- + L *oculus* eye]

binoculars /bɪˈnɒkjʊləz/ n.pl. an optical instrument with a lens for each eye, for viewing distant objects.

binomial /baɪˈnəʊmɪəl/ n. & adj. —n. **1** an algebraic expression of the sum or the difference of two terms. **2** a two-part name, esp. in taxonomy. —adj. consisting of two terms. □ **binomial classification** a system of classification using two terms, the first one indicating the genus and the second the species. **binomial theorem** a formula for finding any power of a binomial without multiplying at length. □ **binomially** adv. [F *binôme* or mod.L *binomium* (as BI-, Gk *nomos* part, portion)]

bint /bɪnt/ n. sl. usu. offens. a girl or woman. [Arab., = daughter, girl]

bio- /ˈbaɪəʊ/ comb. form **1** life (*biography*). **2** biological (*biomathematics*). **3** of living beings (*biophysics*). [Gk *bios* (course of) human life]

biochemistry /ˌbaɪəʊˈkemɪstrɪ/ n. the study of the chemical and physico-chemical processes of living organisms. □ **biochemical** adj. **biochemist** n.

biocoenosis /ˌbaɪəʊsiːˈnəʊsɪs/ n. (US **biocenosis**) (pl. **-noses** /-siːz/) **1** an association of different organisms forming a community. **2** the relationship existing between such organisms. □ **biocoenology** /-ˈnɒlədʒɪ/ n. **biocoenotic** /-ˈnɒtɪk/ adj. [mod.L f. BIO- + Gk *koinōsis* sharing f. *koinos* common]

biodegradable /ˌbaɪəʊdɪˈɡreɪdəb(ə)l/ adj. capable of being decomposed by bacteria or other living organisms. □ **biodegradability** /-ˈbɪlɪtɪ/ n. **biodegradation** /ˌbaɪəʊˌdeɡrəˈdeɪʃ(ə)n/ n.

bioengineering /ˌbaɪəʊˌendʒɪˈnɪərɪŋ/ n. **1** the application of engineering techniques to biological processes. **2** the use of artificial tissues, organs, or organ components to replace damaged or absent parts of the body. □ **bioengineer** n. & v.

biofeedback /ˌbaɪəʊˈfiːdbæk/ n. the technique of using the feedback of a normally automatic bodily response to a stimulus, in order to acquire voluntary control of that response.

biography /baɪˈɒɡrəfɪ/ n. (pl. **-ies**) **1 a** a written account of a person's life, usu. by another. **b** such writing as a branch of literature. **2** the course of a living (usu. human) being's life. □ **biographer** n. **biographical** /ˌbaɪəˈɡræfɪk/ adj. **biographical** /ˌbaɪəˈɡræfɪk(ə)l/ adj. [F *biographie* or mod.L *biographia* f. med.Gk]

biological /ˌbaɪəˈlɒdʒɪk(ə)l/ adj. of or relating to biology or living organisms. □ **biological clock** an innate mechanism controlling the rhythmic physiological activities of an organism. **biological control** the control of a pest by the introduction of a natural enemy. **biological warfare** warfare involving the use of toxins or micro-organisms. □ **biologically** adv.

biology /baɪˈɒlədʒɪ/ n. **1** the study of living organisms. **2** the plants and animals of a particular area. □ **biologist** n. [F *biologie* f. G *Biologie* (as BIO-, -LOGY)]

biomass /ˈbaɪəʊmæs/ n. the total quantity or weight of organisms in a given area or volume. [BIO- + MASS[1]]

biomechanics /ˌbaɪəʊmɪˈkænɪks/ n. the study of the mechanical laws relating to the movement or structure of living organisms.

biometry /baɪˈɒmɪtrɪ/ n. (also **biometrics** /ˌbaɪəʊˈmetrɪks/) the application of statistical analysis to biological data. □ **biometric** /ˌbaɪəʊˈmetrɪk/ adj. **biometrical** /ˌbaɪəʊˈmetrɪk(ə)l/ adj. **biometrician** /ˌbaɪəʊmɪˈtrɪʃ(ə)n/ n.

bionic /baɪˈɒnɪk/ adj. **1** having artificial body parts or the superhuman powers resulting from these. **2** relating to bionics. □ **bionically** adv. [BIO- after ELECTRONIC]

bionics /baɪˈɒnɪks/ n.pl. (treated as sing.) the study of mechanical systems that function like living organisms or parts of living organisms.

bionomics /ˌbaɪəˈnɒmɪks/ n.pl. (treated as sing.) the study of the mode of life of organisms in their natural habitat and their adaptations to their surroundings. □ **bionomic** adj. [BIO- after ECONOMICS]

biophysics /ˌbaɪəʊˈfɪzɪks/ n.pl. (treated as sing.) the science of the application of the laws of physics to biological phenomena. □ **biophysical** adj. **biophysicist** n.

biopsy /ˈbaɪɒpsɪ/ n. (pl. **-ies**) the examination of tissue removed from a living body to discover the presence, cause, or extent of a disease. [F *biopsie* f. Gk *bios* life + *opsis* sight, after *necropsy*]

biorhythm /ˈbaɪəʊˌrɪð(ə)m/ n. **1** any of the recurring cycles of biological processes thought to affect a person's emotional, intellectual, and physical activity. **2** any periodic change in the behaviour or physiology of an organism. □ **biorhythmic** /-ˈrɪðmɪk/ adj. **biorhythmically** /-ˈrɪðmɪkəlɪ/ adv.

bioscope /ˈbaɪəskəʊp/ n. S.Afr. sl. a cinema.

biosphere /ˈbaɪəʊˌsfɪə(r)/ n. the regions of the earth's crust and atmosphere occupied by living organisms. [G *Biosphäre* (as BIO-, SPHERE)]

biosynthesis /ˌbaɪəʊˈsɪnθɪsɪs/ n. the production of organic molecules by living organisms. □ **biosynthetic** /-ˈθetɪk/ adj.

biota /baɪˈəʊtə/ n. the animal and plant life of a region. [mod.L: cf. Gk biotē life]

biotechnology /ˌbaɪəʊtekˈnɒlədʒɪ/ n. the exploitation of biological processes for industrial and other purposes, esp. genetic manipulation of micro-organisms (for the production of antibiotics, hormones, etc.).

biotic /baɪˈɒtɪk/ adj. **1** relating to life or to living things. **2** of biological origin. [F biotique or LL bioticus f. Gk biōtikos f. bios life]

biotin /ˈbaɪətɪn/ n. a vitamin of the B complex, found in egg yolk, liver, and yeast, and involved in the metabolism of carbohydrates, fats, and proteins. [G f. Gk bios life + -IN]

bipartisan /ˌbaɪpɑːtɪˈzæn, baɪˈpɑːtɪz(ə)n/ adj. of or involving two (esp. political) parties. □ **bipartisanship** n.

bipartite /baɪˈpɑːtaɪt/ adj. **1** consisting of two parts. **2** shared by or involving two parties. **3** Law (of a contract, treaty, etc.) drawn up in two corresponding parts or between two parties. [L bipartitus f. bipartire (as BI-, partire PART)]

biped /ˈbaɪped/ n. & adj. —n. a two-footed animal. —adj. two-footed. □ **bipedal** adj. [L bipes -edis (as BI-, pes pedis foot)]

biplane /ˈbaɪpleɪn/ n. an early type of aeroplane having two sets of wings, one above the other.

bipolar /baɪˈpəʊlə(r)/ adj. having two poles or extremities. □ **bipolarity** /-ˈlærɪtɪ/ n.

birch n. & v. —n. **1** any tree of the genus Betula, bearing catkins, and found predominantly in northern temperate regions. **2** (in full **birch-wood**) the hard fine-grained pale wood of these trees. **3** NZ any of various similar trees. **4** (in full **birch-rod**) a bundle of birch twigs used for flogging. —v.tr. beat with a birch (in sense 4). □ **birchen** adj. [OE bi(e)rce f. Gmc]

bird n. **1** a feathered vertebrate with a beak, with two wings and two feet, egg-laying and usu. able to fly. **2** a game-bird. **3** Brit. sl. a young woman. **4** colloq. a person (a wily old bird). **5** sl. a prison. **b** rhyming sl. a prison sentence (short for birdlime = time). □ **bird-** (or **birds'-**) **nesting** hunting for birds' nests, usu. to get eggs. **bird of paradise** any bird of the family Paradiseidae, the males having brilliantly coloured plumage. **bird of passage 1** a migrant. **2** any transient visitor. **bird's-eye view** a general view from above. **birds of a feather** people of like character. **bird table** a raised platform on which food for birds is placed. **bird-watcher** a person who observes birds in their natural surroundings. **for** (or **strictly for**) **the birds** colloq. trivial, uninteresting. **get the bird** sl. **1** be dismissed. **2** be hissed at or booed. **like a bird** without difficulty or hesitation. **a little bird** an unnamed informant. [OE brid, of unkn. orig.]

birdbrain /ˈbɜːdbreɪn/ n. colloq. a stupid or flighty person. □ **birdbrained** adj.

birdcage /ˈbɜːdkeɪdʒ/ n. **1** a cage for birds usu. made of wire or cane. **2** an object of a similar design.

birder /ˈbɜːdə(r)/ n. US a bird-watcher. □ **birding** n.

birdie /ˈbɜːdɪ/ n. & v. —n. **1** colloq. a little bird. **2** Golf a score of one stroke less than par at any

hole. —v.tr. (**birdies, birdied, birdying**) Golf play (a hole) in a birdie.

birdlime /ˈbɜːdlaɪm/ n. sticky material painted on to twigs to trap small birds.

birdseed /ˈbɜːdsiːd/ n. a blend of seed for feeding birds, esp. ones which are caged.

birdsong /ˈbɜːdsɒŋ/ n. the musical cry of a bird or birds.

biretta /bɪˈretə/ n. a square usu. black cap worn by (esp. Roman Catholic) clergymen. [It. berretta or Sp. birreta f. LL birrus cape]

biriani /ˌbɪrɪˈɑːnɪ/ n. (also **biryani**) an orig. Indian dish made with highly seasoned rice, and meat or fish etc. [Urdu]

Biro /ˈbaɪərəʊ/ n. (pl. **-os**) Brit. propr. a kind of ball-point pen. [L. Biró, Hung. inventor d. 1985]

birth /bɜːθ/ n. & v. —n. **1** the emergence of a (usu. fully developed) infant or other young from the body of its mother. **2** rhet. the beginning or coming into existence of something (the birth of civilization; the birth of socialism). **3 a** origin, descent, ancestry (of noble birth). **b** high or noble birth; inherited position. —v.tr. US colloq. **1** to give birth to. **2** to assist (a woman) to give birth. □ **birth certificate** an official document identifying a person by name, place, date of birth, and parentage. **birth control** the control of the number of children one conceives, esp. by contraception. **birth rate** the number of live births per thousand of population per year. **give birth** bear a child etc. **give birth to 1** produce (young) from the womb. **2** cause to begin, found. [ME f. ON byrth f. Gmc: see BEAR¹, -TH²]

birthday /ˈbɜːθdeɪ/ n. **1** the day on which a person etc. was born. **2** the anniversary of this. □ **in one's birthday suit** joc. naked.

birthmark /ˈbɜːθmɑːk/ n. an unusual brown or red mark on one's body at or from birth.

birthplace /ˈbɜːθpleɪs/ n. the place where a person was born.

birthright /ˈbɜːθraɪt/ n. a right of possession or privilege one has from birth, esp. as the eldest son.

birthstone /ˈbɜːθstəʊn/ n. a gemstone popularly associated with the month of one's birth.

biscuit /ˈbɪskɪt/ n. & adj. —n. **1** Brit. a small unleavened cake, usu. flat and crisp and often sweet. **2** fired unglazed pottery. **3** a light brown colour. —adj. biscuit-coloured. [ME f. OF bescoit etc. ult. f. L bis twice + coctus past part. of coquere cook]

bisect /baɪˈsekt/ v.tr. divide into two (strictly, equal) parts. □ **bisection** n. **bisector** n. [BI- + L secare sect- cut]

bisexual /baɪˈseksjʊəl/ adj. & n. —adj. **1** sexually attracted by persons of both sexes. **2** Biol. having characteristics of both sexes. **3** of or concerning both sexes. —n. a bisexual person. □ **bisexuality** /-ˈælɪtɪ/ n.

bishop /ˈbɪʃəp/ n. **1** a senior member of the Christian clergy usu. in charge of a diocese, and empowered to confer holy orders. **2** a chess piece with the top sometimes shaped like a mitre. [OE biscop, ult. f. Gk episkopos overseer (as EPI-, -skopos -looking)]

bishopric /ˈbɪʃəprɪk/ n. **1** the office of a bishop. **2** a diocese. [OE bisceoprīce (as BISHOP, rīce realm)]

bismuth /ˈbɪzməθ/ n. Chem. **1** a brittle reddish-white metallic element, used in alloys. **2** any compound of this element used medicinally. [mod.L *bisemutum*, Latinization of G *Wismut*, of unkn. orig.]

bison /ˈbaɪs(ə)n/ *n.* (*pl.* same) either of two wild hump-backed shaggy-haired oxen of the genus *Bison*, native to N. America (*B. bison*) or Europe (*B. bonasus*). [ME f. L f. Gmc]

bisque[1] /bɪsk/ *n.* a rich shellfish soup, made esp. from lobster. [F]

bisque[2] /bɪsk/ *n.* = BISCUIT *n.* 2.

bistable /baɪˈsteɪb(ə)l/ *adj.* (of an electrical circuit etc.) having two stable states.

bistre /ˈbɪstə(r)/ *n.* & *adj.* (*US* **bister**) —*n.* 1 a brownish pigment made from the soot of burnt wood. 2 the brownish colour of this. —*adj.* of this colour. [F, of unkn. orig.]

bistro /ˈbiːstrəʊ/ *n.* (*pl.* -os) a small restaurant. [F]

bisulphate /baɪˈsʌlfeɪt/ *n.* (*US* **bisulfate**) *Chem.* a salt or ester of sulphuric acid.

bit[1] *n.* 1 a small piece or quantity (*a bit of cheese*; *give me another bit*). 2 (prec. by *a*) **a** a fair amount (*sold quite a bit*; *needed a bit of persuading*). **b** *colloq.* somewhat (*am a bit tired*). **c** (foll. by *of*) *colloq.* rather (*a bit of an idiot*). 3 a short time or distance (*wait a bit*; *move up a bit*). 4 *US sl.* a unit of 12½ cents (used only in even multiples). □ **bit by bit** gradually. **bit on the side** *sl.* an extramarital sexual relationship. **bit part** a minor part in a play or a film. **bits and pieces** (or **bobs**) an assortment of small items. **do one's bit** *colloq.* make a useful contribution to an effort or cause. **not a bit** (or **not a bit of it**) not at all. **to bits** into pieces. [OE *bita* f. Gmc, rel. to BITE]

bit[2] *past* of BITE.

bit[3] *n.* 1 a metal mouthpiece on a bridle, used to control a horse. 2 a (usu. metal) tool or piece for boring or drilling. 3 the cutting or gripping part of a plane, pincers, etc. □ **take the bit between one's teeth 1** take decisive personal action. 2 escape from control. [OE *bite* f. Gmc, rel. to BITE]

bit[4] *n. Computing* a unit of information expressed as a choice between two possibilities; a 0 or 1 in binary notation. [BINARY + DIGIT]

bitch *n.* & *v.* —*n.* 1 a female dog or other canine animal. 2 *sl. offens.* a malicious or spiteful woman. 3 *sl.* a very unpleasant or difficult thing or situation. —*v.* 1 *intr.* (often foll. by *about*) **a** speak scathingly. **b** complain. 2 *tr.* be spiteful or unfair to. [OE *bicce*]

bitchy /ˈbɪtʃɪ/ *adj.* (**bitchier**, **bitchiest**) *sl.* spiteful; bad-tempered. □ **bitchily** *adv.* **bitchiness** *n.*

bite *v.* & *n.* —*v.* (*past* **bit** /bɪt/; *past part.* **bitten** /ˈbɪt(ə)n/) **1** *tr.* cut or puncture using the teeth. **2** *tr.* (foll. by *off*, *away*, etc.) detach with the teeth. **3** *tr.* (of an insect, snake, etc.) wound with a sting, fangs, etc. **4** *intr.* (of a wheel, screw, etc.) grip, penetrate. **5** *intr.* accept bait or an inducement. **6** *intr.* have a (desired) adverse effect. **7** *tr.* (in *passive*) **a** take in; swindle. **b** (foll. by *by*, *with*, etc.) be infected by (enthusiasm etc.). **8** *tr.* (as **bitten** *adj.*) cause a glowing or smarting pain to (*frostbitten*). **9** *intr.* (foll. by *at*) snap at. —*n.* **1** an act of biting. **2** a wound or sore made by biting. **3 a** a mouthful of food. **b** a snack or light meal. **4** the taking of bait by a fish. **5** pungency (esp. of flavour). **6** incisiveness, sharpness. **7** the position of the teeth when the jaws are closed. □ **bite back** restrain (one's speech etc.) by or as if by biting the lips. **bite** (or **bite on**) **the bullet** *sl.* behave bravely or stoically. **bite the dust** *sl.* **1** die. **2** fail; break down. **bite a person's head off** *colloq.* respond fiercely or angrily. **put the bite on** *US sl.* borrow or extort money from. **what's biting you?** *sl.* what is worrying you? □ **biter** *n.* [OE *bītan* f. Gmc]

biting /ˈbaɪtɪŋ/ *adj.* 1 stinging; intensely cold (*a biting wind*). 2 sharp; effective (*biting wit*; *biting sarcasm*). □ **bitingly** *adv.*

bitten *past part.* of BITE.

bitter /ˈbɪtə(r)/ *adj.* & *n.* —*adj.* 1 having a sharp pungent taste; not sweet. 2 **a** caused by or showing mental pain or resentment (*bitter memories*; *bitter rejoinder*). **b** painful or difficult to accept (*bitter disappointment*). 3 **a** harsh; virulent (*bitter animosity*). **b** piercingly cold. —*n.* 1 *Brit.* beer strongly flavoured with hops and having a bitter taste. 2 (in *pl.*) liquor with a bitter flavour used as an additive in cocktails. □ **to the bitter end** to the very end in spite of difficulties. □ **bitterly** *adv.* **bitterness** *n.* [OE *biter* prob. f. Gmc: *to the bitter end* may be assoc. with a Naut. word *bitter* = 'last part of a cable']

bittern /ˈbɪt(ə)n/ *n.* any of a group of wading birds of the heron family, esp. of the genus *Botaurus* with a distinctive booming call. [ME f. OF *butor* ult. f. L *butio* bittern + *taurus* bull; -*n* perh. f. assoc. with HERON]

bitty /ˈbɪtɪ/ *adj.* (**bittier**, **bittiest**) made up of unrelated bits; scrappy. □ **bittily** *adv.* **bittiness** *n.*

bitumen /ˈbɪtjʊmɪn/ *n.* 1 any of various tarlike mixtures of hydrocarbons derived from petroleum and used for road surfacing and roofing. 2 *Austral. colloq.* a tarred road. [L *bitumen* -*minis*]

bituminous /bɪˈtjuːmɪnəs/ *adj.* of, relating to, or containing bitumen. □ **bituminous coal** a form of coal burning with a smoky flame.

bivalent /baɪˈveɪlənt/ *adj.* & *n.* —*adj.* 1 *Chem.* having a valency of two. 2 *Biol.* (of homologous chromosomes) associated in pairs. —*n. Biol.* any pair of homologous chromosomes. □ **bivalency** *n.* [BI- + *valent*- pres. part. stem of *valēre* be strong]

bivalve /ˈbaɪvælv/ *n.* & *adj.* —*n.* any of a group of aquatic molluscs of the class Bivalvia, with bodies enclosed within two hinged shells, e.g. oysters, mussels, etc. —*adj.* 1 with a hinged double shell. 2 *Biol.* having two valves, e.g. of a pea-pod.

bivouac /ˈbɪvʊˌæk/ *n.* & *v.* —*n.* a temporary open encampment without tents, esp. of soldiers. —*v.intr.* (**bivouacked**, **bivouacking**) camp in a bivouac, esp. overnight. [F, prob. f. Swiss G *Beiwacht* additional guard at night]

biweekly /baɪˈwiːklɪ/ *adv.*, *adj.*, & *n.* —*adv.* 1 every two weeks. 2 twice a week. —*adj.* produced or occurring biweekly. —*n.* (*pl.* -**ies**) a biweekly periodical.

biz *n. colloq.* business. [abbr.]

bizarre /bɪˈzɑː(r)/ *adj.* strange in appearance or effect; eccentric; grotesque. □ **bizarrely** *adv.* **bizarreness** *n.* [F, = handsome, brave, f. Sp. & Port. *bizarro* f. Basque *bizarra* beard]

Bk *symb. Chem.* the element berkelium.

blab *v.* & *n.* —*v.* (**blabbed**, **blabbing**) **1** *intr.* **a** talk foolishly or indiscreetly. **b** reveal secrets. **2** *tr.* reveal (a secret etc.) by indiscreet talk. —*n.* a person who blabs. [ME prob. f. Gmc]

blabber /ˈblæbə(r)/ n. & v. —n. (also **blabbermouth** /ˈblæbəˌmaʊθ/) a person who blabs. —v.intr. (often foll. by on) talk foolishly or inconsequentially, esp. at length.

black adj., n., & v. —adj. **1** very dark, having no colour from the absorption of all or nearly all incident light (like coal or soot). **2** completely dark from the absence of a source of light (black night). **3** (**Black**) **a** of the human group having dark-coloured skin, esp. of African or Aboriginal descent. **b** of or relating to Black people (Black rights). **4** (of the sky, a cloud, etc.) dusky; heavily overcast. **5** angry, threatening (a black look). **6** implying disgrace or condemnation (in his black books). **7** wicked, sinister, deadly (black-hearted). **8** gloomy, depressed, sullen (a black mood). **9** portending trouble or difficulty (things looked black). **10** (of hands, clothes, etc.) dirty, soiled. **11** (of humour or its representation) with sinister or macabre, as well as comic, import (black comedy). **12** (of tea or coffee) without milk. **13** Brit. **a** (of industrial labour or its products) boycotted, esp. by a trade union, in an industrial dispute. **b** (of a person) doing work or handling goods that have been boycotted. **14** dark in colour as distinguished from a lighter variety (black bear; black pine). —n. **1** a black colour or pigment. **2** black clothes or material (dressed in black). **3 a** (in a game or sport) a black piece, ball, etc. **b** the player using such pieces. **4** the credit side of an account (in the black). **5** (**Black**) a member of a dark-skinned race, esp. a Negro or Aboriginal. —v.tr. **1** make black (blacked his face). **2** polish with blacking. **3** Brit. declare (goods etc.) 'black'. □ **black and blue** discoloured by bruises. **black and white 1** recorded in writing or print (down in black and white). **2** (of film etc.) not in colour. **3** consisting of extremes only, oversimplified. **the black art** = black magic. **black beetle** the common cockroach, Blatta orientalis. **black belt 1** a black belt worn by an expert in judo, karate, etc. **2** a person qualified to wear this. **black box 1** a flight-recorder in an aircraft. **2** any complex piece of equipment, usu. a unit in an electronic system, with contents which are mysterious to the user. **black bread** a coarse dark-coloured type of rye bread. **Black Country** (usu. prec. by the) a district of the Midlands with heavy industry. **Black Death** (usu. prec. by the) a widespread epidemic of bubonic plague in Europe in the 14th c. **black economy** unofficial economic activity. **Black English** the form of English spoken by many Blacks, esp. as an urban dialect of the US. **black eye** bruised skin around the eye resulting from a blow. **Black Friar** a Dominican friar. **black hole 1** a region of space possessing a strong gravitational field from which matter and radiation cannot escape. **2** a place of confinement for punishment, esp. in the armed services. **black ice** thin hard transparent ice, esp. on a road surface. **black magic** magic involving supposed invocation of evil spirits. **Black Maria** sl. a police vehicle for transporting prisoners. **black mark** a mark of discredit. **black market** an illicit traffic in officially controlled or scarce commodities. **black marketeer** a person who engages in a black market. **Black Mass** a travesty of the Roman Catholic Mass in worship of Satan.

Black Monk a Benedictine monk. **Black Muslim** US a member of an exclusively Black Islamic sect proposing a separate Black community. **Black Nationalism** advocacy of the national civil rights of US (and occas. other) Blacks. **black out 1 a** effect a blackout on. **b** undergo a blackout. **2** obscure windows etc. or extinguish all lights for protection esp. against an air attack. **black pepper** pepper made by grinding the whole dried berry, including the husk, of the pepper plant. **Black Power** a movement in support of rights and political power for Blacks. **black pudding** a black sausage containing pork, dried pig's blood, suet, etc. **Black Rod** Brit. the principal usher of the Lord Chamberlain's department, House of Lords, etc. **black sheep** colloq. an unsatisfactory member of a family, group, etc.; a scoundrel. **black spot** a place of danger or difficulty, esp. on a road (an accident black spot). **black tea** tea that is fully fermented before drying. **black tie 1** a black bow-tie worn with a dinner jacket. **2** colloq. formal evening dress. **black tracker** Austral. an Aboriginal employed to help find persons lost or hiding in the bush. **black velvet** a drink of stout and champagne. **Black Watch** (usu. prec. by the) the Royal Highland Regiment (so called from its dark tartan uniform). **black widow** a venomous spider, Latrodectus mactans, of which the female devours the male. □ **blackish** adj. **blackly** adv. **blackness** n. [OE blæc]

blackamoor /ˈblækəˌmʊə(r), -ˌmɔː(r)/ n. archaic a dark-skinned person, esp. a Negro. [BLACK + MOOR²]

blackball /ˈblækbɔːl/ v.tr. reject (a candidate) in a ballot (orig. by voting with a black ball).

blackberry /ˈblækbəri/ n. & v. —n. (pl. -ies) **1** a climbing thorny rosaceous shrub, Rubus fruticosus, bearing white or pink flowers. **2** a black fleshy edible fruit of this plant. —v.intr. (-ies, -ied) gather blackberries.

blackbird /ˈblækbɜːd/ n. **1** a common thrush, Turdus merula, of which the male is black with an orange beak. **2** US any of various birds, esp. a grackle, with black plumage.

blackboard /ˈblækbɔːd/ n. a board with a smooth usu. dark surface for writing on with chalk.

blackcurrant /blækˈkʌrənt/ n. **1** a widely cultivated shrub, Ribes nigrum, bearing flowers in racemes. **2** the small dark edible berry of this plant.

blacken /ˈblækən/ v. **1** tr. & intr. make or become black or dark. **2** tr. speak evil of, defame (blacken someone's character).

blackfly /ˈblækflaɪ/ n. (pl. -flies) any of various thrips or aphids, esp. Aphis fabae, infesting plants.

blackguard /ˈblægɑːd, -gəd/ n. & v. —n. a villain; a scoundrel; an unscrupulous, unprincipled person. —v.tr. abuse scurrilously. □ **blackguardly** adj. [BLACK + GUARD: orig. applied collectively to menials etc.]

blackhead /ˈblækhed/ n. a black-topped pimple on the skin.

blacking /ˈblækɪŋ/ n. any black paste or polish, esp. for shoes.

blackjack /ˈblækdʒæk/ n. **1** the card-game pontoon. **2** US a flexible leaded bludgeon. [BLACK + JACK]

blacklead /ˈblækled/ n. & v. —n. graphite. —v.tr. polish with graphite.

blackleg /ˈblækleg/ n. & v. —n. (often attrib.) Brit. derog. a person who fails or declines to take part in industrial action. —v.intr. (**-legged**, **-legging**) act as a blackleg.

blacklist /ˈblæklɪst/ n. & v. —n. a list of persons under suspicion, in disfavour, etc. —v.tr. put the name of (a person) on a blacklist.

blackmail /ˈblækmeɪl/ n. & v. —n. **1 a** an extortion of payment in return for not disclosing discreditable information, a secret, etc. **b** any payment extorted in this way. **2** the use of threats or moral pressure. —v.tr. **1** extort or try to extort money etc. from (a person) by blackmail. **2** threaten, coerce. □ **blackmailer** n. [BLACK + obs. mail rent, OE māl f. ON mál agreement]

blackout /ˈblækaʊt/ n. **1** a temporary or complete loss of vision, consciousness, or memory. **2** a loss of power, radio reception, etc. **3** a compulsory period of darkness as a precaution against air raids. **4** a temporary suppression of the release of information, esp. from police or government sources. **5** a sudden darkening of a theatre stage.

blackshirt /ˈblækʃɜːt/ n. a member of a Fascist organization. [f. the colour of the It. Fascist uniform]

blacksmith /ˈblæksmɪθ/ n. a smith who works in iron.

blackthorn /ˈblækθɔːn/ n. a thorny rosaceous shrub, Prunus spinosa, bearing white-petalled flowers before small blue-black fruits.

bladder /ˈblædə(r)/ n. **1 a** any of various membranous sacs in some animals, containing urine (**urinary bladder**), bile (**gall-bladder**), or air (**swim-bladder**). **b** this or part of it or a similar object prepared for various uses. **2** an inflated pericarp or vesicle in various plants. **3** anything inflated and hollow. [OE blǣdre f. Gmc]

bladderwrack /ˈblædəˌræk/ n. a common brown seaweed, Fucus vesiculosus, with fronds containing air bladders which give buoyancy to the plant.

blade n. **1 a** the flat part of a knife, chisel, etc., that forms the cutting edge. **b** = razor-blade. **2** the flattened functional part of an oar, spade, propeller, bat, skate, etc. **3** the flat, narrow, usu. pointed leaf of grass and cereals. **4** (in full **blade-bone**) a flat bone, e.g. in the shoulder. **5** poet. a sword. **6** colloq. (usu. archaic) a carefree young fellow. □ **bladed** adj. (also in comb.). [OE blæd f. Gmc]

blaeberry /ˈbleɪbərɪ/ n. (pl. **-ies**) Brit. = BILBERRY. [ME f. blae (Sc. and N.Engl. dial. f. ME blo f. ON blár f. Gmc: see BLUE¹) + BERRY]

blag /blæg/ n. & v. sl. —n. robbery, esp. with violence; theft. —v.tr. & intr. (**blagged**, **blagging**) rob (esp. with violence); steal. □ **blagger** n. [19th c.: orig. unkn.]

blain n. an inflamed swelling or sore on the skin. [OE blegen f. WG]

blame v. & n. —v.tr. **1** assign fault or responsibility to. **2** (foll. by on) assign the responsibility for (an error or wrong) to a person etc. (blamed his death on a poor diet). —n. **1** responsibility for a bad result; culpability (shared the blame equally; put the blame on the bad weather). **2** the act of blaming or attributing responsibility; censure (she got all the blame). □ **be to blame** (often foll.

by for) be responsible; deserve censure (she is not to blame for the accident). □ **blameable** adj. [ME f. OF bla(s)mer (v.), blame (n.) f. pop.L blastemare f. eccl.L blasphemare reproach f. Gk blasphēmeō blaspheme]

blameful /ˈbleɪmfʊl/ adj. deserving blame; guilty. □ **blamefully** adv.

blameless /ˈbleɪmlɪs/ adj. innocent; free from blame. □ **blamelessly** adv. **blamelessness** n.

blameworthy /ˈbleɪmˌwɜːðɪ/ adj. deserving blame. □ **blameworthiness** n.

blanch /blɑːntʃ/ v. **1** tr. make white or pale by extracting colour. **2** intr. & tr. grow or make pale from shock, fear, etc. **3** tr. Cookery **a** peel (almonds etc.) by scalding. **b** immerse (vegetables or meat) briefly in boiling water. **4** tr. whiten (a plant) by depriving it of light. [ME f. OF blanchir f. blanc white, BLANK]

blancmange /bləˈmɒndʒ/ n. a sweet opaque gelatinous dessert made with flavoured cornflour and milk. [ME f. OF blancmanger f. blanc white, BLANK + manger eat f. L manducare chew]

blanco /ˈblæŋkəʊ/ n. & v. Mil. —n. **1** a white substance for whitening belts etc. **2** a similar coloured substance. —v.tr. (**-oes**, **-oed**) treat with blanco. [F blanc white, BLANK]

bland adj. **1 a** mild, not irritating. **b** tasteless, unstimulating, insipid. **2** gentle in manner; suave. □ **blandly** adv. **blandness** n. [L blandus soft, smooth]

blandish /ˈblændɪʃ/ v.tr. flatter; coax, cajole. [ME f. OF blandir (-ISH²) f. L blandiri f. blandus soft, smooth]

blandishment /ˈblændɪʃmənt/ n. (usu. in pl.) flattery; cajolery.

blank adj., n., & v. —adj. **1 a** (of paper) not written or printed on. **b** (of a document) with spaces left for a signature or details. **2 a** not filled; empty (a blank space). **b** unrelieved; sheer (a blank wall). **3 a** having or showing no interest or expression (a blank face). **b** void of incident or result. **c** puzzled, nonplussed. **d** having (temporarily) no knowledge or understanding (my mind went blank). **4** (with neg. import) complete, downright (a blank refusal; blank despair). **5** euphem. used in place of an adjective regarded as coarse or abusive. —n. **1 a** a space left to be filled in a document. **b** a document having blank spaces to be filled. **2** (in full **blank cartridge**) a cartridge containing gunpowder but no bullet, used for training, etc. **3** an empty space or period of time. **4 a** a dash written instead of a word or letter, esp. instead of an obscenity. **b** euphem. used in place of a noun regarded as coarse. —v.tr. (usu. foll. by off, out) screen, obscure (clouds blanked out the sun). □ **blank cheque 1** a cheque with the amount left for the payee to fill in. **2** colloq. unlimited freedom of action (cf. CARTE BLANCHE). **blank verse** unrhymed verse, esp. iambic pentameters. **draw a blank** elicit no response; fail. □ **blankly** adv. **blankness** n. [ME f. OF blanc white, ult. f. Gmc]

blanket /ˈblæŋkɪt/ n., adj., & v. —n. **1** a large piece of woollen or other material used esp. as a bed-covering or to wrap up a person or an animal for warmth. **2** (usu. foll. by of) a thick mass or layer that covers something (blanket of fog; blanket of silence). —adj. covering all cases or classes; inclusive (blanket condemnation; blanket *agreement*). —*v.tr.* (**blanketed, blanketing**) **1** cover with or as if with a blanket (*snow blanketed the land*). **2** stifle; keep quiet (*blanketed all discussion*). □ **electric blanket** an electrically-wired blanket used for heating a bed. **wet blanket** *colloq.* a gloomy person preventing the enjoyment of others. [ME f. OF *blancquet, blanchet* f. *blanc* white, BLANK]

blare /bleə(r)/ *v. & n.* —*v.* **1** *tr. & intr.* sound or utter loudly. **2** *intr.* make the sound of a trumpet. —*n.* a loud sound resembling that of a trumpet. [ME f. MDu. *blaren, bleren,* imit.]

blarney /ˈblɑːnɪ/ *n. & v.* —*n.* **1** cajoling talk; flattery. **2** nonsense. —*v.* (**-eys, -eyed**) **1** *tr.* flatter (a person) with blarney. **2** *intr.* talk flatteringly. [*Blarney*, an Irish castle near Cork with a stone said to confer a cajoling tongue on whoever kisses it]

blasé /ˈblɑːzeɪ/ *adj.* **1** unimpressed or indifferent because of over-familiarity. **2** tired of pleasure; surfeited. [F]

blaspheme /blæsˈfiːm/ *v.* **1** *intr.* talk profanely, making use of religious names, etc. **2** *tr.* talk profanely about; revile. □ **blasphemer** *n.* [ME f. OF *blasfemer* f. eccl.L *blasphemare* f. Gk *blasphēmeō*: cf. BLAME]

blasphemy /ˈblæsfəmɪ/ *n.* (*pl.* **-ies**) **1** profane talk. **2** an instance of this. □ **blasphemous** *adj.* **blasphemously** *adv.* [ME f. OF *blasfemie* f. eccl.L f. Gk *blasphēmia* slander, blasphemy]

blast /blɑːst/ *n., v., & int.* —*n.* **1** a strong gust of wind. **2 a** a destructive wave of highly compressed air spreading outwards from an explosion. **b** such an explosion. **3** the single loud note of a wind instrument, car horn, whistle, etc. **4** *colloq.* a severe reprimand. **5** a strong current of air used in smelting etc. —*v.* **1** *tr.* blow up (rocks etc.) with explosives. **2** *tr.* **a** wither, shrivel, or blight (a plant, animal, limb, etc.) (*blasted oak*). **b** destroy, ruin (*blasted her hopes*). **c** strike with divine anger; curse. **3** *intr. & tr.* make or cause to make a loud or explosive noise (*blasted away on his trumpet*). **4** *tr. colloq.* reprimand severely. **5** *colloq.* **a** *tr.* shoot; shoot at. **b** *intr.* shoot. —*int.* expressing annoyance. □ **at full blast** *colloq.* working at maximum speed etc. **blast-furnace** a smelting furnace into which compressed hot air is driven. **blast off** (of a rocket etc.) take off from a launching site. **blast-off** *n.* **1** the launching of a rocket etc. **2** the initial thrust for this. [OE *blæst* f. Gmc]

blasted /ˈblɑːstɪd/ *adj. & adv.* —*attrib.adj.* damned; annoying (*that blasted dog!*). —*adv.* *colloq.* damned; extremely (*it's blasted cold*).

blatant /ˈbleɪt(ə)nt/ *adj.* **1** flagrant, unashamed (*blatant attempt to steal*). **2** offensively noisy or obtrusive. □ **blatancy** *n.* **blatantly** *adv.* [a word used by Spenser (1596), perh. after Sc. *bland* = bleating]

blather /ˈblæðə(r)/ *n. & v.* (also **blether** /ˈbleðə(r)/) —*n.* foolish chatter. —*v.intr.* chatter foolishly. [ME *blather,* Sc. *blether,* f. ON *blathra* talk nonsense f. *blathr* nonsense]

blaze[1] *n. & v.* —*n.* **1** a bright flame or fire. **2 a** a bright glaring light. **b** a full light (*a blaze of publicity*). **3** a violent outburst (of passion etc.). **4** **a** a glow of colour (*roses were a blaze of scarlet*). **b** a bright display (*a blaze of glory*). —*v.intr.* **1** burn with a bright flame. **2** be brilliantly lighted. **3** be consumed with anger, excitement, etc. **4 a** show bright colours (*blazing with jewels*). **b** emit

light (*stars blazing*). □ **blaze away** (often foll. by *at*) **1** fire continuously with rifles etc. **2** work enthusiastically. **blaze up 1** burst into flame. **2** burst out in anger. **like blazes** *sl.* **1** with great energy. **2** very fast. **what the blazes!** *sl.* what the hell! □ **blazingly** *adv.* [OE *blæse* torch, f. Gmc: ult. rel. to BLAZE[2]]

blaze[2] *n. & v.* —*n.* **1** a white mark on an animal's face. **2** a mark made on a tree by slashing the bark esp. to mark a route. —*v.tr.* mark (a tree or a path) by chipping bark. □ **blaze a trail 1** mark out a path or route. **2** be the first to do, invent, or study something; pioneer. [17th c.: ult. rel. to BLAZE[1]]

blaze[3] *v.tr.* proclaim as with a trumpet. [ME f. LG or Du. *blāzen* blow, f. Gmc *blǣsan*]

blazer /ˈbleɪzə(r)/ *n.* **1** a coloured, often striped, summer jacket worn by schoolchildren, sportsmen, etc., esp. as part of a uniform. **2** a man's plain jacket, often dark blue, not worn with matching trousers. [BLAZE[1] + -ER[1]]

blazon /ˈbleɪz(ə)n/ *v. & n.* —*v.tr.* **1** proclaim (esp. *blazon abroad*). **2** *Heraldry* **a** describe or paint (arms). **b** inscribe or paint (an object) with arms, names, etc. —*n. Heraldry* **1** a shield, coat of arms, bearings, or a banner. **2** a correct description of these. □ **blazoner** *n.* **blazonment** *n.* [ME f. OF *blason* shield, of unkn. orig.; verb also f. BLAZE[3]]

blazonry /ˈbleɪzənrɪ/ *n. Heraldry* **1 a** the art of describing or painting heraldic devices or armorial bearings. **b** such devices or bearings. **2** brightly coloured display.

bleach *v. & n.* —*v.tr. & intr.* whiten by exposure to sunlight or by a chemical process. —*n.* **1** a bleaching substance. **2** the process of bleaching. [OE *blǣcan* f. Gmc]

bleacher /ˈbliːtʃə(r)/ *n.* **1 a** a person who bleaches (esp. textiles). **b** a vessel or chemical used in bleaching. **2** (usu. in *pl.*) esp. *US* an outdoor uncovered bench-seat at a sports ground.

bleak *adj.* **1** bare, exposed; windswept. **2** unpromising; dreary (*bleak prospects*). □ **bleakly** *adv.* **bleakness** *n.* [16th c.: rel. to obs. adjs. *bleach, blake* (f. ON *bleikr*) pale, ult. f. Gmc: cf. BLEACH]

blear *adj. & v. archaic* —*adj.* **1** (of the eyes or the mind) dim, dull, filmy. **2** indistinct. —*v.tr.* make dim or obscure; blur. [ME, of uncert. orig.]

bleary /ˈblɪərɪ/ *adj.* (**blearier, bleariest**) **1** (of the eyes or mind) dim; blurred. **2** indistinct. □ **blearily** *adv.* **bleariness** *n.*

bleat *v. & n.* —*v.* **1** *intr.* (of a sheep, goat, or calf) make a weak, wavering cry. **2** *intr. & tr.* (often foll. by *out*) speak or say feebly, foolishly, or plaintively. —*n.* **1** the sound made by a sheep, goat, etc. **2** a weak, plaintive, or foolish cry. □ **bleater** *n.* **bleatingly** *adv.* [OE *blǣtan* (imit.)]

bleed *v. & n.* —*v.* (*past* and *past part.* **bled** /bled/) **1** *intr.* emit blood. **2** *tr.* draw blood from surgically. **3** *tr.* **a** extort money from. **b** *intr.* part with money lavishly; suffer extortion. **4** *intr.* (often foll. by *for*) suffer wounds or violent death. **5** *intr.* **a** (of a plant) emit sap. **b** (of dye) come out in water. **6** *tr.* **a** allow (fluid or gas) to escape from a closed system through a valve etc. **b** treat (such a system) in this way. —*n.* an act of bleeding (cf. NOSEBLEED). □ **one's heart bleeds** usu. *iron.* one is very sorrowful. [OE *blēdan* f. Gmc]

bleeder /ˈbliːdə(r)/ n. **1** coarse sl. a person (esp. as a term of contempt or disrespect) (you bleeder; lucky bleeder). **2** colloq. a haemophiliac.

bleeding /ˈbliːdɪŋ/ adj. & adv. Brit. coarse sl. expressing annoyance or antipathy (a bleeding nuisance).

bleep n. & v. —n. an intermittent high-pitched sound made electronically. —v.intr. & tr. make or cause to make such a sound, esp. as a signal. [imit.]

bleeper /ˈbliːpə(r)/ n. a small portable electronic device which emits a bleep when the wearer is contacted.

blemish /ˈblemɪʃ/ n. & v. —n. a physical or moral defect; a stain; a flaw (not a blemish on his character). —v.tr. spoil the beauty or perfection of; stain (spots blemished her complexion). [ME f. OF ble(s)mir (-ISH²) make pale, prob. of Gmc orig.]

blench v.intr. flinch; quail. [ME f. OE blencan, ult. f. Gmc]

blend v. & n. —v. **1** tr. **a** mix (esp. sorts of tea, spirits, tobacco, etc.) together to produce a desired flavour etc. **b** produce by this method (blended whisky). **2** intr. form a harmonious compound; become one. **3 a** tr. & intr. (often foll. by with) mingle or be mingled (blends well with the locals). **b** tr. (often foll. by in, with) mix thoroughly. **4** intr. (esp. of colours): **a** pass imperceptibly into each other. **b** go well together; harmonize. —n. **1** a mixture, esp. of various sorts of tea, spirits, tobacco, fibre, etc. **2** a combination (of different abstract or personal qualities). [ME prob. f. ON blanda mix]

blende /blend/ n. any naturally occurring metal sulphide, esp. zinc blende. [G f. blenden deceive, so called because while often resembling galena it yielded no lead]

blender /ˈblendə(r)/ n. **1** a mixing machine used in food preparation for liquidizing, chopping, or puréeing. **2 a** a thing that blends. **b** a person who blends.

blenny /ˈblenɪ/ n. (pl. -ies) any of a family of small spiny-finned marine fish, esp. of the genus Blennius, having scaleless skins. [L blennius f. Gk blennos mucus, with reference to its mucous coating]

bless /bles/ v.tr. (past and past part. **blessed**, poet. **blest** /blest/) **1** (of a priest etc.) pronounce words, esp. in a religious rite, asking for divine favour; ask God to look favourably on (bless this house). **2 a** consecrate (esp. bread and wine). **b** sanctify by the sign of the cross. **3** call (God) holy; adore. **4** attribute one's good fortune to (an auspicious time, one's fate, etc.); thank (bless the day I met her). **5** (usu. in passive; often foll. by with) make happy or successful (they were truly blessed). **6** euphem. curse; damn (bless the boy!). [OE blǣdsian, blēdsian, blētsian, f. blōd blood (hence mark with blood, consecrate): meaning infl. by its use at the conversion of the English to translate L benedicare praise]

blessed /ˈblesɪd, blest/ adj. (also poet. **blest**) **1 a** consecrated (Blessed Sacrament). **b** revered. **2** /blest/ (usu. foll. by with) often iron. fortunate (in the possession of) (blessed with children). **3** euphem. cursed; damned (blessed nuisance!). **4 a** in paradise. **b** RC Ch. a title given to a dead person as an acknowledgement of his or her holy life; beatified. **5** bringing happiness; blissful (blessed ignorance). □ **blessedly** adv.

blessedness /ˈblesɪdnɪs/ n. **1** happiness. **2** the enjoyment of divine favour.

blessing /ˈblesɪŋ/ n. **1** the act of declaring, seeking, or bestowing (esp. divine) favour (sought God's blessing; mother gave them her blessing). **2** grace said before or after a meal. **3** a gift of God, nature, etc.; a thing one is glad of (what a blessing he brought it!).

blether var. of BLATHER.

blew past of BLOW¹.

blewits /ˈbluːɪts/ n. any fungus of the genus Tricholoma, with edible lilac-stemmed mushrooms. [prob. f BLUE¹]

blight /blaɪt/ n. & v. —n. **1** any plant disease caused by mildews, rusts, smuts, fungi, or insects. **2** any insect or parasite causing such a disease. **3** any obscure force which is harmful. **4** an unsightly or neglected urban area. —v.tr. **1** affect with blight. **2** harm, destroy. **3** spoil. [17th c.: orig. unkn.]

blighter /ˈblaɪtə(r)/ n. Brit. colloq. a person (esp. as a term of contempt or disparagement). [BLIGHT + -ER¹]

blimey /ˈblaɪmɪ/ int. (also **cor blimey** /kɔː/) Brit. coarse sl. an expression of surprise, contempt, etc. [corrupt. of (God) blind me!]

blimp n. **1** (also (**Colonel**) **Blimp**) a proponent of reactionary establishment opinions. **2 a** a small non-rigid airship. **b** a barrage balloon. **3** a soundproof cover for a cine-camera. □ **blimpery** n. **blimpish** adj. [20th. c., of uncert. orig.: in sense 1, a pompous, obese, elderly character invented by cartoonist David Low]

blind /blaɪnd/ adj., v., n., & adv. —adj. **1** lacking the power of sight. **2 a** without foresight, discernment, or adequate information. **b** (often foll. by to) unwilling or unable to appreciate (a factor, circumstance, etc.) (blind to argument). **3** not governed by purpose or reason (blind forces). **4** reckless (blind hitting). **5 a** concealed (blind ditch). **b** (of a door, window, etc.) walled up. **c** closed at one end. **6** Aeron. (of flying) without direct observation, using instruments only. **7** Cookery (of a flan case, pie base, etc.) baked without a filling. —v. **1** tr. deprive of sight, permanently or temporarily (blinded by tears). **2** tr. (often foll. by to) rob of judgement; deceive (blinded them to the danger). —n. **1 a** a screen for a window. **b** an awning over a shop window. **2 a** something designed or used to hide the truth; a pretext. **b** a legitimate business concealing a criminal enterprise. **3** any obstruction to sight or light. —adv. blindly (fly blind; bake it blind). □ **blind alley 1** a cul-de-sac. **2** a course of action leading nowhere. **blind corner** a corner round which a motorist etc. cannot see. **blind date 1** a social engagement between a man and a woman who have not previously met. **2** either of the couple on a blind date. **blind drunk** extremely drunk. **blind side** a direction in which one cannot see the approach of danger etc. **blind spot 1** Anat. the point of entry of the optic nerve on the retina, insensitive to light. **2** an area in which a person lacks understanding or impartiality. **3** a point of unusually weak radio reception. **not a blind bit of** (or **not a blind**) sl. not the slightest; not a single (took not a blind bit of notice). **turn a** (or **one's**) **blind eye to** pretend not to notice. □ **blindly** adv. **blindness** n. [OE f. Gmc]

blinder /ˈblaɪndə(r)/ n. colloq. **1** an excellent piece of play in a game. **2** (in pl.) US blinkers.

blindfold /ˈblaɪndfəʊld/ v., n., adj., & adv. —v.tr. **1** deprive (a person) of sight by covering the eyes, esp. with a tied cloth. **2** deprive of understanding; hoodwink. —n. **1** a bandage or cloth used to blindfold. **2** any obstruction to understanding. —adj. & adv. **1** with eyes bandaged. **2** without care or circumspection (went into it blindfold). [replacing by assoc. with FOLD¹) ME blindfellen, past part. blindfelled (FELL¹) strike blind]

blindworm /ˈblaɪndwɜːm/ n. = SLOW-WORM.

blink v. & n. —v. **1** intr. shut and open the eyes quickly and usu. involuntarily. **2** intr. (often foll. by at) look with eyes opening and shutting. **3** tr. **a** (often foll. by back) prevent (tears) by blinking. **b** (often foll. by away, from) clear (dust etc.) from the eyes by blinking. **4** tr. & (foll. by at) intr. shirk consideration of; ignore; condone. **5** intr. **a** shine with an unsteady or intermittent light. **b** cast a momentary gleam. **6** tr. blink with (eyes). —n. **1** an act of blinking. **2** a momentary gleam or glimpse. □ **on the blink** sl. out of order, esp. intermittently. [partly var. of blenk = BLENCH, partly f. MDu. blinken shine]

blinker /ˈblɪŋkə(r)/ n. & v. —n. **1** (usu. in pl.) either of a pair of screens attached to a horse's bridle to prevent it from seeing sideways. **2** a device that blinks, esp. a vehicle's indicator. —v.tr. **1** obscure with blinkers. **2** (as **blinkered** adj.) having narrow and prejudiced views.

blinking /ˈblɪŋkɪŋ/ adj. & adv. Brit. sl. an intensive, esp. expressing disapproval (a blinking idiot; a blinking awful time). [BLINK + -ING² (euphem. for BLOODY)]

blip n. & v. —n. **1** a minor deviation or error. **2** a quick popping sound, as of dripping water or an electronic device. **3** a small image of an object on a radar screen. —v. intr. (**blipped**, **blipping**) make a blip. [imit.]

bliss n. **1 a** perfect joy or happiness. **b** enjoyment; gladness. **2 a** being in heaven. **b** a state of blessedness. [OE blīths, bliss f. Gmc blīthsjō f. blīthiz BLITHE: sense infl. by BLESS]

blissful /ˈblɪsfʊl/ adj. perfectly happy; joyful. □ **blissfully** adv. **blissfulness** n.

blister /ˈblɪstə(r)/ n. & v. —n. **1** a small bubble on the skin filled with serum and caused by friction, burning, etc. **2** a similar swelling on any other surface. —v. **1** tr. raise a blister on. **2** intr. come up in a blister or blisters. □ **blister pack** a bubble pack. □ **blistery** adj. [ME perh. f. OF blestre, blo(u)stre swelling, pimple]

blithe /blaɪð/ adj. **1** poet. gay, joyous. **2** careless, casual. □ **blithely** adv. **blitheness** n. **blithesome** /-səm/ adj. [OE blīthe f. Gmc]

blithering /ˈblɪðərɪŋ/ adj. colloq. **1** senselessly talkative. **2** (attrib.) utter; hopeless (blithering idiot). [blither, var. of BLATHER + -ING²]

B.Litt. abbr. Bachelor of Letters. [L Baccalaureus Litterarum]

blitz /blɪts/ n. & v. colloq. —n. **1 a** an intensive or sudden (esp. aerial) attack. **b** an energetic intensive attack, usu. on a specific task (must have a blitz on this room). **2** (**the Blitz**) the German air raids on London in 1940. —v.tr. attack, damage, or destroy by a blitz. [abbr. of BLITZKRIEG]

blitzkrieg /ˈblɪtskriːg/ n. an intense military campaign intended to bring about a swift victory. [G, = lightning war]

blizzard /ˈblɪzəd/ n. a severe snowstorm with high winds. [US 'violent blow' (1829), 'snowstorm' (1859), perh. imit.]

bloat /bləʊt/ v. **1** tr. & intr. inflate, swell (bloated with gas). **2** tr. (as **bloated** adj.) **a** swollen, puffed. **b** puffed up with pride or excessive wealth (bloated plutocrat). **3** tr. cure (a herring) by salting and smoking lightly. [obs. bloat swollen, soft and wet, perh. f. ON blautr soaked, flabby]

bloater /ˈbləʊtə(r)/ n. a herring cured by bloating.

blob n. **1** a small roundish mass; a drop of matter. **2** a drop of liquid. **3** a spot of colour. [imit.]

bloc n. a combination of parties, governments, groups, etc. sharing a common purpose. [F, = block]

block n., v., & adj. —n. **1** a solid hewn or unhewn piece of hard material, esp. of rock, stone, or wood (block of ice). **2** a flat-topped block used as a base for chopping, standing something on, hammering on, or for mounting a horse from. **3 a** a large building, esp. when subdivided (block of flats). **b** a compact mass of buildings bounded by (usu. four) streets. **4** an obstruction; anything preventing progress or normal working (a block in the pipe). **5** a pulley or system of pulleys in a case. **6** (in pl.) any of a set of solid cubes etc., used as a child's toy. **7** Printing a piece of wood or metal engraved for printing on paper or fabric. **8** sl. the head (knock his block off). **9** US **a** the area between streets in a town or suburb. **b** the length of such an area, esp. as a measure of distance (lives three blocks away). **10 a** large quantity or allocation of things treated as a unit, esp. shares, seats in a theatre, etc. **11** a set of sheets of paper used for writing, or esp. drawing, glued along one edge. **12** Athletics = starting-block. **13** Amer. Football a blocking action. **14** Austral. **a** a tract of land offered to an individual settler by a government. **b** a large area of land. —v.tr. **1 a** (often foll. by up) obstruct (a passage etc.) (you are blocking my view). **b** put obstacles in the way of (progress etc.). **2** restrict the use or conversion of (currency or any other asset). **3** Cricket stop (a ball) with a bat defensively. **4** Amer. Football intercept (an opponent) with one's body. —attrib.adj. treating (many similar things) as one unit (block booking). □ **block and tackle** a system of pulleys and ropes, esp. for lifting. **block capitals** (or **letters**) letters written with each letter separate and in capitals. **block diagram** a diagram showing the general arrangement of parts of an apparatus. **block in 1** sketch roughly; plan. **2** confine. **block out 1** shut out (light, noise, etc.). **b** exclude from memory, as being too painful. **2** sketch roughly; plan. **block up 1** confine; shut (a person etc.) in. **2** infill (a window, doorway, etc.) with bricks etc. **block vote** a vote proportional in power to the number of people a delegate represents. **mental** (or **psychological**) **block** a particular mental inability due to subconscious emotional factors. □ **blocker** n. [ME f. OF bloc, bloquer f. MDu. blok, of unkn. orig.]

blockade /blɒˈkeɪd/ n. & v. —n. the surrounding or blocking of a place by an enemy to prevent entry and exit of supplies etc. —v.tr.

subject to a blockade. □ **blockader** n. [BLOCK + -ADE¹, prob. after *ambuscade*]

blockage /ˈblɒkɪdʒ/ n. **1** an obstruction. **2** a blocked state.

blockboard /ˈblɒkbɔːd/ n. a plywood board with a core of wooden strips.

blockbuster /ˈblɒkˌbʌstə(r)/ n. *sl.* **1** something of great power or size, esp. an epic film or a book. **2** a huge bomb.

blockhead /ˈblɒkhed/ n. a stupid person. □ **blockheaded** adj.

blockhouse /ˈblɒkhaʊs/ n. **1** a reinforced concrete shelter used as an observation point etc. **2** *hist.* a one-storeyed timber building with loopholes, used as a fort. **3** a house made of squared logs.

bloke n. *Brit. sl.* a man, a fellow. [Shelta]

blond adj. & n. —adj. **1** (of hair) light-coloured; fair. **2** (of the complexion, esp. as an indication of race) light-coloured. —n. a person, esp. a man, with fair hair and skin. □ **blondish** adj. **blondness** n. [ME f. F f. med.L *blondus, blundus* yellow, perh. of Gmc orig.]

blonde /blɒnd/ adj. & n. —adj. (of a woman or a woman's hair) blond. —n. a blond-haired woman. [F fem. of *blond*; see BLOND]

blood /blʌd/ n. & v. —n. **1** a liquid, usually red and circulating in the arteries and veins of vertebrates, that carries oxygen to and carbon dioxide from the tissues of the body. **2** a corresponding fluid in invertebrates. **3** bloodshed, esp. killing. **4** passion, temperament. **5** race, descent, parentage (*of the same blood*). **6** a relationship; relations (*own flesh and blood*). —v.tr. **1** give (a hound) a first taste of blood. **2** initiate (a person) by experience. □ **bad blood** ill feeling. **blood-and-thunder** (*attrib.*) *colloq.* sensational, melodramatic. **blood bank** a place where supplies of blood or plasma for transfusion are stored. **blood bath** a massacre. **blood-brother** a brother by birth or by the ceremonial mingling of blood. **blood count 1** the counting of the number of corpuscles in a specific amount of blood. **2** the number itself. **blood-curdling** horrifying. **blood donor** one who gives blood for transfusion. **blood feud** a feud between families involving killing or injury. **blood group** any one of the various types of human blood determining compatibility in transfusion. **blood-heat** the normal body temperature of a healthy human being, about 37 °C or 98.4 °F. **blood-letting 1** the surgical removal of some of a patient's blood. **2** *joc.* bloodshed. **blood-lust** the desire for shedding blood. **blood-money 1** money paid to the next of kin of a person who has been killed. **2** money paid to a hired murderer. **3** money paid for information about a murder or murderer. **blood orange** an orange with red or red-streaked pulp. **blood-poisoning** a diseased state caused by the presence of micro-organisms in the blood. **blood pressure** the pressure of the blood in the circulatory system, often measured for diagnosis. **blood relation** (or **relative**) a relative by blood, not by marriage. **blood sport** sport involving the wounding or killing of animals, esp. hunting. **blood sugar** the amount of glucose in the blood. **blood test** a scientific examination of blood, esp. for diagnosis. **blood transfusion** the injection of a volume of blood, previously taken from a healthy person, into a patient. **blood-vessel** a vein, artery, or capillary carrying blood. **in one's blood** inherent in one's character. **make one's blood boil** infuriate one. **make one's blood run cold** horrify one. **new** (or **fresh**) **blood** new members admitted to a group, esp. as an invigorating force. [OE *blōd* f. Gmc]

bloodhound /ˈblʌdhaʊnd/ n. **1** a large hound of a breed used in tracking and having a very keen sense of smell. **2** this breed.

bloodless /ˈblʌdlɪs/ adj. **1** without blood. **2** unemotional; cold. **3** pale. **4** without bloodshed (*a bloodless coup*). **5** feeble; lifeless. □ **bloodlessly** adv. **bloodlessness** n.

bloodshed /ˈblʌdʃed/ n. **1** the spilling of blood. **2** slaughter.

bloodshot /ˈblʌdʃɒt/ adj. (of an eyeball) inflamed, tinged with blood.

bloodstain /ˈblʌdsteɪn/ n. a discoloration caused by blood.

bloodstained /ˈblʌdsteɪnd/ adj. **1** stained with blood. **2** guilty of bloodshed.

bloodstock /ˈblʌdstɒk/ n. thoroughbred horses.

bloodstream /ˈblʌdstriːm/ n. blood in circulation.

bloodsucker /ˈblʌdˌsʌkə(r)/ n. **1** an animal or insect that sucks blood, esp. a leech. **2** an extortioner. □ **bloodsucking** adj.

bloodthirsty /ˈblʌdˌθɜːstɪ/ adj. (**bloodthirstier**, **bloodthirstiest**) eager for bloodshed. □ **bloodthirstily** adv. **bloodthirstiness** n.

bloody /ˈblʌdɪ/ adj., adv., & v. —adj. (**bloodier**, **bloodiest**) **1 a** of or like blood. **b** running or smeared with blood (*bloody bandage*). **2 a** involving, loving, or resulting from bloodshed (*bloody battle*). **b** sanguinary; cruel (*bloody butcher*). **3** *coarse sl.* expressing annoyance or antipathy, or as an intensive (*a bloody shame; not a bloody chocolate left*). **4** red. —adv. *coarse sl.* as an intensive (*a bloody good job; I'll bloody thump him*). —v.tr. (**-ies, -ied**) make bloody; stain with blood. □ **Bloody Mary** a drink composed of vodka and tomato juice. **bloody-minded** *colloq.* deliberately uncooperative. □ **bloodily** adv. **bloodiness** n. [OE *blōdig* (as BLOOD, -Y¹)]

bloom /bluːm/ n. & v. —n. **1 a** a flower, esp. one cultivated for its beauty. **b** the state of flowering (*in bloom*). **2** a state of perfection or loveliness; the prime (*in full bloom*). **3 a** (of the complexion) a flush; a glow. **b** a delicate powdery surface deposit on plums, grapes, leaves, etc. **c** a cloudiness on a shiny surface. —v. **1** *intr.* bear flowers; be in flower. **2** *intr.* **a** come into, or remain in, full beauty. **b** flourish; be in a healthy, vigorous state. □ **take the bloom off** make stale. **water-bloom** scum formed by algae on the surface of standing water. [ME f. ON *blóm, blómi* etc. f. Gmc: cf. BLOSSOM]

bloomer¹ /ˈbluːmə(r)/ n. *sl.* a blunder. [= BLOOMING *error*]

bloomer² /ˈbluːmə(r)/ n. *Brit.* an oblong loaf with a rounded diagonally slashed top. [20th c.: orig. uncert.]

bloomer³ /ˈbluːmə(r)/ n. a plant that blooms (in a specified way) (*early autumn bloomer*).

bloomers /ˈbluːməz/ n.pl. **1** women's loose-fitting almost knee-length knickers. **2** *colloq.* any women's knickers. **3** *hist.* women's loose-fitting trousers, gathered at the knee or (orig.) the ankle. [Mrs A. *Bloomer*, Amer. social reformer d. 1894, who advocated a similar costume]

blooming /ˈbluːmɪŋ/ *adj.* & *adv.* —*adj.* **1** flourishing; healthy. **2** *Brit. sl.* an intensive (*a blooming miracle*). —*adv. Brit. sl.* an intensive (*was blooming difficult*). [BLOOM + -ING²: euphem. for BLOODY]

blooper /ˈbluːpə(r)/ *n. esp. US colloq.* an embarrassing error. [imit. *bloop* + -ER¹]

blossom /ˈblɒsəm/ *n.* & *v.* —*n.* **1** a flower or a mass of flowers, esp. of a fruit-tree. **2** the stage or time of flowering (*the cherry tree in blossom*). **3** a promising stage (*the blossom of youth*). —*v.intr.* **1** open into flower. **2** reach a promising stage; mature, thrive. □ **blossomy** *adj.* [OE *blōstm(a)* prob. formed as BLOOM]

blot *n.* & *v.* —*n.* **1** a spot or stain of ink etc. **2** a moral defect in an otherwise good character; a disgraceful act or quality. **3** any disfigurement or blemish. —*v.* (**blotted**, **blotting**) **1** *a tr.* spot or stain with ink; smudge. **b** *intr.* (of a pen, ink, etc.) make blots. **2** *tr.* **a** use blotting-paper or other absorbent material to absorb excess ink. **b** (of blotting-paper etc.) soak up (esp. ink). **3** *tr.* disgrace (*blotted his reputation*). □ **blot one's copybook** damage one's reputation. **blot out 1 a** obliterate (writing). **b** obscure (a view, sound, etc.). **2** obliterate (from the memory) as too painful. **3** destroy. **blotting-paper** unglazed absorbent paper used for soaking up excess ink. [ME prob. f. Scand.: cf. Icel. *blettr* spot, stain]

blotch *n.* & *v.* —*n.* **1** a discoloured patch on the skin. **2** an irregular patch of ink or colour. —*v.tr.* cover with blotches. □ **blotchy** *adj.* (**blotchier**, **blotchiest**). [17th c.: f. obs. *plotch* and BLOT]

blotter /ˈblɒtə(r)/ *n.* a sheet or sheets of blotting-paper, usu. inserted into a frame.

blotto /ˈblɒtəʊ/ *adj. sl.* very drunk, esp. unconscious from drinking. [20th c.: perh. f. BLOT]

blouse /blaʊz/ *n.* & *v.* —*n.* **1** a woman's loose, usu. lightweight, upper garment, usu. buttoned and collared. **2** the upper part of a soldier's or airman's battledress. —*v.tr.* make (a bodice etc.) loose like a blouse. [F, of unkn. orig.]

blouson /ˈbluːzɒn/ *n.* a short blouse-shaped jacket. [F]

blow¹ /bləʊ/ *v.* & *n.* —*v.* (*past* **blew** /bluː/; *past part.* **blown** /bləʊn/) **1 a** *intr.* (of the wind or air, or impersonally) move along; act as an air-current (*it was blowing hard*). **b** *intr.* be driven by an air-current (*waste paper blew along the gutter*). **c** *tr.* blow with an air-current (*blew the door open*). **2 a** *tr.* send out (esp. air) by breathing (*blew cigarette smoke*; *blew a bubble*). **b** *intr.* send a directed air-current from the mouth. **3** *tr.* & *intr.* sound or be sounded by blowing (*the whistle blew*; *they blew the trumpets*). **4** *tr.* **a** direct an air-current at (*blew the embers*). **b** (foll. by *off*, *away*, etc.) clear of by means of an air-current (*blew the dust off*). **5** *tr.* (*past part.* **blowed**) *sl.* (esp. in *imper.*) curse, confound (*blow it!*; *I'll be blowed!*) **6** *tr.* clear (the nose) of mucus by blowing. **7** *intr.* puff, pant. **8** *tr.* shatter or send flying by an explosion (*the bomb blew the tiles off the roof*; *blew them to smithereens*). **9** *tr.* make or shape (glass or a bubble) by blowing air in. **10** *tr.* & *intr.* melt or cause to melt from overloading (*the fuse has blown*). **11** *intr.* (of a whale) eject air and water through a blow-hole. **12** *tr.* break into (a safe etc.) with explosives. **13** *tr. sl.* **a** squander, spend recklessly (*blew £20 on a meal*). **b** spoil, bungle

(an opportunity etc.) (*he's blown his chances of winning*). **c** reveal (a secret etc.). **14** *tr.* (of flies) deposit eggs in. —*n.* **1 a** an act of blowing (e.g. one's nose, a wind instrument). **b** *colloq.* a turn or spell of playing jazz (on any instrument); a musical session. **2 a** gust of wind or air. **b** exposure to fresh air. □ **blow-dry** arrange (the hair) while drying it with a hand-held drier. **blow-drier** (or **-dryer**) a drier used for this. **blow the gaff** reveal a secret inadvertently. **blow-hole 1** the nostril of a whale, on the top of its head. **2** a vent for air, smoke, etc., in a tunnel etc. **blow in 1** break inwards by an explosion. **2** *colloq.* arrive unexpectedly. **blow a kiss** kiss one's hand and wave it to a distant person. **blow a person's mind** *sl.* cause a person to have drug-induced hallucinations or a similar experience. **blow out 1 a** extinguish by blowing. **b** send outwards by an explosion. **2** (of a tyre) burst. **3** (of a fuse etc.) melt. **blow-out** *n. colloq.* **1** a burst tyre. **2** a melted fuse. **3** a huge meal. **blow over** (of trouble etc.) fade away without serious consequences. **blow one's own trumpet** praise oneself. **blow one's top** (*US* **stack**) *colloq.* explode in rage. **blow up 1 a** shatter or destroy by an explosion. **b** explode, erupt. **2** *colloq.* rebuke strongly. **3** inflate (a tyre etc.). **4** *colloq.* **a** enlarge (a photograph). **b** exaggerate. **5** *colloq.* come to notice; arise. **6** *colloq.* lose one's temper. **blow-up** *n.* **1** *colloq.* an enlargement (of a photograph etc.). **2** an explosion. [OE *blāwan* f. Gmc]

blow² /bləʊ/ *n.* **1** a hard stroke with a hand or weapon. **2** a sudden shock or misfortune. □ **blow-by-blow** (of a description etc.) giving all the details in sequence. **come to blows** end up fighting. [15th c.: orig. unkn.]

blower /ˈbləʊə(r)/ *n.* **1** in senses of BLOW¹ *v.* **2** a device for creating a current of air. **3** *colloq.* a telephone.

blowfly /ˈbləʊflaɪ/ *n.* (*pl.* **-flies**) a meat-fly, a bluebottle.

blowlamp /ˈbləʊlæmp/ *n.* a portable device with a hot flame used for burning off paint, soldering, etc.

blowpipe /ˈbləʊpaɪp/ *n.* **1** a tube used esp. by primitive peoples for propelling arrows or darts by blowing. **2** a tube used to intensify the heat of a flame by blowing air or other gas through it at high pressure. **3** a tube used in glass-blowing.

blowtorch /ˈbləʊtɔːtʃ/ *n. US* = BLOWLAMP.

blowy /ˈbləʊɪ/ *adj.* (**blowier**, **blowiest**) windy, windswept. □ **blowiness** *n.*

blowzy /ˈblaʊzɪ/ *adj.* (**blowzier**, **blowziest**) **1** coarse-looking; red-faced. **2** dishevelled, slovenly. □ **blowzily** *adv.* **blowziness** *n.* [obs. *blowze* beggar's wench, of unkn. orig.]

blub *v.intr.* (**blubbed**, **blubbing**) *sl.* sob. [abbr. of BLUBBER¹]

blubber¹ /ˈblʌbə(r)/ *n.* & *v.* —*n.* **1** whale fat. **2** a spell of weeping. —*v.* **1** *intr.* sob loudly. **2** *tr.* sob out (words). □ **blubberer** *n.* **blubberingly** *adv.* **blubbery** *adj.* [ME perh. imit. (obs. meanings 'foaming, bubble')]

blubber² /ˈblʌbə(r)/ *adj.* (of the lips) swollen, protruding. [earlier *blabber*, *blobber*, imit.]

bludge *v.* & *n. Austral.* & *NZ sl.* —*v.intr.* avoid work. —*n.* an easy job or assignment. □ **bludge on** impose on. [back-form. f. BLUDGER]

bludgeon /ˈblʌdʒ(ə)n/ n. & v. —n. a club with a heavy end. —v.tr. **1** beat with a bludgeon. **2** coerce. [18th c.: orig. unkn.]

bludger /ˈblʌdʒə(r)/ n. Austral. & NZ sl. **1** a hanger-on. **2** a loafer. [orig. E sl., = pimp, f. obs. *bludgeoner* f. BLUDGEON]

blue¹ adj., n., & v. —adj. **1** having a colour like that of a clear sky. **2** sad, depressed; (of a state of affairs) gloomy, dismal (*feel blue*; *blue times*). **3** indecent, pornographic (*a blue film*). **4** with bluish skin through cold, fear, anger, etc. **5** Brit. politically conservative. —n. **1** a blue colour or pigment. **2** blue clothes or material (*dressed in blue*). **3** Brit. **a** a person who has represented a university in a sport, esp. Oxford or Cambridge. **b** this distinction. **4** Brit. a supporter of the Conservative party. **5** Austral. sl. **a** an argument or row. **b** (as a nickname) a red-headed person. **6** a blue ball, piece, etc. in a game or sport. **7** (prec. by *the*) the clear sky. —v.tr. (**blues**, **blued**, **bluing** or **blueing**) make blue. □ **blue baby** a baby with a blue complexion from lack of oxygen in the blood due to a congenital defect of the heart or great vessels. **blue blood** noble birth. **blue-blooded** of noble birth. **Blue Book** a report issued by Parliament or the Privy Council. **blue cheese** cheese produced with veins of blue mould. **blue-collar** (*attrib.*) of manual or unskilled work. **blue-eyed boy** esp. Brit. colloq. usu. derog. a favoured person; a favourite. **blue mould** a bluish fungus growing on food and other organic matter. **blue-pencil** (**-pencilled**, **-pencilling**; US **-penciled**, **-penciling**) censor or make cuts in (a manuscript, film, etc.). **Blue Peter** a blue flag with a white square raised on board a ship leaving port. **blue ribbon 1** a high honour. **2** Brit. the ribbon of the Order of the Garter. **blue rinse** a preparation for tinting grey hair. **blue tit** a common tit, *Parus caeruleus*, with a distinct blue crest on a black and white head. **blue whale** a rorqual, *Balaenoptera musculus*, the largest known living mammal. **once in a blue moon** very rarely. **out of the blue** unexpectedly. □ **blueness** n. [ME f. OF *bleu* f. Gmc]

blue² v.tr. (**blues**, **blued**, **bluing** or **blueing**) sl. squander (money). [perh. var. of BLOW¹]

bluebell /ˈbluːbel/ n. **1** a liliaceous plant, *Hyacinthoides nonscripta*, with clusters of bell-shaped blue flowers on a stem arising from a rhizome. **2** Sc. a plant, *Campanula rotundifolia*, with solitary bell-shaped blue flowers on long stalks.

blueberry /ˈbluːbərɪ/ n. (pl. **-ies**) **1** any of several plants of the genus *Vaccinium*, cultivated for their edible fruit. **2** the small blue-black fruit of these plants.

bluebird /ˈbluːbɜːd/ n. any of various N. American songbirds of the thrush family, esp. of the genus *Sialia*, with distinctive blue plumage.

bluebottle /ˈbluːˌbɒt(ə)l/ n. a large buzzing fly, *Calliphora vomitoria*, with a metallic-blue body.

bluegrass /ˈbluːɡrɑːs/ n. US **1** any of several bluish-green grasses, esp. of Kentucky. **2** a kind of country-and-western music characterized by virtuosic playing of banjos, guitars, etc.

bluegum /ˈbluːɡʌm/ n. any tree of the genus *Eucalyptus*, esp. *E. regnans* with blue-green aromatic leaves.

blueprint /ˈbluːprɪnt/ n. & v. —n. **1** a photographic print of the final stage of engineering or other plans in white on a blue background. **2** a detailed plan, esp. in the early stages of a project or idea. —v.tr. US work out (a programme, plan, etc.).

blues /bluːz/ n.pl. **1** (prec. by *the*) a bout of depression (*had a fit of the blues*). **2 a** (prec. by *the*; often treated as *sing.*) melancholic music of Black American folk origin, often in a twelve-bar sequence (*always singing the blues*). **b** (pl. same) (as *sing.*) a piece of such music. □ **bluesy** adj. (in sense 2).

bluestocking /ˈbluːˌstɒkɪŋ/ n. usu. derog. an intellectual or literary woman. [from the (less formal) blue stockings worn by one man at a literary society meeting c.1750]

bluey /ˈbluːɪ/ n. (pl. **-eys**) Austral. colloq. **1** a bundle carried by a bushman. **2** = BLUE n. 5b.

bluff¹ v. & n. —v. **1** intr. make a pretence of strength or confidence to gain an advantage. **2** tr. mislead by bluffing. —n. an act of bluffing; a show of confidence intended to deceive. □ **call a person's bluff** challenge a person thought to be bluffing. □ **bluffer** n. [19th c. (orig. in poker) f. Du. *bluffen* brag]

bluff² adj. & n. —adj. **1** (of a cliff, or a ship's bows) having a vertical or steep broad front. **2** (of a person or manner) blunt, frank, hearty. —n. a steep cliff or headland. □ **bluffly** adv. (in sense 2 of adj.). **bluffness** n. (in sense 2 of adj.). [17th-c. Naut. word: orig. unkn.]

bluish /ˈbluːɪʃ/ adj. somewhat blue.

blunder /ˈblʌndə(r)/ n. & v. —n. a clumsy or foolish mistake, esp. an important one. —v. **1** intr. make a blunder; act clumsily or ineptly. **2** tr. deal incompetently with; mismanage. **3** intr. move about blindly or clumsily; stumble. □ **blunderer** n. **blunderingly** adv. [ME prob. f. Scand.: cf. MSw *blundra* shut the eyes]

blunderbuss /ˈblʌndəˌbʌs/ n. hist. a short large-bored gun. [alt. of Du. *donderbus* thunder gun, assoc. with BLUNDER]

blunt adj. & v. —adj. **1** (of a knife, pencil, etc.) lacking in sharpness; having a worn-down point or edge. **2** (of a person or manner) direct, uncompromising, outspoken. —v.tr. make blunt or less sharp. □ **bluntly** adv. (in sense 2 of adj.). **bluntness** n. [ME perh. f. Scand.: cf. ON *blunda* shut the eyes]

blur v. & n. —v. (**blurred**, **blurring**) **1** tr. & intr. make or become unclear or less distinct. **2** tr. smear; partially efface. **3** tr. make (one's memory, perception, etc.) dim or less clear. —n. something indistinct or unclear. □ **blurry** adj. (**blurrier**, **blurriest**). [16th c.: perh. rel. to BLEAR]

blurb n. a description of a book, esp. printed on its jacket, as promotion by its publishers. [coined by G. Burgess, Amer. humorist d. 1951]

blurt v.tr. (usu. foll. by *out*) utter abruptly, thoughtlessly, or tactlessly. [prob. imit.]

blush /blʌʃ/ v. & n. —v.intr. **1 a** develop a pink tinge in the face from embarrassment or shame. **b** (of the face) redden in this way. **2** feel embarrassed or ashamed. **3** be or become red or pink. —n. **1** the act of blushing. **2** a pink tinge. [ME f. OE *blyscan*]

blusher /ˈblʌʃə(r)/ n. a cosmetic used to give a warmth of colour to the face.

bluster /ˈblʌstə(r)/ v. & n. —v.intr. **1** behave pompously and boisterously; utter empty threats. **2** (of the wind etc.) blow fiercely. —n.

noisily self-assertive talk. **2** empty threats. □
blusterer n. **blustery** adj. [16th c.: ult. imit.]

BM abbr. **1** British Museum. **2** Bachelor of Medicine.

B.Mus. abbr. Bachelor of Music.

BMX /ˌbiːemˈeks/ n. **1** organized bicycle-racing on a dirt-track, esp. for youngsters. **2** a kind of bicycle used for this. [abbr. of bicycle moto-cross]

BO abbr. colloq. body odour.

bo /bəʊ/ int. = BOO. [imit.]

boa /ˈbəʊə/ n. **1** any large non-poisonous snake from tropical America esp. of the genus Boa, which kills its prey by crushing and suffocating it in its coils. **2** any snake which is similar in appearance, such as Old World pythons. **3** a long thin stole made of feathers or fur. □ **boa constrictor** a large snake, Boa constrictor, native to tropical America and the West Indies, which crushes its prey. [L]

boar n. **1** (in full **wild boar**) the tusked wild pig, Sus scrofa, from which domestic pigs are descended. **2** an uncastrated male pig. **3** its flesh. **4** a male guinea-pig etc. [OE bār f. WG]

board n. & v. —n. **1** a a flat thin piece of sawn timber, usu. long and narrow. **b** a piece of material resembling this, made from compressed fibres. **c** a thin slab of wood or a similar substance, often with a covering, used for any of various purposes (chessboard; ironing-board; notice-board). **d** thick stiff card used in bookbinding. **2** the provision of regular meals, usu. with accommodation, for payment. **3** the directors of a company; any other specially constituted administrative body. **4** (in pl.) the stage of a theatre. —v. **1** tr. **a** go on board (a ship, train, aircraft, etc.). **b** force one's way on board (a ship etc.) in attack. **2** a intr. receive regular meals, or (esp. of a schoolchild) meals and lodging, for payment. **b** tr. (often foll. by out) arrange accommodation away from home for (esp. a child). **3** tr. (usu. foll. by up) cover with boards; seal or close. □ **board-game** a game played on a board. **board of trade** US a chamber of commerce. **go by the board** be neglected, omitted, or discarded. **on board** on or on to a ship, aircraft, oil rig, etc. **take on board** consider (a new idea etc.). [OE bord f. Gmc]

boarder /ˈbɔːdə(r)/ n. **1** a person who boards (see BOARD v. 2a), esp. a pupil at a boarding-school. **2** a person who boards a ship, esp. an enemy.

boarding-house /ˈbɔːdɪŋˌhaʊs/ n. an unlicensed establishment providing board and lodging.

boarding-school /ˈbɔːdɪŋˌskuːl/ n. a school where pupils are resident in term-time.

boardroom /ˈbɔːdruːm, -rʊm/ n. a room in which a board of directors etc. meets regularly.

boardsailing /ˈbɔːdˌseɪlɪŋ/ n. = WINDSURFING. □ **boardsailor** n. (also **boardsailer**).

boardwalk /ˈbɔːdwɔːk/ n. US **1** a wooden walkway across sand, marsh, etc. **2** a promenade along a beach.

boast v. & n. —v. **1** intr. declare one's achievements, possessions, or abilities with indulgent pride and satisfaction. **2** tr. own or have as something praiseworthy etc. (the hotel boasts magnificent views). —n. **1** an act of boasting. **2** something one is proud of. □ **boaster** n. **boastingly** adv. [ME f. AF bost, of unkn. orig.]

boastful /ˈbəʊstfʊl/ adj. **1** given to boasting. **2** characterized by boasting (boastful talk). □ **boastfully** adv. **boastfulness** n.

boat n. & v. —n. **1** a small vessel propelled on water by an engine, oars, or sails. **2** (in general use) a ship of any size. **3** an elongated boat-shaped jug used for holding sauce etc. —v.intr. travel or go in a boat, esp. for pleasure. □ **boat-hook** a long pole with a hook and a spike at one end, for moving boats. **boat-house** a shed at the edge of a river, lake, etc., for housing boats. **boat people** refugees who have left a country by sea. **boat-train** a train scheduled to meet or go on a boat. **in the same boat** sharing the same adverse circumstances. **push the boat out** colloq. celebrate lavishly. □ **boatful** n. (pl. -fuls). [OE bāt f. Gmc]

boater /ˈbəʊtə(r)/ n. a flat-topped hardened straw hat with a brim.

boating /ˈbəʊtɪŋ/ n. rowing or sailing in boats as a sport or form of recreation.

boatload /ˈbəʊtləʊd/ n. **1** enough to fill a boat. **2** colloq. a large number of people.

boatman /ˈbəʊtmən/ n. (pl. -men) a person who hires out boats or provides transport by boat.

boatswain /ˈbəʊs(ə)n/ n. (also **bo'sun, bosun, bo's'n**) a ship's officer in charge of equipment and the crew. [OE bātswegen (as BOAT, SWAIN)]

bob¹ v. & n. —v.intr. (**bobbed, bobbing**) **1** move quickly up and down; dance. **2** (usu. foll. by back, up) **a** bounce buoyantly. **b** emerge suddenly; become active or conspicuous again after a defeat etc. **3** curtsy. **4** (foll. by for) try to catch with the mouth alone (fruit etc. floating or hanging). —n. **1** a jerking or bouncing movement, esp. upward. **2** a curtsy. [14th c.: prob. imit.]

bob² n. & v. —n. **1** a short hairstyle for women and children. **2** a weight on a pendulum, plumb-line, or kite-tail. **3** a horse's docked tail. —v. (**bobbed, bobbing**) tr. cut (a woman's or child's hair) so that it hangs clear of the shoulders. [ME: orig. unkn.]

bob³ n. (pl. same) Brit. sl. a former shilling (now = 5 decimal pence). [19th c.: orig. unkn.]

bob⁴ /bɒb/ n. □ **bob's your uncle** Brit. sl. an expression of completion or satisfaction. [pet-form of the name Robert]

bobbin /ˈbɒbɪn/ n. **1** a cylinder or cone holding thread, yarn, wire, etc., used esp. in weaving and machine sewing. **2** a spool or reel. □ **bobbin-lace** lace made by hand with thread wound on bobbins. [F bobine]

bobble /ˈbɒb(ə)l/ n. a small woolly or tufted ball as a decoration or trimming. [dimin. of BOB²]

bobby¹ /ˈbɒbɪ/ n. (pl. -ies) Brit. colloq. a policeman. [Sir Robert Peel, Engl. statesman d. 1850, founder of the metropolitan police force]

bobby² /ˈbɒbɪ/ n. (pl. -ies) (in full **bobby calf**) Austral. & NZ an unweaned calf slaughtered for veal. [Eng. dial.]

bobby-dazzler /ˈbɒbɪˌdæzlə(r)/ n. colloq. a remarkable or excellent person or thing. [dial., rel. to DAZZLE]

bobby-pin /ˈbɒbɪpɪn/ n. US, Austral., & NZ a flat hairpin. [BOB² + -Y²]

bobby socks /ˈbɒbɪ ˌsɒks/ n.pl. esp. US short socks reaching just above the ankle.

bob-sled /ˈbɒbsled/ n. US = BOB-SLEIGH.

bob-sleigh /ˈbɒbsleɪ/ n. & v. —n. a mechanically-steered and -braked sledge used for racing down a steep ice-covered run. —v.intr. race in a bob-sleigh. [BOB² + SLEIGH]

bobtail /ˈbɒbteɪl/ n. a docked tail; a horse or a dog with a bobtail. [BOB² + TAIL¹]

Boche /bɒʃ/ n. & adj. sl. derog. —n. 1 a German, esp. a soldier. 2 (prec. by the) Germans, esp. German soldiers, collectively. —adj. German. [F sl., orig. = rascal: applied to Germans in the war of 1914–18]

bod n. Brit. colloq. a person. [abbr. of BODY]

bode v. tr. portend, foreshow. □ **bode well** (or **ill**) show good (or bad) signs for the future. □ **boding** n. [OE bodian f. boda messenger]

bodge var. of BOTCH.

bodice /ˈbɒdɪs/ n. 1 the part of a woman's dress (excluding sleeves) which is above the waist. 2 a woman's undergarment, like a vest, for the same part of the body. [orig. pair of bodies = stays, corsets]

bodiless /ˈbɒdɪlɪs/ adj. 1 lacking a body. 2 incorporeal, insubstantial.

bodily /ˈbɒdɪlɪ/ adj. & adv. —adj. of or concerning the body. —adv. 1 with the whole bulk; as a whole (threw them bodily). 2 in the body; as a person.

bodkin /ˈbɒdkɪn/ n. 1 a blunt thick needle with a large eye used esp. for drawing tape etc. through a hem. 2 a long pin for fastening hair. 3 a small pointed instrument. [ME perh. f. Celt.]

body /ˈbɒdɪ/ n. & v. —n. (pl. **-ies**) 1 the physical structure, including the bones, flesh, and organs, of a person or an animal, whether dead or alive. 2 the trunk apart from the head and the limbs. 3 a the main or central part of a thing (body of the car; body of the attack). b the bulk or majority; the aggregate (body of opinion). 4 a a group of persons regarded collectively, esp. as having a corporate function (governing body). b (usu. foll. by of) a collection (body of facts). 5 a quantity (body of water). 6 a piece of matter (heavenly body). 7 colloq. a person. 8 a full or substantial quality of flavour, tone, etc. —v.tr. (**-ies**, **-ied**) (usu. foll. by forth) give body or substance to. □ **body-blow** a severe setback. **body language** the process of communicating through conscious or unconscious gestures and poses. **body odour** the smell of the human body, esp. when unpleasant. **body politic** the nation or State as a corporate body. **body shop** a workshop where repairs to the bodywork of vehicles are carried out. **body stocking** a woman's undergarment which covers the torso. **body warmer** a sleeveless quilted or padded jacket worn as an outdoor garment. **in a body** all together. **keep body and soul together** keep alive, esp. barely. □ **-bodied** adj. (in comb.) (able-bodied). [OE bodig, of unkn. orig.]

body-check /ˈbɒdɪˌtʃek/ n. & v. Sport —n. a deliberate obstruction of one player by another. —v.tr. obstruct in this way.

bodyguard /ˈbɒdɪˌɡɑːd/ n. a person or group of persons escorting and protecting another person (esp. a dignitary).

bodywork /ˈbɒdɪwɜːk/ n. the outer shell of a vehicle.

Boer /ˈbəʊə(r), bʊə(r)/ n. & adj. —n. a South African of Dutch descent. —adj. of or relating to the Boers. [Du.: see BOOR]

boffin /ˈbɒfɪn/ n. esp. Brit. colloq. a person engaged in scientific (esp. military) research. [20th c.: orig. unkn.]

bog n. & v. —n. 1 a a wet spongy ground. b a stretch of such ground. 2 Brit. sl. a lavatory. —v.tr. (**bogged**, **bogging**) (foll. by down; usu. in passive) impede (was bogged down by difficulties). □ **bog oak** an ancient oak which has been preserved in a black state in peat. □ **boggy** adj. (**boggier**, **boggiest**). **bogginess** n. [Ir. or Gael. bogach f. bog soft]

bogey¹ /ˈbəʊɡɪ/ n. & v. Golf —n. (pl. **-eys**) a score of one stroke more than par at any hole. —v.tr. (**-eys**, **-eyed**) play (a hole) in one stroke more than par. [perh. f. Bogey as an imaginary player]

bogey² /ˈbəʊɡɪ/ n. (also **bogy**) (pl. **-eys** or **-ies**) 1 an evil or mischievous spirit; a devil. 2 an awkward thing or circumstance. 3 sl. a piece of dried nasal mucus. [19th c., orig. as a proper name]

bogeyman /ˈbəʊɡɪˌmæn/ n. (also **bogyman**) (pl. **-men**) a person (real or imaginary) causing fear or difficulty.

boggle /ˈbɒɡ(ə)l/ v.intr. colloq. 1 be startled or baffled (esp. the mind boggles). 2 (usu. foll. by about, at) hesitate, demur. [prob. f. dial. boggle BOGEY²]

bogie /ˈbəʊɡɪ/ n. esp. Brit. a wheeled undercarriage pivoted below the end of a rail vehicle. [19th-c. north. dial. word: orig. unkn.]

bogus /ˈbəʊɡəs/ adj. sham, spurious. □ **bogusly** adv. **bogusness** n. [19th-c. US word: orig. unkn.]

Bohemian /bəʊˈhiːmɪən/ n. & adj. —n. 1 a native of Bohemia, now part of modern Czechoslovakia; Czech. 2 (also **bohemian**) a socially unconventional person, esp. an artist or writer. —adj. 1 of, relating to, or characteristic of Bohemia or its people. 2 socially unconventional. □ **bohemianism** n. [Bohemia + -AN: sense 2 f. F bohémien gypsy]

boil¹ v. & n. —v. 1 intr. a (of a liquid) start to bubble up and turn into vapour; reach a temperature at which this happens. b (of a vessel) contain boiling liquid (the kettle is boiling). 2 a tr. bring (a liquid or vessel) to a temperature at which it boils. b tr. cook (food) by boiling. c intr. (of food) be cooked by boiling. d tr. subject to the heat of boiling water, e.g. to clean. 3 intr. a (of the sea etc.) undulate or seethe like boiling water. b (of a person or feelings) be greatly agitated, esp. by anger. —n. the act or process of boiling; boiling-point (on the boil; bring to the boil). □ **boil down 1** reduce volume by boiling. 2 reduce to essentials. 3 (foll. by to) amount to; signify basically. **boil over 1** spill over in boiling. 2 lose one's temper; become over-excited. [ME f. AF boiller, OF boillir, f. L bullire to bubble f. bulla bubble]

boil² n. an inflamed pus-filled swelling caused by infection of a hair follicle etc. [OE bȳl(e) f. WG]

boiler /ˈbɔɪlə(r)/ n. 1 a fuel-burning apparatus for heating a hot-water supply. 2 a tank for heating water, esp. for turning it to steam under pressure. 3 a metal tub for boiling laundry etc. 4 a fowl, vegetable, etc., suitable for cooking only by boiling. □ **boiler suit** a one-piece suit worn as overalls for heavy manual work.

boiling /ˈbɔɪlɪŋ/ adj. (also **boiling hot**) colloq. very hot.

boiling-point /ˈbɔɪlɪŋ/ *n.* **1** the temperature at which a liquid starts to boil. **2** high excitement (*feelings reached boiling-point*).

boisterous /ˈbɔɪstərəs/ *adj.* **1** (of a person) rough; noisily exuberant. **2** (of the sea, weather, etc.) stormy, rough. □ **boisterously** *adv.* **boisterousness** *n.* [var. of ME *boist(u)ous*, of unkn. orig.]

bold /bəʊld/ *adj.* **1** confidently assertive; adventurous, courageous. **2** forthright, impudent. **3** vivid, distinct, well-marked (*bold colours; a bold imagination*). **4** *Printing* (in full **bold-face** or **-faced**) printed in a thick black typeface. □ **make** (or **be**) **so bold as to** presume to; venture to. □ **boldly** *adv.* **boldness** *n.* [OE *bald* dangerous f. Gmc]

bole *n.* the stem or trunk of a tree. [ME f. ON *bolr*]

bolero /bəˈlɛərəʊ/ *n.* (*pl.* **-os**) **1 a** a Spanish dance in simple triple time. **b** music in the time of a bolero. **2** [also ˈbɒlərəʊ] a woman's short open jacket. [Sp.]

boll /bəʊl/ *n.* a rounded capsule containing seeds, esp. flax or cotton. □ **boll-weevil** a small weevil, *Anthonomus grandis*, whose larvae destroy cotton bolls. [ME f. MDu. *bolle*: see BOWL¹]

bollard /ˈbɒlɑːd/ *n.* **1** *Brit.* a short metal, concrete, or plastic post in the road, esp. as part of a traffic island. **2** a short post on a quay or ship for securing a rope. [ME perh. f. ON *bolr* BOLE + -ARD]

bollocking /ˈbɒləkɪŋ/ *n.* *coarse sl.* a severe reprimand.

bollocks /ˈbɒləks/ *n.* (also **ballocks**) *coarse sl.* **1** the testicles. **2** (usu. as an exclam. of contempt) nonsense, rubbish. [OE *bealluc*, rel. to BALL¹]

boloney /bəˈləʊnɪ/ *n.* (also **baloney**) (*pl.* **-eys**) *sl.* humbug, nonsense. [20th c.: orig. uncert.]

Bolshevik /ˈbɒlʃəvɪk/ *n.* & *adj.* —*n.* **1** *hist.* a member of the radical faction of the Russian socialist party, which became the communist party in 1918. **2** a Russian communist. **3** (in general use) any revolutionary socialist. —*adj.* **1** of, relating to, or characteristic of the Bolsheviks. **2** communist. □ **Bolshevism** *n.* **Bolshevist** *n.* [Russ., = a member of the majority, one who (in 1903) favoured extreme measures, f. *bolʹshe* greater]

Bolshie /ˈbɒlʃɪ/ *adj.* & *n.* (also **Bolshy**) *sl.* —*adj.* (usu. **bolshie**) **1** uncooperative, bad-tempered. **2** left-wing. —*n.* (*pl.* **-ies**) a Bolshevik. □ **bolshiness** *n.* (in sense 1 of *adj.*). [abbr.]

bolster /ˈbəʊlstə(r)/ *n.* & *v.* —*n.* **1** a long thick pillow. **2** a pad or support, esp. in a machine. —*v.tr.* (usu. foll. by *up*) **1** encourage, reinforce (*bolstered our morale*). **2** support with a bolster; prop up. □ **bolsterer** *n.* [OE f. Gmc]

bolt¹ /bəʊlt/ *n.*, *v.*, & *adv.* —*n.* **1** a sliding bar and socket used to fasten or lock a door, gate, etc. **2** a large usu. metal pin with a head, usu. riveted or used with a nut, to hold things together. **3** a discharge of lightning. **4** an act of bolting (cf. sense 4 of *v.*); a sudden dash for freedom. **5** *hist.* an arrow for shooting from a crossbow. **6** a roll of fabric (orig. as a measure). —*v.* **1** *tr.* fasten or lock with a bolt. **2** *tr.* (foll. by *in*, *out*) keep (a person etc.) from leaving or entering by bolting a door. **3** *tr.* fasten together with bolts. **4** *intr.* **a** dash suddenly away, esp. to escape. **b** (of a horse) suddenly gallop out of control. **5** *tr.* gulp down (food) unchewed; eat hurriedly. **6** *intr.* (of

a plant) run to seed. —*adv.* (usu. in **bolt upright**) rigidly, stiffly. □ **a bolt from the blue** a complete surprise. **bolt-hole 1** a means of escape. **2** a secret refuge. **shoot one's bolt** do all that is in one's power. □ **bolter** *n.* (in sense 4 of *v.*). [OE *bolt* arrow]

bolt² /bəʊlt/ *v.tr.* (also **boult**) sift (flour etc.). □ **bolter** *n.* [ME f. OF *bulter*, *buleter*, of unkn. orig.]

bomb /bɒm/ *n.* & *v.* —*n.* **1 a** a container with explosive, incendiary material, smoke, or gas etc., designed to explode on impact or by means of a time-mechanism or remote-control device. **b** an ordinary object fitted with an explosive device (*letter-bomb*). **2** (prec. by *the*) the atomic or hydrogen bomb. **3** *Brit. sl.* a large sum of money (*cost a bomb*). **4** bad failure (esp. a theatrical one). —*v.* **1** *tr.* attack with bombs; drop bombs on. **2** *tr.* (foll. by *out*) drive (a person etc.) out of a building or refuge by using bombs. **3** *intr.* throw or drop bombs. **4** *intr.* esp. *US sl.* fail badly. **5** *intr. colloq.* (usu. foll. by *along*, *off*) move or go very quickly. □ **bomb-sight** a device in an aircraft for aiming bombs. **bomb-site** an area where buildings have been destroyed by bombs. **go down a bomb** *colloq.*, often *iron.* be very well received. **like a bomb** *Brit. colloq.* **1** often *iron.* very successfully. **2** very fast. [F *bombe* f. It. *bomba* f. L *bombus* f. Gk *bombos* hum]

bombard /bɒmˈbɑːd/ *v.tr.* **1** attack with a number of heavy guns or bombs. **2** (often foll. by *with*) subject to persistent questioning, abuse, etc. **3** *Physics* direct a stream of high-speed particles at (a substance). □ **bombardment** *n.* [F *bombarder* f. *bombarde* f. med.L *bombarda* a stone-throwing engine: see BOMB]

bombardier /ˌbɒmbəˈdɪə(r)/ *n.* **1** *Brit.* a non-commissioned officer in the artillery. **2** *US* a member of a bomber crew responsible for sighting and releasing bombs. [F (as BOMBARD)]

bombast /ˈbɒmbæst/ *n.* pompous or extravagant language. □ **bombastic** /-ˈbæstɪk/ *adj.* **bombastically** /-ˈbæstɪkəlɪ/ *adv.* [earlier *bombace* cotton wool f. F f. med.L *bombax* *-acis* alt. f. *bombyx*; see BOMBAZINE]

Bombay duck /bɒmˈbeɪ dʌk/ *n.* a dried fish, esp. bummalo, usu. eaten with curries dishes. [corrupt. of *bombil*: see BUMMALO]

bombazine /ˈbɒmbəˌziːn, -ˈziːn/ *n.* (also **bombasine**) a twilled dress-material of worsted, esp. formerly used for mourning. [F *bombasin* f. med.L *bombacinum* f. LL *bombycinus* silken f. *bombyx* *-ycis* silk or silkworm f. Gk *bombux*]

bomber /ˈbɒmə(r)/ *n.* **1** an aircraft equipped to carry and drop bombs. **2** a person using bombs, esp. illegally. □ **bomber jacket** a short leather or cloth jacket tightly gathered at the waist and cuffs.

bombshell /ˈbɒmʃel/ *n.* **1** an overwhelming surprise or disappointment. **2** an artillery bomb.

bona fide /ˌbəʊnə ˈfaɪdɪ/ *adj.* & *adv.* —*adj.* genuine; sincere. —*adv.* genuinely; sincerely. [L, ablat. sing. of BONA FIDES]

bona fides /ˌbəʊnə ˈfaɪdiːz/ *n.* **1** esp. *Law* an honest intention; sincerity. **2** (as *pl.*) *colloq.* documentary evidence of acceptability (*his bona fides are in order*). [L, = good faith]

bonanza /bəˈnænzə/ *n.* **1** a source of wealth or prosperity. **2** a large output (esp. of a mine). **3 a** prosperity; good luck. **b** a run of good luck. [orig. US f. Sp., = fair weather, f. L *bonus* good]

bon-bon /ˈbɒnbɒn/ n. a piece of confectionery; a sweet. [F f. *bon* good f. L *bonus*]

bonce n. *Brit. sl.* the head. [19th c.: orig. unkn.]

bond n. & v. —n. **1 a** a thing that ties another down or together. **b** (usu. in *pl.*) a thing restraining bodily freedom (*broke his bonds*). **2** (often in *pl.*) **a** a uniting force (*sisterly bond*). **b** a restraint; a responsibility (*bonds of duty*). **3** a binding engagement; an agreement (*his word is his bond*). **4** *Commerce* a certificate issued by a government or a public company promising to repay borrowed money at a fixed rate of interest at a specified time; a debenture. **5** adhesiveness. **6** *Law* a deed by which a person is bound to make payment to another. **7** *Chem.* linkage between atoms in a molecule or a solid. **8** *Building* the laying of bricks in one of various patterns in a wall in order to ensure strength (*English bond*; *Flemish bond*). —v. **1** *tr.* **a** lay (bricks) overlapping. **b** bind together (resin with fibres, etc.). **2** *intr.* adhere; hold together. **3** *tr.* connect with a bond. **4** *tr.* place (goods) in bond. **5** *intr.* become emotionally attached. □ **bond paper** high-quality writing-paper. **in bond** (of goods) stored in a bonded warehouse until the importer pays the duty owing (see BOND[1]). [ME var. of BAND[1]]

bondage /ˈbɒndɪdʒ/ n. **1** serfdom; slavery. **2** subjection to constraint, influence, obligation, etc. [ME f. AL *bondagium*: infl. by BOND]

bonded /ˈbɒndɪd/ adj. **1** (of goods) placed in bond. **2** (of material) reinforced by or cemented to another. **3** (of a debt) secured by bonds. □ **bonded warehouse** a Customs-controlled warehouse for the retention of imported goods until the duty owed is paid.

bondsman /ˈbɒndzmən/ n. (*pl.* **-men**) **1** a slave. **2** a person in thrall to another. [var. of *bondman* (f. archaic *bond* in serfdom or slavery) as though f. *bond's* genitive of BOND[1]]

bone n. & v. —n. **1** any of the pieces of hard tissue making up the skeleton in vertebrates. **2** (in *pl.*) **a** the skeleton, esp. as remains after death. **b** the body, esp. as a seat of intuitive feeling (*felt it in my bones*). **3 a** the material of which bones consist. **b** a similar substance such as ivory, dentine, or whalebone. **4** a thing made of bone. **5** (in *pl.*) the essential part of a thing (*the bare bones*). —v. **1** *tr.* take out the bones from (meat or fish). **2** *tr.* stiffen (a garment) with bone etc. **3** *tr.* *Brit. sl.* steal. □ **bone china** fine china made of clay mixed with the ash from bones. **bone-dry** quite dry. **bone idle** (or **lazy**) utterly idle or lazy. **bone-meal** crushed or ground bones used esp. as a fertilizer. **bone of contention** a source or ground of dispute. **bone up** (often foll. by *on*) *colloq.* study (a subject) intensively. **close to** (or **near**) **the bone 1** tactless to the point of offensiveness. **2** destitute; hard up. **have a bone to pick** (usu. foll. by *with*) have a cause for dispute (with another person). **make no bones about 1** admit or allow without fuss. **2** not hesitate or scruple. **point the bone** (usu. foll. by *at*) *Austral.* **1** wish bad luck on. **2** cast a spell on in order to kill. **to the bone 1** to the bare minimum. **2** penetratingly. **work one's fingers to the bone** work very hard, esp. thanklessly. □ **boneless** adj. [OE *bān* f. Gmc]

bonehead /ˈbəʊnhed/ n. *sl.* a stupid person. □ **boneheaded** adj.

boneshaker /ˈbəʊnˌʃeɪkə(r)/ n. **1** a decrepit or uncomfortable old vehicle. **2** an old type of bicycle with solid tyres.

bonfire /ˈbɒnfaɪə(r)/ n. a large open-air fire. □ **Bonfire Night** *Brit.* 5 Nov., on which fireworks are displayed and an effigy of Guy Fawkes burnt (see GUY[1]). [earlier *bonefire* f. BONE (bones being the chief material formerly used) + FIRE]

bongo /ˈbɒŋgəʊ/ n. (*pl.* **-os** or **-oes**) either of a pair of small long-bodied drums usu. held between the knees and played with the fingers. [Amer. Sp. *bongó*]

bonhomie /ˌbɒnɒˈmiː/ n. geniality; good-natured friendliness. [F f. *bonhomme* good fellow]

bonhomous /ˈbɒnəməs/ adj. full of *bonhomie*.

bonito /bəˈniːtəʊ/ n. (*pl.* **-os**) any of several tunny-like fish which are striped like mackerel and are common in tropical seas. [Sp.]

bonk /bɒŋk/ v. & n. —v. **1** *tr.* hit resoundingly. **2** *intr.* bang; bump. **3** *coarse sl.* **a** *intr.* have sexual intercourse. **b** *tr.* have sexual intercourse with. —n. an instance of bonking (*a bonk on the head*). □ **bonker** n. [imit.: cf. BANG, BUMP[1], CONK[2]]

bonkers /ˈbɒŋkəz/ adj. *sl.* crazy. [20th c.: orig. unkn.]

bonnet /ˈbɒnɪt/ n. **1 a** a woman's or child's hat tied under the chin and usu. with a brim framing the face. **b** a soft round brimless hat like a beret worn by men and boys in Scotland. **2** *Brit.* a hinged cover over the engine of a motor vehicle. **3** the ceremonial head-dress of an American Indian. □ **bonneted** adj. [ME f. OF *bonet* short for *chapel de bonet* cap of some kind of material (med.L *bonetus*)]

bonny /ˈbɒnɪ/ adj. (**bonnier**, **bonniest**) esp. *Sc.* & *N.Engl.* **1 a** physically attractive. **b** healthy-looking. **2** good, fine, pleasant. □ **bonnily** adv. **bonniness** n. [16th c.: perh. f. F *bon* good]

bonsai /ˈbɒnsaɪ/ n. (*pl.* same) **1** the art of cultivating artificially dwarfed varieties of trees and shrubs. **2** a tree or shrub grown by this method. [Jap.]

bonus /ˈbəʊnəs/ n. **1** an unsought or unexpected extra benefit. **2 a** a usu. seasonal gratuity to employees beyond their normal pay. **b** an extra dividend or issue paid to the shareholders of a company. **c** a distribution of profits to holders of an insurance policy. [L *bonus, bonum* good (thing)]

bon voyage /ˌbɔ̃ vwaːˈjɑːʒ, vɔɪˈjɑːʒ/ int. & n. an expression of good wishes to a departing traveller. [F]

bony /ˈbəʊnɪ/ adj. (**bonier**, **boniest**) **1** (of a person) thin with prominent bones. **2** having many bones. **3** of or like bone. □ **boniness** n.

bonze /bɒnz/ n. a Japanese or Chinese Buddhist priest. [F *bonze* or Port. *bonzo* perh. f. Jap. *bonzō* f. Chin. *fanseng* religious person, or f. Jap. *bō-zi* f. Chin. *fasi* teacher of the law]

bonzer /ˈbɒnzə(r)/ adj. *Austral. sl.* excellent, first-rate. [perh. f. BONANZA]

boo int., n., & v. —int. **1** an expression of disapproval or contempt. **2** a sound, made esp. to a child, intended to surprise. —n. an utterance of *boo*, esp. as an expression of disapproval or contempt made to a performer etc. —v. (**boos**, **booed**) **1** *intr.* utter a boo or boos. **2** *tr.* jeer at (a performer etc.) by booing. [imit.]

boob[1] *n. & v. sl.* —*n.* **1** *Brit.* an embarrassing mistake. **2** a simpleton. —*v.intr. Brit.* make an embarrassing mistake. [abbr. of BOOBY]

boob[2] *n. sl.* a woman's breast. □ **boob tube** *sl.* **1** a woman's low-cut close-fitting usu. strapless top. **2** (usu. prec. by *the*) *US* television; one's television set. [earlier *bubby*, *booby*, of uncert. orig.]

booboo /ˈbuːbuː/ *n. sl.* a mistake. [BOOB[1]]

boobook /ˈbuːbʊk, ˈbʊəbʊək/ *n. Austral.* a brown spotted owl, *Ninox novae-seelandiae*, native to Australia and New Zealand. [imit. of its call]

booby /ˈbuːbɪ/ *n.* (*pl.* **-ies**) **1** a stupid or childish person. **2** a small gannet of the genus *Sula*. □ **booby prize** a prize given to the least successful competitor in any contest. **booby trap 1** a trap intended as a practical joke. **2** *Mil.* an apparently harmless explosive device intended to kill or injure anyone touching it. **booby-trap** *v.tr.* place a booby trap or traps in or on. [prob. f. Sp. *bobo* (in both senses) f. L *balbus* stammering]

boodle /ˈbuːd(ə)l/ *n. sl.* money, esp. when gained or used dishonestly. [Du. *boedel* possessions]

boogie /ˈbuːgɪ/ *v. & n.* —*v.intr.* (**boogies**, **boogied**, **boogying**) *sl.* dance energetically to pop music. —*n.* **1** = BOOGIE-WOOGIE. **2** *sl.* a dance to pop music. [BOOGIE-WOOGIE]

boogie-woogie /ˌbuːgɪˈwuːgɪ/ *n.* a style of playing blues or jazz on the piano, marked by a persistent bass rhythm. [20th c.: orig. unkn.]

book /bʊk/ *n. & v.* —*n.* **1 a** a written or printed work consisting of pages glued or sewn together along one side and bound in covers. **b** a literary composition intended for publication (*is working on her book*). **2** a bound set of blank sheets for writing or keeping records in. **3** a set of tickets, stamps, matches, cheques, samples of cloth, etc., bound up together. **4** (in *pl.*) a set of records or accounts. **5** a main division of a literary work, or of the Bible. **6** (in full **book of words**) a libretto, script of a play, etc. **7** *colloq.* a magazine. **8** a telephone directory (*his number's in the book*). **9** a record of bets made and money paid out at a race meeting by a bookmaker. —*v.* **1** *tr.* **a** engage (a seat etc.) in advance; make a reservation of. **b** engage (a guest, supporter, etc.) for some occasion. **2** *tr.* **a** take the personal details of (an offender or rule-breaker). **b** enter in a book or list. **3** *tr.* issue a railway etc. ticket to. **4** *intr.* make a reservation (*no need to book*). □ **book club** a society which sells its members selected books on special terms. **book-end** a usu. ornamental prop used to keep a row of books upright. **book in** esp. *Brit.* register one's arrival at a hotel etc. **book-plate** a decorative label stuck in the front of a book bearing the owner's name. **book-rest** an adjustable support for an open book on a table. **book token** *Brit.* a voucher which can be exchanged for books to a specified value. **book up 1** buy tickets in advance for a theatre, concert, holiday, etc. **2** (as **booked up**) with all places reserved. **bring to book** call to account. **closed** (or **sealed**) **book** a subject of which one is ignorant. **go by the book** proceed according to the rules. **the good Book** the Bible. **in a person's bad** (or **good**) **books** in disfavour (or favour) with a person. **in my book** in my opinion. **make a book** take bets and pay out winnings at a race meeting. **on the books** contained in a list of members etc. **suits my book** is convenient to me. **take a**

leaf out of a person's book imitate a person. **throw the book at** *colloq.* charge or punish to the utmost. [OE *bōc*, *bōcian*, f. Gmc, usu. taken to be rel. to BEECH (the bark of which was used for writing on)]

bookbinder /ˈbʊkˌbaɪndə(r)/ *n.* a person who binds books professionally. □ **bookbinding** *n.*

bookcase /ˈbʊkkeɪs/ *n.* a set of shelves for books in the form of a cabinet.

bookie /ˈbʊkɪ/ *n. colloq.* = BOOKMAKER.

booking /ˈbʊkɪŋ/ *n.* the act or an instance of booking or reserving a seat, a room in a hotel, etc.; a reservation (see BOOK *v.* 1).

bookish /ˈbʊkɪʃ/ *adj.* **1** studious; fond of reading. **2** acquiring knowledge from books rather than practical experience. **3** (of a word, language, etc.) literary; not colloquial. □ **bookishly** *adv.* **bookishness** *n.*

bookkeeper /ˈbʊkˌkiːpə(r)/ *n.* a person who keeps accounts for a trader, a public office, etc. □ **bookkeeping** *n.*

booklet /ˈbʊklɪt/ *n.* a small book consisting of a few sheets usu. with paper covers.

bookmaker /ˈbʊkˌmeɪkə(r)/ *n.* a person who takes bets, esp. on horse-races, calculates odds, and pays out winnings. □ **bookmaking** *n.*

bookmark /ˈbʊkmaːk/ *n.* (also **bookmarker**) a strip of leather, card, etc., used to mark one's place in a book.

bookseller /ˈbʊkˌselə(r)/ *n.* a dealer in books.

bookshop /ˈbʊkʃɒp/ *n.* a shop where books are sold.

bookstall /ˈbʊkstɔːl/ *n.* a stand for selling books, newspapers, etc., esp. out of doors or at a station.

bookstore /ˈbʊkstɔː(r)/ *n. US* = BOOKSHOP.

bookworm /ˈbʊkwɜːm/ *n.* **1** *colloq.* a person devoted to reading. **2** the larva of a moth or beetle which feeds on the paper and glue used in books.

Boolean /ˈbuːlɪən/ *adj.* denoting a system of algebraic notation to represent logical propositions. □ **Boolean logic** the use of the logical operators 'and', 'or', and 'not' in retrieving information from a computer database. [G. *Boole*, Engl. mathematician d. 1864]

boom[1] /buːm/ *n. & v.* —*n.* a deep resonant sound. —*v.intr.* make or speak with a boom. [imit.]

boom[2] /buːm/ *n. & v.* —*n.* a period of prosperity or sudden activity in commerce. —*v.intr.* (esp. of commercial ventures) be suddenly prosperous or successful. □ **boomlet** *n.* [19th-c. US word, perhaps f. BOOM[1] (cf. *make things hum*)]

boom[3] /buːm/ *n.* **1** *Naut.* a pivoted spar to which the foot of a sail is attached, allowing the angle of the sail to be changed. **2** a long pole over a film or television set, carrying microphones and other equipment. **3** a floating barrier across the mouth of a harbour or river. [Du., = BEAM *n.*]

boomerang /ˈbuːməˌræŋ/ *n. & v.* —*n.* **1** a curved flat hardwood missile used by Australian Aboriginals to kill prey, and often of a kind able to return in flight to the thrower. **2** a plan or scheme that recoils on its originator. —*v.intr.* (of a plan or action) backfire. [Aboriginal name, perh. modified]

boon[1] /buːn/ *n.* **1** an advantage; a blessing. **2** *archaic* **a** a thing asked for; a request. **b** a gift; a favour. [ME, orig. = prayer, f. ON *bón* f. Gmc]

boon[2] /buːn/ adj. close, intimate, favourite (usu. *boon companion*). [ME (orig. = jolly, congenial) f. OF *bon* f. L *bonus* good]

boor /bʊə(r)/ n. 1 a rude, ill-mannered person. 2 a clumsy person. □ **boorish** adj. **boorishly** adv. **boorishness** n. [LG *būr* or Du. *boer* farmer]

boost /buːst/ v. & n. colloq. —v.tr. 1 a promote or increase the reputation of (a person, scheme, commodity, etc.) by praise or advertising; push; increase or assist (*boosted his spirits; boost sales*). b push from behind; assist (*boosted me up the tree*). 2 a raise the voltage in (an electric circuit etc.). b amplify (a radio signal). —n. an act, process, or result of boosting; a push (*asked for a boost up the hill*). [19th-c. US word: orig. unkn.]

booster /ˈbuːstə(r)/ n. 1 a device for increasing electrical power or voltage. 2 an auxiliary engine or rocket used to give initial acceleration. 3 *Med.* a dose of an immunizing agent increasing or renewing the effect of an earlier one.

boot[1] /buːt/ n. & v. —n. 1 an outer covering for the foot, reaching above the ankle. 2 *Brit.* the luggage compartment of a motor car. 3 colloq. a firm kick. 4 (prec. by *the*) colloq. dismissal, esp. from employment (*gave them the boot*). —v.tr. 1 kick, esp. hard. 2 (often foll. by *out*) dismiss (a person) forcefully. 3 (usu. foll. by *up*) put (a computer) in a state of readiness (cf. BOOTSTRAP 2). □ **put the boot in 1** kick brutally. 2 act decisively against a person. □ **booted** adj. [ME f. ON *bóti* or f. OF *bote*, of unkn. orig.]

boot[2] /buːt/ n. □ **to boot** as well; to the good; in addition. [orig. = 'advantage': OE *bōt* f. Gmc]

bootee /buːˈtiː/ n. 1 a soft shoe, esp. a woollen one, worn by a baby. 2 a woman's short boot.

booth /buːð, buːθ/ n. 1 a small temporary roofed structure of canvas, wood, etc., used esp. as a market stall, for puppet shows, etc. 2 an enclosure or compartment for various purposes, e.g. telephoning or voting. 3 a set of a table and benches in a restaurant or bar. [ME f. Scand.]

bootlace /ˈbuːtleɪs/ n. a cord or leather thong for lacing boots.

bootleg /ˈbuːtleg/ adj. & v. —adj. (esp. of liquor) smuggled; illicitly sold. —v.tr. (**-legged**, **-legging**) make, distribute, or smuggle illicit goods (esp. alcohol). □ **bootlegger** n. [f. the smugglers' practice of concealing bottles in their boots]

bootless /ˈbuːtlɪs/ adj. archaic unavailing, useless. [OE *bōtlēas* (as BOOT[2], LESS)]

bootlicker /ˈbuːtˌlɪkə(r)/ n. colloq. a person who behaves obsequiously or servilely; a toady.

bootstrap /ˈbuːtstræp/ n. 1 a loop at the back of a boot used to pull it on. 2 *Computing* a technique of loading a program into a computer by means of a few initial instructions which enable the introduction of the rest of the program from an input device.

booty /ˈbuːtɪ/ n. 1 plunder gained esp. in war or by piracy. 2 colloq. something gained or won. [ME f. MLG *būte, buite* exchange, of uncert. orig.]

booze /buːz/ n. & v. colloq. —n. 1 alcoholic drink. 2 the drinking of this (*on the booze*). —v.intr. drink alcoholic liquor, esp. excessively or habitually. □ **booze-up** sl. a drinking bout. [earlier *bouse, bowse*, f. MDu. *būsen* drink to excess]

boozer /ˈbuːzə(r)/ n. colloq. 1 a person who drinks alcohol, esp. to excess. 2 *Brit.* a public house.

boozy /ˈbuːzɪ/ adj. (**boozier, booziest**) colloq. intoxicated; addicted to drink. □ **boozily** adv. **booziness** n.

bop[1] n. & v. colloq. —n. 1 = BEBOP. 2 a a spell of dancing, esp. to pop music. b an organized social occasion for this. —v.intr. (**bopped, bopping**) dance, esp. to pop music. □ **bopper** n. [abbr. of BEBOP]

bop[2] v. & n. colloq. —v.tr. (**bopped, bopping**) hit, punch lightly. —n. a light blow or hit. [imit.]

boracic /bəˈræsɪk/ adj. of borax; containing boron. □ **boracic acid** = boric acid. [med.L *borax -acis*]

borage /ˈbɒrɪdʒ/ n. any plant of the genus *Borago*, esp. *Borago officinalis* with bright blue flowers and leaves used as flavouring. [OF *bourrache* f. med.L *borrago* f. Arab. *'abu 'āraḳ* father of sweat (from its use as a diaphoretic)]

borak /ˈbɔːræk/ n. *Austral.* & *NZ* sl. banter, ridicule. [Aboriginal Austral.]

borate /ˈbɔːreɪt/ n. a salt or ester of boric acid.

borax /ˈbɔːræks/ n. 1 the mineral salt sodium borate. 2 the purified form of this salt, used in making glass and china, and as an antiseptic. [ME f. OF *boras* f. med.L *borax* f. Arab. *būraḳ* f. Pers. *būrah*]

Bordeaux /bɔːˈdəʊ/ n. (pl. same /-ˈdəʊz/) any of various wines from the district of Bordeaux in SW France. □ **Bordeaux mixture** a fungicide composed of copper sulphate and calcium oxide in water.

bordello /bɔːˈdeləʊ/ n. (pl. **-os**) esp. *US* a brothel. [ME (f. It. *bordello*) f. OF *bordel* small farm, dimin. of *borde* ult. f. Frank.: see BOARD]

border /ˈbɔːdə(r)/ n. & v. —n. 1 the edge or boundary of anything, or the part near it. 2 a the line separating two political or geographical areas, esp. countries. b the district on each side of this. 3 a distinct edging round anything, esp. for strength or decoration. 4 a long narrow bed of flowers or shrubs in a garden. —v. 1 tr. be a border to. 2 tr. provide with a border. 3 intr. (usu. foll. by *on, upon*) a adjoin; come close to being. b approximate, resemble. [ME f. OF *bordure*: cf. BOARD]

borderer /ˈbɔːdərə(r)/ n. a person who lives near a border, esp. that between Scotland and England.

borderland /ˈbɔːdəˌlænd/ n. 1 the district near a border. 2 an intermediate condition between two extremes. 3 an area for debate.

borderline /ˈbɔːdəˌlaɪn/ n. & adj. —n. 1 the line dividing two conditions. 2 a line marking a boundary. —adj. 1 on the borderline. 2 verging on an extreme condition; only just acceptable.

bore[1] v. & n. —v. 1 tr. make a hole in, esp. with a revolving tool. 2 tr. hollow out (a tube etc.). 3 tr. make (a hole) by boring or excavation. 4 intr. drill a well (for oil etc.). —n. 1 the hollow of a firearm barrel or of a cylinder in an internal-combustion engine. 2 the diameter of this; the calibre. 3 = BOREHOLE. □ **borer** n. [OE *borian* f. Gmc]

bore[2] n. & v. —n. a tiresome or dull person or thing. —v.tr. weary by tedious talk or dullness. [18th c.: orig. unkn.]

bore[3] n. a high tidal wave rushing up a narrow estuary. [ME, perh. f. ON *bára* wave]

bore[4] past of BEAR[1].

boreal /ˈbɔːrɪəl/ *adj.* of the North or northern regions. [ME f. F *boréal* or LL *borealis* f. L *Boreas* f. Gk *Boreas* god of the north wind]

boredom /ˈbɔːdəm/ *n.* the state of being bored; ennui.

borehole /ˈbɔːhəʊl/ *n.* a deep narrow hole, esp. one made in the earth to find water, oil, etc.

boric /ˈbɔːrɪk/ *adj.* of or containing boron. □ **boric acid** an acid derived from borax, used as a mild antiseptic and in the manufacture of heat-resistant glass and enamels.

boring /ˈbɔːrɪŋ/ *adj.* that makes one bored; uninteresting, tedious, dull. □ **boringly** *adv.* **boringness** *n.*

born /bɔːn/ *adj.* **1** existing as a result of birth. **2 a** being such or likely to become such by natural ability or quality (*a born leader*). **b** (usu. foll. by to + infin.) having a specified destiny or prospect (*born lucky; born to be king; born to lead men*). **3** (in *comb.*) of a certain status by birth (*French-born; well-born*). □ **born-again** (*attrib.*) converted (esp. to fundamentalist Christianity). [past part. of BEAR[1]]

borne /bɔːn/ **1** *past part.* of BEAR[1]. **2** (in *comb.*) carried or transported by (*airborne*).

boron /ˈbɔːrɒn/ *n. Chem.* a non-metallic element extracted from borax and boracic acid and mainly used for hardening steel. [BORAX + -*on* f. *carbon* (which it resembles in some respects)]

borough /ˈbʌrə/ *n.* **1** *Brit.* **a** a town represented in the House of Commons. **b** a town or district granted the status of a borough. **2** *Brit. hist.* a town with a municipal corporation and privileges conferred by a royal charter. **3** *US* a municipal corporation in certain States. [OE *burg, burh* f. Gmc: cf. BURGH]

borrow /ˈbɒrəʊ/ *v.* **1 a** *tr.* acquire temporarily with the promise or intention of returning. **b** *intr.* obtain money in this way. **2** *tr.* use (an idea, invention, etc.) originated by another; plagiarize. □ **borrowed time** an unexpected extension esp. of life. □ **borrower** *n.* **borrowing** *n.* [OE *borgian* give a pledge]

Borstal /ˈbɔːst(ə)l/ *n. Brit. hist.* an institution for reforming and training young offenders. [*Borstal* in S. England, where the first of these was established]

■ **Usage** This term has now been replaced by *detention centre* and *youth custody centre*.

bortsch /bɔːtʃ/ *n.* (also **borsch** /bɔːʃ/) a highly seasoned Russian or Polish soup with various ingredients including beetroot and cabbage and served with sour cream. [Russ. *borshch*]

borzoi /ˈbɔːzɔɪ/ *n.* **1** a large Russian wolfhound of a breed with a narrow head and silky, usu. white, coat. **2** this breed. [Russ. f. *borzyi* swift]

bosh *n.* & *int. sl.* nonsense; foolish talk. [Turk. *boş* empty]

bosky /ˈbɒskɪ/ *adj.* (**boskier, boskiest**) *literary* wooded, bushy. [ME *bosk* thicket]

bo's'n var. of BOATSWAIN.

bosom /ˈbʊz(ə)m/ *n.* **1 a** a person's breast or chest, esp. a woman's. **b** *colloq.* each of a woman's breasts. **c** the enclosure formed by a person's breast and arms. **2** an emotional centre, esp. as the source of an enfolding relationship (*in the bosom of one's family*). **3** the part of a woman's dress covering the breast. □ **bosom friend** a very close or intimate friend. [OE *bōsm* f. Gmc]

bosomy /ˈbʊzəmɪ/ *adj.* (of a woman) having large breasts.

boss[1] *n.* & *v. colloq.* —*n.* **1** a person in charge; an employer, manager, or overseer. **2** *US* a person who controls or dominates a political organization. —*v.tr.* **1** (usu. foll. by *about, around*) treat domineeringly; give peremptory orders to. **2** be the master or manager of. [orig. US: f. Du. *baas* master]

boss[2] *n.* **1** a round knob, stud, or other protuberance, esp. on the centre of a shield or in ornamental work. **2** *Archit.* a piece of ornamental carving etc. covering the point where the ribs in a vault or ceiling cross. [ME f. OF *boce* f. Rmc]

bossa nova /ˌbɒsə ˈnəʊvə/ *n.* **1** a dance like the samba, originating in Brazil. **2** a piece of music for this or in its rhythm. [Port., = new flair]

boss-eyed /ˈbɒsaɪd/ *adj. Brit. colloq.* **1** having only one good eye; cross-eyed. **2** crooked; out of true. [dial. *boss* miss, bungle]

boss-shot /ˈbɒsʃɒt/ *n. Brit. dial.* & *sl.* **1** a bad shot or aim. **2** an unsuccessful attempt. [as BOSS-EYED]

bossy /ˈbɒsɪ/ *adj.* (**bossier, bossiest**) *colloq.* domineering; tending to boss. □ **bossily** *adv.* **bossiness** *n.*

bosun (also **bo'sun**) var. of BOATSWAIN.

bot *n.* (also **bott**) any of various parasitic larvae of flies of the family Oestridae, infesting horses, sheep, etc. □ **bot-fly** (*pl.* **-flies**) any dipterous fly of the genus *Oestrus*. [prob. of LG orig.]

botanize /ˈbɒtənaɪz/ *v.intr.* (also **-ise**) study plants, esp. in their habitat.

botany /ˈbɒtənɪ/ *n.* **1** the study of the physiology, structure, genetics, ecology, distribution, classification, and economic importance of plants. **2** the plant life of a particular area or time. □ **botanic** /bəˈtænɪk/ *adj.* **botanical** /bəˈtænɪk(ə)l/ *adj.* **botanically** /bəˈtænɪkəlɪ/ *adv.* **botanist** *n.* [*botanic* f. F *botanique* or LL *botanicus* f. Gk *botanikos* f. *botanē* plant]

botch *v.* & *n.* (also **bodge**) —*v.tr.* **1** bungle; do badly. **2** patch or repair clumsily. —*n.* bungled or spoilt work (*made a botch of it*). □ **botcher** *n.* [ME: orig. unkn.]

both /bəʊθ/ *adj.*, *pron.*, & *adv.* —*adj.* & *pron.* the two, not only one (*both boys; both the boys; both of the boys; the boys are both here*). —*adv.* with equal truth in two cases (*both the boy and his sister are here; are both here and hungry*). □ **both ways** = each way. [ME f. ON *báthir*]

bother /ˈbɒðə(r)/ *v.*, *n.*, & *int.* —*v.* **1** *tr.* **a** give trouble to; worry, disturb. **b** *refl.* (often foll. by *about*) be anxious or concerned. **2** *intr.* **a** (often foll. by *about*, or *to* + infin.) worry or trouble oneself (*don't bother about that; didn't bother to tell me*). **b** (foll. by *with*) be concerned. —*n.* **1 a** person or thing that bothers or causes worry. **b** a minor nuisance. **2** trouble, worry, fuss. —*int.* esp. *Brit.* expressing annoyance or impatience. □ **cannot be bothered** will not make the effort needed. [Ir. *bodhraim* deafen]

botheration /ˌbɒðəˈreɪʃ(ə)n/ *n.* & *int. colloq.* = BOTHER *n.*, *int.*

bothersome /ˈbɒðəsəm/ *adj.* causing bother; troublesome.

bo-tree /ˈbəʊtriː/ *n.* the Indian fig-tree, *Ficus religiosa*, regarded as sacred by Buddhists. [repr. Sinh. *bogaha* tree of knowledge (Buddha's enlightenment having occurred beneath such a tree)]

bottle /'bɒt(ə)l/ *n. & v.* —*n.* **1** a container, usu. of glass or plastic and with a narrow neck, for storing liquid. **2** the amount that will fill a bottle. **3** a baby's feeding-bottle. **4** = *hot-water bottle*. **5** a metal cylinder for liquefied gas. **6** *Brit. sl.* courage, confidence. —*v.tr.* **1** put into bottles or jars. **2** preserve (fruit etc.) in jars. **3** (foll. by *up*) **a** conceal or restrain for a time (esp. a feeling). **b** keep (an enemy force etc.) contained or entrapped. □ **bottle bank** a place where used bottles may be deposited for recycling. **bottle-green** a dark shade of green. **bottle party** a party to which guests bring bottles of drink. **hit the bottle** *sl.* drink heavily. **on the bottle** *sl.* drinking (alcoholic drink) heavily. □ **bottleful** *n.* (*pl.* **-fuls**) [ME f. OF *botele*, *botaille* f. med.L *butticula* dimin. of LL *buttis* BUTT⁴]

bottleneck /'bɒt(ə)l₁nek/ *n.* **1** a point at which the flow of traffic, production, etc., is constricted. **2** a narrow place causing constriction.

bottlenose /'bɒt(ə)l₁nəʊz/ *n.* (also **bottlenosed**) a swollen nose. □ **bottlenose dolphin** a dolphin, *Tursiops truncatus*, with a bottle-shaped snout.

bottler /'bɒtlə(r)/ *n.* **1** a person who bottles drinks etc. **2** *Austral. & NZ sl.* an excellent person or thing.

bottom /'bɒtəm/ *n., adj., & v.* —*n.* **1 a** the lowest point or part (*bottom of the stairs*). **b** the part on which a thing rests (*bottom of a saucepan*). **c** the underneath part (*scraped the bottom of the car*). **d** the furthest or inmost part (*bottom of the garden*). **2** *colloq.* **a** the buttocks. **b** the seat of a chair etc. **3 a** the less honourable, important, or successful end of a table, a class, etc. (*at the bottom of the list of requirements*). **b** a person occupying this place (*he's always bottom of the class*). **4** the ground under the water of a lake, a river, etc. (*swam until he touched the bottom*). **5** the basis; the origin (*he's at the bottom of it*). **6** the essential character; reality. **7** *Naut.* **a** the keel or hull of a ship. **b** a ship, esp. as a cargo-carrier. **8** staying power; endurance. —*adj.* **1** lowest (*bottom button*). **2** last (*got the bottom score*). —*v.* **1** *tr.* put a bottom to (a chair, saucepan, etc.). **2** *intr.* (of a ship) reach or touch the bottom. **3** *tr.* find the extent or real nature of; work out. **4** *tr.* touch the bottom or lowest point of. □ **at bottom** basically, essentially. **be at the bottom of** have caused. **bottom falls out** collapse occurs. **bottom line** *colloq.* the underlying or ultimate truth; the ultimate, esp. financial, criterion. **bottom out** reach the lowest level. **bottoms up!** a call to drain one's glass. **bottom up** upside-down. **get to the bottom of** fully investigate and explain. **knock the bottom out of** prove (a thing) worthless. □ **bottommost** /'bɒtəm₁məʊst/ *adj.* [OE *botm* f. Gmc]

bottomless /'bɒtəmlɪs/ *adj.* **1** without a bottom. **2** (of a supply etc.) inexhaustible.

botulism /'bɒtjʊ₁lɪz(ə)m/ *n.* poisoning caused by a toxin produced by the bacillus *Clostridium botulinum* growing in poorly preserved food. [G *Botulismus* f. L *botulus* sausage]

bouclé /'buːkleɪ/ *n.* **1** a looped or curled yarn (esp. wool). **2** a fabric, esp. knitted, made of this. [F, = buckled, curled]

boudoir /'buːdwɑː(r)/ *n.* a woman's small private room or bedroom. [F, lit. sulking-place f. *bouder* sulk]

bouffant /'buːfɑ̃/ *adj.* (of a dress, hair, etc.) puffed out. [F]

bougainvillaea /₁buːgən'vɪlɪə/ *n.* any tropical widely cultivated plant of the genus *Bougainvillaea*, with large coloured bracts. [L. A. de *Bougainville*, Fr. navigator d. 1811]

bough /baʊ/ *n.* a branch of a tree, esp. a main one. [OE *bōg, bōh* f. Gmc]

bought *past* and *past part.* of BUY.

bouillon /'buːjɔ̃, 'buːjɒn/ *n.* thin soup; broth. [F f. *bouillir* to boil]

boulder /'bəʊldə(r)/ *n.* a large stone worn smooth by erosion. [short for *boulderstone*, ME f. Scand.]

boule¹ /buːl/ *n.* (also **boules** *pronunc.* same) a French form of bowls, played on rough ground with usu. metal balls. [F, = BOWL²]

boule² var. of BUHL.

boulevard /'buːləvɑːd, 'buːlvɑː(r)/ *n.* **1** a broad tree-lined avenue. **2** esp. *US* a broad main road. [F f. G *Bollwerk* BULWARK, orig. of a promenade on a demolished fortification]

boulle var. of BUHL.

boult var. of BOLT².

bounce /baʊns/ *v. & n.* —*v.* **1 a** *intr.* (of a ball etc.) rebound. **b** *tr.* cause to rebound. **c** *tr. & intr.* bounce repeatedly. **2** *intr. sl.* (of a cheque) be returned by a bank when there are insufficient funds to meet it. **3** *intr.* **a** (foll. by *about, up*) (of a person, dog, etc.) jump or spring energetically. **b** (foll. by *in, out*, etc.) rush noisily, angrily, enthusiastically, etc. (*bounced into the room*; *bounced out in a temper*). **4** *tr. colloq.* (usu. foll. by *into* + *verbal noun*) hustle, persuade (*bounced him into signing*). —*n.* **1 a** a rebound. **b** the power of rebounding (*this ball has a good bounce*). **2** *colloq.* **a** swagger, self-confidence. **b** liveliness. □ **bounce back** regain one's good health, spirits, prosperity, etc. [ME *bunsen* beat, thump, (perh. imit.), or f. LG *bunsen*, Du. *bons* thump]

bouncer /'baʊnsə(r)/ *n.* **1** *sl.* a person employed to eject troublemakers from a dancehall, club, etc. **2** *Cricket* = BUMPER.

bouncing /'baʊnsɪŋ/ *adj.* **1** (esp. of a baby) big and healthy. **2** boisterous.

bouncy /'baʊnsɪ/ *adj.* (**bouncier, bounciest**) **1** (of a ball etc.) that bounces well. **2** cheerful and lively. **3** resilient, springy (*a bouncy sofa*). □ **bouncily** *adv.* **bounciness** *n.*

bound¹ /baʊnd/ *v. & n.* —*v.intr.* **1 a** spring, leap (*bounded out of bed*). **b** walk or run with leaping strides. **2** (of a ball etc.) recoil from a wall or the ground; bounce. —*n.* **1** a springy movement upwards or outwards; a leap. **2** a bounce. [F *bond, bondir* (orig. of sound) f. LL *bombitare* f. L *bombus* hum]

bound² /baʊnd/ *n. & v.* —*n.* (usu. in *pl.*) **1** a limitation; a restriction (*beyond the bounds of possibility*). **2** a border of a territory; a boundary. —*v.tr.* **1** (esp. in *passive*; foll. by *by*) set bounds to; limit (*views bounded by prejudice*). **2** be the boundary of. □ **out of bounds 1** outside the part of a school etc. in which one is allowed to be. **2** beyond what is acceptable; forbidden. [ME f. AF *bounde*, OF *bonde* etc., f. med.L *bodina*, earlier *butina*, of unkn. orig.]

bound³ /baʊnd/ *adj.* **1** (usu. foll. by *for*) ready to start or having started (*bound for stardom*). **2** (in *comb.*) moving in a specified direction (*north-bound; outward bound*). [ME f. ON *búinn* past part. of *búa* get ready: *-d* euphonic, or partly after BIND¹]

bound⁴ /baʊnd/ *past* and *past part.* of BIND. □ **bound to** certain to (*he's bound to come*).

boundary /'baʊndərɪ, -drɪ/ n. (pl. **-ies**) **1** a line marking the limits of an area, territory, etc. (*the fence is the boundary; boundary between liberty and licence*). **2** *Cricket* a hit crossing the limits of the field, scoring 4 or 6 runs. [dial. *bounder* f. BOUND² + -ER¹ perh. after *limitary*]

bounden /'baʊnd(ə)n/ adj. *archaic* obligatory. □ **bounden duty** solemn responsibility. [archaic past part. of BIND]

bounder /'baʊndə(r)/ n. *colloq.* or *joc.* a cad; an ill-bred person.

boundless /'baʊndlɪs/ adj. unlimited; immense (*boundless enthusiasm*). □ **boundlessly** adv. **boundlessness** n.

bounteous /'baʊntɪəs/ adj. *poet.* **1** generous, liberal. **2** freely given (*bounteous affection*). □ **bounteously** adv. **bounteousness** n. [ME f. OF *bontif* f. *bonté* BOUNTY after *plenteous*]

bountiful /'baʊntɪˌfʊl/ adj. **1** = BOUNTEOUS. **2** ample. □ **bountifully** adv. [BOUNTY + -FUL]

bounty /'baʊntɪ/ n. (pl. **-ies**) **1** liberality; generosity. **2** a gift or reward, made usu. by the State. [ME f. OF *bonté* f. L *bonitas -tatis* f. *bonus* good]

bouquet /buː'keɪ, bɔʊ-/ n. **1** a bunch of flowers, esp. for carrying at a wedding or other ceremony. **2** the scent of wine etc. **3** a favourable comment; a compliment. □ **bouquet garni** /'ɡɑːnɪ/ *Cookery* a bunch of herbs used for flavouring stews etc. [F f. dial. var. of OF *bos*, *bois* wood]

bourbon /'bɜːbən, 'bʊə-/ n. *US* whisky distilled from maize and rye. [*Bourbon* County, Kentucky, where it was first made]

bourgeois /'bʊəʒwɑː/ adj. & n. often *derog.* —adj. **1 a** conventionally middle-class. **b** humdrum, unimaginative. **c** selfishly materialistic. **2** upholding the interests of the capitalist class; non-communist. —n. a bourgeois person. [F: see BURGESS]

bourgeoisie /ˌbʊəʒwɑː'ziː/ n. **1** the capitalist class. **2** the middle class. [F]

bourn¹ /bɔːn, bʊən/ n. a small stream. [ME: S. Engl. var. of BURN²]

bourn² /bɔːn, bʊən/ n. (also **bourne**) *archaic* **1** a goal; a destination. **2** a limit. [F *borne* f. OF *bodne* BOUND²]

bourse /bʊəs/ n. **1** (**Bourse**) the Paris equivalent of the Stock Exchange. **2** a money-market. [F, = purse, f. med.L *bursa*: cf. PURSE¹]

bout /baʊt/ n. (often foll. by *of*) **1 a** a limited period (of intensive work or exercise). **b** a drinking session. **c** a period (of illness) (*a bout of flu*). **2 a** a wrestling- or boxing-match. **b** a trial of strength. [16th c.: app. the same as obs. *bought* bending]

boutique /buː'tiːk/ n. a small shop or department of a store, selling (esp. fashionable) clothes or accessories. [F, = small shop, f. L *apotheca*]

bouzouki /buː'zuːkɪ/ n. a Greek form of mandolin. [mod. Gk]

bovine /'bəʊvaɪn/ adj. **1** of or relating to cattle. **2** stupid, dull. □ **bovinely** adv. [LL *bovinus* f. L *bos bovis* OX]

bovver /'bɒvə(r)/ n. *Brit. sl.* deliberate trouble-making. □ **bovver boot** a heavy laced boot worn typically by skinheads. **bovver boy** a violent hooligan. [cockney pronunc. of BOTHER]

bow¹ /bəʊ/ n. & v. —n. **1 a** a slip-knot with a double loop. **b** a ribbon, shoelace, etc., tied with this. **c** a decoration (on clothing, or painted etc.) in the form of a bow. **2** a device for shooting arrows with a taut string joining the ends of a curved piece of wood etc. **3 a** a rod with horsehair stretched along its length, used for playing the violin, cello, etc. **b** a single stroke of a bow over strings. **4 a** a shallow curve or bend. **b** a rainbow. **5** *US* the side-piece of a spectacle-frame. —v.tr. (also *absol.*) use a bow on (a violin etc.) (*he bowed vigorously*). □ **bow-legged** having bandy legs. **bow-legs** bandy legs. **bow-saw** *Carpentry* a narrow saw stretched like a bowstring on a light frame. **bow-tie** a necktie in the form of a bow (sense 1). **bow-window** a curved bay window. [OE *boga* f. Gmc: cf. BOW²]

bow² /baʊ/ v. & n. —v. **1** *intr.* incline the head or trunk, esp. in greeting or assent or acknowledgement of applause. **2** *intr.* submit (*bowed to the inevitable*). **3** *tr.* cause to incline (*bowed his head; bowed his will to hers*). **4** *tr.* (foll. by *in, out*) usher or escort obsequiously (*bowed us out of the restaurant*). —n. an inclining of the head or body in greeting, assent, or in the acknowledgement of applause, etc. □ **bow down 1** bend or kneel in submission or reverence (*bowed down before the king*). **2** (usu. in *passive*) make stoop; crush (*was bowed down by care*). **bow out 1** make one's exit (esp. formally). **2** retreat, withdraw; retire gracefully. **make one's bow** make a formal exit or entrance. **take a bow** acknowledge applause. [OE *būgan*, f. Gmc: cf. BOW¹]

bow³ /baʊ/ n. *Naut.* **1** (often in *pl.*) the fore-end of a boat or a ship. **2** = BOWMAN². □ **shot across the bows** a warning. [LG *boog*, Du. *boeg*, ship's bow, orig. shoulder: see BOUGH]

bowdlerize /'baʊdləˌraɪz/ v.tr. (also **-ise**) expurgate (a book etc.). □ **bowdlerism** n. **bowdlerization** /-'zeɪʃ(ə)n/ n. [T. *Bowdler* (d. 1825), expurgator of Shakesp.]

bowel /'baʊəl/ n. **1 a** the part of the alimentary canal below the stomach. **b** the intestine. **2** (in *pl.*) the depths; the innermost parts (*the bowels of the earth*). □ **bowel movement 1** discharge from the bowels; defecation. **2** the faeces discharged from the body. [ME f. OF *buel* f. L *botellus* little sausage]

bower /'baʊə(r)/ n. & v. —n. **1 a** a secluded place, esp. in a garden, enclosed by foliage; an arbour. **b** a summer-house. **2** *poet.* an inner room; a boudoir. —v.tr. *poet.* embower. □ **bowery** adj. [OE *būr* f. Gmc]

bowerbird /'baʊəˌbɜːd/ n. **1** any of various birds of the Ptilonorhynchidae family, native to Australia and New Guinea, the males of which construct elaborate bowers of feathers, grasses, shells, etc. during courtship. **2** a person who collects bric-à-brac.

bowery /'baʊərɪ/ n. (also **Bowery**) (pl. **-ies**) *US* a district known as a resort of drunks and down-and-outs. [orig. the Bowery, a street in New York City, f. Du. *bouwerij* farm]

bowhead /'bəʊhed/ n. an Arctic whale, *Balaena mysticetus*.

bowie /'bəʊɪ/ n. (in full **bowie knife**) a long knife with a blade double-edged at the point, used as a weapon by American pioneers. [J. *Bowie*, Amer. soldier d. 1836]

bowl¹ /bəʊl/ n. **1 a** a usu. round deep basin used for food or liquid. **b** the quantity (of soup etc.) a bowl holds. **c** the contents of a bowl. **2 a** any deep-sided container shaped like a bowl (*lavatory* *bowl*). **b** the bowl-shaped part of a tobacco-pipe, spoon, balance, etc. **3** esp. *US* a bowl-shaped region or building, esp. an amphitheatre (*Hollywood Bowl*). □ **bowlful** *n.* (*pl.* **-fuls**). [OE *bolle*, *bolla*, f. Gmc]

bowl² /bəʊl/ *n. & v.* —*n.* **1 a** a wooden or hard rubber ball, slightly asymmetrical so that it runs on a curved course, used in the game of bowls. **b** a wooden ball or disc used in playing skittles. **c** a large ball with indents for gripping, used in tenpin bowling. **2** (in *pl.*; usu. treated as *sing.*) **a** a game played with bowls (sense 1a) on grass. **b** tenpin bowling. **c** skittles. **3** a spell or turn of bowling in cricket. —*v.* **1 a** *tr.* roll (a ball, a hoop, etc.) along the ground. **b** *intr.* play bowls or skittles. **2** *tr.* (also *absol.*) *Cricket* etc. **a** deliver (a ball, an over, etc.) (*bowled six overs*; *bowled well*). **b** (often foll. by *out*) dismiss (a batsman) by knocking down the wicket with a ball. **c** (often foll. by *down*) knock (a wicket) over. **3** *intr.* (often foll. by *along*) go along rapidly by revolving, esp. on wheels (*the cart bowled along the road*). □ **bowl out** *Cricket* dismiss (a batsman or a side). **bowl over 1** knock down. **2** *colloq.* **a** impress greatly. **b** overwhelm (*bowled over by her energy*). [ME & F *boule* f. L *bulla* bubble]

bowler¹ /ˈbəʊlə(r)/ *n.* **1** *Cricket* etc. a member of the fielding side who bowls or is bowling. **2** a player at bowls.

bowler² /ˈbəʊlə(r)/ *n.* (in full **bowler hat**) a man's hard felt hat with a round dome-shaped crown. [*Bowler*, a hatter, who designed it in 1850]

bowline /ˈbəʊlɪn/ *n. Naut.* **1** a rope attaching the weather side of a square sail to the bow. **2** a simple knot for forming a non-slipping loop at the end of a rope. [ME f. MLG *bōlīne* (as BOW³, LINE¹)]

bowling /ˈbəʊlɪŋ/ *n.* the game of bowls as a sport or recreation. □ **bowling-alley 1** an enclosure for skittles or tenpin bowling. **2** a building containing these. **bowling-green** a lawn used for playing bowls.

bowman¹ /ˈbəʊmən/ *n.* (*pl.* **-men**) an archer.

bowman² /ˈbaʊmən/ *n.* (*pl.* **-men**) the rower nearest the bow of esp. a racing boat.

bowser /ˈbaʊzə(r)/ *n.* **1** a tanker used for fuelling aircraft etc. **2** *Austral.* & *NZ* a petrol pump. [trade name, orig. propr.]

bowsprit /ˈbəʊsprɪt/ *n. Naut.* a spar running out from a ship's bow to which the forestays are fastened. [ME f. Gmc (as BOW³, SPRIT)]

bowyer /ˈbəʊjə(r)/ *n.* a maker or seller of archers' bows.

box¹ *n. & v.* —*n.* **1** a container, usu. with flat sides and of firm material such as wood or card, esp. for holding solids. **2** the amount that will fill a box. **3** a separate compartment for any of various purposes, e.g. for a small group in a theatre, for witnesses in a lawcourt, for horses in a stable or vehicle. **4** an enclosure or receptacle for a special purpose (often in *comb.*: *money box*; *telephone box*). **5** a facility at a newspaper office for receiving replies to an advertisement. **6** (prec. by *the*) *colloq.* television; one's television set (*what's on the box?*). **7** an enclosed area or space. **8** a space or area of print on a page, enclosed by a border. **9** a protective casing for a piece of mechanism. **10** a light shield for protecting the genitals in sport, esp. in cricket. **11** (prec. by *the*) *Football colloq.* the penalty area.

12 *Baseball* the area occupied by the batter or the pitcher. **13** a coachman's seat. —*v.tr.* **1** put in or provide with a box. **2** (foll. by *in*, *up*) confine; restrain from movement. □ **box camera** a simple box-shaped hand camera. **box girder** a hollow girder square in cross-section. **box junction** *Brit.* a road area at a junction marked with a yellow grid, which a vehicle should enter only if its exit from it is clear. **box kite** a kite in the form of a long box open at each end. **box number** a number by which replies are made to a private advertisement in a newspaper. **box office 1** an office for booking seats and buying tickets at a theatre, cinema, etc. **2** the commercial aspect of the arts and entertainment (often *attrib.*: *a box-office failure*). **box pleat** a pleat consisting of two parallel creases forming a raised band. **box spanner** a spanner with a box-shaped end fitting over the head of a nut. **box spring** each of a set of vertical springs housed in a frame, e.g. in a mattress. □ **boxful** *n.* (*pl.* **-fuls**). **boxlike** *adj.* [OE f. LL *buxis* f. L *pyxis* f. Gk *puxis* f. *puxos* box]

box² *v. & n.* —*v.* **1 a** *tr.* fight (an opponent) at boxing. **b** *intr.* practise boxing. **2** slap (esp. a person's ears). —*n.* a slap with the hand, esp. on the ears. □ **box clever** *colloq.* act in a clever or effective way. [ME: orig. unkn.]

box³ /bɒks/ *n.* **1** any small evergreen tree or shrub of the genus *Buxus*, esp. *B. sempervirens*, a slow-growing tree with glossy dark green leaves which is often used in hedging. **2** its wood. **3** any of various trees in Australasia which have similar wood or foliage, esp. those of several species of *Eucalyptus*. [OE f. L *buxus*, Gk *puxos*]

Box and Cox /ˌbɒks ənd ˈkɒks/ *n. & v.* —*n.* (often *attrib.*) two persons sharing accommodation etc., and using it at different times. —*v.intr.* share accommodation, duties, etc. by a strictly timed arrangement. [the names of characters in a play (1847) by J. M. Morton]

boxcar /ˈbɒkskɑː(r)/ *n. US* an enclosed railway goods wagon, usu. with sliding doors on the sides.

boxer /ˈbɒksə(r)/ *n.* **1** a person who practises boxing, esp. for sport. **2 a** a medium-size dog of a breed with a smooth brown coat and puglike face. **b** this breed. □ **boxer shorts** men's underpants similar to shorts worn in boxing.

boxing /ˈbɒksɪŋ/ *n.* the practice of fighting with the fists, esp. in padded gloves as a sport. □ **boxing glove** each of a pair of heavily padded gloves used in boxing. **boxing weight** each of a series of fixed weight-ranges at which boxers are matched.

Boxing Day /ˈbɒksɪŋ/ *n.* the first weekday after Christmas. [from the custom of giving tradesmen gifts or money]

boxroom /ˈbɒksruːm, -rʊm/ *n. Brit.* a room or large cupboard for storing boxes, cases, etc.

boxy /ˈbɒksɪ/ *adj.* (**boxier**, **boxiest**) reminiscent of a box; (of a room or space) very cramped.

boy *n. & int.* —*n.* **1** a male child or youth. **2** a young man, esp. regarded as not yet mature. **3** a male servant, attendant, etc. **4** (**the boys**) *colloq.* a group of men mixing socially. —*int.* expressing pleasure, surprise, etc. □ **boyhood** *n.* **boyish** *adj.* **boyishly** *adv.* **boyishness** *n.* [ME = servant, perh. ult. f. L *boia* fetter]

boycott /ˈbɔɪkɒt/ *v. & n.* —*v.tr.* **1** combine in refusing social or commercial relations with (a person, group, country, etc.) usu. as punishment or coercion. **2** refuse to handle (goods) to this end. —*n.* such a refusal. [Capt. C. C. Boycott, Irish land-agent d. 1897, so treated from 1880]

boyfriend /ˈbɔɪfrend/ *n.* a person's regular male companion or lover.

boysenberry /ˈbɔɪzənbərɪ/ *n.* (*pl.* **-ies**) **1** a hybrid of several species of bramble. **2** the large red edible fruit of this plant. [R. *Boysen*, 20th-c. Amer. horticulturalist]

BP *abbr* British Pharmacopoeia.

B.Phil. *abbr.* Bachelor of Philosophy.

Bq *abbr.* becquerel.

Br *symb. Chem.* the element bromine.

bra /brɑː/ *n.* (*pl.* **bras**) *colloq.* = BRASSIÈRE. [abbr.]

brace /breɪs/ *n. & v.* —*n.* **1a** a device that clamps or fastens tightly. **b** a strengthening piece of iron or timber in building. **2** (in *pl.*) *Brit.* straps supporting trousers from the shoulders. **3** a wire device for straightening the teeth. **4** (*pl.* same) a pair (esp. of game). **5** a rope attached to the yard of a ship for trimming the sail. **6 a** a connecting mark { or } used in printing. **b** *Mus.* a similar mark connecting staves to be performed at the same time. —*v.tr.* **1** fasten tightly, give firmness to. **2** make steady by supporting. **3** (esp. as **bracing** *adj.*) invigorate, refresh. **4** (often *refl.*) prepare for a difficulty, shock, etc. □ **brace and bit** a revolving tool with a D-shaped central handle for boring. □ **bracingly** *adv.* **bracingness** *n.* [ME f. OF *brace* two arms, *bracier* embrace, f. L *bra(c)chia* arms]

bracelet /ˈbreɪslɪt/ *n.* **1** an ornamental band, hoop, or chain worn on the wrist or arm. **2** *sl.* a hand-cuff. [ME f. OF, dimin. of *bracel* f. L *bracchiale* f. *bra(c)chium* arm]

bracer /ˈbreɪsə(r)/ *n. colloq.* a tonic.

brachiosaurus /ˌbreɪkɪəˈsɔːrəs, ˌbræk-/ *n.* any huge plant-eating dinosaur of the genus *Brachiosaurus* with forelegs longer than its hind legs. [mod.L f. Gk *brakhiōn* arm + *sauros* lizard]

bracken /ˈbrækən/ *n.* **1** any large coarse fern, esp. *Pteridium aquilinum*, abundant on heaths and moorlands, and in woods. **2** a mass of such ferns. [north. ME f. ON]

bracket /ˈbrækɪt/ *n. & v.* —*n.* **1** a right-angled or other support attached to and projecting from a vertical surface. **2** a shelf fixed with such a support to a wall. **3** each of a pair of marks () [] {} used to enclose words or figures. **4** a group classified as containing similar elements or falling between given limits (*income bracket*). —*v.tr.* (**bracketed, bracketing**) **1** a couple (names etc.) with a brace. **b** imply a connection or equality between. **2 a** enclose in brackets as parenthetic or spurious. **b** *Math.* enclose in brackets as having specific relations to what precedes or follows. [F *braguette* or Sp. *bragueta* codpiece, dimin. of F *brague* f. Prov. *braga* f. L *braca*, pl. *bracae* breeches]

brackish /ˈbrækɪʃ/ *adj.* (of water etc.) slightly salty. □ **brackishness** *n.* [obs. *brack* (adj.) f. MLG, MDu. *brac*]

bract *n.* a modified and often brightly coloured leaf, with a flower or an inflorescence in its axil. □ **bracteal** *adj.* **bracteate** /-tɪɪt/ *adj.* [L *bractea* thin plate, gold-leaf]

brad *n.* a thin flat nail with a head in the form of slight enlargement at the top. [var. of ME

brod goad, pointed instrument, f. ON *broddr* spike]

bradawl /ˈbrædɔːl/ *n.* a small tool with a pointed end for boring holes by hand. [BRAD + AWL]

brae /breɪ/ *n. Sc.* a steep bank or hillside. [ME f. ON *brá* eyelash]

brag *v. & n.* —*v.* (**bragged, bragging**) **1** *intr.* talk boastfully. **2** *tr.* boast about. —*n.* **1** a card-game like poker. **2** a boastful statement; boastful talk. □ **bragger** *n.* **braggingly** *adv.* [ME, orig. adj., = spirited, boastful: orig. unkn.]

braggart /ˈbrægət/ *n. & adj.* —*n.* a person given to bragging. —*adj.* boastful. [F *bragard* f. *braguer* BRAG]

Brahma /ˈbrɑːmə/ *n.* **1** the Hindu Creator. **2** the supreme divine reality in Hindu belief. [Skr., = creator]

Brahman /ˈbrɑːmən/ *n.* (also **brahman**) (*pl.* **-mans**) **1** a member of the highest Hindu class, whose members are traditionally eligible for the priesthood. **2** = BRAHMA 2. □ **Brahmanic** /-ˈmænɪk/ *adj.* **Brahmanical** /-ˈmænɪk(ə)l/ *adj.* **Brahmanism** *n.* [Skr. *brāhmaṇas* f. *brahman* priest]

Brahmin /ˈbrɑːmɪn/ *n.* **1** = BRAHMAN. **2** *US* a socially or intellectually superior person. [var. of BRAHMAN]

braid *n. & v.* —*n.* **1** a woven band of silk or thread used for edging or trimming. **2** a length of entwined hair. —*v.tr.* **1** plait or intertwine (hair or thread). **2** trim or decorate with braid. □ **braider** *n.* [OE *bregdan* f. Gmc]

Braille /breɪl/ *n. & v.* —*n.* a system of writing and printing for the blind, in which characters are represented by patterns of raised dots. —*v.tr.* print or transcribe in Braille. [L. *Braille*, Fr. teacher d. 1852, its inventor]

brain *n. & v.* —*n.* **1** an organ of soft nervous tissue contained in the skull of vertebrates, functioning as the coordinating centre of sensation, and of intellectual and nervous activity. **2** (in *pl.*) the substance of the brain, esp. as food. **3 a** a person's intellectual capacity (*has a poor brain*). **b** (often in *pl.*) intelligence; high intellectual capacity (*has a brain; has brains*). **4** (in *pl.*; prec. by *the*) *colloq.* **a** the cleverest person in a group. **b** a person who originates a complex plan or idea (*the brains behind the robbery*). **5** an electronic device with functions comparable to those of a brain. —*v.tr.* **1** dash out the brains of. **2** strike hard on the head. □ **brain-dead** suffering from brain death. **brain death** irreversible brain damage causing the end of independent respiration, regarded as indicative of death. **brain drain** *colloq.* the loss of skilled personnel by emigration. **brains** (*US* **brain**) **trust** a group of experts who give impromptu answers to questions, usu. publicly. **brain-teaser** (or **-twister**) *colloq.* a puzzle or problem. **brain trust** *US* a group of expert advisers. **on the brain** *colloq.* obsessively in one's thoughts. [OE *bræegen* f. WG]

brainchild /ˈbreɪntʃaɪld/ *n.* (*pl.* **-children**) *colloq.* an idea, plan, or invention regarded as the result of a person's mental effort.

brainless /ˈbreɪnlɪs/ *adj.* stupid, foolish.

brainpower /ˈbreɪnˌpaʊə(r)/ *n.* mental ability or intelligence.

brainstorm /ˈbreɪnstɔːm/ *n.* **1** a violent or excited outburst often as a result of a sudden mental disturbance. **2** *colloq.* mental confusion.

3 *US* a brainwave. **4** a concerted intellectual treatment of a problem by discussing spontaneous ideas about it. □ **brainstorming** *n*. (in sense 4).

brainwash /ˈbreɪnwɒʃ/ *v.tr.* subject (a person) to a prolonged process by which ideas other than and at variance with those already held are implanted in the mind. □ **brainwashing** *n*.

brainwave /ˈbreɪnweɪv/ *n*. **1** (usu. in *pl.*) an electrical impulse in the brain. **2** *colloq.* a sudden bright idea.

brainy /ˈbreɪnɪ/ *adj.* (**brainier, brainiest**) intellectually clever or active. □ **brainily** *adv.* **braininess** *n*.

braise /breɪz/ *v.tr.* fry lightly and then stew slowly with a little liquid in a closed container. [F *braiser* f. *braise* live coals]

brake[1] *n*. & *v.* —*n*. **1** (often in *pl.*) a device for checking the motion of a mechanism, esp. a wheel or vehicle, or for keeping it at rest. **2** anything that has the effect of hindering or impeding (*shortage of money was a brake on their enthusiasm*). —*v.* **1** *intr.* apply a brake. **2** *tr.* retard or stop with a brake. □ **brake drum** a cylinder attached to a wheel on which the brake shoe presses to brake. **brake horsepower** the power of an engine reckoned in terms of the force needed to brake it. **brake lining** a strip of fabric which increases the friction of the brake shoe. **brake shoe** a long curved block which presses on the brake drum to brake. **brake van** *Brit.* a railway coach or vehicle from which the train's brakes can be controlled. □ **brakeless** *adj.* [prob. obs. *brake* in sense 'machine-handle, bridle']

brake[2] *n*. a large estate car. [perh. *brake* framework; 17th c., of unkn. orig.]

brake[3] *n*. **1** a thicket. **2** brushwood. [ME f. OF *bracu*, MLG *brake* branch, stump]

brake[4] *n*. bracken. [ME, perh. shortened f. BRACKEN, -*en* being taken as a pl. ending]

bramble /ˈbræmb(ə)l/ *n*. **1** any of various thorny shrubs bearing fleshy red or black berries, esp. the blackberry bush, *Rubus fructicosus.* **2** the edible berry of these shrubs. **3** any of various other rosaceous shrubs with similar foliage, esp. the dog rose (*Rosa canina*). □ **brambly** *adj.* [OE *bræmbel* (earlier *bræmel*): see BROOM]

brambling /ˈbræmblɪŋ/ *n*. the speckled finch, *Fringilla montifringilla*, native to northern Eurasia, the male having a distinctive red breast. [G *Brämling* f. WG (cf. BRAMBLE)]

bran *n*. grain husks separated from the flour. □ **bran-tub** *Brit.* a lucky dip with prizes concealed in bran. [ME f. OF, of unkn. orig.]

branch /brɑːntʃ/ *n*. & *v.* —*n*. **1** a limb extending from a tree or bough. **2** a lateral extension or subdivision, esp. of a river, road, or railway. **3** a conceptual extension or subdivision, as of a family, knowledge, etc. **4** a local division or office etc. of a large business, as of a bank, library, etc. —*v.intr.* (often foll. by *off*) **1** diverge from the main part. **2** divide into branches. **3** (of a tree) bear or send out branches. □ **branch out** extend one's field of interest. □ **branched** *adj.* **branchlet** *n*. **branchlike** *adj.* **branchy** *adj.* [ME f. OF *branche* f. LL *branca* paw]

brand *n*. & *v.* —*n*. **1 a** a particular make of goods. **b** an identifying trade mark, label, etc. **2** (usu. foll. by *of*) a special or characteristic kind (*brand of humour*). **3** an identifying mark burned

on livestock or (formerly) prisoners etc. with a hot iron. **4** an iron used for this. **5** a piece of burning, smouldering, or charred wood. **6** a stigma; a mark of disgrace. **7** *poet.* **a** a torch. **b** a sword. —*v.tr.* **1** mark with a hot iron. **2** stigmatize; mark with disgrace (*they branded him a liar; was branded for life*). **3** impress unforgettably on one's mind. **4** assign a trademark or label to. □ **brand-new** completely or obviously new. □ **brander** *n*. [OE f. Gmc]

brandish /ˈbrændɪʃ/ *v.tr.* wave or flourish as a threat or in display. □ **brandisher** *n*. [OF *brandir* ult. f. Gmc, rel. to BRAND]

brandy /ˈbrændɪ/ *n*. (*pl.* -**ies**) a strong alcoholic spirit distilled from wine or fermented fruit juice. □ **brandy-snap** a crisp rolled gingerbread wafer usu. filled with cream. [earlier *brand(e)wine* f. Du. *brandewijn* burnt (distilled) wine]

brant *US* var. of BRENT.

brash *adj.* **1** vulgarly or ostentatiously self-assertive. **2** hasty, rash. **3** impudent. □ **brashly** *adv.* **brashness** *n*. [orig. dial., perh. f. RASH[1]]

brass /brɑːs/ *n*. & *adj.* —*n*. **1** a yellow alloy of copper and zinc. **2 a** an ornament or other decorated piece of brass. **b** brass objects collectively. **3** *Mus.* brass wind instruments (including trumpet, horn, trombone) forming a band or a section of an orchestra. **4** *Brit. sl.* money. **5** (in full **horse-brass**) a round flat brass ornament for the harness of a draught-horse. **6** (in full **top brass**) *colloq.* persons in authority or of high (esp. military) rank. **7** an inscribed or engraved memorial tablet of brass. **8** *colloq.* effrontery (*then had the brass to demand money*). —*adj.* made of brass. □ **brass band** a group of musicians playing brass instruments, sometimes also with percussion. **brass hat** *Brit. colloq.* an officer of high rank, usu. one with gold braid on the cap. **brass-rubbing 1** the rubbing of heelball etc. over paper laid on an engraved brass to take an impression of its design. **2** the impression obtained by this. **brass tacks** *sl.* actual details; real business (*get down to brass tacks*). [OE *bræs*, of unkn. orig.]

brasserie /ˈbræsərɪ/ *n*. a restaurant, orig. one serving beer with food. [F, = brewery]

brassica /ˈbræsɪkə/ *n*. any cruciferous plant of the genus *Brassica*, having tap roots and erect branched stems, including cabbage, swede, mustard, cauliflower, kale, and turnip. [L, = cabbage]

brassière /ˈbræzɪə(r), -sɪˌeə(r)/ *n*. an undergarment worn by women to support the breasts. [F, = child's vest]

brassy /ˈbrɑːsɪ/ *adj.* (**brassier, brassiest**) **1** impudent. **2** pretentious, showy. **3** loud and blaring. **4** of or like brass. □ **brassily** *adv.* **brassiness** *n*.

brat *n*. usu. *derog.* a child, esp. an ill-behaved one. □ **brat pack** a rowdy or ostentatious group of young celebrities, esp. film stars. □ **bratty** *adj.* [perh. abbr. of Sc. *bratchart* hound, or f. *brat* rough garment]

bratwurst /ˈbrætvʊəst, -vɜːst/ *n*. a type of small German pork sausage. [G f. *braten* fry, roast + *Wurst* sausage]

bravado /brəˈvɑːdəʊ/ *n*. a bold manner or a show of boldness intended to impress. [Sp. *bravata* f. *bravo*]

brave /breɪv/ *adj., n.,* & *v.* —*adj.* **1** able or ready to face and endure danger or pain. **2** *formal* splendid, spectacular (make a brave show). —n. an American Indian warrior. —v.tr. defy; encounter bravely. □ **bravely** adv. **braveness** n. [ME f. F, ult. f. L barbarus BARBAROUS]

bravery /ˈbreɪvərɪ/ n. 1 brave conduct. 2 a brave nature. [F braverie or It. braveria (as BRAVE)]

bravo[1] /brɑːˈvəʊ/ int. & n. —int. expressing approval of a performer etc. —n. (pl. -os) a cry of bravo. [F f. It.]

bravo[2] /ˈbrɑːvəʊ/ n. (pl. -oes or -os) a hired ruffian or killer. [It.: see BRAVE]

bravura /brəˈvʊərə, -ˈvjʊərə/ n. (often attrib.) 1 a brilliant or ambitious action or display. 2 a a style of (esp. vocal) music requiring exceptional ability. b a passage of this kind. 3 bravado. [It.]

brawl n. & v. —n. a noisy quarrel or fight. —v.intr. 1 quarrel noisily or roughly. 2 (of a stream) run noisily. □ **brawler** n. [ME f. OProv., rel. to BRAY]

brawn n. 1 muscular strength. 2 muscle; lean flesh. 3 Brit. a jellied preparation of the chopped meat from a boiled pig's head. [ME f. AF braun, OF braon f. Gmc]

brawny /ˈbrɔːnɪ/ adj. (**brawnier, brawniest**) muscular, strong. □ **brawniness** n.

bray n. & v. —n. 1 the cry of a donkey. 2 a sound like this cry, e.g. that of a harshly-played brass instrument, a laugh, etc. —v. 1 intr. make a braying sound. 2 tr. utter harshly. [ME f. OF braire, perh. ult. f. Celt.]

braze v. & n. —v.tr. solder with an alloy of brass and zinc at a high temperature. —n. 1 a brazed joint. 2 the alloy used for brazing. [F braser solder f. braise live coals]

brazen /ˈbreɪz(ə)n/ adj. & v. —adj. 1 (also **brazen-faced**) flagrant and shameless; insolent. 2 made of brass. 3 of or like brass, esp. in colour or sound. —v.tr. (foll. by out) face or undergo defiantly. □ **brazen it out** be defiantly unrepentant under censure. □ **brazenly** adv. **brazenness** /ˈbreɪzənnɪs/ n. [OE bræsen f. bræs brass]

brazier[1] /ˈbreɪzɪə(r), -ʒə(r)/ n. a portable heater consisting of a pan or stand for holding lighted coals. [F brasier f. braise hot coals]

brazier[2] /ˈbreɪzɪə(r), -ʒə(r)/ n. a worker in brass. □ **braziery** n. [ME prob. f. BRASS + -IER, after glass, glazier]

Brazil /brəˈzɪl/ n. 1 a a lofty tree, Bertholletia excelsa, forming large forests in S. America. b (in full **Brazil nut**) a large three-sided nut with an edible kernel from this tree. 2 (in full **Brazil-wood**) a hard red wood from any tropical tree of the genus Caesalpina, that yields dyes. [the name of a S.Amer. country, named from Brazil-wood, ult. f. med.L brasilium]

breach /briːtʃ/ n. & v. —n. 1 (often foll. by of) the breaking of or failure to observe a law, contract, etc. 2 a a breaking of relations; an estrangement. b a quarrel. 3 a a broken state. b a gap, esp. one made by artillery in fortifications. —v.tr. 1 break through; make a gap in. 2 break (a law, contract, etc.). □ **breach of the peace** an infringement or violation of the public peace by any disturbance or riot etc. **breach of promise** the breaking of a promise, esp. a promise to marry. **stand in the breach** bear the brunt of an attack. **step into the breach** give help in a crisis, esp. by replacing someone who has dropped out. [ME f. OF breche, ult. f. Gmc]

bread /bred/ n. & v. —n. 1 baked dough made of flour usu. leavened with yeast and moistened, eaten as a staple food. 2 a necessary food. b (also **daily bread**) one's livelihood. 3 sl. money. —v.tr. coat with breadcrumbs for cooking. □ **bread and butter** 1 bread spread with butter. 2 a one's livelihood. b routine work to ensure an income. [OE brēad f. Gmc]

breadboard /ˈbredbɔːd/ n. 1 a board for cutting bread on. 2 a board for making an experimental model of an electric circuit.

breadcrumb /ˈbredkrʌm/ n. 1 a small fragment of bread. 2 (in pl.) bread crumbled for use in cooking.

breadfruit /ˈbredfruːt/ n. 1 a tropical evergreen tree, Artocarpus altilis, bearing edible usu. seedless fruit. 2 the fruit of this tree which when roasted becomes soft like new bread.

breadline /ˈbredlaɪn/ n. 1 subsistence level (esp. on the breadline). 2 US a queue of people waiting to receive free food.

breadth /bredθ/ n. 1 the distance or measurement from side to side of a thing; broadness. 2 a piece (of cloth etc.) of standard or full breadth. 3 extent, distance, room. 4 (usu. foll. by of) freedom from prejudice or intolerance (esp. breadth of mind or view). □ **breadthways** adv. **breadthwise** adv. [obs. brede, OE brǣdu, f. Gmc, rel. to BROAD]

breadwinner /ˈbredˌwɪnə(r)/ n. a person who earns the money to support a family.

break /breɪk/ v. & n. —v. (past **broke** /brəʊk/ or archaic **brake** /breɪk/; past part. **broken** /ˈbrəʊkən/ or archaic **broke**) 1 tr. & intr. a separate into pieces under a blow or strain; shatter. b make or become inoperative, esp. from damage (the toaster has broken). c break a bone in or dislocate (part of the body). d break the skin of (the head or crown). 2 a tr. cause or effect an interruption in (broke our journey; broke the silence). b intr. have an interval between spells of work (let's break now; we broke for tea). 3 tr. fail to observe or keep (a law, promise, etc.). 4 a tr. & intr. make or become subdued or weakened; yield or cause to yield (broke his spirit; he broke under the strain). b tr. weaken the effect of (a fall, blow, etc.). c tr. = break in 3c. d tr. defeat, destroy (broke the enemy's power). e tr. defeat the object of (a strike, e.g. by engaging other personnel). 5 tr. surpass (a record). 6 intr. (foll. by with) quarrel or cease association with (another person etc.). 7 tr. a be no longer subject to (a habit). b (foll. by of) cause (a person) to be free of a habit (broke them of their addiction). 8 tr. & intr. reveal or be revealed; (cause to) become known (broke the news; the story broke on Friday). 9 intr. a (of the weather) change suddenly, esp. after a fine spell. b (of waves) curl over and dissolve into foam. c (of the day) dawn. d (of clouds) move apart; show a gap. e (of a storm) begin violently. 10 tr. Electr. disconnect (a circuit). 11 intr. a (of the voice) change with emotion. b (of a boy's voice) change in register etc. at puberty. 12 tr. ruin (an individual or institution) financially (see also BROKE adj.). 13 tr. penetrate (e.g. a safe) by force. 14 tr. decipher (a code). 15 tr. make (a way, path, etc.) by separating obstacles. 16 intr. burst forth (the sun broke through the clouds). 17 Mil. a intr. (of troops) disperse in confusion. b tr. make a rupture in (ranks). 18 a intr. (usu. foll. by free, loose, out, etc.)

escape from constraint by a sudden effort. **b** *tr.* escape or emerge from (prison, bounds, cover, etc.). **19** *tr. Tennis etc.* win a game against (an opponent's service). **20** *intr. Boxing etc.* (of two fighters, usu. at the referee's command) come out of a clinch. **21** *Mil. tr.* demote (an officer). **22** *intr. esp. Stock Exch.* (of prices) fall sharply. **23** *intr. Cricket* (of a bowled ball) change direction on bouncing. **24** *intr. Billiards etc.* disperse the balls at the beginning of a game. **25** *tr.* disprove (an alibi). —*n.* **1 a** an act or instance of breaking. **b** a point where something is broken; a gap. **2** an interval, an interruption; a pause in work. **3** a sudden dash (esp. to escape). **4** *colloq.* **a** a piece of good luck; a fair chance. **b** (also **bad break**) an unfortunate remark or action, a blunder. **5** *Cricket* a change in direction of a bowled ball on bouncing. **6** *Billiards etc.* **a** a series of points scored during one turn. **b** the opening shot that disperses the balls. **7** *Mus.* (in jazz) a short unaccompanied passage for a soloist, usu. improvised. **8** *Electr.* a discontinuity in a circuit. □ **break away** make or become free or separate (see also BREAKAWAY). **break the back of 1** do the hardest or greatest part of. **2** overburden (a person). **break-dancing** an energetic style of street-dancing, developed by US Blacks. **break down 1 a** fail in mechanical action; cease to function. **b** (of human relationships etc.) fail, collapse. **c** fail in (esp. mental) health. **d** be overcome by emotion; collapse in tears. **2 a** demolish, destroy. **b** suppress (resistance). **c** force (a person) to yield under pressure. **3** analyse into components (see also BREAKDOWN). **break even** emerge from a transaction etc. with neither profit nor loss. **break the ice 1** begin to overcome formality or shyness, esp. between strangers. **2** make a start. **break in 1** enter premises by force, esp. with criminal intent. **2** interrupt. **3 a** accustom to a habit etc. **b** wear etc. until comfortable. **c** tame or discipline (an animal); accustom (a horse) to saddle and bridle etc. **4** *Austral. & NZ* bring (virgin land) into cultivation. **break-in** *n.* an illegal forced entry into premises, esp. with criminal intent. **breaking and entering** (formerly) the illegal entering of a building with intent to commit a felony. **breaking-point** the point of greatest strain, at which a thing breaks or a person gives way. **break in on** disturb; interrupt. **break into 1** enter forcibly or violently. **2 a** suddenly begin, burst forth with (a song, laughter, etc.). **b** suddenly change one's pace for (a faster one) (*broke into a gallop*). **3** interrupt. **break of day** dawn. **break off 1** detach by breaking. **2** bring to an end. **3** cease talking etc. **break open** open forcibly. **break out 1** escape by force, esp. from prison. **2** begin suddenly; burst forth (*then violence broke out*). **3** (foll. by *in*) become covered in (a rash etc.). **4** exclaim. **5** *US* **a** open up (a receptacle) and remove its contents. **b** remove (articles) from a place of storage. **break-out** *n.* a forcible escape. **break point 1** a place or time at which an interruption or change is made. **2** = *breaking-point*. **break step** get out of step. **break up 1** break into small pieces. **2** disperse; disband. **3** end the school term. **4 a** terminate a relationship; disband. **b** cause to do this. **5** (of the weather) change suddenly (esp. after a fine spell). **6** esp. *US* **a** upset or be upset. **b** excite or be excited. **c** convulse or be convulsed (see also

BREAKUP). **break wind** release gas from the anus. [OE *brecan* f. Gmc]

breakable /ˈbreɪkəb(ə)l/ *adj. & n.* —*adj.* that may or is apt to be broken easily. —*n.* (esp. in *pl.*) a breakable thing.

breakage /ˈbreɪkɪdʒ/ *n.* **1 a** a broken thing. **b** damage caused by breaking. **2** an act or instance of breaking.

breakaway /ˈbreɪkəˌweɪ/ *n.* **1** the act or an instance of breaking away or seceding. **2** (*attrib.*) that breaks away or has broken away; separate.

breakdown /ˈbreɪkdaʊn/ *n.* **1 a** a mechanical failure. **b** a loss of (esp. mental) health and strength. **2** a collapse or disintegration (*breakdown of communication*). **3** a detailed analysis (of statistics etc.).

breaker /ˈbreɪkə(r)/ *n.* **1** a person or thing that breaks something, esp. disused machinery. **2** a heavy wave that breaks.

breakfast /ˈbrekfəst/ *n. & v.* —*n.* the first meal of the day. —*v.intr.* have breakfast. □ **breakfaster** *n.* [BREAK interrupt + FAST²]

breakneck /ˈbreɪknek/ *adj.* (of speed) dangerously fast.

breakthrough /ˈbreɪkθruː/ *n.* **1** a major advance or discovery. **2** an act of breaking through an obstacle etc.

breakup /ˈbreɪkʌp/ *n.* **1** disintegration, collapse. **2** dispersal.

breakwater /ˈbreɪkˌwɔːtə(r)/ *n.* a barrier built out into the sea to break the force of waves.

bream *n.* (*pl.* same) **1** a yellowish arch-backed freshwater fish, *Abramis brama*. **2** (in full **sea bream**) a similarly shaped marine fish of the family Sparidae. [ME f. OF *bre(s)me* f. WG]

breast /brest/ *n. & v.* —*n.* **1 a** either of two milk-secreting organs on the upper front of a woman's body. **b** the corresponding usu. rudimentary part of a man's body. **2 a** the upper front part of a human body; the chest. **b** the corresponding part of an animal. **3** the part of a garment that covers the breast. **4** the breast as a source of nourishment or emotion. —*v.tr.* **1** face, meet in full opposition (*breast the wind*). **2** contend with (*breast it out against difficulties*). **3** reach the top of (a hill). □ **breast-feed** (*past* and *past part.* **-fed**) feed (a baby) from the breast. **breast-stroke** a stroke made while swimming on the breast by extending arms forward and sweeping them back in unison. **make a clean breast of** confess fully. □ **breasted** *adj.* (also in *comb.*). **breastless** *adj.* [OE *brēost* f. Gmc]

breastbone /ˈbrestbəʊn/ *n.* a thin flat vertical bone and cartilage in the chest connecting the ribs.

breastplate /ˈbrestpleɪt/ *n.* a piece of armour covering the breast.

breastwork /ˈbrestwɜːk/ *n.* a low temporary defence or parapet.

breath /breθ/ *n.* **1 a** the air taken into or expelled from the lungs. **b** one respiration of air. **c** an exhalation of air that can be seen, smelt, or heard (*breath steamed in the cold air; bad breath*). **2 a** a slight movement of air; a breeze. **b** a whiff of perfume etc. **3 a** a whisper, a murmur (esp. of a scandalous nature). **4** the power of breathing; life (*is there breath in him?*). □ **below** (or **under**) **one's breath** in a whisper. **breath test** *Brit.* a test of a person's alcohol consumption, using a breathalyser. **catch one's breath 1** cease breathing momentarily in surprise, suspense, etc. **2** rest after exercise to restore normal breathing. **draw breath** breathe; live. **hold one's breath** cease breathing temporarily. **out of breath** gasping for air, esp. after exercise. **take one's breath away** astound; surprise; awe; delight. [OE *bræth* f. Gmc]

Breathalyser /ˈbreθəˌlaɪzə(r)/ *n.* (also **Breathalyzer**) *Brit. propr.* an instrument for measuring the amount of alcohol in the breath (and hence in the blood) of a driver. □ **breathalyse** *v.tr.* (also **-lyze**). [BREATH + ANALYSE + -ER¹]

breathe /briːð/ *v.* **1** *intr.* take air into and expel it from the lungs. **2** *intr.* be or seem alive (*is she breathing?*). **3** *tr.* utter; say (esp. quietly) (*breathed her forgiveness*). **b** express; display (*breathed defiance*). **4** *intr.* take breath, pause. **5** *tr.* send out or take in (as if) with breathed air (*breathed new life into them; breathed whisky*). **6** *intr.* (of wine, fabric, etc.) be exposed to fresh air. □ **breathe one's last** die. **breathe upon** tarnish, taint. **not breathe a word** keep quite secret. [ME f. BREATH]

breather /ˈbriːðə(r)/ *n. colloq.* **1** a brief pause for rest. **2** a short spell of exercise.

breathing /ˈbriːðɪŋ/ *n.* **1** the process of taking air into and expelling it from the lungs. **2** *Phonet.* a sign in Greek indicating that an initial vowel or rho is aspirated (**rough breathing**) or not aspirated (**smooth breathing**). □ **breathing-space** time to breathe; a pause.

breathless /ˈbreθlɪs/ *adj.* **1** panting, out of breath. **2** holding the breath because of excitement, suspense, etc. (*a state of breathless expectancy*). **3** unstirred by wind; still. □ **breathlessly** *adv.* **breathlessness** *n.*

breathtaking /ˈbreθˌteɪkɪŋ/ *adj.* astounding; awe-inspiring. □ **breathtakingly** *adv.*

breathy /ˈbreθɪ/ *adj.* (**breathier**, **breathiest**) (of a singing-voice etc.) containing the sound of breathing. □ **breathily** *adv.* **breathiness** *n.*

bred *past* and *past part.* of BREED.

breech *n.* **1 a** the part of a cannon behind the bore. **b** the back part of a rifle or gun barrel. **2** *archaic* the buttocks. □ **breech birth** (or **delivery**) the delivery of a baby with the buttocks or feet foremost. [OE *brōc*, pl. *brēc* (treated as sing. in ME), f. Gmc]

breeches /ˈbrɪtʃɪz/ *n.pl.* (also **pair of breeches** *sing.*) **1** short trousers, esp. fastened below the knee, now used esp. for riding or in court costume. **2** *colloq.* any trousers, knickerbockers, or underpants. □ **breeches buoy** a lifebuoy suspended from a rope which has canvas breeches for the user's legs. [pl. of BREECH]

breed *v.* & *n.* —*v.* (*past* and *past part.* **bred** /bred/) **1** *tr.* & *intr.* bear, generate (offspring). **2** *tr.* & *intr.* propagate or cause to propagate; raise (livestock). **3** *tr.* **a** yield, produce; result in (*war breeds famine*). **b** spread (*discontent bred by rumour*). **4** *intr.* arise; spread (*disease breeds in the Tropics*). **5** *tr.* bring up; train (*bred to the law; Hollywood breeds stars*). **6** *tr.* *Physics* create (fissile material) by nuclear reaction. —*n.* **1** a stock of animals or plants within a species, having a similar appearance, and usu. developed by deliberate selection. **2** a race; a lineage. **3** a sort, a kind. □ **breeder reactor** a nuclear reactor that can create more fissile material than it consumes. □ **breeder** *n.* [OE *brēdan*: rel. to BROOD]

breeding /ˈbriːdɪŋ/ *n.* **1** the process of developing or propagating (animals, plants, etc.). **2** generation; childbearing. **3** the result of training or education; behaviour. **4** good manners (as produced by an aristocratic heredity) (*has no breeding*).

breeze¹ *n.* & *v.* —*n.* **1** a gentle wind. **2** *Meteorol.* a wind of 4–31 m.p.h. and between force 2 and force 6 on the Beaufort scale. **3** a wind blowing from land at night or sea during the day. **4** esp. *US colloq.* an easy task. —*v.intr.* (foll. by *in, out, along,* etc.) *colloq.* come or go in a casual or lighthearted manner. [prob. f. OSp. & Port. *briza* NE wind]

breeze² *n.* small cinders. □ **breeze-block** any lightweight building block, esp. one made from breeze mixed with sand and cement. [F *braise* live coals]

breezy /ˈbriːzɪ/ *adj.* (**breezier**, **breeziest**) **1 a** windswept. **b** pleasantly windy. **2** *colloq.* lively; jovial. **3** *colloq.* careless (*with breezy indifference*). □ **breezily** *adv.* **breeziness** *n.*

Bren *n.* (in full **Bren gun**) a lightweight quick-firing machine-gun. [*Brno* in Czechoslovakia (where orig. made) + *Enfield* in England (where later made)]

brent *n.* (*US* **brant**) (in full **brent-goose**) a small migratory goose, *Branta bernicla*. [16th c.: orig. unkn.]

brethren see BROTHER.

Breton /ˈbret(ə)n, brəˈtɔ̃/ *n.* & *adj.* —*n.* **1** a native of Brittany. **2** the Celtic language of Brittany. —*adj.* of or relating to Brittany or its people or language. [OF, = BRITON]

bretzel var. of PRETZEL.

breve /briːv/ *n.* **1** *Mus.* a note, now rarely used, having the time value of two semibreves. **2** a written or printed mark (˘) indicating a short or unstressed vowel. [ME var. of BRIEF]

breviary /ˈbriːvɪərɪ/ *n.* (*pl.* **-ies**) *RC Ch.* a book containing the service for each day, to be recited by those in orders. [L *breviarium* summary f. *breviare* abridge: see ABBREVIATE]

brevity /ˈbrevɪtɪ/ *n.* **1** economy of expression; conciseness. **2** shortness (of time etc.) (*the brevity of happiness*). [AF *breveté*, OF *brieveté* f. *bref* BRIEF]

brew *v.* & *n.* —*v.* **1** *tr.* **a** make (beer etc.) by infusion, boiling, and fermentation. **b** make (tea etc.) by infusion or (punch etc.) by mixture. **2** *intr.* undergo either of these processes (*the tea is brewing*). **3** *intr.* (of trouble, a storm, etc.) gather force; threaten (*mischief was brewing*). **4** *tr.* bring about; set in train; concoct. —*n.* **1** an amount (of beer etc.) brewed at one time (*this year's brew*). **2** what is brewed (esp. with regard to its quality) (*a good strong brew*). **3** the action or process of brewing. □ **brew up** make tea. **brew-up** *n.* an instance of making tea. □ **brewer** *n.* [OE *brēowan* f. Gmc]

brewery /ˈbruːərɪ/ *n.* (*pl.* **-ies**) a place where beer etc. is brewed commercially.

briar¹ var. of BRIER¹.

briar² var. of BRIER².

bribe /braɪb/ *v.* & *n.* —*v.tr.* (often foll. by *to* + *infin.*) persuade (a person etc.) to act improperly in one's favour by a gift of money, services, etc. —*n.* money or services offered in the process of bribing. □ **bribable** *adj.* **briber** *n.* **bribery** *n.* [ME f. OF *briber, brimber* beg, of unkn. orig.]

bric-à-brac /ˈbrɪkəˌbræk/ *n.* (also **bric-a-brac**, **bricabrac**)   miscellaneous,   often   old, ornaments, trinkets, furniture, etc., of no great value. [F f. obs. *à bric et à brac* at random]

brick *n.*, *v.*, & *adj.* —*n.* **1 a** a small, usu. rectangular, block of fired or sun-dried clay, used in building. **b** the material used to make these. **c** a similar block of concrete etc. **2** *Brit.* a child's toy building-block. **3** a brick-shaped solid object (*a brick of ice-cream*). **4** *sl.* a generous or loyal person. —*v.tr.* (foll. by *in*, *up*) close or block with brickwork. □ —*adj.* **1** built of brick (*brick wall*). **2** of a dull red colour. □ **bricky** *adj.* [ME f. MLG, MDu. bri(c)ke, of unkn. orig.]

brickbat /ˈbrɪkbæt/ *n.* **1** a piece of brick, esp. when used as a missile. **2** an uncomplimentary remark.

brickie /ˈbrɪkɪ/ *n.* *sl.* a bricklayer.

bricklayer /ˈbrɪkˌleɪə(r)/ *n.* a worker who builds with bricks. □ **bricklaying** *n.*

brickwork /ˈbrɪkwɜːk/ *n.* **1** building in brick. **2** a wall, building, etc. made of brick.

bridal /ˈbraɪd(ə)l/ *adj.* of or concerning a bride or a wedding. □ **bridally** *adv.* [orig. as noun, = wedding-feast, f. OE brȳd-ealu f. brȳd BRIDE + ealu ale-drinking]

bride *n.* a woman on her wedding day and for some time before and after it. [OE brȳd f. Gmc]

bridegroom /ˈbraɪdɡruːm, -ɡrʊm/ *n.* a man on his wedding day and for some time before and after it. [OE brȳdguma (as BRIDE, *guma* man, assim. to GROOM)]

bridesmaid /ˈbraɪdzmeɪd/ *n.* a girl or unmarried woman attending a bride on her wedding day. [earlier *bridemaid*, f. BRIDE + MAID]

bridge¹ *n.* & *v.* —*n.* **1 a** a structure carrying a road, path, railway, etc., across a stream, ravine, road, railway, etc. **b** anything providing a connection between different things (*English is a bridge between nations*). **2** the superstructure on a ship from which the captain and officers direct operations. **3** the upper bony part of the nose. **4** *Mus.* an upright piece of wood on a violin etc. over which the strings are stretched. **5** = BRIDGEWORK. **6** *Billiards* etc. **a** a long stick with a structure at the end which is used to support a cue for a difficult shot. **b** a support for a cue formed by a raised hand. —*v.tr.* **1 a** be a bridge over (*a fallen tree bridges the stream*). **b** make a bridge over; span. **2** span as if with a bridge (*bridged their differences with understanding*). □ **bridging loan** a loan from a bank etc. to cover the short interval between buying a house etc. and selling another. □ **bridgeable** *adj.* [OE brycg f. Gmc]

bridge² *n.* a card-game derived from whist, in which one player's cards are exposed and are played by his or her partner (cf. *auction bridge*, *contract bridge*). □ **bridge roll** a small soft bread roll. [19th c.: orig. unkn.]

bridgehead /ˈbrɪdʒhed/ *n.* *Mil.* a fortified position held on the enemy's side of a river or other obstacle.

bridgework /ˈbrɪdʒwɜːk/ *n.* *Dentistry* a dental structure used to cover a gap, joined to and supported by the teeth on either side.

bridle /ˈbraɪd(ə)l/ *n.* & *v.* —*n.* the headgear used to control a horse, consisting of buckled leather straps, a metal bit, and reins. —*v.* **1** *tr.* put a bridle on (a horse etc.). **2** *tr.* bring under control; curb. **3** *intr.* (often foll. by *up*) express offence, resentment, etc., esp. by throwing up the head and drawing in the chin. □ **bridle-path** (or

-road or **-way**) a rough path or road fit only for riders or walkers, not vehicles. [OE brīdel]

Brie /briː/ *n.* a kind of soft cheese. [*Brie* in N. France]

brief /briːf/ *adj.*, *n.*, & *v.* —*adj.* **1** of short duration. **2** concise in expression. **3** abrupt, brusque (*was rather brief with me*). **4** scanty; lacking in substance (*wearing a brief skirt*). —*n.* **1** (in *pl.*) **a** women's brief pants. **b** men's brief underpants. **2** *Law* **a** a summary of the facts and legal points of a case drawn up for counsel. **b** a piece of work for a barrister. **3** instructions given for a task, operation, etc. **4** *RC Ch.* a letter from the Pope to a person or community on a matter of discipline. —*v.tr.* **1** *Brit.* *Law* instruct (a barrister) by brief. **2** instruct (an employee, a participant, etc.) in preparation for a task; inform or instruct in advance (*briefed him for the interview*). □ **hold a brief for 1** argue in favour of. **2** be retained as counsel for. **in brief** in short. **watching brief 1** a brief held by a barrister following a case for a client not directly involved. **2** a state of interest maintained in a proceeding not directly or immediately concerning one. □ **briefly** *adv.* **briefness** *n.* [ME f. AF bref, OF brief, f. L brevis short]

briefcase /ˈbriːfkeɪs/ *n.* a flat rectangular case for carrying documents etc.

briefing /ˈbriːfɪŋ/ *n.* **1** a meeting for giving information or instructions. **2** the information or instructions given; a brief. **3** the action of informing or instructing.

brier¹ /ˈbraɪə(r)/ *n.* (also **briar**) any prickly bush esp. of a wild rose. □ **briery** *adj.* [OE brēr, brēr, of unkn. orig.]

brier² /ˈbraɪə(r)/ *n.* (also **briar**) **1** a white heath, *Erica arborea*, native to S. Europe. **2** a tobacco pipe made from its root. [19th-c. *bruyer* f. F *bruyère* heath]

Brig. *abbr.* Brigadier.

brig *n.* **1** a two-masted square-rigged ship. **2** *US* a prison, esp. on a warship. [abbr. of BRIGANTINE]

brigade /brɪˈɡeɪd/ *n.* & *v.* —*n.* **1** *Mil.* **a** a subdivision of an army. **b** a British infantry unit consisting usu. of 3 battalions and forming part of a division. **c** a corresponding armoured unit. **2** an organized or uniformed band of workers (*fire brigade*). **3** *colloq.* any group of people with a characteristic in common. —*v.tr.* form into a brigade. [F f. It. *brigata* company f. *brigare* be busy with f. *briga* strife]

brigadier /ˌbrɪɡəˈdɪə(r)/ *n.* *Mil.* **1** an officer commanding a brigade. **2 a** a staff officer of similar standing, above a colonel and below a major-general. **b** the titular rank granted to such an officer. □ **brigadier general** *US* an officer ranking next above colonel. [F (as BRIGADE, -IER)]

brigand /ˈbrɪɡənd/ *n.* a member of a robber band living by pillage and ransom. □ **brigandage** *n.* **brigandish** *adj.* **brigandism** *n.* **brigandry** *n.* [ME f. OF f. It. *brigante* f. *brigare*: see BRIGADE]

brigantine /ˈbrɪɡənˌtiːn/ *n.* a two-masted sailing-ship with a square-rigged foremast and a fore-and-aft rigged mainmast. [OF *brigandine* or It. *brigantino* f. *brigante* BRIGAND]

bright /braɪt/ *adj.* & *adv.* —*adj.* **1** emitting or reflecting much light; shining. **2** (of colour) intense, vivid. **3** clever, talented, quick-witted (*a bright idea*; *a bright child*). **4** cheerful, vivacious. —*adv.* esp. *poet.* brightly (*the moon shone bright*).

□ **brightish** adj. **brightly** adv. **brightness** n. [OE beorht, (adv.) beorhte, f. Gmc]

brighten /ˈbraɪt(ə)n/ v.tr. & intr. **1** make or become brighter. **2** make or become more cheerful.

brill[1] n. a European flat-fish, Scophthalmus rhombus, resembling a turbot. [15th c.: orig. unkn.]

brill[2] adj. colloq. = BRILLIANT adj. 4. [abbr.]

brilliance /ˈbrɪlɪəns/ n. (also **brilliancy** /-ənsɪ/) **1** great brightness; sparkling or radiant quality. **2** outstanding talent or intelligence.

brilliant /ˈbrɪlɪənt/ adj. & n. —adj. **1** very bright; sparkling. **2** outstandingly talented or intelligent. **3** showy; outwardly impressive. **4** colloq. excellent, superb. —n. a diamond of the finest cut with many facets. □ **brilliantly** adv. [F brillant part. of briller shine f. It. brillare, of unkn. orig.]

brilliantine /ˈbrɪljənˌtiːn/ n. an oily liquid dressing for making the hair glossy. [F brillantine (as BRILLIANT)]

brim n. & v. —n. **1** the edge or lip of a cup or other vessel, or of a hollow. **2** the projecting edge of a hat. —v.tr. & intr. (**brimmed, brimming**) fill or be full to the brim. □ **brim over** overflow. □ **brimless** adj. **brimmed** adj. (usu. in comb.). [ME brimme, of unkn. orig.]

brim-full /brɪmˈfʊl/ adj. (also **brimful**) (often foll. by of) filled to the brim.

brimstone /ˈbrɪmstəʊn/ n. archaic the element sulphur. [ME prob. f. OE bryne burning + STONE]

brindled /ˈbrɪnd(ə)ld/ adj. (also **brindle**) brownish or tawny with streaks of other colour (esp. of domestic animals). [earlier brinded, brended f. brend, perh. of Scand. orig.]

brine n. & v. —n. **1** water saturated or strongly impregnated with salt. **2** sea water. —v.tr. soak in or saturate with brine. [OE brīne, of unkn. orig.]

bring v.tr. (past and past part. **brought** /brɔːt/) **1 a** come conveying esp. by carrying or leading. **b** come with. **2** cause to come or be present (what brings you here?). **3** cause or result in (war brings misery). **4** be sold for; produce as income. **5 a** prefer (a charge). **b** initiate (legal action). **6** cause to become or to reach a particular state (brings me alive; brought them to their senses; cannot bring myself to agree). **7** adduce (evidence, an argument, etc.). □ **bring about 1** cause to happen. **2** turn (a ship) around. **bring-and-buy sale** Brit. a kind of charity sale at which participants bring items for sale and buy what is brought by others. **bring back** call to mind. **bring down 1** cause to fall. **2** lower (a price). **3** sl. make unhappy or less happy. **4** colloq. damage the reputation of; demean. **bring forth 1** give birth to. **2** produce, emit, cause. **bring forward 1** move to an earlier date or time. **2** transfer from the previous page or account. **3** draw attention to; adduce. **bring home to** cause to realize fully (brought home to me that I was wrong). **bring the house down** receive rapturous applause. **bring in 1** introduce (legislation, a custom, fashion, topic, etc.). **2** yield as income or profit. **bring into play** cause to operate; activate. **bring low** overcome. **bring off** achieve successfully. **bring on 1** cause to happen or appear. **2** accelerate the progress of. **bring out 1** emphasize; make evident. **2** publish. **bring over** convert to one's own side. **bring round 1** restore to consciousness. **2** persuade. **bring through** aid (a person) through adversity, esp. illness. **bring to 1** restore to consciousness (brought him to). **2** check the motion of. **bring to bear** (usu. foll. by on) direct and concentrate (forces). **bring to mind** recall; cause one to remember. **bring to pass** cause to happen. **bring under** subdue. **bring up 1** rear (a child). **2** vomit, regurgitate. **3** call attention to. **4** (absol.) stop suddenly. **bring upon oneself** be responsible for (something one suffers). □ **bringer** n. [OE bringan f. Gmc]

brink n. **1** the extreme edge of land before a precipice, river, etc., esp. when a sudden drop follows. **2** the furthest point before something dangerous or exciting is discovered. □ **on the brink of** about to experience or suffer; in imminent danger of. [ME f. ON: orig. unkn.]

brinkmanship /ˈbrɪŋkmənʃɪp/ n. the art or policy of pursuing a dangerous course to the brink of catastrophe before desisting.

briny /ˈbraɪnɪ/ adj. & n. —adj. (**brinier, briniest**) of brine or the sea; salty. —n. (prec. by the) Brit. sl. the sea. □ **brininess** n.

brio /ˈbriːəʊ/ n. dash, vigour, vivacity. [It.]

brioche /ˈbriːɒʃ/ n. a small rounded sweet roll made with a light yeast dough. [F]

briquette /brɪˈket/ n. (also **briquet**) a block of compressed coal dust used as fuel. [F briquette, dimin. of brique brick]

brisk adj. & v. —adj. **1** quick, lively, keen (a brisk pace; brisk trade). **2** enlivening (a brisk wind). —v.tr. & intr. (often foll. by up) make or grow brisk. □ **brisken** v.tr. & intr. **briskly** adv. **briskness** n. [prob. F brusque BRUSQUE]

brisket /ˈbrɪskɪt/ n. an animal's breast, esp. as a joint of meat. [AF f. OF bruschet, perh. f. ON]

brisling /ˈbrɪzlɪŋ, ˈbrɪs-/ n. a small herring or sprat. [Norw. & Da., = sprat]

bristle /ˈbrɪs(ə)l/ n. & v. —n. **1** a short stiff hair, esp. one of those on an animal's back. **2** this, or a man-made substitute, used in clumps to make a brush. —v. **1 a** intr. (of the hair) stand upright, esp. in anger or pride. **b** tr. make (the hair) do this. **2** intr. show irritation or defensiveness. **3** intr. (usu. foll. by with) be covered or abundant (in). [ME bristel, brestel f. OE byrst]

bristly /ˈbrɪslɪ/ adj. (**bristlier, bristliest**) full of bristles; rough, prickly.

Brit /brɪt/ n. colloq. a British person. [abbr.]

Britannia /brɪˈtænjə/ n. the personification of Britain, esp. as a helmeted woman with shield and trident. □ **Britannia metal** a silvery alloy of tin, antimony, and copper. [L f. Gk Brettania f. Brettanoi Britons]

Britannic /brɪˈtænɪk/ adj. (esp. in His or Her **Britannic Majesty**) of Britain. [L Britannicus (as BRITANNIA)]

Briticism /ˈbrɪtɪˌsɪz(ə)m/ n. (also **Britishism** /-ˌʃɪz(ə)m/) an idiom used in Britain but not in other English-speaking countries. [BRITISH, after GALLICISM]

British /ˈbrɪtɪʃ/ adj. & n. —adj. **1** of or relating to Great Britain or the United Kingdom, or to its people or language. **2** of the British Commonwealth or (formerly) the British Empire (British subject). —n. (prec. by the; treated as pl.) the British people. □ **British Legion** = Royal British Legion. □ **Britishness** n. [OE Brettisc etc. f. Bret f. L Britto or OCelt.]

Britisher /ˈbrɪtɪʃə(r)/ n. a British subject, esp. of British descent.

Briton /ˈbrɪt(ə)n/ n. **1** one of the people of S. Britain before the Roman conquest. **2** a native or inhabitant of Great Britain or (formerly) of the British Empire. [ME & OF *Breton* f. L *Britto -onis* f. OCelt.]

brittle /ˈbrɪt(ə)l/ adj. & n. —adj. hard and fragile; apt to break. —n. a brittle sweet made from nuts and set melted sugar. □ **brittlely** adv. **brittleness** n. **brittly** adv. [ME ult. f. a Gmc root rel. to OE *brēotan* break up]

broach /brəʊtʃ/ v. & n. —v.tr. **1** raise (a subject) for discussion. **2** pierce (a cask) to draw liquor. **3** open and start using contents of (a box, bale, bottle, etc.). —n. **1** a bit for boring. **2** a roasting-spit. □ **broach spire** an octagonal church spire rising from a square tower without a parapet. [ME f. OF *broche* (n.), *brocher* (v.) ult. f. L *brocc(h)us* projecting]

broad /brɔːd/ adj. & n. —adj. **1** large in extent from one side to the other; wide. **2** (following a measurement) in breadth (2 *metres broad*). **3** spacious or extensive (*broad acres*; *a broad plain*). **4** full and clear (*broad daylight*). **5** explicit, unmistakable (*broad hint*). **6** general; not taking account of detail (*a broad inquiry*; *in the broadest sense of the word*). **7** chief or principal (*the broad facts*). **8** tolerant, liberal (*take a broad view*). **9** somewhat coarse (*broad humour*). **10** (of speech) markedly regional (*broad Scots*). —n. **1** the broad part of something (*broad of the back*). **2** US *sl.* a young woman. **3** (**the Broads**) large areas of fresh water in E. Anglia, formed where rivers widen. □ **broad bean 1** a kind of bean, *Vicia faba*, with pods containing large edible flat seeds. **2** one of these seeds. **broad-leaved** (of a tree) deciduous and hard-timbered. □ **broadness** n. **broadways** adv. **broadwise** adv. [OE *brād* f. Gmc]

broadcast /ˈbrɔːdkɑːst/ v., n., adj., & adv. —v. (*past* **broadcast** or **broadcasted**; *past part.* **broadcast**) **1** tr. **a** transmit (programmes or information) by radio or television. **b** disseminate (information) widely. **2** *intr.* undertake or take part in a radio or television transmission. **3** tr. scatter (seed etc.) over a large area, esp. by hand. —n. a radio or television programme or transmission. —adj. **1** transmitted by radio or television. **2 a** scattered widely. **b** (of information etc.) widely disseminated. —adv. over a large area. □ **broadcaster** n. **broadcasting** n. [BROAD + CAST *past part.*]

broadcloth /ˈbrɔːdklɒθ/ n. a fine cloth of wool, cotton, or silk. [orig. with ref. to width and quality]

broaden /ˈbrɔːd(ə)n/ v.tr. & intr. make or become broader.

broadloom /ˈbrɔːdluːm/ adj. (esp. of carpet) woven in broad widths.

broadly /ˈbrɔːdlɪ/ adv. in a broad manner; widely (*grinned broadly*). □ **broadly speaking** disregarding minor exceptions.

broad-minded /brɔːdˈmaɪndɪd/ adj. tolerant or liberal in one's views. □ **broad-mindedly** adv. **broad-mindedness** n.

broadsheet /ˈbrɔːdʃiːt/ n. **1** a large sheet of paper printed on one side only, esp. with information. **2** a newspaper with a large format.

broadside /ˈbrɔːdsaɪd/ n. **1** the firing of all guns from one side of a ship. **2** a vigorous verbal onslaught. **3** the side of a ship above the water

between the bow and quarter. □ **broadside on** sideways on.

broadsword /ˈbrɔːdsɔːd/ n. a sword with a broad blade, for cutting rather than thrusting.

broadway /ˈbrɔːdweɪ/ n. a large open or main road.

brocade /brəˈkeɪd, brɒ-/ n. & v. —n. a rich fabric with a silky finish woven with a raised pattern. —v.tr. weave with this design. [Sp. & Port. *brocado* f. It. *broccato* f. *brocco* twisted thread]

broccoli /ˈbrɒkəlɪ/ n. **1** a variety of cabbage, similar to the cauliflower, with a loose cluster of greenish flower buds. **2** the flower-stalk and head used as a vegetable. [It., pl. of *broccolo* dimin. of *brocco* sprout]

brochure /ˈbrəʊʃə(r), brəʊˈʃjʊə(r)/ n. a pamphlet or leaflet, esp. one giving descriptive information. [F, lit. 'stitching', f. *brocher* stitch]

broderie anglaise /ˌbrəʊdərɪ ɑ̃ˈɡleɪz/ n. open embroidery on white linen or cambric, esp. in floral patterns. [F, = English embroidery]

brogue[1] /brəʊɡ/ n. **1** a strong outdoor shoe with ornamental perforated bands. **2** a rough shoe of untanned leather. [Gael. & Ir. *brōg* f. ON *brók*]

brogue[2] /brəʊɡ/ n. a marked accent, esp. Irish. [18th c.: orig. unkn.: perh. allusively f. BROGUE[1]]

broil v. esp. US **1** tr. cook (meat) on a rack or a gridiron. **2** tr. & intr. make or become very hot, esp. from the sun. [ME f. OF *bruler* burn f. Rmc]

broiler /ˈbrɔɪlə(r)/ n. **1** a young chicken raised for broiling or roasting. **2** a gridiron etc. for broiling. **3** *colloq.* a very hot day. □ **broiler house** a building for rearing broiler chickens in close confinement.

broke past of BREAK. —*predic.adj. colloq.* having no money; financially ruined. □ **go for broke** *sl.* risk everything in a strenuous effort. [(adj.) archaic past part. of BREAK]

broken /ˈbrəʊkən/ past part. of BREAK. —adj. **1** that has been broken; out of order. **2** (of a person) reduced to despair; beaten. **3** (of a language or of speech) spoken falteringly as by a foreigner (*broken English*). **4** disturbed, interrupted (*broken time*). **5** uneven (*broken ground*). □ **broken chord** Mus. a chord in which the notes are played successively. **brokendown 1** worn out by age, use, or ill-treatment. **2** out of order. **broken-hearted** overwhelmed with sorrow or grief. **broken home** a family in which the parents are divorced or separated. **broken reed** a person who has become unreliable or ineffective. □ **brokenly** adv. **brokenness** n.

broker /ˈbrəʊkə(r)/ n. **1** an agent who buys and sells for others; a middleman. **2** a member of the Stock Exchange dealing in stocks and shares. **3** *Brit.* an official appointed to sell or appraise distrained goods. [ME f. AF *brocour*, of unkn. orig.]

■ **Usage** In sense 2 in the UK, brokers have officially been called *broker-dealers* since Oct. 1986, and entitled to act as agents and principals in share dealings.

brokerage /ˈbrəʊkərɪdʒ/ n. a broker's fee or commission.

broking /ˈbrəʊkɪŋ/ n. the trade or business of a broker.

brolly /ˈbrɒlɪ/ n. (pl. **-ies**) *Brit.* **1** *colloq.* an umbrella. **2** *sl.* a parachute. [abbr.]

bromelia /brəʊˈmiːlɪə/ *n.* (also **bromeliad** /-lɪad/) any plant of the family Bromeliaceae (esp. of the genus *Bromelia*), native to the New World, having short stems with rosettes of stiff usu. spiny leaves, e.g. pineapple. [O. *Bromel*, Sw. botanist d. 1705]

bromide /ˈbrəʊmaɪd/ *n.* **1** *Chem.* any binary compound of bromine. **2** *Pharm.* a preparation of usu. potassium bromide, used as a sedative. **3** a trite remark. □ **bromide paper** a photographic printing paper coated with silver bromide emulsion.

bromine /ˈbrəʊmiːn/ *n.* *Chem.* a liquid element with a choking irritating smell, used in the manufacture of chemicals for photography and medicine. □ **bromism** *n.* [F *brome* f. Gk *brōmos* stink]

bronchial /ˈbrɒŋkɪəl/ *adj.* of or relating to the bronchi or bronchioles.

bronchiole /ˈbrɒŋkɪˌəʊl/ *n.* any of the minute divisions of a bronchus. □ **bronchiolar** /-ˈəʊlə(r)/ *adj.*

bronchitis /brɒŋˈkaɪtɪs/ *n.* inflammation of the mucous membrane in the bronchial tubes. □ **bronchitic** /-ˈkɪtɪk/ *adj.* & *n.*

bronchopneumonia /ˌbrɒŋkəʊnjuːˈməʊnɪə/ *n.* inflammation of the lungs, arising in the bronchi or bronchioles.

bronchus /ˈbrɒŋkəs/ *n.* (*pl.* **bronchi** /-kaɪ/) any of the major air passages of the lungs, esp. either of the two main divisions of the windpipe. [LL f. Gk *brogkhos* windpipe]

bronco /ˈbrɒŋkəʊ/ *n.* (*pl.* **-os**) a wild or half-tamed horse of the western US. [Sp., = rough]

brontosaurus /ˌbrɒntəˈsɔːrəs/ *n.* (also **brontosaur** /ˈbrɒntəˌsɔː(r)/) a large plant-eating dinosaur of the genus *Brontosaurus*, with a long whiplike tail and trunk-like legs. [Gk *brontē* thunder + *sauros* lizard]

bronze /brɒnz/ *n., adj.,* & *v.* —*n.* **1** any alloy of copper and tin. **2** its brownish colour. **3** a thing made of bronze, esp. as a work of art. —*adj.* made of or coloured like bronze. —*v.* **1** *tr.* give a bronzelike surface to. **2** *tr.* & *intr.* make or become brown; tan. □ **Bronze Age** *Archaeol.* the period when weapons and tools were usu. made of bronze. **bronze medal** a medal usu. awarded to a competitor who comes third (esp. in sport). □ **bronzy** *adj.* [F f. It. *bronzo*, prob. f. Pers. *birinj* copper]

brooch /brəʊtʃ/ *n.* an ornament fastened to clothing with a hinged pin. [ME *broche* = BROACH *n.*]

brood /bruːd/ *n.* & *v.* —*n.* **1** the young of an animal (esp. a bird) produced at one hatching or birth. **2** *colloq.* the children in a family. **3** a group of related things. **4** bee or wasp larvae. **5** (*attrib.*) kept for breeding (*brood-mare*). —*v.* **1** *intr.* (often foll. by *on, over,* etc.) worry or ponder (esp. resentfully). **2 a** *intr.* sit as a hen on eggs to hatch them. **b** *tr.* sit on (eggs) to hatch them. **3** *intr.* (usu. foll. by *over*) (of silence, a storm, etc.) hang or hover closely. □ **broodingly** *adv.* [OE *brōd* f. Gmc]

brooder /ˈbruːdə(r)/ *n.* **1** a heated house for chicks, piglets, etc. **2** a person who broods.

broody /ˈbruːdɪ/ *adj.* (**broodier, broodiest**) **1** (of a hen) wanting to brood. **2** sullenly thoughtful or depressed. **3** *colloq.* (of a woman) wanting to have a baby. □ **broodily** *adv.* **broodiness** *n.*

brook[1] /brʊk/ *n.* a small stream. □ **brooklet** /-lɪt/ *n.* [OE *brōc*, of unkn. orig.]

brook[2] /brʊk/ *v.tr.* (usu. with *neg.*) *literary* tolerate, allow. [OE *brūcan* f. Gmc]

broom /bruːm/ *n.* **1** a long-handled brush of bristles, twigs, etc. for sweeping (orig. one made of twigs of broom). **2** any of various shrubs, esp. *Cytisus scoparius* bearing bright yellow flowers. □ **new broom** a newly appointed person eager to make changes. [OE *brōm*]

broomstick /ˈbruːmstɪk/ *n.* the handle of a broom, esp. as allegedly ridden on through the air by witches.

Bros. *abbr.* Brothers (esp. in the name of a firm).

broth /brɒθ/ *n.* *Cookery* **1** a thin soup of meat or fish stock. **2** unclarified meat or fish stock. [OE f. Gmc: rel. to BREW]

brothel /ˈbrɒθ(ə)l/ *n.* a house etc. where prostitution takes place. [orig. *brothel-house* f. ME *brothel* worthless man, prostitute, f. OE *brēothan* go to ruin]

brother /ˈbrʌðə(r)/ *n.* **1** a man or boy in relation to other sons and daughters of his parents. **2 a** (often as a form of address) a close male friend or associate. **b** a male fellow member of a trade union etc. **3** (*pl.* also **brethren** /ˈbreðrɪn/) **a** a member of a male religious order, esp. a monk. **b** a fellow member of the Christian Church, a religion, or a guild etc. **4** a fellow human being. □ **brother-in-law** (*pl.* **brothers-in-law**) **1** the brother of one's wife or husband. **2** the husband of one's sister. **3** the husband of one's sister-in-law. □ **brotherless** *adj.* **brotherly** *adj.* & *adv.* **brotherliness** *n.* [OE *brōthor* f. Gmc]

brotherhood /ˈbrʌðəhʊd/ *n.* **1 a** the relationship between brothers. **b** brotherly friendliness; companionship. **2 a** an association, society, or community of people linked by a common interest, religion, trade, etc. **b** its members collectively. **3** *US* a trade union. **4** community of feeling between all human beings. [ME alt. f. *brotherrede* f. OE *brōthor-ræden* (cf. KINDRED) after words in -HOOD, -HEAD]

brought *past* and *past part.* of BRING.

brouhaha /ˈbruːhɑːˌhɑː/ *n.* commotion, sensation; hubbub, uproar. [F]

brow /braʊ/ *n.* **1** the forehead. **2** (usu. in *pl.*) an eyebrow. **3** the summit of a hill or pass. **4** the edge of a cliff etc. □ **browed** *adj.* [OE *brū* f. Gmc]

browbeat /ˈbraʊbiːt/ *v.tr.* (*past* **-beat**; *past part.* **-beaten**) intimidate with stern looks and words. □ **browbeater** *n.*

brown /braʊn/ *adj., n.,* & *v.* —*adj.* **1** having the colour produced by mixing red, yellow, and black, as of dark wood or rich soil. **2** dark-skinned or suntanned. **3** (of bread) made from a dark flour as wholemeal or wheatmeal. —*n.* **1** a brown colour or pigment. **2** brown clothes or material (*dressed in brown*). **3** (in a game or sport) a brown ball, piece, etc. —*v.tr.* & *intr.* make or become brown by cooking, sunburn, etc. □ **brown ale** a dark, mild, bottled beer. **brown bear** a large N. American brown bear, *Ursus arctos*. **brown coal** = LIGNITE. **browned off** *Brit. sl.* fed up, disheartened. **brown owl 1** any of various owls, esp. the tawny owl. **2** (**Brown Owl**) an adult leader of a Brownie Guides pack. **brown rice** unpolished rice with only the husk of the grain removed. **brown sugar** unrefined or partially refined sugar. □ **brownish** adj. **brownness** n. **browny** adj. [OE brūn f. Gmc]

Brownie /ˈbraʊnɪ/ n. **1** (in full **Brownie Guide**) a member of the junior branch of the Guides. **2** (**brownie**) Cookery **a** a small square of rich, usu. chocolate, cake with nuts. **b** Austral. & NZ a sweet currant-bread. **3** (**brownie**) a benevolent elf said to haunt houses and do household work secretly. □ **Brownie point** colloq. a notional credit for something done to please or win favour.

browning /ˈbraʊnɪŋ/ n. Brit. Cookery browned flour or any other additive to colour gravy.

brownstone /ˈbraʊnstəʊn/ n. US **1** a kind of reddish-brown sandstone used for building. **2** a building faced with this.

browse /braʊz/ v. & n. —v. **1** intr. & tr. read or survey desultorily. **2** intr. (often foll. by on) feed (on leaves, twigs, or scanty vegetation). **3** tr. crop and eat. —n. **1** twigs, young shoots, etc., as fodder for cattle. **2** an act of browsing. □ **browser** n. [(n.) f. earlier brouse f. OF brost young shoot, prob. f. Gmc; (v.) f. F broster]

brucellosis /ˌbruːsəˈləʊsɪs/ n. a disease caused by bacteria of the genus Brucella, affecting esp. cattle and causing undulant fever in humans. [Brucella f. Sir D. Bruce, Sc. physician d. 1931 + -OSIS]

bruise /bruːz/ n. & v. —n. **1** an injury appearing as an area of discoloured skin on a human or animal body, caused by a blow or impact. **2** a similar area of damage on a fruit etc. —v. **1** tr. **a** inflict a bruise on. **b** hurt mentally. **2** intr. be susceptible to bruising. **3** tr. crush or pound. [ME f. OE brȳsan crush, reinforced by AF bruser, OF bruisier break]

bruiser /ˈbruːzə(r)/ n. colloq. **1** a large tough-looking person. **2** a professional boxer.

bruit /bruːt/ v. & n. —v.tr. (often foll. by abroad, about) spread (a report or rumour). —n. archaic a report or rumour. [F, = noise f. bruire roar]

Brummagem /ˈbrʌmədʒəm/ adj. **1** cheap and showy (Brummagem goods). **2** counterfeit. [dial. form of Birmingham, England, with ref. to counterfeit coins and plated goods once made there]

Brummie /ˈbrʌmɪ/ n. & adj. (also **Brummy**) colloq. —n. (pl. **-ies**) a native of Birmingham. —adj. of or characteristic of a Brummie (a Brummie accent). [BRUMMAGEM]

brunch n. & v. —n. a late-morning meal eaten as the first meal of the day. —v.intr. eat brunch. [BR(EAKFAST) + (L)UNCH]

brunette /bruːˈnet/ n. & adj. —n. a woman with dark brown hair. —adj. (of a woman) having dark brown hair. [F, fem. of brunet, dimin. of brun BROWN]

brunt n. the chief or initial impact of an attack, task, etc. (esp. bear the brunt of). [ME: orig. unkn.]

brush n. & v. —n. **1** an implement with bristles, hair, wire, etc. varying in firmness set into a block or projecting from the end of a handle, for any of various purposes, esp. cleaning or scrubbing, painting, arranging the hair, etc. **2** the application of a brush; brushing. **3 a** (usu. foll. by with) a short esp. unpleasant encounter (a brush with the law). **b** a skirmish. **4 a** the bushy tail of a fox. **b** a brushlike tuft. **5** Electr. a piece of carbon or metal serving as an electrical contact esp. with a moving part. **6** esp. US & Austral. **a** undergrowth, thicket; small trees and shrubs. **b** land covered with brush. **c** Austral.

dense forest. —v. **1** tr. **a** sweep or scrub or put in order with a brush. **b** treat (a surface) with a brush so as to change its nature or appearance. **2** tr. **a** remove (dust etc.) with a brush. **b** apply (a liquid preparation) to a surface with a brush. **3** tr. & intr. graze or touch in passing. **4** intr. perform a brushing action or motion. □ **brush aside** dismiss or dispose of (a person, idea, etc.) curtly or lightly. **brushed aluminium** aluminium with a lustreless surface. **brushed fabric** fabric brushed so as to raise the nap. **brush off** rebuff; dismiss abruptly. **brush-off** n. a rebuff; an abrupt dismissal. **brush over** paint lightly. **brush up 1** clean up or smarten. **2** revive one's former knowledge of (a subject). **brush-up** n. the process of cleaning up. □ **brushlike** adj. **brushy** adj. [ME f. OF brosse]

brushless /ˈbrʌʃlɪs/ adj. not requiring the use of a brush.

brushwood /ˈbrʌʃwʊd/ n. **1** cut or broken twigs etc. **2** undergrowth; a thicket.

brushwork /ˈbrʌʃwɜːk/ n. **1** manipulation of the brush in painting. **2** a painter's style in this.

brusque /brʊsk, bruːsk, brʌsk/ adj. abrupt or offhand in manner or speech. □ **brusquely** adv. **brusqueness** n. **brusquerie** /ˈbrʊskəˌriː/ n. [F f. It. brusco sour]

Brussels sprout /ˈbrʌs(ə)lz/ n. **1** a variety of cabbage with small compact cabbage-like buds borne close together along a tall single stem. **2** any of these buds used as a vegetable.

brutal /ˈbruːt(ə)l/ adj. **1** savagely or coarsely cruel. **2** harsh, merciless. □ **brutality** /-ˈtælɪtɪ/ n. (pl. **-ies**). **brutally** adv. [F brutal or med.L brutalis f. brutus BRUTE]

brutalism /ˈbruːtəˌlɪz(ə)m/ n. **1** brutality. **2** a heavy plain style of architecture etc.

brutalize /ˈbruːtəˌlaɪz/ v.tr. (also **-ise**) **1** make brutal. **2** treat brutally. □ **brutalization** /-ˈzeɪʃ(ə)n/ n.

brute n. & adj. —n. **1 a** a brutal or violent person or animal. **b** colloq. an unpleasant person. **2** an animal as opposed to a human being. —adj. **1** not possessing the capacity to reason. **2 a** animal-like, cruel. **b** stupid, sensual. **3** unthinking, merely material (brute force; brute matter). □ **brutehood** n. **brutish** adj. **brutishly** adv. **brutishness** n. [F f. L brutus stupid]

bryony /ˈbraɪənɪ/ n. (pl. **-ies**) any climbing plant of the genus Bryonia, esp. B. dioica bearing greenish-white flowers and red berries. □ **black bryony** a similar unrelated plant, Tamus communis, bearing poisonous berries. [L bryonia f. Gk bruōnia]

bryophyte /ˈbraɪəˌfaɪt/ n. any plant of the phylum Bryophyta, including mosses and liverworts. □ **bryophytic** /-ˈfɪtɪk/ adj. [mod.L Bryophyta f. Gk bruon moss + phuton plant]

BS abbr. **1** US Bachelor of Science. **2** Bachelor of Surgery. **3** British Standard(s).

B.Sc. abbr. Bachelor of Science.

BSE abbr. bovine spongiform encephalopathy, a usu. fatal disease of cattle involving the central nervous system and causing extreme agitation.

BSI abbr. British Standards Institution.

B-side /ˈbiːsaɪd/ n. the side of a gramophone record regarded as less important.

BST abbr. British Summer Time.

Bt. abbr. Baronet.

bubble /ˈbʌb(ə)l/ n. & v. —n. **1 a** a thin sphere of liquid enclosing air etc. **b** an air-filled cavity in a liquid or a solidified liquid such as glass or amber. **2** the sound or appearance of boiling. **3** a transparent domed cavity. —v.intr. **1** rise in or send up bubbles. **2** make the sound of boiling. □ **bubble and squeak** Brit. cooked cabbage fried with cooked potatoes or meat. **bubble bath 1** a preparation for adding to bath water to make it foam. **2** a bath with this added. **bubble car** Brit. a small motor car with a transparent dome. **bubble gum** chewing-gum that can be blown into bubbles. **bubble over** (often foll. by with) be exuberant with laughter, excitement, anger, etc. **bubble pack** a small package enclosing goods in a transparent material on a backing. [ME: prob. imit.]

bubbly /ˈbʌblɪ/ adj. & n. —adj. (**bubblier, bubbliest**) **1** having or resembling bubbles. **2** exuberant. —n. colloq. champagne.

bubo /ˈbjuːbəʊ/ n. (pl. **-oes**) a swollen inflamed lymph node in the armpit or groin. [med.L bubo -onis swelling f. Gk boubōn groin]

bubonic /bjuːˈbɒnɪk/ adj. relating to or characterized by buboes. □ **bubonic plague** a contagious bacterial disease characterized by fever, delirium, and the formation of buboes.

buccaneer /ˌbʌkəˈnɪə(r)/ n. & v. —n. **1** a pirate, orig. off the Spanish-American coasts. **2** an unscrupulous adventurer. —v.intr. be a buccaneer. □ **buccaneering** n. & adj. **buccaneerish** adj. [F boucanier f. boucaner cure meat on a barbecue f. boucan f. Tupi mukem]

buck[1] n. & v. —n. **1** the male of various animals, esp. the deer, hare, or rabbit. **2** archaic a fashionable young man. **3** (attrib.) **a** sl. male (buck antelope). **b** US Mil. of the lowest rank (buck private). —v. **1** intr. (of a horse) jump upwards with back arched and feet drawn together. **2** tr. **a** (usu. foll. by off) throw (a rider or burden) in this way. **b** US oppose, resist. **3** tr. & intr. (usu. foll. by up) colloq. **a** make or become more cheerful. **b** hurry. **4** tr. (as **bucked** adj.) colloq. encouraged, elated. □ **buck rarebit** Welsh rarebit with a poached egg on top. **buck-tooth** an upper tooth that projects. **bucker** n. [OE buc male deer, bucca male goat, f. ON]

buck[2] n. US etc. sl. a dollar. [19th c.: orig. unkn.]

buck[3] n. sl. an article placed as a reminder before a player whose turn it is to deal at poker. □ **pass the buck** colloq. shift responsibility (to another). [19th c.: orig. unkn.]

bucket /ˈbʌkɪt/ n. & v. —n. **1 a** a roughly cylindrical open container, esp. of metal, with a handle, used for carrying, drawing, or holding water etc. **b** the amount contained in this (need three buckets to fill the bath). **2** (in pl.) large quantities of liquid, esp. rain or tears (wept buckets). **3** a compartment on the outer edge of a water wheel. **4** the scoop of a dredger or a grain-elevator. —v. (**bucketed, bucketing**) **1** intr. & tr. (often foll. by along) Brit. move or drive jerkily or bumpily. **2** intr. (often foll. by down) (of liquid, esp. rain) pour heavily. □ **bucket seat** a seat with a rounded back to fit one person, esp. in a car. **bucket-shop 1** an office for gambling in stocks, speculating on markets, etc. **2** colloq. a travel agency specializing in cheap air tickets. □ **bucketful** n. (pl. **-fuls**). [ME & AF buket, buquet, perh. f. OE būc pitcher]

buckle /ˈbʌk(ə)l/ n. & v. —n. **1** a flat often rectangular frame with a hinged pin, used for joining the ends of a belt, strap, etc. **2** a similarly shaped ornament, esp. on a shoe. —v. **1** tr. (often foll. by up, on, etc.) fasten with a buckle. **2** tr. & intr. (often foll. by up) give way or cause to give way under longitudinal pressure; crumple up. □ **buckle down** make a determined effort. **buckle to** (or **down to**) prepare for, set about (work etc.). **buckle to** get to work, make a vigorous start. [ME f. OF boucle f. L buccula cheek-strap of a helmet f. bucca cheek: sense 2 of v. f. F boucler bulge]

buckler /ˈbʌklə(r)/ n. hist. a small round shield held by a handle. [ME f. OF bocler lit. 'having a boss' f. boucle BOSS²]

Buckley's /ˈbʌklɪz/ n. (in full **Buckley's chance**) Austral. & NZ colloq. little or no chance. [19th c.: orig. uncert.]

buckling /ˈbʌklɪŋ/ n. a smoked herring. [G Bückling bloater]

buckram /ˈbʌkrəm/ n. a coarse linen or other cloth stiffened with gum or paste, and used as interfacing or in bookbinding. [ME f. AF bukeram, OF boquerant, perh. f. Bokhara in central Asia]

buckshee /bʌkˈʃiː/ adj. & adv. Brit. sl. free of charge. [corrupt. of BAKSHEESH]

buckshot /ˈbʌkʃɒt/ n. coarse lead shot.

buckskin /ˈbʌkskɪn/ n. **1 a** the skin of a buck. **b** leather made from a buck's skin. **2** a thick smooth cotton or woollen cloth.

buckthorn /ˈbʌkθɔːn/ n. any thorny shrub of the genus Rhamnus, esp. R. cathartica with berries formerly used as a cathartic.

buckwheat /ˈbʌkwiːt/ n. any cereal plant of the genus Fagopyrum, esp. F. esculentum with seeds used for fodder and for flour. [MDu. boecweite beech wheat, its grains being shaped like beechmast]

bucolic /bjuːˈkɒlɪk/ adj. & n. —adj. of or concerning shepherds, the pastoral life, etc.; rural. —n. **1** (usu. in pl.) a pastoral poem or poetry. **2** a peasant. □ **bucolically** adv. [L bucolicus f. Gk boukolikos f. boukolos herdsman f. bous OX]

bud[1] n. & v. —n. **1 a** an immature knoblike shoot from which a stem, leaf, or flower develops. **b** a flower or leaf that is not fully open. **2** Biol. an asexual outgrowth from a parent organism that separates to form a new individual. **3** anything still undeveloped. —v. (**budded, budding**) **1** intr. Bot. & Zool. form a bud. **2** intr. begin to grow or develop (a budding cricketer). **3** tr. Hort. graft a bud (of a plant) on to another plant. □ **in bud** having newly formed buds. [ME: orig. unkn.]

bud[2] n. US colloq. (as a form of address) = BUDDY. [abbr.]

Buddha /ˈbʊdə/ n. **1** a title given to successive teachers of Buddhism, esp. to its founder, Gautama. **2** a statue or picture of the Buddha. [Skr., = enlightened, past part. of budh know]

Buddhism /ˈbʊdɪz(ə)m/ n. a widespread Asian religion or philosophy, founded by Gautama Buddha in India in the 5th c. BC, which teaches that elimination of the self and earthly desires is the highest goal (cf. NIRVANA). □ **Buddhist** n. & adj. **Buddhistic** /-ˈdɪstɪk/ adj. **Buddhistical** /-ˈdɪstɪk(ə)l/ adj.

buddleia /ˈbʌdlɪə/ n. any shrub of the genus Buddleia, with fragrant flowers attractive to butterflies. [A. Buddle, Engl. botanist d. 1715]

buddy /ˈbʌdɪ/ n. & v. esp. US colloq. —n. (pl. **-ies**) (often as a form of address) a close friend or mate. —v.intr. (**-ies**, **-ied**) (often foll. by *up*) become friendly. [perh. corrupt. of *brother*]

budge /bʌdʒ/ v. (usu. with *neg.*) **1** intr. **a** make the slightest movement. **b** change one's opinion (*he's stubborn, he won't budge*). **2** tr. cause or compel to budge (*nothing will budge him*). [F *bouger* stir ult. f. L *bullire* boil]

budgerigar /ˈbʌdʒərɪˌɡɑː(r)/ n. a small green parrot, *Melopsittacus undulatus*, native to Australia, and bred in coloured varieties which are often kept as cage-birds. [Aboriginal, = good cockatoo]

budget /ˈbʌdʒɪt/ n. & v. —n. **1** the amount of money needed or available (for a specific item etc.) (*a budget of £200; mustn't exceed the budget*). **2 a** (**the Budget**) *Brit.* the usu. annual estimate of national revenue and expenditure. **b** an estimate or plan of expenditure in relation to income. **c** a private person's or family's similar estimate. **3** (*attrib.*) inexpensive. —v.tr. & intr. (**budgeted**, **budgeting**) (often foll. by *for*) allow or arrange for in a budget (*have budgeted for a new car; can budget £60*). □ **on a budget** avoiding expense; cheap. □ **budgetary** adj. [ME = pouch, f. OF *bougette* dimin. of *bouge* leather bag f. L *bulga* (f. Gaulish) knapsack: cf. BULGE]

budgie /ˈbʌdʒɪ/ n. colloq. = BUDGERIGAR. [abbr.]

buff adj., n., & v. —adj. **1** of a yellowish beige colour (*buff envelope*). —n. **1** a yellowish beige colour. **2** colloq. an enthusiast, esp. for a particular hobby (*railway buff*). **3** colloq. the human skin unclothed. **4 a** a velvety dull-yellow ox-leather. **b** (*attrib.*) (of a garment etc.) made of this (*buff gloves*). —v.tr. **1** polish (metal, fingernails, etc.). **2** make (leather) velvety like buff, by removing the surface. □ **in the buff** colloq. naked. [orig. sense 'buffalo', prob. f. F *buffle*; sense 2 of n. orig. f. buff uniforms formerly worn by New York volunteer firemen, applied to enthusiastic fire-watchers]

buffalo /ˈbʌfəˌləʊ/ n. (pl. same or **-oes**) **1** either of two species of ox, *Synceros caffer*, native to Africa, or *Bubalus arnee*, native to Asia with heavy backswept horns. **2** a N. American bison, *Bison bison*. [prob. f. Port. *bufalo* f. LL *bufalus* f. L *bubalus* f. Gk *boubalos* antelope, wild ox]

buffer[1] /ˈbʌfə(r)/ n. & v. —n. **1 a** a device that protects against or reduces the effect of an impact. **b** *Brit.* such a device (usu. one of a pair) on the front and rear of a railway vehicle or at the end of a track. **2** *Computing* a temporary memory area or queue for data to aid its transfer between devices or programs operating at different speeds etc. —v.tr. act as a buffer to. □ **buffer State** a small State situated between two larger ones potentially hostile to one another and regarded as reducing the likelihood of open hostilities. [prob. f. obs. *buff* (v.), imit. of the sound of a soft body struck]

buffer[2] /ˈbʌfə(r)/ n. *Brit. sl.* a silly or incompetent old man (esp. *old buffer*). [18th c.: prob. formed as BUFFER[1] or with the sense 'stutterer']

buffet[1] /ˈbʊfeɪ, ˈbʌfeɪ/ n. **1** a room or counter where light meals or snacks may be bought (*station buffet*). **2** a meal consisting of several dishes set out from which guests serve themselves (*buffet lunch*). **3** /also bʌfɪt/ a sideboard or recessed cupboard for china etc. [F f. OF *bufet* stool, of unkn. orig.]

buffet[2] /ˈbʌfɪt/ v. & n. —v. (**buffeted**, **buffeting**) **1** tr. **a** strike or knock repeatedly (*wind buffeted the trees*). **b** strike, esp. repeatedly, with the hand or fist. **2** tr. (of fate etc.) treat badly; plague. **3 a** intr. struggle; fight one's way (through difficulties etc.). **b** tr. contend with (waves etc.). —n. **1** a blow, esp. of the hand or fist. **2** a shock. [ME f. OF dimin. of *bufe* blow]

buffoon /bəˈfuːn/ n. **1** a jester; a mocker. **2** a stupid person. □ **buffoonery** n. **buffoonish** adj. [F *bouffon* f. It. *buffone* f. med.L *buffo* clown f. Rmc]

bug n. & v. —n. **1 a** any of various hemipterous insects with oval flattened bodies and mouth-parts modified for piercing and sucking. **b** US any small insect. **2** *sl.* a micro-organism, esp. a bacterium, or a disease caused by it. **3** a concealed microphone. **4** *sl.* an error in a computer program or system etc. **5** *sl.* an obsession, enthusiasm, etc. —v. (**bugged**, **bugging**) **1** tr. *sl.* conceal a microphone in (esp. a building or room). **2** tr. *sl.* annoy, bother. **3** intr. (often foll. by *out*) US *sl.* leave quickly. □ **bug-eyed** with bulging eyes. [17th c.: orig. unkn.]

bugbear /ˈbʌɡbeə(r)/ n. **1** a cause of annoyance or anger; a *bête noire.* **2** an object of baseless fear. [obs. *bug* + BEAR[2]]

bugger /ˈbʌɡə(r)/ n., v., & int. coarse sl. (except in sense 2 of n. and 3 of v.) —n. **1 a** an unpleasant or awkward person or thing (*the bugger won't fit*). **b** a person of a specified kind (*he's a miserable bugger; you clever bugger!*). **2** a person who commits buggery. —v.tr. **1** as an exclamation of annoyance (*bugger the thing!*). **2** (often foll. by *up*) *Brit.* **a** ruin; spoil (*really buggered it up*). **b** exhaust, tire out. **3** commit buggery with. —int. expressing annoyance. □ **bugger about** (or **around**) (often foll. by *with*) **1** mess about. **2** mislead; persecute. **bugger-all** nothing. **bugger off** (often in *imper.*) go away. [ME f. MDu. f. OF *bougre*, orig. 'heretic' f. med.L *Bulgarus* Bulgarian (member of the Greek Church)]

buggery /ˈbʌɡərɪ/ n. **1** anal intercourse. **2** = BESTIALITY 2. [ME f. MDu. *buggerie* f. OF *bougerie*: see BUGGER]

buggy /ˈbʌɡɪ/ n. (pl. **-ies**) **1** a light, horse-drawn, esp. two-wheeled, vehicle for one or two people. **2** a small, sturdy, esp. open, motor vehicle (*beach buggy; dune buggy*). **3** US a pram. [18th c.: orig. unkn.]

bugle[1] /ˈbjuːɡ(ə)l/ n. & v. —n. (also **bugle-horn**) a brass instrument like a small trumpet, used esp. by huntsmen and for military signals. —v. **1** intr. sound a bugle. **2** tr. sound (a note, a call, etc.) on a bugle. □ **bugler** /ˈbjuːɡlə(r)/ n. **buglet** /ˈbjuːɡlɪt/ n. [ME, orig. = 'buffalo', f. OF f. L *buculus* dimin. of *bos* ox]

bugle[2] /ˈbjuːɡ(ə)l/ n. a blue-flowered mat-forming plant, *Ajuga reptans.* [ME f. LL *bugula*]

buhl /buːl/ n. (also **boule**, **boulle**) **1** pieces of brass, tortoiseshell, etc., cut to make a pattern and used as decorative inlays esp. on furniture. **2** work inlaid with buhl. **3** (*attrib.*) inlaid with buhl. [(*buhl* Germanized) f. A. C. *Boule*, Fr. wood-carver d. 1732]

build /bɪld/ v. & n. —v.tr. (*past* and *past. part.* **built** /bɪlt/) **1 a** construct (a house, vehicle, fire, road, model, etc.) by putting parts or material together. **b** commission, finance, and oversee the building of (*the council has built two new* schools). **2 a** (often foll. by *up*) establish, develop, make, or accumulate gradually (*built the business up from nothing*). **b** (often foll. by *on*) base (hopes, theories, etc.) (*ideas built on a false foundation*). **3** (as **built** adj.) having a specified build (*sturdily built*; *brick-built*). —*n.* **1** the proportions of esp. the human body (*a slim build*). **2** a style of construction. □ **build in** incorporate as part of a structure. **build on** add (an extension etc.). **build up 1** increase in size or strength. **2** praise; boost. **3** gradually become established. **build-up 1** a favourable description in advance; publicity. **2** a gradual approach to a climax or maximum (*the build-up was slow but sure*). **built-in 1** forming an integral part of a structure. **2** forming an integral part of a person's character. **built-up 1** (of a locality) densely covered by houses etc. **2** increased in height etc. by the addition of parts. [OE *byldan* f. *bold* dwelling f. Gmc: cf. BOWER, BOOTH]

builder /ˈbɪldə(r)/ *n.* **1** a contractor for building houses etc.; a master builder. **2** a person engaged as a bricklayer etc. on a building site.

building /ˈbɪldɪŋ/ *n.* **1** a permanent fixed structure forming an enclosure and providing protection from the elements etc. (e.g. a house, school, factory, or stable). **2** the constructing of such structures. □ **building line** a limit or boundary between a house and a street beyond which the owner may not build. **building site** an area before or during the construction of a house etc. **building society** *Brit.* a public finance company which accepts investments at interest and lends capital for mortgages on houses etc.

bulb *n.* **1 a** an underground fleshy-leaved storage organ of some plants (e.g. lily, onion) sending roots downwards and leaves upwards. **b** a plant grown from this, e.g. a daffodil. **2** = *light-bulb* (see LIGHT¹). **3** any object or part shaped like a bulb. [L *bulbus* f. Gk *bolbos* onion]

bulbous /ˈbʌlbəs/ *adj.* **1** shaped like a bulb; fat or bulging. **2** having a bulb or bulbs. **3** (of a plant) growing from a bulb.

bulge *n.* & *v.* —*n.* **1 a** a convex part of an otherwise flatter surface. **b** an irregular swelling; a lump. **2** *colloq.* a temporary increase in quantity or number (*baby bulge*). —*v.* **1** *intr.* swell outwards. **2** *intr.* be full or replete. **3** *tr.* swell (a bag, cheeks, etc.) by stuffing. □ **bulgingly** *adv.* **bulgy** *adj.* [ME f. OF *boulge*, *bouge* f. L *bulga*: see BUDGET]

bulgur /ˈbʌlgə(r)/ *n.* (also **bulgar**, **bulghur**) a cereal food of whole wheat partially boiled then dried, eaten esp. in Turkey. [Turk.]

bulimarexia /bjuːˌlɪməˈreksɪə/ *n.* esp. *US* = BULIMIA 2. □ **bulimarexic** *adj.* & *n.* [BULIMIA + ANOREXIA]

bulimia /bjuːˈlɪmɪə/ *n.* *Med.* **1** insatiable overeating. **2** (in full **bulimia nervosa**) an emotional disorder in which bouts of extreme overeating are followed by depression and self-induced vomiting, purging, or fasting. □ **bulimic** *adj.* & *n.* [mod.L f. Gk *boulimia* f. *bous* ox + *limos* hunger]

bulk *n.* & *v.* —*n.* **1 a** size; magnitude (esp. large). **b** a large mass, body, or person. **c** a large quantity. **2 a** large shape, body, or person (*jacket barely covered his bulk*). **3** (usu. prec. by *the*; treated as *pl.*) the greater part or number (*the bulk of the applicants are women*). **4** roughage. —*v.* **1** *intr.*

seem in respect of size or importance (*bulks large in his reckoning*). **2** *tr.* make (a book, a textile yarn, etc.) seem thicker by suitable treatment. □ **bulk-buying 1** buying in large amounts at a discount. **2** the purchase by one buyer of all or most of a producer's output. **in bulk** in large quantities. [sense 'cargo' f. OIcel. *búlki*; sense 'mass' etc. perh. alt. f. obs. *bouk* (cf. BUCK³)]

bulkhead /ˈbʌlkhed/ *n.* an upright partition separating the compartments in a ship, aircraft, vehicle, etc. [*bulk* stall f. ON *bálkr* + HEAD]

bulky /ˈbʌlkɪ/ *adj.* (**bulkier**, **bulkiest**) **1** taking up much space, large. **2** awkwardly large, unwieldy. □ **bulkily** *adv.* **bulkiness** *n.*

bull¹ /bʊl/ *n.* & *adj.* —*n.* **1 a** an uncastrated male bovine animal. **b** a male of the whale, elephant, and other large animals. **2** (**the Bull**) the zodiacal sign or constellation Taurus. **3** *Brit.* the bull's-eye of a target. **4** *Stock Exch.* a person who buys shares hoping to sell them at a higher price later. —*adj.* like that of a bull (*bull neck*). □ **bull-nose** (or **-nosed**) with rounded end. **bull's-eye 1** the centre of a target. **2** a large hard peppermint-flavoured sweet. **3** a hemisphere or thick disc of glass in a ship's deck or side to admit light. **4** a small circular window. **5 a** a hemispherical lens. **b** a lantern fitted with this. **6** a boss of glass at the centre of a blown glass sheet. **bull-terrier 1** a short-haired dog of a breed that is a cross between a bulldog and a terrier. **2** this breed. □ **bullish** *adj.* [ME f. ON *boli* = MLG, MDu *bulle*]

bull² /bʊl/ *n.* a papal edict. [ME f. OF *bulle* f. L *bulla* rounded object, in med.L 'seal']

bull³ /bʊl/ *n.* (also **Irish bull**) an expression containing a contradiction in terms or implying ludicrous inconsistency. **2** *sl.* **a** unnecessary routine tasks or discipline. **b** nonsense. **c** trivial or insincere talk or writing. [17th c.: orig. unkn.]

bulldog /ˈbʊldɒg/ *n.* **1 a** a dog of a sturdy powerful breed with a large head and smooth hair. **b** this breed. **2** a tenacious and courageous person. □ **bulldog clip** a strong sprung clip for papers.

bulldoze /ˈbʊldəʊz/ *v.tr.* **1** clear with a bulldozer. **2** *colloq.* **a** intimidate. **b** make (one's way) forcibly.

bulldozer /ˈbʊlˌdəʊzə(r)/ *n.* a powerful tractor with a broad curved vertical blade at the front for clearing ground. [*bulldose* (or *-doze*) *US* = intimidate, f. BULL¹: second element uncert.]

bullet /ˈbʊlɪt/ *n.* a small round or cylindrical missile with a pointed end, fired from a rifle, revolver, etc. □ **bullet-headed** having a round head. [F *boulet*, *boulette* dimin. of *boule* ball f. L *bulla* bubble]

bulletin /ˈbʊlɪtɪn/ *n.* **1** a short official statement of news. **2** a regular list of information etc. issued by an organization or society. □ **bulletin-board** *US* a notice-board. [F f. It. *bullettino* dimin. of *bulletta* passport, dimin. of *bulla* seal, BULL²]

bullfight /ˈbʊlfaɪt/ *n.* a sport of baiting and (usu.) killing bulls as a public spectacle, esp. in Spain. □ **bullfighter** *n.* **bullfighting** *n.*

bullfinch /ˈbʊlfɪntʃ/ *n.* a finch, *Pyrrhula pyrrhula*, with a short stout beak and bright plumage.

bullfrog /ˈbʊlfrɒg/ *n.* large frog, *Rana catesbiana*, native to N. America, with a deep croak.

bull-headed /bʊlˈhedɪd/ *adj.* obstinate; impetuous; blundering. □ **bull-headedly** *adv.* **bull-headedness** *n.*

bullion /ˈbʊlɪən/ n. a metal (esp. gold or silver) in bulk before coining, or valued by weight. [AF = mint, var. of OF *bouillon* ult. f. L *bullire* boil]

bullock /ˈbʊlək/ n. a castrated bull. [OE *bulluc*, dimin. of BULL¹]

bullring /ˈbʊlrɪŋ/ n. an arena for bullfights.

bullshit /ˈbʊlʃɪt/ n. & v. *coarse sl.* —n. 1 (often as *int.*) nonsense, rubbish. 2 trivial or insincere talk or writing. —v.intr. (**-shitted, -shitting**) talk nonsense; bluff. □ **bullshitter** n. [BULL³ + SHIT]

bully¹ /ˈbʊlɪ/ n. & v. —n. (pl. **-ies**) a person who uses strength or power to coerce others by fear. —v.tr. (**-ies, -ied**) 1 persecute or oppress by force or threats. 2 (foll. by *into* + verbal noun) pressure or coerce (a person) to do something (*bullied him into agreeing*). □ **bully-boy** a hired ruffian. [orig. as a term of endearment, prob. f. MDu. *boele* lover]

bully² /ˈbʊlɪ/ *int. colloq.* (foll. by *for*) expressing admiration or approval, or *iron.* (*bully for them!*). [perh. f BULLY¹]

bully³ /ˈbʊlɪ/ n. & v. (in full **bully off**) —n. (pl. **-ies**) the start of play in hockey in which two opponents strike each other's sticks three times and then go for the ball. —v.intr. (**-ies, -ied**) start play in this way. [19th c.: perh. f. *bully* scrum in Eton football, of unkn. orig.]

bully⁴ /ˈbʊlɪ/ n. (in full **bully beef**) corned beef. [F *bouilli* boiled beef f. *bouillir* BOIL¹]

bulrush /ˈbʊlrʌʃ/ n. 1 = *reed-mace* (see REED). 2 a rushlike water-plant, *Scirpus lacustris*, used for weaving. 3 *Bibl.* a papyrus plant. [perh. f. BULL¹ = large, coarse, as in *bullfrog*, etc.]

bulwark /ˈbʊlwək/ n. 1 a defensive wall, esp. of earth; a rampart; a mole or breakwater. 2 a person, principle, etc., that acts as a defence. 3 (usu. in pl.) a ship's side above deck. [ME f. MLG, MDu. *bolwerk*: see BOLE, WORK]

bum¹ n. *Brit. sl.* the buttocks. □ **bum-bag** a small pouch on a belt worn round the waist or hips and used for carrying money, valuables, etc. **bum-sucking** toadying. [ME *bom*, of unkn. orig.]

bum² n., v., & adj. *US sl.* —n. a habitual loafer or tramp; a lazy dissolute person. —v. (**bummed, bumming**) 1 intr. (often foll. by *about, around*) loaf or wander around; be a bum. 2 tr. get by begging; cadge. —*attrib.adj.* of poor quality. □ **bum's rush** forcible ejection. **bum steer** false information. **on the bum** vagrant, begging. [prob. abbr. or back-form. f. BUMMER]

bumble /ˈbʌmb(ə)l/ v.intr. 1 (foll. by *on*) speak in a rambling incoherent way. 2 (often as **bumbling** adj.) move or act ineptly; blunder. 3 make a buzz or hum. □ **bumbler** n. [BOOM¹ + -LE⁴: partly f. *bumble* = blunderer]

bumble-bee /ˈbʌmb(ə)lˌbiː/ n. any large loud humming bee of the genus *Bombus*. [as BUMBLE]

bumf /bʌmf/ n. (also **bumph**) *Brit. colloq.* 1 usu. *derog.* papers, documents. 2 lavatory paper. [abbr. of *bum-fodder*]

bummalo /ˈbʌməˌləʊ/ n. (pl. same) a small fish, *Harpodon nehereus*, of S. Asian coasts, dried and used as food (see BOMBAY DUCK). [perh. f. Marathi *bombīl(a)*]

bummer /ˈbʌmə(r)/ n. *US sl.* 1 an idler; a loafer. 2 an unpleasant occurrence. [19th c.: perh. f. G *Bummler*]

bump /bʌmp/ n., v., & adv. —n. 1 a dull-sounding blow or collision. 2 a swelling or dent caused by this. 3 an uneven patch on a road, field, etc. 4 *Phrenol.* any of various prominences on the skull thought to indicate different mental faculties. —v. 1 a tr. hit or come against with a bump. b intr. (of two objects) collide. 2 intr. (foll. by *against, into*) hit with a bump; collide with. 3 tr. (often foll. by *against, on*) hurt or damage by striking (*bumped my head on the ceiling; bumped the car while parking*). 4 intr. (usu. foll. by *along*) move or travel with much jolting (*we bumped along the road*). 5 tr. *US* displace, esp. by seniority. —adv. with a bump; suddenly; violently. □ **bump into** *colloq.* meet by chance. **bump off** *sl.* murder. **bump up** *colloq.* increase (prices etc.). [16th c., imit.: perh. f. Scand.]

bumper /ˈbʌmpə(r)/ n. 1 a horizontal bar or strip fixed across the front or back of a motor vehicle to reduce damage in a collision or as a trim. 2 (usu. *attrib.*) an unusually large or fine example (*a bumper crop*). 3 *Cricket* a ball rising high after pitching. □ **bumper car** = DODGEM.

bumpkin /ˈbʌmpkɪn/ n. a rustic or socially inept person. [perh. Du. *boomken* little tree or MDu. *bommekijn* little barrel]

bumptious /ˈbʌmpʃəs/ adj. offensively self-assertive or conceited. □ **bumptiously** adv. **bumptiousness** n. [BUMP, after FRACTIOUS]

bumpy /ˈbʌmpɪ/ adj. (**bumpier, bumpiest**) 1 having many bumps (*a bumpy road*). 2 affected by bumps (*a bumpy ride*). □ **bumpily** adv. **bumpiness** n.

bun /bʌn/ n. 1 a small usu. sweetened bread roll or cake, often with dried fruit. 2 *Sc.* a rich fruit cake or currant bread. 3 hair worn in the shape of a bun. □ **hot cross bun** a bun marked with a cross, traditionally eaten on Good Friday. [ME: orig. unkn.]

bunch /bʌntʃ/ n. & v. —n. 1 a cluster of things growing or fastened together (*bunch of grapes; bunch of keys*). 2 a collection; a set or lot (*best of the bunch*). 3 *colloq.* a group; a gang. —v. 1 tr. make into a bunch or bunches; gather into close folds. 2 intr. form into a group or crowd. □ **bunchy** adj. [ME: orig. unkn.]

bundle /ˈbʌnd(ə)l/ n. & v. —n. 1 a collection of things tied or fastened together. 2 a set of nerve fibres etc. banded together. 3 *sl.* a large amount of money. —v. 1 tr. (usu. foll. by *up*) tie in or make into a bundle (*bundled up my squash kit*). 2 tr. (usu. foll. by *into*) throw or push, esp. quickly or confusedly (*bundled the papers into the drawer*). 3 tr. (usu. foll. by *out, off, away*, etc.) send (esp. a person) away hurriedly or unceremoniously (*bundled them off the premises*). □ **bundle up** dress warmly or cumbersomely. **go a bundle on** *sl.* be very fond of. □ **bundler** n. [ME, perh. f. OE *byndelle* a binding, but also f. LG, Du *bundel*]

bung¹ n. & v. —n. a stopper for closing a hole in a container, esp. a cask. —v.tr. 1 stop with a bung. 2 *Brit. sl.* throw, toss. □ **bunged up** closed, blocked. **bung-hole** a hole for filling or emptying a cask etc. [MDu. *bonghe*]

bung² adj. *Austral.* & *NZ sl.* dead; ruined, useless. □ **go bung** 1 die. 2 fail; go bankrupt. [Aboriginal]

bungalow /ˈbʌŋgəˌləʊ/ n. a one-storeyed house. [Gujarati *bangalo* f. Hind. *banglā* belonging to Bengal]

bungee /ˈbʌndʒɪ/ n. (in full **bungee cord, rope**) elasticated cord or rope used for securing baggage and in bungee jumping. □ **bungee jumping** the sport of jumping from a height while secured by a bungee from the ankles or a harness. [20th c.: orig. unkn.]

bungle /ˈbʌŋg(ə)l/ v. & n. —v. 1 tr. blunder over, mismanage, or fail at (a task). 2 intr. work badly or clumsily. —n. a bungled attempt; bungled work. □ **bungler** n. [imit.: cf. BUMBLE]

bunion /ˈbʌnjən/ n. a swelling on the foot, esp. at the first joint of the big toe. [OF buignon f. buigne bump on the head]

bunk¹ n. a sleeping-berth, esp. a shelflike bed against a wall, e.g. in a ship. □ **bunk-bed** each of two or more beds one above the other, forming a unit. [18th c.: orig. unkn.]

bunk² n. □ **do a bunk** Brit. sl. leave or abscond hurriedly. [19th c.: orig. unkn.]

bunk³ n. sl. nonsense, humbug. [abbr. of BUNKUM]

bunker /ˈbʌŋkə(r)/ n. & v. —n. 1 a large container or compartment for storing fuel. 2 a reinforced underground shelter, esp. for use in wartime. 3 a hollow filled with sand, used as an obstacle in a golf-course. —v.tr. 1 fill the fuel bunkers of (a ship etc.). 2 (usu. in passive) a trap in a bunker (in sense 3). b bring into difficulties. [19th c.: orig. unkn.]

bunkum /ˈbʌŋkəm/ n. (also **buncombe**) nonsense; humbug. [orig. buncombe f. Buncombe County in N. Carolina, mentioned in a nonsense speech by its Congressman, c.1820]

bunny /ˈbʌnɪ/ n. (pl. -ies) a child's name for a rabbit. [dial. bun rabbit]

Bunsen burner /ˈbʌns(ə)n/ n. a small adjustable gas burner used in scientific work. [R. W. Bunsen, Ger. chemist d. 1899]

bunting¹ /ˈbʌntɪŋ/ n. any of numerous seed-eating birds of the family Emberizidae, related to the finches and sparrows. [ME: orig. unkn.]

bunting² /ˈbʌntɪŋ/ n. 1 flags and other decorations. 2 a loosely-woven fabric used for these. [18th c.: orig. unkn.]

bunyip /ˈbʌnjɪp/ n. Austral. 1 a fabulous monster inhabiting swamps and lagoons. 2 an imposter. [Aboriginal]

buoy /bɔɪ/ n. & v. —n. 1 an anchored float serving as a navigation mark or to show reefs etc. 2 a lifebuoy. —v.tr. 1 (usu. foll. by up) a keep afloat. b sustain the courage or spirits of (a person etc.); uplift, encourage. 2 (often foll. by out) mark with a buoy or buoys. [ME prob. f. MDu. bo(e)ye, ult. f. L boia collar f. Gk boeiai ox-hides]

buoyancy /ˈbɔɪənsɪ/ n. 1 the capacity to be or remain buoyant. 2 resilience; recuperative power. 3 cheerfulness.

buoyant /ˈbɔɪənt/ adj. 1 a able or apt to keep afloat or rise to the top of a liquid or gas. b (of a liquid or gas) able to keep something afloat. 2 light-hearted. □ **buoyantly** adv. [F buoyant or Sp. boyante part. of boyar float f. boya BUOY]

bur n. (also **burr**) 1 a a prickly clinging seed-case or flower-head. b any plant producing these. 2 a person hard to shake off. 3 = BURR n. 2a. [ME: cf. Da. burre bur, burdock, Sw. kard-borre burdock]

burble /ˈbɜːb(ə)l/ v. & n. —v.intr. speak ramblingly; make a murmuring noise. —n. 1 a murmuring noise. 2 rambling speech. □ **burbler** n. [19th c.: imit.]

burden /ˈbɜːd(ə)n/ n. & v. —n. 1 a load, esp. a heavy one. 2 an oppressive duty, obligation, expense, emotion, etc. 3 the bearing of loads

(beast of burden). 4 (also archaic **burthen** /ˈbɜːð(ə)n/) a ship's carrying-capacity, tonnage. 5 a the refrain or chorus of a song. b the chief theme or gist of a speech, book, poem, etc. —v.tr. load with a burden; oppress. □ **burden of proof** the obligation to prove one's case. □ **burdensome** adj. [OE byrthen: rel. to BIRTH]

burdock /ˈbɜːdɒk/ n. any plant of the genus Arctium, with prickly flowers and docklike leaves. [BUR + DOCK³]

bureau /ˈbjʊərəʊ, -ˈrəʊ/ n. (pl. **bureaux** or **bureaus** /-rəʊz/) 1 a Brit. a writing-desk with drawers and usu. an angled top opening downwards to form a writing surface. b US a chest of drawers. 2 a an office or department for transacting specific business. b a government department. [F, = desk, orig. its baize covering, f. OF burel f. bure, buire dark brown ult. f. Gk purros red]

bureaucracy /bjʊəˈrɒkrəsɪ/ n. (pl. -ies) 1 a government by central administration. b a State or organization so governed. 2 the officials of such a government, esp. regarded as oppressive and inflexible. 3 conduct typical of such officials. [F bureaucratie: see BUREAU]

bureaucrat /ˈbjʊərəˌkræt, -rəʊˌkræt/ n. 1 an official in a bureaucracy. 2 an inflexible or insensitive administrator. □ **bureaucratic** /-ˈkrætɪk/ adj. **bureaucratically** /-ˈkrætɪkəlɪ/ adv. [F bureaucrate (as BUREAUCRACY)]

burette /bjʊəˈret/ n. (US **buret**) a graduated glass tube with an end-tap for measuring small volumes of liquid in chemical analysis. [F]

burgee /bɜːˈdʒiː/ n. a triangular or swallow-tailed flag bearing the colours or emblem of a sailing-club. [18th c.: perh. = (ship)owner, ult. F bourgeois: see BURGESS]

burgeon /ˈbɜːdʒ(ə)n/ literary v.intr. 1 begin to grow rapidly; flourish. 2 put forth young shoots; bud. [ME f. OF bor-, burjon ult. f. LL burra wool]

burger /ˈbɜːgə(r)/ n. 1 colloq. a hamburger. 2 (in comb.) a certain kind of hamburger or variation of it (beefburger; nutburger). [abbr.]

burgess /ˈbɜːdʒɪs/ n. 1 Brit. an inhabitant of a town or borough. 2 US a borough magistrate or governor. [ME f. OF burgeis ult. f. LL burgus BOROUGH]

burgh /ˈbʌrə/ n. hist. a Scottish borough or chartered town. □ **burghal** /ˈbɜːg(ə)l/ adj. [Sc. form of BOROUGH]

burgher /ˈbɜːgə(r)/ n. a citizen or freeman, esp. of a Continental town. [G Burger or Du. burger f. Burg, burg BOROUGH]

burglar /ˈbɜːglə(r)/ n. a person who commits burglary. □ **burglarious** /-ˈgleərɪəs/ adj. [legal AF burgler, rel. to OF burgier pillage]

burglarize /ˈbɜːgləˌraɪz/ v.tr. & intr. (also -ise) US = BURGLE.

burglary /ˈbɜːglərɪ/ n. (pl. -ies) 1 entry into a building illegally with intent to commit theft, do bodily harm, or do damage. 2 an instance of this. [legal AF burglarie: see BURGLAR]

■ **Usage** Before 1968 in English law, burglary was a crime under statute and common law; since 1968 it has been a statutory crime only: cf. HOUSEBREAKING.

burgle /ˈbɜːg(ə)l/ v. 1 tr. commit burglary on (a building or person). 2 intr. commit burglary. [back-form. f. BURGLAR]

burgomaster /ˈbɜːgəˌmɑːstə(r)/ n. the mayor of a Dutch or Flemish town. [Du. *burgemeester* f. *burg* BOROUGH: assim. to MASTER]

burgundy /ˈbɜːgəndɪ/ n. (pl. **-ies**) **1 a** the wine of Burgundy in E. France. **b** a similar wine from another place. **2** the colour of red Burgundy wine.

burial /ˈberɪəl/ n. **1 a** the burying of a dead body. **b** a funeral. **2** *Archaeol.* a grave or its remains. □ **burial-ground** a cemetery. [ME, erron. formed as sing. of OE *byrgels* f. Gmc: rel. to BURY]

burin /ˈbjʊərɪn/ n. **1** a steel tool for engraving on copper or wood. **2** *Archaeol.* a flint tool with a chisel point. [F]

burk var. of BERK.

burka /ˈbɜːkə/ n. a long enveloping garment worn in public by Muslim women. [Hind. f. Arab. *burḳa*]

burlap /ˈbɜːlæp/ n. **1** coarse canvas esp. of jute used for sacking etc. **2** a similar lighter material for use in dressmaking or furnishing. [17th c.: orig. unkn.]

burlesque /bɜːˈlesk/ n., adj., & v. —n. **1 a** comic imitation, esp. in parody of a dramatic or literary work. **b** a performance or work of this kind. **2** *US* a variety show, often including striptease. —adj. of or in the nature of burlesque. —v.tr. (**burlesques, burlesqued, burlesquing**) make or give a burlesque of. □ **burlesquer** n. [F f. It. *burlesco* f. *burla* mockery]

burly /ˈbɜːlɪ/ adj. (**burlier, burliest**) of stout sturdy build; big and strong. □ **burliness** n. [ME *borli* prob. f. an OE form = 'fit for the bower' (BOWER)]

burn[1] v. & n. —v. (past and past part. **burnt** or **burned**) **1** tr. & intr. be or cause to be consumed or destroyed by fire. **2** intr. **a** blaze or glow with fire. **b** be in the state characteristic of fire. **3** tr. & intr. be or cause to be injured or damaged by fire or great heat or by radiation. **4** tr. & intr. use or be used as a source of heat, light, or other energy. **5** tr. & intr. char or scorch in cooking (*burned the meat; the meat is burning*). **6** tr. produce (a hole, a mark, etc.) by fire or heat. **7** tr. **a** subject (clay, chalk, etc.) to heat for a purpose. **b** harden (bricks) by fire. **c** make (lime or charcoal) by heat. **8** tr. colour, tan, or parch with heat or light (*we were burnt brown by the sun*). **9** tr. & intr. put or be put to death by fire. **10** tr. **a** cauterize, brand. **b** (foll. by *in*) imprint by burning. **11** tr. & intr. make or be hot, give or feel a sensation or pain of or like heat. **12** tr. & intr. (often foll. by *with*) make or be passionate; feel or cause to feel great emotion (*burn with shame*). **13** intr. (foll. by *into*) (of acid etc.) gradually penetrate (into) causing disintegration. —n. **1** a mark or injury caused by burning. **2** the ignition of a rocket engine in flight, giving extra thrust. **3** *US, Austral., & NZ* a forest area cleared by burning. □ **burn one's boats** (or **bridges**) commit oneself irrevocably. **burn the candle at both ends** exhaust one's strength or resources by undertaking too much. **burn down 1 a** destroy (a building) by burning. **b** (of a building) be destroyed by fire. **2** burn less vigorously as fuel fails. **burn one's fingers** suffer for meddling or rashness. **burning-glass** a lens for concentrating the sun's rays on an object to burn it. **burn low** (of fire) be nearly out. **burn the midnight oil** read or work late into the night. **burn out 1** be reduced to

nothing by burning. **2** fail or cause to fail by burning. **3** (usu. *refl.*) esp. *US* suffer physical or emotional exhaustion. **4** consume the contents of by burning. **5** make (a person) homeless by burning his or her house. **burn-out** n. *US* **1** physical or emotional exhaustion, esp. caused by stress. **2** depression, disillusionment. **burnt ochre** (or **sienna** or **umber**) a pigment darkened by burning. **burnt offering** an offering burnt on an altar as a sacrifice. **burnt-out** physically or emotionally exhausted. **burn up 1** get rid of by fire. **2** begin to blaze. [OE *birnan, bærnan* f. Gmc]

burn[2] n. *Sc.* a small stream. [OE *burna* etc. f. Gmc]

burner /ˈbɜːnə(r)/ n. the part of a gas cooker, lamp, etc. that emits and shapes the flame. □ **on the back** (or **front**) **burner** *colloq.* receiving little (or much) attention.

burning /ˈbɜːnɪŋ/ adj. **1** ardent, intense (*burning desire*). **2** hotly discussed, exciting (*burning question*). **3** flagrant (*burning shame*). □ **burningly** adv.

burnish /ˈbɜːnɪʃ/ v.tr. polish by rubbing. □ **burnisher** n. [ME f. OF *burnir* = *brunir* f. *brun* BROWN]

burnous /bɜːˈnuːs/ n. an Arab or Moorish hooded cloak. [F f. Arab. *burnus* f. Gk *birros* cloak]

burnt see BURN[1].

burp /bɜːp/ v. & n. *colloq.* —v. **1** intr. belch. **2** tr. make (a baby) belch, usu. by patting its back. —n. a belch. [imit.]

burr n. & v. —n. **1 a** a whirring sound. **b** a rough sounding of the letter *r*. **2** (also **bur**) **a** a rough edge left on cut or punched metal or paper. **b** a surgeon's or dentist's small drill. —v. **1** tr. pronounce with a burr. **2** intr. make a whirring sound. [var. of BUR]

burrow /ˈbʌrəʊ/ n. & v. —n. a hole or tunnel dug by a small animal, esp. a rabbit, as a dwelling. —v. **1** intr. make or live in a burrow. **2** tr. make (a hole etc.) by digging. **3** intr. hide oneself. **4** intr. (foll. by *into*) investigate, search. □ **burrower** n. [ME, app. var. of BOROUGH]

bursar /ˈbɜːsə(r)/ n. **1** a treasurer, esp. the person in charge of the funds and other property of a college. **2** the holder of a bursary. □ **bursarship** n. [F *boursier* or (in sense 1) med.L *bursarius* f. *bursa* bag]

bursary /ˈbɜːsərɪ/ n. (pl. **-ies**) **1** a grant, esp. a scholarship. **2** the post or room of a bursar. □ **bursarial** /-ˈseərɪəl/ adj. [med.L *bursaria* (as BURSAR)]

burst v. & n. —v. (past and past part. **burst**) **1 a** intr. break suddenly and violently apart by expansion of contents or internal pressure. **b** tr. cause to do this. **c** tr. send (a container etc.) violently apart. **2** tr. open forcibly. **b** intr. come open or be opened forcibly. **3 a** intr. (usu. foll. by *in, out*) make one's way suddenly, dramatically, or by force. **b** tr. break away from or through (*the river burst its banks*). **4** tr. & intr. fill or be full to overflowing. **5** intr. appear or come suddenly (*burst into flame; burst upon the view; sun burst out*). **6** intr. (foll. by *into*) suddenly begin to shed or utter (esp. *burst into tears* or *laughter* or *song*). **7** intr. be as if about to burst because of effort, excitement, etc. **8** tr. suffer bursting of (*burst a blood-vessel*). **9** tr. separate (continuous stationery) into single sheets. —n. **1** the act of or an instance of bursting; a split. **2**

a sudden issuing forth (*burst of flame*). **3** a sudden outbreak (*burst of applause*). **4 a** a short sudden effort; a spurt. **b** a gallop. **5** an explosion. □ **burst out 1** suddenly begin (*burst out laughing*). **2** exclaim. [OE *berstan* f. Gmc]

burthen *archaic* var. of BURDEN *n.* 4.

burton /ˈbɜːt(ə)n/ *n.* □ **go for a burton** *Brit. sl.* be lost or destroyed or killed. [20th c.: perh. *Burton* ale f. *Burton-on-Trent* in England]

bury /ˈberi/ *v.tr.* (-**ies**, -**ied**) **1** place (a dead body) in the earth, in a tomb, or in the sea. **2** lose by death (*has buried three husbands*). **3 a** put under ground (*bury alive*). **b** hide (treasure, a bone, etc.) in the earth. **c** cover up; submerge. **4 a** put out of sight (*buried his face in his hands*). **b** consign to obscurity (*the idea was buried after brief discussion*). **c** put away; forget. **5** involve deeply (*buried himself in his work; was buried in a book*). □ **bury the hatchet** cease to quarrel. [OE *byrgan* f. WG: cf. BURIAL]

bus /bʌs/ *n.* & *v.* —*n.* (*pl.* **buses** or *US* **busses**) **1** a large passenger vehicle, esp. one serving the public on a fixed route. **2** *colloq.* a motor car, aeroplane, etc. **3** *Computing* a defined set of conductors carrying data and control signals within a computer. —*v.* (**buses** or **busses**, **bussed**, **bussing**) **1** *intr.* go by bus. **2** *tr. US* transport by bus, esp. to promote racial integration. □ **bus shelter** a shelter from rain etc. beside a bus stop. **bus station** a centre, esp. in a town, where (esp. long-distance) buses depart and arrive. **bus-stop 1** a regular stopping-place of a bus. **2** a sign marking this. [abbr. of OMNIBUS]

busby /ˈbʌzbi/ *n.* (*pl.* -**ies**) (not in official use) a tall fur hat worn by hussars etc. [18th c.: orig. unkn.]

bush[1] /bʊʃ/ *n.* **1** a shrub or clump of shrubs with stems of moderate length. **2** a thing resembling this, esp. a clump of hair or fur. **3** (esp. in Australia and Africa) a wild uncultivated district; woodland or forest. □ **bush-baby** (*pl.* -**ies**) a small African tree-climbing lemur; a galago. **bush lawyer 1** *Austral.* & *NZ* a person claiming legal knowledge without qualifications for it. **2** *NZ* a bramble. **bush-ranger** *hist.* an Australian outlaw living in the bush. **bush telegraph** rapid spreading of information, a rumour, etc. **go bush** *Austral.* leave one's usual surroundings; run wild. [ME f. OE & ON, ult. f. Gmc]

bush[2] /bʊʃ/ *n.* & *v.* —*n.* **1** a metal lining for a round hole enclosing a revolving shaft etc. **2** a sleeve providing electrical insulation. —*v.tr.* provide with a bush. [MDu. *busse* BOX[1]]

bushed /bʊʃt/ *adj. colloq.* **1** *Austral.* & *NZ* a lost in the bush. **b** bewildered. **2** *US* tired out.

bushel /ˈbʊʃ(ə)l/ *n.* a measure of capacity for corn, fruit, liquids, etc. (*Brit.* 8 gallons, or 36.4 litres; *US* 64 US pints). □ **bushelful** *n.* (*pl.* -**fuls**) [ME f. OF *buissiel* etc., perh. of Gaulish orig.]

bushfire /ˈbʊʃˌfaɪə(r)/ *n.* a fire in a forest or in scrub often spreading widely.

bushman /ˈbʊʃmən/ *n.* (*pl.* -**men**) **1** a person who lives or travels in the Australian bush. **2** (**Bushman**) **a** a member of an aboriginal people in S. Africa. **b** the language of this people. [BUSH[1] + MAN: sense 2 after Du. *boschjesman* f. *bosch* bush]

bushveld /ˈbʊʃfelt/ *n.* open country consisting largely of bush. [BUSH[1] + VELD, after Afrik. *bosveld*]

bushwhack /ˈbʊʃwæk/ *v.* **1** *intr. US, Austral.,* & *NZ* **a** clear woods and bush country. **b** live or travel in bush country. **2** *tr. US* ambush.

bushwhacker /ˈbʊʃˌwækə(r)/ *n.* **1** *US, Austral.,* & *NZ* **a** a person who clears woods and bush country. **b** a person who lives or travels in bush country. **2** *US* a guerrilla fighter (orig. in the American Civil war).

bushy[1] /ˈbʊʃi/ *adj.* (**bushier, bushiest**) **1** growing thickly like a bush. **2** covered with bush. **3** covered with bush. □ **bushily** *adv.* **bushiness** *n.*

bushy[2] /ˈbʊʃi/ *n.* (*pl.* -**ies**) *Austral.* & *NZ colloq.* a person who lives in the bush (as distinct from in a town).

busily /ˈbɪzɪli/ *adv.* in a busy manner.

business /ˈbɪznɪs/ *n.* **1** one's regular occupation, profession, or trade. **2** a thing that is one's concern. **3 a** a task or duty. **b** a reason for coming (*what is your business?*). **4** serious work or activity (*get down to business*). **5** *derog.* **a** an affair, a matter (*sick of the whole business*). **b** a structure (*a lath-and-plaster business*). **6** a thing or series of things needing to be dealt with (*the business of the day*). **7** buying and selling; trade (*good stroke of business*). **8** a commercial house or firm. **9** *Theatr.* action on stage. **10** a difficult matter (*what a business it is!; made a great business of it*). □ **business card** a card printed with one's name and professional details. **the business end** *colloq.* the functional part of a tool or device. **business park** an area designed to accommodate businesses and light industry. **business person** a businessman or businesswoman. **has no business to** has no right to. **in business 1** trading or dealing. **2** able to begin operations. **in the business of 1** engaged in. **2** intending to (*we are not in the business of surrendering*). **mind one's own business** not meddle. **on business** with a definite purpose, esp. one relating to one's regular occupation. [OE *bisignis* (as BUSY, -NESS)]

businesslike /ˈbɪznɪsˌlaɪk/ *adj.* efficient, systematic, practical.

businessman /ˈbɪznɪsmən/ *n.* (*pl.* -**men**; *fem.* **businesswoman**, *pl.* -**women**) a man or woman engaged in trade or commerce, esp. at a senior level.

busk *v.intr.* perform (esp. music) for voluntary donations, usu. in the street or in subways. □ **busker** *n.* **busking** *n.* [*busk* peddle etc. (perh. f. obs. F *busquer* seek)]

busman /ˈbʌsmən/ *n.* (*pl.* -**men**) the driver of a bus. □ **busman's holiday** leisure time spent in an activity similar to one's regular work.

bust[1] *n.* **1 a** the human chest, esp. that of a woman; the bosom. **b** the circumference of the body at bust level (*a 36-inch bust*). **2** a sculpture of a person's head, shoulders, and chest. [F *buste* f. It. *busto*, of unkn. orig.]

bust[2] *v., n.,* & *adj.* —*v.* (*past* and *past part.* **busted** or **bust**) *colloq.* **1** *tr.* & *intr.* burst, break. **2** *tr.* esp. *US* reduce (a soldier etc.) to a lower rank; dismiss. **3** *tr.* esp. *US* a raid, search. **b** arrest. —*n.* **1** a sudden failure; a bankruptcy. **2** a police raid. **3** a worthless thing. —*adj.* (also **busted**) **1** broken, burst, collapsed. **2** bankrupt. □ **bust up 1** bring or come to collapse; explode. **2** (of esp. a married couple) separate. **bust-up** *n.* **1** a quarrel. **2** a collapse; an explosion. **go bust**

become bankrupt; fail. [orig. a (dial.) pronunc. of BURST]

bustard /ˈbʌstəd/ n. any large terrestrial bird of the family Otididae, with long neck, long legs, and stout tapering body. [ME f. OF *bistarde* f. L *avis tarda* slow bird (? = slow on the ground; but possibly a perversion of a foreign word)]

buster /ˈbʌstə(r)/ n. **1** esp. US sl. mate; fellow (used esp. as a disrespectful form of address). **2** a violent gale.

bustier /ˈbʌstɪˌeɪ/ n. a strapless close-fitting bodice, usu. boned. [F]

bustle[1] /ˈbʌs(ə)l/ v. & n. —v. **1** intr. (often foll. by *about*) **a** work etc. showily, energetically, and officiously. **b** hasten (*bustled about the kitchen banging saucepans*). **2** tr. make (a person) hurry or work hard (*bustled him into his overcoat*). **3** intr. (as **bustling** adj.) colloq. full of activity. —n. excited activity; a fuss. □ **bustler** n. [perh. f. *buskle* frequent. of *busk* prepare]

bustle[2] /ˈbʌs(ə)l/ n. hist. a pad or frame worn under a skirt and puffing it out behind. [18th c.: orig. unkn.]

busty /ˈbʌstɪ/ adj. (**bustier**, **bustiest**) (of a woman) having a prominent bust. □ **bustiness** n.

busy /ˈbɪzɪ/ adj. & v. —adj. (**busier**, **busiest**) **1** (often foll. by *in*, *with*, *at*, or pres. part.) occupied or engaged in work etc. with the attention concentrated. **2** full of activity or detail; fussy (*a busy evening*; *a picture busy with detail*). **3** employed continuously; unresting. **4** meddlesome; prying. **5** esp. US (of a telephone line) engaged. —v.tr. (**-ies**, **-ied**) (often refl.) keep busy; occupy (*the work busied him for many hours*; *busied herself with the accounts*). □ **busily** /ˈbɪzɪlɪ/ adv. **busyness** /ˈbɪzɪnɪs/ n. (cf. BUSINESS). [OE *bisig*]

busybody /ˈbɪzɪˌbɒdɪ/ n. (pl. **-ies**) **1** a meddlesome person. **2** a mischief-maker.

but /bʌt, bət/ conj., prep., adv., pron. & n. —conj. **1 a** nevertheless; however (*tried hard but did not succeed*; *I am old, but I am not weak*). **b** on the other hand; on the contrary (*I am old but you are young*). **2** (prec. by *can* etc.; in neg. or interrog.) except, other than, otherwise than (*cannot choose but do it*; *what could we do but run?*). **3** without the result that (*it never rains but it pours*). **4** prefixing an interruption to the speaker's train of thought (*the weather is ideal—but is that a cloud on the horizon?*). —prep. except; apart from; other than (*everyone went but me*; *nothing but trouble*). —adv. **1** only; no more than; only just (*we can but try*; *is but a child*; *had but arrived*; *did it but once*). **2** introducing emphatic repetition; definitely (*wanted to see nobody, but nobody*). **3** Austral. & NZ though; however (*didn't like it, but*). —rel.pron. who not; that not (*there is not a man but feels pity*). —n. an objection (*ifs and buts*). □ **but for** without the help or hindrance etc. of (*but for you I'd be rich by now*). **but one** (or **two** etc.) excluding one (or two etc.) from the number (*next door but one*; *last but one*). **but that** (prec. by neg.) that (*I don't deny but that it's true*). **but that** (or colloq. **what**) other than that; except that; that (*who knows but that it is true?*). **but then** (or **yet**) however, on the other hand (*I won, but then the others were beginners*). [OE *be-ūtan*, *būtan*, *būta* outside, without]

butane /ˈbjuːteɪn, bjuːˈteɪn/ n. Chem. a gaseous hydrocarbon of the alkane series used in liquefied form as fuel. [L *butyrum* BUTTER + -ANE]

butch /bʊtʃ/ adj. sl. masculine; tough-looking. [perh. abbr. of BUTCHER]

butcher /ˈbʊtʃə(r)/ n. & v. —n. **1 a** a person whose trade is dealing in meat. **b** a person who slaughters animals for food. **2** a person who kills or has people killed indiscriminately or brutally. —v.tr. **1** slaughter or cut up (an animal) for food. **2** kill (people) wantonly or cruelly. **3** ruin (esp. a job or a musical composition) through incompetence. □ **butcher's meat** slaughtered fresh meat excluding game, poultry, and bacon. □ **butcherly** adj. [ME f. OF *bo(u)chier* f. *boc* BUCK[1]]

butchery /ˈbʊtʃərɪ/ n. (pl. **-ies**) **1** needless or cruel slaughter (of people). **2** the butcher's trade. **3** a slaughterhouse. [ME f. OF *boucherie* (as BUTCHER)]

butler /ˈbʌtlə(r)/ n. the principal manservant of a household, usu. in charge of the wine cellar, pantry, etc. [ME f. AF *buteler*, OF *bouteillier*: see BOTTLE]

butt[1] v. & n. —v. **1** tr. & intr. push with the head or horns. **2 a** intr. (usu. foll. by *against*, *upon*) come with one end flat against, meet end to end with, abut. **b** tr. (usu. foll. by *against*) place (timber etc.) with the end flat against a wall etc. —n. **1** a push with the head. **2** a join of two edges. □ **butt in** interrupt, meddle. [ME f. AF *buter*, OF *boter* f. Gmc: infl. by BUTT[2] and ABUT]

butt[2] n. **1** (often foll. by *of*) an object (of ridicule etc.) (*the butt of his jokes*; *made them her butt*). **2 a** a mound behind a target. **b** (in pl.) a shooting-range. **c** a target. [ME f. OF *but* goal, of unkn. orig.]

butt[3] n. **1** (also **butt-end**) the thicker end, esp. of a tool or a weapon (*gun butt*). **2 a** the stub of a cigar or a cigarette. **b** (also **butt-end**) a remnant (*the butt of the evening*). **3** esp. US sl. the buttocks. [Du. *bot* stumpy]

butt[4] n. a cask, esp. as a measure of wine or ale. [AL *butta*, *bota*, AF *but*, f. OF *bo(u)t* f. LL *buttis*]

butte /bjuːt/ n. US a high isolated steep-sided hill. [F, = mound]

butter /ˈbʌtə(r)/ n. & v. —n. **1** a pale yellow edible fatty substance made by churning cream and used as a spread or in cooking. **2** a substance of a similar consistency or appearance (*peanut butter*). —v.tr. spread, cook, or serve with butter (*butter the bread*; *buttered carrots*). □ **butter-bean 1** the flat, dried, white lima bean. **2** a yellow-podded bean. **butter-cream** (or **-icing**) a mixture of butter, icing sugar, etc. used as a filling or a topping for a cake. **butter-fingers** colloq. a clumsy person prone to drop things. **butter muslin** a thin, loosely-woven cloth with a fine mesh, orig. for wrapping butter. **butter up** colloq. flatter excessively. [OE *butere* f. L *butyrum* f. Gk *bouturon*]

buttercup /ˈbʌtəˌkʌp/ n. any common yellow-flowered plant of the genus *Ranunculus*.

butterfat /ˈbʌtəˌfæt/ n. the essential fats of pure butter.

butterfly /ˈbʌtəˌflaɪ/ n. (pl. **-flies**) **1** any diurnal insect of the order Lepidoptera, with four usu. brightly coloured wings erect when at rest. **2** a showy or frivolous person. **3** (in pl.) colloq. a nervous sensation felt in the stomach. □ **butterfly net** a fine net attached to a pole, used for catching butterflies. **butterfly nut** a kind of wing-nut. **butterfly stroke** a stroke in swimming, with both arms raised and lifted forwards together. [OE *buttor-flēoge* (as BUTTER, FLY²)]

buttermilk /ˈbʌtəmɪlk/ *n.* a slightly acid liquid left after churning butter.

butterscotch /ˈbʌtəskɒtʃ/ *n.* a brittle sweet made from butter, brown sugar, etc. [SCOTCH]

buttery¹ /ˈbʌtərɪ/ *n.* (*pl.* **-ies**) a room, esp. in a college, where provisions are kept and supplied to students etc. [ME f. AF *boterie* butt-store (as BUTT⁴)]

buttery² /ˈbʌtərɪ/ *adj.* like, containing, or spread with butter. □ **butteriness** *n.*

buttock /ˈbʌtək/ *n.* (usu. in *pl.*) 1 each of two fleshy protuberances on the lower rear part of the human body. 2 the corresponding part of an animal. [*butt* ridge + -OCK]

button /ˈbʌt(ə)n/ *n.* & *v.* —*n.* 1 a small disc or knob sewn on to a garment, either to fasten it by being pushed through a buttonhole, or as an ornament or badge. 2 a knob on a piece of esp. electronic equipment which is pressed to operate it. 3 **a** a small round object (*chocolate buttons*). **b** (*attrib.*) anything resembling a button (*button nose*). 4 **a** a bud. **b** a button mushroom. 5 *Fencing* a terminal knob on a foil making it harmless. —*v.* 1 *tr.* & *intr.* = *button up* 1. 2 *tr.* supply with buttons. □ **buttoned up** *colloq.* 1 formal and inhibited in manner. 2 silent. **button one's lip** esp. *US sl.* remain silent. **button mushroom** a young unopened mushroom. **button-through** (of a dress) fastened with buttons from neck to hem like a coat. **button up** 1 fasten with buttons. 2 *colloq.* complete (a task etc.) satisfactorily. 3 *colloq.* become silent. **on the button** esp. *US sl.* precisely. □ **buttoned** *adj.* **buttonless** *adj.* **buttony** *adj.* [ME f. OF *bouton*, ult. f. Gmc]

buttonhole /ˈbʌt(ə)nˌhəʊl/ *n.* & *v.* —*n.* 1 a slit made in a garment to receive a button for fastening. 2 a flower or spray worn in a lapel buttonhole. —*v.tr.* 1 *colloq.* accost and detain (a reluctant listener). 2 make buttonholes in.

buttons /ˈbʌt(ə)nz/ *n.* *colloq.* a liveried page-boy. [from the rows of buttons on his jacket]

buttress /ˈbʌtrɪs/ *n.* & *v.* —*n.* 1 **a** a projecting support of stone or brick etc. built against a wall. **b** a source of help or encouragement (*she was a buttress to him in his trouble*). 2 a projecting portion of a hill or mountain. —*v.tr.* (often foll. by *up*) 1 support with a buttress. 2 support by argument etc. (*claim buttressed by facts*). [ME f. OF (*ars*) *bouterez* thrusting (arch) f. *bouteret* f. *bouter* BUTT¹]

butty /ˈbʌtɪ/ *n.* (*pl.* **-ies**) *N.Engl.* 1 a sandwich (*bacon butty*). 2 a slice of bread and butter. [BUTTER + -Y²]

buxom /ˈbʌksəm/ *adj.* (esp. of a woman) plump and healthy-looking; large and shapely; busty. □ **buxomly** *adv.* **buxomness** *n.* [earlier sense *pliant*: ME f. stem of OE *būgan* BOW² + -SOME¹]

buy /baɪ/ *v.* & *n.* —*v.* (**buys, buying**; *past* and *past part.* **bought** /bɔːt/) 1 *tr.* **a** obtain in exchange for money etc. **b** (usu. in *neg.*) serve to obtain (*money can't buy happiness*). 2 *tr.* **a** procure (the loyalty etc.) of a person by bribery, promises, etc. **b** win over (a person) in this way. 3 *tr.* *sl.* be got by sacrifice, great effort, etc. (*dearly bought; bought with our sweat*). 4 *tr.* *sl.* accept, believe in, approve of (*it's a good scheme, I'll buy it; he bought it, he's so gullible*). 5 *absol.* be a buyer for a store etc. (*buys for Selfridges*). —*n.* *colloq.* a purchase

(*that sofa was a good buy*). □ **buy in** 1 buy a stock of. 2 withdraw (an item) at auction because of failure to reach the reserve price. **buy into** obtain a share in (an enterprise) by payment. **buy it** (usu. in *past*) *sl.* be killed. **buy off** get rid of (a claim, a claimant, a blackmailer) by payment. **buy oneself out** obtain one's release (esp. from the armed services) by payment. **buy out** pay (a person) to give up an ownership, interest, etc. **buy-out** *n.* the purchase of a controlling share in a company etc. **buy time** delay an event, conclusion, etc., temporarily. **buy up** 1 buy as much as possible of. 2 absorb (another firm etc.) by purchase. [OE *bycgan* f. Gmc]

buyer /ˈbaɪə(r)/ *n.* 1 a person employed to select and purchase stock for a large store etc. 2 a purchaser, a customer. □ **buyer's** (or **buyers'**) **market** an economic position in which goods are plentiful and cheap and buyers have the advantage.

buzz *n.* & *v.* —*n.* 1 the hum of a bee etc. 2 the sound of a buzzer. 3 **a** a confused low sound as of people talking; a murmur. **b** a stir; hurried activity (*a buzz of excitement*). **c** *colloq.* a rumour. 4 *sl.* a telephone call. 5 *sl.* a thrill; a euphoric sensation. —*v.* 1 *intr.* make a humming sound. 2 **a** *tr.* & *intr.* signal or signal to with a buzzer. **b** *tr.* telephone. 3 *intr.* **a** (often foll. by *about*) move or hover busily. **b** (of a place) have an air of excitement or purposeful activity. 4 *tr.* *Aeron.* *colloq.* fly fast and very close to (another aircraft). □ **buzz off** *sl.* go or hurry away. **buzz-saw** *US* a circular saw. **buzz-word** *sl.* 1 a fashionable piece of esp. technical or computer jargon. 2 a catchword; a slogan. [imit.]

buzzard /ˈbʌzəd/ *n.* any of a group of predatory birds of the hawk family, esp. of the genus *Buteo*, with broad wings. [ME f. OF *busard*, *buson* f. L *buteo -onis* falcon]

buzzer /ˈbʌzə(r)/ *n.* 1 an electrical device that makes a buzzing noise. 2 a whistle or hooter.

bwana /ˈbwɑːnə/ *n.* *Afr.* master, sir. [Swahili]

by /baɪ/ *prep.*, *adv.*, & *n.* —*prep.* 1 near, beside, in the region of (*stand by the door; sit by me*). 2 through the agency, means, instrumentality, or causation of (*by proxy; bought by a millionaire; a poem by Donne; went by bus; succeeded by persisting; divide by two*). 3 not later than; as soon as (*by next week; by now; by the time he arrives*). 4 **a** past, beyond (*drove by the church; came by us*). **b** passing through; via (*went by Paris*). 5 in the circumstances of (*by day; by daylight*). 6 to the extent of (*missed by a foot; better by far*). 7 according to; using as a standard or unit (*judge by appearances; paid by the hour*). 8 with the succession of (*worse by the minute; day by day; one by one*). 9 concerning; in respect of (*did our duty by them; Smith by name; all right by me*). 10 used in mild oaths (orig. = as surely as one believes in) (*by God; by gum; swear by all that is sacred*). 11 placed between specified lengths in two directions (*three feet by two*). 12 avoiding, ignoring (*pass by him; passed us by*). 13 inclining to (*north by north-west*). —*adv.* 1 near (*sat by, watching; lives close by*). 2 aside; in reserve (*put £5 by*). 3 past (*they marched by*). —*n.* = BYE. □ **by and by** before long; eventually. **by and large** on the whole, everything considered. **by the by** (or **bye**) incidentally, parenthetically. **by oneself** 1

a unaided. **b** without prompting. **2** alone; without company. [OE *bī, bi, be* f. Gmc]

by- /baɪ/ *prefix* (also **bye-**) subordinate, incidental, secondary (*by-effect; by-road*).

by-blow /ˈbaɪbləʊ/ *n.* **1** a side-blow not at the main target. **2** an illegitimate child.

bye[1] /baɪ/ *n.* **1** *Cricket* a run scored from a ball that passes the batsman without being hit. **2** the status of an unpaired competitor in a sport, who proceeds to the next round as if having won. □ **by the bye** = *by the by.* **leg-bye** *Cricket* a run scored from a ball that touches the batsman. [BY as noun]

bye[2] /baɪ/ *int. colloq.* = GOODBYE. [abbr.]

bye-bye[1] /ˈbaɪbaɪ, bəˈbaɪ/ *int. colloq.* = GOODBYE. [childish corrupt.]

bye-bye[2] /ˈbaɪbaɪ/ *n.* (also **bye-byes** /-baɪz/) (a child's word for) sleep. [ME, f. the sound used in lullabies]

by-election /ˈbaɪɪˌlekʃ(ə)n/ *n.* the election of an MP in a single constituency to fill a vacancy arising during a government's term of office.

bygone /ˈbaɪgɒn/ *adj. & n.* —*adj.* past, antiquated (*bygone years*). —*n.* (in *pl.*) past offences (*let bygones be bygones*).

by-law /ˈbaɪlɔː/ *n.* (also **bye-law**) **1** *Brit.* a regulation made by a local authority or corporation. **2** a rule made by a company or society for its members. [ME prob. f. obs. *byrlaw* local custom (ON *býjar* genitive sing. of *býr* town, but assoc. with BY)]

byline /ˈbaɪlaɪn/ *n.* **1** a line in a newspaper etc. naming the writer of an article. **2** a secondary line of work. **3** a goal-line or touch-line.

bypass /ˈbaɪpɑːs/ *n. & v.* —*n.* **1** a road passing round a town or its centre to provide an alternative route for through traffic. **2 a** a secondary channel or pipe etc. to allow a flow when the main one is closed or blocked. **b** an alternative passage for the circulation of blood during a surgical operation on the heart. —*v.tr.* **1** avoid; go round. **2** provide with a bypass.

byplay /ˈbaɪpleɪ/ *n.* a secondary action or sequence of events, esp. in a play.

by-product /ˈbaɪˌprɒdʌkt/ *n.* **1** an incidental or secondary product made in the manufacture of something else. **2** a secondary result.

byre /ˈbaɪə(r)/ *n.* a cowshed. [OE *bȳre*: perh. rel. to BOWER]

byroad /ˈbaɪrəʊd/ *n.* a minor road.

bystander /ˈbaɪˌstændə(r)/ *n.* a person who stands by but does not take part; a mere spectator.

byte /baɪt/ *n. Computing* a group of eight binary digits, often used to represent one character. [20th c.: perh. based on BIT[4] and BITE]

byway /ˈbaɪweɪ/ *n.* **1** a byroad or bypath. **2** a minor activity.

byword /ˈbaɪwɜːd/ *n.* **1** a person or thing cited as a notable example (*is a byword for luxury*). **2** a familiar saying; a proverb.

Byzantine /bɪˈzæntaɪn, baɪ-, ˈbɪzənˌtiːn, ˈbɪzənˌtaɪn/ *adj. & n.* —*adj.* **1** of Byzantium or the E. Roman Empire. **2** (of a political situation etc.): **a** extremely complicated. **b** inflexible. **c** carried on by underhand methods. **3** *Archit. & Painting* of a highly decorated style developed in the Eastern Empire. —*n.* a citizen of Byzantium or the E. Roman Empire. □ **Byzantinism** *n.* **Byzantinist** *n.* [F *byzantin* or L *Byzantinus* f. *Byzantium*, later Constantinople and now Istanbul]

Cc

C¹ /siː/ n. (also **c**) (pl. **Cs** or **C's**) **1** the third letter of the alphabet. **2** *Mus.* the first note of the diatonic scale of C major (the major scale having no sharps or flats). **3** the third hypothetical person or example. **4** the third highest class or category (of academic marks etc.). **5** *Algebra* (usu. **c**) the third known quantity. **6** (as a Roman numeral) 100. **7** (also ©) copyright.

C² *symb. Chem.* the element carbon.

C³ *abbr.* (also **C.**) Celsius, Centigrade.

c. *abbr.* **1** century; centuries. **2** chapter. **3** cent(s). **4** cold. **5** cubic. **6** *Cricket* caught by. **7** centi-.

c. *abbr. circa*, about.

c/- *abbr. Austral. & NZ* care of.

Ca *symb. Chem.* the element calcium.

ca. *abbr. circa*, about.

cab n. **1** a taxi. **2** the driver's compartment in a lorry, train, or crane. **3** *hist.* a hackney carriage. [abbr. of CABRIOLET]

cabal /kəˈbæl/ n. **1** a secret intrigue. **2** a political clique or faction. [F *cabale* f. med.L *cabala*, CABBALA]

cabaret /ˈkæbəˌreɪ/ n. **1** an entertainment in a nightclub or restaurant while guests eat or drink at tables. **2** a nightclub etc. [F, = wooden structure, tavern]

cabbage /ˈkæbɪdʒ/ n. **1 a** any of several cultivated varieties of *Brassica oleracea*, with thick green or purple leaves forming a round heart or head. **b** this head usu. eaten as vegetable. **2** *colloq. derog.* a person who is inactive or lacks interest. □ **cabbagy** *adj.* [earlier *cabache*, *-oche* f. OF (Picard) *caboche* head, OF *caboce*, of unkn. orig.]

cabbala /kəˈbɑːlə, ˈkæbələ/ n. (also **cabala**, **kabbala**) **1** the Jewish mystical tradition. **2** mystic interpretation; any esoteric doctrine or occult lore. □ **cabbalism** n. **cabbalist** n. **cabbalistic** /-ˈlɪstɪk/ *adj.* [med.L f. Rabbinical Heb. *ḳabbālâ* tradition]

cabby /ˈkæbɪ/ n. (also **cabbie**) (pl. **-ies**) *colloq.* a taxi-driver. [CAB + -Y²]

caber /ˈkeɪbə(r)/ n. a roughly trimmed tree-trunk used in the Scottish Highland sport of tossing the caber. [Gael. *cabar* pole]

cabin /ˈkæbɪn/ n. **1** a small shelter or house, esp. of wood. **2** a room or compartment in an aircraft or ship for passengers or crew. **3** a driver's cab. □ **cabin-boy** a boy who waits on a ship's officers or passengers. **cabin crew** the crew members on an aeroplane attending to passengers and cargo. **cabin cruiser** a large motor boat with living accommodation. [ME f. OF *cabane* f. Prov. *cabana* f. LL *capanna*, *cavanna*]

cabinet /ˈkæbɪnɪt/ n. **1 a** a cupboard or case with drawers, shelves, etc., for storing or displaying articles. **b** a piece of furniture housing a radio or television set etc. **2** (**Cabinet**) the committee of senior ministers responsible for controlling government policy. □ **cabinet-maker** a skilled joiner. **Cabinet Minister** *Brit.* a member of the Cabinet. [CABIN + -ET¹, infl. by F *cabinet*]

cable /ˈkeɪb(ə)l/ n. & v. —n. **1** a thick rope of wire or hemp. **2** an encased group of insulated wires for transmitting electricity or electrical signals. **3** a cablegram. **4** *Naut.* the chain of an anchor. **5** (in full **cable stitch**) a knitted stitch resembling twisted rope. —v. **1 a** tr. transmit (a message) by cablegram. **b** tr. inform (a person) by cablegram. **c** intr. send a cablegram. **2** tr. furnish or fasten with a cable or cables. □ **cable-car 1** a small cabin (often one of a series) suspended on an endless cable and drawn up and down a mountainside etc. by an engine at one end. **2** a carriage drawn along a cable railway. **cable railway** a railway along which carriages are drawn by an endless cable. **cable television** a broadcasting system with signals transmitted by cable to subscribers' sets. [ME f. OF *chable*, ult. f. LL *capulum* halter f. Arab. *ḥabl*]

cablegram /ˈkeɪb(ə)lˌgræm/ n. a telegraph message sent by undersea cable etc.

cabman /ˈkæbmən/ n. (pl. **-men**) the driver of a cab.

cabochon /ˈkæbəˌʃɒn/ n. a gem polished but not faceted. [F dimin. of *caboche*: see CABBAGE]

caboodle /kəˈbuːd(ə)l/ n. □ **the whole caboodle** sl. the whole lot (of persons or things). [19th c. US: perh. f. phr. *kit and boodle*]

caboose /kəˈbuːs/ n. **1** a kitchen on a ship's deck. **2** *US* a guard's van; a car on a freight train for workmen etc. [Du. *cabūse*, of unkn. orig.]

cabriole /ˈkæbrɪˌəʊl/ n. a kind of curved leg characteristic of Queen Anne and Chippendale furniture. [F f. *cabrioler*, *caprioler* f. It. *capriolare* to leap in the air; from the resemblance to a leaping animal's foreleg: see CAPRIOLE]

cabriolet /ˌkæbrɪəʊˈleɪ/ n. **1** a light two-wheeled carriage with a hood, drawn by one horse. **2** a motor car with a folding top. [F f. *cabriole* goat's leap (cf. CABRIOLE), applied to its motion]

cacao /kəˈkɑːəʊ, -ˈkeɪəʊ/ n. (pl. **-os**) **1** a seed pod from which cocoa and chocolate are made. **2** a small widely cultivated evergreen tree, *Theobroma cacao*, bearing these. [Sp. f. Nahuatl *cacauatl* (*uatl* tree)]

cachalot /ˈkæʃəˌlɒt, -ˌləʊt/ n. a sperm whale. [F f. Sp. & Port. *cachalote*, of unkn. orig.]

cache /kæʃ/ n. & v. —n. **1** a hiding-place for treasure, provisions, ammunition, etc. **2** what is hidden in a cache. —v.tr. put in a cache. [F *cacher* to hide]

cachet /ˈkæʃeɪ/ n. **1** a distinguishing mark or seal. **2** prestige. **3** *Med.* a flat capsule enclosing a dose of unpleasant-tasting medicine. [F f. *cacher* press ult. f. L *coactare* constrain]

cachou /ˈkæʃuː/ n. a lozenge to sweeten the breath. [F f. Port. *cachu* f. Malay *kāchu*]

cack-handed /kækˈhændɪd/ *adj. colloq.* **1** awkward, clumsy. **2** left-handed. □ **cack-handedly** *adv.* **cack-handedness** n. [dial. *cack* excrement]

cackle /ˈkæk(ə)l/ n. & v. —n. **1** a clucking sound as of a hen or a goose. **2** a loud silly laugh. **3** noisy inconsequential talk. —v. **1** intr. emit a cackle. **2** intr. talk noisily and inconsequentially. **3** tr. utter or express with a cackle. [ME prob. f. MLG, MDu. kākelen (imit.)]

cacography /kəˈkɒgrəfɪ/ n. **1** bad handwriting. **2** bad spelling. □ **cacographer** n. **cacographic** /ˌkækəˈgræfɪk/ adj. **cacographical** /ˌkækəˈgræfɪk(ə)l/ adj. [Gk kakos bad, after orthography]

cacophony /kəˈkɒfənɪ/ n. (pl. **-ies**) **1** a harsh discordant mixture of sound. **2** dissonance; discord. □ **cacophonous** adj. [F cacophonie f. Gk kakophōnia f. kakophōnos f. kakos bad + phōnē sound]

cactus /ˈkæktəs/ n. (pl. **cacti** /-taɪ/ or **cactuses**) any succulent plant of the family Cactaceae, with a thick fleshy stem and usu. spines but no leaves. □ **cactaceous** /-ˈteɪʃəs/ adj. [L f. Gk kaktos cardoon]

CAD abbr. computer-aided design.

cad n. a person (esp. a man) who behaves dishonourably. □ **caddish** adj. **caddishly** adv. **caddishness** n. [abbr. of CADDIE in sense 'odd-job man']

cadaver /kəˈdeɪvə(r), -ˈdɑːvə(r)/ n. esp. Med. a corpse. □ **cadaveric** /-ˈdævərɪk/ adj. [ME f. L f. cadere fall]

cadaverous /kəˈdævərəs/ adj. **1** corpselike. **2** deathly pale. [L cadaverosus (as CADAVER)]

caddie /ˈkædɪ/ n. & v. (also **caddy**) —n. (pl. **-ies**) a person who assists a golfer during a match, by carrying clubs etc. —v.intr. (**caddies, caddied, caddying**) act as caddie. [orig. Sc. f. F CADET]

caddis-fly /ˈkædɪs/ n. (pl. **-flies**) any small hairy-winged nocturnal insect of the order Trichoptera, living near water. [17th c.: orig. unkn.]

caddis-worm /ˈkædɪs/ n. (also **caddis**) a larva of the caddis-fly, living in water and making protective cylindrical cases of sticks, leaves, etc., and used as fishing-bait. [as CADDIS-FLY]

caddy¹ /ˈkædɪ/ n. (pl. **-ies**) a small container, esp. a box for holding tea. [earlier catty weight of 1⅓ lb., f. Malay kātī]

caddy² var. of CADDIE.

cadence /ˈkeɪd(ə)ns/ n. **1** a fall in pitch of the voice, esp. at the end of a phrase or sentence. **2** intonation, tonal inflection. **3** Mus. the close of a musical phrase. **4** rhythm; the measure or beat of sound or movement. □ **cadenced** adj. [ME f. OF f. It. cadenza, ult. f. L cadere fall]

cadenza /kəˈdenzə/ n. Mus. a virtuosic passage for a solo instrument or voice, usu. near the close of a movement of a concerto, sometimes improvised. [It.: see CADENCE]

cadet /kəˈdet/ n. **1** a young trainee in the armed services or police force. **2** NZ an apprentice in sheep-farming. **3** a younger son. □ **cadetship** n. [F f. Gascon dial. capdet, ult. f. L caput head]

cadge /kædʒ/ v. **1** tr. get or seek by begging. **2** intr. beg. □ **cadger** n. [19th c., earlier = ? bind, carry: orig. unkn.]

cadi /ˈkɑːdɪ, ˈkeɪdɪ/ n. (also **kadi**) (pl. **-is**) a judge in a Muslim country. [Arab. ḳāḍī f. ḳaḍā to judge]

cadmium /ˈkædmɪəm/ n. a soft bluish-white metallic element occurring naturally with zinc ores, and used in the manufacture of solders and in electroplating. [obs. cadmia calamine f. L cadmia f. Gk kadm(e)ia (gē) Cadmean (earth), f. Cadmus legendary founder of Thebes: see -IUM]

cadre /ˈkɑːdə(r), ˈkɑːdrə/ n. **1** a basic unit, esp. of servicemen, forming a nucleus for expansion when necessary. **2** /also ˈkeɪdə(r)/ **a** a group of activists in a communist or any revolutionary party. **b** a member of such a group. [F f. It. quadro f. L quadrus square]

caecum /ˈsiːkəm/ n. (US **cecum**) (pl. **-ca** /-kə/) a blind-ended pouch at the junction of the small and large intestines. □ **caecal** adj. [L for intestinum caecum f. caecus blind, transl. of Gk tuphlon enteron]

Caenozoic var. of CENOZOIC.

Caerphilly /keəˈfɪlɪ, kə-/ n. a kind of mild white cheese orig. made in Caerphilly in Wales.

Caesar /ˈsiːzə(r)/ n. **1** the title of the Roman emperors, from Augustus to Hadrian. **2** an autocrat. [L, family name of Gaius Julius Caesar, Roman statesman d. 44 BC]

Caesarean /sɪˈzeərɪən/ adj. & n. (also **Caesarian**, US **Ces-**) —adj. **1** of Caesar or the Caesars. **2** (of a birth) effected by Caesarean section. —n. a Caesarean section. □ **Caesarean section** an operation for delivering a child by cutting through the wall of the abdomen (Julius Caesar supposedly having been born this way). [L Caesarianus]

caesium /ˈsiːzɪəm/ n. (US **cesium**) a soft silver-white element occurring naturally in a number of minerals, and used in photoelectric cells. [L, neut. of caesius blue (from its spectrum lines)]

caesura /sɪˈzjʊərə/ n. (pl. **caesuras**) Prosody a pause near the middle of a line. □ **caesural** adj. [L f. caedere caes- cut]

café /ˈkæfeɪ, ˈkæfɪ/ n. (also **cafe** /also joc. kæf, keɪf/) **1** a small coffee-house or teashop; a simple restaurant. **2** US a bar. [F, = coffee, coffee-house]

cafeteria /ˌkæfɪˈtɪərɪə/ n. a restaurant in which customers collect their meals on trays at a counter and usu. pay before sitting down to eat. [Amer. Sp. cafetería coffee-shop]

caff /kæf/ n. Brit. sl. = CAFÉ. [abbr.]

caffeine /ˈkæfiːn/ n. an alkaloid drug with stimulant action found in tea leaves and coffee beans. [F caféine f. café coffee]

caftan /ˈkæftæn/ n. (also **kaftan**) **1** a long usu. belted tunic worn by men in countries of the Near East. **2 a** a woman's long loose dress. **b** a loose shirt or top. [Turk. ḳaftān, partly through F cafetan]

cage /keɪdʒ/ n. & v. —n. **1** a structure of bars or wires, esp. for confining animals or birds. **2** any similar open framework, esp. an enclosed platform or lift in a mine or the compartment for passengers in a lift. —v.tr. place or keep in a cage. [ME f. OF f. L cavea]

cagey /ˈkeɪdʒɪ/ adj. (also **cagy**) (**cagier, cagiest**) colloq. cautious and uncommunicative; wary. □ **cagily** adv. **caginess** n. (also **cageyness**). [20th-c. US: orig. unkn.]

cagoule /kəˈguːl/ n. a hooded thin windproof garment worn in mountaineering etc. [F]

cahoots /kəˈhuːts/ n.pl. □ **in cahoots** (often foll. by with) sl. in collusion. [19th c.: orig. uncert.]

caiman var. of CAYMAN.

Cain /keɪn/ n. □ **raise Cain** colloq. make a disturbance; create trouble. [Cain, eldest son of Adam (Gen. 4)]

Cainozoic var. of CENOZOIC.

cairn /keən/ n. 1 a mound of rough stones as a monument or landmark. 2 (in full **cairn terrier**) a a small terrier of a breed with short legs and a shaggy coat. b this breed. [Gael. carn]

cairngorm /ˈkeəngɔːm/ n. a yellow or wine-coloured semi-precious form of quartz. [found on Cairngorm, a mountain in Scotland f. Gael. carn gorm blue cairn]

caisson /ˈkeɪs(ə)n, kəˈsuːn/ n. 1 a watertight chamber in which underwater construction work can be done. 2 a floating vessel used as a floodgate in docks. 3 an ammunition chest or wagon. □ **caisson disease** = decompression sickness. [F (f. It. cassone) assim. to caisse CASE²]

cajole /kəˈdʒəʊl/ v.tr. (often foll. by into, out of) persuade by flattery, deceit, etc. □ **cajolement** n. **cajoler** n. **cajolery** n. [F cajoler]

cake /keɪk/ n. & v. —n. 1 a a mixture of flour, butter, eggs, sugar, etc., baked in the oven. b a quantity of this baked in a flat round or ornamental shape and often iced and decorated. 2 a other food in a flat round shape (fish cake). b = cattle-cake. 3 a flattish compact mass (a cake of soap). —v. 1 tr. & intr. form into a compact mass. 2 tr. (usu. foll. by with) cover (with a hard or sticky mass) (boots caked with mud). □ **have one's cake and eat it** colloq. enjoy both of two mutually exclusive alternatives. **like hot cakes** rapidly or successfully. **a piece of cake** colloq. something easily achieved. **a slice of the cake** participation in benefits. [ME f. ON kaka]

cakewalk /ˈkeɪkwɔːk/ n. 1 a dance developed from an American Black contest in graceful walking with a cake as a prize. 2 colloq. an easy task.

CAL abbr. computer-assisted learning.

calabash /ˈkæləbæʃ/ n. 1 a an evergreen tree, Crescentia cujete, native to tropical America, bearing fruit in the form of large gourds. b a gourd from this tree. 2 the shell of this or a similar gourd used as a vessel for water, to make a tobacco pipe, etc. [F calebasse f. Sp. calabaza perh. f. Pers. karbuz melon]

calaboose /ˌkæləˈbuːs/ n. US a prison. [Black F calabouse f. Sp. calabozo dungeon]

calabrese /ˌkæləˈbriːz, ˌkæləˈbreɪseɪ/ n. a large succulent variety of sprouting broccoli. [It., = Calabrian]

calamary /ˈkæləmərɪ/ n. (pl. -ies) any cephalopod mollusc with a long tapering penlike horny internal shell, esp. a squid of the genus Loligo. [med.L calamarium pen-case f. L calamus pen]

calamine /ˈkæləˌmaɪn/ n. 1 a pink powder consisting of zinc carbonate and ferric oxide used as a lotion or ointment. 2 a zinc mineral usu. zinc carbonate. [ME f. F f. med.L calamina alt. f. L cadmia: see CADMIUM]

calamity /kəˈlæmɪtɪ/ n. (pl. -ies) 1 a disaster, a great misfortune. 2 a adversity. b deep distress. □ **calamitous** adj. **calamitously** adv. [ME f. F calamité f. L calamitas -tatis]

calc- /kælk/ comb. form lime or calcium. [G Kalk f. L CALX]

calcareous /kælˈkeərɪəs/ adj. (also **calcarious**) of or containing calcium carbonate; chalky. [L calcarius (as CALX)]

calceolaria /ˌkælsɪəˈleərɪə/ n. Bot. any plant of the genus Calceolaria, native to S. America, with slipper-shaped flowers. [mod.L f. L calceolus dimin. of calceus shoe + -aria fem. = -ARY¹]

calces pl. of CALX.

calciferol /kælˈsɪfəˌrɒl/ n. one of the D vitamins, routinely added to dairy products, essential for the deposition of calcium in bones. [CALCIFEROUS + -OL¹]

calciferous /kælˈsɪfərəs/ adj. yielding calcium salts, esp. calcium carbonate. [L CALX lime + -FEROUS]

calcify /ˈkælsɪˌfaɪ/ v.tr. & intr. (-ies, -ied) 1 harden or become hardened by deposition of calcium salts; petrify. 2 convert or be converted to calcium carbonate. □ **calcific** /-ˈsɪfɪk/ adj. **calcification** /-fɪˈkeɪʃ(ə)n/ n.

calcine /ˈkælsɪn, -saɪn/ v. 1 tr. a reduce, oxidize, or desiccate by strong heat. b burn to ashes; consume by fire; roast. c reduce to calcium oxide by roasting or burning. 2 tr. consume or purify as if by fire. 3 intr. undergo any of these. □ **calcination** /-ˈneɪʃ(ə)n/ n. [ME f. OF calciner or med.L calcinare f. LL calcina lime f. L CALX]

calcium /ˈkælsɪəm/ n. a soft grey metallic element of the alkaline earth group occurring naturally in limestone, marble, chalk, etc., that is important in industry and essential for normal growth in living organisms. □ **calcium carbide** a greyish solid used in the production of acetylene. **calcium carbonate** a white insoluble solid occurring naturally as chalk, limestone, marble, and calcite, and used in the manufacture of lime and cement. **calcium hydroxide** a white crystalline powder used in the manufacture of plaster and cement; slaked lime. **calcium oxide** a white crystalline solid from which many calcium compounds are manufactured. **calcium phosphate** the main constituent of animal bones, used as bone ash fertilizer. [L CALX lime + -IUM]

calculable /ˈkælkjʊləb(ə)l/ adj. able to be calculated or estimated. □ **calculability** /-ˈbɪlɪtɪ/ n. **calculably** adv.

calculate /ˈkælkjʊˌleɪt/ v. 1 tr. ascertain or determine beforehand, esp. by mathematics or by reckoning. 2 tr. plan deliberately. 3 intr. (foll. by on, upon) rely on; make an essential part of one's reckoning (calculated on a quick response). 4 tr. US colloq. suppose, believe. □ **calculative** /-lətɪv/ adj. [L calculare (as CALCULUS)]

calculated /ˈkælkjʊˌleɪtɪd/ adj. 1 (of an action) done with awareness of the likely consequences. 2 (foll. by to + infin.) designed or suitable; intended. □ **calculatedly** adv.

calculating /ˈkælkjʊˌleɪtɪŋ/ adj. (of a person) shrewd, scheming. □ **calculatingly** adv.

calculation /ˌkælkjʊˈleɪʃ(ə)n/ n. 1 the act or process of calculating. 2 a result got by calculating. 3 a reckoning or forecast. [ME f. OF f. LL calculatio (as CALCULATE)]

calculator /ˈkælkjʊˌleɪtə(r)/ n. 1 a device (esp. a small electronic one) used for making mathematical calculations. 2 a person or thing that calculates. [ME f. L (as CALCULATE)]

calculus /ˈkælkjʊləs/ n. (pl. **calculuses** or **calculi** /-ˌlaɪ/) 1 Math. a a particular method of calculation or reasoning (calculus of probabilities). b the infinitesimal calculuses of integration or differentiation (see integral calculus, differential calculus). 2 Med. a stone or concretion of minerals formed within the body. □ **calculous** adj. (in sense 2). [L, = small stone used in reckoning on an abacus]

caldron var. of CAULDRON.

Caledonian /ˌkælɪˈdəʊnɪən/ adj. & n. —adj. **1** of or relating to Scotland. **2** Geol. of a mountain-forming period in Europe in the Palaeozoic era. —n. a Scotsman. [L Caledonia northern Britain]

calendar /ˈkælɪndə(r)/ n. & v. —n. **1** a system by which the beginning, length, and subdivisions of the year are fixed. **2** a chart or series of pages showing the days, weeks, and months of a particular year, or giving special seasonal information. **3** a timetable or programme of appointments, special events, etc. —v.tr. register or enter in a calendar or timetable etc. □ **calendric** /-ˈlendrɪk/ adj. **calendrical** /-ˈlendrɪk(ə)l/ adj. [ME f. AF calender, OF calendier f. L calendarium account-book (as CALENDS)]

calender /ˈkælɪndə(r)/ n. & v. —n. a machine in which cloth, paper, etc., is pressed by rollers to glaze or smooth it. —v.tr. press in a calender. [F calendre(r), of unkn. orig.]

calends /ˈkælendz/ n.pl. (also **kalends**) the first of the month in the ancient Roman calendar. [ME f. OF calendes f. L kalendae]

calendula /kəˈlendjʊlə/ n. any plant of the genus Calendula, with large yellow or orange flowers, e.g. marigold. [mod.L dimin. of calendae (as CALENDS), perh. = little clock]

calf[1] /kɑːf/ n. (pl. **calves** /kɑːvz/) **1** a young bovine animal, used esp. of domestic cattle. **2** the young of other animals, e.g. elephant, deer, and whale. □ **calf-love** romantic attachment or affection between adolescents. **in** (or **with**) **calf** (of a cow) pregnant. □ **calfhood** n. **calfish** adj. **calflike** adj. [OE cælf f. WG]

calf[2] /kɑːf/ n. (pl. **calves** /kɑːvz/) the fleshy hind part of the human leg below the knee. □ **-calved** /kɑːvd/ adj. (in comb.). [ME f. ON kálfi, of unkn. orig.]

calfskin /ˈkɑːfskɪn/ n. calf-leather, esp. in book-binding and shoemaking.

calibrate /ˈkælɪˌbreɪt/ v.tr. **1** mark (a gauge) with a standard scale of readings. **2** correlate the readings of (an instrument) with a standard. **3** determine the calibre of (a gun). **4** determine the correct capacity or value of. □ **calibration** /-ˈbreɪʃ(ə)n/ n. **calibrator** n. [CALIBRE + -ATE[3]]

calibre /ˈkælɪbə(r)/ n. (US **caliber**) **1 a** the internal diameter of a gun or tube. **b** the diameter of a bullet or shell. **2** strength or quality of character; ability, importance (we need someone of your calibre). □ **calibred** adj. (also in comb.). [F calibre or It. calibro, f. Arab. ḳālib mould]

calico /ˈkælɪˌkəʊ/ n. & adj. —n. (pl. **-oes** or US **-os**) **1** a cotton cloth, esp. plain white or unbleached. **2** US a printed cotton fabric. —adj. **1** made of calico. **2** US multicoloured, piebald. [earlier calicut f. Calicut in India]

californium /ˌkælɪˈfɔːnɪəm/ n. Chem. a trans-uranic radioactive metallic element produced artificially from curium. [California (where it was first made) + -IUM]

caliph /ˈkeɪlɪf, ˈkæl-/ n. esp. hist. the chief Muslim civil and religious ruler, regarded as the successor of Muhammad. □ **caliphate** n. [ME f. OF caliphe f. Arab. ḳalīfa successor]

calix var. of CALYX.

calk US var. of CAULK.

call /kɔːl/ v. & n. —v. **1** intr. **a** (often foll. by out) cry, shout; speak loudly. **b** (of a bird or animal) emit its characteristic note or cry. **2** tr. communicate or converse with by telephone or radio. **3** tr. **a** bring to one's presence by calling; summon (will you call the children?). **b** arrange for (a person or thing) to come or be present (called a taxi). **4** intr. (often foll. by at, in, on) pay a brief visit (called at the house; called in to see you; come and call on me). **5** tr. **a** order to take place; fix a time for (called a meeting). **b** direct to happen; announce (call a halt). **6 a** intr. require one's attention or consideration (duty calls). **b** tr. urge, invite, nominate (call to the bar). **7** tr. name; describe as (call her Della). **8** tr. consider; regard or estimate as (I call that silly). **9** tr. rouse from sleep (call me at 8). **10** intr. guess the outcome of tossing a coin etc. **11** intr. (foll. by for) order, require, demand (called for silence). **12** tr. (foll. by over) read out (a list of names to determine those present). **13** intr. (foll. by on, upon) invoke; appeal to; request or require (called on us to be quiet). **14** tr. Cards specify (a suit or contract) in bidding. —n. **1** a shout or cry; an act of calling. **2 a** the characteristic cry of a bird or animal. **b** an imitation of this. **c** an instrument for imitating it. **3** a brief visit (paid them a call). **4 a** an act of telephoning. **b** a telephone conversation. **5 a** an invitation or summons to appear or be present. **b** an appeal or invitation (from a specific source or discerned by a person's conscience etc.) to follow a certain profession, set of principles, etc. **6** (foll. by for, or to + infin.) a duty, need, or occasion (no call to be rude; no call for violence). **7** (foll. by for, on) a demand (not much call for it these days; a call on one's time). **8** a signal on a bugle etc.; a signalling-whistle. **9** Cards **a** a player's right or turn to make a bid. **b** a bid made. □ **at call** = on call. **call away** divert, distract. **call-box** a public telephone box or kiosk. **call-boy** a theatre attendant who summons actors when needed on stage. **call down 1** invoke. **2** reprimand. **call forth** elicit. **call-girl** a prostitute who accepts appointments by telephone. **call in** tr. **1** withdraw from circulation. **2** seek the advice or services of. **calling-card** US = visiting-card. **call in** (or **into**) **question** dispute; doubt the validity of. **call into play** give scope for; make use of. **call off 1** cancel (an arrangement etc.). **2** order (an attacker or pursuer) to desist. **call of nature** a need to urinate or defecate. **call out 1** summon (troops etc.) to action. **2** order (workers) to strike. **call the shots** (or **tune**) be in control; take the initiative. **call-sign** (or **-signal**) a broadcast signal identifying the radio transmitter used. **call to mind** recollect; cause one to remember. **call to order 1** request to be orderly. **2** declare (a meeting) open. **call up 1** reach by telephone. **2** imagine, recollect. **3** summon, esp. to serve in the army. **call-up** n. the act or process of calling up (sense 3). **on call 1** (of a doctor etc.) available if required but not formally on duty. **2** (of money lent) repayable on demand. **within call** near enough to be summoned by calling. [OE ceallian f. ON kalla]

caller /ˈkɔːlə(r)/ n. a person who calls, esp. one who pays a visit or makes a telephone call.

calligraphy /kəˈlɪgrəfɪ/ n. **1** handwriting, esp. when fine or pleasing. **2** the art of handwriting. □ **calligrapher** n. **calligraphic** /-ˈgræfɪk/ adj. **calligraphist** n. [Gk kalligraphia f. kallos beauty]

calling /ˈkɔːlɪŋ/ n. **1** a profession or occupation. **2** an inwardly felt call or summons; a vocation.

calliper /ˈkælɪpə(r)/ n. & v. (also **caliper**) —n. **1** (in pl.) (also **calliper compasses**) compasses with bowed legs for measuring the diameter of convex bodies, or with out-turned points for measuring internal dimensions. **2** (in full **calliper splint**) a metal splint to support the leg. —v.tr. measure with callipers. [app. var. of CALIBRE]

callisthenics /ˌkælɪsˈθenɪks/ n.pl. (also **calisthenics**) gymnastic exercises to achieve bodily fitness and grace of movement. □ **callisthenic** adj. [Gk kallos beauty + sthenos strength]

callosity /kəˈlɒsɪtɪ/ n. (pl. **-ies**) a hard thick area of skin usu. occurring in parts of the body subject to pressure or friction. [F callosité or L callositas (as CALLOUS)]

callous /ˈkæləs/ adj. & n. —adj. **1** unfeeling, insensitive. **2** (of skin) hardened or hard. —n. = CALLUS 1. □ **callously** adv. (in sense 1 of adj.). **callousness** n. [ME f. L callosus (as CALLOUS) or F calleux]

callow /ˈkæləʊ/ adj. inexperienced, immature. □ **callowly** adv. **callowness** n. [OE calu]

callus /ˈkæləs/ n. **1** a hard thick area of skin or tissue. **2** a hard tissue formed round bone ends after a fracture. **3** Bot. a new protective tissue formed over a wound. [L]

calm /kɑːm/ adj., n., & v. —adj. **1** tranquil, quiet, windless (a calm sea; a calm night). **2** (of a person or disposition) settled; not agitated (remained calm throughout the ordeal). **3** self-assured, confident (his calm assumption that we would wait). —n. **1** a state of being calm; stillness, serenity. **2** a period without wind or storm. —v.tr. & intr. (often foll. by down) make or become calm. □ **calmly** adv. **calmness** n. [ME ult. f. LL cauma f. Gk kauma heat]

calmative /ˈkælmətɪv, ˈkɑːm-/ adj. & n. Med. —adj. tending to calm or sedate. —n. a calmative drug etc.

calomel /ˈkæləˌmel/ n. a compound of mercury, esp. when used medicinally as a cathartic. [mod.L perh. f. Gk kalos beautiful + melas black]

Calor gas /ˈkælə/ n. propr. liquefied butane gas stored under pressure in containers for domestic use and used as a substitute for mains gas. [L calor heat]

caloric /ˈkælərɪk/ adj. & n. —adj. of heat or calories. —n. hist. a supposed material form or cause of heat. [F calorique f. L calor heat]

calorie /ˈkælərɪ/ n. (also **calory**) (pl. **-ies**) a unit of quantity of heat: **1** (in full **small calorie**) the amount needed to raise the temperature of 1 gram of water through 1 °C. **2** (in full **large calorie**) the amount needed to raise the temperature of 1 kilogram of water through 1 °C, often used to measure the energy value of foods. [F, arbitr. f. L calor heat + -ie]

calorific /ˌkæləˈrɪfɪk/ adj. producing heat. □ **calorific value** the amount of heat produced by a specified quantity of fuel, food, etc. □ **calorifically** adv. [L calorificus f. calor heat]

calorimeter /ˌkæləˈrɪmɪtə(r)/ n. any of various instruments for measuring quantity of heat, esp. to find calorific values. □ **calorimetric** /-ˈmetrɪk/ adj. **calorimetry** n. [L calor heat + -METER]

calumet /ˈkæljʊˌmet/ n. a N. American Indian peace-pipe. [F, ult. f. L calamus reed]

calumniate /kəˈlʌmnɪˌeɪt/ v.tr. slander. □ **calumniation** /-ˈeɪʃ(ə)n/ n. **calumniator** n. **calumniatory** adj. [L calumniari]

calumny /ˈkæləmnɪ/ n. & v. —n. (pl. **-ies**) **1** slander; malicious misrepresentation. **2** an instance of this. —v.tr. (**-ies**, **-ied**) slander. □ **calumnious** adj. [L calumnia]

calvados /ˈkælvəˌdɒs/ n. an apple brandy. [Calvados in France]

Calvary /ˈkælvərɪ/ n. the place where Christ was crucified. [ME f. LL calvaria skull, transl. Gk golgotha, Aram. gûlgûltâ (Matt. 27:33)]

calve /kɑːv/ v. **1** intr. give birth to a calf. **2** tr. (esp. in passive) give birth to (a calf). [OE calfian]

calves pl. of CALF[1], CALF[2].

Calvinism /ˈkælvɪˌnɪz(ə)m/ n. the theology of the French theologian J. Calvin (d. 1564) or his followers, in which predestination and justification by faith are important elements. □ **Calvinist** n. **Calvinistic** /-ˈnɪstɪk/ adj. **Calvinistical** /-ˈnɪstɪk(ə)l/ adj. [F calvinisme or mod.L calvinismus]

calx /kælks/ n. (pl. **calces** /ˈkælsiːz/) **1** a powdery metallic oxide formed when an ore or mineral has been heated. **2** calcium oxide. [L calx calcis lime prob. f. Gk khalix pebble, limestone]

calypso /kəˈlɪpsəʊ/ n. (pl. **-os**) a W. Indian song in African rhythm, usu. improvised on a topical theme. [20th c.: orig. unkn.]

calyx /ˈkeɪlɪks, ˈkæl-/ n. (also **calix**) (pl. **calyces** /-lɪˌsiːz/ or **calyxes**) **1** Bot. the sepals collectively, forming the protective layer of a flower in bud. **2** Biol. any cuplike cavity or structure. [L f. Gk kalux case of bud, husk: cf. kaluptō hide]

cam n. a projection on a rotating part in machinery, shaped to impart reciprocal or variable motion to the part in contact with it. [Du. kam comb: cf. Du. kamrad cog-wheel]

camaraderie /ˌkæməˈrɑːdərɪ/ n. mutual trust and sociability among friends. [F]

camber /ˈkæmbə(r)/ n. & v. —n. **1** the slightly convex or arched shape of the surface of a road, ship's deck, aircraft wing, etc. **2** the slight sideways inclination of the front wheel of a motor vehicle. —v. **1** intr. (of a surface) have a camber. **2** tr. give a camber to; build with a camber. [F cambre arched f. L camurus curved inwards]

cambium /ˈkæmbɪəm/ n. (pl. **cambia** /-bɪə/ or **cambiums**) Bot. a cellular plant tissue responsible for the increase in girth of stems and roots. □ **cambial** adj. [med.L, = change, exchange]

Cambrian /ˈkæmbrɪən/ adj. & n. —adj. **1** Welsh. **2** Geol. of or relating to the first period in the Palaeozoic era. —n. this period or system. [L Cambria var. of Cumbria f. Welsh Cymry Welshman or Cymru Wales]

cambric /ˈkæmbrɪk/ n. a fine white linen or cotton fabric. [Kamerijk, Flem. form of Cambrai in N. France, where it was orig. made]

Cambridge blue /ˈkeɪmbrɪdʒ/ n. & adj. a pale blue. [Cambridge in S. England]

camcorder /ˈkæmˌkɔːdə(r)/ n. a combined video camera and sound recorder. [camera + recorder]

came past of COME.

camel /ˈkæm(ə)l/ n. **1** either of two kinds of large cud-chewing mammals having slender cushion-footed legs and one hump (**Arabian camel**, Camelus dromedarius) or two humps

(**Bactrian camel**, *Camelus bactrianus*). **2** a fawn colour. □ **camel** (or **camel's**) **-hair 1** the hair of a camel. **2 a** a fine soft hair used in artists' brushes. **b** a fabric made of this. [OE f. L *camelus* f. Gk *kamēlos*, of Semitic orig.]

camellia /kəˈmiːlɪə/ *n.* any evergreen shrub of the genus *Camellia*, native to E. Asia, with shiny leaves and showy flowers. [J. *Camellus* or *Kamel*, 17th-c. Jesuit botanist]

Camembert /ˈkæməmˌbeə(r)/ *n.* a kind of soft creamy cheese, usu. with a strong flavour. [*Camembert* in N. France, where it was orig. made]

cameo /ˈkæmɪˌəʊ/ *n.* (*pl.* **-os**) **1 a** a small piece of onyx or other hard stone carved in relief with a background of a different colour. **b** a similar relief design using other materials. **2 a** a short descriptive literary sketch or acted scene. **b** a small character part in a play or film. [ME f. OF *camahieu* and med.L *cammaeus*]

camera /ˈkæmrə, -ərə/ *n.* **1** an apparatus for taking photographs, consisting of a lightproof box to hold light-sensitive film, a lens, and a shutter mechanism, either for still photographs or for motion-picture film. **2** *Telev.* a piece of equipment which forms an optical image and converts it into electrical impulses for transmission or storage. □ **camera obscura** /ɒbˈskjʊərə/ an internally darkened box with an aperture for projecting the image of an external object on a screen inside it. **in camera 1** *Law* in a judge's private room. **2** privately; not in public. [orig. = chamber f. L *camera* f. Gk *kamara* vault etc.]

cameraman /ˈkæmrəmən/ *n.* (*pl.* **-men**) a person who operates a camera professionally, esp. in film-making or television.

camiknickers /ˈkæmɪˌnɪkəz/ *n.pl.* *Brit.* a one-piece close-fitting undergarment formerly worn by women. [CAMISOLE + KNICKERS]

camisole /ˈkæmɪˌsəʊl/ *n.* an under-bodice, usu. embroidered. [F f. It. *camiciola* or Sp. *camisola*: see CHEMISE]

camomile /ˈkæməˌmaɪl/ *n.* (also **chamomile**) any aromatic plant of the genus *Anthemis* or *Matricaria*, with daisy-like flowers. [ME f. OF *camomille* f. LL *camomilla* or *chamomilla* f. Gk *khamaimēlon* earth-apple (from the apple-smell of its flowers)]

camouflage /ˈkæməˌflɑːʒ/ *n.* & *v.* —*n.* **1 a** the disguising of military vehicles, aircraft, ships, artillery, and installations by painting them or covering them to make them blend with their surroundings. **b** such a disguise. **2** the natural colouring of an animal which enables it to blend in with its surroundings. **3** a misleading or evasive precaution or expedient. —*v.tr.* hide or disguise by means of camouflage. [F f. *camoufler* disguise f. It. *camuffare* disguise, deceive]

camp[1] *n.* & *v.* —*n.* **1** a place where troops are lodged or trained. **2** temporary overnight lodging in tents etc. in the open. **3 a** temporary accommodation of various kinds, usu. consisting of huts or tents, for detainees, homeless persons, and other emergency use. **b** a complex of buildings for holiday accommodation, usu. with extensive recreational facilities. **4** an ancient fortified site or its remains. **5** the adherents of a particular party or doctrine

regarded collectively (*the Labour camp was jubilant*). —*v.intr.* **1** set up or spend time in a camp (in senses 1 and 2 of *n.*). **2** (often foll. by *out*) lodge in temporary quarters or in the open. **3** *Austral.* (of sheep or cattle) flock together esp. for rest. □ **camp-bed** a folding portable bed of a kind used in camping. **camp-fire** an open-air fire in a camp etc. **camp-follower 1** a civilian worker in a military camp. **2** a disciple or adherent. **camp-site** a place for camping. □ **camping** *n.* [F f. It. *campo* f. L *campus* level ground]

camp[2] *adj.*, *n.*, & *v.* *colloq.* —*adj.* **1** affected, effeminate. **2** homosexual. **3** done in an exaggerated way for effect. —*n.* a camp manner or style. —*v.intr.* & *tr.* behave or do in a camp way. □ **camp it up** overact; behave affectedly. □ **campy** *adj.* (**campier**, **campiest**). **campily** *adv.* **campiness** *n.* [20th c.: orig. uncert.]

campaign /kæmˈpeɪn/ *n.* & *v.* —*n.* **1** an organized course of action for a particular purpose, esp. to arouse public interest (e.g. before a political election). **2 a** a series of military operations in a definite area or to achieve a particular objective. **b** military service in the field (*on campaign*). —*v.intr.* conduct or take part in a campaign. □ **campaigner** *n.* [F *campagne* open country f. It. *campagna* f. LL *campania*]

campanile /ˌkæmpəˈniːlɪ/ *n.* a bell-tower (usu. free-standing), esp. in Italy. [It. f. *campana* bell]

campanology /ˌkæmpəˈnɒlədʒɪ/ *n.* **1** the study of bells. **2** the art or practice of bell-ringing. □ **campanologer** *n.* **campanological** /-nəˈlɒdʒɪk(ə)l/ *adj.* **campanologist** *n.* [mod.L *campanologia* f. LL *campana* bell]

campanula /kæmˈpænjʊlə/ *n.* any plant of the genus *Campanula*, with bell-shaped usu. blue, purple, or white flowers. Also called 'bellflower'. [mod.L dimin. of L *campana* bell]

camper /ˈkæmpə(r)/ *n.* **1** a person who camps out or lives temporarily in a tent, hut, etc., esp. on holiday. **2** a large motor vehicle with accommodation for camping out.

camphor /ˈkæmfə(r)/ *n.* a white translucent crystalline volatile substance with aromatic smell and bitter taste, used to make celluloid and in medicine. □ **camphoric** /-ˈfɒrɪk/ *adj.* [ME f. OF *camphore* or med.L *camphora* f. Arab. *kāfūr* f. Skr. *karpūram*]

camphorate /ˈkæmfəˌreɪt/ *v.tr.* impregnate or treat with camphor.

campion /ˈkæmpɪən/ *n.* **1** any plant of the genus *Silene*, with usu. pink or white notched flowers. **2** any of several similar cultivated plants of the genus *Lychnis*. [perh. f. obs. *campion* f. OF, = CHAMPION: transl. of Gk *lukhnis stephanōmatikē* a plant used for (champions') garlands]

campus /ˈkæmpəs/ *n.* (*pl.* **campuses**) **1** the grounds of a university or college. **2** esp. *US* a university, esp. as a teaching institution. [L, = field]

camshaft /ˈkæmʃɑːft/ *n.* a shaft with one or more cams attached to it.

can[1] /kæn, kən/ *v.aux.* (*3rd sing. present* **can**; *past* **could** /kʊd/) (foll. by *infin.* without *to*, or *absol.*; present and past only in use) **1 a** be able to; know how to (*I can run fast; can he?; can you speak German?*). **b** be potentially capable of (*you can do it if you try*). **2** be permitted to (*can we go to the party?*). [OE *cunnan* know]

can² *n. & v.* —*n.* **1** a metal vessel for liquid. **2** a tin container in which food or drink is hermetically sealed to enable storage over long periods. **3** (prec. by *the*) *sl.* **a** prison (*sent to the can*). **b** *US* lavatory. —*v.tr.* (**canned, canning**) **1** put or preserve in a can. **2** record on film or tape for future use. □ **in the can** *colloq.* completed. □ **canner** *n.* [OE *canne*]

Canada goose /ˈkænədə/ *n.* a wild goose, *Branta canadensis*, of N. America, with a brownish-grey body and white cheeks and breast.

canal /kəˈnæl/ *n.* **1** an artificial waterway for inland navigation or irrigation. **2** any of various tubular ducts in a plant or animal, for carrying food, liquid, or air. □ **canal boat** a long narrow boat for use on canals. [ME f. OF (earlier *chanel*) f. L *canalis* or It. *canale*]

canalize /ˈkænəˌlaɪz/ *v.tr.* (also **-ise**) **1** make a canal through. **2** convert (a river) into a canal. **3** provide with canals. **4** give the desired direction or purpose to. □ **canalization** /-ˈzeɪʃ(ə)n/ *n.* [F *canaliser*: see CANAL]

canapé /ˈkænəpɪ/ *n.* a small piece of bread or pastry with a savoury on top. [F]

canard /kəˈnɑːd, ˈkænɑːd/ *n.* an unfounded rumour or story. [F, = duck]

canary /kəˈneərɪ/ *n.* (*pl.* **-ies**) any of various small finches of the genus *Serinus*, esp. *S. canaria*, a songbird native to the Canary Islands, with mainly yellow plumage. [*Canary Islands* f. F *Canarie* f. Sp. & L *Canaria* f. *canis* dog, one of the islands being noted in Roman times for large dogs]

canasta /kəˈnæstə/ *n.* a card-game using two packs and resembling rummy. [Sp., = basket]

cancan /ˈkænkæn/ *n.* a lively stage-dance with high kicking, performed by women in long skirts and petticoats. [F]

cancel /ˈkæns(ə)l/ *v. & n.* —*v.* (**cancelled, cancelling;** *US* **canceled, canceling**) **1** *tr.* **a** withdraw or revoke (a previous arrangement). **b** discontinue (an arrangement in progress). **2** *tr.* obliterate or delete (writing etc.). **3** *tr.* mark or pierce (a ticket, stamp, etc.) to invalidate it. **4** *tr.* annul; make void; abolish. **5** (often foll. by *out*) **a** *tr.* (of one factor or circumstance) neutralize or counterbalance (another). **b** *intr.* (of two factors or circumstances) neutralize each other. **6** *tr.* *Math.* strike out (an equal factor) on each side of an equation or from the numerator and denominator of a fraction. —*n.* **1** a countermand. **2** the cancellation of a postage stamp. **3** *Mus.* *US* a natural-sign. □ **canceller** *n.* [ME f. F *canceller* f. L *cancellare* f. *cancelli* crossbars, lattice]

cancellation /ˌkænsəˈleɪʃ(ə)n/ *n.* **1** the act or an instance of cancelling or being cancelled. **2** something that has been cancelled, esp. a booking or reservation. [L *cancellatio* (as CANCEL)]

cancer /ˈkænsə(r)/ *n.* **1 a** any malignant growth or tumour from an abnormal and uncontrolled division of body cells. **b** a disease caused by this. **2** an evil influence or corruption spreading uncontrollably. **3** (**Cancer**) **a** a constellation, traditionally regarded as contained in the figure of a crab. **b** the fourth sign of the zodiac (the Crab). **c** a person born when the sun is in this sign. □ **Cancerian** /-ˈsɪərɪən/ *n. & adj.* (in sense 3). **cancerous** *adj.* [ME f. L, = crab, cancer, after Gk *karkinos*]

cancroid /ˈkæŋkrɔɪd/ *adj. & n.* —*adj.* **1** crablike. **2** resembling cancer. —*n.* a disease resembling cancer.

candela /kænˈdiːlə, -ˈdeɪlə/ *n.* the SI unit of luminous intensity. [L, = candle]

candelabrum /ˌkændɪˈlɑːbrəm/ *n.* (also **candelabra** /-brə/) (*pl.* **candelabra,** *US* **candelabrums, candelabras**) a large branched candlestick or lamp-holder. [L f. *candela* CANDLE]

■ **Usage** The form *candelabra* is, strictly speaking, plural. However, *candelabra* (singular) and *candelabras* (plural) are often found in informal use.

candescent /kænˈdes(ə)nt/ *adj.* glowing with or as with white heat. □ **candescence** *n.* [L *candēre* be white]

candid /ˈkændɪd/ *adj.* **1** frank; not hiding one's thoughts. **2** (of a photograph) taken informally, usu. without the subject's knowledge. □ **candidly** *adv.* **candidness** *n.* [F *candide* or L *candidus* white]

candida /ˈkændɪdə/ *n.* any yeastlike parasitic fungus of the genus *Candida*, esp. *C. albicans* causing thrush. [mod.L fem. of L *candidus*: see CANDID]

candidate /ˈkændɪdət, -ˌdeɪt/ *n.* **1** a person who seeks or is nominated for an office, award, etc. **2** a person or thing likely to gain some distinction or position. **3** a person entered for an examination. □ **candidacy** *n.* **candidature** *n. Brit.* [F *candidat* or L *candidatus* white-robed (Roman candidates wearing white)]

candle /ˈkænd(ə)l/ *n.* **1** a cylinder or block of wax or tallow with a central wick, for giving light when burning. **2** = CANDLEPOWER. □ **cannot hold a candle to** cannot be compared with; is much inferior to. **not worth the candle** not justifying the cost or trouble. □ **candler** *n.* [OE *candel* f. L *candela* f. *candēre* shine]

candlelight /ˈkænd(ə)lˌlaɪt/ *n.* **1** light provided by candles. **2** dusk.

Candlemas /ˈkænd(ə)lməs, -ˌmæs/ *n.* a feast with blessing of candles (2 Feb.), commemorating the Purification of the Virgin Mary. [OE *Candelmæsse* (as CANDLE, MASS²)]

candlepower /ˈkænd(ə)lˌpaʊə(r)/ *n.* a unit of luminous intensity.

candlestick /ˈkænd(ə)lstɪk/ *n.* a holder for one or more candles.

candlewick /ˈkænd(ə)lwɪk/ *n.* **1** a thick soft cotton yarn. **2** material made from this, usu. with a tufted pattern.

candour /ˈkændə(r)/ *n.* (*US* **candor**) candid behaviour or action; frankness. [F *candeur* or L *candor* whiteness]

C. & W. *abbr.* country-and-western.

candy /ˈkændɪ/ *n. & v.* —*n.* (*pl.* **-ies**) **1** (in full **sugar-candy**) sugar crystallized by repeated boiling and slow evaporation. **2** *US* sweets; a sweet. —*v.tr.* (**-ies, -ied**) (usu. as **candied** *adj.*) preserve by coating and impregnating with a sugar syrup (*candied fruit*). [F *sucre candi* candied sugar f. Arab. *kand* sugar]

candyfloss /ˈkændɪˌflɒs/ *n. Brit.* a fluffy mass of spun sugar wrapped round a stick.

candystripe /ˈkændɪˌstraɪp/ *n.* a pattern consisting of alternate stripes of white and a colour (usu. pink). □ **candystriped** *adj.*

cane /keɪn/ *n. & v.* —*n.* **1 a** the hollow jointed stem of giant reeds or grasses (*bamboo cane*). **b** the solid stem of slender palms (*malacca cane*). **2**

= *sugar cane*. **3** a raspberry-cane. **4** material of cane used for wickerwork etc. **5 a** a cane used as a walking-stick or a support for a plant or an instrument of punishment. **b** any slender walking-stick. —*v.tr.* **1** beat with a cane. **2** weave cane into (a chair etc.). □ **cane-sugar** sugar obtained from sugar-cane. □ **caner** *n.* (in sense 2 of *v.*). **caning** *n.* [ME f. OF f. L *canna* f. Gk *kanna*]

canine /ˈkeɪnaɪn, ˈkæn-/ *adj.* & *n.* —*adj.* **1** of a dog or dogs. **2** of or belonging to the family Canidae, including dogs, wolves, foxes, etc. —*n.* **1** a dog. **2** (in full **canine tooth**) a pointed tooth between the incisors and premolars. [ME f. *canin -ine* or f. L *caninus* f. *canis* dog]

canister /ˈkænɪstə(r)/ *n.* **1** a small container, usu. of metal and cylindrical, for storing tea etc. **2 a** a cylinder of shot, tear-gas, etc., that explodes on impact. **b** such cylinders collectively. [L *canistrum* f. Gk f. *kanna* CANE]

canker /ˈkæŋkə(r)/ *n.* & *v.* —*n.* **1 a** a destructive fungus disease of trees and plants. **b** an open wound in the stem of a tree or plant. **2** *Zool.* an ulcerous ear disease of animals esp. cats and dogs. **3** a corrupting influence. —*v.tr.* **1** consume with canker. **2** corrupt. **3** (as **cankered** *adj.*) soured, malignant, crabbed. □ **cankerous** *adj.* [OE *cancer* & ONF *cancre*, OF *chancre* f. L *cancer* crab]

canna /ˈkænə/ *n.* any tropical plant of the genus *Canna* with bright flowers and ornamental leaves. [L: see CANE]

cannabis /ˈkænəbɪs/ *n.* **1** any hemp plant of the genus *Cannabis*, esp. Indian hemp. **2** a preparation of parts of this used as an intoxicant or hallucinogen. □ **cannabis resin** a sticky product, esp. from the flowering tops of the female cannabis plant. [L f. Gk]

canned /kænd/ *adj.* **1** pre-recorded (*canned laughter*; *canned music*). **2** supplied in a can (*canned beer*). **3** *sl.* drunk.

cannelloni /ˌkænəˈləʊnɪ/ *n.pl.* tubes or rolls of pasta stuffed with meat or a vegetable mixture. [It. f. *cannello* stalk]

cannery /ˈkænərɪ/ *n.* (pl. **-ies**) a factory where food is canned.

cannibal /ˈkænɪb(ə)l/ *n.* & *adj.* —*n.* **1** a person who eats human flesh. **2** an animal that feeds on flesh of its own species. —*adj.* of or like a cannibal. □ **cannibalism** *n.* **cannibalistic** /-bəˈlɪstɪk/ *adj.* **cannibalistically** /-bəˈlɪstɪkəlɪ/ *adv.* [orig. pl. *Canibales* f. Sp.: var. of *Caribes* name of a W.Ind. nation]

cannibalize /ˈkænɪbəlaɪz/ *v.tr.* (also **-ise**) use (a machine etc.) as a source of spare parts for others. □ **cannibalization** /-ˈzeɪʃ(ə)n/ *n.*

cannon /ˈkænən/ *n.* & *v.* —*n.* **1** *hist.* (pl. same) a large heavy gun installed on a carriage or mounting. **2** an automatic aircraft gun firing shells. **3** *Billiards* the hitting of two balls successively by the cue-ball. —*v.intr.* **1** (usu. foll. by *against*, *into*) collide heavily or obliquely. **2** *Billiards* make a cannon shot. □ **cannon-ball** *hist.* a large usu. metal ball fired by a cannon. **cannon-fodder** soldiers regarded merely as material to be expended in war. [F *canon* f. It. *cannone* large tube f. *canna* CANE: in Billiards sense f. older *carom* f. Sp. *carambola*]

cannonade /ˌkænəˈneɪd/ *n.* & *v.* —*n.* a period of continuous heavy gunfire. —*v.tr.* bombard with a cannonade. [F f. It. *cannonata*]

cannot /ˈkænɒt, kæˈnɒt/ *v.aux.* can not.

canny /ˈkænɪ/ *adj.* (**cannier**, **canniest**) **1 a** shrewd, worldly-wise. **b** thrifty. **c** circumspect. **2** sly, drily humorous. □ **cannily** *adv.* **canniness** *n.* [CAN¹ (in sense 'know') + -Y¹]

canoe /kəˈnuː/ *n.* & *v.* —*n.* a small narrow boat with pointed ends usu. propelled by paddling. —*v.intr.* (**canoes**, **canoed**, **canoeing**) travel in a canoe. □ **canoeist** *n.* [Sp. and Haitian *canoa*]

canon /ˈkænən/ *n.* **1 a** a general law, rule, principle, or criterion. **b** a church decree or law. **2** (*fem.* **canoness**) **a** a member of a cathedral chapter. **b** a member of certain RC orders. **3 a** a collection or list of sacred books etc. accepted as genuine. **b** the recognized genuine works of a particular author; a list of these. **4** the part of the Roman Catholic Mass containing the words of consecration. **5** *Mus.* a piece with different parts taking up the same theme successively, either at the same or at a different pitch. □ **canon law** ecclesiastical law. [OE f. L f. Gk *kanōn*, in ME also f. AF & OF *canun*, *-on*; in sense 2 ME f. OF *canonie* f. eccl.L *canonicus*: cf. CANONICAL]

cañon var. of CANYON.

canonical /kəˈnɒnɪk(ə)l/ *adj.* & *n.* —*adj.* **1 a** according to or ordered by canon law. **b** included in the canon of Scripture. **2** authoritative, standard, accepted. **3** of a cathedral chapter or a member of it. **4** *Mus.* in canon form. —*n.* (in pl.) the canonical dress of the clergy. □ **canonically** *adv.* [med.L *canonicalis* (as CANON)]

canonicity /ˌkænəˈnɪsɪtɪ/ *n.* the status of being canonical. [L *canonicus* canonical]

canonist /ˈkænənɪst/ *n.* an expert in canon law. [ME f. F *canoniste* or f. med.L *canonista*: see CANON]

canonize /ˈkænənaɪz/ *v.tr.* (also **-ise**) **1 a** declare officially to be a saint, usu. with a ceremony. **b** regard as a saint. **2** admit to the canon of Scripture. **3** sanction by Church authority. □ **canonization** /-ˈzeɪʃ(ə)n/ *n.* [ME f. med.L *canonizare*: see CANON]

canonry /ˈkænənrɪ/ *n.* (pl. **-ies**) the office or benefice of a canon.

canoodle /kəˈnuːd(ə)l/ *v.intr.* *colloq.* kiss and cuddle amorously. [19th-c. US: orig. unkn.]

canopy /ˈkænəpɪ/ *n.* & *v.* —*n.* (pl. **-ies**) **1 a** a covering hung or held up over a throne, bed, person, etc. **b** the sky. **c** an overhanging shelter. **2** *Archit.* a rooflike projection over a niche etc. **3** the uppermost layers of foliage etc. in a forest. **4 a** the expanding part of a parachute. **b** the cover of an aircraft's cockpit. —*v.tr.* (**-ies**, **-ied**) supply or be a canopy to. [ME f. med.L *canopeum* f. L *conopeum* f. Gk *kōnōpeion* couch with mosquito-curtains f. *kōnōps* gnat]

cant¹ *n.* & *v.* —*n.* **1** insincere pious or moral talk. **2** ephemeral or fashionable catchwords. **3** language peculiar to a class, profession, sect, etc.; jargon. —*v.intr.* use cant. [earlier of musical sound, of intonation, and of beggars' whining: perh. from the singing of religious mendicants: prob. f. L *canere* sing]

cant² *n.* & *v.* —*n.* **1 a** a slanting surface, e.g. of a bank. **b** a bevel of a crystal etc. **2** an oblique push or movement that upsets or partly upsets something. **3** a tilted or sloping position. —*v.* **1** *tr.* push or pitch out of level; tilt. **2** *intr.* take or lie in a slanting position. **3** *tr.* impart a bevel to.

[ME f. MLG *kant*, *kante*, MDu. *cant*, point, side, edge, ult. f. L *cant(h)us* iron tire]

can't /kɑːnt/ *contr.* can not.

Cantab. /ˈkæntæb/ *abbr.* of Cambridge University. [L *Cantabrigiensis*]

cantabile /kænˈtɑːbɪlɪ/ *adv.*, *adj.*, & *n. Mus.* —*adv.* & *adj.* in a smooth singing style. —*n.* a cantabile passage or movement. [It., = singable]

Cantabrigian /ˌkæntəˈbrɪdʒɪən/ *adj.* & *n.* —*adj.* of Cambridge or Cambridge University. —*n.* **1** a member of Cambridge University. **2** a native of Cambridge. [L *Cantabrigia* Cambridge]

cantaloup /ˈkæntəˌluːp/ *n.* (also **cantaloupe**) a small round ribbed variety of melon with orange flesh. [F *cantaloup* f. *Cantaluppi* near Rome, where it was first grown in Europe]

cantankerous /kænˈtæŋkərəs/ *adj.* bad-tempered, quarrelsome. □ **cantankerously** *adv.* **cantankerousness** *n.* [perh. f. Ir. *cant* out-bidding + *rancorous*]

cantata /kænˈtɑːtə/ *n. Mus.* a short narrative or descriptive composition with vocal solos and usu. chorus and orchestral accompaniment. [It. *cantata* (*aria*) sung (air) f. *cantare* sing]

canteen /kænˈtiːn/ *n.* **1 a** a restaurant for employees in an office or factory etc. **b** a shop selling provisions or liquor in a barracks or camp. **2** a case or box of cutlery. **3** a soldier's or camper's water-flask or set of eating or drinking utensils. [F *cantine* f. It. *cantina* cellar]

canter /ˈkæntə(r)/ *n.* & *v.* —*n.* a gentle gallop. —*v.* **1** *intr.* (of a horse or its rider) go at a canter. **2** *tr.* make (a horse) canter. [short for *Canterbury pace*, from the supposed easy pace of medieval pilgrims to Canterbury]

canterbury /ˈkæntəbərɪ/ *n.* (*pl.* -**ies**) a piece of furniture with partitions for holding music etc. [*Canterbury* in Kent]

Canterbury bell /ˈkæntəbərɪ/ *n.* a cultivated campanula with large flowers. [after the bells of Canterbury pilgrims' horses: see CANTER]

canticle /ˈkæntɪk(ə)l/ *n.* a song or chant with a Biblical text. [ME f. OF *canticle* (var. of *cantique*) or L *canticulum* dimin. of *canticum* f. *canere* sing]

cantilever /ˈkæntɪˌliːvə(r)/ *n.* & *v.* —*n.* **1** a long bracket or beam etc. projecting from a wall to support a balcony etc. **2** a beam or girder fixed at only one end. —*v.intr.* **1** project as a cantilever. **2** be supported by cantilevers. □ **cantilever bridge** a bridge made of cantilevers projecting from the piers and connected by girders. [17th c.: orig. unkn.]

canto /ˈkæntəʊ/ *n.* (*pl.* -**os**) a division of a long poem. [It., = song, f. L *cantus*]

canton *n.* & *v.* —*n.* /ˈkæntɒn/ **1** a subdivision of a country. **2** a State of the Swiss confederation. —*v.tr.* /kænˈtuːn/ put (troops) into quarters. □ **cantonal** /ˈkæntən(ə)l, kænˈtɒn(ə)l/ *adj.* [OF, = corner (see CANT²): (v.) also partly f. F *cantonner*]

Cantonese /ˌkæntəˈniːz/ *adj.* & *n.* —*adj.* of Canton or the Cantonese dialect of Chinese. —*n.* (*pl.* same) **1** a native of Canton. **2** the dialect of Chinese spoken in SE China and Hong Kong. [*Canton* in China]

cantonment /kænˈtuːnmənt/ *n.* **1** a lodging assigned to troops. **2** a permanent military station in India. [F *cantonnement*: see CANTON]

cantor /ˈkæntɔː(r)/ *n.* **1** the leader of the singing in church; a precentor. **2** the precentor in a synagogue. [L, = singer f. *canere* sing]

cantorial /kænˈtɔːrɪəl/ *adj.* **1** of or relating to the cantor. **2** of the north side of the choir in a church (cf. DECANAL).

canvas /ˈkænvəs/ *n.* & *v.* —*n.* **1 a** a strong coarse kind of cloth made from hemp or flax or other coarse yarn and used for sails and tents etc. and as a surface for oil-painting. **b** a piece of this. **2** a painting on canvas, esp. in oils. **3** an open kind of canvas used as a basis for tapestry and embroidery. **4** *sl.* the floor of a boxing or wrestling ring. —*v.tr.* (**canvassed, canvassing**; *US* **canvased, canvasing**) cover with canvas. □ **under canvas 1** in a tent or tents. **2** with sails spread. [ME & ONF *canevas*, ult. f. L *cannabis* hemp]

canvass /ˈkænvəs/ *v.* & *n.* —*v.* **1 a** *intr.* solicit votes. **b** *tr.* solicit votes from (electors in a constituency). **2** *tr.* **a** ascertain opinions of. **b** seek custom from. **c** discuss thoroughly. **3** *tr. Brit.* propose (an idea or plan etc.). **4** *intr. US* check the validity of votes. —*n.* the process of or an instance of canvassing, esp. of electors. □ **canvasser** *n.* [orig. = toss in a sheet, agitate, f. CANVAS]

canyon /ˈkænjən/ *n.* (also **cañon**) a deep gorge, often with a stream or river. [Sp. *cañón* tube, ult. f. L *canna* CANE]

caoutchouc /ˈkaʊtʃʊk/ *n.* raw rubber. [F f. Carib *cahuchu*]

CAP *abbr.* Common Agricultural Policy (of the EC).

cap *n.* & *v.* —*n.* **1 a** a soft brimless head-covering, usu. with a peak. **b** a head-covering worn in a particular profession (*nurse's cap*). **c** esp. *Brit.* a cap awarded as a sign of membership of a sports team. **d** an academic mortarboard or soft hat. **2 a** a cover like a cap in shape or position (*kneecap; toecap*). **b** a device to seal a bottle or protect the point of a pen, lens of a camera, etc. **3 a** = *Dutch cap*. **b** = *percussion cap*. **4** = CROWN *n.* 8b. —*v.tr.* (**capped, capping**) **1 a** put a cap on. **b** cover the top or end of. **c** set a limit to (*rate-capping*). **2 a** esp. *Brit.* award a sports cap to. **b** *Sc.* & *NZ* confer a university degree on. **3 a** lie on top of; form the cap of. **b** surpass, excel. **c** improve on (a story, quotation, etc.) esp. by producing a better or more apposite one. □ **cap in hand** humbly. **cap of maintenance** a cap or hat worn as a symbol of official dignity or carried before the sovereign etc. **cap sleeve** a sleeve extending only a short distance from the shoulder. **if the cap fits** (said of a generalized comment) it seems to be true (of a particular person). **set one's cap at** try to attract as a suitor. □ **capful** *n.* (*pl.* -**fuls**). **capping** *n.* [OE *cæppe* f. LL *cappa*, perh. f. L *caput* head]

capability /ˌkeɪpəˈbɪlɪtɪ/ *n.* (*pl.* -**ies**) **1** (often foll. by *of*, *for*, *to*) ability, power; the condition of being capable. **2** an undeveloped or unused faculty.

capable /ˈkeɪpəb(ə)l/ *adj.* **1** competent, able, gifted. **2** (foll. by *of*) **a** having the ability or fitness or necessary quality for. **b** susceptible or admitting of (explanation or improvement etc.). □ **capably** *adv.* [F f. LL *capabilis* f. L *capere* hold]

capacious /kəˈpeɪʃəs/ *adj.* roomy; able to hold much. □ **capaciously** *adv.* **capaciousness** *n.* [L *capax -acis* f. *capere* hold]

capacitance /kəˈpæsɪt(ə)ns/ *n. Electr.* **1** the ability of a system to store an electric charge. **2** the ratio of the change in an electric charge in a system to the corresponding change in its electric potential. [CAPACITY + -ANCE]

capacitate /kə'pæsɪˌteɪt/ v.tr. **1** (usu. foll. by *for*, or *to* + infin.) render capable. **2** make legally competent.

capacitor /kə'pæsɪtə(r)/ n. *Electr.* a device of one or more pairs of conductors separated by insulators used to store an electric charge.

capacity /kə'pæsɪtɪ/ n. (pl. **-ies**) **1 a** the power of containing, receiving, experiencing, or producing (*capacity for heat, pain,* etc.). **b** the maximum amount that can be contained or produced etc. **c** the volume, e.g. of the cylinders in an internal-combustion engine. **d** (*attrib.*) fully occupying the available space, resources, etc. (*a capacity audience*). **2 a** mental power. **b** a faculty or talent. **3** a position or function (*in a civil capacity; in my capacity as a critic*). **4** legal competence. □ **to capacity** fully; using all resources (*working to capacity*). □ **capacitative** /-tətɪv/ adj. (also **capacitive**) (in sense 5). [ME f. F f. L *capacitas -tatis* (as CAPACIOUS)]

caparison /kə'pærɪs(ə)n/ n. & v. —n. **1** (usu. in pl.) a horse's trappings. **2** equipment, finery. —v.tr. put caparisons on; adorn richly. [obs. F *caparasson* f. Sp. *caparazón* saddle-cloth f. *capa* CAPE¹]

cape¹ n. **1** a sleeveless cloak. **2** a short sleeveless cloak as a fixed or detachable part of a longer cloak or coat. [F f. Prov. *capa* f. LL *cappa* CAP]

cape² n. **1** a headland or promontory. **2** (**the Cape**) **a** the Cape of Good Hope. **b** the S. African province containing it. [ME f. OF *cap* f. Prov. *cap* ult. f. L *caput* head]

caper¹ /'keɪpə(r)/ v. & n. —v.intr. jump or run about playfully. —n. **1** a playful jump or leap. **2 a** a fantastic proceeding; a prank. **b** *sl.* any activity or occupation. □ **caperer** n. [abbr. of CAPRIOLE]

caper² /'keɪpə(r)/ n. **1** a bramble-like S. European shrub, *Capparis spinosa*. **2** (in pl.) its flower buds cooked and pickled. [ME *capres* & F *câpres* f. L *capparis* f. Gk *kapparis*, treated as pl.: cf. CHERRY, PEA]

capercaillie /ˌkæpə'keɪlɪ/ n. (also **capercailzie** /-lzɪ/) a large European grouse, *Tetrao urogallus*. [Gael. *capull coille* horse of the wood]

capillarity /ˌkæpɪ'lærɪtɪ/ n. a phenomenon at liquid boundaries resulting in the rise or depression of liquids in narrow tubes. Also called *capillary action*. [F *capillarité* (as CAPILLARY)]

capillary /kə'pɪlərɪ/ adj. & n. —adj. **1** of or like a hair. **2** (of a tube) of hairlike internal diameter. **3** of one of the delicate ramified blood vessels intervening between arteries and veins. —n. (pl. **-ies**) **1** a capillary tube. **2** a capillary blood vessel. □ **capillary action** = CAPILLARITY. [L *capillaris* f. *capillus* hair]

capital¹ /'kæpɪt(ə)l/ n., adj., & int. —n. **1** the most important town or city of a country or region, usu. its seat of government and administrative centre. **2 a** the money or other assets with which a company starts in business. **b** accumulated wealth, esp. as used in further production. **c** money invested or lent at interest. **3** capitalists generally. **4** a capital letter. —adj. **1 a** principal; most important; leading. **b** *colloq.* excellent, first-rate. **2 a** involving or punishable by death (*capital punishment; a capital offence*). **b** (of an error etc.) vitally harmful; fatal. **3** (of letters of the alphabet) large in size and of the

form used to begin sentences and names etc. —int. expressing approval or satisfaction. □ **capital gain** a profit from the sale of investments or property. **capital levy 1** the appropriation by the State of a fixed proportion of the wealth in the country. **2** a wealth tax. **capital sum** a lump sum of money, esp. payable to an insured person. **capital transfer tax** *hist.* (in the UK) a tax levied on the transfer of capital by gift or bequest etc. **make capital out of** use to one's advantage. □ **capitally** adv. [ME f. OF f. L *capitalis* f. *caput -itis* head]

■ **Usage** Capital transfer tax was replaced in 1986 by *inheritance tax.*

capital² /'kæpɪt(ə)l/ n. *Archit.* the head or cornice of a pillar or column. [ME f. OF *capitel* f. LL *capitellum* dimin. of L *caput* head]

capitalism /'kæpɪtəˌlɪz(ə)m/ n. **1** an economic system in which the production and distribution of goods depend on invested private capital and profit-making. **2** *Polit.* the dominance of private owners of capital and production for profit.

capitalist /'kæpɪtəlɪst/ n. & adj. —n. **1** a person using or possessing capital; a rich person. **2** an advocate of capitalism. —adj. of or favouring capitalism. □ **capitalistic** /-'lɪstɪk/ adj. **capitalistically** /-'lɪstɪkəlɪ/ adv.

capitalize /'kæpɪtəˌlaɪz/ v. (also **-ise**) **1** tr. **a** convert into or provide with capital. **b** calculate or realize the present value of an income. **c** reckon (the value of an asset) by setting future benefits against the cost of maintenance. **2** tr. **a** write (a letter of the alphabet) as a capital. **b** begin (a word) with a capital letter. **3** intr. (foll. by *on*) use to one's advantage; profit from. □ **capitalization** /-'zeɪʃ(ə)n/ n. [F *capitaliser* as CAPITAL¹)]

capitation /ˌkæpɪ'teɪʃ(ə)n/ n. **1** a tax or fee at a set rate per person. **2** the levying of such a tax or fee. □ **capitation grant** a grant of a sum calculated from the number of people to be catered for, esp. in education. [F *capitation* or LL *capitatio* poll-tax f. *caput* head]

capitular /kə'pɪtjʊlə(r)/ adj. of or relating to a cathedral chapter. [LL *capitularis* f. L *capitulum* CHAPTER]

capitulate /kə'pɪtjʊˌleɪt/ v.intr. surrender, esp. on stated conditions. □ **capitulator** n. **capitulatory** /-lətərɪ/ adj. [med.L *capitulare* draw up under headings f. L *caput* head]

capitulation /kəˌpɪtjʊ'leɪʃ(ə)n/ n. **1** the act of capitulating; surrender. **2** a statement of the main divisions of a subject. **3** an agreement or set of conditions.

cap'n /kæpn/ n. *sl.* captain. [contr.]

capo /'kæpəʊ/ n. (in full **capo tasto** /'tæstəʊ/) (pl. **capos** or **capo tastos**) *Mus.* a device secured across the neck of a fretted instrument to raise equally the tuning of all strings by the required amount. [It. *capo tasto* head stop]

capon /'keɪpən/ n. a domestic cock castrated and fattened for eating. □ **caponize** v.tr. (also **-ise**). [OE f. AF *capun*, OF *capon*, ult. f. L *capo -onis*]

cappuccino /ˌkæpʊ'tʃiːnəʊ/ n. (pl. **-os**) coffee with milk made frothy with pressurized steam. [It., = CAPUCHIN]

capriccio /kə'prɪtʃɪəʊ/ n. (pl. **-os**) **1** a lively and usu. short musical composition. **2** a painting etc. representing a fantasy or a mixture of real and imaginary features. [It., = sudden start, orig. 'horror']

caprice /kə'priːs/ n. **1 a** an unaccountable or whimsical change of mind or conduct. **b** a tendency to this. **2** a work of lively fancy in painting, drawing, or music; a capriccio. [F f. It. CAPRICCIO]

capricious /kə'prɪʃəs/ adj. **1** guided by or given to caprice. **2** irregular, unpredictable. □ **capriciously** adv. **capriciousness** n. [F capricieux f. It. capriccioso]

Capricorn /'kæprɪˌkɔːn/ n. (also **Capricornus** /-'kɔːnəs/) **1** a constellation, traditionally regarded as contained in the figure of a goat's horns. **2 a** the tenth sign of the zodiac (the Goat). **b** a person born when the sun is in this sign. □ **Capricornian** n. & adj. [ME f. OF capricorne f. L capricornus f. caper -pri goat + cornu horn]

caprine /'kæpraɪn/ adj. of or like a goat. [ME f. L caprinus f. caper -pri goat]

capriole /'kæprɪˌəʊl/ n. & v. —n. **1** a leap or caper. **2** a trained horse's high leap and kick without advancing. —v. **1** intr. (of a horse or its rider) perform a capriole. **2** tr. make (a horse) capriole. [F f. It. capriola leap, ult. f. caper -pri goat]

capsicum /'kæpsɪkəm/ n. **1** any plant of the genus Capsicum, having edible capsular fruits containing many seeds, esp. C. annuum yielding several varieties of pepper. **2** the fruit of any of these plants. [mod.L, perh. f. L capsa box]

capsize /kæp'saɪz/ v. **1** tr. upset or overturn (a boat). **2** intr. be capsized. □ **capsizal** n. [cap- as in Prov. capvirar, F chavirer: -size unexpl.]

capstan /'kæpst(ə)n/ n. **1 a** thick revolving cylinder with a vertical axis, for winding an anchor cable or a halyard etc. **2** a revolving spindle on a tape recorder, that guides the tape past the head. □ **capstan lathe** a lathe with a revolving tool-holder. [Prov. cabestan, ult. f. L capistrum halter f. capere seize]

capstone /'kæpstəʊn/ n. coping; a coping-stone.

capsule /'kæpsjuːl/ n. **1** a small soluble case of gelatine enclosing a dose of medicine and swallowed with it. **2** a detachable compartment of a spacecraft or nose-cone of a rocket. **3** an enclosing membrane in the body. **4** a dry fruit that releases its seeds when ripe. □ **capsular** adj. **capsulate** adj. [F f. L capsula f. capsa CASE²]

capsulize /'kæpsjuˌlaɪz/ v.tr. (also **-ise**) put (information etc.) in compact form.

Capt. abbr. Captain.

captain /'kæptɪn/ n. & v. —n. **1 a** a chief or leader. **b** the leader of a team, esp. in sports. **c** a powerful or influential person (captain of industry). **2 a** the person in command of a merchant or passenger ship. **b** the pilot of a civil aircraft. **3** (as a title **Captain**) **a** an army or US Air Force officer next above lieutenant. **b** a Navy officer in command of a warship; one ranking below commodore or rear admiral and above commander. **c** US a police officer in charge of a precinct, ranking below Chief Officer. **4 a** a foreman. **b** a head boy or girl in a school. **c** US a supervisor of waiters or bellboys. — v. captain (a team etc.). □ **captaincy** n. (pl. **-ies**). **captainship** n. [ME & OF capitain f. LL capitaneus chief f. L caput capit- head]

caption /'kæpʃ(ə)n/ n. & v. —n. **1** a title or brief explanation appended to an illustration, cartoon, etc. **2** wording appearing on a cinema or television screen as part of a film or broadcast.

3 the heading of a chapter or article etc. —v.tr. provide with a caption. [ME f. L captio f. capere capt- take]

captious /'kæpʃəs/ adj. given to finding fault or raising petty objections. □ **captiously** adv. **captiousness** n. [ME f. OF captieux or L captiosus (as CAPTION)]

captivate /'kæptɪˌveɪt/ v.tr. **1** overwhelm with charm or affection. **2** fascinate. □ **captivatingly** adv. **captivation** /-'veɪʃ(ə)n/ n. [LL captivare take captive (as CAPTIVE)]

captive /'kæptɪv/ n. & adj. —n. a person or animal that has been taken prisoner or confined. —adj. **1 a** taken prisoner. **b** kept in confinement or under restraint. **2 a** unable to escape. **b** in a position of having to comply (captive audience; captive market). **3** of or like a prisoner (captive state). [ME f. L captivus f. capere capt- take]

captivity /kæp'tɪvɪtɪ/ n. (pl. **-ies**) **1** the condition or circumstances of being a captive. **2** a period of captivity.

captor /'kæptə(r), -tɔː(r)/ n. a person who captures (a person, place, etc.). [L (as CAPTURE)]

capture /'kæptʃə(r)/ v. & n. —v.tr. **1 a** take prisoner; seize as a prize. **b** obtain by force or trickery. **2** portray in permanent form (could not capture the likeness). **3** Physics absorb (a subatomic particle). **4** (in board games) make a move that secures the removal of (an opposing piece) from the board. **5** cause (data) to be stored in a computer. —n. **1** the act of capturing. **2** a thing or person captured. □ **capturer** n. [F f. L captura f. capere capt- take]

Capuchin /'kæpjuːtʃɪn/ n. **1** a Franciscan friar of the new rule of 1529. **2** (**capuchin**) any monkey of the genus Cebus of S. America, with cowl-like head hair. [F f. It. cappuccino f. cappuccio cowl f. cappa CAPE¹]

capybara /ˌkæpɪ'bɑːrə/ n. a very large semi-aquatic rodent, Hydrochoerus hydrochaeris, native to S. America. [Tupi]

car n. **1** (in full **motor car**) a road vehicle with an enclosed passenger compartment, powered by an internal-combustion engine. **2** (in comb.) a wheeled vehicle, esp. of a specified kind (tramcar). **b** a railway carriage of a specified type (dining-car). **3** US any railway carriage or van. **4** the passenger compartment of a lift, cableway, balloon, etc. □ **car bomb** a terrorist bomb concealed in or under a parked car. **car-boot sale** an outdoor sale at which participants sell unwanted possessions from the boots of their cars. **car park** an area for parking cars. **car phone** a radio-telephone for use in a motor vehicle. □ **carful** n. (pl. **-fuls**). [ME f. AF & ONF carre ult. f. L carrum, carrus, of OCelt. orig.]

carabineer /ˌkærəbɪ'nɪə(r)/ n. (also **carabinier**) hist. **1** a soldier whose principal weapon is a carbine. **2** (**the Carabineers**) the Royal Scots Dragoon Guards. [F carabinier f. carabine CARBINE]

caracul var. of KARAKUL.

carafe /kə'ræf, -rɑːf/ n. a glass container for water or wine, esp. at a table or bedside. [F f. It. caraffa, ult. f. Arab. ġarrāfa drinking vessel]

carambola /ˌkærəm'bəʊlə/ n. **1** a small tree, Averrhoa carambola, native to SE Asia, bearing golden-yellow ribbed fruit. **2** this fruit. [Port., prob. of Indian or E. Indian orig.]

caramel /'kærəˌmel/ n. **1 a** sugar or syrup heated until it turns brown, then used as a flavouring or to colour spirits etc. **b** a kind of soft toffee made with sugar, butter, etc., melted and further heated. **2** the light-brown colour of caramel. [F f. Sp. *caramelo*]

caramelize /ˈkærəməˌlaɪz/ v. (also **-ise**) **1 a** tr. convert (sugar or syrup) into caramel. **b** intr. (of sugar or syrup) be converted into caramel. **2** tr. coat or cook (food) with caramelized sugar or syrup. □ **caramelization** /-ˈzeɪʃ(ə)n/ n.

carapace /ˈkærəˌpeɪs/ n. the hard upper shell of a tortoise or a crustacean. [F f. Sp. *carapacho*]

carat /ˈkærət/ n. **1** a unit of weight for precious stones, now equivalent to 200 milligrams. **2** (US **karat**) a measure of purity of gold, pure gold being 24 carats. [F f. It. *carato* f. Arab. *ḳīrāṭ* weight of four grains, f. Gk *keration* fruit of the carob (dimin. of *keras* horn)]

caravan /ˈkærəˌvæn/ n. & v. —n. **1** a Brit. a vehicle equipped for living in and usu. towed by a motor vehicle or a horse. **b** US a covered motor vehicle equipped for living in. **2** a company of merchants or pilgrims etc. travelling together, esp. across a desert in Asia or N. Africa. —v.intr. (**caravanned**, **caravanning**) travel or live in a caravan. □ **caravan site** (or **park**) a place where caravans are parked as dwellings, often with special amenities. □ **caravanner** n. [F *caravane* f. Pers. *kārwān*]

caravanette /ˌkærəvæˈnet/ n. a motor vehicle with a caravan-like rear compartment for eating, sleeping, etc.

caravanserai /ˌkærəˈvænsərɪ, -ˌraɪ/ n. an Eastern inn with a central court where caravans (see CARAVAN 2) may rest. [Pers. *kārwānsarāy* f. *sarāy* palace]

caravel /ˈkærəˌvel/ n. (also **carvel** /ˈkɑːv(ə)l/) hist. a small light fast ship, chiefly Spanish and Portuguese of the 15th–17th c. [F *caravelle* f. Port. *caravela* f. Gk *karabos* horned beetle, light ship]

caraway /ˈkærəˌweɪ/ n. an umbelliferous plant, *Carum carvi*, bearing clusters of tiny white flowers. □ **caraway seed** its fruit used as flavouring and as a source of oil. [prob. OSp. *alcarahueya* f. Arab. *alkarāwiyā*, perh. f. Gk *karon*, *kareon* cumin]

carb n. colloq. a carburettor. [abbr.]

carbide /ˈkɑːbaɪd/ n. Chem. **1** a binary compound of carbon. **2** = *calcium carbide*.

carbine /ˈkɑːbaɪn/ n. a short firearm, usu. a rifle, orig. for cavalry use. [F *carabine* (this form also earlier in Engl.), weapon of the *carabin* mounted musketeer]

carbo- /ˈkɑːbəʊ/ comb. form carbon (*carbohydrate*; *carbolic*; *carboxyl*).

carbohydrate /ˌkɑːbəˈhaɪdreɪt/ n. Biochem. any of a large group of energy-producing organic compounds containing carbon, hydrogen, and oxygen, e.g. starch, glucose, and other sugars.

carbolic /kɑːˈbɒlɪk/ n. (in full **carbolic acid**) phenol, esp. when used as a disinfectant. □ **carbolic soap** soap containing this. [CARBO- + -OL¹ + -IC]

carbon /ˈkɑːbən/ n. **1** a non-metallic element occurring naturally as diamond, graphite, and charcoal, and in all organic compounds. **2 a** = *carbon copy*. **b** = *carbon paper*. **3** a rod of carbon in an arc lamp. □ **carbon copy 1** a copy made with carbon paper. **2** a person or thing identical or similar to another (*is a carbon copy of his father*). **carbon cycle** Biol. the cycle in which carbon compounds are inter-converted, usu. by

living organisms. **carbon dating** the determination of the age of an organic object from the ratio of isotopes which changes as carbon-14 decays. **carbon dioxide** a colourless odourless gas occurring naturally in the atmosphere and formed by respiration. **carbon-14** a long-lived radioactive carbon isotope of mass 14, used in radiocarbon dating, and as a tracer in biochemistry. **carbon monoxide** a colourless odourless toxic gas formed by the incomplete burning of carbon. **carbon paper** a thin carbon-coated paper used for making (esp. typed) copies. **carbon steel** a steel with properties dependent on the percentage of carbon present. **carbon tax** a tax on the carbon emissions that result from burning fossil fuels (e.g. in motor vehicles) because of their contribution to the greenhouse effect. [F *carbone* f. L *carbo -onis* charcoal]

carbonaceous /ˌkɑːbəˈneɪʃəs/ adj. **1** consisting of or containing carbon. **2** of or like coal or charcoal.

carbonade /ˌkɑːbəˈneɪd/ n. a rich beef stew made with onions and beer. [F]

carbonate /ˈkɑːbəˌneɪt/ n. & v. —n. Chem. a salt of carbonic acid. —v.tr. **1** impregnate with carbon dioxide; aerate. **2** convert into a carbonate. □ **carbonation** /-ˈneɪʃ(ə)n/ n. [F *carbonat* f. mod.L *carbonatum* (as CARBON)]

carbonic /kɑːˈbɒnɪk/ adj. Chem. containing carbon. □ **carbonic acid** a very weak acid formed from carbon dioxide dissolved in water.

carboniferous /ˌkɑːbəˈnɪfərəs/ adj. & n. —adj. **1** producing coal. **2** (**Carboniferous**) Geol. of or relating to the fifth period in the Palaeozoic era. —n. (**Carboniferous**) Geol. this period or system.

carbonize /ˈkɑːbəˌnaɪz/ v.tr. (also **-ise**) **1** convert into carbon by heating. **2** reduce to charcoal or coke. **3** coat with carbon. □ **carbonization** /-ˈzeɪʃ(ə)n/ n.

carborundum /ˌkɑːbəˈrʌndəm/ n. a compound of carbon and silicon used esp. as an abrasive. [CARBON + CORUNDUM]

carboy /ˈkɑːbɔɪ/ n. a large globular glass bottle usu. protected by a frame, for containing liquids. [Pers. *ḳarāba* large glass flagon]

carbuncle /ˈkɑːbʌŋk(ə)l/ n. **1** a severe abscess in the skin. **2** a bright red gem. □ **carbuncular** /-ˈbʌŋkjʊlə(r)/ adj. [ME f. OF *charbucle* etc. f. L *carbunculus* small coal f. *carbo* coal]

carburation /ˌkɑːbjʊˈreɪʃ(ə)n/ n. the process of charging air with a spray of liquid hydrocarbon fuel, esp. in an internal-combustion engine. [as CARBURET]

carburet /ˌkɑːbjʊˈret/ v.tr. (**carburetted**, **carburetting**; US **carbureted**, **carbureting**) combine (a gas etc.) with carbon. [earlier *carbure* f. f. L *carbo* (as CARBON)]

carburettor /ˌkɑːbjʊˈretə(r), ˌkɑːbə-/ n. (also **carburetter**, US **carburetor**) an apparatus for carburation of petrol and air in an internal-combustion engine. [as CARBURET + -OR¹]

carcass /ˈkɑːkəs/ n. (also **carcase**) **1** a dead body of an animal, esp. a trunk for cutting up as meat. **2** the bones of a cooked bird. **3** derog. the human body, living or dead. **4** the skeleton, framework of a building, ship, etc. **5** worthless remains. [ME f. AF *carcois* (OF *charcois*) & f. F *carcasse*: ult. orig. unkn.]

carcinogen /kɑːˈsɪnədʒ(ə)n/ *n.* any substance that produces cancer. [as CARCINOMA + -GEN]

carcinogenic /ˌkɑːsɪnəˈdʒɛnɪk/ *adj.* producing cancer. □ **carcinogenicity** /-ˈnɪsɪtɪ/ *n.*

carcinoma /ˌkɑːsɪˈnəʊmə/ *n.* (*pl.* **carcinomata** /-tə/ or **carcinomas**) a cancer, esp. one arising in epithelial tissue. □ **carcinomatous** *adj.* [L f. Gk *karkinōma* f. *karkinos* crab]

card[1] *n.* & *v.* —*n.* **1** thick stiff paper or thin pasteboard. **2 a** a flat piece of this, esp. for writing or printing on. **b** = POSTCARD. **c** a card used to send greetings, issue an invitation, etc. (*birthday card*). **d** = *visiting-card*. **e** = *business card*. **f** a ticket of admission or membership. **3 a** = PLAYING-CARD. **b** a similar card in a set designed for particular games, e.g. happy families. **c** (in *pl.*) card-playing; a card-game. **4** (in *pl.*) *colloq.* an employee's documents, esp. for tax and national insurance, held by the employer. **5 a** a programme of events at a race-meeting etc. **b** *Cricket* a score-card. **c** a list of holes on a golf course, on which a player's scores are entered. **6** *colloq.* a person, esp. an odd or amusing one (*what a card!*; *a knowing card*). **7** a plan or expedient. **8** a printed or written notice, set of rules, etc., for display. **9** a small rectangular piece of plastic issued by a bank, building society, etc., with personal (often machine-readable) data on it, chiefly to obtain cash or credit (*cheque card*; *credit card*). —*v.tr.* **1** fix to a card. **2** write on a card, esp. for indexing. □ **ask for** (or **get**) **one's cards** ask (or be told) to leave one's employment. **card-carrying** being a registered member of an organization, esp. a political party or trade union. **card-game** a game in which playing-cards are used. **card index** an index in which each item is entered on a separate card. **card-playing** the playing of card-games. **card-sharp** (or **-sharper**) a swindler at card-games. **card-table** a table for card-playing, esp. a folding one. **card up one's sleeve** a plan in reserve. **card vote** *US* a block vote, esp. in trade-union meetings. **on** (*US* **in**) **the cards** possible or likely. **put** (or **lay**) **one's cards on the table** reveal one's resources, intentions, etc. [ME f. OF *carte* f. L *charta* f. Gk *khartēs* papyrus-leaf]

card[2] *n.* & *v.* —*n.* a toothed instrument, wire brush, etc., for raising a nap on cloth or for disentangling fibres before spinning. —*v.tr.* brush, comb, cleanse, or scratch with a card. □ **carder** *n.* [ME f. OF *carde* f. Prov. *carda* f. *cardar* tease, comb, ult. f. L *carere* card]

cardamom /ˈkɑːdəməm/ *n.* (also **cardamum**) **1** an aromatic SE Asian plant, *Elettaria cardamomum*. **2** the seed-capsules of this used as a spice. [L *cardamomum* or F *cardamome* f. Gk *kardamōmon* f. *kardamon* cress + *amōmon* a spice plant]

cardboard /ˈkɑːdbɔːd/ *n.* & *adj.* —*n.* pasteboard or stiff paper, esp. for making cards or boxes. —*adj.* **1** made of cardboard. **2** flimsy, insubstantial. □ **cardboard city** a place where homeless people gather at night using cardboard boxes etc. for shelter.

cardiac /ˈkɑːdɪˌæk/ *adj.* & *n.* —*adj.* of or relating to the heart. —*n.* a person with heart disease. [F *cardiaque* or L *cardiacus* f. Gk *kardiakos* f. *kardia* heart]

cardigan /ˈkɑːdɪgən/ *n.* a knitted jacket fastening down the front, usu. with long sleeves. [named after the 7th Earl of *Cardigan* d. 1868]

cardinal /ˈkɑːdɪn(ə)l/ *n.* & *adj.* —*n.* (as a title **Cardinal**) a leading dignitary of the RC Church, one of the college electing the Pope. —*adj.* **1** chief, fundamental; on which something hinges. **2** of deep scarlet (like a cardinal's cassock). □ **cardinal numbers** those denoting quantity (one, two, three, etc.), as opposed to ordinal numbers (first, second, third, etc.). **cardinal points** the four main points of the compass (N., S., E., W.). **cardinal virtues** the chief moral attributes: justice, prudence, temperance, and fortitude. □ **cardinalate** /-ˌleɪt/ *n.* (in sense 1 of *n.*). **cardinally** *adv.* **cardinalship** *n.* (in sense 1 of *n.*). [ME f. OF f. L *cardinalis* f. *cardo -inis* hinge: in Eng. first applied to the four virtues on which conduct 'hinges']

cardio- /ˈkɑːdɪəʊ/ *comb. form* heart (*cardiogram*; *cardiology*). [Gk *kardia* heart]

cardiogram /ˈkɑːdɪəʊˌgræm/ *n.* a record of muscle activity within the heart, made by a cardiograph.

cardiograph /ˈkɑːdɪəʊˌgrɑːf/ *n.* an instrument for recording heart muscle activity. □ **cardiographer** /-ˈɒgrəfə(r)/ *n.* **cardiography** /-ˈɒgrəfɪ/ *n.*

cardiology /ˌkɑːdɪˈɒlədʒɪ/ *n.* the branch of medicine concerned with diseases and abnormalities of the heart. □ **cardiologist** *n.*

cardiovascular /ˌkɑːdɪəʊˈvæskjʊlə(r)/ *adj.* of or relating to the heart and blood vessels.

cardphone /ˈkɑːdfəʊn/ *n.* a public telephone operated by the insertion of a prepaid plastic machine-readable card instead of money.

care /keə(r)/ *n.* & *v.* —*n.* **1** worry, anxiety. **2** an occasion for this. **3** serious attention; heed, caution, pains (*assembled with care*; *handle with care*). **4 a** protection, charge. **b** *Brit.* = *child care*. **5** a thing to be done or seen to. —*v.intr.* **1** (usu. foll. by *about, for, whether*) feel concern or interest. **2** (usu. foll. by *for, about*, and with neg. expressed or implied) feel liking, affection, regard, or deference (*don't care for jazz*). **3** (foll. by *to* + infin.) wish or be willing (*should not care to be seen with him*; *would you care to try them?*). □ **care for** provide for; look after. **care of** at the address of (*sent it care of his sister*). **for all one cares** *colloq.* denoting uninterest or unconcern (*for all I care they can leave tomorrow*; *I could be dying for all you care*). **have a care** take care; be careful. **I** (etc.) **couldn't** (*US* **could**) **care less** *colloq.* an expression of complete indifference. **in care** *Brit.* (of a child) taken into the care of a local authority. **take care 1** be careful. **2** (foll. by *to* + infin.) not fail or neglect. **take care of 1** look after; keep safe. **2** deal with. **3** dispose of. [OE *caru, carian*, f. Gmc]

careen /kəˈriːn/ *v.* **1** *tr.* turn (a ship) on one side for cleaning, caulking, or repair. **2** *intr.* tilt; lean over. **b** *tr.* cause to do this. **3** *intr.* *US* swerve about. □ **careenage** *n.* [earlier as noun, = careened position of ship, f. F *carène* f. It. *carena* f. L *carina* keel]

■ **Usage** Sense 3 of *careen* is influenced by the verb *career*.

career /kəˈrɪə(r)/ *n.* & *v.* —*n.* **1 a** one's advancement through life, esp. in a profession. **b** the progress through history of a group or institution. **2** a profession or occupation, esp. as offering advancement. **3** (*attrib.*) **a** pursuing or wishing to pursue a career (*career woman*). **b** working permanently in a specified profession (*career diplomat*). **4** swift course; impetus (*in full career*). —*v.intr.* **1** move or swerve about wildly. **2** go swiftly. [F *carrière* f. It. *carriera* ult. f. L *carrus* CAR]

careerist /kə'rɪərɪst/ *n.* a person predominantly concerned with personal advancement.

carefree /'keəfriː/ *adj.* free from anxiety or responsibility; light-hearted. □ **carefreeness** *n.*

careful /'keəfʊl/ *adj.* **1** painstaking, thorough. **2** cautious. **3** done with care and attention. **4** (usu. foll. by *that* + clause, or *to* + infin.) taking care; not neglecting. **5** (foll. by *for, of*) concerned for; taking care of. □ **carefully** *adv.* **carefulness** *n.* [OE *carful* (as CARE, -FUL)]

careless /'keəlɪs/ *adj.* **1** not taking care or paying attention. **2** unthinking, insensitive. **3** done without care; inaccurate. **4** light-hearted. **5** (foll. by *of*) not concerned about; taking no heed of. **6** effortless. □ **carelessly** *adv.* **carelessness** *n.* [OE *carlēas* (as CARE, -LESS)]

carer /'keərə(r)/ *n.* a person who cares for a sick or elderly person.

caress /kə'res/ *v. & n.* —*v.tr.* **1** touch or stroke gently or lovingly; kiss. **2** treat fondly or kindly. —*n.* a loving or gentle touch or kiss. [F *caresse* (n.), *caresser* (v.), f. It. *carezza* ult. f. L *carus* dear]

caret /'kærət/ *n.* a mark (∧, ⁄) indicating a proposed insertion in printing or writing. [L, = is lacking]

caretaker /'keəteɪkə(r)/ *n.* **1** a person employed to look after something, esp. a house in the owner's absence, or *Brit.* a public building. **2** (*attrib.*) exercising temporary authority (*caretaker government*).

careworn /'keəwɔːn/ *adj.* showing the effects of prolonged worry.

cargo /'kɑːgəʊ/ *n.* (*pl.* **-oes** or **-os**) **1** goods carried on a ship or aircraft. **2** *US* goods carried in a motor vehicle. [Sp. (as CHARGE)]

Carib /'kærɪb/ *n. & adj.* —*n.* **1** an aboriginal inhabitant of the southern W. Indies or the adjacent coasts. **2** the language of this people. —*adj.* of or relating to this people. [Sp. *Caribe* f. Haitian]

Caribbean /ˌkærɪ'biːən, kə'rɪbɪən/ *n. & adj.* —*n.* the part of the Atlantic between the southern W. Indies and Central America. —*adj.* **1** of or relating to this region. **2** of the Caribs or their language or culture.

caribou /'kærɪˌbuː/ *n.* (*pl.* same) a N. American reindeer. [Can. F, prob. f. Amer. Ind.]

caricature /'kærɪkətjʊə(r)/ *n. & v.* —*n.* **1** a grotesque usu. comic representation of a person by exaggeration of characteristic traits, in a picture, writing, or mime. **2** a ridiculously poor or absurd imitation or version. —*v.tr.* make or give a caricature of. □ **caricatural** *adj.* **caricaturist** *n.* [F f. It. *caricatura* f. *caricare* load, exaggerate: see CHARGE]

caries /'keəriːz, -rɪˌiːz/ *n.* (*pl.* same) decay and crumbling of a tooth or bone. [L]

carillon /kə'rɪljən, 'kærɪljən/ *n.* **1** a set of bells sounded either from a keyboard or mechanically. **2** a tune played on bells. [F f. OF *quarregnon* peal of four bells, alt. of Rmc *quaternio* f. L *quattuor* four]

caring /'keərɪŋ/ *adj.* compassionate, esp. with reference to the professional care of the sick or elderly.

carioca /ˌkærɪ'əʊkə/ *n.* **1 a** a Brazilian dance like the samba. **b** the music for this. **2** a native of Rio de Janeiro. [Port.]

cariogenic /ˌkeərɪəʊ'dʒenɪk/ *adj.* causing caries.

carious /'keərɪəs/ *adj.* (of bones or teeth) decayed. [L *cariosus*]

carload /'kɑːləʊd/ *n.* a quantity that can be carried in a car.

Carlovingian var. of CAROLINGIAN.

Carmelite /'kɑːmɪˌlaɪt/ *n. & adj.* —*n.* **1** a friar of the Order of Our Lady of Mount Carmel, following a rule of extreme asceticism. **2** a nun of a similar order. —*adj.* of or relating to the Carmelites. [F *Carmelite* or med.L *carmelita* f. Mt. *Carmel* in Palestine, where the order was founded in the 12th c.]

carminative /'kɑːmɪnətɪv/ *adj. & n.* —*adj.* relieving flatulence. —*n.* a carminative drug. [F *carminatif* -ive or med.L *carminare* heal (by incantation): see CHARM]

carmine /'kɑːmaɪn/ *adj. & n.* —*adj.* of a vivid crimson colour. —*n.* **1** this colour. **2** a vivid crimson pigment made from cochineal. [F *carmin* or med.L *carminium* perh. f. *carmesinum* crimson + *minium* cinnabar]

carnage /'kɑːnɪdʒ/ *n.* great slaughter, esp. of human beings in battle. [F f. It. *carnaggio* f. med.L *carnaticum* f. L *caro carnis* flesh]

carnal /'kɑːn(ə)l/ *adj.* **1** of the body or flesh; worldly. **2** sensual, sexual. □ **carnal knowledge** *Law* sexual intercourse. □ **carnality** /-'nælɪtɪ/ *n.* **carnalize** *v.tr.* (also **-ise**). **carnally** *adv.* [ME f. LL *carnalis* f. *caro carnis* flesh]

carnation[1] /kɑː'neɪʃ(ə)n/ *n.* **1** any of several cultivated varieties of clove-scented pink, with variously coloured showy flowers (see also CLOVE[1] 2). **2** this flower. [orig. uncert.: in early use varying with *coronation*]

carnation[2] /kɑː'neɪʃ(ə)n/ *n. & adj.* —*n.* a rosy pink colour. —*adj.* of this colour. [F f. It. *carnagione* ult. f. L *caro carnis* flesh]

carnelian var. of CORNELIAN.

carnet /'kɑːneɪ/ *n.* **1** a customs permit to take a motor vehicle across a frontier for a limited period. **2** a permit allowing use of a camp-site. [F, = notebook]

carnival /'kɑːnɪv(ə)l/ *n.* **1 a** the festivities usual during the period before Lent in Roman Catholic countries. **b** any festivities, esp. those occurring at a regular date. **2** merrymaking, revelry. **3** *US* a travelling funfair or circus. [It. *carne-, carnovale* f. med.L *carnelevarium* etc. Shrovetide f. L *caro carnis* flesh + *levare* put away]

carnivore /'kɑːnɪvɔː(r)/ *n.* **1 a** any mammal of the order Carnivora, with jaws and teeth adapted for eating flesh, including cats, dogs, and bears. **b** any other flesh-eating mammal. **2** any flesh-eating plant.

carnivorous /kɑː'nɪvərəs/ *adj.* **1** (of an animal) feeding on flesh. **2** (of a plant) digesting trapped insects or other animal substances. **3** of or relating to the order Carnivora. □ **carnivorously** *adv.* **carnivorousness** *n.* [L *carnivorus* f. *caro carnis* flesh + -VOROUS]

carob /'kærəb/ *n.* **1** (in full **carob-tree**) an evergreen tree, *Ceratonia siliqua*, native to the Mediterranean, bearing edible pods. **2** its bean-shaped edible seed pod sometimes used as a substitute for chocolate. [obs. F *carobe* f. med.L *carruba*, *-um* f. Arab. *ḳarrūba*]

carol /ˈkær(ə)l/ *n*. & *v*. —*n*. a joyous song, esp. a Christmas hymn. —*v*. (**carolled, carolling**; *US* **caroled, caroling**) **1** *intr*. sing carols, esp. outdoors at Christmas. **2** *tr*. & *intr*. sing joyfully. □ **caroler** *n*. (also **caroller**). [ME f. OF *carole*, *caroler*, of unkn. orig.]

Caroline /ˈkærəˌlaɪn/ *adj*. **1** (also **Carolean** /-ˈliːən/) of the time of Charles I or II of England. **2** = CAROLINGIAN *adj*. [L *Carolus* Charles]

Carolingian /ˌkærəˈlɪndʒɪən/ *adj*. & *n*. (also **Carlovingian** /ˌkɑːləˈvɪndʒɪən/) —*adj*. of or relating to the second Frankish dynasty, founded by Charlemagne (d. 814). —*n*. a member of the Carolingian dynasty. [F *carlovingien* f. *Karl* Charles after *mérovingien*, reformed after L *Carolus*]

carotene /ˈkærəˌtiːn/ *n*. any of several orange-coloured plant pigments found in carrots, tomatoes, etc., acting as a source of vitamin A. [G *Carotin* f. L *carota* CARROT]

carotid /kəˈrɒtɪd/ *n*. & *adj*. —*n*. each of the two main arteries carrying blood to the head and neck. —*adj*. of or relating to either of these arteries. [F *carotide* or mod.L *carotides* f. Gk *karōtides* (pl.) f. *karoō* stupefy (compression of these arteries being thought to cause stupor)]

carouse /kəˈraʊz/ *v*. & *n*. —*v.intr*. **1** have a noisy or lively drinking-party. **2** drink heavily. —*n*. a noisy or lively drinking-party. □ **carousal** *n*. **carouser** *n*. [orig. as adv. = right out, in phr. *drink carouse* f. G *gar aus trinken*]

carousel /ˌkærəˈsel, -ˈzel/ *n*. (*US* **carrousel**) **1** *US* a merry-go-round or roundabout. **2** a rotating delivery or conveyor system, esp. for passengers' luggage at an airport. [F *carrousel* f. It. *carosello*]

carp[1] *n*. (pl. same) any freshwater fish of the family Cyprinidae, esp. *Cyprinus carpio*. [ME f. OF *carpe* f. Prov. or f. LL *carpa*]

carp[2] *v.intr*. (usu. foll. by *at*) find fault; complain pettily. □ **carper** *n*. [obs. ME senses 'talk, say, sing' f. ON *karpa* to brag: mod. sense (16th c.) from or infl. by L *carpere* pluck at, slander]

carpal /ˈkɑːp(ə)l/ *adj*. & *n*. —*adj*. of or relating to the bones in the wrist. —*n*. any of the bones forming the wrist. [CARPUS + -AL]

carpel /ˈkɑːp(ə)l/ *n*. *Bot*. the female reproductive organ of a flower, consisting of a stigma, style, and ovary. □ **carpellary** *adj*. [F *carpelle* or mod.L *carpellum* f. Gk *karpos* fruit]

carpenter /ˈkɑːpɪntə(r)/ *n*. & *v*. —*n*. a person skilled in woodwork, esp. of a structural kind (cf. JOINER). —*v*. **1** *intr*. do carpentry. **2** *tr*. make by means of carpentry. **3** *tr*. (often foll. by *together*) construct; fit together. [ME & AF; OF *carpentier* f. LL *carpentarius* f. *carpentum* wagon f. Gaulish]

carpentry /ˈkɑːpɪntrɪ/ *n*. **1** the work or occupation of a carpenter. **2** timber-work constructed by a carpenter. [ME f. OF *carpenterie* f. L *carpentaria*: see CARPENTER]

carpet /ˈkɑːpɪt/ *n*. & *v*. —*n*. **1 a** a thick fabric for covering a floor or stairs. **b** a piece of this fabric. **2** an expanse or layer resembling a carpet in being smooth, soft, bright, or thick (*carpet of snow*). —*v.tr*. (**carpeted, carpeting**) **1** cover with or as with a carpet. **2** *colloq*. reprimand, reprove. □ **carpet-bag** a travelling-bag of a kind orig. made of carpet-like material. **carpet-bagger 1** esp. *US* a political candidate in an area where the candidate has no local connections (orig. a northerner in the southern US after the Civil War). **2** an unscrupulous opportunist. **carpet bombing** intensive bombing. **carpet slipper** a kind of slipper with the upper made orig. of carpet-like material. **carpet-sweeper** a household implement with a revolving brush or brushes for sweeping carpets. **on the carpet 1** *colloq*. being reprimanded. **2** under consideration. **sweep under the carpet** conceal (a problem or difficulty) in the hope that it will be forgotten. [ME f. OF *carpite* or med.L *carpita*, f. obs. It. *carpita* woollen counterpane, ult. f. L *carpere* pluck, pull to pieces]

carpeting /ˈkɑːpɪtɪŋ/ *n*. **1** material for carpets. **2** carpets collectively.

carport /ˈkɑːpɔːt/ *n*. a shelter with a roof and open sides for a car, usu. beside a house.

carpus /ˈkɑːpəs/ *n*. (*pl*. **carpi** /-paɪ/) the small bones between the forelimb and metacarpus in terrestrial vertebrates, forming the wrist in humans. [mod.L f. Gk *karpos* wrist]

carrageen /ˈkærəˌgiːn/ *n*. (also **carragheen**) an edible red seaweed, *Chondrus crispus*, of the N. hemisphere. [orig. uncert.: perh. f. Ir. *cosáinín carraige* carrageen, lit. 'little stem of the rock']

carrel /ˈkær(ə)l/ *n*. **1** a small cubicle for a reader in a library. **2** *hist*. a small enclosure or study in a cloister. [OF *carole*, med.L *carola*, of unkn. orig.]

carriage /ˈkærɪdʒ/ *n*. **1** *Brit*. a railway passenger vehicle. **2** a wheeled passenger vehicle, esp. one with four wheels and pulled by horses. **3 a** the conveying of goods. **b** the cost of this (*carriage paid*). **4** the part of a machine (e.g. a typewriter) that carries other parts into the required position. **5** a gun-carriage. **6** a manner of carrying oneself; one's bearing or deportment. [ME f. ONF *cariage* f. *carier* CARRY]

carriageway /ˈkærɪdʒˌweɪ/ *n*. *Brit*. the part of a road intended for vehicles.

carrier /ˈkærɪə(r)/ *n*. **1** a person or thing that carries. **2** a person or company undertaking to convey goods or passengers for payment. **3** = *carrier bag*. **4** a part of a bicycle etc. for carrying luggage or a passenger. **5** a person or animal that may transmit a disease or a hereditary characteristic without suffering from or displaying it. **6** = *aircraft-carrier*. □ **carrier bag** *Brit*. a disposable plastic or paper bag with handles. **carrier pigeon** a pigeon trained to carry messages tied to its neck or leg. **carrier wave** a high-frequency electromagnetic wave modulated in amplitude or frequency to convey a signal.

carrion /ˈkærɪən/ *n*. **1** dead putrefying flesh. **2** something vile or filthy. □ **carrion crow** a black crow, *Corvus corone*, native to Europe, feeding mainly on carrion. [ME f. AF & ONF *caroine*, *-oigne*, OF *charoigne* ult. f. L *caro* flesh]

carrot /ˈkærət/ *n*. **1 a** an umbelliferous plant, *Daucus carota*, with a tapering orange-coloured root. **b** this root as a vegetable. **2** a means of enticement or persuasion. **3** (in *pl*.) *sl*. a red-haired person. □ **carroty** *adj*. [F *carotte* f. L *carota* f. Gk *karōton*]

carry /ˈkærɪ/ *v*. & *n*. —*v*. (**-ies, -ied**) **1** *tr*. support or hold up, esp. while moving. **2** *tr*. convey with one from one place to another. **3** *tr*. have on one's person (*carry a watch*). **4** *tr*. conduct or transmit (*pipe carries water; wire carries electric* current). **5** *tr.* take (a process etc.) to a specified point (*carry into effect*; *carry a joke too far*). **6** *tr.* (foll. by *to*) continue or prolong (*carry modesty to excess*). **7** *tr.* involve, imply; have as a feature or consequence (*carries a two-year guarantee*). **8** *tr.* (in reckoning) transfer (a figure) to a column of higher value. **9** *tr.* hold in a specified way (*carry oneself erect*). **10** *tr.* **a** (of a newspaper or magazine) publish; include in its contents, esp. regularly. **b** (of a radio or television station) broadcast, esp. regularly. **11** *tr.* (of a retailing outlet) keep a regular stock of (particular goods for sale). **12** *intr.* **a** (of sound, esp. a voice) be audible at a distance. **b** (of a missile) travel, penetrate. **13** *tr.* (of a gun etc.) propel to a specified distance. **14** *tr.* **a** win victory or acceptance for (a proposal etc.). **b** win acceptance from (*carried the audience with them*). **c** win, capture (a prize, a fortress, etc.). **d** *US* gain (a State or district) in an election. **15** *tr.* **a** endure the weight of; support (*columns carry the dome*). **b** be the chief cause of the effectiveness of; be the driving force in (*you carry the sales department*). **16** *tr.* be pregnant with (*is carrying twins*). **17** *tr.* **a** (of a motive, money, etc.) cause or enable (a person) to go to a specified place. **b** (of a journey) bring (a person) to a specified point. —*n.* (*pl.* **-ies**) **1** an act of carrying. **2** *Golf* the distance a ball travels before reaching the ground. **3** a portage between rivers etc. **4** the range of a gun etc. □ **carry-all 1** *US* a car with seats placed sideways. **2** *US* a large bag or case. **carry away 1** remove. **2** inspire; affect emotionally or spiritually. **3** deprive of self-control (*got carried away*). **carry the can** *colloq.* bear the responsibility or blame. **carry conviction** be convincing. **carry-cot** a portable cot for a baby. **carry forward** transfer to a new page or account. **carry it off** (or **carry it off well**) do well under difficulties. **carry off 1** take away, esp. by force. **2** win (a prize). **3** (esp. of a disease) kill. **4** render acceptable or passable. **carry on 1** continue (*carry on eating*; *carry on, don't mind me*). **2** engage in (a conversation or a business). **3** *colloq.* behave strangely or excitedly. **4** (often foll. by *with*) *colloq.* flirt or have a love affair. **carry out** put (ideas, instructions, etc.) into practice. **carry-out** *attrib.adj.* & *n.* esp. *Sc.* & *US* = *take-away*. **carry over 1** = *carry forward*. **2** postpone (work etc.). **3** *Stock Exch.* keep over to the next settling-day. **carry through 1** complete successfully. **2** bring safely out of difficulties. **carry weight** be influential or important. [ME f. AF & ONF *carier* (as CAR)]

carsick /ˈkɑːsɪk/ *adj.* affected with nausea caused by the motion of a car. □ **carsickness** *n.*

cart *n.* & *v.* —*n.* **1** a strong vehicle with two or four wheels for carrying loads, usu. drawn by a horse. **2** a light vehicle for pulling by hand. —*v.tr.* **1** convey in or as in a cart. **2** *sl.* carry (esp. a cumbersome thing) with difficulty or over a long distance. □ **cart-horse** a thickset horse suitable for heavy work. **cart-load 1** an amount filling a cart. **2** a large quantity of anything. **cart off** remove, esp. by force. **cart-track** (or **-road**) a track or road too rough for ordinary vehicles. **in the cart** *sl.* in trouble or difficulty. □ **carter** *n.* **cartful** *n.* (*pl.* **-fuls**). [ME f. ON *kartr* cart & OE *cræt*, prob. infl. by AF & ONF *carete* dimin. of *carre* CAR]

carte blanche /kɑːt ˈblɑ̃ʃ/ *n.* full discretionary power given to a person. [F, = blank paper]

cartel /kɑːˈtel/ *n.* **1** an informal association of manufacturers or suppliers to maintain prices at a high level. **2** a political combination between parties. □ **cartelize** /ˈkɑːtəˌlaɪz/ *v.tr.* & *intr.* (also **-ise**). [G *Kartell* f. F *cartel* f. It. *cartello* dimin. of *carta* CARD¹]

Cartesian /kɑːˈtiːzjən, -ʒ(ə)n/ *adj.* & *n.* —*adj.* of or relating to R. Descartes, 17th-c. French philosopher and mathematician. —*n.* a follower of Descartes. □ **Cartesian coordinates** a system for locating a point by reference to its distance from two or three axes intersecting at right angles. □ **Cartesianism** *n.* [mod.L *Cartesianus* f. *Cartesius*, name of *Descartes*]

Carthusian /kɑːˈθjuːzjən/ *n.* & *adj.* —*n.* a monk of a contemplative order founded by St Bruno in 1084. —*adj.* of or relating to this order. [med.L *Carthusianus* f. L *Cart(h)usia* Chartreuse, near Grenoble]

cartilage /ˈkɑːtɪlɪdʒ/ *n.* gristle, a firm flexible connective tissue forming the infant skeleton, which is mainly replaced by bone in adulthood. □ **cartilaginoid** /-ˈlædʒɪˌnɔɪd/ *adj.* **cartilaginous** /-ˈlædʒɪnəs/ *adj.* [F f. L *cartilago* *-ginis*]

cartography /kɑːˈtɒɡrəfɪ/ *n.* the science or practice of map-drawing. □ **cartographer** *n.* **cartographic** /-təˈɡræfɪk/ *adj.* **cartographical** /-təˈɡræfɪk(ə)l/ *adj.* [F *cartographie* f. *carte* map, card]

carton /ˈkɑːt(ə)n/ *n.* a light box or container, esp. one made of cardboard. [F (as CARTOON)]

cartoon /kɑːˈtuːn/ *n.* & *v.* —*n.* **1** a humorous drawing in a newspaper, magazine, etc., esp. as a topical comment. **2** a sequence of drawings, often with speech indicated, telling a story (*strip cartoon*). **3** a filmed sequence of drawings using the technique of animation. **4** a full-size drawing on stout paper as an artist's preliminary design for a painting, tapestry, mosaic, etc. —*v.* **1** *tr.* draw a cartoon of. **2** *intr.* draw cartoons. □ **cartoonist** *n.* [It. *cartone* f. *carta* CARD¹]

cartouche /kɑːˈtuːʃ/ *n.* **1** *Archit.* a scroll-like ornament. **2** *Archaeol.* an oval ring enclosing Egyptian hieroglyphs. [F, = cartridge, f. It. *cartoccio* f. *carta* CARD¹]

cartridge /ˈkɑːtrɪdʒ/ *n.* **1** a case containing a charge of propelling explosive for firearms or blasting, with a bullet or shot if for small arms. **2** a spool of film, magnetic tape, etc., in a sealed container ready for insertion. **3** a component carrying the stylus on the pick-up head of a record-player. **4** an ink-container for insertion in a pen. □ **cartridge-belt** a belt with pockets or loops for cartridges (in sense 1). **cartridge paper** thick rough paper used for cartridges, for drawing, and for strong envelopes. [corrupt. of CARTOUCHE (but recorded earlier)]

cartwheel /ˈkɑːtwiːl/ *n.* **1** the (usu. spoked) wheel of a cart. **2** a circular sideways handspring with the arms and legs extended.

carve *v.* **1** *tr.* produce or shape (a statue, representation in relief, etc.) by cutting into a hard material (*carved a figure out of rock*; *carved it in wood*). **2** *tr.* **a** cut patterns, letters, etc. in (hard material). **b** (foll. by *into*) form a pattern, design, etc., from (*carved it into a bust*). **c** (foll. by *with*) cover or decorate (material) with designs cut in it. **3** *tr.* (*absol.*) cut (meat etc.) into slices for eating. □ **carve out 1** take from a larger whole.

2 establish (a career etc.) purposefully (*carved out a name for themselves*). **carving knife** a knife with a long blade, for carving meat. [OE *ceorfan* cut f. WG]

carvel /ˈkɑːv(ə)l/ *n.* var. of CARAVEL. □ **carvel-built** (of a boat) made with planks flush, not overlapping. [as CARAVEL]

carver /ˈkɑːvə(r)/ *n.* **1** a person who carves. **2 a** a carving knife. **b** (in *pl.*) a knife and fork for carving. **3** *Brit.* the principal chair, with arms, in a set of dining-chairs, intended for the person who carves.

carvery /ˈkɑːvərɪ/ *n.* (*pl.* **-ies**) a buffet or restaurant with joints displayed, and carved as required, in front of customers.

carving /ˈkɑːvɪŋ/ *n.* a carved object, esp. as a work of art.

Casanova /ˌkæsəˈnəʊvə/ *n.* a man notorious for seducing women. [G. J. *Casanova* de Seingalt, It. adventurer d. 1798]

casbah var. of KASBAH.

cascade /kæsˈkeɪd/ *n.* & *v.* —*n.* **1** a small waterfall, forming one in a series or part of a large broken waterfall. **2** a succession of electrical devices or stages in a process. **3** a quantity of material etc. draped in descending folds. —*v.intr.* fall in or like a cascade. [F f. It. *cascata* f. *cascare* to fall ult. f. L *casus*: see CASE¹]

cascara /kæsˈkɑːrə/ *n.* (in full **cascara sagrada** /səgˈrɑːdə/) the bark of a Californian buckthorn, *Rhamnus purshiana*, used as a purgative. [Sp., = sacred bark]

case¹ /keɪs/ *n.* **1** an instance of something occurring. **2** a state of affairs, hypothetical or actual. **3 a** an instance of a person receiving professional guidance, e.g. from a doctor or social worker. **b** this person or the circumstances involved. **4** a matter under official investigation, esp. by the police. **5** *Law* a cause or suit for trial. **6 a** the sum of the arguments on one side, esp. in a lawsuit (*that is our case*). **b** a set of arguments, esp. in relation to persuasiveness (*have a good case*; *have a weak case*). **c** a valid set of arguments (*have no case*). **7** *Gram.* **a** the relation of a word to other words in a sentence. **b** a form of a noun, adjective, or pronoun expressing this. **8** the position or circumstances in which one is. □ **case history** information about a person for use in professional treatment, e.g. by a doctor. **case-law** the law as established by the outcome of former cases (cf. *common law, statute law*). **case-load** the cases with which a doctor etc. is concerned at one time. **case-study 1** an attempt to understand a person, institution, etc., from collected information. **2** a record of such an attempt. **3** the use of a particular instance as an exemplar of general principles. **in any case** whatever the truth is; whatever may happen. **in case 1** in the event that; if. **2** lest; in provision against a stated or implied possibility (*take an umbrella in case it rains*; *took it in case*). **in case of** in the event of. **is** (or **is not**) **the case** is (or is not) so. [ME f. OF *cas* f. L *casus* fall f. *cadere cas-* to fall]

case² /keɪs/ *n.* & *v.* —*n.* **1** a container or covering serving to enclose or contain. **2** a container with its contents. **3** the outer protective covering of a watch, book, seed-vessel, sausage, etc. **4** an item of luggage, esp. a suitcase. **5** a glass box for showing specimens, curiosities, etc. —*v.tr.* **1**

enclose in a case. **2** (foll. by *with*) surround. **3** *sl.* reconnoitre (a house etc.) esp. with a view to robbery. □ **case-bound** (of a book) in a hard cover. **case-harden 1** harden the surface of, esp. give a steel surface to (iron) by carbonizing. **2** make callous. **lower case** small letters. **upper case** capitals. [ME f. OF *casse, chasse*, f. L *capsa* f. *capere* hold]

casebook /ˈkeɪsbʊk/ *n.* a book containing a record of legal or medical cases.

casein /ˈkeɪsiːn, ˈkeɪsɪn/ *n.* the main protein in milk, esp. in coagulated form as in cheese. [L *caseus* cheese]

casement /ˈkeɪsmənt/ *n.* **1** a window or part of a window hinged vertically to open like a door. **2** *poet.* a window. [ME f. AL *cassimentum* f. *cassa* CASE²]

casework /ˈkeɪswɜːk/ *n.* social work concerned with individuals, esp. involving examination of the client's family and background. □ **caseworker** *n.*

cash *n.* & *v.* —*n.* **1** money in coins or notes, as distinct from cheques or orders. **2** (also **cash down**) money paid as full payment at the time of purchase, as distinct from credit. **3** *colloq.* wealth. —*v.tr.* give or obtain cash for (a note, cheque, etc.). □ **cash and carry 1** a system of wholesaling in which goods are paid for in cash and taken away by the purchaser. **2** a store where this system operates. **cash crop** a crop produced for sale, not for use as food etc. **cash dispenser** an automatic machine from which customers of a bank etc. may withdraw cash, esp. by using a cashcard. **cash flow** the movement of money into and out of a business, as a measure of profitability, or as affecting liquidity. **cash in 1** obtain cash for. **2** *colloq.* (usu. foll. by *on*) profit (from); take advantage (of). **3** pay into a bank etc. **4** (in full **cash in one's checks**) *colloq.* die. **cash on delivery** a system of paying the carrier for goods when they are delivered. **cash register** a machine in a shop etc. with a drawer for money, recording the amount of each sale, totalling receipts, etc. **cash up** *Brit.* count and check cash takings at the end of a day's trading. □ **cashable** *adj.* **cashless** *adj.* [obs. F *casse* box or It. *cassa* f. L *capsa* CASE²]

cashcard /ˈkæʃkɑːd/ *n.* a plastic card (see CARD¹ *n.* 9) which enables the holder to draw money from a cash dispenser.

cashew /ˈkæʃuː, kæˈʃuː/ *n.* **1** a bushy evergreen tree, *Anacardium occidentale*, native to Central and S. America, bearing kidney-shaped nuts attached to fleshy fruits. **2** (in full **cashew nut**) the edible nut of this tree. [Port. f. Tupi *(a)caju*]

cashier¹ /kæˈʃɪə(r)/ *n.* a person dealing with cash transactions in a shop, bank, etc. [Du. *cassier* or F *caissier* (as CASH)]

cashier² /kæˈʃɪə(r)/ *v.tr.* dismiss from service, esp. from the armed forces with disgrace. [Flem. *kasseren* disband, revoke, f. F *casser* f. L *quassare* QUASH]

cashmere /ˈkæʃmɪə(r)/ *n.* **1** a fine soft wool, esp. that of a Kashmir goat. **2** a material made from this. [*Kashmir* in Asia]

cashpoint /ˈkæʃpɔɪnt/ *n.* = *cash dispenser*.

casing /ˈkeɪsɪŋ/ *n.* **1** a protective or enclosing cover or shell. **2** the material for this.

casino /kəˈsiːnəʊ/ *n.* (*pl.* **-os**) a public room or building for gambling. [It., dimin. of *casa* house f. L *casa* cottage]

cask /kɑːsk/ n. **1** a large barrel-like container made of wood, metal, or plastic, esp. one for alcoholic liquor. **2** its contents. **3** its capacity. [F *casque* or Sp. *casco* helmet]

casket /ˈkɑːskɪt/ n. **1** a small often ornamental box or chest for jewels, letters, etc. **2 a** a small wooden box for cremated ashes. **b** US a coffin, esp. a rectangular one. [perh. f. AF form of OF *cassette* f. It. *cassetta* dimin. of *cassa* f. L *capsa* CASE²]

Cassandra /kəˈsændrə/ n. a prophet of disaster, esp. one who is disregarded. [L f. Gk *Kassandra*, daughter of Priam King of Troy: she was condemned by Apollo to prophesy correctly but not be believed]

cassava /kəˈsɑːvə/ n. **1 a** any plant of the genus *Manihot*, esp. the cultivated varieties *M. esculenta* (**bitter cassava**) and *M. dulcis* (**sweet cassava**), having starchy tuberous roots. **b** the roots themselves. **2** a starch or flour obtained from these roots. [earlier *cas(s)avi* etc., f. Taino *casavi*, infl. by F *cassave*]

casserole /ˈkæsərəʊl/ n. & v. —n. **1** a covered dish, usu. of earthenware or glass, in which food is cooked, esp. slowly in the oven. **2** food cooked in a casserole. —v.tr. cook in a casserole. [F f. *cassole* dimin. of *casse* f. Prov. *casa* f. LL *cattia* ladle, pan f. Gk *kuathion* dimin. of *kuathos* cup]

cassette /kæˈset, kə-/ n. a sealed case containing a length of tape, ribbon, etc., ready for insertion in a machine, esp.: **1** a length of magnetic tape wound on to spools, ready for insertion in a tape recorder. **2** a length of photographic film, ready for insertion in a camera. [F, dimin. of *casse* CASE²]

cassia /ˈkæsɪə, ˈkæʃə/ n. **1** any tree of the genus *Cassia*, bearing leaves from which senna is extracted. **2** the cinnamon-like bark of this tree used as a spice. [L f. Gk *kasia* f. Heb. ḵᵉṣîʿāh bark like cinnamon]

cassis /kæˈsiːs/ n. a syrupy usu. alcoholic blackcurrant flavouring for drinks etc. [F, = blackcurrant]

cassock /ˈkæsək/ n. a long close-fitting usu. black or red garment worn by clergy, members of choirs, etc. □ **cassocked** adj. [F *casaque* long coat f. It. *casacca* horseman's coat, prob. f. Turkic: cf. COSSACK]

cassowary /ˈkæsəˌweərɪ/ n. (pl. **-ies**) any large flightless Australasian bird of the genus *Casuarius*, with heavy body, stout legs, a wattled neck, and a bony crest on its forehead. [Malay *kasuārī, kasavārī*]

cast /kɑːst/ v. & n. —v. (past and past part. **cast**) **1** tr. throw, esp. deliberately or forcefully. **2** tr. (often foll. by *on, over*) **a** direct or cause to fall (one's eyes, a glance, light, a shadow, a spell, etc.). **b** express (doubts, aspersions, etc.). **3** tr. throw out (a fishing-line) into the water. **4** tr. let down (an anchor or sounding-lead). **5** tr. **a** throw off, get rid of. **b** shed (skin etc.) esp. in the process of growth. **c** (of a horse) lose (a shoe). **6** tr. record, register, or give (a vote). **7** tr. **a** shape (molten metal or plastic material) in a mould. **b** make (a product) in this way. **8** tr. *Printing* make (type). **9** tr. **a** (usu. foll. by *as*) assign (an actor) to play a particular character. **b** allocate roles in (a play, film, etc.). **10** tr. (foll. by *in, into*) arrange or formulate (facts etc.) in a specified form. **11** tr. & intr. reckon, add up, calculate (accounts or figures). **12** tr. calculate and record details of (a horoscope). —n. **1 a** the throwing of a missile etc. **b** the distance reached by this. **2** a throw or a number thrown at dice. **3** a throw of a net, sounding-lead, or fishing-line. **4** *Fishing* **a** that which is cast, esp. the gut with hook and fly. **b** a place for casting (*a good cast*). **5 a** an object of metal, clay, etc., made in a mould. **b** a moulded mass of solidified material, esp. plaster protecting a broken limb. **6** the actors taking part in a play, film, etc. **7** form, type, or quality (*cast of features; cast of mind*). **8** a tinge or shade of colour. **9** (in full **cast in the eye**) a slight squint. **10** a mass of earth excreted by a worm. □ **cast about** (or **around** or **round**) make an extensive search (actually or mentally) (*cast about for a solution*). **cast adrift** leave to drift. **cast aside** give up using; abandon. **cast away 1** reject. **2** (in *passive*) be shipwrecked (cf. CASTAWAY). **cast down** depress, deject (cf. DOWNCAST). **casting vote** a deciding vote usu. given by the chairperson when the votes on two sides are equal. **cast iron** a hard alloy of iron, carbon, and silicon cast in a mould. **cast-iron** adj. **1** made of cast iron. **2** hard, unchallengeable, unchangeable. **cast loose** detach; detach oneself. **cast off 1** abandon. **2** *Knitting* take the stitches off the needle by looping each over the next to finish the edge. **3** *Naut.* **a** set a ship free from a quay etc. **b** loosen and throw off (rope etc.). **cast-off** adj. abandoned, discarded. —n. a cast-off thing, esp. a garment. **cast on** *Knitting* make the first row of loops on the needle. **cast out** expel. **cast up 1** (of the sea) deposit on the shore. **2** add up (figures etc.). [ME f. ON *kasta*]

castanet /ˌkæstəˈnet/ n. (usu. in *pl.*) a small concave piece of hardwood, ivory, etc., in pairs clicked together by the fingers as a rhythmic accompaniment, esp. by Spanish dancers. [Sp. *castañeta* dimin. of *castaña* f. L *castanea* chestnut]

castaway /ˈkɑːstəˌweɪ/ n. & adj. —n. a shipwrecked person. —adj. **1** shipwrecked. **2** cast aside; rejected.

caste /kɑːst/ n. **1** any of the Hindu hereditary classes whose members have no social contact with other classes, but are socially equal with one another and often follow the same occupations. **2** a more or less exclusive social class. **3** a system of such classes. **4** the position it confers. □ **lose caste** descend in the social order. [Sp. and Port. *casta* lineage, race, breed, fem. of *casto* pure, CHASTE]

casteism /ˈkɑːstɪz(ə)m/ n. often *derog.* the caste system.

castellated /ˈkæstəˌleɪtɪd/ adj. **1** having battlements. **2** castle-like. □ **castellation** /-ˈleɪʃ(ə)n/ n. [med.L *castellatus*: see CASTLE]

caster /ˈkɑːstə(r)/ n. **1** var. of CASTOR¹. **2** a person who casts. **3** a machine for casting type.

castigate /ˈkæstɪˌgeɪt/ v.tr. rebuke or punish severely. □ **castigation** /-ˈgeɪʃ(ə)n/ n. **castigator** n. **castigatory** adj. [L *castigare* reprove f. *castus* pure]

Castilian /kəˈstɪlɪən/ n. & adj. —n. **1** a native of Castile in Spain. **2** the language of Castile, standard spoken and literary Spanish. —adj. of or relating to Castile.

casting /ˈkɑːstɪŋ/ n. an object made by casting, esp. of molten metal.

castle /ˈkɑːs(ə)l/ n. & v. —n. **1 a** a large fortified building or group of buildings; a stronghold. **b** a formerly fortified mansion. **2** *Chess* = ROOK².

—*v. Chess* **1** *intr.* make a special move in which the king is moved two squares along the back rank and the nearer rook is moved to the square passed over by the king. **2** *tr.* move (the king) by castling. □ **castled** *adj.* [AF & ONF *castel*, *chastel* f. L *castellum* dimin. of *castrum* fort]

castor[1] /ˈkɑːstə(r)/ *n.* (also **caster**) **1** a small swivelled wheel fixed to a leg (or the underside) of a piece of furniture. **2** a small container with holes in the top for sprinkling the contents. □ **castor sugar** finely granulated white sugar. [orig. a var. of CASTER (in the general sense)]

castor[2] /ˈkɑːstə(r)/ *n.* an oily substance secreted by beavers and used in medicine and perfumes. [F or L f. Gk *kastōr* beaver]

castor oil /ˈkɑːstə(r)/ *n.* an oil from the seeds of a plant, *Ricinus communis*, used as a purgative and lubricant. [18th c.: orig. uncert.: perh. so called as having succeeded CASTOR[2] in the medical sense]

castrate /kæˈstreɪt/ *v.tr.* **1** remove the testicles of; geld. **2** deprive of vigour. □ **castration** *n.* **castrator** *n.* [L *castrare*]

castrato /kæˈstrɑːtəʊ/ *n.* (*pl.* **castrati** /-tɪ/) *hist.* a male singer castrated in boyhood so as to retain a soprano or alto voice. [It., past part. of *castrare*: see CASTRATE]

casual /ˈkæʒʊəl, -zjʊəl/ *adj.* & *n.* —*adj.* **1** accidental; due to chance. **2** not regular or permanent; temporary, occasional (*casual work*; *a casual affair*). **3 a** unconcerned, uninterested (*was very casual about it*). **b** made or done without great care or thought (*a casual remark*). **c** acting carelessly or unmethodically. **4** (of clothes) informal. —*n.* **1** a casual worker. **2** (usu. in *pl.*) casual clothes or shoes. □ **casually** *adv.* **casualness** *n.* [ME f. OF *casuel* & L *casualis* f. *casus* CASE[1]]

casualty /ˈkæʒʊəltɪ, ˈkæzjʊ-/ *n.* (*pl.* **-ies**) **1** a person killed or injured in a war or accident. **2** a thing lost or destroyed. **3** = *casualty department*. **4** an accident, mishap, or disaster. □ **casualty department** (or **ward**) the part of a hospital where casualties are treated. [ME f. med.L *casualitas* (as CASUAL), after ROYALTY etc.]

casuist /ˈkæʒjuːɪst, ˈkæzjʊɪst/ *n.* **1** a person who resolves problems of conscience etc., often with clever but false reasoning. **2** a sophist or quibbler. □ **casuistic** /-ˈɪstɪk/ *adj.* **casuistical** /-ˈɪstɪk(ə)l/ *adj.* **casuistically** /-ˈɪstɪkəlɪ/ *adv.* **casuistry** *n.* [F *casuiste* f. Sp. *casuista* f. L *casus* CASE[1]]

cat *n.* **1** a small soft-furred four-legged domesticated animal, *Felis catus*. **2 a** any wild animal of the genus *Felis*, e.g. a lion, tiger, or leopard. **b** = *wild cat*. **3** a catlike animal of any other species (*civet cat*). **4** *colloq.* a malicious or spiteful woman. **5** *sl.* a jazz enthusiast. **6** = *cat-o'-nine-tails*. □ **cat-and-dog** (of a relationship etc.) full of quarrels. **cat burglar** a burglar who enters by climbing to an upper storey. **cat flap** (or **door**) a small swinging flap in an outer door, for a cat to pass in and out. **cat-o'-nine-tails** *hist.* a rope whip with nine knotted lashes. **cat's cradle** a child's game in which a loop of string is held between the fingers and patterns are formed. **Cat's-eye** *Brit. propr.* one of a series of reflector studs set into a road. **cat's-eye** a precious stone of Sri Lanka and Malabar. **cat's-paw 1** a person used as a tool by another. **2** a slight breeze. **cat's whiskers** (or **pyjamas**)

sl. an excellent person or thing. **let the cat out of the bag** reveal a secret, esp. involuntarily. **like a cat on hot bricks** (or **on a hot tin roof**) very agitated or agitatedly. **put** (or **set**) **the cat among the pigeons** cause trouble. **rain cats and dogs** rain very hard. [OE *catt(e)* f. LL *cattus*]

cata- /ˈkætə/ *prefix* (usu. **cat-** before a vowel or h) **1** down, downwards. **2** wrongly, badly. [Gk *kata* down]

catabolism /kəˈtæbəˌlɪz(ə)m/ *n.* (also **katabolism**) *Biochem.* the breakdown of complex molecules in living organisms to form simpler ones with the release of energy; destructive metabolism. □ **catabolic** /ˌkætəˈbɒlɪk/ *adj.* [Gk *katabolē* descent f. *kata* down + *bolē* f. *ballō* throw]

catachresis /ˌkætəˈkriːsɪs/ *n.* (*pl.* **catachreses** /-siːz/) an incorrect use of words. □ **catachrestic** /-ˈkriːstɪk, -ˈkrestɪk/ *adj.* [L f. Gk *katakhrēsis* f. *khraomai* use]

cataclysm /ˈkætəˌklɪz(ə)m/ *n.* **1 a** a violent, esp. social or political, upheaval or disaster. **b** a great change. **2** a great flood or deluge. □ **cataclysmal** /-ˈklɪzm(ə)l/ *adj.* **cataclysmic** /-ˈklɪzmɪk/ *adj.* **cataclysmically** /-ˈklɪzmɪkəlɪ/ *adv.* [F *cataclysme* f. L *cataclysmus* f. Gk *kataklusmos* f. *klusmos* flood f. *kluzō* wash]

catacomb /ˈkætəˌkuːm, -ˌkəʊm/ *n.* (often in *pl.*) **1** an underground cemetery with recesses for tombs. **2** a cellar. [F *catacombes* f. LL *catacumbas* (name given in the 5th c. to the cemetery of St Sebastian near Rome), of unkn. orig.]

catafalque /ˈkætəˌfælk/ *n.* a decorated wooden framework for supporting the coffin of a distinguished person during a funeral or while lying in state. [F f. It. *catafalco*, of unkn. orig.: cf. SCAFFOLD]

Catalan /ˈkætəlæn/ *n.* & *adj.* —*n.* **1** a native of Catalonia in Spain. **2** the language of Catalonia. —*adj.* of or relating to Catalonia or its people or language. [F f. Sp.]

catalepsy /ˈkætəˌlepsɪ/ *n.* a state of trance or seizure with loss of sensation and consciousness accompanied by rigidity of the body. □ **cataleptic** /-ˈleptɪk/ *adj.* & *n.* [F *catalepsie* or LL *catalepsia* f. Gk *katalēpsis* (as CATA-, *lēpsis* seizure)]

catalogue /ˈkætəˌlɒg/ *n.* & *v.* (*US* **catalog**) —*n.* a complete list of items (e.g. articles for sale, books held by a library), usu. in alphabetical or other systematic order and often with a description of each. —*v.tr.* (**catalogues, catalogued, cataloguing**; *US* **catalogs, cataloged, cataloging**) **1** make a catalogue of. **2** enter in a catalogue. □ **cataloguer** *n.* (*US* **cataloger**). [F f. LL *catalogus* f. Gk. *katalogos* f. *katalegō* enrol (as CATA-, *legō* choose)]

catalpa /kəˈtælpə/ *n.* any tree of the genus *Catalpa*, with heart-shaped leaves, trumpet-shaped flowers, and long pods. [Amer. Ind. (Creek)]

catalyse /ˈkætəˌlaɪz/ *v.tr.* (*US* **catalyze**) *Chem.* produce (a reaction) by catalysis. [as CATALYSIS after *analyse*]

catalysis /kəˈtælɪsɪs/ *n.* (*pl.* **catalyses** /-ˌsiːz/) *Chem.* & *Biochem.* the acceleration of a chemical or biochemical reaction by a catalyst. [Gk *katalusis* dissolution (as CATA-, *luō* set free)]

catalyst /ˈkætəlɪst/ *n.* **1** *Chem.* a substance that, without itself undergoing any permanent chemical change, increases the rate of a reaction. **2** a person or thing that precipitates a change. [as CATALYSIS after *analyst*]

catalytic /ˌkætəˈlɪtɪk/ *adj. Chem.* relating to or involving catalysis. □ **catalytic converter** a device incorporated in the exhaust system of a motor vehicle, with a catalyst for converting pollutant gases into harmless products.

catamaran /ˌkætəməˈræn/ *n.* **1** a boat with twin hulls in parallel. **2** a raft of yoked logs or boats. [Tamil *kaṭṭumaram* tied wood]

catamite /ˈkætəˌmaɪt/ *n.* the passive partner in sodomy. [L *catamitus* through Etruscan f. Gk *Ganumēdēs* Ganymede, cupbearer of Zeus]

catapult /ˈkætəˌpʌlt/ *n. & v.* —*n.* **1** a forked stick etc. with elastic for shooting stones. **2** *hist.* a military machine worked by a lever and ropes for hurling large stones etc. **3** a mechanical device for launching a glider, an aircraft from the deck of a ship, etc. —*v.* **1** *tr.* **a** hurl from or launch with a catapult. **b** fling forcibly. **2** *intr.* leap or be hurled forcibly. [F *catapulte* or L *catapulta* f. Gk *katapeltēs* (as CATA-, *pallō* hurl)]

cataract /ˈkætəˌrækt/ *n.* **1 a** a large waterfall. **b** a downpour; a rush of water. **2** *Med.* a condition in which the eye-lens becomes progressively opaque. [L *cataracta* f. Gk *katarrhaktēs* downrushing; in med. sense prob. f. obs. sense 'portcullis']

catarrh /kəˈtɑː(r)/ *n.* **1** inflammation of the mucous membrane of the nose, air passages, etc. **2** a watery discharge in the nose or throat due to this. □ **catarrhal** *adj.* [F *catarrhe* f. LL *catarrhus* f. Gk *katarrhous* f. *katarrheō* flow down]

catastrophe /kəˈtæstrəfɪ/ *n.* **1** a great and usu. sudden disaster. **2** the denouement of a drama. **3** a disastrous end; ruin. **4** an event producing a subversion of the order of things. □ **catastrophic** /-ˈstrɒfɪk/ *adj.* **catastrophically** /-ˈstrɒfɪkəlɪ/ *adv.* [L *catastropha* f. Gk *katastrophē* (as CATA-, *strophē* turning f. *strephō* turn)]

catastrophism /kəˈtæstrəˌfɪz(ə)m/ *n. Geol.* the theory that changes in the earth's crust have occurred in sudden violent and unusual events. □ **catastrophist** *n.*

catatonia /ˌkætəˈtəʊnɪə/ *n.* **1** schizophrenia with intervals of catalepsy and sometimes violence. **2** catalepsy. □ **catatonic** /-ˈtɒnɪk/ *adj. & n.* [G *Katatonie* (as CATA-, TONE)]

catcall /ˈkætkɔːl/ *n. & v.* —*n.* a shrill whistle of disapproval made at meetings etc. —*v.* **1** *intr.* make a catcall. **2** *tr.* make a catcall at.

catch /kætʃ/ *v. & n.* —*v.* (*past* and *past part.* **caught** /kɔːt/) **1** *tr.* a lay hold of so as to restrain or prevent from escaping; capture in a trap, in one's hands, etc. **b** (also **catch hold of**) get into one's hands so as to retain, operate, etc. (*caught hold of the handle*). **2** *tr.* detect or surprise (a person, esp. in a wrongful or embarrassing act) (*caught him smoking*). **3** *tr.* **a** intercept and hold (a moving thing) in the hands etc. (*failed to catch the ball; a bowl to catch the drips*). **b** *Cricket* dismiss (a batsman) by catching the ball before it reaches the ground. **4** *tr.* **a** contract (a disease) by infection or contagion. **b** acquire (a quality or feeling) from another's example (*caught her enthusiasm*). **5** *tr.* **a** reach in time and board (a train, bus, etc.). **b** be in time to see etc. (a person or thing about to leave or finish). **6** *tr.* **a** apprehend with the senses or the mind (esp. a thing occurring quickly or briefly) (*didn't catch what he said*). **b** (of an artist etc.) reproduce

faithfully. **7 a** *intr.* become fixed or entangled; be checked. **b** *tr.* cause to do this (*caught her tights on a nail*). **c** *tr.* (often foll. by *on*) hit, deal a blow to (*caught him on the nose*). **8** *tr.* draw the attention of; captivate (*caught his eye; caught her fancy*). **9** *intr.* begin to burn. **10** *tr.* (often foll. by *up*) reach or overtake (a person etc. ahead). **11** *tr.* check suddenly (*caught his breath*). **12** *tr.* (foll. by *at*) grasp or try to grasp. —*n.* **1 a** an act of catching. **b** *Cricket* a chance or act of catching the ball. **2 a** an amount of a thing caught, esp. of fish. **b** a thing or person caught or worth catching, esp. in marriage. **3 a** a question, trick, etc., intended to deceive, incriminate, etc. **b** an unexpected or hidden difficulty or disadvantage. **4** a device for fastening a door or window etc. **5** *Mus.* a round, esp. with words arranged to produce a humorous effect. □ **catch-all** (often *attrib.*) a thing designed to be all-inclusive. **catch-as-catch-can** a style of wrestling with few holds barred. **catch crop** a crop grown between two staple crops (in position or time). **catch it** *sl.* be punished or in trouble. **catch me!** etc. (often foll. by *pres. part.*) *colloq.* you may be sure I etc. shall not. **catch on** *colloq.* **1** (of a practice, fashion, etc.) become popular. **2** (of a person) understand what is meant. **catch out 1** detect in a mistake etc. **2** take unawares; cause to be bewildered or confused. **3** = sense 3b of *v.* **catch-phrase** a phrase in frequent use. **catch up 1 a** (often foll. by *with*) reach a person etc. ahead (*he caught up in the end; he caught us up; he caught up with us*). **b** (often foll. by *with, on*) make up arrears (of work etc.) (*must catch up with my correspondence*). **2** snatch or pick up hurriedly. **3** (often in *passive*) involve; entangle (*caught up in suspicious dealings*). □ **catchable** *adj.* [ME f. AF *cachier*, OF *chacier*, ult. f. L *captare* try to catch]

catcher /ˈkætʃə(r)/ *n.* **1** a person or thing that catches. **2** *Baseball* a fielder who stands behind the batter.

catching /ˈkætʃɪŋ/ *adj.* **1 a** (of a disease) infectious. **b** (of a practice, habit, etc.) likely to be imitated. **2** attractive; captivating.

catchment /ˈkætʃmənt/ *n.* the collection of rainfall. □ **catchment area 1** the area from which rainfall flows into a river etc. **2** the area served by a school, hospital, etc.

catchpenny /ˈkætʃˌpenɪ/ *adj.* intended merely to sell quickly; superficially attractive.

catch-22 /ˌkætʃˌtwentɪˈtuː/ *n.* (often *attrib.*) *colloq.* a dilemma or circumstance from which there is no escape because of mutually conflicting or dependent conditions. [title of a novel by J. Heller (1961) featuring a dilemma of this kind]

catchup var. of KETCHUP.

catchweight /ˈkætʃweɪt/ *adj. & n.* —*adj.* unrestricted as regards weight. —*n.* unrestricted weight, as a weight category in sports.

catchword /ˈkætʃwɜːd/ *n.* **1** a word or phrase in common (often temporary) use; a topical slogan. **2** a word so placed as to draw attention.

catchy /ˈkætʃɪ/ *adj.* (**catchier, catchiest**) (of a tune) easy to remember; attractive. □ **catchily** *adv.* **catchiness** *n.* [CATCH + -Y¹]

catechism /ˈkætɪˌkɪz(ə)m/ *n.* **1 a** a summary of the principles of a religion in the form of questions and answers. **b** a book containing this. **2** a series of questions put to anyone. □

catechismal /-ˈkɪzm(ə)l/ adj. [eccl.L catechismus (as CATECHIZE)]

catechist /ˈkætɪkɪst/ n. a religious teacher, esp. one using a catechism.

catechize /ˈkætɪˌkaɪz/ v.tr. (also **-ise**) **1** instruct by means of question and answer, esp. from a catechism. **2** put questions to; examine. □ **catechizer** n. [LL catechizare f. eccl.Gk katēkhizō f. katēkheō make hear (as CATA-, ēkheō sound)]

catechumen /ˌkætɪˈkjuːmən/ n. a Christian convert under instruction before baptism. [ME f. OF catechumene or eccl.L catechumenus f. Gk katēkheō: see CATECHIZE]

categorical /ˌkætɪˈɡɒrɪk(ə)l/ adj. unconditional, absolute; explicit, direct (a categorical refusal). □ **categorically** adv. [F catégorique or LL categoricus f. Gk katēgorikos: see CATEGORY]

categorize /ˈkætɪɡəˌraɪz/ v.tr. (also **-ise**) place in a category or categories. □ **categorization** /-ˈzeɪʃ(ə)n/ n.

category /ˈkætɪɡərɪ/ n. (pl. **-ies**) a class or division. □ **categorial** /-ˈɡɔːrɪəl/ adj. [F catégorie or LL categoria f. Gk katēgoria statement f. katēgoros accuser]

catenary /kəˈtiːnərɪ/ n. & adj. —n. (pl. **-ies**) a curve formed by a uniform chain hanging freely from two points not in the same vertical line. —adj. of or resembling such a curve. □ **catenary bridge** a suspension bridge hung from such chains. [L catenarius f. catena chain]

catenate /ˈkætɪˌneɪt/ v.tr. connect like links of a chain. □ **catenation** /-ˈneɪʃ(ə)n/ n. [L catenare catenat- (as CATENARY)]

cater /ˈkeɪtə(r)/ v.intr. **1** supply food. **2** (foll. by for) **a** provide meals for. **b** provide entertainment for. **3** (foll. by to) pander to (evil inclinations). [obs. noun cater (now caterer), f. acater f. AF acatour buyer f. acater buy f. Rmc]

cater-cornered /ˈkætəˌkɔːnəd/ adj. & adv. (also **cater-corner**, **catty-cornered** /ˈkætɪ-/) US —adj. placed or situated diagonally. —adv. diagonally. [dial. adv. cater diagonally (cf. obs. cater the four on dice f. F quatre f. L quattuor four)]

caterer /ˈkeɪtərə(r)/ n. a person who supplies food for social events, esp. professionally.

catering /ˈkeɪtərɪŋ/ n. the profession or work of a caterer.

caterpillar /ˈkætəˌpɪlə(r)/ n. **1 a** the larva of a butterfly or moth. **b** (in general use) any similar larva of various insects. **2** (**Caterpillar**) **a** (in full **Caterpillar track** or **tread**) propr. a steel band passing round the wheels of a tractor etc. for travel on rough ground. **b** a vehicle with these tracks, e.g. a tractor or tank. [perh. AF var. of OF chatepelose lit. hairy cat, infl. by obs. piller ravager]

caterwaul /ˈkætəˌwɔːl/ v. & n. —v.intr. make the shrill howl of a cat. —n. a caterwauling noise. [ME f. CAT + -waul etc. imit.]

catfish /ˈkætfɪʃ/ n. any of various esp. freshwater fish, usu. having whisker-like barbels round the mouth.

catgut /ˈkætɡʌt/ n. a material used for the strings of musical instruments and surgical sutures, made of the twisted intestines of the sheep, horse, or ass.

catharsis /kəˈθɑːsɪs/ n. (pl. **catharses** /-ˌsiːz/) **1** an emotional release in drama or art. **2** Psychol. the process of freeing repressed emotion by association with the cause, and elimination by abreaction. **3** Med. purgation. [mod.L f. Gk katharsis f. kathairō cleanse: sense 1 f. Aristotle's Poetics]

cathartic /kəˈθɑːtɪk/ adj. & n. —adj. **1** effecting catharsis. **2** purgative. —n. a cathartic drug. □ **cathartically** adv. [LL catharticus f. Gk kathartikos (as CATHARSIS)]

cathedral /kəˈθiːdr(ə)l/ n. the principal church of a diocese, containing the bishop's throne. [ME (as adj.) f. OF cathedral or f. LL cathedralis f. L f. Gk kathedra seat]

Catherine wheel /ˈkæθrɪn/ n. a firework in the form of a flat coil which spins when fixed and lit. [mod.L Catharina f. Gk Aikaterina name of a saint martyred on a spiked wheel]

catheter /ˈkæθɪtə(r)/ n. Med. a tube for insertion into a body cavity for introducing or removing fluid. [LL f. Gk kathetēr f. kathiēmi send down]

catheterize /ˈkæθɪtəˌraɪz/ v.tr. (also **-ise**) Med. insert a catheter into.

cathode /ˈkæθəʊd/ n. (also **kathode**) Electr. **1** the negative electrode in an electrolytic cell or electronic valve or tube. **2** the positive terminal of a primary cell such as a battery. □ **cathode ray** a beam of electrons emitted from the cathode of a high-vacuum tube. **cathode-ray tube** a high-vacuum tube in which cathode rays produce a luminous image on a fluorescent screen. □ **cathodal** adj. **cathodic** /kəˈθɒdɪk/ adj. [Gk kathodos descent f. kata down + hodos way]

catholic /ˈkæθəlɪk, ˈkæθlɪk/ adj. & n. —adj. **1** of interest or use to all; universal. **2** all-embracing; of wide sympathies or interests (has catholic tastes). **3** (**Catholic**) **a** of the Roman Catholic religion. **b** including all Christians. **c** including all of the Western Church. —n. (**Catholic**) a Roman Catholic. □ **catholically** adv. **Catholicism** /kəˈθɒlɪˌsɪz(ə)m/ n. **catholicity** /ˌkæθəˈlɪsɪtɪ/ n. **catholicly** adv. [ME f. OF catholique or LL catholicus f. Gk katholikos universal f. kata in respect of + holos whole]

catholicize /kəˈθɒlɪˌsaɪz/ v.tr. & intr. (also **-ise**) **1** make or become catholic. **2** (**Catholicize**) make or become a Roman Catholic.

cation /ˈkætˌaɪən/ n. a positively charged ion; an ion that is attracted to the cathode in electrolysis. [CATA- + ION]

cationic /ˌkætaɪˈɒnɪk/ adj. **1** of a cation or cations. **2** having an active cation.

catkin /ˈkætkɪn/ n. a spike of usu. downy or silky male or female flowers hanging from a willow, hazel, etc. [obs. Du. katteken kitten]

catmint /ˈkætmɪnt/ n. a white-flowered plant, Nepeta cataria, having a pungent smell attractive to cats.

catnap /ˈkætnæp/ n. & v. —n. a short sleep. —v.intr. (**-napped**, **-napping**) have a catnap.

catnip /ˈkætnɪp/ n. = CATMINT. [CAT + dial. nip catmint, var. of dial. nep]

catsuit /ˈkætsuːt, -sjuːt/ n. a close-fitting garment with trouser legs, covering the body from neck to feet.

catsup /ˈkætsəp/ esp. US var. of KETCHUP.

cattery /ˈkætərɪ/ n. (pl. **-ies**) a place where cats are boarded or bred.

cattish /ˈkætɪʃ/ adj. = CATTY. □ **cattishly** adv. **cattishness** n.

cattle /ˈkæt(ə)l/ n.pl. any bison, buffalo, yak, or domesticated bovine animal, esp. of the genus Bos. □ **cattle-cake** Brit. a concentrated food for cattle, in cake form. **cattle-grid** Brit. a grid covering a ditch, allowing vehicles to pass over but not cattle, sheep, etc. **cattle-guard** US = *cattle-grid*. **cattle-stop** NZ = *cattle-grid*. [ME & AF *catel* f. OF *chatel* CHATTEL]

catty /ˈkætɪ/ *adj*. (**cattier, cattiest**) **1** sly, spiteful; deliberately hurtful in speech. **2** catlike. □ **cattily** *adv*. **cattiness** *n*.

catty-cornered var. of CATER-CORNERED.

catwalk /ˈkætwɔːk/ *n*. **1** a narrow footway along a bridge, above a theatre stage, etc. **2** a narrow platform or gangway used in fashion shows etc.

Caucasian /kɔːˈkeɪʒ(ə)n, -ˈkeɪzɪən/ *adj*. & *n*. —*adj*. **1** of or relating to the White or light-skinned division of mankind. **2** of or relating to the Caucasus. —*n*. a Caucasian person. [*Caucasus*, mountain range between the Black Sea and the Caspian Sea, its supposed place of origin]

Caucasoid /ˈkɔːkəˌsɔɪd/ *adj*. of or relating to the Caucasian division of mankind.

caucus /ˈkɔːkəs/ *n*. **1** US **a** a meeting of the members of a political party, esp. in the Senate etc., to decide policy. **b** a bloc of such members. **2** often *derog*. (esp. in the UK) **a** a usu. secret meeting of a group within a larger organization or party. **b** such a group. [18th-c. US, perh. f. Algonquin *cau'-cau-as'u* adviser]

caudal /ˈkɔːd(ə)l/ *adj*. **1** of or like a tail. **2** of the posterior part of the body. □ **caudally** *adv*. [mod.L *caudalis* f. L *cauda* tail]

caudate /ˈkɔːdeɪt/ *adj*. having a tail. [see CAUDAL]

caught *past* and *past part*. of CATCH.

caul /kɔːl/ *n*. the inner membrane enclosing a foetus. [ME perh. f. OF *cale* small cap]

cauldron /ˈkɔːldrən/ *n*. (also **caldron**) a large deep bowl-shaped vessel for boiling over an open fire; an ornamental vessel resembling this. [ME f. AF & ONF *caudron*, ult. f. L *caldarium* hot bath f. *calidus* hot]

cauliflower /ˈkɒlɪˌflaʊə(r)/ *n*. **1** a variety of cabbage with a large immature flower-head of small usu. creamy-white flower-buds. **2** the flower-head eaten as a vegetable. □ **cauliflower ear** an ear thickened by repeated blows, esp. in boxing. [earlier *cole-florie* etc. f. obs. F *chou fleuri* flowered cabbage, assim. to COLE and FLOWER]

caulk /kɔːk/ *v.tr*. (US **calk**) **1** stop up (the seams of a boat etc.) with oakum etc. and waterproofing material, or by driving plate-junctions together. **2** make (esp. a boat) watertight by this method. □ **caulker** *n*. [OF dial. *cauquer* tread, press with force, f. L *calcare* tread f. *calx* heel]

causal /ˈkɔːz(ə)l/ *adj*. **1** of, forming, or expressing a cause or causes. **2** relating to, or of the nature of, cause and effect. □ **causally** *adv*. [LL *causalis*: see CAUSE]

causality /kɔːˈzælɪtɪ/ *n*. **1** the relation of cause and effect. **2** the principle that everything has a cause.

causation /kɔːˈzeɪʃ(ə)n/ *n*. **1** the act of causing or producing an effect. **2** = CAUSALITY. [F *causation* or L *causatio* pretext etc., in med.L the action of causing, f. *causare* CAUSE]

causative /ˈkɔːzətɪv/ *adj*. **1** acting as cause. **2** (foll. by *of*) producing; having as effect. **3** *Gram*. expressing cause. □ **causatively** *adv*. [ME f. OF *causatif* or f. LL *causativus*: see CAUSATION]

cause /kɔːz/ *n*. & *v*. —*n*. **1 a** that which produces an effect, or gives rise to an action, phenomenon, or condition. **b** a person or thing that occasions something. **c** a reason or motive; a ground that

may be held to justify something (*no cause for complaint*). **2** a reason adjudged adequate (*show cause*). **3** a principle, belief, or purpose which is advocated or supported. **4 a** a matter to be settled at law. **b** an individual's case offered at law. **5** the side taken by any party in a dispute. —*v.tr*. **1** be the cause of, produce, make happen. **2** (foll. by *to* + infin.) induce (*caused me to smile*). □ **in the cause of** to maintain, defend, or support (*in the cause of justice*). **make common cause with** join the side of. □ **causable** *adj*. **causeless** *adj*. **causer** *n*. [ME f. OF f. L *causa*]

cause célèbre /ˌkɔːz seˈlebr/ *n*. (pl. **causes célèbres** pronunc. same) a lawsuit that attracts much attention. [F]

causeway /ˈkɔːzweɪ/ *n*. **1** a raised road or track across low or wet ground or a stretch of water. **2** a raised path by a road. [earlier *cauce, causeway* f. ONF *caucié* ult. f. L CALX lime, limestone]

caustic /ˈkɔːstɪk/ *adj*. & *n*. —*adj*. **1** that burns or corrodes organic tissue. **2** sarcastic, biting. **3** *Chem*. strongly alkaline. —*n*. a caustic substance. □ **caustic potash** potassium hydroxide. **caustic soda** sodium hydroxide. □ **caustically** *adv*. **causticity** /-ˈtɪsɪtɪ/ *n*. [L *causticus* f. Gk *kaustikos* f. *kaustos* burnt f. *kaiō* burn]

cauterize /ˈkɔːtəˌraɪz/ *v.tr*. (also **-ise**) *Med*. burn or coagulate (tissue) with a heated instrument or caustic substance, esp. to stop bleeding. □ **cauterization** /-ˈzeɪʃ(ə)n/ *n*. [F *cautériser* f. LL *cauterizare* f. Gk *kautēriazō* f. *kautērion* branding-iron f. *kaiō* burn]

caution /ˈkɔːʃ(ə)n/ *n*. & *v*. —*n*. **1** attention to safety; prudence, carefulness. **2 a** esp. *Brit*. a warning, esp. a formal one in law. **b** a formal warning and reprimand. **3** *colloq*. an amusing or surprising person. —*v.tr*. **1** (often foll. by *against*, or *to* + infin.) warn or admonish. **2** esp. *Brit*. issue a caution to. [ME f. OF f. L *cautio -onis* f. *cavēre caut-* take heed]

cautionary /ˈkɔːʃənərɪ/ *adj*. that gives or serves as a warning (*a cautionary tale*).

cautious /ˈkɔːʃəs/ *adj*. careful, prudent; attentive to safety. □ **cautiously** *adv*. **cautiousness** *n*. [ME f. OF f. L: see CAUTION]

cavalcade /ˌkævəlˈkeɪd/ *n*. a procession or formal company of riders, motor vehicles, etc. [F f. It. *cavalcata* f. *cavalcare* ride ult. f. L *caballus* pack-horse]

cavalier /ˌkævəˈlɪə(r)/ *n*. & *adj*. —*n*. **1** *hist*. (**Cavalier**) a supporter of Charles I in the Civil War. **2** a courtly gentleman, esp. as a lady's escort. —*adj*. offhand, supercilious, blasé. □ **cavalierly** *adv*. [F f. It. *cavaliere*: see CHEVALIER]

cavalry /ˈkævəlrɪ/ *n*. (pl. **-ies**) (usu. treated as *pl*.) soldiers on horseback or in armoured vehicles. [F *cavallerie* f. It. *cavalleria* f. *cavallo* horse f. L *caballus*]

cave *n*. & *v*. —*n*. a large hollow in the side of a cliff, hill, etc., or underground. —*v.intr*. explore caves, esp. interconnecting or underground. □ **cave in 1 a** (of a wall, earth over a hollow, etc.) subside, collapse. **b** cause (a wall, earth, etc.) to do this. **2** yield or submit under pressure; give up. □ **cavelike** *adj*. **caver** *n*. [ME f. OF f. L *cava* f. *cavus* hollow: *cave in* prob. f. E. Anglian dial. *calve in*]

caveat /ˈkævɪˌæt/ *n*. **1** a warning or proviso. **2** *Law* a process in court to suspend proceedings. [L, = let a person beware]

caveman /ˈkeɪvmæn/ n. (pl. **-men**) **1** a prehistoric man living in a cave. **2** a primitive or crude person.

cavern /ˈkæv(ə)n/ n. a cave, esp. a large or dark one. □ **cavernous** adj. **cavernously** adv. [ME f. OF caverne or f. L caverna f. cavus hollow]

caviare /ˈkævɪˌɑː(r), ˌkævɪˈɑː(r)/ n. (US **caviar**) the pickled roe of sturgeon or other large fish, eaten as a delicacy. [early forms repr. It. caviale, Fr. caviar, prob. f. med.Gk khaviári]

cavil /ˈkævɪl/ v. & n. —v.intr. (**cavilled, cavilling**; US **caviled, caviling**) (usu. foll. by at, about) make petty objections; carp. —n. a trivial objection. □ **caviller** n. [F caviller f. L cavillari f. cavilla mockery]

caving /ˈkeɪvɪŋ/ n. exploring caves as a sport or pastime.

cavity /ˈkævɪtɪ/ n. (pl. **-ies**) **1** a hollow within a solid body. **2** a decayed part of a tooth. □ **cavity wall** a wall formed from two skins of brick or blockwork with a space between. [F cavité or LL cavitas f. L cavus hollow]

cavort /kəˈvɔːt/ v.intr. caper excitedly; gambol, prance. [US, perh. f. CURVET]

caw /kɔː/ n. & v. —n. the harsh cry of a rook, crow, etc. —v.intr. utter this cry. [imit.]

cayenne /keɪˈen/ n. (in full **cayenne pepper**) a pungent red powder obtained from various plants of the genus Capsicum and used for seasoning. [Tupi kyynha assim. to Cayenne capital of French Guiana]

cayman /ˈkeɪmən/ n. (also **caiman**) any of various S. American alligator-like reptilians, esp. of the genus Caiman. [Sp. & Port. caiman, f. Carib acayuman]

CB abbr. **1** citizens' band. **2** (in the UK) Companion of the Order of the Bath.

Cb symb. US Chem. the element columbium.

CBE abbr. Commander of the Order of the British Empire.

CBI abbr. (in the UK) Confederation of British Industry.

cc abbr. cubic centimetre(s).

CD abbr. **1** compact disc. **2** Corps Diplomatique.

Cd symb. Chem. the element cadmium.

cd abbr. candela.

Cdr. abbr. Mil. Commander.

Cdre. abbr. Commodore.

CD-ROM /ˌsiːdiːˈrɒm/ abbr. compact disc readonly memory (for retrieval of text or data on a VDU screen).

Ce symb. Chem. the element cerium.

cease /siːs/ v. & n. —v.tr. & intr. stop; bring or come to an end (ceased breathing). —n. (in **without cease**) unending. □ **cease fire** Mil. stop firing. **cease-fire** n. **1** the order to do this. **2** a period of truce; a suspension of hostilities. [ME f. OF cesser, L cessare frequent. of cedere cess- yield]

ceaseless /ˈsiːslɪs/ adj. without end; not ceasing. □ **ceaselessly** adv.

cecum US var. of CAECUM.

cedar /ˈsiːdə(r)/ n. **1** any spreading evergreen conifer of the genus Cedrus, bearing tufts of small needles and cones of papery scales. **2** any of various similar conifers yielding timber. **3** (in full **cedar wood**) the fragrant durable wood of any cedar tree. □ **cedarn** adj. poet. [ME f. OF cedre f. L cedrus f. Gk kedros]

cede /siːd/ v.tr. give up one's rights to or possession of. [F céder or L cedere yield]

cedilla /sɪˈdɪlə/ n. **1** a mark written under the letter c, esp. in French, to show that it is sibilant (as in façade). **2** a similar mark under s in Turkish and other oriental languages. [Sp. cedilla dimin. of zeda f. Gk zēta letter Z]

Ceefax /ˈsiːfæks/ n. Brit. propr. a teletext service provided by the BBC.

ceilidh /ˈkeɪlɪ/ n. orig. Ir. & Sc. an informal gathering for music, dancing, and stories. [Gael.]

ceiling /ˈsiːlɪŋ/ n. **1 a** the upper interior surface of a room or other similar compartment. **b** the material forming this. **2** an upper limit on prices, wages, performance, etc. **3** Aeron. the maximum altitude a given aircraft can reach. [ME celynge, siling, perh. ult. f. L caelum heaven or celare hide]

celandine /ˈselənˌdaɪn/ n. either of two yellow-flowered plants, the greater celandine, Chelidonium majus, and the lesser celandine, Ranunculus ficaria. [ME and OF celidoine ult. f. Gk khelidōn swallow: the flowering of the plant was associated with the arrival of swallows]

celebrant /ˈselɪbrənt/ n. a person who performs a rite, esp. a priest at the Eucharist. [F célébrant or L celebrare celebrant-: see CELEBRATE]

celebrate /ˈselɪˌbreɪt/ v. **1** tr. mark (a festival or special event) with festivities etc. **2** tr. perform publicly and duly (a religious ceremony etc.). **3 a** tr. officiate at (the Eucharist). **b** intr. officiate, esp. at the Eucharist. **4** intr. engage in festivities, usu. after a special event etc. **5** tr. (as **celebrated** adj.) publicly honoured, widely known. □ **celebration** /-ˈbreɪʃ(ə)n/ n. **celebrator** n. **celebratory** adj. [L celebrare f. celeber -bris frequented, honoured]

celebrity /sɪˈlebrɪtɪ/ n. (pl. **-ies**) **1** a well-known person. **2** fame. [F célébrité or L celebritas f. celeber: see CELEBRATE]

celeriac /sɪˈlerɪˌæk/ n. a variety of celery with a swollen turnip-like stem-base used as a vegetable. [CELERY: -ac is unexplained]

celerity /sɪˈlerɪtɪ/ n. archaic or literary swiftness (esp. of a living creature). [ME f. F célérité f. L celeritas -tatis f. celer swift]

celery /ˈselərɪ/ n. an umbelliferous plant, Apium graveolens, with closely packed succulent leaf-stalks used as a vegetable. [F céleri f. It. dial. selleri f. L selinum f. Gk selinon parsley]

celesta /sɪˈlestə/ n. Mus. a small keyboard instrument resembling a glockenspiel. [pseudo-L f. F céleste heavenly f. L caelestis f. caelum heaven]

celestial /sɪˈlestɪəl/ adj. **1** heavenly; divinely good or beautiful; sublime. **2 a** of the sky; of the part of the sky commonly observed in astronomy etc. **b** of heavenly bodies. □ **celestial equator** the great circle of the sky in the plane perpendicular to the earth's axis. **celestial navigation** navigation by the stars etc. □ **celestially** adv. [ME f. OF f. med.L caelestialis f. L caelestis: see CELESTA]

celibate /ˈselɪbət/ adj. & n. —adj. **1** committed to abstention from sexual relations and from marriage, esp. for religious reasons. **2** abstaining from sexual relations. —n. a celibate person. □ **celibacy** n. [F célibat or L caelibatus unmarried state f. caelebs -ibis unmarried]

cell /sel/ n. **1** a small room, esp. in a prison or monastery. **2** a small compartment, e.g. in a honeycomb. **3** a small group as a nucleus of

political activity, esp. of a subversive kind.
4 *Biol.* **a** the structural and functional usu.
microscopic unit of an organism, consisting
of cytoplasm and a nucleus enclosed in a
membrane. **b** an enclosed cavity in an organism
etc. **5** *Electr.* a vessel for containing electrodes
within an electrolyte for current-generation or
electrolysis. □ **celled** *adj.* (also in *comb.*). [ME f.
OF *celle* or f. L *cella* storeroom etc.]

cellar /ˈselə(r)/ *n.* & *v.* —*n.* **1** a room below
ground level in a house, used for storage. **2** a
stock of wine in a cellar. —*v.tr.* store or put in a
cellar. [ME f. AF *celer*, OF *celier* f. LL *cellarium*
storehouse]

cello /ˈtʃeləʊ/ *n.* (*pl.* **-os**) a bass instrument of
the violin family, held upright on the floor
between the legs of the seated player. □ **cellist**
n. [abbr. of VIOLONCELLO]

Cellophane /ˈseləˌfeɪn/ *n. propr.* a thin transparent wrapping material made from viscose.
[CELLULOSE + -*phane* (cf. DIAPHANOUS)]

cellphone /ˈselfəʊn/ *n.* a small portable radio-
telephone having access to a cellular radio
system.

cellular /ˈseljʊlə(r)/ *adj.* **1** of or having small
compartments or cavities. **2** of open texture;
porous. **3** *Physiol.* of or consisting of cells. □
cellular blanket a blanket of open texture.
cellular radio a system of mobile radio-
telephone transmission with an area divided
into 'cells' each served by its own small transmitter. □ **cellularity** /-ˈlærɪtɪ/ *n.* **cellulate** *adj.*
cellulation /-ˈleɪʃ(ə)n/ *n.* **cellulous** *adj.* [F *cel-
lulaire* f. mod.L *cellularis*: see CELLULE]

cellule /ˈselju:l/ *n. Biol.* a small cell or cavity. [F
cellule or L *cellula* dimin. of *cella* CELL]

cellulite /ˈseljʊlaɪt/ *n.* a lumpy form of fat, esp.
on the hips and thighs of women, causing
puckering of the skin. [F (as CELLULE)]

celluloid /ˈseljʊˌlɔɪd/ *n.* **1** a transparent flammable plastic made from camphor and cellulose
nitrate. **2** cinema film. [irreg. f. CELLULOSE]

cellulose /ˈseljʊˌləʊz, -ˌləʊs/ *n.* **1** *Biochem.* a
carbohydrate forming the main constituent of
plant-cell walls, used in the production of textile
fibres. **2** (in general use) a paint or lacquer
consisting of esp. cellulose acetate or nitrate
in solution. □ **cellulosic** /-ˈləʊsɪk/ *adj.* [F (as
CELLULE)]

Celsius /ˈselsɪəs/ *adj.* of or denoting a temperature on the Celsius scale. □ **Celsius scale**
a scale of temperature on which water freezes
at 0° and boils at 100° under standard conditions. [A. *Celsius*, Sw. astronomer d. 1744]

■ **Usage** See note at **centigrade**.

Celt /kelt, selt/ *n.* (also **Kelt**) a member of a
group of W. European peoples, including the
pre-Roman inhabitants of Britain and Gaul
and their descendants, esp. in Ireland, Wales,
Scotland, Cornwall, Brittany, and the Isle of
Man. [L *Celtae* (pl.) f. Gk *Keltoi*]

Celtic /ˈkeltɪk, ˈseltɪk/ *adj.* & *n.* —*adj.* of or
relating to the Celts. —*n.* a group of languages
spoken by Celtic peoples, including Gaelic,
Welsh, Cornish, and Breton. □ **Celtic cross** a
Latin cross with a circle round the centre. □
Celticism /-ˌsɪz(ə)m/ *n.* [L *celticus* (as CELT) or F
celtique]

cement /sɪˈment/ *n.* & *v.* —*n.* **1** a powdery
substance made by calcining lime and clay,

mixed with water to form mortar or used in
concrete. **2** any similar substance that hardens
and fastens on setting. **3** a uniting factor or
principle. **4** a substance for filling cavities in
teeth. —*v.tr.* **1 a** unite with or as with cement.
b establish or strengthen (a friendship etc.). **2**
apply cement to. **3** line or cover with cement. □
cementation *n.* **cementer** *n.* [ME f. OF *ciment*
f. L *caementum* quarry stone f. *caedere* hew]

cemetery /ˈsemɪtərɪ/ *n.* (*pl.* **-ies**) a burial ground,
esp. one not in a churchyard. [LL *coemeterium* f.
Gk *koimētērion* dormitory f. *koimaō* put to sleep]

cenobite *US* var. of COENOBITE.

cenotaph /ˈsenəˌtɑːf/ *n.* a tomblike monument,
to a person whose body is elsewhere. [F *cénotaphe*
f. LL *cenotaphium* f. Gk *kenos* empty + *taphos*
tomb]

Cenozoic /ˌsiːnəˈzəʊɪk/ (also **Cainozoic** /ˌkaɪnə-/,
Caenozoic /ˌsiːn-/) *adj.* & *n. Geol.* —*adj.* of or
relating to the most recent era of geological
time. —*n.* this era. [Gk *kainos* new + *zōion*
animal]

censer /ˈsensə(r)/ *n.* a vessel in which incense is
burnt, esp. during a religious procession or
ceremony. [ME f. AF *censer*, OF *censier* aphetic of
encensier f. *encens* INCENSE¹]

censor /ˈsensə(r)/ *n.* & *v.* —*n.* an official authorized to examine printed matter, films, news,
etc., before public release, and to suppress any
parts on the grounds of obscenity, a threat to
security, etc. —*v.tr.* **1** act as a censor of. **2** make
deletions or changes in. □ **censorial** /-ˈsɔːrɪəl/
adj. **censorship** *n.* [L f. *censēre* assess: in sense 3
mistransl. of G *Zensur* censorship]

■ **Usage** As a verb, this word is often confused
with *censure*.

censorious /senˈsɔːrɪəs/ *adj.* severely critical;
fault-finding; quick or eager to criticize. □
censoriously *adv.* **censoriousness** *n.* [L *cen-
sorius*: see CENSOR]

censure /ˈsensjə(r)/ *v.* & *n.* —*v.tr.* criticize
harshly; reprove. —*n.* harsh criticism; expression of disapproval. □ **censurable** *adj.* [ME f.
OF f. L *censura* f. *censēre* assess]

■ **Usage** As a verb, this word is often confused
with *censor*.

census /ˈsensəs/ *n.* (*pl.* **censuses**) the official
count of a population or of a class of things,
often with various statistics noted. [L f. *censēre*
assess]

cent /sent/ *n.* **1 a** a monetary unit valued at
one-hundredth of a dollar or other metric unit.
b a coin of this value. **2** *colloq.* a very small sum
of money. **3** see PER CENT. [F *cent* or It. *cento* or L
centum hundred]

centaur /ˈsentɔː(r)/ *n.* a creature in Greek mythology with the head, arms, and torso of a man
and the body and legs of a horse. [ME f. L
centaurus f. Gk *kentauros*, of unkn. orig.]

centenarian /ˌsentɪˈneərɪən/ *n.* & *adj.* —*n.* a
person a hundred or more years old. —*adj.* a
hundred or more years old.

centenary /senˈtiːnərɪ/ *n.* & *adj.* —*n.* (*pl.* **-ies**) **1**
a hundredth anniversary. **2** a celebration of this.
—*adj.* **1** of or relating to a centenary. **2** occurring
every hundred years. [L *centenarius* f. *centeni* a
hundred each f. *centum* a hundred]

centennial /senˈtenɪəl/ *adj.* & *n.* —*adj.* **1** lasting
for a hundred years. **2** occurring every hundred

years. —*n*. US = CENTENARY *n*. [L *centum* a hundred, after BIENNIAL]

center US var. of CENTRE.

centesimal /sen'tesɪm(ə)l/ *adj*. reckoning or reckoned by hundredths. □ **centesimally** *adv*. [L *centesimus* hundredth f. *centum* hundred]

centi- /'sentɪ/ *comb. form* **1** one-hundredth, esp. of a unit in the metric system (*centigram*; *centilitre*). **2** hundred. [L *centum* hundred]

centigrade /'sentɪˌɡreɪd/ *adj*. **1** = CELSIUS. **2** having a scale of a hundred degrees. [F f. L *centum* hundred + *gradus* step]

■ **Usage** In sense 1, *Celsius* is usually preferred in technical contexts.

centigram /'sentɪˌɡræm/ *n*. (also **centi-gramme**) a metric unit of mass, equal to one-hundredth of a gram.

centilitre /'sentɪˌliːtə(r)/ *n*. (US **centiliter**) a metric unit of capacity, equal to one-hundredth of a litre.

centimetre /'sentɪˌmiːtə(r)/ *n*. (US **centimeter**) a metric unit of length, equal to one-hundredth of a metre.

centipede /'sentɪˌpiːd/ *n*. any arthropod of the class Chilopoda, with a wormlike body of many segments each with a pair of legs. [F *centipède* or L *centipeda* f. *centum* hundred + *pes pedis* foot]

central /'sentr(ə)l/ *adj*. **1** of, at, or forming the centre. **2** from the centre. **3** chief, essential, most important. □ **Central America** the isthmus joining North and South America. **central bank** a national bank issuing currency etc. **central heating** a method of warming a building by pipes, radiators, etc., fed from a central source of heat. **central nervous system** *Anat*. the complex of nerve tissues that controls the activities of the body, in vertebrates the brain and spinal cord. **central processor** (or **pro-cessing unit**) the principal operating part of a computer. □ **centrality** /-'trælɪtɪ/ *n*. **centrally** *adv*. [F *central* or L *centralis* f. *centrum* CENTRE]

centralism /'sentrəˌlɪz(ə)m/ *n*. a system that centralizes (esp. an administration). □ **cent-ralist** *n*.

centralize /'sentrəˌlaɪz/ *v*. (also **-ise**) **1** *tr*. & *intr*. bring or come to a centre. **2** *tr*. **a** concentrate (administration) at a single centre. **b** subject (a State) to this system. □ **centralization** /-ˈzeɪʃ(ə)n/ *n*.

centre /'sentə(r)/ *n*. & *v*. (US **center**) —*n*. **1** the middle point, esp. of a line, circle, or sphere, equidistant from the ends or from any point on the circumference or surface. **2** a pivot or axis of rotation. **3 a** a place or group of buildings forming a central point in a district, city, etc., or a main area for an activity (*shopping centre*; *town centre*). **b** (with preceding word) a piece or set of equipment for a number of connected functions (*music centre*). **4** a point of con-centration or dispersion; a nucleus or source. **5** a political party or group holding moderate opinions. **6** the filling in a chocolate etc. **7** *Sport* **a** the middle player in a line or group in some field games. **b** a kick or hit from the side to the centre of the pitch. —*v*. **1** *intr*. (foll. by *in*, *on*; *disp*. foll. by *round*) have as its main centre. **2** *tr*. place in the centre. **3** *tr*. (foll. by *in* etc.) concentrate. **4** *tr*. *Sport* kick or hit (the ball) from the side to the centre of the pitch. □ **centre forward** *Sport* the middle player or position in

a forward line. **centre half** *Sport* the middle player or position in a half-back line. **centre of gravity** (or **mass**) the point at which the weight of a body may be considered to act. **centre-piece 1** an ornament for the middle of a table. **2** a principal item. **centre spread** the two facing middle pages of a newspaper etc. □ **centred** *adj*. (often in *comb*.). **centremost** *adj*. **centric** *adj*. **centrical** *adj*. **centricity** /-'trɪsɪtɪ/ *n*. [ME f. OF *centre* or L *centrum* f. Gk *kentron* sharp point]

■ **Usage** The use of the verb in sense 1 with *round* is common and used by good writers, but is still considered incorrect by some people.

centreboard /'sentəˌbɔːd/ *n*. (US **centerboard**) a board for lowering through a boat's keel to prevent leeway.

centrefold /'sentəˌfəʊld/ *n*. (US **centerfold**) a printed and usu. illustrated sheet folded to form the centre spread of a magazine etc.

-centric /'sentrɪk/ *comb. form* forming adjectives with the sense 'having a (specified) centre' (*anthropocentric*; *eccentric*). [after *concentric* etc. f. Gk *kentrikos*: see CENTRE]

centrifugal /ˌsentrɪ'fjuːɡ(ə)l, sen'trɪfjʊɡ(ə)l/ *adj*. moving or tending to move from a centre. □ **centrifugal force** an apparent force that acts outwards on a body moving about a centre. □ **centrifugally** *adv*. [mod.L *centrifugus* f. L *centrum* centre + *fugere* flee]

centrifuge /'sentrɪˌfjuːdʒ/ *n*. & *v*. —*n*. a machine with a rapidly rotating device designed to separate liquids from solids or other liquids (e.g. cream from milk). —*v.tr*. **1** subject to the action of a centrifuge. **2** separate by centrifuge. □ **centrifugation** /-fjʊ'ɡeɪʃ(ə)n/ *n*.

centripetal /sen'trɪpɪt(ə)l/ *adj*. moving or tend-ing to move towards a centre. □ **centripetal force** the force acting on a body causing it to move about a centre. □ **centripetally** *adv*. [mod.L *centripetus* f. L *centrum* centre + *petere* seek]

centrist /'sentrɪst/ *n*. *Polit*. often *derog*. a person who holds moderate views. □ **centrism** *n*.

centurion /sen'tjʊərɪən/ *n*. the commander of a century in the ancient Roman army. [ME f. L *centurio -onis* (as CENTURY)]

century /'sentʃərɪ, -tjʊrɪ/ *n*. (*pl*. **-ies**) **1 a** a period of one hundred years. **b** any of the centuries reckoned from the birth of Christ (*twentieth century* = 1901–2000; *fifth century* BC = 500–401 BC). **2 a** a score etc. of a hundred in a sporting event, esp. a hundred runs by one batsman in cricket. **b** a group of a hundred things. **3 a** company in the ancient Roman army, orig. of 100 men. [L *centuria* f. *centum* hundred]

■ **Usage** Strictly speaking, since the first century is regarded as running to the year 100, the first year of a given century should be that ending in 01. However, in general use this has been moved back a year, and so the twenty-first century will commonly be regarded as running from 2000–2099.

cep /sep/ *n*. an edible mushroom, *Boletus edulis*, with a stout stalk and brown smooth cap. [F *cèpe* f. Gascon *cep* f. L *cippus* stake]

cephalic /sɪ'fælɪk, ke-/ *adj*. of or in the head. [F *céphalique* f. L *cephalicus* f. Gk *kephalikos* f. *kephalē* head]

cephalopod /ˈsefələˌpɒd/ n. any mollusc of the class Cephalopoda, having a distinct tentacled head, e.g. octopus, squid, and cuttlefish. [Gk *kephalē* head + *pous podos* foot]

ceramic /sɪˈræmɪk, kɪ-/ adj. & n. —adj. **1** made of (esp.) clay and permanently hardened by heat (*a ceramic bowl*). **2** of or relating to ceramics (*the ceramic arts*). —n. **1** a ceramic article or product. **2** a substance, esp. clay, used to make ceramic articles. [Gk *keramikos* f. *keramos* pottery]

ceramics /sɪˈræmɪks, kɪ-/ n.pl. **1** ceramic products collectively (*exhibition of ceramics*). **2** (usu. treated as *sing.*) the art of making ceramic articles.

cereal /ˈsɪərɪəl/ n. & adj —n. **1** (usu. in pl.) **a** any kind of grain used for food. **b** any grass producing this, e.g. wheat, maize, rye, etc. **2** a breakfast food made from a cereal and requiring no cooking. —adj. of edible grain or products of it. [L *cerealis* f. *Ceres* goddess of agriculture]

cerebellum /ˌserɪˈbeləm/ n. (pl. **cerebellums** or **cerebella** /-lə/) the part of the brain at the back of the skull in vertebrates, which coordinates and regulates muscular activity. □ **cerebellar** adj. [L dimin. of CEREBRUM]

cerebral /ˈserɪbr(ə)l/ adj. **1** of the brain. **2** intellectual rather than emotional. □ **cerebral hemisphere** each of the two halves of the vertebrate cerebrum. **cerebral palsy** Med. spastic paralysis from brain damage before or at birth. □ **cerebrally** adv. [L *cerebrum* brain]

cerebration /ˌserɪˈbreɪʃ(ə)n/ n. working of the brain. □ **cerebrate** /ˈserɪˌbreɪt/ v.intr.

cerebro- /ˈserɪbrəʊ/ comb. form brain (*cerebrospinal*).

cerebrospinal /ˌserɪbrəʊˈspaɪn(ə)l/ adj. of the brain and spine.

cerebrovascular /ˌserɪbrəʊˈvæskjʊlə(r)/ adj. of the brain and its blood vessels.

cerebrum /ˈserɪbrəm/ n. (pl. **cerebra** /-brə/) the principal part of the brain in vertebrates, located in the front area of the skull, which integrates complex sensory and neural functions. [L, = brain]

ceremonial /ˌserɪˈməʊnɪəl/ adj. & n. —adj. **1** with or concerning ritual or ceremony. **2** formal (*a ceremonial bow*). —n. **1** a system of rites etc. to be used esp. at a formal or religious occasion. **2** the formalities or behaviour proper to any occasion (*with all due ceremonial*). □ **ceremonialism** n. **ceremonialist** n. **ceremonially** adv. [LL *caerimonialis* (as CEREMONY)]

ceremonious /ˌserɪˈməʊnɪəs/ adj. **1** excessively polite; punctilious. **2** having or showing a fondness for ritualistic observance or formality. □ **ceremoniously** adv. **ceremoniousness** n. [F *cérémonieux* or LL *caerimoniosus* (as CEREMONY)]

ceremony /ˈserɪmənɪ/ n. (pl. **-ies**) **1** a formal religious or public occasion, esp. celebrating a particular event or anniversary. **2** formalities, esp. of an empty or ritualistic kind (*ceremony of exchanging compliments*). **3** excessively polite behaviour (*bowed low with great ceremony*). □ **Master of Ceremonies 1** a person introducing speakers at a banquet, or entertainers in a variety show. **2** a person in charge of ceremonies at a state or public occasion. **stand on ceremony** insist on the observance of formalities. [ME f. OF *ceremonie* or L *caerimonia* religious worship]

cerise /səˈriːz, -ˈriːs/ adj. & n. —adj. of a light clear red. —n. this colour. [F, = CHERRY]

cerium /ˈsɪərɪəm/ n. Chem. a silvery metallic element of the lanthanide series used in the manufacture of lighter flints. [named after the asteroid *Ceres*, discovered (1801) about the same time as this]

cert /sɜːt/ n. sl. (esp. **dead cert**) **1** an event or result regarded as certain to happen. **2** a horse strongly tipped to win. [abbr. of CERTAIN, CERTAINTY]

certain /ˈsɜːt(ə)n, -tɪn/ adj. & pron. —adj. **1 a** (often foll. by *of*, or *that* + clause) confident, convinced (*certain that I put it here*). **b** (often foll. by *that* + clause) indisputable; known for sure (*it is certain that he is guilty*). **2** (often foll. by *to* + infin.) **a** that may be relied on to happen (*it is certain to rain*). **b** destined (*certain to become a star*). **3** definite, unfailing, reliable (*a certain indication of the coming storm; his touch is certain*). **4** (of a person, place, etc.) that might be specified, but is not (*a certain lady; of a certain age*). **5** some though not much (*a certain reluctance*). **6** (of a person, place, etc.) existing, though probably unknown to the reader or hearer (*a certain John Smith*). —pron. (as pl.) some but not all (*certain of them were wounded*). □ **for certain** without doubt. **make certain** = *make sure* (see SURE). [ME f. OF ult. f. L *certus* settled]

certainly /ˈsɜːtənlɪ, -tɪnlɪ/ adv. **1** undoubtedly, definitely. **2** confidently. **3** (in affirmative answer to a question or command) yes; by all means.

certainty /ˈsɜːtəntɪ, -tɪntɪ/ n. (pl. **-ies**) **1 a** an undoubted fact. **b** a certain prospect (*his return is a certainty*). **2** (often foll. by *of*, or *that* + clause) an absolute conviction (*has a certainty of his own worth*). **3** (often foll. by *to* + infin.) a thing or person that may be relied on (*a certainty to win the Derby*). [ME f. AF *certainté*, OF *-eté* (as CERTAIN)]

Cert. Ed. abbr. (in the UK) Certificate in Education.

certifiable /ˌsɜːtɪˈfaɪəb(ə)l, ˈsɜːt-/ adj. **1** able or needing to be certified. **2** colloq. insane.

certificate /səˈtɪfɪkət/ n. & v. —n. a formal document attesting a fact, esp. birth, marriage, or death, a medical condition, a level of achievement, a fulfilment of requirements, ownership of shares, etc. —v.tr. /-ˌkeɪt/ (esp. as **certificated** adj.) provide with or license or attest by a certificate. □ **Certificate of Secondary Education** hist. **1** an examination set for secondary-school pupils in England and Wales. **2** the certificate gained by passing it. □ **certification** /ˌsɜːtɪfɪˈkeɪʃ(ə)n/ n. [F *certificat* or med.L *certificatum* f. *certificare*: see CERTIFY]

■ **Usage** The Certificate of Secondary Education was replaced in 1988 by the *General Certificate of Secondary Education* (GCSE).

certify /ˈsɜːtɪˌfaɪ/ v.tr. (**-ies, -ied**) **1** make a formal statement of; attest; attest to (*certified that he had witnessed the crime*). **2** declare by certificate (that a person is qualified or competent) (*certified as a trained bookkeeper*). **3** officially declare insane (*he should be certified*). □ **certified cheque** a cheque guaranteed by a bank. **certified mail** US = *recorded delivery* (see RECORD). [ME f. OF *certifier* f. med.L *certificare* f. L *certus* certain]

certitude /ˈsɜːtɪˌtjuːd/ n. a feeling of absolute certainty or conviction. [ME f. LL *certitudo* f. *certus* certain]

cerulean /səˈruːlɪən/ adj. & n. *literary* —adj. deep blue like a clear sky. —n. this colour. [L *caeruleus* sky-blue f. *caelum* sky]

cervelat /ˈsɜːvəˌlɑː, -ˌlæt/ n. a kind of smoked pork sausage. [obs. F f. It. *cervellata*]

cervical /sɜːˈvaɪk(ə)l, ˈsɜːvɪk(ə)l/ adj. Anat. **1** of or relating to the neck (*cervical vertebrae*). **2** of or relating to the cervix. □ **cervical screening** examination of a large number of apparently healthy women for cervical cancer. **cervical smear** a specimen of cellular material from the neck of the womb for detection of cancer. [F *cervical* or mod.L *cervicalis* f. L *cervix -icis* neck]

cervix /ˈsɜːvɪks/ n. (pl. **cervices** /-ˌsiːz/) Anat. **1** the neck. **2** any necklike structure, esp. the neck of the womb. [L]

Cesarean (also **Cesarian**) US var. of CAESAREAN.

cesium US var. of CAESIUM.

cessation /seˈseɪʃ(ə)n/ n. **1** a ceasing (*cessation of the truce*). **2** a pause (*resumed fighting after the cessation*). [ME f. L *cessatio* f. *cessare* CEASE]

cession /ˈseʃ(ə)n/ n. **1** (often foll. by *of*) the ceding or giving up (of rights, property, and esp. of territory by a State). **2** the territory etc. so ceded. [ME f. OF *cession* or L *cessio* f. *cedere cess-* go away]

cesspit /ˈsespɪt/ n. **1** a pit for the disposal of refuse. **2** = CESSPOOL. [*cess* in CESSPOOL + PIT¹]

cesspool /ˈsespuːl/ n. **1** an underground container for the temporary storage of liquid waste or sewage. **2** a centre of corruption, depravity, etc. [perh. alt., after POOL¹, f. earlier *cesperalle*, f. *suspiral* vent, water-pipe, f. OF *souspirail* air-hole f. L *suspirare* breathe up, sigh (as SUB-, *spirare* breathe)]

cetacean /sɪˈteɪʃ(ə)n/ n. & adj. —n. any marine mammal of the order Cetacea with streamlined hairless body and dorsal blowhole for breathing, including whales, dolphins, and porpoises. —adj. of cetaceans. □ **cetaceous** adj. [mod.L *Cetacea* f. L *cetus* f. Gk *kētos* whale]

cetane /ˈsiːteɪn/ n. Chem. a colourless liquid hydrocarbon of the alkane series used in standardizing ratings of diesel fuel. [f. SPERMACETI after *methane* etc.]

Cf symb. Chem. the element californium.

cf. abbr. compare. [L *confer* imper. of *conferre* compare]

c.f. abbr. carried forward.

CFC abbr. Chem. chloro-fluorocarbon, any of various usu. gaseous compounds of carbon, hydrogen, chlorine, and fluorine, used in refrigerants, aerosol propellants, etc., and thought to be harmful to the ozone layer in the earth's atmosphere.

CFE abbr. College of Further Education.

cg abbr. centigram(s).

CH abbr. (in the UK) Companion of Honour.

cha var. of CHAR³.

Chablis /ˈʃæblɪ/ n. (pl. same /-lɪz/) a dry white burgundy wine. [*Chablis* in E. France]

cha-cha /ˈtʃɑːtʃɑː/ (also **cha-cha-cha** /ˌtʃɑːtʃɑːˈtʃɑː/) n. & v. —n. **1** a ballroom dance with a Latin-American rhythm. **2** music for or in the rhythm of a cha-cha. —v.intr. (**cha-chas**, **cha-chaed** /-tʃɑːd/ or **cha-cha'd**, **cha-chaing** /-tʃɑːɪŋ/) dance the cha-cha. [Amer. Sp.]

chador /ˈtʃʌdə(r)/ n. (also **chadar**, **chuddar**) a large piece of cloth worn in some countries by Muslim women, wrapped around the body to leave only the face exposed. [Pers. *chador*, Hindi *chador*]

chafe /tʃeɪf/ v. & n. —v. **1** tr. & intr. make or become sore or damaged by rubbing. **2** tr. rub (esp. the skin to restore warmth or sensation). **3** tr. & intr. make or become annoyed; fret (*was chafed by the delay*). —n. **1 a** an act of chafing. **b** a sore resulting from this. **2** a state of annoyance. [ME f. OF *chaufer* ult. f. L *calefacere* f. *calēre* be hot + *facere* make]

chafer /ˈtʃeɪfə(r)/ n. any of various large slow-moving beetles of the family Scarabaeidae, esp. the cockchafer. [OE *ceafor*, *cefer* f. Gmc]

chaff /tʃɑːf/ n. & v. —n. **1** the husks of corn or other seed separated by winnowing or threshing. **2** chopped hay and straw used as fodder. **3** light-hearted joking; banter. **4** worthless things; rubbish. —v. **1** tr. & intr. tease; banter. **2** tr. chop (straw etc.). □ **chaffy** adj. [OE *ceaf*, *cæf* prob. f. Gmc: sense 3 of n. & 1 of v. perh. f. CHAFE]

chaffer /ˈtʃæfə(r)/ v. & n. —v.intr. haggle; bargain. —n. bargaining; haggling. □ **chafferer** n. [ME f. OE *ceapfaru* f. *ceap* bargain + *faru* journey]

chaffinch /ˈtʃæfɪntʃ/ n. Brit. a common European finch, *Fringilla coelebs*, the male of which has a blue-grey head with pinkish cheeks. [OE *ceaffinc*: see CHAFF, FINCH]

chafing-dish /ˈtʃeɪfɪŋ/ n. **1** a cooking pot with an outer pan of hot water, used for keeping food warm. **2** a dish with a spirit-lamp etc. for cooking at table. [obs. sense of CHAFE = warm]

chagrin /ˈʃægrɪn, ʃəˈɡriːn/ n. & v. —n. acute vexation or mortification. —v.tr. affect with chagrin. [F *chagrin(er)*, of uncert. orig.]

chain /tʃeɪn/ n. & v. —n. **1 a** a connected flexible series of esp. metal links as decoration or for a practical purpose. **b** something resembling this (*formed a human chain*). **2** (in pl.) **a** fetters used to confine prisoners. **b** any restraining force. **3** a sequence, series, or set (*chain of events*; *mountain chain*). **4** a group of associated hotels, shops, newspapers, etc. **5** a badge of office in the form of a chain worn round the neck (*mayoral chain*). **6 a** a jointed measuring-line consisting of linked metal rods. **b** its length (66 ft.). —v.tr. **1** (often foll. by *up*) secure or confine with a chain. **2** confine or restrict (a person) (*is chained to the office*). □ **chain-armour** armour made of interlaced rings. **chain bridge** a suspension bridge on chains. **chain-gang** a team of convicts chained together and forced to work in the open air. **chain-letter** one of a sequence of letters the recipient of which is requested to send copies to a specific number of other people. **chain-link** made of wire in a diamond-shaped mesh (*chain-link fencing*). **chain-mail** = *chain-armour*. **chain reaction 1** Physics a self-sustaining nuclear reaction, esp. one in which a neutron from a fission reaction initiates a series of these reactions. **2** Chem. a self-sustaining molecular reaction in which intermediate products initiate further reactions. **3** a series of events, each caused by the previous one. **chain-saw** a motor-driven saw with teeth on an endless chain. **chain-smoker** a person who smokes continually, esp. one who lights a cigarette etc. from the stub of the last one smoked. **chain store** one of a series of shops owned by one firm and selling the same sort of goods. [ME f. OF cha(e)ine f. L catena]

chair /tʃeə(r)/ n. & v. —n. 1 a separate seat for one person, of various forms, usu. having a back and four legs. 2 a a professorship. b a seat of authority, esp. on a board of directors. 3 a a chairperson. b the seat or office of a chairperson (will you take the chair?; I'm in the chair). 4 US = electric chair. —v.tr. 1 act as chairperson of or preside over (a meeting). 2 Brit. carry (a person) aloft in a chair or in a sitting position, in triumph. 3 install in a chair, esp. as a position of authority. □ **chair-lift** a series of chairs on an endless cable for carrying passengers up and down a mountain etc. **take a chair** sit down. [ME f. AF chaere, OF chaiere f. L cathedra: see CATHEDRAL]

chairman /ˈtʃeəmən/ n. (pl. -men; fem. **chairwoman**, pl. -women) 1 a person chosen to preside over a meeting. 2 the permanent president of a committee, a board of directors, a firm, etc. 3 the master of ceremonies at an entertainment etc. □ **chairmanship** n.

chairperson /ˈtʃeəˌpɜːs(ə)n/ n. a chairman or chairwoman (used as a neutral alternative).

chaise /ʃeɪz/ n. esp. hist. a horse-drawn carriage for one or two persons, esp. one with an open top and two wheels. [F var. of chaire, formed as CHAIR]

chaise longue /ʃeɪz ˈlɒŋg/ n. a sofa with only one arm rest. [F, lit. long chair]

chalcedony /kælˈsedənɪ/ n. a type of quartz occurring in several different forms, e.g. onyx, agate, tiger's eye, etc. □ **chalcedonic** /ˌkælsɪˈdɒnɪk/ adj. [ME f. L c(h)alcedonius f. Gk khalkēdōn]

chalet /ˈʃæleɪ/ n. 1 a small suburban house or bungalow, esp. with an overhanging roof. 2 a small, usu. wooden, hut or house on a beach or in a holiday camp. 3 a Swiss cowherd's hut, or wooden cottage, with overhanging eaves. [Swiss F]

chalice /ˈtʃælɪs/ n. 1 literary a goblet. 2 a wine-cup used in the Communion service. [ME f. OF f. L calix -icis cup]

chalk /tʃɔːk/ n. & v. —n. 1 a white soft earthy limestone (calcium carbonate) formed from the skeletal remains of sea creatures. 2 a a similar substance (calcium sulphate), sometimes coloured, used for writing or drawing. b a piece of this (a box of chalks). 3 a series of strata consisting mainly of chalk. 4 = French chalk. —v.tr. 1 rub, mark, draw, or write with chalk. 2 (foll. by up) a write or record with chalk. b register (a success etc.). c charge (to an account). □ **by a long chalk** Brit. by far (from the use of chalk to mark the score in games). **chalk out** sketch or plan a thing to be accomplished. **chalk-pit** a quarry in which chalk is dug. **chalk-stripe** a pattern of thin white stripes on a dark background. **chalk-striped** having chalk-stripes. [OE cealc ult. f. WG f. L CALX]

chalkboard /ˈtʃɔːkbɔːd/ n. US = BLACKBOARD.

chalky /ˈtʃɔːkɪ/ adj. (**chalkier**, **chalkiest**) 1 abounding in chalk. 2 white as chalk. □ **chalkiness** n.

challenge /ˈtʃælɪndʒ/ n. & v. —n. 1 a a summons to take part in a contest or a trial of strength etc., esp. to a duel. b a summons to prove or justify something. 2 a demanding or difficult task (rose to the challenge of the new job). 3 Law an

objection made to a jury member. 4 a call to respond, esp. a sentry's call for a password etc. 5 an invitation to a sporting contest, esp. one issued to a reigning champion. —v.tr. 1 (often foll. by to + infin.) a invite to take part in a contest, game, debate, duel, etc. b invite to prove or justify something. 2 dispute, deny (I challenge that remark). 3 a stretch, stimulate (challenges him to produce his best). b (as **challenging** adj.) demanding; stimulatingly difficult. 4 (of a sentry) call to respond. 5 claim (attention, etc.). 6 Law object to (a jury member, evidence, etc.). □ **challengeable** /-dʒəb(ə)l/ adj. **challenger** n. [ME f. OF c(h)alenge, c(h)alenger f. L calumnia calumniari calumny]

challis /ˈʃælɪs, ˈʃælɪ/ n. a lightweight soft clothing fabric. [perh. f. a surname]

chalybeate /kəˈlɪbɪət/ adj. (of mineral water etc.) impregnated with iron salts. [mod.L chalybeatus f. L chalybs f. Gk khalups -ubos steel]

chamber /ˈtʃeɪmbə(r)/ n. 1 a a hall used by a legislative or judicial body. b the body that meets in it. c any of the houses of a parliament (Chamber of Deputies; second chamber). 2 (in pl.) Brit. Law a rooms used by a barrister or group of barristers, esp. in the Inns of Court. b a judge's room used for hearing cases not needing to be taken in court. 3 poet. or archaic a room, esp. a bedroom. 4 Mus. (attrib.) of or for a small group of instruments (chamber orchestra; chamber music). 5 an enclosed space in machinery etc. (esp. the part of a gun-bore that contains the charge). 6 a a cavity in a plant or in the body of an animal. b a compartment in a structure. □ **Chamber of Commerce** an association to promote local commercial interests. **chamber-pot** a receptacle for urine etc., used in a bedroom. [ME f. OF chambre f. L CAMERA]

chamberlain /ˈtʃeɪmbəlɪn/ n. 1 an officer managing the household of a sovereign or a great noble. 2 the treasurer of a corporation etc. □ **Lord Chamberlain (of the Household)** the official in charge of the Royal Household, formerly the licenser of plays. **Lord Great Chamberlain of England** the hereditary holder of a ceremonial office. □ **chamberlainship** n. [ME f. OF chamberlain etc. f. Frank. f. L camera CAMERA]

chambermaid /ˈtʃeɪmbəˌmeɪd/ n. 1 a housemaid at a hotel etc. 2 US a housemaid.

chambray /ˈʃæmbreɪ/ n. a linen-finished gingham cloth with a white weft and a coloured warp. [irreg. f. Cambrai: see CAMBRIC]

chameleon /kəˈmiːlɪən/ n. 1 any of a family of small lizards having grasping tails, long tongues, protruding eyes, and the power of changing colour. 2 a variable or inconstant person. □ **chameleonic** /-ˈɒnɪk/ adj. [ME f. L f. Gk khamaileōn f. khamai on the ground + leōn lion]

chamfer /ˈtʃæmfə(r)/ v. & n. —v.tr. bevel symmetrically (a right-angled edge or corner). —n. a bevelled surface at an edge or corner. [back-form. f. chamfering f. F chamfrain f. chant edge (CANT²) + fraint broken f. OF fraindre break f. L frangere]

chamois /ˈʃæmwɑː/ n. (pl. same /-wɑːz/) 1 an agile goat antelope, Rupicapra rupicapra, native to the mountains of Europe and Asia. 2 /ˈʃæmɪ, ˈʃæmwɑː/ (in full **chamois leather**) a soft pliable leather from sheep, goats, deer, etc. b a piece of this for polishing etc. [F: cf. Gallo-Roman *camox*]

chamomile var. of CAMOMILE.

champ[1] *v. & n.* —*v.* **1** *tr.* & *intr.* munch or chew noisily. **2** *tr.* (of a horse etc.) work (the bit) noisily between the teeth. **3** *intr.* fret with impatience (*is champing to be away*). —*n.* a chewing noise or motion. □ **champ at the bit** be restlessly impatient. [prob. imit.]

champ[2] *n. sl.* a champion. [abbr.]

champagne /ʃæm'peɪn/ *n.* **1 a** a white sparkling wine from Champagne. **b** (loosely) a similar wine from elsewhere. **2** a pale cream or straw colour. [*Champagne*, former province in E. France]

■ **Usage** The use of this word in sense 1b is, strictly speaking, incorrect.

---

champion /'tʃæmpɪən/ *n., v., adj., & adv.* —*n.* **1** (often *attrib.*) a person (esp. in a sport or game), an animal, plant, etc., that has defeated or surpassed all rivals in a competition etc. **2** a person who fights or argues for a cause or on behalf of another person. —*v.tr.* support the cause of, defend, argue in favour of. —*adj. colloq.* or *dial.* first-class, splendid. —*adv. colloq.* or *dial.* splendidly, well. [ME f. OF f. med.L *campio -onis* fighter f. L *campus* field]

championship /'tʃæmpɪənʃɪp/ *n.* **1** (often in *pl.*) a contest for the position of champion in a sport etc. **2** the position of champion over all rivals. **3** the advocacy or defence (of a cause etc.).

chance /tʃɑːns/ *n., adj., & v.* —*n.* **1 a** a possibility (*just a chance we will catch the train*). **b** (often in *pl.*) probability (*the chances are against it*). **2** a risk (*have to take a chance*). **3 a** an undesigned occurrence (*just a chance that they met*). **b** the absence of design or discoverable cause (*here merely because of chance*). **4** an opportunity (*didn't have a chance to speak to him*). **5** the way things happen; fortune; luck (*we'll just leave it to chance*). **6** (often **Chance**) the course of events regarded as a power; fate. —*adj.* fortuitous, accidental (*a chance meeting*). —*v.* **1** *tr. colloq.* risk (*we'll chance it and go*). **2** *intr.* (often foll. by *that* + clause, or *to* + infin.) happen without intention (*it chanced that I found it*; *I chanced to find it*). □ **by any chance** as it happens; perhaps. **by chance** without design; unintentionally. **chance one's arm** make an attempt though unlikely to succeed. **chance on** (or **upon**) happen to find, meet, etc. **game of chance** a game decided by luck, not skill. **the off chance** the slight possibility. **on the chance** (often foll. by *of*, or *that* + clause) in view of the possibility. **stand a chance** have a prospect of success etc. **take a chance** (or **chances**) behave riskily; risk failure. **take a** (or **one's**) **chance on** (or **with**) consent to take the consequences of; trust to luck. [ME f. AF *ch(e)aunce*, OF *chëance chëoir* fall out. f. L *cadere*]

chancel /'tʃɑːns(ə)l/ *n.* the part of a church near the altar. [ME f. OF f. L *cancelli* lattice]

chancellery /'tʃɑːnsələrɪ/ *n.* (*pl.* **-ies**) **1 a** the position, office, staff, department, etc., of a chancellor. **b** the official residence of a chancellor. **2** US an office attached to an embassy or consulate. [ME f. OF *chancellerie* (as CHANCELLOR)]

chancellor /'tʃɑːnsələ(r)/ *n.* **1** a State or legal official of various kinds. **2** the head of the government in some European countries. **3** the non-resident honorary head of a university. □ **Chancellor of the Exchequer** the finance minister of the United Kingdom. **Lord** (or **Lord High**) **Chancellor** an officer presiding in the House of Lords, the Chancery Division, or the Court of Appeal. □ **chancellorship** *n.* [OE f. AF *c(h)anceler*, OF *-ier* f. LL *cancellarius* porter, secretary, f. *cancelli* lattice]

chancery /'tʃɑːnsərɪ/ *n.* (*pl.* **-ies**) **1** Law (**Chancery**) the Lord Chancellor's court, a division of the High Court of Justice. **2** an office attached to an embassy or consulate. **3** a public record office. [ME, contracted f. CHANCELLERY]

chancre /'ʃæŋkə(r)/ *n.* a painless ulcer developing in venereal disease etc. [F f. L CANCER]

chancy /'tʃɑːnsɪ/ *adj.* (**chancier**, **chanciest**) subject to chance; uncertain; risky. □ **chancily** *adv.* **chanciness** *n.*

chandelier /ˌʃændɪ'lɪə(r)/ *n.* an ornamental branched hanging support for several candles or electric light bulbs. [F (chandelle f. as CANDLE)]

chandler /'tʃɑːndlə(r)/ *n.* a dealer in candles, oil, soap, paint, groceries, etc. □ **corn chandler** a dealer in corn. **ship** (or **ship's**) **chandler** a dealer in cordage, canvas, etc. [ME f. AF *chaundeler*, OF *chandelier* (as CANDLE)]

chandlery /'tʃɑːndlərɪ/ *n.* the goods sold by a chandler.

change /tʃeɪndʒ/ *n. & v.* —*n.* **1 a** the act or an instance of making or becoming different. **b** an alteration or modification (*the change in her expression*). **2 a** money given in exchange for money in larger units or a different currency. **b** money returned as the balance of that given in payment. **c** = *small change*. **3** a new experience; variety (*fancied a change*; *for a change*). **4 a** the substitution of one thing for another; an exchange (*change of scene*). **b** a set of clothes etc. put on in place of another. **5** (in full **change of life**) *colloq.* the menopause. **6** (usu. in *pl.*) the different orders in which a peal of bells can be rung. —*v.* **1** *tr.* & *intr.* undergo, show, or subject to change; make or become different (*the wig changed his appearance*; *changed from a frog into a prince*). **2** *tr.* **a** take or use another instead of; go from one to another (*change one's socks*; *changed trains*). **b** (usu. foll. by *for*) give up or get rid of in exchange (*changed the car for a van*). **3** *tr.* **a** give or get change in smaller denominations for (*can you change a ten-pound note?*). **b** (foll. by *for*) exchange (a sum of money) for (*changed his dollars for pounds*). **4** *tr.* & *intr.* put fresh clothes or coverings on (*changed into something loose*). **5** *tr.* (often foll. by *with*) give and receive, exchange (*changed places with him*; *we changed places*). **6** *intr.* change trains etc. (*changed at Crewe*). □ **change down** engage a lower gear in a vehicle. **change gear** engage a different gear in a vehicle. **change hands 1** pass to a different owner. **2** substitute one hand for another. **change one's mind** adopt a different opinion or plan. **change of air** a different climate; variety. **change of heart** a conversion to a different view. **change over** change from one system or situation to another. **change-over** *n.* such a change. **change step** begin to keep step with the opposite leg when marching etc. **change the subject** begin talking of something different. **change one's tune 1** voice a different opinion from that expressed previously. **2** change one's style of language or manner, esp. from an insolent to a respectful tone. **change up** engage a higher gear in a vehicle. **get no change out of** sl. **1** fail to get information from. **2** fail to get the better of (in business etc.). **ring the changes (on)** vary the ways of expressing, arranging, or doing something. □ **changeful** adj. **changer** n. [ME f. AF chaunge, OF change, changer f. LL cambiare, L cambiare barter, prob. of Celt. orig.]

changeable /ˈtʃeɪndʒəb(ə)l/ adj. **1** irregular, inconstant. **2** that can change or be changed. □ **changeability** /-ˈbɪlɪtɪ/ n. **changeableness** n. **changeably** adv. [ME f. OF, formed as CHANGE]

changeless /ˈtʃeɪndʒlɪs/ adj. unchanging. □ **changelessly** adv. **changelessness** n.

changeling /ˈtʃeɪndʒlɪŋ/ n. a child believed to be substituted for another by stealth, esp. an elf-child left by fairies.

channel /ˈtʃæn(ə)l/ n. & v. —n. **1 a** a length of water wider than a strait, joining two larger areas, esp. seas. **b** (**the Channel**) the English Channel between Britain and France. **2** a medium of communication; an agency for conveying information (through the usual channels). **3** Broadcasting **a** a band of frequencies used in radio and television transmission, esp. as used by a particular station. **b** a service or station using this. **4** the course in which anything moves; a direction. **5 a** a natural or artificial hollow bed of water. **b** the navigable part of a waterway. **6** a tubular passage for liquid. **7** Electronics a lengthwise strip on recording tape etc. **8** a groove or a flute, esp. in a column. —v.tr. (**channelled**, **channelling**; US **channeled**, **channeling**) **1** guide, direct (channelled them through customs). **2** form channels in; groove. [ME f. OF chanel f. L canalis CANAL]

channelize /ˈtʃænəˌlaɪz/ v.tr. (also **-ise**) convey in, or as if in, a channel; guide.

chant /tʃɑːnt/ n. & v. —n. **1** a spoken singsong phrase, esp. one performed in unison by a crowd etc. **2** Mus. **a** a short musical passage in two or more phrases used for singing unmetrical words, e.g. psalms, canticles. **b** the psalm or canticle so sung. —v.tr. & intr. **1** talk or repeat monotonously (a crowd chanting slogans). **2** sing or intone (a psalm etc.). [ME (orig. as verb) f. OF chanter sing f. L cantare frequent. of canere cant- sing]

chanter /ˈtʃɑːntə(r)/ n. Mus. the melody-pipe, with finger-holes, of a bagpipe.

chanterelle /ˌtʃæntəˈrel/ n. an edible fungus, Cantharellus cibarius, with a yellow funnel-shaped cap. [F f. mod.L cantharellus dimin. of cantharus f. Gk kantharos a kind of drinking vessel]

chanteuse /ʃɑːnˈtɜːz/ n. a female singer of popular songs. [F]

chanticleer /ˌtʃæntɪˈklɪə(r), ˌtʃɑːn-, ˌʃæn-, ˌʃɑːn-/ n. literary a name given to a domestic cock, esp. in fairy tales etc. [ME f. OF chantecler (as CHANT, CLEAR), a name in Reynard the Fox]

chantry /ˈtʃɑːntrɪ/ n. (pl. **-ies**) **1** an endowment for a priest or priests to celebrate masses for the founder's soul. **2** the priests, chapel, altar, etc., endowed. [ME f. AF chaunterie, OF chanterie f. chanter CHANT]

chanty var. of SHANTY².

Chanukkah var. of HANUKKAH.

chaos /ˈkeɪɒs/ n. **1** utter confusion. **2** the formless matter supposed to have existed before the creation of the universe. □ **chaos theory** a branch of mathematics dealing with the apparently chaotic behaviour of dynamic systems that are highly sensitive to small changes in external conditions. □ **chaotic** /keɪˈɒtɪk/ adj. **chaotically** /-ˈɒtɪkəlɪ/ adv. [F or L f. Gk khaos: -otic after erotic etc.]

chap¹ v. & n. —v. (**chapped**, **chapping**) **1** intr. (esp. of the skin; also of dry ground etc.) crack in fissures, esp. because of exposure and dryness. **2** tr. (of the wind, cold, etc.) cause to chap. —n. (usu. in pl.) a crack in the skin. [ME, perh. rel. to MLG, MDu. kappen chop off]

chap² n. colloq. a man; a boy; a fellow. [abbr. of CHAPMAN]

chap³ n. the lower jaw or half of the cheek, esp. of a pig as food. □ **chap-fallen** dispirited, dejected (with the lower jaw hanging). [16th c.: var. of CHOP², of unkn. orig.]

chaparejos /ˌʃæpəˈreɪɒs, ˌtʃæp-/ n.pl. US a cowboy's leather protection for the front of the legs. [Mex. Sp.]

chaparral /ˌtʃæpəˈræl, ˌʃæp-/ n. US dense tangled brushwood; undergrowth. [Sp. f. chaparra evergreen oak]

chapati /tʃəˈpɑːtɪ, -ˈpætɪ/ n. (also **chapati**, **chupatty**) (pl. **-is** or **chupatties**) Ind. a flat thin cake of unleavened wholemeal bread. [Hindi capātī]

chapel /ˈtʃæp(ə)l/ n. **1 a** a place for private Christian worship in a large church or esp. a cathedral, with its own altar and dedication (Lady chapel). **b** a place of Christian worship attached to a private house or institution. **2** Brit. **a** a place of worship for nonconformist bodies. **b** (predic.) an attender at or believer in nonconformist worship (they are strictly chapel). **c** a chapel service. **d** attendance at a chapel. **3** the members or branch of a printers' or journalists' trade union. □ **father** (or **mother**) **of chapel** (or **the chapel**) the shop steward of a printers' chapel. [ME f. OF chapele f. med.L cappella dimin. of cappa cloak: the first chapel was a sanctuary in which St Martin's sacred cloak (cappella) was preserved]

chaperon /ˈʃæpəˌrəʊn/ n. & v. (also **chaperone**) —n. **1** a person, esp. an older woman, who ensures propriety by accompanying a young unmarried woman on social occasions. **2** a person who takes charge of esp. young people in public. —v.tr. act as a chaperon to. □ **chaperonage** /ˈʃæpərənɪdʒ/ n. [F. = hood, chaperon, dimin. of chape cope, formed as CAP]

chaplain /ˈtʃæplɪn/ n. a member of the clergy attached to a private chapel, institution, ship, regiment, etc. □ **chaplaincy** n. (pl. **-ies**). [ME f. AF & OF c(h)apelain f. med.L cappellanus, orig. custodian of the cloak of St Martin: see CHAPEL]

chaplet /ˈtʃæplɪt/ n. **1** a garland or circlet for the head. **2** a string of 55 beads (one-third of the rosary number) for counting prayers. □ **chapleted** adj. [ME f. OF chapelet, ult. f. LL cappa CAP]

chapman /ˈtʃæpmən/ n. (pl. **-men**) hist. a pedlar. [OE cēapman f. cēap barter]

chappal /ˈtʃæp(ə)l/ n. an Indian sandal, usu. of leather. [Hindi]

chappie /ˈtʃæpɪ/ n. colloq. = CHAP².

chaps /tʃæps, ʃæps/ n. = CHAPAREJOS. [abbr.]

chapstick /ˈtʃæpstɪk/ n. US a cylinder of a cosmetic substance used to prevent chapping of the lips.

chapter /ˈtʃæptə(r)/ n. **1** a main division of a book. **2** a period of time (in a person's life, a nation's history, etc.). **3** a series or sequence (a *chapter of misfortunes*). **4** **a** the canons of a cathedral or other religious community or knightly order. **b** a meeting of these. **5** *US* a local branch of a society. □ **chapter house 1** a building used for the meetings of a chapter. **2** *US* the place where a college fraternity or sorority meets. [ME f. OF *chapitre* f. L *capitulum* dimin. of *caput -itis* head]

char¹ v.tr. & intr. (**charred**, **charring**) **1** make or become black by burning; scorch. **2** burn or be burnt to charcoal. [app. back-form. f. CHARCOAL]

char² n. & v. Brit. colloq. —n. = CHARWOMAN. —v.intr. (**charred**, **charring**) work as a charwoman. [earlier *chare* f. OE *cerr* a turn, *cierran* to turn]

char³ n. (also **cha** /tʃɑː/) Brit. sl. tea. [Chin. *cha*]

char⁴ n. (also **charr**) (pl. same) any small troutlike fish of the genus *Salvelinus*. [17th c.: orig. unkn.]

charabanc /ˈʃærəˌbæŋ/ n. Brit. hist. an early form of motor coach. [F *char à bancs* seated carriage]

character /ˈkærɪktə(r)/ n. **1** the collective qualities or characteristics, esp. mental and moral, that distinguish a person or thing. **2 a** moral strength (*has a weak character*). **b** reputation, esp. good reputation. **3 a** a person in a novel, play, etc. **b** a part played by an actor; a role. **4** colloq. a person, esp. an eccentric or outstanding individual (*he's a real character*). **5 a** a printed or written letter, symbol, or distinctive mark (*Chinese characters*). **b** Computing any of a group of symbols representing a letter etc. **6** a written description of a person's qualities; a testimonial. **7** a characteristic (esp. of a biological species). □ **character assassination** a malicious attempt to harm or destroy a person's good reputation. **in** (or **out of**) **character** consistent (or inconsistent) with a person's character. □ **characterful** adj. **characterfully** adv. **characterless** adj. [ME f. OF *caractere* f. L *character* f. Gk *kharaktēr* stamp, impress]

characteristic /ˌkærɪktəˈrɪstɪk/ adj. & n. —adj. typical, distinctive (*with characteristic expertise*). —n. a characteristic feature or quality. □ **characteristically** adv. [F *caractéristique* or med.L *characterizare* f. Gk *kharaktērizō*]

characterize /ˈkærɪktəˌraɪz/ v.tr. (also -**ise**) **1 a** describe the character of. **b** (foll. by *as*) describe as. **2** be characteristic of. **3** impart character to. □ **characterization** /-ˈzeɪʃ(ə)n/ n. [F *caractériser* or med.L *characterizare* f. Gk *kharaktērizō*]

charade /ʃəˈrɑːd/ n. **1** (usu. in pl., treated as sing.) a game of guessing a word from written or acted clues. **2** an absurd pretence. [F f. mod.Prov. *charrado* conversation f. *charra* chatter]

charcoal /ˈtʃɑːkəʊl/ n. **1 a** an amorphous form of carbon consisting of a porous black residue from partially burnt wood, bones, etc. **b** (usu. in pl.) a piece of this used for drawing. **2** a drawing in charcoal. **3** (in full **charcoal grey**) a dark grey colour. [ME COAL = charcoal: first element perh. *chare* turn (cf. CHAR¹, CHAR²)]

chard n. a kind of beet, *Beta vulgaris*, with edible broad white leaf-stalks and green blades. [F *carde*, and *chardon* thistle, ult. f. L *cardu(u)s*]

charge v. & n. —v. **1** tr. **a** ask (an amount) as a price (*charges £5 a ticket*). **b** ask (a person) for an

amount as a price (*you forgot to charge me*). **2** tr. **a** (foll. by *to, up to*) debit the cost of to (a person or account) (*charge it to my account; charge it up to me*). **b** debit (a person or an account) (*bought a new car and charged the company*). **3** tr. **a** (often foll. by *with*) accuse (of an offence) (*charged him with theft*). **b** (foll. by *that* + clause) make an accusation that. **4** tr. (foll. by *to* + infin.) instruct or urge. **5** (foll. by *with*) **a** tr. entrust with. **b** refl. undertake. **6 a** intr. make a rushing attack; rush headlong. **b** tr. make a rushing attack on; throw oneself against. **7** tr. (often foll. by *up*) **a** give an electric charge to (a body). **b** store energy in (a battery). **8** tr. (often foll. by *with*) load or fill (a vessel, gun, etc.) to the full or proper extent. **9** tr. (usu. as **charged** adj.) **a** (foll. by *with*) saturated with (*air charged with vapour*). **b** (usu. foll. by *with*) pervaded (with strong feelings etc.) (*atmosphere charged with emotion*). —n. **1 a** a price asked for goods or services. **b** a financial liability or commitment. **2** an accusation, esp. against a prisoner brought to trial. **3 a** a task, duty, or commission. **b** care, custody, responsible possession. **c** a person or thing entrusted. **4 a** an impetuous rush or attack, esp. in a battle. **b** the signal for this. **5** the appropriate amount of material to be put into a receptacle, mechanism, etc. at one time, esp. of explosive for a gun. **6 a** a property of matter that is a consequence of the interaction between its constituent particles and exists in a positive or negative form, causing electrical phenomena. **b** the quantity of this carried by a body. **c** energy stored chemically for conversion into electricity. **d** the process of charging a battery. **7** an exhortation; directions, orders. **8** Heraldry a device; a bearing. □ **charge account** *US* a credit account at a shop etc. **charge card** a credit card for which the account must be paid in full when a statement is issued. **charge-hand** Brit. a worker, ranking below a foreman, in charge of others on a particular job. **charge-nurse** Brit. a nurse in charge of a ward etc. **charge-sheet** Brit. a record of cases and charges made at a police station. **free of charge** gratis. **give a person in charge** hand a person over to the police. **in charge** having command. **lay to a person's charge** accuse a person of. **put a person on a charge** charge a person with a specified offence. **take charge** (often foll. by *of*) assume control or direction. □ **chargeable** adj. [ME f. OF *charger* f. LL *car(ri)care* load f. L *carrus* CAR]

chargé d'affaires /ˌʃɑːʒeɪ dæˈfeə(r)/ n. (also **chargé**) (pl. **chargés** pronunc. same) **1** an ambassador's deputy. **2** an envoy to a minor country. [F, = in charge (of affairs)]

charger¹ /ˈtʃɑːdʒə(r)/ n. **1 a** a cavalry horse. **b** poet. any horse. **2** an apparatus for charging a battery. **3** a person or thing that charges.

charger² /ˈtʃɑːdʒə(r)/ n. archaic a large flat dish. [ME f. AF *chargeour*]

chariot /ˈtʃærɪət/ n. **1** hist. a two-wheeled vehicle drawn by horses, used in ancient warfare and racing. **2** poet. a stately or triumphal vehicle. [ME f. OF, augment. of *char* CAR]

charioteer /ˌtʃærɪəˈtɪə(r)/ n. a chariot-driver.

charisma /kəˈrɪzmə/ n. (pl. **charismata** /kəˈrɪzmətə/) **1 a** the ability to inspire followers with devotion and enthusiasm. **b** an attractive aura; great charm. **2** a divinely conferred power or talent. [eccl.L f. Gk *kharisma* f. *kharis* favour, grace]

charismatic /ˌkærɪzˈmætɪk/ *adj.* **1** having charisma; inspiring enthusiasm. **2** (of Christian worship) characterized by spontaneity, ecstatic utterances, etc. □ **charismatically** *adv.*

charitable /ˈtʃærɪtəb(ə)l/ *adj.* **1** generous in giving to those in need. **2** of, relating to, or connected with a charity or charities. **3** apt to judge favourably of persons, acts, and motives. □ **charitableness** *n.* **charitably** *adv.* [ME f. OF f. *charité* CHARITY]

charity /ˈtʃærɪtɪ/ *n.* (*pl.* **-ies**) **1 a** a giving voluntarily to those in need. **b** the help, esp. money, so given. **2** an institution or organization for helping those in need. **3 a** kindness, benevolence. **b** tolerance in judging others. **c** love of one's fellow men. [OE f. OF *charité* f. L *caritas -tatis* f. *carus* dear]

charlady /ˈtʃɑːˌleɪdɪ/ *n.* (*pl.* **-ies**) = CHARWOMAN.

charlatan /ˈʃɑːlət(ə)n/ *n.* a person falsely claiming a special knowledge or skill. □ **charlatanism** *n.* **charlatanry** *n.* [F f. It. *ciarlatano* f. *ciarlare* babble]

Charles's Wain /ˌtʃɑːlzɪz ˈweɪn/ *n.* the constellation Ursa Major or its seven bright stars. [OE *Carles wægn* the wain of Carl (Charles the Great, Charlemagne), perh. by assoc. of the star Arcturus with legends of King Arthur and Charlemagne]

charleston /ˈtʃɑːlst(ə)n/ *n.* & *v.* (also **Charleston**) —*n.* a lively American dance of the 1920s with side-kicks from the knee. —*v.intr.* dance the charleston. [*Charleston* in S. Carolina, US]

charley horse /ˈtʃɑːlɪ/ *n.* US sl. stiffness or cramp in an arm or leg. [19th c.: orig. uncert.]

charlock /ˈtʃɑːlɒk/ *n.* a wild mustard, *Sinapis arvensis*, with yellow flowers. [OE *cerlic*, of unkn. orig.]

charlotte /ˈʃɑːlɒt/ *n.* a pudding made of stewed fruit with a casing or layers or covering of bread, cake, biscuits, or breadcrumbs (*apple charlotte*). [F]

charm /tʃɑːm/ *n.* & *v.* —*n.* **1 a** the power or quality of giving delight or arousing admiration. **b** fascination, attractiveness. **c** (usu. in *pl.*) an attractive or enticing quality. **2** a trinket on a bracelet etc. **3 a** an object, act, or word(s) supposedly having occult or magic power; a spell. **b** a thing worn to avert evil etc.; an amulet. **4** *Physics* a property of matter manifested by some elementary particles. —*v.tr.* **1** delight, captivate (*charmed by the performance*). **2** influence or protect as if by magic (*leads a charmed life*). **3 a** gain by charm (*charmed agreement out of him*). **b** influence by charm (*charmed her into consenting*). **4** cast a spell on, bewitch. □ **charmer** *n.* [ME f. OF *charme*, *charmer* f. L *carmen* song]

charming /ˈtʃɑːmɪŋ/ *adj.* **1** delightful, attractive, pleasing. **2** (often as *int.*) *iron.* expressing displeasure or disapproval. □ **charmingly** *adv.*

charmless /ˈtʃɑːmlɪs/ *adj.* lacking charm; unattractive. □ **charmlessly** *adv.* **charmlessness** *n.*

charnel-house /ˈtʃɑːn(ə)lˌhaʊs/ *n.* a house or vault in which dead bodies or bones are piled. [ME & OF *charnel* burying-place f. med.L *carnale* f. LL *carnalis* CARNAL]

charr var. of CHAR⁴.

chart /tʃɑːt/ *n.* & *v.* —*n.* **1** a geographical map or plan, esp. for navigation by sea or air. **2** a sheet

of information in the form of a table, graph, or diagram. **3** (usu. in *pl.*) *colloq.* a listing of the currently most popular gramophone records. —*v.tr.* make a chart of, map. [F *charte* f. L *charta* CARD¹]

charter /ˈtʃɑːtə(r)/ *n.* & *v.* —*n.* **1 a** a written grant of rights, by the sovereign or legislature, esp. the creation of a borough, company, university, etc. **b** a written constitution or description of an organization's functions etc. **2** a contract to hire an aircraft, ship, etc., for a special purpose. —*v.tr.* **1** grant a charter to. **2** hire (an aircraft, ship, etc.). □ **chartered accountant, engineer, librarian, surveyor,** etc. *Brit.* a member of a professional body that has a royal charter. **charter flight** a flight by a chartered aircraft. □ **charterer** *n.* [ME f. OF *chartre* f. L *chartula* dimin. of *charta* CARD¹]

Chartism /ˈtʃɑːtɪz(ə)m/ *n. hist.* the principles of the UK Parliamentary reform movement of 1837–48. □ **Chartist** *n.* [L *charta* charter + -ISM: name taken from the manifesto 'People's Charter']

chartreuse /ʃɑːˈtrɜːz/ *n.* **1** a pale green or yellow liqueur of brandy and aromatic herbs etc. **2** the pale yellow or pale green colour of this. [La Grande *Chartreuse* (Carthusian monastery near Grenoble)]

charwoman /ˈtʃɑːˌwʊmən/ *n.* (*pl.* **-women**) a woman employed as a cleaner in houses or offices.

chary /ˈtʃeərɪ/ *adj.* (**charier, chariest**) **1** cautious, wary (*chary of employing such people*). **2** sparing; ungenerous (*chary of giving praise*). **3** shy. □ **charily** *adv.* **chariness** *n.* [OE *cearig*]

Charybdis see SCYLLA AND CHARYBDIS.

chase¹ /tʃeɪs/ *v.* & *n.* —*v.* **1** *tr.* pursue in order to catch. **2** *tr.* (foll. by *from, out of, to,* etc.) drive. **3** *intr.* **a** (foll. by *after*) hurry in pursuit of (a person). **b** (foll. by *round* etc.) *colloq.* act or move about hurriedly. **4** *tr.* (usu. foll. by *up*) *colloq.* pursue (overdue work, payment, etc. or the person responsible for it). **5** *tr. colloq.* **a** try to attain. **b** court persistently and openly. —*n.* **1** pursuit. **2** unenclosed hunting-land. **3** (prec. by *the*) hunting, esp. as a sport. **4** an animal etc. that is pursued. **5** = STEEPLECHASE. [ME f. OF *chace chacier*, ult. f. L *capere* take]

chase² /tʃeɪs/ *v.tr.* emboss or engrave (metal). [app. f. earlier *enchase* f. F *enchâsser* (as EN-¹, CASE²)]

chaser /ˈtʃeɪsə(r)/ *n.* **1** a person or thing that chases. **2** a horse for steeplechasing. **3** *colloq.* a drink taken after another of a different kind, e.g. beer after spirits. **4** *US colloq.* an amorous pursuer of women.

chasm /ˈkæz(ə)m/ *n.* **1** a deep fissure or opening in the earth, rock, etc. **2** a wide difference of feeling, interests, etc.; a gulf. □ **chasmic** *adj.* [L *chasma* f. Gk *khasma* gaping hollow]

chassé /ˈʃæseɪ/ *n.* & *v.* —*n.* a gliding step in dancing. —*v.intr.* (**chasséd; chasséing**) make this step. [F, = chasing]

chassis /ˈʃæsɪ/ *n.* (*pl.* same /-sɪz/) **1** the base-frame of a motor vehicle, carriage, etc. **2** a frame to carry radio etc. components. [F *châssis* ult. f. L *capsa* CASE²]

chaste /tʃeɪst/ *adj.* **1** abstaining from extramarital, or from all, sexual intercourse. **2** (of behaviour, speech, etc.) pure, virtuous, decent. **3** (of artistic etc. style) simple, unadorned. □

chastely *adv.* **chasteness** *n.* [ME f. OF f. L *castus*]

chasten /ˈtʃeɪs(ə)n/ *v.tr.* **1** (esp. as **chastening**, **chastened** *adjs.*) subdue, restrain (*a chastening experience*; *chastened by his failure*). **2** discipline, punish. **3** moderate. □ **chastener** *n.* [obs. *chaste* (v.) f. OF *chastier* f. L *castigare* CASTIGATE]

chastise /tʃæsˈtaɪz/ *v.tr.* **1** rebuke or reprimand severely. **2** punish, esp. by beating. □ **chastisement** *n.* **chastiser** *n.* [ME, app. irreg. formed f. obs. verbs *chaste, chasty*: see CHASTEN]

chastity /ˈtʃæstɪtɪ/ *n.* **1** being chaste. **2** sexual abstinence; virginity. **3** simplicity of style or taste. □ **chastity belt** *hist.* a garment designed to prevent a woman from having sexual intercourse. [ME f. OF *chasteté* f. L *castitas -tatis* f. *castus* CHASTE]

chasuble /ˈtʃæzjʊb(ə)l/ *n.* a loose sleeveless usu. ornate outer vestment worn by a priest celebrating Mass or the Eucharist. [ME f. OF *chesible*, later *-uble*, ult. f. L *casula* hooded cloak, little cottage, dimin. of *casa* cottage]

chat *v. & n.* —*v.intr.* (**chatted, chatting**) talk in a light familiar way. —*n.* **1** informal conversation or talk. **2** an instance of this. □ **chat show** *Brit.* a television or radio programme in which celebrities are interviewed informally. **chat up** *Brit. colloq.* chat to, esp. flirtatiously or with an ulterior motive. [ME: shortening of CHATTER]

château /ˈʃætəʊ/ *n.* (*pl.* **châteaux** /-təʊz/) a large French country house or castle, often giving its name to wine made in its neighbourhood. [F f. OF *chastel* CASTLE]

chatelaine /ˈʃætəleɪn/ *n.* the mistress of a large house. [F *châtelaine*, fem. of *-ain* lord of a castle, f. med.L *castellanus*: see CASTLE]

chattel /ˈtʃæt(ə)l/ *n.* (usu. in *pl.*) a moveable possession; any possession or piece of property other than real estate or a freehold. □ **goods and chattels** personal possessions. [ME f. OF *chatel*: see CATTLE]

chatter /ˈtʃætə(r)/ *v. & n.* —*v.intr.* **1** talk quickly, incessantly, trivially, or indiscreetly. **2** (of a bird) emit short quick notes. **3** (of the teeth) click repeatedly together (usu. from cold). —*n.* chattering talk or sounds. □ **chatterer** *n.* **chattery** *adj.* [ME: imit.]

chatterbox /ˈtʃætəbɒks/ *n.* a talkative person.

chatty /ˈtʃætɪ/ *adj.* (**chattier, chattiest**) **1** fond of chatting; talkative. **2** resembling chat; informal and lively. □ **chattily** *adv.* **chattiness** *n.*

chauffeur /ˈʃəʊfə(r), -ˈfɜː(r)/ *n. & v.* —*n.* (*fem.* **chauffeuse** /-ˈfɜːz/) a person employed to drive a private or hired motor car. —*v.tr.* drive (a car or a person) as a chauffeur. [F, = stoker]

chautauqua /tʃɔːˈtɔːkwə, ʃɔː-/ *n.* *US* a summer school or similar educational course. [*Chautauqua* in New York State]

chauvinism /ˈʃəʊvɪˌnɪz(ə)m/ *n.* **1** exaggerated or aggressive patriotism. **2** excessive or prejudiced support or loyalty for one's cause or group or sex (*male chauvinism*). [*Chauvin*, a Napoleonic veteran in the Cogniards' *Cocarde Tricolore* (1831)]

chauvinist /ˈʃəʊvɪnɪst/ *n.* **1** a person exhibiting chauvinism. **2** (in full **male chauvinist**) a man showing excessive loyalty to men and prejudice against women. □ **chauvinistic** /-ˈnɪstɪk/ *adj.* **chauvinistically** /-ˈnɪstɪkəlɪ/ *adv.*

Ch.B. *abbr.* Bachelor of Surgery. [L *Chirurgiae Baccalaureus*]

cheap *adj. & adv.* —*adj.* **1** low in price; worth more than its cost (*a cheap holiday*; *cheap labour*). **2** charging low prices; offering good value. **3** of poor quality; inferior. **4 a** costing little effort or acquired by discreditable means and hence of little worth (*cheap popularity*; *a cheap joke*). **b** contemptible; despicable (*a cheap criminal*). —*adv.* cheaply (*got it cheap*). □ **dirt cheap** very cheap. **on the cheap** cheaply. □ **cheapish** *adj.* **cheaply** *adv.* **cheapness** *n.* [obs. phr. *good cheap* f. *cheap* a bargain f. OE *cēap* barter, ult. f. L *caupo* innkeeper]

cheapen /ˈtʃiːpən/ *v.tr. & intr.* make or become cheap or cheaper; depreciate, degrade.

cheapjack /ˈtʃiːpdʒæk/ *n. & adj.* —*n.* a seller of inferior goods at low prices. —*adj.* inferior, shoddy. [CHEAP + JACK]

cheapo /ˈtʃiːpəʊ/ *attrib.adj.* *sl.* cheap.

cheapskate /ˈtʃiːpskeɪt/ *n.* esp. *US colloq.* a mean or contemptible person.

cheat *v. & n.* —*v.* **1** *tr.* **a** (often foll. by *into, out of*) deceive or trick (*cheated into parting with his savings*). **b** (foll. by *of*) deprive of (*cheated of a chance to reply*). **2** *intr.* gain unfair advantage by deception or breaking rules, esp. in a game or examination. **3** *tr.* avoid (something undesirable) by luck or skill (*cheated the bad weather*). —*n.* **1** a person who cheats. **2** a trick, fraud, or deception. **3** an act of cheating. □ **cheat on** *colloq.* be sexually unfaithful to. □ **cheatingly** *adv.* [ME *chete* f. *achete*, var. of ESCHEAT]

cheater /ˈtʃiːtə(r)/ *n.* **1** a person who cheats. **2** (in *pl.*) *US sl.* spectacles.

check[1] *v., n., & int.* —*v.* **1** *tr.* (also *absol.*) **a** examine the accuracy, quality, or condition of. **b** (often foll. by *that* + clause) make sure; verify; establish to one's satisfaction (*checked that the doors were locked*; *checked the train times*). **2** *tr.* **a** stop or slow the motion of; curb, restrain (*progress was checked by bad weather*). **b** *colloq.* find fault with; rebuke. **3** *tr.* *Chess* move a piece into a position that directly threatens (the opposing king). **4** *intr.* *US* agree or correspond when compared. **5** *tr.* *US* mark with a tick etc. **6** *tr.* *US* deposit (luggage etc.) for storage or dispatch. —*n.* **1** a means or act of testing or ensuring accuracy, quality, satisfactory condition, etc. **2 a** a stopping or slowing of motion; a restraint on action. **b** a rebuff or rebuke. **c** a person or thing that restrains. **3** *Chess* (also as *int.*) **a** the exposure of a king to direct attack from an opposing piece. **b** an announcement of this by the attacking player. **4** *US* a bill in a restaurant. **5** esp. *US* a token of identification for left luggage etc. —*int.* *US* expressing assent or agreement. □ **check in 1** arrive or register at a hotel, airport, etc. **2** record the arrival of. **check-in** *n.* the act or place of checking in. **check into** register one's arrival at (a hotel etc.). **check-list** a list for reference and verification. **check off** mark on a list etc. as having been examined or dealt with. **check on** examine carefully or in detail; ascertain the truth about; keep a watch on (a person, work done, etc.). **check out 1** (often foll. by *of*) leave a hotel etc. with due formalities. **2** *US* investigate; examine for authenticity or suitability. **check over** examine for errors; verify. **check through** inspect or examine exhaustively; verify successive items of. **check up** ascertain, verify, make sure. **check-up** n. a thorough (esp. medical) examination. **check up on** = *check on*. **in check** under control, restrained. □ **checkable** adj. [ME f. OF *eschequier* play chess, give check to, and OF *eschec*, ult. f. Pers. *šāh* king]

check[2] n. **1** a pattern of small squares. **2** fabric having this pattern. [ME, prob. f. CHEQUER]

check[3] US var. of CHEQUE.

checked /tʃekt/ adj. having a check pattern.

checker[1] /ˈtʃekə(r)/ n. **1** a person or thing that verifies or examines, esp. in a factory etc. **2** US a cashier in a supermarket etc.

checker[2] /ˈtʃekə(r)/ n. **1** var. of CHEQUER. **2** US (in pl., usu. treated as *sing.*) the game of draughts.

checkerboard /ˈtʃekəbɔːd/ n. US = DRAUGHTBOARD.

checking account /ˈtʃekɪŋ/ n. US a current account at a bank. [CHECK[3]]

checkmate /ˈtʃekmeɪt/ n. & v. —n. **1** (also as *int.*) *Chess* a check from which a king cannot escape. **b** an announcement of this. **2** a defeat or deadlock. —v.tr. **1** *Chess* put into checkmate. **2** defeat; frustrate. [ME f. OF *eschec mat* f. Pers. *šāh māt* the king is dead]

checkout /ˈtʃekaʊt/ n. **1** an act of checking out. **2** a point at which goods are paid for in a supermarket etc.

checkpoint /ˈtʃekpɔɪnt/ n. a place, esp. a barrier or manned entrance, where documents, vehicles, etc., are inspected.

Cheddar /ˈtʃedə(r)/ n. a kind of firm smooth cheese orig. made in Cheddar in S. England.

cheek n. & v. —n. **1** a the side of the face below the eye. **b** the side-wall of the mouth. **2** a impertinent speech. **b** impertinence; cool confidence (*had the cheek to ask for more*). **3** sl. either buttock. —v.tr. speak impertinently to. □ **cheek-bone** the bone below the eye. **cheek by jowl** close together; intimate. **turn the other cheek** accept attack etc. meekly; refuse to retaliate. [OE *cē(a)ce*, *cēoce*]

cheeky /ˈtʃiːkɪ/ adj. (**cheekier**, **cheekiest**) impertinent, impudent. □ **cheekily** adv. **cheekiness** n.

cheep n. & v. —n. the weak shrill cry of a young bird. —v.intr. make such a cry. [imit.: cf. PEEP[2]]

cheer n. & v. —n. **1** a shout of encouragement or applause. **2** mood, disposition (*full of good cheer*). **3** (in pl.; as int.) *Brit. colloq.* a expressing good wishes on parting or before drinking. **b** expressing gratitude. —v. **1** tr. **a** applaud with shouts. **b** (usu. foll. by *on*) urge or encourage with shouts. **2** intr. shout for joy. **3** tr. gladden; comfort. □ **cheer-leader** a person who leads cheers of applause etc. **cheer up** make or become less depressed. [ME f. AF *chere* face etc., OF *chiere* f. LL *cara* face f. Gk *kara* head]

cheerful /ˈtʃɪəfʊl/ adj. **1** in good spirits, noticeably happy (*a cheerful disposition*). **2** bright, pleasant (*a cheerful room*). **3** willing, not reluctant. □ **cheerfully** adv. **cheerfulness** n.

cheerio /ˌtʃɪərɪˈəʊ/ int. *Brit. colloq.* expressing good wishes on parting or before drinking.

cheerless /ˈtʃɪəlɪs/ adj. gloomy, dreary, miserable. □ **cheerlessly** adv. **cheerlessness** n.

cheery /ˈtʃɪərɪ/ adj. (**cheerier**, **cheeriest**) lively; in good spirits; genial, cheering. □ **cheerily** adv. **cheeriness** n.

cheese[1] /tʃiːz/ n. **1** a a food made from the pressed curds of milk. **b** a complete cake of this

with rind. **2** a conserve having the consistency of soft cheese (*lemon cheese*). □ **cheese-paring** adj. stingy. —n. stinginess. **cheese plant** = Swiss cheese plant. **hard cheese** sl. bad luck. [OE *cēse* etc. ult. f. L *caseus*]

cheese[2] /tʃiːz/ v.tr. *Brit. sl.* (as **cheesed** adj.) (often foll. by *off*) bored, fed up. □ **cheese it** stop it, leave off. [19th c.: orig. unkn.]

cheese[3] /tʃiːz/ n. (also **big cheese**) sl. an important person. [perh. f. Hind. *chīz* thing]

cheeseboard /ˈtʃiːzbɔːd/ n. **1** a board from which cheese is served. **2** a selection of cheeses.

cheeseburger /ˈtʃiːzbɜːgə(r)/ n. a hamburger with cheese in or on it.

cheesecake /ˈtʃiːzkeɪk/ n. **1** a tart filled with sweetened curds etc. **2** sl. the portrayal of women in a sexually attractive manner.

cheesecloth /ˈtʃiːzklɒθ/ n. thin loosely woven cloth, used orig. for wrapping cheese.

cheesemonger /ˈtʃiːzˌmʌŋgə(r)/ n. a dealer in cheese, butter, etc.

cheesy /ˈtʃiːzɪ/ adj. (**cheesier**, **cheesiest**) **1** like cheese in taste, smell, appearance, etc. **2** sl. inferior; cheap and nasty. □ **cheesiness** n.

cheetah /ˈtʃiːtə/ n. a swift-running feline, Acinonyx jubatus, with a leopard-like spotted coat. [Hindi *cītā*, perh. f. Skr. *citraka* speckled]

chef /ʃef/ n. a (usu. male) cook, esp. the chief cook in a restaurant etc. [F, = head]

cheiro- comb. form var. of CHIRO-.

Chelsea bun /ˈtʃelsɪ/ n. a kind of currant bun in the form of a flat spiral. [*Chelsea* in London]

Chelsea pensioner /ˈtʃelsɪ/ n. an inmate of the Chelsea Royal Hospital for old or disabled soldiers.

chemi- comb. form var. of CHEMO-.

chemical /ˈkemɪk(ə)l/ adj. & n. —adj. of, made by, or employing chemistry or chemicals. —n. a substance obtained or used in chemistry. □ **chemical bond** the force holding atoms together in a molecule or crystal. **chemical engineer** one engaged in chemical engineering, esp. professionally. **chemical engineering** the design, manufacture, and operation of industrial chemical plants. **chemical reaction** a process that involves change in the structure of atoms, molecules, or ions. **chemical warfare** warfare using poison gas and other chemicals. □ **chemically** adv. [*chemic* alchemic f. F *chimique* or mod.L *chimicus*, *chymicus*, f. med.L *alchymicus*: see ALCHEMY]

chemico- /ˈkemɪkəʊ/ comb. form chemical; chemical and (*chemico-physical*).

chemin de fer /ʃəˌmæ̃ də ˈfeə(r)/ n. a form of baccarat. [F, = railway, lit. road of iron]

chemise /ʃəˈmiːz/ n. *hist.* a woman's loose-fitting under-garment or dress hanging straight from the shoulders. [ME f. OF f. LL *camisia* shirt]

chemist /ˈkemɪst/ n. **1** *Brit.* a a dealer in medicinal drugs, usu. also selling other medical goods and toiletries. **b** an authorized dispenser of medicines. **2** a person practising or trained in chemistry. [earlier *chymist* f. F *chimiste* f. mod.L *chimista* f. *alchimista* ALCHEMIST (see ALCHEMY)]

chemistry /ˈkemɪstrɪ/ n. (pl. -ies) **1** the study of the elements and the compounds they form and the reactions they undergo. **2** any complex (esp. emotional) change or process (*the chemistry of fear*). **3** colloq. a person's personality or temperament.

chemo- /ˈkiːməʊ/ *comb. form* (also **chemi-** /ˈkemɪ/) chemical.

chemotherapy /ˌkiːməˈθerəpɪ/ *n.* the treatment of disease, esp. cancer, by use of chemical substances. □ **chemotherapist** *n.*

chenille /ʃəˈniːl/ *n.* **1** a tufty velvety cord or yarn. **2** fabric made from this. [F, = hairy caterpillar f. L *canicula* dimin. of *canis* dog]

cheongsam /tʃɪɒŋˈsæm/ *n.* a Chinese woman's garment with a high neck and slit skirt. [Chin.]

cheque /tʃek/ *n.* (US **check**) **1** a written order to a bank to pay the stated sum from the drawer's account. **2** the printed form on which such an order is written. □ **cheque-book** a book of forms for writing cheques. **cheque card** a card issued by a bank to guarantee the honouring of cheques up to a stated amount. [special use of CHECK¹ to mean 'device for checking the amount of an item']

chequer /ˈtʃekə(r)/ *n. & v.* (also **checker**) —*n.* **1** (often in *pl.*) a pattern of squares often alternately coloured. **2** (in *pl.*) (usu. as **checkers**) US the game of draughts. —*v.tr.* **1** mark with chequers. **2** variegate; break the uniformity of. **3** (as **chequered** *adj.*) with varied fortunes (a *chequered career*). □ **chequer-board 1** a chessboard. **2** a pattern resembling it. [ME f. EXCHEQUER]

cherish /ˈtʃerɪʃ/ *v.tr.* **1** protect or tend (a child, plant, etc.) lovingly. **2** hold dear, cling to (hopes, feelings, etc.). [ME f. OF *cherir* f. *cher* f. L *carus* dear]

cheroot /ʃəˈruːt/ *n.* a cigar with both ends open. [F *cheroute* f. Tamil *shuruṭṭu* roll]

cherry /ˈtʃerɪ/ *n. & adj.* —*n.* (*pl.* **-ies**) **1 a** a small soft round stone-fruit. **b** any of several trees of the genus *Prunus* bearing this or grown for its ornamental flowers. **2** (in full **cherry wood**) the wood of a cherry. **3** US *sl.* a virginity. **b** a virgin. —*adj.* of a light red colour. □ **cherry brandy** a dark-red liqueur of brandy in which cherries have been steeped. **cherry tomato** a miniature tomato with a strong flavour. [ME f. ONF *cherise* (taken as *pl.*: cf. PEA) f. med.L *ceresia* perh. f. L f. Gk *kerasos*]

cherub /ˈtʃerəb/ *n.* **1** (*pl.* **cherubim** /-bɪm/) an angelic being of the second order of the celestial hierarchy. **2 a** a representation of a winged child or the head of a winged child. **b** a beautiful or innocent child. □ **cherubic** /tʃɪˈruːbɪk/ *adj.* **cherubically** /tʃɪˈruːbɪkəlɪ/ *adv.* [ME f. OE *cherubin* and f. Heb. *keruḇ*, pl. *keruḇîm*]

chervil /ˈtʃɜːvɪl/ *n.* an umbelliferous plant, *Anthriscus cerefolium*, used as a herb in cooking. [OE *cerfille* f. L *chaerephylla* f. Gk *khairephullon*]

Cheshire /ˈtʃeʃə(r)/ *n.* a kind of firm crumbly cheese, orig. made in Cheshire. □ **like a Cheshire cat** with a broad fixed grin. [*Cheshire*, a county in England]

chess /tʃes/ *n.* a game for two with 16 men each, played on a chessboard. [ME f. OF *esches* pl. of *eschec* CHECK¹]

chessboard /ˈtʃesbɔːd/ *n.* a chequered board of 64 squares on which chess and draughts are played.

chessman /ˈtʃesmæn/ *n.* (*pl.* **-men**) any of the 32 pieces and pawns with which chess is played.

chest /tʃest/ *n.* **1** a large strong box, esp. for storage or transport e.g. of blankets, tea, etc. **2 a** the part of a human or animal body enclosed by the ribs. **b** the front surface of the body from neck to waist. **3** a small cabinet for medicines etc. □ **chest of drawers** a piece of furniture consisting of a set of drawers in a frame. **get a thing off one's chest** *colloq.* disclose a fact, secret, etc., to relieve one's anxiety about it. **play (one's cards, a thing,** etc.) **close to one's chest** *colloq.* be cautious or secretive about. □ **-chested** *adj.* (in *comb.*). [OE *cest, cyst* f. Gmc f. L f. Gk *kistē*]

chesterfield /ˈtʃestəˌfiːld/ *n.* **1** a sofa with arms and back of the same height. **2** a man's plain overcoat usu. with a velvet collar. [19th-c. Earl of *Chesterfield*]

chestnut /ˈtʃesnʌt/ *n. & adj.* —*n.* **1 a** a glossy hard brown edible nut. **b** the tree *Castanea sativa*, bearing flowers in catkins and nuts enclosed in a spiny fruit. **2** any other tree of the genus *Castanea*. **3** = horse chestnut. **4** (in full **chestnut-wood**) the heavy wood of any chestnut tree. **5** a horse of a reddish-brown or yellowish-brown colour. **6** *colloq.* a stale joke or anecdote. **7** a reddish-brown colour. —*adj.* of the colour chestnut. [obs. *chesten* f. OF *chastaine* f. L *castanea* f. Gk *kastanea*]

chesty /ˈtʃestɪ/ *adj.* (**chestier, chestiest**) **1** *Brit. colloq.* inclined to or symptomatic of chest disease. **2** *colloq.* having a large chest or prominent breasts. **3** US *sl.* arrogant. □ **chestily** *adv.* **chestiness** *n.*

cheval-glass /ʃəˈvæl/ *n.* a tall mirror swung on an upright frame. [F *cheval* horse, frame]

chevalier /ʃeˈvælɪə(r)/ *n.* a member of certain orders of knighthood, and of modern French orders, as the Legion of Honour. [ME f. AF *chevaler*, OF *chevalier* f. med.L *caballarius* f. L *caballus* horse]

chèvre /ʃevr/ *n.* a variety of goat's-milk cheese. [F, = goat, she-goat]

chevron /ˈʃevrən/ *n.* **1** a badge in a V shape on the sleeve of a uniform indicating rank or length of service. **2** *Heraldry & Archit.* a bent bar of an inverted V shape. **3** any V-shaped line or stripe. [ME f. OF ult. f. L *caper* goat: cf. L *capreoli* pair of rafters]

chevy var. of CHIVVY.

chew /tʃuː/ *v. & n.* —*v.tr.* (also *absol.*) work (food etc.) between the teeth; crush or indent with the teeth. —*n.* **1** an act of chewing. **2** something for chewing, esp. a chewy sweet. □ **chew the cud** reflect, ruminate. **chew the fat** (or **rag**) *sl.* **1** chat. **2** grumble. **chewing-gum** flavoured gum, esp. chicle, for chewing. **chew on 1** work continuously between the teeth (*chewed on a piece of string*). **2** think about; meditate on. **chew out** US *colloq.* reprimand. **chew over 1** discuss, talk over. **2** think about; meditate on. □ **chewable** *adj.* **chewer** *n.* [OE *cēowan*]

chewy /ˈtʃuːɪ/ *adj.* (**chewier, chewiest**) **1** needing chewing. **2** suitable for chewing. □ **chewiness** *n.*

chez /ʃeɪ/ *prep.* at the house or home of. [F f. OF *chiese* f. L *casa* cottage]

chi /kaɪ/ *n.* the twenty-second letter of the Greek alphabet (X, χ). □ **chi-rho** a monogram of chi and rho as the first two letters of Greek *Khristos* Christ. **chi-square test** a method of comparing observed and theoretical values in statistics. [ME f. Gk *khi*]

Chianti /kɪˈæntɪ/ *n.* (*pl.* **Chiantis**) a dry red Italian wine. [*Chianti*, an area in Tuscany, Italy]

chiaroscuro /kɪˌɑːrəˈskʊərəʊ/ n. **1** the treatment of light and shade in drawing and painting. **2** the use of contrast in literature etc. **3** (attrib.) half-revealed. [It. f. chiaro CLEAR + oscuro dark, OBSCURE]

chic /ʃiːk/ adj. & n. —adj. (**chic-er, chic-est**) stylish, elegant (in dress or appearance). —n. stylishness, elegance. □ **chicly** adv. [F]

chicane /ʃɪˈkeɪn/ n. & v. —n. **1** chicanery. **2** an artificial barrier or obstacle on a motor racecourse. —v. archaic **1** intr. use chicanery. **2** tr. (usu. foll. by into, out of, etc.) cheat (a person). [F chicane(r) quibble]

chicanery /ʃɪˈkeɪnərɪ/ n. (pl. **-ies**) **1** clever but misleading talk; a false argument. **2** trickery, deception. [F chicanerie (as CHICANE)]

chicano /tʃɪˈkɑːnəʊ/ n. (pl. **-os**) US an American of Mexican origin. [Sp. mejicano Mexican]

chichi /ˈʃiːʃiː/ adj. & n. —adj. **1** (of a thing) frilly, showy. **2** (of a person or behaviour) fussy, affected. —n. over-refinement, pretentiousness, fussiness. [F]

chick n. **1** a young bird, esp. one newly hatched. **2** sl. **a** a young woman. **b** a child. [ME: shortening of CHICKEN]

chickadee /ˈtʃɪkəˌdiː/ n. US any of various small birds of the tit family, esp. Parus atricapillus. [imit.]

chicken /ˈtʃɪkɪn/ n., adj., & v. —n. (pl. same or **chickens**) **1** a young bird of a domestic fowl. **2** **a** a domestic fowl prepared as food. **b** its flesh. **3** a youthful person (usu. with neg.: is no chicken). **4** colloq. a children's pastime testing courage, usu. recklessly. —adj. colloq. cowardly. —v.intr. (foll. by out) colloq. withdraw from or fail in some activity through fear or lack of nerve. □ **chicken-feed 1** food for poultry. **2** colloq. an unimportant amount, esp. of money. **chicken-hearted** (or **-livered**) easily frightened; lacking nerve or courage. **chicken-wire** a light wire netting with a hexagonal mesh. [OE cīcen, cȳcen f. Gmc]

chickenpox /ˈtʃɪkɪnˌpɒks/ n. an infectious disease, esp. of children, with a rash of small blisters.

chick-pea /ˈtʃɪkpiː/ n. **1** a leguminous plant, Cicer arietinum, with short swollen pods containing yellow beaked seeds. **2** this seed used as a vegetable. [orig. ciche pease f. L cicer: see PEASE]

chickweed /ˈtʃɪkwiːd/ n. any of numerous small plants, esp. Stellaria media, a garden weed with slender stems and tiny white flowers.

chicle /ˈtʃɪk(ə)l, ˈtʃiːkliː/ n. the milky juice of the sapodilla tree, used in the manufacture of chewing-gum. [Amer. Sp. f. Nahuatl tzictli]

chicory /ˈtʃɪkərɪ/ n. (pl. **-ies**) **1** a blue-flowered plant, Cichorium intybus, cultivated for its salad leaves and its root. **2** its root, roasted and ground for use with or instead of coffee. **3** US = ENDIVE. [ME f. obs. F cicorée endive f. med.L cic(h)orea f. L cichorium f. Gk kikhorion]

chide /tʃaɪd/ v.tr. & intr. (past **chided** or **chid** /tʃɪd/; past part. **chided** or **chidden** /ˈtʃɪd(ə)n/) archaic or literary scold, rebuke. □ **chider** n. **chidingly** adv. [OE cīdan, of unkn. orig.]

chief /tʃiːf/ n. & adj. —n. **1 a** a leader or ruler. **b** the head of a tribe, clan, etc. **2** the head of a department; the highest official. —adj. (usu. attrib.) **1** first in position, importance, influence, etc. (chief engineer). **2** prominent, leading. □ **Chief of Staff** the senior staff officer of a service or command. **-in-Chief** supreme (Commander-in-Chief). □ **chiefdom** n. [ME f. OF ch(i)ef ult. f. L caput head]

chiefly /ˈtʃiːflɪ/ adv. above all; mainly but not exclusively.

chieftain /ˈtʃiːft(ə)n/ n. (fem. **chieftainess** /-nɪs/) the leader of a tribe, clan, etc. □ **chieftaincy** /-sɪ/ n. (pl. **-ies**). **chieftainship** n. [ME f. OF chevetaine f. LL capitaneus CAPTAIN: assim. to CHIEF]

chiffchaff /ˈtʃɪftʃæf/ n. a small European bird, Phylloscopus collybita, of the warbler family. [imit.]

chiffon /ˈʃɪfɒn/ n. & adj. —n. a light diaphanous fabric of silk, nylon, etc. —adj. **1** made of chiffon. **2** (of a pie-filling, dessert, etc.) light-textured. [F f. chiffe rag]

chiffonier /ˌʃɪfəˈnɪə(r)/ n. a movable low cupboard with a sideboard top. [F chiffonnier, -ière rag-picker, chest of drawers for odds and ends]

chigger /ˈtʃɪgə(r)/ n. **1** = CHIGOE. **2** any harvest mite of the genus Leptotrombidium with parasitic larvae. [var. of CHIGOE]

chignon /ˈʃiːnjɔ̃/ n. a coil or mass of hair at the back of a woman's head. [F, orig. = nape of the neck]

chigoe /ˈtʃɪgəʊ/ n. a tropical flea, Tunga penetrans, the females of which burrow beneath the skin causing painful sores. [Carib]

chihuahua /tʃɪˈwɑːwə/ n. **1** a very small dog of a smooth-haired large-eyed breed originating in Mexico. **2** this breed. [Chihuahua State and city in Mexico]

chilblain /ˈtʃɪlbleɪn/ n. a painful itching swelling of the skin usu. on a hand, foot, etc., caused by exposure to cold and by poor circulation. □ **chilblained** adj. [CHILL + BLAIN]

child /tʃaɪld/ n. (pl. **children** /ˈtʃɪldrən/) **1 a** a young human being below the age of puberty. **b** an unborn or newborn human being. **2** one's son or daughter (at any age). **3** (foll. by of) a descendant, follower, adherent, or product of (children of Israel; child of nature). **4** a childish person. □ **child abuse** maltreatment of a child, esp. by physical violence or sexual interference. **child benefit** (in the UK) regular payment by the State to the parents of a child up to a certain age. **child care** the care of children, esp. by a local authority. **child-minder** a person who looks after children for payment. **child's play** an easy task. □ **childless** adj. **childlessness** n. [OE cild]

childbirth /ˈtʃaɪldbɜːθ/ n. the act of giving birth to a child.

childhood /ˈtʃaɪldhʊd/ n. the state or period of being a child. □ **second childhood** a person's dotage. [OE cildhād]

childish /ˈtʃaɪldɪʃ/ adj. **1** of, like, or proper to a child. **2** immature, silly. □ **childishly** adv. **childishness** n.

childlike /ˈtʃaɪldlaɪk/ adj. having the good qualities of a child as innocence, frankness, etc.

childproof /ˈtʃaɪldpruːf/ adj. that cannot be damaged or operated by a child.

children pl. of CHILD.

chill n., v., & adj. —n. **1 a** an unpleasant cold sensation; lowered body temperature. **b** a feverish cold (catch a chill). **2** unpleasant coldness (of air, water, etc.). **3 a** a depressing influence (cast a chill over). **b** a feeling of fear accompanied by coldness. **4** coldness of manner. —*v*. **1** *tr*. & *intr*. make or become cold. **2** *tr*. depress, dispirit. **3** *tr*. cool (food or drink); preserve by cooling. **4** *tr*. harden (molten metal) by contact with cold material. —*adj*. *literary* chilly. □ **chiller** *n*. **chillingly** *adv*. **chillness** *n*. **chillsome** *adj*. *literary*. [OE *cele*, *ciele*, etc.: in mod. use the verb is the oldest (ME), and is of obscure orig.]

chilli /ˈtʃɪlɪ/ *n*. (*pl*. **-ies**) (also *US* **chili**) a small hot-tasting dried red pod of a capsicum, *Capsicum frutescens*, used as seasoning and in cayenne pepper, etc. □ **chilli con carne** /kɒn ˈkɑːnɪ/ a stew of chilli-flavoured minced beef and beans. [Sp. *chile, chili*, f. Aztec *chilli*]

chilly /ˈtʃɪlɪ/ *adj*. (**chillier, chilliest**) **1** (of the weather or an object) somewhat cold. **2** (of a person or animal) feeling somewhat cold; sensitive to the cold. **3** unfriendly; unemotional. □ **chilliness** *n*.

Chiltern Hundreds /ˈtʃɪlt(ə)n/ *n.pl*. a Crown manor, whose administration is a nominal office for which an MP applies as a way of resigning from the House of Commons. [*Chiltern* Hills in S. England]

chime *n*. & *v*. —*n*. **1 a** a set of attuned bells. **b** the series of sounds given by this. **c** (usu. in *pl*.) a set of attuned bells as a door bell. **2** agreement, correspondence, harmony. —*v*. **1 a** *intr*. (of bells) ring. **b** *tr*. sound (a bell or chime) by striking. **2** *tr*. show (the hour) by chiming. **3** *intr*. (usu. foll. by *together, with*) be in agreement, harmonize. □ **chime in 1** interject a remark. **2** join in harmoniously. **3** (foll. by *with*) agree with. □ **chimer** *n*. [ME, prob. f. *chym(b)e* bell f. OE *cimbal* f. L *cymbalum* f. Gk *kumbalon* CYMBAL]

chimera /kaɪˈmɪərə, kɪ-/ (also **chimaera**) *n*. **1** (in Greek mythology) a fire-breathing female monster with a lion's head, a goat's body, and a serpent's tail. **2** a fantastic or grotesque product of the imagination; a bogey. **3** any fabulous beast with parts taken from various animals. □ **chimeric** /-ˈmerɪk/ *adj*. **chimerical** /-ˈmerɪk(ə)l/ *adj*. **chimerically** /-ˈmerɪkəlɪ/ *adv*. [L f. Gk *khimaira* she-goat, chimera]

chimney /ˈtʃɪmnɪ/ *n*. (*pl*. **-eys**) **1** a vertical channel conducting smoke or combustion gases etc. up and away from a fire, furnace, engine, etc. **2** the part of this which projects above a roof. **3** a glass tube protecting the flame of a lamp. **4** a narrow vertical crack in a rock-face, often used by mountaineers to ascend. □ **chimney-breast** a projecting interior wall surrounding a chimney. **chimney-piece** an ornamental structure around an open fireplace; a mantelpiece. **chimney-pot** an earthenware or metal pipe at the top of a chimney, narrowing the aperture and increasing the up draught. **chimney-stack 1** a number of chimneys grouped in one structure. **2** = sense 2. **chimney-sweep** a person whose job is removing soot from inside chimneys. [ME f. OF *cheminée* f. LL *caminata* having a fire-place, f. L *caminus* f. Gk *kaminos* oven]

chimp *n*. *colloq*. = CHIMPANZEE. [abbr.]

chimpanzee /ˌtʃɪmpənˈziː/ *n*. a small African anthropoid ape, *Pan troglodytes*. [F *chimpanzé* f. Kongo]

chin *n*. the front of the lower jaw. □ **chin-wag** *sl*. *n*. a talk or chat. —*v.intr*. have a gossip. **keep one's chin up** *colloq*. remain cheerful, esp. in adversity. **take on the chin 1**

suffer a severe blow from (a misfortune etc.). **2** endure courageously. □ **-chinned** *adj*. (in *comb*.). [OE *cin(n)* f. Gmc]

china /ˈtʃaɪnə/ *n*. & *adj*. —*n*. **1** a kind of fine white or translucent ceramic ware, porcelain, etc. **2** things made from ceramic, esp. household tableware. —*adj*. made of china. □ **china clay** kaolin. **China tea** smoke-cured tea from a small-leaved tea plant grown in China. [orig. *China ware* (from China in Asia): name f. Pers. *chīnī*]

Chinagraph /ˈtʃaɪnəˌɡrɑːf/ *n*. *propr*. a waxy coloured pencil used to write on china, glass, etc.

Chinaman /ˈtʃaɪnəmən/ *n*. (*pl*. **-men**) **1** *archaic* or *derog*. (now usu. *offens*.) a native of China. **2** *Cricket* a ball bowled by a left-handed bowler that spins from off to leg.

Chinatown /ˈtʃaɪnəˌtaʊn/ *n*. a district of any non-Chinese town, esp. a city or seaport, in which the population is predominantly Chinese.

chinchilla /tʃɪnˈtʃɪlə/ *n*. **1 a** any small rodent of the genus *Chinchilla*, native to S. America, having soft silver-grey fur and a bushy tail. **b** its highly valued fur. **2** a breed of cat or rabbit. [Sp. prob. f. S. Amer. native name]

chine[1] *n*. & *v*. —*n*. **1 a** a backbone, esp. of an animal. **b** a joint of meat containing this. **2** a ridge or arête. —*v.tr*. cut (meat) across or along the backbone. [ME f. OF *eschine* f. L *spina* SPINE]

chine[2] *n*. a deep narrow ravine in the Isle of Wight or Dorset. [OE *cinu* chink etc. f. Gmc]

Chinese /tʃaɪˈniːz/ *adj*. & *n*. —*adj*. **a** of or relating to China. **b** of Chinese descent. —*n*. **1** the Chinese language. **2** (*pl*. same) **a** a native or national of China. **b** a person of Chinese descent. □ **Chinese cabbage** = *Chinese leaf*. **Chinese gooseberry** = *kiwi fruit*. **Chinese lantern 1** a collapsible paper lantern. **2** a solanaceous plant, *Physalis alkekengi*, bearing globular orange fruits enclosed in an orange-red papery calyx. **Chinese leaf** a lettuce-like cabbage, *Brassica chinensis*. **Chinese white** zinc oxide as a white pigment.

chink[1] *n*. **1** an unintended crack that admits light or allows an attack. **2** a narrow opening; a slit. [16th c.: rel. to CHINE[2]]

chink[2] *v*. & *n*. —*v*. **1** *intr*. make a slight ringing sound, as of glasses or coins striking together. **2** *tr*. cause to make this sound. —*n*. this sound. [imit.]

Chink *n*. *sl*. *offens*. a Chinese. □ **Chinky** *adj*. [abbr.]

chinless /ˈtʃɪnlɪs/ *adj*. *colloq*. weak or feeble in character. □ **chinless wonder** *Brit*. an ineffectual esp. upper class person.

Chino- /ˈtʃaɪnəʊ/ *comb. form* = SINO-.

chino /ˈtʃiːnəʊ/ *n*. *US* (*pl*. **-os**) **1** a cotton twill fabric, usu. khaki-coloured. **2** (in *pl*.) a garment, esp. trousers, made from this. [Amer. Sp., = toasted]

chinoiserie /ʃiːnˈwɑːzərɪ/ *n*. **1** the imitation of Chinese motifs in painting and in decorating furniture. **2** an object or objects in this style. [F]

chinook /ʃəˈnʊk, tʃə-, -ˈnuːk/ *n*. **1** a warm dry wind which blows east of the Rocky Mountains. **2** a warm wet southerly wind west of the Rocky Mountains. [Amer. Ind. name of a tribe]

chintz *n*. & *adj*. —*n*. a printed multicoloured cotton fabric with a glazed finish. —*adj*. made from or upholstered with this fabric. [earlier *chints* (pl.) f. Hindi *chīnt* f. Skr. *citra* variegated]

chintzy /ˈtʃɪntsɪ/ *adj.* (**chintzier, chintziest**) **1** like chintz. **2** gaudy, cheap. **3** characteristic of the décor associated with chintz soft furnishings. □ **chintzily** *adv.* **chintziness** *n.*

chip *n. & v.* —*n.* **1** a small piece removed by or in the course of chopping, cutting, or breaking, esp. from hard material such as wood or stone. **2** the place where such a chip has been made. **3 a** (usu. in *pl.*) a strip of potato, deep fried. **b** (in *pl.*) *US* potato crisps. **4** a counter used in some gambling games to represent money. **5** *Electronics* = MICROCHIP. **6** *Football* etc. & *Golf* a short shot, kick, or pass with the ball describing an arc. —*v.* (**chipped, chipping**) **1** *tr.* (often foll. by *off, away*) cut or break (a piece) from a hard material. **2** *intr.* (often foll. by *at, away at*) cut pieces off (a hard material) to alter its shape, break it up, etc. **3** *intr.* (of stone, china, etc.) be susceptible to being chipped; be apt to break at the edge. **4** *tr.* (also *absol.*) *Football* etc. & *Golf* strike or kick (the ball) with a chip (cf. sense 6 of *n.*). **5** *tr.* (usu. as **chipped** *adj.*) cut (potatoes) into chips. □ **chip heater** *Austral.* & *NZ* a domestic water-heater that burns wood chips. **chip in** *colloq.* **1** interrupt or contribute abruptly to a conversation (*chipped in with a reminiscence*). **2** contribute (money or resources). **a chip off the old block** a child who resembles a parent, esp. in character. **a chip on one's shoulder** *colloq.* a disposition or inclination to feel resentful or aggrieved. **have had one's chips** *Brit. colloq.* be unable to avoid defeat, punishment, etc. **when the chips are down** *colloq.* when it comes to the point. [ME f. OF *cipp, cyp* beam]

chipboard /ˈtʃɪpbɔːd/ *n.* a rigid sheet or panel made from compressed wood chips and resin.

chipmunk /ˈtʃɪpmʌŋk/ *n.* any ground squirrel of the genus *Tamias* or *Eutamias*, having alternate light and dark stripes down the body. [Algonquian]

chipolata /ˌtʃɪpəˈlɑːtə/ *n. Brit.* a small thin sausage. [F f. It. *cipollata* a dish of onions f. *cipolla* onion]

chipper /ˈtʃɪpə(r)/ *adj. esp. US colloq.* **1** cheerful. **2** smartly dressed. [perh. f. N.Engl. dial. *kipper* lively]

chipping /ˈtʃɪpɪŋ/ *n.* **1** a small fragment of stone, wood, etc. **2** (in *pl.*) these used as a surface for roads, roofs, etc.

chippy /ˈtʃɪpɪ/ *n.* (also **chippie**) (*pl.* **-ies**) *Brit. colloq.* **1** a fish-and-chip shop. **2** a carpenter.

chiro- /ˈkaɪərəʊ/ (also **cheiro-**) *comb. form* of the hand. [Gk *kheir* hand]

chirography /kaɪəˈrɒɡrəfɪ/ *n.* handwriting, calligraphy.

chiromancy /ˈkaɪərəʊˌmænsɪ/ *n.* palmistry.

chiropody /kɪˈrɒpədɪ/ *n.* the treatment of the feet and their ailments. □ **chiropodist** *n.* [CHIRO- + Gk *pous podos* foot]

chiropractic /ˌkaɪərəʊˈpræktɪk/ *n.* the diagnosis and manipulative treatment of mechanical disorders of the joints, esp. of the spinal column. □ **chiropractor** /ˈkaɪərəʊ-/ *n.* [CHIRO- + Gk *praktikos*: see PRACTICAL]

chirp *v. & n.* —*v.* **1** *intr.* (usu. of small birds, grasshoppers, etc.) utter a short sharp high-pitched note. **2** *tr. & intr.* (esp. of a child) speak or utter in a lively or jolly way. —*n.* a chirping

sound. □ **chirper** *n.* [ME, earlier *chirk, chirt*: imit.]

chirpy /ˈtʃɜːpɪ/ *adj. colloq.* (**chirpier, chirpiest**) cheerful, lively. □ **chirpily** *adv.* **chirpiness** *n.*

chirr *v. & n.* (also **churr**) —*v.intr.* (esp. of insects) make a prolonged low trilling sound. —*n.* this sound. [imit.]

chirrup /ˈtʃɪrəp/ *v. & n.* —*v.intr.* (**chirruped, chirruping**) (esp. of small birds) chirp, esp. repeatedly; twitter. —*n.* a chirruping sound. □ **chirrupy** *adj.* [trilled form of CHIRP]

chisel /ˈtʃɪz(ə)l/ *n. & v.* —*n.* a hand tool with a squared bevelled blade for shaping wood, stone, or metal. —*v.* **1** *tr.* (**chiselled, chiselling**; *US* **chiseled, chiseling**) cut or shape with a chisel. **2** *tr.* (as **chiselled** *adj.*) (of facial features) clear-cut, fine. **3** *tr. & intr. sl.* cheat, swindle. □ **chiseller** *n.* [ME f. ONF ult. f. LL *cisorium* f. L *caedere caes-* cut]

chit[1] *n.* **1** *derog.* or *joc.* a young, small, or frail girl or woman (esp. *a chit of a girl*). **2** a young child. [ME, = whelp, cub, kitten, perh. = dial. *chit* sprout]

chit[2] *n.* a note of requisition; a note of a sum owed, esp. for food or drink. [earlier *chitty*: Anglo-Ind. f. Hindi *ciṭṭhī* pass f. Skr. *citra* mark]

chit-chat /ˈtʃɪttʃæt/ *n. & v. colloq.* —*n.* light conversation; gossip. —*v.intr.* (**-chatted, -chatting**) talk informally; gossip. [redupl. of CHAT]

chitin /ˈkaɪtɪn/ *n. Chem.* a polysaccharide forming the major constituent in the exoskeleton of arthropods and in the cell walls of fungi. □ **chitinous** *adj.* [F *chitine* irreg. f. Gk *khitōn* tunic]

chitterling /ˈtʃɪtəlɪŋ/ *n.* (usu. in *pl.*) the smaller intestines of pigs etc., esp. as cooked for food. [ME: orig. uncert.]

chivalrous /ˈʃɪvəlrəs/ *adj.* **1** (usu. of a male) gallant, honourable, courteous. **2** involving or showing chivalry. □ **chivalrously** *adv.* [ME f. OF *chevalerous*: see CHEVALIER]

chivalry /ˈʃɪvəlrɪ/ *n.* **1** the medieval knightly system with its religious, moral, and social code. **2** the combination of qualities expected of an ideal knight, esp. courage, honour, courtesy, justice, and readiness to help the weak. **3** a man's courteous behaviour, esp. towards women. □ **chivalric** *adj.* [ME f. OF *chevalerie* etc. f. med.L *caballerius* for LL *caballarius* horseman: see CAVALIER]

chive /tʃaɪv/ *n.* a small alliaceous plant, *Allium schoenoprasum*, having dense tufts of long tubular leaves which are used as a herb. [ME f. OF *cive* f. L *cepa* onion]

chivvy /ˈtʃɪvɪ/ *v.tr.* (**-ies, -ied**) (also **chivy, chevy** /ˈtʃevɪ/) harass, nag; pursue. [*chevy* (n. & v.), prob. f. the ballad of *Chevy Chase*, a place on the Scottish border]

chlor- var. of CHLORO-.

chloral /ˈklɔːr(ə)l/ *n.* **1** a colourless liquid aldehyde used in making DDT. **2** (in full **chloral hydrate**) *Pharm.* a colourless crystalline solid made from chloral and used as a sedative. [F f. *chlore* chlorine + *alcool* alcohol]

chloride /ˈklɔːraɪd/ *n. Chem.* **1** any compound of chlorine with another element or group. **2** any bleaching agent containing chloride. [CHLORO- + -IDE]

chlorinate /ˈklɔːrɪˌneɪt/ v.tr. **1** impregnate or treat with chlorine. **2** Chem. cause to react or combine with chlorine. □ **chlorinator** n.

chlorination /ˌklɔːrɪˈneɪʃ(ə)n/ n. **1** the treatment of water with chlorine to disinfect it. **2** Chem. a reaction in which chlorine is introduced into a compound.

chlorine /ˈklɔːriːn/ n. Chem. a poisonous greenish-yellow gaseous element of the halogen group used for purifying water, bleaching, and the manufacture of many organic chemicals. [Gk khlōros green + -INE⁴]

chloro- /ˈklɔːrəʊ/ comb. form (also **chlor-** esp. before a vowel) **1** Bot. & Mineral. green. **2** Chem. chlorine. [Gk khlōros green: in sense 2 f. CHLORINE]

chloro-fluorocarbon see CFC.

chloroform /ˈklɒrəˌfɔːm, ˈklɔːrə-/ n. & v. —n. a colourless volatile sweet-smelling liquid used as a solvent and formerly used as a general anaesthetic. —v.tr. render (a person) unconscious with this. [F chloroforme formed as CHLORO- + formyle: see FORMIC (ACID)]

chlorophyll /ˈklɒrəfɪl/ n. the green pigment found in most plants, responsible for light absorption to provide energy for photosynthesis. □ **chlorophyllous** /-ˈfɪləs/ adj. [F chlorophylle f. Gk phullon leaf: see CHLORO-]

Ch.M. abbr. Master of Surgery. [L Chirurgiae Magister]

choc /tʃɒk/ n. & adj. colloq. chocolate. □ **choc-ice** a bar of ice-cream covered with a thin coating of chocolate. [abbr.]

chock /tʃɒk/ n., v., & adv. —n. a block or wedge of wood to check motion, esp. of a cask or a wheel. —v.tr. **1** fit or make fast with chocks. **2** (usu. foll. by up) Brit. cram full. —adv. as closely or tightly as possible. [prob. f. OF couche, çoche, of unkn. orig.]

chock-a-block /ˈtʃɒkəˌblɒk/ adj. & adv. crammed close together; crammed full (a street chock-a-block with cars). [orig. Naut., with ref. to tackle with the two blocks run close together]

chock-full /ˈtʃɒkfʊl, -ˈfʊl/ adj. & adv. = CHOCK-A-BLOCK (chock-full of rubbish). [CHOCK + FULL¹: ME chokkefulle (rel. to CHOKE¹) is doubtful]

chocolate /ˈtʃɒkələt, ˈtʃɒklət/ n. & adj. —n. **1 a** a food preparation in the form of a paste or solid block made from roasted and ground cacao seeds, usually sweetened. **b** a sweet made of or coated with this. **c** a drink made with chocolate. **2** a deep brown colour. —adj. **1** made from or of chocolate. **2** chocolate-coloured. □ **chocolatey** adj. (also **chocolaty**). [F chocolat or Sp. chocolate f. Aztec chocolatl]

choice n. & adj. —n. **1 a** the act or an instance of choosing. **b** a thing or person chosen (not a good choice). **2** a range from which to choose. **3** (usu. foll. by of) the élite, the best. **4** the power or opportunity to choose (what choice have I?). —adj. of superior quality; carefully chosen. □ **choicely** adv. **choiceness** n. [ME f. OF chois f. choisir CHOOSE]

choir /ˈkwaɪə(r)/ n. **1** a regular group of singers, esp. taking part in church services. **2** the part of a cathedral or large church between the altar and the nave. **3** a company of singers, birds, angels, etc. (a heavenly choir). [ME f. OF quer f. L chorus: see CHORUS]

choirboy /ˈkwaɪəˌbɔɪ/ n. a boy who sings in a church or cathedral choir.

choke¹ v. & n. —v. **1** tr. hinder or impede the breathing of (a person or animal) esp. by constricting the windpipe or (of gas, smoke, etc.) by being unbreathable. **2** intr. suffer a hindrance or stoppage of breath. **3** tr. & intr. make or become speechless from emotion. **4** tr. retard the growth of or kill (esp. plants) by the deprivation of light, air, nourishment, etc. **5** tr. (often foll. by back) suppress (feelings) with difficulty. **6** tr. block or clog (a passage, tube, etc.). **7** tr. (as **choked** adj.) colloq. disgusted, disappointed. —n. **1** the valve in the carburettor of an internal-combustion engine that controls the intake of air, esp. to enrich the fuel mixture. **2** Electr. an inductance coil used to smooth the variations of an alternating current or to alter its phase. □ **choke-chain** a chain looped round a dog's neck to exert control by pressure on its windpipe when the dog pulls. **choke down** swallow with difficulty. **choke up** block (a channel etc.). [ME f. OE ācēocian f. cēoce, cēce CHEEK]

choke² n. the centre part of an artichoke. [prob. confusion of the ending of artichoke with CHOKE¹]

choker /ˈtʃəʊkə(r)/ n. **1** a close-fitting necklace or ornamental neckband. **2** a clerical or other high collar.

choko /ˈtʃəʊkəʊ/ n. (pl. **-os**) Austral. & NZ a succulent green pear-shaped vegetable like a cucumber in flavour. [Braz. Ind. chocho]

choky¹ /ˈtʃəʊkɪ/ n. (also **chokey**) (pl. **-ies** or **-eys**) Brit. sl. prison. [orig. Anglo-Ind., f. Hindi caukī shed]

choky² /ˈtʃəʊkɪ/ adj. (**chokier**, **chokiest**) tending to choke or to cause choking.

chole- /ˈkɒlɪ/ comb. form (also **chol-** esp. before a vowel) Med. & Chem. bile. [Gk kholē gall, bile]

cholecalciferol /ˌkɒlɪkælˈsɪfəˌrɒl/ n. one of the D vitamins, produced by the action of sunlight on a cholesterol derivative in the skin. [CHOLE- + CALCIFEROL]

choler /ˈkɒlə(r)/ n. **1** hist. one of the four humours, bile. **2** poet. or archaic anger, irascibility. [ME f. OF colere bile, anger f. L cholera f. Gk kholera diarrhoea, in LL = bile, anger, f. Gk kholē bile]

cholera /ˈkɒlərə/ n. Med. an infectious and often fatal disease of the small intestine caused by the bacterium Vibrio cholerae, resulting in severe vomiting and diarrhoea. □ **choleraic** /-ˈreɪɪk/ adj. [ME f. L f. Gk kholera: see CHOLER]

choleric /ˈkɒlərɪk/ adj. irascible, angry. □ **cholerically** adv. [ME f. OF cholerique f. L cholericus f. Gk kholerikos: see CHOLER]

cholesterol /kəˈlestəˌrɒl/ n. Biochem. a sterol found in most body tissues, including the blood, where high concentrations promote arteriosclerosis. [cholesterin f. Gk kholē bile + stereos stiff]

choline /ˈkəʊliːn, -lɪn/ n. Biochem. a basic nitrogenous organic compound occurring widely in living matter. [G Cholin f. Gk kholē bile]

chomp v.tr. = CHAMP¹. [imit.]

choo-choo /ˈtʃuːtʃuː/ n. colloq. (esp. as a child's word) a railway train or locomotive, esp. a steam engine. [imit.]

chook /tʃʊk/ n. (also **chookie**) Austral. & NZ colloq. **1** a chicken or fowl. **2** sl. an older woman. [E dial. chuck chicken]

choose /tʃuːz/ v. (past **chose** /tʃəʊz/; past part. **chosen** /ˈtʃəʊz(ə)n/) **1** tr. select out of a greater number. **2** intr. (usu. foll. by between, from) take or select one or another. **3** *tr.* (usu. foll. by *to* + infin.) decide, be determined (*chose to stay behind*). **4** *tr.* (foll. by complement) select as (*was chosen king*). □ **chooser** *n.* [OE *cēosan* f. Gmc]

choosy /'tʃuːzɪ/ *adj.* (**choosier, choosiest**) *colloq.* fastidious. □ **choosily** *adv.* **choosiness** *n.*

chop[1] *v.* & *n.* —*v.tr.* (**chopped, chopping**) **1** (usu. foll. by *off, down,* etc.) cut or fell by a blow, usu. with an axe. **2** (often foll. by *up*) cut (esp. meat or vegetables) into small pieces. **3** strike (esp. a ball) with a short heavy edgewise blow. **4** *Brit. colloq.* dispense with; shorten or curtail. —*n.* **1** a cutting blow, esp. with an axe. **2** a thick slice of meat (esp. pork or lamb) usu. including a rib. **3** a short heavy edgewise stroke or blow in tennis, cricket, boxing, etc. **4** the broken motion of water, usu. owing to the action of the wind against the tide. **5** (prec. by *the*) *Brit. sl.* **a** dismissal from employment. **b** the action of killing or being killed. □ **chop logic** argue pedantically. [ME, var. of CHAP[1]]

chop[2] *n.* (usu. in *pl.*) the jaw of an animal etc. [16th-c. var. (occurring earlier) of CHAP[3], of unkn. orig.]

chop[3] *v.intr.* (**chopped, chopping**) □ **chop and change** vacillate; change direction frequently. [ME, perh. rel. to *chap* f. OE *cēapian* (as CHEAP)]

chop-chop /tʃɒp'tʃɒp/ *adv.* & *int.* (pidgin English) quickly, quick. [f. Chin. dial. *k'wâi-k'wâi*]

chopper /'tʃɒpə(r)/ *n.* **1 a** *Brit.* a short axe with a large blade. **b** a butcher's cleaver. **2** *colloq.* a helicopter. **3** *colloq.* a type of bicycle or motor cycle with high handlebars. **4** (in *pl.*) *Brit. sl.* teeth.

choppy /'tʃɒpɪ/ *adj.* (**choppier, choppiest**) (of the sea, the weather, etc.) fairly rough. □ **choppily** *adv.* **choppiness** *n.* [CHOP[1] + -Y[1]]

chopstick /'tʃɒpstɪk/ *n.* each of a pair of small thin sticks of wood or ivory etc., held both in one hand as eating utensils by the Chinese, Japanese, etc. [pidgin Engl. f. *chop* = quick + STICK[1] equivalent of Cantonese *k'wâi-tsze* nimble ones]

chopsuey /tʃɒp'suːɪ/ *n.* (*pl.* **-eys**) a Chinese-style dish of meat fried with bean sprouts and vegetables served with rice. [Cantonese *shap sui* mixed bits]

choral /'kɔːr(ə)l/ *adj.* of, for, or sung by a choir or chorus. □ **choral society** a group which meets regularly to sing choral music. □ **chorally** *adv.* [med.L *choralis* f. L *chorus*: see CHORUS]

chorale /kɔːˈrɑː/ *n.* (also **choral**) **1** a stately and simple hymn tune; a harmonized version of this. **2** esp. *US* a choir or choral society. [G *Choral(gesang)* f. med.L *cantus choralis*]

chord[1] /kɔːd/ *n.* *Mus.* a group of notes sounded together, as a basis of harmony. □ **chordal** *adj.* [orig. *cord* f. ACCORD: later confused with CHORD[2]]

chord[2] /kɔːd/ *n.* **1** *Math.* & *Aeron.* etc. a straight line joining the ends of an arc, the wings of an aeroplane, etc. **2** *Anat.* = CORD. □ **strike a chord 1** recall something to a person's memory. **2** elicit sympathy. **touch the right chord** appeal skilfully to the emotions. □ **chordal** *adj.* [16th-c. refashioning of CORD after L *chorda*]

chordate /'kɔːdeɪt/ *n.* & *adj.* —*n.* any animal of the phylum Chordata, possessing a notochord at some stage during its development. —*adj.* of or relating to the chordates. [mod.L *chordata* f. L *chorda* CHORD[2] after *Vertebrata* etc.]

chore /tʃɔː(r)/ *n.* a tedious or routine task, esp. domestic. [orig. dial. & US form of CHAR[2]]

chorea /kɒ'rɪə/ *n.* *Med.* a disorder characterized by jerky involuntary movements affecting esp. the shoulders, hips, and face. □ **Huntington's chorea** chorea accompanied by a progressive dementia. [L f. Gk *khoreia* (as CHORUS)]

choreograph /'kɒrɪəˌɡrɑːf/ *v.tr.* compose the choreography for (a ballet etc.). □ **choreographer** /-ɪˈɒɡrəfə(r)/ *n.* [back-form. f. CHOREOGRAPHY]

choreography /ˌkɒrɪˈɒɡrəfɪ/ *n.* **1** the design or arrangement of a ballet or other staged dance. **2** the sequence of steps and movements in dance. **3** the written notation for this. □ **choreographic** /ˌkɒrɪəˈɡræfɪk/ *adj.* **choreographically** /ˌkɒrɪəˈɡræfɪkəlɪ/ *adv.* [Gk *khoreia* dance + -GRAPHY]

choric /'kɔːrɪk/ *adj.* of, like, or for a chorus in drama or recitation. [LL *choricus* f. Gk *khorikos* (as CHORUS)]

chorine /'kɔːriːn/ *n.* *US* a chorus girl. [CHORUS + -INE[3]]

chorister /'kɒrɪstə(r)/ *n.* **1** a member of a choir, esp. a choirboy. **2** *US* the leader of a church choir. [ME, ult. f. OF *cueriste* f. *quer* CHOIR]

chorology /kəˈrɒlədʒɪ/ *n.* the study of the geographical distribution of animals and plants. □ **chorological** /ˌkɔːrəˈlɒdʒɪk(ə)l/ *adj.* **chorologist** *n.* [Gk *khōra* region + -LOGY]

chortle /'tʃɔːt(ə)l/ *v.* & *n.* —*v.intr.* *colloq.* chuckle gleefully. —*n.* a gleeful chuckle. [portmanteau word coined by Lewis Carroll, prob. f. CHUCKLE + SNORT]

chorus /'kɔːrəs/ *n.* & *v.* —*n.* (*pl.* **choruses**) **1** a group (esp. a large one) of singers; a choir. **2** a piece of music composed for a choir. **3** the refrain or the main part of a popular song, in which a chorus participates. **4** any simultaneous utterance by many persons etc. (*a chorus of disapproval followed*). **5** a group of singers and dancers performing in concert in a musical comedy, opera, etc. **6** *Gk Antiq.* **a** in Greek tragedy, a group of performers who comment together in voice and movement on the main action. **b** an utterance of the chorus. **7** esp. in Elizabethan drama, a character who speaks the prologue and other linking parts of the play. **8** the part spoken by this character. —*v.tr.* & *intr.* (of a group) speak or utter simultaneously. □ **chorus girl** a young woman who sings or dances in the chorus of a musical comedy etc. **in chorus** (uttered) together; in unison. [L f. Gk *khoros*]

chose past of CHOOSE.

chosen past part. of CHOOSE.

chough /tʃʌf/ *n.* any corvine bird of the genus *Pyrrhocorax*, with a glossy blue-black plumage and red legs. [ME, prob. orig. imit.]

choux pastry /ʃuː/ *n.* very light pastry enriched with eggs. [F, pl. of *chou* cabbage, rosette]

chow /tʃaʊ/ *n.* **1** *sl.* food. **2 a** a dog of a Chinese breed with long hair and bluish-black tongue. **b** this breed. [shortened f. pidgin Engl. *chow-chow*]

chowder /'tʃaʊdə(r)/ *n.* *US* a soup or stew usu. of fresh fish, clams, or corn with bacon, onions, etc. [perh. F *chaudière* pot: see CAULDRON]

chow mein /tʃaʊ 'meɪn/ *n.* a Chinese-style dish of fried noodles with shredded meat or shrimps etc. and vegetables. [Chin. *chao mian* fried flour]

chrism /ˈkrɪz(ə)m/ n. a consecrated oil or unguent used esp. for anointing in Catholic and Greek Orthodox rites. [OE crisma f. eccl.L f. Gk khrisma anointing]

Christ /kraɪst/ n. & int. —n. 1 the title, also now treated as a name, given to Jesus of Nazareth, believed by Christians to have fulfilled the Old Testament prophecies of a coming Messiah. 2 the Messiah as prophesied in the Old Testament. 3 an image or picture of Jesus. —int. sl. expressing surprise, anger, etc. □ **Christhood** n. **Christlike** adj. **Christly** adj. [OE Crīst f. L Christus f. Gk khristos anointed one f. khriō anoint: transl. of Heb. māšîaḥ MESSIAH]

christen /ˈkrɪs(ə)n/ v.tr. 1 give a Christian name to at baptism as a sign of admission to a Christian Church. 2 give a name to anything, esp. formally or with a ceremony. 3 colloq. use for the first time. □ **christener** n. **christening** n. [OE crīstnian make Christian]

Christendom /ˈkrɪsəndəm/ n. Christians worldwide, regarded as a collective body. [OE crīstendōm f. cristen CHRISTIAN + -DOM]

Christian /ˈkrɪstɪən, ˈkrɪstʃ(ə)n/ adj. & n. —adj. 1 of Christ's teaching or religion. 2 believing in or following the religion of Jesus Christ. 3 showing the qualities associated with Christ's teaching. 4 colloq. (of a person) kind, fair, decent. —n. 1 a a person who has received Christian baptism. b an adherent of Christ's teaching. 2 a person exhibiting Christian qualities. □ **Christian era** the era reckoned from the traditional date of Christ's birth. **Christian name** a forename, esp. as given at baptism. **Christian Science** a Christian sect believing in the power of healing by prayer alone. **Christian Scientist** an adherent of Christian Science. □ **Christianize** v.tr. & intr. (also -ise). **Christianization** /ˌkrɪstɪənaɪˈzeɪʃ(ə)n/ n. **Christianly** adv. [Christianus f. Christus CHRIST]

Christianity /ˌkrɪstɪˈænɪtɪ/ n. 1 the Christian religion; its beliefs and practices. 2 being a Christian; Christian quality or character. 3 = CHRISTENDOM. [ME cristianite f. OF crestienté f. crestien CHRISTIAN]

Christingle /ˈkrɪstɪŋɡ(ə)l/ n. a lighted candle symbolizing Christ as the light of the world, held by children esp. at Advent services. [perh. f. G Christkindl dimin. of Christkind Christ child]

Christmas /ˈkrɪsməs/ n. (pl. **Christmases**) 1 (also **Christmas Day**) the annual festival of Christ's birth, celebrated on 25 Dec. 2 the season in which this occurs; the time immediately before and after 25 Dec. □ **Christmas-box** a present or gratuity given at Christmas esp. to tradesmen and employees. **Christmas cake** Brit. a rich fruit cake usu. covered with marzipan and icing and eaten at Christmas. **Christmas card** a card sent with greetings at Christmas. **Christmas Eve** the day or the evening before Christmas Day. **Christmas pudding** Brit. a rich boiled pudding eaten at Christmas, made with flour, suet, dried fruit, etc. **Christmas rose** a white-flowered winter-blooming evergreen, Helleborus niger. **Christmas tree** an evergreen (usu. spruce) or artificial tree set up with decorations at Christmas. □ **Christmassy** adj. [OE Crīstes mæsse (MASS²)]

Christo- /ˈkrɪstəʊ/ comb. form Christ.

chroma /ˈkrəʊmə/ n. purity or intensity of colour. [Gk khrōma colour]

chromatic /krəˈmætɪk/ adj. 1 of or produced by colour; in (esp. bright) colours. 2 Mus. **a** of or having notes not belonging to a diatonic scale. **b** (of a scale) ascending or descending by semitones. □ **chromatically** adv. **chromaticism** /-tɪˌsɪz(ə)m/ n. [F chromatique or L chromaticus f. Gk khrōmatikos f. khrōma -atos colour]

chromaticity /ˌkrəʊməˈtɪsɪtɪ/ n. the quality of colour regarded independently of brightness.

chromatin /ˈkrəʊmətɪn/ n. the material in a cell nucleus that stains with basic dyes and consists of protein, RNA, and DNA. [G f. Gk khrōma -atos colour]

chromato- /ˈkrəʊmətəʊ/ comb. form (also **chromo-** /ˈkrəʊməʊ/) colour (chromatography). [Gk khrōma -atos colour]

chromatography /ˌkrəʊməˈtɒɡrəfɪ/ n. Chem. the separation of the components of a mixture by slow passage through or over a material which adsorbs them differently. □ **chromatograph** /-ˈmætəˌɡrɑːf/ n. **chromatographic** /-mətəʊˈɡræfɪk/ adj. [G Chromatographie (as CHROMATO-, -GRAPHY)]

chrome /krəʊm/ n. 1 chromium, esp. as plating. 2 (in full **chrome yellow**) a yellow pigment obtained from a compound of chromium. □ **chrome steel** a hard fine-grained steel containing much chromium and used for tools etc. [F, = chromium, f. Gk khrōma colour]

chromite /ˈkrəʊmaɪt/ n. Mineral. a black mineral of chromium and iron oxides, which is the principal ore of chromium.

chromium /ˈkrəʊmɪəm/ n. Chem. a hard white metallic transition element, occurring naturally as chromite and used as a shiny decorative electroplated coating. □ **chromium steel** = chrome steel. [mod.L f. F CHROME]

chromium-plate /ˌkrəʊmɪəmˈpleɪt/ n. & v. —n. an electrolytically deposited protective coating of chromium. —v.tr. 1 coat with this. 2 (as **chromium-plated** adj.) pretentiously decorative.

chromo-¹ /ˈkrəʊməʊ/ comb. form Chem. chromium.

chromo-² comb. form var. of CHROMATO-.

chromolithograph /ˌkrəʊməʊˈlɪθəˌɡrɑːf/ n. & v. —n. a coloured picture printed by lithography. —v.tr. print or produce by this process. □ **chromolithographer** /-ˈθɒɡrəfə(r)/ n. **chromolithographic** /-ˌlɪθəˈɡræfɪk/ adj. **chromolithography** /-lɪˈθɒɡrəfɪ/ n.

chromosome /ˈkrəʊməˌsəʊm/ n. Biochem. one of the threadlike structures, usu. found in the cell nucleus, that carry the genetic information in the form of genes. □ **chromosomal** adj. [G Chromosom (as CHROMO-², -SOME³)]

chronic /ˈkrɒnɪk/ adj. 1 persisting for a long time (usu. of an illness or a personal or social problem). 2 having a chronic complaint. 3 colloq. disp. habitual, inveterate (a chronic liar). 4 Brit. colloq. very bad; intense, severe. □ **chronically** adv. **chronicity** /krɒˈnɪsɪtɪ/ n. [F chronique f. L chronicus (in LL of disease) f. Gk khronikos f. khronos time]

■ **Usage** The use of chronic in sense 4 is very informal, and its use in sense 3 is considered incorrect by some people.

chronicle /ˈkrɒnɪk(ə)l/ n. & v. —n. 1 a register of events in order of their occurrence. 2 a narrative, a full account. —*v.tr.* record (events) in the order of their occurrence. □ **chronicler** *n.* [ME f. AF *cronicle* ult. f. L *chronica* f. Gk *khronika* annals: see CHRONIC]

chrono- /ˈkrɒnəʊ/ *comb. form* time. [Gk *khronos* time]

chronograph /ˈkrɒnəˌgrɑːf, ˈkrəʊnə-, -ˌgræf/ *n.* **1** an instrument for recording time with extreme accuracy. **2** a stopwatch. □ **chronographic** /-ˈgræfɪk/ *adj.*

chronological /ˌkrɒnəˈlɒdʒɪk(ə)l/ *adj.* **1** (of a number of events) arranged or regarded in the order of their occurrence. **2** of or relating to chronology. □ **chronologically** *adv.*

chronology /krəˈnɒlədʒɪ/ *n.* (*pl.* **-ies**) **1** the study of historical records to establish the dates of past events. **2 a** the arrangement of events, dates, etc. in the order of their occurrence. **b** a table or document displaying this. □ **chronologist** *n.* **chronologize** *v.tr.* (also **-ise**). [mod.L *chronologia* (as CHRONO-, -LOGY)]

chronometer /krəˈnɒmɪtə(r)/ *n.* a time-measuring instrument, esp. one keeping accurate time at all temperatures and used in navigation.

chronometry /krəˈnɒmɪtrɪ/ *n.* the science of accurate time-measurement. □ **chronometric** /ˌkrɒnəˈmetrɪk/ *adj.* **chronometrical** /ˌkrɒnəˈmetrɪk(ə)l/ *adj.* **chronometrically** /ˌkrɒnəˈmetrɪkəlɪ/ *adv.*

chrysalis /ˈkrɪsəlɪs/ *n.* (*pl.* **chrysalises** or **chrysalides** /krɪˈsælɪˌdiːz/) **1 a** a quiescent pupa of a butterfly or moth. **b** the hard outer case enclosing it. **2** a preparatory or transitional state. [L f. Gk *khrusallis -idos* f. *khrusos* gold]

chrysanthemum /krɪˈsænθəməm/ *n.* any composite plant of the genus *Chrysanthemum*, having brightly coloured flowers. [L f. Gk *khrusanthemon* f. *khrusos* gold + *anthemon* flower]

chrysoberyl /ˈkrɪsəˌberɪl/ *n.* a yellowish-green gem consisting of a beryllium salt. [L *chrysoberyllus* f. Gk *khrusos* gold + *bērullos* beryl]

chrysolite /ˈkrɪsəˌlaɪt/ *n.* a precious stone, a yellowish-green or brownish variety of olivine. [ME f. OF *crisolite* f. med.L *crisolitus* f. L *chrysolithus* f. Gk *khrusolithos* f. *khrusos* gold + *lithos* stone]

chrysoprase /ˈkrɪsəˌpreɪz/ *n.* an apple-green variety of chalcedony containing nickel and used as a gem. [ME f. OF *crisopace* f. L *chrysopassus* var. of L *chrysoprasus* f. Gk *khrusoprasos* f. *khrusos* gold + *prason* leek]

chthonic /ˈkθɒnɪk, ˈθɒnɪk/ (also **chthonian** /ˈkθəʊnɪən, ˈθəʊ-/) *adj.* of, relating to, or inhabiting the underworld. [Gk *khthōn* earth]

chub *n.* a thick-bodied coarse-fleshed river fish, *Leuciscus cephalus*. [15th c.: orig. unkn.]

chubby /ˈtʃʌbɪ/ *adj.* (**chubbier**, **chubbiest**) plump and rounded (esp. of a person or a part of the body). □ **chubbily** *adv.* **chubbiness** *n.* [CHUB]

chuck[1] *v.* & *n.* —*v.tr.* **1** *colloq.* fling or throw carelessly or with indifference. **2** *colloq.* (often foll. by *in*, *up*) give up; reject (*chucked in my job*). **3** touch playfully, esp. under the chin. —*n.* a playful touch under the chin. □ **the chuck** *sl.* dismissal (*he got the chuck*). **chuck it** *sl.* stop, desist. **chuck out** *colloq.* **1** expel (a person) from a gathering etc. **2** get rid of, discard. [16th c., perh. f. F *chuquer, choquer* to knock]

chuck[2] *n.* & *v.* —*n.* **1** a cut of beef between the neck and the ribs. **2** a device for holding a

workpiece in a lathe or a tool in a drill. —*v.tr.* fix (wood, a tool, etc.) to a chuck. [var. of CHOCK]

chuck[3] *n.* US *colloq.* food. □ **chuck-wagon 1** a provision-cart on a ranch etc. **2** a roadside eating-place. [19th c.: perh. f. CHUCK[2]]

chuckle /ˈtʃʌk(ə)l/ *v.* & *n.* —*v.intr.* laugh quietly or inwardly. —*n.* a quiet or suppressed laugh. □ **chuckler** *n.* [*chuck* cluck]

chuddar var. of CHADOR.

chuff /tʃʌf/ *v.intr.* (of a steam engine etc.) work with a regular sharp puffing sound. [imit.]

chuffed /tʃʌft/ *adj.* Brit. *sl.* delighted. [dial. *chuff* pleased]

chug /tʃʌg/ *v.* & *n.* —*v.intr.* (**chugged**, **chugging**) **1** emit a regular muffled explosive sound, as of an engine running slowly. **2** move with this sound. —*n.* a chugging sound. [imit.]

chukker /ˈtʃʌkə(r)/ *n.* (also **chukka**) each of the periods of play into which a game of polo is divided. □ **chukka boot** an ankle-high leather boot as worn for polo. [Hindi *cakkar* f. Skr. *cakra* wheel]

chum *n.* & *v.* —*n.* *colloq.* (esp. among school-children) a close friend. —*v.intr.* (often foll. by *with*) share rooms. □ **chum up** (often foll. by *with*) become a close friend (of). □ **chummy** *adj.* (**chummier**, **chummiest**). **chummily** *adv.* **chumminess** *n.* [17th c.: prob. short for *chamber-fellow*]

chump *n.* **1** *colloq.* a foolish person. **2** Brit. the thick end, esp. of a loin of lamb or mutton (*chump chop*). **3** a short thick block of wood. **4** Brit. *sl.* the head. □ **off one's chump** Brit. *sl.* crazy. [18th c.: blend of CHUNK and LUMP[1]]

chunder /ˈtʃʌndə(r)/ *v.intr.* & *n.* Austral. *sl.* vomit. [20th c.: orig. unkn.]

chunk *n.* **1** a thick solid slice or piece of something firm or hard. **2** a substantial amount or piece. [prob. var. of CHUNK[2]]

chunky /ˈtʃʌŋkɪ/ *adj.* (**chunkier**, **chunkiest**) **1** containing or consisting of chunks. **2** short and thick; small and sturdy. **3** (of clothes) made of a thick material. □ **chunkiness** *n.*

Chunnel /ˈtʃʌn(ə)l/ *n. colloq.* a tunnel under the English Channel linking England and France. [portmanteau word f. *Channel tunnel*]

chunter /ˈtʃʌntə(r)/ *v.intr.* Brit. *colloq.* mutter, grumble. [prob. imit.]

chupatty var. of CHAPATTI.

church *n.* & *v.* —*n.* **1** a building for public (usu. Christian) worship. **2** a meeting for public worship in such a building (*go to church; met after church*). **3** (**Church**) the body of all Christians. **4** (**Church**) the clergy or clerical profession (*went into the Church*). **5** (**Church**) an organized Christian group or society of any time, country, or distinct principles of worship (*Church of Scotland; High Church*). **6** (**Church**) institutionalized religion as a political or social force (*Church and State*). —*v.tr.* bring (esp. a woman after child-birth) to church for a service of thanksgiving. □ **Church of England** the English Church, recognized by the State and having the sovereign as its head. **church school** a school founded by or associated with the Church of England. [OE *cirice, circe*, etc. f. med. Gk *kurikon* f. Gk *kuriakon* (*dōma*) Lord's (house) f. *kurios* Lord: cf. KIRK]

churchgoer /ˈtʃɜːˌtʃˌgəʊə(r)/ *n.* a person who goes to church, esp. regularly. □ **churchgoing** *n.* & *adj.*

churchman /ˈtʃɜːtʃmən/ n. (pl. **-men**) **1** a member of the clergy or of a church. **2** a supporter of the church.

churchwarden /tʃɜːtʃˈwɔːd(ə)n/ n. **1** either of two elected lay representatives of a parish, assisting with routine administration. **2** a long-stemmed clay pipe.

churchwoman /ˈtʃɜːtʃˌwʊmən/ n. (pl. **-women**) **1** a woman member of the clergy or of a church. **2** a woman supporter of the Church.

churchy /ˈtʃɜːtʃɪ/ adj. **1** obtrusively or intolerantly devoted to the Church or opposed to religious dissent. **2** like a church. □ **churchiness** n.

churchyard /ˈtʃɜːtʃjɑːd/ n. the enclosed ground around a church, esp. as used for burials.

churl n. **1** an ill-bred person. **2** archaic a peasant; a person of low birth. **3** archaic a surly or mean person. [OE ceorl f. a WG root, = man]

churlish /ˈtʃɜːlɪʃ/ adj. surly; mean. □ **churlishly** adv. **churlishness** n. [OE cierlisc, ceorlisc f. ceorl CHURL]

churn n. & v. —n. **1** Brit. a large milk-can. **2** a machine for making butter by agitating milk or cream. —v. **1** tr. agitate (milk or cream) in a churn. **2** tr. produce (butter) in this way. **3** tr. (usu. foll. by up) cause distress to; upset, agitate. **4** intr. (of a liquid) seethe, foam violently (the churning sea). **5** tr. agitate or move (liquid) vigorously, causing it to foam. □ **churn out** produce routinely or mechanically, esp. in large quantities. [OE cyrin f. Gmc]

churr var. of CHIRR.

chute[1] /ʃuːt/ n. **1** a sloping channel or slide, with or without water, for conveying things to a lower level. **2** a slide into a swimming-pool. [F chute fall (of water etc.), f. OF cheoite fem. past part. of cheoir fall f. L cadere; in some senses = SHOOT]

chute[2] /ʃuːt/ n. colloq. parachute. □ **chutist** n. [abbr.]

chutney /ˈtʃʌtnɪ/ n. (pl. **-eys**) a pungent orig. Indian condiment made of fruits or vegetables, vinegar, spices, sugar, etc. [Hindi caṭnī]

chutzpah /ˈxʊtzpə/ n. sl. shameless audacity; cheek. [Yiddish]

chyle /kaɪl/ n. a milky fluid consisting of lymph and absorbed food materials from the intestine after digestion. □ **chylous** adj. [LL chylus f. Gk khulos juice]

chyme /kaɪm/ n. the acidic semisolid and partly digested food produced by the action of gastric secretion. □ **chymous** adj. [LL chymus f. Gk khumos juice]

Ci abbr. curie.

CIA abbr. (in the US) Central Intelligence Agency.

ciao /tʃaʊ/ int. colloq. **1** goodbye. **2** hello. [It.]

cicada /sɪˈkɑːdə, -ˈkeɪdə/ n. (also **cicala** /sɪˈkɑːlə/) any transparent-winged large insect of the family Cicadidae, the males of which make a loud rhythmic chirping sound. [L cicada, It. f. L cicala, It. cigala]

cicatrice /ˈsɪkətrɪs/ n. (also **cicatrix** /ˈsɪkətrɪks/) (pl. **cicatrices** /ˌsɪkəˈtraɪsiːz/) any mark left by a healed wound; a scar. □ **cicatricial** /ˌsɪkəˈtrɪʃ(ə)l/ adj. [ME f. OF cicatrice or L cicatrix -icis]

cicatrize /ˈsɪkətraɪz/ v. (also **-ise**) **1** tr. heal (a wound) by scar formation. **2** intr. (of a wound) heal by scar formation. □ **cicatrization** /-ˈzeɪʃ(ə)n/ n. [F cicatriser: see CICATRICE]

CID abbr. (in the UK) Criminal Investigation Department.

-cide /saɪd/ suffix forming nouns meaning: **1** a person or substance that kills (regicide; insecticide). **2** the killing of (infanticide; suicide). [F f. L -cida (sense 1), -cidium (sense 2), caedere kill]

cider /ˈsaɪdə(r)/ n. (also **cyder**) **1** Brit. an alcoholic drink made from fermented apple-juice. **2** US an unfermented drink made from apple-juice. □ **cider-press** a press for crushing apples to make cider. [ME f. OF sidre, ult. f. Heb. šēkār strong drink]

cigala /sɪˈgɑːlə/ n. = CICADA. [F cigale, It. & Prov. cigala f. L cicada]

cigar /sɪˈgɑː(r)/ n. a cylinder of tobacco rolled in tobacco leaves for smoking. [F cigare or Sp. cigarro]

cigarette /ˌsɪɡəˈret/ n. (US also **cigaret**) **1** a thin cylinder of finely-cut tobacco rolled in paper for smoking. **2** a similar cylinder containing a narcotic or medicated substance. □ **cigarette card** a small picture card of a kind formerly included in a packet of cigarettes. **cigarette-end** the unsmoked remainder of a cigarette. [F, dimin. of cigare CIGAR]

cigarillo /ˌsɪɡəˈrɪləʊ/ n. (pl. **-os**) a small cigar. [Sp., dimin. of cigarro CIGAR]

cilium /ˈsɪlɪəm/ n. (pl. **cilia** /-lɪə/) **1** a short minute hairlike vibrating structure on the surface of some cells, causing currents in the surrounding fluid. **2** an eyelash. □ **ciliary** adj. **ciliate** /-eɪt, -ət/ adj. **ciliated** adj. **ciliation** /-ˈeɪʃ(ə)n/ n. [L, = eyelash]

cill var. of SILL.

cimbalom /ˈsɪmbələm/ n. a dulcimer. [Magyar f. It. cembalo]

C.-in-C. abbr. Commander-in-Chief.

cinch /sɪntʃ/ n. & v. —n. **1** colloq. **a** a sure thing; a certainty. **b** an easy task. **2** a firm hold. **3** esp. US a girth for a saddle or pack. —v.tr. **1** **a** tighten as with a cinch (cinched at the waist with a belt). **b** secure a grip on. **2** sl. make certain of. **3** esp. US put a cinch (sense 3) on. [Sp. cincha]

cinchona /sɪŋˈkəʊnə/ n. **1** **a** any evergreen tree or shrub of the genus Cinchona, native to S. America, with fragrant flowers and yielding cinchona bark. **b** the bark of this tree, containing quinine. **2** any drug from this bark formerly used as a tonic and to stimulate the appetite. □ **cinchonic** /-ˈkɒnɪk/ adj. **cinchonine** /ˈsɪŋkəˌniːn/ n. [mod.L f. Countess of Chinchón d. 1641, introducer of drug into Spain]

cincture /ˈsɪŋktʃə(r)/ n. literary a girdle, belt, or border. [L cinctura f. cingere cinct- gird]

cinder /ˈsɪndə(r)/ n. **a** the residue of coal or wood etc. that has stopped giving off flames but still has combustible matter in it. **b** slag. **c** (in pl.) ashes. □ **burnt to a cinder** made useless by burning. □ **cindery** adj. [OE sinder, assim. to the unconnected F cendre and L cinis ashes]

Cinderella /ˌsɪndəˈrelə/ n. **1** a person or thing of unrecognized or disregarded merit or beauty. **2** a neglected or despised member of a group. [the name of a girl in a fairy-tale]

cine- /ˈsɪnɪ/ comb. form cinematographic (cine-camera; cinephotography). [abbr.]

cineaste /ˈsɪnɪˌæst/ n. (also **cineast**) a cinema enthusiast. [F cinéaste (as CINE-): cf. ENTHUSIAST]

cinema /ˈsɪnɪˌmɑː, -mə/ n. **1** Brit. a theatre where motion-picture films (see FILM n. 3) are shown.

2 a films collectively. **b** the production of films as an art or industry; cinematography.[F *cinéma*: see CINEMATOGRAPH]

cinematic /ˌsɪnɪˈmætɪk/ *adj.* **1** having the qualities characteristic of the cinema. **2** of or relating to the cinema. □ **cinematically** *adv.*

cinematograph /ˌsɪnɪˈmætəˌgrɑːf/ (also **kine-matograph** /ˌkɪn-/) *n.* an apparatus for showing motion-picture films. [F *cinématographe* f. Gk *kīnēma -atos* movement f. *kineō* move]

cinematography /ˌsɪnɪməˈtɒgrəfɪ/ *n.* the art of making motion-picture films. □ **cine-matographer** *n.* **cinematographic** /-ˌmætəˈgræfɪk/ *adj.* **cinematographically** /-ˌmætəˈgræfɪkəlɪ/ *adv.*

cineraria /ˌsɪnəˈreərɪə/ *n.* any of several varieties of the composite plant, *Cineraria cruentus*, having bright flowers and ash-coloured down on its leaves. [mod.L, fem. of L *cinerarius* of ashes f. *cinis -eris* ashes, from the ash-coloured down on the leaves]

cinerary /ˈsɪnərərɪ/ *adj.* of ashes. □ **cinerary urn** an urn for holding the ashes after cremation. [L *cinerarius*: see CINERARIA]

cinnabar /ˈsɪnəˌbɑː(r)/ *n.* **1 a** a bright red mineral form of mercuric sulphide from which mercury is obtained. **2** vermilion. [ME f. L *cinnabaris* f. Gk *kinnabari*, of oriental orig.]

cinnamon /ˈsɪnəmən/ *n.* **1** an aromatic spice from the peeled, dried, and rolled bark of a SE Asian tree. **2** any tree of the genus *Cinnamomum*, esp. *C. zeylanicum* yielding the spice. **3** yellowish-brown. [ME f. OF *cinnamome* f. L *cinnamomum* f. Gk *kinnamōmon*, and L *cinnamon* f. Gk *kinnamon*, f. Semitic (cf. Heb. *ḳinnāmôn*)]

cinquefoil /ˈsɪŋkfɔɪl/ *n.* **1** any plant of the genus *Potentilla*, with compound leaves of five leaflets. **2** *Archit.* a five-cusped ornament in a circle or arch. [ME f. L *quinquefolium* f. *quinque* five + *folium* leaf]

Cinque Ports /sɪŋk ˈpɔːts/ *n.pl.* a group of ports (orig. five only) on the SE coast of England with ancient privileges. [ME f. OF *cink porz*, L *quinque portus* five ports]

cion US var. of SCION 1.

cipher /ˈsaɪfə(r)/ *n. & v.* (also **cypher**) —*n.* **1 a** a secret or disguised way of writing. **b** a thing written in this way. **c** the key to it. **2** the arithmetical symbol (0) denoting no amount but used to occupy a vacant place in decimal etc. numeration (as in 12.05). **3** a person or thing of no importance. **4** the interlaced initials of a person or company etc.; a monogram. —*v. tr.* put into secret writing, encipher. [ME, f. OF *cifre* f. Arab *ṣifr* ZERO]

circa /ˈsɜːkə/ *prep.* (preceding a date) about. [L]

circadian /sɜːˈkeɪdɪən/ *adj. Physiol.* occurring or recurring about once per day. [irreg. f. L *circa* about + *dies* day]

circle /ˈsɜːk(ə)l/ *n. & v.* —*n.* **1 a** a round plane figure whose circumference is everywhere equidistant from its centre. **b** the line enclosing a circle. **2** a roundish enclosure or structure. **3** a ring. **4** a curved upper tier of seats in a theatre etc. (*dress circle*). **5** a circular route. **6** *Archaeol.* a group of (usu. large embedded) stones arranged in a circle. **7** persons grouped round a centre of interest. **8** a set or class or restricted group (*literary circles; not done in the best circles*). **9** (in full **vicious circle**) **a** an unbroken sequence of reciprocal cause and effect. **b** an action and

reaction that intensify each other. **c** the fallacy of proving a proposition from another which depends on the first for its own proof. —*v.* **1** *intr.* (often foll. by *round*, *about*) move in a circle. **2** *tr.* **a** revolve round. **b** form a circle round. □ **circle back** move in a wide loop towards the starting-point. **come full circle** return to the starting-point. **go round in circles** make no progress despite effort. **great** (or **small**) **circle** a circle on the surface of a sphere whose plane passes (or does not pass) through the sphere's centre. **run round in circles** *colloq.* be fussily busy with little result. □ **circler** *n.* [ME f. OF *cercle* f. L *circulus* dimin. of *circus* ring]

circlet /ˈsɜːklɪt/ *n.* **1** a small circle. **2** a circular band, esp. of gold or jewelled etc., as an ornament.

circuit /ˈsɜːkɪt/ *n.* **1 a** a line or course enclosing an area; the distance round. **b** the area enclosed. **2** *Electr.* **a** the path of a current. **b** the apparatus through which a current passes. **3 a** the journey of a judge in a particular district to hold courts. **b** this district. **c** the lawyers following a circuit. **4** a chain of theatres or cinemas etc. under a single management. **5** *Brit.* a motor-racing track. **6 a** a sequence of sporting events (*the US tennis circuit*). **b** a sequence of athletic exercises. **7** a roundabout journey. **8 a** a group of local Methodist churches forming a minor administrative unit. **b** the journey of an itinerant minister within this. □ **circuit-breaker** an automatic device for stopping the flow of current in an electrical circuit. [ME f. OF, f. L *circuitus* f. CIRCUM- + *ire* it- go]

circuitous /sɜːˈkjuːɪtəs/ *adj.* **1** indirect (and usu. long). **2** going a long way round. □ **circuitously** *adv.* **circuitousness** *n.* [med.L *circuitosus* f. *circuitus* CIRCUIT]

circuitry /ˈsɜːkɪtrɪ/ *n.* (*pl.* **-ies**) **1** a system of electric circuits. **2** the equipment forming this.

circular /ˈsɜːkjʊlə(r)/ *adj. & n.* —*adj.* **1 a** having the form of a circle. **b** moving or taking place along a circle (*circular tour*). **2** *Logic* (of reasoning) depending on a vicious circle. **3** (of a letter or advertisement etc.) printed for distribution to a large number of people. —*n.* a circular letter, leaflet, etc. □ **circular saw** a power saw with a rapidly rotating toothed disc. □ **circularity** /-ˈlærɪtɪ/ *n.* **circularly** *adv.* [ME f. AF *circuler*, OF *circulier*, *cerclier* f. LL *circularis* f. L *circulus* CIRCLE]

circularize /ˈsɜːkjʊləˌraɪz/ *v.tr.* (also **-ise**) **1** distribute circulars to. **2** *US* seek opinions of (people) by means of a questionnaire. □ **circularization** /-ˈzeɪʃ(ə)n/ *n.*

circulate /ˈsɜːkjʊˌleɪt/ *v.* **1** *intr.* go round from one place or person etc. to the next and so on; be in circulation. **2** *tr.* **a** cause to go round; put into circulation. **b** give currency to (a report etc.). **c** circularize. **3** *intr.* be actively sociable at a party, gathering, etc. □ **circulating library** a small library with books lent to a group of subscribers in turn. □ **circulative** *adj.* **circulator** *n.* [L *circulare circulat-* f. *circulus* CIRCLE]

circulation /ˌsɜːkjʊˈleɪʃ(ə)n/ *n.* **1 a** a movement to and fro, or from and back to a starting point, esp. of a fluid in a confined area or circuit. **b** the movement of blood from and to the heart. **c** a similar movement of sap etc. **2 a** the transmission or distribution (of news or information or books etc.). **b** the number of copies sold, esp. of journals and newspapers. **3 a** currency, coin, etc. **b** the movement or exchange of this in a country etc. □ **in** (or **out of**) **circulation** participating (or not participating) in activities etc. [F *circulation* or L *circulatio* f. *circulare* CIRCULATE]

circulatory /ˌsɜːkjʊˈleɪtərɪ, ˈsɜːkjʊlətərɪ/ *adj.* of or relating to the circulation of blood or sap.

circum- /ˈsɜːkəm/ *comb. form* round, about, around, used: **1** adverbially (*circumambient*; *circumfuse*). **2** prepositionally (*circumlunar*; *circumocular*). [from or after L *circum* prep. = round, about]

circumambient /ˌsɜːkəmˈæmbɪənt/ *adj.* (esp. of air or another fluid) surrounding. □ **circumambience** *n.* **circumambiency** *n.*

circumcise /ˈsɜːkəmˌsaɪz/ *v.tr.* **1** cut off the foreskin, as a Jewish or Muslim rite or a surgical operation. **2** cut off the clitoris (and sometimes the labia), usu. as a religious rite. [ME f. OF f. L *circumcidere circumcis-* (as CIRCUM-, *caedere* cut)]

circumcision /ˌsɜːkəmˈsɪʒ(ə)n/ *n.* the act or rite of circumcising or being circumcised. [ME f. OF *circoncision* f. LL *circumcisio -onis* (as CIRCUMCISE)]

circumference /sɜːˈkʌmfərəns/ *n.* **1** the enclosing boundary, esp. of a circle or other figure enclosed by a curve. **2** the distance round. □ **circumferential** /ˌsɜːkəmfəˈrenʃ(ə)l/ *adj.* **circumferentially** /ˌsɜːkəmfəˈrenʃəlɪ/ *adv.* [ME f. OF *circonference* f. L *circumferentia* (as CIRCUM-, *ferre* bear)]

circumflex /ˈsɜːkəmˌfleks/ *n.* (in full **circumflex accent**) a mark (ˆ or ˜) placed over a vowel in some languages to indicate a contraction, length, or a special quality. [L *circumflexus* (as CIRCUM-, *flectere flex-* bend), transl. of Gk *perispōmenos* drawn around]

circumlocution /ˌsɜːkəmləˈkjuːʃ(ə)n/ *n.* **1 a** a roundabout expression. **b** evasive talk. **2** the use of many words where fewer would do; verbosity. □ **circumlocutional** *adj.* **circumlocutionary** *adj.* **circumlocutionist** *n.* **circumlocutory** /-ˈlɒkjʊtərɪ/ *adj.* [ME f. F *circumlocution* or L *circumlocutio* (as CIRCUM-, LOCUTION), transl. of Gk PERIPHRASIS]

circumnavigate /ˌsɜːkəmˈnævɪˌgeɪt/ *v.tr.* sail round (esp. the world). □ **circumnavigation** /-ˈgeɪʃ(ə)n/ *n.* **circumnavigator** *n.* [L *circumnavigare* (as CIRCUM-, NAVIGATE)]

circumpolar /ˌsɜːkəmˈpəʊlə(r)/ *adj.* **1** *Geog.* around or near one of the earth's poles. **2** *Astron.* (of a star or motion etc.) above the horizon at all times in a given latitude.

circumscribe /ˈsɜːkəmˌskraɪb/ *v.tr.* **1** (of a line etc.) enclose or outline. **2** lay down the limits of; confine, restrict. **3** *Geom.* draw (a figure) round another, touching it at points but not cutting it. □ **circumscribable** /-ˈskraɪbəb(ə)l/ *adj.* **circumscriber** *n.* **circumscription** /-ˈskrɪpʃ(ə)n/ *n.* [L *circumscribere* (as CIRCUM-, *scribere script-* write)]

circumspect /ˈsɜːkəmˌspekt/ *adj.* wary, cautious; taking everything into account. □ **circumspection** /-ˈspekʃ(ə)n/ *n.* **circumspectly** *adv.* [ME f. L *circumspicere circumspect-* (as CIRCUM-, *specere spect-* look)]

circumstance /ˈsɜːkəmst(ə)ns/ *n.* **1 a** a fact, occurrence, or condition, esp. (in *pl.*) the time, place, manner, cause, occasion, etc., or surroundings of an act or event. **b** (in *pl.*) the external conditions that affect or might affect

an action. **2** (often foll. by *that* + clause) an incident, occurrence, or fact, as needing consideration (*the circumstance that he left early*). **3** (in *pl.*) one's state of financial or material welfare (*in reduced circumstances*). **4** ceremony, fuss (*pomp and circumstance*). **5** full detail in a narrative (*told it with much circumstance*). □ **in** (or **under**) **the** (or **these**) **circumstances** the state of affairs being what it is. **in** (or **under**) **no circumstances** not at all; never. □ **circumstanced** *adj.* [ME f. OF *circonstance* or L *circumstantia* (as CIRCUM-, *stantia* f. *sto* stand)]

circumstantial /ˌsɜːkəmˈstænʃ(ə)l/ *adj.* **1** given in full detail (*a circumstantial account*). **2** (of evidence, a legal case, etc.) tending to establish a conclusion by inference from known facts hard to explain otherwise. **3 a** depending on circumstances. **b** adventitious, incidental. □ **circumstantiality** /-ʃɪˈælɪtɪ/ *n.* **circumstantially** *adv.* [L *circumstantia:* see CIRCUMSTANCE]

circumvent /ˌsɜːkəmˈvent/ *v.tr.* **1 a** evade (a difficulty); find a way round. **b** baffle, outwit. **2** entrap (an enemy) by surrounding. □ **circumvention** *n.* [L *circumvenire circumvent-* (as CIRCUM-, *venire* come)]

circus /ˈsɜːkəs/ *n.* (*pl.* **circuses**) **1** a travelling show of performing animals, acrobats, clowns, etc. **2** *colloq.* **a** a scene of lively action; a disturbance. **b** a group of people in a common activity, esp. sport. **3** *Brit.* an open space in a town, where several streets converge (*Piccadilly Circus*). **4** *Rom. Antiq.* a rounded or oval arena with tiers of seats, for equestrian and other sports and games. [L, = ring]

cirque /sɜːk/ *n.* *Geol.* a deep bowl-shaped hollow at the head of a valley or on a mountainside. [F f. L CIRCUS]

cirrhosis /sɪˈrəʊsɪs/ *n.* a chronic disease of the liver as a result of alcoholism, hepatitis, etc. □ **cirrhotic** /sɪˈrɒtɪk/ *adj.* [mod.L f. Gk *kirrhos* tawny]

cirriped /ˈsɪrɪˌped/ *n.* (also **cirripede** /ˈsɪrɪˌpiːd/) any marine crustacean of the class Cirripedia, having a valved shell, e.g. a barnacle. [mod.L *Cirripedia* f. L *cirrus* curl (from the form of the legs) + *pes pedis* foot]

cirro- /ˈsɪrəʊ/ *comb. form* cirrus (cloud).

cirrus /ˈsɪrəs/ *n.* (*pl.* **cirri** /-raɪ/) **1** *Meteorol.* a form of white wispy cloud, esp. at high altitude. **2** *Bot.* a tendril. **3** *Zool.* a long slender appendage or filament. □ **cirrose** *adj.* **cirrous** *adj.* [L, = curl]

cis- /sɪs/ *prefix* (opp. TRANS- or ULTRA-). on this side of; on the side nearer to the speaker or writer (*cisatlantic*). [L *cis* on this side of]

cisalpine /sɪsˈælpaɪn/ *adj.* on the southern side of the Alps.

cisatlantic /ˌsɪsətˈlæntɪk/ *adj.* on this side of the Atlantic.

cispontine /sɪsˈpɒntaɪn/ *adj.* on the north side of the Thames in London. [CIS- (orig. the better-known side) + L *pons pont-* bridge]

cissy var. of SISSY.

Cistercian /sɪˈstɜːʃ(ə)n/ *n. & adj.* —*n.* a monk or nun of an order founded as a stricter branch of the Benedictines. —*adj.* of the Cistercians. [F *cistercien* f. L *Cistercium* Cîteaux near Dijon in France, where the order was founded]

cistern /ˈsɪst(ə)n/ *n.* **1** a tank for storing water, esp. one in a roof-space supplying taps or as part of a flushing lavatory. **2** an underground reservoir for rainwater. [ME f. OF *cisterne* f. L *cisterna* f. *cista* f. Gk *kistē* box]

cistus /ˈsɪstəs/ *n.* any shrub of the genus *Cistus*, with large white or red flowers. [mod.L f. Gk *kistos*]

citadel /ˈsɪtəd(ə)l, -ˌdel/ *n.* **1** a fortress, usu. on high ground protecting or dominating a city. **2** a meeting-hall of the Salvation Army. [F *citadelle* or It. *citadella*, ult. f. L *civitas -tatis* city]

citation /saɪˈteɪʃ(ə)n/ *n.* **1** the citing of a book or other source; a passage cited. **2** a mention in an official dispatch. **3** a note accompanying an award, describing the reasons for it.

cite /saɪt/ *v.tr.* **1** adduce as an instance. **2** quote (a passage, book, or author) in support of an argument etc. **3** mention in an official dispatch. **4** summon to appear in a lawcourt. □ **citable** *adj.* [ME f. F f. L *citare* f. *ciēre* set moving]

citified /ˈsɪtɪˌfaɪd/ *adj.* (also **cityfied**) usu. *derog.* city-like or urban in appearance or behaviour.

citizen /ˈsɪtɪz(ə)n/ *n.* **1** a member of a State or Commonwealth, either native or naturalized (*British citizen*). **2** (usu. foll. by *of*) **a** an inhabitant of a city. **b** a freeman of a city. **3** *US* a civilian. □ **Citizens' Advice Bureau** (in the UK) an office at which the public can receive free advice and information on civil matters. **citizen's arrest** an arrest by an ordinary person without a warrant. **citizen's band** a system of local intercommunication by individuals on special radio frequencies. □ **citizenhood** *n.* **citizenry** *n.* **citizenship** *n.* [ME f. AF *citesein*, OF *citeain* ult. f. L *civitas -tatis* city: cf. DENIZEN]

citric /ˈsɪtrɪk/ *adj.* derived from citrus fruit. □ **citric acid** a sharp-tasting water-soluble organic acid found in the juice of lemons and other sour fruits. □ **citrate** *n.* [F *citrique* f. L *citrus* citron]

citrine /ˈsɪtrɪn/ *adj.* & *n.* —*adj.* lemon-coloured. —*n.* a transparent yellow variety of quartz. [ME f. OF *citrin* (as CITRUS)]

citron /ˈsɪtrən/ *n.* **1** a shrubby tree, *Citrus medica*, bearing large lemon-like fruits with thick fragrant peel. **2** this fruit. [F f. L CITRUS, after *limon* lemon]

citronella /ˌsɪtrəˈnelə/ *n.* **1** any fragrant grass of the genus *Cymbopogon*, native to S. Asia. **2** the scented oil from these, used in insect repellent, and perfume and soap manufacture. [mod.L, formed as CITRON + dimin. suffix]

citrus /ˈsɪtrəs/ *n.* **1** any tree of the genus *Citrus*, including citron, lemon, lime, orange, and grapefruit. **2** (in full **citrus fruit**) a fruit from such a tree. □ **citrous** *adj.* [L, = citron-tree or thuja]

city /ˈsɪtɪ/ *n.* (*pl.* **-ies**) **1 a** a large town. **b** *Brit.* (strictly) a town created a city by charter and containing a cathedral. **c** *US* a municipal corporation occupying a definite area. **2** (**the City**) **a** the part of London governed by the Lord Mayor and the Corporation. **b** the business part of this. **c** commercial circles; high finance. **3** (*attrib.*) of a city or the City. □ **city father** (usu. in *pl.*) a person concerned with or experienced in the administration of a city. **city hall** *US* municipal offices or officers. **city slicker** usu. *derog.* **1** a smart and sophisticated city-dweller. **2** a plausible rogue as found in cities. **city-state** esp. *hist.* a city that with its surrounding

territory forms an independent state. □ **cityward** *adj.* & *adv.* **citywards** *adv.* [ME f. OF *cité* f. L *civitas -tatis* f. *civis* citizen]

cityfied var. of CITIFIED.

cityscape /ˈsɪtɪˌskeɪp/ *n.* **1** a view of a city (actual or depicted). **2** city scenery.

civet /ˈsɪvɪt/ *n.* **1** (in full **civet-cat**) any catlike animal of the mongoose family, esp. *Civettictis civetta* of Central Africa, having well developed anal scent glands. **2** a strong musky perfume obtained from the secretions of these scent glands. [F *civette* f. It. *zibetto* f. med.L *zibethum* f. Arab. *azzabād* f. *al* the + *zabād* this perfume]

civic /ˈsɪvɪk/ *adj.* **1** of a city; municipal. **2** of or proper to citizens (*civic virtues*). **3** of citizenship, civil. □ **civic centre** *Brit.* the area where municipal offices and other public buildings are situated; the buildings themselves. □ **civically** *adv.* [F *civique* or L *civicus* f. *civis* citizen]

civics /ˈsɪvɪks/ *n.pl.* (usu. treated as *sing.*) the study of the rights and duties of citizenship.

civil /ˈsɪv(ə)l, -ɪl/ *adj.* **1** of or belonging to citizens. **2** of ordinary citizens and their concerns, as distinct from military or naval or ecclesiastical matters. **3** polite, obliging, not rude. **4** *Law* relating to civil law (see below), not criminal or political matters (*civil court; civil lawyer*). **5** (of the length of a day, year, etc.) fixed by custom or law, not natural or astronomical. □ **civil aviation** non-military, esp. commercial aviation. **civil commotion** a riot or similar disturbance. **civil defence** the organization and training of civilians for the protection of lives and property during and after attacks in wartime. **civil disobedience** the refusal to comply with certain laws or to pay taxes etc. as a peaceful form of political protest. **civil engineer** an engineer who designs or maintains roads, bridges, dams, etc. **civil engineering** this work. **civil law 1** law concerning private rights (opp. *criminal law*). **2** *hist.* Roman or non-ecclesiastical law. **civil liberty** (often in *pl.*) freedom of action and speech subject to the law. **civil list** (in the UK) an annual allowance voted by Parliament for the royal family's household expenses. **civil marriage** a marriage solemnized as a civil contract without religious ceremony. **civil rights** the rights of citizens to political and social freedom and equality. **civil servant** a member of the civil service. **civil service** the permanent professional branches of State administration, excluding military and judicial branches and elected politicians. **civil war** a war between citizens of the same country. □ **civilly** *adv.* [ME f. OF f. L *civilis* f. *civis* citizen]

civilian /sɪˈvɪlɪən/ *n.* & *adj.* —*n.* a person not in the armed services or the police force. —*adj.* of or for civilians.

civilianize /sɪˈvɪlɪəˌnaɪz/ *v.tr.* (also **-ise**) make civilian in character or function. □ **civilianization** /-ˈzeɪʃ(ə)n/ *n.*

civility /sɪˈvɪlɪtɪ/ *n.* (*pl.* **-ies**) **1** politeness. **2** an act of politeness. [ME f. OF *civilité* f. L *civilitas -tatis* (as CIVIL)]

civilization /ˌsɪvɪlaɪˈzeɪʃ(ə)n, ˌsɪvɪlɪ-/ *n.* (also **-isation**) **1** an advanced stage or system of social development. **2** those peoples of the world regarded as having this. **3** a people or nation (esp. of the past) regarded as an element of social evolution (*ancient civilizations; the Inca civilization*). **4** making or becoming civilized.

civilize /ˈsɪvɪˌlaɪz/ *v.tr.* (also **-ise**) **1** bring out of a barbarous or primitive stage of society. **2** enlighten; refine and educate. □ **civilizable** *adj.* **civilizer** *n.* [F *civiliser* (as CIVIL)]

civvies /ˈsɪvɪz/ *n.pl. sl.* civilian clothes. [abbr.]

Civvy Street /ˈsɪvɪ/ *n. sl.* civilian life. [abbr.]

Cl *symb. Chem.* the element chlorine.

cl *abbr.* centilitre(s).

clack *v.* & *n.* —*v.intr.* **1** make a sharp sound as of boards struck together. **2** chatter, esp. loudly. —*n.* **1** a clacking sound. **2** clacking talk. □ **clacker** *n.* [ME, = to chatter, prob. f. ON *klaka*, of imit. orig.]

clad[1] *adj.* **1** clothed. **2** provided with cladding. [past part. of CLOTHE]

clad[2] *v.tr.* (**cladding**; *past* and *past part.* **cladded** or **clad**) provide with cladding. [app. f. CLAD[1]]

cladding /ˈklædɪŋ/ *n.* a covering or coating on a structure or material etc.

clade *n. Biol.* a group of organisms evolved from a common ancestor. [Gk *klados* branch]

cladistics /kləˈdɪstɪks/ *n.pl.* (usu. treated as *sing.*) *Biol.* a method of classification of animals and plants on the basis of shared characteristics, which are assumed to indicate common ancestry. □ **cladism** /ˈklædɪz(ə)m/ *n.* [as CLADE + -IST + -ICS]

claim *v.* & *n.* —*v.tr.* **1 a** (often foll. by *that* + clause) demand as one's due or property. **b** (usu. *absol.*) submit a request for payment under an insurance policy. **2 a** represent oneself as having or achieving (*claim victory; claim accuracy*). **b** (foll. by *to* + infin.) profess (*claimed to be the owner*). **c** assert, contend (*claim that one knows*). **3** have an achievement or a consequence (*could then claim five wins; the fire claimed many victims*). **4** (of a thing) deserve (*one's attention etc.*). —*n.* **1 a** a demand or request for something considered one's due (*lay claim to; put in a claim*). **b** an application for compensation under the terms of an insurance policy. **2** (foll. by *to*, *on*) a right or title to a thing (*his only claim to fame; have many claims on my time*). **3** a contention or assertion. **4** a thing claimed. **5** *Mining* a piece of land allotted or taken. □ **no claim** (or **claims**) **bonus** a reduction of an insurance premium after an agreed period without a claim under the terms of the policy. □ **claimable** *adj.* **claimer** *n.* [ME f. OF *claime* f. *clamer* call out f. L *clamare*]

claimant /ˈkleɪmənt/ *n.* a person making a claim, esp. in a lawsuit or for a State benefit.

clairvoyance /kleəˈvɔɪəns/ *n.* **1** the supposed faculty of perceiving things or events in the future or beyond normal sensory contact. **2** exceptional insight. [F *clairvoyance* f. *clair* CLEAR + *voir* voy- see]

clairvoyant /kleəˈvɔɪənt/ *n.* & *adj.* —*n.* (*fem.* **clairvoyante**) a person having clairvoyance. —*adj.* having clairvoyance. □ **clairvoyantly** *adv.*

clam *n.* & *v.* —*n.* **1** any bivalve mollusc, esp. the edible N. American hard or round clam (*Mercenaria mercenaria*) or the soft or long clam (*Mya arenaria*). **2** *colloq.* a shy or withdrawn person. —*v.intr.* (**clammed**, **clamming**) **1** dig for clams. **2** (foll. by *up*) *colloq.* refuse to talk. [16th c.: app. f. *clam* a clamp]

clamant /ˈkleɪmənt/ *adj. literary* noisy; insistent, urgent. □ **clamantly** *adv.* [L *clamare clamant-* cry out]

clamber /ˈklæmbə(r)/ *v.* & *n.* —*v.intr.* climb with hands and feet, esp. with difficulty or laboriously. —*n.* a difficult climb. [ME, prob. f. *clamb*, obs. past tense of CLIMB]

clammy /ˈklæmɪ/ *adj.* (**clammier**, **clammiest**) **1** unpleasantly damp and sticky or slimy. **2** (of weather) cold and damp. □ **clammily** *adv.* **clamminess** *n.* [ME f. *clam* to daub]

clamour /ˈklæmə(r)/ *n.* & *v.* (US **clamor**) —*n.* **1** loud or vehement shouting or noise. **2** a protest or complaint; an appeal or demand. —*v.* **1** *intr.* make a clamour. **2** *tr.* utter with a clamour. □ **clamorous** *adj.* **clamorously** *adv.* **clamorousness** *n.* [ME f. OF f. L *clamor -oris* f. *clamare* cry out]

clamp[1] *n.* & *v.* —*n.* **1** a device, esp. a brace or band of iron etc., for strengthening other materials or holding things together. **2** a device for immobilizing an illegally parked car. —*v.tr.* **1** strengthen or fasten with a clamp. **2** place or hold firmly. **3** immobilize (an illegally parked car) by fixing a clamp to one of its wheels. □ **clamp down 1** (often foll. by *on*) be rigid in enforcing a rule etc. **2** (foll. by *on*) try to suppress. **clamp-down** *n.* severe restriction or suppression. [ME prob. f. MDu., MLG *klamp(e)*]

clamp[2] *n.* **1** a heap of potatoes or other root vegetables stored under straw or earth. **2** a pile of bricks for burning. [16th c.: prob. f. Du. *klamp* heap (in sense 2 related to CLUMP)]

clan *n.* **1** a group of people with a common ancestor, esp. in the Scottish Highlands. **2** a large family as a social group. **3** a group with a strong common interest. [ME f. Gael. *clann* f. L *planta* sprout]

clandestine /klænˈdestɪn/ *adj.* surreptitious, secret. □ **clandestinely** *adv.* **clandestinity** /-ˈtɪnɪtɪ/ *n.* [F *clandestin* or L *clandestinus* f. *clam* secretly]

clang *n.* & *v.* —*n.* a loud resonant metallic sound as of a bell or hammer etc. —*v.* **1** *intr.* make a clang. **2** *tr.* cause to clang. [imit.: infl. by L *clangere* resound]

clanger /ˈklæŋə(r)/ *n. sl.* a mistake or blunder. □ **drop a clanger** commit a conspicuous indiscretion.

clangour /ˈklæŋgə(r)/ *n.* (US **clangor**) **1** a prolonged or repeated clanging noise. **2** an uproar or commotion. □ **clangorous** *adj.* **clangorously** *adv.* [L *clangor* noise of trumpets etc.]

clank *n.* & *v.* —*n.* a sound as of heavy pieces of metal meeting or a chain rattling. —*v.* **1** *intr.* make a clanking sound. **2** *tr.* cause to clank. □ **clankingly** *adv.* [imit.: cf. CLANG, CLINK[1], Du. *klank*]

clannish /ˈklænɪʃ/ *adj.* usu. *derog.* **1** (of a family or group) tending to hold together. **2** of or like a clan. □ **clannishly** *adv.* **clannishness** *n.*

clansman /ˈklænzmən/ *n.* (pl. **-men**; *fem.* **clanswoman**, pl. **-women**) a member or fellow-member of a clan.

clap[1] *v.* & *n.* —*v.* (**clapped**, **clapping**) **1 a** *intr.* strike the palms of one's hands together as a signal or repeatedly as applause. **b** *tr.* strike (the hands) together in this way. **2** *tr.* applaud or show one's approval of (esp. a person) in this way. **3** *tr.* (of a bird) flap (its wings) audibly. **4** *tr.* put or place quickly or with determination (*clapped him in prison*; *clap a tax on whisky*). —*n.* **1** the act of clapping, esp. as applause. **2** an explosive sound, esp. of thunder. **3** a slap, a pat. □ **clap eyes on** *colloq.* see. **clapped out** *Brit. sl.* worn out (esp. of machinery etc.); exhausted. [OE *clappian* throb, beat, of imit. orig.]

clap[2] *n. coarse sl.* venereal disease, esp. gonorrhoea. [OF *clapoir* venereal bubo]

clapboard /ˈklæpbɔːd, ˈklæbəd/ *n.* US = WEATHERBOARD. [Anglicized f. LG *klappholt* cask-stave]

clapper /ˈklæpə(r)/ *n.* the tongue or striker of a bell. □ **like the clappers** *Brit. sl.* very fast or hard.

clapperboard /ˈklæpəˌbɔːd/ *n. Cinematog.* a device of hinged boards struck together to synchronize the starting of picture and sound machinery in filming.

claptrap /ˈklæptræp/ *n.* **1** insincere or pretentious talk, nonsense. **2** language used or feelings expressed only to gain applause. [CLAP[1] + TRAP[1]]

claque /klæk, klɑːk/ *n.* a group of people hired to applaud in a theatre etc. [F f. *claquer* to clap]

claret /ˈklærət/ *n.* & *adj.* —*n.* **1** red wine, esp. from Bordeaux. **2** a deep purplish-red. **3** *archaic sl.* blood. —*adj.* claret-coloured. [ME f. OF (*vin*) *claret* f. med.L *claratum* (*vinum*) f. L *clarus* clear]

clarify /ˈklærɪˌfaɪ/ *v.* (**-ies, -ied**) **1** *tr.* & *intr.* make or become clearer. **2** *tr.* **a** free (liquid, butter, etc.) from impurities. **b** make transparent. **c** purify. □ **clarification** /-fɪˈkeɪʃ(ə)n/ *n.* **clarificatory** /-fɪˈkeɪtərɪ/ *n.* **clarifier** *n.* [ME f. OF *clarifier* f. L *clarus* clear]

clarinet /ˌklærɪˈnet/ *n.* **1** a woodwind instrument with a single-reed mouthpiece, a cylindrical tube with a flared end, holes, and keys. **2** its player. □ **clarinettist** *n.* (US **clarinetist**). [F *clarinette*, dimin. of *clarine* a kind of bell]

clarion /ˈklærɪən/ *n.* & *adj.* —*n.* **1** a clear rousing sound. **2** *hist.* a shrill narrow-tubed war trumpet. —*adj.* clear and loud. [ME f. med.L *clario -onis* f. L *clarus* clear]

clarity /ˈklærɪtɪ/ *n.* the state or quality of being clear, esp. of sound or expression. [ME f. L *claritas* f. *clarus* clear]

clash *n.* & *v.* —*n.* **1 a** a loud jarring sound as of metal objects being struck together. **b** a collision, esp. with force. **2 a** a conflict or disagreement. **b** a discord of colours etc. —*v.* **1 a** *intr.* make a clashing sound. **b** *tr.* cause to clash. **2** *intr.* collide; coincide awkwardly. **3** *intr.* (often foll. by *with*) **a** come into conflict or be at variance. **b** (of colours) be discordant. □ **clasher** *n.* [imit.: cf. *clack, clang, crack, crash*]

clasp /klɑːsp/ *n.* & *v.* —*n.* **1 a** a device with interlocking parts for fastening. **b** a buckle or brooch. **c** a metal fastening on a book-cover. **2 a** an embrace; a person's reach. **b** a grasp or handshake. **3** a bar of silver on a medal-ribbon with the name of the battle etc. at which the wearer was present. —*v.* **1** *tr.* fasten with or as with a clasp. **2** *tr.* **a** grasp, hold closely. **b** embrace, encircle. **3** *intr.* fasten a clasp. □ **clasp hands** shake hands with fervour or affection. **clasp one's hands** interlace one's fingers. **clasp-knife** a folding knife, usu. with a catch holding the blade when open. □ **clasper** *n.* [ME: orig. unkn.]

class /klɑːs/ *n.* & *v.* —*n.* **1** any set of persons or things grouped together, or graded or differentiated from others esp. by quality (*first class*; *economy class*). **2 a** a division or order of society (*upper class*; *professional classes*). **b** a caste system, a system of social classes. **3** *colloq.* distinction or high quality in appearance, behaviour, etc.; stylishness. **4 a** a group of students or pupils taught together. **b** the occasion when they meet. **c** their course of instruction. **5** US all the college or school students of the same standing or graduating in a given year (*the class of 1990*). **6** *Brit.* a division of candidates according to merit in an examination. **8** *Biol.* a grouping of organisms, the next major rank below a division or phylum. —*v.tr.* assign to a class or category. □ **class-conscious** aware of and reacting to social divisions or one's place in a system of social class. **class-list** *Brit.* a list of candidates in an examination with the class achieved by each. **class war** conflict between social classes. **in a class of** (or **on**) **its** (or **one's**) **own** unequalled. [L *classis* assembly]

classic /ˈklæsɪk/ *adj.* & *n.* —*adj.* **1 a** of the first class; of acknowledged excellence. **b** remarkably typical; outstandingly important (*a classic case*). **2 a** of ancient Greek and Latin literature, art, or culture. **b** (of style in art, music, etc.) simple, harmonious, well-proportioned; in accordance with established forms (cf. ROMANTIC). **3** having literary or historic associations (*classic ground*). **4** (of clothes) made in a simple elegant style not much affected by changes in fashion. —*n.* **1 a** a classic writer, artist, work, or example. **2 a** an ancient Greek or Latin writer. **b** (in *pl.*) the study of ancient Greek and Latin literature and history. **3** a garment in classic style. [F *classique* or L *classicus* f. *classis* class]

classical /ˈklæsɪk(ə)l/ *adj.* **1** of ancient Greek or Latin literature or art. **b** (of language) having the form used by the ancient standard authors (*classical Hebrew*). **c** based on the study of ancient Greek and Latin (*a classical education*). **2 a** (of music) serious or conventional; following traditional principles and intended to be of permanent rather than ephemeral value (cf. POPULAR, LIGHT). **b** of the period from *c.*1750–1800 (cf. ROMANTIC). **3 a** in or following the restrained style of classical antiquity (cf. ROMANTIC). **b** in or relating to a long-established style. **4** *Physics* relating to the concepts which preceded relativity and quantum theory. □ **classicalism** *n.* **classicalist** *n.* **classicality** /-ˈkælɪtɪ/ *n.* **classically** *adv.* [L *classicus* (as CLASSIC)]

classicism /ˈklæsɪˌsɪz(ə)m/ *n.* **1** the following of a classic style. **2** classical scholarship. □ **classicist** *n.*

classicize /ˈklæsɪˌsaɪz/ *v.* (also **-ise**) **1** *tr.* make classic. **2** *intr.* imitate a classical style.

classified /ˈklæsɪˌfaɪd/ *adj.* **1** arranged in classes or categories. **2** (of information etc.) designated as officially secret. **3** *Brit.* (of a road) assigned to a category according to its importance. **4** *Brit.* (of newspaper advertisements) arranged in columns according to various categories.

classify /ˈklæsɪˌfaɪ/ *v.tr.* (**-ies, -ied**) **1 a** arrange in classes or categories. **b** assign (a thing) to a class or category. **2** designate as officially secret or not for general disclosure. □ **classifiable** *adj.* **classification** /-fɪˈkeɪʃ(ə)n/ *n.* **classificatory**

/-'keɪtərɪ/ adj. **classifier** n. [back-form. f. *classification* f. F (as CLASS)]

classless /'klɑːslɪs/ adj. making or showing no distinction of classes (*classless society*; *classless accent*). □ **classlessness** n.

classmate /'klɑːsmeɪt/ n. a fellow-member of a class, esp. at school.

classroom /'klɑːsruːm, -rʊm/ n. a room in which a class of students is taught, esp. in a school.

classy /'klɑːsɪ/ adj. (**classier**, **classiest**) colloq. superior, stylish. □ **classily** adv. **classiness** n.

clatter /'klætə(r)/ n. & v. —n. **1** a rattling sound as of many hard objects struck together. **2** noisy talk. —v. **1** intr. **a** make a clatter. **b** fall or move etc. with a clatter. **2** tr. cause (plates etc.) to clatter. [OE, of imit. orig.]

clause /klɔːz/ n. **1** Gram. a distinct part of a sentence, including a subject and predicate. **2** a single statement in a treaty, law, bill, or contract. □ **clausal** adj. [ME f. OF f. L *clausula* conclusion f. *claudere claus-* shut]

claustral /'klɔːstr(ə)l/ adj. **1** of or associated with the cloister; monastic. **2** narrow-minded. [ME f. LL *claustralis* f. *claustrum* CLOISTER]

claustrophobia /ˌklɔːstrə'fəʊbɪə/ n. an abnormal fear of confined places. □ **claustrophobe** /'klɔːstrəfəʊb/ n. [mod.L f. L *claustrum*: see CLOISTER]

claustrophobic /ˌklɔːstrə'fəʊbɪk/ adj. **1** suffering from claustrophobia. **2** inducing claustrophobia. □ **claustrophobically** adv.

clave past of CLEAVE[2].

clavichord /'klævɪˌkɔːd/ n. a small keyboard instrument with a very soft tone. [ME f. med.L *clavichordium* f. L *clavis* key, *chorda* string: see CHORD[2]]

clavicle /'klævɪk(ə)l/ n. the collar-bone. □ **clavicular** /klə'vɪkjʊlə(r)/ adj. [L *clavicula* dimin. of *clavis* key (from its shape)]

clavier /klə'vɪə(r), 'klævɪə(r)/ n. Mus. **1** any keyboard instrument. **2** its keyboard. [F *clavier* or G *Klavier* f. med.L *claviarius*, orig. = key-bearer, f. L *clavis* key]

claw n. & v. —n. **1 a** a pointed horny nail on an animal's or bird's foot. **b** a foot armed with claws. **2** the pincers of a shellfish. **3** a device for grappling, holding, etc. —v. tr. & intr. scratch, maul, or pull (a person or thing) with claws. □ **claw back 1** regain laboriously or gradually. **2** recover (money paid out) from another source (e.g. taxation). **claw-hammer** a hammer with one side of the head forked for extracting nails. □ **clawed** adj. (also in comb.). **clawer** n. **clawless** adj. [OE *clawu, clawian*]

clay n. **1** a stiff sticky earth, used for making bricks, pottery, ceramics, etc. **2** poet. the substance of the human body. □ **clay pigeon** a breakable disc thrown up from a trap as a target for shooting. □ **clayey** adj. **clayish** adj. **claylike** adj. [OE *clæg* f. WG]

claymore /'kleɪmɔː(r)/ n. **1** hist. **a** a Scottish two-edged broadsword. **b** a broadsword, often with a single edge, having a hilt with a basketwork design. **2** US a type of anti-personnel mine. [Gael. *claidheamh mór* great sword]

-cle /k(ə)l/ suffix forming (orig. diminutive) nouns (*article*; *particle*). [as -CULE]

clean adj., adv., v., & n. —adj. **1** (often foll. by *of*) free from dirt or contaminating matter, unsoiled. **2** clear; unused or unpolluted; preserving what is regarded as the original state

(*clean air*; *clean page*). **3** free from obscenity or indecency. **4 a** attentive to personal hygiene and cleanliness. **b** (of children and animals) toilet-trained or house-trained. **5** complete, clear-cut, unobstructed, even. **6 a** (of a ship, aircraft, or car) streamlined, smooth. **b** well-formed, slender and shapely (*clean-limbed*; *the car has clean lines*). **7** adroit, skilful (*clean fielding*). **8** (of a nuclear weapon) producing relatively little fallout. **9 a** free from ceremonial defilement or from disease. **b** (of food) not prohibited. **10 a** free from any record of a crime, offence, etc. (*a clean driving-licence*). **b** sl. free from suspicion; not carrying incriminating material. **11** (of a taste, smell, etc.) sharp, fresh, distinctive. —adv. **1** completely, outright, simply (*clean bowled*; *clean forgot*). **2** in a clean manner. —v. **1** tr. (also foll. by *of*) & intr. make or become clean. **2** tr. Cookery remove the innards of (fish or fowl). —n. the act or process of cleaning or being cleaned (*give it a clean*). □ **clean break** a quick and final separation. **clean-cut** sharply outlined. **clean hands** freedom from guilt. **clean-living** of upright character. **clean out 1** clean thoroughly. **2** sl. empty or deprive (esp. of money). **clean-shaven** without beard, whiskers, moustache. **clean sheet** (or **slate**) freedom from commitments or imputations; the removal of these from one's record. **clean up 1 a** clear (a mess) away. **b** (also absol.) put (things) tidy. **c** make (oneself) clean. **2** restore order or morality to. **3** sl. **a** acquire as gain or profit. **b** make a gain or profit. **clean-up** n. an act of cleaning up. **come clean** colloq. own up; confess everything. **make a clean job of** colloq. do thoroughly. □ **cleanable** adj. **cleanish** adj. **cleanness** n. [OE *clǣne* (adj. & adv.), *clēne* (adv.), f. WG]

cleaner /'kliːnə(r)/ n. **1** a person employed to clean the interior of a building. **2** (usu. in pl.) a commercial establishment for cleaning clothes. **3** a device or substance for cleaning. □ **take to the cleaners** sl. **1** defraud or rob (a person) of all his or her money. **2** criticize severely.

cleanly[1] /'kliːnlɪ/ adv. **1** in a clean way. **2** efficiently; without difficulty. [OE *clǣnlīce*: see CLEAN, -LY[2]]

cleanly[2] /'klenlɪ/ adj. (**cleanlier**, **cleanliest**) habitually clean; with clean habits. □ **cleanlily** adv. **cleanliness** n. [OE *clǣnlic*: see CLEAN, -LY[1]]

cleanse /klenz/ v.tr. **1** usu. formal make clean. **2** (often foll. by *of*) purify from sin or guilt. □ **cleansing cream** cream for removing unwanted matter from the face, hands, etc. **cleansing department** Brit. a local service of refuse collection etc. □ **cleanser** n. [OE *clǣnsian* (see CLEAN)]

clear adj., adv., & v. —adj. **1** free from dirt or contamination. **2** (of weather, the sky, etc.) not dull or cloudy. **3 a** transparent. **b** lustrous, shining; free from obscurity. **4** (of soup) not containing solid ingredients. **5 a** distinct, easily perceived by the senses. **b** unambiguous, easily understood (*make a thing clear*; *make oneself clear*). **c** manifest; not confused or doubtful (*clear evidence*). **6** that discerns or is able to discern readily and accurately (*clear thinking*; *clear-sighted*). **7** (usu. foll. by *about*, *on*, or *that* + clause) confident, convinced, certain. **8** (of a conscience) free from guilt. **9** (of a road etc.) unobstructed, open. **10 a** net, without deduction (*a clear £1000*). **b** complete (*three clear days*). **11**

(often foll. by *of*) free, unhampered; unencumbered by debt, commitments, etc. **12** (foll. by *of*) not obstructed by. —*adv.* **1** clearly (*speak loud and clear*). **2** completely (*he got clear away*). **3** apart, out of contact (*keep clear; stand clear of the doors*). **4** (foll. by *to*) US all the way. —*v.* **1** *tr.* & *intr.* make or become clear. **2 a** *tr.* (often foll. by *of*) free from prohibition or obstruction. **b** *tr.* & *intr.* make or become empty or unobstructed. **c** *tr.* free (land) for cultivation or building by cutting down trees etc. **d** *tr.* cause people to leave (a room etc.). **3** *tr.* (often foll. by *of*) show or declare (a person) to be innocent (*cleared them of complicity*). **4** *tr.* approve (a person) for special duty, access to information, etc. **5** *tr.* pass over or by safely or without touching, esp. by jumping. **6** *tr.* make (an amount of money) as a net gain or to balance expenses. **7** *tr.* pass (a cheque) through a clearing-house. **8** *tr.* pass through (a customs office etc.). **9** *tr.* remove (an obstruction, an unwanted object, etc.) (*clear them out of the way*). **10** *intr.* (often foll. by *away, up*) (of physical phenomena) disappear, gradually diminish (*mist cleared by lunchtime; my cold has cleared up*). □ **clear the air 1** make the air less sultry. **2** disperse an atmosphere of suspicion, tension, etc. **clear away 1** remove completely. **2** remove the remains of a meal from the table. **clear-cut** sharply defined. **clear the decks** prepare for action, esp. fighting. **clear off 1** get rid of. **2** *colloq.* go away. **clear out 1** empty. **2** remove. **3** *colloq.* go away. **clear one's throat** cough slightly to make one's voice clear. **clear up 1** tidy up. **2** solve (a mystery etc.). **3** (of weather) become fine. **clear the way 1** remove obstacles. **2** stand aside. **in the clear** free from suspicion or difficulty. □ **clearable** *adj.* **clearer** *n.* **clearly** *adv.* **clearness** *n.* [ME f. OF *cler* f. L *clarus*]

clearance /ˈklɪərəns/ *n.* **1** the removal of obstructions etc., esp. removal of buildings, persons, etc., so as to clear land. **2** clear space allowed for the passing of two objects or two parts in machinery etc. **3** special authorization or permission (esp. for an aircraft to take off or land, or for access to information etc.). **4 a** the clearing of a person, ship, etc., by customs. **b** a certificate showing this. **5** the clearing of cheques. □ **clearance sale** *Brit.* a sale to get rid of superfluous stock.

clearing /ˈklɪərɪŋ/ *n.* **1** in senses of CLEAR *v.* **2** an area in a forest cleared for cultivation. □ **clearing bank** *Brit.* a bank which is a member of a clearing-house. **clearing-house 1** a bankers' establishment where cheques and bills from member banks are exchanged, so that only the balances need be paid in cash. **2** an agency for collecting and distributing information etc.

clearstory US var. of CLERESTORY.

clearway /ˈklɪəweɪ/ *n. Brit.* a main road (other than a motorway) on which vehicles are not normally permitted to stop.

cleat *n.* **1** a piece of metal, wood, etc., bolted on for fastening ropes to, or to strengthen woodwork etc. **2** a projecting piece on a spar, gangway, boot, etc., to give footing or prevent a rope from slipping. **3** a wedge. [OE: cf. CLOT]

cleavage /ˈkliːvɪdʒ/ *n.* **1** the hollow between a woman's breasts, esp. as exposed by a low-cut garment. **2** a division or splitting. **3** the splitting of rocks, crystals, etc., in a preferred direction.

cleave[1] *v.* (*past* **clove** /kləʊv/ or **cleft** /kleft/ or **cleaved**; *past part.* **cloven** /ˈkləʊv(ə)n/ or **cleft** or **cleaved**) *literary* **1 a** *tr.* chop or break apart, split, esp. along the grain or the line of cleavage. **b** *intr.* come apart in this way. **2** *tr.* make one's way through (air or water). □ **cleavable** *adj.* [OE *clēofan* f. Gmc]

cleave[2] *v.intr.* (*past* **cleaved** or **clave** /kleɪv/) (foll. by *to*) *literary* stick fast; adhere. [OE *cleofian, clifian* f. WG: cf. CLAY]

cleaver /ˈkliːvə(r)/ *n.* a tool for cleaving, esp. a heavy chopping tool used by butchers.

clef *n. Mus.* any of several symbols placed at the beginning of a staff, indicating the pitch of the notes written on it. [F f. L *clavis* key]

cleft[1] *adj.* split, partly divided. □ **cleft lip (and) palate** a congenital split in the roof of the mouth (and the upper lip). **in a cleft stick** in a difficult position, esp. one allowing neither retreat nor advance. [past part. of CLEAVE[1]]

cleft[2] *n.* a split or fissure; a space or division made by cleaving. [OE (rel. to CLEAVE[1]): assim. to CLEFT[1]]

clematis /ˈklemətɪs, kləˈmeɪtɪs/ *n.* any erect or climbing plant of the genus *Clematis*, bearing white, pink, or purple flowers and feathery seeds. [L f. Gk *klēmatis* f. *klēma* vine branch]

clement /ˈklemənt/ *adj.* **1** mild (*clement weather*). **2** merciful. □ **clemency** *n.* [ME f. L *clemens -entis*]

clementine /ˈklemənˌtiːn, -ˌtaɪn/ *n.* a small citrus fruit, thought to be a hybrid between a tangerine and sweet orange. [F *clémentine*]

clench /klentʃ/ *v.* & *n.* —*v.tr.* **1** close (the teeth or fingers) tightly. **2** grasp firmly. **3** = CLINCH *v.* **4.** —*n.* **1** a clenching action. **2** a clenched state. [OE f. Gmc: cf. CLING]

clerestory /ˈklɪəstərɪ, -ˌstɔːrɪ/ *n.* (US **clearstory**) (*pl.* **-ies**) an upper row of windows in a cathedral or large church, above the level of the aisle roofs. [ME f. CLEAR + STOREY]

clergy /ˈklɜːdʒɪ/ *n.* (*pl.* **-ies**) (usu. treated as *pl.*) (usu. prec. by *the*) the body of all persons ordained for religious duties in the Christian churches. [ME, partly f. OF *clergé* f. eccl.L *clericatus*, partly f. OF *clergie* f. *clerc* CLERK]

clergyman /ˈklɜːdʒɪmən/ *n.* (*pl.* **-men**) a member of the clergy, esp. of the Church of England.

cleric /ˈklerɪk/ *n.* a member of the clergy. [(orig. adj.) f. eccl.L f. Gk *klērikos* f. *klēros* lot, heritage, as in Acts 1:17]

clerical /ˈklerɪk(ə)l/ *adj.* **1** of the clergy or clergymen. **2** of or done by a clerk or clerks. □ **clerical collar** a stiff upright white collar fastening at the back. **clerical error** an error made in copying or writing out. □ **clericalism** *n.* **clericalist** *n.* **clerically** *adv.* [eccl.L *clericalis* (as CLERIC)]

clerihew /ˈklerɪˌhjuː/ *n.* a short comic or nonsensical verse, usu. in two rhyming couplets with lines of unequal length and referring to a famous person. [E. *Clerihew* Bentley, Engl. writer d. 1956, its inventor]

clerk /klɑːk/ *n.* & *v.* —*n.* **1** a person employed in an office, bank, shop, etc., to keep records, accounts, etc. **2** a secretary, agent, or record-keeper of a local council (*town clerk*), court, etc. **3** a lay officer of a church (*parish clerk*), college chapel, etc. —*v.intr.* work as a clerk. □ **clerk in holy orders** *formal* a clergyman. **clerk of the course** the judges' secretary etc. in horse or motor racing. **clerk of the works** (or **of works**) an overseer of building works etc. □ **clerkdom** *n.* **clerkess** *n. Sc.* **clerkish** *adj.* **clerkly** *adj.* **clerkship** *n.* [OE *cleric, clerc,* & OF *clerc,* f. eccl.L *clericus* CLERIC]

clever /ˈklevə(r)/ *adj.* (**cleverer, cleverest**) **1** skilful, talented; quick to understand and learn. **2** adroit, dextrous. **3** (of the doer or the thing done) ingenious, cunning. □ **cleverly** *adv.* **cleverness** *n.* [ME, = adroit: perh. rel. to CLEAVE², with sense 'apt to seize']

clew *n.* & *v.* —*n.* **1** *Naut.* **a** a lower or after corner of a sail. **b** a set of small cords suspending a hammock. **2** *archaic* a ball of thread or yarn. —*v.tr. Naut.* **1** (foll. by *up*) draw the lower ends of (a sail) to the upper yard or the mast ready for furling. **2** (foll. by *down*) let down (a sail) by the clews in unfurling. [OE *cliwen, cleowen*]

cliché /ˈkliːʃeɪ/ *n.* **1** a hackneyed phrase or opinion. **2** *Brit.* a metal casting of a stereotype or electrotype. [F f. *clicher* to stereotype]

clichéd /ˈkliːʃeɪd/ *adj.* (also **cliché'd**) hackneyed; full of clichés.

click /klɪk/ *n.* & *v.* —*n.* **1** a slight sharp sound as of a switch being operated. **2** a catch in machinery acting with a slight sharp sound. —*v.* **1 a** *intr.* make a click. **b** *tr.* cause (one's tongue, heels, etc.) to click. **2** *intr. colloq.* **a** become clear or understandable (often prec. by *it* as subject: *when I saw them it all clicked*). **b** be successful, secure one's object. **c** (foll. by *with*) become friendly, esp. with a person of the opposite sex. □ **clicker** *n.* [imit.: cf. Du. *klikken*, F *cliquer*]

client /ˈklaɪənt/ *n.* **1** a person using the services of a lawyer, architect, social worker, or other professional person. **2** a customer. **3** *archaic* a dependant or hanger-on. □ **clientship** *n.* [ME f. L *cliens -entis* f. *cluere* hear, obey]

clientele /ˌkliːɒnˈtel/ *n.* **1** clients collectively. **2** customers, esp. of a shop. **3** the patrons of a theatre etc. [L *clientela* clientship & F *clientèle*]

cliff /klɪf/ *n.* a steep rock-face, esp. at the edge of the sea. □ **cliff-hanger** a story etc. with a strong element of suspense; a suspenseful ending to an episode of a serial. □ **clifflike** *adj.* **cliffy** *adj.* [OE *clif* f. Gmc]

climacteric /klaɪˈmæktərɪk, ˌklaɪmækˈterɪk/ *n.* & *adj.* —*n.* **1** *Med.* the period of life when fertility and sexual activity are in decline. **2** a supposed critical period in life. —*adj.* **1** *Med.* occurring at the climacteric. **2** constituting a crisis; critical. [F *climatérique* or L *climactericus* f. Gk *klimaktērikos* f. *klimaktēr* critical period f. *klimax -akos* ladder]

climactic /klaɪˈmæktɪk/ *adj.* of or forming a climax. □ **climactically** *adv.* [CLIMAX + -IC, perh. after SYNTACTIC or CLIMACTERIC]

climate /ˈklaɪmɪt/ *n.* **1** the prevailing weather conditions of an area. **2** a region with particular weather conditions. **3** the prevailing trend of opinion or public feeling. □ **climatic** /-ˈmætɪk/ *adj.* **climatical** /-ˈmætɪk(ə)l/ *adj.* **climatically** /-ˈmætɪkəlɪ/ *adv.* [ME f. OF *climat* or LL *clima climat-* f. Gk *klima* f. *klinō* slope]

climatology /ˌklaɪməˈtɒlədʒɪ/ *n.* the scientific study of climate. □ **climatological** /-təˈlɒdʒɪk(ə)l/ *adj.* **climatologist** *n.*

climax /ˈklaɪmæks/ *n.* & *v.* —*n.* **1** the event or point of greatest intensity or interest; a culmination or apex. **2** a sexual orgasm. **3** *Ecol.* a state of equilibrium reached by a plant community. —*v.tr.* & *intr. colloq.* bring or come

to a climax. [LL f. Gk *klimax -akos* ladder, climax]

climb /klaɪm/ *v.* & *n.* —*v.* **1** *tr.* & *intr.* (often foll. by *up*) ascend, mount, go or come up, esp. by using one's hands. **2** *intr.* (of a plant) grow up a wall, tree, trellis, etc. by clinging with tendrils or by twining. **3** *intr.* make progress from one's own efforts, esp. in social rank, intellectual or moral strength, etc. **4** *intr.* (of an aircraft, the sun, etc.) go upwards. **5** *intr.* slope upwards. —*n.* **1** an ascent by climbing. **2 a** a place, esp. a hill, climbed or to be climbed. **b** a recognized route up a mountain etc. □ **climb down 1** descend with the help of one's hands. **2** withdraw from a stance taken up in argument, negotiation, etc. □ **climbable** *adj.* [OE *climban* f. WG, rel. to CLEAVE²]

climber /ˈklaɪmə(r)/ *n.* **1** a mountaineer. **2** a climbing plant. **3** a person with strong social etc. aspirations.

clime *n. literary* **1** a region. **2** a climate. [LL *clima*: see CLIMATE]

clinch *v.* & *n.* —*v.* **1** *tr.* confirm or settle (an argument, bargain, etc.) conclusively. **2** *intr. Boxing* & *Wrestling* (of participants) become too closely engaged. **3** *intr. colloq.* embrace. **4** *tr.* secure (a nail or rivet) by driving the point sideways when through. **5** *tr. Naut.* fasten (a rope) with a particular half hitch. —*n.* **1 a** a clinching action. **b** a clinched state. **2** *colloq.* an (esp. amorous) embrace. **3** *Boxing* & *Wrestling* an action or state in which participants become too closely engaged. [16th-c. var. of CLENCH]

clincher /ˈklɪntʃ(ə)r/ *n. colloq.* a remark or argument that settles a matter conclusively.

clincher-built var. of CLINKER-BUILT.

cling *v.intr.* (*past* and *past part.* **clung**) **1** (foll. by *to*) adhere, stick, or hold on. **2** (foll. by *to*) remain persistently or stubbornly faithful. **3** maintain one's grasp; keep hold; resist separation. □ **cling film** a very thin clinging transparent plastic film, used as a covering esp. for food. □ **clinger** *n.* **clingingly** *adv.* [OE *clingan* f. Gmc: cf. CLENCH]

clingy /ˈklɪŋɪ/ *adj.* (**clingier, clingiest**) liable to cling. □ **clinginess** *n.*

clinic /ˈklɪnɪk/ *n.* **1** *Brit.* a private or specialized hospital. **2** a place or occasion for giving specialist medical treatment or advice (*eye clinic*; *fertility clinic*). **3** a gathering at a hospital bedside for the teaching of medicine or surgery. □ **clinician** /klɪˈnɪʃ(ə)n/ *n.* [F *clinique* f. Gk *klinikē* (*tekhnē*) clinical, lit. bedside (art)]

clinical /ˈklɪnɪk(ə)l/ *adj.* **1** *Med.* **a** of or for the treatment of patients. **b** taught or learnt at the hospital bedside. **2** dispassionate, coldly detached. □ **clinical death** death judged by observation of a person's condition. **clinical medicine** medicine dealing with the observation and treatment of patients. **clinical thermometer** a thermometer with a small range, for taking a person's temperature. □ **clinically** *adv.* [L *clinicus* f. Gk *klinikos* f. *klinē* bed]

clink¹ *n.* & *v.* —*n.* a sharp ringing sound. —*v.* **1** *intr.* make a clink. **2** *tr.* cause (glasses etc.) to clink. [ME, prob. f. MDu. *klinken*; cf. CLANG, CLANK]

clink² *n.* (often prec. by *in*) *sl.* prison. [16th c.: orig. unkn.]

clinker /ˈklɪŋkə(r)/ *n.* **1** a mass of slag or lava. **2** a stony residue from burnt coal. [earlier *clincard* etc. f. obs. Du. *klinkaerd* f. *klinken* CLINK¹]

clinker-built /ˈklɪŋkəˌbɪlt/ *adj.* (also **clincher-built** /ˈklɪntʃəˌbɪlt/) (of a boat) having external planks overlapping downwards and secured with clinched copper nails. [*clink* N.Engl. var. of CLINCH + -ER¹]

clip¹ *n.* & *v.* —*n.* **1** a device for holding things together or for attachment to an object as a marker. **2** a piece of jewellery fastened by a clip. **3** a set of attached cartridges for a firearm. —*v.tr.* (**clipped**, **clipping**) **1** fix with a clip. **2** grip tightly. **3** surround closely. [OE *clyppan* embrace f. WG]

clip² *v.* & *n.* —*v.tr.* (**clipped**, **clipping**) **1** cut with shears or scissors, esp. cut short or trim (hair, wool, etc.). **2** trim or remove the hair or wool of (a person or animal). **3** *colloq.* hit smartly. **4 a** omit (a letter etc.) from a word. **b** omit letters or syllables of (words pronounced). **5** *Brit.* remove a small piece of (a ticket) to show that it has been used. **6** cut (an extract) from a newspaper etc. —*n.* **1** an act of clipping, esp. shearing or hair-cutting. **2** *colloq.* a smart blow, esp. with the hand. **3** a short sequence from a motion picture. **4** the quantity of wool clipped from a sheep, flock, etc. **5** *colloq.* speed, esp. rapid. □ **clip-joint** *sl.* a club etc. charging exorbitant prices. □ **clippable** *adj.* [ME f. ON *klippa*, prob. imit.]

clipboard /ˈklɪpbɔːd/ *n.* a small board with a spring clip for holding papers etc. and providing support for writing.

clipper /ˈklɪpə(r)/ *n.* **1** (usu. in *pl.*) any of various instruments for clipping hair, fingernails, hedges, etc. **2** a fast sailing-ship, esp. one with raking bows and masts. **3** a fast horse.

clipping /ˈklɪpɪŋ/ *n.* a piece clipped or cut from something, esp. from a newspaper.

clique /kliːk/ *n.* a small exclusive group of people. □ **cliquey** *adj.* (**cliquier**, **cliquiest**). **cliquish** *adj.* **cliquishness** *n.* **cliquism** *n.* [F f. *cliquer* CLICK]

clitoris /ˈklɪtərɪs, ˈklaɪ-/ *n.* a small erectile part of the female genitals at the upper end of the vulva. □ **clitoral** *adj.* [mod.L f. Gk *kleitoris*]

cloak *n.* & *v.* —*n.* **1** an outdoor over-garment, usu. sleeveless, hanging loosely from the shoulders. **2** a covering (*cloak of snow*). —*v.tr.* **1** cover with a cloak. **2** conceal, disguise. □ **cloak-and-dagger** involving intrigue and espionage. [ME f. OF *cloke*, dial. var. of *cloche* bell, cloak (from its bell shape) f. med.L *clocca* bell: see CLOCK¹]

cloakroom /ˈkləʊkruːm, -rʊm/ *n.* **1** a room where outdoor clothes or luggage may be left by visitors, clients, etc. **2** *Brit. euphem.* a lavatory.

clobber¹ /ˈklɒbə(r)/ *n. Brit. sl.* clothing or personal belongings. [19th c.: orig. unkn.]

clobber² /ˈklɒbə(r)/ *v.tr. sl.* **1** hit repeatedly; beat up. **2** defeat. **3** criticize severely. [20th c.: orig. unkn.]

cloche /klɒʃ, kləʊʃ/ *n.* **1** a small translucent cover for protecting or forcing outdoor plants. **2** (in full **cloche hat**) a woman's close-fitting bell-shaped hat. [F, = bell, f. med.L *clocca*: see CLOCK¹]

clock¹ *n.* & *v.* —*n.* **1** an instrument for measuring time, indicating hours, minutes, etc., by hands on a dial or by displayed figures. **2 a** any measuring device resembling a clock. **b** *colloq.* a speedometer, taximeter, or stopwatch. **3** time taken as an element in competitive sports etc.

(*ran against the clock*). **4** a downy seed-head, esp. that of a dandelion. —*v.tr.* **1** *colloq.* **a** (often foll. by *up*) attain or register (a stated time, distance, or speed, esp. in a race). **b** time (a race) with a stopwatch. **2** *Brit. sl.* hit, esp. on the head. □ **clock in** (or **on**) register one's arrival at work, esp. by means of an automatic recording clock. **clock off** (or **out**) register one's departure similarly. **clock radio** a combined radio and alarm clock. **round the clock** all day and (usu.) night. [ME f. MDu., MLG *klocke* f. med.L *clocca* bell, perh. f. Celt.]

clock² *n.* an ornamental pattern on the side of a stocking or sock. [16th c.: orig. unkn.]

clockwise /ˈklɒkwaɪz/ *adj.* & *adv.* in a curve corresponding in direction to the movement of the hands of a clock.

clockwork /ˈklɒkwɜːk/ *n.* **1** a mechanism like that of a mechanical clock, with a spring and gears. **2** (*attrib.*) **a** driven by clockwork. **b** regular, mechanical. □ **like clockwork** smoothly, regularly, automatically.

clod *n.* **1** a lump of earth, clay, etc. **2** *sl.* a silly or foolish person. □ **cloddy** *adj.* [ME: var. of CLOT]

cloddish /ˈklɒdɪʃ/ *adj.* loutish, foolish, clumsy. □ **cloddishly** *adv.* **cloddishness** *n.*

clodhopper /ˈklɒdˌhɒpə(r)/ *n.* **1** (usu. in *pl.*) *colloq.* a large heavy shoe. **2** = CLOD 2.

clodhopping /ˈklɒdˌhɒpɪŋ/ *adj.* = CLODDISH.

clog *n.* & *v.* —*n.* **1** a shoe with a thick wooden sole. **2** *archaic* an encumbrance or impediment. —*v.* (**clogged**, **clogging**) **1** (often foll. by *up*) **a** *tr.* obstruct, esp. by accumulation of glutinous matter. **b** *intr.* become obstructed. **2** *tr.* impede, hamper. **3** *tr.* & *intr.* (often foll. by *up*) fill with glutinous or choking matter. [ME: orig. unkn.]

cloister /ˈklɔɪstə(r)/ *n.* & *v.* —*n.* **1** a covered walk, often with a wall on one side and a colonnade open to a quadrangle on the other, esp. in a convent, monastery, college, or cathedral. **2** monastic life or seclusion. —*v.tr.* seclude or shut up usu. in a convent or monastery. □ **cloistral** *adj.* [ME f. OF *cloistre* f. L *claustrum, clostrum* lock, enclosed place f. *claudere* claus-CLOSE²]

cloistered /ˈklɔɪstəd/ *adj.* **1** secluded, sheltered. **2** monastic.

clomp var. of CLUMP *v.* 2.

clone *n.* & *v.* —*n.* **1 a** a group of organisms produced asexually from one stock or ancestor. **b** one such organism. **2** a person or thing regarded as identical with another. —*v.tr.* propagate as a clone. □ **clonal** *adj.* [Gk *klōn* twig, slip]

clonk *n.* & *v.* —*n.* an abrupt heavy sound of impact. —*v.* **1** *intr.* make such a sound. **2** *tr. colloq.* hit. [imit.]

clop *n.* & *v.* —*n.* the sound made by a horse's hooves. —*v.intr.* (**clopped**, **clopping**) make this sound. [imit.]

close¹ /kləʊs/ *adj., adv.,* & *n.* —*adj.* **1** (often foll. by *to*) situated at only a short distance or interval. **2 a** having a strong or immediate relation or connection (*close friend; close relative*). **b** in intimate friendship or association (*were very close*). **c** corresponding almost exactly (*close resemblance*). **3** in or almost in contact (*close combat; close proximity*). **4** dense, compact, with no or only slight intervals (*close texture; close formation*). **5** in which competitors are almost equal (*close contest; close election*). **6** leaving no gaps or weaknesses, rigorous (*close reasoning*). **7** concentrated, searching (*close examination*; *close attention*). **8** (of air etc.) stuffy or humid. **9** closed, shut. **10** limited or restricted to certain persons etc. (*close corporation*). **11 a** hidden, secret, covered. **b** secretive. **12** (of a danger etc.) directly threatening, narrowly avoided (*that was close*). **13** niggardly. —*adv.* **1** (often foll. by *by*, *on*, *to*, *upon*) at only a short distance or interval (*they live close by*; *close to the church*). **2** closely, in a close manner (*shut close*). —*n.* **1** an enclosed space. **2** *Brit.* a street closed at one end. **3** *Brit.* the precinct of a cathedral. **4** *Brit.* a school playing-field or playground. **5** *Sc.* an entry from the street to a common stairway or to a court at the back. □ **at close quarters** very close together. **close-fisted** niggardly. **close-fitting** (of a garment) fitting close to the body. **close harmony** harmony in which the notes of the chord are close together. **close-knit** tightly bound or interlocked; closely united in friendship. **close season** *Brit.* the season when something, esp. the killing of game etc., is illegal. **close-set** separated only by a small interval or intervals. **close shave** *colloq.* a narrow escape. **close-up** **1** a photograph etc. taken at close range. **2** an intimate description. □ **closely** *adv.* **closeness** *n.* **closish** *adj.* [ME f. OF *clos* f. L *clausum* enclosure & *clausus* past part. of *claudere* shut]

close² /kləʊz/ *v.* & *n.* —*v.* **1 a** *tr.* shut (a lid, box, door, room, house, etc.). **b** *intr.* be shut (*the door closed slowly*). **c** *tr.* block up. **2 a** *tr.* & *intr.* bring or come to an end. **b** *intr.* finish speaking. **c** *tr.* settle (a bargain etc.). **3 a** *intr.* end the day's business. **b** *tr.* end the day's business at (a shop, office, etc.). **4** *tr.* & *intr.* bring or come closer or into contact (*close ranks*). **5** *tr.* make (an electric circuit etc.) continuous. **6** *intr.* (foll. by *with*) express agreement (with an offer, terms, or the person offering them). **7** *intr.* (often foll. by *with*) come within striking distance; grapple. **8** *intr.* (foll. by *on*) (of a hand, box, etc.) grasp or entrap. —*n.* a conclusion, an end. □ **close down 1** (of a shop, factory, etc.) discontinue business, esp. permanently. **2** *Brit.* (of a broadcasting station) end transmission esp. until the next day. **close in 1** enclose. **2** come nearer. **3** (of days) get successively shorter. **close out** *US* discontinue, terminate, dispose of (a business). **close up 1** (often foll. by *to*) move closer. **2** shut, esp. temporarily. **3** block up. **4** (of an aperture) grow smaller. □ **closable** *adj.* **closer** *n.* [ME f. OF *clos*-stem of *clore* f. L *claudere* shut]

closed /kləʊzd/ *adj.* **1** not giving access; shut. **2** (of a shop etc.) having ceased business temporarily. **3** (of a society, system, etc.) self-contained; not communicating with others. □ **closed-circuit** (of television) transmitted by wires to a restricted set of receivers. **closed season** *US* = **close season** (see CLOSE¹). **closed shop 1** a place of work etc. where all employees must belong to an agreed trade union. **2** this system.

closet /ˈklɒzɪt/ *n.* & *v.* —*n.* **1** a small or private room. **2** a cupboard or recess. **3** = *water-closet*. **4** (*attrib.*) secret, covert (*closet homosexual*). —*v.tr.* (**closeted**, **closeting**) shut away, esp. in private conference or study. [ME f. OF, dimin. of *clos*: see CLOSE¹]

closure /ˈkləʊʒə(r)/ *n.* & *v.* —*n.* **1** the act or process of closing. **2** a closed condition. **3** something that closes or seals, e.g. a cap or tie. **4** a procedure for ending a debate and taking a vote, esp. in Parliament. —*v.tr.* apply the closure to (a motion, speakers, etc.). [ME f. OF f. LL *clausura* f. *claudere claus*- CLOSE²]

clot *n.* & *v.* —*n.* **1 a** a thick mass of coagulated liquid, esp. of blood exposed to air. **b** a mass of material stuck together. **2** *Brit. colloq.* a foolish person. —*v.tr.* & *intr.* (**clotted**, **clotting**) form into clots. □ **clotted cream** esp. *Brit.* thick cream obtained by slow scalding. [OE *clot(t)* f. WG: cf. CLEAT]

cloth /klɒθ/ *n.* (pl. **cloths** /klɒθs, klɒðz/) **1** woven or felted material. **2** a piece of this. **3** a piece of cloth for a particular purpose; a tablecloth, dishcloth, etc. **4** woollen woven fabric as used for clothes. **5 a** a profession or status, esp. of the clergy, as shown by clothes (*respect due to his cloth*). **b** (prec. by *the*) the clergy. [OE *clāth*, of unkn. orig.]

clothe /kləʊð/ *v.tr.* (*past* and *past part.* **clothed** or *formal* **clad**) **1** put clothes on; provide with clothes. **2** cover as with clothes. [OE: rel. to CLOTH]

clothes /kləʊðz/ *n.pl.* **1** garments worn to cover the body and limbs. **2** bedclothes. □ **clothes-horse** a frame for airing washed clothes. **2** *colloq.* an affectedly fashionable person. **clothes-line** a rope or wire etc. on which washed clothes are hung to dry. **clothes-peg** *Brit.* a clip or forked device for securing clothes to a clothes-line. **clothes-pin** *US* a clothes-peg. [OE *clāthas* pl. of *clāth* CLOTH]

clothier /ˈkləʊðɪə(r)/ *n.* a seller of men's clothes. [ME *clother* f. CLOTH]

clothing /ˈkləʊðɪŋ/ *n.* clothes collectively.

cloud /klaʊd/ *n.* & *v.* —*n.* **1** a visible mass of condensed watery vapour floating in the atmosphere high above the ground. **2** a mass of smoke or dust. **3** (foll. by *of*) a great number of insects, birds, etc., moving together. **4** a state of gloom, trouble, or suspicion. —*v.* **1** *tr.* cover or darken with clouds or gloom or trouble. **2** *intr.* (often foll. by *over*, *up*) become overcast or gloomy. **3** *tr.* make unclear. □ **in the clouds 1** unreal, imaginary, mystical. **2** (of a person) abstracted, inattentive. **under a cloud** out of favour, discredited, under suspicion. **with one's head in the clouds** day-dreaming, unrealistic. □ **cloudless** *adj.* **cloudlessly** *adv.* **cloudlet** *n.* [OE *clūd* mass of rock or earth, prob. rel. to CLOD]

cloudburst /ˈklaʊdbɜːst/ *n.* a sudden violent rainstorm.

cloud-cuckoo-land /klaʊdˈkʊkuːˌlænd/ *n.* a fanciful or ideal place. [transl. of Gk *Nephelo-kokkugia* f. *nephelē* cloud + *kokkux* cuckoo (in Aristophanes' *Birds*)]

cloudy /ˈklaʊdɪ/ *adj.* (**cloudier**, **cloudiest**) **1 a** (of the sky) covered with clouds, overcast. **b** (of weather) characterized by clouds. **2** not transparent; unclear. □ **cloudily** *adv.* **cloudiness** *n.*

clout /klaʊt/ *n.* & *v.* —*n.* **1** a heavy blow. **2** *colloq.* influence, power of effective action esp. in politics or business. **3** *dial.* a piece of cloth or clothing (*cast not a clout*). **4** *Archery hist.* a piece of canvas on a frame, used as a mark. **5** a nail with a large flat head. **6** a patch. —*v.tr.* **1** hit hard. **2** mend with a patch. [OE *clūt*, rel. to CLEAT, CLOT]

clove[1] *n.* **1 a** a dried flower-bud of a tropical plant, *Eugenia aromatica*, used as a pungent aromatic spice. **b** this plant. **2** (in full **clove gillyflower** or **clove pink**) a clove-scented pink, *Dianthus caryophyllus*. [ME f. OF *clou* (*de girofle*) nail (of gillyflower), from its shape, GILLYFLOWER being orig. the name of the spice; later applied to the similarly scented pink]

clove[2] *n.* any of the small bulbs making up a compound bulb of garlic, shallot, etc. [OE *clufu*, rel. to CLEAVE[1]]

clove[3] *past* of CLEAVE[1].

clove hitch /kləʊv/ *n.* a knot by which a rope is secured to a spar or rope. [old past part. of CLEAVE[1], as showing parallel separate lines]

cloven /ˈkləʊv(ə)n/ *adj.* split, partly divided. □ **cloven hoof** (or **foot**) the divided hoof of ruminant quadrupeds (e.g. oxen, sheep, goats). □ **cloven-footed** /-ˈfʊtɪd/ *adj.* **cloven-hoofed** /-ˈhuːfd/ *adj.* [past part. of CLEAVE[1]]

clover /ˈkləʊvə(r)/ *n.* any leguminous fodder plant of the genus *Trifolium*, having dense flower heads and leaves each consisting of usu. three leaflets. □ **in clover** in ease and luxury. [OE *clǣfre* f. Gmc]

clown /klaʊn/ *n.* & *v.* —*n.* **1** a comic entertainer, esp. in a pantomime or circus, usu. with traditional costume and make-up. **2** a silly, foolish, or playful person. —*v. intr.* (often foll. by *about*, *around*) behave like a clown; act foolishly or playfully. □ **clownery** *n.* **clownish** *adj.* **clownishly** *adv.* **clownishness** *n.* [16th c.: perh. of LG orig.]

cloy *v.tr.* (usu. foll. by *with*) satiate or sicken with an excess of sweetness, richness, etc. □ **cloyingly** *adv.* [ME f. obs. *acloy* f. AF *acloyer*, OF *encloyer* f. Rmc: cf. ENCLAVE]

club[1] *n.* & *v.* —*n.* **1** a heavy stick with a thick end, used as a weapon etc. **2** a stick used in a game, esp. a stick with a head used in golf. **3 a** a playing-card of a suit denoted by a black trefoil. **b** (in *pl.*) this suit. **4** an association of persons united by a common interest, usu. meeting periodically for a shared activity (*tennis club; yacht club*). **5** an organization or premises offering members social amenities, meals and temporary residence, etc. **6** an organization offering subscribers certain benefits (*book club*). **7** a group of persons, nations, etc., having something in common. —*v.* (**clubbed, clubbing**) **1** *tr.* beat with or as with a club. **2** *intr.* (foll. by *together*, *with*) combine for joint action, esp. making up a sum of money for a purpose. **3** *tr.* contribute (money etc.) to a common stock. □ **club-foot** a congenitally deformed foot. **club-root** a disease of cabbages etc. with swelling at the base of the stem. **club sandwich** *US* a sandwich with two layers of filling between three slices of toast or bread. **in the club** *Brit. sl.* pregnant. □ **clubber** *n.* [ME f. ON *klubba* assim. form of *klumba* club, rel. to CLUMP]

clubbable /ˈklʌbəb(ə)l/ *adj.* sociable; fit for membership of a club. □ **clubbability** /-ˈbɪlɪtɪ/ *n.* **clubbableness** *n.*

clubby /ˈklʌbɪ/ *adj.* (**clubbier, clubbiest**) esp. *US* sociable; friendly.

clubhouse /ˈklʌbhaʊs/ *n.* the premises used by a club.

cluck *n.* & *v.* —*n.* **1** a guttural cry like that of a hen. **2** *sl.* a silly or foolish person (*dumb cluck*). —*v.intr.* emit a cluck or clucks. [imit.]

clue *n.* & *v.* —*n.* **1** a fact or idea that serves as a guide, or suggests a line of inquiry, in a problem or investigation. **2** a piece of evidence etc. in the detection of a crime. **3** a verbal formula serving as a hint as to what is to be inserted in a crossword. —*v.tr.* (**clues, clued, cluing** or **clueing**) provide a clue to. □ **clue in** (or **up**) *sl.* inform. **not have a clue** *colloq.* be ignorant or incompetent. [var. of CLEW]

clueless /ˈkluːlɪs/ *adj. colloq.* ignorant, stupid. □ **cluelessly** *adv.* **cluelessness** *n.*

clump *n.* & *v.* —*n.* **1** (foll. by *of*) a cluster of plants. **2** an agglutinated mass. —*v.* **1 a** *intr.* form a clump. **b** *tr.* heap or plant together. **2** *intr.* (also **clomp** /klɒmp/) walk with heavy tread. **3** *tr. colloq.* hit. □ **clumpy** *adj.* (**clumpier, clumpiest**). [MLG *klumpe*, MDu. *klompe*: see CLUB]

clumsy /ˈklʌmzɪ/ *adj.* (**clumsier, clumsiest**) **1** awkward in movement or shape; ungainly. **2** difficult to handle or use. **3** tactless. □ **clumsily** *adv.* **clumsiness** *n.* [obs. *clumse* be numb with cold (prob. f. Scand.)]

clung *past* and *past part.* of CLING.

clunk *n.* & *v.* —*n.* a dull sound as of thick pieces of metal meeting. —*v.intr.* make such a sound. [imit.]

cluster /ˈklʌstə(r)/ *n.* & *v.* —*n.* **1** a close group or bunch of similar things growing together. **2** a close group or swarm of people, animals, gems, etc. **3** a group of successive consonants or vowels. —*v.* **1** *tr.* bring into a cluster or clusters. **2** *intr.* be or come into a cluster or clusters. **3** *intr.* (foll. by *round*, *around*) gather, congregate. □ **cluster bomb** an anti-personnel bomb spraying pellets on impact. [OE *clyster*: cf. CLOT]

clutch[1] *v.* & *n.* —*v.* **1** *tr.* seize eagerly; grasp tightly. **2** *intr.* (foll. by *at*) snatch suddenly. —*n.* **1 a** a tight grasp. **b** (foll. by *at*) grasping. **2** (in *pl.*) grasping hands, esp. as representing a cruel or relentless grasp or control. **3 a** (in a motor vehicle) a device for connecting and disconnecting the engine to the transmission. **b** the pedal operating this. □ **clutch bag** a slim flat handbag without handles. [ME *clucche, clicche* f. OE *clyccan* crook, clench, f. Gmc]

clutch[2] *n.* **1** a set of eggs for hatching. **2** a brood of chickens. [18th c.: prob. S.Engl. var. of *cletch* f. *cleck* to hatch f. ON *klekja*, assoc. with CLUTCH[1]]

clutter /ˈklʌtə(r)/ *n.* & *v.* —*n.* **1** a crowded and untidy collection of things. **2** an untidy state. —*v.tr.* (often foll. by *up*, *with*) crowd untidily, fill with clutter. [partly var. of *clotter* coagulate, partly assoc. with CLUSTER, CLATTER]

Cm *symb. Chem.* the element curium.

cm *abbr.* centimetre(s).

Cmdr. *abbr.* Commander.

Cmdre. *abbr.* Commodore.

CMG *abbr.* (in the UK) Companion (of the Order) of St Michael and St George.

CND *abbr.* (in the UK) Campaign for Nuclear Disarmament.

CO *abbr.* **1** Commanding Officer. **2** conscientious objector.

Co *symb. Chem.* the element cobalt.

Co. *abbr.* **1** company. **2** county.

co- /kəʊ/ *prefix* **1** added to: **a** nouns, with the sense 'joint, mutual, common' (*co-author*; *coequality*). **b** adjectives and adverbs, with the sense 'jointly, mutually' (*co-belligerent*; *coequal*; *coequally*). **c** verbs, with the sense 'together with another or others' (*cooperate*; *co-author*). **2** *Math.* of the complement of an angle (*cosine*). [orig. a form of COM-]

c/o *abbr.* care of.

coach *n.* & *v.* —*n.* **1** a single-decker bus, usu. comfortably equipped for longer journeys. **2** a railway carriage. **3** a horse-drawn carriage, usu. closed, esp. a State carriage or a stagecoach. **4 a** an instructor or trainer in sport. **b** a private tutor. —*v.tr.* **1** train or teach (a pupil, sports team, etc.) as a coach. **2** prime with facts. □ **coach-house** an outhouse for carriages. **coach station** a stopping-place for a number of coaches, usu. with buildings and amenities. [F *coche* f. Magyar *kocsi* (adj.) f. *Kocs* in Hungary]

coachman /ˈkəʊtʃmən/ *n.* (*pl.* **-men**) the driver of a horse-drawn carriage.

coachwork /ˈkəʊtʃwɜːk/ *n.* the bodywork of a road or rail vehicle.

coagulant /kəʊˈægjʊlənt/ *n.* a substance that produces coagulation.

coagulate /kəʊˈægjʊˌleɪt/ *v.tr.* & *intr.* **1** change from a fluid to a solid or semisolid state. **2** clot, curdle. □ **coagulable** *adj.* **coagulative** /-lətɪv/ *adj.* **coagulator** *n.* [ME f. L *coagulare* f. *coagulum* rennet]

coagulation /ˌkəʊægjʊˈleɪʃ(ə)n/ *n.* the process by which a liquid changes to a semisolid mass. [as COAGULATE]

coal *n.* & *v.* —*n.* **1 a** a hard black or blackish rock, mainly carbonized plant matter, found in underground seams and used as a fuel and in the manufacture of gas, tar, etc. **b** *Brit.* a piece of this for burning. **2** a red-hot piece of coal, wood, etc. in a fire. —*v.* **1** *intr.* take in a supply of coal. **2** *tr.* put coal into (an engine, fire, etc.). □ **coal gas** mixed gases extracted from coal and used for lighting and heating. **coal-hole** *Brit.* a compartment or small cellar for storing coal. **coal measures** a series of rocks formed by seams of coal with intervening strata. **coalscuttle** a container for coal to supply a domestic fire. **coals to Newcastle** something brought or sent to a place where it is already plentiful. **coal tar** a thick black oily liquid distilled from coal and used as a source of benzene. **coal-tit** (or **cole-tit**) a small greyish bird, *Parus ater*, with a black head. **haul** (or **call**) **over the coals** reprimand. □ **coaly** *adj.* [OE *col* f. Gmc]

coalesce /ˌkəʊəˈles/ *v.intr.* **1** come together and form one whole. **2** combine in a coalition. □ **coalescence** *n.* **coalescent** *adj.* [L *coalescere* (as CO-, *alescere* alit- grow f. *alere* nourish)]

coalface /ˈkəʊlfeɪs/ *n.* an exposed surface of coal in a mine.

coalfield /ˈkəʊlfiːld/ *n.* an extensive area with strata containing coal.

coalition /ˌkəʊəˈlɪʃ(ə)n/ *n.* **1** *Polit.* a temporary alliance, esp. of distinct parties forming a government, or of States. **2** fusion into one whole. □ **coalitionist** *n.* [med.L *coalitio* (as COALESCE)]

coalmine /ˈkəʊlmaɪn/ *n.* a mine in which coal is dug. □ **coalminer** *n.*

coaming /ˈkəʊmɪŋ/ *n.* a raised border round the hatches etc. of a ship to keep out water. [17th c.: orig. unkn.]

coarse /kɔːs/ *adj.* **1 a** rough or loose in texture or grain; made of large particles. **b** (of a person's features) rough or large. **2** lacking refinement or delicacy; crude, obscene (*coarse humour*). **3** inferior, common. □ **coarse fish** *Brit.* any fresh-water fish other than salmon and trout. □ **coarsely** *adv.* **coarseness** *n.* **coarsish** *adj.* [ME: orig. unkn.]

coarsen /ˈkɔːs(ə)n/ *v.tr.* & *intr.* make or become coarse.

coast *n.* & *v.* —*n.* the border of the land near the sea; the seashore. —*v.intr.* **1** ride or move, usu. downhill, without use of power, free-wheel. **2** make progress without much effort. **3** sail along the coast. □ **the coast is clear** there is no danger of being observed or caught. □ **coastal** *adj.* [ME f. OF *coste*, *costeier* f. L *costa* rib, flank, side]

coaster /ˈkəʊstə(r)/ *n.* **1** a ship that travels along the coast from port to port. **2** a small tray or mat for a bottle or glass.

coastguard /ˈkəʊstgɑːd/ *n.* **1** an organization keeping watch on the coasts and on local shipping to save life, prevent smuggling, etc. **2** a member of this.

coastline /ˈkəʊstlaɪn/ *n.* the line of the seashore, esp. with regard to its shape (*a rugged coastline*).

coat *n.* & *v.* —*n.* **1** an outer garment with sleeves and often extending below the hips; an overcoat or jacket. **2 a** an animal's fur, hair, etc. **b** *Physiol.* a structure, esp. a membrane, enclosing or lining an organ. **c** a skin, rind, or husk. **3 a** a layer or covering. **b** a covering of paint etc. laid on a surface at one time. —*v.tr.* **1** (usu. foll. by *with*, *in*) **a** apply a coat of paint etc. to; provide with a layer or covering. **b** (as **coated** *adj.*) covered with. **2** (of paint etc.) form a covering to. □ **coat of arms** the heraldic bearings or shield of a person, family, or corporation. **coat of mail** a jacket of mail armour. **on a person's coat-tails** undeservedly benefiting from another's success. □ **coated** *adj.* (also in *comb.*). [ME f. OF *cote* f. Rmc f. Frank., of unkn. orig.]

coating /ˈkəʊtɪŋ/ *n.* **1** a thin layer or covering of paint etc. **2** material for making coats.

co-author /ˌkəʊˈɔːθə(r)/ *n.* & *v.* —*n.* a joint author. —*v.tr.* be a joint author of.

coax *v.tr.* **1** (usu. foll. by *into*, or *to* + infin.) persuade (a person) gradually or by flattery. **2** (foll. by *out of*) obtain (a thing from a person) by coaxing. **3** manipulate (a thing) carefully or slowly. □ **coaxer** *n.* **coaxingly** *adv.* [16th c.: f. 'make a *cokes* of' f. obs. *cokes* simpleton, of unkn. orig.]

coaxial /kəʊˈæksɪəl/ *adj.* **1** having a common axis. **2** *Electr.* (of a cable or line) transmitting by means of two concentric conductors separated by an insulator. □ **coaxially** *adv.*

cob *n.* **1** a roundish lump of coal etc. **2** *Brit.* a domed loaf of bread. **3** *Brit.* = *corn-cob* (see CORN[1]). **4** (in full **cob-nut**) a large hazelnut. **5** a sturdy horse with short legs. **6** a male swan. [ME: orig. unkn.]

cobalt /ˈkəʊbɔːlt, -bɒlt/ *n.* *Chem.* a silvery-white magnetic metallic element and used in many alloys. □ **cobalt blue 1** a pigment containing a cobalt salt. **2** the deep-blue colour of this. □ **cobaltic** /kəˈbɔːltɪk/ *adj.* **cobaltous** /kəˈbɔːltəs/

adj. [G *Kobalt* etc., prob. = *Kobold* an underground spirit in mines]

cobber /ˈkɒbə(r)/ *n. Austral. & NZ colloq.* a companion or friend. [19th c.: perh. rel. to E dial. *cob* take a liking to]

cobble[1] /ˈkɒb(ə)l/ *n. & v.* —*n.* (in full **cobblestone**) a small rounded stone of a size used for paving. —*v.tr.* pave with cobbles. [ME *cobel(-ston)*, f. COB]

cobble[2] /ˈkɒb(ə)l/ *v.tr.* **1** mend or patch up (esp. shoes). **2** (often foll. by *together*) join or assemble roughly. [back-form. f. COBBLER]

cobbler /ˈkɒblə(r)/ *n.* **1** a person who mends shoes, esp. professionally. **2** an iced drink of wine etc., sugar, and lemon (*sherry cobbler*). **3** a fruit pie topped with scones. **4** (in *pl.*) *Brit. sl.* nonsense. [ME, of unkn. orig.: sense 4 f. rhyming sl. *cobbler's awls* = *balls*]

COBOL /ˈkəʊbɒl/ *n. Computing* a programming language designed for use in commerce. [common business oriented language]

cobra /ˈkəʊbrə, ˈkɒbrə/ *n.* any venomous snake of the genus *Naja*, native to Africa and Asia, with a neck dilated like a hood when excited. [Port. f. L *colubra* snake]

cobweb /ˈkɒbweb/ *n.* **1** a fine network of threads spun by a spider from a liquid secreted by it, used to trap insects etc. **2** the thread of this. □ **cobwebbed** *adj.* **cobwebby** *adj.* [ME *cop(pe)web* f. obs. *coppe* spider]

coca /ˈkəʊkə/ *n.* **1** a S. American shrub, *Erythroxylum coca*. **2** its dried leaves, chewed as a stimulant. [Sp. f. Quechua *cuca*]

cocaine /kəˈkeɪn, kəʊ-/ *n.* a drug derived from coca or prepared synthetically, used as a local anaesthetic and as a stimulant. [COCA + -INE[4]]

coccus /ˈkɒkəs/ *n.* (*pl.* **cocci** /-kɪ/) any spherical or roughly spherical bacterium. □ **coccal** *adj.* **coccoid** *adj.* [mod.L f. Gk *kokkos* berry]

coccyx /ˈkɒksɪks/ *n.* (*pl.* **coccyges** /-ˌdʒiːz/ or **coccyxes**) the small triangular bone at the base of the spinal column in humans and some apes. □ **coccygeal** /kɒkˈsɪdʒɪəl/ *adj.* [L f. Gk *kokkux -ugos* cuckoo (from being shaped like its bill)]

cochineal /ˈkɒtʃɪniːl, -ˈniːl/ *n.* **1** a scarlet dye used esp. for colouring food. **2** the dried bodies of the female of the Mexican insect, *Dactylopius coccus*, yielding this. [F *cochenille* or Sp. *cochinilla* f. L *coccinus* scarlet f. Gk *kokkos* berry]

cochlea /ˈkɒklɪə/ *n.* (*pl.* **cochleae** /-klɪˌiː/) the spiral cavity of the internal ear. □ **cochlear** *adj.* [L, = snail-shell, f. Gk *kokhlias*]

cock[1] *n. & v.* —*n.* **1 a** a male bird, esp. a domestic fowl. **b** a male lobster, crab, or salmon. **2** *Brit. sl.* (usu. **old cock** as a form of address) a friend; a fellow. **3** *coarse sl.* the penis. **4** *Brit. sl.* nonsense. **5 a** a firing lever in a gun which can be raised to be released by the trigger. **b** the cocked position of this (*at full cock*). **6** a tap or valve controlling flow. —*v.tr.* **1** raise or make upright or erect. **2** turn or move (the eye or ear) attentively or knowingly. **3** set aslant, or turn up the brim of (a hat). **4** raise the cock of (a gun). □ **at half cock** only partly ready. **cock-a-doodle-doo** a cock's crow. **cock-and-bull story** an absurd or incredible account. **cock crow** dawn. **cocked hat** a brimless triangular hat that pointed at the front, back, and top. **cock-fight** a fight between cocks as sport. **cock-of-the-walk** a dominant or arrogant person. **cock sparrow 1** a male

sparrow. **2** a lively quarrelsome person. **cock up** *Brit. sl.* bungle; make a mess of. **cock-up** *n. Brit. sl.* a muddle or mistake. **knock into a cocked hat** defeat utterly. [OE *cocc* and OF *coq* prob. f. med.L *coccus*]

cock[2] *n.* a small pile of hay, straw, etc. with vertical sides and a rounded top. [ME, perh. of Scand. orig.]

cockade /kɒˈkeɪd/ *n.* a rosette etc. worn in a hat as a badge of office or party, or as part of a livery. □ **cockaded** *adj.* [F *cocarde* orig. in *bonnet à la coquarde*, f. fem. of obs. *coquard* saucy f. *coq* COCK[1]]

cock-a-hoop /ˌkɒkəˈhuːp/ *adj. & adv.* —*adj.* exultant; crowing boastfully. —*adv.* exultantly. [16th c.: orig. in phr. *set cock a hoop* denoting some action preliminary to hard drinking]

cock-a-leekie /ˌkɒkəˈliːkɪ/ *n.* (also **cocky-leeky** /ˌkɒkɪ-/) a soup traditionally made in Scotland with boiling fowl and leeks. [COCK[1] + LEEK]

cockatoo /ˌkɒkəˈtuː/ *n.* **1** any of several parrots of the family Cacatuinae, having powerful beaks and erectile crests. **2** *Austral. & NZ colloq.* a small farmer. [Du. *kaketoe* f. Malay *kakatua*, assim. to COCK[1]]

cockchafer /ˈkɒkˌtʃeɪfə(r)/ *n.* a large nocturnal beetle, *Melolontha melolontha*, whose larva feeds on roots of crops etc. [perh. f. COCK[1] as expressing size or vigour + CHAFER]

cocker /ˈkɒkə(r)/ *n.* (in full **cocker spaniel**) **1** a small spaniel of a breed with a silky coat. **2** this breed. [as COCK[1], from use in hunting woodcocks etc.]

cockerel /ˈkɒkər(ə)l/ *n.* a young cock. [ME: dimin. of COCK[1]]

cock-eyed /ˈkɒkaɪd/ *adj. colloq.* **1** crooked, askew, not level. **2** (of a scheme etc.) absurd, not practical. **3** drunk. **4** squinting. [19th c.: app. f. COCK[1] + EYE]

cockle[1] /ˈkɒk(ə)l/ *n.* **1 a** any edible mollusc of the genus *Cardium*, having a chubby ribbed bivalve shell. **b** its shell. **2** (in full **cockle-shell**) a small shallow boat. □ **warm the cockles of one's heart** make one contented; be satisfying. [ME f. OF *coquille* shell ult. f. Gk *kogkhulion* f. *kogkhē* CONCH]

cockle[2] /ˈkɒk(ə)l/ *v. & n.* —*v.* **1** *intr.* pucker, wrinkle. **2** *tr.* cause to cockle. —*n.* a pucker or wrinkle in paper, glass, etc. [F *coquiller* blister (bread in cooking) f. *coquille*: see COCKLE[1]]

cockney /ˈkɒknɪ/ *n. & adj.* —*n.* (*pl.* **-eys**) **1** a native of East London, esp. one born within hearing of Bow Bells. **2** the dialect or accent typical of this area. —*adj.* of or characteristic of cockneys or their dialect or accent. □ **cockneyism** *n.* [ME *cokeney* cock's egg, later derog. for 'townsman']

cockpit /ˈkɒkpɪt/ *n.* **1 a** a compartment for the pilot (or the pilot and crew) of an aircraft or spacecraft. **b** a similar compartment for the driver in a racing car. **c** a space for the helmsman in some small yachts. **2** an arena of war or other conflict. **3** a place where cock-fights are held. [orig. in sense 3, f. COCK[1] + PIT[1]]

cockroach /ˈkɒkrəʊtʃ/ *n.* any of various flat brown insects, esp. *Blatta orientalis*, infesting kitchens, bathrooms, etc. [Sp. *cucaracha*, assim. to COCK[1], ROACH[1]]

cockscomb /ˈkɒkskəʊm/ *n.* the crest or comb of a cock.

cocksure /ˌkɒkˈʃʊə(r), -ˈʃɔː(r)/ adj. **1** presumptuously or arrogantly confident. **2** (foll. by *of, about*) absolutely sure. □ **cocksurely** adv. **cocksureness** n. [*cock* = God + SURE]

cocktail /ˈkɒkteɪl/ n. **1 a** usu. alcoholic drink made by mixing various spirits, fruit juices, etc. **2** a dish of mixed ingredients (*fruit cocktail*; *shellfish cocktail*). **3** any hybrid mixture. □ **cocktail stick** a small pointed stick for serving an olive, cherry, small sausage, etc. [orig. unkn.: cf. earlier sense 'docked horse' f. COCK¹: the connection is unclear]

cocky¹ /ˈkɒkɪ/ adj. (**cockier, cockiest**) **1** conceited, arrogant. **2** saucy, impudent. □ **cockily** adv. **cockiness** n. [COCK¹ + -Y¹]

cocky² /ˈkɒkɪ/ n. (pl. **-ies**) Austral. & NZ colloq. = COCKATOO 2. [abbr.]

coco /ˈkəʊkəʊ/ n. (also **cocoa**) (pl. **cocos** or **cocoas**) a tall tropical palm tree, *Cocos nucifera*, bearing coconuts. [Port. & Sp. *coco* grimace: the base of the shell resembles a face]

cocoa /ˈkəʊkəʊ/ n. **1** a powder made from crushed cacao seeds. **2** a drink made from this. □ **cocoa bean** a cacao seed. **cocoa butter** a fatty substance obtained from cocoa beans and used for confectionery, cosmetics, etc. [alt. of CACAO]

coconut /ˈkəʊkəˌnʌt/ n. (also **cocoanut**) **1** a large ovate brown seed of the coco, with a hard shell and edible white fleshy lining enclosing a milky juice. **2** = COCO. **3** the edible white fleshy lining of a coconut. □ **coconut butter** a solid oil obtained from the lining of the coconut, and used in soap, candles, ointment, etc. **coconut ice** a sweet of sugar and desiccated coconut. **coconut matting** a matting made of fibre from coconut husks. **coconut shy** a fairground sideshow where balls are thrown to dislodge coconuts. [COCO + NUT]

cocoon /kəˈkuːn/ n. & v. —n. **1 a** a silky case spun by many insect larvae for protection as pupae. **b** a similar structure made by other animals. **2** a protective covering. —v. **1** tr. & intr. wrap in or form a cocoon. **2** tr. spray with a protective coating. [F *cocon* f. mod. Prov. *coucoun* dimin. of *coca* shell]

cocotte /kəˈkɒt/ n. **1 a** a small fireproof dish for cooking and serving an individual portion of food. **b** a deep cooking pot with a tight-fitting lid and handles. **2** archaic a fashionable prostitute. [F]

COD abbr. **1 a** cash on delivery. **b** US collect on delivery. **2** Concise Oxford Dictionary.

cod¹ n. (pl. same) any large marine fish of the family Gadidae, esp. *Gadus morhua*. □ **cod-liver oil** an oil pressed from the fresh liver of cod, which is rich in vitamins D and A. [ME: orig. unkn.]

cod² n. & v. Brit. sl. —n. **1** a parody. **2** a hoax. **3** (attrib.) = MOCK adj. —v. (**codded, codding**) **1 a** intr. perform a hoax. **b** tr. play a trick on; fool. **2** tr. parody. [19th c.: orig. unkn.]

cod³ n. sl. nonsense. [abbr. of CODSWALLOP]

coda /ˈkəʊdə/ n. **1** Mus. the concluding passage of a piece or movement, usu. forming an addition to the basic structure. **2** Ballet the concluding section of a dance. **3** a concluding event or series of events. [It. f. L *cauda* tail]

coddle /ˈkɒd(ə)l/ v.tr. **1 a** treat as an invalid; protect attentively. **b** (foll. by *up*) strengthen by feeding. **2** cook (an egg) in water below boiling

point. □ **coddler** n. [prob. dial. var. of *caudle* invalids' gruel]

code /kəʊd/ n. & v. —n. **1** a system of words, letters, figures, or symbols, used to represent others for secrecy or brevity. **2** a system of prearranged signals, esp. used to ensure secrecy in transmitting messages. **3** Computing a piece of program text. **4 a** a systematic collection of statutes, a body of laws. **b** a set of rules on any subject. **5 a** the prevailing morality of a society or class (*code of honour*). **b** a person's standard of moral behaviour. —v.tr. put (a message, program, etc.) into code. □ **code-name** (or **-number**) a word or symbol (or number) used for secrecy or convenience instead of the usual name. □ **coder** n. [ME f. OF f. L CODEX]

codeine /ˈkəʊdiːn/ n. an alkaloid derived from morphine and used to relieve pain. [Gk *kōdeia* poppy-head + -INE⁴]

codependency /ˌkəʊdɪˈpendənsɪ/ n. addiction to a supportive role in a relationship. □ **codependent** adj. & n. [CO- + DEPENDENCY]

codex /ˈkəʊdeks/ n. (pl. **codices** /ˈkəʊdɪˌsiːz, ˈkɒd-/) **1** an ancient manuscript text in book form. **2** a collection of pharmaceutical descriptions of drugs etc. [L, = block of wood, tablet, book]

codfish /ˈkɒdfɪʃ/ n. = COD¹.

codger /ˈkɒdʒə(r)/ n. (usu. in **old codger**) colloq. a person, esp. an old or strange one. [perh. var. of *cadger*: see CADGE]

codicil /ˈkəʊdɪsɪl, ˈkɒd-/ n. an addition explaining, modifying, or revoking a will or part of one. □ **codicillary** /ˌkɒdɪˈsɪlərɪ/ adj. [L *codicillus*, dimin. of CODEX]

codify /ˈkəʊdɪfaɪ, ˈkɒd-/ v.tr. (**-ies, -ied**) arrange (laws etc.) systematically into a code. □ **codification** /-fɪˈkeɪʃ(ə)n/ n. **codifier** n.

codling¹ /ˈkɒdlɪŋ/ n. (also **codlin**) **1** any of several varieties of cooking-apple, having a long tapering shape. **2** a small moth, *Carpocapsa pomonella*, the larva of which feeds on apples. [ME f. AF *quer de lion* lion-heart]

codling² /ˈkɒdlɪŋ/ n. a small codfish.

codpiece /ˈkɒdpiːs/ n. hist. an appendage like a small bag or flap at the front of a man's breeches. [ME, f. *cod* scrotum + PIECE]

co-driver /kəʊˈdraɪvə(r)/ n. a person who shares the driving of a vehicle with another, esp. in a race, rally, etc.

codswallop /ˈkɒdzˌwɒləp/ n. Brit. sl. nonsense. [20th c.: orig. unkn.]

coed /ˈkəʊed, kəʊˈed/ n. & adj. colloq. —n. **1** a coeducational system or institution. **2** esp. US a female student at a coeducational institution. —adj. coeducational. [abbr.]

coeducation /ˌkəʊedjuːˈkeɪʃ(ə)n/ n. the education of pupils of both sexes together. □ **coeducational** adj.

coefficient /ˌkəʊɪˈfɪʃ(ə)nt/ n. **1** Math. a quantity placed before and multiplying an algebraic expression (e.g. 4 in $4x^y$). **2** Physics a multiplier or factor that measures some property (*coefficient of expansion*). [mod.L *coefficiens* (as CO-, EFFICIENT)]

coelacanth /ˈsiːləˌkænθ/ n. a large marine fish, *Latimeria chalumnae*, formerly thought to be extinct. [mod.L *Coelacanthus* f. Gk *koilos* hollow + *akantha* spine]

coeliac /ˈsiːlɪæk/ adj. (US **celiac**) of or affecting the belly. □ **coeliac disease** a digestive disease of the small intestine brought on by contact with dietary gluten. [L *coeliacus* f. Gk *koiliakos* f. *koilia* belly]

coenobite /ˈsiːnəˌbaɪt/ n. (US **cenobite**) a member of a monastic community. □ **coenobitic** /-ˈbɪtɪk/ adj. **coenobitical** /-ˈbɪtɪk(ə)l/ adj. [OF *cenobite* or eccl.L *coenobita* f. LL *coenobium* f. Gk *koinobion* convent f. *koinos* common + *bios* life]

coenzyme /ˈkəʊˌenzaɪm/ n. *Biochem.* a nonproteinaceous compound that assists in the action of an enzyme.

coequal /kəʊˈiːkw(ə)l/ adj. & n. *archaic* or *literary* —adj. equal with one another. —n. an equal. □ **coequality** /ˌkəʊiːˈkwɒlɪtɪ/ n. **coequally** adv. [ME f. L or eccl.L *coaequalis* (as CO-, EQUAL)]

coerce /kəʊˈɜːs/ v.tr. (often foll. by *into*) persuade or restrain (an unwilling person) by force (*coerced you into signing*). □ **coercible** adj. [ME f. L *coercēre* restrain (as CO-, *arcēre* restrain)]

coercion /kəʊˈɜːʃ(ə)n/ n. **1** the act or process of coercing. **2** government by force. □ **coercive** adj. **coercively** adv. **coerciveness** n. [OF *coercion*, *-tion* f. L *coer(c)tio*, *coercitio -onis* (as COERCE)]

coeval /kəʊˈiːv(ə)l/ adj. & n. —adj. **1** having the same age or date of origin. **2** living or existing at the same epoch. **3** having the same duration. —n. a coeval person, a contemporary. □ **coevality** /-ˈvælɪtɪ/ n. **coevally** adv. [LL *coaevus* (as CO-, L *aevum* age)]

coexist /ˌkəʊɪgˈzɪst/ v.intr. (often foll. by *with*) **1** exist together (in time or place). **2** (esp. of nations) exist in mutual tolerance though professing different ideologies etc. □ **coexistence** n. **coexistent** adj. [LL *coexistere* (as CO-, EXIST)]

coextensive /ˌkəʊɪkˈstensɪv/ adj. extending over the same space or time.

C. of E. abbr. Church of England.

coffee /ˈkɒfɪ/ n. **1 a** a drink made from the roasted and ground beanlike seeds of a tropical shrub. **b** a cup of this. **2 a** any shrub of the genus *Coffea*, yielding berries containing one or more seeds. **b** these seeds raw, or roasted and ground. **3** a pale brown colour, of coffee mixed with milk. □ **coffee bar** a bar or café serving coffee and light refreshments from a counter. **coffee bean** the beanlike seeds of the coffee shrub. **coffee-house** a place serving coffee and other refreshments. **coffee-mill** a small machine for grinding roasted coffee beans. **coffee-morning** a morning gathering at which coffee is served. **coffee-shop** a small informal restaurant, esp. in a hotel or department store. **coffee-table** a small low table. **coffee-table book** a large lavishly illustrated book. [ult. f. Turk. *kahveh* f. Arab. *ḳahwa*, the drink]

coffer /ˈkɒfə(r)/ n. **1** a box, etc. a large strongbox for valuables. **2** (in *pl.*) a treasury or store of funds. **3** a sunken panel in a ceiling etc. □ **coffer-dam** a watertight enclosure pumped dry to permit work below the waterline on building bridges etc., or for repairing a ship. □ **coffered** adj. [ME f. OF *coffre* f. L *cophinus* f. Gk *kophinos* basket]

coffin /ˈkɒfɪn/ n. & v. —n. a long narrow usu. wooden box in which a corpse is buried or cremated. —v.tr. (**coffined**, **coffining**) put in a coffin. [ME f. OF *cof(f)in* little basket etc. f. L *cophinus*: see COFFER]

cog n. **1** each of a series of projections on the edge of a wheel or bar transferring motion by engaging with another series. **2** an unimportant

member of an organization etc. □ **cog-wheel** a wheel with cogs. □ **cogged** adj. [ME: prob. of Scand. orig.]

cogent /ˈkəʊdʒ(ə)nt/ adj. (of arguments, reasons, etc.) convincing, compelling. □ **cogency** n. **cogently** adv. [L *cogere* compel (as CO-, *agere* act-drive)]

cogitate /ˈkɒdʒɪˌteɪt/ v.tr. & intr. ponder, meditate. □ **cogitation** /-ˈteɪʃ(ə)n/ n. **cogitative** /-tətɪv/ adj. **cogitator** n. [L *cogitare* think (as CO-, AGITATE)]

cognac /ˈkɒnjæk/ n. a high-quality brandy, properly that distilled in Cognac in W. France.

cognate /ˈkɒgneɪt/ adj. & n. —adj. **1** related to or descended from a common ancestor. **2** *Philol.* (of a word) having the same linguistic family or derivation (as another). —n. **1** a relative. **2** a cognate word. □ **cognately** adv. **cognateness** n. [L *cognatus* (as CO-, *natus* born)]

cognition /kɒgˈnɪʃ(ə)n/ n. **1** *Philos.* knowing, perceiving, or conceiving as an act or faculty distinct from emotion and volition. **2** a result of this. □ **cognitional** adj. **cognitive** /ˈkɒgnɪtɪv/ adj. [L *cognitio* (as CO-, *gnoscere gnit-* apprehend)]

cognizance /ˈkɒgnɪz(ə)ns, ˈkɒn-/ n. (also **cognisance** /-z(ə)ns/) **1** knowledge or awareness; perception, notice. **2** the sphere of one's observation or concern. **3** *Law* the right of a court to deal with a matter. □ **have cognizance of** know, esp. officially. **take cognizance of** attend to; take account of. [ME f. OF *conoisance* ult. f. L *cognoscent-* f. *cognitio*: see COGNITION]

cognizant /ˈkɒgnɪz(ə)nt, ˈkɒn-/ adj. (also **cognisant** /-z(ə)nt/) (foll. by *of*) having knowledge of or being aware of.

cognomen /kɒgˈnəʊmen/ n. **1** a nickname. **2** an ancient Roman's personal name or epithet, as in Marcus Tullius *Cicero*. [L]

cognoscente /ˌkɒnjəˈʃentɪ/ n. (pl. **cognoscenti** /-tɪ/) (usu. in pl.) a connoisseur. [It., lit. one who knows]

cohabit /kəʊˈhæbɪt/ v.intr. (**cohabited**, **cohabiting**) live together, esp. as husband and wife without being married to one another. □ **cohabitant** n. **cohabitation** /-ˈteɪʃ(ə)n/ n. **cohabitee** /-ˈtiː/ n. **cohabiter** n. [L *cohabitare* (as CO-, *habitare* dwell)]

cohere /kəʊˈhɪə(r)/ v.intr. **1** (of parts or a whole) stick together, remain united. **2** (of reasoning etc.) be logical or consistent. [L *cohaerēre cohaes-* (as CO-, *haerēre* stick)]

coherent /kəʊˈhɪərənt/ adj. **1** (of a person) able to speak intelligibly and articulately. **2** (of speech, an argument, etc.) logical and consistent; easily followed. **3** cohering; sticking together. **4** *Physics* (of waves) having a constant phase relationship. □ **coherence** n. **coherency** n. **coherently** adv. [L *cohaerēre cohaerent-* (as COHERE)]

cohesion /kəʊˈhiːʒ(ə)n/ n. **1 a** the act or condition of sticking together. **b** a tendency to cohere. **2** *Chem.* the force with which molecules cohere. □ **cohesive** /-sɪv/ adj. **cohesively** /-sɪvlɪ/ adv. **cohesiveness** /-sɪvnɪs/ n. [L *cohaes-* (see COHERE) after *adhesion*]

cohort /ˈkəʊhɔːt/ n. **1** an ancient Roman military unit, equal to one-tenth of a legion. **2** a band of warriors. **3 a** persons banded or grouped together, esp. in a common cause. **b** a group of persons with a common statistical characteristic. **4** *US* a companion or colleague. [ME f. F *cohorte* or L *cohors cohort-* enclosure, company]

coif /kɔɪf/ *n. hist.* a close-fitting cap, esp. as worn by nuns under a veil. [ME f. OF *coife* f. LL *cofia* helmet]

coiffeur /kwɑːˈfɜː(r)/ *n.* (*fem.* **coiffeuse** /-ˈfɜːz/) a hairdresser. [F]

coiffure /kwɑːˈfjʊə(r)/ *n.* the way hair is arranged; a hairstyle. [F]

coign /kɔɪn/ *n.* □ **coign of vantage** a favourable position for observation or action. [earlier spelling of COIN in the sense 'cornerstone']

coil[1] *n. & v.* —*n.* **1** anything arranged in a joined sequence of concentric circles. **2** a length of rope, a spring, etc., arranged in this way. **3** a single turn of something coiled, e.g. a snake. **4** a lock of hair twisted and coiled. **5** an intra-uterine contraceptive device. **6** *Electr.* a device consisting of a coiled wire for converting low voltage to high voltage, esp. for transmission to the sparking plugs of an internal-combustion engine. —*v.* **1** *tr.* arrange in a series of concentric loops or rings. **2** *tr. & intr.* twist or be twisted into a circular or spiral shape. **3** *intr.* move sinuously. [OF *coillir* f. L *colligere* COLLECT[1]]

coil[2] *n.* □ **this mortal coil** the difficulties of earthly life (with ref. to Shakesp. *Hamlet* III. i. 67). [16th c.: orig. unkn.]

coin *n. & v.* —*n.* **1** a piece of flat usu. round metal stamped and issued by authority as money. **2** (*collect.*) metal money. —*v.tr.* **1** make (coins) by stamping. **2** make (metal) into coins. **3** invent or devise (esp. a new word or phrase). □ **coin-box 1** a telephone operated by inserting coins. **2** the receptacle for these. **coin money** make much money quickly. □ **coiner** *n.* [ME f. OF, = stamping-die, f. L *cuneus* wedge]

coinage /ˈkɔɪnɪdʒ/ *n.* **1** the act or process of coining. **2 a** coins collectively. **b** a system or type of coins in use (*decimal coinage*; *bronze coinage*). **3** an invention, esp. of a new word or phrase. [ME f. OF *coigniage*]

coincide /ˌkəʊɪnˈsaɪd/ *v.intr.* **1** occur at or during the same time. **2** occupy the same portion of space. **3** (often foll. by *with*) be in agreement; have the same view. [med.L *coincidere* (as CO-, INCIDENT)]

coincidence /kəʊˈɪnsɪd(ə)ns/ *n.* **1 a** occurring or being together. **b** an instance of this. **2** a remarkable concurrence of events or circumstances without apparent causal connection. [med.L *coincidentia* (as COINCIDE)]

coincident /kəʊˈɪnsɪd(ə)nt/ *adj.* **1** occurring together in space or time. **2** (foll. by *with*) in agreement; harmonious. □ **coincidently** *adv.*

coincidental /kəʊˌɪnsɪˈdent(ə)l/ *adj.* **1** in the nature of or resulting from a coincidence. **2** happening or existing at the same time. □ **coincidentally** *adv.*

coir /ˈkɔɪə(r)/ *n.* fibre from the outer husk of the coconut, used for ropes, matting, etc. [Malayalam *kāyar* cord f. *kāyaru* be twisted]

coition /kəʊˈɪʃ(ə)n/ *n. Med.* = COITUS. [L *coitio* f. *coire coit-* go together]

coitus /ˈkəʊɪtəs/ *n. Med.* sexual intercourse. □ **coitus interruptus** /ˌɪntəˈrʌptəs/ sexual intercourse in which the penis is withdrawn before ejaculation. □ **coital** *adj.* [L (as COITION)]

coke[1] *n. & v.* —*n.* **1** a solid substance left after the gases have been extracted from coal. **2** a residue left after the incomplete combustion of petrol etc. —*v.tr.* convert (coal) into coke. [prob. f. N.Engl. dial. *colk* core, of unkn. orig.]

coke[2] *n. sl.* cocaine. [abbr.]

Col. *abbr.* Colonel.

col *n.* a depression in the summit-line of a chain of mountains. [F, = neck, f. L *collum*]

col. *abbr.* column.

cola /ˈkəʊlə/ *n.* (also **kola**) **1** any small tree of the genus *Cola*, native to W. Africa, bearing seeds containing caffeine. **2** a carbonated drink usu. flavoured with these seeds. [W.Afr.]

colander /ˈkʌləndə(r)/ *n.* a perforated vessel used to strain off liquid in cookery. [ME, ult. f. L *colare* strain]

cold /kəʊld/ *adj., n., & adv.* —*adj.* **1** of or at a low or relatively low temperature, esp. when compared with the human body. **2** not heated; cooled after being heated. **3** (of a person) feeling cold. **4** lacking ardour, friendliness, or affection; undemonstrative, apathetic. **5** depressing, uninteresting (*cold facts*). **6 a** dead. **b** *colloq.* unconscious. **7** *colloq.* at one's mercy (*had me cold*). **8** sexually frigid. **9** (of a scent in hunting) having become weak. **10** (in children's games) far from finding or guessing what is sought. **11** without preparation or rehearsal. —*n.* **1 a** the prevalence of a low temperature, esp. in the atmosphere. **b** cold weather; a cold environment (*went out into the cold*). **2** an infection in which the mucous membrane of the nose and throat becomes inflamed, causing running at the nose, sneezing, sore throat, etc. —*adv.* esp. *US* completely, entirely (*was stopped cold mid-sentence*). □ **catch a cold 1** become infected with a cold. **2** encounter trouble or difficulties. **cold call** *v.* sell goods or services by making unsolicited calls on prospective customers by telephone or in person. **cold chisel** a chisel suitable for cutting metal. **cold comfort** poor or inadequate consolation. **cold cream** ointment for cleansing and softening the skin. **cold cuts** slices of cold cooked meats. **cold feet** *colloq.* loss of nerve or confidence. **cold frame** an unheated frame with a glass top for growing small plants. **cold front** the forward edge of an advancing mass of cold air. **cold fusion** nuclear fusion at room temperature, esp. as a possible energy source. **cold shoulder** a show of intentional unfriendliness. **cold-shoulder** *v.tr.* be deliberately unfriendly to. **cold sore** inflammation and blisters in and around the mouth, caused by a virus infection. **cold storage 1** storage in a refrigerator or other cold place for preservation. **2** a state in which something (esp. an idea) is put aside temporarily. **cold sweat** a state of sweating induced by fear or illness. **cold table** a selection of dishes of cold food. **cold turkey** *US sl.* **1** a series of blunt statements or behaviour. **2** abrupt withdrawal from addictive drugs; the symptoms of this. **cold war** a state of hostility between nations without actual fighting. **in cold blood** without feeling or passion; deliberately, ruthlessly. **throw** (or **pour**) **cold water on** be discouraging or depreciatory about. □ **coldish** *adj.* **coldly** *adv.* **coldness** *n.* [OE *cald* f. Gmc, rel. to L *gelu* frost]

cold-blooded /kəʊldˈblʌdɪd/ *adj.* **1** (of fish etc.) having a body temperature varying with that of the environment. **2** callous; deliberately cruel. □ **cold-bloodedly** *adv.* **cold-bloodedness** *n.*

cole /kəʊl/ *n.* (usu. in *comb.*) **1** cabbage. **2** = RAPE². [ME f. ON *kál* f. L *caulis* stem, cabbage]

coleopteron /ˌkɒlɪˈɒptəˌrɒn/ *n.* any insect of the order Coleoptera, with front wings modified into sheaths to protect the hinder wings, e.g. a beetle or weevil. □ **coleopterist** *n.* **coleopterous** *adj.* [mod.L *Coleoptera* f. Gk *koleopteros* f. *koleon* sheath + *pteron* wing]

coleoptile /ˌkɒlɪˈɒptaɪl/ *n.* *Bot.* a sheath protecting a young shoot tip in grasses. [Gk *koleon* sheath + *ptilon* feather]

coleslaw /ˈkəʊlslɔː/ *n.* a dressed salad of sliced raw cabbage, etc. [Du. *koolsla*: see COLE, SLAW]

cole-tit var. of *coal-tit*.

colic /ˈkɒlɪk/ *n.* a severe spasmodic abdominal pain. □ **colicky** *adj.* [ME f. F *colique* f. LL *colicus*: see COLON²]

colitis /kəˈlaɪtɪs/ *n.* inflammation of the lining of the colon.

collaborate /kəˈlæbəˌreɪt/ *v.intr.* (often foll. by *with*) **1** work jointly, esp. in a literary or artistic production. **2** cooperate traitorously with an enemy. □ **collaboration** /-ˈreɪʃ(ə)n/ *n.* **collaborationist** /-ˈreɪʃənɪst/ *n.* & *adj.* **collaborative** /-rətɪv/ *adj.* **collaborator** *n.* [L *collaborare collaborat-* (as COM-, *laborare* work)]

collage /ˈkɒlɑːʒ, kəˈlɑːʒ/ *n.* **1** a form of art in which various materials (e.g. photographs, pieces of paper, matchsticks) are arranged and glued to a backing. **2** a work of art done in this way. **3** a collection of unrelated things. □ **collagist** *n.* [F, = gluing]

collagen /ˈkɒlədʒ(ə)n/ *n.* a protein found in animal connective tissue, yielding gelatin on boiling. [F *collagène* f. Gk *kolla* glue + *-gène* f. *-GEN*]

collapse /kəˈlæps/ *n.* & *v.* —*n.* **1** the tumbling down or falling in of a structure; folding up; giving way. **2** a sudden failure of a plan, undertaking, etc. **3** a physical or mental breakdown. —*v.* **1 a** *intr.* undergo or experience a collapse. **b** *tr.* cause to collapse. **2** *intr.* *colloq.* lie or sit down and relax, esp. after prolonged effort (*collapsed into a chair*). **3 a** *intr.* (of furniture etc.) be foldable into a small space. **b** *tr.* fold (furniture) in this way. □ **collapsible** *adj.* **collapsibility** /-ˈbɪlɪtɪ/ *n.* [L *collapsus* past part. of *collabi* (as COM-, *labi* slip)]

collar /ˈkɒlə(r)/ *n.* & *v.* —*n.* **1** the part of a shirt, dress, coat, etc., that goes round the neck, either upright or turned over. **2** a band of linen, lace, etc., completing the upper part of a costume. **3** a band of leather or other material put round an animal's (esp. a dog's) neck. **4** a restraining or connecting band, ring, or pipe in machinery. **5** a coloured marking resembling a collar round the neck of a bird or animal. —*v.tr.* **1** seize (a person) by the collar or neck. **2** capture, apprehend. **3** *colloq.* accost. **4** *sl.* take, esp. illicitly. □ **collar-bone** either of two bones joining the breastbone and the shoulder-blades. □ **collared** *adj.* (also in *comb.*). **collarless** *adj.* [ME f. AF *coler*, OF *colier*, f. L *collare* f. *collum* neck]

collate /kəˈleɪt/ *v.tr.* **1** analyse and compare (texts, statements, etc.) to identify points of agreement and difference. **2** assemble (information) from different sources. □ **collator** *n.* [L *collat-* past part. stem of *conferre* compare]

collateral /kəˈlætər(ə)l/ *n.* & *adj.* —*n.* **1** security pledged as a guarantee for repayment of a loan. **2** a person having the same descent as another but by a different line. —*adj.* **1** descended from the same stock but by a different line. **2** side by side; parallel. **3 a** additional but subordinate. **b** contributory. **c** connected but aside from the main subject, course, etc. □ **collaterality** /-ˈrælɪtɪ/ *n.* **collaterally** *adv.* [ME f. med.L *collateralis* (as COM-, LATERAL)]

collation /kəˈleɪʃ(ə)n/ *n.* **1** the act or an instance of collating. **2** a light informal meal. [ME f. OF f. L *collatio -onis* (see COLLATE): sense 2 f. Cassian's *Collationes Patrum* (= *Lives of the Fathers*) read by Benedictines and followed by a light meal]

colleague /ˈkɒliːg/ *n.* a fellow official or worker, esp. in a profession or business. [F *collègue* f. L *collega* (as COM-, *legare* depute)]

collect¹ /kəˈlekt/ *v.*, *adj.*, & *adv.* —*v.* **1** *tr.* & *intr.* bring or come together; assemble, accumulate. **2** *tr.* systematically seek and acquire (books, stamps, etc.), esp. as a continuing hobby. **3 a** *tr.* obtain (taxes, contributions, etc.) from a number of people. **b** *intr.* *colloq.* receive money. **4** *tr.* call for; fetch (*went to collect the laundry*). **5 a** *refl.* regain control of oneself esp. after a shock. **b** *tr.* concentrate (one's energies, thoughts, etc.). **c** *tr.* (as **collected** *adj.*) calm and cool; not perturbed or distracted. —*adj.* & *adv.* *US* to be paid for by the receiver (of a telephone call, parcel, etc.). □ **collectable** *adj.* **collectedly** *adv.* [F *collecter* or med.L *collectare* f. L *collectus* past part. of *colligere* (as COM-, *legere* pick)]

collect² /ˈkɒlekt, -ɪkt/ *n.* a short prayer of the Anglican and Roman Catholic Church. [ME f. OF *collecte* f. L *collecta* fem. past part. of *colligere*: see COLLECT¹]

collectible /kəˈlektɪb(ə)l/ *adj.* & *n.* —*adj.* worth collecting. —*n.* an item sought by collectors.

collection /kəˈlekʃ(ə)n/ *n.* **1** the act or process of collecting or being collected. **2** a group of things collected together, esp. systematically. **3** (foll. by *of*) an accumulation; a mass or pile (*a collection of dust*). **4 a** the collecting of money, esp. in church or for a charitable cause. **b** the amount collected. **5** the regular removal of mail, esp. from a postbox, for dispatch. [ME f. OF f. L *collectio -onis* (as COLLECT¹)]

collective /kəˈlektɪv/ *adj.* & *n.* —*adj.* **1** formed by or constituting a collection. **2** taken as a whole; aggregate (*our collective opinion*). **3** of or from several or many individuals; common. —*n.* **1 a** = *collective farm*. **b** any cooperative enterprise. **c** its members. **2** = *collective noun*. □ **collective bargaining** negotiation of wages etc. by an organized body of employees. **collective farm** a jointly-operated esp. State-owned amalgamation of several smallholdings. **collective noun** *Gram.* a noun that is grammatically singular and denotes a collection or number of individuals (e.g. *assembly*, *family*, *troop*). **collective ownership** ownership of land, means of production, etc., by all for the benefit of all. □ **collectively** *adv.* **collectiveness** *n.* **collectivity** /-ˈtɪvɪtɪ/ *n.* [F *collectif* or L *collectivus* (as COLLECT¹)]

collectivism /kəˈlektɪˌvɪz(ə)m/ *n.* the theory and practice of the collective ownership of land and the means of production. □ **collectivist** *n.* **collectivistic** /-ˈvɪstɪk/ *adj.*

collectivize /kə'lektɪˌvaɪz/ v.tr. (also **-ise**) organize on the basis of collective ownership. □ **collectivization** /-'zeɪʃ(ə)n/ n.

collector /kə'lektə(r)/ n. **1** a person who collects, esp. things of interest as a hobby. **2** a person who collects money etc. due (*tax-collector*; *ticket-collector*). □ **collector's item** (or **piece**) a valuable object, esp. one of interest to collectors. [ME f. AF *collectour* f. med.L *collector* (as COLLECT¹)]

colleen /kɒ'liːn/ n. Ir. a girl. [Ir. *cailín*, dimin. of *caile* country-woman]

college /'kɒlɪdʒ/ n. **1** an establishment for further or higher education, sometimes part of a university. **2** an establishment for specialized professional education (*business college*; *college of music*). **3** the buildings or premises of a college. **4** the students and teachers in a college. **5** Brit. a public school. **6** an organized body of persons with shared functions and privileges (*College of Physicians*). □ **college of education** Brit. a training college for schoolteachers. □ **collegial** /kə'liːdʒ(ə)l/ adj. [ME f. OF *college* or L *collegium* f. *collega* (as COLLEAGUE)]

collegian /kə'liːdʒ(ə)n/ n. a member of a college. [med.L *collegianus* (as COLLEGE)]

collegiate /kə'liːdʒət/ adj. constituted as or belonging to a college; corporate. □ **collegiate church 1** a church endowed for a chapter of canons but without a bishop's see. **2** US & Sc. a church or group of churches established under a joint pastorate. □ **collegiately** adv. [LL *collegiatus* (as COLLEGE)]

collide /kə'laɪd/ v.intr. (often foll. by *with*) **1** come into abrupt or violent impact. **2** be in conflict. [L *collidere collis-* (as COM-, *laedere* strike, damage)]

collie /'kɒlɪ/ n. **1** a sheepdog orig. of a Scottish breed. **2** this breed. [perh. f. *coll* COAL (as being orig. black)]

collier /'kɒlɪə(r)/ n. **1** a coalminer. **2 a** a coal-ship. **b** a member of its crew. [ME, f. COAL + -IER]

colliery /'kɒlɪərɪ/ n. (pl. **-ies**) a coalmine and its associated buildings.

collision /kə'lɪʒ(ə)n/ n. **1** a violent impact of a moving body, esp. a vehicle or ship, with another or with a fixed object. **2** the clashing of opposed interests or considerations. **3** Physics the action of particles striking or coming together. □ **collision course** a course or action that is bound to cause a collision or conflict. □ **collisional** adj. [ME f. LL *collisio* (as COLLIDE)]

collocate /'kɒləˌkeɪt/ v.tr. **1** place together or side by side. **2** arrange; set in a particular place. □ **collocation** /-'keɪʃ(ə)n/ n. [L *collocare collocat-* (as COM-, *locare* to place)]

colloid /'kɒlɔɪd/ n. **1** Chem. **a** a substance consisting of ultramicroscopic particles. **b** a mixture of such a substance uniformly dispersed through a second substance esp. to form a viscous solution. **2** Med. a substance of a homogeneous gelatinous consistency. □ **colloidal** /-'lɔɪd(ə)l/ adj. [Gk *kolla* glue + -OID]

collop /'kɒləp/ n. a slice, esp. of meat or bacon; an escalope. [ME, = fried bacon and eggs, of Scand. orig.]

colloquial /kə'ləʊkwɪəl/ adj. belonging to or proper to ordinary or familiar conversation, not formal or literary. □ **colloquially** adv. [L *colloquium* COLLOQUY]

colloquialism /kə'ləʊkwɪəˌlɪz(ə)m/ n. **1** a colloquial word or phrase. **2** the use of colloquialisms.

colloquium /kə'ləʊkwɪəm/ n. (pl. **colloquiums** or **colloquia** /-kwɪə/) an academic conference or seminar. [L: see COLLOQUY]

colloquy /'kɒləkwɪ/ n. (pl. **-quies**) **1** the act of conversing. **2** a conversation. [L *colloquium* (as COM-, *loqui* speak)]

collude /kə'luːd, -'ljuːd/ v.intr. come to an understanding or conspire together, esp. for a fraudulent purpose. □ **colluder** n. [L *colludere collus-* (as COM-, *ludere lus-* play)]

collusion /kə'luːʒ(ə)n, -'ljuːʒ(ə)n/ n. **1** a secret understanding, esp. for a fraudulent purpose. **2** Law such an understanding between ostensible opponents in a lawsuit. □ **collusive** adj. **collusively** adv. [ME f. OF *collusion* or L *collusio* (as COLLUDE)]

collywobbles /'kɒlɪˌwɒb(ə)lz/ n.pl. colloq. **1** a rumbling or pain in the stomach. **2** a feeling of strong apprehension. [fanciful, f. COLIC + WOBBLE]

colobus /'kɒləbəs/ n. any leaf-eating monkey of the genus *Colobus*, native to Africa, having shortened thumbs. [mod.L f. Gk *kolobos* docked]

cologne /kə'ləʊn/ n. (in full **cologne water**) eau-de-Cologne or a similar scented toilet water. [abbr.]

colon¹ /'kəʊlən, -lɒn/ n. a punctuation mark (:), used esp. to introduce a quotation or a list or to separate clauses when the second expands or illustrates the first. [L f. Gk *kōlon* limb, clause]

colon² /'kəʊlən, -lɒn/ n. Anat. the lower and greater part of the large intestine. □ **colonic** /kə'lɒnɪk/ adj. [ME, ult. f. Gk *kolon*]

colonel /'kɜːn(ə)l/ n. **1** an army officer in command of a regiment, immediately below a brigadier in rank. **2** US an officer of corresponding rank in the Air Force. **3** = *lieutenant-colonel*. □ **colonelcy** n. (pl. **-ies**). [obs. F *coronel* f. It. *colonnello* f. *colonna* COLUMN]

colonial /kə'ləʊnɪəl/ adj. & n. —adj. **1** of, relating to, or characteristic of a colony or colonies, esp. of a British Crown Colony. **2** (esp. of architecture or furniture) built or designed in, or in a style characteristic of, the period of the British colonies in America before independence. —n. **1** a native or inhabitant of a colony. **2** a house built in colonial style. □ **colonially** adv.

colonialism /kə'ləʊnɪəˌlɪz(ə)m/ n. **1** a policy of acquiring or maintaining colonies. **2** derog. this policy regarded as the esp. economic exploitation of weak or backward peoples by a larger power. □ **colonialist** n.

colonist /'kɒlənɪst/ n. a settler in or inhabitant of a colony.

colonize /'kɒləˌnaɪz/ v. (also **-ise**) **1** tr. **a** establish a colony or colonies in (a country or area). **b** settle as colonists. **2** intr. establish or join a colony. **3** tr. Biol. (of plants and animals) become established (in an area). □ **colonization** /-'zeɪʃ(ə)n/ n. **colonizer** n.

colonnade /ˌkɒlə'neɪd/ n. a row of columns, esp. supporting an entablature or roof. □ **colonnaded** adj. [F f. *colonne* COLUMN]

colony /'kɒlənɪ/ n. (pl. **-ies**) **1 a** a group of settlers in a new country (whether or not already inhabited) fully or partly subject to the mother country. **b** the settlement or its territory. **2 a** people of one nationality or race or occupation in a city, esp. if living more or less in isolation or in a special quarter. **b** a separate or segregated group (*nudist colony*). **3** Biol. a collection of animals, plants, etc., connected, in contact, or living close together. [ME f. L *colonia* f. *colonus* farmer f. *colere* cultivate]

colophon /ˈkɒləˌfon, -fən/ *n.* **1** a publisher's device or imprint, esp. on the title-page. **2** a tailpiece in a manuscript or book, often ornamental, giving the writer's or printer's name, the date, etc. [LL f. Gk *kolophōn* summit, finishing touch]

color etc. *US* var. of COLOUR etc.

Colorado beetle /ˌkɒləˈrɑːdəʊ/ *n.* a yellow and black striped beetle, *Leptinotarsa decemlineata*, the larva of which is highly destructive to the potato plant. [*Colorado* in the US]

coloration /ˌkʌləˈreɪʃ(ə)n/ *n.* (also **colouration**) **1** colouring; a scheme or method of applying colour. **2** the natural colour of living things or animals. [F *coloration* or LL *coloratio* f. *colorare* COLOUR]

coloratura /ˌkɒlərəˈtʊərə/ *n.* **1** elaborate ornamentation of a vocal melody. **2** a singer (esp. a soprano) skilled in coloratura singing. [It. f. L *colorare* COLOUR]

colossal /kəˈlɒs(ə)l/ *adj.* **1** of immense size; huge, gigantic. **2** *colloq.* remarkable, splendid. □ **colossally** *adv.* [F f. *colosse* COLOSSUS]

colossus /kəˈlɒsəs/ *n.* (*pl.* **colossi** /-saɪ/ or **colossuses**) **1** a statue much bigger than life size. **2** a gigantic person, animal, building, etc. **3** an imperial power personified. [L f. Gk *kolossos*]

colostomy /kəˈlɒstəmɪ/ *n.* (*pl.* **-ies**) *Surgery* an operation on the colon to make an opening in the abdominal wall to provide an artificial anus. [as COLON² + Gk *stoma* mouth]

colostrum /kəˈlɒstrəm/ *n.* the first secretion from the mammary glands occurring after giving birth. [L]

colour /ˈkʌlə(r)/ *n. & v.* (*US* **color**) —*n.* **1 a** the sensation produced on the eye by rays of light when resolved as by a prism, selective reflection, etc., into different wavelengths. **b** perception of colour; a system of colours. **2** one, or any mixture, of the constituents into which light can be separated as in a spectrum or rainbow, sometimes including (loosely) black and white. **3** a colouring substance, esp. paint. **4** the use of all colours, not only black and white, as in photography and television. **5 a** pigmentation of the skin, esp. when dark. **b** this as a ground for prejudice or discrimination. **6** ruddiness of complexion (*a healthy colour*). **7** (in *pl.*) appearance or aspect (*see things in their true colours*). **8** (in *pl.*) **a** *Brit.* a coloured ribbon or uniform etc. worn to signify membership of a school, club, team, etc. **b** the flag of a regiment or ship. **c** a national flag. **9** quality, mood, or variety in music, literature, speech, etc.; distinctive character or timbre. **10** a show of reason; a pretext (*lend colour to*; *under colour of*). —*v.* **1** *tr.* apply colour to, esp. by painting or dyeing or with coloured pens or pencils. **2** *tr.* influence (*an attitude coloured by experience*). **3** *tr.* misrepresent, exaggerate, esp. with spurious detail (*a highly coloured account*). **4** *intr.* take on colour; blush. □ **colour bar** the denial of services and facilities to non-White people. **colour-blind** unable to distinguish certain colours. **colour code** use of colours as a standard means of identification. **colour-code** *v.tr.* identify by means of a colour code. **colour-fast** dyed in colours that will not fade or be washed out. **colour scheme** an arrangement

or planned combination of colours esp. in interior design. **colour-sergeant** the senior sergeant of an infantry company. **colour supplement** *Brit.* a magazine with coloured illustrations, issued as a supplement to a newspaper. **Queen's** (or **King's** or **regimental**) **colour** a flag carried by a regiment. **show one's true colours** reveal one's true character or intentions. **under false colours** falsely, deceitfully. [ME f. OF *color*, *colorer* f. L *color*, *colorare*]

colourable /ˈkʌlərəb(ə)l/ *adj.* (*US* **colorable**) **1** specious, plausible. **2** counterfeit. □ **colourably** *adv.*

colourant /ˈkʌlərənt/ *n.* (*US* **colorant**) a colouring substance.

coloured /ˈkʌləd/ *adj. & n.* (*US* **colored**) —*adj.* **1** having colour(s). **2** (**Coloured**) **a** wholly or partly of non-White descent. **b** *S.Afr.* of mixed White and non-White descent. **c** of or relating to Coloured people (*a Coloured audience*). —*n.* (**Coloured**) **1** a Coloured person. **2** *S.Afr.* a person of mixed descent speaking Afrikaans or English as the mother tongue.

colourful /ˈkʌləfʊl/ *adj.* (*US* **colorful**) **1** having much or varied colour; bright. **2** full of interest; vivid, lively. □ **colourfully** *adv.* **colourfulness** *n.*

colouring /ˈkʌlərɪŋ/ *n.* (*US* **coloring**) **1** the process of or skill in using colour(s). **2** the style in which a thing is coloured, or in which an artist uses colour. **3** facial complexion.

colourist /ˈkʌlərɪst/ *n.* (*US* **colorist**) a person who uses colour, esp. in art.

colourless /ˈkʌləlɪs/ *adj.* (*US* **colorless**) **1** without colour. **2** lacking character or interest. **3** dull or pale in hue. **4** neutral, impartial, indifferent. □ **colourlessly** *adv.*

colt /kəʊlt/ *n.* **1** a young uncastrated male horse, usu. less than four years old. **2** *Sport* a young or inexperienced player; a member of a junior team. □ **colthood** *n.* **coltish** *adj.* **coltishly** *adv.* **coltishness** *n.* [OE, = young ass or camel]

colter *US* var. of COULTER.

columbine /ˈkɒləmˌbaɪn/ *n.* any plant of the genus *Aquilegia*, esp. *A. vulgaris*, having purple-blue flowers. [ME f. OF *colombine* f. med.L *colombina herba* dovelike plant f. L *columba* dove (from the supposed resemblance of the flower to a cluster of 5 doves)]

columbium /kəˈlʌmbɪəm/ *n. US Chem.* = NIOBIUM.

column /ˈkɒləm/ *n.* **1** *Archit.* an upright cylindrical pillar often slightly tapering and usu. supporting an entablature or arch, or standing alone as a monument. **2** a structure or part shaped like a column. **3** a vertical cylindrical mass of liquid or vapour. **4 a** a vertical division of a page, chart, etc., containing a sequence of figures or words. **b** the figures or words themselves. **5** a part of a newspaper regularly devoted to a particular subject (*gossip column*). **6 a** *Mil.* an arrangement of troops in successive lines, with a narrow front. **b** *Naut.* a similar arrangement of ships. □ **column-inch** a quantity of print (esp. newsprint) occupying a one-inch length of a column. □ **columnar** /kəˈlʌmnə(r)/ *adj.* **columned** *adj.* [ME f. OF *columpne* & L *columna* pillar]

columnist /ˈkɒləmnɪst, -mɪst/ *n.* a journalist contributing regularly to a newspaper.

colza /ˈkɒlzə/ n. = RAPE². [F kolza(t) f. LG kōlsāt (as COLE, SEED)]

com- /kɒm, kəm, kʌm/ prefix (also **co-, col-, con-, cor-**) with, together, jointly, altogether. [L com-, cum with]

■ **Usage** com- is used before b, m, p, and occasionally before vowels and f; co- esp. before vowels, h, and gn; col- before l, cor- before r, and con- before other consonants.

coma /ˈkəʊmə/ n. (pl. **comas**) a prolonged deep unconsciousness, caused esp. by severe injury or excessive use of drugs. [med.L f. Gk kōma deep sleep]

comatose /ˈkəʊmətəʊz/ adj. **1** in a coma. **2** drowsy, sleepy, lethargic.

comb /kəʊm/ n. & v. —n. **1** a toothed strip of rigid material for tidying and arranging the hair, or for keeping it in place. **2** a part of a machine having a similar design or purpose. **3 a** the red fleshy crest of a fowl, esp. a cock. **b** an analogous growth in other birds. **4** a honeycomb. —v.tr. **1** arrange or tidy (the hair) by drawing a comb through. **2** curry (a horse). **3** dress (wool or flax) with a comb. **4** search (a place) thoroughly. □ **comb out 1** tidy and arrange (hair) with a comb. **2** remove with a comb. **3** search out and get rid of (anything unwanted). □ **combed** adj. **comber** n. [OE camb f. Gmc]

combat /ˈkɒmbæt, ˈkʌm-/ n. & v. —n. a fight, struggle, or contest. —v. (**combated, combating**) **1** intr. engage in combat. **2** tr. engage in combat with. **3** tr. oppose; strive against. [F combat f. combattre f. LL (as COM-, L battuere fight)]

combatant /ˈkɒmbət(ə)nt, ˈkʌm-/ n. & adj. —n. a person engaged in fighting. —adj. **1** fighting. **2** for fighting.

combative /ˈkɒmbətɪv, ˈkʌm-/ adj. ready or eager to fight; pugnacious. □ **combatively** adv. **combativeness** n.

combe var. of COOMB.

combination /ˌkɒmbɪˈneɪʃ(ə)n/ n. **1** the act or an instance of combining; the process of being combined. **2** a combined state (in combination with). **3** a combined set of things or people. **4** a sequence of numbers or letters used to open a combination lock. **5** Brit. a motor cycle with side-car attached. **6** (in pl.) Brit. a single undergarment for the body and legs. **7** Chem. a union of substances in a compound with new properties. □ **combination lock** a lock that can be opened only by a specific sequence of movements. □ **combinative** /ˈkɒmbɪnətɪv/ adj. **combinational** adj. **combinatory** /ˈkɒmbɪnətərɪ/ adj. [obs. F combination or LL combinatio (as COMBINE)]

combine v. & n. /kəmˈbaɪn/ **1** tr. & intr. join together; unite for a common purpose. **2** tr. possess (qualities usually distinct) together (combines charm and authority). **3 a** intr. coalesce in one substance. **b** tr. cause to do this. **c** intr. form a chemical compound. **4** intr. cooperate. **5** /ˈkɒmbaɪn/ tr. harvest (crops etc.) by means of a combine harvester. —n. /ˈkɒmbaɪn/ a combination of esp. commercial interests to control prices etc. □ **combine harvester** a mobile machine that reaps and threshes in one operation. **combining form** Gram. a linguistic element used in combination with another element to form a word (e.g. Anglo- = English, bio- = life, -graphy = writing). □ **combinable** adj. [ME f. OF combiner or LL combinare (as COM-, L bini two)]

combing /ˈkəʊmɪŋ/ n. (in pl.) hairs combed off.

combo /ˈkɒmbəʊ/ n. (pl. **-os**) sl. a small jazz or dance band. [abbr. of COMBINATION + -o]

combs /kɒmz/ n.pl. colloq. combinations (see COMBINATION 6).

combust /kəmˈbʌst/ v.tr. subject to combustion. [obs. combust (adj.) f. L combustus past part. (as COMBUSTION)]

combustible /kəmˈbʌstɪb(ə)l/ adj. & n. —adj. **1** capable of or used for burning. **2** excitable; easily irritated. —n. a combustible substance. □ **combustibility** /-ˈbɪlɪtɪ/ n. [F combustible or med.L combustibilis (as COMBUSTION)]

combustion /kəmˈbʌstʃ(ə)n/ n. **1** burning; consumption by fire. **2** Chem. the development of light and heat from the chemical combination of a substance with oxygen. □ **combustive** adj. [ME f. F combustion or LL combustio f. L comburere combust- burn up]

come /kʌm/ v.intr. (past **came** /keɪm/; past part. **come**) **1** move, be brought towards, or reach a place thought of as near or familiar to the speaker or hearer (come and see me; shall we come to your house?; the books have come). **2** reach or be brought to a specified situation or result (you'll come to no harm; have come to believe it; came into prominence). **3** reach or extend to a specified point (the road comes within a mile of us). **4** traverse or accomplish (with compl.: have come a long way). **5** occur, happen; become present instead of future (how did you come to break your leg?). **6** take or occupy a specified position in space or time (it comes on the third page; Nero came after Claudius). **7** become perceptible or known (the church came into sight; the news comes as a surprise). **8** be available (the dress comes in three sizes). **9** become (with compl.: the handle has come loose). **10** (foll. by of) **a** be descended from (comes of a rich family). **b** be the result of (that comes of complaining). **11** colloq. play the part of; behave like (with compl.: don't come the bully with me). **12** sl. have a sexual orgasm. **13** (in subj.) colloq. when a specified time is reached (come next month). **14** (as int.) expressing caution or reserve (come, it cannot be that bad). □ **as ... as they come** typically or supremely so (is as tough as they come). **come about** happen; take place. **come across 1** be effective or understood. **2** (foll. by with) sl. hand over what is wanted. **3** meet or find by chance (came across an old jacket). **come again** colloq. **1** make a further effort. **2** (as imper.) what did you say? **come along 1** make progress; move forward. **2** (as imper.) hurry up. **come and go 1** pass to and fro; be transitory. **2** pay brief visits. **come apart** fall or break into pieces, disintegrate. **come at 1** reach, discover; get access to. **2** attack (came at me with a knife). **come away 1** become detached or broken off (came away in my hands). **2** (foll. by with) be left with a feeling, impression, etc. (came away with many misgivings). **come back 1** return. **2** recur to one's memory. **3** become fashionable or popular again. **4** US reply, retort. **come before** be dealt with by (a judge etc.). **come between 1** interfere with the relationship of. **2** separate; prevent contact between. **come by 1** pass; go past. **2** call on a visit (why not come by tomorrow?). **3** acquire, obtain (came by a new bicycle). **come**

down 1 come to a place or position regarded as lower. **2** lose position or wealth (*has come down in the world*). **3** be handed down by tradition or inheritance. **4** be reduced; show a downward trend (*prices are coming down*). **5** (foll. by *against*, in favour of) reach a decision or recommendation (*the report came down against change*). **6** (foll. by *to*) signify or betoken basically; be dependent on (a factor) (*it comes down to who is willing to go*). **7** (foll. by *on*) criticize harshly; rebuke, punish. **8** (foll. by *with*) begin to suffer from (a disease). **come for 1** come to collect or receive. **2** attack (*came for me with a hammer*). **come forward 1** advance. **2** offer oneself for a task, post, etc. **come-hither** *attrib.adj. colloq.* (of a look or manner) enticing, flirtatious. **come in 1** enter a house or room. **2** take a specified position in a race etc. (*came in third*). **3** become fashionable or seasonable. **4 a** have a useful role or function. **b** (with compl.) prove to be (*came in very handy*). **c** have a part to play (*where do I come in?*). **5** be received (*more news has just come in*). **6** begin speaking, esp. in radio transmission. **7** be elected; come to power. **8** *Cricket* begin an innings. **9** (foll. by *for*) receive; be the object of (usu. something unwelcome) (*came in for much criticism*). **10** (foll. by *on*) join (an enterprise etc.). **11** (of a tide) turn to high tide. **12** (of a train, ship, or aircraft) approach its destination. **come into 1** see senses 2, 7. **2** receive, esp. as heir. **come off 1** *colloq.* (of an action) succeed; be accomplished. **2** (with compl.) fare; turn out (*came off badly; came off the winner*). **3** be detached or detachable (from). **4** fall (from). **5** be reduced or subtracted from (*£5 came off the price*). **come off it** (as *imper.*) *colloq.* an expression of disbelief or refusal to accept another's opinion, behaviour, etc. **come on 1** continue to come. **2** advance, esp. to attack. **3** make progress; thrive (*is really coming on*). **4** (foll. by *to* + *infin.*) begin (*it came on to rain*). **5** appear on the stage, field of play, etc. **6** be heard or seen on television, on the telephone, etc. **7** arise to be discussed. **8** (as *imper.*) expressing encouragement. **9** = come upon. **come-on** *n. sl.* a lure or enticement. **come out 1** emerge; become known (*it came out that he had left*). **2** appear or be published (*comes out every Saturday*). **3 a** declare oneself; make a decision (*came out in favour of joining*). **b** openly declare that one is a homosexual. **4** *Brit.* go on strike. **5 a** be satisfactorily visible in a photograph etc., or present in a specified way (*the dog didn't come out; he came out badly*). **b** (of a photograph) be produced satisfactorily or in a specified way (*only three have come out*). **6** attain a specified result in an examination etc. **7** (of a stain etc.) be removed. **8** make one's début on stage or in society. **9** (foll. by *in*) be covered with (*came out in spots*). **10** (of a problem) be solved. **11** (foll. by *with*) declare openly; disclose. **come over 1** come from some distance or nearer to the speaker (*came over from Paris; come over here a moment*). **2** change sides or one's opinion. **3 a** (of a feeling etc.) overtake or affect (a person). **b** *colloq.* feel suddenly (*came over faint*). **4** appear or sound in a specified way (*you came over very well; the ideas came over clearly*). **5** affect or influence (*I don't know what came over me*). **come round 1** pay an informal visit. **2** recover consciousness. **3** be converted to another person's opinion. **4** (of a date or regular occurrence) recur; be

imminent again. **come through 1** be successful; survive. **2** be received by telephone. **3** survive or overcome (a difficulty) (*came through the ordeal*). **come to 1** recover consciousness. **2** *Naut.* bring a vessel to a stop. **3** reach in total; amount to. **4** *refl.* **a** recover consciousness. **b** stop being foolish. **5** have as a destiny; reach (*what is the world coming to?*). **come to hand** become available; be recovered. **come to nothing** have no useful result in the end; fail. **come to pass** happen, occur. **come to rest** cease moving. **come to that** *colloq.* in fact; if that is the case. **come under 1** be classified as or among. **2** be subject to (influence or authority). **come up 1** come to a place or position regarded as higher. **2** attain wealth or position (*come up in the world*). **3** (of an issue, problem, etc.) arise; present itself; be mentioned or discussed. **4** (often foll. by *to*) **a** approach a person, esp. to talk. **b** approach or draw near to a specified time, event, etc. (*is coming up to eight o'clock*). **5** (foll. by *to*) match (a standard etc.). **6** (foll. by *with*) produce (an idea etc.), esp. in response to a challenge. **7** (of a plant etc.) spring up out of the ground. **8** become brighter (e.g. with polishing); shine more brightly. **come up against** be faced with or opposed by. **come upon 1** meet or find by chance. **2** attack by surprise. **come what may** no matter what happens. **have it coming to one** *colloq.* be about to get one's deserts. **how come?** *colloq.* how did that happen? **if it comes to that** in that case. **to come** future; in the future (*the year to come; many problems were still to come*). [OE *cuman* f. Gmc]

comeback /ˈkʌmbæk/ *n.* **1** a return to a previous (esp. successful) state. **2** *sl.* a retaliation or retort.

comedian /kəˈmiːdɪən/ *n.* **1** a humorous entertainer on stage, television, etc. **2** an actor in comedy. [F *comédien* f. *comédie* COMEDY]

comedienne /kəˌmiːdɪˈen/ *n.* a female comedian. [F fem. (as COMEDIAN)]

comedown /ˈkʌmdaʊn/ *n.* **1** a loss of status; decline or degradation. **2** a disappointment.

comedy /ˈkɒmɪdɪ/ *n.* (*pl.* **-ies**) **1 a** a play, film, etc., of an amusing or satirical character, usu. with a happy ending. **b** the dramatic genre consisting of works of this kind. **2** an amusing or farcical incident or series of incidents in everyday life. **3** humour, esp. in a work of art etc. □ **comedic** /kəˈmiːdɪk/ *adj.* [ME f. OF *comedie* f. L *comoedia* f. Gk *kōmōidia* f. *kōmōidos* comic poet f. *kōmos* revel]

comely /ˈkʌmlɪ/ *adj.* (**comelier**, **comeliest**) pleasant to look at. □ **comeliness** /ˈkʌmlɪnɪs/ *n.* [ME *cumelich, cumli* prob. f. *becumelich* f. BECOME]

comer /ˈkʌmə(r)/ *n.* **1** a person who comes, esp. as an applicant, participant, etc. (*offered the job to the first comer*). **2** *colloq.* a person likely to be a success.

comestible /kəˈmestɪb(ə)l/ *n.* (usu. in *pl.*) *formal* or *joc.* food. [ME f. F f. med.L *comestibilis* f. L *comedere comest-* eat up]

comet /ˈkɒmɪt/ *n.* a hazy object usu. with a nucleus of ice and dust surrounded by gas and with a tail pointing away from the sun, moving about the sun in an eccentric orbit. □ **cometary** *adj.* [ME f. OF *comete* f. L *cometa* f. Gk *komētēs* long-haired (star)]

comeuppance /kʌmˈʌpəns/ *n. colloq.* one's deserved fate or punishment (*got his comeuppance*). [COME + UP + -ANCE]

comfit /ˈkʌmfɪt/ n. archaic a sweet consisting of a nut, seed, etc., coated in sugar. [ME f. OF confit f. L confectum past part. of conficere prepare: see CONFECTION]

comfort /ˈkʌmfət/ n. & v. —n. 1 consolation; relief in affliction. 2 a a state of physical well-being; being comfortable (live in comfort). b (usu. in pl.) things that make life easy or pleasant. 3 a cause of satisfaction (a comfort to me that you are here). 4 a person who consoles or helps one (he's a comfort to her in her old age). —v.tr. 1 soothe in grief; console. 2 make comfortable (comforted by the warmth of the fire). [ME f. OF confort(er) f. LL confortare strengthen (as COM-, L fortis strong)]

comfortable /ˈkʌmftəb(ə)l, -fətəb(ə)l/ adj. 1 ministering to comfort; giving ease (a comfortable pair of shoes). 2 free from discomfort; at ease (I'm quite comfortable thank you). 3 colloq. having an adequate standard of living; free from financial worry. 4 having an easy conscience. 5 with a wide margin (a comfortable win). □ **comfortableness** n. **comfortably** adv. [ME f. AF confortable (as COMFORT)]

comforter /ˈkʌmfətə(r)/ n. 1 a person who comforts. 2 a baby's dummy. 3 archaic a woollen scarf. 4 US a warm quilt. [ME f. AF confortour, OF -éor (as COMFORT)]

comfrey /ˈkʌmfrɪ/ n. (pl. **-eys**) any of various plants of the genus Symphytum, esp. S. officinale having large hairy leaves and bell-shaped flowers. [ME f. AF cumfirie, ult. f. L conferva (as COM-, fervēre boil)]

comfy /ˈkʌmfɪ/ adj. (**comfier, comfiest**) colloq. comfortable. □ **comfily** adv. **comfiness** n. [abbr.]

comic /ˈkɒmɪk/ adj. & n. —adj. 1 (often attrib.) of, or in the style of, comedy (a comic actor; comic opera). 2 causing or meant to cause laughter; funny (comic to see his struggles). —n. 1 a professional comedian. 2 a a children's periodical, mainly in the form of comic strips. b a similar publication intended for adults. □ **comic opera** 1 an opera with much spoken dialogue, usu. with humorous treatment. 2 this genre of opera. **comic strip** a series of drawings in a comic, newspaper, etc., telling a story. [L comicus f. Gk kōmikos f. kōmos revel]

comical /ˈkɒmɪk(ə)l/ adj. funny; causing laughter. □ **comicality** /-ˈkælɪtɪ/ n. **comically** adv. [COMIC]

coming /ˈkʌmɪŋ/ adj. & n. —attrib.adj. 1 approaching, next (in the coming week; this coming Sunday). 2 of potential importance (a coming man). —n. arrival; approach.

comity /ˈkɒmɪtɪ/ n. (pl. **-ies**) 1 courtesy, civility; considerate behaviour towards others. 2 a an association of nations etc. for mutual benefit. b (in full **comity of nations**) the mutual recognition by nations of the laws and customs of others. [L comitas f. comis courteous]

comma /ˈkɒmə/ n. a punctuation mark (,) indicating a pause between parts of a sentence, or dividing items in a list, string of figures, etc. [L f. Gk komma clause]

command /kəˈmɑːnd/ v. & n. —v.tr. 1 (often foll. by to + infin., or that + clause) give formal order or instructions to (commands us to obey; commands that it be done). 2 (also absol.) have authority or control over. 3 a (often refl.) restrain, master. b gain the use of; have at one's disposal

or within reach (skill, resources, etc.). 4 deserve and get (sympathy, respect, etc.). 5 Mil. dominate (a strategic position) from a superior height; look down over. —n. 1 an authoritative order; an instruction. 2 mastery, control, possession (a good command of languages). 3 the exercise or tenure of authority, esp. naval or military (has command of this ship). 4 Mil. a a body of troops etc. (Bomber Command). b a district under a commander (Western Command). 5 Computing a an instruction causing a computer to perform one of its basic functions. b a signal initiating such an operation. □ **command module** the control compartment in a spacecraft. **Command Paper** (in the UK) a paper laid before Parliament by command of the Crown. **command performance** (in the UK) a theatrical or film performance given by royal command. **in command of** commanding; having under control. **under command of** commanded by. [ME f. AF comaunder, OF comander f. LL commandare COMMEND]

commandant /ˌkɒmənˈdænt, -ˈdɑːnt, ˈkɒm-/ n. a commanding officer, esp. of a particular force, military academy, etc. □ **commandantship** n. [F commandant, or It. or Sp. commandante (as COMMAND)]

commandeer /ˌkɒmənˈdɪə(r)/ v.tr. 1 seize (men or goods) for military purposes. 2 take possession of without authority. [S.Afr. Du. kommanderen f. F commander COMMAND]

commander /kəˈmɑːndə(r)/ n. 1 a person who commands, esp.: a a naval officer next in rank below captain. b = wing commander. 2 an officer in charge of a London police district. 3 (in full **knight commander**) a member of a higher class in some orders of knighthood. □ **commander-in-chief** the supreme commander, esp. of a nation's forces. □ **commandership** n. [ME f. OF comandere, -éor f. Rmc (as COMMAND)]

commanding /kəˈmɑːndɪŋ/ adj. 1 dignified, exalted, impressive. 2 (of a hill or other high point) giving a wide view. 3 (of an advantage, a position, etc.) controlling; superior (has a commanding lead). □ **commandingly** adv.

commandment /kəˈmɑːndmənt/ n. a divine command. □ **the Ten Commandments** the divine rules of conduct given by God to Moses on Mount Sinai, according to Exod. 20:1–17. [ME f. OF comandement (as COMMAND)]

commando /kəˈmɑːndəʊ/ n. (pl. **-os**) Mil. 1 a a unit of British amphibious shock troops. b a member of such a unit. c a similar unit or member of such a unit elsewhere. 2 a a party of men called out for military service. b a body of troops. [Port. f. commandar COMMAND]

commemorate /kəˈmeməˌreɪt/ v.tr. 1 celebrate in speech or writing. 2 a preserve in memory by some celebration. b (of a stone, plaque, etc.) be a memorial of. □ **commemoration** n. **commemorative** /kəˈmemərətɪv/ adj. **commemorator** n. [L commemorare (as COM-, memorare relate f. memor mindful)]

commence /kəˈmens/ v.tr. & intr. formal begin. [ME f. OF com(m)encier f. Rmc (as COM-, L initiare INITIATE)]

commencement /kəˈmensmənt/ n. formal 1 a beginning. 2 esp. US a ceremony of degree conferment. [ME f. OF (as COMMENCE)]

commend /kə'mend/ v.tr. **1** (often foll. by to) entrust, commit (commends his soul to God). **2** praise (commends her singing voice). **3** recommend (method commends itself). □ **commendation** /ˌkɒmen'deɪʃ(ə)n/ n. [ME f. L commendare (as COM-, mendare = mandare entrust: see MANDATE)]

commendable /kə'mendəb(ə)l/ adj. praiseworthy. □ **commendably** adv. [ME f. OF f. L commendabilis (as COMMEND)]

commendatory /kə'mendətərɪ/ adj. commending, recommending. [LL commendatorius (as COMMEND)]

commensal /kə'mens(ə)l/ adj. & n. —adj. Biol. of, relating to, or exhibiting commensalism. —n. Biol. a commensal organism. □ **commensality** /ˌkɒmen'sælɪtɪ/ n. [ME f. F commensal or med.L commensalis (in sense 2) (as COM-, mensa table)]

commensalism /kə'mensəˌlɪz(ə)m/ n. Biol. an association between two organisms in which one benefits and the other derives no benefit or harm.

commensurable /kə'menʃərəb(ə)l, -sjərəb(ə)l/ adj. **1** (often foll. by with, to) measurable by the same standard. **2** (foll. by to) proportionate to. **3** Math. (of numbers) in a ratio equal to the ratio of integers. □ **commensurability** /-'bɪlɪtɪ/ n. **commensurably** adv. [LL commensurabilis (as COM-, MEASURE)]

commensurate /kə'menʃərət, -sjərət/ adj. **1** (usu. foll. by with) having the same size, duration, etc.; coextensive. **2** (often foll. by to, with) proportionate. □ **commensurately** adv. [LL commensuratus (as COM-, MEASURE)]

comment /'kɒment/ n. & v. —n. **1 a** a remark, esp. critical; an opinion (passed a comment on her hat). **b** commenting; criticism (his behaviour aroused much comment). **2** an explanatory note (e.g. on a written text). —v.intr. **1** (often foll. by on, upon, or that + clause) make (esp. critical) remarks (commented on her choice of friends). **2** (often foll. by on, upon) write explanatory notes. □ **commenter** n. [ME f. L commentum contrivance (in LL also = interpretation), neut. past part. of comminisci devise, or F commenter (v.)]

commentary /'kɒməntərɪ/ n. (pl. -ies) **1** a set of explanatory or critical notes on a text etc. **2** a descriptive spoken account (esp. on radio or television) of an event or a performance as it happens. [L commentarius, -ium adj. used as noun (as COMMENT)]

commentate /'kɒmənˌteɪt/ v.intr. disp. act as a commentator. [back-form. f. COMMENTATOR]

commentator /'kɒmənˌteɪtə(r)/ n. **1** a person who provides a commentary on an event etc. **2** the writer of a commentary. **3** a person who writes or speaks on current events. [L f. commentari frequent. of comminisci devise]

commerce /'kɒmɜːs/ n. financial transactions, esp. the buying and selling of merchandise, on a large scale. [F commerce or L commercium (as COM-, mercium f. merx mercis merchandise)]

commercial /kə'mɜːʃ(ə)l/ adj. & n. —adj. **1** of, engaged in, or concerned with, commerce. **2** having profit as a primary aim rather than artistic etc. value; philistine. —n. a television or radio advertisement. □ **commercial broadcasting** television or radio broadcasting in which programmes are financed by advertisements. **commercial traveller** a firm's travelling salesman or saleswoman who visits shops

to get orders. □ **commercialism** n. **commerciality** /-ʃɪ'ælɪtɪ/ n. **commercially** adv.

commercialize /kə'mɜːʃəˌlaɪz/ v.tr. (also **-ise**) **1** exploit for the purpose of gaining profit. **2** make commercial. □ **commercialization** /-'zeɪʃ(ə)n/ n.

Commie /'kɒmɪ/ n. sl. derog. a Communist. [abbr.]

commination /ˌkɒmɪ'neɪʃ(ə)n/ n. the threatening of divine vengeance. [ME f. L comminatio f. comminari threaten]

comminatory /'kɒmɪnətərɪ/ adj. threatening, denunciatory. [med.L comminatorius (as COMMINATION)]

commingle /kə'mɪŋɡ(ə)l/ v.tr. & intr. literary mingle together.

comminute /'kɒmɪˌnjuːt/ v.tr. **1** reduce to small fragments. **2** divide (property) into small portions. □ **comminution** /-'njuːʃ(ə)n/ n. [L comminuere comminut- (as COM-, minuere lessen)]

commiserate /kə'mɪzəˌreɪt/ v. intr. (usu. foll. by with) express or feel pity. □ **commiseration** /-'reɪʃ(ə)n/ n. **commiserative** /-rətɪv/ adj. **commiserator** n. [L commiserari (as COM-, miserari pity f. miser wretched)]

commissar /'kɒmɪˌsɑː(r)/ n. hist. an official of the former Soviet Communist Party responsible for political education and organization. [Russ. komissar f. F commissaire (as COMMISSARY)]

commissariat /ˌkɒmɪ'seərɪət, -'særɪˌæt/ n. esp. Mil. **1** a department for the supply of food etc. **2** the food supplied. [F commissariat & med.L commissariatus (as COMMISSARY)]

commissary /'kɒmɪsərɪ, kə'mɪs-/ n. (pl. -ies) **1 a** deputy or delegate. **2** US **a** a restaurant in a film studio etc. **b** the food supplied. **3** US Mil. a store for the supply of food etc. to soldiers. □ **commissarial** /-'seərɪəl/ adj. **commissaryship** n. [ME f. med.L commissarius person in charge (as COMMIT)]

commission /kə'mɪʃ(ə)n/ n. & v. —n. **1 a** the authority to perform a task or certain duties. **b** a person or group entrusted esp. by a government with such authority (set up a commission to look into it). **c** an instruction, command, or duty given to such a group or person (their commission was to simplify the procedure; my commission was to find him). **2** an order for something, esp. a work of art, to be produced specially. **3** Mil. **a** a warrant conferring the rank of officer in the army, navy, or air force. **b** the rank so conferred. **4 a** the authority to act as agent for a company etc. in trade. **b** a percentage paid to the agent from the profits of goods etc. sold, or business obtained (his wages are low, but he gets 20 per cent commission). **5** the act of committing (a crime, sin, etc.). **6** the office or department of a commissioner. —v.tr. **1** authorize or empower by a commission. **2 a** give (an artist etc.) a commission for a piece of work. **b** order (a work) to be written (commissioned a new concerto). **3** Naut. **a** give (an officer) the command of a ship. **b** prepare (a ship) for active service. **4** bring (a machine, equipment, etc.) into operation. □ **in commission** (of a warship etc.) manned, armed, and ready for service. **out of commission** (esp. of a ship) not in service, not in working order. **Royal Commission 1** a commission of inquiry appointed by the Crown at the instance of the Government. **2** a committee so appointed. [ME f. OF f. L *commissio -onis* (as COMMIT)]

commissionaire /kəˌmɪʃəˈneə(r)/ *n.* esp. *Brit.* a uniformed door-attendant at a theatre, cinema, etc. [F (as COMMISSIONER)]

commissioner /kəˈmɪʃənə(r)/ *n.* **1** a person appointed by a commission to perform a specific task, e.g. the head of the London police. **2** a person appointed as a member of a government commission. **3** a representative of the supreme authority in a district, department, etc. □ **Commissioner for Oaths** a solicitor authorized to administer an oath to a person making an affidavit. [ME f. med.L *commissionarius* (as COMMISSION)]

commissure /ˈkɒmɪˌsjʊə(r)/ *n.* a junction, joint, or seam. □ **commissural** /kəmɪˈsjʊərəl/ *adj.* [ME f. L *commissura* junction (as COMMIT)]

commit /kəˈmɪt/ *v.tr.* (**committed, committing**) **1** (usu. foll. by *to*) entrust or consign for: **a** safe keeping (*I commit him to your care*). **b** treatment, usu. destruction (*committed the book to the flames*). **2** perpetrate, do (esp. a crime, sin, or blunder). **3** pledge, involve, or bind (esp. oneself) to a certain course or policy. **4** (as **committed** *adj.*) (often foll. by *to*) **a** morally dedicated or politically aligned. **b** obliged (*felt committed to staying there*). □ **commit to memory** memorize. **commit to prison** consign officially to custody, esp. on remand. □ **committable** *adj.* **committer** *n.* [ME f. L *committere* join, entrust (as COM-, *mittere miss-* send)]

commitment /kəˈmɪtmənt/ *n.* **1** an engagement or (esp. financial) obligation that restricts freedom of action. **2** the process or an instance of committing oneself; a pledge or undertaking.

committal /kəˈmɪt(ə)l/ *n.* **1** the act of committing a person to an institution, esp. prison or a mental hospital. **2** the burial of a dead body.

committee /kəˈmɪtɪ/ *n.* **1** a body of persons appointed for a specific function by, and usu. out of, a larger body. **2** such a body appointed by Parliament etc. to consider the details of proposed legislation. **3** (**Committee**) *Brit.* the whole House of Commons when sitting as a committee. □ **select committee** a small parliamentary committee appointed for a special purpose. **standing committee** a committee that is permanent during the existence of the appointing body. [COMMIT + -EE]

commode /kəˈməʊd/ *n.* **1** a chest of drawers. **2 a** a bedside table with a cupboard containing a chamber-pot. **b** a chamber-pot concealed in a chair with a hinged cover. [F, adj. (as noun) f. L *commodus* convenient (as COM-, *modus* measure)]

commodious /kəˈməʊdɪəs/ *adj.* roomy and comfortable. □ **commodiously** *adv.* **commodiousness** *n.* [F *commodieux* or f. med.L *commodiosus* f. L *commodus* (as COMMODE)]

commodity /kəˈmɒdɪtɪ/ *n.* (pl. **-ies**) **1** *Commerce* an article or raw material that can be bought and sold, esp. a product as opposed to a service. **2** a useful thing. [ME f. OF *commodité* or f. L *commoditas* (as COMMODE)]

commodore /ˈkɒmədɔː(r)/ *n.* **1** a naval officer above a captain and below a rear-admiral. **2** the commander of a squadron or other division of a fleet. **3** the president of a yacht-club. □

Commodore-in-Chief the supreme officer in the air force. [prob. f. Du. *komandeur* f. F *commandeur* COMMANDER]

common /ˈkɒmən/ *adj.* & *n.* —*adj.* (**commoner, commonest**) **1 a** occurring often (*a common mistake*). **b** ordinary; of ordinary qualities; without special rank or position (*common soldier; the common people*). **2 a** shared by, coming from, or done by, more than one (*common knowledge; by common consent*). **b** belonging to, open to, or affecting, the whole community or the public (*common land*). **3** *derog.* low-class; vulgar; inferior. **4** of the most familiar type (*common cold; common nightshade*). **5** *Math.* belonging to two or more quantities (*common factor*). **6** *Gram.* (of gender) referring to individuals of either sex (e.g. *teacher*). **7** *Mus.* having two or four beats, esp. four crotchets, in a bar. —*n.* a piece of open public land, esp. in a village or town. □ **Common Era** the Christian era. **common ground** a point or argument accepted by both sides in a dispute. **common law** law derived from custom and judicial precedent rather than statutes. **common-law husband** (or **wife**) a partner in a marriage recognized by common law, esp. after a period of cohabitation. **Common Market** the European Economic Community. **common noun** (or **name**) *Gram.* a name denoting a class of objects or a concept as opposed to a particular object (e.g. *boy, chocolate, beauty*). **common or garden** *colloq.* ordinary. **Common Prayer** the Church of England liturgy orig. set forth in the *Book of Common Prayer* of Edward VI (1549). **common-room 1** a room in some colleges, schools, etc., which members may use for relaxation or work. **2** the members who use this. **common sense** sound practical sense, esp. in everyday matters. **common stock** *US* = *ordinary shares*. **common weal** public welfare. **in common 1** in joint use; shared. **2** of joint interest (*have little in common*). **in common with** in the same way as. **out of the common** unusual. □ **commonly** *adv.* **commonness** *n.* [ME f. OF *comun* f. L *communis*]

commonality /ˌkɒməˈnælɪtɪ/ *n.* (pl. **-ies**) **1** the sharing of an attribute. **2** a common occurrence. **3** = COMMONALTY. [var. of COMMONALTY]

commonalty /ˈkɒmənəltɪ/ *n.* (pl. **-ies**) **1** the common people. **2** the general body (esp. of mankind). **3** a corporate body. [ME f. OF *comunalté* f. med.L *communalitas -tatis* (as COMMON)]

commoner /ˈkɒmənə(r)/ *n.* one of the common people, as opposed to the aristocracy. [ME f. med.L *communarius* f. *communa* (as COMMUNE¹)]

commonplace /ˈkɒmənˌpleɪs/ *adj.* & *n.* —*adj.* lacking originality; trite. —*n.* **1 a** an everyday saying; a platitude (*uttered a commonplace about the weather*). **b** an ordinary topic of conversation. **2** anything usual or trite. □ **commonplace-book** a book into which notable extracts from other works are copied for personal use. □ **commonplaceness** *n.* [transl. of L *locus communis* = Gk *koinos topos* general theme]

commons /ˈkɒmənz/ *n.pl.* **1** (**the Commons**) = *House of Commons*. **2 a** the common people. **b** (prec. by *the*) the common people regarded as a part of a political, esp. British, system. **3** provisions shared in common; daily fare. □ **short commons** insufficient food. [ME pl. of COMMON]

commonsensical /ˌkɒmən'sensɪk(ə)l/ adj. possessing or marked by common sense. [common sense (see COMMON)]

commonwealth /'kɒmənˌwelθ/ n. **1 a** an independent State or community, esp. a democratic republic. **b** such a community or organization of shared interests in a non-political field (the commonwealth of learning). **2** (**the Commonwealth**) **a** (in full **the British Commonwealth of Nations**) an international association consisting of the UK together with States that were previously part of the British Empire. **b** the republican period of government in Britain 1649–60. **c** US a part of the title of some of the States of the US. **d** the title of the federated Australian States. [COMMON + WEALTH]

commotion /kə'məʊʃ(ə)n/ n. **1** a confused and noisy disturbance or outburst. **2** loud and confusing noise. [ME f. OF commotion or L commotio (as COM-, MOTION)]

communal /'kɒmjʊn(ə)l/ adj. relating to or benefiting a community; for common use (communal baths). □ **communality** /-'nælɪtɪ/ n. **communally** adv. [F f. LL communalis (as COMMUNE¹)]

communalism /'kɒmjʊnəˌlɪz(ə)m/ n. **1** a principle of political organization based on federated communes. **2** the principle of communal ownership etc. □ **communalist** n. **communalistic** /-'lɪstɪk/ adj.

communard /'kɒmjʊˌnɑːd/ n. **1** a member of a commune. **2** (also **Communard**) hist. a supporter of the Paris Commune. [F (as COMMUNE¹)]

commune¹ /'kɒmjuːn/ n. **1 a** a group of people, not necessarily related, sharing living accommodation, goods, etc., esp. as a political act. **b** a communal settlement esp. for the pursuit of shared interests. **2 a** the smallest French territorial division for administrative purposes. **b** a similar division elsewhere. [F f. med.L communia neut. pl. of L communis common]

commune² /kə'mjuːn/ v.intr. (usu. foll. by with) **1** speak confidentially and intimately (communed together about their loss; communed with his heart). **2** feel in close touch (with nature etc.) (communed with the hills). [ME f. OF comuner share f. comun COMMON]

communicable /kə'mjuːnɪkəb(ə)l/ adj. (esp. of a disease) able to be passed on. □ **communicability** /-'bɪlɪtɪ/ n. **communicably** adv. [ME f. OF communicable or LL communicabilis (as COMMUNICATE)]

communicant /kə'mjuːnɪkənt/ n. **1** a person who receives Holy Communion, esp. regularly. **2** a person who imparts information. [L communicare communicant- (as COMMON)]

communicate /kə'mjuːnɪˌkeɪt/ v. **1** tr. **a** transmit or pass on by speaking or writing. **b** transmit (heat, motion, etc.). **c** pass on (an infectious illness). **d** impart (feelings etc.) non-verbally. **2** intr. succeed in conveying information, evoking understanding, etc. (he communicates well). **3** intr. (often foll. by with) share a feeling or understanding; relate socially. **4** intr. (often foll. by with) (of a room etc.) have a common door (my room communicates with yours). **5 a** tr. administer Holy Communion to. **b** intr. receive Holy Communion. □ **communicator** n. **communicatory** adj. [L communicare communicat- (as COMMON)]

communication /kəˌmjuːnɪ'keɪʃ(ə)n/ n. **1 a** the act of imparting, esp. news. **b** an instance of this. **c** the information etc. communicated. **2** a means of connecting different places. **3** social intercourse (it was difficult to maintain communication in the uproar). **4** (in pl.) the science and practice of transmitting information esp. by electronic or mechanical means. □ **communication cord** Brit. a cord or chain in a railway carriage that may be pulled to stop the train in an emergency. **communication** (or **communications**) **satellite** an artificial satellite used to relay telephone circuits or broadcast programmes.

communicative /kə'mjuːnɪkətɪv/ adj. **1** open, talkative, informative. **2** ready to communicate. □ **communicatively** adv. [LL communicativus (as COMMUNICATE)]

communion /kə'mjuːnɪən/ n. **1** a sharing, esp. of thoughts etc.; fellowship. **2** participation; a sharing in common (communion of interests). **3** (**Communion, Holy Communion**) **a** the Eucharist. **b** participation in the Communion service. **4** a body or group within the Christian faith (the Methodist communion). [ME f. OF communion or L communio f. communis common]

communiqué /kə'mjuːnɪˌkeɪ/ n. an official communication, esp. a news report. [F, = communicated]

communism /'kɒmjʊˌnɪz(ə)m/ n. **1** a political theory advocating class war and leading to a society in which all property is publicly owned and each person is paid and works according to his or her needs and abilities. **2** (usu. **Communism**) **a** the communistic form of society. **b** any movement or political doctrine advocating communism. **3** = COMMUNALISM. [F communisme f. commun COMMON]

communist /'kɒmjʊnɪst/ n. & adj. —n. **1** a person advocating or practising communism. **2** (**Communist**) a member of a Communist Party. —adj. of or relating to communism (a communist play). □ **communistic** /-'nɪstɪk/ adj. [COMMUNISM]

community /kə'mjuːnɪtɪ/ n. (pl. **-ies**) **1 a** all the people living in a specific locality. **b** a specific locality, including its inhabitants. **2** a body of people having a religion, a profession, etc., in common (the immigrant community). **3** fellowship of interests etc.; similarity (community of intellect). **4** a monastic, socialistic, etc. body practising common ownership. **5** joint ownership or liability (community of goods). **6** (prec. by the) the public. **7** a body of nations unified by common interests. **8** Ecol. a group of animals or plants living or growing together in the same area. □ **community centre** a place providing social etc. facilities for a neighbourhood. **community charge** (in the UK) a tax levied locally on every adult in a community. **community chest** US a fund for charity and welfare work in a community. **community service order** an order for a convicted offender to perform a period of unpaid work in the community. **community singing** singing by a large crowd or group, esp. of old popular songs or hymns. [ME f. OF comuneté f. L communitas -tatis (as COMMON)]

■ **Usage** The community charge, or poll tax, replaced household rates in the UK in 1989–90 and is itself to be replaced by a council tax in 1993.

commutable /kəˈmjuːtəb(ə)l/ adj. **1** convertible into money; exchangeable. **2** Law (of a punishment) able to be commuted. **3** within commuting distance. □ **commutability** /-ˈbɪlɪtɪ/ n. [L commutabilis (as COMMUTE)]

commutate /ˈkɒmjuːteɪt/ v.tr. Electr. **1** regulate the direction of (an alternating current), esp. to make it a direct current. **2** reverse the direction (of an electric current). [L commutare commutat- (as COMMUTE)]

commutation /ˌkɒmjuːˈteɪʃ(ə)n/ n. **1** the act or process of commuting or being commuted (in legal and exchange senses). **2** Electr. the act or process of commutating or being commutated. **3** Math. the reversal of the order of two quantities. [F commutation or L commutatio (as COMMUTE)]

commutative /kəˈmjuːtətɪv/ adj. **1** relating to or involving substitution. **2** Math. unchanged in result by the interchange of the order of quantities. [F commutatif or med.L commutativus (as COMMUTE)]

commutator /ˈkɒmjuːˌteɪtə(r)/ n. Electr. a device for reversing electric current.

commute /kəˈmjuːt/ v. **1** intr. travel to and from one's daily work, usu. in a city, esp. by car or train. **2** tr. Law (usu. foll. by to) change (a judicial sentence etc.) to another less severe. **3** tr. (often foll. by into, for) **a** change (one kind of payment) for another. **b** make a payment etc. to change (an obligation etc.) for another. **4** tr. **a** exchange; interchange (two things). **b** change (to another thing). [L commutare commutat- (as COM-, mutare change)]

commuter /kəˈmjuːtə(r)/ n. a person who travels some distance to work, usu. by car or train.

compact[1] adj., v., & n. —adj. /kəmˈpækt/ **1** closely or neatly packed together. **2** (of a piece of equipment, a room, etc.) well-fitted and practical though small. **3** (of style etc.) condensed; brief. **4** (esp. of the human body) small but well-proportioned. —v.tr. /kəmˈpækt/ **1** join or press firmly together. **2** condense. —n. /ˈkɒmpækt/ **1** a small flat case for face-powder, a mirror, etc. **2** US a medium-sized motor car. □ **compact disc** /ˈkɒmpækt/ a disc on which information or sound is recorded digitally and reproduced by reflection of laser light. □ **compaction** n. **compactly** adv. **compactness** n. **compactor** n. [ME f. L compingere compact- (as COM-, pangere fasten)]

compact[2] /ˈkɒmpækt/ n. an agreement or contract between two or more parties. [L compactum f. compacisci compact- (as COM-, pacisci covenant): cf. PACT]

companion[1] /kəmˈpænjən/ n. **1 a** (often foll. by in, of) a person who accompanies, associates with, or shares with, another (a companion in adversity; they were close companions). **b** a person, esp. an unmarried or widowed woman, employed to live with and assist another. **2** a handbook or reference book on a particular subject. **3** a thing that matches another. **4** (**Companion**) a member of the lowest grade of some orders of knighthood (Companion of the Bath). [ME f. OF compaignon ult. f. L panis bread]

companion[2] /kəmˈpænjən/ n. Naut. **1** a raised frame on a quarterdeck used for lighting the cabins etc. below. **2** = companion-way. □ **companion-way** a staircase to a cabin. [obs. Du. kompanje quarterdeck f. OF compagne f. It.

(camera della) compagna pantry, prob. ult. rel. to COMPANION[1]]

companionable /kəmˈpænjənəb(ə)l/ adj. agreeable as a companion; sociable. □ **companionableness** n. **companionably** adv.

companionate /kəmˈpænjənɪt/ adj. **1** well-suited; (of clothes) matching. **2** of or like a companion.

companionship /kəmˈpænjənʃɪp/ n. good fellowship; friendship.

company /ˈkʌmpənɪ/ n. (pl. -ies) **1 a** a number of people assembled; a crowd; an audience (addressed the company). **b** guests or a guest (am expecting company). **2 a** a state of being a companion or fellow; companionship, esp. of a specific kind (enjoys low company; do not care for his company). **3** a commercial business. **4** a troupe of actors or entertainers. **5** Mil. a subdivision of an infantry battalion usu. commanded by a major or a captain. **6** a group of Guides. □ **good** (or **bad**) **company 1** a pleasant (or dull) companion. **2** a suitable (or unsuitable) associate or group of friends. **in company** not alone. **in company with** together with. **keep company** (often foll. by with) associate habitually. **keep a person company** accompany a person; be sociable. **part company** (often foll. by with) cease to associate. **ship's company** the entire crew. [ME f. AF compainie, OF compai(g)nie f. Rmc (as COMPANION[1])]

comparable /ˈkɒmpərəb(ə)l/ adj. **1** (often foll. by with) able to be compared. **2** (often foll. by to) fit to be compared; worth comparing. □ **comparability** /-ˈbɪlɪtɪ/ n. **comparableness** n. **comparably** adv. [ME f. OF f. L comparabilis (as COMPARE)]

■ **Usage** Use of this word with to and with corresponds to the senses of compare: to is more common.

comparative /kəmˈpærətɪv/ adj. & n. —adj. **1** perceptible by comparison; relative (in comparative comfort). **2** estimated by comparison (the comparative merits of the two ideas). **3** of or involving comparison (esp. of sciences etc.). **4** Gram. (of an adjective or adverb) expressing a higher degree of a quality, but not the highest possible (e.g. braver, more fiercely). —n. Gram. **1** the comparative expression or form of an adjective or adverb. **2** a word in the comparative. □ **comparatively** adv. [ME f. L comparativus (as COMPARE)]

compare /kəmˈpeə(r)/ v. & n. —v. **1** tr. (usu. foll. by to) express similarities in; liken (compared the landscape to a painting). **2** tr. (often foll. by to, with) estimate the similarity or dissimilarity of; assess the relation between (compared radio with television; that lacks quality compared to this). **3** intr. (often foll. by with) bear comparison (compares favourably with the rest). **4** intr. (often foll. by with) be equal or equivalent to. —n. literary comparison (beyond compare; without compare; has no compare). □ **compare notes** exchange ideas or opinions. [ME f. OF comparer f. L comparare (as COM-, parare f. par equal)]

■ **Usage** In current use of the verb, to and with are generally interchangeable, but with often implies a greater element of formal analysis.

comparison /kəmˈpærɪs(ə)n/ n. **1** the act or an instance of comparing. **2** a simile or semantic illustration. **3** capacity for being likened; similarity (*there's no comparison*). **4** (in full **degrees of comparison**) *Gram.* the positive, comparative, and superlative forms of adjectives and adverbs. □ **bear** (or **stand**) **comparison** (often foll. by *with*) be able to be compared favourably. **beyond comparison 1** totally different in quality. **2** greatly superior; excellent. **in comparison with** compared to. [ME f. OF *comparesoun* f. L *comparatio -onis* (as COMPARE)]

compartment /kəmˈpɑːtmənt/ *n.* **1** a space within a larger space, separated from the rest by partitions. **2** *Naut.* a watertight division of a ship. □ **compartmentation** /-ˈteɪʃ(ə)n/ *n.* [F *compartiment* f. It. *compartimento* f. LL *compartiri* (as COM-, *partiri* share)]

compartmental /ˌkɒmpɑːtˈment(ə)l/ *adj.* consisting of or relating to compartments or a compartment. □ **compartmentally** *adv.*

compartmentalize /ˌkɒmpɑːtˈmentəˌlaɪz/ *v.tr.* (also **-ise**) divide into compartments or categories. □ **compartmentalization** /-ˈzeɪʃ(ə)n/ *n.*

compass /ˈkʌmpəs/ *n. & v.* —*n.* **1** (in full **magnetic compass**) an instrument showing the direction of magnetic north and bearings from it. **2** (usu. in *pl.*) an instrument for taking measurements and describing circles, with two arms connected at one end by a movable joint. **3** a circumference or boundary. **4** area, extent; scope (e.g. of knowledge or experience) (*beyond my compass*). **5** the range of tones of a voice or a musical instrument. —*v.tr. literary* **1** hem in. **2** grasp mentally. **3** contrive, accomplish. □ **compassable** *adj.* [ME f. OF *compas* ult. f. L *passus* PACE[1]]

compassion /kəmˈpæʃ(ə)n/ *n.* pity inclining one to help or be merciful. □ **compassion fatigue** indifference to others' suffering brought about by overexposure to charitable appeals. [ME f. OF f. eccl.L *compassio -onis* f. *compati* (as COM-, *pati pass-* suffer)]

compassionate /kəmˈpæʃənət/ *adj.* sympathetic, pitying. □ **compassionate leave** *Brit.* leave granted on grounds of bereavement etc. □ **compassionately** *adv.* [obs. F *compassioné* f. *compassioner* feel pity (as COMPASSION)]

compatible /kəmˈpætəb(ə)l/ *adj.* **1** (often foll. by *with*) **a** able to coexist; well-suited; mutually tolerant (*a compatible couple*). **b** consistent (*their views are not compatible with their actions*). **2** (of equipment, machinery, etc.) capable of being used in combination. □ **compatibility** /-ˈbɪlɪtɪ/ *n.* **compatibly** *adv.* [F f. med.L *compatibilis* (as COMPASSION)]

compatriot /kəmˈpætrɪət/ *n.* a fellow-countryman. □ **compatriotic** /-ˈɒtɪk/ *adj.* [F *compatriote* f. LL *compatriota* (as COM-, *patriota* PATRIOT)]

compeer /ˈkɒmpɪə(r), -ˈpɪə(r)/ *n.* **1** an equal, a peer. **2** a comrade. [ME f. OF *comper* (as COM-, PEER[2])]

compel /kəmˈpel/ *v.tr.* (**compelled**, **compelling**) **1** (usu. foll. by *to* + infin.) force, constrain (*compelled them to admit it*). **2** bring about (an action) by force (*compel submission*). **3** (as **compelling** *adj.*) rousing strong interest, attention, conviction, or admiration. □ **compellable** *adj.* **compellingly** *adv.* [ME f. L *compellere compuls-* (as COM-, *pellere* drive)]

compendious /kəmˈpendɪəs/ *adj.* (esp. of a book etc.) comprehensive but fairly brief. □

compendiously *adv.* **compendiousness** *n.* [ME f. OF *compendieux* f. L *compendiosus* brief (as COMPENDIUM)]

compendium /kəmˈpendɪəm/ *n.* (*pl.* **compendiums** or **compendia** /-dɪə/) **1** esp. *Brit.* a usu. one-volume handbook or encyclopaedia. **2 a** a summary or abstract of a larger work. **b** an abridgement. **3** a collection of games in a box. [L, = what is weighed together, f. *compendere* (as COM-, *pendere* weigh)]

compensate /ˈkɒmpenˌseɪt/ *v.* **1** *tr.* (often foll. by *for*) recompense (a person) (*compensated him for his loss*). **2** *intr.* (usu. foll. by *for* a thing, *to* a person) make amends (*compensated for the insult*). **3** *tr.* counterbalance. **4** *intr. Psychol.* offset a disability or frustration by development in another direction. □ **compensative** /-sətɪv/ *adj.* **compensator** *n.* **compensatory** /-ˈpensətərɪ, -ˈseɪtərɪ/ *adj.* [L *compensare* (as COM-, *pensare* frequent. of *pendere pens-* weigh)]

compensation /ˌkɒmpenˈseɪʃ(ə)n/ *n.* **1 a** the act of compensating. **b** the process of being compensated. **2** something, esp. money, given as a recompense. **3** *US* a salary or wages. □ **compensational** *adj.* [ME f. OF f. L *compensatio* (as COMPENSATE)]

compère /ˈkɒmpeə(r)/ *n. & v. Brit.* —*n.* a person who introduces and links the artistes in a variety show etc.; a master of ceremonies. —*v.* **1** *tr.* act as a compère to. **2** *intr.* act as compère. [F, = godfather f. Rmc (as COM-, L *pater* father)]

compete /kəmˈpiːt/ *v.intr.* **1** (often foll. by *with*, *against* a person, *for* a thing) strive for superiority or supremacy. **2** (often foll. by *in*) take part (in a contest etc.). [L *competere competit-*, in late sense 'strive after or contend for (something)' (as COM-, *petere* seek)]

competence /ˈkɒmpɪt(ə)ns/ *n.* (also **competency** /ˈkɒmpɪtənsɪ/) **1** (often foll. by *for*, or *to* + infin.) ability; the state of being competent. **2** an income large enough to live on, usu. unearned. **3** *Law* the legal capacity (of a court, a magistrate, etc.) to deal with a matter.

competent /ˈkɒmpɪt(ə)nt/ *adj.* **1 a** (usu. foll. by *to* + infin. or *for*) adequately qualified or capable (*not competent to drive*). **b** effective (*a competent batsman*). **2** *Law* (of a judge, court, or witness) legally qualified or qualifying. □ **competently** *adv.* [ME f. OF *competent* or L *competent-* (as COMPETE)]

competition /ˌkɒmpəˈtɪʃ(ə)n/ *n.* **1** (often foll. by *for*) competing, esp. in an examination, in trade, etc. **2** an event or contest in which people compete. **3 a** the people competing against a person. **b** the opposition they represent. [LL *competitio* rivalry (as COMPETITIVE)]

competitive /kəmˈpetɪtɪv/ *adj.* **1** involving, offered for, or by competition (*competitive contest*). **2** (of prices etc.) low enough to compare well with those of rival traders. **3** (of a person) having a strong urge to win; keen to compete. □ **competitively** *adv.* **competitiveness** *n.* [*competit-*, past part. stem of L *competere* COMPETE]

competitor /kəmˈpetɪtə(r)/ *n.* a person who competes; a rival, esp. in business or commerce. [F *compétiteur* or L *competitor* (as COMPETE)]

compilation /ˌkɒmpɪˈleɪʃ(ə)n/ *n.* **1 a** the act of compiling. **b** the process of being compiled. **2** something compiled, esp. a book etc. composed of separate articles, stories, etc. [ME f. OF f. L *compilatio -onis* (as COMPILE)]

compile /kəm'paɪl/ v.tr. **1 a** collect (material) into a list, volume, etc. **b** make up (a volume etc.) from such material. **2** accumulate (a large number of) (*compiled a score of 160*). **3** *Computing* produce (a machine-coded form of a high-level program). [ME f. OF *compiler* or its apparent source, L *compilare* plunder, plagiarize]

compiler /kəm'paɪlə(r)/ n. **1** *Computing* a program for translating a high-level programming language into machine code. **2** a person who compiles.

complacency /kəm'pleɪsənsɪ/ n. (also **complacence**) **1** smug self-satisfaction. **2** tranquil pleasure. [med.L *complacentia* f. L *complacēre* (as COM-, *placēre* please)]

complacent /kəm'pleɪs(ə)nt/ adj. **1** smugly self-satisfied. **2** calmly content. □ **complacently** adv. [L *complacēre*: see COMPLACENCY]

■ **Usage** This word is often confused with *complaisant*.

complain /kəm'pleɪn/ v.intr. **1** (often foll. by *about, at,* or *that* + clause) express dissatisfaction (*is always complaining*). **2** (foll. by *of*) **a** announce that one is suffering from (an ailment). **b** state a grievance concerning. □ **complainer** n. **complainingly** adv. [ME f. OF *complaindre* (stem *complaign-*) f. med.L *complangere* bewail (as COM-, *plangere planct-* lament)]

complainant /kəm'pleɪnənt/ n. *Law* a plaintiff in certain lawsuits.

complaint /kəm'pleɪnt/ n. **1** an act of complaining. **2** a grievance. **3** an ailment or illness. [ME f. OF *complainte* f. *complaint* past part. of *complaindre*: see COMPLAIN]

complaisant /kəm'pleɪz(ə)nt/ adj. **1** politely deferential. **2** willing to please; acquiescent. □ **complaisance** n. [F f. *complaire* (stem *complais-*) acquiesce to please, f. L *complacēre*: see COMPLACENCY]

■ **Usage** This word is often confused with *complacent*.

complement n. & v. —n. /'kɒmplɪmənt/ **1 a** something that completes. **b** one of a pair, or one of two things that go together. **2** (often **full complement**) the full number needed to man a ship, fill a conveyance, etc. **3** *Gram.* a word or phrase added to a verb to complete the predicate of a sentence. **4** *Geom.* the amount by which an angle is less than 90°. —v.tr. /'kɒmplɪˌment/ **1** complete. **2** form a complement to (*the scarf complements her dress*). □ **complemental** /-'ment(ə)l/ adj. [ME f. L *complementum* (as COMPLETE)]

complementary /ˌkɒmplɪ'mentərɪ/ adj. **1** completing; forming a complement. **2** (of two or more things) complementing each other. □ **complementary angle** either of two angles making up 90°. **complementary colour** a colour that combined with a given colour makes white or black. **complementary medicine** alternative medicine. □ **complementarily** adv. **complementariness** n.

complete /kəm'pliːt/ adj. & v. —adj. **1** having all its parts; entire (*the set is complete*). **2** finished (*my task is complete*). **3** of the maximum extent or degree (*a complete surprise; a complete stranger*). —v.tr. **1** finish. **2 a** make whole or perfect. **b** make up the amount of (*completes the quota*). **3** fill in the answers to (a questionnaire etc.). **4** (usu. *absol.*) *Law* conclude a sale of property. □ **complete with** having (as an important accessory) (*comes complete with instructions*). □ **completely** adv. **completeness** n. **completion** /-'pliːʃ(ə)n/ n. [ME f. OF *complet* or L *completus* past part. of *complēre* fill up]

complex /'kɒmpleks/ n. & adj. —n. **1** a building, a series of rooms, a network, etc. made up of related parts (*the arts complex*). **2** *Psychol.* a related group of usu. repressed feelings or thoughts which cause abnormal behaviour or mental states. **3** (in general use) a preoccupation or obsession. —adj. **1** consisting of related parts; composite. **2** complicated (*a complex problem*). □ **complexity** /kəm'pleksɪtɪ/ n. (pl. **-ies**). **complexly** adv. [F *complexe* or L *complexus* past part. of *complectere* embrace, assoc. with *complexus* plaited]

complexion /kəm'plekʃ(ə)n/ n. **1** the natural colour, texture, and appearance, of the skin, esp. of the face. **2** an aspect; a character (*puts a different complexion on the matter*). □ **complexioned** adj. (also in comb.). [ME f. OF f. L *complexio -onis* (as COMPLEX): orig. = combination of supposed qualities determining the nature of a body]

compliance /kəm'plaɪəns/ n. **1** the act or an instance of complying; obedience to a request, command, etc. **2** unworthy acquiescence. □ **in compliance with** according to (a wish, command, etc.).

compliant /kəm'plaɪənt/ adj. disposed to comply; yielding, obedient. □ **compliantly** adv.

complicate /'kɒmplɪˌkeɪt/ v.tr. & intr. **1** (often foll. by *with*) make or become difficult, confused, or complex. **2** (as **complicated** adj.) complex; intricate. □ **complicatedly** adv. **complicatedness** n. [L *complicare complicat-* (as COM-, *plicare* fold)]

complication /ˌkɒmplɪ'keɪʃ(ə)n/ n. **1 a** an involved or confused condition or state. **b** a complicating circumstance; a difficulty. **2** *Med.* a secondary disease or condition aggravating a previous one. [F *complication* or LL *complicatio* (as COMPLICATE)]

complicity /kəm'plɪsɪtɪ/ n. partnership in a crime or wrongdoing. [*complice* (see ACCOMPLICE) + -ITY]

compliment n. & v. —n. /'kɒmplɪmənt/ **1 a** a spoken or written expression of praise. **b** an act or circumstance implying praise (*their success was a compliment to their efforts*). **2** (in pl.) **a** formal greetings, esp. as a written accompaniment to a gift etc. (*with the compliments of the management*). **b** praise (*my compliments to the cook*). —v.tr. /'kɒmplɪˌment/ (often foll. by *on*) congratulate; praise (*complimented him on his roses*). □ **compliments slip** a printed slip of paper sent with a gift etc., esp. from a business firm. **pay a compliment to** praise. **return the compliment 1** give a compliment in return for another. **2** retaliate or recompense in kind. [F *complimenter* f. It. *complimento* ult. f. L (as COMPLEMENT)]

complimentary /ˌkɒmplɪ'mentərɪ/ adj. **1** expressing a compliment. **2** (of a ticket for a play etc.) given free of charge. □ **complimentarily** adv.

compline /'kɒmplɪn, -plaɪn/ n. *Eccl.* **1** the last of the canonical hours of prayer. **2** the service taking place during this. [ME f. OF *complie*, fem.

past part. of obs. *complir* complete, ult. f. L *complēre* fill up]

comply /kəm'plaɪ/ *v.intr.* (**-ies, -ied**) act in accordance (with a wish, command, etc.) (*complied with her expectation*; *had no choice but to comply*). [It. *complire* f. Cat. *complir*, Sp. *cumplir* f. L *complēre* fill up]

component /kəm'pəʊnənt/ *n.* & *adj.* —*n.* a part of a larger whole, esp. part of a motor vehicle. —*adj.* being part of a larger whole (*assembled the component parts*). □ **componential** /ˌkɒmpə'nenʃ(ə)l/ *adj.* [L *componere* component- (as COM-, *ponere* put)]

comport /kəm'pɔːt/ *v.refl. literary* conduct oneself. □ **comport with** suit, befit. □ **comportment** *n.* [L *comportare* (as COM-, *portare* carry)]

compose /kəm'pəʊz/ *v.* **1 a** *tr.* construct or create (a work of art, esp. literature or music). **b** *intr.* compose music (*gave up composing in 1917*). **2** *tr.* constitute; make up (*six tribes which composed the German nation*). **3** *tr.* put together to form a whole, esp. artistically; order; arrange. **4** *tr.* a (often *refl.*) calm; settle (*compose your expression*; *composed himself to wait*). **b** (as **composed** *adj.*) calm, settled. **5** *tr.* settle (a dispute etc.). **6** *tr. Printing* **a** set up (type) to form words and blocks of words. **b** set up (a manuscript etc.) in type. □ **composed of** made up of, consisting of (*a flock composed of sheep and goats*). □ **composedly** /-zɪdlɪ/ *adv.* [F *composer*, f. L *componere* (as COM-, *ponere* put)]

■ **Usage** In sense 2, *compose* is preferred to *comprise*.

composer /kəm'pəʊzə(r)/ *n.* a person who composes (esp. music).

composite /'kɒmpəzɪt, -ˌzaɪt/ *adj.* & *n.* —*adj.* **1** made up of various parts; blended. **2** *Archit.* consisting of elements of the Ionic and Corinthian orders. **3** *Bot.* of the plant family Compositae. —*n.* **1** a thing made up of several parts or elements. **2** *Bot.* any plant of the family Compositae, having a head of many small flowers forming one bloom, e.g. the daisy or the dandelion. **3** *Polit.* a resolution composed of two or more related resolutions. □ **compositely** *adv.* **compositeness** *n.* [F f. L *compositus* past part. of *componere* (as COM-, *ponere posit-* put)]

composition /ˌkɒmpə'zɪʃ(ə)n/ *n.* **1 a** the act of putting together; formation or construction. **b** something so composed; a mixture. **c** the constitution of such a mixture; the nature of its ingredients (*the composition is two parts oil to one part vinegar*). **2 a** a literary or musical work. **b** the act or art of producing such a work. **c** an essay, esp. written by a schoolchild. **d** an artistic arrangement (of parts of a picture, subjects for a photograph, etc.). **3** (often *attrib.*) a compound artificial substance, esp. one serving the purpose of a natural one. **4** *Printing* the setting-up of type. □ **compositional** *adj.* **compositionally** *adv.* [ME f. OF, f. L *compositio -onis* (as COMPOSITE)]

compositor /kəm'pɒzɪtə(r)/ *n. Printing* a person who sets up type for printing. [ME f. AF *compositour* f. L *compositor* (as COMPOSITE)]

compos mentis /ˌkɒmpɒs 'mentɪs/ *adj.* (also *compos*) having control of one's mind; sane. [L]

compost /'kɒmpɒst/ *n.* & *v.* —*n.* **1** mixed manure, esp. of organic origin. **2** a loam soil or other medium with added compost, used for growing plants. —*v.tr.* **1** treat (soil) with compost. **2** make (manure, vegetable matter, etc.) into compost. □ **compost heap** (or **pile**) a layered structure of garden refuse, soil, etc., which decays to become compost. [ME f. OF *composte* f. L *compos(i)tum* (as COMPOSITE)]

composure /kəm'pəʊʒə(r)/ *n.* a tranquil manner; calmness. [COMPOSE + -URE]

compote /'kɒmpəʊt, -pɒt/ *n.* fruit preserved or cooked in syrup. [F f. OF *composte* (as COMPOSITE)]

compound[1] /'kɒmpaʊnd/ *n., adj.,* & *v.* —*n.* **1** a mixture of two or more things, qualities, etc. **2** (also **compound word**) a word made up of two or more existing words. **3** *Chem.* a substance formed from two or more elements chemically united in fixed proportions. —*adj.* **1 a** made up of several ingredients. **b** consisting of several parts. **2** combined; collective. **3** *Zool.* consisting of individual organisms. **4** *Biol.* consisting of several or many parts. —*v.* /kəm'paʊnd/ **1** *tr.* mix or combine (ingredients, ideas, motives, etc.) (*grief compounded with fear*). **2** *tr.* increase or complicate (difficulties etc.) (*anxiety compounded by discomfort*). **3** *tr.* make up (a composite whole). **4** *tr. Law* **a** condone (a liability or offence) in exchange for money etc. **b** forbear from prosecuting (a felony) from private motives. **5** *tr.* combine (words or elements) into a word. □ **compound eye** an eye consisting of numerous visual units, as found in insects and crustaceans. **compound fracture** a fracture complicated by a skin wound. **compound interest** interest payable on capital and its accumulated interest. **compound leaf** a leaf consisting of several or many leaflets. **compound sentence** a sentence with more than one subject or predicate. **compound time** *Mus.* music having more than one group of simple-time units in each bar. □ **compoundable** /kəm'paʊndəb(ə)l/ *adj.* [ME *compoun(e)* f. OF *compondre* f. L *componere* (as COM-, *ponere* put: *-d* as in *expound*)]

compound[2] /'kɒmpaʊnd/ *n.* **1** a large open enclosure for housing workers etc. **2** an enclosure, esp. in India, China, etc., in which a factory or a house stands. **3** a large enclosed space in a prison or prison camp. **4** = POUND[3]. [Port. *campon* or Du. *kampong* f. Malay]

comprehend /ˌkɒmprɪ'hend/ *v.tr.* **1** grasp mentally; understand (a person or a thing). **2** include; take in. [ME f. OF *comprehender* or L *comprehendere comprehens-* (as COM-, *prehendere* grasp)]

comprehensible /ˌkɒmprɪ'hensɪb(ə)l/ *adj.* **1** that can be understood; intelligible. **2** that can be included or contained. □ **comprehensibility** /-'bɪlɪtɪ/ *n.* **comprehensibly** *adv.* [F *compréhensible* or L *comprehensibilis* (as COMPREHEND)]

comprehension /ˌkɒmprɪ'henʃ(ə)n/ *n.* **1 a** the act or capability of understanding, esp. writing or speech. **b** an extract from a text set as an examination, with questions designed to test understanding of it. **2** inclusion. [F *compréhension* or L *comprehensio* (as COMPREHENSIBLE)]

comprehensive /ˌkɒmprɪ'hensɪv/ *adj.* & *n.* —*adj.* **1** complete; including all or nearly all elements, aspects, etc. (*a comprehensive grasp of the subject*). **2** of or relating to understanding (*the comprehensive faculty*). **3** (of motor-vehicle insurance) providing complete protection. —*n.* (in full **comprehensive school**) *Brit.* a secondary school catering for children of all abilities from a given area. □ **comprehensively** *adv.* **comprehensiveness** *n.* [F *compréhensif -ive* or LL *comprehensivus* (as COMPREHENSIBLE)]

compress *v. & n.* —*v.tr.* /kəm'pres/ **1** squeeze together. **2** bring into a smaller space or shorter extent. —*n.* /'kɒmpres/ a pad of lint etc. pressed on to part of the body to relieve inflammation, stop bleeding, etc. □ **compressed air** air at more than atmospheric pressure. □ **compressible** /kəm'presɪb(ə)l/ *adj.* **compressibility** /-'bɪlɪtɪ/ *n.* **compressive** /kəm'presɪv/ *adj.* [ME f. OF *compresser* or LL *compressare* frequent. of L *comprimere* compress- (as COM-, *premere* press)]

compression /kəm'preʃ(ə)n/ *n.* **1** the act of compressing or being compressed. **2** the reduction in volume (causing an increase in pressure) of the fuel mixture in an internal-combustion engine before ignition. [F f. L *compressio* (as COMPRESS)]

compressor /kəm'presə(r)/ *n.* an instrument or device for compressing, esp. a machine used for increasing the pressure of air or other gases.

comprise /kəm'praɪz/ *v.tr.* **1** include; comprehend. **2** consist of, be composed of (*the book comprises 350 pages*). **3** *disp.* make up, compose (*the essays comprise his total work*). □ **comprisable** *adj.* [ME f. F, fem. past part. of *comprendre* COMPREHEND]

■ **Usage** The use of this word in sense 3 is considered incorrect and *compose* is generally preferred.

compromise /'kɒmprə,maɪz/ *n. & v.* —*n.* **1** the settlement of a dispute by mutual concession (*reached a compromise by bargaining*). **2** (often foll. by *between*) an intermediate state between conflicting opinions, actions, etc. (*a compromise between ideals and material necessity*). —*v.* **1** *intr.* settle a dispute by mutual concession (*compromised over the terms*). **2** *tr.* bring into disrepute or danger esp. by indiscretion or folly. □ **compromiser** *n.* **compromisingly** *adv.* [ME f. OF *compromis* f. LL *compromissum* neut. past part. of *compromittere* (as COM-, *promittere* PROMISE)]

comptroller /kən'trəʊlə(r)/ *n.* a controller (used in the title of some financial officers). [var. of CONTROLLER, by erron. assoc. with COUNT[1], L *computus*]

compulsion /kəm'pʌlʃ(ə)n/ *n.* **1** a constraint; an obligation. **2** *Psychol.* an irresistible urge to a form of behaviour, esp. against one's conscious wishes. [ME f. F f. LL *compulsio -onis* (as COMPEL)]

compulsive /kəm'pʌlsɪv/ *adj.* **1** compelling. **2** resulting or acting from, or as if from, compulsion (*a compulsive gambler*). **3** *Psychol.* resulting or acting from compulsion against one's conscious wishes. **4** irresistible (*compulsive entertainment*). □ **compulsively** *adv.* **compulsiveness** *n.* [med.L *compulsivus* (as COMPEL)]

compulsory /kəm'pʌlsərɪ/ *adj.* required by law or a rule. □ **compulsory purchase** the enforced purchase of land or property by a local authority etc., for public use. □ **compulsorily** *adv.* **compulsoriness** *n.* [med.L *compulsorius* (as COMPEL)]

compunction /kəm'pʌŋkʃ(ə)n/ *n.* (usu. with *neg.*) **1** the pricking of the conscience. **2** a slight regret; a scruple. □ **compunctious** /-'ʃəs/ *adj.* **compunctiously** /-'ʃəslɪ/ *adv.* [ME f. OF *componction* f. eccl.L *compunctio -onis* f. L *compungere compunct-* (as COM-, *pungere* prick)]

compute /kəm'pju:t/ *v.* **1** *tr.* (often foll. by *that* + clause) reckon or calculate (a number, an amount, etc.). **2** *intr.* make a reckoning, esp. using a computer. □ **computability** /-tə'bɪlɪtɪ/ *n.* **computable** /-'pju:təb(ə)l, 'kɒm-/ *adj.* **computation** /,kɒmpju:'teɪʃ(ə)n/ *n.* **computational** /,kɒmpju:'teɪʃən(ə)l/ *adj.* [F *computer* or L *computare* (as COM-, *putare* reckon)]

computer /kəm'pju:tə(r)/ *n.* **1** a usu. electronic device for storing and processing data (usu. in binary form), according to instructions given to it in a variable program. **2** a person who computes or makes calculations. □ **computer-literate** able to use computers; familiar with the operation of computers. **computer science** the study of the principles and use of computers. **computer virus** a hidden code within a computer program intended to corrupt a system or destroy data stored in it.

computerize /kəm'pju:tə,raɪz/ *v.tr.* (also **-ise**) **1** equip with a computer; install a computer in. **2** store, perform, or produce by computer. □ **computerization** /-'zeɪʃ(ə)n/ *n.*

comrade /'kɒmreɪd, -rɪd/ *n.* **1 a** a workmate, friend, or companion. **b** (also **comrade-in-arms**) a fellow soldier etc. **2** *Polit.* a fellow socialist or communist (often as a form of address). □ **comradely** *adj.* **comradeship** *n.* [earlier *cama- camerade* f. F *camerade, camarade* (orig. fem.) f. Sp. *camarada* room-mate (as CHAMBER)]

Comsat /'kɒmsæt/ *n. propr.* a communication satellite. [abbr.]

con[1] *n. & v. sl.* —*n.* a confidence trick. —*v.tr.* (**conned, conning**) swindle; deceive (*conned him into thinking he had won*). □ **con man** = *confidence man.* [abbr.]

con[2] *n., prep., & adv.* —*n.* (usu. in *pl.*) a reason against. —*prep. & adv.* against (cf. PRO[2]). [L *contra* against]

con[3] *n. sl.* a convict. [abbr.]

con[4] *v.tr.* (US **conn**) (**conned, conning**) *Naut.* direct the steering of (a ship). [app. weakened form of obs. *cond, condie,* f. F *conduire* f. L *conducere* CONDUCT]

con[5] *v.tr.* (**conned, conning**) *archaic* (often foll. by *over*) study, learn by heart (*conned his part well*). [ME *cunn-, con,* forms of CAN[1]]

concatenate /kɒn'kætɪ,neɪt/ *v. & adj.* —*v.tr.* link together (a chain of events, things, etc.). —*adj.* joined; linked. □ **concatenation** /-'neɪʃ(ə)n/ *n.* [LL *concatenare* (as COM-, *catenare* f. *catena* chain)]

concave /'kɒnkeɪv/ *adj.* having an outline or surface curved like the interior of a circle or sphere. □ **concavely** *adv.* **concavity** /-'kævɪtɪ/ *n.* [L *concavus* (as COM-, *cavus* hollow), or through F *concave*]

conceal /kən'si:l/ *v.tr.* **1** (often foll. by *from*) keep secret. **2** not allow to be seen; hide. □ **concealer** *n.* **concealment** *n.* [ME f. OF *conceler* f. L *concelare* (as COM-, *celare* hide)]

concede /kən'si:d/ *v.tr.* **1 a** (often foll. by *that* + clause) admit (a defeat etc.) to be true. **b** admit defeat in. **2** (often foll. by *to*) grant, yield, or surrender (a right, a privilege, etc.). **3** *Sport* allow an opponent to score (a goal) or to win (a match), etc. □ **conceder** *n.* [F *concéder* or L *concedere concess-* (as COM-, *cedere* yield)]

conceit /kən'si:t/ *n.* **1** personal vanity; pride. **2** *literary* **a** a far-fetched comparison, esp. as a stylistic affectation. **b** a fanciful notion. [ME f. CONCEIVE after *deceit*, *deceive*, etc.]

conceited /kən'si:tɪd/ *adj.* vain, proud. □ **conceitedly** *adv.* **conceitedness** *n.*

conceivable /kən'si:vəb(ə)l/ *adj.* capable of being grasped or imagined; understandable. □ **conceivability** /-'bɪlɪtɪ/ *n.* **conceivably** *adv.*

conceive /kən'si:v/ *v.* **1** *intr.* become pregnant. **2** *tr.* become pregnant with (a child). **3** *tr.* (often foll. by *that* + clause) imagine, think (*can't conceive that he could be guilty*). □ **conceive of** form in the mind; imagine. [ME f. OF *conceiv*-stressed stem of *concevoir* f. L *concipere* *concept*- (as COM-, *capere* take)]

concentrate /'kɒnsən,treɪt/ *v.* & *n.* —*v.* **1** *intr.* (often foll. by *on*, *upon*) focus all one's attention or mental ability. **2** *tr.* bring together (troops, power, attention, etc.) to one point; focus. **3** *tr.* increase the strength of (a liquid etc.) by removing water or any other diluting agent. **4** *tr.* (as **concentrated** *adj.*) (of hate etc.) intense, strong. —*n.* **1** a concentrated substance. **2** a concentrated form of esp. food. □ **concentratedly** *adv.* **concentrative** *adj.* **concentrator** *n.* [after *concentre* f. F *concentrer* (as COM- + CENTRE)]

concentration /,kɒnsən'treɪʃ(ə)n/ *n.* **1 a** the act or power of concentrating (*needs to develop concentration*). **b** an instance of this (*interrupted my concentration*). **2** something concentrated (*a concentration of resources*). **3** the weight of substance in a given weight or volume of material. □ **concentration camp** a camp for the detention of political prisoners, internees, etc.

concentric /kən'sentrɪk/ *adj.* (often foll. by *with*) (esp. of circles) having a common centre. □ **concentrically** *adv.* **concentricity** /,kɒnsen'trɪsɪtɪ/ *n.* [ME f. OF *concentrique* or med.L *concentricus* (as COM-, *centricus* as CENTRE)]

concept /'kɒnsept/ *n.* **1** a general notion; an abstract idea (*the concept of evolution*). **2** *colloq.* an idea or invention to help sell or publicize a commodity (*a new concept in swimwear*). [LL *conceptus* f. *concept*-: see CONCEIVE]

conception /kən'sepʃ(ə)n/ *n.* **1** the act or an instance of conceiving; the process of being conceived. **2** an idea or plan, esp. as being new or daring (*the whole conception showed originality*). □ **conceptional** *adj.* [ME f. OF f. L *conceptio* -*onis* (as CONCEPT)]

conceptual /kən'septjʊəl/ *adj.* of mental conceptions or concepts. □ **conceptually** *adv.* [med.L *conceptualis* (*conceptus* as CONCEPT)]

conceptualize /kən'septjʊə,laɪz/ *v.tr.* (also **-ise**) form a concept or idea of. □ **conceptualization** /-'zeɪʃ(ə)n/ *n.*

concern /kən'sɜ:n/ *v.* & *n.* —*v.tr.* **1 a** be relevant or important to (*this concerns you*). **b** relate to; be about. **2** (usu. *refl.*; often foll. by *with*, *in*, *about*, or *to* + *infin.*) interest or involve oneself (*don't concern yourself with my problems*). **3** worry, affect (*it concerns me that he is always late*). —*n.* **1** anxiety, worry (*felt a deep concern*). **2 a** a matter of interest or importance to one (*no concern of mine*). **b** (usu. in pl.) affairs, private business (*meddling in my concerns*). **3** a business, a firm (*quite a prosperous concern*). [F *concerner* or LL *concernere* (as COM-, *cernere* sift, discern)]

concerned /kən'sɜ:nd/ *adj.* **1** involved, interested (*the people concerned*; *concerned with proving his innocence*). **2** (often foll. by *that*, *about*, *at*, *for*, or *to* + *infin.*) troubled, anxious. □ **be concerned** (often foll. by *in*) take part. □ **concernedly** /-'sɜ:nɪdlɪ/ *adv.* **concernedness** /-'sɜ:nɪdnɪs/ *n.*

concerning /kən'sɜ:nɪŋ/ *prep.* about, regarding.

concert *n.* & *v.* —*n.* /'kɒnsət/ **1** a musical performance of usu. several separate compositions. **2** agreement, accordance, harmony. **3** a combination of voices or sounds. —*v.tr.* /kən'sɜ:t/ arrange (by mutual agreement or coordination). □ **concert-master** esp. *US* the leading first-violin player in some orchestras.

concert pitch 1 *Mus.* the pitch internationally agreed in 1960 whereby the A above middle C = 440 Hz. **2** a state of unusual readiness, efficiency, and keenness (for action etc.). **in concert 1** (often foll. by *with*) acting jointly and accordingly. **2** (*predic.*) (of a musician) in a performance. [F *concert* (n.), *concerter* (v.) f. It. *concertare* harmonize]

concerted /kən'sɜ:tɪd/ *adj.* **1** combined together; jointly arranged or planned (*a concerted effort*). **2** *Mus.* arranged in parts for voices or instruments.

concertina /,kɒnsə'ti:nə/ *n.* & *v.* —*n.* a musical instrument held in the hands and stretched and squeezed like bellows, having reeds and a set of buttons at each end to control the valves. —*v.tr.* & *intr.* (**concertinas, concertinaed** /-nəd/ or **concertina'd, concertinaing**) compress or collapse in folds like those of a concertina dimin. suffix -*ina*. [CONCERT + dimin. suffix -*ina*]

concerto /kən'tʃeətəʊ, -'tʃɜ:təʊ/ *n.* (pl. **-os** or **concerti** /-tɪ/) *Mus.* a composition for a solo instrument or instruments accompanied by an orchestra. [It. (see CONCERT): *grosso* big]

concession /kən'seʃ(ə)n/ *n.* **1 a** the act or an instance of conceding (*made the concession that we were right*). **b** a thing conceded. **2** a reduction in price for a certain category of person. **3 a** the right to use land or other property, granted esp. by a government or local authority, esp. for a specific use. **b** the right, given by a company, to sell goods, esp. in a particular territory. **c** the land or property used or given. □ **concessionary** *adj.* (also **concessional**). [F *concession* f. L *concessio* (as CONCEDE)]

concessionaire /kən,seʃə'neə(r)/ *n.* (also **concessionnaire**) the holder of a concession or grant. [F *concessionnaire* (as CONCESSION)]

concessive /kən'sesɪv/ *adj.* **1** of or tending to concession. **2** *Gram.* **a** (of a preposition or conjunction) introducing a phrase or clause which might be expected to preclude the action of the main clause, but does not (e.g. *in spite of*, *although*). **b** (of a phrase or clause) introduced by a concessive preposition or conjunction. [LL *concessivus* (as CONCEDE)]

conch /kɒŋk, kɒntʃ/ *n.* (pl. **conchs** /kɒŋks/ or **conches** /'kɒntʃɪz/) **1** a thick heavy spiral shell, occasionally bearing long projections, of various marine gastropod molluscs of the family Strombidae. **2** any of these gastropods. [L *concha* shell f. Gk *kogkhē*]

conchology /kɒŋ'kɒlədʒɪ/ *n.* *Zool.* the scientific study of shells. □ **conchological** /-kə'lɒdʒɪk(ə)l/ *adj.* **conchologist** *n.* [Gk *kogkhē* shell + -LOGY]

concierge /,kɒsi'eəʒ, ,kɒn-/ *n.* (esp. in France) a door-keeper or porter of a block of flats etc. [F, prob. ult. f. L *conservus* fellow slave]

conciliar /kən'sɪlɪə(r)/ *adj.* of or concerning a council, esp. an ecclesiastical council. [med.L *consiliarius* counsellor]

conciliate /kən'sɪlɪˌeɪt/ v.tr. **1** make calm and amenable; pacify. **2** gain (esteem or goodwill). □ **conciliative** /-'sɪlɪətɪv/ adj. **conciliator** n. **conciliatory** /-'sɪlɪətərɪ/ adj. **conciliatoriness** /-'sɪlɪətərɪnɪs/ n. [L conciliare combine, gain (concilium COUNCIL)]

conciliation /kənˌsɪlɪ'eɪʃ(ə)n/ n. the use of conciliating measures; reconcilement. [L conciliatio (as CONCILIATE)]

concise /kən'saɪs/ adj. (of speech, writing, style, or a person) brief but comprehensive in expression. □ **concisely** adv. **conciseness** n. **concision** n. [F concis or L concisus past part. of concidere (as COM-, caedere cut)]

conclave /'kɒnkleɪv/ n. **1** a private meeting. **2** RC Ch. **a** the assembly of cardinals for the election of a pope. **b** the meeting-place for a conclave. [ME f. OF f. L conclave lockable room (as COM-, clavis key)]

conclude /kən'kluːd/ v. **1** tr. & intr. bring or come to an end. **2** tr. (often foll. by from, or that + clause) infer (from given premisses) (what did you conclude?; concluded from the evidence that he had been mistaken). **3** tr. settle, arrange (a treaty etc.). [ME f.L concludere (as COM-, claudere shut)]

conclusion /kən'kluːʒ(ə)n/ n. **1** a final result; a termination. **2** a judgement reached by reasoning. **3** the summing-up of an argument, article, book, etc. **4** a settling; an arrangement (the conclusion of peace). **5** Logic a proposition that is reached from given premisses. □ **in conclusion** lastly, to conclude. [ME OF conclusion or L conclusio (as CONCLUDE)]

conclusive /kən'kluːsɪv/ adj. decisive, convincing. □ **conclusively** adv. **conclusiveness** n. [LL conclusivus (as CONCLUSION)]

concoct /kən'kɒkt/ v.tr. **1** make by mixing ingredients. **2** invent (a story, a lie, etc.). □ **concocter** n. **concoction** /-'kɒkʃ(ə)n/ n. **concoctor** n. [L concoquere concoct- (as COM-, coquere cook)]

concomitance /kən'kɒmɪt(ə)ns/ n. (also **concomitancy**) coexistence. [med.L concomitantia (as CONCOMITANT)]

concomitant /kən'kɒmɪt(ə)nt/ adj. & n. —adj. going together; associated (concomitant circumstances). —n. an accompanying thing. □ **concomitantly** adv. [LL concomitari (as COM-, comitari f. L comes -mitis companion)]

concord /'kɒnkɔːd, 'kɒŋ-/ n. **1** agreement or harmony between people or things. **2** a treaty. **3** Mus. a chord that is pleasing or satisfactory in itself. **4** Gram. agreement between words in gender, number, etc. [ME f. OF concorde f. L concordia f. concors of one mind (as COM-, cors f. cor cordis heart)]

concordance /kən'kɔːd(ə)ns, kɒŋ-/ n. **1** agreement. **2** a book containing an alphabetical list of the important words used in a book or by an author, usu. with citations of the passages concerned. [ME f. OF f. med.L concordantia (as CONCORDANT)]

concordant /kən'kɔːd(ə)nt/ adj. **1** (often foll. by with) agreeing, harmonious. **2** Mus. in harmony. □ **concordantly** adv. [ME f. OF f. L concordare f. concors (as CONCORD)]

concordat /kən'kɔːdæt/ n. an agreement, esp. between the Roman Catholic Church and a State. [F concordat or L concordatum neut. past part. of concordare (as CONCORDANCE)]

concourse /'kɒnkɔːs, 'kɒŋ-/ n. **1** a crowd. **2** a coming together; a gathering (a concourse of ideas). **3** an open central area in a large public building. [ME f. OF concours f. L concursus (as CONCUR)]

concrete /'kɒnkriːt, 'kɒŋ-/ adj., n., & v. —adj. **1 a** existing in a material form; real. **b** specific, definite. **2** Gram. (of a noun) denoting a material object as opposed to an abstract quality, state, or action. —n. (often attrib.) a composition of gravel, sand, cement, and water, used for building. —v. **1** tr. **a** cover with concrete. **b** embed in concrete. **2 a** tr. & intr. form into a mass; solidify. **b** tr. make concrete instead of abstract. □ **concrete-mixer** a machine, usu. with a revolving drum, used for mixing concrete. **concrete music** music constructed by mixing recorded sounds. **concrete poetry** poetry using unusual typographical layout to enhance the effect on the page. □ **concretely** adv. **concreteness** n. [F concret or L concretus past part. of concrescere (as COM-, crescere cret- GROW)]

concretion /kən'kriːʃ(ə)n/ n. **1** a hard solid concreted mass. **2** the forming of this by coalescence. □ **concretionary** adj. [F f. L concretio (as CONCRETE)]

concubinage /kən'kjuːbɪnɪdʒ/ n. **1** the cohabitation of a man and woman not married to each other. **2** the state of being or having a concubine. [ME f. F (as CONCUBINE)]

concubine /'kɒŋkjʊˌbaɪn/ n. **1** a woman who lives with a man as his wife. **2** (among polygamous peoples) a secondary wife. □ **concubinary** /kən'kjuːbɪnərɪ/ adj. [ME f. OF f. L concubina (as COM-, cubina f. cubare lie)]

concupiscence /kən'kjuːpɪs(ə)ns/ n. formal sexual desire. □ **concupiscent** adj. [ME f. OF f. LL concupiscentia f. L concupiscere begin to desire (as COM-, inceptive f. cupere desire)]

concur /kən'kɜː(r)/ v.intr. (**concurred, concurring**) **1** happen together; coincide. **2** (often foll. by with) **a** agree in opinion. **b** express agreement. [L concurrere (as COM-, currere run)]

concurrent /kən'kʌrənt/ adj. **1** (often foll. by with) **a** existing in or operation at the same time (served two concurrent sentences). **b** existing or acting together. **2** Geom. (of three or more lines) meeting at or tending towards one point. □ **concurrence** n. **concurrently** adv.

concuss /kən'kʌs/ v.tr. **1** subject to concussion. **2** shake violently. [L concutere concuss- (as COM-, cutere = quatere shake)]

concussion /kən'kʌʃ(ə)n/ n. **1** Med. temporary unconsciousness or incapacity due to injury to the head. **2** violent shaking; shock. [L concussio (as CONCUSS)]

condemn /kən'dem/ v.tr. **1** express utter disapproval of; censure (was condemned for his irresponsible behaviour). **2 a** find guilty; convict. **b** (usu. foll. by to) sentence to (a punishment, esp. death). **c** bring about the conviction of (his looks condemn him). **3** pronounce (a building etc.) unfit for use or habitation. **4** (usu. foll. by to) doom or assign to (something unwelcome or painful). □ **condemnable** /-'demnəb(ə)l/ adj. **condemnation** /ˌkɒndem'neɪʃ(ə)n/ n. **condemnatory** /-'demnətərɪ/ adj. [ME f. OF condem(p)ner f. L condemnare (as COM-, damnare DAMN)]

condensation /ˌkɒnden'seɪʃ(ə)n/ n. **1** the act of condensing. **2** any condensed material (esp.

water on a cold surface). **3** an abridgement. [LL *condensatio* (as CONDENSE)]

condense /kənˈdens/ v. **1** tr. make denser or more concentrated. **2** tr. express in fewer words; make concise. **3** tr. & intr. reduce or be reduced from a gas or solid to a liquid. □ **condensed milk** milk thickened by evaporation and sweetened. □ **condensable** adj. [F *condenser* or L *condensare* (as COM-, *densus* thick)]

condenser /kənˈdensə(r)/ n. **1** an apparatus or vessel for condensing vapour. **2** *Electr.* = CAPACITOR. **3** a lens or system of lenses for concentrating light.

condescend /ˌkɒndɪˈsend/ v.intr. **1** (usu. foll. by *to* + infin.) be gracious enough (to do a thing) esp. while showing one's sense of dignity or superiority (*condescended to attend the meeting*). **2** (foll. by *to*) behave as if one is on equal terms with (an inferior), usu. while maintaining an attitude of superiority. **3** (as **condescending** adj.) patronizing; kind to inferiors. □ **condescendingly** adv. [ME f. OF *condescendre* f. eccl.L *condescendere* (as COM-, DESCEND)]

condescension /ˌkɒndɪˈsenʃ(ə)n/ n. **1** a patronizing manner. **2** affability towards inferiors. [obs. F f. eccl.L *condescensio* (as CONDESCEND)]

condign /kənˈdaɪn/ adj. (of a punishment etc.) severe and well-deserved. □ **condignly** adv. [ME f. OF *condigne* f. L *condignus* (as COM-, *dignus* worthy)]

condiment /ˈkɒndɪmənt/ n. a seasoning or relish for food. [ME f. L *condimentum* f. *condire* pickle]

condition /kənˈdɪʃ(ə)n/ n. & v. —n. **1** a stipulation; something upon the fulfilment of which something else depends. **2 a** the state of being or fitness of a person or thing. **b** an ailment or abnormality (*a heart condition*). **3** (in *pl.*) circumstances, esp. those affecting the functioning or existence of something (*working conditions are good*). **4** *Gram.* a clause expressing a condition. —v.tr. **1 a** bring into a good or desired state or condition. **b** make fit (esp. dogs or horses). **2** teach or accustom to adopt certain habits etc. (*conditioned by society*). **3** govern, determine (*his behaviour was conditioned by his drunkenness*). **4 a** impose conditions on. **b** be essential to (*the two things condition each other*). □ **conditioned reflex** a reflex response to a non-natural stimulus, established by training. **in** (or **out of**) **condition** in good (or bad) condition. **on condition that** with the stipulation that. [ME f. OF *condicion* (n.), *condicionner* (v.) or med.L *condicionare* f. L *condicio -onis* f. *condicere* (as COM-, *dicere* say)]

conditional /kənˈdɪʃən(ə)l/ adj. & n. —adj. **1** (often foll. by *on*) dependent; not absolute; containing a condition or stipulation (*a conditional offer*). **2** *Gram.* (of a clause, mood, etc.) expressing a condition. —n. *Gram.* **1** a conditional clause etc. **2** the conditional mood. □ **conditional discharge** *Law* an order made by a criminal court whereby an offender will not be sentenced for an offence unless a further offence is committed within a stated period. □ **conditionality** /-ˈnælɪtɪ/ n. **conditionally** adv. [ME f. OF *condicionel* or f. LL *conditionalis* (as CONDITION)]

conditioner /kənˈdɪʃənə(r)/ n. an agent that brings something into good condition, esp. a substance applied to the hair.

condo /ˈkɒndəʊ/ n. (pl. **-os**) US colloq. a condominium. [abbr.]

condole /kənˈdəʊl/ v.intr. (foll. by *with*) express sympathy with a person over a loss, grief, etc. [LL *condolēre* (as COM-, *dolēre* suffer)]

■ **Usage** This word is often confused with *console*[1].

condolence /kənˈdəʊləns/ n. (often in *pl.*) an expression of sympathy (*sent my condolences*).

condom /ˈkɒndɒm/ n. a rubber sheath worn on the penis during sexual intercourse as a contraceptive or to prevent infection. [18th c.: orig. unkn.]

condominium /ˌkɒndəˈmɪnɪəm/ n. **1** the joint control of a State's affairs by other States. **2** *US* a building containing flats which are individually owned. [mod.L (as COM-, *dominium* DOMINION)]

condone /kənˈdəʊn/ v.tr. **1** forgive or overlook (an offence or wrongdoing). **2** approve or sanction, usu. reluctantly. □ **condonation** /ˌkɒndəˈneɪʃ(ə)n/ n. **condoner** n. [L *condonare* (as COM-, *donare* give)]

condor /ˈkɒndɔː(r)/ n. a large vulture, *Vultur gryphus*, of S. America, having black plumage with a white neck ruff and a fleshy wattle on the forehead. [Sp. f. Quechua *cuntur*]

conduce /kənˈdjuːs/ v.intr. (foll. by *to*) (usu. of an event or attribute) lead or contribute to (a result). [L *conducere* conduct- (as COM-, *ducere* duct- lead)]

conducive /kənˈdjuːsɪv/ adj. (often foll. by *to*) contributing or helping (towards something) (*not a conducive atmosphere for negotiation*).

conduct n. & v. —n. /ˈkɒndʌkt/ **1** behaviour (esp. in its moral aspect). **2** the action or manner of directing or managing (business, war, etc.). —v. /kənˈdʌkt/ **1** tr. lead or guide (a person or persons). **2** tr. direct or manage (business etc.). **3** tr. (also *absol.*) be the conductor of (an orchestra etc.). **4** tr. *Physics* transmit (heat, electricity, etc.) by conduction. **5** *refl.* behave (*conducted himself appropriately*). □ **conducted tour** a tour led by a guide on a fixed itinerary. □ **conductible** /kənˈdʌktɪb(ə)l/ adj. **conductibility** /kənˌdʌktɪˈbɪlɪtɪ/ n. [ME f. L *conductus* (as COM-, *ducere* duct- lead): (v.) f. OF *conduite* past part. of *conduire*]

conductance /kənˈdʌkt(ə)ns/ n. *Physics* the power of a specified material to conduct electricity.

conduction /kənˈdʌkʃ(ə)n/ n. **1 a** the transmission of heat through a substance from a region of higher temperature to a region of lower temperature. **b** the transmission of electricity through a substance by the application of an electric field. **2** the transmission of impulses along nerves. [F *conduction* or L *conductio* (as CONDUCT)]

conductive /kənˈdʌktɪv/ adj. having the property of conducting (esp. heat, electricity, etc.). □ **conductively** adv.

conductivity /ˌkɒndʌkˈtɪvɪtɪ/ n. the conducting power of a specified material.

conductor /kənˈdʌktə(r)/ n. **1** a person who directs the performance of an orchestra or choir etc. **2** (*fem.* **conductress** /-trɪs/) **a** a person who collects fares in a bus etc. **b** *US* an official in charge of a train. **3** *Physics* **a** a thing that conducts or transmits heat or electricity, esp. regarded in terms of its capacity to do this (*a poor conductor*). **b** = *lightning-conductor*. □

conductorship *n.* [ME f. F *conducteur* f. L *conductor* (as CONDUCTOR)]

conduit /ˈkɒndɪt, -djʊɪt/ *n.* **1** a channel or pipe for conveying liquids. **2 a** a tube or trough for protecting insulated electric wires. **b** a length or stretch of this. [ME f. OF *conduit* f. med.L *conductus* CONDUCT *n.*]

cone *n.* & *v.* —*n.* **1** a solid figure with a circular (or other curved) plane base, tapering to a point. **2** a thing of a similar shape, solid or hollow, e.g. as used to mark off areas of roads. **3** the dry fruit of a conifer. **4** an ice-cream cornet. **5** any of the minute cone-shaped structures in the retina. —*v.tr.* **1** shape like a cone. **2** (foll. by *off*) *Brit.* mark off (a road etc.) with cones. [F *cône* f. L *conus* f. Gk *kōnos*]

coney var. of CONY.

confab /ˈkɒnfæb/ *n.* & *v. colloq.* —*n.* = CON-FABULATION (see CONFABULATE). —*v.intr.* (**confabbed, confabbing**) = CONFABULATE. [abbr.]

confabulate /kənˈfæbjʊˌleɪt/ *v.intr.* converse, chat. □ **confabulation** /-ˈleɪʃ(ə)n/ *n.* **confabulatory** *adj.* [L *confabulari* (as COM-, *fabulari* f. *fabula* tale)]

confection /kənˈfekʃ(ə)n/ *n.* **1** a dish or delicacy made with sweet ingredients. **2** mixing, compounding. □ **confectionary** *adj.* [ME f. OF f. L *confectio -onis* f. *conficere confect-* put together]

confectioner /kənˈfekʃənə(r)/ *n.* a maker or retailer of confectionery.

confectionery /kənˈfekʃənərɪ/ *n.* sweets and other confections.

confederacy /kənˈfedərəsɪ/ *n.* (*pl.* **-ies**) **1** a league or alliance, esp. of confederate States. **2** the condition or fact of being confederate; alliance; conspiracy. [ME, AF, OF *confederacie* (as CONFEDERATE)]

confederate /kənˈfedərət/ *adj.*, *n.*, & *v.* —*adj.* esp. *Polit.* allied; joined by an agreement or treaty. —*n.* **1** an ally, esp. (in a bad sense) an accomplice. **2** (**Confederate**) a supporter of the Confederate States. —*v.* /-ˌreɪt/ (often foll. by *with*) **1** *tr.* bring (a person, State, or oneself) into alliance. **2** *intr.* come into alliance. □ **Confederate States** States which seceded from the US in 1860–1. [LL *confoederatus* (as COM-, FEDERATE)]

confederation /kənˌfedəˈreɪʃ(ə)n/ *n.* **1** a union or alliance of States etc. **2** the act or an instance of confederating; the state of being confederated. [F *confédération* (as CONFEDERATE)]

confer /kənˈfɜː(r)/ *v.* (**conferred, conferring**) **1** *tr.* (often foll. by *on, upon*) grant or bestow (a title, degree, favour, etc.). **2** *intr.* (often foll. by *with*) converse, consult. □ **conferrable** *adj.* [L *conferre* (as COM-, *ferre* bring)]

conference /ˈkɒnfərəns/ *n.* **1** consultation, discussion. **2** a meeting for discussion, esp. a regular one held by an association or organization. □ **in conference** engaged in discussion. □ **conferential** /ˌkɒnfəˈrenʃ(ə)l/ *adj.* [F *conférence* or med.L *conferentia* (as CONFER)]

conferment /kənˈfɜːmənt/ *n.* **1** the conferring of a degree, honour, etc. **2** an instance of this.

conferral /kənˈfɜːr(ə)l/ *n.* esp. *US* = CONFERMENT.

confess /kənˈfes/ *v.* **1 a** *tr.* (also *absol.*) acknowledge or admit (a fault, wrongdoing, etc.). **b** *intr.* (foll. by *to*) admit to (*confessed to having lied*). **2** *tr.* admit reluctantly (*confessed it would be difficult*). **3 a** *tr.* (also *absol.*) declare (one's sins) to a priest. **b** *tr.* (of a priest) hear the confession of. [ME f. OF

confesser f. Rmc f. L *confessus* past part. of *confitēri* (as COM-, *fatēri* declare, avow)]

confessedly /kənˈfesɪdlɪ/ *adv.* by one's own or general admission.

confession /kənˈfeʃ(ə)n/ *n.* **1 a** a confessing or acknowledgement of a fault, wrongdoing, a sin to a priest, etc. **b** an instance of this. **c** a thing confessed. **2** (in full **confession of faith**) **a** a declaration of one's religious beliefs. **b** a statement of one's principles. □ **confessionary** *adj.* [ME f. OF f. L *confessio -onis* (as CONFESS)]

confessional /kənˈfeʃən(ə)l/ *n.* & *adj.* —*n.* an enclosed stall in a church in which a priest hears confessions. —*adj.* of or relating to confession. [F f. It. *confessionale* f. med.L, neut. of *confessionalis* (as CONFESSION)]

confessor /kənˈfesə(r)/ *n.* **1** a person who makes a confession. **2** /also ˈkɒn-/ a priest who hears confessions and gives spiritual counsel. [ME f. AF *confessur*, OF *-our*, f. eccl.L *confessor* (as CONFESS)]

confetti /kənˈfetɪ/ *n.* small bits of coloured paper thrown by wedding guests at the bride and groom. [It., = sweetmeats f. L (as COMFIT)]

confidant /ˌkɒnfɪˈdænt, ˈkɒn-/ *n.* (*fem.* **confidante** *pronunc.* same) a person trusted with knowledge of one's private affairs. [18th-c. for earlier CONFIDENT *n.*, prob. to represent the pronunc. of F *confidente* (as CONFIDE)]

confide /kənˈfaɪd/ *v.* **1** *tr.* (usu. foll. by *to*) tell (a secret etc.) in confidence. **2** *tr.* (foll. by *to*) entrust (an object of care, a task, etc.) to. **3** *intr.* (foll. by *in*) talk confidentially to. □ **confidingly** *adv.* [L *confidere* (as COM-, *fidere* trust)]

confidence /ˈkɒnfɪd(ə)ns/ *n.* **1** firm trust (*have confidence in his ability*). **2 a** a feeling of reliance or certainty. **b** a sense of self-reliance; boldness. **3** something told confidentially. □ **confidence man** a man who robs by means of a confidence trick. **confidence trick** (*US* **game**) a swindle in which the victim is persuaded to trust the swindler in some way. **in confidence** as a secret. **in a person's confidence** trusted with a person's secrets. **take into one's confidence** confide in. [ME f. L *confidentia* (as CONFIDE)]

confident /ˈkɒnfɪd(ə)nt/ *adj.* **1** feeling or showing confidence; bold (*spoke with a confident air*). **2** (often foll. by *of*, or *that* + clause) assured, trusting. □ **confidently** *adv.* [F f. It. *confidente* (as CONFIDE)]

confidential /ˌkɒnfɪˈdenʃ(ə)l/ *adj.* **1** spoken or written in confidence. **2** entrusted with secrets (*a confidential secretary*). **3** confiding. □ **confidentiality** /-ʃɪˈælɪtɪ/ *n.* **confidentially** *adv.*

configuration /kənˌfɪgjʊˈreɪʃ(ə)n, -gəˈreɪʃ(ə)n/ *n.* **1** an arrangement of parts or elements in a particular form or figure. **2** the form, shape, or figure resulting from such an arrangement. □ **configurational** *adj.* **configure** *v.tr.* [LL *configuratio* f. L *configurare* (as COM-, *figurare* fashion)]

confine *v.* & *n.* —*v.tr.* /kənˈfaɪn/ (often foll. by *in, to, within*) **1** keep or restrict (within certain limits etc.). **2** hold captive; imprison. —*n.* /ˈkɒnfaɪn/ (usu. in *pl.*) a limit or boundary (*within the confines of the town*). □ **be confined** be in childbirth. [(v.) f. F *confiner*, (n.) ME f. F *confins* (pl.), f. L *confinia* (as COM-, *finia* neut. pl. f. *finis* end, limit)]

confinement /kənˈfaɪnmənt/ n. **1** the act or an instance of confining; the state of being confined. **2** the time of a woman's giving birth.

confirm /kənˈfɜːm/ v.tr. **1** provide support for the truth or correctness of; make definitely valid (*confirmed my suspicions*). **2** (foll. by *in*) encourage (a person) in (an opinion etc.). **3** establish more firmly (power, possession, etc.). **4** make formally valid. **5** administer the religious rite of confirmation to. □ **confirmative** adj. **confirmatory** adj. [ME f. OF *confermer* f. L *confirmare* (as COM-, FIRM¹)]

confirmation /ˌkɒnfəˈmeɪʃ(ə)n/ n. **1 a** the act or an instance of confirming; the state of being confirmed. **b** an instance of this. **2 a** a religious rite confirming a baptized person as a member of the Christian Church. **b** a ceremony of confirming persons in the Jewish faith. [ME f. OF f. L *confirmatio -onis* (as CONFIRM)]

confirmed /kənˈfɜːmd/ adj. firmly settled in some habit or condition (*a confirmed bachelor*).

confiscate /ˈkɒnfɪˌskeɪt/ v.tr. **1** take or seize by authority. **2** appropriate to the public treasury (by way of a penalty). □ **confiscable** /kənˈfɪskəb(ə)l/ adj. **confiscation** /-ˈskeɪʃ(ə)n/ n. **confiscator** n. **confiscatory** /kənˈfɪskətəri/ adj. [L *confiscare* (as COM-, *fiscare* f. *fiscus* treasury)]

conflagration /ˌkɒnfləˈɡreɪʃ(ə)n/ n. a great and destructive fire. [L *conflagratio* f. *conflagrare* (as COM-, *flagrare* blaze)]

conflate /kənˈfleɪt/ v.tr. blend or fuse together (esp. two variant texts into one). □ **conflation** /-ˈfleɪʃ(ə)n/ n. [L *conflare* (as COM-, *flare* blow)]

conflict n. & v. —n. /ˈkɒnflɪkt/ **1 a** a state of opposition or hostilities. **b** a fight or struggle. **2** (often foll. by *of*) **a** the clashing of opposed principles etc. **b** an instance of this. —v.intr. /kənˈflɪkt/ **1** clash; be incompatible. **2** (often foll. by *with*) struggle or contend. **3** (as **conflicting** adj.) contradictory. □ **confliction** /kənˈflɪkʃ(ə)n/ n. **conflictual** /kənˈflɪktʃʊəl/ adj. [ME f. L *confligere conflict-* (as COM-, *fligere* strike)]

confluence /ˈkɒnfluəns/ n. **1** a place where two rivers meet. **2 a** a coming together. **b** a crowd of people. [L *confluere* (as COM-, *fluere* flow)]

confluent /ˈkɒnfluənt/ adj. & n. —adj. flowing together, uniting. —n. a stream joining another.

conform /kənˈfɔːm/ v. **1** intr. comply with rules or general custom. **2** intr. & tr. (often foll. by *to*) be or make accordant or suitable. **3** tr. (often foll. by *to*) form according to a pattern; make similar. **4** intr. (foll. by *to, with*) comply with; be in accordance with. □ **conformer** n. [ME f. OF *conformer* f. L *conformare* (as COM-, FORM)]

conformable /kənˈfɔːməb(ə)l/ adj. **1** (often foll. by *to*) similar. **2** (often foll. by *with*) consistent. **3** (often foll. by *to*) adapted. **4** tractable; submissive. □ **conformability** /-ˈbɪlɪti/ n. **conformably** adv. [med.L *conformabilis* (as CONFORM)]

conformation /ˌkɒnfɔːˈmeɪʃ(ə)n/ n. the way in which a thing is formed; shape, structure. [L *conformatio* (as CONFORM)]

conformist /kənˈfɔːmɪst/ n. & adj. —n. a person who conforms to an established practice; a conventional person. —adj. (of a person) conforming to established practices; conventional. □ **conformism** n.

conformity /kənˈfɔːmɪti/ n. **1** (often foll. by *to, with*) action or behaviour in accordance with established practice; compliance. **2** (often foll.

by *to, with*) likeness, agreement. [ME f. OF *conformité* or LL *conformitas* (as CONFORM)]

confound /kənˈfaʊnd/ v. & int. —v.tr. **1** throw into perplexity or confusion. **2** mix up; confuse (in one's mind). **3** *archaic* defeat, overthrow. —int. expressing annoyance (*confound you!*). [ME f. AF *confu(o)undre*, OF *confondre* f. L *confundere* mix up (as COM-, *fundere fus-* pour)]

confounded /kənˈfaʊndɪd/ adj. *colloq.* damned (*a confounded nuisance!*). □ **confoundedly** adv.

confrère /ˈkɒnfreə(r)/ n. a fellow member of a profession, scientific body, etc. [ME f. OF f. med.L *confrater* (as COM-, *frater* brother)]

confront /kənˈfrʌnt/ v.tr. **1 a** face in hostility or defiance. **b** face up to and deal with (a problem, difficulty, etc.). **2** (of a difficulty etc.) present itself to (*countless obstacles confronted us*). **3** (foll. by *with*) **a** bring (a person) face to face with (a circumstance), esp. by way of accusation (*confronted them with the evidence*). **b** set (a thing) face to face with (another) for comparison. □ **confrontation** /ˌkɒnfrʌnˈteɪʃ(ə)n/ n. **confrontational** /ˌkɒnfrʌnˈteɪʃən(ə)l/ adj. [F *confronter* f. med.L *confrontare* (as COM-, *frontare* f. *frons frontis* face)]

Confucian /kənˈfjuːʃ(ə)n/ adj. & n. —adj. of or relating to Confucius, Chinese philosopher d. 479 BC, or his philosophy. —n. a follower of Confucius. □ **Confucianism** n. **Confucianist** n. [*Confucius*, Latinization of *Kongfuze* Kong the master]

confusable /kənˈfjuːzəb(ə)l/ adj. that is able or liable to be confused. □ **confusability** /-ˈbɪlɪti/ n.

confuse /kənˈfjuːz/ v.tr. **1 a** disconcert, perplex, bewilder. **b** embarrass. **2** mix up in the mind; mistake (one for another). **3** make indistinct (*that point confuses the issue*). **4** (as **confused** adj.) mentally decrepit. **5** (often as **confused** adj.) throw into disorder (*a confused jumble of clothes*). □ **confusedly** /kənˈfjuːzɪdli/ adv. **confusing** adj. **confusingly** adv. [19th-c. back-form. f. *confused* (14th c.) f. OF *confus* f. L *confusus*: see CONFOUND]

confusion /kənˈfjuːʒ(ə)n/ n. **1 a** the act of confusing (*the confusion of fact and fiction*). **b** an instance of this; a misunderstanding. **2 a** the result of confusing; a confused state; disorder (*thrown into confusion by his words*). **b** (foll. by *of*) a disorderly jumble (*a confusion of ideas*). [ME f. OF *confusion* or L *confusio* (as CONFUSE)]

confute /kənˈfjuːt/ v.tr. **1** prove (a person) to be in error. **2** prove (an argument) to be false. □ **confutation** /ˌkɒnfjuːˈteɪʃ(ə)n/ n. [L *confutare* restrain]

conga /ˈkɒŋɡə/ n. & v. —n. a Latin-American dance of African origin, usu. with several persons in a single line, one behind the other. —v.intr. (**congas, congaed** /-ɡəd/ or **conga'd, congaing** /-ɡəɪŋ/) perform the conga. [Amer. Sp. f. Sp. *conga* (fem.) of the Congo]

congeal /kənˈdʒiːl/ v.tr. & intr. **1** make or become semi-solid by cooling. **2** (of blood etc.) coagulate. □ **congealable** adj. **congealment** n. [ME f. OF *congeler* f. L *congelare* (as COM-, *gelare* f. *gelu* frost)]

congelation /ˌkɒndʒɪˈleɪʃ(ə)n/ n. **1** the process of congealing. **2** a congealed state. **3** a congealed substance. [ME f. OF *congelation* or L *congelatio* (as CONGEAL)]

congener /kənˈdʒiːnə(r)/ n. a thing or person of the same kind or category as another, esp. animals or plants of a specified genus (*the *goldfinch is a congener of the canary).* [L (as COM-, GENUS)]

congenial /kən'dʒi:nɪəl/ *adj.* **1** (often foll. by *with*, *to*) (of a person, character, etc.) pleasant because akin to oneself in temperament or interests. **2** (often foll. by *to*) suited or agreeable. □ **congeniality** /-ˈælɪtɪ/ *n.* **congenially** *adv.* [COM- + GENIAL]

congenital /kən'dʒenɪt(ə)l/ *adj.* **1** (esp. of a disease, defect, etc.) existing from birth. **2** that is (or as if) such from birth. □ **congenitally** *adv.* [L *congenitus* (as COM-, *genitus* past part. of *gigno* beget)]

conger /ˈkɒŋgə(r)/ *n.* (in full **conger eel**) any large marine eel of the family Congridae. [ME f. OF *congre* f. L *conger, congrus,* f. Gk *goggros*]

congeries /kən'dʒɪərɪːz, -'dʒerɪ,iːz/ *n.* (*pl.* same) a disorderly collection; a mass or heap. [L, formed as CONGEST]

■ **Usage** The form *congery*, formed under the misapprehension that *congeries* is plural only, is incorrect.

congest /kən'dʒest/ *v.tr.* (esp. as **congested** *adj.*) affect with congestion; obstruct, block (*congested streets; congested lungs*). □ **congestive** *adj.* [L *congerere congest-* (as COM-, *gerere* bring)]

congestion /kən'dʒestʃ(ə)n/ *n.* abnormal accumulation, crowding, or obstruction, esp. of traffic etc. or of blood or mucus in a part of the body. [F f. L *congestio -onis* (as CONGEST)]

conglomerate /kən'glɒmərət/ *adj., n.,* & *v.* —*adj.* gathered into a rounded mass. —*n.* **1** a number of things or parts forming a heterogeneous mass. **2** a group or corporation formed by the merging of separate and diverse firms. —*v.tr.* & *intr.* /kən'glɒmə,reɪt/ collect into a coherent mass. □ **conglomeration** /kən,glɒmə'reɪʃ(ə)n/ *n.* [L *conglomeratus* past part. of *conglomerare* (as COM-, *glomerare* f. *glomus -eris* ball)]

congratulate /kən'grætjʊ,leɪt/ *v.tr.* & *refl.* (often foll. by *on, upon*) **1** *tr.* express pleasure at the happiness or excellence of (a person) (*congratulated them on their success*). **2** *refl.* think oneself fortunate or clever. □ **congratulant** *adj.* & *n.* **congratulator** *n.* **congratulatory** /-lətərɪ/ *adj.* [L *congratulari* (as COM-, *gratulari* show joy f. *gratus* pleasing)]

congratulation /kən,grætjʊ'leɪʃ(ə)n/ *n.* **1** congratulating. **2** (also as *int.*; usu. in *pl.*) an expression of this (*congratulations on winning!*). [L *congratulatio* (as CONGRATULATE)]

congregate /ˈkɒŋgrɪ,geɪt/ *v.intr.* & *tr.* collect or gather into a crowd or mass. [ME f. L *congregare* (as COM-, *gregare* f. *grex gregis* flock)]

congregation /,kɒŋgrɪ'geɪʃ(ə)n/ *n.* **1** the process of congregating; collection into a crowd or mass. **2** a crowd or mass gathered together. **3 a** a body assembled for religious worship. **b** a body of persons regularly attending a particular church etc. □ **congregational** *adj.* [ME f. OF *congregation* or L *congregatio* (as CONGREGATE)]

Congregationalism /,kɒŋgrɪ'geɪʃənə,lɪz(ə)m/ *n.* a system of ecclesiastical organization whereby individual churches are largely self-governing. □ **Congregationalist** *n.* **Congregationalize** *v.tr.* (also -**ise**).

congress /ˈkɒŋgres/ *n.* **1** a formal meeting of delegates for discussion. **2** (**Congress**) a national legislative body, esp. that of the US. **3**

coming together, meeting. □ **congressional** /kɒŋ'greʃən(ə)l/ *adj.* [L *congressus* f. *congredi* (as COM-, *gradi* walk)]

congressman /ˈkɒŋgresmən/ *n.* (*pl.* **-men**; *fem.* **congresswoman**, *pl.* **-women**) a member of the US Congress.

congruence /ˈkɒŋgrʊəns/ *n.* (also **congruency** /-ənsɪ/) **1** agreement, consistency. **2** *Geom.* the state of being congruent. [ME f. L *congruentia* (as CONGRUENT)]

congruent /ˈkɒŋgrʊənt/ *adj.* **1** (often foll. by *with*) suitable, agreeing. **2** *Geom.* (of figures) coinciding exactly when superimposed. □ **congruently** *adv.* [ME f. L *congruere* agree]

congruous /ˈkɒŋgrʊəs/ *adj.* (often foll. by *with*) suitable, agreeing; fitting. □ **congruity** /-'gruːɪtɪ/ *n.* **congruously** *adv.* [L *congruus* (as CONGRUENT)]

conic /ˈkɒnɪk/ *adj.* of a cone. □ **conic section** a figure formed by the intersection of a cone and a plane. [mod.L *conicus* f. Gk *kōnikos* (as CONE)]

conical /ˈkɒnɪk(ə)l/ *adj.* cone-shaped. □ **conically** *adv.*

conifer /ˈkɒnɪfə(r), ˈkəʊn-/ *n.* any evergreen tree of a group usu. bearing cones. □ **coniferous** /kə'nɪfərəs/ *adj.* [L (as CONE, -FEROUS)]

conjectural /kən'dʒektʃər(ə)l/ *adj.* based on, involving, or given to conjecture. □ **conjecturally** *adv.* [F f. L *conjecturalis* (as CONJECTURE)]

conjecture /kən'dʒektʃə(r)/ *n.* & *v.* —*n.* **1** the formation of an opinion on incomplete information; guessing. **2** an opinion or conclusion reached in this way. —*v. tr.* & *intr.* guess. □ **conjecturable** *adj.* [ME f. OF *conjecture* or L *conjectura* f. *conjicere* (as COM-, *jacere* throw)]

conjoin /kən'dʒɔɪn/ *v.tr.* & *intr.* join, combine. [ME f. OF *conjoign-* pres. stem of *conjoindre* f. L *conjungere* (as COM-, *jungere junct-* join)]

conjoint /kən'dʒɔɪnt/ *adj.* associated, conjoined. □ **conjointly** *adv.* [ME f. OF, past part. (as CONJOIN)]

conjugal /ˈkɒndʒʊg(ə)l/ *adj.* of marriage or the relation between husband and wife. □ **conjugality** /-'gælɪtɪ/ *n.* **conjugally** *adv.* [L *conjugalis* f. *conjux* consort (as COM-, *-jux -jugis* f. root of *jungere* join)]

conjugate *v., adj.,* & *n.* —*v.* /ˈkɒndʒʊ,geɪt/ **1** *tr. Gram.* give the different forms of (a verb). **2** *intr.* **a** unite sexually. **b** (of gametes) become fused. —*adj.* /ˈkɒndʒʊgət/ **1** joined together, esp. as a pair. **2** *Biol.* fused. —*n.* /ˈkɒndʒʊgət/ a conjugate word or thing. □ **conjugately** /ˈkɒndʒʊgətlɪ/ *adv.* [L *conjugare* yoke together (as COM-, *jugare* f. *jugum* yoke)]

conjugation /,kɒndʒʊ'geɪʃ(ə)n/ *n.* **1** *Gram.* a system of verbal inflection. **2 a** the act or an instance of conjugating. **b** an instance of this. **3** *Biol.* the fusion of two gametes in reproduction. □ **conjugational** *adj.* [L *conjugatio* (as CONJUGATE)]

conjunct /kən'dʒʌŋkt/ *adj.* joined together; combined; associated. [ME f. L *conjunctus* (as CONJOIN)]

conjunction /kən'dʒʌŋkʃ(ə)n/ *n.* **1 a** the action of joining; the condition of being joined. **b** an instance of this. **2** *Gram.* a word used to connect clauses or sentences or words in the same clause (e.g. *and, but, if*). **3 a** a combination (of events or circumstances). **b** a number of associated persons or things. **4** *Astron.* & *Astrol.*

the alignment of two bodies in the solar system as seen from the earth. □ **in conjunction with** together with. □ **conjunctional** *adj.* [ME f. OF *conjonction* f. L *conjunctio -onis* (as CONJUNCT)]

conjunctiva /ˌkɒndʒʌŋkˈtaɪvə, kənˈdʒʌŋktɪvə/ *n.* (*pl.* **conjunctivas**) *Anat.* the mucous membrane that covers the front of the eye and lines the inside of the eyelids. □ **conjunctival** *adj.* [med.L (*membrana*) *conjunctiva* (as CONJUNCTIVE)]

conjunctive /kənˈdʒʌŋktɪv/ *adj.* & *n.* —*adj.* **1** serving to join; connective. **2** *Gram.* of the nature of a conjunction. —*n.* *Gram.* a conjunctive word. □ **conjunctively** *adv.* [LL *conjunctivus* (as CONJOIN)]

conjunctivitis /kənˌdʒʌŋktɪˈvaɪtɪs/ *n.* inflammation of the conjunctiva.

conjuncture /kənˈdʒʌŋktʃə(r)/ *n.* a combination of events; a state of affairs. [obs. F f. It. *congiuntura* (as CONJOIN)]

conjure /ˈkʌndʒə(r)/ *v.* **1** *intr.* perform tricks which are seemingly magical, esp. by rapid movements of the hands. **2** *tr.* (usu. foll. by *out of*, *away*, *to*, etc.) cause to appear or disappear as if by magic (*conjured a rabbit out of a hat*; *his pain was conjured away*). **3** *tr.* call upon (a spirit) to appear. □ **conjure up 1** bring into existence or cause to appear as if by magic. **2** cause to appear to the eye or mind; evoke. [ME f. OF *conjurer* plot, exorcise f. L *conjurare* band together by oath (as COM-, *jurare* swear)]

conjuror /ˈkʌndʒərə(r)/ *n.* (also **conjurer**) a performer of conjuring tricks. [CONJURE + -ER[1] & AF *conjurour* (OF *-eor*) f. med.L *conjurator* (as CONJURE)]

conk[1] *v.intr.* (usu. foll. by *out*) *colloq.* **1** (of a machine etc.) break down. **2** (of a person) become exhausted and give up; faint; die. [20th c.: orig. unkn.]

conk[2] *n.* & *v. sl.* —*n.* **1 a** the nose. **b** the head. **2 a** a punch on the nose or head. **b** a blow. —*v.tr.* punch on the nose; hit on the head etc. [19th c.: perh. = CONCH]

conker /ˈkɒŋkə(r)/ *n.* **1** the hard fruit of a horse chestnut. **2** (in *pl.*) *Brit.* a children's game played with conkers on strings, one hit against another to try to break it. [dial. *conker* snail-shell (orig. used in the game), assoc. with CONQUER]

conn US var. of CON[4].

connect /kəˈnekt/ *v.* **1 a** *tr.* (often foll. by *to*, *with*) join (one thing with another) (*connected the hose to the tap*). **b** *tr.* join (two things) (*a track connected the two villages*). **c** *intr.* be joined or joinable (*the two parts do not connect*). **2** *tr.* (often foll. by *with*) associate mentally or practically (*never connected her with the theatre*). **3** *intr.* (foll. by *with*) (of a train etc.) be synchronized at its destination with another train etc., so that passengers can transfer (*the train connects with the boat*). **4** *tr.* put into communication by telephone. **5 a** *tr.* (usu. in *passive*; foll. by *with*) unite or associate with others in relationships etc. (*am connected with the royal family*). **b** *intr.* form a logical sequence; be meaningful. □ **connecting-rod** the rod between the piston and the crankpin etc. in an internal-combustion engine or between the wheels of a locomotive. □ **connectable** *adj.* **connector** *n.* [L *connectere connex-* (as COM-, *nectere* bind)]

connected /kəˈnektɪd/ *adj.* **1** joined in sequence. **2** (of ideas etc.) coherent. **3** related or associated. □ **well-connected** associated with persons

of good social position. □ **connectedly** *adv.* **connectedness** *n.*

connection /kəˈnekʃ(ə)n/ *n.* (also *Brit.* **connexion**) **1 a** the act of connecting; the state of being connected. **b** an instance of this. **2** the point at which two things are connected (*broke at the connection*). **3 a** a thing or person that connects; a link (*cannot see the connection between the two ideas*). **b** a telephone link (*got a bad connection*). **4** arrangement or opportunity for catching a connecting train etc.; the train etc. itself (*missed the connection*). **5** *Electr.* **a** the linking up of an electric current by contact. **b** a device for effecting this. **6** (often in *pl.*) a relative or associate, esp. one with influence (*heard it through a business connection*). **7** a relation of ideas; a context. □ **in connection with** with reference to. □ **connectional** *adj.* [L *connexio* (as CONNECT): spelling *-ct-* after CONNECT]

connective /kəˈnektɪv/ *adj.* & *n.* —*adj.* serving or tending to connect. —*n.* something that connects. □ **connective tissue** *Anat.* a fibrous tissue that supports, binds, or separates more specialized tissue.

conning tower /ˈkɒnɪŋ/ *n.* **1** the superstructure of a submarine, which contains the periscope. **2** the armoured pilot-house of a warship. [CON[4] + -ING[1]]

connivance /kəˈnaɪv(ə)ns/ *n.* **1** conniving. **2** tacit permission (*done with his connivance*). [F *connivence* or L *conniventia* (as CONNIVE)]

connive /kəˈnaɪv/ *v.intr.* **1** (foll. by *at*) disregard or tacitly consent to (a wrongdoing). **2** (usu. foll. by *with*) conspire. □ **conniver** *n.* [F *conniver* or L *connivēre* shut the eyes (to)]

connoisseur /ˌkɒnəˈsɜː(r)/ *n.* (often foll. by *of*, *in*) an expert judge in matters of taste. □ **connoisseurship** *n.* [F, obs. spelling of *connaisseur* f. pres. stem of *connaître* know + *-eur* -OR[1]: cf. *reconnoitre*]

connotation /ˌkɒnəˈteɪʃ(ə)n/ *n.* that which is implied by a word etc. in addition to its literal or primary meaning (*a letter with sinister connotations*).

connote /kəˈnəʊt/ *v.tr.* **1** (of a word etc.) imply in addition to the literal or primary meaning. **2** (of a fact) imply as a consequence or condition. **3** mean, signify. □ **connotative** /ˈkɒnəˌteɪtɪv, kəˈnəʊtətɪv/ *adj.* [med.L *connotare* mark in addition (as COM-, *notare* f. *nota* mark)]

connubial /kəˈnjuːbɪəl/ *adj.* of or relating to marriage or the relationship of husband and wife. □ **connubiality** /-bɪˈælɪtɪ/ *n.* **connubially** *adv.* [L *connubialis* f. *connubium* (*nubium* f. *nubere* marry)]

conquer /ˈkɒŋkə(r)/ *v.tr.* **1 a** overcome and control (an enemy or territory) by military force. **b** *absol.* be victorious. **2** overcome by effort (*conquered his fear*). □ **conquerable** *adj.* **conqueror** *n.* [ME f. OF *conquerre* f. Rmc f. L *conquirere* (as COM-, *quaerere* seek, get)]

conquest /ˈkɒŋkwest/ *n.* **1** the act or an instance of conquering; the state of being conquered. **2 a** conquered territory. **b** something won. **3** a person whose affection or favour has been won. **4** (**the Conquest** or **Norman Conquest**) the conquest of England by William of Normandy in 1066. [ME f. OF *conquest(e)* f. Rmc (as CONQUER)]

consanguineous /ˌkɒnsæŋ'gwɪnɪəs/ adj. descended from the same ancestor; akin. □ **consanguinity** n. [L consanguineus (as COM-, sanguis -inis blood)]

conscience /'kɒnʃ(ə)ns/ n. **1** a moral sense of right and wrong. **2** an inner feeling as to the goodness or otherwise of one's behaviour (has a guilty conscience). □ **conscience clause** a clause in a law, ensuring respect for the consciences of those affected. **conscience money** a sum paid to relieve one's conscience, esp. about a payment previously evaded. **conscience-stricken** (or **-struck**) made uneasy by a bad conscience. **freedom of conscience** a system allowing all citizens a free choice of religion. **in all conscience** colloq. by any reasonable standard; by all that is fair. **on one's conscience** causing one feelings of guilt. **prisoner of conscience** a person imprisoned by a State for holding political or religious views it does not tolerate. □ **conscienceless** adj. [ME f. OF f. L conscientia f. conscire be privy to (as COM-, scire know)]

conscientious /ˌkɒnʃɪ'enʃəs/ adj. (of a person or conduct) diligent and scrupulous. □ **conscientious objector** a person who for reasons of conscience objects to military service etc. □ **conscientiously** adv. **conscientiousness** n. [F consciencieux f. med.L conscientiosus (as CONSCIENCE)]

conscious /'kɒnʃəs/ adj. & n. —adj. **1** awake and aware of one's surroundings and identity. **2** (usu. foll. by of, or that + clause) aware, knowing (conscious of his inferiority). **3** (of actions, emotions, etc.) realized or recognized by the doer; intentional (made a conscious effort not to laugh). —n. (prec. by the) the conscious mind. □ **consciously** adv. [L conscius knowing with others or in oneself f. conscire (as COM-, scire know)]

consciousness /'kɒnʃəsnɪs/ n. **1** the state of being conscious (lost consciousness during the fight). **2** awareness, perception (had no consciousness of being ridiculed).

conscript v. & n. —v.tr. /kən'skrɪpt/ enlist by conscription. —n. /'kɒnskrɪpt/ a person enlisted by conscription. [(v.) back-form. f. CONSCRIPTION: (n.) f. F conscrit f. L conscriptus (as CONSCRIPTION)]

conscription /kən'skrɪpʃ(ə)n/ n. compulsory enlistment for State service, esp. military service. [F f. LL conscriptio levying of troops f. L conscribere conscript- enrol (as COM-, scribere write)]

consecrate /'kɒnsɪkreɪt/ v.tr. **1** make or declare sacred; dedicate formally to a religious or divine purpose. **2** (foll. by to) devote to (a purpose). **3** ordain (esp. a bishop) to a sacred office. □ **consecration** /-'kreɪʃ(ə)n/ n. **consecrator** n. **consecratory** adj. [ME f. L consecrare (as COM-, secrare = sacrare dedicate f. sacer sacred)]

consecutive /kən'sekjʊtɪv/ adj. **1** following continuously. **b** in unbroken or logical order. **2** Gram. expressing consequence. □ **consecutively** adv. **consecutiveness** n. [F consécutif -ive f. med.L consecutivus f. consequi consecut- overtake]

consensual /kən'sensjʊəl, -'senʃʊəl/ adj. of or by consent or consensus. □ **consensually** adv. [L consensus (see CONSENSUS) + -AL]

consensus /kən'sensəs/ n. (often foll. by of) **1 a** general agreement of opinion, testimony, etc. **b** an instance of this. **2** (attrib.) majority view, collective opinion. [L, = agreement (as CONSENT)]

consent /kən'sent/ v. & n. —v.intr. (often foll. by to) express willingness, give permission, agree. —n. voluntary agreement, permission, compliance. □ **age of consent** the age at which consent to sexual intercourse is valid in law. **consenting adult 1** an adult who consents to something, esp. a homosexual act. **2** a homosexual. [ME f. OF consentir f. L consentire (as COM-, sentire sens- feel)]

consequence /'kɒnsɪkwəns/ n. **1** the result or effect of an action or condition. **2 a** importance (it is of no consequence). **b** social distinction (persons of consequence). □ **in consequence** as a result. **take the consequences** accept the results of one's choice. [ME f. OF f. L consequentia (as CONSEQUENT)]

consequent /'kɒnsɪkwənt/ adj. & n. —adj. **1** (often foll. by on, upon) following as a result or consequence. **2** logically consistent. —n. a thing that follows another. [ME f. OF f. L consequi (as CONSECUTIVE)]

consequential /ˌkɒnsɪ'kwenʃ(ə)l/ adj. **1** following as a result or consequence. **2** resulting indirectly (consequential damage). **3** (of a person) self-important. □ **consequentiality** /-ʃɪ'ælɪtɪ/ n. **consequentially** adv. [L consequentia]

consequently /'kɒnsɪ,kwentlɪ/ adv. & conj. as a result; therefore.

conservancy /kən'sɜːvənsɪ/ n. (pl. **-ies**) **1** Brit. a commission etc. controlling a port, river, etc. (Thames Conservancy). **2** a body concerned with the preservation of natural resources (Nature Conservancy). [18th-c. alt. of obs. conservacy f. AF conservacie f. AL conservatia f. L conservatio (as CONSERVE)]

conservation /ˌkɒnsə'veɪʃ(ə)n/ n. preservation, esp. of the natural environment. □ **conservation area** an area containing a noteworthy environment and specially protected by law against undesirable changes. **conservation of energy** (or **mass** or **momentum** etc.) Physics the principle that the total quantity of energy etc. of any system not subject to external action remains constant. □ **conservational** adj. [ME f. OF conservation or L conservatio (as CONSERVE)]

conservationist /ˌkɒnsə'veɪʃənɪst/ n. a supporter or advocate of environmental conservation.

conservative /kən'sɜːvətɪv/ adj. & n. —adj. **1 a** averse to rapid change. **b** (of views, taste, etc.) moderate, avoiding extremes (conservative in his dress). **2** (of an estimate etc.) purposely low; moderate, cautious. **3** (**Conservative**) of or characteristic of Conservatives or the Conservative Party. **4** tending to conserve. —n. **1** a conservative person. **2** (**Conservative**) a supporter or member of the Conservative Party. □ **Conservative Party 1** a British political party promoting free enterprise and private ownership. **2** a similar party elsewhere. □ **conservatism** n. **conservatively** adv. **conservativeness** n. [ME f. LL conservativus (as CONSERVE)]

conservatoire /kən'sɜːvə,twɑː(r)/ n. (usu. European) school of music or other arts. [F f. It. conservatorio (as CONSERVATORY)]

conservator /'kɒnsə,veɪtə(r), kən'sɜːvətə(r)/ n. a person who preserves something; an official custodian (of a museum etc.). [ME f. AF conservatour, OF -ateur f. L conservator -oris (as CONSERVE)]

conservatory /kən'sɜːvətəri/ n. (pl. **-ies**) **1** a greenhouse for tender plants, esp. one attached to and communicating with a house. **2** esp. US = CONSERVATOIRE. [LL *conservatorium* (as CONSERVE): sense 2 through It. *conservatorio*]

conserve /kən'sɜːv/ v. & n. —v.tr. **1** store up; keep from harm or damage, esp. for later use. **2** *Physics* maintain a quantity of (heat etc.). —n. /also 'kɒnsɜːv/ **1** fruit etc. preserved in sugar. **2** jam. [ME f. OF *conserver* f. L *conservare* (as COM-, *servare* keep)]

consider /kən'sɪdə(r)/ v.tr. (often *absol.*) **1** contemplate mentally, esp. in order to reach a conclusion. **2** examine the merits of. **3** give attention to. **4** reckon with; take into account. **5** (foll. by *that* + clause) have the opinion. **6** believe; regard as (*consider it to be genuine; consider it settled*). **7** (as **considered** adj.) formed after careful thought (*a considered opinion*). [ME f. OF *considerer* f. L *considerare* examine]

considerable /kən'sɪdərəb(ə)l/ adj. **1** enough in amount or extent to need consideration. **2** much; a lot of (*considerable pain*). **3** notable, important. □ **considerably** adv.

considerate /kən'sɪdərət/ adj. thoughtful towards other people; careful not to cause hurt or inconvenience. □ **considerately** adv.

consideration /kən,sɪdə'reɪʃ(ə)n/ n. **1** the act of considering; careful thought. **2** being considerate. **3** a fact or a thing taken into account in deciding or judging something. **4** compensation; a payment or reward. □ **in consideration of** in return for; on account of. **take into consideration** include as a factor, reason, etc.; make allowance for. **under consideration** being considered. [ME f. OF f. L *consideratio -onis* (as CONSIDER)]

considering /kən'sɪdərɪŋ/ prep. **1** in view of; taking into consideration. **2** (without compl.) *colloq.* all in all; taking everything into account (*not so bad, considering*).

consign /kən'saɪn/ v.tr. (often foll. by *to*) **1** hand over; deliver to a person's possession or trust. **2** assign; commit decisively or permanently (*consigned it to the dustbin; consigned to years of misery*). **3** transmit or send (goods). □ **consignee** /,kɒnsaɪ'niː/ n. **consignor** n. [ME f. F *consigner* or L *consignare* mark with a seal (as COM-, SIGN)]

consignment /kən'saɪnmənt/ n. **1** the act or an instance of consigning; the process of being consigned. **2** a batch of goods consigned.

consist /kən'sɪst/ v.intr. **1** (foll. by *of*) be composed; have specified ingredients or elements. **2** (foll. by *in*, *of*) have its essential features as specified (*its beauty consists in the use of colour*). [L *consistere* exist (as COM-, *sistere* stop)]

consistency /kən'sɪstənsɪ/ n. (also **consistence**) (pl. **-ies** or **-es**) **1** the degree of density, firmness, or viscosity, esp. of thick liquids. **2** the state of being consistent; conformity with other or earlier attitudes, practice, etc. **3** the state or quality of holding or sticking together and retaining shape. [F *consistence* or LL *consistentia* (as CONSIST)]

consistent /kən'sɪst(ə)nt/ adj. (usu. foll. by *with*) **1** compatible or in harmony. **2** (of a person) constant to the same principles of thought or action. □ **consistently** adv. [L *consistere* (as CONSIST)]

consistory /kən'sɪstərɪ/ n. (pl. **-ies**) *RC Ch.* the council of cardinals (with or without the pope).

□ **consistorial** /,kɒnsɪ'stɔːrɪəl/ adj. [ME f. AF *consistorie*, OF *-oire* f. LL *consistorium* (as CONSIST)]

consolation /,kɒnsə'leɪʃ(ə)n/ n. **1** the act or an instance of consoling; the state of being consoled. **2** a consoling thing, person, or circumstance. □ **consolation prize** a prize given to a competitor who just fails to win a main prize. □ **consolatory** /kən'sɒlətəri/ adj. [ME f. OF f. L *consolatio -onis* (as CONSOLE[1])]

console[1] /kən'səʊl/ v.tr. comfort, esp. in grief or disappointment. □ **consolable** adj. **consoler** n. **consolingly** adv. [F *consoler* f. L *consolari*]

■ **Usage** This word is often confused with *condole*.

console[2] /'kɒnsəʊl/ n. **1** a panel or unit accommodating a set of switches, controls, etc. **2** a cabinet for television or radio equipment etc. **3** *Mus.* a cabinet with the keyboards, stops, pedals, etc., of an organ. **4** an ornamented bracket supporting a shelf etc. □ **console table** a table supported by a bracket against a wall. [F, perh. f. *consolider* (as CONSOLIDATE)]

consolidate /kən'sɒlɪ,deɪt/ v. **1** tr. & intr. make or become strong or solid. **2** tr. reinforce or strengthen (one's position, power, etc.). **3** tr. combine (territories, companies, debts, etc.) into one whole. □ **consolidation** /kən,sɒlɪ'deɪʃ(ə)n/ n. **consolidator** n. **consolidatory** adj. [L *consolidare* (as COM-, *solidare* f. *solidus* solid)]

consols /'kɒnsɒlz/ n.pl. British government securities without redemption date and with fixed annual interest. [abbr. of *consolidated annuities*]

consommé /kən'sɒmeɪ/ n. a clear soup made with meat stock. [F, past part. of *consommer* f. L *consummare* (as CONSUMMATE)]

consonance /'kɒnsənəns/ n. agreement, harmony. [ME f. OF *consonance* or L *consonantia* (as CONSONANT)]

consonant /'kɒnsənənt/ n. & adj. —n. **1** a speech sound in which the breath is at least partly obstructed, and which to form a syllable must be combined with a vowel. **2** a letter or letters representing this. —adj. (foll. by *with*, *to*) consistent; in agreement or harmony. □ **consonantal** /-'nænt(ə)l/ adj. **consonantly** adv. [ME f. F f. L *consonare* (as COM-, *sonare* sound f. *sonus*)]

consort[1] n. & v. —n. /'kɒnsɔːt/ **1** a wife or husband, esp. of royalty (*prince consort*). **2** a ship sailing with another. —v. /kən'sɔːt/ **1** intr. (usu. foll. by *with*, *together*) **a** keep company; associate. **b** harmonize. **2** tr. class or bring together. [ME f. F f. L *consors* sharer, comrade (as COM-, *sors sortis* lot, destiny)]

consort[2] /'kɒnsɔːt/ n. *Mus.* a group of players or instruments. [earlier form of CONCERT]

consortium /kən'sɔːtɪəm/ n. (pl. **consortia** /-tɪə/ or **consortiums**) an association, esp. of several business companies. [L, = partnership (as CONSORT[1])]

conspectus /kən'spektəs/ n. **1** a general or comprehensive survey. **2** a summary or synopsis. [L f. *conspicere conspect-* (as COM-, *spicere* look at)]

conspicuous /kən'spɪkjʊəs/ adj. **1** clearly visible; attracting notice. **2** remarkable of its kind. □ **conspicuously** adv. **conspicuousness** n. [L *conspicuus* (as CONSPECTUS)]

conspiracy /kən'spɪrəsɪ/ n. (pl. **-ies**) **1** a secret plan to commit a crime or do harm; a plot. **2**

the act of conspiring. □ **conspiracy of silence** an agreement to say nothing. [ME f. AF *conspiracie*, alt. form of OF *conspiration* f. L *conspiratio -onis* (as CONSPIRE)]

conspirator /kənˈspɪrətə(r)/ *n.* a person who takes part in a conspiracy. □ **conspiratorial** /-ˈtɔːrɪəl/ *adj.* **conspiratorially** /-ˈtɔːrɪəlɪ/ *adv.* [ME f. AF *conspiratour*, OF *-teur* (as CONSPIRE)]

conspire /kənˈspaɪə(r)/ *v.intr.* **1** combine secretly to plan and prepare an unlawful or harmful act. **2** (often foll. by *against*, or *to* + infin.) (of events or circumstances) seem to be working together, esp. disadvantageously. [ME f. OF *conspirer* f. L *conspirare* agree, plot (as COM-, *spirare* breathe)]

constable /ˈkʌnstəb(ə)l/ *n.* **1** *Brit.* **a** a policeman or policewoman. **b** (also **police constable**) a police officer of the lowest rank. **2** the governor of a royal castle. **3** *hist.* the principal officer in a royal household. □ **Chief Constable** the head of the police force of a county or other region. [ME f. OF *conestable* f. LL *comes stabuli* count of the stable]

constabulary /kənˈstæbjʊlərɪ/ *n. & adj.* —*n.* (pl. **-ies**) an organized body of police; a police force. —*attrib.adj.* of or concerning the police force. [med.L *constabularius* (as CONSTABLE)]

constancy /ˈkɒnstənsɪ/ *n.* **1** the quality of being unchanging and dependable; faithfulness. **2** firmness, endurance. [L *constantia* (as CONSTANT)]

constant /ˈkɒnst(ə)nt/ *adj. & n.* —*adj.* **1** continuous (*needs constant attention*). **2** occurring frequently (*receive constant complaints*). **3** (often foll. by *to*) unchanging, faithful, dependable. —*n.* **1** anything that does not vary. **2** *Math.* a component of a relationship between variables that does not change its value. **3** *Physics* **a** a number expressing a relation, property, etc., and remaining the same in all circumstances. **b** such a number that remains the same for a substance in the same conditions. □ **constantly** *adv.* [ME f. OF f. L *constare* (as COM-, *stare* stand)]

constellation /ˌkɒnstəˈleɪʃ(ə)n/ *n.* **1** a group of fixed stars. **2** a group of associated persons, ideas, etc. [ME f. OF f. LL *constellatio -onis* (as COM-, *stella* star)]

consternation /ˌkɒnstəˈneɪʃ(ə)n/ *n.* anxiety or dismay causing mental confusion. [F *consternation* or L *consternatio* f. L *consternare* (as COM-, *sternere* throw down)]

constipate /ˈkɒnstɪˌpeɪt/ *v.tr.* (esp. as **constipated** *adj.*) affect with constipation. [L *constipare* (as COM-, *stipare* press)]

constipation /ˌkɒnstɪˈpeɪʃ(ə)n/ *n.* a condition with hardened faeces and difficulty in emptying the bowels. [ME f. OF *constipation* or LL *constipatio* (as CONSTIPATE)]

constituency /kənˈstɪtjʊənsɪ/ *n.* (pl. **-ies**) **1** a body of voters in a specified area who elect a representative member to a legislative body. **2** the area represented in this way. **3** a body of customers, supporters, etc.

constituent /kənˈstɪtjʊənt/ *adj. & n.* —*adj.* **1** composing or helping to make up a whole. **2** able to make or change a (political etc.) constitution (*constituent assembly*). **3** appointing or electing. —*n.* **1** a member of a constituency (esp. political). **2** a component part. [L *constituent-* partly through F *-ant* (as CONSTITUTE)]

constitute /ˈkɒnstɪˌtjuːt/ *v.tr.* **1** be the components or essence of; make up, form. **2 a** be

equivalent or tantamount to (*this constitutes an official warning*). **b** formally establish (*does not constitute a precedent*). **3** give legal or constitutional form to; establish by law. □ **constitutor** *n.* [L *constituere* (as COM-, *statuere* set up)]

constitution /ˌkɒnstɪˈtjuːʃ(ə)n/ *n.* **1** the act or method of constituting; the composition (of something). **2** the body of fundamental principles or established precedents according to which a State or other organization is acknowledged to be governed. **3** a person's physical state as regards health, strength, etc. **4** a person's psychological make-up. [ME f. OF *constitution* or L *constitutio* (as CONSTITUTE)]

constitutional /ˌkɒnstɪˈtjuːʃən(ə)l/ *adj. & n.* —*adj.* **1** of, consistent with, authorized by, or limited by a political constitution (*a constitutional monarchy*). **2** inherent in, stemming from, or affecting the physical or mental constitution. —*n.* a walk taken regularly to maintain or restore good health. □ **constitutionalism** /-ˈnælɪtɪ/ *n.* **constitutionalize** *v.tr.* (also **-ise**). **constitutionally** *adv.*

constitutive /ˈkɒnstɪˌtjuːtɪv/ *adj.* **1** able to form or appoint. **2** component. **3** essential. □ **constitutively** *adv.* [LL *constitutivus* (as CONSTITUTE)]

constrain /kənˈstreɪn/ *v.tr.* **1** compel; urge irresistibly or by necessity. **2 a** confine forcibly; imprison. **b** restrict severely as regards action, behaviour, etc. **3** bring about by compulsion. **4** (as **constrained** *adj.*) forced, embarrassed (*a constrained manner*). □ **constrainedly** /kənˈstreɪnɪdlɪ/ *adv.* [ME f. OF *constraindre* f. L *constringere* (as COM-, *stringere* strict- tie)]

constraint /kənˈstreɪnt/ *n.* **1** the act or result of constraining or being constrained; restriction of liberty. **2** something that constrains; a limitation on motion or action. **3** the restraint of natural feelings or their expression; a constrained manner. [ME f. OF *constreinte*, fem. past part. (as CONSTRAIN)]

constrict /kənˈstrɪkt/ *v.tr.* make narrow or tight; compress. □ **constriction** *n.* **constrictive** *adj.* [L (as CONSTRAIN)]

constrictor /kənˈstrɪktə(r)/ *n.* **1** any snake that kills by coiling round its prey and compressing it. **2** *Anat.* any muscle that compresses or contracts an organ or part of the body. [mod.L (as CONSTRICT)]

construct *v. & n.* —*v.tr.* /kənˈstrʌkt/ **1** make by fitting parts together; build, form (something physical or abstract). **2** *Geom.* draw or delineate (*construct a triangle*). —*n.* /ˈkɒnstrʌkt/ a thing constructed, esp. by the mind. □ **constructor** *n.* [L *construere* *construct-* (as COM-, *struere* pile, build)]

construction /kənˈstrʌkʃ(ə)n/ *n.* **1** the act or a mode of constructing. **2** a thing constructed. **3** an interpretation or explanation (*they put a generous construction on his act*). **4** *Gram.* an arrangement of words according to syntactical rules. □ **constructional** *adj.* **constructionally** *adv.* [ME f. OF f. L *constructio -onis* (as CONSTRUCT)]

constructive /kənˈstrʌktɪv/ *adj.* **1 a** of construction; tending to construct. **b** tending to form a basis for ideas. **2** helpful, positive (*a constructive approach*). **3** derived by inference; not expressed (*constructive permission*). □ **constructively** *adv.* **constructiveness** *n.* [LL *constructivus* (as CONSTRUCT)]

construe /kən'stru:/ v.tr. (**construes, construed, construing**) 1 interpret (words or actions). 2 (often foll. by *with*) combine (words) grammatically ('*rely*' is construed with '*on*'). 3 analyse the syntax of (a sentence). 4 translate word for word. □ **construable** adj. **construal** n. [ME f. L *construere* CONSTRUCT]

consubstantial /ˌkɒnsəb'stænʃ(ə)l/ adj. *Theol.* of the same substance (esp. of the three persons of the Trinity). □ **consubstantiality** /-ʃɪ'ælɪtɪ/ n. [ME f. eccl.L *consubstantialis*, transl. Gk *homoousios* (as COM-, SUBSTANTIAL)]

consubstantiation /ˌkɒnsəbˌstænʃɪ'eɪʃ(ə)n/ n. *Theol.* the real substantial presence of the body and blood of Christ together with the bread and wine in the Eucharist. [mod.L *consubstantiatio*, after *tran- substantiatio* TRANSUBSTANTIATION]

consul /'kɒns(ə)l/ n. 1 an official appointed by a State to live in a foreign city and protect the State's citizens and interests there. 2 *hist.* either of two annually elected chief magistrates in ancient Rome. □ **consular** /'kɒnsjʊlə(r)/ adj. **consulship** n. [ME f. L, rel. to *consulere* take counsel]

consulate /'kɒnsjʊlət/ n. 1 the building officially used by a consul. 2 the office, position, or period of office of a consul. [ME f. L *consulatus* (as CONSUL)]

consult /kən'sʌlt/ v. 1 tr. seek information or advice from (a person, book, watch, etc.). 2 intr. (often foll. by *with*) refer to a person for advice, etc. 3 tr. seek permission or approval from (a person) for a proposed action. 4 tr. take into account (feelings etc.). □ **consultative** /-tətɪv/ adj. [F consulter f. L consultare frequent. of consulere consult- take counsel]

consultancy /kən'sʌltənsɪ/ n. (pl. **-ies**) the professional practice or position of a consultant.

consultant /kən'sʌlt(ə)nt/ n. 1 a person providing professional advice etc., esp. for a fee. 2 a senior specialist in a branch of medicine. [prob. F (as CONSULT)]

consultation /ˌkɒnsəl'teɪʃ(ə)n/ n. 1 a meeting arranged to consult. 2 the act or an instance of consulting. [ME f. OF *consultation* or L *consultatio* (as CONSULTANT)]

consulting /kən'sʌltɪŋ/ attrib.adj. giving professional advice to others working in the same field or subject (*consulting physician*).

consumable /kən'sju:məb(ə)l/ adj. & n. —adj. that can be consumed; intended for consumption. —n. (usu. in pl.) a commodity that is eventually used up.

consume /kən'sju:m/ v.tr. 1 eat or drink. 2 completely destroy; reduce to nothing or to tiny particles. 3 (as **consumed** adj., foll. by *with*) possessed by or entirely taken up. 4 use up. □ **consumingly** adv. [ME f. L *consumere* (as COM-, *sumere sumpt-* take up): partly through F *consumer*]

consumer /kən'sju:mə(r)/ n. 1 a person who consumes, esp. one who uses a product. 2 a purchaser of goods or services.

consumerism /kən'sju:məˌrɪz(ə)m/ n. the protection or promotion of consumers' interests in relation to the producer. □ **consumerist** adj. & n.

consummate v. & adj. —v.tr. /'kɒnsəˌmeɪt/ 1 complete; make perfect. 2 complete (a marriage) by sexual intercourse. —adj. /kən'sʌmɪt, 'kɒnsəmɪt/ complete, perfect; fully skilled. □

consummately adv. **consummative** adj. **consummator** /'kɒnsəˌmeɪtə(r)/ n. [L *consummare* (as COM-, *summare* complete f. *summus* utmost)]

consummation /ˌkɒnsə'meɪʃ(ə)n/ n. 1 completion, esp. of a marriage by sexual intercourse. 2 a desired end or goal; perfection. [ME f. OF *consommation* or L *consummatio* (as CONSUMMATE)]

consumption /kən'sʌmpʃ(ə)n/ n. 1 the act or an instance of consuming; the process of being consumed. 2 any disease causing wasting of tissues, esp. pulmonary tuberculosis. 3 an amount consumed. 4 the purchase and use of goods etc. [ME f. OF *consomption* f. L *consumptio* (as CONSUME)]

consumptive /kən'sʌmptɪv/ adj. & n. —adj. 1 of or tending to consumption. 2 tending to or affected with pulmonary tuberculosis. —n. a consumptive patient. □ **consumptively** adv. [med.L *consumptivus* (as CONSUMPTION)]

contact /'kɒntækt/ n. & v. —n. 1 the state or condition of touching, meeting, or communicating. 2 a person who is or may be communicated with for information, supplies, assistance, etc. 3 *Electr.* a a connection for the passage of a current. b a device for providing this. 4 a person likely to carry a contagious disease through being associated with an infected person. 5 (usu. in pl.) *colloq.* a contact lens. —v.tr. /'kɒntækt, kən'tækt/ 1 get into communication with (a person). 2 begin correspondence or personal dealings with. □ **contact lens** a small lens placed directly on the eyeball to correct the vision. **contact sport** a sport in which participants necessarily come into bodily contact with one another. □ **contactable** adj. [L *contactus* f. *contingere* (as COM-, *tangere* touch)]

contagion /kən'teɪdʒ(ə)n/ n. 1 a the communication of disease from one person to another by bodily contact. b a contagious disease. 2 a contagious or harmful influence. [ME f. L *contagio* (as COM-, *tangere* touch)]

contagious /kən'teɪdʒəs/ adj. 1 a (of a person) likely to transmit disease by contact. b (of a disease) transmitted in this way. 2 (of emotions, reactions, etc.) likely to affect others (*contagious enthusiasm*). □ **contagiously** adv. **contagiousness** n. [ME f. LL *contagiosus* (as CONTAGION)]

contain /kən'teɪn/ v.tr. 1 hold or be capable of holding within itself; include, comprise. 2 (of measures) consist of or be equal to (*a gallon contains eight pints*). 3 prevent (an enemy, difficulty, etc.) from moving or extending. 4 control or restrain (feelings etc.). 5 (of a number) be divisible by (a factor) without a remainder. □ **containable** adj. [ME f. OF *contenir* f. L *continēre content-* (as COM-, *tenēre* hold)]

container /kən'teɪnə(r)/ n. 1 a vessel, box, etc., for holding particular things. 2 a large boxlike receptacle of standard design for the transport of goods.

containerize /kən'teɪnəˌraɪz/ v.tr. (also **-ise**) 1 pack in or transport by container. 2 adapt to transport by container. □ **containerization** /-'zeɪʃ(ə)n/ n.

containment /kən'teɪnmənt/ n. the action or policy of preventing the expansion of a hostile country or influence.

contaminate /kən'tæmɪˌneɪt/ v.tr. 1 pollute, esp. with radioactivity. 2 infect. □ **contaminant** n.

contamination /-ˈneɪʃ(ə)n/ n. **contaminator** n. [L *contaminare* (as COM-, *tamen-* rel. to *tangere* touch)]

contemn /kənˈtem/ v.tr. *literary* despise; treat with disregard. □ **contemner** /-ˈtemə(r), -ˈtemnə(r)/ n. [ME f. OF *contemner* or L *contemnere* (as COM-, *temnere* tempt- despise)]

contemplate /ˈkɒntəmˌpleɪt/ v. **1** tr. survey with the eyes or in the mind. **2** tr. regard (an event) as possible. **3** tr. intend; have as one's purpose. **4** intr. meditate. □ **contemplation** /-ˈpleɪʃ(ə)n/ n. **contemplator** n. [L *contemplari* (as COM-, *templum* place for observations)]

contemplative /kənˈtemplətɪv/ adj. & n. —adj. of or given to (esp. religious) contemplation; meditative. —n. a person devoted to religious contemplation. □ **contemplatively** adv. [ME f. OF *contemplatif -ive*, or L *contemplativus* (as CONTEMPLATE)]

contemporaneous /kənˌtempəˈreɪnɪəs/ adj. (usu. foll. by *with*) **1** existing or occurring at the same time. **2** of the same period. □ **contemporaneity** /-ˈniːɪtɪ/ n. **contemporaneously** adv. **contemporaneousness** n. [L *contemporaneus* (as COM-, *temporaneus* f. *tempus -oris* time)]

contemporary /kənˈtempərərɪ/ adj. & n. —adj. **1** living or occurring at the same time. **2** approximately equal in age. **3** following modern ideas or fashion in style or design. —n. (pl. **-ies**) **1** a person or thing living or existing at the same time as another. **2** a person of roughly the same age as another. □ **contemporarily** adv. **contemporariness** n. **contemporarize** v.tr. (also **-ise**). [med.L *contemporarius* (as CONTEMPORANEOUS)]

contempt /kənˈtempt/ n. **1** a feeling that a person or a thing is beneath consideration or deserving scorn. **2** the condition of being held in contempt. **3** (in full **contempt of court**) disobedience to or disrespect for a court of law and its officers. [ME f. L *contemptus* (as CONTEMN)]

contemptible /kənˈtemptɪb(ə)l/ adj. deserving contempt; despicable. □ **contemptibility** n. **contemptibly** adv. [ME f. OF or LL *contemptibilis* (as CONTEMN)]

contemptuous /kənˈtemptjʊəs/ adj. (often foll. by *of*) showing contempt; scornful; insolent. □ **contemptuously** adv. [med.L *contemptuosus* f. L *contemptus* (as CONTEMPT)]

contend /kənˈtend/ v. **1** intr. (usu. foll. by *with*) strive, fight. **2** intr. compete (*contending emotions*). **3** tr. (usu. foll. by *that* + clause) assert, maintain. □ **contender** n. [OF *contendre* or L *contendere* (as COM-, *tendere* tent- stretch, strive)]

content[1] /kənˈtent/ adj., v., & n. —predic.adj. **1** satisfied; adequately happy; in agreement. **2** (foll. by *to* + infin.) willing. —v.tr. make content; satisfy. —n. a contented state; satisfaction. □ **to one's heart's content** to the full extent of one's desires. [ME f. OF f. L *contentus* satisfied, past part. of *continēre* (as CONTAIN)]

content[2] /ˈkɒntent/ n. **1** (usu. in *pl.*) what is contained in something, esp. in a vessel, book, or house. **2** the amount of a constituent contained (*low sodium content*). **3** the substance or material dealt with (in a speech, work of art, etc.) as distinct from its form or style. **4** the capacity or volume of a thing. [ME f. med.L *contentum* (as CONTAIN)]

contented /kənˈtentɪd/ adj. (often foll. by *with*, or *to* + infin.) **1** happy, satisfied. **2** (foll. by *with*) willing to be content. □ **contentedly** adv. **contentedness** n.

contention /kənˈtenʃ(ə)n/ n. **1** a dispute or argument; rivalry. **2** a point contended for in an argument (*it is my contention that you are wrong*). □ **in contention** competing. [ME f. OF *contention* or L *contentio* (as CONTEND)]

contentious /kənˈtenʃəs/ adj. **1** argumentative, quarrelsome. **2** likely to cause an argument; disputed, controversial. □ **contentiously** adv. **contentiousness** n. [ME f. OF *contentieux* f. L *contentiosus* (as CONTENTION)]

contentment /kənˈtentmənt/ n. a satisfied state; tranquil happiness.

conterminous /kɒnˈtɜːmɪnəs/ adj. (often foll. by *with*) **1** having a common boundary. **2** coextensive, coterminous. □ **conterminously** adv. [L *conterminus* (as COM-, *terminus* boundary)]

contest n. & v. —n. /ˈkɒntest/ **1** a process of contending; a competition. **2** a dispute; a controversy. —v.tr. /kənˈtest/ **1** challenge or dispute (a decision etc.). **2** debate (a point, statement, etc.). **3** contend or compete for (a prize, parliamentary seat, etc.); compete in (an election). □ **contestable** /kənˈtestəb(ə)l/ adj. **contester** /kənˈtestə(r)/ n. [L *contestari* (as COM-, *testis* witness)]

contestant /kənˈtest(ə)nt/ n. a person who takes part in a contest or competition.

context /ˈkɒntekst/ n. **1** the parts of something written or spoken that immediately precede and follow a word or passage and clarify its meaning. **2** the circumstances relevant to something under consideration (*must be seen in context*). □ **out of context** without the surrounding words or circumstances and so not fully understandable. □ **contextual** /kənˈtekstjʊəl/ adj. **contextualize** /kənˈtekstjʊəˌlaɪz/ v.tr. (also **-ise**). **contextualization** /kənˌtekstjʊəlaɪˌzeɪʃ(ə)n/ n. **contextually** /kənˈtekstjʊəl/ adv. [ME f. L *contextus* (as COM-, *texere* text- weave)]

contiguous /kənˈtɪɡjʊəs/ adj. (usu. foll. by *with*, *to*) touching, esp. along a line; in contact. □ **contiguity** n. **contiguously** adv. [L *contiguus* (as COM-, *tangere* touch)]

continent[1] /ˈkɒntɪnənt/ n. **1** any of the main continuous expanses of land (Europe, Asia, Africa, N. and S. America, Australia, Antarctica). **2** (**the Continent**) *Brit.* the mainland of Europe as distinct from the British Isles. [L *terra continens* (see CONTAIN) continuous land]

continent[2] /ˈkɒntɪnənt/ adj. **1** able to control movements of the bowels and bladder. **2** exercising self-restraint, esp. sexually. □ **continence** n. **continently** adv. [ME f. L (as CONTAIN)]

continental /ˌkɒntɪˈnent(ə)l/ adj. & n. —adj. **1** of or characteristic of a continent. **2** (**Continental**) *Brit.* of, relating to, or characteristic of mainland Europe. —n. an inhabitant of mainland Europe. □ **continental breakfast** a light breakfast of coffee, rolls, etc. **continental drift** *Geol.* the hypothesis that the continents are moving slowly over the surface of the earth. **continental quilt** *Brit.* a duvet. **continental shelf** an area of relatively shallow seabed between the shore of a continent and the deeper ocean. □ **continentally** adv.

contingency /kən'tɪndʒənsɪ/ n. (pl. **-ies**) **1** a future event or circumstance regarded as likely to occur, or as influencing present action. **2** something dependent on another uncertain event or occurrence. □ **contingency fund** a fund to cover incidental or unforeseen expenses. [earlier *contingence* f. LL *contingentia* (as CONTINGENT)]

contingent /kən'tɪndʒ(ə)nt/ adj. & n. —adj. **1** (usu. foll. by *on, upon*) conditional, dependent (on an uncertain event or circumstance). **2** associated. **3** (usu. foll. by *to*) incidental. **4 a** that may or may not occur. **b** fortuitous; occurring by chance. —n. a body (esp. of troops, ships, etc.) forming part of a larger group. □ **contingently** adv. [L *contingere* (as COM-, *tangere* touch)]

continual /kən'tɪnjʊəl/ adj. constantly or frequently recurring; always happening. □ **continually** adv. [ME f. OF *continuel* f. *continuer* (as CONTINUE)]

■ **Usage** This word is often confused with *continuous. Continual* is used of something happening very frequently (e.g. *there were continual interruptions*) while *continuous* is used of something happening without a pause (e.g. *there was continuous rain all day*).

continuance /kən'tɪnjʊəns/ n. **1** a state of continuing in existence or operation. **2** the duration of an event or action. [ME f. OF (as CONTINUE)]

continuation /kən,tɪnjʊ'eɪʃ(ə)n/ n. **1** the act or an instance of continuing; the process of being continued. **2** a part that continues something else. [ME f. OF f. L *continuatio -onis* (as CONTINUE)]

continue /kən'tɪnjuː/ v. (**continues, continued, continuing**) **1** tr. (often foll. by verbal noun, or *to* + infin.) persist in, maintain, not stop (an action etc.). **2 a** tr. (also *absol.*) resume or prolong (a narrative, journey, etc.). **b** intr. recommence after a pause (*the concert will continue shortly*). **3** tr. be a sequel to. **4** intr. **a** remain in existence or unchanged. **b** (with compl.) remain in a specified state (*the weather continued fine*). □ **continuable** adj. **continuer** n. [ME f. OF *continuer* f. L *continuare* make or be CONTINUOUS]

continuity /kɒntɪ'njuːɪtɪ/ n. (pl. **-ies**) **1 a** the state of being continuous. **b** an unbroken succession. **c** a logical sequence. **2** the detailed and self-consistent scenario of a film or broadcast. **3** the linking of broadcast items. [F *continuité* f. L *continuitas -tatis* (as CONTINUOUS)]

continuo /kən'tɪnjʊəʊ/ n. (pl. **-os**) Mus. an accompaniment providing a bass line and harmonies which are indicated by figures, usu. played on a keyboard instrument. [*basso continuo* (It., = continuous bass)]

continuous /kən'tɪnjʊəs/ adj. unbroken, uninterrupted, connected throughout in space or time. □ **continuous stationery** a continuous ream of paper, usu. perforated to form single sheets. □ **continuously** adv. **continuousness** n. [L *continuus* uninterrupted f. *continēre* (as COM-, *tenēre* hold)]

■ **Usage** See note at *continual.*

continuum /kən'tɪnjʊəm/ n. (pl. **continua** /-jʊə/) anything seen as having a continuous, not discrete, structure (*space-time continuum*). [L, neut. of *continuus*: see CONTINUOUS]

contort /kən'tɔːt/ v.tr. twist or force out of normal shape. [L *contorquēre contort-* (as COM-, *torquēre* twist)]

contortion /kən'tɔːʃ(ə)n/ n. **1** the act or process of twisting. **2** a twisted state, esp. of the face or body. [L *contortio* (as CONTORT)]

contortionist /kən'tɔːʃənɪst/ n. an entertainer who adopts contorted postures.

contour /'kɒntʊə(r)/ n. & v. —n. **1** an outline, esp. representing or bounding the shape or form of something. **2** the outline of a natural feature, e.g. a coast or mountain mass. —v.tr. **1** mark with contour lines. **2** carry (a road or railway) round the side of a hill. □ **contour line** a line on a map joining points of equal altitude. [F f. It. *contorno* f. *contornare* draw in outline (as COM-, *tornare* turn)]

contra- /'kɒntrə/ comb. form against, opposite (*contradict*). [L *contra* against]

contraband /'kɒntrə,bænd/ n. & adj. —n. **1** goods that have been smuggled, or imported or exported illegally. **2** prohibited trade; smuggling. —adj. forbidden to be imported or exported (at all or without payment of duty). □ **contrabandist** n. [Sp. *contrabanda* f. It. (as CONTRA-, *bando* proclamation)]

contraception /,kɒntrə'sepʃ(ə)n/ n. the intentional prevention of pregnancy. [CONTRA- + CONCEPTION]

contraceptive /,kɒntrə'septɪv/ adj. & n. —adj. preventing pregnancy. —n. a contraceptive device or drug.

contract n. & v. —n. /'kɒntrækt/ **1** a written or spoken agreement between two or more parties, intended to be enforceable by law. **2** a document recording this. —v. /kən'trækt/ **1** tr. & intr. make or become smaller. **2 a** intr. (usu. foll. by *with*) make a contract. **b** intr. (usu. foll. by *for*, or *to* + infin.) enter formally into a business or legal arrangement. **c** tr. (often foll. by *out*) arrange (work) to be done by contract. **3** tr. catch or develop (a disease). **4** tr. form or develop (a friendship, habit, etc.). **5** tr. enter into (marriage). **6** tr. incur (a debt etc.). **7** tr. shorten (a word) by combination or elision. **8** tr. draw (one's muscles, brow, etc.) together. □ **contract bridge** the most common form of bridge, in which only tricks bid and won count towards the game. **contract in** (or **out**) (also *refl.*) Brit. choose to be involved in (or withdraw or remain out of) a scheme or commitment. □ **contractive** adj. [earlier as adj., = contracted: OF, f. L *contractus* (as COM-, *trahere tract-* draw)]

contractable /kən'træktəb(ə)l/ adj. (of a disease) that can be contracted.

contractible /kən'træktɪb(ə)l/ adj. that can be shrunk or drawn together.

contractile /kən'træktaɪl/ adj. capable of or producing contraction. □ **contractility** /,kɒntræk'tɪlɪtɪ/ n.

contraction /kən'trækʃ(ə)n/ n. **1** the act of contracting. **2** Med. (usu. in *pl.*) shortening of the uterine muscles during childbirth. **3** shrinking, diminution. **4 a** a shortening of a word by combination or elision. **b** a contracted word or group of words. [F f. L *contractio -onis* (as CONTRACT)]

contractor /kən'træktə(r)/ n. a person who undertakes a contract, esp. to provide materials, conduct building operations, etc. [LL (as CONTRACT)]

contractual /kənˈtræktjʊəl/ adj. of or in the nature of a contract. □ **contractually** adv.

contradict /ˌkɒntrəˈdɪkt/ v.tr. **1** deny or express the opposite of (a statement). **2** deny or express the opposite of a statement made by (a person). **3** be in opposition to or in conflict with (new evidence contradicted our theory). □ **contradictor** n. [L contradicere contradict- (as CONTRA-, dicere say)]

contradiction /ˌkɒntrəˈdɪkʃ(ə)n/ n. **1 a** statement of the opposite; denial. **b** an instance of this. **2** inconsistency. □ **contradiction in terms** a self-contradictory statement or group of words. [ME f. OF f. L contradictio -onis (as CONTRADICT)]

contradictory /ˌkɒntrəˈdɪktərɪ/ adj. **1** expressing a denial or opposite statement. **2** (of statements etc.) mutually opposed or inconsistent. **3** (of a person) inclined to contradict. □ **contradictorily** adv. **contradictoriness** n. [ME f. LL contradictorius (as CONTRADICT)]

contradistinction /ˌkɒntrədɪˈstɪŋkʃ(ə)n/ n. a distinction made by contrasting.

contraflow /ˈkɒntrəˌfləʊ/ n. Brit. a flow (esp. of road traffic) alongside, and in a direction opposite to, an established or usual flow, esp. as a temporary or emergency arrangement.

contraindicate /ˌkɒntrəˈɪndɪˌkeɪt/ v.tr. Med. act as an indication against (the use of a particular substance or treatment). □ **contraindication** /-ˈkeɪʃ(ə)n/ n.

contralto /kənˈtræltəʊ/ n. (pl. -os) **1 a** the lowest female singing-voice. **b** a singer with this voice. **2** a part written for contralto. [It. (as CONTRA-, ALTO)]

contraption /kənˈtræpʃ(ə)n/ n. often derog. or joc. a machine or device, esp. a strange or cumbersome one. [19th c.: perh. f. CONTRIVE, INVENTION: assoc. with TRAP[1]]

contrapuntal /ˌkɒntrəˈpʌnt(ə)l/ adj. Mus. of or in counterpoint. □ **contrapuntally** adv. **contrapuntist** n. [It. contrappunto counterpoint]

contrariwise /kənˈtreərɪˌwaɪz/ adv. **1** on the other hand. **2** in the opposite way. **3** perversely. [ME f. CONTRARY + -WISE]

contrary /ˈkɒntrərɪ/ adj., n., & adv. —adj. **1** (usu. foll. by to) opposed in nature or tendency. **2** /kənˈtreərɪ/ colloq. perverse, self-willed. **3** (of a wind) unfavourable, impeding. **4** mutually opposed. **5** opposite in position or direction. —n. (pl. -ies) (prec. by the) the opposite. —adv. (foll. by to) in opposition or contrast. □ **on the contrary** intensifying a denial of what has just been implied or stated. **to the contrary** to the opposite effect (can find no indication to the contrary). □ **contrarily** /ˈkɒntrərɪlɪ/ (/kənˈtreərɪlɪ/ in sense 2 of adj.) adv. **contrariness** /ˈkɒntrərɪnɪs/ (/kənˈtreərɪnɪs/ in sense 2 of adj.) n. [ME f. AF contrarie, OF contraire, f. L contrarius f. contra against]

contrast n. & v. —n. /ˈkɒntrɑːst/ **1 a** a juxtaposition or comparison showing striking differences. **b** a difference so revealed. **2** (often foll. by to) a thing or person having qualities noticeably different from another. **3 a** the degree of difference between tones in a television picture or a photograph. **b** the change of apparent brightness or colour of an object caused by the juxtaposition of other objects. —v. /kənˈtrɑːst/ (often foll. by with) **1** tr. distinguish or set together so as to reveal a contrast. **2** intr.

have or show a contrast. □ **contrastingly** /kənˈtrɑːstɪŋlɪ/ adv. **contrastive** /kənˈtrɑːstɪv/ adj. [F f. contraste, contraster, f. It. contrasto f. med.L contrastare (as CONTRA-, stare stand)]

contravene /ˌkɒntrəˈviːn/ v.tr. **1** infringe (a law or code of conduct). **2** (of things) conflict with. □ **contravener** n. [LL contravenire (as CONTRA-, venire vent- come)]

contravention /ˌkɒntrəˈvenʃ(ə)n/ n. **1** infringement. **2** an instance of this. □ **in contravention of** infringing, violating (a law etc.). [F f. med.L contraventio (as CONTRAVENE)]

contretemps /ˈkɔːntrəˌtɑ̃/ n. **1** an awkward or unfortunate occurrence. **2** an unexpected mishap. [F]

contribute /kənˈtrɪbjuːt, disp. ˈkɒntrɪˌbjuːt/ v. (often foll. by to) **1** tr. give (money, an idea, help, etc.) towards a common purpose. **2** intr. help to bring about a result etc. **3** tr. (also absol.) supply (an article etc.) for publication with others in a journal etc. □ **contributive** /kənˈtrɪb-/ adj. **contributor** n. [L contribuere contribut- (as COM-, tribuere bestow)]

━━━━━━━━━━━━━━━━━━━━━━━━━

■ **Usage** The second pronunciation, stressed on the first syllable, is considered incorrect by some people.

━━━━━━━━━━━━━━━━━━━━━━━━━

contribution /ˌkɒntrɪˈbjuːʃ(ə)n/ n. **1** the act of contributing. **2** something contributed. [ME f. OF contribution or LL contributio (as CONTRIBUTE)]

contributory /kənˈtrɪbjʊtərɪ/ adj. **1** that contributes. **2** operated by means of contributions (contributory pension scheme). [med.L contributorius (as CONTRIBUTE)]

contrite /ˈkɒntraɪt, kənˈtraɪt/ adj. **1** completely penitent. **2** feeling remorse or penitence; affected by guilt. □ **contritely** adv. **contriteness** n. **contrition** /kənˈtrɪʃ(ə)n/ n. [ME f. OF contrit f. L contritus bruised (as COM-, terere trit- rub)]

contrivance /kənˈtraɪv(ə)ns/ n. **1** something contrived, esp. a mechanical device or a plan. **2** an act of contriving, esp. deceitfully. **3** inventive capacity.

contrive /kənˈtraɪv/ v.tr. **1** devise; plan or make resourcefully or with skill. **2** (often foll. by to + infin.) manage (contrived to make matters worse). □ **contrivable** adj. **contriver** n. [ME f. OF controver find, imagine f. med.L contropare compare]

contrived /kənˈtraɪvd/ adj. planned so carefully as to seem unnatural; artificial, forced (the plot seemed contrived).

control /kənˈtrəʊl/ n. & v. —n. **1** the power of directing; command (under the control of). **2** the power of restraining, esp. self-restraint. **3** a means of restraint; a check. **4** (usu. in pl.) switches and other devices by which a machine, esp. an aircraft or vehicle, is controlled (also attrib.: control panel). **5 a** a place where something is controlled or verified. **b** a person or group that controls something. **6** a standard of comparison for checking the results of a survey or experiment. —v.tr. (**controlled, controlling**) **1** have control or command of; dominate. **2** exert control over; regulate. **3** hold in check; restrain (told him to control himself). **4** serve as control to. **5** check, verify. □ **control tower** a tall building at an airport etc. from which air traffic is controlled. **in control** (often foll. by of) directing an activity. **out of control** no longer subject to containment, restraint, or guidance. **under**

control being controlled; in order. □ **controllability** /-ˈbɪlɪtɪ/ n. **controllable** adj. **controllably** adv. [ME f. AF contreroller keep a copy of a roll of accounts, f. med.L contrarotulare (as CONTRA-, rotulus ROLL n.): (n.) perh. f. F contrôle]

controller /kənˈtrəʊlə(r)/ n. **1** a person or thing that controls. **2** a person in charge of expenditure. □ **controllership** n. [ME counterroller f. AF contrerollour (as CONTROL)]

controversial /ˌkɒntrəˈvɜːʃ(ə)l/ adj. **1** causing or subject to controversy. **2** of controversy. **3** given to controversy. □ **controversialism** n. **controversialist** n. **controversially** adv. [LL controversialis (as CONTROVERSY)]

controversy /ˈkɒntrəˌvɜːsɪ, disp. kənˈtrɒvəsɪ/ n. (pl. **-ies**) a prolonged argument or dispute, esp. when conducted publicly. [ME f. L controversia (as CONTROVERT)]

■ **Usage** The second pronunciation, stressed on the second syllable, is considered incorrect by some people.

controvert /ˈkɒntrəˌvɜːt, -ˈvɜːt/ v.tr. dispute, deny. □ **controvertible** adj. [orig. past part.; f. F controvers(e) f. L controversus (as CONTRA-, vertere vers- turn)]

contumacious /ˌkɒntjuːˈmeɪʃəs/ adj. insubordinate; stubbornly or wilfully disobedient, esp. to a court order. □ **contumaciously** adv. [L contumax, perh. rel. to tumēre swell]

contumacy /ˈkɒntjʊməsɪ/ n. stubborn refusal to obey or comply. [L contumacia f. contumax: see CONTUMACIOUS]

contumelious /ˌkɒntjuːˈmiːlɪəs/ adj. reproachful, insulting, or insolent. □ **contumeliously** adv. [ME f. OF contumelieus f. L contumeliosus (as CONTUMELY)]

contumely /ˈkɒntjuːmlɪ/ n. **1** insolent or reproachful language or treatment. **2** disgrace. [ME f. OF contumelie f. L contumelia (as COM-, tumēre swell)]

contuse /kənˈtjuːz/ v.tr. injure without breaking the skin; bruise. □ **contusion** n. [L contundere contus- (as COM-, tundere thump)]

conundrum /kəˈnʌndrəm/ n. **1** a riddle, esp. one with a pun in its answer. **2** a hard or puzzling question. [16th c.: orig. unkn.]

conurbation /ˌkɒnɜːˈbeɪʃ(ə)n/ n. an extended urban area, esp. one consisting of several towns and merging suburbs. [COM- + L urbs urbis city + -ATION]

convalesce /ˌkɒnvəˈles/ v.intr. recover one's health after illness or medical treatment. [ME f. L convalescere (as COM-, valēre be well)]

convalescent /ˌkɒnvəˈles(ə)nt/ adj. & n. —adj. recovering from an illness. —n. a convalescent person. □ **convalescence** n.

convection /kənˈvekʃ(ə)n/ n. transference of heat in a gas or liquid by upward movement of the heated and less dense medium. □ **convectional** adj. **convective** adj. [LL convectio f. L convehere convect- (as COM-, vehere vect- carry)]

convector /kənˈvektə(r)/ n. a heating appliance that circulates warm air by convection.

convene /kənˈviːn/ v. **1** tr. summon or arrange (a meeting etc.). **2** intr. assemble. **3** tr. summon (a person) before a tribunal. □ **convenable** adj. **convener** n. **convenor** n. [ME f. L convenire convent- assemble, agree, fit (as COM-, venire come)]

convenience /kənˈviːnɪəns/ n. **1** the quality of being convenient; suitability. **2** freedom from difficulty or trouble; material advantage. **3** an advantage (a great convenience). **4** a useful thing, esp. an installation or piece of equipment. **5** Brit. a lavatory, esp. a public one. □ **at one's convenience** at a time or place that suits one. **convenience food** food, esp. complete meals, sold in convenient form and requiring very little preparation. **convenience store** US a large shop with extended opening hours. [ME f. L convenientia (as CONVENE)]

convenient /kənˈviːnɪənt/ adj. **1** (often foll. by for, to) **a** serving one's comfort or interests; easily accessible. **b** suitable. **c** free of trouble or difficulty. **2** available or occurring at a suitable time or place (will try to find a convenient moment). **3** well situated for some purpose (convenient for the shops). □ **conveniently** adv. [ME (as CONVENE)]

convent /ˈkɒnv(ə)nt, -vent/ n. **1** a religious community, esp. of nuns, under vows. **2** the premises occupied by this. **3** (in full **convent school**) a school attached to and run by a convent. [ME f. AF covent, OF convent f. L conventus assembly (as CONVENE)]

conventicle /kənˈventɪk(ə)l/ n. esp. hist. a secret or unlawful religious meeting, esp. of dissenters. [ME f. L conventiculum (place of) assembly, dimin. of conventus (as CONVENE)]

convention /kənˈvenʃ(ə)n/ n. **1 a** general agreement, esp. agreement on social behaviour etc. by implicit consent of the majority. **b** a custom or customary practice, esp. an artificial or formal one. **2 a** a formal assembly or conference for a common purpose. **b** US an assembly of the delegates of a political party to select candidates for office. **3 a** a formal agreement. **b** an agreement between States, esp. one less formal than a treaty. [ME f. OF f. L conventio -onis (as CONVENE)]

conventional /kənˈvenʃ(ə)n(ə)l/ adj. **1** depending on or according with convention. **2** (of a person) attentive to social conventions. **3** usual; of agreed significance. **4** not spontaneous or sincere or original. **5** (of weapons or power) non-nuclear. □ **conventionalism** n. **conventionalist** n. **conventionality** /-ˈnalɪtɪ/ n. **conventionalize** v.tr. (also **-ise**). **conventionally** adv. [F conventionnel or LL conventionalis (as CONVENTION)]

converge /kənˈvɜːdʒ/ v.intr. **1** come together as if to meet or join. **2** (of lines) tend to meet at a point. **3** (foll. by on, upon) approach from different directions. □ **convergence** n. **convergency** n. **convergent** adj. [LL convergere (as COM-, vergere incline)]

conversant /kənˈvɜːs(ə)nt, ˈkɒnvəs(ə)nt/ adj. (foll. by with) well experienced or acquainted with a subject, person, etc. □ **conversance** n. **conversancy** n. [ME f. OF, pres. part. of converser CONVERSE[1]]

conversation /ˌkɒnvəˈseɪʃ(ə)n/ n. **1** the informal exchange of ideas by spoken words. **2** an instance of this. [ME f. OF f. L conversatio -onis (as CONVERSE[1])]

conversational /ˌkɒnvəˈseɪʃən(ə)l/ adj. **1** of or in conversation. **2** fond of or good at conversation. **3** colloquial. □ **conversationally** adv.

conversationalist /ˌkɒnvəˈseɪʃənəlɪst/ n. one who is good at or fond of conversing.

converse[1] v. & n. —v.intr. /kənˈvɜːs/ (often foll. by with) engage in conversation. —n. /ˈkɒnvɜːs/

archaic conversation. □ **converser** /kən'vɜːsə(r)/ *n.* [ME f. OF *converser* f. L *conversari* keep company (with), frequent. of *convertere* (CONVERT)]

converse² /'kɒnvɜːs/ *adj.* & *n.* —*adj.* opposite, contrary, reversed. —*n.* **1** something that is opposite or contrary. **2** a statement formed from another statement by the transposition of certain words, e.g. *some philosophers are men* from *some men are philosophers*. □ **conversely** /'kɒnvɜːslɪ, kən'vɜːslɪ/ *adv.* [L *conversus*, past part. of *convertere* (CONVERT)]

conversion /kən'vɜːʃ(ə)n/ *n.* **1** the act or an instance of converting or the process of being converted, esp. in belief or religion. **2 a** an adaptation of a building for new purposes. **b** a converted building. **3** *Rugby Football* the scoring of points by a successful kick at goal after scoring a try. [ME f. OF f. L *conversio -onis* (as CONVERT)]

convert *v.* & *n.* —*v.* /kən'vɜːt/ **1** *tr.* (usu. foll. by *into*) change in form, character, or function. **2** *tr.* cause (a person) to change beliefs, opinion, party, etc. **3** *tr.* change (moneys, stocks, units in which a quantity is expressed, etc.) into others of a different kind. **4** *tr.* make structural alterations in (a building) to serve a new purpose. **5** *tr.* (also *absol.*) **a** *Rugby Football* score extra points from (a try) by a successful kick at goal. **b** *Amer. Football* complete (a touchdown) by kicking a goal or crossing the goal-line. **6** *intr.* be converted or convertible (*the sofa converts into a bed*). —*n.* /'kɒnvɜːt/ (often foll. by *to*) a person who has been converted to a different belief, opinion, etc. [ME f. OF *convertir* ult. f. L *convertere convers-* turn about (as COM-, *vertere* turn)]

converter /kən'vɜːtə(r)/ *n.* (also **convertor**) **1** a person or thing that converts. **2** *Electr.* **a** an electrical apparatus for the interconversion of alternating current and direct current. **b** *Electronics* an apparatus for converting a signal from one frequency to another.

convertible /kən'vɜːtɪb(ə)l/ *adj.* & *n.* —*adj.* **1** that may be converted. **2** (of currency etc.) that may be converted into other forms, esp. into gold or US dollars. **3** (of a car) having a folding or detachable roof. —*n.* a car with a folding or detachable roof. □ **convertibility** /-'bɪlɪtɪ/ *n.* **convertibly** *adv.* [OF f. L *convertibilis* (as CONVERT)]

convex /'kɒnveks/ *adj.* having an outline or surface curved like the exterior of a circle or sphere. □ **convexity** /-'veksɪtɪ/ *n.* **convexly** *adv.* [L *convexus* vaulted, arched]

convey /kən'veɪ/ *v.tr.* **1** transport or carry (goods, passengers, etc.). **2** communicate (an idea, meaning, etc.). **3** *Law* transfer the title to (property). **4** transmit (sound, smell, etc.). □ **conveyable** *adj.* [ME f. OF *conveier* f. med.L *conviare* (as COM-, L *via* way)]

conveyance /kən'veɪəns/ *n.* **1 a** the act or process of carrying. **b** the communication (of ideas etc.). **2** a means of transport; a vehicle. **3** *Law* **a** the transfer of property from one owner to another. **b** a document effecting this. □ **conveyancer** *n.* (in sense 3). **conveyancing** *n.* (in sense 3).

conveyor /kən'veɪə(r)/ *n.* (also **conveyer**) a person or thing that conveys. □ **conveyor belt** an endless moving belt for conveying articles or materials, esp. in a factory.

convict *v.* & *n.* —*v.tr.* /kən'vɪkt/ **1** (often foll. by *of*) prove to be guilty (of a crime etc.). **2** declare guilty by the verdict of a jury or the decision of a judge. —*n.* /'kɒnvɪkt/ **1** a person found guilty of a criminal offence. **2** *chiefly hist.* a person serving a prison sentence, esp. in a penal colony. [ME f. L *convincere convict-* (as COM-, *vincere* conquer): noun f. obs. *convict* convicted]

conviction /kən'vɪkʃ(ə)n/ *n.* **1 a** the act or process of proving or finding guilty. **b** an instance of this (*has two previous convictions*). **2 a** the action or resulting state of being convinced. **b** a firm belief or opinion. [L *convictio* (as CONVICT)]

convince /kən'vɪns/ *v.tr.* **1** (often foll. by *of*, or *that* + clause) persuade (a person) to believe or realize. **2** (as **convinced** *adj.*) firmly persuaded (*a convinced pacifist*). □ **convincer** *n.* **convincible** *adj.* [L (as CONVICT)]

convincing /kən'vɪnsɪŋ/ *adj.* **1** able to or such as to convince. **2** leaving no margin of doubt, substantial (*a convincing victory*). □ **convincingly** *adv.*

convivial /kən'vɪvɪəl/ *adj.* **1** fond of good company; sociable and lively. **2** festive (*a convivial atmosphere*). □ **conviviality** /-'ælɪtɪ/ *n.* **convivially** *adv.* [L *convivialis* f. *convivium* feast (as COM-, *vivere* live)]

convocation /ˌkɒnvə'keɪʃ(ə)n/ *n.* **1** the act of calling together. **2** a large formal gathering of people, esp.: **a** *Brit.* a provincial synod of the Anglican clergy. **b** *Brit.* a legislative or deliberative assembly of a university. □ **convocational** *adj.* [ME f. L *convocatio* (as CONVOKE)]

convoke /kən'vəʊk/ *v.tr. formal* call (people) together to a meeting etc.; summon to assemble. [L *convocare convocat-* (as COM-, *vocare* call)]

convoluted /'kɒnvəˌluːtɪd/ *adj.* **1** coiled, twisted. **2** complex, intricate. □ **convolutedly** *adv.* [past part. of *convolute* f. L *convolutus* (as COM-, *volvere volut-* roll)]

convolution /ˌkɒnvə'luːʃ(ə)n/ *n.* **1** coiling, twisting. **2** a coil or twist. **3** complexity. **4** a sinuous fold in the surface of the brain. □ **convolutional** *adj.* [med.L *convolutio* (as CONVOLUTED)]

convolvulus /kən'vɒlvjʊləs/ *n.* any twining plant of the genus *Convolvulus*, with trumpet-shaped flowers, e.g. bindweed. [L]

convoy /'kɒnvɔɪ/ *n.* & *v.* —*n.* **1** a group of ships travelling together or under escort. **2** a group of vehicles travelling on land together or under escort. —*v.tr.* **1** (of a warship) escort (a merchant or passenger vessel). **2** escort, esp. with armed force. [OF *convoyer* var. of *conveier* CONVEY]

convulse /kən'vʌls/ *v.tr.* **1** (usu. in *passive*) affect with convulsions. **2** cause to laugh uncontrollably. **3** shake violently; agitate, disturb. [L *convellere convuls-* (as COM-, *vellere* pull)]

convulsion /kən'vʌlʃ(ə)n/ *n.* **1** (usu. in *pl.*) violent irregular motion of a limb or limbs or the body caused by involuntary contraction of muscles, esp. as a disorder of infants. **2** a violent natural disturbance, esp. an earthquake. **3** violent social or political agitation. **4** (in *pl.*) uncontrollable laughter. □ **convulsionary** *adj.* [F *convulsion* or L *convulsio* (as CONVULSE)]

convulsive /kən'vʌlsɪv/ *adj.* **1** characterized by or affected with convulsions. **2** producing convulsions. □ **convulsively** *adv.*

cony /'kəʊnɪ/ *n.* (also **coney**) (*pl.* **-ies** or **-eys**) **1 a** a rabbit. **b** its fur. **2** *Bibl.* a hyrax. [ME *cunin(g)* f. AF *coning*, OF *conin*, f. L *cuniculus*]

coo *n.*, *v.*, & *int.* —*n.* a soft murmuring sound like that of a dove or pigeon. —*v.* (**coos**, **cooed**)

1 *intr.* make the sound of a coo. **2** *intr.* & *tr.* talk or say in a soft or amorous voice. —*int. Brit. sl.* expressing surprise or incredulity. □ **cooingly** *adv.* [imit.]

cooee /ˈkuːiː/ *n.*, *int.*, & *v. colloq.* —*n.* & *int.* a sound used to attract attention, esp. at a distance. —*v.intr.* (**cooees, cooeed, cooeeing**) make this sound. □ **within cooee** (or **a cooee**) **of** *Austral.* & *NZ colloq.* very near to. [imit. of a signal used by Australian Aboriginals and copied by settlers]

cook /kʊk/ *v.* & *n.* —*v.* **1** *tr.* prepare (food) by heating it. **2** *intr.* (of food) undergo cooking. **3** *tr. colloq.* falsify (accounts etc.); alter to produce a desired result. **4** *intr.* (as **be cooking**) *colloq.* be happening or about to happen (*went to find out what was cooking*). —*n.* a person who cooks, esp. professionally or in a specified way (*a good cook*). □ **cook-chill 1** the process of cooking and refrigerating food ready for reheating at a later time. **2** (*attrib.*) (of food) prepared in this way. **cook a person's goose** ruin a person's chances. **cook up** *colloq.* invent or concoct (a story, excuse, etc.). □ **cookable** *adj.* & *n.* [OE *cōc* f. pop.L *cocus* for L *coquus*]

cookbook /ˈkʊkbʊk/ *n. US* a cookery book.

cooker /ˈkʊkə(r)/ *n.* **1 a** a container or device for cooking food. **b** *Brit.* an appliance powered by gas, electricity, etc., for cooking food. **2** *Brit.* a fruit etc. (esp. an apple) that is more suitable for cooking than for eating raw.

cookery /ˈkʊkərɪ/ *n.* (*pl.* **-ies**) the art or practice of cooking. □ **cookery book** *Brit.* a book containing recipes and other information about cooking.

cookie /ˈkʊkɪ/ *n.* **1** *US* a small sweet biscuit. **2** *US sl.* a person. [Du. *koekje* dimin. of *koek* cake]

cooking /ˈkʊkɪŋ/ *n.* **1** the art or process by which food is cooked. **2** (*attrib.*) suitable for or used in cooking (*cooking apple; cooking utensils*).

cookware /ˈkʊkweə(r)/ *n.* utensils for cooking.

cool /kuːl/ *adj.*, *n.*, & *v.* —*adj.* **1** of or at a fairly low temperature, fairly cold (*a cool day; a cool bath*). **2** suggesting or achieving coolness (*cool colours; cool clothes*). **3** calm, unexcited. **4** lacking zeal or enthusiasm. **5** unfriendly; lacking cordiality (*got a cool reception*). **6** (prec. by *a*) *colloq.* at least; not less than (*cost me a cool thousand*). **7** *sl.* esp. *US* excellent, marvellous. —*n.* **1** coolness. **2** cool air; a cool place. **3** *sl.* calmness, composure (*keep one's cool; lose one's cool*). —*v.tr.* & *intr.* (often foll. by *down, off*) make or become cool. □ **cool-bag** (or **-box**) an insulated container for keeping food cool. **cooling-off period** an interval to allow for a change of mind before commitment to action. **cooling tower** a tall structure for cooling hot water before reuse, esp. in industry. **cool it** *sl.* relax, calm down. □ **coolish** *adj.* **coolly** /ˈkuːllɪ/ *adv.* **coolness** *n.* [OE *cōl, cōlian,* f. Gmc: cf. COLD]

coolant /ˈkuːlənt/ *n.* a cooling agent, esp. fluid, to remove heat from an engine, nuclear reactor, etc. **2** a fluid used to lessen the friction of a cutting tool. [COOL + -ANT after *lubricant*]

cooler /ˈkuːlə(r)/ *n.* **1** a vessel in which a thing is cooled. **2** *US* a refrigerator. **3** a long drink, esp. a spritzer. **4** *sl.* prison or a prison cell.

coolie /ˈkuːlɪ/ *n.* (also **cooly**) (*pl.* **-ies**) an unskilled native labourer in Eastern countries. □ **coolie hat** a broad conical hat as worn by coolies. [perh. f. *Kulī,* an aboriginal tribe of Gujarat, India]

coomb /kuːm/ *n.* (also **combe**) *Brit.* **1** a valley or hollow on the side of a hill. **2** a short valley running up from the coast. [OE *cumb:* cf. CWM]

coon /kuːn/ *n.* **1** *US* a racoon. **2** *sl. offens.* a Black. [abbr.]

coop /kuːp/ *n.* & *v.* —*n.* **1** a cage placed over sitting or fattening fowls. **2** a fowl-run. **3** a small place of confinement, esp. a prison. —*v.tr.* **1** put or keep (a fowl) in a coop. **2** (often foll. by *up, in*) confine (a person) in a small space. [ME *cupe* basket f. MDu., MLG *kūpe,* ult. f. L *cupa* cask]

co-op /ˈkəʊɒp/ *n. colloq.* **1** *Brit.* a cooperative society or shop. **2** a cooperative enterprise. [abbr.]

cooper /ˈkuːpə(r)/ *n.* & *v.* —*n.* a maker or repairer of casks, barrels, etc. —*v.tr.* make or repair (a cask). [ME f. MDu., MLG *kūper* f. *kūpe* COOP]

cooperate /kəʊˈɒpəˌreɪt/ *v.intr.* (also **co-operate**) **1** (often foll. by *with*) work or act together. **2** (of things) concur in producing an effect. □ **cooperant** *adj.* **cooperation** *n.* **cooperator** *n.* [eccl.L *cooperari* (as CO-, *operari* f. *opus operis* work)]

cooperative /kəʊˈɒpərətɪv/ *adj.* & *n.* (also **co-operative**) —*adj.* **1** of or affording cooperation. **2** willing to cooperate. **3** *Econ.* (of a farm, shop, or other business) owned and run jointly by its members, with profits shared among them. —*n.* a cooperative farm or society or business. □ **cooperatively** *adv.* **cooperativeness** *n.* [LL *cooperativus* (as COOPERATE)]

co-opt /kəʊˈɒpt/ *v.tr.* appoint to membership of a body by invitation of the existing members. □ **co-optation** /-ˈteɪʃ(ə)n/ *n.* **co-option** *n.* **co-optive** *adj.* [L *cooptare* (as CO-, *optare* choose)]

coordinate *v.*, *adj.*, & *n.* (also **co-ordinate**) —*v.* /kəʊˈɔːdɪˌneɪt/ **1** *tr.* bring (various parts, movements, etc.) into a proper or required relation. **2** *intr.* work or act together effectively. **3** *tr.* make coordinate. —*adj.* /kəʊˈɔːdɪnət/ **1** equal in rank or importance. **2** in which the parts are coordinated; involving coordination. **3** *Gram.* (of parts of a compound sentence) equal in status. —*n.* /kəʊˈɔːdɪnət/ **1** *Math.* each of a system of magnitudes used to fix the position of a point, line, or plane. **2** a person or thing equal in rank or importance. **3** (in *pl.*) matching items of clothing. □ **coordinately** /-nətlɪ/ *adv.* **coordination** /-ˈneɪʃ(ə)n/ *n.* **coordinative** /-ˌneɪtɪv/ *adj.* **coordinator** /-ˌneɪtə(r)/ *n.* [CO- + L *ordinare ordinat-* f. *ordo -inis* order]

coot /kuːt/ *n.* **1** any black aquatic bird of the genus *Fulica,* esp. *F. atra* with a white plate on the forehead. **2** *colloq.* a stupid person. [ME, prob. f. LG]

cop *n.* & *v. sl.* —*n.* **1** a policeman. **2** *Brit.* a capture or arrest (*it's a fair cop*). —*v.tr.* (**copped, copping**) **1** catch or arrest (an offender). **2** receive, suffer. **3** take, seize. □ **cop it 1** get into trouble; be punished. **2** be killed. **cop out** withdraw; give up an attempt. **2** go back on a promise. **3** escape. **cop-out** *n.* **1** a cowardly or feeble evasion. **2** an escape; a way of escape. **not much** (or **no**) **cop** *Brit.* of little or no value or use. [perh. f. obs. *cap* arrest f. OF *caper* seize f. L *capere:* (n.) cf. COPPER²]

copal /ˈkəʊp(ə)l/ *n.* a resin from any of various tropical trees, used for varnish. [Sp. f. Aztec *copalli* incense]

copartner /kəʊˈpɑːtnə(r)/ *n.* a partner or associate, esp. when sharing equally. □ **copartnership** *n.*

cope[1] *v.intr.* **1** (foll. by *with*) deal effectively or contend successfully with a person or task. **2** manage successfully; deal with a situation or problem (*found they could no longer cope*). [ME f. OF *coper, colper* f. *cop, colp* blow f. med.L *colpus* f. L *colaphus* f. Gk *kolaphos* blow with the fist]

cope[2] *n. & v. —n. Eccl.* a long cloaklike vestment worn by a priest or bishop in ceremonies and processions. *—v.tr.* cover with a cope or coping. [ME ult. f. LL *cappa* CAP, CAPE[1]]

copeck /ˈkəʊpek, ˈkɒpek/ *n.* (also **kopeck, kopek**) a Russian coin and monetary unit worth one-hundredth of a rouble. [Russ. *kopeĭka* dimin. of *kopʹë* lance (from the figure of Ivan IV bearing a lance instead of a sword in 1535)]

Copernican system /kəˈpɜːnɪkən/ *n.* (also **Copernican theory**) *Astron.* the theory that the planets (including the earth) move round the sun. [*Copernicus* latinized f. M. *Kopernik*, Polish astronomer d. 1543]

copiable /ˈkɒpɪəb(ə)l/ *adj.* that can or may be copied.

copier /ˈkɒpɪə(r)/ *n.* a machine or person that copies (esp. documents).

copilot /ˈkəʊˌpaɪlət/ *n.* a second pilot in an aircraft.

coping /ˈkəʊpɪŋ/ *n.* the top (usu. sloping) course of masonry in a wall or parapet. □ **coping-stone** a stone used in a coping.

copious /ˈkəʊpɪəs/ *adj.* **1** abundant, plentiful. **2** producing much. **3** providing much information. **4** profuse in speech. □ **copiously** *adv.* **copiousness** *n.* [ME f. OF *copieux* or f. L *copiosus* f. *copia* plenty]

copper[1] /ˈkɒpə(r)/ *n., adj., & v. —n.* **1** *Chem.* a malleable red-brown metallic element occurring naturally esp. in cuprite and malachite, and used esp. for electrical cables and apparatus. **2** a bronze coin. **3** a large metal vessel for boiling esp. laundry. *—adj.* made of or coloured like copper. *—v.tr.* cover (a ship's bottom, a pan, etc.) with copper. □ **copper beech** a variety of beech with copper-coloured leaves. **copper belt** a copper-mining area of Central Africa. **copper-bottomed 1** having a bottom sheathed with copper (esp. of a ship or pan). **2** genuine or reliable (esp. financially). [OE *copor, coper*, ult. f. L *cyprium aes* Cyprus metal]

copper[2] /ˈkɒpə(r)/ *n. Brit. sl.* a policeman. [COP + ER[1]]

copperhead /ˈkɒpəˌhed/ *n.* **1** a venomous viper, *Agkistrodon contortrix*, native to N. America. **2** a venomous cobra, *Denisonia superba*, native to Australia.

copperplate /ˈkɒpəˌpleɪt/ *n. & adj. —n.* **1 a** a polished copper plate for engraving or etching. **b** a print made from this. **2** an ornate style of handwriting. *—adj.* of or in copperplate writing.

coppery /ˈkɒpərɪ/ *adj.* of or like copper, esp. in colour.

coppice /ˈkɒpɪs/ *n. & v. —n.* an area of undergrowth and small trees, grown for periodic cutting. *—v.tr.* cut back (young trees) periodically to stimulate growth of shoots. □ **coppiced** *adj.* [OF *copeiz* ult. f. med.L *colpus* blow: see COPE[1]]

copra /ˈkɒprə/ *n.* the dried kernels of the coconut. [Port. f. Malayalam *koppara* coconut]

copro- /ˈkɒprəʊ/ *comb. form* dung, faeces. [Gk *kopros* dung]

co-production /ˌkəʊprəˈdʌkʃ(ə)n/ *n.* a production of a play, broadcast, etc., jointly by more than one company.

copse /kɒps/ *n.* **1** = COPPICE. **2** (in general use) a small wood. □ **copsy** *adj.* [shortened f. COPPICE]

copsewood /ˈkɒpswʊd/ *n.* undergrowth.

Copt *n.* **1** a native Egyptian in the Hellenistic and Roman periods. **2** a native Christian of the independent Egyptian Church. [F *Copte* or mod.L *Coptus* f. Arab. *al-ḳibṭ, al-ḳubṭ* Copts f. Coptic *Gyptios* f. Gk *Aiguptios* Egyptian]

Coptic /ˈkɒptɪk/ *n. & adj. —n.* the language of the Copts, now used only in the Coptic Church. *—adj.* of or relating to the Copts.

copula /ˈkɒpjʊlə/ *n.* (*pl.* **copulas**) *Logic & Gram.* a connecting word, esp. a part of the verb *be* connecting a subject and predicate. □ **copular** *adj.* [L (as CO-, *apere* fasten)]

copulate /ˈkɒpjʊˌleɪt/ *v.intr.* (often foll. by *with*) have sexual intercourse. □ **copulation** *n.* **copulatory** *adj.* [L *copulare* fasten together (as COPULA)]

copy /ˈkɒpɪ/ *n. & v. —n.* (*pl.* **-ies**) **1** a thing made to imitate or be identical to another. **2** a single specimen of a publication or issue (*ordered twenty copies*). **3 a** matter to be printed. **b** material for a newspaper or magazine article (*scandals make good copy*). **c** the text of an advertisement. *—v.* (**-ies, -ied**) **1** *tr.* **a** make a copy of. **b** (often foll. by *out*) transcribe. **2** *intr.* make a copy, esp. clandestinely. **3** *tr.* (foll. by *to*) send a copy of (a letter) to a third party. **4** *tr.* do the same as; imitate. □ **copy-edit** edit (copy) for printing. **copy editor** a person who edits copy for printing. **copy-typist** a person who makes typewritten transcripts of documents. [ME f. OF *copie, copier*, ult. f. L *copia* abundance (in med.L = transcript)]

copybook /ˈkɒpɪˌbʊk/ *n.* **1** a book containing models of handwriting for learners to imitate. **2** (*attrib.*) **a** tritely conventional. **b** accurate, exemplary.

copycat /ˈkɒpɪˌkæt/ *n. colloq.* (esp. as a child's word) a person who copies another, esp. slavishly.

copyist /ˈkɒpɪɪst/ *n.* **1** a person who makes (esp. written) copies. **2** an imitator. [earlier *copist* f. F *copiste* or med.L *copista* f. *copia*]

copyright /ˈkɒpɪˌraɪt/ *n., adj., & v. —n.* the exclusive legal right granted for a specified period to an author, designer, etc., or another appointed person, to print, publish, perform, film, or record original literary, artistic, or musical material. *—adj.* (of such material) protected by copyright. *—v.tr.* secure copyright for (material).

copywriter /ˈkɒpɪˌraɪtə(r)/ *n.* a person who writes or prepares copy (esp. of advertising material) for publication. □ **copywriting** *n.*

coquetry /ˈkɒkɪtrɪ, ˈkəʊk-/ *n.* (*pl.* **-ies**) **1** coquettish behaviour. **2** a coquettish act. **3** trifling with serious matters. [F *coquetterie* f. *coqueter* (as COQUETTE)]

coquette /kɒˈket, kəˈket/ *n.* a woman who flirts. □ **coquettish** *adj.* **coquettishly** *adv.* **coquettishness** *n.* [F, fem. of *coquet* wanton, dimin. of *coq* cock]

cor *int. Brit. sl.* expressing surprise, alarm, exasperation, etc. [corrupt. of *God*]

coracle /ˈkɒrək(ə)l/ *n. Brit.* a small boat of wickerwork covered with watertight material, used on Welsh and Irish lakes and rivers. [Welsh *corwgl* (*corwg* = Ir. *currach* boat)]

coral /ˈkɒr(ə)l/ *n. & adj.* —*n.* **1 a** a hard red, pink, or white calcareous substance secreted by various marine polyps for support and habitation. **b** any of these usu. colonial organisms. **2** the unimpregnated roe of a lobster or scallop. —*adj.* **1** like coral, esp. in colour. **2** made of coral. □ **coral island** (or **reef**) one formed by the growth of coral. [ME f. OF f. L *corallum* f. Gk *korallion*, prob. of Semitic orig.]

coralline /ˈkɒrəlaɪn/ *n. & adj.* —*n.* any seaweed of the genus *Corallina* having a calcareous jointed stem. —*adj.* **1** coral-red. **2** of or like coral. [F *corallin* & It. *corallina* f. LL *corallinus* (as CORAL)]

cor anglais /kɔːr ˈɒŋgleɪ, ɑ̃ˈgleɪ/ *n.* (*pl.* **cors anglais** *pronunc.* same) *Mus.* **1** an alto woodwind instrument of the oboe family. **2** its player. [F, = English horn]

corbel /ˈkɔːb(ə)l/ *n. Archit.* a projection of stone, timber, etc., jutting out from a wall to support a weight. [ME f. OF, dimin. of *corp*: see CORBIE]

corbie /ˈkɔːbɪ/ *n. Sc.* **1** a raven. **2** a carrion crow. [ME f. OF *corb*, *corp* f. L *corvus* crow]

cord *n. & v.* —*n.* **1 a** long thin flexible material made from several twisted strands. **b** a piece of this. **2** *Anat.* a structure in the body resembling a cord (*spinal cord*). **3 a** ribbed fabric, esp. corduroy. **b** (in *pl.*) corduroy trousers. **c** a cordlike rib on fabric. **4** an electric flex. **5** a measure of cut wood (usu. 128 cu.ft., 3.6 cubic metres). —*v.tr.* **1** fasten or bind with cord. **2** (as **corded** *adj.*) **a** (of cloth) ribbed. **b** provided with cords. **c** (of muscles) standing out like taut cords. □ **cordlike** *adj.* [ME f. OF *corde* f. L *chorda* f. Gk *khordē* gut, string of musical instrument]

cordate /ˈkɔːdeɪt/ *adj.* heart-shaped. [mod.L *cordatus* f. L *cor cordis* heart]

cordial /ˈkɔːdɪəl/ *adj. & n.* —*adj.* **1** heartfelt, sincere. **2** warm, friendly. —*n.* **1** a fruit-flavoured drink. **2** a comforting or pleasant-tasting medicine. □ **cordiality** /-ˈælɪtɪ/ *n.* **cordially** *adv.* [ME f. med.L *cordialis* f. L *cor cordis* heart]

cordite /ˈkɔːdaɪt/ *n.* a smokeless explosive made from cellulose nitrate and nitroglycerine. [CORD (from its appearance) + -ITE¹]

cordless /ˈkɔːdlɪs/ *adj.* (of an electrical appliance, telephone, etc.) working from an internal source of energy etc. (esp. a battery) and without a connection to a mains supply or central unit.

cordon /ˈkɔːd(ə)n/ *n. & v.* —*n.* **1** a line or circle of police, soldiers, guards, etc., esp. preventing access to or from an area. **2** an ornamental cord or braid. **3** a fruit-tree trained to grow as a single stem. —*v.tr.* (often foll. by *off*) enclose or separate with a cordon of police etc. [It. *cordone* augmentative of *corda* CORD, & F *cordon* (as CORD)]

cordon bleu /ˌkɔːdɒn ˈblɜː, ˌkɔːˈdɜː/ *adj. & n.* *Cookery* —*adj.* of the highest class. —*n.* a cook of this class. [F, = blue ribbon]

corduroy /ˈkɔːdərɔɪ, -djʊˌrɔɪ/ *n.* **1** a thick cotton fabric with velvety ribs. **2** (in *pl.*) corduroy trousers. [18th c.: prob. f. CORD ribbed fabric + obs. *duroy* coarse woollen fabric]

core *n. & v.* —*n.* **1** the horny central part of various fruits, containing the seeds. **2 a** the central or most important part of anything (also *attrib.*: *core curriculum*). **b** the central part, of different character from the surroundings. **3** the central region of the earth. **4** the central part of a nuclear reactor, containing the fissile material. **5** a magnetic structural unit in a computer, storing one bit of data. **6** the inner strand of an electric cable, rope, etc. **7** a piece of soft iron forming the centre of an electromagnet or an induction coil. —*v.tr.* remove the core from. □ **core memory** *Computing* the memory of a computer consisting of many cores. **core time** (in a flexitime system) the central part of the working day, when all employees must be present. □ **corer** *n.* [ME: orig. unkn.]

corelation var. of CORRELATION.

co-religionist /ˌkəʊrɪˈlɪdʒənɪst/ *n.* (*US* **coreligionist**) an adherent of the same religion.

coreopsis /ˌkɒrɪˈɒpsɪs/ *n.* any composite plant of the genus *Coreopsis*, having rayed usu. yellow flowers. [mod.L f. Gk *koris* bug + *opsis* appearance, with ref. to the shape of the seed]

co-respondent /ˌkəʊrɪˈspɒnd(ə)nt/ *n.* (*US* **corespondent**) a person cited in a divorce case as having committed adultery with the respondent.

corgi /ˈkɔːgɪ/ *n.* (*pl.* **corgis**) (in full **Welsh corgi**) **1** a dog of a short-legged breed with foxlike head. **2** this breed. [Welsh f. *cor* dwarf + *ci* dog]

coriander /ˌkɒrɪˈændə(r)/ *n.* **1** a plant, *Coriandrum sativum*, with leaves used for flavouring and small round aromatic fruits. **2** (also **coriander seed**) the dried fruit used for flavouring. [ME f. OF *coriandre* f. L *coriandrum* f. Gk *koriannon*]

Corinthian /kəˈrɪnθɪən/ *adj.* **1** of ancient Corinth in southern Greece. **2** *Archit.* of an order characterized by ornate decoration and flared capitals with acanthus leaves. [L *Corinthius* f. Gk *Korinthios* + -AN]

cork *n. & v.* —*n.* **1** the buoyant light-brown bark of the cork-oak. **2** a bottle-stopper of cork or other material. **3** a float of cork used in fishing etc. **4** (*attrib.*) made of cork. —*v.tr.* (often foll. by *up*) **1** stop or confine. **2** restrain (feelings etc.). □ **cork-oak** a S. European oak, *Quercus suber*. □ **corklike** *adj.* [ME f. Du. & LG *kork* f. Sp. *alcorque* cork sole, perh. f. Arab.]

corkage /ˈkɔːkɪdʒ/ *n.* a charge made by a restaurant or hotel for serving wine etc. when brought in by customers.

corked /kɔːkt/ *adj.* **1** stopped with a cork. **2** (of wine) spoilt by a decayed cork.

corker /ˈkɔːkə(r)/ *n. sl.* an excellent or astonishing person or thing.

corkscrew /ˈkɔːkskruː/ *n. & v.* —*n.* **1** a spirally twisted steel device for extracting corks from bottles. **2** (often *attrib.*) a thing with a spiral shape. —*v.tr. & intr.* move spirally; twist.

corky /ˈkɔːkɪ/ *adj.* (**corkier**, **corkiest**) **1** corklike. **2** (of wine) corked.

corm *n. Bot.* an underground swollen stem base of some plants, e.g. crocus. [mod.L *cormus* f. Gk *kormos* trunk with boughs lopped off]

cormorant /ˈkɔːmərənt/ *n.* any diving sea bird of the family Phalacrocoracidae, esp. *Phalacrocorax carbo* having lustrous black plumage. [ME f. OF *cormaran* f. med.L *corvus marinus* sea-raven: for ending -*ant* cf. *peasant*, *tyrant*]

corn¹ *n. & v.* —*n.* **1 a** any cereal before or after harvesting, esp. the chief crop of a region: wheat, oats, or (in the US and Australia) maize. **b** a grain or seed of a cereal plant. **2** *colloq.* something corny or trite. —*v.tr.* (as **corned** *adj.*) sprinkled or preserved with salt or brine (*corned* *beef*). □ **corn-cob** the cylindrical centre of the maize ear to which rows of grains are attached. **corn dolly** a symbolic or decorative figure made of plaited straw. **corn exchange** a place for trade in corn. **corn on the cob** maize cooked and eaten from the corn-cob. [OE f. Gmc: rel. to L *granum* grain]

corn² *n.* a small area of horny usu. tender skin esp. on the toes, extending into subcutaneous tissue. [ME f. AF f. L *cornu* horn]

corncrake /ˈkɔːnkreɪk/ *n.* a rail, *Crex crex*, inhabiting grassland and nesting on the ground.

cornea /ˈkɔːnɪə/ *n.* the transparent circular part of the front of the eyeball. □ **corneal** *adj.* [med.L *cornea tela* horny tissue, f. L *corneus* horny f. *cornu* horn]

cornel /ˈkɔːn(ə)l/ *n.* any plant of the genus *Cornus*, esp. a dwarf kind, *C. suecica*. [ME f. L *cornus*]

cornelian /kɔːˈniːlɪən/ *n.* (also **carnelian** /kɑː-/) **1** a dull red variety of chalcedony. **2** this colour. [ME f. OF *corneline*; car- after L *caro carnis* flesh]

corner /ˈkɔːnə(r)/ *n.* & *v.* —*n.* **1** a place where converging sides or edges meet. **2** a projecting angle, esp. where two streets meet. **3** the internal space or recess formed by the meeting of two sides, esp. of a room. **4** a difficult position, esp. one from which there is no escape (*driven into a corner*). **5** a secluded or remote place. **6** a region or quarter, esp. a remote one (*from the four corners of the earth*). **7** the action or result of buying or controlling the whole available stock of a commodity, thereby dominating the market. **8** *Boxing & Wrestling* **a** an angle of the ring, esp. one where a contestant rests between rounds. **b** a contestant's supporters offering assistance at the corner between rounds. **9** *Football & Hockey* a free kick or hit from a corner of the pitch after the ball has been kicked over the goal-line by a defending player. —*v.* **1** *tr.* force (a person or animal) into a difficult or inescapable position. **2** *tr.* **a** establish a corner in (a commodity). **b** dominate (dealers or the market) in this way. **3** *intr.* (esp. of or in a vehicle) go round a corner. [ME f. AF ult. f. L *cornu* horn]

cornerstone /ˈkɔːnəˌstəʊn/ *n.* **1 a** a stone in a projecting angle of a wall. **b** a foundation-stone. **2** an indispensable part or basis of something.

cornet /ˈkɔːnɪt/ *n.* **1** *Mus.* **a** a brass instrument resembling a trumpet but shorter and wider. **b** its player. **2** *Brit.* a conical wafer for holding ice-cream. □ **cornetist** /kɔːˈnetɪst, ˈkɔːnɪtɪst/ *n.* **cornettist** /kɔːˈnetɪst/ *n.* [ME f. OF ult. f. L *cornu* horn]

cornfield /ˈkɔːnfiːld/ *n.* a field in which corn is being grown.

cornflake /ˈkɔːnfleɪk/ *n.* **1** (in *pl.*) a breakfast cereal of toasted flakes made from maize flour. **2** a flake of this cereal.

cornflour /ˈkɔːnˌflaʊə(r)/ *n.* **1** a fine-ground maize flour. **2** a flour of rice or other grain.

cornflower /ˈkɔːnˌflaʊə(r)/ *n.* any plant of the genus *Centaurea* growing among corn, esp. *C. cyanus*, with deep-blue flowers.

cornice /ˈkɔːnɪs/ *n.* *Archit.* **1** an ornamental moulding round the wall of a room just below the ceiling. **2** a horizontal moulded projection crowning a building or structure. □ **corniced** *adj.* [F *corniche* etc. f. It. *cornice*, perh. f. L *cornix -icis* crow]

Cornish /ˈkɔːnɪʃ/ *adj.* & *n.* —*adj.* of or relating to Cornwall in SW England. —*n.* the ancient Celtic language of Cornwall. □ **Cornish pasty** seasoned meat and vegetables baked in a pastry envelope.

cornstarch /ˈkɔːnstɑːtʃ/ *n.* = CORNFLOUR.

cornucopia /ˌkɔːnjʊˈkəʊpɪə/ *n.* **1 a** a symbol of plenty consisting of a goat's horn overflowing with flowers, fruit, and corn. **b** an ornamental vessel shaped like this. **2** an abundant supply. □ **cornucopian** *adj.* [LL f. L *cornu copiae* horn of plenty]

corny /ˈkɔːnɪ/ *adj.* (**cornier**, **corniest**) **1** *colloq.* **a** trite. **b** feebly humorous. **c** sentimental. **d** old-fashioned; out of date. **2** of or abounding in corn. □ **cornily** *adv.* **corniness** *n.* [CORN¹ + -Y¹: sense 1 f. sense 'rustic']

corolla /kəˈrɒlə/ *n.* *Bot.* a whorl or whorls of petals forming the inner envelope of a flower. [L, dimin. of *corona* crown]

corollary /kəˈrɒlərɪ/ *n.* (*pl.* **-ies**) **1 a** a proposition that follows from (and is often appended to) one already proved. **b** an immediate deduction. **2** (often foll. by *of*) a natural consequence or result. [ME f. L *corollarium* money paid for a garland, gratuity: neut. adj. f. COROLLA]

corona¹ /kəˈrəʊnə/ *n.* (*pl.* **coronae** /-niː/) **1 a** a small circle of light round the sun or moon. **b** the rarefied gaseous envelope of the sun, seen as an irregularly shaped area of light around the moon's disc during a total solar eclipse. **2** *Anat.* a crown or crownlike structure. **3** *Bot.* a crownlike outgrowth from the inner side of a corolla. **4** *Electr.* the glow around a conductor at high potential. [L, = crown]

corona² /kəˈrəʊnə/ *n.* a long cigar with straight sides. [Sp. *La Corona* the crown]

coronal /kəˈrəʊn(ə)l, ˈkɒrən(ə)l/ *adj.* **1** *Astron.* & *Bot.* of a corona. **2** *Anat.* of the crown of the head. [F *coronal* or L *coronalis* (as CORONA¹)]

coronary /ˈkɒrənərɪ/ *adj.* & *n.* —*adj.* *Anat.* resembling or encircling like a crown. —*n.* (*pl.* **-ies**) = *coronary thrombosis*. □ **coronary artery** an artery supplying blood to the heart. **coronary thrombosis** *Med.* a blockage of the blood flow caused by a blood clot in a coronary artery. [L *coronarius* f. *corona* crown]

coronation /ˌkɒrəˈneɪʃ(ə)n/ *n.* the ceremony of crowning a sovereign or a sovereign's consort. [ME f. OF f. med.L *coronatio -onis* f. *coronare* to crown f. CORONA¹]

coroner /ˈkɒrənə(r)/ *n.* an officer of a county, district, or municipality, holding inquests on deaths thought to be violent or accidental, and inquiries in cases of treasure trove. □ **coronership** *n.* [ME f. AF *cor(o)uner* f. *coro(u)ne* CROWN]

coronet /ˈkɒrənɪt, -ˌnet/ *n.* **1** a small crown (esp. as worn, or used as a heraldic device, by a peer or peeress). **2** a circlet of precious materials, esp. as a woman's head-dress or part of one. **3** a garland for the head. □ **coroneted** *adj.* [OF *coronet(t)e* dimin. of *corone* CROWN]

Corp. *abbr.* **1** Corporal. **2** *US* Corporation.

corpora *pl.* of CORPUS.

corporal¹ /ˈkɔːpər(ə)l/ *n.* a non-commissioned army or air-force officer ranking next below sergeant. [obs. F. var. of *caporal* f. It. *caporale* prob. f. L *corporalis* (as CORPORAL²), confused with It. *capo* head]

corporal[2] /ˈkɔːpər(ə)l/ adj. of or relating to the human body. □ **corporal punishment** punishment inflicted on the body, esp. by beating. □ **corporally** adv. [ME f. OF f. L corporalis f. corpus -oris body]

corporality /ˌkɔːpəˈrælɪtɪ/ n. (pl. **-ies**) **1** material existence. **2** a body. [ME f. LL corporalitas (as CORPORAL[2])]

corporate /ˈkɔːpərət/ adj. **1** forming a corporation (corporate body; body corporate). **2** forming one body of many individuals. **3** of or belonging to a corporation or group (corporate responsibility). **4** corporative. □ **corporate raider** US a person who mounts an unwelcome takeover bid by buying up a company's shares on the stock market. □ **corporately** adv. **corporatism** n. [L corporare corporat- form into a body (corpus -oris)]

corporation /ˌkɔːpəˈreɪʃ(ə)n/ n. **1** a group of people authorized to act as an individual and recognized in law as a single entity, esp. in business. **2** the municipal authorities of a borough, town, or city. **3** joc. a protruding stomach. [LL corporatio (as CORPORATE)]

corporative /ˈkɔːpərətɪv/ adj. **1** of a corporation. **2** governed by or organized in corporations, esp. of employers and employed. □ **corporativism** n.

corporeal /kɔːˈpɔːrɪəl/ adj. bodily, physical, material, esp. as distinct from spiritual. □ **corporeality** /-ˈælɪtɪ/ n. **corporeally** adv. [LL corporealis f. L corporeus f. corpus -oris body]

corps /kɔː(r)/ n. (pl. **corps** /kɔːz/) **1** Mil. **a** a body of troops with special duties (intelligence corps; Royal Army Medical Corps). **b** a main subdivision of an army in the field, consisting of two or more divisions. **2** a body of people engaged in a special activity (diplomatic corps; press corps). [F (as CORPSE)]

corps de ballet /ˌkɔː də ˈbæleɪ/ n. the company of ensemble dancers in a ballet. [F]

corps diplomatique /ˌkɔː dɪpləmæˈtiːk/ n. a diplomatic corps. [F]

corpse /kɔːps/ n. a dead (usu. human) body. [ME corps, var. spelling of cors (CORSE), f. OF cors f. L corpus body]

corpulent /ˈkɔːpjʊlənt/ adj. bulky in body, fat. □ **corpulence** n. **corpulency** n. [ME f. L corpulentus f. corpus body]

corpus /ˈkɔːpəs/ n. (pl. **corpora** /ˈkɔːpərə/ or **corpuses**) a body or collection of writings, texts, spoken material, etc. [ME f. L, = body]

corpuscle /ˈkɔːpʌs(ə)l/ n. a minute body or cell in an organism, esp. (in pl.) the red or white cells in the blood of vertebrates. □ **corpuscular** /kɔːˈpʌskjʊlə(r)/ adj. [L corpusculum (as CORPUS)]

corral /kɒˈrɑːl/ n. & v. —n. **1** US a pen for cattle, horses, etc. **2** an enclosure for capturing wild animals. **3** esp. US hist. a defensive enclosure of wagons in an encampment. —v.tr. (**corralled**, **corralling**) **1** put or keep in a corral. **2** form (wagons) into a corral. **3** US colloq. acquire. [Sp. & OPort. (as KRAAL)]

correct /kəˈrekt/ adj. & v. —adj. **1** true, right, accurate. **2** (of conduct, manners, etc.) proper, right. **3** in accordance with good standards of taste etc. —v.tr. **1** set right; amend (an error, omission, etc., or the person responsible for it). **2** mark the errors in (written or printed work etc.). **3** substitute the right thing for (the wrong one). **4 a** admonish or rebuke (a person). **b**

punish (a person or fault). **5** counteract (a harmful quality). **6** adjust (an instrument etc.) to function accurately or accord with a standard. □ **correctly** adv. **correctness** n. [ME (adj. through F) f. L corrigere correct- (as COM-, regere guide)]

correction /kəˈrekʃ(ə)n/ n. **1 a** the act or process of correcting. **b** an instance of this. **2** a thing substituted for what is wrong. □ **correctional** adj. [ME f. OF f. L correctio -onis (as CORRECT)]

correctitude /kəˈrektɪˌtjuːd/ n. correctness, esp. conscious correctness of conduct. [19th c., f. CORRECT + RECTITUDE]

corrective /kəˈrektɪv/ adj. & n. —adj. serving or tending to correct or counteract something undesired or harmful. —n. a corrective measure or thing. □ **correctively** adv. [F correctif -ive or LL correctivus (as CORRECT)]

corrector /kəˈrektə(r)/ n. a person who corrects or points out faults. [ME f. AF correctour f. L corrector (as CORRECT)]

correlate /ˈkɒrəˌleɪt, ˈkɒrɪ-/ v. & n. —v. **1** intr. (foll. by with, to) have a mutual relation. **2** tr. (usu. foll. by with) bring into a mutual relation. —n. each of two related or complementary things (esp. so related that one implies the other). [back-form. f. CORRELATION, CORRELATIVE]

correlation /ˌkɒrəˈleɪʃ(ə)n, ˌkɒrɪ-/ n. (also **corelation** /ˌkəʊrɪ-/) **1** a mutual relation between two or more things. **2 a** interdependence of variable quantities. **b** a quantity measuring the extent of this. **3** the act of correlating. □ **correlational** adj. [med.L correlatio (as CORRELATIVE)]

correlative /kɒˈrelətɪv, kə-/ adj. & n. —adj. **1** (often foll. by with, to) having a mutual relation. **2** Gram. (of words) corresponding to each other and regularly used together (as neither and nor). —n. a correlative word or thing. □ **correlatively** adv. **correlativity** /-ˈtɪvɪtɪ/ n. [med.L correlativus (as COM-, RELATIVE)]

correspond /ˌkɒrɪˈspɒnd/ v.intr. **1 a** (usu. foll. by to) be analogous or similar. **b** (usu. foll. by to) agree in amount, position, etc. **c** (usu. foll. by with, to) be in harmony or agreement. **2** (usu. foll. by with) communicate by interchange of letters. □ **correspondingly** adv. [F correspondre f. med.L correspondere (as COM-, RESPOND)]

correspondence /ˌkɒrɪˈspɒnd(ə)ns/ n. **1** (usu. foll. by with, to, between) agreement, similarity, or harmony. **2 a** communication by letters. **b** letters sent or received. □ **correspondence column** the part of a newspaper etc. that contains letters from readers. **correspondence course** a course of study conducted by post. [ME f. OF f. med.L correspondentia (as CORRESPOND)]

correspondent /ˌkɒrɪˈspɒnd(ə)nt/ n. & adj. —n. **1** a person who writes letters to a person or a newspaper, esp. regularly. **2** a person employed to contribute material for publication in a periodical or for broadcasting. —adj. (often foll. by to, with) archaic corresponding. □ **correspondently** adv. [ME f. OF correspondant or med.L (as CORRESPOND)]

corrida /kɒˈriːdə/ n. **1** a bullfight. **2** bullfighting. [Sp. corrida de toros running of bulls]

corridor /ˈkɒrɪˌdɔː(r)/ n. **1** a passage from which doors lead into rooms. **2** a passage in a railway carriage from which doors lead into compartments. **3** a strip of the territory of one State passing through that of another, esp. securing access to the sea. **4** a route to which aircraft are restricted, esp. over a foreign country. [F f. It. *corridore* corridor for *corridojo* running-place f. *correre* run, by confusion with *corridore* runner]

corrie /ˈkɒrɪ/ *n. Sc.* a circular hollow on a mountainside; a cirque. [Gael. *coire* cauldron]

corrigendum /ˌkɒrɪˈgendəm, -ˈdʒendəm/ *n. (pl.* **corrigenda** /-də/) a thing to be corrected, esp. an error in a printed book. [L, neut. gerundive of *corrigere*: see CORRECT]

corrigible /ˈkɒrɪdʒɪb(ə)l/ *adj.* **1** capable of being corrected. **2** (of a person) submissive; open to correction. □ **corrigibly** *adv.* [ME f. F f. med.L *corrigibilis* (as CORRECT)]

corroborate /kəˈrɒbəˌreɪt/ *v.tr.* confirm or give support to (a statement or belief, or the person holding it), esp. in relation to witnesses in a lawcourt. □ **corroboration** /-ˈreɪʃ(ə)n/ *n.* **corroborative** /-rətɪv/ *adj.* **corroborator** *n.* **corroboratory** /-rətərɪ/ *adj.* [L *corroborare* strengthen (as COM-, *roborare* f. *robur -oris* strength)]

corroboree /kəˈrɒbərɪ/ *n.* **1** a festive or warlike dance-drama with song of Australian Aboriginals. **2** a noisy party. [Aboriginal dial.]

corrode /kəˈrəʊd/ *v.* **1 a** *tr.* wear away, esp. by chemical action. **b** *intr.* be worn away; decay. **2** *tr.* destroy gradually (*optimism corroded by recent misfortunes*). □ **corrodible** *adj.* [ME f. L *corrodere corros-* (as COM-, *rodere* gnaw)]

corrosion /kəˈrəʊʒ(ə)n/ *n.* **1** the process of corroding, esp. of a rusting metal. **2 a** damage caused by corroding. **b** a corroded area.

corrosive /kəˈrəʊsɪv/ *adj. & n.* —*adj.* tending to corrode or consume. —*n.* a corrosive substance. □ **corrosively** *adv.* **corrosiveness** *n.* [ME f. OF *corosif -ive* (as CORRODE)]

corrugate /ˈkɒrʊˌgeɪt/ *v.* **1** *tr.* (esp. as **corrugated** *adj.*) form into alternate ridges and grooves, esp. to strengthen (*corrugated iron; corrugated paper*). **2** *tr. & intr.* contract into wrinkles or folds. □ **corrugation** /-ˈgeɪʃ(ə)n/ *n.* [L *corrugare* (as COM-, *rugare* f. *ruga* wrinkle)]

corrupt /kəˈrʌpt/ *adj. & v.* —*adj.* **1** morally depraved; wicked. **2** influenced by or using bribery or fraudulent activity. **3** (of a text, language, etc.) harmed (esp. made suspect or unreliable) by errors or alterations. **4** rotten. —*v.* **1** *tr. & intr.* make or become corrupt or depraved. **2** *tr.* affect or harm by errors or alterations. **3** *tr.* infect, taint. □ **corrupter** *n.* **corruptible** *adj.* **corruptibility** /-ˈbɪlɪtɪ/ *n.* **corruptive** *adj.* **corruptly** *adv.* **corruptness** *n.* [ME f. OF *corrupt* or L *corruptus* past part. of *corrumpere corrupt-* (as COM-, *rumpere* break)]

corruption /kəˈrʌpʃ(ə)n/ *n.* **1** moral deterioration, esp. widespread. **2** use of corrupt practices, esp. bribery or fraud. **3 a** irregular alteration (of a text, language, etc.) from its original state. **b** an irregularly altered form of a word. **4** decomposition, esp. of a corpse or other organic matter. [ME f. OF *corruption* or L *corruptio* (as CORRUPT)]

corsage /kɔːˈsɑːʒ/ *n.* **1** a small bouquet worn by a woman. **2** the bodice of a woman's dress. [ME f. OF f. *cors* body: see CORPSE]

corsair /ˈkɔːseə(r)/ *n.* **1** a pirate ship. **2** a pirate. [F *corsaire* f. med.L *cursarius* f. *cursus* inroad f. *currere* run]

corselette /ˈkɔːslɪt, ˌkɔːsəˌlet/ *n.* (also **corselet**) a woman's foundation garment combining corset and brassière.

corset /ˈkɔːsɪt/ *n. & v.* —*n.* **1** a closely-fitting undergarment worn by women to support the abdomen. **2** a similar garment worn by men and women because of injury, weakness, or deformity. —*v.tr.* (**corseted, corseting**) **1** provide with a corset. **2** control closely. □ **corseted** *adj.* **corsetry** *n.* [ME OF, dimin. of *cors* body: see CORPSE]

corslet /ˈkɔːslɪt/ *n.* (also **corselet**) **1** a garment (usu. tight-fitting) covering the trunk but not the limbs. **2** *hist.* a piece of armour covering the trunk. [OF *corselet*, dimin. formed as CORSET]

cortège /kɔːˈteɪʒ/ *n.* **1** a procession, esp. for a funeral. **2** a train of attendants. [F]

cortex /ˈkɔːteks/ *n. (pl.* **cortices** /-tɪˌsiːz/) **1** *Anat.* the outer part of an organ, esp. of the brain (**cerebral cortex**) or kidneys (**renal cortex**). **2** *Bot.* **a** an outer layer of tissue immediately below the epidermis. **b** bark. □ **cortical** /ˈkɔːtɪk(ə)l/ *adj.* [L *cortex, -icis* bark]

cortisone /ˈkɔːtɪˌzəʊn/ *n. Biochem.* a steroid hormone used medicinally esp. against inflammation and allergy. [Chem. name 17-hydroxy-11-dehydrocorticosterone]

corundum /kəˈrʌndəm/ *n. Mineral.* extremely hard crystallized alumina, used esp. as an abrasive, and varieties of which are used for gemstones. [Tamil *kurundam* f. Skr. *kuruvinda* ruby]

coruscate /ˈkɒrəˌskeɪt/ *v.intr.* **1** give off flashing light; sparkle. **2** be showy or brilliant. □ **coruscation** /-ˈskeɪʃ(ə)n/ *n.* [L *coruscare* glitter]

corvette /kɔːˈvet/ *n. Naut.* **1** a small naval escort-vessel. **2** *hist.* a flush-decked warship with one tier of guns. [F f. MDu. *korf* kind of ship + dimin. -ETTE]

corymb /ˈkɒrɪmb/ *n. Bot.* a flat-topped cluster of flowers with the flower-stalks proportionally longer lower down the stem. □ **corymbose** *adj.* [F *corymbe* or L *corymbus* f. Gk *korumbos* cluster]

cos[1] /kɒs/ *n.* a variety of lettuce with crisp narrow leaves forming a long upright head. [L f. Gk *Kōs*, island in the Aegean, where it originated]

cos[2] /kɒs, kɒz/ *abbr.* cosine.

cos[3] /kɒz/ *conj. & adv.* (also **'cos**) *colloq.* because. [abbr.]

cosh /kɒʃ/ *n. & v. Brit. colloq.* —*n.* a heavy blunt weapon. —*v.tr.* hit with a cosh. [19th c.: orig. unkn.]

co-signatory /kəʊˈsɪgnətərɪ/ *n. & adj.* (US **cosignatory**) —*n. (pl.* **-ies**) a person or State signing (a treaty etc.) jointly with others. —*adj.* signing jointly.

cosine /ˈkəʊsaɪn/ *n. Math.* the ratio of the side adjacent to an acute angle (in a right-angled triangle) to the hypotenuse. [mod.L *cosinus* (as CO-, SINE)]

cosmetic /kɒzˈmetɪk/ *adj. & n.* —*adj.* **1** intended to adorn or beautify the body, esp. the face. **2** intended to improve only appearances; superficially improving or beneficial (*a cosmetic change*). **3** (of surgery or a prosthetic device) imitating, restoring, or enhancing the normal appearance. —*n.* a cosmetic preparation, esp. for the face. □ **cosmetically** *adv.* [F *cosmétique* f. Gk *kosmētikos* f. *kosmeō* adorn f. *kosmos* order, adornment]

cosmic /ˈkɒzmɪk/ *adj.* **1** of the universe or cosmos, esp. as distinct from the earth. **2** of or for space travel. □ **cosmic rays** (or **radiation**) radiations from space etc. that reach the earth from all directions, usu. with high energy and penetrative power. □ **cosmical** *adj.* **cosmically** *adv.*

cosmogony /kɒz'mɒgənɪ/ *n.* (*pl.* **-ies**) **1** the origin of the universe. **2** a theory about this. □ **cosmogonic** /-mə'gɒnɪk/ *adj.* **cosmogonical** /-mə'gɒnɪk(ə)l/ *adj.* **cosmogonist** *n.* [Gk *kosmogonia* f. *kosmos* world + -*gonia* -begetting]

cosmography /kɒz'mɒgrəfɪ/ *n.* (*pl.* **-ies**) a description or mapping of general features of the universe. □ **cosmographer** *n.* **cosmographic** /-mə'græfɪk/ *adj.* **cosmographical** /-mə'græfɪk(ə)l/ *adj.* [ME f. F *cosmographie* or f. LL f. Gk *kosmographia* (as COSMOS¹, -GRAPHY)]

cosmology /kɒz'mɒlədʒɪ/ *n.* the science or theory of the universe. □ **cosmological** /-mə'lɒdʒɪk(ə)l/ *adj.* **cosmologist** *n.* [F *cosmologie* or mod.L *cosmologia* (as COSMOS¹, -LOGY)]

cosmonaut /'kɒzmə,nɔːt/ *n. hist.* a Soviet astronaut. [Russ. *kosmonavt*, as COSMOS¹, after *astronaut*]

cosmopolitan /,kɒzmə'pɒlɪt(ə)n/ *adj.* & *n.* —*adj.* **1 a** of, from, or knowing many parts of the world. **b** consisting of people from many or all parts. **2** free from national limitations or prejudices. **3** *Ecol.* (of a plant, animal, etc.) widely distributed. —*n.* **1** a cosmopolitan person. **2** *Ecol.* a widely distributed animal or plant. □ **cosmopolitanism** *n.* **cosmopolitanize** *v.tr.* & *intr.* (also **-ise**). [Gk *kosmopolitēs* f. *kosmos* world + *politēs* citizen + -AN]

cosmos¹ /'kɒzmɒs/ *n.* **1** the universe, esp. as a well-ordered whole. **2 a** an ordered system of ideas etc. **b** a sum total of experience. [Gk *kosmos*]

cosmos² /'kɒzmɒs/ *n.* any composite plant of the genus *Cosmos*, bearing single dahlia-like blossoms of various colours. [mod.L f. Gk *kosmos* in sense 'ornament']

Cossack /'kɒsæk/ *n.* & *adj.* —*n.* **1** a member of a people of southern Imperial Russia, orig. famous for their military skill. **2** a member of a Cossack military unit. —*adj.* of, relating to, or characteristic of the Cossacks. [F *cosaque* f. Russ. *kazak* f. Turki *quzzāq* nomad, adventurer]

cosset /'kɒsɪt/ *v.tr.* (**cosseted**, **cosseting**) pamper. [dial. *cosset* = pet lamb, prob. f. AF *coscet, cozet* f. OE *cotsǣta* cottager (as COT², SIT)]

cost *v.* & *n.* —*v.* (*past* and *past part.* **cost**) **1** *tr.* be obtainable for (a sum of money); have as a price (*what does it cost?*; *it cost me £50*). **2** *tr.* involve as a loss or sacrifice (*it cost them much effort*; *it cost him his life*). **3** *tr.* (*past* and *past part.* **costed**) fix or estimate the cost or price of. **4** *colloq.* **a** *tr.* be costly to (*it'll cost you*). **b** *intr.* be costly. —*n.* **1** what a thing costs; the price paid or to be paid. **2** a loss or sacrifice; an expenditure of time, effort, etc. **3** (in *pl.*) legal expenses, esp. those allowed in favour of the winning party or against the losing party in a suit. □ **at all costs** (or **at any cost**) no matter what the cost or risk may be. **cost-effective** effective or productive in relation to its cost. **cost of living** the level of prices esp. of the basic necessities of life. **cost-plus** calculated as the basic cost plus a profit factor. **cost price** the price paid for a thing by one who later sells it. **to a person's cost** at a person's expense; with loss or disadvantage to a person. [ME f. OF *coster, couster*,

coust ult. f. L *constare* stand firm, stand at a price (as COM-, *stare* stand)]

costal /'kɒst(ə)l/ *adj.* of the ribs. [F f. mod.L *costalis* f. L *costa* rib]

co-star /'kəʊstɑː(r)/ *n.* & *v.* —*n.* a cinema or stage star appearing with another or others of equal importance. —*v.* (**-starred**, **-starring**) **1** *intr.* take part as a co-star. **2** *tr.* (of a production) include as a co-star.

costard /'kɒstəd/ *n. Brit.* a large ribbed variety of apple. [ME f. AF f. *coste* rib f. L *costa*]

coster /'kɒstə(r)/ *n. Brit.* = COSTERMONGER. [abbr.]

costermonger /'kɒstə,mʌŋgə(r)/ *n. Brit.* a person who sells fruit, vegetables, etc., in the street from a barrow. [COSTARD + MONGER]

costive /'kɒstɪv/ *adj.* **1** constipated. **2** niggardly. □ **costively** *adv.* **costiveness** *n.* [ME f. OF *costivé* f. L *constipatus*: see CONSTIPATE]

costly /'kɒstlɪ/ *adj.* (**costlier**, **costliest**) **1** costing much; expensive. **2** of great value. □ **costliness** *n.*

costume /'kɒstjuːm/ *n.* & *v.* —*n.* **1** a style or fashion of dress, esp. that of a particular place, time, or class. **2** a set of clothes. **3** clothing for a particular activity (*swimming-costume*). **4** an actor's clothes for a part. **5** a woman's matching jacket and skirt. —*v.tr.* provide with a costume. □ **costume jewellery** artificial jewellery worn to adorn clothes. **costume play** (or **piece**) a play in which the actors wear historical costume. [F f. It. f. L *consuetudo* CUSTOM]

costumier /kɒ'stjuːmɪə(r)/ *n.* (also **costumer** /-mə(r)/) a person who makes or deals in costumes, esp. for theatrical use. [F *costumier* (as COSTUME)]

cosy /'kəʊzɪ/ *adj., n.,* & *v.* (*US* **cozy**) —*adj.* (**cosier**, **cosiest**) **1** comfortable and warm; snug. **2** *derog.* complacent. **3** warm and friendly. —*n.* (*pl.* **-ies**) a cover to keep something hot, esp. a teapot or a boiled egg. —*v.tr.* (**-ies**, **-ied**) (often foll. by *along*) *colloq.* reassure, esp. deceptively. □ **cosily** *adv.* **cosiness** *n.* [18th c. f. Sc., of unkn. orig.]

cot¹ *n.* **1** *Brit.* a small bed with high sides, esp. for a baby or very young child. **2** a hospital bed. **3** *US* a small folding bed. **4** *Ind.* a light bedstead. **5** *Naut.* a kind of swinging bed hung from deck beams, formerly used by officers. □ **cot-death** the unexplained death of a baby while sleeping. [Anglo-Ind., f. Hindi *khāt* bedstead, hammock]

cot² *n.* **1** a small shelter; a cote (*bell-cot*; *sheep-cot*). **2** *poet.* a cottage. [OE f. Gmc, rel. to COTE]

cote /kəʊt/ *n.* a shelter, esp. for animals or birds; a shed or stall (*sheep-cote*). [OE f. Gmc, rel. to COT²]

coterie /'kəʊtərɪ/ *n.* **1** an exclusive group of people sharing interests. **2** a select circle in society. [F, orig. = association of tenants, ult. f. MLG *kote* COTE]

coterminous /kəʊ'tɜːmɪnəs/ *adj.* (often foll. by *with*) having the same boundaries or extent (in space, time, or meaning). [CO- + TERMINUS + -OUS]

cotoneaster /kə,təʊnɪ'æstə(r)/ *n.* any rosaceous shrub of the genus *Cotoneaster*, bearing usu. bright red berries. [mod.L f. L *cotoneum* QUINCE + -ASTER]

cottage /'kɒtɪdʒ/ *n.* **1** a small simple house, esp. in the country. **2** a dwelling forming part of a farm establishment, used by a worker. □ **cottage cheese** soft white cheese made from curds of skimmed milk without pressing. **cottage hospital** Brit. a small hospital not having resident medical staff. **cottage industry** a business activity partly or wholly carried on at home. **cottage loaf** a loaf formed of two round masses, the smaller on top of the larger. **cottage pie** Brit. a dish of minced meat topped with browned mashed potato. □ **cottagey** adj. [ME f. AF, formed as COT², COTE]

cottager /ˈkɒtɪdʒə(r)/ n. a person who lives in a cottage.

cotter /ˈkɒtə(r)/ n. 1 a bolt or wedge for securing parts of machinery etc. 2 (in full **cotter pin**) a split pin that opens after passing through a hole. [17th c. (rel. to earlier cotterel): orig. unkn.]

cotton /ˈkɒt(ə)n/ n. & v. —n. 1 a soft white fibrous substance covering the seeds of certain plants. 2 a (in full **cotton plant**) such a plant, esp. any of the genus Gossypium. b cotton-plants cultivated as a crop for the fibre or the seeds. 3 thread or cloth made from the fibre. 4 (attrib.) made of cotton. —v.intr. (foll. by to) be attracted by (a person). □ **cotton candy** US candyfloss. **cotton on** (often foll. by to) colloq. begin to understand. **cotton-picking** US sl. unpleasant, wretched. **cotton wool 1** esp. Brit. fluffy wadding of a kind orig. made from raw cotton. 2 US raw cotton. □ **cottony** adj. [ME f. OF coton f. Arab. ḳuṭn]

cotyledon /ˌkɒtɪˈliːd(ə)n/ n. an embryonic leaf in seed-bearing plants. □ **cotyledonary** adj. **cotyledonous** adj. [L, = pennywort, f. Gk kotulēdōn cup-shaped cavity f. kotulē cup]

couch¹ /kaʊtʃ/ n. & v. —n. 1 an upholstered piece of furniture for several people; a sofa. 2 a long padded seat with a headrest at one end. —v. 1 tr. (foll. by in) express in words of a specified kind (couched in simple language). 2 tr. lay on or as on a couch. 3 intr. a (of an animal) lie, esp. in its lair. b lie in ambush. 4 tr. lower (a spear etc.) to the position for attack. □ **couch potato** US sl. a person who watches television to excess. [ME f. OF couche, coucher f. L collocare (as COM-, locare place)]

couch² /kuːtʃ, kaʊtʃ/ n. (in full **couch grass**) any of several grasses of the genus Agropyron, esp. A. repens, having long creeping roots. [var. of QUITCH]

couchant /ˈkaʊtʃ(ə)nt/ adj. (placed after noun) Heraldry (of an animal) lying with the body resting on the legs and the head raised. [F, pres. part. of coucher: see COUCH¹]

couchette /kuːˈʃet/ n. 1 a railway carriage with seats convertible into sleeping-berths. 2 a berth in this. [F, = little bed, dimin. of couche COUCH¹]

cougar /ˈkuːgə(r)/ n. US a puma. [F, repr. Guarani guaçu ara]

cough /kɒf/ v. & n. —v.intr. 1 expel air from the lungs with a sudden sharp sound produced by abrupt opening of the glottis, to remove an obstruction or congestion. 2 (of an engine, gun, etc.) make a similar sound. 3 sl. confess. —n. 1 an act of coughing. 2 a condition of the respiratory organs causing coughing. 3 a tendency to cough. □ **cough drop** (or **sweet**) a medicated lozenge to relieve a cough. **cough mixture** a liquid medicine to relieve a cough. **cough out 1** eject by coughing. 2 say with a cough. **cough up 1** = cough out. 2 sl. bring out or give (money or information) reluctantly. □

cougher n. [ME coghe, cowhe, rel. to MDu. kuchen, MHG küchen, of imit. orig.]

could past of CAN¹.

couldn't /ˈkʊd(ə)nt/ contr. could not.

coulomb /ˈkuːlɒm/ n. Electr. the SI unit of electric charge, equal to the quantity of electricity conveyed in one second by a current of one ampere. [C. A. de Coulomb, Fr. physicist d. 1806]

coulter /ˈkəʊltə(r)/ n. (US **colter**) a vertical cutting blade fixed in front of a ploughshare. [OE f. L culter]

council /ˈkaʊns(ə)l/ n. 1 a an advisory, deliberative, or administrative body of people formally constituted and meeting regularly. b a meeting of such a body. 2 a the elected local administrative body of a parish, district, town, city, or administrative county and its paid officers and workforce. b (attrib.) (esp. of housing) provided by a local council (council flat; council estate). 3 a body of persons chosen as advisers (Privy Council). 4 an ecclesiastical assembly (ecumenical council). □ **council of war 1** an assembly of officers called in a special emergency. 2 any meeting held to plan a response to an emergency. [ME f. AF cuncile f. L concilium convocation, assembly f. calare summon: cf. COUNSEL]

councillor /ˈkaʊnsələ(r)/ n. an elected member of a council, esp. a local one. □ **councillorship** n. [ME, alt. of COUNSELLOR: assim. to COUNCIL]

councilman /ˈkaʊns(ə)lmən/ n. (pl. **-men**; fem. **councilwoman**, pl. **-women**) esp. US a member of a council; a councillor.

counsel /ˈkaʊns(ə)l/ n. & v. —n. 1 advice, esp. formally given. 2 consultation, esp. to seek or give advice. 3 (pl. same) a barrister or other legal adviser; a body of these advising in a case. 4 a plan of action. —v.tr. (**counselled**, **counselling**; US **counseled**, **counseling**) 1 (often foll. by to + infin.) advise (a person). 2 a give advice to (a person) on social or personal problems, esp. professionally. b assist or guide (a person) in resolving personal difficulties. 3 (often foll. by that) recommend (a course of action). □ **counsel of despair** action to be taken when all else fails. **counsel of perfection 1** advice that is ideal but not feasible. 2 advice guiding towards moral perfection. **keep one's own counsel** not confide in others. **Queen's** (or **King's**) **Counsel** Brit. a counsel to the Crown, taking precedence over other barristers. **take counsel** (usu. foll. by with) consult. [ME f. OF c(o)unseil, conseiller f. L consilium consultation, advice]

counselling /ˈkaʊnsəlɪŋ/ n. (US **counseling**) 1 the act or process of giving counsel. 2 the process of assisting and guiding clients, esp. by a trained person on a professional basis, to resolve esp. personal, social, or psychological problems and difficulties (cf. COUNSEL v. 2b).

counsellor /ˈkaʊnsələ(r)/ n. (US **counselor**) 1 a person who gives counsel; an adviser. 2 a person trained to give guidance on personal, social, or psychological problems. 3 (also **counselor-at-law**) US a barrister. [ME f. OF conseiller (f. L consiliarius), conseillour, -eur (f. L consiliator): see COUNSEL]

count¹ /kaʊnt/ v. & n. —v. 1 tr. determine the total number or amount of, esp. by assigning successive numbers (count the stations). 2 intr. repeat numbers in ascending order; conduct a reckoning. **3 a** *tr.* (often foll. by *in*) include in one's reckoning or plan (*fifteen people, counting the guide*). **b** *intr.* be included in a reckoning or plan. **4** *tr.* consider (a thing or a person) to be (lucky etc.) (*count no man happy until he is dead*). **5** *intr.* (often foll. by *for*) have value; matter (*his opinion counts for a great deal*). —*n.* **1 a** the act of counting; a reckoning (*after a count of fifty*). **b** the sum total of a reckoning (*blood count; pollen count*). **2** *Law* each charge in an indictment (*guilty on ten counts*). **3** a count of up to ten seconds by a referee when a boxer is knocked down. **4** *Polit.* the act of counting the votes after a general or local election. **5** one of several points under discussion. □ **count against** be reckoned to the disadvantage of. **count one's chickens** be over-optimistic or hasty in anticipating good fortune. **count the cost** consider the risks before taking action. **count down** recite numbers backwards to zero, esp. as part of a rocket-launching procedure. **counting-house** a place where accounts are kept. **count noun** a countable noun (see COUNTABLE 2). **count on** (or **upon**) depend on, rely on; expect confidently. **count out 1** count while taking from a stock. **2** complete a count of ten seconds over (a fallen boxer etc.), indicating defeat. **3** *colloq.* exclude from a plan or reckoning (*I'm too tired, count me out*). **count up** find the sum of. **keep count** take note of how many there have been etc. **lose count** fail to take note of the number etc. **not counting** excluding from the reckoning. **out for the count 1** *Boxing* defeated by being unable to rise within ten seconds. **2 a** defeated or demoralized. **b** soundly asleep. [ME f. OF *co(u)nter*, *co(u)nte* f. LL *computus*, *computare* COMPUTE]

count² /kaʊnt/ *n.* a foreign noble corresponding to an earl. □ **countship** *n.* [OF *conte* f. L *comes comitis* companion]

countable /ˈkaʊntəb(ə)l/ *adj.* **1** that can be counted. **2** *Gram.* (of a noun) that can form a plural or be used with the indefinite article (e.g. *book, kindness*).

countdown /ˈkaʊntdaʊn/ *n.* **1 a** the act of counting down, esp. at the launching of a rocket etc. **b** the procedures carried out during this time. **2** the final moments before any significant event.

countenance /ˈkaʊntɪnəns/ *n.* & *v.* —*n.* **1 a** the face. **b** the facial expression. **2** composure. **3** moral support. —*v.tr.* **1** give approval to (an act etc.) (*cannot countenance this breach of the rules*). **2** (often foll. by *in*) encourage (a person or a practice). □ **keep one's countenance** maintain composure, esp. by refraining from laughter. **out of countenance** disconcerted. [ME f. AF *c(o)untenance*, OF *contenance* bearing f. *contenir*: see CONTAIN]

counter¹ /ˈkaʊntə(r)/ *n.* **1 a** a long flat-topped fitment in a shop, bank, etc., across which business is conducted with customers. **b** a similar structure used for serving food etc. in a cafeteria or bar. **2 a** a small disc used for keeping the score etc. esp. in table-games. **b** a token representing a coin. **c** something used in bargaining; a pawn (*a counter in the struggle for power*). **3** an apparatus used for counting. **4** a person or thing that counts. □ **over the counter** by ordinary retail purchase. **under the counter** (esp. of the sale of scarce goods) surreptitiously,

esp. illegally. [AF *count(e)our*, OF *conteo(i)r*, f. med.L *computatorium* (as COMPUTE)]

counter² /ˈkaʊntə(r)/ *v., adv., adj.,* & *n.* —*v.* **1** *tr.* **a** oppose, contradict (*countered our proposal with their own*). **b** meet by a countermove. **2** *intr.* **a** make a countermove. **b** make an opposing statement. —*adv.* **1** in the opposite direction (*ran counter to the fox*). **2** contrary (*his action was counter to my wishes*). —*adj.* **1** opposed; opposite. **2** duplicate; serving as a check. —*n.* **1** a parry; a countermove. **2** something opposite or opposed. □ **run counter to** act contrary to. [ME f. OF *countre* f. L *contra* against: see COUNTER-]

counter- /ˈkaʊntə(r)/ *comb. form* denoting: **1** retaliation, opposition, or rivalry (*counter-threat; counter-cheers*). **2** opposite direction (*counter-current*). **3** correspondence, duplication, or substitution (*counterpart; countersign*). [from or after AF *countre-*, OF *contre* f. L *contra* against]

counteract /ˌkaʊntəˈrækt/ *v.tr.* **1** hinder or oppose by contrary action. **2** neutralize. □ **counteraction** *n.* **counteractive** *adj.*

counter-attack /ˈkaʊntərəˌtæk/ *n.* & *v.* —*n.* an attack in reply to an attack by an enemy or opponent. —*v.tr.* & *intr.* attack in reply.

counter-attraction /ˈkaʊntərəˌtrækʃ(ə)n/ *n.* **1** a rival attraction. **2** the attraction of a contrary tendency.

counterbalance /ˈkaʊntəˌbæləns/ *n.* & *v.* —*n.* **1** a weight balancing another. **2** an argument, force, etc., balancing another. —*v.tr.* act as a counterbalance to.

counterblast /ˈkaʊntəˌblɑːst/ *n.* (often foll. by *to*) an energetic or violent verbal or written reply to an argument etc.

countercharge /ˈkaʊntəˌtʃɑːdʒ/ *n.* & *v.* —*n.* a charge or accusation in return for one received. —*v.tr.* make a countercharge against.

counter-claim /ˈkaʊntəˌkleɪm/ *n.* & *v.* —*n.* **1** a claim made against another claim. **2** *Law* a claim made by a defendant in a suit against the plaintiff. —*v.tr.* & *intr.* make a counter-claim (for).

counter-clockwise /ˌkaʊntəˈklɒkwaɪz/ *adv.* & *adj.* US = ANTICLOCKWISE.

counter-culture /ˈkaʊntəˌkʌltʃə(r)/ *n.* a way of life etc. opposed to that usually considered normal.

counter-espionage /ˌkaʊntərˈespɪəˌnɑːʒ, -ɪdʒ/ *n.* action taken to frustrate enemy spying.

counterfeit /ˈkaʊntəfɪt, -ˌfiːt/ *adj., n.,* & *v.* —*adj.* **1** (of a coin, writing, etc.) made in imitation; not genuine; forged. **2** (of a claimant etc.) pretended. —*n.* a forgery; an imitation. —*v.tr.* **1 a** imitate fraudulently (a coin, handwriting, etc.); forge. **b** make an imitation of. **2** simulate (feelings etc.) (*counterfeited interest*). **3** resemble closely. □ **counterfeiter** *n.* [ME f. OF *countrefet, -fait*, past part. of *contrefaire* f. Rmc]

counterfoil /ˈkaʊntəˌfɔɪl/ *n.* the part of a cheque, receipt, etc., retained by the payer and containing details of the transaction.

counter-intelligence /ˌkaʊntərɪnˈtelɪdʒ(ə)ns/ *n.* = COUNTER-ESPIONAGE.

countermand /ˌkaʊntəˈmɑːnd/ *v.* & *n.* —*v.tr.* **1** *Mil.* **a** revoke (an order or command). **b** recall (forces etc.) by a contrary order. **2** cancel an order for (goods etc.). —*n.* an order revoking a previous one. [ME f. OF *contremander* f. med.L *contramandare* (as CONTRA-, *mandare* order)]

countermarch /ˈkaʊntəˌmɑːtʃ/ v. & n. —v.intr. & tr. esp. Mil. march or cause to march in the opposite direction, e.g. with the front marchers turning and marching back through the ranks. —n. an act of countermarching.

countermeasure /ˈkaʊntəˌmeʒə(r)/ n. an action taken to counteract a danger, threat, etc.

countermove /ˈkaʊntəˌmuːv/ n. & v. —n. a move or action in opposition to another. —v.intr. make a countermove. □ **countermovement** n.

counter-offensive /ˈkaʊntərəˌfensɪv/ n. 1 Mil. an attack made from a defensive position in order to effect an escape. 2 any attack made from a defensive position.

counterpane /ˈkaʊntəˌpeɪn/ n. a bedspread. [alt. (with assim. to pane in obs. sense 'cloth') f. obs. counterpoint f. OF contrepointe alt. f. cou(l)tepointe f. med.L culcita puncta quilted mattress]

counterpart /ˈkaʊntəˌpɑːt/ n. 1 a person or thing extremely like another. 2 a person or thing forming a natural complement or equivalent to another.

counterplot /ˈkaʊntəˌplɒt/ n. & v. —n. a plot intended to defeat another plot. —v. (-plotted, -plotting) 1 intr. make a counterplot. 2 tr. make a counterplot against.

counterpoint /ˈkaʊntəˌpɔɪnt/ n. & v. —n. 1 Mus. **a** the art or technique of setting, writing, or playing a melody or melodies in conjunction with another, according to fixed rules. **b** a melody played in conjunction with another. 2 a contrasting argument, plot, idea, or literary theme, etc., used to set off the main element. —v.tr. 1 Mus. add counterpoint to. 2 set (an argument, plot, etc.) in contrast to (a main element). [OF contrepoint f. med.L contrapunctum pricked or marked opposite, i.e. to the original melody (as CONTRA-, pungere punct- prick)]

counterpoise /ˈkaʊntəˌpɔɪz/ n. & v. —n. 1 a force etc. equivalent to another on the opposite side. 2 a state of equilibrium. 3 a counterbalancing weight. —v.tr. 1 counterbalance. 2 compensate. 3 bring into or keep in equilibrium. [ME f. OF contrepeis, -pois, contrepeser (as COUNTER-, peis, pois f. L pensum weight: cf. POISE)]

counter-productive /ˌkaʊntəprəˈdʌktɪv/ adj. having the opposite of the desired effect.

counter-revolution /ˌkaʊntəˌrevəˈluːʃ(ə)n/ n. a revolution opposing a former one or reversing its results. □ **counter-revolutionary** adj. & n. (pl. -ies).

countersign /ˈkaʊntəˌsaɪn/ v. & n. —v.tr. 1 add a signature to (a document already signed by another). 2 ratify. —n. 1 a watchword or password spoken to a person on guard. 2 a mark used for identification etc. □ **countersignature** /-ˈsɪɡnətʃə(r)/ n. [F contresigner (v.), contresigne (n.) f. It. contrasegno (as COUNTER-, SIGN)]

countersink /ˈkaʊntəˌsɪŋk/ v.tr. (past and past part. -sunk) 1 enlarge and bevel (the rim of a hole) so that a screw or bolt can be inserted flush with the surface. 2 sink (a screw etc.) in such a hole.

counterstroke /ˈkaʊntəˌstrəʊk/ n. a blow given in return for another.

counter-tenor /ˈkaʊntəˌtenə(r)/ n. Mus. 1 **a** a male alto singing-voice. **b** a singer with this voice. 2 a part written for counter-tenor. [ME f. F contre-teneur f. obs. It. contratenore (as CONTRA-, TENOR)]

countervail /ˌkaʊntəˈveɪl, ˈkaʊntə-/ v. 1 tr. counterbalance. 2 tr. & intr. (often foll. by against) oppose (with a force) and usu. successfully. [ME f. AF contrevaloir f. L contra valēre be of worth against]

counterweight /ˈkaʊntəˌweɪt/ n. a counterbalancing weight.

countess /ˈkaʊntɪs/ n. 1 the wife or widow of a count or an earl. 2 a woman holding the rank of count or earl. [ME f. OF contesse, cuntesse, f. LL comitissa fem. of comes COUNT²]

countless /ˈkaʊntlɪs/ adj. too many to be counted.

countrified /ˈkʌntrɪˌfaɪd/ adj. (also **countryfied**) often derog. rural or rustic, esp. of manners, appearance, etc. [past part. of countrify f. COUNTRY]

country /ˈkʌntrɪ/ n. (pl. -ies) 1 **a** the territory of a nation with its own government; a State. **b** a territory possessing its own language, people, culture, etc. 2 (often attrib.) rural districts as opposed to towns or the capital (a cottage in the country; a country town). 3 the land of a person's birth or citizenship; a fatherland. 4 **a** a territory, esp. an area of interest or knowledge. **b** a region associated with a particular person, esp. a writer (Hardy country). 5 Brit. a national population, esp. as voters (the country won't stand for it). □ **across country** not keeping to roads. **country-and-western** rural or cowboy songs originating in the US, and usu. accompanied by a guitar etc. **country club** a sporting and social club in a rural setting. **country cousin** often derog. a person with a countrified appearance or manners. **country music** = country-and-western. **country party** a political party supporting agricultural interests. **country-wide** extending throughout a nation. **go** (or **appeal**) **to the country** Brit. test public opinion by dissolving Parliament and holding a general election. **line of country** a subject about which a person is knowledgeable. [ME f. OF cuntree, f. med.L contrata (terra) (land) lying opposite (CONTRA)]

countryman /ˈkʌntrɪmən/ n. (pl. -men; fem. **countrywoman**, pl. -women) 1 a person living in a rural area. 2 **a** (also **fellow-countryman**) a person of one's own country or district. **b** (often in comb.) a person from a specified country or district (north-countryman).

countryside /ˈkʌntrɪˌsaɪd/ n. 1 a rural area. 2 rural areas in general.

county /ˈkaʊntɪ/ n. & adj. —n. (pl. -ies) 1 **a** any of the territorial divisions of some countries, forming the chief unit of local administration. **b** US a political and administrative division of a State. 2 the people of a county, esp. the leading families. —adj. having the social status or characteristics of county families. □ **county council** the elected governing body of an administrative county. **county court** a judicial court for civil cases (in the US for civil and criminal cases). **county cricket** cricket matches between teams representing counties. **county family** an aristocratic family with an ancestral seat in a county. **county town** (US **seat**) the administrative capital of a county. [ME f. AF counté, OF conté, cunté, f. L comitatus (as COUNT²)]

coup /kuː/ n. (pl. **coups** /kuːz/) 1 a notable or successful stroke or move. 2 = COUP D'ÉTAT. [F f. med.L colpus blow: see COPE¹]

coup de grâce /ˌkuː də ˈɡrɑːs/ n. a finishing stroke, esp. to kill a wounded animal or person. [F, lit. stroke of grace]

coup d'état /ˌkuː deɪˈtɑː/ n. a violent or illegal seizure of power. [F, lit. stroke of the State]

coupé /ˈkuːpeɪ/ n. (US **coupe** /kuːp/) a car with a hard roof, esp. one with two seats and a sloping rear. [F, past part. of *couper* cut (formed as COUP)]

couple /ˈkʌp(ə)l/ n. & v. —n. **1** (usu. foll. by *of*; often as *sing.*) **a** two (*a couple of girls*). **b** about two (*a couple of hours*). **2** (often as *sing.*) **a** a married or engaged pair. **b** a pair of partners in a dance, a game, etc. —v. **1** tr. fasten or link together; connect (esp. railway carriages). **2** tr. (often foll. by *together*, with) associate in thought or speech (*papers coupled their names*). **3** intr. copulate. [ME f. OF *cople*, *cuple*, *copler*, *cupler* f. L *copulare*, L COPULA]

coupler /ˈkʌplə(r)/ n. anything that connects two things, esp. a transformer used for connecting electric circuits.

couplet /ˈkʌplɪt/ n. *Prosody* two successive lines of verse, usu. rhyming and of the same length. [F dimin. of *couple*, formed as COUPLE]

coupling /ˈkʌplɪŋ/ n. **1 a** a link connecting railway carriages etc. **b** a device for connecting parts of machinery. **2** *Mus.* **a** the arrangement of items on a gramophone record. **b** each such item.

coupon /ˈkuːpɒn/ n. **1** a form etc. in a newspaper, magazine, etc., which may be filled in and sent as an application for a purchase, information, etc. **2** *Brit.* an entry form for a football pool or other competition. **3** a voucher given with a retail purchase, a certain number of which entitle the holder to a discount etc. **4 a** a detachable ticket entitling the holder to a ration of food, clothes, etc., esp. in wartime. **b** a similar ticket entitling the holder to payment, goods, services, etc. [F, = piece cut off f. *couper* cut: see COUPÉ]

courage /ˈkʌrɪdʒ/ n. the ability to disregard fear; bravery. □ **courage of one's convictions** the courage to act on one's beliefs. **lose courage** become less brave. **pluck up** (or **take**) **courage** muster one's courage. [ME f. OF *corage*, f. L *cor* heart]

courageous /kəˈreɪdʒəs/ adj. brave, fearless. □ **courageously** adv. **courageousness** n. [ME f. AF *corageous*, OF *corageus* (as COURAGE)]

courgette /kʊəˈʒet/ n. a small green variety of vegetable marrow. [F, dimin. of *courge* gourd]

courier /ˈkʊrɪə(r)/ n. **1** a person employed, usu. by a travel company, to guide and assist a group of tourists. **2** a special messenger. [ME f. obs. F, f. It. *corriere*, & f. OF *coreor*, both f. L *currere* run]

course /kɔːs/ n. & v. —n. **1** a continuous onward movement or progression. **2 a** a line along which a person or thing moves; a direction taken (*has changed course*; *the course of the winding river*). **b** a correct or intended direction or line of movement. **c** the direction taken by a ship or aircraft. **3 a** the ground on which a race (or other sport involving extensive linear movement) takes place. **b** a series of fences, hurdles, or other obstacles to be crossed in a race etc. **4 a** a series of lectures, lessons, etc., in a particular subject. **b** a book for such a course. **5** any of the successive parts of a meal. **6** *Med.* a sequence of medical treatment etc. (*prescribed a course of*

antibiotics). **7** a line of conduct (*disappointed by the course he took*). **8** *Archit.* a continuous horizontal layer of brick, stone, etc., in a building. **9** a channel in which water flows. **10** the pursuit of game (esp. hares) with hounds, esp. greyhounds, by sight rather than scent. —v. **1** intr. (esp. of liquid) run, esp. fast (*blood coursed through his veins*). **2** tr. (also *absol.*) **a** use (hounds) to hunt. **b** pursue (hares etc.) in hunting. □ **the course of nature** ordinary events or procedure. **in course of** in the process of. **in the course of** during. **a matter of course** the natural or expected thing. **of course** naturally; as is or was to be expected; admittedly. **on** (or **off**) **course** following (or deviating from) the desired direction or goal. □ **courser** n. (in sense 2 of v.). [ME f. OF *cours* f. L *cursus* f. *currere curs-* run]

courser /ˈkɔːsə(r)/ n. *poet.* a swift horse. [ME f. OF *corsier* f. Rmc]

court /kɔːt/ n. & v. —n. **1** (in full **court of law**) **a** an assembly of judges or other persons acting as a tribunal in civil and criminal cases. **b** = COURTROOM. **2 a** an enclosed quadrangular area for games, which may be open or covered (*tennis-court*; *squash-court*). **b** an area marked out for lawn tennis etc. (*hit the ball out of court*). **3 a** a small enclosed street in a town, having a yard surrounded by houses, and adjoining a larger street. **b** *Brit.* = COURTYARD. **c** (**Court**) the name of a large house, block of flats, street, etc. (*Grosvenor Court*). **d** (at Cambridge University) a college quadrangle. **4 a** the establishment, retinue, and courtiers of a sovereign. **b** a sovereign and his or her councillors, constituting a ruling power. **c** a sovereign's residence. **d** an assembly held by a sovereign; a State reception. **5** attention paid to a person whose favour, love, or interest is sought (*paid court to her*). —v.tr. **1 a** try to win the affection or favour of (a person). **b** pay amorous attention to (*courting couples*). **2** seek to win (applause, fame, etc.). **3** invite (misfortune) by one's actions (*you are courting disaster*). □ **court-card** a playing-card that is a king, queen, or jack. **court-house 1** a building in which a judicial court is held. **2** *US* a building containing the administrative offices of a county. **Court of Appeal** a court of law hearing appeals against judgements in the Crown Court, High Court, County Court, etc. **Court of St James's** the British sovereign's court. **Court of Session** the supreme civil court in Scotland. **court order** a direction issued by a court or a judge, usu. requiring a person to do or not do something. **court shoe** a woman's light, usu. high-heeled, shoe with a low-cut upper. **go to court** take legal action. **in court** appearing as a party or an advocate in a court of law. **out of court 1** (of a plaintiff) not entitled to be heard. **2** (of a settlement) arranged before a hearing or judgement can take place. **3** not worthy of consideration (*that suggestion is out of court*). [ME f. AF *curt*, OF *cort*, ult. f. L *cohors*, *-hortis* yard, retinue: (v.) after OIt. *corteare*, OF *courtoyer*]

courteous /ˈkɜːtɪəs/ adj. polite, kind, or considerate in manner; well-mannered. □ **courteously** adv. **courteousness** n. [ME f. OF *corteis*, *curteis* f. Rmc (as COURT): assim. to words in -OUS]

courtesan /ˌkɔːtɪˈzæn, ˈkɔːt-/ n. *literary* **1** a prostitute, esp. one with wealthy or upper-class clients. **2** the mistress of a wealthy man. [F *courtisane* f. It. *cortigiana*, fem. of *cortigiano* courtier f. *corte* COURT]

courtesy /ˈkɜːtɪsɪ/ *n.* (*pl.* **-ies**) **1** courteous behaviour; good manners. **2** a courteous act. **3** *archaic* = CURTSY. □ **by courtesy** by favour, not by right. **by courtesy of** with the formal permission of (a person etc.). **courtesy light** a light in a car that is switched on by opening a door. **courtesy title** a title held by courtesy, usu. having no legal validity, e.g. a title given to the heir of a duke etc. [ME f. OF *curtesie*, *co(u)rtesie* f. *curteis* etc. COURTEOUS]

courtier /ˈkɔːtɪə(r)/ *n.* a person who attends or frequents a sovereign's court. [ME f. AF *courte(i)our*, f. OF f. *cortoyer* be present at court]

courtly /ˈkɔːtlɪ/ *adj.* (**courtlier**, **courtliest**) polished or refined in manners. □ **courtliness** *n.* [COURT]

court martial /ˌkɔːt ˈmɑːʃ(ə)l/ *n.* & *v.* —*n.* (*pl.* **courts martial**) a judicial court for trying members of the armed services. —*v.tr.* (**court-martial**) (**-martialled**, **-martialling**; *US* **-martialed**, **-martialing**) try by a court martial.

courtroom /ˈkɔːtruːm, -rʊm/ *n.* the place or room in which a court of law meets.

courtship /ˈkɔːtʃɪp/ *n.* **1 a** courting with a view to marriage. **b** the courting behaviour of male animals, birds, etc. **c** a period of courting. **2** an attempt to gain advantage by flattery, attention, etc.

courtyard /ˈkɔːtjɑːd/ *n.* an area enclosed by walls or buildings, often opening off a street.

couscous /ˈkuːskuːs/ *n.* a N. African dish of wheat grain or coarse flour steamed over broth, often with meat added. [F f. Arab. *kuskus* f. *kaskasa* to pound]

cousin /ˈkʌz(ə)n/ *n.* **1** (also **first cousin, cousin-german**) the child of one's uncle or aunt. **2** (usu. in *pl.*) applied to the people of kindred races or nations (*our American cousins*). **3** *hist.* a title formerly used by a sovereign in addressing another. □ **second cousin** a child of one's parent's first cousin. □ **cousinhood** *n.* **cousinly** *adj.* **cousinship** *n.* [ME f. OF *cosin*, *cusin*, f. L *consobrinus* mother's sister's child]

■ **Usage** There is often confusion about the difference between *cousin*, *first cousin*, *second cousin*, *first cousin once removed*, etc. For definitions see *cousin*, *second cousin*, and *remove* v.7.

couture /kuːˈtjʊə(r)/ *n.* the design and manufacture of fashionable clothes; = HAUTE COUTURE. [F, = sewing, dressmaking]

couturier /kuːˈtjʊərɪˌeɪ/ *n.* (*fem.* **couturière** /-ˌrɪˈeə(r)/) a fashion designer or dressmaker. [F]

covalency /kəʊˈveɪlənsɪ/ *n. Chem.* **1** the linking of atoms by a covalent bond. **2** the number of pairs of electrons an atom can share with another.

covalent /kəʊˈveɪlənt/ *adj. Chem.* of, relating to, or characterized by covalency. □ **covalent bond** *Chem.* a bond formed by sharing of electrons usu. in pairs by two atoms in a molecule. □ **covalence** *n.* **covalently** *adv.* [CO- + *valent*, after *trivalent* etc.]

cove¹ *n.* & *v.* —*n.* **1** a small, esp. sheltered, bay or creek. **2** a sheltered recess. **3** *Archit.* a concave arch or arched moulding, esp. one formed at the junction of a wall with a ceiling. —*v.tr.*

Archit. **1** provide (a room, ceiling, etc.) with a cove. **2** slope (the sides of a fireplace) inwards. [OE *cofa* chamber f. Gmc]

cove² *n. Brit. sl. archaic* a fellow; a chap. [16th-c. cant: orig. unkn.]

coven /ˈkʌv(ə)n/ *n.* an assembly of witches. [var. of *covent*; see CONVENT]

covenant /ˈkʌvənənt/ *n.* & *v.* —*n.* **1** an agreement; a contract. **2** *Law* **a** a contract drawn up under a seal, esp. undertaking to make regular payments to a charity. **b** a clause of a covenant. **3** (**Covenant**) *Bibl.* the agreement between God and the Israelites (see *Ark of the Covenant*). —*v.tr.* & *intr.* agree, esp. by legal covenant. □ **covenantal** /-ˈnænt(ə)l/ *adj.* **covenantor** *n.* [ME f. OF, pres. part. of *co(n)venir*, formed as CONVENE]

covenanter /ˈkʌvənəntə(r)/ *n.* **1** a person who covenants. **2** (**Covenanter**) *hist.* an adherent of the National Covenant or the Solemn League and Covenant in 17th-c. Scotland, in support of Presbyterianism.

Coventry /ˈkɒvəntrɪ/ *n.* □ **send a person to Coventry** refuse to associate with or speak to a person. [*Coventry* in W. Midlands]

cover /ˈkʌvə(r)/ *v.* & *n.* —*v.tr.* **1** (often foll. by *with*) protect or conceal by means of a cloth, lid, etc. **2 a** extend over; occupy the whole surface of (*covered in dirt*; *covered with writing*). **b** (often foll. by *with*) strew thickly or thoroughly (*covered the floor with straw*). **c** lie over; be a covering to (*the blanket scarcely covered him*). **3 a** protect; clothe. **b** (as **covered** *adj.*) wearing a hat; having a roof. **4** include; comprise; deal with (*the talk covered recent discoveries*). **5** travel (a specified distance) (*covered sixty miles*). **6** *Journalism* report (events, a meeting, etc.). **b** investigate as a reporter. **7** be enough to defray (expenses, a bill, etc.). **8 a** *refl.* take precautionary measures so as to protect oneself (*had covered myself by saying I might be late*). **b** (*absol.*; foll. by *for*) deputize or stand in for (a colleague etc.) (*will you cover for me?*). **9** *Mil.* **a** aim a gun etc. at. **b** (of a fortress, guns, etc.) command (a territory). **c** protect (an exposed person etc.) by being able to return fire. **10 a** esp. *Cricket* stand behind (another player) to stop any missed balls. **b** (in team games) mark (a corresponding player of the other side). **11** (of a stallion, a bull, etc.) copulate with. —*n.* **1** something that covers or protects, esp.: **a** a lid. **b** the binding of a book. **c** either board of this. **d** an envelope or the wrapper of a parcel (*under separate cover*). **e** (in *pl.*) bedclothes. **2** a hiding-place; a shelter. **3** woods or undergrowth sheltering game or covering the ground (see COVERT). **4 a** a pretence; a screen (*under cover of humility*). **b** a spy's pretended identity or activity, intended as concealment. **c** *Mil.* a supporting force protecting an advance party from attack. **5 a** funds, esp. obtained by insurance, to meet a liability or secure against a contingent loss. **b** the state of being protected (*third-party cover*). **6** a place setting at table, esp. in a restaurant. **7** *Cricket* = *cover-point*. □ **break cover** (of an animal, esp. game, or a hunted person) leave a place of shelter, esp. vegetation. **cover charge** an extra charge levied per head in a restaurant, nightclub, etc. **cover girl** a female model whose picture appears on magazine covers etc. **cover in** provide with a roof etc. **covering letter** (or **note**) an explanatory letter sent with an enclosure. **cover note** *Brit.* a temporary certificate of current insurance. **cover-point** *Cricket* **1** a fielding position on the off side and halfway to the boundary. **2** a fielder at this position. **cover story** a news story in a magazine, that is illustrated or advertised on the front cover. **cover one's tracks** conceal evidence of what one has done. **cover up 1** completely cover or conceal. **2** conceal (circumstances etc., esp. illicitly) (also *absol.: refused to cover up for them*). **cover-up** *n.* an act of concealing circumstances, esp. illicitly. **take cover** use a natural or prepared shelter against an attack. □ **coverable** *adj.* **coverer** *n.* [ME f. OF *covrir, cuvrir* f. L *cooperire* (as CO-, *operire opert-* cover)]

coverage /ˈkʌvərɪdʒ/ *n.* **1** an area or an amount covered. **2** *Journalism* the amount of press etc. publicity received by a particular story, person, etc. **3** a risk covered by an insurance policy.

coverall /ˈkʌvərɔːl/ *n.* & *adj.* esp. *US* —*n.* **1** something that covers entirely. **2** (usu. in *pl.*) a full-length protective outer garment often zipped up the front. —*attrib.adj.* covering entirely (*a coverall term*).

covering /ˈkʌvərɪŋ/ *n.* something that covers, esp. a bedspread, blanket, etc., or clothing.

coverlet /ˈkʌvəlɪt/ *n.* a bedspread. [ME f. AF *covrelet, -lit* f. OF *covrir* cover + *lit* bed]

covert /ˈkʌvət/ *adj.* & *n.* —*adj.* secret or disguised (*a covert glance*). —*n.* **1** a shelter, esp. a thicket hiding game. **2** a feather covering the base of a bird's flight-feather. □ **covertly** *adv.* **covertness** *n.* [ME f. OF *covert* past part. of *covrir* COVER]

covet /ˈkʌvɪt/ *v.tr.* (**coveted, coveting**) desire greatly (esp. something belonging to another person). □ **covetable** *adj.* [ME f. OF *cu-, coveitier* f. Rmc]

covetous /ˈkʌvɪtəs/ *adj.* (usu. foll. by *of*) **1** greatly desirous (esp. of another person's property). **2** grasping, avaricious. □ **covetously** *adv.* **covetousness** *n.* [ME f. OF *coveitous* f. Gallo-Roman]

covey /ˈkʌvɪ/ *n.* (*pl.* -**eys**) **1** a brood of partridges. **2** a small party or group of people or things. [ME f. OF *covee* f. Rmc f. L *cubare* lie]

coving *n.* = COVE[1] *n.* 3.

cow[1] /kaʊ/ *n.* **1** a fully grown female of any bovine animal, esp. of the genus *Bos*, used as a source of milk and beef. **2** the female of other large animals, esp. the elephant, whale, and seal. **3** *derog. sl.* **a** a woman esp. a coarse or unpleasant one. **b** *Austral.* & *NZ* an unpleasant person, thing, situation, etc. □ **cow-heel** the foot of a cow or an ox stewed to a jelly. **cow-lick** a projecting lock of hair. **cow-parsley** a hedgerow plant *Anthriscus sylvestris*, having lacelike umbels of flowers. **cow-pat** a flat round piece of cow-dung. **till the cows come home** *colloq.* an indefinitely long time. [OE *cū* f. Gmc, rel. to L *bos*, Gk *bous*]

cow[2] /kaʊ/ *v.tr.* (usu. in *passive*) intimidate or dispirit (*cowed by ill-treatment*). [prob. f. ON *kúga* oppress]

coward /ˈkaʊəd/ *n.* & *adj.* —*n.* a person who is easily frightened or intimidated by danger or pain. —*adj. poet.* easily frightened. [ME f. OF *cuard, couard* ult. f. L *cauda* tail]

cowardice /ˈkaʊədɪs/ *n.* a lack of bravery. [ME f. OF *couardise* (as COWARD)]

cowardly /ˈkaʊədlɪ/ *adj.* & *adv.* —*adj.* **1** of or like a coward; lacking courage. **2** (of an action) done against one who cannot retaliate.

—*adv. archaic* like a coward; with cowardice. □ **cowardliness** *n.*

cowbell /ˈkaʊbel/ *n.* **1** a bell worn round a cow's neck for easy location of the animal. **2** a similar bell used as a percussion instrument.

cowboy /ˈkaʊbɔɪ/ *n.* **1** (*fem.* **cowgirl**) a person who herds and tends cattle, esp. in the western US. **2** this as a conventional figure in American folklore, esp. in films. **3** *colloq.* an unscrupulous or reckless person in business, esp. an unqualified one.

cowcatcher /ˈkaʊˌkætʃə(r)/ *n.* *US* a peaked metal frame at the front of a locomotive for pushing aside obstacles on the line.

cower /ˈkaʊə(r)/ *v.intr.* **1** crouch or shrink back, esp. in fear; cringe. **2** stand or squat in a bent position. [ME f. MLG *kūren* lie in wait, of unkn. orig.]

cowherd /ˈkaʊhɜːd/ *n.* a person who tends cattle.

cowhide /ˈkaʊhaɪd/ *n.* **1 a** a cow's hide. **b** leather made from this. **2** a leather whip made from cowhide.

cowl /kaʊl/ *n.* **1 a** the hood of a monk's habit. **b** a loose hood. **c** a monk's hooded habit. **2** the hood-shaped covering of a chimney or ventilating shaft. **3** the removable cover of a vehicle or aircraft engine. □ **cowled** *adj.* (in sense 1). [OE *cugele, cūle* f. eccl.L *cuculla* f. L *cucullus* hood of a cloak]

cowling /ˈkaʊlɪŋ/ *n.* = COWL 3.

cowman /ˈkaʊmən/ *n.* (*pl.* -**men**) **1** = COWHERD. **2** *US* a cattle-owner.

co-worker /kəʊˈwɜːkə(r)/ *n.* a person who works in collaboration with another.

cowpox /ˈkaʊpɒks/ *n.* a disease of cows, of which the virus was formerly used in vaccination against smallpox.

cowrie /ˈkaʊrɪ/ *n.* (also **cowry**) (*pl.* -**ies**) **1** any gastropod mollusc of the family Cypraeidae, having a smooth glossy and usu. brightly-coloured shell. **2** its shell, esp. used as money in parts of Africa and S. Asia. [Urdu & Hindi *kaurī*]

cowshed /ˈkaʊʃed/ *n.* **1** a shed for cattle that are not at pasture. **2** a milking-shed.

cowslip /ˈkaʊslɪp/ *n.* **1** a primula, *Primula veris*, with fragrant yellow flowers and growing in pastures. **2** *US* a marsh marigold. [OE *cūslyppe* f. *cū* COW[1] + *slyppe* slimy substance, i.e. cow-dung]

Cox /kɒks/ *n.* (in full **Cox's orange pippin**) a variety of eating-apple with a red-tinged green skin. [R. *Cox*, amateur Eng. fruit grower d. 1825]

cox /kɒks/ *n.* & *v.* —*n.* a coxswain, esp. of a racing-boat. —*v.* **1** *intr.* act as a cox (*coxed for Cambridge*). **2** *tr.* act as cox for (*coxed the winning boat*). [abbr.]

coxcomb /ˈkɒkskəʊm/ *n.* an ostentatiously conceited man; a dandy. □ **coxcombry** /-kəmrɪ/ *n.* (*pl.* -**ies**). [= *cock's comb* (see COCK[1]), orig. (a cap worn by) a jester]

coxswain /ˈkɒkswein, -s(ə)n/ *n.* & *v.* —*n.* **1** a person who steers, esp. in a rowing-boat. **2** the senior petty officer in a small ship. —*v.* **1** *intr.* act as a coxswain. **2** *tr.* act as a coxswain of. □ **coxswainship** *n.* [ME f. obs. *cock* small boat (f. OF *coque*) + swain: cf. BOATSWAIN]

coy /kɔɪ/ *adj.* (**coyer, coyest**) **1** archly or affectedly shy. **2** irritatingly reticent (*always coy about her age*). **3** (esp. of a girl) modest or shy. □ **coyly** *adv.* **coyness** *n.* [ME f. OF *coi, quei* f. L *quietus* QUIET]

coyote /kɔɪˈəʊtɪ, ˈkɔɪəʊt/ n. (pl. same or **coyotes**) a wolflike wild dog, *Canis latrans*, native to N. America. [Mex. Sp. f. Aztec *coyotl*]

coypu /ˈkɔɪpuː/ n. (pl. **coypus**) an aquatic beaver-like rodent, *Myocastor coypus*, native to S. America. [Araucan]

cozen /ˈkʌz(ə)n/ v. *literary* 1 tr. (often foll. by *of*, *out of*) cheat, defraud. 2 tr. (often foll. by *into*) beguile; persuade. 3 intr. act deceitfully. □ **cozenage** n. [16th-c. cant, perh. rel. to COUSIN]

cozy *US* var. of COSY.

c.p. abbr. candlepower.

Cpl. abbr. Corporal.

CPO abbr. Chief Petty Officer.

cps abbr. (also **c.p.s.**) 1 *Computing* characters per second. 2 cycles per second.

Cr symb. *Chem.* the element chromium.

crab[1] n. 1 a any of numerous ten-footed crustaceans having the first pair of legs modified as pincers. b the flesh of a crab, esp. *Cancer pagurus*, as food. 2 (**the Crab**) the zodiacal sign or constellation Cancer. 3 (in full **crab-louse**) (often in *pl.*) a parasitic louse, *Phthirus pubis*, infesting hairy parts of the body. □ **catch a crab** *Rowing* effect a faulty stroke in which the oar is jammed under water or misses the water altogether. **crab-grass** *US* a creeping grass infesting lawns. □ **crablike** adj. [OE *crabba*, rel. to ON *krafla* scratch]

crab[2] n. 1 (in full **crab-apple**) a small sour apple-like fruit. 2 (in full **crab tree** or **crab-apple tree**) any of several trees bearing this fruit. [ME, perh. alt. (after CRAB[1] or CRABBED) of earlier *scrab*, prob. of Scand. orig.]

crab[3] v. (**crabbed**, **crabbing**) *colloq.* 1 tr. & intr. criticize adversely or captiously; grumble. 2 tr. act so as to spoil (*the mistake crabbed his chances*). [orig. of hawks fighting, f. MLG *krabben*]

crabbed /ˈkræbɪd/ adj. 1 irritable or morose. 2 (of handwriting) ill-formed and hard to decipher. 3 perverse or cross-grained. □ **crabbedly** adv. **crabbedness** n. [ME f. CRAB[1], assoc. with CRAB[2]]

crabby /ˈkræbɪ/ adj. (**crabbier**, **crabbiest**) = CRABBED 1,3. □ **crabbily** adv. **crabbiness** n.

crabwise /ˈkræbwaɪz/ adv. & attrib.adj. (of movement) sideways or backwards like a crab.

crack n., v., & adj. —n. 1 a a sudden sharp or explosive noise (*the crack of a whip; a rifle crack*). b (in a voice) a sudden harshness or change in pitch. 2 a sharp blow (*a crack on the head*). 3 a a narrow opening formed by a break (*entered through a crack in the wall*). b a partial fracture, with the parts still joined (*the teacup has a crack in it*). c a chink (*looked through the crack formed by the door; a crack of light*). 4 *colloq.* a mischievous or malicious remark or aside (*a nasty crack about my age*). 5 *colloq.* an attempt (*I'll have a crack at it*). 6 the exact moment (*at the crack of noon; the crack of dawn*). 7 *colloq.* a first-rate player, horse, etc. 8 *dial. colloq.* conversation; good company; fun (*only went there for the crack*). 9 *sl.* a crystalline form of cocaine inhaled or smoked for its stimulating effect. —v. 1 tr. & intr. break without a complete separation of the parts (*cracked the window; the cup cracked on hitting the floor*). 2 intr. & tr. make or cause to make a sudden sharp or explosive sound. 3 intr. & tr. break or cause to break with a sudden sharp sound. 4 intr. & tr. give way or cause to give way (under torture etc.); yield. 5 intr. (of the voice, esp. of an adolescent boy or a person under strain) become

dissonant; break. 6 tr. *colloq.* find a solution to (a problem, code, etc.). 7 tr. say (a joke etc.) in a jocular way. 8 tr. *colloq.* hit sharply or hard (*cracked her head on the ceiling*). 9 tr. *Chem.* decompose (heavy oils) to produce lighter hydrocarbons (such as petrol). 10 tr. break (wheat) into coarse pieces. —attrib.adj. *colloq.* excellent; first-rate (*a crack regiment; a crack shot*). □ **crack a bottle** open a bottle, esp. of wine, and drink it. **crack-brained** crazy. **crack-down** *colloq.* severe measures (esp. against law-breakers etc.). **crack down on** *colloq.* take severe measures against. **crack up** *colloq.* 1 collapse under strain. 2 praise. **crack-up** n. *colloq.* a mental breakdown. **get cracking** *colloq.* begin promptly and vigorously. [OE *cracian* resound]

cracked /krækt/ adj. 1 having cracks. 2 (*predic.*) *sl.* crazy. □ **cracked wheat** wheat that has been crushed into small pieces.

cracker /ˈkrækə(r)/ n. 1 a paper cylinder both ends of which are pulled at Christmas etc. making a sharp noise and releasing a small toy etc. 2 a firework exploding with a sharp noise. 3 (usu. in *pl.*) an instrument for cracking (*nutcrackers*). 4 a thin dry biscuit often eaten with cheese. 5 *sl. Brit.* a notable or attractive person. 6 *US* a biscuit. □ **cracker-barrel** *US* (of philosophy etc.) homespun; unsophisticated.

crackers /ˈkrækəz/ predic.adj. *Brit. sl.* crazy.

cracking /ˈkrækɪŋ/ adj. & adv. *sl.* —adj. 1 outstanding; very good (*a cracking performance*). 2 (*attrib.*) fast and exciting (*a cracking speed*). —adv. outstandingly (*a cracking good time*).

crackle /ˈkræk(ə)l/ v. & n. —v.intr. make a repeated slight cracking sound. —n. 1 such a sound. 2 a paintwork, china, or glass decorated with a pattern of minute surface cracks. b the smooth surface of such paintwork etc. □ **crackly** adj. [CRACK + -LE[4]]

crackling /ˈkræklɪŋ/ n. 1 the crisp skin of roast pork. 2 *joc.* or *offens.* attractive women regarded collectively as objects of sexual desire.

cracknel /ˈkrækn(ə)l/ n. a light crisp biscuit. [ME f. F *craquelin* f. MDu. *krākelinc* f. *krāken* CRACK]

crackpot /ˈkrækpɒt/ n. & adj. *sl.* —n. an eccentric or impractical person. —adj. mad, unworkable (*a crackpot scheme*).

-cracy /krəsɪ/ comb. form denoting a particular form of government, rule, or influence (*aristocracy; bureaucracy*). [from or after F *-cratie* f. med.L *-cratia* f. Gk *-kratia* f. *kratos* strength, power]

cradle /ˈkreɪd(ə)l/ n. & v. —n. 1 a a child's bed or cot, esp. one mounted on rockers. b a place in which a thing begins, esp. a civilization etc., or is nurtured in its infancy. 2 a framework resembling a cradle, esp.: a that on which a ship, a boat, etc., rests during construction or repairs. b that on which a worker is suspended to work on a ceiling, a ship, the vertical side of a building, etc. c the part of a telephone on which the receiver rests when not in use. —v.tr. 1 contain or shelter as if in a cradle (*cradled his head in her arms*). 2 place in a cradle. □ **from the cradle** from infancy. **from the cradle to the grave** from infancy till death (esp. of State welfare). [OE *cradol*, perh. rel. to OHG *kratto* basket]

craft /krɑːft/ n. & v. —n. 1 skill, esp. in practical arts. 2 a (esp. in *comb.*) a trade or an art (*statecraft; handicraft; the craft of pottery*). b the members of a craft. **3** (*pl.* **craft**) **a** a boat or vessel. **b** an aircraft or spacecraft. **4** cunning or deceit. —*v.tr.* make in a skilful way (*a well-crafted piece of work*). [OE cræft]

craftsman /ˈkrɑːftsmən/ *n.* (*pl.* **-men**; *fem.* **craftswoman**, *pl.* **-women**) **1** a skilled and usu. time-served worker. **2** a person who practises a handicraft. **3** a private soldier in the Royal Electrical and Mechanical Engineers. □ **craftsmanship** *n.* [ME, orig. *craft's man*]

crafty /ˈkrɑːftɪ/ *adj.* (**craftier**, **craftiest**) cunning, artful, wily. □ **craftily** *adv.* **craftiness** *n.* [OE cræftig]

crag *n. Brit.* a steep or rugged rock. [ME, of Celt. orig.]

craggy /ˈkrægɪ/ *adj.* (**craggier**, **craggiest**) **1** (esp. of a person's face) rugged; rough-textured. **2** (of a landscape) having crags. □ **craggily** *adv.* **cragginess** *n.*

crake *n.* any rail (see RAIL³), esp. a corncrake. [ME f. ON *kráka* (imit.): cf. CROAK]

cram *v.* (**crammed**, **cramming**) **1** *tr.* **a** fill to bursting; stuff (*the room was crammed*). **b** (foll. by *in*, *into*) force a (thing) into (*cram the sandwiches into the bag*). **2** *tr. & intr.* prepare for an examination by intensive study. **3** *tr.* (often foll. by *with*) feed (poultry etc.) to excess. □ **cram-full** as full as possible. [OE *crammian* f. Gmc]

crammer /ˈkræmə(r)/ *n.* a person or institution that crams pupils for examinations.

cramp /kræmp/ *n. & v.* —*n.* **1 a** a painful involuntary contraction of a muscle or muscles from the cold, exertion, etc. **b** = *writer's cramp.* **2** (also **cramp-iron**) a metal bar with bent ends for holding masonry etc. together. **3** a portable tool for holding two planks etc. together; a clamp. **4** a restraint. —*v.tr.* **1** affect with cramp. **2** confine narrowly. **3** restrict (energies etc.). **4** (as **cramped** *adj.*) (of handwriting) small and difficult to read. **5** fasten with a cramp. □ **cramp a person's style** prevent a person from acting freely or naturally. [ME f. OF *crampe* f. MDu., MLG *krampe*, OHG *krampfo* f. adj. meaning 'bent': cf. CRIMP]

crampon /ˈkræmpən/ *n.* (*US* **crampoon** /-ˈpuːn/) (usu. in *pl.*) an iron plate with spikes fixed to a boot for walking on ice, climbing, etc. [ME f. F (as CRAMP)]

cranberry /ˈkrænbərɪ/ *n.* (*pl.* **-ies**) **1** any evergreen shrub of the genus *Vaccinium*, esp. *V. macrocarpon* of America and *V. oxycoccos* of Europe, yielding small red acid berries. **2** a berry from this used in cooking. [17th c.: named by Amer. colonists f. G *Kranbeere*, LG *kranebere* crane-berry]

crane /kreɪn/ *n. & v.* —*n.* **1** a machine for moving heavy objects, usu. by suspending them from a projecting arm or beam. **2** any tall wading bird of the family Gruidae, with long legs, long neck, and straight bill. **3** a moving platform supporting a television camera or cine-camera. —*v.tr.* **1** (also *absol.*) stretch out (one's neck) in order to see something. **2** *tr.* move (an object) by a crane. □ **crane-fly** (*pl.* **-flies**) any fly of the family Tipulidae, having two wings and long legs. [OE *cran*, rel. to L *grus*, Gk *geranos*]

cranesbill /ˈkreɪnzbɪl/ *n.* any of various plants of the genus *Geranium*, having beaked fruits.

cranial /ˈkreɪnɪəl/ *adj.* of or relating to the skull. □ **cranial index** the ratio of the width and length of a skull. [CRANIUM + -AL]

cranio- /ˈkreɪnɪəʊ/ *comb. form* cranium.

craniology /ˌkreɪnɪˈɒlədʒɪ/ *n.* the scientific study of the shape and size of the human skull. □ **craniological** /ˌkreɪnɪəˈlɒdʒɪk(ə)l/ *adj.* **craniologist** *n.*

cranium /ˈkreɪnɪəm/ *n.* (*pl.* **craniums** or **crania** /-nɪə/) **1** the skull. **2** the part of the skeleton that encloses the brain. [ME f. med.L f. Gk *kranion* skull]

crank¹ *n. & v.* —*n.* part of an axle or shaft bent at right angles for interconverting reciprocal and circular motion. —*v.tr.* cause to move by means of a crank. □ **crank up 1** start (a car engine) by turning a crank. **2** *sl.* increase (speed etc.) by intensive effort. [OE *cranc*, app. f. *crincan*, rel. to *cringan* fall in battle, orig. 'curl up']

crank² *n.* **1** an eccentric person, esp. one obsessed by a particular theory (*health-food crank*). **2** *US* a bad-tempered person. [back-form. f. CRANKY]

crankcase /ˈkræŋkkeɪs/ *n.* a case enclosing a crankshaft.

crankpin /ˈkræŋkpɪn/ *n.* a pin by which a connecting-rod is attached to a crank.

crankshaft /ˈkræŋkʃɑːft/ *n.* a shaft driven by a crank (see CRANK¹ *n.*).

cranky /ˈkræŋkɪ/ *adj.* (**crankier**, **crankiest**) **1** *colloq.* eccentric, esp. obsessed with a particular theory. **2** shaky. **3** esp. *US* ill-tempered or crotchety. □ **crankily** *adv.* **crankiness** *n.* [perh. f. obs. *crank* rogue feigning sickness]

cranny /ˈkrænɪ/ *n.* (*pl.* **-ies**) a chink, a crevice, a crack. □ **crannied** /-ɪd/ *adj.* [ME f. OF *crané* past part. of *craner* f. *cran* f. pop.L *crena* notch]

crap *n. & v. coarse sl.* —*n.* **1** (often as *int.*) nonsense, rubbish (*he talks crap*). **2** faeces. —*v.intr.* (**crapped**, **crapping**) defecate. [earlier senses 'chaff, refuse from fat-boiling': ME f. Du. *krappe*]

crape *n.* crêpe, usu. of black silk or imitation silk, formerly used for mourning clothes. □ **crape hair** artificial hair used in stage make-up. □ **crapy** *adj.* [earlier *crispe*, *crespe* f. F *crespe* CRÊPE]

crappy /ˈkræpɪ/ *adj.* (**crappier**, **crappiest**) *coarse sl.* **1** rubbishy, cheap. **2** disgusting.

craps *n.pl. US* a gambling game played with dice. □ **shoot craps** play craps. [19th c.: perh. f. *crab* lowest throw at dice]

crapulent /ˈkræpjʊlənt/ *adj.* **1** given to indulging in alcohol. **2** resulting from drunkenness. **3 a** drunk. **b** suffering from the effects of drunkenness. □ **crapulence** *n.* **crapulous** *adj.* [LL *crapulentus* very drunk f. L *crapula* inebriation f. Gk *kraipalē* drunken headache]

crash¹ *v., n., & adv.* —*v.* **1** *intr. & tr.* make or cause to make a loud smashing noise (*the cymbals crashed; crashed the plates together*). **2** *tr. & intr.* throw, drive, move, or fall with a loud smashing noise. **3** *intr. & tr.* **a** collide or cause (a vehicle) to collide violently with another vehicle, obstacle, etc.; overturn at high speed. **b** fall or cause (an aircraft) to fall violently on to the land or the sea. **4** *intr.* (usu. foll. by *into*) collide violently (*crashed into the window*). **5** *intr.* undergo financial ruin. **6** *tr. colloq.* enter without permission (*crashed the cocktail party*). **7** *intr. colloq.* be heavily defeated (*crashed to a 4–0 defeat*). **8** *intr. Computing* (of a machine or system) fail suddenly. **9** *tr.* *colloq.* pass (a red traffic-light etc.). **10** *intr.* (often foll. by *out*) *sl.* sleep for a night, esp. in an improvised setting. —*n.* **1 a** a loud and sudden smashing noise (*a thunder crash*; *the crash of crockery*). **b** a breakage (esp. of crockery, glass, etc.). **2 a** a violent collision, esp. of one vehicle with another or with an object. **b** the violent fall of an aircraft on to the land or sea. **3** ruin, esp. financial. **4** *Computing* a sudden failure which puts a system out of action. **5** (*attrib.*) done rapidly or urgently (*a crash course in first aid*). —*adv.* with a crash (*the window went crash*). □ **crash barrier** a barrier intended to prevent a car from leaving the road etc. **crash-dive** —*v.* **1** *intr.* **a** (of a submarine or its pilot) dive hastily and steeply in an emergency. **b** (of an aircraft or airman) dive and crash. **2** *tr.* cause to crash-dive. —*n.* such a dive. **crash-helmet** a helmet worn esp. by a motorcyclist to protect the head in a crash. **crash-land 1** *intr.* (of an aircraft or airman) land hurriedly with a crash, usu. without lowering the undercarriage. **2** *tr.* cause (an aircraft) to crash-land. **crash landing** a hurried landing with a crash. [ME: imit.]

crash² *n.* a coarse plain linen, cotton, etc., fabric. [Russ. *krashenina* coloured linen]

crashing /ˈkræʃɪŋ/ *adj. colloq.* overwhelming (*a crashing bore*).

crass *adj.* **1** grossly stupid (*a crass idea*). **2** gross (*crass stupidity*). □ **crassitude** *n.* **crassly** *adv.* **crassness** *n.* [L *crassus* solid, thick]

-crat /kræt/ *comb. form* a member or supporter of a particular form of government or rule (*autocrat*; *democrat*). [from or after F *-crate*: see -CRACY]

crate *n. & v.* —*n.* **1** a large wickerwork basket or slatted wooden case etc. for packing esp. fragile goods for transportation. **2** *sl.* an old aeroplane or other vehicle. —*v.tr.* pack in a crate. □ **crateful** *n.* (*pl.* **-fuls**). [ME, perh. f. Du. *krat* basket etc.]

crater /ˈkreɪtə(r)/ *n. & v.* —*n.* **1** the mouth of a volcano. **2** a bowl-shaped cavity, esp. that made by the explosion of a shell or bomb. **3** *Astron.* a hollow with a raised rim on the surface of a planet or moon, caused by the impact of a meteorite. —*v.tr.* form a crater in. □ **craterous** *adj.* [L f. Gk *kratēr* mixing-bowl]

-cratic /ˈkrætɪk/ *comb. form* (also **-cratical**) denoting a particular kind of government or rule (*autocratic*; *democratic*). □ **-cratically** *comb. form* (*adv.*) [from or after F *-cratique*: see -CRACY]

cravat /krəˈvæt/ *n.* a scarf worn by men inside an open-necked shirt. □ **cravatted** *adj.* [F *cravate* f. G *Krawat*, *Kroat* f. Serbo-Croatian *Hrvat* Croat]

crave *v.* **1** *tr.* **a** long for (*craved affection*). **b** beg for (*craves a blessing*). **2** *intr.* (foll. by *for*) long for; beg for (*craved for comfort*). □ **craver** *n.* [OE *crafian*, rel. to ON *krefja*]

craven /ˈkreɪv(ə)n/ *adj. & n.* —*adj.* (of a person, behaviour, etc.) cowardly; abject. —*n.* a cowardly person. □ **cravenly** *adv.* **cravenness** *n.* [ME *cravand* etc. perh. f. OF *cravanté* defeated, past part. of *cravanter* ult. f. L *crepare* burst; assim. to -EN³]

craving /ˈkreɪvɪŋ/ *n.* (usu. foll. by *for*) a strong desire or longing.

craw *n. Zool.* the crop of a bird or insect. □ **stick in one's craw** be unacceptable. [ME, rel. to MDu. *crāghe*, MLG *krage*, MHG *krage* neck, throat]

crawfish /ˈkrɔːfɪʃ/ *n.* (*pl.* same) a large marine spiny lobster. [var. of CRAYFISH]

crawl *v. & n.* —*v.intr.* **1** move slowly, esp. on hands and knees. **2** (of an insect, snake, etc.) move slowly with the body close to the ground etc. **3** walk or move slowly (*the train crawled into the station*). **4** (often foll. by *to*) *colloq.* behave obsequiously or ingratiatingly in the hope of advantage. **5** (often foll. by *with*) be covered or filled with crawling or moving things, or with people etc. compared to this. **6** (esp. of the skin) feel a creepy sensation. —*n.* **1** an act of crawling. **2** a slow rate of movement. **3** a high-speed swimming stroke with alternate overarm movements and rapid straight-legged kicks. □ **crawlingly** *adv.* **crawly** *adj.* (in senses 5, 6 of *v.*). [ME: orig. unkn.: cf. Sw. *kravla*, Da. *kravle*]

crawler /ˈkrɔːlə(r)/ *n.* **1** *sl.* a person who behaves obsequiously in the hope of advantage. **2** anything that crawls, esp. an insect.

cray *n. Austral. & NZ* = CRAYFISH.

crayfish /ˈkreɪfɪʃ/ *n.* (*pl.* same) **1** a small lobster-like freshwater crustacean. **2** a crawfish. [ME f. OF *crevice*, *crevis*, ult. f. OHG *krebiz* CRAB¹: assim. to FISH¹]

crayon /ˈkreɪən, -ɒn/ *n. & v.* —*n.* **1** a stick or pencil of coloured chalk, wax, etc. used for drawing. **2** a drawing made with this. —*v.tr.* draw with crayons. [F f. *craie* f. L *creta* chalk]

craze *v. & n.* —*v.* **1** *tr.* (usu. as **crazed** *adj.*) make insane (*crazed with grief*). **2 a** *tr.* produce fine surface cracks on (pottery glaze etc.). **b** *intr.* develop such cracks. —*n.* **1** a usu. temporary enthusiasm (*a craze for hula hoops*). **2** the object of this. [ME, orig. = break, shatter, perh. f. ON]

crazy /ˈkreɪzɪ/ *adj.* (**crazier**, **craziest**) **1** *colloq.* (of a person, an action, etc.) insane or mad; foolish. **2** *colloq.* (usu. foll. by *about*) extremely enthusiastic. **3** *sl.* **a** exciting, unrestrained. **b** excellent. **4** (*attrib.*) (of paving, a quilt, etc.) made of irregular pieces fitted together. □ **like crazy** *colloq.* = *like mad.* □ **crazily** *adv.* **craziness** *n.*

creak *n. & v.* —*n.* a harsh scraping or squeaking sound. —*v.intr.* **1** make a creak. **2 a** move with a creaking noise. **b** move stiffly and awkwardly. **c** show weakness or frailty under strain. □ **creakingly** *adv.* [ME, imit.: cf. CRAKE, CROAK]

creaky /ˈkriːkɪ/ *adj.* (**creakier**, **creakiest**) **1** liable to creak. **2 a** stiff or frail (*creaky joints*). **b** (of a practice, institution, etc.) decrepit, dilapidated, outmoded. □ **creakily** *adv.* **creakiness** *n.*

cream *n., v., & adj.* —*n.* **1** the fatty content of milk which gathers at the top and can be made into butter by churning. **2** the part of a liquid that gathers at the top. **3** (usu. prec. by *the*) best or choicest part of something, esp.: **a** the point of an anecdote. **b** an élite group of people (*the cream of the nation*). **4** a creamlike preparation, esp. a cosmetic (*hand cream*). **5** a very pale yellow or off-white colour. **6 a** a dish or sweet like or made with cream. **b** a soup or sauce containing milk or cream. **c** a full-bodied mellow sweet sherry. **d** a biscuit with a creamy sandwich filling. **e** a chocolate-covered usu. fruit-flavoured fondant. —*v.* **1** *tr.* **a** take the cream from (milk). **b** take the best or a specified part from. **2** *tr.* work (butter etc.) to a creamy consistency. **3** *tr.* treat (the skin etc.) with cosmetic cream. **4** *intr.* (of milk or any other liquid) form a cream or scum. —*adj.* pale yellow; off-white. □ **cream cheese** a soft rich cheese made from unskimmed milk and cream. **cream cracker** *Brit.* a crisp dry unsweetened biscuit usu. eaten with cheese. **cream off** take (the best or a specified part) from a whole (*creamed off the brightest pupils*). **cream of tartar** purified and crystallized potassium hydrogen tartrate, used in medicine, baking powder, etc. **cream soda** a carbonated vanilla-flavoured soft drink. **cream tea** afternoon tea with scones, jam, and cream. [ME f. OF *cre(s)me* f. LL *cramum* (perh. f. Gaulish) & eccl.L *chrisma* CHRISM]

creamer /ˈkriːmə(r)/ *n.* **1** a flat dish used for skimming the cream off milk. **2** a machine used for separating cream from milk. **3** *US* a jug for cream.

creamery /ˈkriːmərɪ/ *n.* (*pl.* **-ies**) **1** a factory producing butter and cheese. **2** a shop where milk, cream, etc., are sold; a dairy. [CREAM, after F *crémerie*]

creamy /ˈkriːmɪ/ *adj.* (**creamier**, **creamiest**) **1** like cream in consistency or colour. **2** rich in cream. □ **creamily** *adv.* **creaminess** *n.*

crease /kriːs/ *n.* & *v.* —*n.* **1 a** a line in paper etc. caused by folding. **b** a fold or wrinkle. **2** *Cricket* a line marking the position of the bowler or batsman. —*v.* **1** *tr.* make creases in (material). **2** *intr.* become creased (*linen creases badly*). **3** *tr.* & *intr. sl.* (often foll. by *up*) make or become incapable through laughter. **4** *tr. esp. US sl.* **a** tire out. **b** stun or kill. [earlier *creast* = CREST ridge in material]

create /kriːˈeɪt/ *v.* **1** *tr.* **a** (of natural or historical forces) bring into existence; cause (*poverty creates resentment*). **b** (of a person or persons) make or cause (*create a diversion*). **2** *tr.* originate (*an actor creates a part*). **3** *tr.* invest (a person) with a rank (*created him a lord*). **4** *intr. sl. Brit.* make a fuss; grumble. □ **creatable** *adj.* [ME f. L *creare*]

creation /kriːˈeɪʃ(ə)n/ *n.* **1 a** the act of creating. **b** an instance of this. **2 a** (usu. **the Creation**) the creating of the universe regarded as an act of God. **b** (usu. **Creation**) everything so created; the universe. **3** a product of human intelligence, esp. of imaginative thought or artistic ability. [ME f. OF f. L *creatio -onis* (as CREATE)]

creationism /kriːˈeɪʃ(ə)nɪz(ə)m/ *n. Theol.* a theory attributing all matter, biological species, etc., to separate acts of creation, rather than to evolution. □ **creationist** *n.*

creative /kriːˈeɪtɪv/ *adj.* **1** inventive and imaginative. **2** creating or able to create. □ **creatively** *adv.* **creativeness** *n.* **creativity** /-ˈtɪvɪtɪ/ *n.*

creator /kriːˈeɪtə(r)/ *n.* **1** a person who creates. **2** (as **the Creator**) God. [ME f. OF *creat(o)ur* f. L *creator -oris* (as CREATE)]

creature /ˈkriːtʃə(r)/ *n.* **1 a** an animal, as distinct from a human being. **b** any living being (*we are all God's creatures*). **2** a person of a specified kind (*poor creature*). **3** a person owing status to and obsequiously subservient to another. **4** anything created; a creation. □ **creature comforts** material comforts such as good food, warmth, etc. □ **creaturely** *adj.* [ME f. OF f. LL *creatura* (as CREATE)]

crèche /kreʃ, kreɪʃ/ *n.* a day nursery for babies and young children. [F f. Gmc: rel. to CRIB]

credence /ˈkriːd(ə)ns/ *n.* **1** belief. **2** (in full **credence table**) a small side-table etc. which holds the elements of the Eucharist before they are consecrated. □ **give credence to** believe. [ME f. OF f. med.L *credentia* f. *credere* believe]

credential /krɪˈdenʃ(ə)l/ *n.* (usu. in *pl.*) **1** evidence of a person's achievements or trustworthiness, usu. in the form of certificates, references, etc. **2** a letter or letters of introduction. [med.L *credentialis* (as CREDENCE)]

credibility /ˌkredɪˈbɪlɪtɪ/ *n.* **1** the condition of being credible or believable. **2** reputation, status. □ **credibility gap** an apparent difference between what is said and what is true.

credible /ˈkredɪb(ə)l/ *adj.* **1** (of a person or statement) believable or worthy of belief. **2** (of a threat etc.) convincing. □ **credibly** *adv.* [ME f. L *credibilis* f. *credere* believe]

■ **Usage** This word is sometimes confused with *credulous.*

credit /ˈkredɪt/ *n.* & *v.* —*n.* **1** (usu. of a person) a source of honour, pride, etc. (*is a credit to the school*). **2** the acknowledgement of merit (*must give him credit for consistency*). **3** a good reputation (*his credit stands high*). **4 a** belief or trust (*I place credit in that*). **b** something believable or trustworthy (*that statement has credit*). **5 a** a person's financial standing; the sum of money at a person's disposal in a bank etc. **b** the power to obtain goods etc. before payment (based on the trust that payment will be made). **6** (usu. in *pl.*) an acknowledgement of a contributor's services to a film, television programme, etc. **7** a grade above a pass in an examination. **8** a reputation for solvency and honesty in business. **9 a** (in bookkeeping) the acknowledgement of being paid by an entry on the credit side of an account. **b** the sum entered. **c** the credit side of an account. **10** *US* a certificate indicating that a student has completed a course. —*v.tr.* (**credited**, **crediting**) **1** believe (*cannot credit it*). **2** (usu. foll. by *to*, *with*) enter on the credit side of an account. □ **credit card** a card from a bank etc. authorizing the obtaining of goods on credit. **credit a person with** ascribe (a good quality) to a person. **do credit to** (or **do a person credit**) enhance the reputation of. **on credit** with an arrangement to pay later. **to one's credit** in one's praise, commendation, or defence (*to his credit, he refused the offer*). [F *crédit* f. It. *credito* or L *creditum* f. *credere* credit- believe, trust]

creditable /ˈkredɪtəb(ə)l/ *adj.* (often foll. by *to*) bringing credit or honour. □ **creditability** /-ˈbɪlɪtɪ/ *n.* **creditably** *adv.*

creditor /ˈkredɪtə(r)/ *n.* **1** a person to whom a debt is owing. **2** a person or company that gives credit for money or goods. [ME f. AF *creditour* (OF *-eur*) f. L *creditor -oris* (as CREDIT)]

creditworthy /ˈkredɪtˌwɜːðɪ/ *adj.* considered suitable to receive commercial credit. □ **creditworthiness** *n.*

credo /ˈkreɪdəʊ, ˈkriː-/ *n.* (*pl.* **-os**) a statement of belief; a creed. [ME f. L, = I believe]

credulous /ˈkredjʊləs/ *adj.* **1** too ready to believe; gullible. **2** (of behaviour) showing such gullibility. □ **credulity** /krɪˈdjuːlɪtɪ/ *n.* **credulously** *adv.* **credulousness** *n.* [L *credulus* f. *credere* believe]

■ **Usage** This word is sometimes confused with *credible.*

creed *n.* **1** a set of principles or opinions, esp. as a philosophy of life. **2** (often **the Creed**) a formal statement of belief used in Christian worship, esp. in one of the forms developed by the early church (*Apostles' Creed, Nicene Creed*). □ **credal** /ˈkriːd(ə)l/ *adj.* **creedal** *adj.* [OE *crēda* f. L CREDO]

creek *n.* **1** *Brit.* **a** a small bay or harbour on a sea-coast. **b** a narrow inlet on a sea-coast or in a river-bank. **2** esp. *US* a tributary of a river; a stream. **3** *Austral.* & *NZ* a stream or brook. □ **up the creek** *sl.* **1** in difficulties or trouble. **2** crazy. [ME *crike* f. ON *kriki* nook (or partly f. OF *crique* f. ON), & ME *crēke* f. MDu. *krēke* (or f. *crike* by lengthening): ult. orig. unkn.]

creel *n.* **1** a large wicker basket for fish. **2** an angler's fishing-basket. [ME, orig. Sc.: ult. orig. unkn.]

creep *v.* & *n.* —*v.intr.* (*past* and *past part.* **crept**) **1** move with the body prone and close to the ground; crawl. **2** (often foll. by *in, out, up,* etc.) come, go, or move slowly and stealthily or timidly (*crept out without being seen*). **3** enter slowly (into a person's affections, life, awareness, etc.). **4** *colloq.* act abjectly or obsequiously in the hope of advancement. **5** (of a plant) grow along the ground or up a wall by means of tendrils etc. **6** (as **creeping** *adj.*) developing slowly and steadily (*creeping inflation*). **7** (of the flesh) feel as if insects etc. were creeping over it, as a result of fear, horror, etc. —*n.* **1 a** the act of creeping. **b** an instance of this. **2** (in *pl.*; prec. by *the*) *colloq.* a nervous feeling of revulsion or fear (*gives me the creeps*). **3** *sl.* an unpleasant person. [OE *crēopan*]

creeper /ˈkriːpə(r)/ *n.* **1** *Bot.* any climbing or creeping plant. **2** *sl.* a soft-soled shoe.

creepy /ˈkriːpɪ/ *adj.* (**creepier, creepiest**) **1** *colloq.* having or producing a creeping of the flesh (*I feel creepy; a creepy film*). **2** given to creeping. □ **creepily** *adv.* **creepiness** *n.* [CREEP]

creepy-crawly /ˌkriːpɪˈkrɔːlɪ/ *n.* & *adj.* *Brit. colloq.* —*n.* (*pl.* **-ies**) an insect, worm, etc. —*adj.* creeping and crawling.

cremate /krɪˈmeɪt/ *v.tr.* consume (a corpse etc.) by fire. □ **cremation** /-ˈmeɪʃ(ə)n/ *n.* **cremator** *n.* [L *cremare* burn]

crematorium /ˌkreməˈtɔːrɪəm/ *n.* (*pl.* **crematoria** or **crematoriums**) a place for cremating corpses in a furnace. [mod.L (as CREMATE, -ORY)]

crematory /ˈkremətərɪ/ *adj.* & *n.* —*adj.* of or relating to cremation. —*n.* (*pl.* **-ies**) *US* = CREMATORIUM.

crème de menthe /krem də ˈmãt, ˈmɒnt/ *n.* a peppermint-flavoured liqueur. [F, = cream of mint]

crenellate /ˈkrenəleɪt/ *v.tr.* provide (a tower etc.) with battlements and loopholes. □ **crenellation** /-ˈleɪʃ(ə)n/ *n.* [F *créneler* f. *crenel* ult. f. pop.L *crena* notch]

Creole /ˈkriːəʊl/ *n.* & *adj.* —*n.* **1 a** a descendant of European (esp. Spanish) settlers in the W. Indies or Central or S. America. **b** a White descendant of French settlers in the southern US. **c** a person of mixed European and Black descent. **2** a language formed from the contact of a European language (esp. English, French, or Portuguese) with another (esp. African) language. —*adj.* **1** of or relating to a Creole or Creoles. **2** (usu. **creole**) of Creole origin or production (*creole cooking*). [F *créole, criole* f. Sp.

criollo, prob. f. Port. *crioulo* home-born slave f. *criar* breed f. L *creare* CREATE]

creosote /ˈkriːəˌsəʊt/ *n.* & *v.* —*n.* **1** (in full **creosote oil**) a dark-brown oil distilled from coal tar, used as a wood-preservative. **2** a colourless oily fluid distilled from wood tar, used as an antiseptic. —*v.tr.* treat with creosote. [G *Kreosote* f. Gk *kreas* flesh + *sōtēr* preserver, with ref. to its antiseptic properties]

crêpe /kreɪp/ *n.* **1** a fine often gauzelike fabric with a wrinkled surface. **2** a thin pancake, usu. with a savoury or sweet filling. **3** (also **crêpe rubber**) a very hard-wearing wrinkled sheet rubber used for the soles of shoes etc. □ **crêpe de Chine** /də ˈʃiːn/ a fine silk crêpe. **crêpe paper** thin crinkled paper. □ **crêpey** *adj.* **crêpy** *adj.* [F f. OF *crespe* curled f. L *crispus*]

crepitate /ˈkrepɪˌteɪt/ *v.intr.* make a crackling sound. □ **crepitant** *adj.* **crepitation** *n.* [L *crepitare* frequent. of *crepare* creak]

crept *past* and *past part.* of CREEP.

crepuscular /krɪˈpʌskjʊlə(r)/ *adj.* **1 a** of twilight. **b** dim. **2** *Zool.* appearing or active in twilight. [L *crepusculum* twilight]

crescendo /krɪˈʃendəʊ/ *n., adv., adj.,* & *v.* —*n.* (*pl.* **-os**) **1** *Mus.* a passage gradually increasing in loudness. **2 a** progress towards a climax (*a crescendo of emotions*). **b** *disp.* a climax (*reached a crescendo*). —*adv.* & *adj.* with a gradual increase in loudness. —*v.intr.* (**-oes, -oed**) increase gradually in loudness or intensity. [It., part. of *crescere* grow (as CRESCENT)]

■ **Usage** This word is sometimes wrongly used to mean the climax itself rather than progress towards it.

crescent /ˈkrez(ə)nt, ˈkres-/ *n.* & *adj.* —*n.* **1** the curved sickle shape of the waxing or waning moon. **2** anything of this shape, esp. *Brit.* a street forming an arc. **3 a** the crescent-shaped emblem of Islam or Turkey. **b** (**the Crescent**) the world or power of Islam. —*adj.* **1** *poet.* increasing. **2** crescent-shaped. □ **crescentic** /-ˈsentɪk/ *adj.* [ME f. AF *cressaunt*, OF *creissant*, f. L *crescere* grow]

cress *n.* any of various cruciferous plants usu. with pungent edible leaves. [OE *cresse* f. WG]

crest *n.* & *v.* —*n.* **1 a** a comb or tuft of feathers, fur, etc. on a bird's or animal's head. **b** something resembling this, esp. a plume of feathers on a helmet. **2** the top of something, esp. of a mountain, wave, roof, etc. **3** *Heraldry* **a** a device above the shield and helmet of a coat of arms. **b** such a device signifying a family. —*v.* **1** *tr.* reach the crest of (a hill, wave, etc.). **2** *tr.* **a** provide with a crest. **b** serve as a crest to. **3** *intr.* (of a wave) form into a crest. □ **on the crest of a wave** at the most favourable moment in one's progress. □ **crested** *adj.* (also in *comb.*). **crestless** *adj.* [ME f. OF *creste* f. L *crista* tuft]

crestfallen /ˈkrestˌfɔːlən/ *adj.* **1** dejected, dispirited. **2** with a fallen or drooping crest.

cretaceous /krɪˈteɪʃəs/ *adj.* & *n.* —*adj.* **1** of the nature of chalk. **2** (**Cretaceous**) *Geol.* of or relating to the last period of the Mesozoic era. —*n.* *Geol.* this era or system. [L *cretaceus* f. *creta* chalk]

cretin /ˈkretɪn/ *n.* **1** a person who is deformed and mentally retarded as the result of a thyroid deficiency. **2** *colloq.* a stupid person. □ **cretinism** *n.* **cretinize** *v.tr.* (also **-ise**). **cretinous** *adj.* [F crétin f. Swiss F. creitin, crestin f. L Christianus CHRISTIAN]

cretonne /kreˈtɒn, ˈkre-/ n. (often attrib.) a heavy cotton fabric with a usu. floral pattern, used for upholstery. [F f. Creton in Normandy]

crevasse /krəˈvæs/ n. a deep open crack, esp. in a glacier. [F f. OF crevace: see CREVICE]

crevice /ˈkrevɪs/ n. a narrow opening or fissure, esp. in a rock or building etc. [ME f. OF crevace f. crever burst f. L crepare]

crew[1] n. & v. —n. (often treated as pl.) **1 a** a body of people manning a ship, aircraft, train, etc. **b** such a body as distinguished from the captain or officers. **c** a body of people working together; a team. **2** colloq. a company of people; a gang (a motley crew). —v. **1** act as a crew or member of a crew for. **2** intr. act as a crew or member of a crew. □ **crew cut** an orig. man's haircut which is short all over the head. **crew neck** a close-fitting round neckline, esp. on a sweater. [ME f. OF creüe increase, fem. past part. of croistre grow f. L crescere]

crew[2] past of CROW[2].

crewel /ˈkruːəl/ n. a thin worsted yarn used for tapestry and embroidery. [ME crule etc., of unkn. orig.]

crewman /ˈkruːmən/ n. (pl. **-men**) a member of a crew.

crib n. & v. —n. **1 a** a child's bed; a cot. **b** a model of the Nativity of Christ, with a manger as a bed. **2** a barred container or rack for animal fodder. **3** colloq. **a** a translation of a text for the use of students. **b** plagiarized work etc. **4** colloq. cribbage. **5** Austral. & NZ a light meal; food. —v.tr. (also absol.) (**cribbed, cribbing**) **1** colloq. copy (another person's work) unfairly or without acknowledgement. **2** confine in a small space. **3** colloq. pilfer, steal. □ **cribber** n. [OE crib(b)]

cribbage /ˈkrɪbɪdʒ/ n. a card game for two, three, or four players. □ **cribbage-board** a board with pegs and holes used for scoring at cribbage. [17th c.: orig. unkn.]

crick n. & v. —n. a sudden painful stiffness in the neck or the back etc. —v.tr. produce a crick in (the neck etc.). [ME: orig. unkn.]

cricket[1] /ˈkrɪkɪt/ n. & v. —n. a game played on a grass pitch with two teams of 11 players taking turns to bowl at a wicket defended by a batting player of the other team. —v.intr. (**cricketed, cricketing**) play cricket. □ **cricket-bag** a long bag used for carrying a cricketer's bat etc. **not cricket** Brit. colloq. underhand or unfair behaviour. □ **cricketer** n. [16th c.: orig. uncert.]

cricket[2] /ˈkrɪkɪt/ n. any of various grasshopper-like insects of the order Orthoptera, the males of which produce a characteristic chirping sound. [ME f. OF criquet f. criquer creak etc. (imit.)]

cried past and past part. of CRY.

crier /ˈkraɪə(r)/ n. (also **cryer**) **1** a person who cries. **2** an officer who makes public announcements in a court of justice. □ **town** (or **common**) **crier** hist. an officer employed by a town council etc. to make public announcements in the streets or market-place. [ME f. AF criour, OF criere f. crier CRY]

crikey /ˈkraɪkɪ/ int. sl. an expression of astonishment. [euphem. for CHRIST]

crim n. & adj. Austral. sl. = CRIMINAL. [abbr.]

crime n. **1 a** an offence punishable by law. **b** illegal acts as a whole (resorted to crime). **2** an evil act (a crime against humanity). □ **crime wave** a sudden increase in crime. **crime-writer** a writer of detective fiction or thrillers. [ME f. OF f. L crimen -minis judgement, offence]

criminal /ˈkrɪmɪn(ə)l/ n. & adj. —n. a person who has committed a crime or crimes. —adj. **1** of, involving, or concerning crime (criminal records). **2** having committed (and usu. been convicted of) a crime. **3** Law relating to or expert in criminal law rather than civil or political matters (criminal lawyer). **4** colloq. scandalous, deplorable. □ **criminal law** law concerned with punishment of offenders. —v. **criminality** /-ˈnælɪtɪ/ n. **criminally** adv. [ME f. LL criminalis (as CRIME)]

criminology /ˌkrɪmɪˈnɒlədʒɪ/ n. the scientific study of crime. □ **criminological** /-nəˈlɒdʒɪk(ə)l/ adj. **criminologist** n. [L crimen -minis CRIME + -OLOGY]

crimp v. & n. —v.tr. **1** compress into small folds or ridges; frill. **2** make narrow wrinkles or flutings in; corrugate. **3** make waves in (the hair) with a hot iron. —n. a crimped thing or form. □ **crimper** n. **crimpy** adj. **crimpily** adv. **crimpiness** n. [ME, prob. ult. f. OHG krimphan]

crimson /ˈkrɪmz(ə)n/ adj., n., & v. —adj. of a rich deep red inclining to purple. —n. this colour. —v.tr. & intr. make or become crimson. [ME cremesin, crimesin, ult. f. Arab. ḳirmizī KERMES]

cringe v. & n. —v.intr. **1** shrink back in fear or apprehension; cower. **2** (often foll. by to) behave obsequiously. —n. the act or an instance of cringing. □ **cringer** n. [ME crenge, crenche, OE cringan, crincan: see CRANK[1]]

crinkle /ˈkrɪŋk(ə)l/ n. & v. —n. a wrinkle or crease in paper, cloth, etc. —v. **1** tr. form crinkles in. **2** tr. form crinkles in. □ **crinkle-cut** (of vegetables) cut with wavy edges. □ **crinkly** adj. [ME f. OE crincan: see CRANK[1]]

crinoline /ˈkrɪnəlɪn/ n. a stiffened or hooped petticoat formerly worn to make a long skirt stand out. [F f. L crinis hair + linum thread]

cripple /ˈkrɪp(ə)l/ n. & v. —n. a person who is permanently lame. —v.tr. **1** make a cripple of; lame. **2** disable, impair. **3** weaken or damage (an institution, enterprise, etc.) seriously. □ **crippledom** n. **cripplehood** n. **crippler** n. [OE crypel, rel. to CREEP]

crisis /ˈkraɪsɪs/ n. (pl. **crises** /-siːz/) **1 a** a decisive moment. **b** a time of danger or great difficulty. **2** the turning-point, esp. of a disease. [L f. Gk krisis decision f. krinō decide]

crisp /krɪsp/ adj., n., & v. —adj. **1** hard but brittle. **2 a** (of air) bracing. **b** (of a style or manner) lively, brisk and decisive. **c** (of features etc.) neat and clear-cut. **d** (of paper) stiff and crackling. **e** (of hair) closely curling. —n. **1** (in full **potato crisp**) Brit. a thin fried slice of potato sold in packets etc. and eaten as a snack or appetizer. **2** a thing overdone in roasting etc. (burnt to a crisp). —v.tr. & intr. **1** make or become crisp. **2** curl in short stiff folds or waves. □ **crisply** adv. **crispness** n. [OE f. L crispus curled]

crispbread /ˈkrɪspbred/ n. **1** a thin crisp biscuit of crushed rye etc. **2** these collectively (a packet of crispbread).

crisper /ˈkrɪspə(r)/ n. a compartment in a refrigerator used for storing fruit and vegetables.

crispy /ˈkrɪspɪ/ adj. (**crispier, crispiest**) **1** crisp, brittle. **2** curly. **3** brisk. □ **crispiness** n.

criss-cross /ˈkrɪskrɒs/ *n., adj., adv.,* & *v.* —*n.* **1** a pattern of crossing lines. **2** the crossing of lines or currents etc. —*adj.* crossing; in cross lines (*criss-cross marking*). —*adv.* crosswise; at cross purposes. —*v.* **1** *intr.* **a** intersect repeatedly. **b** move crosswise. **2** *tr.* mark or make with a criss-cross pattern. [15th c., f. *Christ's cross*: later treated as redupl. of CROSS]

criterion /kraɪˈtɪərɪən/ *n.* (*pl.* **criteria** /-rɪə/) a principle or standard that a thing is judged by. □ **criterial** *adj.* [Gk *kritērion* means of judging (cf. CRITIC)]

■ **Usage** The plural form of this word, *criteria*, is often used incorrectly as the singular. In the singular *criterion* should always be used.

critic /ˈkrɪtɪk/ *n.* **1** a person who censures. **2** a person who reviews or judges the merits of literary, artistic, or musical works etc. [L *criticus* f. Gk *kritikos* f. *kritēs* judge f. *krinō* judge, decide]

critical /ˈkrɪtɪk(ə)l/ *adj.* **1 a** making or involving adverse or censorious comments or judgements. **b** expressing or involving criticism. **2** skilful at or engaged in criticism. **3** providing textual criticism (*a critical edition of Milton*). **4 a** of or at a crisis; involving risk or suspense (*in a critical condition; a critical operation*). **b** decisive, crucial (*of critical importance; at the critical moment*). **5 a** *Math.* & *Physics* marking transition from one state etc. to another (*critical angle*). **b** *Physics* (of a nuclear reactor) maintaining a self-sustaining chain reaction. □ **critical mass** *Physics* the amount of fissile material needed to maintain a nuclear chain reaction. **critical path** the sequence of stages determining the minimum time needed for an operation. □ **criticality** /-ˈkælɪtɪ/ *n.* (in sense 5). **critically** *adv.* **criticalness** *n.* [L *criticus*: see CRITIC]

criticism /ˈkrɪtɪˌsɪz(ə)m/ *n.* **1 a** finding fault; censure. **b** a statement or remark expressing this. **2 a** the work of a critic. **b** an article, essay, etc., expressing or containing an analytical evaluation of something. [CRITIC or L *criticus* + -ISM]

criticize /ˈkrɪtɪˌsaɪz/ *v.tr.* (also **-ise**) (also *absol.*) **1** find fault with; censure. **2** discuss critically. □ **criticizable** *adj.* **criticizer** *n.*

critique /krɪˈtiːk/ *n.* & *v.* —*n.* a critical essay or analysis; an instance or the process of formal criticism. —*v.tr.* (**critiques, critiqued, critiquing**) discuss critically. [F f. Gk *kritikē tekhnē* critical art]

croak *n.* & *v.* —*n.* **1** a deep hoarse sound as of a frog or a raven. **2** a sound resembling this. —*v.* **1 a** *intr.* utter a croak. **b** *tr.* utter with a croak or in a dismal manner. **2** *sl.* **a** *intr.* die. **b** *tr.* kill. □ **croaker** *n.* [ME: imit.]

croaky /ˈkrəʊkɪ/ *adj.* (**croakier, croakiest**) (of a voice) croaking; hoarse. □ **croakily** *adv.* **croakiness** *n.*

crochet /ˈkrəʊʃeɪ, -ʃɪ/ *n.* & *v.* —*n.* **1** a handicraft in which yarn is made up into a patterned fabric by means of a hooked needle. **2** work made in this way. —*v.* (**crocheted** /-ʃeɪd/; **crocheting** /-ʃeɪɪŋ/) **1** *tr.* make by crocheting. **2** *intr.* do crochet. □ **crocheter** /ˈkrəʊʃeɪə(r)/ *n.* [F, dimin. of *croc* hook]

crock[1] *n.* & *v. colloq.* —*n.* **1** an inefficient, broken-down, or worn-out person. **2** a worn-out vehicle, ship, etc. —*v.* **1** *intr.* (foll. by *up*) break

down, collapse. **2** *tr.* (often foll. by *up*) disable, cause to collapse. [orig. Sc., perh. f. Flem.]

crock[2] *n.* **1** an earthenware pot or jar. **2** a broken piece of earthenware. [OE *croc(ca)*]

crockery /ˈkrɒkərɪ/ *n.* earthenware or china dishes, plates, etc. [obs. *crocker* potter: see CROCK[2]]

crocket /ˈkrɒkɪt/ *n. Archit.* a small carved ornament (usu. a bud or curled leaf) on the inclined side of a pinnacle etc. [ME f. var. of OF *crochet*: see CROCHET]

crocodile /ˈkrɒkəˌdaɪl/ *n.* **1 a** any large tropical amphibious reptile of the order Crocodilia, with thick scaly skin, long tail, and long jaws. **b** leather from its skin, used to make bags, shoes, etc. **2** *Brit. colloq.* a line of schoolchildren etc. walking in pairs. □ **crocodile tears** insincere grief (from the belief that crocodiles wept while devouring or alluring their prey). □ **crocodilian** /-ˈdɪlɪən/ *adj.* [ME f. OF *cocodrille* f. med.L *cocodrillus* f. L *crocodilus* f. Gk *krokodilos* f. *krokē* pebble + *drilos* worm]

crocus /ˈkrəʊkəs/ *n.* (*pl.* **crocuses**) any dwarf plant of the genus *Crocus*, having brilliant usu. yellow or purple flowers. [ME, = saffron, f. L f. Gk *krokos* crocus, of Semitic orig.]

Croesus /ˈkriːsəs/ *n.* a person of great wealth. [name of a king of Lydia (6th c. BC)]

croft *n.* & *v. Brit.* —*n.* **1** an enclosed piece of (usu. arable) land. **2** a small rented farm in Scotland or N. England. —*v.intr.* farm a croft; live as a crofter. [OE: orig. unkn.]

crofter /ˈkrɒftə(r)/ *n. Brit.* a person who rents a smallholding, esp. a joint tenant of a divided farm in parts of Scotland.

croissant /ˈkrwʌsɑ̃/ *n.* a crescent-shaped roll made of rich yeast pastry. [F, formed as CRESCENT]

cromlech /ˈkrɒmlek/ *n.* **1** a dolmen; a megalithic tomb. **2** a circle of upright prehistoric stones. [Welsh f. *crom* fem. of *crwm* bent + *llech* flat stone]

crone *n.* **1** a withered old woman. **2** an old ewe. [ME, ult. f. ONF *carogne* CARRION]

crony /ˈkrəʊnɪ/ *n.* (*pl.* **-ies**) a close friend or companion. [17th-c. *chrony*, university sl. f. Gk *khronios* long-standing f. *khronos* time]

crook /krʊk/ *n., v.,* & *adj.* —*n.* **1** the hooked staff of a shepherd or bishop. **2 a** a bend, curve, or hook. **b** anything hooked or curved. **3** *colloq.* **a** a rogue; a swindler. **b** a professional criminal. —*v.tr.* & *intr.* bend, curve. —*adj.* **1** crooked. **2** *Austral.* & *NZ colloq.* **a** unsatisfactory, out of order; (of a person) unwell, injured. **b** unpleasant. **c** dishonest, unscrupulous. **d** bad-tempered, irritable, angry. □ **go crook** (usu. foll. by *at, on*) *Austral.* & *NZ colloq.* lose one's temper; become angry. □ **crookery** *n.* [ME f. ON *krókr* hook]

crooked /ˈkrʊkɪd/ *adj.* (**crookeder, crookedest**) **1 a** not straight or level; bent, curved, twisted. **b** deformed, bent with age. **2** *colloq.* not straightforward; dishonest. **3** /krʊkt/ *Austral.* & *NZ sl.* = CROOK *adj.* 2. **4** (foll. by *on*) *Austral. sl.* hostile to. □ **crookedly** *adv.* **crookedness** *n.* [ME f. CROOK, prob. after ON *krókóttr*]

croon /kruːn/ *v.* & *n.* —*v.tr.* & *intr.* hum or sing in a low subdued voice, esp. in a sentimental manner. —*n.* such singing. □ **crooner** *n.* [ME (orig. Sc. & N.Engl.) f. MDu. & MLG *krōnen* groan, lament]

crop *n. & v. —n.* **1 a** the produce of cultivated plants, esp. cereals. **b** the season's total yield of this (*a good crop*). **2 a** a group or an amount produced or appearing at one time (*this year's crop of students*). **3** (in full **hunting crop**) the stock or handle of a whip. **4** a style of hair cut very short. **5** *Zool.* **a** the pouch in a bird's gullet where food is prepared for digestion. **b** a similar organ in other animals. —*v.* (**cropped**, **cropping**) **1** *tr.* **a** cut off. **b** (of animals) bite off (the tops of plants). **2** *tr.* cut (hair, cloth, etc.) short. **3** *tr.* gather or reap (produce). **4** *tr.* (foll. by *with*) sow or plant (land) with a crop. **5** *intr.* (of land) bear a crop. □ **crop circle** a circular area of crops that has been inexplicably flattened. **crop-eared** having the ears (esp. of animals) or hair cut short. **crop-full** having a full crop or stomach. **crop up** (of a subject, circumstance, etc.) appear or come to one's notice unexpectedly. [OE *crop(p)*]

cropper /ˈkrɒpə(r)/ *n.* a crop-producing plant of specified quality (*a good cropper*; *a heavy cropper*). □ **come a cropper** *sl.* **1** fall heavily. **2** fail badly.

croquet /ˈkrəʊkeɪ, -kɪ/ *n. & v. —n.* a game played on a lawn, with wooden balls which are driven through a series of hoops with mallets. —*v.tr.* (**croqueted** /-keɪd/; **croqueting** /-keɪɪŋ/) drive away (one's opponent's ball in croquet) by placing one's own against it and striking one's own. [perh. dial. form of F CROCHET hook]

croquette /krəˈket/ *n.* a fried breaded roll or ball of mashed potato or minced meat etc. [F f. *croquer* crunch]

crore /krɔː(r)/ *n. Ind.* **1** ten million. **2** one hundred lakhs. [Hindi *k(a)rōr*, ult. f. Skr. *koṭi* apex]

crosier /ˈkrəʊzɪə(r), -ʒə(r)/ *n.* (also **crozier**) **1** a hooked staff carried by a bishop as a symbol of pastoral office. **2** a crook. [orig. = bearer of a crook, f. OF *crocier* & OF *croisier* f. *crois* CROSS]

cross *n., v., & adj. —n.* **1** an upright post with a transverse bar, as used in antiquity for crucifixion. **2 a** (**the Cross**) in Christianity, the cross on which Christ was crucified. **b** a representation of this as an emblem of Christianity. **3** a staff surmounted by a cross and borne before an archbishop or in a religious procession. **4 a** a thing or mark shaped like a cross, esp. a figure made by two short intersecting lines (+ or ×). **b** a monument in the form of a cross, esp. one in the centre of a town or on a tomb. **5** a cross-shaped decoration indicating rank in some orders of knighthood or awarded for personal valour. **6 a** an intermixture of animal breeds or plant varieties. **b** an animal or plant resulting from this. **7** (foll. by *between*) a mixture or compromise of two things. **8 a** a crosswise movement, e.g. of an actor on stage. **b** *Football* etc. a pass of the ball across the direction of play. **c** *Boxing* a blow with a crosswise movement of the fist. **9** a trial or affliction; something to be endured (*bear one's crosses*). —*v.* **1** *tr.* (often foll. by *over*; also *absol.*) go across or to the other side of (a road, river, sea, etc.). **2 a** *intr.* intersect or be across one another (*the roads cross near the bridge*). **b** *tr.* cause to do this; place crosswise (*cross one's legs*). **3** *tr.* **a** draw a line or lines across. **b** *Brit.* mark (a cheque) with two parallel lines, and often an annotation, to indicate that it must be paid into a named bank account. **4** *tr.* (foll. by *off*, *out*, *through*) cancel or obliterate or remove from a

list with lines drawn across. **5** *tr.* (often *refl.*) make the sign of the cross on or over. **6** *intr.* **a** pass in opposite or different directions. **b** (of letters between two correspondents) each be dispatched before receipt of the other. **c** (of telephone lines) become wrongly interconnected so that intrusive calls can be heard. **7** *tr.* **a** cause to interbreed. **b** cross-fertilize (plants). **8** *tr.* thwart or frustrate (*crossed in love*). **9** *tr. sl.* cheat. —*adj.* **1** (often foll. by *with*) peevish, angry. **2** (usu. *attrib.*) transverse; reaching from side to side. **3** (usu. *attrib.*) intersecting. **4** (usu. *attrib.*) contrary, opposed, reciprocal. □ **at cross purposes** misunderstanding or conflicting with one another. **cross one's mind** (of a thought etc.) occur to one, esp. transiently. **on the cross 1** diagonally. **2** *sl.* fraudulently, dishonestly. □ **crossly** *adv.* **crossness** *n.* [OE *cros* f. ON *kross* f. OIr. *cros* f. L *crux cruc-*]

cross- *comb. form* **1** denoting movement or position across something (*cross-channel*; *cross-country*). **2** denoting interaction (*cross-breed*; *cross-cultural*; *cross-fertilize*). **3 a** passing from side to side; transverse (*crossbar*; *cross-current*). **b** having a transverse part (*crossbow*). **4** describing the form or shape of a cross (*cross-keys*; *crossroads*).

crossbar /ˈkrɒsbɑː(r)/ *n.* a horizontal bar, esp. held on a pivot or between two upright bars etc., e.g. of a bicycle or of a football goal.

cross-bench /ˈkrɒsbentʃ/ *n. Brit.* a seat in Parliament (now only the House of Lords) occupied by a member not taking the whip from a political party. □ **cross-bencher** *n.*

crossbones /ˈkrɒsbəʊnz/ *n.* a representation of two crossed thigh-bones (SEE SKULL).

crossbow /ˈkrɒsbəʊ/ *n.* chiefly *hist.* a bow fixed across a wooden stock, with a groove for an arrow and a mechanism for drawing and releasing the string. □ **crossbowman** *n.* (*pl.* **-men**)

cross-breed /ˈkrɒsbriːd/ *n. & v. —n.* **1** a breed of animals or plants produced by crossing. **2** an individual animal or plant of a cross-breed. —*v.tr.* (*past* and *past part.* **-bred**) produce by crossing.

cross-check /ˈkrɒstʃek/ *v. & n. —v.tr.* check by a second or alternative method, or by several methods. —*n.* an instance of cross-checking.

cross-country /krɒsˈkʌntrɪ/ *adj. & adv.* **1** across fields or open country. **2** not keeping to main or direct roads.

cross-cut /ˈkrɒskʌt/ *adj. & n. —adj.* cut across the main grain or axis. —*n.* a diagonal cut, path, etc. □ **cross-cut saw** a saw for cutting across the grain of wood.

crosse /krɒs/ *n.* a stick with a triangular net at the end for conveying the ball in lacrosse. [F f. OF *croce*, *croc* hook]

cross-examine /ˌkrɒsɪgˈzæmɪn/ *v.tr.* examine (esp. a witness in a lawcourt) to check or extend testimony already given. □ **cross-examination** /-ˈneɪʃ(ə)n/ *n.* **cross-examiner** *n.*

cross-eyed /ˈkrɒsaɪd/ *adj.* (as a disorder) having one or both eyes turned permanently inwards towards the nose.

cross-fertilize /krɒsˈfɜːtɪˌlaɪz/ *v.tr.* (also **-ise**) **1** fertilize (an animal or plant) from one of a different species. **2** help by the interchange of ideas etc. □ **cross-fertilization** /-ˈzeɪʃ(ə)n/ *n.*

crossfire /ˈkrɒsˌfaɪə(r)/ n. **1** firing in two crossing directions simultaneously. **2 a** attack or criticism from several sources at once. **b** a lively or combative exchange of views etc.

cross-grain /ˈkrɒsgreɪn/ n. a grain in timber, running across the regular grain.

cross-grained /ˈkrɒsgreɪnd/ adj. **1** (of timber) having a cross-grain. **2** perverse, intractable.

cross-hatch /ˈkrɒshætʃ/ v.tr. shade with intersecting sets of parallel lines.

crossing /ˈkrɒsɪŋ/ n. **1** a place where things (esp. roads) cross. **2** a place at which one may cross a street etc. (pedestrian crossing). **3** a journey across water (had a smooth crossing). **4** the intersection of a church nave and transepts. **5** Biol. mating.

cross-legged /krɒsˈlegd, -ˈlegɪd, ˈkrɒs-/ adj. with one leg crossed over the other.

crossover /ˈkrɒsˌəʊvə(r)/ n. & adj. —n. a point or place of crossing from one side to the other. —adj. having a crossover.

crosspatch /ˈkrɒspætʃ/ n. colloq. a bad-tempered person. [CROSS adj. 1 + obs. patch fool, clown]

crosspiece /ˈkrɒspiːs/ n. a transverse beam or other component of a structure etc.

cross-ply /ˈkrɒsplaɪ/ adj. (of a tyre) having fabric layers with cords lying crosswise.

cross-pollinate /krɒsˈpɒlɪˌneɪt/ v.tr. pollinate (a plant) from another. □ **cross-pollination** /-ˈneɪʃ(ə)n/ n.

cross-question /krɒsˈkwestʃ(ə)n/ v.tr. = CROSS-EXAMINE.

cross-refer /ˌkrɒsrɪˈfɜː(r)/ v.intr. (**-referred**, **-referring**) refer from one part of a book, article, etc., to another.

cross-reference /ˈkrɒsˌrefərəns/ n. & v. —n. a reference from one part of a book, article, etc., to another. —v.tr. provide with cross-references.

crossroad /ˈkrɒsrəʊd/ n. **1** (usu. in pl.) an intersection of two or more roads. **2** US a road that crosses a main road or joins two main roads. □ **at the crossroads** at a critical point in one's life.

cross-section /krɒsˈsekʃ(ə)n/ n. **1 a** a cutting of a solid at right angles to an axis. **b** a plane surface produced in this way. **c** a representation of this. **2** a representative sample, esp. of people. □ **cross-sectional** adj.

cross-stitch /ˈkrɒsstɪtʃ/ n. **1** a stitch formed of two stitches crossing each other. **2** needlework done using this stitch.

crosstalk /ˈkrɒstɔːk/ n. **1** unwanted transfer of signals between communication channels. **2** Brit. witty talk; repartee.

crosswalk /ˈkrɒswɔːk/ n. US a pedestrian crossing.

crossways /ˈkrɒsweɪz/ adv. = CROSSWISE.

crosswind /ˈkrɒswɪnd/ n. a wind blowing across one's direction of travel.

crosswise /ˈkrɒswaɪz/ adj. & adv. **1** in the form of a cross; intersecting. **2** transverse or transversely.

crossword /ˈkrɒswɜːd/ n. (also **crossword puzzle**) a puzzle of a grid of squares and blanks into which words crossing vertically and horizontally have to be filled from clues.

crotch n. a place where something forks, esp. the legs of the human body or a garment. [perh. = ME & OF croc(he) hook, formed as CROOK]

crotchet /ˈkrɒtʃɪt/ n. **1** Mus. a note having the time value of a quarter of a semibreve and usu.

representing one beat, drawn as a large dot with a stem. **2** a whimsical fancy. **3** a hook. [ME f. OF crochet dimin. of croc hook (see CROTCH)]

crotchety /ˈkrɒtʃɪtɪ/ adj. peevish, irritable. □ **crotchetiness** n. [CROTCHET + -Y[1]]

crouch /kraʊtʃ/ v. & n. —v.intr. lower the body with the limbs close to the chest, esp. for concealment, or (of an animal) before pouncing; be in this position. —n. an act of crouching; a crouching position. [ME, perh. f. OF crochir be bent f. croc hook: cf. CROOK]

croup[1] /kruːp/ n. an inflammation of the larynx and trachea in children, with a hard cough and difficulty in breathing. □ **croupy** adj. [croup to croak (imit.)]

croup[2] /kruːp/ n. the rump or hindquarters esp. of a horse. [ME f. OF croupe, rel. to CROP]

croupier /ˈkruːpɪə(r), -ɪˌeɪ/ n. the person in charge of a gaming-table, raking in and paying out money etc. [F, orig. = rider on the croup: see CROUP[2]]

croûton /ˈkruːtɒn/ n. a small piece of fried or toasted bread served with soup or used as a garnish. [F f. croûte CRUST]

crow[1] /krəʊ/ n. **1** any large black bird of the genus Corvus, having a powerful black beak. **2** any similar bird of the family Corvidae, e.g. the raven, rook, and jackdaw. **3** sl. derog. a woman, esp. an old or ugly one. □ **as the crow flies** in a straight line. **crow's-foot** (pl. -feet) (usu. in pl.) a wrinkle at the outer corner of a person's eye. **crow's-nest** a barrel or platform fixed at the masthead of a sailing vessel as a shelter for a lookout man. **eat crow** US submit to humiliation. [OE crāwe ult. f. WG]

crow[2] /krəʊ/ v. & n. —v.intr. **1** (past **crowed** or **crew** /kruː/) (of a cock) utter its characteristic loud cry. **2** (of a baby) utter happy cries. **3** (usu. foll. by over) express unrestrained gleeful satisfaction. —n. **1** the cry of a cock. **2** a happy cry of a baby. [OE crāwan, of imit. orig.]

crowbar /ˈkrəʊbɑː(r)/ n. an iron bar with a flattened end, used as a lever.

crowd /kraʊd/ n. & v. —n. **1** a large number of people gathered together, usu. without orderly arrangement. **2** a mass of spectators; an audience. **3** colloq. a particular company or set of people. **4** (prec. by the) the mass or multitude of people. **5** a large number (of things). —v. **1 a** intr. come together in a crowd. **b** tr. cause to do this. **c** intr. force one's way. **2** tr. **a** (foll. by into) force or compress into a confined space. **b** (often foll. by with; usu. in passive) fill or make abundant with (was crowded with tourists). **3** tr. **a** (of a number of people) come aggressively close to. **b** colloq. harass or pressure (a person). □ **crowd out** exclude by crowding. □ **crowdedness** n. [OE crūdan press, drive]

crown /kraʊn/ n. & v. —n. **1** a monarch's ornamental and usu. jewelled head-dress. **2** (**the Crown**) **a** the monarch, esp. as head of State. **b** the power or authority residing in the monarchy. **3 a** a wreath of leaves or flowers etc. worn on the head, esp. as an emblem of victory. **b** an award or distinction gained by a victory or achievement, esp. in sport. **4** a crown-shaped thing, esp. a device or ornament. **5** the top part of a thing, esp. of the head or a hat. **6 a** the highest or central part of an arched or curved thing (crown of the road). **b** a thing that completes or forms the summit. **7** the part of a plant just above and below the ground. **8 a** the part of a tooth projecting from the gum. **b** an artificial replacement or covering for this. **9 a** a former British coin equal to five shillings (25p). **b** any of several foreign coins with a name meaning 'crown', esp. the krona or krone. —*v.tr.* **1** put a crown on (a person or a person's head). **2** invest (a person) with a royal crown or authority. **3** be a crown to; encircle or rest on the top of. **4 a** (often as **crowning** *adj.*) be or cause to be the consummation, reward, or finishing touch to (*the crowning glory*). **b** bring (efforts) to a happy issue. **5** fit a crown to (a tooth). **6** *sl.* hit on the head. □ **crown cap** a cork-lined metal cap for a bottle. **Crown Colony** a British colony controlled by the Crown. **Crown Court** a court of criminal jurisdiction in England and Wales. **crown green** a kind of bowling-green rising towards the middle. **crown jewels** the regalia and other jewellery worn by the sovereign on certain State occasions. **Crown prince** a male heir to a sovereign throne. **Crown princess 1** the wife of a Crown prince. **2** a female heir to a sovereign throne. **crown roast** a roast of rib-pieces of pork or lamb arranged like a crown. **crown wheel** a wheel with teeth set at right angles to its plane, esp. in the gears of motor vehicles. [ME f. AF *corune*, OF *corone* f. L *corona*]

crozier var. of CROSIER.

CRT *abbr.* cathode-ray tube.

cruces *pl.* of CRUX.

crucial /ˈkruːʃ(ə)l/ *adj.* **1** decisive, critical. **2** *colloq. disp.* very important. □ **cruciality** /-ʃɪˈælɪtɪ/ *n.* (*pl.* **-ies**). **crucially** *adv.* [F f. L *crux crucis* cross]

■ **Usage** Sense 2 should only be used informally.

crucible /ˈkruːsɪb(ə)l/ *n.* **1** a melting-pot for metals etc. **2** a severe test or trial. [ME f. med.L *crucibulum* night-lamp, crucible, f. L *crux crucis* cross]

cruciferous /kruːˈsɪfərəs/ *adj. Bot.* of the family Cruciferae, having flowers with four petals arranged in a cross. [LL *crucifer* (as CRUCIAL, -FEROUS)]

crucifix /ˈkruːsɪfɪks/ *n.* a model or image of a cross with a figure of Christ on it. [ME f. OF f. eccl.L *crucifixus* f. L *cruci fixus* fixed to a cross]

crucifixion /ˌkruːsɪˈfɪkʃ(ə)n/ *n.* **1 a** crucifying or being crucified. **b** an instance of this. **2** (**Crucifixion**) **a** the crucifixion of Christ. **b** a representation of this. [eccl.L *crucifixio* (as CRUCIFIX)]

cruciform /ˈkruːsɪfɔːm/ *adj.* cross-shaped (esp. of a church with transepts). [L *crux crucis* cross + -FORM]

crucify /ˈkruːsɪfaɪ/ *v.tr.* (**-ies, -ied**) **1** put to death by fastening to a cross. **2 a** cause extreme pain to. **b** persecute, torment. **c** *sl.* defeat thoroughly in an argument, match, etc. □ **crucifier** *n.* [ME f. OF *crucifier* f. LL *crucifigere* (as CRUCIFIX)]

crud *n. sl.* a deposit of unwanted impurities, grease, etc. □ **cruddy** *adj.* (**cruddier, cruddiest**). [var. of CURD]

crude *adj. & n.* —*adj.* **1 a** in the natural or raw state; not refined. **b** rough, unpolished; lacking finish. **2 a** (of an action, statement, or manners) rude, blunt. **b** offensive, indecent (*a crude gesture*). **3 a** *Statistics* (of figures) not adjusted or corrected. **b** rough (*a crude estimate*). —*n.* natural mineral

oil. □ **crudely** *adv.* **crudeness** *n.* **crudity** *n.* [ME f. L *crudus* raw, rough]

cruel /ˈkruːəl/ *adj.* (**crueller, cruellest** or **crueler, cruelest**) **1** indifferent to or gratified by another's suffering. **2** causing pain or suffering, esp. deliberately. □ **cruelly** *adv.* **cruelness** *n.* [ME f. OF f. L *crudelis*, rel. to *crudus* (as CRUDE)]

cruelty /ˈkruːəltɪ/ *n.* (*pl.* **-ies**) **1** a cruel act or attitude; indifference to another's suffering. **2** a succession of cruel acts; a continued cruel attitude (*suffered much cruelty*). □ **cruelty-free** *adj.* (of cosmetics etc.) produced without involving any cruelty to animals in the development or manufacturing process. [OF *crualté* ult. f. L *crudelitas*]

cruet /ˈkruːɪt/ *n.* **1** a small container for salt, pepper, oil, or vinegar for use at table. **2** (in full **cruet-stand**) a stand holding cruets. [ME through AF f. OF *crue* pot f. OS *krūka*: rel. to CROCK²]

cruise /kruːz/ *v. & n.* —*v.* **1** *intr.* make a journey by sea calling at a series of ports usu. according to a predetermined plan, esp. for pleasure. **2** *intr.* sail about without a precise destination. **3** *intr.* **a** (of a motor vehicle or aircraft) travel at a moderate or economical speed. **b** (of a vehicle or its driver) travel at random, esp. slowly. —*n.* a cruising voyage, esp. as a holiday. □ **cruise missile** one able to fly at a low altitude and guide itself by reference to the features of the region it traverses. **cruising speed** a comfortable and economical speed for a motor vehicle, below its maximum speed. [prob. f. Du. *kruisen* f. *kruis* CROSS]

cruiser /ˈkruːzə(r)/ *n.* **1** a warship of high speed and medium armament. **2** = *cabin cruiser*. **3** *US* a police patrol car. [Du. *kruiser* (as CRUISE)]

cruiserweight /ˈkruːzəweɪt/ *n.* esp. Brit. = *light heavyweight* (see HEAVYWEIGHT).

crumb /krʌm/ *n. & v.* —*n.* **1 a** a small fragment, esp. of bread. **b** a small particle (*a crumb of comfort*). **2** the soft inner part of a loaf of bread. **3** *sl.* an objectionable person. —*v.tr.* **1** cover with breadcrumbs. **2** break into crumbs. [OE *cruma*]

crumble /ˈkrʌmb(ə)l/ *v. & n.* —*v.* **1** *tr. & intr.* break or fall into crumbs or fragments. **2** *intr.* (of power, a reputation, etc.) gradually disintegrate. —*n.* a mixture of flour and fat, rubbed to the texture of breadcrumbs and cooked as a topping for fruit etc. (*apple crumble*; *vegetable crumble*). [ME f. OE, formed as CRUMB]

crumbly /ˈkrʌmblɪ/ *adj.* (**crumblier, crumbliest**) consisting of, or apt to fall into, crumbs or fragments. □ **crumbliness** *n.*

crumbs /krʌmz/ *int. Brit. sl.* expressing dismay or surprise. [euphem. for *Christ*]

crumby /ˈkrʌmɪ/ *adj.* (**crumbier, crumbiest**) **1** like or covered in crumbs. **2** = CRUMMY.

crummy /ˈkrʌmɪ/ *adj.* (**crummier, crummiest**) *colloq.* dirty, squalid; inferior, worthless. □ **crummily** *adv.* **crumminess** *n.* [var. of CRUMBY]

crumpet /ˈkrʌmpɪt/ *n.* **1** a soft flat cake of a yeast mixture cooked on a griddle and eaten toasted and buttered. **2** *Brit. joc.* or *offens.* **a** a sexually attractive person, esp. a woman. **b** women regarded collectively, esp. as objects of sexual desire. [17th c.: orig. uncert.]

crumple /ˈkrʌmp(ə)l/ *v. & n.* —*v.* **1** *tr. & intr.* (often foll. by *up*) **a** crush or become crushed into creases. **b** ruffle, wrinkle. **2** *intr.* (often foll.

by *up*) collapse, give way. —*n.* a crease or wrinkle. □ **crumple zone** a part of a motor vehicle, esp. the extreme front and rear, designed to crumple easily in a crash and absorb impact. □ **crumply** *adj.* (obs. *crump* (v. & adj.) (make or become) curved)

crunch /krʌntʃ/ *v. & n.* —*v.* **1** *tr.* **a** crush noisily with the teeth. **b** grind (gravel, dry snow, etc.) under foot, wheels, etc. **2** *intr.* (often foll. by *up*, *through*) make a crunching sound in walking, moving, etc. —*n.* **1** crunching; a crunching sound. **2** *colloq.* a decisive event or moment. [earlier *cra(u)nch*, assim. to *munch*]

crunchy /ˈkrʌntʃɪ/ *adj.* (**crunchier, crunchiest**) that can be or has been crunched or crushed into small pieces; hard and crispy. □ **crunchily** *adv.* **crunchiness** *n.*

crupper /ˈkrʌpə(r)/ *n.* **1** a strap buckled to the back of a saddle and looped under the horse's tail to hold the harness back. **2** the hindquarters of a horse. [ME f. OF *cropiere* (cf. CROUP²)]

crusade /kruːˈseɪd/ *n. & v.* —*n.* **1 a** any of several medieval military expeditions made by Europeans to recover the Holy Land from the Muslims. **b** a war instigated by the Church for alleged religious ends. **2** a vigorous campaign in favour of a cause. —*v.intr.* engage in a crusade. □ **crusader** *n.* [earlier *croisade* (F f. *croix* cross) or *crusado* (Sp. f. *cruz* cross)]

cruse /kruːz/ *n. archaic* an earthenware pot or jar. [OE *crūse*, of unkn. orig.]

crush /krʌʃ/ *v. & n.* —*v.tr.* **1** compress with force or violence, so as to break, bruise, etc. **2** reduce to powder by pressure. **3** crease or crumple by rough handling. **4** defeat or subdue completely (*crushed by my reply*). —*n.* **1** an act of crushing. **2** a crowded mass of people. **3** a drink made from the juice of crushed fruit. **4** *colloq.* (usu. foll. by *on*) a (usu. passing) infatuation. □ **crushable** *adj.* **crusher** *n.* **crushingly** *adv.* [ME f. AF *cruissir*, *corussier*, OF *croissir*, *cruissir*, gnash (teeth), crack, f. Rmc]

crust /krʌst/ *n. & v.* —*n.* **1 a** the hard outer part of a loaf of bread. **b** a piece of this with some soft bread attached. **c** a hard dry scrap of bread. **2** the pastry covering of a pie. **3** a hard casing of a softer thing, e.g. a harder layer over soft snow. **4** *Geol.* the outer portion of the earth. **5 a** a coating or deposit on the surface of anything. **b** a hard dry formation on the skin, a scab. **6** a deposit of tartar formed in bottles of old wine. **7** *sl.* impudence (*you have a crust!*). —*v.tr. & intr.* **1** cover or become covered with a crust. **2** form into a crust. □ **crustal** *adj.* (in sense 4 of *n.*). [ME f. OF *crouste* f. L *crusta* rind, shell]

crustacean /krʌˈsteɪʃ(ə)n/ *n. & adj.* —*n.* any arthropod of the class Crustacea, having a hard shell and usu. aquatic, e.g. the crab, lobster, and shrimp. —*adj.* of or relating to crustaceans. □ **crustaceology** /-ʃɪˈɒlədʒɪ/ *n.* **crustaceous** /-ʃəs/ *adj.* [mod.L *crustaceus* f. *crusta*: see CRUST]

crusted /ˈkrʌstɪd/ *adj.* **1 a** having a crust. **b** (of wine) having deposited a crust. **2** antiquated, venerable.

crusty /ˈkrʌstɪ/ *adj.* (**crustier, crustiest**) **1** having a crisp crust (*a crusty loaf*). **2** irritable, curt. **3** hard, crustlike. □ **crustily** *adv.* **crustiness** *n.*

crutch *n.* **1** a support for a lame person, usu. with a crosspiece at the top fitting under the armpit (*pair of crutches*). **2** any support or prop. **3** the crotch of the human body or garment. [OE *cryc(c)* f. Gmc]

crux *n.* (*pl.* **cruxes** or **cruces** /ˈkruːsiːz/) **1** the decisive point at issue. **2** a difficult matter; a puzzle. [L, = cross]

cruzado /kruːˈzɑːdəʊ/ *n.* (*pl.* **-os**) the chief monetary unit of Brazil from 1986. [Port. *cruzado*, *crusado*, = marked with the cross]

cry *v. & n.* —*v.* (**cries, cried**) **1** *intr.* (often foll. by *out*) make a loud or shrill sound, esp. to express pain, grief, etc., or to appeal for help. **2 a** *intr.* shed tears; weep. **b** *tr.* shed (tears). **3** *tr.* (often foll. by *out*) say or exclaim loudly or excitedly. **4** *intr.* (of an animal, esp. a bird) make a loud call. **5** *tr.* (of a hawker etc.) proclaim (wares etc.) in the street. —*n.* (*pl.* **cries**) **1** a loud inarticulate utterance of grief, pain, fear, joy, etc. **2** a loud excited utterance of words. **3** an urgent appeal or entreaty. **4** a spell of weeping. **5 a** public demand; a strong movement of opinion. **b** a watchword or rallying call. **6** the natural utterance of an animal, esp. of hounds on the scent. **7** the street-call of a hawker etc. □ **cry-baby** a person, esp. a child, who sheds tears frequently. **cry down** disparage, belittle. **cry off** *colloq.* withdraw from a promise or undertaking. **cry out for** demand as a self-evident requirement or solution. **cry up** praise, extol. **a far cry 1** a long way. **2** a very different thing. **in full cry** (of hounds) in keen pursuit. [ME f. OF *crier*, *cri* f. L *quiritare* wail]

cryer var. of CRIER.

crying /ˈkraɪɪŋ/ *attrib.adj.* (of an injustice or other evil) flagrant, demanding redress (*a crying need*; *a crying shame*).

cryo- /ˈkraɪəʊ/ *comb. form* (extreme) cold. [Gk *kruos* frost]

cryogenics /ˌkraɪəʊˈdʒɛnɪks/ *n.* the branch of physics dealing with the production and effects of very low temperatures. □ **cryogenic** *adj.*

cryosurgery /ˌkraɪəʊˈsɜːdʒərɪ/ *n.* surgery using the local application of intense cold for anaesthesia or therapy.

crypt /krɪpt/ *n.* an underground room or vault, esp. one beneath a church, used usu. as a burial-place. [ME f. L *crypta* f. Gk *kruptē* f. *kruptos* hidden]

cryptic /ˈkrɪptɪk/ *adj.* **1 a** obscure in meaning. **b** (of a crossword clue etc.) indirect; indicating the solution in a way that is not obvious. **c** secret, mysterious, enigmatic. **2** *Zool.* (of coloration etc.) serving for concealment. □ **cryptically** *adv.* [LL *crypticus* f. Gk *kruptikos* (as CRYPTO-)]

crypto- /ˈkrɪptəʊ/ *comb. form* concealed, secret (*crypto-communist*). [Gk *kruptos* hidden]

cryptogam /ˈkrɪptəˌgæm/ *n.* a plant that has no true flowers or seeds, e.g. ferns, mosses, algae, and fungi. □ **cryptogamic** /-ˈgæmɪk/ *adj.* **cryptogamous** /-ˈtɒgəməs/ *adj.* [F *cryptogame* f. mod.L *cryptogamia* (*plantae*) formed as CRYPTO- + Gk *gamos* marriage]

cryptogram /ˈkrɪptəˌgræm/ *n.* a text written in cipher.

cryptography /krɪpˈtɒgrəfɪ/ *n.* the art of writing or solving ciphers. □ **cryptographer** *n.* **cryptographic** /-təˈgræfɪk/ *adj.* **cryptographically** /-təˈgræfɪkəlɪ/ *adv.*

crystal /ˈkrɪst(ə)l/ *n. & adj.* —*n.* **1 a** a clear transparent mineral, esp. rock crystal. **b** a piece of this. **2** (in full **crystal glass**) a highly transparent glass; flint glass. **b** articles made of this. **3** *Electronics* a crystalline piece of semi-conductor. **5** *Chem.* an aggregation of molecules with a definite internal structure and the external form of a solid enclosed by symmetrically arranged plane faces. —*adj.* (usu. *attrib.*) made of, like, or clear as crystal. □ **crystal ball** a glass globe used in crystal-gazing. **crystal clear** unclouded, transparent. **crystal-gazing** the process of concentrating one's gaze on a crystal ball supposedly in order to obtain a picture of future events etc. [OE f. OF *cristal* f. L *crystallum* f. Gk *krustallos* ice, crystal]

crystalline /ˈkrɪstəlaɪn/ *adj.* **1** of, like, or clear as crystal. **2** *Chem.* & *Mineral.* having the structure and form of a crystal. □ **crystallinity** /-ˈlɪnɪtɪ/ *n.* [ME f. OF *cristallin* f. L *crystallinus* f. Gk *krustallinos* (as CRYSTAL)]

crystallize /ˈkrɪstəlaɪz/ *v.* (also **-ise**) **1** *tr.* & *intr.* form or cause to form crystals. **2** (often foll. by *out*) **a** *intr.* (of ideas or plans) become definite. **b** *tr.* make definite. **3** *tr.* & *intr.* coat or impregnate or become coated or impregnated with sugar (*crystallized fruit*). □ **crystallizable** *adj.* **crystallization** /-ˈzeɪʃ(ə)n/ *n.*

crystallography /ˌkrɪstəˈlɒgrəfɪ/ *n.* the science of crystal form and structure. □ **crystallographer** *n.* **crystallographic** /-ləˈgræfɪk/ *adj.*

crystalloid /ˈkrɪstəlɔɪd/ *adj.* **1** crystal-like. **2** having a crystalline structure.

Cs *symb. Chem.* the element caesium.

c/s *abbr.* cycles per second.

CSE *abbr. hist.* (in the UK) Certificate of Secondary Education.

■ **Usage** This examination was replaced in 1988 by GCSE.

CS gas /siːˈes/ *n.* a gas causing tears and choking, used to control riots etc. [B. B. Corson & R. W. Stoughton, Amer. chemists]

Cu *symb. Chem.* the element copper.

cu. *abbr.* cubic.

cub *n.* & *v.* —*n.* **1** the young of a fox, bear, lion, etc. **2** an ill-mannered young man. **3** (**Cub**) (in full **Cub Scout**) a member of the junior branch of the Scout Association. **4** (in full **cub reporter**) *colloq.* a young or inexperienced newspaper reporter. **5** *US* an apprentice. —*v.tr.* (**cubbed, cubbing**) (also *absol.*) give birth to (cubs). □ **cubhood** *n.* [16th c.: orig. unkn.]

cubby /ˈkʌbɪ/ *n.* (pl. **-ies**) (in full **cubby-hole**) **1** a very small room. **2** a snug or confined space. [dial. *cub* stall, pen, of LG orig.]

cube *n.* & *v.* —*n.* **1** a solid contained by six equal squares. **2** a cube-shaped block. **3** *Math.* the product of a number multiplied by its square. —*v.tr.* **1** find the cube of (a number). **2** cut (food for cooking etc.) into small cubes. □ **cube root** the number which produces a given number when cubed. □ **cuber** *n.* [F *cube* or L *cubus* f. Gk *kubos*]

cubic /ˈkjuːbɪk/ *adj.* **1** cube-shaped. **2** of three dimensions. **3** involving the cube (and no higher power) of a number (*cubic equation*). □ **cubic content** the volume of a solid expressed in cubic metres. **cubic metre** etc. the volume of a cube whose edge is one metre etc. [F *cubique* or L *cubicus* f. Gk *kubikos* (as CUBE)]

cubical /ˈkjuːbɪk(ə)l/ *adj.* cube-shaped. □ **cubically** *adv.*

cubicle /ˈkjuːbɪk(ə)l/ *n.* **1** a small partitioned space, screened for privacy. **2** a small separate sleeping-compartment. [L *cubiculum* f. *cubare* lie down]

cubiform /ˈkjuːbɪfɔːm/ *adj.* cube-shaped.

cubism /ˈkjuːbɪz(ə)m/ *n.* a style and movement in art, esp. painting, in which objects are represented as an assemblage of geometrical forms. □ **cubist** *n.* & *adj.* [F *cubisme* (as CUBE)]

cubit /ˈkjuːbɪt/ *n.* an ancient measure of length, approximately equal to the length of a forearm. [ME f. L *cubitum* elbow, cubit]

cuboid /ˈkjuːbɔɪd/ *adj.* & *n.* —*adj.* cube-shaped; like a cube. —*n.* *Geom.* a rectangular parallelepiped. □ **cuboidal** /-ˈbɔɪd(ə)l/ *adj.* [mod.L *cuboides* f. Gk *kuboeidēs* (as CUBE)]

cuckold /ˈkʌkəʊld/ *n.* & *v.* —*n.* the husband of an adulteress. —*v.tr.* make a cuckold of. □ **cuckoldry** *n.* [ME *cukeweld, cokewold,* f. OF *cucu* cuckoo]

cuckoo /ˈkʊkuː/ *n.* & *adj.* —*n.* any bird of the family Cuculidae, esp. *Cuculus canorus,* having a characteristic cry, and depositing its eggs in the nests of small birds. —*predic.adj.* *sl.* crazy, foolish. □ **cuckoo clock** a clock that strikes the hour with a sound like a cuckoo's call. **cuckoo-spit** froth exuded by larvae of insects of the family Cercopidae on leaves, stems, etc. [ME f. OF *cucu,* imit.]

cucumber /ˈkjuːkʌmbə(r)/ *n.* **1** a long green fleshy fruit, used in salads. **2** the climbing plant, *Cucumis sativus,* yielding this fruit. [ME f. OF *co(u)combre* f. L *cucumer*]

cud *n.* half-digested food returned from the first stomach of ruminants to the mouth for further chewing. [OE *cwidu, cudu* what is chewed, corresp. to OHG *kuti, quiti* glue]

cuddle /ˈkʌd(ə)l/ *v.* & *n.* —*v.* **1** *tr.* hug, embrace, fondle. **2** *intr.* nestle together, lie close and snug. —*n.* a prolonged and fond hug. □ **cuddlesome** *adj.* [16th c.: perh. f. dial. *couth* snug]

cuddly /ˈkʌdlɪ/ *adj.* (**cuddlier, cuddliest**) tempting to cuddle; given to cuddling.

cudgel /ˈkʌdʒ(ə)l/ *n.* & *v.* —*n.* a short thick stick used as a weapon. —*v.tr.* (**cudgelled, cudgelling;** *US* **cudgeled, cudgeling**) beat with a cudgel. □ **cudgel one's brains** think hard about a problem. **take up the cudgels** (often foll. by *for*) make a vigorous defence. [OE *cycgel,* of unkn. orig.]

cue[1] *n.* & *v.* —*n.* **1 a** the last words of an actor's speech serving as a signal to another actor to enter or speak. **b** a similar signal to a singer or player etc. **2 a** a stimulus to perception etc. **b** a signal for action. **c** a hint on how to behave in particular circumstances. —*v.tr.* (**cues, cued, cueing** or **cuing**) **1** give a cue to. **2** put (a piece of audio equipment, esp. a record-player or tape recorder) in readiness to play a particular part of the recorded material. □ **cue in** insert a cue for. **2** give information to. **on cue** at the correct moment. **take one's cue from** follow the example or advice of. [16th c.: orig. unkn.]

cue[2] /kjuː/ *n.* & *v.* *Billiards* etc. —*n.* a long straight tapering rod for striking the ball. —*v.* (**cues, cued, cueing** or **cuing**) **1** *tr.* strike (a ball) with a cue. **2** *intr.* use a cue. □ **cue-ball** the ball that is to be struck with the cue. □ **cueist** *n.* [var. of QUEUE]

cuff[1] *n.* **1 a** the end part of a sleeve. **b** a separate band of linen worn round the wrist so as to appear under the sleeve. **c** the part of a glove covering the wrist. **2** *US* a trouser turn-up. **3** (in *pl.*) *colloq.* handcuffs. □ **cuff-link** a device of two joined studs etc. to fasten the sides of a cuff together. **off the cuff** *colloq.* without preparation, extempore. □ **cuffed** *adj.* (also in *comb.*). [ME: orig. unkn.]

cuff[2] *v.* & *n.* —*v.tr.* strike with an open hand. —*n.* such a blow. [16th c.: perh. imit.]

Cufic var. of KUFIC.

cuirass /kwɪˈræs/ *n.* **1** *hist.* a piece of armour consisting of breastplate and back-plate fastened together. **2** a device for artificial respiration. [ME f. OF *cuirace*, ult. f. LL *coriaceus* f. *corium* leather]

cuisine /kwɪˈziːn/ *n.* a style or method of cooking, esp. of a particular country or establishment. [F f. L *coquina* f. *coquere* to cook]

cul-de-sac /ˈkʌldəˌsæk, ˈkʊl-/ *n.* (*pl.* **culs-de-sac** *pronunc.* same) **1** a street or passage closed at one end. **2** a route or course leading nowhere; a position from which one cannot escape. [F, = sack-bottom]

-cule /kjuːl/ *suffix* forming (orig. diminutive) nouns (*molecule*). [F *-cule* or L *-culus*]

culinary /ˈkʌlɪnərɪ/ *adj.* of or for cooking or the kitchen. □ **culinarily** *adv.* [L *culinarius* f. *culina* kitchen]

cull /kʌl/ *v.* & *n.* —*v.tr.* **1** select, choose, or gather from a large quantity or amount (*knowledge culled from books*). **2** pick or gather (flowers, fruit, etc.). **3** select (animals) according to quality, esp. poor surplus specimens for killing. —*n.* **1** an act of culling. **2** an animal or animals culled. □ **culler** *n.* [ME f. OF *coillier* etc. ult. f. L *colligere* COLLECT[1]]

cullet /ˈkʌlɪt/ *n.* recycled waste or broken glass used in glass-making. [var. of *collet*, F dimin. of *col* neck]

culminate /ˈkʌlmɪˌneɪt/ *v.* **1** *intr.* (usu. foll. by *in*) reach its highest or final point (*the antagonism culminated in war*). **2** *tr.* bring to its highest or final point. □ **culmination** /-ˈneɪʃ(ə)n/ *n.* [LL *culminare culminat-* f. *culmen* summit]

culottes /kjuːˈlɒts/ *n.pl.* women's (usu. short) trousers cut to resemble a skirt. [F, = knee-breeches]

culpable /ˈkʌlpəb(ə)l/ *adj.* deserving blame. □ **culpability** /-ˈbɪlɪtɪ/ *n.* **culpably** *adv.* [ME f. OF *coupable* f. L *culpabilis* f. *culpare* f. *culpa* blame]

culprit /ˈkʌlprɪt/ *n.* a person accused of or guilty of an offence. [17th c.: orig. in the formula *Culprit, how will you be tried?*, said by the Clerk of the Crown to a prisoner pleading Not Guilty: perh. abbr. of AF *Culpable: prest d'averrer* etc. (You are) guilty: (I am) ready to prove etc.]

cult /kʌlt/ *n.* **1** a system of religious worship, esp. as expressed in ritual. **2 a** devotion or homage to a person or thing (*the cult of aestheticism*). **b** a popular fashion, esp. followed by a specific section of society. **3** (*attrib.*) denoting a person or thing popularized in this way (*cult film*; *cult figure*). □ **cultic** *adj.* **cultism** *n.* **cultist** *n.* [F *culte* or L *cultus* worship f. *colere cult-* inhabit, till, worship]

cultivar /ˈkʌltɪˌvɑː(r)/ *n.* *Bot.* a plant variety produced by cultivation. [CULTIVATE + VARIETY]

cultivate /ˈkʌltɪˌveɪt/ *v.tr.* **1 a** prepare and use (soil etc.) for crops or gardening. **b** break up (the ground) with a cultivator. **2 a** raise or produce (crops). **b** culture (bacteria etc.). **3 a** (often as **cultivated** *adj.*) apply oneself to improving or developing (the mind, manners, etc.). **b** pay attention to or nurture (a person or a person's friendship). □ **cultivable** *adj.* **cultivatable** *adj.* **cultivation** /-ˈveɪʃ(ə)n/ *n.* [med.L *cultivare* f. *cultiva* (*terra*) arable (land) (as CULT)]

cultivator /ˈkʌltɪˌveɪtə(r)/ *n.* **1** a mechanical implement for breaking up the ground and uprooting weeds. **2** a person or thing that cultivates.

cultural /ˈkʌltʃər(ə)l/ *adj.* of or relating to the cultivation of the mind or manners, esp. through artistic or intellectual activity. □ **culturally** *adv.*

culture /ˈkʌltʃə(r)/ *n.* & *v.* —*n.* **1 a** the arts and other manifestations of human intellectual achievement regarded collectively. **b** a refined understanding of this; intellectual development. **2** the customs, civilization, and achievements of a particular time or people (*studied Chinese culture*). **3** improvement by mental or physical training. **4 a** the cultivation of plants; the rearing of bees, silkworms, etc. **b** the cultivation of the soil. **5** a quantity of micro-organisms and the nutrient material supporting their growth. —*v.tr.* maintain (bacteria etc.) in conditions suitable for growth. [ME f. F *culture* or L *cultura* (as CULT): (v.) from med.L *culturare*]

cultured /ˈkʌltʃəd/ *adj.* having refined taste and manners and a good education. □ **cultured pearl** a pearl formed by an oyster after the insertion of a foreign body into its shell.

culvert /ˈkʌlvət/ *n.* **1** an underground channel carrying water across a road etc. **2** a channel for an electric cable. [18th c.: orig. unkn.]

cum /kʌm/ *prep.* (usu. in *comb.*) with, combined with, also used as (*a bedroom-cum-study*). [L]

cumber /ˈkʌmbə(r)/ *v.* & *n.* —*v.tr.* *literary* hamper, hinder, inconvenience. —*n.* a hindrance, obstruction, or burden. [ME, prob. f. ENCUMBER]

cumbersome /ˈkʌmbəsəm/ *adj.* inconvenient in size, weight, or shape; unwieldy. □ **cumbersomely** *adv.* **cumbersomeness** *n.* [ME f. CUMBER + -SOME[1]]

cumbrous /ˈkʌmbrəs/ *adj.* = CUMBERSOME. □ **cumbrously** *adv.* **cumbrousness** *n.* [CUMBER + -OUS]

cumin /ˈkʌmɪn/ *n.* (also **cummin**) **1** an umbelliferous plant, *Cuminum cyminum*, bearing aromatic seeds. **2** these seeds used as flavouring. [ME f. OF *cumin, comin* f. L *cuminum* f. Gk *kuminon*, prob. of Semitic orig.]

cummerbund /ˈkʌməˌbʌnd/ *n.* a waist sash. [Hind. & Pers. *kamar-band* loin-band]

cumquat var. of KUMQUAT.

cumulate *v.* & *adj.* —*v.tr.* & *intr.* /ˈkjuːmjʊˌleɪt/ accumulate, amass; combine. —*adj.* /ˈkjuːmjʊlət/ heaped up, massed. □ **cumulation** /-ˈleɪʃ(ə)n/ *n.* [L *cumulare* f. *cumulus* heap]

cumulative /ˈkjuːmjʊlətɪv/ *adj.* **1** increasing or increased in amount, force, etc., by successive additions (*cumulative evidence*). **2** formed by successive additions (*learning is a cumulative process*). □ **cumulatively** *adv.* **cumulativeness** *n.*

cumulo- /ˈkjuːmjʊləʊ/ *comb. form* cumulus (cloud).

cumulus /ˈkjuːmjʊləs/ *n.* (*pl.* **cumuli** /-ˌlaɪ/) a cloud formation consisting of rounded masses heaped on each other above a horizontal base. □ **cumulous** *adj.* [L, = heap]

cuneiform /ˈkjuːnɪˌfɔːm/ adj. & n. —adj. 1 wedge-shaped. 2 of, relating to, or using the wedge-shaped writing impressed usu. in clay in ancient Babylonian etc. inscriptions. —n. cuneiform writing. [F cunéiforme or mod.L cuneiformis f. L cuneus wedge]

cunnilingus /ˌkʌnɪˈlɪŋɡəs/ n. (also **cunnilinctus** /-ˈlɪŋktəs/) oral stimulation of the female genitals. [L f. cunnus vulva + lingere lick]

cunning /ˈkʌnɪŋ/ adj. & n. —adj. (**cunninger**, **cunningest**) 1 a skilled in ingenuity or deceit. b selfishly clever or crafty. 2 ingenious (a cunning device). 3 US attractive, quaint. —n. 1 craftiness; skill in deceit. 2 skill, ingenuity. □ **cunningly** adv. **cunningness** n. [ME f. ON kunnandi knowing f. kunna know: cf. CAN¹]

cunt /kʌnt/ n. coarse sl. 1 the female genitals. 2 offens. an unpleasant or stupid person. [ME f. Gmc]

■ **Usage** This is considered a highly taboo word.

cup n. & v. —n. 1 a small bowl-shaped container, usu. with a handle for drinking from. 2 a its contents (a cup of tea). b = CUPFUL. 3 a cup-shaped thing, esp. the calyx of a flower or the socket of a bone. 4 flavoured wine, cider, etc., usu. chilled. 5 an ornamental cup-shaped trophy as a prize for victory or prowess, esp. in a sports contest. 6 one's fate or fortune (a bitter cup). 7 either of the two cup-shaped parts of a brassière. —v.tr. (**cupped**, **cupping**) 1 form (esp. one's hands) into the shape of a cup. 2 take or hold as in a cup. □ **Cup Final** a final match in a competition for a cup. **one's cup of tea** colloq. what interests or suits one. **cup-tie** a match in a competition for a cup. **in one's cups** while drunk; drunk. [OE cuppe f. med.L cuppa cup, prob. differentiated from L cupa tub]

cupboard /ˈkʌbəd/ n. a recess or piece of furniture with a door and (usu.) shelves, in which things are stored. □ **cupboard love** a display of affection meant to secure own gain. [ME f. CUP + BOARD]

cupful /ˈkʌpfʊl/ n. (pl. **-fuls**) 1 the amount held by a cup, esp. US a half-pint or 8-ounce measure in cookery. 2 a cup full of a substance (drank a cupful of water).

■ **Usage** A cupful is a measure, and so three cupfuls is a quantity regarded in terms of a cup; three cups full denotes the actual cups as in they brought us three cups full of water.

Cupid /ˈkjuːpɪd/ n. 1 (in Roman mythology) the Roman god of love represented as a naked winged boy with a bow and arrows. 2 (also **cupid**) a representation of Cupid. [ME f. L Cupido f. cupere desire]

cupidity /kjuːˈpɪdɪtɪ/ n. greed for gain; avarice. [ME f. OF cupidité or L cupiditas f. cupidus desirous]

cupola /ˈkjuːpələ/ n. 1 a a rounded dome forming a roof or ceiling. b a small rounded dome adorning a roof. 2 a revolving dome protecting mounted guns on a warship or in a fort. 3 (in full **cupola-furnace**) a furnace for melting metals. □ **cupolaed** /-ləd/ adj. [It. f. LL cupula dimin. of cupa cask]

cuppa /ˈkʌpə/ n. (also **cupper** /ˈkʌpə(r)/) Brit. colloq. 1 a cup of. 2 a cup of tea. [corruption]

cupreous /ˈkjuːprɪəs/ adj. of or like copper. [LL cupreus f. cuprum copper]

cupric /ˈkjuːprɪk/ adj. of copper, esp. divalent copper. □ **cupriferous** /-ˈprɪfərəs/ adj. [LL cuprum copper]

cupro-nickel /ˌkjuːprəʊˈnɪk(ə)l/ n. an alloy of copper and nickel, esp. in the proportions 3:1 as used in 'silver' coins.

cuprous /ˈkjuːprəs/ adj. of copper, esp. monovalent copper. [LL cuprum copper]

cur n. 1 a worthless or snappy dog. 2 a contemptible person. [ME, prob. orig. in cur-dog, perh. f. ON kurr grumbling]

curable /ˈkjʊərəb(ə)l/ adj. that can be cured. □ **curability** /-ˈbɪlɪtɪ/ n. [CURE]

curaçao /ˌkjʊərəˈsəʊ/ n. (also **curaçoa** /-ˈsəʊə/) (pl. **-os** or **curaçaos**) a liqueur of spirits flavoured with the peel of bitter oranges. [F Curaçao, name of the Caribbean island producing these oranges]

curacy /ˈkjʊərəsɪ/ n. (pl. **-ies**) a curate's office or the tenure of it.

curare /kjʊəˈrɑːrɪ/ n. a resinous bitter substance prepared from S. American plants of the genera Strychnos and Chondodendron, paralysing the motor nerves. [Carib]

curate /ˈkjʊərət/ n. a member of the clergy engaged as assistant to a parish priest. □ **curate's egg** a thing that is partly good and partly bad. [ME f. med.L curatus f. L cura CURE]

curative /ˈkjʊərətɪv/ adj. & n. —adj. tending or able to cure (esp. disease). —n. a curative medicine or agent. [F curatif -ive f. med.L curativus f. L curare CURE]

curator /kjʊəˈreɪtə(r)/ n. a keeper or custodian of a museum or other collection. □ **curatorial** /ˌkjʊərəˈtɔːrɪəl/ adj. **curatorship** n. [ME f. AF curatour (OF -eur) or L curator (as CURATIVE)]

curb n. & v. —n. 1 a check or restraint. 2 a strap etc. fastened to the bit and passing under a horse's lower jaw, used as a check. 3 an enclosing border or edging. 4 = KERB. —v.tr. 1 restrain. 2 put a curb on (a horse). [ME f. OF courber f. L curvare bend, CURVE]

curd n. 1 (often in pl.) a coagulated substance formed by the action of acids on milk, which may be made into cheese or eaten as food. 2 the edible head of a cauliflower. □ **curds and whey** the result of acidulating milk. □ **curdy** adj. [ME: orig. unkn.]

curdle /ˈkɜːd(ə)l/ v.tr. & intr. make into or become curds; congeal. □ **make one's blood curdle** fill one with horror. □ **curdler** n. [frequent. form of CURD]

cure v. & n. —v. 1 tr. (often foll. by of) restore (a person or animal) to health (was cured of pleurisy). 2 tr. eliminate (a disease, evil, etc.). 3 tr. preserve (meat, fruit, tobacco, or skins) by salting, drying, etc. 4 tr. a vulcanize (rubber). b harden (concrete or plastic). 5 intr. effect a cure. 6 intr. undergo a process of curing. —n. 1 restoration to health. 2 a thing that effects a cure. 3 a course of medical or healing treatment. □ **cure-all** a panacea; a universal remedy. □ **curer** n. [ME f. OF curer f. med.L curare take care of f. cura care]

curé /ˈkjʊəreɪ/ n. a parish priest in France etc. [F f. med.L curatus: see CURATE]

curettage /kjʊəˈretɪdʒ, -rɪˈtɑːdʒ/ n. the use of or an operation involving the use of a curette. [F (as CURETTE)]

curette /kjʊəˈret/ n. & v. —n. a surgeon's small scraping-instrument. —v.tr. & intr. clean or scrape with a curette. [F, f. curer cleanse (as CURE)]

curfew /ˈkɜːfjuː/ n. 1 a a regulation restricting or forbidding the public circulation of people, esp. requiring people to remain indoors between specified hours. b the hour designated as the beginning of such a restriction. c a daily signal indicating this. 2 hist. a medieval regulation requiring people to extinguish fires at a fixed hour in the evening. 3 the ringing of a bell at a fixed evening hour. [ME f. AF coeverfu, OF cuevrefeu f. the stem of couvrir COVER + feu fire]

Curia /ˈkjʊərɪə/ n. (also **curia**) the papal court; the government departments of the Vatican. □ **Curial** adj. [L: orig. a division of an ancient Roman tribe, the senate house at Rome, a feudal court of justice]

curie /ˈkjʊərɪ/ n. 1 a unit of radioactivity, corresponding to 3.7 × 10¹⁰ disintegrations per second. 2 a quantity of radioactive substance having this activity. [P. Curie, Fr. scientist d. 1906]

curio /ˈkjʊərɪəʊ/ n. (pl. **-os**) a rare or unusual object or person. [19th-c. abbr. of CURIOSITY]

curiosity /ˌkjʊərɪˈɒsɪtɪ/ n. (pl. **-ies**) 1 an eager desire to know; inquisitiveness. 2 strangeness. 3 a strange, rare, or interesting object. [ME f. OF curiouseté f. L curiositas -tatis (as CURIOUS)]

curious /ˈkjʊərɪəs/ adj. 1 eager to learn; inquisitive. 2 strange, surprising, odd. □ **curiously** adv. **curiousness** n. [ME f. OF curios f. L curiosus careful f. cura care]

curium /ˈkjʊərɪəm/ n. an artificially made transuranic radioactive metallic element. [M. Curie d. 1934 and P. Curie d. 1906, Fr. scientists]

curl v. & n. —v. 1 tr. & intr. (often foll. by up) bend or coil into a spiral; form or cause to form curls. 2 intr. move in a spiral form (smoke curling upwards). 3 a intr. (of the upper lip) be raised slightly on one side as an expression of contempt or disapproval. b tr. cause (the lip) to do this. 4 intr. play curling. —n. 1 a lock of curled hair. 2 anything spiral or curved inwards. 3 a a curling movement or act. b the state of being curled. □ **curl up** 1 lie or sit with the knees drawn up. 2 colloq. writhe with embarrassment or horror. [ME; earliest form crolled, crulled f. obs. adj. crolle, crulle curly f. MDu. krul]

curler /ˈkɜːlə(r)/ n. 1 a pin or roller etc. for curling the hair. 2 a player in the game of curling.

curlew /ˈkɜːljuː/ n. any wading bird of the genus Numenius, esp. N. arquatus, possessing a usu. long slender down-curved bill. [ME f. OF courlieu, courlis orig. imit., but assim. to courliu courier f. courre run + lieu place]

curlicue /ˈkɜːlɪˌkjuː/ n. a decorative curl or twist. [CURLY + CUE² (= pigtail) or Q¹]

curling /ˈkɜːlɪŋ/ n. 1 in senses of CURL v. 2 a game played on ice, in which large round flat stones are slid across the surface towards a mark. □ **curling-tongs** (or **-iron** or **-pins**) a heated device for twisting the hair into curls.

curly /ˈkɜːlɪ/ adj. (**curlier**, **curliest**) 1 having or arranged in curls. 2 moving in curves. □ **curliness** n.

curmudgeon /kɜːˈmʌdʒ(ə)n/ n. a bad-tempered person. □ **curmudgeonly** adj. [16th c.: orig. unkn.]

currant /ˈkʌrənt/ n. 1 a dried fruit of a small seedless variety of grape grown in the Levant and much used in cookery. 2 a any of various shrubs of the genus Ribes producing red, white, or black berries. b a berry of these shrubs. [ME raysons of coraunce f. AF, = grapes of Corinth (the orig. source)]

currency /ˈkʌrənsɪ/ n. (pl. **-ies**) 1 a the money in general use in a country. b any other commodity used as a medium of exchange. 2 the condition of being current; prevalence (e.g. of words or ideas). 3 the time during which something is current.

current /ˈkʌrənt/ adj. & n. —adj. 1 belonging to the present time; happening now (current events; the current week). 2 (of money, opinion, a rumour, a word, etc.) in general circulation or use. —n. 1 a body of water, air, etc., moving in a definite direction, esp. through a stiller surrounding body. 2 an ordered movement of electrically charged particles. 3 (usu. foll. by of) a general tendency or course (of events, opinions, etc.). □ **current account** a bank account from which money may be drawn without notice. □ **currentness** n. [ME f. OF corant f. L currere run]

currently /ˈkʌrəntlɪ/ adv. at the present time; now.

curriculum /kəˈrɪkjʊləm/ n. (pl. **curricula** /-lə/) 1 the subjects that are prescribed for study in a school. 2 any programme of activities. □ **curricular** adj. [L, = course, race-chariot, f. currere run]

curriculum vitae /kəˈrɪkjʊləm ˈviːtaɪ/ n. a brief account of one's education, qualifications, and previous occupations. [L, = course of life]

curry¹ /ˈkʌrɪ/ n. & v. —n. (pl. **-ies**) a dish of meat, vegetables, etc., cooked in a sauce of hot-tasting spices, usu. served with rice. —v.tr. (**-ies**, **-ied**) prepare or flavour with a sauce of hot-tasting spices (curried eggs). □ **curry-powder** a preparation of spices for making curry. [Tamil]

curry² /ˈkʌrɪ/ v.tr. (**-ies**, **-ied**) 1 groom (a horse) with a curry-comb. 2 treat (tanned leather) to improve its properties. □ **curry-comb** a hand-held metal serrated device for grooming horses. **curry favour** ingratiate oneself. [ME f. OF correier ult. f. Gmc]

curse /kɜːs/ n. & v. —n. 1 a solemn utterance intended to invoke a supernatural power to inflict destruction or punishment on a person or thing. 2 the evil supposedly resulting from a curse. 3 a violent exclamation of anger; a profane oath. 4 a thing that causes evil or harm. 5 (prec. by the) colloq. menstruation. —v. 1 tr. utter a curse against. 2 tr. (usu. in passive; foll. by with) afflict with (cursed with blindness). 3 intr. utter expletive curses; swear. 4 tr. excommunicate. □ **curser** n. [OE curs, cursian, of unkn. orig.]

cursed /ˈkɜːsɪd, kɜːst/ adj. damnable, abominable. □ **cursedly** adv. **cursedness** n.

cursive /ˈkɜːsɪv/ adj. & n. —adj. (of writing) done with joined characters. —n. cursive writing. □ **cursively** adv. [med.L (scriptura) cursiva f. L currere curs- run]

cursor /ˈkɜːsə(r)/ n. 1 Math. etc. a transparent slide engraved with a hairline and forming part of a slide-rule. 2 Computing a movable indicator on a VDU screen identifying a particular position in the display, esp. the position that the program will operate on with the next keystroke. [L. = runner (as CURSIVE)]

cursory /ˈkɜːsərɪ/ adj. hasty, hurried (a cursory glance). □ **cursorily** adv. **cursoriness** n. [L cursorius of a runner (as CURSOR)]

curt adj. noticeably or rudely brief. □ **curtly** adv. **curtness** n. [L curtus cut short, abridged]

curtail /kɜːˈteɪl/ v.tr. cut short; reduce; terminate esp. prematurely (curtailed his visit to America). □ **curtailment** n. [obs. curtal horse with docked tail f. F courtault f. court short f. L curtus: assim. to tail]

curtain /ˈkɜːt(ə)n/ n. & v. —n. 1 a piece of cloth etc. hung up as a screen, usu. moveable sideways or upwards, esp. at a window or between the stage and auditorium of a theatre. 2 Theatr. **a** the rise or fall of the stage curtain at the beginning or end of an act or scene. **b** = curtain-call. 3 (in pl.) sl. the end. —v.tr. 1 furnish or cover with a curtain or curtains. 2 (foll. by off) shut off with a curtain or curtains. □ **curtain-call** Theatr. an audience's summons to actor(s) to take a bow after the fall of the curtain. **curtain-raiser 1** Theatr. a piece prefaced to the main performance. 2 a preliminary event. **curtain-wall 1** Fortification the plain wall of a fortified place, connecting two towers etc. 2 Archit. a piece of plain wall not supporting a roof. [ME f. OF cortine f. LL cortina transl. Gk aulaia f. aulē court]

curtsy /ˈkɜːtsɪ/ n. & v. (also **curtsey**) —n. (pl. **-ies** or **-eys**) a woman's or girl's formal greeting or salutation made by bending the knees and lowering the body. —v.intr. (**-ies, -ied** or **-eys, -eyed**) make a curtsy. [var. of COURTESY]

curvaceous /kɜːˈveɪʃəs/ adj. colloq. (esp. of a woman) having a shapely curved figure.

curvature /ˈkɜːvətʃə(r)/ n. 1 the act or state of curving. 2 a curved form. 3 Geom. **a** the deviation of a curve from a straight line, or of a curved surface from a plane. **b** the quantity expressing this. [OF f. L curvatura (as CURVE)]

curve n. & v. —n. 1 a line or surface having along its length a regular deviation from being straight or flat, as exemplified by the surface of a sphere or lens. 2 a curved form or thing. 3 a curved line on a graph. 4 Baseball a ball caused to deviate by the pitcher's spin. —v.tr. & intr. bend or shape so as to form a curve. □ **curved** adj. [orig. as adj. (in curve line) f. L curvus bent: (v.) f. L curvare]

curvet /kɜːˈvet/ n. & v. —n. a horse's leap with the forelegs raised together and the hind legs raised with a spring before the forelegs reach the ground. —v.intr. (**curvetted, curvetting** or **curveted, curveting**) (of a horse or rider) make a curvet. [It. corvetta dimin. of corva CURVE]

curvi- /ˈkɜːvɪ/ comb. form curved. [L curvus curved]

curvilinear /ˌkɜːvɪˈlɪnɪə(r)/ adj. contained by or consisting of curved lines. □ **curvilinearly** adv. [CURVI- after rectilinear]

curvy /ˈkɜːvɪ/ adj. (**curvier, curviest**) 1 having many curves. 2 (of a woman's figure) shapely. □ **curviness** n.

cushion /ˈkʊʃ(ə)n/ n. & v. —n. 1 a bag of cloth etc. stuffed with a mass of soft material, used as a soft support for sitting or leaning on etc. 2 a means of protection against shock. 3 the elastic lining of the sides of a billiard-table, from which the ball rebounds. 4 a body of air supporting a hovercraft etc. —v.tr. 1 provide or

protect with a cushion or cushions. 2 provide with a defence; protect. 3 mitigate the adverse effects of (cushioned the blow). □ **cushiony** adj. [ME f. OF co(i)ssin, cu(i)ssin f. Gallo-Roman f. L culcita mattress, cushion]

cushy /ˈkʊʃɪ/ adj. (**cushier, cushiest**) colloq. 1 (of a job etc.) easy and pleasant. 2 US (of a seat, surroundings, etc.) soft, comfortable. □ **cushiness** n. [Anglo-Ind. f. Hind. k̲h̲ūsh pleasant]

cusp n. 1 an apex or peak. 2 the horn of a crescent moon etc. 3 Astrol. the initial point of a house. 4 Archit. a projecting point between small arcs in Gothic tracery. 5 a cone-shaped prominence on the surface of a tooth. □ **cuspate** /-speɪt/ adj. **cusped** adj. **cuspidal** adj. [L cuspis, -idis point, apex]

cuspidor /ˈkʌspɪˌdɔː(r)/ n. US a spittoon. [Port., = spitter f. cuspir spit f. L conspuere]

cuss n. & v. colloq. —n. 1 a curse. 2 usu. derog. a person; a creature. —v.tr. & intr. curse. □ **cuss-word** US a swear-word. [var. of CURSE]

cussed /ˈkʌsɪd/ adj. colloq. awkward and stubborn. □ **cussedly** adv. **cussedness** n. [var. of CURSED]

custard /ˈkʌstəd/ n. 1 a dish made with milk and eggs, usu. sweetened. 2 a sweet sauce made with milk and flavoured cornflour. □ **custard-pie 1** a pie containing custard, commonly thrown in slapstick comedy. 2 (attrib.) denoting slapstick comedy. **custard powder** a preparation of cornflour etc. for making custard. [ME, earlier crusta(r)de f. AF f. OF crouste CRUST]

custodian /kʌˈstəʊdɪən/ n. a guardian or keeper, esp. of a public building etc. □ **custodianship** n. [CUSTODY + -AN, after guardian]

custody /ˈkʌstədɪ/ n. 1 guardianship; protective care. 2 imprisonment. □ **take into custody** arrest. □ **custodial** /kʌˈstəʊdɪəl/ adj. [L custodia f. custos -odis guardian]

custom /ˈkʌstəm/ n. 1 **a** the usual way of behaving or acting. **b** a particular established way of behaving (our customs seem strange to foreigners). 2 Law established usage having the force of law. 3 business patronage; regular dealings or customers (lost a lot of custom). 4 (in pl.; also treated as sing.) **a** a duty levied on certain imported and exported goods. **b** the official department that administers this. **c** the area at a port, frontier, etc., where customs officials deal with incoming goods, baggage, etc. □ **custom-built** (or **-made** etc.) made to a customer's order. **custom-house** the office at a port or frontier etc. at which customs duties are levied. [ME and OF custume ult. f. L consuetudo -dinis f. consuetus accustomed]

customary /ˈkʌstəmərɪ/ adj. 1 usual; in accordance with custom. 2 Law in accordance with custom. □ **customarily** adv. **customariness** n. [med.L custumarius f. custuma f. AF custume (as CUSTOM)]

customer /ˈkʌstəmə(r)/ n. 1 a person who buys goods or services from a shop or business. 2 a person one has to deal with (an awkward customer). [ME f. AF custumer (as CUSTOMARY), or f. CUSTOM + -ER¹]

customize /ˈkʌstəˌmaɪz/ v.tr. (also **-ise**) make to order or modify according to individual requirements.

cut /kʌt/ v. & n. —v. (**cutting**; past and past part. **cut**) 1 tr. (also absol.) penetrate or wound with a sharp-edged instrument (cut his finger; the knife won't cut). 2 tr. & intr. (often foll. by into) divide or be divided with a knife etc. (*cut the bread; cut the cloth into metre lengths*). **3** *tr.* **a** trim or reduce the length of (hair, a hedge, etc.) by cutting. **b** detach all or the significant part of (flowers, corn, etc.) by cutting. **4** *tr.* (foll. by *loose, open,* etc.) make loose, open, etc. by cutting. **5** *tr.* (esp. as **cutting** *adj.*) cause sharp physical or mental pain to (*a cutting wind; was cut to the quick*). **6** *tr.* (often foll. by *down*) **a** reduce (wages, prices, time, etc.). **b** reduce or cease (services etc.). **7** *tr.* shape or fashion (a coat, gem, key, record, etc.) by cutting. **8** *tr.* perform, execute, make (*cut a caper; cut a sorry figure*). **9** *tr.* (also *absol.*) cross, intersect (*the line cuts the circle at two points*). **10** *intr.* (foll. by *across, through,* etc.) pass or traverse, esp. in a hurry or as a shorter way (*cut across the grass*). **11** *tr.* **a** ignore or refuse to recognize (a person). **b** renounce (a connection). **12** *tr.* esp. *US* deliberately fail to attend (a class etc.). **13** *Cards* **a** *tr.* divide (a pack) into two parts. **b** *intr.* select a dealer etc. by dividing the pack. **14** *Cinematog.* **a** *tr.* edit (a film or tape). **b** *intr.* (often in *imper.*) stop filming or recording. **c** *intr.* (foll. by *to*) go quickly to (another shot). **15** *tr.* switch off (an engine etc.). **16** *tr.* hit (a ball) with a chopping motion. **17** *tr.* *US* dilute, adulterate. **18** *tr.* castrate. —*n.* **1** an act of cutting. **2** a division or wound made by cutting. **3** a stroke with a knife, sword, whip, etc. **4 a** a reduction (in prices, wages, etc.). **b** a cessation (of a power supply etc.). **5** an excision of part of a play, film, book, etc. **6** a wounding remark or act. **7** the way or style in which a garment, the hair, etc., is cut. **8** a piece of meat etc. cut from a carcass. **9** *colloq.* commission; a share of profits. **10** *Tennis* & *Cricket* etc. a stroke made by cutting. **11** ignoring of or refusal to recognize a person. □ **a cut above** *colloq.* noticeably superior to. **be cut out** (foll. by *for*, or *to* + infin.) be suited (*was not cut out to be a teacher*). **cut and dried 1** completely decided; prearranged; inflexible. **2** (of opinions etc.) ready-made, lacking freshness. **cut and run** *sl.* run away. **cut and thrust** a lively interchange of argument etc. **cut back 1** reduce (expenditure etc.). **2** prune (a tree etc.). **cut-back** *n.* an instance or the act of cutting back, esp. a reduction in expenditure. **cut both ways 1** serve both sides of an argument etc. **2** (of an action) have both good and bad effects. **cut a corner** go across and not round it. **cut corners** do a task etc. perfunctorily or incompletely, esp. to save time. **cut dead** completely refuse to recognize (a person). **cut down 1 a** bring or throw down by cutting. **b** kill by means of a sword or disease. **2** see sense 6 of *v.* **3** reduce the length of (*cut down the trousers to make shorts*). **4** (often foll. by *on*) reduce one's consumption (*tried to cut down on beer*). **cut glass** glass with patterns and designs cut on it. **cut in 1** interrupt. **2** pull in too closely in front of another vehicle (esp. having overtaken it). **3** give a share of profits etc. to (a person). **cut into 1** make a cut in (*they cut into the cake*). **2** interfere with and reduce (*travelling cuts into my free time*). **cut it out** (usu. in *imper.*) *sl.* stop doing that (esp. quarrelling). **cut-line 1** a caption to an illustration. **2** the line in squash above which a served ball must strike the wall. **cut loose 1** begin to act freely. **2** see sense 4 of *v.* **cut one's losses** (or **a loss**) abandon an unprofitable enterprise before losses become too great. **cut the mustard** *US sl.* reach the required standard.

cut no ice *sl.* **1** have no influence or importance. **2** achieve little or nothing. **cut off 1** remove (an appendage) by cutting. **2 a** (often in *passive*) bring to an abrupt end or (esp. early) death. **b** intercept, interrupt; prevent from continuing (*cut off supplies; cut off the gas*). **c** disconnect (a person engaged in a telephone conversation) (*was suddenly cut off*). **3 a** prevent from travelling or venturing out (*was cut off by the snow*). **b** (as **cut off** *adj.*) isolated, remote (*felt cut off in the country*). **4** disinherit (*was cut off without a penny*). **cut-off** *n.* **1** the point at which something is cut off. **2** a device for stopping a flow. **3** *US* a short cut. **cut out 1** remove from the inside by cutting. **2** make by cutting from a larger whole. **3** omit; leave out. **4** *colloq.* stop doing or using (something). **5** cease or cause to cease functioning (*the engine cut out*). **6** outdo or supplant (a rival). **cut-out 1** a figure cut out of paper etc. **2** a device for automatic disconnection, the release of exhaust gases, etc. **cut-out box** *US* = *fuse-box.* **cut-price** (or **-rate**) selling or sold at a reduced price. **cut short** interrupt; terminate prematurely (*cut short his visit*). **cut one's teeth on** acquire initial practice or experience from (something). **cut a tooth** have it appear through the gum. **cut up 1** cut into pieces. **2** destroy utterly. **3** (usu. in *passive*) distress greatly (*was very cut up about it*). **4** criticize severely. **5** *US* behave in a comical or unruly manner. **cut up rough** *Brit. sl.* show anger or resentment. [ME *cutte, kitte, kette,* perh. f. OE *cyttan* (unrecorded)]

cutaneous /kjuːˈteɪnɪəs/ *adj.* of the skin. [mod.L *cutaneus* f. L *cutis* skin]

cutaway /ˈkʌtəˌweɪ/ *adj.* **1** (of a diagram etc.) with some parts left out to reveal the interior. **2** (of a coat) with the front below the waist cut away.

cutch var. of COUCH².

cute /kjuːt/ *adj. colloq.* **1** esp. *US* attractive, quaint. **b** affectedly attractive. **2** clever, ingenious. □ **cutely** *adv.* **cuteness** *n.* [shortening of ACUTE]

cuticle /ˈkjuːtɪk(ə)l/ *n.* **1 a** the dead skin at the base of a fingernail or toenail. **b** the epidermis or other superficial skin. **2** *Bot.* a thin surface film on plants. □ **cuticular** /-ˈtɪkjʊlə(r)/ *adj.* [L *cuticula,* dimin. of *cutis* skin]

cutis /ˈkjuːtɪs/ *n.* *Anat.* the true skin or dermis, underlying the epidermis. [L, = skin]

cutlass /ˈkʌtləs/ *n.* a short sword with a slightly curved blade, esp. of the type formerly used by sailors. [F *coutelas* ult. f. L *cultellus:* see CUTLER]

cutler /ˈkʌtlə(r)/ *n.* a person who makes or deals in knives and similar utensils. [ME f. AF *cotillere,* OF *coutelier* f. *coutel* f. L *cultellus* dimin. of *culter* COULTER]

cutlery /ˈkʌtləri/ *n.* knives, forks, and spoons for use at table. [OF & F *coutel(l)erie* (as CUTLER)]

cutlet /ˈkʌtlɪt/ *n.* **1** a neck-chop of mutton or lamb. **2** a small piece of veal etc. for frying. **3** a flat cake of minced meat or nuts and breadcrumbs etc. [F *côtelette,* OF *costelet* dimin. of *coste* rib f. L *costa*]

cutter /ˈkʌtə(r)/ *n.* **1** a tailor etc. who takes measurements and cuts cloth. **2** *Naut.* **a** a small fast sailing-ship. **b** a small boat carried by a large ship.

cutthroat /ˈkʌtθrəʊt/ *n.* & *adj.* —*n.* **1** a murderer. **2** (in full **cutthroat razor**) a razor having a long blade set in a handle and usu. folding like a penknife. —*adj.* (of competition) ruthless and intense.

cutting /ˈkʌtɪŋ/ *n. & adj.* —*n.* **1** a piece cut from a newspaper etc. **2** a piece cut from a plant for propagation. **3** an excavated channel through high ground for a railway or road. —*adj.* see CUT *v.* 5. □ **cuttingly** *adv.*

cuttlefish /ˈkʌt(ə)lfɪʃ/ *n.* any marine cephalopod mollusc of the genera *Sepia* and *Sepiola*, having ten arms and ejecting a black fluid when threatened or pursued. [OE *cudele*, ME *codel*, rel. to *cod* bag, with ref. to its ink-bag]

cutwater /ˈkʌtˌwɔːtə(r)/ *n.* **1** the forward edge of a ship's prow. **2** a wedge-shaped projection from a pier or bridge.

cutworm /ˈkʌtwɜːm/ *n.* any of various caterpillars that eat through the stems of young plants level with the ground.

c.v. *abbr.* curriculum vitae.

cwm /kuːm/ *n.* **1** (in Wales) = COOMB. **2** *Geog.* a cirque. [Welsh]

cwt. *abbr.* hundredweight.

-cy /sɪ/ *suffix* (see also -ACY, -ANCY, -CRACY, -ENCY, -MANCY). **1** denoting state or condition (*bankruptcy*; *idiocy*). **2** denoting rank or status (*captaincy*). [from or after L -*cia*, -*tia*, Gk -*k(e)ia*, -*t(e)ia*]

cyanide /ˈsaɪənaɪd/ *n.* any of the highly poisonous salts or esters of hydrocyanic acid. [CYANOGEN + -IDE]

cyanobacterium /ˌsaɪæˌnəʊbækˈtɪərɪəm/ *n.* any prokaryotic organism of the division Cyanobacteria, found in many environments and capable of photosynthesizing. [CYANOGEN + BACTERIUM]

cyanocabalamin /ˌsaɪəˌnəʊkəˈbæləmɪn/ *n.* a vitamin of the B complex, found in foods of animal origin such as liver, fish, and eggs.

cyanogen /saɪˈænədʒ(ə)n/ *n. Chem.* a colourless highly poisonous gas intermediate in the preparation of many fertilizers. [F *cyanogène* f. Gk *kuanos* dark-blue mineral, as being a constituent of Prussian blue]

cyanosis /ˌsaɪəˈnəʊsɪs/ *n. Med.* a bluish discoloration of the skin due to the presence of oxygen-deficient blood. □ **cyanotic** /-ˈnɒtɪk/ *adj.* [mod.L f. Gk *kuanōsis* blueness (as CYANOGEN)]

cybernetics /ˌsaɪbəˈnetɪks/ *n.pl.* (usu. treated as *sing.*) the science of communications and automatic control systems in both machines and living things. □ **cybernetic** *adj.* **cybernetician** /-ˈtɪʃ(ə)n/ *n.* **cyberneticist** /-sɪst/ *n.* [Gk *kubernētēs* steersman]

cycad /ˈsaɪkæd/ *n. Bot.* any of the palmlike plants of the order Cycadales (including fossil forms) inhabiting tropical and subtropical regions and often growing to a great height. [mod.L *cycas*, *cycad-* f. supposed Gk *kukas*, scribal error for *koikas*, pl. of *koix* Egyptian palm]

cyclamate /ˈsaɪkləmeɪt, ˈsɪk-/ *n.* any of various salts or esters of sulphamic acid formerly used as artificial sweetening agents. [Chem. name *cyclohexyl- sulphamate*]

cyclamen /ˈsɪkləmən/ *n.* any plant of the genus Cyclamen, originating in Europe, having pink, red, or white flowers with reflexed petals. [med.L f. Gk *kuklaminos*, perh. f. *kuklos* circle, with ref. to its bulbous roots]

cycle /ˈsaɪk(ə)l/ *n. & v.* —*n.* **1 a** a recurrent round or period (of events, phenomena, etc.). **b** the

time needed for one such round or period. **2 a** *Physics* etc. a recurrent series of operations or states. **b** *Electr.* = HERTZ. **3** a series of songs, poems, etc., usu. on a single theme. **4** a bicycle, tricycle, or similar machine. —*v.intr.* **1** ride a bicycle etc. **2** move in cycles. □ **cycle-track** (or **-way**) a path or road for bicycles. [ME f. OF, or f. LL *cyclus* f. Gk *kuklos* circle]

cyclic /ˈsaɪklɪk/ *adj.* **1 a** recurring in cycles. **b** belonging to a chronological cycle. **2** *Chem.* with constituent atoms forming a ring. **3** of a cycle of songs etc. [F *cyclique* or L *cyclicus* f. Gk *kuklikos* (as CYCLE)]

cyclical /ˈsaɪklɪk(ə)l, ˈsɪk-/ *adj.* = CYCLIC 1. □ **cyclically** *adv.*

cyclist /ˈsaɪklɪst/ *n.* a rider of a bicycle.

cyclo- /ˈsaɪkləʊ/ *comb. form* circle, cycle, or cyclic (*cyclometer*; *cyclorama*). [Gk *kuklos* circle]

cyclo-cross /ˈsaɪkləʊˌkrɒs/ *n.* cross-country racing on bicycles.

cycloid /ˈsaɪklɔɪd/ *n. Math.* a curve traced by a point on a circle when the circle is rolled along a straight line. □ **cycloidal** /-ˈklɔɪd(ə)l/ *adj.* [Gk *kukloeidēs* (as CYCLE, -OID)]

cyclometer /saɪˈklɒmɪtə(r)/ *n.* **1** an instrument for measuring circular arcs. **2** an instrument for measuring the distance traversed by a bicycle etc.

cyclone /ˈsaɪkləʊn/ *n.* **1** a system of winds rotating inwards to an area of low barometric pressure; a depression. **2** a violent hurricane of limited diameter. □ **cyclonic** /-ˈklɒnɪk/ *adj.* **cyclonically** /-ˈklɒnɪkəlɪ/ *adv.* [prob. repr. Gk *kuklōma* wheel, coil of a snake]

cyclopedia /ˌsaɪkləˈpiːdɪə/ *n.* (also **cyclopaedia**) an encyclopedia. □ **cyclopedic** *adj.* [shortening of ENCYCLOPEDIA]

Cyclopean /ˌsaɪkləˈpiːən, -ˈkləʊpɪən/ *adj.* (also **Cyclopian**) (of ancient masonry) made with massive irregular blocks.

cyclostyle /ˈsaɪkləˌstaɪl/ *n. & v.* —*n.* an apparatus for printing copies of writing from a stencil. —*v.tr.* print or reproduce with this.

cyclotron /ˈsaɪkləˌtrɒn/ *n. Physics* an apparatus in which charged atomic and subatomic particles are accelerated by an alternating electric field while following an outward spiral or circular path in a magnetic field.

cyder var. of CIDER.

cygnet /ˈsɪgnɪt/ *n.* a young swan. [ME f. AF *cignet* dimin. of OF *cigne* swan f. med.L *cycnus* f. Gk *kuknos*]

cylinder /ˈsɪlɪndə(r)/ *n.* **1 a** a uniform solid or hollow body with straight sides and a circular section. **b** a thing of this shape, e.g. a container for liquefied gas. **2** a cylinder-shaped part of various machines, esp. a piston-chamber in an engine. □ **cylindrical** /-ˈlɪndrɪk(ə)l/ *adj.* **cylindrically** /-ˈlɪndrɪkəlɪ/ *adv.* [L *cylindrus* f. Gk *kulindros* f. *kulindō* roll]

cymbal /ˈsɪmb(ə)l/ *n.* a musical instrument consisting of a concave brass or bronze plate, struck with another or with a stick etc. to make a ringing sound. □ **cymbalist** *n.* [ME f. L *cymbalum* f. Gk *kumbalon* f. *kumbē* cup]

cyme /saɪm/ *n. Bot.* an inflorescence in which the primary axis bears a single terminal flower that develops first. □ **cymose** *adj.* [F, var. of *cime* summit, ult. f. Gk *kuma* wave]

Cymric /ˈkɪmrɪk/ *adj.* Welsh. [Welsh *Cymru* Wales]

cynic /ˈsɪnɪk/ n. & adj. —n. **1** a person who has little faith in human sincerity and goodness. **2** (**Cynic**) one of a school of ancient Greek philosophers founded by Antisthenes, marked by ostentatious contempt for ease and pleasure. —adj. **1** (**Cynic**) of the Cynics. **2** = CYNICAL. □ **cynicism** /-ˌsɪz(ə)m/ n. [L cynicus f. Gk kunikos f. kuōn kunos dog, nickname for a Cynic]

cynical /ˈsɪnɪk(ə)l/ adj. **1** of or characteristic of a cynic; incredulous of human goodness. **2** (of behaviour etc.) disregarding normal standards. **3** sneering, mocking. □ **cynically** adv.

cynosure /ˈsaɪnəˌzjʊə(r), ˈsɪn-/ n. **1** a centre of attraction or admiration. **2** a guiding star. [F cynosure or L cynosura f. Gk kunosoura dog's tail, Ursa Minor f. kuōn kunos dog + oura tail]

cypher var. of CIPHER.

cypress /ˈsaɪprəs/ n. **1** any coniferous tree of the genus Cupressus or Chamaecyparis, with hard wood and dark foliage. **2** this, or branches from it, as a symbol of mourning. [ME f. OF cipres f. LL cypressus f. Gk kuparissos]

Cypriot /ˈsɪprɪət/ n. & adj. (also **Cypriote** /-əʊt/) —n. a native or national of Cyprus. —adj. of Cyprus. [Gk Kupriōtes f. Kupros Cyprus in E. Mediterranean]

Cyrillic /sɪˈrɪlɪk/ adj. & n. —adj. denoting the alphabet used by the Slavonic peoples of the Orthodox Church; now used esp. for Russian and Bulgarian. —n. this alphabet. [St Cyril d. 869, its reputed inventor]

cyst /sɪst/ n. **1** Med. a sac containing morbid matter, a parasitic larva, etc. **2** Biol. a hollow organ, bladder, etc., in an animal or plant, containing a liquid secretion. [LL cystis f. Gk kustis bladder]

cystic /ˈsɪstɪk/ adj. **1** of the urinary bladder. **2** of the gall-bladder. **3** of the nature of a cyst. □ **cystic fibrosis** Med. a hereditary disease affecting the exocrine glands and usu. resulting in respiratory infections. [F cystique or mod.L cysticus (as CYST)]

cystitis /sɪˈstaɪtɪs/ n. an inflammation of the urinary bladder, usu. accompanied by frequent painful urination.

cysto- /ˈsɪstəʊ/ comb. form the urinary bladder (cystoscope; cystotomy). [Gk kustē, kustis bladder]

-cyte /saɪt/ comb. form Biol. a mature cell (leucocyte). [Gk kutos vessel]

cyto- /ˈsaɪtəʊ/ comb. form Biol. cells or a cell. [as -CYTE]

cytogenetics /ˌsaɪtəʊdʒɪˈnetɪks/ n. the study of inheritance in relation to the structure and function of cells. □ **cytogenetic** adj. **cytogenetical** adj. **cytogenetically** adv. **cytogeneticist** /-sɪst/ n.

cytology /saɪˈtɒlədʒɪ/ n. the study of cells. □ **cytological** /ˌsaɪtəˈlɒdʒɪk(ə)l/ adj. **cytologically** /ˌsaɪtəˈlɒdʒɪkəlɪ/ adv. **cytologist** n.

cytoplasm /ˈsaɪtəʊˌplæz(ə)m/ n. the protoplasmic content of a cell apart from its nucleus. □ **cytoplasmic** /-ˈplæzmɪk/ adj.

czar etc. var. of TSAR etc.

Czech /tʃek/ n. & adj. —n. **1** a native or national of Czechoslovakia. **2** one of the two official languages of Czechoslovakia (cf. SLOVAK). —adj. of or relating to Czechoslovakia or its people or language. [Pol. spelling of Bohemian Čech]

Czechoslovak /ˌtʃekəˈsləʊvæk/ n. & adj. (also **Czechoslovakian** /-sləˈvækɪən/) —n. a native or national of Czechoslovakia. —adj. of or relating to Czechoslovakia. [CZECH + SLOVAK]

Dd

D¹ /diː/ *n.* (also **d**) (*pl.* **Ds** or **D's**) **1** the fourth letter of the alphabet. **2** *Mus.* the second note of the diatonic scale of C major. **3** (as a Roman numeral) 500. **4** = DEE. **5** the fourth highest class or category (of academic marks etc.).

D² *symb. Chem.* the element deuterium.

d. *abbr.* **1** died. **2** daughter. **3** *Brit.* (pre-decimal) penny. **4** deci-. [sense 3 f. L *denarius* silver coin]

'd *v. colloq.* (usu. after pronouns) had, would (*I'd; he'd*). [abbr.]

da *abbr.* deca-.

dab¹ *v. & n.* —*v.* (**dabbed, dabbing**) **1** *tr.* press (a surface) briefly with a cloth, sponge, etc., without rubbing, esp. in cleaning or to apply a substance. **2** *tr.* press (a sponge etc.) lightly on a surface. **3** *tr.* (foll. by *on*) apply (a substance) by dabbing a surface. **4** *intr.* (usu. foll. by *at*) aim a feeble blow; tap. **5** *tr.* strike lightly; tap. —*n.* **1** a brief application of a cloth, sponge, etc., to a surface without rubbing. **2** a small amount of something applied in this way (*a dab of paint*). **3** a light blow or tap. **4** (in *pl.*) *Brit. sl.* fingerprints. □ **dabber** *n.* [ME, imit.]

dab² *n.* any flat-fish of the genus *Limanda*. [15th c.: orig. unkn.]

dab³ *adj.* esp. *Brit. colloq.* □ **dab hand** (usu. foll. by *at*) a person especially skilled (in) (*a dab hand at cooking*). [17th c.: orig. unkn.]

dabble /ˈdæb(ə)l/ *v.* **1** *intr.* (usu. foll. by *in*, *at*) take a casual or superficial interest or part (in a subject or activity). **2** *intr.* move the feet, hands, etc. about in (usu. a small amount of) liquid. **3** *tr.* wet partly or intermittently; moisten, stain, splash. □ **dabbler** *n.* [16th c.: f. Du. *dabbelen* or DAB¹]

dace *n.* (*pl.* same) any small freshwater fish, esp. of the genus *Leuciscus*, related to the carp. [OF *dars*: see DART]

dacha /ˈdætʃə/ *n.* a country house or cottage in Russia. [Russ., = gift]

dachshund /ˈdækshʊnd/ *n.* **1** a dog of a short-legged long-bodied breed. **2** this breed. [G, = badger-dog]

dactyl /ˈdæktɪl/ *n.* a metrical foot (‒ ⌣ ⌣) consisting of one long (or stressed) syllable followed by two short (or unstressed). □ **dactylic** /dækˈtɪlɪk/ *adj.* [ME f. L *dactylus* f. Gk *daktulos* finger, the three bones corresponding to the three syllables]

dad *n. colloq.* father. [perh. imit. of a child's *da, da* (cf. DADDY)]

Dada /ˈdɑːdɑː/ *n.* an early 20th-c. international movement in art, literature, music, and film, repudiating and mocking artistic and social conventions □ **Dadaism** /-də‚ɪz(ə)m/ *n.* **Dadaist** /-dəɪst/ *n. & adj.* **Dadaistic** /-ɪstɪk/ *adj.* [F (the title of an early 20th-c. review) f. *dada* hobby-horse]

daddy /ˈdædɪ/ *n.* (*pl.* **-ies**) *colloq.* **1** father. **2** (usu. foll. by *of*) the oldest or supreme example. □ **daddy-long-legs 1** a crane-fly. **2** *US* a harvestman. [DAD + -Y³]

dado /ˈdeɪdəʊ/ *n.* (*pl.* **-os**) **1** the lower part of the wall of a room when visually distinct from the upper part. **2** the plinth of a column. **3** the cube of a pedestal between the base and the cornice. [It., = DIE²]

daffodil /ˈdæfədɪl/ *n.* **1 a** a bulbous plant, *Narcissus pseudonarcissus*, with a yellow trumpet-shaped crown. **b** any of various other large-flowered plants of the genus *Narcissus*. **c** a flower of any of these plants. **2** a pale-yellow colour. [earlier *affodill*, as ASPHODEL]

daffy /ˈdæfɪ/ *adj.* (**daffier, daffiest**) *sl.* = DAFT. □ **daffily** *adv.* **daffiness** *n.* [*daff* simpleton + -Y²]

daft /dɑːft/ *adj.* esp. *Brit. colloq.* silly, foolish, crazy. [ME *daffte* = OE *gedæfte* mild, meek, f. Gmc]

dag *n. Austral. & NZ sl.* an eccentric or noteworthy person; a character (*he's a bit of a dag*). [orig. Engl. dial., = a dare, challenge]

dagger /ˈdægə(r)/ *n.* **1** a short stabbing-weapon with a pointed and edged blade. **2** *Printing* = OBELUS. □ **at daggers drawn** in bitter enmity. **look daggers at** glare angrily or venomously at. [ME, perh. f. obs. *dag* pierce, infl. by OF *dague* long dagger]

dago /ˈdeɪgəʊ/ *n.* (*pl.* **-os**) *sl. offens.* a foreigner, esp. a Spaniard, Portuguese, or Italian. [Sp. *Diego* = James]

daguerreotype /dəˈgerəʊ‚taɪp/ *n.* a photograph taken by an early photographic process employing an iodine-sensitized silvered plate and mercury vapour. [L. *Daguerre*, Fr. inventor d. 1851]

dahlia /ˈdeɪlɪə/ *n.* any composite garden plant of the genus *Dahlia*, cultivated for its many-coloured flowers. [A. *Dahl*, Sw. botanist d. 1789]

Dáil /dɔɪl/ *n.* (in full **Dáil Éireann** /ˈeɪrən/) the lower house of parliament in the Republic of Ireland. [Ir., = assembly (of Ireland)]

daily /ˈdeɪlɪ/ *adj., adv., & n.* —*adj.* **1** done, produced, or occurring every day or every weekday. **2** constant, regular. —*adv.* **1** every day; from day to day. **2** constantly. —*n.* (*pl.* **-ies**) *colloq.* **1** a daily newspaper. **2** *Brit.* a charwoman or domestic help working daily. □ **daily bread** necessary food; a livelihood. [ME f. DAY + -LY¹, -LY²]

dainty /ˈdeɪntɪ/ *adj. & n.* —*adj.* (**daintier, daintiest**) **1** delicately pretty. **2** delicate of build or in movement. **3** (of food) choice. **4** fastidious; having delicate taste and sensibility. —*n.* (*pl.* **-ies**) a choice morsel; a delicacy. □ **daintily** *adv.* **daintiness** *n.* [AF *dainté*, OF *daintié, deintié* f. L *dignitas -tatis* f. *dignus* worthy]

daiquiri /ˈdækərɪ, ˈdaɪ-/ *n.* (*pl.* **daiquiris**) a cocktail of rum, lime-juice, etc. [*Daiquiri* in Cuba]

dairy /ˈdeərɪ/ *n.* (*pl.* **-ies**) **1** a building or room for the storage, processing, and distribution of milk and its products. **2** a shop where milk and milk products are sold. **3** (*attrib.*) of, containing, or concerning milk and its products (and sometimes eggs). [ME *deierie* f. *deie* maidservant f. OE *dæge* kneader of dough]

dairymaid /ˈdeərɪˌmeɪd/ n. a woman employed in a dairy.

dairyman /ˈdeərɪmən/ n. (pl. **-men**) **1** a man dealing in dairy products. **2** a man employed in a dairy.

dais /ˈdeɪɪs/ n. a low platform, usu. at the upper end of a hall. [ME f. OF *deis* f. L *discus* disc, dish, in med.L = table]

daisy /ˈdeɪzɪ/ n. (pl. **-ies**) **1** a small composite plant, *Bellis perennis*, bearing flowers each with a yellow disc and white rays. **2** any other plant with daisy-like flowers. □ **daisy wheel** *Computing* a disc of spokes extending radially from a central hub, each terminating in a printing character, used as a printer in word processors and typewriters. [OE *dæges ēage* day's eye, the flower opening in the morning]

dal var. of DHAL.

Dalai lama /ˌdælaɪ ˈlɑːmə/ n. the spiritual head of Tibetan Buddhism, formerly also the chief ruler of Tibet. [Mongolian *dalai* ocean; see LAMA]

dale n. a valley, esp. in N. England. [OE *dæl* f. Gmc]

dalesman /ˈdeɪlzmən/ n. (pl. **-men**) an inhabitant of the dales in Northern England.

dalliance /ˈdælɪəns/ n. a leisurely or frivolous passing of time. [DALLY + -ANCE]

dally /ˈdælɪ/ v.intr. (**-ies**, **-ied**) **1** delay; waste time, esp. frivolously. **2** (often foll. by *with*) play about; flirt, treat frivolously. [ME f. OF *dalier* chat]

Dalmatian /dælˈmeɪʃ(ə)n/ n. **1** a dog of a large white short-haired breed with dark spots. **2** this breed. [*Dalmatia* in Yugoslavia]

dam¹ n. & v. —n. **1** a barrier constructed to hold back water and raise its level, forming a reservoir or preventing flooding. **2** a barrier constructed in a stream by a beaver. —v.tr. (**dammed, damming**) **1** furnish or confine with a dam. **2** (often foll. by *up*) block up; hold back; obstruct. [ME f. MLG, MDu.]

dam² n. the female parent of an animal, esp. a four-footed one. [ME: var. of DAME]

damage /ˈdæmɪdʒ/ n. & v. —n. **1** harm or injury impairing the value or usefulness of something, or the health or normal function of a person. **2** (in pl.) *Law* a sum of money claimed or awarded in compensation for a loss or an injury. **3** the loss of what is desirable. **4** (prec. by *the*) *sl.* cost (*what's the damage?*). —v.tr. **1** inflict damage on. **2** (esp. as **damaging** *adj.*) detract from the reputation of (*a most damaging admission*). □ **damagingly** adv. [ME f. OF *damage* (n.), *damagier* (v.), f. *dam(me)* loss f. L *damnum* loss, damage]

damascene /ˈdæməˌsiːn, ˌdæməˈsiːn/ v.tr. decorate (metal, esp. iron or steel) by etching or inlaying esp. with gold or silver, or with a watered pattern produced in welding. [*Damascene* of Damascus, f. L *Damascenus* f. Gk *Damaskēnos*]

damask /ˈdæməsk/ n., adj., & v. —n. **1** a figured woven fabric (esp. silk or linen) with a pattern visible on both sides. **2** twilled table linen with woven designs shown by the reflection of light. —adj. **1** made of or resembling damask. **2** coloured like a damask rose, velvety pink. —v.tr. weave with figured designs. □ **damask**

rose an old sweet-scented variety of rose. [ME, ult. f. L *Damascus*]

dame n. **1** (**Dame**) **a** (in the UK) the title given to a woman with the rank of Knight Commander or holder of the Grand Cross in the Orders of Chivalry. **b** a woman holding this title. **2** *Brit.* a comic middle-aged woman in modern pantomime, usu. played by a man. **3** *US sl.* a woman. [ME f. OF f. L *domina* mistress]

damn /dæm/ v., n., adj., & adv. —v.tr. **1** (often *absol.* or as *int.* of anger or annoyance, = *may God damn*) curse (a person or thing). **2** doom to hell; cause the damnation of. **3** condemn, censure (*a review damning the performance*). **4** (often as **damning** *adj.*) (of a circumstance, piece of evidence, etc.) show or prove to be guilty; bring condemnation upon (*evidence against them was damning*). —n. **1** an uttered curse. **2** *sl.* a negligible amount (*not worth a damn*). —adj. & adv. *colloq.* = DAMNED. □ **damn all** *sl.* nothing at all. □ **damningly** adv. [ME f. OF *damner* f. L *damnare* inflict loss on f. *damnum* loss]

damnable /ˈdæmnəb(ə)l/ adj. hateful, annoying. □ **damnably** adv. [ME f. OF *damnable* (as DAMN)]

damnation /dæmˈneɪʃ(ə)n/ n. & int. —n. condemnation to eternal punishment, esp. in hell. —int. expressing anger or annoyance. [ME f. OF *damnation* (as DAMN)]

damnatory /ˈdæmnətərɪ/ adj. conveying or causing censure or damnation. [L *damnatorius* (as DAMN)]

damned /dæmd/ adj. & adv. *colloq.* —adj. damnable, infernal, unwelcome. —adv. extremely (*damned hot*; *damned lovely*). □ **do one's damnedest** do one's utmost.

damp adj., n., & v. —adj. slightly wet; moist. —n. diffused moisture in the air, on a surface, or in a solid, esp. as a cause of inconvenience or danger. —v.tr. **1** make damp; moisten. **2** (often foll. by *down*) **a** take the force or vigour out of (*damp one's enthusiasm*). **b** make flaccid or spiritless. **c** make (a fire) burn less strongly by reducing the flow of air to it. **3** reduce or stop the vibration of (esp. the strings of a musical instrument). **4** quieten. □ **damp** (or **damp-proof**) **course** a layer of waterproof material in the wall of a building near the ground, to prevent rising damp. □ **dampness** n. [ME f. MLG, = vapour etc., OHG *dampf* steam f. WG]

dampen /ˈdæmpən/ v. **1** v.tr. & intr. make or become damp. **2** tr. make less forceful or vigorous. □ **dampener** n.

damper /ˈdæmpə(r)/ n. **1** a person or thing that discourages, or tempers enthusiasm. **2** a device that reduces shock or noise. **3** a metal plate in a flue to control the draught, and so the rate of combustion. **4** *Mus.* a pad silencing a piano string except when removed by means of a pedal or by the note's being struck. **5** esp. *Austral.* & *NZ* unleavened bread or cake of flour and water baked in wood ashes. □ **put a damper on** take the vigour or enjoyment out of.

damsel /ˈdæmz(ə)l/ n. *archaic* or *literary* a young unmarried woman. [ME f. OF *dam(e)isele* ult. f. L *domina* mistress]

damselfly /ˈdæmz(ə)lˌflaɪ/ n. (pl. **-flies**) any of various insects of the order Odonata, like a dragonfly but with its wings folded over the body when resting.

damson /'dæmz(ə)n/ *n.* & *adj.* —*n.* **1** (in full **damson plum**) **a** a small dark-purple plumlike fruit. **b** the small deciduous tree, *Prunus institia*, bearing this. **2** a dark-purple colour. —*adj.* damson-coloured. □ **damson cheese** a solid preserve of damsons and sugar. [ME *damacene*, *-scene*, *-sene* f. L *damascenum* (*prunum plum*) of *Damascus*: see DAMASCENE]

dan *n.* **1** any of twelve degrees of advanced proficiency in judo. **2** a person who has achieved any of these. [Jap.]

dance /dɑːns/ *v.* & *n.* —*v.* **1** *intr.* move about rhythmically alone or with a partner or in a set. **2** *intr.* move in a lively way; skip or jump about. **3** *tr.* **a** perform (a specified dance or form of dancing). **b** perform (a specified role) in a ballet etc. **4** *intr.* move up and down (on water, in the field of vision, etc.). **5** *tr.* move (esp. a child) up and down; dandle. —*n.* **1 a** a piece of dancing; a sequence of steps in dancing. **b** a special form of this. **2** a single round or turn of a dance. **3** a social gathering for dancing, a ball. **4** a piece of music for dancing to or in a dance rhythm. **5** a dancing or lively motion. □ **dance attendance on** follow or wait on (a person) obsequiously. **lead a person a dance** (or **merry dance**) *Brit.* cause a person much trouble in following a course one has instigated. □ **danceable** *adj.* [ME f. OF *dance*, *danse* (n.), *dancer*, *danser* (v.), f. Rmc, of unkn. orig.]

dancehall /'dɑːnshɔːl/ *n.* a public hall for dancing.

dancer /'dɑːnsə(r)/ *n.* **1** a person who performs a dance. **2** a person whose profession is dancing.

d. and c. *n.* dilatation and curettage.

dandelion /'dændɪˌlaɪən/ *n.* a composite plant, *Taraxacum officinale*, with jagged leaves and a large bright-yellow flower. □ **dandelion clock** the downy seed-head of a dandelion. [F *dent-de-lion* transl. med.L *dens leonis* lion's tooth]

dander /'dændə(r)/ *n. colloq.* temper, anger, indignation. □ **get one's dander up** lose one's temper; become angry. [19th c.: orig. uncert.]

dandify /'dændɪˌfaɪ/ *v.tr.* (**-ies**, **-ied**) cause to resemble a dandy.

dandle /'dænd(ə)l/ *v.tr.* dance (a child) on one's knees or in one's arms. [16th c.: orig. unkn.]

dandruff /'dændrʌf/ *n.* **1** dead skin in small scales among the hair. **2** the condition of having this. [16th c.: *-ruff* perh. rel. to ME *rove* scurfiness f. ON *hrufa* or MLG, MDu. *rōve*]

dandy /'dændɪ/ *n.* & *adj.* —*n.* (pl. **-ies**) **1** a man unduly devoted to style, smartness, and fashion in dress and appearance. **2** *colloq.* an excellent thing. —*adj.* (**dandier**, **dandiest**) esp. *US colloq.* very good of its kind; splendid, first-rate. □ **dandyish** *adj.* **dandyism** *n.* [18th c.: perh. orig. = *Andrew*, in *Jack-a-dandy*]

Dane /deɪn/ *n.* **1** a native or national of Denmark. **2** *hist.* a Viking invader of England in the 9th–11th c. □ **Great Dane 1** a dog of a very large short-haired breed. **2** this breed. [ME f. ON *Danir* (pl.), LL *Dani*]

danger /'deɪndʒə(r)/ *n.* **1** liability or exposure to harm. **2** a thing that causes or is likely to cause harm. □ **danger list** a list of those dangerously ill. **danger money** extra payment for dangerous work. **in danger of** likely to incur or to suffer from. [earlier sense 'jurisdiction, power': ME f. OF *dangier* ult. f. L *dominus* lord]

dangerous /'deɪndʒərəs/ *adj.* involving or causing danger. □ **dangerously** *adv.* **dangerousness** *n.* [ME f. AF *dangerous*, *daungerous*, OF *dangereus* (as DANGER)]

dangle /'dæŋg(ə)l/ *v.* **1** *intr.* be loosely suspended, so as to be able to sway to and fro. **2** *tr.* hold or carry loosely suspended. **3** *tr.* hold out (a hope, temptation, etc.) enticingly. □ **dangler** *n.* [16th c. (imit.): cf. Sw. *dangla*, Da. *dangle*]

Danish /'deɪnɪʃ/ *adj.* & *n.* —*adj.* of or relating to Denmark or the Danes. —*n.* **1** the Danish language. **2** (prec. by *the*; treated as *pl.*) the Danish people. □ **Danish blue** a soft salty white cheese with blue veins. **Danish pastry** a cake of sweetened yeast pastry topped with icing, fruit, nuts, etc. [ME f. AF *danes*, OF *daneis* f. med.L *Danensis* (as DANE)]

dank /dæŋk/ *adj.* disagreeably damp and cold. □ **dankly** *adv.* **dankness** *n.* [ME prob. f. Scand.: cf. Sw. *dank* marshy spot]

daphne /'dæfnɪ/ *n.* any flowering shrub of the genus *Daphne*, e.g. the spurge laurel or mezereon. [ME, = laurel, f. Gk *daphnē*]

dapper /'dæpə(r)/ *adj.* **1** neat and precise, esp. in dress or movement. **2** sprightly. □ **dapperly** *adv.* **dapperness** *n.* [ME f. MLG, MDu. *dapper* strong, stout]

dapple /'dæp(ə)l/ *v.* & *n.* —*v.* **1** *tr.* mark with spots or rounded patches of colour or shade. **2** *intr.* become marked in this way. —*n.* **1** a dappled effect. **2** a dappled animal, esp. a horse. □ **dapple grey 1** (of an animal's coat) grey or white with darker spots. **2** a horse of this colour. [ME *dappled*, *dappeld*, (adj.), of unkn. orig.]

Darby and Joan /'dɑːbɪ ənd 'dʒəʊn/ *n.* a devoted old married couple. □ **Darby and Joan club** *Brit.* a club for people over 60. [18th c.: perh. f. a poem of 1735 in the *Gentleman's Magazine*]

dare /deə(r)/ *v.* & *n.* —*v.tr.* (*3rd sing.* present usu. **dare** before an expressed or implied infinitive without *to*) **1** (foll. by infin. with or without *to*) venture to; have the courage or impudence (to) (*dare he do it?*; *how dare you?*; *I do not dare to jump*). **2** (usu. foll. by *to* + infin.) defy or challenge (a person) (*I dare you to own up*). —*n.* **1** an act of daring. **2** a challenge, esp. to prove courage. □ **I dare say 1** (often foll. by *that* + clause) it is probable. **2** probably; I grant that much (*I dare say, but you are still wrong*). □ **darer** *n.* [OE *durran* with Gmc cognates: cf. Skr. *dhṛsh*, Gk *tharseō* be bold]

daredevil /'deəˌdev(ə)l/ *n.* & *adj.* —*n.* a recklessly daring person. —*adj.* recklessly daring. □ **daredevilry** *n.* **daredeviltry** *n.*

daring /'deərɪŋ/ *n.* & *adj.* —*n.* adventurous courage. —*adj.* adventurous, bold; prepared to take risks. □ **daringly** *adv.*

dariole /'dærɪˌəʊl/ *n.* a savoury or sweet dish cooked and served in a small mould usu. shaped like a flowerpot. [ME f. OF]

dark *adj.* & *n.* —*adj.* **1** with little or no light. **2** of a deep or sombre colour. **3** (of a person) with deep brown or black hair, complexion, or skin. **4** gloomy, depressing, dismal (*dark thoughts*). **5** evil, sinister (*dark deeds*). **6** sullen, angry (*a dark mood*). **7** remote, secret, mysterious, little-known (*the dark and distant past*; *keep it dark*). **8** ignorant, unenlightened. —*n.* **1** absence of light. **2** nightfall (*don't go out after dark*). **3** a lack of knowledge. **4** a dark area or colour, esp. in painting. □ **the Dark Ages** (or **Age**) **1** the period of European history preceding the Middle Ages, esp. the 5th–10th c. **2** any period of supposed unenlightenment. **the Dark Continent** a name for Africa, esp. when little known to Europeans. **dark glasses** spectacles with dark-tinted lenses. **dark horse** a little-known person who is unexpectedly successful or prominent. **dark star** an invisible star known to exist from reception of physical data other than light. **in the dark** lacking information. □ **darkish** adj. **darkly** adv. **darkness** n. **darksome** poet. adj. [OE deorc prob. f. Gmc]

darken /ˈdɑːkən/ v. **1** tr. make dark or darker. **2** intr. become dark or darker. □ **darkener** n.

darkroom /ˈdɑːkruːm, -rʊm/ n. a room for photographic work, with normal light excluded.

darling /ˈdɑːlɪŋ/ n. & adj. —n. **1** a beloved or lovable person or thing. **2** a favourite. **3** colloq. a pretty or endearing person or thing. —adj. **1** beloved, lovable. **2** favourite. **3** colloq. charming or pretty. [OE déorling (as DEAR, -LING¹)]

darn¹ v. & n. —v.tr. **1** mend (esp. knitted material, or a hole in it) by interweaving yarn across the hole with a needle. **2** embroider with a large running stitch. —n. a darned area in material. □ **darning needle** a long needle with a large eye, used in darning. [16th c.: perh. f. obs. dern hide]

darn² v.tr., int., adj., & adv. (US **durn** /dɜːn/) colloq. = DAMN (in imprecatory senses). [corrupt. of DAMN]

darned /dɑːnd/ adj. & adv. (US **durned** /dɜːnd/) colloq. = DAMNED.

darnel /ˈdɑːn(ə)l/ n. any of several grasses of the genus Lolium, growing as weeds among cereal crops. [ME: cf. Walloon darnelle]

darner /ˈdɑːnə(r)/ n. a person or thing that darns, esp. a darning needle.

darning /ˈdɑːnɪŋ/ n. **1** the action of a person who darns. **2** things to be darned.

dart n. & v. —n. **1** a small pointed missile used as a weapon or in a game. **2** (in pl.; usu. treated as sing.) an indoor game in which light feathered darts are thrown at a circular target. **3** a sudden rapid movement. **4** Zool. a dartlike structure, such as an insect's sting. **5** a tapering tuck stitched in a garment. —v. **1** intr. (often foll. by out, in, past, etc.) move or go suddenly or rapidly (darted into the shop). **2** tr. throw (a missile). **3** tr. direct suddenly (a glance etc.). [ME f. OF darz, dars, f. Frank.]

dartboard /ˈdɑːtbɔːd/ n. a circular board marked with numbered segments, used as a target in darts.

Darwinian /dɑːˈwɪnɪən/ adj. & n. —adj. of or relating to Darwin's theory of the evolution of species by the action of natural selection. —n. an adherent of this theory. □ **Darwinism** /ˈdɑː-/ n. **Darwinist** /ˈdɑː-/ n. [C. Darwin, Engl. naturalist d. 1882]

dash v. & n. —v. **1** intr. rush hastily or forcefully (dashed up the stairs). **2** tr. strike or fling with great force, esp. so as to shatter (dashed it to the ground). **3** tr. frustrate, daunt, dispirit (dashed their hopes). **4** tr. colloq. (esp. **dash it** or **dash it all**) = DAMN v. 1. —n. **1** a rush or onset; a sudden advance (made a dash for shelter). **2** a horizontal stroke in writing or printing to mark a pause or break in sense or to represent omitted letters or words. **3** impetuous vigour

or the capacity for this. **4** showy appearance or behaviour. **5** US a sprinting-race. **6** the longer signal of the two used in Morse code. **7** a slight admixture, esp. of a liquid. **8** = DASHBOARD. □ **cut a dash** make a brilliant show. **dash down** (or **off**) write or finish hurriedly. [ME, prob. imit.]

dashboard /ˈdæʃbɔːd/ n. the surface below the windscreen of a motor vehicle or aircraft, containing instruments and controls.

dashiki /ˈdæʃiki/ n. a loose brightly-coloured shirt worn by American Blacks. [W. Afr.]

dashing /ˈdæʃɪŋ/ adj. **1** spirited, lively. **2** showy. □ **dashingly** adv. **dashingness** n.

dastardly /ˈdæstədlɪ/ adj. cowardly, despicable. □ **dastardliness** n. [dastard base coward, prob. f. dazed past part. + -ARD, or obs. dasart dullard, DOTARD]

DAT abbr. digital audio tape.

data /ˈdeɪtə/ n.pl. **1** known facts or things used as a basis for inference or reckoning. **2** quantities or characters operated on by a computer etc. □ **data bank 1** a store or source of data. **2** = DATABASE. **data capture** the action or process of entering data into a computer. **data processing** a series of operations on data, esp. by a computer, to retrieve or classify etc. information. **data processor** a machine, esp. a computer, that carries out data processing. **data protection** legal control over access to data stored in computers. [pl. of DATUM]

■ **Usage** (1) In scientific, philosophical, and general use, this word is usually considered to denote a number of items and is thus treated as plural with datum as the singular. (2) In computing and allied subjects (and sometimes in general use), this word is treated as a mass (or collective) noun and used with words like this, that, and much, with singular verbs, e.g. useful data has been collected. Some people consider use (2) to be incorrect but it is more common than use (1). However, data is not a singular countable noun and cannot be preceded by a, every, each, either, or neither, or be given a plural form datas.

database /ˈdeɪtəbeɪs/ n. a structured set of data held in a computer, esp. one that is accessible in various ways.

datable /ˈdeɪtəb(ə)l/ adj. (often foll. by to) capable of being dated (to a particular time).

date¹ n. & v. —n. **1** a day of the month, esp. specified by a number. **2** a particular day or year, esp. when a given event occurred. **3** a statement (usu. giving the day, month, and year) in a document or inscription etc., of the time of composition or publication. **4** the period to which a work of art etc. belongs. **5** the time when an event happens or is to happen. **6** colloq. **a** an engagement or appointment, esp. with a person of the opposite sex. **b** US a person with whom one has a social engagement. —v. **1** tr. mark with a date. **2** tr. **a** assign a date to (an object, event, etc.). **b** (foll. by to) assign to a particular time, period, etc. **3** intr. (often foll. by from, back to, etc.) have its origins at a particular time. **4** intr. be recognizable as from a past or particular period; become evidently out of date (a design that does not date). **5** tr. indicate or expose as being out of date (that hat really dates you). **6** colloq. **a** tr. make an arrangement with (a person) to meet socially. **b** *intr.* meet socially by agreement (*they are now dating regularly*). □ **date-line 1** the line from north to south partly along the meridian 180° from Greenwich, to the east of which the date is a day earlier than it is to the west. **2** a line at the head of a dispatch or special article in a newspaper showing the date and place of writing. **date-stamp** *n.* **1** an adjustable rubber stamp etc. used to record a date. **2** the impression made by this. —*v.tr.* mark with a date-stamp. **out of date** (*attrib.* **out-of-date**) old-fashioned, obsolete. **to date** until now. **up to date** (*attrib.* **up-to-date**) meeting or according to the latest requirements, knowledge, or fashion; modern. [ME f. OF f. med.L *data*, fem. past part. of *dare* give: from the L formula used in dating letters, *data* (*epistola*) (letter) given or delivered (at a particular time or place)]

date² *n.* **1** a dark oval single-stoned fruit. **2** (in full **date-palm**) the tall tree *Phoenix dactylifera*, native to W. Asia and N. Africa, bearing this fruit. [ME f. OF f. L *dactylus* f. Gk *daktulos* finger, from the shape of its leaf]

dative /ˈdeɪtɪv/ *n.* & *adj.* *Gram.* —*n.* the case of nouns and pronouns (and words in grammatical agreement with them) indicating an indirect object or recipient. —*adj.* of or in the dative. □ **datival** /dəˈtaɪv(ə)l/ *adj.* **datively** /dəˈtaɪvəlɪ/ *adv.* [ME f. L (*casus*) *dativus* f. *dare dat-* give]

datum /ˈdeɪtəm, ˈdɑːtəm/ *n.* (*pl.* **data**: see DATA as main entry). **1** a piece of information. **2** a thing known or granted; an assumption or premiss from which inferences may be drawn. **3** a fixed starting-point of a scale etc. (*datum-line*). [L, = thing given, neut. past part. of *dare* give]

daub *v.* & *n.* —*v.tr.* **1** spread (paint, plaster, or some other thick substance) crudely or roughly on a surface. **2** coat or smear (a surface) with paint etc. **3** (also *absol.*) paint crudely or unskilfully. **b** lay (colours) on crudely and clumsily. —*n.* **1** paint or other substance daubed on a surface. **2** plaster, clay, etc., for coating a surface, esp. mixed with straw and applied to laths or wattles to form a wall. **3** a crude painting. □ **dauber** *n.* [ME f. OF *dauber* f. L *dealbare* whitewash f. *albus* white]

daube /dəʊb/ *n.* a stew of braised meat (usu. beef) with wine etc. [F]

daughter /ˈdɔːtə(r)/ *n.* **1** a girl or woman in relation to either or both of her parents. **2** a female descendant. **3** (foll. by *of*) a female member of a family, nation, etc. **4** (foll. by *of*) a woman who is regarded as the spiritual descendant of, or as spiritually attached to, a person or thing. □ **daughter-in-law** (*pl.* **daughters-in-law**) the wife of one's son. □ **daughterhood** *n.* **daughterly** *adj.* [OE *dohtor* f. Gmc]

daunt *v.tr.* discourage, intimidate. □ **daunting** *adj.* **dauntingly** *adv.* [ME f. AF *daunter*, OF *danter*, *donter* f. L *domitare* frequent. of *domare* tame]

dauntless /ˈdɔːntlɪs/ *adj.* intrepid, persevering. □ **dauntlessly** *adv.* **dauntlessness** *n.*

dauphin /ˈdɔːfɪn, ˈdəʊfæ/ *n.* *hist.* the eldest son of the King of France. [ME f. F, ult. f. L *delphinus* DOLPHIN, as a family name]

Davenport /ˈdævənˌpɔːt/ *n.* **1** *Brit.* an ornamental writing-desk. **2** *US* a large heavily upholstered sofa. [19th c.: from the name *Davenport*]

davit /ˈdævɪt, ˈdeɪvɪt/ *n.* a small crane on board a ship, esp. one of a pair for suspending or lowering a lifeboat. [AF & OF *daviot* dimin. of *Davi* David]

Davy /ˈdeɪvɪ/ *n.* (*pl.* **-ies**) (in full **Davy lamp**) a miner's safety lamp with the flame enclosed by wire gauze. [Sir H. *Davy*, Engl. chemist d. 1829, who invented it]

Davy Jones's locker /ˌdeɪvɪ ˈdʒəʊnzɪz/ *n.* *sl.* the bottom of the sea, esp. regarded as the grave of those drowned at sea. [18th c.: orig. unkn.]

daw *n.* = JACKDAW. [ME: cf. OHG *tāha*]

dawdle /ˈdɔːd(ə)l/ *v.* **1** *intr.* **a** walk slowly and idly. **b** delay; waste time. **2** *tr.* (foll. by *away*) waste (time). □ **dawdler** *n.* [perh. rel. to dial. *daddle*, *doddle* idle, dally]

dawn *n.* & *v.* —*n.* **1** the first light of day; daybreak. **2** the beginning or incipient appearance of something. —*v.intr.* **1** (of a day) begin; grow light. **2** (often foll. by *on*, *upon*) begin to become evident or understood (by a person). □ **dawn chorus** the singing of many birds at the break of day. [orig. as verb: back-form. f. *dawning*, ME f. earlier *dawing* after Scand. (as DAY)]

dawning /ˈdɔːnɪŋ/ *n.* **1** daybreak. **2** the first beginning of something.

day *n.* **1** the time between sunrise and sunset. **2** a period of 24 hours as a unit of time, esp. from midnight to midnight, corresponding to a complete revolution of the earth on its axis. **3** daylight (*clear as day*). **4** the time in a day during which work is normally done (*an eight-hour day*). **5 a** (also *pl.*) a period of the past or present (*the modern day*; *the old days*). **b** (prec. by *the*) the present time (*the issues of the day*). **6** the lifetime of a person or thing, esp. regarded as useful or productive (*have had my day*; *in my day things were different*). **7** a point of time (*will do it one day*). **8 a** the date of a specific festival. **b** a day associated with a particular event or purpose (*payday*; *Christmas day*). **9** a particular day; a date agreed on. **10** a day's endeavour, or the period of an endeavour, esp. as bringing success (*win the day*). □ **day-boy** (or **-girl**) *Brit.* a boy or girl who goes daily from home to school, esp. a school that also has boarders. **day by day** gradually. **day care** the supervision of young children during the working day. **day centre** a place providing care for the elderly or handicapped during the day. **day-dream** *n.* a pleasant fantasy or reverie. —*v.intr.* indulge in this. **day-dreamer** a person who indulges in day-dreams. **day in, day out** routinely, constantly. **day labourer** an unskilled labourer hired by the day. **day nursery** a nursery where children are looked after during the working day. **day off** a day's holiday from work. **Day of Judgement** = Judgement Day. **day of rest** the Sabbath. **day out** a trip or excursion for a day. **day release** *Brit.* a system of allowing employees days off work for education. **day return** a fare or ticket at a reduced rate for a journey out and back in one day. **day-room** a room, esp. a communal room in an institution, used during the day. **day-school** a school for pupils living at home. **day-to-day** mundane, routine. **day-trip** a trip or excursion completed in one day. **day-tripper** a person who goes on a day-trip. **one of these days** before very long. **some day** at some point in the future. **that will be the day** *colloq.* that will never happen.

this day and age the present time or period. □

dayless *adj.* [OE dæg f. Gmc]

daybreak /ˈdeɪbreɪk/ *n.* the first appearance of light in the morning.

Day-Glo /ˈdeɪgləʊ/ *n. & adj.* —*n. propr.* a make of fluorescent paint or other colouring. —*adj.* coloured with or like this. [DAY + GLOW]

daylight /ˈdeɪlaɪt/ *n.* **1** the light of day. **2** dawn (*before daylight*). **3 a** openness, publicity. **b** open knowledge. **4** a visible gap or interval. **5** (usu. in *pl.*) *sl.* one's life or consciousness (orig. the internal organs) esp. as representing vulnerability to fear, attack, etc. (*scared the daylights out of me; beat the living daylights out of them*). □ **daylight robbery** *colloq.* a blatantly excessive charge. **daylight saving** the achieving of longer evening daylight, esp. in summer, by setting the time an hour ahead of the standard time. **see daylight** begin to understand what was previously obscure.

daytime /ˈdeɪtaɪm/ *n.* the part of the day when there is natural light.

daze *v. & n.* —*v.tr.* stupefy, bewilder. —*n.* a state of confusion or bewilderment (*in a daze*). □ **dazedly** /-zɪdlɪ/ *adv.* [ME *dased* past part., f. ON *dasathr* weary]

dazzle /ˈdæz(ə)l/ *v. & n.* —*v.tr.* **1** blind temporarily or confuse the sight of by an excess of light. **2** impress or overpower (a person) with any brilliant display or prospect. —*n.* bright confusing light. □ **dazzlement** *n.* **dazzler** *n.* **dazzling** *adj.* **dazzlingly** *adv.* [ME, f. DAZE + -LE⁴]

dB *abbr.* decibel(s).

DC *abbr.* **1** (also **d.c.**) direct current. **2** District of Columbia.

DCL *abbr.* Doctor of Civil Law.

DD *abbr.* Doctor of Divinity.

D-Day /ˈdiːdeɪ/ *n.* **1** the day (6 June 1944) on which British and American forces invaded N. France. **2** the day on which an important operation is to begin or a change to take effect. [D for *day* + DAY]

DDT *abbr.* dichlorodiphenyltrichloroethane, a colourless chlorinated hydrocarbon used as an insecticide.

de- /dɪ, diː/ *prefix* **1** forming verbs and their derivatives: **a** down, away (*descend; deduct*). **b** completely (*declare; denude; deride*). **2** added to verbs and their derivatives to form verbs and nouns implying removal or reversal (*decentralize; de-ice; demoralization*). [from or after L *de* (adv. & prep.) = off, from: sense 2 through OF *des-* f. L *dis-*]

deacon /ˈdiːkən/ *n.* **1** (in Episcopal churches) a minister of the third order, below bishop and priest. **2** (in Nonconformist churches) a lay officer attending to a congregation's secular affairs. **3** (in the early Church) an appointed minister of charity. □ **deaconate** *n.* **deaconship** *n.* [OE *diacon* f. eccl.L *diaconus* f. Gk *diakonos* servant]

deaconess /ˌdiːkəˈnes, ˈdiːkənɪs/ *n.* a woman in the early Church and in some modern Churches with functions analogous to a deacon's. [DEACON, after LL *diaconissa*]

deactivate /diːˈæktɪˌveɪt/ *v.tr.* make inactive or less reactive. □ **deactivation** /-ˈveɪʃ(ə)n/ *n.* **deactivator** *n.*

dead /ded/ *adj., adv., & n.* —*adj.* **1** no longer alive. **2** *colloq.* extremely tired or unwell. **3** benumbed; affected by loss of sensation (*my fingers are dead*). **4** (foll. by *to*) unappreciative or unconscious of; insensitive to. **5** no longer effective or in use; obsolete, extinct. **6** (of a match, of coal, etc.) no longer burning; extinguished. **7** inanimate. **8 a** lacking force or vigour; dull, lustreless, muffled. **b** (of sound) not resonant. **9** quiet; lacking activity (*the dead season*). **10 a** (of a microphone, telephone, etc.) not transmitting any sound, esp. because of a fault. **b** (of a circuit, conductor, etc.) carrying or transmitting no current; not connected to a source of electricity (*a dead battery*). **11** (of the ball in a game) out of play. **12** abrupt, complete, exact, unqualified, unrelieved (*come to a dead stop; a dead faint; in dead silence*). —*adv.* **1** absolutely, exactly, completely (*dead on target; dead level; dead tired*). **2** *colloq.* very, extremely (*dead easy*). —*n.* (*prec. by the*) **1** (treated as *pl.*) those who have died. **2** a time of silence or inactivity (*the dead of night*). □ **dead beat** *colloq.* exhausted. **dead-beat** *n.* **1** *colloq.* a penniless person. **2** *US sl.* a person constantly in debt. **dead duck** *sl.* an unsuccessful or useless person or thing. **dead end 1** a closed end of a road, passage, etc. **2** (often with hyphen) *attrib.*) a situation offering no prospects of progress or advancement. **dead hand** an oppressive persisting influence, esp. posthumous control. **dead heat 1** a race in which two or more competitors finish exactly level. **2** the result of such a race. **dead language** a language no longer commonly spoken, e.g. Latin. **dead letter** a law or practice no longer observed or recognized. **dead loss 1** *colloq.* a useless person or thing. **2** a complete loss. **dead man's handle** (or **pedal** etc.) a controlling-device on an electric train, allowing power to be connected only as long as the operator presses on it. **dead march** a funeral march. **dead men** *colloq.* bottles after the contents have been drunk. **dead-nettle** any plant of the genus *Lamium*, having nettle-like leaves but without stinging hairs. **dead-on** exactly right. **dead reckoning** *Naut.* calculation of a ship's position from the log, compass, etc., when observations are impossible. **dead shot** one who is extremely accurate. **dead to the world** *colloq.* fast asleep; unconscious. **dead weight** (or **dead-weight**) **1 a** an inert mass. **b** a heavy weight or burden. **2** a debt not covered by assets. **3** the total weight carried on a ship. **dead wood** *colloq.* one or more useless people or things. □ **deadness** *n.* [OE *dēad* f. Gmc, rel. to DIE¹]

deadbolt /ˈdedbəʊlt/ *n.* esp. *US* a bolt engaged by turning a knob or key, rather than by spring action.

deaden /ˈded(ə)n/ *v.* **1** *tr. & intr.* deprive of or lose vitality, force, brightness, sound, feeling, etc. **2** *tr.* (foll. by *to*) make insensitive. □ **deadener** *n.*

deadhead /ˈdedhed/ *n. & v.* —*n.* **1** a faded flower-head. **2** a passenger or member of an audience who has made use of a free ticket. **3** a useless or unenterprising person. —*v.tr.* remove deadheads from (a plant).

deadline /ˈdedlaɪn/ *n.* a time-limit for the completion of an activity etc.

deadlock /ˈdedlɒk/ *n. & v.* —*n.* **1** a situation, esp. one involving opposing parties, in which no progress can be made. **2** a type of lock requiring a key to open or close it. —*v.tr.* & *intr.* bring or come to a standstill.

deadly /ˈdedlɪ/ *adj.* & *adv.* —*adj.* (**deadlier, deadliest**) **1 a** causing or able to cause fatal injury or serious damage. **b** poisonous (*deadly snake*). **2** intense, extreme (*deadly dullness*). **3** (of an aim etc.) extremely accurate. **4** deathlike (*deadly pale*). **5** *colloq.* dreary, dull. **6** implacable. —*adv.* **1** like death; as if dead (*deadly faint*). **2** extremely, intensely (*deadly serious*). □ **deadly nightshade** = BELLADONNA. **deadly sin** a sin regarded as leading to damnation. □ **deadliness** *n.* [OE *dēadlic, dēadlīce* (as DEAD, -LY¹)]

deadpan /ˈdedpæn/ *adj.* & *adv.* with a face or manner totally lacking expression or emotion.

deaf /def/ *adj.* **1** wholly or partly without hearing (*deaf in one ear*). **2** (foll. by *to*) refusing to listen or comply. **3** insensitive to harmony, rhythm, etc. (*tone-deaf*). □ **deaf-aid** *Brit.* a hearing-aid. **deaf-and-dumb alphabet** (or **language** etc.) = *sign language*. **deaf mute** a deaf and dumb person. **fall on deaf ears** be ignored. **turn a deaf ear** (usu. foll. by *to*) be unresponsive. □ **deafly** *adv.* **deafness** *n.* [OE *dēaf* f. Gmc]

deafen /ˈdef(ə)n/ *v.tr.* **1** (often as **deafening** *adj.*) overpower with sound. **2** deprive of hearing by noise, esp. temporarily. □ **deafeningly** *adv.*

deal¹ *v.* & *n.* —*v.* (*past* and *past part.* **dealt** /delt/) **1** *intr.* (foll. by *with*) **a** take measures concerning (a problem, person, etc.), esp. in order to put something right. **b** do business with; associate with. **c** discuss or treat (a subject). **d** (often foll. by *by*) behave in a specified way towards a person (*dealt honourably by them*). **2** *intr.* (foll. by *in*) to sell or be concerned with commercially (*deals in insurance*). **3** *tr.* (often foll. by *out, round*) distribute or apportion to several people etc. **4** *tr.* (also *absol.*) distribute (cards) to players for a game or round. **5** *tr.* cause to be received; administer (*deal a heavy blow*). **6** *tr.* assign as a share or deserts to a person (*Providence dealt them much happiness*). —*n.* **1** (usu. **a good** or **great deal**) *colloq.* **a** a large amount (*a good deal of trouble*). **b** to a considerable extent (*is a great deal better*). **2** *colloq.* a business arrangement; a transaction. **3** a specified form of treatment given or received (*gave them a rough deal*). **4 a** the distribution of cards by dealing. **b** a player's turn to do this (*it's my deal*). **c** the round of play following this. **d** a set of hands dealt to players. □ **it's a deal** *colloq.* expressing assent to an agreement. [OE *dǣl, dǣlan,* f. Gmc]

deal² *n.* **1** fir or pine timber, esp. sawn into boards of a standard size. **2** a board of this timber. [ME f. MLG, MDu. *dele* plank f. Gmc]

dealer /ˈdiːlə(r)/ *n.* **1** a person or business dealing in (esp. retail) goods (*car-dealer; a dealer in tobacco*). **2** the player dealing at cards. **3** a jobber on the Stock Exchange. □ **dealership** *n.* (in sense 1).

■ **Usage** In sense 3, this name has been merged with *broker* since Oct. 1986 (see BROKER 2, JOBBER 1).

dealings /ˈdiːlɪŋz/ *n.pl.* contacts or transactions, esp. in business. □ **have dealings with** associate with.

dealt *past* and *past part.* of DEAL¹.

dean¹ *n.* **1 a** the head of the chapter of a cathedral or collegiate church. **b** (usu. **rural dean**) *Brit.* a member of the clergy exercising supervision over a group of parochial clergy

within a division of an archdeaconry. **2 a** a college or university official, with disciplinary and advisory functions. **b** the head of a university faculty or department or of a medical school. [ME f. AF *deen,* OF *deien,* f. LL *decanus* f. *decem* ten; orig. = chief of a group of ten]

dean² var. of DENE.

deanery /ˈdiːnərɪ/ *n.* (*pl.* **-ies**) **1** a dean's house or office. **2** *Brit.* the group of parishes presided over by a rural dean.

dear /dɪə(r)/ *adj., n., adv.,* & *int.* —*adj.* **1 a** beloved or much esteemed. **b** as a merely polite or ironic form (*my dear man*). **2** used as a formula of address, esp. at the beginning of letters (*Dear Sir*). **3** (often foll. by *to*) precious; much cherished. **4** (usu. in *superl.*) earnest, deeply felt (*my dearest wish*). **5 a** high-priced relative to its value. **b** having high prices. —*n.* (esp. as a form of address) dear person. —*adv.* at a high price or great cost (*will pay dear*). —*int.* expressing surprise, dismay, pity, etc. (*dear me!; oh dear!*). □ **Dear John** *colloq.* a letter terminating a personal relationship. □ **dearly** *adv.* (esp. in sense 3 of *adj.*). **dearness** *n.* [OE *dēore* f. Gmc]

dearth /dɜːθ/ *n.* scarcity or lack, esp. of food. [ME, formed as DEAR]

death /deθ/ *n.* **1** the final cessation of vital functions in an organism; the ending of life. **2** the event that terminates life. **3 a** the fact or process of being killed or killing (*stone to death; fight to the death*). **b** the fact or state of being dead (*eyes closed in death; their deaths caused rioting*). **4** the destruction or permanent cessation of something (*was the death of our hopes*). **5** (usu. **Death**) a personification of death, esp. as a destructive power. **6** a lack of religious faith or spiritual life. □ **at death's door** close to death. **catch one's death** *colloq.* catch a serious chill etc. **death certificate** an official statement of the cause and date and place of a person's death. **death duty** *Brit. hist.* a tax levied on property after the owner's death. **death-mask** a cast taken of a dead person's face. **death penalty** punishment by being put to death. **death rate** the number of deaths per thousand of population per year. **death-rattle** a gurgling sound sometimes heard in a dying person's throat. **death row** *US* a prison block or section for prisoners sentenced to death. **death's head** a human skull as an emblem of mortality. **death squad** an armed paramilitary group formed to kill political enemies etc. **death tax** *US* a tax on property payable on the owner's death. **death-toll** the number of people killed in an accident, battle, etc. **death-trap** *colloq.* a dangerous or unhealthy building, vehicle, etc. **death-warrant** an order for the execution of a condemned person. **2** anything that causes the end of an established practice etc. **death-watch** (in full **death-watch beetle**) a small beetle (*Xestobium rufovillosum*) which makes a sound like a watch ticking, once supposed to portend death, and whose larva bores in old wood. **death-wish** *Psychol.* a desire (usu. unconscious) for the death of oneself or another. **do to death 1** kill. **2** overdo. **put to death** kill or cause to be killed. **to death** to the utmost, extremely (*bored to death; worked to death*). □ **deathless** *adj.* **deathlessness** *n.* **deathlike** *adj.* [OE *dēath* f. Gmc: rel. to DIE¹]

deathbed /ˈdeθbed/ n. a bed as the place where a person is dying or has died.

deathblow /ˈdeθbləʊ/ n. **1** a blow or other action that causes death. **2** an event or circumstance that abruptly ends an activity, enterprise, etc.

deathly /ˈdeθlɪ/ adj. & adv. —adj. (**deathlier**, **deathliest**) suggestive of death (*deathly silence*). —adv. in a deathly way (*deathly pale*).

deb /deb/ n. colloq. a débutante. [abbr.]

débâcle /deɪˈbɑːk(ə)l/ n. (US **debacle**) **1 a** an utter defeat or failure. **b** a sudden collapse or downfall. **2** a confused rush or rout. [F f. débâcler unbar]

debag /diːˈbæg/ v.tr. (**debagged**, **debagging**) Brit. sl. remove the trousers of (a person), esp. as a joke.

debar /dɪˈbɑː(r)/ v.tr. (**debarred**, **debarring**) (foll. by from) exclude from admission or from a right; prohibit from an action (*was debarred from entering*). □ **debarment** n. [ME f. F débarrer, OF desbarrer (as DE-, BAR¹)]

debark[1] /diːˈbɑːk, dɪ-/ v.tr. & intr. land from a ship. □ **debarkation** /-ˈkeɪʃ(ə)n/ n. [F débarquer (as DE-, BARQUE)]

debark[2] /diːˈbɑːk/ v.tr. remove the bark from (a tree).

debase /dɪˈbeɪs/ v.tr. **1** lower in quality, value, or character. **2** depreciate (coin) by alloying etc. □ **debasement** n. **debaser** n. [DE- + obs. base for ABASE]

debatable /dɪˈbeɪtəb(ə)l/ adj. **1** questionable; subject to dispute. **2** capable of being debated. □ **debatably** adv. [OF debatable or AL debatabilis (as DEBATE)]

debate /dɪˈbeɪt/ v. & n. —v. **1** tr. (also absol.) discuss or dispute about (an issue, proposal, etc.) esp. formally in a legislative assembly, public meeting, etc. **2 a** tr. consider, ponder (a matter). **b** intr. consider different sides of a question. —n. **1** a formal discussion on a particular matter, esp. in a legislative assembly etc. **2** debating, discussion (*open to debate*). □ **debater** n. [ME f. OF debatre, debat f. Rmc (as DE-, BATTLE)]

debauch /dɪˈbɔːtʃ/ v. & n. —v.tr. **1** corrupt morally. **2** make intemperate or sensually indulgent. **3** deprave or debase (taste or judgement). **4** (as **debauched** adj.) dissolute. **5** seduce (a woman). —n. **1** a bout of sensual indulgence. **2** debauchery. □ **debaucher** n. [F débauche(r), OF desbaucher, of unkn. orig.]

debauchee /ˌdiːbɔːˈtʃiː, ˌdeb-/ n. a person addicted to excessive sensual indulgence. [F débauché past part.: see DEBAUCH]

debauchery /dɪˈbɔːtʃərɪ/ n. excessive sensual indulgence.

debenture /dɪˈbentʃə(r)/ n. **1** Brit. an acknowledgement of indebtedness, esp. a bond of a company or corporation acknowledging a debt and providing for payment of interest at fixed intervals. **2** US (in full **debenture bond**) a fixed-interest bond of a company or corporation, backed by general credit rather than specified assets. [ME f. L debentur are owing f. debēre owe: assim. to -URE]

debilitate /dɪˈbɪlɪteɪt/ v.tr. enfeeble, enervate. □ **debilitatingly** adv. **debilitation** /-ˈteɪʃ(ə)n/ n. **debilitative** /-tətɪv/ adj. [L debilitare (as DEBILITY)]

debility /dɪˈbɪlɪtɪ/ n. feebleness, esp. of health. [ME f. OF debilité f. L debilitas -tatis f. debilis weak]

debit /ˈdebɪt/ n. & v. —n. **1** an entry in an account recording a sum owed. **2** the sum recorded. **3** the total of such sums. **4** the debit side of an account. —v.tr. (**debited, debiting**) **1** (foll. by against, to) enter (an amount) on the debit side of an account (*debited £500 against me*). **2** (foll. by with) enter (a person) on the debit side of an account (*debited me with £500*). [F débit f. L debitum DEBT]

debonair /ˌdebəˈneə(r)/ adj. carefree, cheerful, self-assured. □ **debonairly** adv. [ME f. OF debonaire = de bon aire of good disposition]

debouch /dɪˈbaʊtʃ, -ˈbuːʃ/ v.intr. **1** (of troops or a stream) issue from a ravine, wood, etc., into open ground. **2** (often foll. by into) (of a river, road, etc.) merge into a larger body or area. □ **debouchment** n. [F déboucher (as DE-, bouche mouth)]

debrief /diːˈbriːf/ v.tr. colloq. interrogate (a person, e.g. a diplomat or pilot) about a completed mission or undertaking. □ **debriefing** n.

debris /ˈdebriː, ˈdeɪ-/ n. scattered fragments, esp. of something wrecked or destroyed. [F débris f. obs. débriser break down (as DE-, briser break)]

debt /det/ n. **1** something that is owed, esp. money. **2** a state of obligation to pay something owed (*in debt*). □ **debt of honour** a debt not legally recoverable, esp. a sum lost in gambling. **in a person's debt** under an obligation to a person. [ME det(te) f. OF dette (later debte) ult. f. L debitum past part. of debēre owe]

debtor /ˈdetə(r)/ n. a person who owes a debt, esp. money. [ME f. OF det(t)or, -our f. L debitor (as DEBT)]

debug /diːˈbʌg/ v.tr. (**debugged, debugging**) **1** colloq. trace and remove concealed listening devices from (a room etc.). **2** colloq. identify and remove defects from (a machine, computer program, etc.). **3** remove bugs from.

debunk /diːˈbʌŋk/ v.tr. colloq. **1** show the good reputation or aspirations of (a person, institution, etc.) to be spurious. **2** expose the falseness of (a claim etc.). □ **debunker** n.

début /ˈdeɪbjuː, -buː/ n. (US **debut**) **1** the first public appearance of a performer on stage etc. **2** the first appearance of a débutante in society. [F f. débuter lead off]

débutante /ˈdebjuːˌtɑːnt, ˈdeɪb-/ n. (US **debutante**) a (usu. wealthy) young woman making her social début. [F, fem. part. of débuter: see DÉBUT]

Dec. abbr. December.

deca- /ˈdekə/ comb. form (also **dec-** before a vowel) **1** having ten. **2** tenfold. **3** ten, esp. of a metric unit (*decagram; decalitre*). [Gk deka ten]

decade /ˈdekeɪd, disp. dɪˈkeɪd/ n. **1** a period of ten years. **2** a set, series, or group of ten. □ **decadal** /ˈdekəd(ə)l/ adj. [ME f. F décade f. LL decas -adis f. Gk f. deka ten]

■ **Usage** The second pronunciation given, with the stress on the second syllable, is considered incorrect by some people though much heard in the media.

decadence /ˈdekəd(ə)ns/ n. **1** moral or cultural deterioration, esp. after a peak or culmination of achievement. **2** decadent behaviour; a state of decadence. [F décadence f. med.L decadentia f. decadere DECAY]

decadent /ˈdekəd(ə)nt/ adj. & n. —adj. **1 a** in a state of moral or cultural deterioration; showing or characterized by decadence. **b** of a period of decadence. **2** self-indulgent. —*n.* a decadent person. □ **decadently** *adv.* [F *décadent* (as DECADENCE)]

decaffeinate /diːˈkæfɪˌneɪt/ *v.tr.* **1** remove the caffeine from. **2** reduce the quantity of caffeine in (usu. coffee).

decagon /ˈdekəgən/ *n.* a plane figure with ten sides and angles. □ **decagonal** /dɪˈkægən(ə)l/ *adj.* [med.L *decagonum* f. Gk *dekagōnon* (as DECA-, -GON)]

decahedron /ˌdekəˈhiːdrən/ *n.* a solid figure with ten faces. □ **decahedral** *adj.* [DECA- + -HEDRON after POLYHEDRON]

decalcify /diːˈkælsɪˌfaɪ/ *v.tr.* (**-ies**, **-ied**) remove lime or calcareous matter from (a bone, tooth, etc.). □ **decalcification** /-fɪˈkeɪʃ(ə)n/ *n.* **decalcifier** *n.*

decalitre /ˈdekəˌliːtə(r)/ *n.* a metric unit of capacity, equal to 10 litres.

Decalogue /ˈdekəˌlɒg/ *n.* the Ten Commandments. [ME f. F *décalogue* or eccl.L *decalogus* f. Gk *dekalogos* (after *hoi deka logoi* the Ten Commandments)]

decametre /ˈdekəˌmiːtə(r)/ *n.* a metric unit of length, equal to 10 metres.

decamp /dɪˈkæmp/ *v.intr.* **1** break up or leave a camp. **2** depart suddenly; abscond. □ **decampment** *n.* [F *décamper* (as DE-, CAMP[1])]

decanal /dɪˈkeɪn(ə)l, ˈdekə-/ *adj.* **1** of a dean or deanery. **2** of the south side of a choir, the side on which the dean sits. [med.L *decanalis* f. LL *decanus* DEAN[1]]

decant /dɪˈkænt/ *v.tr.* gradually pour off (liquid, esp. wine or a solution) from one container to another, esp. without disturbing the sediment. [med.L *decanthare* (as DE-, L *canthus* f. Gk *kanthos* canthus, used of the lip of a beaker)]

decanter /dɪˈkæntə(r)/ *n.* a stoppered glass container into which wine or spirit is decanted.

decapitate /dɪˈkæpɪˌteɪt/ *v.tr.* **1** behead. **2** cut the head or end from. □ **decapitation** /-ˈteɪʃ(ə)n/ *n.* **decapitator** *n.* [LL *decapitare* (as DE-, *caput -itis* head)]

decapod /ˈdekəˌpɒd/ *n.* **1** any crustacean of the order Decapoda, characterized by five pairs of walking legs, e.g. shrimps, crabs, and lobsters. **2** any of various molluscs of the class Cephalopoda, having ten tentacles, e.g. squids and cuttlefish. □ **decapodan** /dɪˈkæpəd(ə)n/ *adj.* [F *dé- capode* f. Gk *deka* ten + *pous podos* foot]

decarbonize /diːˈkɑːbəˌnaɪz/ *v.tr.* (also **-ise**) remove carbon or carbonaceous deposits from (an internal-combustion engine etc.). □ **decarbonization** /-ˈzeɪʃ(ə)n/ *n.*

decathlon /dɪˈkæθlən/ *n.* an athletic contest in which each competitor takes part in ten events. □ **decathlete** /-liːt/ *n.* [DECA- + Gk *athlon* contest]

decay /dɪˈkeɪ/ *v.* & *n.* —*v.* **1 a** *intr.* rot, decompose. **b** *tr.* cause to rot or decompose. **2** *intr.* & *tr.* decline or cause to decline in quality, power, wealth, energy, beauty, etc. **3** *intr. Physics* (usu. foll. by *to*) (of a substance etc.) undergo change by radioactivity. —*n.* **1** a rotten or ruinous state; a process of wasting away. **2** decline in health, quality, etc. **3** *Physics* change into another substance etc. by radioactivity. □ **decayable** *adj.* [ME f. OF *decair* f. Rmc (as DE-, L *cadere* fall)]

decease /dɪˈsiːs/ *n.* & *v.* *formal* esp. *Law* —*n.* death. —*v.intr.* die. [ME f. OF *deces* f. L *decessus* f. *decedere* (as DE-, *cedere cess-* go)]

deceased /dɪˈsiːst/ *adj.* & *n.* *formal* —*adj.* dead. —*n.* (usu. prec. by *the*) a person who has died, esp. recently.

deceit /dɪˈsiːt/ *n.* **1** the act or process of deceiving or misleading, esp. by concealing the truth. **2** a dishonest trick or stratagem. **3** willingness to deceive. [ME f. OF f. past part. of *deceveir* f. L *decipere* deceive (as DE-, *capere* take)]

deceitful /dɪˈsiːtfʊl/ *adj.* **1** (of a person) using deceit, esp. habitually. **2** (of an act, practice, etc.) intended to deceive. □ **deceitfully** *adv.* **deceitfulness** *n.*

deceive /dɪˈsiːv/ *v.* **1** *tr.* make (a person) believe what is false, mislead purposely. **2** *tr.* be unfaithful to, esp. sexually. **3** *intr.* use deceit. **4** *tr. archaic* disappoint (esp. hopes). □ **be deceived** be mistaken or deluded. **deceive oneself** persist in a mistaken belief. □ **deceivable** *adj.* **deceiver** *n.* [ME f. OF *deceivre* or *deceiv-* stressed stem of *deceveir* (as DECEIT)]

decelerate /diːˈseləˌreɪt/ *v.* **1** *intr.* & *tr.* begin or cause to begin to reduce speed. **2** *tr.* make slower (*decelerated motion*). □ **deceleration** /-ˈreɪʃ(ə)n/ *n.* **decelerator** *n.* **decelerometer** /-ˈrɒmɪtə(r)/ *n.* [DE-, after ACCELERATE]

December /dɪˈsembə(r)/ *n.* the twelfth month of the year. [ME f. OF *decembre* f. L *December* f. *decem* ten: orig. the tenth month of the Roman year]

decency /ˈdiːsənsɪ/ *n.* (*pl.* **-ies**) **1** correct and tasteful standards of behaviour as generally accepted. **2** conformity with current standards of behaviour or propriety. **3** avoidance of obscenity. **4** (in *pl.*) the requirements of correct behaviour. [L *decentia* f. *decēre* be fitting]

decennial /dɪˈsenɪ(ə)l/ *adj.* **1** lasting ten years. **2** recurring every ten years. □ **decennially** *adv.* [L *decennis* of ten years f. *decem* ten + *annus* year]

decent /ˈdiːs(ə)nt/ *adj.* **1 a** conforming with current standards of behaviour or propriety. **b** avoiding obscenity. **2** respectable. **3** acceptable, passable; good enough. **4** *Brit.* kind, obliging, generous (*was decent enough to apologize*). □ **decently** *adv.* [F *décent* or L *decēre* be fitting]

decentralize /diːˈsentrəˌlaɪz/ *v.tr.* (also **-ise**) **1** transfer (powers etc.) from a central to a local authority. **2** reorganize (a centralized institution, organization, etc.) on the basis of greater local autonomy. □ **decentralist** /-lɪst/ *n.* & *adj.* **decentralization** /-ˈzeɪʃ(ə)n/ *n.*

deception /dɪˈsepʃ(ə)n/ *n.* **1** the act or an instance of deceiving; the process of being deceived. **2** a thing that deceives; a trick or sham. [ME f. OF or LL *deceptio* f. *decipere* (as DECEIT)]

deceptive /dɪˈseptɪv/ *adj.* apt to deceive; easily mistaken for something else or as having a different quality. □ **deceptively** *adv.* **deceptiveness** *n.* [OF *deceptif -ive* or LL *deceptivus* (as DECEPTION)]

deci- /ˈdesɪ/ *comb. form* one-tenth, esp. of a unit in the metric system (*decilitre*; *decimetre*). [L *decimus* tenth]

decibel /ˈdesɪˌbel/ *n.* a unit (one-tenth of a bel) used in the comparison of two power levels relating to electrical signals or sound intensities, one of the pair usually being taken as a standard.

decide /dɪˈsaɪd/ *v.* **1 a** *intr.* (often foll. by *on*, *about*) come to a resolution as a result of consideration. **b** *tr.* (usu. foll. by *to* + infin., or that + clause) have or reach as one's resolution about something (*decided to stay*; *decided that we should leave*). **2** *tr.* **a** cause (a person) to reach a resolution (*was unsure about going but the weather decided me*). **b** resolve or settle (a question, dispute, etc.). **3** *intr.* give a judgement concerning a matter. □ **decidable** *adj.* [ME f. F *décider* or f. L *decidere* (as DE-, *cædere* cut)]

decided /dɪˈsaɪdɪd/ *adj.* **1** (usu. *attrib.*) definite, unquestionable (*a decided difference*). **2** (of a person, esp. as a characteristic) having clear opinions, resolute, not vacillating. □ **decidedness** *n.*

decidedly /dɪˈsaɪdɪdlɪ/ *adv.* undoubtedly, undeniably.

decider /dɪˈsaɪdə(r)/ *n.* **1** a game, race, etc., to decide between competitors finishing equal in a previous contest. **2** any person or thing that decides.

deciduous /dɪˈsɪdjʊəs/ *adj.* **1** (of a tree) shedding its leaves annually. **2** (of leaves, horns, teeth, etc.) shed periodically. □ **deciduousness** *n.* [L *deciduus* f. *decidere* f. *cadere* fall]

decigram /ˈdesɪˌɡræm/ *n.* (also **decigramme**) a metric unit of mass, equal to 0.1 gram.

decilitre /ˈdesɪˌliːtə(r)/ *n.* a metric unit of capacity, equal to 0.1 litre.

decimal /ˈdesɪm(ə)l/ *adj.* & *n.* —*adj.* **1** (of a system of numbers, weights, measures, etc.) based on the number ten, in which the smaller units are related to the principal units as powers of ten (units, tens, hundreds, thousands, etc.). **2** of tenths or ten; reckoning or proceeding by tens. —*n.* a decimal fraction. □ **decimal fraction** a fraction whose denominator is a power of ten, esp. when expressed positionally by units to the right of a decimal point. **decimal point** a full point or dot placed before a numerator in a decimal fraction. □ **decimally** *adv.* [mod.L *decimalis* f. L *decimus* tenth]

decimalize /ˈdesɪməˌlaɪz/ *v.tr.* (also **-ise**) **1** express as a decimal. **2** convert to a decimal system (esp. of coinage). □ **decimalization** /-ˈzeɪʃ(ə)n/ *n.*

decimate /ˈdesɪˌmeɪt/ *v.tr.* **1** *disp.* destroy a large proportion of. **2** *orig. Mil.* kill or remove one in every ten of. □ **decimation** /-ˈmeɪʃ(ə)n/ *n.* **decimator** *n.* [L *decimare* take the tenth man f. *decimus* tenth]

■ **Usage** Sense 1 is now the usual sense but it is considered inappropriate by some people. This word should not be used to mean 'defeat utterly'.

decimetre /ˈdesɪˌmiːtə(r)/ *n.* a metric unit of length, equal to 0.1 metre.

decipher /dɪˈsaɪfə(r)/ *v.tr.* **1** convert (a text written in cipher) into an intelligible script or language. **2** determine the meaning of (anything obscure or unclear). □ **decipherable** *adj.* **decipherment** *n.*

decision /dɪˈsɪʒ(ə)n/ *n.* **1** the act or process of deciding. **2** a conclusion or resolution reached after consideration (*have made my decision*). **3** (often foll. by *of*) **a** the settlement of a question. **b** a formal judgement. **4** a tendency to decide firmly; resoluteness. [ME f. OF *decision* or L *decisio* (as DECIDE)]

decisive /dɪˈsaɪsɪv/ *adj.* **1** that decides an issue; conclusive. **2** (of a person, esp. as a characteristic) able to decide quickly and effectively.

□ **decisively** *adv.* **decisiveness** *n.* [F *décisif* -*ive* f. med.L *decisivus* (as DECIDE)]

deck *n.* & *v.* —*n.* **1 a** a platform in a ship covering all or part of the hull's area at any level and serving as a floor. **b** the accommodation on a particular deck of a ship. **2** anything compared to a ship's deck, e.g. the floor or compartment of a bus. **3** a component, usu. a flat horizontal surface, that carries a particular recording medium (such as a disc or tape) in sound-reproduction equipment. **4** *US* a pack of cards. **5** *sl.* the ground. **6** any floor or platform, esp. the floor of a pier or a platform for sunbathing. —*v.tr.* **1** (often foll. by *out*) decorate, adorn. **2** furnish with or cover as a deck. □ **below deck** (or **decks**) in or into the space below the main deck. **deck-chair** a folding chair of wood and canvas, of a kind used on deck on passenger ships. **deck-hand** a person employed in cleaning and odd jobs on a ship's deck. **on deck 1** in the open air on a ship's main deck. **2** esp. *US* ready for action, work, etc. [ME, = covering f. MDu. *dec* roof, cloak]

-decker /ˈdekə(r)/ *comb. form* having a specified number of decks or layers (*double-decker*).

declaim /dɪˈkleɪm/ *v.* **1** *intr.* & *tr.* speak or utter rhetorically or affectedly. **2** *intr.* practise oratory or recitation. **3** *intr.* (foll. by *against*) protest forcefully. □ **declaimer** *n.* [ME f. F *déclamer* or f. L *declamare* (as DE-, CLAIM)]

declamation /ˌdekləˈmeɪʃ(ə)n/ *n.* **1** the act or art of declaiming. **2** an impassioned speech; a harangue. □ **declamatory** /dɪˈklæmətərɪ/ *adj.* [F *déclamation* or L *declamatio* (as DECLAIM)]

declaration /ˌdekləˈreɪʃ(ə)n/ *n.* **1** the act or process of declaring. **2** a formal, emphatic, or deliberate statement or announcement. **3** a written public announcement of intentions, terms of an agreement, etc. [ME f. L *declaratio* (as DECLARE)]

declare /dɪˈkleə(r)/ *v.* **1** *tr.* announce openly or formally (*declare war*; *declare a dividend*). **2** *tr.* pronounce (a person or thing) to be something (*declared him to be an impostor*). **3** *tr.* (usu. foll. by *that* + clause) assert emphatically; state explicitly. **4** *tr.* acknowledge possession of (dutiable goods, income, etc.). **5** *tr.* (as **declared** *adj.*) who admits to be such (*a declared atheist*). **6** *tr.* (also *absol.*) *Cricket* close (an innings) voluntarily before all the wickets have fallen. **7** *tr.* *Cards* **a** (also *absol.*) name (the trump suit). **b** announce that one holds (certain combinations of cards etc.). **8** *tr.* (of things) make evident, prove (*your actions declare your honesty*). **9** *intr.* (foll. by *for*, *against*) take the side of one party or another. □ **declare oneself** reveal one's intentions or identity. □ **declarable** *adj.* **declarative** /-ˈklærətɪv/ *adj.* **declaratively** /-ˈklærətɪvlɪ/ *adv.* **declaratory** /-ˈklærətərɪ/ *adj.* **declaredly** /-rɪdlɪ/ *adv.* **declarer** *n.* [ME f. L *declarare* (as DE-, *clarare* f. *clarus* clear)]

declassify /diːˈklæsɪˌfaɪ/ *v.tr.* (**-ies**, **-ied**) declare (information etc.) to be no longer secret. □ **declassification** /-fɪˈkeɪʃ(ə)n/ *n.*

declension /dɪˈklenʃ(ə)n/ *n.* **1** *Gram.* **a** the variation of the form of a noun, pronoun, or adjective, by which its grammatical case, number, and gender are identified. **b** the class in which a noun etc. is put according to the exact form of this variation. **2** deterioration, declining. □ **declensional** *adj.* [OF *déclinaison* f.

decliner DECLINE after L *declinatio*: assim. to ASCENSION etc.]

declination /ˌdeklɪ'neɪʃ(ə)n/ *n.* **1** a downward bend or turn. **2** *Astron.* the angular distance of a star etc. north or south of the celestial equator. **3** *Physics* the angular deviation of a compass needle from true north. **4** *US* a formal refusal. □ **declinational** *adj.* [ME f. L *declinatio* (as DECLINE)]

decline /dɪ'klaɪn/ *v.* & *n.* —*v.* **1** *intr.* deteriorate; lose strength or vigour; decrease. **2 a** *tr.* reply with formal courtesy that one will not accept (an invitation, honour, etc.). **b** *tr.* refuse, esp. formally and courteously. **c** *tr.* turn away from (a challenge, discussion, etc.). **d** *intr.* give or send a refusal. **3** *intr.* slope downwards. **4** *intr.* bend down, droop. **5** *tr. Gram.* state the forms of (a noun, pronoun, or adjective) corresponding to cases, number, and gender. **6** *intr.* (of a day, life, etc.) draw to a close. **7** *intr.* decrease in price etc. **8** *tr.* bend down. —*n.* **1** gradual loss of vigour or excellence (*on the decline*). **2** decay, deterioration. **3** setting; the last part of the course (of the sun, of life, etc.). **4** a fall in price. □ **declining years** old age. □ **declinable** *adj.* **decliner** *n.* [ME f. OF *decliner* f. L *declinare* (as DE-, *clinare* bend)]

declivity /dɪ'klɪvɪtɪ/ *n.* (*pl.* **-ies**) a downward slope, esp. a piece of sloping ground. □ **declivitous** *adj.* [L *declivitas* f. *declivis* (as DE-, *clivus* slope)]

declutch /diː'klʌtʃ/ *v.intr.* disengage the clutch of a motor vehicle.

decoction /dɪ'kɒkʃ(ə)n/ *n.* **1** a process of boiling down so as to extract some essence. **2** the extracted liquor resulting from this. [ME f. OF *decoction* or LL *decoctio* (as DE-, L *coquere coct-* boil)]

decode /diː'kəʊd/ *v.tr.* convert (a coded message) into intelligible language. □ **decodable** *adj.*

decoder /diː'kəʊdə(r)/ *n.* **1** a person or thing that decodes. **2** an electronic device for analysing signals and feeding separate amplifier-channels.

decoke *v.* & *n. Brit. colloq.* —*v.tr.* /diː'kəʊk/ remove carbon or carbonaceous material from (an internal-combustion engine). —*n.* /'diː'kəʊk/ the process of decoking.

décolletage /ˌdeɪkɒl'tɑːʒ/ *n.* a low neckline of a woman's dress etc. [F (as DE-, *collet* collar of a dress)]

décolleté /deɪ'kɒlteɪ/ *adj.* & *n.* —*adj.* (also **décolletée**) **1** (of a dress etc.) having a low neckline. **2** (of a woman) wearing a dress with a low neckline. —*n.* a low neckline. [F (as DÉCOLLETAGE)]

decolonize /diː'kɒləˌnaɪz/ *v.tr.* (also **-ise**) (of a State) withdraw from (a colony), leaving it independent. □ **decolonization** /-'zeɪʃ(ə)n/ *n.*

decommission /ˌdiːkə'mɪʃ(ə)n/ *v.tr.* **1** close down (a nuclear reactor etc.). **2** take (a ship) out of service.

decompose /ˌdiːkəm'pəʊz/ *v.* **1** *intr.* decay, rot. **2** *tr.* separate (a substance, light, etc.) into its elements or simpler constituents. **3** *intr.* disintegrate; break up. □ **decomposition** /ˌdiːkɒmpə'zɪʃ(ə)n/ *n.* [F *dé- composer* (as DE-, COMPOSE)]

decompress /ˌdiːkəm'pres/ *v.tr.* subject to decompression; relieve or reduce the compression on.

decompression /ˌdiːkəm'preʃ(ə)n/ *n.* **1** release from compression. **2** a gradual reduction of air pressure on a person who has been subjected to high pressure (esp. underwater). □ **decompression chamber** an enclosed space for subjecting a person to decompression. **decompression sickness** a condition caused by the sudden lowering of air pressure and formation of bubbles in the blood.

decompressor /ˌdiːkəm'presə(r)/ *n.* a device for reducing pressure in the engine of a motor vehicle.

decongestant /ˌdiːkən'dʒest(ə)nt/ *adj.* & *n.* —*adj.* that relieves (esp. nasal) congestion. —*n.* a medicinal agent that relieves nasal congestion.

deconsecrate /diː'kɒnsɪˌkreɪt/ *v.tr.* transfer (esp. a building) from sacred to secular use. □ **deconsecration** /-'kreɪʃ(ə)n/ *n.*

deconstruct /ˌdiːkən'strʌkt/ *v.tr.* subject to deconstruction. □ **deconstructive** *adj.* [backform. f. DECONSTRUCTION]

deconstruction /ˌdiːkən'strʌkʃ(ə)n/ *n.* a method of critical analysis of philosophical and literary language. □ **deconstructionism** *n.* **deconstructionist** *adj.* & *n.* [F *déconstruction* (as DE-, CONSTRUCTION)]

decontaminate /ˌdiːkən'tæmɪˌneɪt/ *v.tr.* remove contamination from (an area, person, clothes, etc.). □ **decontamination** /-'neɪʃ(ə)n/ *n.*

décor /'deɪkɔː(r), 'de-/ *n.* **1** the furnishing and decoration of a room etc. **2** the decoration and scenery of a stage. [F f. *décorer* (as DECORATE)]

decorate /'dekəˌreɪt/ *v.tr.* **1** provide with adornments. **2** provide (a room or building) with new paint, wallpaper, etc. **3** serve as an adornment to. **4** confer an award or distinction on. □ **Decorated style** *Archit.* the second stage of English Gothic (14th c.), with increasing use of decoration and geometrical tracery. [L *decorare decorat-* f. *decus -oris* beauty]

decoration /ˌdekə'reɪʃ(ə)n/ *n.* **1** the process or art of decorating. **2** a thing that decorates or serves as an ornament. **3** a medal etc. conferred and worn as an honour. **4** (in *pl.*) flags etc. put up on an occasion of public celebration. [F *décoration* or LL *decoratio* (as DECORATE)]

decorative /'dekərətɪv/ *adj.* serving to decorate. □ **decoratively** *adv.* **decorativeness** *n.* [F *décoratif* (as DECORATE)]

decorator /'dekəˌreɪtə(r)/ *n.* a person who decorates, esp. one who paints or papers houses professionally.

decorous /'dekərəs/ *adj.* **1** respecting good taste or propriety. **2** dignified and decent. □ **decorously** *adv.* **decorousness** *n.* [L *decorus* seemly]

decorum /dɪ'kɔːrəm/ *n.* **1 a** seemliness, propriety. **b** behaviour required by politeness or decency. **2** etiquette. [L, neut. of *decorus* seemly]

decouple /diː'kʌp(ə)l/ *v.tr* separate, disengage, dissociate.

decoy *n.* & *v.* —*n.* /'diːkɔɪ, dɪ'kɔɪ/ **1** a person or thing used to lure an animal or person into a trap or danger. **2** a bait or enticement. —*v.tr.* /dɪ'kɔɪ, 'diːkɔɪ/ (often foll. by *into*, *out of*) allure or entice, esp. by means of a decoy. [17th c.: perh. f. Du. *de kooi* the decoy f. *de* THE + *kooi* f. L *cavea* cage]

decrease *v.* & *n.* —*v.tr.* & *intr.* /dɪ'kriːs/ make or become smaller or fewer. —*n.* /'diːkriːs/ **1** the act or an instance of decreasing. **2** the amount by which a thing decreases. □ **decreasingly** *adv.* [ME f. OF *de(s)creiss-*, pres. stem of *de(s)creistre* ult. f. L *decrescere* (as DE-, *crescere cret-* grow)]

decree /dɪˈkriː/ n. & v. —n. **1** an official order issued by a legal authority. **2** a judgement or decision of certain lawcourts, esp. in matrimonial cases. —v.tr. (**decrees, decreed, decreeing**) ordain by decree. □ **decree absolute** a final order for divorce, enabling either party to remarry. **decree nisi** a provisional order for divorce, made absolute unless cause to the contrary is shown within a fixed period. [ME f. OF *decré* f. L *decretum* neut. past part. of *decernere* decide (as DE-, *cernere* sift)]

decrepit /dɪˈkrɛpɪt/ adj. **1** weakened or worn out by age and infirmity. **2** worn out by long use; dilapidated. □ **decrepitude** n. [ME f. L *decrepitus* (as DE-, *crepitus* past part. of *crepare* creak)]

decretal /dɪˈkriːt(ə)l/ n. **1** a papal decree. **2** (in pl.) a collection of these, forming part of canon law. [ME f. med.L *decretale* f. LL (*epistola*) *decretalis* (letter) of decree f. L *decernere*: see DECREE]

decriminalize /diːˈkrɪmɪnəˌlaɪz/ v.tr. (also **-ise**) cease to treat (an action etc.) as criminal. □ **decriminalization** /-ˈzeɪʃ(ə)n/ n.

decry /dɪˈkraɪ/ v.tr. (**-ies, -ied**) disparage, belittle. □ **decrier** n. [after F *décrier*: cf. *cry down*]

decrypt /diːˈkrɪpt/ v.tr. decipher (a cryptogram), with or without knowledge of its key. □ **decryption** n. [DE- + CRYPTOGRAM]

dedicate /ˈdɛdɪˌkeɪt/ v.tr. **1** (foll. by *to*) devote (esp. oneself) to a special task or purpose. **2** (foll. by *to*) address (a book, piece of music, etc.) as a compliment to a friend, patron, etc. **3** (often foll. by *to*) devote (a building etc.) to a deity or a sacred person or purpose. **4** (as **dedicated** adj.) **a** (of a person) devoted to an aim or vocation; having single-minded loyalty or integrity. **b** (of equipment, esp. a computer) designed for a specific purpose. □ **dedicatee** /-kəˈtiː/ n. **dedicative** adj. **dedicator** n. **dedicatory** adj. [L *dedicare* (DE-, *dicare* declare, dedicate)]

dedication /ˌdɛdɪˈkeɪʃ(ə)n/ n. **1** the act or an instance of dedicating; the process of being dedicated. **2** the words with which a book etc. is dedicated. **3** a dedicatory inscription. [ME f. OF *dedicacion* or L *dedicatio* (as DEDICATE)]

deduce /dɪˈdjuːs/ v.tr. (often foll. by *from*) infer; draw as a logical conclusion. □ **deducible** adj. [L *deducere* (as DE-, *ducere duct-* lead)]

deduct /dɪˈdʌkt/ v.tr. (often foll. by *from*) subtract, take away, withhold (an amount, portion, etc.). [L (as DEDUCE)]

deductible /dɪˈdʌktɪb(ə)l/ adj. & n. —adj. that may be deducted, esp. from tax to be paid or taxable income. —n. US = EXCESS n. 6.

deduction /dɪˈdʌkʃ(ə)n/ n. **1 a** the act of deducting. **b** an amount deducted. **2 a** the inferring of particular instances from a general law. **b** a conclusion deduced. [ME f. OF *deduction* or L *deductio* (as DEDUCE)]

deductive /dɪˈdʌktɪv/ adj. of or reasoning by deduction. □ **deductively** adv. [med.L *deductivus* (as DEDUCE)]

dee n. **1** the letter D. **2** a thing shaped like this. [the name of the letter]

deed n. & v. —n. **1** a thing done intentionally or consciously. **2** a brave, skilful, or conspicuous act. **3** actual fact or performance (*kind in word and deed*; *in deed and not in name*). **4** *Law* a written or printed document often used for a legal transfer of ownership and bearing the disposer's signature. —v.tr. US convey or transfer by legal deed. □ **deed-box** a strong box for keeping deeds and other documents. **deed of covenant** an agreement to pay a specified amount regularly to a charity etc., enabling the recipient to recover the tax paid by the donor on an equivalent amount of income. **deed poll** a deed made and executed by one party only, esp. to change one's name. [OE *dǣd* f. Gmc: cf. DO[1]]

deejay /ˈdiːˌdʒeɪ/ n. sl. a disc jockey. [abbr. *DJ*]

deem v.tr. formal regard, consider, judge (*deem it my duty*; *was deemed sufficient*). [OE *dēman* f. Gmc, rel. to DOOM]

de-emphasize /diːˈɛmfəˌsaɪz/ v.tr. (also **-ise**) **1** remove emphasis from. **2** reduce emphasis on.

deemster /ˈdiːmstə(r)/ n. a judge in the Isle of Man. [DEEM + -STER]

deep /diːp/ adj., n., & adv. —adj. **1 a** extending far down from the top (*deep hole*; *deep water*). **b** extending far in from the surface or edge (*deep wound*; *deep plunge*; *deep shelf*; *deep border*). **2** (*predic.*) **a** extending to or lying at a specified depth (*water 6 feet deep*; *ankle-deep in mud*). **b** in a specified number of ranks one behind another (*soldiers drawn up six deep*). **3** situated far down or back or in (*hands deep in his pockets*). **4** coming or brought from far down or in (*deep breath*; *deep sigh*). **5** low-pitched, full-toned, not shrill (*deep voice*; *deep note*; *deep bell*). **6** intense, vivid, extreme (*deep disgrace*; *deep sleep*; *deep colour*; *deep secret*). **7** heartfelt, absorbing (*deep affection*; *deep feelings*; *deep interest*). **8** (*predic.*) fully absorbed or overwhelmed (*deep in a book*; *deep in debt*). **9** profound, penetrating, not superficial; difficult to understand (*deep thinker*; *deep thought*; *deep insight*; *deep learning*). **10** sl. cunning or secretive (*a deep one*). —n. **1** (prec. by *the*) poet. the sea. **2** a deep part of the sea. **3** an abyss, pit, or cavity. **4** (prec. by *the*) *Cricket* the position of a fielder distant from the batsman. **5** a deep state (*deep of the night*). **6** poet. a mysterious region of thought or feeling. —adv. deeply; far down or in (*dig deep*; *read deep into the night*). □ **deep-fry** (**-fries, -fried**) fry (food) in an amount of fat or oil sufficient to cover it. **deep-laid** (of a scheme) secret and elaborate. **deep-rooted** (esp. of convictions) firmly established. **deep sea** the deeper parts of the ocean. **deep-seated** (of emotion, disease, etc.) firmly established, profound. **deep space** the regions beyond the solar system or the earth's atmosphere. **go off** (or **go in off**) **the deep end** *colloq.* give way to anger or emotion. **in deep water** (or **waters**) in trouble or difficulty. **jump** (or **be thrown**) **in at the deep end** face a difficult problem, undertaking, etc., with little experience of it. □ **deeply** adv. **deepness** n. [OE *dēop* (adj.), *dīope*, *dēope* (adv.), f. Gmc: rel. to DIP]

deepen /ˈdiːp(ə)n/ v.tr. & intr. make or become deep or deeper.

deepening /ˈdiːpənɪŋ/ n. the act or process of making deeper; esp. the implementation of measures (such as economic and monetary union) to deepen and strengthen the ties among EC countries.

deep-freeze /diːpˈfriːz/ n. & v. —n. **1** a refrigerator in which food can be quickly frozen and kept for long periods at a very low temperature. **2** a suspension of activity. —v.tr. (**-froze, -frozen**) freeze or store (food) in a deep-freeze.

deer /dɪə(r)/ n. (pl. same) any four-hoofed grazing animal of the family Cervidae, the males of which usu. have deciduous branching antlers. [OE *dēor* animal, deer]

deerskin /ˈdɪəskɪn/ n. & adj. —n. leather from a deer's skin. —adj. made from a deer's skin.

deerstalker /ˈdɪəˌstɔːkə(r)/ n. 1 a soft cloth cap with peaks in front and behind and ear-flaps often joined at the top. 2 a person who stalks deer.

de-escalate /diːˈeskəˌleɪt/ v.tr. reduce the level or intensity of. □ **de-escalation** /-ˈleɪʃ(ə)n/ n.

def /def/ adj. sl. excellent. [Corrupt. of DEATH or shortened f. DEFINITIVE]

deface /dɪˈfeɪs/ v.tr. 1 spoil the appearance of; disfigure. 2 make illegible. □ **defaceable** adj. **defacement** n. **defacer** n. [ME f. F *défacer* f. OF *desfacier* (as DE-, FACE)]

de facto /diː ˈfæktəʊ, deɪ/ adv. & adj. —adv. in fact, whether by right or not. —adj. that exists or is such in fact (*a de facto ruler*). [L]

defalcate /ˈdiːfælˌkeɪt/ v.intr. formal misappropriate property in one's charge, esp. money. □ **defalcator** n. [med.L *defalcare* lop (as DE-, L *falx -cis* sickle)]

defalcation /ˌdiːfælˈkeɪʃ(ə)n/ n. formal 1 Law **a** a misappropriation of money. **b** an amount misappropriated. 2 a shortcoming. [ME f. med.L *defalcatio* (as DEFALCATE)]

defame /dɪˈfeɪm/ v.tr. attack the good reputation of; speak ill of. □ **defamation** /ˌdefəˈmeɪʃ(ə)n, ˌdiːf-/ n. **defamatory** /dɪˈfæmətərɪ/ adj. **defamer** n. [ME f. OF *diffamer* etc. f. L *diffamare* spread evil report (as DIS-, *fama* report)]

default /dɪˈfɔːlt, -ˈfɒlt/ n. & v. —n. 1 failure to fulfil an obligation, esp. to appear, pay, or act in some way. 2 lack, absence. 3 a preselected option adopted by a computer program when no alternative is specified by the user or programmer. —v. 1 intr. fail to fulfil an obligation, esp. to pay money or to appear in a lawcourt. 2 tr. declare (a party) in default and give judgement against that party. □ **go by default** 1 be ignored because of absence. 2 be absent. [ME f. OF *defaut(e)* f. *defaillir* fail f. Rmc (as DE-, L *fallere* deceive); cf. FAIL]

defaulter /dɪˈfɔːltə(r), -ˈfɒltə(r)/ n. a person who defaults, esp. Brit. a soldier guilty of a military offence.

defeat /dɪˈfiːt/ v. & n. —v.tr. 1 overcome in a battle or other contest. 2 frustrate, baffle. 3 reject (a motion etc.) by voting. —n. the act or process of defeating or being defeated. [ME f. OF *deffait, desfait* past part. of *desfaire* f. med.L *disfacere* (as DIS-, L *facere* do)]

defeatism /dɪˈfiːtɪz(ə)m/ n. 1 an excessive readiness to accept defeat. 2 conduct conducive to this. □ **defeatist** n. & adj. [F *défaitisme* f. *défaite* DEFEAT]

defecate /ˈdefɪˌkeɪt/ v.intr. discharge faeces from the body. □ **defecation** /-ˈkeɪʃ(ə)n/ n. [earlier as adj., = purified, f. L *defaecare* (as DE-, *faex faecis* dregs)]

defect /ˈdiːfekt/ n. & v. —n. /also ˈdiːfekt/ 1 lack of something essential; imperfection. 2 a shortcoming or failing. 3 a blemish. —v.intr. /dɪˈfekt/ abandon one's country or cause in favour of another. □ **defector** n. [L *defectus* f. *deficere* desert, fail (as DE-, *facere* do)]

defection /dɪˈfekʃ(ə)n/ n. 1 the abandonment of one's country or cause. 2 ceasing in allegiance

to a leader, party, religion, or duty. [L *defectio* (as DEFECT)]

defective /dɪˈfektɪv/ adj. & n. —adj. 1 having a defect or defects; incomplete, imperfect, faulty. 2 mentally subnormal. 3 (usu. foll. by *in*) lacking, deficient. —n. a mentally defective person. □ **defectively** adv. **defectiveness** n. [ME f. OF *defectif -ive* or LL *defectivus* (as DEFECT)]

defence /dɪˈfens/ n. (*US* **defense**) 1 the act of defending from or resisting attack. 2 **a** a means of resisting attack. **b** a thing that protects. **c** the military resources of a country. 3 (in *pl.*) fortifications. 4 **a** justification, vindication. **b** a speech or piece of writing used to this end. 5 **a** the defendant's case in a lawsuit. **b** the counsel for the defendant. 6 **a** the action or role of defending one's goal etc. against attack. **b** the players in a team who perform this role. □ **defenceless** adj. **defencelessly** adv. **defencelessness** n. [ME f. OF *defens(e)* f. LL *defensum, -a,* past part. of *defendere*: see DEFEND]

defend /dɪˈfend/ v.tr. (also *absol.*) 1 (often foll. by *against, from*) resist an attack made on; protect (a person or thing) from harm or danger. 2 support or uphold by argument; speak or write in favour of. 3 conduct the case for (a defendant in a lawsuit). □ **defendable** adj. **defender** n. [ME f. OF *defendre* f. L *defendere* (cf. OFFEND]

defendant /dɪˈfend(ə)nt/ n. a person etc. sued or accused in a court of law. [ME f. OF, part. of *defendre*: see DEFEND]

defensible /dɪˈfensɪb(ə)l/ adj. 1 justifiable; supportable by argument. 2 that can be easily defended militarily. □ **defensibility** /-ˈbɪlɪtɪ/ n. **defensibly** adv. [ME f. LL *defensibilis* (as DEFEND)]

defensive /dɪˈfensɪv/ adj. 1 done or intended for defence or to defend. 2 (of a person or attitude) concerned to challenge criticism. □ **on the defensive** 1 expecting criticism. 2 in an attitude or position of defence. □ **defensively** adv. **defensiveness** n. [ME f. F *défensif -ive* f. med.L *defensivus* (as DEFEND)]

defer[1] /dɪˈfɜː(r)/ v.tr. (**deferred, deferring**) put off to a later time; postpone. □ **deferment** n. **deferrable** adj. **deferral** n. [ME, orig. the same as DIFFER]

defer[2] /dɪˈfɜː(r)/ v.intr. (**deferred, deferring**) (foll. by *to*) yield or make concessions. □ **deferrer** n. [ME f. F *déférer* f. L *deferre* (as DE-, *ferre* bring)]

deference /ˈdefərəns/ n. 1 courteous regard, respect. 2 compliance with the advice or wishes of another (*pay deference to*). [F *déférence* (as DEFER[2])]

deferential /ˌdefəˈrenʃ(ə)l/ adj. showing deference; respectful. □ **deferentially** adv. [DEFERENCE, after PRUDENTIAL etc.]

defiance /dɪˈfaɪəns/ n. 1 open disobedience; bold resistance. 2 a challenge to fight or maintain a cause, assertion, etc. □ **in defiance of** disregarding; in conflict with. [ME f. OF (as DEFY)]

defiant /dɪˈfaɪənt/ adj. 1 showing defiance. 2 openly disobedient. □ **defiantly** adv.

deficiency /dɪˈfɪʃənsɪ/ n. (pl. **-ies**) 1 the state or condition of being deficient. 2 (usu. foll. by *of*) a lack or shortage. 3 a thing lacking. 4 the amount by which a thing, esp. revenue, falls short. □ **deficiency disease** a disease caused by the lack of some essential or important element in the diet.

deficient /dɪˈfɪʃ(ə)nt/ *adj.* **1** (usu. foll. by *in*) incomplete; not having enough of a specified quality or ingredient. **2** insufficient in quantity, force, etc. **3** (in full **mentally deficient**) incapable of adequate social or intellectual behaviour through imperfect mental development. □ **deficiently** *adv.* [L *deficiens* part. of *deficere* (as DEFECT)]

deficit /ˈdefɪsɪt/ *n.* **1** the amount by which a thing (esp. a sum of money) is too small. **2** an excess of liabilities over assets in a given period, esp. a financial year. [F *déficit* f. L *deficit* 3rd sing. pres. of *deficere* (as DEFECT)]

defier /dɪˈfaɪə(r)/ *n.* a person who defies.

defile[1] /dɪˈfaɪl/ *v.tr.* **1** make dirty; pollute, befoul. **2** corrupt. **3** desecrate, profane. □ **defilement** *n.* **defiler** *n.* [ME *defoul* f. OF *defouler* trample down, outrage (as DE-, *fouler* tread, trample) altered after obs. *befile* f. OE *befylan* (BE-, *fūl* FOUL)]

defile[2] /dɪˈfaɪl/ *n.* & *v.* —*n.* [also ˈdiːfaɪl] **1** a narrow way through which troops can only march in file. **2** a gorge. —*v.intr.* march in file. [F *défiler* and *défilé* past part. (as DE-, FILE[2])]

define /dɪˈfaɪn/ *v.tr.* **1** give the exact meaning of (a word etc.). **2** describe or explain the scope of (*define one's position*). **3** make clear, esp. in outline (*well-defined image*). **4** mark out the boundary or limits of. **5** (of properties) make up the total character of. □ **definable** *adj.* **definer** *n.* [ME f. OF *definer* ult. f. L *definire* (as DE-, *finire* finish, f. *finis* end)]

definite /ˈdefɪnɪt/ *adj.* **1** having exact and discernible limits. **2** clear and distinct; not vague. □ **definiteness** *n.* [L *definitus* past part. of *definire* (as DEFINE)]

■ **Usage** See note at *definitive*.

definitely /ˈdefɪnɪtlɪ/ *adv.* & *int.* —*adv.* **1** in a definite manner. **2** certainly; without doubt (*they were definitely there*). —*int. colloq.* yes, certainly.

definition /ˌdefɪˈnɪʃ(ə)n/ *n.* **1 a** the act or process of defining. **b** a statement of the meaning of a word or the nature of a thing. **2** the degree of distinctness in outline of an object or image. [ME f. OF f. L *definitio* (as DEFINE)]

definitive /dɪˈfɪnɪtɪv/ *adj.* **1** (of an answer, treaty, verdict, etc.) decisive, unconditional, final. **2** (of an edition of a book etc.) most authoritative. □ **definitively** *adv.* [ME f. OF *definitif* -*ive* f. L *definitivus* (as DEFINE)]

■ **Usage** In sense 1, this word is often confused with *definite*, which does not imply authority and conclusiveness. A *definite no* is a firm refusal, while a *definitive no* is an authoritative judgement or decision that something is not the case.

deflate /dɪˈfleɪt/ *v.* **1 a** *tr.* let air or gas out of (a tyre, balloon, etc.). **b** *intr.* be emptied of air or gas. **2 a** *tr.* cause to lose confidence or conceit. **b** *intr.* lose confidence. **3** *Econ.* **a** *tr.* subject (a currency or economy) to deflation. **b** *intr.* pursue a policy of deflation. **4** *tr.* reduce the importance of, depreciate. □ **deflator** *n.* [DE- + INFLATE]

deflation /dɪˈfleɪʃ(ə)n/ *n.* **1** the act or process of deflating or being deflated. **2** *Econ.* reduction of the amount of money in circulation to increase its value as a measure against inflation. □ **deflationary** *adj.* **deflationist** *n.*

deflect /dɪˈflekt/ *v.* **1** *tr.* & *intr.* bend or turn aside from a straight course or intended purpose. **2** (often foll. by *from*) **a** *tr.* cause to deviate. **b** *intr.* deviate. [L *deflectere* (as DE-, *flectere flex-* bend)]

deflection /dɪˈflekʃ(ə)n/ *n.* (also **deflexion**) **1** the act or process of deflecting or being deflected. **2** a lateral bend or turn; a deviation. [LL *deflexio* (as DEFLECT)]

deflector /dɪˈflektə(r)/ *n.* a thing that deflects, esp. a device for deflecting a flow of air etc.

deflower /dɪˈflaʊə(r)/ *v.tr.* **1** deprive (esp. a woman) of virginity. **2** ravage, spoil. **3** strip of flowers. [ME f. OF *deflourer, des-*, ult. f. LL *deflorare* (as DE-, L *flos floris* flower)]

defoliate /diːˈfəʊlɪˌeɪt/ *v.tr.* remove leaves from, esp. as a military tactic. □ **defoliant** *n.* & *adj.* **defoliation** /-ˈeɪʃ(ə)n/ *n.* **defoliator** *n.* [LL *defoliare* f. *folium* leaf]

deforest /diːˈfɒrɪst/ *v.tr.* clear of forests or trees. □ **deforestation** /-ˈsteɪʃ(ə)n/ *n.*

deform /dɪˈfɔːm/ *v.* **1** *tr.* make ugly, deface. **2** *tr.* put out of shape, misshape. **3** *intr.* undergo deformation; be deformed. □ **deformable** *adj.* **deformation** /diːfɔːˈmeɪʃ(ə)n/ *n.* [ME f. OF *deformer* etc. f. med.L *difformare* ult. f. L *deformare* (as DE-, *formare* f. *forma* shape)]

deformed /dɪˈfɔːmd/ *adj.* (of a person or limb) misshapen.

deformity /dɪˈfɔːmɪtɪ/ *n.* (pl. **-ies**) **1** the state of being deformed; disfigurement. **2** a malformation, esp. of body or limb. [ME f. OF *deformité* etc. f. L *deformitas -tatis* f. *deformis* (as DE-, *forma* shape)]

defraud /dɪˈfrɔːd/ *v.tr.* (often foll. by *of*) cheat by fraud. □ **defrauder** *n.* [ME f. OF *defrauder* or L *defraudare* (as DE-, FRAUD)]

defray /dɪˈfreɪ/ *v.tr.* provide money to pay (a cost or expense). □ **defrayable** *adj.* **defrayal** *n.* **defrayment** *n.* [F *défrayer* (as DE-, obs. *frai*(*t*) cost, f. med.L *fredum, -us* fine for breach of the peace)]

defrock /diːˈfrɒk/ *v.tr.* deprive (a person, esp. a priest) of ecclesiastical status. [F *défroquer* (as DE-, FROCK)]

defrost /diːˈfrɒst/ *v.* **1** *tr.* **a** free (the interior of a refrigerator) of excess frost, usu. by turning it off for a period. **b** remove frost or ice from (esp. the windscreen of a motor vehicle). **2** *tr.* unfreeze (frozen food). **3** *intr.* become unfrozen. □ **defroster** *n.*

deft /deft/ *adj.* neatly skilful or dextrous; adroit. □ **deftly** *adv.* **deftness** *n.* [ME, var. of DAFT in obs. sense 'meek']

defunct /dɪˈfʌŋkt/ *adj.* **1** no longer existing. **2** no longer used or in fashion. **3** dead or extinct. □ **defunctness** *n.* [L *defunctus* dead, past part. of *defungi* (as DE-, *fungi* perform)]

defuse /diːˈfjuːz/ *v.tr.* **1** remove the fuse from (an explosive device). **2** reduce the tension or potential danger in (a crisis, difficulty, etc.).

defy /dɪˈfaɪ/ *v.tr.* (**-ies, -ied**) **1** resist openly; refuse to obey. **2** (of a thing) present insuperable obstacles to (*defies solution*). **3** (foll. by *to* + infin.) challenge (a person) to do or prove something. [ME f. OF *defier* f. Rmc (as DIS-, L *fidus* faithful)]

degenerate *adj., n.,* & *v.* —*adj.* /dɪˈdʒenərət/ having lost the qualities that are normal and desirable or proper to its kind; fallen from former excellence. —*n.* /dɪˈdʒenərət/ a degenerate person or animal. —*v.intr.* /dɪˈdʒenəˌreɪt/

become degenerate. □ **degeneracy** n. **degenerately** adv. [L degeneratus past part. of degenerare (as DE-, genus -eris race)]

degeneration /dɪˌdʒenəˈreɪʃ(ə)n/ n. **1 a** the process of becoming degenerate. **b** the state of being degenerate. **2** Med. morbid deterioration of tissue or change in its structure. [ME f. F dégéneration or f. LL degeneratio (as DEGENERATE)]

degenerative /dɪˈdʒenərətɪv/ adj. **1** of or tending to degeneration. **2** (of disease) characterized by progressive often irreversible deterioration.

degrade /dɪˈgreɪd/ v. **1** tr. reduce to a lower rank, esp. as a punishment. **2** tr. bring into dishonour or contempt. **3** tr. Chem. reduce to a simpler molecular structure. **4** tr. Physics reduce (energy) to a less convertible form. □ **degradable** adj. **degradation** /ˌdegrəˈdeɪʃ(ə)n/ n. **degradative** /-dətɪv/ adj. **degrader** n. [ME f. OF degrader f. eccl.L degradare (as DE-, L gradus step)]

degrading /dɪˈgreɪdɪŋ/ adj. humiliating; causing a loss of self-respect. □ **degradingly** adv.

degree /dɪˈgriː/ n. **1** a stage in an ascending or descending scale, series, or process. **2** a stage in intensity or amount (to a high degree; in some degree). **3** relative condition (each is good in its degree). **4** Math. a unit of measurement of angles. **5** Physics a unit in a scale of temperature, hardness, etc. **6** Med. an extent of burns on a scale characterized by the destruction of the skin. **7** an academic rank conferred by a college or university after completion of a course, or conferred as an honour. **8** a grade of crime or criminality (murder in the first degree). **9** a step in direct genealogical descent. **10** social or official rank. □ **by degrees** a little at a time; gradually. **to a degree** colloq. considerably. □ **degreeless** adj. [ME f. OF degré f. Rmc (as DE-, L gradus step)]

dehire /diːˈhaɪə(r)/ v.tr. US colloq. dismiss (a person) from employment; sack, fire.

dehorn /diːˈhɔːn/ v.tr. remove the horns from (an animal).

dehumanize /diːˈhjuːməˌnaɪz/ v.tr. (also **-ise**) **1** deprive of human characteristics. **2** make impersonal or machine-like. □ **dehumanization** /-ˈzeɪʃ(ə)n/ n.

dehumidify /ˌdiːhjuːˈmɪdɪˌfaɪ/ v.tr. (**-ies, -ied**) reduce the degree of humidity of; remove moisture from (a gas, esp. air). □ **dehumidification** /-fɪˈkeɪʃ(ə)n/ n. **dehumidifier** n.

dehydrate /diːˈhaɪdreɪt, ˌdiːhaɪˈdreɪt/ v. **1** tr. **a** remove water from (esp. foods for preservation and storage in bulk). **b** make dry, esp. make (the body) deficient in water. **c** render lifeless or uninteresting. **2** intr. lose water. □ **dehydration** /-ˈdreɪʃ(ə)n/ n. **dehydrator** n.

de-ice /diːˈaɪs/ v.tr. **1** remove ice from. **2** prevent the formation of ice on.

de-icer /diːˈaɪsə(r)/ n. a device or substance for de-icing, esp. a windscreen or ice on an aircraft.

deify /ˈdiːɪˌfaɪ, ˈdeɪɪ-/ v.tr. (**-ies, -ied**) **1** make a god of. **2** regard or worship as a god. □ **deification** /-fɪˈkeɪʃ(ə)n/ n. [ME f. OF deifier f. eccl.L deificare f. deus god]

deign /deɪn/ v. **1** intr. (foll. by to + infin.) think fit, condescend. **2** tr. (usu. with neg.) archaic condescend to give (an answer etc.). [ME f. OF degnier, deigner, daigner f. L dignare, -ari deem worthy f. dignus worthy]

deinstitutionalize /diːˌɪnstɪˈtjuːʃənəˌlaɪz/ v.tr. (also **-ise**) (usu. as **deinstitutionalized** adj.) remove from an institution or from the effects of institutional life. □ **deinstitutionalization** /-ˈzeɪʃ(ə)n/ n.

deism /ˈdiːɪz(ə)m, ˈdeɪ-/ n. belief in the existence of a supreme being arising from reason rather than revelation. □ **deist** n. **deistic** /-ˈɪstɪk/ adj. **deistical** /-ˈɪstɪk(ə)l/ adj. [L deus god + -ISM]

deity /ˈdiːɪtɪ, ˈdeɪɪ-/ n. (pl. **-ies**) **1** a god or goddess. **2** divine status, quality, or nature. **3** (**the Deity**) the Creator, God. [ME f. OF deité f. eccl.L deitas -tatis transl. Gk theotēs f. theos god]

déjà vu /ˌdeɪʒɑː ˈvuː/ n. **1** Psychol. an illusory feeling of having already experienced a present situation. **2** something tediously familiar. [F, = already seen]

deject /dɪˈdʒekt/ v.tr. (usu. as **dejected** adj.) make sad or dispirited; depress. □ **dejectedly** adv. [ME f. L dejicere (DE-, jacĕre throw)]

dejection /dɪˈdʒekʃ(ə)n/ n. a dejected state; low spirits. [ME f. L dejectio (as DEJECT)]

de jure /diː ˈdʒʊərɪ, deɪ ˈjʊəreɪ/ adj. & adv. —adj. rightful. —adv. rightfully; by right. [L]

delay /dɪˈleɪ/ v. & n. —v. **1** tr. postpone; defer. **2** tr. make late (was delayed at the traffic lights). **3** intr. loiter; be late (don't delay!). —n. **1** the act or an instance of delaying; the process of being delayed. **2** time lost by inaction or the inability to proceed. **3** a hindrance. □ **delayer** n. [ME f. OF delayer (v.), delai (n.), prob. f. des- DIS- + laier leave: see RELAY]

delectable /dɪˈlektəb(ə)l/ adj. esp. literary. delightful, pleasant. □ **delectability** /-ˈbɪlɪtɪ/ n. **delectably** adv. [ME f. OF f. L delectabilis f. delectare DELIGHT]

delectation /ˌdiːlekˈteɪʃ(ə)n/ n. literary pleasure, enjoyment (sang for his delectation). [ME f. OF (as DELECTABLE)]

delegacy /ˈdelɪgəsɪ/ n. (pl. **-ies**) **1** a system of delegating. **2 a** an appointment as a delegate. **b** a body of delegates; a delegation.

delegate n. & v. —n. /ˈdelɪgət/ **1** an elected representative sent to a conference. **2** a member of a committee. **3** a member of a deputation. —v.tr. /ˈdelɪˌgeɪt/ **1** (often foll. by to) **a** commit (authority, power, etc.) to an agent or deputy. **b** entrust (a task) to another person. **2** send or authorize (a person) as a representative; depute. □ **delegable** /ˈdelɪgəb(ə)l/ adj. [ME f. L delegatus (as DE-, legare depute)]

delegation /ˌdelɪˈgeɪʃ(ə)n/ n. **1** a body of delegates; a deputation. **2** the act or process of delegating or being delegated. [L delegatio (as DELEGATE)]

delete /dɪˈliːt/ v.tr. remove or obliterate (written or printed matter), esp. by striking out. □ **deletion** /-ˈliːʃ(ə)n/ n. [L delēre delet- efface]

deleterious /ˌdelɪˈtɪərɪəs/ adj. harmful (to the mind or body). □ **deleteriously** adv. [med.L deleterius f. Gk dēlētērios noxious]

delft /delft/ n. (also **delftware** /ˈdelftweə(r)/) glazed, usu. blue and white, earthenware, made in Delft in Holland.

deli /ˈdelɪ/ n. (pl. **delis**) esp. US colloq. a delicatessen shop. [abbr.]

deliberate adj. & v. —adj. /dɪˈlɪbərət/ **1 a** intentional (a deliberate foul). **b** fully considered; not impulsive (made a deliberate choice). **2** slow in deciding; cautious. **3** (of movement etc.) leisurely and unhurried. —v. /dɪˈlɪbəˌreɪt/ **1** intr. think carefully; take counsel. **2** tr. consider, discuss carefully. □ **deliberately** /dɪˈlɪbərətlɪ/ adv. **deliberateness** /dɪˈlɪbərətnɪs/ n. **deliberator**

/dɪˈlɪbəˌreɪtə(r)/ n. [L *deliberatus* past part. of *deliberare* (as DE-, *librare* weigh f. *libra* balance)]

deliberation /dɪˌlɪbəˈreɪʃ(ə)n/ n. **1** careful consideration. **2 a** the discussion of reasons for and against. **b** a debate or discussion. **3 a** caution and care. **b** (of movement) slowness or ponderousness. [ME f. OF f. L *deliberatio -onis* (as DELIBERATE)]

deliberative /dɪˈlɪbərətɪv/ adj. of, or appointed for the purpose of, deliberation or debate (a *deliberative assembly*). □ **deliberatively** adv.

deliberativeness n. [F *délibératif -ive* or L *deliberativus* (as DELIBERATE)]

delicacy /ˈdelɪkəsɪ/ n. (pl. **-ies**) **1** fineness or intricacy of structure or texture; gracefulness. **2** susceptibility to injury or disease; weakness. **3** the quality of requiring discretion or sensitivity. **4** a choice or expensive food. **5 a** consideration for the feelings of others. **b** avoidance of immodesty or vulgarity. [ME f. DELICATE + -ACY]

delicate /ˈdelɪkət/ adj. **1 a** fine in texture or structure; soft, slender, or slight. **b** of exquisite quality or workmanship. **c** (of colour) subtle or subdued; not bright. **d** subtle, hard to appreciate. **2** (of a person) easily injured; susceptible to illness. **3 a** requiring careful handling; tricky (a *delicate situation*). **b** (of an instrument) highly sensitive. **4** deft (a *delicate touch*). **5** (of a person) avoiding the immodest or offensive. **6** (esp. of actions) considerate. **7** (of food) dainty; suitable for an invalid. □ **delicately** adv. **delicateness** n. [ME f. OF *delicat* or L *delicatus*, of unkn. orig.]

delicatessen /ˌdelɪkəˈtes(ə)n/ n. **1** a shop selling cooked meats, cheeses, and unusual or foreign prepared foods. **2** (often *attrib.*) such foods collectively (a *delicatessen counter*). [G *Delikatessen* or Du. *delicatessen* f. F *délicatesse* f. *délicat* (as DELICATE)]

delicious /dɪˈlɪʃəs/ adj. **1** highly delightful and enjoyable to the taste or sense of smell. **2** (of a joke etc.) very witty. □ **deliciously** adv. **deliciousness** n. [ME f. OF f. LL *deliciosus* f. L *deliciae* delight]

delight /dɪˈlaɪt/ v. & n. —v. **1** tr. (often foll. by *with*) please greatly. **2** intr. (often foll. by *in*, or *to* + infin.) take great pleasure; be highly pleased. —n. **1** great pleasure. **2** something giving pleasure. □ **delighted** adj. **delightedly** adv. [ME f. OF *delitier*, *delit*, f. L *delectare* frequent. of *delicere*: alt. after *light* etc.]

delightful /dɪˈlaɪtfʊl/ adj. causing great delight; pleasant, charming. □ **delightfully** adv. **delightfulness** n.

delimit /dɪˈlɪmɪt/ v.tr. (**delimited**, **delimiting**) **1** determine the limits of. **2** fix the territorial boundary of. □ **delimitation** /-ˈteɪʃ(ə)n/ n. [F *délimiter* f. L *delimitare* (as DE-, *limitare* f. *limes -itis* boundary)]

delineate /dɪˈlɪnɪˌeɪt/ v.tr. portray by drawing etc. or in words (*delineated her character*). □ **delineation** /-ˈeɪʃ(ə)n/ n. **delineator** n. [L *delineare delineat-* (as DE-, *lineare* f. *linea* line)]

delinquency /dɪˈlɪŋkwənsɪ/ n. (pl. **-ies**) **1 a** a crime, usu. not of a serious kind; a misdeed. **b** minor crime in general, esp. that of young people (*juvenile delinquency*). **2** wickedness (*moral delinquency*). [eccl. L *delinquentia* f. L *delinquens* part. of *delinquere* offend]

delinquent /dɪˈlɪŋkwənt/ n. & adj. —n. an offender (*juvenile delinquent*). —adj. **1** guilty of a

minor crime or a misdeed. **2** failing in one's duty. **3** US in arrears. □ **delinquently** adv.

deliquesce /ˌdelɪˈkwes/ v.intr. **1** become liquid, melt. **2** Chem. dissolve in water absorbed from the air. □ **deliquescence** n. **deliquescent** adj. [L *deliquescere* (as DE-, *liquescere* incept. of *liquēre* be liquid)]

delirious /dɪˈlɪrɪəs/ adj. **1** affected with delirium; temporarily or apparently mad; raving. **2** wildly excited, ecstatic. **3** (of behaviour) betraying delirium or ecstasy. □ **deliriously** adv.

delirium /dɪˈlɪrɪəm/ n. **1** an acutely disordered state of mind involving incoherent speech, hallucinations, and frenzied excitement. **2** great excitement, ecstasy. □ **delirium tremens** /ˈtriːmenz/ a psychosis of chronic alcoholism involving tremors and hallucinations. [L f. *delirare* be deranged (as DE-, *lira* ridge between furrows)]

deliver /dɪˈlɪvə(r)/ v.tr. **1 a** distribute (letters, parcels, ordered goods, etc.) to the addressee or the purchaser. **b** (often foll. by *to*) hand over (*delivered the boy safely to his teacher*). **2** (often foll. by *from*) save, rescue, or set free (*delivered him from his enemies*). **3 a** give birth to (*delivered a girl*). **b** (in *passive*; often foll. by *of*) give birth (*was delivered of a child*). **c** assist at the birth of (*delivered six babies that week*). **4 a** (often *refl.*) utter or recite (an opinion, a speech, etc.) (*delivered himself of the observation*; *delivered the sermon well*). **b** (of a judge) pronounce (a judgement). **5** (often foll. by *up*, *over*) abandon; hand over (*delivered his soul up to God*). **6** present or render (an account). **7** launch or aim (a blow, a ball, or an attack). **8** colloq. = *deliver the goods*. □ **deliver the goods** colloq. carry out one's part of an agreement. □ **deliverable** adj. **deliverer** n. [ME f. OF *delivrer* f. Gallo-Roman (as DE-, LIBERATE)]

deliverance /dɪˈlɪvərəns/ n. **1** the act or an instance of rescuing; the process of being rescued. **2** a rescue. [ME f. OF *delivrance* (as DELIVER)]

delivery /dɪˈlɪvərɪ/ n. (pl. **-ies**) **1 a** the delivering of letters etc. **b** a regular distribution of letters etc. (*two deliveries a day*). **c** something delivered. **2 a** the process of childbirth. **b** an act of this. **3** deliverance. **4** an act of throwing, esp. of a cricket ball. **5** the act of giving or surrendering (*delivery of the town to the enemy*). **6 a** the uttering of a speech etc. **b** the manner or style of such a delivery (a *measured delivery*). [ME f. AF *delivree* fem. past part. of *delivrer* (as DELIVER)]

dell n. a small usu. wooded hollow or valley. [OE f. Gmc]

delocalize /diːˈləʊkəˌlaɪz/ v.tr. (also **-ise**) **1** detach or remove (a thing) from its place. **2** not limit to a particular location. □ **delocalization** /-ˈzeɪʃ(ə)n/ n.

delouse /diːˈlaʊs/ v.tr. rid (a person or animal) of lice.

Delphic /ˈdelfɪk/ adj. (also **Delphian** /-fɪən/) **1** (of an utterance, prophecy, etc.) obscure, ambiguous, or enigmatic. **2** of or concerning the ancient Greek oracle at Delphi.

delphinium /delˈfɪnɪəm/ n. any ranunculaceous garden plant of the genus *Delphinium*, with tall spikes of usu. blue flowers. [mod.L f. Gk *delphinion* larkspur f. *delphin* dolphin]

delphinoid /ˈdelfɪˌnɔɪd/ adj. & n. —adj. **1** of the family that includes dolphins, porpoises, grampuses, etc. **2** dolphin-like. —*n.* **1** a member of the delphinoid family of aquatic mammals. **2** a dolphin-like animal. [Gk *delphinoeidēs* f. *delphin* dolphin]

delta /ˈdeltə/ *n.* **1** a triangular tract of deposited earth, alluvium, etc., at the mouth of a river, formed by its diverging outlets. **2** the fourth letter of the Greek alphabet (Δ, δ). □ **delta wing** the triangular swept-back wing of an aircraft. □ **deltaic** /delˈteɪɪk/ *adj.* [ME f. Gk f. Phoen. *daleth*]

deltoid /ˈdeltɔɪd/ *adj.* & *n.* —*adj.* triangular; like a river delta. —*n.* (in full **deltoid muscle**) a thick triangular muscle covering the shoulder joint and used for raising the arm away from the body. [F *deltoïde* or mod.L *deltoides* f. Gk *deltoeidēs* (as DELTA, -OID)]

delude /dɪˈluːd, -ˈljuːd/ *v.tr.* deceive or mislead (*deluded by false optimism*). □ **deluder** *n.* [ME f. L *deludere* mock (as DE-, *ludere lus-* play)]

deluge /ˈdeljuːdʒ/ *n.* & *v.* —*n.* **1** a great flood. **2** (**the Deluge**) the biblical Flood (Gen. 6–8). **3** a great outpouring (of words, paper, etc.). **4** a heavy fall of rain. —*v.tr.* **1** flood. **2** inundate with a great number or amount (*deluged with complaints*). [ME f. OF f. L *diluvium*, rel. to *lavare* wash]

delusion /dɪˈluːʒ(ə)n, -ˈljuːʒ(ə)n/ *n.* **1** a false belief or impression. **2** *Psychol.* this as a symptom or form of mental disorder. □ **delusional** *adj.* [ME f. LL *delusio* (as DELUDE)]

delusive /dɪˈluːsɪv, -ˈljuːsɪv/ *adj.* **1** deceptive or unreal. **2** disappointing. □ **delusively** *adv.* **delusiveness** *n.*

de luxe /də ˈlʌks, ˈlʊks/ *adj.* **1** luxurious or sumptuous. **2** of a superior kind. [F, = of luxury]

delve /delv/ *v.* **1** *intr.* (often foll. by *in, into*) **a** search energetically (*delved into his pocket*). **b** make a laborious search in documents etc.; research (*delved into his family history*). **2** *tr.* & *intr. poet.* dig. □ **delver** *n.* [OE *delfan* f. WG]

demagnetize /diːˈmægnɪˌtaɪz/ *v.tr.* (also **-ise**) remove the magnetic properties of. □ **demagnetization** /-ˈzeɪʃ(ə)n/ *n.* **demagnetizer** *n.*

demagogue /ˈdeməˌɡɒɡ/ *n.* (US **-gog**) a political agitator appealing to the basest instincts of a mob. □ **demagogic** /-ˈɡɒɡɪk/ *adj.* **demagoguery** /-ˈɡɒɡərɪ/ *n.* **demagogy** /-ˈɡɒɡɪ/ *n.* [Gk *dēmagōgos* f. *dēmos* the people + *agōgos* leading]

demand /dɪˈmɑːnd/ *n.* & *v.* —*n.* **1** an insistent and peremptory request, made as of right. **2** *Econ.* the desire of purchasers or consumers for a commodity. **3** an urgent claim (*care of her mother makes demands on her*). —*v.tr.* **1** (often foll. by *of, from, or to* + infin., or *that* + clause) ask for (something) insistently and urgently, as of right. **2** require or need (*a task demanding skill*). **3** insist on being told (*demanded her business*). **4** (as **demanding** *adj.*) making demands; requiring skill, effort, etc. (*a demanding but worthwhile job*). □ **in demand** sought after. **on demand** as soon as a demand is made. □ **demandable** *adj.* **demander** *n.* **demandingly** *adv.* [ME f. OF *demande* (n.), *demander* (v.) f. L *demandare* entrust (as DE-, *mandare* order: see MANDATE)]

demarcation /ˌdiːmɑːˈkeɪʃ(ə)n/ *n.* **1** the act of marking a boundary or limits. **2** the trade-union practice of strictly assigning specific jobs to different unions. □ **demarcation dispute** an inter-union dispute about who does a particular job. □ **demarcate** /ˈdiː-/ *v.tr.* **demarcator** /ˈdiː-/

n. [Sp. *demarcación* f. *demarcar* mark the bounds of (as DE-, MARK[1])]

dematerialize /ˌdiːməˈtɪərɪəˌlaɪz/ *v.tr.* & *intr.* (also **-ise**) make or become non-material or spiritual (esp. of psychic phenomena etc.). □ **dematerialization** /-ˈzeɪʃ(ə)n/ *n.*

demean /dɪˈmiːn/ *v.tr.* (usu. *refl.*) lower the dignity of (*would not demean myself to take it*). [DE- + MEAN[2], after *debase*]

demeanour /dɪˈmiːnə(r)/ *n.* (US **demeanor**) outward behaviour or bearing. [ME f. OF *demener* f. Rmc (as DE-, L *minare* drive animals f. *minari* threaten): prob. after obs. *havour* behaviour]

demented /dɪˈmentɪd/ *adj.* mad; crazy. □ **dementedly** *adv.* **dementedness** *n.* [past part. of *dement* verb f. OF *dementer* or f. LL *dementare* f. *demens* out of one's mind (as DE-, *mens mentis* mind)]

dementia /dɪˈmenʃə/ *n.* *Med.* a chronic or persistent disorder of the mental processes due to brain disease or injury. □ **dementia praecox** /ˈpriːkɒks/ schizophrenia. [L f. *demens* (as DEMENTED)]

demerara /ˌdeməˈreərə/ *n.* light-brown cane sugar coming orig. and chiefly from Demerara. [*Demerara* in Guyana]

demerit /diːˈmerɪt/ *n.* **1** a quality or action deserving blame; a fault. **2** *US* a mark given to an offender. □ **demeritorious** /-ˈtɔːrɪəs/ *adj.* [ME f. OF *de(s)merite* or L *demeritum* neut. past part. of *demerēri* deserve]

demersal /dɪˈmɜːs(ə)l/ *adj.* (of a fish etc.) being or living near the sea-bottom (cf. PELAGIC). [L *demersus* past part. of *demergere* (as DE-, *mergere* plunge)]

demesne /dɪˈmiːn, -ˈmeɪn/ *n.* **1 a** a sovereign's or State's territory; a domain. **b** land attached to a mansion etc. **c** landed property; an estate. **2** (usu. foll. by *of*) a region or sphere. [ME f. AF, OF *demeine* (later AF *demesne*) belonging to a lord f. L *dominicus* f. *dominus* lord]

demi- /ˈdemɪ/ *prefix* **1** half; half-size. **2** partially or imperfectly such (*demigod*). [ME f. F f. med.L *dimedius* half, for L *dimidius*]

demigod /ˈdemɪˌɡɒd/ *n.* (*fem.* **-goddess** /-ˌɡɒdɪs/) **1** a partly divine being. **2** the offspring of a god or goddess and a mortal.

demijohn /ˈdemɪˌdʒɒn/ *n.* a bulbous narrow-necked bottle holding from 3 to 10 gallons and usu. in a wicker cover. [prob. corrupt. of F *dame-jeanne* Lady Jane, assim. to DEMI- + the name *John*]

demilitarize /diːˈmɪlɪtəˌraɪz/ *v.tr.* (also **-ise**) remove a military organization or forces from (a frontier, a zone, etc.). □ **demilitarization** /-ˈzeɪʃ(ə)n/ *n.*

demi-monde /ˈdemɪˌmɒnd, -ˈmɔ̃d/ *n.* **1** a class of women considered to be of doubtful social standing and morality. **2** any group considered to be on the fringes of respectable society. [F, = half-world]

demineralize /diːˈmɪnərəˌlaɪz/ *v.tr.* (also **-ise**) remove salts from (sea water etc.). □ **demineralization** /-ˈzeɪʃ(ə)n/ *n.*

demise /dɪˈmaɪz/ *n.* & *v.* —*n.* **1** death (*left a will on her demise; the demise of the agreement*). **2** *Law* conveyance or transfer (of property, a title, etc.) by demising. —*v.tr. Law* **1** convey or grant (an estate) by will or lease. **2** transmit (a title etc.) by death. [AF use of past part. of OF *de(s)mettre* DISMISS, in refl. abdicate]

demisemiquaver /ˌdemɪˈsemɪˌkweɪvə(r), ˈdemɪ-/ n. Mus. a note having the time value of half a semiquaver and represented by a large dot with a three-hooked stem.

demist /diːˈmɪst/ v.tr. clear mist from (a windscreen etc.). □ **demister** n.

demo /ˈdeməʊ/ n. (pl. -os) colloq. = DEMONSTRATION 2, 3. [abbr.]

demob /diːˈmɒb/ v. & n. Brit. colloq. —v.tr. (**demobbed, demobbing**) demobilize. —n. demobilization. [abbr.]

demobilize /diːˈməʊbɪˌlaɪz/ v.tr. (also -ise) disband (troops, ships, etc.). □ **demobilization** /-ˈzeɪʃ(ə)n/ n. [F démobiliser (as DE-, MOBILIZE)]

democracy /dɪˈmɒkrəsɪ/ n. (pl. -ies) 1 a a system of government by the whole population, usu. through elected representatives. b a State so governed. c any organization governed on democratic principles. 2 a classless and tolerant form of society. [F démocratie f. LL democratia f. Gk dēmokratia f. dēmos the people + -CRACY]

democrat /ˈdeməˌkræt/ n. 1 an advocate of democracy. 2 (**Democrat**) (in the US) a member of the Democratic Party. □ **democratism** /dɪˈmɒkrəˌtɪz(ə)m/ n. [F démocrate (as DEMOCRACY), after aristocrate]

democratic /ˌdeməˈkrætɪk/ adj. 1 of, like, practising, advocating, or constituting democracy or a democracy. 2 favouring social equality. □ **democratically** adv. [F dé- mocratique f. med.L democraticus f. Gk dēmokratikos f. dēmokratia DEMOCRACY]

democratize /dɪˈmɒkrəˌtaɪz/ v.tr. (also -ise) make (a State, institution, etc.) democratic. □ **democratization** /-ˈzeɪʃ(ə)n/ n.

demodulate /diːˈmɒdjʊˌleɪt/ v.tr. Physics extract (a modulating signal) from its carrier. □ **demodulation** /ˌdiːmɒdjʊˈleɪʃ(ə)n/ n. **demodulator** n.

demography /dɪˈmɒgrəfɪ/ n. the study of the statistics of births, deaths, disease, etc., as illustrating the conditions of life in communities. □ **demographer** n. **demographic** /ˌdeməˈgræfɪk/ adj. **demographical** /ˌdeməˈgræfɪk(ə)l/ adj. **demographically** /ˌdeməˈgræfɪkəlɪ/ adv. [Gk dēmos the people + -GRAPHY]

demolish /dɪˈmɒlɪʃ/ v.tr. 1 a pull down (a building). b completely destroy or break. 2 overthrow (an institution). 3 refute (an argument, theory, etc.). 4 joc. eat up completely and quickly. □ **demolisher** n. **demolition** /ˌdeməˈlɪʃ(ə)n/ n. **demolitionist** /ˌdeməˈlɪʃənɪst/ n. [F démolir f. L demoliri (as DE-, moliri molit- construct f. moles mass)]

demon /ˈdiːmən/ n. 1 a an evil spirit or devil. b the personification of evil passion. 2 a malignant supernatural being; the Devil. 3 (often attrib.) a forceful, fierce, or skilful performer (a demon on the tennis court; a demon player). 4 a cruel or destructive person. 5 an inner or attendant spirit; a genius (the demon of creativity). [ME f. med.L demon f. L daemon f. Gk daimōn deity]

demonetize /diːˈmʌnɪˌtaɪz/ v.tr. (also -ise) withdraw (a coin etc.) from use as money. □ **demonetization** /-ˈzeɪʃ(ə)n/ n. [F démonétiser (as DE-, L moneta MONEY)]

demoniac /dɪˈməʊnɪˌæk/ adj. & n. —adj. 1 fiercely energetic or frenzied. 2 supposedly possessed by an evil spirit. 3 of or like demons. —n. a person possessed by an evil spirit. □

demoniacal /ˌdiːməˈnaɪək(ə)l/ adj. **demoniacally** /ˌdiːməˈnaɪəkəlɪ/ adv. [ME f. OF demoniaque f. eccl.L daemoniacus f. daemonium f. Gk daimonion dimin. of daimōn: see DEMON)]

demonic /dɪˈmɒnɪk/ adj. 1 = DEMONIAC. 2 having or seeming to have supernatural genius or power. [LL daemonicus f. Gk daimonikos (as DEMON)]

demonism /ˈdiːməˌnɪz(ə)m/ n. belief in the power of demons.

demonize /ˈdiːməˌnaɪz/ v.tr. (also -ise) 1 make into or like a demon. 2 represent as a demon.

demonolatry /ˌdiːməˈnɒlətrɪ/ n. the worship of demons.

demonology /ˌdiːməˈnɒlədʒɪ/ n. the study of demons etc. □ **demonologist** n.

demonstrable /ˈdemənstrəb(ə)l, dɪˈmɒnstrəb(ə)l/ adj. capable of being shown or logically proved. □ **demonstrability** /-ˈbɪlɪtɪ/ n. **demonstrably** adv. [ME f. L demonstrabilis (as DEMONSTRATE)]

demonstrate /ˈdemənˌstreɪt/ v. 1 tr. show evidence of (feelings etc.). 2 tr. describe and explain (a scientific proposition, machine, etc.) by experiment, practical use, etc. 3 tr. a logically prove the truth of. b be proof of the existence of. 4 intr. take part in or organize a public demonstration. [L demonstrare (as DE-, monstrare show)]

demonstration /ˌdemənˈstreɪʃ(ə)n/ n. 1 (foll. by of) a the outward showing of feeling etc. b an instance of this. 2 a public meeting, march, etc., for a political or moral purpose. 3 a the exhibiting or explaining of specimens or experiments as a method of esp. scientific teaching. b an instance of this. 4 proof provided by logic, argument, etc. 5 Mil. a show of military force. □ **demonstrational** adj. [ME f. OF demonstration or L demonstratio (as DEMONSTRATE)]

demonstrative /dɪˈmɒnstrətɪv/ adj. & n. —adj. 1 given to or marked by an open expression of feeling, esp. of affection. 2 (usu. foll. by of) logically conclusive; giving proof (the work is demonstrative of their skill). 3 Gram. (of an adjective or pronoun) indicating the person or thing referred to (e.g. this, that, those). —n. Gram. a demonstrative adjective or pronoun. □ **demonstratively** adv. **demonstrativeness** n. [ME f. OF demonstratif -ive f. L demonstrativus (as DEMONSTRATION)]

demonstrator /ˈdemənˌstreɪtə(r)/ n. 1 a person who takes part in a political demonstration etc. 2 a person who demonstrates, esp. machines, equipment, etc., to prospective customers. 3 a person who teaches by demonstration, esp. in a laboratory etc. [L (as DEMONSTRATE)]

demoralize /dɪˈmɒrəˌlaɪz/ v.tr. (also -ise) destroy (a person's) morale; make hopeless. □ **demoralization** /-ˈzeɪʃ(ə)n/ n. **demoralizing** adj. **demoralizingly** adv. [F démoraliser (as DE-, MORAL)]

demote /dɪˈməʊt, diː-/ v.tr. reduce to a lower rank or class. □ **demotion** /-ˈməʊʃ(ə)n/ n. [DE- + PROMOTE]

demotic /dɪˈmɒtɪk/ n. & adj. —n. the popular colloquial form of a language. —adj. (esp. of language) popular, colloquial, or vulgar. [Gk dēmotikos f. dēmotēs one of the people (dēmos)]

demotivate /diːˈməʊtɪˌveɪt/ v.tr. (also absol.) cause to lose motivation; discourage. □ **demotivation** /-ˈveɪʃ(ə)n/ n.

demur /dɪ'mɜ:(r)/ v. & n. —v.intr. (**demurred**, **demurring**) (often foll. by *to*, *at*) raise scruples or objections. —n. (also **demurral** /dɪ'mʌr(ə)l/) (usu. in *neg.*) **1** an objection (*agreed without demur*). **2** the act or process of objecting. □ **demurrant** /dɪ'mʌrənt/ n. (in sense 2 of v.). [ME f. OF *demeure* (n.), *demeurer* (v.) f. Rmc (as DE-, L *morari* delay)]

demure /dɪ'mjʊə(r)/ adj. (**demurer**, **demurest**) **1** composed, quiet, and reserved; modest. **2** affectedly shy and quiet; coy. **3** decorous (*a demure high collar*). □ **demurely** adv. **demureness** n. [ME, perh. f. AF *demuré* f. OF *demoré* past part. of *demorer* remain, stay (as DEMUR): infl. by OF *meür* f. L *maturus* ripe]

demurrer /dɪ'mʌrə(r)/ n. *Law* an objection raised or exception taken. [AF (infin. as noun), = DEMUR]

demystify /di:'mɪstɪ,faɪ/ v.tr. (**-ies**, **-ied**) **1** clarify (obscure beliefs or subjects etc.). **2** reduce or remove the irrationality in (a person). □ **demystification** /-fɪ'keɪʃ(ə)n/ n.

demythologize /ˌdi:mɪ'θɒlə,dʒaɪz/ v.tr. (also **-ise**) remove mythical elements from (a legend, famous person's life, etc.).

den n. **1** a wild animal's lair. **2** a place of crime or vice (*den of iniquity*; *opium den*). **3** a small private room for pursuing a hobby etc. [OE *denn* f. Gmc, rel. to DEAN²]

denarius /dɪ'neərɪəs/ n. (pl. **denarii** /-rɪ,aɪ/) an ancient Roman silver coin. [L, = (coin) of ten *asses* (a Roman copper coin), as DENARY]

denary /'di:nərɪ/ adj. of ten; decimal. [L *denarius* containing ten (*deni* by tens)]

denationalize /di:'næʃənə,laɪz/ v.tr. (also **-ise**) transfer (a nationalized industry or institution etc.) from public to private ownership. □ **denationalization** /-'zeɪʃ(ə)n/ n. [F *dénationaliser* (as DE-, NATIONAL)]

denature /di:'neɪtʃə(r)/ v.tr. **1** change the properties of (a protein etc.) by heat, acidity, etc. **2** make (alcohol) unfit for drinking esp. by the addition of another substance. □ **denaturant** n. **denaturation** /di:,nætʃə'reɪʃ(ə)n/ n. [F *dénaturer* (as DE-, NATURE)]

dendrochronology /ˌdendrəʊkrə'nɒlədʒɪ/ n. a system of dating using the characteristic patterns of annual growth rings of trees to assign dates to timber. □ **dendrochronological** /-ˌkrɒnə'lɒdʒɪk(ə)l/ adj. **dendrochronologist** n. [Gk *dendron* tree + CHRONOLOGY]

dendrology /den'drɒlədʒɪ/ n. the scientific study of trees. □ **dendrological** /-drə'lɒdʒɪk(ə)l/ adj. **dendrologist** n. [Gk *dendron* tree + -LOGY]

dene /di:n/ n. (also **dean**) *Brit.* **1** a narrow wooded valley. **2** a vale (esp. as the ending of place-names). [OE *denu*, rel. to DEN]

dengue /'dengɪ/ n. an infectious viral disease of the tropics causing a fever and acute pains in the joints. [W. Ind. Sp., f. Swahili *denga*, *dinga*, with assim. to Sp. *dengue* fastidiousness, with ref. to the stiffness of the patient's neck and shoulders]

deniable /dɪ'naɪəb(ə)l/ adj. that may be denied. □ **deniability** n.

denial /dɪ'naɪəl/ n. **1** the act or an instance of denying. **2** a refusal of a request or wish. **3** a statement that a thing is not true; a rejection (*denial of the accusation*).

denier /'denjə(r)/ n. a unit of weight by which the fineness of silk, rayon, or nylon yarn is measured. (orig. the name of a small coin: ME f. OF f. L *denarius*)

denigrate /'denɪ,greɪt/ v.tr. defame or disparage the reputation of (a person). □ **denigration** /-'ɡreɪʃ(ə)n/ n. **denigrator** n. **denigratory** /-'ɡreɪtərɪ/ adj. [L *denigrare* (as DE-, *nigrare* f. *niger* black)]

denim /'denɪm/ n. **1** (often *attrib.*) a usu. blue hard-wearing cotton twill fabric. **2** (in *pl.*) *colloq.* jeans, overalls, etc. made of this. [for *serge de Nim* f. *Nîmes* in S. France]

denitrify /di:'naɪtrɪ,faɪ/ v.tr. (**-ies**, **-ied**) remove the nitrates or nitrites from (soil etc.). □ **denitrification** /-fɪ'keɪʃ(ə)n/ n.

denizen /'denɪz(ə)n/ n. **1** a foreigner admitted to certain rights in his or her adopted country. **2** a naturalized foreign word, animal, or plant. **3** (usu. foll. by *of*) *poet.* an inhabitant or occupant. □ **denizenship** n. [ME f. AF *deinzein* f. OF *deinz* within f. L *de* from + *intus* within + *-ein* f. L *-aneus*: see -ANEOUS]

denominate /dɪ'nɒmɪ,neɪt/ v.tr. **1** give a name to. **2** call or describe (a person or thing) as. [L *denominare* (as DE-, NOMINATE)]

denomination /dɪ,nɒmɪ'neɪʃ(ə)n/ n. **1** a Church or religious sect. **2** a class of units within a range or sequence of numbers, weights, money, etc. (*money of small denominations*). **3 a** a name or designation, esp. a characteristic or class name. **b** a class or kind having a specific name. **4** the rank of a playing-card within a suit, or of a suit relative to others. □ **denominational** adj. [ME f. OF *denomination* or L *denominatio* (as DENOMINATE)]

denominator /dɪ'nɒmɪ,neɪtə(r)/ n. *Math.* the number below the line in a vulgar fraction; a divisor. □ **common denominator 1** a common multiple of the denominators of several fractions. **2** a common feature of members of a group. **least** (or **lowest**) **common denominator** the lowest common multiple as above. [F *dénominateur* f. med.L *denominator* (as DE-, NOMINATE)]

denote /dɪ'nəʊt/ v.tr. **1** be a sign of; indicate. **2** (usu. foll. by + clause) mean, convey. **3** stand as a name for; signify. □ **denotation** /ˌdi:nə'teɪʃ(ə)n/ n. **denotative** /-tətɪv/ adj. [F *dénoter* or f. L *denotare* (as DE-, *notare* mark f. *nota* NOTE)]

denouement /deɪ'nu:mɑ̃/ n. (also **dénouement**) the final unravelling of a plot or complicated situation. [F *dénouement* f. *dénouer* unknot (as DE-, L *nodare* f. *nodus* knot)]

denounce /dɪ'naʊns/ v.tr. **1** accuse publicly; condemn (*denounced him as a traitor*). **2** inform against (*denounced her to the police*). **3** give notice of the termination of (an armistice, treaty, etc.). □ **denouncement** n. **denouncer** n. [ME f. OF *denoncier* f. L *denuntiare* (as DE-, *nuntiare* make known f. *nuntius* messenger)]

dense /dens/ adj. **1** closely compacted in substance; thick (*dense fog*). **2** crowded together (*the population is less dense on the outskirts*). **3** *colloq.* stupid. □ **densely** adv. **denseness** n. [F *dense* or L *densus*]

density /'densɪtɪ/ n. (pl. **-ies**) **1** the degree of compactness of a substance. **2** *Physics* degree of consistency measured by the quantity of mass per unit volume. **3** the opacity of a photographic image. [F *densité* or L *densitas* (as DENSE)]

dent *n. & v.* **—n. 1** a slight mark or hollow in a surface made by, or as if by, a blow with a hammer etc. **2** a noticeable effect (*lunch made a dent in our funds*). **—v.tr. 1** mark with a dent. **2** have (esp. an adverse) effect on (*the news dented our hopes*). [ME, prob. f INDENT¹]

dental /ˈdent(ə)l/ *adj.* **1** of the teeth; of or relating to dentistry. **2** *Phonet.* (of a consonant) produced with the tongue-tip against the upper front teeth (as *th*) or the ridge of the teeth (as *n, s, t*). □ **dental floss** a thread of floss silk etc. used to clean between the teeth. **dental mechanic** a person who makes and repairs artificial teeth. **dental surgeon** a dentist. □ **dentalize** *v.tr.* (also **-ise**). [LL *dentalis* f. L *dens dentis* tooth]

dentate /ˈdenteɪt/ *adj.* Bot. & Zool. toothed; with toothlike notches; serrated. [L *dentatus* f. *dens dentis* tooth]

dentifrice /ˈdentɪfrɪs/ *n.* a paste or powder for cleaning the teeth. [F f. L *dentifricium* f. *dens dentis* tooth + *fricare* rub]

dentine /ˈdentiːn/ *n.* (US **dentin** /-tɪn/) a hard dense bony tissue forming the bulk of a tooth. □ **dentinal** /ˈdentɪn(ə)l/ *adj.* [L *dens dentis* tooth + -INE⁴]

dentist /ˈdentɪst/ *n.* a person who is qualified to treat the diseases and conditions that affect the mouth, esp. the repair and extraction of teeth and the insertion of artificial ones. □ **dentistry** *n.* [F *dentiste* f. *dent* tooth]

dentition /denˈtɪʃ(ə)n/ *n.* **1** the type, number, and arrangement of teeth in a species etc. **2** the cutting of teeth; teething. [L *dentitio* f. *dentire* to teethe]

denture /ˈdentʃə(r)/ *n.* a removable artificial replacement for one or more teeth carried on a removable plate or frame. [F f. *dent* tooth]

denuclearize /diːˈnjuːklɪəˌraɪz/ *v.tr.* (also **-ise**) remove nuclear armaments from (a country etc.). □ **denuclearization** /-ˈzeɪʃ(ə)n/ *n.*

denude /dɪˈnjuːd/ *v.tr.* **1** make naked or bare. **2** (foll. by *of*) **a** strip of clothing, a covering, etc. **b** deprive of a possession or attribute. **3** *Geol.* lay (rock or a formation etc.) bare by removing what lies above. □ **denudation** /ˌdiːnjuːˈdeɪʃ(ə)n/ *n.* **denudative** /-dətɪv/ *adj.* [L *denudare* (as DE-, *nudus* naked)]

denunciation /dɪˌnʌnsɪˈeɪʃ(ə)n/ *n.* **1** the act of denouncing (a person, policy, etc.); public condemnation. **2** an instance of this. □ **denunciate** /-ˈnʌnsɪˌeɪt/ *v.tr.* **denunciative** /-ˈnʌnsɪətɪv/ *adj.* **denunciator** /-ˈnʌnsɪˌeɪtə(r), -ˈnʌnʃɪˌeɪtə(r)/ *n.* **denunciatory** /dɪˈnʌnsɪətərɪ, -ˈnʌnʃɪətərɪ/ *adj.* [F *dénonciation* or L *denunciatio* (as DENOUNCE)]

deny /dɪˈnaɪ/ *v.tr.* (**-ies, -ied**) **1** declare untrue or non-existent (*denied the charge; denied that it is so*). **2** repudiate or disclaim (*denied his faith*). **3** (often foll. by *to*) refuse (a person or thing, or something to a person) (*denied him the satisfaction*). □ **deny oneself** be abstinent. □ **denier** *n.* [ME f. OF *denier* f. L *denegare* (as DE-, *negare* say no)]

deodar /ˈdiːəˌdɑː(r)/ *n.* the Himalayan cedar *Cedrus deodara*. [Hindi *dē' odār* f. Skr. *deva-dāru* divine tree]

deodorant /diːˈəʊdərənt/ *n.* (often *attrib.*) a substance sprayed or rubbed on to the body or sprayed into the air to remove or conceal unpleasant smells (*has a deodorant effect*). [as DEODORIZE + -ANT]

deodorize /diːˈəʊdəˌraɪz/ *v.tr.* (also **-ise**) remove or destroy the (usu. unpleasant) smell of. □ **deodorization** /-ˈzeɪʃ(ə)n/ *n.* **deodorizer** *n.* [DE- + L *odor* smell]

deoxygenate /diːˈɒksɪdʒəˌneɪt/ *v.tr.* remove oxygen, esp. free oxygen, from. □ **deoxygenation** /-ˈneɪʃ(ə)n/ *n.*

deoxyribonucleic acid /ˌdiːˈɒksɪˌraɪbəʊnjʊˈkleɪɪk/ *n.* see DNA. [DE- + OXYGEN + RIBONUCLEIC (ACID)]

dep. *abbr.* **1** departs. **2** deputy.

depart /dɪˈpɑːt/ *v.* **1** *intr.* **a** go away; leave (*the train departs from this platform*). **b** start; set out (*trains depart for Crewe every hour*). **2** *intr.* diverge; deviate (*departs from standard practice*). **3 a** *intr.* die. **b** *tr.* formal or literary leave by death (*departed this life*). [ME f. OF *departir* ult. f. L *dispertire* divide]

departed /dɪˈpɑːtɪd/ *adj. & n.* **—adj.** bygone (*departed greatness*). **—n.** (prec. by *the*) euphem. a particular dead person or dead people.

department /dɪˈpɑːtmənt/ *n.* **1** a separate part of a complex whole, esp.: **a** a branch of municipal or State administration (*Department of Social Security*). **b** a branch of study and its administration at a university, school, etc. (*the physics department*). **c** a specialized section of a large store (*hardware department*). **2** *colloq.* an area of special expertise. **3** an administrative district in France and other countries. □ **department store** a large shop stocking many varieties of goods in different departments. [F *département* (as DEPART)]

departmental /ˌdiːpɑːtˈment(ə)l/ *adj.* of or belonging to a department. □ **departmentalism** *n.* **departmentalize** *v.tr.* (also **-ise**). **departmentalization** /-ˈzeɪʃ(ə)n/ *n.* **departmentally** *adv.*

departure /dɪˈpɑːtʃə(r)/ *n.* **1** the act or an instance of departing. **2** (often foll. by *from*) a deviation (from the truth, a standard, etc.). **3** (often *attrib.*) the starting of a train, an aircraft, etc. **4** a new course of action or thought (*driving a car is rather a departure for him*). [OF *departeüre* (as DEPART)]

depend /dɪˈpend/ *v.intr.* **1** (often foll. by *on, upon*) be controlled or determined by (*success depends on hard work; it depends how you tackle the problem*). **2** (foll. by *on, upon*) **a** be unable to do without (*depends on her mother*). **b** rely on (*I'm depending on you to come*). □ **depend upon it!** you may be sure! **it** (or **it all** or **that**) **depends** expressing uncertainty or qualification in answering a question. [ME f. OF *dependre* ult. f. L *dependēre* (as DE-, *pendēre* hang)]

dependable /dɪˈpendəb(ə)l/ *adj.* reliable. □ **dependability** /-ˈbɪlɪtɪ/ *n.* **dependableness** *n.* **dependably** *adv.*

dependant /dɪˈpend(ə)nt/ *n.* (US **dependent**) **1** a person who relies on another esp. for financial support. **2** a servant. [F *dépendant* pres. part. of *dépendre* (as DEPEND)]

dependence /dɪˈpend(ə)ns/ *n.* **1** the state of being dependent, esp. on financial or other support. **2** reliance; trust; confidence. [F *dépendance* (as DEPEND)]

dependency /dɪˈpendənsɪ/ *n.* (pl. **-ies**) **1** a country or province controlled by another. **2** anything subordinate or dependent.

dependent /dɪˈpend(ə)nt/ *adj. & n.* —*adj.* **1** (usu. foll. by *on*) depending, conditional, or subordinate. **2** unable to do without (esp. a drug). **3** maintained at another's cost. **4** *Gram.* (of a clause, phrase, or word) subordinate to a sentence or word. —*n.* *US* var. of DEPENDANT. □ **dependently** *adv.* [ME, earlier *-ant* = DEPENDANT]

depersonalize /diːˈpɜːsənəˌlaɪz/ *v.tr.* (also **-ise**) **1** make impersonal. **2** deprive of personality. □ **depersonalization** *n.*

depict /dɪˈpɪkt/ *v.tr.* **1** represent in a drawing or painting etc. **2** portray in words; describe. □ **depicter** *n.* **depiction** /-ˈpɪkʃ(ə)n/ *n.* **depictive** *adj.* **depictor** *n.* [L *depingere depict-* (as DE-, *pingere* paint)]

depilate /ˈdepɪˌleɪt/ *v.tr.* remove the hair from. □ **depilation** /-ˈleɪʃ(ə)n/ *n.* [L *depilare* (as DE-, *pilare* f. *pilus* hair)]

depilatory /dɪˈpɪlətərɪ/ *adj. & n.* —*adj.* that removes unwanted hair. —*n.* (*pl.* **-ies**) a depilatory substance.

deplane /diːˈpleɪn/ *v.* esp. *US* **1** *intr.* disembark from an aeroplane. **2** *tr.* remove from an aeroplane.

deplete /dɪˈpliːt/ *v.tr.* (esp. in *passive*) **1** reduce in numbers or quantity (*depleted forces*). **2** empty out; exhaust (*their energies were depleted*). □ **depletion** /-ˈpliːʃ(ə)n/ *n.* [L *deplēre* (as DE-, *plēre* *plet-* fill)]

deplorable /dɪˈplɔːrəb(ə)l/ *adj.* **1** exceedingly bad (*a deplorable meal*). **2** that can be deplored. □ **deplorably** *adv.*

deplore /dɪˈplɔː(r)/ *v.tr.* **1** grieve over; regret. **2** be scandalized by; find exceedingly bad. □ **deploringly** *adv.* [F *déplorer* or It. *deplorare* f. L *deplorare* (as DE-, *plorare* bewail)]

deploy /dɪˈplɔɪ/ *v.* **1** *Mil.* **a** *tr.* cause (troops) to spread out from a column into a line. **b** *intr.* (of troops) spread out in this way. **2** *tr.* bring (arguments, forces, etc.) into effective action. □ **deployment** *n.* [F *déployer* f. L *displicare* (as DIS-, *plicare* fold) & LL *deplicare* explain]

depoliticize /ˌdiːpəˈlɪtɪˌsaɪz/ *v.tr.* (also **-ise**) **1** make (a person, an organization, etc.) non-political. **2** remove from political activity or influence. □ **depoliticization** /-ˈzeɪʃ(ə)n/ *n.*

deponent /dɪˈpəʊnənt/ *n.* *Law* **1** a person making a deposition under oath. **2** a witness giving written testimony for use in court etc. [L *deponere* (as DE-, *ponere posit-* place)]

depopulate /diːˈpɒpjʊˌleɪt/ *v.* **1** *tr.* reduce the population of. **2** *intr.* decline in population. □ **depopulation** /-ˈleɪʃ(ə)n/ *n.* [L *depopulari* (as DE-, *populari* lay waste f. *populus* people)]

deport /dɪˈpɔːt/ *v.tr.* **1 a** remove (an immigrant or foreigner) forcibly to another country; banish. **b** exile (a native) to another country. **2** *refl.* conduct (oneself) or behave (in a specified manner) (*deported himself well*). □ **deportable** *adj.* **deportation** /ˌdiːpɔːˈteɪʃ(ə)n/ *n.* [OF *deporter* and (sense 1) F *déporter* (as DE-, L *portare* carry)]

deportee /ˌdiːpɔːˈtiː/ *n.* a person who has been or is being deported.

deportment /dɪˈpɔːtmənt/ *n.* bearing, demeanour, or manners, esp. of a cultivated kind. [F *déportement* (as DEPORT)]

depose /dɪˈpəʊz/ *v.* **1** *tr.* remove from office, esp. dethrone. **2** *intr.* *Law* (usu. foll. by *to*, or *that* + clause) bear witness, esp. on oath in court. [ME

f. OF *deposer* after L *deponere*: see DEPONENT, POSE[1]]

deposit /dɪˈpɒzɪt/ *n. & v.* —*n.* **1 a** *Brit.* a sum of money kept in an account in a bank. **b** anything stored or entrusted for safe keeping, usu. in a bank. **2 a** a sum payable as a first instalment on an item bought on hire purchase, or as a pledge for a contract. **b** a returnable sum payable on the short-term hire of a car, boat, etc. **3 a** a natural layer of sand, rock, coal, etc. **b** a layer of precipitated matter on a surface, e.g. fur on a kettle. —*v.tr.* (**deposited**, **depositing**) **1 a** put or lay down in a (usu. specified) place (*deposited the book on the floor*). **b** (of water, wind, etc.) leave (matter etc.) lying in a displaced position. **2 a** store or entrust for keeping. **b** pay (a sum of money) into a bank account, esp. a deposit account. **3** pay (a sum) as a deposit. □ **deposit account** *Brit.* a bank account that pays interest but from which money cannot usu. be withdrawn without notice or loss of interest. **on deposit** (of money) placed in a deposit account. [L *depositum* (n.), med.L *depositare* f. L *deponere deposit-* (as DEPONENT)]

depositary /dɪˈpɒzɪtərɪ/ *n.* (*pl.* **-ies**) a person to whom something is entrusted; a trustee. [LL *depositarius* (as DEPOSIT)]

deposition /ˌdiːpəˈzɪʃ(ə)n, ˌdep-/ *n.* **1** the act or an instance of deposing, esp. a monarch; dethronement. **2** *Law* the process of giving sworn evidence; allegation. **b** an instance of this. **c** evidence given under oath; a testimony. **3** (**the Deposition**) the taking down of the body of Christ from the Cross. [ME f. OF f. L *depositio -onis* f. *deponere*: see DEPOSIT]

depositor /dɪˈpɒzɪtə(r)/ *n.* a person who deposits money, property, etc.

depository /dɪˈpɒzɪtərɪ/ *n.* (*pl.* **-ies**) **1 a** a storehouse for furniture etc. **b** a store (of wisdom, knowledge, etc.) (*the book is a depository of wit*). **2** = DEPOSITARY. [LL *depositorium* (as DEPOSIT)]

depot /ˈdepəʊ/ *n.* **1** a storehouse. **2** *Mil.* **a** a storehouse for equipment etc. **b** the head-quarters of a regiment. **3 a** a building for the servicing, parking, etc. of esp. buses, trains, or goods vehicles. **b** *US* a railway or bus station. [F *dépôt*, OF *depost* f. L (as DEPOSIT)]

deprave /dɪˈpreɪv/ *v.tr.* pervert or corrupt, esp. morally. □ **depravation** /ˌdeprəˈveɪʃ(ə)n/ *n.* [ME f. OF *depraver* or L *depravare* (as DE-, *pravare* f. *pravus* crooked)]

depravity /dɪˈprævɪtɪ/ *n.* (*pl.* **-ies**) moral corruption; wickedness. [DE- + obs. *pravity* f. L *pravitas* (as DEPRAVE)]

deprecate /ˈdeprɪˌkeɪt/ *v.tr.* express disapproval of or a wish against; deplore (*deprecate hasty action*). □ **deprecatingly** *adv.* **deprecation** /-ˈkeɪʃ(ə)n/ *n.* **deprecative** /ˈdeprɪkətɪv/ *n.* **deprecator** *n.* **deprecatory** /-ˈkeɪtərɪ/ *adj.* [L *deprecari* (as DE-, *precari* pray)]

■ **Usage** This word is often confused with *depreciate*.

depreciate /dɪˈpriːʃɪˌeɪt, -sɪˌeɪt/ *v.* **1** *tr. & intr.* diminish in value (*the car has depreciated*). **2** *tr.* disparage; belittle (*they are always depreciating his taste*). **3** *tr.* reduce the purchasing power of (money). □ **depreciatingly** *adv.* **depreciatory**

/dɪˈpriːʃɪətərɪ/ adj. [LL depretiare (as DE-, pretiare f. pretium price)]

■ **Usage** This word is often confused with *deprecate*.

depreciation /dɪˌpriːʃɪˈeɪʃ(ə)n, -sɪˈeɪʃ(ə)n/ n. **1** the amount of wear and tear (of a property etc.) for which a reduction may be made in a valuation, an estimate, or a balance sheet. **2** *Econ.* a decrease in the value of a currency. **3** the act or an instance of depreciating; belittlement.

depredation /ˌdeprɪˈdeɪʃ(ə)n/ n. (usu. in pl.) **1** despoiling, ravaging, or plundering. **2** an instance or instances of this. [F *déprédation* f. LL *depraedatio* (as DE-, *praedatio -onis* f. L *praedari* plunder)]

depress /dɪˈpres/ v.tr. **1** push or pull down; lower (*depressed the lever*). **2** make dispirited or dejected. **3** *Econ.* reduce the activity of (esp. trade). **4** (as **depressed** adj.) **a** dispirited or miserable. **b** *Psychol.* suffering from depression. □ **depressed area** an area suffering from economic depression. □ **depressible** adj. **depressing** adj. **depressingly** adv. [ME f. OF *depresser* f. LL *depressare* (as DE-, *pressare* frequent. of *premere* press)]

depressant /dɪˈpres(ə)nt/ adj. & n. —adj. **1** that depresses. **2** *Med.* sedative. —n. **1** *Med.* an agent, esp. a drug, that sedates. **2** an influence that depresses.

depression /dɪˈpreʃ(ə)n/ n. **1** *Psychol.* a state of extreme dejection or morbidly excessive melancholy; a mood of hopelessness and feelings of inadequacy. **2** a long period of financial and industrial decline; a slump. **3** *Meteorol.* a lowering of atmospheric pressure, esp. the centre of a region of minimum pressure or the system of winds round it. **4** a sunken place or hollow on a surface. **5** pressing down. [ME f. OF or L *depressio* (as DE-, *premere press-* press)]

depressive /dɪˈpresɪv/ adj. & n. —adj. **1** tending to depress. **2** *Psychol.* involving or characterized by depression. —n. *Psychol.* a person suffering or with a tendency to suffer from depression. [F *dépressif -ive* or med.L *depressivus* (as DEPRESSION)]

depressor /dɪˈpresə(r)/ n. *Anat.* (in full **depressor muscle**) a muscle that causes the lowering of some part of the body. [L (as DEPRESSION)]

depressurize /diːˈpreʃəˌraɪz/ v.tr. (also **-ise**) cause an appreciable drop in the pressure of the gas inside (a container), esp. to the ambient level. □ **depressurization** /-ˈzeɪʃ(ə)n/ n.

deprivation /ˌdeprɪˈveɪʃ(ə)n, ˌdiːpraɪ-/ n. (usu. foll. by *of*) the act or an instance of depriving; the state of being deprived (*deprivation of liberty*; *suffered many deprivations*). [med.L *deprivatio* (as DEPRIVE)]

deprive /dɪˈpraɪv/ v.tr. **1** (usu. foll. by *of*) strip, dispossess; debar from enjoying (*illness deprived him of success*). **2** (as **deprived** adj.) **a** (of a child etc.) suffering from the effects of a poor or loveless home. **b** (of an area) with inadequate housing, facilities, employment, etc. □ **deprivable** adj. **deprival** n. [ME f. OF *depriver* f. med.L *deprivare* (as DE-, L *privare* deprive)]

Dept. abbr. Department.

depth /depθ/ n. **1 a** deepness (*the depth is not great at the edge*). **b** the measurement from the top down, from the surface inwards, or from the front to the back (*depth of the drawer is 12*

inches). **2** difficulty; abstruseness. **3 a** sagacity; wisdom. **b** intensity of emotion etc. (*the poem has little depth*). **4** an intensity of colour, darkness, etc. **5** (in pl.) **a** deep water, a deep place; an abyss. **b** a low, depressed state. **c** the lowest or inmost part (*the depths of the country*). **6** the middle (*in the depth of winter*). □ **depth-bomb** (or **-charge**) a bomb capable of exploding under water, esp. for dropping on a submerged submarine etc. **in depth** comprehensively, thoroughly, or profoundly. **in-depth** adj. thorough; done in depth. **out of one's depth 1** in water over one's head. **2** engaged in a task or on a subject too difficult for one. [ME (as DEEP, -TH²)]

deputation /ˌdepjʊˈteɪʃ(ə)n/ n. a group of people appointed to represent others. [ME f. LL *deputatio* (as DEPUTE)]

depute v. & n. —v.tr. /dɪˈpjuːt/ (often foll. by *to*) **1** appoint as a deputy. **2** delegate (a task, authority, etc.) (*deputed the leadership to her*). —n. /ˈdepjuːt/ *Sc.* a deputy. [ME f. OF *député* past part. of *deputer* f. L *deputare* regard as, allot (as DE-, *putare* think)]

deputize /ˈdepjʊˌtaɪz/ v.intr. (also **-ise**) (usu. foll. by *for*) act as a deputy or understudy.

deputy /ˈdepjʊtɪ/ n. (pl. **-ies**) **1** a person appointed or delegated to act for another or others (also *attrib.*: *deputy manager*). **2** *Polit.* a parliamentary representative in certain countries, e.g. France. □ **deputyship** n. [ME var. of DEPUTE n.]

derail /dɪˈreɪl, diː-/ v.tr. (usu. in *passive*) cause (a train etc.) to leave the rails. □ **derailment** n. [F *dérailler* (as DE-, RAIL¹)]

derange /dɪˈreɪndʒ/ v.tr. **1** throw into confusion; disorganize; cause to act irregularly. **2** (esp. as **deranged** adj.) make insane (*deranged by the tragic events*). **3** disturb; interrupt. □ **derangement** n. [F *déranger* (as DE-, *rang* RANK¹)]

Derby /ˈdɑːbɪ/ n. (pl. **-ies**) **1 a** an annual horse-race run on the flat at Epsom. **b** a similar race elsewhere (*Kentucky Derby*). **2** any important sporting contest. **3** (**derby**) US a bowler hat. □ **local Derby** a match between two teams from the same district. [the 12th Earl of *Derby* d. 1834, founder of the horse-race]

deregister /diːˈredʒɪstə(r)/ v.tr. remove from a register. □ **deregistration** /-ˈstreɪʃ(ə)n/ n.

derelict /ˈderəlɪkt, ˈderɪ-/ adj. & n. —adj. **1** abandoned, ownerless (esp. of a ship at sea or an empty decrepit property). **2** (esp. of property) ruined; dilapidated. **3** US negligent (of duty etc.). —n. **1** a person without a home, a job, or property. **2** abandoned property, esp. a ship. [L *derelictus* past part. of *derelinquere* (as DE-, *relinquere* leave)]

dereliction /ˌderɪˈlɪkʃ(ə)n/ n. **1** (usu. foll. by *of*) **a** neglect; failure to carry out one's obligations (*dereliction of duty*). **b** an instance of this. **2** the act or an instance of abandoning; the process of being abandoned. [L *derelictio* (as DERELICT)]

derestrict /ˌdiːrɪˈstrɪkt/ v.tr. **1** remove restrictions from. **2** remove speed restrictions from (a road, area, etc.). □ **derestriction** n.

deride /dɪˈraɪd/ v.tr. laugh scornfully at; mock. □ **derider** n. **deridingly** adv. [L *deridēre* (as DE-, *ridēre ris-* laugh)]

de rigueur /də rɪˈɡɜː(r)/ predic.adj. required by custom or etiquette. [F. = of strictness]

derision /dɪˈrɪʒ(ə)n/ n. ridicule; mockery (*bring into derision*). □ **derisible** /dɪˈrɪzɪb(ə)l/ adj. [ME f. OF f. LL *derisio -onis* (as DERIDE)]

derisive /dɪˈraɪsɪv/ adj. = DERISORY. □ **derisively** adv. **derisiveness** n.

derisory /dɪˈraɪsərɪ/ adj. **1** scoffing; ironical; scornful (*derisory cheers*). **2** so small or unimportant as to be ridiculous (*derisory offer; derisory costs*). [LL *derisorius* (as DERISION)]

derivation /ˌderɪˈveɪʃ(ə)n/ n. **1** the act or an instance of deriving or obtaining from a source; the process of being derived. **2 a** the formation of a word from another word or from a root. **b** the tracing of the origin of a word. **3** extraction, descent. □ **derivational** adj. [F *dérivation* or L *derivatio* (as DERIVE)]

derivative /dəˈrɪvətɪv, dɪ-/ adj. & n. —adj. derived from another source; not original. —n. **1** something derived from another source, esp.: **a** a word derived from another or from a root (e.g. *quickly* from *quick*). **b** *Chem.* a chemical compound that is derived from another. **2** *Math.* a quantity measuring the rate of change of another. □ **derivatively** adv. [F *dérivatif -ive* f. L *derivativus* (as DERIVE)]

derive /dɪˈraɪv/ v. **1** tr. (usu. foll. by *from*) get, obtain, or form (*derived satisfaction from work*). **2** intr. (foll. by *from*) arise from, be descended or obtained from (*happiness derives from many things*). **3** tr. **a** trace the descent of (a person). **b** show the origin of (a thing). **4** tr. (usu. foll. by *from*) show or state the origin or formation of (a word etc.) (*derived the word from Latin*). **5** tr. *Math.* obtain (a function) by differentiation. □ **derivable** adj. [ME f. OF *deriver* or f. L *derivare* (as DE-, *rivus* stream)]

dermatitis /ˌdɜːməˈtaɪtɪs/ n. inflammation of the skin. [Gk *derma -atos* skin + -ITIS]

dermatology /ˌdɜːməˈtɒlədʒɪ/ n. the study of the diagnosis and treatment of skin disorders. □ **dermatological** /-təˈlɒdʒɪk(ə)l/ adj. **dermatologist** n. [as DERMATITIS + -LOGY]

dermis /ˈdɜːmɪs/ n. (also **derm** /dɜːm/ or **derma** /ˈdɜːmə/) **1** (in general use) the skin. **2** *Anat.* the true skin, the thick layer of living tissue below the epidermis. □ **dermal** adj. **dermic** adj. [mod.L, after EPIDERMIS]

derogate /ˈderəˌɡeɪt/ v.intr. (foll. by *from*) *formal* take away a part from; detract from (a merit, a right, etc.). □ **derogative** /dɪˈrɒɡətɪv/ adj. [L *derogare* (as DE-, *rogare* ask)]

derogation /ˌderəˈɡeɪʃ(ə)n/ n. **1** (foll. by *of*) lessening or impairment of (a law, authority, position, dignity, etc.). **2** deterioration; debasement. [ME f. F *dérogation* or L *derogatio* (as DEROGATE)]

derogatory /dɪˈrɒɡətərɪ/ adj. (often foll. by *to*) involving disparagement or discredit; insulting, depreciatory (*made a derogatory remark*). □ **derogatorily** adv. [LL *derogatorius* (as DEROGATE)]

derrick /ˈderɪk/ n. **1** a kind of crane for moving or lifting heavy weights, having a movable pivoted arm. **2** the framework over an oil well or similar excavation, holding the drilling machinery. [obs. senses *hangman, gallows*, f. the name of a London hangman *c.*1600]

derring-do /ˌderɪŋˈduː/ n. *literary joc.* heroic courage or action. [ME, = *daring to do*, misinterpreted by Spenser and by Scott]

derris /ˈderɪs/ n. **1** any woody tropical climbing leguminous plant of the genus *Derris*, bearing leathery pods. **2** an insecticide made from the powdered root of some kinds of derris. [mod.L f. Gk, = leather covering (with ref. to its pod)]

derv /dɜːv/ n. *Brit.* diesel oil for road vehicles. [f. diesel-engined road-vehicle]

dervish /ˈdɜːvɪʃ/ n. a member of any of several Muslim fraternities vowed to poverty and austerity. □ **whirling** (or **dancing** or **howling**) **dervish** a dervish performing a wild dance, or howling, according to which sect he belongs to. [Turk. *derviş* f. Pers. *darvēsh* poor, a mendicant]

desalinate /diːˈsælɪneɪt/ v.tr. remove salt from (esp. sea water). □ **desalination** /-ˈneɪʃ(ə)n/ n.

desalt /diːˈsɔːlt/ v.tr. = DESALINATE.

desaparecido /ˌdezəpærəˈsiːdəʊ/ n. a person who has 'disappeared' in a totalitarian state, esp. in South America. [Sp., lit. 'disappeared']

descale /diːˈskeɪl/ v.tr. remove the scale from.

descant /ˈdeskænt/ n. & v. —n. **1** *Mus.* an independent treble melody usu. sung or played above a basic melody. **2** *poet.* a melody; a song. —v.intr. /dɪsˈkænt/ (foll. by *on, upon*) talk lengthily and prosily, esp. in praise of. □ **descant recorder** the most common size of recorder, with a range of two octaves. [ME f. OF *deschant* f. med.L *discantus* (as DIS-, *cantus* song, CHANT)]

descend /dɪˈsend/ v. **1** tr. & intr. go or come down (a hill, stairs, etc.). **2** intr. (of a thing) sink, fall (*rain descended heavily*). **3** intr. slope downwards, lie along a descending slope (*fields descended to the beach*). **4** intr. (usu. foll. by *on*) **a** make a sudden attack. **b** make an unexpected and usu. unwelcome visit. **5** intr. (usu. foll. by *from, to*) (of property, qualities, rights, etc.) be passed by inheritance (*the property descended to me*). **6** intr. **a** sink in rank, quality, etc. **b** (foll. by *to*) degrade oneself morally to (an unworthy act) (*descend to violence*). □ **be descended from** have as an ancestor. □ **descendent** adj. [ME f. OF *descendre* f. L *descendere* (as DE-, *scandere* climb)]

descendant /dɪˈsend(ə)nt/ n. (often foll. by *of*) a person or thing descended from another. [F, part. of *descendre* (as DESCEND)]

descent /dɪˈsent/ n. **1 a** the act of descending. **b** an instance of this. **c** a downward movement. **2 a** a way or path etc. by which one may descend. **b** a downward slope. **3** being descended; lineage, family origin. **4 a** a decline; a fall. **b** a lowering (of pitch, temperature, etc.). **5** a sudden violent attack. [ME f. OF *descente* f. *descendre* DESCEND]

describe /dɪˈskraɪb/ v.tr. **1 a** state the characteristics, appearance, etc. of, in spoken or written form (*described the landscape*). **b** (foll. by *as*) assert to be; call (*described him as a habitual liar*). **2 a** mark out or draw (esp. a geometrical figure). **b** move in (a specified way, esp. a curve) (*described a parabola through the air*). □ **describable** adj. **describer** n. [L *describere* (as DE-, *scribere script-* write)]

description /dɪˈskrɪpʃ(ə)n/ n. **1 a** the act or an instance of describing; the process of being described. **b** a spoken or written representation (of a person, object, or event). **2** a sort, kind, or class (*no food of any description*). [ME f. OF f. L *descriptio -onis* (as DESCRIBE)]

descriptive /dɪˈskrɪptɪv/ adj. **1** serving or seeking to describe (*a descriptive writer*). **2** describing or classifying without expressing feelings or judging (*a purely descriptive account*). □ **descriptively** adv. **descriptiveness** n. [LL *descriptivus* (as DESCRIBE)]

descry /dɪˈskraɪ/ v.tr. (**-ies, -ied**) *literary* catch sight of; discern. [ME (earlier senses 'proclaim,

DECRY') f. OF descrier: prob. confused with var. of obs. descrive f. OF descrivre DESCRIBE]

desecrate /ˈdesɪˌkreɪt/ v.tr. violate (a sacred place or thing) with violence, profanity, etc. □ **desecration** /-ˈkreɪʃ(ə)n/ n. **desecrator** n. [DE- + CONSECRATE]

deseed /diːˈsiːd/ v.tr. remove the seeds from (a plant, vegetable, etc.).

desegregate /diːˈsegrɪˌgeɪt/ v.tr. abolish racial segregation in (schools etc.) or of (people etc.). □ **desegregation** /-ˈgeɪʃ(ə)n/ n.

deselect /ˌdiːsɪˈlekt/ v.tr. Polit. decline to select or retain as a constituency candidate in an election. □ **deselection** n.

desensitize /diːˈsensɪˌtaɪz/ v.tr. (also **-ise**) reduce or destroy the sensitiveness of (photographic materials, an allergic person, etc.). □ **desensitization** /-ˈzeɪʃ(ə)n/ n. **desensitizer** n.

desert[1] /dɪˈzɜːt/ v. 1 tr. abandon, give up, leave. 2 tr. forsake or abandon (a cause or a person, people, etc., having claims on one). 3 tr. fail (his presence of mind deserted him). 4 intr. Mil. run away (esp. from military service). 5 tr. (as **deserted** adj.) empty, abandoned (a deserted house). □ **deserter** n. (in sense 4 of v.). **desertion** /-ˈzɜːʃ(ə)n/ n. [F déserter f. LL desertare f. L desertus (as DESERT[2])]

desert[2] /ˈdezət/ n. & adj. —n. a dry barren often sand-covered area of land, characteristically desolate, waterless, and without vegetation; an uninteresting or barren subject, period, etc. (a cultural desert). —adj. 1 uninhabited, desolate. 2 uncultivated, barren. [ME f. OF f. L desertus, eccl.L desertum (n.), past part. of deserere leave, forsake]

desert[3] /dɪˈzɜːt/ n. 1 (in pl.) **a** acts or qualities deserving reward or punishment. **b** such reward or punishment (has got his deserts). 2 the fact of being worthy of reward or punishment; deservingness. [ME f. OF f. deservir DESERVE]

desertification /dɪˌsɜːtɪfɪˈkeɪʃ(ə)n/ n. the process of making or becoming a desert.

deserve /dɪˈzɜːv/ v.tr. (often foll. by to + infin.) show conduct or qualities worthy of (reward, punishment, etc.). □ **deservedly** /-vɪdlɪ/ adv. **deservedness** /-vɪdnɪs/ n. **deserver** n. [ME f. OF deservir f. L deservire (as DE-, servire serve)]

deserving /dɪˈzɜːvɪŋ/ adj. meritorious. □ **deservingly** adv. **deservingness** n.

desexualize /diːˈseksjʊəˌlaɪz/ v.tr. (also **-ise**) deprive of sexual character.

déshabillé /ˌdezæˈbiːeɪ/ n. (also **déshabille** /ˌdeɪzæˈbiːl/, **dishabille** /ˌdɪsæˈbiːl/) a state of being only partly or carelessly clothed. [F, = undressed]

desiccate /ˈdesɪˌkeɪt/ v.tr. remove the moisture from, dry (esp. food for preservation) (desiccated coconut). □ **desiccation** /-ˈkeɪʃ(ə)n/ n. **desiccative** /-kətɪv/ adj. [L desiccare (as DE-, siccus dry)]

desideratum /dɪˌzɪdəˈrɑːtəm, dɪˌsɪd-/ n. (pl. **desiderata** /-tə/) something lacking but needed or desired. [L neut. past part. of desiderare DESIRE]

design /dɪˈzaɪn/ n. & v. —n. 1 **a** a preliminary plan or sketch for the making or production of a building, machine, garment, etc. **b** the art of producing these. 2 a scheme of lines or shapes forming a pattern or decoration. 3 a plan, purpose, or intention. 4 **a** the general arrangement or layout of a product. **b** an established version of a product (one of our most popular designs). —v. 1 tr. produce a design for (a

building, machine, picture, garment, etc.). 2 tr. intend, plan, or purpose (the remark was designed to offend; a course designed for beginners; designed an attack). 3 absol. be a designer. □ **by design** on purpose. **have designs on** plan to harm or appropriate. [F désigner appoint or obs. F desseing ult. f. L designare DESIGNATE]

designate v. & adj. —v.tr. /ˈdezɪgˌneɪt/ 1 (often foll. by as) appoint to an office or function. 2 specify or particularize (receives guests at designated times). 3 (often foll. by as) describe as; entitle, style. 4 serve as the name or distinctive mark of (English uses French words to designate ballet steps). —adj. /ˈdezɪgnət/ (placed after noun) appointed to an office but not yet installed (bishop designate). □ **designator** /-ˌneɪtə(r)/ n. [L designare, past part. designatus (as DE-, signare f. signum mark)]

designation /ˌdezɪgˈneɪʃ(ə)n/ n. 1 a name, description, or title. 2 the act or process of designating. [ME f. OF designation or L designatio (as DESIGNATE)]

designedly /dɪˈzaɪnɪdlɪ/ adv. by design; on purpose.

designer /dɪˈzaɪnə(r)/ n. 1 a person who makes artistic designs or plans for construction, e.g. for clothing, machines, theatre sets. 2 (attrib.) (of clothing etc.) bearing the name or label of a famous designer; prestigious. □ **designer drug** a synthetic analogue, not itself illegal, of an illegal drug.

designing /dɪˈzaɪnɪŋ/ adj. crafty, artful, or scheming. □ **designingly** adv.

desirable /dɪˈzaɪərəb(ə)l/ adj. 1 worth having or wishing for. 2 arousing sexual desire; very attractive. □ **desirability** /-ˈbɪlɪtɪ/ n. **desirableness** n. **desirably** adv. [ME f. OF (as DESIRE)]

desire /dɪˈzaɪə(r)/ n. & v. —n. 1 **a** an unsatisfied longing or craving. **b** an expression of this; a request (expressed a desire to rest). 2 lust. 3 something desired (achieved his heart's desire). —v.tr. 1 (often foll. by to + infin., or that + clause) long for; crave. 2 request (desires a cup of tea). 3 archaic pray, entreat, or command (desire him to wait). [ME f. OF desir f. desirer f. L desiderare]

desirous /dɪˈzaɪərəs/ predic.adj. 1 (usu. foll. by of) ambitious, desiring (desirous of stardom). 2 (usu. foll. by to + infin., or that + clause) wishful; hoping (desirous to do the right thing). [ME f. AF desirous, OF desireus f. Rmc (as DESIRE)]

desist /dɪˈzɪst/ v.intr. (often foll. by from) literary abstain; cease. [OF desister f. L desistere (as DE-, sistere stop, redupl. f. stare stand)]

desk n. 1 a piece of furniture or a portable box with a flat or sloped surface for writing on, and often drawers. 2 a counter in a hotel, bank, etc., which separates the customer from the assistant. 3 a section of a newspaper office etc. dealing with a specified topic (the sports desk; the features desk). 4 Mus. a music stand in an orchestra regarded as a unit of two players. [ME f. med.L desca f. L DISCUS disc]

desktop /ˈdesktɒp/ n. 1 the working surface of a desk. 2 (attrib.) (esp. of a microcomputer) suitable for use at an ordinary desk. □ **desktop publishing** the production of printed matter with a desktop computer and printer.

desolate adj. & v. —adj. /ˈdesələt/ 1 left alone; solitary. 2 (of a building or place) uninhabited, ruined, neglected, barren, dreary, empty (a *desolate moor*). **3** forlorn; wretched; miserable (*was left desolate and weeping*). —*v.tr.* /ˈdesəˌleɪt/ **1** depopulate or devastate; lay waste to. **2** (esp. as **desolated** *adj.*) make wretched or forlorn (*desolated by grief*). □ **desolately** /-lətlɪ/ *adv.* **desolateness** /-lətnɪs/ *n.* **desolator** /-ˌleɪtə(r)/ *n.* [ME f. L *desolatus* past part. of *desolare* (as DE-, *solare* f. *solus* alone)]

desolation /ˌdesəˈleɪʃ(ə)n/ *n.* **1 a** the act of desolating. **b** the process of being desolated. **2** loneliness, grief, or wretchedness. **3** a neglected, ruined, or empty state. [ME f. LL *desolatio* (as DESOLATE)]

despair /dɪˈspeə(r)/ *n. & v.* —*n.* the complete loss or absence of hope. —*v.intr.* **1** (often foll. by *of*) lose or be without hope (*despaired of ever seeing her again*). **2** (foll. by *of*) lose hope about (*his life is despaired of*). □ **be the despair of** be the cause of despair by badness or unapproachable excellence. □ **despairingly** *adv.* [ME f. OF *desespeir, desperer* f. L *desperare* (as DE-, *sperare* hope)]

despatch var. of DISPATCH.

desperado /ˌdespəˈrɑːdəʊ/ *n.* (*pl.* -**oes** or US -**os**) a desperate or reckless person, esp. a criminal. [after DESPERATE (obs. n.)]

desperate /ˈdespərət/ *adj.* **1** reckless from despair; violent and lawless. **2 a** extremely dangerous or serious (*a desperate situation*). **b** staking all on a small chance (*a desperate remedy*). **3** very bad (*desperate poverty*). **4** (usu. foll. by *for*) needing or desiring very much (*desperate for recognition*). □ **desperately** *adv.* **desperateness** *n.* **desperation** /-ˈreɪʃ(ə)n/ *n.* [ME f. L *desperatus* past part. of *desperare* (as DE-, *sperare* hope)]

despicable /ˈdespɪkəb(ə)l, dɪˈspɪk-/ *adj.* vile; contemptible, esp. morally. □ **despicably** *adv.* [LL *despicabilis* f. *despicari* (as DE-, *specere* look at)]

despise /dɪˈspaɪz/ *v.tr.* look down on as inferior, worthless, or contemptible. □ **despiser** *n.* [ME f. *despis-* pres. stem of OF *despire* f. L *despicere* (as DE-, *specere* look at)]

despite /dɪˈspaɪt/ *prep.* in spite of. [ME f. OF *despit* f. L *despectus* noun f. *despicere* (as DESPISE)]

despoil /dɪˈspɔɪl/ *v.tr. literary* (often foll. by *of*) plunder; rob; deprive (*despoiled the roof of its lead*). □ **despoiler** *n.* **despoilment** *n.* **despoliation** /dɪˌspəʊlɪˈeɪʃ(ə)n/ *n.* [ME f. OF *despoill(i)er* f. L *despoliare* (as DE-, *spoliare* SPOIL)]

despond /dɪˈspɒnd/ *v. & n.* —*v.intr.* lose heart or hope; be dejected. —*n. archaic* despondency. [L *despondēre* give up, abandon (as DE-, *spondēre* promise)]

despondent /dɪˈspɒnd(ə)nt/ *adj.* in low spirits, dejected. □ **despondence** *n.* **despondency** *n.* **despondently** *adv.*

despot /ˈdespɒt/ *n.* **1** an absolute ruler. **2** a tyrant or oppressor. □ **despotic** /-ˈspɒtɪk/ *adj.* **despotically** /-ˈspɒtɪkəlɪ/ *adv.* [F *despote* f. med.L *despota* f. Gk *despotēs* master, lord]

despotism /ˈdespəˌtɪz(ə)m/ *n.* **1 a** rule by a despot. **b** a country ruled by a despot. **2** absolute power or control; tyranny.

des res /dez ˈrez/ *n. sl.* a desirable residence. [abbr.]

dessert /dɪˈzɜːt/ *n.* **1** the sweet course of a meal, served at or near the end. **2** *Brit.* a course of fruit, nuts, etc., served after a meal. □ **dessert wine** usu. sweet wine drunk with or following dessert. [F, past part. of *desservir* clear the table (as DIS-, *servir* SERVE)]

dessertspoon /dɪˈzɜːtspuːn/ *n.* **1** a spoon used for dessert, smaller than a tablespoon and larger than a teaspoon. **2** the amount held by this. □ **dessertspoonful** *n.* (*pl.* -**fuls**).

destabilize /diːˈsteɪbɪˌlaɪz/ *v.tr.* (also -**ise**) **1** render unstable. **2** subvert (esp. a foreign government). □ **destabilization** /-ˈzeɪʃ(ə)n/ *n.*

destination /ˌdestɪˈneɪʃ(ə)n/ *n.* a place to which a person or thing is going. [OF *destination* or L *destinatio* (as DESTINE)]

destine /ˈdestɪn/ *v.tr.* (often foll. by *to, for,* or *to* + infin.) set apart; appoint; preordain; intend. □ **be destined to** be fated or preordained to. [ME f. F *destiner* f. L *destinare* (as DE-, *stanare* (unrecorded) settle f. *stare* stand)]

destiny /ˈdestɪnɪ/ *n.* (*pl.* -**ies**) **1 a** the predetermined course of events; fate. **b** this regarded as a power. **2** what is destined to happen to a particular person etc. (*it was their destiny to be rejected*). [ME f. OF *destinée* f. Rmc, past part. of *destinare*: see DESTINE]

destitute /ˈdestɪˌtjuːt/ *adj.* **1** without food, shelter, etc.; completely impoverished. **2** (usu. foll. by *of*) lacking (*destitute of friends*). □ **destitution** /-ˈtjuːʃ(ə)n/ *n.* [ME f. L *destitutus* past part. of *destituere* forsake (as DE-, *statuere* place)]

destroy /dɪˈstrɔɪ/ *v.tr.* **1** pull or break down; demolish. **2** end the existence of (*the accident destroyed her confidence*). **3** kill (esp. a sick or savage animal). **4** make useless; spoil utterly. **5** ruin financially, professionally, or in reputation. [ME f. OF *destruire* ult. f. L *destruere* (as DE-, *struere struct-* build)]

destroyer /dɪˈstrɔɪə(r)/ *n.* **1** a person or thing that destroys. **2** *Naut.* a fast warship with guns and torpedoes used to protect other ships.

destruct /dɪˈstrʌkt/ *v. & n.* US esp. *Astronaut.* —*v.* **1** *tr.* destroy (one's own rocket etc.) deliberately, esp. for safety reasons. **2** *intr.* be destroyed in this way. —*n.* an act of destructing. [L *destruere* (as DESTROY) or as back-form. f. DESTRUCTION]

destructible /dɪˈstrʌktɪb(ə)l/ *adj.* able to be destroyed. □ **destructibility** /-ˈbɪlɪtɪ/ *n.* [F *destructible* or LL *destructibilis* (as DESTROY)]

destruction /dɪˈstrʌkʃ(ə)n/ *n.* **1** the act or an instance of destroying; the process of being destroyed. **2** a cause of ruin; something that destroys (*greed was their destruction*). [ME f. OF f. L *destructio -onis* (as DESTROY)]

destructive /dɪˈstrʌktɪv/ *adj.* **1** (often foll. by *of*) destroying or tending to destroy (*destructive of her peace of mind; a destructive child*). **2** negative in attitude or criticism; refuting without suggesting, helping, amending, etc. □ **destructively** *adv.* **destructiveness** *n.* [ME f. OF *destructif -ive* f. LL *destructivus* (as DESTROY)]

desuetude /dɪˈsjuːɪˌtjuːd, ˈdeswɪ-/ *n.* a state of disuse (*the custom fell into desuetude*). [F *désuétude* or L *desuetudo* (as DE-, *suescere suet-* be accustomed)]

desultory /ˈdezəltərɪ/ *adj.* **1** going constantly from one subject to another, esp. in a half-hearted way. **2** disconnected; unmethodical; superficial. □ **desultorily** *adv.* **desultoriness** *n.* [L *desultorius* superficial f. *desultor* vaulter f. *desult-* (as DE-, *salt-* past part. stem of *salire* leap)]

detach /dɪˈtætʃ/ *v.tr.* **1** (often foll. by *from*) unfasten or disengage and remove (*detached the buttons; detached himself from the group*). **2** *Mil.* send (a ship, regiment, officer, messenger, etc.)

on a separate mission. **3** (as **detached** adj.) **a** impartial; unemotional (*a detached viewpoint*). **b** (esp. of a house) not joined to another or others; separate. □ **detachable** adj. **detachedly** /dɪˈtætʃɪdlɪ/ adv. [F *détacher* (as DE-, ATTACH)]

detachment /dɪˈtætʃmənt/ n. **1 a** a state of aloofness from or indifference to other people, one's surroundings, public opinion, etc. **b** disinterested independence of judgement. **2 a** the act or process of detaching or being detached. **b** an instance of this. **3** Mil. a separate group or unit of an army etc. used for a specific purpose. [F *détachement* (as DETACH)]

detail /ˈdiːteɪl/ n. & v. —n. **1** a small or subordinate particular; an item. **2** small items or particulars (esp. in an artistic work) regarded collectively (*has an eye for detail*). **3** (often in pl.) a number of particulars; an aggregate of small items (*filled in the details on the form*). **4 a** a minor decoration on a building, in a picture, etc. **b** a small part of a picture etc. shown alone. **5** Mil. **a** the distribution of orders for the day. **b** a small detachment of soldiers etc. for special duty. —v.tr. **1** give particulars of (*detailed the plans*). **2** relate circumstantially (*detailed the anecdote*). **3** Mil. assign for special duty. **4** (as **detailed** adj.) **a** (of a picture, story, etc.) having many details. **b** itemized (*a detailed list*). □ **go into detail** give all the items or particulars. **in detail** item by item, minutely. [F *détail, détailler* (as DE-, *tailler* cut, formed as TAIL²)]

detain /dɪˈteɪn/ v.tr. **1** keep in confinement or under restraint. **2** keep waiting; delay. □ **detainment** n. [ME f. OF *detenir* ult. f. L *detinēre* detent- (as DE-, *tenēre* hold)]

detainee /ˌdiːteɪˈniː/ n. a person detained in custody, esp. for political reasons.

detect /dɪˈtekt/ v.tr. **1 a** (often foll. by *in*) reveal the guilt of; discover (*detected him in his crime*). **b** discover (a crime). **2** discover or perceive the existence or presence of (*detected a smell of burning*). □ **detectable** adj. **detectably** adv. **detector** n. [L *detegere* detect- (as DE-, *tegere* cover)]

detection /dɪˈtekʃ(ə)n/ n. **1 a** the act or an instance of detecting; the process of being detected. **b** an instance of this. **2** the work of a detective. [LL *detectio* (as DETECT)]

detective /dɪˈtektɪv/ n. & adj. —n. (often attrib.) a person, esp. a member of a police force, employed to investigate crime. —adj. serving to detect. □ **private detective** a usu. freelance detective carrying out investigations for a private employer. [DETECT]

détente /deɪˈtɑ̃t/ n. an easing of strained relations esp. between States. [F, = relaxation]

detention /dɪˈtenʃ(ə)n/ n. **1** detaining or being detained. **2 a** being kept in school after hours as a punishment. **b** an instance of this. **3** custody; confinement. □ **detention centre** Brit. an institution for the brief detention of young offenders. [F *détention* or LL *detentio* (as DETAIN)]

deter /dɪˈtɜː(r)/ v.tr. (**deterred, deterring**) **1** (often foll. by *from*) discourage or prevent (a person) through fear or dislike of the consequences. **2** discourage, check, or prevent (a thing, process, etc.). □ **determent** n. [L *deterrēre* (as DE-, *terrēre* frighten)]

detergent /dɪˈtɜːdʒ(ə)nt/ n. & adj. —n. a cleansing agent, esp. a synthetic substance (usu. other than soap) used with water as a means of

removing dirt etc. —adj. cleansing, esp. in the manner of a detergent. [L *detergēre* (as DE-, *tergēre* ters- wipe)]

deteriorate /dɪˈtɪərɪəreɪt/ v.tr. & intr. make or become bad or worse. □ **deterioration** /-ˈreɪʃ(ə)n/ n. **deteriorative** /-rətɪv/ adj. [LL *deteriorare deteriorat-* f. L *deterior* worse]

determinant /dɪˈtɜːmɪnənt/ adj. & n. —adj. serving to determine or define. —n. **1** a determining factor, element, word, etc. **2** Math. a quantity obtained by the addition of products of the elements of a square matrix according to a given rule. [L *determinare* (as DETERMINE)]

determinate /dɪˈtɜːmɪnət/ adj. **1** limited in time, space, or character. **2** of definite scope or nature. □ **determinacy** n. **determinately** adv. **determinateness** n. [ME f. L *determinatus* past part. (as DETERMINE)]

determination /dɪˌtɜːmɪˈneɪʃ(ə)n/ n. **1** firmness of purpose; resoluteness. **2** the process of deciding, determining, or calculating. [ME f. OF f. L *determinatio -onis* (as DETERMINE)]

determine /dɪˈtɜːmɪn/ v. **1** tr. find out or establish precisely (*have to determine the extent of the problem*). **2** tr. decide or settle (*determined who should go*). **3** tr. be a decisive factor in regard to (*demand determines supply*). **4** intr. & tr. make or cause (a person) to make a decision (*what determined you to do it?*). □ **be determined** be resolved (*was determined not to give up*). □ **determinable** adj. **determiner** n. [ME f. OF *determiner* f. L *determinare* (as DE-, *terminus* end)]

determined /dɪˈtɜːmɪnd/ adj. showing determination; resolute, unflinching. □ **determinedly** adv. **determinedness** n.

determinism /dɪˈtɜːmɪˌnɪz(ə)m/ n. Philos. the doctrine that all events, including human action, are determined by causes regarded as external to the will. □ **determinist** n. **deterministic** /-ˈnɪstɪk/ adj. **deterministically** /-ˈnɪstɪkəlɪ/ adv.

deterrent /dɪˈterənt/ adj. & n. —adj. that deters. —n. a deterrent thing or factor, esp. a nuclear weapon regarded as deterring an enemy from attack. □ **deterrence** n.

detest /dɪˈtest/ v.tr. hate, loathe. □ **detester** n. [L *detestari* (as DE-, *testari* call to witness f. *testis* witness)]

detestable /dɪˈtestəb(ə)l/ adj. intensely disliked; hateful. □ **detestably** adv.

detestation /ˌdiːteˈsteɪʃ(ə)n/ n. **1** intense dislike, hatred. **2** a detested person or thing. [ME f. OF f. L *detestatio -onis* (as DETEST)]

dethrone /diːˈθrəʊn/ v.tr. **1** remove from the throne, depose. **2** remove from a position of authority or influence. □ **dethronement** n.

detonate /ˈdetəneɪt/ v.intr. & tr. explode with a loud noise. □ **detonation** n. **detonative** adj. [L *detonare detonat-* (as DE-, *tonare* thunder)]

detonator /ˈdetəneɪtə(r)/ n. a device for detonating an explosive.

detour /ˈdiːtʊə(r)/ n. & v. —n. a divergence from a direct or intended route; a roundabout course. —v.intr. & tr. make or cause to make a detour. [F *détour* change of direction f. *détourner* turn away (as DE-, TURN)]

detoxify /diːˈtɒksɪfaɪ/ v.tr. remove the poison from. □ **detoxification** /-fɪˈkeɪʃ(ə)n/ n. [DE- + L *toxicum* poison]

detract /dɪˈtrækt/ v.tr. (usu. foll. by *from*) take away (a part of something); reduce, diminish (*self-interest detracted nothing from their achievement*). □ **detraction** *n*. **detractive** *adj*. **detractor** *n*. [L *detrahere detract-* (as DE-, *trahere* draw)]

detrain /diːˈtreɪn/ *v.intr.* & *tr.* alight or cause to alight from a train. □ **detrainment** *n*.

detriment /ˈdetrɪmənt/ *n*. **1** harm, damage. **2** something causing this. [ME f. OF *détriment* or L *detrimentum* (as DE-, *terere trit-* rub, wear)]

detrimental /ˌdetrɪˈment(ə)l/ *adj*. harmful; causing loss. □ **detrimentally** *adv*.

detritus /dɪˈtraɪtəs/ *n*. matter produced by erosion, such as gravel, sand, silt, rock-debris, etc.; debris. □ **detrital** /dɪˈtraɪt(ə)l/ *adj*. [after F *détritus* f. L *detritus* (n.) = wearing down (as DETRIMENT)]

de trop /də ˈtrəʊ/ *predic.adj.* not wanted, unwelcome, in the way. [F, = excessive]

deuce¹ /djuːs/ *n*. **1** the two on dice or playing cards. **2** (in lawn tennis) the score of 40 all, at which two consecutive points are needed to win. [OF *deus* f. L *duo* (accus. *duos*) two]

deuce² /djuːs/ *n*. misfortune, the Devil, used esp. *colloq.* as an exclamation of surprise or annoyance (*who the deuce are you?*). [LG *duus*, formed as DEUCE¹, two aces at dice being the worst throw]

deuced /ˈdjuːsɪd, djuːst/ *adj*. & *adv. archaic* damned, confounded (*a deuced liar*). □ **deucedly** /ˈdjuːsɪdlɪ/ *adv*.

deus ex machina /ˌdeɪʊs eks ˈmækɪnə, ˌdiːəs/ *n*. an unexpected power or event saving a seemingly hopeless situation, esp. in a play or novel. [mod.L transl. of Gk *theos ek mēkhanēs*, = god from the machinery (by which in the Greek theatre the gods were suspended above the stage)]

deuterium /djuːˈtɪərɪəm/ *n. Chem.* a stable isotope of hydrogen with a mass about double that of the usual isotope. [mod.L, formed as DEUTERO- + -IUM]

deutero- /ˈdjuːtərəʊ/ *comb. form* second. [Gk *deuteros* second]

deuteron /ˈdjuːtəˌrɒn/ *n. Physics* the nucleus of a deuterium atom, consisting of a proton and a neutron. [DEUTERIUM + -ON]

Deutschmark /ˈdɔɪtʃmɑːk/ *n*. (also **Deutsche Mark** /ˈdɔɪtʃə mɑːk/ the chief monetary unit of Germany. [G, = German mark (see MARK²)]

devalue /diːˈvæljuː/ *v.tr.* (**devalues, devalued, devaluing**) **1** reduce the value of. **2** *Econ.* reduce the value of (a currency) in relation to other currencies or to gold. □ **devaluation** /-ˈeɪʃ(ə)n/ *n*.

devastate /ˈdevəˌsteɪt/ *v.tr.* **1** lay waste; cause great destruction to. **2** (often in *passive*) overwhelm with shock or grief; upset deeply. □ **devastation** /-ˈsteɪʃ(ə)n/ *n*. **devastator** *n*. [L *devastare devastat-* (as DE-, *vastare* lay waste)]

devastating /ˈdevəˌsteɪtɪŋ/ *adj*. crushingly effective; overwhelming. □ **devastatingly** *adv*.

develop /dɪˈveləp/ *v*. (**developed, developing**) **1** *tr.* & *intr.* **a** make or become bigger or fuller or more elaborate or systematic. **b** bring or come to an active or visible state or to maturity (*developed a plan of action*). **2** *tr.* begin to exhibit or suffer from (*developed a rattle*). **3** *tr.* **a** construct new buildings on (land). **b** convert (land) to a new purpose so as to use its resources more fully. **4** *tr.* treat (photographic film etc.) to make the latent image visible. □ **developing country**

a poor or primitive country that is developing better economic and social conditions. □ **developable** *adj*. **developer** *n*. [F *développer* f. Rmc (as DIS-, orig. of second element unknown)]

development /dɪˈveləpmənt/ *n*. **1** the act or an instance of developing; the process of being developed. **2 a** a stage of growth or advancement. **b** a thing that has developed, esp. an event or circumstance (*the latest developments*). **3** a full-grown state. **4** the process of developing a photograph. **5** a developed area of land.

developmental /dɪˌveləpˈment(ə)l/ *adj*. **1** incidental to growth (*developmental diseases*). **2** evolutionary. □ **developmentally** *adv*.

deviant /ˈdiːvɪənt/ *adj*. & *n*. —*adj*. that deviates from the normal, esp. with reference to sexual practices. —*n*. a deviant person or thing. □ **deviance** *n*. **deviancy** *n*. [ME (as DEVIATE)]

deviate /ˈdiːvɪˌeɪt/ —*v.intr.* (often foll. by *from*) turn aside or diverge (from a course of action, rule, truth, etc.); digress. □ **deviator** *n*. **deviatory** /-ˈvɪətərɪ/ *adj*. [LL *deviare deviat-* (as DE-, *via* way)]

deviation /ˌdiːvɪˈeɪʃ(ə)n/ *n*. **1 a** deviating, digressing. **b** an instance of this. **2** *Statistics* the amount by which a single measurement differs from the mean. □ **standard deviation** *Statistics* a quantity calculated to indicate the extent of deviation for a group as a whole. □ **deviational** *adj*. **deviationism** *n*. **deviationist** *n*. [F *déviation* f. med.L *deviatio -onis* (as DEVIATE)]

device /dɪˈvaɪs/ *n*. **1** a thing made or adapted for a particular purpose, esp. a mechanical contrivance. **2** a plan, scheme, or trick. **3** an emblematic or heraldic design. □ **leave a person to his** or **her own devices** leave a person to do as he or she wishes. [ME f. OF *devis* ult. f. L (as DIVIDE)]

devil /ˈdev(ə)l/ *n*. & *v*. —*n*. **1** (usu. **the Devil**) (in Christian and Jewish belief) the supreme spirit of evil; Satan. **2 a** an evil spirit; a demon; a superhuman malignant being. **b** a personified evil force or attribute. **3 a** a wicked or cruel person. **b** a mischievously energetic, clever, or self-willed person. **4** *colloq.* a person, a fellow (*lucky devil*). **5** fighting spirit, mischievousness (*the devil is in him tonight*). **6** *colloq.* something difficult or awkward (*this door is a devil to open*). **7** (**the devil** or **the Devil**) *colloq.* used as an exclamation of surprise or annoyance (*who the devil are you?*). **8** a literary hack exploited by an employer. **9** *Brit.* a junior legal counsel. —*v*. (**devilled, devilling**; *US* **deviled, deviling**) **1** *tr.* cook (food) with hot seasoning. **2** *intr.* act as a devil for an author or barrister. **3** *tr. US* harass, worry. □ **devil-may-care** cheerful and reckless. **a devil of** *colloq.* a considerable, difficult, or remarkable. **devil's advocate** a person who tests a proposition by arguing against it. **devil's own** *colloq.* very difficult or unusual (*the devil's own job*). **the devil to pay** trouble to be expected. **go to the devil 1** be damned. **2** (in *imper.*) depart at once. **like the devil** with great energy. **play the devil with** cause severe damage to. **speak** (or **talk**) **of the devil** said when a person appears just after being mentioned. **the very devil** (*predic.*) *colloq.* a great difficulty or nuisance. [OE *dēofol* f. LL *diabolus* f. Gk *diabolos* accuser, slanderer f. *dia* across + *ballō* to throw)]

devilish /ˈdevəlɪʃ/ adj. & adv. —adj. **1** of or like a devil; wicked. **2** mischievous. —adv. colloq. very, extremely. □ **devilishly** adv. **devilishness** n.

devilment /ˈdevəlmənt/ n. mischief, wild spirits.

devilry /ˈdevɪlrɪ/ n. (also **deviltry**) (pl. **-ies**) **1** wickedness; reckless mischief. **2** black magic. [OF diablerie: -try wrongly after harlotry etc.]

devious /ˈdiːvɪəs/ adj. **1** (of a person etc.) not straightforward, underhand. **2** winding, circuitous. **3** erring, straying. □ **deviously** adv. **deviousness** n. [L devius f. DE- + via way]

devise /dɪˈvaɪz/ —v.tr. **1** plan or invent by careful thought. **2** Law leave (real estate) by the terms of a will. □ **devisable** adj. **devisee** /-ˈziː/ n. (in sense 2). **deviser** n. **devisor** n. (in sense 2 of v.). [ME f. OF deviser ult. f. L dividere divis- DIVIDE: (n.) f. OF devise f. med.L divisa fem. past part. of dividere]

devitalize /diːˈvaɪtəlaɪz/ v.tr. (also **-ise**) take away strength and vigour from. □ **devitalization** /-ˈzeɪʃ(ə)n/ n.

devoid /dɪˈvɔɪd/ predic.adj. (foll. by of) quite lacking or free from (a book devoid of all interest). [ME, past part. of obs. devoid f. OF devoidier (as DE-, VOID)]

devolution /ˌdiːvəˈluːʃ(ə)n, -ˈljuːʃ(ə)n/ n. **1** the delegation of power, esp. by central government to local or regional administration. **2 a** descent or passing on through a series of stages. **b** descent by natural or due succession from one to another of property or qualities. □ **devolutionary** adj. **devolutionist** n. [LL devolutio (as DEVOLVE)]

devolve /dɪˈvɒlv/ v. **1** (foll. by on, upon, etc.) **a** tr. pass (work or duties) to (a deputy etc.). **b** intr. (of work or duties) pass to (a deputy etc.). **2** intr. (foll. by on, to, upon) Law (of property etc.) descend or fall by succession to. □ **devolvement** n. [ME f. L devolvere devolut- (as DE-, volvere roll)]

Devonian /dɪˈvəʊnɪən/ adj. & n. —adj. **1** of or relating to Devon in SW England. **2** Geol. of or relating to the fourth period of the Palaeozoic era. —n. **1** this period or system. **2** a native of Devon. [med.L Devonia Devonshire]

devote /dɪˈvəʊt/ v.tr. & refl. (foll. by to) apply or give over (resources etc. or oneself) to (a particular activity or purpose or person) (devoted their time to reading; devoted himself to his guests). □ **devotement** n. [L devovēre devot- (as DE-, vovēre vow)]

devoted /dɪˈvəʊtɪd/ adj. very loving or loyal. □ **devotedly** adv. **devotedness** n.

devotee /ˌdevəˈtiː/ n. **1** (usu. foll. by of) a zealous enthusiast or supporter. **2** a zealously pious or fanatical person.

devotion /dɪˈvəʊʃ(ə)n/ n. **1** (usu. foll. by to) enthusiastic attachment or loyalty (to a person or cause); great love. **2 a** religious worship. **b** (in pl.) prayers. □ **devotional** adj. [ME f. OF devotion or L devotio (as DEVOTE)]

devour /dɪˈvaʊə(r)/ v.tr. **1** eat hungrily or greedily. **2** (of fire etc.) engulf, destroy. **3** take in greedily with the eyes or ears (devoured book after book). □ **devourer** n. **devouringly** adv. [ME f. OF devorer f. L devorare (as DE-, vorare swallow)]

devout /dɪˈvaʊt/ adj. **1** earnestly religious. **2** earnestly sincere (devout hope). □ **devoutly** adv. **devoutness** n. [ME f. OF devot f. L devotus past part. (as DEVOTE)]

dew n. & v. —n. **1** atmospheric vapour condensing in small drops on cool surfaces at night.

2 beaded or glistening moisture resembling this. **3** freshness, refreshing quality. —v.tr. wet with or as with dew. □ **dew-fall 1** the time when dew begins to form. **2** evening. **dew-point** the temperature at which dew forms. **dew-pond** a shallow usu. artificial pond once supposed to have been fed by atmospheric condensation. [OE dēaw f. Gmc]

dewberry /ˈdjuːbərɪ/ n. (pl. **-ies**) **1** a bluish fruit like the blackberry. **2** the shrub, Rubus caesius, bearing this.

dewdrop /ˈdjuːdrɒp/ n. a drop of dew.

dewlap /ˈdjuːlæp/ n. **1** a loose fold of skin hanging from the throat of cattle, dogs, etc. **2** similar loose skin round the throat of an elderly person. [ME f. DEW + LAP¹, perh. after ON (unrecorded) dögglepþr]

dewy /ˈdjuːɪ/ adj. (**dewier**, **dewiest**) **1 a** wet with dew. **b** moist as if with dew. **2** of or like dew. □ **dewy-eyed** innocently trusting; naïvely sentimental. □ **dewily** adv. **dewiness** n. [OE dēawig (as DEW, -Y¹)]

dexter /ˈdekstə(r)/ adj. esp. Heraldry on or of the right-hand side (the observer's left) of a shield etc. [L, = on the right]

dexterity /dekˈsterɪtɪ/ n. **1** skill in handling. **2** manual or mental adroitness. **3** right-handedness, using the right hand. [F dextérité f. L dexteritas (as DEXTER)]

dexterous /ˈdekstrəs/ adj. (also **dextrous**) having or showing dexterity. □ **dexterously** adv. **dexterousness** n. [L DEXTER + -OUS]

dextro- /ˈdekstrəʊ/ comb. form on or to the right (dextrose). [L dexter, dextra on or to the right]

dextrose /ˈdekstrəʊs/ n. Chem. a form of glucose. [formed as DEXTRO- + -OSE²]

DFC abbr. Brit. Distinguished Flying Cross.

DFM abbr. Brit. Distinguished Flying Medal.

dhal /dɑːl/ n. (also **dal**) **1** a kind of split pulse, a common foodstuff in India. **2** a dish made with this. [Hindi]

dharma /ˈdɑːmə/ n. Ind. **1** social custom; the right behaviour. **2** the Buddhist truth. **3** the Hindu social or moral law. [Skr., = decree, custom]

dhoti /ˈdəʊtɪ/ n. (pl. **dhotis**) the loincloth worn by male Hindus. [Hindi dhotī]

dhow /daʊ/ n. a lateen-rigged ship used on the Arabian sea. [19th c.: orig. unkn.]

di-¹ /daɪ/ comb. form **1** twice, two-, double. **2** Chem. containing two atoms, molecules, or groups of a specified kind (dichromate; dioxide). [Gk f. dis twice]

di-² /daɪ, dɪ/ prefix form of DIS- occurring before l, m, n, r, s (foll. by a consonant), v, usu. g, and sometimes j. [L var. of dis-]

di-³ /daɪ/ prefix form of DIA- before a vowel.

dia. abbr. diameter.

dia- /ˈdaɪə/ prefix (also **di-** before a vowel) **1** through (diaphanous). **2** apart (diacritical). **3** across (diameter). [Gk f. dia through]

diabetes /ˌdaɪəˈbiːtiːz/ n. **1** any disorder of the metabolism with excessive thirst and the production of large amounts of urine. **2** (in full **diabetes mellitus**) the commonest form of diabetes in which sugar and starch are not properly absorbed from the blood. [orig. = siphon: L f. Gk f. diabainō go through]

diabetic /ˌdaɪəˈbetɪk/ adj. & n. —adj. **1** of or relating to or having diabetes. **2** for use by diabetics. —n. a person suffering from diabetes.

diabolic /ˌdaɪəˈbɒlɪk/ adj. (also **diabolical** /-ˈbɒlɪk(ə)l/) **1** of the Devil. **2** devilish; inhumanly cruel or wicked. **3** fiendishly clever or cunning or annoying. □ **diabolically** adv. [ME f. OF diabolique or LL diabolicus f. L diabolus (as DEVIL)]

diabolism /daɪˈæbəˌlɪz(ə)m/ n. **1 a** belief in or worship of the Devil. **b** sorcery. **2** devilish conduct or character. □ **diabolist** n. [Gk diabolos DEVIL]

diachronic /ˌdaɪəˈkrɒnɪk/ adj. Linguistics etc. concerned with the historical development of a subject (esp. a language). □ **diachronically** adv. **diachronism** /daɪˈækrəˌnɪz(ə)m/ n. **diachronistic** /daɪˌækrəˈnɪstɪk/ adj. **diachronous** /daɪˈækrənəs/ adj. **diachrony** /daɪˈækrənɪ/ n. [F diachronique (as DIA-, CHRONIC)]

diaconal /daɪˈækən(ə)l/ adj. of a deacon. [eccl.L diaconalis f. diaconus DEACON]

diaconate /daɪˈækəˌneɪt, -nət/ n. **1 a** the office of deacon. **b** a person's time as deacon. **2** a body of deacons. [eccl.L diaconatus (as DIACONAL)]

diacritic /ˌdaɪəˈkrɪtɪk/ n. & adj. —n. a sign (e.g. an accent, diaeresis, cedilla) used to indicate different sounds or values of a letter. —adj. = DIACRITICAL. [Gk diakritikos (as DIA-, CRITIC)]

diacritical /ˌdaɪəˈkrɪtɪk(ə)l/ adj. & n. —adj. distinguishing, distinctive. —n. (in full **diacritical mark** or **sign**) = DIACRITIC.

diadem /ˈdaɪəˌdem/ n. & v. —n. **1** a crown or headband worn as a sign of sovereignty. **2** a wreath of leaves or flowers worn round the head. **3** sovereignty. **4** a crowning distinction or glory. —v.tr. (esp. as **diademed** adj.) adorn with or as with a diadem. [ME f. OF diademe f. L diadema f. Gk diadēma (as DIA-, deō bind)]

diaeresis /daɪˈɪərəsɪs/ n. (US **dieresis**) (pl. -**ses** /-ˌsiːz/) a mark (as in naïve) over a vowel to indicate that it is sounded separately. [L f. Gk, = separation]

diagnose /ˈdaɪəgˌnəʊz/ v.tr. make a diagnosis of (a disease, a mechanical fault, etc.) from its symptoms. □ **diagnosable** adj.

diagnosis /ˌdaɪəgˈnəʊsɪs/ n. (pl. **diagnoses** /-ˌsiːz/) **1 a** the identification of a disease by means of a patient's symptoms. **b** an instance or formal statement of this. **2 a** the identification of the cause of a mechanical fault etc. **b** an instance of this. [mod.L f. Gk (as DIA-, gignōskō recognize)]

diagnostic /ˌdaɪəgˈnɒstɪk/ adj. & n. —adj. of or assisting diagnosis. —n. a symptom. □ **diagnostically** adv. **diagnostician** /-nɒˈstɪʃ(ə)n/ n. [Gk diagnōstikos (as DIAGNOSIS)]

diagnostics /ˌdaɪəgˈnɒstɪks/ n. **1** (treated as pl.) Computing programs and other mechanisms used to detect and identify faults in hardware or software. **2** (treated as sing.) the science or study of diagnosing disease.

diagonal /daɪˈægən(ə)l/ adj. & n. —adj. **1** crossing a straight-sided figure from corner to corner. **2** slanting, oblique. —n. a straight line joining two non-adjacent corners. □ **diagonally** adv. [L diagonalis f. Gk diagōnios (as DIA-, gōnia angle)]

diagram /ˈdaɪəˌgræm/ n. & v. —n. **1** a drawing showing the general scheme or outline of an object and its parts. **2** a graphic representation of the course or results of an action or process. —v.tr. (**diagrammed**, **diagramming**; US **diagramed**, **diagraming**) represent by means of a diagram. □ **diagrammatic** /-grəˈmætɪk/ adj.

diagrammatically /-grəˈmætɪkəlɪ/ adv. [L diagramma f. Gk (as DIA-, -GRAM)]

dial /ˈdaɪ(ə)l/ n. & v. —n. **1** the face of a clock or watch, marked to show the hours etc. **2** a similar flat plate marked with a scale for measuring weight, volume, pressure, consumption, etc., indicated by a pointer. **3** a movable disc on a telephone, with finger-holes and numbers for making a connection. **4 a** a plate or disc etc. on a radio or television set for selecting wavelength or channel. **b** a similar selecting device on other equipment, e.g. a washing machine. **5** Brit. sl. a person's face. —v. (**dialled, dialling**; US **dialed, dialing**) **1** tr. (also absol.) select (a telephone number) by means of a dial or set of buttons (dialled 999). **2** tr. measure, indicate, or regulate by means of a dial. □ **dialling code** a sequence of numbers dialled to connect a telephone with the exchange of the telephone being called. **dialling tone** (US **dial tone**) a sound indicating that a caller may start to dial. □ **dialler** n. [ME, = sundial, f. med.L diale clock-dial ult. f. L dies day]

dialect /ˈdaɪəˌlekt/ n. **1** a form of speech peculiar to a particular region. **2** a subordinate variety of a language with non-standard vocabulary, pronunciation, or grammar. □ **dialectal** /-ˈlekt(ə)l/ adj. **dialectology** /-ˈtɒlədʒɪ/ n. **dialectologist** /-ˈtɒlədʒɪst/ n. [F dialecte or L dialectus f. Gk dialektos discourse f. dialegomai converse]

dialectic /ˌdaɪəˈlektɪk/ n. Philos. **1 a** the art of investigating the truth of opinions; the testing of truth by discussion. **b** logical disputation. **2 a** inquiry into metaphysical contradictions and their solutions. **b** the existence or action of opposing social forces etc. [ME f. OF dialectique or L dialectica f. Gk dialektikē (tekhnē) (art) of debate (as DIALECT)]

dialectical /ˌdaɪəˈlektɪk(ə)l/ adj. of dialectic or dialectics. □ **dialectically** adv.

dialectician /ˌdaɪəlekˈtɪʃ(ə)n/ n. a person skilled in dialectic. [F dialecticien f. L dialecticus]

dialectics /ˌdaɪəˈlektɪks/ n. (treated as sing. or pl.) = DIALECTIC n. 1.

dialogue /ˈdaɪəˌlɒg/ n. (US **dialog**) **1 a** conversation. **b** conversation in written form; this as a form of composition. **2 a** a discussion, esp. one between representatives of two political groups. **b** a conversation, a talk (long dialogues between the two main characters). [ME f. OF dialoge f. L dialogus f. Gk dialogos f. dialegomai converse]

dialyse /ˈdaɪəˌlaɪz/ v.tr. (US **dialyze**) separate by means of dialysis.

dialysis /daɪˈælɪsɪs/ n. (pl. **dialyses** /-ˌsiːz/) **1** Chem. the separation of particles in a liquid by differences in their ability to pass through a membrane into another liquid. **2** Med. the clinical purification of blood by this technique. □ **dialytic** /ˌdaɪəˈlɪtɪk/ adj. [L f. Gk dialusis (as DIA-, luō set free)]

diamanté /dɪəˈmɒ̃teɪ/ adj. & n. —adj. decorated with powdered crystal or another sparkling substance. —n. fabric or costume jewellery so decorated. [F, past part. of diamanter set with diamonds f. diamant DIAMOND]

diamantine /ˌdaɪəˈmæntaɪn/ adj. of or like diamonds. [F diamantin f. diamant DIAMOND]

diameter /daɪˈæmɪtə(r)/ n. **1 a** a straight line passing from side to side through the centre of a body or figure, esp. a circle or sphere. **b** the length of this line. **2** a transverse measurement;

width, thickness. **3** a unit of linear measurement of magnifying power (*a lens magnifying 2000 diameters*). □ **diametral** *adj*. [ME f. OF *diametre* f. L *diametrus* f. Gk *diametros* (*grammē*) (line) measuring across f. *metron* measure]

diametrical /ˌdaɪəˈmetrɪk(ə)l/ *adj*. (also **diametric**) **1** of or along a diameter. **2** (of opposition, difference, etc.) complete, like that between opposite ends of a diameter. □ **diametrically** *adv*. [Gk *diametrikos* (as DIAMETER)]

diamond /ˈdaɪəmənd/ *n.*, *adj.*, & *v.* —*n.* **1** a precious stone of pure carbon crystallized in octahedrons etc., the hardest naturally-occurring substance. **2** a figure shaped like the cross-section of a diamond; a rhombus. **3** **a** a playing-card of a suit denoted by a red rhombus. **b** (in *pl.*) this suit. **4** *Baseball* **a** the space delimited by the bases. **b** the entire field. —*adj.* **1** made of or set with diamonds or a diamond. **2** rhombus-shaped. —*v.tr.* adorn with or as with diamonds. □ **diamond jubilee** the 60th (or 75th) anniversary of an event, esp. a sovereign's accession. **diamond wedding** a 60th (or 75th) wedding anniversary. □ **diamondiferous** /-ˈdɪfərəs/ *adj*. [ME f. OF *diamant* f. med.L *diamas diamant*- var. of L *adamas* ADAMANT f. Gk]

dianthus /daɪˈænθəs/ *n.* any flowering plant of the genus *Dianthus*, e.g. a carnation or pink. [Gk *Dios* of Zeus + *anthos* flower]

diapason /ˌdaɪəˈpeɪz(ə)n, -ˈpeɪs(ə)n/ *n.* *Mus.* **1** the compass of a voice or musical instrument. **2** a fixed standard of musical pitch. **3** (in full **open** or **stopped diapason**) either of two main organ-stops extending through the organ's whole compass. **4** an entire compass, range, or scope. [ME in sense 'octave' f. L *diapason* f. Gk *dia pasōn* (*khordōn*) through all (notes)]

diaper /ˈdaɪəpə(r)/ *n.* **1** *US* a baby's nappy. **2 a** a linen or cotton fabric with a small diamond pattern. **b** this pattern. [ME f. OF *diapre* f. med.L *diasprum* f. med.Gk *diaspros* (adj.) (as DIA-, *aspros* white)]

diaphanous /daɪˈæfənəs/ *adj*. (of fabric etc.) light and delicate, and almost transparent. □ **diaphanously** *adv*. [med.L *diaphanus* f. Gk *diaphanes* (as DIA-, *phainō* show)]

diaphragm /ˈdaɪəˌfræm/ *n.* **1** a muscular partition separating the thorax from the abdomen in mammals. **2** a partition in animal and plant tissues. **3** a disc pierced by one or more holes in optical and acoustic systems etc. **4** a device for varying the effective aperture of the lens in a camera etc. **5** a thin contraceptive cap fitting over the cervix. **6** a thin sheet of material used as a partition etc. □ **diaphragmatic** /-fræɡˈmætɪk/ *adj*. [ME f. LL *diaphragma* f. Gk (as DIA-, *phragma -atos* f. *phrassō* fence in)]

diarist /ˈdaɪərɪst/ *n.* a person who keeps a diary. □ **diaristic** /-ˈrɪstɪk/ *adj*.

diarrhoea /ˌdaɪəˈrɪə/ *n.* (esp. *US* **diarrhea**) a condition of excessively frequent and loose bowel movements. □ **diarrhoeal** *adj*. **diarrhoeic** *adj*. [ME f. LL f. Gk *diarrhoia* (as DIA-, *rheō* flow)]

diary /ˈdaɪərɪ/ *n.* (*pl.* **-ies**) **1** a daily record of events or thoughts. **2** a book for this or for noting future engagements, usu. printed and with a calendar and other information. [L *diarium* f. *dies* day]

Diaspora /daɪˈæspərə/ *n.* **1** (prec. by *the*) **a** the dispersion of the Jews among the Gentiles

mainly in the 8th–6th c. BC. **b** Jews dispersed in this way. **2** (also **diaspora**) **a** any group of people similarly dispersed. **b** their dispersion. [Gk f. *diaspeirō* (as DIA-, *speirō* scatter)]

diastase /ˈdaɪəˌsteɪz/ *n.* *Biochem.* = AMYLASE. □ **diastasic** /-ˈsteɪzɪk/ *adj*. **diastatic** /-ˈstætɪk/ *adj*. [F f. Gk *diastasis* separation (as DIA-, *stasis* placing)]

diastole /daɪˈæstəlɪ/ *n.* *Physiol.* the period between two contractions of the heart when the heart muscle relaxes and allows the chambers to fill with blood (cf. SYSTOLE). □ **diastolic** /ˌdaɪəˈstɒlɪk/ *adj*. [LL f. Gk *diastellō* (as DIA-, *stellō* place)]

diatom /ˈdaɪətəm/ *n.* a microscopic unicellular alga with a siliceous cell-wall, found as plankton and forming fossil deposits. □ **diatomaceous** /-ˈmeɪʃəs/ *adj*. [mod.L *Diatoma* (genus-name) f. Gk *diatomos* (as DIA-, *temnō* cut)]

diatomic /ˌdaɪəˈtɒmɪk/ *adj*. consisting of two atoms. [DI-[1] + ATOM]

diatonic /ˌdaɪəˈtɒnɪk/ *adj*. *Mus.* **1** (of a scale, interval, etc.) involving only notes proper to the prevailing key without chromatic alteration. **2** (of a melody or harmony) constructed from such a scale. [F *diatonique* or LL *diatonicus* f. Gk *diatonikos* at intervals of a tone (as DIA-, TONIC)]

diatribe /ˈdaɪəˌtraɪb/ *n.* a forceful verbal attack; a piece of bitter criticism. [F f. L *diatriba* f. Gk *diatribē* spending of time, discourse f. *diatribō* (as DIA-, *tribō* rub)]

dibber /ˈdɪbə(r)/ *n.* = DIBBLE.

dibble /ˈdɪb(ə)l/ *n.* & *v.* —*n.* a hand-tool for making holes in the ground for seeds or young plants. —*v.* **1** *tr.* sow or plant with a dibble. **2** *tr.* prepare (soil) with a dibble. **3** *intr.* use a dibble. [ME: perh. rel. to DIBS]

dibs *n.pl.* *sl.* money. [earlier sense 'pebbles for game', also *dib-stones*, perh. f. *dib* dip lightly]

dice *n.* & *v.* —*n.pl.* **1** a small cubes with faces bearing 1–6 spots used in games of chance. **b** (treated as *sing.*) one of these cubes (see DIE[2]). **2** a game played with one or more such cubes. **3** food cut into small cubes for cooking. —*v.* **1** *intr.* play dice. **b** *intr.* take great risks, gamble (*dicing with death*). **c** *tr.* (foll. by *away*) gamble away. **2** *tr.* cut (food) into small cubes. □ **no dice** *sl.* no success or prospect of it. □ **dicer** *n.* (in sense 1 of *v.*). [pl. of DIE[2]]

■ **Usage** See note at DIE[2].

dicey /ˈdaɪsɪ/ *adj*. (**dicier**, **diciest**) *sl.* risky, unreliable. [DICE + -Y[1]]

dichotomy /daɪˈkɒtəmɪ/ *n.* (*pl.* **-ies**) **1 a** a division into two, esp. a sharply defined one. **b** the result of such a division. **2** binary classification. □ **dichotomic** /-kəˈtɒmɪk/ *adj*. **dichotomize** *v.* **dichotomous** *adj*. [mod.L *dichotomia* f. Gk *dikhotomia* f. *dikho-* apart + -TOMY]

■ **Usage** This word should not be used to mean *dilemma* or *ambivalence*.

dichromatic /ˌdaɪkrəʊˈmætɪk/ *adj*. **1** two-coloured. **2 a** (of animal species) having individuals that show different colorations. **b** having vision sensitive to only two of the three primary colours. □ **dichromatism** /daɪˈkrəʊməˌtɪz(ə)m/ *n.* [DI-[1] + Gk *khrōmatikos* f. *khrōma -atos* colour]

dick[1] *n.* **1** *Brit. colloq.* (in certain set phrases) fellow; person (*clever dick*). **2** *coarse sl.* the penis. [pet form of the name *Richard*]

dick | diesel

dick² *n. sl.* a detective. [perh. abbr.]

dicken /ˈdɪkən/ *int. Austral. sl.* an expression of disgust or disbelief. [usu. assoc. with DICKENS or the name *Dickens*]

dickens /ˈdɪkɪnz/ *n.* (usu. prec. by *how, what, why,* etc., *the*) *colloq.* (esp. in exclamations) deuce; the Devil (*what the dickens are you doing here?*). [16th c.: prob. a use of the surname *Dickens*]

Dickensian /dɪˈkenzɪən/ *adj.* & *n.* —*adj.* **1** of or relating to Charles Dickens, Engl. novelist d. 1870, or his work. **2** resembling or reminiscent of the situations, poor social conditions, or comically repulsive characters described in Dickens's work. —*n.* an admirer or student of Dickens or his work. □ **Dickensianly** *adv.*

dicker /ˈdɪkə(r)/ *v.* & *n.* esp. *US* —*v.* **1 a** *intr.* bargain, haggle. **b** *tr.* barter, exchange. **2** *intr.* dither, hesitate. —*n.* a deal, a barter. □ **dickerer** *n.* [perh. f. *dicker* set of ten (hides), as a unit of trade]

dicky¹ /ˈdɪkɪ/ *n.* (also **dickey**) (*pl.* **-ies** or **-eys**) *colloq.* **1** a false shirt-front. **2** (in full **dicky-bird**) a child's word for a little bird. [some senses f. *Dicky* (as DICK¹)]

dicky² /ˈdɪkɪ/ *adj.* (**dickier, dickiest**) *Brit. sl.* unsound, likely to collapse or fail. [19th c.: perh. f. 'as queer as Dick's hatband']

dicotyledon /ˌdaɪkɒtɪˈliːd(ə)n/ *n.* any flowering plant having two cotyledons. □ **dicotyledonous** *adj.* [mod.L *dicotyledones* (as DI-¹, COTYLEDON)]

dicta *pl.* of DICTUM.

Dictaphone /ˈdɪktəˌfəʊn/ *n. propr.* a machine for recording and playing back dictated words. [DICTATE + PHONE]

dictate /dɪkˈteɪt/ *v.* & *n.* —*v.* **1** *tr.* say or read aloud (words to be written down or recorded). **2 a** *tr.* prescribe or lay down authoritatively (terms, things to be done). **b** *intr.* lay down the law; give orders. —*n.* /ˈdɪk-/ (usu. in *pl.*) an authoritative instruction (*dictates of conscience*). [L *dictare dictat-* frequent. of *dicere dict-* say]

dictation /dɪkˈteɪʃ(ə)n/ *n.* **1 a** the saying of words to be written down or recorded. **b** an instance of this, esp. as a school exercise. **c** the material that is dictated. **2 a** authoritative prescription. **b** an instance of this. **c** a command.

dictator /dɪkˈteɪtə(r)/ *n.* **1** a ruler with (often usurped) unrestricted authority. **2** a person with supreme authority in any sphere. **3** a domineering person. [ME f. L (as DICTATE)]

dictatorial /ˌdɪktəˈtɔːrɪəl/ *adj.* **1** of or like a dictator. **2** imperious, overbearing. □ **dictatorially** *adv.* [L *dictatorius* (as DICTATOR)]

dictatorship /dɪkˈteɪtəʃɪp/ *n.* **1** a State ruled by a dictator. **2 a** the position, rule, or period of rule of a dictator. **b** rule by a dictator. **3** absolute authority in any sphere.

diction /ˈdɪkʃ(ə)n/ *n.* **1** the manner of enunciation in speaking or singing. **2** the choice of words or phrases in speech or writing. [F *diction* or L *dictio* f. *dicere dict-* say]

dictionary /ˈdɪkʃənrɪ, -nərɪ/ *n.* (*pl.* **-ies**) **1** a book that lists (usu. in alphabetical order) and explains the words of a language or gives equivalent words in another language. **2** a reference book on any subject, the items of which are arranged in alphabetical order. [med.L *dictionarium* (*manuale* manual) & *dictionarius* (*liber* book) f. L *dictio* (as DICTION)]

dictum /ˈdɪktəm/ *n.* (*pl.* **dicta** /-tə/ or **dictums**) **1** a formal utterance or pronouncement. **2** a

saying or maxim. [L, = neut. past part. of *dicere* say]

did *past* of DO¹.

didactic /daɪˈdæktɪk, dɪ-/ *adj.* **1** meant to instruct. **2** (of a person) tediously pedantic. □ **didactically** *adv.* **didacticism** /-tɪˌsɪz(ə)m/ *n.* [Gk *didaktikos* f. *didaskō* teach]

diddle /ˈdɪd(ə)l/ *v. colloq.* **1** *tr.* cheat, swindle. **2** *intr. US* waste time. □ **diddler** *n.* [prob. back-form. f. Jeremy *Diddler* in Kenney's 'Raising the Wind' (1803)]

diddums /ˈdɪdəmz/ *int.* expressing commiseration esp. to a child. [= *did 'em,* i.e. did they (tease you etc.)?]

didgeridoo /ˌdɪdʒərɪˈduː/ *n.* (also **didjeridoo**) an Australian Aboriginal musical wind instrument of long tubular shape. [imit.]

didn't /ˈdɪd(ə)nt/ *contr.* did not.

die¹ /daɪ/ *v.* (**dies, died, dying** /ˈdaɪɪŋ/) **1** *intr.* (often foll. by *of*) (of a person, animal, or plant) cease to live; expire, lose vital force (*died of hunger*). **2** *intr.* **a** come to an end, cease to exist, fade away (*the project died within six months*). **b** cease to function; break down (*the engine died*). **c** (of a flame) go out. **3** *intr.* (foll. by *on*) die or cease to function while in the presence or charge of (a person). **4** *intr.* (usu. foll. by *of, from, with*) be exhausted or tormented (*nearly died of boredom; was dying from the heat*). **5** *tr.* suffer (a specified death) (*died a natural death*). □ **be dying** (foll. by *for,* or *to* + infin.) wish for longingly or intently (*was dying for a drink; am dying to see you*). **die away** become weaker or fainter to the point of extinction. **die back** (of a plant) decay from the tip towards the root. **die down** become less loud or strong. **die hard** die reluctantly, not without a struggle (*old habits die hard*). **die-hard** *n.* a conservative or stubborn person. **die off** die one after another until few or none are left. **die out** become extinct, cease to exist. **never say die** keep up courage, not give in. [ME, prob. f. ON *deyja* f. Gmc]

die² /daɪ/ *n.* **1** *sing.* of DICE *n.* 1a. **2** (*pl.* **dies**) **a** an engraved device for stamping a design on coins, medals, etc. **b** a device for stamping, cutting, or moulding material into a particular shape. □ **as straight** (or **true**) **as a die 1** quite straight. **2** entirely honest or loyal. **die-cast** cast (hot metal) in a die or mould. **die-casting** the process or product of casting from metal moulds. **the die is cast** an irrevocable step has been taken. **die-stamping** embossing paper etc. with a die. [ME f. OF *de* f. L *datum* neut. past part. of *dare* give, play]

■ **Usage** *Dice,* rather than *die,* is now the standard singular as well as plural form in the games sense (*one dice, two dice*).

dieldrin /dɪˈeldrɪn/ *n.* a crystalline insecticide produced by the oxidation of aldrin. [O. *Diels,* Ger. chemist d. 1954 + ALDRIN]

dielectric /ˌdaɪɪˈlektrɪk/ *adj.* & *n. Electr.* —*adj.* insulating. —*n.* an insulating medium or substance. □ **dielectrically** *adv.* [DI-³ + ELECTRIC = through which electricity is transmitted (without conduction)]

dieresis *US* var. of DIAERESIS.

diesel /ˈdiːz(ə)l/ *n.* **1** (in full **diesel engine**) an internal-combustion engine in which the heat produced by the compression of air in the cylinder ignites the fuel. **2** a vehicle driven by a

diesel engine. **3** fuel for a diesel engine. □
diesel-electric n. a vehicle driven by the
electric current produced by a diesel-engined
generator. —*adj.* of or powered by this means.
diesel oil a heavy petroleum fraction used as
fuel in diesel engines. □ **dieselize** *v.tr.* (also
-ise). [R. *Diesel*, Ger. engineer d. 1913]

diet[1] /ˈdaɪət/ n. & v. —n. **1** the kinds of food that
a person or animal habitually eats. **2** a special
course of food to which a person is restricted,
esp. for medical reasons or to control weight.
—v. (**dieted**, **dieting**) **1** *intr.* restrict oneself to
small amounts or special kinds of food, esp. to
control one's weight. **2** *tr.* restrict (a person or
animal) to a special diet. □ **dieter** n. [ME f. OF
diete (n.), *dieter* (v.) f. L *diaeta* f. Gk *diaita* a way of
life]

diet[2] /ˈdaɪət/ n. **1** a legislative assembly in certain
countries. **2** *hist.* a national or international
conference. [ME f. med.L *dieta* day's work, wages,
etc.]

dietary /ˈdaɪətrɪ/ adj. & n. —adj. of or relating
to a diet. —n. (pl. **-ies**) a regulated or restricted
diet. [ME f. med.L *dietarium* (as DIET[1])]

dietetic /ˌdaɪəˈtɛtɪk/ adj. of or relating to diet. □
dietetically adv. [L *dieteticus* f. Gk *diaitētikos* (as
DIET[1])]

dietetics /ˌdaɪəˈtɛtɪks/ n.pl. (usu. treated as *sing.*)
the scientific study of diet and nutrition.

dietitian /ˌdaɪəˈtɪʃ(ə)n/ n. (also **dietician**) an
expert in dietetics.

dif- /dɪf/ prefix assim. form of DIS- before *f*. [L
var. of DIS-]

differ /ˈdɪfə(r)/ v.intr. **1** (often foll. by *from*) be
unlike or distinguishable. **2** (often foll. by *with*)
disagree; be at variance (with a person). [ME f.
OF *differer* f. L *differre*, differ, DEFER[1], (as DIS-, *ferre*
bear, tend)]

difference /ˈdɪfrəns/ n. **1** the state or condition
of being different or unlike. **2** a point in
which things differ; a distinction. **3** a degree of
unlikeness. **4 a** the quantity by which amounts
differ; a deficit (*will have to make up the difference*).
b the remainder left after subtraction. **5 a** a
disagreement, quarrel, or dispute. **b** the grounds
of disagreement (*put aside their differences*). □
make a (or **all the** etc.) **difference** (often foll.
by *to*) have a significant effect or influence (on a
person, situation, etc.). **make no difference**
(often foll. by *to*) have no effect (on a person,
situation, etc.). [ME f. OF f. L *differentia* (as
DIFFERENT)]

different /ˈdɪfrənt/ adj. **1** (often foll. by *from, to,
than*) unlike, distinguishable in nature, form, or
quality (from another). **2** distinct, separate; not
the same one (as another). **3** *colloq.* unusual
(*wanted to do something different*). □ **differently**
adv. **differentness** n. [ME f. OF *different* f. L
different- (as DIFFER)]

■ **Usage** In sense 1, *different from* is regarded
as more acceptable than *different to* which is
common in less formal use.

---

differential /ˌdɪfəˈrɛnʃ(ə)l/ adj. & n. —adj. **1**
of, exhibiting, or depending on a difference. **b**
varying according to circumstances. **2** *Math.*
relating to infinitesimal differences. **3** constituting a specific difference; distinctive; relating to specific differences (*differential diagnosis*).
4 *Physics & Mech.* concerning the difference of
two or more motions, pressures, etc. —n. **1** a

difference between individuals or examples of
the same kind. **2** *Brit.* a difference in wage
or salary between industries or categories of
employees in the same industry. **3** a difference
between rates of interest etc. **4** *Math.* **a** an
infinitesimal difference between successive values of a variable. **b** a function expressing this
as a rate of change with respect to another
variable. **5** (in full **differential gear**) a gear
allowing a vehicle's driven wheels to revolve at
different speeds in cornering. □ **differential
calculus** *Math.* a method of calculating rates of
change, maximum or minimum values, etc. □
differentially adv. [med. & mod.L *differentialis*
(as DIFFERENTIAL)]

differentiate /ˌdɪfəˈrɛnʃɪˌeɪt/ v. **1** *tr.* constitute a
difference between or in. **2** *tr.* & (often foll. by
between) *intr.* find differences (between); discriminate. **3** *tr.* & *intr.* make or become different
in the process of growth or development
(species, word-forms, etc.). **4** *tr. Math.* transform
(a function) into its derivative. □ **differentiation** /-ˈeɪʃ(ə)n/ n. **differentiator** n. [med.L
differentiare differentiat- (as DIFFERENCE)]

difficult /ˈdɪfɪkəlt/ adj. **1 a** needing much effort
or skill. **b** troublesome, perplexing. **2** (of a
person): **a** not easy to please or satisfy. **b**
uncooperative, troublesome. **3** characterized by
hardships or problems (*a difficult period in his
life*). □ **difficultly** adv. **difficultness** n. [ME,
back-form. f. DIFFICULTY]

difficulty /ˈdɪfɪkəltɪ/ n. (pl. **-ies**) **1** the state or
condition of being difficult. **2 a** a difficult thing;
a problem or hindrance. **b** (often in pl.) a cause
of distress or hardship (*in financial difficulties*). □
make difficulties be intransigent or unaccommodating. **with difficulty** not easily. [ME
f. L *difficultas* (as DIS-, *facultas* FACULTY)]

diffident /ˈdɪfɪd(ə)nt/ adj. **1** shy, lacking self-
confidence. **2** excessively modest and reticent. □
diffidence n. **diffidently** adv. [L *diffidere* (as
DIS-, *fidere* trust)]

diffract /dɪˈfrækt/ v.tr. *Physics* (of the edge of an
opaque body, a narrow slit, etc.) break up (a
beam of light) into a series of dark or light bands
or coloured spectra, or (a beam of radiation or
particles) into a series of alternately high and
low intensities. □ **diffraction** n. **diffractive**
adj. **diffractively** adv. [L *diffringere diffract-* (as
DIS-, *frangere* break)]

diffuse adj. & v. —adj. /dɪˈfjuːs/ **1** (of light,
inflammation, etc.) spread out, diffused, not
concentrated. **2** (of prose, speech, etc.) not
concise, long-winded, verbose. —v.tr. & intr.
/dɪˈfjuːz/ **1** disperse or be dispersed from a
centre. **2** spread or be spread widely; reach a
large area. **3** *Physics* (esp. of fluids) intermingle
by diffusion. □ **diffusely** /dɪˈfjuːslɪ/ adv.
diffuseness /dɪˈfjuːsnɪs/ n. **diffusible** /dɪˈfjuː-
zɪb(ə)l/ adj. **diffusive** /dɪˈfjuːsɪv/ adj. [ME f. F
diffus or L *diffusus* extensive (as DIS-, *fusus* past
part. of *fundere* pour)]

diffuser /dɪˈfjuːzə(r)/ n. (also **diffusor**) a person
or thing that diffuses, esp. a device for diffusing
light.

diffusion /dɪˈfjuːʒ(ə)n/ n. **1** the act or an instance
of diffusing; the process of being diffused. **2**
Physics & Chem. the interpenetration of substances by the natural movement of their
particles. □ **diffusionist** n. [ME f. L *diffusio* (as
DIFFUSE)]

dig *v. & n.* —*v.* (**digging**; *past* and *past part.* **dug**) **1** *intr.* break up and remove or turn over soil, ground, etc., with a tool, one's hands, (of an animal) claws, etc. **2** *tr.* break up and displace (the ground etc.) in this way. **3** *tr.* make (a hole, grave, tunnel, etc.) by digging. **4** *tr.* (often foll. by *up*, *out*) **a** obtain or remove by digging. **b** find or discover after searching. **5** *tr.* (also *absol.*) excavate (an archaeological site). **6** *tr. sl.* like, appreciate, or understand. **7** *tr. & intr.* (foll. by *in*, *into*) thrust or poke into or down into. **8** *intr.* make one's way by digging (*dug through the mountainside*). —*n.* **1** a piece of digging. **2** a thrust or poke (*a dig in the ribs*). **3** *colloq.* (often foll. by *at*) a pointed or critical remark. **4** an archaeological excavation. **5** (in *pl.*) *Brit. colloq.* lodgings. [ME *digge*, of uncert. orig.: cf. OE *dīc* ditch]

digest *v. & n.* —*v.tr.* /daɪˈdʒest, dɪ-/ **1** assimilate (food) in the stomach and bowels. **2** understand and assimilate mentally. **3** *Chem.* treat (a substance) with heat, enzymes, or a solvent in order to decompose it, extract the essence, etc. **4** a reduce to a systematic or convenient form; classify; summarize. **b** think over; arrange in the mind. —*n.* /ˈdaɪdʒest/ **1** a methodical summary esp. of a body of laws. **2** a regular or occasional synopsis of current literature or news. □ **digester** *n.* **digestible** *adj.* **digestibility** /-ˈbɪlɪti/ *n.* [ME f. L *digerere digest-* distribute, dissolve, digest (as DI-², *gerere* carry)]

digestion /daɪˈdʒestʃ(ə)n/ *n.* **1** the process of digesting. **2** the capacity to digest food (*has a weak digestion*). **3** digesting a substance by means of heat, enzymes, or a solvent. [ME f. OF f. L *digestio -onis* (as DIGEST)]

digestive /dɪˈdʒestɪv, daɪ-/ *adj. & n.* —*adj.* **1** of or relating to digestion. **2** aiding or promoting digestion. —*n.* **1** a substance that aids digestion. **2** (in full **digestive biscuit**) *Brit.* a usu. round semi-sweet wholemeal biscuit. □ **digestively** *adv.* [ME f. OF *digestif -ive* or L *digestivus* (as DIGEST)]

digger /ˈdɪɡə(r)/ *n.* **1** a person or machine that digs, esp. a mechanical excavator. **2** a miner, esp. a gold-digger. **3** *colloq.* an Australian or New Zealander, esp. a private soldier.

digit /ˈdɪdʒɪt/ *n.* **1** any numeral from 0 to 9, esp. when forming part of a number. **2** *Anat. & Zool.* a finger, thumb, or toe. [ME f. L *digitus*]

digital /ˈdɪdʒɪt(ə)l/ *adj.* **1** of or using a digit or digits. **2** (of a clock, watch, etc.) that gives a reading by means of displayed digits instead of hands. **3** (of a computer) operating on data represented as a series of usu. binary digits or in similar discrete form. **4 a** (of a recording) with sound-information represented in digits for more reliable transmission. **b** (of a recording medium) using this process. □ **digital audio tape** magnetic tape on which sound is recorded digitally. □ **digitalize** *v.tr.* (also **-ise**). **digitally** *adv.* [L *digitalis* (as DIGIT)]

digitalin /ˌdɪdʒɪˈteɪlɪn/ *n.* the pharmacologically active constituent(s) of the foxglove. [DIGITALIS + -IN]

digitalis /ˌdɪdʒɪˈteɪlɪs/ *n.* a drug prepared from the dried leaves of foxgloves and containing substances that stimulate the heart muscle. [mod.L, genus-name of foxglove after G *Fingerhut* thimble: see DIGITAL]

digitize /ˈdɪdʒɪˌtaɪz/ *v.tr.* (also **-ise**) convert (data etc.) into digital form, esp. for processing by a computer. □ **digitization** /-ˈzeɪʃ(ə)n/ *n.*

dignified /ˈdɪɡnɪˌfaɪd/ *adj.* having or expressing dignity; noble or stately in appearance or manner. □ **dignifiedly** *adv.*

dignify /ˈdɪɡnɪˌfaɪ/ *v.tr.* (**-ies**, **-ied**) **1** give dignity or distinction to. **2** ennoble; make worthy or illustrious. **3** give the form or appearance of dignity to (*dignified the house with the name of mansion*). [obs. F *dignifier* f. OF *dignefier* f. LL *dignificare* f. *dignus* worthy]

dignitary /ˈdɪɡnɪtəri/ *n.* (*pl.* **-ies**) a person holding high rank or office. [DIGNITY + -ARY¹, after PROPRIETARY]

dignity /ˈdɪɡnɪti/ *n.* (*pl.* **-ies**) **1** a composed and serious manner or style. **2** the state of being worthy of honour or respect. **3** worthiness, excellence (*the dignity of work*). **4** a high or honourable rank or position. □ **beneath one's dignity** not considered worthy enough for one to do. **stand on one's dignity** insist (esp. by one's manner) on being treated with due respect. [ME f. OF *digneté*, *dignité* f. L *dignitas -tatis* f. *dignus* worthy]

digraph /ˈdaɪɡrɑːf/ *n.* a group of two letters representing one sound, as in *ph* and *ey*. □ **digraphic** /-ˈɡræfɪk/ *adj.*

■ **Usage** This word is sometimes confused with *ligature* which means two or more letters joined together.

digress /daɪˈɡres/ *v.intr.* depart from the main subject temporarily in speech or writing. □ **digresser** *n.* **digression** *n.* **digressive** *adj.* **digressively** *adv.* **digressiveness** *n.* [L *digredi digress-* (as DI-², *gradi* walk)]

digs see DIG n. 5.

dike¹ var. of DYKE¹.

dike² var. of DYKE².

diktat /ˈdɪktæt/ *n.* a categorical statement or decree, esp. terms imposed after a war by a victor. [G, = DICTATE]

dilapidated /dɪˈlæpɪˌdeɪtɪd/ *adj.* in a state of disrepair or ruin, esp. as a result of age or neglect. [L *dilapidare* demolish, squander (as DI-², *lapis lapid-* stone)]

dilapidation /dɪˌlæpɪˈdeɪʃ(ə)n/ *n.* **1 a** the process of dilapidating. **b** a state of disrepair. **2** (in *pl.*) repairs required at the end of a tenancy or lease. [ME f. LL *dilapidatio* (as DILAPIDATED)]

dilatation /ˌdaɪləˈteɪʃ(ə)n/ *n.* **1** the widening or expansion of a hollow organ or cavity. **2** the process of dilating. □ **dilatation and curettage** an operation in which the cervix is expanded and the womb-lining scraped off with a curette, performed after a miscarriage or for the removal of cysts, tumours, etc.

dilate /daɪˈleɪt/ *v.* **1** *tr.* make or become wider or larger (esp. of an opening in the body) (*dilated pupils*). **2** *intr.* (often foll. by *on*, *upon*) speak or write at length. □ **dilatable** *adj.* **dilation** *n.* [ME f. OF *dilater* f. L *dilatare* spread out (as DI-², *latus* wide)]

dilatory /ˈdɪlətəri/ *adj.* given to or causing delay. □ **dilatorily** *adv.* **dilatoriness** *n.* [LL *dilatorius* (as DI-², *dilat-* past part. stem of *differre* DEFER¹)]

dildo /ˈdɪldəʊ/ *n.* (*pl.* **-os**) an object shaped like an erect penis and used, esp. by women, for sexual stimulation. [17th c.: orig. unkn.]

dilemma /daɪˈlemə, dɪ-/ n. **1** a situation in which a choice has to be made between two equally undesirable alternatives. **2** a state of indecision between two alternatives. **3** disp. a difficult situation. [L f. Gk (as DI-¹, lēmma premiss)]

■ **Usage** The use of this word in sense 3 is considered incorrect by some people.

dilettante /ˌdɪlɪˈtæntɪ/ n. (pl. **dilettanti** /-tɪ/ or **dilettantes**) a person who studies a subject or area of knowledge superficially. □ **dilettantish** adj. **dilettantism** n. [It. f. pres. part. of dilettare delight f. L delectare]

diligence /ˈdɪlɪdʒ(ə)ns/ n. **1** careful and persistent application or effort. **2** (as a characteristic) industriousness. [ME f. OF f. L diligentia (as DILIGENT)]

diligent /ˈdɪlɪdʒ(ə)nt/ adj. **1** careful and steady in application to one's work or duties. **2** showing care and effort. □ **diligently** adv. [ME f. OF f. L diligens assiduous, part. of diligere love, take delight in (as DI-², legere choose)]

dill¹ n. **1** an umbelliferous herb, Anethum graveolens, with yellow flowers and aromatic seeds. **2** the leaves or seeds of this plant used for flavouring and medicinal purposes. □ **dill pickle** pickled cucumber etc. flavoured with dill. [OE dile]

dill² n. Austral. sl. **1** a fool or simpleton. **2** the victim of a trickster. [app. back-form. f. dilly perh. f. DAFT, SILLY]

dilly /ˈdɪlɪ/ n. (pl. **-ies**) esp. US sl. a remarkable or excellent person or thing. [dilly (adj.) f. DELIGHTFUL or DELICIOUS]

dilly-dally /ˌdɪlɪˈdælɪ/ v.intr. (**-ies**, **-ied**) colloq. **1** dawdle, loiter. **2** vacillate. [redupl. of DALLY]

dilute /daɪˈljuːt/ v. & adj. —v.tr. **1** reduce the strength of (a fluid) by adding water or another solvent. **2** weaken or reduce the strength or forcefulness of, esp. by adding something. —adj. /also ˈdaɪ-/ (esp. of a fluid) diluted, weakened. □ **diluter** n. **dilution** n. [L diluere dilut- (as DI-², luere wash)]

diluvial /daɪˈluːvɪəl, dɪ-, -ˈljuːvɪəl/ adj. of a flood, esp. of the Flood in Genesis. [LL diluvialis f. diluvium DELUGE]

dim adj. & v. —adj. (**dimmer**, **dimmest**) **1 a** only faintly luminous or visible; not bright. **b** obscure; ill-defined. **2** not clearly perceived or remembered. **3** colloq. stupid; slow to understand. **4** (of the eyes) not seeing clearly. —v. (**dimmed**, **dimming**) **1** tr. & intr. make or become dim or less bright. **2** tr. US dip (headlights). □ **dim-wit** colloq. a stupid person. **dim-witted** colloq. stupid, unintelligent. **take a dim view of** colloq. **1** disapprove of. **2** feel gloomy about. □ **dimly** adv. **dimmish** adj. **dimness** n. [OE dim, dimm, of unkn. orig.]

dime /daɪm/ n. US & Can. colloq. **1** a ten-cent coin. **2** a small amount of money. [ME (orig. = tithe) f. OF disme f. L decima pars tenth part]

dimension /daɪˈmenʃ(ə)n, dɪ-/ n. **1** a measurable extent of any kind, as length, breadth, depth, area, and volume. **2** (in pl.) size, scope, extent. **3** an aspect or facet of a situation, problem, etc. □ **dimensional** adj. (also in comb.). **dimensionless** adj. [ME f. OF f. L dimensio -onis (as DI-², metiri mensus measure)]

dimer /ˈdaɪmə(r)/ n. Chem. a compound consisting of two identical molecules linked together. □ **dimeric** /-ˈmerɪk/ adj. [DI-¹ + -mer after POLYMER]

diminish /dɪˈmɪnɪʃ/ v. **1** tr. & intr. make or become smaller or less. **2** tr. lessen the reputation or influence of (a person). □ **law of diminishing returns** Econ. the fact that the increase of expenditure, investment, taxation, etc., beyond a certain point ceases to produce a proportionate yield. □ **diminishable** adj. [ME, blending of earlier minish f. OF menusier (formed as MINCE) and diminue f. OF diminuer f. L diminuere diminut- break up small]

diminished /dɪˈmɪnɪʃt/ adj. **1** reduced; made smaller or less. **2** Mus. (of an interval, usu. a seventh or fifth) less by a semitone than the corresponding minor or perfect interval. □ **diminished responsibility** Law the limitation of criminal responsibility on the ground of mental weakness or abnormality.

diminuendo /dɪˌmɪnjʊˈendəʊ/ adv. & n. Mus. —adv. with a gradual decrease in loudness. —n. (pl. **-os**) a passage to be played in this way. [It., part. of diminuire DIMINISH]

diminution /ˌdɪmɪˈnjuːʃ(ə)n/ n. **1** the act or an instance of diminishing. **2** the amount by which something diminishes. [ME f. OF f. L diminutio -onis (as DIMINISH)]

diminutive /dɪˈmɪnjʊtɪv/ adj. & n. —adj. **1** remarkably small; tiny. **2** Gram. (of a word or suffix) implying smallness, either actual or imputed in token of affection, scorn, etc. (e.g. -let, -kins). —n. Gram. a diminutive word or suffix. □ **diminutival** /-ˈtaɪv(ə)l/ adj. **diminutively** adv. **diminutiveness** n. [ME f. OF diminutif, -ive f. LL diminutivus (as DIMINISH)]

dimmer /ˈdɪmə(r)/ n. **1** a device for varying the brightness of an electric light. **2** US **a** (in pl.) small parking lights on a motor vehicle. **b** a headlight on low beam.

dimorphic /daɪˈmɔːfɪk/ adj. (also **dimorphous** /daɪˈmɔːfəs/) Biol., Chem., & Mineral. exhibiting, or occurring in, two distinct forms. □ **dimorphism** n. [Gk dimorphos (as DI-¹, morphē form)]

dimple /ˈdɪmp(ə)l/ n. & v. —n. a small hollow or dent in the flesh, esp. in the cheeks or chin. —v. **1** intr. produce or show dimples. **2** tr. produce dimples in (a cheek etc.). □ **dimply** adj. [ME prob. f. OE dympel (unrecorded) f. a Gmc root dump-, perh. a nasalized form rel. to DEEP]

DIN /dɪn/ n. any of a series of technical standards originating in Germany and used internationally, esp. to designate electrical connections, film speeds, and paper sizes. [G, f. Deutsche Industrie-Norm]

din /dɪn/ n. & v. —n. a prolonged loud and distracting noise. —v. (**dinned**, **dinning**) **1** tr. (foll. by into) instil (something to be learned) by constant repetition. **2** intr. make a din. [OE dyne, dynn, dynian f. Gmc]

dinar /ˈdiːnɑː(r)/ n. **1** the chief monetary unit of Yugoslavia. **2** the chief monetary unit of certain countries of the Middle East and N. Africa. [Arab. & Pers. dīnār f. Gk dēnarion f. L denarius: see DENIER]

dine /daɪn/ v. **1** intr. eat dinner. **2** tr. give dinner to. □ **dine out 1** dine away from home. **2** (foll. by on) be entertained to dinner etc. on account of (one's ability to relate an interesting event, story, etc.). **dining-car** a railway carriage equipped as a restaurant. **dining-room** a room in which meals are eaten. [ME f. OF *diner*, *disner*, ult. f. DIS- + LL *jejunare* f. *jejunus* fasting]

diner /ˈdaɪnə(r)/ n. **1** a person who dines, esp. in a restaurant. **2** a railway dining-car. **3** *US* a small restaurant. **4** a small dining-room.

dinette /daɪˈnet/ n. a small room or part of a room used for eating meals.

dingbat /ˈdɪŋbæt/ n. *sl.* **1** *US* & *Austral.* a stupid or eccentric person. **2** (in *pl.*) *Austral.* & *NZ* **a** madness. **b** discomfort, unease (*gives me the dingbats*). [19th c.: perh. f. *ding* to beat + BAT¹]

ding-dong /ˈdɪŋdɒŋ/ n., adj., & adv. —n. **1** the sound of alternate chimes, as of two bells. **2** *colloq.* an intense argument or fight. —adj. (of a contest etc.) evenly matched and intensely waged; thoroughgoing. —adv. with vigour and energy (*hammer away at it ding-dong*). [16th c.: imit.]

dinghy /ˈdɪŋɪ, ˈdɪŋgɪ/ n. (pl. **-ies**) **1** a small boat carried by a ship. **2** a small pleasure-boat. **3** a small inflatable rubber boat. [orig. a rowing-boat used on Indian rivers, f. Hindi *ḍĩgī*, *ḍẽgī*]

dingle /ˈdɪŋg(ə)l/ n. a deep wooded valley or dell. [ME: orig. unkn.]

dingo /ˈdɪŋgəʊ/ n. (pl. **-oes**) a wild or half-domesticated Australian dog, *Canis dingo*. [Aboriginal]

dingy /ˈdɪndʒɪ/ adj. (**dingier**, **dingiest**) dirty-looking, drab, dull-coloured. □ **dingily** adv. **dinginess** n. [perh. ult. f. OE *dynge* DUNG]

dinkum /ˈdɪŋkəm/ adj. & n. *Austral.* & *NZ colloq.* —adj. genuine, right. —n. work, toil. □ **dinkum oil** the honest truth. [19th c.: orig. unkn.]

dinky /ˈdɪŋkɪ/ adj. (**dinkier**, **dinkiest**) *colloq.* **1** *Brit. colloq.* (esp. of a thing) neat and attractive; small, dainty. **2** *US* trifling, insignificant. [Sc. *dink* neat, trim, of unkn. orig.]

dinner /ˈdɪnə(r)/ n. **1** the main meal of the day, taken either at midday or in the evening. **2** a formal evening meal, often in honour of a person or event. □ **dinner-jacket** a man's short usu. black formal jacket for evening wear. **dinner lady** a woman who supervises children's lunch in a school. **dinner service** a set of usu. matching crockery for serving a meal. [ME f. OF *diner*, *disner*: see DINE]

dinosaur /ˈdaɪnəsɔː(r)/ n. **1** an extinct reptile of the Mesozoic era, often of enormous size. **2** a large unwieldy system or organization, esp. one not adapting to new conditions. □ **dinosaurian** /-ˈsɔːrɪən/ adj. & n. [mod.L *dinosaurus* f. Gk *deinos* terrible + *sauros* lizard]

dinothere /ˈdaɪnəθɪə(r)/ n. any elephant-like animal of the extinct genus *Deinotherium*, having downward curving tusks. [mod.L *dinotherium* f. Gk *deinos* terrible + *thērion* wild beast]

dint /dɪnt/ n. & v. —n. **1** a dent. **2** *archaic* a blow or stroke. —v.tr. mark with dints. □ **by dint of** by force or means of. [ME f. OE *dynt*, and partly f. cogn. ON *dyntr*: ult. orig. unkn.]

diocesan /daɪˈɒsɪs(ə)n/ adj. & n. —adj. of or concerning a diocese. —n. the bishop of a diocese. [ME f. F *diocésain* f. LL *diocesanus* (as DIOCESE)]

diocese /ˈdaɪəsɪs/ n. a district under the pastoral care of a bishop. [ME f. OF *diocise* f. LL *diocesis* f. L *dioecesis* f. Gk *dioikēsis* administration (as DI-³, *oikeō* inhabit)]

diode /ˈdaɪəʊd/ n. *Electronics* **1** a semiconductor allowing the flow of current in one direction only and having two terminals. **2** a thermionic

valve having two electrodes. [DI-¹ + ELECTRODE]

Dionysiac /ˌdaɪəˈnɪsɪˌæk/ adj. (also **Dionysian** /-sɪən/) **1** wildly sensual; unrestrained. **2** (in Greek mythology) of or relating to Dionysus, the Greek god of wine, or his worship. [LL *Dionysiacus* f. L *Dionysus* f. Gk *Dionusos*]

dioptre /daɪˈɒptə(r)/ n. (*US* **diopter**) *Optics* a unit of refractive power of a lens. [F *dioptre* f. L *dioptra* f. Gk *dioptra*: see DIOPTRIC]

dioptric /daɪˈɒptrɪk/ adj. *Optics* **1** serving as a medium for sight; assisting sight by refraction (*dioptric glass*; *dioptric lens*). **2** of refraction; refractive. [Gk *dioptrikos* f. *dioptra* a kind of theodolite]

diorama /ˌdaɪəˈrɑːmə/ n. **1** a scenic painting in which changes in colour and direction of illumination simulate a sunrise etc. **2** a small representation of a scene with three-dimensional figures, viewed through a window etc. **3** a small-scale model or film-set. □ **dioramic** /-ˈræmɪk/ adj. [DI-³ + Gk *horama* -*atos* f. *horaō* see]

dioxide /daɪˈɒksaɪd/ n. *Chem.* an oxide containing two atoms of oxygen which are not linked together (*carbon dioxide*).

Dip. abbr. Diploma.

dip v. & n. —v. (**dipped**, **dipping**) **1** tr. put or let down briefly into liquid etc.; immerse. **2** intr. **a** go below a surface or level (*the sun dipped below the horizon*). **b** (of a level of income, activity, etc.) decline slightly, esp. briefly (*profits dipped in May*). **3** intr. extend downwards; take or have a downward slope (*the road dips after the bend*). **4** intr. go under water and emerge quickly. **5** intr. (foll. by *into*) **a** read briefly from (a book etc.). **b** take a cursory interest in (a subject). **6** (foll. by *into*) **a** intr. put a hand, ladle, etc., into a container to take something out. **b** tr. put (a hand etc.) into a container to do this. **c** intr. spend from or make use of one's resources (*dipped into our savings*). **7** tr. & intr. lower or be lowered, esp. in salute. **8** tr. *Brit.* lower the beam of (a vehicle's headlights) to reduce dazzle. **9** tr. colour (a fabric) by immersing it in dye. **10** tr. wash (sheep) by immersion in a vermin-killing liquid. **11** tr. make (a candle) by immersing a wick briefly in hot tallow. —n. **1** an act of dipping or being dipped. **2** a liquid into which something is dipped. **3** a brief bathe in the sea, river, etc. **4** a brief downward slope, followed by an upward one, in a road etc. **5** a sauce or dressing into which food is dipped before eating. [OE *dyppan* f. Gmc: rel. to DEEP]

Dip. A.D. abbr. *Brit.* Diploma in Art and Design.

Dip. Ed. abbr. Diploma in Education.

Dip. H.E. abbr. *Brit.* Diploma of Higher Education.

diphtheria /dɪfˈθɪərɪə, disp. dɪp-/ n. an acute infectious bacterial disease with inflammation of a mucous membrane esp. of the throat. □ **diphtherial** adj. **diphtheric** /-ˈθerɪk/ adj. **diphtheritic** /-θəˈrɪtɪk/ adj. **diphtheroid** /ˈdɪfθəˌrɔɪd/ adj. [mod.L f. F *diphthérie*, earlier *diphthérite* f. Gk *diphthera* skin, hide]

■ **Usage** The second pronunciation is considered incorrect by some people.

diphthong /ˈdɪfθɒŋ/ n. **1** a speech sound in one syllable in which the articulation begins as for one vowel and moves as for another (as in *coin*, *loud*, and *side*). **2** a digraph representing the sound of a diphthong or single vowel (as in *feat*). □ **diphthongal** /-ˈθɒŋg(ə)l/ *adj.* [F *diphtongue* f. LL *diphthongus* f. Gk *diphthoggos* (as DI-¹, *phthoggos* voice)]

diplo- /ˈdɪpləʊ/ *comb. form* double. [Gk *diplous* double]

diplodocus /dɪpˈlɒdəkəs, ˌdɪpləʊˈdəʊkəs/ *n.* a giant plant-eating dinosaur of the order Sauropoda, with a long neck and tail. [DIPLO- + Gk *dokos* wooden beam]

diploid /ˈdɪplɔɪd/ *adj. & n. Biol.* —*adj.* (of an organism or cell) having two complete sets of chromosomes per cell. —*n.* a diploid cell or organism. [G (as DIPLO-, -OID)]

diploidy /ˈdɪplɔɪdɪ/ *n. Biol.* the condition of being diploid.

diploma /dɪˈpləʊmə/ *n.* 1 a certificate of qualification awarded by a college etc. 2 a document conferring an honour or privilege. □ **diplomaed** /-məd/ *adj.* (also **diploma'd**). [L f. Gk *diplōma -atos* folded paper f. *diploō* to fold f. *diplous* double]

diplomacy /dɪˈpləʊməsɪ/ *n.* 1 a the management of international relations. b expertise in this. 2 adroitness in personal relations; tact. [F *diplomatie* f. *diplomatique* DIPLOMATIC after *aristocratie*]

diplomat /ˈdɪpləˌmæt/ *n.* 1 an official representing a country abroad; a member of a diplomatic service. 2 a tactful person. [F *diplomate*, back-form. f. *diplomatique*: see DIPLOMATIC]

diplomate /ˈdɪpləˌmeɪt/ *n.* esp. *US* a person who holds a diploma, esp. in medicine.

diplomatic /ˌdɪpləˈmætɪk/ *adj.* 1 a of or involved in diplomacy. b skilled in diplomacy. 2 tactful; adroit in personal relations. □ **diplomatic bag** a container in which official mail etc. is dispatched to or from an embassy, not usu. subject to customs inspection. **diplomatic corps** the body of diplomats representing other countries at a seat of government. **diplomatic immunity** the exemption of diplomatic staff abroad from arrest, taxation, etc. **diplomatic service** *Brit.* the branch of public service concerned with the representation of a country abroad. □ **diplomatically** *adv.* [mod.L *diplomaticus* and F *diplomatique* f. L DIPLOMA]

diplomatist /dɪˈpləʊmətɪst/ *n.* = DIPLOMAT.

dipole /ˈdaɪpəʊl/ *n.* 1 *Physics* two equal and oppositely charged or magnetized poles separated by a distance. 2 *Chem.* a molecule in which a concentration of positive charges is separated from a concentration of negative charges. 3 an aerial consisting of a horizontal metal rod with a connecting wire at its centre.

dipper /ˈdɪpə(r)/ *n.* 1 a diving bird, *Cinclus cinclus.* 2 a ladle.

dipso /ˈdɪpsəʊ/ *n.* (*pl.* **-os**) *colloq.* a dipsomaniac. [abbr.]

dipsomania /ˌdɪpsəˈmeɪnɪə/ *n.* an abnormal craving for alcohol. □ **dipsomaniac** /-ˈmeɪnɪˌæk/ *n.* [Gk *dipso-* f. *dipsa* thirst + -MANIA]

dipstick /ˈdɪpstɪk/ *n.* a graduated rod for measuring the depth of a liquid, esp. in a vehicle's engine.

dipterous /ˈdɪptərəs/ *adj.* (of an insect) of the order Diptera, having two membranous wings, e.g. the fly, gnat, or mosquito. [mod.L *dipterus* f. Gk *dipteros* (as DI-², *pteron* wing)]

diptych /ˈdɪptɪk/ *n.* a painting, esp. an altarpiece, on two hinged usu. wooden panels which may be closed like a book. [LL *diptycha* f. Gk *diptukha* (as DI-¹, *ptukhē* fold)]

dire *adj.* 1 a calamitous, dreadful (*in dire straits*). b ominous (*dire warnings*). 2 urgent (*in dire need*). □ **direly** *adv.* **direness** *n.* [L *dirus*]

direct /daɪˈrekt, dɪ-/ *adj., adv., & v.* —*adj.* 1 extending or moving in a straight line or by the shortest route; not crooked or circuitous. 2 a straightforward; going straight to the point. b frank; not ambiguous. 3 without intermediaries or the intervention of other factors (*direct rule*; *made a direct approach*). 4 (of descent) lineal, not collateral. 5 exact, complete, greatest possible (esp. where contrast is implied) (*the direct opposite*). —*adv.* 1 in a direct way or manner; without an intermediary or intervening factor (*dealt with them direct*). 2 frankly; without evasion. 3 by a direct route (*send it direct to London*). —*v.tr.* 1 control, guide; govern the movements of. 2 (foll. by *to* + infin., or *that* + clause) give a formal order or command to. 3 (foll. by *to*) a address or give indications for the delivery of (a letter etc.). b tell or show (a person) the way to a destination. 4 (foll. by *at, to, towards*) a point, aim, or cause (a blow or missile) to move in a certain direction. b point or address (one's attention, a remark, etc.). 5 guide as an adviser, as a principle, etc. (*I do as duty directs me*). 6 a (also *absol.*) supervise the performing, staging, etc., of (a film, play, etc.). b supervise the performance of (an actor etc.). 7 (also *absol.*) guide the performance of (a group of musicians), esp. as a participant. □ **direct action** action such as a strike or sabotage directly affecting the community and meant to reinforce demands on a government, employer, etc. **direct current** an electric current flowing in one direction only. **direct debit** an arrangement for the regular debiting of a bank account at the request of the payee. **direct-grant school** *hist.* (in the UK) a school receiving funds from the Government and not from a local authority. **direct object** *Gram.* the primary object of the action of a transitive verb. **direct proportion** a relation between quantities whose ratio is constant. **direct speech** (or **oration**) words actually spoken, not reported in the third person. **direct tax** a tax levied on the person who ultimately bears the burden of it, esp. on income. □ **directness** *n.* [ME f. L *directus* past part. of *dirigere direct-* (as DI-², *regere* put straight)]

direction /daɪˈrekʃ(ə)n, dɪ-/ *n.* 1 the act or process of directing; supervision. 2 (usu. in *pl.*) an order or instruction, esp. each of a set guiding use of equipment etc. 3 a the course or line along which a person or thing moves or looks, or which must be taken to reach a destination. b (in *pl.*) guidance on how to reach a destination. c the point to or from which a person or thing moves or looks. 4 the tendency or scope of a theme, subject, or inquiry. □ **directionless** *adj.* [ME f. F *direction* or L *directio* (as DIRECT)]

directional /daɪˈrekʃən(ə)l, dɪ-/ *adj.* 1 of or indicating direction. 2 *Electronics* a concerned with the transmission of radio or sound waves in a particular direction. b (of equipment) designed to receive radio or sound waves most effectively from a particular direction or directions and not others. □ **directionality** /-ˈnælɪtɪ/ *n.* **directionally** *adv.*

directive /daɪ'rektɪv, dɪ-/ n. & adj. —n. a general instruction from one in authority. —adj. serving to direct. [ME f. med.L *directivus* (as DIRECT)]

directly /daɪ'rektlɪ, dɪ-/ adv. & conj. —adv. 1 **a** at once; without delay. **b** presently, shortly. 2 exactly, immediately (*directly opposite*; *directly after lunch*). 3 in a direct manner. —conj. colloq. as soon as (*will tell you directly they come*).

director /daɪ'rektə(r), dɪ-/ n. 1 a person who directs or controls something. 2 a member of the managing board of a commercial company. 3 a person who directs a film etc., esp. professionally. 4 esp. US = CONDUCTOR 1. □ **director-general** the chief executive of a large (esp. public) organization. **director of public prosecutions** Brit. = *public prosecutor*. □ **directorial** /-'tɔːrɪəl/ adj. **directorship** n. (esp. in sense 2). [AF *directorium* f. LL *director* governor (as DIRECT)]

directorate /daɪ'rektərət, dɪ-/ n. 1 a board of directors. 2 the office of director.

directory /daɪ'rektərɪ, dɪ-/ n. (pl. **-ies**) a book listing alphabetically or thematically a particular group of individuals (e.g. telephone subscribers) or organizations with various details. [LL *directorium* (as DIRECT)]

direful /'daɪə,fʊl/ adj. literary terrible, dreadful. □ **direfully** adv. [DIRE + -FUL]

dirge n. 1 a lament for the dead, esp. forming part of a funeral service. 2 any mournful song or lament. □ **dirgeful** adj. [ME f. L *dirige* (imper.) direct, the first word in the Latin antiphon (from Ps. 5:8) in the Matins part of the Office for the Dead]

dirigible /'dɪrɪdʒɪb(ə)l, dɪ'rɪdʒ-/ adj. & n. —adj. capable of being guided. —n. a dirigible balloon or airship. [L *dirigere* arrange, direct: see DIRECT]

dirk n. a long dagger, esp. as formerly worn by Scottish Highlanders. [17th-c. *durk*, of unkn. orig.]

dirndl /'dɜː:nd(ə)l/ n. 1 a woman's dress styled in imitation of Alpine peasant costume, with close-fitting bodice, tight waistband, and full skirt. 2 a full skirt of this kind. [G dial., dimin. of *Dirne* girl]

dirt n. 1 unclean matter that soils. 2 **a** earth, soil. **b** earth, cinders, etc., used to make a surface for a road etc. (usu. *attrib.*: *dirt track*). 3 foul or malicious words or talk. 4 excrement. 5 a dirty condition. 6 a person or thing considered worthless. □ **dirt bike** a motor cycle designed for use on unmade roads and tracks, esp. in scrambling. **dirt cheap** colloq. extremely cheap. **dirt-track** a course made of rolled cinders, soil, etc., for motor-cycle racing or flat racing. **do a person dirt** sl. harm or injure a person's reputation maliciously. **treat like dirt** treat (a person) contemptuously; abuse. [ME f. ON *drit* excrement]

dirty /dɜː:tɪ/ adj., adv., & v. —adj. (**dirtier, dirtiest**) 1 soiled, unclean. 2 causing one to become dirty (*a dirty job*). 3 sordid, lewd; morally illicit or questionable (*dirty joke*). 4 unpleasant, nasty. 5 dishonest, dishonourable, unfair (*dirty play*). 6 (of weather) rough, squally. 7 (of a colour) not pure or clear, dingy. —adv. sl. (with adjectives expressing magnitude) very (*a dirty great diamond*). —v.tr. & intr. (**-ies, -ied**) make or become dirty. □ **dirty linen** (or **washing**) colloq. intimate secrets, esp. of a scandalous nature. **dirty look** colloq. a look of disapproval,

anger, or disgust. **dirty trick 1** a dishonourable and deceitful act. 2 (in *pl.*) underhand political activity, esp. to discredit an opponent. **dirty weekend** colloq. a weekend spent clandestinely with a lover. **dirty word 1** an offensive or indecent word. 2 a word for something which is disapproved of (*profit is a dirty word*). **dirty work** dishonourable or illegal activity, esp. done clandestinely. **do the dirty on** colloq. play a mean trick on. □ **dirtily** adv. **dirtiness** n.

dis- /dɪs/ prefix forming nouns, adjectives, and verbs: 1 expressing negation (*dishonest*). 2 indicating reversal or absence of an action or state (*disengage*; *disbelieve*). 3 indicating removal of a thing or quality (*dismember*; *disable*). 4 indicating separation (*distinguish*; *dispose*). 5 indicating completeness or intensification of the action (*disembowel*; *disgruntled*). 6 indicating expulsion from (*disbar*). [L *dis-*, sometimes through OF *des-*]

disability /,dɪsə'bɪlɪtɪ/ n. (pl. **-ies**) 1 physical incapacity, either congenital or caused by injury, disease, etc. 2 a lack of some asset, quality, or attribute, that prevents one's doing something. 3 a legal disqualification.

disable /dɪs'eɪb(ə)l/ v.tr. 1 render unable to function; deprive of an ability. 2 (often as **disabled** adj.) deprive of or reduce the power of to walk or do other normal activities. □ **disablement** n.

disabuse /,dɪsə'bjuːz/ v.tr. 1 (foll. by *of*) free from a mistaken idea. 2 disillusion, undeceive.

disaccord /,dɪsə'kɔːd/ n. & v. —n. disagreement, disharmony. —v.intr. (usu. foll. by *with*) disagree; be at odds. [ME f. F *désaccorder* (as ACCORD)]

disadvantage /,dɪsəd'vɑːntɪdʒ/ n. & v. —n. 1 an unfavourable circumstance or condition. 2 damage to one's interest or reputation. —v.tr. cause disadvantage to. □ **at a disadvantage** in an unfavourable position or aspect. [ME f. OF *desavantage*: see ADVANTAGE]

disadvantaged /,dɪsəd'vɑːntɪdʒd/ adj. placed in unfavourable circumstances (esp. of a person lacking the normal social opportunities).

disadvantageous /dɪsˌædvən'teɪdʒəs/ adj. 1 involving disadvantage or discredit. 2 derogatory. □ **disadvantageously** adv.

disaffected /,dɪsə'fektɪd/ adj. 1 disloyal, esp. to one's superiors. 2 estranged; no longer friendly; discontented. □ **disaffectedly** adv. [past part. of *disaffect* (v.), orig. = dislike, disorder (as DIS-, AFFECT)]

disaffection /,dɪsə'fekʃ(ə)n/ n. 1 disloyalty. 2 political discontent.

disaffiliate /,dɪsə'fɪlɪ,eɪt/ v. 1 tr. end the affiliation of. 2 intr. end one's affiliation. 3 tr. & intr. detach. □ **disaffiliation** /-'eɪʃ(ə)n/ n.

disafforest /,dɪsə'fɒrɪst/ v.tr. Brit. clear of forests or trees. □ **disafforestation** /-'steɪʃ(ə)n/ n. [ME f. AL *disafforestare* (as DIS-, AFFOREST)]

disagree /,dɪsə'griː/ v.intr. (**-agrees, -agreed, -agreeing**) (often foll. by *with*) 1 hold a different opinion. 2 quarrel. 3 (of factors or circumstances) not correspond. 4 have an adverse effect upon (a person's health, digestion, etc.). □ **disagreement** n. [ME f. OF *desagreer* (as DIS-, AGREE)]

disagreeable /,dɪsə'griːəb(ə)l/ adj. 1 unpleasant, not to one's liking. 2 quarrelsome; rude or bad-tempered. □ **disagreeableness** n. **disagreeably** adv. [ME f. OF *desagreable* (as DIS-, AGREEABLE)]

disallow /ˌdɪsəˈlaʊ/ v.tr. refuse to allow or accept as valid; prohibit. □ **disallowance** n. [ME f. OF desalouer (as DIS-, ALLOW)]

disappear /ˌdɪsəˈpɪə(r)/ v.intr. **1** cease to be visible; pass from sight. **2** cease to exist or be in circulation or use. □ **disappearance** n.

disappoint /ˌdɪsəˈpɔɪnt/ v.tr. **1** (also absol.) fail to fulfil a desire or expectation of (a person). **2** frustrate (hopes etc.); cause the failure of (a plan etc.). □ **be disappointed** (foll. by with, at, in, or to + infin., or that + clause) fail to have one's expectation etc. fulfilled in some regard (was disappointed with you; am disappointed to be last). □ **disappointedly** adv. **disappointing** adj. **disappointingly** adv. [ME f. F désappointer (as DIS-, APPOINT)]

disappointment /ˌdɪsəˈpɔɪntmənt/ n. **1** an event, thing, or person that disappoints. **2** a feeling of distress, vexation, etc., resulting from this (I cannot hide my disappointment).

disapprobation /dɪsˌæprəˈbeɪʃ(ə)n/ n. strong (esp. moral) disapproval.

disapprove /ˌdɪsəˈpruːv/ v. **1** intr. (usu. foll. by of) have or express an unfavourable opinion. **2** tr. be displeased with. □ **disapproval** n. **disapprover** n. **disapproving** adj. **disapprovingly** adv.

disarm /dɪsˈɑːm/ v. **1** tr. take weapons away from (a person, State, etc.) (often foll. by of: were disarmed of their rifles). **2** intr. (of a State etc.) disband or reduce its armed forces. **3** tr. remove the fuse from (a bomb etc.). **4** tr. deprive of the power to injure. **5** tr. pacify or allay the hostility or suspicions of; mollify; placate. □ **disarmer** n. **disarming** adj. (esp. in sense 5). **disarmingly** adv. [ME f. OF desarmer (as DIS-, ARM²)]

disarmament /dɪsˈɑːməmənt/ n. the reduction by a State of its military forces and weapons.

disarrange /ˌdɪsəˈreɪndʒ/ v.tr. bring into disorder. □ **disarrangement** n.

disarray /ˌdɪsəˈreɪ/ n. & v. —n. (often prec. by in, into) disorder, confusion (esp. among people). —v.tr. throw into disorder.

disassemble /ˌdɪsəˈsemb(ə)l/ v.tr. take (a machine etc.) to pieces. □ **disassembly** n.

disassociate /ˌdɪsəˈsəʊʃɪˌeɪt, -sɪˌeɪt/ v.tr. & intr. = DISSOCIATE. □ **disassociation** /-ˈeɪʃ(ə)n/ n.

disaster /dɪˈzɑːstə(r)/ n. **1** a great or sudden misfortune. **2** a complete failure. **b** a person or enterprise ending in failure. □ **disastrous** adj. **disastrously** adv. [orig. 'unfavourable aspect of a star', f. F désastre or It. disastro (as DIS-, astro f. L astrum star)]

disavow /ˌdɪsəˈvaʊ/ v.tr. disclaim knowledge of, responsibility for, or belief in. □ **disavowal** n. [ME f. OF desavouer (as DIS-, AVOW)]

disband /dɪsˈbænd/ v. **1** intr. (of an organized group etc.) cease to work or act together; disperse. **2** tr. cause (such a group) to disband. □ **disbandment** n. [obs. F desbander (as DIS-, ON band bond)]

disbar /dɪsˈbɑː(r)/ v.tr. (**disbarred**, **disbarring**) deprive (a barrister) of the right to practise; expel from the Bar. □ **disbarment** n.

disbelieve /ˌdɪsbɪˈliːv/ v. **1** tr. be unable or unwilling to believe (a person or statement). **2** intr. have no faith. □ **disbelief** n. **disbeliever** n. **disbelievingly** adv.

disbud /dɪsˈbʌd/ v.tr. (**disbudded**, **disbudding**) remove (esp. superfluous) buds from.

disburden /dɪsˈbɜːd(ə)n/ v.tr. **1** relieve (a person, one's mind, etc.) of a burden (often foll. by of: was disburdened of all worries). **2** get rid of, discharge (a duty, anxiety, etc.).

disburse /dɪsˈbɜːs/ v. **1** tr. expend (money). **2** tr. defray (a cost). **3** intr. pay money. □ **disbursal** n. **disbursement** n. **disburser** n. [OF desbourser (as DIS-, BOURSE)]

disc n. (also **disk** esp. US and in sense 4) **1 a** a flat thin circular object. **b** a round flat or apparently flat surface (the sun's disc). **c** a mark of this shape. **2** a layer of cartilage between vertebrae. **3** a gramophone record. **4 a** (usu. **disk**; in full **magnetic disk**) a computer storage device consisting of several flat circular magnetically coated plates formed into a rotatable disc. **b** (in full **optical disc**) a smooth nonmagnetic disc with large storage capacity for data recorded and read by laser. □ **disc brake** a brake employing the friction of pads against a disc. **disk drive** Computing a mechanism for rotating a disk and reading or writing data from or to it. **disc jockey** the presenter of a selection of gramophone records of popular music, esp. in a broadcast. [F disque or L discus: see DISCUS]

discard v. & n. —v.tr. /dɪsˈkɑːd/ reject or get rid of as unwanted or superfluous. —n. /ˈdɪskɑːd/ a discarded item. □ **discardable** /-ˈkɑːdəb(ə)l/ adj. [DIS- + CARD¹]

discern /dɪˈsɜːn/ v.tr. **1** perceive clearly with the mind or the senses. **2** make out by thought or by gazing, listening, etc. □ **discerner** n. **discernible** adj. **discernibly** adv. [ME f. OF discerner f. L (as DIS-, cernere cret- separate)]

discerning /dɪˈsɜːnɪŋ/ adj. having or showing good judgement or insight. □ **discerningly** adv.

discernment /dɪˈsɜːnmənt/ n. good judgement or insight.

discharge v. & n. —v. /dɪsˈtʃɑːdʒ/ **1** tr. **a** let go, release, esp. from a duty, commitment, or period of confinement. **b** relieve (a bankrupt) of residual liability. **2** tr. dismiss from office, employment, army commission, etc. **3** tr. **a** fire (a gun etc.). **b** (of a gun etc.) fire (a bullet etc.). **4 a** tr. (also absol.) pour out or cause to pour out (pus, liquid, etc.) (the wound was discharging). **b** tr. throw; eject. **c** intr. (foll. by into) (of a river etc.) flow into (esp. the sea). **5** tr. **a** carry out, perform (a duty or obligation). **b** relieve oneself of (a financial commitment) (discharged his debt). **6** tr. Law cancel (an order of court). **7** tr. Physics release an electrical charge from. **8** tr. **a** relieve (a ship etc.) of its cargo. **b** unload (a cargo) from a ship. —n. /ˈdɪstʃɑːdʒ, dɪsˈtʃɑːdʒ/ **1** the act or an instance of discharging; the process of being discharged. **2** a dismissal, esp. from the armed services. **3 a** a release, exemption, acquittal, etc. **b** a written certificate of release etc. **4** an act of firing a gun etc. **5 a** an emission (of pus, liquid, etc.). **b** the liquid or matter so discharged. **6** (usu. foll. by of) **a** the payment (of a debt). **b** the performance (of a duty etc.). **7** Physics **a** the release of a quantity of electric charge from an object. **b** a flow of electricity through the air or other gas esp. when accompanied by the emission of light. **8** the unloading (of a ship or a cargo). □ **dischargeable** adj. **discharger** n. (in sense 7 of v.). [ME f. OF descharger (as DIS-, CHARGE)]

disciple /dɪˈsaɪp(ə)l/ n. **1** a follower or pupil of a leader, teacher, philosophy, etc. (*a disciple of Zen Buddhism*). **2** any early believer in Christ, esp. one of the twelve Apostles. □ **discipleship** n.

discipular /dɪˈsɪpjʊlə(r)/ adj. [OE *discipul* f. L *discipulus* f. *discere* learn]

disciplinarian /ˌdɪsɪplɪˈneərɪən/ n. a person who upholds or practises firm discipline (*a strict disciplinarian*).

disciplinary /ˈdɪsɪplɪnərɪ, -ˈplɪnərɪ/ adj. of, promoting, or enforcing discipline. [med.L *disciplinarius* (as DISCIPLINE)]

discipline /ˈdɪsɪplɪn/ n. & v. —n. **1 a** control or order exercised over people or animals, esp. children, prisoners, military personnel, church members, etc. **b** the system of rules used to maintain this control. **c** the behaviour of groups subjected to such rules (*poor discipline in the ranks*). **2** mental, moral, or physical training. **3** a branch of instruction or learning. **4** punishment. —v.tr. **1** punish, chastise. **2** bring under control by training in obedience; drill. □ **disciplinable** adj. **disciplinal** /ˌdɪsɪˈplaɪn(ə)l, ˈdɪsɪplɪn(ə)l/ adj. [ME f. OF *discipliner* or LL & med.L *disciplinare*, *disciplina* f. *discipulus* DISCIPLE]

disclaim /dɪsˈkleɪm/ v.tr. **1** deny or disown (*disclaim all responsibility*). **2** (often *absol.*) Law renounce a legal claim to (property etc.). [ME f. AF *desclaim-* stressed stem of *desclamer* (as DIS-, CLAIM)]

disclaimer /dɪsˈkleɪmə(r)/ n. a renunciation or disavowal, esp. of responsibility. [ME f. AF (= DISCLAIM as noun)]

disclose /dɪsˈkləʊz/ v.tr. **1** make known; reveal (*disclosed the truth*). **2** remove the cover from; expose to view. □ **discloser** n. [ME f. OF *desclos-* stem of *desclore* f. Gallo-Roman (as DIS-, CLOSE²)]

disclosure /dɪsˈkləʊʒə(r)/ n. **1** the act or an instance of disclosing; the process of being disclosed. **2** something disclosed; a revelation. [DISCLOSE + -URE after *closure*]

disco /ˈdɪskəʊ/ n. & v. colloq. —n. (pl. **-os**) = DISCOTHÈQUE. —v.intr. (**-oes**, **-oed**) attend a discothèque. [abbr.]

discography /dɪsˈkɒɡrəfɪ/ n. (pl. **-ies**) **1** a descriptive catalogue of gramophone records, esp. of a particular performer or composer. **2** the study of gramophone records. □ **discographer** n. [DISC f. DISCO + -GRAPHY after *biography*]

discoid /ˈdɪskɔɪd/ adj. disc-shaped. [Gk *diskoeidēs* (as DISCUS, -OID)]

discolour /dɪsˈkʌlə(r)/ v.tr. & intr. (US **discolor**) spoil or cause to spoil the colour of; stain; tarnish. □ **discoloration** /-ˈreɪʃ(ə)n/ n. (also **discolouration**). [ME f. OF *descolorer* or med.L *discolorare* (as DIS-, COLOUR)]

discombobulate /ˌdɪskəmˈbɒbjʊˌleɪt/ v.tr. US joc. disturb; disconcert. [prob. based on *discompose* or *discomfit*]

discomfit /dɪsˈkʌmfɪt/ v.tr. (**discomfited**, **discomfiting**) **1** disconcert or baffle. **2** thwart. □ **discomfiture** n. [ME f. OF *disconfit* f. OF past part. of *desconfire* f. Rmc (as DIS-, L *conficere* put together: see CONFECTION)]

■ **Usage** This word is sometimes confused with *discomfort*.

discomfort /dɪsˈkʌmfət/ n. & v. —n. **1 a** a lack of ease; slight pain (*tight collar caused discomfort*). **b** mental uneasiness (*his presence caused her discomfort*). **2** a lack of comfort. —v.tr. make uneasy. [ME f. OF *desconfort(er)* (as DIS-, COMFORT)]

■ **Usage** As a verb, this word is sometimes confused with *discomfit*.

discommode /ˌdɪskəˈməʊd/ v.tr. inconvenience (a person etc.). □ **discommodious** adj. [obs. F *discommoder* var. of *incommoder* (as DIS-, INCOMMODE)]

discompose /ˌdɪskəmˈpəʊz/ v.tr. disturb the composure of; agitate; disturb. □ **discomposure** /-ˈpəʊʒə(r)/ n.

disconcert /ˌdɪskənˈsɜːt/ v.tr. **1** disturb the composure of; agitate; fluster (*disconcerted by his expression*). **2** spoil or upset (plans etc.). □ **disconcertedly** adv. **disconcerting** adj. **disconcertingly** adv. **disconcertion** /-ˈsɜːʃ(ə)n/ n. **disconcertment** n. [obs. F *desconcerter* (as DIS-, CONCERT)]

disconnect /ˌdɪskəˈnekt/ v.tr. **1** (often foll. by *from*) break the connection of (things, ideas, etc.). **2** put (an electrical device) out of action by disconnecting the parts, esp. by pulling out the plug.

disconnected /ˌdɪskəˈnektɪd/ adj. (of speech, writing, argument, etc.) incoherent and illogical. □ **disconnectedly** adv. **disconnectedness** n.

disconnection /ˌdɪskəˈnekʃ(ə)n/ n. (also **disconnexion**) the act or an instance of disconnecting; the state of being disconnected.

disconsolate /dɪsˈkɒnsələt/ adj. **1** forlorn or inconsolable. **2** unhappy or disappointed. □ **disconsolately** adv. **disconsolateness** n. **disconsolation** /-ˈleɪʃ(ə)n/ n. [ME f. med.L *disconsolatus* (as DIS-, *consolatus* past part. of L *consolari* console)]

discontent /ˌdɪskənˈtent/ n., adj., & v. —n. lack of contentment; restlessness, dissatisfaction. —adj. dissatisfied (*was discontent with his lot*). —v.tr. (esp. as **discontented** adj.) make dissatisfied. □ **discontentedly** adv. **discontentedness** n. **discontentment** n.

discontinue /ˌdɪskənˈtɪnjuː/ v. (**-continues**, **-continued**, **-continuing**) **1** intr. & tr. cease or cause to cease to exist or be made (*a discontinued line*). **2** tr. give up, cease from (*discontinued his visits*). **3** tr. cease taking or paying (a newspaper, a subscription, etc.). □ **discontinuance** n. **discontinuation** /-ˈeɪʃ(ə)n/ n. [ME f. OF *discontinuer* f. med.L *discontinuare* (as DIS-, CONTINUE)]

discontinuous /ˌdɪskənˈtɪnjʊəs/ adj. lacking continuity in space or time; intermittent. □ **discontinuity** /-ˌkɒntɪˈnjuːɪtɪ/ n. **discontinuously** adv. [med.L *discontinuus* (as DIS-, CONTINUOUS)]

discord n. /ˈdɪskɔːd/ **1** disagreement; strife. **2** harsh clashing noise; clangour. **3** Mus. **a** a lack of harmony between notes sounding together. **b** an unpleasing or unfinished chord needing to be completed by another. [ME f. OF *descord* f. L *discordare* f. *discors* discordant (as DIS-, *cor cord-* heart)]

discordant /dɪsˈkɔːd(ə)nt/ adj. (usu. foll. by *to*, *from*, *with*) **1** disagreeing; at variance. **2** (of sounds) not in harmony; dissonant. □ **discordance** n. **discordancy** n. **discordantly** adv. [ME f. OF, part. of *discorder*: see DISCORD]

discothèque /ˈdɪskəˌtek/ n. **1** a club etc. for dancing to recorded popular music. **2 a** the professional lighting and sound equipment used at a discothèque. **b** a business that provides this. **3** a party with dancing to popular music, esp. using such equipment. [F, = record-library]

discount n. & v. —n. /ˈdɪskaʊnt/ **1** a deduction from a bill or amount due. **2** a deduction from the amount of a bill of exchange etc. by a person who gives value for it before it is due. **3** the act or an instance of discounting. —v.tr. /dɪˈskaʊnt/ **1** disregard as being unreliable or unimportant (discounted his story). **2** reduce the effect of (an event etc.) by previous action. **3** detract from; lessen; deduct (esp. an amount from a bill etc.). **4** give or get the present worth of (a bill not yet due). □ **at a discount 1** below the nominal or usual price. **2** not in demand; depreciated. □ **discountable** /-ˈskaʊntəb(ə)l/ adj. **discounter** /-ˈskaʊntə(r)/ n. [obs. F descompte, -conte, descompter or It. (di)scontare (as DIS-, COUNT¹)]

discountenance /dɪˈskaʊntɪnəns/ v.tr. **1** (esp. in passive) disconcert. **2** refuse to countenance; show disapproval of.

discourage /dɪˈskʌrɪdʒ/ v.tr. **1** deprive of courage, confidence, or energy. **2** (usu. foll. by from) dissuade (discouraged him from going). **3** show disapproval of (smoking is discouraged). □ **discouragement** n. **discouragingly** adv. [ME f. OF descouragier (as DIS-, COURAGE)]

discourse n. & v. —n. /ˈdɪskɔːs, -ˈskɔːs/ **1** literary **a** conversation; talk. **b** a dissertation or treatise on an academic subject. **c** a lecture or sermon. **2** Linguistics a connected series of utterances; a text. —v. /dɪˈskɔːs/ **1** intr. talk; converse. **2** intr. (usu. foll. by of, on, upon) speak or write learnedly or at length (on a subject). [ME f. L discursus (as DIS-, COURSE): (v.) after F discourir]

discourteous /dɪsˈkɜːtɪəs/ adj. impolite; rude. □ **discourteously** adv. **discourteousness** n.

discourtesy /dɪsˈkɜːtəsɪ/ n. (pl. -ies) **1** bad manners; rudeness. **2** an impolite act or remark.

discover /dɪˈskʌvə(r)/ v.tr. **1** (often foll. by that + clause) **a** find out or become aware of, whether by research or searching or by chance. **b** be the first to find or find out (who discovered America?). **2** (in show business) find and promote as a new singer, actor, etc. □ **discoverable** adj. **discoverer** n. [ME f. OF descovrir f. LL discooperire (as DIS-, COVER)]

discovery /dɪˈskʌvərɪ/ n. (pl. -ies) **1 a** the act or process of discovering or being discovered. **b** an instance of this (the discovery of a new planet). **2** a person or thing discovered. [DISCOVER after recover, recovery]

discredit /dɪsˈkredɪt/ n. & v. —n. **1** harm to reputation (brought discredit on the enterprise). **2** a person or thing causing this (he is a discredit to his family). **3** lack of credibility; doubt (throws discredit on her story). —v.tr. (-credited, -crediting) **1** harm the good reputation of. **2** cause to be disbelieved. **3** refuse to believe.

discreditable /dɪsˈkredɪtəb(ə)l/ adj. bringing discredit; shameful. □ **discreditably** adv.

discreet /dɪˈskriːt/ adj. (**discreeter, discreetest**) **1 a** circumspect in speech or action, esp. to avoid social disgrace or embarrassment. **b** tactful; trustworthy. **2** unobtrusive (a discreet touch of rouge). □ **discreetly** adv. **discreetness** n. [ME f. OF discret -ete f. L discretus separate (as DIS-, cretus past part. of cernere sift), with LL sense f. its derivative discretio discernment]

discrepancy /dɪsˈkrepənsɪ/ n. (pl. -ies) **1** difference; failure to correspond; inconsistency. **2** an

instance of this. □ **discrepant** adj. [L discrepare be discordant (as DIS-, crepare creak)]

discrete /dɪˈskriːt/ adj. individually distinct; separate, discontinuous. □ **discretely** adv. **discreteness** n. [ME f. L discretus: see DISCREET]

discretion /dɪˈskreʃ(ə)n/ n. **1** being discreet; discreet behaviour (treats confidences with discretion). **2** prudence; self-preservation. **3** the freedom to act and think as one wishes, usu. within legal limits (it is within his discretion to leave). **4** Law a court's freedom to decide a sentence etc. □ **years** (or **age**) **of discretion** the esp. legal age at which a person is able to manage his or her own affairs. □ **discretionary** adj. [ME f. OF f. L discretio -onis (as DISCREET)]

discriminate /dɪˈskrɪmɪˌneɪt/ v. **1** intr. (often foll. by between) make or see a distinction; differentiate (cannot discriminate between right and wrong). **2** intr. make a distinction, esp. unjustly and on the basis of race, colour, or sex. **3** intr. (foll. by against) select for unfavourable treatment. **4** tr. (usu. foll. by from) make or see or constitute a difference in or between (many things discriminate one person from another). **5** intr. observe distinctions carefully; have good judgement. **6** tr. mark as distinctive; be a distinguishing feature of. □ **discriminately** /-nətlɪ/ adv. **discriminative** /-nətɪv/ adj. **discriminator** n. **discriminatory** /-nətərɪ/ adj. [L discriminare f. discrimen -minis distinction f. discernere DISCERN]

discriminating /dɪˈskrɪmɪˌneɪtɪŋ/ adj. **1** able to discern, esp. distinctions. **2** having good taste. □ **discriminatingly** adv.

discrimination /dɪˌskrɪmɪˈneɪʃ(ə)n/ n. **1** unfavourable treatment based on prejudice, esp. regarding race, colour, or sex. **2** good taste or judgement in artistic matters etc. **3** the power of discriminating or observing differences. **4** a distinction made with the mind or in action.

discursive /dɪˈskɜːsɪv/ adj. rambling or digressive. □ **discursively** adv. **discursiveness** n. [med.L discursivus f. L discurrere discurs- (as DIS-, currere run)]

discus /ˈdɪskəs/ n. (pl. **discuses**) **1** a heavy thick-centred disc thrown in ancient Greek games. **2** a similar disc thrown in modern athletic field events. [L f. Gk diskos]

discuss /dɪˈskʌs/ v.tr. **1** hold a conversation about (discussed their holidays). **2** examine by argument, esp. written; debate. □ **discussable** adj. **discussant** n. **discusser** n. **discussible** adj. [ME f. L discutere discuss- disperse (as DIS-, quatere shake)]

discussion /dɪˈskʌʃ(ə)n/ n. **1** a conversation, esp. on specific subjects; a debate (had a discussion about what they should do). **2** an examination by argument, written or spoken. [ME f. OF f. LL discussio -onis (as DISCUSS)]

disdain /dɪsˈdeɪn/ n. & v. —n. scorn; contempt. —v.tr. **1** regard with disdain. **2** think oneself superior to; reject (disdained his offer; disdained to enter; disdained answering). [ME f. OF desdeign(ier) ult. f. L dedignari (as DE-, dignari f. dignus worthy)]

disdainful /dɪsˈdeɪnfʊl/ adj. showing disdain or contempt. □ **disdainfully** adv. **disdainfulness** n.

disease /dɪˈziːz/ n. **1** an unhealthy condition of the body (or a part of it) or the mind; illness, sickness. **2** a corresponding physical condition of plants. **3** a particular kind of disease with special symptoms or location. [ME f. OF desaise]

diseased /dɪˈziːzd/ adj. **1** affected with disease. **2** abnormal, disordered. [ME, past part. of *disease* (v.) f. OF *desaisier* (as DISEASE)]

disembark /ˌdɪsɪmˈbɑːk/ v.tr. & intr. put or go ashore or land from a ship or an aircraft. □ **disembarkation** /-ˈkeɪʃ(ə)n/ n. [F *désembarquer* (as DIS-, EMBARK)]

disembarrass /ˌdɪsɪmˈbærəs/ v.tr. **1** (usu. foll. by *of*) relieve (of a load etc.). **2** free from embarrassment. □ **disembarrassment** n.

disembody /ˌdɪsɪmˈbɒdɪ/ v.tr. (**-ies**, **-ied**) **1** separate or free (esp. the soul) from the body or a concrete form (*disembodied spirit*). **2** *archaic* disband (troops). □ **disembodiment** n.

disembowel /ˌdɪsɪmˈbaʊəl/ v.tr. (**-embowelled**, **-embowelling**; US **-emboweled**, **-emboweling**) remove the bowels or entrails of. □ **disembowelment** n.

disenchant /ˌdɪsɪnˈtʃɑːnt/ v.tr. free from enchantment; disillusion. □ **disenchantingly** adv. **disenchantment** n. [F *désenchanter* (as DIS-, ENCHANT)]

disencumber /ˌdɪsɪnˈkʌmbə(r)/ v.tr. free from encumbrance.

disenfranchise /ˌdɪsɪnˈfræntʃaɪz/ v.tr. (also **disfranchise** /dɪsˈfræntʃaɪz/) **1 a** deprive (a person) of the right to vote. **b** deprive (a place) of the right to send a representative to parliament. **2** deprive (a person) of rights as a citizen or of a franchise held. □ **disenfranchisement** n.

disengage /ˌdɪsɪnˈɡeɪdʒ/ v. **1** tr. detach, free, loosen, or separate (parts etc.) (*disengaged the clutch*). **2** tr. Mil. remove (troops) from a battle or a battle area. **3** intr. become detached. **4** intr. (as **disengaged** adj.) a unoccupied; free; vacant. **b** uncommitted, esp. politically.

disengagement /ˌdɪsɪnˈɡeɪdʒmənt/ n. **1 a** the act of disengaging. **b** an instance of this. **2** freedom from ties; detachment.

disentangle /ˌdɪsɪnˈtæŋɡ(ə)l/ v. **1** tr. **a** unravel, untwist. **b** free from complications; extricate (*disentangled her from the difficulty*). **2** intr. become disentangled. □ **disentanglement** n.

disestablish /ˌdɪsɪˈstæblɪʃ/ v.tr. **1** deprive (a Church) of State support. **2** depose from an official position. **3** terminate the establishment of. □ **disestablishment** n.

disfavour /dɪsˈfeɪvə(r)/ n. & v. (US **disfavor**) —n. **1** disapproval or dislike. **2** the state of being disliked (*fell into disfavour*). —v.tr. regard or treat with disfavour.

disfigure /dɪsˈfɪɡə(r)/ v.tr. spoil the beauty of; deform; deface. □ **disfigurement** n. [ME f. OF *desfigurer* f. Rmc (as DIS-, FIGURE)]

disforest /dɪsˈfɒrɪst/ v.tr. Brit. = DISAFFOREST. □ **disforestation** /-ˈsteɪʃ(ə)n/ n.

disfranchise var. of DISENFRANCHISE.

disgorge /dɪsˈɡɔːdʒ/ v.tr. **1** eject from the throat or stomach. **2** pour forth, discharge (contents, ill-gotten gains, etc.). □ **disgorgement** n. [ME f. OF *desgorger* (as DIS-, GORGE)]

disgrace /dɪsˈɡreɪs/ n. & v. —n. **1** the loss of reputation; shame; ignominy (*brought disgrace on his family*). **2** a dishonourable, inefficient, or shameful person, thing, state of affairs, etc. (*the bus service is a disgrace*). —v.tr. **1** bring shame or discredit on; be a disgrace to. **2** degrade from a position of honour; dismiss from favour. □ **in disgrace** having lost respect or reputation; out of favour. [F *disgrâce*, *disgracier* f. It. *disgrazia*, *disgraziare* (as DIS-, GRACE)]

disgraceful /dɪsˈɡreɪsfʊl/ adj. shameful; dishonourable; degrading. □ **disgracefully** adv.

disgruntled /dɪsˈɡrʌnt(ə)ld/ adj. discontented; moody; sulky. □ **disgruntlement** n. [DIS- + *gruntle* obs. frequent. of GRUNT]

disguise /dɪsˈɡaɪz/ v. & n. —v.tr. **1** (often foll. by *as*) alter the appearance, sound, smell, etc., of so as to conceal the identity; make unrecognizable. **2** misrepresent or cover up (*disguised their intentions*). —n. **1 a** a costume, false beard, make-up, etc., used to alter the appearance so as to conceal or deceive. **b** any action, manner, etc., used for deception. **2 a** the act or practice of disguising; the concealment of reality. **b** an instance of this. □ **in disguise 1** wearing a concealing costume etc. **2** appearing to be the opposite (*a blessing in disguise*). □ **disguisement** n. [ME f. OF *desguis(i)er* (as DIS-, GUISE)]

disgust /dɪsˈɡʌst/ n. & v. —n. (usu. foll. by *at, for*) **1** strong aversion; repugnance. **2** indignation. —v.tr. cause disgust in (*their behaviour disgusts me*; *was disgusted to find a slug*). □ **in disgust** as a result of disgust (*left in disgust*). □ **disgustedly** adv. [OF *degoust*, *desgouster*, or It. *disgusto*, *disgustare* (as DIS-, GUSTO)]

disgusting /dɪsˈɡʌstɪŋ/ adj. arousing aversion or indignation (*disgusting behaviour*). □ **disgustingly** adv. **disgustingness** n.

dish n. & v. —n. **1 a** a shallow, usu. flat-bottomed container for cooking or serving food. **b** the food served in a dish (*all the dishes were delicious*). **c** a particular kind of food (*a meat dish*). **2** (in pl.) dirty plates, cutlery, cooking pots, etc. after a meal. **3 a** a dish-shaped receptacle, object, or cavity. **b** = satellite dish. **4** sl. a sexually attractive person. —v.tr. **1** put (food) into a dish ready for serving. **2** colloq. **a** outmanœuvre. **b** Brit. destroy (one's hopes, chances, etc.). **3** make concave or dish-shaped. □ **dish out** sl. distribute, esp. carelessly or indiscriminately. **dish up 1** serve or prepare to serve (food). **2** colloq. seek to present (facts, argument, etc.) attractively. □ **dishful** n. (pl. **-fuls**). **dishlike** adj. [OE *disc* plate, bowl (with Gmc and ON cognates) f. L *discus* DISC]

dishabille var. of DÉSHABILLÉ.

disharmony /dɪsˈhɑːmənɪ/ n. a lack of harmony; discord. □ **disharmonious** /-ˈməʊnɪəs/ adj. **disharmoniously** /-ˈməʊnɪəslɪ/ adv. **disharmonize** /-ˌnaɪz/ v.tr.

dishcloth /ˈdɪʃklɒθ/ n. a usu. open-weave cloth for washing dishes.

dishearten /dɪsˈhɑːt(ə)n/ v.tr. cause to lose courage or confidence; make despondent. □ **dishearteningly** adv. **disheartenment** n.

dishevelled /dɪˈʃev(ə)ld/ adj. (US **disheveled**) (of the hair, a person, etc.) untidy; ruffled; disordered. □ **dishevel** v.tr. (**dishevelled**, **dishevelling**; US **disheveled**, **disheveling**) **dishevelment** n. [ME *dischevelee* f. OF *deschevelé* past part. (as DIS-, *chevel* hair f. L *capillus*)]

dishonest /dɪsˈɒnɪst/ adj. (of a person, act, or statement) fraudulent or insincere. □ **dishonestly** adv. [ME f. OF *deshoneste* (as DIS-, HONEST)]

dishonesty /dɪsˈɒnɪstɪ/ n. (pl. **-ies**) **1 a** a lack of honesty. **b** deceitfulness; fraud. **2** a dishonest or fraudulent act. [ME f. OF *deshon(n)esté* (as DISHONEST)]

dishonour /dɪsˈɒnə(r)/ n. & v. (US **dishonor**) —n. **1** a state of shame or disgrace; discredit. **2**

something that causes dishonour (*a dishonour to his profession*). —*v.tr.* **1** treat without honour or respect. **2** disgrace (*dishonoured his name*). **3** refuse to accept or pay (a cheque or a bill of exchange). [ME f. OF *deshonor, deshonorer* f. med.L *dishonorare* (as DIS-, HONOUR)]

dishonourable /dɪsˈɒnərəb(ə)l/ *adj.* (US **dishonorable**) **1** causing disgrace; ignominious. **2** unprincipled. □ **dishonourableness** *n.* **dishonourably** *adv.*

dishrag /ˈdɪʃræg/ *n.* = DISHCLOTH.

dishwasher /ˈdɪʃˌwɒʃə(r)/ *n.* **1** a machine for automatically washing dishes. **2** a person employed to wash dishes.

dishwater /ˈdɪʃˌwɔːtə(r)/ *n.* water in which dishes have been washed.

dishy /ˈdɪʃɪ/ *adj.* (**dishier, dishiest**) *Brit. colloq.* sexually attractive. [DISH *n.* 4 + -Y¹]

disillusion /ˌdɪsɪˈluːʒ(ə)n, -ˈljuːʒ(ə)n/ *n.* & *v.* —*n.* freedom from illusions; disenchantment. —*v.tr.* rid of illusions; disenchant. □ **disillusionize** *v.tr.* (also **-ise**). **disillusionment** *n.*

disincentive /ˌdɪsɪnˈsentɪv/ *n.* & *adj.* —*n.* **1** something that tends to discourage a particular action etc. **2** *Econ.* a source of discouragement to productivity or progress. —*adj.* tending to discourage.

disinclination /ˌdɪsɪnklɪˈneɪʃ(ə)n/ *n.* (usu. foll. by *for*, or *to* + infin.) the absence of willingness; a reluctance (*a disinclination for work*).

disincline /ˌdɪsɪnˈklaɪn/ *v.tr.* (usu. foll. by *to* + infin. or *for*) make unwilling or reluctant.

disinfect /ˌdɪsɪnˈfekt/ *v.tr.* cleanse (a wound, a room, clothes, etc.) of infection, esp. with a disinfectant. □ **disinfection** *n.* [F *désinfecter* (as DIS-, INFECT)]

disinfectant /ˌdɪsɪnˈfekt(ə)nt/ *n.* & *adj.* —*n.* **1** usu. commercially produced chemical liquid that destroys germs etc. —*adj.* causing disinfection.

disinfest /ˌdɪsɪnˈfest/ *v.tr.* rid (a person, a building, etc.) of vermin, infesting insects, etc. □ **disinfestation** /-ˈsteɪʃ(ə)n/ *n.*

disinflation /ˌdɪsɪnˈfleɪʃ(ə)n/ *n.* *Econ.* a policy designed to counteract inflation without causing deflation. □ **disinflationary** *adj.*

disinformation /ˌdɪsɪnfəˈmeɪʃ(ə)n/ *n.* false information, intended to mislead.

disingenuous /ˌdɪsɪnˈdʒenjʊəs/ *adj.* having secret motives; insincere. □ **disingenuously** *adv.* **disingenuousness** *n.*

disinherit /ˌdɪsɪnˈherɪt/ *v.tr.* (**disinherited, disinheriting**) reject as one's heir; deprive of the right of inheritance. □ **disinheritance** *n.* [ME f. DIS- + INHERIT in obs. sense 'make heir']

disintegrate /dɪsˈɪntɪˌgreɪt/ *v.* **1** *tr.* & *intr.* separate into component parts or fragments. **b** lose or cause to lose cohesion. **2** *intr. colloq.* deteriorate mentally or physically. **3** *intr.* & *tr.* *Physics* undergo or cause to undergo disintegration. □ **disintegrator** *n.*

disintegration /dɪsˌɪntɪˈgreɪʃ(ə)n/ *n.* **1** the act or an instance of disintegrating. **2** *Physics* any process in which a nucleus emits a particle or particles or divides into smaller nuclei.

disinter /ˌdɪsɪnˈtɜː(r)/ *v.tr.* (**disinterred, disinterring**) remove (esp. a corpse) from the ground; unearth; exhume. □ **disinterment** *n.* [F *désenterrer* (as DIS-, INTER)]

disinterest /dɪsˈɪntrɪst/ *n.* **1** impartiality. **2** *disp.* lack of interest; unconcern.

disinterested /dɪsˈɪntrɪstɪd/ *adj.* **1** not influenced by one's own advantage; impartial. **2** *disp.* uninterested. □ **disinterestedly** *adv.* **disinterestedness** *n.* [past part. of *disinterest* (v.) divest of interest]

■ **Usage** Use of this word in sense 2 is common in informal use but widely regarded as incorrect. The use of the noun *disinterest* to mean 'lack of interest' is also objected to but it is rarely used in any other sense and the alternative *uninterest* is rare.

disinvest /ˌdɪsɪnˈvest/ *v.intr.* (foll. by *from*, or *absol.*) reduce or dispose of one's investment (in a place, company, etc.). □ **disinvestment** *n.*

disjoin /dɪsˈdʒɔɪn/ *v.tr.* separate or disunite; part. [ME f. OF *desjoindre* f. L *disjungere* (as DIS-, *jungere junct-* join)]

disjoint /dɪsˈdʒɔɪnt/ *v.tr.* **1** take apart at the joints. **2** (as **disjointed** *adj.*) (esp. of conversation) incoherent; desultory. **3** disturb the working or connection of; dislocate. □ **disjointedly** *adv.* **disjointedness** *n.* [ME f. obs. *disjoint* (adj.) f. past part. of OF *desjoindre* (as DISJOIN)]

disjunction /dɪsˈdʒʌŋkʃ(ə)n/ *n.* **1** the process of disjoining; separation. **2** an instance of this. [ME f. OF *disjunction* or L *disjunctio* (as DISJOIN)]

disjunctive /dɪsˈdʒʌŋktɪv/ *adj.* & *n.* —*adj.* **1** involving separation; disjoining. **2** *Gram.* (esp. of a conjunction) expressing a choice between two words etc. —*n.* *Gram.* a disjunctive conjunction or other word. □ **disjunctively** *adv.* [ME f. L *disjunctivus* (as DISJOIN)]

disk var. of DISC (US & *Computing*).

diskette /dɪˈsket/ *n.* *Computing* = *floppy disk.*

dislike /dɪsˈlaɪk/ *v.* & *n.* —*v.tr.* have an aversion or objection to; not like. —*n.* **1** a feeling of repugnance or not liking. **2** an object of dislike. □ **dislikable** *adj.* (also **dislikeable**).

dislocate /ˈdɪsləˌkeɪt/ *v.tr.* **1** disturb the normal connection of (esp. a joint in the body). **2** disrupt; put out of order. **3** displace. [prob. back-form. f. DISLOCATION]

dislocation /ˌdɪsləˈkeɪʃ(ə)n/ *n.* the act or result of dislocating. [ME f. OF *dislocation* or med.L *dislocatio* f. *dislocare* (as DIS-, *locare* place)]

dislodge /dɪsˈlɒdʒ/ *v.tr.* remove from an established or fixed position. □ **dislodgement** *n.* (also **dislodgment**). [ME f. OF *dislog(i)er* (as DIS-, LODGE)]

disloyal /dɪsˈlɔɪəl/ *adj.* (often foll. by *to*) **1** not loyal; unfaithful. **2** untrue to one's allegiance; treacherous to one's government etc. □ **disloyalist** *n.* **disloyally** *adv.* **disloyalty** *n.* [ME f. OF *desloial* (as DIS-, LOYAL)]

dismal /ˈdɪzm(ə)l/ *adj.* **1** causing or showing gloom; miserable. **2** dreary or sombre. **3** *colloq.* feeble or inept (*a dismal performance*). □ **dismally** *adv.* **dismalness** *n.* [orig. noun = unlucky days: ME f. AF *dis mal* f. med.L *dies mali* two days in each month held to be unpropitious]

dismantle /dɪsˈmænt(ə)l/ *v.tr.* **1** take to pieces; pull down. **2** deprive of defences or equipment. □ **dismantlement** *n.* **dismantler** *n.* [OF *desmanteler* (as DIS-, MANTLE)]

dismay /dɪsˈmeɪ/ *v.* & *n.* —*v.tr.* fill with consternation or anxiety; reduce to despair. —*n.* **1** consternation or anxiety. **2** depression or despair. [ME f. OF *desmaiier* (unrecorded) ult. f. a Gmc root = deprive of power (as DIS-, MAY)]

dismember /dɪsˈmembə(r)/ v.tr. **1** tear or cut the limbs from. **2** partition or divide up (an empire, country, etc.). □ **dismemberment** n. [ME f. OF *desmembrer* f. Rmc (as DIS-, L *membrum* limb)]

dismiss /dɪsˈmɪs/ v. **1 a** tr. send away, cause to leave one's presence, disperse; disband (an assembly or army). **b** intr. (of an assembly etc.) disperse; break ranks. **2** tr. discharge from employment, office, etc., esp. dishonourably. **3** tr. put out of one's thoughts; cease to feel or discuss (*dismissed him from memory*). **4** tr. treat (a subject) summarily (*dismissed his application*). **5** tr. Law refuse further hearing to (a case); send out of court. **6** tr. Cricket put (a batsman or a side) out (*was dismissed for 75 runs*). **7** intr. (in imper.) Mil. a word of command at the end of drilling. □ **dismissal** n. **dismissible** adj. **dismission** n. [ME, orig. as past part. after OF *desmis* f. med.L *dismissus* (as DIS-, L *mittere* miss-send)]

dismissive /dɪsˈmɪsɪv/ adj. tending to dismiss from consideration; disdainful. □ **dismissively** adv. **dismissiveness** n.

dismount /dɪsˈmaʊnt/ v. **1 a** intr. alight from a horse, bicycle, etc. **b** tr. (usu. in passive) throw from a horse, unseat. **2** tr. remove (a thing) from its mounting (esp. a gun from its carriage).

disobedient /ˌdɪsəˈbiːdɪənt/ adj. disobeying; rebellious, rule-breaking. □ **disobedience** n. **disobediently** adv. [ME f. OF *desobedient* (as DIS-, OBEDIENT)]

disobey /ˌdɪsəˈbeɪ/ v.tr. (also absol.) fail or refuse to obey; disregard (orders); break (rules). □ **disobeyer** n. [ME f. OF *desobeir* f. Rmc (as DIS-, OBEY)]

disoblige /ˌdɪsəˈblaɪdʒ/ v.tr. **1** refuse to consider the convenience or wishes of. **2** (as **disobliging** adj.) uncooperative. [F *désobliger* f. Rmc (as DIS-, OBLIGE)]

disorder /dɪsˈɔːdə(r)/ n. & v. —n. **1** a lack of order; confusion. **2** a riot; a commotion. **3** Med. a usu. minor ailment or disease. —v.tr. **1** throw into confusion; disarrange. **2** Med. put out of good health; upset. [ME, alt. after ORDER v. of earlier *disordain* f. OF *desordener* (as DIS-, ORDAIN)]

disorderly /dɪsˈɔːdəlɪ/ adj. **1** untidy; confused. **2** irregular; unruly; riotous. **3** Law contrary to public order or morality. □ **disorderly house** Law a brothel. □ **disorderliness** n.

disorganize /dɪsˈɔːgənaɪz/ v.tr. (also **-ise**) **1** destroy the system or order of; throw into confusion. **2** (as **disorganized** adj.) lacking organization or system. □ **disorganization** /-ˈzeɪʃ(ə)n/ n. [F *désorganiser* (as DIS-, ORGANIZE)]

disorient /dɪsˈɔːrɪənt/ v.tr. = DISORIENTATE. [F *désorienter* (as DIS-, ORIENT v.)]

disorientate /dɪsˈɔːrɪənˌteɪt/ v.tr. **1** confuse (a person) as to his or her whereabouts or bearings. **2** confuse (a person). □ **disorientation** /-ˈteɪʃ(ə)n/ n.

disown /dɪsˈəʊn/ v.tr. **1** refuse to recognize; repudiate; disclaim. **2** renounce one's connection with or allegiance to. □ **disowner** n.

disparage /dɪsˈpærɪdʒ/ v.tr. **1** speak slightingly of; depreciate. **2** bring discredit on. □ **disparagement** n. **disparagingly** adv. [ME f. OF *desparagier* marry unequally (as DIS-, *parage* equality of rank ult. f. L *par* equal)]

disparate /ˈdɪspərət/ adj. essentially different in kind; without comparison or relation. □ **disparately** adv. **disparateness** n. [L *disparatus* separated (as DIS-, *paratus* past part. of *parare* prepare), infl. in sense by L *dispar* unequal]

disparity /dɪsˈpærɪtɪ/ n. (pl. **-ies**) **1** inequality; difference; incongruity. **2** an instance of this. [F *disparité* f. LL *disparitas -tatis* (as DIS-, PARITY)]

dispassionate /dɪsˈpæʃənət/ adj. free from passion; calm; impartial. □ **dispassionately** adv. **dispassionateness** n.

dispatch /dɪsˈpætʃ/ v. & n. (also **despatch**) —v.tr. **1** send off to a destination or for a purpose (*dispatched him with the message*). **2** perform (business, a task, etc.) promptly; finish off. **3** kill, execute (*dispatched him with the revolver*). **4** colloq. eat (food, a meal, etc.) quickly. —n. **1** the act or an instance of sending (a messenger, letter, etc.). **2** the act or an instance of killing; execution. **3 a** an official written message on State or esp. military affairs. **b** a report sent in by a newspaper's correspondent. **4** promptness, efficiency (*done with dispatch*). □ **dispatch-box** (or **-case**) a container for esp. official State or military documents or dispatches. **dispatch-rider** a motor cyclist or rider on horseback carrying military dispatches. □ **dispatcher** n. [It. *dispacciare* or Sp. *despachar* expedite (as DIS-, It. *impacciare* and Sp. *empachar* hinder, of uncert. orig.)]

dispel /dɪsˈpel/ v.tr. (**dispelled, dispelling**) dissipate; disperse; scatter. □ **dispeller** n. [L *dispellere* (as DIS-, *pellere* drive)]

dispensable /dɪsˈpensəb(ə)l/ adj. able to be done without; unnecessary. □ **dispensability** /-ˈbɪlɪtɪ/ n. [med.L *dispensabilis* (as DISPENSE)]

dispensary /dɪsˈpensərɪ/ n. (pl. **-ies**) a place where medicines etc. are dispensed. [med.L *dispensarius* (as DISPENSE)]

dispensation /ˌdɪspenˈseɪʃ(ə)n/ n. **1 a** the act or an instance of dispensing or distributing. **b** something distributed. **2** (usu. foll. by *from*) **a** exemption from a penalty or duty; an instance of this. **b** exemption from a religious observance; an instance of this. **3** a religious or political system obtaining in a nation etc. (*the Christian dispensation*). **4 a** the ordering or management of the world by Providence. **b** a specific example of such ordering (of a community, a person, etc.). □ **dispensational** adj. [ME f. OF *dispensation* or L *dispensatio* (as DISPENSE)]

dispense /dɪsˈpens/ v. **1** tr. distribute; deal out. **2** tr. administer (a sacrament, justice, etc.). **3** tr. make up and give out (medicine etc.) according to a doctor's prescription. **4** intr. (foll. by *with*) **a** do without; render needless. **b** give exemption from (a rule). □ [ME f. OF *despenser* f. L *dispensare* frequent. of *dispendĕre* weigh or pay out (as DIS-, *pendĕre pens-* weigh)]

dispenser /dɪsˈpensə(r)/ n. **1** a person or thing that dispenses something, e.g. medicine, good advice. **2** an automatic machine that dispenses an item or a specific amount of something (e.g. cash).

disperse /dɪsˈpɜːs/ v. **1** intr. & tr. go, send, drive, or distribute in different directions or over a wide area. **2 a** intr. (of people at a meeting etc.) leave and go their various ways. **b** tr. cause to do this. **3** tr. send to or station at separate points. **4** tr. put in circulation; disseminate.

□ **dispersable** *adj.* **dispersal** *n.* **disperser** *n.* **dispersible** *adj.* **dispersive** *adj.* [ME f. L *dispergere dispers-* (as DIS-, *spargere* scatter)]

dispersion /dɪˈspɜːʃ(ə)n/ *n.* **1** the act or an instance of dispersing; the process of being dispersed. **2** *Statistics* the extent to which values of a variable differ from the mean. **3** (**the Dispersion**) the Jews dispersed among the Gentiles after the Captivity in Babylon. [ME f. LL *dispersio* (as DISPERSE), transl. Gk *diaspora*: see DIASPORA]

dispirit /dɪˈspɪrɪt/ *v.tr.* **1** (esp. as **dispiriting** *adj.*) make despondent; discourage. **2** (as **dispirited** *adj.*) dejected; discouraged. □ **dispiritedly** *adv.* **dispiritedness** *n.* **dispiritingly** *adv.*

displace /dɪsˈpleɪs/ *v.tr.* **1** shift from its accustomed place. **2** remove from office. **3** take the place of; oust. □ **displaced person** a person who is forced to leave his or her home country because of war, persecution, etc.; a refugee.

displacement /dɪsˈpleɪsmənt/ *n.* **1 a** the act or an instance of displacing; the process of being displaced. **b** an instance of this. **2** *Physics* the amount of a fluid displaced by a solid floating or immersed in it (*a ship with a displacement of 11,000 tons*). **3** the amount by which a thing is shifted from its place.

display /dɪsˈpleɪ/ *v.* & *n.* —*v.tr.* **1** expose to view; exhibit; show. **2** show ostentatiously. **3** allow to appear; reveal; betray (*displayed his ignorance*). —*n.* **1** the act or an instance of displaying. **2** an exhibition or show. **3** ostentation; flashiness. **4** the distinct behaviour of some birds and fish, esp. used to attract a mate. **5 a** the presentation of signals or data on a visual display unit etc. **b** the information so presented. □ **displayer** *n.* [ME f. OF *despleier* f. L *displicare* (as DIS-, *plicare* fold): cf. DEPLOY]

displease /dɪsˈpliːz/ *v.tr.* make indignant or angry; offend; annoy. □ **displeasing** *adj.* **displeasingly** *adv.* [ME f. OF *desplaisir* (as DIS-, L *placēre* please)]

displeasure /dɪsˈpleʒə(r)/ *n.* disapproval; anger; dissatisfaction. [ME f. OF (as DISPLEASE): assim. to PLEASURE]

disport /dɪsˈpɔːt/ *v.intr.* & *refl.* frolic; gambol; enjoy oneself (*disported on the sand; disported themselves in the sea*). [ME f. AF & OF *desporter* (as DIS-, *porter* carry f. L *portare*)]

disposable /dɪsˈpəʊzəb(ə)l/ *adj.* & *n.* —*adj.* **1** intended to be used once and then thrown away (*disposable nappies*). **2** that can be got rid of, made over, or used. **3** (esp. of financial assets) at the owner's disposal. —*n.* a thing designed to be thrown away after one use. □ **disposable income** income after tax etc. □ **disposability** /-ˈbɪlɪtɪ/ *n.*

disposal /dɪsˈpəʊz(ə)l/ *n.* (usu. foll. by *of*) **1** the act or an instance of disposing of something. **2** the arrangement, disposition, or placing of something. **3** control or management (of a person, business, etc.). **4** (esp. as **waste disposal**) the disposing of rubbish. □ **at one's disposal 1** available for one's use. **2** subject to one's orders or decisions.

■ **Usage** This word is the noun corresponding to the verb *dispose of* (get rid of, deal with, etc.). *Disposition* is the noun from *dispose* (arrange, incline).

dispose /dɪsˈpəʊz/ *v.* **1** *tr.* (usu. foll. by *to*, or *to* + infin.) **a** make willing; incline (*disposed him to the idea; was disposed to release them*). **b** give a tendency to (*the wheel was disposed to buckle*). **2** *tr.* place suitably or in order (*disposed the pictures in sequence*). **3** *tr.* (as **disposed** *adj.*) have a specified mental inclination (usu. in *comb.*: *ill-disposed*). **4** *intr.* determine the course of events (*man proposes, God disposes*). □ **dispose of 1** deal with. **b** get rid of. **c** finish. **d** kill. **2** sell. **3** consume (food). □ **disposer** *n.* [ME f. OF *disposer* (as DIS-, POSE[1]) after L *disponere disposit-*]

disposition /ˌdɪspəˈzɪʃ(ə)n/ *n.* **1** (often foll. by *to*) a natural tendency; an inclination; a person's temperament (*a happy disposition; a disposition to overeat*). **2 a** setting in order; arranging. **b** the relative position of parts; an arrangement. **3** (usu. in *pl.*) preparations; plans. [ME f. OF f. L *dispositio* (as DIS-, *ponere posit-* place)]

■ **Usage** See note at *disposal*.

dispossess /ˌdɪspəˈzes/ *v.tr.* **1** dislodge; oust (a person). **2** (usu. foll. by *of*) deprive. □ **dispossession** /-ˈzeʃ(ə)n/ *n.* [OF *despossesser* (as DIS-, POSSESS)]

disproof /dɪsˈpruːf/ *n.* **1** something that disproves. **2** a refutation. **b** an instance of this.

disproportion /ˌdɪsprəˈpɔːʃ(ə)n/ *n.* **1** a lack of proportion. **2** an instance of this. □ **disproportional** *adj.* **disproportionally** *adv.*

disproportionate /ˌdɪsprəˈpɔːʃənət/ *adj.* **1** lacking proportion. **2** relatively too large or small, long or short, etc. □ **disproportionately** *adv.* **disproportionateness** *n.*

disprove /dɪsˈpruːv/ *v.tr.* prove false; refute. □ **disprovable** *adj.* **disproval** *n.* [ME f. OF *desprover* (as DIS-, PROVE)]

disputable /dɪsˈpjuːtəb(ə)l, ˈdɪspjʊ-/ *adj.* open to question; uncertain. □ **disputably** *adv.* [F or f. L *disputabilis* (as DISPUTE)]

disputation /ˌdɪspjuːˈteɪʃ(ə)n/ *n.* **1 a** disputing, debating. **b** an argument; a controversy. **2** a formal debate. [ME f. F *disputation* or L *disputatio* (as DISPUTE)]

disputatious /ˌdɪspjuːˈteɪʃ(ə)s/ *adj.* fond of or inclined to argument. □ **disputatiously** *adv.* **disputatiousness** *n.*

dispute *v.* & *n.* —*v.* /dɪsˈpjuːt/ **1** *intr.* (usu. foll. by *with*, *against*) a debate, argue. **b** quarrel. **2** *tr.* discuss, esp. heatedly (*disputed whether it was true*). **3** *tr.* question the truth or correctness or validity of (a statement, alleged fact, etc.). **4** *tr.* contend for; strive to win (*disputed the crown*). **5** *tr.* resist (a landing, advance, etc.). —*n.* /dɪˈspjuːt, ˈdɪspjuːt/ **1** a controversy; a debate. **2** a quarrel. **3** a disagreement between management and employees, esp. one leading to industrial action. □ **in dispute 1** being argued about. **2** (of a workforce) involved in industrial action. □ **disputant** /-ˈspjuːt(ə)nt/ *n.* **disputer** *n.* [ME f. OF *desputer* f. L *disputare* estimate (as DIS-, *putare* reckon)]

disqualification /dɪsˌkwɒlɪfɪˈkeɪʃ(ə)n/ *n.* **1** the act or an instance of disqualifying; the state of being disqualified. **2** something that disqualifies.

disqualify /dɪsˈkwɒlɪˌfaɪ/ *v.tr.* (**-ies**, **-ied**) **1** (often foll. by *from*) debar from a competition or pronounce ineligible as a winner. **2** (often foll. by *for*, *from*) make or pronounce ineligible or unsuitable (*his age disqualifies him for the job*).

disquiet /dɪsˈkwaɪət/ v. & n. —v.tr. deprive of peace; worry. —n. anxiety; unrest. □ **disquieting** adj. **disquietingly** adv.

disquietude /dɪsˈkwaɪəˌtjuːd/ n. a state of uneasiness; anxiety.

disquisition /ˌdɪskwɪˈzɪʃ(ə)n/ n. a long or elaborate treatise or discourse on a subject. □ **disquisitional** adj. [F f. L disquisitio (as DIS-, quaerere quaesit- seek)]

disregard /ˌdɪsrɪˈɡɑːd/ v. & n. —v.tr. **1** pay no attention to; ignore. **2** treat as of no importance. —n. (often foll. by of, for) indifference; neglect. □ **disregardful** adj. **disregardfully** adv.

disrepair /ˌdɪsrɪˈpeə(r)/ n. poor condition due to neglect (in disrepair; in a state of disrepair).

disreputable /dɪsˈrepjʊtəb(ə)l/ adj. **1** of bad reputation; discreditable. **2** not respectable in appearance; dirty, untidy. □ **disreputableness** n. **disreputably** adv.

disrepute /ˌdɪsrɪˈpjuːt/ n. a lack of good reputation or respectability; discredit (esp. fall into disrepute).

disrespect /ˌdɪsrɪˈspekt/ n. a lack of respect; discourtesy. □ **disrespectful** adj. **disrespectfully** adv.

disrobe /dɪsˈrəʊb/ v.tr. & refl. (also absol.) divest (oneself or another) of a robe or a garment; undress.

disrupt /dɪsˈrʌpt/ v.tr. **1** interrupt the flow or continuity of (a meeting, speech, etc.); bring disorder to. **2** separate forcibly; shatter. □ **disrupter** n. (also **disruptor**). **disruption** n. **disruptive** adj. **disruptively** adv. **disruptiveness** n. [L disrumpere disrupt- (as DIS-, rumpere break)]

diss /dɪs/ v.tr. US sl. put (a person) down verbally; bad-mouth. [shortened f. DISRESPECT]

dissatisfy /dɪsˈsætɪsˌfaɪ/ v.tr. (-ies, -ied) make discontented; fail to satisfy. □ **dissatisfaction** /-ˈfækʃ(ə)n/ n. **dissatisfactory** /-ˈfæktərɪ/ adj. **dissatisfiedly** adv.

dissect /dɪˈsekt/ v.tr. **1** cut into pieces. **2** cut up (a plant or animal) to examine its parts, structure, etc., or (a corpse) for a post mortem. **3** analyse; criticize or examine in detail. □ **dissection** n. **dissector** n. [L dissecare dissect- (as DIS-, secare cut)]

dissemble /dɪˈsemb(ə)l/ v. **1** intr. conceal one's motives; talk or act hypocritically. **2** tr. **a** disguise or conceal (a feeling, intention, act, etc.). **b** simulate (dissembled grief in public). □ **dissemblance** n. **dissembler** n. **dissemblingly** adv. [ME, alt. after semblance of obs. dissimule f. OF dissimuler f. L dissimulare (as DIS-, SIMULATE)]

disseminate /dɪˈsemɪˌneɪt/ v.tr. scatter about, spread (esp. ideas) widely. □ **dissemination** /-ˈneɪʃ(ə)n/ n. **disseminator** n. [L disseminare (as DIS-, semen -inis seed)]

dissension /dɪˈsenʃ(ə)n/ n. disagreement giving rise to discord. [ME f. OF f. L dissensio (as DIS-, sentire sens- feel)]

dissent /dɪˈsent/ v. & n. —v.intr. (often foll. by from) **1** think differently, disagree; express disagreement. **2** differ in religious opinion, esp. from the doctrine of an established or orthodox church. —n. **1 a** a difference of opinion. **b** an expression of this. **2** the refusal to accept the doctrines of an established or orthodox church; nonconformity. □ **dissenting** adj. **dissentingly** adv. [ME f. L dissentire (as DIS-, sentire feel)]

dissenter /dɪˈsentə(r)/ n. **1** a person who dissents. **2** (**Dissenter**) Brit. a member of a non-established church; a Nonconformist.

dissentient /dɪˈsenʃ(ə)nt/ adj. & n. —adj. disagreeing with a majority or official view. —n. a person who dissents. [L dissentire (as DIS-, sentire feel)]

dissertation /ˌdɪsəˈteɪʃ(ə)n/ n. a detailed discourse on a subject, esp. one submitted in partial fulfilment of the requirements of a degree or diploma. □ **dissertational** adj. [L dissertatio f. dissertare discuss, frequent. of disserere dissert- examine (as DIS-, serere join)]

disservice /dɪsˈsɜːvɪs/ n. an ill turn; an injury, esp. done when trying to help. □ **disserve** v.tr. archaic.

dissidence /ˈdɪsɪd(ə)ns/ n. disagreement; dissent. [F dissidence or L dissidentia (as DISSIDENT)]

dissident /ˈdɪsɪd(ə)nt/ adj. & n. —adj. disagreeing, esp. with an established government, system, etc. —n. a dissident person. [F or f. L dissidēre disagree (as DIS-, sedēre sit)]

dissimilar /dɪˈsɪmɪlə(r)/ adj. (often foll. by to) unlike, not similar. □ **dissimilarity** /-ˈlærɪtɪ/ n. (pl. -ies). **dissimilarly** adv.

dissimulate /dɪˈsɪmjʊˌleɪt/ v.tr. & intr. dissemble. □ **dissimulation** /-ˈleɪʃ(ə)n/ n. **dissimulator** n. [L dissimulare (as DIS-, SIMULATE)]

dissipate /ˈdɪsɪˌpeɪt/ v. **1 a** tr. cause (a cloud, vapour, fear, darkness, etc.) to disappear or disperse. **b** intr. disperse, scatter, disappear. **2** intr. & tr. break up; bring or come to nothing. **3** tr. squander or fritter away (money, energy, etc.). **4** intr. (as **dissipated** adj.) given to dissipation, dissolute. □ **dissipater** n. **dissipative** adj. **dissipator** n. [L dissipare dissipat- (as DIS-, sipare (unrecorded) throw)]

dissipation /ˌdɪsɪˈpeɪʃ(ə)n/ n. **1** dissolute or debauched living. **2** (usu. foll. by of) wasteful expenditure (dissipation of resources). **3** scattering, dispersion, or disintegration. **4** a frivolous amusement. [F dissipation or L dissipatio (as DISSIPATE)]

dissociate /dɪˈsəʊʃɪˌeɪt, -sɪˌeɪt/ v. tr. & intr. (usu. foll. by from) disconnect or become disconnected; separate (dissociated her from their guilt). □ **dissociate oneself from 1** declare oneself unconnected with. **2** decline to support or agree with (a proposal etc.). □ **dissociation** n. **dissociative** /-ətɪv/ adj. [L dissociare (as DIS-, socius companion)]

dissoluble /dɪˈsɒljʊb(ə)l/ adj. able to be disintegrated, loosened, or disconnected; soluble. □ **dissolubility** /-ˈbɪlɪtɪ/ n. **dissolubly** adv. [F dissoluble or L dissolubilis (as DIS-, SOLUBLE)]

dissolute /ˈdɪsəˌluːt, -ˌljuːt/ adj. lax in morals; licentious. □ **dissolutely** adv. **dissoluteness** n. [ME f. L dissolutus past part. of dissolvere DISSOLVE]

dissolution /ˌdɪsəˈluːʃ(ə)n, -ˈljuːʃ(ə)n/ n. **1** disintegration; decomposition. **2** (usu. foll. by of) the undoing or relaxing of a bond, esp.: **a** a marriage. **b** a partnership. **c** an alliance. **3** the dismissal or dispersal of an assembly, esp. of a parliament at the end of its term. **4** death. [ME f. OF dissolution or L dissolutio (as DISSOLVE)]

dissolve /dɪˈzɒlv/ v. tr. & intr. make or become liquid, esp. by immersion or dispersion in a liquid. **2** intr. & tr. disappear or cause to disappear gradually. **3 a** tr. dismiss or disperse (an assembly, esp. parliament). **b** intr. (of an assembly) be dissolved. **4** tr. annul or put an end to (a partnership, marriage, etc.). **5** intr. (of a person) become enfeebled or emotionally overcome (*dissolved into tears*). □ adj. [ME f. L *dissolvere dissolut-* (as DIS-, *solvere* loosen)]

dissonant /ˈdɪsənənt/ adj. **1** Mus. harsh-toned; unharmonious. **2** incongruous; clashing. □ **dissonance** n. **dissonantly** adv. [ME f. OF *dissonant* or L *dissonare* (as DIS-, *sonare* sound)]

dissuade /dɪˈsweɪd/ v.tr. (often foll. by *from*) discourage (a person); persuade against. □ **dissuader** n. **dissuasion** /-ˈsweɪʒ(ə)n/ n. **dissuasive** /-ˈsweɪsɪv/ adj. [L *dissuadēre* (as DIS-, *suadēre suaspersuade*)]

distaff /ˈdɪstɑːf/ n. a cleft stick holding wool or flax wound for spinning by hand. □ **distaff side** the female branch of a family. [OE *distæf* (as STAFF), the first element being app. rel. to LG *diesse*, MLG *dise(ne)* bunch of flax]

distance /ˈdɪst(ə)ns/ n. & v. —n. **1** the condition of being far off; remoteness. **2 a** a space or interval between two things. **b** the length of this (*a distance of twenty miles*). **3** a distant point or place (*came from a distance*). **4** the avoidance of familiarity; aloofness; reserve. **5** a remoter field of vision (*saw him in the distance*). **6** an interval of time (*can't remember what happened at this distance*). —v.tr. (often *refl.*) **1** place far off (*distanced herself from them*). **2** leave far behind in a race or competition. □ **at a distance** far off. **distance runner** an athlete who competes in long- or middle-distance races. **go the distance 1** Boxing complete a fight without being knocked out. **2** complete, esp. a hard task; endure an ordeal. **keep one's distance** maintain one's reserve. [ME f. OF *distance*, *destance* f. L *distantia* f. *distare* stand apart (as DI-², *stare* stand)]

distant /ˈdɪst(ə)nt/ adj. **1 a** far away in space or time. **b** (usu. *predic.*; often foll. by *from*) at a specified distance (*three miles distant from them*). **2** remote or far apart in position, time, resemblance, etc. (*a distant prospect; a distant relation*). **3** not intimate; reserved; cool. **4** remote; abstracted. **5** faint, vague (*he was a distant memory to her*). □ **distantly** adv. [ME f. OF *distant* or L *distant-* part. stem of *distare*: see DISTANCE]

distaste /dɪsˈteɪst/ n. (usu. foll. by *for*) dislike; repugnance; aversion, esp. slight. □ **distasteful** adj. **distastefully** adv. **distastefulness** n.

distemper¹ /dɪsˈtempə(r)/ n. & v. —n. **1** a kind of paint using glue or size instead of an oil-base. **2** a method of mural and poster painting using this. —v.tr. paint (walls etc.) with distemper. [earlier as verb, f. OF *destremper* or LL *distemperare* soak, macerate: see DISTEMPER²]

distemper² /dɪsˈtempə(r)/ n. a disease of some animals, esp. dogs, causing fever, coughing, and catarrh. [earlier as verb, = upset, derange: ME f. LL *distemperare* (as DIS-, *temperare* mingle correctly)]

distend /dɪˈstend/ v.tr. & intr. swell out by pressure from within (*distended stomach*). □ **distensible** /-ˈstensɪb(ə)l/ adj. **distensibility** /-ˈbɪlɪtɪ/ n. **distension** /-ˈstenʃ(ə)n/ n. [ME f. L *distendere* (as DIS-, *tendere tens-* stretch)]

distich /ˈdɪstɪk/ n. Prosody a verse couplet. [L *distichon* f. Gk *distikhon* (as DI-¹, *stikhos* line)]

distil /dɪˈstɪl/ v. (US **distill**) (**distilled**, **distilling**) **1** tr. Chem. purify (a liquid) by vaporizing it with heat, then condensing it with cold and collecting the result. **2** tr.extract the essential meaning or implications of (an idea etc.). **3** tr. make (whisky, essence, etc.) by distilling raw materials. **4** tr. &

intr. come as or give forth in drops; exude. □ **distillatory** adj. [ME f. L *distillare* f. *destillare* (as DE-, *stilla* drop)]

distillate /ˈdɪstɪˌleɪt/ n. a product of distillation.

distillation /ˌdɪstɪˈleɪʃ(ə)n/ n. **1** the process of distilling or being distilled (in various senses). **2** something distilled.

distiller /dɪˈstɪlə(r)/ n. a person who distils, esp. a manufacturer of alcoholic liquor.

distillery /dɪˈstɪlərɪ/ n. (pl. **-ies**) a place where alcoholic liquor is distilled.

distinct /dɪˈstɪŋkt/ adj. **1** (often foll. by *from*) **a** not identical; separate. **b** different in kind or quality; unlike. **2 a** clearly perceptible. **b** clearly understandable. **3** unmistakable (*had a distinct impression of being watched*). □ **distinctly** adv. **distinctness** n. [ME f. L *distinctus* past part. of *distinguere* DISTINGUISH]

distinction /dɪˈstɪŋkʃ(ə)n/ n. **1 a** the act or an instance of discriminating or distinguishing. **b** an instance of this. **c** the difference made by distinguishing. **2 a** something that differentiates, e.g. a mark, name, or title. **b** the fact of being different. **3** special consideration or honour. **4** distinguished character; eminence (*shows distinction in his bearing*). [ME f. OF f. L *distinctio -onis* (as DISTINGUISH)]

distinctive /dɪˈstɪŋktɪv/ adj. distinguishing, characteristic. □ **distinctively** adv. **distinctiveness** n.

distingué /dɪˈstæŋɡeɪ, dɪstæ̃ˈɡeɪ/ adj. (fem. **distinguée** pronunc. same) having a distinguished air, manner, etc. [F, past part. of *distinguer*: see DISTINGUISH]

distinguish /dɪˈstɪŋɡwɪʃ/ v. **1** tr. (often foll. by *from*) **a** see or point out the difference of; draw distinctions (*cannot distinguish one from the other*). **b** constitute such a difference (*the mole distinguishes him from his twin*). **c** draw distinctions between; differentiate. **2** tr. be a mark or property of; characterize (*distinguished by his greed*). **3** tr. discover by listening, looking, etc. (*could distinguish two voices*). **4** tr. (usu. *refl.*; often foll. by *by*) make prominent or noteworthy (*distinguished himself by winning first prize*). **5** intr. (foll. by *between*) make or point out a difference between. □ **distinguishable** adj. [F *distinguer* or L *distinguere* (as DIS-, *stinguere stinct-* extinguish): cf. EXTINGUISH]

distinguished /dɪˈstɪŋɡwɪʃt/ adj. **1** (often foll. by *for*, *by*) of high standing; eminent; famous. **2** = DISTINGUÉ.

distort /dɪˈstɔːt/ v.tr. **1 a** put out of shape; make crooked or unshapely. **b** distort the appearance of, esp. by curved mirrors etc. **2** misrepresent (motives, facts, statements, etc.). □ **distortedly** adv. **distortedness** n. [L *distorquēre distort-* (as DIS-, *torquēre* twist)]

distortion /dɪˈstɔːʃ(ə)n/ n. **1** the act or an instance of distorting; the process of being distorted. **2** Electronics a change in the form of a signal during transmission etc. usu. with some impairment of quality. □ **distortional** adj. **distortionless** adj. [L *distortio* (as DISTORT)]

distract /dɪˈstrækt/ v.tr. **1** (often foll. by *from*) draw away the attention of (a person, the mind, etc.). **2** bewilder, perplex. **3** (as **distracted** adj.) mad or angry. **4** amuse. □ **distractedly** adv. [ME f. L *distrahere distract-* (as DIS-, *trahere* draw)]

distraction /dɪˈstrækʃ(ə)n/ n. **1 a** the act of distracting, esp. the mind. **b** something that distracts; an interruption. **2** a relaxation from work; an amusement. **3** a lack of concentration. **4** confusion; perplexity. **5** frenzy; madness. □ **to distraction** almost to a state of madness. [ME f. OF *distraction* or L *distractio* (as DISTRACT)]

distrain /dɪˈstreɪn/ *v.intr. Law* (usu. foll. by *upon*) impose distraint (on a person, goods, etc.). □ **distrainee** /-ˈniː/ *n.* **distrainer** *n.* **distrainment** *n.* **distrainor** *n.* [ME f. OF *destreindre* f. L *distringere* (as DIS-, *stringere* strict- draw tight)]

distraint /dɪˈstreɪnt/ *n. Law* the seizure of chattels to make a person pay rent etc. or meet an obligation. [DISTRAIN, after *constraint*]

distrait /dɪˈstreɪ/ *adj.* (fem. *distraite* /-ˈstreɪt/) not paying attention; absent-minded; distraught. [ME f. OF *destrait* past part. of *destraire* (as DISTRACT)]

distraught /dɪˈstrɔːt/ *adj.* distracted with worry, fear, etc. [ME, alt. of obs. *distract* (adj.) (as DISTRACT), after *straught* obs. past part. of STRETCH]

distress /dɪˈstres/ *n. & v.* —*n.* **1** severe pain, sorrow, anguish, etc. **2** the lack of money or comforts. **3** *Law* = DISTRAINT. **4** breathlessness; exhaustion. —*v.tr.* **1** subject to distress; exhaust, afflict. **2** cause anxiety to; make unhappy; vex. □ **in distress 1** suffering or in danger. **2** (of a ship, aircraft, etc.) in danger or damaged. □ **distressful** *adj.* **distressingly** *adv.* [ME f. OF *destresse* etc., AF *destresser*, OF *-ecier* f. Gallo-Roman (as DISTRAIN)]

distressed /dɪˈstrest/ *adj.* **1** suffering from distress. **2** impoverished. **3** (of furniture, leather, etc.) having simulated marks of age and wear.

distribute /dɪˈstrɪbjuːt, ˈdɪ-/ *v.tr.* **1** give shares of; deal out. **2** spread about; scatter. **3** divide into parts; arrange; classify. □ **distributable** *adj.* [ME f. L *distribuere distribut-* (as DIS-, *tribuere* assign)]

■ **Usage** The second pronunciation given, with the stress on the first syllable, is considered incorrect by some people.

distribution /ˌdɪstrɪˈbjuːʃ(ə)n/ *n.* **1** the act or an instance of distributing; the process of being distributed. **2** *Statistics* the way in which a characteristic is spread over members of a class. □ **distributional** *adj.* [ME f. OF *distribution* or L *distributio* (as DISTRIBUTE)]

distributive /dɪˈstrɪbjʊtɪv/ *adj. & n.* —*adj.* **1** of, concerned with, or produced by distribution. **2** *Logic & Gram.* (of a pronoun etc.) referring to each individual of a class, not to the class collectively (e.g. *each*, *either*). —*n. Gram.* a distributive word. □ **distributively** *adv.* [ME f. F *distributif -ive* or LL *distributivus* (as DISTRIBUTE)]

distributor /dɪˈstrɪbjʊtə(r)/ *n.* **1** a person or thing that distributes. **2** an agent who supplies goods. **3** *Electr.* a device in an internal-combustion engine for passing current to each spark-plug in turn.

district /ˈdɪstrɪkt/ *n.* **1 a** (often *attrib.*) a territory marked off for special administrative purposes. **b** *Brit.* a division of a county or region electing its own councillors. **2** an area which has common characteristics; a region (*the wine-growing district*). □ **district attorney** (in the US) the prosecuting officer of a district. **district nurse** *Brit.* a peripatetic nurse serving a rural or urban area. [F f. med.L *districtus* (territory of) jurisdiction (as DISTRAIN)]

distrust /dɪsˈtrʌst/ *n. & v.* —*n.* a lack of trust; doubt; suspicion. —*v.tr.* have no trust or confidence in; doubt. □ **distruster** *n.* **distrustful** *adj.* **distrustfully** *adv.*

disturb /dɪˈstɜːb/ *v.tr.* **1** break the rest, calm, or quiet of; interrupt. **2** agitate; worry (*your story disturbs me*). **3** move from a settled position, disarrange (*the papers had been disturbed*). **4** (as **disturbed** *adj.*) *Psychol.* emotionally or mentally unstable or abnormal. □ **disturber** *n.* **disturbing** *adj.* **disturbingly** *adv.* [ME f. OF *desto(u)rber* f. L *disturbare* (as DIS-, *turbare* f. *turba* tumult)]

disturbance /dɪˈstɜːbəns/ *n.* **1** the act or an instance of disturbing; the process of being disturbed. **2** a tumult; an uproar. **3** agitation; worry. **4** an interruption. [ME f. OF *desto(u)rbance* (as DISTURB)]

disunion /dɪsˈjuːnɪən/ *n.* a lack of union; separation; dissension. □ **disunite** /-ˈnaɪt/ *v.tr. & intr.* **disunity** *n.*

disuse *n. & v.* —*n.* /dɪsˈjuːs/ **1** lack of use or practice; discontinuance. **2** a disused state. —*v.tr.* /-ˈjuːz/ cease to use. □ **fall into disuse** cease to be used. [ME f. OF *desuser* (as DIS-, USE)]

disyllable /dɪˈsɪləb(ə)l, ˈdaɪ-/ *n. Prosody* a word or metrical foot of two syllables. □ **disyllabic** /-ˈlæbɪk/ *adj.* [F *disyllabe* f. L *disyllabus* f. Gk *disullabos* (as DI-[1], SYLLABLE)]

ditch *n. & v.* —*n.* a long narrow excavated channel esp. for drainage or to mark a boundary. —*v.* **1** *intr.* make or repair ditches. **2** *tr. sl.* leave in the lurch; abandon. **4** *tr. colloq.* **a** bring (an aircraft) down on the sea in an emergency. **b** drive (a vehicle) into a ditch. **5** *intr. colloq.* (of an aircraft) make a forced landing on the sea. **6** *tr. sl.* defeat; frustrate. □ **last ditch** a place of final desperate defence (*fight to the last ditch*). □ **ditcher** *n.* [OE *dīc*, of unkn. orig.: cf. DIKE[1]]

dither /ˈdɪðə(r)/ *v. & n.* —*v.intr.* hesitate; be indecisive. —*n. colloq.* **1** a state of agitation or apprehension. **2** a state of hesitation; indecisiveness. □ **ditherer** *n.* **dithery** *adj.* [var. of *didder*, DODDER]

dithyramb /ˈdɪθɪˌræm, -ˌræmb/ *n.* **1** a wild choral hymn in ancient Greece, esp. to Dionysus. **2** any passionate or inflated poem, speech, etc. □ **dithyrambic** /-ˈræmbɪk/ *adj.* [L *dithyrambus* f. Gk *dithurambos*, of unkn. orig.]

ditto /ˈdɪtəʊ/ *n.* (pl. **-os**) **1** (in accounts, inventories, lists, etc.) the aforesaid, the same. **2** *colloq.* (replacing a word or phrase to avoid repetition) the same (*came in late last night and ditto the night before*). **3** a similar thing; a duplicate. □ **ditto marks** inverted commas etc. representing 'ditto'. [It. dial. f. L *dictus* past part. of *dicere* say]

■ **Usage** In sense 1, this word is often replaced by " under the word or sum to be repeated.

ditty /ˈdɪtɪ/ *n.* (pl. **-ies**) a short simple song. [ME f. OF *dité* composition f. L *dictatum* neut. past part. of *dictare* DICTATE]

diuretic /ˌdaɪjʊˈretɪk/ *adj. & n.* —*adj.* causing increased output of urine. —*n.* a diuretic drug. [ME f. OF *diuretique* or LL *diureticus* f. Gk *diourētikos* f. *dioureō* urinate]

diurnal /daɪˈɜːn(ə)l/ *adj.* **1** of or during the day; not nocturnal. **2** daily; of each day. **3** *Astron.* occupying one day. **4** *Zool.* (of animals) active in the daytime. **5** *Bot.* (of plants) open only during the day. □ **diurnally** adv. [ME f. LL diurnalis f. L diurnus f. dies day]

diva /ˈdiːvə/ n. (pl. **divas**) a great or famous woman singer; a prima donna. [It. f. L, = goddess]

divalent /daɪˈveɪlənt, ˈdaɪ-/ adj. Chem. 1 having a valency of two; bivalent. 2 having two valencies. □ **divalency** n. [DI-¹ + valent- part. stem (as VALENCY)]

divan /dɪˈvæn, daɪ-, ˈdaɪ-/ n. 1 a long, low, padded seat set against a room-wall; a backless sofa. 2 a bed consisting of a sprung base and mattress. [F divan or It. divano f. Turk. dīvān f. Arab. dīwān f. Pers. dīvān anthology, register, court, bench]

dive v. & n. —v. (**dived** or US **dove** /dəʊv/) 1 intr. plunge head first into water, esp. as a sport. 2 intr. **a** Aeron. (of an aircraft) plunge steeply downwards at speed. **b** Naut. (of a submarine) submerge. **c** (of a person) plunge downwards. 3 intr. (foll. by into) colloq. **a** put one's hand into (a pocket, handbag, vessel, etc.) quickly and deeply. **b** occupy oneself suddenly and enthusiastically with (a subject, meal, etc.). —n. 1 an act of diving; a plunge. 2 **a** the submerging of a submarine. **b** the steep descent of an aircraft. 3 a sudden darting movement. 4 colloq. a disreputable nightclub etc. 5 Boxing sl. a pretended knockout (took a dive in the second round). □ **dive-bomb** bomb (a target) while diving in an aircraft. **dive in** colloq. help oneself (to food). **diving-bell** an open-bottomed box or bell, supplied with air, in which a person can descend into deep water. **diving-board** an elevated board used for diving from. **diving-suit** a watertight suit usu. with a helmet and an air-supply, worn for working under water. [OE dūfan (v.intr.) dive, sink, and dȳfan (v.tr.) immerse, f. Gmc: rel. to DEEP, DIP]

diver /ˈdaɪvə(r)/ n. 1 a person who dives. 2 a person who wears a diving-suit to work under water for long periods. 3 any of various diving birds, esp. large water-birds of the family Gaviidae.

diverge /daɪˈvɜːdʒ/ v. 1 intr. **a** proceed in a different direction or in different directions from a point (diverging rays; the path diverges here). **b** take a different course or different courses (their interests diverged). 2 intr. **a** (often foll. by from) depart from a set course (diverged from the track; diverged from his parents' wishes). **b** differ markedly (they diverged as to the best course). 3 tr. cause to diverge; deflect. □ **divergence** n. **divergency** n. **divergent** adj. **divergently** adv. [med.L divergere (as DI-², L vergere incline)]

divers /ˈdaɪvɜːz/ adj. archaic or literary sundry; several. [ME f. OF f. L diversus DIVERSE (as DI-², versus past part. of vertere turn)]

diverse /daɪˈvɜːs, ˈdaɪ-, dɪ-/ adj. unlike in nature or qualities; varied. □ **diversely** adv. [ME as DIVERS]

diversify /daɪˈvɜːsɪˌfaɪ/ v. (**-ies**, **-ied**) 1 tr. make diverse; vary; modify. 2 tr. Commerce **a** spread (investment) over several enterprises or products, esp. to reduce the risk of loss. **b** introduce a spread of investment in (an enterprise etc.). 3 intr. (often foll. by into) esp. Commerce (of a firm etc.) expand the range of products handled. □ **diversification** /-fɪˈkeɪʃ(ə)n/ n. [ME f. OF diversifier f. med.L diversificare (as DIVERS)]

diversion /daɪˈvɜːʃ(ə)n, dɪ-/ n. 1 **a** the act of diverting; deviation. **b** an instance of this. 2 **a**

the diverting of attention deliberately. **b** a stratagem for this purpose (created a diversion to secure their escape). 3 a recreation or pastime. 4 Brit. an alternative route when a road is temporarily closed to traffic. □ **diversional** adj. **diversionary** adj. [LL diversio (as DIVERT)]

diversity /daɪˈvɜːsɪtɪ, dɪ-/ n. (pl. **-ies**) being diverse; variety. [ME f. OF diversité f. L diversitas -tatis (as DIVERS)]

divert /daɪˈvɜːt, dɪ-/ v.tr. 1 (often foll. by from, to) **a** turn aside; deflect. **b** draw the attention of; distract. 2 (often as **diverting** adj.) entertain; amuse. □ **divertingly** adv. [ME f. F divertir f. L divertere (as DI-², vertere turn)]

diverticular /ˌdaɪvəˈtɪkjʊlə(r)/ adj. Med. of or relating to a diverticulum. □ **diverticular disease** a condition with abdominal pain as a result of muscle spasms in the presence of diverticula.

diverticulum /ˌdaɪvəˈtɪkjʊləm/ n. (pl. **diverticula** /-lə/) Anat. a blind tube forming at weak points in a cavity or passage esp. of the alimentary tract. □ **diverticulosis** /-ˈləʊsɪs/ n. [med.L, var. of L deverticulum byway f. devertere (as DE-, vertere turn)]

divest /daɪˈvest/ v.tr. 1 (usu. foll. by of; often refl.) unclothe; strip (divested himself of his jacket). 2 deprive; dispossess; free, rid. □ **divestiture** n. **divestment** n. **divesture** n. [earlier devest f. OF desvestir etc. (as DIS-, L vestire f. vestis garment)]

divi var. of DIVVY.

divide /dɪˈvaɪd/ v. & n. —v. 1 tr. & intr. (often foll. by in, into) separate or be separated into parts; break up; split (the river divides into two; divided them into three groups). 2 tr. & intr. (often foll. by out) distribute; deal; share (divided it out between them). 3 tr. a cut off; separate; part (divide the sheep from the goats). **b** mark out into parts (a ruler divided into inches). **c** specify different kinds of, classify (people can be divided into two types). 4 tr. cause to disagree; set at variance (religion divided them). 5 Math. **a** tr. find how many times (a number) contains another (divide 20 by 4). **b** intr. (of a number) be contained in (a number) without a remainder (4 divides into 20). **c** intr. be susceptible of division (10 divides by 2 and 5). **d** tr. find how many times (a number) is contained in another (divide 4 into 20). 6 Parl. **a** intr. (of a legislative assembly etc.) part into two groups for voting (the House divided). **b** tr. so divide (a Parliament etc.) for voting. —n. 1 a dividing or boundary line (the divide between rich and poor). 2 a watershed. □ **divided highway** US a dual carriageway. **divided skirt** culottes. [ME f. L dividere divis- (as DI-², vid- separate)]

dividend /ˈdɪvɪˌdend/ n. 1 **a** a sum of money to be divided among a number of persons, esp. that paid by a company to shareholders. **b** a similar sum payable to winners in a football pool, to members of a cooperative, or to creditors of an insolvent estate. **c** an individual's share of a dividend. 2 Math. a number to be divided by a divisor. 3 a benefit from any action (their long training paid dividends). [AF dividende f. L dividendum (as DIVIDE)]

divider /dɪˈvaɪdə(r)/ n. 1 a screen, piece of furniture, etc., dividing a room into two parts. 2 (in pl.) a measuring-compass, esp. with a screw for setting small intervals.

divination /ˌdɪvɪˈneɪʃ(ə)n/ n. 1 supposed insight into the future or the unknown gained by supernatural means. **2 a** a skilful and accurate forecast. **b** a good guess. □ **divinatory** adj. [ME f. OF divination or L divinatio (as DIVINE)]

divine /dɪˈvaɪn/ adj., v., & n. —adj. (**diviner, divinest**) **1 a** of, from, or like God or a god. **b** devoted to God; sacred (divine service). **2 a** more than humanly excellent, gifted, or beautiful. **b** colloq. excellent; delightful. —v. **1** tr. discover by guessing, intuition, inspiration, or magic. **2** tr. foresee, predict, conjecture. **3** intr. practise divination. —n. **1** a cleric, usu. an expert in theology. **2** (**the Divine**) providence or God. □ **divining-rod** = dowsing-rod (see DOWSE¹). □ **divinely** adv. **divineness** n. **diviner** n. **divinize** /ˈdɪvɪ-/ v.tr. (also **-ise**). [ME f. OF devin -ine f. L divinus f. divus godlike]

divinity /dɪˈvɪnɪtɪ/ n. (pl. **-ies**) **1** the state or quality of being divine. **2 a** a god; a divine being. **b** (as **the Divinity**) God. **3** the study of religion; theology. [ME f. OF divinité f. L divinitas -tatis (as DIVINE)]

divisible /dɪˈvɪzɪb(ə)l/ adj. **1** capable of being divided. **2** (foll. by by) Math. containing (a number) a number of times without a remainder (15 is divisible by 3 and 5). □ **divisibility** /-ˈbɪlɪtɪ/ n. [F divisible or LL divisibilis (as DIVIDE)]

division /dɪˈvɪʒ(ə)n/ n. **1** the act or an instance of dividing; the process of being divided. **2** Math. the process of dividing one number by another. **3** disagreement or discord (division of opinion). **4** Parl. the separation of members of a legislative body into two sets for counting votes for and against. **5** one of two or more parts into which a thing is divided. **6** a major unit of administration or organization, esp.: **a** a group of army brigades or regiments. **b** Sport a grouping of teams within a league, usu. by ability. **7** a district defined for administrative purposes. □ **division sign** the sign (÷) indicating that one quantity is to be divided by another. □ **divisional** adj. **divisionally** adv. **divisionary** adj. [ME f. OF divisiun f. L divisio -onis (as DIVIDE)]

divisive /dɪˈvaɪsɪv/ adj. tending to divide, esp. in opinion; causing disagreement. □ **divisively** adv. **divisiveness** n. [LL divisivus (as DIVIDE)]

divisor /dɪˈvaɪzə(r)/ n. Math. **1** a number by which another is to be divided. **2** a number that divides another without a remainder. [ME f. F diviseur or L divisor (as DIVIDE)]

divorce /dɪˈvɔːs/ n. & v. —n. **1 a** the legal dissolution of a marriage. **b** a legal decree of this. **2** a severance or separation (a divorce between thought and feeling). —v. **1 a** tr. (usu. as **divorced** adj.) (often foll. by from) legally dissolve the marriage of. **b** intr. separate by divorce (they divorced last year). **c** tr. end one's marriage with (divorced him for neglect). **2** tr. (often foll. by from) detach, separate (divorced from reality). □ **divorcement** n. [ME f. OF divorce (n.), divorcer (v.) f. LL divortiare f. L divortium f. divortere (as DI-², vertere turn)]

divorcee /ˌdɪvɔːˈsiː/ n. (also masc. **divorcé**, fem. **divorcée** /-ˈseɪ/) a divorced person.

divot /ˈdɪvət/ n. a piece of turf cut out by a golf club in making a stroke. [16th c.: orig. unkn.]

divulge /daɪˈvʌldʒ, dɪ-/ v.tr. disclose; reveal (a secret etc.). □ **divulgation** /-ˈgeɪʃ(ə)n/ n. **divulgement** n. **divulgence** n. [L divulgare (as DI-², vulgare publish f. vulgus common people)]

divvy /ˈdɪvɪ/ n. & v. (also **divi**) colloq. —n. (pl. **-ies**) **1** Brit. a dividend; a share, esp. of profits earned by a cooperative. **2** a distribution. —v.tr. (**-ies, -ied**) (often foll. by up) share out; divide. [abbr. of DIVIDEND]

Diwali /dɪˈwɑːlɪ/ n. a Hindu festival with illuminations, held between September and November. [Hind. dīwalī f. Skr. dīpāvalī row of lights f. dīpa lamp]

Dixie /ˈdɪksɪ/ n. the southern States of the US. [19th c.: orig. uncert.]

dixie /ˈdɪksɪ/ n. a large iron cooking pot used by campers etc. [Hind. degchī cooking pot f. Pers. degcha dimin. of deg pot]

Dixieland /ˈdɪksɪˌlænd/ n. **1** = DIXIE. **2** a kind of jazz with a strong two-beat rhythm and collective improvisation. [DIXIE]

DIY abbr. Brit. do-it-yourself.

dizzy /ˈdɪzɪ/ adj. & v. —adj. (**dizzier, dizziest**) **1 a** giddy, unsteady. **b** feeling confused. **2** causing giddiness (dizzy heights; dizzy speed). —v.tr. **1** make dizzy. **2** bewilder. □ **dizzily** adv. **dizziness** n. [OE dysig f. WG]

DJ abbr. **1** Brit. dinner-jacket. **2** disc jockey.

djinn var. of JINNEE.

dl abbr. decilitre(s).

D-layer /ˈdiːˌleɪə(r)/ n. the lowest layer of the ionosphere able to reflect low-frequency radio waves. [D (arbitrary)]

D.Litt. abbr. Doctor of Letters. [L Doctor Litterarum]

dm abbr. decimetre(s).

D.Mus. abbr. Doctor of Music.

DNA abbr. deoxyribonucleic acid, the self-replicating material present in nearly all living organisms, esp. as a constituent of chromosomes, which is the carrier of genetic information.

D-notice /ˈdiːˌnəʊtɪs/ n. Brit. a government notice to news editors not to publish items on specified subjects, for reasons of security. [defence + NOTICE]

do¹ /duː, də/ v. & n. —v. (3rd sing. present **does** /dʌz/; past **did** /dɪd/; past part. **done** /dʌn/) **1** tr. perform, carry out, achieve, complete (work etc.) (did his homework; there's a lot to do). **2** tr. produce, make (she was doing a painting; I did a translation). **3** tr. provide (do you do lunches?). **3** tr. bestow, grant; have a specified effect on (a walk would do you good; do me a favour). **4** intr. act, behave, proceed (do as I do). **5** tr. work at, study; be occupied with (he did chemistry at university). **6 a** intr. be suitable or acceptable; suffice (a sandwich will do until we get home; that will never do). **b** tr. satisfy; be suitable for (that hotel will do me nicely). **7** tr. deal with; put in order (the garden needs doing; I must do my hair before we go). **8** intr. a fare; get on (the patients were doing excellently; he did badly in the test). **b** perform, work (could do better). **9** tr. a solve; work out (we did the puzzle). **b** (prec. by can or be able to) be competent at (can you do cartwheels?; I never could do maths). **10** tr. a traverse (a certain distance) (we did fifty miles today). **b** travel at a specified speed (he overtook us doing about eighty). **11** tr. colloq. act or behave like (did a Houdini). **12** intr. **a** colloq. finish (I've done in the bathroom). **b** (as **done** adj.) be over (the day is done). **13** tr. produce or give a performance of (we've never done 'Pygmalion'). **14** tr. cook, esp. to the right degree (do it in the oven; the potatoes aren't done yet). **15** intr. be in progress (what's doing?). **16** tr. colloq. visit; see the sights of (we did all the art galleries). **17** tr. colloq. **a** (often as

done adj.) exhaust; tire out (*the climb has completely done me*). **b** beat up, defeat, kill. **c** ruin (*now you've done it*). **18** tr. (foll. by *into*) translate or transform (*the book was done into French*). **19** tr. colloq. (with qualifying adverb) provide food etc. for in a specified way (*they do one very well here*). **20** tr. sl. **a** rob (*they did a shop in Soho*). **b** swindle (*I was done at the market*). **21** tr. sl. prosecute, convict (*they were done for shoplifting*). **22** tr. sl. undergo (a specified term of imprisonment) (*he did two years for fraud*). —*v.aux.* **1 a** (except with *be, can, may, ought, shall, will*) in questions and negative statements (*do you understand?; I don't smoke*). **b** (except with *can, may, ought, shall, will*) in negative commands (*don't be silly; do not come tomorrow*). **2** ellipt. or in place of verb or verb and object (*you know her better than I do; I wanted to go and I did so; tell me, do!*). **3** forming emphatic present and past tenses (*I do want to; they did go but she was out*). **4** in inversion for emphasis (*rarely does it happen; did he but know it*). —*n.* (pl. **dos** or **do's**) **1** colloq. an elaborate event, party, or operation. **2** Brit. sl. a swindle or hoax. □ **do away with** colloq. **1** abolish. **2** kill. □ **do battle** enter into combat. **do by** treat or deal with in a specified way (*do as you would be done by*). **do down** colloq. **1** cheat, swindle. **2** get the better of; overcome. **do for 1** be satisfactory or sufficient for. **2** colloq. (esp. as **done for** adj.) destroy, ruin, kill (*he knew he was done for*). **3** colloq. act as housekeeper for. **do one's head** (or **nut**) sl. be extremely angry or agitated. **do in 1** sl. **a** kill. **b** ruin, do injury to. **2** colloq. exhaust, tire out. **do-it-yourself** adj. (of work, esp. building, painting, decorating, etc.) done or to be done by an amateur at home. —*n.* such work. **do nothing for** (or **to**) colloq. detract from the appearance or quality of (*such behaviour does nothing for our reputation*). **do out** colloq. clean or redecorate (a room). **do a person out of** colloq. unjustly deprive a person of; swindle out of (*he was done out of his holiday*). **do over 1** sl. attack; beat up. **2** colloq. redecorate, refurbish. **3** US colloq. do again. **dos and don'ts** rules of behaviour. **do something for** (or **to**) colloq. enhance the appearance or quality of (*that carpet does something for the room*). **do to** (*archaic* **unto**) = *do by*. **do up 1** fasten, secure. **2** colloq. **a** refurbish, renovate. **b** adorn, dress up. **3** sl. **a** ruin, get the better of. **b** beat up. **do well for oneself** prosper. **do well out of** profit by. **do with** (prec. by *could*) would be glad to have; would profit by (*I could do with a rest*). **do without** manage without; forgo (also *absol.*: *we shall just have to do without*). [OE *dōn* f. Gmc: rel. to Skr *dádhami* put, Gk *tithemi* place, L *facere* do]

do² var. of DOH.

do. abbr. ditto.

doable /ˈduːəb(ə)l/ adj. that can be done.

Dobermann /ˈdəʊbəmən/ n. (in full **Dobermann pinscher** /ˈpɪnʃə(r)/) **1** a large dog of a German breed with a smooth coat. **2** this breed. [L. *Dobermann*, 19th-c. Ger. dog-breeder + G *Pinscher* terrier]

doc n. colloq. doctor. [abbr.]

docile /ˈdəʊsaɪl/ adj. **1** submissive, easily managed. **2** archaic teachable. □ **docilely** /ˈdəʊsaɪlɪ/ adv. **docility** /-ˈsɪlɪtɪ/ n. [ME f. L *docilis* f. *docēre* teach]

dock¹ n. & v. —*n.* **1** an artificially enclosed body of water for the loading, unloading, and repair of ships. **2** (in pl.) a range of docks with wharves and offices; a dockyard. **3** US a ship's berth, a wharf. —*v.* **1** tr. & intr. bring or come into a dock. **2 a** tr. join (spacecraft) together in space. **b** intr. (of spacecraft) be joined. □ **in dock** Brit. colloq. in hospital or (of a vehicle) laid up for repairs. [MDu. *docke*, of unkn. orig.]

dock² n. the enclosure in a criminal court for the accused. □ **in the dock** on trial. [16th c.: prob. orig. cant = Flem. *dok* cage, of unkn. orig.]

dock³ n. any weed of the genus *Rumex*, with broad leaves. [OE *docce*]

dock⁴ v. & n. —*v.tr.* **1 a** cut short (an animal's tail). **b** cut short the tail of (an animal). **2 a** (often foll. by *from*) deduct (a part) from wages, supplies, etc. **b** reduce (wages etc.) in this way. □ **dock-tailed** having a docked tail. [ME, of uncert. orig.]

docker /ˈdɒkə(r)/ n. a person employed to load and unload ships.

docket /ˈdɒkɪt/ n. & v. —*n.* **1** Brit. a document or label listing goods delivered or the contents of a package, or recording payment of customs dues etc. **2** US a list of causes for trial or persons having causes pending. —*v.tr.* (**docketed, docketing**) label with a docket. [15th c.: orig. unkn.]

dockland /ˈdɒklənd/ n. a district near docks. [DOCK¹]

dockyard /ˈdɒkjɑːd/ n. an area with docks and equipment for building and repairing ships, esp. for naval use.

doctor /ˈdɒktə(r)/ n. & v. —*n.* **1 a** a qualified practitioner of medicine; a physician. **b** US a qualified dentist or veterinary surgeon. **2** a person who holds a doctorate (*Doctor of Civil Law*). —*v.* colloq. **1** tr. treat medically. **b** intr. (esp. as **doctoring** n.) practise as a physician. **2** tr. castrate or spay. **3** tr. patch up (machinery etc.); mend. **4** tr. adulterate. **5** tr. tamper with, falsify. **6** tr. confer a degree of doctor on. □ **Doctor of Philosophy** a doctorate in any faculty except law, medicine, or sometimes theology. **what the doctor ordered** colloq. something beneficial or desirable. □ **doctorhood** n. **doctorial** /-ˈtɔːrɪəl/ adj. **doctorly** adj. **doctorship** n. [ME f. OF *doctour* f. L *doctor* f. *docēre* doct- teach]

doctoral /ˈdɒktər(ə)l/ adj. of or for a degree of doctor.

doctorate /ˈdɒktərət/ n. the highest university degree in any faculty, often honorary.

doctrinaire /ˌdɒktrɪˈneə(r)/ adj. & n. —*adj.* seeking to apply a theory or doctrine in all circumstances without regard to practical considerations; theoretical and impractical. —*n.* a doctrinaire person. □ **doctrinairism** n. **doctrinarian** n. [F f. *doctrine* DOCTRINE + -*aire* -ARY¹]

doctrinal /dɒkˈtraɪn(ə)l, ˈdɒktrɪn(ə)l/ adj. of or inculcating a doctrine or doctrines. □ **doctrinally** adv. [LL *doctrinalis* (as DOCTRINE)]

doctrine /ˈdɒktrɪn/ n. **1** what is taught; a body of instruction. **2 a** a principle of religious or political etc. belief. **b** a set of such principles; dogma. □ **doctrinism** n. **doctrinist** n. [ME f. OF f. L *doctrina* teaching (as DOCTOR)]

docudrama /ˈdɒkjʊˌdrɑːmə/ n. a dramatized television film based on real events. [DOCUMENTARY + DRAMA]

document /ˈdɒkjʊmənt/ n. & v. Law —*n.* a piece of written or printed matter that provides a record or evidence of events, an agreement,

ownership, identification, etc. —v.tr.
/ˈdɒkjʊˌment/ 1 prove by or provide with documents or evidence. 2 record in a document. □
documental /-ˈment(ə)l/ adj. [ME f. OF f. L documentum proof f. docēre teach]

documentary /ˌdɒkjʊˈmentərɪ/ adj. & n. —adj.
1 consisting of documents (documentary evidence).
2 providing a factual record or report. —n. (pl.
-ies) a documentary film etc. □ **documentarily** adv.

documentation /ˌdɒkjʊmenˈteɪʃ(ə)n/ n. 1 the accumulation, classification, and dissemination of information. 2 the material collected or disseminated. 3 the collection of documents relating to a process or event, esp. the written specification and instructions accompanying a computer program.

dodder /ˈdɒdə(r)/ v.intr. tremble or totter, esp. from age. □ **dodderer** n. [17th c.: var. of obs. dial. dadder]

doddery /ˈdɒdərɪ/ adj. tending to tremble or totter, esp. from age. □ **dodderiness** n. [DODDER + -Y¹]

doddle /ˈdɒd(ə)l/ n. Brit. colloq. an easy task. [perh. f. doddle = TODDLE]

dodeca- /ˈdəʊdekə/ comb. form twelve. [Gk dōdeka twelve]

dodecagon /dəʊˈdekəgən/ n. a plane figure with twelve sides.

dodecahedron /ˌdəʊdekəˈhiːdrən/ n. a solid figure with twelve faces. □ **dodecahedral** adj.

dodge v. & n. —v. 1 intr. (often foll. by about, behind, round) move quickly to one side or quickly change position, to elude a pursuer, blow, etc. (dodged behind the chair). 2 tr. **a** evade by cunning or trickery (dodged paying the fare). **b** elude (a pursuer, opponent, blow, etc.) by a sideward movement etc. —n. 1 a quick movement to avoid or evade something. 2 a clever trick or expedient. □ **dodger** n. [16th c.: orig. unkn.]

dodgem /ˈdɒdʒəm/ n. each of a number of small electrically-driven cars in an enclosure at a funfair, driven round and bumped into each other. [DODGE + 'EM]

dodgy /ˈdɒdʒɪ/ adj. (**dodgier, dodgiest**) 1 colloq. awkward, unreliable, tricky. 2 Brit. cunning, artful.

dodo /ˈdəʊdəʊ/ n. (pl. **-os** or **-oes**) any large flightless bird of the extinct family Raphidae, formerly native to Mauritius. □ **as dead as the** (or **a**) **dodo** 1 completely or unmistakably dead. 2 entirely obsolete. [Port. doudo simpleton]

doe n. a female fallow deer, reindeer, hare, or rabbit. [OE dā]

doer /ˈduːə(r)/ n. 1 a person who does something. 2 one who acts rather than merely talking or thinking.

does 3rd sing. present of DO¹.

doesn't /ˈdʌz(ə)nt/ contr. does not.

doff v.tr. literary take off (one's hat, clothing). [ME, = do off]

dog n. & v. —n. 1 any four-legged flesh-eating animal of the genus Canis, of many breeds domesticated and wild, kept as pets or for work or sport. 2 the male of the dog, or of the fox (also **dog-fox**) or wolf (also **dog-wolf**). 3 colloq. **a** a despicable person. **b** a person or fellow of a specified kind (a lucky dog). **c** US & Austral. sl. an informer; a traitor. 4 a mechanical device for

gripping. 5 US sl. something poor; a failure. 6 = FIREDOG. 7 (in pl.; prec. by the) Brit. colloq. greyhound-racing. —v.tr. (**dogged, dogging**) follow closely and persistently; pursue, track. □
dog-biscuit a hard thick biscuit for feeding dogs. **dog-box** Austral. sl. a compartment in a railway carriage without a corridor. **dog-collar** 1 a collar for a dog. 2 colloq. a clerical collar. **dog days** the hottest period of the year. **dog-eared** (of a book etc.) with the corners worn or battered with use. **dog-end** sl. a cigarette-end. **dog in the manger** a person who prevents others from using something, although that person has no use for it. **dog-leg** (or **-legged**) bent like a dog's hind leg. **dog-paddle** n. an elementary swimming-stroke like that of a dog. —v.intr. swim using this stroke. **dog-rose** a wild hedge-rose, Rosa canina. **dog's breakfast** (or **dinner**) colloq. a mess. **dog's life** a life of misery or harassment. **dog's meat** horse's or other flesh as food for dogs; carrion. **dog-star** the chief star of the constellation Canis Major or Minor, esp. Sirius. **dog-tired** tired out. **dog-tooth** 1 a small pointed ornament or moulding esp. in Norman and Early English architecture. 2 a broken check pattern used esp. in cloth for suits. **dog trials** Austral. & NZ a public competitive display of the skills of sheepdogs. **go to the dogs** sl. deteriorate, be ruined. **hair of the dog** further drink to cure the effects of drink. **like a dog's dinner** colloq. smartly or flashily (dressed, arranged, etc.). **not a dog's chance** no chance at all. **put on dog** colloq. behave pretentiously. □ **doglike** adj. [OE docga, of unkn. orig.]

dogcart /ˈdɒgkɑːt/ n. a two-wheeled driving-cart with cross seats back to back.

doge /dəʊdʒ/ n. hist. the chief magistrate of Venice or Genoa. [F f. It. f. Venetian doze f. L dux ducis leader]

dogfight /ˈdɒgfaɪt/ n. 1 a close combat between fighter aircraft. 2 uproar; a fight like that between dogs.

dogfish /ˈdɒgfɪʃ/ n. (pl. same or **dogfishes**) any of various small sharks esp. of the families Scyliorhinidae or Squalidae.

dogged /ˈdɒgɪd/ adj. tenacious; grimly persistent. □ **doggedly** adv. **doggedness** n. [ME f. DOG + -ED¹]

doggerel /ˈdɒgər(ə)l/ n. poor or trivial verse. [ME, app. f. DOG + derog. suffix -rel]

doggie var. of DOGGY.

doggish /ˈdɒgɪʃ/ adj. 1 of or like a dog. 2 currish, malicious, snappish. □ **doggishly** adv. **doggishness** n.

doggo /ˈdɒgəʊ/ adv. □ **lie doggo** sl. lie motionless or hidden, making no sign. [prob. f. DOG: cf. -o]

doggone /ˈdɒgɒn/ adj., adv., & int. esp. US sl. —adj. & adv. damned. —int. expressing annoyance. [prob. f. dog on it = God damn it]

doggy /ˈdɒgɪ/ adj. & n. —adj. 1 of or like a dog. 2 devoted to dogs. —n. (also **doggie**) (pl. **-ies**) a little dog; a pet name for a dog. □ **doggy bag** a bag given to a customer in a restaurant or to a guest at a party etc. for putting leftovers in to take home. □ **dogginess** n.

doghouse /ˈdɒghaʊs/ n. US a dog's kennel. □ **in the doghouse** sl. in disgrace or disfavour.

dogma /ˈdɒgmə/ n. 1 **a** a principle, tenet, or system of these, esp. as laid down by the authority of a Church. **b** such principles collectively. **2** an arrogant declaration of opinion. [L f. Gk *dogma -matos* opinion f. *dokeō* seem]

dogmatic /dɒgˈmætɪk/ *adj.* **1 a** (of a person) given to asserting or imposing personal opinions; arrogant. **b** intolerantly authoritative. **2** of or in the nature of dogma; doctrinal. □ **dogmatically** *adv.* [LL *dogmaticus* f. Gk *dogmatikos* (as DOGMA)]

dogmatism /ˈdɒgməˌtɪz(ə)m/ *n.* a tendency to be dogmatic. □ **dogmatist** *n.* [F *dogmatisme* f. med.L *dogmatismus* (as DOGMA)]

dogmatize /ˈdɒgməˌtaɪz/ *v.* (also **-ise**) **1** *intr.* make positive unsupported assertions; speak dogmatically. **2** *tr.* express (a principle etc.) as a dogma. [F *dogmatiser* or f. LL *dogmatizare* f. Gk (as DOGMA)]

do-gooder /duːˈɡʊdə(r)/ *n.* a well-meaning but unrealistic philanthropist or reformer. □ **do-good** /ˈduːɡʊd/ *adj. & n.* **do-goodery** *n.* **do-goodism** *n.*

dogsbody /ˈdɒgzˌbɒdɪ/ *n.* (pl. **-ies**) **1** *colloq.* a drudge. **2** *Naut. sl.* a junior officer.

dogwood /ˈdɒgwʊd/ *n.* **1** any of various shrubs of the genus *Cornus*, esp. the wild cornel with dark red branches and purple berries. **2** any of various similar trees. **3** the wood of the dogwood.

doh *n.* (also **do**) *Mus.* **1** (in tonic sol-fa) the first and eighth note of a major scale. **2** the note C in the fixed-doh system. [18th c.: f. It. *do*]

doily /ˈdɔɪlɪ/ *n.* (also **doyley**) (pl. **-ies** or **-eys**) a small ornamental mat of paper, lace, etc., on a plate for cakes etc. [orig. the name of a fabric: f. *Doiley*, the name of a draper]

doing /ˈduːɪŋ/ *n.* **1 a** an action; the performance of a deed (*famous for his doings; it was my doing*). **b** activity, effort (*it takes a lot of doing*). **2** *colloq.* a scolding; a beating.

Dolby /ˈdɒlbɪ/ *n. propr.* an electronic noise-reduction system used esp. in tape-recording to reduce hiss. [R. M. *Dolby*, US inventor]

dolce vita /ˌdɒltʃeɪ ˈviːtə/ *n.* a life of pleasure and luxury. [It., = sweet life]

doldrums /ˈdɒldrəmz/ *n.pl.* (usu. prec. by *the*) **1** low spirits; a feeling of boredom or depression. **2** a period of inactivity or state of stagnation. **3** an equatorial ocean region of calms, sudden storms, and light unpredictable winds. [prob. after *dull* and *tantrum*]

dole *n. & v.* —*n.* **1** (usu. prec. by *the*) *Brit. colloq.* benefit claimable by the unemployed from the State. **2 a** a charitable distribution. **b** a charitable (esp. sparing, niggardly) gift of food, clothes, or money. —*v.tr.* (usu. foll. by *out*) deal out sparingly. □ **on the dole** *Brit. colloq.* receiving State benefit for the unemployed. [OE *dāl* f. Gmc]

doleful /ˈdəʊlfʊl/ *adj.* **1** mournful, sad. **2** dreary, dismal. □ **dolefully** *adv.* **dolefulness** *n.* [ME f. OF *do(e)l* etc. f. pop.L *dolus* f. L *dolēre* grieve + -FUL]

doll *n. & v.* —*n.* **1** a small model of a human figure, esp. a baby or a child, as a child's toy. **2 a** *colloq.* a pretty but silly young woman. **b** *sl.* a young woman, esp. an attractive one. **3** a ventriloquist's dummy. —*v.* (foll. by *up*) dress up smartly. □ **doll's house 1** a miniature toy house for dolls. **2** a very small house. [pet form of the name *Dorothy*]

dollar /ˈdɒlə(r)/ *n.* **1** the chief monetary unit in the US, Canada, and Australia. **2** the chief monetary unit of certain countries in the Pacific, West Indies, SE Asia, Africa, and S. America. □ **dollar area** the area in which currency is linked to the US dollar. **dollar mark** (or **sign**) the sign \$, representing a dollar. [LG *daler* f. G *Taler*, short for *Joachimstaler*, a coin from the silver-mine of *Joachimstal* in Czechoslovakia]

dollhouse /ˈdɒlhaʊs/ *n. US* = *doll's house* (see DOLL).

dollop /ˈdɒləp/ *n. & v.* —*n.* a shapeless lump of food etc. —*v.tr.* (**dolloped**, **dolloping**) (usu. foll. by *out*) serve out in large shapeless quantities. [perh. f. Scand.]

dolly /ˈdɒlɪ/ *n.* (pl. **-ies**) **1** a child's name for a doll. **2** a movable platform for a cine-camera. **3** *Cricket colloq.* an easy catch or hit. □ **dolly mixture** any of a mixture of small variously shaped and coloured sweets.

dolman /ˈdɒlmən/ *n.* **1** a long Turkish robe open in front. **2** a hussar's jacket worn with the sleeves hanging loose. □ **dolman sleeve** a loose sleeve cut in one piece with the body of the coat etc. [ult. f. Turk. *dolama*]

dolmen /ˈdɒlmən/ *n.* a megalithic tomb with a large flat stone laid on upright ones. [F, perh. f. Cornish *tolmên* hole of stone]

dolorous /ˈdɒlərəs/ *adj. literary* or *joc.* **1** distressing, painful; doleful, dismal. **2** distressed, sad. □ **dolorously** *adv.* [ME f. OF *doleros* f. LL *dolorosus* (as DOLOUR)]

dolour /ˈdɒlə(r)/ *n.* (*US* **dolor**) *literary* sorrow, distress. [ME f. OF f. L *dolor -oris* pain, grief]

dolphin /ˈdɒlfɪn/ *n.* any of various porpoise-like sea mammals of the family Delphinidae having a slender beaklike snout. [ME, also *delphin* f. L *delphinus* f. Gk *delphis -inos*]

dolphinarium /ˌdɒlfɪˈneərɪəm/ *n.* (pl. **dolphinariums**) an aquarium for dolphins.

dolt /dəʊlt/ *n.* a stupid person. □ **doltish** *adj.* **doltishly** *adv.* **doltishness** *n.* [app. related to *dol*, *dold*, obs. var. of DULL]

Dom *n.* **1** a title prefixed to the names of some Roman Catholic dignitaries, and Benedictine and Carthusian monks. **2** the Portuguese equivalent of *Don* (see DON¹). [L *dominus* master: sense 2 through Port.]

-dom /dəm/ *suffix* forming nouns denoting: **1** state or condition (*freedom*). **2** rank or status (*earldom*). **3** domain (*kingdom*). **4** a class of people (or the attitudes etc. associated with them) regarded collectively (*officialdom*). [OE *-dōm*, orig. = DOOM]

domain /dəˈmeɪn/ *n.* **1** an area under one rule; a realm. **2** an estate or lands under one control. **3** a sphere of control or influence. **4** *Math.* the set of possible values of an independent variable. □ **domanial** /dəˈmeɪnɪəl/ *adj.* [ME f. F *domaine*, OF *demeine* DEMESNE, assoc. with L *dominus* lord]

dome *n. & v.* —*n.* **1 a** a rounded vault as a roof, with a circular, elliptical, or polygonal base. **2 a** a natural vault or canopy (of the sky, trees, etc.). **b** the rounded summit of a hill etc. **3** *sl.* the head. —*v.tr.* (usu. as **domed** *adj.*) cover with or shape as a dome. □ **domelike** *adj.* [F *dôme* f. It. *duomo* cathedral, dome f. L *domus* house]

domestic /dəˈmestɪk/ *adj. & n.* —*adj.* **1** of the home, household, or family affairs. **2 a** of one's own country, not foreign or international. **b** home-grown or home-made. **3** (of an animal) kept by or living with man. **4** fond of home life. —*n.* a household servant. □ **domestic science** the study of household management. □ **domestically** *adv.* [F *domestique* f. L *domesticus* f. *domus* home]

domesticate /dəˈmestɪˌkeɪt/ *v.tr.* **1** tame (an animal) to live with humans. **2** accustom to home life and management. **3** naturalize (a plant or animal). □ **domesticable** /-kəb(ə)l/ *adj.* **domestication** /-ˈkeɪʃ(ə)n/ *n.* [med.L *domesticare* (as DOMESTIC)]

domesticity /ˌdɒməˈstɪsɪtɪ, ˌdəʊ-/ *n.* **1** the state of being domestic. **2** domestic or home life.

domicile /ˈdɒmɪˌsaɪl, -sɪl/ *n.* & *v.* (also **domicil** /-sɪl/) —*n.* **1** a dwelling-place; one's home. **2** *Law* **a** a place of permanent residence. **b** the fact of residing. —*v.tr.* (usu. as **domiciled** *adj.*) (usu. foll. by *at, in*) establish or settle in a place. [ME f. OF f. L *domicilium* f. *domus* home]

domiciliary /ˌdɒmɪˈsɪlɪərɪ/ *adj.* of a dwelling-place (esp. of a doctor's, official's, etc., visit to a person's home). [F *domiciliaire* f. med.L *domiciliarius* (as DOMICILE)]

dominance /ˈdɒmɪnəns/ *n.* **1** the state of being dominant. **2** control, authority.

dominant /ˈdɒmɪnənt/ *adj.* & *n.* —*adj.* **1** dominating, prevailing, most influential. **2** (of a high place) prominent, overlooking others. **3 a** (of an allele) expressed even when inherited from only one parent. **b** (of an inherited characteristic) appearing in an individual even when its allelic counterpart is also inherited. —*n.* *Mus.* the fifth note of the diatonic scale of any key. □ **dominantly** *adv.* [F f. L *dominari* (as DOMINATE)]

dominate /ˈdɒmɪˌneɪt/ *v.* **1** *tr.* & (foll. by *over*) *intr.* have a commanding influence on; exercise control over (*fear dominated them for years; dominates over his friends*). **2** *intr.* (of a person, sound, feature of a scene, etc.) be the most influential or conspicuous. **3** *tr.* & (foll. by *over*) *intr.* (of a building etc.) have a commanding position over; overlook. □ **dominator** *n.* [L *dominari dominat-* f. *dominus* lord]

domination /ˌdɒmɪˈneɪʃ(ə)n/ *n.* **1** command, control. **2** the act or an instance of dominating; the process of being dominated. [ME f. OF f. L *dominatio -onis* (as DOMINATE)]

domineer /ˌdɒmɪˈnɪə(r)/ *v.intr.* (often as **domineering** *adj.*) behave in an arrogant and overbearing way. □ **domineeringly** *adv.* [Du. *domineren* f. F *dominer*]

Dominican /dəˈmɪnɪkən/ *adj.* & *n.* —*adj.* **1** of or relating to St Dominic or the order of friars which he founded. **2** of or relating to either of the two orders of female religious founded on Dominican principles. —*n.* a Dominican friar, nun, or sister. [med.L *Dominicanus* f. *Dominicus* L name of *Domingo* de Guzmán (St Dominic)]

dominion /dəˈmɪnɪən/ *n.* **1** sovereignty, control. **2** the territory of a sovereign or government; a domain. **3** *hist.* the title of each of the self-governing territories of the British Commonwealth. [ME f. OF f. med.L *dominio -onis* f. L *dominium* f. *dominus* lord]

domino /ˈdɒmɪˌnəʊ/ *n.* (pl. **-oes**) **1 a** any of 28 small oblong pieces marked with 0–6 pips in each half. **b** (in pl., usu. treated as *sing.*) a game played with these. **2** a loose cloak with a mask for the upper part of the face, worn at masquerades. □ **domino theory** the theory that a political event etc. in one country will cause similar events in neighbouring countries. [F, prob. f. L *dominus* lord, but unexplained]

don[1] *n.* **1** a university teacher, esp. a senior member of a college at Oxford or Cambridge. **2** (**Don**) **a** a Spanish title prefixed to a forename. **b** a Spanish gentleman; a Spaniard. [Sp. f. L *dominus* lord]

don[2] *v.tr.* (**donned, donning**) put on (clothing). [= *do on*]

donate /dəʊˈneɪt/ *v.tr.* give or contribute (money etc.), esp. voluntarily to a fund or institution. □ **donator** *n.* [back-form. f. DONATION]

donation /dəʊˈneɪʃ(ə)n/ *n.* **1** the act or an instance of donating. **2** something, esp. an amount of money, donated. [ME f. OF f. L *donatio -onis* f. *donare* give f. *donum* gift]

done /dʌn/ *past part.* of DO[1]. —*adj.* **1** *colloq.* socially acceptable (*the done thing; it isn't done*). **2** (often with *in, up*) *colloq.* tired out. **3** (esp. as *int.* in reply to an offer etc.) accepted. □ **be done with** have finished with, be finished with. **done for** *colloq.* in serious trouble. **have done** have ceased or finished. **have done with** be rid of; have finished dealing with.

donjon /ˈdɒndʒ(ə)n, ˈdʌn-/ *n.* the great tower or innermost keep of a castle. [archaic spelling of DUNGEON]

donkey /ˈdɒŋkɪ/ *n.* (pl. **-eys**) **1** a domestic ass. **2** *colloq.* a stupid or foolish person. □ **donkey engine** a small auxiliary engine. **donkey jacket** a thick weatherproof jacket worn by workers and as a fashion garment. **donkey's years** *colloq.* a very long time. **donkey-work** the laborious part of a job; drudgery. [earlier with pronunc. as *monkey*: perh. f. DUN[1], or the Christian name *Duncan*]

donna /ˈdɒnə/ *n.* **1** an Italian, Spanish, or Portuguese lady. **2** (**Donna**) the title of such a lady. [It. f. L *domina* mistress fem. of *dominus*: cf. DON[1]]

donnish /ˈdɒnɪʃ/ *adj.* like or resembling a college don, esp. in supposed pedantry. □ **donnishly** *adv.* **donnishness** *n.*

donor /ˈdəʊnə(r)/ *n.* **1** a person who gives or donates something (e.g. to a charity). **2** one who provides blood for a transfusion, semen for insemination, or an organ or tissue for transplantation. □ **donor card** an official card authorizing use of organs for transplant, carried by the donor. [ME f. AF *donour*, OF *doneur* f. L *donator -oris* f. *donare* give]

don't /dəʊnt/ *contr.* do not. —*n.* a prohibition (*dos and don'ts*).

donut US var. of DOUGHNUT.

doodad /ˈduːdæd/ *n.* US = DOODAH. [20th c.: orig. unkn.]

doodah /ˈduːdɑː/ *n.* **1** a fancy article; a trivial ornament. **2** a gadget or 'thingummy'. □ **all of a doodah** excited, dithering. [from the refrain of the song *Camptown Races*]

doodle /ˈduːd(ə)l/ *v.* & *n.* —*v.intr.* scribble or draw, esp. absent-mindedly. —*n.* a scrawl or drawing made. □ **doodler** *n.* [orig. = foolish person; cf. LG *dudeldopf*]

doohickey /ˈduːˌhɪkɪ/ *n.* (pl. **-eys**) US *colloq.* a small object, esp. mechanical. [DOODAD + HICKEY]

doom /duːm/ *n.* & *v.* —*n.* **1 a** a grim fate or destiny. **b** death or ruin. **2 a** a condemnation; a judgement or sentence. **b** the Last Judgement (*the crack of doom*). —*v.tr.* **1** (usu. foll. by *to*) condemn or destine (*a city doomed to destruction*). **2** (esp. as **doomed** *adj.*) consign to misfortune or destruction. [OE *dōm* statute, judgement f. Gmc: rel. to DO¹]

doomsday /ˈduːmzdeɪ/ *n.* the day of the Last Judgement. □ **till doomsday** for ever. [OE *dōmes dæg*: see DOOM]

doomwatch /ˈduːmwɒtʃ/ *n.* organized vigilance or observation to avert danger, esp. from environmental pollution. □ **doomwatcher** *n.*

door /dɔː(r)/ *n.* **1 a** a hinged, sliding, or revolving barrier for closing and opening an entrance to a building, room, cupboard, etc. **b** this as representing a house etc. (*lives two doors away*). **2 a** an entrance or exit; a doorway. **b** a means of access or approach. □ **door-case** (or **-frame**) the structure into which a door is fitted. **door-keeper** = DOORMAN. **door-to-door** (of selling etc.) done at each house in turn. **lay** (or **lie**) **at the door of** impute (or be imputable) to. **next door** in or to the next house or room. **next door to 1** in the next house to. **2** nearly, almost, near to. **out of doors** in or into the open air. □ **doored** *adj.* (also in *comb.*). [OE *duru, dor* f. Gmc]

doorbell /ˈdɔːbel/ *n.* a bell in a house etc. rung by visitors outside to signal their arrival.

doorknob /ˈdɔːnɒb/ *n.* a knob for turning to release the latch of a door.

doorman /ˈdɔːmən/ *n.* (*pl.* **-men**) a person on duty at the door to a large building; a janitor or porter.

doormat /ˈdɔːmæt/ *n.* **1** a mat at an entrance for wiping mud etc. from the shoes. **2** a feebly submissive person.

doornail /ˈdɔːneɪl/ *n.* a nail with which doors were studded for strength or ornament. □ **dead as a doornail** completely or unmistakably dead.

doorpost /ˈdɔːpəʊst/ *n.* each of the uprights of a door-frame, on one of which the door is hung.

doorstep /ˈdɔːstep/ *n.* & *v.* —*n.* **1** a step leading up to the outer door of a house etc. **2** *sl.* a thick slice of bread. —*v.intr.* (**-stepped, -stepping**) go from door to door selling, canvassing, etc. □ **on one's** (or **the**) **doorstep** very close.

doorstop /ˈdɔːstɒp/ *n.* a device for keeping a door open or to prevent it from striking a wall etc. when opened.

doorway /ˈdɔːweɪ/ *n.* an opening filled by a door.

dooryard /ˈdɔːjɑːd/ *n.* US a yard or garden near a house-door.

dopa /ˈdəʊpə/ *n. Pharm.* a crystalline amino acid derivative used in the treatment of Parkinsonism. [G f. Dioxyphenylalanine, former name of the compound]

dope *n.* & *v.* —*n.* **1** a varnish applied to the cloth surface of aeroplane parts to strengthen them, keep them airtight, etc. **2** a thick liquid used as a lubricant etc. **3** a substance added to petrol etc. to increase its effectiveness. **4 a** *sl.* a narcotic; a stupefying drug. **b** a drug etc. given to a horse or greyhound, or taken by an athlete, to affect performance. **5** *sl.* a stupid person. **6** *sl.* **a** information about a subject, esp. if not generally known. **b** misleading information. —*v.* **1** *tr.* administer dope to, drug. **2** *tr.* smear, daub; apply dope to. **3** *intr.* take addictive drugs. □ **doper** *n.* [Du. *doop* sauce f. *doopen* to dip]

dopey /ˈdəʊpɪ/ *adj.* (also **dopy**) (**dopier, dopiest**) *colloq.* **1 a** half asleep. **b** stupefied by or as if by a drug. **2** stupid, silly. □ **dopily** *adv.* **dopiness** *n.*

doppelgänger /ˈdɒp(ə)lˌgeŋə(r)/ *n.* an apparition or double of a living person. [G, = double-goer]

Doppler effect /ˈdɒplə(r)/ *n.* (also **Doppler shift**) *Physics* an increase (or decrease) in the frequency of sound, light, or other waves as the source and observer move towards (or away) from each other. [C. J. Doppler, Austrian physicist d. 1853]

dorado /dəˈrɑːdəʊ/ *n.* (*pl.* **-os**) a blue and silver marine fish, *Coryphaena hippurus*, showing brilliant colours when dying out of water. [Sp. f. LL *deauratus* gilt f. *aurum* gold]

Doric /ˈdɒrɪk/ *adj.* & *n.* —*adj.* **1** (of a dialect) broad, rustic. **2** *Archit.* of the oldest, sturdiest, and simplest of the Greek orders. —*n.* **1** rustic English or esp. Scots. **2** *Archit.* the Doric order. [L *Doricus* f. Gk *Dōrikos* f. *Dōros* mythical ancient Greek]

dorm *n. colloq.* dormitory. [abbr.]

dormant /ˈdɔːmənt/ *adj.* **1** lying inactive as in sleep; sleeping. **2 a** (of a volcano etc.) temporarily inactive. **b** (of potential faculties etc.) in abeyance. **3** (of plants) alive but not actively growing. □ **dormancy** *n.* [ME f. OF, pres. part. of *dormir* f. L *dormire* sleep]

dormer /ˈdɔːmə(r)/ *n.* (in full **dormer window**) a projecting upright window in a sloping roof. [OF *dormēor* (as DORMANT)]

dormitory /ˈdɔːmɪtərɪ/ *n.* (*pl.* **-ies**) **1** a sleeping-room with several beds, esp. in a school or institution. **2** (in full **dormitory town** etc.) a small town or suburb from which people travel to work in a city etc. **3** US a university or college hall of residence or hostel. [ME f. L *dormitorium* f. *dormire* dormit- sleep]

dormouse /ˈdɔːmaʊs/ *n.* (*pl.* **dormice**) any small mouselike hibernating rodent of the family Gliridae, having a long bushy tail. [ME: orig. unkn.]

dormy /ˈdɔːmɪ/ *adj.* Golf (of a player or side) ahead by as many holes as there are holes left to play (*dormy five*). [19th c.: orig. unkn.]

dorp *n.* S.Afr. a village or small township. [Du. (as THORP)]

dorsal /ˈdɔːs(ə)l/ *adj. Anat., Zool., & Bot.* **1** of, on, or near the back. **2** ridge-shaped. □ **dorsally** *adv.* [F *dorsal* or LL *dorsalis* f. L *dorsum* back]

dory /ˈdɔːrɪ/ *n.* (*pl.* **-ies**) any of various marine fish having a compressed body and flat head, esp. the John Dory, used as food. [ME f. F *dorée* fem. past part. of *dorer* gild (as DORADO)]

DOS /dɒs/ *n. Computing* a program for manipulating information on a disk. [abbr. of disk operating system]

dosage /ˈdəʊsɪdʒ/ *n.* **1** the giving of medicine in doses. **2** the size of a dose.

dose /dəʊs/ *n.* & *v.* —*n.* **1** an amount of a medicine or drug for taking or taken at one time. **2** a quantity of something administered or allocated (e.g. work, praise, punishment, etc.). **3** the amount of ionizing radiation received by a person or thing. **4** *sl.* a venereal infection. —*v.tr.* **1** treat (a person or animal) with doses of medicine. **2** give a dose or doses to. □ **like a dose of salts** *colloq.* very fast and efficiently. [F f. LL *dosis* f. Gk *dosis* gift f. *didōmi* give]

dosh *n. sl.* money. [20th c.: orig. unkn.]

dosimeter /dəʊˈsɪmɪtə(r)/ n. a device used to measure an absorbed dose of ionizing radiation. □ **dosimetric** /-ˈmetrɪk/ adj. **dosimetry** n.

doss v. & n. Brit. sl. —v.intr. (often foll. by down) sleep, esp. roughly or in cheap lodgings. —n. a bed, esp. in cheap lodgings. □ **doss-house** a cheap lodging-house, esp. for vagrants. [prob. = doss ornamental covering for a seat-back etc. f. OF dos ult. f. L dorsum back]

dosser /ˈdɒsə(r)/ n. Brit. sl. 1 a person who dosses. 2 = doss-house.

dossier /ˈdɒsɪə(r), -ɪ,eɪ/ n. a set of documents, esp. a collection of information about a person, event, or subject. [F, so called from the label on the back, f. dos back f. L dorsum]

dot n. & v. —n. 1 a a small spot, speck, or mark. b such a mark written or printed as part of an i or j, as a diacritical mark, as one of a series of marks to signify omission, or as a full stop. c a decimal point. 2 Mus. a dot used to denote the lengthening of a note or rest, or to indicate staccato. 3 the shorter signal of the two used in Morse code. —v.tr. (**dotted**, **dotting**) 1 a mark with a dot or dots. b place a dot over (a letter). 2 Mus. mark (a note or rest) to show that the time value is increased by half. 3 (often foll. by about) scatter like dots. 4 partly cover as with dots (a sea dotted with ships). 5 sl. hit (dotted him one in the eye). □ **dot the i's and cross the t's** colloq. 1 be minutely accurate, emphasize details. 2 add the final touches to a task, exercise, etc. **dot matrix printer** Computing a printer with characters formed from dots printed by configurations of the tips of small wires. **dotted line** a line of dots on a document, esp. to show a place left for a signature. **on the dot** exactly on time. **the year dot** Brit. colloq. far in the past. □ **dotter** n. [OE dott head of a boil, perh. infl. by Du. dot knot]

dotage /ˈdəʊtɪdʒ/ n. feeble-minded senility (in his dotage).

dotard /ˈdəʊtəd/ n. a person who is feeble-minded, esp. from senility. [ME f. DOTE + -ARD]

dote /dəʊt/ v.intr. 1 (foll. by on, upon) be foolishly or excessively fond of. 2 be silly or feeble-minded, esp. from old age. □ **doter** n. **dotingly** adv. [ME, corresp. to MDu. doten be silly]

dotterel /ˈdɒtər(ə)l/ n. a small migrant plover, Eudromias morinellus. [ME f. DOTE + dimin. suffix -rel, named from the ease with which it is caught, taken to indicate stupidity]

dottle /ˈdɒt(ə)l/ n. a remnant of unburnt tobacco in a pipe. [DOT + -LE¹]

dotty /ˈdɒtɪ/ adj. (**dottier**, **dottiest**) colloq. 1 feeble-minded, silly. 2 eccentric. 3 absurd. 4 (foll. by about, on) infatuated with; obsessed by. □ **dottily** adv. **dottiness** n. [earlier = unsteady: f. DOT + -Y¹]

double /ˈdʌb(ə)l/ adj., adv., n., & v. —adj. 1 a consisting of two usu. equal parts or things; twofold. b consisting of two identical parts. 2 twice as much or many (double the amount; double the number; double thickness). 3 having twice the usual size, quantity, strength, etc. (double whisky). 4 designed for two people (double bed). 5 a having some part double. b (of a flower) having more than one circle of petals. 6 having two different roles or interpretations, esp. implying confusion or deceit (double meaning; leads a double life). —adv. 1 at or to twice the amount etc. (counts double). 2 two together (sleep double). —n. 1 a a

double quantity or thing; twice as much or many. b colloq. a double measure of spirits. 2 a a counterpart of a person or thing; a person who looks exactly like another. b an understudy. 3 (in pl.) Sport (in lawn tennis) a game between two pairs of players. 4 Sport a pair of victories over the same team, a pair of championships at the same game, etc. 5 a system of betting in which the winnings and stake from the first bet are transferred to a second. 6 Bridge the doubling of an opponent's bid. 7 Darts a hit on the narrow ring enclosed by the two outer circles of a dartboard, scoring double. —v. 1 tr. & intr. make or become twice as much or many; increase twofold; multiply by two. 2 tr. amount to twice as much as. 3 a tr. fold or bend (paper, cloth, etc.) over on itself. b intr. become folded. 4 a tr. (of an actor) play (two parts) in the same piece. b intr. (often foll. by for) be understudy etc. 5 intr. (usu. foll. by as) play a twofold role. 6 intr. turn sharply in flight or pursuit; take a tortuous course. 7 tr. Naut. sail round (a headland). 8 tr. Bridge make a call increasing the value of the points to be won or lost on (an opponent's bid). 9 Mus. intr. (often foll. by on) play two or more musical instruments (the clarinettist doubles on tenor sax). 10 tr. clench (a fist). □ **at the double** running, hurrying. **bent double** folded, stooping. **double agent** one who spies simultaneously for two rival countries etc. **double back** take a new direction opposite to the previous one. **double-barrelled** 1 (of a gun) having two barrels. 2 Brit. (of a surname) having two parts joined by a hyphen. 3 twofold. **double-bass** 1 the largest and lowest-pitched instrument of the violin family. 2 its player. **double bill** a programme with two principal items. **double bind** a dilemma. **double-blind** adj. (of a test or experiment) in which neither the tester nor the subject has knowledge of identities etc. that might lead to bias. —n. such a test or experiment. **double bluff** an action or statement intended to appear as a bluff, but in fact genuine. **double boiler** a saucepan with a detachable upper compartment heated by boiling water in the lower one. **double-breasted** (of a coat etc.) having two fronts overlapping across the body. **double-check** verify twice or in two ways. **double chin** a chin with a fold of loose flesh below it. **double cream** thick cream with a high fat-content. **double-cross** v.tr. deceive or betray (a person one is supposedly helping). —n. an act of doing this. **double-dealing** n. deceit, esp. in business. —adj. deceitful; practising deceit. **double-decker** 1 esp. Brit. a bus having an upper and lower deck. 2 colloq. anything consisting of two layers. **double Dutch** Brit. colloq. incomprehensible talk. **double-dyed** deeply affected with guilt. **double eagle** a figure of a two-headed eagle. **double-edged** 1 having two functions or (often contradictory) applications. 2 (of a knife etc.) having two cutting-edges. **double entry** a system of bookkeeping in which each transaction is entered as a debit in one account and a credit in another. **double exposure** Photog. the accidental or deliberate repeated exposure of a plate, film, etc. **double-faced** 1 insincere. 2 (of a fabric or material) finished on both sides so that either may be used as the right side. **double fault** (in lawn tennis) two consecutive faults in serving. **double feature** a cinema programme with two full-length films. **double figures** the numbers from 10 to 99. **double first** Brit. **1** first-class honours in two subjects or examinations at a university. **2** a person achieving this. **double-fronted** (of a house) with principal windows on either side of the front door. **double glazing 1** a window consisting of two layers of glass with a space between them, designed to reduce loss of heat and exclude noise. **2** the provision of this. **double Gloucester** a kind of hard cheese orig. made in Gloucestershire. **double helix** a pair of parallel helices with a common axis, esp. in the structure of the DNA molecule. **double-jointed** having joints that allow unusual bending of the fingers, limbs, etc. **double negative** Gram. a negative statement containing two negative elements (e.g. didn't say nothing). **double or quits** a gamble to decide whether a player's loss or debt be doubled or cancelled. **double-park** park (a vehicle) alongside one that is already parked at the roadside. **double play** Baseball putting out two runners. **double pneumonia** pneumonia affecting both lungs. **double-quick** very quick or quickly. **double saucepan** Brit. = double boiler. **double standard** a rule or principle applied more strictly to some people than to others (or to oneself). **double-stopping** Mus. the sounding of two strings at once on a violin etc. **double take** a delayed reaction to a situation etc. immediately after one's first reaction. **double-talk** verbal expression that is (usu. deliberately) ambiguous or misleading. **double-think** the mental capacity to accept contrary opinions or beliefs at the same time esp. as a result of political indoctrination. **double time 1** payment of an employee at twice the normal rate. **2** Mil. the regulation running-pace. **double up 1 a** bend or curl up. **b** cause to do this, esp. by a blow. **2** be overcome with pain or laughter. **3** share or assign to a room, quarters, etc., with another or others. **4** fold or become folded. **5** use winnings from a bet as stake for another. □ **doubler** n. **doubly** adv. [ME f. OF doble, duble (n.), dobler, dubler (v.) f. L duplus DUPLE]

■ **Usage** The double negative is considered incorrect in standard English.

---

double entendre /ˌduːbˈ(ə)l ɑːnˈtɑːndrə/ n. **1** a word or phrase open to two interpretations, one usu. risqué or indecent. **2** humour using such words or phrases. [obs. F, = double understanding]

doublet /ˈdʌblɪt/ n. **1** either of a pair of similar things, esp. either of two words of the same derivation but different sense (e.g. fashion and faction, cloak and clock). **2** hist. a man's short close-fitting jacket, with or without sleeves. [ME f. OF f. double: see DOUBLE]

doubloon /dʌbˈluːn, dəb-/ n. hist. a Spanish gold coin. [F doublon or Sp. doblón (as DOUBLE)]

doubt /daʊt/ n. & v. —n. **1** a feeling of uncertainty; an undecided state of mind (be in no doubt about; have no doubt that). **2** (often foll. by of, about) an inclination to disbelieve (have one's doubts about). **3** an uncertain state of things. **4** a lack of full proof or clear indication (benefit of the doubt). —v. **1** tr. (often foll. by whether, if, that + clause; also foll. (after neg. or interrog.) by but, but that) feel uncertain or undecided about (I doubt that you are right; I do not doubt but that you are wrong). **2** tr. hesitate to believe or trust. **3** intr. (often foll. by of) feel uncertain or undecided; have doubts (never doubted of success). **4** tr. call in question. □ **in doubt** uncertain; open to question. **no doubt** certainly; probably; admittedly. **without doubt** (or **a doubt**) certainly. □ **doubtable** adj. **doubter** n. **doubtingly** adv. [ME doute f. OF doute (n.), douter (v.) f. L dubitare hesitate; mod. spelling after L]

doubtful /ˈdaʊtfʊl/ adj. **1** feeling doubt or misgivings; unsure or guarded in one's opinion. **2** causing doubt; ambiguous; uncertain in meaning etc. **3** unreliable (a doubtful ally). □ **doubtfully** adv. **doubtfulness** n.

doubtless /ˈdaʊtlɪs/ adv. (often qualifying a sentence) **1** certainly; no doubt. **2** probably. □ **doubtlessly** adv.

douche /duːʃ/ n. & v. —n. **1** a jet of liquid applied to part of the body for cleansing or medicinal purposes. **2** a device for producing such a jet. —v. **1** tr. treat with a douche. **2** intr. use a douche. [F f. It. doccia pipe f. docciare pour by drops ult. f. L ductus: see DUCT]

dough /dəʊ/ n. **1** a thick mixture of flour etc. and liquid (usu. water), for baking into bread, pastry, etc. **2** sl. money. [OE dāg f. Gmc]

doughnut /ˈdəʊnʌt/ n. (US **donut**) a small fried cake of sweetened dough, usu. in the shape of a ball or ring.

doughty /ˈdaʊtɪ/ adj. (**doughtier, doughtiest**) archaic or joc. valiant, stout-hearted. □ **doughtily** adv. **doughtiness** n. [OE dohtig var. of dyhtig f. Gmc]

doughy /ˈdəʊɪ/ adj. (**doughier, doughiest**) **1** having the form or consistency of dough. **2** pale and sickly in colour. □ **doughiness** n.

dour /dʊə(r)/ adj. severe, stern, or sullenly obstinate in manner or appearance. □ **dourly** adv. **dourness** n. [ME (orig. Sc.), prob. f. Gael. dúr dull, obstinate, perh. f. L durus hard]

douse /daʊs/ v.tr. (also **dowse**) **1 a** throw water over. **b** plunge into water. **2** extinguish (a light). [16th c.: perh. rel. to MDu., LG dossen strike]

dove[1] /dʌv/ n. **1** any bird of the family Columbidae, with short legs, small head, and large breast. **2** a gentle or innocent person. **3** Polit. an advocate of peace or peaceful policies. **4** a soft grey colour. □ **dovelike** adj. [ME f. ON dúfa f. Gmc]

dove[2] US past and past part. of DIVE.

dovecote /ˈdʌvkɒt/ n. (also **dovecot**) a shelter with nesting-holes for domesticated pigeons.

dovetail /ˈdʌvteɪl/ n. & v. —n. **1** a joint formed by a mortise with a tenon shaped like a dove's spread tail or a reversed wedge. **2** such a tenon. —v. **1** tr. join together by means of a dovetail. **2** tr. & intr. (often foll. by with, into) fit readily together; combine neatly or compactly.

dowager /ˈdaʊədʒə(r)/ n. **1** a widow with a title or property derived from her late husband (Queen dowager; dowager duchess). **2** colloq. a dignified elderly woman. [OF douag(i)ere f. douage (as DOWER)]

dowdy /ˈdaʊdɪ/ adj. & n. —adj. (**dowdier, dowdiest**) **1** (of clothes) unattractively dull; unfashionable. **2** (of a person, esp. a woman) dressed in dowdy clothes. —n. (pl. **-ies**) a dowdy woman. □ **dowdily** adv. **dowdiness** n. [ME dowd slut, of unkn. orig.]

dowel /ˈdaʊəl/ n. & v. —n. a headless peg of wood, metal, or plastic for holding together components of a structure. —v.tr. (**dowelled**, **dowelling**; US **doweled**, **doweling**) fasten with a dowel or dowels. [ME f. MLG *dovel*: cf. THOLE]

dowelling /ˈdaʊəlɪŋ/ n. (US **doweling**) round rods for cutting into dowels.

dower /ˈdaʊə(r)/ n. & v. —n. 1 a widow's share for life of her husband's estate. 2 *archaic* a dowry. 3 a natural gift or talent. —v.tr. 1 *archaic* give a dowry to. 2 (foll. by *with*) endow with talent etc. □ **dower house** *Brit.* a smaller house near a big one, forming part of a widow's dower. □ **dowerless** adj. [ME f. OF *douaire* f. med.L *dotarium* f. L *dos dotis*]

Dow–Jones index /daʊˈdʒəʊnz/ n. (also **Dow–Jones average**) a figure based on the average price of selected stocks, indicating the relative price of shares on the New York Stock Exchange. [C. H. *Dow* d. 1902 & E. D. *Jones* d. 1920, Amer. economists]

down[1] /daʊn/ adv., prep., adj., v., & n. —adv. (*superl.* **downmost**) 1 into or towards a lower place, esp. to the ground (*fall down*; *knelt down*). 2 in a lower place or position (*blinds were down*). 3 to or in a place regarded as lower, esp.: **a** southwards. **b** *Brit.* away from a major city or a university. 4 **a** in or into a low or weaker position or condition (*hit a man when he's down*; *many down with colds*). **b** *Brit.* in a position of lagging or loss (*our team was three goals down*; *£5 down on the transaction*). **c** (of a computer system) out of action or unavailable for use (esp. temporarily). 5 from an earlier to a later time (*customs handed down*; *down to 1600*). 6 to a finer or thinner consistency or a smaller amount or size (*grind down*; *water down*; *boil down*). 7 cheaper; lower in price or value (*bread is down*; *shares are down*). 8 into a more settled state (*calm down*). 9 in writing; in or into recorded or listed form (*copy it down*; *I got it down on tape*). 10 (of part of a larger whole) paid, dealt with (*£5 down, £20 to pay*). 11 *Naut.* with the current or wind. 12 inclusively of the lower limit in a series (*read down to the third paragraph*). 13 (as *int.*) lie down, put (something) down, etc. 14 downstairs, esp. after rising (*is not down yet*). 15 swallowed (*could not get the pill down*). 16 *Amer.* Football (of the ball) out of play. —prep. 1 downwards along, through, or into. 2 from top to bottom of. 3 along (*walk down the road*; *cut down the middle*). 4 at or in a lower part of (*situated down the river*). —adj. (*superl.* **downmost**) 1 directed downwards. 2 *Brit.* of travel away from a capital or centre (*the down train*). —v.tr. *colloq.* 1 knock or bring down. 2 swallow (a drink). —n. 1 an act of putting down (esp. an opponent in wrestling, or the ball in American football). 2 a reverse of fortune (*ups and downs*). 3 *colloq.* a period of depression. □ **be** (or **have a**) **down on** *colloq.* disapprove of; show animosity towards. **be down to 1** be attributable to. 2 be the responsibility of. 3 have used up everything except (*down to their last tin of rations*). **down and out 1** penniless, destitute. 2 *Boxing* unable to resume the fight. **down-and-out** n. a destitute person. **down at heel 1** (of a shoe) with the heel worn down. 2 (of a person) wearing such shoes; shabby, slovenly. **down in the mouth** *colloq.* looking unhappy. **down-market** adj. & adv. *colloq.* towards or relating to the cheaper or less affluent sector of

the market. **down on one's luck** *colloq.* 1 temporarily unfortunate. 2 dispirited by misfortune. **down payment** a partial payment made at the time of purchase. **down stage** *Theatr.* at or to the front of the stage. **down time** time during which a machine, esp. a computer, is out of action or unavailable for use. **down-to-earth** practical, realistic. **down to the ground** *colloq.* completely. **down tools** *colloq.* cease work, esp. to go on strike. **down town 1** into a town from a higher or outlying part. 2 *US* to or in the business part of a city (see also DOWNTOWN). **down under** *colloq.* in the antipodes, esp. Australia. **down wind** in the direction in which the wind is blowing (see also DOWNWIND). **down with** *int.* expressing strong disapproval or rejection of a specified person or thing. [OE *dūn(e)* f. *adūne* ADOWN]

down[2] /daʊn/ n. 1 **a** the first covering of young birds. **b** a bird's under-plumage, used in cushions etc. **c** a layer of fine soft feathers. 2 fine soft hair esp. on the face. 3 short soft hairs on some leaves, fruit, seeds, etc. 4 a fluffy substance. [ME f. ON *dúnn*]

down[3] /daʊn/ n. 1 an area of open rolling land. 2 (in *pl.*; usu. prec. by *the*) undulating chalk and limestone uplands esp. in S. England, with few trees and used mainly for pasture. □ **downy** adj. [OE *dūn* perh. f. OCelt.]

downbeat /ˈdaʊnbiːt/ n. & adj. —n. *Mus.* an accented beat, usu. the first of the bar. —adj. 1 pessimistic, gloomy. 2 relaxed.

downcast /ˈdaʊnkɑːst/ adj. 1 (of eyes) looking downwards. 2 (of a person) dejected.

downer /ˈdaʊnə(r)/ n. *sl.* 1 a depressant or tranquillizing drug, esp. a barbiturate. 2 a depressing person or experience; a failure. 3 = DOWNTURN.

downfall /ˈdaʊnfɔːl/ n. 1 **a** a fall from prosperity or power. **b** the cause of this. 2 a sudden heavy fall of rain etc.

downgrade /ˈdaʊngreɪd/ v. & n. —v.tr. 1 make lower in rank or status. 2 speak disparagingly of. —n. *US* a downward grade. □ **on the downgrade** *US* in decline.

downhearted /daʊnˈhɑːtɪd/ adj. in low spirits. □ **downheartedly** adv. **downheartedness** n.

downhill adv., adj., & n. —adv. /daʊnˈhɪl/ in a descending direction, esp. towards the bottom of an incline. —adj. /ˈdaʊnhɪl/ 1 sloping down, descending. 2 declining; deteriorating. —n. /ˈdaʊnhɪl/ 1 *Skiing* a downhill race. 2 a downward slope. 3 a decline. □ **go downhill** *colloq.* decline, deteriorate (in health, state of repair, moral state, etc.).

downland /ˈdaʊnlənd/ n. = DOWN.

download /daʊnˈləʊd/ v.tr. *Computing* transfer (data) from one storage device or system to another (esp. smaller remote one).

downpipe /ˈdaʊnpaɪp/ n. *Brit.* a pipe to carry rainwater from a roof to a drain or to ground level.

downplay /daʊnˈpleɪ/ v.tr. play down; minimize the importance of.

downpour /ˈdaʊnpɔː(r)/ n. a heavy fall of rain.

downright /ˈdaʊnraɪt/ adj. & adv. —adj. 1 plain, definite, straightforward, blunt. 2 utter, complete (*downright nonsense*). —adv. completely, positively (*downright rude*). □ **downrightness** n.

downscale /ˈdaʊnskeɪl/ v. & adj. *US* —v.tr. reduce or restrict in size, scale, or extent. —adj. at the lower end of a scale, esp. a social scale; inferior.

downspout /ˈdaʊnspaʊt/ n. US = DOWNPIPE.

Down's syndrome /daʊnz/ n. Med. a congenital disorder due to a chromosome defect, characterized by mental retardation and physical abnormalities. [J. L. H. *Down*, Engl. physician d. 1896]

downstairs adv., adj., & n. —adv. /daʊnˈsteəz/ 1 down a flight of stairs. 2 to or on a lower floor. —adj. /ˈdaʊnsteəz/ (also **downstair**) situated downstairs. —n. /daʊnˈsteəz/ the lower floor.

downstream /ˈdaʊnstriːm/ adv. & adj. —adv. in the direction of the flow of a stream etc. —adj. moving downstream.

downtown /ˈdaʊntaʊn/ adj., n., & adv. US —adj. of or in the lower or more central part, or the business part, of a town or city. —n. a downtown area. —adv. in or into a downtown area.

downtrodden /ˈdaʊnˌtrɒd(ə)n/ adj. oppressed; badly treated; kept under.

downturn /ˈdaʊntɜːn/ n. a decline, esp. in economic or business activity.

downward /ˈdaʊnwəd/ adv. & adj. —adv. (also **downwards**) towards what is lower, inferior, less important, or later. —adj. moving, extending, pointing, or leading downward. □ **downwardly** adv.

downwind /ˈdaʊnwɪnd/ adj. & adv. in the direction in which the wind is blowing.

downy /ˈdaʊnɪ/ adj. (**downier, downiest**) 1 a of, like, or covered with down. b soft and fluffy. 2 Brit. sl. aware, knowing. □ **downily** adv. **downiness** n.

dowry /ˈdaʊərɪ/ n. (pl. **-ies**) 1 property or money brought by a bride to her husband. 2 a talent, a natural gift. [ME f. AF *dowarie*, OF *douaire* DOWER]

dowse[1] /daʊz/ v.intr. search for underground water or minerals by holding a Y-shaped stick or rod which dips abruptly when over the right spot. □ **dowsing-rod** such a stick or rod. □ **dowser** n. [17th c.: orig. unkn.]

dowse[2] var. of DOUSE.

doxology /dɒkˈsɒlədʒɪ/ n. (pl. **-ies**) a liturgical formula of praise to God. □ **doxological** /-səˈlɒdʒɪk(ə)l/ adj. [med.L *doxologia* f. Gk *doxologia* f. *doxa* glory + -LOGY]

doyen /ˈdɔɪən, ˈdwɑːjæ̃/ n. (fem. **doyenne** /dɔɪˈen, dwɑːˈjen/) the senior member of a body of colleagues, esp. the senior ambassador at a court. [F (as DEAN[1])]

doyley var. of DOILY.

doz. abbr. dozen.

doze /dəʊz/ v. & n. —v.intr. sleep lightly; be half asleep. —n. a short light sleep. □ **doze off** fall lightly asleep. □ **dozer** n. [17th c.: cf. Da. *døse* make drowsy]

dozen /ˈdʌz(ə)n/ n. 1 (prec. by a or a number) (pl. **dozen**) twelve, regarded collectively (a dozen eggs; two dozen packets). 2 a set or group of twelve (packed in dozens). 3 colloq. about twelve, a fairly large indefinite number. 4 (in pl.; usu. foll. by of) colloq. very many (made dozens of mistakes). □ **talk nineteen to the dozen** Brit. talk incessantly. □ **dozenth** adj. & n. [ME f. OF *dozeine*, ult. f. L *duodecim* twelve]

dozy /ˈdəʊzɪ/ adj. (**dozier, doziest**) 1 drowsy; tending to doze. 2 Brit. colloq. stupid or lazy. □ **dozily** adv. **doziness** n.

D.Phil. abbr. Doctor of Philosophy.

DPP abbr. (in the UK) Director of Public Prosecutions.

Dr abbr. 1 Doctor. 2 Drive. 3 debtor.

drab[1] adj. & n. —adj. (**drabber, drabbest**) 1 dull, uninteresting. 2 of a dull brownish colour. —n. 1 drab colour. 2 monotony. □ **drably** adv. **drabness** n. [prob. f. obs. *drap* cloth f. OF f. LL *drappus*, perh. of Celt. orig.]

drab[2] see DRIBS AND DRABS.

drachm /dræm/ n. Brit. a weight or measure formerly used by apothecaries, equivalent to 60 grains or one eighth of an ounce. [ME *dragme* f. OF *dragme* or LL *dragma* f. L *drachma* f. Gk *drakhmē* Attic weight and coin]

drachma /ˈdrækmə/ n. (pl. **drachmas** or **drachmae** /-miː/) 1 the chief monetary unit of Greece. 2 a silver coin of ancient Greece. [L f. Gk *drakhmē*]

drack /dræk/ adj. Austral. sl. 1 (esp. of a woman) unattractive. 2 dismal, dull. [20th c.: orig. unkn.]

Draconian /drəˈkəʊnɪən, dreɪ-/ adj. (also **Draconic** /-ˈkɒnɪk/) very harsh or severe (esp. of laws and their application). [*Drakōn*, 7th-c. BC Athenian legislator]

draft /drɑːft/ n. & v. —n. 1 a a preliminary written version of a speech, document, etc. b a rough preliminary outline of a scheme. c a sketch of work to be carried out. 2 a a written order for payment of money by a bank. b the drawing of money by means of this. 3 a a party detached from a larger group for a special duty or purpose. b the selection of this. 4 US compulsory military service. 5 US = DRAUGHT. —v.tr. 1 prepare a draft of (a document, scheme, etc.). 2 select for a special duty or purpose. 3 US conscript for military service. □ **draftee** /-ˈtiː/ n.

drafter n. [phonetic spelling of DRAUGHT]

draftsman /ˈdrɑːftsmən/ n. (pl. **-men**) 1 a person who drafts documents. 2 = DRAUGHTSMAN 1. [phonetic spelling of DRAUGHTSMAN]

drafty US var. of DRAUGHTY.

drag v. & n. —v. (**dragged, dragging**) 1 tr. pull along with effort or difficulty. 2 a tr. allow (one's feet, tail, etc.) to trail along the ground. b intr. trail along the ground. c intr. (of time etc.) go or pass heavily or slowly or tediously. 3 a intr. (usu. foll. by for) use a grapnel or drag (to find a drowned person or lost object). b intr. search the bottom of (a river etc.) with grapnels, nets, or drags. 4 tr. (often foll. by to) colloq. take (a person to a place etc., esp. against his or her will). 5 intr. (foll. by on, at) draw on (a cigarette etc.). 6 intr. (often foll. by on) continue at tedious length. —n. 1 an obstruction to progress. 2 colloq. a boring or dreary person, duty, performance, etc. 3 a a strong-smelling lure drawn before hounds as a substitute for a fox. b a hunt using this. 4 an apparatus for dredging or recovering drowned persons etc. from under water. 5 = drag-net. 6 sl. a draw on a cigarette etc. 7 sl. women's clothes worn by men. 8 an act of dragging. 9 a (in full **drag race**) an acceleration race between cars usu. for a quarter of a mile. 10 US sl. a street or road (the main drag). □ **drag one's feet** (or **heels**) be deliberately slow or reluctant to act. **drag in** introduce (a subject) irrelevantly. **drag-net** 1 a net drawn through a river or across ground to trap fish or game. 2 a systematic hunt for criminals etc. **drag out** protract. **drag queen** sl. a male homosexual transvestite. **drag up** *colloq.* **1** deliberately mention (an unwelcome subject). **2** rear (a child) roughly and without proper training. [ME f. OE *dragan* or ON *draga* DRAW]

dragée /ˈdrɑːʒeɪ/ *n.* **1** a sugar-coated almond etc. **2** a small silver ball for decorating a cake. **3** a chocolate-coated sweet. [F: see DREDGE²]

draggle /ˈdræg(ə)l/ *v.* **1** *tr.* make dirty or wet or limp by trailing. **2** *intr.* hang trailing. **3** *intr.* lag; straggle in the rear. [DRAG + -LE⁴]

draggy /ˈdrægɪ/ *adj.* (**draggier**, **draggiest**) *colloq.* **1** tedious. **2** unpleasant.

dragon /ˈdrægən/ *n.* **1** a mythical monster like a reptile, usu. with wings and claws and able to breathe out fire. **2** a fierce person, esp. a woman. [ME f. OF f. L *draco -onis* f. Gk *drakōn* serpent]

dragonfly /ˈdrægənˌflaɪ/ *n.* (*pl.* **-ies**) any of various insects of the order Odonata, having a long slender body and two pairs of large transparent wings.

dragoon /drəˈguːn/ *n. & v.* —*n.* **1** a cavalryman (orig. a mounted infantryman armed with a carbine). **2** a rough fierce fellow. —*v.tr.* (foll. by *into*) coerce into doing something, esp. by use of strong force. [orig. = carbine (thought of as breathing fire) f. F *dragon* DRAGON]

dragster /ˈdrægstə(r)/ *n.* a car built or modified to take part in drag races.

drain *v. & n.* —*v.* **1** *tr.* draw off liquid from, esp.: **a** make (land etc.) dry by providing an outflow for moisture. **b** (of a river) carry off the superfluous water of (a district). **c** remove purulent matter from (an abscess). **2** *tr.* (foll. by *off, away*) draw off (liquid) esp. by a pipe. **3** *intr.* (foll. by *away, off, through*) flow or trickle away. **4** *intr.* (of a wet cloth, a vessel, etc.) become dry as liquid flows away (*put it there to drain*). **5** *tr.* (often foll. by *of*) exhaust or deprive (a person or thing) of strength, resources, property, etc. **6** *tr.* **a** drink (liquid) to the dregs. **b** empty (a vessel) by drinking the contents. —*n.* **1 a** a channel, conduit, or pipe carrying off liquid, esp. an artificial conduit for water or sewage. **b** a tube for drawing off the discharge from an abscess etc. **2** a constant outflow, withdrawal, or expenditure (*a great drain on my resources*). □ **down the drain** *colloq.* lost, wasted. **laugh like a drain** laugh copiously; guffaw. [OE *drē(a)hnian* f. Gmc]

drainage /ˈdreɪnɪdʒ/ *n.* **1** the process or means of draining (*the land has poor drainage*). **2** a system of drains, artificial or natural. **3** what is drained off, esp. sewage.

drainboard /ˈdreɪnbɔːd/ *n.* US = DRAINING-BOARD.

drainer /ˈdreɪnə(r)/ *n.* **1** a device for draining; anything on which things are put to drain, e.g. a draining-board. **2** a person who drains.

draining-board /ˈdreɪnɪŋˌbɔːd/ *n.* a sloping usu. grooved surface beside a sink, on which washed dishes etc. are left to drain.

drake *n.* a male duck. [ME prob. f. Gmc]

dram *n.* **1** a small drink of spirits. **2** = DRACHM. [ME f. OF *drame* or med.L *drama, dragma*: cf. DRACHM]

drama /ˈdrɑːmə/ *n.* **1** a play for acting on stage or for broadcasting. **2** (often prec. by *the*) the art of writing and presenting plays. **3** an exciting or emotional event, set of circumstances, etc. **4** dramatic quality (*the drama of the situation*). [LL f. Gk *drama -atos* f. *draō* do]

dramatic /drəˈmætɪk/ *adj.* **1** of drama or the study of drama. **2** (of an event, circumstance, etc.) sudden and exciting or unexpected. **3** vividly striking. **4** (of a gesture etc.) theatrical, overdone, absurd. □ **dramatic irony** = *tragic irony*. □ **dramatically** *adv.* [LL *dramaticus* f. Gk *dramatikos* (as DRAMA)]

dramatics /drəˈmætɪks/ *n.pl.* (often treated as *sing.*) **1** the production and performance of plays. **2** exaggerated or showy behaviour.

dramatis personae /ˌdræmətɪs pɜːˈsəʊnaɪ, -niː/ *n.pl.* (often treated as *sing.*) **1** the characters in a play. **2** a list of these. [L, = persons of the drama]

dramatist /ˈdræmətɪst/ *n.* a writer of dramas.

dramatize /ˈdræməˌtaɪz/ *v.* (also **-ise**) **1 a** *tr.* adapt (a novel etc.) to form a stage play. **b** *intr.* admit of such adaptation. **2** *tr.* make a drama or dramatic scene of. **3** *tr.* (also *absol.*) express or react to in a dramatic way. □ **dramatization** /-ˈzeɪʃ(ə)n/ *n.*

drank *past* of DRINK.

drape *v. & n.* —*v.tr.* **1** hang, cover loosely, or adorn with cloth etc. **2** arrange (clothes or hangings) carefully in folds. —*n.* **1** (often in *pl.*) a curtain or drapery. **2** a piece of drapery. **3** the way in which a garment or fabric hangs. [ME f. OF *draper* f. *drap* f. LL *drappus* cloth]

draper /ˈdreɪpə(r)/ *n.* *Brit.* a retailer of textile fabrics. [ME f. AF, OF *drapier* (as DRAPE)]

drapery /ˈdreɪpərɪ/ *n.* (*pl.* **-ies**) **1** clothing or hangings arranged in folds. **2** (often in *pl.*) a curtain or hanging. **3** *Brit.* cloth; textile fabrics. **4** *Brit.* the trade of a draper. **5** the arrangement of clothing in sculpture or painting. [ME f. OF *draperie* f. *drap* cloth]

drastic /ˈdræstɪk, ˈdrɑː-/ *adj.* having a strong or far-reaching effect; severe. □ **drastically** *adv.* [Gk *drastikos* f. *draō* do]

drat *v. & int.* *colloq.* —*v.tr.* (**dratted**, **dratting** (usu. as an exclam.)) curse, confound (*drat the thing!*). —*int.* expressing anger or annoyance. □ **dratted** *adj.* [for 'od (= God) *rot*]

draught /drɑːft/ *n. & v.* (*US* **draft**) —*n.* **1** a current of air in a confined space (e.g. a room or chimney). **2** pulling, traction. **3** *Naut.* the depth of water needed to float a ship. **4** the drawing of liquor from a cask etc. **5 a** a single act of drinking. **b** the amount drunk in this. **c** a dose of liquid medicine. **6** (in *pl.*; usu. treated as *sing.*) *Brit.* a game for two played with 12 pieces each on a draughtboard. **7** = DRAFT. —*v.tr.* = DRAFT. □ **draught beer** beer drawn from a cask, not bottled. **draught-horse** a horse used for pulling heavy loads, esp. a cart or plough. [ME *draht*, perh. f. ON *drahtr*, *dráttr* f. Gmc, rel. to DRAW]

draughtboard /ˈdrɑːftbɔːd/ *n.* a chequered board, identical to a chessboard, used in draughts.

draughtsman /ˈdrɑːftsmən/ *n.* (*pl.* **-men**) **1** a person who makes drawings or plans. **2** /ˈdrɑːftsmæn/ a piece in the game of draughts. **3** = DRAFTSMAN. □ **draughtsmanship** *n.* [*draught's* + MAN]

draughty /ˈdrɑːftɪ/ *adj.* (*US* **drafty**) (**-ier**, **-iest**) (of a room etc.) letting in sharp currents of air. □ **draughtily** *adv.* **draughtiness** *n.*

draw v. & n. —v. (past **drew**; past part. **drawn**) **1** tr. pull or cause to move towards or after one. **2** tr. pull (a thing) up, over, or across. **3** tr. pull (curtains etc.) open or shut. **4** tr. take (a person) aside, esp. to talk to. **5** tr. attract; bring to oneself or to something; take in (drew a deep breath; I felt drawn to her; drew my attention to the matter). **6** intr. (foll. by at, on) suck smoke from (a cigarette, pipe, etc.). **7** tr. (also absol.) take out; remove (e.g. a tooth, a gun from a holster, etc.). **8** tr. obtain or take from a source (draw a salary; draw inspiration). **9** tr. trace (a line, mark, furrow, or figure). **10 a** tr. produce (a picture) by tracing lines and marks. **b** tr. represent (a thing) by this means. **c** absol. make a drawing. **11** tr. (also absol.) finish (a contest or game) with neither side winning. **12** intr. make one's or its way, proceed, move, come (drew near the bridge; draw to a close). **13** tr. infer, deduce (a conclusion). **14** tr. **a** elicit, evoke. **b** bring about, entail (draw criticism; draw ruin upon oneself). **c** induce (a person) to reveal facts, feelings, or talent (refused to be drawn). **d** (foll. by to + infin.) induce (a person) to do something. **e** Cards cause to be played (drew all the trumps). **15** tr. haul up (water) from a well. **16** tr. bring out (liquid from a vessel or blood from a wound). **17** tr. extract a liquid essence from. **18** intr. (of a chimney or pipe) promote or allow a draught. **19** intr. (of tea) infuse. **20 a** tr. obtain by lot (drew the winner). **b** absol. draw lots. **21** intr. (foll. by on) make a demand on a person, a person's skill, memory, imagination, etc. **22** tr. write out (a bill, cheque, or draft) (drew a cheque on the bank). **23** tr. frame (a document) in due form, compose. **24** tr. formulate or perceive (a comparison or distinction). **25** tr. (of a ship) require (a specified depth of water) to float in. **26** tr. disembowel (hang, draw, and quarter). **27** tr. Hunting search (cover) for game. **28** tr. drag (a badger or fox) from a hole. **29** tr. **a** protract, stretch, elongate (long-drawn agony). **b** make (wire) by pulling a piece of metal through successively smaller holes. —n. **1** an act of drawing. **2 a** a person or thing that draws custom, attention, etc. **b** the power to attract attention. **3** the drawing of lots, esp. a raffle. **4** a drawn game. **5** a suck on a cigarette etc. **6** the act of removing a gun from its holster in order to shoot (quick on the draw). **7** strain, pull. □ **draw back** withdraw from an undertaking. **draw a person's fire** attract hostility, criticism, etc., away from a more important target. **draw in 1 a** (of successive days) become shorter because of the changing seasons. **b** (of a day) approach its end. **c** (of successive evenings or nights) start earlier because of the changing seasons. **2** persuade to join, entice. **3** (of a train etc.) arrive at a station. **draw in one's horns** become less assertive or ambitious; draw back. **draw the line at** set a limit (of tolerance etc.) at. **draw off** withdraw (troops). **draw on 1** approach, come near. **2** lead to, bring about. **3** allure. **4** put (gloves, boots, etc.) on. **draw out 1** prolong. **2** elicit. **3** induce to talk. **4** (of successive days) become longer because of the changing seasons. **5** (of a train etc.) leave a station etc. **6** write out in proper form. **7** lead out, detach, or array (troops). **draw-sheet** a sheet that can be taken from under a patient without remaking the bed. **draw-string** a string that can be pulled to tighten the mouth of a bag, the waist of a garment, etc. **draw stumps** Cricket take the stumps out of the ground at the close of play. **draw up 1** compose or draft (a document etc.). **2** bring or come into regular order. **3** come to a halt. **4** make (oneself) stiffly erect. **5** (foll. by with, to) gain on or overtake. □ **quick on the draw** quick to act or react. [OE dragan f. Gmc]

drawback /ˈdrɔːbæk/ n. a thing that impairs satisfaction; a disadvantage.

drawbridge /ˈdrɔːbrɪdʒ/ n. a bridge, esp. over water, hinged at one end so that it may be raised to prevent passage or to allow ships etc. to pass.

drawer /ˈdrɔːə(r)/ n. **1** a person or thing that draws, esp. a person who draws a cheque etc. **2** /drɔː(r), ˈdrɔːə(r)/ a boxlike storage compartment without a lid, sliding in and out of a frame, table, etc. (chest of drawers). **3** (in pl.) an undergarment worn next to the body below the waist. □ **drawerful** n. (pl. **-fuls**).

drawing /ˈdrɔːɪŋ/ n. **1 a** the art of representing by line. **b** delineation without colour or with a single colour. **c** the art of representing with pencils, pens, crayons, etc., rather than paint. **2** a picture produced in this way. □ **drawing-board** a board for spreading paper on for drawing. **drawing-pin** Brit. a flat-headed pin for fastening paper etc. (orig. drawing-paper) to a surface.

drawing-room /ˈdrɔːɪŋˌruːm, -ˌrʊm/ n. **1** a room for comfortable sitting or entertaining in a private house. **2** US a private compartment in a train. [earlier withdrawing-room, because orig. used for women to withdraw to after dinner]

drawl v. & n. —v. **1** intr. speak with drawn-out vowel sounds. **2** tr. utter in this way. —n. a drawling utterance or way of speaking. □ **drawler** n. [16th c.: prob. orig. cant, f. LG, Du. dralen delay, linger]

drawn past part. of DRAW. —adj. looking strained from fear, anxiety, or pain.

dray[1] n. **1** a low cart without sides for heavy loads, esp. beer-barrels. **2** Austral. & NZ a two-wheeled cart. □ **dray-horse** a large, powerful horse. [ME f. OE dræge drag-net, dragan DRAW]

dray[2] var. of DREY.

dread /dred/ v., n., & adj. —v.tr. **1** (foll. by that, or to + infin.) fear greatly. **2** shrink from; look forward to with great apprehension. **3** be in great fear of. —n. **1** great fear, apprehension, awe. **2** an object of fear or awe. —adj. **1** dreaded. **2** archaic awe-inspiring, revered. [OE ādrǣdan, ondrǣdan]

dreadful /ˈdredfʊl/ adj. **1** terrible; inspiring fear or awe. **2** colloq. troublesome, disagreeable; very bad. □ **dreadfully** adv. **dreadfulness** n.

dreadlocks /ˈdredlɒks/ n.pl. a Rastafarian hairstyle in which the hair is twisted into tight braids or ringlets hanging down on all sides.

dream n. & v. —n. **1 a** a series of pictures or events in the mind of a sleeping person. **b** the act or time of seeing this. **2** a day-dream or fantasy. **3** an ideal, aspiration, or ambition, esp. of a nation. **4** a beautiful or ideal person or thing. **5** a state of mind without proper perception of reality (goes about in a dream). —v. (past and past part. **dreamt** /dremt, drempt/ or **dreamed**) **1** intr. experience a dream. **2** tr. imagine in or as if in a dream. **3** (usu. with neg.) **a** intr. (foll. by of) contemplate the possibility of, have any conception or intention of (would not dream of upsetting them). **b** tr. (often foll. by that + clause) think of as a possibility (never dreamt that he would come). **4** tr. (foll. by away) spend (time) unprofitably. **5** intr. be inactive or unpractical. □ **dream-time** Austral. the alcheringa. **dream up** imagine, invent. **like a dream** colloq. easily, effortlessly. □ **dreamful** adj. **dreamless** adj. **dreamlike** adj. [ME f. OE drēam joy, music]

dreamboat /ˈdriːmbəʊt/ n. colloq. a very attractive or ideal person, esp. of the opposite sex.

dreamer /ˈdriːmə(r)/ n. **1** a person who dreams. **2** a romantic or unpractical person.

dreamland /ˈdriːmlænd/ n. an ideal or imaginary land.

dreamy /ˈdriːmɪ/ adj. (**dreamier**, **dreamiest**) **1** given to day-dreaming; fanciful; unpractical. **2** dreamlike; vague; misty. **3** colloq. delightful; marvellous. □ **dreamily** adv. **dreaminess** n.

drear /drɪə(r)/ adj. poet. = DREARY. [abbr.]

dreary /ˈdrɪərɪ/ adj. (**drearier**, **dreariest**) dismal, dull, gloomy. □ **drearily** adv. **dreariness** n. [OE drēorig f. drēor gore: rel. to drēosan to drop f. Gmc]

dredge¹ /dredʒ/ v. & n. —v. **1** tr. **a** (often foll. by up) bring up (lost or hidden material) as if with a dredge (don't dredge all that up again). **b** (often foll. by away, up, out) bring up or clear (mud etc.) from a river, harbour, etc. with a dredge. **2** tr. clean (a harbour, river, etc.) with a dredge. **3** intr. use a dredge. —n. an apparatus used to scoop up oysters, specimens, etc., or to clear mud etc., from a river or sea bed. [15th-c. Sc. dreg, perh. rel. to MDu. dregghe]

dredge² /dredʒ/ v.tr. **1** sprinkle with flour, sugar, etc. **2** (often foll. by over) sprinkle (flour, sugar, etc.) on. [obs. dredge sweetmeat f. OF dragie, dragee, perh. f. L tragemata f. Gk tragēmata spices]

dredger¹ /ˈdredʒə(r)/ n. **1** a machine used for dredging rivers etc. **2** a boat containing this.

dredger² /ˈdredʒə(r)/ n. a container with a perforated lid used for sprinkling flour, sugar, etc.

dreg n. (in pl.) **1** a sediment; grounds, lees, etc. **2** a worthless part; refuse (the dregs of humanity). □ **drain** (or **drink**) **to the dregs** consume leaving nothing (drained life to the dregs). □ **dreggy** adj. colloq. [ME prob. f. ON dreggjar]

drench /drentʃ/ v. & n. —v.tr. **1 a** wet thoroughly (was drenched by the rain). **b** saturate; soak (in liquid). **2** force (an animal) to take medicine. —n. **1** a soaking; a downpour. **2** medicine administered to an animal. [OE drencan, drenc f. Gmc: rel. to DRINK]

dress v. & n. —v. **1 a** tr. clothe; array (dressed in rags; dressed her quickly). **b** intr. wear clothes of a specified kind or in a specified way (dresses well). **2** intr. **a** put on clothes. **b** put on formal or evening clothes, esp. for dinner. **3** tr. decorate or adorn. **4** tr. Med. **a** treat (a wound) with ointment etc. **b** apply a dressing to (a wound). **5** tr. trim, comb, brush, or smooth (the hair). **6** tr. **a** clean and prepare (poultry, a crab, etc.) for cooking or eating. **b** add a dressing to (a salad etc.). **7** tr. apply manure etc. to a field, garden, etc. **8** tr. finish the surface of (fabric, building-stone, etc.). —n. **1** a one-piece woman's garment consisting of a bodice and skirt. **2** clothing, esp. a whole outfit etc. (wore the dress of a highlander). **3** formal or ceremonial costume (evening dress). **4** an external covering; the outward form (birds in their winter dress). □ **dress circle** the first

gallery in a theatre. **dress down** colloq. reprimand or scold. **dress out** attire conspicuously. **dress rehearsal** the final rehearsal of a play etc., wearing costume. **dress up 1** dress (oneself or another) elaborately for a special occasion. **2** dress in fancy dress. **3** disguise (unwelcome facts) by embellishment. [ME f. OF dresser ult. f. L directus DIRECT]

dressage /ˈdresɑːʒ, -sɑːdʒ/ n. the training of a horse in obedience and deportment. [F f. dresser to train]

dresser¹ /ˈdresə(r)/ n. **1** a kitchen sideboard with shelves above for displaying plates etc. **2** US a dressing-table or chest of drawers. [ME f. OF dresseur f. dresser prepare: cf. med.L directorium]

dresser² /ˈdresə(r)/ n. **1** a person who assists actors to dress. **2** Med. a surgeon's assistant in operations. **3** a person who dresses elegantly or in a specified way (a snappy dresser).

dressing /ˈdresɪŋ/ n. **1** in senses of DRESS v. **2 a** an accompaniment to salads, usu. a mixture of oil with other ingredients; a sauce or seasoning. **b** US stuffing. **3 a** a bandage for a wound. **b** ointment etc. used to dress a wound. **4** size or stiffening used to finish fabrics. **5** compost etc. spread over land (a top dressing of peat). □ **dressing-down** colloq. a scolding; a severe reprimand. **dressing-gown** a loose usu. belted robe worn over nightwear or while resting. **dressing-room 1** a room for changing the clothes etc. in a theatre, sports-ground, etc. **2** a small room attached to a bedroom, containing clothes. **dressing-table** a table with a mirror, drawers, etc., used while applying make-up etc.

dressmaker /ˈdres.meɪkə(r)/ n. a woman who makes clothes professionally. □ **dressmaking** n.

dressy /ˈdresɪ/ adj. (**dressier**, **dressiest**) **1** fond of smart clothes. **2** (of clothes) stylish or elaborate. □ **dressiness** n.

drew past of DRAW.

drey n. (also **dray**) a squirrel's nest. [17th c.: orig. unkn.]

dribble /ˈdrɪb(ə)l/ v. & n. —v. **1** intr. allow saliva to flow from the mouth. **2** intr. & tr. flow or allow to flow in drops or a trickling stream. **3** tr. (also absol.) esp. Football & Hockey move (the ball) forward with slight touches of the feet, the stick, etc. —n. **1** the act or an instance of dribbling. **2** a small trickling stream. □ **dribbler** n. **dribbly** adj. [frequent. of obs. drib, var. of DRIP]

driblet /ˈdrɪblɪt/ n. **1** a small quantity. **2** a thin stream; a dribble. [drib (see DRIBBLE) + -LET]

dribs and drabs /ˌdrɪbz ənd ˈdræbz/ n.pl. colloq. small scattered amounts (did the work in dribs and drabs). [as DRIBBLE + drab redupl.]

dried past and past part. of DRY.

drier¹ compar. of DRY.

drier² /ˈdraɪə(r)/ n. (also **dryer**) a machine for drying the hair, laundry, etc.

driest superl. of DRY.

drift n. & v. —n. **1 a** a slow movement or variation. **b** such movement caused by a slow current. **2** the intention, meaning, scope, etc. of what is said etc. (didn't understand his drift). **3** a large mass of snow, sand, etc., accumulated by the wind. **4** a state of inaction. **5 a** Naut. a ship's deviation from its course, due to currents. **b** Aeron. an aircraft's deviation due to side winds. **c** a projectile's deviation due to its rotation. **6 a**

large mass of esp. flowering plants (*a drift of bluebells*). **7** *Geol.* material deposited by the wind, a current of water, etc. **8** *S.Afr.* a ford. —*v.* **1** *intr.* be carried by or as if by a current of air or water. **2** *intr.* move or progress passively, casually, or aimlessly (*drifted into teaching*). **3** *tr.* & *intr.* pile or be piled by the wind into drifts. □ **drift-net** a large net for herrings etc., allowed to drift with the tide. □ **driftage** *n.* [ME f. ON & MDu., MHG *trift* movement of cattle: rel. to DRIVE]

drifter /ˈdrɪftə(r)/ *n.* **1** an aimless or rootless person. **2** a boat used for drift-net fishing.

driftwood /ˈdrɪftwʊd/ *n.* wood etc. driven or deposited by water or wind.

drill¹ *n.* & *v.* —*n.* **1** a pointed, esp. revolving, steel tool or machine used for boring cylindrical holes, sinking wells, etc. **2 a** esp. *Mil.* instruction or training in military exercises. **b** rigorous discipline or methodical instruction, esp. when learning or performing tasks. **c** routine procedure to be followed in an emergency (*fire-drill*). **3** *colloq.* a recognized procedure (*I expect you know the drill*). —*v.* **1** *tr.* (also *absol.*) **a** (of a person or a tool) make a hole with a drill through or into (wood, metal, etc.). **b** make (a hole) with a drill. **2** *tr.* & *intr.* esp. *Mil.* subject to or undergo discipline by drill. **3** *tr.* impart (knowledge etc.) by a strict method. **4** *tr.* *sl.* shoot with a gun (*drilled him full of holes*). □ **driller** *n.* [earlier as verb, f. MDu. *drillen* bore, of unkn. orig.]

drill² *n.* & *v.* —*n.* **1** a machine used for making furrows, sowing, and covering seed. **2** a small furrow for sowing seed in. **3** a row of plants so sown. —*v.tr.* **1** sow (seed) with a drill. **2** plant (the ground) in drills. [perh. f. obs. *drill* rill (17th c., of unkn. orig.)]

drill³ *n.* a W. African baboon, *Papio leucophaeus*, related to the mandrill. [prob. a native name: cf. MANDRILL]

drill⁴ *n.* a coarse twilled cotton or linen fabric. [earlier *drilling* f. G *Drillich* f. L *trilix* *-licis* f. *tri-* three + *licium* thread]

drily /ˈdraɪlɪ/ *adv.* (also **dryly**) **1** (said) in a dry manner; humorously. **2** in a dry way or condition.

drink *v.* & *n.* —*v.* (*past* **drank**; *past part.* **drunk**) **1 a** *tr.* swallow (a liquid). **b** *tr.* swallow the liquid contents of (a vessel). **c** *intr.* swallow liquid, take draughts (*drank from the stream*). **2** *intr.* take alcohol, esp. to excess (*I have heard that he drinks*). **3** *tr.* (of a plant, porous material, etc.) absorb (moisture). **4** *refl.* bring (oneself etc.) to a specified condition by drinking (*drank himself into a stupor*). **5** *tr.* (usu. foll. by *away*) spend (wages etc.) on drink (*drank away the money*). **6** *tr.* wish (a person's good health, luck, etc.) by drinking (*drank his health*). —*n.* **1 a** a liquid for drinking (*milk is a sustaining drink*). **b** a draught or specified amount of this (*had a drink of milk*). **2 a** alcoholic liquor (*got the drink in for Christmas*). **b** a portion, glass, etc. of this (*have a drink*). **c** excessive indulgence in alcohol (*drink is his vice*). **3** (as **the drink**) *colloq.* the sea. □ **drink in** listen to closely or eagerly (*drank in his every word*). **drink to** toast; wish success to. **drink up** drink the whole of; empty. □ **drinkable** *adj.* **drinker** *n.* [OE *drincan* (v.), *drinc*(a) (n.) f. Gmc]

drip *v.* & *n.* —*v.* (**dripped**, **dripping**) **1** *intr.* & *tr.* fall or let fall in drops. **2** *intr.* (often foll. by *with*) be so wet as to shed drops (*dripped with blood*). —*n.* **1 a** the act or an instance of dripping (*the steady drip of rain*). **b** a drop of liquid (*a drip of paint*). **c** a sound of dripping. **2** *colloq.* a stupid, dull, or ineffective person. **3** (*Med.* **drip-feed**) the drip-by-drip intravenous administration of a solution of salt, sugar, etc. □ **drip-dry** *v.* (**-dries**, **-dried**) **1** *intr.* (of fabric etc.) dry crease-free when hung up to drip. **2** *tr.* leave (a garment etc.) hanging up to dry. —*adj.* able to be drip-dried. [MDa. *drippe* f. Gmc (cf. DROP)]

dripping /ˈdrɪpɪŋ/ *n.* **1** fat melted from roasted meat and used for cooking or as a spread. **2** (in *pl.*) water, grease, etc., dripping from anything.

drippy /ˈdrɪpɪ/ *adj.* (**drippier**, **drippiest**) **1** tending to drip. **2** *sl.* (of a person) ineffectual; sloppily sentimental. □ **drippily** *adv.* **drippiness** *n.*

drive *v.* & *n.* —*v.* (*past* **drove** /drəʊv/; *past part.* **driven** /ˈdrɪv(ə)n/) **1** *tr.* (usu. foll. by *away*, *back*, *in*, *out*, *to*, etc.) urge in some direction, esp. forcibly (*drove back the wolves*). **2** *tr.* **a** (usu. foll. by *to* + infin., or *to* + verbal noun) compel or constrain forcibly (*was driven to complain*). **b** (often foll. by *to*) force into a specified state (*drove him mad*; *driven to despair*). **c** (often *refl.*) urge to overwork (*drives himself too hard*). **3 a** *tr.* (also *absol.*) operate and direct the course of (a vehicle, a locomotive, etc.). **b** *tr.* & *intr.* convey or be conveyed in a vehicle (*drove them to the station*; *drove to the station in a bus*). **c** *tr.* (also *absol.*) urge and direct the course of (an animal drawing a vehicle or plough). **4** *tr.* (of wind, water, etc.) carry along, propel, send, or cause to go in some direction. **5** *tr.* **a** (often foll. by *into*) force (a stake, nail, etc.) into place by blows (*drove the nail home*). **b** *Mining* bore (a tunnel, horizontal cavity, etc.). **6** *tr.* effect or conclude forcibly (*drove a hard bargain*). **7** *tr.* (of steam or other power) set or keep (machinery) going. **8** *intr.* (usu. foll. by *at*) work hard; dash, rush, or hasten. **9** *tr.* *Cricket* & *Tennis* hit (the ball) hard from a freely swung bat or racket. **10** *tr.* (often *absol.*) *Golf* strike (a ball) with a driver from the tee. **11** *tr.* chase or frighten (game, wild beasts, an enemy in warfare, etc.) from a large area to a smaller, to kill or capture; corner. —*n.* **1** an act of driving in a motor vehicle; a journey or excursion in such a vehicle (*went for a pleasant drive*; *lives an hour's drive from us*). **2 a** the capacity for achievement; motivation and energy (*lacks the drive needed to succeed*). **b** *Psychol.* an inner urge to attain a goal or satisfy a need. **3 a** a usu. landscaped street or road. **b** a usu. private road through a garden or park to a house. **4** *Cricket*, *Golf*, & *Tennis* a driving stroke of the bat etc. **5** an organized effort to achieve a usu. charitable purpose (*a famine-relief drive*). **6 a** the transmission of power to machinery, the wheels of a motor vehicle, etc. (*front-wheel drive*). **b** the position of a steering-wheel in a motor vehicle (*left-hand drive*). **c** *Computing* = disk drive (DISC). **7** *Brit.* an organized competition of whist, bingo, etc. **8** an act of driving game or an enemy. □ **drive at** seek, intend, or mean (*what is he driving at?*). **drive-by** *attrib. adj.* (of a crime etc.) carried out from a moving vehicle. **drive-in** *attrib.adj.* (of a bank, cinema, etc.) able to be used while sitting in one's car. —*n.* such a bank, cinema, etc. **drive-on** (of a ship) on to which motor vehicles may be driven. **drive out** take the place of; oust; exorcize, cast out (*evil spirits* etc.). **driving-licence** a licence permitting a person to drive a motor vehicle. **driving rain** an excessive windblown downpour. **driving test** an official test of a motorist's competence which must be passed to obtain a driving licence. **driving-wheel 1** the large wheel of a locomotive. **2** a wheel communicating motive power in machinery. □ **drivable** adj. [OE *drīfan* f. Gmc]

drivel /ˈdrɪv(ə)l/ n. & v. —n. silly nonsense; twaddle. —v. (**drivelled, drivelling**; US **driveled, driveling**) **1** intr. run at the mouth or nose; dribble. **2** intr. talk childishly or idiotically. □ **driveller** n. (US **driveler**). [OE *dreflian* (v.)]

driven past part. of DRIVE.

driver /ˈdraɪvə(r)/ n. **1** (often in comb.) a person who drives a vehicle (*bus-driver; engine-driver*). **2** Golf a club with a flat face and wooden head, used for driving from the tee. □ **driverless** adj.

driveway /ˈdraɪvweɪ/ n. = DRIVE n. 3b.

drizzle /ˈdrɪz(ə)l/ n. & v. —n. very fine rain. —v.intr. (esp. of rain) fall in very fine drops. □ **drizzly** adj. [prob. f. ME *drēse*, OE *drēosan* fall]

droll /drəʊl/ adj. & n. —adj. **1** quaintly amusing. **2** odd; surprising. —n. a quaintly amusing person. □ **drollery** n. (pl. **-ies**). **drolly** /ˈdrəʊllɪ/ adv. **drollness** n. [F *drôle*, perh. f. MDu. *drolle* little man]

-drome /drəʊm/ comb. form forming nouns denoting: **1** a place for running, racing, or other forms of movement (*aerodrome; hippodrome*). **2** a thing that runs or proceeds in a certain way (*palindrome; syndrome*). [Gk *dromos* course, running]

dromedary /ˈdrɒmɪdərɪ, ˈdrʌm-/ n. (pl. **-ies**) a one-humped camel, *Camelus dromedarius*, bred for riding and racing. [ME f. OF *dromedaire* or LL *dromedarius* ult. f. Gk *dromas -ados* runner]

drone n. & v. —n. **1** a non-working male of the honey-bee, whose sole function is to mate with fertile females. **2** an idler. **3** a deep humming sound. **4** a monotonous speech or speaker. **5** a pipe, esp. of a bagpipe, sounding a continuous note of fixed low pitch. —v. **1** intr. make a deep humming sound. **2** intr. & tr. speak or utter monotonously. **3** intr. be idle. [OE *drān, drǣn* prob. f. WG]

drongo /ˈdrɒŋɡəʊ/ n. (pl. **-os** or **-oes**) **1** any black bird of the family Dicruridae, native to India, Africa, and Australia, having a long forked tail. **2** Austral. & NZ sl. derog. a simpleton. [Malagasy]

drool v. & n. —v.intr. **1** drivel; slobber. **2** (often foll. by over) show much pleasure or infatuation. —n. slobbering; drivelling. [contr. of *drivel*]

droop v. & n. —v. **1** intr. & tr. hang or allow to hang down; languish, decline, or sag, esp. from weariness. **2** intr. (of the eyes) look downwards. **3** intr. lose heart; be dejected; flag. —n. **1** a drooping attitude. **2** a loss of spirit or enthusiasm. [ME f. ON *drūpa* hang the head f. Gmc: cf. DROP]

droopy /ˈdruːpɪ/ adj. (**droopier, droopiest**) **1** drooping. **2** dejected, gloomy. □ **droopily** adv. **droopiness** n.

drop n. & v. —n. **1 a** a small round or pear-shaped portion of liquid that hangs or falls or adheres to a surface. **b** a very small amount of usu. drinkable liquid (*just a drop left in the glass*). **c** a glass etc. of alcoholic liquor (*take a drop with us*). **2 a** an abrupt fall or slope. **b** the amount of this

(*a drop of fifteen feet*). **c** an act of falling or dropping (*had a nasty drop*). **d** a reduction in prices, temperature, etc. **e** a deterioration or worsening (*a drop in status*). **3** something resembling a drop, esp.: **a** a pendant or earring. **b** a crystal ornament on a chandelier etc. **c** (often in comb.) a sweet or lozenge (*pear-drop; cough drop*). **4** something that drops or is dropped, esp.: **a** Theatr. a painted curtain or scenery let down on to the stage. **b** a platform or trapdoor on a gallows, the opening of which causes the victim to fall. **5** Med. **a** the smallest separable quantity of a liquid. **b** (in pl.) liquid medicine to be measured in drops (*eye drops*). **6** a minute quantity (*not a drop of pity*). **7** sl. **a** a hiding-place for stolen or illicit goods. **b** a secret place where documents etc. may be left or passed on in espionage. **8** sl. a bribe. **9** US a box for letters etc. —v. (**dropped, dropping**) **1** intr. & tr. fall or let fall in drops. **2** intr. & tr. fall or allow to fall; relinquish; let go. **3 a** intr. & tr. sink or cause to sink or fall to the ground from exhaustion, a blow, a wound, etc. **b** intr. die. **4 a** intr. & tr. cease or cause to cease; lapse or let lapse; abandon (*dropped the friendship; drop everything and come at once*). **b** tr. colloq. cease to associate with. **5** tr. set down (a passenger etc.) (*drop me at the station*). **6** tr. & intr. utter or be uttered casually (*dropped a hint; the remark dropped into the conversation*). **7** tr. send casually (*drop me a postcard*). **8 a** intr. & tr. fall or allow to fall in direction, amount, condition, degree, pitch, etc. (*the wind dropped; we dropped the price by £20*). **b** intr. (of a person) jump down lightly; let oneself fall. **c** tr. remove (clothes, esp. trousers) rapidly, allowing them to fall to the ground. **9** tr. omit (a letter, esp. aitch, a syllable etc.) in speech. **10** tr. (as **dropped** adj.) in a lower position than usual (*dropped handlebars; dropped waist*). **11** tr. give birth to (esp. a lamb, a kitten, etc.). **12** tr. Sport lose (a game, a point, a contest, a match, etc.). **13** tr. Aeron. deliver (supplies etc.) by parachute. **14** tr. Football **a** send (a ball) by a drop-kick. **b** score (a goal) by a drop-kick. **15** tr. colloq. dismiss or omit (*was dropped from the team*). □ **at the drop of a hat** given the slightest excuse. **drop anchor** anchor ship. **drop away** decrease or depart gradually. **drop back** (or **behind** or **to the rear**) fall back; get left behind. **drop back into** return to (a habit etc.). **drop a brick** colloq. make an indiscreet or embarrassing remark. **drop-curtain** (or **-scene**) Theatr. a painted curtain or scenery (cf. sense 4 of n.). **drop a curtsy** make a curtsy. **drop down** descend a hill etc. **drop in** (or **by**) colloq. call casually as a visitor. **drop into 1** call casually at (a place). **2** fall into (a habit etc.). **drop it!** sl. stop that! **drop-kick** Football a kick made by dropping the ball and kicking it on the bounce. **drop-leaf** (of a table etc.) having a hinged flap. **drop off 1** decline gradually. **2** colloq. fall asleep. **3** = sense 5 of v. **drop on** reprimand or punish. **drop out** colloq. cease to participate, esp. in a race, a course of study, or in conventional society. **drop-out** n. **1** colloq. a person who has dropped out. **2** the restarting of a game by a drop-kick. **drop scone** Brit. a small thick pancake made by dropping batter into a frying pan etc. **drop-shot** (in lawn tennis) a shot dropping abruptly over the net. **drop a stitch** let a stitch fall off the end of a knitting-needle. □ **droplet** *n.* [OE *dropa, drop-(p)ian* ult. f. Gmc: cf. DRIP, DROOP]

dropper /ˈdrɒpə(r)/ *n.* **1** a device for administering liquid, esp. medicine, in drops. **2** *Austral., NZ, & S.Afr.* a light vertical stave in a fence.

droppings /ˈdrɒpɪŋz/ *n.pl.* **1** the dung of animals or birds. **2** something that falls or has fallen in drops, e.g. wax from candles.

dropsy /ˈdrɒpsɪ/ *n.* (*pl.* **-ies**) **1** = OEDEMA. **2** *sl.* a tip or bribe. □ **dropsical** *adj.* (in sense 1). [ME f. *idrop(e)sie* f. OF *idropesie* ult. f. L *hydropisis* f. Gk *hudrōps* dropsy (as HYDRO-)]

dross *n.* **1** rubbish, refuse. **2 a** the scum separated from metals in melting. **b** foreign matter mixed with anything; impurities. □ **drossy** *adj.* [OE *drōs*: cf. MLG *drōsem*, OHG *truosana*]

drought /draʊt/ *n.* **1** the continuous absence of rain; dry weather. **2** the prolonged lack of something. □ **droughty** *adj.* [OE *drūgath* f. *drȳge* DRY]

drove[1] *past of* DRIVE.

drove[2] /drəʊv/ *n.* **1 a** a large number (of people etc.) moving together; a crowd; a multitude; a shoal. **b** (in *pl.*) *colloq.* a great number (*people arrived in droves*). **2** a herd or flock being driven or moving together. [OE *drāf* f. *drīfan* DRIVE]

drover /ˈdrəʊvə(r)/ *n.* a person who drives herds to market; a cattle-dealer. □ **drove** *v.tr.* **droving** *n.*

drown /draʊn/ *v.* **1** *tr.* & *intr.* kill or be killed by submersion in liquid. **2** *tr.* submerge; flood; drench (*drowned the fields in six feet of water*). **3** *tr.* (often foll. by *in*) deaden (grief etc.) with drink. **4** *tr.* (often foll. by *out*) make (a sound) inaudible by means of a louder sound. □ **drown out** drive out by flood. [ME (orig. north.) *drun(e), droun(e)*, perh. f. OE *drūnian* (unrecorded), rel. to DRINK]

drowse /draʊz/ *v. intr.* be dull and sleepy or half asleep. [back-form. f. DROWSY]

drowsy /ˈdraʊzɪ/ *adj.* (**drowsier, drowsiest**) **1** half asleep; dozing. **2** soporific; lulling. **3** sluggish. □ **drowsily** *adv.* **drowsiness** *n.* [prob. rel. to OE *drūsian* be languid or slow, *drēosan* fall: cf. DREARY]

drub *v.tr.* (**drubbed, drubbing**) **1** thump; belabour. **2** beat in a fight. □ **drubbing** *n.* [ult. f. Arab. *ḍaraba* beat]

drudge *n.* & *v.* —*n.* a servile worker, esp. at menial tasks; a hack. —*v.intr.* (often foll. by *at*) work slavishly (at menial, hard, or dull work). □ **drudgery** /ˈdrʌdʒərɪ/ *n.* [15th c.: perh. rel. to DRAG]

drug *n.* & *v.* —*n.* **1** a medicinal substance. **2** a narcotic, hallucinogen, or stimulant, esp. one causing addiction. —*v.* (**drugged, drugging**) **1** *tr.* add a drug to (food or drink). **2** *tr.* administer a drug to. **b** stupefy with a drug. **3** *intr.* take drugs as an addict. □ **drug addict** a person who is addicted to a narcotic drug. **drug on the market** a commodity that is plentiful but no longer in demand. **drug peddler** (*colloq.* **pusher**) a person who sells esp. addictive drugs illegally. **drug squad** a division of a police force investigating crimes involving illegal drugs. [ME *drogges, drouges* f. OF *drogue*, of unkn. orig.]

drugget /ˈdrʌgɪt/ *n.* **1** a coarse woven fabric used as a floor or table covering. **2** such a covering. [F *droguet*, of unkn. orig.]

druggist /ˈdrʌgɪst/ *n.* esp. *US* a pharmacist. [F *droguiste* (as DRUG)]

drugstore /ˈdrʌgstɔː(r)/ *n.* *US* a chemist's shop also selling light refreshments and other articles.

Druid /ˈdruːɪd/ *n.* (*fem.* **Druidess**) **1** an ancient Celtic priest, magician, or soothsayer of Gaul, Britain, or Ireland. **2** a member of a Welsh etc. Druidic order. □ **Druidism** *n.* **Druidic** /-ˈɪdɪk/ *adj.* **Druidical** /-ˈɪdɪk(ə)l/ *adj.* [F *druide* or L *pl. druidae, -des*, Gk *druidai* f. Gaulish *druides*]

drum *n.* & *v.* —*n.* **1 a** a percussion instrument or toy made of a hollow cylinder or hemisphere covered at one or both ends with stretched skin or parchment and sounded by striking (*bass drum*; *kettledrum*). **b** (often in *pl.*) a drummer or percussion section (*the drums are playing too loud*). **c** a sound made by or resembling that of a drum. **2** something resembling a drum in shape, esp.: **a** a cylindrical container or receptacle for oil etc. **b** a cylinder or barrel in machinery on which something is wound etc. **c** *Archit.* a stone block forming a section of a shaft. **3** *Zool.* & *Anat.* the membrane of the middle ear; the eardrum. —*v.* (**drummed, drumming**) **1** *intr.* & *tr.* play on a drum. **2** *tr.* & *intr.* beat, tap, or thump (knuckles, feet, etc.) continuously (on something) (*drummed on the table*; *drummed his feet*). **3** *intr.* (of a bird or an insect) make a loud, hollow noise with quivering wings. □ **drum brake** a brake in which shoes on a vehicle press against the drum on a wheel. **drum into** drive (a lesson) into (a person) by persistence. **drum machine** an electronic device that imitates the sound of percussion instruments. **drum major** the leader of a marching band. **drum majorette** esp. *US* a member of a female baton-twirling parading group. **drum out** *Mil.* cashier (a soldier) by the beat of a drum; dismiss with ignominy. **drum up** summon, gather, or call up (*needs to drum up more support*). [obs. *drombslade, drombyllsclad*, f. LG *trommelslag* drum-beat f. *trommel* drum + *slag* beat]

drumhead /ˈdrʌmhed/ *n.* **1** the skin or membrane of a drum. **2** an eardrum. **3** (*attrib.*) improvised (*drumhead court martial*).

drummer /ˈdrʌmə(r)/ *n.* **1** a person who plays a drum or drums. **2** esp. *US colloq.* a commercial traveller.

drumstick /ˈdrʌmstɪk/ *n.* **1** a stick used for beating a drum. **2** the lower joint of the leg of a cooked chicken, turkey, etc.

drunk *adj.* & *n.* —*adj.* **1** rendered incapable by alcohol. **2** (often foll. by *with*) overcome or elated with joy, success, power, etc. —*n.* **1** a habitually drunk person. **2** *sl.* a drinking-bout; a period of drunkenness. [past part. of DRINK]

drunkard /ˈdrʌŋkəd/ *n.* a person who is drunk, esp. habitually.

drunken /ˈdrʌŋkən/ *adj.* (usu. *attrib.*) **1** = DRUNK. **2** caused by or exhibiting drunkenness (*a drunken brawl*). **3** fond of drinking; often drunk. □ **drunkenly** *adv.* **drunkenness** *n.*

drupe /druːp/ *n.* any fleshy or pulpy fruit enclosing a stone containing one or a few seeds, e.g. an olive, plum, or peach. □ **drupaceous** /-ˈpeɪʃəs/ *adj.* [L *drupa* f. Gk *druppa* olive]

dry *adj., v.,* & *n.* —*adj.* (**drier** /ˈdraɪə(r)/; **driest** /ˈdraɪɪst/) **1** free from moisture, not wet, esp.: **a** with any moisture having evaporated, drained, or been wiped away (*the clothes are not dry yet*). **b** (of the eyes) free from tears. **c** (of a climate etc.) with insufficient rainfall; not rainy (*a dry spell*).

d (of a river, well, etc.) dried up; not yielding water. **e** (of a liquid) having disappeared by evaporation etc. **f** not connected with or for use without moisture (*dry shampoo*). **g** (of a shave) with an electric razor. **2** (of wine etc.) not sweet (*dry sherry*). **3 a** meagre, plain, or bare (*dry facts*). **b** uninteresting; dull. **4** (of a sense of humour, a joke, etc.) subtle, ironic, and quietly expressed; not obvious. **5** (of a country, of legislation, etc.) prohibiting the sale of alcoholic drink. **6** (of toast, bread, etc.) without butter, margarine, etc. **7** (of provisions, groceries, etc.) solid, not liquid (*dry goods*). **8** impassive, unsympathetic; hard; cold. **9** (of a cow etc.) not yielding milk. **10** *colloq.* thirsty or thirst-making (*feel dry; this is dry work*). **11** *Polit. colloq.* of or being a political 'dry'. —*v.* (**dries, dried**) **1** *tr.* & *intr.* make or become dry by wiping, evaporation, draining, etc. **2** *tr.* (usu. as **dried** *adj.*) preserve (food etc.) by removing the moisture (*dried fruit; dried flowers*). **3** *intr.* (often foll. by *up*) *Theatr. colloq.* forget one's lines. —*n.* (*pl.* **dries**) **1** the process or an instance of drying. **2** *sl.* a politician, esp. a Conservative, who advocates individual responsibility, free trade, and economic stringency, and opposes high government spending. □ **dry battery** *Electr.* an electric battery consisting of dry cells. **dry cell** *Electr.* a cell in which the electrolyte is absorbed in a solid and cannot be spilled. **dry-clean** clean (clothes etc.) with organic solvents without using water. **dry dock** an enclosure for the building or repairing of ships, from which water can be pumped out. **dry-fly** *adj.* (of fishing) with an artificial fly floating on the surface. **dry ice** solid carbon dioxide. **dry land** land as opposed to the sea, a river, etc. **dry measure** a measure of capacity for dry goods. **dry out 1** become fully dry. **2** (of a drug addict, alcoholic, etc.) undergo treatment to cure addiction. **dry rot 1** a decayed state of wood when not ventilated, caused by certain fungi. **2** these fungi. **dry run** *colloq.* a rehearsal. **dry-shod** without wetting the shoes. **dry up 1** make utterly dry. **2** dry dishes. **3** (of moisture) disappear utterly. **4** (of a well etc.) cease to yield water. **5** *colloq.* (esp. in *imper.*) cease talking. □ **dryish** *adj.* **dryness** *n.* [OE *drȳge, drygan*, rel. to MLG *dröge*, MDu. *drōghe*, f. Gmc]

dryad /ˈdraɪæd, ˈdraɪəd/ *n. Mythol.* a nymph inhabiting a tree; a wood nymph. [ME f. OF *dryade* f. L f. Gk *druas -ados* f. *drus* tree]

dryer var. of DRIER².

dryly var. of DRILY.

drystone /ˈdraɪstəʊn/ *adj.* (of a wall etc.) built without mortar.

DSC *abbr.* Distinguished Service Cross.

D.Sc. *abbr.* Doctor of Science.

DSM *abbr.* Distinguished Service Medal.

DSO *abbr.* (in the UK) Distinguished Service Order.

DT *abbr.* (also **DT's** /diːˈtiːz/) delirium tremens.

DTP *abbr.* desktop publishing.

dual /ˈdjuːəl/ *adj., n.,* & *v.* —*adj.* **1** of two; twofold. **2** divided in two; double (*dual ownership*). **3** *Gram.* (in some languages) denoting two persons or things (additional to singular and plural). —*n.* (also **dual number**) *Gram.* a dual form of a noun, verb, etc. —*v.tr.* (**dualled, dualling**) *Brit.* convert (a road) into a dual carriageway. □ **dual carriageway** *Brit.* a road with a dividing strip between the traffic in opposite directions. **dual**

control (of a vehicle or an aircraft) having two sets of controls, one of which is used by the instructor. **dual-purpose** (of a vehicle) usable for passengers or goods. □ **duality** /-ˈælɪtɪ/ *n.* **dualize** *v.tr.* (also **-ise**). **dually** *adv.* [L *dualis* f. *duo* two]

dualism /ˈdjuːəlɪz(ə)m/ *n.* being twofold; duality. □ **dualist** *n.* **dualistic** /-ˈlɪstɪk/ *adj.* **dualistically** /-ˈlɪstɪkəlɪ/ *adv.*

dub¹ *v.tr.* (**dubbed, dubbing**) **1** make (a person) a knight by touching his shoulders with a sword. **2** give (a person) a name, nickname, or title (*dubbed him a crank*). **3** smear (leather) with grease. [OE f. AF *duber, aduber*, OF *adober* equip with armour, repair, of unkn. orig.]

dub² *v.tr.* (**dubbed, dubbing**) **1** provide (a film etc.) with an alternative soundtrack, esp. in a different language. **2** add (sound effects or music) to a film or a broadcast. [abbr. of DOUBLE]

dubbin /ˈdʌbɪn/ *n.* & *v.* —*n.* (also **dubbing** /ˈdʌbɪŋ/) prepared grease for softening and waterproofing leather. —*v.tr.* (**dubbined, dubbining**) apply dubbin to (boots etc.). [see DUB¹ 3]

dubbing /ˈdʌbɪŋ/ *n.* an alternative soundtrack to a film etc.

dubiety /djuːˈbaɪətɪ/ *n.* (*pl.* **-ies**) *literary* **1** a feeling of doubt. **2** a doubtful matter. [LL *dubietas* f. *dubium* doubt]

dubious /ˈdjuːbɪəs/ *adj.* **1** hesitating or doubting (*dubious about going*). **2** of questionable value or truth (*a dubious claim*). **3** unreliable; suspicious (*dubious company*). **4** of doubtful result (*a dubious undertaking*). □ **dubiously** *adv.* **dubiousness** *n.* [L *dubiosus* f. *dubium* doubt]

ducal /ˈdjuːk(ə)l/ *adj.* of, like, or bearing the title of a duke. [F f. *duc* DUKE]

ducat /ˈdʌkət/ *n.* **1** *hist.* a gold coin, formerly current in most European countries. **2 a** a coin. **b** (in *pl.*) money. [ME f. It. *ducato* or med.L *ducatus* DUCHY]

duchess /ˈdʌtʃɪs/ *n.* (as a title usu. **Duchess**) **1** a duke's wife or widow. **2** a woman holding the rank of duke in her own right. [ME f. OF *duchesse* f. med.L *ducissa* (as DUKE)]

duchy /ˈdʌtʃɪ/ *n.* (*pl.* **-ies**) **1** the territory of a duke or duchess; a dukedom. **2** (often as the **Duchy**) the royal dukedom of Cornwall or Lancaster. [ME f. OF *duché(e)* f. med.L *ducatus* f. L *dux ducis* leader]

duck¹ *n.* (*pl.* same or **ducks**) **1 a** any of various swimming-birds of the family Anatidae, esp. the domesticated form of the mallard or wild duck. **b** the female of this. **c** the flesh of a duck as food. **2** *Cricket* (in full **duck's-egg**) the score of a batsman dismissed for nought. **3** (also **ducks**) *Brit. colloq.* (esp. as a form of address) dear, darling. □ **ducks and drakes** a game of making a flat stone skim along the surface of water. **like water off a duck's back** *colloq.* (of remonstrances etc.) producing no effect. **play ducks and drakes with** *colloq.* squander. [OE *duce, dūce*: rel. to DUCK²]

duck² *v.* **1** *intr.* & *tr.* plunge, dive, or dip under water and emerge (*ducked him in the pond*). **2** *intr.* & *tr.* bend (the head or the body) quickly to avoid a blow or being seen, or as a bow or curtsy; bob (*ducked out of sight; ducked his head under the beam*). **3** *tr.* & *intr. colloq.* avoid or dodge; withdraw (from) (*ducked out of the engagement;*

ducked the meeting). □ **ducker** *n.* [OE *dūcan* (unrecorded) f. Gmc]

duck³ *n.* **1** a strong untwilled linen or cotton fabric used for small sails and the outer clothing of sailors. **2** (in *pl.*) trousers made of this (*white ducks*). [MDu. *doek*, of unkn. orig.]

duckbill /ˈdʌkbɪl/ *n.* (also **duck-billed platypus**) = PLATYPUS.

duckboard /ˈdʌkbɔːd/ *n.* (usu. in *pl.*) a path of wooden slats placed over muddy ground or in a trench.

duckling /ˈdʌklɪŋ/ *n.* **1** a young duck. **2** its flesh as food.

duckweed /ˈdʌkwiːd/ *n.* any of various aquatic plants, esp. of the genus *Lemna*, growing on the surface of still water.

ducky /ˈdʌkɪ/ *n.* & *adj.* Brit. *colloq.* —*n.* (*pl.* -**ies**) darling, dear. —*adj.* sweet, pretty; splendid.

duct *n.* & *v.* —*n.* **1** a channel or tube for conveying fluid, cable, etc. **2** a tube in the body conveying secretions such as tears etc. —*v.tr.* convey through a duct. [L *ductus* leading, aqueduct f. *ducere* duct- lead]

ductile /ˈdʌktaɪl/ *adj.* **1** (of a metal) capable of being drawn into wire; pliable, not brittle. **2** (of a substance) easily moulded. **3** (of a person) docile, gullible. □ **ductility** /-ˈtɪlɪtɪ/ *n.* [ME f. OF *ductile* or L *ductilis* f. *ducere* duct- lead]

ducting /ˈdʌktɪŋ/ *n.* **1** a system of ducts. **2** material in the form of a duct or ducts.

ductless /ˈdʌktlɪs/ *adj.* lacking or not using a duct or ducts. □ **ductless gland** a gland secreting directly into the bloodstream.

dud *n.* & *adj.* *sl.* —*n.* **1** a futile or ineffectual person or thing (*a dud at the job*). **2** a counterfeit article. **3** a shell etc. that fails to explode. **4** (in *pl.*) clothes. —*adj.* **1** useless, worthless, unsatisfactory or futile. **2** counterfeit. [ME: orig. unkn.]

dude /djuːd, duːd/ *n.* US *sl.* **1** a fastidious aesthetic person, usu. male; a dandy. **2** a fellow; a guy. □ **dude ranch** a cattle ranch converted to a holiday centre for tourists etc. □ **dudish** *adj.* [19th c.: prob. f. G dial. *dude* fool]

dudgeon /ˈdʌdʒ(ə)n/ *n.* a feeling of offence; resentment. □ **in high dudgeon** very angry or angrily. [16th c.: orig. unkn.]

due *adj.*, *n.*, & *adv.* —*adj.* **1** (*predic.*) owing or payable as a debt or an obligation (*our thanks are due to him; £500 was due on the 15th*). **2** (often foll. by *to*) merited; appropriate; fitting (*his due reward; received the applause due to a hero*). **3** rightful; proper; adequate (*after due consideration*). **4** (*predic.*; foll. by *to*) to be ascribed to (a cause, an agent, etc.) (*the discovery was due to Newton*). **5** (*predic.*) intended to arrive at a certain time (*a train is due at 7.30*). **6** (foll. by *to* + *infin.*) under an obligation or agreement to do something (*due to speak tonight*). —*n.* **1** a person's right; what is owed to a person (*a fair hearing is my due*). **2** (in *pl.*) **a** what one owes (*pays his dues*). **b** a legally demandable toll or fee (*harbour dues*). —*adv.* (of a point of the compass) exactly, directly (*a due north wind*). □ **due to** *disp.* because of, owing to (*was late due to an accident*) (cf. sense 4 of *adj.*). **fall** (or **become**) **due** (of a bill etc.) be immediately payable. **in due course 1** at about the appropriate time. **2** in the natural order.

[ME f. OF *deü* ult. f. L *debitus* past part. of *debēre* owe]

■ **Usage** The use of *due to* to mean 'because of' as in the example given is regarded as unacceptable by some people and could be avoided by substituting *his lateness was due to an accident*. Alternatively, *owing to* could be used.

duel /ˈdjuːəl/ *n.* & *v.* —*n.* **1** *hist.* a contest with deadly weapons between two people, in the presence of two seconds, to settle a point of honour. **2** any contest between two people, parties, causes, animals, etc. —*v.intr.* (**duelled, duelling;** US **dueled, dueling**) fight a duel or duels. □ **dueller** *n.* (US **dueler**). **duellist** *n.* (US **duelist**). [It. *duello* or L *duellum* (archaic form of *bellum* war), in med.L = single combat]

duenna /djuːˈenə/ *n.* an older woman acting as a governess and companion in charge of girls, esp. in a Spanish family; a chaperon. [Sp. *dueña* f. L *domina* mistress]

duet /djuːˈet/ *n.* **1** *Mus.* **a** a performance by two voices, instrumentalists, etc. **b** a composition for two performers. **2** a dialogue. □ **duettist** *n.* [G *Duett* or It. *duetto* dimin. of *duo* duet f. L *duo* two]

duff¹ *n.* a boiled pudding. [N.Engl. form of DOUGH]

duff² *adj.* Brit. *sl.* **1** worthless, counterfeit. **2** useless, broken. [perh. = DUFF¹]

duff³ *v.tr.* *sl.* Brit. Golf mishit (a shot, a ball); bungle. □ **duff up** *sl.* beat; thrash. [perh. back-form. f. DUFFER]

duffer /ˈdʌfə(r)/ *n.* *sl.* an inefficient, useless, or stupid person. [perh. f. Sc. *doofart* stupid person f. *douf* spiritless]

duffle /ˈdʌf(ə)l/ *n.* (also **duffel**) **1** a coarse woollen cloth with a thick nap. **2** US a sportsman's or camper's equipment. □ **duffle bag** a cylindrical canvas bag closed by a draw-string and carried over the shoulder. **duffle-coat** a hooded overcoat of duffle, usu. fastened with toggles. [*Duffel* in Belgium]

dug¹ past and past part. of DIG.

dug² /dʌg/ *n.* the udder, breast, teat, or nipple of a female animal. [16th c.: orig. unkn.]

dugong /ˈduːgɒŋ/ *n.* (*pl.* same or **dugongs**) a marine mammal, *Dugong dugon*, of Asian seas and coasts. [ult. f. Malay *dūyong*]

dugout /ˈdʌgaʊt/ *n.* **1 a** a roofed shelter esp. for troops in trenches. **b** an underground air-raid or nuclear shelter. **2** a canoe made from a hollowed tree-trunk.

duke *n.* (as a title usu. **Duke**) **1** a person holding the highest hereditary title of the nobility. **2** a sovereign prince ruling a duchy or small State. □ **royal duke** a duke who is also a royal prince. [ME f. OF *duc* f. L *dux ducis* leader]

dukedom /ˈdjuːkdəm/ *n.* **1** a territory ruled by a duke. **2** the rank of duke.

dulcet /ˈdʌlsɪt/ *adj.* (esp. of sound) sweet and soothing. [ME, earlier *doucet* f. OF dimin. of *doux* f. L *dulcis* sweet]

dulcimer /ˈdʌlsɪmə(r)/ *n.* a musical instrument with strings stretched over a sounding-board or box, played by being struck with hammers. [OF *doulcemer*, said to repr. L *dulce* sweet, *melos* song]

dull *adj.* & *v.* —*adj.* **1** slow to understand; stupid. **2** tedious; boring. **3** (of the weather) overcast; gloomy. **4 a** (esp. of a knife edge etc.) blunt. **b**

(of colour, light, sound, or taste) not bright, vivid, or keen. **5** (of a pain etc.) usu. prolonged and indistinct; not acute (*a dull ache*). **6 a** (of a person, an animal, trade, etc.) sluggish, slow-moving, or stagnant. **b** (of a person) listless; depressed. **7** (of the ears, eyes, etc.) without keen perception. —*v.tr. & intr.* make or become dull. □ **dull the edge of** make less sensitive, interesting, effective, amusing, etc.; blunt. □ **dullish** *adj.* **dullness** *n.* (also **dulness**). **dully** /'dʌllı/ *adv.* [ME f. MLG, MDu. *dul,* corresp. to OE *dol* stupid]

dullard /'dʌləd/ *n.* a stupid person.

dulse /dʌls/ *n.* an edible seaweed, *Rhodymenia palmata,* with red wedge-shaped fronds. [Ir. & Gael. *duileasg*]

duly /'dju:lı/ *adv.* **1** in due time or manner. **2** rightly, properly, fitly.

dumb /dʌm/ *adj.* **1 a** (of a person) unable to speak, usu. because of a congenital defect or deafness. **b** (of an animal) naturally unable to speak (*our dumb friends*). **2** silenced by surprise, shyness, etc. (*struck dumb by this revelation*). **3** taciturn or reticent, esp. insultingly (*dumb insolence*). **4** (of an action etc.) performed without speech. **5** *colloq.* esp. *US* stupid; ignorant. **6** (usu. of a class, population, etc.) having no voice in government; inarticulate (*the dumb masses*). **7** (of a computer terminal etc.) able only to transmit data to or receive data from a computer; not programmable. □ **dumb-bell** a short bar with a weight at each end, used for exercise, muscle-building, etc. **dumb cluck** *sl.* a stupid person. **dumb show 1** significant gestures or mime, used when words are inappropriate. **2** a part of a play in early drama, acted in mime. **dumb waiter 1** a small lift for carrying food, plates, etc., between floors. **2** a movable table, esp. with revolving shelves, used in a dining-room. □ **dumbly** /'dʌmlı/ *adv.* **dumbness** /'dʌmnıs/ *n.* [OE: orig. unkn.: sense 6 f. G *dumm*]

dumbfound /dʌm'faʊnd/ *v.tr.* (also **dumfound**) strike dumb; confound; nonplus. [DUMB, CONFOUND]

dumbo /'dʌmbəʊ/ *n.* (*pl.* **-os**) *sl.* a stupid person; a fool. [DUMB + -O]

dumbstruck /'dʌmstrʌk/ *adj.* greatly shocked or surprised and so lost for words.

dumdum /'dʌmdʌm/ *n.* (in full **dumdum bullet**) a kind of soft-nosed bullet that expands on impact and inflicts laceration. [*Dum-Dum* in India, where it was first produced]

dummy /'dʌmı/ *n., adj., & v.* —*n.* (*pl.* **-ies**) **1** a model of a human being, esp.: **a** a ventriloquist's doll. **b** a figure used to model clothes in a shop window etc. **c** a target used for firearms practice. **2** (often *attrib.*) a counterfeit object used to replace or resemble a real or normal one. **3** *colloq.* a stupid person. **4** a person taking no significant part; a figurehead. **5** *Brit.* a rubber or plastic teat for a baby to suck on. **6** an imaginary fourth player at whist, whose hand is turned up and played by a partner. **7** *Bridge* the partner of the declarer, whose cards are exposed after the first lead. —*adj.* sham; counterfeit. —*v.intr.* (**-ies, -ied**) *Football* make a pretended pass or swerve etc. □ **dummy run 1** a practice attack, etc.; a trial run. **2** a rehearsal. **dummy up** *US sl.* keep quiet; give no information. **sell the** (or a) **dummy** *Rugby Football colloq.* deceive (an

opponent) by pretending to pass the ball. [DUMB + -Y²]

dump *n. & v.* —*n.* **1 a** a place for depositing rubbish. **b** a heap of rubbish. **2** *colloq.* an unpleasant or dreary place. **3** *Mil.* a temporary store of ammunition, provisions, etc. **4** an accumulated pile of ore, earth, etc. **5** *Computing* **a** a printout of stored data. **b** the process or result of dumping data. —*v.tr.* **1** put down firmly or clumsily (*dumped the shopping on the table*). **2** shoot or deposit (rubbish etc.). **3** *colloq.* abandon, desert. **4** *Mil.* leave (ammunition etc.) in a dump. **5** *Econ.* send (goods unsaleable at a high price in the home market) to a foreign market for sale at a low price. **6** *Computing* **a** copy (stored data) to a different location. **b** reproduce the contents of (a store) externally. □ **dump truck** a truck with a body that tilts or opens at the back for unloading. □ **dumper** *n.* **dumping** *n.* [ME perh. f. Norse; cf. Da., Norw. *dumpe* fall suddenly]

dumpling /'dʌmplıŋ/ *n.* **1 a** a small ball of usu. suet, flour, and water, boiled in stew or water, and eaten. **b** a pudding consisting of apple or other fruit enclosed in dough and baked. **2** a small fat person. [app. dimin., of *dump* small round object, but recorded much earlier]

dumps /dʌmps/ *n.pl. colloq.* depression; melancholy (*in the dumps*). [prob. f. LG or Du., fig. use of MDu. *domp* exhalation, haze, mist: rel. to DAMP]

dumpy /'dʌmpı/ *adj.* (**dumpier, dumpiest**) short and stout. □ **dumpily** *adv.* **dumpiness** *n.* [*dump* (cf. DUMPLING) + -Y¹]

dun¹ *adj. & n.* —*adj.* dull greyish-brown. —*n.* **1** a dun colour. **2** a dun horse. [OE *dun, dunn*]

dun² *n. & v.* —*n.* **1** a debt-collector; an importunate creditor. **2** a demand for payment. —*v.tr.* (**dunned, dunning**) importune for payment of a debt; pester. [abbr. of obs. *dunkirk* privateer, f. *Dunkirk* in France]

dunce *n.* a person slow at learning; a dullard. □ **dunce's cap** a paper cone formerly put on the head of a dunce at school as a mark of disgrace. [John *Duns* Scotus, scholastic theologian d. 1308, whose followers were ridiculed by 16th-c. humanists and reformers as enemies of learning]

dunderhead /'dʌndəhed/ *n.* a stupid person. □ **dunderheaded** *adj.* [17th c.: perh. rel. to dial. *dunner* resounding noise]

dune *n.* a mound or ridge of loose sand etc. formed by the wind. □ **dune buggy** = *beach buggy*. [F f. MDu. *dūne*: cf. DOWN³]

dung *n. & v.* —*n.* the excrement of animals; manure. —*v.tr.* apply dung to; manure (land). □ **dung-beetle** any of a family of beetles whose larvae develop in dung. [OE, rel. to OHG *tunga,* Icel. *dyngja,* of unkn. orig.]

dungaree /ˌdʌŋgə'riː/ *n.* **1** a coarse Indian calico. **2** (in *pl.*) **a** overalls etc. made of dungaree or similar material. **b** trousers with a bib. [Hindi *dungrī*]

dungeon /'dʌndʒ(ə)n/ *n.* a strong underground cell for prisoners. [orig. = *donjon*: ME f. OF *donjon* ult. f. L *dominus* lord]

dunghill /'dʌŋhıl/ *n.* a heap of dung or refuse, esp. in a farmyard.

dunk *v.tr.* **1** dip (bread, a biscuit, etc.) into soup, coffee, etc. while eating. **2** immerse, dip (*was* dunked in the river). [Pennsylvanian G dunke to dip f. G tunken]

dunlin /ˈdʌnlɪn/ n. a long-billed sandpiper, Calidris alpina. [prob. f. DUN¹ + -LING¹]

dunnock /ˈdʌnək/ n. Brit. the hedge sparrow. [app. f. DUN¹ + -OCK, from its brown and grey plumage]

dunny /ˈdʌnɪ/ n. (pl. -ies) 1 Sc. an underground passage or cellar, esp. in a tenement. 2 esp. Austral. & NZ sl. an earth-closet; an outdoor privy. [20th c.: orig. uncert.]

duo /ˈdjuːəʊ/ n. (pl. -os) 1 a pair of actors, entertainers, singers, etc. (a comedy duo). 2 Mus. a duet. [It. f. L, = two]

duodecimal /ˌdjuːəʊˈdesɪm(ə)l/ adj. & n. —adj. relating to or using a system of numerical notation that has 12 as a base. —n. 1 the duodecimal system. 2 duodecimal notation. □ **duodecimally** adv. [L duodecimus twelfth f. duodecim twelve]

duodenum /ˌdjuːəʊˈdiːnəm/ n. Anat. the first part of the small intestine immediately below the stomach. □ **duodenal** adj. **duodenitis** /-ˈnaɪtɪs/ n. [ME f. med.L f. duodeni distrib. of duodecim twelve from its length of about 12 fingers' breadth]

duologue /ˈdjuːəˌlɒg/ n. 1 a conversation between two people. 2 a play or part of a play for two actors. [irreg. f. L duo or Gk duo two, after monologue]

duopoly /djuːˈɒpəlɪ/ n. (pl. -ies) Econ. the possession of trade in a commodity etc. by only two sellers. [Gk duo two + pōleō sell, after monopoly]

dupe n. & v. —n. a victim of deception. —v.tr. make a fool of; cheat; gull. □ **dupable** adj. **duper** n. **dupery** n. [F f. dial. F dupe hoopoe, from the bird's supposedly stupid appearance]

dupion /ˈdjuːpɪən/ n. 1 a rough silk fabric woven from the threads of double cocoons. 2 an imitation of this with other fibres. [F doupion f. It. doppione f. doppio double]

duple /ˈdjuːp(ə)l/ adj. of two parts. □ **duple time** Mus. that with two beats to the bar. [L duplus f. duo two]

duplex /ˈdjuːpleks/ n. & adj. —n. esp. US 1 a flat or maisonette on two levels. 2 a house subdivided for two families. —adj. 1 having two elements; twofold. 2 esp. US a (of a flat) two-storeyed. b (of a house) for two families. [L duplex duplicis f. duo two + plic- fold]

duplicate adj., n., & v. —adj. /ˈdjuːplɪkət/ 1 exactly like something already existing; copied (esp. in large numbers). 2 a having two corresponding parts. b existing in two examples; paired. c twice as large or many; doubled. —n. /ˈdjuːplɪkət/ 1 a one of two identical things, esp. a copy of an original. b one of two or more specimens of a thing exactly or almost identical. 2 Law a second copy of a letter or document. —v.tr. /ˈdjuːplɪˌkeɪt/ 1 multiply by two; double. 2 a make or be an exact copy of. b make or supply copies of (duplicated the leaflet for distribution). 3 repeat (an action etc.), esp. unnecessarily. □ **in duplicate** consisting of two exact copies. □ **duplicable** /-kəb(ə)l/ adj. **duplication** /-ˈkeɪʃ(ə)n/ n. [L duplicatus past part. of duplicare (as DUPLEX)]

duplicator /ˈdjuːplɪˌkeɪtə(r)/ n. 1 a machine for making copies of a document, leaflet, etc. 2 a person or thing that duplicates.

duplicity /djuːˈplɪsɪtɪ/ n. double-dealing; deceitfulness. □ **duplicitous** adj. [ME f. OF duplicité or LL duplicitas (as DUPLEX)]

durable /ˈdjʊərəb(ə)l/ adj. & n. —adj. 1 capable of lasting; hard-wearing. 2 (of goods) not for immediate consumption; able to be kept. —n. (in pl.) durable goods. □ **durability** /-ˈbɪlɪtɪ/ n. **durableness** n. **durably** adv. [ME f. OF f. L durabilis f. durare endure f. durus hard]

durance /ˈdjʊərəns/ n. archaic imprisonment (in durance vile). [ME f. F f. durer last f. L durare: see DURABLE]

duration /djʊəˈreɪʃ(ə)n/ n. 1 the length of time for which something continues. 2 a specified length of time (after the duration of a minute). □ **for the duration** 1 until the end of the war. 2 for a very long time. □ **durational** adj. [ME f. OF f. med.L duratio -onis (as DURANCE)]

duress /djʊəˈres, ˈdjʊə-/ n. 1 compulsion, esp. imprisonment, threats, or violence, illegally used to force a person to act against his or her will (under duress). 2 forcible restraint or imprisonment. [ME f. OF duresse f. L duritia f. durus hard]

during /ˈdjʊərɪŋ/ prep. 1 throughout the course or duration of (read during the meal). 2 at some point in the duration of (came in during the evening). [ME f. OF durant ult. f. L durare last, continue]

durn US var. of DARN².

durned US var. of DARNED.

durum /ˈdjʊərəm/ n. a kind of wheat, Triticum turgidum, having hard seeds and yielding a flour used in the manufacture of spaghetti etc. [L, neut. of durus hard]

dusk n. 1 the darker stage of twilight. 2 shade; gloom. [ME dosk, dusk f. OE dox dark, swarthy, doxian darken in colour]

dusky /ˈdʌskɪ/ adj. (**duskier**, **duskiest**) 1 shadowy; dim. 2 dark-coloured, darkish. □ **duskily** adv. **duskiness** n.

dust n. & v. —n. 1 a finely powdered earth, dirt, etc., lying on the ground or on surfaces, and blown about by the wind. b fine powder of any material (pollen dust; gold-dust). c a cloud of dust. 2 a dead person's remains (honoured dust). 3 confusion or turmoil (raised quite a dust). —v. 1 tr. (also absol.) clear (furniture etc.) of dust etc. by wiping, brushing, etc. 2 tr. a sprinkle (esp. a cake) with powder, dust, sugar, etc. b sprinkle or strew (sugar, powder, etc.). 3 tr. make dusty. □ **dust-bath** a bird's rolling in dust to freshen its feathers. **dust bowl** an area denuded of vegetation by drought or erosion and reduced to desert. **dust cover** 1 = dust-sheet. 2 = dust-jacket. **dust devil** S.Afr. a whirlwind visible as a column of dust. **dust down** 1 dust the clothes of (a person). 2 colloq. reprimand. 3 = dust off. **dusting-powder** 1 talcum powder. 2 any dusting or drying powder. **dust-jacket** a usu. decorated paper cover used to protect a book from dirt etc. **dust off** 1 remove the dust from (an object on which it has long been allowed to settle). 2 use and enjoy again after a long period of neglect. **dust-sheet** Brit. a cloth put over furniture to protect it from dust. **dust-storm** a storm with clouds of dust carried in the air. **dust-up** colloq. a fight. **dust-wrapper** = dust-jacket. □ **dustless** adj. [OE dūst: cf. LG dunst vapour]

dustbin /ˈdʌstbɪn, ˈdʌsbɪn/ n. Brit. a container for household refuse, esp. one kept outside.

dustcart /ˈdʌstkɑːt/ n. Brit. a vehicle used for collecting household refuse.

duster /ˈdʌstə(r)/ n. **1** a cloth for dusting furniture etc. **2** a person or contrivance that dusts.

dustman /ˈdʌstmən, ˈdʌsmən/ n. (pl. -**men**) Brit. a man employed to clear household refuse.

dustpan /ˈdʌstpæn/ n. a small pan into which dust etc. is brushed from the floor.

dusty /ˈdʌstɪ/ adj. (**dustier, dustiest**) **1** full of, covered with, or resembling dust. **2** dry as dust; uninteresting. **3** (of a colour) dull or muted. □ **dusty answer** a curt rejection of a request. □ **dustily** adv. **dustiness** n. [OE dūstig (as DUST)]

Dutch adj. & n. —adj. **1** of, relating to, or associated with the Netherlands. **2** US sl. German. **3** S.Afr. of Dutch descent. —n. **1 a** the language of the Netherlands. **b** S.Afr. usu. derog. Afrikaans. **2** (prec. by the; treated as pl.) **a** the people of the Netherlands. **b** S.Afr. Afrikaans-speakers. □ **Dutch barn** Brit. a barn roof over hay etc., set on poles and having no walls. **Dutch cap 1** a contraceptive diaphragm. **2** a woman's lace cap with triangular flaps on each side. **Dutch courage** false courage gained from alcohol. **Dutch doll** a jointed wooden doll. **Dutch door** a door divided into two parts horizontally allowing one part to be shut and the other open. **Dutch elm disease** a disease affecting elms caused by the fungus Ceratocystis ulmi, first found in the Netherlands. **Dutch hoe** a hoe pushed forward by the user. **Dutch interior** a painting of Dutch domestic life. **Dutch oven 1** a metal box the open side of which is turned towards a fire. **2** a covered cooking pot for braising etc. **Dutch treat** a party, outing, etc. to which each person makes a contribution. **Dutch uncle** a person giving advice with benevolent firmness. **go Dutch** share expenses equally. [MDu. dutsch etc. Hollandish, Netherlandish, German, OHG diutisc national]

dutch /dʌtʃ/ n. Brit. sl. a wife (esp. old dutch). [abbr. of duchess (also in this sense)]

Dutchman /ˈdʌtʃmən/ n. (pl. -**men**; fem. **Dutchwoman**, pl. -**women**) **1** a native or national of the Netherlands. **2** a person of Dutch descent.

duteous /ˈdjuːtɪəs/ adj. literary (of a person or conduct) dutiful; obedient. □ **duteously** adv. **duteousness** n. [DUTY + -OUS: cf. beauteous]

dutiable /ˈdjuːtɪəb(ə)l/ adj. liable to customs or other duties.

dutiful /ˈdjuːtɪˌfʊl/ adj. doing or observant of one's duty; obedient. □ **dutifully** adv. **dutifulness** n.

duty /ˈdjuːtɪ/ n. (pl. -**ies**) **1 a** a moral or legal obligation; a responsibility (his duty to report it). **b** the binding force of what is right (strong sense of duty). **c** what is required of one (do one's duty). **2** payment to the public revenue, esp.: **a** that levied on the import, export, manufacture, or sale of goods (customs duty). **b** that levied on the transfer of property, licences, the legal recognition of documents, etc. (death duty; probate duty). **3** a job or function (his duties as caretaker). **4** the behaviour due to a superior; deference, respect. □ **do duty for** serve as or pass for (something else). **duty-bound** obliged by duty. **duty-free** (of goods) on which duty is not leviable. **duty-free shop** a shop at an airport etc. at which duty-free goods can be bought. **duty-officer** the officer currently on duty. **duty-paid** (of goods) on which duty has been paid. **on** (or **off**) **duty** engaged (or not engaged) in one's work. [AF deweté, dueté (as DUE)]

duvet /ˈduːveɪ/ n. a thick soft quilt used instead of an upper sheet and blankets. [F]

dwarf /dwɔːf/ n. & v. —n. (pl. **dwarfs** or **dwarves** /dwɔːvz/) **1 a** a person of abnormally small stature, esp. one with a normal-sized head and body but short limbs. **b** an animal or plant much below the ordinary size for the species. **2** a small mythological being with supernatural powers. **3** (in full **dwarf star**) a small usu. dense star. **4** (attrib.) **a** of a kind very small in size (dwarf bean). **b** puny, stunted. —v.tr. **1** stunt in growth. **2** cause (something similar or comparable) to seem small or insignificant (efforts dwarfed by their rivals' achievements). □ **dwarfish** adj. [OE dweorg f. Gmc]

■ **Usage** In sense 1, with regard to people, the term person of restricted growth is now often preferred.

dwarfism /ˈdwɔːfɪz(ə)m/ n. the condition of being a dwarf.

dweeb /dwiːb/ n. US sl. a studious or boring person; a nerd. [orig. unkn.]

dwell /dwel/ v.intr. (past and past part. **dwelt** or **dwelled**) literary (usu. foll. by in, at, near, on, etc.) live, reside (dwelt in the forest). □ **dwell on** (or **upon**) spend time on, linger over; write, brood, or speak at length on (a specified subject) (always dwells on his grievances). □ **dweller** n. [OE dwellan lead astray, later 'continue in a place', f. Gmc]

dwelling /ˈdwelɪŋ/ n. (also **dwelling-place**) formal a house; a residence; an abode. □ **dwelling-house** a house used as a residence, not as an office etc.

dwindle /ˈdwɪnd(ə)l/ v.intr. **1** become gradually smaller; shrink. **2** lose importance; decline; degenerate. [dwine fade away f. OE dwīnan, ON dvína]

Dy symb. Chem. the element dysprosium.

dye /daɪ/ n. & v. —n. **1 a** a substance used to change the colour of hair, fabric, wood, etc. **b** a colour produced by this. **2** (in full **dyestuff**) a substance yielding a dye, esp. for colouring materials in solution. —v.tr. (**dyeing**) **1** impregnate with dye. **2** make (a thing) a specified colour with dye (dyed it yellow). □ **dyed in the wool** (or **grain**) out and out; unchangeable, inveterate. □ **dyeable** adj. [OE deag, deagian]

dyer /ˈdaɪə(r)/ n. a person who dyes cloth etc.

dying /ˈdaɪɪŋ/ adj. connected with, or at the time of, death (his dying words). □ **to one's dying day** for the rest of one's life. [pres. part. of DIE¹]

dyke¹ n. & v. (also **dike**) —n. **1** a long wall or embankment built to prevent flooding, esp. from the sea. **2 a** a ditch or artificial watercourse. **b** Brit. a natural watercourse. **3 a** a low wall, esp. of turf. **b** a causeway. **4** a barrier or obstacle; a defence. —v.tr. provide or defend with a dyke or dykes. [ME f. ON dík or MLG dīk dam, MDu. dijc ditch, dam: cf. DITCH]

dyke² n. (also **dike**) sl. a lesbian. [20th c.: orig. unkn.]

dyn abbr. dyne.

dynamic /daɪˈnæmɪk/ *adj.* & *n.* —*adj.* (also **dynamical**) **1** energetic; active; potent. **2** *Physics* **a** concerning motive force. **b** concerning force in actual operation. **3** of or concerning dynamics. **4** *Mus.* relating to the volume of sound. **5** *Philos.* relating to dynamism. —*n.* **1** an energizing or motive force. **2** *Mus.* = DYNAMICS 3. □ **dynamically** *adv.* [F *dynamique* f. Gk *dunamikos* f. *dunamis* power]

dynamics /daɪˈnæmɪks/ *n.pl.* **1** (usu. treated as *sing.*) **a** *Mech.* the branch of mechanics concerned with the motion of bodies under the action of forces. **b** the branch of any science in which forces or changes are considered (*aerodynamics*; *population dynamics*). **2** the motive forces, physical or moral, affecting behaviour and change in any sphere. **3** *Mus.* the varying degree of volume of sound in musical performance. □ **dynamicist** /-sɪst/ *n.* (in sense 1).

dynamism /ˈdaɪnəˌmɪz(ə)m/ *n.* energizing or dynamic action or power. □ **dynamist** *n.* [Gk *dunamis* power + -ISM]

dynamite /ˈdaɪnəˌmaɪt/ *n.* & *v.* —*n.* **1** a high explosive consisting of nitroglycerine mixed with an absorbent. **2** a potentially dangerous person, thing, or situation. —*v.tr.* charge or shatter with dynamite. □ **dynamiter** *n.* [formed as DYNAMISM + -ITE¹]

dynamo /ˈdaɪnəˌməʊ/ *n.* (*pl.* **-os**) **1** a machine converting mechanical into electrical energy, esp. by rotating coils of copper wire in a magnetic field. **2** *colloq.* an energetic person. [abbr. of *dynamo-electric machine* f. Gk *dunamis* power, force]

dynamometer /ˌdaɪnəˈmɒmɪtə(r)/ *n.* an instrument measuring energy expended. [F *dynamomètre* f. Gk *dunamis* power, force]

dynast /ˈdɪnæst, ˈdaɪ-/ *n.* **1** a ruler. **2** a member of a dynasty. [L f. Gk *dunastēs* f. *dunamai* be able]

dynasty /ˈdɪnəstɪ/ *n.* (*pl.* **-ies**) **1** a line of hereditary rulers. **2** a succession of leaders in any

field. □ **dynastic** /-ˈnæstɪk/ *adj.* **dynastically** /-ˈnæstɪkəlɪ/ *adv.* [F *dynastie* or LL *dynastia* f. Gk *dunasteia* lordship (as DYNAST)]

dyne /daɪn/ *n. Physics* a unit of force that, acting on a mass of one gram, increases its velocity by one centimetre per second every second along the direction that it acts. [F f. Gk *dunamis* force, power]

dys- /dɪs/ *comb. form esp. Med.* bad, difficult. [Gk *dus-* bad]

dysentery /ˈdɪsəntərɪ, -trɪ/ *n.* a disease with inflammation of the intestines, causing severe diarrhoea with blood and mucus. □ **dysenteric** /-ˈterɪk/ *adj.* [OF *dissenterie* or L *dysenteria* f. Gk *dusenteria* (as DYS-, *enteria* f. *entera* bowels)]

dysfunction /dɪsˈfʌŋkʃ(ə)n/ *n.* an abnormality or impairment of function. □ **dysfunctional** *adj.*

dyslexia /dɪsˈleksɪə/ *n.* an abnormal difficulty in reading and spelling, caused by a condition of the brain. □ **dyslexic** *adj.* & *n.* **dyslectic** /-ˈlektɪk/ *adj.* & *n.* [G *Dyslexie* (as DYS-, Gk *lexis* speech)]

dyspepsia /dɪsˈpepsɪə/ *n.* indigestion. [L *dyspepsia* f. Gk *duspepsia* (as DYS-, *peptos* cooked, digested)]

dyspeptic /dɪsˈpeptɪk/ *adj.* & *n.* —*adj.* of or relating to dyspepsia or the resulting depression. —*n.* a person suffering from dyspepsia.

dysphasia /ˌdɪsˈfeɪzɪə/ *n. Med.* lack of coordination in speech, owing to brain damage. □ **dysphasic** *adj.* [Gk *dusphatos* hard to utter f. DYS-, *phatos* spoken f. *phēmi phan-* speak]

dysprosium /dɪsˈprəʊzɪəm/ *n. Chem.* a naturally occurring soft metallic element of the lanthanide series. [mod.L f. Gk *dusprositos* hard to get at + -IUM]

dystrophy /ˈdɪstrəfɪ/ *n.* defective nutrition. □ **muscular dystrophy** a hereditary progressive weakening and wasting of the muscles. □ **dystrophic** /dɪsˈtrɒfɪk/ *adj.* [mod.L *dystrophia* formed as DYS- + Gk *-trophia* nourishment]

Ee

E[1] /iː/ *n.* (also **e**) (*pl.* **Es** or **E's**) **1** the fifth letter of the alphabet. **2** *Mus.* the third note of the diatonic scale of C major.

E[2] *abbr.* (also **E.**) **1** East, Eastern. **2** see E-NUMBER.

e *symb.* used on packaging (in conjunction with specification of weight, size, etc.) to indicate compliance with EC regulations.

e- /ɪ, e/ *prefix* form of EX-[1] 1 before some consonants.

each *adj. & pron.* —*adj.* every one of two or more persons or things, regarded separately (*each person; five in each class*). —*pron.* each person or thing (*each of us; have two books each; cost a penny each*). □ **each other** one another (*they hate each other; they wore each other's hats*). **each way** *Brit.* (of a bet) backing a horse etc. for both a win and a place. [OE *ǣlc* f. WG (as AYE, ALIKE)]

eager /ˈiːgə(r)/ *adj.* **1 a** full of keen desire, enthusiastic. **b** (of passions etc.) keen, impatient. **2** keen, impatient, strongly desirous (*eager to learn; eager for news*). □ **eager beaver** *colloq.* a very or excessively diligent person. □ **eagerly** *adv.* **eagerness** *n.* [ME f. AF *egre*, OF *aigre* keen, ult. f. L *acer acris*]

eagle /ˈiːg(ə)l/ *n.* **1 a** any of various large birds of prey of the family Accipitridae, with keen vision and powerful flight. **b** a figure of an eagle, esp. as a symbol of the US, or formerly as a Roman or French ensign. **2** *Golf* a score of two strokes under par at any hole. □ **eagle eye** keen sight, watchfulness. **eagle-eyed** keen-sighted, watchful. [ME f. AF *egle*, OF *aigle* f. L *aquila*]

eaglet /ˈiːglɪt/ *n.* a young eagle.

ear[1] *n.* **1 a** the organ of hearing and balance in man and vertebrates, esp. the external part of this. **b** an organ sensitive to sound in other animals. **2** the faculty for discriminating sounds (*an ear for music*). **3** an ear-shaped thing, esp. the handle of a jug. **4** listening, attention. □ **all ears** listening attentively. **ear lobe** the lower soft pendulous external part of the ear. **ear-piercing** loud and shrill. **ear-splitting** excessively loud. **ear-trumpet** a trumpet-shaped device formerly used as a hearing-aid. **have a person's ear** receive a favourable hearing. □ **eared** *adj.* (also in *comb.*). **earless** *adj.* [OE *ēare* f. Gmc: rel. to L *auris*, Gk *ous*]

ear[2] *n.* the seed-bearing head of a cereal plant. [OE *ēar* f. Gmc]

earache /ˈɪəreɪk/ *n.* a pain in the ear.

earbash /ˈɪəbæʃ/ *v.tr.* esp. *Austral. sl.* talk inordinately to; harangue. □ **earbasher** *n.* **earbashing** *n.*

eardrum /ˈɪədrʌm/ *n.* the membrane of the middle ear.

earful /ˈɪəfʊl/ *n.* (*pl.* **-fuls**) *colloq.* **1** a copious or prolonged amount of talking. **2** a strong reprimand.

earl /ɜːl/ *n.* a British nobleman ranking between a marquess and a viscount. □ **Earl Marshal** (in the UK) the officer presiding over the College of Heralds, with ceremonial duties on various royal occasions. □ **earldom** *n.* [OE *eorl*, of unkn. orig.]

early /ˈɜːlɪ/ *adj., adv., & n.* —*adj. & adv.* (**earlier**, **earliest**) **1** before the due, usual, or expected time (*was early for my appointment; the train arrived early*). **2 a** not far on in the day or night, or in time (*early evening; at the earliest opportunity*). **b** prompt (*early payment appreciated*). **3 a** not far on in a period, development, or process of evolution; being the first stage (*Early English architecture; early Spring*). **b** of the distant past (*early man*). **c** not far on in a sequence or serial order (*appears early in the list*). **4 a** of childhood, esp. the preschool years (*early learning*). **b** (of a piece of writing, music, etc.) immature, youthful (*an early work*). **5** forward in flowering, ripening, etc. (*early peaches*). —*n.* (*pl.* **-ies**) (usu. in *pl.*) an early fruit or vegetable, esp. potatoes. □ **early bird** *colloq.* one who arrives, gets up, etc. early. **early days** early in time for something to happen etc. **early hours** the very early morning, usu. before dawn. **early** (or **earlier**) **on** at an early (or earlier) stage. **early warning** advance warning of an imminent (esp. nuclear) attack. □ **earliness** *n.* [orig. as *adv.*, f. OE *ǣrlīce*, *ārlīce* (ǣr ERE)]

earmark /ˈɪəmɑːk/ *n. & v.* —*n.* **1** an identifying mark. **2** an owner's mark on the ear of an animal. —*v.tr.* **1** set aside (money etc.) for a special purpose. **2** mark (sheep etc.) with such a mark.

earmuff /ˈɪəmʌf/ *n.* a wrap or cover for the ears, protecting them from cold, noise, etc.

earn /ɜːn/ *v.tr.* **1** (also *absol.*) **a** (of a person) obtain (income) in the form of money in return for labour or services. **b** (of capital invested) bring in as interest or profit. **2 a** deserve; obtain as the reward for hard work or merit (*have earned a holiday; earned our admiration*). **b** incur (a reproach, reputation, etc.). [OE *earnian* f. WG, rel. to Gmc roots assoc. with reaping]

earner /ˈɜːnə(r)/ *n.* **1** a person or thing that earns (often in *comb.*: *wage-earner*). **2** *sl.* a lucrative job or enterprise.

earnest[1] /ˈɜːnɪst/ *adj. & n.* —*adj.* ardently or intensely serious; zealous; not trifling or joking. —*n.* seriousness. □ **in** (or **in real**) **earnest** serious(ly), not joking(ly); with determination. □ **earnestly** *adv.* **earnestness** *n.* [OE *eornust*, *eornost* (with Gmc cognates): cf. ON *ern* vigorous]

earnest[2] /ˈɜːnɪst/ *n.* **1** money paid as an instalment, esp. to confirm a contract etc. **2** a token or foretaste (*in earnest of what is to come*). [ME *ernes*, prob. var. of *erles*, *arles* prob. f. med.L *arrhula* (unrecorded) f. *arr(h)a* pledge]

earnings /ˈɜːnɪŋz/ *n.pl.* money earned.

earphone /ˈɪəfəʊn/ *n.* a device applied to the ear to aid hearing or receive radio or telephone communications.

earpiece /ˈɪəpiːs/ n. the part of a telephone etc. applied to the ear during use.

earplug /ˈɪəplʌg/ n. a piece of wax etc. placed in the ear to protect against cold air, water, or noise.

earring /ˈɪərɪŋ/ n. a piece of jewellery worn in or on (esp. the lobe of) the ear.

earshot /ˈɪəʃɒt/ n. the distance over which something can be heard (esp. *within* or *out of earshot*).

earth /ɜːθ/ n. & v. —n. **1 a** (also **Earth**) the planet on which we live. **b** land and sea, as distinct from sky. **2 a** dry land; the ground (*fell to earth*). **b** soil, clay, mould. **3** *Relig.* the present abode of mankind, as distinct from heaven or hell; the world. **4** *Brit. Electr.* the connection to the earth as an arbitrary reference voltage in an electrical circuit. **5** the hole of a badger, fox, etc. **6** (prec. by *the*) *colloq.* a huge amount; everything (*cost the earth; want the earth*). —v. **1** tr. (foll. by *up*) cover (the roots and lower stems of plants) with heaped-up earth. **2 a** tr. drive (a fox) to its earth. **b** intr. (of a fox etc.) run to its earth. **3** tr. *Brit. Electr.* connect to the earth. □ **come back** (or **down**) **to earth** return to realities. **earth-closet** a lavatory with dry earth used to cover excreta. **earth sciences** the sciences concerned with the earth or part of it, or its atmosphere (e.g. geology, oceanography, meteorology). **earth-shattering** *colloq.* having a traumatic or devastating effect. **earth-shatteringly** *colloq.* devastatingly, remarkably. **gone to earth** in hiding. **on earth** *colloq.* existing anywhere; whatever (*the happiest man on earth; what on earth?*). □ **earthward** adj. & adv. **earthwards** adv. [OE *eorthe* f. Gmc]

earthbound /ˈɜːθbaʊnd/ adj. **1** attached to the earth or earthly things. **2** moving towards the earth.

earthen /ˈɜːθ(ə)n/ adj. **1** made of earth. **2** made of baked clay.

earthenware /ˈɜːθ(ə)nˌweə(r)/ n. & adj. —n. pottery, vessels, etc., made of clay fired to a porous state which can be made impervious to liquids by the use of a glaze. —adj. made of fired clay. [EARTHEN + WARE¹]

earthling /ˈɜːθlɪŋ/ n. an inhabitant of the earth, esp. as regarded in fiction by outsiders.

earthly /ˈɜːθlɪ/ adj. **1** of the earth or human life on earth; terrestrial. **2** (usu. with *neg.*) *colloq.* remotely possible or conceivable (*is no earthly use; there wasn't an earthly reason*). □ **not an earthly** *colloq.* no chance whatever. □ **earthliness** n.

earthquake /ˈɜːθkweɪk/ n. **1** a convulsion of the superficial parts of the earth due to the release of accumulated stress as a result of faults in strata or volcanic action. **2** a social etc. disturbance.

earthwork /ˈɜːθwɜːk/ n. **1** an artificial bank of earth in fortification or road-building etc. **2** the process of excavating soil in civil engineering work.

earthworm /ˈɜːθwɜːm/ n. any of various annelid worms, esp. of the genus *Lumbricus* or *Allolobophora*, living and burrowing in the ground.

earthy /ˈɜːθɪ/ adj. (**earthier**, **earthiest**) **1** of or like earth or soil. **2** somewhat coarse or crude; unrefined (*earthy humour*). □ **earthily** adv. **earthiness** n.

earwax /ˈɪəwæks/ n. a yellow waxy secretion produced by the ear..

earwig /ˈɪəwɪg/ n. **1** any small insect of the order Dermaptera, with a pair of terminal appendages in the shape of forceps. **2** *US* a small centipede. [OE *ēarwicga* f. *ēare* EAR¹ + *wicga* earwig, prob. rel. to *wiggle*: once thought to enter the head through the ear]

ease /iːz/ n. & v. —n. **1** absence of difficulty; facility, effortlessness (*did it with ease*). **2** a freedom or relief from pain, anxiety, or trouble. **b** freedom from embarrassment or awkwardness. **c** freedom or relief from constraint or formality. —v. **1** tr. relieve from pain or anxiety etc. (often foll. by *of: eased my mind; eased me of the burden*). **2** intr. (often foll. by *off, up*) **a** become less painful or burdensome. **b** relax; begin to take it easy. **c** slow down; moderate one's behaviour, habits, etc. **3** intr. *Meteorol.* become less severe (*the wind will ease tonight*). **4 a** tr. relax; slacken; make a less tight fit. **b** tr. & intr. (foll. by *through, into,* etc.) move or be moved carefully into place (*eased it into the hole*). **5** intr. (often foll. by *off*) *Stock Exch.* (of shares etc.) descend in price or value. □ **at ease 1** free from anxiety or constraint. **2** *Mil.* in a relaxed attitude, with the feet apart. **at one's ease** free from embarrassment, awkwardness, or undue formality. **ease away** (or **down** or **off**) *Naut.* slacken (a rope, sail, etc.). □ **easer** n. [ME f. AF *ese*, OF *eise*, ult. f. L *adjacens* ADJACENT]

easel /ˈiːz(ə)l/ n. a standing frame, usu. of wood, for supporting an artist's work, a blackboard, etc. [Du. *ezel* = G *Esel* ASS¹]

easement /ˈiːzmənt/ n. *Law* a right of way or a similar right over another's land. [ME f. OF *aisement*]

easily /ˈiːzɪlɪ/ adv. **1** without difficulty. **2** by far (*easily the best*). **3** very probably (*it could easily snow*).

east n., adj., & adv. —n. **1 a** the point of the horizon where the sun rises at the equinoxes. **b** the compass point corresponding to this. **c** the direction in which this lies. **2** (usu. **the East**) **a** the regions or countries lying to the east of Europe. **b** eastern Europe. **3** the eastern part of a country, town, etc. —adj. **1** towards, at, near, or facing east. **2** coming from the east (*east wind*). —adv. **1** towards, at, or near the east. **2** (foll. by *of*) further east than. □ **East End** the part of London east of the City. **East Indies** the islands etc. east of India, esp. the Malay archipelago. **east-north** (or **-south**) **-east** the direction or compass point midway between east and north-east (or south-east). **to the east** (often foll. by *of*) in an easterly direction. [OE *ēast-* f. Gmc]

eastbound /ˈiːstbaʊnd/ adj. travelling or leading eastwards.

Easter /ˈiːstə(r)/ n. **1** (also **Easter Day** or **Sunday**) the festival (held on a variable Sunday in March or April) commemorating Christ's resurrection. **2** the season in which this occurs, esp. the weekend from Good Friday to Easter Monday. □ **Easter egg** an artificial usu. chocolate egg given at Easter, esp. to children. **Easter week** the week beginning on Easter Sunday. [OE *ēastre* app. f. *Ēostre*, a goddess associated with spring, f. Gmc]

easterly /ˈiːstəlɪ/ adj., adv., & n. —adj. & adv. **1** in an eastern position or direction. **2** (of a wind) blowing from the east. —n. (pl. -ies) an easterly wind.

eastern /ˈiːst(ə)n/ adj. 1 of or in the east; inhabiting the east. 2 lying or directed towards the east. 3 (Eastern) of or in the Far, Middle, or Near East. □ Eastern Church the Orthodox Church. □ easternmost adj. [OE ēasterne (as EAST, -ERN)]

easterner /ˈiːstənə(r)/ n. a native or inhabitant of the east.

eastward /ˈiːstwəd/ adj., adv., & n. —adj. & adv. (also eastwards) towards the east. —n. an eastward direction or region. □ eastwardly adj. & adv.

easy /ˈiːzɪ/ adj., adv., & int. (easier, easiest) —adj. 1 not difficult; achieved without great effort. 2 a free from pain, discomfort, anxiety, etc. b comfortably off, affluent (easy circumstances). 3 free from embarrassment, awkwardness, constraint, etc.; relaxed and pleasant (an easy manner). 4 compliant, obliging; easily persuaded (an easy mark). —adv. with ease; in an effortless or relaxed manner. —int. go carefully; move gently. □ easy chair a large comfortable chair, usu. an armchair. easy money money got without effort (esp. of dubious legality). easy on the eye (or ear etc.) colloq. pleasant to look at (or listen to etc.). Easy Street colloq. affluence. easy terms payment by instalments. go easy (foll. by with, on) be sparing or cautious. I'm easy colloq. I have no preference. of easy virtue (of a woman) sexually promiscuous. stand easy! Brit. Mil. permission to a squad standing at ease to relax their attitude further. take it easy 1 proceed gently or carefully. 2 relax; avoid overwork. □ easiness n. [ME f. AF aisé, OF aisié past part. of aisier EASE]

easygoing /ˌiːzɪˈgəʊɪŋ/ adj. placid and tolerant; relaxed in manner; accepting things as they are.

eat v. (past ate /et, eɪt/; past part. eaten /ˈiːt(ə)n/) 1 a tr. take into the mouth, chew, and swallow (food). b intr. consume food; take a meal. c tr. devour (eaten by a lion). 2 intr. (foll. by (away) at, into) a destroy gradually, esp. by corrosion, erosion, disease, etc. b begin to consume or diminish (resources etc.). 3 tr. colloq. trouble, vex (what's eating you?). □ eat one's heart out suffer from excessive longing or envy. eat out have a meal away from home, esp. in a restaurant. eat up 1 (also absol.) eat or consume completely. 2 use or deal with rapidly or wastefully (eats up petrol; eats up the miles). 3 encroach upon or annex (eating up the neighbouring States). 4 absorb, preoccupy (eaten up with pride). eat one's words admit that one was wrong. [OE etan f. Gmc]

eatable /ˈiːtəb(ə)l/ adj. & n. —adj. that is in a condition to be eaten (cf. EDIBLE). —n. (usu. in pl.) food.

eater /ˈiːtə(r)/ n. 1 a person who eats (a big eater). 2 Brit. an eating apple etc.

eatery /ˈiːtərɪ/ n. US (pl. -ies) colloq. a restaurant or eating-place.

eating /ˈiːtɪŋ/ adj. 1 suitable for eating (eating apple). 2 used for eating (eating-house).

eats /iːts/ n.pl. colloq. food.

eau-de-Cologne /ˌəʊdəkəˈləʊn/ n. an alcohol-based perfume of a kind made orig. at Cologne. [F, lit. 'water of Cologne']

eaves /iːvz/ n.pl. the underside of a projecting roof. [orig. sing., f. OE efes: prob. rel. to OVER]

eavesdrop /ˈiːvzdrɒp/ v.intr. (-dropped, -dropping) listen secretly to a private conversation. □ eavesdropper n. [eavesdropper orig. 'one who listens under walls' prob. f. ON upsardropi (cf. OE yfæsdrype): eavesdrop by back-form.]

ebb /eb/ n. & v. —n. 1 the movement of the tide out to sea (also attrib.: ebb tide). 2 the process of draining away of flood-water etc. —v.intr. (often foll. by away) 1 (of tidewater) flow out to sea; recede; drain away. 2 decline; run low (his life was ebbing away). □ at a low ebb in a poor condition or state of decline. ebb and flow a continuing process of decline and upturn in circumstances. [OE ebba, ebbian]

ebonite /ˈebəˌnaɪt/ n. = VULCANITE. [EBONY + -ITE¹]

ebony /ˈebənɪ/ n. & adj. —n. (pl. -ies) 1 a heavy hard dark wood used for furniture. 2 any of various trees of the genus Diospyros producing this. —adj. 1 made of ebony. 2 black like ebony. [earlier hebeny f. (h)eben(e) = ebon, perh. after ivory]

ebullient /ɪˈbʌlɪənt, disp. ɪˈbʊlɪənt/ adj. exuberant, high-spirited. □ ebullience n. ebulliency n. ebulliently adv. [L ebullire ebullient- bubble out (as E-, bullire boil)]

EC abbr. 1 East Central (London postal district). 2 a European Community. b European Commission.

ecad /ˈiːkæd/ n. Ecol. an organism modified by its environment. [Gk oikos house + -AD]

eccentric /ɪkˈsentrɪk, ek-/ adj. & n. —adj. 1 odd or capricious in behaviour or appearance; whimsical. 2 a not placed, not having its axis etc. placed centrally. b (often foll. by to) (of a circle) not concentric (to another). c (of an orbit) not circular. —n. 1 an eccentric person. 2 Mech. an eccentric contrivance for changing rotatory into backward-and-forward motion, e.g. the cam used in an internal-combustion engine. □ eccentrically adv. eccentricity /-ˈtrɪsɪtɪ/ n. (pl. -ies). [LL eccentricus f. Gk ekkentros f. ek out of + kentros CENTRE]

ecclesiastic /ɪˌkliːzɪˈæstɪk/ n. & adj. —n. a priest or clergyman. —adj. = ECCLESIASTICAL. □ ecclesiasticism /-ˌsɪz(ə)m/ n. [F ecclésiastique or LL ecclesiasticus f. Gk ekklēsiastikos f. ekklēsia assembly, church f. ekklētos summoned out f. ek out + kaleō call]

ecclesiastical /ɪˌkliːzɪˈæstɪk(ə)l/ adj. of the Church or the clergy. □ ecclesiastically adv.

ECG abbr. electrocardiogram.

echelon /ˈeʃəˌlɒn, ˈeɪʃəˌlɔ̃/ n. 1 a level or rank in an organization, in society, etc.; those occupying it (often in pl.: the upper echelons). 2 Mil. a formation of troops, ships, aircraft, etc., in parallel rows with the end of each row projecting further than the one in front (in echelon). [F échelon f. échelle ladder f. L scala]

echidna /ɪˈkɪdnə/ n. any of several egg-laying pouch-bearing mammals native to Australia and New Guinea, with a covering of spines. [mod.L f. Gk ekhidna viper]

echinoderm /ɪˈkaɪnəˌdɜːm, ˈekɪn-/ n. any marine invertebrate of the phylum Echinodermata, e.g. starfish and sea urchins. [f. Gk ekhinos hedgehog, sea urchin + Gk derma -atos skin]

echo /ˈekəʊ/ n. & v. —n. (pl. -oes) 1 a the repetition of a sound by the reflection of sound waves. b the secondary sound produced. 2 a reflected radio or radar beam. 3 a close imitation or repetition of something already done. **4 a** a person who slavishly repeats the words or opinions of another. **5** (often in *pl.*) circumstances or events reminiscent of or remotely connected with earlier ones. —*v.* (**-oes**, **-oed**) **1** *intr.* **a** (of a place) resound with an echo. **b** (of a sound) be repeated; resound. **2** *tr.* repeat (a sound) by an echo. **3** *tr.* **a** repeat (another's words). **b** imitate the words, opinions, or actions of (a person). □ **echo chamber** an enclosure with sound-reflecting walls. **echo location** the location of objects by reflected sound. **echo-sounder** sounding apparatus for determining the depth of the sea beneath a ship by measuring the time taken for an echo to be received. **echo-sounding** the use of an echo-sounder. □ **echoer** *n.* **echoless** *adj.* [ME f. OF or L f. Gk *ēkhō*, rel. to *ēkhē* a sound]

echogram /ˈekəʊˌgræm/ *n.* a record made by an echo-sounder.

echograph /ˈekəʊˌgrɑːf/ *n.* a device for automatically recording echograms.

echoic /eˈkəʊɪk/ *adj. Phonet.* (of a word) imitating the sound it represents; onomatopoeic. □ **echoically** *adv.*

éclair /eɪˈkleə(r), ɪˈkleə(r)/ *n.* a small elongated cake of choux pastry filled with cream and iced with chocolate or coffee icing. [F, lit. lightning, flash]

eclampsia /ɪˈklæmpsɪə/ *n.* a condition involving convulsions leading to coma, occurring esp. in pregnant women. □ **eclamptic** *adj.* [mod.L f. F *eclampsie* f. Gk *eklampsis* sudden development f. *eklampō* shine forth]

éclat /eɪˈklɑː, ˈeɪklɑː/ *n.* **1** brilliant display; dazzling effect. **2** social distinction; conspicuous success; universal approbation. [F f. *éclater* burst out]

eclectic /ɪˈklektɪk/ *adj. & n.* —*adj.* deriving ideas, tastes, style, etc., from various sources. —*n.* an eclectic person. □ **eclectically** *adv.* **eclecticism** /-ɪsɪz(ə)m/ *n.* [Gk *eklektikos* f. *eklegō* pick out]

eclipse /ɪˈklɪps/ *n. & v.* —*n.* **1** the obscuring of the reflected light from one celestial body by the passage of another between it and the eye or between it and its source of illumination. **2** a deprivation of light or the period of this. **3** a rapid or sudden loss of importance or prominence, esp. in relation to a newly-arrived person or thing. —*v.tr.* **1** (of a celestial body) obscure the light from or to (another). **2** intercept (light, esp. of a lighthouse). **3** deprive of prominence or importance; outshine, surpass. □ **eclipser** *n.* [ME f. OF f. L f. Gk *ekleipsis* f. *ekleipō* fail to appear, be eclipsed f. *leipō* leave]

ecliptic /ɪˈklɪptɪk/ *n. & adj.* —*n.* the sun's apparent path among the stars during the year. —*adj.* of an eclipse or the ecliptic. [ME f. L f. Gk *ekleiptikos* (as ECLIPSE)]

eclogue /ˈeklɒg/ *n.* a short poem, esp. a pastoral dialogue. [L *ecloga* f. Gk *eklogē* selection f. *eklegō* pick out]

eco- /ˈiːkəʊ/ *comb. form* ecology, ecological.

ecoclimate /ˈiːkəʊˌklaɪmɪt, -mət/ *n.* climate considered as an ecological factor.

ecology /ɪˈkɒlədʒɪ/ *n.* **1** the branch of biology dealing with the relations of organisms to one another and to their physical surroundings. **2** (in full **human ecology**) the study of the interaction of people with their environment. □ **ecological** /ˌiːkəˈlɒdʒɪk(ə)l/ *adj.* **ecologically**

/ˌiːkəˈlɒdʒɪkəlɪ/ *adv.* **ecologist** *n.* [G *Ökologie* f. Gk *oikos* house]

econometrics /ɪˌkɒnəˈmetrɪks/ *n.pl.* (usu. treated as *sing.*) a branch of economics concerned with the application of mathematical economics to economic data by the use of statistics. □ **econometric** *adj.* **econometrical** *adj.* **econometrician** /-məˈtrɪʃ(ə)n/ *n.* **econometrist** *n.* [ECONOMY + METRIC]

economic /ˌiːkəˈnɒmɪk, ˌek-/ *adj.* **1** of or relating to economics. **2** maintained for profit; on a business footing. **3** adequate to repay or recoup expenditure with some profit (*an economic rent*). **4** practical; considered or studied with regard to human needs (*economic geography*). □ **economically** *adv.* [ME f. OF *economique* or L *oeconomicus* f. Gk *oikonomikos* (as ECONOMY)]

economical /ˌiːkəˈnɒmɪk(ə)l, ˌek-/ *adj.* sparing in the use of resources; avoiding waste. □ **economically** *adv.*

economics /ˌiːkəˈnɒmɪks, ˌek-/ *n.pl.* (treated as *sing.*) **1 a** the science of the production and distribution of wealth. **b** the application of this to a particular subject (*the economics of publishing*). **2** the condition of a country etc. as regards material prosperity.

economist /ɪˈkɒnəmɪst/ *n.* an expert in or student of economics. [Gk *oikonomos* (as ECONOMY) + -IST]

economize /ɪˈkɒnəmaɪz/ *v.intr.* (also **-ise**) **1** be economical; make economies; reduce expenditure. **2** (foll. by *on*) use sparingly; spend less on. □ **economization** /-ˈzeɪʃ(ə)n/ *n.* **economizer** *n.*

economy /ɪˈkɒnəmɪ/ *n.* (*pl.* **-ies**) **1 a** the wealth and resources of a community, esp. in terms of the production and consumption of goods and services. **b** a particular kind of this (*a capitalist economy*). **c** the administration or condition of an economy. **2 a** the careful management of (esp. financial) resources; frugality. **b** (often in *pl.*) an instance of this (*made many economies*). **3** sparing or careful use (*economy of language*). **4** (also **economy class**) the cheapest class of air travel. **5** (*attrib.*) (also **economy-size**) (of goods) consisting of a large quantity for a proportionally lower cost. [F *économie* or L *oeconomia* f. Gk *oikonomia* household management f. *oikos* house + *nemō* manage]

ecosphere /ˈiːkəʊˌsfɪə(r)/ *n.* the region of space including planets where conditions are such that living things can exist.

ecosystem /ˈiːkəʊˌsɪstəm/ *n.* a biological community of interacting organisms and their physical environment.

ecru /ˈeɪkruː/ *n.* the colour of unbleached linen; light fawn. [F *écru* unbleached]

ecstasy /ˈekstəsɪ/ *n.* (*pl.* **-ies**) **1** an overwhelming feeling of joy or rapture. **2** *Psychol.* an emotional or religious frenzy or trancelike state. **3** *sl.* methylenedioxymethamphetamine, a powerful stimulant and hallucinatory drug. [ME f. OF *extasie* f. LL *extasis* f. Gk *ekstasis* standing outside oneself f. *ek* out + *histēmi* to place]

ecstatic /ɪkˈstætɪk/ *adj.* **1** in a state of ecstasy. **2** very enthusiastic or excited (*was ecstatic about his new job*). **3** producing ecstasy; sublime (*an ecstatic embrace*). □ **ecstatically** *adv.* [F *extatique* f. Gk *ekstatikos* (as ECSTASY)]

ECT *abbr.* electroconvulsive therapy.

ecto- /ˈektəʊ/ *comb. form* outside. [Gk *ekto-* stem of *ektos* outside]

ectomorph /ˈektəʊˌmɔːf/ n. a person with a lean and delicate build of body and large skin surface in comparison with weight. □ **ectomorphic** /-ˈmɔːfɪk/ adj. **ectomorphy** n. [ECTO- + Gk morphē form]

-ectomy /ˈektəmɪ/ comb. form denoting a surgical operation in which a part of the body is removed (appendectomy). [Gk ektomē excision f. ek out + temnō cut]

ectopic /ˈektɒpɪk/ adj. Med. in an abnormal place or position. □ **ectopic pregnancy** a pregnancy occurring outside the womb. [mod.L ectopia f. Gk ektopos out of place]

ectoplasm /ˈektəʊˌplæz(ə)m/ n. 1 the dense outer layer of the cytoplasm. 2 the supposed viscous substance exuding from the body of a spiritualistic medium during a trance. □ **ectoplasmic** /-ˈplæzmɪk/ adj.

ECU abbr. (also **ecu** /ˈekjuː/) European currency unit.

ecumenical /ˌiːkjuːˈmenɪk(ə)l, ˈek-/ adj. 1 of or representing the whole Christian world. 2 seeking or promoting worldwide Christian unity. □ **ecumenically** adv. [LL oecumenicus f. Gk oikoumenikos of the inhabited earth (oikoumenē)]

ecumenicalism /ˌiːkjuːˈmenɪkəˌlɪz(ə)m, ˌek-/ n. (also **ecumenism** /iːˈkjuːmənɪz(ə)m/) the principle or aim of the unity of Christians worldwide.

eczema /ˈeksɪmə/ n. inflammation of the skin, with itching and discharge from blisters. □ **eczematous** /ekˈziːmətəs, ekˈzem-/ adj. [mod.L f. Gk ekzema -atos f. ek out + zeō boil]

ed. abbr. 1 edited by. 2 edition. 3 editor. 4 educated; education.

-ed¹ /əd, ɪd/ suffix forming adjectives: 1 from nouns, meaning 'having, wearing, affected by, etc.' (talented; trousered; diseased). 2 from phrases of adjective and noun (good-humoured; three-cornered). [OE -ede]

-ed² /əd, ɪd/ suffix forming: 1 the past tense and past participle of weak verbs (needed; risked). 2 participial adjectives (escaped prisoner; a pained look). [OE -ed, -ad, -od]

Edam /ˈiːdæm/ n. a round Dutch cheese, usu. pale yellow with a red rind. [Edam in Holland]

edaphic /ɪˈdæfɪk/ adj. 1 Bot. of the soil. 2 Ecol. produced or influenced by the soil. [G edaphisch f. Gk edaphos floor]

eddy /ˈedɪ/ n. & v. —n. (pl. **-ies**) 1 a circular movement of water causing a small whirlpool. 2 a movement of wind, fog, or smoke resembling this. —v.tr. & intr. (**-ies**, **-ied**) whirl round in eddies. [prob. OE ed- again, back, perh. of Scand. orig.]

edelweiss /ˈeɪd(ə)lˌvaɪs/ n. an Alpine plant, Leontopodium alpinum, with woolly white bracts around the flower-heads. [G f. edel noble + weiss white]

edema US var. of OEDEMA.

Eden /ˈiːd(ə)n/ n. (also **Garden of Eden**) a place or state of great happiness; paradise (with reference to the abode of Adam and Eve in the biblical account of the Creation). [ME f. LL f. Gk Ēdēn f. Heb. ʿēden, orig. = delight]

edentate /ɪˈdenteɪt/ adj. & n. —adj. having no or few teeth. —n. any mammal, esp. of the order Edentata, having no or few teeth, e.g. an anteater or sloth. [L edentatus (as E-, dens dentis tooth)]

edge n. & v. —n. 1 a boundary line or margin of an area or surface. 2 a narrow surface of a thin object. 3 the meeting-line of two surfaces of a solid. 4 a the sharpened side of the blade of a cutting instrument or weapon. b the sharpness of this (the knife has lost its edge). 5 the area close to a steep drop (along the edge of the cliff). 6 anything compared to an edge, esp. the crest of a ridge. 7 a (as a personal attribute) incisiveness, excitement. b keenness, excitement (esp. as an element in an otherwise routine situation). —v. 1 tr. & intr. (often foll. by in, into, out, etc.) move gradually or furtively towards an objective (edged it into the corner; they all edged towards the door). 2 tr. a provide with an edge or border. b form a border to. c trim the edge of. 3 tr. sharpen (a knife, tool, etc.). □ **have the edge on** (or **over**) have a slight advantage over. **on edge** 1 tense and restless or irritable. 2 eager, excited. **on the edge of** almost involved in or affected by. **set a person's teeth on edge** (of a taste or sound) cause an unpleasant nervous sensation. **take the edge off** dull, weaken; make less effective or intense. □ **edgeless** adj. **edger** n. [OE ecg f. Gmc]

edgeways /ˈedʒweɪz/ adv. (also **edgewise** /-waɪz/) 1 with the edge uppermost or towards the viewer. 2 edge to edge. □ **get a word in edgeways** contribute to a conversation when the dominant speaker pauses briefly.

edging /ˈedʒɪŋ/ n. 1 something forming an edge or border, e.g. a fringe or lace. 2 the process of making an edge.

edgy /ˈedʒɪ/ adj. (**edgier**, **edgiest**) irritable; nervously anxious. □ **edgily** adv. **edginess** n.

edible /ˈedɪb(ə)l/ adj. & n. —adj. fit or suitable to be eaten (cf. EATABLE). —n. (in pl.) food. □ **edibility** /-ˈbɪlɪtɪ/ n. [LL edibilis f. edere eat]

edict /ˈiːdɪkt/ n. an order proclaimed by authority. □ **edictal** /ɪˈdɪkt(ə)l/ adj. [ME f. L edictum f. edicere proclaim]

edifice /ˈedɪfɪs/ n. 1 a building, esp. a large imposing one. 2 a complex organizational or conceptual structure. [ME f. OF f. L aedificium f. aedis dwelling + -ficium f. facere make]

edify /ˈedɪˌfaɪ/ v.tr. (**-ies**, **-ied**) (of a circumstance, experience, etc.) instruct and improve morally or intellectually. □ **edification** /-fɪˈkeɪʃ(ə)n/ n. **edifying** adj. **edifyingly** adv. [ME f. OF edifier f. L aedificare (as EDIFICE)]

edit /ˈedɪt/ v. & n. —v.tr. (**edited**, **editing**) 1 a assemble, prepare, or modify (written material, esp. the work of another or others) for publication. b prepare an edition of (an author's work). 2 be in overall charge of the content and arrangement of (a newspaper, journal, etc.). 3 take extracts from and collate (films, tape-recordings, etc.) to form a unified sequence. 4 a prepare (data) for processing by a computer. b alter (a text entered in a word processor etc.). 5 a reword to correct, or to alter the emphasis. b (foll. by out) remove (part) from a text etc. —n. 1 a piece of editing. 2 an edited item. [F éditer (as EDITION): partly a back-form. f. EDITOR]

edition /ɪˈdɪʃ(ə)n/ n. 1 a one of the particular forms in which a literary work etc. is published (paperback edition; pocket edition). b a copy of a book in a particular form (a first edition). 2 a whole number of copies of a book, newspaper, etc., issued at one time. 3 a particular version or instance of a broadcast, esp. of a regular

programme or feature. **4** a person or thing
similar to or resembling another (*a miniature
edition of her mother*). [F *édition* f. L *editio -onis* f.
edere edit- put out (as E-, *dare* give)]

editor /ˈedɪtə(r)/ *n.* **1** a person who edits material
for publication or broadcasting. **2** a person who
directs the preparation of a newspaper or
periodical, or a particular section of one (*sports
editor*). **3** a person who selects or commissions
material for publication. **4** a person who edits
film, sound track, etc. **5** a computer program
for modifying data. □ **editorship** *n.* [LL, =
producer (of games), publisher (as EDIT)]

editorial /ˌedɪˈtɔːrɪəl/ *adj. & n.* —*adj.* of or
concerned with editing or editors. —*n.* a newspaper article written by or on behalf of an
editor, esp. one giving an opinion on a topical
issue. □ **editorialist** *n.* **editorialize** *v.intr.* (also
-**ise**) **editorially** *adv.*

educate /ˈedjʊˌkeɪt/ *v.tr.* (also *absol.*) **1** give
intellectual, moral, and social instruction to (a
pupil, esp. a child), esp. as a formal and
prolonged process. **2** provide education for. **3**
(often foll. by *in*, or *to* + infin.) train or
instruct for a particular purpose. **4** advise;
give information to. □ **educable** /-kəb(ə)l/ *adj.*
educability /-kəˈbɪlɪtɪ/ *n.* **educatable** *adj.* **edu-
cative** /-kətɪv/ *adj.* **educator** *n.* [L *educare educat-*,
rel. to *educere* EDUCE]

educated /ˈedjʊˌkeɪtɪd/ *adj.* **1** having had an
education, esp. to a higher level than average. **2**
resulting from a (good) education (*an educated
accent*). **3** based on experience or study (*an
educated guess*).

education /ˌedjʊˈkeɪʃn/ *n.* **1** the act or process
of educating or being educated; systematic
instruction. **2** a particular kind of or stage in
education (*further education; a classical education*).
3 development of character or mental powers.
□ **educational** *adj.* **educationalist** *n.* **educationally** *adv.* **educationist** *n.* [F *éducation* or
L *educatio* (as EDUCATE)]

educe /ɪˈdjuːs/ *v.tr.* bring out or develop from
latent or potential existence; elicit. □ **educible**
adj. **eduction** /ɪˈdʌkʃ(ə)n/ *n.* **eductive** /ɪˈdʌktɪv/ *adj.*
[ME f. L *educere educt-* lead out (as E-, *ducere* lead)]

Edwardian /edˈwɔːdɪən/ *adj. & n.* —*adj.* of,
characteristic of, or associated with the reign
of King Edward VII (1901–10). —*n.* a person
belonging to this period.

-ee *suffix* forming nouns denoting: **1** the person
affected by the verbal action (*addressee; employee;
lessee*). **2** a person concerned with or described
as (*absentee; bargee; refugee*). **3** an object of smaller
size (*bootee*). [from or after AF past part. in *-é* f. L
-atus]

EEC *abbr.* European Economic Community.

■ **Usage** EC is now the officially preferred term.

EEG *abbr.* electroencephalogram.

eel *n.* **1** any of various snakelike fish, with
slender body and poorly developed fins. **2** a
slippery or evasive person or thing. □ **eel-like**
adj. **eely** *adj.* [OE *ǣl* f. Gmc]

eelworm /ˈiːlwɜːm/ *n.* any of various small
nematode worms infesting plant roots.

-een /iːn/ *suffix Ir.* forming diminutive nouns
(*colleen*). [Ir. *-ín* dimin. suffix]

-eer /ɪə(r)/ *suffix* forming: **1** nouns meaning
'person concerned or engaged in' (*auctioneer; mountaineer; profiteer*). **2** verbs meaning

'be concerned with' (*electioneer*). [from or after F
-ier f. L *-arius*: cf. -IER, -ARY[1]]

eerie /ˈɪərɪ/ *adj.* (**eerier**, **eeriest**) gloomy and
strange; weird; frightening (*an eerie silence*). □
eerily *adv.* **eeriness** *n.* [orig. N.Engl. and Sc. *eri*,
of obscure orig.: cf. OE *earg* cowardly]

ef- /ɪf, ef/ *prefix* assim. form of EX-[1] 1 before *f*.

efface /ɪˈfeɪs/ *v.* **1** *tr.* rub or wipe out (a mark
etc.). **2** (in abstract senses) obliterate; wipe
out (*effaced it from his memory*). **3** *tr.* utterly
surpass; eclipse (*success has effaced all previous
attempts*). **4** *refl.* treat or regard oneself as
unimportant (*self-effacing*). □ **effacement** *n.* [F
effacer (as EX-[1], FACE)]

effect /ɪˈfekt/ *n. & v.* —*n.* **1** the result or
consequence of an action etc. **2** efficacy (*had
little effect*). **3** an impression produced on a
spectator, hearer, etc. (*lights had a pretty effect*). **4**
(in *pl.*) property, luggage. **5** (in *pl.*) the lighting,
sound, etc., used to accompany a play, film,
broadcast, etc. **6** *Physics* a physical phenomenon,
usually named after its discoverer (*Doppler effect*).
7 the state of being operative. —*v.tr.* **1** bring
about; accomplish. **2** cause to exist or occur. □
bring (or **carry**) **into effect** accomplish. **for
effect** to create an impression. **give effect to**
make operative. **in effect** for practical purposes;
in reality. **take effect** become operative. **to the
effect that** the general substance or gist being.
to that effect having that result or implication.
with effect from coming into operation at or
on (a stated time or day). [ME f. OF *effect* or L
effectus (as EX-[1], *facere* make)]

■ **Usage** This word should not be confused with
affect which, as a verb, has more meanings and
is more common but which only exists as a
noun in specialized use.

effective /ɪˈfektɪv/ *adj.* **1** having a definite or
desired effect. **2** powerful in effect; impressive.
3 a actual; existing in fact rather than officially
or theoretically (*took effective control in their
absence*). **b** actually usable; realizable; equivalent
in its effect (*effective money; effective demand*). **4**
coming into operation (*effective as from 1 May*). □
effectively *adv.* **effectiveness** *n.* [ME f. L *effect-
ivus* (as EFFECT)]

effectual /ɪˈfektʃʊəl, -tjʊəl/ *adj.* **1** capable of
producing the required result or effect; answering its purpose. **2** valid. □ **effectuality** /-ˈælɪtɪ/
n. **effectually** *adv.* **effectualness** *n.* [ME f. med.L
effectualis (as EFFECT)]

effeminate /ɪˈfemɪnət/ *adj.* (of a man) feminine
in appearance or manner; unmasculine. □
effeminacy *n.* **effeminately** *adv.* [ME f. L
effeminatus past part. of *effeminare* (as EX-[1], *femina*
woman)]

efferent /ˈefərənt/ *adj. Physiol.* conducting outwards (*efferent nerves; efferent vessels*). □ **efference**
n. [L *efferre* (as EX-[1], *ferre* carry)]

effervesce /ˌefəˈves/ *v.intr.* **1** give off bubbles of
gas; bubble. **2** (of a person) be lively or energetic.
□ **effervescence** *n.* **effervescency** *n.* **effervescent** *adj.* [L *effervescere* (as EX-[1], *fervēre* be hot)]

effete /ɪˈfiːt/ *adj.* **1** feeble and incapable. **2** worn
out; exhausted of its essential quality or vitality.
□ **effeteness** *n.* [L *effetus* worn out by bearing
young (as EX-[1], FOETUS)]

efficacious /ˌefɪˈkeɪʃəs/ *adj.* (of a thing) producing or sure to produce the desired effect. □

efficaciously adv. **efficaciousness** n. **efficacy** /ˈefɪkəsɪ/ n. [L efficax (as EFFICIENT)]

efficiency /ɪˈfɪʃənsɪ/ n. (pl. **-ies**) **1** the state or quality of being efficient. **2** Mech. & Physics the ratio of useful work performed to the total energy expended or heat taken in. [L efficientia (as EFFICIENT)]

efficient /ɪˈfɪʃ(ə)nt/ adj. **1** productive with minimum waste or effort. **2** (of a person) capable; acting effectively. □ **efficiently** adv. [ME f. L efficere (as EX-¹, facere make, accomplish)]

effigy /ˈefɪdʒɪ/ n. (pl. **-ies**) a sculpture or model of a person. □ **in effigy** in the form of a representation of a person. [L effigies f. effingere to fashion]

effloresce /ˌeflɔːˈres/ v.intr. **1** burst out into flower. **2** Chem. **a** (of a substance) turn to a fine powder on exposure to air. **b** (of salts) come to the surface and crystallize on it. **c** (of a surface) become covered with salt particles. □ **efflorescence** n. **efflorescent** adj. [L efflorescere (as EX-¹, florēre to bloom f. flos floris flower)]

effluence /ˈefluəns/ n. **1** a flowing out (of light, electricity, etc.). **2** that which flows out. [F effluence or med.L effluentia f. L effluere efflux- flow out (as EX-¹, fluere flow)]

effluent /ˈefluənt/ adj. & n. —adj. flowing forth or out. —n. **1** sewage or industrial waste discharged into a river, the sea, etc. **2** a stream or lake flowing from a larger body of water.

effluvium /ɪˈfluːvɪəm/ n. (pl. **effluvia** /-vɪə/) an unpleasant or noxious odour or exhaled substance affecting the lungs or the sense of smell etc. [L (as EFFLUENT)]

efflux /ˈeflʌks/ n. = EFFLUENCE. □ **effluxion** /eˈflʌkʃ(ə)n/ n. [med.L effluxus (as EFFLUENT)]

effort /ˈefət/ n. **1** strenuous physical or mental exertion. **2** a vigorous or determined attempt. **3** Mech. a force exerted. **4** colloq. the result of an attempt; something accomplished (not bad for a first effort). □ **effortful** adj. [F f. OF esforcier ult. f. L fortis strong]

effortless /ˈefətlɪs/ adj. **1** seemingly without effort; natural, easy. **2** requiring no effort. □ **effortlessly** adv. **effortlessness** n.

effrontery /ɪˈfrʌntərɪ/ n. (pl. **-ies**) **1** shameless insolence; impudent audacity (esp. have the effrontery to). **2** an instance of this. [F effronterie f. effronté ult. f. LL effrons -ontis shameless (as EX-¹, frons forehead)]

effulgent /ɪˈfʌldʒ(ə)nt/ adj. literary radiant; shining brilliantly. □ **effulgence** n. **effulgently** adv. [L effulgēre shine forth (as EX-¹, fulgēre shine)]

effuse /ɪˈfjuːz/ v.tr. **1** pour forth (liquid, light, etc.). **2** give out (ideas etc.). [ME f. L effusus past part. of effundere effus- pour out (as EX-¹, fundere pour)]

effusion /ɪˈfjuːʒ(ə)n/ n. **1** a copious outpouring. **2** usu. derog. an unrestrained flow of speech or writing. [ME f. OF effusion or L effusio (as EFFUSE)]

effusive /ɪˈfjuːsɪv/ adj. gushing, demonstrative, exuberant (effusive praise). □ **effusively** adv. **effusiveness** n.

EFL abbr. English as a foreign language.

eft n. a newt. [OE efeta, of unkn. orig.]

Efta /ˈeftə/ n. (also **EFTA**) European Free Trade Association. [abbr.]

EFTPOS /ˈeftpɒz/ abbr. electronic funds transfer at point-of-sale.

e.g. abbr. for example. [L exempli gratia]

egalitarian /ɪˌɡælɪˈteərɪən/ adj. & n. —adj. **1** of or relating to the principle of equal rights and opportunities for all (an egalitarian society). **2** advocating this principle. —n. a person who advocates or supports egalitarian principles. □ **egalitarianism** n. [F égalitaire f. égal EQUAL]

egg¹ /eɡ/ n. **1 a** the spheroidal reproductive body produced by females of animals such as birds, reptiles, fish, etc., enclosed in a protective layer and capable of developing into a new individual. **b** the egg of the domestic hen, used for food. **2** Biol. the female reproductive cell in animals and plants. **3** colloq. a person or thing qualified in some way (a tough egg). **4** anything resembling or imitating an egg, esp. in shape or appearance. □ **egg-flip** (or **-nog**) a drink of alcoholic spirit with beaten egg, milk, etc. **egg-timer** a device for timing the cooking of an egg. **egg-tooth** a projection of an embryo bird or reptile used for breaking out of the shell. **egg-white** the white of an egg. **have** (or **put**) **all one's eggs in one basket** colloq. risk everything on a single venture. **with egg on one's face** colloq. made to look foolish. □ **eggless** adj. **eggy** adj. (**eggier, eggiest**). [ME f. ON, rel. to OE æg]

egg² /eɡ/ v.tr. (foll. by on) urge (egged us on to it; egged them on to do it). [ME f. ON eggja = EDGE]

eggcup /ˈeɡkʌp/ n. a cup for holding a boiled egg.

egghead /ˈeɡhed/ n. colloq. an intellectual; an expert.

eggplant /ˈeɡplɑːnt/ n. = AUBERGINE.

eggshell /ˈeɡʃel/ n. & adj. —n. **1** the shell of an egg. **2** anything very fragile. —adj. **1** (of china) thin and fragile. **2** (of paint) with a slight gloss finish.

ego /ˈiːɡəʊ/ n. (pl. **-os**) **1** Metaphysics a conscious thinking subject. **2** Psychol. the part of the mind that reacts to reality and has a sense of individuality. **3** self-esteem. □ **ego-trip** colloq. activity etc. devoted entirely to one's own interests or feelings. [L, = I]

egocentric /ˌiːɡəʊˈsentrɪk/ adj. **1** centred in the ego. **2** self-centred, egoistic. □ **egocentrically** adv. **egocentricity** /-ˈtrɪsɪtɪ/ n. [EGO + -CENTRIC after geocentric etc.]

egoism /ˈiːɡəʊˌɪz(ə)m/ n. **1** an ethical theory that treats self-interest as the foundation of morality. **2** systematic selfishness. **3** self-opinionatedness. **4** = EGOTISM. □ **egoist** n. **egoistic** /-ˈɪstɪk/ adj. **egoistical** /-ˈɪstɪk(ə)l/ adj. [F égoïsme ult. f. mod.L egoismus (as EGO)]

■ **Usage** The senses of egoism and egotism overlap, but egoism alone is used as a term in philosophy and psychology to mean self-interest (often contrasted with altruism).

egomania /ˌiːɡəʊˈmeɪnɪə/ n. morbid egotism. □ **egomaniac** /-ˈmeɪnɪˌæk/ n. **egomaniacal** /-məˈnaɪək(ə)l/ adj.

egotism /ˈiːɡəˌtɪz(ə)m/ n. **1** excessive use of 'I' and 'me'. **2** the practice of talking about oneself. **3** conceit. **4** selfishness. □ **egotist** n. **egotistic** /-ˈtɪstɪk/ adj. **egotistical** /-ˈtɪstɪk(ə)l/ adj. **egotistically** /-ˈtɪstɪkəlɪ/ adv. **egotize** v.intr. (also **-ise**). [EGO + -ISM with intrusive -t-]

■ **Usage** See note at egoism.

egregious /ɪˈɡriːdʒəs/ adj. **1** outstandingly bad; shocking (egregious folly; an egregious ass). **2** archaic or joc. remarkable. □ **egregiously** adv.

egregiousness *n.* [L *egregius* illustrious, lit. 'standing out from the flock' f. *grex gregis* flock]

egress /ˈiːgres/ *n.* **1 a** going out. **b** the right of going out. **2** an exit; a way out. □ **egression** /iːˈgreʃ(ə)n/ *n.* [L *egressus* f. *egredi egress-* (as E-, *gradi* to step)]

egret /ˈiːgrɪt/ *n.* any of various herons of the genus *Egretta* or *Bulbulcus*, usu. having long white feathers in the breeding season. [ME, var. of AIGRETTE]

Egyptian /ɪˈdʒɪpʃ(ə)n/ *adj. & n.* —*adj.* **1** of or relating to Egypt in NE Africa. **2** of or for Egyptian antiquities (e.g. in a museum). —*n.* **1** a native of ancient or modern Egypt; a national of the Arab Republic of Egypt. **2** the Hamitic language used in ancient Egypt until the 3rd c. AD. □ **Egyptianize** *v.tr.* (also **-ise**) **Egyptianization** /-ˈzeɪʃ(ə)n/ *n.*

Egyptology /ˌiːdʒɪpˈtɒlədʒɪ/ *n.* the study of the language, history, and culture of ancient Egypt. □ **Egyptologist** *n.*

eh /eɪ/ *int. colloq.* **1** expressing enquiry or surprise. **2** inviting assent. **3** asking for something to be repeated or explained. [ME *ey*, instinctive exclam.]

-eian /ɪən/ *suffix* corresp. to *-ey* (or *-y*) + *-an* (*Bodleian*; *Rugbeian*).

eider /ˈaɪdə(r)/ *n.* **1** (in full **eider duck**) any of various large northern ducks, esp. of the genus *Somateria*. **2** (in full **eider-down**) small soft feathers from the breast of the eider duck. [Icel. *aethr*]

eiderdown /ˈaɪdəˌdaʊn/ *n.* a quilt stuffed with down (orig. from the eider) or some other soft material, esp. as the upper layer of bedclothes.

eight /eɪt/ *n. & adj.* —*n.* **1** one more than seven. **2** a symbol for this (8, viii, VIII). **3** a figure resembling the form of 8. **4** a size etc. denoted by eight. **5** an eight-oared rowing-boat or its crew. **6** the time of eight o'clock (*is it eight yet?*). —*adj.* that amount to eight. □ **have one over the eight** *sl.* get slightly drunk. [OE *ehta*, *eahta*]

eighteen /eɪˈtiːn/ *n. & adj.* —*n.* **1** one more than seventeen. **2** a symbol for this (18, xviii, XVIII). **3** a size etc. denoted by eighteen. **4** a set or team of eighteen individuals. **5** (**18**) *Brit.* (of films) classified as suitable for persons of 18 years and over. —*adj.* that amount to eighteen. □ **eighteenth** *adj. & n.* [OE *ehtatēne*, *eaht-*]

eightfold /ˈeɪtfəʊld/ *adj. & adv.* **1** eight times as much or as many. **2** consisting of eight parts. **3** amounting to eight.

eighth /eɪtθ/ *n. & adj.* —*n.* **1** the position in a sequence corresponding to the number 8 in the sequence 1–8. **2** something occupying this position. **3** one of eight equal parts of a thing. —*adj.* that is the eighth. □ **eighthly** *adv.*

eightsome /ˈeɪtsəm/ *n.* (in full **eightsome reel**) a lively Scottish reel for eight dancers.

eighty /ˈeɪtɪ/ *n. & adj.* —*n.* (*pl.* **-ies**) **1** the product of eight and ten. **2** a symbol for this (80, lxxx, LXXX). **3** (in *pl.*) the numbers from 80 to 89, esp. the years of a century or of a person's life. —*adj.* that amount to eighty. □ **eightieth** *adj. & n.* **eightyfold** *adj. & adv.* [OE *-eahtatig* (as EIGHT, -TY²)]

einsteinium /aɪnˈstaɪnɪəm/ *n. Chem.* a transuranic radioactive metallic element produced artificially from plutonium. [A. *Einstein*, Ger.-Amer. physicist d. 1955]

eisteddfod /aɪˈsteðvɒd, -ˈstedfəd/ *n.* (*pl.* **eisteddfods** or **eisteddfodau** /-ˌdaɪ/) a congress of Welsh bards; a national or local festival for musical competitions etc. □ **eisteddfodic** /-ˈfɒdɪk/ *adj.* [Welsh, lit. = session, f. *eistedd* sit]

either /ˈaɪðə(r), ˈiːðə(r)/ *adj., pron., adv., & conj.* —*adj. & pron.* **1** one or the other of two (*either of you can go; you may have either book*). **2** each of two (*houses on either side of the road; either will do*). —*adv. & conj.* **1** as one possibility (*is either black or white*). **2** as one choice or alternative; which way you will (*either come in or go out*). **3** (with *neg.* or *interrog.*) **a** any more than the other (*I didn't like it either*). **b** moreover (*there is no time to lose, either*). [OE *ægther* f. Gmc]

ejaculate *v. & n.* —*v.tr.* /ɪˈdʒækjʊˌleɪt/ (also *absol.*) **1** utter suddenly (words esp. of prayer or other emotion). **2** eject (fluid etc., esp. semen) from the body. —*n.* /ɪˈdʒækjʊlət/ semen that has been ejaculated from the body. □ **ejaculation** /-ˈleɪʃ(ə)n/ *n.* **ejaculator** /ɪˈdʒækjʊˌleɪtə(r)/ *n.* **ejaculatory** /ɪˈdʒækjʊˌleɪtərɪ/ *adj.* [L *ejaculari* to dart (as E-, *jaculum* javelin)]

eject /ɪˈdʒekt/ *v.tr.* **1** send or drive out precipitately or by force, esp. from a building or other property; compel to leave. **2 a** cause (the pilot etc.) to be propelled from an aircraft or spacecraft in an emergency. **b** (*absol.*) (of the pilot etc.) be ejected in this way (*they both ejected at 1,000 feet*). **3** cause to be removed or drop out (e.g. a spent cartridge from a gun). **4** dispossess (a tenant etc.) by legal process. **5** dart forth; emit. □ **ejective** *adj.* **ejectment** *n.* [L *ejicere eject-* (as E-, *jacere* throw)]

ejection /ɪˈdʒekʃ(ə)n/ *n.* the act or an instance of ejecting; the process of being ejected.

ejector /ɪˈdʒektə(r)/ *n.* a device for ejecting. □ **ejector seat** a device for the automatic ejection of the pilot etc. of an aircraft or spacecraft in an emergency.

eke /iːk/ *v.tr.* □ **eke out 1** (foll. by *with*, *by*) supplement; make the best use of (defective means etc.). **2** contrive to make (a livelihood) or support (an existence). [OE *ēacan*, rel. to L *augēre* increase]

-el var. of -LE².

elaborate *adj. & v.* —*adj.* /ɪˈlæbərət/ **1** carefully or minutely worked out. **2** highly developed or complicated. —*v.tr.* /ɪˈlæbəˌreɪt/ **1** work out or explain in detail. **2** (*absol.*) go into details (*I need not elaborate*). □ **elaborately** /-rətlɪ/ *adv.* **elaborateness** /-rətnɪs/ *n.* **elaboration** /-ˈreɪʃ(ə)n/ *n.* **elaborative** /-rətɪv/ *adj.* **elaborator** /-ˌreɪtə(r)/ *n.* [L *elaboratus* past part. of *elaborare* (as E-, *labor* work)]

élan /eɪˈlɑ̃/ *n.* vivacity, dash. [F f. *élancer* launch]

eland /ˈiːlənd/ *n.* any antelope of the genus *Taurotragus*, native to Africa, having spirally twisted horns. [Du., = elk]

elapse /ɪˈlæps/ *v.intr.* (of time) pass by. [L *elabor elaps-* slip away]

elastic /ɪˈlæstɪk, ɪˈlɑːstɪk/ *adj. & n.* —*adj.* **1** able to resume its normal bulk or shape spontaneously after contraction, dilatation, or distortion. **2** springy. **3** (of a person or feelings) buoyant. **4** flexible, adaptable (*elastic conscience*). —*n.* elastic cord or fabric, usu. woven with strips of rubber. □ **elastic band** = *rubber band*. □□ **elastically** *adv.* **elasticity** /ɪlæsˈtɪsɪtɪ/ *n.* **elasticize** /ɪˈlæstɪˌsaɪz/ *v.tr.* (also **-ise**). [mod.L *elasticus* f. Gk *elastikos* propulsive f. *elaunō* drive]

elasticated /ɪˈlæstɪˌkeɪtɪd, ɪˈlɑːst-/ *adj.* (of a fabric) made elastic by weaving with rubber thread.

elastomer /ɪˈlæstəmə(r)/ *n.* a natural or synthetic rubber or rubber-like plastic. □ **elastomeric** /-ˈmerɪk/ *adj.* [ELASTIC, after *isomer*]

elate /ɪˈleɪt/ *v.tr.* 1 (esp. as **elated** *adj.*) inspirit, stimulate. 2 make proud. □ **elatedly** *adv.* **elatedness** *n.* **elation** *n.* [ME f. L *efferre elat-* raise]

E-layer /ˈiːˌleɪə(r)/ *n.* a layer of the ionosphere able to reflect medium-frequency radio waves. [E (arbitrary) + LAYER]

elbow /ˈelbəʊ/ *n.* & *v.* —*n.* 1 **a** the joint between the forearm and the upper arm. **b** the part of the sleeve of a garment covering the elbow. 2 an elbow-shaped bend or corner; a short piece of piping bent through a right angle. —*v.tr.* (foll. by *in, out, aside,* etc.) 1 thrust or jostle (a person or oneself). 2 make (one's way) by thrusting or jostling. □ **elbow-grease** *colloq.* vigorous polishing; hard work. **elbow-room** plenty of room to move or work in. **give a person the elbow** *colloq.* send a person away; dismiss or reject a person. [OE *elboga, elnboga,* f. Gmc (as ELL, BOW[1])]

elder[1] /ˈeldə(r)/ *adj.* & *n.* —*attrib.adj.* (of two indicated persons, esp. when related) senior; of a greater age (*my elder brother*). —*n.* (often prec. by *the*) 1 the older or more senior of two indicated (esp. related) persons (*which is the elder?; is my elder by ten years*). 2 (in *pl.*) **a** persons of greater age or seniority (*respect your elders*). **b** persons venerable because of age. 3 a person advanced in life. 4 an official in the early Christian, Presbyterian, or Mormon Churches. □ **elder statesman** an influential experienced person, esp. a politician, of advanced age. □ **eldership** *n.* [OE *eldra,* rel. to OLD]

elder[2] /ˈeldə(r)/ *n.* any shrub or tree of the genus *Sambucus,* with white flowers and usu. blue-black or red berries. [OE *ellærn*]

elderberry /ˈeldəˌberɪ/ *n.* (*pl.* **-ies**) the berry of the elder, esp. common elder (*Sambucus nigra*).

elderly /ˈeldəlɪ/ *adj.* 1 somewhat old. 2 (of a person) past middle age. □ **elderliness** *n.*

eldest /ˈeldɪst/ *adj.* & *n.* —*adj.* first-born or oldest surviving (member of a family, son, daughter, etc.). —*n.* (often prec. by *the*) the eldest of three or more indicated (*who is the eldest?*). [OE (as ELDER[1])]

eldorado /ˌeldəˈrɑːdəʊ/ *n.* (*pl.* **-os**) 1 any imaginary country or city abounding in gold. 2 a place of great abundance. [Sp. *el dorado* the gilded]

eldritch /ˈeldrɪtʃ/ *adj.* Sc. 1 weird. 2 hideous. [16th c.: perh. f. OE *elfrīce* (unrecorded) 'fairy realm']

elecampane /ˌelɪkæmˈpeɪn/ *n.* a sunflower-like plant, *Inula helenium,* with bitter aromatic leaves and roots. [corrupt. of med.L *enula* (for L *inula* f. Gk *helenion*) *campana* (prob. = of the fields)]

elect /ɪˈlekt/ *v.* & *adj.* —*v.tr.* (usu. foll. by *to* + infin.) 1 choose (*the principles they elected to follow*). 2 choose (a person) by vote (*elected a new chairman*). —*adj.* 1 chosen. 2 select, choice. 3 (after a noun designating office) chosen but not yet in office (*president elect*). [ME f. L *electus* past part. of *eligere elect-* (as E-, *legere* pick)]

election /ɪˈlekʃ(ə)n/ *n.* 1 the process of electing or being elected, esp. of members of a political body. 2 the act or an instance of electing. [ME f. OF f. L *electio -onis* (as ELECT)]

electioneer /ɪˌlekʃəˈnɪə(r)/ *v.* & *n.* —*v.intr.* take part in an election campaign. —*n.* a person who electioneers.

elective /ɪˈlektɪv/ *adj.* & *n.* —*adj.* 1 **a** (of an office or its holder) filled or appointed by election. **b** (of authority) derived from election. 2 (of a body) having the power to elect. 3 (of a course of study) chosen by the student; optional. 4 (of a surgical operation etc.) optional; not urgently necessary. —*n.* US an elective course of study. □ **electively** *adv.* [F *électif -ive* f. LL *electivus* (as ELECT)]

elector /ɪˈlektə(r)/ *n.* 1 a person who has the right of voting to elect an MP etc. 2 US a member of an electoral college. □ **electorship** *n.* [ME f. F *électeur* f. L *elector* (as ELECT)]

electoral /ɪˈlektər(ə)l/ *adj.* relating to or ranking as electors. □ **electoral college** 1 a body of persons representing the States of the US, who cast votes for the election of the President. 2 a body of electors. □ **electorally** *adv.*

electorate /ɪˈlektərət/ *n.* 1 a body of electors. 2 *Austral.* & *NZ* an area represented by one member of parliament.

electric /ɪˈlektrɪk/ *adj.* & *n.* —*adj.* 1 of, worked by, or charged with electricity; producing or capable of generating electricity. 2 causing or charged with sudden and dramatic excitement (*the atmosphere was electric*). —*n.* 1 an electric light, vehicle, etc. 2 (in *pl.*) electrical equipment. □ **electric blanket** a blanket that can be heated electrically by an internal element. **electric blue** a steely or brilliant light blue. **electric chair** (in the US) an electrified chair used for capital punishment. **electric eel** an eel-like freshwater fish, *Electrophorus electricus,* native to S. America, that kills its prey by electric shock. **electric eye** *colloq.* a photoelectric cell operating a relay when the beam of light illuminating it is obscured. **electric field** a region of electrical influence. **electric fire** an electrically operated incandescent or convector heater. **electric shock** the effect of a sudden discharge of electricity on a person or animal, usually with stimulation of the nerves and contraction of the muscles. **electric storm** a violent disturbance of the electrical condition of the atmosphere. □ **electrically** *adv.* [mod.L *electricus* f. L *electrum* f. Gk *ēlektron* amber, the rubbing of which causes electrostatic phenomena]

electrical /ɪˈlektrɪk(ə)l/ *adj.* 1 of or concerned with or of the nature of electricity. 2 operating by electricity. 3 suddenly or dramatically exciting.

electrician /ˌɪlekˈtrɪʃ(ə)n/ *n.* a person who installs or maintains electrical equipment, esp. professionally.

electricity /ˌɪlekˈtrɪsɪtɪ, ˌel-/ *n.* 1 a form of energy resulting from the existence of charged particles (electrons, protons, etc.), either statically as an accumulation of charge or dynamically as a current. 2 the branch of physics dealing with electricity. 3 a supply of electric current for heating, lighting, etc.

electrify /ɪˈlektrɪˌfaɪ/ *v.tr.* (**-ies, -ied**) 1 charge (a body) with electricity. 2 convert (machinery or the place or system employing it) to the use of electric power. **3** cause dramatic or sudden excitement in. □ **electrification** /-fɪˈkeɪʃ(ə)n/ n. **electrifier** n.

electro- /ɪˈlektrəʊ/ comb. form Electr. of, relating to, or caused by electricity (electrocute; electromagnet). [Gk ēlektron amber: see ELECTRIC]

electrocardiogram /ɪˌlektrəʊˈkɑːdɪəˌgræm/ n. a record of the heartbeat traced by an electrocardiograph. [G Elektrocardiogramm (as ELECTRO-, CARDIO-, -GRAM)]

electrocardiograph /ɪˌlektrəʊˈkɑːdɪəgrɑːf/ n. an instrument recording the electric currents generated by a person's heartbeat. □ **electrocardiographic** /-ˈgræfɪk/ adj. **electrocardiography** /-ˈɒgrəfɪ/ n.

electroconvulsive /ɪˌlektrəʊkənˈvʌlsɪv/ adj. (of a therapy) employing the use of the convulsive response to the application of electric shocks.

electrocute /ɪˈlektrəˌkjuːt/ v.tr. **1** kill by electricity (as a form of capital punishment). **2** cause death of by electric shock. □ **electrocution** /-ˈkjuːʃ(ə)n/ n. [ELECTRO-, after EXECUTE]

electrode /ɪˈlektrəʊd/ n. a conductor through which electricity enters or leaves an electrolyte, gas, vacuum, etc. [ELECTRIC + Gk hodos way]

electrodynamics /ɪˌlektrəʊdaɪˈnæmɪks/ n.pl. (usu. treated as sing.) the branch of mechanics concerned with electric current applied to motive forces. □ **electrodynamic** adj.

electroencephalogram /ɪˌlektrəʊɪnˈsefələˌgræm/ n. a record of the brain's activity traced by an electroencephalograph. [G Elektrenkephalogramm (as ELECTRO-, ENCEPHALO-, -GRAM)]

electroencephalograph /ɪˌlektrəʊɪnˈsefələgrɑːf/ n. an instrument recording the electrical activity of the brain. □ **electroencephalography** /-ˈlɒgrəfɪ/ n.

electrolyse /ɪˈlektrəˌlaɪz/ v.tr. (US -yze) subject to or treat by electrolysis. □ **electrolyser** n. [ELECTROLYSIS after analyse]

electrolysis /ˌɪlekˈtrɒlɪsɪs, ˌel-/ n. **1** Chem. the decomposition of a substance by the application of an electric current. **2** Surgery this process applied to the destruction of tumours, hairroots, etc. □ **electrolytic** /ɪˌlektrəʊˈlɪtɪk/ adj. **electrolytical** /-ˈlɪtɪk(ə)l/ adj. **electrolytically** /-ˈlɪtɪkəlɪ/ adv. [ELECTRO- + -LYSIS]

electrolyte /ɪˈlektrəˌlaɪt/ n. **1** a substance which conducts electricity when molten or in solution, esp. in an electric cell or battery. **2** a solution of this. [ELECTRO- + Gk lutos released f. luō loosen]

electromagnet /ɪˌlektrəʊˈmægnɪt/ n. a soft metal core made into a magnet by the passage of electric current through a coil surrounding it. □ **electromagnetically** /-ˈnetɪkəlɪ/ adv.

electromagnetic /ɪˌlektrəʊmægˈnetɪk/ adj. having both an electrical and a magnetic character or properties. □ **electromagnetic radiation** a kind of radiation including visible light, radio waves, gamma rays, X-rays, etc., in which electric and magnetic fields vary simultaneously.

electromagnetism /ɪˌlektrəʊˈmægnɪˌtɪz(ə)m/ n. **1** the magnetic forces produced by electricity. **2** the study of these.

electromechanical /ɪˌlektrəʊmɪˈkænɪk(ə)l/ adj. relating to the application of electricity to mechanical processes, devices, etc.

electrometer /ˌɪlekˈtrɒmɪtə(r), ˌel-/ n. an instrument for measuring electrical potential without

drawing any current from the circuit. □ **electrometric** /-ˈmetrɪk/ adj. **electrometry** n.

electromotive /ɪˌlektrəʊˈməʊtɪv/ adj. producing or tending to produce an electric current. □ **electromotive force** a force set up in an electric circuit by a difference in potential.

electron /ɪˈlektrɒn/ n. a stable elementary particle with a charge of negative electricity, found in all atoms and acting as the primary carrier of electricity in solids. □ **electron beam** a stream of electrons in a gas or vacuum. **electron gun** a device for producing a narrow stream of electrons from a heated cathode. **electron lens** a device for focusing a stream of electrons by means of electric or magnetic fields. **electron microscope** a microscope with high magnification and resolution, employing electron beams in place of light and using electron lenses. **electron pair** an electron and a positron. [ELECTRIC + -ON]

electronic /ˌɪlekˈtrɒnɪk, ˌel-/ adj. **1 a** produced by or involving the flow of electrons. **b** of or relating to electrons or electronics. **2** (of a device) using electronic components. **3 a** (of music) produced by electronic means and usu. recorded on tape. **b** (of a musical instrument) producing sounds by electronic means. □ **electronic mail** messages distributed by electronic means esp. from one computer system to one or more recipients. **electronic publishing** the publication of books etc. in machine-readable form (on disk or tape) rather than on paper. □ **electronically** adv.

electronics /ˌɪlekˈtrɒnɪks, ˌel-/ n.pl. (treated as sing.) **1** a branch of physics and technology concerned with the behaviour and movement of electrons in a vacuum, gas, semiconductor, etc. **2** the circuits used in this.

electronvolt /ɪˈlektrɒnˌvɒlt/ n. a unit of energy equal to the work done on an electron in accelerating it through a potential difference of one volt.

electrophorus /ˌɪlekˈtrɒfərəs, el-/ n. a device for repeatedly generating static electricity by induction. [mod.L f. ELECTRO- + Gk -phoros bearing]

electroplate /ɪˈlektrəˌpleɪt/ v. & n. —v.tr. (a utensil etc.) by electrolytic deposition with chromium, silver, etc. —n. electroplated articles. □ **electroplater** n.

electroscope /ɪˈlektrəˌskəʊp/ n. an instrument for detecting and measuring electricity, esp. as an indication of the ionization of air by radioactivity. □ **electroscopic** /-ˈskɒpɪk/ adj.

electro-shock /ɪˈlektrəʊˌʃɒk/ attrib.adj. (of medical treatment) by means of electric shocks.

electrostatic /ɪˌlektrəʊˈstætɪk/ adj. of electricity at rest. □ **electrostatic units** a system of units based primarily on the forces between electric charges. [ELECTRO- + STATIC after hydrostatic]

electrostatics /ɪˌlektrəʊˈstætɪks/ n.pl. (treated as sing.) the study of electricity at rest.

electrotechnology /ɪˌlektrəʊtekˈnɒlədʒɪ/ n. the science of the application of electricity in technology. □ **electrotechnic** /-ˈteknɪk/ adj. **electrotechnical** /-ˈteknɪk(ə)l/ adj. **electrotechnics** /-ˈteknɪks/ n.

electrotherapy /ɪˌlektrəʊˈθerəpɪ/ n. the treatment of diseases by the use of electricity.

□ **electrotherapeutic** /-'pjuːtɪk/ *adj.* **electrotherapeutical** /-'pjuːtɪk(ə)l/ *adj.* **electrotherapist** *n.*

electrovalent /ɪˌlektrəʊ'veɪlənt/ *adj. Chem.* linking ions by a bond resulting from electrostatic attraction. □ **electrovalence** *n.* **electrovalency** *n.* [ELECTRO- + -valent after trivalent etc.]

elegant /'elɪɡənt/ *adj.* **1** graceful in appearance or manner. **2** tasteful, refined. **3** (of a mode of life etc.) of refined luxury. **4** ingeniously simple and pleasing. **5** *US* excellent. □ **elegance** *n.* **elegantly** *adv.* [F *élégant* or L *elegant-*, rel. to *eligere*: see ELECT]

elegiac /ˌelɪ'dʒaɪək/ *adj. & n.* —*adj.* **1** (of a metre) used for elegies. **2** mournful. —*n.* (in *pl.*) verses in an elegiac metre. □ **elegiac couplet** a pair of lines consisting of a dactylic hexameter and a pentameter. □ **elegiacally** *adv.* [F *élégiaque* or f. LL *elegiacus* f. Gk *elegeiakos*: see ELEGY]

elegize /'elɪˌdʒaɪz/ *v.* (also **-ise**) **1** *intr.* (often foll. by *upon*) write an elegy. **2** *intr.* write in a mournful strain. **3** *tr.* write an elegy upon. □ **elegist** *n.*

elegy /'elɪdʒɪ/ *n.* (*pl.* **-ies**) **1** a song of lament, esp. for the dead (sometimes vaguely used of other poems). **2** a poem in elegiac metre. [F *élégie* or L *elegia* f. Gk *elegeia* f. *elegos* mournful poem]

element /'elɪmənt/ *n.* **1** a component part; a contributing factor or thing. **2** *Chem. & Physics* any of the hundred or so substances that cannot be resolved by chemical means into simpler substances. **3 a** any of the four substances (earth, water, air, and fire) in ancient and medieval philosophy. **b** any of these as a being's natural abode or environment. **4** *Electr.* a resistance wire that heats up in an electric heater, cooker, etc.; an electrode. **5** (in *pl.*) atmospheric agencies, esp. wind and storm. **6** (in *pl.*) the rudiments of learning or of a branch of knowledge. **7** (in *pl.*) the bread and wine of the Eucharist. **8** *Math. & Logic* an entity that is a single member of a set. □ **in** (or **out of**) **one's element** in (or out of) one's accustomed or preferred surroundings. [ME f. OF f. L *elementum*]

elemental /ˌelɪ'ment(ə)l/ *adj.* **1** of the four elements. **2** of the powers of nature (*elemental worship*). **3** comparable to a force of nature (*elemental grandeur; elemental tumult*). **4** uncompounded (*elemental oxygen*). **5** essential. □ **elementalism** *n.* (in senses 1, 2). [med.L *elementalis* (as ELEMENT)]

elementary /ˌelɪ'mentərɪ/ *adj.* **1 a** dealing with or arising from the simplest facts of a subject; rudimentary, introductory. **b** simple. **2** *Chem.* not decomposable. □ **elementary particle** *Physics* any of several subatomic particles supposedly not decomposable into simpler ones. **elementary school** a school in which elementary subjects are taught to young children. □ **elementarily** *adv.* **elementariness** *n.* [ME f. L *elementarius* (as ELEMENT)]

elephant /'elɪfənt/ *n.* (*pl.* same or **elephants**) the largest living land animal, of which two species survive, the larger African (*Loxodonta africana*) and the smaller Indian (*Elephas maximus*), both with a trunk and long curved ivory tusks. □ **elephantoid** /-'fæntɔɪd/ *adj.* [ME *olifaunt* etc. f. OF *oli-, elefant* ult. f. L *elephantus, elephans* f. Gk *elephas -antos* ivory, elephant]

elephantiasis /ˌelɪfən'taɪəsɪs/ *n.* gross enlargement of the body, esp. the limbs, due to lymphatic obstruction esp. by a nematode parasite. [L f. Gk (as ELEPHANT)]

elephantine /ˌelɪ'fæntaɪn/ *adj.* **1** of elephants. **2 a** huge. **b** clumsy, unwieldy. [L *elephantinus* f. Gk *elephantinos* (as ELEPHANT)]

elevate /'elɪˌveɪt/ *v.tr.* **1** bring to a higher position. **2** raise, lift. **3** exalt in rank etc. **4** (usu. as **elevated** *adj.*) raise morally or intellectually (*elevated style*). □ **elevatory** *adj.* [L *elevare* raise (as E-, *levis* light)]

elevation /ˌelɪ'veɪʃ(ə)n/ *n.* **1 a** the process of elevating or being elevated. **b** the angle with the horizontal, esp. of a gun or of the direction of a heavenly body. **c** the height above a given level, esp. sea level. **d** a high place or position. **2 a** a drawing or diagram made by projection on a vertical plane. **b** a flat drawing of the front, side, or back of a house etc. **3** *Ballet* the capacity of a dancer to attain height in springing movements. □ **elevational** *adj.* (in sense 2). [ME f. OF *elevation* or L *elevatio*: see ELEVATE]

elevator /'elɪˌveɪtə(r)/ *n.* **1** a hoisting machine. **2** *Aeron.* the movable part of a tailplane for changing the pitch of an aircraft. **3** *US* **a** = LIFT *n.* 3. **b** a place for lifting and storing quantities of grain. [mod.L (as ELEVATE)]

eleven /ɪ'lev(ə)n/ *n. & adj.* —*n.* **1** one more than ten. **2** a symbol for this (11, xi, XI). **3** a size etc. denoted by eleven. **4** a set or team of eleven individuals. **5** the time of eleven o'clock (*is it eleven yet?*). —*adj.* that amount to eleven. [OE *endleofon* f. Gmc]

elevenfold /ɪ'lev(ə)nˌfəʊld/ *adj. & adv.* **1** eleven times as much or as many. **2** consisting of eleven parts.

elevenses /ɪ'levənzɪz/ *n.* (usu. in *pl.*) *Brit. colloq.* light refreshment, usu. with tea or coffee, taken about 11 a.m.

eleventh /ɪ'levənθ/ *n. & adj.* —*n.* **1** the position in a sequence corresponding to the number 11 in the sequence 1–11. **2** something occupying this position. **3** one of eleven equal parts of a thing. —*adj.* that is the eleventh. □ **the eleventh hour** the last possible moment.

elf *n.* (*pl.* **elves** /elvz/) a mythological being, esp. one that is small and mischievous. **2** a sprite or little creature. □ **elf-lock** a tangled mass of hair. □ **elfish** *adj.* **elvish** *adj.* [OE f. Gmc]

elfin /'elfɪn/ *adj.* of elves; elflike. [ELF, perh. infl. by ME *elvene* genit. pl. of *elf*, and by *Elphin* in Arthurian romance]

elicit /ɪ'lɪsɪt, e'lɪsɪt/ *v.tr.* (**elicited**, **eliciting**) **1** draw out, evoke (an admission, response, etc.). **2** draw forth (what is latent). □ **elicitation** /-'teɪʃ(ə)n/ *n.* **elicitor** *n.* [L *elicere elicit-* (as E-, *lacere* entice)]

elide /ɪ'laɪd/ *v.tr.* omit (a vowel or syllable) by elision. [L *elidere elis-* crush out (as E-, *laedere* knock)]

eligible /'elɪdʒɪb(ə)l/ *adj.* **1** (often foll. by *for*) fit or entitled to be chosen (*eligible for a rebate*). **2** desirable or suitable, esp. as a partner in marriage. □ **eligibility** /-'bɪlɪtɪ/ *n.* **eligibly** *adv.* [F *éligible* f. LL *eligibilis* (as ELECT)]

eliminate /ɪ'lɪmɪˌneɪt/ *v.tr.* **1** remove, get rid of. **2** exclude from consideration; ignore as irrelevant. **3** exclude from further participation in a competition etc. on defeat. □ **eliminable**

/-nəb(ə)l/ *adj.* **elimination** /-ˈneɪʃ(ə)n/ *n.* **eliminator** *n.* **eliminatory** /-nətərɪ/ *adj.* [L *eliminare* (as E-, *limen liminis* threshold)]

elision /ɪˈlɪʒ(ə)n/ *n.* the omission of a vowel or syllable in pronouncing (as in *I'm, let's, e'en*). [LL *elisio* (as ELIDE)]

élite /eɪˈliːt, ɪ-/ *n.* **1** (prec. by *the*) the best or choice part of a larger body or group. **2** a select group or class. [F f. past part. of *élire* f. Rmc: rel. to ELECT]

élitism /eɪˈliːtɪz(ə)m, ɪ-/ *n.* **1** advocacy of or reliance on leadership or dominance by a select group. **2** a sense of belonging to an élite. □ **élitist** *n.* & *adj.*

elixir /ɪˈlɪksɪə(r)/ *n.* **1** *Alchemy* **a** a preparation supposedly able to change metals into gold. **b** (in full **elixir of life**) a preparation supposedly able to prolong life indefinitely. **c** a supposed remedy for all ills. **2** *Pharm.* an aromatic solution used as a medicine or flavouring. [ME f. med.L f. Arab. *al-iksīr* f. *al* the + *iksīr* prob. f. Gk *xērion* powder for drying wounds f. *xēros* dry]

Elizabethan /ɪˌlɪzəˈbiːθ(ə)n/ *adj.* & *n.* —*adj.* of the time of Queen Elizabeth I (1558–1603) or of Queen Elizabeth II (1952–). —*n.* a person, esp. a writer, of the time of Queen Elizabeth I or II.

elk *n.* (*pl.* same or **elks**) **1** a large deer, *Alces alces*, of N. Europe and Asia, with palmate antlers; a moose. **2** *US* a wapiti. [ME, prob. repr. OE *elh, eolh*]

ell *n. hist.* a former measure of length, about 45 inches. [OE *eln*, rel. to L *ulna*: see ULNA]

ellipse /ɪˈlɪps/ *n.* a regular oval, traced by a point moving in a plane so that the sum of its distances from two other points is constant, or resulting when a cone is cut by a plane which does not intersect the base and makes a smaller angle with the base than the side of the cone makes. [F f. L *ellipsus* f. Gk *elleipsis* f. *elleipō* come short f. *en* in + *leipō* leave]

ellipsis /ɪˈlɪpsɪs/ *n.* (also **ellipse**) (*pl.* **ellipses** /-siːz/) **1** the omission from a sentence of words needed to complete the construction or sense. **2** a set of three dots etc. indicating an omission.

ellipsoid /ɪˈlɪpsɔɪd/ *n.* a solid of which all the plane sections normal to one axis are circles and all the other plane sections are ellipses. □ **ellipsoidal** /ˌelɪpˈsɔɪd(ə)l/ *adj.*

elliptic /ɪˈlɪptɪk/ *adj.* (also **elliptical**) of, relating to, or having the form of an ellipse or ellipsis. □ **elliptically** *adv.* **ellipticity** /ˌelɪpˈtɪsɪtɪ/ *n.* [Gk *elleiptikos* defective f. *elleipō* (as ELLIPSE)]

elm *n.* **1** any tree of the genus *Ulmus*, esp. *U. procera* with rough serrated leaves. **2** (in full **elmwood**) the wood of the elm. □ **elmy** *adj.* [OE, rel. to L *ulmus*]

elocution /ˌeləˈkjuːʃ(ə)n/ *n.* **1** the art of clear and expressive speech, esp. of distinct pronunciation and articulation. **2** a particular style of speaking. □ **elocutionary** *adj.* **elocutionist** *n.* [L *elocutio* f. *eloqui elocut-* speak out (as E-, *loqui* speak)]

elongate /ˈiːlɒŋˌgeɪt/ *v. tr.* lengthen, prolong. □ **elongation** /-ˈgeɪʃ(ə)n/ *n.* [LL *elongare* (as E-, L *longus* long)]

elope /ɪˈləʊp/ *v.intr.* **1** run away to marry secretly, esp. without parental consent. **2** run away with a lover. □ **elopement** *n.* **eloper** *n.* [AF *aloper* perh. f. a ME form *alope*, rel. to LEAP]

eloquence /ˈeləkwəns/ *n.* **1** fluent and effective use of language. **2** rhetoric. [ME f. OF f. L *eloquentia* f. *eloqui* speak out (as E-, *loqui* speak)]

eloquent /ˈeləkwənt/ *adj.* **1** possessing or showing eloquence. **2** (often foll. by *of*) clearly expressive or indicative. □ **eloquently** *adv.* [ME f. OF f. L *eloqui* (as ELOQUENCE)]

Elsan /ˈelsæn/ *n. Brit. propr.* a type of transportable chemical lavatory. [app. f. E. L. Jackson (its manufacturer) + SANITATION]

else /els/ *adv.* **1** (prec. by indef. or interrog. pron.) besides; in addition (*nowhere else; who else*). **2** instead; other, different (*what else could I say?*). **3** otherwise; if not (*run, (or) else you will be late*). [OE *elles*, rel. to L *alius*, Gk *allos*]

elsewhere /ˈelsweə(r), elsˈweə(r)/ *adv.* in or to some other place. [OE *elles hwǣr* (as ELSE, WHERE)]

elucidate /ɪˈluːsɪˌdeɪt, ɪˈljuː-/ *v.tr.* throw light on; explain. □ **elucidation** /-ˈdeɪʃ(ə)n/ *n.* **elucidative** *adj.* **elucidator** *n.* **elucidatory** *adj.* [LL *elucidare* (as E-, LUCID)]

elude /ɪˈluːd, ɪˈljuːd/ *v.tr.* **1** escape adroitly from (a danger, difficulty, pursuer, etc.); dodge. **2** avoid compliance with (a law, request, etc.) or fulfilment of (an obligation). **3** (of a fact, solution, etc.) escape from or baffle (a person's memory or understanding). □ **elusion** /-ʒ(ə)n/ *n.* **elusory** *adj.* [L *eludere elus-* (as E-, *ludere* play)]

elusive /ɪˈluːsɪv, ɪˈljuːsɪv/ *adj.* **1** difficult to find or catch; tending to elude. **2** difficult to remember or recall. **3** (of an answer etc.) avoiding the point raised; seeking to elude. □ **elusively** *adv.* **elusiveness** *n.*

elver /ˈelvə(r)/ *n.* a young eel. [var. of *eel-fare* (see FARE) = a brood of young eels]

elves *pl.* of ELF.

elvish see ELF.

Elysium /ɪˈlɪzɪəm/ *n.* **1** (also **Elysian Fields**) (in Greek mythology) the abode of the blessed after death. **2** a place or state of ideal happiness. □ **Elysian** *adj.* [L f. Gk *Elusion* (*pedion* plain)]

em /em/ *n. Printing* **1** a unit for measuring the amount of printed matter in a line, usually equal to the nominal width of capital M. **2** a unit of measurement equal to 12 points. [name of the letter M]

em- /ɪm, em/ *prefix* assim. form of EN-¹, EN-² before *b, p.*

'em /əm/ *pron. colloq.* them (*let 'em all come*). [orig. a form of ME *hem*, dative and accus. 3rd pers. pl. pron.: now regarded as an abbr. of THEM]

emaciate /ɪˈmeɪsɪˌeɪt, ɪˈmeɪʃɪˌeɪt/ *v.tr.* (esp. as **emaciated** *adj.*) make abnormally thin or feeble. □ **emaciation** /-ˈeɪʃ(ə)n/ *n.* [L *emaciare emaciat-* (as E-, *macies* leanness)]

email /ˈiːmeɪl/ *n.* (also **e-mail**) = *electronic mail*.

emanate /ˈeməˌneɪt/ *v.* **1** *intr.* (usu. foll. by *from*) (of an idea, rumour, etc.) issue, originate (from a source). **2** *intr.* (usu. foll. by *from*) (of gas, light, etc.) proceed, issue. **3** *tr.* emit; send forth. [L *emanare* flow out]

emanation /ˌeməˈneɪʃ(ə)n/ *n.* **1** the act or process of emanating. **2** something that emanates from a source (esp. of virtues, qualities, etc.). □ **emanative** *adj.* [LL *emanatio* (as EMANATE)]

emancipate /ɪˈmænsɪˌpeɪt/ *v.tr.* **1** free from restraint, esp. legal, social, or political. **2** (usu. as **emancipated** *adj.*) cause to be less inhibited by moral or social convention. **3** free from slavery. □ **emancipation** /-ˈpeɪʃ(ə)n/ *n.* **emancipator** *n.* **emancipatory** *adj.* [L *emancipare* transfer property (as E-, *manus* hand + *capere* take)]

emasculate v. & adj. —v.tr. /ɪˈmæskjʊˌleɪt/ 1 deprive of force or vigour; make feeble or ineffective. 2 castrate. —adj. /ɪˈmæskjʊlət/ 1 deprived of force or vigour. 2 castrated. 3 effeminate. □ **emasculation** /-ˈleɪʃ(ə)n/ n. **emasculator** n. **emasculatory** /-lətərɪ/ adj. [L emasculatus past part. of emasculare (as E-, masculus dimin. of mas male)]

embalm /ɪmˈbɑːm/ v.tr. 1 preserve (a corpse) from decay. 2 preserve from oblivion. □ **embalmer** n. **embalmment** n. [ME f. OF embaumer (as EN-¹, BALM)]

embank /ɪmˈbæŋk/ v.tr. shut in or confine (a river etc.) with an artificial bank.

embankment /ɪmˈbæŋkmənt/ n. an earth or stone bank for keeping back water, or for carrying a road or railway.

embargo /emˈbɑːgəʊ, ɪm-/ n. & v. —n. (pl. -oes) 1 an order of a State forbidding foreign ships to enter, or any ships to leave, its ports. 2 an official suspension of commerce or other activity. —v.tr. (-oes, -oed) 1 place (ships, trade, etc.) under embargo. 2 seize (a ship, goods) for State service. [Sp. f. embargar arrest f. Rmc (as IN-², BAR¹)]

embark /ɪmˈbɑːk/ v. 1 tr. & intr. (often foll. by for) put or go on board a ship or aircraft (to a destination). 2 intr. (foll. by on, upon) engage in an activity or undertaking. □ **embarkation** /ˌembɑːˈkeɪʃ(ə)n/ n. (in sense 1). [F embarquer (as IN-², BARQUE)]

embarrass /ɪmˈbærəs/ v.tr. 1 cause (a person) to feel awkward or self-conscious or ashamed. 2 (as **embarrassed** adj.) encumbered with debts. 3 encumber, impede. □ **embarrassedly** adv. **embarrassingly** adv. **embarrassment** n. [F embarrasser (orig. = hamper) f. Sp. embarazar f. It. imbarrare bar in (as IN-², BAR¹)]

embassy /ˈembəsɪ/ n. (pl. -ies) 1 a the residence or offices of an ambassador. b the ambassador and staff attached to an embassy. 2 a deputation or mission to a foreign country. [earlier ambassy f. OF ambassée etc. f. med.L ambasciata f. Rmc (as AMBASSADOR)]

embattle /ɪmˈbæt(ə)l/ v.tr. 1 a set (an army etc.) in battle array. b fortify against attack. 2 provide (a building or wall) with battlements. 3 (as **embattled** adj.) a prepared or arrayed for battle. b involved in a conflict or difficult undertaking. [ME f. OF embataillier (as EN-¹, BATTLE): see BATTLEMENT]

embed /ɪmˈbed/ v.tr. (also **imbed**) (**-bedded**, **-bedding**) 1 (esp. as **embedded** adj.) fix firmly in a surrounding mass. 2 (of a mass) surround so as to fix firmly. □ **embedment** n.

embellish /ɪmˈbelɪʃ/ v.tr. 1 beautify, adorn. 2 add interest to (a narrative) with fictitious additions. □ **embellisher** n. **embellishment** n. [ME f. OF embellir (as EN-¹, bel handsome f. L bellus)]

ember /ˈembə(r)/ n. (usu. in pl.) a small piece of glowing coal or wood in a dying fire. [OE ǣmyrge f. Gmc]

ember days /ˈembə(r)/ n.pl. any of the days traditionally reserved for fasting and prayer in the Christian Church, now associated with ordinations. [OE ymbren (n.), perh. f. ymbryne period f. ymb about + ryne course]

embezzle /ɪmˈbez(ə)l/ v.tr. (also absol.) divert (money etc.) fraudulently to one's own use. □ **embezzlement** n. **embezzler** n. [AF embesiler

(as EN-¹, OF besillier maltreat, ravage, of unkn. orig.)]

embitter /ɪmˈbɪtə(r)/ v.tr. 1 arouse bitter feelings in (a person). 2 make more bitter or painful. 3 render (a person or feelings) hostile. □ **embitterment** n.

emblazon /ɪmˈbleɪz(ə)n/ v.tr. 1 a portray conspicuously, as on a heraldic shield. b adorn (a shield) with heraldic devices. 2 adorn brightly and conspicuously. □ **emblazonment** n.

emblem /ˈembləm/ n. 1 a symbol or representation typifying or identifying an institution, quality, etc. 2 (foll. by of) (of a person) the type (the very emblem of courage). 3 a symbolic object as a distinctive badge. □ **emblematic** /-ˈmætɪk/ adj. **emblematical** /-ˈmætɪk(ə)l/ adj. **emblematically** /-ˈmætɪkəlɪ/ adv. [ME f. L emblema f. Gk emblēma -matos insertion f. emballō throw in (as EN-¹, ballō throw)]

emblematize /ɪmˈblemǝˌtaɪz/ v.tr. (also **-ise**) 1 serve as an emblem of. 2 represent by an emblem.

embody /ɪmˈbɒdɪ/ v.tr. (**-ies**, **-ied**) 1 give a concrete or discernible form to (an idea, concept, etc.). 2 (of a thing or person) be an expression of (an idea etc.). 3 express tangibly (courage embodied in heroic actions). 4 include, comprise. □ **embodiment** n.

embolden /ɪmˈbəʊld(ə)n/ v.tr. (often foll. by to + infin.) make bold; encourage.

embolism /ˈembǝˌlɪz(ə)m/ n. an obstruction of any artery by a clot of blood, air-bubble, etc. [ME, = 'intercalation' f. LL embolismus f. Gk embolismos f. emballō (as EMBLEM)]

embolus /ˈembǝlǝs/ n. (pl. **emboli** /-ˌlaɪ/) an object causing an embolism. [L, = piston, f. Gk embolos peg, stopper]

emboss /ɪmˈbɒs/ v.tr. 1 carve or mould in relief. 2 form figures etc. so that they stand out on a surface). 3 make protuberant. □ **embosser** n. **embossment** n. [ME, f. OF (as EN-¹, BOSS²)]

embrace /ɪmˈbreɪs/ v. & n. —v.tr. 1 a hold (a person) closely in the arms, esp. as a sign of affection. b (absol., of two people) hold each other closely. 2 clasp, enclose. 3 accept eagerly (an offer, opportunity, etc.). 4 adopt (a course of action, doctrine, cause, etc.). 5 include, comprise. 6 take in with the eye or mind. —n. an act of embracing; holding in the arms. □ **embraceable** adj. **embracement** n. **embracer** n. [ME f. OF embracer, ult. f. L in- IN-¹ + bracchium arm]

embrasure /ɪmˈbreɪʒǝ(r)/ n. 1 the bevelling of a wall at the sides of a door or window; splaying. 2 a small opening in a parapet of a fortified building. □ **embrasured** adj. [F f. embraser splay, of unkn. orig.]

embrocation /ˌembrǝʊˈkeɪʃ(ə)n/ n. a liquid used for rubbing on the body to relieve muscular pain etc. [F embrocation or med.L embrocatio ult. f. Gk embrokhē lotion]

embroider /ɪmˈbrɔɪdǝ(r)/ v.tr. 1 (also absol.) a decorate (cloth etc.) with needlework. b create (a design) in this way. 2 add interest to (a narrative) with fictitious additions. □ **embroiderer** n. [ME f. AF enbrouder (as EN-¹, OF brouder, broisder f. Gmc)]

embroidery /ɪmˈbrɔɪdǝrɪ/ n. (pl. **-ies**) 1 the art of embroidering. 2 embroidered work; a piece of this. 3 unnecessary or extravagant ornament. [ME f. AF enbrouderie (as EMBROIDER)]

embroil /ɪmˈbrɔɪl/ v.tr. **1** (often foll. by with) involve (a person) in conflict or difficulties. **2** bring (affairs) into a state of confusion. □ **embroilment** n. [F embrouiller (as EN-¹ + obs. broil to muddle)]

embryo /ˈembrɪəʊ/ n. (pl. **-os**) **1 a** an unborn or unhatched offspring. **b** a human offspring in the first eight weeks from conception. **2** a rudimentary plant contained in a seed. **3** a thing in a rudimentary stage. **4** (attrib.) undeveloped, immature. □ **in embryo** undeveloped. □ **embryoid** adj. **embryonal** /ˈembrɪən(ə)l/ adj. **embryonic** /ˌembrɪˈɒnɪk/ adj. **embryonically** /-ˈɒnɪkəlɪ/ adv. [LL embryo -onis f. Gk embruon foetus (as EN-², bruō swell, grow)]

embryology /ˌembrɪˈɒlədʒɪ/ n. the study of embryos. □ **embryologic** /-brɪəˈlɒdʒɪk/ adj. **embryological** /-brɪəˈlɒdʒɪk(ə)l/ adj. **embryologically** /-brɪəˈlɒdʒɪkəlɪ/ adv. **embryologist** n.

emcee /emˈsiː/ n. & v. colloq. —n. a master of ceremonies or compère. —v.tr. & intr. (**emcees, emceed**) compère. [the letters MC]

emend /ɪˈmend/ v.tr. edit (a text etc.) to remove errors and corruptions. □ **emendation** /ˌiːmenˈdeɪʃ(ə)n/ n. **emendator** /ˈiːmenˌdeɪtə(r)/ n. **emendatory** adj. [ME f. L emendare (as E-, menda fault)]

■ **Usage** See note at amend.

emerald /ˈemər(ə)ld/ n. **1** a bright-green precious stone, a variety of beryl. **2** (also **emerald green**) the colour of this. □ **Emerald Isle** literary Ireland. □ **emeraldine** /-ˌdaɪn, -dɪn/ adj. [ME f. OF emeraude, esm-, ult. f. Gk smaragdos]

emerge /ɪˈmɜːdʒ/ v.intr. (often foll. by from) **1** come up or out into view, esp. when formerly concealed. **2** come up out of a liquid. **3** (of facts, circumstances, etc.) come to light, become known, esp. as a result of inquiry etc. **4** become recognized or prominent (emerged as a leading contender). **5** (of a question, difficulty, etc.) become apparent. □ **emergence** n. [L emergere emers- (as E-, mergere dip)]

emergency /ɪˈmɜːdʒ(ə)nsɪ/ n. (pl. **-ies**) **1** a sudden state of danger, conflict, etc., requiring immediate action. **2 a** a medical condition requiring immediate treatment. **b** a patient with such a condition. **3** (attrib.) characterized by or for use in an emergency. **4** Austral. Sport a reserve player. □ **state of emergency** a condition of danger or disaster affecting a country, esp. with normal constitutional procedures suspended. [med.L emergentia (as EMERGE)]

emergent /ɪˈmɜːdʒ(ə)nt/ adj. **1** becoming apparent; emerging. **2** (of a nation) newly formed or made independent.

emeritus /ɪˈmerɪtəs/ adj. retired and retaining one's title as an honour (emeritus professor; professor emeritus). [L, past part. of emerēri (as E-, merēri earn)]

emery /ˈemərɪ/ n. **1** a coarse rock of corundum and magnetite or haematite used for polishing metal or other hard materials. **2** (attrib.) covered with emery. [F émeri(l) f. It. smeriglio ult. f. Gk smuris, smēris polishing powder]

emetic /ɪˈmetɪk/ adj. & n. —adj. that causes vomiting. —n. an emetic medicine. [Gk emetikos f. emeō vomit]

EMF abbr. electromotive force.

emigrant /ˈemɪɡrənt/ n. & adj. —n. a person who emigrates. —adj. emigrating.

emigrate /ˈemɪˌɡreɪt/ v. intr. leave one's own country to settle in another. □ **emigration** /-ˈɡreɪʃ(ə)n/ n. **emigratory** adj. [L emigrare emigrat- (as E-, migrare depart)]

émigré /ˈemɪˌɡreɪ/ n. an emigrant, esp. a political exile. [F, past part. of émigrer EMIGRATE]

eminence /ˈemɪnəns/ n. **1** distinction; recognized superiority. **2** a piece of rising ground. **3** (**Eminence**) a title used in addressing or referring to a cardinal (Your Eminence; His Eminence). **4** an important person. [L eminentia (as EMINENT)]

éminence grise /ˌeɪmɪˌnɑːs ˈɡriːz/ n. a person who exercises power or influence without holding office. [F, = grey cardinal (see EMINENCE): orig. applied to Cardinal Richelieu's private secretary, Père Joseph d. 1638]

eminent /ˈemɪnənt/ adj. **1** distinguished, notable. **2** (of qualities) remarkable in degree. □ **eminently** adv. [ME f. L eminēre eminent- jut]

emir /eˈmɪə(r)/ n. a title of various Muslim rulers. [F émir f. Arab. 'amīr: cf. AMIR]

emirate /ˈemɪərət/ n. the rank, domain, or reign of an emir.

emissary /ˈemɪsərɪ/ n. (pl. **-ies**) a person sent on a special mission (usu. diplomatic, formerly usu. odious or underhand). [L emissarius scout, spy (as EMIT)]

emission /ɪˈmɪʃ(ə)n/ n. **1** (often foll. by of) the process or an act of emitting. **2** a thing emitted. [L emissio (as EMIT)]

emit /ɪˈmɪt/ v.tr. (**emitted, emitting**) **1 a** send out (heat, light, vapour, etc.). **b** discharge from the body. **2** utter (a cry etc.). [L emittere emiss- (as E-, mittere send)]

Emmental /ˈemənˌtɑːl/ n. (also **Emmenthal**) a kind of hard Swiss cheese, similar to Gruyère. [G Emmentaler f. Emmental in Switzerland]

emollient /ɪˈmɒlɪənt/ adj. & n. —adj. that softens or soothes the skin. —n. an emollient agent. □ **emollience** n. [L emollire (as E-, mollis soft)]

emolument /ɪˈmɒljʊmənt/ n. a salary, fee, or profit from employment or office. [ME f. OF emolument or L emolumentum, orig. prob. 'payment for corn-grinding', f. emolere (as E-, molere grind)]

emote /ɪˈməʊt/ v.intr. colloq. show excessive emotion. □ **emoter** n. [back-form. f. EMOTION]

emotion /ɪˈməʊʃ(ə)n/ n. a strong mental or instinctive feeling such as love or fear. [earlier = agitation, disturbance of the mind, f. F émotion f. émouvoir excite]

emotional /ɪˈməʊʃən(ə)l/ adj. **1** of or relating to the emotions. **2** (of a person) liable to excessive emotion. **3** expressing or based on emotion (an emotional appeal). **4** likely to excite emotion (an emotional issue). □ **emotionalism** n. **emotionalist** n. **emotionality** /-ˈnælɪtɪ/ n. **emotionalize** v.tr. (also **-ise**). **emotionally** adv.

■ **Usage** See note at emotive.

emotive /ɪˈməʊtɪv/ adj. **1** of or characterized by emotion. **2** tending to excite emotion. **3** arousing feeling; not purely descriptive. □ **emotively** adv. **emotiveness** n. **emotivity** /ˌiːməʊˈtɪvɪtɪ/ n. [L emovere emot- (as E-, movēre move)]

■ **Usage** Although the senses of emotive and emotional overlap, emotive is more common in the sense 'arousing emotion', as in an emotive issue, and is not used at all in sense 2 of *emotional.*

empanel /ɪmˈpæn(ə)l/ *v.tr.* (also **impanel**) (**-panelled, -panelling**; *US* **-paneled, -paneling**) enrol or enter on a panel (those eligible for jury service). □ **empanelment** *n*. [AF *empaneller* (as EN-[1], PANEL)]

empathize /ˈempəˌθaɪz/ *v. Psychol.* **1** *intr.* (usu. foll. by *with*) exercise empathy. **2** *tr.* treat with empathy.

empathy /ˈempəθɪ/ *n. Psychol.* the power of identifying oneself mentally with (and so fully comprehending) a person or object of contemplation. □ **empathetic** /-ˈθetɪk/ *adj.* **empathetically** /-ˈθetɪkəlɪ/ *adv.* **empathic** /emˈpæθɪk/ *adj.* **empathically** /emˈpæθ-/ *adv.* **empathist** *n.* [transl. G *Einfühlung* f. *ein* in + *Fühlung* feeling, after Gk *empatheia*: see SYMPATHY]

emperor /ˈempərə(r)/ *n.* **1** the sovereign of an empire. **2** a sovereign of higher rank than a king. □ **emperor penguin** the largest known penguin, *Aptenodytes forsteri.* □ **emperorship** *n*. [ME f. OF *emperere, empereor* f. L *imperator -oris* f. *imperare* command]

emphasis /ˈemfəsɪs/ *n.* (*pl.* **emphases** /-ˌsiːz/) **1** special importance or prominence attached to a thing, fact, idea, etc. (*emphasis on economy*). **2** stress laid on a word or words to indicate special meaning or importance. **3** vigour or intensity of expression, feeling, action, etc. [L f. Gk f. *emphainō* exhibit (as EN-[2], *phainō* show)]

emphasize /ˈemfəˌsaɪz/ *v.tr.* (also **-ise**) **1** bring (a thing, fact, etc.) into special prominence. **2** lay stress on (a word in speaking).

emphatic /ɪmˈfætɪk/ *adj.* **1** (of language, tone, or gesture) forcibly expressive. **2** of words: **a** bearing the stress. **b** used to give emphasis. **3** expressing oneself with emphasis. **4** (of an action or process) forcible, significant. □ **emphatically** *adv.* [LL *emphaticus* f. Gk *emphatikos* (as EMPHASIS)]

emphysema /ˌemfɪˈsiːmə/ *n.* **1** enlargement of the air sacs of the lungs causing breathlessness. **2** a swelling caused by the presence of air in the connective tissues of the body. [LL f. Gk *emphusēma* f. *emphusaō* puff up]

empire /ˈempaɪə(r)/ *n.* **1** an extensive group of States or countries under a single supreme authority, esp. an emperor. **2** supreme dominion. **3** a large commercial organization etc. owned or directed by one person or group. **4** a type or period of government in which the sovereign is called emperor. □ **empire-builder** a person who deliberately acquires extra territory, authority, etc. esp. unnecessarily. [ME f. OF f. L *imperium* rel. to *imperare*: see EMPEROR]

empirical /ɪmˈpɪrɪk(ə)l/ *adj.* **1** based or acting on observation or experiment, not on theory. **2** deriving knowledge from experience alone. □ **empirically** *adv.* [L *empiricus* f. Gk *empeirikos* f. *empeiria* experience f. *empeiros* skilled]

emplacement /ɪmˈpleɪsmənt/ *n.* **1** the act or an instance of putting in position. **2** a platform or defended position where a gun is placed for firing. **3** situation, position. [F (as EN-[1], PLACE)]

employ /ɪmˈplɔɪ/ *v.* & *n.* —*v.tr.* **1** use the services of (a person) in return for payment; keep (a person) in one's service. **2** (often foll. by *for, in, on*) use (a thing, time, energy, etc.) esp. to good effect. **3** (often foll. by *in*) keep (a person) occupied. —*n.* the state of being employed, esp. for wages. □ **in the employ of** employed by. □ **employable** *adj.* **employability** /-ˈbɪlɪtɪ/ *n.*

employer *n.* [ME f. OF *employer* ult. f. L *implicare* be involved f. *implicare* enfold: see IMPLICATE]

employee /ˌemplɔɪˈiː, -ˈplɔɪɪ/ *n.* (*US* **employe**) a person employed for wages or salary.

employment /ɪmˈplɔɪmənt/ *n.* **1** the act of employing or the state of being employed. **2** a person's regular trade or profession. □ **employment agency** a business that finds employers or employees for those seeking them. **employment office** (formerly **employment exchange**) *Brit.* any of a number of government offices concerned with advising and finding work for the unemployed.

emporium /emˈpɔːrɪəm/ *n.* (*pl.* **emporia** /-rɪə/ or **-ums**) **1** a large retail store selling a wide variety of goods. **2** a centre of commerce, a market. [L f. Gk *emporion* f. *emporos* merchant]

empower /ɪmˈpaʊə(r)/ *v.tr.* (foll. by *to* + infin.) **1** authorize, license. **2** give power to; make able. □ **empowerment** *n.*

empress /ˈemprɪs/ *n.* **1** the wife or widow of an emperor. **2** a woman emperor. [ME f. OF *emperesse* fem. of *emperere* EMPEROR]

empty /ˈemptɪ/ *adj., v.,* & *n.* —*adj.* (**emptier, emptiest**) **1** containing nothing. **2** (of a house etc.) unoccupied or unfurnished. **3** (of a transport vehicle etc.) without a load, passengers, etc. **4 a** meaningless, hollow, insincere (*empty threats; an empty gesture*). **b** without substance or purpose (*an empty existence*). **5** *colloq.* hungry. **6** (foll. by *of*) devoid, lacking. —*v.* (**-ies, -ied**) **1** *tr.* **a** make empty; remove the contents of. **b** (foll. by *of*) deprive of certain contents (*emptied the room of its chairs*). **2** *tr.* (often foll. by *into*) transfer (the contents of a container). **3** *intr.* become empty. **4** *intr.* (usu. foll. by *into*) (of a river) discharge itself (into the sea etc.). —*n.* (*pl.* **-ies**) *colloq.* a container (esp. a bottle) left empty of its contents. □ **empty-handed 1** bringing or taking nothing. **2** having achieved or obtained nothing. **empty-headed** foolish; lacking common sense. **empty-nester** *US* either of a couple whose children have grown up and left home. □ **emptily** *adv.* **emptiness** *n.* [OE *ǣmtig, ǣmetig* f. *ǣmetta* leisure]

empurple /ɪmˈpɜːp(ə)l/ *v.tr.* **1** make purple or red. **2** make angry.

empyrean /ˌempaɪˈriːən, ˌempɪ-/ *n.* & *adj.* —*n.* **1** the highest heaven, as the sphere of fire or as the abode of God. **2** the visible heavens. —*adj.* of the empyrean. □ **empyreal** /empaɪˈriːəl, ˌempɪ-, emˈpɪ-/ *adj.* [med.L *empyreus* f. Gk *empurios* (as EN-[2], *pur* fire)]

EMS *abbr.* European Monetary System.

EMU /ˌiːemˈjuː, ˈiːmjuː/ *abbr.* economic and monetary union (of the EC); European monetary union.

emu /ˈiːmjuː/ *n.* a large flightless bird, *Dromaius novaehollandiae*, native to Australia. [earlier *emia, eme* f. Port. *ema*]

emulate /ˈemjʊˌleɪt/ *v.tr.* **1** try to equal or excel. **2** imitate zealously. **3** rival. □ **emulation** /-ˈleɪʃ(ə)n/ *n.* **emulative** /-lətɪv/ *adj.* **emulator** *n.* [L *aemulari* (as EMULOUS)]

emulous /ˈemjʊləs/ *adj.* **1** (usu. foll. by *of*) seeking to emulate. **2** actuated by a spirit of rivalry. □ **emulously** *adv.* [ME f. L *aemulus* rival]

emulsifier /ɪˈmʌlsɪˌfaɪə(r)/ n. **1** any substance that stabilizes an emulsion, esp. a food additive used to stabilize processed foods. **2** an apparatus used for producing an emulsion.

emulsify /ɪˈmʌlsɪˌfaɪ/ v.tr. (-ies, -ied) convert into an emulsion. □ **emulsifiable** adj. **emulsification** /-fɪˈkeɪʃ(ə)n/ n.

emulsion /ɪˈmʌlʃ(ə)n/ n. **1** a fine dispersion of one liquid in another, esp. as paint, medicine, etc. **2** a mixture of a silver compound suspended in gelatin etc. for coating plates or films. □ **emulsion paint** a water-thinned paint containing a non-volatile substance as its binding medium. □ **emulsionize** v.tr. (also -ise). **emulsive** adj. [F émulsion or mod.L emulsio f. emulgēre (as E-, mulgēre muls- to milk)]

en /en/ n. Printing a unit of measurement equal to half an em. [name of the letter N]

en-[1] /en, ɪn/ prefix (also **em-** before b, p) forming verbs, = IN-[1]: **1** from nouns, meaning 'put into or on' (engulf; entrust; embed). **2** from nouns or adjectives, meaning 'bring into the condition of' (enslave); often with the suffix -en (enlighten). **3** from verbs: **a** in the sense 'in, into, on' (enfold). **b** as an intensive (entangle). [from or after F en- f. L in-]

en-[2] /en, ɪn/ prefix (also **em-** before b, p) in, inside (energy; enthusiasm). [Gk]

-en[1] /ən/ suffix forming verbs: **1** from adjectives, usu. meaning 'make or become so or more so' (deepen; fasten; moisten). **2** from nouns (happen; strengthen). [OE -nian f. Gmc]

-en[2] /ən/ suffix (also **-n**) forming adjectives from nouns, meaning: **1** made or consisting of (often with extended and figurative senses) (wooden). **2** resembling; of the nature of (golden; silvern). [OE f. Gmc]

-en[3] /ən/ suffix (also **-n**) forming past participles of strong verbs: **1** as a regular inflection (spoken; sworn). **2** with restricted sense (drunken). [OE f. Gmc]

-en[4] /ən/ suffix forming the plural of a few nouns (children; brethren; oxen). [ME reduction of OE -an]

-en[5] /ən/ suffix forming diminutives of nouns (chicken; maiden). [OE f. Gmc]

-en[6] /ən/ suffix **1** forming feminine nouns (vixen). **2** forming abstract nouns (burden). [OE f. Gmc]

enable /ɪˈneɪb(ə)l/ v.tr. **1** (foll. by to + infin.) give (a person etc.) the means or authority to do something. **2** make possible. **3** esp. Computing make (a device) operational; switch on. □ **enabler** n.

enact /ɪˈnækt/ v.tr. **1 a** (often foll. by that + clause) ordain, decree. **b** make (a bill etc.) law. **2** play (a part or scene on stage or in life). □ **enactable** adj. **enaction** n. **enactive** adj. **enactor** n. **enactory** adj.

enactment /ɪˈnæktmənt/ n. **1** a law enacted. **2** the process of enacting.

enamel /ɪˈnæm(ə)l/ n. & v. —n. **1** a glasslike opaque or semi-transparent coating on metallic or other hard surfaces for ornament or as a preservative lining. **2 a** a smooth hard coating. **b** a cosmetic simulating this. **3** the hard glossy natural coating over the crown of a tooth. **4** painting done in enamel. —v.tr. (**enamelled**, **enamelling**; US **enameled**, **enameling**) **1** inlay or encrust (a metal etc.) with enamel. **2** portray (figures etc.) with enamel. □ **enamel paint** a paint that dries to give a smooth hard coat. □

enameller n. **enamelwork** n. [ME f. AF enameler, enamailler (as EN-[1], OF esmail f. Gmc)]

enamour /ɪˈnæmə(r)/ v.tr. (US **enamor**) (usu. in passive; foll. by of) **1** inspire with love or liking. **2** charm, delight. [ME f. OF enamourer f. amourer (as EN-[1], AMOUR)]

en bloc /ɑ̃ ˈblɒk/ adv. in a block; all at the same time; wholesale. [F]

encamp /ɪnˈkæmp/ v.tr. & intr. **1** settle in a military camp. **2** lodge in the open in tents.

encampment /ɪnˈkæmpmənt/ n. **1** a place where troops etc. are encamped. **2** the process of setting up a camp.

encapsulate /ɪnˈkæpsjʊˌleɪt/ v.tr. **1** enclose in or as in a capsule. **2** summarize; express the essential features of. **3** isolate. □ **encapsulation** /-ˈleɪʃ(ə)n/ n. [EN-[1] + L capsula CAPSULE)]

encase /ɪnˈkeɪs/ v.tr. (also **incase**) **1** put into a case. **2** surround as with a case. □ **encasement** n.

encash /ɪnˈkæʃ/ v.tr. Brit. **1** convert (bills etc.) into cash. **2** receive in the form of cash; realize. □ **encashable** adj. **encashment** n.

encaustic /ɪnˈkɔːstɪk/ adj. & n. —adj. **1** (in painting, ceramics, etc.) using pigments mixed with hot wax, which are burned in as an inlay. **2** (of bricks and tiles) inlaid with differently coloured clays burnt in. —n. **1** the art of encaustic painting. **2** a painting done with this technique. [L encausticus f. Gk egkaustikos (as EN-[2], CAUSTIC)]

-ence /əns/ suffix forming nouns expressing: **1** a quality or state or an instance of one (patience; an impertinence). **2** an action (reference; reminiscence). [from or after F -ence f. L -entia, -antia (cf. -ANCE) f. pres. part. stem -ent-, -ant-]

encephalin var. of ENKEPHALIN.

encephalitis /enˌkefəˈlaɪtɪs, enˌsef-/ n. inflammation of the brain. □ **encephalitic** /-ˈlɪtɪk/ adj.

encephalo- /enˈkefələʊ, enˈsef-/ comb. form brain. [Gk egkephalos brain (as EN-[2], kephalē head)]

encephalogram /enˈkefələʊˌgræm, enˈsef-/ n. an X-ray photograph of the brain.

encephalograph /enˈkefələʊˌgrɑːf, enˈsef-/ n. an instrument for recording the electrical activity of the brain.

encephalopathy /enˌkefəˈlɒpəθɪ, enˌsef-/ n. disease of the brain.

enchain /ɪnˈtʃeɪn/ v.tr. **1** chain up, fetter. **2** hold fast (the attention, emotions, etc.). □ **enchainment** n. [ME f. F enchaîner ult. f. L catena chain]

enchant /ɪnˈtʃɑːnt/ v.tr. **1** charm, delight. **2** bewitch. □ **enchantedly** adv. **enchanting** adj. **enchantingly** adv. **enchantment** n. [ME f. F enchanter f. L incantare (as IN-[2], canere cant- sing)]

enchanter /ɪnˈtʃɑːntə(r)/ n. (fem. **enchantress**) a person who enchants, esp. by supposed use of magic.

enchilada /ˌentʃɪˈlɑːdə/ n. a tortilla with chilli sauce and usu. a filling, esp. meat. [Amer. Sp., fem. past part. of enchilar season with chilli]

encipher /ɪnˈsaɪfə(r)/ v.tr. **1** write (a message etc.) in cipher. **2** convert into coded form using a cipher. □ **encipherment** n.

encircle /ɪnˈsɜːk(ə)l/ v.tr. **1** (usu. foll. by with) surround, encompass. **2** form a circle round. □ **encirclement** n.

enclave /ˈenkleɪv/ n. **1** a portion of territory of one State surrounded by territory of another or others, as viewed by the surrounding territory. **2** a group of people who are culturally or socially distinct from those surrounding them. [F f. *enclaver* ult. f. L *clavis* key]

enclitic /en'klɪtɪk/ *adj.* & *n.* Gram. —*adj.* (of a word) pronounced with so little emphasis that it forms part of the preceding word. —*n.* such a word, e.g. *not* in *cannot*. □ **enclitically** *adv.* [LL *encliticus* f. Gk *egklitikos* (as EN-², *klīnō* lean)]

enclose /ɪn'kləʊz/ *v.tr.* (also **inclose**) **1** (often foll. by *with*, *in*) **a** surround with a wall, fence, etc. **b** shut in on all sides. **2** fence in (common land) so as to make it private property. **3** put in a receptacle (esp. in an envelope together with a letter). **4** (usu. as **enclosed** *adj.*) seclude (a religious community) from the outside world. [ME f. OF *enclos* past part. of *enclore* ult. f. L *includere* (as INCLUDE)]

enclosure /ɪn'kləʊʒə(r)/ *n.* (also **inclosure**) **1** the act of enclosing, esp. of common land. **2** *Brit.* an enclosed space or area. **3** a thing enclosed with a letter. [AF & OF (as ENCLOSE)]

encode /ɪn'kəʊd/ *v.tr.* put (a message etc.) into code or cipher. □ **encoder** *n.*

encomium /en'kəʊmɪəm/ *n.* (*pl.* **encomiums** or **encomia** /-mɪə/) a formal or high-flown expression of praise. [L f. Gk *egkōmion* (as EN-², *kōmos* revelry)]

encompass /ɪn'kʌmpəs/ *v.tr.* **1** surround or form a circle about, esp. to protect or attack. **2** contain. □ **encompassment** *n.*

encore /'ɒŋkɔː(r)/ *n.*, *v.*, & *int.* —*n.* **1** a call by an audience or spectators for the repetition of an item, or for a further item. **2** such an item. —*v.tr.* **1** call for the repetition of (an item). **2** call back (a performer) for this. —*int.* /also ˌɒŋ'kɔː(r)/ again, once more. [F, = once again]

encounter /ɪn'kaʊntə(r)/ *v.* & *n.* —*v.tr.* **1** meet by chance or unexpectedly. **2** meet as an adversary. —*n.* **1** a meeting by chance. **2** a meeting in conflict. [ME f. OF *encontrer*, *encontre* ult. f. L *contra* against]

encourage /ɪn'kʌrɪdʒ/ *v.tr.* **1** give courage, confidence, or hope to. **2** (foll. by *to* + infin.) urge, advise. **3** stimulate by help, reward, etc. **4** promote or assist (an enterprise, opinion, etc.). □ **encouragement** *n.* **encourager** *n.* **encouraging** *adj.* **encouragingly** *adv.* [ME f. F *encourager* (as EN¹, COURAGE)]

encroach /ɪn'krəʊtʃ/ *v.intr.* **1** (foll. by *on*, *upon*) intrude, esp. on another's territory or rights. **2** advance gradually beyond due limits. □ **encroacher** *n.* **encroachment** *n.* [ME f. OF *encrochier* (as EN-¹, *crochier* f. *croc* hook: see CROOK)]

encrust /ɪn'krʌst/ *v.* (also **incrust**) **1** *tr.* cover with a crust. **2** *tr.* overlay with an ornamental crust of precious material. □ **encrustment** *n.* [F *incruster* f. L *incrustare* (as IN-², *crustare* f. *crusta* CRUST)]

encrypt /ɪn'krɪpt/ *v.tr.* convert (data) into code, esp. to prevent unauthorized access. □ **encryption** *n.* [EN-¹ + Gk *kruptos* hidden]

encumber /ɪn'kʌmbə(r)/ *v.tr.* **1** be a burden to. **2** hamper, impede. **3** burden (a person or estate) with debts, esp. mortgages. □ **encumberment** *n.* [ME f. OF *encombrer* block up f. Rmc]

encumbrance /ɪn'kʌmbrəns/ *n.* **1** a burden. **2** an impediment. **3** a mortgage or other charge on property. [ME f. OF *encombrance* (as ENCUMBER)]

-ency /ənsɪ/ *suffix* forming nouns denoting a quality (*efficiency*; *fluency*) or state (*presidency*) but not action (cf. -ENCE). [L *-entia* (cf. -ANCY)]

encyclical /en'sɪklɪk(ə)l/ *n.* & *adj.* —*n.* a papal letter sent to all bishops of the Roman Catholic Church. —*adj.* (of a letter) for wide circulation. [LL *encyclicus* f. Gk *egkuklios* (as EN-², *kuklos* circle)]

encyclopaedia /enˌsaɪklə'piːdɪə, ɪn-/ *n.* (also **encyclopedia**) a book, often in several volumes, giving information on many subjects, or on many aspects of one subject, usu. arranged alphabetically. [mod.L f. spurious Gk *egkuklopaideia* for *egkuklios paideia* all-round education: cf. ENCYCLICAL]

encyclopaedic /enˌsaɪklə'piːdɪk, ɪn-/ *adj.* (also **encyclopedic**) (of knowledge or information) comprehensive.

end *n.* & *v.* —*n.* **1 a** the extreme limit; the point beyond which a thing does not continue. **b** an extremity of a line, or of the greatest dimension of an object. **c** the furthest point (*to the ends of the earth*). **2** the surface bounding a thing at either extremity; an extreme part. **3 a** conclusion, finish. **b** the latter or final part. **c** death, destruction, downfall (*met an untimely end*). **d** result, outcome. **e** an ultimate state or condition. **4 a** a thing one seeks to attain; a purpose (*to what end?*). **b** the object for which a thing exists. **5** a remnant; a piece left over (*cigarette-end*). **6** (prec. by *the*) *colloq.* the limit of endurability. **7** the half of a sports pitch or court occupied by one team or player. **8** the part or share with which a person is concerned (*no problem at my end*). —*v.* **1** *tr.* & *intr.* bring or come to an end. **2** *tr.* put an end to; destroy. **3** *intr.* (foll. by *in*) have as its result (*will end in tears*). **4** *intr.* (foll. by *by*) do or achieve eventually (*ended by marrying an heiress*). □ **at an end** exhausted or completed. **come to a bad** (or **sticky**) **end** meet with ruin or disgrace. **come to an end 1** be completed or finished. **2** become exhausted. **end-game** the final stage of a game (esp. chess), when few pieces remain. **end on** with the end facing one, or with the end adjoining the end of the next object. **end-product** the final product of manufacture, radioactive decay, etc. **end result** final outcome. **end to end** with the end of each of a series adjoining the end of the next. **end up** reach a specified state, action, or place eventually (*ended up a drunkard*; *ended up making a fortune*). **end-user** the person, customer, etc., who is the ultimate user of a product. **in the end** finally; after all. **keep one's end up** do one's part despite difficulties. **make an end of** put a stop to. **make ends** (or **both ends**) **meet** live within one's income. **no end** *colloq.* to a great extent, very much. **no end of** *colloq.* much or many of. **on end 1** upright (*hair stood on end*). **2** continuously (*for three weeks on end*). **put an end to 1** stop (an activity etc.). **2** abolish, destroy. □ **ender** *n.* [OE *ende*, *endian*, f. Gmc]

-end /end, ənd/ *suffix* forming nouns in the sense 'person or thing to be treated in a specified way' (*dividend*; *reverend*). [L gerundive ending *-endus*]

endanger /ɪn'deɪndʒə(r)/ *v.tr.* place in danger. □ **endangered species** a species about to die of extinction. □ **endangerment** *n.*

endear /ɪn'dɪə(r)/ *v.tr.* (usu. foll. by *to*) make dear to or beloved by.

endearing /ɪnˈdɪərɪŋ/ *adj.* inspiring affection. □ **endearingly** *adv.*

endearment /ɪnˈdɪəmənt/ *n.* **1** an expression of affection. **2** liking, affection.

endeavour /ɪnˈdevə(r)/ *v.* & *n.* (US **endeavor**) —*v. tr.* (foll. by *to* + infin.) try earnestly. —*n.* (often foll. by *at*, or *to* + infin.) an earnest attempt. [ME f. phr. *put oneself in devoir*, f. OF *deveir* owe]

endemic /enˈdemɪk/ *adj.* & *n.* —*adj.* regularly or only found among a particular people or in a certain region. —*n.* an endemic disease or plant. □ **endemically** *adv.* **endemicity** /ˌendɪˈmɪsɪtɪ/ *n.* **endemism** /ˈendɪˌmɪz(ə)m/ *n.* [F *endémique* or mod.L *endemicus* f. Gk *endēmos* native (as EN-², *dēmos* the people)]

ending /ˈendɪŋ/ *n.* **1** an end or final part, esp. of a story. **2** an inflected final part of a word. [OE (as END, -ING¹)]

endive /ˈendaɪv, -dɪv/ *n.* **1** a curly-leaved plant, *Cichorium endivia*, used in salads. **2** US a chicory crown. [ME f. OF f. LL *endivia* ult. f. Gk *entubon*]

endless /ˈendlɪs/ *adj.* **1** infinite; without end; eternal. **2** continual, incessant (*tired of their endless complaints*). **3** *colloq.* innumerable. **4** (of a belt, chain, etc.) having the ends joined for continuous action over wheels etc. □ **endlessly** *adv.* **endlessness** *n.* [OE *endelēas* (as END, -LESS)]

endmost /ˈendməʊst/ *adj.* nearest the end.

endo- /ˈendəʊ/ *comb. form* internal. [Gk *endon* within]

endocrine /ˈendəʊˌkraɪn, -ˌkrɪn/ *adj.* (of a gland) secreting directly into the blood; ductless. [ENDO- + Gk *krinō* sift]

endocrinology /ˌendəʊkrɪˈnɒlədʒɪ/ *n.* the study of the structure and physiology of endocrine glands. □ **endocrinological** /-nəˈlɒdʒɪk(ə)l/ *adj.* **endocrinologist** *n.*

endogenous /enˈdɒdʒɪnəs/ *adj.* growing or originating from within. □ **endogenesis** /ˌendəˈdʒenɪsɪs/ *n.* **endogeny** /enˈdɒdʒɪnɪ/ *n.*

endomorph /ˈendəʊˌmɔːf/ *n.* **1** a person with a soft round build of body and a high proportion of fat tissue. □ **endomorphic** /-ˈmɔːfɪk/ *adj.* **endomorphy** *n.* [ENDO- + Gk *morphē* form]

endoplasm /ˈendəʊˌplæz(ə)m/ *n.* the inner fluid layer of the cytoplasm.

endorphin /enˈdɔːfɪn/ *n.* *Biochem.* any of a group of peptide neurotransmitters occurring naturally in the brain and having pain-relieving properties. [F *endorphine* f. *endogène* endogenous + MORPHINE]

endorse /ɪnˈdɔːs/ *v.tr.* (also **indorse**) **1 a** confirm (a statement or opinion). **b** declare one's approval of. **2** sign or write on the back of (a document), esp. the back of (a bill, cheque, etc.) as the payee or to specify another as payee. **3** write (an explanation or comment) on the back of a document. **4** *Brit.* enter details of a conviction for a motoring offence on (a driving licence). □ **endorsable** *adj.* **endorsee** /ˌendɔːˈsiː/ *n.* **endorser** *n.* [med.L *indorsare* (as IN-², L *dorsum* back)]

endorsement /ɪnˈdɔːsmənt/ *n.* **1** the act or an instance of endorsing. **2** something with which a document etc. is endorsed, esp. a signature. **3** a record in a driving licence of a conviction for a motoring offence.

endoskeleton /ˈendəʊˌskelɪt(ə)n/ *n.* an internal skeleton, as found in vertebrates.

endosperm /ˈendəʊˌspɜːm/ *n.* albumen enclosed with the germ in seeds.

endothermic /ˌendəʊˈθɜːmɪk/ *adj.* occurring or formed with the absorption of heat.

endow /ɪnˈdaʊ/ *v.tr.* **1** bequeath or give a permanent income to (a person, institution, etc.). **2** (esp. as **endowed** *adj.*) (usu. foll. by *with*) provide (a person) with talent, ability, etc. □ **endower** *n.* [ME f. AF *endouer* (as EN-¹, OF *douer* f. L *dotare* f. *dos dotis* DOWER)]

endowment /ɪnˈdaʊmənt/ *n.* **1** the act or instance of endowing. **2** assets, esp. property or income with which a person or body is endowed. **3** (usu. in *pl.*) skill, talent, etc., with which a person is endowed. **4** (*attrib.*) denoting forms of life insurance involving payment by the insurer of a fixed sum on a specified date, or on the death of the insured person if earlier. □ **endowment mortgage** a mortgage linked to endowment insurance of the mortgagor's life, the capital being paid from the sum insured.

endpaper /ˈendˌpeɪpə(r)/ *n.* a usu. blank leaf of paper at the beginning and end of a book, fixed to the inside of the cover.

endue /ɪnˈdjuː/ *v.tr.* (also **indue**) (foll. by *with*) invest or provide (a person) with qualities, powers, etc. [earlier = induct, put on clothes: ME f. OF *enduire* f. L *inducere* lead in, assoc. in sense with L *induere* put on (clothes)]

endurance /ɪnˈdjʊərəns/ *n.* **1** the power or habit of enduring (*beyond endurance*). **2** the ability to withstand prolonged strain (*endurance test*). **3** the act of enduring. [OF f. *endurer*: see ENDURE]

endure /ɪnˈdjʊə(r)/ *v.* **1** *tr.* undergo (a difficulty, hardship, etc.). **2** *tr.* **a** tolerate (a person) (*cannot endure him*). **b** (esp. with *neg.*; foll. by *to* + infin.) bear. **3** *intr.* remain in existence; last. **4** *tr.* submit to. □ **endurable** *adj.* **endurability** /-ˈbɪlɪtɪ/ *n.* **enduringly** *adv.* [ME f. OF *endurer* f. L *indurare* harden (as IN-², *durus* hard)]

endways /ˈendweɪz/ *adv.* **1** with its end uppermost or foremost. **2** end to end.

endwise /ˈendwaɪz/ *adv.* = ENDWAYS.

-ene /iːn/ *suffix* **1** forming names of inhabitants of places (*Nazarene*). **2** *Chem.* forming names of unsaturated hydrocarbons containing a double bond (*benzene*; *ethylene*). [from or after Gk *-ēnos*]

enema /ˈenɪmə/ *n.* (*pl.* **enemas** or **enemata** /ɪˈnemətə/) **1** the injection of liquid or gas into the rectum, esp. to expel its contents. **2** a liquid or syringe used for this. [LL f. Gk *enema* f. *eniēmi* inject (as EN-², *hiēmi* send)]

enemy /ˈenəmɪ/ *n.* (*pl.* **-ies**) **1** a person or group actively opposing or hostile to another, or to a cause etc. **2 a** a hostile nation or army, esp. in war. **b** a member of this. **c** a hostile ship or aircraft. **3** (usu. foll. by *of*, *to*) an adversary or opponent. **4** a thing that harms or injures. **5** (*attrib.*) of or belonging to an enemy (*destroyed by enemy action*). [ME f. OF *enemi* f. L *inimicus* (as IN-¹, *amicus* friend)]

energetic /ˌenəˈdʒetɪk/ *adj.* **1** strenuously active. **2** forcible, vigorous. **3** powerfully operative. □ **energetically** *adv.* [Gk *energētikos* f. *energeō* (as EN-², *ergon* work)]

energize /ˈenəˌdʒaɪz/ *v.tr.* (also **-ise**) **1** infuse energy into (a person or work). **2** provide energy for the operation of (a device). □ **energizer** *n.*

energy /ˈenədʒɪ/ *n.* (*pl.* **-ies**) **1** force, vigour; capacity for activity. **2** (in *pl.*) individual powers in use (*devote your energies to this*). **3** *Physics* the capacity of matter or radiation to do work. **4** the means of doing work by utilizing matter or radiation. [F *énergie* or LL *energia* f. Gk *energeia* f. *ergon* work]

enervate *v. & adj.* —*v.tr.* /ˈenəˌveɪt/ deprive of vigour or vitality. —*adj.* /ɪˈnɜːvət/ enervated. □ **enervation** /ˌenəˈveɪʃ(ə)n/ *n.* [L *enervatus* past part. of *enervare* (as E-, *nervus* sinew)]

enfant terrible /ˌɑ̃fɑ̃ teˈriːbl/ *n.* a person who causes embarrassment by indiscreet or unruly behaviour. [F, = terrible child]

enfeeble /ɪnˈfiːb(ə)l/ *v.tr.* make feeble. □ **enfeeblement** *n.* [ME f. OF *enfeblir* (as EN-¹, FEEBLE)]

enfilade /ˌenfɪˈleɪd/ *n. & v.* —*n.* gunfire directed along a line from end to end. —*v.tr.* direct an enfilade at (troops, a road, etc.). [F f. *enfiler* (as EN-¹, *fil* thread)]

enfold /ɪnˈfəʊld/ *v.tr.* (also **infold**) **1** (usu. foll. by *in, with*) wrap up; envelop. **2** clasp, embrace.

enforce /ɪnˈfɔːs/ *v.tr.* **1** compel observance of (a law etc.). **2** (foll. by *on, upon*) impose (an action, conduct, one's will). **3** persist in (a demand or argument). □ **enforceable** *adj.* **enforceability** /-səˈbɪlɪtɪ/ *n.* **enforcedly** /-sɪdlɪ/ *adv.* **enforcement** *n.* **enforcer** *n.* [ME f. OF *enforcir, -ier* ult. f. L *fortis* strong]

enfranchise /ɪnˈfræntʃaɪz/ *v.tr.* **1** give (a person) the right to vote. **2** give (a town) municipal rights, esp. that of representation in parliament. **3** *hist.* free (a slave, villein, etc.). □ **enfranchisement** /-ɪzmənt/ *n.* [OF *enfranchir* (as EN-¹, *franc franche* FRANK)]

engage /ɪnˈɡeɪdʒ/ *v.* **1** *tr.* employ or hire (a person). **2** *tr.* **a** (usu. in *passive*) employ busily; occupy (*are you engaged tomorrow?*). **b** hold fast (a person's attention). **3** *tr.* (usu. in *passive*) bind by a promise, esp. of marriage. **4** *tr.* (usu. foll. by + infin.) bind by a contract. **5** *tr.* arrange beforehand to occupy (a room, seat, etc.). **6** (usu. foll. by *with*) *Mech.* **a** *tr.* interlock (parts of a gear etc.); cause (a part) to interlock. **b** *intr.* (of a part, gear, etc.) interlock. **7 a** *intr.* (usu. foll. by *with*) (of troops etc.) come into battle. **b** *tr.* bring (troops) into battle. **c** *tr.* come into battle with (an enemy etc.). **8** *intr.* take part (*engage in politics*). **9** *intr.* (foll. by *that* + clause or *to* + infin.) pledge oneself. □ **engager** *n.* [F *engager, rel. to GAGE¹]*

engaged /ɪnˈɡeɪdʒd/ *adj.* **1** under a promise to marry. **2 a** occupied, busy. **b** reserved, booked. **3** *Brit.* (of a telephone line) unavailable because already in use.

engagement /ɪnˈɡeɪdʒmənt/ *n.* **1** the act or state of engaging or being engaged. **2** an appointment with another person. **3** a betrothal. **4** an encounter between hostile forces. [F f. *engager*: see ENGAGE]

engaging /ɪnˈɡeɪdʒɪŋ/ *adj.* attractive, charming. □ **engagingly** *adv.* **engagingness** *n.*

engender /ɪnˈdʒendə(r)/ *v.tr.* give rise to; bring about (a feeling etc.). [ME f. OF *engendrer* f. L *ingenerare* (as IN-², *generare* GENERATE)]

engine /ˈendʒɪn/ *n.* **1** a mechanical contrivance consisting of several parts working together, esp. as a source of power. **2 a** a railway locomotive. **b** = *fire-engine*. **c** = *steam engine*. **3** *archaic* a machine or instrument, esp. a contrivance used in warfare. □ **engined** *adj.* (also in *comb.*). **engineless** *adj.* [OF *engin* f. L *ingenium* talent, device: cf. INGENIOUS]

engineer /ˌendʒɪˈnɪə(r)/ *n. & v.* —*n.* **1** a person qualified in a branch of engineering, esp. as a professional. **2** = *civil engineer*. **3** a person who

makes or is in charge of engines. **4** *US* the driver of a locomotive. **5** a person who designs and constructs military works; a soldier trained for this purpose. —*v.* **1** *tr.* arrange, contrive, or bring about, esp. artfully. **2** *intr.* act as an engineer. **3** *tr.* construct or manage as an engineer. □ **engineership** *n.* [ME f. OF *engigneor* f. med.L *ingeniator -oris* f. *ingeniare* (as ENGINE)]

engineering /ˌendʒɪˈnɪərɪŋ/ *n.* the application of science to the design, building, and use of machines, constructions, etc.

English /ˈɪŋɡlɪʃ/ *adj. & n.* —*adj.* of or relating to England or its people or language. —*n.* **1** the language of England, now used in many varieties in the British Isles, the United States, and most Commonwealth or Ex-Commonwealth countries. **2** (prec. by *the*; treated as *pl.*) the people of England. □ **the Queen's** (or **King's**) **English** the English language as correctly written or spoken in Britain. □ **Englishness** *n.* [OE *englisc, ænglisc* (as ANGLE, -ISH¹)]

Englishman /ˈɪŋɡlɪʃmən/ *n.* (*pl.* -**men**) a man who is English by birth or descent.

Englishwoman /ˈɪŋɡlɪʃˌwʊmən/ *n.* (*pl.* -**women**) a woman who is English by birth or descent.

engorged /ɪnˈɡɔːdʒd/ *adj.* crammed; congested with blood. □ **engorgement** *n.* [F *engorger* (as EN-¹, GORGE, -ED²)]

engraft /ɪnˈɡrɑːft/ *v.tr.* (also **ingraft**) **1** *Bot.* (usu. foll. by *into, upon*) insert (a scion of one tree into another). **2** (usu. foll. by *in*) implant (principles etc.) in a person's mind. **3** (usu. foll. by *into*) incorporate permanently. □ **engraftment** *n.*

engrave /ɪnˈɡreɪv/ *v.tr.* **1** (often foll. by *on*) inscribe, cut, or carve (a text or design) on a hard surface. **2** (often foll. by *with*) inscribe or ornament (a surface) in this way. **3** cut (a design) as lines on a metal plate for printing. **4** (often foll. by *on*) impress deeply on a person's memory etc. □ **engraver** *n.* [EN-¹ + GRAVE³]

engraving /ɪnˈɡreɪvɪŋ/ *n.* a print made from an engraved plate.

engross /ɪnˈɡrəʊs/ *v.tr.* **1** absorb the attention of; occupy fully (*engrossed in studying*). **2** make a fair copy of (a legal document). **3** reproduce (a document etc.) in larger letters or larger format. □ **engrossing** *adj.* (in sense 1). **engrossment** *n.* [ME f. AF *engrosser*: senses 2 and 3 f. *en* in + *grosse* large writing: sense 1 f. *en gros* wholesale]

engulf /ɪnˈɡʌlf/ *v.tr.* (also **ingulf**) **1** flow over and swamp; overwhelm. **2** swallow or plunge into a gulf. □ **engulfment** *n.*

enhance /ɪnˈhɑːns/ *v.tr.* heighten or intensify (qualities, powers, value, etc.); improve (something already of good quality). □ **enhancement** *n.* **enhancer** *n.* [ME f. AF *enhauncer*, prob. alt. f. OF *enhaucier* ult. f. L *altus* high]

enharmonic /ˌenhɑːˈmɒnɪk/ *adj. Mus.* of or having intervals smaller than a semitone. □ **enharmonically** *adv.* [LL *enharmonicus* f. Gk *enarmonikos* (as EN-², *harmonia* HARMONY)]

enigma /ɪˈnɪɡmə/ *n.* **1** a puzzling thing or person. **2** a riddle or paradox. □ **enigmatic** /ˌenɪɡˈmætɪk/ *adj.* **enigmatical** /ˌenɪɡˈmætɪk(ə)l/ *adj.* **enigmatically** /ˌenɪɡˈmætɪkəlɪ/ *adv.* **enigmatize** *v.tr.* (also -**ise**). [L *aenigma* f. Gk *ainigma -matos* f. *ainissomai* speak allusively f. *ainos* fable]

enjoin /ɪnˈdʒɔɪn/ *v.tr.* **1 a** (foll. by *to* + infin.) command or order (a person). **b** (foll. by *that* +

clause) issue instructions. **2** (often foll. by *on*) impose or prescribe (an action or conduct). **3** (usu. foll. by *from*) *Law* prohibit (a person) by order. □ **enjoinment** *n.* [ME f. OF *enjoindre* f. L *injungere* (as IN-², *jungere* join)]

enjoy /ɪnˈdʒɔɪ/ *v.tr.* **1** take delight or pleasure in. **2** have the use or benefit of. **3** *iron.* experience (*enjoy poor health*). □ **enjoy oneself** experience pleasure. □ **enjoyer** *n.* **enjoyment** *n.* [ME f. OF *enjoier* give joy to or *enjoïr* enjoy, ult. f. L *gaudēre* rejoice]

enjoyable /ɪnˈdʒɔɪəb(ə)l/ *adj.* pleasant; giving enjoyment. □ **enjoyability** /-ˈbɪlɪtɪ/ *n.* **enjoyableness** *n.* **enjoyably** *adv.*

enkephalin /enˈkefəlɪn/ *n.* (also **encephalin** /enˈsef-/) *Biochem.* either of two morphine-like peptides occurring naturally in the brain and thought to control levels of pain. [Gk *egkephalos* brain]

enkindle /ɪnˈkɪnd(ə)l/ *v.tr. literary* **1 a** cause (flames) to flare up. **b** stimulate (feeling, passion, etc.). **2** inflame with passion.

enlarge /ɪnˈlɑːdʒ/ *v.* **1** *tr.* & *intr.* make or become larger or wider. **2 a** *tr.* describe in greater detail. **b** *intr.* (usu. foll. by *upon*) expatiate. **3** *tr. Photog.* produce an enlargement of (a negative). [ME f. OF *enlarger* (as EN-¹, LARGE)]

enlargement /ɪnˈlɑːdʒmənt/ *n.* **1** the act or an instance of enlarging; the state of being enlarged. **2** *Photog.* a print that is larger than the negative from which it is produced.

enlarger /ɪnˈlɑːdʒə(r)/ *n. Photog.* an apparatus for enlarging or reducing negatives or positives.

enlighten /ɪnˈlaɪt(ə)n/ *v.tr.* **1** (often foll. by *on*) instruct or inform (about a subject). **2** (esp. as **enlightened** *adj.*) free from prejudice or superstition. **3** *rhet.* or *poet.* **a** shed light on (an object). **b** give spiritual insight to (a person). □ **enlightener** *n.*

enlightenment /ɪnˈlaɪt(ə)nmənt/ *n.* **1** the act or an instance of enlightening; the state of being enlightened. **2** (**the Enlightenment**) the 18th-c. philosophy emphasizing reason and individualism rather than tradition.

enlist /ɪnˈlɪst/ *v.* **1** *intr.* & *tr.* enrol in the armed services. **2** *tr.* secure as a means of help or support. □ **enlisted man** *US* a soldier or sailor below the rank of officer. □ **enlister** *n.* **enlistment** *n.*

enliven /ɪnˈlaɪv(ə)n/ *v.tr.* **1** give life or spirit to. **2** make cheerful, brighten (a picture or scene). □ **enlivener** *n.* **enlivenment** *n.*

en masse /ɑ̃ ˈmæs/ *adv.* **1** all together. **2** in a mass. [F]

enmesh /ɪnˈmeʃ/ *v.tr.* entangle in or as in a net. □ **enmeshment** *n.*

enmity /ˈenmɪtɪ/ *n.* (*pl.* **-ies**) **1** the state of being an enemy. **2** a feeling of hostility. [ME f. OF *enemitié* f. Rmc (as ENEMY)]

ennoble /ɪˈnəʊb(ə)l/ *v.tr.* **1** make (a person) a noble. **2** make noble; elevate. □ **ennoblement** *n.* [F *ennoblir* (as EN-¹, NOBLE)]

ennui /ɒnˈwiː/ *n.* mental weariness from lack of occupation or interest; boredom. [F f. L *in odio*: cf. ODIUM]

enormity /ɪˈnɔːmɪtɪ/ *n.* (*pl.* **-ies**) **1** extreme wickedness. **2** an act of extreme wickedness. **3** a serious error. **4** great size; enormousness.

[ME f. F *énormité* f. L *enormitas* *-tatis* f. *enormis* (as ENORMOUS)]

■ **Usage** Sense 4, 'great size', is commonly found but is regarded as incorrect by some people.

enormous /ɪˈnɔːməs/ *adj.* very large; huge. □ **enormously** *adv.* **enormousness** *n.* [L *enormis* (as E-, *norma* pattern, standard)]

enough /ɪˈnʌf/ *adj.*, *n.*, *adv.*, & *int.* —*adj.* as much or as many as required (*we have enough apples; earned enough money to buy a house*). —*n.* an amount or quantity that is enough (*we have enough of everything now*). —*adv.* **1** to the required degree, adequately (*are you warm enough?*). **2** fairly (*she sings well enough*). **3** very, quite (*you know well enough what I mean*). —*int.* that is enough (in various senses, esp. to put an end to an action, thing said, etc.). □ **have had enough of** want no more of; be satiated with or tired of. [OE *genog* f. Gmc]

en passant /ɑ̃ pæˈsɑ̃/ *adv.* by the way. [F, = in passing]

enprint /ˈenprɪnt/ *n.* a standard-sized photographic print. [*enlarged print*]

enquire /ɪnˈkwaɪə(r), ɪŋ-/ *v.* **1** *intr.* (often foll. by *of*) seek information; ask a question (of a person). **2** *intr.* = INQUIRE. **3** *intr.* (foll. by *after, for*) ask about a person, a person's health, etc. **4** *intr.* (foll. by *for*) ask about the availability of. **5** *tr.* ask for information as to (*enquired my name; enquired whether we were coming*). □ **enquirer** *n.* [ME *enquere* f. OF *enquerre* ult. f. L *inquirere* (as IN-², *quaerere quaesit-* seek)]

enquiry /ɪnˈkwaɪərɪ, ɪŋ-/ *n.* (*pl.* **-ies**) **1** the act or an instance of asking or seeking information. **2** = INQUIRY.

enrage /ɪnˈreɪdʒ/ *v.tr.* (often foll. by *at, by, with*) make furious. □ **enragement** *n.* [F *enrager* (as EN-¹, RAGE)]

enrapture /ɪnˈræptʃə(r)/ *v.tr.* give intense delight to.

enrich /ɪnˈrɪtʃ/ *v.tr.* **1** make rich or richer. **2** make richer in quality, flavour, nutritive value, etc. **3** add to the contents of (a collection, museum, or book). **4** increase the content of an isotope in (material) esp. enrich uranium with isotope U-235. □ **enrichment** *n.* [ME f. OF *enrichir* (as EN-¹, RICH)]

enrol /ɪnˈrəʊl/ *v.* (*US* **enroll**) (**enrolled, enrolling**) **1** *intr.* enter one's name on a list, esp. as a commitment to membership. **2** *tr.* **a** write the name of (a person) on a list. **b** (usu. foll. by *in*) incorporate (a person) as a member of a society etc. **3** *tr.* record. □ **enrollee** /-ˈliː/ *n.* **enroller** *n.* [ME f. OF *enroller* (as EN-¹, *rolle* ROLL)]

enrolment /ɪnˈrəʊlmənt/ *n.* (*US* **enrollment**) **1** the act or an instance of enrolling; the state of being enrolled. **2** *US* the number of persons enrolled, esp. at a school or college.

en route /ɑ̃ ˈruːt/ *adv.* (usu. foll. by *to, for*) on the way. [F]

ensconce /ɪnˈskɒns/ *v.tr.* (usu. *refl.* or in *passive*) establish or settle comfortably, safely, or secretly.

ensemble /ɒnˈsɒmb(ə)l/ *n.* **1 a** a thing viewed as the sum of its parts. **b** the general effect of this. **2** a set of clothes worn together; an outfit. **3** a group of actors, dancers, musicians, etc. performing together. **4** *Mus.* a concerted passage for an ensemble. [F, ult. f. L *insimul* (as IN-², *simul* at the same time)]

enshrine /ɪnˈʃraɪn/ v.tr. **1** enclose in or as in a shrine. **2** serve as a shrine for. **3** preserve or cherish. □ **enshrinement** n.

enshroud /ɪnˈʃraʊd/ v.tr. literary **1** cover with or as with a shroud. **2** cover completely; hide from view.

ensign /ˈensaɪn, -s(ə)n/ n. **1 a** a banner or flag, esp. the military or naval flag of a nation. **b** Brit. a flag with the union in the corner. **2** a standard-bearer. **3** a hist. the lowest commissioned infantry officer. **b** US the lowest commissioned officer in the navy. □ **ensigncy** n. [ME f. OF enseigne f. L insignia: see INSIGNIA]

ensilage /ˈensɪlɪdʒ/ n. & v. —n. = SILAGE. —v.tr. treat (fodder) by ensilage. [F (as ENSILE)]

ensile /ɪnˈsaɪl/ v.tr. **1** put (fodder) into a silo. **2** preserve (fodder) in a silo. [F ensiler f. Sp. ensilar (as EN-¹, SILO)]

enslave /ɪnˈsleɪv/ v.tr. make (a person) a slave. □ **enslavement** n. **enslaver** n.

ensnare /ɪnˈsneə(r)/ v.tr. catch in or as in a snare; entrap. □ **ensnarement** n.

ensue /ɪnˈsjuː/ v.intr. **1** happen afterwards. **2** (often foll. by from, on) occur as a result. [ME f. OF ensuivre ult. f. L sequi follow]

en suite /ɑ̃ ˈswiːt/ adv. forming a single unit (bedroom with bathroom en suite). [F, = in sequence]

ensure /ɪnˈʃʊə(r)/ v.tr. **1** (often foll. by that + clause) make certain. **2** (usu. foll. by to, for) secure (a thing for a person etc.). **3** (usu. foll. by against) make safe. □ **ensurer** n. [ME f. AF enseürer f. OF aseürer ASSURE]

ENT abbr. ear, nose, and throat.

-ent /ənt, ent/ suffix **1** forming adjectives denoting attribution of an action (consequent) or state (existent). **2** forming nouns denoting an agent (coefficient; president). [from or after F -ent or L -ent- pres. part. stem of verbs (cf. -ANT)]

entablature /ɪnˈtæblətʃə(r)/ n. Archit. the upper part of a classical building supported by columns or a colonnade, comprising architrave, frieze, and cornice. [It. intavolatura f. intavolare board up (as IN-², tavola table)]

entail /ɪnˈteɪl, en-/ v. & n. —v.tr. **1** necessitate or involve unavoidably (the work entails much effort). **2** Law bequeath (property etc.) so that it remains within a family. **3** (usu. foll. by on) bestow (a thing) inalienably. —n. Law **1** an entailed estate. **2** the succession to such an estate. □ **entailment** n. [ME, f. EN-¹ + AF taille TAIL²]

entangle /ɪnˈtæŋg(ə)l/ v.tr. **1** cause to get caught in a snare or among obstacles. **2** cause to become tangled. **3** involve in difficulties or illicit activities. **4** make (a thing) tangled or intricate; complicate. □ **entanglement** n.

entente /ɒnˈtɒnt/ n. **1** = ENTENTE CORDIALE. **2** a group of States in such a relation. [F, = understanding (as INTENT)]

entente cordiale /ɑ̃ˌtɑ̃t kɔːdrˈɑːl/ n. a friendly understanding between States, esp. (often **Entente Cordiale**) that reached in 1904 between Britain and France. [F, = cordial understanding: see ENTENTE]

enter /ˈentə(r)/ v. **1 a** intr. (often foll. by into) go or come in. **b** tr. go or come into. **c** intr. come on stage (as a direction: enter Macbeth). **2** tr. penetrate; go through (a bullet entered his chest). **3** tr. (often foll. by up) write (a name, details, etc.) in a list, book, etc. **4 a** intr. register or announce oneself as a competitor (entered for the long jump). **b** tr. become a competitor in (an event). **c** tr. record the name of (a person etc.) as a competitor (entered two horses for the Derby). **5** tr. **a** become a member of (a society etc.). **b** enrol as a member or prospective member of a society, school, etc.; admit or obtain admission for. **6** tr. make known; present for consideration (entered a protest). **7** tr. put into an official record. **8** intr. (foll. by into) engage in (conversation, relations, an undertaking, etc.). **b** subscribe to; bind oneself by (an agreement etc.). **c** form part of (one's calculations, plans, etc.). **d** sympathize with (feelings etc.). **9** intr. (foll. by on, upon) **a** begin, undertake; begin to deal with (a subject). **b** assume the functions of (an office). **c** assume possession of (property). □ **enterer** n. [ME f. OF entrer f. L intrare]

enteric /enˈterɪk/ adj. & n. —adj. of the intestines. —n. (in full **enteric fever**) typhoid. □ **enteritis** /ˌentəˈraɪtɪs/ n. [Gk enterikos (as ENTERO-)]

entero- /ˈentərəʊ/ comb. form intestine. [Gk enteron intestine]

enterprise /ˈentəˌpraɪz/ n. **1** an undertaking, esp. a bold or difficult one. **2** (as a personal attribute) readiness to engage in such undertakings (has no enterprise). **3** a business firm. □ **enterpriser** n. [ME f. OF entreprise fem. past part. of entreprendre var. of emprendre ult. f. L prendere, prehendere take]

enterprising /ˈentəˌpraɪzɪŋ/ adj. **1** ready to engage in enterprises. **2** resourceful, imaginative, energetic. □ **enterprisingly** adv.

entertain /ˌentəˈteɪn/ v.tr. **1** amuse; occupy agreeably. **2 a** receive or treat as a guest. **b** (absol.) receive guests (they entertain a great deal). **3** give attention or consideration to (an idea, feeling, or proposal). [ME f. F entretenir ult. f. L tenēre hold]

entertainer /ˌentəˈteɪnə(r)/ n. a person who entertains, esp. professionally on stage etc.

entertaining /ˌentəˈteɪnɪŋ/ adj. amusing, diverting.

entertainment /ˌentəˈteɪnmənt/ n. **1** the act or an instance of entertaining; the process of being entertained. **2** a public performance or show. **3** diversions or amusements for guests etc. **4** amusement (much to my entertainment). **5** hospitality.

enthral /ɪnˈθrɔːl/ v.tr. (US **enthrall**, **inthrall**) (**-thralled**, **-thralling**) **1** captivate, please greatly. **2** enslave. □ **enthralment** n. (US **enthrallment**). [EN-¹ + THRALL]

enthrone /ɪnˈθrəʊn/ v.tr. **1** install (a king, bishop, etc.) on a throne, esp. ceremonially. **2** exalt. □ **enthronement** n.

enthuse /ɪnˈθjuːz, -ˈθuːz/ v.intr. & tr. colloq. be or make enthusiastic. [back-form. f. ENTHUSIASM]

enthusiasm /ɪnˈθjuːzɪˌæz(ə)m, -ˈθuːzɪˌæz(ə)m/ n. **1** (often foll. by for, about) **a** strong interest or admiration. **b** great eagerness. **2** an object of enthusiasm. [F enthousiasme or LL enthusiasmus f. Gk enthousiasmos f. entheos possessed by a god, inspired (as EN-², theos god)]

enthusiast /ɪnˈθjuːzɪˌæst, -ˈθuːzɪˌæst/ n. (often foll. by for) a person who is full of enthusiasm. [F enthousiaste or eccl.L enthusiastes f. Gk (as ENTHUSIASM)]

enthusiastic /ɪnˌθjuːzɪˈæstɪk, -ˌθuːzɪˈæstɪk/ *adj.* having or showing enthusiasm. □ **enthusiastically** *adv.* [Gk *enthousiastikos* (as ENTHUSIASM)]

entice /ɪnˈtaɪs/ *v.tr.* (often foll. by *from, into,* or *to* + infin.) persuade by the offer of pleasure or reward. □ **enticement** *n.* **enticer** *n.* **enticingly** *adv.* [ME f. OF *enticier* prob. f. Rmc]

entire /ɪnˈtaɪə(r)/ *adj.* 1 whole, complete. 2 not broken or decayed. 3 unqualified, absolute (*an entire success*). 4 in one piece; continuous. [ME f. AF *enter,* OF *entier* f. L *integer* (as IN-², *tangere* touch)]

entirely /ɪnˈtaɪəlɪ/ *adv.* 1 wholly, completely (*the stock is entirely exhausted*). 2 solely, exclusively (*did it entirely for my benefit*).

entirety /ɪnˈtaɪərətɪ/ *n.* (pl. **-ies**) 1 completeness. 2 (usu. foll. by *of*) the sum total. □ **in its entirety** in its complete form; completely. [ME f. OF *entiereté* f. L *integritas -tatis* f. *integer*: see ENTIRE]

entitle /ɪnˈtaɪt(ə)l/ *v.tr.* 1 a (usu. foll. by *to*) give (a person etc.) a just claim. b (foll. by *to* + infin.) give (a person etc.) a right. 2 give (a book etc.) the title of. □ **entitlement** *n.* [ME f. AF *entitler,* OF *entiteler* f. LL *intitulare* (as IN-², TITLE)]

entity /ˈentɪtɪ/ *n.* (pl. **-ies**) 1 a thing with distinct existence, as opposed to a quality or relation. 2 a thing's existence regarded distinctly. □ **entitative** /-tətɪv/ *adj.* [F *entité* or med.L *entitas* f. LL *ens* being]

entomb /ɪnˈtuːm/ *v.tr.* 1 place in or as in a tomb. 2 serve as a tomb for. □ **entombment** *n.* [OF *entomber* (as EN-¹, TOMB)]

entomo- /ˈentəməʊ/ *comb. form* insect. [Gk *entomos* cut up (in neut. = INSECT) f. EN-² + *temnō* cut]

entomology /ˌentəˈmɒlədʒɪ/ *n.* the study of the forms and behaviour of insects. □ **entomological** /-məˈlɒdʒɪk(ə)l/ *adj.* **entomologist** *n.* [F *entomologie* or mod.L *entomologia* (as ENTOMO-, -LOGY)]

entourage /ˌɒntʊəˈrɑːʒ/ *n.* 1 people attending an important person. 2 surroundings. [F f. *entourer* surround]

entr'acte /ˈɒntrækt/ *n.* 1 an interval between two acts of a play. 2 a piece of music or a dance performed during this. [F f. *entre* between + *acte* act]

entrails /ˈentreɪlz/ *n.pl.* 1 the bowels and intestines of a person or animal. 2 the innermost parts (*entrails of the earth*). [ME f. OF *entrailles* f. med.L *intralia* alt. f. L *interaneus* internal f. *inter* among]

entrance¹ /ˈentrəns/ *n.* 1 the act or an instance of going or coming in. 2 a door, passage, etc., by which one enters. 3 right of admission. 4 the coming of an actor on stage. [OF (as ENTER, -ANCE)]

entrance² /ɪnˈtrɑːns/ *v.tr.* 1 enchant, delight. 2 put into a trance. □ **entrancement** *n.* **entrancing** *adj.* **entrancingly** *adv.*

entrant /ˈentrənt/ *n.* a person who enters (esp. an examination, profession, etc.). [F, part. of *entrer*: see ENTER]

entrap /ɪnˈtræp/ *v.tr.* (**entrapped, entrapping**) 1 catch in or as in a trap. 2 (often foll. by *into* + verbal noun) beguile or trick (a person). □ **entrapper** *n.* [OF *entraper* (as EN-¹, TRAP¹)]

entrapment /ɪnˈtræpmənt/ *n.* 1 the act or an instance of entrapping; the process of being entrapped. 2 *Law* inducement to commit a

crime, esp. by the authorities to secure a prosecution.

entreat /ɪnˈtriːt/ *v.tr.* 1 (foll. by *to* + infin. or *that* + clause) ask (a person) earnestly. 2 ask earnestly for (a thing). □ **entreatingly** *adv.* [ME f. OF *entraiter* (as EN-¹, *traiter* TREAT)]

entreaty /ɪnˈtriːtɪ/ *n.* (pl. **-ies**) an earnest request; a supplication. [ENTREAT, after TREATY]

entrecôte /ˈɒntrəˌkəʊt/ *n.* a boned steak cut off the sirloin. [F f. *entre* between + *côte* rib]

entrée /ˈɒntreɪ, ˈɑːtreɪ/ *n.* 1 *Cookery* a *Brit.* a dish served between the fish and meat courses. b esp. *US* the main dish of a meal. 2 the right or privilege of admission, esp. at Court. [F, = ENTRY]

entrench /ɪnˈtrentʃ/ *v.* (also **intrench**) 1 *tr.* establish firmly (in a defensible position, in office, etc.). 2 *tr.* surround (a post, army, town, etc.) with a trench as a fortification. 3 *intr.* entrench oneself. □ **entrenchment** *n.*

entrepôt /ˈɒntrəˌpəʊ/ *n.* 1 a warehouse for temporary storage of goods in transit. 2 a commercial centre for import and export, and for collection and distribution. [F f. *entreposer* store f. *entre-* INTER- + *poser* place]

entrepreneur /ˌɒntrəprəˈnɜː(r)/ *n.* 1 a person who undertakes an enterprise or business, with the chance of profit or loss. 2 a contractor acting as an intermediary. 3 the person in effective control of a commercial undertaking. □ **entrepreneurial** /-ˈnɜːrɪəl, -ˈnjʊərɪəl/ *adj.* **entrepreneurialism** /-ˈnɜːrɪəˌlɪz(ə)m, -ˈnjʊərɪəˌlɪz(ə)m/ *n.* (also **entrepreneurism**). **entrepreneurially** /-ˈnɜːrɪəlɪ, -ˈnjʊərɪəlɪ/ *adv.* **entrepreneurship** *n.* [F f. *entreprendre* undertake: see ENTERPRISE]

entropy /ˈentrəpɪ/ *n.* 1 *Physics* a measure of the unavailability of a system's thermal energy for conversion into mechanical work. 2 *Physics* a measure of the disorganization or degradation of the universe. □ **entropic** /-ˈtrɒpɪk/ *adj.* **entropically** /-ˈtrɒpɪkəlɪ/ *adv.* [G *Entropie* (as EN-², Gk *tropē* transformation)]

entrust /ɪnˈtrʌst/ *v.tr.* (also **intrust**) 1 (foll. by *to*) give responsibility for (a person or a thing) to a person in whom one has confidence. 2 (foll. by *with*) assign responsibility for a thing to (a person). □ **entrustment** *n.*

entry /ˈentrɪ/ *n.* (pl. **-ies**) 1 a the act or an instance of going or coming in. b the coming of an actor on stage. c ceremonial entrance. 2 liberty to go or come in. 3 a a place of entrance; a door, gate, etc. b a lobby. 4 *Brit.* a passage between buildings. 5 the mouth of a river. 6 a an item entered in a diary, list, account-book, etc. b the recording of this. 7 a a person or thing competing in a race, contest, etc. b a list of competitors. 8 the start or resumption of music for a particular instrument in an ensemble. 9 *Law* the act of taking possession. [ME f. OF *entree* ult. f. L *intrare* ENTER]

entryism /ˈentrɪˌɪz(ə)m/ *n.* (also **entrism**) infiltration into a political organization to change or subvert its policies or objectives. □ **entrist** *n.* **entryist** *n.*

Entryphone /ˈentrɪˌfəʊn/ *n. propr.* an intercom device at an entrance to a building by which callers may identify themselves to gain admission.

entwine /ɪnˈtwaɪn/ *v.tr.* (also **intwine**) 1 (foll. by *with, about, round*) twine together (a thing with or round another). **2** interweave. □ **entwinement** *n.*

E-number /ˈiːˌnʌmbə(r)/ *n.* the letter E followed by a code number, designating food additives according to EC directives.

enumerate /ɪˈnjuːməˌreɪt/ *v.tr.* **1** specify (items); mention one by one. **2** count; establish the number of. □ **enumerable** *adj.* **enumeration** /-ˈreɪʃ(ə)n/ *n.* **enumerative** /-rətɪv/ *adj.* [L *enumerare* (as E-, NUMBER)]

enumerator /ɪˈnjuːməˌreɪtə(r)/ *n.* **1** a person who enumerates. **2** a person employed in census-taking.

enunciate /ɪˈnʌnsɪˌeɪt/ *v.tr.* **1** pronounce (words) clearly. **2** express (a proposition or theory) in definite terms. **3** proclaim. □ **enunciation** /-ˈeɪʃ(ə)n/ *n.* **enunciative** /-sɪətɪv/ *adj.* **enunciator** *n.* [L *enuntiare* (as E-, *nuntiare* announce f. *nuntius* messenger)]

enure /ɪˈnjʊə(r)/ *v.intr. Law* take effect. [var. of INURE]

enuresis /ˌenjʊəˈriːsɪs/ *n. Med.* involuntary urination. □ **enuretic** /-ˈretɪk/ *adj.* & *n.* [mod.L f. Gk *enoureō* urinate in (as EN-2, *ouron* urine)]

envelop /ɪnˈveləp/ *v.tr.* (**enveloped, enveloping**) (often foll. by *in*) **1** wrap up or cover completely. **2** make obscure; conceal (*was enveloped in mystery*). □ **envelopment** *n.* [ME f. OF *envoluper* (as EN-1: cf. DEVELOP)]

envelope /ˈenvəˌləʊp, ˈɒn-/ *n.* **1** a folded paper container, usu. with a sealable flap, for a letter etc. **2** a wrapper or covering. **3** the structure within a balloon or airship containing the gas. **4** the outer metal or glass housing of a vacuum tube, electric light, etc. [F *enveloppe* (as ENVELOP)]

envenom /ɪnˈvenəm/ *v.tr.* **1** put poison on or into; make poisonous. **2** infuse venom or bitterness into (feelings, words, or actions). [ME f. OF *envenimer* (as EN-1, *venim* VENOM)]

enviable /ˈenvɪəb(ə)l/ *adj.* (of a person or thing) exciting or likely to excite envy. □ **enviably** *adv.*

envious /ˈenvɪəs/ *adj.* (often foll. by *of*) feeling or showing envy. □ **enviously** *adv.* [ME f. AF *envious*, OF *envieus* f. *envie* ENVY]

environment /ɪnˈvaɪərənmənt/ *n.* **1** physical surroundings and conditions, esp. as affecting people's lives. **2** conditions or circumstances of living. **3** *Ecol.* external conditions affecting the growth of plants and animals. **4** *Computing* the overall structure within which a user, computer, or program operates. □ **environment-friendly** *adj.* not harmful to the environment. □ **environmental** /-ˈment(ə)l/ *adj.* **environmentally** /-ˈmentəlɪ/ *adv.* [ME f. OF *environ* surroundings f. *en* in + *viron* circuit f. *virer* turn, VEER]

environmentalist /ɪnˌvaɪərənˈmentəlɪst/ *n.* a person who is concerned with or advocates the protection of the environment. □ **environmentalism** *n.*

environs /ɪnˈvaɪərɒnz, ˈenvɪrɒnz/ *n.pl.* a surrounding district, esp. round an urban area.

envisage /ɪnˈvɪzɪdʒ/ *v.tr.* **1** have a mental picture of (a thing or conditions not yet existing). **2** contemplate or conceive, esp. as possible or desirable. □ **envisagement** *n.* [F *envisager* (as EN-1, VISAGE)]

envision /ɪnˈvɪʒ(ə)n/ *v.tr.* envisage, visualize.

envoy /ˈenvɔɪ/ *n.* **1** a messenger or representative, esp. on a diplomatic mission. **2** (in full **envoy extraordinary**) a minister plenipotentiary,

ranking below ambassador and above chargé d'affaires. □ **envoyship** *n.* [F *envoyé*, past part. of *envoyer* send f. *en voie* on the way f. L *via*]

envy /ˈenvɪ/ *n.* & *v.* —*n.* (pl. **-ies**) **1** a feeling of discontented or resentful longing aroused by another's better fortune etc. **2** the object or ground of this feeling (*their house is the envy of the neighbourhood*). —*v.tr.* (**-ies, -ied**) feel envy of (a person, circumstances, etc.) (*I envy you your position*). □ **envier** *n.* [ME f. OF *envie* f. L *invidia* f. *invidēre* envy (as IN-1, *vidēre* see)]

enwrap /ɪnˈræp/ *v.tr.* (also **inwrap**) (**-wrapped, -wrapping**) (often foll. by *in*) *literary* wrap or enfold.

Enzed /enˈzed/ *n. Austral.* & *NZ colloq.* a popular written form of: **1** New Zealand. **2** a New Zealander. □ **Enzedder** *n.* [pronunc. of NZ]

enzyme /ˈenzaɪm/ *n. Biochem.* a protein acting as a catalyst in a specific biochemical reaction. □ **enzymatic** /-ˈmætɪk/ *adj.* **enzymic** /-ˈzaɪmɪk/ *adj.* **enzymology** /-ˈmɒlədʒɪ/ *n.* [G *Enzym* f. med. Gk *enzumos* leavened f. Gk *en* in + *zumē* leaven]

Eocene /ˈiːəʊˌsiːn/ *adj.* & *n. Geol.* —*adj.* of or relating to the second epoch of the Tertiary period. —*n.* this epoch or system. [Gk *ēōs* dawn + *kainos* new]

eolian *US* var. of AEOLIAN.

eolithic /ˌiːəˈlɪθɪk/ *adj. Archaeol.* of the period preceding the palaeolithic age, thought to include the earliest use of flint tools. [F *éolithique* f. Gk *ēōs* dawn + *lithos* stone]

eon var. of AEON.

-eous /ɪəs/ *suffix* forming adjectives meaning 'of the nature of' (*erroneous; gaseous*).

EP *abbr.* **1** electroplate. **2** extended-play (gramophone record).

ep- /ep, ɪp, iːp/ *prefix* form of EPI- before a vowel or *h*.

epaulette /ˈepələt, ˈepɔːˌlet, ˈepəʊˌlet, ˌepəˈlet/ *n.* (*US* **epaulet**) an ornamental shoulder-piece on a coat, dress, etc., esp. on a uniform. [F *épaulette* dimin. of *épaule* shoulder f. L *spatula*: see SPATULA]

épée /eɪˈpeɪ/ *n.* a sharp-pointed duelling-sword, used (with the end blunted) in fencing. □ **épéeist** *n.* [F, = sword, f. OF *espee*: see SPAY]

ephedrine /ˈefədrɪn/ *n.* an alkaloid drug used to relieve asthma, etc. [f. *ephedra* evergreen shrub yielding drug + -INE4]

ephemera[1] /ɪˈfemərə, ɪˈfiːm-/ *n.* (pl. **ephemeras** or **ephemerae** /-ˌriː/) **1 a** an insect living only a day or a few days. **b** any insect of the order Ephemeroptera, e.g. the mayfly. **2** = EPHEMERON. [mod.L f. Gk *ephēmeros* lasting only a day (as EPI-, *hēmera* day)]

ephemera[2] *pl.* of EPHEMERON 1.

ephemeral /ɪˈfemər(ə)l, ɪˈfiːm-/ *adj.* **1** lasting or of use for only a short time; transitory. **2** lasting only a day. **3** (of an insect, flower, etc.) lasting a day or a few days. □ **ephemerality** /-ˈrælɪtɪ/ *n.* **ephemerally** *adv.* **ephemeralness** *n.* [Gk *ephēmeros*: see EPHEMERA1]

ephemerist /ɪˈfemərɪst/ *n.* a collector of ephemera.

ephemeron /ɪˈfemərən, ɪˈfiːm-/ *n.* **1** (pl. **ephemera** /-rə/) (usu. in pl.) **a** a thing (esp. a printed item) of short-lived interest or usefulness. **b** a short-lived thing. **2** (pl. **ephemerons**) = EPHEMERA1 1. [as EPHEMERA1]

epi- /ˈepɪ-/ *prefix* (usu. **ep-** before a vowel or *h*) **1** upon. **2** above. **3** in addition. [Gk *epi* (prep.)]

epic /ˈepɪk/ n. & adj. —n. **1** a long poem narrating the adventures or deeds of one or more heroic or legendary figures. **2** an imaginative work of any form, embodying a nation's conception of its past history. **3** a book or film based on an epic narrative or heroic in type or scale. **4** a subject fit for recital in an epic. —adj. **1** of or like an epic. **2** grand, heroic. □ **epical** adj. **epically** adv. [L epicus f. Gk epikos f. epos word, song]

epicene /ˈepɪˌsiːn/ adj. & n. —adj. **1** Gram. denoting either sex without change of gender. **2** of, for, or used by both sexes. **3** having characteristics of both sexes. **4** having no characteristics of either sex. **5** effete, effeminate. —n. an epicene person. [ME f. LL epicoenus f. Gk epikoinos (as EPI-, koinos common)]

epicentre /ˈepɪˌsentə(r)/ n. (US **epicenter**) **1** Geol. the point at which an earthquake reaches the earth's surface. **2** the central point of a difficulty. □ **epicentral** /-ˈsentr(ə)l/ adj. [Gk epikentros (adj.) (as EPI-, CENTRE)]

epicure /ˈepɪˌkjʊə(r)/ n. a person with refined tastes, esp. in food and drink. □ **epicurism** n. [med.L epicurus one preferring sensual enjoyment: see EPICUREAN]

Epicurean /ˌepɪkjʊəˈriːən/ n. & adj. —n. **1** a disciple or student of the Greek philosopher Epicurus (d. 270 BC), who taught that the highest good is personal happiness. **2** (**epicurean**) a person devoted to (esp. sensual) enjoyment. —adj. **1** of or concerning Epicurus or his ideas. **2** (**epicurean**) characteristic of an epicurean. □ **Epicureanism** n. [F épicurien or L epicureus f. Gk epikoureios f. Epikouros Epicurus]

epidemic /ˌepɪˈdemɪk/ n. & adj. —n. **1** a widespread occurrence of a disease in a community at a particular time. **2** such a disease. **3** (foll. by of) a wide prevalence of something usu. undesirable. —adj. in the nature of an epidemic. □ **epidemically** adv. [F épidémique f. épidémie f. LL epidemia f. Gk epidēmia prevalence of disease f. epidēmios (adj.) (as EPI-, dēmos the people)]

epidemiology /ˌepɪdiːmɪˈɒlədʒɪ/ n. the study of the incidence and distribution of diseases, and of their control and prevention. □ **epidemiological** /-mɪəˈlɒdʒɪk(ə)l/ adj. **epidemiologist** n.

epidermis /ˌepɪˈdɜːmɪs/ n. **1** the outer cellular layer of the skin. **2** Bot. the outer layer of cells of leaves, stems, roots, etc. □ **epidermal** adj. **epidermic** adj. **epidermoid** adj. [LL f. Gk (as EPI-, DERMIS)]

epidiascope /ˌepɪˈdaɪəˌskəʊp/ n. an optical projector capable of giving images of both opaque and transparent objects. [EPI- + DIA- + -SCOPE]

epididymis /ˌepɪˈdɪdɪmɪs/ n. (pl. **epididymides** /-ˈdɪmɪˌdiːz/) Anat. a convoluted duct behind the testis, along which sperm passes to the vas deferens. [Gk epididumis (as EPI-, didumoi testicles)]

epidural /ˌepɪˈdjʊər(ə)l/ adj. & n. —adj. **1** Anat. on or around the dura mater. **2** (of an anaesthetic) introduced into the space around the dura mater of the spinal cord. —n. an epidural anaesthetic, used esp. in childbirth to produce loss of sensation below the waist. [EPI- + DURA (MATER)]

epifauna /ˈepɪˌfɔːnə/ n. animals living on the seabed, either attached to animals, plants, etc., or free-living. [Da. (as EPI-, FAUNA)]

epiglottis /ˌepɪˈglɒtɪs/ n. Anat. a flap of cartilage at the root of the tongue, which is depressed during swallowing to cover the windpipe. □ **epiglottal** adj. **epiglottic** adj. [Gk epiglōttis (as EPI-, glōtta tongue)]

epigram /ˈepɪˌgræm/ n. **1** a short poem with a witty ending. **2** a pointed saying. **3** a pointed mode of expression. □ **epigrammatic** /-grəˈmætɪk/ adj. **epigrammatically** /-grəˈmætɪkəlɪ/ adv. **epigrammatist** /-ˈgræmətɪst/ n. **epigrammatize** /-ˈgræməˌtaɪz/ v.tr. & intr. (also **-ise**). [F épigramme or L epigramma f. Gk epigramma -atos (as EPI-, -GRAM)]

epigraph /ˈepɪˌgrɑːf/ n. an inscription on a statue or coin, at the head of a chapter, etc. [Gk epigraphē f. epigraphō (as EPI-, graphō write)]

epigraphy /eˈpɪgrəfɪ/ n. the study of (esp. ancient) inscriptions. □ **epigraphic** /-ˈgræfɪk/ adj. **epigraphical** /-ˈgræfɪk(ə)l/ adj. **epigraphically** /-ˈgræfɪkəlɪ/ adv. **epigraphist** n.

epilate /ˈepɪˌleɪt/ v.tr. remove hair from. □ **epilation** /-ˈleɪʃ(ə)n/ n. [F épiler (cf. DEPILATE)]

epilepsy /ˈepɪˌlepsɪ/ n. a nervous disorder with convulsions and often loss of consciousness. [F épilepsie or LL epilepsia f. Gk epilēpsia f. epilambanō attack (as EPI-, lambanō take)]

epileptic /ˌepɪˈleptɪk/ adj. & n. —adj. of or relating to epilepsy. —n. a person with epilepsy. [F épileptique f. LL epilepticus f. Gk epilēptikos (as EPILEPSY)]

epilogue /ˈepɪˌlɒg/ n. **1 a** the concluding part of a literary work. **b** an appendix. **2** a speech or short poem addressed to the audience by an actor at the end of a play. [ME f. F épilogue f. L epilogus f. Gk epilogos (as EPI-, logos speech)]

epiphany /eˈpɪfənɪ, ɪˈpɪf-/ n. (pl. **-ies**) **1** (**Epiphany**) **a** the manifestation of Christ to the Magi according to the biblical account. **b** the festival commemorating this on 6 January. **2** any manifestation of a god or demigod. □ **epiphanic** /ˌepɪˈfænɪk/ adj. [ME f. Gk epiphaneia manifestation f. epiphainō reveal (as EPI-, phainō show): sense 1 through OF epiphanie and eccl.L epiphania]

epiphyte /ˈepɪˌfaɪt/ n. a plant growing but not parasitic on another, e.g. a moss. □ **epiphytal** /-ˈfaɪt(ə)l/ adj. **epiphytic** /ˌepɪˈfɪtɪk/ adj. [EPI- + Gk phuton plant]

episcopacy /ɪˈpɪskəpəsɪ/ n. (pl. **-ies**) **1** government of a Church by bishops. **2** (prec. by the) the bishops.

episcopal /ɪˈpɪskəp(ə)l/ adj. **1** of a bishop or bishops. **2** (of a Church) constituted on the principle of government by bishops. □ **Episcopal Church** the Anglican Church in Scotland and the US, with elected bishops. □ **episcopalism** n. **episcopally** adv. [ME f. F épiscopal or eccl.L episcopalis f. episcopus BISHOP]

episcopalian /ɪˌpɪskəˈpeɪlɪən/ adj. & n. —adj. **1** of or advocating government of a Church by bishops. **2** of or belonging to an episcopal Church or (**Episcopalian**) the Episcopal Church. —n. **1** an adherent of episcopacy. **2** (**Episcopalian**) a member of the Episcopal Church. □ **episcopalianism** n.

episcopate /ɪˈpɪskəpət/ n. **1** the office or tenure of a bishop. **2** (prec. by the) the bishops collectively. [eccl.L episcopatus f. episcopus BISHOP]

episiotomy /eˌpɪsɪˈɒtəmɪ, eˌpiːz-/ n. (pl. **-ies**) a surgical cut made at the opening of the vagina during childbirth, to aid delivery. [Gk *epision* pubic region]

episode /ˈepɪˌsəʊd/ n. **1** one event or a group of events as part of a sequence. **2** each of the parts of a serial story or broadcast. **3** an incident or set of incidents in a narrative. **4** an incident that is distinct but contributes to a whole (*a romantic episode in her life*). [Gk *epeisodion* (as EPI- + *eisodos* entry f. *eis* into + *hodos* way)]

episodic /ˌepɪˈsɒdɪk/ adj. (also **episodical** /-ˈsɒdɪk(ə)l/) **1** in the nature of an episode. **2** sporadic; occurring at irregular intervals. □ **episodically** adv.

epistemology /ɪˌpɪstɪˈmɒlədʒɪ/ n. the theory of knowledge, esp. with regard to its methods and validation. □ **epistemological** /-məˈlɒdʒɪk(ə)l/ adj. **epistemologically** /-məˈlɒdʒɪkəlɪ/ adv. **epistemologist** n.

epistle /ɪˈpɪs(ə)l/ n. **1** formal or joc. a letter, esp. a long one on a serious subject. **2** (**Epistle**) **a** any of the letters of the apostles in the New Testament. **b** an extract from an Epistle read in a church service. **3** a poem or other literary work in the form of a letter or series of letters. [ME f. OF f. L *epistola* f. Gk *epistolē* f. *epistellō* send news (as EPI-, *stellō* send)]

epistolary /ɪˈpɪstələrɪ/ adj. **1** in the style or form of a letter or letters. **2** of, carried by, or suited to letters. [F *épistolaire* or L *epistolaris* (as EPISTLE)]

epitaph /ˈepɪˌtɑːf/ n. words written in memory of a person who has died, esp. as a tomb inscription. [ME f. OF *epitaphe* f. L *epitaphium* f. Gk *epitaphion* funeral oration (as EPI-, *taphos* tomb)]

epithelium /ˌepɪˈθiːlɪəm/ n. (pl. **epitheliums** or **epithelia** /-lɪə/) the tissue forming the outer layer of the body surface and lining many hollow structures. □ **epithelial** adj. [mod.L f. EPI- + Gk *thēlē* teat]

epithet /ˈepɪˌθet/ n. **1** an adjective or other descriptive word expressing a quality or attribute, esp. used with or as a name. **2** such a word as a term of abuse. □ **epithetic** /-ˈθetɪk/ adj. **epithetical** /-ˈθetɪk(ə)l/ adj. **epithetically** /-ˈθetɪkəlɪ/ adv. [F *épithète* or L *epitheton* f. Gk *epitheton* f. *epitithēmi* add (as EPI-, *tithēmi* place)]

epitome /ɪˈpɪtəmɪ/ n. **1** a person or thing embodying a quality, class, etc. **2** a thing representing another in miniature. **3** a summary of a written work; an abstract. □ **epitomist** n. [L f. Gk *epitomē* f. *epitemnō* abridge (as EPI-, *temnō* cut)]

epitomize /ɪˈpɪtəˌmaɪz/ v.tr. (also **-ise**) **1** be a perfect example of (a quality etc.); typify. **2** make an epitome of (a work). □ **epitomization** /-ˈzeɪʃ(ə)n/ n.

EPNS abbr. electroplated nickel silver.

epoch /ˈiːpɒk/ n. **1** a period of history or of a person's life marked by notable events. **2** the beginning of an era. **3** Geol. a division of a period, corresponding to a set of strata. □ **epoch-making** remarkable, historic; of major importance. □ **epochal** /ˈepɒk(ə)l/ adj. [mod.L *epocha* f. Gk *epokhē* stoppage]

eponym /ˈepənɪm/ n. **1** a person (real or imaginary) after whom a discovery, invention, place, institution, etc., is named or thought to be named. **2** the name given. □ **eponymous** /ɪˈpɒnɪməs/ adj. [Gk *epōnumos* (as EPI-, *-ōnumos* f. *onoma* name)]

EPOS /ˈiːpɒs/ abbr. electronic point-of-sale (of retail outlets recording information electronically).

epoxide /ɪˈpɒksaɪd/ n. Chem. a compound containing an oxygen atom bonded in a triangular arrangement to two carbon atoms. [EPI- + OXIDE]

epoxy /ɪˈpɒksɪ/ adj. Chem. relating to or derived from an epoxide. □ **epoxy resin** a synthetic thermosetting resin containing epoxy groups. [EPI- + OXY-]

epsilon /ˈepsɪˌlɒn/ n. the fifth letter of the Greek alphabet (E, ϵ). [ME f. Gk, = bare E f. *psilos* bare]

Epsom salts /ˈepsəm/ n. a preparation of magnesium sulphate used as a purgative etc. [*Epsom* in Surrey, where it was first found occurring naturally]

equable /ˈekwəb(ə)l/ adj. **1** even; not varying. **2** uniform and moderate (*an equable climate*). **3** (of a person) not easily disturbed or angered. □ **equability** /-ˈbɪlɪtɪ/ n. **equably** adv. [L *aequabilis* (as EQUATE)]

equal /ˈiːkw(ə)l/ adj., n., & v. —adj. **1** (often foll. by *to*, *with*) the same in quantity, quality, size, degree, rank, level, etc. **2** evenly balanced (*an equal contest*). **3** having the same rights or status (*human beings are essentially equal*). **4** uniform in application or effect (*equal opportunities*). —n. a person or thing equal to another, esp. in rank, status, or characteristic quality (*their treatment of the subject has no equal*; *is the equal of any man*). —v.tr. (**equalled**, **equalling**; US **equaled**, **equaling**) **1** be equal to in number, quality, etc. **2** achieve something that is equal to (an achievement) or to the achievement of (a person). □ **be equal to** have the ability or resources for. **equal opportunity** (often in pl.) the opportunity or right to be employed, paid, etc., without discrimination on grounds of sex, race, etc. **equal** (or **equals**) **sign** the symbol =. [ME f. L *aequalis* f. *aequus* even]

equality /ɪˈkwɒlɪtɪ/ n. the state of being equal. [ME f. OF *equalité* f. L *aequalitas -tatis* (as EQUAL)]

equalize /ˈiːkwəˌlaɪz/ v. (also **-ise**) **1** tr. & intr. make or become equal. **2** intr. reach one's opponent's score in a game, after being behind. □ **equalization** /-ˈzeɪʃ(ə)n/ n.

equalizer /ˈiːkwəˌlaɪzə(r)/ n. **1** an equalizing score or goal etc. in a game. **2** sl. a weapon, esp. a gun. **3** Electr. a connection in a system which compensates for any undesirable frequency or phase response with the system.

equally /ˈiːkwəlɪ/ adv. **1** in an equal manner (*treated them all equally*). **2** to an equal degree (*is equally important*).

■ **Usage** In sense 2, the construction with *as* (*equally as important*) is often found but is considered incorrect by many people.

equanimity /ˌekwəˈnɪmɪtɪ, ˌiːk-/ n. mental composure, evenness of temper, esp. in misfortune. □ **equanimous** /ɪˈkwænɪməs/ adj. [L *aequanimitas* f. *aequanimis* f. *aequus* even + *animus* mind]

equate /ɪˈkweɪt/ v. **1** tr. (usu. foll. by *to*, *with*) regard as equal or equivalent. **2** intr. (foll. by *with*) **a** be equal or equivalent to. **b** agree or correspond. □ **equatable** adj. [ME f. L *aequare aequat-* f. *aequus* equal]

equation /ɪˈkweɪʒ(ə)n/ n. **1** the process of equating or making equal; the state of being equal.

2 *Math.* a statement that two mathematical expressions are equal (indicated by the sign =). **3** *Chem.* a formula indicating a chemical reaction by means of symbols for the elements taking part. □ **equational** *adj.* [ME f. OF *equation* or L *aequatio* (as EQUATE)]

equator /ɪˈkweɪtə(r)/ *n.* **1** an imaginary line round the earth or other body, equidistant from the poles. **2** *Astron.* = *celestial equator*. [ME f. OF *equateur* or med.L *aequator* (as EQUATION)]

equatorial /ˌekwəˈtɔːrɪəl, ˌiːk-/ *adj.* of or near the equator. □ **equatorially** *adv.*

equerry /ˈekwərɪ, ɪˈkwerɪ/ *n.* (pl. **-ies**) an officer of the British royal household attending members of the royal family. [earlier *esquiry* f. OF *esquierie* company of squires, prince's stables, f. OF *esquier* ESQUIRE: perh. assoc. with L *equus* horse]

equestrian /ɪˈkwestrɪən/ *adj. & n.* —*adj.* **1** of or relating to horses and horse-riding. **2** on horseback. —*n.* (*fem.* **equestrienne** /-trɪˈen/) a rider or performer on horseback. □ **equestrianism** *n.* [L *equestris* f. *eques* horseman, knight, f. *equus* horse]

equi- /ˈiːkwɪ/ *comb. form* equal. [L *aequi-* f. *aequus* equal]

equiangular /ˌiːkwɪˈæŋɡjʊlə(r)/ *adj.* having equal angles.

equidistant /ˌiːkwɪˈdɪst(ə)nt/ *adj.* at equal distances. □ **equidistantly** *adv.*

equilateral /ˌiːkwɪˈlætər(ə)l/ *adj.* having all its sides equal in length.

equilibrium /ˌiːkwɪˈlɪbrɪəm/ *n.* (pl. **equilibria** /-rɪə/ or **equilibriums**) **1** a state of physical balance. **2** a state of mental or emotional equanimity. **3** a state in which the energy in a system is evenly distributed and forces, influences, etc., balance each other. [L (as EQUI-, *libra* balance)]

equine /ˈiːkwaɪn, ˈek-/ *adj.* of or like a horse. [L *equinus* f. *equus* horse]

equinoctial /ˌiːkwɪˈnɒkʃ(ə)l, ˌek-/ *adj. & n.* —*adj.* **1** happening at or near the time of an equinox (*equinoctial gales*). **2** of or relating to equal day and night. **3** at or near the (terrestrial) equator. —*n.* (in full **equinoctial line**) = *celestial equator*. [ME f. OF *equinoctial* or L *aequinoctialis* (as EQUINOX)]

equinox /ˈiːkwɪˌnɒks, ˈek-/ *n.* the time or date (twice each year) at which the sun crosses the celestial equator, when day and night are of equal length. □ **autumn** (or **autumnal**) **equinox** about 22 Sept. **spring** (or **vernal**) **equinox** about 20 March. [ME f. OF *equinoxe* or med.L *equinoxium* for L *aequinoctium* (as EQUI-, *nox noctis* night)]

equip /ɪˈkwɪp/ *v.tr.* (**equipped, equipping**) supply with what is needed. □ **equipper** *n.* [F *équiper*, prob. f. ON *skipa* to man (a ship) f. *skip* SHIP]

equipage /ˈekwɪpɪdʒ/ *n.* **1 a** requisites for an undertaking. **b** an outfit for a special purpose. **2** a carriage and horses with attendants. [F *équipage* (as EQUIP)]

equipment /ɪˈkwɪpmənt/ *n.* **1** the necessary articles, clothing, etc., for a purpose. **2** the process of equipping or being equipped. [F *équipement* (as EQUIP)]

equipoise /ˈekwɪˌpɔɪz, ˈiː-/ *n. & v.* —*n.* **1** equilibrium; a balanced state. **2** a counterbalancing thing. —*v.tr.* counterbalance.

equiprobable /ˌiːkwɪˈprɒbəb(ə)l/ *adj.* *Logic* equally probable. □ **equiprobability** /-ˈbɪlɪtɪ/ *n.*

equitable /ˈekwɪtəb(ə)l/ *adj.* **1** fair, just. **2** *Law* valid in equity as distinct from law. □ **equitableness** *n.* **equitably** *adv.* [F *équitable* (as EQUITY)]

equitation /ˌekwɪˈteɪʃ(ə)n/ *n.* the art and practice of horsemanship and horse-riding. [F *équitation* or L *equitatio* f. *equitare* ride a horse f. *eques equitis* horseman f. *equus* horse]

equity /ˈekwɪtɪ/ *n.* (pl. **-ies**) **1** fairness. **2** the application of the principles of justice to correct or supplement the law. **3 a** the value of the shares issued by a company. **b** (in pl.) stocks and shares not bearing fixed interest. **4** the net value of a mortgaged property after the deduction of charges. [ME f. OF *equité* f. L *aequitas -tatis* f. *aequus* fair]

equivalent /ɪˈkwɪvələnt/ *adj. & n.* —*adj.* **1** (often foll. by *to*) equal in value, amount, importance, etc. **2** corresponding. **3** (of words) having the same meaning. **4** having the same result. —*n.* an equivalent thing, amount, word, etc. □ **equivalence** *n.* **equivalency** *n.* **equivalently** *adv.* [ME f. OF f. LL *aequivalēre* (as EQUI-, *valēre* be worth)]

equivocal /ɪˈkwɪvək(ə)l/ *adj.* **1** of double or doubtful meaning; ambiguous. **2** of uncertain nature. **3** (of a person, character, etc.) questionable, suspect. □ **equivocality** /-ˈkælɪtɪ/ *n.* **equivocally** *adv.* **equivocalness** *n.* [LL *aequivocus* (as EQUI-, *vocare* call)]

equivocate /ɪˈkwɪvəˌkeɪt/ *v.intr.* use ambiguity to conceal the truth. □ **equivocation** /-ˈkeɪʃ(ə)n/ *n.* **equivocator** *n.* **equivocatory** *adj.* [ME f. LL *aequivocare* (as EQUIVOCAL)]

ER *abbr.* **1** Queen Elizabeth. **2** King Edward. [L *Elizabetha Regina, Edwardus Rex*]

Er *symb. Chem.* the element erbium.

er /ɜː(r)/ *int.* expressing hesitation or a pause in speech. [imit.]

-er¹ /ə(r)/ *suffix* forming nouns from nouns, adjectives, and many verbs, denoting: **1** a person, animal, or thing that performs a specified action or activity (*lover; executioner; computer; eye-opener*). **2** a person or thing that has a specified attribute or form (*foreigner; four-wheeler; second-rater*). **3** a person concerned with a specified thing or subject (*hatter; geographer*). **4** a person belonging to a specified place or group (*villager; New Zealander; sixth-former*). [orig. 'one who has to do with': OE *-ere* f. Gmc]

-er² /ə(r)/ *suffix* forming the comparative of adjectives (*wider; hotter*) and adverbs (*faster*). [OE *-ra* (adj.), *-or* (adv.) f. Gmc]

-er³ /ə(r)/ *suffix* used in slang formations usu. distorting the root word (*rugger; soccer*). [prob. an extension of -ER¹]

-er⁴ /ə(r)/ *suffix* forming iterative and frequentative verbs (*blunder; glimmer; twitter*). [OE *-erian, -rian* f. Gmc]

-er⁵ /ə(r)/ *suffix* **1** forming nouns and adjectives through OF or AF, corresponding to: **a** L *-aris* (*sampler*) (cf. -AR¹). **b** L *-arius, -arium* (*butler; carpenter; danger*). **c** (through OF *-eüre*) L *-atura* or (through OF *-eör*) L *-atorium* (see COUNTER¹, FRITTER²). **2** = -OR.

-er⁶ /ə(r)/ *suffix* esp. *Law* forming nouns denoting verbal action or a document effecting this (*cesser; disclaimer; misnomer*). [AF infin. ending of verbs]

era /'ɪərə/ n. **1** a system of chronology reckoning from a noteworthy event (*the Christian era*). **2** a large distinct period of time, esp. regarded historically (*the pre-Roman era*). **3** a date at which an era begins. **4** *Geol.* a major division of time. [LL *aera* number expressed in figures (pl. of *aes aeris* money, treated as fem. sing.)]

eradicate /ɪ'rædɪˌkeɪt/ v.tr. root out; destroy completely; get rid of. □ **eradicable** adj. **eradication** /-'keɪʃ(ə)n/ n. **eradicator** n. [ME f. L *eradicare* tear up by the roots (as E-, *radix -icis* root)]

erase /ɪ'reɪz/ v.tr. **1** rub out; obliterate. **2** remove all traces of (*erased it from my memory*). **3** remove recorded material from (a magnetic tape or medium). □ **erasable** adj. **erasure** n. [L *eradere eras-* (as E-, *radere* scrape)]

eraser /ɪ'reɪzə(r)/ n. *US* a thing that erases, esp. a piece of rubber or plastic used for removing pencil and ink marks.

erbium /'ɜːbɪəm/ n. *Chem.* a soft silvery metallic element of the lanthanide series. [mod.L f. *Ytterby* in Sweden]

ere /eə(r)/ prep. & conj. *poet.* or *archaic* before (of time) (*ere noon; ere they come*). [OE *ær* f. Gmc]

erect /ɪ'rekt/ adj. & v. —adj. **1** upright, vertical. **2** (of the penis, clitoris, or nipples) enlarged and rigid, esp. in sexual excitement. **3** (of hair) bristling, standing up from the skin. —v.tr. **1** raise; set upright. **2** build. **3** establish (*erect a theory*). □ **erectable** adj. **erectly** adv. **erectness** n. **erector** n. [ME f. L *erigere erect-* set up (as E-, *regere* direct)]

erectile /ɪ'rektaɪl/ adj. that can be erected or become erect. □ **erectile tissue** *Physiol.* animal tissue that is capable of becoming rigid, esp. with sexual excitement. [F *érectile* (as ERECT)]

erection /ɪ'rekʃ(ə)n/ n. **1** the act or an instance of erecting; the state of being erected. **2** a building or structure. **3** *Physiol.* an enlarged and erect state of erectile tissue, esp. of the penis. [F *érection* or L *erectio* (as ERECTILE)]

erg /ɜːg/ n. *Physics* a unit of work or energy, equal to the work done by a force of one dyne when its point of application moves one centimetre in the direction of action of the force. [Gk *ergon* work]

ergo /'ɜːgəʊ/ adv. therefore. [L]

ergonomics /ˌɜːgə'nɒmɪks/ n. the study of the efficiency of persons in their working environment. □ **ergonomic** adj. **ergonomist** /ɜː'gɒnəmɪst/ n. [Gk *ergon* work: cf. ECONOMICS]

ergot /'ɜːgət/ n. **1** a disease of rye and other cereals caused by the fungus *Claviceps purpurea*. **2 a** this fungus. **b** the dried spore-containing structures of this, used as a medicine to aid childbirth. [F f. OF *argot* cock's spur, from the appearance produced]

ergotism /'ɜːgəˌtɪz(ə)m/ n. poisoning produced by eating food affected by ergot.

erica /'erɪkə/ n. any shrub or heath of the genus *Erica*, with small leathery leaves and bell-like flowers. □ **ericaceous** /-'keɪʃəs/ adj. [L f. Gk *ereikē* heath]

Erin /'erɪn, 'ɪərɪn/ n. *archaic* or *poet.* Ireland. [Ir.]

ERM abbr. exchange-rate mechanism.

ermine /'ɜːmɪn/ n. (pl. same or **ermines**) **1** the stoat, esp. when in its white winter fur. **2** its white fur, used as trimming for the robes of judges, peers, etc. □ **ermined** adj. [ME f. OF

(h)*ermine* prob. f. med.L (*mus*) *Armenius* Armenian (mouse)]

-ern /ən/ suffix forming adjectives (*northern*). [OE *-erne* f. Gmc]

erne /ɜːn/ n. (*US* **ern**) *poet.* a sea eagle. [OE *earn* f. Gmc]

Ernie /'ɜːnɪ/ n. (in the UK) a device for drawing prize-winning numbers of Premium Bonds. [initial letters of *electronic random number indicator equipment*]

erode /ɪ'rəʊd/ v. tr. & intr. wear away, destroy or be destroyed gradually. □ **erodible** adj. [F *éroder* or L *erodere eros-* (as E-, *rodere ros-* gnaw)]

erogenous /ɪ'rɒdʒɪnəs/ adj. **1** (esp. of a part of the body) sensitive to sexual stimulation. **2** giving rise to sexual desire or excitement. [as EROTIC + -GENOUS]

erosion /ɪ'rəʊʒ(ə)n/ n. **1** *Geol.* the wearing away of the earth's surface by the action of water, wind, etc. **2** the act or an instance of eroding; the process of being eroded. □ **erosional** adj. **erosive** adj. [F *érosion* f. L *erosio* (as ERODE)]

erotic /ɪ'rɒtɪk/ adj. of or causing sexual love, esp. tending to arouse sexual desire or excitement. □ **erotically** adv. [F *érotique* f. Gk *erōtikos* f. *erōs erōtos* sexual love]

erotica /ɪ'rɒtɪkə/ n.pl. erotic literature or art.

eroticism /ɪ'rɒtɪˌsɪz(ə)m/ n. **1** erotic nature or character. **2** the use of or response to erotic images or stimulation.

erotism /'erəˌtɪz(ə)m/ n. sexual desire or excitement; eroticism.

eroto- /ɪˌrɒtəʊ, ɪˌrəʊt-/ comb. form erotic, eroticism. [Gk *erōs erōtos* sexual love]

erotogenic /ɪˌrɒtə'dʒenɪk/ adj. (also **erotogenous** /ˌerə'tɒdʒɪnəs/) = EROGENOUS.

erotomania /ɪˌrəʊtə'meɪnɪə/ n. **1** excessive or morbid erotic desire. **2** a preoccupation with sexual passion. □ **erotomaniac** /-nɪæk/ n.

err /ɜː(r)/ v.intr. **1** be mistaken or incorrect. **2** do wrong; sin. [ME f. OF *errer* f. L *errare* stray: rel. to Goth. *airzei* error, *airzjan* lead astray]

errand /'erənd/ n. **1** a short journey, esp. on another's behalf, to take a message, collect goods, etc. **2** the object of such a journey. □ **errand of mercy** a journey to relieve suffering etc. [OE *ærende* f. Gmc]

errant /'erənt/ adj. **1** erring; deviating from an accepted standard. **2** *literary* or *archaic* travelling in search of adventure (*knight errant*). □ **errancy** n. (in sense 1). **errantry** n. (in sense 2). [ME: sense 1 formed as ERR: sense 2 f. OF *errer* ult. f. LL *itinerare* f. *iter* journey]

erratic /ɪ'rætɪk/ adj. **1** inconsistently variable in conduct, opinions, etc. **2** uncertain in movement. □ **erratically** adv. [ME f. OF *erratique* f. L *erraticus* (as ERR)]

erratum /ɪ'rɑːtəm/ n. (pl. **errata** /-tə/) an error in printing or writing, esp. (in pl.) a list of corrected errors attached to a book etc. [L, neut. past part. (as ERR)]

erroneous /ɪ'rəʊnɪəs/ adj. incorrect; arising from error. □ **erroneously** adv. **erroneousness** n. [ME f. OF *erroneus* or L *erroneus* f. *erro -onis* vagabond (as ERR)]

error /'erə(r)/ n. **1** a mistake. **2** the condition of being wrong in conduct or judgement (*led into error*). **3** a wrong opinion or judgement. **4** the amount by which something is incorrect or inaccurate in a calculation or measurement. □

errorless adj. [ME f. OF *errour* f. L *error -oris* (as ERR)]

ersatz /ˈɜːzæts, ˈeə-/ adj. & n. —adj. substitute, imitation (esp. of inferior quality). —n. an ersatz thing. [G, = replacement]

Erse /ɜːs/ adj. & n. —adj. Irish or Highland Gaelic. —n. the Gaelic language. [early Sc. form of IRISH]

erst /ɜːst/ adv. archaic formerly; of old. [OE *ǣrest* superl. of *ǣr*: see ERE]

erstwhile /ˈɜːstwaɪl/ adj. & adv. —adj. former, previous. —adv. archaic = ERST.

eructation /ˌiːrʌkˈteɪʃ(ə)n/ n. the act or an instance of belching. [L *eructatio* f. *eructare* (as E-, *ructare* belch)]

erudite /ˈeruːˌdaɪt/ adj. 1 (of a person) learned. 2 (of writing etc.) showing great learning. □ **eruditely** adv. **erudition** /-ˈdɪʃ(ə)n/ n. [ME f. L *eruditus* past part. of *erudire* instruct, train (as E-, *rudis* untrained)]

erupt /ɪˈrʌpt/ v.intr. 1 break out suddenly or dramatically. 2 (of a volcano) become active and eject lava etc. 3 a (of a rash, boil, etc.) appear on the skin. b (of the skin) produce a rash etc. 4 (of the teeth) break through the gums in normal development. □ **eruption** n. **eruptive** adj. [L *erumpere erupt-* (as E-, *rumpere* break)]

-ery /ərɪ/ suffix forming nouns denoting: 1 a class or kind (*greenery; machinery; citizenry*). 2 employment; state or condition (*archery; dentistry; slavery; bravery*). 3 a place of work or cultivation or breeding (*brewery; orangery; rookery*). 4 behaviour (*mimicry*). 5 often derog. all that has to do with (*knavery; popery; tomfoolery*). [ME, from or after F *-erie*, *-ere* ult. f. L *-ario-*, *-ator*]

erysipelas /ˌerɪˈsɪpɪləs/ n. Med. a streptococcal infection producing inflammation and a deep red colour on the skin, esp. of the face and scalp. [ME f. L f. Gk *erusipelas*, perh. rel. to *eruthros* red + a root *pel-* skin]

erythro- /ɪˈrɪθrəʊ/ comb. form red. [Gk *eruthros* red]

erythrocyte /ɪˈrɪθrəʊsaɪt/ n. a red blood cell, which contains the pigment haemoglobin and transports oxygen and carbon dioxide to and from the tissues. □ **erythrocytic** /-ˈsɪtɪk/ adj.

Es symb. Chem. the element einsteinium.

-es¹ /ɪz/ suffix forming plurals of nouns ending in sibilant sounds (such words in -e dropping the e) (*kisses; cases; boxes; churches*). [var. of -s¹]

-es² /ɪz, z/ suffix forming the 3rd person sing. present of verbs ending in sibilant sounds (such words in -e dropping the e) and ending in -o (but not -oo) (*goes; places; pushes*). [var. of -s²]

escalate /ˈeskəˌleɪt/ v. 1 intr. & tr. increase or develop (usu. rapidly) by stages. 2 tr. cause (an action, activity, or process) to become more intense. □ **escalation** /-ˈleɪʃ(ə)n/ n. [back-form. f. ESCALATOR]

escalator /ˈeskəˌleɪtə(r)/ n. a moving staircase consisting of a circulating belt forming steps. [f. the stem of *escalade* 'climb a wall by ladder' + -ATOR]

escallop /ɪˈskæləp/ n. 1 = SCALLOP n. 1, 2. 2 = ESCALOPE. 3 (in pl.) = SCALLOP n. 3. [formed as ESCALOPE]

escalope /ˈeskəˌlɒp/ n. a thin slice of meat without any bone, esp. from a leg of veal. [F (in OF = shell): see SCALLOP]

escapade /ˈeskəˌpeɪd, ˌeskəˈpeɪd/ n. a piece of daring or reckless behaviour. [F f. Prov. or Sp. *escapada* (as ESCAPE)]

escape /ɪˈskeɪp/ v. & n. —v. 1 intr. (often foll. by *from*) get free of the restriction or control of a place, person, etc. 2 intr. (of a gas, liquid, etc.) leak from a container or pipe etc. 3 intr. succeed in avoiding danger, punishment, etc.; get off safely. 4 tr. get completely free of (a person, grasp, etc.). 5 tr. avoid or elude (a commitment, danger, etc.). 6 tr. elude the notice or memory of (*nothing escapes you; the name escaped me*). 7 tr. (of words etc.) issue unawares from (a person, a person's lips). —n. 1 the act or an instance of escaping; avoidance of danger, injury, etc. 2 the state of having escaped (*was a narrow escape*). 3 a means of escaping (often attrib.: *escape hatch*). 4 a leakage of gas etc. 5 a temporary relief from reality or worry. 6 a garden plant running wild. □ **escape clause** Law a clause specifying the conditions under which a contracting party is free from an obligation. **escape velocity** the minimum velocity needed to escape from the gravitational field of a body. □ **escapable** adj. **escaper** n. [ME f. AF, ONF *escaper* ult. f. med.L (as EX-¹, *cappa* cloak)]

escapee /ɪskeɪˈpiː/ n. a person, esp. a prisoner, who has escaped.

escapement /ɪˈskeɪpmənt/ n. the part of a clock or watch that connects and regulates the motive power. [F *échappement* f. *échapper* ESCAPE]

escapism /ɪˈskeɪpɪz(ə)m/ n. the tendency to seek distraction and relief from reality, esp. in the arts or through fantasy. □ **escapist** n. & adj.

escapology /ˌeskəˈpɒlədʒɪ/ n. the methods and techniques of escaping from confinement, esp. as a form of entertainment. □ **escapologist** n.

escarpment /ɪˈskɑːpmənt/ n. (also **escarp**) Geol. a long steep slope at the edge of a plateau etc. [F *escarpement* f. *escarpe* SCARP]

eschatology /ˌeskəˈtɒlədʒɪ/ n. the part of theology concerned with death and final destiny. □ **eschatological** /-təˈlɒdʒɪk(ə)l/ adj. **eschatologist** n. [Gk *eskhatos* last + -LOGY]

escheat /ɪsˈtʃiːt/ n. & v. hist. —n. 1 the reversion of property to the State, or (in feudal law) to a lord, on the owner's dying without legal heirs. 2 property affected by this. —v. 1 tr. hand over (property) as an escheat. 2 tr. confiscate. 3 intr. revert by escheat. [ME f. OF *eschete*, ult. f. L *excidere* (as EX-¹, *cadere* fall)]

eschew /ɪsˈtʃuː/ v.tr. literary avoid; abstain from. □ **eschewal** n. [ME f. OF *eschiver*, ult. f. Gmc: rel. to SHY¹]

escort n. & v. —n. /ˈeskɔːt/ 1 one or more persons, vehicles, ships, etc., accompanying a person, vehicle, etc., esp. for protection or security or as a mark of rank or status. 2 a person accompanying a person of the opposite sex socially. —v.tr. /ɪˈskɔːt/ act as an escort to. [F *escorte*, *escorter* f. It. *scorta* fem. past part. of *scorgere* conduct]

escritoire /ˌeskrɪˈtwɑː(r)/ n. a writing-desk with drawers etc. [F f. L *scriptorium* writing-room: see SCRIPTORIUM]

escrow /eˈskrəʊ/ n. & v. Law —n. 1 money, property, or a written bond, kept in the custody of a third party until a specified condition has been fulfilled. 2 the status of this (*in escrow*). —v.tr. place in escrow. [AF *escrowe*, OF *escroe* scrap, scroll, f. med.L *scroda* f. Gmc]

escudo /eˈskjuːdəʊ/ n. (pl. -os) the principal monetary unit of Portugal and Chile. [Sp. & Port. f. L scutum shield]

esculent /ˈeskjʊlənt/ adj. & n. —adj. fit to eat; edible. —n. an edible substance. [L esculentus f. esca food]

escutcheon /ɪˈskʌtʃ(ə)n/ n. 1 a shield or emblem bearing a coat of arms. 2 the middle part of a ship's stern where the name is placed. 3 the protective plate around a keyhole or door-handle. □ **escutcheoned** adj. [AF & ONF escuchon ult. f. L scutum shield]

-ese /iːz/ suffix forming adjectives and nouns denoting: 1 an inhabitant or language of a country or city (Japanese; Milanese; Viennese). 2 often derog. character or style, esp. of language (officialese). [OF -eis ult. f. L -ensis]

■ **Usage** Singular and plural forms in sense 1 are the same.

Eskimo /ˈeskɪˌməʊ/ n. & adj. —n. (pl. same or -os) 1 a member of a people inhabiting N. Canada, Alaska, Greenland, and E. Siberia. 2 the language of this people. —adj. of or relating to the Eskimos or their language. [Da. f. F Esquimaux (pl.) f. Algonquian]

■ **Usage** The people themselves prefer the name Inuit.

Esky /ˈeskɪ/ n. (pl. -ies) Austral. propr. a portable insulated container for keeping food or drink cool. [prob. f. ESKIMO, with ref. to their cold climate]

ESN abbr. educationally subnormal.

esophagus US var. of OESOPHAGUS.

esoteric /ˌiːsəʊˈterɪk, ˌe-/ adj. intelligible only to those with special knowledge. □ **esoterical** adj. **esoterically** adv. **esotericism** /-ˌsɪz(ə)m/ n. **esotericist** /-sɪst/ n. [Gk esōterikos f. esōterō compar. of esō within]

ESP abbr. extrasensory perception.

espadrille /ˌespəˈdrɪl/ n. a light canvas shoe with a plaited fibre sole. [F f. Prov. espardillo f. espart ESPARTO]

espalier /ɪˈspælɪə(r)/ n. 1 a lattice-work along which the branches of a tree or shrub are trained to grow flat against a wall etc. 2 a tree or shrub trained in this way. [F f. It. spalliera f. spalla shoulder]

esparto /eˈspaːtəʊ/ n. (pl. -os) (in full **esparto grass**) a coarse grass, Stipa tenacissima, native to Spain and N. Africa, used to make ropes, wickerwork, and paper. [Sp. f. L spartum f. Gk sparton rope]

especial /ɪˈspeʃ(ə)l/ adj. 1 notable, exceptional. 2 attributed or belonging chiefly to one person or thing (your especial charm). [ME f. OF f. L specialis special]

especially /ɪˈspeʃəlɪ, -ʃlɪ/ adv. chiefly; much more than in other cases.

Esperanto /ˌespəˈræntəʊ/ n. an artificial universal language devised in 1887. □ **Esperantist** n. [the pen-name (f. L sperare hope) of its inventor, L. L. Zamenhof, Polish physician d. 1917]

espial /ɪˈspaɪəl/ n. 1 the act or an instance of catching sight of or of being seen. 2 archaic spying. [ME f. OF espiaille f. espier: see ESPY]

espionage /ˈespɪəˌnɑːʒ/ n. the practice of spying or of using spies, esp. by governments. [F espionnage f. espionner f. espion SPY]

esplanade /ˌespləˈneɪd/ n. 1 a long open level area for walking on, esp. beside the sea. 2 a level space separating a fortress from a town. [F f. Sp. esplanada f. esplanar make level f. L explanare (as EX-[1], planus level)]

espousal /ɪˈspaʊz(ə)l/ n. 1 (foll. by of) the espousing of a cause etc. 2 archaic a marriage or betrothal. [ME f. OF espousailles f. L sponsalia neut. pl. of sponsalis (as ESPOUSE)]

espouse /ɪˈspaʊz/ v.tr. 1 adopt or support (a cause, doctrine, etc.). 2 archaic a (of a man) marry. b (usu. foll. by to) give (a woman) in marriage. □ **espouser** n. [ME f. OF espouser f. L sponsare f. sponsus past part. of spondēre betroth]

espresso /eˈspresəʊ/ n. (also **expresso** /ekˈspresəʊ/) (pl. -os) 1 strong concentrated black coffee made under steam pressure. 2 a machine for making this. [It., = pressed out]

esprit /eˈspriː, ˈespriː/ n. sprightliness, wit. □ **esprit de corps** /də ˈkɔː(r)/ a feeling of devotion to and pride in the group one belongs to. [F f. L spiritus SPIRIT (+ corps body, escalier stairs)]

espy /ɪˈspaɪ/ v.tr. (-ies, -ied) literary catch sight of; perceive. [ME f. OF espier: see SPY]

Esq. abbr. Esquire.

-esque /esk/ suffix forming adjectives meaning 'in the style of' or 'resembling' (romanesque; Schumannesque; statuesque). [F f. It. -esco f. med.L -iscus]

esquire /ɪˈskwaɪə(r)/ n. 1 (usu. as abbr. **Esq.**) Brit. a title appended to a man's surname when no other form of address is used, esp. as a form of address for letters. 2 archaic = SQUIRE. [ME f. OF esquier f. L scutarius shield-bearer f. scutum shield]

-ess[1] /ɪs/ suffix forming nouns denoting females (actress; lioness; mayoress). [from or after F -esse f. LL -issa f. Gk -issa]

-ess[2] /es/ suffix forming abstract nouns from adjectives (duress). [ME f. F -esse f. L -itia; cf. -ICE]

essay n. & v. —n. /ˈeseɪ/ 1 a composition, usu. short and in prose, on any subject. 2 (often foll. by at, in) formal an attempt. —v.tr. /eˈseɪ/ formal attempt, try. □ **essayist** n. [ME f. ASSAY, assim. to F essayer ult. f. LL exagium weighing f. exigere weigh: see EXACT]

essence /ˈes(ə)ns/ n. 1 the indispensable quality or element identifying a thing or determining its character; fundamental nature or inherent characteristics. 2 a an extract obtained by distillation etc., esp. a volatile oil. b a perfume or scent, esp. made from a plant or animal substance. 3 the constituent of a plant that determines its chemical properties. □ **in essence** fundamentally. **of the essence** indispensable, vital. [ME f. OF f. L essentia f. esse be]

essential /ɪˈsenʃ(ə)l/ adj. & n. —adj. 1 absolutely necessary; indispensable. 2 fundamental, basic. 3 of or constituting the essence of a person or thing. —n. (esp. in pl.) a basic or indispensable element or thing. □ **essential element** any of various elements required by living organisms for normal growth. **essential oil** a volatile oil derived from a plant etc. with its characteristic odour. □ **essentiality** /-ʃɪˈælɪtɪ/ n. **essentially** adv. **essentialness** n. [ME f. LL essentialis (as ESSENCE)]

-est /ɪst/ suffix forming the superlative of adjectives (widest; nicest; happiest) and adverbs (soonest). [OE -ost, -ust-, -ast-]

establish /ɪˈstæblɪʃ/ v.tr. 1 set up or consolidate (a business, system, etc.) on a permanent basis. 2 (foll. by in) settle (a person or oneself) in some capacity. **3** (esp. as **established** adj.) achieve permanent acceptance for (a custom, belief, practice, institution, etc.). **4** validate; place beyond dispute (a fact etc.). □ **Established Church** the Church recognized by the State as the national Church. □ **establisher** n. [ME f. OF establir (stem establiss-) f. L stabilire f. stabilis STABLE¹]

establishment /ɪˈstæblɪʃmənt/ n. **1** the act or an instance of establishing; the process of being established. **2 a** a business organization or public institution. **b** a place of business. **c** a residence. **3 a** the staff or equipment of an organization. **b** a household. **4** any organized body permanently maintained for a purpose. **5** a Church system organized by law. **6** (**the Establishment**) **a** the group in a society exercising authority or influence, and seen as resisting change. **b** any influential or controlling group (the literary Establishment).

estate /ɪˈsteɪt/ n. **1** a property consisting of an extensive area of land usu. with a large house. **2** Brit. a modern residential or industrial area with integrated design or purpose. **3** all of a person's assets and liabilities, esp. at death. **4** a property where rubber, tea, grapes, etc., are cultivated. **5** (in full **estate of the realm**) an order or class forming (or regarded as) a part of the body politic. **6** archaic or literary a state or position in life (the estate of holy matrimony; poor man's estate). **7** colloq. = estate car. □ **estate agent** Brit. **1** a person whose business is the sale or lease of buildings and land on behalf of others. **2** the steward of an estate. **estate car** Brit. a car with the passenger area extended and combined with space for luggage, usu. with an extra door at the rear. **estate duty** Brit. hist. death duty levied on property. **the Three Estates** Lords Spiritual (the heads of the Church), Lords Temporal (the peerage), and the Commons. [ME f. OF estat (as STATUS)]

esteem /ɪˈstiːm/ v. & n. —v.tr. **1** (usu. in passive) have a high regard for; greatly respect; think favourably of. **2** formal consider, deem (esteemed it an honour). —n. high regard; respect; favour (held them in esteem). [ME f. OF estimer f. L aestimare fix the price of]

ester /ˈestə(r)/ n. Chem. any of a class of organic compounds produced by replacing the hydrogen of an acid by an alkyl, aryl, etc. radical, many of which occur naturally as oils and fats. □ **esterify** /eˈsterɪˌfaɪ/ v.tr. (**-ies, -ied**). [G, prob. f. Essig vinegar + Äther ether]

esthete US var. of AESTHETE.

esthetic US var. of AESTHETIC.

estimable /ˈestɪməb(ə)l/ adj. worthy of esteem. □ **estimably** adv. [F f. L aestimabilis (as ESTEEM)]

estimate n. & v. —n. /ˈestɪmət/ **1** an approximate judgement, esp. of cost, value, size, etc. **2** a price specified as that likely to be charged for work to be undertaken. —v.tr. (also absol.) /ˈestɪˌmeɪt/ **1** form an estimate or opinion of. **2** (foll. by that + clause) make a rough calculation. **3** (often foll. by at) form an estimate; adjudge. **4** fix (a price etc.) by estimate. □ **estimative** /-mətɪv/ adj. **estimator** /-ˌmeɪtə(r)/ n. [L aestimare aestimat- fix the price of]

estimation /ˌestɪˈmeɪʃ(ə)n/ n. **1** the process or result of estimating. **2** judgement or opinion of worth. [ME f. OF estimation or L aestimatio (as ESTIMATE)]

estival US var. of AESTIVAL.

estivate US var. of AESTIVATE.

estrange /ɪˈstreɪndʒ/ v.tr. (usu. in passive; often foll. by from) cause (a person or group) to turn away in feeling or affection; alienate. □ **estrangement** n. [ME f. AF estraunger, OF estranger f. L extraneare treat as a stranger f. extraneus stranger]

estrogen US var. of OESTROGEN.

estrus etc. US var. of OESTRUS etc.

estuary /ˈestjʊərɪ/ n. (pl. **-ies**) a wide tidal mouth of a river. □ **estuarine** /-ˌraɪn/ adj. [L aestuarium tidal channel f. aestus tide]

-et¹ /ɪt/ suffix forming nouns (orig. diminutives) (baronet; bullet; sonnet). [OF -et -ete]

-et² /ɪt/ suffix (also **-ete** /iːt/) forming nouns usu. denoting persons (comet; poet; athlete). [Gk -ētēs]

ETA¹ abbr. estimated time of arrival.

ETA² /ˈetə/ n. a Basque separatist movement. [Basque abbr., f. Euzkadi ta Azkatasuna Basque homeland and liberty]

eta /ˈiːtə/ n. the seventh letter of the Greek alphabet (H, η). [Gk]

et al. /et ˈæl/ abbr. and others. [L et alii, et alia, etc.]

etc. abbr. = ET CETERA.

et cetera /et ˈsetərə, ˈsetrə/ adv. & n. (also **etcetera**) —adv. **1 a** and the rest; and similar things or people. **b** or similar things or people. **2** and so on. —n. (in pl.) the usual sundries or extras. [ME f. L]

etch /etʃ/ v. **1** tr. reproduce (a picture etc.) by engraving a design on a metal plate with acid (esp. to print copies). **b** tr. engrave (a plate) in this way. **2** intr. practise this craft. **3** tr. (foll. by on, upon) impress deeply (esp. on the mind). □ **etcher** n. [Du. etsen f. G ätzen etch f. OHG azzen cause to eat or to be eaten f. Gmc]

etching /ˈetʃɪŋ/ n. **1** a print made from an etched plate. **2** the art of producing these plates.

-ete suffix var. of -ET².

eternal /ɪˈtɜːn(ə)l/ adj. **1** existing always; without an end or (usu.) beginning in time. **2** essentially unchanging (eternal truths). **3** colloq. constant; seeming not to cease (your eternal nagging). □ **the Eternal** God. **Eternal City** Rome. **eternal triangle** a complex of emotional relationships involving two people of one sex and one of the other sex. □ **eternality** /-ˈnælɪtɪ/ n. **eternalize** v.tr. (also **-ise**). **eternally** adv. **eternalness** n. **eternize** v.tr. (also **-ise**). [ME f. OF f. LL aeternalis f. L aeternus f. aevum age]

eternity /ɪˈtɜːnɪtɪ/ n. (pl. **-ies**) **1** infinite or unending (esp. future) time. **2** Theol. endless life after death. **3** the state of being eternal. **4** colloq. (often prec. by an) a very long time. □ **eternity ring** a finger-ring set with gems all round. [ME f. OF eternité f. L aeternitas -tatis f. aeternus: see ETERNAL]

-eth var. of -TH¹.

ethane /ˈeθeɪn, ˈiːθ-/ n. Chem. a gaseous hydrocarbon of the alkane series, occurring in natural gas. [ETHER + -ANE²]

ethanol /ˈeθənɒl/ n. Chem. = ALCOHOL 1. [ETHANE + ALCOHOL]

ethene /ˈeθiːn, ˈiːθ-/ n. Chem. = ETHYLENE. [ETHER + -ENE]

ether /ˈiːθə(r)/ n. **1** Chem. **a** a colourless volatile organic liquid used as an anaesthetic or solvent. **b** any of a class of organic compounds with a similar structure to this, having an oxygen joined to two alkyl etc. groups. **2** a clear sky; the upper regions of air beyond the clouds. **3** *hist.* **a** a medium formerly assumed to permeate space and fill the interstices between particles of matter. **b** a medium through which electromagnetic waves were formerly thought to be transmitted. □ **etheric** /iːˈθerɪk/ *adj.* [ME f. OF *ether* or L *aether* f. Gk *aithēr* f. root of *aithō* burn, shine]

ethereal /ɪˈθɪərɪəl/ *adj.* (also **etherial**) **1** light, airy. **2** highly delicate, esp. in appearance. **3** heavenly, celestial. □ **ethereality** /-ˈælɪtɪ/ *n.* **ethereally** *adv.* [L *aethereus, -ius* f. Gk *aitherios* (as ETHER)]

ethic /ˈeθɪk/ *n.* & *adj.* —*n.* a set of moral principles (*the Quaker ethic*). —*adj.* = ETHICAL. [ME f. OF *éthique* or L *ethicus* f. Gk *ēthikos* (as ETHOS)]

ethical /ˈeθɪk(ə)l/ *adj.* **1** relating to morals, esp. as concerning human conduct. **2** morally correct; honourable. **3** (of a medicine or drug) not advertised to the general public, and usu. available only on a doctor's prescription. □ **ethical investment** investment in companies that meet ethical and moral criteria specified by the investor. □ **ethicality** /-ˈkælɪtɪ/ *n.* **ethically** *adv.*

ethics /ˈeθɪks/ *n.pl.* (also treated as *sing.*) **1** the science of morals in human conduct. **2 a** moral principles; rules of conduct. **b** a set of these (*medical ethics*). □ **ethicist** /-sɪst/ *n.*

ethnic /ˈeθnɪk/ *adj.* & *n.* —*adj.* **1 a** (of a social group) having a common national or cultural tradition. **b** (of clothes etc.) resembling those of a non-European exotic people. **2** denoting origin by birth or descent rather than nationality (*ethnic Turks*). **3** relating to race or culture (*ethnic group*; *ethnic origins*). —*n.* **1** US a member of an (esp. minority) ethnic group. **2** (in *pl.*, usu. treated as *sing.*) = ETHNOLOGY. □ **ethnic minority** a (usu. identifiable) group differentiated from the main population of a community by racial origin or cultural background. □ **ethnically** *adv.* **ethnicity** /-ˈnɪsɪtɪ/ *n.* [ME f. eccl.L *ethnicus* f. Gk *ethnikos* heathen f. *ethnos* nation]

ethno- /ˈeθnəʊ/ *comb. form* ethnic, ethnological. [Gk *ethnos* nation]

ethnocentric /ˌeθnəʊˈsentrɪk/ *adj.* evaluating other races and cultures by criteria specific to one's own. □ **ethnocentrically** *adv.* **ethnocentricity** /-ˈtrɪsɪtɪ/ *n.* **ethnocentrism** *n.*

ethnography /eθˈnɒɡrəfɪ/ *n.* the scientific description of races and cultures of mankind. □ **ethnographer** *n.* **ethnographic** /-nəˈɡræfɪk/ *adj.* **ethnographical** /-nəˈɡræfɪk(ə)l/ *adj.*

ethnology /eθˈnɒlədʒɪ/ *n.* the comparative scientific study of human peoples. □ **ethnologic** /-nəˈlɒdʒɪk/ *adj.* **ethnological** /-nəˈlɒdʒɪk(ə)l/ *adj.* **ethnologist** *n.*

ethology /iːˈθɒlədʒɪ/ *n.* **1** the science of animal behaviour. **2** the science of character-formation in human behaviour. □ **ethological** /ˌiːθəˈlɒdʒɪk(ə)l/ *adj.* **ethologist** *n.* [L *ethologia* f. Gk *ēthologia* (as ETHOS)]

ethos /ˈiːθɒs/ *n.* the characteristic spirit or attitudes of a community, people, or system, or of a literary work etc. [mod.L f. Gk *ēthos* nature, disposition]

ethyl /ˈiːθaɪl, ˈeθɪl/ *n.* (*attrib.*) *Chem.* the univalent radical derived from ethane by removal of a hydrogen atom (*ethyl alcohol*). [G (as ETHER, -YL)]

ethylene /ˈeθɪˌliːn/ *n.* *Chem.* a gaseous hydrocarbon of the alkene series, occurring in natural gas and used in the manufacture of polythene. □ **ethylene glycol** *Chem.* a colourless viscous hygroscopic liquid used as an antifreeze and in the manufacture of polyesters. □ **ethylenic** /-ˈliːnɪk/ *adj.*

-etic /ˈetɪk/ *suffix* forming adjectives and nouns (*ascetic*; *emetic*; *genetic*; *synthetic*). [Gk *-ētikos* or *-ētikos*: cf. -IC]

etiolate /ˈiːtɪəʊˌleɪt/ *v.tr.* **1** make (a plant) pale by excluding light. **2** give a sickly hue to (a person). □ **etiolation** /-ˈleɪʃ(ə)n/ *n.* [F *étioler* f. Norman F *étieuler* make into haulm f. *éteule* ult. f. L *stipula* straw]

etiology US var. of AETIOLOGY.

etiquette /ˈetɪˌket, -ˈket/ *n.* **1** the conventional rules of social behaviour. **2 a** the customary behaviour of members of a profession towards each other. **b** the unwritten code governing this (*medical etiquette*). [F *étiquette* label, etiquette]

Etruscan /ɪˈtrʌskən/ *adj.* & *n.* —*adj.* of ancient Etruria in Italy, esp. its pre-Roman civilization and physical remains. —*n.* **1** a native of Etruria. **2** the language of Etruria. □ **Etruscology** /-ˈkɒlədʒɪ/ *n.* [L *Etruscus*]

et seq. *abbr.* (also **et seqq.**) and the following (pages etc.). [L *et sequentia*]

-ette /et/ *suffix* forming nouns meaning: **1** small (*kitchenette*; *cigarette*). **2** imitation or substitute (*leatherette*; *flannelette*). **3** female (*usherette*; *suffragette*). [from or after OF *-ette*, fem. of -ET¹]

étude /ˈeɪtjuːd, -ˈtjuː/ *n.* a short musical composition or exercise, usu. for one instrument, designed to improve the technique of the player. [F, = study]

etymologize /ˌetɪˈmɒləˌdʒaɪz/ *v.* (also **-ise**) **1** *tr.* give or trace the etymology of. **2** *intr.* study etymology. [med.L *etymologizare* f. L *etymologia* (as ETYMOLOGY)]

etymology /ˌetɪˈmɒlədʒɪ/ *n.* (*pl.* **-ies**) **1 a** the historically verifiable sources of the formation of a word and the development of its meaning. **b** an account of these. **2** the branch of linguistic science concerned with etymologies. □ **etymological** /-məˈlɒdʒɪk(ə)l/ *adj.* **etymologically** /-məˈlɒdʒɪkəlɪ/ *adv.* **etymologist** *n.* [OF *ethimologie* f. L *etymologia* f. Gk *etumologia* (as ETYMON, -LOGY)]

etymon /ˈetɪmən/ *n.* (*pl.* **etyma** /-mə/) the word that gives rise to a derivative or a borrowed or later form. [L f. Gk *etumon* (neut. of *etumos* true), the literal sense or original form of a word]

Eu *symb.* *Chem.* the element europium.

eu- /juː/ *comb. form* well, easily. [Gk]

eucalyptus /ˌjuːkəˈlɪptəs/ *n.* (also **eucalypt**) (*pl.* **eucalyptuses** or **eucalypti** /-taɪ/ or **eucalypts**) **1** any tree of the genus *Eucalyptus*, native to Australasia, cultivated for its timber and for the oil from its leaves. **2** (in full **eucalyptus oil**) this oil used as an antiseptic etc. [mod.L f. EU- + Gk *kaluptos* covered f. *kaluptō* to cover, the unopened flower being protected by a cap]

Eucharist /ˈjuːkərɪst/ *n.* **1** the Christian sacrament commemorating the Last Supper, in which bread and wine are consecrated and consumed. **2** the consecrated elements, esp. the bread (*receive the Eucharist*). □ **Eucharistic**

/-ˈrɪstɪk/ adj. **Eucharistical** /-ˈrɪstɪk(ə)l/ adj. [ME f. OF eucariste, ult. f. eccl.Gk eukharistia thanksgiving f. Gk eukharistos grateful (as EU-, kharizomai offer willingly)]

euchre /ˈjuːkə(r)/ n. & v. —n. an American card-game for two, three, or four players. —v.tr. **1** (in euchre) gain the advantage over (another player) when that player fails to take three tricks. **2** deceive, outwit. **3** Austral. exhaust, ruin. [19th c.: orig. unkn.]

Euclidean /juːˈklɪdɪən/ adj. of or relating to Euclid, 3rd-c. BC Alexandrian geometrician, esp. the system of geometry based on his principles. □ **Euclidean space** space for which Euclidean geometry is valid. [L Euclideus f. Gk Eukleideios]

eugenics /juːˈdʒenɪks/ n.pl. (also treated as sing.) the science of improving the (esp. human) population by controlled breeding for desirable inherited characteristics. □ **eugenic** adj. **eugenically** adv. **eugenicist** /juːˈdʒenɪsɪst/ n. **eugenist** /ˈjuːdʒɪnɪst/ n.

eulogize /ˈjuːləˌdʒaɪz/ v.tr. (also **-ise**) praise in speech or writing. □ **eulogist** n. **eulogistic** /-ˈdʒɪstɪk/ adj. **eulogistically** /-ˈdʒɪstɪkəlɪ/ adv.

eulogy /ˈjuːlədʒɪ/ n. (pl. **-ies**) **1 a** a speech or writing in praise of a person. **b** an expression of praise. **2** US a funeral oration in praise of a person. [med.L eulogium f. (app. by confusion with L elogium epitaph) LL eulogia praise f. Gk]

eunuch /ˈjuːnək/ n. **1** a castrated man, esp. one formerly employed at an oriental harem or court. **2** a person lacking effectiveness (political eunuch). [ME f. L eunuchus f. Gk eunoukhos lit. bedchamber attendant f. eunē bed + second element rel. to ekhō hold]

euphemism /ˈjuːfɪˌmɪz(ə)m/ n. **1** a mild or vague expression substituted for one thought to be too harsh or direct (e.g. pass over for die). **2** the use of such expressions. □ **euphemist** n. **euphemistic** /-ˈmɪstɪk/ adj. **euphemistically** /-ˈmɪstɪkəlɪ/ adv. **euphemize** v.tr. & intr. (also **-ise**). [Gk euphēmismos f. euphēmos (as EU-, phēmē speaking)]

euphonious /juːˈfəʊnɪəs/ adj. **1** sounding pleasant, harmonious. **2** concerning euphony. □ **euphoniously** adv.

euphonium /juːˈfəʊnɪəm/ n. a brass wind instrument of the tuba family. [mod.L f. Gk euphōnos (as EUPHONY)]

euphony /ˈjuːfənɪ/ n. (pl. **-ies**) **1 a** pleasantness of sound, esp. of a word or phrase; harmony. **b** a pleasant sound. **2** the tendency to make a phonetic change for ease of pronunciation. □ **euphonic** /-ˈfɒnɪk/ adj. **euphonize** v.tr. (also **-ise**). [F euphonie f. LL euphonia f. Gk euphōnia (as EU-, phōnē sound)]

euphorbia /juːˈfɔːbɪə/ n. any plant of the genus Euphorbia, including spurges. [ME f. L euphorbea f. Euphorbus, 1st-c. Gk physician]

euphoria /juːˈfɔːrɪə/ n. a feeling of well-being, esp. one based on over-confidence or over-optimism. □ **euphoric** /-ˈfɒrɪk/ adj. **euphorically** /-ˈfɒrɪkəlɪ/ adv. [Gk f. euphoros well-bearing (as EU-, pherō bear)]

euphuism /ˈjuːfjuːˌɪz(ə)m/ n. an affected or high-flown style of writing or speaking. □ **euphuist** n. **euphuistic** /-ˈɪstɪk/ adj. **euphuistically** /-ˈɪstɪkəlɪ/ adv. [Gk euphuēs well endowed by nature: orig. of writing imitating Lyly's Euphues (1578–80)]

Eurasian /jʊəˈreɪʒ(ə)n/ adj. & n. —adj. **1** of mixed European and Asian parentage. **2** of Europe and Asia. —n. a Eurasian person.

Euratom /jʊəˈrætəm/ n. European Atomic Energy Community. [abbr.]

eureka /jʊəˈriːkə/ int. & n. —int. I have found it! (announcing a discovery etc.). —n. the exultant cry of 'eureka'. [Gk heurēka 1st pers. sing. perfect of heuriskō find: attributed to Archimedes]

eurhythmic /jʊəˈrɪðmɪk/ adj. of or in harmonious proportion (esp. of architecture). [eurhythmy harmony of proportions f. L eur(h)ythmia f. Gk eurhuthmia (as EU-, rhuthmos proportion, rhythm)]

eurhythmics /jʊəˈrɪðmɪks/ n.pl. (also treated as sing.) (US **eurythmics**) harmony of bodily movement, esp. as developed with music and dance into a system of education.

Euro- /ˈjʊərəʊ/ comb. form Europe, European. [abbr.]

Eurocrat /ˈjʊərəʊˌkræt/ n. usu. derog. a bureaucrat in the administration of the European Economic Community.

Eurodollar /ˈjʊərəʊˌdɒlə(r)/ n. a dollar held in a bank in Europe.

European /jʊərəˈpɪən/ adj. & n. —adj. **1** of or in Europe. **2 a** descended from natives of Europe. **b** originating in or characteristic of Europe. **3 a** happening in or extending over Europe. **b** concerning Europe as a whole rather than its individual countries. **4** of or relating to the European Economic Community. —n. **1 a** a native or inhabitant of Europe. **b** a person descended from natives of Europe. **c** a White person. **2** a person concerned with European matters. □ **European Economic Community** (or **European Community**) an economic and political association of certain European countries as a unit with internal free trade and common external tariffs. □ **Europeanism** n. **Europeanize** v.tr. & intr. (also **-ise**). **Europeanization** /-ˈzeɪʃ(ə)n/ n. [F européen f. L europaeus f. L Europa f. Gk Eurōpē Europe]

europium /jʊˈrəʊpɪəm/ n. Chem. a soft silvery metallic element of the lanthanide series. [mod.L f. Europe]

Eurovision /ˈjʊərəʊˌvɪʒ(ə)n/ n. a network of European television production administered by the European Broadcasting Union.

Eustachian tube /juːˈsteɪʃ(ə)n/ n. Anat. a tube leading from the pharynx to the cavity of the middle ear and equalizing the pressure on each side of the eardrum. [L Eustachius = B. Eustachio, It. anatomist d. 1574]

eustasy /ˈjuːstəsɪ/ n. a change in sea level throughout the world caused by tectonic movements, melting of glaciers, etc. □ **eustatic** /-ˈstætɪk/ adj. [back-form. f. G eustatisch (adj.) (as EU-, STATIC)]

euthanasia /juːθəˈneɪzɪə/ n. **1** the bringing about of a gentle and easy death in the case of incurable and painful disease. **2** such a death. [Gk (as EU-, thanatos death)]

eutrophic /juːˈtrɒfɪk, -ˈtrəʊfɪk/ adj. (of a lake etc.) rich in nutrients and therefore supporting a dense plant population, which kills animal life by depriving it of oxygen. □ **eutrophicate** v.tr. **eutrophication** /-ˈkeɪʃ(ə)n/ n. **eutrophy** /ˈjuːtrəfɪ/ n. [eutrophy f. Gk eutrophia (as EU-, trephō nourish)]

eV abbr. electronvolt.

evacuate /ɪˈvækjʊˌeɪt/ v.tr. **1 a** remove (people) from a place of danger to stay elsewhere for the duration of the danger. **b** empty (a place) in this way. **2** make empty (a vessel of air etc.). **3** (of troops) withdraw from (a place). **4 a** empty (the bowels or other bodily organ). **b** discharge (faeces etc.). □ **evacuant** n. & adj. **evacuation** /-ˈeɪʃ(ə)n/ n. **evacuative** /-kjʊətɪv/ adj. & n. **evacuator** n. [L evacuare (as E-, vacuus empty)]

evacuee /ɪˌvækjuːˈiː/ n. a person evacuated from a place of danger.

evade /ɪˈveɪd/ v.tr. **1 a** escape from, avoid, esp. by guile or trickery. **b** avoid doing (one's duty etc.). **c** avoid answering (a question) or yielding to (an argument). **2 a** fail to pay (tax due). **b** defeat the intention of (a law etc.), esp. while complying with its letter. **3** (of a thing) elude or baffle (a person). □ **evadable** adj. **evader** n. [F évader f. L evadere (as E-, vadere vas- go)]

evaluate /ɪˈvæljʊˌeɪt/ v.tr. **1** assess, appraise. **2 a** find or state the number or amount of. **b** find a numerical expression for. □ **evaluation** /-ˈeɪʃ(ə)n/ n. **evaluative** /-ətɪv/ adj. **evaluator** n. [back-form. f. evaluation f. F évaluation f. évaluer (as E-, VALUE)]

evanesce /ˌiːvəˈnes, ˌe-/ v.intr. **1** fade from sight; disappear. **2** become effaced. [L evanescere (as E-, vanus empty)]

evanescent /ˌiːvəˈnes(ə)nt, ˌe-/ adj. (of an impression or appearance etc.) quickly fading. □ **evanescence** n. **evanescently** adv.

evangelic /ˌiːvænˈdʒelɪk/ adj. = EVANGELICAL.

evangelical /ˌiːvænˈdʒelɪk(ə)l/ adj. & n. —adj. **1** of or according to the teaching of the gospel or the Christian religion. **2** of the Protestant school maintaining that the doctrine of salvation by faith is the essence of the gospel. —n. a member of the evangelical school. □ **evangelicalism** n. **evangelically** adv. [eccl.L evangelicus f. eccl.Gk euaggelikos f. euaggelion good news (as EU-, ANGEL)]

evangelism /ɪˈvændʒəˌlɪz(ə)m/ n. **1** the preaching or promulgation of the gospel. **2** evangelicalism.

evangelist /ɪˈvændʒəlɪst/ n. **1** any of the writers of the four Gospels (Matthew, Mark, Luke, John). **2** a preacher of the gospel. **3** a lay person doing missionary work.

evangelistic /ɪˌvændʒəˈlɪstɪk/ adj. **1** = EVANGELICAL. **2** of preachers of the gospel. **3** of the four evangelists.

evangelize /ɪˈvændʒəˌlaɪz/ v.tr. (also **-ise**) **1** (also absol.) preach the gospel to. **2** convert (a person) to Christianity. □ **evangelization** /-ˈzeɪʃ(ə)n/ n. **evangelizer** n. [ME f. eccl.L evangelizare f. Gk euaggelizomai f. euaggelion good news]

evaporate /ɪˈvæpəˌreɪt/ v. **1** intr. turn from solid or liquid into vapour. **2** intr. & tr. lose or cause to lose moisture as vapour. **3** intr. & tr. disappear or cause to disappear (our courage evaporated). □ **evaporated milk** milk concentrated by partial evaporation. □ **evaporable** adj. **evaporation** /-ˈreɪʃ(ə)n/ n. **evaporative** /-rətɪv/ adj. **evaporator** n. [L evaporare (as E-, vaporare as VAPOUR)]

evasion /ɪˈveɪʒ(ə)n/ n. **1** the act or a means of evading. **2 a** a subterfuge or prevaricating excuse. **b** an evasive answer. [ME f. OF f. L evasio -onis (as EVADE)]

evasive /ɪˈveɪsɪv/ adj. **1** seeking to evade something. **2** not direct in one's answers etc. **3** enabling or effecting evasion (evasive action). **4** (of a person) tending to evasion; habitually practising evasion. □ **evasively** adv. **evasiveness** n.

eve n. **1** the evening or day before a church festival or any date or event (Christmas Eve; the eve of the funeral). **2** the time just before anything (the eve of the election). **3** archaic evening. [ME, = EVEN²]

even¹ /ˈiːv(ə)n/ adj., adv., & v. —adj. (**evener**, **evenest**) **1** level; flat and smooth. **2 a** uniform in quality; constant. **b** equal in number or amount or value etc. **c** equally balanced. **3** (usu. foll. by with) in the same plane or line. **4** (of a person's temper etc.) equable, calm. **5 a** (of a number such as 4, 6) divisible by two without a remainder. **b** bearing such a number (no parking on even dates). **c** not involving fractions; exact (in even dozens). —adv. **1** used to invite comparison of the stated assertion, negation, etc., with an implied one that is less strong or remarkable (never even opened [let alone read] the letter; does he even suspect [not to say realize] the danger?; ran even faster [not just as fast as before]; even if my watch is right we shall be late [later if it is slow]). **2** used to introduce an extreme case (even you must realize it; it might even cost £100). —v. tr. & intr. (often foll. by up) make or become even. □ **even as** at the very moment that. **even break** colloq. an equal chance. **even chance** an equal chance of success or failure. **even money** betting odds offering the gambler the chance of winning the amount he or she staked. **even now 1** now as well as before. **2** at this very moment. **even so 1** notwithstanding that; nevertheless. **2** quite so. **get** (or **be**) **even with** have one's revenge on. □ **evenly** adv. **evenness** n. [OE efen, efne]

even² /ˈiːv(ə)n/ n. poet. evening. [OE æfen]

even-handed /ˌiːv(ə)nˈhændɪd/ adj. impartial, fair. □ **even-handedly** adv. **even-handedness** n.

evening /ˈiːvnɪŋ/ n. & int. —n. **1** the end part of the day, esp. from about 6 p.m. to bedtime (this evening; during the evening; evening meal). **2** this time spent in a particular way (had a lively evening). **3** a time compared with this, esp. the last part of a person's life. —int. good evening. □ **evening dress** formal dress for evening wear. **evening primrose** any plant of the genus Oenothera with pale yellow flowers that open in the evening. **evening star** a planet, esp. Venus, conspicuous in the west after sunset. [OE æfnung, rel. to EVEN²]

evens /ˈiːv(ə)nz/ n.pl. Brit. = even money.

evensong /ˈiːv(ə)nˌsɒŋ/ n. a service of evening prayer in the Church of England. [EVEN² + SONG]

event /ɪˈvent/ n. **1** a thing that happens or takes place, esp. one of importance. **2 a** the fact of a thing's occurring. **b** a result or outcome. **3** an item in a sports programme, or the programme as a whole. □ **at all events** (or **in any event**) whatever happens. **in the event** as it turns (or turned) out. **in the event of** if (a specified thing) happens. [L eventus f. evenire event- happen (as E-, venire come)]

eventful /ɪˈventfʊl/ adj. marked by noteworthy events. □ **eventfully** adv. **eventfulness** n.

eventide /ˈiːv(ə)nˌtaɪd/ n. archaic or poet. = EVENING. □ **eventide home** a home for the elderly. [OE æfentīd (as EVEN², TIDE)]

eventing /ɪˈventɪŋ/ n. Brit. participation in equestrian competitions, esp. dressage and show-jumping. [EVENT 3 as in *three-day event*]

eventual /ɪˈventjʊəl/ adj. occurring or existing in due course or at last; ultimate. □ **eventually** adv. [as EVENT, after *actual*]

eventuality /ɪˌventjʊˈælɪtɪ/ n. (pl. **-ies**) a possible event or outcome.

eventuate /ɪˈventjʊˌeɪt/ v.intr. formal **1** turn out in a specified way as the result. **2** (often foll. by *in*) result. □ **eventuation** /-ˈeɪʃ(ə)n/ n. [as EVENT, after *actuate*]

ever /ˈevə(r)/ adv. **1** at all times; always (*ever hopeful; ever after*). **2** at any time (*have you ever been to Paris?; nothing ever happens; as good as ever*). **3** as an emphatic word: **a** in any way; at all (*how ever did you do it?; when will they ever learn?*). **b** (prec. by *as*) in any manner possible (*be as quick as ever you can*). **4** (in comb.) constantly (*ever-present; ever-recurring*). **5** (foll. by *so, such*) Brit. colloq. very; very much (*is ever so easy; was ever such a nice man*). **6** (foll. by compar.) constantly, increasingly (*grew ever larger*). □ **ever since** throughout the period since. **for ever 1** for all future time. **2** colloq. for a long time (cf. FOREVER). [OE *æfre*]

■ **Usage** When *ever* is used with a question word for emphasis it is written separately (see sense 2). When used with a relative pronoun or adverb to give it indefinite or general force, *ever* is written as one word with it, e.g. *however it's done, it's difficult.*

evergreen /ˈevəˌɡriːn/ adj. & n. —adj. **1** always green or fresh. **2** (of a plant) retaining green leaves throughout the year. —n. an evergreen plant.

everlasting /ˌevəˈlɑːstɪŋ/ adj. & n. —adj. **1** lasting for ever. **2** lasting for a long time. **3** (of flowers) keeping their shape and colour when dried. —n. **1** eternity. **2** = IMMORTELLE. □ **everlastingly** adv. **everlastingness** n.

evermore /ˌevəˈmɔː(r)/ adv. for ever; always.

every /ˈevrɪ/ adj. **1** each single (*heard every word; watched her every movement*). **2** each at a specified interval in a series (*take every third one; comes every four days*). **3** all possible; the utmost degree of (*there is every prospect of success*). □ **every bit as** colloq. (in comparisons) quite as (*every bit as good*). **every now and again** (or **now and then**) from time to time. **every other** each second in a series (*every other day*). **every so often** at intervals; occasionally. **every which way** US colloq. **1** in all directions. **2** in a disorderly manner. [OE *æfre ælc* ever each]

everybody /ˈevrɪˌbɒdɪ/ pron. every person.

everyday /ˈevrɪˌdeɪ, -ˌdeɪ/ adj. **1** occurring every day. **2** suitable for or used on ordinary days. **3** commonplace, usual.

Everyman /ˈevrɪˌmæn/ n. the ordinary or typical human being; the 'man in the street'. [the principal character in a 15th-c. morality play]

everyone /ˈevrɪˌwʌn/ pron. every person; everybody.

everything /ˈevrɪθɪŋ/ pron. **1** all things; all the things of a group or class. **2** colloq. a great deal (*gave me everything*). **3** an essential consideration (*speed is everything*).

everywhere /ˈevrɪˌweə(r)/ adv. **1** in every place. **2** colloq. in many places.

evict /ɪˈvɪkt/ v.tr. expel (a tenant) from a property by legal process. □ **eviction** n. **evictor** n. [L *evincere evict-* (as E-, *vincere* conquer)]

evidence /ˈevɪd(ə)ns/ n. & v. —n. **1** (often foll. by *for, of*) the available facts, circumstances, etc. supporting or otherwise a belief, proposition, etc., or indicating whether or not a thing is true or valid. **2** Law **a** information given personally or drawn from a document etc. and tending to prove a fact or proposition. **b** statements or proofs admissible as testimony in a lawcourt. **3** clearness, obviousness. —v.tr. be evidence of; attest. □ **in evidence** noticeable, conspicuous. **Queen's** (or **King's** or **State's**) **evidence** Law evidence for the prosecution given by a participant in or accomplice to the crime at issue. [ME f. OF f. L *evidentia* (as EVIDENT)]

evident /ˈevɪd(ə)nt/ adj. **1** plain or obvious (visually or intellectually); manifest. **2** seeming, apparent (*his evident anxiety*). [ME f. OF *evident* or L *evidēre evident-* (as E-, *vidēre* see)]

evidential /ˌevɪˈdenʃ(ə)l/ adj. of or providing evidence. □ **evidentially** adv.

evidently /ˈevɪˌd(ə)ntlɪ/ adv. **1** as shown by evidence. **2** seemingly; as it appears (*was evidently unwilling to go*).

evil /ˈiːv(ə)l, -ɪl/ adj. & n. —adj. **1** morally bad; wicked. **2** harmful or tending to harm, esp. intentionally or characteristically. **3** disagreeable or unpleasant (*has an evil temper*). **4** unlucky; causing misfortune (*evil days*). —n. **1** an evil thing; an instance of something evil. **2** evil quality; wickedness, harm. □ **evil eye** a gaze or stare superstitiously believed to be able to cause material harm. **speak evil of** slander. □ **evilly** adv. **evilness** n. [OE *yfel* f. Gmc]

evince /ɪˈvɪns/ v.tr. **1** indicate or make evident. **2** show that one has (a quality). □ **evincible** adj. **evincive** adj. [L *evincere*: see EVICT]

eviscerate /ɪˈvɪsəˌreɪt/ v.tr. formal **1** disembowel. **2** empty or deprive of essential contents. □ **evisceration** /-ˈreɪʃ(ə)n/ n. [L *eviscerare eviscerat-* (as E-, VISCERA)]

evocative /ɪˈvɒkətɪv/ adj. tending to evoke (esp. feelings or memories). □ **evocatively** adv. **evocativeness** n.

evoke /ɪˈvəʊk/ v.tr. **1** inspire or draw forth (memories, feelings, a response, etc.). **2** summon (a supposed spirit from the dead). □ **evocation** /ˌevəˈkeɪʃ(ə)n/ n. **evoker** n. [L *evocare* (as E-, *vocare* call)]

evolution /ˌiːvəˈluːʃ(ə)n, -ˈljuːʃ(ə)n/ n. **1** gradual development, esp. from a simple to a more complex form. **2** a process by which species develop from earlier forms, as an explanation of their origins. **3** the appearance or presentation of events etc. in due succession (*the evolution of the plot*). **4** a change in the disposition of troops or ships. **5** the giving off or evolving of gas, heat, etc. **6** an opening out. □ **evolutional** adj. **evolutionally** adv. **evolutionary** adj. **evolutionarily** adv. [L *evolutio* unrolling (as EVOLVE)]

evolutionist /ˌiːvəˈluːʃənɪst, -ˈljuːʃənɪst/ n. a person who believes in evolution as explaining the origin of species. □ **evolutionism** n. **evolutionistic** /-ˈnɪstɪk/ adj.

evolve /ɪˈvɒlv/ v. **1** intr. & tr. develop gradually by a natural process. **2** tr. work out or devise (a theory, plan, etc.). **3** intr. & tr. unfold; open out. **4** tr. give off (gas, heat, etc.). □ **evolvable** adj.

evolvement *n*. [L *evolvere evolut-* (as E-, *volvere* roll)]

ewe /juː/ *n*. a female sheep. □ **ewe lamb** one's most cherished possession (2 Sam. 12). [OE *ēowu* f. Gmc]

ewer /ˈjuːə(r)/ *n*. a large pitcher or water-jug with a wide mouth. [ME f. ONF *eviere*, OF *aiguiere*, ult. f. L *aquarius* of water f. *aqua* water]

ex[1] *prep*. **1** (of goods) sold from (*ex-works*). **2** (of stocks or shares) without, excluding. [L, = out of]

ex[2] *n*. *colloq*. a former husband or wife. [absol. use of EX-[1] 2]

ex-[1] *prefix* (also **e-** before some consonants, **ef-** before *f*) **1** forming verbs meaning: **a** out, forth (*exclude*; *exit*). **b** upward (*extol*). **c** thoroughly (*excruciate*). **d** bring into a state (*exasperate*). **e** remove or free from (*expatriate*; *exonerate*). **2** forming nouns from titles of office, status, etc., meaning 'formerly' (*ex-convict*; *ex-president*; *ex-wife*). [L f. *ex* out of]

ex-[2] *prefix* out (*exodus*). [Gk f. *ex* out of]

exacerbate /ekˈsæsəˌbeɪt, ɪg-/ *v.tr*. **1** make (pain, anger, etc.) worse. **2** irritate (a person). □ **exacerbation** /-ˈbeɪʃ(ə)n/ *n*. [L *exacerbare* as EX-[1], *acerbus* bitter)]

exact /ɪgˈzækt/ *adj*. & *v*. —*adj*. **1** accurate; correct in all details (*an exact description*). **2 a** precise. **b** (of a person) tending to precision. —*v.tr*. (often foll. by *from*, *of*) **1** demand and enforce payment of (money, fees, etc.) from a person. **2 a** demand; insist on. **b** (of circumstances) require urgently. □ **exact science** a science admitting of absolute or quantitative precision. □ **exactable** *adj*. **exactitude** *n*. **exactness** *n*. **exactor** *n*. [L *exigere exact-* (as EX-[1], *agere* drive)]

exacting /ɪgˈzæktɪŋ/ *adj*. **1** making great demands. **2** calling for much effort. □ **exactingly** *adv*. **exactingness** *n*.

exaction /ɪgˈzækʃ(ə)n/ *n*. **1** the act or an instance of exacting; the process of being exacted. **2 an** illegal or exorbitant demand; an extortion. **b** a sum or thing exacted. [ME f. L *exactio* (as EXACT)]

exactly /ɪgˈzæktlɪ/ *adv*. **1** accurately, precisely; in an exact manner (*worked it out exactly*). **2** in exact terms (*exactly when did it happen?*). **3** (said in reply) quite so; I quite agree.

exaggerate /ɪgˈzædʒəˌreɪt/ *v.tr*. (also *absol*.) give an impression of (a thing), esp. in speech or writing, that makes it seem larger or greater etc. than it really is. **2** enlarge or alter beyond normal or due proportions (*spoke with exaggerated politeness*). □ **exaggeratedly** *adv*. **exaggeratingly** *adv*. **exaggeration** /-ˈreɪʃ(ə)n/ *n*. **exaggerative** /-rətɪv/ *adj*. **exaggerator** *n*. [L *exaggerare* (as EX-[1], *aggerare* heap up f. *agger* heap)]

exalt /ɪgˈzɔːlt/ *v.tr*. **1** raise in rank or power etc. **2** praise highly. **3** (usu. as **exalted** *adj*.) make lofty or noble (*exalted aims*; *an exalted style*). □ **exaltedly** *adv*. **exaltedness** *n*. **exalter** *n*. [ME f. L *exaltare* (as EX-[1], *altus* high)]

exaltation /ˌegzɔːlˈteɪʃ(ə)n/ *n*. **1** the act or an instance of exalting; the state of being exalted. **2** elation; rapturous emotion. [ME f. OF *exaltation* or LL *exaltatio* (as EXALT)]

exam /ɪgˈzæm/ *n*. = EXAMINATION 3.

examination /ɪgˌzæmɪˈneɪʃ(ə)n/ *n*. **1** the act or an instance of examining; the state of being examined. **2** a detailed inspection. **3** the testing of the proficiency or knowledge of students or

other candidates for a qualification by oral or written questions. **4** an instance of examining or being examined medically. **5** *Law* the formal questioning of the accused or of a witness in court. □ **examinational** *adj*. [ME f. OF f. L *examinatio -onis* (as EXAMINE)]

examine /ɪgˈzæmɪn/ *v*. **1** *tr*. inquire into the nature or condition etc. of. **2** *tr*. look closely or analytically at. **3** *tr*. test the proficiency of, esp. by examination. **4** *tr*. check the health of (a patient) by inspection or experiment. **5** *tr*. *Law* formally question (the accused or a witness) in court. □ **examinable** *adj*. **examinee** /-ˈniː/ *n*. **examiner** *n*. [ME f. OF *examiner* f. L *examinare* weigh, test f. *examen* tongue of a balance, ult. f. *exigere* examine, weigh: see EXACT]

example /ɪgˈzɑːmp(ə)l/ *n*. **1** a thing characteristic of its kind or illustrating a general rule. **2** a person, thing, or piece of conduct, regarded in terms of its fitness to be imitated (*you are a bad example*). **3** a circumstance or treatment seen as a warning to others; a person so treated (*shall make an example of you*). **4** a problem or exercise designed to illustrate a rule. □ **for example** by way of illustration. [ME f. OF f. L *exemplum* (as EXEMPT)]

exasperate /ɪgˈzɑːspəˌreɪt/ *v.tr*. (often as **exasperated** *adj*. or **exasperating** *adj*.) irritate intensely. □ **exasperatedly** *adv*. **exasperatingly** *adv*. **exasperation** /-ˈreɪʃ(ə)n/ *n*. [L *exasperare exasperat-* (as EX-[1], *asper* rough)]

ex cathedra /ˌeks kəˈθiːdrə/ *adj*. & *adv*. with full authority (esp. of a papal pronouncement). [L, = from the (teacher's) chair]

excavate /ˈekskəˌveɪt/ *v.tr*. **1 a** make (a hole or channel) by digging. **b** dig out material from (the ground). **2** reveal or extract by digging. **3** (also *absol*.) *Archaeol*. dig systematically into the ground to explore (a site). □ **excavation** /-ˈveɪʃ(ə)n/ *n*. **excavator** *n*. [L *excavare* (as EX-[1], *cavus* hollow)]

exceed /ɪkˈsiːd/ *v.tr*. **1** (often foll. by *by* an amount) be more or greater than (in number, extent, etc.). **2** go beyond or do more than is warranted by (a set limit, esp. of one's instructions or rights). **3** surpass, excel (a person or achievement). [ME f. OF *exceder* f. L *excedere* (as EX-[1], *cedere cess-* go)]

exceeding /ɪkˈsiːdɪŋ/ *adj*. & *adv*. —*adj*. **1** surpassing in amount or degree. **2** pre-eminent. —*adv*. *archaic* = EXCEEDINGLY 2.

exceedingly /ɪkˈsiːdɪŋlɪ/ *adv*. **1** very; to a great extent. **2** surpassingly, pre-eminently.

excel /ɪkˈsel/ *v*. (**excelled**, **excelling**) (often foll. by *in*, *at*) **1** *tr*. be superior to. **2** *intr*. be pre-eminent or the most outstanding (*excels at games*). □ **excel oneself** surpass one's previous performance. [ME f. L *excellere* (as EX-[1], *celsus* lofty)]

excellence /ˈeksələns/ *n*. **1** the state of excelling; surpassing merit or quality. **2** the activity etc. in which a person excels. [ME f. OF *excellence* f. L *excellentia* (as EXCEL)]

Excellency /ˈeksələnsɪ/ *n*. (*pl*. **-ies**) (usu. prec. by *Your*, *His*, *Her*, *Their*) a title used in addressing or referring to certain high officials, e.g. ambassadors and governors. [ME f. L *excellentia* (as EXCEL)]

excellent /ˈeksələnt/ *adj*. extremely good; pre-eminent. □ **excellently** *adv*. [ME f. OF (as EXCEL)]

except /ɪkˈsept/ v., prep., & conj. —v.tr. (often as **excepted** adj. placed after object) exclude from a general statement, condition, etc. (*excepted him from the amnesty; present company excepted*). —prep. (often foll. by *for*) not including; other than (*all failed except him; all here except for John; is all right except that it is too long*). —conj. archaic unless (*except he be born again*). [ME f. L *excipere except-* (as EX-¹, *capere* take)]

excepting /ɪkˈseptɪŋ/ prep. = EXCEPT prep.

■ **Usage** This word is only used after *not* and *always*.

exception /ɪkˈsepʃ(ə)n/ n. **1** the act or an instance of excepting; the state of being excepted (*made an exception in my case*). **2** a thing that has been or will be excepted. **3** an instance that does not follow a rule. □ **take exception** (often foll. by *to*) object; be resentful (about). **with the exception of** except; not including. [ME f. OF f. L *exceptio -onis* (as EXCEPT)]

exceptionable /ɪkˈsepʃ(ə)nəb(ə)l/ adj. open to objection. □ **exceptionably** adv.

■ **Usage** This word is sometimes confused with *exceptional*.

exceptional /ɪkˈsepʃ(ə)n(ə)l/ adj. **1** forming an exception. **2** unusual; not typical (*exceptional circumstances*). **3** unusually good; outstanding. □ **exceptionality** /-ˈnælɪtɪ/ n. **exceptionally** adv.

■ **Usage** See note at *exceptionable*.

excerpt n. & v. —n. /ˈeksɜːpt/ a short extract from a book, film, piece of music, etc. —v.tr. /ɪkˈsɜːpt/ (also *absol.*) **1** take an excerpt or excerpts from (a book etc.). **2** take (an extract) from a book etc. □ **excerptible** /-ˈsɜːptɪb(ə)l/ adj. **excerption** /-ˈsɜːpʃ(ə)n/ n. [L *excerpere excerpt-* (as EX-¹, *carpere* pluck)]

excess /ɪkˈses, ˈekses/ n. & adj. —n. **1** the state or an instance of exceeding. **2** the amount by which one quantity or number exceeds another. **3** exceeding of a proper or permitted limit. **4** a the overstepping of the accepted limits of moderation, esp. intemperance in eating or drinking. **b** (in *pl.*) outrageous or immoderate behaviour. **5** an extreme or improper degree or extent (*an excess of cruelty*). **6** part of an insurance claim to be paid by the insured, esp. by prior agreement. —attrib.adj. /ˈusu. ˈekses/ **1** that exceeds a limited or prescribed amount (*excess weight*). **2** required as extra payment (*excess postage*). □ **in** (or *to*) **excess** exceeding the proper amount or degree. **in excess of** more than; exceeding. [ME f. OF *exces* f. L *excessus* (as EXCEED)]

excessive /ɪkˈsesɪv/ adj. **1** too much or too great. **2** more than what is normal or necessary. □ **excessively** adv. **excessiveness** n.

exchange /ɪksˈtʃeɪndʒ/ n. & v. —n. **1** the act or an instance of giving one thing and receiving another in its place. **2** the giving of money for its equivalent in the money of the same or another country. **3** the central telephone office of a district, where connections are effected. **4** a place where merchants, bankers, etc. gather to transact business. **5 a** an office where certain information is given or a service provided, usu. involving two parties. **b** an employment office. **6** a system of settling debts between persons (esp. in different countries) without the use of money, by bills of exchange (see BILL¹). **7 a** a short conversation, esp. a disagreement or quarrel. **b** a sequence of letters between correspondents. **8** (*attrib.*) forming part of an exchange, e.g. of personnel between institutions (*an exchange student*). —v. **1** tr. (often foll. by *for*) give or receive (one thing) in place of another. **2** tr. give and receive as equivalents (e.g. things or people, blows, information, etc.); give one and receive another of. **3** intr. (often foll. by *with*) make an exchange. □ **exchange rate** the value of one currency in terms of another. **in exchange** (often foll. by *for*) as a thing exchanged (for). □ **exchangeable** adj. **exchangeability** /-ˈbɪlɪtɪ/ n. **exchanger** n. [ME f. OF *eschangier* f. Rmc (as EX-¹, CHANGE)]

exchequer /ɪksˈtʃekə(r)/ n. **1** Brit. the former government department in charge of national revenue. **2** a royal or national treasury. **3** the money of a private individual or group. [ME f. AF *escheker*, OF *eschequier* f. med.L *scaccarium* chessboard (its orig. sense, with ref. to keeping accounts on a chequered cloth)]

■ **Usage** With reference to sense 1, the functions of this department now belong to the Treasury, although the name formally survives, esp. in the title *Chancellor of the Exchequer*.

excise¹ /ˈeksaɪz/ n. & v. —n. **1 a** a duty or tax levied on goods and commodities produced or sold within the country of origin. **b** a tax levied on certain licences. **2** Brit. a former government office collecting excise. —v.tr. **1** charge excise on (goods). **2** force (a person) to pay excise. [MDu. *excijs, accijs*, perh. f. Rmc: rel. to CENSUS]

excise² /ɪkˈsaɪz, ek-/ v.tr. **1** remove (a passage of a book etc.). **2** cut out (an organ etc.) by surgery. □ **excision** /ɪkˈsɪʒ(ə)n/ n. [L *excidere excis-* (as EX-¹, *caedere* cut)]

excitable /ɪkˈsaɪtəb(ə)l/ adj. (esp. of a person) easily excited. □ **excitability** /-ˈbɪlɪtɪ/ n. **excitably** adv.

excitation /ˌeksɪˈteɪʃ(ə)n/ n. **1** the act or an instance of exciting; the state of being excited; excitement.

excite /ɪkˈsaɪt/ v.tr. **1 a** rouse the feelings or emotions of (a person); bring into play; rouse up (feelings, faculties, etc.). **c** arouse sexually. **2** provoke; bring about (an action or active condition). **3** promote the activity of (an organism, tissue, etc.) by stimulus. □ **excitant** /ˈeksɪt(ə)nt, ɪkˈsaɪt(ə)nt/ adj. & n. **excitative** /-tətɪv/ adj. **excitatory** /-tətərɪ/ adj. **excitedly** adv. **excitedness** n. **excitement** n. **exciter** n. [ME f. OF *exciter* or L *excitare* frequent. of *exciēre* (as EX-¹, *ciēre* set in motion)]

exciting /ɪkˈsaɪtɪŋ/ adj. arousing great interest or enthusiasm. □ **excitingly** adv. **excitingness** n.

exclaim /ɪkˈskleɪm/ v. **1** intr. cry out suddenly, esp. in anger, surprise, pain, etc. **2** tr. (foll. by *that*) utter by exclaiming. [F *exclamer* or L *exclamare* (as EX-¹; cf. CLAIM)]

exclamation /ˌekskləˈmeɪʃ(ə)n/ n. **1** the act or an instance of exclaiming. **2** words exclaimed; a strong sudden cry. □ **exclamation mark** (US **point**) a punctuation mark (!) indicating an exclamation. [ME f. OF *exclamation* or L *exclamatio* (as EXCLAIM)]

exclamatory /ɪkˈsklæmətərɪ/ adj. of or serving as an exclamation.

exclude /ɪkˈskluːd/ v.tr. **1** shut or keep out (a person or thing) from a place, group, privilege, etc. **2** expel and shut out. **3** remove from consideration (*no theory can be excluded*). **4** prevent the occurrence of; make impossible (*excluded all doubt*). □ **excludable** *adj.* **excluder** *n.* [ME f. L *excludere exclus-* (as EX-¹, *claudere* shut)]

exclusion /ɪkˈsklu:ʒ(ə)n/ *n.* the act or an instance of excluding; the state of being excluded. □ **to the exclusion of** so as to exclude. □ **exclusionary** *adj.* [L *exclusio* (as EXCLUDE)]

exclusive /ɪkˈsklu:sɪv/ *adj.* & *n.* —*adj.* **1** excluding other things. **2** (*predic.*; foll. by *of*) not including; except for. **3** tending to exclude others, esp. socially; select. **4** catering for few or select customers; high-class. **5 a** (of a commodity) not obtainable elsewhere. **b** (of a newspaper article) not published elsewhere. **6** (*predic.*; foll. by *to*) restricted or limited to; existing or available only in. **7** (of terms etc.) excluding all but what is specified. **8** employed or followed or held to the exclusion of all else (*my exclusive occupation*; *exclusive rights*). —*n.* an article or story published by only one newspaper or periodical. □ **exclusively** *adv.* **exclusiveness** *n.* **exclusivity** /-ˈsɪvɪtɪ/ *n.* [med.L *exclusivus* (as EXCLUDE)]

excogitate /eksˈkɒdʒɪˌteɪt/ *v.tr.* think out; contrive. □ **excogitation** /-ˈteɪʃ(ə)n/ *n.* [L *excogitare excogitat-* (as EX-¹, *cogitare* COGITATE)]

excommunicate *v.*, *adj.*, & *n.* *Eccl.* —*v.tr.* /ˌekskəˈmju:nɪˌkeɪt/ officially exclude (a person) from participation in the sacraments, or from formal communion with the Church. —*adj.* /ˌekskəˈmju:nɪkət/ excommunicated. —*n.* /ˌekskəˈmju:nɪkət/ an excommunicated person. □ **excommunication** /-ˈkeɪʃ(ə)n/ *n.* **excommunicative** /-kətɪv/ *adj.* **excommunicator** *n.* **excommunicatory** /-ˈkeɪtərɪ/ *adj.* [L *excommunicare -atus* (as EX-¹, *communis* COMMON)]

excoriate /eksˈkɔ:rɪˌeɪt/ *v.tr.* **1 a** remove part of the skin of (a person etc.) by abrasion. **b** strip or peel off (skin). **2** censure severely. □ **excoriation** /-ˈeɪʃ(ə)n/ *n.* [L *excoriare excoriat-* (as EX-¹, *corium* hide)]

excrement /ˈekskrɪmənt/ *n.* (in *sing.* or *pl.*) faeces. □ **excremental** /-ˈment(ə)l/ *adj.* [F *excrément* or L *excrementum* (as EXCRETE)]

excrescence /ɪkˈskres(ə)ns/ *n.* **1** an abnormal or morbid outgrowth on the body or a plant. **2** an ugly addition. □ **excrescent** *adj.* **excrescential** /ˌekskrɪˈsenʃ(ə)l/ *adj.* [L *excrescentia* (as EX-¹, *crescere* grow)]

excreta /eksˈkri:tə, ɪk-/ *n.pl.* waste discharged from the body, esp. faeces and urine. [L neut. pl.: see EXCRETE]

excrete /ɪkˈskri:t/ *v.tr.* (of an animal or plant) separate and expel waste matter as a result of metabolism. □ **excreter** *n.* **excretion** *n.* **excretive** *adj.* **excretory** *adj.* [L *excernere excret-* (as EX-¹, *cernere* sift)]

excruciate /ɪkˈskru:ʃɪˌeɪt/ *v.tr.* (esp. as **excruciating** *adj.*) torment acutely (a person's senses); torture mentally. □ **excruciatingly** *adv.* **excruciation** /-ˈeɪʃ(ə)n/ *n.* [L *excruciare excruciat-* (as EX-¹, *cruciare* torment f. *crux crucis* cross)]

exculpate /ˈekskʌlˌpeɪt/ *v.tr.* *formal* **1** free from blame. **2** (foll. by *from*) clear (a person) of a charge. □ **exculpation** /-ˈpeɪʃ(ə)n/ *n.* **exculpatory** /-ˈkʌlpətərɪ/ *adj.* [med.L *exculpare exculpat-* (as EX-¹, *culpa* blame)]

excursion /ɪkˈskɜ:ʃ(ə)n/ *n.* a short journey or ramble for pleasure, with return to the starting-point. □ **excursional** *adj.* **excursionary** *adj.*

excursionist *n.* [L *excursio* f. *excurrere excurs-* (as EX-¹, *currere* run)]

excursive /ɪkˈskɜ:sɪv/ *adj.* digressive; diverse. □ **excursively** *adv.* **excursiveness** *n.*

excuse *v.* & *n.* —*v.tr.* /ɪkˈskju:z/ **1** attempt to lessen the blame attaching to (a person, act, or fault). **2** (of a fact or circumstance) serve in mitigation of (a person or act). **3** obtain exemption for (a person or oneself). **4** (foll. by *from*) release (a person) from a duty etc. **5** overlook or forgive (a fault or offence). **6** (foll. by *for*) forgive (a person) for a fault. **7** not insist upon (what is due). **8** *refl.* apologize for leaving. —*n.* /ɪkˈskju:s, ek-/ **1** a reason put forward to mitigate or justify an offence, fault, etc. **2** an apology (*made my excuses*). **3** (foll. by *for*) a poor or inadequate example of. □ **be excused** be allowed to leave a room etc., e.g. to go to the lavatory. **excuse me** a polite apology for lack of ceremony, for an interruption etc., or for disagreeing. □ **excusable** /-ˈkju:zəb(ə)l/ *adj.* **excusably** /-ˈkju:zəblɪ/ *adv.* **excusatory** /-ˈkju:zətərɪ/ *adj.* [ME f. OF *escuser* f. L *excusare* (as EX-¹, *causa* CAUSE, accusation)]

ex-directory /ˌeksdaɪˈrektərɪ/ *adj.* *Brit.* not listed in a telephone directory, at the wish of the subscriber.

ex dividend /eksˈdɪvɪˌdend/ *adj.* & *adv.* (of stocks or shares) not including the next dividend.

execrable /ˈeksɪkrəb(ə)l/ *adj.* abominable, detestable. □ **execrably** *adv.* [ME f. OF f. L *execrabilis* (as EXECRATE)]

execrate /ˈeksɪˌkreɪt/ *v.* **1** *tr.* express or feel abhorrence for. **2** *tr.* curse (a person or thing). **3** *intr.* utter curses. □ **execration** /-ˈkreɪʃ(ə)n/ *n.* **execrative** *adj.* **execratory** *adj.* [L *exsecrare* (as EX-¹, *sacrare* devote f. *sacer* sacred, accursed)]

executant /ɪɡˈzekjʊt(ə)nt/ *n.* *formal* **1** a performer, esp. of music. **2** one who carries something into effect. [F *exécutant* pres. part. (as EXECUTE)]

execute /ˈeksɪˌkju:t/ *v.tr.* **1 a** carry out a sentence of death on (a condemned person). **b** kill as a political act. **2** carry into effect, perform (a plan, duty, command, operation, etc.). **3 a** carry out a design for (a product of art or skill). **b** perform (a musical composition, dance, etc.). **4** make (a legal instrument) valid by signing, sealing, etc. **5** put into effect (a judicial sentence, the terms of a will, etc.). □ **executable** *adj.* [ME f. OF *executer* f. med.L *executare* f. L *exsequi exsecut-* (as EX-¹, *sequi* follow)]

execution /ˌeksɪˈkju:ʃ(ə)n/ *n.* **1** the carrying out of a sentence of death. **2** the act or an instance of carrying out or performing something. **3** technique or style of performance in the arts, esp. music. □ **executionary** *adj.* [ME f. OF f. L *executio -onis* (as EXECUTE)]

executioner /ˌeksɪˈkju:ʃənə(r)/ *n.* an official who carries out a sentence of death.

executive /ɪɡˈzekjʊtɪv/ *n.* & *adj.* —*n.* **1** a person or body with managerial or administrative responsibility in a business organization etc.; a senior businessman. **2** a branch of a government or organization concerned with executing laws, agreements, etc., or with other administration or management. —*adj.* **1** concerned with executing laws, agreements, etc., or with other administration or management. **2** relating to or having the function of executing. □ **executively** *adv.* [med.L *executivus* (as EXECUTE)]

executor /ɪgˈzekjʊtə(r)/ n. (fem. **executrix** /-trɪks/) a person appointed by a testator to carry out the terms of his or her will. □ **literary executor** a person entrusted with a writer's papers, unpublished works, etc. □ **executorial** /-ˈtɔːrɪəl/ adj. **executorship** n. **executory** adj. [ME f. AF executor, -our f. L executor -oris (as EXECUTE)]

exegesis /ˌeksɪˈdʒiːsɪs/ n. (pl. **exegeses** /-siːz/) critical explanation of a text, esp. of Scripture. □ **exegete** /ˈeksɪˌdʒiːt/ n. **exegetic** /-ˈdʒetɪk/ adj. **exegetical** /-ˈdʒetɪk(ə)l/ adj. **exegetist** /-ˈdʒiːtɪst/ n. [Gk exēgēsis f. exēgeomai interpret (as EX-[2], hēgeomai lead)]

exemplar /ɪgˈzemplə(r), -plɑː(r)/ n. 1 a model or pattern. 2 a typical instance of a class of things. 3 a parallel instance. [ME f. OF exemplaire f. LL exemplarium (as EXAMPLE)]

exemplary /ɪgˈzemplərɪ/ adj. 1 fit to be imitated; outstandingly good. 2 serving as a warning. 3 illustrative, representative. □ **exemplarily** adv. **exemplariness** n. [LL exemplaris (as EXAMPLE)]

exemplify /ɪgˈzemplɪˌfaɪ/ v.tr. (**-ies, -ied**) 1 illustrate by example. 2 be an example of. □ **exemplification** /-fɪˈkeɪʃ(ə)n/ n. [ME f. med.L exemplificare (as EXAMPLE)]

exempt /ɪgˈzempt/ adj. & v. —adj. 1 free from an obligation or liability etc. imposed on others. 2 (foll. by from) not liable to. —v.tr. (foll. by from) free from an obligation, esp. one imposed on others. □ **exemption** n. [ME f. L exemptus past part. of eximere exempt- (as EX-[1], emere take)]

exequies /ˈeksɪkwɪz/ n.pl. formal funeral rites. [ME f. OF f. L exsequiae (as EX-[1], sequi follow)]

exercise /ˈeksəˌsaɪz/ n. & v. —n. 1 activity requiring physical effort, done esp. as training or to sustain or improve health. 2 mental or spiritual activity, esp. as practice to develop a skill. 3 (often in pl.) a particular task or set of tasks devised as practice in a technique etc. 4 a the use or application of a mental faculty, right, etc. b practice of an ability, quality, etc. 5 (often in pl.) military drill or manoeuvres. 6 (foll. by in) a process directed at or concerned with something specified (was an exercise in public relations). —v. 1 tr. use or apply (a faculty, right, influence, restraint, etc.). 2 tr. perform (a function). 3 a intr. take (esp. physical) exercise; do exercises. b tr. provide (an animal) with exercise. c tr. train (a person). 4 tr. a tax the powers of. b perplex, worry. □ **exercise book** 1 a book containing exercises. 2 a book for writing school work, notes, etc., in. □ **exercisable** adj. **exerciser** n. [ME f. OF exercice f. L exercitium f. exercere exercit- keep at work (as EX-[1], arcēre restrain)]

exert /ɪgˈzɜːt/ v.tr. 1 exercise, bring to bear (a quality, force, influence, etc.). 2 refl. (often foll. by for, or to + infin.) use one's efforts or endeavours; strive. □ **exertion** n. [L exserere exsert- put forth (as EX-[1], serere bind)]

exeunt /ˈeksɪˌʌnt/ v.intr. (as a stage direction) (actors) leave the stage. □ **exeunt omnes** all leave the stage. [L, = they all go out: 3rd pers. pl. pres. of exire go out: see EXIT]

exfoliate /eksˈfəʊlɪˌeɪt/ v.intr. 1 (of bone, the skin, a mineral, etc.) come off in scales or layers. 2 (of a tree) throw off layers of bark. □ **exfoliation** /-ˈeɪʃ(ə)n/ n. **exfoliative** /-lɪətɪv/ adj. [LL exfoliare exfoliat- (as EX-[1], folium leaf)]

ex gratia /eks ˈgreɪʃə/ adv. & adj. —adv. as a favour rather than from an (esp. legal) obligation. —adj. granted on this basis. [L, = from favour]

exhalation /ˌekshəˈleɪʃ(ə)n/ n. 1 a an expiration of air. b a puff of breath. 2 a mist, vapour. [ME f. L exhalatio (as EXHALE)]

exhale /eksˈheɪl, ɪgz-/ v. 1 tr. breathe out (esp. air or smoke) from the lungs. 2 tr. & intr. give off or be given off in vapour. □ **exhalable** adj. [ME f. OF exhaler f. L exhalare (as EX-[1], halare breathe)]

exhaust /ɪgˈzɔːst/ v. & n. —v.tr. 1 consume or use up the whole of. 2 (often as **exhausted** adj. or **exhausting** adj.) use up the strength or resources of; tire out. 3 study or expound on (a subject) completely. 4 (often foll. by of) empty (a vessel etc.) of its contents. —n. 1 waste gases etc. expelled from an engine after combustion. 2 (also **exhaust-pipe**) the pipe or system by which these are expelled. □ **exhauster** n. **exhaustible** adj. **exhaustibility** /-ˈbɪlɪtɪ/ n. **exhaustibly** adv. [L exhaurire exhaust- (as EX-[1], haurire draw (water), drain)]

exhaustion /ɪgˈzɔːstʃ(ə)n/ n. 1 the act or an instance of exhausting; the state of being exhausted. 2 a total loss of strength. [LL exhaustio (as EXHAUST)]

exhaustive /ɪgˈzɔːstɪv/ adj. 1 thorough, comprehensive. 2 tending to exhaust a subject. □ **exhaustively** adv. **exhaustiveness** n.

exhibit /ɪgˈzɪbɪt/ v. & n. —v.tr. (**exhibited**, **exhibiting**) 1 show or reveal publicly (for amusement, in competition, etc.). 2 a show, display. b manifest (a quality). 3 submit for consideration. —n. 1 a thing or collection of things forming part or all of an exhibition. 2 a document or other item or object produced in a lawcourt as evidence. □ **exhibitory** adj. [L exhibēre exhibit- (as EX-[1], habēre hold)]

exhibition /ˌeksɪˈbɪʃ(ə)n/ n. 1 a display (esp. public) of works of art, industrial products, etc. 2 the act or an instance of exhibiting; the state of being exhibited. 3 Brit. a scholarship, esp. from the funds of a school, college, etc. [ME f. OF f. LL exhibitio -onis (as EXHIBIT)]

exhibitioner /ˌeksɪˈbɪʃənə(r)/ n. Brit. a student who has been awarded an exhibition.

exhibitionism /ˌeksɪˈbɪʃəˌnɪz(ə)m/ n. 1 a tendency towards display or extravagant behaviour. 2 Psychol. a mental condition characterized by the compulsion to display one's genitals indecently in public. □ **exhibitionist** n. **exhibitionistic** /-ˈnɪstɪk/ adj. **exhibitionistically** /-ˈnɪstɪkəlɪ/ adv.

exhibitor /ɪgˈzɪbɪtə(r)/ n. a person who provides an item or items for an exhibition.

exhilarate /ɪgˈzɪləˌreɪt/ v.tr. (often as **exhilarating** adj. or **exhilarated** adj.) affect with great liveliness or joy; raise the spirits of. □ **exhilarant** adj. & n. **exhilaratingly** adv. **exhilaration** /-ˈreɪʃ(ə)n/ n. **exhilarative** /-rətɪv/ adj. [L exhilarare (as EX-[1], hilaris cheerful)]

exhort /ɪgˈzɔːt/ v.tr. (often foll. by to + infin.) urge or advise strongly or earnestly. □ **exhortation** /-ˈteɪʃ(ə)n/ n. **exhortative** /-tətɪv/ adj. **exhortatory** /-tətərɪ/ adj. **exhorter** n. [ME f. OF exhorter or L exhortari (as EX-[1], hortari exhort)]

exhume /eksˈhjuːm, ɪgˈzjuːm/ v.tr. dig out, unearth (esp. a buried corpse). □ **exhumation**

/-'meɪʃ(ə)n/ *n.* [F *exhumer* f. med.L *exhumare* (as EX-[1], *humus* ground)]

ex hypothesi /ˌeks haɪ'pɒθəsɪ/ *adv.* according to the hypothesis proposed. [mod.L]

exigency /'eksɪdʒənsɪ, ɪg'zɪdʒ-/ *n.* (*pl.* **-ies**) (also **exigence** /'eksɪdʒ(ə)ns/) **1** an urgent need or demand. **2** an emergency. [F *exigence* & LL *exigentia* (as EXIGENT)]

exigent /'eksɪdʒ(ə)nt/ *adj.* **1** requiring much; exacting. **2** urgent, pressing. [ME f. L *exigere* EXACT]

exiguous /eg'zɪgjʊəs, ɪg-/ *adj.* scanty, small. □ **exiguity** /-'gjuːɪtɪ/ *n.* **exiguously** *adv.* **exiguousness** *n.* [L *exiguus* scanty f. *exigere* weigh exactly: see EXACT]

exile /'eksaɪl, 'egz-/ *n.* & *v.* —*n.* **1** expulsion, or the state of being expelled, from one's native land or (**internal exile**) native town etc. **2** long absence abroad, esp. enforced. **3** a person expelled or long absent from his or her native country. —*v.tr.* (foll. by *from*) officially expel (a person) from his or her native country or town etc. □ **exilic** /-'sɪlɪk, -'zɪlɪk/ *adj.* [ME f. OF *exil*, *exiler* f. L *exilium* banishment]

exist /ɪg'zɪst/ *v.intr.* **1** have a place as part of objective reality. **2 a** have being under specified conditions. **b** (foll. by *as*) exist in the form of. **3** (of circumstances etc.) occur; be found. **4** be alive, live. [prob. back-form. f. EXISTENCE; cf. LL *existere*]

existence /ɪg'zɪst(ə)ns/ *n.* **1** the fact or condition of being or existing. **2** the manner of one's existing or living. **3** all that exists. [ME f. OF *existence* or LL *existentia* f. L *exsistere* (as EX-[1], *stare* stand)]

existent /ɪg'zɪst(ə)nt/ *adj.* existing, actual, current.

existential /ˌegzɪ'stenʃ(ə)l/ *adj.* **1** of or relating to existence. **2** *Philos.* concerned with existence, esp. with human existence as viewed by existentialism. □ **existentially** *adv.* [LL *existentialis* (as EXISTENCE)]

existentialism /ˌegzɪ'stenʃəˌlɪz(ə)m/ *n.* a philosophical theory emphasizing the existence of the individual person as a free and responsible agent determining his or her own development. □ **existentialist** *n.* [G *Existentialismus* (as EXISTENTIAL)]

exit /'eksɪt, 'egzɪt/ *n.* & *v.* —*n.* **1** a passage or door by which to leave a room, building, etc. **2 a** the act of going out. **b** the right to go out. **3** a place where vehicles can leave a motorway or major road. **4** the departure of an actor from the stage. —*v.intr.* (**exited, exiting**) **1** go out of a room, building, etc. **2** (as a stage direction) (an actor) leaves the stage (*exit Macbeth*). [L, 3rd sing. pres. of *exire* go out (as EX-[1], *ire* go): cf. L *exitus* going out]

exo- /'eksəʊ/ *comb. form* external. [Gk *exō* outside]

exocrine /'eksəʊˌkraɪn/ *adj.* (of a gland) secreting through a duct. [EXO- + Gk *krinō* sift]

exodus /'eksədəs/ *n.* **1** a mass departure of people (esp. emigrants). **2** (**Exodus**) *Bibl.* **a** the departure of the Israelites from Egypt. **b** the book of the Old Testament relating this. [eccl.L f. Gk *exodos* (as EX-[2], *hodos* way)]

ex officio /ˌeks ə'fɪʃɪəʊ/ *adv.* & *adj.* by virtue of one's office or status. [L]

exonerate /ɪg'zɒnəˌreɪt/ *v.tr.* (often foll. by *from*) **1** free or declare free from blame etc. **2** release from a duty etc. □ **exoneration** /-'reɪʃ(ə)n/ *n.*

exonerative /-rətɪv/ *adj.* [L *exonerare exonerat-* (as EX-[1], *onus, oneris* burden)]

exophthalmos /ˌeksɒf'θælmɒs/ *n.* (also **exophthalmus, exophthalmia** /-mɪə/) *Med.* abnormal protrusion of the eyeball. □ **exophthalmic** *adj.* [mod.L f. Gk *exophthalmos* having prominent eyes (as EX-[2], *ophthalmos* eye)]

exorbitant /ɪg'zɔːbɪt(ə)nt/ *adj.* (of a price, demand, etc.) grossly excessive. □ **exorbitance** *n.* **exorbitantly** *adv.* [LL *exorbitare* (as EX-[1], *orbita* ORBIT)]

exorcize /'eksɔːˌsaɪz/ *v.tr.* (also **-ise**) **1** expel (a supposed evil spirit) by invocation or by use of a holy name. **2** (often foll. by *of*) free (a person or place) of a supposed evil spirit. □ **exorcism** *n.* **exorcist** *n.* **exorcization** /-'zeɪʃ(ə)n/ *n.* [F *exorciser* or eccl.L *exorcizare* f. Gk *exorkizō* (as EX-[2], *horkos* oath)]

exoskeleton /ˌeksəʊ'skelɪt(ə)n/ *n.* a rigid external covering for the body in certain animals, esp. arthropods. □ **exoskeletal** *adj.*

exosphere /'eksəʊˌsfɪə(r)/ *n.* the layer of atmosphere furthest from the earth.

exothermic /ˌeksəʊ'θɜːmɪk/ *adj.* (also **exothermal** /-m(ə)l/) esp. *Chem.* occurring or formed with the evolution of heat. □ **exothermally** *adv.* **exothermically** *adv.*

exotic /ɪg'zɒtɪk/ *adj.* & *n.* —*adj.* **1** introduced from or originating in a foreign (esp. tropical) country (*exotic fruits*). **2** attractively or remarkably strange or unusual; bizarre. —*n.* an exotic person or thing. □ **exotically** *adv.* **exoticism** /-tɪˌsɪz(ə)m/ *n.* [L *exoticus* f. Gk *exōtikos* f. *exō* outside]

exotica /ɪg'zɒtɪkə/ *n.pl.* remarkably strange or rare objects. [L, neut. pl. of *exoticus*: see EXOTIC]

expand /ɪk'spænd/ *v.* **1** *tr.* & *intr.* increase in size or bulk or importance. **2** *intr.* (often foll. by *on*) give a fuller description or account. **3** *intr.* become more genial or effusive; discard one's reserve. **4** *tr.* set or write out in full (something condensed or abbreviated). **5** *tr.* & *intr.* spread out flat. □ **expandable** *adj.* **expander** *n.* **expansible** *adj.* **expansibility** /-'bɪlɪtɪ/ *n.* [ME f. L *expandere expans-* spread out (as EX-[1], *pandere* spread)]

expanse /ɪk'spæns/ *n.* a wide continuous area or extent of land, space, etc. [mod.L *expansum* neut. past part. (as EXPAND)]

expansile /ɪk'spænsaɪl/ *adj.* **1** of expansion. **2** capable of expansion.

expansion /ɪk'spænʃ(ə)n/ *n.* **1** the act or an instance of expanding; the state of being expanded. **2** enlargement of the scale or scope of (esp. commercial) operations. **3** increase in the amount of a State's territory or area of control. □ **expansionary** *adj.* **expansionism** *n.* **expansionist** *n.* **expansionistic** /-'nɪstɪk/ *adj.* (all in senses 2, 3). [LL *expansio* (as EXPAND)]

expansive /ɪk'spænsɪv/ *adj.* **1** able or tending to expand. **2** extensive, wide-ranging. **3** (of a person, feelings, or speech) effusive, open. □ **expansively** *adv.* **expansiveness** *n.* **expansivity** /-'sɪvɪtɪ/ *n.*

expat /eks'pæt/ *n.* & *adj. colloq.* = EXPATRIATE. [abbr.]

expatiate /ɪk'speɪʃɪˌeɪt/ *v.intr.* (usu. foll. by *on*, *upon*) speak or write at length or in detail. □ **expatiation** /-'eɪʃ(ə)n/ *n.* **expatiatory** /-ʃɪətərɪ/ *adj.* [L *exspatiari* digress (as EX-[1], *spatium* SPACE)]

expatriate *adj.*, *n.*, & *v.* —*adj.* /eksˈpætrɪət, -ˈpeɪtrɪət/ **1** living abroad, esp. for a long period. **2** expelled from one's country; exiled. —*n.* /eksˈpætrɪət, -ˈpeɪtrɪət/ an expatriate person. —*v.tr.* /eksˈpætrɪˌeɪt, -ˈpeɪtrɪˌeɪt/ expel or remove (a person) from his or her native country. □ **expatriation** /-ˈeɪʃ(ə)n/ *n.* [med.L *expatriare* (as EX-¹, *patria* native country)]

expect /ɪkˈspekt/ *v.tr.* **1** (often foll. by *to* + infin., or *that* + clause) **a** regard as likely; assume as a future event or occurrence. **b** (often foll. by *of*) look for as appropriate or one's due (from a person) (*I expect cooperation*; *expect you to be here*). **2** *colloq.* (often foll. by *that* + clause) think, suppose (*I expect we'll be on time*). **3** be shortly to have (a baby) (*is expecting twins*). □ **expectable** *adj.* [L *exspectare* (as EX-¹, *spectare* look, frequent. of *specere* see)]

expectancy /ɪkˈspektənsɪ/ *n.* (pl. -**ies**) **1** a state of expectation. **2** a prospect, esp. of future possession. **3** (foll. by *of*) a prospective chance. [L *exspectantia*, *exp-* (as EXPECT)]

expectant /ɪkˈspekt(ə)nt/ *adj.* **1** (often foll. by *of*) expecting. **2** having the expectation of possession, status, etc. **3** expecting a baby (said of the mother or father). □ **expectantly** *adv.*

expectation /ˌekspekˈteɪʃ(ə)n/ *n.* **1** the act or an instance of expecting or looking forward. **2** something expected or hoped for. **3** (foll. by *of*) the probability of an event. **4** (in *pl.*) one's prospects of inheritance. [L *expectatio* (as EXPECT)]

expectorant /ekˈspektərənt/ *adj.* & *n.* —*adj.* causing the coughing out of phlegm etc. —*n.* an expectorant medicine.

expectorate /ekˈspektəˌreɪt/ *v.tr.* (also *absol.*) cough or spit out (phlegm etc.) from the chest or lungs. □ **expectoration** /-ˈreɪʃ(ə)n/ *n.* **expectorator** *n.* [L *expectorare expectorat-* (as EX-¹, *pectus -oris* breast)]

expedient /ɪkˈspiːdɪənt/ *adj.* & *n.* —*adj.* **1** advantageous; advisable on practical rather than moral grounds. **2** suitable, appropriate. —*n.* a means of attaining an end; a resource. □ **expedience** *n.* **expediency** *n.* **expediently** *adv.* [ME f. L *expedire*: see EXPEDITE]

expedite /ˈekspɪˌdaɪt/ *v.tr.* **1** assist the progress of; hasten (an action, process, etc.). **2** accomplish (business) quickly. □ **expediter** *n.* [L *expedire expedit-* extricate, put in order (as EX-¹, *pes pedis* foot)]

expedition /ˌekspɪˈdɪʃ(ə)n/ *n.* **1** a journey or voyage for a particular purpose, esp. exploration, scientific research, or war. **2** the personnel or ships etc. undertaking this. **3** promptness, speed. □ **expeditionist** *n.* [ME f. OF f. L *expeditio -onis* (as EXPEDITE)]

expeditionary /ˌekspɪˈdɪʃənərɪ/ *adj.* of or used in an expedition, esp. military.

expeditious /ˌekspɪˈdɪʃəs/ *adj.* acting or done with speed and efficiency. □ **expeditiously** *adv.* **expeditiousness** *n.* [EXPEDITION + -OUS]

expel /ɪkˈspel/ *v.tr.* (**expelled**, **expelling**) (often foll. by *from*) **1** deprive (a person) of the membership of or involvement in (a school, society, etc.). **2** force out or eject (a thing from its container etc.). **3** order or force to leave a building etc. □ **expellable** *adj.* **expellee** /-ˈliː/ *n.* **expellent** *adj.* **expeller** *n.* [ME f. L *expellere expuls-* (as EX-¹, *pellere* drive)]

expend /ɪkˈspend/ *v.tr.* spend or use up (money, time, etc.). [ME f. L *expendere expens-* (as EX-¹, *pendere* weigh)]

expendable /ɪkˈspendəb(ə)l/ *adj.* **1** that may be sacrificed or dispensed with, esp. to achieve a purpose. **2 a** not regarded as worth preserving or saving. **b** unimportant, insignificant. □ **expendability** /-ˈbɪlɪtɪ/ *n.* **expendably** *adv.*

expenditure /ɪkˈspendɪtʃə(r)/ *n.* **1** the process or an instance of spending or using up. **2** a thing (esp. a sum of money) expended. [EXPEND, after obs. *expenditor* officer in charge of expenditure, f. med.L f. *expenditus* irreg. past part. of L *expendere*]

expense /ɪkˈspens/ *n.* **1** cost incurred; payment of money. **2** (usu. in *pl.*) **a** costs incurred in doing a particular job etc. (*will pay your expenses*). **b** an amount paid to reimburse this (*offered me £40 per day expenses*). **3** a thing that is a cause of much expense (*the house is a real expense to run*). □ **at the expense of** so as to cause loss or damage or discredit to. **expense account** a list of an employee's expenses payable by the employer. [ME f. AF, alt. of OF *espense* f. LL *expensa* (money) spent, past part. of L *expendere* EXPEND]

expensive /ɪkˈspensɪv/ *adj.* **1** costing much. **2** making a high charge. **3** causing much expense (*has expensive tastes*). □ **expensively** *adv.* **expensiveness** *n.*

experience /ɪkˈspɪərɪəns/ *n.* & *v.* —*n.* **1** actual observation of or practical acquaintance with facts or events. **2** knowledge or skill resulting from this. **3 a** an event regarded as affecting one (*an unpleasant experience*). **b** the fact or process of being so affected (*learnt by experience*). —*v.tr.* **1** have experience of; undergo. **2** feel or be affected by (an emotion etc.). □ **experienceable** *adj.* [ME f. OF f. L *experientia* f. *experiri expert-* try]

experienced /ɪkˈspɪərɪənst/ *adj.* **1** having had much experience. **2** skilled from experience (*an experienced driver*).

experiential /ɪkˌspɪərɪˈenʃ(ə)l/ *adj.* involving or based on experience. □ **experientially** *adv.*

experiment /ɪkˈsperɪmənt, -ˌment/ *n.* & *v.* —*n.* **1** a procedure adopted on the chance of its succeeding, for testing a hypothesis etc., or to demonstrate a known fact. **2** (foll. by *of*) a test or trial of. —*v.intr.* (often foll. by *on*, *with*) make an experiment. □ **experimentation** /-menˈteɪʃ(ə)n/ *n.* **experimenter** *n.* [ME f. OF *experiment* or L *experimentum* (as EXPERIENCE)]

experimental /ɪkˌsperɪˈment(ə)l/ *adj.* **1** based on or making use of experiment (*experimental psychology*). **2 a** used in experiments. **b** serving or resulting from experiment; tentative, provisional. □ **experimentalism** *n.* **experimentalist** *n.* **experimentalize** *v.intr.* (also *-ise*). **experimentally** *adv.* [ME f. med.L *experimentalis* (as EXPERIMENT)]

expert /ˈekspɜːt/ *adj.* & *n.* —*adj.* **1** (often foll. by *at*, *in*) having special knowledge or skill in a subject. **2** involving or resulting from this (*expert evidence*; *an expert piece of work*). —*n.* (often foll. by *at*, *in*) a person having special knowledge or skill. □ **expertly** *adv.* **expertness** *n.* [ME f. OF f. L *expertus* past part. of *experiri*: see EXPERIENCE]

expertise /ˌekspɜːˈtiːz/ *n.* expert skill, knowledge, or judgement. [F (as EXPERT)]

expiate /ˈekspɪˌeɪt/ *v.tr.* **1** pay the penalty for (wrongdoing). **2** make amends for. □ **expiable**

/ˈekspɪrəb(ə)l/ adj. **expiatory** /-pɪətərɪ, -pɪˌeɪtərɪ/ adj. **expiation** /-ˈeɪʃ(ə)n/ n. **expiator** n. [L expiare expiat- (as EX-¹, pius devout)]

expiration /ˌekspɪˈreɪʃ(ə)n/ n. **1** breathing out. **2** expiry. [L expiratio (as EXPIRE)]

expire /ɪkˈspaɪə(r)/ v. **1** intr. (of a period of time, validity, etc.) come to an end. **2** intr. (of a document, authorization, etc.) cease to be valid; become void. **3** intr. (of a person) die. **4** tr. (usu. foll. by from; also absol.) exhale (air etc.) from the lungs. □ **expiratory** adj. (in sense 4). [ME f. OF expirer f. L exspirare (as EX-¹, spirare breathe)]

expiry /ɪkˈspaɪərɪ/ n. the end of the validity or duration of something.

explain /ɪkˈspleɪn/ v.tr. **1** make clear or intelligible with detailed information etc. (also absol.: let me explain). **2** (foll. by that + clause) say by way of explanation. **3** account for (one's conduct etc.). □ **explain away** minimize the significance of (a difficulty or mistake) by explanation. **explain oneself 1** make one's meaning clear. **2** give an account of one's motives or conduct. □ **explainable** adj. **explainer** n. [L explanare (as EX-¹, planus flat, assim. to PLAIN)]

explanation /ˌekspləˈneɪʃ(ə)n/ n. **1** the act or an instance of explaining. **2** a statement or circumstance that explains something. **3** a declaration made with a view to mutual understanding or reconciliation. [ME f. L explanatio (as EXPLAIN)]

explanatory /ɪkˈsplænətərɪ/ adj. serving or intended to serve to explain. □ **explanatorily** adv. [LL explanatorius (as EXPLAIN)]

expletive /ɪkˈspliːtɪv/ n. & adj. —n. **1** an oath, swear-word, or other expression, used in an exclamation. **2** a word used to fill out a sentence etc., esp. in verse. —adj. serving to fill out (esp. a sentence, line of verse, etc.). [LL expletivus (as EX-¹, plēre plet- fill)]

explicable /ɪkˈsplɪkəb(ə)l, ˈek-/ adj. that can be explained.

explicate /ˈeksplɪˌkeɪt/ v.tr. **1** develop the meaning or implication of (an idea, principle, etc.). **2** make clear, explain (esp. a literary text). □ **explication** /-ˈkeɪʃ(ə)n/ n. **explicative** /ekˈsplɪkətɪv, ˈeksplɪˌkeɪtɪv/ adj. **explicator** n. **explicatory** /ekˈsplɪkətərɪ, ˈeksplɪˌkeɪtərɪ/ adj. [L explicare explicat- unfold (as EX-¹, plicare plicat- or plicit- fold)]

explicit /ɪkˈsplɪsɪt/ adj. **1** expressly stated, leaving nothing merely implied; stated in detail. **2** (of knowledge, a notion, etc.) definite, clear. **3** (of a person, book, etc.) expressing views unreservedly; outspoken. □ **explicitly** adv. **explicitness** n. [F explicite or L explicitus (as EXPLICATE)]

explode /ɪkˈspləʊd/ v. **1 a** intr. (of gas, gunpowder, a bomb, a boiler, etc.) expand suddenly with a loud noise owing to a release of internal energy. **b** tr. cause (a bomb etc.) to explode. **2** intr. give vent suddenly to emotion, esp. anger. **3** intr. (of a population etc.) increase suddenly or rapidly. **4** tr. show (a theory etc.) to be false or baseless. **5** tr. (as **exploded** adj.) (of a drawing etc.) showing the components of a mechanism as if separated by an explosion but in the normal relative positions. □ **exploder** n. [earliest in sense 4: L explodere hiss off the stage (as EX-¹, plodere plos- = plaudere clap)]

exploit n. & v. —n. /ˈeksplɔɪt/ a bold or daring feat. —v.tr. /ɪkˈsplɔɪt/ **1** make use of (a resource etc.); derive benefit from. **2** usu. derog. utilize or take advantage of (esp. a person) for one's own ends. □ **exploitable** /ɪkˈsplɔɪtəb(ə)l/ adj. **exploitation** /ˌeksplɔɪˈteɪʃ(ə)n/ n. **exploitative** /ɪkˈsplɔɪtətɪv/ adj. **exploiter** n. **exploitive** /ɪkˈsplɔɪtɪv/ adj. [ME f. OF esploit, exploiter ult. f. L explicare: see EXPLICATE]

exploration /ˌekspləˈreɪʃ(ə)n/ n. **1** an act or instance of exploring. **2** the process of exploring. □ **explorational** adj.

exploratory /ɪkˈsplɒrətərɪ/ adj. **1** (of discussion etc.) preliminary, serving to establish procedure etc. **2** of or concerning exploration or investigation (exploratory surgery).

explore /ɪkˈsplɔː(r)/ v.tr. **1** travel extensively through (a country etc.) in order to learn or discover about it. **2** inquire into; investigate thoroughly. □ **explorative** /ɪkˈsplɒrətɪv/ adj. [F explorer f. L explorare]

explorer /ɪkˈsplɔːrə(r)/ n. a traveller into undiscovered or uninvestigated territory, esp. to get scientific information.

explosion /ɪkˈspləʊʒ(ə)n/ n. **1** the act or an instance of exploding. **2** a loud noise caused by something exploding. **3 a** a sudden outburst of noise. **b** a sudden outbreak of feeling, esp. anger. **4** a rapid or sudden increase, esp. of population. [L explosio scornful rejection (as EXPLODE)]

explosive /ɪkˈspləʊsɪv/ adj. & n. —adj. **1** able or tending or likely to explode. **2** likely to cause a violent outburst etc.; (of a situation etc.) dangerously tense. —n. an explosive substance. □ **explosively** adv. **explosiveness** n.

exponent /ɪkˈspəʊnənt/ n. **1** a person who favours or promotes an idea etc. **2** a representative or practitioner of an activity, profession, etc. **3** a person who explains or interprets something. **4** a type or representative. **5** Math. a raised symbol or expression beside a numeral indicating how many times it is to be multiplied by itself (e.g. $2^3 = 2 \times 2 \times 2$). [L exponere (as EX-¹, ponere posit- put)]

exponential /ˌekspəˈnenʃ(ə)l/ adj. **1** Math. of or indicated by a mathematical exponent. **2** (of an increase etc.) more and more rapid. □ **exponential growth** Biol. a form of population growth in which the rate of growth is related to the number of individuals present. [F exponentiel (as EXPONENT)]

export v. & n. —v.tr. /ekˈspɔːt, ˈek-/ send out (goods or services) esp. for sale in another country. —n. /ˈekspɔːt/ **1** the process of exporting. **2 a** an exported article or service. **b** (in pl.) an amount exported (exports exceeded £50m.). **3** (attrib.) suitable for export, esp. of better quality. □ **exportable** adj. **exportability** /-ˈbɪlɪtɪ/ n. **exportation** /-ˈteɪʃ(ə)n/ n. **exporter** /-ˈspɔːtə(r)/ n. [L exportare (as EX-¹, portare carry)]

expose /ɪkˈspəʊz/ v.tr. **1** leave uncovered or unprotected, esp. from the weather. **2** (foll. by to) cause to be liable to or in danger of (was exposed to great danger). **3** (as **exposed** adj.) **a** (foll. by to) open to; unprotected from (exposed to the east). **b** vulnerable, risky. **4** Photog. subject (a film) to light, esp. by operation of a camera. **5** reveal the identity or fact of (esp. a person or thing disapproved of or guilty of crime etc.). **6** disclose; make public. **7** exhibit, display. □ **expose oneself** display one's body, esp. the genitals, publicly and indecently. □ **exposer** n.

[ME f. OF *exposer* after L *exponere*: see EXPONENT, POSE[1]]

exposé /ek'spəʊzeɪ/ *n.* **1** an orderly statement of facts. **2** the act or an instance of revealing something discreditable. [F, past part. of *exposer* (as EXPOSE)]

exposition /ˌekspə'zɪʃ(ə)n/ *n.* **1** an explanatory statement or account. **2** an explanation or commentary. **3** a large public exhibition. □ **expositional** *adj.* **expositive** /-'spɒzɪtɪv/ *adj.* [ME f. OF *exposition*, or L *expositio* (as EXPONENT)]

expositor /ɪk'spɒzɪtə(r)/ *n.* an expounder or interpreter. □ **expository** *adj.*

ex post facto /ˌeks pəʊst 'fæktəʊ/ *adj. & adv.* with retrospective action or force. [L *ex postfacto* in the light of subsequent events]

expostulate /ɪk'spɒstjʊ,leɪt/ *v.intr.* (often foll. by *with* a person) make a protest; remonstrate earnestly. □ **expostulation** /-'leɪʃ(ə)n/ *n.* **expostulatory** /-lətərɪ/ *adj.* [L *expostulare expostulat-* (as EX-[1], *postulare* demand)]

exposure /ɪk'spəʊʒə(r)/ *n.* (foll. by *to*) **1** the act or condition of exposing or being exposed (to air, cold, danger, etc.). **2** the condition of being exposed to the elements, esp. in severe conditions (*died from exposure*). **3** the revelation of an identity or fact, esp. when concealed or likely to find disapproval. **4** *Photog.* **a** the action of exposing a film etc. to the light. **b** the duration of this action. **c** the area of film etc. affected by it. [EXPOSE after *enclosure* etc.]

expound /ɪk'spaʊnd/ *v.tr.* **1** set out in detail (a doctrine etc.). **2** explain or interpret (esp. Scripture). □ **expounder** *n.* [ME f. OF *espondre* (as EXPONENT)]

express[1] /ɪk'spres/ *v.tr.* **1** represent or make known (thought, feelings, etc.) in words or by gestures, conduct, etc. **2** *refl.* say what one thinks or means. **3** esp. *Math.* represent by symbols. **4** squeeze out (liquid or air). □ **expresser** *n.* **expressible** *adj.* [ME f. OF *expresser* f. Rmc (as EX-[1], PRESS[1])]

express[2] /ɪk'spres/ *adj., adv., n., & v.* —*adj.* **1** operating at high speed. **2** /also 'ekspres/ definitely stated, not merely implied. **3 a** done, made, or sent for a special purpose. **b** (of messages or goods) delivered by a special messenger or service. —*adv.* **1** at high speed. **2** by express messenger or train. —*n.* **1** an express train or messenger. **2** *US* a company undertaking the transport of parcels etc. —*v.tr.* send by express messenger or delivery. □ **express train** a fast train, stopping at few intermediate stations. □ **expressly** *adv.* (in sense 2 of *adj.*). [ME f. OF *expres* f. L *expressus* distinctly shown, past part. of *exprimere* (as EX-[1], *premere* press)]

expression /ɪk'spreʃ(ə)n/ *n.* **1** the act or an instance of expressing. **2** a word or phrase expressed. **3** *Math.* a collection of symbols expressing a quantity. **4** a person's facial appearance or intonation of voice, esp. as indicating feeling. **5** depiction of feeling, movement, etc., in art. **6** conveying of feeling in the performance of a piece of music. □ **expressional** *adj.* **expressionless** *adj.* **expressionlessly** *adv.* **expressionlessness** *n.* [ME f. OF *expression* or L *expressio* f. *exprimere*: see EXPRESS[1]]

expressionism /ɪk'spreʃə,nɪz(ə)m/ *n.* a style of painting, music, drama, etc., in which an artist or writer seeks to express emotional experience rather than impressions of the external world.

□ **expressionist** *n. & adj.* **expressionistic** /-'nɪstɪk/ *adj.* **expressionistically** /-'nɪstɪkəlɪ/ *adv.*

expressive /ɪk'spresɪv/ *adj.* **1** full of expression (*an expressive look*). **2** (foll. by *of*) serving to express (*words expressive of contempt*). □ **expressively** *adv.* **expressiveness** *n.* **expressivity** /-'sɪvɪtɪ/ *n.* [ME f. F *expressif -ive* or med.L *expressivus* (as EXPRESSION)]

expresso var. of ESPRESSO.

expressway /ɪk'spresweɪ/ *n.* *US* an urban motorway.

expropriate /eks'prəʊprɪ,eɪt/ *v.tr.* **1** (esp. of the State) take away (property) from its owner. **2** (foll. by *from*) dispossess. □ **expropriation** /-'eɪʃ(ə)n/ *n.* **expropriator** *n.* [med.L *expropriare expropriat-* (as EX-[1], *proprium* property: see PROPER)]

expulsion /ɪk'spʌlʃ(ə)n/ *n.* the act or an instance of expelling; the process of being expelled. □ **expulsive** /-sɪv/ *adj.* [ME f. L *expulsio* (as EXPEL)]

expunge /ɪk'spʌndʒ/ *v.tr.* (foll. by *from*) erase, remove (esp. a passage from a book or a name from a list). □ **expunction** /ɪk'spʌŋkʃ(ə)n/ *n.* **expunger** *n.* [L *expungere expunct-* (as EX-[1], *pungere* prick)]

expurgate /'ekspə,geɪt/ *v.tr.* **1** remove matter thought to be objectionable from (a book etc.). **2** remove (such matter). □ **expurgation** /-'geɪʃ(ə)n/ *n.* **expurgator** *n.* **expurgatorial** /ˌekspɜ:gə'tɔ:rɪəl/ *adj.* **expurgatory** /ek'spɜ:gətərɪ/ *adj.* [L *expurgare expurgat-* (as EX-[1], *purgare* cleanse)]

exquisite /'ekskwɪzɪt, ek'skwɪzɪt/ *adj. & n.* —*adj.* **1** extremely beautiful or delicate. **2** acute; keenly felt (*exquisite pleasure*). **3** keen; highly sensitive or discriminating (*exquisite taste*). —*n.* a person of refined (esp. affected) tastes. □ **exquisitely** *adv.* **exquisiteness** *n.* [ME f. L *exquirere exquisit-* (as EX-[1], *quaerere* seek)]

ex-service /eks'sɜ:vɪs/ *adj.* **1** having formerly been a member of the armed forces. **2** relating to former servicemen and -women.

ex-serviceman /eks'sɜ:vɪsmən/ *n.* (*pl.* **-men**) a former member of the armed forces.

ex-servicewoman /eks'sɜ:vɪs,wʊmən/ *n.* (*pl.* **-women**) a former woman member of the armed forces.

extant /ek'stænt, ɪk'st-, 'ekst(ə)nt/ *adj.* (esp. of a document etc.) still existing, surviving. [L *exstare exstant-* (as EX-[1], *stare* stand)]

extemporaneous /ɪk,stempə'reɪnɪəs/ *adj.* spoken or done without preparation. □ **extemporaneously** *adv.* **extemporaneousness** *n.*

extemporary /ɪk'stempərərɪ/ *adj.* = EXTEMPORANEOUS. □ **extemporarily** *adv.* **extemporariness** *n.*

extempore /ɪk'stempərɪ/ *adj. & adv.* **1** without preparation. **2** offhand. [L *ex tempore* on the spur of the moment, lit. out of the time f. *tempus* time]

extemporize /ɪk'stempə,raɪz/ *v.tr.* (also **-ise**) (also *absol.*) compose or produce (music, a speech, etc.) without preparation; improvise. □ **extemporization** /-'zeɪʃ(ə)n/ *n.*

extend /ɪk'stend/ *v.* **1** *tr. & intr.* lengthen or make larger in space or time. **2** *tr.* stretch or lay out at full length. **3** *intr. & tr.* (foll. by *to, over*) reach or be or make continuous over a certain area. **4** *intr.* (foll. by *to*) have a certain scope (*the permit does not extend to camping*). **5** *tr.* offer or accord (an invitation, hospitality, kindness, etc.). **6** *tr.* (usu. *refl.* or in *passive*) tax the powers of (an athlete, horse, etc.) to the utmost. □ **extended family** a family including relatives living near. **extended-play** (of a gramophone record) playing for longer than most singles, usu. at 45 r.p.m. □ **extendable** *adj.* **extendability** /-dəˈbɪlɪtɪ/ *n.* **extender** *n.* **extendible** *adj.* **extendibility** /-dɪˈbɪlɪtɪ/ *n.* **extensible** /-sɪb(ə)l/ *adj.* **extensibility** /-sɪˈbɪlɪtɪ/ *n.* [ME f. L *extendere extens-* or *extent-* stretch out (as EX-[1], *tendere* stretch)]

extensile /ɪkˈstensaɪl/ *adj.* capable of being stretched out or protruded.

extension /ɪkˈstenʃ(ə)n/ *n.* **1** the act or an instance of extending; the process of being extended. **2** prolongation; enlargement. **3** a part enlarging or added on to a main structure or building. **4** an additional part of anything. **5** a subsidiary telephone on the same line as the main one. **6** an additional period of time. **7** extramural instruction by a university or college (*extension course*). **8** extent, range. □ **extensional** *adj.* [ME f. LL *extensio* (as EXTEND)]

extensive /ɪkˈstensɪv/ *adj.* **1** covering a large area in space or time. **2** having a wide scope; far-reaching, comprehensive. □ **extensively** *adv.* **extensiveness** *n.* [F *extensif -ive* or LL *extensivus* (as EXTENSION)]

extensor /ɪkˈstensə(r)/ *n.* (in full **extensor muscle**) *Anat.* a muscle that extends or straightens out part of the body. [mod.L (as EXTEND)]

extent /ɪkˈstent/ *n.* **1** the space over which a thing extends. **2** the width or limits of application; scope. [ME f. AF *extente* f. med.L *extenta* past part. of L *extendere*: see EXTEND]

extenuate /ɪkˈstenjʊˌeɪt/ *v.tr.* (often as **extenuating** *adj.*) lessen the seeming seriousness of (guilt or an offence) by reference to some mitigating factor. □ **extenuatingly** *adv.* **extenuation** /-ˈeɪʃ(ə)n/ *n.* **extenuatory** /-jʊətərɪ/ *adj.* [L *extenuare extenuat-* (as EX-[1], *tenuis* thin)]

exterior /ɪkˈstɪərɪə(r)/ *adj.* & *n.* —*adj.* **1** of or on the outer side. **2** (foll. by *to*) situated on the outside of (a building etc.). **3** coming from outside. —*n.* **1** the outward aspect or surface of a building etc. **2** the outward or apparent behaviour or demeanour of a person. **3** *Cinematog.* an outdoor scene. □ **exteriority** /-ˈɒrɪtɪ/ *n.* **exteriorize** *v.tr.* (also **-ise**). **exteriorly** *adv.* [L, *compar.* of *exterus* outside]

exterminate /ɪkˈstɜːmɪˌneɪt/ *v.tr.* **1** destroy utterly (esp. something living). **2** get rid of; eliminate (a pest, disease, etc.). □ **extermination** /-ˈneɪʃ(ə)n/ *n.* **exterminator** *n.* **exterminatory** /-nətərɪ/ *adj.* [L *exterminare exterminat-* (as EX-[1], *terminus* boundary)]

external /ɪkˈstɜːn(ə)l/ *adj.* & *n.* —*adj.* **1 a** of or situated on the outside or visible part. **b** coming or derived from the outside or an outside source. **2** relating to a country's foreign affairs. **3** outside the conscious subject (*the external world*). **4** (of medicine etc.) for use on the outside of the body. **5** for or concerning students taking the examinations of a university without attending it. —*n.* (in *pl.*) **1** the outward features or aspect. **2** external circumstances. **3** inessentials. □ **externality** /ˌekstɜːˈnælɪtɪ/ *n.* (*pl.* **-ies**). **externally** *adv.* [med.L f. L *externus* f. *exterus* outside]

externalize /ɪkˈstɜːnəˌlaɪz/ *v.tr.* (also **-ise**) give or attribute external existence to. □ **externalization** /-ˈzeɪʃ(ə)n/ *n.*

extinct /ɪkˈstɪŋkt/ *adj.* **1** (of a family, class, or species) that has died out. **2 a** (of fire etc.) no longer burning. **b** (of a volcano) that no longer erupts. **3** (of life, hope, etc.) terminated, quenched. [ME f. L *exstinguere exstinct-* (as EX-[1], *stinguere* quench)]

extinction /ɪkˈstɪŋkʃ(ə)n/ *n.* **1** the act of making extinct; the state of being or process of becoming extinct. **2** the act of extinguishing; the state of being extinguished. **3** total destruction or annihilation. □ **extinctive** *adj.* [L *extinctio* (as EXTINCT)]

extinguish /ɪkˈstɪŋgwɪʃ/ *v.tr.* **1** cause (a flame, light, etc.) to die out; put out. **2** make extinct; annihilate, destroy (*a programme to extinguish disease*). **3** put an end to; terminate; obscure utterly (a feeling, quality, etc.). **4** abolish; wipe out (a debt). □ **extinguishable** *adj.* **extinguishment** *n.* [irreg. f. L *extinguere* (as EXTINCT): cf. *distinguish*]

extinguisher /ɪkˈstɪŋgwɪʃə(r)/ *n.* a person or thing that extinguishes, esp. = *fire extinguisher*.

extirpate /ˈekstəˌpeɪt/ *v.tr.* root out; destroy completely. □ **extirpation** /-ˈpeɪʃ(ə)n/ *n.* **extirpator** *n.* [L *exstirpare exstirpat-* (as EX-[1], *stirps* stem)]

extol /ɪkˈstəʊl, ɪkˈstɒl/ *v.tr.* (**extolled**, **extolling**) praise enthusiastically. □ **extoller** *n.* **extolment** *n.* [L *extollere* (as EX-[1], *tollere* raise)]

extort /ɪkˈstɔːt/ *v.tr.* obtain by force, threats, persistent demands, etc. □ **extorter** *n.* **extortive** *adj.* [L *extorquēre extort-* (as EX-[1], *torquēre* twist)]

extortion /ɪkˈstɔːʃ(ə)n/ *n.* **1** the act or an instance of extorting, esp. money. **2** illegal exaction. □ **extortioner** *n.* **extortionist** *n.* [ME f. LL *extortio* (as EXTORT)]

extortionate /ɪkˈstɔːʃənət/ *adj.* **1** (of a price etc.) exorbitant. **2** using or given to extortion (*extortionate methods*). □ **extortionately** *adv.*

extra /ˈekstrə/ *adj.*, *adv.*, & *n.* —*adj.* additional; more than is usual or necessary or expected. —*adv.* **1** more than usually. **2** additionally (*was charged extra*). —*n.* **1** an extra thing. **2** a thing for which an extra charge is made. **3** a person engaged temporarily to fill out a scene in a film or play, esp. as one of a crowd. **4** a special issue of a newspaper etc. **5** *Cricket* a run scored other than from a hit with the bat. □ **extra time** *Sport* a further period of play at the end of a match when the scores are equal. [prob. a shortening of EXTRAORDINARY]

extra- /ˈekstrə/ *comb. form* **1** outside, beyond (*extragalactic*). **2** beyond the scope of (*extracurricular*). [med.L f. L *extra* outside]

extract *v.* & *n.* —*v.tr.* /ɪkˈstrækt/ **1** remove or take out, esp. by effort or force (anything firmly rooted). **2** obtain (money, an admission, etc.) with difficulty or against a person's will. **3** obtain (a natural resource) from the earth. **4** select or reproduce for quotation or performance (a passage of writing, music, etc.). **5** obtain (juice etc.) by suction, pressure, distillation, etc. **6** derive (pleasure etc.). **7** *Math.* find (the root of a number). —*n.* /ˈekstrækt/ **1** a short passage taken from a book etc.; an excerpt. **2** a preparation containing the active principle of a substance in concentrated form (*malt extract*). □ **extractable** *adj.* **extractability**

/-'bɪlɪtɪ/ *n.* [L *extrahere* extract- (as EX-¹, *trahere* draw)]

extraction /ɪk'strækʃ(ə)n/ *n.* **1** the act or an instance of extracting; the process of being extracted. **2** the removal of a tooth. **3** origin, lineage, descent (*of Indian extraction*). [ME f. F f. LL *extractio -onis* (as EXTRACT)]

extractive /ɪk'stræktɪv/ *adj.* of or involving extraction, esp. extensive extracting of natural resources without provision for their renewal.

extractor /ɪk'stræktə(r)/ *n.* **1** a person or machine that extracts. **2** (*attrib.*) (of a device) that extracts bad air etc. or ventilates a room.

extracurricular /ˌekstrəkə'rɪkjʊlə(r)/ *adj.* (of a subject of study) not included in the normal curriculum.

extraditable /'ekstrəˌdaɪtəb(ə)l/ *adj.* **1** liable to extradition. **2** (of a crime) warranting extradition.

extradite /'ekstrəˌdaɪt/ *v.tr.* hand over (a person accused or convicted of a crime) to the foreign State etc. in which the crime was committed. □ **extradition** *n.*

extrajudicial /ˌekstrədʒuː'dɪʃ(ə)l/ *adj.* **1** not legally authorized. **2** (of a confession) not made in court. □ **extrajudicially** *adv.*

extramarital /ˌekstrə'mærɪt(ə)l/ *adj.* (esp. of sexual relations) occurring outside marriage. □ **extramaritally** *adv.*

extramural /ˌekstrə'mjʊər(ə)l/ *adj.* **1** taught or conducted off the premises of a university, college, or school. **2** additional to normal teaching or studies, esp. for non-resident students. □ **extramurally** *adv.* [L *extra muros* outside the walls]

extraneous /ɪk'streɪnɪəs/ *adj.* **1** of external origin. **2** (often foll. by *to*) **a** separate from the object to which it is attached etc. **b** external to; irrelevant or unrelated to. □ **extraneously** *adv.* **extraneousness** *n.* [L *extraneus*]

extraordinary /ɪk'strɔːdɪnərɪ, ˌekstrə'ɔːdɪnərɪ/ *adj.* **1** unusual or remarkable; out of the usual course. **2** unusually great (*an extraordinary talent*). **3 a** (of an official etc.) additional; specially employed (*envoy extraordinary*). **b** (of a meeting) specially convened. □ **extraordinarily** *adv.* **extraordinariness** *n.* [L *extraordinarius* f. *extra ordinem* outside the usual order]

extrapolate /ɪk'stræpəˌleɪt/ *v.tr.* (also *absol.*) **1** *Math.* & *Philos.* calculate approximately from known values, data, etc. (others which lie outside the range of those known). **2** infer more widely from a limited range of known facts. □ **extrapolation** /-'leɪʃ(ə)n/ *n.* **extrapolative** /-lətɪv/ *adj.* **extrapolator** *n.* [EXTRA- + INTERPOLATE]

extrasensory /ˌekstrə'sensərɪ/ *adj.* regarded as derived by means other than the known senses, e.g. by telepathy, clairvoyance, etc. □ **extrasensory perception** a person's supposed faculty of perceiving by such means.

extraterrestrial /ˌekstrətɪ'restrɪəl/ *adj.* & *n.* —*adj.* **1** outside the earth or its atmosphere. **2** (in science fiction) from outer space. —*n.* (in science fiction) a being from outer space.

extravagance /ɪk'strævəgəns/ *n.* **1** excessive spending or use of resources; being extravagant. **2** an instance or item of this. □ **extravagancy** *n.* (*pl.* -**ies**). [F (as EXTRAVAGANT)]

extravagant /ɪk'strævəgənt/ *adj.* **1** spending (esp. money) excessively; immoderate or wasteful in use of resources. **2** exorbitant; costing much. **3** exceeding normal restraint or sense; unreasonable, absurd (*extravagant claims*). □ **extravagantly** *adv.* [ME f. med.L *extravagari* (as EXTRA-, *vagari* wander)]

extravaganza /ɪkˌstrævə'gænzə/ *n.* **1** a fanciful literary, musical, or dramatic composition. **2** a spectacular theatrical or television production, esp. of light entertainment. [It. *estravaganza* extravagance]

extravasate /ɪk'strævəˌseɪt/ *v.* **1** *tr.* force out (a fluid, esp. blood) from its proper vessel. **2** *intr.* (of blood, lava, etc.) flow out. □ **extravasation** /-'seɪʃ(ə)n/ *n.* [L *extra* outward + *vas* vessel]

extreme /ɪk'striːm/ *adj.* & *n.* —*adj.* **1** reaching a high or the highest degree; exceedingly great or intense (*extreme old age; in extreme danger*). **2 a** severe, lacking restraint or moderation (*take extreme measures; an extreme reaction*). **b** (of a person, opinion, etc.) going to great lengths; advocating immoderate measures. **3** outermost; furthest from the centre; situated at either end (*the extreme edge*). **4** *Polit.* on the far left or right of a party. **5** utmost; last. —*n.* **1** (often in *pl.*) one or other of two things as remote or as different as possible. **2** a thing at either end of anything. **3** the highest degree of anything. **4** *Math.* the first or the last term of a ratio or series. □ **extreme unction** the last rites in the Roman Catholic and Orthodox Churches. **go to extremes** take an extreme course of action. **go to the other extreme** take a diametrically opposite course of action. **in the extreme** to an extreme degree. □ **extremely** *adv.* **extremeness** *n.* [ME f. OF f. L *extremus* superl. of *exterus* outward]

extremist /ɪk'striːmɪst/ *n.* (also *attrib.*) a person who holds extreme or fanatical political or religious views. □ **extremism** *n.*

extremity /ɪk'stremɪtɪ/ *n.* (*pl.* -**ies**) **1** the extreme point; the very end. **2** (in *pl.*) the hands and feet. **3** a condition of extreme adversity or difficulty. [ME f. OF *extremité* or L *extremitas* (as EXTREME)]

extricate /'ekstrɪˌkeɪt/ *v.tr.* (often foll. by *from*) free or disentangle from a constraint or difficulty. □ **extricable** *adj.* **extrication** /-'keɪʃ(ə)n/ *n.* [L *extricare* extricat- (as EX-¹, *tricae* perplexities)]

extrinsic /ek'strɪnsɪk/ *adj.* **1** not inherent or intrinsic; not essential. **2** (often foll. by *to*) extraneous; lying outside; not belonging (to). □ **extrinsically** *adv.* [LL *extrinsicus* outward f. L *extrinsecus* (adv.) f. *exter* outside + *secus* beside]

extrovert /'ekstrəˌvɜːt/ *n.* & *adj.* —*n.* **1** *Psychol.* a person predominantly concerned with external things or objective considerations. **2** an outgoing or sociable person. —*adj.* typical or characteristic of an extrovert. □ **extroversion** /-'vɜːʃ(ə)n/ *n.* **extroverted** *adj.* [*extro-* = EXTRA- (after *intro-*) + L *vertere* turn]

extrude /ɪk'struːd/ *v.tr.* **1** (foll. by *from*) thrust or force out. **2** shape metal, plastics, etc. by forcing them through a die. □ **extrusion** /-ʒ(ə)n/ *n.* **extrusile** /-saɪl/ *adj.* **extrusive** /-sɪv/ *adj.* [L *extrudere* extrus- (as EX-¹, *trudere* thrust)]

exuberant /ɪg'zjuːbərənt/ *adj.* **1** lively, high-spirited. **2** (of a plant etc.) prolific; growing copiously. **3** (of feelings etc.) abounding, lavish, effusive. □ **exuberance** *n.* **exuberantly** *adv.* [F exubérant f. L exuberare (as EX-¹, uberare be fruitful f. uber fertile)]

exude /ɪgˈzjuːd/ v. **1** tr. & intr. (of a liquid, moisture, etc.) escape or cause to escape gradually; ooze out; give off. **2** tr. emit (a smell). **3** tr. display (an emotion etc.) freely or abundantly (exuded displeasure). □ **exudate** /ˈegzjʊˌdeɪt/ n. **exudation** /-ˈdeɪʃ(ə)n/ n. **exudative** /ɪgˈzjuːdətɪv/ adj. [L exsudare (as EX-¹, sudare sweat)]

exult /ɪgˈzʌlt/ v.intr. (often foll. by at, in, over, or to + infin.) **1** be greatly joyful. **2** (often foll. by over) have a feeling of triumph (over a person). □ **exultancy** n. **exultation** /-ˈteɪʃ(ə)n/ n. **exultant** adj. **exultantly** adv. **exultingly** adv. [L exsultare (as EX-¹, saltare frequent. of salire salt- leap)]

-ey /ɪ/ suffix var. of -Y².

eye /aɪ/ n. & v. —n. **1 a** the organ of sight in man and other animals. **b** the light-detecting organ in some invertebrates. **2** the eye characterized by the colour of the iris (has blue eyes). **3** the region round the eye (eyes red from weeping). **4** (in sing. or pl.) sight; the faculty of sight (demonstrate to the eye). **5** a particular visual faculty or talent; visual appreciation (cast an expert eye over). **6** (in sing. or pl.) a look, gaze, or glance, esp. as indicating the disposition of the viewer (a friendly eye). **7** a thing like an eye, esp.: **a** a spot on a peacock's tail. **b** the leaf bud of a potato. **8** the centre of something circular, e.g. a flower or target. **9** the relatively calm region at the centre of a storm or hurricane. **10** an aperture in an implement, esp. a needle, for the insertion of something, e.g. thread. **11** a ring or loop for a bolt or hook etc. to pass through. —v.tr. (**eyes, eyed, eyeing** or **eying**) watch or observe closely, esp. admiringly or with curiosity or suspicion. □ **all eyes 1** watching intently. **2** general attention (all eyes were on us). **do a person in the eye** colloq. defraud or thwart a person. **eye-catching** colloq. striking, attractive. **eye contact** looking directly into another person's eyes. **an eye for an eye** retaliation in kind (Exodus 21:24). **eye-liner** a cosmetic applied as a line round the eye. **eye-opener** colloq. **1** an enlightening experience; an unexpected revelation. **2** US an alcoholic drink taken on waking up. **eye-rhyme** a correspondence of words in spelling but not in pronunciation (e.g. love and move). **eye-shade** a device to protect the eyes, esp. from strong light. **eye-shadow** a coloured cosmetic applied to the skin round the eyes. **eye strain** fatigue of the (internal or external) muscles of the eye. **eye-tooth** a canine tooth just under or next to the eye, esp. in the upper jaw. **get one's eye in** Sport accustom oneself to the conditions of play so as to judge speed, distance, etc. **have an eye for** be capable of perceiving or appreciating. **have one's eye on** wish or plan to procure. **have eyes for** be interested in; wish to acquire. **have an eye to** have as one's objective; prudently consider. **keep an eye on 1** pay attention to. **2** look after; take care of. **keep an eye open** (or **out**) (often foll. by for) watch carefully. **keep one's eyes open** (or **peeled** or **skinned**) watch out; be on the alert. **make eyes** (or **sheep's eyes**) (foll. by at) look amorously or

flirtatiously at. **my** (or **all my**) **eye** sl. nonsense. **one in the eye** (foll. by for) a disappointment or setback. **open a person's eyes** be enlightening or revealing to a person. **see eye to eye** (often foll. by with) be in full agreement. **set eyes on** catch sight of. **take one's eyes off** (usu. in neg.) stop watching; stop paying attention to. **under the eye of** under the supervision or observation of. **up to the** (or **one's**) **eyes in 1** deeply engaged or involved in; inundated with. **2** to the utmost limit (mortgaged up to the eyes). **with one's eyes open** deliberately; with full awareness. **with one's eyes shut** (or **closed**) **1** easily; with little effort. **2** without awareness; unobservant. **with an eye to** with a view to; prudently considering. **with a friendly** (or **jealous** etc.) **eye** with a feeling of friendship, jealousy, etc. **with one eye on** directing one's attention partly to. □ **eyed** adj. (also in comb.). **eyeless** adj. [OE ēage f. Gmc]

eyeball /ˈaɪbɔːl/ n. & v. —n. the ball of the eye within the lids and socket. —v. US sl. **1** tr. look or stare at. **2** intr. look or stare. □ **eyeball to eyeball** colloq. confronting closely. **to** (or **up to**) **the eyeballs** colloq. completely (permeated, soaked, etc.).

eyebath /ˈaɪbɑːθ/ n. (also **eyecup** /ˈaɪkʌp/) a small glass or vessel for applying lotion etc. to the eye.

eyebrow /ˈaɪbraʊ/ n. the line of hair growing on the ridge above the eye-socket. □ **raise one's eyebrows** show surprise, disbelief, or mild disapproval.

eyeful /ˈaɪfʊl/ n. (pl. **-fuls**) colloq. **1** a long steady look. **2** a visually striking person or thing.

eyeglass /ˈaɪglɑːs/ n. **1** a lens for correcting or assisting defective sight. **2** (in pl.) a pair of these held in the hand or kept in position on the nose by means of a frame or a spring.

eyehole /ˈaɪhəʊl/ n. a hole to look through.

eyelash /ˈaɪlæʃ/ n. each of the hairs growing on the edges of the eyelids.

eyelet /ˈaɪlɪt/ n. & v. —n. **1** a small hole in paper, leather, cloth, etc., for string or rope etc. to pass through. **2** a metal ring reinforcement for this. —v.tr. (**eyeleted, eyeleting**) provide with eyelets. [ME f. OF oillet dimin. of oil eye f. L oculus]

eyelid /ˈaɪlɪd/ n. the upper or lower fold of skin closing to cover the eye.

eyepiece /ˈaɪpiːs/ n. the lens or lenses to which the eye is applied at the end of a microscope, telescope, etc.

eyesight /ˈaɪsaɪt/ n. the faculty or power of seeing.

eyesore /ˈaɪsɔː(r)/ n. a visually offensive or ugly thing, esp. a building.

eyewash /ˈaɪwɒʃ/ n. **1** lotion for the eye. **2** sl. nonsense, bunkum; pretentious or insincere talk.

eyewitness /ˈaɪˌwɪtnɪs/ n. a person who has personally seen a thing done or happen and can give evidence of it.

eyrie /ˈaɪərɪ, ˈɪərɪ, ˈɜːrɪ/ n. (also **aerie**) **1** a nest of a bird of prey, esp. an eagle, built high up. **2** a house etc. perched high up. [med.L aeria, aerea etc. prob. f. OF aire lair ult. f. L agrum piece of ground]

Ff

F¹ /ef/ n. (also **f**) (pl. **Fs** or **F's**) **1** the sixth letter of the alphabet. **2** *Mus.* the fourth note of the diatonic scale of C major.

F² abbr. (also **F.**) **1** Fahrenheit. **2** farad(s). **3** female. **4** fine (pencil-lead). **5** *Biol.* filial generation (as F_1 for the first filial generation, F_2 for the second, etc.).

F³ symb. *Chem.* the element fluorine.

f abbr. (also **f.**) **1** female. **2** feminine. **3** following page etc. **4** *Mus.* forte. **5** folio. **6** focal length.

FA abbr. **1** (in the UK) Football Association. **2** = FANNY ADAMS.

fa var. of FAH.

fab adj. colloq. fabulous, marvellous. [abbr.]

Fabian /'feɪbɪən/ n. & adj. —n. a member or supporter of the Fabian Society, an organization of socialists aiming at a gradual rather than revolutionary achievement of socialism. —adj. Relating to or characteristic of the Fabians. □ **Fabianism** n. **Fabianist** n. [L *Fabianus* f. the name of Q. *Fabius Maximus Cunctator* (= delayer), Roman general of the 3rd c. BC, noted for cautious strategies]

fable /'feɪb(ə)l/ n. & v. —n. **1 a** a story, esp. a supernatural one, not based on fact. **b** a tale, esp. with animals as characters, conveying a moral. **2** (collect.) myths and legendary tales (in fable). **3 a** a false statement; a lie. **b** a thing only supposed to exist. —v.tr. (as **fabled** adj.) celebrated in fable; famous, legendary. □ **fabler** /'feɪblə(r)/ n. [ME f. OF fabler f. L fabulari f. fabula discourse f. fari speak]

fabric /'fæbrɪk/ n. **1 a** a woven material; a textile. **b** other material resembling woven cloth. **2** a structure or framework, esp. the walls, floor, and roof of a building. **3** (in abstract senses) the essential structure or essence of a thing (the fabric of society). [ME f. F fabrique f. L fabrica f. faber metal-worker etc.]

fabricate /'fæbrɪkeɪt/ v.tr. **1** construct or manufacture, esp. from prepared components. **2** invent or concoct (a story, evidence, etc.). **3** forge (a document). □ **fabrication** /-'keɪʃ(ə)n/ n. **fabricator** n. [L fabricare fabricat- (as FABRIC)]

fabulous /'fæbjʊləs/ adj. **1** incredible, exaggerated, absurd (fabulous wealth). **2** colloq. marvellous (looking fabulous). **3 a** celebrated in fable. **b** legendary, mythical. □ **fabulosity** /-'lɒsɪtɪ/ n. **fabulously** adv. **fabulousness** n. [F fabuleux or L fabulosus (as FABLE)]

façade /fə'sɑːd/ n. **1** the face of a building, esp. its principal front. **2** an outward appearance or front, esp. a deceptive one. [F (as FACE)]

face n. & v. —n. **1** the front of the head from the forehead to the chin. **2** the expression of the facial features (had a happy face). **3** composure, coolness, effrontery. **4** the surface of a thing, esp. as regarded or approached, esp.: **a** the visible part of a celestial body. **b** a side of a mountain etc. (the north face). **c** the (usu. vertical) surface of a coal-seam. **d** *Geom.* each surface of a solid. **e** the façade of a building. **f** the plate of a clock or watch bearing the digits, hands, etc. **5 a** the functional or working side of a tool etc. **b** the distinctive side of a playing card. **c** the obverse of a coin. **6** = TYPEFACE. **7** the outward appearance or aspect (the unacceptable face of capitalism). —v. **1** tr. & intr. look or be positioned towards or in a certain direction (face towards the window; the room faces north). **2** tr. be opposite (facing page 20). **3** tr. **a** (often foll. by out) meet resolutely or defiantly; confront (face one's critics). **b** not shrink from (face the facts). **4** tr. present itself to; confront (the problem that faces us; faces us with a problem). **5** tr. **a** cover the surface of (a thing) with a coating, extra layer, etc. **b** put a facing on (a garment). **6** intr. & tr. turn or cause to turn in a certain direction. □ **face-card** = court-card. **face-cloth 1** a cloth for washing one's face. **2** a smooth-surfaced woollen cloth. **face down** (or **downwards**) with the face or surface turned towards the ground, floor, etc. **face-flannel** = face-cloth 1. **face-lift 1** (also **face-lifting**) cosmetic surgery to remove wrinkles etc. by tightening the skin of the face. **2** a procedure to improve the appearance of a thing. **face the music** colloq. put up with or stand up to unpleasant consequences, esp. criticism. **face-saving** preserving one's reputation, credibility, etc. **face to face** (often foll. by with) facing; confronting each other. **face up** (or **upwards**) with the face or surface turned upwards to view. **face up to** accept bravely; confront; stand up to. **face value 1** the nominal value as printed or stamped on money. **2** the superficial appearance or implication of a thing. **face-worker** a miner who works at the coalface. **have the face** be shameless enough. **in face** (or **the face**) **of 1** despite. **2** confronted by. **on the face of it** as it would appear. **put a bold** (or **brave**) **face on it** accept difficulty etc. cheerfully or with courage. **put a good face on** make (a matter) look well. **put a new face on** alter the aspect of. **save face** preserve esteem; avoid humiliation. **save a person's face** enable a person to save face; forbear from humiliating a person. **set one's face against** oppose or resist with determination. **to a person's face** openly in a person's presence. □ **faced** adj. (also in comb.). **facing** adj. (also in comb.). [ME f. OF ult. f. L facies]

faceless /'feɪslɪs/ adj. **1** without identity; purposely not identifiable. **2** lacking character. **3** without a face. □ **facelessly** adv. **facelessness** n.

facer /'feɪsə(r)/ n. colloq. a sudden difficulty or obstacle.

facet /'fæsɪt/ n. **1** a particular aspect of a thing. **2** one side of a many-sided body, esp. of a cut gem. **3** one segment of a compound eye. □ **faceted** adj. (also in comb.). [F facette dimin. (as FACE, -ETTE)]

facetious /fə'si:ʃəs/ adj. **1** characterized by flippant or inopportune humour. **2** (of a person) intending to be amusing, esp. inopportunely. □ **facetiously** adv. **facetiousness** n. [F *facétieux* f. *facétie* f. L *facetia* jest]

facia var. of FASCIA.

facial /'feɪʃ(ə)l/ adj. & n. —adj. of or for the face. —n. a beauty treatment for the face. □ **facially** adv. [med.L *facialis* (as FACE)]

facile /'fæsaɪl/ adj. usu. derog. **1** easily achieved but of little value. **2** (of speech, writing, etc.) fluent, ready, glib. □ **facilely** adv. **facileness** n. [F *facile* or L *facilis* f. *facere* do]

facilitate /fə'sɪlɪˌteɪt/ v.tr. make easy or less difficult or more easily achieved. □ **facilitation** /-ˈteɪʃ(ə)n/ n. **facilitative** /-tətɪv/ adj. **facilitator** n. [F *faciliter* f. It. *facilitare* f. *facile* easy f. L *facilis*]

facility /fə'sɪlɪtɪ/ n. (pl. **-ies**) **1** ease; absence of difficulty. **2** fluency, dexterity, aptitude (*facility of expression*). **3** (esp. in pl.) an opportunity, the equipment, or the resources for doing something. **4** US a plant, installation, or establishment. [F *facilité* or L *facilitas* (as FACILE)]

facing /'feɪsɪŋ/ n. **1 a** a layer of material covering part of a garment etc. for contrast or strength. **b** (in pl.) the cuffs, collar, etc., of a military jacket. **2** an outer layer covering the surface of a wall etc.

facsimile /fæk'sɪmɪlɪ/ n. & v. —n. **1** an exact copy, esp. of writing, printing, a picture, etc. (often attrib.: *facsimile edition*). **2 a** production of an exact copy of a document etc. by electronic scanning and transmission of the resulting data (see also FAX). **b** a copy produced in this way. —v.tr. (**facsimiled, facsimileing**) make a facsimile of. □ **in facsimile** as an exact copy. [mod.L f. L *fac* imper. of *facere* make + *simile* neut. of *similis* like]

fact /fækt/ n. **1** a thing that is known to have occurred, to exist, or to be true. **2** a datum of experience (often foll. by an explanatory clause or phrase: *the fact that fire burns; the fact of my having seen them*). **3** (usu. in pl.) an item of verified information; a piece of evidence. **4** truth, reality. **5** a thing assumed as the basis for argument or inference. □ **a fact of life** something that must be accepted. **facts and figures** precise details. **fact-sheet** a paper setting out relevant information. **the facts of life** information about sexual functions and practices. **in** (or **in point of**) **fact 1** in reality; as a matter of fact. **2** (in summarizing) in short. [L *factum* f. *facere* do]

faction[1] /'fækʃ(ə)n/ n. **1** a small organized dissentient group within a larger one, esp. in politics. **2** a state of dissension within an organization. [F f. L *factio -onis* f. *facere* fact- do, make]

faction[2] /'fækʃ(ə)n/ n. a book, film, etc., using real events as a basis for a fictional narrative or dramatization. [blend of FACT and FICTION]

-faction /'fækʃ(ə)n/ comb. form forming nouns of action from verbs in -fy (*petrifaction; satisfaction*). [from or after L *-factio -factionis* f. *-facere* do, make]

factional /'fækʃən(ə)l/ adj. **1** of or characterized by faction. **2** belonging to a faction. □ **factionalism** n. **factionalize** v.tr. & intr. (also **-ise**). **factionally** adv. [FACTION[1]]

factious /'fækʃəs/ adj. of, characterized by, or inclined to faction. □ **factiously** adv. **factiousness** n.

factitious /fæk'tɪʃəs/ adj. **1** specially contrived, not genuine (*factitious value*). **2** artificial, not natural (*factitious joy*). □ **factitiously** adv. **factitiousness** n. [L *facticius* f. *facere* fact- do, make]

factoid /'fæktɔɪd/ n. an assumption or speculation that is reported and repeated so often that it becomes accepted as fact.

factor /'fæktə(r)/ n. **1** a circumstance, fact, or influence contributing to a result. **2** Math. a whole number etc. that when multiplied with another produces a given number or expression. **3** Biol. a gene etc. determining hereditary character. **4** (foll. by identifying number) Med. any of several substances in the blood contributing to coagulation (*factor eight*). **5 a** a business agent; a merchant buying and selling on commission. **b** Sc. a land-agent or steward. **c** an agent or a deputy. [F *facteur* or L *factor* f. *facere* fact- do, make]

factorial /fæk'tɔːrɪəl/ n. & adj. Math. —n. the product of a number and all the whole numbers below it (*factorial four = 4 × 3 × 2 × 1*). —adj. of a factor or factorial. □ **factorially** adv.

factorize /'fæktəˌraɪz/ v. (also **-ise**) Math. **1** tr. resolve into factors. **2** intr. be capable of resolution into factors. □ **factorization** /-ˈzeɪʃ(ə)n/ n.

factory /'fæktərɪ/ n. (pl. **-ies**) a building or buildings containing plant or equipment for manufacturing machinery or goods. □ **factory farming** a system of rearing livestock using industrial or intensive methods. **factory floor** workers in industry as distinct from management. **factory ship** Brit. a fishing ship with facilities for immediate processing of the catch. [Port. *feitoria* and LL *factorium*]

factotum /fæk'təʊtəm/ n. (pl. **factotums**) an employee who does all kinds of work. [med.L f. L *fac* imper. of *facere* do, make + *totum* neut. of *totus* whole]

factual /'fæktjʊəl/ adj. **1** based on or concerned with fact or facts. **2** actual, true. □ **factuality** /-ˈælɪtɪ/ n. **factually** adv. **factualness** n. [FACT, after *actual*]

faculty /'fækəltɪ/ n. (pl. **-ies**) **1** an aptitude or ability for a particular activity. **2** an inherent mental or physical power. **3 a** a group of university departments concerned with a major division of knowledge (*faculty of arts*). **b** US the staff of a university or college. [ME f. OF *faculté* f. L *facultas -tatis* f. *facilis* easy]

fad n. **1** a craze. **2** a peculiar notion or idiosyncrasy. □ **faddish** adj. **faddishly** adv. **faddishness** n. **faddism** n. **faddist** n. [19th c. (orig. dial.): prob. f. *fidfad* f. FIDDLE-FADDLE]

faddy /'fædɪ/ adj. (**faddier, faddiest**) having arbitrary likes and dislikes, esp. about food. □ **faddily** adv. **faddiness** n.

fade v. & n. —v. **1** intr. & tr. lose or cause to lose colour. **2** intr. lose freshness or strength; (of flowers etc.) droop, wither. **3** intr. **a** (of colour, light, etc.) grow pale or dim. **b** (of sound) grow faint. **4** intr. (of a feeling etc.) diminish. **5** intr. (foll. by away, out) (of a person etc.) disappear or depart gradually. **6** tr. (foll. by in, out) Cinematog. & Broadcasting **a** cause (a picture) to come gradually in or out of view on a screen, or to merge into another shot. **b** make (the sound) more or less audible. —n. the action or an instance of fading. □ **fade away** colloq. languish, grow thin. □ **fadeless** adj. **fader** n. (in sense 6 of *v*.). [ME f. OF *fader* f. *fade* dull, insipid prob. ult. f. L *fatuus* silly + *vapidus* VAPID]

faeces /ˈfiːsiːz/ *n.pl.* (*US* **feces**) waste matter discharged from the bowels. □ **faecal** /ˈfiːk(ə)l/ *adj.* [L, pl. of *faex* dregs]

faff *v.* & *n. Brit. colloq.* —*v.intr.* (often foll. by *about, around*) fuss, dither. —*n.* a fuss. [imit.]

fag[1] *n.* & *v.* —*n.* **1** esp. *Brit. colloq.* a piece of drudgery; a wearisome or unwelcome task. **2** *sl.* a cigarette. **3** *Brit.* (at public schools) a junior pupil who runs errands for a senior. —*v.* (**fagged, fagging**) **1 a** *tr.* (often foll. by *out*) tire out; exhaust. **b** *intr.* toil. **2** *intr. Brit.* (in public schools) act as a fag. □ **fag-end** *sl.* **1** *Brit.* a cigarette-end. **2** an inferior or useless remnant. [orig. unkn.: cf. FLAG[1]]

fag[2] *n. US sl.* often *offens.* a male homosexual. [abbr. of FAGGOT]

faggot /ˈfægət/ *n.* (*US* **fagot**) **1** (usu. in *pl.*) a ball or roll of seasoned chopped liver etc., baked or fried. **2** a bundle of sticks or twigs bound together as fuel. **3** a bundle of iron rods for heat treatment. **4** a bunch of herbs. **5** *sl. derog.* **a** an unpleasant woman. **b** *US* often *offens.* a male homosexual. □ **faggoty** *adj.* [ME f. OF *fagot*, of uncert. orig.]

fah *n.* (also **fa**) *Mus.* **1** (in tonic sol-fa) the fourth note of a major scale. **2** the note F in the fixed-doh system. [ME *fa* f. L *famuli*: see GAMUT]

Fahrenheit /ˈfærənˌhaɪt/ *adj.* of or measured on a scale of temperature on which water freezes at 32° and boils at 212° under standard conditions. [G. *Fahrenheit*, Ger. physicist d. 1736]

faience /ˈfaɪɑ̃s/ *n.* decorated and glazed earthenware and porcelain, e.g. delftware or majolica. [F *faïence* f. Faenza in Italy]

fail *v.* & *n.* —*v.* **1** *intr.* not succeed (*failed in persuading; failed to qualify*). **2 a** *tr.* & *intr.* be unsuccessful in (an examination, test, interview, etc.). **b** *tr.* (of a commodity etc.) not pass (a test of quality). **c** *tr.* reject (a candidate etc.); adjudge unsuccessful. **3** *intr.* be unable to; neglect to; choose not to (*I fail to see the reason; he failed to appear*). **4** *tr.* disappoint; let down; not serve when needed. **5** *intr.* (of supplies, crops, etc.) be or become lacking or insufficient. **6** *intr.* become weaker; cease functioning; break down. **7** *intr.* **a** (of an enterprise) collapse; come to nothing. **b** become bankrupt. —*n.* a failure in an examination or test. □ **fail-safe** reverting to a safe condition in the event of a breakdown etc. **without fail** for certain, whatever happens. [ME f. OF *faillir* (v.), *fail(l)e* (n.) ult. f. L *fallere* deceive]

failed /feɪld/ *adj.* **1** unsuccessful; not good enough (*a failed actor*). **2** weak, deficient; broken down (*a failed crop; a failed battery*).

failing /ˈfeɪlɪŋ/ *n.* & *prep.* —*n.* **1** a fault or shortcoming; a weakness, esp. in character. —*prep.* in default of; if not.

failure /ˈfeɪljə(r)/ *n.* **1** lack of success; failing. **2** an unsuccessful person, thing, or attempt. **3** non-performance, non-occurrence. **4** breaking down or ceasing to function (*heart failure; engine failure*). **5** running short of supply etc. **6** bankruptcy, collapse. [earlier *failer* f. AF, = OF *faillir* FAIL]

fain *adj.* & *adv. archaic* —*predic.adj.* (foll. by *to* + infin.) **1** willing under the circumstances to. **2** left with no alternative but to. —*adv.* gladly (esp. *would fain*). [OE *fægen* f. Gmc]

faint *adj.*, *v.*, & *n.* —*adj.* **1** indistinct, pale, dim; not clearly perceived. **2** (of a person) weak or giddy; inclined to faint. **3** slight, remote, inadequate (*a faint chance*). **4** feeble, half-hearted (*faint praise*). **5** timid (*a faint heart*). **6** (also **feint**) (of ruled paper) with inconspicuous lines to guide writing. —*v.intr.* **1** lose consciousness. **2** become faint. —*n.* a sudden loss of consciousness; fainting. □ **faint-hearted** cowardly, timid. □ **faintness** *n.* [ME f. OF, past part. of *faindre* FEIGN]

faintly /ˈfeɪntlɪ/ *adv.* **1** very slightly (*faintly amused*). **2** indistinctly, feebly.

fair[1] *adj.* & *adv.* —*adj.* **1** just, unbiased, equitable; in accordance with the rules. **2** blond; light or pale in colour or complexion. **3 a** of (only) moderate quality or amount; average. **b** considerable, satisfactory (*a fair chance of success*). **4** (of weather) fine and dry; (of the wind) favourable. **5** clean, clear, unblemished (*fair copy*). **6** beautiful, attractive. **7** *Austral.* & *NZ* complete, unquestionable. —*adv.* **1** in a fair manner (*play fair*). **2** exactly, completely (*was hit fair on the jaw*). □ **fair and square** *adv.* & *adj.* **1** exactly. **2** straightforward, honest, above-board. **a fair deal** equitable treatment. **fair dos** /duːz/ *colloq.* fair shares. **fair enough** *colloq.* that is reasonable or acceptable. **fair game** a thing or person one may legitimately pursue, exploit, etc. **fair play** reasonable treatment or behaviour. **the fair sex** women. **fair's fair** *colloq.* all involved should act fairly. **fair-weather friend** a friend or ally who is unreliable in times of difficulty. **for fair** *US sl.* completely. **in a fair way** to likely to. □ **fairish** *adj.* **fairness** *n.* [OE *fæger* f. Gmc]

fair[2] *n.* **1** a gathering of stalls, amusements, etc., for public (usu. outdoor) entertainment. **2** a periodical gathering for the sale of goods, often with entertainments. **3** an exhibition, esp. to promote particular products. [ME f. OF *feire* f. LL *feria* sing. f. L *feriae* holiday]

fairground /ˈfeəgraʊnd/ *n.* an outdoor area where a fair is held.

Fair Isle /ˈfeərʌɪl/ *n.* (also *attrib.*) a piece of knitwear knitted in a characteristic particoloured design. [*Fair Isle* in the Shetlands, where the design was first devised]

fairly /ˈfeəlɪ/ *adv.* **1** in a fair manner; justly. **2** moderately, acceptably (*fairly good*). **3** to a noticeable degree (*fairly narrow*). **4** utterly, completely (*fairly beside himself*). **5** actually (*fairly jumped for joy*). □ **fairly and squarely** = *fair and square* (see FAIR[1]).

fairway /ˈfeəweɪ/ *n.* **1** a navigable channel; a regular course or track of a ship. **2** the part of a golf-course between a tee and its green, kept free of rough grass.

fairy /ˈfeərɪ/ *n.* & *adj.* —*n.* (pl. **-ies**) **1** a small imaginary being with magical powers. **2** *sl. derog.* a male homosexual. —*adj.* of fairies, fairy-like, delicate, small. □ **fairy cake** a small individual iced sponge cake. **fairy cycle** a small bicycle for a child. **fairy godmother** a benefactress. **fairy lights** small coloured lights esp. for outdoor decoration. **fairy ring** a ring of darker grass caused by fungi. **fairy story** (or **tale**) **1** a tale about fairies. **2** an incredible story; a fabrication. □ **fairy-like** *adj.* [ME f. OF *faerie* f. *fae* FAY]

fairyland /ˈfeərɪˌlænd/ n. 1 the imaginary home of fairies. 2 an enchanted region.

fait accompli /ˌfeɪt əˈkɒmpliː, əˈkɔ̃pliː/ n. a thing that has been done and is past arguing against or altering. [F]

faith n. 1 complete trust or confidence. 2 firm belief, esp. without logical proof. 3 a a system of religious belief (*the Christian faith*). b belief in religious doctrines. c spiritual apprehension of divine truth apart from proof. d things believed or to be believed. 4 duty or commitment to fulfil a trust, promise, etc. (*keep faith*). 5 (*attrib.*) concerned with a supposed ability to cure by faith rather than treatment (*faith-healing*). □ **bad faith** intent to deceive. **good faith** honesty or sincerity of intention. [ME f. AF *fed* f. OF *feid* f. L *fides*]

faithful /ˈfeɪθfʊl/ adj. 1 showing faith. 2 (often foll. by *to*) loyal, trustworthy, constant. 3 accurate; true to fact (*a faithful account*). 4 (**the Faithful**) the believers in a religion, esp. Muslims and Christians. □ **faithfulness** n.

faithfully /ˈfeɪθfʊlɪ/ adv. in a faithful manner. □ **yours faithfully** a formula for ending a business or formal letter.

faithless /ˈfeɪθlɪs/ adj. 1 false, unreliable, disloyal. 2 without religious faith. □ **faithlessly** adv. **faithlessness** n.

fake n., adj., & v. —n. 1 a thing or person that is not genuine. 2 a trick. —adj. counterfeit; not genuine. —v.tr. 1 make (a false thing) appear genuine; forge, counterfeit. 2 make a pretence of having (a feeling, illness, etc.). □ **faker** n. **fakery** n. [obs. *feak*, *feague* thrash f. G *fegen* sweep, thrash]

fakir /ˈfeɪkɪə(r), fəˈkɪə(r)/ n. a Muslim or (rarely) Hindu religious mendicant or ascetic. [Arab. *faḳīr* needy man]

falcon /ˈfɔːlkən, ˈfɒlkən/ n. any diurnal bird of prey of the family Falconidae, sometimes trained to hunt small game for sport. [ME f. OF *faucon* f. LL *falco -onis*, perh. f. L *falx* scythe or f. Gmc]

falconer /ˈfɔːlkənə(r), ˈfɒl-/ n. 1 a keeper and trainer of hawks. 2 a person who hunts with hawks. [ME f. AF *fauconer*, OF *fauconier* (as FALCON)]

falconry /ˈfɔːlkənrɪ, ˈfɒl-/ n. the breeding and training of hawks; the sport of hawking. [F *fauconnerie* (as FALCON)]

fall /fɔːl/ v. & n. —v.intr. (past **fell** /fel/; past part. **fallen** /ˈfɔːlən/) 1 a go or come down freely; descend rapidly from a higher to a lower level (*fell from the top floor; rain was falling*). b drop or be dropped (*supplies fell by parachute; the curtain fell*). 2 a (often foll. by *over*) cease to stand; come suddenly to the ground from loss of balance etc. b collapse forwards or downwards esp. of one's own volition (*fell into my arms; fell over the chair*). 3 become detached and descend or disappear. 4 take a downward direction: a (of hair, clothing, etc.) hang down. b (of ground etc.) slope. c (foll. by *into*) (of a river etc.) discharge into. 5 a find a lower level; sink lower. b subside, abate. 6 (of a barometer, thermometer, etc.) show a lower reading. 7 occur; become apparent or present (*darkness fell*). 8 decline, diminish (*demand is falling; standards have fallen*). 9 a (of the face) show dismay or disappointment. b (of the eyes or a glance) look downwards. 10 a lose power or status (*the government will fall*). b lose esteem, moral integrity, etc. 11 commit sin; yield to temptation. 12 take or have a particular direction or place (*his eye fell on me; the accent falls on the first syllable*). 13 a find a place; be naturally divisible (*the subject falls into three parts*). b (foll. by *under, within*) be classed among. 14 occur at a specified time (*Easter falls early this year*). 15 come by chance or duty (*it fell to me to answer*). 16 a pass into a specified condition (*fall into decay; fell ill*). b become (*fall asleep*). 17 a (of a position etc.) be overthrown or captured; succumb to attack. b be defeated; fail. 18 die (*fall in battle*). 19 (foll. by *on, upon*) a attack. b meet with. c embrace or embark upon avidly. 20 (foll. by *to* + verbal noun) begin (*fell to wondering*). 21 (foll. by *to*) lapse, revert (*revenues fall to the Crown*). —n. 1 the act or an instance of falling; a sudden rapid descent. 2 that which falls or has fallen, e.g. snow, rocks, etc. 3 the recorded amount of rainfall etc. 4 a decline or diminution. 5 overthrow, downfall (*the fall of Rome*). 6 a succumbing to temptation. b (**the Fall**) the sin of Adam and its consequences, as described in Genesis. 7 (of material, land, light, etc.) a downward direction; a slope. 8 (also **Fall**) US autumn. 9 (esp. in *pl.*) a waterfall, cataract, or cascade. 10 a a wrestling-bout; a throw in wrestling which keeps the opponent on the ground for a specified time. b a controlled act of falling, esp. as a stunt or in judo etc. □ **fall about** *colloq.* be helpless, esp. with laughter. **fall apart** (or **to pieces**) 1 break into pieces. 2 (of a situation etc.) disintegrate; be reduced to chaos. 3 lose one's capacity to cope. **fall away** 1 (of a surface) incline abruptly. 2 become few or thin; gradually vanish. 3 desert, revolt; abandon one's principles. **fall back** retreat. **fall back on** have recourse to in difficulty. **fall behind** 1 be outstripped by one's competitors etc.; lag. 2 be in arrears. **fall down** (often foll. by *on*) *colloq.* fail; perform poorly; fail to deliver (payment etc.). **fall for** *colloq.* 1 be captivated or deceived by. 2 admire; yield to the charms or merits of. **fall foul of** come into conflict with; quarrel with. **fall guy** *sl.* 1 an easy victim. 2 a scapegoat. **fall in** 1 a take one's place in military formation. b (as *int.*) the order to do this. 2 collapse inwards. **falling star** a meteor. **fall into line** 1 take one's place in the ranks. 2 conform or collaborate with others. **fall into place** begin to make sense or cohere. **fall in with** 1 meet by chance. 2 agree with; accede to; humour. 3 coincide with. **fall off** 1 (of demand etc.) decrease, deteriorate. 2 withdraw. **fall-off** n. a decrease, deterioration, withdrawal, etc. **fall out** 1 quarrel. 2 (of the hair, teeth, etc.) become detached. 3 *Mil.* come out of formation. 4 result; come to pass; occur. **fall over oneself** *colloq.* 1 be eager or competitive. 2 be awkward, stumble through haste, confusion, etc. **fall short** 1 be or become deficient or inadequate. 2 (of a missile etc.) not reach its target. **fall short of** fail to reach or obtain. **fall through** fail; come to nothing; miscarry. **fall to** begin an activity, e.g. eating or working. [OE *fallan, feallan* f. Gmc]

fallacy /ˈfæləsɪ/ n. (pl. **-ies**) 1 a mistaken belief, esp. based on unsound argument. 2 faulty reasoning; misleading or unsound argument. □ **fallacious** /fəˈleɪʃəs/ adj. **fallaciously**

/fəˈleɪʃəslɪ/ adv. **fallaciousness** /fəˈleɪʃəsnɪs/ n. [L *fallacia* f. *fallax -acis* deceiving f. *fallere* deceive]

fallen past part. of FALL v. —adj. **1** (*attrib.*) having lost one's honour or reputation. **2** killed in war. □ **fallenness** n.

fallible /ˈfælɪb(ə)l/ adj. **1** capable of making mistakes. **2** liable to be erroneous. □ **fallibility** /-ˈbɪlɪtɪ/ n. **fallibly** adv. [med.L *fallibilis* f. L *fallere* deceive]

Fallopian tube /fəˈləʊpɪən/ n. *Anat.* either of two tubes in female mammals along which ova travel from the ovaries to the uterus. [*Fallopius*, Latinized name of G. *Fallopio*, It. anatomist d. 1562]

fallout /ˈfɔːlaʊt/ n. **1** radioactive debris caused by a nuclear explosion or accident. **2** the adverse side-effects of a situation etc.

fallow[1] /ˈfæləʊ/ adj. & n. —adj. **1 a** (of land) ploughed and harrowed but left unsown for a year. **b** uncultivated. **2** inactive. —n. fallow or uncultivated land. □ **fallowness** n. [ME f. OE *fealh* (n.), *fealgian* (v.)]

fallow[2] /ˈfæləʊ/ adj. of a pale brownish or reddish yellow. □ **fallow deer** any small deer of the genus *Dama*, having a white-spotted reddish-brown coat in the summer. [OE *falu, fealu* f. Gmc]

false /fɔls, fɔːls/ adj. & adv. —adj. **1** not according with fact; wrong, incorrect (*a false idea*). **2 a** spurious, sham, artificial (*false gods; false teeth; false modesty*). **b** acting as such; appearing to be such, esp. deceptively (*a false lining*). **3** illusory; not actually so (*a false economy*). **4** improperly so called (*a false acacia*). **5** deceptive. **6** (foll. by *to*) deceitful, treacherous, or unfaithful. **7** illegal (*false imprisonment*). —adv. in a false manner (esp. *play false*). □ **false alarm** an alarm given needlessly. **false colours** deceitful pretence. **false dawn** a transient light in the east before dawn. **false pretences** misrepresentations made with intent to deceive (esp. *under false pretences*). **false start 1** an invalid or disallowed start in a race. **2** an unsuccessful attempt to begin something. **false step** a slip; a mistake. □ **falsely** adv. **falseness** n. **falsity** n. (pl. **-ies**). [OE *fals* and OF *fals, faus* f. L *falsus* past part. of *fallere* deceive]

falsehood /ˈfɔlshʊd, ˈfɔːls-/ n. **1** the state of being false, esp. untrue. **2** a false or untrue thing. **3 a** the act of lying. **b** a lie or lies.

falsetto /fɒlˈsetəʊ, fɔːl-/ n. (pl. **-os**) **1** a method of voice production used by male singers, esp. tenors, to sing notes higher than their normal range. **2** a singer using this method. [It., dimin. of *falso* FALSE]

falsies /ˈfɒlsɪz, ˈfɔːl-/ n.pl. *colloq.* padded material to increase the apparent size of the breasts.

falsify /ˈfɒlsɪˌfaɪ, ˈfɔːls-/ v.tr. (**-ies, -ied**) **1** fraudulently alter or make false (a document, evidence, etc.). **2** misrepresent. **3** make wrong; pervert. □ **falsifiable** adj. **falsifiability** /-ˌfaɪəˈbɪlɪtɪ/ n. **falsification** /-fɪˈkeɪʃ(ə)n/ n. [ME f. F *falsifier* or med.L *falsificare* f. L *falsificus* making false f. *falsus* false]

falter /ˈfɔltə(r), ˈfɒl-/ v. **1** intr. stumble, stagger; go unsteadily. **2** intr. waver; lose courage. **3** tr. & intr. stammer; speak hesitatingly. □ **falterer** n. **falteringly** adv. [ME: orig. uncert.]

fame n. **1** renown; the state of being famous. **2** reputation. [ME f. OF f. L *fama*]

famed /feɪmd/ adj. (foll. by *for*) famous; much spoken of (*famed for its good food*).

familial /fəˈmɪlɪəl/ adj. of, occurring in, or characteristic of a family or its members. [F f. L *familia* FAMILY]

familiar /fəˈmɪlɪə(r)/ adj. & n. —adj. **1 a** (often foll. by *to*) well known; no longer novel. **b** common, usual; often encountered or experienced. **2** (foll. by *with*) knowing a thing well or in detail (*am familiar with all the problems*). **3** (often foll. by *with*) well acquainted (with a person); in close friendship; intimate. **4** excessively informal; impertinent. **5** unceremonious, informal. —n. **1** a close friend or associate. **2** (in full **familiar spirit**) a demon supposedly attending and obeying a witch etc. □ **familiarly** adv. [ME f. OF *familier* f. L *familiaris* (as FAMILY)]

familiarity /fəˌmɪlɪˈærɪtɪ/ n. (pl. **-ies**) **1** the state of being well known (*the familiarity of the scene*). **2** (foll. by *with*) close acquaintance. **3** a close relationship. **4** familiar or informal behaviour, esp. excessively so. [ME f. OF *familiarité* f. L *familiaritas -tatis* (as FAMILIAR)]

familiarize /fəˈmɪlɪəˌraɪz/ v.tr. (also **-ise**) **1** (foll. by *with*) make (a person) conversant or well acquainted. **2** make (a thing) well known. □ **familiarization** /-ˌzeɪʃ(ə)n/ n. [F *familiariser* f. *familiaire* (as FAMILIAR)]

family /ˈfæmɪlɪ, ˈfæmlɪ/ n. (pl. **-ies**) **1** a set of parents and children, or of relations. **2 a** the members of a household, esp. parents and their children. **b** a person's children. **c** (*attrib.*) serving the needs of families (*family butcher*). **3 a** all the descendants of a common ancestor. **b** a race or group of peoples from a common stock. **4** all the languages ultimately derived from a particular early language, regarded as a group. **5** a group of objects distinguished by common features. **6** *Biol.* a group of related genera of organisms within an order in taxonomic classification. □ **Family Division** (in the UK) a division of the High Court dealing with adoption, divorce, etc. **family man** a man having a wife and children, esp. one fond of family life. **family name** a surname. **family planning** birth control. **family tree** a chart showing relationships and lines of descent. **in the family way** *colloq.* pregnant. [ME f. L *familia* household f. *famulus* servant]

famine /ˈfæmɪn/ n. **1** extreme scarcity of food. **2** a shortage of something specified (*water famine*). [ME f. OF f. *faim* f. L *fames* hunger]

famish /ˈfæmɪʃ/ v.tr. & intr. (usu. in *passive*) **1** reduce or be reduced to extreme hunger. **2** *colloq.* feel very hungry. [ME f. obs. *fame* f. OF *afamer* ult. f. L *fames* hunger]

famous /ˈfeɪməs/ adj. **1** (often foll. by *for*) celebrated; well known. **2** *colloq.* excellent. □ **famousness** n. [ME f. AF, OF *fameus* f. L *famosus* f. *fama* fame]

famously /ˈfeɪməslɪ/ adv. *colloq.* **1** excellently (*got on famously*). **2** notably.

fan[1] n. & v. —n. **1** an apparatus, usu. with rotating blades, giving a current of air for ventilation etc. **2** a device, usu. folding and forming a semicircle when spread out, for agitating the air to cool oneself. **3** anything spread out like a fan. —v. (**fanned, fanning**) **1** tr. **a** blow a current of air on, with or as with a fan. **b** agitate (the air) with a fan. **2** tr. (of a breeze) blow gently on; cool. **3** intr. & tr. (usu.

foll. by *out*) spread out in the shape of a fan. □ **fan belt** a belt that drives a fan to cool the radiator in a motor vehicle. **fan heater** an electric heater in which a fan drives air over an element. □ **fanlike** *adj*. **fanner** *n*. [OE *fann* f. L *vannus* winnowing-fan]

fan² *n*. a devotee of a particular activity, performer, etc. (*film fan; football fan*). □ **fan club** an organized group of devotees. **fan mail** letters from fans. □ **fandom** *n*. [abbr. of FANATIC]

fanatic /fə'nætɪk/ *n*. & *adj*. —*n*. a person filled with excessive and often misguided enthusiasm for something. —*adj*. excessively enthusiastic. □ **fanatical** *adj*. **fanatically** *adv*. **fanaticism** /-tɪ,sɪz(ə)m/ *n*. **fanaticize** /-tɪ,saɪz/ *v.intr*. & *tr*. (also **-ise**). [F *fanatique* or L *fanaticus* f. *fanum* temple (orig. in religious sense)]

fancier /'fænsɪə(r)/ *n*. a connoisseur or follower of some activity or thing (*dog-fancier*).

fanciful /'fænsɪ,fʊl/ *adj*. **1** existing only in the imagination or fancy. **2** indulging in fancies; whimsical, capricious. **3** fantastically designed, ornamented, etc. □ **fancifully** *adv*. **fancifulness** *n*.

fancy /'fænsɪ/ *n*., *adj*., & *v*. —*n*. (*pl*. **-ies**) **1** an individual taste or inclination (*take a fancy to*). **2** a caprice or whim. **3** a thing favoured, e.g. a horse to win a race. **4** an arbitrary supposition. **5 a** the faculty of using imagination or of inventing imagery. **b** a mental image. **6** delusion; unfounded belief. —*adj*. (usu. *attrib*.) (**fancier, fanciest**) **1** ornamental; not plain. **2** capricious, whimsical, extravagant (*at a fancy price*). **3** based on imagination, not fact. **4** *US* (of foods etc.) above average quality. —*v.tr*. (**-ies, -ied**) **1** (foll. by *that* + clause) be inclined to suppose; rather think. **2** *Brit. colloq*. feel a desire for (*do you fancy a drink?*). **3** *Brit. colloq*. find sexually attractive. **4** *colloq*. have an unduly high opinion of (oneself, one's ability, etc.). **5** (in *imper*.) an exclamation of surprise (*fancy their doing that!*). **6** picture to oneself; conceive, imagine. □ **catch** (or **take**) **the fancy of** please; appeal to. **fancy dress** fanciful costume, esp. for masquerading as a different person or as an animal etc. at a party. **fancy-free** without (esp. emotional) commitments. **fancy goods** ornamental novelties etc. **fancy man** *sl. derog*. **1** a woman's lover. **2** a pimp. **fancy woman** *sl. derog*. a mistress. □ **fanciable** *adj*. (in sense 3 of *v*.). **fancily** *adv*. **fanciness** *n*. [contr. of FANTASY]

fandango /fæn'dæŋgəʊ/ *n*. (*pl*. **-oes** or **-os**) a lively Spanish dance for two. [Sp.: orig. unkn.]

fanfare /'fænfeə(r)/ *n*. **1** a short showy or ceremonious sounding of trumpets, bugles, etc. **2** an elaborate welcome. [F, imit.]

fang /fæŋ/ *n*. **1** a canine tooth, esp. of a dog or wolf. **2** the tooth of a venomous snake, by which poison is injected. **3** the root of a tooth or its prong. □ **fanged** *adj*. (also in *comb*.). **fangless** *adj*. [OE f. ON *fang* f. a Gmc root = to catch]

fanlight /'fænlaɪt/ *n*. a small, orig. semicircular window over a door or another window.

fanny /'fænɪ/ *n*. (*pl*. **-ies**) **1** *Brit. coarse sl*. the female genitals. **2** *US sl*. the buttocks. □ **fanny pack** *US sl*. = *bum-bag*. [20th c.: orig. unkn.]

Fanny Adams /,fænɪ 'ædəmz/ *n*. *Brit. sl*. (also **sweet Fanny Adams**) nothing at all. [name of a murder victim *c*.1870]

fantail /'fænteɪl/ *n*. a pigeon with a broad tail. □ **fantailed** *adj*.

fantasia /fæn'teɪzɪə, ,fæntə'zɪə/ *n*. a musical or other composition free in form and often in improvisatory style, or which is based on several familiar tunes. [It., = FANTASY]

fantasize /'fæntə,saɪz/ *v*. (also **phantasize, -ise**) **1** *intr*. have a fantasy or fanciful vision. **2** *tr*. imagine; create a fantasy about. □ **fantasist** *n*.

fantastic /fæn'tæstɪk/ *adj*. (also **fantastical**) **1** *colloq*. excellent, extraordinary. **2** extravagantly fanciful; capricious, eccentric. **3** grotesque or quaint in design etc. □ **fantasticality** /-'kælɪtɪ/ *n*. **fantastically** *adv*. [ME f. OF *fantastique* f. med.L *fantasticus* f. LL *phantasticus* f. Gk *phantastikos* f. *phantazomai* make a show f. *phainō* show]

fantasy /'fæntəsɪ, -zɪ/ *n*. (also **phantasy**) (*pl*. **-ies**) **1** the faculty of inventing images, esp. extravagant or visionary ones. **2** a fanciful mental image; a day-dream. **3** a whimsical speculation. **4** a fantastic invention or composition; a fantasia. [ME f. OF *fantasie* f. L *phantasia* appearance f. Gk (as FANTASTIC)]

far *adv*. & *adj*. (**further, furthest** or **farther, farthest**) —*adv*. **1** at or to or by a great distance (*far away; far off; far out*). **2** a long way (off) in space or time (*are you travelling far?; we talked far into the night*). **3** to a great extent or degree; by much (*far better; far the best; far too early*). —*adj*. **1** situated at or extending over a great distance in space or time; remote (*a far cry; a far country*). **2** more distant (*the far end of the hall*). □ **as far as 1** to the distance of (a place). **2** to the extent that (*travel as far as you like*). **by far** by a great amount. **far and away** by a very large amount. **far and near** everywhere. **far and wide** over a large area. **far-away 1** remote; long-past. **2** (of a look) dreamy. **3** (of a voice) sounding as if from a distance. **far cry** a long way. **the Far East** China, Japan, and other countries of E. Asia. **far-fetched** (of an explanation etc.) strained, unconvincing. **far-flung** extending far; widely distributed. **far from** very different from being; tending to the opposite of (*the problem is far from being solved*). **far gone 1** advanced in time. **2** *colloq*. in an advanced state of illness, drunkenness, etc. **far-off** remote. **far-out 1** distant. **2** avant-garde, unconventional, excellent. **far-reaching 1** widely applicable. **2** having important consequences or implications. **far-seeing** shrewd in judgement; prescient. **go far 1** achieve much. **2** contribute greatly. **3** be adequate. **go too far** go beyond the limits of what is reasonable, polite, etc. **how far** to what extent. **so far 1** to such an extent or distance; to this point. **2** until now. **so** (or **in so**) **far as** (or **that**) to the extent that. **so far so good** progress has been satisfactory up to now. □ **farness** *n*. [OE *feorr*]

farad /'færəd/ *n*. *Electr*. the SI unit of capacitance, such that one coulomb of charge causes a potential difference of one volt. [shortening of *Faraday*, f. M. Faraday, Engl. physicist d. 1867]

farce *n*. **1 a** a coarsely comic dramatic work based on ludicrously improbable events. **b** this branch of drama. **2** absurdly futile proceedings; pretence, mockery. [F, orig. = stuffing, f. OF *farsir* f. L *farcire* to stuff, used metaph. of interludes etc.]

farcical /'fɑːsɪk(ə)l/ *adj*. **1** extremely ludicrous or futile. **2** of or like farce. □ **farcicality** /-'kælɪtɪ/ *n*. **farcically** *adv*.

fare /feə(r)/ *n. & v.* —*n.* **1 a** the price a passenger has to pay to be conveyed by bus, train, etc. **b** a passenger paying to travel in a public vehicle. **2** a range of food provided by a restaurant etc. —*v.intr.* literary progress; get on (*how did you fare?*). □ **fare-stage** *Brit.* **1** a section of a bus etc. route for which a fixed fare is charged. **2** a stop marking this. [OE *fær, faru* journeying, *faran* (v.), f. Gmc]

farewell /feə'wel/ *int. & n.* —*int.* goodbye, adieu. —*n.* leave-taking, departure (also *attrib.: a farewell kiss*). [ME f. imper. of FARE + WELL¹]

farina /fə'raɪnə, -'riːnə/ *n.* the flour or meal of cereal, nuts, or starchy roots. □ **farinaceous** /ˌfærɪ'neɪʃəs/ *adj.* [L f. *far* corn]

farm *n. & v.* —*n.* **1** an area of land and its buildings used under one management for growing crops, rearing animals, etc. **2** a place or establishment for breeding a particular type of animal, growing fruit, etc. (*trout-farm; mink-farm*). **3** = FARMHOUSE. —*v.* **1 a** *tr.* use (land) for growing crops, rearing animals, etc. **b** *intr.* be a farmer; work on a farm. **2** *tr.* breed (fish etc.) commercially. **3** *tr.* (often foll. by *out*) **a** delegate or subcontract (work) to others. **b** contract (the collection of taxes) to another for a fee. **c** arrange for (a person, esp. a child) to be looked after by another, with payment. □ **farm-hand** a worker on a farm. □ **farmable** *adj.* **farming** *n.* [ME f. OF *ferme* f. med.L *firma* fixed payment f. L *firmus* FIRM¹: orig. applied only to leased land]

farmer /ˈfɑːmə(r)/ *n.* **1** a person who cultivates a farm. **2** a person to whom the collection of taxes is contracted for a fee. **3** a person who looks after children for payment. [ME f. AF *fermer,* OF *fermier* f. med.L *firmarius, firmator* f. *firma* FIRM²]

farmhouse /ˈfɑːmhaʊs/ *n.* a dwelling-place (esp. the main one) attached to a farm.

farmstead /ˈfɑːmsted/ *n.* a farm and its buildings regarded as a unit.

farmyard /ˈfɑːmjɑːd/ *n.* a yard or enclosure attached to a farmhouse.

faro /ˈfeərəʊ/ *n.* a gambling card-game in which bets are placed on the order of appearance of the cards. [F *pharaon* PHARAOH (said to have been the name of the king of hearts)]

farrago /fə'rɑːɡəʊ/ *n.* (*pl.* **-os** or *US* **-oes**) a medley or hotchpotch. □ **farraginous** /-'rædʒɪnəs/ *adj.* [L *farrago farraginis* mixed fodder f. *far* corn]

farrier /ˈfærɪə(r)/ *n. Brit.* **1** a smith who shoes horses. **2** a horse-doctor. □ **farriery** *n.* [OF *ferrier* f. L *ferrarius* f. *ferrum* iron, horseshoe]

farrow /ˈfærəʊ/ *n. & v.* —*n.* **1** a litter of pigs. **2** the birth of a litter. —*v.tr.* (also *absol.*) (of a sow) produce (pigs). [OE *fearh, færh* pig f. WG]

Farsi /ˈfɑːsiː/ *n.* the modern Persian language. [Pers.: cf. PARSEE]

far-sighted /fɑː'saɪtɪd, ˈfɑː-/ *adj.* **1** having foresight, prudent. **2** esp. *US* = LONG-SIGHTED. □ **far-sightedly** *adv.* **far-sightedness** *n.*

fart /fɑːt/ *v. & n. coarse sl.* —*v.intr.* **1** emit wind from the anus. **2** (foll. by *about, around*) behave foolishly; waste time. —*n.* **1** an emission of wind from the anus. **2** an unpleasant person. [OE (recorded in *feorting* verbal noun) f. Gmc]

farther var. of FURTHER (esp. with ref. to physical distance).

farthest var. of FURTHEST (esp. with ref. to physical distance).

farthing /ˈfɑːðɪŋ/ *n.* (in the UK) a coin and monetary unit formerly worth a quarter of an old penny. [OE *feorthing* f. *feortha* fourth]

■ **Usage** The farthing was withdrawn from circulation in 1961.

farthingale /ˈfɑːðɪŋɡeɪl/ *n. hist.* a hooped petticoat or a stiff curved roll to extend a woman's skirt. [earlier *vardingale,* verd- f. F *verdugale* f. Sp. *verdugado* f. *verdugo* rod]

fasces /ˈfæsiːz/ *n.pl.* **1** *Rom.Hist.* a bundle of rods with a projecting axe-blade, carried by a lictor as a symbol of a magistrate's power. **2** *hist.* (in Fascist Italy) emblems of authority. [L, pl. of *fascis* bundle]

fascia /ˈfeɪʃə/ *n.* (also **facia**) **1** *Brit.* **a** the instrument panel of a motor vehicle. **b** any similar panel or plate for operating machinery. **2** the upper part of a shop-front with the proprietor's name etc. **3** *Archit.* **a** a long flat surface between mouldings on the architrave in classical architecture. **b** a flat surface, usu. of wood, covering the ends of rafters. **4** a stripe or band. □ **fascial** *adj.* [L, = band, door-frame, etc.]

fascicle /ˈfæsɪk(ə)l/ *n.* (also **fascicule** /-ˌkjuːl/) a separately published instalment of a book, usu. not complete in itself. [L *fasciculus* bundle, dimin. of *fascis:* see FASCES]

fascinate /ˈfæsɪneɪt/ *v.tr.* **1** capture the interest of; attract irresistibly. **2** (esp. of a snake) paralyse (a victim) with fear. □ **fascinated** *adj.* **fascinating** *adj.* **fascinatingly** *adv.* **fascination** /-'neɪʃ(ə)n/ *n.* **fascinator** *n.* [L *fascinare* f. *fascinum* spell]

Fascism /ˈfæʃɪz(ə)m/ *n.* **1** the totalitarian principles and organization of the extreme right-wing nationalist movement in Italy (1922–43). **2** (also **fascism**) any similar nationalist and authoritarian movement. □ **Fascist** *n. & adj.* (also **fascist**). **Fascistic** /-'ʃɪstɪk/ *adj.* (also **fascistic**). [It. *fascismo* f. *fascio* political group f. L *fascis* bundle: see FASCES]

fashion /ˈfæʃ(ə)n/ *n. & v.* —*n.* **1** the current popular custom or style, esp. in dress or social conduct. **2** a manner or style of doing something (*in a peculiar fashion*). **3** (in *comb.*) in a specified manner (*walk crab-fashion*). **4** fashionable society (*a woman of fashion*). —*v.tr.* (often foll. by *into*) make into a particular or the required form. □ **after** (or **in**) **a fashion** as well as is practicable, though not satisfactorily. **in** (or **out of**) **fashion** fashionable (or not fashionable) at the time in question. □ **fashioner** *n.* [ME f. AF *fasun,* OF *façon,* f. L *factio -onis* f. *facere fact-* do, make]

fashionable /ˈfæʃnəb(ə)l/ *adj.* **1** following, suited to, or influenced by the current fashion. **2** characteristic of or favoured by those who are leaders of social fashion. □ **fashionableness** *n.* **fashionably** *adv.*

fast¹ /fɑːst/ *adj. & adv.* —*adj.* **1** rapid, quick-moving. **2** capable of high speed (*a fast car*). **3** enabling or causing or intended for high speed (*a fast road; fast lane*). **4** (of a clock etc.) showing a time ahead of the correct time. **5** (of a photographic film) needing only a short exposure. **6 a** firmly fixed or attached. **b** secure; firmly established (*a fast friendship*). **7** (of a colour) not fading in light or when washed. **8** (of a person) immoral, dissipated. —*adv.* **1** quickly; in quick succession. **2** firmly, fixedly, tightly, securely (*stand fast; eyes fast shut*). **3** soundly, completely *(fast asleep)*. □ **fast breeder** (or **fast breeder reactor**) a reactor using fast neutrons to produce the same fissile material as it uses. **fast food** food that can be prepared and served quickly and easily, esp. in a snack bar or restaurant. **fast neutron** a neutron with high kinetic energy, esp. not slowed by a moderator etc. **fast reactor** a nuclear reactor using mainly fast neutrons. **fast-talk** *US colloq.* persuade by rapid or deceitful talk. **pull a fast one** *colloq.* try to deceive or gain an unfair advantage. [OE *fæst* f. Gmc]

fast² /fɑːst/ *v. & n.* —*v.intr.* abstain from all or some kinds of food or drink, esp. as a religious observance. —*n.* an act or period of fasting. □ **faster** *n.* [ON *fasta* f. Gmc (as FAST¹)]

fastback /ˈfɑːstbæk/ *n.* **1** a motor car with the rear sloping continuously down to the bumper. **2** such a rear.

fasten /ˈfɑːs(ə)n/ *v.* **1** *tr.* make or become fixed or secure. **2** *tr.* (foll. by *in*, *up*) lock securely; shut in. **3** *tr.* **a** (foll. by *on*, *upon*) direct (a look, thoughts, etc.) fixedly or intently. **b** focus or direct the attention fixedly upon *(fastened him with her eyes)*. **4** *tr.* (foll. by *on*, *upon*) fix (a designation or imputation etc.). **5** *intr.* (foll. by *on*, *upon*) **a** take hold of. **b** single out. □ **fastener** *n.* [OE *fæstnian* f. Gmc]

fastening /ˈfɑːsnɪŋ/ *n.* a device that fastens something; a fastener.

fastidious /fæˈstɪdɪəs/ *adj.* **1** very careful in matters of choice or taste; fussy. **2** easily disgusted; squeamish. □ **fastidiously** *adv.* **fastidiousness** *n.* [ME f. L *fastidiosus* f. *fastidium* loathing]

fastness /ˈfɑːstnɪs/ *n.* **1** a stronghold or fortress. **2** the state of being secure. [OE *fæstnes* (as FAST¹)]

fat *n.*, *adj.*, *& v.* —*n.* **1** a natural oily or greasy substance occurring esp. in animal bodies. **2** the part of anything containing this. **3** excessive presence of fat in a person or animal; corpulence. —*adj.* (**fatter**, **fattest**) **1** (of a person or animal) having excessive fat; corpulent. **2** (of an animal) made plump for slaughter; fatted. **3** containing much fat. **4** greasy, oily, unctuous. **5** (of land or resources) fertile, rich; yielding abundantly. **6 a** thick, substantial in content (*a fat book*). **b** substantial as an asset or opportunity (*a fat cheque*; *was given a fat part in the play*). —*v.tr. & intr.* (**fatted**, **fatting**) make or become fat. □ **fat-head** *colloq.* a stupid person. **fat-headed** stupid. **kill the fatted calf** celebrate, esp. at a prodigal's return (Luke 15). **live off** (or **on**) **the fat of the land** have the best of everything. □ **fatless** *adj.* **fatly** *adv.* **fatness** *n.* **fattish** *adj.* [OE *fæt* (adj.), *fættian* (v.) f. Gmc]

fatal /ˈfeɪt(ə)l/ *adj.* **1** causing or ending in death (*a fatal accident*). **2** (often foll. by *to*) destructive; ruinous; ending in disaster (*made a fatal mistake*). **3** fateful, decisive. □ **fatally** *adv.* **fatalness** *n.* [ME f. OF *fatal* or L *fatalis* (as FATE)]

fatalism /ˈfeɪtəˌlɪz(ə)m/ *n.* **1** the belief that all events are predetermined and therefore inevitable. **2** a submissive attitude to events as being inevitable. □ **fatalist** *n.* **fatalistic** /-ˈlɪstɪk/ *adj.* **fatalistically** /-ˈlɪstɪkəlɪ/ *adv.*

fatality /fəˈtælətɪ/ *n.* (*pl.* **-ies**) **1 a** an occurrence of death by accident or in war etc. **b** a person killed in this way. **2** a fatal influence. **3** a predestined liability to disaster. [F *fatalité* or LL *fatalitas* f. *fatalis* FATAL]

fate *n. & v.* —*n.* **1** a power regarded as predetermining events unalterably. **2 a** the future regarded as determined by such a power. **b** an individual's appointed lot. **3** death, destruction. **4** (usu. **Fate**) a goddess of destiny. —*v.tr.* **1** (usu. in *passive*) preordain (*was fated to win*). **2** (as **fated** *adj.*) doomed to destruction. [ME f. It. *fato* & L *fatum* that which is spoken, f. *fari* speak]

fateful /ˈfeɪtfʊl/ *adj.* **1** important, decisive; having far-reaching consequences. **2** controlled as if by fate. **3** causing or likely to cause disaster. □ **fatefully** *adv.* **fatefulness** *n.*

father /ˈfɑːðə(r)/ *n. & v.* —*n.* **1 a** a man in relation to a child or children born from his fertilization of an ovum. **b** (in full **adoptive father**) a man who has continuous care of the child, esp. by adoption. **2** any male animal in relation to its offspring. **3** (usu. in *pl.*) a progenitor or forefather. **4** an originator, designer, or early leader. **5** a person who deserves special respect (*the father of his country*). **6** (**Fathers** or **Fathers of the Church**) early Christian theologians whose writings were regarded as especially authoritative. **7** (also **Father**) **a** (often as a title or form of address) a priest, esp. of a religious order. **b** a religious leader. **8** (**the Father**) (in Christian belief) the first person of the Trinity. **9** (**Father**) a venerable person, esp. as a title in personifications (*Father Time*). **10** the oldest member or doyen (*Father of the House*). —*v.tr.* **1** beget; be the father of. **2** behave as a father towards. **3** originate (a scheme etc.). **4** (foll. by *on*) assign the paternity of (a child, book) to a person. □ **father-figure** an older man who is respected like a father; a trusted leader. **father-in-law** (*pl.* **fathers-in-law**) the father of one's husband or wife. **Father's Day** a day (usu. the third Sunday in June) established for a special tribute to fathers. □ **fatherhood** *n.* **fatherless** *adj.* **fatherlessness** *n.* **fatherlike** *adj. & adv.* **fathership** *n.* [OE *fæder* with many Gmc cognates: rel. to L *pater*, Gk *patēr*]

fatherland /ˈfɑːðəlænd/ *n.* one's native country.

fatherly /ˈfɑːðəlɪ/ *adj.* **1** like or characteristic of a father in affection, care, etc. (*fatherly concern*). **2** of or proper to a father. □ **fatherliness** *n.*

fathom /ˈfæð(ə)m/ *n. & v.* —*n.* (*pl.* often **fathom** when prec. by a number) a measure of six feet, esp. used in taking depth soundings. —*v.tr.* **1** grasp or comprehend (a problem or difficulty). **2** measure the depth of (water) with a sounding-line. □ **fathomable** *adj.* **fathomless** *adj.* [OE *fæthm* outstretched arms f. Gmc]

fatigue /fəˈtiːg/ *n. & v.* —*n.* **1** extreme tiredness after exertion. **2** weakness in materials, esp. metal, caused by repeated variations of stress. **3** a reduction in the efficiency of a muscle, organ, etc., after prolonged activity. **4** a non-military duty in the army, often as a punishment. —*v.tr.* (**fatigues**, **fatigued**, **fatiguing**) cause fatigue in; tire, exhaust. □ **fatiguable** *adj.* (also **fatigable**). **fatiguability** /-gəˈbɪlɪtɪ/ *n.* (also **fatigability**). **fatigueless** *adj.* [F *fatigue*, *fatiguer* f. L *fatigare* tire out]

fatstock /ˈfætstɒk/ *n.* livestock fattened for slaughter.

fatten /ˈfæt(ə)n/ *v. tr. & intr.* (esp. with ref. to meat-producing animals) make or become fat.

fatty /ˈfætɪ/ *adj.* —*adj.* (**fattier**, **fattiest**) **1** like fat; oily, greasy. **2** consisting of or containing fat; adipose. **3** marked by abnormal deposition of fat, esp. in fatty degeneration. —*n. (pl.* **-ies**) *colloq.* a fat person (esp. as a nickname). □ **fatty acid** *Chem.* any of a class of organic compounds occurring as constituents of lipids. □ **fattily** *adv.* **fattiness** *n.*

fatuous /ˈfætjʊəs/ *adj.* vacantly silly; purposeless, idiotic. □ **fatuity** /fəˈtjuːɪtɪ/ *n. (pl.* **-ies**). **fatuously** *adv.* **fatuousness** *n.* [L *fatuus* foolish]

fatwa /ˈfætwaː/ *n.* (in Islamic countries) an authoritative ruling on a religious matter. [Arab. *fatwa*]

faucet /ˈfɔːsɪt/ *n.* esp. *US* a tap. [ME f. OF *fausset* vent-peg f. Prov. *falset* f. *falsar* to bore]

fault /fɒlt, fɔːlt/ *n. & v.* —*n.* **1** a defect or imperfection of character or of structure, appearance, etc. **2** a break or other defect in an electric circuit. **3** a transgression, offence, or thing wrongly done. **4 a** *Tennis* etc. a service of the ball not in accordance with the rules. **b** (in showjumping) a penalty for an error. **5** responsibility for wrongdoing, error, etc. (*it will be your own fault*). **6** a defect regarded as the cause of something wrong (*the fault lies in the teaching methods*). **7** *Geol.* an extended break in the continuity of strata or a vein. —*v.* **1** *tr.* find fault with; blame. **2** *tr.* declare to be faulty. **3** *tr. Geol.* break the continuity of (strata or a vein). **4** *intr.* commit a fault. **5** *intr. Geol.* show a fault. □ **at fault** guilty; to blame. **find fault** (often foll. by *with*) make an adverse criticism; complain. **to a fault** (usu. of a commendable quality etc.) excessively (*generous to a fault*). [ME *faut(e)* f. OF ult. f. L *fallere* FAIL]

faultless /ˈfɒltlɪs, ˈfɔːlt-/ *adj.* without fault; free from defect or error. □ **faultlessly** *adv.* **faultlessness** *n.*

faulty /ˈfɒltɪ, ˈfɔːltɪ/ (**faultier**, **faultiest**) *adj.* having faults; imperfect, defective. □ **faultily** *adv.* **faultiness** *n.*

faun *n.* a Latin rural deity with a human face and torso and a goat's horns, legs, and tail. [ME f. OF *faune* or L *Faunus*, a Latin god identified with Gk Pan]

fauna /ˈfɔːnə/ *n. (pl.* **faunae** /-niː/ or **faunas**) the animal life of a region or geological period. □ **faunal** *adj.* **faunist** *n.* **faunistic** /-ˈnɪstɪk/ *adj.* [mod.L f. the name of a rural goddess, sister of Faunus: see FAUN]

faux pas /fəʊ ˈpɑː/ *n. (pl.* same /ˈpɑːz/) **1** a tactless mistake; a blunder. **2** a social indiscretion. [F, = false step]

favour /ˈfeɪvə(r)/ *n. & v.* (*US* **favor**) —*n.* **1** an act of kindness beyond what is due or usual (*did it as a favour*). **2** esteem, liking, approval, goodwill; friendly regard (*look with favour on*). **3** partiality; too lenient or generous treatment. **4** aid, support (*under favour of night*). **5** a thing given or worn as a mark of favour or support, e.g. a badge or a knot of ribbons. —*v.tr.* **1** regard or treat with favour or partiality. **2** give support or approval to; promote, prefer. **3 a** be to the advantage of (a person). **b** facilitate (a process etc.). **4** tend to confirm (an idea or theory). **5** (foll. by *with*) oblige (*favour me with a reply*). **6** (as **favoured** *adj.*) having special advantages. **7** *colloq.* resemble in features. □ **in favour 1** meeting with approval. **2** (foll. by *of*) in support of. **b** to the advantage of. **out of favour** lacking approval. □ **favourer** *n.* [ME f. OF f. L *favor -oris* f. *favēre* show kindness to]

favourable /ˈfeɪvərəb(ə)l/ *adj.* (*US* **favorable**) **1 a** well-disposed; propitious. **b** commendatory, approving. **2** giving consent (*a favourable answer*). **3** promising, auspicious, satisfactory (*a favourable aspect*). **4** (often foll. by *to*) helpful, suitable. □ **favourableness** *n.* **favourably** *adv.* [ME f. OF *favorable* f. L *favorabilis* (as FAVOUR)]

favourite /ˈfeɪvərɪt/ *adj. & n.* (*US* **favorite**) —*adj.* preferred to all others (*my favourite book*). —*n.* **1** a specially favoured person. **2** *Sport* a competitor thought most likely to win. [obs. F *favorit* f. It. *favorito* past part. of *favorire* favour]

favouritism /ˈfeɪvərɪˌtɪz(ə)m/ *n.* (*US* **favoritism**) the unfair favouring of one person or group at the expense of another.

fawn[1] *n., adj., & v.* —*n.* **1** a young deer in its first year. **2** a light yellowish brown. —*adj.* fawn-coloured. —*v.tr.* (also *absol.*) (of a deer) bring forth (young). [ME f. OF *faon* etc. ult. f. L *fetus* offspring: cf. FOETUS]

fawn[2] *v.intr.* **1** (often foll. by *on, upon*) (of a person) behave servilely, cringe. **2** (of an animal, esp. a dog) show extreme affection. □ **fawner** *n.* **fawning** *adj.* **fawningly** *adv.* [OE *fagnian, fægnian* (as FAIN)]

fax *n. & v.* —*n.* **1** facsimile transmission (see FACSIMILE *n.* 2). **2 a** a copy produced by this. **b** a machine for transmitting and receiving these. —*v.tr.* transmit (a document) in this way. [abbr. of FACSIMILE]

fay *n. literary* a fairy. [ME f. OF *fae, faie* f. L *fata* (pl.) the Fates]

faze *v.tr.* (often as **fazed** *adj.*) *colloq.* disconcert, perturb, disorientate. [var. of *feeze* drive off, f. OE *fēsian*, of unkn. orig.]

FBA *abbr.* Fellow of the British Academy.

FBI *abbr.* (in the US) Federal Bureau of Investigation.

Fe *symb. Chem.* the element iron.

fealty /ˈfiːəltɪ/ *n. (pl.* **-ies**) **1** *hist.* **a** a feudal tenant's or vassal's fidelity to a lord. **b** an acknowledgement of this. **2** allegiance. [ME f. OF *feaulté* f. L *fidelitas -tatis* f. *fidelis* faithful f. *fides* faith]

fear *n. & v.* —*n.* **1 a** an unpleasant emotion caused by exposure to danger, expectation of pain, etc. **b** a state of alarm (*be in fear*). **2** a cause of fear (*all fears removed*). **3** (often foll. by *of*) dread or fearful respect (towards) (*had a fear of heights*). **4** anxiety for the safety of (*in fear of their lives*). **5** danger (*there is little fear of failure*). —*v.* **1 a** *tr.* feel fear about or towards (a person or thing). **b** *intr.* feel fear. **2** *intr.* (foll. by *for*) feel anxiety or apprehension about (*feared for my life*). **3** *tr.* (usu. foll. by *that* + clause) apprehend with fear or regret (*I fear that you are wrong*). **5** *tr.* **a** (foll. by *to* + infin.) hesitate. **b** (foll. by verbal noun) shrink from; be apprehensive about (*he feared meeting his ex-wife*). **6** *tr.* show reverence towards. □ **for fear of** (or **that**) to avoid the risk of (or that). **never fear** there is no danger of that. **no fear** *colloq.* expressing strong denial or refusal. **without fear or favour** impartially. [OE f. Gmc]

fearful /ˈfɪəfʊl/ *adj.* **1** (usu. foll. by *of*, or *that* + clause) afraid. **2** terrible, awful. **3** *colloq.* extremely unwelcome or unpleasant (*a fearful row*). □ **fearfully** *adv.* **fearfulness** *n.*

fearless /ˈfɪəlɪs/ *adj.* **1** courageous, brave. **2** (foll. by *of*) without fear. □ **fearlessly** *adv.* **fearlessness** *n.*

fearsome /ˈfɪəsəm/ adj. appalling or frightening, esp. in appearance. □ **fearsomely** adv. **fearsomeness** n.

feasibility /ˌfiːzɪˈbɪlɪtɪ/ n. the state or degree of being feasible. □ **feasibility study** a study of the practicability of a proposed project.

feasible /ˈfiːzɪb(ə)l/ adj. practicable, possible; easily or conveniently done. □ **feasibly** adv. [ME f. OF faisable, -ible f. fais- stem of faire f. L facere do, make]

■ **Usage** This word should not be used to mean 'possible' or 'probable' in the sense 'likely'. 'Possible' or 'probable' should be used instead.

feast n. & v. —n. **1** a large or sumptuous meal. **2** a gratification to the senses or mind. **3** an annual religious celebration. —v. **1** intr. partake of a feast; eat and drink sumptuously. **2** tr. **a** regale. **b** pass (time) in feasting. □ **feast one's eyes on** take pleasure in beholding. □ **feaster** n. [ME f. OF feste, fester f. L festus joyous]

feat n. a noteworthy act or achievement. [ME f. OF fait, fet (as FACT)]

feather /ˈfeðə(r)/ n. & v. —n. **1** any of the appendages growing from a bird's skin, with a horny hollow stem and fine strands. **2** one or more of these as decoration etc. **3** (collect.) **a** plumage. **b** game-birds. —v. **1** tr. cover or line with feathers. **2** tr. Rowing turn (an oar) so that it passes through the air edgeways. □ **feather bed** a bed with a mattress stuffed with feathers. **feather-bed** v.tr. (**-bedded, -bedding**) provide with (esp. financial) advantages. **feather-bedding** the employment of excess staff. **feather-brained** (or **-headed**) silly, absent-minded. **a feather in one's cap** an achievement to one's credit. **feather one's nest** enrich oneself. **in fine** (or **high**) **feather** colloq. in good spirits. □ **feathered** adj. (also in comb.). **featherless** adj. **feathery** adj. **featheriness** n. [OE fether, gefithrian, f. Gmc]

feathering /ˈfeðərɪŋ/ n. **1** bird's plumage. **2** the feathers of an arrow. **3** a feather-like structure in an animal's coat. **4** Archit. cusps in tracery.

featherweight /ˈfeðəˌweɪt/ n. **1 a** a weight in certain sports intermediate between bantamweight and lightweight. **b** a sportsman of this weight. **2** a very light person or thing. **3** (usu. attrib.) a trifling or unimportant thing.

feature /ˈfiːtʃə(r)/ n. & v. —n. **1** a distinctive or characteristic part of a thing. **2** (usu. in pl.) a distinctive part of the face, esp. with regard to shape and visual effect. **3** a distinctive or regular article in a newspaper or magazine. **4 a** (in full **feature film**) a full-length film intended as the main item in a cinema programme. **b** (in full **feature programme**) a broadcast devoted to a particular topic. —v. **1** tr. make a special display or attraction of; give special prominence to. **2** tr. & intr. have as or be an important actor, participant, or topic in a film, broadcast, etc. **3** intr. be a feature. □ **featured** adj. (also in comb.). **featureless** adj. [ME f. OF feiture, faiture form f. L factura formation f. facere fact- do, make]

Feb. abbr. February.

febrile /ˈfiːbraɪl/ adj. of or relating to fever; feverish. □ **febrility** /fɪˈbrɪlɪtɪ/ n. [F fébrile or med.L febrilis f. L febris fever]

February /ˈfebrʊərɪ/ n. (pl. **-ies**) the second month of the year. [ME f. OF fevrier ult. f. L februarius f. februa a purification feast held in this month]

feces US var. of FAECES.

feckless /ˈfeklɪs/ adj. **1** feeble, ineffective. **2** unthinking, irresponsible (feckless gaiety). □ **fecklessly** adv. **fecklessness** n. [Sc. feck f. effeck var. of EFFECT]

fecund /ˈfiːkənd, ˈfek-/ adj. **1** prolific, fertile. **2** fertilizing. □ **fecundability** /ˈfiːkʌndəˈbɪlɪtɪ/ n. **fecundity** /fɪˈkʌndɪtɪ/ n. [ME f. F fécond or L fecundus]

fecundate /ˈfiːkənˌdeɪt, ˈfek-/ v.tr. **1** make fruitful. **2** = FERTILIZE. □ **fecundation** /-ˈdeɪʃ(ə)n/ n. [L fecundare f. fecundus fruitful]

fed past and past part. of FEED. □ **fed up** (often foll. by with) discontented or bored, esp. from a surfeit of something.

federal /ˈfedər(ə)l/ adj. **1** of a system of government in which several States form a unity but remain independent in internal affairs. **2** relating to or affecting such a federation (federal laws). **3** relating to or favouring centralized government. **4** (**Federal**) US of the Northern States in the Civil War. □ **federalism** n. **federalist** n. **federalize** v.tr. (also **-ise**). **federalization** /-ˈzeɪʃ(ə)n/ n. **federally** adv. [L foedus -eris league, covenant]

federate v. & adj. —v.tr. & intr. /ˈfedəˌreɪt/ organize or be organized on a federal basis. —adj. /ˈfedərət/ having a federal organization. □ **federative** /ˈfedərətɪv/ adj. [LL foederare foederat- (as FEDERAL)]

federation /ˌfedəˈreɪʃ(ə)n/ n. **1** a federal group of States. **2** a federated society or group. **3** the act or an instance of federating. □ **federationist** n. [F fédération f. LL foederatio (as FEDERAL)]

fedora /fɪˈdɔːrə/ n. a low soft felt hat with a crown creased lengthways. [Fédora, drama by V. Sardou (1882)]

fee n. & v. —n. **1** a payment made to a professional person or to a professional or public body in exchange for advice or services. **2** money paid as part of a special transaction, for a privilege, admission to a society, etc. (enrolment fee). **3** (in pl.) money regularly paid (esp. to a school) for continuing services. **4** Law an inherited estate, unlimited (**fee simple**) or limited (**fee tail**) as to the category of heir. —v.tr. (**fee'd** or **feed**) **1** pay a fee to. **2** engage for a fee. [ME f. AF, = OF feu, fieu, etc. f. med.L feodum, feudum, perh. f. Frank.: cf. FEUD², FIEF]

feeble /ˈfiːb(ə)l/ adj. **1** weak, infirm. **2** lacking energy, force, or effectiveness. **3** dim, indistinct. **4** deficient in character or intelligence. □ **feebleness** n. **feeblish** adj. **feebly** adv. [ME f. AF & OF feble, fieble, fleible f. L flebilis lamentable f. flēre weep]

feeble-minded /ˌfiːb(ə)lˈmaɪndɪd/ adj. **1** unintelligent. **2** mentally deficient. □ **feeble-mindedly** adv. **feeble-mindedness** n.

feed v. & n. —v. (past and past part. **fed** /fed/) **1** tr. **a** supply with food. **b** put food into the mouth of. **2** tr. **a** give as food, esp. to animals. **b** graze (cattle). **3** tr. serve as food for. **4** intr. (usu. foll. by on) (esp. of animals, or colloq. of people) take food; eat. **5** tr. nourish; make grow. **6 a** tr. maintain supply of raw material, fuel, etc., to (a fire, machine, etc.). **b** tr. (foll. by into) supply (material) to a machine etc. **c** intr. (often foll. by into) (of a river etc.) flow into another body of water. **d** tr. insert further coins into (a meter) to continue its function, validity, etc. **7** *intr.* (foll. by *on*) **a** be nourished by. **b** derive benefit from. **8** *tr.* use (land) as pasture. **9** *tr. Theatr. sl.* supply (an actor etc.) with cues. **10** *tr. Sport* send passes to (a player) in a ball-game. —*n.* **1** an amount of food, esp. for animals or infants. **2** the act or an instance of feeding; the giving of food. **3** *colloq.* a meal. **4** pasturage; green crops. **5 a** a supply of raw material to a machine etc. **b** the provision of this or a device for it. **6** *Theatr. sl.* an actor who supplies another with cues. □ **feed back** produce feedback. □ **feedable** *adj.* [OE *fēdan* f. Gmc]

feedback /ˈfiːdbæk/ *n.* **1** information about the result of an experiment etc.; response. **2** *Electronics* **a** the return of a fraction of the output signal from one stage of a circuit, amplifier, etc., to the input of the same or a preceding stage. **b** a signal so returned. **3** *Biol.* etc. the modification or control of a process or system by its results or effects.

feeder /ˈfiːdə(r)/ *n.* **1** a person or thing that feeds. **2** a person who eats in a specified manner. **3** a child's feeding-bottle. **4** *Brit.* a bib for an infant. **5** a tributary stream. **6** a branch road, railway line, etc., linking outlying districts with a main communication system. **7** *Electr.* a main carrying electricity to a distribution point. **8** a hopper or feeding apparatus in a machine.

feel *v. & n.* —*v.* (*past* and *past part.* **felt** /felt/) **1** *tr.* **a** examine or search by touch. **b** (*absol.*) have the sensation of touch (*was unable to feel*). **2** *tr.* perceive or ascertain by touch; have a sensation of (*could feel the warmth; felt that it was cold*). **3** *tr.* **a** undergo, experience (*shall feel my anger*). **b** exhibit or be conscious of (an emotion, sensation, conviction, etc.). **4 a** *intr.* have a specified feeling or reaction (*felt strongly about it*). **b** *tr.* be emotionally affected by (*felt the rebuke deeply*). **5** *tr.* (foll. by *that* + clause) have a vague or unreasoned impression (*I feel that I am right*). **6** *tr.* consider, think (*I feel it useful to go*). **7** *intr.* seem; give an impression of being; be perceived as (*the air feels chilly*). **8** *intr.* be consciously; consider oneself (*I feel happy; do not feel well*). **9** *intr.* **a** (foll. by *with*) have sympathy with. **b** (foll. by *for*) have pity or compassion for. —*n.* **1** the act or an instance of feeling; testing by touch. **2** the sensation characterizing a material, situation, etc. **3** the sense of touch. □ **feel like** have a wish for; be inclined towards. **feel oneself** be fit or confident etc. **feel out** investigate cautiously. **feel up to** be ready to face or deal with. **feel one's way** proceed carefully; act cautiously. **get the feel of** become accustomed to using. **make one's influence** (or **presence** etc.) **felt** assert one's influence; make others aware of one's presence etc. [OE *fēlan* f. WG]

feeler /ˈfiːlə(r)/ *n.* **1** an organ in certain animals for testing things by touch or for searching for food. **2** a tentative proposal or suggestion, esp. to elicit a response (*put out feelers*).

feeling /ˈfiːlɪŋ/ *n. & adj.* —*n.* **1 a** the capacity to feel; a sense of touch (*lost all feeling in his arm*). **b** a physical sensation. **2 a** (often foll. by *of*) a particular emotional reaction (*a feeling of despair*). **b** (in *pl.*) emotional susceptibilities or sympathies (*hurt my feelings; had strong feelings about it*). **3** a particular sensitivity (*had a feeling for literature*). **4 a** an opinion or notion, esp. a vague or irrational one (*had a feeling she would be*

there). **b** vague awareness. **c** sentiment (*the general feeling was against it*). **5** readiness to feel sympathy or compassion. **6 a** the general emotional response produced by a work of art, piece of music, etc. **b** emotional commitment or sensibility in artistic execution (*played with feeling*). —*adj.* **1** sensitive, sympathetic. **2** showing emotion or sensitivity. □ **feelingless** *adj.* **feelingly** *adv.*

feet *pl.* of FOOT.

feign /feɪn/ *v.* **1** *tr.* simulate; pretend to be affected by (*feign madness*). **2** *intr.* indulge in pretence. [ME f. *feign-* stem of OF *feindre* f. L *fingere* mould, contrive]

feint[1] /feɪnt/ *n. & v.* —*n.* **1** a sham attack or blow etc. to divert attention or fool an opponent or enemy. **2** pretence. —*v.intr.* make a feint. [F *feinte*, fem. past part. of *feindre* FEIGN]

feint[2] /feɪnt/ *adj.* esp. *Printing* = FAINT *adj.* 6 (*feint lines*). [ME f. OF (as FEINT[1]): see FAINT]

feisty /ˈfaɪstɪ/ *adj.* (**feistier, feistiest**) *US sl.* **1** aggressive, exuberant. **2** touchy. □ **feistiness** *n.* [*feist* (= *fist*) small dog]

feldspar /ˈfeldspɑː(r)/ *n.* (also **felspar** /ˈfelspɑː(r)/) *Mineral.* any of a group of aluminium silicates of potassium, sodium, or calcium. □ **feldspathic** /-ˈspæθɪk/ *adj.* **feldspathoid** /ˈfeldspəθɔɪd/ *n.* [G *Feldspat, -spath* f. *Feld* FIELD + *Spat, Spath* SPAR[3]: *felspar* by false assoc. with G *Fels* rock]

felicitate /fəˈlɪsɪteɪt/ *v.tr.* (usu. foll. by *on*) congratulate. □ **felicitation** /-ˈteɪʃ(ə)n/ *n.* (usu. in *pl.*). [LL *felicitare* make happy f. L *felix -icis* happy]

felicitous /fəˈlɪsɪtəs/ *adj.* (of an expression, quotation, civilities, or a person making them) strikingly apt. □ **felicitously** *adv.* **felicitousness** *n.*

felicity /fəˈlɪsɪtɪ/ *n.* (*pl.* **-ies**) **1** intense happiness; being happy. **2** a cause of happiness. **3 a** a capacity for apt expression; appropriateness. **b** an appropriate or well-chosen phrase. **4** a fortunate trait. [ME f. OF *felicité* f. L *felicitas -tatis* f. *felix -icis* happy]

feline /ˈfiːlaɪn/ *adj. & n.* —*adj.* **1** of or relating to the cat family. **2** catlike, esp. in beauty or slyness. —*n.* an animal of the cat family Felidae. □ **felinity** /fɪˈlɪnɪtɪ/ *n.* [L *felinus* f. *feles* cat]

fell[1] *past* of FALL *v.*

fell[2] *v.tr.* **1** cut down (esp. a tree). **2** strike or knock down (a person or animal). **3** stitch down (the edge of a seam) to lie flat. □ **feller** *n.* [OE *fellan* f. Gmc, rel. to FALL]

fell[3] *n. N.Engl.* **1** a hill. **2** a stretch of hills or moorland. [ME f. ON *fjall, fell* hill]

fell[4] *adj.* *poet.* or *rhet.* **1** fierce, ruthless. **2** terrible, destructive. □ **at** (or **in**) **one fell swoop** in a single action. [ME f. OF *fel* f. Rmc FELON]

fellatio /fɪˈleɪʃɪəʊ, feˈlɑːtɪəʊ/ *n.* oral stimulation of the penis. □ **fellate** /fɪˈleɪt/ *v.tr.* **fellator** /fɪˈleɪtə(r)/ *n.* [mod.L f. L *fellare* suck]

fellow /ˈfeləʊ/ *n.* **1** *colloq.* a man or boy (*poor fellow!; my dear fellow*). **2** *derog.* a person regarded with contempt. **3** (usu. in *pl.*) a person associated with another; a comrade (*were separated from their fellows*). **4** a counterpart or match; the other of a pair. **5** an equal; one of the same class. **6** a contemporary. **7 a** an incorporated senior member of a college. **b** an elected graduate receiving a stipend for a period of research. **8** a member of a learned society. **9** (*attrib.*) belonging to the same class or activity (*fellow soldier; fellow-countryman*). □ **fellow-feeling** sympathy

from common experience. **fellow-traveller**
1 a person who travels with another. **2** a
sympathizer with, or a secret member of, the
Communist Party. [OE *fēolaga* f. ON *félagi* f. *fé*
cattle, property, money: see LAY¹]

fellowship /ˈfeləʊʃɪp/ *n.* **1** companionship,
friendliness. **2** participation, sharing; community of interest. **3** a body of associates; a
company. **4** a brotherhood or fraternity. **5** the
status or emoluments of a fellow of a college or
society.

felon /ˈfelən/ *n.* a person who has committed a
felony. □ **felonry** *n.* [ME f. OF f. med.L *felo -onis*,
of unkn. orig.]

felonious /fɪˈləʊnɪəs/ *adj.* **1** criminal. **2** *Law* **a** of
or involving felony. **b** who has committed
felony. □ **feloniously** *adv.*

felony /ˈfelənɪ/ *n.* (*pl.* **-ies**) a crime regarded by
the law as grave, and usu. involving violence.
[ME f. OF *felonie* (as FELON)]

felspar var. of FELDSPAR.

felt¹ *n.* & *v.* —*n.* **1** a kind of cloth made by
rolling and pressing wool etc., or by weaving
and shrinking it. **2** a similar material made
from other fibres. —*v.* **1** *tr.* make into felt; mat
together. **2** *tr.* cover with felt. **3** *intr.* become
matted. □ **felt-tipped** (or **felt-tip**) **pen** a pen
with a writing-point made of felt or fibre. □
felty *adj.* [OE f. WG]

felt² *past* and *past part.* of FEEL.

felucca /fɪˈlʌkə/ *n.* a small Mediterranean coasting vessel with oars or lateen sails or both. [It.
felucca f. obs. Sp. *faluca* f. Arab. *fulk*, perh. f. Gk
epholkion sloop]

female /ˈfiːmeɪl/ *adj.* & *n.* —*adj.* **1** of the sex that
can bear offspring or produce eggs. **2** (of plants
or their parts) fruit-bearing; having a pistil and
no stamens. **3** of or consisting of women or
female animals or female plants. **4** (of a screw,
socket, etc.) manufactured hollow to receive a
corresponding inserted part. —*n.* a female
person, animal, or plant. □ **femaleness** *n.* [ME
f. OF *femelle* (n.) f. L *femella* dimin. of *femina* a
woman, assim. to *male*]

feminine /ˈfemɪnɪn/ *adj.* & *n.* —*adj.* **1** of or
characteristic of women. **2** having qualities
associated with women. **3** womanly, effeminate.
4 *Gram.* of or denoting the gender proper to
women's names. —*n.* *Gram.* a feminine gender
or word. □ **femininely** *adv.* **feminineness** *n.*
femininity /-ˈnɪnɪtɪ/ *n.* [ME f. OF *feminin -ine* or
L *femininus* f. *femina* woman]

feminism /ˈfemɪnɪz(ə)m/ *n.* the advocacy of
women's rights on the ground of the equality
of the sexes. □ **feminist** *n.* [F *féminisme* f. L
femina woman]

feminity /feˈmɪnɪtɪ/ *n.* = FEMININITY (see FEMININE). [ME f. OF *feminité* f. med.L *feminitas -tatis*
f. L *femina* woman]

feminize /ˈfemɪnaɪz/ *v.tr.* & *intr.* (also **-ise**) make
or become feminine or female. □ **feminization**
/-ˈzeɪʃ(ə)n/ *n.*

femme fatale /ˌfæm fæˈtɑːl/ *n.* (*pl.* *femmes
fatales* pronunc. same) a seductively attractive
woman. [F]

femur /ˈfiːmə(r)/ *n.* (*pl.* **femurs** or **femora**
/ˈfemərə/) *Anat.* the thigh-bone, the thick bone
between the hip and the knee. □ **femoral**
/ˈfemər(ə)l/ *adj.* [L *femur femoris* thigh]

fen *n.* **1** a low marshy or flooded area of land. **2**
(**the Fens**) flat low-lying areas in and around
Cambridgeshire. □ **fenny** *adj.* [OE *fenn* f. Gmc]

fence *n.* & *v.* —*n.* **1** a barrier or railing or other
upright structure enclosing an area of ground,
esp. to prevent or control access. **2** a large
upright obstacle in steeplechasing or showjumping. **3** *sl.* a receiver of stolen goods. **4** a
guard or guide in machinery. —*v.* **1** *tr.* surround
with or as with a fence. **2** *tr.* **a** (foll. by *in*, *off*)
enclose or separate with or as with a fence. **b**
(foll. by *up*) seal with or as with a fence. **3** *tr.*
(foll. by *from*, *against*) screen, shield, protect. **4**
tr. (foll. by *out*) exclude with or as with a fence;
keep out. **5** *tr.* (also *absol.*) *sl.* deal in (stolen
goods). **6** *intr.* practise the sport of fencing; use
a sword. **7** *intr.* (foll. by *with*) evade answering (a
person or question). □ **sit on the fence** remain
neutral or undecided in a dispute etc. □ **fenceless** *adj.* **fencer** *n.* [ME f. DEFENCE]

fencing /ˈfensɪŋ/ *n.* **1** a set or extent of fences. **2**
material for making fences. **3** the art or sport
of swordplay.

fend /fend/ *v.* **1** *intr.* (foll. by *for*) look after (esp.
oneself). **2** *tr.* (usu. foll. by *off*) keep away; ward
off (an attack etc.). [ME f. DEFEND]

fender /ˈfendə(r)/ *n.* **1** a low frame bordering a
fireplace to keep in falling coals etc. **2** *Naut.* a
piece of old cable, matting, etc., hung over a
vessel's side to protect it against impact. **3 a** a
thing used to keep something off, prevent a
collision, etc. **b** *US* a bumper or mudguard of a
motor vehicle.

fenestration /ˌfenɪˈstreɪʃ(ə)n/ *n.* *Archit.* the
arrangement of windows in a building. [f. L
fenestra window]

fennel /ˈfen(ə)l/ *n.* **1** a yellow-flowered fragrant
umbelliferous plant, *Foeniculum vulgare*, with
leaves or leaf-stalks used in salads, soups, etc. **2**
the seeds of this used as flavouring. [OE *finugl*
etc. & OF *fenoil* f. L *feniculum* f. *fenum* hay]

fenugreek /ˈfenjuːˌɡriːk/ *n.* **1** a leguminous plant,
Trigonella foenum-graecum, having aromatic seeds.
2 these seeds used as flavouring, esp. ground
and used in curry powder. [OE *fenogrecum*,
superseded in ME f. OF *fenugrec* f. L *faenugraecum*
(*fenum graecum* Greek hay), used by the Romans
as fodder]

feral /ˈfɪər(ə)l, ˈfer(ə)l/ *adj.* **1** (of an animal or
plant) wild, untamed, uncultivated. **2 a** (of an
animal) in a wild state after escape from
captivity. **b** born in the wild of such an animal.
3 brutal. [L *ferus* wild]

ferial /ˈfɪərɪəl, ˈfer-/ *adj.* *Eccl.* **1** (of a day) ordinary;
not appointed for a festival or fast. **2** (of a
service etc.) for use on a ferial day. [ME f. OF
ferial or med.L *ferialis* f. *feriae*: see FAIR²]

ferment *n.* & *v.* —*n.* /ˈfɜːment/ **1** agitation,
excitement, tumult. **2 a** fermenting, fermentation. **b** a fermenting-agent or leaven. —*v.*
/fəˈment/ **1** *intr.* & *tr.* undergo or subject to
fermentation. **2** *intr.* & *tr.* effervesce or cause
to effervesce. **3** *tr.* excite; stir up; foment.
□ **fermentable** /-ˈmentəb(ə)l/ *adj.* **fermenter**
/-ˈmentə(r)/ *n.* [ME f. OF *ferment* or L *fermentum* f.
L *fervēre* boil]

fermentation /ˌfɜːmenˈteɪʃ(ə)n/ *n.* **1** the breakdown of a substance by micro-organisms, such
as yeasts and bacteria, usu. in the absence of
oxygen, esp. of sugar to ethyl alcohol in making
beers, wines, and spirits. **2** agitation, excitement.

□ **fermentative** /-'mentətɪv/ adj. [ME f. LL *fermentatio* (as FERMENT)]

fermium /'fɜːmɪəm/ n. Chem. a transuranic radioactive metallic element produced artificially. [E. *Fermi*, Ital.-Amer. physicist d. 1954 + -IUM]

fern n. (pl. same or **ferns**) any flowerless plant of the order Filicales, reproducing by spores and usu. having feathery fronds. □ **fernery** n. (pl. **-ies**). **fernless** adj. **ferny** adj. [OE *fearn* f. WG]

ferocious /fə'rəʊʃəs/ adj. fierce, savage; wildly cruel. □ **ferociously** adv. **ferociousness** n. [L *ferox -ocis*]

ferocity /fə'rɒsɪtɪ/ n. (pl. **-ies**) a ferocious nature or act. [F *férocité* or L *ferocitas* (as FEROCIOUS)]

-ferous /fərəs/ comb. form (usu. **-iferous**) forming adjectives with the sense 'bearing', 'having' (*auriferous*; *odoriferous*). □ **-ferously** suffix **-ferousness** suffix [from or after F *-fère* or L *-fer* producing f. *ferre* bear]

ferret /'ferɪt/ n. & v. —n. 1 a small half-domesticated polecat, *Mustela putorius furo*, used in catching rabbits, rats, etc. 2 a person who searches assiduously. —v. 1 intr. hunt with ferrets. 2 intr. rummage; search about. 3 tr. (often foll. by *about, away, out,* etc.) a clear out (holes or an area of ground) with ferrets. b take or drive away (rabbits etc.) with ferrets. 4 tr. (foll. by *out*) search out (secrets, criminals, etc.). □ **ferreter** n. **ferrety** adj. [ME f. OF *fu(i)ret* alt. f. *fu(i)ron* f. LL *furo -onis* f. L *fur* thief]

ferri- /ferɪ/ comb. form Chem. containing iron, esp. in ferric compounds. [L *ferrum* iron]

ferric /'ferɪk/ adj. 1 of iron. 2 Chem. containing iron in a trivalent form (cf. FERROUS).

Ferris wheel /'ferɪs/ n. a fairground ride consisting of a tall revolving vertical wheel with passenger cars suspended on its outer edge. [G. W. G. *Ferris*, Amer. engineer d. 1896]

ferrite /'feraɪt/ n. Chem. 1 a salt of (the hypothetical) ferrous acid, often with magnetic properties. 2 an allotrope of pure iron occurring in low-carbon steel. □ **ferritic** /fe'rɪtɪk/ adj. [L *ferrum* iron]

ferro- /'ferəʊ/ comb. form Chem. 1 iron, esp. in ferrous compounds. 2 (of alloys) containing iron (*ferrocyanide*; *ferromanganese*). [L *ferrum* iron]

ferroconcrete /ˌferəʊ'kɒŋkriːt/ n. & adj. —n. concrete reinforced with steel. —adj. made of reinforced concrete.

ferrous /'ferəs/ adj. 1 containing iron (*ferrous and non-ferrous metals*). 2 Chem. containing iron in a divalent form (cf. FERRIC). [L *ferrum* iron]

ferrule /'feruːl/ n. (also **ferrel** /'fer(ə)l/) a ring or cap strengthening the end of a stick or tube. [earlier *verrel* etc. f. OF *virelle, virol(e)*, f. L *viriola* dimin. of *viriae* bracelet: assim. to L *ferrum* iron]

ferry /'ferɪ/ n. & v. —n. (pl. **-ies**) 1 a boat or aircraft etc. for conveying passengers and goods, esp. across water and as a regular service. 2 the service itself or the place where it operates. —v. (**-ies, -ied**) 1 tr. & intr. convey or go in a boat etc. across water. 2 intr. (of a boat etc.) pass to and fro across water. 3 tr. transport from one place to another, esp. as a regular service. □ **ferryman** n. (pl. **-men**). [ME f. ON *ferja* f. Gmc]

fertile /'fɜːtaɪl/ adj. 1 a (of soil) producing abundant vegetation or crops. b fruitful. 2 a (of a seed, egg, etc.) capable of becoming a new individual. b (of animals and plants) able to

conceive young or produce fruit. 3 (of the mind) inventive. 4 (of nuclear material) able to become fissile by the capture of neutrons. □ **fertility** /-'tɪlɪtɪ/ n. [ME f. F f. L *fertilis*]

fertilization /ˌfɜːtɪlaɪ'zeɪʃ(ə)n/ n. (also **-isation**) 1 Biol. the fusion of male and female gametes during sexual reproduction to form a zygote. 2 a the act or an instance of fertilizing. b the process of being fertilized.

fertilize /'fɜːtɪˌlaɪz/ v.tr. (also **-ise**) 1 make (soil etc.) fertile or productive. 2 cause (an egg, female animal, or plant) to develop a new individual by introducing male reproductive material. □ **fertilizable** adj. **fertilizer** n.

fervent /'fɜːv(ə)nt/ adj. 1 ardent, impassioned, intense. 2 hot, glowing. □ **fervency** n. **fervently** adv. [ME f. OF f. L *fervēre* boil]

fervid /'fɜːvɪd/ adj. 1 ardent, intense. 2 poet. hot, glowing. □ **fervidly** adv. [L *fervidus* (as FERVENT)]

fervour /'fɜːvə(r)/ n. (US **fervor**) 1 vehemence, passion, zeal. 2 a glowing condition; intense heat. [ME f. OF f. L *fervor -oris* (as FERVENT)]

fescue /'feskjuː/ n. any grass of the genus *Festuca*, valuable for pasture and fodder. [ME *festu(e)* f. OF *festu* ult. f. L *festuca* stalk, straw]

festal /'fest(ə)l/ adj. 1 joyous, merry. 2 engaging in holiday activities. 3 of a feast. □ **festally** adv. [OF f. LL *festalis* (as FEAST)]

fester /'festə(r)/ v. 1 tr. & intr. make or become septic. 2 intr. cause continuing annoyance. 3 intr. rot, stagnate. [ME f. obs. *fester* (n.) or OF *festrir*, f. OF *festre* f. L *fistula*: see FISTULA]

festival /'festɪv(ə)l/ n. & adj. —n. 1 a day or period of celebration, religious or secular. 2 a concentrated series of concerts, plays, etc., held regularly in a town etc. (*Bath Festival*). —attrib.adj. of or concerning a festival. [earlier as adj.: ME f. OF f. med.L *festivalis* (as FESTIVE)]

festive /'festɪv/ adj. 1 of or characteristic of a festival. 2 joyous. 3 fond of feasting, jovial. □ **festively** adv. **festiveness** n. [L *festivus* f. *festum* (as FEAST)]

festivity /fe'stɪvɪtɪ/ n. (pl. **-ies**) 1 gaiety, rejoicing. 2 a a festive celebration. b (in pl.) festive proceedings. [ME f. OF *festivité* or L *festivitas* (as FESTIVE)]

festoon /fe'stuːn/ n. & v. —n. 1 a chain of flowers, leaves, ribbons, etc., hung in a curve as a decoration. 2 a carved or moulded ornament representing this. —v.tr. (often foll. by *with*) adorn with or form into festoons; decorate elaborately. □ **festoonery** n. [F *feston* f. It. *festone* f. *festa* FEAST]

Festschrift /'festʃrɪft/ n. (also **festschrift**) (pl. **-schriften** or **-schrifts**) a collection of writings published in honour of a scholar. [G f. *Fest* celebration + *Schrift* writing]

feta /'fetə/ n. (also **fetta**) a soft white ewe's-milk or goat's-milk cheese made esp. in Greece. [mod.Gk *pheta*]

fetch v. & n. —v.tr. 1 go for and bring back (a person or thing) (*fetch a doctor*). 2 be sold for; realize (a price) (*fetched £10*). 3 cause (blood, tears, etc.) to flow. 4 draw (breath), heave (a sigh). 5 colloq. give (a blow, slap, etc.) (*fetched him a slap on the face*). —n. 1 an act of fetching. 2 a dodge or trick. □ **fetch and carry** run backwards and forwards with things, be a mere servant. **fetch up** colloq. 1 arrive, come to rest. 2 vomit. □ **fetcher** n. [OE *fecc(e)an* var. of *fetian*, prob. rel. to a Gmc root = grasp]

fetching /ˈfetʃɪŋ/ adj. attractive. □ **fetchingly** adv.

fête /feɪt/ n. & v. —n. 1 an outdoor function with the sale of goods, amusements, etc., esp. to raise funds for charity. 2 a great entertainment; a festival. 3 a saint's day. —v.tr. honour or entertain lavishly. [F fête (as FEAST)]

fetid /ˈfetɪd, ˈfiːtɪd/ adj. (also **foetid**) stinking. □ **fetidly** adv. **fetidness** n. [L fetidus f. fetēre stink]

fetish /ˈfetɪʃ/ n. 1 Psychol. a thing abnormally stimulating or attracting sexual desire. 2 a an inanimate object worshipped by primitive peoples for its supposed inherent magical powers or as being inhabited by a spirit. b a thing evoking irrational devotion or respect. □ **fetishism** n. **fetishist** n. **fetishistic** /-ˈʃɪstɪk/ adj. [F fétiche f. Port. feitiço charm: orig. adj. = made by art, f. L factitius FACTITIOUS]

fetlock /ˈfetlɒk/ n. part of the back of a horse's leg above the hoof where a tuft of hair grows. [ME fetlak etc. rel. to G Fessel fetlock f. Gmc]

fetter /ˈfetə(r)/ n. & v. —n. 1 a a shackle for holding a prisoner by the ankles. b any shackle or bond. 2 (in pl.) captivity. 3 a restraint or check. —v.tr. 1 put into fetters. 2 restrict, restrain. [OE feter f. Gmc]

fettle /ˈfet(ə)l/ n. & v. —n. condition or trim (in fine fettle). —v.tr. trim or clean (the rough edge of a metal casting, pottery before firing, etc.). [earlier as verb, f. dial. fettle (n.) = girdle, f. OE fetel f. Gmc]

fetus US var. of FOETUS.

feu /fjuː/ n. & v. Sc. —n. 1 a perpetual lease at a fixed rent. 2 a piece of land so held. —v.tr. (**feus, feued, feuing**) grant (land) on feu. [OF: see FEE]

feud[1] /fjuːd/ n. & v. —n. 1 prolonged mutual hostility, esp. between two families, tribes, etc. 2 a prolonged or bitter quarrel or dispute. —v.intr. conduct a feud. [ME fede f. OF feide, fede f. MDu., MLG vēde f. Gmc, rel. to FOE]

feud[2] /fjuːd/ n. a piece of land held under the feudal system or in fee; a fief. [med.L feudum: see FEE]

feudal /ˈfjuːd(ə)l/ adj. 1 of, according to, or resembling the feudal system. 2 of a feud or fief. 3 outdated (had a feudal attitude). □ **feudal system** the social system in medieval Europe whereby a vassal held land from a superior in exchange for allegiance and service. □ **feudalism** n. **feudalist** n. **feudalistic** /-ˈlɪstɪk/ adj. **feudalize** v.tr. (also **-ise**). **feudalization** /-ˈzeɪʃ(ə)n/ n. **feudally** adv. [med.L feudalis, feodalis f. feudum, feodum FEE, perh. f. Gmc]

fever /ˈfiːvə(r)/ n. & v. —n. 1 a an abnormally high body temperature, often with delirium etc. b a disease characterized by this (scarlet fever; typhoid fever). 2 nervous excitement; agitation. —v.tr. (esp. as **fevered** adj.) affect with fever or excitement. □ **fever pitch** a state of extreme excitement. [OE fefor & AF fevre, OF fievre f. L febris]

feverfew /ˈfiːvəfjuː/ n. an aromatic bushy plant, Tenacetum parthenium, with feathery leaves and white daisy-like flowers. [OE feferfuge f. L febrifuga f. febris fever, -fugus f. fugare put to flight]

feverish /ˈfiːvərɪʃ/ adj. 1 having the symptoms of a fever. 2 excited, fitful, restless. □ **feverishly** adv. **feverishness** n.

few adj. & n. —adj. not many (few doctors smoke; visitors are few). —n. (as pl.) 1 (prec. by a) some but not many (a few words should be added; a few

of his friends were there). 2 a small number, not many (many are called but few are chosen). 3 (prec. by the) a the minority. b the elect. 4 (**the Few**) colloq. the RAF pilots who took part in the Battle of Britain. □ **every few** once in every small group of (every few days). **few and far between** scarce. **no fewer than** as many as (a specified number). **some few** some but not at all many. □ **fewness** n. [OE fēawe, fēawa f. Gmc]

fey adj. 1 a strange, other-worldly; elfin; whimsical. b clairvoyant. 2 Sc. fated to die soon. □ **feyly** adv. **feyness** n. [OE fǣge f. Gmc]

fez n. (pl. **fezzes**) a flat-topped conical red cap with a tassel, worn by men in some Muslim countries. □ **fezzed** adj. [Turk., perh. f. Fez (now Fès) in Morocco]

ff abbr. Mus. fortissimo.

ff. abbr. 1 following pages etc. 2 folios.

fiancé /fɪˈɒnseɪ, fɪˈɑ̃seɪ/ n. (fem. **fiancée** pronunc. same) a person to whom another is engaged to be married. [F, past part. of fiancer betroth f. OF fiance a promise, ult. f. L fidere to trust]

fiasco /fɪˈæskəʊ/ n. (pl. **-os**) a ludicrous or humiliating failure or breakdown; an ignominious result. [It., = bottle (with unexplained allusion): see FLASK]

fiat /ˈfaɪæt, ˈfaɪət/ n. 1 an authorization. 2 a decree or order. [L, = let it be done]

fib n. & v. —n. a trivial or venial lie. —v.intr. (**fibbed, fibbing**) tell a fib. □ **fibber** n. **fibster** n. [perh. f. obs. fible-fable nonsense, redupl. of FABLE]

fibre /ˈfaɪbə(r)/ n. (US **fiber**) 1 Biol. any of the threads or filaments forming animal or vegetable tissue and textile substances. 2 a piece of glass in the form of a thread. 3 a a substance formed of fibres. b a substance that can be spun, woven, or felted. 4 the structure, grain, or character of something (lacks moral fibre). 5 dietary material that is resistant to the action of digestive enzymes; roughage. □ **fibre optics** optics employing thin glass fibres, usu. for the transmission of light, esp. modulated to carry signals. □ **fibred** adj. (also in comb.). **fibreless** adj. **fibriform** /ˈfaɪbrɪˌfɔːm/ adj. [ME f. F f. L fibra]

fibreboard /ˈfaɪbəbɔːd/ n. (US **fiberboard**) a building material made of wood or other plant fibres compressed into boards.

fibreglass /ˈfaɪbəˌɡlɑːs/ n. (US **fiberglass**) 1 a textile fabric made from woven glass fibres. 2 a plastic reinforced by glass fibres.

fibril /ˈfaɪbrɪl/ n. 1 a small fibre. 2 a subdivision of a fibre. □ **fibrillar** adj. **fibrillary** adj. [mod.L fibrilla dimin. of L fibra fibre]

fibro /ˈfaɪbrəʊ/ n. (pl. **-os**) Austral. 1 fibro-cement. 2 a house constructed mainly of this. [abbr.]

fibro- /ˈfaɪbrəʊ/ comb. form fibre.

fibro-cement /ˌfaɪbrəʊsɪˈment/ n. a mixture of any of various fibrous materials and cement, used in sheets for building etc.

fibroid /ˈfaɪbrɔɪd/ adj. & n. —adj. 1 of or characterized by fibrous tissue. 2 resembling or containing fibres. —n. a benign tumour of muscular and fibrous tissues, one or more of which may develop in the wall of the womb.

fibrosis /faɪˈbrəʊsɪs/ n. Med. a thickening and scarring of connective tissue, usu. as a result of injury. □ **fibrotic** /-ˈbrɒtɪk/ adj. [mod.L f. L fibra fibre + -OSIS]

fibrositis /ˌfaɪbrəˈsaɪtɪs/ n. an inflammation of fibrous connective tissue, usu. rheumatic. □ **fibrositic** /-ˈsɪtɪk/ adj. [mod.L f. L fibrosus fibrous + -ITIS]

fibrous /ˈfaɪbrəs/ adj. consisting of or like fibres. □ **fibrously** adv. **fibrousness** n.

fibula /ˈfɪbjʊlə/ n. (pl. **fibulae** /-ˌliː/ or **fibulas**) Anat. the smaller and outer of the two bones between the knee and the ankle in terrestrial vertebrates. □ **fibular** adj. [L, perh. rel. to figere fix]

-fic /fɪk/ suffix (usu. as **-ific**) forming adjectives meaning 'producing', 'making' (prolific; pacific). □ **-fically** suffix forming adverbs. [from or after F -fique or L -ficus f. facere do, make]

-fication /fɪˈkeɪʃ(ə)n/ suffix (usu. as **-ification**) forming nouns of action from verbs in -fy (acidification; purification; simplification). [from or after F -fication or L -ficatio -onis f. -ficare: see -FY]

fiche /fiːʃ/ n. (pl. same or **fiches**) a microfiche. [F, = slip of paper]

fickle /ˈfɪk(ə)l/ adj. inconstant, changeable, esp. in loyalty. □ **fickleness** n. **fickly** adv. [OE ficol:; cf. befician deceive, fǣcne deceitful]

fiction /ˈfɪkʃ(ə)n/ n. 1 an invented idea or statement or narrative; an imaginary thing. 2 literature, esp. novels, describing imaginary events and people. 3 a conventionally accepted falsehood (legal fiction; polite fiction). □ **fictional** adj. **fictionality** /-ˈnælɪtɪ/ n. **fictionalize** v.tr. (also **-ise**). **fictionalization** /-ˈzeɪʃ(ə)n/ n. **fictionally** adv. **fictionist** n. [ME f. OF f. L fictio -onis f. fingere fict- fashion]

fictitious /fɪkˈtɪʃəs/ adj. 1 imaginary, unreal. 2 counterfeit; not genuine. 3 (of a name or character) assumed. □ **fictitiously** adv. **fictitiousness** n. [L ficticius (as FICTION)]

fictive /ˈfɪktɪv/ adj. 1 creating or created by imagination. 2 not genuine. □ **fictively** adv. **fictiveness** n. [F fictif -ive or med.L fictivus (as FICTION)]

fiddle /ˈfɪd(ə)l/ n. & v. —n. 1 colloq. or derog. a stringed instrument played with a bow, esp. a violin. 2 colloq. an instance of cheating or fraud. —v. 1 intr. **a** (often foll. by with, at) play restlessly. **b** (often foll. by about) move aimlessly. **c** act idly or frivolously. **d** (usu. foll. by with) make minor adjustments; tinker. 2 tr. sl. **a** cheat, swindle. **b** falsify. **c** get by cheating. 3 **a** intr. play the fiddle. **b** tr. play (a tune etc.) on the fiddle. □ **play second fiddle** take a subordinate role. [OE fithele f. Gmc f. a Rmc root rel. to VIOL]

fiddle-faddle /ˈfɪd(ə)lˌfæd(ə)l/ n., v., int., & adj. —n. trivial matters. —v.intr. fuss, trifle. —int. nonsense! —adj. (of a person or thing) petty, fussy. [redupl. of FIDDLE]

fiddler /ˈfɪdlə(r)/ n. 1 a fiddle-player. 2 sl. a swindler, a cheat. [OE fithelere (as FIDDLE)]

fiddlestick /ˈfɪd(ə)lstɪk/ n. 1 (usu. in pl.; as int.) nonsense! 2 colloq. a bow for a fiddle.

fiddling /ˈfɪdlɪŋ/ adj. 1 **a** petty, trivial. **b** contemptible, futile. 2 colloq. = FIDDLY. 3 that fiddles.

fiddly /ˈfɪdlɪ/ adj. (**fiddlier**, **fiddliest**) colloq. intricate, awkward, or tiresome to do or use.

fidelity /fɪˈdelɪtɪ/ n. 1 (often foll. by to) faithfulness, loyalty. 2 strict conformity to truth or fact. 3 exact correspondence to the original. 4 precision in reproduction of sound (high fidelity). [F fidélité or L fidelitas (as FEALTY)]

fidget /ˈfɪdʒɪt/ v. & n. —v. (**fidgeted**, **fidgeting**) 1 intr. move or act restlessly or nervously, usu. while maintaining basically the same posture. 2 intr. be uneasy, worry. 3 tr. make (a person) uneasy or uncomfortable. —n. 1 a person who fidgets. 2 (usu. in pl.) **a** bodily uneasiness seeking relief in spasmodic movements; such movements. **b** a restless mood. □ **fidgety** adj. **fidgetiness** n. [obs. or dial. fidge to twitch]

fiduciary /fɪˈdjuːʃərɪ/ adj. & n. —adj. 1 **a** of a trust, trustee, or trusteeship. **b** held or given in trust. 2 (of a paper currency) depending for its value on public confidence or securities. —n. (pl. **-ies**) a trustee. [L fiduciarius f. fiducia trust f. fidere to trust]

fie int. expressing disgust, shame, or a pretence of outraged propriety. [ME f. OF f. L fi exclam. of disgust at a stench]

fief /fiːf/ n. 1 a piece of land held under the feudal system or in fee. 2 a person's sphere of operation or control. [F (as FEE)]

fiefdom /ˈfiːfdəm/ n. a fief.

field /fiːld/ n. & v. —n. 1 an area of open land, esp. one used for pasture or crops, often bounded by hedges, fences, etc. 2 an area rich in some natural product (gas field; diamond field). 3 a piece of land for a specified purpose, esp. an area marked out for games (football field). 4 **a** the participants in a contest or sport. **b** all the competitors in a race or all except those specified. 5 Cricket the side fielding. **a** a fielder. 6 an expanse of ice, snow, sea, sky, etc. 7 **a** the ground on which a battle is fought; a battlefield (left his rival in possession of the field). **b** the scene of a campaign. **c** (attrib.) (of artillery etc.) light and mobile for use on campaign. **d** a battle. 8 an area of operation or activity; a subject of study. 9 **a** the region in which a force is effective (magnetic field). **b** the force exerted in such an area. 10 a range of perception (field of view; wide field of vision). 11 (attrib.) **a** (of an animal or plant) found in the countryside, wild (field mouse). **b** carried out or working in the natural environment, not in a laboratory etc. (field test). 12 the background of a picture, coin, flag, etc. 13 Computing a part of a record, representing an item of data. —v. 1 Cricket, Baseball, etc. **a** intr. act as a fieldsman. **b** tr. stop (and return) (the ball). 2 tr. select (a team or individual) to play in a game. 3 tr. deal with (a succession of questions etc.). □ **field-day** 1 wide scope for action or success; a time occupied with exciting events (when crowds form, pickpockets have a field-day). 2 Mil. an exercise, esp. in manoeuvring; a review. **field events** athletic sports other than races. **field-glasses** binoculars for outdoor use. **field hockey** US = HOCKEY¹. **field hospital** a temporary hospital near a battlefield. **Field Marshal** Brit. an army officer of the highest rank. **field mouse** a small rodent, Apodemus sylvaticus, with a long tail. **field mushroom** the edible fungus Agaricus campestris. **field officer** an army officer of field rank. **field of honour** the place where a duel or battle is fought. **field rank** any rank in the army above captain and below general. **field sports** outdoor sports, esp. hunting, shooting, and fishing. **hold the field** not be superseded. **in the field** 1 campaigning. 2 working etc. away from one's laboratory, headquarters, etc. **keep the field** continue a campaign. **play the field** colloq. avoid exclusive attachment to one person or activity etc. **take the field 1** begin a campaign. **2** (of a sports team) go on to a pitch to begin a game. [OE *feld* f. WG]

fielder /'fiːldə(r)/ *n.* = FIELDSMAN.

fieldfare /'fiːldfeə(r)/ *n.* a thrush, *Turdus pilaris*, having grey plumage with a speckled breast. [ME *feldefare*, perh. as FIELD + FARE]

fieldsman /'fiːldzmən/ *n.* (*pl.* **-men**) *Cricket, Baseball*, etc. a member (other than the bowler or pitcher) of the side that is fielding.

fieldwork /'fiːldwɜːk/ *n.* **1** the practical work of a surveyor, collector of scientific data, sociologist, etc., conducted in the natural environment rather than a laboratory, office, etc. **2** a temporary fortification. □ **fieldworker** *n.*

fiend /fiːnd/ *n.* **1 a** an evil spirit, a demon. **b** (prec. by *the*) the Devil. **2 a** a very wicked or cruel person. **b** a person causing mischief or annoyance. **3** (with a qualifying word) *sl.* a devotee or addict (*a fitness fiend*). **4** something difficult or unpleasant. □ **fiendish** *adj.* **fiendishly** *adv.* **fiendishness** *n.* **fiendlike** *adj.* [OE *fēond* f. Gmc]

fierce /fɪəs/ *adj.* (**fiercer, fiercest**) **1** vehemently aggressive or frightening in temper or action, violent. **2** eager, intense, ardent. **3** unpleasantly strong or intense; uncontrolled (*fierce heat*). □ **fiercely** *adv.* **fierceness** *n.* [ME f. AF *fers*, OF *fiers fier* proud f. L *ferus* savage]

fiery /'faɪərɪ/ *adj.* (**fierier, fieriest**) **1 a** consisting of or flaming with fire. **b** (of an arrow etc.) fire-bearing. **2** like fire in appearance, bright red. **3 a** hot as fire. **b** acting like fire; producing a burning sensation. **4 a** flashing, ardent (*fiery eyes*). **b** eager, pugnacious, spirited, irritable (*fiery temper*). **c** (of a horse) mettlesome. □ **fierily** *adv.* **fieriness** *n.*

fiesta /fɪ'estə/ *n.* **1** a holiday or festivity. **2** a religious festival in Spanish-speaking countries. [Sp., = feast]

fife *n.* **1** a kind of small shrill flute used with the drum in military music. **2** its player. □ **fifer** *n.* [G *Pfeife* PIPE, or F *fifre* f. Swiss G *Pfifre* piper]

fifteen /fɪf'tiːn, 'fɪf-/ *n. & adj.* —*n.* **1** one more than fourteen. **2** a symbol for this (15, xv, XV). **3** a size etc. denoted by fifteen. **4** a team of fifteen players, esp. in Rugby football. **5** (15) *Brit.* (of films) classified as suitable for persons of 15 years and over. —*adj.* that amount to fifteen. □ **fifteenth** *adj. & n.* [OE *fīftēne* (as FIVE, -TEEN)]

fifth /fɪfθ/ *n. & adj.* —*n.* **1** the position in a sequence corresponding to that of the number 5 in the sequence 1–5. **2** something occupying this position. **3** the fifth person etc. in a race or competition. **4** any of five equal parts of a thing. **5** *Mus.* **a** an interval or chord spanning five consecutive notes in the diatonic scale (e.g. C to G). **b** a note separated from another by this interval. **6** *US colloq.* **a** a fifth of a gallon of liquor. **b** a bottle containing this. —*adj.* that is the fifth. □ **fifth column** a group working for an enemy within a country at war etc. **fifth-columnist** a member of a fifth column; a traitor or spy. **fifth generation** *Computing* a stage in computer design involving machines that make use of artificial intelligence. **fifth wheel 1** an extra wheel of a coach. **2** a superfluous person or thing. **take the fifth** (in the US) exercise the right guaranteed by the Fifth Amendment to the Constitution of refusing to answer questions in order to avoid incriminating oneself. □ **fifthly** *adv.* [earlier and dial. *fift* f. OE *fīfta* f. Gmc, assim. to FOURTH]

fifty /'fɪftɪ/ *n. & adj.* —*n.* (*pl.* **-ies**) **1** the product of five and ten. **2** a symbol for this (50, l, L). **3** (in *pl.*) the numbers from 50 to 59, esp. the years of a century or of a person's life. **4** a set of fifty persons or things. —*adj.* that amount to fifty. □ **fifty-fifty** *adj.* equal, with equal shares or chances (*on a fifty-fifty basis*). —*adv.* equally, half and half (*go fifty-fifty*). □ **fiftieth** *adj. & n.* **fiftyfold** *adj. & adv.* [OE *fīftig* (as FIVE, -TY²)]

fig[1] *n.* **1 a** a soft pear-shaped fruit with many seeds, eaten fresh or dried. **b** (in full **fig-tree**) any deciduous tree of the genus *Ficus*, esp. *F. carica*, having broad leaves and bearing figs. **2** a valueless thing (*don't care a fig for*). □ **fig-leaf 1** a leaf of a fig-tree. **2** a device for concealing something, esp. the genitals (Gen. 3:7). [ME f. OF *figue* f. Prov. *figa* ult. f. L *ficus*]

fig[2] *n.* **1** dress or equipment (*in full fig*). **2** condition or form (*in good fig*). [var. of obs. *feague* (v.) f. G *fegen*: see FAKE]

fig. *abbr.* figure.

fight /faɪt/ *v. & n.* —*v.* (*past* and *past part.* **fought** /fɔːt/) **1** *intr.* (often foll. by *against, with*) contend or struggle in war, battle, single combat, etc. **2** *tr.* contend with (an opponent) in this way. **3** *tr.* take part or engage in (a battle, war, duel, etc.). **4** *tr.* contend about (an issue, an election); maintain (a lawsuit, cause, etc.) against an opponent. **5** *intr.* campaign or strive determinedly to achieve something. **6** *tr.* strive to overcome (disease, fire, fear, etc.). **7** *tr.* make (one's way) by fighting. —*n.* **1 a** a combat, esp. unpremeditated, between two or more persons, animals, or parties. **b** a boxing-match. **c** a battle. **2** a conflict or struggle; a vigorous effort in the face of difficulty. **3** power or inclination to fight (*has no fight left; showed fight*). □ **fight back 1** counter-attack. **2** suppress (one's feelings, tears, etc.). **fight down** suppress (one's feelings, tears, etc.). **fight for 1** fight on behalf of. **2** fight to secure (a thing). **fighting chance** an opportunity of succeeding by great effort. **fighting fit** fit enough to fight; at the peak of fitness. **fighting fund** money raised to support a campaign. **fighting words** *colloq.* words indicating a willingness to fight. **fight off** repel with effort. **fight out** (usu. **fight it out**) settle (a dispute etc.) by fighting. **fight shy of** avoid; be unwilling to approach (a person, task, etc.). [OE *feohtan, feoht(e)*, f. WG]

fighter /'faɪtə(r)/ *n.* **1** a person or animal that fights. **2** a fast military aircraft designed for attacking other aircraft.

figment /'fɪgmənt/ *n.* a thing invented or existing only in the imagination. [ME f. L *figmentum*, rel. to *fingere* fashion]

figuration /ˌfɪgjʊ'reɪʃ(ə)n/ *n.* **1 a** the act of formation. **b** a mode of formation; a form. **c** a shape or outline. **2 a** ornamentation by designs. **b** *Mus.* ornamental patterns of scales, arpeggios, etc. [ME f. F or f. L *figuratio* (as FIGURE)]

figurative /'fɪgjʊrətɪv, 'fɪgər-/ *adj.* **1 a** metaphorical, not literal. **b** metaphorically so called. **2** characterized by or addicted to figures of speech. **3** of pictorial or sculptural representation. □ **figuratively** *adv.* **figurativeness** *n.* [ME f. LL *figurativus* (as FIGURE)]

figure /'fɪgə(r)/ *n. & v.* —*n.* **1 a** the external form or shape of a thing. **b** bodily shape (*has a* *well-developed figure*). **2 a** a person as seen in outline but not identified (*saw a figure leaning against the door*). **b** a person as contemplated mentally (*a public figure*). **3** appearance as giving a certain impression (*cut a poor figure*). **4 a** a representation of the human form in drawing, sculpture, etc. **b** an image or likeness. **c** an emblem or type. **5** *Geom.* a two-dimensional space enclosed by a line or lines, or a three-dimensional space enclosed by a surface or surfaces; any of the classes of these, e.g. the triangle, the sphere. **6 a** a numerical symbol, esp. any of the ten in Arabic notation. **b** a number so expressed. **c** an amount of money, a value (*cannot put a figure on it*). **d** (in *pl.*) arithmetical calculations. **7** a diagram or illustrative drawing. **8** a decorative pattern. **9 a** a division of a set dance. **b** (in skating) a prescribed pattern of movements from a stationary position. **10** *Mus.* a short succession of notes producing a single impression. **11** (in full **figure of speech**) a recognized form of rhetorical expression, esp. metaphor or hyperbole. —*v.* **1** *intr.* appear or be mentioned, esp. prominently. **2** *tr.* represent in a diagram or picture. **3** *tr.* imagine; picture mentally. **4** *tr.* **a** embellish with a pattern (*figured satin*). **b** *Mus.* embellish with figures. **5** *tr.* mark with numbers or prices. **6 a** *tr.* calculate. **b** *intr.* do arithmetic. **7** *tr.* be a symbol of, represent typically. **8** esp. *US* a *tr.* understand, ascertain, consider. **b** *intr. colloq.* be likely or understandable (*that figures*). □ **figure of fun** a ridiculous person. **figure on** *US* count on, expect. **figure out 1** work out by arithmetic or logic. **2** estimate. **3** understand. **figure-skating** skating in prescribed patterns from a stationary position. □ **figureless** *adj.* [ME f. OF *figure* (n.), *figurer* (v.) f. L *figura*, *figurare*, rel. to *fingere* fashion]

figurehead /ˈfɪɡəˌhed/ *n.* **1** a nominal leader or head without real power. **2** a carving, usu. a bust or a full-length figure, at a ship's prow.

figurine /ˌfɪɡjʊˈriːn, ˈfɪɡ-/ *n.* a statuette. [F f. It. *figurina* dimin. of *figura* FIGURE]

filament /ˈfɪləmənt/ *n.* **1** a slender threadlike body or fibre (esp. in animal or vegetable structures). **2** a conducting wire or thread with a high melting-point in an electric bulb or thermionic valve, heated or made incandescent by an electric current. □ **filamentary** /-ˈmentərɪ/ *adj.* **filamented** *adj.* **filamentous** /-ˈmentəs/ *adj.* [F *filament* or mod.L *filamentum* f. LL *filare* spin f. L *filum* thread]

filbert /ˈfɪlbət/ *n.* **1** the cultivated hazel, *Corylus maxima*, bearing edible ovoid nuts. **2** this nut. [ME *philiberd* etc. f. AF *philbert*, dial. F *noix de filbert*, a nut ripe about St Philibert's day (20 Aug.)]

filch *v.tr.* pilfer, steal. □ **filcher** *n.* [16th-c. thieves' sl.: orig. unkn.]

file¹ *n. & v.* —*n.* **1** a folder, box, etc., for holding loose papers, esp. arranged for reference. **2** a set of papers kept in this. **3** *Computing* a collection of (usu. related) data stored under one name. **4** a series of issues of a newspaper etc. in order. **5** a stiff pointed wire on which documents etc. are impaled for keeping. —*v.tr.* **1** place (papers) in a file or among (esp. public) records. **2** submit (a petition for divorce, an application for a patent, etc.) to the appropriate

authority. **3** (of a reporter) send (a story, information, etc.) to a newspaper. □ **filing cabinet** a case with drawers for storing documents. □ **filer** *n.* [F *fil* f. L *filum* thread]

file² *n. & v.* —*n.* **1** a line of persons or things one behind another. **2** *Chess* a line of squares from player to player (cf. RANK¹). —*v.intr.* walk in a file. [F *file* f. LL *filare* spin or L *filum* thread]

file³ *n. & v.* —*n.* a tool with a roughened surface or surfaces, usu. of steel, for smoothing or shaping wood, fingernails, etc. —*v.tr.* **1** smooth or shape with a file. **2** elaborate or improve (a thing, esp. a literary work). □ **file away** remove (roughness etc.) with a file. □ **filer** *n.* [OE *fīl* f. WG]

filial /ˈfɪlɪəl/ *adj.* **1** of or due from a son or daughter. **2** *Biol.* bearing the relation of offspring (cf. F² 5). □ **filially** *adv.* [ME f. OF *filial* or LL *filialis* f. *filius* son, *filia* daughter]

filibuster /ˈfɪlɪˌbʌstə(r)/ *n. & v.* —*n.* **1 a** the obstruction of progress in a legislative assembly, esp. by prolonged speaking. **b** esp. *US* a person who engages in a filibuster. **2** esp. *hist.* a person engaging in unauthorized warfare against a foreign State. —*v.* **1** *intr.* act as a filibuster. **2** *tr.* act in this way against (a motion etc.). □ **filibusterer** *n.* [ult. f. Du. *vrijbuiter* FREEBOOTER, infl. by F *flibustier*, Sp. *filibustero*]

filigree /ˈfɪlɪˌɡriː/ *n.* (also **filagree** /ˈfɪləˌɡriː/) **1** ornamental work of gold or silver or copper as fine wire formed into delicate tracery; fine metal openwork. **2** anything delicate resembling this. □ **filigreed** *adj.* [earlier *filligreen*, *filligrane* f. F *filigrane* f. It. *filigrana* f. L *filum* thread + *granum* seed]

filing /ˈfaɪlɪŋ/ *n.* (usu. in *pl.*) a particle rubbed off by a file.

Filipino /ˌfɪlɪˈpiːnəʊ/ *n. & adj.* —*n.* (*pl.* **-os**; *fem.* **Filipina** /-nə/) a native or national of the Philippines, a group of islands in the SW Pacific. —*adj.* of or relating to the Philippines or the Filipinos. [Sp., = Philippine]

fill *v. & n.* —*v.* **1** *tr. & intr.* (often foll. by *with*) make or become full. **2** *tr.* occupy completely; spread over or through; pervade. **3** *tr.* block up (a cavity or hole in a tooth) with cement, amalgam, gold, etc.; drill and put a filling into (a decayed tooth). **4** *tr.* appoint a person to hold (a vacant post). **5** *tr.* hold (a position); discharge the duties of (an office). **6** *tr.* carry out or supply (an order, commission, etc.). **7** *tr.* occupy (vacant time). **8** *intr.* (of a sail) be distended by wind. **9** *tr.* (usu. as **filling** *adj.*) (esp. of food) satisfy, satiate. —*n.* **1** (prec. by possessive) as much as one wants or can bear (*eat your fill*). **2** enough to fill something (*a fill of tobacco*). □ **fill the bill** be suitable or adequate. **fill in 1** add information to complete (a form, document, blank cheque, etc.). **2 a** complete (a drawing etc.) within an outline. **b** fill (an outline) in this way. **3** fill (a hole etc.) completely. **4** (often foll. by *for*) act as a substitute. **5** occupy oneself during (time between other activities). **6** *colloq.* inform (a person) more fully. **7** *sl.* thrash, beat. **fill out 1** enlarge to the required size. **2** become enlarged or plump. **3** *US* fill in (a document etc.). **fill up 1** make or become completely full. **2** fill in (a document etc.). **3** fill the petrol tank of (a car etc.). [OE *fyllan* f. Gmc, rel. to FULL¹]

filler /ˈfɪlə(r)/ *n.* **1** material or an object used to fill a cavity or increase bulk. **2** an item filling space in a newspaper etc. **3** a person or thing that fills. □ **filler cap** a cap closing the filling-pipe leading to the petrol tank of a motor vehicle.

fillet /ˈfɪlɪt/ n. & v. —n. **1 a** a fleshy boneless piece of meat from near the loins or the ribs. **b** (in full **fillet steak**) the undercut of a sirloin. **c** a boned longitudinal section of a fish. **2 a** a headband, ribbon, string, or narrow band, for binding the hair or worn round the head. **b** a band or bandage. **3 a** a thin narrow strip of anything. **b** a raised rim or ridge on any surface. **4** Archit. **a** a narrow flat band separating two mouldings. **b** a small band between the flutes of a column. —v.tr. (**filleted, filleting**) **1 a** remove bones from (fish or meat). **b** divide (fish or meat) into fillets. **2** bind or provide with a fillet or fillets. **3** encircle with an ornamental band. □ **filleter** n. [ME f. OF *filet* f. Rmc dimin. of L *filum* thread]

filling /ˈfɪlɪŋ/ n. **1** any material that fills or is used to fill, esp.: **a** a piece of material used to fill a cavity in a tooth. **b** the edible substance between the bread in a sandwich or between the pastry in a pie. **2** US weft. □ **filling-station** an establishment selling petrol etc. to motorists.

fillip /ˈfɪlɪp/ n. & v. —n. **1** a stimulus or incentive. **2 a** a sudden release of a finger or thumb when it has been bent and checked by a thumb or finger. **b** a slight smart stroke given in this way. —v. (**filliped, filliping**) **1** tr. stimulate (*fillip one's memory*). **2** tr. strike slightly and smartly. **3** tr. propel (a coin, marble, etc.) with a fillip. **4** intr. make a fillip. [imit.]

filly /ˈfɪlɪ/ n. (pl. **-ies**) **1** a young female horse, usu. before it is four years old. **2** colloq. a girl or young woman. [ME, prob. f. ON *fylja* f. Gmc (as FOAL)]

film /fɪlm/ n. & v. —n. **1** a thin coating or covering layer. **2** Photog. a strip or sheet of plastic or other flexible base coated with light-sensitive emulsion for exposure in a camera, either as individual visual representations or as a sequence which form the illusion of movement when shown in rapid succession. **3 a** a representation of a story, episode, etc., on a film, with the illusion of movement. **b** a story represented in this way. **c** (in pl.) the cinema industry. **4** a slight veil or haze etc. **5** a dimness or morbid growth affecting the eyes. **6** a fine thread or filament. —v. **1 a** tr. make a photographic film of (a scene, person, etc.). **b** tr. (also absol.) make a cinema or television film of (a book etc.). **2** tr. & intr. cover or become covered with or as with a film. □ **film star** a celebrated actor or actress in films. **film-strip** a series of transparencies in a strip for projection. [OE *filmen* membrane f. WG]

filmic /ˈfɪlmɪk/ adj. of or relating to films or cinematography.

filmset /ˈfɪlmset/ v.tr. (**-setting**; past and past part. **-set**) Printing set (material for printing) by filmsetting. □ **filmsetter** n.

filmsetting /ˈfɪlmˌsetɪŋ/ n. Printing typesetting using characters on photographic film.

filmy /ˈfɪlmɪ/ adj. (**filmier, filmiest**) **1** thin and translucent. **2** covered with or as with a film. □ **filmily** adv. **filminess** n.

Filofax /ˈfaɪləʊˌfæks/ n. propr. a portable loose-leaf filing system for personal or office use. [FILE¹ + *facts* pl. of FACT]

filter /ˈfɪltə(r)/ n. & v. —n. **1** a porous device for removing impurities or solid particles from a liquid or gas passed through it. **2** = *filter tip*. **3** a screen or attachment for absorbing or modifying light, X-rays, etc. **4** a device for suppressing electrical or sound waves of frequencies not required. **5** Brit. **a** an arrangement for filtering traffic. **b** a traffic-light signalling this. —v.intr. & tr. **1** pass or cause to pass through a filter. **2** (foll. by through, into, etc.) make way gradually. **3** (foll. by out) leak or cause to leak. **4** Brit. allow (traffic) or (of traffic) be allowed to pass to the left or right at a junction while traffic going straight ahead is halted (esp. at traffic lights). □ **filter-bed** a tank or pond containing a layer of sand etc. for filtering large quantities of liquid. **filter-paper** porous paper for filtering. **filter tip 1** a filter attached to a cigarette for removing impurities from the inhaled smoke. **2** a cigarette with this. **filter-tipped** having a filter tip. □ **filterable** adj. **filtrable** adj. [F *filtre* f. med.L *filtrum* felt used as a filter, f. WG]

filth n. **1** repugnant or extreme dirt. **2** vileness, corruption, obscenity. **3** foul or obscene language. **4** (prec. by the) sl. the police. [OE *fylth* (as FOUL, -TH²)]

filthy /ˈfɪlθɪ/ adj. & adv. —adj. (**filthier, filthiest**) **1** extremely or disgustingly dirty. **2** obscene. **3** colloq. (of weather) very unpleasant. **4** vile. —adv. **1** filthily (*filthy dirty*). **2** colloq. extremely (*filthy rich*). □ **filthy lucre 1** dishonourable gain (Tit. 1:11). **2** joc. money. □ **filthily** adv. **filthiness** n.

filtrate /ˈfɪltreɪt/ v. & n. —v.tr. filter. —n. filtered liquid. □ **filtration** /-ˈtreɪʃ(ə)n/ n. [mod.L *filtrare* (as FILTER)]

fin n. **1** an organ on various parts of the body of many aquatic vertebrates and some invertebrates, including fish and cetaceans, for propelling, steering, and balancing. **2** a small projecting surface or attachment on an aircraft, rocket, or motor car for ensuring aerodynamic stability. **3** an underwater swimmer's flipper. **4** a finlike projection on any device, for improving heat transfer etc. □ **fin-back** (or **fin whale**) a rorqual, *Balaenoptera physalus*. □ **finless** adj. **finned** adj. (also in comb.). [OE *fin(n)*]

finable see FINE².

finagle /fɪˈneɪg(ə)l/ v.intr. & tr. colloq. act or obtain dishonestly. □ **finagler** n. [dial. *fainaigue* cheat]

final /ˈfaɪn(ə)l/ adj. & n. —adj. **1** situated at the end, coming last. **2** conclusive, decisive, unalterable, putting an end to doubt. **3** concerned with the purpose or end aimed at. —n. **1** the last or deciding heat or game in sports or in a competition (*Cup Final*). **2** the edition of a newspaper published latest in the day. **3** (usu. in pl.) the series of examinations at the end of a degree course. □ **final cause** Philos. the end towards which a thing naturally develops or at which an action aims. **final clause** Gram. a clause expressing purpose, introduced by in order that, lest, etc. □ **finally** adv. [ME f. OF or f. L *finalis* f. *finis* end]

finale /fɪˈnɑːlɪ, -leɪ/ n. **1 a** the last movement of an instrumental composition. **b** a piece of music closing an act in an opera. **2** the close of a drama etc. **3** a conclusion. [It. (as FINAL)]

finalist /ˈfaɪnəlɪst/ n. a competitor in the final of a competition etc.

finality /faɪˈnælɪti/ n. (pl. **-ies**) the quality or fact of being final. [F *finalité* f. LL *finalitas -tatis* (as FINAL)]

finalize /ˈfaɪnəˌlaɪz/ v.tr. (also **-ise**) **1** put into final form. **2** complete; bring to an end. **3** approve the final form or details of. □ **finalization** /-ˈzeɪʃ(ə)n/ n.

finance /ˈfaɪnæns, fɪˈnæns, faɪˈnæns/ n. & v. —n. **1** the management of (esp. public) money. **2** monetary support for an enterprise. **3** (in pl.) the money resources of a State, company, or person. —v.tr. provide capital for (a person or enterprise). □ **finance company** (or **house**) a company concerned with providing money for hire-purchase transactions. [ME f. OF f. *finer* settle a debt f. *fin* end: see FINE²]

financial /faɪˈnænʃ(ə)l, fɪ-/ adj. **1** of finance. **2** Austral. & NZ sl. possessing money. □ **financial year** a year as reckoned for taxing or accounting. □ **financially** adv.

financier n. /faɪˈnænsɪə(r), fɪ-/ a person engaged in large-scale finance. [F (as FINANCE)]

finch n. any small seed-eating passerine bird of the family Fringillidae (esp. one of the genus *Fringilla*), including crossbills, canaries, and chaffinches. [OE *finc* f. WG]

find /faɪnd/ v. & n. —v.tr. (past and past part. **found** /faʊnd/) **1 a** discover by chance or effort (*found a key*). **b** become aware of. **c** (absol.) discover game, esp. a fox. **2 a** get possession of by chance (*found a treasure*). **b** obtain, receive (*idea found acceptance*). **c** succeed in obtaining (*cannot find the money; can't find time to read*). **d** summon up (*found courage to protest*). **3 a** seek out and provide (*will find you a book*). **b** supply, furnish (*each finds his own equipment*). **4** ascertain by study or calculation or inquiry (*could not find the answer*). **5 a** perceive or experience (*find no sense in it; find difficulty in breathing*). **b** (often in passive) recognize or discover to be present (*the word is not found in Shakespeare*). **c** regard or discover from experience (*finds England too cold; you'll find it pays*). **6** Law (of a jury, judge, etc.) decide and declare (*found him guilty; found that he had done it; found it murder*). **7** reach by a natural or normal process (*water finds its own level*). —n. **1 a** a discovery of treasure, minerals, etc. **b** Hunting the finding of a fox. **2** a thing or person discovered, esp. when of value. □ **all found** (of an employee's wages) with board and lodging provided free. **find against** Law decide against (a person), judge to be guilty. **find favour** prove acceptable. **find one's feet 1** become able to walk. **2** develop one's independent ability. **find for** Law decide in favour of (a person), judge to be innocent. **find it in one's heart** (esp. with neg.; foll. by to + infin.) prevail upon oneself, be willing. **find out 1** discover or detect (a wrongdoer etc.). **2** (often foll. by about) get information (*find out about holidays abroad*). **3** discover (*find out where we are*). **4** (often foll. by about) discover the truth, a fact, etc. (*he never found out*). **find one's way 1** (often foll. by to) manage to reach a place. **2** (often foll. by into) be brought or get. □ **findable** adj. [OE *findan* f. Gmc]

finder /ˈfaɪndə(r)/ n. **1** a person who finds. **2** a small telescope attached to a large one to locate

an object for observation. **3** the viewfinder of a camera.

finding /ˈfaɪndɪŋ/ n. (often in pl.) a conclusion reached by an inquiry.

fine¹ adj., n., adv., & v. —adj. **1** of high quality. **2 a** excellent; of notable merit (*a fine painting*). **b** good, satisfactory (*that will be fine*). **c** fortunate (*has been a fine thing for him*). **d** well conceived or expressed (*a fine saying*). **3 a** pure, refined. **b** (of gold or silver) containing a specified proportion of pure metal. **4** of handsome appearance or size; imposing, dignified (*fine buildings; a person of fine presence*). **5** in good health (*I'm fine, thank you*). **6** (of weather etc.) bright and clear with sunshine; free from rain. **7 a** thin; sharp. **b** in small particles. **c** worked in slender thread. **d** (esp. of print) small. **e** (of a pen) narrow-pointed. **8** ornate, showy, smart. **9** fastidious, dainty, pretending refinement; (of speech or writing) affectedly ornate. **10 a** capable of delicate perception or discrimination. **b** perceptible only with difficulty (*a fine distinction*). **11 a** delicate, subtle, exquisitely fashioned. **b** (of feelings) refined, elevated. **12** (of wine or other goods) of a high standard; conforming to a specified grade. —n. **1** fine weather (*in rain or fine*). **2** (in pl.) very small particles in mining, milling, etc. —adv. **1** finely. **2** colloq. very well (*suits me fine*). —v. **1** (often foll. by down) **a** tr. make (beer or wine) clear. **b** intr. (of liquid) become clear. **2** tr. & intr. (often foll. by away, down, off) make or become finer, thinner, or less coarse; dwindle or taper, or cause to do so. □ **cut** (or **run**) **it fine** allow very little margin of time etc. **fine arts** those appealing to the mind or to the sense of beauty, as poetry, music, and esp. painting, sculpture, and architecture. **fine-drawn 1** extremely thin. **2** subtle. **fine print** detailed printed information, esp. in legal documents, instructions, etc. **fine-spun 1** delicate. **2** (of a theory etc.) too subtle, unpractical. **fine-tooth comb** a comb with narrow close-set teeth. **fine-tune** make small adjustments to (a mechanism etc.) in order to obtain the best possible results. **fine up** Austral. colloq. (of the weather) become fine. **not to put too fine a point on it** (as a parenthetic remark) to speak bluntly. □ **finely** adv. **fineness** n. [ME f. OF *fin* ult. f. L *finire* finish]

fine² n. & v. —n. a sum of money exacted as a penalty. —v.tr. punish by a fine (*fined him £5*). □ **in fine** to sum up; in short. □ **finable** /ˈfaɪnəb(ə)l/ adj. [ME f. OF *fin* f. med.L *finis* sum paid on settling a lawsuit f. L *finis* end]

finery /ˈfaɪnəri/ n. showy dress or decoration. [FINE¹ + -ERY, after BRAVERY]

fines herbes /fiːnz ˈeəb/ n.pl. mixed herbs used in cooking, esp. chopped as omelette-flavouring. [F, = fine herbs]

finesse /fɪˈnes/ n. & v. —n. **1** refinement. **2** subtle or delicate manipulation. **3** artfulness, esp. in handling a difficulty tactfully. **4** Cards an attempt to win a trick with a card that is not the highest held. —v. **1** intr. & tr. use or achieve by finesse. **2** Cards intr. make a finesse. [F, rel. to FINE¹]

finger /ˈfɪŋɡə(r)/ n. & v. —n. **1** any of the terminal projections of the hand (including or excluding the thumb). **2** the part of a glove etc. intended to cover a finger. **3 a** a finger-like object (*fish finger*). **b** a long narrow structure. **4** colloq. a measure of liquor in a glass, based on the breadth of a finger. —*v.tr.* **1** touch, feel, or turn about with the fingers. **2** *Mus.* play (a passage) with fingers used in a particular way. **3** *US sl.* indicate (a victim, or a criminal to the police). □ **all fingers and thumbs** clumsy. **finger alphabet** a form of sign language using the fingers. **finger-board** a flat strip at the top end of a stringed instrument, against which the strings are pressed to determine tones. **finger-bowl** (or **-glass**) a small bowl for rinsing the fingers during a meal. **finger-dry** *v.tr.* dry and style (the hair) by running one's fingers through it. **finger language** language expressed by means of the finger alphabet. **finger-mark** a mark left on a surface by a finger. **finger-paint** *n.* paint that can be applied with the fingers. —*v.intr.* apply paint with the fingers. **finger-plate** a plate fixed to a door above the handle to prevent finger-marks. **finger-post** a signpost at a road junction. **finger-stall** a cover to protect a finger, esp. when injured. **get** (or **pull**) **one's finger out** *sl.* cease prevaricating and start to act. **have a finger in the pie** be (esp. officiously) concerned in the matter. **lay a finger on** touch however slightly. **put one's finger on** locate or identify exactly. **put the finger on** *sl.* **1** inform against. **2** identify (an intended victim). □ **fingered** *adj.* (also in *comb.*). **fingerless** *adj.* [OE f. Gmc]

fingering[1] /ˈfɪŋgərɪŋ/ *n.* **1** a manner or technique of using the fingers, esp. to play an instrument. **2** an indication of this in a musical score.

fingering[2] /ˈfɪŋgərɪŋ/ *n.* fine wool for knitting. [earlier *fingram*, perh. f. F *fin grain*, as GROGRAM f. *gros grain*]

fingernail /ˈfɪŋgəˌneɪl/ *n.* the nail at the tip of each finger.

fingerprint /ˈfɪŋgəprɪnt/ *n.* & *v.* —*n.* **1** an impression made on a surface by the fingertips, esp. as used for identifying individuals. **2** a distinctive characteristic. —*v.tr.* record the fingerprints of (a person).

fingertip /ˈfɪŋgətɪp/ *n.* the tip of a finger. □ **have at one's fingertips** be thoroughly familiar with (a subject etc.).

finial /ˈfɪnɪəl/ *n. Archit.* an ornament finishing off the apex of a roof, pediment, gable, tower-corner, canopy, etc. [ME f. OF *fin* f. L *finis* end]

finical /ˈfɪnɪk(ə)l/ *adj.* = FINICKY. □ **finicality** /-ˈkælɪtɪ/ *n.* **finically** *adv.* **finicalness** *n.* [16th c.: prob. orig. university sl. f. FINE[1] + -ICAL]

finicking /ˈfɪnɪkɪŋ/ *adj.* = FINICKY. [FINICAL + -ING[2]]

finicky /ˈfɪnɪkɪ/ *adj.* **1** over-particular, fastidious. **2** needing much attention to detail; fiddly. □ **finickiness** *n.*

finis /ˈfɪnɪs, ˈfiːnɪs, ˈfaɪnɪs/ *n.* **1** (at the end of a book) the end. **2** the end of anything, esp. of life. [L]

finish /ˈfɪnɪʃ/ *v.* & *n.* —*v.* **1** *tr.* **a** (often foll. by *off*) bring to an end; come to the end of; complete. **b** (usu. foll. by *off*) *colloq.* kill; overcome completely. **c** (often foll. by *off, up*) consume or get through the whole or the remainder of (food or drink) (*finish up your dinner*). **2** *intr.* **a** come to an end, cease. **b** reach the end, esp. of a race. **c** = *finish up*. **3** *tr.* **a** complete the manufacture of (cloth, woodwork, etc.) by surface treatment. **b** put the final touches to; make perfect or highly accomplished (*finished manners*). —*n.* **1 a** the end, the last stage. **b** the point at which a race etc.

ends. **c** the death of a fox in a hunt (*be in at the finish*). **2** a method, material, or texture used for surface treatment of wood, cloth, etc. (*mahogany finish*). **3** what serves to give completeness. **4** an accomplished or completed state. □ **fight to a finish** fight till one party is completely beaten. **finishing-school** a private college where girls are prepared for entry into fashionable society. **finish off** provide with an ending. **finish up** (often foll. by *in, by*) end in something, end by doing something (*the plan finished up in the waste-paper basket; finished up by apologizing*). **finish with** have no more to do with, complete one's use of or association with. [ME f. OF *fenir* f. L *finire* f. *finis* end]

finisher /ˈfɪnɪʃə(r)/ *n.* **1** a person who finishes something. **2** a worker or machine doing the last operation in manufacture. **3** *colloq.* a discomfiting thing, a crushing blow, etc.

finite /ˈfaɪnaɪt/ *adj.* **1** limited, bounded; not infinite. **2** *Gram.* (of a part of a verb) having a specific number and person. **3** not infinitely small. □ **finitely** *adv.* **finiteness** *n.* **finitude** /ˈfɪnɪˌtjuːd/ *n.* [L *finitus* past part. of *finire* FINISH]

fink *n.* & *v. US sl.* —*n.* **1** an unpleasant person. **2** an informer. **3** a strikebreaker; a blackleg. —*v.intr.* (foll. by *on*) inform on. [20th c.: orig. unkn.]

Finn *n.* a native or national of Finland; a person of Finnish descent. [OE *Finnas* pl.]

finnan /ˈfɪnən/ *n.* (in full **finnan haddock**) a haddock cured with the smoke of green wood, turf, or peat. [*Findhorn* or *Findon* in Scotland]

Finnish /ˈfɪnɪʃ/ *adj.* & *n.* —*adj.* of the Finns or their language. —*n.* the language of the Finns.

finny /ˈfɪnɪ/ *adj.* **1** having fins; like a fin. **2** *poet.* of or teeming with fish.

fiord /fjɔːd/ *n.* (also **fjord**) a long narrow inlet of sea between high cliffs, as in Norway. [Norw. *fjord* f. ON *fjörthr* f. Gmc: cf. FIRTH, FORD]

fipple /ˈfɪp(ə)l/ *n.* a plug at the mouth-end of a wind instrument. □ **fipple flute** a flute played by blowing endwise, e.g. a recorder. [17th c.: orig. unkn.]

fir *n.* **1** (in full **fir-tree**) any evergreen coniferous tree, esp. of the genus *Abies*, with needles borne singly on the stems. **2** the wood of the fir. □ **fir-cone** the fruit of the fir. □ **firry** *adj.* [ME, prob. f. ON *fyri-* f. Gmc]

fire *n.* & *v.* —*n.* **1 a** the state or process of combustion, in which substances combine chemically with oxygen from the air and usu. give out bright light and heat. **b** the active principle operative in this. **c** flame or incandescence. **2** a conflagration, a destructive burning (*forest fire*). **3** a burning fuel in a grate, furnace, etc. **b** = *electric fire*. **c** = *gas fire*. **4** firing of guns. **5 a** fervour, spirit, vivacity. **b** poetic inspiration, lively imagination. **c** vehement emotion. **6** burning heat, fever. **7** luminosity, glow (*St Elmo's fire*). —*v.* **1 a** *tr.* discharge (a gun etc.). **b** *tr.* propel (a missile) from a gun etc. **c** *intr.* (often foll. by *at, into, on*) fire a gun or missile. **d** *tr.* produce (a broadside, salute, etc.) by discharge of guns. **e** *intr.* (of a gun etc.) be discharged. **2** *tr.* cause (explosive) to explode. **3** *tr.* deliver or utter in rapid succession (*fired insults at us*). **4** *tr. sl.* dismiss (an employee) from a job. **5** *tr.* **a** set fire to with the intention of destroying. **6** *intr.* kindle (explosives). **6** *intr.* catch fire. **7** *intr.* (of an internal-combustion engine, or a cylinder in one) undergo ignition of its fuel. **8** *tr.* supply (a furnace, engine, boiler, or power station) with fuel. **9** *tr.* **a** stimulate (the imagination). **b** fill (a person) with enthusiasm. **10** *tr.* **a** bake or dry (pottery, bricks, etc.). **b** cure (tea or tobacco) by artificial heat. **11** *intr.* become heated or excited. **12** *tr.* cause to glow or redden. □ **catch fire** begin to burn. **fire-alarm** a device for giving warning of fire. **fire away** *colloq.* begin; go ahead. **fire-ball 1** a large meteor. **2** a ball of flame, esp. from a nuclear explosion. **3** an energetic person. **fire-bomb** an incendiary bomb. **fire-break** an obstacle to the spread of fire in a forest etc., esp. an open space. **fire-brick** a fireproof brick used in a grate. **fire brigade** esp. *Brit.* an organized body of firemen trained and employed to extinguish fires. **fire-bug** *colloq.* a pyromaniac. **fire department** *US* = fire brigade. **fire door** a fire-resistant door to prevent the spread of fire. **fire-drill** a rehearsal of the procedures to be used in case of fire. **fire-eater 1** a conjuror who appears to swallow fire. **2** a person fond of quarrelling or fighting. **fire-engine** a vehicle carrying equipment for fighting large fires. **fire-escape** an emergency staircase or apparatus for escape from a building on fire. **fire extinguisher** an apparatus with a jet for discharging liquid chemicals, water, or foam to extinguish a fire. **fire-fighter** a person whose task is to extinguish fires. **fire-guard 1** a protective screen or grid placed in front of a fireplace. **2** *US* a fire-watcher. **3** *US* a fire-break. **fire-hose** a hose-pipe used in extinguishing fires. **fire-irons** tongs, poker, and shovel, for tending a domestic fire. **fire-lighter** *Brit.* a piece of inflammable material to help start a fire in a grate. **fire-power 1** the destructive capacity of guns etc. **2** financial, intellectual, or emotional strength. **fire-practice** a fire-drill. **fire-raiser** *Brit.* an arsonist. **fire-screen 1** a screen to keep off the direct heat of a fire. **2** a fire-guard. **fire station** the headquarters of a fire brigade. **fire-storm** a high wind or storm following a fire caused by bombs. **fire-tongs** tongs for picking up pieces of coal etc. in tending a fire. **fire-trap** a building without proper provision for escape in case of fire. **fire up** show sudden anger. **fire-walking** the (often ceremonial) practice of walking barefoot over white-hot stones, wood-ashes, etc. **fire warden** *US* a person employed to prevent or extinguish fires. **fire-watcher** a person keeping watch for fires, esp. those caused by bombs. **fire-water** *colloq.* strong alcoholic liquor. **go on fire** *Sc.* & *Ir.* catch fire. **on fire 1** burning. **2** excited. **set fire to** (or **set on fire**) ignite, kindle, cause to burn. **take fire** catch fire. **under fire 1** being shot at. **2** being rigorously criticized or questioned. □ **fireless** *adj.* **firer** *n.* [OE *fȳr, fȳrian,* f. WG]

firearm /ˈfaɪərˌɑːm/ *n.* (usu. in *pl.*) a gun, esp. a pistol or rifle.

firebox /ˈfaɪəˌbɒks/ *n.* the fuel-chamber of a steam engine or boiler.

firebrand /ˈfaɪəˌbrænd/ *n.* **1** a piece of burning wood. **2** a cause of trouble, esp. a person causing unrest.

fireclay /ˈfaɪəˌkleɪ/ *n.* clay capable of withstanding high temperatures, often used to make fire-bricks.

firecracker /ˈfaɪəˌkrækə(r)/ *n.* *US* an explosive firework.

firedog /ˈfaɪəˌdɒg/ *n.* a metal support for burning wood or for a grate or fire-irons.

firefly /ˈfaɪəˌflaɪ/ *n.* (*pl.* **-flies**) any soft-bodied beetle of the family Lampyridae, emitting phosphorescent light, including glow-worms.

firehouse /ˈfaɪəˌhaʊs/ *n.* *US* a fire station.

firelight /ˈfaɪəˌlaɪt/ *n.* light from a fire in a fireplace. [OE *fȳr-leoht* (as FIRE, LIGHT¹)]

fireman /ˈfaɪəmən/ *n.* (*pl.* **-men**) **1** a member of a fire brigade; a person employed to extinguish fires. **2** a person who tends a furnace or the fire of a steam engine or steamship.

fireplace /ˈfaɪəˌpleɪs/ *n.* *Archit.* **1** a place for a domestic fire, esp. a grate or hearth at the base of a chimney. **2** a structure surrounding this. **3** the area in front of this.

fireproof /ˈfaɪəˌpruːf/ *adj.* & *v.* —*adj.* able to resist fire or great heat. —*v.tr.* make fireproof.

fireside /ˈfaɪəˌsaɪd/ *n.* **1** the area round a fireplace. **2** a person's home or home-life. □ **fireside chat** an informal talk.

firewood /ˈfaɪəˌwʊd/ *n.* wood for use as fuel.

firework /ˈfaɪəˌwɜːk/ *n.* **1** a device containing combustible chemicals that cause explosions or spectacular effects. **2** (in *pl.*) **a** an outburst of passion, esp. anger. **b** a display of wit or brilliance.

firing /ˈfaɪərɪŋ/ *n.* **1** the discharging of guns. **2** material for a fire, fuel. **3** the heating process which hardens clay into pottery etc. □ **firing-line 1** the front line in a battle. **2** the leading part in an activity etc. **firing-party** a group detailed to fire the salute at a military funeral. **firing-squad 1** a group detailed to shoot a condemned person. **2** a firing-party.

firkin /ˈfɜːkɪn/ *n.* **1** a small cask for liquids, butter, fish, etc. **2** *Brit.* (as a measure) half a kilderkin (8 or 9 gallons). [ME *ferdekyn,* prob. f. MDu. *vierdekijn* (unrecorded) dimin. of *vierde* fourth]

firm¹ *adj., adv.,* & *v.* —*adj.* **1 a** of solid or compact structure. **b** fixed, stable. **c** steady; not shaking. **2 a** resolute, determined. **b** not easily shaken (*firm belief*). **c** steadfast, constant (*a firm friend*). **3** (of an offer etc.) not liable to cancellation after acceptance. —*adv.* firmly (*stand firm; hold firm to*). —*v.* **1** *tr.* & *intr.* make or become firm, secure, compact, or solid. **2** *tr.* fix (plants) firmly in the soil. □ **firmly** *adv.* **firmness** *n.* [ME f. OF *ferme* f. L *firmus*]

firm² *n.* **1 a** a business concern. **b** the partners in such a concern. **2** a group of persons working together, esp. of hospital doctors and assistants. [earlier = signature, style: Sp. & It. *firma* f. med.L. f. L *firmare* confirm f. *firmus* FIRM¹]

firmament /ˈfɜːməmənt/ *n.* *literary* the sky regarded as a vault or arch. □ **firmamental** /-ˈment(ə)l/ *adj.* [ME f. OF f. L *firmamentum* f. *firmare* (as FIRM²)]

firry see FIR.

first *adj., n.,* & *adv.* —*adj.* **1 a** earliest in time or order. **b** coming next after a specified or implied time (*shall take the first train; the first cuckoo*). **2** foremost in position, rank, or importance (*First Lord of the Treasury; first mate*). **3** *Mus.* performing the highest or chief of two or more parts for the same instrument or voice. **4** most willing or likely (*should be the first to admit the difficulty*). **5** basic or evident (*first principles*). —*n.* **1** (prec. by *the*) the person or thing first mentioned or occurring. **2** the first occurrence of something notable. **3 a** a place in the first class in an examination. **b** a person having this. **4** the first day of a month. **5** first gear. **6 a** first place in a race. **b** the winner of this. —*adv.* **1** before any other person or thing (*first of all*; *first come first served*). **2** before someone or something else (*must get this done first*). **3** for the first time (*when did you first see her?*). **4** in preference; rather (*will see him damned first*). **5** first-class (*I usually travel first*). □ **at first** at the beginning. **at first hand** directly from the original source. **first aid** help given to an injured person until proper medical treatment is available. **first-born** *adj.* eldest. —*n.* the eldest child of a person. **first class 1** a set of persons or things grouped together as the best. **2** the best accommodation in a train, ship, etc. **3** the class of mail given priority in handling. **4 a** the highest division in an examination list. **b** a place in this. **first-class** *adj.* **1** belonging to or travelling by the first class. **2** of the best quality; very good. —*adv.* by the first class (*travels first-class*). **first-day cover** an envelope with stamps postmarked on their first day of issue. **first-degree** *Med.* denoting burns that affect only the surface of the skin, causing reddening. **first finger** the finger next to the thumb. **first-foot** *Sc. n.* the first person to cross a threshold in the New Year. —*v.intr.* be a first-foot. **first-fruit** (usu. in *pl.*) **1** the first agricultural produce of a season, esp. as offered to God. **2** the first results of work etc. **First Lady** (in the US) the wife of the President. **first lesson** the first of several passages from the Bible read at a service in the Church of England. **first lieutenant** *US* an army or air force officer next below captain. **first light** the time when light first appears in the morning. **first mate** (on a merchant ship) the officer second in command to the master. **first name** a personal or Christian name. **first night** the first public performance of a play etc. **first off** *US colloq.* at first, first of all. **first offender** a criminal against whom no previous conviction is recorded. **first officer** the mate on a merchant ship. **first past the post 1** winning a race etc. by being the first to reach the finishing line. **2** (of an electoral system) selecting a candidate or party by simple majority. **first-rate** *adj.* of the highest class, excellent. —*adv. colloq.* **1** very well (*feeling first-rate*). **2** excellently. **first reading** the occasion when a Bill is presented to a legislature to permit its introduction. **first school** *Brit.* a school for children from 5 to 9 years old. **first sergeant** *US* the highest-ranking non-commissioned officer in a company. **first-strike** denoting a first aggressive attack with nuclear weapons. **first thing** *colloq.* before anything else; very early in the morning (*shall do it first thing*). **the first thing** even the most elementary fact or principle (*does not know the first thing about it*). **first up** *Austral.* first of all; at the first attempt. **from the first** from the beginning. **from first to last** throughout. **get to first base** *US* achieve the first step towards an objective. **in the first place** as the first consideration. [OE *fyrst* f. Gmc]

firsthand /fɜːstˈhænd, *attrib.* ˈfɜːst-/ *adj.* & *adv.* from the original source; direct.

firstly /ˈfɜːstlɪ/ *adv.* (in enumerating topics, arguments, etc.) in the first place, first (cf. FIRST *adv.*).

firth *n.* (also **frith** /frɪθ/) **1** a narrow inlet of the sea. **2** an estuary. [ME (orig. Sc.) f. ON *fjörthr* FIORD]

fiscal /ˈfɪsk(ə)l/ *adj.* & *n.* —*adj.* of public revenue. —*n.* **1** a legal official in some countries. **2** *Sc.* = *procurator fiscal.* □ **fiscal year** = *financial year.* □ **fiscally** *adv.* [F *fiscal* or L *fiscalis* f. *fiscus* rush-basket, purse, treasury]

fish[1] *n.* & *v.* —*n.* (*pl.* same or **fishes**) **1** a vertebrate cold-blooded animal with gills and fins living wholly in water. **2** any animal living wholly in water, e.g. cuttlefish, shellfish, jellyfish. **3** the flesh of fish as food. **4** *colloq.* a person remarkable in some way (usu. unfavourable) (*an odd fish*). **5** (**the Fish** or **Fishes**) the zodiacal sign or constellation Pisces. —*v.* **1** *intr.* try to catch fish, esp. with a line or net. **2** *tr.* fish for (a certain kind of fish) or in (a certain stretch of water). **3** *intr.* (foll. by *for*) **a** a search for in water or a concealed place. **b** seek by indirect means (*fishing for compliments*). **4** *tr.* (foll. by *up*, *out*, etc.) retrieve with careful or awkward searching. □ **fish-bowl** a usu. round glass bowl for keeping pet fish in. **fish cake** a cake of shredded fish and mashed potato, usu. eaten fried. **fish-eye lens** a very wide-angle lens with a curved front. **fish farm** a place where fish are bred for food. **fish finger** *Brit.* a small oblong piece of fish in batter or breadcrumbs. **fish-hook** a barbed hook for catching fish. **fish-kettle** an oval pan for boiling fish. **fish-meal** ground dried fish used as fertilizer or animal feed. **fish out of water** a person in an unsuitable or unwelcome environment or situation. **fish-pond** (or **-pool**) a pond or pool in which fish are kept. **fish-slice** a flat utensil for lifting fish and fried foods during and after cooking. [OE *fisc*, *fiscian* f. Gmc]

fish[2] *n.* **1** a flat plate of iron, wood, etc., to strengthen a beam or joint. **2** *Naut.* a piece of wood, convex and concave, used to strengthen a mast etc. □ **fish-plate a** a flat piece of iron etc. connecting railway rails. **b** a flat piece of metal with ends like a fish's tail, used to position masonry. □ **fishlike** *adj.* [orig. as verb: f. F *ficher* fix ult. f. L *figere*]

fisher /ˈfɪʃə(r)/ *n.* **1** an animal that catches fish. **2** *archaic* a fisherman. [OE *fiscere* f. Gmc (as FISH[1])]

fisherman /ˈfɪʃəmən/ *n.* (*pl.* **-men**) a person who catches fish as a livelihood or for sport.

fishery /ˈfɪʃərɪ/ *n.* (*pl.* **-ies**) **1** a place where fish are caught or reared. **2** the occupation or industry of catching or rearing fish.

fishing /ˈfɪʃɪŋ/ *n.* the activity of catching fish, esp. for food or as a sport. □ **fishing-line** a long thread of silk etc. with a baited hook, sinker, float, etc., used for catching fish. **fishing-rod** a long tapering usu. jointed rod to which a fishing-line is attached.

fishmonger /ˈfɪʃˌmʌŋɡə(r)/ *n.* esp. *Brit.* a dealer in fish.

fishnet /ˈfɪʃnet/ *n.* (often *attrib.*) an open-meshed fabric (*fishnet stockings*).

fishtail /ˈfɪʃteɪl/ *n.* & *v.* —*n.* a device etc. shaped like a fish's tail. —*v.intr.* move the tail of a vehicle from side to side.

fishwife /ˈfɪʃwaɪf/ *n.* (*pl.* **-wives**) **1** a coarse-mannered or noisy woman. **2** a woman who sells fish.

fishy /ˈfɪʃɪ/ adj. (**fishier, fishiest**) **1 a** smelling or tasting like fish. **b** like that of a fish. **c** (of an eye) dull, vacant-looking. **d** consisting of fish (a *fishy repast*). **e** joc. or poet. abounding in fish. **2** sl. of dubious character, questionable, suspect. □ **fishily** adv. **fishiness** n.

fissile /ˈfɪsaɪl/ adj. **1** capable of undergoing nuclear fission. **2** cleavable; tending to split. □ **fissility** /-ˈsɪlɪtɪ/ n. [L *fissilis* (as FISSURE)]

fission /ˈfɪʃ(ə)n/ n. & v. —n. **1** *Physics* the spontaneous or impact-induced splitting of a heavy atomic nucleus, accompanied by a release of energy. **2** *Biol.* the division of a cell etc. into new cells etc. as a mode of reproduction. —v.intr. & tr. undergo or cause to undergo fission. □ **fission bomb** an atomic bomb. □ **fissionable** adj. [L *fissio* (as FISSURE)]

fissure /ˈfɪʃə(r)/ n. & v. —n. **1** an opening, usu. long and narrow, made esp. by cracking, splitting, or separation of parts. **2** a cleavage. —v.tr. & intr. split or crack. [ME f. OF *fissure* or L *fissura* f. *findere fiss-* cleave]

fist n. **1** a tightly closed hand. **2** sl. handwriting (*writes a good fist; I know his fist*). □ **make a good** (or **poor** etc.) **fist** (foll. by *at, of*) colloq. make a good (or poor etc.) attempt at. □ **fisted** adj. (also in comb.). **fistful** n. (pl. **-fuls**). [OE *fȳst* f. WG]

fisticuffs /ˈfɪstɪˌkʌfs/ n.pl. fighting with the fists. [prob. obs. *fisty* adj. or *fistic* pugilistic, + CUFF²]

fistula /ˈfɪstjʊlə/ n. (pl. **fistulas** or **fistulae** /-ˌliː/) **1** an abnormal or surgically made passage between a hollow organ and the body surface or between two hollow organs. **2** a natural pipe or spout in whales, insects, etc. □ **fistular** adj. **fistulous** adj. [L, = pipe, flute]

fit¹ adj., v., n., & adv. —adj. (**fitter, fittest**) **1 a** (usu. foll. by *for*, or *to* + infin.) well adapted or suited. **b** (foll. by *to* + infin.) qualified, competent, worthy. **c** (foll. by *for*, or *to* + infin.) in a suitable condition, ready. **d** (foll. by *for*) good enough (a *dinner fit for a king*). **e** (foll. by *to* + infin.) sufficiently exhausted, troubled, or angry (*fit to drop*). **2** in good health or athletic condition. **3** proper, becoming, right (*it is fit that*). —v. (**fitted, fitting**) **1 a** tr. (also *absol.*) be of the right shape and size for (*the key doesn't fit the lock; these shoes don't fit*). **b** tr. make, fix, or insert (a thing) so that it is of the right size or shape (*fitted shelves in the alcoves*). **c** intr. (often foll. by *in, into*) (of a component) be correctly positioned (*that bit fits here*). **d** tr. find room for (*can't fit another person on the bench*). **2** tr. (foll. by *for*, or *to* + infin.) **a** make suitable; adapt. **b** make competent (*fitted him to be a priest*). **3** tr. (usu. foll. by *with*) supply, furnish (*fitted the boat with a new rudder*). **4** tr. fix in place (*fit a lock on the door*). **5** tr. = fit on. **6** tr. be in harmony with, befit, become (*the punishment fits the crime*). —n. the way in which a garment, component, etc., fits (a *bad fit; a tight fit*). —adv. (foll. by *to* + infin.) colloq. in a suitable manner, appropriately (*was laughing fit to bust*). □ **fit the bill** = fill the bill. **fit in 1** (often foll. by *with*) be (esp. socially) compatible or accommodating (*tried to fit in with their plans*). **2** find space or time for (an object, engagement, etc.). **fit on** try on (a garment). **fit out** (or **up**) (often foll. by *with*) equip. **see** (or **think**) **fit** (often foll. by *to* + infin.) decide or choose (a specified course of action). □ **fitly** adv. **fitness** n. [ME: orig. unkn.]

fit² n. **1** a sudden seizure of epilepsy, hysteria, apoplexy, fainting, or paralysis, with unconsciousness or convulsions. **2** a sudden brief attack of an illness or of symptoms (*fit of coughing*). **3** a sudden short bout or burst (*fit of energy; fit of giggles*). **4** colloq. an attack of strong feeling (*fit of rage*). **5** a capricious impulse; a mood (*when the fit was on him*). □ **by** (or **in**) **fits and starts** spasmodically. **give a person a fit** colloq. surprise or outrage him or her. **have a fit** colloq. be greatly surprised or outraged. **in fits** laughing uncontrollably. [ME, = position of danger, perh. = OE *fitt* conflict (?)]

fitful /ˈfɪtfʊl/ adj. active or occurring spasmodically or intermittently. □ **fitfully** adv. **fitfulness** n.

fitment /ˈfɪtmənt/ n. (usu. in pl.) a fixed item of furniture.

fitted /ˈfɪtɪd/ adj. **1** made or shaped to fill a space or cover something closely or exactly (a *fitted carpet*). **2** provided with appropriate equipment, fittings, etc. (a *fitted kitchen*). **3** built-in; filling an alcove etc. (*fitted cupboards*).

fitter /ˈfɪtə(r)/ n. **1** a person who supervises the cutting, fitting, altering, etc. of garments. **2** a mechanic who fits together and adjusts machinery.

fitting /ˈfɪtɪŋ/ n. & adj. —n. **1** the process or an instance of having a garment etc. fitted (*needed several fittings*). **2 a** (in pl.) the fixtures and fitments of a building. **b** a piece of apparatus or furniture. —adj. proper, becoming, right. □ **fittingly** adv. **fittingness** n.

five n. & adj. —n. **1** one more than four. **2** a symbol for this (5, v, V). **3** a size etc. denoted by five. **4** a set or team of five individuals. **5** the time of five o'clock (*is it five yet?*). —adj. that amount to five. □ **five-eighth** Austral. & NZ Rugby Football either of two players between the scrum-half and the centre three-quarter. **five o'clock shadow** beard-growth visible on a man's face in the latter part of the day. **five-star** of the highest class. [OE *fīf* f. Gmc]

fivefold /ˈfaɪvfəʊld/ adj. & adv. **1** five times as much or as many. **2** consisting of five parts. **3** amounting to five.

fiver /ˈfaɪvə(r)/ n. colloq. **1** Brit. a five-pound note. **2** US a five-dollar bill.

fives /faɪvz/ n. a game in which a ball is hit with a gloved hand or a bat against the walls of a court with three walls (**Eton fives**) or four walls (**Rugby fives**). [pl. of FIVE used as sing.: significance unkn.]

fix v. & n. —v. **1** tr. make firm or stable; fasten, secure (*fixed a picture to the wall*). **2** tr. decide, settle, specify (a price, date, etc.). **3** tr. mend, repair. **4** tr. implant (an idea or memory) in the mind (*couldn't get the rules fixed in his head*). **5** tr. **a** (foll. by *on, upon*) direct steadily, set (one's eyes, gaze, attention, or affection). **b** attract and hold (a person's attention, eyes, etc.). **c** (foll. by *with*) single out with one's eyes etc. **6** tr. place definitely or permanently, establish, station. **7** tr. determine the exact nature, position, etc., of; refer (a thing or person) to a definite place or time; identify, locate. **8 a** tr. make (eyes, features, etc.) rigid. **b** intr. (of eyes, features, etc.) become rigid. **9** tr. US colloq. prepare (food or drink) (*fixed me a drink*). **10 a** tr. deprive of fluidity or volatility; congeal. **b** intr. lose fluidity or volatility, become congealed. **11** tr. colloq. punish, kill, silence, deal with (a person). **12** *tr. colloq.* **a** secure the support of (a person) fraudulently, esp. by bribery. **b** arrange the result of (a race, match, etc.) fraudulently (*the competition was fixed*). **13** *sl.* **a** *tr.* inject (a person, esp. oneself) with a narcotic. **b** *intr.* take an injection of a narcotic. **14** *tr.* make (a colour, photographic image, or microscope-specimen) fast or permanent. **15** *tr.* (of a plant or micro-organism) assimilate (nitrogen or carbon dioxide) by forming a non-gaseous compound. —*n.* **1** *colloq.* a position hard to escape from; a dilemma or predicament. **2 a** the act of finding one's position by bearings or astronomical observations. **b** a position found in this way. **3** *sl.* a dose of a narcotic drug to which one is addicted. **4** *US sl.* bribery. □ **be fixed** (usu. foll. by *for*) be disposed or affected (regarding) (*how is he fixed for money?*; *how are you fixed for Friday?*). **fixed-doh** *Mus.* applied to a system of sight-singing in which C is called 'doh', D is called 'ray', etc., irrespective of the key in which they occur. **fixed income** income deriving from a pension, investment at fixed interest, etc. **fixed point** *Physics* a well-defined reproducible temperature. **fixed star** *Astron.* a star so far from the earth as to appear motionless. **fix on** (or **upon**) choose, decide on. **fix up 1** arrange, organize, prepare. **2** accommodate. **3** (often foll. by *with*) provide (a person) (*fixed me up with a job*). □ **fixable** *adj.* **fixedly** /ˈfiksɪdlɪ/ *adv.* **fixedness** /ˈfiksɪdnɪs/ *n.* [ME, partly f. obs. *fix* fixed f. OF *fix* or L *fixus* past part. of *figere* fix, fasten, partly f. med.L *fixare* f. *fixus*]

fixate /fikˈseɪt/ *v.tr.* **1** direct one's gaze on. **2** *Psychol.* (usu. in *passive*; often foll. by *on*, *upon*) cause (a person) to acquire an abnormal attachment to persons or things (*was fixated on his son*). [L *fixus* (see FIX) + -ATE³]

fixation /fikˈseɪʃ(ə)n/ *n.* **1** the act or an instance of being fixated. **2** an obsession, concentration on a single idea. **3** fixing or being fixed. **4** the process of rendering solid; coagulation. **5** the process of assimilating a gas to form a solid compound. [ME f. med.L *fixatio* f. *fixare*: see FIX]

fixative /ˈfiksətɪv/ *adj. & n.* —*adj.* tending to fix or secure. —*n.* a substance used to fix colours, hair, microscope-specimens, etc.

fixer /ˈfiksə(r)/ *n.* **1** a person or thing that fixes. **2** *Photog.* a substance used for fixing a photographic image etc. **3** *colloq.* a person who makes arrangements, esp. of an illicit kind.

fixings /ˈfiksɪŋz/ *n.pl. US* **1** apparatus or equipment. **2** the trimmings for a dish. **3** the trimmings of a dress etc.

fixity /ˈfiksɪtɪ/ *n.* **1** a fixed state. **2** stability; permanence. [obs. *fix* fixed: see FIX]

fixture /ˈfikstʃə(r)/ *n.* **1 a** something fixed or fastened in position. **b** (usu. *predic.*) *colloq.* a person or thing confined to or established in one place (*he seems to be a fixture*). **2 a** a sporting event, esp. a match, race, etc. **b** the date agreed for this. **3** (in *pl.*) *Law* articles attached to a house or land and regarded as legally part of it. [alt. of obs. *fixure* f. LL *fixura* f. L *figere fix-* fix]

fizz *v. & n.* —*v.intr.* **1** make a hissing or spluttering sound. **2** (of a drink) make bubbles; effervesce. —*n.* **1** effervescence. **2** *colloq.* an effervescent drink, esp. champagne. [imit.]

fizzle /ˈfiz(ə)l/ *v. & n.* —*v.intr.* make a feeble hissing or spluttering sound. —*n.* such a sound. □ **fizzle out** end feebly. [formed as FIZZ + -LE⁴]

fizzy /ˈfizɪ/ *adj.* (**fizzier**, **fizziest**) effervescent. □ **fizzily** *adv.* **fizziness** *n.*

fjord var. of FIORD.

fl. *abbr.* **1** floor. **2** floruit. **3** fluid.

flab *n. colloq.* fat; flabbiness. [imit., or back-form. f. FLABBY]

flabbergast /ˈflæbəˌɡɑːst/ *v.tr.* (esp. as **flabbergasted** *adj.*) *colloq.* overwhelm with astonishment; dumbfound. [18th c.: perh. f. FLABBY + AGHAST]

flabby /ˈflæbɪ/ *adj.* (**flabbier**, **flabbiest**) **1** (of flesh etc.) hanging down; limp; flaccid. **2** (of language or character) feeble. □ **flabbily** *adv.* **flabbiness** *n.* [alt. of earlier *flappy* f. FLAP]

flaccid /ˈflæksɪd, ˈflæsɪd/ *adj.* **1 a** (of flesh etc.) hanging loose or wrinkled; limp, flabby. **b** (of plant tissue) soft; less rigid. **2** relaxed, drooping. **3** lacking vigour; feeble. □ **flaccidity** /-ˈsɪdɪtɪ/ *n.* **flaccidly** *adv.* [F *flaccide* or L *flaccidus* f. *flaccus* flabby]

flag¹ *n. & v.* —*n.* **1 a** a piece of cloth, usu. oblong or square, attachable by one edge to a pole or rope and used as a country's emblem or as a standard, signal, etc. **b** a small toy, device, etc., resembling a flag. **2** *Brit.* an oblong strip of metal etc. that can be raised or lowered to indicate whether a taxi is for hire or occupied. —*v.* (**flagged**, **flagging**) **1** *intr.* **a** grow tired; lose vigour; lag (*his energy flagged after the first lap*). **b** hang down; droop; become limp. **2** *tr.* **a** place a flag on or over. **b** mark out with or as if with a flag or flags. **3** *tr.* (often foll. by *that*) **a** inform (a person) by flag-signals. **b** communicate (information) by flagging. □ **flag-day** *Brit.* a day on which money is raised for a charity by the sale of small paper flags etc. in the street. **Flag Day** *US* 14 June, the anniversary of the adoption of the Stars and Stripes in 1777. **flag down** signal to (a vehicle or driver) to stop. **flag-lieutenant** *Naut.* an admiral's ADC. **flag of convenience** a foreign flag under which a ship is registered, usu. to avoid financial charges etc. **flag-officer** *Naut.* an admiral, vice admiral, or rear admiral, or the commodore of a yacht-club. **flag of truce** a white flag indicating a desire for a truce. **flag-pole** = FLAGSTAFF. **keep the flag flying** continue the fight. □ **flagger** *n.* [16th c.: perh. f. obs. *flag* drooping]

flag² *n. & v.* —*n.* (also **flagstone**) **1** a flat usu. rectangular stone slab used for paving. **2** (in *pl.*) a pavement made of these. —*v.tr.* (**flagged**, **flagging**) pave with flags. [ME, = sod: cf. Icel. *flag* spot from which a sod has been cut out, ON *flaga* slab of stone, and FLAKE]

flag³ *n.* any plant with a bladed leaf (esp. several of the genus *Iris*) growing on moist ground. [ME: cf. MDu. *flag*, Da. *flæg*]

flagellant /ˈflædʒələnt, fləˈdʒelənt/ *n. & adj.* —*n.* **1** a person who scourges himself or herself or others as a religious discipline. **2** a person who engages in flogging as a sexual stimulus. —*adj.* of or concerning flagellation. [L *flagellare* to whip f. FLAGELLUM]

flagellate¹ /ˈflædʒəˌleɪt/ *v.tr.* scourge, flog (cf. FLAGELLANT). □ **flagellation** /-ˈleɪʃ(ə)n/ *n.* **flagellator** *n.* **flagellatory** /-ˈlətərɪ/ *adj.*

flagellate² /ˈflædʒɪlɪt/ *adj. & n.* —*adj.* having flagella (see FLAGELLUM). —*n.* a protozoan having one or more flagella.

flagellum /fləˈdʒeləm/ *n.* (*pl.* **flagella** /-lə/) **1** *Biol.* a long lashlike appendage found principally on microscopic organisms. 2 *Bot.* a runner; a creeping shoot. □ **flagellar** *adj.* **flagelliform** *adj.* [L, = whip, dimin. of *flagrum* scourge]

flageolet[1] /ˌflædʒəˈlet, ˈflædʒ-/ *n.* a small flute blown at the end, like a recorder but with two thumb-holes. [F, dimin. of OF *flag(e)ol* f. Prov. *flajol*, of unkn. orig.]

flageolet[2] /ˌflædʒəʊˈleɪ, -ˈlet/ *n.* a kind of French kidney bean. [F]

flagon /ˈflægən/ *n.* 1 a large bottle in which wine, cider, etc., are sold, usu. holding 1.13 litres. 2 a large vessel usu. with a handle, spout, and lid, to hold wine etc. [ME *flakon* f. OF *facon* ult. f. LL *flasco -onis* FLASK]

flagrant /ˈfleɪgrənt/ *adj.* (of an offence or an offender) glaring; notorious; scandalous. □ **flagrancy** /-grənsɪ/ *n.* **flagrantly** *adv.* [F *flagrant* or L *flagrant-* part. stem of *flagrare* blaze]

flagship /ˈflægʃɪp/ *n.* 1 a ship having an admiral on board. 2 something that is held to be the best or most important of its kind; a leader.

flagstaff /ˈflægstɑːf/ *n.* a pole on which a flag may be hoisted.

flagstone /ˈflægstəʊn/ *n.* = FLAG[2].

flail *n. & v.* —*n.* a threshing-tool consisting of a wooden staff with a short heavy stick swinging from it. —*v.* 1 *tr.* beat or strike with or as if with a flail. 2 *intr.* wave or swing wildly or erratically. [OE prob. f. L FLAGELLUM]

flair *n.* 1 an instinct for selecting or performing what is excellent, useful, etc.; a talent. 2 talent or ability, esp. artistic or stylistic. [F *flairer* to smell ult. f. L *fragrare*: see FRAGRANT]

flak *n.* (also **flack**) 1 anti-aircraft fire. 2 adverse criticism; abuse. □ **flak jacket** a protective jacket of heavy camouflage fabric reinforced with metal, worn by soldiers etc. [abbr. of G *Fliegerabwehrkanone*, lit. aviator-defence-gun]

flake *n. & v.* —*n.* 1 a a small thin light piece of snow. b a similar piece of another material. 2 a thin broad piece of material peeled or split off. 3 a natural division of the flesh of some fish. 4 the dogfish or other shark as food. 5 esp. *US sl.* a crazy or eccentric person. —*v.tr. & intr.* (often foll. by *away, off*) 1 take off or come away in flakes. 2 sprinkle with or fall in snowlike flakes. □ **flake out** *colloq.* fall asleep or drop from exhaustion; faint. [ME: orig. unkn.: cf. ON *flakna* flake off]

flaky /ˈfleɪkɪ/ *adj.* (**flakier**, **flakiest**) 1 of or like flakes; separating easily into flakes. 2 esp. *US sl.* crazy, eccentric. □ **flakily** *adv.* **flakiness** *n.*

flambé /ˈflɒmbeɪ/ *adj.* (of food) covered with alcohol and set alight briefly. [F, past part. of *flamber* singe f. *flambe* f. L *flammula* dimin. of *flamma* flame]

flamboyant /flæmˈbɔɪənt/ *adj.* 1 ostentatious; showy. 2 floridly decorated. 3 gorgeously coloured. □ **flamboyance** *n.* **flamboyancy** *n.* **flamboyantly** *adv.* [F (in Archit. sense), pres. part. of *flamboyer* f. *flambe*: see FLAMBÉ]

flame *n. & v.* —*n.* 1 a ignited gas (*the fire burnt with a steady flame*). b one portion of this (*the flame flickered and died*). c (usu. in *pl.*) visible combustion (*burst into flames*). 2 a a bright light; brilliant colouring. b a brilliant orange-red colour. 3 a strong passion, esp. love (*fan the flame*). b *colloq.* a boyfriend or girlfriend. —*v.* 1 *intr. & tr.* (often foll. by *away, forth, out, up*) emit or cause to emit flames. 2 *intr.* (often foll. by *out, up*) a (of passion) break out. b (of a person)

become angry. 3 *intr.* shine or glow like flame (*leaves flamed in the autumn sun*). 4 *tr.* subject to the action of flame. □ **flame gun** a device for throwing flames to destroy weeds etc. **flame-proof** (esp. of a fabric) treated so as to be non-flammable. **flame-thrower** (or **-projector**) a weapon for throwing a spray of flame. **go up in flames** be consumed by fire. □ **flameless** *adj.* **flamelike** *adj.* **flamy** *adj.* [ME f. OF *flame, flam(m)e* f. L *flamma*]

flamenco /fləˈmeŋkəʊ/ *n.* (*pl.* **-os**) 1 a style of music played (esp. on the guitar) and sung by Spanish gypsies. 2 a dance performed to this music. [Sp., = Flemish]

flaming /ˈfleɪmɪŋ/ *adj.* 1 emitting flames. 2 very hot (*flaming June*). 3 *colloq.* a passionate; intense (*a flaming row*). b expressing annoyance, or as an intensifier (*that flaming dog*). 4 bright-coloured (*flaming red hair*).

flamingo /fləˈmɪŋgəʊ/ *n.* (*pl.* **-os** or **-oes**) any tall web-footed wading bird of the family Phoenicopteridae, with pink, scarlet, and black plumage. [Port. *flamengo* f. Prov. *flamenc* f. *flama* flame + *-enc* = -ING[3]]

flammable /ˈflæməb(ə)l/ *adj.* inflammable. □ **flammability** /-ˈbɪlɪtɪ/ *n.* [L *flammare* f. *flamma* flame]

■ **Usage** *flammable* is often used because *inflammable* can be mistaken for a negative (the true negative being *non-flammable*).

flan *n.* 1 a pastry case with a savoury or sweet filling. 2 a sponge base with a sweet topping. [F (orig. = round cake) f. OF *flaon* f. med.L *flado -onis* f. Frank.]

flange /flændʒ/ *n. & v. Engin.* —*n.* a projecting flat rim, collar, or rib, used for strengthening or attachment. —*v.tr.* provide with a flange. □ **flangeless** *n.* [17th c.: perh. f. *flange* widen out f. OF *flangir* f. *flanche, flanc* FLANK]

flank *n. & v.* —*n.* 1 a the side of the body between the ribs and the hip. b the side of an animal carved as meat (*flank of beef*). 2 the side of a mountain, building, etc. 3 the right or left side of an army or other body of persons. —*v.tr.* 1 (often in *passive*) be situated at both sides of (*a road flanked by mountains*). 2 *Mil.* guard or strengthen on the flank. [ME f. OF *flanc* f. Frank.]

flannel /ˈflæn(ə)l/ *n. & v.* —*n.* 1 a a kind of woven woollen fabric, usu. without a nap. b (in *pl.*) flannel garments, esp. trousers. 2 *Brit.* a small usu. towelling cloth, used for washing oneself. 3 *Brit. sl.* nonsense; flattery. —*v.* (**flannelled, flannelling**; *US* **flanneled, flanneling**) 1 *Brit. sl.* a *tr.* flatter. b *intr.* use flattery. 2 *tr.* wash or clean with a flannel. □ **flannelly** *adj.* [perh. f. Welsh *gwlanen* f. *gwlân* wool]

flannelette /ˌflænəˈlet/ *n.* a napped cotton fabric imitating flannel. [FLANNEL]

flannelled /ˈflæn(ə)ld/ *adj.* (*US* also **flanneled**) wearing flannel trousers. [FLANNEL]

flap *v. & n.* —*v.* (**flapped, flapping**) 1 a *tr.* move (wings, the arms, etc.) up and down when flying, or as if flying. b *intr.* (of wings, the arms, etc.) move up and down; beat. 2 *intr. colloq.* be agitated or panicky. 3 *intr.* (esp. of curtains, loose cloth, etc.) swing or sway about; flutter. 4 *tr.* (usu. foll. by *away, off*) strike (flies etc.) with something broad; drive. 5 *intr. colloq.* (of ears) listen intently. —*n.* 1 a piece of cloth, wood, paper, etc. hinged or attached by one side only and often used to cover a gap. **2** one up-and-down motion of a wing, an arm, etc. **3** *colloq.* a state of agitation; panic (*don't get into a flap*). **4** a hinged or sliding section of a wing used to control lift; an aileron. **5** a light blow with something broad. **6** an open mushroom-top. □ **flappy** *adj.* [ME, prob. imit.]

flapdoodle /ˈflæpˈduːd(ə)l, ˈflæp-/ *n. colloq.* nonsense. [19th c.: orig. unkn.]

flapjack /ˈflæpdʒæk/ *n.* **1** a cake made from oats and golden syrup etc. **2** *esp. US* a pancake. [FLAP + JACK]

flapper /ˈflæpə(r)/ *n.* **1** a person or thing that flaps. **2** an instrument that is flapped to kill flies, scare birds, etc. **3** a person who panics easily or is easily agitated. **4** *sl.* (in the 1920s) a young unconventional or lively woman.

flare *v. & n.* —*v.* **1** *intr. & tr.* widen or cause to widen gradually towards the top or bottom (*flared trousers*). **2** *intr. & tr.* burn or cause to burn suddenly with a bright unsteady flame. **3** *intr.* burst into anger; burst forth. —*n.* **1 a** a dazzling irregular flame or light, esp. in the open air. **b** a sudden outburst of flame. **2 a** a signal light used at sea. **b** a bright light used as a signal. **c** a flame dropped from an aircraft to illuminate a target etc. **3 a** a gradual widening, esp. of a skirt or trousers. **b** (in *pl.*) wide-bottomed trousers. □ **flare-path** an area illuminated to enable an aircraft to land or take off. **flare up 1** burst into a sudden blaze. **2** become suddenly angry or active. **flare-up** *n.* an outburst of flame, anger, activity, etc. [16th c.: orig. unkn.]

flash *v., n., & adj.* —*v.* **1** *intr. & tr.* emit or reflect or cause to emit or reflect light briefly, suddenly, or intermittently; gleam or cause to gleam. **2** *intr.* break suddenly into flame; give out flame or sparks. **3** *tr.* send or reflect like a sudden flame or blaze (*his eyes flashed fire*). **4** *intr.* **a** burst suddenly into view or perception (*the explanation flashed upon me*). **b** move swiftly (*the train flashed through the station*). **5** *tr.* **a** send (news etc.) by radio, telegraph, etc. (*flashed a message to her*). **b** signal to (a person) by shining lights or headlights briefly. **6** *tr. colloq.* show ostentatiously (*flashed her engagement ring*). **7** *intr. sl.* indecently expose oneself. —*n.* **1** a sudden bright light or flame, e.g. of lightning. **2** a very brief time; an instant (*all over in a flash*). **3 a** a brief, sudden burst of feeling (*a flash of hope*). **b** a sudden display (of wit, understanding, etc.). **4** = NEWSFLASH. **5** *Photog.* = FLASHLIGHT 1. **6** *Brit. Mil.* a coloured patch of cloth on a uniform etc. as a distinguishing emblem. **7** vulgar display, ostentation. **8** a bright patch of colour. —*adj. colloq.* **1** gaudy; showy; vulgar (*a flash car*). **2** connected with thieves, the underworld, etc. □ **flash bulb** *Photog.* a bulb for a flashlight. **flash burn** a burn caused by sudden intense heat, esp. from a nuclear explosion. **flash-cube** *Photog.* a set of four flash bulbs arranged as a cube and operated in turn. **flash-flood** a sudden local flood due to heavy rain etc. **flash-gun** *Photog.* a device used to operate a camera flashlight. **flash in the pan** a promising start followed by failure (from the priming of old guns). **flash-lamp** a portable flashing electric lamp. **flash out** (or **up**) show sudden passion. [ME orig. with ref. to the rushing of water: cf. SPLASH]

flashback /ˈflæʃbæk/ *n. Cinematog.* a scene set in a time earlier than the main action.

flasher /ˈflæʃə(r)/ *n.* **1** *Brit. sl.* a man who indecently exposes himself. **2 a** an automatic device for switching lights rapidly on and off. **b** a sign or signal using this. **3** a person or thing that flashes.

flashing /ˈflæʃɪŋ/ *n.* a usu. metallic strip used to prevent water penetration at the junction of a roof with a wall etc. [dial. *flash* seal with lead sheets or obs. *flash* flashing]

flashlight /ˈflæʃlaɪt/ *n.* **1 a** a light giving an intense flash, used for photographing by night, indoors, etc. **b** a picture so taken. **2** *US* an electric torch.

flashpoint /ˈflæʃpɔɪnt/ *n.* **1** the temperature at which vapour from oil etc. will ignite in air. **2** the point at which anger, indignation, etc. becomes uncontrollable.

flashy /ˈflæʃɪ/ *adj.* (**flashier**, **flashiest**) showy; gaudy; cheaply attractive. □ **flashily** *adv.* **flashiness** *n.*

flask /flɑːsk/ *n.* **1** a narrow-necked bulbous bottle for wine etc. or as used in chemistry. **2** = *hip-flask.* **3** = *vacuum flask.* [F *flasque* & (prob.) It. *fiasco* f. med.L *flasca, flasco*: cf. FLAGON]

flat[1] *adj., adv., n., & v.* —*adj.* (**flatter**, **flattest**) **1 a** horizontally level (*a flat roof*). **b** even; smooth; unbroken; without projection or indentation (*a flat stomach*). **c** with a level surface and little depth; shallow (*a flat cap; a flat heel*). **2** unqualified; plain; downright (*a flat refusal; a flat denial*). **3 a** dull; lifeless; monotonous (*spoke in a flat tone*). **b** without energy; dejected. **4** (of a fizzy drink) having lost its effervescence. **5** (of an accumulator, a battery, etc.) having exhausted its charge. **6** *Mus.* **a** below true or normal pitch (*the violins are flat*). **b** (of a key) having a flat or flats in the signature. **c** (as B, E, etc. **flat**) a semitone lower than B, E, etc. **7** (of a tyre) punctured; deflated. **8** (of a market, prices, etc.) inactive; sluggish. **9** of or relating to flat-racing. —*adv.* **1** lying at full length; spread out, esp. on another surface (*lay flat on the floor; the ladder was flat against the wall*). **2** *colloq.* **a** completely, absolutely (*turned it down flat; flat broke*). **b** exactly (*in five minutes flat*). **3** *Mus.* below the true or normal pitch (*always sings flat*). —*n.* **1** the flat part of anything; something flat (*the flat of the hand*). **2** level ground, esp. a plain or swamp. **3** *Mus.* **a** a note lowered a semitone below natural pitch. **b** the sign (♭) indicating this. **4** (as **the flat**) *Brit.* **a** flat racing. **b** the flat racing season. **5** *Theatr.* a flat section of scenery mounted on a frame. **6** *esp. US colloq.* a flat tyre. —*v.tr.* (**flatted**, **flatting**) **1** make flat, flatten (esp. in technical use). **2** *US Mus.* make (a note) flat. □ **fall flat** fail to live up to expectations; not win applause. **flat-fish** any marine fish of various families having an asymmetric appearance with both eyes on one side of a flattened body, including sole, turbot, plaice, etc. **flat foot** a foot with a less than normal arch. **flat-iron** *hist.* an iron heated externally and used for pressing clothes etc. **flat out 1** at top speed. **2** using all one's strength, energy, or resources. **flat race** a horse race over level ground, as opposed to a steeplechase or hurdles. **flat-racing** the racing of horses in flat races. **flat rate** a rate that is the same in all cases, not proportional. **flat spin 1** *Aeron.* a nearly horizontal spin. **2** *colloq.* a state of agitation or panic. **flat-top 1** US Aeron. sl. an aircraft-carrier. **2** sl. a man's short flat haircut. **that's flat** colloq. let there be no doubt about it. □ **flatly** adv. **flatness** n. **flattish** adj. [ME f. ON flatr f. Gmc]

flat² n. & v. —n. a set of rooms, usu. on one floor, used as a residence. —v.intr. (**flatted**, **flatting**) (often foll. by with) Austral. share a flat with. □ **flatlet** n. [alt. f. obs. flet floor, dwelling f. Gmc (as FLAT¹)]

flat-footed /ˈflætˌfʊtɪd/ adj. **1** having flat feet. **2** colloq. downright, positive. **3** colloq. unprepared; off guard (was caught flat-footed). □ **flat-footedly** adv. **flat-footedness** n.

flatmate /ˈflætmeɪt/ n. Brit. a person in relation to one or more others living in the same flat.

flatten /ˈflæt(ə)n/ v. **1** tr. & intr. make or become flat. **2** tr. colloq. **a** humiliate. **b** knock down. □ **flattener** n.

flatter /ˈflætə(r)/ v.tr. **1** compliment unduly; overpraise. esp. for gain or advantage. **2** (usu. refl.; usu. foll. by that + clause) please, congratulate, or delude (oneself etc.) (I flatter myself that I can sing). **3 a** (of a colour, a style, etc.) make (a person) appear to the best advantage (that blouse flatters you). **b** (esp. of a portrait, a painter, etc.) represent too favourably. **4** gratify the vanity of; make (a person) feel honoured. □ **flatterer** n. **flattering** adj. **flatteringly** adv. [ME, perh. rel. to OF flater to smooth]

flattery /ˈflætərɪ/ n. (pl. **-ies**) **1** exaggerated or insincere praise. **2** the act or an instance of flattering.

flattie /ˈflætɪ/ n. (also **flatty**) (pl. **-ies**) colloq. a flat-heeled shoe.

flatulent /ˈflætjʊlənt/ adj. **1 a** causing formation of gas in the alimentary canal. **b** caused by or suffering from this. **2** (of speech etc.) inflated, pretentious. □ **flatulence** n. **flatulency** n. **flatulently** adv. [F f. mod.L flatulentus (as FLATUS)]

flatus /ˈfleɪtəs/ n. wind in or from the stomach or bowels. [L, = blowing f. flare blow]

flatware /ˈflætweə(r)/ n. **1** plates, saucers, etc. **2** US domestic cutlery.

flatworm /ˈflætwɜːm/ n. any worm of the phylum Platyhelminthes, having a flattened body and no body-cavity or blood vessels.

flaunt v.tr. & intr. **1** (often refl.) display ostentatiously (oneself or one's finery); show off; parade (liked to flaunt his gold cuff-links; flaunted themselves before the crowd). **2** wave or cause to wave proudly (flaunted the banner). □ **flaunter** n. **flaunty** adj. [16th c.: orig. unkn.]

■ **Usage** This word is often confused with flout which means 'to disobey contemptuously'.

flautist /ˈflɔːtɪst/ n. a flute-player. [It. flautista f. flauto FLUTE]

flavorous /ˈfleɪvərəs/ adj. having a pleasant or pungent flavour.

flavour /ˈfleɪvə(r)/ n. & v. (US **flavor**) —n. **1** a distinctive mingled sensation of smell and taste (has a cheesy flavour). **2** an indefinable characteristic quality (music with a romantic flavour). **3** (usu. foll. by of) a slight admixture of a usu. undesirable quality (the flavour of failure hangs over the enterprise). **4** esp. US = FLAVOURING. —v.tr. give flavour to; season. □ **flavour of the month** (or **week**) a temporary trend or fashion. □ **flavourful** adj. **flavourless** adj. **flavoursome** adj. [ME f. OF flaor perh. f. L flatus blowing & foetor stench: assim. to savour]

flavouring /ˈfleɪvərɪŋ/ n. a substance used to flavour food or drink.

flaw¹ n. & v. —n. **1** an imperfection; a blemish (has a character without a flaw). **2** a crack or similar fault (the cup has a flaw). **3** Law an invalidating defect in a legal matter. —v.tr. & intr. crack; damage; spoil. □ **flawless** adj. **flawlessly** adv. **flawlessness** n. [ME perh. f. ON flaga slab f. Gmc: cf. FLAKE, FLAG²]

flaw² n. a squall of wind; a short storm. [prob. f. MDu. vlāghe, MLG vlāge, perh. = stroke]

flax n. **1 a** a blue-flowered plant, Linum usitatissimum, cultivated for its textile fibre and its seeds. **b** a plant resembling this. **2** dressed or undressed flax fibres. □ **flax-seed** linseed. [OE flæx f. WG]

flaxen /ˈflæks(ə)n/ adj. **1** of flax. **2** (of hair) coloured like dressed flax; pale yellow.

flay v.tr. **1** strip the skin or hide off, esp. by beating. **2** criticize severely. **3** peel off (skin, bark, peel, etc.). □ **flayer** n. [OE flēan f. Gmc]

F-layer /ˈefˌleɪə(r)/ n. the highest and most strongly ionized region of the ionosphere. [F (arbitrary) + LAYER]

flea n. a small wingless jumping insect of the order Siphonaptera, feeding on human and other blood. □ **flea-bite 1** the bite of a flea. **2** a trivial injury or inconvenience. **flea-bitten 1** bitten by or infested with fleas. **2** shabby. **flea-circus** a show of performing fleas. **flea-collar** an insecticidal collar for pets. **a flea in one's ear** a sharp reproof. **flea market** a street market selling second-hand goods etc. **flea-pit** a dingy dirty place, esp. a run-down cinema. [OE flēa, flēah f. Gmc]

fleabag /ˈfliːbæg/ n. sl. a shabby or unattractive person or thing.

fleck n. & v. —n. **1** a small patch of colour or light (eyes with green flecks). **2** a small particle or speck, esp. of dust. **3** a spot on the skin; a freckle. —v.tr. mark with flecks; dapple; variegate. [perh. f. ON flekkr (n.), flekka (v.), or MLG, MDu. vlecke, OHG flec, fleccho]

flection US var. of FLEXION.

fled past and past part. of FLEE.

fledge v. **1** intr. (of a bird) grow feathers. **2** tr. provide (an arrow) with feathers. **3** tr. bring up (a young bird) until it can fly. **4** tr. (as **fledged** adj.) **a** able to fly. **b** independent; mature. **5** tr. deck or provide with feathers or down. [obs. fledge (adj.) 'fit to fly', f. OE flycge (recorded in unfligge) f. a Gmc root rel. to FLY¹]

fledgling /ˈfledʒlɪŋ/ n. (also **fledgeling**) **1** a young bird. **2** an inexperienced person. [FLEDGE + -LING¹]

flee v. (past and past part. **fled** /fled/) **1** intr. (often foll. by from, before) **a** run away. **b** seek safety by fleeing. **2** tr. run away from; leave abruptly; shun (fled the room; fled his attentions). **3** intr. vanish; pass away. □ **fleer** /ˈfliːə(r)/ n. [OE flēon f. Gmc]

fleece n. & v. —n. **1 a** the woolly covering of a sheep or a similar animal. **b** the amount of wool sheared from a sheep at one time. **2** something resembling a fleece, esp. a soft warm fabric with a pile, used for lining coats etc. —v.tr. **1** (often foll. by of) strip (a person) of money, valuables, etc.; swindle. **2** remove the fleece from (a sheep etc.); shear. **3** cover as if with a

fleece (*a sky fleeced with clouds*). □ **fleeceable** *adj.*
fleeced *adj.* (also in *comb.*). [OE *flēos, flēs* f. WG]
fleecy /ˈfliːsɪ/ *adj.* (**fleecier, fleeciest**) **1** of or like a fleece. **2** covered with a fleece. □ **fleecily** *adv.* **fleeciness** *n.*
fleet[1] *n.* **1 a** a number of warships under one commander-in-chief. **b** (prec. by *the*) all the warships and merchant-ships of a nation. **2 a** number of ships, aircraft, buses, lorries, taxis, etc. operating together or owned by one proprietor. □ **Fleet Air Arm** *hist.* the aviation service of the Royal Navy. [OE *flēot* ship, shipping f. *flēotan* float, FLEET[4]]
fleet[2] *adj. poet. literary* swift; nimble. □ **fleetly** *adv.* **fleetness** *n.* [prob. f. ON *fljótr* f. Gmc: cf. FLEET[4]]
fleet[3] *n. dial.* **1** a creek; an inlet. **2 (the Fleet) a** an underground stream running into the Thames east of Fleet St. **b** *hist.* a prison that stood near it. □ **Fleet Street 1** the London press. **2** British journalism or journalists. [OE *flēot* f. Gmc: cf. FLEET[4]]
fleet[4] *v.intr. archaic* **1** glide away; vanish; be transitory. **2** (usu. foll. by *away*) (of time) pass rapidly; slip away. **3** move swiftly; fly. [OE *flēotan* float, swim f. Gmc]
fleeting /ˈfliːtɪŋ/ *adj.* transitory; brief. □ **fleetingly** *adv.* [FLEET[4] + -ING[2]]
Fleming /ˈflemɪŋ/ *n.* **1** a native of medieval Flanders in the Low Countries. **2** a member of a Flemish-speaking people inhabiting N. and W. Belgium. [OE f. ON *Flæmingi* & MDu. *Vlāming* f. root of *Vlaanderen* Flanders]
Flemish /ˈflemɪʃ/ *adj. & n.* —*adj.* of or relating to Flanders. —*n.* the language of the Flemings. [MDu. *Vlāmisch* (as FLEMING)]
flesh *n. & v.* —*n.* **1 a** the soft, esp. muscular, substance between the skin and bones of an animal or a human. **b** plumpness; fat (*has put on flesh*). **c** *archaic* meat, esp. excluding poultry, game, and offal. **2** the body as opposed to the mind or the soul, esp. considered as sinful. **3** the pulpy substance of a fruit or a plant. **4 a** the visible surface of the human body with ref. to its colour or appearance. **b** (also **flesh-colour**) a yellowish pink colour. **5** animal or human life. —*v.tr.* embody in flesh. □ **flesh and blood** —*n.* **1** the body or its substance. **2** humankind. **3** human nature, esp. as being fallible. —*adj.* actually living, not imaginary or supernatural. **flesh out** make or become substantial. **flesh tints** flesh-colours as rendered by a painter. **flesh-wound** a wound not reaching a bone or a vital organ. **in the flesh** in bodily form, in person. **lose** (or **put on**) **flesh** grow thinner or fatter. **one flesh** (of two people) intimately united, esp. by virtue of marriage (Gen. 2:24). **one's own flesh and blood** near relatives; descendants. **sins of the flesh** unchastity. **the way of all flesh** experience common to all mankind. □ **fleshless** *adj.* [OE *flæsc* f. Gmc]
fleshly /ˈfleʃlɪ/ *adj.* (**fleshlier, fleshliest**) **1** (of desire etc.) bodily; lascivious; sensual. **2** mortal, not divine. **3** worldly. □ **fleshliness** *n.* [OE *flæsclic* (as FLESH)]
fleshpots /ˈfleʃpɒts/ *n.pl.* luxurious living (Exod. 16:3).
fleshy /ˈfleʃɪ/ *adj.* (**fleshier, fleshiest**) **1** plump, fat. **2** of flesh, without bone. **3** (of plant or fruit tissue) pulpy. **4** like flesh. □ **fleshiness** *n.*

fleur-de-lis /ˌflɜː.dəˈliː/ *n.* (also **fleur-de-lys**) (*pl.* **fleurs-** *pronunc.* same) **1** the iris flower. **2** *Heraldry* **a** a lily composed of three petals bound together near their bases. **b** the former royal arms of France. [ME f. OF *flour de lys* flower of lily]
flew *past* of FLY[1].
flex[1] *v.* **1** *tr. & intr.* bend (a joint, limb, etc.) or be bent. **2** *tr. & intr.* move (a muscle) or (of a muscle) be moved to a joint. [L *flectere flex-bend*]
flex[2] *n. Brit.* a flexible insulated cable used for carrying electric current to an appliance. [abbr. of FLEXIBLE]
flexible /ˈfleksɪb(ə)l/ *adj.* **1** able to bend without breaking; pliable; pliant. **2** easily led; manageable; docile. **3** adaptable; versatile; variable (*works flexible hours*). □ **flexibility** /-ˈbɪlɪtɪ/ *n.* **flexibly** *adv.* [ME f. OF *flexible* or L *flexibilis* (as FLEX[1])]
flexion /ˈflekʃ(ə)n/ *n.* (US **flection**) **1** the act of bending or the condition of being bent, esp. of a limb or joint. **2** a bent part; a curve. [L *flexio* (as FLEX[1])]
flexitime /ˈfleksɪˌtaɪm/ *n. Brit.* **1** a system of working a set number of hours with the starting and finishing times chosen within agreed limits by the employee. **2** the hours worked in this way. [FLEXIBLE + TIME]
flexor /ˈfleksə(r)/ *n.* (in full **flexor muscle**) a muscle that bends part of the body. [mod.L (as FLEX[1])]
flibbertigibbet /ˌflɪbətɪˈdʒɪbɪt, ˈflɪb-/ *n.* a gossiping, frivolous, or restless person. [imit. of chatter]
flick *n. & v.* —*n.* **1 a** a light, sharp, quickly retracted blow with a whip etc. **b** the sudden release of a bent finger or thumb, esp. to propel a small object. **2** a sudden movement or jerk. **3** a quick turn of the wrist in playing games, esp. in throwing or striking a ball. **4** a slight, sharp sound. **5** *Brit. colloq.* **a** a cinema film. **b** (in *pl.*; prec. by *the*) the cinema. —*v.* **1** *tr.* (often foll. by *away, off*) strike or move with a flick (*flicked the ash off his cigar*). **2** *tr.* give a flick with (a whip, towel, etc.). **3** *intr.* make a flicking movement or sound. □ **flick-knife** a weapon with a blade that springs out from the handle when a button is pressed. **flick through 1** turn over (cards, pages, etc.). **2 a** turn over the pages etc. of, by a rapid movement of the fingers. **b** look cursorily through (a book etc.). [ME, imit.]
flicker /ˈflɪkə(r)/ *v. & n.* —*v.intr.* **1** (of light) shine unsteadily or fitfully. **2** (of a flame) burn unsteadily, alternately flaring and dying down. **3 a** (of a flag, a reptile's tongue, an eyelid, etc.) move or wave to and fro; quiver; vibrate. **b** (of the wind) blow lightly and unsteadily. **4** (of hope etc.) increase and decrease unsteadily and intermittently. —*n.* a flickering movement or light. □ **flicker out** die away after a final flicker. [OE *flicorian, flycerian*]
flier var. of FLYER.
flight[1] /flaɪt/ *n.* **1 a** the act or manner of flying through the air (*studied swallows' flight*). **b** the swift movement or passage of a projectile etc. through the air (*the flight of an arrow*). **2 a** a journey made through the air or in space. **b** a timetabled journey made by an airline. **c** an RAF unit of about six aircraft. **3 a** a flock or large body of birds, insects, etc., esp. when

migrating. **b** a migration. **4** (usu. foll. by *of*) a series, esp. of stairs between floors, or of hurdles across a race track (*lives up six flights*). **5** an extravagant soaring, a mental or verbal excursion or sally (of wit etc.) (*a flight of fancy*). **6** the trajectory and pace of a ball in games. **7** the distance that a bird, aircraft, or missile can fly. **8** (usu. foll. by *of*) a volley (*a flight of arrows*). **9** the tail of a dart. □ **flight bag** a small, zipped, shoulder bag carried by air travellers. **flight control** an internal or external system directing the movement of aircraft. **flight-deck 1** the deck of an aircraft-carrier used for take-off and landing. **2** the accommodation for the pilot, navigator, etc. in an aircraft. **flight lieutenant** an RAF officer next in rank below squadron leader. **flight officer** a rank in the WRAF, corresponding to flight lieutenant. **flight path** the planned course of an aircraft or spacecraft. **flight-recorder** a device in an aircraft to record technical details during a flight, that may be used in the event of an accident to discover its cause. **flight sergeant** *Mil.* an RAF rank next above sergeant. **in the first** (or **top**) **flight** taking a leading place. [OE *flyht* f. WG: rel to FLY¹]

flight² /flaɪt/ *n.* **1** the act or manner of fleeing. **2** a hasty retreat. □ **put to flight** cause to flee. **take** (or **take to**) **flight** flee. [OE f. Gmc: rel. to FLEE]

flightless /ˈflaɪtlɪs/ *adj.* (of a bird etc.) naturally unable to fly.

flighty /ˈflaɪtɪ/ *adj.* (**flightier, flightiest**) **1** (usu. of a girl) frivolous, fickle, changeable. **2** crazy. □ **flightily** *adv.* **flightiness** *n.* [FLIGHT¹ + -Y¹]

flimflam /ˈflɪmflæm/ *n.* & *v.* —*n.* **1** a trifle; nonsense; idle talk. **2** humbug; deception. —*v.tr.* (**flimflammed, flimflamming**) cheat; deceive. □ **flimflammer** *n.* **flimflammery** *n.* (*pl.* **-ies**). [imit. redupl.]

flimsy /ˈflɪmzɪ/ *adj.* & *n.* —*adj.* (**flimsier, flimsiest**) **1** lightly or carelessly assembled; insubstantial, easily damaged (*a flimsy structure*). **2** (of an excuse etc.) unconvincing (*a flimsy pretext*). **3** paltry; trivial; superficial (*a flimsy play*). **4** (of clothing) thin (*a flimsy blouse*). —*n.* (*pl.* **-ies**) **1 a** very thin paper. **b** a document, esp. a copy, made on this. **2** a flimsy thing, esp. women's underwear. □ **flimsily** *adv.* **flimsiness** *n.* [17th c.: prob. f. FLIMFLAM: cf. TIPSY]

flinch /flɪntʃ/ *v.* & *n.* —*v.intr.* **1** draw back in pain or expectation of a blow etc.; wince. **2** (often foll. by *from*) give way; shrink, turn aside (*flinched from his duty*). —*n.* an act or instance of flinching. □ **flincher** *n.* **flinchingly** *adv.* [OF *flenchir, flainchir* f. WG]

fling *v.* & *n.* —*v.* (*past* and *past part.* **flung** /flʌŋ/) **1** *tr.* throw or hurl (an object) forcefully. **2** *refl.* **a** (usu. foll. by *into*) rush headlong (into a person's arms, a train, etc.). **b** (usu. foll. by *into*) embark wholeheartedly (on an enterprise). **3** *tr.* utter (words) forcefully. **4** *tr.* (usu. foll. by *out*) suddenly spread (the arms). **5** *tr.* (foll. by *on, off*) put on or take off (clothes) carelessly or rapidly. **6** *intr.* go angrily or violently; rush (*flung out of the room*). **7** *tr.* put or send suddenly or violently (*was flung into jail*). **8** *tr.* (foll. by *away*) discard or put aside thoughtlessly or rashly (*flung away their reputation*). —*n.* **1** an act or instance of flinging; a throw; a plunge. **2** a spell of indulgence or wild behaviour (*he's had his fling*). **3** an impetuous,

whirling Scottish dance, esp. the Highland fling. □ **have a fling at** make an attempt at. □ **flinger** *n.* [ME, perh. f. ON]

flint *n.* **1 a** a hard grey stone of nearly pure silica occurring naturally as nodules or bands in chalk. **b** a piece of this esp. as flaked or ground to form a primitive tool or weapon. **2** a piece of hard alloy of rare-earth metals used to give an igniting spark in a cigarette-lighter etc. **3** a piece of flint used with steel to produce fire, esp. in a flintlock gun. **4** anything hard and unyielding. □ **flinty** *adj.* (**flintier, flintiest**). **flintily** *adv.* **flintiness** *n.* [OE]

flintlock /ˈflɪntlɒk/ *n. hist.* **1** an old type of gun fired by a spark from a flint. **2** the lock producing such a spark.

flip¹ *v., n.,* & *adj.* —*v.* (**flipped, flipping**) **1** *tr.* **a** flick or toss (a coin, pellet, etc.) with a quick movement so that it spins in the air. **b** remove (a small object) from a surface with a flick of the fingers. **2** *tr.* **a** strike or flick (a person's ear, cheek, etc.) lightly or smartly. **b** move (a fan, whip, etc.) with a sudden jerk. **3** *tr.* turn (a small object) over. **4** *intr.* **a** make a fillip or flicking noise with the fingers. **b** (foll. by *at*) strike smartly at. **5** *intr. sl.* become suddenly excited or enthusiastic. —*n.* **1** a smart light blow; a flick. **2** *colloq.* **a** a short pleasure flight in an aircraft. **b** a quick tour etc. **3** an act of flipping over (*gave the stone a flip*). —*adj. colloq.* glib; flippant. □ **flip chart** a large pad erected on a stand and bound so that one page can be turned over at the top to reveal the next. **flip one's lid** *sl.* **1** lose self-control. **2** go mad. **flip side** *colloq.* the less important side of a gramophone record. **flip through** = *flick through.* [prob. f. FILLIP]

flip² *n.* **1** a drink of heated beer and spirit. **2** = *egg-flip.* [perh. f. FLIP¹ in the sense *whip up*]

flip-flop /ˈflɪpflɒp/ *n.* & *v.* —*n.* **1** a usu. rubber sandal with a thong between the big and second toe. **2** an electronic switching circuit changed from one stable state to another, by a triggering pulse. —*v.intr.* (**-flopped, -flopping**) move with a sound or motion suggested by 'flip-flop'. [imit.]

flippant /ˈflɪpənt/ *adj.* lacking in seriousness; treating serious things lightly; disrespectful. □ **flippancy** *n.* **flippantly** *adv.* [FLIP¹ + -ANT]

flipper /ˈflɪpə(r)/ *n.* **1** a broadened limb of a turtle, penguin, etc., used in swimming. **2** a flat rubber etc. attachment worn on the foot for underwater swimming.

flipping /ˈflɪpɪŋ/ *adj.* & *adv. Brit. sl.* expressing annoyance, or as an intensifier (*where's the flipping towel?; he flipping beat me*). [FLIP¹ + -ING²]

flirt *v.* & *n.* —*v.* **1** *intr.* (usu. foll. by *with*) behave in a frivolously amorous or sexually enticing manner. **2** *intr.* (usu. foll. by *with*) **a** superficially interest oneself (with an idea etc.). **b** trifle (with danger etc.) (*flirted with disgrace*). —*n.* a person who indulges in flirting. □ **flirtation** /-ˈteɪʃ(ə)n/ *n.* **flirtatious** /-ˈteɪʃəs/ *adj.* **flirtatiously** /-ˈteɪʃəslɪ/ *adv.* **flirtatiousness** /-ˈteɪʃəsnɪs/ *n.* **flirty** *adj.* (**flirtier, flirtiest**). [imit.]

flit *v.* & *n.* —*v.intr.* (**flitted, flitting**) **1** move lightly, softly, or rapidly (*flitted from one room to another*). **2** fly lightly; make short flights (*flitted from branch to branch*). **3** *Brit. colloq.* leave one's house etc. secretly to escape creditors or obligations. **4** esp. *Sc.* & *N.Engl.* change one's home; move. —*n.* **1** an act of flitting. **2** (also **moonlight flit**) a secret change of abode in order to escape creditors etc. □ **flitter** *n*. [ME f. ON *flytja*: rel. to FLEET⁴]

flitch *n*. a side of bacon. [OE *flicce* f. Gmc]

flitter /ˈflɪtə(r)/ *v.intr*. flit about; flutter. □ **flitter-mouse** = BAT². [FLIT + -ER⁴]

float *v*. & *n*. —*v*. **1** *intr*. & *tr*. **a** rest at or move or cause (a buoyant object) to rest or move on the surface of a liquid without sinking. **b** get afloat or set (a stranded ship) afloat. **2** *intr*. move with a liquid or current of air; drift (*the clouds floated high up*). **3** *intr*. *colloq*. **a** move in a leisurely or casual way (*floated about humming quietly*). **b** (often foll. by *before*) hover before the eye or mind (*the prospect of lunch floated before them*). **4** *intr*. (often foll. by *in*) move or be suspended freely in a liquid or a gas. **5** *tr*. **a** bring (a company, scheme, etc.) into being; launch. **b** offer (stock, shares, etc.) on the stock market. **6** *Commerce* **a** *intr*. (of currency) be allowed to have a fluctuating exchange rate. **b** *tr*. cause (currency) to float. **7** *intr*. & *tr*. circulate or cause (a rumour or idea) to circulate. —*n*. **1** a thing that floats, esp.: **a** a raft. **b** a cork or quill on a fishing-line as an indicator of a fish biting. **c** a cork supporting the edge of a fishing-net. **d** the hollow or inflated part or organ supporting a fish etc. in the water; an air bladder. **e** a hollow structure fixed underneath an aircraft enabling it to float on water. **f** a floating device on the surface of water, petrol, etc., controlling the flow. **2** a small vehicle or cart, esp. one powered by electricity (*milk float*). **3** a platform mounted on a lorry and carrying a display in a procession etc. **4 a** a sum of money used at the beginning of a period of selling in a shop, a fête, etc. to provide change. **b** a small sum of money for minor expenditure; petty cash. **5** *Theatr*. (in *sing*. or *pl*.) footlights. **6** a tool used for smoothing plaster. □ **floatable** *adj*. **floatability** /-ˈbɪlɪtɪ/ *n*. [OE *flot, flotian* float, OE *flota* ship, ON *flota, floti* rel. to FLEET⁴: in ME infl. by OF *floter*]

floatation var. of FLOTATION.

floater /ˈfləʊtə(r)/ *n*. **1** a person or thing that floats. **2** a floating voter. **3** *sl*. a mistake; a gaffe.

floating /ˈfləʊtɪŋ/ *adj*. not settled in a definite place; fluctuating; variable (*the floating population*). □ **floating bridge 1** a bridge on pontoons etc. **2** a ferry working on chains. **floating dock** a floating structure usable as a dry dock. **floating kidney 1** an abnormal condition in which the kidneys are unusually movable. **2** such a kidney. **floating point** *Computing* a decimal etc. point that does not occupy a fixed position in the numbers processed. **floating rib** any of the lower ribs, which are not attached to the breastbone. **floating voter** a voter without allegiance to any political party. □ **floatingly** *adv*.

floaty /ˈfləʊtɪ/ *adj*. (esp. of a woman's garment or a fabric) light and airy. [FLOAT]

flocculent /ˈflɒkjʊlənt/ *adj*. **1** like tufts of wool. **2** consisting of or showing tufts, downy. □ **flocculence** *n*. [L *floccus* FLOCK²]

flock¹ *n*. & *v*. —*n*. **1 a** a number of animals of one kind, esp. birds, feeding or travelling together. **b** a number of domestic animals, esp. sheep, goats, or geese, kept together. **2** a large crowd of people. **3 a** a Christian congregation or body of believers, esp. in relation to one minister. **b** a family of children, a number of pupils, etc. —*v.intr*. **1** congregate; mass. **2** (usu.

foll. by *to, in, out, together*) go together in a crowd. [OE *flocc*]

flock² *n*. **1** a lock or tuft of wool, cotton, etc. **2 a** (also in *pl*.; often *attrib*.) material for quilting and stuffing made of wool-refuse or torn-up cloth (*a flock pillow*). **b** powdered wool or cloth. □ **flock-paper** (or **-wallpaper**) wallpaper sized and sprinkled with powdered wool to make a raised pattern. □ **flocky** *adj*. [ME f. OF *floc* f. L *floccus*]

floe *n*. a sheet of floating ice. [prob. f. Norw. *flo* f. ON *fló* layer]

flog *v*. (**flogged, flogging**) **1** *tr*. **a** beat with a whip, stick, etc. (as a punishment or to urge on). **b** make work through violent effort (*flogged the engine*). **2** *tr*. *Brit*. *sl*. sell. **3** *intr*. & *refl*. *sl*. proceed by violent or painful effort. □ **flog a dead horse** waste energy on something unalterable. **flog to death** *colloq*. talk about or promote at tedious length. □ **flogger** *n*. [17th-c. cant: prob. imit. or f. L *flagellare* to whip]

flood /flʌd/ *n*. & *v*. —*n*. **1 a** an overflowing or influx of water beyond its normal confines, esp. over land; an inundation. **b** the water that overflows. **2 a** an outpouring of water; a torrent (*a flood of rain*). **b** something resembling a torrent (*a flood of tears; a flood of relief*). **3** the inflow of the tide (also in *comb*.: flood-tide). **4** *colloq*. a floodlight. —*v*. **1** *tr*. **a** cover with or overflow in a flood (*rain flooded the cellar*). **b** overflow as if with a flood (*the market was flooded with foreign goods*). **2** *tr*. irrigate (*flooded the paddy fields*). **3** *tr*. deluge (a burning house, a mine, etc.) with water. **4** *intr*. (often foll. by *in, through*) arrive in great quantities (*complaints flooded in; fear flooded through them*). **5** *intr*. become inundated (*the bathroom flooded*). **6** *tr*. overfill (a carburettor) with petrol. **7** *intr*. experience a uterine haemorrhage. **8** *tr*. (of rain etc.) fill (a river) to overflowing. □ **flood out** drive out (of one's home etc.) with a flood. **flood-tide** the periodical exceptional rise of the tide because of lunar or solar attraction. [OE *flōd* f. Gmc]

floodgate /ˈflʌdgeɪt/ *n*. **1** a gate opened or closed to admit or exclude water, esp. the lower gate of a lock. **2** (usu. in *pl*.) a last restraint holding back tears, rain, anger, etc.

floodlight /ˈflʌdlaɪt/ *n*. & *v*. —*n*. **1** a large powerful light (usu. one of several) to illuminate a building, sportsground, stage, etc. **2** the illumination so provided. —*v.tr*. illuminate with floodlight.

floor /flɔː(r)/ *n*. & *v*. —*n*. **1 a** the lower surface of a room. **b** the boards etc. of which it is made. **2 a** the bottom of the sea, a cave, a cavity, etc. **b** any level area. **3** all the rooms etc. on the same level of a building; a storey (*lives on the ground floor; walked up to the sixth floor*). **4 a** (in a legislative assembly) the part of the house in which members sit and from which they speak. **b** the right to speak next in debate (*gave him the floor*). **5** *Stock Exch*. the large central hall where trading takes place. **6** the minimum of prices, wages, etc. **7** *colloq*. the ground. —*v.tr*. **1** furnish with a floor; pave. **2** bring to the ground; knock (a person) down. **3** *colloq*. confound; baffle. **4** *colloq*. get the better of; overcome. **5** serve as the floor of. □ **first** (*US* **second**) **floor** the floor above the ground floor. **floor show** an entertainment presented on the floor (as opposed to the stage) of a nightclub etc. **take the floor 1** begin to dance on a dance-floor etc. **2** speak in a debate. □ **floorless** *adj*. [OE *flōr* f. Gmc]

floorboard /'flɔːbɔːd/ *n*. a long wooden board used for flooring.

floorcloth /'flɔːklɒθ/ *n*. a cloth for washing the floor.

flooring /'flɔːrɪŋ/ *n*. the boards etc. of which a floor is made.

floozie /'fluːzɪ/ *n*. (also **floozy**) (*pl*. **-ies**) *colloq*. a girl or a woman, esp. a disreputable one. [20th c.: cf. FLOSSY and dial. *floosy* fluffy]

flop *v.*, *n.*, & *adv.* —*v.intr.* (**flopped**, **flopping**) **1** sway about heavily or loosely (*hair flopped over his face*). **2** move in an ungainly way (*flopped along the beach in flippers*). **3** (often foll. by *down*, *on*, *into*) sit, kneel, lie, or fall awkwardly or suddenly (*flopped down on to the bench*). **4** *sl.* (esp. of a play, film, book, etc.) fail; collapse (*flopped on Broadway*). **5** make a dull sound as of a soft body landing, or of a flat thing slapping water. —*n.* **1 a** a flopping movement. **b** the sound made by it. **2** *sl.* a failure. —*adv.* with a flop. □ **flop-house** *sl.* esp. *US* a doss-house. [var. of FLAP]

floppy /'flɒpɪ/ *adj.* & *n.* —*adj.* (**floppier**, **floppiest**) tending to flop; not firm or rigid. —*n.* (*pl.* **-ies**) (in full **floppy disk**) *Computing* a flexible removable magnetic disc for the storage of data. □ **floppily** *adv.* **floppiness** *n.*

flora /'flɔːrə/ *n.* (*pl.* **floras** or **florae** /-riː/) the plants of a particular region, geological period, or environment. [mod.L f. the name of the goddess of flowers f. L *flos floris* flower]

floral /'flɔːr(ə)l, 'flɒ-/ *adj.* **1** of flowers. **2** decorated with or depicting flowers. □ **florally** *adv.* [L *floralis* or *flos floris* flower]

Florentine /'flɒrən,taɪn/ *adj.* & *n.* —*adj.* **1** of or relating to Florence in Italy. **2** (**florentine** /-,tiːn/) (of a dish) served on a bed of spinach. —*n.* a native or citizen of Florence. [F *Florentin -ine* or L *Florentinus* f. *Florentia* Florence]

florescence /flɔː'res(ə)ns, flɒ-/ *n.* the process, state, or time of flowering. [mod.L *florescentia* f. L *florescere* f. *florēre* bloom]

floret /'flɒrɪt, 'flɔː-/ *n. Bot.* **1** each of the small flowers making up a composite flower-head. **2** each of the flowering stems making up a head of cauliflower, broccoli, etc. **3** a small flower. [L *flos floris* flower]

floribunda /,flɒrɪ'bʌndə, ,flɔː-/ *n.* a plant, esp. a rose, bearing dense clusters of flowers. [mod.L f. *floribundus* freely flowering f. L *flos floris* flower, infl. by L *abundus* copious]

florid /'flɒrɪd/ *adj.* **1** ruddy; flushed; high-coloured (*a florid complexion*). **2** (of a book, a picture, music, architecture, etc.) elaborately ornate; ostentatious; showy. **3** adorned with or as with flowers; flowery. □ **floridity** /-'rɪdɪtɪ/ *n.* **floridly** *adv.* **floridness** *n.* [F *floride* or L *floridus* f. *flos floris* flower]

florin /'flɒrɪn/ *n. hist.* **1 a** a British silver or alloy two-shilling coin of the 19th–20th c. (now worth 10 pence at face value). **b** an English gold coin of the 14th c., worth 6s. 8d. (33 pence). **2** a foreign coin of gold or silver, esp. a Dutch guilder. [ME f. OF f. It. *fiorino* dimin. of *fiore* flower f. L *flos floris*, the orig. coin having a figure of a lily on it]

florist /'flɒrɪst/ *n.* a person who deals in or grows flowers. □ **floristry** *n.* [L *flos floris* flower + -IST]

floruit /'flɒruɪt, 'flɔː-/ *v.* & *n.* —*v.intr.* (he or she) was alive and working; flourished (used of a person, esp. a painter, a writer, etc., whose exact dates are unknown). —*n.* the period or date at which a person lived or worked. [L, = he or she flourished]

floss *n.* & *v.* —*n.* **1** the rough silk enveloping a silkworm's cocoon. **2** untwisted silk thread used in embroidery. **3** = *dental floss*. —*v.tr.* (also *absol.*) clean (the teeth) with dental floss. □ **floss silk** a rough silk used in cheap goods. [F (*soie*) *floche* floss(-silk) f. OF *flosche* down, nap of velvet]

flossy /'flɒsɪ/ *adj.* (**flossier**, **flossiest**) **1** of or like floss. **2** *colloq.* fancy, showy.

flotation /fləʊ'teɪʃ(ə)n/ *n.* (also **floatation**) the process of launching or financing a commercial enterprise. [alt. of *floatation* f. FLOAT, after *rotation* etc.]

flotilla /flə'tɪlə/ *n.* **1** a small fleet. **2** a fleet of boats or small ships. [Sp., dimin. of *flota* fleet, OF *flote* multitude]

flotsam /'flɒtsəm/ *n.* wreckage found floating. □ **flotsam and jetsam 1** odds and ends; rubbish. **2** vagrants etc. [AF *floteson* f. *floter* FLOAT]

flounce[1] *v.* & *n.* —*v.intr.* (often foll. by *away*, *about*, *off*, *out*) go or move with an agitated, violent, or impatient motion (*flounced out in a huff*). —*n.* a flouncing movement. [16th c.: orig. unkn.: perh. imit., as *bounce*, *pounce*]

flounce[2] *n.* & *v.* —*n.* a wide ornamental strip of material gathered and sewn to a skirt, dress, etc.; a frill. —*v.tr.* trim with a flounce or flounces. [alt. of earlier *frounce* fold, pleat, f. OF *fronce* f. *froncir* wrinkle]

flounder[1] /'flaʊndə(r)/ *v.* & *n.* —*v.intr.* **1** struggle in mud, or as if in mud, or when wading. **2** perform a task badly or without knowledge; be out of one's depth. —*n.* an act of floundering. □ **flounderer** *n.* [imit.: perh. assoc. with *founder*, *blunder*]

flounder[2] /'flaʊndə(r)/ *n.* **1** an edible flat-fish, *Pleuronectes flesus*, native to European shores. **2** any of various flat-fish native to N. American shores. [ME f. AF *floundre*, OF *flondre*, prob. of Scand. orig.]

flour /'flaʊə(r)/ *n.* & *v.* —*n.* **1** a meal or powder obtained by grinding and usu. sifting cereals, esp. wheat. **2** any fine powder. —*v.tr.* **1** sprinkle with flour. **2** *US* grind into flour. □ **floury** *adj.* (**flourier**, **flouriest**). **flouriness** *n.* [ME, different. spelling of FLOWER in the sense 'finest part']

flourish /'flʌrɪʃ/ *v.* & *n.* —*v.* **1** *intr.* **a** grow vigorously; thrive. **b** prosper; be successful. **c** be in one's prime. **d** be in good health. **2** *intr.* (usu. foll. by *in*, *at*, *about*) spend one's life; be active (at a specified time) (*flourished in the Middle Ages*). **3** *tr.* show ostentatiously (*flourished his cheque-book*). **4** *tr.* wave (a weapon, one's limbs, etc.) vigorously. —*n.* **1** an ostentatious gesture with a weapon, a hand, etc. (*removed his hat with a flourish*). **2** an ornamental curving decoration of handwriting. **3** a florid verbal expression; a rhetorical embellishment. **4** *Mus.* **a** a fanfare played by brass instruments. **b** an ornate musical passage. □ **flourisher** *n.* **flourishy** *adj.* [ME f. OF *florir* ult. f. L *florēre* f. *flos floris* flower]

flout *v.* & *n.* —*v.* *tr.* express contempt for (the law, rules, etc.) by word or action; mock; insult (*flouted convention by shaving her head*). —*n.* a flouting speech or act. [perh. f. Du. *fluiten* whistle, hiss: cf. FLUTE]

■ **Usage** This word is often confused with *flaunt* which means 'to display proudly, show off'.

flow /fləʊ/ v. & n. —v.intr. **1** glide along as a stream (*the Thames flows under London Bridge*). **2 a** (of a liquid, esp. water) gush out; spring. **b** (of blood, liquid, etc.) be spilt. **3** (of blood, money, electric current, etc.) circulate. **4** (of people or things) come or go in large numbers or smoothly (*traffic flowed down the hill*). **5** (of talk, literary style, etc.) proceed easily and smoothly. **6** (of a garment, hair, etc.) hang easily or gracefully; undulate. **7** (often foll. by *from*) result from; be caused by (*his failure flows from his diffidence*). **8** (esp. of the tide) be in flood; run full. **9** (of wine) be poured out copiously. **10** (foll. by *with*) archaic be plentifully supplied with (*land flowing with milk and honey*). —n. **1 a** a flowing movement in a stream. **b** the manner in which a thing flows (*a sluggish flow*). **c** a flowing liquid (*couldn't stop the flow*). **d** a copious outpouring; a stream (*a continuous flow of complaints*). **2** the rise of a tide or a river (*ebb and flow*). □ **flow chart** (or **diagram** or **sheet**) **1** a diagram of the movement or action of things or persons engaged in a complex activity. **2** a graphical representation of a computer program in relation to its sequence of functions. [OE *flōwan* f. Gmc, rel. to FLOOD]

flower /ˈflaʊə(r)/ n. & v. —n. **1** the part of a plant from which the fruit or seed is developed. **2** the reproductive organ in a plant containing one or more pistils or stamens or both, and usu. a corolla and calyx. **3** a blossom, esp. on a stem and used in bunches for decoration. **4** a plant cultivated or noted for its flowers. **5** (in *pl.*) ornamental phrases (*flowers of speech*). —v. **1** intr. (of a plant) produce flowers; bloom or blossom. **2** intr. reach a peak. **3** tr. cause or allow (a plant) to flower. **4** tr. decorate with worked flowers or a floral design. □ **flower-bed** a garden bed in which flowers are grown. **the flower of** the best or best part of. **flowers of sulphur** *Chem.* a fine powder produced when sulphur evaporates and condenses. **in flower** with the flowers out. □ **flowered** adj. (also in *comb.*). **flowerless** adj. **flowerlike** adj. [ME f. AF *flur*, OF *flour*, *flor*, f. L *flos floris*]

flowering /ˈflaʊərɪŋ/ adj. (of a plant) capable of producing flowers.

flowerpot /ˈflaʊəˌpɒt/ n. a pot in which a plant may be grown.

flowery /ˈflaʊərɪ/ adj. **1** decorated with flowers or floral designs. **2** (of literary style, manner of speech, etc.) high-flown; ornate. **3** full of flowers (*a flowery meadow*). □ **floweriness** n.

flowing /ˈfləʊɪŋ/ adj. **1** (of literary style etc.) fluent; easy. **2** (of a line, a curve, or a contour) smoothly continuous, not abrupt. **3** (of hair, a garment, a sail, etc.) unconfined. □ **flowingly** adv.

flown past part. of FLY¹.

Flt. Lt. abbr. Flight Lieutenant.

Flt. Off. abbr. Flight Officer.

Flt. Sgt. abbr. Flight Sergeant.

flu /fluː/ n. colloq. influenza. [abbr.]

fluctuate /ˈflʌktjʊˌeɪt/ v.intr. vary irregularly; be unstable, vacillate; rise and fall, move to and fro. □ **fluctuation** /-ˈeɪʃ(ə)n/ n. [L *fluctuare* f. *fluctus* flow, wave f. *fluere fluct-* flow]

flue /fluː/ n. **1** a smoke-duct in a chimney. **2** a channel for conveying heat, esp. a hot-air passage in a wall; a tube for heating water in some kinds of boiler. [16th c.: orig. unkn.]

fluence /ˈfluːəns/ n. colloq. influence. □ **put the fluence on** apply hypnotic etc. power to (a person). [shortening of INFLUENCE]

fluency /ˈfluːənsɪ/ n. **1** a smooth, easy flow, esp. in speech or writing. **2** a ready command of words or of a specified foreign language.

fluent /ˈfluːənt/ adj. **1 a** (of speech or literary style) flowing naturally and readily. **b** having command of a foreign language (*is fluent in German*). **c** able to speak quickly and easily. **2** flowing easily or gracefully (*the fluent line of her arabesque*). □ **fluently** adv. [L *fluere* flow]

fluff n. & v. —n. **1** soft, light, feathery material coming off blankets etc. **2** soft fur or feathers. **3** sl. **a** a mistake in delivering theatrical lines, in playing music, etc. **b** a mistake in playing a game. —v. **1** tr. & intr. (often foll. by *up*) shake into or become a soft mass. **2** tr. & intr. colloq. make a mistake in (a theatrical part, a game, playing music, a speech, etc.); blunder (*fluffed his opening line*). [prob. dial. alt. of *flue* fluff]

fluffy /ˈflʌfɪ/ adj. (**fluffier**, **fluffiest**) **1** of or like fluff. **2** covered in fluff; downy. □ **fluffily** adv. **fluffiness** n.

flugelhorn /ˈfluːg(ə)lˌhɔːn/ n. a valved brass wind instrument like a cornet but with a broader tone. [G *Flügelhorn* f. *Flügel* wing + *Horn* horn]

fluid /ˈfluːɪd/ n. & adj. —n. **1** a substance, esp. a gas or liquid, lacking definite shape and capable of flowing and yielding to the slightest pressure. **2** a fluid part or secretion. —adj. **1** able to flow and alter shape freely. **2** constantly changing or fluctuating (*the situation is fluid*). □ **fluidify** /-ˈɪdɪˌfaɪ/ v.tr. (**-ies**, **-ied**). **fluidity** /-ˈɪdɪtɪ/ n. **fluidly** adv. **fluidness** n. [F *fluide* or L *fluidus* f. *fluere* flow]

fluidounce /ˈfluːɪdˌaʊns/ n. US a fluid ounce (see OUNCE¹).

fluke¹ n. & v. —n. **1** a lucky accident (*won by a fluke*). **2** a chance breeze. —v.tr. achieve by a fluke (*fluked that shot*). [19th c.: perh. f. dial. *fluke* guess]

fluke² n. **1** any parasitic flatworm of the class Digenea or Monogenea, including liver flukes and blood flukes. **2** a flat-fish, esp. a flounder. [OE *flōc*]

fluke³ n. **1** Naut. a broad triangular plate on the arm of an anchor. **2** the barbed head of a lance, harpoon, etc. **3** Zool. either of the lobes of a whale's tail. [16th c.: perh. f. FLUKE²]

fluky /ˈfluːkɪ/ adj. (**flukier**, **flukiest**) of the nature of a fluke; obtained more by chance than skill. □ **flukily** adv. **flukiness** n.

flummery /ˈflʌmərɪ/ n. (*pl.* **-ies**) **1** empty compliments; trifles; nonsense. **2** a sweet dish made with beaten eggs, sugar, etc. [Welsh *llymru*, of unkn. orig.]

flummox /ˈflʌməks/ v.tr. colloq. bewilder, confound, disconcert. [19th c.: prob. dial., imit.]

flung past and past part. of FLING.

flunk v. & n. US colloq. —v. **1** tr. **a** fail (an examination etc.). **b** fail (an examination candidate). **2** intr. (often foll. by *out*) fail utterly; give up. —n. an instance of flunking. □ **flunk out** be dismissed from school etc. after failing an examination. [cf. FUNK[1] and obs. *flink* be a coward]

flunkey /ˈflʌŋkɪ/ *n.* (also **flunky**) (*pl.* **-eys** or **-ies**) usu. *derog.* **1** a liveried servant; a footman. **2** a toady; a snob. **3** *US* a cook, waiter, etc. □ **flunkeyism** *n.* [18th c. (orig. Sc.): perh. f. FLANK with the sense 'sidesman, flanker']

fluoresce /flʊəˈres/ *v.intr.* be or become fluorescent.

fluorescence /flʊəˈres(ə)ns/ *n.* **1** the visible or invisible radiation produced from certain substances as a result of incident radiation of a shorter wavelength as X-rays, ultraviolet light, etc. **2** the property of absorbing light of short (invisible) wavelength and emitting light of longer (visible) wavelength. [FLUORSPAR (which fluoresces) after *opalescence*]

fluorescent /flʊəˈres(ə)nt/ *adj.* (of a substance) having or showing fluorescence. □ **fluorescent lamp** (or **bulb**) a lamp or bulb radiating largely by fluorescence, esp. a tubular lamp in which phosphor on the inside surface of the tube is made to fluoresce by ultraviolet radiation from mercury vapour. **fluorescent screen** a screen coated with fluorescent material to show images from X-rays etc.

fluoridate /ˈflʊərɪˌdeɪt/ *v.tr.* add traces of fluoride to (drinking-water etc.).

fluoridation /ˌflʊərɪˈdeɪʃ(ə)n/ *n.* (also **fluoridization** /-daɪˈzeɪʃ(ə)n/) the addition of traces of fluoride to drinking-water in order to prevent or reduce tooth-decay.

fluoride /ˈflʊəraɪd/ *n.* any binary compound of fluorine.

fluorinate /ˈflʊərɪˌneɪt/ *v.tr.* **1** = FLUORIDATE. **2** introduce fluorine into (a compound) (*fluorinated hydrocarbons*). □ **fluorination** /-ˈneɪʃ(ə)n/ *n.*

fluorine /ˈflʊəriːn/ *n.* a poisonous pale-yellow gaseous element of the halogen group. [F (as FLUORSPAR)]

fluorite /ˈflʊəraɪt/ *n.* a mineral form of calcium fluoride. [It. (as FLUORSPAR)]

fluoro- /ˈflʊərəʊ/ *comb. form* **1** fluorine (*fluorocarbon*). **2** fluorescence (*fluoroscope*). [FLUORINE, FLUORESCENCE]

fluorocarbon /ˌflʊərəʊˈkɑːbən/ *n.* a compound formed by replacing one or more of the hydrogen atoms in a hydrocarbon with fluorine atoms.

fluorspar /ˈflʊəspɑː(r)/ *n.* = FLUORITE. [*fluor* a flow, any of the minerals used as fluxes, fluorspar, f. L *fluor* f. *fluere* flow + SPAR[3]]

flurry /ˈflʌrɪ/ *n.* & *v.* —*n.* (*pl.* **-ies**) **1** a gust or squall (of snow, rain, etc.). **2** a sudden burst of activity. **3** a commotion; excitement; nervous agitation (*a flurry of speculation*). —*v.tr.* (**-ies**, **-ied**) confuse by haste or noise; agitate. [imit.: cf. obs. *flurr* ruffle, *hurry*]

flush[1] *v.* & *n.* —*v.* **1** *intr.* **a** blush, redden (*he flushed with embarrassment*). **b** glow with a warm colour (*sky flushed pink*). **2** *tr.* (usu. as **flushed** *adj.*) cause to glow or blush (often foll. by *with*: *flushed with pride*). **3** *tr.* **a** cleanse (a drain, lavatory, etc.) by a rushing flow of water. **b** (often foll. by *away*, *down*) dispose of (an object) in this way (*flushed away the cigarette*). **4** *intr.* rush out, spurt. —*n.* **1 a** a blush. **b** a glow of light or colour. **2 a** a rush of water. **b** the cleansing of a drain, lavatory, etc. by flushing. **3 a** a rush of emotion. **b** the elation produced by a victory etc. (*the flush of triumph*). **4** sudden abundance. **5** freshness; vigour (*in the first flush of womanhood*). **6 a** (also **hot flush**) a sudden sensation of heat. **b** a feverish temperature. **c** facial redness, esp. caused by fever, alcohol, etc. □ **flusher** *n.* [ME, perh. = FLUSH[4] infl. by *flash* and *blush*]

flush[2] *adj.* & *v.* —*adj.* **1** (often foll. by *with*) in the same plane; level; even (*the sink is flush with the cooker; fitted it flush with the wall*). **2** (usu. *predic.*) *colloq.* **a** having plenty of money. **b** (of money) abundant, plentiful. **3** full to overflowing; in flood. —*v.tr.* **1** make (surfaces) level. **2** fill in (a joint) level with a surface. □ **flushness** *n.* [prob. f. FLUSH[1]]

flush[3] *n.* a hand of cards all of one suit, esp. in poker. □ **royal flush** a straight poker flush headed by an ace. **straight flush** a flush that is a numerical sequence. [OF *flus*, *flux* f. L *fluxus* FLUX]

flush[4] *v.* **1** *tr.* cause (esp. a game bird) to fly up. **2** *intr.* (of a bird) fly up and away. □ **flush out 1** reveal. **2** drive out. [ME, imit.: cf. *fly*, *rush*]

fluster /ˈflʌstə(r)/ *v.* & *n.* —*v. tr.* & *intr.* make or become nervous or confused; flurry (*was flustered by the noise; he flusters easily*). —*n.* a confused or agitated state. [ME: orig. unkn.: cf. Icel. *flaustr(a)* hurry, bustle]

flute *n.* & *v.* —*n.* **1 a** a high-pitched woodwind instrument of metal or wood, having holes along it stopped by the fingers or keys, and held across the body. **b** any of various wind instruments resembling a flute. **c** a flute-player. **2 a** *Archit.* an ornamental vertical groove in a column. **b** any similar cylindrical groove. **3** a tall narrow wineglass. —*v.* **1** *intr.* play the flute. **2** *intr.* speak, sing, or whistle in a fluting way. **3** *tr.* make flutes or grooves in. □ **flutelike** *adj.* **fluting** *n.* **flutist** *n. US* (cf. FLAUTIST). **fluty** *adj.* (in sense 1a of *n.*). [ME f. OF *fleüte*, *flaüte*, *flahute*, prob. f. Prov. *flaüt*]

flutter /ˈflʌtə(r)/ *v.* & *n.* —*v.* **1 a** *intr.* flap the wings in flying or trying to fly (*butterflies fluttered in the sunshine*). **b** *tr.* flap (the wings). **2** *intr.* fall with a quivering motion (*leaves fluttered to the ground*). **3** *intr.* & *tr.* move or cause to move irregularly or tremblingly (*the wind fluttered the flag*). **4** *intr.* go about restlessly; flit; hover. **5** *tr.* agitate, confuse. **6** *intr.* (of a pulse or heartbeat) beat feebly or irregularly. **7** *intr.* tremble with excitement or agitation. —*n.* **1 a** the act of fluttering. **b** an instance of this. **2** tremulous excitement; a sensation (*was in a flutter; caused a flutter with his behaviour*). **3** *Brit. sl.* a small bet, esp. on a horse. **4** an abnormally rapid but regular heartbeat. **5** *Electronics* a rapid variation of pitch, esp. of recorded sound. **6** a vibration. □ **flutterer** *n.* **fluttery** *adj.* [OE *floterian*, *flotorian*, frequent. form rel. to FLEET[4]]

fluvial /ˈfluːvɪəl/ *adj.* of or found in a river or rivers. [ME f. L *fluvialis* f. *fluvius* river f. *fluere* flow]

flux *n.* & *v.* —*n.* **1** a process of flowing or flowing out. **2** an issue or discharge. **3** continuous change (*in a state of flux*). **4** *Metallurgy* a substance mixed with a metal etc. to promote fusion. **5** *Physics* **a** the rate of flow of any fluid across a given area. **b** the amount of fluid crossing an area in a given time. **6** *Physics* the amount of radiation or particles incident on an area in a given time. **7** *Electr.* the total electric or magnetic field passing through a surface. —*v.* **1** *tr.* & *intr.* make or become fluid. **2** *tr.* **a** fuse. **b** treat with a fusing flux. [ME f. OF *flux* or L *fluxus* f. *fluere flux-* flow]

fly[1] *v. & n.* —*v.* (**flies**; *past* **flew** /fluː/; *past part.* **flown** /fləʊn/) **1** *intr.* move through the air under control, esp. with wings. **2** (of an aircraft or its occupants): **a** *intr.* travel through the air or through space. **b** *tr.* traverse (a region or distance) (*flew the Channel*). **3** *tr.* **a** control the flight of (esp. an aircraft). **b** transport in an aircraft. **4 a** *tr.* cause to fly or remain aloft. **b** *intr.* (of a flag, hair, etc.) wave or flutter. **5** *intr.* pass or rise quickly through the air or over an obstacle. **6** *intr.* go or move quickly; pass swiftly (*time flies*). **7** *intr.* **a** flee. **b** *colloq.* depart hastily. **8** *intr.* be driven or scattered; be forced off suddenly (*sent me flying*; *the door flew open*). **9** *intr.* (foll. by *at, upon*) **a** hasten or spring violently. **b** attack or criticize fiercely. **10** *tr.* flee from; escape in haste. —*n.* (*pl.* **-ies**) **1** (usu. in *pl.*) **a** a flap on a garment, esp. trousers, to contain or cover a fastening. **b** this fastening. **2** a flap at the entrance of a tent. **3** (in *pl.*) the space over the proscenium in a theatre. **4** the act or an instance of flying. □ **fly-away** (of hair etc.) tending to fly out or up; streaming. **fly-by-night** *adj.* unreliable. —*n.* an unreliable person. **fly-half** *Rugby Football* a stand-off half. **fly high** pursue a high ambition. **2** excel, prosper. **fly in the face of** openly disregard or disobey; conflict roundly with (probability, the evidence, etc.). **fly into a rage** (or **temper** etc.) become suddenly or violently angry. **fly a kite** try something out; test public opinion. **fly off the handle** *colloq.* lose one's temper suddenly and unexpectedly. **fly-past** a ceremonial flight of aircraft past a person or a place. **fly-pitching** *sl.* street-trading. □ **flyable** *adj.* [OE *flēogan* f. Gmc]

fly[2] *n.* (*pl.* **flies**) **1** any insect of the order Diptera with two usu. transparent wings. **2** any other winged insect, e.g. a firefly or mayfly. **3** a disease of plants or animals caused by flies. **4** a natural or artificial fly used as bait in fishing. □ **fly agaric** a poisonous fungus *Amanita Muscaria*, forming bright-red mushrooms with white flecks. **fly-blown** *adj.* tainted, esp. by flies' eggs. **fly-fish** *v.intr.* fish with a fly. **fly in the ointment** a minor irritation that spoils enjoyment. **fly on the wall** an unnoticed observer. **fly-paper** sticky treated paper for catching flies. **fly-post** display (posters etc.) rapidly in unauthorized places. **fly-tip** illegally dump (waste). **fly-tipper** a person who engages in fly-tipping. **fly-trap** any of various plants that catch flies, esp. the Venus fly-trap. **like flies** in large numbers (usu. of people dying in an epidemic etc.). **no flies on** *colloq.* nothing to diminish (a person's) astuteness. [OE *flȳge, flēoge* f. WG]

fly[3] *adj. Brit. sl.* knowing, clever, alert. □ **flyness** *n.* [19th c.: orig. unkn.]

flycatcher /ˈflaɪˌkætʃə(r)/ *n.* any bird of the families Tyrannidae and Muscicapidae, catching insects esp. in short flights from a perch.

flyer /ˈflaɪə(r)/ *n.* (also **flier**) *colloq.* **1** an airman or airwoman. **2** a thing that flies in a specified way (*a poor flyer*). **3** a fast-moving animal or vehicle. **4** an ambitious or outstanding person. **5** *US* a small handbill.

flying /ˈflaɪɪŋ/ *adj. & n.* —*adj.* **1** fluttering or waving in the air; hanging loose. **2** hasty, brief

(*a flying visit*). **3** designed for rapid movement. **4** (of an animal) able to make very long leaps by using winglike membranes etc. —*n.* flight, esp. in an aircraft. □ **flying boat** a seaplane with a boatlike fuselage. **flying buttress** a buttress slanting from a separate column, usu. forming an arch with the wall it supports. **flying doctor** a doctor (esp. in a large sparsely populated area) who visits distant patients by aircraft. **flying fish** any tropical fish of the family Exocoetidae, with winglike pectoral fins for gliding through the air. **flying fox** any of various fruit-eating bats. **flying officer** the RAF rank next below flight lieutenant. **flying picket** an industrial picket that can be moved rapidly from one site to another, esp. to reinforce local pickets. **flying saucer** any unidentified, esp. circular, flying object, popularly supposed to have come from space. **flying squad** a police detachment or other body organized for rapid movement. **flying start 1** a start (of a race etc.) in which the starting-point is passed at full speed. **2** a vigorous start giving an initial advantage. **with flying colours** with distinction.

flyleaf /ˈflaɪliːf/ *n.* (*pl.* **-leaves**) a blank leaf at the beginning or end of a book.

flyover /ˈflaɪˌəʊvə(r)/ *n.* **1** *Brit.* a bridge carrying one road or railway over another. **2** *US* = *fly-past*.

flysheet /ˈflaɪʃiːt/ *n.* **1** a tract or circular of two or four pages. **2** a canvas cover pitched outside and over a tent to give extra protection against bad weather.

flyweight /ˈflaɪweɪt/ *n.* **1** a weight in certain sports intermediate between light flyweight and bantamweight. **2** a sportsman of this weight. □ **light flyweight 1** a weight in amateur boxing up to 48 kg. **2** an amateur boxer of this weight.

flywheel /ˈflaɪwiːl/ *n.* a heavy wheel on a revolving shaft used to regulate machinery or accumulate power.

FM *abbr.* **1** Field Marshal. **2** frequency modulation.

Fm *symb. Chem.* the element fermium.

f-number /ˈefˌnʌmbə(r)/ *n. Photog.* the ratio of the focal length to the effective diameter of a lens. [*f* (denoting focal length) + NUMBER]

FO *abbr.* Flying Officer.

foal /fəʊl/ *n. & v.* —*n.* the young of a horse or related animal. —*v.tr.* (of a mare etc.) give birth to (a foal). □ **in** (or **with**) **foal** (of a mare etc.) pregnant. [OE *fola* f. Gmc: cf. FILLY]

foam /fəʊm/ *n. & v.* —*n.* **1** a mass of small bubbles formed on or in liquid by agitation, fermentation, etc. **2** a froth of saliva or sweat. **3** a substance resembling these, e.g. rubber or plastic in a cellular mass. —*v.intr.* **1** emit foam; froth. **2** run with foam. **3** (of a vessel) be filled and overflow with foam. □ **foam at the mouth** be very angry. □ **foamless** *adj.* **foamy** *adj.* (**foamier, foamiest**). [OE *fām* f. WG]

fob[1] *n.* **1** (in full **fob-chain**) a chain attached to a watch for carrying in a waistcoat or waistband pocket. **2** a small pocket for carrying a watch. **3** a tab on a key-ring. [orig. cant, prob. f. G]

fob[2] *v.tr.* (**fobbed, fobbing**) □ **fob off 1** (often foll. by *with* a thing) deceive into accepting something inferior. **2** (often foll. by *on* to a person) palm or pass off (an inferior thing). [16th c.: cf. obs. *fop* to dupe, G *foppen* to banter]

f.o.b. *abbr.* free on board.

focal /ˈfəʊk(ə)l/ *adj.* of, at, or in terms of a focus. □ **focal distance** (or **length**) the distance between the centre of a mirror or lens and its focus. **focal point** = FOCUS *n.* 1. [mod.L *focalis* (as FOCUS)]

fo'c's'le var. of FORECASTLE.

focus /ˈfəʊkəs/ *n. & v.* —*n.* (pl. **focuses** or **foci** /ˈfəʊsaɪ/) **1** *Physics* **a** the point at which rays or waves meet after reflection or refraction. **b** the point from which diverging rays or waves appear to proceed. **2 a** *Optics* the point at which an object must be situated for an image of it given by a lens or mirror to be well defined (*bring into focus*). **b** the adjustment of the eye or a lens necessary to produce a clear image (*the binoculars were not in focus*). **c** a state of clear definition (*the photograph was out of focus*). **3** the centre of interest or activity (*focus of attention*). **4** *Med.* the principal site of an infection or other disease. **5** *Geol.* the place of origin of an earthquake. —*v.* (**focused**, **focusing** or **focussed**, **focussing**) **1** *tr.* bring into focus. **2** *tr.* adjust the focus of (a lens, the eye, etc.). **3** *tr. & intr.* (often foll. by *on*) concentrate or be concentrated on. **4** *intr. & tr.* converge or make converge to a focus. □ **focuser** *n.* [L, = hearth]

fodder /ˈfɒdə(r)/ *n. & v.* —*n.* dried hay or straw etc. for cattle, horses, etc. —*v.tr.* give fodder to. [OE *fōdor* f. Gmc, rel. to FOOD]

foe *n.* esp. *poet.* or *formal* an enemy or opponent. [OE *fāh* hostile, rel. to FEUD¹]

foetid var. of FETID.

foetus /ˈfiːtəs/ *n.* (US **fetus**) an unborn or unhatched offspring of a mammal esp. a human one more than eight weeks after conception. □ **foetal** *adj.* **foeticide** /-tɪˌsaɪd/ *n.* [ME f. L *fetus* offspring]

fog /fɒɡ/ *n. & v.* —*n.* **1 a** a thick cloud of water droplets or smoke suspended in the atmosphere at or near the earth's surface restricting or obscuring visibility. **b** obscurity in the atmosphere caused by this. **2** *Photog.* cloudiness on a developed negative etc. obscuring the image. **3** an uncertain or confused position or state. —*v.* (**fogged**, **fogging**) **1** *tr.* **a** envelop or cover with fog or condensed vapour. **b** bewilder or confuse as if with a fog. **2** *intr.* become covered with fog or condensed vapour. **3** *tr. Photog.* make (a negative etc.) obscure or cloudy. □ **fog-bank** a mass of fog at sea. **fog-bound** unable to proceed because of fog. **fog-lamp** a lamp used to improve visibility in fog. **in a fog** puzzled; at a loss. [perh. back-form. f. FOGGY]

foggy /ˈfɒɡɪ/ *adj.* (**foggier, foggiest**) **1** (of the atmosphere) thick or obscure with fog. **2** of or like fog. **3** confused, unclear. □ **not have the foggiest** *colloq.* have no idea at all. □ **foggily** *adv.* **fogginess** *n.*

foghorn /ˈfɒɡhɔːn/ *n.* **1** a deep-sounding instrument for warning ships in fog. **2** *colloq.* a loud penetrating voice.

fogy /ˈfəʊɡɪ/ *n.* (also **fogey**) (pl. **-ies** or **-eys**) a dull old-fashioned person (esp. *old fogy*). □ **fogydom** *n.* **fogyish** *adj.* [18th c.: rel. to sl. *fogram*, of unkn. orig.]

foible /ˈfɔɪb(ə)l/ *n.* a minor weakness or idiosyncrasy. [F, obs. form of *faible* (as FEEBLE)]

foie gras /fwɑː ˈɡrɑː/ *n. colloq.* = *pâté de foie gras*.

foil¹ *v.* frustrate, baffle, defeat. [ME, = trample down, perh. f. OF *fouler* to full cloth, trample, ult. f. L *fullo* FULLER]

foil² *n.* **1** metal hammered or rolled into a thin sheet (*tin foil*). **2** a person or thing that enhances the qualities of another by contrast. [ME f. OF f. L *folium* leaf, and f. OF *foille* f. L *folia* (pl.)]

foil³ *n.* a light blunt-edged sword with a button on its point used in fencing. □ **foilist** *n.* [16th c.: orig. unkn.]

foist *v.tr.* (foll. by (*off*) *on*, (*off*) *upon*) **1** present (a thing) falsely as genuine or superior. **2** falsely fix the ownership of. **3** (foll. by *in*, *into*) introduce surreptitiously or unwarrantably. [orig. of palming a false die, f. Du. dial. *vuisten* take in the hand f. *vuist* FIST]

fold¹ *v. & n.* —*v.* **1** *tr.* **a** bend or close (a flexible thing) over upon itself. **b** (foll. by *back*, *over*, *down*) bend a part of (a flexible thing) in the manner specified (*fold down the flap*). **2** *intr.* become or be able to be folded. **3** *tr.* (foll. by *away*, *up*) make compact by folding. **4** *intr.* (often foll. by *up*) *colloq.* **a** collapse, disintegrate. **b** (of an enterprise) fail; go bankrupt. **5** *tr. poet.* embrace (esp. *fold in the arms* or *to the breast*). **6** *tr.* (foll. by *about*, *round*) clasp (the arms); wrap, envelop. **7** *tr.* (foll. by *in*) mix (an ingredient with others) using a gentle cutting and turning motion. —*n.* **1** the act or an instance of folding. **2** a line made by or for folding. **3** a folded part. **4** a hollow among hills. **5** *Geol.* a curvature of strata. □ **fold one's arms** place one's arms across the chest, side by side or entwined. **fold one's hands** clasp them. **folding money** esp. US *colloq.* banknotes. **fold-out** an oversize page in a book etc. to be unfolded by the reader. □ **foldable** *adj.* [OE *falden, fealden* f. Gmc]

fold² /fəʊld/ *n. & v.* —*n.* **1** = SHEEPFOLD. **2** a body of believers or members of a Church. —*v.tr.* enclose (sheep) in a fold. [OE *fald*]

-fold /fəʊld/ *suffix* forming adjectives and adverbs from cardinal numbers, meaning: **1** in an amount multiplied by (*repaid tenfold*). **2** consisting of so many parts (*threefold blessing*). [OE *-fald, -feald*, rel. to FOLD¹: orig. sense 'folded in so many layers']

folder /ˈfəʊldə(r)/ *n.* **1** a folding cover or holder for loose papers. **2** a folded leaflet.

foliaceous /ˌfəʊlɪˈeɪʃəs/ *adj.* **1** of or like leaves. **2** having organs like leaves. **3** laminated. [L *foliaceus* leafy f. *folium* leaf f. Gmc]

foliage /ˈfəʊlɪɪdʒ/ *n.* leaves, leafage. [ME f. F *feuillage* f. *feuille* leaf f. OF *foille*: see FOIL²]

foliar /ˈfəʊlɪə(r)/ *adj.* of or relating to leaves. □ **foliar feed** feed supplied to leaves of plants. [mod.L *foliaris* f. L *folium* leaf]

foliate *adj. & v.* —*adj.* /ˈfəʊlɪət/ **1** leaflike. **2** having leaves. —*v.* /ˈfəʊlɪˌeɪt/ *intr.* split into laminae. □ **foliation** /-ˈeɪʃ(ə)n/ *n.* [L *foliatus* leaved f. *folium* leaf]

folic acid /ˈfəʊlɪk/ *n.* a vitamin of the B complex, found in leafy green vegetables, liver, and kidney, a deficiency of which causes pernicious anaemia. [L *folium* leaf (because found esp. in green leaves) + -IC]

folio /ˈfəʊlɪəʊ/ *n. & adj.* —*n.* (pl. **-os**) **1** a leaf of paper etc., esp. one numbered only on the front. **2** a sheet of paper folded once making two leaves of a book. **3** a book made of such sheets. **4** a book made of folios, of the largest size. □ **in folio** made of folios. —*adj.* (of a book) made of folios, of the largest size. [L, ablat. of *folium* leaf, = *on leaf* (as specified)]

folk /fəʊk/ *n.* (pl. **folk** or **folks**) **1** (treated as *pl.*) people in general or of a specified class (*few folk* *about*; *townsfolk*). **2** (in *pl.*) (usu. **folks**) one's parents or relatives. **3** (treated as *sing.*) a people. **4** (treated as *sing.*) *colloq.* traditional music. **5** (*attrib.*) of popular origin; traditional (*folk art*). □ **folk-dance** a dance of popular origin. **folk memory** recollection of the past persisting among a people. **folk-singer** a singer of folksongs. **folk-song** a song of popular or traditional origin or style. **folk-tale** a popular or traditional story. [OE *folc* f. Gmc]

folklore /ˈfəʊklɔː(r)/ *n.* the traditional beliefs and stories of a people; the study of these. □ **folkloric** *adj.* **folklorist** *n.* **folkloristic** /-ˈrɪstɪk/ *adj.*

folksy /ˈfəʊksɪ/ *adj.* (**folksier, folksiest**) **1** friendly, sociable, informal. **2** having the characteristics of folk art, culture, etc. □ **folksiness** *n.*

folkweave /ˈfəʊkwiːv/ *n.* a rough loosely woven fabric.

follicle /ˈfɒlɪk(ə)l/ *n.* **1** a small sac or vesicle. **2** a small sac-shaped secretory gland or cavity. □ **follicular** /fɒˈlɪkjʊlə(r)/ *adj.* **folliculate** /fɒˈlɪkjʊlət/ *adj.* **folliculated** /fɒˈlɪkjʊˌleɪtɪd/ *adj.* [L *folliculus* dimin. of *follis* bellows]

follow /ˈfɒləʊ/ *v.* **1** *tr.* or (foll. by *after*) *intr.* go or come after (a person or thing proceeding ahead). **2** *tr.* go along (a route, path, etc.). **3** *tr.* & *intr.* come after in order or time (*Nero followed Claudius; my reasons are as follows*). **4** *tr.* take as a guide or leader. **5** *tr.* conform to (*follow your example*). **6** *tr.* practise (a trade or profession). **7** *tr.* undertake (a course of study etc.). **8** *tr.* understand the meaning or tendency of (a speaker or argument). **9** *tr.* maintain awareness of the current state or progress of (events etc. in a particular sphere). **10** *tr.* (foll. by *with*) provide with a sequel or successor. **11** *intr.* happen after something else; ensue. **12** *intr.* **a** be necessarily true as a result of something else. **b** (foll. by *from*) be a result of. **13** *tr.* strive after; aim at; pursue (*followed fame and fortune*). □ **follow-my-leader** a game in which players must do as the leader does. **follow on 1** continue. **2** (of a cricket team) have to bat again immediately after the first innings. **follow out** carry out; adhere precisely to (instructions etc.). **follow suit 1** *Cards* play a card of the suit led. **2** conform to another person's actions. **follow through 1** continue (an action etc.) to its conclusion. **2** *Sport* continue the movement of a stroke after the ball has been struck. **follow up** (foll. by *with*) **1** pursue, develop, supplement. **2** make further investigation of. **follow-up** *n.* a subsequent or continued action, measure, experience, etc. [OE *folgian* f. Gmc]

follower /ˈfɒləʊə(r)/ *n.* **1** an adherent or devotee. **2** a person or thing that follows.

following /ˈfɒləʊɪŋ/ *prep., n., & adj.* —*prep.* coming after in time; as a sequel to. —*n.* a body of adherents or devotees. —*adj.* that follows or comes after.

folly /ˈfɒlɪ/ *n.* (*pl.* **-ies**) **1** foolishness; lack of good sense. **2** a foolish act, behaviour, idea, etc. **3** an ornamental building, usu. a tower or mock Gothic ruin. [ME f. OF *folie* f. *fol* mad, FOOL¹]

foment /fəˈment, fəʊ-/ *v.tr.* **1** instigate or stir up (trouble, sedition, etc.). **2 a** bathe with warm or medicated liquid. **b** apply warmth to. □ **fomenter** *n.* [ME f. F *fomenter* f. LL *fomentare* f. L *fomentum* poultice, lotion f. *fovēre* heat, cherish]

fomentation /ˌfəʊmenˈteɪʃ(ə)n/ *n.* **1** the act or an instance of fomenting. **2** materials prepared for application to a wound etc. [ME f. OF or LL *fomentatio* (as FOMENT)]

fond *adj.* **1** (foll. by *of*) having affection or a liking for. **2** affectionate, loving, doting. **3** (of beliefs etc.) foolishly optimistic or credulous; naïve. □ **fondly** *adv.* **fondness** *n.* [ME f. obs. *fon* fool, be foolish]

fondant /ˈfɒnd(ə)nt/ *n.* a soft sweet of flavoured sugar. [F, pres. part. of *fondre* melt f. L *fundere* pour]

fondle /ˈfɒnd(ə)l/ *v.tr.* touch or stroke lovingly; caress. □ **fondler** *n.* [back-form. f. *fondling* fondled person (as FOND, -LING¹)]

fondue /ˈfɒndjuː, -dju:/ *n.* a dish of flavoured melted cheese. [F, fem. past part. of *fondre* melt f. L *fundere* pour]

font¹ *n.* a receptacle in a church for baptismal water. □ **fontal** *adj.* [OE *font, fant* f. OIr. *fant, font* f. L *fons fontis* fountain, baptismal water]

font² var. of FOUNT².

fontanelle /ˌfɒntəˈnel/ *n.* (*US* **fontanel**) a membranous space in an infant's skull at the angles of the parietal bones. [F *fontanelle* f. mod.L *fontanella* f. OF *fontenelle* dimin. of *fontaine* fountain]

food /fuːd/ *n.* **1** a nutritious substance, esp. solid in form, that can be taken into an animal or a plant to maintain life and growth. **2** ideas as a resource for or stimulus to mental work (*food for thought*). □ **food additive** a substance added to food to enhance its colour, flavour, or presentation. **food-chain** *Ecol.* a series of organisms each dependent on the next for food. **food poisoning** illness due to bacteria or other toxins in food. **food processor** a machine for chopping and mixing food materials. **food value** the relative nourishing power of a food. [OE *fōda* f. Gmc: cf. FEED]

foodie /ˈfuːdɪ/ *n.* (also **foody**) (*pl.* **-ies**) *colloq.* a person who is particular about food; a gourmet.

foodstuff /ˈfuːdstʌf/ *n.* any substance suitable as food.

fool¹ *n., v., & adj.* —*n.* **1** a person who acts unwisely or imprudently; a stupid person. **2** *hist.* a jester; a clown. **3** a dupe. —*v.* **1** *tr.* deceive so as to cause to appear foolish. **2** *tr.* (foll. by *into* + verbal noun, or *out of*) trick; cause to do something foolish. **3** *tr.* play tricks on; dupe. **4** *intr.* act in a joking, frivolous, or teasing way. **5** *intr.* (foll. by *about, around*) behave in a playful or silly way. —*adj. US colloq.* foolish, silly. □ **act** (or **play**) **the fool** behave in a silly way. **fool's errand** a fruitless venture. **fool's paradise** happiness founded on an illusion. **make a fool of** make (a person or oneself) look foolish; trick or deceive. **no** (or **nobody's**) **fool** a shrewd or prudent person. [ME f. OF *fol* f. L *follis* bellows, empty-headed person]

fool² *n.* a dessert of fruit crushed and mixed with cream, custard, etc. [16th c.: perh. f. FOOL¹]

foolery /ˈfuːlərɪ/ *n.* (*pl.* **-ies**) **1** foolish behaviour. **2** a foolish act.

foolhardy /ˈfuːlˌhɑːdɪ/ *adj.* (**foolhardier, foolhardiest**) rashly or foolishly bold; reckless. □ **foolhardily** *adv.* **foolhardiness** *n.* [ME f. OF *folhardi* f. *fol* foolish + *hardi* bold]

foolish /ˈfuːlɪʃ/ *adj.* (of a person, action, etc.) lacking good sense or judgement; unwise. □ **foolishly** *adv.* **foolishness** *n.*

foolproof /ˈfuːlpruːf/ adj. (of a procedure, mechanism, etc.) so straightforward or simple as to be incapable of misuse or mistake.

foolscap /ˈfuːlskæp/ n. Brit. a size of paper, about 330 × 200 (or 400) mm. [named from the former watermark representing a fool's cap]

foot /fʊt/ n. & v. —n. (pl. **feet**) **1 a** the lower extremity of the leg below the ankle. **b** the part of a sock etc. covering the foot. **2 a** the lower or lowest part of anything, e.g. a mountain, a page, stairs, etc. **b** the lower end of a table. **c** the end of a bed where the user's feet normally rest. **3** the base, often projecting, of anything extending vertically. **4** a step, pace, or tread; a manner of walking (fleet of foot). **5** (pl. **feet** or **foot**) a unit of linear measure equal to 12 inches (30.48 cm). **6** Prosody a group of syllables (one usu. stressed) constituting a metrical unit. **7** Brit. hist. infantry (a regiment of foot). **8** Zool. the locomotive or adhesive organ of invertebrates. **9** Bot. the part by which a petal is attached. **10** a device on a sewing-machine for holding the material steady as it is sewn. —v.tr. **1** (usu. as **foot it**) a traverse (esp. a long distance) by foot. **b** dance. **2** pay (a bill, esp. one considered large). □ **feet of clay** a fundamental weakness in a person otherwise revered. **foot-and-mouth disease** a contagious viral disease of cattle etc. **foot-pound** the amount of energy required to raise 1 lb. a distance of 1 foot. **foot-soldier** a soldier who fights on foot. **have one's** (or **both**) **feet on the ground** be practical. **have a foot in the door** have a prospect of success. **have one foot in the grave** be near death or very old. **my foot!** int. expressing strong contradiction. **not put a foot wrong** make no mistakes. **on foot** walking, not riding etc. **put one's feet up** colloq. take a rest. **put one's foot down** colloq. **1** be firmly insistent or repressive. **2** accelerate a motor vehicle. **put one's foot in it** colloq. commit a blunder or indiscretion. **set foot on** (or **in**) enter; go into. **set on foot** put (an action, process, etc.) in motion. **under one's feet** in the way. **under foot** on the ground. □ **footed** adj. (also in comb.). **footless** adj. [OE fōt f. Gmc]

footage /ˈfʊtɪdʒ/ n. **1** length or distance in feet. **2** an amount of film made for showing, broadcasting, etc.

football /ˈfʊtbɔːl/ n. & v. —n. **1** any of several outdoor games between two teams played with a ball on a pitch with goals at each end, esp. = Association Football. **2** a large inflated ball of a kind used in these. **3** a topical issue or problem that is the subject of continued argument or controversy. —v.intr. play football. □ **football pool** (or **pools**) a form of gambling on the results of football matches, the winners receiving sums accumulated from entry money. □ **footballer** n.

footboard /ˈfʊtbɔːd/ n. **1** a board to support the feet or a foot. **2** an upright board at the foot of a bed.

footbrake /ˈfʊtbreɪk/ n. a brake operated by the foot in a motor vehicle.

footbridge /ˈfʊtbrɪdʒ/ n. a bridge for use by pedestrians.

-footer /ˈfʊtə(r)/ comb. form a person or thing of so many feet in length or height (six-footer).

footfall /ˈfʊtfɔːl/ n. the sound of a footstep.

foothill /ˈfʊthɪl/ n. (often in pl.) any of the low hills around the base of a mountain.

foothold /ˈfʊthəʊld/ n. **1** a place, esp. in climbing, where a foot can be supported securely. **2** a secure initial position or advantage.

footing /ˈfʊtɪŋ/ n. **1** a foothold; a secure position (lost his footing). **2** the basis on which an enterprise is established or operates; the position or status of a person in relation to others (on an equal footing).

footlights /ˈfʊtlaɪts/ n.pl. a row of lights along the front of a stage at the level of the actors' feet.

footling /ˈfuːtlɪŋ/ adj. colloq. trivial, silly.

footloose /ˈfʊtluːs/ adj. free to go where or act as one pleases.

footman /ˈfʊtmən/ n. (pl. **-men**) a liveried servant attending at the door, at table, or on a carriage.

footmark /ˈfʊtmaːk/ n. a footprint.

footnote /ˈfʊtnəʊt/ n. & v. —n. a note printed at the foot of a page. —v.tr. supply with a footnote or footnotes.

footpad /ˈfʊtpæd/ n. hist. an unmounted highwayman.

footpath /ˈfʊtpɑːθ/ n. a path for pedestrians; a pavement.

footplate /ˈfʊtpleɪt/ n. esp. Brit. the platform in the cab of a locomotive for the crew.

footprint /ˈfʊtprɪnt/ n. **1** the impression left by a foot or shoe. **2** Computing the area of desk space etc. occupied by a microcomputer or other piece of hardware. **3** the ground area covered by a communications satellite or affected by noise etc. from aircraft.

footrest /ˈfʊtrest/ n. a support for the feet or a foot.

footslog /ˈfʊtslɒg/ v. & n. —v.intr. (**-slogged**, **-slogging**) walk or march, esp. laboriously for a long distance. —n. a laborious walk or march. □ **footslogger** n.

footsore /ˈfʊtsɔː(r)/ adj. having sore feet, esp. from walking.

footstep /ˈfʊtstep/ n. **1** a step taken in walking. **2** the sound of this. □ **follow** (or **tread**) **in a person's footsteps** do as another person did before.

footstool /ˈfʊtstuːl/ n. a stool for resting the feet on when sitting.

footway /ˈfʊtweɪ/ n. a path or way for pedestrians.

footwear /ˈfʊtweə(r)/ n. shoes, socks, etc.

footwork /ˈfʊtwɜːk/ n. the use of the feet, esp. skilfully, in sports, dancing, etc.

fop n. an affectedly elegant or fashionable man; a dandy. □ **foppery** n. **foppish** adj. **foppishly** adv. **foppishness** n. [17th c.: perh. f. earlier fop fool]

for /fə(r), fɔː(r)/ prep. & conj. —prep. **1** in the interest or to the benefit of; intended to go to (these flowers are for you; wish to see it for myself). **2** in defence, support, or favour of (fight for one's rights). **3** suitable or appropriate to (a dance for beginners; not for me to say). **4** in respect of or with reference to; regarding; so far as concerns (usual for ties to be worn; don't care for him at all; MP for Lincoln). **5** representing or in place of (here for my uncle). **6** in exchange against (swopped it for a bigger one). **7 a** as the price of (give me £5 for it). **b** at the price of (bought it for £5). **c** to the amount of (a bill for £100; all out for 45). **8** as the penalty of (fined them heavily for it). **9** in requital of (*that's for upsetting my sister*). **10** as a reward for (*here's £5 for your trouble*). **11 a** with a view to; in the hope or quest of; in order to get (*go for a walk; did it for the money*). **b** on account of (*could not speak for laughing*). **12** corresponding to (*word for word*). **13** to reach; in the direction of; towards (*left for Rome*). **14** conducive or conducively to; in order to achieve (*take the pills for a sound night's sleep*). **15** so as to start promptly at (*seven-thirty for eight*). **16** through or over (a distance or period); during (*walked for miles; sang for two hours*). **17** in the character of; as being (*for the last time; know it for a lie*). **18** in spite of; notwithstanding (*for all your fine words*). **19** considering or making due allowance in respect of (*good for a beginner*). **20** in order to be (*gone for a soldier*). —*conj.* because, since, seeing that. □ **be for it** *Brit. colloq.* be in imminent danger of punishment or other trouble. **o** (or **oh**) **for** I wish I had. [OE, prob. a reduction of Gmc *fora* (unrecorded) BEFORE (of place and time)]

for- /fɔː, fə/ *prefix* forming verbs and their derivatives meaning: **1** away, off, apart (*forget; forgive*). **2** prohibition (*forbid*). **3** abstention or neglect (*forgo; forsake*). **4** excess or intensity (*forlorn*). [OE *for-, fær-*]

f.o.r. *abbr.* free on rail.

forage /ˈfɒrɪdʒ/ *n. & v.* —*n.* **1** food for horses and cattle. **2** the act or an instance of searching for food. —*v.* **1** *intr.* go searching; rummage (esp. for food). **2** *tr.* collect food from; ravage. **3** *tr.* get by foraging. □ **forage cap** an infantry undress cap. □ **forager** *n.* [ME f. OF *fourrage, fourrager*, rel. to FODDER]

forasmuch as /ˌfɒrəzˈmʌtʃ/ *conj. archaic* because, since. [= for as much]

foray /ˈfɒreɪ/ *n. & v.* —*n.* a sudden attack; a raid or incursion. —*v.intr.* make or go on a foray. [ME, prob. earlier as verb: back-form. f. *forayer* f. OF *forrier* forager, rel. to FODDER]

forbade (also **forbad**) *past* of FORBID.

forbear[1] /fɔːˈbeə(r)/ *v.intr. & tr.* (*past* **forbore** /-ˈbɔː(r)/; *past part.* **forborne** /-ˈbɔːn/) (often foll. by *from*, or *to* + infin.) *literary* abstain or desist (from) (*could not forbear (from) speaking out; forbore to mention it*). [OE *forberan* (as FOR-, BEAR[1])]

forbear[2] var. of FOREBEAR.

forbearance /fɔːˈbeərəns/ *n.* patient self-control; tolerance.

forbid /fəˈbɪd/ *v.tr.* (**forbidding**; *past* **forbade** /-ˈbæd, -ˈbeɪd/ or **forbad** /-ˈbæd/; *past part.* **forbidden** /-ˈbɪd(ə)n/) **1** (foll. by *to* + infin.) order not (*I forbid you to go*). **2** refuse to allow (a thing, or a person to have a thing) (*I forbid it; was forbidden any wine*). **3** refuse a person entry to (*the gardens are forbidden to children*). □ **forbidden fruit** something desired or enjoyed all the more because not allowed. [OE *forbēodan* (as FOR-, BID)]

forbidding /fəˈbɪdɪŋ/ *adj.* uninviting, repellent, stern. □ **forbiddingly** *adv.*

forbore *past* of FORBEAR[1].

forborne *past part.* of FORBEAR[1].

force *n. & v.* —*n.* **1** power; exerted strength or impetus; intense effort. **2** coercion or compulsion, esp. with the use or threat of violence. **3 a** military strength. **b** (in *pl.*) troops; fighting resources. **c** an organized body of people, esp. soldiers, police, or workers. **4** binding power; validity. **5** effect; precise significance (*the force of their words*). **6 a** mental or moral strength; influence, efficacy (*force of habit*). **b** vividness of

effect (*described with much force*). **7** *Physics* **a** an influence tending to cause the motion of a body. **b** the intensity of this equal to the mass of the body and its acceleration. **8** a person or thing regarded as exerting influence (*is a force for good*). —*v.* **1** *tr.* constrain (a person) by force or against his or her will. **2** *tr.* make a way through or into by force; break open by force. **3** *tr.* (usu. with prep. or adv.) drive or propel violently or against resistance (*the wind forced them back*). **4** *tr.* (foll. by *on, upon*) impose or press (on a person) (*forced their views on us*). **5** *tr.* **a** cause or produce by effort (*forced a smile*). **b** attain by strength or effort (*forced an entry; must force a decision*). **6** *tr.* strain or increase to the utmost; overstrain. **7** *tr.* artificially hasten the development or maturity of (a plant). **8** *tr.* seek or demand quick results from; accelerate the process of (*force the pace*). □ **by force of** by means of. **forced labour** compulsory labour, esp. under harsh conditions. **forced landing** the unavoidable landing of an aircraft in an emergency. **forced march** a long and vigorous march esp. by troops. **force-feed** force (esp. a prisoner) to take food. **force field** (in science fiction) an invisible barrier of force. **force a person's hand** make a person act prematurely or unwillingly. **force the issue** render an immediate decision necessary. **in force 1** valid, effective. **2** in great strength or numbers. **join forces** combine efforts. □ **forceable** *adj.* **forceably** *adv.* **forcer** *n.* [ME f. OF *force, forcer* ult. f. L *fortis* strong]

forceful /ˈfɔːsfʊl/ *adj.* **1** vigorous, powerful. **2** (of speech) compelling, impressive. □ **forcefully** *adv.* **forcefulness** *n.*

force majeure /ˌfɔːs mæˈʒɜː(r)/ *n.* **1** irresistible compulsion or coercion. **2** an unforeseeable course of events excusing a person from the fulfilment of a contract. [F, = superior strength]

forcemeat /ˈfɔːsmiːt/ *n.* meat etc. chopped and seasoned for use as a stuffing or a garnish. [obs. *force, farce* stuff f. OF *farsir*: see FARCE]

forceps /ˈfɔːseps/ *n.* (*pl.* same) surgical pincers, used for grasping and holding. □ **forcipate** /-sɪpət/ *adj.* [L *forceps forcipis*]

forcible /ˈfɔːsɪb(ə)l/ *adj.* done by or involving force; forceful. □ **forcibleness** *n.* **forcibly** *adv.* [ME f. AF & OF (as FORCE)]

ford *n. & v.* —*n.* a shallow place where a river or stream may be crossed by wading or in a vehicle. —*v.tr.* cross (water) at a ford. □ **fordable** *adj.* **fordless** *adj.* [OE f. WG]

fore *adj., n., int., & prep.* —*adj.* situated in front. —*n.* the front part, esp. of a ship; the bow. —*int. Golf* a warning to a person in the path of a ball. □ **fore and aft** at bow and stern; all over the ship. **fore-and-aft** *adj.* (of a sail or rigging) set lengthwise. **to the fore** in front; conspicuous. [OE f. Gmc.: (adj. & n.) ME f. compounds with FORE-]

fore- /fɔː(r)/ *prefix* forming: **1** verbs meaning: **a** in front (*foreshorten*). **b** beforehand; in advance (*forewarn*). **2** nouns meaning: **a** situated in front of (*forecourt*). **b** the front part of (*forehead*). **c** of or near the bow of a ship (*forecastle*). **d** preceding (*forerunner*).

forearm[1] /ˈfɔːrɑːm/ *n.* the part of the arm from the elbow to the wrist or the fingertips.

forearm[2] /fɔːrˈɑːm/ *v.tr.* prepare or arm beforehand.

forebear /ˈfɔːbeə(r)/ n. (also **forbear**) (usu. in pl.) an ancestor. [FORE + obs. bear, beer (as BE, -ER[1])]

forebode /fɔːˈbəʊd/ v.tr. 1 betoken; be an advance warning of (an evil or unwelcome event). 2 have a presentiment of (usu. evil).

foreboding /fɔːˈbəʊdɪŋ/ n. an expectation of trouble or evil; a presage or omen. □ **forebodingly** adv.

forecast /ˈfɔːkɑːst/ v. & n. —v.tr. (past and past part. **-cast** or **-casted**) predict; estimate or calculate beforehand. —n. a calculation or estimate of something future, esp. coming weather. □ **forecaster** n.

forecastle /ˈfəʊks(ə)l/ n. (also **fo'c's'le**) Naut. the forward part of a ship where the crew has quarters.

foreclose /fɔːˈkləʊz/ v.tr. 1 (also absol.; foll. by on) stop (a mortgage) from being redeemable or (a mortgager) from redeeming, esp. as a result of defaults in payment. 2 exclude, prevent. 3 shut out; bar. □ **foreclosure** n. [ME f. OF forclos past part. of forclore f. for- out f. L foras + CLOSE[2]]

forecourt /ˈfɔːkɔːt/ n. 1 an enclosed space in front of a building. 2 the part of a filling-station where petrol is supplied.

foredoom /fɔːˈduːm/ v.tr. (often foll. by to) doom or condemn beforehand.

forefather /ˈfɔːˌfɑːðə(r)/ n. (usu. in pl.) 1 an ancestor. 2 a member of a past generation of a family or people.

forefinger /ˈfɔːˌfɪŋgə(r)/ n. the finger next to the thumb.

forefoot /ˈfɔːfʊt/ n. (pl. **-feet**) either of the front feet of a four-footed animal.

forefront /ˈfɔːfrʌnt/ n. 1 the foremost part. 2 the leading position.

foregather var. of FORGATHER.

forego[1] /fɔːˈgəʊ/ v.tr. & intr. (**-goes**; past **-went** /-ˈwent/; past part. **-gone** /-ˈgɒn/) precede in place or time. □ **foregoer** n. [OE foregān]

forego[2] var. of FORGO.

foregoing /fɔːˈgəʊɪŋ, ˈfɔː-/ adj. preceding; previously mentioned.

foregone /fɔːˈgɒn/ past part. of FOREGO[1]. —attrib.adj. /ˈfɔːgɒn/ previous, preceding, completed. □ **foregone conclusion** an easily foreseen or predictable result.

foreground /ˈfɔːgraʊnd/ n. 1 the part of a view, esp. in a picture, that is nearest the observer. 2 the most conspicuous position. [Du. voorgrond (as FORE-, GROUND[1])]

forehand /ˈfɔːhænd/ n. Tennis etc. 1 a stroke played with the palm of the hand facing the opponent. 2 (attrib.) (also **forehanded**) of or made with a forehand.

forehead /ˈfɒrɪd, ˈfɔːhed/ n. the part of the face above the eyebrows. [OE forhēafod (as FORE-, HEAD)]

foreign /ˈfɒrɪn, ˈfɒrən/ adj. 1 of or from or situated in or characteristic of a country or a language other than one's own. 2 dealing with other countries (foreign service). 3 of another district, society, etc. 4 (often foll. by to) unfamiliar, strange, uncharacteristic (his behaviour is foreign to me). 5 coming from outside (a foreign body lodged in my eye). □ **foreign exchange 1** the currency of other countries. 2 dealings in these. **foreign legion** a body of foreign volunteers in an army (esp. the French army).

foreign minister (or **secretary**) a government minister in charge of his or her country's relations with other countries. **foreign office** a government department dealing with other countries. □ **foreignness** n. [ME f. OF forein, forain ult. f. L foras, -is outside: for -g- cf. sovereign]

foreigner /ˈfɒrɪnə(r), ˈfɒrənə(r)/ n. a person born in or coming from a foreign country or place.

foreknow /fɔːˈnəʊ/ v.tr. (past **-knew** /-ˈnjuː/; past part. **-known** /-ˈnəʊn/) know beforehand; have prescience of. □ **foreknowledge** /fɔːˈnɒlɪdʒ/ n.

foreland /ˈfɔːlænd/ n. a cape or promontory.

foreleg /ˈfɔːleg/ n. each of the front legs of a quadruped.

forelimb /ˈfɔːlɪm/ n. any of the front limbs of an animal.

forelock /ˈfɔːlɒk/ n. a lock of hair growing just above the forehead. □ **take time by the forelock** seize an opportunity.

foreman /ˈfɔːmən/ n. (pl. **-men**) 1 a worker with supervisory responsibilities. 2 the member of a jury who presides over its deliberations and speaks on its behalf.

foremast /ˈfɔːmɑːst, -məst/ n. the forward (lower) mast of a ship.

foremost /ˈfɔːməʊst/ adj. & adv. —adj. 1 the chief or most notable. 2 the most advanced in position; the front. —adv. before anything else in position; in the first place (first and foremost). [earlier formost, formest, superl. of OE forma first, assim. to FORE, MOST]

forename /ˈfɔːneɪm/ n. a first or Christian name.

forenoon /ˈfɔːnuːn/ n. Naut. or Law or archaic the part of the day before noon.

forensic /fəˈrensɪk/ adj. 1 of or used in connection with courts of law (forensic science). 2 of or involving forensic science (sent for forensic examination). □ **forensic medicine** the application of medical knowledge to legal problems. □ **forensically** adv. [L forensis f. FORUM]

■ **Usage** Use of this word in sense 2 is common but considered an illogical extension of sense 1 by some people.

foreordain /ˌfɔːrɔːˈdeɪn/ v.tr. predestinate; ordain beforehand. □ **foreordination** /-dɪˈneɪʃ(ə)n/ n.

forepaw /ˈfɔːpɔː/ n. either of the front paws of a quadruped.

foreplay /ˈfɔːpleɪ/ n. stimulation preceding sexual intercourse.

forerunner /ˈfɔːˌrʌnə(r)/ n. 1 a predecessor. 2 an advance messenger.

foresail /ˈfɔːseɪl, -s(ə)l/ n. Naut. the principal sail on a foremast.

foresee /fɔːˈsiː/ v.tr. (past **-saw** /-ˈsɔː/; past part. **-seen** /-ˈsiːn/) (often foll. by that + clause) see or be aware of beforehand. □ **foreseeable** adj. **foreseeability** /-ˈbɪlɪtɪ/ n. **foreseer** /-ˈsiːə(r)/ n. [OE foreseon (as FORE- + SEE[1])]

foreshadow /fɔːˈʃædəʊ/ v.tr. be a warning or indication of (a future event).

foreshore /ˈfɔːʃɔː(r)/ n. the part of the shore between high- and low-water marks.

foreshorten /fɔːˈʃɔːt(ə)n/ v.tr. show or portray (an object) with the apparent shortening due to visual perspective.

foreshow /fɔːˈʃəʊ/ v.tr. (past part. **-shown** /-ˈʃəʊn/) 1 foretell. 2 foreshadow, portend, prefigure.

foresight /ˈfɔːsaɪt/ n. **1** regard or provision for the future. **2** the process of foreseeing. **3** the front sight of a gun. □ **foresighted** /-ˈsaɪtɪd/ adj. **foresightedly** /-ˈsaɪtɪdlɪ/ adv. **foresightedness** /-ˈsaɪtɪdnɪs/ n. [ME, prob. after ON forsjá, forsjó (as FORE-, SIGHT)]

foreskin /ˈfɔːskɪn/ n. the fold of skin covering the end of the penis.

forest /ˈforɪst/ n. & v. —n. **1 a** (often attrib.) a large area covered chiefly with trees and undergrowth. **b** the trees growing in it. **c** a large number or dense mass of vertical objects (a forest of masts). **2** a district formerly a forest but now cultivated (Sherwood Forest). —v.tr. **1** plant with trees. **2** convert into a forest. [ME f. OF f. LL forestis silva wood outside the walls of a park f. L foris outside]

forestall /fɔːˈstɔːl/ v.tr. **1** act in advance of in order to prevent. **2** anticipate (the action of another, or an event). **3** anticipate the action of. **4** deal with beforehand. □ **forestaller** n. **forestalment** n. [ME: cf. AL forestallare f. OE foresteall an ambush (as FORE-, STALL)]

forester /ˈforɪstə(r)/ n. **1** a person in charge of a forest or skilled in forestry. **2** a person or animal living in a forest. [ME f. OF forestier (as FOREST)]

forestry /ˈforɪstrɪ/ n. the science or management of forests.

foretaste n. & v. —n. /ˈfɔːteɪst/ partial enjoyment or suffering in advance; anticipation. —v.tr. /fɔːˈteɪst/ taste beforehand; anticipate the experience of.

foretell /fɔːˈtel/ v.tr. (past and past part.-**told** /-ˈtəʊld/) **1** tell of (an event etc.) before it takes place; predict, prophesy. **2** presage; be a precursor of. □ **foreteller** n.

forethought /ˈfɔːθɔːt/ n. **1** care or provision for the future. **2** deliberate intention.

foretold past and past part. of FORETELL.

forever /fəˈrevə(r)/ adv. continually, persistently (is forever complaining) (cf. for ever).

forewarn /fɔːˈwɔːn/ v.tr. warn beforehand. □ **forewarner** n.

forewent past of FOREGO¹, FOREGO².

forewoman /ˈfɔːˌwʊmən/ n. (pl. -**women**) **1** a female worker with supervisory responsibilities. **2** a woman who presides over a jury's deliberations and speaks on its behalf.

foreword /ˈfɔːwɜːd/ n. introductory remarks at the beginning of a book, often by a person other than the author. [FORE- + WORD after G Vorwort]

forfeit /ˈfɔːfɪt/ n., adj., & v. —n. **1** a penalty for a breach of contract or neglect; a fine. **2** a trivial fine for a breach of rules in clubs etc. or in games. **3** something surrendered as a penalty. —adj. lost or surrendered as a penalty. —v.tr. (**forfeited**, **forfeiting**) lose the right to, be deprived of, or have to pay as a penalty. □ **forfeitable** adj. **forfeiter** n. **forfeiture** n. [ME (= crime) f. OF forfet, forfait past part. of forfaire transgress (f. L foris outside) + faire f. L facere do]

forfend /fɔːˈfend/ v.tr. **1** US protect by precautions. **2** archaic avert; keep off.

forgather /fɔːˈgæðə(r)/ v.intr. (also **foregather**) assemble; meet together; associate. [16th-c. Sc. f. Du. vergaderen, assim. to FOR-, GATHER]

forgave past of FORGIVE.

forge¹ v. & n. —v.tr. **1 a** make (money etc.) in fraudulent imitation. **b** write (a document or signature) in order to pass it off as written by another. **2** fabricate, invent. **3** shape (esp. metal) by heating in a fire and hammering. —n. **1** a blacksmith's workshop; a smithy. **2 a** a furnace or hearth for melting or refining metal. **b** a workshop containing this. □ **forgeable** adj. **forger** n. [ME f. OF forge (n.), forger (v.) f. L fabricare FABRICATE]

forge² v.intr. move forward gradually or steadily. □ **forge ahead 1** take the lead in a race. **2** move forward or make progress rapidly. [18th c.: perh. an aberrant pronunc. of FORCE]

forgery /ˈfɔːdʒərɪ/ n. (pl. -**ies**) **1** the act or an instance of forging, counterfeiting, or falsifying a document etc. **2** a forged or spurious thing, esp. a document or signature.

forget /fəˈget/ v. (**forgetting**; past **forgot** /-ˈgɒt/; past part. **forgotten** /-ˈgɒt(ə)n/ or esp. US **forgot**) **1** tr. & (often foll. by about) intr. lose the remembrance of; not remember (a person or thing). **2** tr. (foll. by clause or to + infin.) not remember; neglect (forgot to come; forgot how to do it). **3** tr. inadvertently omit to bring or mention or attend to. **4** tr. (also absol.) put out of mind; cease to think of (forgive and forget). □ **forget-me-not** any plant of the genus Myosotis, esp. M. alpestris with small bright blue flowers. **forget oneself 1** neglect one's own interests. **2** act unbecomingly or unworthily. □ **forgettable** adj. **forgetter** n. [OE forgietan f. WG (as FOR-, GET)]

forgetful /fəˈgetfʊl/ adj. **1** apt to forget, absent-minded. **2** (often foll. by of) forgetting, neglectful. □ **forgetfully** adv. **forgetfulness** n.

forgive /fəˈgɪv/ v.tr. (also absol. or with double object) (past **forgave**; past part. **forgiven**) **1** cease to feel angry or resentful towards; pardon (an offender or offence) (forgive us our mistakes). **2** remit (a debt). □ **forgivable** adj. **forgivably** adv. **forgiver** n. [OE forgiefan (as FOR-, GIVE)]

forgiveness /fəˈgɪvnɪs/ n. the act of forgiving; the state of being forgiven. [OE forgiefenes (as FORGIVE)]

forgiving /fəˈgɪvɪŋ/ adj. inclined readily to forgive. □ **forgivingly** adv.

forgo /fɔːˈgəʊ/ v.tr. (also **forego**) (-**goes**; past -**went** /-ˈwent/; past part. -**gone** /-ˈgɒn/) **1** abstain from; go without; relinquish. **2** omit or decline to take or use. [OE forgān (as FOR-, GO¹)]

forgot past of FORGET.

forgotten past part. of FORGET.

fork n. & v. —n. **1** an instrument with two or more prongs used in eating or cooking. **2** a similar much larger instrument used for digging, lifting, etc. **3** any pronged device or component (tuning-fork). **4** a forked support for a bicycle wheel. **5** a divergence of anything, e.g. a stick or road, or US a river, into two parts. **b** the place where this occurs. **c** either of the two parts (take the left fork). **6** a flash of forked lightning. —v. **1** intr. form a fork or branch by separating into two parts. **2** intr. take one or other road etc. at a fork (fork left for Banbury). **3** tr. dig or lift etc. with a fork. □ **fork-lift truck** a vehicle with a horizontal fork in front for lifting and carrying loads. **fork out** (or **up**) sl. hand over or pay, usu. reluctantly. [OE forca, force f. L furca]

forked /fɔːkt/ adj. **1** having a fork or forklike end or branches. **2** divergent, cleft.

forlorn /fɔːˈlɔːn/ *adj.* **1** sad and abandoned or lonely. **2** in a pitiful state; of wretched appearance. **3** desperate, hopeless, forsaken. □ **forlorn hope 1** a faint remaining hope or chance. **2** a desperate enterprise. □ **forlornly** *adv.* **forlornness** *n.* [past part. of obs. *forlese* f. OE *forlēosan* (as FOR-, LOSE): *forlorn hope* f. Du. *verloren hoop* lost troop, orig. of a storming-party etc.]

form *n. & v.* —*n.* **1 a** a shape; an arrangement of parts. **b** the outward aspect (esp. apart from colour) or shape of a body. **2** a person or animal as visible or tangible (*the familiar form of the postman*). **3** the mode in which a thing exists or manifests itself (*took the form of a book*). **4** a species, kind, or variety. **5 a** a printed document with blank spaces for information to be inserted. **b** a regularly drawn document. **6** esp. *Brit.* a class in a school. **7** a customary method; what is usually done (*common form*). **8** a set order of words; a formula. **9** behaviour according to a rule or custom. **10** (prec. by *the*) correct procedure (*knows the form*). **11 a** (of an athlete, horse, etc.) condition of health and training (*is in top form*). **b** *Racing* details of previous performances. **12** general state or disposition (*was in great form*). **13** *sl.* a criminal record. **14** formality or mere ceremony. **15** *Gram.* one of the ways in which a word may be spelt or pronounced or inflected. **16** arrangement and style in literary or musical composition. **17** a long bench without a back. **18** a hare's lair. —*v.* **1** *tr.* make or fashion into a certain shape or form. **2** *intr.* take a certain shape; be formed. **3** *tr.* be the material of; make up or constitute (*together form a unit*; *forms part of the structure*). **4** *tr.* train or instruct. **5** *tr.* develop or establish as a concept, institution, or practice (*form an idea*; *formed an alliance*). **6** *tr.* (foll. by *into*) embody, organize. **7** *tr.* articulate (a word). **8** *tr. & intr.* (often foll. by *up*) esp. *Mil.* bring or be brought into a certain arrangement or formation. **9** *tr.* construct (a new word) by derivation, inflection, etc. □ **bad form** an offence against current social conventions. **form letter** a standardized letter to deal with frequently occurring matters. **good form** what complies with current social conventions. **in form** fit for racing etc. **off form** not playing or performing well. **on form** playing or performing well. **out of form** not fit for racing etc. [ME f. OF *forme* f. L *forma* mould, form]

-form /fɔːm/ *comb. form* (usu. as **-iform**) forming adjectives meaning: **1** having the form of (*cruciform*; *cuneiform*). **2** having such a number of (*uniform*; *multiform*). [from or after F *-forme* f. L *-formis* f. *forma* FORM]

formal /ˈfɔːm(ə)l/ *adj.* **1** used or done or held in accordance with rules, convention, or ceremony (*formal dress*; *a formal occasion*). **2** ceremonial; required by convention (*a formal call*). **3** precise or symmetrical (*a formal garden*). **4** prim or stiff in manner. **5** perfunctory, having the form without the spirit. **6** valid or correctly so called because of its form; explicit and definite (*a formal agreement*). **7** in accordance with recognized forms or rules. **8** of or concerned with (outward) form or appearance, esp. as distinct from content or matter. □ **formally** *adv.* **formalness** *n.* [ME f. L *formalis* (as FORM)]

formaldehyde /fɔːˈmældɪˌhaɪd/ *n.* a colourless pungent gas used as a disinfectant and preservative and in the manufacture of synthetic resins. [FORMIC (ACID) + ALDEHYDE]

formalin /ˈfɔːməlɪn/ *n.* a colourless solution of formaldehyde in water used as a preservative for biological specimens etc.

formalism /ˈfɔːməˌlɪz(ə)m/ *n.* **1** excessive adherence to prescribed forms. **2** *derog.* an artist's concentration on form at the expense of content. □ **formalist** *n.* **formalistic** /-ˈlɪstɪk/ *adj.*

formality /fɔːˈmælɪtɪ/ *n.* (*pl.* **-ies**) **1 a** a formal or ceremonial act, requirement of etiquette, regulation, or custom (often with an implied lack of real significance). **b** a thing done simply to comply with a rule. **2** the rigid observance of rules or convention. **3** ceremony; elaborate procedure. **4** being formal; precision of manners. [F *formalité* or med.L *formalitas* (as FORMAL)]

formalize /ˈfɔːməˌlaɪz/ *v.tr.* (also **-ise**) **1** give definite shape or legal formality to. **2** make ceremonious, precise, or rigid. □ **formalization** /-ˈzeɪʃ(ə)n/ *n.*

format /ˈfɔːmæt/ *n. & v.* —*n.* **1** the shape and size of a book, periodical, etc. **2** the style or manner of an arrangement or procedure. **3** *Computing* a defined structure for holding data etc. in a record. —*v.tr.* (**formatted, formatting**) **1** arrange or put into a format. **2** *Computing* prepare (a storage medium) to receive data. [F f. G f. L *formatus* (*liber*) shaped (book), past part. of *formare* FORM]

formate see FORMIC ACID.

formation /fɔːˈmeɪʃ(ə)n/ *n.* **1** the act or an instance of forming; the process of being formed. **2** a thing formed. **3** a structure or arrangement of parts. **4** a particular arrangement, e.g. of troops, aircraft in flight, etc. **5** *Geol.* an assemblage of rocks or series of strata having some common characteristic. □ **formational** *adj.* [ME f. OF *formation* or L *formatio* (as FORM)]

formative /ˈfɔːmətɪv/ *adj.* serving to form or fashion; of formation. □ **formatively** *adv.* [ME f. OF *formatif -ive* or med.L *formativus* (as FORM)]

former[1] /ˈfɔːmə(r)/ *attrib.adj.* **1** of or occurring in the past or an earlier period (*in former times*). **2** having been previously (*her former husband*). **3** (prec. by *the*; often *absol.*) the first or first mentioned of two. [ME f. *forme* first, after FOREMOST]

former[2] /ˈfɔːmə(r)/ *n.* **1** a person or thing that forms. **2** (in *comb.*) a pupil of a specified form in a school (*fourth-former*).

formerly /ˈfɔːməlɪ/ *adv.* in the past; in former times.

Formica /fɔːˈmaɪkə/ *n. propr.* a hard durable plastic laminate used for working surfaces, cupboard doors, etc. [20th c.: orig. uncert.]

formic acid /ˈfɔːmɪk/ *n.* a colourless irritant volatile acid contained in the fluid emitted by some ants. □ **formate** /-meɪt/ *n.* [L *formica* ant]

formidable /ˈfɔːmɪdəb(ə)l, disp. fɔːˈmɪd-/ *adj.* **1** inspiring fear or dread. **2** inspiring respect or awe. **3** likely to be hard to overcome, resist, or deal with. □ **formidableness** *n.* **formidably** *adv.* [F *formidable* or L *formidabilis* f. *formidare* fear]

──────────

■ **Usage** The second pronunciation given, with the stress on the second syllable, is common but considered incorrect by some people.

formless /ˈfɔːmlɪs/ *adj.* shapeless; without determinate or regular form. □ **formlessly** *adv.* **formlessness** *n.*

formula /ˈfɔːmjʊlə/ n. (pl. **formulas** or (esp. in senses 1, 2) **formulae** /-ˌliː/) **1** Chem. a set of chemical symbols showing the constituents of a substance and their relative proportions. **2** Math. a mathematical rule expressed in symbols. **3 a** a fixed form of words, esp. one used on social or ceremonial occasions. **b** a rule unintelligently or slavishly followed; an established or conventional usage. **c** a form of words embodying or enabling agreement, resolution of a dispute, etc. **4 a** a list of ingredients; a recipe. **b** US an infant's food made up from a recipe. **5** a classification of racing car, esp. by the engine capacity. □ **formulaic** /-ˈleɪɪk/ adj. **formularize** v.tr. (also **-ise**). **formulize** v.tr. (also **-ise**). [L, dimin. of forma FORM]

formulary /ˈfɔːmjʊlərɪ/ n. (pl. **-ies**) a collection of formulas or set forms, esp. for religious use. [F formulaire or f. med.L formularius (liber book) f. L (as FORMULA)]

formulate /ˈfɔːmjʊˌleɪt/ v.tr. **1** express in a formula. **2** express clearly and precisely. □ **formulation** /-ˈleɪʃ(ə)n/ n.

fornicate /ˈfɔːnɪˌkeɪt/ v.intr. archaic or joc. (of people not married or not married to each other) have sexual intercourse voluntarily. □ **fornication** /-ˈkeɪʃ(ə)n/ n. **fornicator** n. [eccl.L fornicari f. L fornix -icis brothel]

forsake /fəˈseɪk, fɔː-/ v.tr. (past **forsook** /-ˈsʊk/; past part. **forsaken** /-ˈseɪkən/) **1** give up; break off from; renounce. **2** withdraw one's help, friendship, or companionship from; desert, abandon. □ **forsakenness** n. **forsaker** n. [OE forsacan deny, renounce, refuse, f. WG; cf. OE sacan quarrel]

forsooth /fəˈsuːθ, fɔː-/ adv. archaic or joc. truly; in truth; no doubt. [OE forsōth (as FOR, SOOTH)]

forswear /fɔːˈsweə(r)/ v.tr. (past **forswore** /-ˈswɔː(r)/; past part. **forsworn** /-ˈswɔːn/) **1** abjure; renounce on oath. **2** (as **forsworn** adj.) perjured. □ **forswear oneself** swear falsely; perjure oneself. [OE forswerian (as FOR-, SWEAR)]

forsythia /fɔːˈsaɪθɪə/ n. any ornamental shrub of the genus Forsythia bearing bright-yellow flowers. [mod.L f. W. Forsyth, Engl. botanist d. 1804]

fort n. **1** a fortified building or position. **2** hist. a trading-station, orig. fortified. [F fort or It. forte f. L fortis strong]

forte[1] /ˈfɔːteɪ/ n. a person's strong point; a thing in which a person excels. [F fort strong f. L fortis]

forte[2] /ˈfɔːtɪ/ adj., adv., & n. Mus. —adj. performed loudly. —adv. loudly. —n. a passage to be performed loudly. [It., = strong, loud]

fortepiano /ˌfɔːtɪpɪˈænəʊ/ n. (pl. **-os**) Mus. = PIANOFORTE esp. with ref. to an instrument of the 18th to early 19th c. [FORTE[2] + PIANO[2]]

forth adv. archaic except in set phrases and after certain verbs, esp. bring, come, go, and set **1** forward; into view. **2** onwards in time (from this time forth; henceforth). **3** forwards. **4** out from a starting-point (set forth). □ **and so forth** and so on; and the like. [OE f. Gmc]

forthcoming /fɔːθˈkʌmɪŋ, attrib. ˈfɔːθ-/ adj. **1 a** about or likely to appear or become available. **b** approaching. **2** produced when wanted (no reply was forthcoming). **3** (of a person) informative, responsive. □ **forthcomingness** n.

forthright adj. /ˈfɔːθraɪt/ **1** direct and outspoken; straightforward. **2** decisive, unhesitating. □

forthrightly adv. **forthrightness** n. [OE forthriht (as FORTH, RIGHT)]

forthwith /fɔːθˈwɪθ, -ˈwɪð/ adv. immediately; without delay. [earlier forthwithal (as FORTH, WITH, ALL)]

fortification /ˌfɔːtɪfɪˈkeɪʃ(ə)n/ n. **1** the act or an instance of fortifying; the process of being fortified. **2** Mil. **a** the art or science of fortifying. **b** (usu. in pl.) defensive works fortifying a position. [ME f. F f. LL fortificatio -onis act of strengthening (as FORTIFY)]

fortify /ˈfɔːtɪˌfaɪ/ v.tr. (**-ies**, **-ied**) **1** provide or equip with defensive works so as to strengthen against attack. **2** strengthen or invigorate mentally or morally; encourage. **3** strengthen the structure of. **4** strengthen (wine) with alcohol. **5** increase the nutritive value of (food, esp. with vitamins). □ **fortifiable** adj. **fortifier** n. [ME f. OF fortifier f. LL fortificare f. L fortis strong]

fortissimo /fɔːˈtɪsɪˌməʊ/ adj., adv., & n. Mus. —adj. performed very loudly. —adv. very loudly. —n. (pl. **-os** or **fortissimi** /-ˌmiː/) a passage to be performed very loudly. [It., superl. of FORTE[2]]

fortitude /ˈfɔːtɪˌtjuːd/ n. courage in pain or adversity. [ME f. F f. L fortitudo -dinis f. fortis strong]

fortnight /ˈfɔːtnaɪt/ n. **1** a period of two weeks. **2** (prec. by a specified day) two weeks after (that day) (Tuesday fortnight). [OE fēowertīene niht fourteen nights]

fortnightly /ˈfɔːtˌnaɪtlɪ/ adj., adv., & n. —adj. done, produced, or occurring once a fortnight. —adv. every fortnight. —n. (pl. **-ies**) a magazine etc. issued every fortnight.

Fortran /ˈfɔːtræn/ n. (also **FORTRAN**) Computing a high-level programming language used esp. for scientific calculations. [formula translation]

fortress /ˈfɔːtrɪs/ n. a military stronghold, esp. a strongly fortified town fit for a large garrison. [ME f. OF forteresse, ult. f. L fortis strong]

fortuitous /fɔːˈtjuːɪtəs/ adj. due to or characterized by chance; accidental, casual. □ **fortuitously** adv. **fortuitousness** n. [L fortuitus f. forte by chance]

fortunate /ˈfɔːtjʊnət, -tʃənət/ adj. **1** favoured by fortune; lucky, prosperous. **2** auspicious, favourable. [ME f. L fortunatus (as FORTUNE)]

fortunately /ˈfɔːtjʊnətlɪ, -tʃənətlɪ/ adv. **1** luckily, successfully. **2** (qualifying a whole sentence) it is fortunate that.

fortune /ˈfɔːtjuːn, -tʃuːn/ n. **1 a** chance or luck as a force in human affairs. **b** a person's destiny. **2** (**Fortune**) this force personified, often as a deity. **3** (in sing. or pl.) luck (esp. favourable) that befalls a person or enterprise. **4** good luck. **5** prosperity; a prosperous condition. **6** (also colloq. **small fortune**) great wealth; a huge sum of money. □ **fortune-teller** a person who claims to predict future events in a person's life. [ME f. OF f. L fortuna luck, chance]

forty /ˈfɔːtɪ/ n. & adj. —n. (pl. **-ies**) **1** the product of four and ten. **2** a symbol for this (40, xl, XL). **3** (in pl.) the numbers from 40 to 49, esp. the years of a century or of a person's life. —adj. that amount to forty. □ **forty-five** a gramophone record played at 45 r.p.m. **forty winks** colloq. a short sleep. □ **fortieth** adj. & n. **fortyfold** adj. & adv. [OE fēowertig (as FOUR, -TY[2])]

forum /ˈfɔːrəm/ n. **1** a place of or meeting for public discussion. **2** a periodical etc. giving an opportunity for discussion. **3** a court or tribunal. **4** hist. a public square or market-place in an ancient Roman city used for judicial and other business. [L, in sense 4]

forward /ˈfɔːwəd/ adj., n., adv., & v. —adj. **1** lying in one's line of motion. **2** onward or towards the front. **3** precocious; bold in manner; presumptuous. **4 a** advanced; progressing towards or approaching maturity or completion. **b** (of a plant etc.) well advanced or early. —n. an attacking player positioned near the front of a team in football, hockey, etc. —adv. **1** to the front; into prominence (come forward; move forward). **2** in advance; ahead (sent them forward). **3** onward so as to make progress (not getting any further forward). **4** towards the future; continuously onwards (from this time forward). **5** (also **forwards**) **a** towards the front in the direction one is facing. **b** in the normal direction of motion or of traversal. **c** with continuous forward motion (backwards and forwards; rushing forward). —v.tr. **1 a** send (a letter etc.) on to a further destination. **b** dispatch (goods etc.). **2** help to advance; promote. □ □ **forwarder** n. **forwardly** adv. **forwardness** n. (esp. in sense 3 of adj.). [OE forweard, var. of forthweard (as FORTH, -WARD)]

forwards var. of FORWARD adv. 5.

forwent past of FORGO.

fosse /fɒs/ n. a long narrow trench or excavation, esp. in a fortification. [ME f. OF f. L fossa ditch, fem. past part. of fodere dig]

fossick /ˈfɒsɪk/ v.intr. Austral. & NZ colloq. (foll. by about, around) rummage, search. □ **fossicker** n. [19th c.: cf. dial. fossick bustle about]

fossil /ˈfɒs(ə)l/ n. & adj. —n. **1** the remains or impression of a (usu. prehistoric) plant or animal hardened in rock (often attrib.: fossil shells). **2** colloq. an antiquated or unchanging person or thing. —adj. **1** of or like a fossil. **2** antiquated; out of date. □ **fossil fuel** a natural fuel such as coal or gas formed in the geological past from the remains of living organisms. □ **fossiliferous** /ˌfɒsɪˈlɪfərəs/ adj. **fossilize** v.tr. & intr. (also **-ise**). **fossilization** /-ˈzeɪʃ(ə)n/ n. [F fossile f. L fossilis f. fodere foss- dig]

foster /ˈfɒstə(r)/ v. & adj. —v.tr. **1 a** promote the growth or development of. **b** encourage or harbour (a feeling). **2** (of circumstances) be favourable to. **3 a** bring up (a child that is not one's own by birth). **b** Brit. (of a local authority etc.) assign (a child) to be fostered. **4** cherish; have affectionate regard for (an idea, scheme, etc.). —adj. **1** having a family connection by fostering and not by birth (foster-brother; foster-parent). **2** involving or concerned with fostering a child (foster care; foster home). □ **fosterage** n. (esp. in sense 3 of v.). **fosterer** n. [OE fōstrian, fōster, rel. to FOOD]

fought past and past part. of FIGHT.

foul /faʊl/ adj., n., adv., & v. —adj. **1** offensive to the senses; loathsome, stinking. **2** dirty, soiled, filthy. **3** colloq. revolting, disgusting. **4 a** containing or charged with noxious matter (foul air). **b** clogged, choked. **5** morally polluted; disgustingly abusive or offensive (foul language; foul deeds). **6** unfair; against the rules of a game etc. (by fair means or foul). **7** (of the weather) wet, rough, stormy. **8** (of a rope etc.) entangled. **9**

(of a ship's bottom) overgrown with weeds, barnacles, etc. —n. **1** Sport an unfair or invalid stroke or piece of play. **2** a collision or entanglement. **3** a foul thing. —adv. unfairly; contrary to the rules. —v. **1** tr. & intr. make or become foul or dirty. **2** tr. (of an animal) make dirty with excrement. **3** a tr. Sport commit a foul against (a player). **b** intr. commit a foul. **4 a** tr. (often foll. by up) cause (an anchor, cable, etc.) to become entangled or muddled. **b** intr. become entangled. **5** tr. (usu. foll. by up) colloq. spoil or bungle. □ **foul mouth** a person who uses foul language. **foul play 1** unfair play in games. **2** treacherous or violent activity, esp. murder. **foul-up** a muddled or bungled situation. □ **foully** adv. **foulness** n. [OE fūl f. Gmc]

foulard /fuːˈlɑːd/ n. **1** a thin soft material of silk or silk and cotton. **2** an article made of this. [F]

found[1] past and past part. of FIND.

found[2] /faʊnd/ v. **1** tr. **a** establish (esp. with an endowment). **b** originate or initiate (an institution). **2** tr. be the original builder or begin the building of (a town etc.). **3** tr. lay the base of (a building etc.). **4** (foll. by on, upon) tr. construct or base (a story, theory, rule, etc.) according to a specified principle or ground. [ME f. OF fonder f. L fundare f. fundus bottom]

found[3] /faʊnd/ v.tr. **1 a** melt and mould (metal). **b** fuse (materials for glass). **2** make by founding. □ **founder** n. [ME f. OF fondre f. L fundere fuspour]

foundation /faʊnˈdeɪʃ(ə)n/ n. **1 a** the solid ground or base, natural or artificial, on which a building rests. **b** (usu. in pl.) the lowest load-bearing part of a building, usu. below ground level. **2** a body or ground on which other parts are overlaid. **3** a basis or underlying principle; groundwork (the report has no foundation). **4 a** the act or an instance of establishing or constituting (esp. an endowed institution) on a permanent basis. **b** such an institution, e.g. a monastery, college, or hospital. **5** (in full **foundation garment**) a woman's supporting undergarment, e.g. a corset. □ **foundation cream** a cream used as a base for applying cosmetics. **foundation-stone 1** a stone laid with ceremony to celebrate the founding of a building. **2** the main ground or basis of something. □ **foundational** adj. [ME f. OF fondation f. L fundatio -onis (as FOUND[2])]

founder[1] /ˈfaʊndə(r)/ n. a person who founds an institution. □ **foundership** n.

founder[2] /ˈfaʊndə(r)/ v. **1 a** intr. (of a ship) fill with water and sink. **b** tr. cause (a ship) to founder. **2** intr. (of a plan etc.) fail. **3** intr. (of earth, a building, etc.) fall down or in, give way. **4** intr. (of a horse or its rider) fall to the ground, fall from lameness, stick fast in mud etc. [ME f. OF fondrer, esfondrer submerge, collapse, ult. f. L fundus bottom]

foundling /ˈfaʊndlɪŋ/ n. an abandoned infant of unknown parentage. [ME, perh. f. obs. funding (as FIND, -ING[3]), assim. to -LING[1]]

foundry /ˈfaʊndrɪ/ n. (pl. **-ies**) a workshop for or a business of casting metal.

fount[1] /faʊnt/ n. poet. a spring or fountain; a source. [back-form. f. FOUNTAIN after MOUNT[2]]

fount[2] /faʊnt, fɒnt/ n. (also **font** /fɒnt/) Printing a set of type of one face or size. [F fonte f. fondre FOUND[3]]

fountain /ˈfaʊntɪn/ n. **1 a** a jet or jets of water made to spout for ornamental purposes or for drinking. **b** a structure provided for this. **2** a natural spring of water. **3** a source (in physical or abstract senses). □ **fountain-head** an original source. **fountain-pen** a pen with a reservoir or cartridge holding ink. □ **fountained** adj. (also in comb.). [ME f. OF fontaine f. LL fontana fem. of L fontanus (adj.) f. fons fontis a spring]

four /fɔː(r)/ n. & adj. —n. **1** one more than three. **2** a symbol for this (4, iv, IV, rarely iiii, IIII). **3** a size etc. denoted by four. **4** a four-oared rowing-boat or its crew. **5** the time of four o'clock (is it four yet?). **6** a hit at cricket scoring four runs. —adj. that amount to four. □ **four-in-hand** a vehicle with four horses driven by one person. **four-letter word** any of several short words referring to sexual or excretory functions, regarded as coarse or offensive. **four-poster** a bed with a post at each corner supporting a canopy. **four-square** adj. **1** solidly based. **2** steady, resolute; forthright. **3** square-shaped. —adv. steadily, resolutely. **four-stroke** (of an internal-combustion engine) having a cycle of four strokes (intake, compression, combustion, and exhaust). **four-wheel drive** drive acting on all four wheels of a vehicle. **on all fours** on hands and knees. [OE fēower f. Gmc]

fourfold /ˈfɔːfəʊld/ adj. & adv. **1** four times as much or as many. **2** consisting of four parts. **3** amounting to four.

fourscore /fɔːˈskɔː(r)/ n. archaic eighty.

foursome /ˈfɔːsəm/ n. **1** a group of four persons. **2** a golf match between two pairs with partners playing the same ball.

fourteen /fɔːˈtiːn/ n. & adj. —n. **1** one more than thirteen. **2** a symbol for this (14, xiv, XIV). **3** a size etc. denoted by fourteen. —adj. that amount to fourteen. □ **fourteenth** adj. & n. [OE fēowertīene (as FOUR, -TEEN)]

fourth /fɔːθ/ n. & adj. —n. **1** the position in a sequence corresponding to that of the number 4 in the sequence 1–4. **2** something occupying this position. **3** the fourth person etc. in a race or competition. **4** each of four equal parts of a thing; a quarter. **5** the fourth (and often highest) in a sequence of gears. **6** Mus. **a** an interval or chord spanning four consecutive notes in the diatonic scale (e.g. C to F). **b** a note separated from another by this interval. —adj. that is the fourth. □ **fourth dimension 1** a postulated dimension additional to those determining area and volume. **2** time regarded as equivalent to linear dimensions. **fourth estate** joc. the press; journalism. □ **fourthly** adv. [OE fēortha, fēowertha f. Gmc]

fowl /faʊl/ n. & v. (pl. same or **fowls**) —n. **1** any domestic cock or hen of various gallinaceous birds, kept for eggs and flesh. **2** the flesh of birds, esp. a domestic cock or hen, as food. **3** archaic (except in comb. or collect.) a bird (guinea-fowl; wildfowl). —v.intr. catch or hunt wildfowl. □ **fowl pest** an infectious virus disease of fowls. □ **fowler** n. **fowling** n. [OE fugol f. Gmc]

fox n. & v. —n. **1 a** any of various wild flesh-eating mammals of the dog family, esp. of the genus Vulpes, with a bushy tail and red or grey fur. **b** the fur of a fox. **2** a cunning or sly person. **3** US sl. an attractive young woman. —v. **1 a** intr. act craftily. **b** tr. deceive, baffle, trick. **2** tr. (usu. as **foxed** adj.) discolour (the leaves of a book,

engraving, etc.) with brownish marks. □ **fox-terrier 1** a terrier of a short-haired breed originally used for unearthing foxes. **2** this breed. □ **foxing** n. (in sense 2 of v.). **foxlike** adj. [OE f. WG]

foxglove /ˈfɒksɡlʌv/ n. any tall plant of the genus Digitalis, with erect spikes of purple or white flowers like glove-fingers.

foxhole /ˈfɒkshəʊl/ n. **1** Mil. a hole in the ground used as a shelter against enemy fire or as a firing-point. **2** a place of refuge or concealment.

foxhound /ˈfɒkshaʊnd/ n. a kind of hound bred and trained to hunt foxes.

fox-hunt /ˈfɒkshʌnt/ n. & v. —n. **1** the hunting of foxes with hounds. **2** a particular group of people engaged in this. —v.intr. engage in a fox-hunt. □ **fox-hunter** n. **fox-hunting** n. & adj.

foxtrot /ˈfɒkstrɒt/ n. & v. —n. **1** a ballroom dance with slow and quick steps. **2** the music for this. —v.intr. (**foxtrotted, foxtrotting**) perform this dance.

foxy /ˈfɒksɪ/ adj. (**foxier, foxiest**) **1** of or like a fox. **2** sly or cunning. **3** reddish-brown. **4** (of paper) damaged, esp. by mildew. **5** US sl. (of a woman) sexually attractive. □ **foxily** adv. **foxiness** n.

foyer /ˈfɔɪeɪ/ n. the entrance hall or other large area in a hotel, theatre, etc. [F, = hearth, home, ult. f. L focus fire]

Fr symb. Chem. the element francium.

Fr. abbr. (also **Fr**) **1** Father. **2** French.

fr. abbr. franc(s).

fracas /ˈfrækɑː/ n. (pl. same /-kɑːz/) a noisy disturbance or quarrel. [F. f. fracasser f. It. fracassare make an uproar]

fraction /ˈfrækʃ(ə)n/ n. **1** a numerical quantity that is not a whole number (e.g. ½, 0.5). **2** a small, esp. very small, part, piece, or amount. **3** a portion of a mixture separated by distillation etc. □ **fractionary** adj. **fractionize** v.tr. (also **-ise**). [ME f. OF f. LL fractio -onis f. L frangere fract-break]

fractional /ˈfrækʃən(ə)l/ adj. **1** of or relating to or being a fraction. **2** very slight; incomplete. **3** Chem. relating to the separation of parts of a mixture by making use of their different physical properties (fractional distillation). □ **fractionalize** v.tr. (also **-ise**). **fractionally** adv. (esp. in sense 2).

fractious /ˈfrækʃəs/ adj. **1** irritable, peevish. **2** unruly. □ **fractiously** adv. **fractiousness** n. [FRACTION in obs. sense 'brawling', prob. after factious etc.]

fracture /ˈfræktʃə(r)/ n. & v. —n. **1** breakage or breaking, esp. of a bone or cartilage. **2** the result of breaking; a crack or split. —v.intr. & tr. **1** Med. undergo or cause to undergo a fracture. **2** break or cause to break. [ME f. F fracture or f. L fractura (as FRACTION)]

fragile /ˈfrædʒaɪl, -dʒɪl/ adj. **1** easily broken; weak. **2** of delicate frame or constitution; not strong. □ **fragilely** adv. **fragility** /frəˈdʒɪlɪtɪ/ n. [F fragile or L fragilis f. frangere break]

fragment n. & v. —n. /ˈfræɡmənt/ **1** a part broken off; a detached piece. **2** an isolated or incomplete part. **3** the remains of an otherwise lost or destroyed whole, esp. the extant remains or unfinished portion of a book or work of art. —v.tr. & intr. /fræɡˈment/ break or separate into fragments. □ **fragmental** /-ˈment(ə)l/ adj.

fragmentize /ˈfrægmənˌtaɪz/ v.tr. (also **-ise**). [ME f. F *fragment* or L *fragmentum* (as FRAGILE)]

fragmentary /ˈfrægməntərɪ/ adj. **1** consisting of fragments. **2** disconnected. □ **fragmentarily** adv.

fragmentation /ˌfrægmənˈteɪʃ(ə)n/ n. the process or an instance of breaking into fragments. □ **fragmentation bomb** a bomb designed to break up into small rapidly-moving fragments when exploded.

fragrance /ˈfreɪɡrəns/ n. **1** sweetness of smell. **2** a sweet scent. [F *fragrance* or L *fragrantia* (as FRAGRANT)]

fragrant /ˈfreɪɡrənt/ adj. sweet-smelling. □ **fragrantly** adv. [ME f. F *fragrant* or L *fragrare* smell sweet]

frail adj. **1** fragile, delicate. **2** in weak health. **3** morally weak; unable to resist temptation. □ **frailly** adv. **frailness** n. [ME f. OF *fraile*, *frele* f. L *fragilis* FRAGILE]

frailty /ˈfreɪltɪ/ n. (pl. **-ies**) **1** the condition of being frail. **2** liability to err or yield to temptation. **3** a fault, weakness, or foible. [ME f. OF *frailete* f. L *fragilitas -tatis* (as FRAGILE)]

frame /freɪm/ n. & v. —n. **1** a case or border enclosing a picture, window, door, etc. **2** the basic rigid supporting structure of anything, e.g. of a building, motor vehicle, or aircraft. **3** (in pl.) the structure of spectacles holding the lenses. **4** a human or animal body, esp. with reference to its size or structure (*his frame shook with laughter*). **5** construction, constitution, build. **6** a temporary state (esp. in **frame of mind**). **7** a single complete image or picture on a cinema film or transmitted in a series of lines by television. **8 a** a triangular structure for positioning the balls in snooker etc. **b** a round of play in snooker etc. **9** *Hort.* a boxlike structure of glass etc. for protecting plants. **10** *US sl.* = *frame-up*. —v.tr. **1 a** set in or provide with a frame. **b** serve as a frame for. **2** construct by a combination of parts or in accordance with a design or plan. **3** formulate or devise the essentials of (a complex thing, idea, theory, etc.). **4** (foll. by *to*, *into*) adapt or fit. **5** *sl.* concoct a false charge or evidence against; devise a plot with regard to. **6** articulate (words). □ **frame of reference 1** a set of standards or principles governing behaviour, thought, etc. **2** *Geom.* a system of geometrical axes for defining position. **frame-up** *colloq.* a conspiracy, esp. to make an innocent person appear guilty. □ **framable** adj. **frameless** adj. **framer** n. [OE *framian* be of service f. *fram* forward: see FROM]

framework /ˈfreɪmwɜːk/ n. **1** an essential supporting structure. **2** a basic system.

franc /fræŋk/ n. the chief monetary unit of France, Belgium, Switzerland, Luxemburg, and several other countries. [ME f. OF f. *Francorum Rex* king of the Franks, the legend on the earliest gold coins so called (14th c.): see FRANK]

franchise /ˈfræntʃaɪz/ n. & v. —n. **1 a** the right to vote at State (esp. parliamentary) elections. **b** the principle of qualification for this. **2** full membership of a corporation or State; citizenship. **3** authorization granted to an individual or group by a company to sell its goods or services in a particular way. **4** a right or privilege granted to a corporation or person. —v.tr. grant a franchise to. □ **franchisee** /-ˈziː/ n. **franchiser**

n. (also **franchisor**). [ME f. OF f. *franc, franche* free: see FRANK]

Franciscan /frænˈsɪskən/ n. & adj. —n. a friar, nun, or sister of an order founded by St Francis of Assisi. —adj. of St Francis or his order. [F *franciscain* f. mod.L *Franciscanus* f. *Franciscus* Francis]

francium /ˈfræŋkɪəm/ n. *Chem.* a radioactive metallic element occurring naturally in uranium and thorium ores. [mod.L f. *France* (the discoverer's country)]

Franco- /ˈfræŋkəʊ/ comb. form **1** French; French and (*Franco-German*). **2** regarding France or the French (*Francophile*). [med.L *Francus* FRANK]

francophone /ˈfræŋkəˌfəʊn/ n. & adj. —n. a French-speaking person. —adj. French-speaking. [FRANCO- + Gk *phōnē* voice]

frangipane /ˈfrændʒɪˌpeɪn/ n. **1** an almond-flavoured cream or paste. **2** = FRANGIPANI. [F prob. f. Marquis *Frangipani*, 16th-c. It. inventor of the perfume]

frangipani /ˌfrændʒɪˈpɑːnɪ/ n. (pl. **frangipanis**) **1** any tree or shrub of the genus *Plumeria*, native to tropical America, esp. *P. rubra* with clusters of fragrant white, pink, or yellow flowers. **2** the perfume from this plant. [var. of FRANGIPANE]

franglais /ˈfrɒŋleɪ/ n. a corrupt version of French using many words and idioms borrowed from English. [F f. *français* French + *anglais* English]

Frank n. a member of the Germanic nation or coalition that conquered Gaul in the 6th c. □ **Frankish** adj. [OE *Franca*, OHG *Franko*, perh. f. the name of a weapon: cf. OE *franca* javelin]

frank adj., v., & n. —adj. **1** candid, outspoken (a *frank opinion*). **2** undisguised, avowed (*frank admiration*). **3** ingenuous, open (a *frank face*). —v.tr. stamp (a letter) with an official mark (esp. other than a normal postage stamp) to record the payment of postage. —n. **1** a franking signature or mark. **2** a franked cover. □ **frankable** adj. **franker** n. **frankness** n. [ME f. OF *franc* f. med.L *francus* free, f. FRANK (since only Franks had full freedom in Frankish Gaul)]

Frankenstein /ˈfræŋkənˌstaɪn/ n. (in full **Frankenstein's monster**) a thing that becomes terrifying to its maker; a monster. [Baron *Frankenstein*, a character in and the title of a novel (1818) by Mary Shelley]

frankfurter /ˈfræŋkˌfɜːtə(r)/ n. a seasoned smoked sausage made of beef and pork. [G *Frankfurter Wurst* Frankfurt sausage]

frankincense /ˈfræŋkɪnˌsens/ n. an aromatic gum resin used for burning as incense. [ME f. OF *franc encens* pure incense]

frankly /ˈfræŋklɪ/ adv. **1** in a frank manner. **2** (qualifying a whole sentence) to be frank.

frantic /ˈfræntɪk/ adj. **1** wildly excited; frenzied. **2** characterized by great hurry or anxiety; desperate, violent. □ **frantically** adv. **franticly** adv. **franticness** n. [ME *frentik*, *frantik* f. OF *frenetique* f. L *phreneticus*: see PHRENETIC]

frappé /ˈfræpeɪ/ adj. (of wine) iced, cooled. [F, past part. of *frapper* strike, ice (drinks)]

fraternal /frəˈtɜːn(ə)l/ adj. **1** of a brother or brothers. **2** suitable to a brother; brotherly. **3** (of twins) developed from separate ova and not necessarily closely similar. □ **fraternalism** n. **fraternally** adv. [med.L *fraternalis* f. L *fraternus* f. *frater* brother]

fraternity /frə'tɜːnɪtɪ/ n. (pl. **-ies**) **1** a religious brotherhood. **2** a group or company with common interests, or of the same professional class. **3** US a male students' society in a university or college. **4** being fraternal; brotherliness. [ME f. OF *fraternité* f. L *fraternitas -tatis* (as FRATERNAL)]

fraternize /'frætəˌnaɪz/ v.intr. (also **-ise**) (often foll. by *with*) **1** associate; make friends; behave as intimates. **2** (of troops) enter into friendly relations with enemy troops or the inhabitants of an occupied country. □ **fraternization** /-'zeɪʃ(ə)n/ n. [F *fraterniser* & med.L *fraternizare* f. L *fraternus*: see FRATERNAL]

fratricide /'frætrɪˌsaɪd/ n. **1** the killing of one's brother or sister. **2** a person who does this. □ **fratricidal** /-'saɪd(ə)l/ adj. [F *fratricide* or LL *fratricidium*, L *fratricida*, f. *frater fratris* brother]

Frau /frau/ n. (pl. **Frauen** /'frauən/) (often as a title) a married or widowed German woman. [G]

fraud n. **1** criminal deception; the use of false representations to gain an unjust advantage. **2** a dishonest artifice or trick. **3** a person or thing not fulfilling what is claimed or expected of it. [ME f. OF *fraude* f. L *fraus fraudis*]

fraudulent /'frɔːdjʊlənt/ adj. **1** characterized by or achieved by fraud. **2** guilty of fraud; intending to deceive. □ **fraudulence** n. **fraudulently** adv. [ME f. OF *fraudulent* or L *fraudulentus* (as FRAUD)]

fraught /frɔːt/ adj. **1** (foll. by *with*) filled or attended with (*fraught with danger*). **2** colloq. causing or affected by great anxiety or distress. [ME, past part. of obs. *fraught* (v.) load with cargo f. MDu. *vrachten* f. *vracht* FREIGHT]

Fräulein /'frɔɪlaɪn/ n. (often as a title or form of address) an unmarried (esp. young) German woman. [G, dimin. of FRAU]

fray[1] v. **1** tr. & intr. wear through or become worn, esp. (of woven material) unweave at the edges. **2** intr. (of nerves, temper, etc.) become strained; deteriorate. [F *frayer* f. L *fricare* rub]

fray[2] n. **1** conflict, fighting (*eager for the fray*). **2** a noisy quarrel or brawl. [ME f. *fray* to quarrel f. *affray* (v.) (as AFFRAY)]

frazzle /'fræz(ə)l/ n. & v. colloq. —n. a worn or exhausted state (*burnt to a frazzle*). —v.tr. (usu. as **frazzled** adj.) wear out; exhaust. [orig. uncert.]

freak n. & v. —n. **1** (also **freak of nature**) a monstrosity; an abnormally developed individual or thing. **2** (often *attrib.*) an abnormal, irregular, or bizarre occurrence (*a freak storm*). **3** colloq. **a** an unconventional person. **b** a person with a specified enthusiasm or interest (*health freak*). **4 a** a caprice or vagary. **b** capriciousness. —v. (often foll. by *out*) colloq. **1** intr. & tr. become or make very angry. **2** intr. & tr. undergo or cause to undergo hallucinations or a strong emotional experience, esp. from use of narcotics. **3** intr. adopt a wildly unconventional lifestyle. [16th c.: prob. f. dial.]

freakish /'friːkɪʃ/ adj. **1** of or like a freak. **2** bizarre, unconventional. □ **freakishly** adv. **freakishness** n.

freaky /'friːkɪ/ adj. (**freakier, freakiest**) = FREAKISH. □ **freakily** adv. **freakiness** n.

freckle /'frek(ə)l/ n. & v. —n. (often in pl.) a light brown spot on the skin, usu. caused by exposure to the sun. —v. **1** tr. (usu. as **freckled** adj.) spot with freckles. **2** intr. be spotted with freckles. □

freckly adj. [ME *fracel* etc. f. dial. *freken* f. ON *freknur* (pl.)]

free adj., adv., & v. —adj. (**freer** /'friːə(r)/; **freest** /'friːɪst/) **1** not in bondage to or under the control of another; having personal rights and social and political liberty. **2** (of a State, or its citizens or institutions) subject neither to foreign domination nor to despotic government; having national and civil liberty (*a free press; a free society*). **3 a** unrestricted, unimpeded; not restrained or fixed. **b** at liberty; not confined or imprisoned. **c** released from ties or duties; unimpeded. **d** unrestrained as to action; independent (*set free*). **4** (foll. by *of, from*) **a** not subject to; exempt from (*free of tax*). **b** not containing or subject to a specified (usu. undesirable) thing (*free of preservatives; free from disease*). **5** (foll. by *to* + infin.) able or permitted to take a specified action (*you are free to choose*). **6** unconstrained (*free gestures*). **7 a** available without charge; costing nothing. **b** not subject to tax, duty, trade-restraint, or fees. **8 a** clear of engagements or obligations (*are you free tomorrow?*). **b** not occupied or in use (*the bathroom is free now*). **c** clear of obstructions. **9** spontaneous, unforced (*free compliments*). **10** open to all comers. **11** lavish, profuse; using or used without restraint (*very free with their money*). **12** frank, unreserved. **13** (of a literary style) not observing the strict laws of form. **14** (of a translation) conveying the broad sense; not literal. **15** forward, familiar, impudent. **16** (of talk, stories, etc.) slightly indecent. **17** *Physics* **a** not modified by an external force. **b** not bound in an atom or molecule. **18** *Chem.* not combined (*free oxygen*). —adv. **1** in a free manner. **2** without cost or payment. —v.tr. **1** make free; set at liberty. **2** (foll. by *of, from*) relieve from (something undesirable). **3** disengage, disentangle. □ **free agent** a person with freedom of action. **free and easy** informal, unceremonious. **free-born** inheriting a citizen's rights and liberty. **Free Church** a Church dissenting or seceding from an established Church. **free enterprise** a system in which private business operates in competition and largely free of State control. **free fall** movement under the force of gravity only, esp.: **1** the part of a parachute descent before the parachute opens. **2** the movement of a spacecraft in space without thrust from the engines. **free fight** a general fight in which all present join. **free-for-all** a free fight, unrestricted discussion, etc. **free hand** freedom to act at one's own discretion (see also FREEHAND). **free-handed** generous. **free house** *Brit.* an inn or public house not controlled by a brewery and therefore not restricted to selling particular brands of beer or liquor. **free kick** *Football* a set kick allowed to be taken by one side without interference from the other. **free love** sexual relations according to choice and unrestricted by marriage. **free market** a market in which prices are determined by unrestricted competition. **free on board** (or **rail**) without charge for delivery to a ship or railway wagon. **free port 1** a port area where goods in transit are exempt from customs duty. **2** a port open to all traders. **free radical** *Chem.* an unchanged atom or group of atoms with one or more unpaired electrons. **free-range** esp. *Brit.* (of hens etc.) kept in natural conditions with freedom of movement. **free speech** the right to express opinions freely. **free-spoken** speaking candidly; not concealing one's opinions. **free-standing** not supported by another structure. **free trade** international trade left to its natural course without restriction on imports or exports. **free verse** = VERS LIBRE. **free vote** a Parliamentary vote not subject to party discipline. **free wheel** the driving wheel of a bicycle, able to revolve with the pedals at rest. **free-wheel** *v.intr.* **1** ride a bicycle with the pedals at rest, esp. downhill. **2** move or act without constraint or effort. **free will 1** the power of acting without the constraint of necessity or fate. **2** the ability to act at one's own discretion (*I did it of my own free will*). □ **freely** *adv.* **freeness** *n.* [OE *frēo, frēon* f. Gmc]

-free /friː/ *comb. form* free of or from (*duty-free; fancy-free*).

freebie /ˈfriːbɪ/ *n. esp. US colloq.* a thing provided free of charge. [arbitrary f. FREE]

freebooter /ˈfriːˌbuːtə(r)/ *n.* a pirate or lawless adventurer. □ **freeboot** *v.intr.* [Du. *vrijbuiter* (as FREE, BOOTY): cf. FILIBUSTER]

freedman /ˈfriːdmən/ *n.* (*pl.* **-men**) an emancipated slave.

freedom /ˈfriːdəm/ *n.* **1** the condition of being free or unrestricted. **2** personal or civic liberty; absence of slave status. **3** the power of self-determination; independence of fate or necessity. **4** the state of being free to act (often foll. by *to* + *infin.*: *we have the freedom to leave*). **5** frankness, outspokenness; undue familiarity. **6** (foll. by *from*) the condition of being exempt from or not subject to (a defect, burden, etc.). **7** (foll. by *of*) **a** full or honorary participation in (membership, privileges, etc.). **b** unrestricted use of (facilities etc.). **8** a privilege possessed by a city or corporation. **9** facility or ease in action. **10** boldness of conception. □ **freedom fighter** a person who takes part in violent resistance to an established political system etc. [OE *frēodōm* (as FREE, -DOM)]

freehand /ˈfriːhænd/ *adj.* & *adv.* —*adj.* (of a drawing or plan etc.) done by hand without special instruments or guides. —*adv.* in a freehand manner.

freehold /ˈfriːhəʊld/ *n.* & *adj.* —*n.* **1** tenure of land or property in fee simple or fee tail or for life. **2** land or property or an office held by such tenure. —*adj.* held by or having the status of freehold. □ **freeholder** *n.*

freelance /ˈfriːlɑːns/ *n., v.,* & *adv.* —*n.* **1** (also **freelancer**) a person, usu. self-employed, offering services on a temporary basis, esp. to several businesses etc. for particular assignments. **2** (*attrib.*) (*a freelance editor*). —*v.intr.* act as a freelance. —*adv.* as a freelance. [19th c.: orig. in sense 2 of *n.*]

freeloader /ˈfriːˌləʊdə(r)/ *n. US sl.* a person who eats or drinks at others' expense; a sponger. □ **freeload** /-ˈləʊd/ *v.intr.*

freeman /ˈfriːmən/ *n.* (*pl.* **-men**) **1** a person who has the freedom of a city, company, etc. **2** a person who is not a slave or serf.

Freemason /ˈfriːˌmeɪs(ə)n/ *n.* a member of an international fraternity for mutual help and fellowship, with elaborate secret rituals.

Freemasonry /ˈfriːˌmeɪsənrɪ/ *n.* **1** the system and institutions of the Freemasons. **2** (**freemasonry**) instinctive sympathy or understanding.

freepost /ˈfriːpəʊst/ *n.* a system of sending business post with postage paid by the recipient.

freer *compar.* of FREE.

freesia /ˈfriːzjə, -ʒə/ *n.* any plant of the genus *Freesia*, native to Africa, having fragrant coloured flowers. [mod.L f. F. H. T. *Freese*, Ger. physician d. 1876]

freest *superl.* of FREE.

freestyle /ˈfriːstaɪl/ *adj.* (of a race or contest) in which all styles are allowed, esp.: **1** *Swimming* in which any stroke may be used. **2** *Wrestling* with few restrictions on the holds permitted.

freethinker /friːˈθɪŋkə(r)/ *n.* a person who rejects dogma or authority, esp. in religious belief. □ **freethinking** *n.* & *adj.*

freeware /ˈfriːweə(r)/ *n. Computing* software that is distributed free and without technical support to users. [FREE + SOFTWARE]

freeway /ˈfriːweɪ/ *n. US* **1** an express highway, esp. with controlled access. **2** a toll-free highway.

freeze *v.* & *n.* —*v.* (*past* **froze** /frəʊz/; *past part.* **frozen** /ˈfrəʊz(ə)n/) **1** *tr.* & *intr.* **a** turn or be turned into ice or another solid by cold. **b** (often foll. by *over, up*) make or become rigid or solid as a result of the cold. **2** *intr.* be or feel very cold. **3** *tr.* & *intr.* cover or become covered with ice. **4** *intr.* (foll. by *to, together*) adhere or be fastened by frost (*the curtains froze to the window*). **5** *tr.* preserve (food) by refrigeration below freezing-point. **6** *tr.* & *intr.* **a** make or become motionless or powerless through fear, surprise, etc. **b** react or cause to react with sudden aloofness or detachment. **7** *tr.* stiffen or harden, injure or kill, by chilling (*frozen to death*). **8** *tr.* make (credits, assets, etc.) temporarily or permanently unrealizable. **9** *tr.* fix or stabilize (prices, wages, etc.) at a certain level. **10** *tr.* arrest (an action) at a certain stage of development. **11** *tr.* arrest (a movement in a film) by repeating a frame or stopping the film at a frame. —*n.* **1** a state of frost; a period or the coming of frost or very cold weather. **2** the fixing or stabilization of prices, wages, etc. □ **freeze-dry** (**-dries, -dried**) freeze and dry by the sublimation of ice in a high vacuum. **freeze on to** *colloq.* take or keep tight hold of. **freeze out** *US colloq.* exclude from business, society, etc. by competition or boycott etc. **freeze up** obstruct or be obstructed by the formation of ice. **freeze-up** *n.* a period or conditions of extreme cold. **freezing-point** the temperature at which a liquid, esp. water, freezes. □ **freezable** *adj.* **frozenly** *adv.* [OE *frēosan* f. Gmc]

freezer /ˈfriːzə(r)/ *n.* a refrigerated cabinet or room for preserving food at very low temperatures; = DEEP-FREEZE *n.*

freight /freɪt/ *n.* & *v.* —*n.* **1** the transport of goods in containers or by water or air or *US* by land. **2** goods transported; cargo. **3** a charge for transportation of goods. —*v.tr.* **1** transport (goods) as freight. **2** load with freight. [MDu., MLG *vrecht* var. of *vracht*: cf. FRAUGHT]

freighter /ˈfreɪtə(r)/ *n.* **1** a ship or aircraft designed to carry freight. **2** *US* a wagon for freight.

freightliner /ˈfreɪtˌlaɪnə(r)/ *n.* a train carrying goods in containers.

French adj. & n. —adj. **1** of or relating to France or its people or language. **2** having the characteristics attributed to the French people. —n. **1** the language of France, also used in Belgium, Switzerland, Canada, and elsewhere. **2** (**the French**) (pl.) the people of France. **3** colloq. bad language (excuse my French). **4** colloq. dry vermouth (gin and French). □ **French bean** Brit. **1** a beanplant, Phaseolus vulgaris, having many varieties cultivated for their pods and seeds. **2 a** the pod used as food. **b** the seed used as food. **French bread** white bread in a long crisp loaf. **French Canadian** n. a Canadian whose principal language is French. —adj. of or relating to French-speaking Canadians. **French chalk** a kind of steatite used for marking cloth and removing grease and as a dry lubricant. **French door** = French window. **French dressing** a salad dressing of vinegar and oil, usu. seasoned. **French fried potatoes** (US **French fries**) potato chips. **French horn** a coiled brass wind instrument with a wide bell. **French kiss** a kiss with one partner's tongue inserted in the other's mouth. **French knickers** wide-legged knickers. **French leave** absence without permission. **French letter** Brit. colloq. a condom. **French polish** shellac polish for wood. **French-polish** v.tr. polish with this. **French window** a glazed door in an outside wall, serving as a window and door. □ **Frenchness** n. [OE francisc f. Gmc]

Frenchify /ˈfrentʃɪˌfaɪ/ v.tr. (-ies, -ied) (usu. as **Frenchified** adj.) make French in form, character, or manners.

Frenchman /ˈfrentʃmən/ n. (pl. -men) a man who is French by birth or descent.

Frenchwoman /ˈfrentʃˌwʊmən/ n. (pl. -women) a woman who is French by birth or descent.

frenetic /frəˈnetɪk/ adj. **1** frantic, frenzied. **2** fanatic. □ **frenetically** adv. [ME f. OF frenetique f. L phreneticus f. Gk phrenitikos f. phrenitis delirium f. phrēn phrenos mind]

frenzy /ˈfrenzɪ/ n. & v. —n. (pl. -ies) **1** mental derangement; wild excitement or agitation. **2** delirious fury. —v.tr. (-ies, -ied) (usu. as **frenzied** adj.) drive to frenzy; infuriate. □ **frenziedly** adv. [ME f. OF frenesie f. med.L phrenesia f. L phrenesis f. Gk phrēn mind]

Freon /ˈfriːɒn/ n. propr. any of a group of halogenated hydrocarbons containing fluorine, chlorine, and sometimes bromine, used in aerosols, refrigerants, etc.

frequency /ˈfriːkwənsɪ/ n. (pl. -ies) **1** commonness of occurrence. **2 a** the state of being frequent; frequent occurrence. **b** the process of being repeated at short intervals. **3** Physics the rate of recurrence of a vibration, oscillation, cycle, etc.; the number of repetitions in a given time, esp. per second. □ **frequency band** Electronics = BAND n. 3a. **frequency modulation** Electronics a modulation in which the frequency of the carrier wave is varied. [L frequentia (as FREQUENT)]

frequent adj. & v. —adj. /ˈfriːkwənt/ **1** occurring often or in close succession. **2** habitual, constant (a frequent caller). —v.tr. /frɪˈkwent/ attend or go to habitually. □ **frequentation** /ˌfriːkwenˈteɪʃ(ə)n/ n. **frequenter** /frɪˈkwentə(r)/ n. **frequently** /ˈfriːkwəntlɪ/ adv. [F fréquent or L frequens -entis crowded]

frequentative /frɪˈkwentətɪv/ adj. & n. Gram. —adj. expressing frequent repetition or intensity of action. —n. a verb or verbal form or conjugation expressing this (e.g. chatter, twinkle). [F fréquentatif -ive or L frequentativus (as FREQUENT)]

fresco /ˈfreskəʊ/ n. (pl. -os or -oes) **1** a painting done in water-colour on a wall or ceiling while the plaster is still wet. **2** this method of painting (esp. in fresco). □ **frescoed** adj. [It., = cool, fresh]

fresh adj. & adv. —adj. **1** newly made or obtained (fresh sandwiches). **2 a** other, different; not previously known or used (start a fresh page). **b** additional (fresh supplies). **3** (foll. by from) lately arrived from (a specified place or situation). **4** not stale or musty or faded (fresh flowers; fresh memories). **5** (of food) not preserved by salting, tinning, freezing, etc. **6** not salty (fresh water). **7 a** pure, untainted, refreshing, invigorating (fresh air). **b** bright and pure in colour (a fresh complexion). **8** (of the wind) brisk; of fair strength. **9** alert, vigorous, fit. **10** colloq. **a** cheeky, presumptuous. **b** amorously impudent. **11** young and inexperienced. —adv. newly, recently (esp. in comb.: fresh-baked; fresh-cut). □ **freshly** adv. **freshness** n. [ME f. OF freis fresche ult. f. Gmc]

freshen /ˈfreʃ(ə)n/ v. **1** tr. & intr. make or become fresh or fresher. **2** intr. & tr. (foll. by up) **a** wash, change one's clothes, etc. **b** revive, refresh, renew.

fresher /ˈfreʃə(r)/ n. Brit. colloq. = FRESHMAN.

freshet /ˈfreʃɪt/ n. **1** a rush of fresh water flowing into the sea. **2** the flood of a river from heavy rain or melted snow. [prob. f. OF freschete f. frais FRESH]

freshman /ˈfreʃmən/ n. (pl. -men) a first-year student at university or US at high school.

freshwater /ˈfreʃˌwɔːtə(r)/ adj. of or found in fresh water; not of the sea.

fret[1] v. & n. —v. (fretted, fretting) **1** intr. **a** be greatly and visibly worried or distressed. **b** be irritated or resentful. **2** tr. **a** cause anxiety or distress to. **b** irritate, annoy. **3** tr. wear or consume by gnawing or rubbing. **4** tr. form (a channel or passage) by wearing away. —n. irritation, vexation, querulousness (esp. in a fret). [OE fretan f. Gmc, rel. to EAT]

fret[2] n. & v. —n. an ornamental pattern made of continuous combinations of straight lines joined usu. at right angles. —v.tr. (fretted, fretting) **1** embellish or decorate with a fret. **2** adorn (esp. a ceiling) with carved or embossed work. [ME f. OF frete trellis-work and freter (v.)]

fret[3] n. each of a sequence of bars or ridges on the finger-board of some stringed musical instruments (esp. the guitar) fixing the positions of the fingers to produce the desired notes. □ **fretless** adj. [15th c.: orig. unkn.]

fretful /ˈfretfʊl/ adj. visibly anxious, distressed, or irritated. □ **fretfully** adv. **fretfulness** n.

fretsaw /ˈfretsɔː/ n. a saw consisting of a narrow blade stretched on a frame, for cutting thin wood in patterns.

fretwork /ˈfretwɜːk/ n. ornamental work in wood, done with a fretsaw.

Freudian /ˈfrɔɪdɪən/ adj. & n. Psychol. —adj. of or relating to the Austrian psychologist Sigmund Freud (d. 1939) or his methods of psychoanalysis. —n. a follower of Freud or his methods. □ **Freudian slip** an unintentional error regarded as revealing subconscious feelings. □ **Freudianism** n.

Fri. *abbr.* Friday.

friable /ˈfraɪəb(ə)l/ *adj.* easily crumbled. □ **friability** /-ˈbɪlɪti/ *n.* **friableness** *n.* [F *friable* or L *friabilis* f. *friare* crumble]

friar /ˈfraɪə(r)/ *n.* a member of any of certain religious orders of men, esp. the four mendicant orders (Augustinians, Carmelites, Dominicans, and Franciscans). □ **friar's** (or **friars'**) **balsam** a tincture of benzoin etc. used esp. as an inhalant. □ **friarly** *adj.* [ME & OF *frere* f. L *frater fratris* brother]

friary /ˈfraɪərɪ/ *n.* (*pl.* **-ies**) a convent of friars.

fricassee /ˈfrɪkəˌsiː, -ˈsiː/ *n.* & *v.* —*n.* a dish of stewed or fried pieces of meat served in a thick white sauce. —*v.tr.* (**fricassees, fricasseed**) make a fricassee of. [F, fem. past part. of *fricasser* (v.)]

fricative /ˈfrɪkətɪv/ *adj.* & *n.* Phonet. —*adj.* made by the friction of breath in a narrow opening. —*n.* a consonant made in this way, e.g. *f* and *th*. [mod.L *fricativus* f. L *fricare* rub]

friction /ˈfrɪkʃ(ə)n/ *n.* 1 the action of one object rubbing against another. 2 the resistance an object encounters in moving over another. 3 a clash of wills, temperaments, or opinions. □ **frictional** *adj.* **frictionless** *adj.* [F f. L *frictio -onis* f. *fricare* *frict-* rub]

Friday /ˈfraɪdeɪ, -dɪ/ *n.* & *adv.* —*n.* the sixth day of the week, following Thursday. —*adv. colloq.* 1 on Friday. 2 (**Fridays**) on Fridays; each Friday. □ **girl** (or **man**) **Friday** a helper or follower (after Man Friday in Defoe's *Robinson Crusoe*). [OE *frīgedæg* f. Gmc (named after *Frigg* the wife of Odin)]

fridge /frɪdʒ/ *n.* Brit. colloq. = REFRIGERATOR. □ **fridge-freezer** an upright unit comprising a refrigerator and a freezer, each self-contained. [abbr.]

friend /frend/ *n.* 1 a person with whom one enjoys mutual affection and regard (usu. exclusive of sexual or family bonds). 2 a sympathizer, helper, or patron (*no friend to virtue; a friend of order*). 3 a person who is not an enemy or who is on the same side (*friend or foe?*). 4 a person already mentioned or under discussion (*my friend at the next table then left the room*). 5 (usu. in *pl.*) a regular contributor of money or other assistance to an institution. 6 (**Friend**) a member of the Society of Friends, a Quaker. □ **friended** *adj.* **friendless** *adj.* [OE *frēond* f. Gmc]

friendly /ˈfrendlɪ/ *adj., n.,* & *adv.* —*adj.* (**friendlier, friendliest**) 1 acting as or like a friend, well-disposed, kindly. 2 a (often foll. by *with*) on amicable terms. b not hostile. 3 characteristic of friends, showing or prompted by kindness. 4 favourably disposed, ready to approve or help. 5 a (of a thing) serviceable, convenient, opportune. b = user-friendly. —*n.* (*pl.* **-ies**) = friendly match. —*adv.* in a friendly manner. □ **friendly fire** *Mil.* fire coming from one's own side in a conflict, esp. as the cause of accidental injury or damage to one's forces. **friendly match** a match played for enjoyment and not in competition for a cup etc. □ **friendlily** *adv.* **friendliness** *n.*

friendship /ˈfrendʃɪp/ *n.* 1 being friends, the relationship between friends. 2 a friendly disposition felt or shown. [OE *frēondscipe* (as FRIEND, -SHIP)]

frier var. of FRYER.

Friesian /ˈfriːʒ(ə)n, -zɪən/ *n.* & *adj.* Brit. —*n.* 1 a large animal of a usu. black and white breed of dairy cattle orig. from Friesland. 2 this breed. —*adj.* of or concerning Friesians. [var. of FRISIAN]

frieze /friːz/ *n.* 1 the part of an entablature between the architrave and the cornice. 2 a horizontal band of sculpture filling this. 3 a band of decoration elsewhere, esp. along a wall near the ceiling. [F *frise* f. med.L *frisium, frigium* f. L *Phrygium* (*opus*) (work) of Phrygia]

frigate /ˈfrɪgɪt/ *n.* 1 a Brit. a naval escort-vessel between a corvette and a destroyer in size. b US a similar ship between a destroyer and a cruiser in size. 2 *hist.* a warship next in size to ships of the line. [F *frégate* f. It. *fregata*, of unkn. orig.]

fright /fraɪt/ *n.* 1 a sudden or extreme fear. b an instance of this (*gave me a fright*). 2 a person or thing looking grotesque or ridiculous. □ **take fright** become frightened. [OE *fryhto*, metathetic form of *fyrhto*, f. Gmc]

frighten /ˈfraɪt(ə)n/ *v.tr.* 1 fill with fright; terrify. 2 (foll. by *away, off, out, into*) drive or force by fright (*frightened it out of the room; frightened them into submission*). □ **frightening** *adj.* **frighteningly** *adv.*

frightener /ˈfraɪtənə(r)/ *n.* a person or thing that frightens. □ **put the frighteners on** *sl.* intimidate.

frightful /ˈfraɪtfʊl/ *adj.* 1 a dreadful, shocking, revolting. b ugly, hideous. 2 *colloq.* extremely bad (*a frightful idea*). 3 *colloq.* very great, extreme. □ **frightfully** *adv.* **frightfulness** *n.*

frigid /ˈfrɪdʒɪd/ *adj.* 1 a lacking friendliness or enthusiasm; formal, forced. b dull, flat, insipid. 2 (of a woman) sexually unresponsive. 3 (esp. of climate or air) cold. □ **frigidity** /-ˈdʒɪdɪti/ *n.* **frigidly** *adv.* **frigidness** *n.* [L *frigidus* f. *frigēre* be cold f. *frigus* (n.) cold]

frill *n.* & *v.* —*n.* 1 a a strip of material with one side gathered or pleated and the other left loose with a fluted appearance, used as an ornamental edging. b a similar paper ornament on a ham-knuckle, chop, etc. c a natural fringe of feathers, hair, etc., on an animal (esp. a bird) or a plant. 2 (in *pl.*) a unnecessary embellishments or accomplishments. b airs, affectation (*put on frills*). —*v.tr.* 1 decorate with a frill. 2 form into a frill. □ **frilled** *adj.* **frillery** *n.* [16th c.: orig. unkn.]

frilly /ˈfrɪlɪ/ *adj.* (**frillier, frilliest**) 1 having a frill or frills. 2 resembling a frill. □ **frilliness** *n.*

fringe *n.* & *v.* —*n.* 1 a an ornamental bordering of threads left loose or formed into tassels or twists. b such a bordering made separately. c any border or edging. 2 a a portion of the front hair hanging over the forehead. b a natural border of hair etc. in an animal or plant. 3 an outer edge or margin; the outer limit of an area, population, etc. (often *attrib.*: *fringe theatre*). 4 a thing, part, or area of secondary or minor importance. 5 a band of contrasting brightness or darkness produced by diffraction or interference of light. —*v.tr.* 1 adorn or encircle with a fringe. 2 serve as a fringe to. □ **fringe benefit** an employee's benefit supplementing a money wage or salary. **fringe medicine** systems of treatment of disease etc. not regarded as orthodox by the medical profession. □ **fringeless** *adj.* **fringy** *adj.* [ME & OF *frenge* ult. f. LL *fimbria* (earlier only in *pl.*) fibres, fringe]

frippery /ˈfrɪpərɪ/ n. (pl. **-ies**) **1** showy, tawdry, or unnecessary finery or ornament, esp. in dress. **2** empty display in speech, literary style, etc. **3 a** knick-knacks, trifles. **b** a knick-knack or trifle. [F *friperie* f. OF *freperie* f. *frepe* rag]

Frisbee /ˈfrɪzbɪ/ n. *propr.* a concave plastic disc for skimming through the air as an outdoor game. [perh. f. *Frisbie* bakery (Bridgeport, Conn.), whose pie-tins could be used similarly]

Frisian /ˈfrɪzɪən/ adj. & n. —adj. of Friesland (an area comprising the NW Netherlands and adjacent islands). —n. **1** a native or inhabitant of Friesland. **2** the language of Friesland. [L *Frisii* pl. f. OFris. *Frīsa*, *Frēsa*]

frisk v. & n. —v. **1** intr. leap or skip playfully. **2** tr. sl. feel over or search (a person) for a weapon etc. (usu. rapidly). —n. **1** a playful leap or skip. **2** sl. the frisking of a person. □ **frisker** n. [obs. *frisk* (adj.) f. OF *frisque* lively, of unkn. orig.]

frisky /ˈfrɪskɪ/ adj. (**friskier, friskiest**) lively, playful. □ **friskily** adv. **friskiness** n.

frisson /ˈfriːsɒn, -sɔ̃/ n. an emotional thrill. [F, = shiver]

frith var. of FIRTH.

fritillary /frɪˈtɪlərɪ, ˈfrɪ-/ n. (pl. **-ies**) **1** any liliaceous plant of the genus *Fritillaria*, esp. snake's head, having pendent bell-like flowers. **2** any of various butterflies, esp. of the genus *Argynnis*, having red-brown wings chequered with black. [mod.L *fritillaria* f. L *fritillus* dice-box]

fritter[1] /ˈfrɪtə(r)/ v.tr. (usu. foll. by *away*) waste (money, time, energy, etc.) triflingly, indiscriminately, or on divided aims. [obs. n. *fritter(s)* fragments = obs. *fitters* (n.pl.), perh. rel. to MHG *vetze* rag]

fritter[2] /ˈfrɪtə(r)/ n. a piece of fruit, meat, etc., coated in batter and deep-fried (*apple fritter*). [ME f. OF *friture* ult. f. L *frigere* *frict-* FRY[1]]

frivol /ˈfrɪv(ə)l/ v. (**frivolled, frivolling**; US **frivoled, frivoling**) **1** intr. be a trifler; trifle. **2** tr. (foll. by *away*) spend (money or time) foolishly. [back-form. f. FRIVOLOUS]

frivolous /ˈfrɪvələs/ adj. **1** paltry, trifling, trumpery. **2** lacking seriousness; given to trifling; silly. □ **frivolity** /-ˈvɒlɪtɪ/ n. (pl. **-ies**). **frivolously** adv. **frivolousness** n. [L *frivolus* silly, trifling]

frizz v. & n. —v.tr. form (hair) into a mass of small curls. —n. **1** frizzed hair. **2** a row of curls. [F *friser*, perh. f. the stem of *frire* FRY[1]]

frizzle[1] /ˈfrɪz(ə)l/ v.intr. & tr. **1** fry, toast, or grill, with a sputtering noise. **2** (often foll. by *up*) burn or shrivel. [*frizz* (in the same sense) f. FRY[1], with imit. ending + -LE[4]]

frizzle[2] /ˈfrɪz(ə)l/ v. & n. —v. **1** tr. form (hair) into tight curls. **2** intr. (often foll. by *up*) (of hair etc.) curl tightly. —n. frizzled hair. [16th c.: orig. unkn. (earlier form FRIZZ)]

frizzly /ˈfrɪzlɪ/ adj. in tight curls.

frizzy /ˈfrɪzɪ/ adj. (**frizzier, frizziest**) in a mass of small curls. □ **frizziness** n.

fro /frəʊ/ adv. back (now only in *to and fro*: see TO). [ME f. ON *frá* FROM]

frock n. & v. —n. **1** a woman's or girl's dress. **2 a** a monk's or priest's long gown with loose sleeves. **b** priestly office. **3** a smock. —v.tr. invest with priestly office. □ **frock-coat** a man's long-skirted coat not cut away in front. [ME f. OF *froc* f. Frank.]

frog[1] n. **1** any of various small amphibians of the order Anura, having a tailless smooth-skinned body with legs developed for jumping. **2** (**Frog**) *Brit. sl. offens.* a Frenchman. □ **frog in the** (or **one's) throat** *colloq.* hoarseness. **frog-spawn** the spawn of a frog. [OE *frogga* f. Gmc]

frog[2] n. an elastic horny substance in the sole of a horse's foot. [17th c.: orig. uncert. (perh. a use of FROG[1])]

frog[3] n. an ornamental coat-fastening of a spindle-shaped button and loop. □ **frogged** adj. **frogging** n. [18th c.: orig. unkn.]

froggy /ˈfrɒgɪ/ adj. & n. —adj. **1** of or like a frog or frogs. **2** *Brit. sl. offens.* French. —n. (**Froggy**) (pl. **-ies**) *sl. derog.* a Frenchman.

froghopper /ˈfrɒgˌhɒpə(r)/ n. any jumping insect of the family Cercopidae, sucking sap and as larvae producing a protective mass of froth.

frogman /ˈfrɒgmən/ n. (pl. **-men**) a person equipped with a rubber suit, flippers, and an oxygen supply for underwater swimming.

frogmarch /ˈfrɒgmɑːtʃ/ v. & n. esp. *Brit.* —v.tr. **1** hustle (a person) forward holding and pinning the arms from behind. **2** carry (a person) in a frogmarch. —n. the carrying of a person face downwards by four others each holding a limb.

frolic /ˈfrɒlɪk/ v. & n. —v.intr. (**frolicked, frolicking**) play about cheerfully, gambol. —n. **1** cheerful play. **2** a prank. **3** a merry party. □ **frolicker** n. [Du. *vrolijk* (adj.) f. *vro* glad + -*lijk* -LY[1]]

frolicsome /ˈfrɒlɪksəm/ adj. merry, playful. □ **frolicsomely** adv. **frolicsomeness** n.

from /frɒm, frəm/ prep. expressing separation or origin, followed by: **1** a person, place, time, etc., that is the starting-point of motion or action, or of extent in place or time (*rain comes from the clouds; repeated from mouth to mouth; dinner is served from 8; from start to finish*). **2** a place, object, etc. whose distance or remoteness is reckoned or stated (*ten miles from Rome; I am far from admitting it; absent from home*). **3 a** a source (*dig gravel from a pit; a man from Italy; quotations from Shaw*). **b** a giver or sender (*presents from Father Christmas; have not heard from her*). **4 a** a thing or person avoided, escaped, lost, etc. (*released him from prison; cannot refrain from laughing*). **b** a person or thing deprived (*took his gun from him*). **5** a reason, cause, or motive (*died from fatigue; suffering from mumps; did it from jealousy*). **6** a thing distinguished or unlike (*know black from white*). **7** a lower limit (*saw from 10 to 20 boats; tickets from £5*). **8** a state changed for another (*raised the penalty from a fine to imprisonment*). **9** an adverb or preposition of time or place (*from long ago; from abroad*). **10** the position of a person who observes or considers (*saw it from the roof; from his point of view*). **11** a model (*painted it from nature*). □ **from a child** since childhood. **from time to time** occasionally. [OE *fram*, *from* f. Gmc]

fromage frais /ˌfrɒmɑːˈʒ ˈfreɪ/ n. a kind of smooth low-fat soft cheese. [Fr., lit. 'fresh cheese']

frond n. *Bot.* a large usu. divided foliage leaf in various flowerless plants, esp. ferns and palms. □ **frondage** n. **frondose** adj. [L *frons frondis* leaf]

front /frʌnt/ n., adj., & v. —n. **1** the side or part normally nearer or towards the spectator or the direction of motion (*the front of the car; the front of the chair*). **2** any face of a building, esp.

that of the main entrance. **3** Mil. **a** the foremost line or part of an army etc. **b** line of battle. **c** the part of the ground towards a real or imaginary enemy. **d** a scene of actual fighting (go to the front). **4 a** a sector of activity regarded as resembling a military front. **b** an organized political group. **5 a** demeanour, bearing (show a bold front). **b** outward appearance. **6** a forward or conspicuous position (come to the front). **7 a** a bluff. **b** a pretext. **8** a person etc. serving to cover subversive or illegal activities. **9** (prec. by the) the promenade of a seaside resort. **10** Meteorol. the forward edge of an advancing mass of cold or warm air. **11** (prec. by the) the auditorium of a theatre. **12** impudence. —attrib.adj. **1** of the front. **2** situated in front. —v. **1** intr. (foll. by on, to, towards, upon) have the front facing or directed. **2** intr. (foll. by for) sl. act as a front or cover for. **3** tr. furnish with a front (fronted with stone). **4** tr. lead (a band). **5** tr. **a** stand opposite to, front towards. **b** have its front on the side of (a street etc.). □ **front bench** Brit. the foremost seats in Parliament, occupied by leading members of the government and opposition. **front-bencher** Brit. such a member. **front door 1** the chief entrance of a house. **2** a chief means of approach or access to a place, situation, etc. **front line** Mil. = sense 3 of n. **front man** a person acting as a front or cover. **front office** a main office, esp. police headquarters. **front page** the first page of a newspaper, esp. as containing important or remarkable news. **front runner 1** the contestant most likely to succeed. **2** an athlete or horse running best when in the lead. **in front 1** in an advanced position. **2** facing the spectator. **in front of 1** ahead of, in advance of. **2** in the presence of, confronting. □ **frontless** adj. **frontward** adj. & adv. **frontwards** adv. [ME f. OF front (n.), fronter (v.) f. L frons frontis]

frontage /ˈfrʌntɪdʒ/ n. **1** the front of a building. **2 a** land abutting on a street or on water. **b** the land between the front of a building and the road. **3** extent of front (a shop with little frontage). **4 a** the way a thing faces. **b** outlook. □ **frontager** n.

frontal /ˈfrʌnt(ə)l/ adj. **1 a** of, at, or on the front (a frontal attack). **b** of the front as seen by an onlooker (a frontal view). **2** of the forehead or front part of the skull (frontal bone). □ **frontally** adv. [mod.L frontalis (as FRONT)]

frontier /ˈfrʌntɪə(r), -ˈtɪə(r)/ n. **1 a** the border between two countries. **b** the district on each side of this. **2** the limits of attainment or knowledge in a subject. **3** US the borders between settled and unsettled country. □ **frontierless** adj. [ME f. AF frounter, OF frontiere ult. f. L frons frontis FRONT]

frontiersman /ˈfrʌntɪəzmən, -ˈtɪəzmən/ n. (pl. -men) a person living in the region of a frontier, esp. between settled and unsettled country.

frontispiece /ˈfrʌntɪsˌpiːs/ n. an illustration facing the title-page of a book or of one of its divisions. [F frontispice or LL frontispicium façade f. L frons frontis FRONT + -spicium f. specere look: assim. to PIECE]

frost n. & v. —n. **1 a** (also **white frost**) a white frozen dew coating esp. the ground at night. **b** a consistent temperature below freezing-point causing frost to form. **2** a chilling dispiriting atmosphere. **3** sl. a failure. —v. **1** intr. (usu. foll.

by over, up) become covered with frost. **2** tr. **a** cover with or as if with frost, powder, etc. **b** injure (a plant etc.) with frost. **3** tr. give a roughened or finely granulated surface to (glass, metal) (frosted glass). **4** tr. US cover or decorate (a cake etc.) with icing. □ **degrees of frost** Brit. degrees below freezing-point (ten degrees of frost tonight). □ **frostless** adj. [OE f. Gmc]

frostbite /ˈfrɒstbaɪt/ n. injury to body tissues, esp. the nose, fingers, or toes, due to freezing.

frosting /ˈfrɒstɪŋ/ n. **1** US icing. **2** a rough surface on glass etc.

frosty /ˈfrɒstɪ/ adj. (**frostier**, **frostiest**) **1** cold with frost. **2** covered with or as with hoar-frost. **3** unfriendly in manner, lacking in warmth of feeling. □ **frostily** adv. **frostiness** n.

froth n. & v. —n. **1 a** a collection of small bubbles in liquid, caused by shaking, fermenting, etc.; foam. **b** impure matter on liquid, scum. **2 a** idle talk or ideas. **b** anything unsubstantial or of little worth. —v. **1** intr. emit or gather froth (frothing at the mouth). **2** tr. cause (beer etc.) to foam. □ **frothily** adv. **frothiness** n. **frothy** adj. (**frothier**, **frothiest**). [ME f. ON frotha, frauth f. Gmc]

froward /ˈfrəʊəd/ adj. archaic perverse; difficult to deal with. □ **frowardly** adv. **frowardness** n. [ME f. FRO + -WARD]

frown /fraʊn/ v. & n. —v. **1** intr. wrinkle one's brows, esp. in displeasure or deep thought. **2** intr. (foll. by at, on, upon) express disapproval. **3** intr. (of a thing) present a gloomy aspect. —n. **1** an action of frowning; a vertically furrowed or wrinkled state of the brow. **2** a look expressing severity, disapproval, or deep thought. □ **frowner** n. **frowningly** adv. [ME f. OF frongnier, froignier f. froigne surly look f. Celt.]

frowst /fraʊst/ n. & v. Brit. colloq. —n. fusty warmth in a room. —v.intr. stay in or enjoy frowst. □ **frowster** n. [back-form. f. FROWSTY]

frowsty /ˈfraʊstɪ/ adj. Brit. (**frowstier**, **frowstiest**) fusty, stuffy. □ **frowstiness** n. [var. of FROWZY]

frowzy /ˈfraʊzɪ/ adj. (also **frowsy**) (-**ier**, -**iest**) **1** fusty, musty, ill-smelling, close. **2** slatternly, unkempt, dingy. □ **frowziness** n. [17th c.: orig. unkn.: cf. earlier frowy]

froze past of FREEZE.

frozen past part. of FREEZE.

FRS abbr. (in the UK) Fellow of the Royal Society.

fructify /ˈfrʌktɪˌfaɪ/ v. (-**ies**, -**ied**) **1** intr. bear fruit. **2** tr. make fruitful; impregnate. □ **fructification** /-ˈkeɪʃ(ə)n/ n. [ME f. OF fructifier f. L fructificare f. fructus FRUIT]

fructose /ˈfrʌktəʊz, -əʊs, ˈfrʊk-/ n. Chem. a simple sugar found in honey and fruits. [L fructus FRUIT + -OSE²]

frugal /ˈfruːg(ə)l/ adj. **1** (often foll. by of) sparing or economical, esp. as regards food. **2** sparingly used or supplied; meagre, costing little. □ **frugality** /-ˈɡælɪtɪ/ n. **frugally** adv. **frugalness** n. [L frugalis f. frugi economical]

fruit /fruːt/ n. & v. —n. **1 a** the usu. sweet and fleshy edible product of a plant or tree, containing seed. **b** (in sing.) these in quantity (eats fruit). **2** the seed of a plant or tree with its covering, e.g. an acorn, pea pod, cherry, etc. **3** (usu. in pl.) vegetables, grains, etc. used for food (fruits of the earth). **4** (usu. in pl.) the result of action etc., esp. as financial reward (fruits of his labours). **5** Bibl. an offspring (the fruit of the womb;

the fruit of his loins). —v.intr. & tr. bear or cause to bear fruit. □ **fruit-bat** any large bat of the suborder Megachiroptera, feeding on fruit. **fruit cake 1** a cake containing dried fruit. **2** sl. an eccentric or mad person. **fruit fly** (pl. **flies**) any of various flies, esp. of the genus *Drosophila*, having larvae that feed on fruit. **fruit machine** Brit. a coin-operated gaming machine giving random combinations of symbols often representing fruit. **fruit salad** various fruits cut up and served in syrup, juice, etc. **fruit sugar** fructose. □ **fruitage** n. **fruited** adj. (also in comb.). **fruiter** n. [ME f. OF f. L *fructus* fruit, enjoyment f. *frui* enjoy]

fruiterer /ˈfruːtərə(r)/ n. esp. Brit. a dealer in fruit.

fruitful /ˈfruːtfʊl/ adj. **1** producing much fruit; fertile; causing fertility. **2** producing good results, successful; beneficial, remunerative. **3** producing offspring, esp. prolifically. □ **fruitfully** adv. **fruitfulness** n.

fruition /fruːˈɪʃ(ə)n/ n. **1 a** the bearing of fruit. **b** the production of results. **2** the realization of aims or hopes. **3** enjoyment. [ME f. OF f. LL *fruitio -onis* f. *frui* enjoy, erron. assoc. with FRUIT]

fruitless /ˈfruːtlɪs/ adj. **1** not bearing fruit. **2** useless, unsuccessful, unprofitable. □ **fruitlessly** adv. **fruitlessness** n.

fruity /ˈfruːtɪ/ adj. (**fruitier, fruitiest**) **1 a** of fruit. **b** tasting or smelling like fruit, esp. (of wine) tasting of the grape. **2** (of a voice etc.) of full rich quality. **3** colloq. full of rough humour or (usu. scandalous) interest; suggestive. □ **fruitily** adv. **fruitiness** n.

frump n. a dowdy unattractive old-fashioned woman. □ **frumpish** adj. **frumpishly** adv. [16th c.: perh. f. dial. *frumple* (v.) wrinkle f. MDu. *verrompelen* (as FOR-, RUMPLE)]

frumpy /ˈfrʌmpɪ/ adj. (**frumpier, frumpiest**) dowdy, unattractive, and old-fashioned. □ **frumpily** adv. **frumpiness** n.

frustrate v. & adj. —v.tr. /frʌˈstreɪt, ˈfrʌs-/ **1** make (efforts) ineffective. **2** prevent (a person) from achieving a purpose. **3** (as **frustrated** adj.) **a** discontented because unable to achieve one's desire. **b** sexually unfulfilled. **4** disappoint (a hope). —adj. /ˈfrʌstreɪt/ archaic frustrated. □ **frustratedly** adv. **frustrater** n. **frustrating** adj. **frustratingly** adv. **frustration** n. [ME f. L *frustrari frustrat-* f. *frustra* in vain]

fry[1] v. & n. —v. (**fries, fried**) **1** tr. & intr. cook or be cooked in hot fat. **2** tr. & intr. sl. electrocute or be electrocuted. —n. (pl. **fries**) **1** various internal parts of animals usu. eaten fried (*lamb's fry*). **2** a dish of fried food, esp. meat. **3** US a social gathering to eat fried food. □ **frying-** (US **fry-**) **pan** a shallow pan used in frying. **fry up** heat or reheat (food) in a frying-pan. **fry-up** n. Brit. colloq. a dish of miscellaneous fried food. [ME f. OF *frire* f. L *frigere*]

fry[2] n.pl. **1** young or newly hatched fishes. **2** the young of other creatures produced in large numbers, e.g. bees or frogs. □ **small fry** people of little importance; children. [ME f. ON *frjó*]

fryer /ˈfraɪə(r)/ n. (also **frier**) **1** a person who fries. **2** a vessel for frying fish. **3** US a chicken suitable for frying.

ft. abbr. foot, feet.

fuchsia /ˈfjuːʃə/ n. any shrub of the genus *Fuchsia*, with drooping red or purple or white flowers. [mod.L f. L. *Fuchs*, Ger. botanist d. 1566]

fuck v., int., & n. coarse sl. —v. **1** tr. & intr. have sexual intercourse (with). **2** intr. (foll. by about, around) mess about; fool around. **3** tr. (usu. as an exclam.) curse, confound (*fuck the thing!*). **4** intr. (as **fucking** adj., adv.) used as an intensive to express annoyance etc. —int. expressing anger or annoyance. —n. **1 a** an act of sexual intercourse. **b** a partner in sexual intercourse. **2** the slightest amount (*don't give a fuck*). □ **fuck all** nothing. **fuck off** go away. **fuck up** make a mess of. **fuck-up** n. a mess or muddle. □ **fucker** n. (often as a term of abuse). [16th c.: orig. unkn.]

■ **Usage** This is considered a highly taboo word.

fuddle /ˈfʌd(ə)l/ v. & n. —v. **1** tr. confuse or stupefy, esp. with alcoholic liquor. **2** intr. tipple, booze. —n. **1** confusion. **2** intoxication. **3** a spell of drinking (*on the fuddle*). [16th c.: orig. unkn.]

fuddy-duddy /ˈfʌdɪˌdʌdɪ/ adj. & n. sl. —adj. old-fashioned or quaintly fussy. —n. (pl. **-ies**) a fuddy-duddy person. [20th c.: orig. unkn.]

fudge n. & v. —n. **1 a** a soft toffee-like sweet made with milk, sugar, butter, etc. **2** nonsense. **3** a piece of dishonesty or faking. —v. **1** tr. put together in a makeshift or dishonest way; fake. **2** tr. deal with incompetently. **3** intr. practise such methods. [perh. f. obs. *fadge* (v.) fit]

fuel /ˈfjuːəl/ n. & v. —n. **1** material, esp. coal, wood, oil, etc., burnt or used as a source of heat or power. **2** food as a source of energy. **3** material used as a source of nuclear energy. **4** anything that sustains or inflames emotion or passion. —v. (**fuelled, fuelling**; US **fueled, fueling**) **1** tr. supply with fuel. **2** tr. sustain or inflame (an argument, feeling, etc.) (*drink fuelled his anger*). **3** intr. take in or get fuel. □ **fuel cell** a cell producing an electric current direct from a chemical reaction. **fuel element** an element of nuclear fuel etc. for use in a reactor. **fuel injection** the direct introduction of fuel under pressure into the combustion units of an internal-combustion engine. **fuel oil** oil used as fuel in an engine or furnace. [ME f. AF *fuaille*, *fewaile*, OF *fouaille*, ult. f. L *focus* hearth]

fug n. & v. colloq. —n. stuffiness or fustiness of the air in a room. —v.intr. (**fugged, fugging**) stay in or enjoy a fug. □ **fuggy** adj. [19th c.: orig. unkn.]

fugal /ˈfjuːg(ə)l/ adj. of the nature of a fugue. □ **fugally** adv.

fugitive /ˈfjuːdʒɪtɪv/ adj. & n. —adj. **1** fleeing; that runs or has run away. **2** transient, fleeting; of short duration. **3** (of literature) of passing interest, ephemeral. **4** flitting, shifting. —n. **1** (often foll. by *from*) a person who flees, esp. from justice, an enemy, danger, or a master. **2** an exile or refugee. □ **fugitively** adv. [ME f. OF *fugitif -ive* f. L *fugitivus* f. *fugere fugit-* flee]

fugue /fjuːg/ n. Mus. a contrapuntal composition in which a short melody or phrase (the subject) is introduced by one part and successively taken up by others and developed by interweaving the parts. □ **fuguist** n. [F or It. f. L *fuga* flight]

fugued /fjuːgd/ adj. in the form of a fugue.

führer /ˈfjʊərə(r)/ n. (also **fuehrer**) a leader, esp. a tyrannical one. [G, = leader: part of the title assumed by Adolf Hitler in Germany in 1934]

-ful /fʊl/ comb. form forming: **1** adjectives from nouns, meaning: **a** full of (*beautiful*). **b** having the qualities of (*masterful*). **2** adjectives from adjectives or Latin stems with little change of sense (*direful; grateful*). **3** adjectives from verbs, meaning 'apt to', 'able to', 'accustomed to' (*forgetful*; *mournful*; *useful*). **4** nouns (pl. **-fuls**) meaning 'the amount needed to fill' (*handful*; *spoonful*).

fulcrum /ˈfʊlkrəm, ˈfʌl-/ *n.* (pl. **fulcra** /-rə/ or **fulcrums**) **1** the point against which a lever is placed to get a purchase or on which it turns or is supported. **2** the means by which influence etc. is brought to bear. [L, = post of a couch, f. *fulcire* to prop]

fulfil /fʊlˈfɪl/ *v.tr.* (*US* **fulfill**) (**fulfilled, fulfilling**) **1** bring to consummation, carry out (a prophecy or promise). **2** satisfy (a desire or prayer). **3 a** execute, obey (a command or law). **b** perform, carry out (a task). **4** comply with (conditions). **5** answer (a purpose). **6** bring to an end, finish, complete (a period or piece of work). □ **fulfil oneself** develop one's gifts and character to the full. □ **fulfillable** *adj.* **fulfiller** *n.* **fulfilment** *n.* (*US* **fulfillment**). [OE *fullfyllan* (as FULL¹, FILL)]

full¹ /fʊl/ *adj.* & *adv.* —*adj.* **1** (often foll. by *of*) holding all its limits will allow (*the bucket is full*; *full of water*). **2** having eaten to one's limits or satisfaction. **3** abundant, copious, satisfying, sufficient (*led a full life*; *give full details*; *the book is very full on this point*). **4** (foll. by *of*) having or holding an abundance of, showing marked signs of (*full of vitality*; *full of mistakes*). **5** (foll. by *of*) **a** engrossed in thinking about (*full of himself*). **b** unable to refrain from talking about (*full of the news*). **6** complete, perfect, reaching the specified or usual or utmost limit (*full membership*; *full daylight*; *waited a full hour*). **7 a** (of tone or colour) deep and clear, mellow. **b** (of light) intense. **c** (of motion etc.) vigorous (*a full pulse*; *at full gallop*). **8** plump, rounded, protuberant (*a full figure*). **9** (of clothes) made of much material arranged in folds or gathers. **10** (of the heart etc.) overcharged with emotion. —*adv.* **1** very (*you know full well*). **2** quite, fully (*full six miles*; *full ripe*). **3** exactly (*hit him full on the nose*). **4** more than sufficiently (*full early*). □ **at full length 1** lying stretched out. **2** without abridgement. **full back** a defensive player, or a position near the goal, in football, hockey, etc. **full-blooded 1** vigorous, hearty, sensual. **2** not hybrid. **full-blown** fully developed, complete, (of flowers) quite open. **full board** provision of accommodation and all meals at a hotel etc. **full-bodied** rich in quality, tone, etc. **full-bottomed** (of a wig) long at the back. **full brother** a brother born of the same parents. **full-cream** of or made from unskimmed milk. **full-dress** *adj.* (of a debate etc.) of major importance. **full face** with all the face visible to the spectator. **full-frontal 1** (of nudity or a nude figure) with full exposure at the front. **2** unrestrained, explicit; with nothing concealed. **full-grown** having reached maturity. **full house 1** a maximum or large attendance at a theatre, in Parliament, etc. **2** *Poker* a hand with three of a kind and a pair. **full-length 1** not shortened or abbreviated. **2** (of a mirror, portrait, etc.) showing the whole height of the human figure. **full marks** the maximum award in an examination, in assessment of a person, etc. **full measure** not less than the professed amount. **full moon 1** the moon with its whole disc illuminated. **2** the time when this occurs. **full pitch** = *full toss*. **full point** = *full stop* 1.

full professor a professor of the highest grade in a university etc. **full-scale** not reduced in size, complete. **full sister** a sister born of the same parents. **full speed** (or **steam**) **ahead!** an order to proceed at maximum speed or to pursue a course of action energetically. **full stop 1** a punctuation mark (.) used at the end of a sentence or an abbreviation. **2** a complete cessation. **full term** the completion of a normal pregnancy. **full time 1** the total normal duration of work etc. **2** the end of a football etc. match. **full-time** *adj.* occupying or using the whole of the available working time. **full-timer** a person who does a full-time job. **full toss** *Cricket n.* a ball pitched right up to the batsman. —*adv.* without the ball's having touched the ground. **full up** *colloq.* completely full. **in full 1** without abridgement. **2** to or for the full amount (*paid in full*). **in full swing** at the height of activity. **in full view** entirely visible. **to the full** to the utmost extent. [OE f. Gmc]

full² /fʊl/ *v.tr.* cleanse and thicken (cloth). [ME, back-form. f. FULLER: cf. OF *fouler* (FOIL¹)]

fuller /ˈfʊlə(r)/ *n.* a person who fulls cloth. □ **fuller's earth** a type of clay used in fulling cloth and as an adsorbent. [OE *fullere* f. L *fullo*]

fullness /ˈfʊlnɪs/ *n.* (also **fulness**) **1** being full. **2** (of sound, colour, etc.) richness, volume, body. **3** all that is contained (in the world etc.). □ **the fullness of the heart** emotion, genuine feelings. **the fullness of time** the appropriate or destined time.

fully /ˈfʊlɪ/ *adv.* **1** completely, entirely (*am fully aware*). **2** no less or fewer than (*fully 60*). □ **fully-fashioned** (of women's clothing) shaped to fit the body. **fully-fledged** mature. [OE *fullīce* (as FULL¹, -LY²)]

-fully /ˈfʊlɪ/ *comb. form* forming adverbs corresp. to adjectives in *-ful*.

fulmar /ˈfʊlmə(r)/ *n.* any medium-sized sea bird of the genus *Fulmarus*, with stout body, robust bill, and rounded tail. [orig. Hebridean dial.: perh. f. ON *fúll* FOUL (with ref. to its smell) + *már* gull (cf. MEW²)]

fulminant /ˈfʌlmɪnənt, ˈfʊl-/ *adj.* **1** fulminating. **2** *Med.* (of a disease or symptom) developing suddenly. [F *fulminant* or L *fulminant-* (as FULMINATE)]

fulminate /ˈfʌlmɪˌneɪt, ˈfʊl-/ *v.intr.* **1** (often foll. by *against*) express censure loudly and forcefully. **2** explode violently; flash like lightning (*fulminating mercury*). **3** *Med.* (of a disease or symptom) develop suddenly. □ **fulmination** /-ˈneɪʃ(ə)n/ *n.* **fulminatory** *adj.* [L *fulminare fulminat-* f. *fulmen -minis* lightning]

fulsome /ˈfʊlsəm/ *adj.* disgusting by excess of flattery, servility, or expressions of affection; excessive, cloying. □ **fulsomely** *adv.* **fulsomeness** *n.* [ME f. FULL¹ + -SOME¹]

■ **Usage** The phrase *fulsome praise* is sometimes wrongly used to mean generous praise rather than excessive praise.

fumble /ˈfʌmb(ə)l/ *v.* & *n.* —*v.* **1** *intr.* (often foll. by *at, with, for, after*) use the hands awkwardly, grope about. **2** *tr.* **a** handle or deal with clumsily or nervously. **b** *Sport* fail to stop (a ball) cleanly. —*n.* an act of fumbling. □ **fumbler** *n.* **fumblingly** *adv.* [LG *fummeln, fommeln*, Du. *fommelen*]

fume *n.* & *v.* —*n.* **1** (usu. in *pl.*) exuded gas or smoke or vapour, esp. when harmful or unpleasant. **2** a fit of anger (*in a fume*). —*v.* **1 a** *intr.* emit fumes. **b** *tr.* give off as fumes. **2** *intr.* (often foll. by *at*) be affected by (esp. suppressed) anger (*was fuming at their inefficiency*). **3** *tr.* **a** fumigate. **b** subject to fumes esp. those of ammonia (to darken tints in oak, photographic film, etc.). □ **fumeless** *adj.* **fumingly** *adv.* **fumy** *adj.* (in sense 1 of *n.*). [ME f. OF *fum* f. L *fumus* smoke & OF *fume* f. *fumer* f. L *fumare* to smoke]

fumigate /ˈfjuːmɪˌɡeɪt/ *v.tr.* **1** disinfect or purify with fumes. **2** apply fumes to. □ **fumigant** *n.* **fumigation** /-ˈɡeɪʃ(ə)n/ *n.* **fumigator** *n.* [L *fumigare fumigat-* f. *fumus* smoke]

fun *n.* & *adj.* —*n.* **1** amusement, esp. lively or playful. **2** a source of this. **3** (in full **fun and games**) exciting or amusing goings-on. —*adj.* *disp. colloq.* amusing, entertaining, enjoyable (*a fun thing to do*). □ **for fun** (or **for the fun of it**) not for a serious purpose. **fun run** *colloq.* an uncompetitive run, esp. for sponsored runners in support of a charity. **have fun** enjoy oneself. **in fun** as a joke, not seriously. **is great** (or **good**) **fun** is very amusing. **like fun 1** vigorously, quickly. **2** much. **3** *iron.* not at all. [obs. *fun* (v.) var. of *fon* befool: cf. FOND]

■ **Usage** The use of *fun* as an attributive adjective is common in informal use but considered incorrect by some people.

funambulist /fjuːˈnæmbjʊlɪst/ *n.* a rope-walker. [F *funambule* or L *funambulus* f. *funis* rope + *ambulare* walk]

function /ˈfʌŋkʃ(ə)n/ *n.* & *v.* —*n.* **1 a** an activity proper to a person or institution. **b** a mode of action or activity by which a thing fulfils its purpose. **c** an official or professional duty; an employment, profession, or calling. **2 a** a public ceremony or occasion. **b** a social gathering, esp. a large, formal, or important one. **3** *Math.* a variable quantity regarded in relation to another or others in terms of which it may be expressed or on which its value depends (*x is a function of y and z*). —*v.intr.* fulfil a function, operate; be in working order. □ **functionless** *adj.* [F *fonction* f. L *functio -onis* f. *fungi funct-* perform]

functional /ˈfʌŋkʃ(ə)n(ə)l/ *adj.* **1** of or serving a function. **2** (esp. of buildings) designed or intended to be practical rather than attractive; utilitarian. **3** *Physiol.* **a** (esp. of disease) of or affecting only the functions of an organ etc., not structural or organic. **b** (of mental disorder) having no discernible organic cause. **c** (of an organ) having a function, not functionless or rudimentary. **4** *Math.* of a function. □ **functionality** /-ˈnælɪtɪ/ *n.* **functionally** *adv.*

functionalism /ˈfʌŋkʃ(ə)nəˌlɪz(ə)m/ *n.* belief in or stress on the practical application of a thing. □ **functionalist** *n.*

functionary /ˈfʌŋkʃ(ə)nərɪ/ *n.* (pl. **-ies**) a person who has to perform official functions or duties; an official.

fund /fʌnd/ *n.* & *v.* —*n.* **1** a permanent stock of something ready to be drawn upon (*a fund of knowledge*). **2** a stock of money, esp. one set apart for a purpose. **3** (in *pl.*) money resources. —*v.tr.* **1** provide with money. **2** convert (a floating debt) into a more or less permanent debt at fixed interest. □ **fund-raiser** a person who seeks financial support for a cause, enterprise, etc. **fund-raising** the seeking of financial

support. **in funds** *colloq.* having money to spend. [L *fundus* bottom, piece of land]

fundament /ˈfʌndəmənt/ *n.* *joc.* the buttocks. [ME f. OF *fondement* f. L *fundamentum* (as FOUND[2])]

fundamental /ˌfʌndəˈment(ə)l/ *adj.* & *n.* —*adj.* of, affecting, or serving as a base or foundation, essential, primary, original (*a fundamental change; the fundamental form*). —*n.* (usu. in *pl.*) a fundamental rule, principle, or article. **2** *Mus.* a fundamental note or tone. □ **fundamental note** *Mus.* the lowest note of a chord. **fundamental particle** an elementary particle. □ **fundamentality** /-ˈtælɪtɪ/ *n.* **fundamentally** *adv.* [ME f. F *fondamental* or LL *fundamentalis* (as FUNDAMENT)]

fundamentalism /ˌfʌndəˈmentəˌlɪz(ə)m/ *n.* **1** strict maintenance of traditional Protestant beliefs. **2** strict maintenance of ancient or fundamental doctrines of any religion, esp. Islam. □ **fundamentalist** *n.*

funeral /ˈfjuːnər(ə)l/ *n.* & *adj.* —*n.* **1 a** the burial or cremation of a dead person with its ceremonies. **b** a burial or cremation procession. **c** *US* a burial or cremation service. **2** *sl.* one's (usu. unpleasant) concern (*that's your funeral*). —*attrib.adj.* of or used etc. at a funeral (*funeral oration*). □ **funeral director** an undertaker. **funeral parlour** (*US* **home**) an establishment where the dead are prepared for burial or cremation. **funeral pile** (or **pyre**) a pile of wood etc. on which a corpse is burnt. **funeral urn** an urn holding the ashes of a cremated body. [ME f. OF *funeraille* f. med.L *funeralia* neut. pl. of LL *funeralis* f. L *funus -eris* funeral: (adj.) OF f. L *funeralis*]

funerary /ˈfjuːnərərɪ/ *adj.* of or used at a funeral or funerals. [LL *funerarius* (as FUNERAL)]

funereal /fjuːˈnɪərɪəl/ *adj.* **1** of or appropriate to a funeral. **2** gloomy, dismal, dark. □ **funereally** *adv.* [L *funereus* (as FUNERAL)]

funfair /ˈfʌnfeə(r)/ *n.* *Brit.* a fair, or part of one, consisting of amusements and sideshows.

fungi *pl.* of FUNGUS.

fungicide /ˈfʌndʒɪˌsaɪd/ *n.* a fungus-destroying substance. □ **fungicidal** /-ˈsaɪd(ə)l/ *adj.*

fungoid /ˈfʌŋɡɔɪd/ *adj.* & *n.* —*adj.* **1** resembling a fungus in texture or in rapid growth. **2** *Brit.* of a fungus or fungi. —*n.* a fungoid plant.

fungous /ˈfʌŋɡəs/ *adj.* **1** having the nature of a fungus. **2** springing up like a mushroom; transitory. [ME f. L *fungosus* (as FUNGUS)]

fungus /ˈfʌŋɡəs/ *n.* (pl. **fungi** /-ɡaɪ, -dʒaɪ/ or **funguses**) **1** any of a group of non-photosynthetic organisms feeding on organic matter, which include moulds, yeast, mushrooms, and toadstools. **2** anything similar usu. growing suddenly and rapidly. **3** *Med.* a spongy morbid growth. **4** *sl.* a beard. □ **fungal** *adj.*

fungiform /ˈfʌndʒɪˌfɔːm/ *adj.* **fungivorous** /-ˈdʒɪvərəs/ *adj.* [L, perh. f. Gk *sp(h)oggos* SPONGE]

funicular /fjuːˈnɪkjʊlə(r)/ *adj.* & *n.* —*adj.* (of a railway, esp. on a mountainside) operating by cable with ascending and descending cars counterbalanced. —*n.* a funicular railway. [L *funiculus* f. *funis* rope]

funk[1] *n.* & *v.* —*n.* **1** fear, panic. **2** a coward. —*v.* *Brit.* **1** *intr.* flinch, shrink, show cowardice. **2** *tr.* try to evade (an undertaking), shirk. **3** *tr.* be afraid of. [18th-c. Oxford sl.: perh. f. sl. FUNK[2] = tobacco-smoke]

funk[2] *n. sl.* **1** funky music. **2** *US* a strong smell. [*funk* blow smoke on, perh. f. F dial. *funkier* f. L (as FUMIGATE)]

funky /ˈfʌŋkɪ/ *adj.* (**funkier, funkiest**) *sl.* **1** (esp. of jazz or rock music) earthy, bluesy, with a heavy rhythmical beat. **2** fashionable. **3** *US* having a strong smell. □ **funkily** *adv.* **funkiness** *n.*

funnel /ˈfʌn(ə)l/ *n. & v.* —*n.* **1** a narrow tube or pipe widening at the top, for pouring liquid, powder, etc., into a small opening. **2** a metal chimney on a steam engine or ship. **3** something resembling a funnel in shape or use. —*v.tr. & intr.* (**funnelled, funnelling;** *US* **funneled, funneling**) guide or move through or as through a funnel. □ **funnel-like** *adj.* [ME f. Prov. *fonilh* f. LL *fundibulum* f. L *infundibulum* f. *infundere* (as IN-[2], *fundere* pour)]

funny /ˈfʌnɪ/ *adj. & n.* —*adj.* (**funnier, funniest**) **1** amusing, comical. **2** strange, perplexing, hard to account for. **3** *colloq.* slightly unwell, eccentric, etc. —*n.* (*pl.* **-ies**) (usu. in *pl.*) *colloq.* **1** a comic strip in a newspaper. **2** a joke. □ **funny-bone** the part of the elbow over which the ulnar nerve passes. **funny business 1** *sl.* misbehaviour or deception. **2** comic behaviour, comedy. **funny paper** a newspaper etc. containing humorous matter. □ **funnily** *adv.* **funniness** *n.* [FUN + -Y[1]]

fur *n. & v.* —*n.* **1 a** the short fine soft hair of certain animals, distinguished from the longer hair. **b** the skin of such an animal with the fur on it; a pelt. **2 a** the coat of certain animals as material for making, trimming, or lining clothes. **b** a trimming or lining made of the dressed coat of such animals, or of material imitating this. **c** a garment made of or trimmed or lined with fur. **3** (*collect.*) furred animals. **4 a** a coating formed on the tongue in sickness. **b** *Brit.* a coating formed on the inside surface of a pipe, kettle, etc., by hard water. —*v.* (**furred, furring**) **1** *tr.* (esp. as **furred** *adj.*) **a** line or trim (a garment) with fur. **b** provide (an animal) with fur. **c** clothe (a person) with fur. **d** coat (a tongue, the inside of a kettle) with fur. **2** *intr.* (often foll. by *up*) (of a kettle etc.) become coated with fur. □ **furless** *adj.* [ME (earlier as v.) f. OF *forrer* f. *forre, fuerre* sheath f. Gmc]

furbelow /ˈfɜːbɪˌləʊ/ *n. & v.* —*n.* **1** a gathered strip or pleated border of a skirt or petticoat. **2** (in *pl.*) *derog.* showy ornaments. —*v.tr.* adorn with a furbelow or furbelows. [18th-c. var. of *falbala* flounce, trimming]

furbish /ˈfɜːbɪʃ/ *v.tr.* (often foll. by *up*) **1** remove rust from, polish, burnish. **2** give a new look to, renovate, revive (something antiquated). □ **furbisher** *n.* [ME f. OF *forbir* f. Gmc]

furcate /ˈfɜːkeɪt/ *adj. & v.* —*adj.* /also ˈfɜːkət/ forked, branched. —*v.intr.* form a fork, divide. □ **furcation** /fɜːˈkeɪʃ(ə)n/ *n.* [L *furca* fork: (adj.) f. LL *furcatus*]

furious /ˈfjʊərɪəs/ *adj.* **1** extremely angry. **2** full of fury. **3** raging, violent, intense. □ **furiously** *adv.* **furiousness** *n.* [ME f. OF *furieus* f. L *furiosus* (as FURY)]

furl *v.* **1** *tr.* roll up and secure (a sail, umbrella, flag, etc.). **2** *intr.* become furled. **3** *tr.* **a** close (a fan). **b** fold up (wings). □ **furlable** *adj.* [F *ferler* f. OF *fer(m)* FIRM[1] + *lier* bind f. L *ligare*]

furlong /ˈfɜːlɒŋ/ *n.* an eighth of a mile, 220 yards. [OE *furlang* f. *furh* FURROW + *lang* LONG[1]: orig. = length of a furrow in a common field]

furlough /ˈfɜːləʊ/ *n. & v.* —*n.* leave of absence, esp. granted to a member of the services or to a missionary. —*v.* *US* **1** *tr.* grant furlough to. **2** *intr.* spend furlough. [Du. *verlof* after G *Verlaub* (as FOR-, LEAVE[2])]

furnace /ˈfɜːnɪs/ *n.* **1** an enclosed structure for intense heating by fire, esp. of metals or water. **2** a very hot place. [ME f. OF *fornais* f. L *fornax* *-acis* f. *fornus* oven]

furnish /ˈfɜːnɪʃ/ *v.tr.* **1** provide (a house, room, etc.) with all necessary contents, esp. movable furniture. **2** (foll. by *with*) cause to have possession or use of. **3** provide, afford, yield. [OF *furnir* ult. f. WG]

furnished /ˈfɜːnɪʃt/ *adj.* (of a house, flat, etc.) let with furniture.

furnisher /ˈfɜːnɪʃə(r)/ *n.* **1** a person who sells furniture. **2** a person who furnishes.

furnishings /ˈfɜːnɪʃɪŋz/ *n.pl.* the furniture and fitments in a house, room, etc.

furniture /ˈfɜːnɪtʃə(r)/ *n.* **1** the movable equipment of a house, room, etc., e.g. tables, chairs, and beds. **2** *Naut.* a ship's equipment, esp. tackle etc. **3** accessories, e.g. the handles and lock of a door. □ **furniture beetle** a beetle, *Anobium punctatum*, the larvae of which bore into wood. **furniture van** a large van used to move furniture from one house to another. **part of the furniture** *colloq.* a person or thing taken for granted. [F *fourniture* f. *fournir* (as FURNISH)]

furore /fjʊˈrɔːrɪ/ *n.* (*US* **furor** /ˈfjʊərɔː(r)/) **1** uproar; an outbreak of fury. **2** a wave of enthusiastic admiration, a craze. [It. f. L *furor* *-oris* f. *furere* be mad]

furrier /ˈfʌrɪə(r)/ *n.* a dealer in or dresser of furs. [ME *furrour* f. OF *forreor* f. *forrer* trim with fur, assim. to -IER]

furriery /ˈfʌrɪərɪ/ *n.* the work of a furrier.

furrow /ˈfʌrəʊ/ *n. & v.* —*n.* **1** a narrow trench made in the ground by a plough. **2** a rut, groove, or deep wrinkle. **3** a ship's track. —*v.tr.* **1** plough. **2 a** make furrows, grooves, etc. in. **b** mark with wrinkles. □ **furrowless** *adj.* **furrowy** *adj.* [OE *furh* f. Gmc]

furry /ˈfɜːrɪ/ *adj.* (**furrier, furriest**) **1** of or like fur. **2** covered with or wearing fur. □ **furriness** *n.*

further /ˈfɜːðə(r)/ *adv., adj., & v.* —*adv.* (also **farther** /ˈfɑːðə(r)/) esp. with ref. to physical distance) **1** to or at a more advanced point in space or time (*unsafe to proceed further*). **2** at a greater distance (*nothing was further from his thoughts*). **3** to a greater extent, more (*will enquire further*). **4** in addition; furthermore (*I may add further*). —*adj.* (also **farther** /ˈfɑːðə(r)/) **1** more distant or advanced (*on the further side*). **2** more, additional, going beyond what exists or has been dealt with (*threats of further punishment*). —*v.tr.* promote, favour, help on (a scheme, undertaking, movement, or cause). □ **further education** *Brit.* education for persons above school age but usu. below degree level. **further to** *formal* following on from (esp. an earlier letter etc.). **further notice** (or **orders**) to continue until explicitly changed. □ **furtherer** *n.* **furthermost** *adj.* [OE *furthor* (adv.), *furthra* (adj.), *fyrthrian* (v.), formed as FORTH, -ER[3]]

■ **Usage** The form *farther* is used esp. with reference to physical distance, although *further* is preferred by many people even in this sense.

furtherance /ˈfɜːðərəns/ *n.* furthering or being furthered; the advancement of a scheme etc.

furthermore /ˌfɜːðəˈmɔː(r)/ adv. in addition, besides (esp. introducing a fresh consideration in an argument).

furthest /ˈfɜːðɪst/ adj. & adv. (also **farthest** /ˈfɑːðɪst/ esp. with ref. to physical distance) —adj. most distant. —adv. to or at the greatest distance. □ **at the furthest** (or **at furthest**) at the greatest distance; at the latest; at most. [ME, superl. f. FURTHER]

■ **Usage** The form *farthest* is used esp. with reference to physical distance, although *furthest* is preferred by many people even in this sense.

furtive /ˈfɜːtɪv/ adj. 1 done by stealth, clandestine, meant to escape notice. 2 sly, stealthy. 3 stolen, taken secretly. 4 thievish, pilfering. □ **furtively** adv. **furtiveness** n. [F furtif -ive or L furtivus f. furtum theft]

fury /ˈfjʊərɪ/ n. (pl. **-ies**) 1 a wild and passionate anger, rage. b a fit of rage (in a blind fury). c impetuosity in battle etc. 2 violence of a storm, disease, etc. 3 (**Fury**) (usu. in pl.) (in Greek mythology) each of three goddesses sent from Tartarus to avenge crime. 4 an avenging spirit. 5 an angry or malignant woman, a virago. □ **like fury** colloq. with great force or effect. [ME f. OF furie f. L furia f. furere be mad]

furze n. Brit. = GORSE. □ **furzy** /ˈfɜːzɪ/ adj. [OE fyrs, of unkn. orig.]

fuse[1] /fjuːz/ v. & n. —v. 1 tr. & intr. melt with intense heat; liquefy. 2 tr. & intr. blend or amalgamate into one whole by or as by melting. 3 tr. provide (a circuit, plug, etc.) with a fuse. 4 a intr. (of an appliance) cease to function when a fuse blows. b tr. cause (an appliance) to do this. —n. a device or component for protecting an electric circuit, containing a strip of wire of easily melted metal and placed in the circuit so as to break it by melting when an excessive current passes through. □ **fuse-box** a box housing the fuses for circuits in a building. [L fundere fus- pour, melt]

fuse[2] /fjuːz/ n. & v. (also **fuze**) —n. 1 a device for igniting a bomb or explosive charge, consisting of a tube or cord etc. filled or saturated with combustible matter. 2 a component in a shell, mine, etc., designed to detonate an explosive charge on impact, after an interval, or when subjected to a magnetic or vibratory stimulation. —v.tr. fit a fuse to. □ **fuseless** adj. [It. fuso f. L fusus spindle]

fuselage /ˈfjuːzəˌlɑːʒ, -lɪdʒ/ n. the body of an aeroplane. [F f. fuseler cut into a spindle f. fuseau spindle f. OF fusel ult. f. L fusus]

fusible /ˈfjuːzɪb(ə)l/ adj. that can be easily fused or melted. □ **fusibility** /-ˈbɪlɪtɪ/ n.

fusil /ˈfjuːzɪl/ n. hist. a light musket. [F ult. f. L focus hearth, fire]

fusilier /ˌfjuːzɪˈlɪə(r), -zəˈlɪə(r)/ n. (US **fusileer**) a member of any of several British regiments formerly armed with fusils.

fusillade /ˌfjuːzɪˈleɪd/ n. 1 a continuous discharge of firearms. 2 a sustained outburst of criticism etc. [F f. fusiller shoot]

fusion /ˈfjuːʒ(ə)n/ n. 1 the act or an instance of fusing or melting. 2 a fused mass. 3 the blending of different things into one. 4 a coalition. 5 Physics = nuclear fusion. □ **fusion bomb** a bomb involving nuclear fusion, esp. a hydrogen bomb. □ **fusional** adj. [F fusion or L fusio (as FUSE[1])]

fuss n. & v. —n. 1 excited commotion, bustle, ostentatious or nervous activity. 2 a excessive concern about a trivial thing. b abundance of petty detail. 3 a sustained protest or dispute. 4 a person who fusses. —v. 1 intr. a make a fuss. b busy oneself restlessly with trivial things. c (often foll. by about, up and down) move fussily. 2 tr. agitate, worry. □ **make a fuss** complain vigorously. **make a fuss of** (or **over**) treat (a person or animal) with great or excessive attention. □ **fusser** n. [18th c.: perh. Anglo-Ir.]

fusspot /ˈfʌspɒt/ n. colloq. a person given to fussing.

fussy /ˈfʌsɪ/ adj. (**fussier, fussiest**) 1 inclined to fuss. 2 full of unnecessary detail or decoration. 3 fastidious. □ **fussily** adv. **fussiness** n.

fustian /ˈfʌstɪən/ n. & adj. —n. 1 thick twilled cotton cloth with a short nap, usu. dyed in dark colours. 2 turgid speech or writing, bombast. —adj. 1 made of fustian. 2 bombastic. 3 worthless. [ME f. OF fustaigne f. med.L fustaneus (adj.) relating to cloth from Fostat a suburb of Cairo]

fusty /ˈfʌstɪ/ adj. (**fustier, fustiest**) 1 stale-smelling, musty, mouldy. 2 stuffy, close. 3 antiquated, old-fashioned. □ **fustily** adv. **fustiness** n. [ME f. OF fusté smelling of the cask f. fust cask, tree-trunk, f. L fustis cudgel]

futile /ˈfjuːtaɪl/ adj. 1 useless, ineffectual, vain. 2 frivolous, trifling. □ **futilely** adv. **futility** /-ˈtɪlɪtɪ/ n. [L futilis leaky, futile, rel. to fundere pour]

futon /ˈfuːtɒn/ n. a Japanese quilted mattress rolled out on the floor for use as a bed; a type of low-slung wooden bed using this kind of mattress. [Jap.]

future /ˈfjuːtʃə(r)/ adj. & n. —adj. 1 a going or expected to happen or be or become (his future career). b that will be something specified (my future wife). c that will be after death (a future life). 2 a of time to come (future years). b Gram. (of a tense or participle) describing an event yet to happen. —n. 1 time to come (past, present, and future). 2 what will happen in the future (the future is uncertain). 3 the future condition of a person, country, etc. 4 a prospect of success etc. (there's no future in it). 5 Gram. the future tense. 6 (in pl.) Stock Exch. a goods and stocks sold for future delivery. b contracts for these. □ **in future** from now onwards. □ **futureless** adj. [ME f. OF futur -ure f. L futurus future part. of esse be f. stem fu- be]

futurism /ˈfjuːtʃəˌrɪz(ə)m/ n. a movement in art, literature, music, etc., with violent departure from traditional forms so as to express movement and growth. □ **futurist** n. [FUTURE + -ISM, after It. futurismo, F futurisme]

futuristic /ˌfjuːtʃəˈrɪstɪk/ adj. 1 suitable for the future; ultra-modern. 2 of futurism. 3 relating to the future. □ **futuristically** adv.

futurity /fjuːˈtjʊərɪtɪ/ n. (pl. **-ies**) 1 future time. 2 (in sing. or pl.) future events. 3 future condition; existence after death.

futurology /ˌfjuːtʃəˈrɒlədʒɪ/ n. systematic forecasting of the future esp. from present trends in society. □ **futurologist** n.

fuze var. of FUSE[2].

fuzz n. 1 fluff. 2 fluffy or frizzled hair. 3 sl. a the police. b a policeman. [17th c.: prob. f. LG or Du.: sense 3 perh. a different word]

fuzzy /ˈfʌzɪ/ *adj.* (**fuzzier, fuzziest**) **1 a** like fuzz. **b** frayed, fluffy. **c** frizzy. **2** blurred, indistinct. □ **fuzzily** *adv.* **fuzziness** *n.*

-fy /faɪ/ *suffix* forming: **1** verbs from nouns, meaning: **a** make, produce (*pacify*; *satisfy*). **b** make into (*deify*; *petrify*). **2** verbs from adjectives, meaning 'bring or come into such a state' (*Frenchify*; *solidify*). **3** verbs in causative sense (*horrify*; *stupefy*). [from or after F *-fier* f. L *-ficare*, *-facere* f. *facere* do, make]

Gg

G[1] /dʒiː/ n. (also **g**) (pl. **Gs** or **G's**) **1** the seventh letter of the alphabet. **2** Mus. the fifth note in the diatonic scale of C major.

G[2] abbr. (also **G.**) **1** gauss. **2** giga-. **3** gravitational constant. **4** US sl. = GRAND n. 2.

g abbr. (also **g.**) **1** gelding. **2** gram(s). **3 a** gravity. **b** acceleration due to gravity.

Ga symb. Chem. the element gallium.

gab n. colloq. talk, chatter, twaddle. □ **gift of the gab** the facility of speaking eloquently or profusely. □ **gabber** n. [17th-c. var. of GOB[1]]

gabardine /ˈgæbəˌdiːn, -ˈdiːn/ n. (also **gaberdine**) **1** a smooth durable twill-woven cloth esp. of worsted or cotton. **2** a garment made of this, esp. a raincoat. [f. OF gauvardine]

gabble /ˈgæb(ə)l/ v. & n. —v. **1** intr. **a** talk volubly or inarticulately. **b** read aloud too fast. **2** tr. utter too fast, esp. in reading aloud. —n. fast unintelligible talk. □ **gabbler** n. [MDu. gabbelen (imit.)]

gabbro /ˈgæbrəʊ/ n. (pl. **-os**) a dark granular plutonic rock of crystalline texture. □ **gabbroic** /-ˈbrəʊɪk/ adj. **gabbroid** adv. [It. f. Gabbro in Tuscany]

gabby /ˈgæbɪ/ adj. (**gabbier**, **gabbiest**) colloq. talkative. [GAB + -Y[1]]

gable /ˈgeɪb(ə)l/ n. **1 a** the triangular upper part of a wall at the end of a ridged roof. **b** (in full **gable-end**) a gable-topped wall. **2** a gable-shaped canopy over a window or door. □ **gabled** adj. (also in comb.). [ME gable F. ON gafl]

gad[1] v.intr. (**gadded**, **gadding**) (foll. by about, around) go about idly or in search of pleasure. [back-form. f. obs. gadling companion f. OE gædeling f. gæd fellowship]

gad[2] int. (also **by gad**) an expression of surprise or emphatic assertion. [= God]

gadabout /ˈgædəˌbaʊt/ n. a person who gads about; an idle pleasure-seeker.

gadfly /ˈgædflaɪ/ n. (pl. **-flies**) **1** a cattle-biting fly. **2** an irritating or harassing person. [obs. gad goad, spike f. ON gaddr, rel. to YARD[1]]

gadget /ˈgædʒɪt/ n. any small and usu. ingenious mechanical device or tool. □ **gadgeteer** /-ˈtɪə(r)/ n. **gadgetry** n. **gadgety** adj. [19th-c. Naut.: orig. unkn.]

gadolinium /ˌgædəˈlɪnɪəm/ n. Chem. a soft silvery metallic element of the lanthanide series. [mod.L f. J. Gadolin, Finnish mineralogist d. 1852]

gadwall /ˈgædwɔːl/ n. a brownish-grey freshwater duck, Anas strepera. [17th c.: orig. unkn.]

Gael /geɪl/ n. **1** a Scottish Celt. **2** a Gaelic-speaking Celt. □ **Gaeldom** n. [Gael. Gaidheal]

Gaelic /ˈgeɪlɪk, ˈgæ-/ n. & adj. —n. any of the Celtic languages spoken in Ireland, Scotland, and the Isle of Man. —adj. of or relating to the Celts or the Celtic languages.

Gaeltacht /ˈgeɪltəxt/ n. any of the regions in Ireland where the vernacular language is Irish. [Ir.]

gaff[1] n. & v. —n. **1 a** a stick with an iron hook for landing large fish. **b** a barbed fishing-spear. **2** a spar to which the head of a fore-and-aft sail is bent. —v.tr. seize with a gaff. [ME f. Prov. gaf hook]

gaff[2] n. Brit. sl. □ **blow the gaff** let out a plot or secret. [19th c., = nonsense: orig. unkn.]

gaffe /gæf/ n. a blunder; an indiscretion. [F]

gaffer /ˈgæfə(r)/ n. **1** an old fellow; an elderly rustic. **2** Brit. colloq. a foreman or boss. **3** colloq. the chief electrician in a film or television production unit. [prob. contr. of GODFATHER]

gag n. & v. —n. **1** a piece of cloth etc. thrust into or held over the mouth to prevent speaking or crying out, or to hold it open in surgery. **2** a joke or comic scene in a play, film, etc., or as part of a comedian's act. **3** a thing or circumstance restricting free speech. **4 a** a joke or hoax. **b** a humorous action or situation. **5** Parl. a closure or guillotine. —v. (**gagged**, **gagging**) **1** tr. apply a gag to. **2** tr. silence; deprive of free speech. **3** tr. apply a gag-bit to (a horse). **4 a** intr. choke or retch. **b** tr. cause to do this. **5** intr. Theatr. make gags. □ **gag-bit** a specially powerful bit for horse-breaking. [ME, orig. as verb: orig. uncert.]

gaga /ˈgɑːgɑː/ adj. sl. **1** senile. **2** fatuous; slightly crazy. [F, = senile]

gage[1] n. **1** a pledge; a thing deposited as security. **2 a** a challenge to fight. **b** a symbol of this, esp. a glove thrown down. [ME f. OF gage ult. f. Gmc, rel. to WED]

gage[2] US var. of GAUGE.

gage[3] n. = GREENGAGE. [abbr.]

gaggle /ˈgæg(ə)l/ n. **1** a flock of geese. **2** colloq. a disorderly group of people. [ME, imit.: cf. gabble, cackle]

gaiety /ˈgeɪətɪ/ n. (US **gayety**) **1** the state of being light-hearted or merry. **2** merrymaking. **3** a bright appearance. [F gaieté (as GAY)]

gaily /ˈgeɪlɪ/ adv. **1** in a gay or light-hearted manner. **2** with a bright or colourful appearance.

gain v. & n. —v. **1** tr. obtain or secure (usu. something desired or favourable) (gain an advantage; gain recognition). **2** tr. acquire (a sum) as profits or as a result of changed conditions; earn. **3** tr. obtain as an increment or addition (gain momentum; gain weight). **4** tr. **a** win (a victory). **b** reclaim (land from the sea). **5** intr. (foll. by in) make a specified advance or improvement (gained in stature). **6** intr. & tr. (of a clock etc.) become fast, or be fast by (a specified amount of time). **7** intr. (often foll. by on, upon) come closer to a person or thing pursued. **8** tr. **a** bring over to one's interest or views. **b** (foll. by over) win by persuasion etc. **9** tr. reach or arrive at (a desired place). —n. **1** something gained, achieved, etc. **2** an increase of possessions etc.; a profit, advance, or improvement. **3** the acquisition of wealth. **4** (in pl.) sums of money acquired by trade etc., emoluments, winnings. **5** an increase in amount. □ **gain ground** see

GROUND¹. **gain time** improve one's chances by causing or accepting delay. □ **gainable** *adj.*

gainer *n.* **gainings** *n.pl.* [OF *gaigner, gaaignier* to till, acquire, ult. f. Gmc]

gainful /ˈɡeɪnfʊl/ *adj.* **1** (of employment) paid. **2** lucrative, remunerative. □ **gainfully** *adv.* **gainfulness** *n.*

gainsay /ɡeɪnˈseɪ/ *v.tr.* (*past* and *past part.* **gainsaid** /-ˈsed/) *archaic* or *literary* deny, contradict. □ **gainsayer** *n.* [ME f. obs. *gain-* against f. ON *gegn* straight f. Gmc + SAY]

gait *n.* **1** a manner of walking; one's bearing as one walks. **2** the manner of forward motion of a runner, horse, vehicle, etc. [var. of GATE²]

gaiter /ˈɡeɪtə(r)/ *n.* a covering of cloth, leather, etc. for the leg below the knee, for the ankle, for part of a machine, etc. □ **gaitered** *adj.* [F *guêtre*, prob. rel. to WRIST]

gal *n. sl.* a girl. [repr. var. pronunc.]

gal. *abbr.* gallon(s).

gala /ˈɡɑːlə/ *n.* **1** a festive occasion. **2** *Brit.* a festive gathering for sports, esp. swimming. [F or It. f. Sp. f. OF *gale* rejoicing f. Gmc]

galactic /ɡəˈlæktɪk/ *adj.* of or relating to a galaxy or galaxies, esp. the Galaxy. [Gk *galaktias*, var. of *galaxias*: see GALAXY]

galago /ɡəˈleɪɡəʊ/ *n.* (*pl.* **-os**) any small tree-climbing primate of the genus *Galago*, found in southern Africa, with large eyes and ears and a long tail. [mod.L]

galah /ɡəˈlɑː/ *n. Austral.* **1** a small rose-breasted grey-backed cockatoo, *Cacatua roseicapilla*. **2** *sl.* a fool or simpleton. [Aboriginal]

galantine /ˈɡælənˌtiːn/ *n.* white meat or fish boned, cooked, pressed, and served cold in aspic etc. [ME f. OF, alt. f. *galatine* jellied meat f. med.L *galatina*]

galaxy /ˈɡæləksɪ/ *n.* (*pl.* **-ies**) **1** any of many independent systems of stars, gas, dust, etc., held together by gravitational attraction. **2** (**the Galaxy**) the galaxy of which the solar system is a part. **3** (**the Galaxy**) the irregular luminous band of stars indistinguishable to the naked eye encircling the heavens, the Milky Way. **4** (foll. by *of*) a brilliant company or gathering. [ME f. OF *galaxie* f. med.L *galaxia*, LL *galaxias* f. Gk f. *gala galaktos* milk]

gale *n.* **1** a very strong wind, esp. (on the Beaufort scale) one of 32–54 m.p.h. **2** *Naut.* a storm. **3** an outburst, esp. of laughter. [16th c.: orig. unkn.]

galena /ɡəˈliːnə/ *n.* a bluish, grey or black mineral ore of lead sulphide. [L, = lead ore (in a partly purified state)]

galenic /ɡəˈlenɪk/ *adj. & n.* (also **galenical** /-ˈlenɪk(ə)l/) —*adj.* **1** of or relating to Galen, a Greek physician of the 2nd c. AD, or his methods. **2** made of natural as opposed to synthetic components. —*n.* a drug or medicament produced directly from animal or vegetable tissues.

Galilean¹ /ˌɡælɪˈliːən/ *adj.* of or relating to Galileo, Italian astronomer d. 1642, or his methods.

Galilean² /ˌɡælɪˈliːən/ *adj. & n.* —*adj.* **1** of Galilee in Palestine. **2** Christian. —*n.* **1** a native of Galilee. **2** a Christian. **3** (prec. by *the*) *derog.* Christ.

gall¹ /ɡɔːl/ *n.* **1** *sl.* impudence. **2** asperity, rancour. **3** bitterness; anything bitter (*gall and wormwood*). **4** the bile of animals. **5** the gall-bladder and its contents. □ **gall-bladder** the vessel storing bile

after its secretion by the liver and before release into the intestine. [ON, corresp. to OE *gealla*, f. Gmc]

gall² /ɡɔːl/ *n. & v.* —*n.* **1** a sore on the skin made by chafing. **2 a** mental soreness or vexation. **b** a cause of this. **3** a place rubbed bare. —*v.tr.* **1** rub sore; injure by rubbing. **2** vex, annoy, humiliate. □ **gallingly** *adv.* [ME f. LG or Du. *galle*, corresp. to OE *gealla* sore on a horse]

gall³ /ɡɔːl/ *n.* **1** a growth produced by insects or fungus etc. on plants and trees, esp. on oak. **2** (*attrib.*) of insects producing galls (*gall-fly*). [ME f. OF *galle* f. L *galla*]

gall. *abbr.* gallon(s).

gallant *adj. & n.* —*adj.* /ˈɡælənt/ **1** brave, chivalrous. **2 a** (of a ship, horse, etc.) grand, fine, stately. **b** *archaic* finely dressed. **3** /ˈɡælənt, ɡəˈlænt/ markedly attentive to women. —*n.* /ˈɡælənt, ɡəˈlænt/ **1** a ladies' man; a lover or paramour. **2** *archaic* a man of fashion; a fine gentleman. □ **gallantly** /ˈɡæləntlɪ/ *adv.* [ME f. OF *galant* part. of *galer* make merry]

gallantry /ˈɡæləntrɪ/ *n.* (*pl.* **-ies**) **1** bravery; dashing courage. **2** courtliness; devotion to women. **3** a polite act or speech. **4** sexual intrigue; immorality. [F *galanterie* (as GALLANT)]

galleon /ˈɡælɪən/ *n. hist.* **1** a ship of war (usu. Spanish). **2** a large Spanish ship used in American trade. **3** a vessel shorter and higher than a galley. [MDu. *galjoen* f. F *galion* f. *galie* galley, or f. Sp. *galeón*]

galleria /ˌɡælɪˈriːə/ *n.* a collection of small shops under a single roof; an arcade. [It.]

gallery /ˈɡælərɪ/ *n.* (*pl.* **-ies**) **1** a room or building for showing works of art. **2** a balcony, esp. a platform projecting from the inner wall of a church, hall, etc., providing extra room for spectators etc. or reserved for musicians etc. (*minstrels' gallery*). **3 a** the highest balcony in a theatre. **b** its occupants. **4 a** a covered space for walking in, partly open at the side; a portico or colonnade. **b** a long narrow passage in the thickness of a wall or supported on corbels, open towards the interior of the building. **5 a** long narrow room, passage, or corridor. **6** *Mil. & Mining* a horizontal underground passage. **7** a group of spectators at a golf-match etc. □ **play to the gallery** seek to win approval by appealing to popular taste. □ **galleried** *adj.* [F *galerie* f. It. *galleria* f. med.L *galeria*]

galley /ˈɡælɪ/ *n.* (*pl.* **-eys**) **1** *hist.* **a** a low flat single-decked vessel using sails and oars, and usu. rowed by slaves or criminals. **b** an ancient Greek or Roman warship with one or more banks of oars. **2** a ship's or aircraft's kitchen. **3** *Printing* **a** an oblong tray for set type. **b** (in full **galley proof**) a proof in the form of single-column strips as from type in a galley, not in sheets or pages. □ **galley-slave 1** *hist.* a person condemned to row in a galley. **2** a drudge. [ME f. OF *galie* f. med.L *galea*, med.Gk *galaia*]

galliard /ˈɡælɪˌɑːd/ *n. hist.* **1** a lively dance usu. in triple time for two persons. **2** the music for this. [ME f. OF *gaillard* valiant]

Gallic /ˈɡælɪk/ *adj.* **1** French or typically French. **2** of the Gauls; Gaulish. □ **Gallicize** /-ˌsaɪz/ *v.tr. & intr.* (also **-ise**). [L *Gallicus* f. *Gallus* a Gaul]

Gallicism /ˈɡælɪˌsɪz(ə)m/ *n.* a French idiom, esp. one adopted in another language. [F *gallicisme* (as GALLIC)]

gallimaufry /ˌgælɪˈmɔːfrɪ/ n. (pl. -ies) a heterogeneous mixture; a jumble or medley. [F *galimafrée*, of unkn. orig.]

gallinaceous /ˌgælɪˈneɪʃəs/ adj. of or relating to the order Galliformes, which includes domestic poultry, pheasants, partridges, etc. [L *gallinaceus* f. *gallina* hen f. *gallus* cock]

gallium /ˈgælɪəm/ n. Chem. a soft bluish-white metallic element occurring naturally in zinc blende, bauxite, and kaolin. [mod.L f. L *Gallia* France (so named patriotically by its discoverer Lecoq de Boisbaudran d. 1912)]

gallivant /ˈgælɪˌvænt/ v.intr. colloq. 1 gad about. 2 flirt. [orig. uncert.]

Gallo- /ˈgæləʊ/ comb. form 1 French; French and. 2 Gaul (*Gallo-Roman*). [L *Gallus* a Gaul]

gallon /ˈgælən/ n. 1 a (in full **imperial gallon**) Brit. a measure of capacity equal to eight pints and equivalent to 4546 cc, used for liquids and corn etc. b US a measure of capacity equivalent to 3785 cc, used for liquids. 2 (usu. in pl.) colloq. a large amount. □ **gallonage** n. [ME f. ONF *galon*, OF *jalon*, f. base of med.L *gallēta, gallētum*, perh. of Celtic orig.]

gallop /ˈgæləp/ n. & v. —n. 1 the fastest pace of a horse or other quadruped, with all the feet off the ground together in each stride. 2 a ride at this pace. 3 a track or ground for this. —v. (**galloped, galloping**) 1 a intr. (of a horse etc. or its rider) go at the pace of a gallop. b tr. make (a horse etc.) gallop. 2 intr. (foll. by *through, over*) read, recite, or talk at great speed. 3 intr. move or progress rapidly (*galloping inflation*). □ **at a gallop** at the pace of a gallop. □ **galloper** n. [OF *galop, galoper*: see WALLOP]

gallows /ˈgæləʊz/ n.pl. (usu. treated as *sing.*) 1 a structure, usu. of two uprights and a crosspiece, for the hanging of criminals. 2 (prec. by *the*) execution by hanging. □ **gallows humour** grim and ironical humour. [ME f. ON *gálgi*]

gallstone /ˈgɔːlstəʊn/ n. a small hard mass forming in the gall-bladder.

Gallup poll /ˈgæləp/ n. an assessment of public opinion by questioning a representative sample, esp. as the basis for forecasting the results of voting. [G. H. *Gallup*, Amer. statistician d. 1984]

galop /ˈgæləp/ n. & v. —n. 1 a lively dance in duple time. 2 the music for this. —v.intr. (**galoped, galoping**) perform this dance. [F: see GALLOP]

galore /gəˈlɔː(r)/ adv. in abundance (placed after noun: *flowers galore*). [Ir. *go leór* to sufficiency]

galosh /gəˈlɒʃ/ n. (also **golosh**) (usu. in pl.) a waterproof overshoe, usu. of rubber. [ME f. OF *galoche* f. LL *gallicula* small Gallic shoe]

galumph /gəˈlʌmf/ v.intr. colloq. 1 move noisily or clumsily. 2 go prancing in triumph. [coined by Lewis Carroll (in sense 2), perh. f. GALLOP + TRIUMPH]

galvanic /gælˈvænɪk/ adj. 1 a sudden and remarkable (*had a galvanic effect*). b stimulating; full of energy. 2 of or producing an electric current by chemical action. □ **galvanically** adv.

galvanism /ˈgælvəˌnɪz(ə)m/ n. hist. 1 electricity produced by chemical action. 2 the use of electricity for medical purposes. □ **galvanist** n. [F *galvanisme* f. L. *Galvani*, It. physiologist d. 1798]

galvanize /ˈgælvəˌnaɪz/ v.tr. (also -**ise**) 1 (often foll. by *into*) rouse forcefully, esp. by shock or excitement (*was galvanized into action*). 2

stimulate by or as if by electricity. 3 coat (iron) with zinc (usu. without the use of electricity) as a protection against rust. □ **galvanization** /-ˈzeɪʃ(ə)n/ n. **galvanizer** n. [F *galvaniser*: see GALVANISM]

galvanometer /ˌgælvəˈnɒmɪtə(r)/ n. an instrument for detecting and measuring small electric currents. □ **galvanometric** /-nəˈmetrɪk/ adj.

gambit /ˈgæmbɪt/ n. 1 a chess opening in which a player sacrifices a piece or pawn to secure an advantage. 2 an opening move in a discussion etc. 3 a trick or device. [earlier *gambett* f. It. *gambetto* tripping up f. *gamba* leg]

gamble /ˈgæmb(ə)l/ v. & n. —v. 1 intr. play games of chance for money, esp. for high stakes. 2 tr. a bet (a sum of money) in gambling. b (often foll. by *away*) lose (assets) by gambling. 3 intr. take great risks in the hope of substantial gain. 4 intr. (foll. by *on*) act in the hope or expectation of (*gambled on fine weather*). —n. 1 a risky undertaking or attempt. 2 a spell of gambling. □ **gambler** n. [obs. *gamel* to sport, *gamene* GAME¹]

gamboge /gæmˈbəʊʒ, -ˈbuːʒ/ n. a gum resin used as a yellow pigment and as a purgative. [mod.L *gambaugium* f. *Cambodia* in SE Asia]

gambol /ˈgæmb(ə)l/ v. & n. —v.intr. (**gambolled, gambolling**; US **gamboled, gamboling**) skip or frolic playfully. —n. a playful frolic. [f. It. & Sp. *gamba* leg]

game¹ n., adj., & v. —n. 1 a form or spell of play or sport, esp. a competitive one played according to rules and decided by skill, strength, or luck. 2 a single portion of play forming a scoring unit in some contests, e.g. bridge or tennis. 3 (in pl.) a athletics or sports as organized in a school etc. b a meeting for athletic etc. contests (*Olympic Games*). 4 a winning score in a game; the state of the score in a game (*the game is two all*). 5 the equipment for a game. 6 one's level of achievement in a game, as specified (*played a good game*). 7 a a piece of fun; a jest. b (in pl.) dodges, tricks (*none of your games!*). 8 a scheme or undertaking etc. regarded as a game (*so that's your game*). 9 a policy or line of action. 10 (collect.) a wild animals or birds hunted for sport or food. b the flesh of these. 11 a hunted animal; a quarry or object of pursuit or attack. —adj. 1 spirited; eager and willing. 2 (foll. by *for*, or to + infin.) having the spirit or energy; eagerly prepared. —v.intr. play at games of chance for money; gamble. □ **the game is up** the scheme is revealed or foiled. **game** (or **games**) **theory** the mathematical analysis of conflict in war, economics, games of skill, etc. **gaming-house** a place frequented for gambling; a casino. **gaming-table** a table used for gambling. **make game** (or **a game**) **of** mock, taunt. **off** (or **on**) **one's game** playing badly (or well). **on the game** Brit. sl. involved in prostitution or thieving. **play the game** behave fairly or according to the rules. □ **gamely** adv. **gameness** n. **gamester** n. [OE *gamen*]

game² adj. (of a leg, arm, etc.) lame, crippled. [18th-c. dial.: orig. unkn.]

gamekeeper /ˈgeɪmˌkiːpə(r)/ n. a person employed to breed and protect game.

gamelan /ˈgæməˌlæn/ n. 1 a type of orchestra found in SE Asia (esp. Indonesia), with string and woodwind instruments, and a wide range of percussion instruments. **2** a kind of xylophone used in this. [Jav.]

gamesmanship /ˈgeɪmzmənʃɪp/ n. the art or practice of winning games or other contests by gaining a psychological advantage over an opponent.

gamete /ˈgæmiːt, gəˈmiːt/ n. Biol. a mature germ cell able to unite with another in sexual reproduction. □ **gametic** /gəˈmetɪk/ adj. [mod.L gameta f. Gk gametē wife f. gamos marriage]

gametogenesis /gəˌmiːtəʊˈdʒenɪsɪs/ n. Biol. the process by which cells undergo meiosis to form gametes.

gametophyte /gəˈmiːtəʊˌfaɪt/ n. the gamete-producing form of a plant that has alternation of generations between this and the asexual form. □ **gametophytic** /-ˈfɪtɪk/ adj.

gamin /ˈgæmɪn/ n. **1** a street urchin. **2** an impudent child. [F]

gamine /gæˈmiːn/ n. **1** a girl gamin. **2** a girl with mischievous or boyish charm. [F]

gamma /ˈgæmə/ n. **1** the third letter of the Greek alphabet (Γ, γ). **2** the third member of a series. □ **gamma radiation** (or **rays**) electromagnetic radiation of very short wavelength. [ME f. Gk]

gammon¹ /ˈgæmən/ n. & v. —n. **1** the bottom piece of a flitch of bacon including a hind leg. **2** the ham of a pig cured like bacon. —v.tr. cure (bacon). [ONF gambon f. gambe leg: cf. JAMB]

gammon² /ˈgæmən/ n. & v. colloq. —n. humbug, deception. —v. **1** intr. **a** talk speciously. **b** pretend. **2** tr. hoax, deceive. [18th c.: orig. uncert.]

gammy /ˈgæmɪ/ adj. (**gammier, gammiest**) Brit. sl. (esp. of a leg) lame; permanently injured. [dial. form of GAME²]

gamp n. Brit. colloq. an umbrella, esp. a large one. [Mrs Gamp in Dickens's Martin Chuzzlewit]

gamut /ˈgæmət/ n. **1** the whole series or range or scope of anything (the whole gamut of crime). **2** Mus. **a** the whole series of notes used in medieval or modern music. **b** a major diatonic scale. **c** a people's or a period's recognized scale. **d** a voice's or instrument's compass. [med.L gamma ut f. GAMMA taken as the name for a note one tone lower than A of the classical scale + ut the first of six arbitrary names of notes forming the hexachord, being syllables (ut, re, mi, fa, so, la) of the Latin hymn beginning Ut queant laxis]

gamy /ˈgeɪmɪ/ adj. (**gamier, gamiest**) **1** having the flavour or scent of game kept till it is high. **2** US scandalous. □ **gamily** adv. **gaminess** n.

gander /ˈgændə(r)/ n. **1** a male goose. **2** sl. a look, a glance (take a gander). [OE gandra, rel. to GANNET]

gang¹ n. **1 a** a band of persons acting or going about together, esp. for criminal purposes. **b** colloq. such a band pursuing a purpose causing disapproval. **2** a set of workers, slaves, or prisoners. □ **gang-bang** sl. an occasion on which several men successively have sexual intercourse with one woman. **gang up** colloq. **1** (often foll. by with) act in concert. **2** (foll. by on) combine against. [orig. = going, journey, f. ON gangr, ganga GOING, corresp. to OE gang]

gang² v.intr. Sc. go. □ **gang agley** (of a plan etc.) go wrong. [OE gangan: cf. GANG¹]

ganger /ˈgæŋə(r)/ n. Brit. the foreman of a gang of workers, esp. navvies.

gangling /ˈgæŋglɪŋ/ adj. (of a person) loosely built; lanky. □ **gangle** v.intr. [frequent. of GANG²]

ganglion /ˈgæŋglɪən/ n. (pl. **ganglia** /-lɪə/ or **ganglions**) **1 a** an enlargement or knot on a nerve etc. containing an assemblage of nerve-cells. **b** a mass of grey matter in the central nervous system forming a nerve-nucleus. **2** Med. a cyst, esp. on a tendon sheath. **3** a centre of activity or interest. □ **gangliar** adj. **gangliform** adj. **ganglionated** adj. **ganglionic** /-ˈɒnɪk/ adj. [Gk gagglion]

gangly /ˈgæŋglɪ/ adj. (**ganglier, gangliest**) = GANGLING.

gangplank /ˈgæŋplæŋk/ n. a movable plank usu. with cleats nailed on it for boarding or disembarking from a ship etc.

gangrene /ˈgæŋgriːn/ n. & v. —n. **1** Med. death and decomposition of a part of the body tissue, usu. resulting from obstructed circulation. **2** moral corruption. —v.tr. & intr. affect or become affected with gangrene. □ **gangrenous** /ˈgæŋgrɪnəs/ adj. [F gangrène f. L gangraena f. Gk gaggraina]

gangster /ˈgæŋstə(r)/ n. a member of a gang of violent criminals. □ **gangsterism** n.

gangue /gæŋ/ n. valueless earth etc. in which ore is found. [F f. G Gang lode = GANG¹]

gangway /ˈgæŋweɪ/ n. & int. —n. **1** Brit. a passage, esp. between rows of seats. **2 a** an opening in the bulwarks by which a ship is entered or left. **b** a bridge laid from ship to shore. **c** a passage on a ship, esp. a platform connecting the quarterdeck and forecastle. **3** a temporary bridge on a building site etc. —int. make way!

ganja /ˈgændʒə/ n. marijuana. [Hindi gānjhā]

gannet /ˈgænɪt/ n. **1** any sea bird of the genus Sula, esp. Sula bassana, catching fish by plunge-diving. **2** sl. a greedy person. □ **gannetry** n. (pl. **-ies**). [OE ganot f. Gmc, rel. to GANDER]

gantry /ˈgæntrɪ/ n. (pl. **-ies**) **1** an overhead structure with a platform supporting a travelling crane, or railway or road signals. **2** a structure supporting a space rocket prior to launching. [prob. f. gawn, dial. form of GALLON + TREE]

gaol Brit. var. of JAIL.

gaoler Brit. var. of JAILER.

gap n. **1** an unfilled space or interval; a blank; a break in continuity. **2** a wide divergence in views, sympathies, development, etc. (generation gap). **3** a gorge or pass. □ **gapped** adj. **gappy** adj. [ME f. ON, = chasm, rel. to GAPE]

gape v. & n. —v.intr. **1 a** open one's mouth wide, esp. in amazement or wonder. **b** be or become wide open. **2** (foll. by at) gaze curiously or wondrously. **3** split. **4** yawn. —n. **1** an open-mouthed stare. **2** a yawn. **3** an expanse of open mouth or beak. **4** a rent or opening. □ **gapingly** adv. [ME f. ON gapa]

garage /ˈgærɑːdʒ, -rɑːʒ, -rɪdʒ/ n. & v. —n. **1** a building or shed for the storage of a motor vehicle or vehicles. **2** an establishment selling petrol etc., or repairing and selling motor vehicles. —v.tr. put or keep (a motor vehicle) in a garage. □ **garage sale** US a sale of miscellaneous household goods, usu. for charity, held in the garage of a private house. [F f. garer shelter]

garb n. & v. —n. **1** clothing, esp. of a distinctive kind. **2** the way a person is dressed. —v.tr. (usu. in passive or refl.) put (esp. distinctive) clothes on (a person). [obs. F *garbe* f. It. *garbo* f. Gmc, rel. to GEAR]

garbage /ˈgɑːbɪdʒ/ n. **1 a** refuse, filth. **b** domestic waste. **2** foul or rubbishy literature etc. □ **garbage can** US a dustbin. [AF: orig. unkn.]

garble /ˈgɑːb(ə)l/ v.tr. **1** unintentionally distort or confuse (facts, messages, etc.). **2** make (usu. unfair or malicious) selections from (facts, statements, etc.). □ **garbler** n. [It. *garbellare* f. Arab. *ġarbala* sift, perh. f. LL *cribellare* to sieve f. L *cribrum* sieve]

Garda /ˈgɑːdə/ n. **1** the State police force of the Irish Republic. **2** (also **garda**) (pl. **-dai** /-diː/) a member of this. [Ir. *Garda Síochána* Civic Guard]

garden /ˈgɑːd(ə)n/ n. & v. —n. **1** esp. *Brit.* a piece of ground, usu. adjoining a private house, used for growing flowers, fruit, or vegetables, and as a place of recreation. **2** (esp. in pl.) ornamental grounds laid out for public enjoyment. **3** (attrib.) **a** (of plants) cultivated, not wild. **b** for use in a garden (*garden seat*). **4** (usu. in pl. prec. by a name) *Brit.* a street, square, etc. (*Onslow Gardens*). **5** an especially fertile region. **6** US a large public hall. —v.intr. cultivate or work in a garden. □ **garden centre** an establishment where plants and garden equipment etc. are sold. **garden city** an industrial or other town laid out systematically with spacious surroundings, parks, etc. **garden party** a social event held on a lawn or in a garden. **garden suburb** *Brit.* a suburb laid out spaciously with open spaces, parks, etc. □ **gardenesque** /-ˈnesk/ adj. **gardening** n. [ME f. ONF *gardin* (OF *jardin*) ult. f. Gmc: cf. YARD²]

gardener /ˈgɑːdnə(r)/ n. a person who gardens or is employed to tend a garden. [ME ult. f. OF *jardinier* (as GARDEN)]

gardenia /gɑːˈdiːnɪə/ n. any tree or shrub of the genus *Gardenia*, with large white or yellow flowers and usu. a fragrant scent. [mod.L f. Dr A. *Garden*, Sc. naturalist d. 1791]

garfish /ˈgɑːfɪʃ/ n. (pl. same) **1** any mainly marine fish of the family *Belonidae*, esp. *Belone belone*, having long beaklike jaws with sharp teeth. **2** US any similar freshwater fish of the genus *Lepisosteus*. [app. f. OE *gār* spear + *fisc* FISH¹]

garganey /ˈgɑːgənɪ/ n. (pl. **-eys**) a small duck, *Anas querquedula*, the drake of which has a white stripe from the eye to the neck. [It., dial. var. of *garganello*]

gargantuan /gɑːˈgæntjʊən/ adj. enormous, gigantic. [the name of a giant in Rabelais' book *Gargantua* (1534)]

gargle /ˈgɑːg(ə)l/ v. & n. —v. **1** tr. (also *absol.*) wash (one's mouth and throat) with a liquid kept in motion by breathing through it. **2** intr. make a sound as when doing this. —n. a liquid used for gargling. [F *gargouiller* f. *gargouille*: see GARGOYLE]

gargoyle /ˈgɑːgɔɪl/ n. a grotesque carved human or animal face or figure projecting from the gutter of (esp. a Gothic) building usu. as a spout to carry water clear of a wall. [OF *gargouille* throat, gargoyle]

garibaldi /ˌgærɪˈbɔːldɪ/ n. (pl. **garibaldis**) **1** a kind of woman's or child's loose blouse, orig. of bright red material. **2** *Brit.* a biscuit containing a layer of currants. [G. *Garibaldi*, It. patriot d. 1882]

garish /ˈgeərɪʃ/ adj. **1** obtrusively bright; showy. **2** gaudy; over-decorated. □ **garishly** adv. **garishness** n. [16th-c. *gaurish* app. f. obs. *gaure* stare]

garland /ˈgɑːlənd/ n. & v. —n. **1** a wreath of flowers, leaves, etc., worn on the head or hung as a decoration. **2** a prize or distinction. —v.tr. **1** adorn with garlands. **2** crown with a garland. [ME f. OF *garlande*, of unkn. orig.]

garlic /ˈgɑːlɪk/ n. **1** any of various alliaceous plants, esp. *Allium sativum*. **2** the strong-smelling pungent-tasting bulb of this plant, used as a flavouring in cookery. □ **garlicky** adj. [OE *gārlēac* f. *gār* spear + *lēac* LEEK]

garment /ˈgɑːmənt/ n. **1 a** an article of dress. **b** (in pl.) clothes. **2** the outward and visible covering of anything. [ME f. OF *garnement* (as GARNISH)]

garner /ˈgɑːnə(r)/ v. & n. —v.tr. **1** collect. **2** store, deposit. —n. *literary* a storehouse or granary. [ME (orig. as noun) f. OF *gernier* f. L *granarium* GRANARY]

garnet /ˈgɑːnɪt/ n. a vitreous silicate mineral, esp. a transparent deep-red kind used as a gem. [ME f. OF *grenat* f. med.L *granatum* POMEGRANATE, from its resemblance to the pulp of the fruit]

garnish /ˈgɑːnɪʃ/ v. & n. —v.tr. decorate or embellish (esp. food). —n. (also **garnishing**) a decoration or embellishment, esp. to food. [ME f. OF *garnir* f. Gmc]

garniture /ˈgɑːnɪtʃə(r)/ n. **1** decoration or trimmings, esp. of food. **2** accessories, appurtenances. [F (as GARNISH)]

garret /ˈgærɪt/ n. **1** a top-floor or attic room, esp. a dismal one. **2** an attic. [ME f. OF *garite* watch-tower f. Gmc]

garrison /ˈgærɪs(ə)n/ n. & v. —n. **1** the troops stationed in a fortress, town, etc., to defend it. **2** the building occupied by them. —v.tr. **1** provide (a place) with or occupy as a garrison. **2** place on garrison duty. □ **garrison town** a town having a permanent garrison. [ME f. OF *garison* f. *garir* defend, furnish f. Gmc]

garrotte /gəˈrɒt/ v. & n. (also **garotte**; US **garrote**) —v.tr. execute or kill by strangulation, esp. with an iron or wire collar etc. —n. **1** a Spanish method of execution by garrotting. **2** the apparatus used for this. [F *garrotter* or Sp. *garrotear* f. *garrote* a cudgel, of unkn. orig.]

garrulous /ˈgærʊləs/ adj. **1** talkative, esp. on trivial matters. **2** loquacious, wordy. □ **garrulity** /gəˈruːlɪtɪ/ n. **garrulously** adv. **garrulousness** n. [L *garrulus* f. *garrire* chatter]

garter /ˈgɑːtə(r)/ n. & v. —n. **1** a band worn to keep a sock or stocking up. **2** (**the Garter**) *Brit.* **a** the highest order of English knighthood. **b** the badge of this. **c** membership of this. **3** US a suspender for a sock or stocking. —v.tr. fasten (a stocking) or encircle (a leg) with a garter. □ **garter-belt** US a suspender belt. **garter stitch** a plain knitting stitch or pattern, forming ridges in alternate rows. [ME f. OF *gartier* f. *garet* bend of the knee]

garth /gɑːθ/ n. *Brit.* an open space within cloisters. [ME f. ON *garthr* = OE *geard* YARD²]

gas /gæs/ n. & v. —n. (pl. **gases**) **1** any airlike substance which moves freely to fill any space available, irrespective of its quantity. **2** such a substance (esp. found naturally or extracted from coal) used as a domestic or industrial fuel (also *attrib.*: *gas cooker*; *gas fire*). **3** nitrous oxide or another gas used as an anaesthetic. **4** a gas or vapour used as a poisonous agent in warfare. **5** *US colloq.* petrol, gasoline. **6** *sl.* pointless idle talk; boasting. **7** *sl.* an enjoyable, attractive, or amusing thing or person. —*v.* (**gases, gassed, gassing**) **1** *tr.* expose to gas, esp. to kill or make unconscious. **2** *intr.* give off gas. **3** *colloq.* talk idly or boastfully. □ **gas chamber** an airtight chamber that can be filled with poisonous gas to kill people or animals. **gas chromatography** chromatography employing gas as the eluent. **gas mask** a respirator used as a defence against poison gas. **gas meter** an apparatus recording the amount of gas consumed. **gas oil** a type of fuel oil distilled from petroleum and heavier than paraffin oil. **gas-permeable** *adj.* (esp. of a contact lens) allowing the diffusion of gases. **gas ring** a hollow ring perforated with gas jets, used esp. for cooking. **gas station** *US* a filling-station. [invented by J. B. van Helmont, Belgian chemist d. 1644, after Gk *khaos* chaos]

gasbag /ˈgæsbæg/ *n.* **1** a container of gas, esp. for holding the gas for a balloon or airship. **2** *sl.* an idle talker.

Gascon /ˈgæskən/ *n.* **1** a native of Gascony. **2** (**gascon**) a braggart. [F f. L *Vasco -onis*]

gaseous /ˈgæsɪəs/ *adj.* of or like gas. □ **gaseousness** *n.*

gash *n.* & *v.* —*n.* **1** a long and deep slash, cut, or wound. **2 a** a cleft such as might be made by a slashing cut. **b** the act of making such a cut. —*v.tr.* make a gash in; cut. [var. of ME *garse* f. OF *garcer* scarify, perh. ult. f. Gk *kharassō*]

gasholder /ˈgæsˌhəʊldə(r)/ *n.* a large receptacle for storing gas; a gasometer.

gasify /ˈgæsɪˌfaɪ/ *v.tr.* & *intr.* (**-ies, -ied**) convert or be converted into gas. □ **gasification** /-fɪˈkeɪʃ(ə)n/ *n.*

gasket /ˈgæskɪt/ *n.* **1** a sheet or ring of rubber etc., shaped to seal the junction of metal surfaces. **2** a small cord securing a furled sail to a yard. [perh. f. F *garcette* thin rope (orig. little girl)]

gaslight /ˈgæslaɪt/ *n.* **1** a jet of burning gas, usu. heating a mantle, to provide light. **2** light emanating from this.

gasoline /ˈgæsəˌliːn/ *n.* (also **gasolene**) **1** a volatile inflammable liquid distilled from petroleum and used for heating and lighting. **2** *US* petrol. [GAS + -OL² + -INE⁴, -ENE]

gasometer /gæˈsɒmɪtə(r)/ *n.* a large tank in which gas is stored for distribution by pipes to users. [F *gazomètre* f. gaz gas + *-mètre* -METER]

gasp /gɑːsp/ *v.* & *n.* —*v.* **1** *intr.* catch one's breath with an open mouth as in exhaustion or astonishment. **2** *intr.* (foll. by *for*) strain to obtain by gasping (*gasped for air*). **3** *tr.* (often foll. by *out*) utter with gasps. —*n.* a convulsive catching of breath. □ **at one's last gasp 1** at the point of death. **2** exhausted. [ME f. ON *geispa*: cf. *geip* idle talk]

gasper /ˈgɑːspə(r)/ *n.* **1** a person who gasps. **2** *Brit. sl.* a cigarette.

gasser /ˈgæsə(r)/ *n.* **1** *colloq.* an idle talker. **2** *sl.* a very attractive or impressive person or thing.

gassy /ˈgæsɪ/ *adj.* (**gassier, gassiest**) **1 a** of or like gas. **b** full of gas. **2** *colloq.* (of talk etc.) pointless, verbose. □ **gassiness** *n.*

gastrectomy /gæˈstrektəmɪ/ *n.* (*pl.* **-ies**) a surgical operation in which the whole or part of the stomach is removed. [GASTRO- + -ECTOMY]

gastric /ˈgæstrɪk/ *adj.* of the stomach. □ **gastric flu** a popular name for an intestinal disorder of unknown cause. **gastric juice** a thin clear virtually colourless acid fluid secreted by the stomach glands and active in promoting digestion. [mod.L *gastricus* f. Gk *gastēr gast(e)ros* stomach]

gastritis /gæˈstraɪtɪs/ *n.* inflammation of the lining of the stomach.

gastro- /ˈgæstrəʊ/ *comb. form* (also **gastr-** before a vowel) stomach. [Gk *gastēr gast(e)ros* stomach]

gastro-enteritis /ˌgæstrəʊˌentəˈraɪtɪs/ *n. Med.* inflammation of the stomach and intestines.

gastronome /ˈgæstrəˌnəʊm/ *n.* a gourmet. [F f. *gastronomie* GASTRONOMY]

gastronomy /gæˈstrɒnəmɪ/ *n.* the practice, study, or art of eating and drinking well. □ **gastronomic** /ˌgæstrəˈnɒmɪk/ *adj.* **gastronomical** /ˌgæstrəˈnɒmɪk(ə)l/ *adj.* **gastronomically** /ˌgæstrəˈnɒmɪkəlɪ/ *adv.* [F *gastronomie* f. Gk *gastronomia* (as GASTRO-, *-nomia* f. *nomos* law)]

gastropod /ˈgæstrəˌpɒd/ *n.* (also **gasteropod**) any mollusc of the class Gastropoda that moves along by means of a large muscular foot, e.g. a snail, slug, etc. □ **gastropodous** /gæˈstrɒpədəs/ *adj.* [F *gastéropode* f. mod.L *gasteropoda* (as GASTRO-, Gk *pous podos* foot)]

gasworks /ˈgæswɜːks/ *n.* a place where gas is manufactured and processed.

gate¹ *n.* & *v.* —*n.* **1** a barrier, usu. hinged, used to close an opening made for entrance and exit through a wall, fence, etc. **2** such an opening, esp. in the wall of a city or enclosure. **3** a means of entrance or exit. **4** a numbered place of access to aircraft at an airport. **5** an arrangement of slots into which the gear lever of a motor vehicle moves to engage the required gear. **6** a device for holding the frame of a cine film momentarily in position behind the lens of a camera or projector. **7 a** an electrical signal that causes or controls the passage of other signals. **b** an electrical circuit with an output which depends on the combination of several inputs. **8** a device regulating the passage of water in a lock etc. **9 a** the number of people entering by payment at the gates of a sports ground etc. **b** (in full **gate-money**) the proceeds taken for admission. **10** = *starting-gate.* —*v.tr.* **1** *Brit.* confine to college or school entirely or after certain hours. **2** (as **gated** *adj.*) (of a road) having a gate or gates to control the movement of traffic or animals. [OE *gæt, geat*, pl. *gatu*, f. Gmc]

gate² *n.* (prec. or prefixed by a name) *Brit.* a street (*Westgate*). [ME f. ON *gata*, f. Gmc]

gateau /ˈgætəʊ/ *n.* (*pl.* **gateaus** or **gateaux**) any of various rich cakes, usu. containing cream or fruit. [F *gâteau* cake]

gatecrasher /ˈgeɪtˌkræʃə(r)/ *n.* an uninvited guest at a party etc. □ **gatecrash** *v.tr.* & *intr.*

gatefold /ˈgeɪtfəʊld/ *n.* a page in a book or magazine etc. that folds out to be larger than the page-format.

gatehouse /ˈgeɪthaʊs/ *n.* **1** a house standing by a gateway, esp. to a large house or park. **2** *hist.* a room over a city gate, often used as a prison.

gatekeeper /ˈgeɪtˌkiːpə(r)/ *n.* an attendant at a gate, controlling entrance and exit.

gateleg /ˈgeɪtleg/ *n.* (in full **gateleg table**) a table with folding flaps supported by legs swung open like a gate. □ **gatelegged** *adj.*

gatepost /ˈgeɪtpəʊst/ n. a post on which a gate is hung or against which it shuts.

gateway /ˈgeɪtweɪ/ n. **1** an entrance with or opening for a gate. **2** a frame or structure built over a gate.

gather /ˈgæðə(r)/ v. & n. —v. **1** tr. & intr. bring or come together; assemble, accumulate. **2** tr. (usu. foll. by up) **a** bring together from scattered places or sources. **b** take up together from the ground, a surface, etc. **c** draw into a smaller compass. **3** tr. acquire by gradually collecting; amass. **4** tr. **a** pick a quantity of (flowers etc.). **b** collect (grain etc.) as a harvest. **5** tr. (often foll. by that + clause) infer or understand. **6** tr. be subjected to or affected by the accumulation or increase of (gathering dust; gather speed). **7** tr. (often foll. by up) summon up (one's thoughts, energy, etc.) for a purpose. **8** tr. gain or recover (one's breath). **9** tr. **a** draw (material, or one's brow) together in folds or wrinkles. **b** pucker or draw together (part of a dress) by running a thread through. **10** intr. come to a head; develop a purulent swelling. —n. (in pl.) a part of a garment that is gathered or drawn in. □ **gatherer** n. [OE gaderian f. WG]

gathering /ˈgæðərɪŋ/ n. **1** an assembly or meeting. **2** a purulent swelling. **3** a group of leaves taken together in bookbinding.

GATT /gæt/ abbr. (also **Gatt**) General Agreement on Tariffs and Trade.

gauche /gəʊʃ/ adj. **1** lacking ease or grace; socially awkward. **2** tactless. □ **gauchely** adv. **gaucheness** n. [F, = left-handed, awkward]

gaucherie /ˈgəʊʃəˌriː/ n. **1** gauche manners. **2** a gauche action. [F]

gaucho /ˈgaʊtʃəʊ/ n. (pl. -os) a cowboy from the S. American pampas. [Sp. f. Quechua]

gaud /gɔːd/ n. a gaudy thing; a showy ornament. [perh. through AF f. OF gaudir rejoice f. L gaudēre]

gaudy /ˈgɔːdɪ/ adj. (**gaudier, gaudiest**) tastelessly or extravagantly bright or showy. □ **gaudily** adv. **gaudiness** n. [prob. f. GAUD + -Y¹]

gauge /geɪdʒ/ n. & v. (US **gage**: see also sense 7) —n. **1** a standard measure to which certain things must conform, esp.: **a** the measure of the capacity or contents of a barrel. **b** the fineness of a textile. **c** the diameter of a bullet. **d** the thickness of sheet metal. **2** any of various instruments for measuring or determining this, or for measuring length, thickness, or other dimensions or properties. **3** the distance between a pair of rails or the wheels on one axle. **4** the capacity, extent, or scope of something. **5** a means of estimating; a criterion or test. **6** a graduated instrument measuring the force or quantity of rainfall, stream, tide, wind, etc. **7** (usu. **gage**) Naut. a relative position with respect to the wind. —v.tr. **1** measure exactly (esp. objects of standard size). **2** determine the capacity or content of. **3** estimate or form a judgement of (a person, temperament, situation, etc.). **4** make uniform; bring to a standard size or shape. □ **gauge pressure** the amount by which a pressure exceeds that of the atmosphere. **take the gauge of** estimate. □ **gaugeable** adj. **gauger** n. [ME f. ONF gauge, gauger, of unkn. orig.]

Gaul /gɔːl/ n. a native or inhabitant of ancient Gaul. [Gaul the country f. F Gaule f. Gmc]

gauleiter /ˈgaʊˌlaɪtə(r)/ n. **1** an official governing a district under Nazi rule. **2** a local or petty tyrant. [G f. Gau administrative district + Leiter leader]

Gaulish /ˈgɔːlɪʃ/ adj. & n. —adj. of or relating to the ancient Gauls. —n. their language.

gaunt /gɔːnt/ adj. **1** lean, haggard. **2** grim or desolate in appearance. □ **gauntly** adv. **gauntness** n. [ME: orig. unkn.]

gauntlet¹ /ˈgɔːntlɪt/ n. **1** a stout glove with a long loose wrist. **2** hist. an armoured glove. **3** the part of a glove covering the wrist. **4** a challenge (esp. in **throw down the gauntlet**). [ME f. OF gantelet dimin. of gant glove f. Gmc]

gauntlet² /ˈgɔːntlɪt/ n. (US **gantlet** /ˈgænt-/) □ **run the gauntlet 1** be subjected to harsh criticism. **2** pass between two rows of people and receive blows from them, as a punishment or ordeal. [earlier gantlope f. Sw. gatlopp f. gata lane, lopp course, assim. to GAUNTLET¹]

gauss /gaʊs/ n. (pl. same or **gausses**) a unit of magnetic induction, equal to one ten-thousandth of a tesla. [K. Gauss, Ger. mathematician d. 1855]

gauze /gɔːz/ n. **1** a thin transparent fabric of silk, cotton, etc. **2** a fine mesh of wire etc. **3** a slight haze. [F gaze f. Gaza in Palestine]

gauzy /ˈgɔːzɪ/ adj. (**gauzier, gauziest**) **1** like gauze; thin and translucent. **2** flimsy, delicate. □ **gauzily** adv. **gauziness** n.

gave past of GIVE.

gavel /ˈgæv(ə)l/ n. a small hammer used by an auctioneer, or for calling a meeting to order. [19th c.: orig. unkn.]

gavotte /gəˈvɒt/ n. **1** an old French dance in common time beginning on the third beat of the bar. **2** the music for this, or a piece of music in the rhythm of this as a movement in a suite. [F f. Prov. gavoto f. Gavot native of a region in the Alps]

gawk v. & n. —v.intr. colloq. stare stupidly. —n. an awkward or bashful person. □ **gawkish** adj. [rel. to obs. gaw gaze f. ON gá heed]

gawky /ˈgɔːkɪ/ adj. (**gawkier, gawkiest**) awkward or ungainly. □ **gawkily** adv. **gawkiness** n.

gawp v.intr. Brit. colloq. stare stupidly or obtrusively. □ **gawper** n. [earlier gaup, galp f. ME galpen yawn, rel. to YELP]

gay adj. & n. —adj. **1** light-hearted and carefree; mirthful. **2** brightly coloured; showy, brilliant (a gay scarf). **3** colloq. **a** homosexual. **b** intended for or used by homosexuals (a gay bar). **4** colloq. dissolute, immoral. —n. colloq. a homosexual, esp. male. □ **gayness** n. [ME f. OF gai, of unkn. orig.]

■ **Usage** Sense 3 is generally informal in tone, but favoured by homosexual groups.

gayety US var. of GAIETY.

gaze v. & n. —v.intr. (foll. by at, into, on, upon, etc.) look fixedly. —n. a fixed or intent look. □ **gazer** n. [ME: orig. unkn.; cf. obs. gaw GAWK]

gazebo /gəˈziːbəʊ/ n. (pl. -os or -oes) a small building or structure such as a summer-house or turret, designed to give a wide view. [perh. joc. f. GAZE, in imitation of L futures in -ēbo: cf. LAVABO]

gazelle /gəˈzel/ n. any of various small graceful soft-eyed antelopes of Asia or Africa, esp. of the genus Gazella. [F prob. f. Sp. gacela f. Arab. ġazāl]

gazette /gə'zet/ n. & v. —n. **1** a newspaper, esp. the official one of an organization or institution. **2** *hist.* a news-sheet; a periodical publication giving current events. **3** *Brit.* an official journal with a list of government appointments, bankruptcies, and other public notices. —*v.tr. Brit.* announce or publish in an official gazette. [F f. It. *gazzetta* f. *gazeta*, a Venetian small coin]

gazetteer /ˌgæzɪ'tɪə(r)/ n. a geographical index or dictionary. [earlier = journalist, for whom such an index was provided: f. F *gazettier* f. It. *gazzettiere* (as GAZETTE)]

gazpacho /gæ'spætʃəʊ/ n. (pl. **-os**) a Spanish soup made with tomatoes, oil, garlic, onions, etc., and served cold. [Sp.]

gazump /gə'zʌmp/ v.tr. (also *absol.*) *Brit. colloq.* **1** (of a seller) raise the price of a property after having accepted an offer by (an intending buyer). **2** swindle. □ **gazumper** n. [20th c.: orig. uncert.]

gazunder /gə'zʌndə(r)/ v.tr. (also *absol.*) *Brit. colloq.* (of a buyer) lower the amount of an offer made to (the seller for a property), esp. just before exchange of contracts. [GAZUMP + UNDER]

GB *abbr.* Great Britain.

GBH *abbr.* grievous bodily harm.

GC *abbr.* (in the UK) George Cross.

GCE *abbr.* (in the UK) General Certificate of Education.

GCHQ *abbr.* (in the UK) Government Communications Headquarters.

GCSE *abbr.* (in the UK) General Certificate of Secondary Education.

Gd *symb. Chem.* the element gadolinium.

GDP *abbr.* gross domestic product.

Ge *symb. Chem.* the element germanium.

gear n. & v. —n. **1** (often in *pl.*) **a** a set of toothed wheels that work together to transmit and control motion from an engine, esp. to the road wheels of a vehicle. **b** a mechanism for doing this. **2** a particular function or state of adjustment of engaged gears (*low gear; second gear*). **3** a mechanism of wheels, levers, etc., usu. for a special purpose (*winding-gear*). **4** a particular apparatus or mechanism, as specified (*landing-gear*). **5** equipment or tackle for a special purpose. **6** *colloq.* clothing, esp. when modern or fashionable. **7** goods; household utensils. **8** rigging. **9** a harness for a draught animal. —v. **1** tr. (foll. by *to*) adjust or adapt to suit a special purpose or need. **2** tr. (often foll. by *up*) equip with gears. **3** tr. (foll. by *up*) make ready or prepared. **4** tr. put (machinery) in gear. **5** intr. **a** be in gear. **b** (foll. by *with*) work smoothly with. □ **be geared** (or **all geared**) **up** (often foll. by *for*, or *to* + infin.) *colloq.* be ready or enthusiastic. **first** (or **bottom**) **gear** the lowest gear in a series. **gear down** (or **up**) provide with a low (or high) gear. **gear lever** (or **shift**) a lever used to engage or change gear, esp. in a motor vehicle. **high** (or **low**) **gear** a gear such that the driven end of a transmission revolves faster (or slower) than the driving end. **in gear** with a gear engaged. **out of gear 1** with no gear engaged. **2** out of order. **top gear** the highest gear in a series. □ **gearing** n. [ME f. ON *gervi* f. Gmc]

gearbox /'gɪəbɒks/ n. **1** the casing that encloses a set of gears. **2** a set of gears with its casing, esp. in a motor vehicle.

gearwheel /'gɪəwiːl/ n. **1** a toothed wheel in a set of gears. **2** (in a bicycle) the cog-wheel driven directly by the chain.

gecko /'gekəʊ/ n. (pl. **-os** or **-oes**) any of various house lizards found in warm climates, with adhesive feet for climbing vertical surfaces. [Malay *chichak* etc., imit. of its cry]

gee[1] /dʒiː/ int. (also **gee whiz** /wɪz/) *US colloq.* a mild expression of surprise, etc. [perh. abbr. of the name *Jesus* used as an oath]

gee[2] /dʒiː/ int. (often foll. by *up*) a command to a horse etc., esp. to go faster. [17th c.: orig. unkn.]

gee[3] /dʒiː/ n. *US sl.* (usu. in *pl.*) a thousand dollars. [the letter *G*, as initial of GRAND]

gee-gee /'dʒiːdʒiː/ n. *Brit. colloq.* a horse. [orig. a child's word, f. GEE[2]]

geese *pl.* of GOOSE.

geezer /'giːzə(r)/ n. *sl.* a person, esp. an old man. [dial. pronunc. of *guiser* mummer]

Geiger counter /'gaɪgə(r)/ n. a device for measuring radioactivity by detecting and counting ionizing particles. [H. *Geiger*, Ger. physicist d. 1945]

geisha /'geɪʃə/ n. (pl. same or **geishas**) **1** a Japanese hostess trained in entertaining men with dance and song. **2** a Japanese prostitute. [Jap.]

gel /dʒel/ n. & v. —n. a semi-solid colloidal suspension or jelly, of a solid dispersed in a liquid. —v.intr. (**gelled**, **gelling**) form a gel. □ **gelation** /-'leɪʃ(ə)n/ n. [abbr. of GELATIN]

gelatin /'dʒelətɪn/ n. (also **gelatine** /-ˌtiːn/) a virtually colourless tasteless transparent water-soluble protein derived from collagen and used in food preparation, photography, etc. □ **gelatinize** /dʒɪ'lætɪˌnaɪz/ v.tr. & intr. (also **-ise**). **gelatinization** /dʒɪˌlætɪnaɪ'zeɪʃ(ə)n/ n. [F *gélatine* f. It. *gelatina* f. *gelata* JELLY]

gelatinous /dʒɪ'lætɪnəs/ adj. **1** of or like gelatin. **2** of a jelly-like consistency. □ **gelatinously** adv.

gelation /dʒɪ'leɪʃ(ə)n/ n. solidification by freezing. [L *gelatio* f. *gelare* freeze]

geld /geld/ v.tr. **1** deprive (usu. a male animal) of the ability to reproduce. **2** castrate or spay; excise the testicles or ovaries of. [ME f. ON *gelda* f. *geldr* barren f. Gmc]

gelding /'geldɪŋ/ n. a gelded animal, esp. a male horse. [ME f. ON *geldingr*: see GELD]

gelid /'dʒelɪd/ adj. **1** icy, ice-cold. **2** chilly, cool. [L *gelidus* f. *gelu* frost]

gelignite /'dʒelɪgˌnaɪt/ n. an explosive made from nitroglycerine, cellulose nitrate, sodium nitrate, and wood pulp. [GELATIN + L *ignis* fire + -ITE[1]]

gelly /'dʒelɪ/ n. *Brit. sl.* gelignite. [abbr.]

gem /dʒem/ n. & v. —n. **1** a precious stone, esp. when cut and polished or engraved. **2** an object or person of great beauty or worth. —v.tr. (**gemmed**, **gemming**) adorn with or as with gems. □ **gemlike** adj. **gemmy** adj. [ME f. OF *gemme* f. L *gemma* bud, jewel]

geminate adj. & v. —adj. /'dʒemɪnət/ combined in pairs. —v.tr. /'dʒemɪˌneɪt/ **1** double, repeat. **2** arrange in pairs. □ **gemination** /-'neɪʃ(ə)n/ n. [L *geminatus* past part. of *geminare* f. *geminus* twin]

Gemini /'dʒemɪˌnaɪ, -ˌniː/ n. **1** a constellation, traditionally regarded as contained in the figures of twins. **2 a** the third sign of the zodiac (the Twins). **b** a person born when the sun is in this sign. □ **Geminean** /ˌdʒemɪˈniːən/ n. & adj. [ME f. L, = twins]

gemmiferous /dʒeˈmɪfərəs/ adj. **1** producing precious stones. **2** bearing buds. [L gemmifer f. gemma bud, jewel]

gemmology /dʒeˈmɒlədʒɪ/ n. the study of gems. □ **gemmologist** n. [L gemma gem + -LOGY]

gemstone /ˈdʒemstəʊn/ n. a precious stone used as a gem.

Gen. abbr. General.

gen /dʒen/ n. & v. Brit. sl. —n. information. —v.tr. & intr. (**genned, genning**) (foll. by up) provide with or obtain information. [perh. f. first syll. of general information]

-gen /dʒ(ə)n/ comb. form **1** Chem. that which produces (hydrogen; antigen). **2** Bot. growth (endogen; exogen; acrogen). [F -gène f. Gk -genēs -born, of a specified kind f. gen- root of gignomai be born, become]

gendarme /ˈʒɒndɑːm/ n. a soldier, mounted or on foot, employed in police duties esp. in France. [F f. gens d'armes men of arms]

gendarmerie /ʒɒnˈdɑːmərɪ/ n. **1** a force of gendarmes. **2** the headquarters of such a force.

gender /ˈdʒendə(r)/ n. **1 a** the grammatical classification of nouns and related words, roughly corresponding to the two sexes and sexlessness. **b** each of the classes of nouns (see MASCULINE, FEMININE, NEUTER, COMMON adj. 6). **2** (of nouns and related words) the property of belonging to such a class. **3** colloq. a person's sex. [ME f. OF gendre ult. f. L GENUS]

gene /dʒiːn/ n. a unit of heredity composed of DNA or RNA and forming part of a chromosome etc., that determines a particular characteristic of an individual. □ **gene therapy** Med. the introduction of normal genes into cells in place of defective or missing ones in order to correct genetic disorders. [G Gen: see -GEN]

genealogical /ˌdʒiːnɪəˈlɒdʒɪk(ə)l/ adj. **1** of or concerning genealogy. **2** tracing family descent. □ **genealogical tree** a chart like an inverted branching tree showing the descent of a family or of an animal species. □ **genealogically** adv. [F généalogique f. Gk genealogikos (as GENEALOGY)]

genealogy /ˌdʒiːnɪˈælədʒɪ/ n. (pl. **-ies**) **1 a** a line of descent traced continuously from an ancestor. **b** an account or exposition of this. **2** the study and investigation of lines of descent. **3** a plant's or animal's line of development from earlier forms. □ **genealogist** n. **genealogize** v.tr. & intr. (also -ise). [ME f. OF genealogie f. LL genealogia f. Gk genealogia f. genea race]

genera pl. of GENUS.

general /ˈdʒenər(ə)l/ adj. & n. —adj. **1 a** completely or almost universal. **b** including or affecting all or nearly all parts or cases of things. **2** prevalent, widespread, usual. **3** not partial, particular, local, or sectional. **4** not limited in application; relating to whole classes or all cases. **5** including points common to the individuals of a class and neglecting the differences (a general term). **6** not restricted or specialized (general knowledge). **7 a** roughly corresponding or adequate. **b** sufficient for practical purposes. **8** not detailed (a general resemblance). **9** vague, indefinite (spoke only in general terms). **10** chief or principal; having overall authority (general manager; Secretary-General). —n. **1 a** an army officer ranking next below Field Marshal or above lieutenant-general. **b** US = lieutenant-general, major-general. **2** a commander of an army. **3** a tactician or strategist of specified merit (a great general). **4** the head of a religious order, e.g. of the Jesuits or Dominicans or the Salvation Army. □ **General American** a form of US speech not markedly dialectal or regional. **General Certificate of Education 1** an examination set esp. for secondary-school pupils at advanced level in England, Wales and N. Ireland. **2** the certificate gained by passing it. **General Certificate of Secondary Education** an examination set esp. for secondary-school pupils in England, Wales, and N. Ireland. **general election** the election of representatives to a legislature from constituencies throughout the country. **general meeting** a meeting open to all the members of a society etc. **general practice** the work of a general practitioner. **general practitioner** a doctor working in the community and treating cases of all kinds, as distinct from a consultant or specialist. **general staff** the staff assisting a military commander in planning and administration. **general strike** a strike of workers in all or most trades. **General Synod** the highest governing body in the Church of England. **in general 1** as a normal rule; usually. **2** for the most part. □ **generalness** n. [ME f. OF f. L generalis (as GENUS)]

generalissimo /ˌdʒenərəˈlɪsɪməʊ/ n. (pl. **-os**) the commander of a combined military force consisting of army, navy, and air-force units. [It., superl. of generale GENERAL]

generalist /ˈdʒenərəlɪst/ n. a person competent in several different fields or activities (opp. SPECIALIST).

generality /ˌdʒenəˈrælɪtɪ/ n. (pl. **-ies**) **1** a statement or principle etc. having general validity or force. **2** applicability to a whole class of instances. **3** vagueness; lack of detail. **4** the state of being general. **5** (foll. by of) the main body or majority. [F généralité f. LL generalitas -tatis (as GENERAL)]

generalization /ˌdʒenərəlaɪˈzeɪʃ(ə)n/ n. (also **-isation**) **1** a general notion or proposition obtained by inference from (esp. limited or inadequate) particular cases. **2** the act or an instance of generalizing. [F généralisation (as GENERALIZE)]

generalize /ˈdʒenərəlaɪz/ v. (also **-ise**) **1** intr. **a** speak in general or indefinite terms. **b** form general principles or notions. **2** tr. reduce to a general statement, principle, or notion. **3** tr. give a general character to. **b** call by a general name. **4** tr. infer (a law or conclusion) by induction. **5** tr. Math. & Philos. express in a general form; extend the application of. **6** tr. bring into general use. □ **generalizable** adj. **generalizability** /-zəˈbɪlɪtɪ/ n. **generalizer** n. [F généraliser (as GENERAL)]

generally /ˈdʒenərəlɪ/ adv. **1** usually; in most cases. **2** in a general sense; without regard to particulars or exceptions (generally speaking). **3** for the most part; extensively (not generally known). **4** in most respects (they were generally well-behaved).

generalship /ˈdʒenər(ə)lʃɪp/ n. **1** the art or practice of exercising military command. **2** military skill; strategy. **3** skilful management; tact, diplomacy.

generate /ˈdʒenəˌreɪt/ v.tr. bring into existence; produce, evolve. □ **generable** /-rəb(ə)l/ adj. [L generare beget (as GENUS)]

generation /ˌdʒenəˈreɪʃ(ə)n/ n. **1** all the people born at a particular time, regarded collectively (my generation; the rising generation). **2** a single step in descent or pedigree (have known them for three generations). **3** a stage in (esp. technological) development (fourth-generation computers). **4** the average time in which children are ready to take the place of their parents (usu. reckoned at about 30 years). **5** production by natural or artificial process, esp. the production of electricity or heat. **6** procreation; the propagation of species. □ **generation gap** differences of outlook or opinion between those of different generations. □ **generational** adj. [ME f. OF f. L generatio -onis (as GENERATE)]

generative /ˈdʒenərətɪv/ adj. **1** of or concerning procreation. **2** able to produce, productive. [ME f. OF generatif or LL generativus (as GENERATE)]

generator /ˈdʒenəˌreɪtə(r)/ n. **1** a machine for converting mechanical into electrical energy; a dynamo. **2** an apparatus for producing gas, steam, etc. **3** a person who generates an idea etc.; an originator.

generic /dʒɪˈnerɪk/ adj. **1** characteristic of or relating to a class; general, not specific or special. **2** Biol. characteristic of or belonging to a genus. **3** (of goods, esp. a drug) having no brand name; not protected by a registered trade mark. □ **generically** adv. [F générique f. L GENUS]

generous /ˈdʒenərəs/ adj. **1** giving or given freely. **2** magnanimous, noble-minded, unprejudiced. **3** ample, abundant, copious. □ **generosity** /-ˈrɒsɪtɪ/ n. **generously** adv. **generousness** n. [OF generous f. L generosus noble, magnanimous (as GENUS)]

genesis /ˈdʒenɪsɪs/ n. **1** the origin, or mode of formation or generation, of a thing. **2** (**Genesis**) the first book of the Old Testament. [L f. Gk f. gen- be produced, root of gignomai become]

genetic /dʒɪˈnetɪk/ adj. **1** of genetics or genes; inherited. **2** of, in, or concerning origin; causal. □ **genetic code** Biochem. the means by which genetic information is stored as sequences of nucleotide bases in the chromosomal DNA. **genetic engineering** the deliberate modification of the characters of an organism by the manipulation of DNA and the transformation of certain genes. **genetic fingerprinting** (or **profiling**) the analysis of characteristic patterns in DNA as a means of identifying individuals. □ **genetically** adv. [GENESIS after antithetic]

genetics /dʒɪˈnetɪks/ n.pl. (treated as sing.) the study of heredity and the variation of inherited characteristics. □ **geneticist** /-tɪsɪst/ n.

Geneva Convention /dʒɪˈniːvə/ n. an international agreement first made at Geneva in 1864 and later revised, governing the status and treatment of captured and wounded military personnel in wartime. [Geneva in Switzerland]

genial /ˈdʒiːnɪəl/ adj. **1** jovial, sociable, kindly, cheerful. **2** (of the climate) mild and warm; conducive to growth. **3** cheering, enlivening. □ **geniality** /-ˈælɪtɪ/ n. **genially** adv. [L genialis (as GENIUS)]

genic /ˈdʒiːnɪk/ adj. of or relating to genes.

-genic /ˈdʒenɪk/ comb. form forming adjectives meaning: **1** producing (carcinogenic; pathogenic).

2 well suited to (photogenic; radiogenic). **3** produced by (iatrogenic). □ **-genically** suffix forming adverbs. [-GEN + -IC]

genie /ˈdʒiːnɪ/ n. (pl. usu. **genii** /ˈdʒiːnɪˌaɪ/) a jinnee, goblin, or familiar spirit of Arabian folklore. [F génie f. L GENIUS: cf. JINNEE]

genii pl. of GENIE, GENIUS.

genista /dʒɪˈnɪstə/ n. any almost leafless shrub of the genus Genista, with a profusion of yellow pea-shaped flowers, e.g. dyer's broom. [L]

genital /ˈdʒenɪt(ə)l/ adj. & n. —adj. of or relating to animal reproduction. —n. (in pl.) the external reproductive organs. [OF génital or L genitalis f. gignere genit- beget]

genitalia /ˌdʒenɪˈteɪlɪə/ n.pl. the genitals. [L, neut. pl. of genitalis: see GENITAL]

genitive /ˈdʒenɪtɪv/ n. & adj. Gram. —n. the case of nouns and pronouns (and words in grammatical agreement with them) corresponding to of, from, and other prepositions and indicating possession or close association. —adj. of or in the genitive. □ **genitival** /-ˈtaɪv(ə)l/ adj. **genitivally** /-ˈtaɪvəlɪ/ adv. [ME f. OF genetif, -ive or L genitivus f. gignere genit- beget]

genito- /ˈdʒenɪtəʊ/ comb. form genital.

genito-urinary /ˌdʒenɪtəʊˈjʊərɪnərɪ/ adj. of the genital and urinary organs.

genius /ˈdʒiːnɪəs/ n. (pl. **geniuses** or **genii** /-nɪˌaɪ/) **1** (pl. **geniuses**) **a** an exceptional intellectual or creative power or other natural ability or tendency. **b** a person having this. **2** the tutelary spirit of a person, place, institution, etc. **3** a person or spirit regarded as powerfully influencing a person for good or evil. [L (in sense 2) f. the root of gignere beget]

genocide /ˈdʒenəˌsaɪd/ n. the deliberate extermination of a people or nation. □ **genocidal** /-ˈsaɪd(ə)l/ adj. [Gk genos race + -CIDE]

genome /ˈdʒiːnəʊm/ n. **1** the haploid set of chromosomes of an organism. **2** the genetic material of an organism. [GENE + CHROMOSOME]

genotype /ˈdʒiːnəˌtaɪp/ n. Biol. the genetic constitution of an individual. □ **genotypic** /-ˈtɪpɪk/ adj. [G Genotypus (as GENE, TYPE)]

-genous /ˈdʒenəs/ comb. form forming adjectives meaning 'produced' (endogenous).

genre /ˈʒɑ̃rə/ n. **1** a kind or style, esp. of art or literature (e.g. novel, drama, satire). **2** (in full **genre painting**) the painting of scenes from ordinary life. [F, = a kind (as GENDER)]

gent /dʒent/ n. colloq. (often joc.) a gentleman. [abbr.]

genteel /dʒenˈtiːl/ adj. **1** affectedly or ostentatiously refined or stylish. **2** often iron. of or appropriate to the upper classes. □ **genteelly** adv. **genteelness** n. [earlier gentile, readoption of F gentil GENTLE]

genteelism /dʒenˈtiːlɪz(ə)m/ n. a word used because it is thought to be less vulgar than the commoner word (e.g. perspire for sweat).

gentian /ˈdʒenʃ(ə)n, -ʃɪən/ n. any plant of the genus Gentiana or Gentianella, found esp. in mountainous regions, and having usu. vivid blue flowers. □ **gentian violet** a violet dye used as an antiseptic, esp. in the treatment of burns. [OE f. L gentiana f. Gentius king of Illyria]

gentile /ˈdʒentaɪl/ adj. & n. —adj. **1** (**Gentile**) not Jewish; heathen. **2** of or relating to a nation or tribe. —n. (**Gentile**) a person who is not

Jewish. [ME f. L *gentilis* f. *gens gentis* family f. the root of *gignere* beget]

gentility /dʒenˈtɪlɪtɪ/ n. **1** social superiority. **2** good manners; habits associated with the nobility. **3** people of noble birth. [ME f. OF *gentilité* (as GENTLE)]

gentle /ˈdʒent(ə)l/ adj. & n. —adj. (**gentler**, **gentlest**) **1** not rough; mild or kind, esp. in temperament. **2** moderate; not severe or drastic (*a gentle rebuke; a gentle breeze*). **3** (of birth, pursuits, etc.) honourable, of or fit for people of good social position. **4** quiet; requiring patience (*gentle art*). —n. a maggot, the larva of the meat-fly or bluebottle used as fishing-bait. □ **gentleness** n. **gently** adv. [ME f. OF *gentil* f. L *gentilis*: see GENTILE]

gentlefolk /ˈdʒent(ə)lˌfəʊk/ n.pl. *literary* people of good family.

gentleman /ˈdʒent(ə)lmən/ n. (pl. **-men**) **1** a man (in polite or formal use). **2** a chivalrous or well-bred man. **3** a man of good social position or of wealth and leisure (*country gentleman*). **4** a man of gentle birth attached to a royal household (*gentleman in waiting*). **5** (in pl. as a form of address) a male audience or the male part of an audience. □ **gentleman-at-arms** one of a sovereign's bodyguard. **gentleman farmer** a country gentleman who farms. **gentleman's** (or **-men's**) **agreement** one which is binding in honour but not legally enforceable. [GENTLE + MAN after OF *gentilz hom*]

gentlemanly /ˈdʒent(ə)lmənlɪ/ adj. like a gentleman in looks or behaviour; befitting a gentleman. □ **gentlemanliness** n.

gentlewoman /ˈdʒent(ə)lˌwʊmən/ n. (pl. **-women**) *archaic* a woman of good birth or breeding.

gentoo /ˈdʒentuː/ n. a penguin, *Pygoscelis papua*, esp. abundant in the Falkland Islands. [perh. f. Anglo-Ind. *Gentoo* = Hindu, f. Port. *gentio* GENTILE]

gentrification /ˌdʒentrɪfɪˈkeɪʃ(ə)n/ n. the social advancement of an inner urban area by the arrival of affluent middle-class residents. □ **gentrify** /-ˌfaɪ/ v.tr. (**-ies, -ied**).

gentry /ˈdʒentrɪ/ n.pl. **1** the people next below the nobility in position and birth. **2** *derog.* people (*these gentry*). [prob. f. obs. *gentrice* f. OF *genterise* var. of *gentelise* nobility f. *gentil* GENTLE]

genuflect /ˈdʒenjʊˌflekt/ v.intr. bend the knee, esp. in worship or as a sign of respect. □ **genuflection** /-ˈflekʃ(ə)n/ n. (also **genuflexion**). **genuflector** n. [eccl.L *genuflectere genuflex-* f. L *genu* the knee + *flectere* bend]

genuine /ˈdʒenjʊɪn/ adj. **1** really coming from its stated, advertised, or reputed source. **2** properly so called; not sham. **3** pure-bred. □ **genuinely** adv. **genuineness** n. [L *genuinus* f. *genu* knee, with ref. to a father's acknowledging a new-born child by placing it on his knee: later associated with GENUS]

genus /ˈdʒiːnəs, ˈdʒenəs/ n. (pl. **genera** /ˈdʒenərə/) **1** *Biol.* a taxonomic grouping of organisms having common characteristics distinct from those of other genera, usu. containing several or many species and being one of a series constituting a taxonomic family). **2** a kind or class having common characteristics. [L *genus -eris* birth, race, stock]

-geny /dʒənɪ/ *comb. form* forming nouns meaning 'mode of production or development of' (*anthropogeny; ontogeny; pathogeny*). [F *-génie* (as -GEN, -Yᶾ)]

geo- /ˈdʒiːəʊ/ *comb. form* earth. [Gk *geō-* f. *gē* earth]

geocentric /ˌdʒiːəʊˈsentrɪk/ adj. **1** considered as viewed from the centre of the earth. **2** having or representing the earth as the centre; not heliocentric. □ **geocentrically** adv.

geochronology /ˌdʒiːəʊkrəˈnɒlədʒɪ/ n. **1** the study and measurement of geological time by means of geological events. **2** the ordering of geological events. □ **geochronological** /-ˌkrɒnəˈlɒdʒɪk(ə)l/ adj. **geochronologist** n.

geode /ˈdʒiːəʊd/ n. **1** a small cavity lined with crystals or other mineral matter. **2** a rock containing such a cavity. □ **geodic** /dʒiːˈɒdɪk/ adj. [L *geodes* f. Gk *geōdēs* earthy f. *gē* earth]

geodesic /ˌdʒiːəʊˈdiːzɪk/ adj. (also **geodetic** /-ˈdetɪk/) **1** of or relating to geodesy. **2** of, involving, or consisting of a geodesic line. □ **geodesic dome** a dome constructed of short struts along geodesic lines. **geodesic line** the shortest possible line between two points on a curved surface.

geodesy /dʒiːˈɒdɪsɪ/ n. the branch of mathematics dealing with the figures and areas of the earth or large portions of it. □ **geodesist** n. [mod.L f. Gk *geōdaisia* (as GEO-, *daiō* divide)]

geographical /ˌdʒiːəˈɡræfɪk(ə)l/ adj. (also **geographic** /-ˈɡræfɪk/) of or relating to geography. □ **geographical mile** a distance equal to one minute of longitude or latitude at the equator (about 1850 metres). □ **geographically** adv. [*geographic* f. F *géographique* or L *geographicus* f. Gk *geōgraphikos* (as GEO-, -GRAPHIC)]

geography /dʒɪˈɒɡrəfɪ/ n. **1** the study of the earth's physical features, resources, and climate, and the physical aspects of its population. **2** the main physical features of an area. **3** the layout or arrangement of rooms in a building. □ **geographer** n. [F *géographie* or L *geographia* f. Gk *geōgraphia* (as GEO-, -GRAPHY)]

geoid /ˈdʒiːɔɪd/ n. the shape of the earth. [Gk *geōeidēs* (as GEO-, -OID)]

geology /dʒɪˈɒlədʒɪ/ n. **1** the science of the earth, including the composition, structure, and origin of its rocks. **2** this science applied to any other planet or celestial body. **3** the geological features of a district. □ **geologic** /ˌdʒiːəˈlɒdʒɪk/ adj. **geological** /ˌdʒiːəˈlɒdʒɪk(ə)l/ adj. **geologically** /ˌdʒiːəˈlɒdʒɪkəlɪ/ adv. **geologist** n. **geologize** v.tr. & intr. (also **-ise**). [mod.L *geologia* (as GEO-, -LOGY)]

geometer /dʒɪˈɒmɪtə(r)/ n. **1** a person skilled in geometry. **2** any moth, esp. of the family *Geometridae*, having twiglike larvae which move in a looping fashion, seeming to measure the ground. [ME f. LL *geometra* f. L *geometres* f. Gk *geōmetrēs* (as GEO-, *metrēs* measurer)]

geometric /ˌdʒɪəˈmetrɪk/ adj. (also **geometrical**) **1** of, according to, or like geometry. **2** (of a design, architectural feature, etc.) characterized by or decorated with regular lines and shapes. □ **geometric mean** the central number in a geometric progression. **geometric progression** a progression of numbers with a constant ratio between each number and the one before (as 1, 3, 9, 27, 81). □ **geometrically** adv. [F *géométrique* f. L *geometricus* f. Gk *geōmetrikos* (as GEOMETER)]

geometry /dʒɪˈɒmɪtrɪ/ n. **1** the branch of mathematics concerned with the properties and relations of points, lines, surfaces, and solids. **2** the relative arrangement of objects or parts. □ **geometrician** /ˌdʒiːəmɪˈtrɪʃ(ə)n/ n. [ME f. OF *geometrie* f. L *geometria* f. Gk (as GEO-, -METRY)]

geomorphology /ˌdʒiːəmɔːˈfɒlədʒɪ/ n. the study of the physical features of the surface of the earth and their relation to its geological structures. □ **geomorphological** /-fəˈlɒdʒɪk(ə)l/ adj. **geomorphologist** n.

geophysics /ˌdʒiːəʊˈfɪzɪks/ n. the physics of the earth. □ **geophysical** adj. **geophysicist** /-sɪst/ n.

geopolitics /ˌdʒiːəʊˈpɒlɪtɪks/ n. **1** the politics of a country as determined by its geographical features. **2** the study of this. □ **geopolitical** /-pəˈlɪtɪk(ə)l/ adj. **geopolitically** /-pəˈlɪtɪkəlɪ/ adv. **geopolitician** /-ˈtɪʃ(ə)n/ n.

Geordie /ˈdʒɔːdɪ/ n. Brit. colloq. a native of Tyneside. [the name *George* + -IE]

George Cross /dʒɔːdʒ/ n. (also **George Medal**) (in the UK) decorations for bravery awarded esp. to civilians, instituted in 1940 by King George VI.

georgette /dʒɔːˈdʒet/ n. a thin silk or crêpe dress-material. [*Georgette* de la Plante, Fr. dressmaker]

Georgian[1] /ˈdʒɔːdʒ(ə)n/ adj. **1** of or characteristic of the time of Kings George I–IV (1714–1830). **2** of or characteristic of the time of Kings George V and VI (1910–52), esp. of the literature of 1910–20.

Georgian[2] /ˈdʒɔːdʒ(ə)n/ adj. & n. —adj. of or relating to Georgia in the Caucasus. —n. **1** a native of Georgia; a person of Georgian descent. **2** the language of Georgia.

Georgian[3] /ˈdʒɔːdʒ(ə)n/ adj. & n. —adj. of or relating to Georgia in the US. —n. a native of Georgia.

geosphere /ˈdʒiːəˌsfɪə(r)/ n. **1** the solid surface of the earth. **2** any of the almost spherical concentric regions of the earth and its atmosphere.

geostationary /ˌdʒiːəʊˈsteɪʃənərɪ/ adj. Electronics (of an artificial satellite of the earth) moving in such an orbit as to remain above the same point on the earth's surface (see also GEOSYNCHRONOUS).

geosynchronous /ˌdʒiːəʊˈsɪŋkrənəs/ adj. (of an artificial satellite of the earth) moving in an orbit equal to the earth's period of rotation (see also GEOSTATIONARY).

geothermal /ˌdʒiːəʊˈθɜːm(ə)l/ adj. relating to, originating from, or produced by the internal heat of the earth.

geotropism /dʒɪˈɒtrəˌpɪz(ə)m/ n. plant growth in relation to gravity. □ **negative geotropism** the tendency of stems etc. to grow away from the centre of the earth. **positive geotropism** the tendency of roots to grow towards the centre of the earth. □ **geotropic** /ˌdʒiːəʊˈtrɒpɪk/ adj. [GEO- + Gk *tropikos* f. *tropē* a turning f. *trepō* to turn]

geranium /dʒəˈreɪnɪəm/ n. **1** any herb or shrub of the genus *Geranium* bearing fruit shaped like the bill of a crane. **2** (in general use) a cultivated pelargonium. [L f. Gk *geranion* f. *geranos* crane]

gerbil /ˈdʒɜːbɪl/ n. (also **jerbil**) a mouselike desert rodent of the subfamily Gerbillinae, with long hind legs. [F *gerbille* f. mod.L *gerbillus* dimin. of *gerbo* JERBOA]

geriatric /ˌdʒerɪˈætrɪk/ adj. & n. —adj. **1** of or relating to old people. **2** colloq. old, outdated. —n. **1** an old person, esp. one receiving special care. **2** colloq. a person or thing considered as relatively old or outdated. [Gk *gēras* old age + *iatros* doctor]

geriatrics /ˌdʒerɪˈætrɪks/ n.pl. (usu. treated as sing.) a branch of medicine or social science dealing with the health and care of old people. □ **geriatrician** /-əˈtrɪʃ(ə)n/ n.

germ /dʒɜːm/ n. **1** a micro-organism, esp. one which causes disease. **2 a** a portion of an organism capable of developing into a new one; the rudiment of an animal or plant. **b** an embryo of a seed (*wheat germ*). **3** an original idea etc. from which something may develop; an elementary principle. □ **germ-cell** a cell containing half the number of chromosomes of a somatic cell and able to unite with one from the opposite sex to form a new individual; a gamete. **germ warfare** the systematic spreading of micro-organisms to cause disease in an enemy population. □ **germy** adj. [F *germe* f. L *germen germinis* sprout]

German /ˈdʒɜːmən/ n. & adj. —n. **1** a native or national of Germany; a person of German descent. **2** the language of Germany, also used in Austria and Switzerland. —adj. of or relating to Germany or its people or language. □ **German measles** a contagious disease, rubella, with symptoms like mild measles. **German shepherd** (or **shepherd dog**) an Alsatian. **High German** a literary and cultured form of German. **Low German** German dialects other than High German. [L *Germanus* with ref. to related peoples of Central and N. Europe, a name perh. given by Celts to their neighbours: cf. OIr. *gair* neighbour]

german /ˈdʒɜːmən/ adj. (placed after *brother*, *sister*, or *cousin*) **1** having both parents the same (*brother german*). **2** having both grandparents the same on one side (*cousin german*). [ME f. OF *germain* f. L *germanus* genuine, of the same parents]

germander /dʒɜːˈmændə(r)/ n. any plant of the genus *Teucrium*. □ **germander speedwell** a creeping plant, *Veronica chamaedrys*, with germander-like leaves. [ME f. med.L *germandra* ult. f. Gk *khamaidrus* f. *khamai* on the ground + *drus* oak]

germane /dʒɜːˈmeɪn/ adj. (usu. foll. by *to*) relevant (to a subject under consideration). □ **germanely** adv. **germaneness** n. [var. of GERMAN]

Germanic /dʒɜːˈmænɪk/ adj. & n. —adj. **1** having German characteristics. **2** hist. of the Germans. **3** of the Scandinavians, Anglo-Saxons, or Germans. **4** of the languages or language group called Germanic. —n. **1** the branch of Indo-European languages including English, German, Dutch, and the Scandinavian languages. **2** the (unrecorded) early language from which other Germanic languages developed. [L *Germanicus* (as GERMAN)]

germanium /dʒɜːˈmeɪnɪəm/ n. Chem. a lustrous brittle semi-metallic element occurring naturally in sulphide ores and used in semi-conductors. [mod.L f. *Germanus* GERMAN]

Germanize /'dʒɜːmənaɪz/ v.tr. & intr. (also **-ise**) make or become German; adopt or cause to adopt German customs etc. □ **Germanization** /-'zeɪʃ(ə)n/ n. **Germanizer** n.

germicide /'dʒɜːmɪˌsaɪd/ n. a substance destroying germs, esp. those causing disease. □ **germicidal** /-'saɪd(ə)l/ adj.

germinal /'dʒɜːmɪn(ə)l/ adj. **1** relating to or of the nature of a germ or germs (see GERM 1). **2** in the earliest stage of development. **3** productive of new ideas. □ **germinally** adv. [L germen germin- sprout: see GERM]

germinate /'dʒɜːmɪˌneɪt/ v. **1 a** intr. sprout, bud, or put forth shoots. **b** tr. cause to sprout or shoot. **2 a** tr. cause (ideas etc.) to originate or develop. **b** intr. come into existence. □ **germination** /-'neɪʃ(ə)n/ n. **germinative** /-nətɪv/ adj. **germinator** n. [L germinare germinat- (as GERM)]

gerontology /ˌdʒerɒn'tɒlədʒɪ/ n. the scientific study of old age, the process of ageing, and the special problems of old people. □ **gerontological** /-tə'lɒdʒɪk(ə)l/ adj. **gerontologist** n. [Gk gerōn -ontos old man + -LOGY]

-gerous /dʒərəs/ comb. form forming adjectives meaning 'bearing' (lanigerous).

gerrymander /ˌdʒerɪ'mændə(r)/ v.tr. (also **jerrymander**). **1** manipulate the boundaries of a constituency etc.) so as to give undue influence to some party or class. **2** manipulate (a situation etc.) to gain advantage. □ **gerrymanderer** n. [the name of Governor Gerry of Massachusetts + (SALA)MANDER, from the shape of a district on a political map drawn when he was in office (1812)]

gerund /'dʒerənd/ n. Gram. a form of a verb functioning as a noun, in English ending in -ing and used distinctly as a part of a verb (e.g. do you mind my asking you?). [LL gerundium f. gerundum var. of gerendum, the gerund of L gerere do]

gesso /'dʒesəʊ/ n. (pl. **-oes**) plaster of Paris or gypsum as used in painting or sculpture. [It. f. L gypsum: see GYPSUM]

gestalt /gə'stɑːlt/ n. Psychol. an organized whole that is perceived as more than the sum of its parts. □ **gestalt psychology** a system maintaining that perceptions, reactions, etc., are gestalts. □ **gestaltism** n. **gestaltist** n. [G, = form, shape]

Gestapo /ge'stɑːpəʊ/ n. **1** the German secret police under Nazi rule. **2** derog. an organization compared to this. [G, f. Geheime Staatspolizei]

gestation /dʒe'steɪʃ(ə)n/ n. **1 a** the process of carrying or being carried in the womb between conception and birth. **b** this period. **2** the private development of a plan, idea, etc. [L gestatio f. gestare frequent. of gerere carry]

gesticulate /dʒe'stɪkjʊˌleɪt/ v. **1** intr. use gestures instead of or in addition to speech. **2** tr. express with gestures. □ **gesticulation** /-'leɪʃ(ə)n/ n. **gesticulative** /-lətɪv/ adj. **gesticulator** n. **gesticulatory** /-lətərɪ/ adj. [L gesticulari f. gesticulus dimin. of gestus GESTURE]

gesture /'dʒestʃə(r)/ n. & v. —n. **1** a significant movement of a limb or the body. **2** the use of such movements esp. to convey feeling or as a rhetorical device. **3** an action to evoke a response or convey intention, usu. friendly. —v.tr. & intr. gesticulate. □ **gestural** adj. **gesturer** n. [ME f. med.L gestura f. L gerere gest- wield]

get /get/ v. (**getting**; past **got** /gɒt/; past part. **got** or US (and in comb.) **gotten** /'gɒt(ə)n/) **1** tr. come into the possession of; receive or earn (get a job; got £200 a week). **2** tr. fetch, obtain, procure, purchase (get my book for me; got a new car). **3** tr. go to reach or catch (a bus, train, etc.). **4** tr. prepare (a meal etc.). **5** intr. & tr. reach or cause to reach a certain state or condition; become or cause to become (get rich; get one's feet wet; get to be famous; got them ready; cannot get the key into the lock). **6** tr. obtain as a result of calculation. **7** tr. contract (a disease etc.). **8** tr. establish or be in communication with via telephone or radio; receive (a radio signal). **9** tr. experience or suffer; have inflicted on one (got four years in prison). **10 a** tr. succeed in bringing, placing, etc. (get it on to the agenda; flattery will get you nowhere). **b** intr. & tr. succeed or cause to succeed in coming or going (will get you there somehow; got absolutely nowhere). **11** tr. (prec. by have) **a** possess (have not got a penny). **b** (foll. by to + infin.) be bound or obliged (have got to see you). **12** tr. (foll. by to + infin.) induce; prevail upon (got them to help me). **13** tr. colloq. understand (a person or an argument) (have you got that?; I get your point). **14** tr. colloq. inflict punishment on, esp. in retaliation (I'll get you for that). **15** tr. colloq. **a** annoy. **b** move; affect emotionally. **c** attract, obsess. **d** amuse. **16** tr. (foll. by to + infin.) develop an inclination as specified (am getting to like it). **17** intr. (foll. by verbal noun) begin (get going). **18** tr. (esp. in past or perfect) catch in an argument; corner, puzzle. **19** tr. establish (an idea etc.) in one's mind. □ **get about** (or **around**) **1** travel extensively or fast; go from place to place. **2** manage to walk, move about, etc. (esp. after illness). **3** (of news) be circulated, esp. orally. **get across 1** manage to communicate (an idea etc.). **2** (of an idea etc.) be communicated successfully. **3** colloq. annoy, irritate. **get along** (or **on**) **1** (foll. by together, with) live harmoniously, accord. **2** be off! nonsense! **get at 1** reach; get hold of. **2** colloq. imply (what are you getting at?). **get away 1** escape. **2** (foll. by with) escape blame or punishment for. **get back at** colloq. retaliate against. **get by** colloq. **1** just manage, even with difficulty. **2** be acceptable. **get down 1** alight, descend (from a vehicle, ladder, etc.). **2** record in writing. **get a person down** depress or deject him or her. **get down to** begin working on or discussing. **get even** (often foll. by with) achieve revenge; act in retaliation. **get hold of 1** grasp (physically). **2** grasp (intellectually); understand. **3** make contact with (a person). **4** acquire. **get in 1** enter. **2** be elected. **get into** become interested or involved in. **get it** sl. be punished or in trouble. **get it into one's head** (foll. by that + clause) firmly believe or maintain; realize. **get off 1** colloq. be acquitted; escape with little or no punishment. **2** start. **3** alight; alight from (a bus etc.). **4** go, or cause to go, to sleep. **5** (foll. by with, together) Brit. colloq. form an amorous or sexual relationship, esp. abruptly or quickly. **get a person off** colloq. cause a person to be acquitted. **get on 1** make progress; manage. **2** enter (a bus etc.). **3** = get along 1. **get on to** colloq. **1** make contact with. **2** understand; become aware of. **get out 1** leave or escape. **2** manage to go outdoors. **3** alight from a vehicle. **4** become known. **5** succeed in uttering, publishing, etc. **6** solve or finish (a puzzle etc.). **7**

Cricket be dismissed. **get-out** *n.* a means of avoiding something. **get a person out 1** help a person to leave or escape. **2** *Cricket* dismiss (a batsman). **get out of 1** avoid or escape (a duty etc.). **2** abandon (a habit) gradually. **get a thing out of** manage to obtain it from (a person) esp. with difficulty. **get over 1** recover from (an illness, upset, etc.). **2** overcome (a difficulty). **3** manage to communicate (an idea etc.). **get a thing over** (or **over with**) complete (a tedious task) promptly. **get one's own back** *colloq.* have one's revenge. **get round** (*US* **around**) **1** successfully coax or cajole (a person) esp. to secure a favour. **2** evade (a law etc.). **get round to** deal with (a task etc.) in due course. **get somewhere** make progress; be initially successful. **get there** *colloq.* **1** succeed. **2** understand what is meant. **get through 1** pass or assist in passing (an examination, an ordeal, etc.). **2** finish or use up (esp. resources). **3** make contact by telephone. **4** (foll. by *to*) succeed in making (a person) listen or understand. **get a thing through** cause it to overcome obstacles, difficulties, etc. **get to 1** reach. **2** = *get down to*. **get together** gather, assemble. **get-together** *n.* *colloq.* a social gathering. **get up 1** rise or cause to rise from sitting etc., or from bed after sleeping or an illness. **2** ascend or mount, e.g. on horseback. **3** (of fire, wind, or the sea) begin to be strong or agitated. **4** prepare or organize. **5** enhance or refine one's knowledge of (a subject). **6** work up (a feeling, e.g. anger). **7** produce or stimulate (*get up steam*; *get up speed*). **8** (often *refl.*) dress or arrange elaborately; make presentable; arrange the appearance of. **9** (foll. by *to*) *colloq.* indulge or be involved in (*always getting up to mischief*). **get-up** *n.* *colloq.* a style or arrangement of dress etc., esp. an elaborate one. □ **gettable** *adj.* **getter** *n.* [ME f. ON *geta* obtain, beget, guess, corresp. to OE *gietan* (recorded only in compounds), f. Gmc]

getaway /ˈgetəˌweɪ/ *n.* an escape, esp. after committing a crime.

geum /ˈdʒiːəm/ *n.* any rosaceous plant of the genus *Geum* including herb bennet. [mod.L, var. of L *gaeum*]

gewgaw /ˈgjuːgɔː/ *n.* a gaudy plaything or ornament; a bauble. [ME: orig. unkn.]

geyser /ˈgaɪzə(r), ˈgiː-/ *n.* **1** an intermittently gushing hot spring that throws up a tall column of water. **2** /ˈgiːzə(r)/ *Brit.* an apparatus for heating water rapidly for domestic use. [Icel. *Geysir*, the name of a particular spring in Iceland, rel. to *geysa* to gush]

ghastly /ˈgɑːstlɪ/ *adj.* & *adv.* —*adj.* (**ghastlier**, **ghastliest**) **1** horrible, frightful. **2** *colloq.* objectionable, unpleasant. **3** deathlike, pallid. —*adv.* in a ghastly or sickly way (*ghastly pale*). □ **ghastlily** *adv.* **ghastliness** *n.* [ME *gastlich* f. obs. *gast* terrify: *gh* after *ghost*]

ghat /gɑːt/ *n.* (also **ghaut**) in India: **1** steps leading down to a river. **2** a landing-place. [Hindi *ghāṭ*]

ghee /giː/ *n.* (also **ghi**) Indian clarified butter esp. from the milk of a buffalo or cow. [Hindi *ghī* f. Skr. *ghṛtá*- sprinkled]

gherkin /ˈgɜːkɪn/ *n.* **1** a small variety of cucumber, or a young green cucumber, used for pickling. **2 a** a trailing plant, *Cucumis sativus*, with cucumber-like fruits used for pickling. **b**

this fruit. [Du. *gurkkijn* (unrecorded), dimin. of *gurk*, f. Slavonic, ult. f. med. Gk *aggourion*]

ghetto /ˈgetəʊ/ *n.* & *v.* —*n.* (pl. **-os**) **1** a part of a city, esp. a slum area, occupied by a minority group or groups. **2** *hist.* the Jewish quarter in a city. **3** a segregated group or area. —*v.tr.* (**-oes**, **-oed**) put or keep (people) in a ghetto. □ **ghetto-blaster** *sl.* a large portable radio, esp. used to play loud pop music. [perh. f. It. *getto* foundry (applied to the site of the first ghetto in Venice in 1516)]

ghillie var. of GILLIE.

ghost /gəʊst/ *n.* & *v.* —*n.* **1** the supposed apparition of a dead person or animal; a disembodied spirit. **2** a shadow or mere semblance (*not a ghost of a chance*). **3** an emaciated or pale person. **4** a secondary or duplicated image produced by defective television reception or by a telescope. —*v.* **1** *intr.* (often foll. by *for*) act as ghost-writer. **2** *tr.* act as ghost-writer of (a work). □ **ghost town** a deserted town with few or no remaining inhabitants. **ghost-write** *v.intr.* & *intr.* act as ghost-writer (of). **ghost-writer** a person who writes on behalf of the credited author of a work. □ **ghostlike** *adj.* [OE *gāst* f. WG: *gh-* occurs first in Caxton, prob. infl. by Flem. *gheest*]

ghosting /ˈgəʊstɪŋ/ *n.* the appearance of a 'ghost' (see GHOST *n.* 4) or secondary image in a television picture.

ghostly /ˈgəʊstlɪ/ *adj.* (**ghostlier**, **ghostliest**) like a ghost. □ **ghostliness** *n.* [OE *gāstlic* (as GHOST)]

ghoul /guːl/ *n.* **1** a person morbidly interested in death etc. **2** a spirit in Muslim folklore preying on corpses. □ **ghoulish** *adj.* **ghoulishly** *adv.* **ghoulishness** *n.* [Arab. *ġūl* protean desert demon]

GHQ *abbr.* General Headquarters.

ghyll *Brit.* var. of GILL³.

GI /dʒiːˈaɪ/ *n.* & *adj.* —*n.* a private soldier in the US Army. —*adj.* of or for US servicemen. [abbr. of *government* (or *general*) *issue*]

giant /ˈdʒaɪənt/ *n.* & *adj.* —*n.* **1** an imaginary or mythical being of human form but superhuman size. **2** an abnormally tall or large person, animal, or plant. **3** a person of exceptional ability, integrity, courage, etc. **4** a large star. —*attrib.adj.* **1** of extraordinary size or force, gigantic; monstrous. **2** *colloq.* extra large (*giant packet*). **3** (of a plant or animal) of a very large kind. □ **giantism** *n.* **giant-like** *adj.* [ME *geant* (later infl. by L) f. OF, ult. f. L *gigas gigant-* f. Gk]

gibber /ˈdʒɪbə(r)/ *v.* & *n.* —*v.intr.* speak fast and inarticulately; chatter incoherently. —*n.* such speech or sound. [imit.]

gibberellin /ˌdʒɪbəˈrelɪn/ *n.* one of a group of plant hormones that stimulate the growth of leaves and shoots. [*Gibberella* a genus of fungi, dimin. of genus-name *Gibbera* f. L *gibber* hump]

gibberish /ˈdʒɪbərɪʃ/ *n.* unintelligible or meaningless speech; nonsense. [perh. f. GIBBER (but attested earlier) + -ISH¹ as used in *Spanish*, *Swedish*, etc.]

gibbet /ˈdʒɪbɪt/ *n.* & *v.* —*n.* *hist.* **1 a** a gallows. **b** an upright post with an arm on which the bodies of executed criminals were hung up. **2** (prec. by *the*) death by hanging. —*v.tr.* (**gibbeted**, **gibbeting**) **1** put to death by hanging. **2 a** expose on a gibbet. **b** hang up as on a gibbet. **3** hold up to contempt. [ME f. OF *gibet* gallows dimin. of *gibe* club, prob. f. Gmc]

gibbon /ˈgɪbən/ n. any small ape of the genus *Hylobates*, native to SE Asia. [F f. a native name]

gibbous /ˈgɪbəs/ adj. **1** convex or protuberant. **2** (of a moon or planet) having the bright part greater than a semicircle and less than a circle. □ **gibbosity** /-ˈbɒsɪtɪ/ n. **gibbously** adv. **gibbousness** n. [ME f. LL *gibbosus* f. *gibbus* hump]

gibe /dʒaɪb/ v. & n. (also **jibe**) —v.intr. (often foll. by *at*) jeer, mock. —n. an instance of gibing; a taunt. □ **giber** n. [perh. f. OF *giber* handle roughly]

giblets /ˈdʒɪblɪts/ n.pl. the liver, gizzard, neck, etc., of a bird, usu. removed and kept separate when the bird is prepared for cooking. [OF *gibelet* game stew, perh. f. *gibier* game]

giddy /ˈgɪdɪ/ adj. & v. —adj. (**giddier, giddiest**) **1** having a sensation of whirling and a tendency to fall, stagger, or spin round. **2 a** overexcited. **b** excitable, frivolous. **3** tending to make one giddy. —v.tr. & intr. (**-ies, -ied**) make or become giddy. □ **giddily** adv. **giddiness** n. [OE *gidig* insane, lit. 'possessed by a god']

gift n. & v. —n. **1** a thing given; a present. **2** a natural ability or talent. **3** the power to give (*in his gift*). **4** the act or an instance of giving. **5** *colloq.* an easy task. —v.tr. **1** endow with gifts. **2 a** (foll. by *with*) give to as a gift. **b** bestow as a gift. □ **gift token** (or **voucher**) a voucher used as a gift and exchangeable for goods. **gift-wrap** (**-wrapped, -wrapping**) wrap attractively as a gift. **look a gift-horse in the mouth** (usu. *neg.*) find fault with what has been given. [ME f. ON *gipt* f. Gmc, rel. to GIVE]

gifted /ˈgɪftɪd/ adj. exceptionally talented or intelligent. □ **giftedly** adv. **giftedness** n.

gig¹ /gɪg/ n. **1** a light two-wheeled one-horse carriage. **2** a light boat for rowing or sailing. [ME in var. senses: prob. imit.]

gig² /gɪg/ n. an engagement of an entertainer, esp. of musicians to play jazz or dance music, usu. for a single appearance. [20th c.: orig. unkn.]

giga- /ˈgaɪgə, ˈgɪgə/ comb. form denoting a factor of 10^9. [Gk *gigas* giant]

gigantic /dʒaɪˈgæntɪk/ adj. **1** very large; enormous. **2** like or suited to a giant. □ **gigantesque** /-ˈtesk/ adj. **gigantically** adv. [L *gigas gigantis* GIANT]

gigantism /ˈdʒaɪgənˌtɪz(ə)m/ n. abnormal largeness, esp. *Med.* excessive growth due to hormonal imbalance, or to polyploidy in plants.

giggle /ˈgɪg(ə)l/ v. & n. —v.intr. laugh in half-suppressed spasms. —n. **1** such a laugh. **2** *colloq.* an amusing person or thing. □ **giggler** n. **giggly** adj. (**gigglier, giggliest**). **giggliness** n. [imit.: cf. Du. *gichelen*, G *gickeln*]

gigolo /ˈʒɪgəˌləʊ, ˈdʒɪg-/ n. (pl. **-os**) **1** a young man paid by an older woman to be her escort or lover. **2** a professional male dancing-partner or escort. [F, formed as masc. of *gigole* dance-hall woman]

gigot /ˈdʒɪgət/ n. a leg of mutton or lamb. [F, dimin. of dial. *gigue* leg]

gild¹ /gɪld/ v.tr. (past part. **gilded** or as adj. in sense 1 **gilt**) **1** cover thinly with gold. **2** tinge with a golden colour or light. **3** give a specious or false brilliance to. □ **gilded cage** luxurious but restrictive surroundings. **gilded youth** young people of wealth, fashion, and flair. **gild**

the lily try to improve what is already beautiful or excellent. □ **gilder** n. [OE *gyldan* f. Gmc]

gild² var. of GUILD.

gilding /ˈgɪldɪŋ/ n. **1** the act or art of applying gilt. **2** material used in applying gilt.

gilet /dʒɪˈleɪ/ n. a light often padded waistcoat, usu. worn for warmth by women. [F, = waistcoat]

gill¹ /gɪl/ n. (usu. in pl.) **1** the respiratory organ in fishes and other aquatic animals. **2** the vertical radial plates on the underside of mushrooms and other fungi. **3** the flesh below a person's jaws and ears (*green about the gills*). □ **gilled** adj. (also in comb.). [ME f. ON *gil* (unrecorded) f. Gmc]

gill² /dʒɪl/ n. **1** a unit of liquid measure, equal to a quarter of a pint. **2** *Brit. dial.* half a pint. [ME f. OF *gille*, med.L *gillo* f. LL *gello, gillo* water-pot]

gill³ /gɪl/ n. (also **ghyll**) *Brit.* **1** a deep usu. wooded ravine. **2** a narrow mountain torrent. [ME f. ON *gil* glen]

gillie /ˈgɪlɪ/ n. (also **ghillie**) *Sc.* a man or boy attending a person hunting or fishing. [Gael. *gille* lad, servant]

gillyflower /ˈdʒɪlɪˌflaʊə(r)/ n. **1** (in full **clove gillyflower**) a clove-scented pink (see CLOVE¹ 2). **2** any of various similarly scented flowers such as the wallflower or white stock. [ME *gilofre, gerofle* f. OF *gilofre, girofle*, f. med.L f. Gk *karuophullon* clove-tree f. *karuon* nut + *phullon* leaf, assim. to FLOWER]

gilt¹ /gɪlt/ adj. & n. —adj. **1** covered thinly with gold. **2** gold-coloured. —n. **1** gold or a goldlike substance applied in a thin layer to a surface. **2** (often in pl.) a gilt-edged security. □ **gilt-edged 1** (of securities, stocks, etc.) having a high degree of reliability as an investment. **2** having a gilded edge. [past part. of GILD¹]

gilt² /gɪlt/ n. a young unbred sow. [ME f. ON *gyltr*]

gimbals /ˈdʒɪmb(ə)lz/ n.pl. a contrivance, usu. of rings and pivots, for keeping instruments such as a compass and chronometer horizontal at sea, in the air, etc. [var. of earlier *gimmal* f. OF *gemel* double finger-ring f. L *gemellus* dimin. of *geminus* twin]

gimcrack /ˈdʒɪmkræk/ adj. showy but flimsy and worthless. □ **gimcrackery** n. **gimcracky** adj. [ME *gibecrake* a kind of ornament, of unkn. orig.]

gimlet /ˈgɪmlɪt/ n. a small tool with a screw-tip for boring holes. [ME f. OF *guimbelet*, dimin. of *guimble*]

gimmick /ˈgɪmɪk/ n. *colloq.* a trick or device, esp. to attract attention, publicity, or trade. □ **gimmickry** n. **gimmicky** adj. [20th-c. US: orig. unkn.]

gimp /gɪmp/ n. (also **guimp, gymp**) **1** a twist of silk etc. with cord or wire running through it, used esp. as trimming. **2** fishing-line of silk etc. bound with wire. [Du.: orig. unkn.]

gin¹ /dʒɪn/ n. an alcoholic spirit distilled from grain or malt and flavoured with juniper berries. □ **gin rummy** a form of the card-game rummy. [f. Du. *genever* f. OF *genevre* f. L *juniperus*]

gin² /dʒɪn/ n. **1** a snare or trap. **2** a machine for separating cotton from its seeds. **3** a kind of crane and windlass. □ **ginner** n. [ME f. OF *engin* ENGINE]

ginger /ˈdʒɪndʒə(r)/ n., adj., & v. —n. **1 a** a hot spicy root usu. powdered for use in cooking, or preserved in syrup, or candied. **b** the plant, *Zingiber officinale*, of SE Asia, having this root. **2** a light reddish-yellow colour. **3** spirit, mettle. **4** stimulation. —*adj.* of a ginger colour. —*v.tr.* **1** flavour with ginger. **2** (foll. by *up*) rouse or enliven. □ **ginger ale** an effervescent non-alcoholic clear drink flavoured with ginger extract. **ginger beer** an effervescent mildly alcoholic cloudy drink, made by fermenting a mixture of ginger and syrup. **ginger group** *Brit.* a group within a party or movement that presses for stronger or more radical policy or action. **ginger-nut** a ginger-flavoured biscuit. **ginger-snap** a thin brittle biscuit flavoured with ginger. **ginger wine** a drink of fermented sugar, water, and bruised ginger. □ **gingery** *adj.* [ME f. OE *gingiber* & OF *gingi(m)bre*, both f. med.L *gingiber* ult. f. Skr. *śṛṅgaveram* f. *śṛṅgam* horn + *-vera* body, with ref. to the antler-shape of the root]

gingerbread /ˈdʒɪndʒəˌbred/ *n.* a cake made with treacle or syrup and flavoured with ginger.

gingerly /ˈdʒɪndʒəli/ *adv.* & *adj.* —*adv.* in a careful or cautious manner. —*adj.* showing great care or caution. □ **gingerliness** *n.* [perh. f. OF *gensor* delicate, compar. of *gent* graceful f. L *genitus* (well-)born]

gingham /ˈɡɪŋəm/ *n.* a plain-woven cotton cloth esp. striped or checked. [Du. *gingang* f. Malay *ginggang* (orig. adj. = striped)]

gingivitis /ˌdʒɪndʒɪˈvaɪtɪs/ *n.* inflammation of the gums.

ginkgo /ˈɡɪŋkɡəʊ/ *n.* (also **gingko** /ˈɡɪŋkəʊ/) (pl. **-os** or **-oes**) an orig. Chinese and Japanese tree, *Ginkgo biloba*, with fan-shaped leaves and yellow flowers. [Jap. *ginkyo* f. Chin. *yinxing* silver apricot]

ginseng /ˈdʒɪnseŋ/ *n.* **1** any of several medicinal plants of the genus *Panax*, found in E. Asia and N. America. **2** the root of this. [Chin. *renshen* perh. = man-image, with allusion to its forked root]

gippy tummy /ˈdʒɪpɪ/ *n.* (also **gyppy tummy**) *colloq.* diarrhoea affecting visitors to hot countries. [abbr. of EGYPTIAN]

gipsy var. of GYPSY.

giraffe /dʒɪˈrɑːf, -ˈræf/ *n.* (pl. same or **giraffes**) a ruminant mammal, *Giraffa camelopardalis* of Africa, the tallest living animal, with a long neck and forelegs. [F *girafe*, It. *giraffa*, ult. f. Arab. *zarāfa*]

gird /ɡɜːd/ *v.tr.* (*past* and *past part.* **girded** or **girt**) *literary* **1** encircle, attach, or secure with a belt or band. **2** secure (clothes) on the body with a girdle or belt. **3** enclose or encircle. **4** (foll. by *round*) place (cord etc.) round. □ **gird** (or **gird up**) **one's loins** prepare for action. [OE *gyrdan* f. Gmc (as GIRTH)]

girder /ˈɡɜːdə(r)/ *n.* a large iron or steel beam or compound structure for bearing loads, esp. in bridge-building. [GIRD + -ER¹]

girdle¹ /ˈɡɜːd(ə)l/ *n.* & *v.* —*n.* **1** a belt or cord worn round the waist. **2** a woman's corset extending from waist to thigh. **3** a thing that surrounds like a girdle. **4** the bony support for a limb (*pelvic girdle*). —*v.tr.* surround with a girdle. [OE *gyrdel*: see GIRD]

girdle² /ˈɡɜːd(ə)l/ *n.* Sc. & N.Engl. a circular iron plate placed over a fire or otherwise heated for baking, toasting, etc. [var. of GRIDDLE]

girl /ɡɜːl/ *n.* **1** a female child or youth. **2** *colloq.* a young (esp. unmarried) woman. **3** *colloq.* a girlfriend or sweetheart. **4** a female servant. □ **girl Friday** see FRIDAY. □ **girlhood** *n.* [ME *gurle*, *girle*, perh. rel. to LG *gör* child]

girlfriend /ˈɡɜːlfrend/ *n.* **1** a regular female companion or lover. **2** a female friend.

girlie /ˈɡɜːlɪ/ *adj. colloq.* (of a magazine etc.) depicting nude or partially nude young women in erotic poses.

girlish /ˈɡɜːlɪʃ/ *adj.* of or like a girl. □ **girlishly** *adv.* **girlishness** *n.*

giro /ˈdʒaɪrəʊ/ *n.* & *v.* —*n.* (pl. **-os**) **1** a system of credit transfer between banks, post offices, etc. **2** a cheque or payment by giro. —*v.tr.* (**-oes**, **-oed**) pay by giro. [G f. It., = circulation (of money)]

girt *past part.* of GIRD.

girth /ɡɜːθ/ *n.* (also **girt** /ɡɜːt/) **1** the distance around a thing. **2** a band round the body of a horse to secure the saddle etc. [ME f. ON *gjörth*, Goth. *gaírda* f. Gmc]

gismo /ˈɡɪzməʊ/ *n.* (also **gizmo**) (pl. **-os**) *sl.* a gadget. [20th c.: orig. unkn.]

gist /dʒɪst/ *n.* the substance or essence of a matter. [OF, 3rd sing. pres. of *gesir* lie f. L *jacēre*]

give /ɡɪv/ *v.* & *n.* (*past* **gave** /ɡeɪv/; *past part.* **given** /ˈɡɪv(ə)n/) **1** *tr.* (also *absol.*; often foll. by *to*) transfer the possession of freely; hand over as a present (*gave them her old curtains; gives to cancer research*). **2** *tr.* **a** transfer the ownership of with or without actual delivery; bequeath (*gave him £200 in her will*). **b** transfer, esp. temporarily or for safe keeping; hand over; provide with (*gave him the dog to hold; gave them a drink*). **c** administer (medicine). **d** deliver (a message) (*give her my best wishes*). **3** *tr.* (usu. foll. by *for*) make over in exchange or payment; pay; sell (*gave him £30 for the bicycle*). **4** *tr.* **a** confer; grant (a benefit, an honour, etc.). **b** accord; bestow (one's affections, confidence, etc.). **c** award; administer (one's approval, blame, etc.); tell, offer (esp. something unpleasant) (*gave him my blessing; gave him the sack*). **d** pledge, assign as a guarantee (*gave his word*). **5** *tr.* **a** effect or perform (an action etc.) (*gave him a kiss; gave a jump*). **b** utter (*gave a shriek*). **6** *tr.* allot; assign; grant (*was given the contract*). **7** *tr.* (in passive; foll. by *to*) be inclined to or fond of (*is given to speculation*). **8** *tr.* state as a product or result (*the lamp gives a bad light*). **9** *intr.* **a** yield to pressure; become relaxed; lose firmness (*this elastic doesn't give properly*). **b** collapse (*the roof gave under the pressure*). **10** *intr.* (usu. foll. by *of*) grant; bestow (*gave freely of his time*). **11** *tr.* **a** commit, consign, or entrust (*give her into your care*). **b** sanction the marriage of (a daughter etc.). **12** *tr.* devote; dedicate (*gave his life to table tennis; shall give it my attention*). **13** *tr.* present; show; hold out (*gives no sign of life; gave her his arm; give him your ear*). **14** *tr. Theatr.* read, recite, perform, act, etc. (*gave them Hamlet's soliloquy*). **15** *tr.* impart; be a source of (*gave its name to the battle; gives him a right to complain*). **16** *tr.* allow (esp. a fixed amount of time) (*can give you five minutes*). **17** *tr.* (usu. foll. by *for*) value (something) (*gives nothing for their opinions*). **18** *tr.* concede; yield (*I give you the victory*). **19** *tr.* deliver (a judgement etc.) authoritatively (*gave her verdict*). **20** *tr. Cricket* (of an umpire) declare (a batsman) out or not out. **21** *tr.* toast (a person, cause, etc.) (*I give you our*

President). **22** tr. provide (a party, meal, etc.) as host (gave a banquet). —n. **1** capacity to yield or bend under pressure; elasticity (there is no give in a stone floor). **2** ability to adapt or comply (no give in his attitudes). □ **give and take** v.tr. exchange (words, blows, or concessions). —n. an exchange of words etc.; a compromise. **give away 1** transfer as a gift. **2** hand over (a bride) ceremonially to a bridegroom. **3** betray or expose to ridicule or detection. **4** Austral. abandon, desist from, give up, lose faith or interest in. **give-away** n. colloq. **1** an inadvertent betrayal or revelation. **2** an act of giving away. **3** a free gift; a low price. **give back** return (something) to its previous owner or in exchange. **give chase** pursue a person, animal, etc.; hunt. **give the game** (or **show**) **away** reveal a secret or intention. **give in 1** cease fighting or arguing; yield. **2** hand in (a document etc.) to an official etc. **give me** I prefer or admire. **give off** emit (vapour etc.). **give oneself** (of a woman) yield sexually. **give oneself airs** act pretentiously or snobbishly. **give oneself up to 1** abandon oneself to an emotion, esp. despair. **2** addict oneself to. **give on to** (or **into**) (of a window, corridor, etc.) overlook or lead into. **give or take** colloq. add or subtract (a specified amount or number) in estimating. **give out 1** announce; emit; distribute. **2** cease or break down from exhaustion etc. **3** run short. **give over 1** colloq. cease from doing; abandon (a habit etc.); (give over sniffing). **2** hand over. **3** devote. **give rise to** cause, induce, suggest. **give tongue 1** speak one's thoughts. **2** (of hounds) bark, esp. on finding a scent. **give a person to understand** inform authoritatively. **give up 1** resign; surrender. **2** part with. **3** deliver (a wanted person etc.). **4** pronounce incurable or insoluble; renounce hope of. **5** renounce or cease (an activity). **give up the ghost** archaic or colloq. die. **give a person what for** colloq. punish or scold severely. **give one's word** (or **word of honour** etc.) promise solemnly. **not give a damn** (or **monkey's** or **toss** etc.) colloq. not care at all. **what gives?** colloq. what is the news?; what's happening? □ **giveable** adj. **giver** n. [OE g(i)efan f. Gmc]

given /ˈgɪv(ə)n/ adj. & n. —adj. **1** as previously stated or assumed; granted; specified (given that he is a liar, we cannot trust him; a given number of people). **2** Law (of a document) signed and dated (given this day the 30th June). —n. a known fact or situation. □ **given name** US a name given at, or as if at, baptism; a Christian name. [past part. of GIVE]

gizzard /ˈgɪzəd/ n. **1** the second part of a bird's stomach, for grinding food usu. with grit. **2** a muscular stomach of some fish, insects, molluscs, and other invertebrates. □ **stick in one's gizzard** colloq. be distasteful. [ME giser f. OF giser, gesier etc., ult. f. L gigeria cooked entrails of fowl]

glacé /ˈglæseɪ/ adj. **1** (of fruit, esp. cherries) preserved in sugar, usu. resulting in a glossy surface. **2** (of cloth, leather, etc.) smooth; polished. □ **glacé icing** icing made with icing sugar and water. [F, past part. of glacer to ice, gloss f. glace ice: see GLACIER]

glacial /ˈgleɪʃ(ə)l, -sɪəl/ adj. **1** of ice; icy. **2** Geol. characterized or produced by the presence or agency of ice. □ **glacial epoch** (or **period**) a period when ice-sheets were exceptionally extensive. □ **glacially** adv. [F glacial or L glacialis icy f. glacies ice]

glaciated /ˈgleɪsɪˌeɪtɪd, ˈglæs-/ adj. **1** marked or polished by the action of ice. **2** covered or having been covered by glaciers. □ **glaciation** /-ˈeɪʃ(ə)n/ n. [past part. of glaciate f. L glaciare freeze f. glacies ice]

glacier /ˈglæsɪə(r)/ n. a mass of land ice formed by the accumulation of snow on high ground. [F f. glace ice ult. f. L glacies]

glad adj. (**gladder**, **gladdest**) **1** (predic.; usu. foll. by of, about, or to + infin.) pleased; willing (shall be glad to come; would be glad of a chance to talk about it). **2 a** marked by, filled with, or expressing, joy (a glad expression). **b** (of news, events, etc.) giving joy (glad tidings). **3** (of objects) bright; beautiful. □ **the glad eye** colloq. an amorous glance. **glad hand** the hand of welcome. **glad-hand** v.tr. greet cordially; welcome. **glad rags** colloq. best clothes; evening dress. □ **gladly** adv. **gladness** n. **gladsome** adj. poet. [OE glæd f. Gmc]

gladden /ˈglæd(ə)n/ v.tr. & intr. make or become glad. □ **gladdener** n.

glade n. an open space in a wood or forest. [16th c.: orig. unkn.]

gladiator /ˈglædɪˌeɪtə(r)/ n. hist. a man trained to fight with a sword or other weapons in ancient Roman shows. □ **gladiatorial** /-ɪəˈtɔːrɪəl/ adj. [L f. gladius sword]

gladiolus /ˌglædɪˈəʊləs/ n. (pl. **gladioli** /-laɪ/ or **gladioluses**) any iridaceous plant of the genus Gladiolus with usu. brightly coloured flower-spikes. [L, dimin. of gladius sword]

Gladstone bag /ˈglædst(ə)n/ n. a bag like a briefcase having two equal compartments joined by a hinge. [W. E. Gladstone, Engl. statesman d. 1898]

glam adj., n., & v. colloq. —adj. glamorous. —n. glamour. —v.tr. (**glammed**, **glamming**) glamorize. [abbr.]

glamorize /ˈglæməˌraɪz/ v.tr. (also **glamourize**, **-ise**) make glamorous or attractive. □ **glamorization** /-ˈzeɪʃ(ə)n/ n.

glamour /ˈglæmə(r)/ n. & v. (US **glamor**) —n. **1** physical attractiveness, esp. when achieved by make-up etc. **2** alluring or exciting beauty or charm (the glamour of New York). —v.tr. **1** poet. affect with glamour; bewitch; enchant. **2** colloq. make glamorous. □ **glamour girl** (or **boy**) an attractive young woman (or man), esp. a model etc. □ **glamorous** adj. **glamorously** adv. [18th c.: var. of GRAMMAR, with ref. to the occult practices associated with learning in the Middle Ages]

glance /glɑːns/ v. & n. —v. **1** intr. (often foll. by down, up, etc.) cast a momentary look (glanced up at the sky). **2** intr. (often foll. by off) (esp. of a weapon) glide or bounce (off an object). **3** intr. (usu. foll. by over, off, from) (of talk or a reader) pass quickly over a subject or subjects (glanced over the question of payment). **4** intr. (of a bright object or light) flash, dart, or gleam; reflect (the sun glanced off the knife). **5** tr. (esp. of a weapon) strike (an object) obliquely. **6** tr. Cricket deflect (the ball) with an oblique stroke. —n. **1** (usu. foll. by at, into, over, etc.) a brief look (took a glance at the paper; threw a glance over her shoulder). **2 a** a flash or gleam (a glance of sunlight). **b** a sudden movement producing this. **3** a swift oblique movement or impact. **4** *Cricket* a stroke with the bat's face turned slantwise to deflect the ball. □ **at a glance** immediately upon looking. **glance at 1** give a brief look at. **2** make a passing and usu. sarcastic allusion to. **glance over** (or **through**) read cursorily. □ **glancingly** *adv.* [ME *glence* etc., prob. a nasalized form of obs. *glace* in the same sense, f. OF *glacier* to slip.]

gland *n.* **1 a** an organ in an animal body secreting substances for use in the body or for ejection. **b** a structure resembling this, such as a lymph gland. **2** *Bot.* a secreting cell or group of cells on the surface of a plant-structure. [F *glande* f. OF *glandre* f. L *glandulae* throat-glands]

glanders /ˈglændəz/ *n.pl.* (also treated as *sing.*) **1** a contagious disease of horses. □ **glandered** *adj.* **glanderous** *adj.* [OF *glandre*: see GLAND]

glandular /ˈglændjʊlə(r)/ *adj.* of or relating to a gland or glands. □ **glandular fever** an infectious viral disease characterized by swelling of the lymph glands and prolonged lassitude. [F *glandulaire* (as GLAND)]

glans /glænz/ *n.* (*pl.* **glandes** /ˈglændiːz/) the rounded part forming the end of the penis or clitoris. [L, = acorn]

glare /gleə(r)/ *v.* & *n.* —*v.* **1** *intr.* look fiercely or fixedly. **2** *intr.* shine dazzlingly or disagreeably. **3** *tr.* express (hate, defiance, etc.) by a look. **4** *intr.* be over-conspicuous or obtrusive. —*n.* **1 a** strong fierce light, esp. sunshine. **b** oppressive public attention (*the glare of fame*). **2 a** fierce or fixed look. □ **glary** *adj.* [ME, prob. ult. rel. to GLASS: cf. MDu. and MLG *glaren* gleam, glare]

glaring /ˈgleərɪŋ/ *adj.* **1** obvious, conspicuous (*a glaring error*). **2** shining oppressively. **3** staring fiercely. □ **glaringly** *adv.* **glaringness** *n.*

glasnost /ˈglæznɒst, ˈglɑːs-/ *n.* the policy or practice of more open consultative government and wider dissemination of information that contributed to the democratization and eventual breakup of the Soviet Union. [Russ. *glasnost'*, lit. = publicity, openness]

glass /glɑːs/ *n.*, *v.*, & *adj.* —*n.* **1 a** (often *attrib.*) a hard, brittle, usu. transparent, translucent, or shiny substance, made by fusing sand with soda and lime. **b** a substance of similar properties or composition. **2** (often *collect.*) an object or objects made from, or partly from, glass, esp.: **a** a drinking vessel. **b** a mirror; a looking-glass. **c** an hour- or sand-glass. **d** a window. **e** glass ornaments. **f** a barometer. **g** a glass disc covering a watch-face. **h** a magnifying lens. **i** a monocle. **3** (in *pl.*) **a** spectacles. **b** field-glasses; opera-glasses. **4** the amount of liquid contained in a glass; a drink (*he likes a glass*). —*v.tr.* (usu. as **glassed** *adj.*) fit with glass; glaze. —*adj.* of or made from glass. □ **glass-blower** a person who blows semi-molten glass to make glassware. **glass-blowing** this occupation. **glass-cloth 1** a linen cloth for drying glasses. **2** a cloth covered with powdered glass or abrasive. **glass cloth 1** a woven fabric of fine-spun glass. **glass-cutter 1** a worker who cuts glass. **2** a tool used for cutting glass. **glass eye** a false eye made from glass. **glass fibre 1** a filament or filaments of glass made into fabric. **2** such filaments embedded in plastic as reinforcement. **glass-paper** paper covered with glass-dust or abrasive. **glass wool** glass in the form of fine fibres used for packing and insulation. □ **glassful** *n.*

(*pl.* **-fuls**). **glassless** *adj.* **glasslike** *adj.* [OE *glæs* f. Gmc: cf. GLAZE]

glasshouse /ˈglɑːshaʊs/ *n.* **1** a greenhouse. **2** *Brit. sl.* a military prison.

glassware /ˈglɑːsweə(r)/ *n.* articles made from glass, esp. drinking glasses, tableware, etc.

glasswort /ˈglɑːswɜːt/ *n.* any plant of the genus *Salicornia* or *Salsola*.

glassy /ˈglɑːsɪ/ *adj.* (**glassier, glassiest**) **1** of or resembling glass, esp. in smoothness. **2** (of the eye, the expression, etc.) abstracted; dull; fixed (*fixed her with a glassy stare*). □ **glassily** *adv.* **glassiness** *n.*

Glaswegian /glæzˈwiːdʒ(ə)n, glɑː-/ *adj.* & *n.* —*adj.* of or relating to Glasgow in Scotland. —*n.* a native of Glasgow. [*Glasgow* after *Norwegian* etc.]

glaucoma /glɔːˈkəʊmə/ *n.* an eye-condition with increased pressure within the eyeball, causing gradual loss of sight. □ **glaucomatous** *adj.* [L f. Gk *glaukōma -atos*, ult. f. *glaukos*: see GLAUCOUS]

glaucous /ˈglɔːkəs/ *adj.* **1** of a dull greyish green or blue. **2** covered with a powdery bloom as of grapes. [L *glaucus* f. Gk *glaukos*]

glaze *v.* & *n.* —*v.* **1** *tr.* **a** fit (a window, picture, etc.) with glass. **b** provide (a building) with glass windows. **2** *tr.* **a** cover (pottery etc.) with a glaze. **b** fix (paint) on pottery with a glaze. **3** *tr.* cover (pastry, meat, etc.) with a glaze. **4** *intr.* (often foll. by *over*) (of the eyes) become fixed or glassy. **5** *tr.* cover (cloth, paper, leather, a painted surface, etc.) with a glaze. **6** *tr.* give a glassy surface to. —*n.* **1** a vitreous substance, usu. a special glass, used to glaze pottery. **2** a smooth shiny coating of milk, sugar, gelatine, etc., on food. **3** a thin topcoat of transparent paint used to modify the tone of the underlying colour. **4** a smooth surface formed by glazing. □ **glaze in** enclose (a building, a window frame, etc.) with glass. □ **glazer** *n.* **glazy** *adj.* [ME f. an oblique form of GLASS]

glazier /ˈgleɪzjə(r)/ *n.* a person whose trade is glazing windows etc. □ **glaziery** *n.*

glazing /ˈgleɪzɪŋ/ *n.* **1** the act or an instance of glazing. **2** windows (see also **double glazing**). **3** material used to produce a glaze.

gleam *n.* & *v.* —*n.* **1** a faint or brief light (*a gleam of sunlight*). **2** a faint, sudden, intermittent, or temporary show (*not a gleam of hope*). —*v.intr.* **1** emit gleams. **2** shine with a faint or intermittent brightness. **3** (of a quality) be indicated (*fear gleamed in his eyes*). □ **gleamingly** *adv.* **gleamy** *adj.* [OE *glǣm*: cf. GLIMMER]

glean *v.* **1** *tr.* collect or scrape together (news, facts, gossip, etc.) in small quantities. **2 a** *tr.* (also *absol.*) gather (ears of corn etc.) after the harvest. **b** *tr.* strip (a field etc.) after a harvest. □ **gleaner** *n.* [ME f. OF *glener* f. LL *glennare*, prob. of Celt. orig.]

gleanings /ˈgliːnɪŋz/ *n.pl.* things gleaned, esp. facts.

glebe *n.* **1** a piece of land serving as part of a clergyman's benefice and providing income. **2** *poet.* earth; land; a field. [ME f. L *gl(a)eba* clod, soil]

glee *n.* **1** mirth; delight. **2** a song for three or more, esp. adult male, voices, singing different parts simultaneously, usu. unaccompanied. □ **glee club** a society for singing part-songs. □ **gleesome** *adj.* [OE *glīo*, *glēo* minstrelsy, jest f. Gmc]

gleeful /ˈgliːfʊl/ *adj.* joyful. □ **gleefully** *adv.* **gleefulness** *n.*

glen *n.* a narrow valley. [Gael. & Ir. *gleann*]

glengarry /glenˈgærɪ/ *n.* (*pl.* **-ies**) a brimless Scottish hat with a cleft down the centre and usu. two ribbons hanging at the back. [*Glengarry* in Scotland]

glib *adj.* (**glibber**, **glibbest**) (of a speaker, speech, etc.) fluent and voluble but insincere and shallow. □ **glibly** *adv.* **glibness** *n.* [rel. to obs. *glibbery* slippery f. Gmc: perh. imit.]

glide *v.* & *n.* —*v.* **1** (of a stream, bird, snake, ship, train, skater, etc.) move with a smooth continuous motion. **2** *intr.* (of an aircraft, esp. a glider) fly without engine-power. **3** *intr.* of time etc.: **a** pass gently and imperceptibly. **b** (often foll. by *into*) pass and change gradually and imperceptibly (*night glided into day*). **4** *intr.* move quietly or stealthily. **5** *tr.* cause to glide (*breezes glided the ship on its course*). **6** *tr.* cross in a glider. —*n.* **1** the act of gliding. **2** an instance of this. □ **glide path** an aircraft's line of descent to land, esp. as indicated by ground radar. □ **glidingly** *adv.* [OE *glīdan* f. WG]

glider /ˈglaɪdə(r)/ *n.* **1** an aircraft that flies without an engine. **2** a person or thing that glides.

glimmer /ˈglɪmə(r)/ *v.* & *n.* —*v.intr.* shine faintly or intermittently. —*n.* **1** a feeble or wavering light. **2** (usu. foll. by *of*) a faint gleam (of hope, understanding, etc.). **3** a glimpse. □ **glimmeringly** *adv.* [ME prob. f. Scand. f. WG: see GLEAM]

glimmering /ˈglɪmərɪŋ/ *n.* **1** = GLIMMER *n.* **2** an act of glimmering.

glimpse /glɪmps/ *n.* & *v.* —*n.* (often foll. by *of*) **1** a momentary or partial view (*caught a glimpse of her*). **2** a faint and transient appearance (*glimpses of the truth*). —*v.* **1** *tr.* see faintly or partly (*glimpsed his face in the crowd*). **2** *intr.* (often foll. by *at*) cast a passing glance. **3** *intr.* **a** shine faintly or intermittently. **b** *poet.* appear faintly; dawn. [ME *glimse* corresp. to MHG *glimsen* f. WG (as GLIMMER)]

glint *v.* & *n.* —*v.intr.* & *tr.* flash or cause to flash; sparkle; reflect (*eyes glinted with amusement; the sword glinted fire*). —*n.* a brief flash of light; a sparkle. [alt. of ME *glent*, prob. of Scand. orig.]

glissade /glɪˈsɑːd, -ˈseɪd/ *n.* & *v.* —*n.* **1** an act of sliding down a steep slope of snow or ice, usu. on the feet with the support of an ice-axe etc. **2** a gliding step in ballet. —*v.intr.* perform a glissade. [F f. *glisser* slip, slide]

glissando /glɪˈsændəʊ/ *n.* (*pl.* **glissandi** /-dɪ/ or **-os**) *Mus.* a continuous slide of adjacent notes upwards or downwards. [It. f. F *glissant* sliding (as GLISSADE)]

glisten /ˈglɪs(ə)n/ *v.* & *n.* —*v.intr.* shine, esp. like a wet object, snow, etc.; glitter. —*n.* a glitter; a sparkle. [OE *glisnian* f. *glisian* shine]

glister /ˈglɪstə(r)/ *v.* & *n. archaic* —*v.intr.* sparkle; glitter. —*n.* a sparkle; a gleam. [ME f. MLG *glistern*, MDu *glisteren*, rel. to GLISTEN]

glitch *n. colloq.* a sudden irregularity or malfunction (of equipment etc.). [20th c.: orig. unkn.]

glitter /ˈglɪtə(r)/ *v.* & *n.* —*v.intr.* **1** shine, esp. with a bright reflected light; sparkle. **2** (usu. foll. by *with*) **a** be showy or splendid (*glittered with diamonds*). **b** be ostentatious or flashily brilliant (*glittering rhetoric*). —*n.* **1** a gleam; a

sparkle. **2** showiness; splendour. **3** tiny pieces of sparkling material. □ **glitteringly** *adv.* **glittery** *adj.* [ME f. ON *glitra* f. Gmc]

glitterati /ˌglɪtəˈrɑːtɪ/ *n.pl. sl.* the fashionable set of literary or show-business people. [GLITTER + LITERATI]

glitzy /ˈglɪtsɪ/ *adj.* (**glitzier**, **glitziest**) *sl.* extravagant, ostentatious; tawdry, gaudy. □ **glitz** *n.* **glitzily** *adv.* **glitziness** *n.* [GLITTER, after RITZY: cf. G *glitzerig* glittering]

gloaming /ˈgləʊmɪŋ/ *n. poet.* twilight; dusk. [OE *glōmung* f. *glōm* twilight, rel. to GLOW]

gloat *v.* & *n.* —*v.intr.* (often foll. by *on, upon, over*) consider or contemplate with lust, greed, malice, triumph, etc. (*gloated over his collection*). —*n.* **1** the act of gloating. **2** a look or expression of triumphant satisfaction. □ **gloater** *n.* **gloatingly** *adv.* [16th c.: orig. unkn., but perh. rel. to ON *glotta* grin, MHG *glotzen* stare]

glob *n.* a mass or lump of semi-liquid substance, e.g. mud. [20th c.: perh. f. BLOB and GOB[1]]

global /ˈgləʊb(ə)l/ *adj.* **1** worldwide (*global conflict*). **2** relating to or embracing a group of items etc.; total. □ **global warming** the increase in temperature of the earth's atmosphere caused by the greenhouse effect. □ **globally** *adv.* [F (as GLOBE)]

globe *n.* **1 a** (prec. by *the*) the planet earth. **b** a planet, star, or sun. **c** any spherical body; a ball. **2** a spherical representation of the earth or of the constellations with a map on the surface. **3** a golden sphere as an emblem of sovereignty; an orb. **4** any spherical glass vessel. □ **globe artichoke** the partly edible head of the artichoke plant. **globe-trotter** a person who travels widely. **globe-trotting** such travel. □ **globelike** *adj.* **globoid** *adj.* & *n.* **globose** *adj.* [F *globe* or L *globus*]

globular /ˈglɒbjʊlə(r)/ *adj.* **1** globe-shaped, spherical. **2** composed of globules. □ **globularity** /-ˈlærɪtɪ/ *n.* **globularly** *adv.*

globule /ˈglɒbjuːl/ *n.* a small globe or round particle; a drop. □ **globulous** *adj.* [F *globule* or L *globulus* (as GLOBE)]

globulin /ˈglɒbjʊlɪn/ *n.* any of a group of proteins found in plant and animal tissues and esp. responsible for the transport of molecules etc.

glockenspiel /ˈglɒkənˌspiːl, -ˌʃpiːl/ *n.* a musical instrument consisting of a series of bells or metal bars or tubes struck by hammers. [G, = bell-play]

glomerate /ˈglɒmərət/ *adj. Bot.* & *Anat.* compactly clustered. [L *glomeratus* past part. of *glomerare* f. *glomus -eris* ball]

gloom *n.* & *v.* —*n.* **1** darkness; obscurity. **2** melancholy; despondency. **3** *poet.* a dark place. —*v.* **1** *intr.* be gloomy or melancholy; frown. **2** *intr.* (of the sky etc.) be dull or threatening; lour. **3** *intr.* appear darkly or obscurely. **4** *tr.* cover with gloom; make dark or dismal. [ME *gloum(b)e*, of unkn. orig.: cf. GLUM]

gloomy /ˈgluːmɪ/ *adj.* (**gloomier**, **gloomiest**) **1** dark; unlighted. **2** depressed; sullen. **3** dismal; depressing. □ **gloomily** *adv.* **gloominess** *n.*

glop *n. US sl.* a liquid or sticky mess, esp. inedible food. [imit.: cf. obs. *glop* swallow greedily]

glorify /ˈglɔːrɪfaɪ/ *v.tr.* (**-ies**, **-ied**) **1** exalt to heavenly glory; make glorious. **2** transform into something more splendid. **3** extol; praise. **4** (as **glorified** *adj.*) seeming or pretending to be more splendid than in reality (*just a glorified office* boy). □ **glorification** /-fɪˈkeɪʃ(ə)n/ n. **glorifier** n. [ME f. OF glorifier f. eccl.L glorificare f. LL glorificus f. L gloria glory]

gloriole /ˈglɔːrɪˌəʊl/ n. an aureole; a halo. [F f. L gloriola dimin. of gloria glory]

glorious /ˈglɔːrɪəs/ adj. **1** possessing glory; illustrious. **2** conferring glory; honourable. **3** colloq. splendid; magnificent; delightful (a glorious day; glorious fun). □ **gloriously** adv. **gloriousness** n. [ME f. AF glorious, OF glorios, -eus f. L gloriosus (as GLORY)]

glory /ˈglɔːrɪ/ n. & v. —n. (pl. -ies) **1** high renown or fame; honour. **2** adoring praise and thanksgiving (Glory to the Lord). **3** resplendent majesty or magnificence; great beauty. **4** a thing that brings renown or praise; a distinction. **5** the bliss and splendour of heaven. **6** an aureole, a halo. —v.intr. (often foll. by in, or to + infin.) pride oneself; exult (glory in their skill). □ **glory be! 1** a devout cry. **2** colloq. an exclamation of surprise or delight. **glory-box** Austral. & NZ a box for women's clothes etc., stored in preparation for marriage. **glory-hole 1** colloq. an untidy room, drawer, or receptacle. **2** US an open quarry. **go to glory** sl. die; be destroyed. [ME f. AF & OF glorie f. L gloria]

gloss[1] n. & v. —n. **1 a** surface shine or lustre. **b** an instance of this; a smooth finish. **2 a** deceptively attractive appearance. **b** an instance of this. **3** (in full **gloss paint**) paint formulated to give a hard glossy finish. —v.tr. make glossy. □ **gloss over** conceal or evade by mentioning briefly or misleadingly. □ **glosser** n. [16th c.: orig. unkn.]

gloss[2] n. & v. —n. **1** an explanatory word or phrase inserted between the lines or in the margin of a text. **2** a comment, explanation, interpretation, or paraphrase. —v. **1** tr. **a** add a gloss or glosses to (a text, word, etc.). **b** read a different sense into; explain away. **2** intr. (often foll. by on) make (esp. unfavourable) comments. □ **glosser** n. [alt. of GLOZE after med.L glossa]

glossal /ˈglɒs(ə)l/ adj. Anat. of the tongue; lingual. [Gk glōssa tongue]

glossary /ˈglɒsərɪ/ n. (pl. -ies) (also **gloss**) an alphabetical list of terms or words found in or relating to a specific subject or text, esp. dialect, with explanations; a brief dictionary. □ **glossarial** /glɒˈseərɪəl/ adj. **glossarist** n. [L glossarium f. glossa GLOSS[2]]

glossitis /glɒˈsaɪtɪs/ n. inflammation of the tongue. [Gk glōssa tongue + -ITIS]

glossolalia /ˌglɒsəˈleɪlɪə/ n. = gift of tongues (see TONGUE). [mod.L f. Gk glōssa tongue + -lalia speaking]

glossy /ˈglɒsɪ/ adj. & n. —adj. (**glossier, glossiest**) **1** having a shine; smooth. **2** (of a magazine etc.) printed on smooth and shiny paper. —n. (pl. -ies) colloq. **1** a glossy magazine. **2** a photograph with a glossy surface. □ **glossily** adv. **glossiness** n.

glottal /ˈglɒt(ə)l/ adj. of or produced by the glottis. □ **glottal stop** a sound produced by the sudden opening or shutting of the glottis.

glottis /ˈglɒtɪs/ n. the space at the upper end of the windpipe and between the vocal cords, affecting voice modulation. □ **glottic** adj. [mod.L f. Gk glōttis f. glōtta var. of glōssa tongue]

Gloucester /ˈglɒstə(r)/ n. (usu. **double Gloucester**, orig. a richer kind) a kind of hard cheese orig. made in Gloucestershire in S. England.

glove /glʌv/ n. & v. —n. **1** a covering for the hand, of wool, leather, cotton, etc., worn esp. for protection against cold or dirt, and usu. having separate fingers. **2** a padded protective glove. —v.tr. cover or provide with a glove or gloves. □ **glove box 1** a box for gloves. **2** a closed chamber with sealed-in gloves for handling radioactive material etc. **3** = glove compartment. **glove compartment** a recess for small articles in the dashboard of a motor vehicle. **glove puppet** a small cloth puppet fitted on the hand and worked by the fingers. **throw down** (or **take up**) **the glove** issue (or accept) a challenge. **with the gloves off** mercilessly; unfairly. □ **gloveless** adj. **glover** n. [OE glōf, corresp. to ON glófi, perh. f. Gmc]

glow /gləʊ/ v. & n. —v.intr. **1 a** throw out light and heat without flame; be incandescent. **b** shine like something heated in this way. **2** (of the cheeks) redden, esp. from cold or exercise. **3** (often foll. by with) **a** (of the body) be heated, esp. from exertion; sweat. **b** express or experience strong emotion (glowed with pride; glowing with indignation). **4** show a warm colour (the painting glows with warmth). **5** (as **glowing** adj.) expressing pride or satisfaction (a glowing report). —n. **1** a glowing state. **2** a bright warm colour, esp. the red of cheeks. **3** ardour; passion. **4** a feeling induced by good health, exercise, etc.; well-being. □ **glow-worm** any beetle of the genus Lampyris whose wingless female emits light from the end of the abdomen. □ **glowingly** adv. [OE glōwan f. Gmc]

glower /ˈglaʊə(r)/ v. & n. —v.intr. (often foll. by at) stare or scowl, esp. angrily. —n. a glowering look. □ **gloweringly** adv. [orig. uncert.: perh. Sc. var. of ME glore f. LG or Scand.; or f. obs. (ME) glow stare + -ER[4]]

gloxinia /glɒkˈsɪnɪə/ n. any tropical plant of the genus Gloxinia, with large bell flowers. [mod.L f. B. P. Gloxin, 18th-c. Ger. botanist]

gloze v.tr. (also **gloze over**) explain away; extenuate; palliate. [ME f. OF gloser f. glose f. med.L glosa, gloza f. L glossa tongue, GLOSS[2]]

glucose /ˈgluːkəʊs, -kəʊz/ n. a simple sugar containing six carbon atoms, found in fruit juice etc., which is an important energy source in living organisms. [F f. Gk gleukos sweet wine, rel. to glukus sweet]

glue n. & v. —n. an adhesive substance used for sticking objects or materials together. —v.tr. (**glues, glued, gluing** or **glueing**) **1** fasten or join with glue. **2** keep or put very close (an eye glued to the keyhole). □ **glue-sniffer** a person who inhales the fumes from adhesives as a drug. □ **gluelike** adj. **gluer** n. **gluey** /ˈgluːɪ/ adj. (**gluier, gluiest**). **glueyness** n. [ME f. OF glu (n.), gluer (v.), f. LL glus glutis f. L gluten]

glum adj. (**glummer, glummest**) looking or feeling dejected; sullen; displeased. □ **glumly** adv. **glumness** n. [rel. to dial. glum (v.) frown, var. of gloume GLOOM[1]]

glut v. & n. —v.tr. (**glutted, glutting**) **1** feed (a person etc.) or indulge (an appetite etc.) to the full; satiate; cloy. **2** fill to excess; choke up. **3** Econ. overstock (a market) with goods. —n. **1** Econ. supply exceeding demand; a surfeit. **2** full indulgence; one's fill. [ME prob. f. OF gloutir swallow f. L gluttire: cf. GLUTTON]

glutamate /ˈgluːtəˌmeɪt/ n. any salt or ester of glutamic acid, esp. a sodium salt used to enhance the flavour of food.

glutamic acid /gluːˈtæmɪk/ n. a naturally occurring amino acid, a constituent of many proteins. [GLUTEN + AMINE + -IC]

gluten /ˈgluːt(ə)n/ n. a mixture of proteins in cereal grains. [F f. L gluten glutinis glue]

gluteus /ˈgluːtɪəs/ n. (pl. **glutei** /-tɪˌaɪ/) any of the three muscles in each buttock. □ **gluteal** adj. [mod.L f. Gk gloutos buttock]

glutinous /ˈgluːtɪnəs/ adj. sticky; like glue. □ **glutinously** adv. **glutinousness** n. [F glutineux or L glutinosus (as GLUTEN)]

glutton /ˈglʌt(ə)n/ n. 1 an excessively greedy eater. 2 (often foll. by for) colloq. a person insatiably eager (a glutton for work). 3 a voracious animal Gulo gulo, of the weasel family. □ **gluttonize** v.intr. (also **-ise**). **gluttonous** adj. **gluttonously** adv. [ME f. OF gluton, gloton f. L glutto -onis f. gluttire swallow, gluttus greedy]

gluttony /ˈglʌtənɪ/ n. habitual greed or excess in eating. [OF glutonie (as GLUTTON)]

glycerine /ˈglɪsəˌriːn/ n. (US **glycerin** /-rɪn/) = GLYCEROL. [F glycerin f. Gk glukeros sweet]

glycerol /ˈglɪsəˌrɒl/ n. a colourless sweet viscous liquid, used as an emollient and laxative, in explosives, etc. [GLYCERINE + -OL¹]

glyco- /ˈglaɪkəʊ/ comb. form sugar. [Gk glukus sweet]

glycogen /ˈglaɪkədʒ(ə)n/ n. a polysaccharide serving as a store of carbohydrates, esp. in animal tissues, and yielding glucose on hydrolysis. □ **glycogenic** /-ˈdʒenɪk/ adj.

glycol /ˈglaɪkɒl/ n. a diol, esp. ethylene glycol. □ **glycolic** /-ˈkɒlɪk/ adj. **glycollic** /-ˈkɒlɪk/ adj. [GLYCERINE + -OL¹, orig. as being intermediate between glycerine and alcohol]

glycolysis /glaɪˈkɒlɪsɪs/ n. Biochem. the breakdown of glucose by enzymes in most living organisms to release energy and pyruvic acid.

glycosuria /ˌglaɪkəˈsjʊərɪə/ n. a condition characterized by an excess of sugar in the urine, associated with diabetes, kidney disease, etc. □ **glycosuric** adj. [F glycose glucose + -uria f. Gk -ouria denoting something present in urine]

glyph /glɪf/ n. 1 a sculptured character or symbol. 2 a vertical groove, esp. that on a Greek frieze. □ **glyphic** adj. [F glyphe f. Gk gluphē carving f. gluphō carve]

gm abbr. gram(s).

G-man /ˈdʒiːmæn/ n. (pl. **G-men**) 1 US colloq. a federal criminal-investigation officer. 2 Ir. a political detective. [Government + MAN]

GMT abbr. Greenwich Mean Time.

gnarled /nɑːld/ adj. (also **gnarly** /ˈnɑːlɪ/) (of a tree, hands, etc.) knobbly, twisted, rugged. [var. of knarled, rel. to KNURL]

gnash /næʃ/ v. & n. —v. 1 tr. grind (the teeth). 2 intr. (of the teeth) strike together; grind. —n. an act of grinding the teeth. [var. of obs. gnacche or gnast, rel. to ON gnastan a gnashing (imit.)]

gnat /næt/ n. 1 any small two-winged biting fly of the genus Culex, esp. C. pipiens. 2 an insignificant annoyance. 3 a tiny thing. [OE gnætt]

gnathic /ˈnæθɪk/ adj. of or relating to the jaws. [Gk gnathos jaw]

gnaw /nɔː/ v. (past part. **gnawed** or **gnawn**) 1 a tr. (usu. foll. by away, off, in two, etc.) bite persistently; wear away by biting. **b** intr. (often foll. by at, into) bite, nibble. 2 a intr. (often foll. by at, into) (of a destructive agent, pain, fear, etc.) corrode; waste away; consume; torture. **b** tr. corrode, consume, torture, etc. with pain, fear, etc. (was gnawed by doubt). 3 tr. (as **gnawing** adj.) persistent; worrying. □ **gnawingly** adv. [OE gnagen, ult. imit.]

gneiss /naɪs/ n. a usu. coarse-grained metamorphic rock foliated by mineral layers, principally of feldspar, quartz, and ferromagnesian minerals. □ **gneissic** adj. **gneissoid** adj. **gneissose** adj. [G]

gnocchi /ˈnɒkɪ, ˈnjɒkɪ/ n.pl. an Italian dish of small dumplings usu. made from potato, semolina flour, etc., or from spinach and cheese. [It., pl. of gnocco f. nocchio knot in wood]

gnome /nəʊm/ n. 1 a a dwarfish legendary creature supposed to guard the earth's treasures underground; a goblin. **b** a figure of a gnome, esp. as a garden ornament. 2 (esp. in pl.) colloq. a person with sinister influence, esp. financial (gnomes of Zurich). □ **gnomish** adj. [F f. mod.L gnomus (word invented by Paracelsus)]

gnomic /ˈnəʊmɪk/ adj. of, consisting of, or using maxims or aphorisms; sententious. □ **gnomically** adv. [Gk gnōmikos f. gnōmē opinion f. gignōskō know]

gnomon /ˈnəʊmɒn/ n. 1 the rod or pin etc. on a sundial that shows the time by the position of its shadow. 2 Astron. a column etc. used in observing the sun's meridian altitude. □ **gnomonic** /-ˈmɒnɪk/ adj. [F or L gnomon f. Gk gnōmōn indicator etc. f. gignōskō know]

gnostic /ˈnɒstɪk/ adj. & n. —adj. 1 relating to knowledge, esp. esoteric mystical knowledge. 2 (**Gnostic**) concerning the Gnostics; occult; mystic. —n. (**Gnostic**) (usu. in pl.) a Christian heretic of the 1st–3rd c. □ **Gnosticism** /-ˌsɪz(ə)m/ n. **gnosticize** /-ˌsaɪz/ v.tr. & intr. [eccl.L gnosticus f. Gk gnōstikos f. gnōsis knowledge (as GNOMIC)]

GNP abbr. gross national product.

gnu /nuː, njuː/ n. any antelope of the genus Connochaetes, native to S. Africa. [Bushman nqu, prob. through Du. gnoe]

go¹ /gəʊ/ v., n., & adj. —v. (3rd sing. present **goes** /gəʊz/; past **went** /went/; past part. **gone** /gɒn/) 1 intr. **a** start moving or be moving from one place or point in time to another; travel, proceed. **b** (foll. by to + infin., or and + verb) proceed in order to (go to find him; go and buy some bread). **c** (foll. by and + verb) colloq. expressing annoyance (you went and told him; they've gone and broken it. 2 intr. (foll. by verbal noun) make a special trip for; participate in; proceed to do (went skiing; then went shopping). 3 intr. lie or extend in a certain direction (the road goes to London). 4 intr. leave; depart (they had to go). 5 intr. move, act, work, etc. (the clock doesn't go; his brain is going all the time). 6 intr. **a** make a specified movement (go like this). **b** make a sound (often of a specified kind) (the gun went bang; the bell went). **c** (of an animal) make (its characteristic cry) (the cow went 'moo'). 7 intr. be in a specified state (go hungry; went in fear of his life). 8 intr. **a** pass into a specified condition (gone bad; went to sleep). **b** colloq. die. **c** proceed or escape in a specified condition (the poet went unrecognized; the crime went unnoticed). 9 intr. (of time or distance) pass, elapse; be traversed (ten days to go before Easter; the last mile went quickly). 10 intr.

a (of a document, verse, song, etc.) have a specified content or wording; run (*the tune goes like this*). **b** be current or accepted (*so the story goes*). **c** be suitable; fit; match (*the shoes don't go with the hat*). **d** be regularly kept or put (*the forks go here*). **e** find room; fit (*this won't go into the cupboard*). **11** *intr.* **a** turn out, proceed; take a course or view (*things went well; Liverpool went Labour*). **b** be successful (*make the party go; went like a bomb*). **c** progress (*we've still a long way to go*). **12** *intr.* **a** be sold (*went for £1*). **b** (of money) be spent (*£200 went on a new jacket*). **13** *intr.* **a** be relinquished, dismissed, or abolished (*the car will have to go*). **b** fail, decline; give way, collapse (*his sight is going; the bulb has gone*). **14** *intr.* be acceptable or permitted; be accepted without question (*anything goes; what I say goes*). **15** *intr.* (often foll. by *by, with, on, upon*) be guided by; judge or act on or in harmony with (*have nothing to go on; a good rule to go by*). **16** *intr.* attend or visit or travel to regularly (*goes to church; this train goes to Bristol*). **17** *intr.* (foll. by pres. part.) *colloq.* proceed (often foolishly) to do (*went running to the police; don't go making him angry*). **18** *intr.* act or proceed to a certain point (*will go so far and no further; went as high as £100*). **19** *intr.* (of a number) be capable of being contained in another (*6 into 12 goes twice; 6 into 5 won't go*). **20** *tr. Cards* bid; declare (*go nap; has gone two spades*). **21** *intr.* (usu. foll. by *to*) be allotted or awarded; pass (*first prize went to the girl; the job went to his rival*). **22** *intr.* (foll. by *to, towards*) amount to; contribute to (*12 inches go to make a foot; this will go towards your holiday*). **23** *intr.* (in *imper.*) begin motion (a starter's order in a race) (*ready, steady, go!*). **24** *intr.* (usu. foll. by *to*) refer or appeal (*go to him for help*). **25** *intr.* (often foll. by *on*) take up a specified profession (*went on the stage; gone soldiering*). **26** *intr.* (usu. foll. by *by, under*) be known or called (*goes by the name of Droopy*). **27** *tr. colloq.* proceed to (*go jump in the lake*). **28** *intr.* (foll. by *for*) apply to; have relevance for (*that goes for me too*). —*n.* (pl. **goes**) **1** the act or an instance of going. **2** mettle; spirit; dash; animation (*has a lot of go*). **3** vigorous activity (*it's all go*). **4** *colloq.* a success (*made a go of it*). **5** *colloq.* a turn; an attempt (*I'll have a go; all in one go*). **6** *colloq.* a state of affairs (*a rum go*). **7** *colloq.* an attack of illness (*a bad go of flu*). **8** *colloq.* a quantity of liquor, food, etc. served at one time. —*adj. colloq.* functioning properly (*all systems are go*). □ **all the go** *colloq.* in fashion. **go about 1** busy oneself with; set to work at. **2** be socially active. **3** (foll. by pres. part.) make a habit of doing (*goes about telling lies*). **4** *Naut.* change to an opposite tack. **go ahead** proceed without hesitation. **go-ahead** *n.* permission to proceed. —*adj.* enterprising. **go along with** agree to; take the same view as. **go around 1** (foll. by *with*) be regularly in the company of. **2** = **go about** 3. **go at** take in hand energetically; attack. **go away** depart, esp. from home for a holiday etc. **go back on** fail to keep (one's word, promise, etc.). **go-between** an intermediary; a negotiator. **go by 1** pass. **2** be dependent on; be guided by. **go-by** *colloq.* a snub; a slight (*gave it the go-by*). **go-cart 1** a handcart; a pushchair. **2** = **go-kart**. **go down 1 a** (of an amount) become less (*the coffee has gone down a lot*). **b** subside (*the flood went down*). **c** decrease in price; lose value. **2 a** (of a ship) sink. **b** (of the sun) set. **3** (usu. foll. by *to*) be continued to a specified point. **4**

deteriorate; fail; (of a computer network etc.) cease to function. **5** be recorded in writing. **6** be swallowed. **7** (often foll. by *with*) find acceptance. **8** *Brit. colloq.* leave university. **9** *colloq.* be sent to prison (*went down for ten years*). **10** (often foll. by *before*) fall (before a conqueror). **go down with** *Brit.* begin to suffer from (a disease). **go far** be very successful. **go for 1** go to fetch. **2** be accounted as or achieve (*went for nothing*). **3** prefer; choose (*that's the one I go for*). **4** *colloq.* strive to attain (*go for it!*). **5** *colloq.* attack (*the dog went for him*). **go-getter** *colloq.* an aggressively enterprising person, esp. a businessman. **go-go** *colloq.* **1** (of a dancer, music, etc.) in modern style, lively and rhythmic. **2** unrestrained; energetic. **3** (of investment) speculative. **go halves** (or **shares**) (often foll. by *with*) share equally. **go in 1** enter a room, house, etc. **2** (usu. foll. by *for*) enter as a competitor. **3** *Cricket* take or begin an innings. **4** (of the sun etc.) become obscured by cloud. **go in for** take as one's object, style, pursuit, principle, etc. **going!**, **gone!** an auctioneer's announcement that bidding is closing or closed. **go into 1** enter (a profession, Parliament, etc.). **2** take part in; be a part of. **3** investigate. **4** allow oneself to pass into (hysterics etc.). **5** dress oneself in (mourning etc.). **6** frequent (society). **go it** *colloq.* **1** act vigorously, furiously, etc. **2** indulge in dissipation. **go it strong** *colloq.* go to great lengths; exaggerate. **go-kart** a miniature racing car with a skeleton body. **go a long way 1** (often foll. by *towards*) have a great effect. **2** (of food, money, etc.) last a long time, buy much. **3** = **go far**. **go off 1** explode. **2** leave the stage. **3** gradually cease to be felt. **4** (esp. of foodstuffs) deteriorate; decompose. **5** go to sleep; become unconscious. **6** begin. **7** die. **8** be got rid of by sale etc. **9** *Brit. colloq.* begin to dislike (*I've gone off him*). **go-off** *colloq.* a start (*at the first go-off*). **go off at** *Austral. & NZ sl.* reprimand, scold. **go off well** (or **badly** etc.) (of an enterprise etc.) be received or accomplished well (or badly etc.). **go on 1** (often foll. by pres. part.) continue, persevere (*decided to go on with it; went on trying; unable to go on*). **2** *colloq.* a talk at great length. **b** (foll. by *at*) admonish (*went on and on at him*). **3** (foll. by *to* + *infin.*) proceed (*went on to become a star*). **4** happen. **5** conduct oneself (*shameful, the way they went on*). **6** *Theatr.* appear on stage. **7** *Cricket* begin bowling. **8** (of a garment) be large enough for its wearer. **9** take one's turn to do something. **10** (also **go upon**) *colloq.* use as evidence (*police don't have anything to go on*). **11** *colloq.* (esp. in *neg.*) **a** concern oneself about. **b** care for (*don't go much on red hair*). **go out 1** leave a room, house, etc. **2** be broadcast. **3** be extinguished. **4** (often foll. by *with*) be courting. **5** (of a government) leave office. **6** cease to be fashionable. **7** (usu. foll. by *to*) depart, esp. to a colony etc. **8** *colloq.* lose consciousness. **9** (of workers) strike. **10** (usu. foll. by *to*) (of the heart etc.) expand with sympathy etc. towards (*my heart goes out to them*). **11** *Golf* play the first nine holes in a round. **12** *Cards* be the first to dispose of one's hand. **13** (of a tide) turn to low tide. **go over 1** inspect the details of; rehearse; retouch. **2** (often foll. by *to*) change one's allegiance or religion. **3** (of a play etc.) be successful (*went over well in Dundee*). **go round 1** spin, revolve. **2** be long enough to encompass. **3** (of food etc.) suffice for everybody. **4** (usu. foll. by *to*) visit informally. **5** = **go around**.

go slow work slowly, as a form of industrial action. **go-slow** *Brit.* such industrial action. **go through 1** be dealt with or completed. **2** discuss in detail; scrutinize in sequence. **3** perform (a ceremony, a recitation, etc.). **4** undergo. **5** *colloq.* use up; spend (money etc.). **6** make holes in. **7** (of a book) be successively published (in so many editions). **8** *Austral. sl.* abscond. **go through with** not leave unfinished; complete. **go to the bar** become a barrister. **go to blazes** (or **hell** or **Jericho** etc.) *sl.* an exclamation of dismissal, contempt, etc. **go together 1** match; fit. **2** be courting. **go to it!** *colloq.* begin work! **go under** sink; fail; succumb. **go up 1** increase in price. **2** *Brit. colloq.* enter university. **3** be consumed (in flames etc.); explode. **go well** (or **ill** etc.) (often foll. by *with*) turn out well, (or ill etc.). **go with 1** be harmonious with; match. **2** agree to; take the same view as. **3 a** be a pair with. **b** be courting. **4** follow the drift of. **go without** manage without; forgo (also *absol.: we shall just have to go without*). **go with the tide** (or **times**) do as others do; follow the drift. **have a go at 1** attack, criticize. **2** attempt, try. **on the go** *colloq.* **1** in constant motion. **2** constantly working. **to go** *US* (of refreshments etc.) to be eaten or drunk off the premises. **who goes there?** a sentry's challenge. [OE *gān* f. Gmc: *went* orig. past of WEND]

go² /gəʊ/ *n.* a Japanese board game of territorial possession and capture. [Jap.]

goad *n. & v. —n.* **1** a spiked stick used for urging cattle forward. **2** anything that torments, incites, or stimulates. —*v.tr.* **1** urge on with a goad. **2** (usu. foll. by *on, into*) irritate; stimulate (*goaded him into retaliating; goaded me on to win*). [OE *gād*, rel. to Lombard *gaida* arrowhead f. Gmc]

goal *n.* **1** the object of a person's ambition or effort; a destination; an aim (*fame is his goal; London was our goal*). **2 a** *Football* a pair of posts with a crossbar between which the ball has to be sent to score. **b** a cage or basket used similarly in other games. **c** a point won (*scored 3 goals*). **3** a point marking the end of a race. □ **goal average** *Football* the ratio of the numbers of goals scored for and against a team in a series of matches. **goal difference** *Football* the difference of goals scored for and against. **goal-kick 1** *Assoc. Football* a kick by the defending side after attackers send the ball over the goal-line without scoring. **2** *Rugby Football* an attempt to kick a goal. **goal-line** *Football* a line between each pair of goalposts, extended to form the end-boundary of a field of play (cf. *touch-line*). **goal-mouth** *Football* the space between or near the goalposts. **in goal** in the position of goalkeeper. □ **goalless** *adj.* [16th c.: orig. unkn.: perh. identical with ME *gol* boundary]

goalball /ˈgəʊlbɔːl/ *n.* a team ball game for blind and visually handicapped players.

goalkeeper /ˈgəʊlˌkiːpə(r)/ *n.* a player stationed to protect the goal in various sports.

goalpost /ˈgəʊlpəʊst/ *n.* either of the two upright posts of a goal. □ **move the goalposts** alter the basis or scope of a procedure during its course, so as to fit adverse circumstances encountered.

goanna /gəʊˈænə/ *n. Austral.* a monitor lizard. [corrupt. of IGUANA]

goat *n.* **1 a** a hardy lively frisky short-haired domesticated mammal, *Capra aegagrus*, having horns and (in the male) a beard, and kept for its milk and meat. **b** either of two similar mammals, the mountain goat and the Spanish goat. **2** any other mammal of the genus *Capra*, including the ibex. **3** a lecherous man. **4** *colloq.* a foolish person. **5** (**the Goat**) the zodiacal sign or constellation Capricorn. **6** *US* a scapegoat. □ **get a person's goat** *colloq.* irritate a person. □ **goatish** *adj.* **goaty** *adj.* [OE *gāt* she-goat f. Gmc]

goatee /gəʊˈtiː/ *n.* a small pointed beard like that of a goat.

goatherd /ˈgəʊthɜːd/ *n.* a person who tends goats.

goatskin /ˈgəʊtskɪn/ *n.* **1** the skin of a goat. **2** a garment or bottle made out of goatskin.

gob¹ *n. esp. Brit. sl.* the mouth. □ **gob-stopper** a large hard sweet. [perh. f. Gael. & Ir., = beak, mouth]

gob² *n. & v. Brit. sl.* —*n.* a clot of slimy matter. —*v.intr.* (**gobbed, gobbing**) spit. [ME f. OF *go(u)be* mouthful]

gobbet /ˈgɒbɪt/ *n.* **1** a piece or lump of raw meat, flesh, food, etc. **2** an extract from a text, esp. one set for translation or comment in an examination. [ME f. OF *gobet* (as GOB²)]

gobble¹ /ˈgɒb(ə)l/ *v.tr. & intr.* eat hurriedly and noisily. □ **gobbler** *n.* [prob. dial. f. GOB²]

gobble² /ˈgɒb(ə)l/ *v.intr.* **1** (of a turkeycock) make a characteristic swallowing sound in the throat. **2** make such a sound when speaking, esp. when excited, angry, etc. [imit.: perh. based on GOBBLE¹]

gobbledegook /ˈgɒb(ə)ldɪˌguːk, -ˌgʊk/ *n.* (also **gobbledygook**) *colloq.* pompous or unintelligible jargon. [prob. imit. of a turkeycock]

goblet /ˈgɒblɪt/ *n.* **1** a drinking-vessel with a foot and a stem, usu. of glass. **2** *archaic* a metal or glass bowl-shaped drinking-cup without handles. [ME f. OF *gobelet* dimin. of *gobel* cup, of unkn. orig.]

goblin /ˈgɒblɪn/ *n.* a mischievous ugly dwarflike creature of folklore. [ME prob. f. AF *gobelin*, med.L *gobelinus*, prob. f. name dimin. of *Gobel*, rel. to G *Kobold*: see COBALT]

gobsmacked /ˈgɒbsmækt/ *adj. sl.* astounded, flabbergasted. [GOB¹ + SMACK¹]

goby /ˈgəʊbɪ/ *n.* (*pl.* **-ies**) any small marine fish of the family Gabiidae, having ventral fins joined to form a sucker or disc. [L *gobius, cobius* f. Gk *kōbios*]

god *n.* **1 a** (in many religions) a superhuman being or spirit worshipped as having power over nature, human fortunes, etc.; a deity. **b** an image, idol, animal, or other object worshipped as divine or symbolizing a god. **2** (**God**) (in Christian and other monotheistic religions) the creator and ruler of the universe; the supreme being. **3 a** an adored, admired, or influential person. **b** something worshipped like a god (*makes a god of success*). **4** *Theatr.* (in *pl.*) **a** the gallery. **b** the people sitting in it. □ **god-daughter** a female godchild. **God the Father, Son, and Holy Ghost** (in the Christian tradition) the Persons of the Trinity. **God-fearing** earnestly religious. **God-forsaken** devoid of all merit; dismal; dreary. **God's own country** an earthly paradise, esp. the United States. **God squad** *sl.* **1** a religious organization, esp. an evangelical Christian group. **2** its members.

with God dead and in Heaven. □ **godhood** n. **godship** n. **godward** adj. & adv. **godwards** adv. [OE f. Gmc]

godchild /ˈgɒdtʃaɪld/ n. a person in relation to a godparent.

goddess /ˈgɒdɪs/ n. **1** a female deity. **2** a woman who is adored, esp. for her beauty.

godet /ˈgəʊdeɪ/ n. a triangular piece of material inserted in a dress, glove, etc. [F]

godetia /gəˈdiːʃə/ n. any plant of the genus *Godetia*, having showy rose-purple or reddish flowers. [mod.L f. C. H. *Godet*, Swiss botanist d. 1879]

godfather /ˈgɒdˌfɑːðə(r)/ n. **1** a male godparent. **2** esp. US a person directing an illegal organization, esp. the Mafia.

godhead /ˈgɒdhed/ n. (also **Godhead**) **1 a** the state of being God or a god. **b** divine nature. **2** a deity. **3** (**the Godhead**) God.

godless /ˈgɒdlɪs/ adj. **1** impious; wicked. **2** without a god. **3** not recognizing God. □ **godlessness** n.

godlike /ˈgɒdlaɪk/ adj. **1** resembling God or a god in some quality, esp. in physical beauty. **2** befitting or appropriate to a god.

godly /ˈgɒdlɪ/ adj. religious, pious, devout. □ **godliness** n.

godmother /ˈgɒdˌmʌðə(r)/ n. a female godparent.

godown /gəʊˈdaʊn/ n. a warehouse in parts of E. Asia. [Port. *gudão* f. Malay *godong* perh. f. Telugu *giḍangi* place where goods lie f. *kiḍu* lie]

godparent /ˈgɒdˌpeərənt/ n. a person who presents a child at baptism and responds on the child's behalf.

godsend /ˈgɒdsend/ n. an unexpected but welcome event or acquisition.

godson /ˈgɒdsʌn/ n. a male godchild.

godwit /ˈgɒdwɪt/ n. any wading bird of the genus *Limosa*, with long legs and a long straight or slightly upcurved bill. [16th c.: of unkn. orig.]

goer /ˈgəʊə(r)/ n. **1** a person or thing that goes (a *slow goer*). **2** (often in *comb.*) a person who attends, esp. regularly (a *churchgoer*). **3** colloq. **a** a lively or persevering person. **b** a sexually promiscuous person. **4** Austral. colloq. a project likely to be accepted or to succeed.

goes 3rd sing. present of GO[1].

gofer /ˈgəʊfə(r)/ n. esp. US sl. a person who runs errands, a dogsbody. [*go for* (see GO[1])]

goffer /ˈgəʊfə(r), ˈgɒf-/ v. & n. —v.tr. make wavy, flute, or crimp (a lace edge, a trimming, etc.) with heated irons. —n. an iron used for goffering. [F *gaufrer* stamp with a patterned tool f. *gaufre* honeycomb, rel. to WAFER, WAFFLE[2]]

goggle /ˈgɒg(ə)l/ v., adj., & n. —v. **1** intr. **a** (often foll. by *at*) look with wide-open eyes. **b** (of the eyes) be rolled about; protrude. **2** tr. turn (the eyes) sideways or from side to side. —adj. (usu. *attrib.*) (of the eyes) protuberant or rolling. —n. (in *pl.*) **1** spectacles for protecting the eyes from glare, dust, water, etc. **2** colloq. spectacles. **3** a goggling expression. □ **goggle-box** Brit. colloq. a television set. **goggle-eyed** having staring or protuberant eyes. [ME, prob. from a base *gog* (unrecorded) expressive of oscillating movement]

going /ˈgəʊɪŋ/ n. & adj. —n. **1 a** the act or process of going. **b** an instance of this; a departure. **2 a** the condition of the ground for walking, riding, etc. **b** progress affected by this (*found the going hard*). —adj. **1** in or into action (*set the clock going*). **2** existing, available; to be had (*there's cold beef going*). **3** current, prevalent (*the going rate*). □ **get going** start steadily talking, working, etc. (*can't stop him when he gets going*). **going concern** a thriving business. **going for one** colloq. acting in one's favour (*he has got a lot going for him*). **going on fifteen** etc. esp. US approaching one's fifteenth etc. birthday. **going on for** approaching (a time, an age, etc.) (*must be going on for 6 years*). **going-over 1** colloq. an inspection or overhaul. **2** sl. a thrashing. **3** US colloq. a scolding. **goings-on** /ˌgəʊɪŋzˈɒn/ behaviour, esp. morally suspect. **going to** intending or intended to; about to; likely to. **heavy going** slow or difficult to progress with. **to be going on with** to start with; for the time being. **while the going is good** while conditions are favourable. [GO[1]: in some senses f. earlier *a-going*: see A[2]]

goitre /ˈgɔɪtə(r)/ n. (US **goiter**) Med. a swelling of the neck resulting from enlargement of the thyroid gland. □ **goitred** adj. **goitrous** adj. [F, back-form. f. *goitreux* or f. Prov. *goitron*, ult. f. L *guttur* throat]

gold /gəʊld/ n. & adj. —n. **1 a** a yellow malleable ductile high density metallic element resistant to chemical reaction, occurring naturally in quartz veins and gravel, and precious as a monetary medium, in jewellery, etc. **2** the colour of gold. **3 a** coins or articles made of gold. **b** money in large sums, wealth. **4** something precious, beautiful, or brilliant (*all that glitters is not gold*). **5** = **gold medal**. **6** the bull's-eye of an archery target (usu. gilt). —adj. **1** made wholly or chiefly of gold. **2** coloured like gold. □ **gold brick** sl. **1** a thing with only a surface appearance of value, a sham or fraud. **2** US a lazy person. **gold card** a kind of preferential charge card giving privileges and benefits not available to holders of the standard card. **gold-digger 1** sl. a woman who wheedles money out of men. **2** a person who digs for gold. **gold-dust 1** gold in fine particles as often found naturally. **2** a plant, *Alyssum saxatile*, with many small yellow flowers. **gold-field** a district in which gold is found as a mineral. **gold foil** gold beaten into a thin sheet. **gold leaf** gold beaten into a very thin sheet. **gold medal** a medal of gold, usu. awarded as first prize. **gold-mine 1** a place where gold is mined. **2** colloq. a source of wealth. **gold plate 1** vessels made of gold. **2** material plated with gold. **gold-plate** v.tr. plate with gold. **gold reserve** a reserve of gold coins or bullion held by a central bank etc. **gold-rush** a rush to a newly-discovered gold-field. **gold standard** a system by which the value of a currency is defined in terms of gold, for which the currency may be exchanged. [OE f. Gmc]

goldcrest /ˈgəʊldkrest/ n. a small bird, *Regulus regulus*, with a golden crest.

golden /ˈgəʊld(ə)n/ adj. **1 a** made or consisting of gold. **b** yielding gold. **2** coloured or shining like gold (*golden hair*). **3** precious; valuable; excellent; important (a *golden memory*; a *golden opportunity*). □ **golden age 1** a supposed past age when people were happy and innocent. **2** the period of a nation's greatest prosperity, literary merit, etc. **golden-ager** US an old person. **golden balls** a pawnbroker's sign.

golden boy (or **girl**) *colloq.* a popular or successful person. **golden calf** wealth as an object of worship (Exod. 32). **golden delicious** a variety of dessert apple. **golden disc** an award given to a performer after the sale of 500,000 copies of a record. **golden eagle** a large eagle, *Aquila chrysaetos*, with yellow-tipped head-feathers. **Golden Fleece** (in Greek mythology) a fleece of gold sought and won by Jason. **golden goose** a continuing source of wealth or profit. **golden handshake** *colloq.* a payment given on redundancy or early retirement. **golden hello** *colloq.* a payment made by an employer to a keenly sought recruit. **golden jubilee 1** the fiftieth anniversary of a sovereign's accession. **2** any other fiftieth anniversary. **golden mean 1** the principle of moderation, as opposed to excess. **2** = *golden section.* **golden oldie** *colloq.* an old hit record or film etc. that is still well known and popular. **golden opinions** high regard. **golden retriever** a retriever with a thick golden-coloured coat. **golden rule** a basic principle of action, esp. 'do as you would be done by'. **golden section** the division of a line so that the whole is to the greater part as that part is to the smaller part. **golden share** the controlling interest in a company, often retained by the government after a nationalized industry is privatized. **golden syrup** *Brit.* a pale treacle. **golden wedding** the fiftieth anniversary of a wedding. □ **goldenly** *adv.* **goldenness** *n.*

goldfinch /ˈgəʊldfɪntʃ/ *n.* any of various bright-coloured songbirds of the genus *Carduelis*, esp. the Eurasian *C. carduelis*, with a yellow band across each wing. [OE *goldfinc* (as GOLD, FINCH)]

goldfish /ˈgəʊldfɪʃ/ *n.* a small reddish-golden Chinese carp kept for ornament, *Carassius auratus.* □ **goldfish bowl 1** a globular glass container for goldfish. **2** a situation lacking privacy.

goldsmith /ˈgəʊldsmɪθ/ *n.* a worker in gold, a manufacturer of gold articles. [OE (as GOLD, SMITH)]

golf /gɒlf/ *n.* & *v.* —*n.* a game played on a course set in open country, in which a small hard ball is driven with clubs into a series of 18 or 9 holes with the fewest possible strokes. —*v.intr.* play golf. □ **golf-bag** a bag used for carrying clubs and balls. **golf ball 1** a ball used in golf. **2** *colloq.* a small ball used in some electric typewriters to carry the type. **golf cart 1** a trolley used for carrying clubs in golf. **2** a motorized cart for golfers and equipment. **golf club 1** a club used in golf. **2** an association for playing golf. **3** the premises used by a golf club. **golf-course** (or **-links**) the course on which golf is played. □ **golfer** *n.* [15th-c. Sc.: orig. unkn.]

golliwog /ˈgɒlɪˌwɒg/ *n.* a black-faced brightly dressed soft doll with fuzzy hair. [19th c.: perh. f. GOLLY¹ + US dial. *polliwog* tadpole]

gollop /ˈgɒləp/ *v.* & *n.* *colloq.* —*v.tr.* (**golloped**, **golloping**) swallow hastily or greedily. —*n.* a hasty gulp. [perh. f. GULP, infl. by GOBBLE¹]

golly¹ /ˈgɒlɪ/ *int.* expressing surprise. [euphem. for GOD]

golly² /ˈgɒlɪ/ *n.* (*pl.* **-ies**) *colloq.* = GOLLIWOG. [abbr.]

golosh *Brit.* var. of GALOSH.

-gon /gən/ *comb. form* forming nouns denoting plane figures with a specified number of angles (*hexagon; polygon; n-gon*). [Gk *-gōnos* -angled]

gonad /ˈgəʊnæd/ *n.* an animal organ producing gametes, e.g. the testis or ovary. □ **gonadal** /gəʊˈneɪd(ə)l/ *adj.* [mod.L *gonas gonad-* f. Gk *gonē, gonos* generation, seed]

gondola /ˈgɒndələ/ *n.* **1** a light flat-bottomed boat used on Venetian canals, worked by one oar at the stern. **2** a car suspended from an airship or balloon. **3** an island of shelves used to display goods in a supermarket. **4** a car attached to a ski-lift. [Venetian It., of obscure orig.]

gondolier /ˌgɒndəˈlɪə(r)/ *n.* the oarsman on a gondola. [F f. It. *gondoliere* (as GONDOLA)]

gone /gɒn/ *adj.* **1** (of time) past (*not until gone nine*). **2 a** lost; hopeless. **b** dead. **3** *colloq.* pregnant for a specified time (*already three months gone*). **4** *sl.* completely entranced. □ **be gone** depart; leave temporarily. **gone goose** (or **gosling**) *colloq.* a person or thing beyond hope. **gone on** *sl.* infatuated with. [past part. of GO¹]

goner /ˈgɒnə(r)/ *n.* *sl.* a person or thing that is doomed, ended, irrevocably lost, etc.; a dead person.

gonfalon /ˈgɒnfələn/ *n.* a banner, often with streamers, hung from a crossbar. □ **gonfalonier** /ˌgɒnfələˈnɪə(r)/ *n.* [It. *gonfalone* f. Gmc (cf. VANE)]

gong *n.* **1** a metal disc with a turned rim, giving a resonant note when struck. **2** a saucer-shaped bell. **3** *Brit. sl.* a medal; a decoration. [Malay *gong, gung* of imit. orig.]

gonorrhoea /ˌgɒnəˈrɪə/ *n.* (*US* **gonorrhea**) a venereal disease with inflammatory discharge from the urethra or vagina. □ **gonorrhoeal** *adj.* [LL f. Gk *gonorrhoia* f. *gonos* semen + *rhoia* flux]

goo *n.* **1** a sticky or slimy substance. **2** sickly sentiment. [20th c.: perh. f. *burgoo* (Naut. sl.) = porridge]

good /gʊd/ *adj., n.,* & *adv.* —*adj.* (**better, best**) **1** having the right or desired qualities; satisfactory, adequate. **2 a** (of a person) efficient, competent (*good at French; a good driver*). **b** (of a thing) reliable, efficient (*good brakes*). **c** (of health etc.) strong (*good eyesight*). **3 a** kind, benevolent (*good of you to come*). **b** morally excellent; virtuous (*a good deed*). **c** charitable (*good works*). **d** well-behaved (*a good child*). **4** enjoyable, agreeable (*a good party; good news*). **5** thorough, considerable (*a good wash*). **6 a** not less than (*waited a good hour*). **b** considerable in number, quality, etc. (*a good many people*). **7** healthy, beneficial (*milk is good for you*). **8 a** valid, sound (*a good reason*). **b** financially sound (*his credit is good*). **9** in exclamations of surprise (*good heavens!*). **10** right, proper, expedient (*thought it good to try*). **11** fresh, eatable, untainted (*is the meat still good?*). **12** (sometimes patronizing) commendable, worthy (*good old George; my good man*). **13** well shaped, attractive (*has good legs; good looks*). **14** in courteous greetings and farewells (*good afternoon*). —*n.* **1** (only in *sing.*) that which is good; what is beneficial or morally right (*only good can come of it; did it for your own good; what good will it do?*). **2** (only in *sing.*) a desirable end or object; a thing worth attaining (*sacrificing the present for a future good*). **3** (in *pl.*) **a** movable property or merchandise. **b** *Brit.* things to be transported, as distinct from passengers. **c** (prec. by *the*) *colloq.* what one has undertaken to supply (esp.

deliver the goods). **d** (prec. by *the*) *sl.* the real thing; the genuine article. **4** (as *pl.*; prec. by *the*) virtuous people. —*adv. US colloq.* well (*doing pretty good*). □ **as good as** practically (*he as good as told me*). **be so good as** (or **be good enough**) **to** (often in a request) be kind and do (a favour) (*be so good as to open the window*). **be (a certain amount) to the good** have as net profit or advantage. **do good** show kindness. **do a person good** be beneficial to. **for good (and all)** finally, permanently. **good and** *colloq.* used as an intensifier before an adj. or adv. (*raining good and hard*). **the good book** the Bible. **good breeding** correct or courteous manners. **good for 1** beneficial to; having a good effect on. **2** able to perform; inclined for (*good for a ten-mile walk*). **3** able to be trusted to pay (*is good for £100*). **good-for-nothing** (or **-nought**) *adj.* worthless. —*n.* a worthless person. **good for you!** (or **him!, her!,** etc.) exclamation of approval towards a person. **Good Friday** the Friday before Easter Sunday commemorating the Crucifixion of Christ. **good-hearted** kindly, well-meaning. **good humour** a genial mood. **a good job** a fortunate state of affairs (*it's a good job you came early*). **good-looker** a handsome or attractive person. **good-looking** handsome; attractive. **good luck 1** good fortune, happy chance. **2** exclamation of well-wishing. **good money 1** genuine money; money that might usefully have been spent elsewhere. **2** *colloq.* high wages. **good nature** a friendly disposition. **good on you!** (or **him!** etc.) = *good for you!* **good-time** recklessly pursuing pleasure. **good times** a period of prosperity. **good will** the intention and hope that good will result (see also GOODWILL). **a good word** (often in phr. **put in a good word for**) words in recommendation or defence of a person. **good works** charitable acts. **have the goods on a person** *sl.* have advantageous information about a person. **have a good time** enjoy oneself. **in good time 1** with no risk of being late. **2** (also **all in good time**) in due course but without haste. **make good 1** make up for, compensate for, pay (an expense). **2** fulfil (a promise); effect (a purpose or an intended action). **3** demonstrate the truth of (a statement); substantiate (a charge). **4** gain and hold (a position). **5** replace or restore (a thing lost or damaged). **6** (*absol.*) accomplish what one intended. **no good 1** mischief (*is up to no good*). **2** useless; to no advantage (*it is no good arguing*). **no-good** —*adj.* useless. —*n.* a useless thing or person. **take in good part** not be offended by. **to the good** having as profit or benefit. □ **goodish** *adj.* [OE *gōd* f. Gmc]

goodbye /gʊd'baɪ/ *int.* & *n.* (*US* **goodby**) —*int.* expressing good wishes on parting, ending a telephone conversation, etc., or said with reference to a thing got rid of or irrevocably lost. —*n.* (*pl.* **goodbyes** or *US* **goodbys**) the saying of 'goodbye'; a parting; a farewell. [contr. of *God be with you!* with *good* substituted after *good night* etc.]

good-humoured /gʊd'hjuːməd/ *adj.* genial, cheerful, amiable. □ **good-humouredly** *adv.*

goodly /'gʊdlɪ/ *adj.* (**goodlier, goodliest**) **1** comely, handsome. **2** of imposing size etc. □ **goodliness** *n.* [OE *gōdlic* (as GOOD, -LY¹)]

good-natured /gʊd'neɪtʃəd/ *adj.* kind, patient; easygoing. □ **good-naturedly** *adv.*

goodness /'gʊdnɪs/ *n.* & *int.* —*n.* **1** virtue; excellence, esp. moral. **2** kindness, generosity (*had the goodness to wait*). **3** what is good or beneficial in a thing (*vegetables with all the goodness boiled out*). —*int.* expressing surprise, anger, etc. [OE *gōdnes* (as GOOD, -NESS)]

goodo /'gʊdəʊ/ *adj. Austral.* & *NZ* = GOOD *adj.* 10.

good-tempered /gʊd'tempəd/ *adj.* having a good temper; not easily annoyed. □ **good-temperedly** *adv.*

goodwill /gʊd'wɪl/ *n.* **1** kindly feeling. **2** the established reputation of a business etc. as enhancing its value. **3** cheerful acquiescence; zeal.

goody /'gʊdɪ/ *n.* & *int.* —*n.* (also **goodie**) (*pl.* **-ies**) **1** *colloq.* a good or favoured person, esp. a hero in a story, film, etc. **2** (usu. in *pl.*) something good or attractive, esp. to eat. **3** = GOODY-GOODY *n.* —*int.* expressing childish delight.

goody-goody /'gʊdɪ,gʊdɪ/ *n.* & *adj. colloq.* —*n.* a smug or obtrusively virtuous person. —*adj.* obtrusively or smugly virtuous.

gooey /'guːɪ/ *adj.* (**gooier, gooiest**) *sl.* **1** viscous, sticky. **2** sickly, sentimental. □ **gooeyness** *n.* (also **gooiness**). [GOO + -Y²]

goof /guːf/ *n.* & *v. sl.* —*n.* **1** a foolish or stupid person. **2** a mistake. —*v.* **1** *tr.* bungle. **2** *intr.* make a mistake. **3** *intr.* (often foll. by *off*) idle. [var. of dial. *goff* f. F *goffe* f. It. *goffo* f. med.L *gufus* coarse]

goofy /'guːfɪ/ *adj.* (**goofier, goofiest**) **1** stupid, silly, daft. **2** having protruding or crooked front teeth. □ **goofily** *adv.* **goofiness** *n.*

googly /'guːglɪ/ *n.* (*pl.* **-ies**) *Cricket* an off-break ball bowled with apparent leg-break action. [20th c.: orig. unkn.]

googol /'guːgɒl/ *n.* ten raised to the hundredth power (10^{100}). [arbitrary formation]

goolie /'guːlɪ/ *n.* (also **gooly**) (*pl.* **-ies**) (usu. in *pl.*) *sl.* a testicle. [app. of Ind. orig.; cf. Hind. *golī* bullet, ball, pill]

goon *n. sl.* **1** a stupid or playful person. **2** esp. *US* a person hired by racketeers etc. to terrorize political or industrial opponents. [perh. f. dial. *gooney* booby: infl. by the subhuman cartoon character 'Alice the *Goon*']

goopy /'guːpɪ/ *adj. sl.* (**goopier, goopiest**) stupid, fatuous. □ **goop** *n.* **goopiness** *n.*

goosander /guː'sændə(r)/ *n.* a large diving duck, *Mergus merganser*, with a narrow serrated bill. [prob. f. GOOSE + -ander in *bergander* sheldrake]

goose /guːs/ *n.* & *v.* —*n.* (*pl.* **geese** /giːs/) **1 a** any of various large water-birds of the family Anatidae, with short legs, webbed feet, and a broad bill. **b** the female of this (opp. GANDER). **c** the flesh of a goose as food. **2** *colloq.* a simpleton. —*v.tr. sl.* poke (a person) in the bottom. □ **goose-egg** *US* a zero score in a game. **goose-flesh** (or **-pimples** or **-skin** or *US* **bumps**) a bristling state of the skin produced by cold or fright. **goose-step** a military marching step in which the knees are kept stiff. [OE *gōs* f. Gmc]

gooseberry /'gʊzbərɪ/ *n.* (*pl.* **-ies**) **1** a round edible yellowish-green berry. **2** the thorny shrub, *Ribes grossularia*, bearing this fruit. □ **play gooseberry** *Brit. colloq.* be an unwanted extra (usu. third) person. [perh. f. GOOSE + BERRY]

goosefoot /ˈguːsfʊt/ n. (pl. **-foots**) any plant of the genus *Chenopodium*, having leaves shaped like the foot of a goose.

goosegrass /ˈguːsgrɑːs/ n. cleavers.

gopher¹ /ˈɡəʊfə(r)/ n. 1 (in full **pocket gopher**) any burrowing rodent of the family Geomyidae, native to N. America, having external cheek pouches and sharp front teeth. 2 a N. American ground squirrel. 3 a tortoise, *Gopherus polyphemus*, native to the southern US. [18th c.: orig. uncert.]

gopher² /ˈɡəʊfə(r)/ n. 1 *Bibl.* a tree from the wood of which Noah's ark was made. 2 (in full **gopher-wood**) a tree, *Cladrastis lutea*, yielding yellowish timber. [Heb. *gōper*]

gorblimey /ɡɔːˈblaɪmɪ/ *int.* & n. *Brit. colloq.* —*int.* an expression of surprise, indignation, etc. —n. (pl. **-eys**) a soft service cap. [corrupt. of *God blind me*]

Gordian knot /ˈɡɔːdɪən/ n. **cut the Gordian knot** solve a problem by force or by evasion. [*Gordius*, king of Phrygia, who tied an intricate knot that remained tied until cut by Alexander the Great]

gore¹ /ɡɔː(r)/ n. blood shed and clotted. [OE *gor* dung, dirt]

gore² /ɡɔː(r)/ v.tr. pierce with a horn, tusk, etc. [ME: orig. unkn.]

gore³ /ɡɔː(r)/ n. & v. —n. a wedge-shaped piece in a garment or umbrella etc. —v.tr. shape with a gore. [OE *gāra* triangular piece of land, rel. to OE *gār* spear, a spearhead being triangular]

gorge /ɡɔːdʒ/ n. & v. —n. 1 a narrow opening between hills or a rocky ravine, often with a stream running through it. 2 an act of gorging; a feast. 3 the contents of the stomach; what has been swallowed. —v. 1 *intr.* feed greedily. 2 *tr.* a (often *refl.*) satiate, glut. b swallow, devour greedily. □ **one's gorge rises at** one is sickened by. □ **gorger** n. [ME f. OF *gorge* throat ult. f. L *gurges* whirlpool]

gorgeous /ˈɡɔːdʒəs/ adj. 1 richly coloured, sumptuous, magnificent. 2 *colloq.* very pleasant, splendid (*gorgeous weather*). 3 *colloq.* strikingly beautiful. □ **gorgeously** adv. **gorgeousness** n. [earlier *gorgayse*, *-yas* f. OF *gorgias* fine, elegant, of unkn. orig.]

gorgon /ˈɡɔːɡən/ n. 1 (in Greek mythology) each of three snake-haired sisters (esp. Medusa) with the power to turn anyone who looked at them to stone. 2 a frightening or repulsive person, esp. a woman. □ **gorgonian** /ɡɔːˈɡəʊnɪən/ adj. [L *Gorgo -onis* f. Gk *Gorgō* f. *gorgos* terrible]

Gorgonzola /ˌɡɔːɡənˈzəʊlə/ n. a type of rich cheese with bluish-green veins. [*Gorgonzola* in Italy]

gorilla /ɡəˈrɪlə/ n. the largest anthropoid ape, *Gorilla gorilla*, native to Central Africa. [adopted as the specific name in 1847 f. Gk *Gorillai* an African tribe noted for hairiness]

gormandize /ˈɡɔːməndaɪz/ v. (also **-ise**) 1 *intr.* & *tr.* eat or devour voraciously. 2 *intr.* indulge in good eating. □ **gormandizer** n. [as GOURMANDISE]

gormless /ˈɡɔːmlɪs/ adj. esp. *Brit. colloq.* foolish, lacking sense. □ **gormlessly** adv. **gormlessness** n. [orig. *gaumless* f. dial. *gaum* understanding]

gorse /ɡɔːs/ n. any spiny yellow-flowered shrub of the genus *Ulex*. □ **gorsy** adj. [OE *gors*(t) rel. to OHG *gersta*, L *hordeum*, barley]

gory /ˈɡɔːrɪ/ adj. (**gorier, goriest**) 1 involving bloodshed; bloodthirsty (*a gory film*). 2 covered in gore. □ **gorily** adv. **goriness** n.

gosh /ɡɒʃ/ int. expressing surprise. [euphem. for GOD]

goshawk /ˈɡɒshɔːk/ n. a large short-winged hawk, *Accipiter gentilis*. [OE *gōs-hafoc* (as GOOSE, HAWK¹)]

gosling /ˈɡɒzlɪŋ/ n. a young goose. [ME, orig. *gesling* f. ON *gǽslingr*]

gospel /ˈɡɒsp(ə)l/ n. 1 the teaching or revelation of Christ. 2 (**Gospel**) a the record of Christ's life and teaching in the first four books of the New Testament. b each of these books. c a portion from one of them read at a service. 3 a thing regarded as absolutely true (*take my word as gospel*). 4 a principle one acts on or advocates. 5 (in full **gospel music**) Black American evangelical religious singing. □ **gospel truth** something as true as the Gospel. [OE *gōdspel* (as GOOD, *spel* news, SPELL¹), rendering eccl.L *bona annuntiatio*, *bonus nuntius* = *evangelium* good news: assoc. with GOD]

gospeller /ˈɡɒspələ(r)/ n. the reader of the Gospel in a Communion service. □ **hot gospeller** a zealous puritan; a rabid propagandist.

gossamer /ˈɡɒsəmə(r)/ n. & adj. —n. 1 a filmy substance of small spiders' webs. 2 delicate filmy material. —adj. light and flimsy as gossamer. □ **gossamered** adj. **gossamery** adj. [ME *gos(e)somer(e)*, app. f. GOOSE + SUMMER (*goose summer* = St Martin's summer, i.e. early November when geese were eaten, gossamer being common then)]

gossip /ˈɡɒsɪp/ n. & v. —n. 1 a easy or unconstrained talk or writing esp. about persons or social incidents. b idle talk; groundless rumour. 2 an informal chat, esp. about persons or social incidents. 3 a person who indulges in gossip. —v.intr. (**gossiped, gossiping**) talk or write gossip. □ **gossip column** a section of a newspaper devoted to gossip about well-known people. □ **gossiper** n. **gossipy** adj. [earlier sense 'godparent': f. OE *godsibb* person related to one in GOD: see SIB]

got past and past part. of GET.

Goth /ɡɒθ/ n. a member of a Germanic tribe that invaded the Roman Empire in the 3rd–5th c. [LL *Gothi* (pl.) f. Gk *Go(t)thoi* f. Goth.]

goth /ɡɒθ/ n. 1 a style of rock music with an intense or droning blend of guitars, bass, and drums, often with apocalyptic or mystical lyrics. 2 a performer or devotee of this music or a member of the subculture favouring black clothing and white-painted faces with black make-up.

Gothic /ˈɡɒθɪk/ adj. & n. —adj. 1 of the Goths or their language. 2 in the style of architecture prevalent in W. Europe in the 12th–16th c., characterized by pointed arches. 3 (of a novel etc.) in a style popular in the 18th–19th c., with supernatural or horrifying events. 4 *Printing* (of type) old-fashioned German, black letter, or sanserif. —n. 1 the Gothic language. 2 Gothic architecture. 3 *Printing* Gothic type. □ **Gothically** adv. **Gothicism** /-ˌsɪz(ə)m/ n. **Gothicize** /-ˌsaɪz/ v.tr. & intr. (also **-ise**). [F *gothique* or LL *gothicus* f. *Gothi*: see GOTH]

gotten US past part. of GET.

gouache /ɡʊˈɑːʃ, gwɑːʃ/ n. 1 a method of painting in opaque pigments ground in water and thickened with a gluelike substance. **2** these pigments. **3** a picture painted in this way. [F f. It. *guazzo*]

Gouda /ˈgaʊdə/ n. a flat round usu. Dutch cheese with a yellow rind. [*Gouda* in Holland, where orig. made]

gouge /gaʊdʒ/ n. & v. —*n.* **1** a chisel with a concave blade, used in carpentry, sculpture, and surgery. **2** an indentation or groove made with or as with this. —*v.* **1** *tr.* cut with or as with a gouge. **2** *tr.* **a** (foll. by *out*) force out (esp. an eye with the thumb) with or as with a gouge. **b** force out the eye of (a person). □ **gouger** n. [F f. LL *gubia*, perh. of Celt. orig.]

goulash /ˈguːlæʃ/ n. a highly-seasoned Hungarian dish of meat and vegetables, usu. flavoured with paprika. [Magyar *gulyás-hús* f. *gulyás* herdsman + *hús* meat]

gourd /gʊəd/ n. **1 a** any of various fleshy usu. large fruits with a hard skin. **b** any of various climbing or trailing plants of the family Cucurbitaceae bearing this fruit. **2** the hollow hard skin of the gourd-fruit, dried and used as a drinking-vessel, water container, etc. □ **gourdful** n. (pl. **-fuls**). [ME f. AF *gurde*, OF *gourde* ult. f. L *cucurbita*]

gourmand /ˈgʊəmænd/ n. & adj. —*n.* a glutton. —*adj.* gluttonous; fond of eating, esp. to excess. □ **gourmandism** n. [ME f. OF, of unkn. orig.]

■ **Usage** This word is sometimes used to mean GOURMET, but the use is considered incorrect by some people.

gourmandise /ˈgʊəmɑ̃diːz/ n. the habits of a gourmand; gluttony. [F (as GOURMAND)]

gourmet /ˈgʊəmeɪ/ n. a connoisseur of good or delicate food. [F, = wine-taster: sense infl. by GOURMAND]

gout /gaʊt/ n. **1** a disease with inflammation of the smaller joints, esp. the toe, as a result of excess uric acid salts in the blood. **2** *archaic* **a** a drop, esp. of blood. **b** a splash or spot. □ **gouty** adj. **goutily** adv. **goutiness** n. [ME f. OF *goute* f. L *gutta* drop, with ref. to the medieval theory of the flowing down of humours]

govern /ˈgʌv(ə)n/ v. **1 a** *tr.* rule or control (a State, subject, etc.) with authority; conduct the policy and affairs of (an organization etc.). **b** *intr.* be in government. **2 a** *tr.* influence or determine (a person or a course of action). **b** *intr.* be the predominating influence. **3** *tr.* be a standard or principle for; constitute a law for; serve to decide (a case). **4** *tr.* check or control (esp. passions). **5** *tr. Gram.* (esp. of a verb or preposition) have (a noun or pronoun or its case) depending on it. □ **governable** adj. **governability** /-nəˈbɪlɪtɪ/ n. **governableness** n. [ME f. OF *governer* f. L *gubernare* steer, rule f. Gk *kubernaō*]

governance /ˈgʌvənəns/ n. **1** the act or manner of governing. **2** the office or function of governing. **3** sway, control. [ME f. OF (as GOVERN)]

governess /ˈgʌvənɪs/ n. a woman employed to teach children in a private household. [earlier *governeress* f. OF *governeresse* (as GOVERNOR)]

governessy /ˈgʌvənɪsɪ/ adj. characteristic of a governess; prim.

government /ˈgʌvənmənt/ n. **1** the act or manner of governing. **2** the system by which a State or community is governed. **3 a** a body of persons governing a State. **b** (usu. **Government**) a

particular ministry in office. **4** the State as an agent. □ **governmental** /-ˈment(ə)l/ adj. **governmentally** /-ˈmentəlɪ/ adv. [ME f. OF *governement* (as GOVERN)]

governor /ˈgʌvənə(r)/ n. **1** a person who governs; a ruler. **2 a** an official governing a province, town, etc. **b** a representative of the Crown in a colony. **3** the executive head of each State of the US. **4** an officer commanding a fortress or garrison. **5** the head or a member of a governing body of an institution. **6** the official in charge of a prison. **7 a** *sl.* one's employer. **b** *sl.* one's father. **8** *Mech.* an automatic regulator controlling the speed of an engine etc. □ **Governor-General** the representative of the Crown in a Commonwealth country that regards the Queen as Head of State. □ **governorate** /-rət/ n. **governorship** n. [ME f. AF *gouvernour*, OF *governēo(u)r* f. L *gubernator -oris* (as GOVERN)]

gown /gaʊn/ n. & v. —*n.* **1** a loose flowing garment, esp. a long dress worn by a woman. **2** the official robe of an alderman, judge, cleric, member of a university, etc. **3** a surgeon's overall. —*v.tr.* (usu. as **gowned** adj.) attire in a gown. [ME f. OF *goune*, *gon(n)e* f. LL *gunna* fur garment: cf. med. Gk *gouna* fur]

goy /gɔɪ/ n. (pl. **goyim** /ˈgɔɪɪm/ or **goys**) *sl. derog.* a Jewish name for a non-Jew. □ **goyish** adj. (also **goyisch**). [Heb. *gōy* people, nation]

GP abbr. general practitioner.

Gp. Capt. abbr. (in the RAF) Group Captain.

GPO abbr. **1** General Post Office. **2** US Government Printing Office.

gr abbr. (also **gr.**) **1** gram(s). **2** grains. **3** gross.

grab v. & n. —*v.* (**grabbed**, **grabbing**) **1** *tr.* **a** seize suddenly. **b** capture, arrest. **2** *tr.* take greedily or unfairly. **3** *tr. sl.* attract the attention of, impress. **4** *intr.* (foll. by *at*) make a sudden snatch at. **5** *intr.* (of the brakes of a motor vehicle) act harshly or jerkily. —*n.* **1** a sudden clutch or attempt to seize. **2** a mechanical device for clutching. **3** the practice of grabbing. □ **grab-bag** US a lucky dip. **grab handle** (or **rail** etc.) a handle or rail etc. to steady passengers in a moving vehicle. **up for grabs** *sl.* easily obtainable; inviting capture. □ **grabber** n. [MLG, MDu. *grabben*: cf. GRIP, GRIPE, GROPE]

grabby /ˈgræbɪ/ adj. *colloq.* tending to grab; greedy, grasping.

graben /ˈgrɑːbən/ n. (pl. same or **grabens**) *Geol.* a depression of the earth's surface between faults. [G, orig. = ditch]

grace n. & v. —*n.* **1** attractiveness, esp. in elegance of proportion or manner or movement; gracefulness. **2** courteous good will (*had the grace to apologize*). **3** an attractive feature; an accomplishment (*social graces*). **4 a** (in Christian belief) the unmerited favour of God; a divine saving and strengthening influence. **b** the state of receiving this. **c** a divinely given talent. **5** goodwill, favour (*fall from grace*). **6** delay granted as a favour (*a year's grace*). **7** a short thanksgiving before or after a meal. **8** (**Grace**) (in Greek mythology) each of three beautiful sister goddesses, bestowers of beauty and charm. **9** (**Grace**) (prec. by *His*, *Her*, *Your*) forms of description or address for a duke, duchess, or archbishop. —*v.tr.* (often foll. by *with*) add grace to, enhance; confer honour or dignity on (*graced us with his presence*). □ **days of grace** the time allowed by law for payment of a sum due.

grace-note *Mus.* an extra note as an embellishment not essential to the harmony or melody. **in a person's good** (or **bad**) **graces** regarded by a person with favour (or disfavour). **with good** (or **bad**) **grace** as if willingly (or reluctantly). [ME f. OF f. L *gratia* f. *gratus* pleasing: cf. GRATEFUL]

graceful /ˈgreɪsfʊl/ *adj.* having or showing grace or elegance. □ **gracefully** *adv.* **gracefulness** *n.*

graceless /ˈgreɪslɪs/ *adj.* lacking grace or elegance or charm. □ **gracelessly** *adv.* **gracelessness** *n.*

gracile /ˈgræsaɪl, -sɪl/ *adj.* slender; gracefully slender. □ **gracility** *n.* [L *gracilis* slender]

gracious /ˈgreɪʃəs/ *adj.* & *int.* —*adj.* **1** kind; indulgent and beneficent to inferiors. **2** (of God) merciful, benign. —*int.* expressing surprise. □ **gracious living** an elegant way of life. □ **graciosity** /ˌgreɪsɪˈɒsɪtɪ/ *n.* **graciously** *adv.* **graciousness** *n.* [ME f. OF f. L *gratiosus* (as GRACE)]

grackle /ˈgræk(ə)l/ *n.* **1** any of various orioles, esp. of the genus *Quiscalus*, native to America. **2** any of various minas, esp. of the genus *Gracula*, native to Asia. [mod.L *Gracula* f. L *graculus* jackdaw]

gradate /grəˈdeɪt/ *v.* **1** *v.intr.* & *tr.* pass or cause to pass by gradations from one shade to another. **2** *tr.* arrange in steps or grades of size etc. [back-form. f. GRADATION]

gradation /grəˈdeɪʃ(ə)n/ *n.* (usu. in *pl.*) **1** a stage of transition or advance. **2 a** a certain degree in rank, intensity, merit, divergence, etc. **b** such a degree; an arrangement in such degrees. **3** (of paint etc.) the gradual passing from one shade, tone, etc., to another. □ **gradational** *adj.* **gradationally** *adv.* [L *gradatio* f. *gradus* step]

grade *n.* & *v.* —*n.* **1 a** a certain degree in rank, merit, proficiency, quality, etc. **b** a class of persons or things of the same grade. **2 a** a mark indicating the quality of a student's work. **b** an examination, esp. in music. **3** US a class in school, concerned with a particular year's work and usu. numbered from the first upwards. **4 a** a gradient or slope. **b** the rate of ascent or descent. —*v.* **1** *tr.* arrange in or allocate to grades; class, sort. **2** *intr.* (foll. by *up, down, off, into,* etc.) pass gradually between grades, or into a grade. **3** *tr.* give a grade to (a student). **4** *tr.* blend so as to affect the grade of colour with tints passing into each other. □ **grade crossing** US = *level crossing.* **grade school** US elementary school. **make the grade** *colloq.* succeed; reach the desired standard. [F *grade* or L *gradus* step]

grader /ˈgreɪdə(r)/ *n.* **1** a person or thing that grades. **2** (in *comb.*) US a pupil in a specified school grade.

gradient /ˈgreɪdɪənt/ *n.* **1 a** a stretch of road, railway, etc., that slopes from the horizontal. **b** the amount of such a slope. **2** the rate of rise or fall of temperature, pressure, etc., in passing from one region to another. [prob. formed on GRADE after *salient*]

gradual /ˈgrædjʊəl/ *adj.* **1** taking place or progressing slowly or by degrees. **2** not rapid or steep or abrupt. □ **gradually** *adv.* **gradualness** *n.* [med.L *gradualis, -ale* f. L *gradus* step]

gradualism /ˈgrædjʊəˌlɪz(ə)m/ *n.* a policy of gradual reform rather than sudden change or revolution. □ **gradualist** *n.* **gradualistic** /-ˈlɪstɪk/ *adj.*

graduate *n.* & *v.* —*n.* /ˈgrædjʊət/ **1** a person who has been awarded an academic degree (also *attrib.*: *graduate student*). **2** US a person who has completed a school course. —*v.* /ˈgrædjʊˌeɪt/ **1 a** *intr.* take an academic degree. **b** *tr.* US admit to an academic degree or a certificate of completion of School Studies. **2** *intr.* **a** (foll. by *from*) be a graduate of a specified university. **b** (foll. by *in*) be a graduate in a specified subject. **3** *tr.* US send out as a graduate from a university etc. **4** *intr.* a (foll. by *to*) move up to (a higher grade of activity etc.). **b** (foll. by *as, in*) gain specified qualifications. **5** *tr.* mark out in degrees or parts. **6** *tr.* arrange in gradations; apportion (e.g. tax) according to a scale. **7** *intr.* (foll. by *into, away*) pass by degrees. □ **graduated pension** (in the UK) a system of pension contributions by employees in proportion to their wages or salary. **graduate school** a department of a university for advanced work by graduates. □ **graduator** *n.* [med.L *graduari* take a degree f. L *gradus* step]

graduation /ˌgrædjʊˈeɪʃ(ə)n/ *n.* **1** the act or an instance of graduating or being graduated. **2** a ceremony at which degrees are conferred. **3** each or all of the marks on a vessel or instrument indicating degrees of quantity etc.

Graecism /ˈgriːkɪz(ə)m, -sɪz(ə)m/ *n.* (also **Grecism**) **1** a Greek idiom, esp. as imitated in another language. **2** the Greek spirit, style, mode of expression, etc. [F *grécisme* or med.L *Graecismus* f. *Graecus* GREEK]

Graeco- /ˈgriːkəʊ/ *comb. form* (also **Greco-**) Greek; Greek and. [L *Graecus* GREEK]

graffito /grəˈfiːtəʊ/ *n.* (*pl.* **graffiti** /-tiː/) (usu. in *pl.*) a piece of writing or drawing scribbled, scratched, or sprayed on a surface. [It. f. *graffio* a scratch]

■ **Usage** The singular or collective use of the form *graffiti* is considered incorrect by some people but is frequently found, e.g. *graffiti has appeared.*

graft¹ /grɑːft/ *n.* & *v.* —*n.* **1** *Bot.* **a** a shoot or scion inserted into a slit of stock, from which it receives sap. **b** the place where a graft is inserted. **2** *Surgery* a piece of living tissue, organ, etc., transplanted surgically. **3** *sl.* hard work. —*v.* **1** *tr.* **a** (often foll. by *into, on, together,* etc.) insert (a scion) as a graft. **b** insert a graft on (a stock). **2** *intr.* insert a graft. **3** *tr. Surgery* transplant (living tissue). **4** *tr.* (foll. by *in, on*) insert or fix (a thing) permanently to another. **5** *intr. sl.* work hard. □ **grafter** *n.* [ME (earlier *graff*) f. OF *grafe, grefe* f. L *graphium* f. Gk *graphion* stylus f. *graphō* write]

graft² /grɑːft/ *n.* & *v. colloq.* —*n.* **1** practices, esp. bribery, used to secure illicit gains in politics or business. **2** such gains. —*v.intr.* seek or make such gains. □ **grafter** *n.* [19th c.: orig. unkn.]

Grail *n.* (in full **Holy Grail**) (in medieval legend) the cup or platter used by Christ at the Last Supper, and in which Joseph of Arimathea received Christ's blood at the Cross, esp. as the object of quests by medieval knights. [ME f. OF *graal* etc. f. med.L *gradalis* dish, of unkn. orig.]

grain *n.* & *v.* —*n.* **1** a fruit or seed of a cereal. **2 a** (*collect.*) wheat or any allied grass used as food, corn. **b** (*collect.*) their fruit. **c** any particular species of corn. **3 a** a small hard particle of salt, sand, etc. **b** a discrete particle or crystal, usu.

small, in a rock or metal. **4** The smallest unit of weight in the troy system (equivalent to $\frac{1}{480}$ of an ounce), and in the avoirdupois system (equivalent to $\frac{1}{437.5}$ of an ounce). **5** the smallest possible quantity (*not a grain of truth in it*). **6 a** roughness of surface. **b** *Photog.* a granular appearance on a photograph or negative. **7** the texture of skin, wood, stone, etc.; the arrangement and size of constituent particles. **8 a** a pattern of lines of fibre in wood or paper. **b** lamination or planes of cleavage in stone, coal, etc. **9** nature, temper, tendency. —*v.* **1** *tr.* paint in imitation of the grain of wood or marble. **2** *tr.* give a granular surface to. **3** *tr.* & *intr.* form into grains. □ **against the grain** contrary to one's natural inclination or feeling. **in grain** thorough, genuine, by nature, downright, indelible. □ **grained** *adj.* (also in comb.). **grainer** *n.* **grainless** *adj.* [ME f. OF f. L *granum*]

grainy /ˈgreɪnɪ/ *adj.* (**grainier, grainiest**) **1** granular. **2** resembling the grain of wood. **3** *Photog.* having a granular appearance. □ **graininess** *n.*

grallatorial /ˌgræləˈtɔːrɪəl/ *adj.* *Zool.* of or relating to long-legged wading birds, e.g. storks. [mod.L *grallatorius* f. L *grallator* stilt-walker f. *grallae* stilts]

gram *n.* (also **gramme**) a metric unit of mass equal to one-thousandth of a kilogram. □ **gram-atom** *Chem.* the quantity of a chemical element equal to its relative atomic mass in grams. **gram-equivalent** *Chem.* the quantity of a substance equal to its equivalent weight in grams. **gram-molecule** *Chem.* the quantity of a substance equal to its relative molecular mass in grams. [F *gramme* f. Gk *gramma* small weight]

-gram /græm/ *comb. form* forming nouns denoting a thing written or recorded (often in a certain way) (*anagram; monogram; telegram*). □ **-grammatic** /grəˈmætɪk/ *comb. form* forming adjectives. [from or after Gk *gramma -atos* thing written, letter of the alphabet, f. *graphō* write]

graminaceous /ˌgræmɪˈneɪʃəs/ *adj.* of or like grass; grassy. [L *gramen -inis* grass]

gramineous /grəˈmɪnɪəs/ *adj.* = GRAMINACEOUS. [L *gramineus* f. *gramen -inis* grass]

graminivorous /ˌgræmɪˈnɪvərəs/ *adj.* feeding on grass, cereals, etc. [L *gramen -inis* grass + -VOROUS]

grammar /ˈgræmə(r)/ *n.* **1** the study or rules of a language's inflections or other means of showing the relation between words, including its phonetic system. **2** a person's manner or quality of observance or application of the rules of grammar (*bad grammar*). **3** a book on grammar. **4** the elements or rudiments of an art or science. **5** *Brit. colloq.* = grammar school. □ **grammar school** *Brit.* esp. *hist.* a selective State secondary school with a mainly academic curriculum. □ **grammarless** *adj.* [ME f. AF *gramere*, OF *gramaire* f. L *grammatica* f. Gk *grammatikē* (*tekhnē*) (art) of letters f. *gramma -atos* letter of the alphabet]

grammarian /grəˈmeərɪən/ *n.* an expert in grammar or linguistics; a philologist. [ME f. OF *gramarien*]

grammatical /grəˈmætɪk(ə)l/ *adj.* **1 a** of or relating to grammar. **b** determined by grammar, esp. by form or inflection (*grammatical gender*). **2** conforming to the rules of grammar, or to the formal principles of an art, science, etc. □

grammatically *adv.* **grammaticalness** *n.* [F *grammatical* or LL *grammaticalis* f. L *grammaticus* f. Gk *grammatikos* (as GRAMMAR)]

gramophone /ˈgræməˌfəʊn/ *n.* an instrument reproducing recorded sound by a stylus resting on a rotating grooved disc. □ **gramophonic** /-ˈfɒnɪk/ *adj.* [formed by inversion of the word *phonogram*]

grampus /ˈgræmpəs/ *n.* (*pl.* **grampuses**) **1** a dolphin, *Grampus griseus*, with a blunt snout and long pointed black flippers. **2** a person breathing heavily and loudly. [earlier *graundepose, grapeys* f. OF *grapois* etc. f. med.L *craspiscis* f. L *crassus piscis* fat fish]

gran *n.* *colloq.* grandmother (cf. GRANNY). [abbr.]

granadilla /ˌgrænəˈdɪlə/ *n.* (also **grenadilla** /ˌgren-/) a passion-fruit. [Sp., dimin. of *granada* pomegranate]

granary /ˈgrænərɪ/ *n.* (*pl.* **-ies**) **1** a storehouse for threshed grain. **2** a region producing, and esp. exporting, much corn. [L *granarium* f. *granum* grain]

grand /grænd/ *adj.* & *n.* —*adj.* **1 a** splendid, magnificent, imposing, dignified. **b** solemn or lofty in conception, execution, or expression; noble. **2** main; of chief importance (*grand staircase; grand entrance*). **3** (**Grand**) of the highest rank, esp. in official titles (*Grand Cross; grand vizier; Grand Inquisitor*). **4** *colloq.* excellent, enjoyable (*had a grand time; in grand condition*). **5** belonging to high society; wealthy (*the grand folk at the big house*). **6** (in comb.) in names of family relationships, denoting the second degree of ascent or descent (*granddaughter*). —*n.* **1** = grand piano. **2** (*pl.* same) (usu. in *pl.*) esp. *US sl.* a thousand dollars or pounds. □ **grand jury** esp. *US Law* a jury selected to examine the validity of an accusation prior to trial. **grand master 1** a chess-player of the highest class. **2** the head of a military order of knighthood, of Freemasons, etc. **Grand National** a steeplechase held annually at Aintree, Liverpool. **grand opera** opera on a serious theme, or in which the entire libretto (including dialogue) is sung. **grand piano** a large full-toned piano standing on three legs, with the body, strings, and soundboard arranged horizontally and in line with the keys. **grand slam 1** *Sport* the winning of all of a group of championships. **2** *Bridge* the winning of 13 tricks. **grand total** the final amount after everything is added up; the sum of other totals. □ **grandly** *adv.* **grandness** *n.* [ME f. AF *graunt*, OF *grant* f. L *grandis* full-grown]

grandad /ˈgrændæd/ *n.* (also **grand-dad**) *colloq.* **1** grandfather. **2** an elderly man.

grandchild /ˈgræntʃaɪld, ˈgrænd-/ *n.* (*pl.* **-children**) a child of one's son or daughter.

granddaughter /ˈgrænˌdɔːtə(r)/ *n.* a female grandchild.

grandee /grænˈdiː/ *n.* **1** a Spanish or Portuguese nobleman of the highest rank. **2** a person of high rank or eminence. [Sp. & Port. *grande*, assim. to -EE]

grandeur /ˈgrændjə(r), -ndʒə(r)/ *n.* **1** majesty, splendour; dignity of appearance or bearing. **2** high rank, eminence. **3** nobility of character. [F f. *grand* great, GRAND]

grandfather /ˈgrænˌfɑːðə(r), ˈgrænd-/ *n.* a male grandparent. □ **grandfather clock** a clock in a tall wooden case, driven by weights. □ **grandfatherly** *adj.*

grandiflora /ˌɡrændɪˈflɔːrə/ adj. bearing large flowers. [mod.L (often used in specific names of large-flowered plants) f. L grandis great + FLORA]

grandiloquent /ˌɡrænˈdɪləkwənt/ adj. 1 pompous or inflated in language. 2 given to boastful talk. □ **grandiloquence** n. **grandiloquently** adv. [L grandiloquus (as GRAND, -loquus -speaking f. loqui speak), after eloquent etc.]

grandiose /ˈɡrændɪˌəʊs/ adj. 1 producing or meant to produce an imposing effect. 2 planned on an ambitious or magnificent scale. □ **grandiosely** adv. **grandiosity** /-ˈɒsɪtɪ/ n. [F f. It. grandioso (as GRAND, -OSE¹)]

grandma /ˈɡrænmɑː, ˈɡrænd-/ n. colloq. grandmother.

grand mal /ɡrɑ̃ ˈmæl/ n. a serious form of epilepsy with loss of consciousness (cf. PETIT MAL). [F, = great sickness]

grandmother /ˈɡrænˌmʌðə(r), ˈɡrænd-/ n. a female grandparent. □ **grandmother clock** a clock like a grandfather clock but in a smaller case. □ **grandmotherly** adj.

grandpa /ˈɡrænpɑː, ˈɡrænd-/ n. colloq. grandfather.

grandparent /ˈɡrænˌpeərənt, ˈɡrænd-/ n. a parent of one's father or mother.

Grand Prix /ɡrɑ̃ ˈpriː/ n. any of several important international motor or motor-cycle racing events. [F, = great or chief prize]

grandsire /ˈɡrænˌsaɪə(r)/ n. archaic grandfather, old man, ancestor.

grandson /ˈɡrænsʌn, ˈɡrænd-/ n. a male grandchild.

grandstand /ˈɡrænstænd, ˈɡrænd-/ n. the main stand, usu. roofed, for spectators at a racecourse etc. □ **grandstand finish** a close and exciting finish to a race etc.

grange /ɡreɪndʒ/ n. a country house with farmbuildings. [ME f. AF graunge, OF grange f. med.L granica (villa) ult. f. L granum GRAIN]

graniferous /ɡrəˈnɪfərəs/ adj. producing grain or a grainlike seed. □ **graniform** /ˈɡrænɪˌfɔːm/ adj. [L granum GRAIN]

granite /ˈɡrænɪt/ n. 1 a granular crystalline igneous rock of quartz, mica, feldspar, etc., used for building. 2 a determined or resolute quality, attitude, etc. □ **granitic** /ɡrəˈnɪtɪk/ adj. **granitoid** adj. & n. [It. granito, lit. grained f. grano f. L granum GRAIN]

granivorous /ɡrəˈnɪvərəs/ adj. feeding on grain. □ **granivore** /ˈɡrænɪˌvɔː(r)/ n. [L granum GRAIN]

granny /ˈɡrænɪ/ n. (also **grannie**) (pl. **-ies**) colloq. grandmother. □ **granny flat** (or **annexe**) Brit. part of a house made into self-contained accommodation for an elderly relative. **granny knot** a reef-knot crossed the wrong way and therefore insecure. [obs. grannam f. AF graund dame (as GRAND, DAME) + -Y²]

Granny Smith /ˌɡrænɪ ˈsmɪθ/ n. an Australian green variety of apple. [Maria Ann ('Granny') Smith d. 1870]

grant /ɡrɑːnt/ v. & n. —v.tr. 1 **a** consent to fulfil (a request, wish, etc.) (granted all he asked). **b** allow (a person) to have (a thing) (granted me my freedom). **c** (as **granted**) colloq. apology accepted; pardon given. 2 give (rights, property, etc.) formally; transfer legally. 3 (often foll. by that + clause) admit as true; concede, esp. as a basis for argument. —n. 1 the process of granting or a thing granted. 2 a sum of money given by the State for any of various purposes, esp. to finance education. 3 Law **a** a legal conveyance by written instrument. **b** formal conferment. □ **grant-in-aid** (pl. **grants-in-aid**) a grant by central government to local government or an institution. **take for granted** 1 assume something to be true or valid. 2 cease to appreciate through familiarity. □ **grantable** adj. **grantee** /-ˈtiː/ n. (esp. in sense 2 of v.). **granter** n. **grantor** /-ˈtɔː(r)/ n. (esp. in sense 2 of v.). [ME f. OF gr(e)anter var. of creanter ult. f. part. of L credere entrust]

Granth /ɡrʌnt/ n. (also **Grunth**) the sacred scriptures of the Sikhs. [Hindi, = book, code f. Skr. grantha tying, literary composition]

granular /ˈɡrænjʊlə(r)/ adj. 1 of or like grains or granules. 2 having a granulated surface or structure. □ **granularity** /-ˈlærɪtɪ/ n. **granularly** adv. [LL granulum GRANULE]

granulate /ˈɡrænjʊˌleɪt/ v. 1 tr. & intr. form into grains (granulated sugar). 2 tr. roughen the surface of. 3 intr. (of a wound etc.) form small prominences as the beginning of healing; heal, join. □ **granulation** /-ˈleɪʃ(ə)n/ n. **granulator** n.

granule /ˈɡrænjuːl/ n. a small grain. [LL granulum, dimin. of L granum grain]

grape /ɡreɪp/ n. 1 a berry (usu. green, purple, or black) growing in clusters on a vine, used as fruit and in making wine. 2 (prec. by the) colloq. wine. □ **grape hyacinth** any liliaceous plant of the genus Muscari, with clusters of usu. blue flowers. □ **grapey** adj. (also **grapy**). [ME f. OF grape bunch of grapes prob. f. graper gather (grapes) f. grap(p)e hook, ult. f. Gmc]

grapefruit /ˈɡreɪpfruːt/ n. (pl. same) 1 a large round yellow citrus fruit with an acid juicy pulp. 2 the tree, Citrus paradisi, bearing this fruit.

grapeshot /ˈɡreɪpʃɒt/ n. hist. small balls used as charge in a cannon and scattering when fired.

grapevine /ˈɡreɪpvaɪn/ n. 1 any of various vines of the genus Vitis, esp. Vitis vinifera. 2 colloq. the means of transmission of unofficial information or rumour (heard it through the grapevine).

graph /ɡrɑːf, ɡræf/ n. & v. —n. a diagram showing the relation between variable quantities, usu. of two variables, each measured along one of a pair of axes at right angles. —v.tr. plot or trace on a graph. □ **graph paper** paper printed with a network of lines as a basis for drawing graphs. [abbr. of graphic formula]

-graph /ɡrɑːf/ comb. form forming nouns and verbs meaning: 1 a thing written or drawn etc. in a specified way (autograph; photograph). 2 an instrument that records (heliograph; seismograph; telegraph).

-grapher /ɡrəfə(r)/ comb. form forming nouns denoting a person concerned with a subject (geographer; radiographer). [from or after Gk -graphos writer + -ER¹]

graphic /ˈɡræfɪk/ adj. & n. —adj. 1 of or relating to the visual or descriptive arts, esp. writing and drawing. 2 vividly descriptive. 3 = GRAPHICAL. —n. a product of the graphic arts (cf. GRAPHICS). □ **graphic arts** the visual and technical arts involving design, writing, drawing, printing, etc. **graphic equalizer** a device for the separate control of the strength and quality of selected frequency bands. **graphic novel** an adult novel in comic-strip format. □ **graphically** adv.

graphicness *n.* [L *graphicus* f. Gk *graphikos* f. *graphē* writing]

-graphic /ˈɡræfɪk/ *comb. form* (also **-graphical**) forming adjectives corresponding to nouns in *-graphy* (see **-GRAPHY**). □ **-graphically** *comb. form* forming adverbs. [from or after Gk *-graphikos* (as **GRAPHIC**)]

graphical /ˈɡræfɪk(ə)l/ *adj.* 1 of or in the form of graphs. 2 graphic. □ **graphically** *adv.*

graphics /ˈɡræfɪks/ *n.pl.* (usu. treated as *sing.*) 1 the products of the graphic arts, esp. commercial design or illustration. 2 the use of diagrams in calculation and design. 3 (in full **computer graphics**) *Computing* a mode of processing and output in which a significant part of the information is in pictorial form.

graphite /ˈɡræfaɪt/ *n.* a crystalline allotropic form of carbon used as a solid lubricant, in pencils, and as a moderator in nuclear reactors etc. □ **graphitic** /-ˈfɪtɪk/ *adj.* **graphitize** /-ˈfɪˌtaɪz/ *v.tr. & intr.* (also **-ise**). [G *Graphit* f. Gk *graphō* write]

graphology /ɡrəˈfɒlədʒɪ/ *n.* 1 the study of handwriting esp. as a supposed guide to character. 2 notation for graphs. □ **graphological** /-fəˈlɒdʒɪk(ə)l/ *adj.* **graphologist** *n.* [Gk *graphē* writing]

-graphy /ɡrəfɪ/ *comb. form* forming nouns denoting: 1 a descriptive science (*bibliography*; *geography*). 2 a technique of producing images (*photography*; *radiography*). 3 a style or method of writing, drawing, etc. (*calligraphy*). [from or after F or G *-graphie* f. L *-graphia* f. Gk *-graphia* writing]

grapnel /ˈɡræpn(ə)l/ *n.* 1 a device with iron claws, attached to a rope and used for dragging or grasping. 2 a small anchor with several flukes. [ME f. AF f. OF *grapon* f. Gmc: cf. **GRAPE**]

grapple /ˈɡræp(ə)l/ *v. & n.* 1 *intr.* (often foll. by *with*) fight at close quarters or in close combat. 2 *intr.* (foll. by *with*) try to manage or overcome a difficult problem etc. 3 *tr.* a grip with the hands; come to close quarters with. b seize with or as with a grapnel; grasp. —*n.* 1 a a hold or grip in or as in wrestling. b a contest at close quarters. 2 a clutching-instrument; a grapnel. □ **grappling-iron** (or **-hook**) = **GRAPNEL**. □ **grappler** *n.* [OF *grapil* (n.) f. Prov., dimin. of *grapa* hook (as **GRAPNEL**)]

grasp /ɡrɑːsp/ *v. & n.* —*v.* 1 *tr.* a clutch at; seize greedily. b hold firmly; grip. 2 *intr.* (foll. by *at*) try to seize; accept avidly. 3 *tr.* understand or realize (a fact or meaning). —*n.* 1 a firm hold; a grip. 2 (foll. by *of*) a mastery or control (a grasp of the situation). b a mental hold or understanding (a grasp of the facts). 3 mental agility (a quick grasp). □ **grasp the nettle** tackle a difficulty boldly. □ **graspable** *adj.* **grasper** *n.* [ME *graspe, grapse* perh. f. OE *græpsan* (unrecorded) f. Gmc, rel. to **GROPE**: cf. LG *grapsen*]

grasping /ˈɡrɑːspɪŋ/ *adj.* avaricious, greedy. □ **graspingly** *adv.* **graspingness** *n.*

grass /ɡrɑːs/ *n. & v.* —*n.* 1 a vegetation belonging to a group of small plants with green blades. b any species of this. c any plant of the family Gramineae, which includes cereals, reeds, and bamboos. 2 pasture land. 3 grass-covered ground, a lawn (*keep off the grass*). 4 grazing (*out to grass; be at grass*). 5 *sl.* marijuana. 6 *Brit. sl.* an informer, esp. a police informer. —*v.* 1 *tr.* cover with turf. 2 *tr.* *US* provide with pasture. 3 *Brit. sl.* a *tr.* betray, esp. to the police. b *intr.* inform the

police. □ **grass roots** 1 a fundamental level or source. 2 ordinary people, esp. as voters; the rank and file of an organization, esp. a political party. **grass snake** 1 *Brit.* the common ringed snake, *Natrix natrix*. 2 *US* the common greensnake, *Opheodrys vernalis*. **grass widow** (or **widower**) a person whose husband (or wife) is away for a prolonged period. □ **grassless** *adj.* **grasslike** *adj.* [OE *græs* f. Gmc, rel. to **GREEN**, **GROW**]

grasshopper /ˈɡrɑːsˌhɒpə(r)/ *n.* a jumping and chirping plant-eating insect of the order Saltatoria.

grassland /ˈɡrɑːslænd/ *n.* a large open area covered with grass, esp. one used for grazing.

grassy /ˈɡrɑːsɪ/ *adj.* (**grassier, grassiest**) 1 covered with or abounding in grass. 2 resembling grass. 3 of grass. □ **grassiness** *n.*

grate[1] *v.* 1 *tr.* reduce to small particles by rubbing on a serrated surface. 2 *intr.* (often foll. by *against, on*) rub with a harsh scraping sound. 3 *tr.* utter in a harsh tone. 4 *intr.* (often foll. by *on*) **a** sound harshly or discordantly. **b** have an irritating effect. 5 *tr.* grind (one's teeth). 6 *intr.* (of a hinge etc.) creak. [ME f. OF *grater* ult. f. WG]

grate[2] *n.* 1 the recess of a fireplace or furnace. 2 a metal frame confining fuel in a grate. [ME, = grating f. OF ult. f. L *cratis* hurdle]

grateful /ˈɡreɪtfʊl/ *adj.* 1 thankful; feeling or showing gratitude. 2 pleasant. □ **gratefully** *adv.* **gratefulness** *n.* [obs. *grate* (adj.) f. L *gratus* + **-FUL**]

grater /ˈɡreɪtə(r)/ *n.* a device for reducing cheese or other food to small particles.

graticule /ˈɡrætɪˌkjuːl/ *n.* fine lines or fibres incorporated in a telescope or other optical instrument as a measuring scale or as an aid in locating objects. [F f. med.L *graticula* for *craticula* gridiron f. L *cratis* hurdle]

gratify /ˈɡrætɪˌfaɪ/ *v.tr.* (**-fies, -fied**) 1 a please, delight. b please by compliance; assent to the wish of. 2 indulge in or yield to (a feeling or desire). □ **gratification** /-fɪˈkeɪʃ(ə)n/ *n.* **gratifier** *n.* **gratifying** *adj.* **gratifyingly** *adv.* [F *gratifier* or L *gratificari* do a favour to, make a present of, f. *gratus* pleasing]

grating[1] /ˈɡreɪtɪŋ/ *adj.* 1 sounding harsh or discordant (a grating laugh). 2 having an irritating effect. □ **gratingly** *adv.*

grating[2] /ˈɡreɪtɪŋ/ *n.* a framework of parallel or crossed metal bars.

gratis /ˈɡrɑːtɪs, ˈɡreɪ-/ *adv. & adj.* free; without charge. [L, contracted ablat. pl. of *gratia* favour]

gratitude /ˈɡrætɪˌtjuːd/ *n.* being thankful; readiness to show appreciation for and to return kindness. [F *gratitude* or med.L *gratitudo* f. *gratus* thankful]

gratuitous /ɡrəˈtjuːɪtəs/ *adj.* 1 given or done free of charge. 2 uncalled for; unwarranted; lacking good reason. □ **gratuitously** *adv.* **gratuitousness** *n.* [L *gratuitus* spontaneous: cf. *fortuitous*]

gratuity /ɡrəˈtjuːɪtɪ/ *n.* (pl. **-ies**) money given in recognition of services; a tip. [OF *gratuité* or med.L *gratuitas* gift f. L *gratus* grateful]

graunch /ɡrɔːntʃ/ *v.intr. & tr.* make or cause to make a crunching or grinding sound. [imit.]

gravamen /ɡrəˈveɪmen/ *n.* (pl. **gravamens** or **gravamina** /-mɪnə/) 1 the essence or most serious part of an argument. 2 a grievance. [LL,

= inconvenience. f. L *gravare* to load f. *gravis* heavy]

grave[1] *n.* **1 a** a trench dug in the ground to receive a coffin on burial. **b** a mound or memorial stone placed over this. **2** (prec. by *the*) death, esp. as indicating mortal finality. **3** something compared to or regarded as a grave. □ **graveless** *adj.* **graveward** *adv.* & *adj.* [OE *græf* f. WG]

grave[2] *adj.* & *n.* —*adj.* **1 a** serious, weighty, important (*a grave matter*). **b** dignified, solemn, sombre (*a grave look*). **2** extremely serious or threatening (*grave danger*). **3** /grɑːv/ (of sound) low-pitched, not acute. —*n.* /grɑːv/ = *grave accent.* □ **grave accent** /grɑːv/ a mark (ˋ) placed over a vowel in some languages to denote pronunciation, length, etc., orig. indicating low or falling pitch. □ **gravely** *adv.* **graveness** *n.* [F *grave* or L *gravis* heavy, serious]

grave[3] *v.tr.* (*past part.* **graven** or **graved**) **1** (foll. by *in*, *on*) fix indelibly (on one's memory). **2** *archaic* engrave, carve. □ **graven image** an idol. [OE *grafan* dig, engrave f. Gmc: cf. GROOVE]

grave[4] *v.tr.* clean (a ship's bottom) by burning off accretions and by tarring. □ **graving dock** = *dry dock.* [perh. F dial. *grave* = OF *greve* shore]

gravel /ˈgræv(ə)l/ *n.* & *v.* —*n.* **1 a** a mixture of coarse sand and small water-worn or pounded stones, used for paths and roads and as an aggregate. **b** *Geol.* a stratum of this. **2** *Med.* aggregations of crystals formed in the urinary tract. —*v.tr.* (**gravelled, gravelling**; US **graveled, graveling**) **1** lay or strew with gravel. **2** perplex, puzzle, nonplus. [ME f. OF *gravel(e)* dimin. of *grave* (as GRAVE[4])]

gravelly /ˈgrævəlɪ/ *adj.* **1** of or like gravel. **2** having or containing gravel. **3** (of a voice) deep and rough-sounding.

graven *past part.* of GRAVE[3].

gravestone /ˈgreɪvstəʊn/ *n.* a stone (usu. inscribed) marking a grave.

graveyard /ˈgreɪvjɑːd/ *n.* a burial-ground, esp. by a church.

gravid /ˈgrævɪd/ *adj.* *literary* or *Zool.* pregnant. [L *gravidus* f. *gravis* heavy]

gravimeter /grəˈvɪmɪtə(r)/ *n.* an instrument for measuring the difference in the force of gravity from one place to another. [F *gravimètre* f. L *gravis* heavy]

gravimetric /ˌgrævɪˈmetrɪk/ *adj.* **1** of or relating to the measurement of weight. **2** denoting chemical analysis based on weight.

gravimetry /grəˈvɪmɪtrɪ/ *n.* the measurement of weight.

gravitate /ˈgrævɪˌteɪt/ *v.* **1** *intr.* (foll. by *to*, *towards*) move or be attracted to some source of influence. **2** *tr.* & *intr.* **a** move or tend by force of gravity towards. **b** sink by or as if by gravity. [mod.L *gravitare* f. *gravis* heavy]

gravitation /ˌgrævɪˈteɪʃ(ə)n/ *n.* *Physics* **1** a force of attraction between any particle of matter in the universe and any other. **2** the effect of this, esp. the falling of bodies to the earth. [mod.L *gravitatio* (as GRAVITY)]

gravitational /ˌgrævɪˈteɪʃən(ə)l/ *adj.* of or relating to gravitation. □ **gravitational field** the region of space surrounding a body in which another body experiences a force of attraction. □ **gravitationally** *adv.*

gravity /ˈgrævɪtɪ/ *n.* **1 a** the force that attracts a body to the centre of the earth or other celestial body. **b** the degree of intensity of this measured by acceleration. **c** gravitational force. **2** the property of having weight. **3 a** importance, seriousness; the quality of being grave. **b** solemnity, sobriety; serious demeanour. [F *gravité* or L *gravitas* f. *gravis* heavy]

gravy /ˈgreɪvɪ/ *n.* (*pl.* **-ies**) **1 a** the juices exuding from meat during and after cooking. **b** a dressing or sauce for food, made from these or from other materials, e.g. stock. **2** *sl.* unearned or unexpected money. □ **gravy-boat** a boat-shaped vessel for serving gravy. **gravy train** *sl.* a source of easy financial benefit. [ME, perh. from a misreading as *gravé* of OF *grané*, prob. f. *grain* spice: see GRAIN]

gray[1] /greɪ/ *n.* *Physics* the SI unit of the absorbed dose of ionizing radiation, corresponding to one joule per kilogram. [L. H. *Gray*, Engl. radiobiologist d. 1965]

gray[2] *US* var. of GREY.

grayling /ˈgreɪlɪŋ/ *n.* any silver-grey freshwater fish of the genus *Thymallus*, with a long high dorsal fin. [*gray* var. of GREY + -LING[2]]

graze[1] *v.* **1** *intr.* (of cattle, sheep, etc.) eat growing grass. **2** *tr.* **a** feed (cattle etc.) on growing grass. **b** feed on (grass). **3** *intr.* pasture cattle. □ **grazer** *n.* [OE *grasian* f. *græs* GRASS]

graze[2] *v.* & *n.* —*v.* **1** *tr.* rub or scrape (a part of the body, esp. the skin) so as to break the surface without causing bleeding. **2 a** *tr.* touch lightly in passing. **b** *intr.* (foll. by *against, along*, etc.) move with a light passing contact. —*n.* an act or instance of grazing. [perh. a specific use of GRAZE[1], as if 'take off the grass close to the ground' (of a shot etc.)]

grazier /ˈgreɪzɪə(r)/ *n.* **1** a person who feeds cattle for market. **2** *Austral.* a large-scale sheep-farmer or cattle-farmer. □ **graziery** *n.* [GRASS + -IER]

grazing /ˈgreɪzɪŋ/ *n.* grassland suitable for pasturage.

grease /griːs/ *n.* & *v.* —*n.* **1** oily or fatty matter esp. as a lubricant. **2** the melted fat of a dead animal. —*v.tr.* /griːs, griːz/ smear or lubricate with grease. □ **grease-gun** a device for pumping grease under pressure to a particular point. **grease the palm of** *colloq.* bribe. □ **greaser** *n.* **greaseless** *adj.* [ME f. AF *grece, gresse*, OF *graisse* ult. f. L *crassus* (adj.) fat]

greasepaint /ˈgriːspeɪnt/ *n.* a waxy composition used as make-up for actors.

greaseproof /ˈgriːspruːf/ *adj.* impervious to the penetration of grease.

greasy /ˈgriːsɪ, -zɪ/ *adj.* (**greasier, greasiest**) **1 a** of or like grease. **b** smeared or covered with grease. **c** containing or having too much grease. **2 a** slippery. **b** (of a person or manner) unpleasantly unctuous, smarmy. **c** objectionable. □ **greasily** *adv.* **greasiness** *n.*

great /greɪt/ *adj.* & *n.* —*adj.* **1 a** of a size, amount, extent, or intensity considerably above the normal or average; big (*made a great hole*; *take great care*). **b** also with implied surprise, admiration, contempt, etc., esp. in exclamations (*look at that great wasp*). **c** reinforcing other words denoting size, quantity, etc. (*a great big hole*; *a great many*). **2** important, pre-eminent; worthy or most worthy of consideration (*the great thing is not to get caught*). **3** grand, imposing (*a great occasion*; *the great hall*). **4 a** (esp. of a public or historic figure) distinguished; prominent. **b** (**the**

Great) as a title denoting the most important of the name (*Alfred the Great*). **5 a** (of a person) remarkable in ability, character, achievement, etc. (*great men; a great thinker*). **b** (of a thing) outstanding of its kind (*the Great Fire*). **6** (foll. by *at, on*) competent, skilled, well-informed. **7** fully deserving the name of; doing a thing habitually or extensively (*a great reader; not a great one for travelling*). **8** (also **greater**) the larger of the name, species, etc. (*great auk; greater celandine*). **9** (**Greater**) (of a city etc.) including adjacent urban areas (*Greater Manchester*). **10** *colloq.* **a** very enjoyable or satisfactory; attractive, fine (*had a great time; it would be great if we won*). **b** (as an exclam.) fine, very good. **11** (in *comb.*) (in names of family relationships) denoting one degree further removed upwards or downwards (*great-uncle; great-great-grandmother*). —*n.* a great or outstanding person or thing. □ **Great Britain** England, Wales, and Scotland. **Great Russian** *n.* a member or the language of the principal East Slavonic people; Russian. —*adj.* of or relating to this people or language. **great tit** *n.* a Eurasian songbird, *Parus major*, with black and white head markings. **Great War** the world war of 1914–18. □ **greatness** *n.* [OE *grēat* f. WG]

greatcoat /ˈgreɪtkəʊt/ *n.* a long heavy overcoat.

greatly /ˈgreɪtlɪ/ *adv.* by a considerable amount; much (*greatly admired; greatly superior*).

greave *n.* (usu. in *pl.*) armour for the shin. [ME f. OF *greve* shin, greave, of unkn. orig.]

grebe *n.* any diving bird of the family Podicipedidae, with a long neck, lobed toes, and almost no tail. [F *grèbe*, of unkn. orig.]

Grecian /ˈgriːʃ(ə)n/ *adj.* (of architecture or facial outline) following Greek models or ideals. [OF *grecien* or med.L *graecianus* (unrecorded) f. L *Graecia* Greece]

Grecism var. of GRAECISM.

Greco- var. of GRAECO-.

greed *n.* an excessive desire, esp. for food or wealth. [back-form. f. GREEDY]

greedy /ˈgriːdɪ/ *adj.* (**greedier, greediest**) **1** having or showing an excessive appetite for food or drink. **2** wanting wealth or pleasure to excess. **3** (foll. by *for*, or *to* + infin.) very keen or eager; needing intensely. □ **greedily** *adv.* **greediness** *n.* [OE *grǣdig* f. Gmc]

Greek *n.* & *adj.* —*n.* **1 a** a native or national of modern Greece; a person of Greek descent. **b** a native or citizen of any of the ancient States of Greece; a member of the Greek people. **2** the Indo-European language of Greece. —*adj.* of Greece or its people or language; Hellenic. □ **Greek cross** a cross with four equal arms. □ **Greekness** *n.* [OE *Grēcas* (pl.) f. Gmc f. L *Graecus* Greek f. Gk *Graikoi*, the prehistoric name of the Hellenes (in Aristotle)]

green *adj.*, *n.*, & *v.* —*adj.* **1** of the colour between blue and yellow in the spectrum; coloured like grass, emeralds, etc. **2 a** covered with leaves or grass. **b** mild and without snow (*a green Christmas*). **3** (of fruit etc. or wood) unripe or unseasoned. **4** not dried, smoked, or tanned. **5** inexperienced, naïve, gullible. **6 a** (of the complexion) pale, sickly-hued. **b** jealous, envious. **7** young, flourishing. **8** not withered or worn out (*a green old age*). **9** vegetable (*green food; green salad*). **10** (also **Green**) concerned with or supporting protection of the environment as a political principle. —*n.* **1** a green colour or

pigment. **2** green clothes or material (*dressed in green*). **3 a** a piece of public or common grassy land (*village green*). **b** a grassy area used for a special purpose (*putting-green; bowling-green*). **c** *Golf* a putting-green. **d** *Golf* a fairway. **4** (in *pl.*) green vegetables. **5** a green light. **6** a green ball, piece, etc., in a game or sport. **7** (also **Green**) a member or supporter of an environmentalist group or party. **8** green foliage or growing plants. —*v. tr.* & *intr.* make or become green. □ **green belt** an area of open land round a city, designated for preservation. **Green Beret** *colloq.* a British or American commando. **green card** an international insurance document for motorists. **green crop** a crop used as fodder in a green state rather than as hay etc. **green-eyed** jealous. **the green-eyed monster** jealousy. **green fingers** skill in growing plants. **green light 1** a signal to proceed on a road, railway, etc. **2** *colloq.* permission to go ahead with a project. **green manure** growing plants ploughed into the soil as fertilizer. **Green Paper** (in the UK) a preliminary report of Government proposals, for discussion. **green pound** the exchange rate for the pound for payments for agricultural produce in the EC. **green revolution** greatly increased crop production in underdeveloped countries. **green-room** a room in a theatre for actors and actresses who are off stage. **green-stick fracture** a bone-fracture, esp. in children, in which one side of the bone is broken and one only bent. **green tea** tea made from steam-dried, not fermented, leaves. **green thumb** = *green fingers*. □ **greenish** *adj.* **greenly** *adv.* **greenness** *n.* [OE *grēne* (adj. & n.), *grēnian* (v.), f. Gmc, rel. to GROW]

greenback /ˈgriːnbæk/ *n.* *US* a US legal-tender note.

greenery /ˈgriːnərɪ/ *n.* green foliage or growing plants.

greenfeed /ˈgriːnfiːd/ *n.* *Austral.* & *NZ* forage grown to be fed fresh to livestock.

greenfield /ˈgriːnfiːld/ *n.* (*attrib.*) (of a site, in terms of its potential development) having no previous building development on it.

greenfinch /ˈgriːnfɪntʃ/ *n.* a finch, *Carduelis chloris*, with green and yellow plumage.

greenfly /ˈgriːnflaɪ/ *n.* (*pl.* **-flies**) *Brit.* **1** a green aphid. **2** these collectively.

greengage /ˈgriːngeɪdʒ/ *n.* a roundish green fine-flavoured variety of plum. [Sir W. *Gage* d. 1727]

greengrocer /ˈgriːnˌgrəʊsə(r)/ *n.* *Brit.* a retailer of fruit and vegetables.

greengrocery /ˈgriːnˌgrəʊsərɪ/ *n.* (*pl.* **-ies**) *Brit.* **1** the business of a greengrocer. **2** goods sold by a greengrocer.

greenhorn /ˈgriːnhɔːn/ *n.* an inexperienced or foolish person; a new recruit.

greenhouse /ˈgriːnhaʊs/ *n.* a light structure with the sides and roof mainly of glass, for rearing delicate plants or hastening the growth of plants. □ **greenhouse effect** the trapping of the sun's warmth in the lower atmosphere of the earth caused by an increase in carbon dioxide, which is more transparent to solar radiation than to the reflected radiation from the earth. **greenhouse gas** any of various gases, esp. carbon dioxide, that contribute to the greenhouse effect.

greensand /ˈgriːnsænd/ n. **1** a greenish kind of sandstone, often imperfectly cemented. **2** a stratum largely formed of this sandstone.

greenstone /ˈgriːnstəʊn/ n. **1** a greenish igneous rock containing feldspar and hornblende. **2** a variety of jade found in New Zealand, used for tools, ornaments, etc.

greenstuff /ˈgriːnstʌf/ n. vegetation; green vegetables.

greensward /ˈgriːnswɔːd/ n. **1** grassy turf. **2** an expanse of this.

Greenwich Mean Time /ˈgrenɪtʃ, ˈgrɪnɪdʒ/ n. (also **Greenwich Time**) the local time on the meridian of Greenwich, used as an international basis of time-reckoning. [*Greenwich* in London, former site of the Royal Observatory]

greenwood /ˈgriːnwʊd/ n. a wood in summer, esp. as the scene of outlaw life.

greeny /ˈgriːnɪ/ adj. greenish (*greeny-yellow*).

greet[1] v.tr. **1** address politely or welcomingly on meeting or arrival. **2** receive or acknowledge in a specified way (*was greeted with derision*). **3** (of a sight, sound, etc.) become apparent to or noticed by. □ **greeter** n. [OE *grētan* handle, attack, salute f. WG]

greet[2] v.intr. Sc. weep. [OE *grētan*, *grēotan*, of uncert. orig.]

greeting /ˈgriːtɪŋ/ n. **1** the act or an instance of welcoming or addressing politely. **2** words, gestures, etc., used to greet a person. **3** (often in pl.) an expression of goodwill. □ **greetings card** a decorative card sent to convey greetings.

gregarious /grɪˈgeərɪəs/ adj. **1** fond of company. **2** living in flocks or communities. **3** growing in clusters. □ **gregariously** adv. **gregariousness** n. [L *gregarius* f. *grex gregis* flock]

Gregorian calendar /grɪˈgɔːrɪən/ n. the calendar introduced in 1582 by Pope Gregory XIII, as a correction of the Julian calendar. [med.L *Gregorianus* f. LL *Gregorius* f. Gk *Grēgorios* Gregory]

Gregorian chant /grɪˈgɔːrɪən/ n. plainsong ritual music, named after Pope Gregory I.

gremlin /ˈgremlɪn/ n. colloq. **1** an imaginary mischievous sprite regarded as responsible for mechanical faults, esp. in aircraft. **2** any similar cause of trouble. [20th c.: orig. unkn., but prob. after *goblin*]

grenade /grɪˈneɪd/ n. a small bomb thrown by hand (**hand-grenade**) or shot from a rifle. [F f. OF *grenate* and Sp. *granada* POMEGRANATE]

grenadier /ˌgrenəˈdɪə(r)/ n. **1** Brit. (**Grenadiers** or **Grenadier Guards**) the first regiment of the royal household infantry. **2** hist. a soldier armed with grenades. [F (as GRENADE)]

grenadilla var. of GRANADILLA.

grenadine /ˌgrenəˈdiːn/ n. a French cordial syrup of pomegranates etc. [F f. *grenade*: see GRENADE]

grew past of GROW.

grey /greɪ/ adj., n., & v. (US **gray**) —adj. **1** of a colour intermediate between black and white, as of ashes or lead. **2 a** (of the weather etc.) dull, dismal; heavily overcast. **b** bleak, depressing; (of a person) depressed. **3 a** (of hair) turning white with age etc. **b** (of a person) having grey hair. **4** anonymous, nondescript, unidentifiable. —n. **1 a** a grey colour or pigment. **b** grey clothes or material (*dressed in grey*). **2** a cold sunless light. **3** a grey or white horse. —v.tr. & intr. make or become grey. □ **grey area** a situation or topic sharing features of more than one category and

not clearly attributable to any one category. **grey eminence** = ÉMINENCE GRISE. **Grey Friar** a Franciscan friar. **grey goose** = GREYLAG. **grey-hen** the female of the black grouse. **grey matter 1** the darker tissues of the brain and spinal cord consisting of nerve-cell bodies and branching dendrites. **2** colloq. intelligence. **grey squirrel** an American squirrel, *Sciurus carolinensis*, brought to Europe in the 19th c. □ **greyish** adj. **greyly** adv. **greyness** n. [OE *græg* f. Gmc]

greybeard /ˈgreɪbɪəd/ n. archaic **1** an old man. **2** Brit. clematis in seed.

greyhound /ˈgreɪhaʊnd/ n. **1** a dog of a tall slender breed having keen sight and capable of high speed, used in racing and coursing. **2** this breed. [OE *grīghund* f. *grīeg* bitch (unrecorded: cf. ON *grey*) + *hund* dog, rel. to HOUND]

greylag /ˈgreɪlæg/ n. (in full **greylag goose**) a wild goose, *Anser anser*, native to Europe. [GREY + LAG[1] (because of its late migration)]

greywacke /ˈgreɪˌwækə, -wæk/ n. (US **graywacke**) Geol. a dark and coarse-grained sandstone, usu. with an admixture of clay. [Anglicized f. G *Grauwacke* f. *grau* grey: see WACKE]

grid n. **1** a framework of spaced parallel bars; a grating. **2** a system of numbered squares printed on a map and forming the basis of map references. **3** a network of lines, electric-power connections, gas-supply lines, etc. **4** a pattern of lines marking the starting-places on a motor-racing track. **5** an arrangement of town streets in a rectangular pattern. □ **gridded** adj. [back-form. f. GRIDIRON]

griddle /ˈgrɪd(ə)l/ n. & v. —n. = GIRDLE[2]. —v.tr. cook with a griddle; grill. [ME f. OF *gredil*, *gridil* gridiron ult. f. L *craticula* dimin. of *cratis* hurdle; cf. GRATE[2], GRILL]

gridiron /ˈgrɪdˌaɪən/ n. **1** a cooking utensil of metal bars for broiling or grilling. **2** US a football field (with parallel lines marking out the area of play). **3** = GRID 5. [ME *gredire*, var. of *gredil* GRIDDLE, later assoc. with IRON]

grief /griːf/ n. **1** deep or intense sorrow or mourning. **2** the cause of this. □ **come to grief** meet with disaster; fail. **good** (or **great**) **grief!** an exclamation of surprise, alarm, etc. [ME f. AF *gref*, OF *grief* f. *grever* GRIEVE]

grievance /ˈgriːv(ə)ns/ n. a real or fancied cause for complaint. [ME, = injury, f. OF *grevance* (as GRIEF)]

grieve /griːv/ v. **1** tr. cause grief or great distress to. **2** intr. suffer grief, esp. at another's death. □ **griever** n. [ME f. OF *grever* ult. f. L *gravare* f. *gravis* heavy]

grievous /ˈgriːvəs/ adj. **1** (of pain etc.) severe. **2** causing grief or suffering. **3** injurious. **4** flagrant, heinous. □ **grievous bodily harm** Law serious injury inflicted intentionally on a person. □ **grievously** adv. **grievousness** n. [ME f. OF *grevos* (as GRIEVE)]

griffin /ˈgrɪfɪn/ n. (also **gryphon** /-f(ə)n/) a mythical creature with an eagle's head and wings and a lion's body. [ME f. OF *grifoun* ult. f. LL *gryphus* f. L *gryps* f. Gk *grups*]

griffon /ˈgrɪf(ə)n/ n. **1 a** a dog of a small terrier-like breed with coarse or smooth hair. **b** this breed. **2** (in full **griffon vulture**) a large vulture, *Gyps fulvus*. **3** = GRIFFIN. [F (in sense 1) or var. of GRIFFIN]

grig *n.* **1** a small eel. **2** a grasshopper or cricket. □ **merry** (or **lively**) **as a grig** full of fun; extravagantly lively. [ME, orig. = dwarf: orig. unkn.]

grill *n. & v.* —*n.* **1 a** a device on a cooker for radiating heat downwards. **b** = GRIDIRON 1. **2** a dish of food cooked on a grill. **3** (in full **grill room**) a restaurant serving grilled food. —*v.* **1** *tr. & intr.* cook or be cooked under a grill or on a gridiron. **2** *tr. & intr.* subject or be subjected to extreme heat, esp. from the sun. **3** *tr.* subject to severe questioning or interrogation. □ **griller** *n.* **grilling** *n.* (in sense 3 of *v.*). [F *gril* (n.), *griller* (v.), f. OF forms of GRILLE]

grille /grɪl/ *n.* (also **grill**) **1** a grating or latticed screen, used as a partition or to allow discreet vision. **2** a metal grid protecting the radiator of a motor vehicle. [F f. OF *graille* f. med.L *graticula, craticula*: see GRIDDLE]

grilse /grɪls/ *n.* a young salmon that has returned to fresh water from the sea for the first time. [ME: orig. unkn.]

grim *adj.* (**grimmer, grimmest**) **1** of a stern or forbidding appearance. **2** harsh, merciless, severe. **3** ghastly, joyless, sinister (*has a grim truth in it*). **4** unpleasant, unattractive. □ **grimly** *adv.* **grimness** *n.* [OE f. Gmc]

grimace /ˈgrɪməs, grɪˈmeɪs/ *n. & v.* —*n.* a distortion of the face made in disgust etc. or to amuse. —*v.intr.* make a grimace. □ **grimacer** *n.* [F f. Sp. *grimazo* f. *grima* fright]

grime *n. & v.* —*n.* soot or dirt ingrained in a surface. —*v.tr.* blacken with grime. [orig. as verb: f. MLG & MDu.]

grimy /ˈgraɪmɪ/ *adj.* (**grimier, grimiest**) covered with grime; dirty. □ **grimily** *adv.* **griminess** *n.*

grin *v. & n.* —*v.* (**grinned, grinning**) **1** *intr.* **a** smile broadly, showing the teeth. **b** make a forced, unrestrained, or stupid smile. **2** *tr.* express by grinning (*grinned his satisfaction*). —*n.* the act or action of grinning. □ **grinner** *n.* **grinningly** *adv.* [OE *grennian* f. Gmc]

grind /graɪnd/ *v. & n.* —*v.* (*past* and *past part.* **ground** /graʊnd/) **1 a** *tr.* reduce to small particles or powder by crushing etc. **b** by passing through a mill. **b** *intr.* (of a mill, machine, etc.) move with a crushing action. **2 a** *tr.* reduce, sharpen, or smooth by friction. **b** *tr. & intr.* rub or rub together gratingly (*grind one's teeth*). **3** *tr.* (often foll. by *down*) oppress; harass with exactions (*grinding poverty*). **4** *intr.* **a** (often foll. by *away*) work or study hard. **b** (foll. by *out*) produce with effort (*grinding out verses*). **c** (foll. by *on*) (of a sound) continue gratingly or monotonously. **5** *tr.* turn the handle of e.g. a coffee-mill, barrel-organ, etc. **6** *intr. sl.* (of a dancer) rotate the hips. —*n.* **1** the act or an instance of grinding. **2** *colloq.* hard dull work; a laborious task (*the daily grind*). **3** the size of ground particles. **4** *sl.* a dancer's rotary movement of the hips. □ **ground glass 1** glass made non-transparent by grinding etc. **2** glass ground to a powder. □ **grindingly** *adv.* [OE *grindan*, of unkn. orig.]

grinder /ˈgraɪndə(r)/ *n.* **1** a person or thing that grinds, esp. a machine (often in *comb.*: *coffee-grinder, organ-grinder*). **2** a molar tooth.

grindstone /ˈgraɪndstəʊn/ *n.* **1** a thick revolving disc used for grinding, sharpening, and polishing. **2** a kind of stone used for this. □ **keep**

one's nose to the grindstone work hard and continuously.

gringo /ˈgrɪŋgəʊ/ *n.* (*pl.* **-os**) *colloq.* a foreigner, esp. a British or N. American person, in a Spanish-speaking country. [Sp., = gibberish]

grip *v. & n.* —*v.* (**gripped, gripping**) **1 a** *tr.* grasp tightly; take a firm hold of. **b** *intr.* take a firm hold, esp. by friction. **2** *tr.* (of a feeling or emotion) deeply affect (a person) (*was gripped by fear*). **3** *tr.* compel the attention or interest of (a *gripping story*). —*n.* **1 a** a firm hold; a tight grasp or clasp. **b** a manner of grasping or holding. **2** the power of holding attention. **3 a** mental or intellectual understanding or mastery. **b** effective control of a situation or one's behaviour etc. (*lose one's grip*). **4 a** a part of a machine that grips or holds something. **b** a part or attachment by which a tool, component, weapon, etc., is held in the hand. **5** = HAIRGRIP. **6** a travelling bag. **7** an assistant in a theatre, film studio, etc. □ **come** (or **get**) **to grips with** approach purposefully; begin to deal with. □ **gripper** *n.* **grippingly** *adv.* [OE *gripe, gripa* handful (as GRIPE)]

gripe *v. & n.* —*v.* **1** *intr. colloq.* complain, esp. peevishly. **2** *tr.* affect with gastric or intestinal pain. —*n.* **1** (usu. in *pl.*) gastric or intestinal pain; colic. **2** *colloq.* a complaint. **b** the act of griping. □ **Gripe Water** *propr.* a carminative solution to relieve colic and stomach ailments in infants. □ **griper** *n.* **gripingly** *adv.* [OE *grīpan* f. Gmc: cf. GROPE]

grisaille /grɪˈzeɪl, -ˈzaɪl/ *n.* **1** a method of painting in grey monochrome, often to imitate sculpture. **2** a painting or stained-glass window of this kind. [F f. *gris* grey]

grisly /ˈgrɪzlɪ/ *adj.* (**grislier, grisliest**) causing horror, disgust, or fear. □ **grisliness** *n.* [OE *grislic* terrifying]

grist *n.* **1** corn to grind. **2** malt crushed for brewing. □ **grist to the** (or **a person's**) **mill** a source of profit or advantage. [OE f. Gmc, rel. to GRIND]

gristle /ˈgrɪs(ə)l/ *n.* tough flexible tissue in vertebrates; cartilage. □ **gristly** /-slɪ/ *adj.* [OE *gristle*]

grit *n. & v.* —*n.* **1** particles of stone or sand, esp. as causing discomfort, clogging machinery, etc. **2** coarse sandstone. **3** *colloq.* pluck, endurance; strength of character. —*v.* (**gritted, gritting**) **1** *tr.* spread grit on (icy roads etc.). **2** *tr.* clench (the teeth). **3** *intr.* make or move with a grating sound. □ **gritter** *n.* **gritty** *adj.* (**grittier, grittiest**). **grittily** *adv.* **grittiness** *n.* [OE *grēot* f. Gmc: cf. GRITS, GROATS]

grits *n.pl.* **1** coarsely ground grain, esp. oatmeal. **2** oats that have been husked but not ground. [OE *grytt(e)*: cf. GRIT, GROATS]

grizzle /ˈgrɪz(ə)l/ *v.intr. Brit. colloq.* **1** (esp. of a child) cry fretfully. **2** complain whiningly. □ **grizzler** *n.* **grizzly** *adj.* [19th c.: orig. unkn.]

grizzled /ˈgrɪz(ə)ld/ *adj.* having, or streaked with, grey hair. [*grizzle* grey f. OF *grisel* f. *gris* grey]

grizzly /ˈgrɪzlɪ/ *adj. & n.* —*adj.* (**grizzlier, grizzliest**) grey, greyish, grey-haired. —*n.* (*pl.* **-ies**) (in full **grizzly bear**) a large variety of brown bear, found in N. America and N. Russia.

groan *v. & n.* —*v.* **1 a** *intr.* make a deep sound expressing pain, grief, or disapproval. **b** *tr.* utter with groans. **2** *intr.* (usu. foll. by *under, beneath, with*) be loaded or oppressed. —*n.* the sound made in groaning. □ **groaner** *n.* **groaningly** *adv.* [OE *grānian* f. Gmc, rel. to GRIN]

groat *n. hist.* a silver coin worth four old pence. [ME f. MDu. *groot*, orig. = great, i.e. thick (penny)]

groats *n.pl.* hulled or crushed grain, esp. oats. [OE *grotan* (pl.): cf. *grot* fragment, *grēot* GRIT, *grytt* bran]

grocer /ˈgrəʊsə(r)/ *n.* a dealer in food and household provisions. [ME & AF *grosser*, orig. one who sells in the gross, f. OF *grossier* f. med.L *grossarius* (as GROSS)]

grocery /ˈgrəʊsərɪ/ *n.* (*pl.* **-ies**) **1** a grocer's trade or shop. **2** (in *pl.*) provisions, esp. food, sold by a grocer.

grog *n.* **1** a drink of spirit (orig. rum) and water. **2** *Austral. & NZ colloq.* alcoholic liquor, esp. beer. [said to be from 'Old *Grog*', the reputed nickname (f. his GROGRAM cloak) of Admiral Vernon, who in 1740 first had diluted instead of neat rum served out to sailors]

groggy /ˈgrɒgɪ/ *adj.* (**groggier, groggiest**) incapable or unsteady from being dazed or semiconscious. □ **groggily** *adv.* **grogginess** *n.*

grogram /ˈgrɒgrəm/ *n.* a coarse fabric of silk, mohair, and wool, or a mixture of these. [F *gros grain* coarse grain (as GROSS, GRAIN)]

groin[1] *n. & v.* —*n.* **1** the depression between the belly and the thigh. **2** *Archit.* **a** an edge formed by intersecting vaults. **b** an arch supporting a vault. —*v.tr. Archit.* build with groins. [ME *grynde*, perh. f. OE *grynde* depression]

groin[2] US var. of GROYNE.

grommet /ˈgrɒmɪt/ *n.* (also **grummet** /ˈgrʌmɪt/) a metal, plastic, or rubber eyelet placed in a hole to protect or insulate a rope or cable etc. passed through it. [obs. F *grommette* f. *gourmer* to curb, of unkn. orig.]

groom /gruːm/ *n. & v.* —*n.* **1** a person employed to take care of horses. **2** = BRIDEGROOM. **3** *Brit. Mil.* any of certain officers of the Royal Household. —*v.tr.* **1 a** curry or tend (a horse). **b** give a neat appearance to (a person etc.). **2** (of an ape or monkey etc.) clean and comb the fur of (its fellow) with the fingers. **3** prepare or train (a person) for a particular purpose or activity (*was groomed for the top job*). [ME, orig. = boy: orig. unkn.]

groove /gruːv/ *n. & v.* —*n.* **1 a** a channel or hollow, esp. one made to guide motion or receive a corresponding ridge. **b** a spiral track cut in a gramophone record. **2** an established routine or habit, esp. a monotonous one. —*v.* **1** *tr.* make a groove or grooves in. **2** *intr. sl.* enjoy oneself. □ **in the groove** *sl.* doing or performing well. [ME, = mine-shaft, f. obs. Du. *groeve* furrow f. Gmc]

groovy /ˈgruːvɪ/ *adj.* (**groovier, grooviest**) **1** *sl.* fashionable and exciting; enjoyable, excellent. **2** of or like a groove. □ **groovily** *adv.* **grooviness** *n.*

grope *v. & n.* —*v.* **1** *intr.* (usu. foll. by *for*) feel about or search uncertainly with the hands. **2** *intr.* (foll. by *for, after*) search mentally (*groping for the answer*). **3** *tr.* feel (one's way) towards something. **4** *tr. sl.* fondle clumsily for sexual pleasure. —*n.* the process or an instance of groping. □ **groper** *n.* **gropingly** *adv.* [OE *grāpian* f. Gmc]

grosbeak /ˈgrəʊsbiːk/ *n.* any of various finches of the families Cardinalidae and Fringillidae, having stout conical bills. [F *grosbec* (as GROSS)]

grosgrain /ˈgrəʊgreɪn/ *n.* a corded fabric of silk etc. [F, = coarse grain (as GROSS, GRAIN)]

gros point /grəʊ ˈpwæ̃/ *n.* cross-stitch embroidery on canvas. [F (as GROSS, POINT)]

gross /grəʊs/ *adj., v., & n.* —*adj.* **1** overfed; repulsively fat. **2** (of a person, manners, or morals) noticeably coarse or indecent. **3** flagrant; conspicuously wrong (*gross negligence*). **4** total; without deductions; not net (*gross tonnage*; *gross income*). **5 a** luxuriant, rank. **b** thick, solid, dense. **6** (of the senses etc.) dull; lacking sensitivity. —*v.tr.* produce or earn as gross profit or income. —*n.* (*pl.* same) an amount equal to twelve dozen. □ **gross domestic product** the total value of goods produced and services provided in a country in one year. **gross national product** the gross domestic product plus the total of net income from abroad. **gross out** *US sl.* disgust. **gross up** increase (a net amount) to its value before deductions. □ **grossly** *adv.* **grossness** *n.* [ME f. OF *gros grosse* large f. LL *grossus*: (n.) f. F *grosse douzaine* large dozen]

grotesque /grəʊˈtesk/ *adj. & n.* —*adj.* **1** comically or repulsively distorted; monstrous, unnatural. **2** incongruous, ludicrous, absurd. —*n.* **1** a decorative form interweaving human and animal features. **2** a comically distorted figure or design. □ **grotesquely** *adv.* **grotesqueness** *n.* **grotesquerie** /-ˈteskərɪ/ *n.* [earlier *crotesque* f. F *crotesque* f. It. *grottesca* grotto-like (painting etc.) fem. of *grottesco* (as GROTTO, -ESQUE)]

grotto /ˈgrɒtəʊ/ *n.* (*pl.* **-oes** or **-os**) **1** a small picturesque cave. **2** an artificial ornamental cave. □ **grottoed** *adj.* [It. *grotta* ult. f. L *crypta* f. Gk *kruptē* CRYPT]

grotty /ˈgrɒtɪ/ *adj.* (**grottier, grottiest**) *Brit. sl.* unpleasant, dirty, shabby, unattractive. □ **grottiness** *n.* [shortening of GROTESQUE + -Y[1]]

grouch /graʊtʃ/ *v. & n. colloq.* —*v.intr.* grumble. —*n.* **1** a discontented person. **2** a fit of grumbling or the sulks. **3** a cause of discontent. [var. of *grutch*: see GRUDGE]

grouchy /ˈgraʊtʃɪ/ *adj.* (**grouchier, grouchiest**) *colloq.* discontented, grumpy. □ **grouchily** *adv.* **grouchiness** *n.*

ground[1] /graʊnd/ *n. & v.* —*n.* **1 a** the surface of the earth, esp. as contrasted with the air around it. **b** a part of this specified in some way (*low ground*). **2** the substance of the earth's surface; soil, earth (*stony ground*; *dug deep into the ground*). **3 a** a position, area, or distance on the earth's surface. **b** the extent of activity etc. achieved or of a subject dealt with (*the book covers a lot of ground*). **4** (often in *pl.*) a foundation, motive, or reason (*there is ground for concern*; *there are grounds for believing*; *excused on the grounds of ill-health*). **5** an area of a special kind or use (often in *comb.*: *cricket-ground*; *fishing-grounds*). **6** (in *pl.*) an area of usu. enclosed land attached to a house etc. **7** an area or basis for consideration, agreement, etc. (*common ground*; *on firm ground*). **8 a** (in painting) the prepared surface giving the predominant colour or tone. **b** (in embroidery, ceramics, etc.) the undecorated surface. **9** (in full **ground bass**) *Mus.* a short theme in the bass constantly repeated with the upper parts of the music varied. **10** (in *pl.*) solid particles, esp. of coffee, forming a residue. **11** *Electr.* =

EARTH. **12** the bottom of the sea (*the ship touched ground*). **13** *Brit.* the floor of a room etc. **14** (*attrib.*) **a** (of animals) living on or in the ground; (of fish) living at the bottom of water; (of plants) dwarfish or trailing. **b** relating to or concerned with the ground (*ground staff*). —*v.* **1** *tr.* refuse authority for (a pilot or an aircraft) to fly. **2 a** *tr.* run (a ship) aground; strand. **b** *intr.* (of a ship) run aground. **3** *tr.* (foll. by *in*) instruct thoroughly (in a subject). **4** *tr.* (often as **grounded** *adj.*) (foll. by *on*) base (a principle, conclusion, etc.) on. **5** *tr. Electr.* = EARTH *v.* **6** *intr.* alight on the ground. **7** *tr.* place or lay (esp. weapons) on the ground. □ **break new** (or **fresh**) **ground** treat a subject previously not dealt with. **fall to the ground** (of a plan etc.) fail. **gain** (or **make**) **ground 1** advance steadily; make progress. **2** (foll. by *on*) catch (a person) up. **get off the ground** *colloq.* make a successful start. **give** (or **lose**) **ground 1** retreat, decline. **2** lose the advantage or one's position in an argument, contest, etc. **go to ground 1** (of a fox etc.) enter its earth or burrow etc. **2** (of a person) become inaccessible for a prolonged period. **ground-bait** bait thrown to the bottom of a fishing-ground. **ground control** the personnel directing the landing etc. of aircraft or spacecraft. **ground elder** a garden weed, *Aegopodium podagraria*, spreading by means of underground stems. **ground floor** the floor of a building at ground level. **ground frost** frost on the surface of the ground or in the top layer of soil etc. **ground-plan 1** the plan of a building at ground level. **2** the general outline of a scheme. **ground-rent** rent for land leased for building. **ground rule** a basic principle. **ground speed** an aircraft's speed relative to the ground. **ground swell 1** a heavy sea caused by a distant or past storm or an earthquake. **2** an increasingly forceful presence (esp. of public opinion). **ground zero** the point on the ground under an exploding (usu. nuclear) bomb. **hold one's ground** not retreat or give way. **on the ground** at the point of production or operation; in practical conditions. **on one's own ground** on one's own territory or subject; on one's own terms. □ **grounder** *n.* [OE *grund* f. Gmc]

ground² past and past part. of GRIND.

groundhog /ˈɡraʊndhɒɡ/ *n.* **1** = AARDVARK. **2** *US* a marmot; a woodchuck.

grounding /ˈɡraʊndɪŋ/ *n.* basic training or instruction in a subject.

groundless /ˈɡraʊndlɪs/ *adj.* without motive or foundation. □ **groundlessly** *adv.* **groundlessness** *n.* [OE *grundlēas* (as GROUND¹, -LESS)]

groundnut /ˈɡraʊndnʌt/ *n.* **1** *Brit.* = PEANUT. **2 a** a N. American wild bean. **b** its edible tuber.

groundsel /ˈɡraʊns(ə)l/ *n.* any composite plant of the genus *Senecio*, esp. *S. vulgaris*. [OE *grundeswylige*, *gundæswelgiæ* (perh. = pus-absorber f. *gund* pus, with ref. to use for poultices)]

groundsheet /ˈɡraʊndʃiːt/ *n.* a waterproof sheet for spreading on the ground, esp. in a tent.

groundsman /ˈɡraʊndzmən/ *n.* (pl. **-men**) a person who maintains a sports ground.

groundwater /ˈɡraʊndˌwɔːtə(r)/ *n.* water found in soil or in pores, crevices, etc., in rock.

groundwork /ˈɡraʊndwɜːk/ *n.* **1** preliminary or basic work. **2** a foundation or basis.

group /ɡruːp/ *n.* & *v.* —*n.* **1** a number of persons or things located close together, or considered

or classed together. **2** (*attrib.*) concerning or done by a group (*a group photograph; group sex*). **3** a number of people working together or sharing beliefs. **4** a number of commercial companies under common ownership. **5** an ensemble playing popular music. **6** a division of an air force or air-fleet. **7** *Math.* a set of elements, together with an associative binary operation, which contains an inverse for each element and an identity element. **8** *Chem.* **a** a set of ions or radicals giving a characteristic qualitative reaction. **b** a set of elements having similar properties. **c** a combination of atoms having a recognizable identity in a number of compounds. —*v.* **1** *tr.* & *intr.* form or be formed into a group. **2** *tr.* (often foll. by *with*) place in a group or groups. **3** *tr.* form (colours, figures, etc.) into a well-arranged and harmonious whole. **4** *tr.* classify. □ **group captain** an RAF officer next below air commodore. **group practice** a medical practice in which several doctors are associated. **group therapy** therapy in which patients with a similar condition are brought together to assist one another. □ **groupage** *n.* [F *groupe* f. It. *gruppo* f. Gmc, rel. to CROP]

grouper /ˈɡruːpə(r)/ *n.* any marine fish of the family Serranidae, with heavy body and big head. [Port. *garupa*, prob. f. native name in S. America]

groupie /ˈɡruːpɪ/ *n.* *sl.* an ardent follower of touring pop groups, esp. a young woman seeking sexual relations with them.

grouse¹ /ɡraʊs/ *n.* (*pl.* same) **1** any of various game-birds of the family Tetraonidae, with a plump body and feathered legs. **2** the flesh of a grouse used as food. [16th c.: orig. uncert.]

grouse² /ɡraʊs/ *v.* & *n.* *colloq.* —*v.intr.* grumble or complain pettily. —*n.* a complaint. □ **grouser** *n.* [19th c.: orig. unkn.]

grout /ɡraʊt/ *n.* & *v.* —*n.* a thin fluid mortar for filling gaps in tiling etc. —*v.tr.* provide or fill with grout. □ **grouter** *n.* [perh. f. OE *grūt* rel. to GRITS, but cf. F dial. *grouter* grout a wall]

grove *n.* a small wood or group of trees. □ **grovy** *adj.* [OE *grāf*, rel. to *græfa* brushwood]

grovel /ˈɡrɒv(ə)l/ *v.intr.* (**grovelled, grovelling;** *US* **groveled, groveling**) **1** behave obsequiously in seeking favour or forgiveness. **2** lie prone in abject humility. □ **groveller** *n.* **grovelling** *adj.* **grovellingly** *adv.* [back-form. f. obs. *grovelling* (adv.) f. *gruf* face down f. *on grufe* f. ON *á grúfu*, later taken as pres. part.]

grow /ɡrəʊ/ *v.* (*past* **grew** /ɡruː/; *past part.* **grown** /ɡrəʊn/) **1** *intr.* increase in size, height, quantity, degree, or in any way regarded as measurable (e.g. authority or reputation) (often foll. by *in*: *grew in stature*). **2** *intr.* **a** develop or exist as a living plant or natural product. **b** develop in a specific way or direction (*began to grow sideways*). **c** germinate, sprout; spring up. **3** *intr.* be produced; come naturally into existence; arise. **4** *intr.* (as **grown** *adj.*) fully matured; adult. **5** *intr.* **a** become gradually (*grow rich; grow less*). **b** (foll. by *to* + infin.) come by degrees (*grew to like it*). **6** *intr.* (foll. by *into*) **a** become, having grown or developed (*the acorn has grown into a tall oak; will grow into a fine athlete*). **b** become large enough for or suited to (*will grow into the coat; grew into her new job*). **7** *intr.* (foll. by *on*) become gradually more favoured by. **8** *tr.* **a** produce (plants, fruit, wood, etc.) by cultivation. **b** bring forth. **c** cause (a beard etc.) to develop. **9** *tr.* (in *passive*; foll. by *over*, *up*) be covered with a growth. □ **grown-up** *adj.* adult. —*n.* an adult person. **grow out of 1** become too large to wear (a garment). **2** become too mature to retain (a childish habit etc.). **3** be the result or development of. **grow up 1** advance to maturity. **2** (of a custom) arise, become common. □ **growable** *adj.* [OE *grōwan* f. Gmc, rel. to GRASS, GREEN]

grower /ˈgrəʊə(r)/ *n.* **1** (often in *comb.*) a person growing produce (*fruit-grower*). **2** a plant that grows in a specified way (*a fast grower*).

growl /graʊl/ *v. & n.* —*v.* **1** *intr.* **a** (often foll. by *at*) (esp. of a dog) make a low guttural sound, usu. of anger. **b** murmur angrily. **2** *intr.* rumble. **3** *tr.* (often foll. by *out*) utter with a growl. —*n.* **1** a growling sound, esp. made by a dog. **2** an angry murmur; complaint. **3** a rumble. □ **growler** *n.* **growlingly** *adv.* [prob. imit.]

grown *past part.* of GROW.

growth /grəʊθ/ *n.* **1** the act or process of growing. **2** an increase in size or value. **3** something that has grown or is growing. **4** *Med.* a morbid formation. **5** the cultivation of produce. **6** a crop or yield of grapes. □ **growth industry** an industry that is developing rapidly. **growth stock** etc. stock etc. that tends to increase in capital value rather than yield high income.

groyne /grɔɪn/ *n.* (*US* **groin**) a timber framework or low broad wall built out from a shore to check erosion of a beach. [dial. *groin* snout f. OF *groign* f. LL *grunium* pig's snout]

grub *n. & v.* —*n.* **1** the larva of an insect, esp. of a beetle. **2** *colloq.* food. —*v.* (**grubbed, grubbing**) **1** *tr. & intr.* dig superficially. **2** *tr.* **a** clear (the ground) of roots and stumps. **b** clear away (roots etc.). **3** *tr.* (foll. by *up, out*) a fetch by digging (*grubbing up weeds*). **b** extract (information etc.) by searching in books etc. **4** *intr.* search, rummage. □ **grub-screw** a small headless screw. □ **grubber** *n.* (also in *comb.*). [ME, (v.) perh. corresp. to OE *grybban* (unrecorded) f. Gmc]

grubby /ˈgrʌbɪ/ *adj.* (**grubbier, grubbiest**) **1** dirty, grimy, slovenly. **2** of or infested with grubs. □ **grubbily** *adv.* **grubbiness** *n.*

grudge *n. & v.* —*n.* a persistent feeling of resentment, esp. one due to an insult or injury (*bears a grudge against me*). —*v.tr.* **1** be resentfully unwilling to give or allow (a thing). **2** (foll. by verbal noun) be reluctant to do (a thing). □ **grudger** *n.* [ME *grutch* f. OF *grouchier* murmur, of unkn. orig.]

grudging /ˈgrʌdʒɪŋ/ *adj.* reluctant; not willing. □ **grudgingly** *adv.* **grudgingness** *n.*

gruel /ˈgruːəl/ *n.* a liquid food of oatmeal etc. boiled in milk or water chiefly for invalids. [ME f. OF, ult. f. Gmc, rel. to GROUT]

gruelling /ˈgruːəlɪŋ/ *adj.* (*US* **grueling**) extremely demanding, severe, or tiring. □ **gruellingly** *adv.* [GRUEL as verb, = exhaust, punish]

gruesome /ˈgruːsəm/ *adj.* horrible, grisly, disgusting. □ **gruesomely** *adv.* **gruesomeness** *n.* [Sc. *grue* to shudder f. Scand. + -SOME¹]

gruff *adj.* **1 a** (of a voice) low and harsh. **b** (of a person) having a gruff voice. **2** surly, laconic, rough-mannered. □ **gruffly** *adv.* **gruffness** *n.* [Du., MLG *grof* coarse f. WG (rel. to ROUGH)]

grumble /ˈgrʌmb(ə)l/ *v. & n.* —*v.* **1** *intr.* **a** (often foll. by *at, about, over*) complain peevishly. **b** be

discontented. **2** *intr.* **a** utter a dull inarticulate sound; murmur, growl faintly. **b** rumble. **3** *tr.* utter complainingly. **4** *intr.* (as **grumbling** *adj.*) *colloq.* giving intermittent discomfort without causing illness (*a grumbling appendix*). —*n.* **1** a complaint. **2 a** a dull inarticulate sound. **b** a rumble. □ **grumbler** *n.* **grumbling** *adj.* **grumblingly** *adv.* **grumbly** *adj.* [obs. *grumme*: cf. MDu. *grommen*, MLG *grommelen*, f. Gmc]

grummet var. of GROMMET.

grumpy /ˈgrʌmpɪ/ *adj.* (**grumpier, grumpiest**) morosely irritable; surly. □ **grumpily** *adv.* **grumpiness** *n.* [imit.]

grunt /grʌnt/ *n. & v.* —*n.* **1** a low guttural sound made by a pig. **2** a sound resembling this. —*v.* **1** *intr.* (of a pig) make a grunt or grunts. **2** *intr.* (of a person) make a low inarticulate sound resembling this, esp. to express discontent, fatigue, etc. **3** *tr.* utter with a grunt. □ **grunter** *n.* [OE *grunnettan*, prob. orig. imit.]

Grunth var. of GRANTH.

Gruyère /ˈgruːjeə(r)/ *n.* a firm pale cheese made from cow's milk. [*Gruyère*, a district in Switzerland where it was first made]

gryphon var. of GRIFFIN.

G-string /ˈdʒiːstrɪŋ/ *n.* **1** *Mus.* a string sounding the note G. **2** (also **gee-string**) a narrow strip of cloth etc. covering only the genitals and attached to a string round the waist.

G-suit /ˈdʒiːsuːt, -sjuːt/ *n.* a garment with inflatable pressurized pouches, worn by pilots and astronauts to enable them to withstand high acceleration. [g = gravity + SUIT]

GT /dʒiːˈtiː/ *n.* a high-performance saloon car. [abbr. f. It. *gran turismo* great touring]

guacamole /ˌgwɑːkəˈməʊlɪ/ *n.* a dish of mashed avocado pears. [Amer. Sp. f. Nahuatl *ahuacamolli* f. *ahuacatl* avocado + *molli* sauce]

guanaco /gwəˈnɑːkəʊ/ *n.* (*pl.* -os) a llama-like camelid, *Lama guanicoe*, with a coat of soft pale-brown hair used for wool. [Quechua *huanaco*]

guanine /ˈgwɑːniːn/ *n.* *Biochem.* a purine derivative found in all living organisms as a component base of DNA and RNA. [GUANO + -INE⁴]

guano /ˈgwɑːnəʊ/ *n. & v.* (*pl.* -os) —*n.* **1** the excrement of sea-fowl, found esp. in the islands off Peru and used as manure. **2** an artificial manure, esp. that made from fish. —*v.tr.* (-oes, -oed) fertilize with guano. [Sp. f. Quechua *huanu* dung]

guarantee /ˌgærənˈtiː/ *n. & v.* —*n.* **1 a** a formal promise or assurance, esp. that an obligation will be fulfilled or that something is of a specified quality and durability. **b** a document giving such an undertaking. **2** = GUARANTY. **3** a person making a guaranty or giving a security. —*v.tr.* (**guarantees, guaranteed**) **1 a** give or serve as a guarantee for; answer for the due fulfilment of (a contract etc.) or the genuineness of (an article). **b** assure the permanence etc. of. **c** provide with a guarantee. **2** (foll. by *that* + clause, or to + infin.) give a promise or assurance. **3 a** (foll. by *to*) secure the possession of (a thing) for a person. **b** make (a person) secure against a risk or in possession of a thing. [earlier *garante*, perh. f. Sp. *garante* = F *garant* WARRANT: later infl. by F *garantie* guaranty]

guarantor /ˌgærənˈtɔː(r), ˈgærəntə(r)/ *n.* a person who gives a guarantee or guaranty.

guaranty /ˈgærəntɪ/ n. (pl. **-ies**) **1** a written or other undertaking to answer for the payment of a debt or for the performance of an obligation by another person liable in the first instance. **2** a thing serving as security for a guaranty. [AF *guarantie*, var. of *warantie* WARRANTY]

guard /gɑːd/ v. & n. —v. **1** tr. (often foll. by *from*, *against*) watch over and defend or protect from harm. **2** tr. keep watch by (a door etc.) so as to control entry or exit. **3** tr. supervise (prisoners etc.) and prevent from escaping. **4** tr. provide (machinery) with a protective device. **5** tr. keep (thoughts or speech) in check. **6** tr. provide with safeguards. **7** intr. (foll. by *against*) take precautions. —n. **1** a state of vigilance or watchfulness. **2** a person who protects or keeps watch. **3** a body of soldiers etc. serving to protect a place or person; an escort. **4** US a prison warder. **5** a part of an army detached for some purpose (*advance guard*). **6** (in pl.) (usu. **Guards**) any of various bodies of troops variously employed to guard a monarch. **7** a thing that protects or defends. **8** (often in *comb.*) a device fitted to a machine, vehicle, weapon, etc., to prevent injury or accident to the user (*fire-guard*). **9** Brit. an official who rides with and is in general charge of a train. □ **be on** (or **keep** or **stand**) **guard** (of a sentry etc.) keep watch. **guard's van** Brit. a coach or compartment occupied by a guard. **lower one's guard** reduce vigilance against attack. **off** (or **off one's**) **guard** unprepared for some surprise or difficulty. **on** (or **on one's**) **guard** prepared for all contingencies; vigilant. **raise one's guard** become vigilant against attack. □ **guarder** n. **guardless** adj. [ME f. OF *garde*, *garder* ult. f. WG, rel. to WARD n.]

guarded /ˈgɑːdɪd/ adj. (of a remark etc.) cautious, avoiding commitment. □ **guardedly** adv. **guardedness** n.

guardhouse /ˈgɑːdhaʊs/ n. a building used to accommodate a military guard or to detain prisoners.

guardian /ˈgɑːdɪən/ n. **1** a defender, protector, or keeper. **2** a person having legal custody of another person and his or her property when that person is incapable of managing his or her own affairs. □ **guardian angel** a spirit conceived as watching over a person or place. □ **guardianship** n. [ME f. AF *gardein*, OF *garden* f. Frank., rel. to WARD, WARDEN]

guardroom /ˈgɑːdruːm, -rʊm/ n. a room with the same purpose as a guardhouse.

guardsman /ˈgɑːdzmən/ n. (pl. **-men**) **1** a soldier belonging to a body of guards. **2** (in the UK) a soldier of a regiment of Guards.

guava /ˈgwɑːvə/ n. **1** a small tropical American tree, *Psidium guajava*, bearing an edible pale yellow fruit with pink juicy flesh. **2** this fruit. [Sp. *guayaba* prob. f. a S.Amer. name]

gubbins /ˈgʌbɪnz/ n. Brit. **1** a set of equipment or paraphernalia. **2** a gadget. **3** something of little value. [orig. = fragments, f. obs. *gobbon*: perh. rel. to GOBBET]

gubernatorial /ˌgjuːbənəˈtɔːrɪəl/ adj. esp. US of or relating to a governor. [L *gubernator* governor]

gudgeon¹ /ˈgʌdʒ(ə)n/ n. a small European freshwater fish, *Gobio gobio*, often used as bait. [ME f. OF *goujon* f. L *gobio -onis* GOBY]

gudgeon² /ˈgʌdʒ(ə)n/ n. **1** any of various kinds of pivot working a wheel, bell, etc. **2** the tubular part of a hinge into which the pin fits to effect the joint. **3** a socket at the stern of a boat, into which a rudder is fitted. **4** a pin holding two blocks of stone etc. together. □ **gudgeon-pin** (in an internal-combustion engine) a pin holding a piston-rod and a connecting-rod together. [ME f. OF *goujon* dimin. of *gouge* GOUGE]

guelder rose /ˈgeldə(r)/ n. a deciduous shrub, *Viburnum opulus*, with round bunches of creamy-white flowers. [Du. *geldersch* f. *Gelderland* a province in the Netherlands]

Guernsey /ˈgɜːnzɪ/ n. (pl. **-eys**) **1 a** an animal of a breed of dairy cattle from Guernsey in the Channel Islands. **b** this breed. **2** (**guernsey**) **a** a thick (usu. blue) woollen sweater of a distinctive pattern. **b** Austral. a football shirt.

guerrilla /gəˈrɪlə/ n. (also **guerilla**) a member of a small independently acting group taking part in irregular fighting, esp. against regular forces. □ **guerrilla war** (or **warfare**) fighting by or with guerrillas. [Sp. *guerrilla*, dimin. of *guerra* war]

guess /ges/ v. & n. —v. **1** tr. (often *absol.*) estimate without calculation or measurement, or on the basis of inadequate data. **2** tr. (often foll. by *that* etc. + clause, or *to* + infin.) form a hypothesis or opinion about; conjecture; think likely (*cannot guess how you did it; guess them to be Italian*). **3** tr. conjecture or estimate correctly by guessing (*you have to guess the weight*). **4** intr. (foll. by *at*) make a conjecture about. —n. an estimate or conjecture reached by guessing. □ **I guess** colloq. I think it likely; I suppose. □ **guessable** adj. **guesser** n. [ME *gesse*, of uncert. orig.: cf. OSw. *gissa*, MLG, MDu. *gissen*: f. the root of GET v.]

guesswork /ˈgeswɜːk/ n. the process of or results got by guessing.

guest /gest/ n. & v. —n. **1** a person invited to visit another's house or have a meal etc. at the expense of the inviter. **2** a person lodging at a hotel, boarding-house, etc. **3 a** an outside performer invited to take part with a regular body of performers. **b** a person who takes part by invitation in a radio or television programme (often *attrib.*: *guest artist*). **4** (*attrib.*) **a** a serving or set aside for guests (*guest-room; guest-night*). **b** acting as a guest (*guest speaker*). **5** an organism living in close association with another. —v.intr. be a guest on a radio or television show or in a theatrical performance etc. □ **guest-house** a private house offering paid accommodation. □ **guestship** n. [ME f. ON *gestr* f. Gmc]

guestimate /ˈgestɪmət/ n. (also **guesstimate**) colloq. an estimate based on a mixture of guesswork and calculation. [GUESS + ESTIMATE]

guff n. sl. empty talk; nonsense. [19th c., orig. = 'puff': imit.]

guffaw /gʌˈfɔː/ n. & v. —n. a coarse or boisterous laugh. —v. **1** intr. utter a guffaw. **2** tr. say with a guffaw. [orig. Sc.: imit.]

guidance /ˈgaɪd(ə)ns/ n. **1** advice or information aimed at resolving a problem, difficulty, etc. **2** the process of guiding or being guided.

guide /gaɪd/ n. & v. —n. **1** a person who leads or shows the way, or directs the movements of a person or group. **2** a person who conducts travellers on tours etc. **3** a professional mountain-climber in charge of a group. **4** an adviser. **5** a directing principle or standard (*one's feelings are a bad guide*). **6** a book with essential information on a subject, esp. = GUIDEBOOK. **7**

a thing marking a position or guiding the eye. **8 (Guide)** *Brit.* a member of a girls' organization similar to the Scouts. —*v.tr.* **1 a** act as guide to; lead or direct. **b** arrange the course of (events). **2** be the principle, motive, or ground of (an action, judgement, etc.). **3** direct the affairs of (a State etc.). □ **guided missile** a missile directed to its target by remote control or by equipment within itself. **guide-dog** a dog trained to guide a blind person. **guide-rope** a rope guiding the movement of a crane, airship, etc. □ **guidable** *adj.* **guider** *n.* [ME f. OF *guide* (n.), *guider* (v.), earlier *guier* ult. f. Gmc, rel. to WIT²]

guidebook /ˈgaɪdbʊk/ *n.* a book of information about a place for visitors, tourists, etc.

guideline /ˈgaɪdlaɪn/ *n.* a principle or criterion guiding or directing action.

Guider /ˈgaɪdə(r)/ *n.* an adult leader of Guides (see GUIDE *n.* 8).

guidon /ˈgaɪd(ə)n/ *n.* a pennant narrowing to a point or fork at the free end. [F f. It. *guidone* f. *guida* GUIDE]

guild /gɪld/ *n.* (also **gild**) **1** an association of people for mutual aid or the pursuit of a common goal. **2** a medieval association of craftsmen or merchants. [ME prob. f. MLG, MDu. *gilde* f. Gmc: rel. to OE *gild* payment, sacrifice]

guilder /ˈgɪldə(r)/ *n.* the chief monetary unit of the Netherlands. [ME, alt. of Du. *gulden* GOLDEN]

guildhall /gɪldˈhɔːl, ˈgɪld-/ *n.* **1** the meeting-place of a guild or corporation; a town hall. **2 (the Guildhall)** the hall of the Corporation of the City of London, used for ceremonial occasions.

guile /gaɪl/ *n.* treachery, deceit; cunning or sly behaviour. □ **guileful** *adj.* **guilefully** *adv.* **guilefulness** *n.* **guileless** *adj.* **guilelessly** *adv.* **guilelessness** *n.* [ME f. OF, prob. f. Gmc]

guillemot /ˈgɪlɪˌmɒt/ *n.* any fast-flying sea bird of the genus *Uria* or *Cepphus*, nesting on cliffs or islands. [F f. *Guillaume* William]

guillotine /ˈgɪləˌtiːn/ *n.* & *v.* —*n.* **1** a machine with a heavy knife-blade sliding vertically in grooves, used for beheading. **2** a device for cutting paper, metal, etc. **3** *Parl.* a method of preventing delay in the discussion of a legislative bill by fixing times at which various parts of it must be voted on. —*v.tr.* use a guillotine on. □ **guillotiner** *n.* [F f. J.-I. *Guillotin*, Fr. physician d. 1814, who recommended its use for executions in 1789]

guilt /gɪlt/ *n.* **1** the fact of having committed a specified or implied offence. **2 a** culpability. **b** the feeling of this. [OE *gylt*, of unkn. orig.]

guiltless /ˈgɪltlɪs/ *adj.* **1** (often foll. by *of* an offence) innocent. **2** (foll. by *of*) not having knowledge or possession of. □ **guiltlessly** *adv.* **guiltlessness** *n.* [OE *gyltlēas* (as GUILT, -LESS)]

guilty /ˈgɪltɪ/ *adj.* (**guiltier, guiltiest**) **1** culpable of or responsible for a wrong. **2** conscious of or affected by guilt (*a guilty conscience; a guilty look*). **3** concerning guilt (*a guilty secret*). **4 a** (often foll. by *of*) having committed a (specified) offence. **b** *Law* adjudged to have committed a specified offence, esp. by a verdict in a trial. □ **guiltily** *adv.* **guiltiness** *n.* [OE *gyltig* (as GUILT, -Y¹)]

guimp var. of GIMP.

guinea /ˈgɪnɪ/ *n.* **1** *Brit. hist.* the sum of 21 old shillings (£1.05). **2** *hist.* a former British gold coin worth 21 shillings, first coined for the African trade. □ **guinea-fowl** any African fowl

of the family Numididae, esp. *Numida meleagris*, with slate-coloured white-spotted plumage. **guinea-pig 1** a domesticated S. American cavy, *Cavia porcellus*, kept as a pet or for research in biology etc. **2** a person or thing used as a subject for experiment. [*Guinea* in W. Africa]

guipure /ˈgiːpjʊə(r)/ *n.* a heavy lace of linen pieces joined by embroidery. [F f. *guiper* cover with silk etc. f. Gmc]

guise /gaɪz/ *n.* **1** an assumed appearance; a pretence (*in the guise of; under the guise of*). **2** external appearance. [ME f. OF ult. f. Gmc]

guitar /gɪˈtɑː(r)/ *n.* a usu. six-stringed musical instrument with a fretted finger-board, played by plucking with the fingers or a plectrum. □ **guitarist** *n.* [Sp. *guitarra* (partly through F *guitare*) f. Gk *kithara* a kind of harp]

gulch /gʌltʃ/ *n.* *US* a ravine, esp. one in which a torrent flows. [perh. dial. *gulch* to swallow]

gulf *n.* & *v.* —*n.* **1** a stretch of sea consisting of a deep inlet with a narrow mouth. **2 (the Gulf)** the Persian Gulf. **3** a deep hollow; a chasm. **4** a wide difference of feelings, opinion, etc. —*v.tr.* engulf; swallow up. □ **Gulf Stream** an oceanic warm current flowing from the Gulf of Mexico. [ME f. OF *golfe* f. It. *golfo* ult. f. Gk *kolpos* bosom, gulf]

gull¹ /gʌl/ *n.* any of various long-winged web-footed sea birds of the family Laridae, usu. having white plumage. □ **gullery** *n.* (*pl.* -ies). [ME ult. f. OCelt.]

gull² /gʌl/ *v.tr.* (usu. in *passive*, foll. by *into*) dupe, fool. [perh. f. obs. *gull* yellow f. ON *gulr*]

gullet /ˈgʌlɪt/ *n.* **1** the food-passage extending from the mouth to the stomach; the oesophagus. **2** the throat. [ME f. OF dimin. of *go(u)le* throat f. L *gula*]

gullible /ˈgʌlɪb(ə)l/ *adj.* easily persuaded or deceived, credulous. □ **gullibility** /-ˈbɪlɪtɪ/ *n.* **gullibly** *adv.* [GULL² + -IBLE]

gully /ˈgʌlɪ/ *n.* (*pl.* -ies) **1** a water-worn ravine. **2** a deep artificial channel; a gutter or drain. **3** *Austral.* & *NZ* a river valley. **4** *Cricket* **a** the fielding position between point and slips. **b** a fielder in this position. [F *goulet* bottle-neck (as GULLET)]

gulp *v.* & *n.* —*v.* **1** *tr.* (often foll. by *down*) swallow hastily, greedily, or with effort. **2** *intr.* swallow with difficulty; choke. **3** *tr.* (foll. by *down, back*) stifle, suppress (esp. tears). —*n.* **1** an act of gulping (*drained it at one gulp*). **2** an effort to swallow. **3** a large mouthful of a drink. □ **gulper** *n.* **gulpingly** *adv.* **gulpy** *adj.* [ME prob. f. MDu. *gulpen* (imit.)]

gum¹ *n.* & *v.* —*n.* **1 a** a viscous secretion of some trees and shrubs that hardens on drying but is soluble in water. **b** an adhesive substance made from this. **2** *US* chewing gum. **3** = GUMDROP. **4** = *gum arabic*. **5** = *gum-tree*. **6** a secretion collecting in the corner of the eye. —*v.* (**gummed, gumming**) **1** *tr.* smear or cover with gum. **2** *tr.* (usu. foll. by *down, together*, etc.) fasten with gum. □ **gum arabic** a gum exuded by some kinds of acacia and used as glue and in incense. **gum resin** a vegetable secretion of resin mixed with gum, e.g. gamboge. **gum-tree** a tree exuding gum, esp. a eucalyptus. **gum up 1** (of a mechanism etc.) become clogged or obstructed with stickiness. **2** *colloq.* interfere with the smooth running of (*gum up the works*). **up a gum-tree** *colloq.* in great difficulties. [ME

f. OF *gomme* ult. f. L *gummi, cummi* f. Gk *kommi* f. Egypt. *kemai*]

gum² *n.* (usu. in *pl.*) the firm flesh around the roots of the teeth. □ **gum-shield** a pad protecting a boxer's teeth and gums. [OE *gōma* rel. to OHG *guomo*, ON *gómr* roof or floor of the mouth]

gum³ /gʌm/ *n. colloq.* (in oaths) God (*by gum!*). [corrupt. of *God*]

gumbo /ˈgʌmbəʊ/ *n.* (*pl.* **-os**) US **1** okra. **2** a soup thickened with okra pods. [of Afr. orig.]

gumboil /ˈgʌmbɔɪl/ *n.* a small abscess on the gums.

gumboot /ˈgʌmbuːt/ *n.* a rubber boot; a wellington.

gumdrop /ˈgʌmdrɒp/ *n.* a soft coloured sweet made with gelatin or gum arabic.

gummy¹ /ˈgʌmɪ/ *adj.* (**gummier, gummiest**) **1** viscous, sticky. **2** abounding in or exuding gum. □ **gumminess** *n.* [ME f. GUM¹ + -Y¹]

gummy² /ˈgʌmɪ/ *adj.* (**gummier, gummiest**) toothless. □ **gummily** *adv.* [GUM² + -Y¹]

gumption /ˈgʌmpʃ(ə)n/ *n. colloq.* **1** resourcefulness, initiative; enterprising spirit. **2** common sense. [18th-c. Sc.: orig. unkn.]

gumshoe /ˈgʌmʃuː/ *n.* US **1** a galosh. **2** *sl.* a detective.

gun *n.* & *v.* —*n.* **1** any kind of weapon consisting of a metal tube and often held in the hand with a grip at one end, from which bullets or other missiles are propelled with great force, esp. by a contained explosion. **2** any device imitative of this, e.g. a starting pistol. **3** a device for discharging insecticide, grease, electrons, etc., in the required direction (often in *comb.*: *grease-gun*). **4** a member of a shooting-party. **5** US a gunman. **6** the firing of a gun. —*v.* (**gunned, gunning**) **1** *tr.* **a** (usu. foll. by *down*) shoot (a person) with a gun. **b** shoot at with a gun. **2** *tr. colloq.* accelerate (an engine or vehicle). **3** *intr.* go shooting. **4** *intr.* (foll. by *for*) seek out determinedly to attack or rebuke. □ **go great guns** *colloq.* proceed forcefully or vigorously or successfully. **gun-carriage** a wheeled support for a gun. **gun-cotton** an explosive used for blasting, made by steeping cotton in nitric and sulphuric acids. **gun dog** a dog trained to follow sportsmen using guns. **jump the gun** *colloq.* start before a signal is given, or before an agreed time. **stick to one's guns** *colloq.* maintain one's position under attack. □ **gunless** *adj.* **gunned** *adj.* [ME *gunne, gonne*, perh. f. the Scand. name *Gunnhildr*]

gunboat /ˈgʌnbəʊt/ *n.* a small vessel of shallow draught and with relatively heavy guns. □ **gunboat diplomacy** political negotiation supported by the use or threat of military force.

gunfight /ˈgʌnfaɪt/ *n.* US a fight with firearms. □ **gunfighter** *n.*

gunfire /ˈgʌnˌfaɪə(r)/ *n.* **1** the firing of a gun or guns, esp. repeatedly. **2** the noise from this.

gunge /gʌndʒ/ *n.* & *v. Brit. colloq.* —*n.* sticky or viscous matter, esp. when messy or indeterminate. —*v.tr.* (usu. foll. by *up*) clog or obstruct with gunge. □ **gungy** *adj.* [20th c.: orig. uncert.: cf. GOO, GUNK]

gung-ho /gʌŋˈhəʊ/ *adj.* enthusiastic, eager. [Chin. *gonghe* work together, slogan adopted by US Marines in 1942]

gunk *n. sl.* viscous or liquid material. [20th c.: orig. the name of a detergent (propr.)]

gunman /ˈgʌnmən/ *n.* (*pl.* **-men**) a man armed with a gun, esp. in committing a crime.

gun-metal /ˈgʌnˌmet(ə)l/ *n.* **1** a dull bluish-grey colour. **2** an alloy of copper and tin or zinc (formerly used for guns).

gunnel var. of GUNWALE.

gunner /ˈgʌnə(r)/ *n.* **1** an artillery soldier (esp. as an official term for a private). **2** *Naut.* a warrant-officer in charge of a battery, magazine, etc. **3** a member of an aircraft crew who operates a gun. **4** a person who hunts game with a gun.

gunnera /ˈgʌnərə/ *n.* any plant of the genus *Gunnera*, having large leaves. [J. E. *Gunnerus*, Norw. botanist d. 1773]

gunnery /ˈgʌnərɪ/ *n.* **1** the construction and management of large guns. **2** the firing of guns.

gunpoint /ˈgʌnpɔɪnt/ *n.* the point of a gun. □ **at gunpoint** threatened with a gun or an ultimatum etc.

gunpowder /ˈgʌnˌpaʊdə(r)/ *n.* **1** an explosive of saltpetre, sulphur, and charcoal. **2** a fine green tea.

gunroom /ˈgʌnruːm, -rʊm/ *n. Brit.* **1** a room in a house for storing sporting-guns. **2** quarters for junior officers (orig. for gunners) in a warship.

gunrunner /ˈgʌnˌrʌnə(r)/ *n.* a person engaged in the illegal sale or importing of firearms. □ **gunrunning** *n.*

gunship /ˈgʌnʃɪp/ *n.* a heavily-armed helicopter or other aircraft.

gunshot /ˈgʌnʃɒt/ *n.* **1** a shot fired from a gun. **2** the range of a gun (*within gunshot*).

gunslinger /ˈgʌnˌslɪŋə(r)/ *n.* esp. US *sl.* a gunman. □ **gunslinging** *n.*

gunsmith /ˈgʌnsmɪθ/ *n.* a person who makes, sells, and repairs small firearms.

gunwale /ˈgʌn(ə)l/ *n.* (also **gunnel**) the upper edge of the side of a boat or ship. [GUN + WALE (because formerly used to support guns)]

guppy /ˈgʌpɪ/ *n.* (*pl.* **-ies**) a freshwater fish, *Poecilia reticulata*, of the W. Indies and S. America. [R. J. L. *Guppy*, 19th-c. Trinidad clergyman who sent the first specimen to the British Museum]

gurdwara /gɜːˈdwɑːrə/ *n.* a Sikh temple. [Punjabi *gurduārā* f. Skr. *guru* teacher + *dvāra* door]

gurgle /ˈgɜːg(ə)l/ *v.* & *n.* —*v.* **1** *intr.* make a bubbling sound as of water from a bottle. **2** *tr.* utter with such a sound. —*n.* a gurgling sound. □ **gurgler** *n.* [imit., or f. Du. *gorgelen*, G *gurgeln*, or med.L *gurgulare* f. L *gurgulio* gullet]

Gurkha /ˈgɜːkə/ *n.* **1** a member of the dominant Hindu race in Nepal. **2** a Nepalese soldier serving in the British army. [native name, f. Skr. *gāus* cow + *raksh* protect]

gurnard /ˈgɜːnəd/ *n.* (also **gurnet** /ˈgɜːnɪt/) any marine fish of the family Triglidae, having three finger-like pectoral rays used for walking on the sea bed etc. [ME f. OF *gornart* f. *grondir* to grunt f. L *grunnire*]

guru /ˈgʊruː, ˈguːruː/ *n.* **1** a Hindu spiritual teacher or head of a religious sect. **2** an influential teacher. [Hindi *gurū* teacher f. Skr. *gurús* grave, dignified]

gush /gʌʃ/ *v.* & *n.* —*v.* **1** *tr.* & *intr.* emit or flow in a sudden and copious stream. **2** *intr.* speak or behave with effusiveness or sentimental affectation. —*n.* **1** a sudden or copious stream. **2** an effusive or sentimental manner. □ **gushing** *adj.* **gushingly** *adv.* [ME *gosshe, gusche*, prob. imit.]

gusher /ˈgʌʃə(r)/ n. **1** an oil well from which oil flows without being pumped. **2** an effusive person.

gushy /ˈgʌʃɪ/ adj. (**gushier, gushiest**) excessively effusive. □ **gushily** adv. **gushiness** n.

gusset /ˈgʌsɪt/ n. **1** a piece let into a garment etc. to strengthen or enlarge a part. **2** a bracket strengthening an angle of a structure. □ **gusseted** adj. [ME f. OF gousset flexible piece filling up a joint in armour f. gousse pod, shell]

gust n. & v. —n. **1** a sudden strong rush of wind. **2** a burst of rain, fire, smoke, or sound. **3** a passionate or emotional outburst. —v.intr. blow in gusts. [ON gustr, rel. to gjósa to gush]

gustation /gʌˈsteɪʃ(ə)n/ n. the act or capacity of tasting. □ **gustative** /ˈgʌstətɪv/ adj. **gustatory** /ˈgʌstətərɪ/ adj. [F gustation or L gustatio f. gustare f. gustus taste]

gusto /ˈgʌstəʊ/ n. (pl. **-oes**) zest; enjoyment or vigour in doing something. [It. f. L gustus taste]

gusty /ˈgʌstɪ/ adj. (**gustier, gustiest**) **1** characterized by or blowing in strong winds. **2** characterized by gusto. □ **gustily** adv. **gustiness** n.

gut n. & v. —n. **1** the lower alimentary canal or a part of this; the intestine. **2** (in pl.) the bowel or entrails, esp. of animals. **3** (in pl.) colloq. personal courage and determination; vigorous application and perseverance. **4** (in pl.) colloq. the belly as the source of appetite. **5** (in pl.) a the contents of anything, esp. representing substantiality. **b** the essence of a thing, e.g. of an issue or problem. **6 a** material for violin or racket strings or surgical use made from the intestines of animals. **b** material for fishing-lines made from the silk-glands of silkworms. **7** (attrib.) **a** instinctive (a gut reaction). **b** fundamental (a gut issue). —v.tr. (**gutted, gutting**) **1** remove or destroy (esp. by fire) the internal fittings of (a house etc.). **2** take out the guts of (a fish). **3** extract the essence of (a book etc.). □ **gut-rot** colloq. **1** = rot-gut. **2** a stomach upset. **hate a person's guts** colloq. dislike a person intensely. [OE guttas (pl.), prob. rel. to gēotan pour]

gutless /ˈgʌtlɪs/ adj. colloq. lacking courage or determination. □ **gutlessly** adv. **gutlessness** n.

gutsy /ˈgʌtsɪ/ adj. (**gutsier, gutsiest**) colloq. **1** courageous. **2** greedy. □ **gutsily** adv. **gutsiness** n.

gutta-percha /ˌgʌtəˈpɜːtʃə/ n. a tough plastic substance obtained from the latex of various Malaysian trees. [Malay getah gum + percha name of a tree]

gutted /ˈgʌtɪd/ adj. sl. utterly exhausted or devastated; shattered.

gutter /ˈgʌtə(r)/ n. & v. —n. **1** a shallow trough below the eaves of a house, or a channel at the side of a street, to carry off rainwater. **2** (prec. by the) a poor or degraded background or environment. **3** an open conduit along which liquid flows out. **4** a groove. —v. intr. flow in streams. □ **gutter press** sensational journalism. [ME f. AF gotere, OF gotiere ult. f. L gutta drop]

guttering /ˈgʌtərɪŋ/ n. **1 a** the gutters of a building etc. **b** a section of a gutter. **2** material for gutters.

guttersnipe /ˈgʌtəˌsnaɪp/ n. a street urchin.

guttural /ˈgʌtər(ə)l/ adj. & n. —adj. **1** throaty, harsh-sounding. **2 a** Phonet. (of a consonant) produced in the throat or by the back of the tongue and palate. **b** (of a sound) coming from the throat. **c** of the throat. —n. Phonet. a guttural consonant (e.g. k, g). □ **gutturally** adv. [F guttural or med.L gutturalis f. L guttur throat]

guv /gʌv/ n. Brit. sl. = GOVERNOR 7. [abbr.]

guy[1] /gaɪ/ n. & v. —n. **1** colloq. a man; a fellow. **2** (usu. in pl.) US a person of either sex. **3** Brit. an effigy of Guy Fawkes in ragged clothing, burnt on a bonfire on 5 Nov. **4** Brit. a grotesquely dressed person. —v.tr. **1** ridicule. **2** exhibit in effigy. [Guy Fawkes, conspirator in the Gunpowder Plot to blow up Parliament in 1605]

guy[2] /gaɪ/ n. & v. —n. a rope or chain to secure a tent or steady a crane-load etc. —v.tr. secure with a guy or guys. [prob. of LG orig.: cf. LG & Du. gei brail etc.]

guzzle /ˈgʌz(ə)l/ v.tr. & intr. eat, drink, or consume excessively or greedily. □ **guzzler** n. [perh. f. OF gosiller chatter, vomit f. gosier throat]

Gy abbr. = GRAY[1].

gybe /dʒaɪb/ v. & n. (US **jibe**) —v. **1** intr. (of a fore-and-aft sail or boom) swing across in wearing or running before the wind. **2** tr. cause (a sail) to do this. **3** intr. (of a ship or its crew) change course so that this happens. —n. a change of course causing gybing. [obs. Du. gijben]

gym /dʒɪm/ n. colloq. **1** a gymnasium. **2** gymnastics. [abbr.]

gymkhana /dʒɪmˈkɑːnə/ n. a meeting for competition or display in sport, esp. horse-riding. [Hind. gendkhāna ball-house, racket-court, assim. to GYMNASIUM]

gymnasium /dʒɪmˈneɪzɪəm/ n. (pl. **gymnasiums** or **gymnasia** /-zɪə/) a room or building equipped for gymnastics. □ **gymnasial** adj. [L f. Gk gumnasion f. gumnazō exercise f. gumnos naked]

gymnast /ˈdʒɪmnæst/ n. an expert in gymnastics. [F gymnaste or Gk gumnastēs athlete-trainer f. gumnazō: see GYMNASIUM]

gymnastic /dʒɪmˈnæstɪk/ adj. of or involving gymnastics. □ **gymnastically** adv. [L gymnasticus f. Gk gumnastikos (as GYMNASIUM)]

gymnastics /dʒɪmˈnæstɪks/ n.pl. (also treated as sing.) **1** exercises developing or displaying physical agility and coordination, usu. in competition. **2** other forms of physical or mental agility.

gymno- /ˈdʒɪmnəʊ/ comb. form Biol. bare, naked. [Gk gumnos naked]

gymnosperm /ˈdʒɪmnəʊˌspɜːm/ n. any of various plants having seeds unprotected by an ovary, including conifers, cycads, and ginkgos (opp. ANGIOSPERM). □ **gymnospermous** /-ˈspɜːməs/ adj.

gymp var. of GIMP.

gymslip /ˈdʒɪmslɪp/ n. a sleeveless tunic, usu. belted, worn by schoolgirls.

gynaeco- /ˈgaɪnɪkəʊ/ comb. form (US **gyneco-**) woman, women; female. [Gk gunē gunaikos woman]

gynaecology /ˌgaɪnɪˈkɒlədʒɪ/ n. (US **gynecology**) the science of the physiological functions and diseases of women and girls, esp. those affecting the reproductive system. □ **gynaecological** /-kəˈlɒdʒɪk(ə)l/ adj. **gynaecologically** /-kəˈlɒdʒɪkəlɪ/ adv. **gynaecologist** n. **gynecologic** /-kəˈlɒdʒɪk/ adj. US.

-gynous /ˈgɪnəs, ˈdʒɪnəs/ *comb. form Bot.* forming adjectives meaning 'having specified female organs or pistils' (*monogynous*). [Gk *-gunos* f. *gunē* woman]

gyp[1] /dʒɪp/ *n. Brit. colloq.* pain or severe discomfort. [19th c.: perh. f. *gee-up* (see GEE²)]

gyp[2] /dʒɪp/ *v. & n. sl.* —*v.tr.* (**gypped, gypping**) cheat, swindle. —*n.* an act of cheating; a swindle. [19th c.: perh. f. obs. *gippo* scullion]

gyppy tummy var. of GIPPY TUMMY.

gypsophila /dʒɪpˈsɒfɪlə/ *n.* any plant of the genus *Gypsophila*, with a profusion of small flowers. [mod.L f. Gk *gupsos* chalk + *philos* loving]

gypsum /ˈdʒɪpsəm/ *n.* a hydrated form of calcium sulphate occurring naturally and used to make plaster of Paris and in the building industry. □ **gypseous** *adj.* **gypsiferous** /-ˈsɪfərəs/ *adj.* [L f. Gk *gupsos*]

Gypsy /ˈdʒɪpsɪ/ *n.* (also **Gipsy**) (*pl.* **-ies**) **1** a member of a nomadic people of Europe and N. America, of Hindu origin, and speaking a language related to Hindi. **2** (**gypsy**) a person resembling or living like a Gypsy. □ **Gypsyfied** *adj.* **Gypsyhood** *n.* **Gypsyish** *adj.* [earlier *gipcyan, gipsen* f. EGYPTIAN, from the supposed origin of Gypsies when they appeared in England in the early 16th c.]

gyrate *v. intr.* /ˌdʒaɪəˈreɪt/ go in a circle or spiral; revolve, whirl. □ **gyration** /-ˈreɪʃ(ə)n/ *n.* **gyrator** /ˌdʒaɪəˈreɪtə(r)/ *n.* **gyratory** /-rətərɪ, -ˈreɪtərɪ/ *adj.* [L *gyrare gyrat-* revolve f. *gyrus* ring f. Gk *guros*]

gyro /ˈdʒaɪərəʊ/ *n.* (*pl.* **-os**) *colloq.* **1** = GYROSCOPE. **2** = GYROCOMPASS. [abbr.]

gyro- /ˈdʒaɪərəʊ/ *comb. form* rotation. [Gk *guros* ring]

gyrocompass /ˈdʒaɪərəʊˌkʌmpəs/ *n.* a non-magnetic compass giving true north and bearings from it by means of a gyroscope.

gyroscope /ˈdʒaɪərəˌskəʊp/ *n.* a rotating wheel whose axis is free to turn but maintains a fixed direction unless perturbed, esp. used for stabilization or with the compass in an aircraft, ship, etc. □ **gyroscopic** /-ˈskɒpɪk/ *adj.* **gyroscopically** /-ˈskɒpɪkəlɪ/ *adv.* [F (as GYRO-, SCOPE²)]

Hh

H¹ /eɪtʃ/ *n.* (also **h**) (*pl.* **Hs** or **H's**) **1** the eighth letter of the alphabet (see AITCH). **2** anything having the form of an H (esp. in *comb.*: *H-girder*).

H² *abbr.* (also **H.**) **1** hardness. **2** (of a pencil-lead) hard. **3** henry, henrys.

H³ *symb. Chem.* the element hydrogen.

h. *abbr.* **1** hecto-. **2** height. **3** hot. **4** hour(s).

Ha *symb. Chem.* the element hahnium.

ha¹ /hɑː/ *int.* & *v.* (also **hah**) —*int.* expressing surprise, suspicion, triumph, etc. (cf. HA HA). —*v. intr.* (in **hum and ha**: see HUM¹) [ME]

ha² *abbr.* hectare(s).

habanera /ˌhæbəˈneərə/ *n.* **1** a Cuban dance in slow duple time. **2** the music for this. [Sp., fem. of *habanero* of Havana in Cuba]

habeas corpus /ˌheɪbɪəs ˈkɔːpəs/ *n.* a writ requiring a person to be brought before a judge or into court, esp. to investigate the lawfulness of his or her detention. [L, = you must have the body]

haberdasher /ˈhæbəˌdæʃə(r)/ *n.* **1** *Brit.* a dealer in dress accessories and sewing-goods. **2** *US* a dealer in men's clothing. □ **haberdashery** *n.* (*pl.* **-ies**). [ME prob. ult. f. AF *hapertas* perh. the name of a fabric]

habiliment /həˈbɪlɪmənt/ *n.* (usu. in *pl.*) clothes suited to a particular purpose. [ME f. OF *habillement* f. *habiller* fit out f. *habile* ABLE]

habit /ˈhæbɪt/ *n.* **1** a settled or regular tendency or practice (often foll. by *of* + verbal noun: *has a habit of ignoring me*). **2** a practice that is hard to give up. **3** a mental constitution or attitude. **4** *colloq.* an addictive practice, esp. of taking drugs. **5 a** the dress of a particular class, esp. of a religious order. **b** (in full **riding-habit**) a woman's riding-dress. **6** *Biol.* & *Crystallog.* a mode of growth. □ **habit-forming** causing addiction. **make a habit of** do regularly. [ME f. OF *abit* f. L *habitus* f. *habēre* habit- have, be constituted]

habitable /ˈhæbɪtəb(ə)l/ *adj.* that can be inhabited. □ **habitability** /-ˈbɪlɪtɪ/ *n.* **habitableness** *n.* **habitably** *adv.* [ME f. OF f. L *habitabilis* (as HABITANT)]

habitant /ˈhæbɪt(ə)nt/ *n.* an inhabitant. [F f. OF *habiter* f. L *habitare* inhabit (as HABIT)]

habitat /ˈhæbɪˌtæt/ *n.* **1** the natural home of an organism. **2** a habitation. [L, = it dwells: see HABITANT]

habitation /ˌhæbɪˈteɪʃ(ə)n/ *n.* **1** the process of inhabiting (*fit for human habitation*). **2** a house or home. [ME f. OF f. L *habitatio -onis* (as HABITANT)]

habitual /həˈbɪtjʊəl/ *adj.* **1** done constantly or as a habit. **2** regular, usual. **3** given to a (specified) habit (*a habitual smoker*). □ **habitually** *adv.* **habitualness** *n.* [med.L *habitualis* (as HABIT)]

habituate /həˈbɪtjʊˌeɪt/ *v.tr.* (often foll. by *to*) accustom; make used to something. □ **habituation** /-ˈeɪʃ(ə)n/ *n.* [LL *habituare* (as HABIT)]

habitué /həˈbɪtjʊˌeɪ/ *n.* a habitual visitor or resident. [F, past part. of *habituer* as HABITUATE)]

háček /ˈhætʃek/ *n.* a diacritic mark (ˇ) placed over letters to modify the sound in some Slavonic and Baltic languages. [Czech, dimin. of *hák* hook]

hachures /hæˈfjʊə(r)/ *n.pl.* parallel lines used in hill-shading on maps, their closeness indicating the steepness of gradient. [F f. *hacher* HATCH³]

hacienda /ˌhæsɪˈendə/ *n.* in Spanish-speaking countries: **1** an estate or plantation with a dwelling-house. **2** a factory. [Sp. f. L *facienda* things to be done]

hack¹ *v.* & *n.* —*v.* **1** *tr.* cut or chop roughly; mangle. **2** *tr.* kick the shin of (an opponent at football). **3** *intr.* (often foll. by *at*) deliver cutting blows. **4** *tr.* cut (one's way) through thick foliage etc. **5** *tr. colloq.* gain unauthorized access to (data in a computer). **6** *tr. sl.* **a** manage, cope with. **b** tolerate. —*n.* **1** a kick with the toe of a boot. **2** a gash or wound, esp. from a kick. **3 a** a mattock. **b** a miner's pick. □ **hacking cough** a short dry frequent cough. [OE *haccian* cut in pieces f. WG]

hack² *n., adj.,* & *v.* —*n.* **1 a** a horse for ordinary riding. **b** a horse let out for hire. **2** a dull, uninspired writer. **3** a person hired to do dull routine work. —*attrib.adj.* **1** used as a hack. **2** typical of a hack; commonplace (*hack work*). —*v.* **1** *intr.* ride on horseback on a road at an ordinary pace. **2** *tr.* ride (a horse) in this way. [abbr. of HACKNEY]

hacker /ˈhækə(r)/ *n.* **1** a person or thing that hacks or cuts roughly. **2** *colloq.* a person who uses computers for a hobby, esp. to gain unauthorized access to data.

hackle /ˈhæk(ə)l/ *n.* **1** a long feather or series of feathers on the neck or saddle of a domestic cock and other birds. **2** (in *pl.*) the erectile hairs along the back of a dog, which rise when it is angry or alarmed. □ **make one's hackles rise** cause one to be angry or indignant. [ME *hechele*, *hakele*, prob. f. OE f. WG]

hackney /ˈhæknɪ/ *n.* (*pl.* **-eys**) **1** a horse of average size and quality for ordinary riding. **2** (*attrib.*) designating any of various vehicles kept for hire. [ME, perh. f. *Hackney* (formerly *Hakenei*) in London, where horses were pastured]

■ **Usage** Sense 2 is no longer used except in *hackney carriage*, still in official use as a term for 'taxi'.

hackneyed /ˈhæknɪd/ *adj.* (of a phrase etc.) made commonplace or trite by overuse.

hacksaw /ˈhæksɔː/ *n.* a saw with a narrow blade set in a frame, for cutting metal.

had *past* and *past part.* of HAVE.

haddock /ˈhædək/ *n.* (*pl.* same) a marine fish, *Melanogrammus aeglefinus*, of the N. Atlantic, allied to cod, but smaller. [ME, prob. f. AF *hadoc*, OF *(h)adot*, of unkn. orig.]

Hades /ˈheɪdiːz/ *n.* (in Greek mythology) the underworld. [Gk *haidēs*, orig. a name of Pluto]

hadj var. of HAJJ.

hadji var. of HAJJI.

hadn't /'hæd(ə)nt/ *contr.* had not.

hadron /'hædrɒn/ *n. Physics* any strongly interacting elementary particle. □ **hadronic** /-'drɒnɪk/ *adj.* [Gk *hadros* bulky]

haemal /'hiːm(ə)l/ *adj.* (US **hemal**) *Anat.* of or concerning the blood. [Gk *haima* blood]

haematic /hiː'mætɪk/ *adj.* (US **hematic**) *Med.* of or containing blood. [Gk *haimatikos* f. *haima* *-matos* blood]

haematite /'hiːmə,taɪt/ *n.* (US **hematite** /'hiːm-, 'hem-/) a ferric oxide ore. [L *haematites* f. Gk *haimatitēs* (*lithos*) bloodlike (stone) (as HAEMATIC)]

haemato- /'hiːmətəʊ/ *comb. form* (US **hemato-**) blood. [Gk *haima haimat-* blood]

haematology /,hiːmə'tɒlədʒɪ/ *n.* (US **hematology** /'hiː-/, 'he-/) the study of the physiology of the blood. □ **haematologic** /-tə'lɒdʒɪk/ *adj.* **haematological** /-tə'lɒdʒɪk(ə)l/ *adj.* **haematologist** *n.*

haemo- /'hiːməʊ/ *comb. form* (US **hemo-**) = HAEMATO-. [abbr.]

haemodialysis /,hiːməʊdaɪ'ælɪsɪs/ *n.* = DIALYSIS 2.

haemoglobin /,hiːmə'gləʊbɪn/ *n.* (US **hemoglobin** /,hiː-, ,he-/) a red oxygen-carrying substance containing iron, present in the red blood-cells of vertebrates. [shortened f. *haematoglobin*, compound of HAEMATIN + GLOBULIN]

haemophilia /,hiːmə'fɪlɪə/ *n.* (US **hemophilia** /,hiː-, ,he-/) *Med.* a usu. hereditary disorder with a tendency to bleed severely from even a slight injury, through the failure of the blood to clot normally. □ **haemophilic** *adj.* [mod.L (as HAEMO-, -PHILIA)]

haemophiliac /,hiːmə'fɪlɪ,æk/ *n.* (US **hemophiliac** /,hiː-, ,he-/) a person suffering from haemophilia.

haemorrhage /'hemərɪdʒ/ *n.* & *v.* (US **hemorrhage**) —*n.* 1 an escape of blood from a ruptured blood-vessel, esp. when profuse. 2 an extensive damaging loss suffered by a State, organization, etc., esp. of people or assets. —*v.intr.* undergo a haemorrhage. □ **haemorrhagic** /,hemə'rædʒɪk/ *adj.* [earlier *haemorrhagy* f. F *hémorr(h)agie* f. L *haemorrhagia* f. Gk *haimorrhagia* f. *haima* blood + stem of *rhēgnumi* burst]

haemorrhoid /'hemə,rɔɪd/ *n.* (US **hemorrhoid**) (usu. in *pl.*) swollen veins at or near the anus; piles. □ **haemorrhoidal** /-'rɔɪd(ə)l/ *adj.* [ME *emeroudis* (Bibl. *emerods*) f. OF *emeroyde* f. L f. Gk *haimorrhoides* (*phlebes*) bleeding (veins) f. *haima* blood, *-rhoos* -flowing]

haere mai /'haɪrə ,maɪ/ *int. NZ* welcome. [Maori, lit. 'come hither']

hafnium /'hæfnɪəm/ *n. Chem.* a silvery lustrous metallic element occurring naturally with zirconium. [mod.L f. *Hafnia* Copenhagen]

haft /hɑːft/ *n.* & *v.* —*n.* the handle of a dagger or knife etc. —*v.tr.* provide with a haft. [OE *hæft* f. Gmc]

hag *n.* 1 an ugly old woman. 2 a witch. □ **haggish** *adj.* [ME *hegge, hagge*, perh. f. OE *hægtesse*, OHG *hagazissa*, of unkn. orig.]

haggard /'hægəd/ *adj.* looking exhausted and distraught, esp. from fatigue, worry, privation, etc. □ **haggardly** *adv.* **haggardness** *n.* [F *hagard*, of uncert. orig.: later infl. by HAG]

haggis /'hægɪs/ *n.* a Scottish dish consisting of a sheep's or calf's offal mixed with suet, oatmeal, etc., and boiled in a bag made from the animal's stomach or in an artificial bag. [ME: orig. unkn.]

haggle /'hæg(ə)l/ *v.* & *n.* —*v.intr.* (often foll. by *about, over*) dispute or bargain persistently. —*n.* a dispute or wrangle. □ **haggler** *n.* [earlier sense 'hack' f. ON *höggva* HEW]

hagio- /'hægɪəʊ/ *comb. form* of saints or holiness. [Gk *hagios* holy]

hagiographer /,hægɪ'ɒgrəfə(r)/ *n.* a writer of the lives of saints.

hagiography /,hægɪ'ɒgrəfɪ/ *n.* the writing of the lives of saints. □ **hagiographic** /-ə'græfɪk/ *adj.* **hagiographical** /-ə'græfɪk(ə)l/ *adj.*

hagiolatry /,hægɪ'ɒlətrɪ/ *n.* the worship of saints.

hagiology /,hægɪ'ɒlədʒɪ/ *n.* literature dealing with the lives and legends of saints. □ **hagiological** /-ɪə'lɒdʒɪk(ə)l/ *adj.* **hagiologist** *n.*

hagridden /'hæg,rɪd(ə)n/ *adj.* afflicted by nightmares or anxieties.

hah var. of HA.

ha ha /hɑː'hɑː/ *int.* repr. laughter. [OE: cf. HA¹]

ha-ha /'hɑːhɑː/ *n.* a ditch with a wall on its inner side below ground level, forming a boundary to a park or garden without interrupting the view. [F, perh. from the cry of surprise on encountering it]

hahnium /'hɑːnɪəm/ *n. Chem.* an artificially produced radioactive element. [O. *Hahn*, Ger. chemist d. 1968 + -IUM]

haiku /'haɪkuː/ *n.* (*pl.* same) 1 a Japanese three-part poem of usu. 17 syllables. 2 an English imitation of this. [Jap.]

hail¹ *n.* & *v.* —*n.* 1 pellets of frozen rain falling in showers from cumulonimbus clouds. 2 (foll. by *of*) a barrage or onslaught (of missiles, curses, questions, etc.). —*v.* 1 *intr.* (prec. by *it* as subject) hail falls (*it is hailing; if it hails*). 2 a *tr.* pour down (blows, words, etc.). b *intr.* come down forcefully. [OE *hagol, hægl, hagalian* f. Gmc]

hail² *v., int.,* & *n.* —*v.* 1 *tr.* greet enthusiastically. 2 *tr.* signal to or attract the attention of (*hailed a taxi*). 3 *tr.* acclaim (*hailed him king*). 4 *intr.* (foll. by *from*) have one's home or origins in (a place) (*hails from Mauritius*). —*int.* expressing greeting. —*n.* 1 a greeting or act of hailing. 2 distance as affecting the possibility of hailing (*was within hail*). □ **hail-fellow-well-met** intimate, esp. too intimate. **Hail Mary** the Ave Maria. □ **hailer** *n.* [ellipt. use of obs. *hail* (adj.) f. ON *heill* sound, WHOLE]

hailstone /'heɪlstəʊn/ *n.* a pellet of hail.

hailstorm /'heɪlstɔːm/ *n.* a period of heavy hail.

hair /heə(r)/ *n.* 1 a any of the fine threadlike strands growing from the skin of mammals, esp. from the human head. b these collectively (*his hair is falling out*). 2 a an artificially produced hairlike strand, e.g. in a brush. b a mass of such hairs. 3 anything resembling a hair. 4 an elongated cell growing from the epidermis of a plant. 5 a very small quantity or extent (also *attrib.*: *a hair crack*). □ **get in a person's hair** *colloq.* encumber or annoy a person. **hair-drier** (or **-dryer**) an electrical device for drying the hair by blowing warm air over it. **hair-raising** extremely alarming; terrifying. **hair's breadth** a very small amount or margin. **hair shirt** a shirt of haircloth, worn formerly by penitents and ascetics. **hair-shirt** *adj.* (*attrib.*) austere, harsh, self-sacrificing. **hair-slide** Brit. a (usu. ornamental) clip for keeping the hair in position. **hair-splitting** adj. & n. making over-fine distinctions; quibbling. **hair-trigger** a trigger of a firearm set for release at the slightest pressure. **keep one's hair on** Brit. colloq. remain calm; not get angry. **let one's hair down** colloq. abandon restraint; behave freely or wildly. **make one's hair stand on end** alarm or horrify one. **not turn a hair** remain apparently unmoved or unaffected. □ **haired** adj. (also in comb.). **hairless** adj. **hairlike** adj. [OE hǣr f. Gmc]

hairbreadth /ˈheəbredθ/ n. = hair's breadth; (esp. attrib.: a hairbreadth escape).

hairbrush /ˈheəbrʌʃ/ n. a brush for arranging or smoothing the hair.

haircloth /ˈheəklɒθ/ n. stiff cloth woven from hair, used e.g. in upholstery.

haircut /ˈheəkʌt/ n. 1 a cutting of the hair. 2 the style in which the hair is cut.

hairdo /ˈheədu:/ n. (pl. -dos) colloq. the style of or an act of styling a woman's hair.

hairdresser /ˈheəˌdresə(r)/ n. 1 a person who cuts and styles hair, esp. professionally. 2 the business or establishment of a hairdresser. □ **hairdressing** n.

hairgrip /ˈheəgrɪp/ n. Brit. a flat hairpin with the ends close together.

hairline /ˈheəlaɪn/ n. 1 the edge of a person's hair, esp. on the forehead. 2 a very thin line or crack etc.

hairnet /ˈheənet/ n. a piece of fine mesh-work for confining the hair.

hairpiece /ˈheəpi:s/ n. a quantity or switch of detached hair used to augment a person's natural hair.

hairpin /ˈheəpɪn/ n. a U-shaped pin for fastening the hair. □ **hairpin bend** a sharp U-shaped bend in a road.

hairspray /ˈheəspreɪ/ n. a solution sprayed on to the hair to keep it in place.

hairspring /ˈheəsprɪŋ/ n. a fine spring regulating the balance-wheel in a watch.

hairstyle /ˈheəstaɪl/ n. a particular way of arranging or dressing the hair. □ **hairstyling** n. **hairstylist** n.

hairy /ˈheərɪ/ adj. (**hairier**, **hairiest**) 1 made of or covered with hair. 2 having the feel of hair. 3 sl. alarmingly unpleasant or difficult. □ **hairily** adv. **hairiness** n.

hajj /hædʒ/ n. (also **hadj**) the Islamic pilgrimage to Mecca. [Arab. ḥajj pilgrimage]

hajji /ˈhædʒɪ/ n. (also **hadji**) (pl. **-is**) a Muslim who has been to Mecca as a pilgrim: also (**Hajji**) used as a title. [Pers. ḥājī (partly through Turk. hacı) f. Arab. ḥājjī: see HAJJ]

haka /ˈhɑːkə/ n. NZ 1 a Maori ceremonial war-dance accompanied by chanting. 2 an imitation of this by members of a sports team before a match. [Maori]

hake /heɪk/ n. any marine fish of the genus Merluccius, esp. M. merluccius with an elongate body and large head. [ME perh. ult. f. dial. hake hook + FISH¹]

halal /hɑːˈlɑːl/ v. & n. (also **hallal**) —v.tr. (**halal-led**, **halalling**) kill (an animal) as prescribed by Muslim law. —n. (often attrib.) meat prepared in this way; lawful food. [Arab. ḥalāl lawful]

halberd /ˈhælbəd/ n. (also **halbert**) hist. a combined spear and battleaxe. [ME f. F hallebarde f. It alabarda f. MHG helmbarde f. helm handle + barde hatchet]

halcyon /ˈhælsɪən/ adj. & n. —adj. 1 calm, peaceful (halcyon days). 2 (of a period) happy, prosperous. —n. 1 any kingfisher of the genus Halcyon, with brightly-coloured plumage. 2 Mythol. a bird thought in antiquity to breed in a nest floating at sea at the winter solstice, charming the wind and waves into calm. [ME f. L (h)alcyon f. Gk (h)alkuōn kingfisher]

hale¹ adj. (esp. of an old person) strong and healthy (esp. in **hale and hearty**). □ **haleness** n. [OE hāl WHOLE]

hale² v.tr. drag or draw forcibly. [ME f. OF haler f. ON hala]

half /hɑːf/ n., adj., & adv. —n. (pl. **halves** /hɑːvz/) 1 either of two equal or corresponding parts or groups into which a thing is or might be divided. 2 colloq. = half-back. 3 colloq. half a pint, esp. of beer etc. 4 either of two equal periods of play in sports. 5 colloq. a half-price fare or ticket, esp. for a child. —adj. 1 of an amount or quantity equal to a half, or loosely to a part thought of as roughly a half (take half the men; spent half the time reading; half-price). 2 forming a half (a half share). —adv. 1 (often in comb.) to the extent of half; partly (only half cooked; half-laughing). 2 to a certain extent; somewhat (esp. in idiomatic phrases: half dead; am half inclined to agree). 3 (in reckoning time) by the amount of half (an hour etc.) (half past two). □ **by half** (prec. by too + adj.) excessively (too clever by half). **by halves** imperfectly or incompletely (never does things by halves). **half-and-half** being half one thing and half another. **half-back** (in some sports) a player between the forwards and full backs. **half-baked 1** incompletely considered or planned. **2** (of enthusiasm etc.) only partly committed. **3** foolish. **half-binding** a type of bookbinding in which the spine and corners are bound in one material (usu. leather) and the sides in another. **half-blood 1** a person having one parent in common with another. **2** this relationship. **3** = half-breed. **half board** provision of bed, breakfast, and one main meal at a hotel etc. **half-breed** often offens. a person of mixed race. **half-brother** a brother with only one parent in common. **half-caste** often offens. n. a person whose parents are of different races. —adj. of or relating to such a person. **half a chance** colloq. the slightest opportunity (esp. given half a chance). **half-crown** (or **half a crown**) (in the UK) a former coin and monetary unit worth 2s. 6d. (12½p). **half-cut** Brit. sl. fairly drunk. **half-dozen** (or **half a dozen**) colloq. six, or about six. **half an eye** the slightest degree of perceptiveness. **half-hardy** (of a plant) able to grow in the open air at all times except in severe frost. **half hitch** a noose or knot formed by passing the end of a rope round its standing part and then through the loop. **half holiday** a day of which half (usu. the afternoon) is taken as a holiday. **half-hour 1** (also **half an hour**) a period of 30 minutes. **2** a point of time 30 minutes after any hour o'clock. **half-hourly** at intervals of 30 minutes. **half-landing** a landing part of the way up a flight of stairs, whose length is twice the width of the flight plus the width of the well. **half-life** Physics & Biochem.

etc. the time taken for the radioactivity or some other property of a substance to fall to half its original value. **half-light** a dim imperfect light. **half-mast** the position of a flag halfway down the mast, as a mark of respect for a person who has died. **half measures** an unsatisfactory compromise or inadequate policy. **half moon 1** the moon when only half its illuminated surface is visible from earth. **2** the time when this occurs. **3** a semicircular object. **half-note** esp. *US Mus.* = MINIM 1. **the half of it** *colloq.* the rest or more important part of something (usu. after *neg.*: *you don't know the half of it*). **half pay** reduced income, esp. on retirement. **half-sister** a sister with only one parent in common. **half-term** *Brit.* a period about halfway through a school term, when a short holiday is usually taken. **half-timbered** *Archit.* having walls with a timber frame and a brick or plaster filling. **half-time 1** the time at which half of a game or contest is completed. **2** a short interval occurring at this time. **half-title** the title or short title of a book, printed on the recto of the leaf preceding the title-page. **half-tone 1** a reproduction printed from a block (produced by photographic means) in which the various tones of grey are produced from small and large black dots. **2** *US Mus.* a semitone. **half-track 1** a propulsion system for land vehicles with wheels at the front and an endless driven belt at the back. **2** a vehicle equipped with this. **half-truth** a statement that (esp. deliberately) conveys only part of the truth. **half-volley** (*pl.* **-eys**) (in ball games) the playing of a ball as soon as it bounces off the ground. **half-yearly** at intervals of six months. **not half 1** not nearly (*not half long enough*). **2** *colloq.* not at all (*not half bad*). **3** *Brit. sl.* to an extreme degree (*he didn't half get angry*). [OE *half*, *healf* f. Gmc, orig. = 'side']

■ **Usage** In sense 3 of the adverb, the word 'past' is often omitted in colloquial usage, e.g. *came at half two*. In some parts of Scotland and Ireland this means 'half past one'.

half-hearted /hɑːˈhɑːtɪd/ *adj.* lacking enthusiasm; feeble. □ **half-heartedly** *adv.* **half-heartedness** *n.*

halfpenny /ˈheɪpnɪ/ *n.* (also **ha'penny** /ˈheɪpnɪ/) (*pl.* **-pennies** or **-pence** /ˈheɪpəns/) (in the UK) a former bronze coin worth half a penny.

■ **Usage** The halfpenny was withdrawn from circulation in 1984.

halfpennyworth /ˈheɪpəθ/ *n.* (also **ha'p'orth** /ˈheɪpəθ/) **1** as much as could be bought for a halfpenny. **2** *colloq.* a negligible amount (esp. after *neg.*: *doesn't make a halfpennyworth of difference*).

halfway /hɑːˈfweɪ, ˈhɑːfweɪ/ *adv. & adj.* —*adv.* **1** at a point equidistant between two others (*we were halfway to Rome*). **2** *US* to some extent; more or less (*is halfway decent*). —*adj.* situated halfway (*reached a halfway point*). □ **halfway house 1** a compromise. **2** a centre for rehabilitating ex-prisoners, mental patients, or others unused to normal life. **halfway line** a line midway between the ends of a pitch, esp. in football.

halfwit /ˈhɑːfwɪt/ *n.* **1** *colloq.* an extremely foolish or stupid person. **2** a person who is mentally deficient. □ **halfwitted** /-ˈwɪtɪd/ *adj.* **halfwittedly** /-ˈwɪtɪdlɪ/ *adv.* **halfwittedness** /-ˈwɪtɪdnɪs/ *n.*

halibut /ˈhælɪbət/ *n.* (also **holibut** /ˈhɒl-/) (*pl.* same) a large marine flat-fish, *Hippoglossus vulgaris*, used as food. [ME f. *haly* HOLY + *butt* flat-fish, perh. because eaten on holy days]

halide /ˈhælaɪd, ˈheɪl-/ *n. Chem.* **1** a binary compound of a halogen with another group or element. **2** any organic compound containing a halogen.

halite /ˈhælaɪt/ *n.* rock-salt. [mod.L *halites* f. Gk *hals* salt]

halitosis /ˌhælɪˈtəʊsɪs/ *n.* = *bad breath*. [mod.L f. L *halitus* breath]

hall /hɔːl/ *n.* **1 a** a space or passage into which the front entrance of a house etc. opens. **b** *US* a corridor or passage in a building. **2** a large room or building for meetings, meals, concerts, etc. **3** a large country house, esp. with a landed estate. **4** (in full **hall of residence**) a university residence for students. **5 a** (in a college etc.) a common dining-room. **b** dinner in this. **6** the building of a guild (*Fishmongers' Hall*). **7** a large public room in a palace etc. □ **Hall of Fame** *US* a building with memorials of celebrated people. **hall porter** *Brit.* a porter who carries baggage etc. in a hotel. **hall-stand** a stand in the hall of a house, with a mirror, pegs, etc. [OE = *hall* f. Gmc, rel. to HELL]

hallal var. of HALAL.

hallelujah var. of ALLELUIA.

halliard var. of HALYARD.

hallmark /ˈhɔːlmɑːk/ *n. & v.* —*n.* **1** a mark used for marking the standard of gold, silver, and platinum. **2** any distinctive feature esp. of excellence. —*v.tr.* **1** stamp with a hallmark. **2** designate as excellent.

hallo var. of HELLO.

halloo /həˈluː/ *int., n., & v.* —*int.* **1** inciting dogs to the chase. **2** calling attention. **3** expressing surprise. —*n.* the cry 'halloo'. —*v.* (**halloos, hallooed**) **1** *intr.* cry 'halloo', esp. to dogs. **2** *intr.* shout to attract attention. **3** *tr.* urge on (dogs etc.) with shouts. [perh. f. *hallow* pursue with shouts f. OF *halloer* (imit.)]

hallow /ˈhæləʊ/ *v.tr.* **1** make holy, consecrate. **2** honour as holy. □ **All Hallows** All Saints' Day, 1 Nov. [OE *hālgian, hālga* f. Gmc]

Hallowe'en /ˌhæləʊˈiːn/ *n.* the eve of All Saints' Day, 31 Oct. [HALLOW + EVEN²]

hallucinate /həˈluːsɪneɪt/ *v.* **1** *tr.* produce illusions in the mind of (a person). **2** *intr.* experience hallucinations. □ **hallucinant** *adj. & n.* **hallucinator** *n.* [L *(h)allucinari* wander in mind f. Gk *alussō* be uneasy]

hallucination /həˌluːsɪˈneɪʃ(ə)n/ *n.* the apparent or alleged perception of an object not actually present. □ **hallucinatory** /həˈluːsɪnətərɪ/ *adj.* [L *hallucinatio* (as HALLUCINATE)]

hallucinogen /həˈluːsɪnədʒ(ə)n/ *n.* a drug causing hallucinations. □ **hallucinogenic** /-ˈdʒenɪk/ *adj.*

hallway /ˈhɔːlweɪ/ *n.* an entrance-hall or corridor.

halm var. of HAULM.

halma /ˈhælmə/ *n.* a game played by two or four persons on a board of 256 squares, with men advancing from one corner to the opposite corner by being moved over other men into vacant squares. [Gk, = leap]

halo /ˈheɪləʊ/ *n. & v.* —*n.* (*pl.* **-oes**) **1** a disc or circle of light shown surrounding the head of a sacred person. **2** the glory associated with an idealized person etc. **3** a circle of white or coloured light round a luminous body, esp. the sun or moon. **4** a circle or ring. —*v.tr.* (**-oes, -oed**) surround with a halo. [med.L f. L f. Gk *halōs* threshing-floor, disc of the sun or moon]

halogen /ˈhælədʒ(ə)n/ *n. Chem.* any of the group of non-metallic elements: fluorine, chlorine, bromine, iodine, and astatine, which form halides (e.g. sodium chloride) by simple union with a metal. □ **halogenic** /-ˈdʒenɪk/ *adj.* [Gk *hals halos* salt]

halon /ˈheɪlɒn/ *n. Chem.* any of various gaseous compounds of carbon, bromine, and other halogens, used to extinguish fires. [as HALOGEN + -ON]

halt[1] /hɒlt, hɔːlt/ *n. & v.* —*n.* **1** a stop (usu. temporary); an interruption of progress (*come to a halt*). **2** a temporary stoppage on a march or journey. **3** *Brit.* a minor stopping-place on a local railway line. —*v.intr.* & *tr.* stop; come or bring to a halt. □ **call a halt (to)** decide to stop. [orig. in phr. *make halt* f. G *Halt machen* f. *halten* hold, stop]

halt[2] /hɒlt, hɔːlt/ *v. & adj.* —*v.intr.* **1** (esp. as **halting** *adj.*) lack smooth progress. **2** walk hesitatingly. **3** *archaic* be lame. —*adj. archaic* lame or crippled. □ **haltingly** *adv.* [OE *halt, healt, healtian* f. Gmc]

halter /ˈhɒltə(r), ˈhɔːl-/ *n. & v.* —*n.* **1** a rope or strap with a noose or headstall for horses or cattle. **2 a** a strap round the back of a woman's neck holding her dress-top and leaving her shoulders and back bare. **b** a dress-top held by this. **3 a** a rope with a noose for hanging a person. **b** death by hanging. —*v.tr.* put a halter on (a horse etc.). [OE *hælftre*: cf. HELVE]

halva /ˈhælvɑː/ *n.* (also **halvah**) a sweet confection of sesame flour and honey. [Yiddish f. Turk. *helva* f. Arab. *ḥalwa*]

halve /hɑːv/ *v.tr.* **1** divide into two halves or parts. **2** reduce by half. **3** share equally (with another person etc.). **4** *Golf* use the same number of strokes as one's opponent in (a hole or match). [ME *halfen* f. HALF]

halves *pl.* of HALF.

halyard /ˈhæljəd/ *n.* (also **halliard, haulyard** /ˈhɔːljəd/) *Naut.* a rope or tackle for raising or lowering a sail or yard etc. [ME *halier* f. HALE[2] + -IER, assoc. with YARD[1]]

ham *n. & v.* —*n.* **1 a** the upper part of a pig's leg salted and dried or smoked for food. **b** the meat from this. **2** the back of the thigh; the thigh and buttock. **3** *sl.* (often *attrib.*) an inexpert or unsubtle actor or piece of acting. **4** (in full **radio ham**) *colloq.* the operator of an amateur radio station. —*v.intr.* & (often foll. by *up*) *tr.* (**hammed, hamming**) *sl.* overact; act or treat emotionally or sentimentally. [OE *ham, hom* f. a Gmc root meaning 'be crooked']

hamburger /ˈhæmˌbɜːgə(r)/ *n.* a cake of minced beef usu. fried or grilled and eaten in a soft bread roll. [G, = of Hamburg in Germany]

ham-fisted /hæmˈfɪstɪd/ *adj. colloq.* clumsy, heavy-handed, bungling. □ **ham-fistedly** *adv.* **ham-fistedness** *n.*

ham-handed /hæmˈhændɪd/ *adj. colloq.* = HAM-FISTED. □ **ham-handedly** *adv.* **ham-handedness** *n.*

Hamitic /həˈmɪtɪk/ *n. & adj.* —*n.* a group of African languages including ancient Egyptian and Berber. —*adj.* **1** of or relating to this group of languages. **2** of or relating to the Hamites, a group of peoples in Egypt and N. Africa, by tradition descended from Noah's son Ham (Gen. 10:6 ff.).

hamlet /ˈhæmlɪt/ *n.* a small village, esp. one without a church. [ME f. AF *hamelet(t)e*, OF *hamelet* dimin. of *hamel* dimin. of *ham* f. MLG *hamm*]

hammer /ˈhæmə(r)/ *n. & v.* —*n.* **1 a** a tool with a heavy metal head at right angles to the handle, used for breaking, driving nails, etc. **b** a machine with a metal block serving the same purpose. **c** a similar contrivance, as for exploding the charge in a gun, striking the strings of a piano, etc. **2** an auctioneer's mallet, indicating by a rap that an article is sold. **3 a** a metal ball of about 7 kg, attached to a wire for throwing in an athletic contest. **b** the sport of throwing the hammer. —*v.* **1 a** *tr.* & *intr.* hit or beat with or as with a hammer. **b** *intr.* strike loudly; knock violently (esp. on a door). **2** *tr.* a drive in (nails) with a hammer. **b** fasten or secure by hammering (*hammered the lid down*). **3** *tr.* (often foll. by *in*) inculcate (ideas, knowledge, etc.) forcefully or repeatedly. **4** *tr. colloq.* utterly defeat; inflict heavy damage on. **5** *intr.* (foll. by *at, away at*) work hard or persistently at. □ **come under the hammer** be sold at an auction. **hammer and sickle** the symbols of the industrial worker and the peasant formerly used as the emblem of the USSR and of international communism. **hammer and tongs** *colloq.* with great vigour and commotion. **hammer out 1** make flat or smooth by hammering. **2** work out the details of (a plan, agreement, etc.) laboriously. **3** play (a tune, esp. on the piano) loudly or clumsily. **hammer-toe** a deformity in which the toe is bent permanently downwards. □ **hammering** *n.* (esp. in sense 4 of *v.*). **hammerless** *adj.* [OE *hamor, hamer*]

hammerhead /ˈhæməˌhed/ *n.* any shark of the family Sphyrinidae, with a flattened head and eyes in lateral extensions of it.

hammock /ˈhæmək/ *n.* a bed of canvas or rope network, suspended by cords at the ends, used esp. on board ship. [earlier *hamaca* f. Sp., of Carib orig.]

hammy /ˈhæmɪ/ *adj.* (**hammier, hammiest**) **1** of or like ham. **2** *colloq.* (of an actor or acting) over-theatrical.

hamper[1] /ˈhæmpə(r)/ *n.* **1** a large basket usu. with a hinged lid and containing food (*picnic hamper*). **2** *Brit.* a selection of food, drink, etc., for an occasion. [ME f. obs. *hanaper*, AF f. OF *hanapier* case for a goblet f. *hanap* goblet]

hamper[2] /ˈhæmpə(r)/ *v.tr.* **1** prevent the free movement or activity of. **2** impede, hinder. [ME: orig. unkn.]

hamster /ˈhæmstə(r)/ *n.* any of various rodents of the subfamily Cricetinae, esp. *Cricetus cricetus*, having a short tail and large cheek pouches for storing food, kept as a pet or laboratory animal. [G f. OHG *hamustro* corn-weevil]

hamstring /ˈhæmstrɪŋ/ *n. & v. Anat.* —*n.* **1** each of five tendons at the back of the knee in humans. **2** the great tendon at the back of the hock in quadrupeds. —*v.tr.* (*past and past part.* **hamstrung** or **hamstringed**) **1** cripple by cutting the hamstrings of (a person or animal).

2 prevent the activity or efficiency of (a person or enterprise).

hand *n. & v.* —*n.* **1 a** the end part of the human arm beyond the wrist, including the fingers and thumb. **b** in other primates, the end part of a forelimb, also used as a foot. **2 a** (often in *pl.*) control, management, custody, disposal (*is in good hands*). **b** agency or influence (*suffered at their hands*). **c** a share in an action; active support. **3** a thing compared with a hand or its functions, esp. the pointer of a clock or watch. **4** the right or left side or direction relative to a person or thing. **5 a** a skill, esp. in something practical (*a hand for making pastry*). **b** a person skilful in some respect. **6** a person who does or makes something, esp. distinctively (*a picture by the same hand*). **7** an individual's writing or the style of this; a signature (*a legible hand*; *in one's own hand*; *witness the hand of . . .*). **8** a person etc. as the source of information etc. (*at first hand*). **9** a pledge of marriage. **10** a person as a source of manual labour esp. in a factory, on a farm, or on board ship. **11 a** the playing-cards dealt to a player. **b** the player holding these. **c** a round of play. **12** *colloq.* applause (*got a big hand*). **13** the unit of measure of a horse's height, equal to 4 inches (10.16 cm). **14** a forehock of pork. **15** a bunch of bananas. **16** (*attrib.*) **a** operated or held in the hand (*hand-drill*; *hand-luggage*). **b** done by hand and not by machine (*hand-knitted*). —*v.tr.* **1** (foll. by *in, to, over,* etc.) deliver; transfer by hand or otherwise. **2** convey verbally (*handed me a lot of abuse*). □ **all hands 1** the entire crew of a ship. **2** the entire workforce. **at hand 1** close by. **2** about to happen. **by hand 1** by a person and not a machine. **2** delivered privately and not by the public post. **from hand to mouth** satisfying only one's immediate needs (also *attrib.*: *a hand-to-mouth existence*). **get** (or **have** or **keep**) **one's hand in** become (or be or remain) practised in something. **give** (or **lend**) **a hand** assist in an action or enterprise. **hand down 1** pass the ownership or use of to another. **2 a** transmit (a decision) from a higher court etc. **b** *US* express (an opinion or verdict). **hand in glove** in collusion or association. **hand in hand** in close association. **hand it to** *colloq.* acknowledge the merit of (a person). **hand-me-down** an article of clothing etc. passed on from another person. **hand on** pass (a thing) to the next in a series or succession. **hand out 1** serve, distribute. **2** award, allocate (*the judges handed out stiff sentences*). **hand-out 1** something given free to a needy person. **2** a statement given to the press etc. **hand over** deliver; surrender possession of. **hand-over** *n.* the act or an instance of handing over. **hand-over-fist** *colloq.* with rapid progress. **hand-pick** choose carefully or personally. **hand-picked** carefully or personally chosen. **hand round** distribute. **hands down** (esp. of winning) with no difficulty. **hands off 1** a warning not to touch or interfere with something. **2** *Computing* etc. not requiring manual use of controls. **hands on** *Computing* or requiring personal operation at a keyboard. **hands up!** an instruction to raise one's hands in surrender or to signify assent or participation. **hand-to-hand** (of fighting) at close quarters. **have** (or **take**) **a hand in** share or take part in. **have one's hands full** be fully occupied. **in hand 1** receiving attention. **2** in reserve; at

one's disposal. **3** under one's control. **off one's hands** no longer one's responsibility. **on every hand** (or **all hands**) to or from all directions. **on hand** available. **on one's hands** resting on one as a responsibility. **on the one** (or **the other**) **hand** from one (or another) point of view. **out of hand 1** out of control. **2** peremptorily (*refused out of hand*). **put** (or **set**) **one's hand to** start work on; engage in. **to hand 1** within easy reach. **2** (of a letter) received. **turn one's hand to** undertake (as a new activity). □ **handed** *adj.* **handless** *adj.* [OE *hand, hond*]

handbag /ˈhændbæg/ *n.* a small bag for a purse etc., carried esp. by a woman.

handball *n.* **1** /ˈhændbɔːl/ a game with a ball thrown by hand among players or against a wall. **2** /hændˈbɔːl/ *Football* intentional touching of the ball with the hand or arm by a player other than the goalkeeper in the goal area, constituting a foul.

handbell /ˈhændbel/ *n.* a small bell, usu. tuned to a particular note and rung by hand, esp. one of a set giving a range of notes.

handbill /ˈhændbɪl/ *n.* a printed notice distributed by hand.

handbook /ˈhændbʊk/ *n.* a short manual or guidebook.

handbrake /ˈhændbreɪk/ *n.* a brake operated by hand.

h. & c. *abbr.* hot and cold (water).

handcart /ˈhændkɑːt/ *n.* a small cart pushed or drawn by hand.

handclap /ˈhændklæp/ *n.* a clapping of the hands.

handcraft /ˈhændkrɑːft/ *n. & v.* —*n.* = HANDICRAFT. —*v.tr.* make by handicraft.

handcuff /ˈhændkʌf/ *n. & v.* —*n.* (in *pl.*) a pair of lockable linked metal rings for securing a prisoner's wrists. —*v.tr.* put handcuffs on.

-handed /ˈhændɪd/ *adj.* (in *comb.*) **1** for or involving a specified number of hands (in various senses) (*two-handed*). **2** using chiefly the hand specified (*left-handed*). □ **-handedly** *adv.* **-handedness** *n.* (both in sense 2).

handful /ˈhændfʊl/ *n.* (*pl.* **-fuls**) **1** a quantity that fills the hand. **2** a small number or amount. **3** *colloq.* a troublesome person or task.

handgrip /ˈhændgrɪp/ *n.* **1** a grasp with the hand. **2** a handle designed for easy holding.

handgun /ˈhændgʌn/ *n.* a small firearm held in and fired with one hand.

handhold /ˈhændhəʊld/ *n.* something for the hands to grip on (in climbing, sailing, etc.).

handicap /ˈhændɪˌkæp/ *n. & v.* —*n.* **1 a** a disadvantage imposed on a superior competitor in order to make the chances more equal. **b** a race or contest in which this is imposed. **2** the number of strokes by which a golfer normally exceeds par for the course. **3** a thing that makes progress or success difficult. **4** a physical or mental disability. —*v.tr.* (**handicapped**, **handicapping**) **1** impose a handicap on. **2** place (a person) at a disadvantage. □ **handicapper** *n.* [prob. from the phrase *hand i'* (= in) *cap* describing a kind of sporting lottery]

handicapped /ˈhændɪˌkæpt/ *adj.* suffering from a physical or mental disability.

handicraft /ˈhændɪˌkrɑːft/ *n.* work that requires both manual and artistic skill. [ME, alt. of earlier HANDCRAFT after HANDIWORK]

handiwork /ˈhændɪˌwɜːk/ n. work done or a thing made by hand, or by a particular person. [OE handgeweorc]

handkerchief /ˈhæŋkətʃɪf, -ˌtʃiːf/ n. (pl. **handkerchiefs** or **-chieves** /-ˌtʃiːvz/) a square of cotton, linen, silk, etc., usu. carried in the pocket for wiping one's nose, etc.

handle /ˈhænd(ə)l/ n. & v. —n. **1** the part by which a thing is held, carried, or controlled. **2** a fact that may be taken advantage of (gave a handle to his critics). **3** colloq. a personal title. **4** the feel of goods, esp. textiles, when handled. —v.tr. **1** touch, feel, operate, or move with the hands. **2** manage or deal with; treat in a particular or correct way (unable to handle the situation). **3** deal in (goods). **4** discuss or write about (a subject). □ **handleable** adj. **handleability** /-ˈbɪlɪtɪ/ n. **handled** adj. (also in comb.). [OE handle, handlian (as HAND)]

handlebar /ˈhænd(ə)lˌbɑːr/ n. (often in pl.) the steering bar of a bicycle etc., with a handgrip at each end. □ **handlebar moustache** a thick moustache with curved ends.

handler /ˈhændlə(r)/ n. **1** a person who handles or deals in certain commodities. **2** a person who trains and looks after an animal (esp. a police dog).

handmade /hændˈmeɪd/ adj. made by hand and not by machine, esp. as designating superior quality.

handmaid /ˈhændmeɪd/ n. (also **handmaiden** /-ˌmeɪd(ə)n/) archaic a female servant or helper.

handrail /ˈhændreɪl/ n. a narrow rail for holding as a support on stairs etc.

handsaw /ˈhændsɔː/ n. a saw worked by one hand.

handset /ˈhændset/ n. a telephone mouthpiece and earpiece forming one unit.

handshake /ˈhændʃeɪk/ n. the shaking of a person's hand with one's own as a greeting etc.

handsome /ˈhænsəm/ adj. (**handsomer**, **handsomest**) **1** (of a person) good-looking. **2** (of a building etc.) imposing, attractive. **3 a** generous, liberal (a handsome present; handsome treatment). **b** (of a price, fortune, etc., as assets gained) considerable. □ **handsomeness** n. [ME, = easily handled, f. HAND + -SOME¹]

handsomely /ˈhænsəmlɪ/ adv. **1** generously, liberally. **2** finely, beautifully.

handspring /ˈhændsprɪŋ/ n. a somersault in which one lands first on the hands and then on the feet.

handstand /ˈhændstænd/ n. balancing on one's hands with the feet in the air or against a wall.

handwork /ˈhændwɜːk/ n. work done with the hands, esp. as opposed to machinery. □ **handworked** adj.

handwriting /ˈhændˌraɪtɪŋ/ n. **1** writing with a pen, pencil, etc. **2** a person's particular style of writing. □ **handwritten** /-ˌrɪt(ə)n/ adj.

handy /ˈhændɪ/ adj. (**handier**, **handiest**) **1** convenient to handle or use; useful. **2** ready to hand; placed or occurring conveniently. **3** clever with the hands. □ **handily** adv. **handiness** n.

handyman /ˈhændɪˌmæn/ n. (pl. **-men**) a person able or employed to do occasional domestic repairs and minor renovations.

hang v. & n. —v. (past and past part. **hung** /hʌŋ/ except in sense 7) **1** tr. **a** secure or cause to be supported from above, esp. with the lower part free. **b** (foll. by up, on, on to, etc.) attach loosely by suspending from the top. **2** tr. set up (a door, gate, etc.) on its hinges so that it moves freely. **3** tr. place (a picture) on a wall or in an exhibition. **4** tr. attach (wallpaper) in vertical strips to a wall. **5** tr. (foll. by on) colloq. attach the blame for (a thing) to (a person) (you can't hang that on me). **6** tr. (foll. by with) decorate by hanging pictures or decorations etc. (a hall hung with tapestries). **7** tr. & intr. (past and past part. **hanged**) **a** suspend or be suspended by the neck with a noosed rope until dead, esp. as a form of capital punishment. **b** as a mild oath (hang the expense; let everything go hang). **8** tr. let droop (hang one's head). **9** tr. suspend (meat or game) from a hook and leave it until dry or tender or high. **10** intr. be or remain hung (in various senses). **11** intr. remain static in the air. **12** intr. (often foll. by over) be present or imminent, esp. oppressively or threateningly (a hush hung over the room). **13** intr. (foll. by on) **a** be contingent or dependent on (everything hangs on the discussions). **b** listen closely to (hangs on their every word). —n. **1** the way a thing hangs or falls. **2** a downward droop or bend. □ **get the hang of** colloq. understand the technique or meaning of. **hang about** (or **around**) **1** loiter or dally; not move away. **2** (foll. by with) associate with (a person etc.). **hang back 1** show reluctance to act or move. **2** remain behind. **hang fire** be slow in taking action or in progressing. **hang heavily** (or **heavy**) (of time) pass slowly. **hang in** US colloq. **1** persist, persevere. **2** linger. **hang on** colloq. **1** continue or persevere, esp. with difficulty. **2** (foll. by to) continue to hold or grasp. **3** (foll. by to) retain; fail to give back. **4 a** wait for a short time. **b** (in telephoning) continue to listen during a pause in the conversation. **hang out 1** hang from a window, clothes-line, etc. **2** protrude or cause to protrude downwards. **3** sl. reside or be often present. **4** (foll. by of) lean out of (a window etc.). **hang-out** n. sl. a place one lives in or frequently visits. **hang together 1** make sense. **2** remain associated. **hang up 1** hang from a hook, peg, etc. **2** (often foll. by on) end a telephone conversation, esp. abruptly (then he hung up on me). **3** cause delay or difficulty to. **4** (usu. in passive, foll. by on) sl. be a psychological or emotional obsession or problem to (is really hung up on her father). **hang-up** n. sl. an emotional problem or inhibition. **hung-over** colloq. suffering from a hangover. **hung parliament** a parliament in which no party has a clear majority. **not care** (or **give**) **a hang** colloq. not care at all. [ON hanga (tr.) = OE hōn, & f. OE hangian (intr.), f. Gmc]

hangar /ˈhæŋə(r)/ n. a building with extensive floor area, for housing aircraft etc. □ **hangarage** n. [F, of unkn. orig.]

hangdog /ˈhæŋdɒg/ adj. having a dejected or guilty appearance; shamefaced.

hanger /ˈhæŋə(r)/ n. **1** a person or thing that hangs. **2** (in full **coat-hanger**) a shaped piece of wood or plastic etc. from which clothes may be hung. □ **hanger-on** (pl. **hangers-on**) a follower or dependant, esp. an unwelcome one.

hang-glider /ˈhæŋˌglaɪdə(r)/ n. a frame with a fabric aerofoil stretched over it, from which the operator is suspended and controls flight by body movement. □ **hang-glide** v.intr. **hang-gliding** n.

hanging /'hæŋɪŋ/ n. & adj. —n. **1 a** the practice or an act of executing by hanging a person. **b** (attrib.) meriting or causing this (a hanging offence). **2** (usu. in pl.) draperies hung on a wall etc. —adj. that hangs or is hung; suspended.

hangman /'hæŋmən/ n. (pl. **-men**) **1** an executioner who hangs condemned persons. **2** a word-game for two players, in which the tally of failed guesses is kept by drawing a representation of a gallows.

hangnail /'hæŋneɪl/ n. = AGNAIL. [alt. of AGNAIL, infl. by HANG and taking nail as = NAIL n. 2a]

hangover /'hæŋ,əʊvə(r)/ n. **1** a severe headache or other after-effects caused by drinking an excess of alcohol. **2** a survival from the past.

hank n. a coil or skein of wool or thread etc. [ME f. ON hönk: cf. Sw. hank string, Da. hank handle]

hanker /'hæŋkə(r)/ v.intr. (foll. by for, after, or to + infin.) long for; crave. □ **hankerer** n. **hankering** n. [obs. hank, prob. rel. to HANG]

hanky /'hæŋkɪ/ n. (also **hankie**) (pl. **-ies**) colloq. a handkerchief. [abbr.]

hanky-panky /,hæŋkɪ'pæŋkɪ/ n. sl. **1** naughtiness, esp. sexual misbehaviour. **2** dishonest dealing; trickery. [19th c.: perh. based on hocus-pocus]

Hanoverian /,hænə'vɪərɪən/ adj. of or relating to the British sovereigns from George I to Victoria (1714–1901). [Hanover in Germany, whose Elector became George I in 1714]

Hansard /'hænsɑːd/ n. the official verbatim record of debates in the British Parliament. [T. C. Hansard, Engl. printer d. 1833, who first printed it]

Hansen's disease /'hæns(ə)nz/ n. leprosy. [G. H. A. Hansen, Norw. physician d. 1912]

hansom /'hænsəm/ n. (in full **hansom cab**) hist. a two-wheeled horse-drawn cab accommodating two inside, with the driver seated behind. [J. A. Hansom, Engl. architect d. 1822, who designed it]

Hanukkah /'hɑːnəkə, -xə/ n. (also **Chanukkah**) the Jewish festival of lights, commemorating the purification of the Temple in 165 BC. [Heb. ḥănukkāh consecration]

hap n. & v. archaic —n. **1** chance, luck. **2** a chance occurrence. —v.intr. (**happed, happing**) **1** come about by chance. **2** (foll. by to + infin.) happen to. [ME f. ON happ]

ha'penny var. of HALFPENNY.

haphazard /hæp'hæzəd/ adj. & adv. —adj. done etc. by chance; random. —adv. at random. □ **haphazardly** adv. **haphazardness** n. [HAP + HAZARD]

hapless /'hæplɪs/ adj. unlucky. □ **haplessly** adv. **haplessness** n. [HAP + -LESS]

haploid /'hæplɔɪd/ adj. & n. —adj. Biol. (of an organism or cell) with a single set of chromosomes. —n. a haploid organism or cell. [G f. Gk haplous single + eidos form]

ha'p'orth Brit. var. of HALFPENNYWORTH.

happen /'hæpən/ v. & adv. —v.intr. **1** occur (by chance or otherwise). **2** (foll. by to + infin.) have the (good or bad) fortune to (I happened to meet her). **3** (foll. by to) be the (esp. unwelcome) fate or experience of (what happened to you?; I hope nothing happens to them). **4** (foll. by on) encounter

or discover by chance. —adv. N.Engl. dial. perhaps, maybe (happen it'll rain). □ **as it happens** in fact; in reality (as it happens, it turned out well). [ME f. HAP + -EN¹]

happening /'hæpənɪŋ, -pnɪŋ/ n. & adj. —n. **1** an event or occurrence. **2** an improvised or spontaneous theatrical etc. performance. —adj. sl. exciting, fashionable, trendy.

happenstance /'hæpənst(ə)ns/ n. US a thing that happens by chance. [HAPPEN + CIRCUMSTANCE]

happy /'hæpɪ/ adj. (**happier, happiest**) **1** feeling or showing pleasure or contentment. **2 a** fortunate; characterized by happiness. **b** (of words, behaviour, etc.) apt, pleasing. **3** colloq. slightly drunk. **4** (in comb.) colloq. inclined to use excessively or at random (trigger-happy). □ **happy event** colloq. the birth of a child. **happy families** a card-game the object of which is to acquire four members of the same 'family'. **happy-go-lucky** cheerfully casual. **happy hour** esp. US a period of the day when drinks are sold at reduced prices in bars, hotels, etc. **happy hunting-ground** a place where success or enjoyment is obtained. **happy medium** a compromise; the avoidance of extremes. □ **happily** adv. **happiness** n. [ME f. HAP + -Y¹]

hara-kiri /,hærə'kɪrɪ/ n. ritual suicide by disembowelment with a sword, formerly practised by Samurai to avoid dishonour. [colloq. Jap. f. hara belly + kiri cutting]

harangue /hə'ræŋ/ n. & v. —n. a lengthy and earnest speech. —v.tr. lecture or make a harangue to. □ **haranguer** n. [ME f. F f. OF arenge f. med.L harenga, perh. f. Gmc]

harass /'hærəs, disp. hə'ræs/ v.tr. **1** trouble and annoy continually or repeatedly. **2** make repeated attacks on (an enemy or opponent). □ **harasser** n. **harassingly** adv. **harassment** n. [F harasser f. OF harer set a dog on]

■ **Usage** The second pronunciation given, with the stress on the second syllable, is common but considered incorrect by some people.

harbinger /'hɑːbɪndʒə(r)/ n. **1** a person or thing that announces or signals the approach of another. **2** a forerunner. [earlier = 'one who provides lodging': ME herbergere f. OF f. herberge lodging f. Gmc]

harbour /'hɑːbə(r)/ n. & v. (US **harbor**) —n. **1** a place of shelter for ships. **2** a shelter; a place of refuge or protection. —v. **1** tr. give shelter to (esp. a criminal or wanted person). **2** tr. keep in one's mind, esp. resentfully (harbour a grudge). **3** intr. come to anchor in a harbour. □ **harbour-master** an official in charge of a harbour. □ **harbourless** adj. [OE herebeorg perh. f. ON, rel. to HARBINGER]

hard adj., adv., & n. —adj. **1** (of a substance, material, etc.) firm and solid; unyielding to pressure; not easily cut. **2 a** difficult to understand or explain (a hard problem). **b** difficult to accomplish (a hard decision). **c** (foll. by to + infin.) not easy to (hard to believe; hard to please). **3** difficult to bear; entailing suffering (a hard life). **4** (of a person) unfeeling; severely critical. **5** (of a season or the weather) severe, harsh (a hard winter; a hard frost). **6** harsh or unpleasant to the senses (a hard voice; hard colours). **7 a** strenuous, enthusiastic, intense (a hard worker; a hard fight). **b** severe, uncompromising (a hard blow; a hard bargain; hard words). **c** Polit. extreme;

most radical (*the hard right*). **8 a** (of liquor) strongly alcoholic. **b** (of drugs) potent and addictive. **c** (of radiation) highly penetrating. **d** (of pornography) highly suggestive and explicit. **9** (of water) containing mineral salts that make lathering difficult. **10** established; not disputable; reliable (*hard facts; hard data*). **11** *Stock Exch.* (of currency, prices, etc.) high; not likely to fall in value. **12** *Phonet.* (of a consonant) guttural (as *c* in *cat*, *g* in *go*). —*adv.* **1** strenuously, intensely, copiously; with one's full effort (*try hard; look hard at; is raining hard; hard-working*). **2** with difficulty or effort (*hard-earned*). **3** so as to be hard or firm (*hard-baked; the jelly set hard*). —*n.* *Brit.* **1** a sloping roadway across a foreshore. **2** *sl.* = hard labour (*got two years hard*). □ **be hard on 1** be difficult for. **2** be severe in one's treatment or criticism of. **3** be unpleasant to (the senses). **be hard put to it** (usu. foll. by *to* + infin.) find it difficult. **go hard with** turn out to (a person's) disadvantage. **hard and fast** (of a rule or a distinction made) definite, unalterable, strict. **hard at it** *colloq.* busily working or occupied. **hard-boiled 1** (of an egg) boiled until the white and the yolk are solid. **2** (of a person) tough, shrewd. **hard by** near; close by. **a hard case 1** *colloq.* **a** an intractable person. **b** *Austral.* & *NZ* an amusing or eccentric person. **2** a case of hardship. **hard cash** negotiable coins and banknotes. **hard copy** printed material produced by computer, usu. on paper, suitable for ordinary reading. **hard core 1** an irreducible nucleus. **2** *colloq.* **a** the most active or committed members of a society etc. **b** a conservative or reactionary minority. **3** *Brit.* solid material, esp. rubble, forming the foundation of a road etc. **hard-core** *adj.* blatant, uncompromising, esp.: **1** (of pornography) explicit, obscene. **2** (of drug addiction) relating to 'hard' drugs, esp. heroin. **hard disk** *Computing* a large-capacity rigid usu. magnetic storage disk. **hard-done-by** harshly or unfairly treated. **hard feelings** feelings of resentment. **hard hat** *colloq.* **1** protective headgear worn on building-sites etc. **2** a reactionary person. **hard labour** heavy manual work as a punishment, esp. in a prison. **hard line** unyielding adherence to a firm policy. **hard-liner** a person who adheres rigidly to a policy. **hard lines** *Brit. colloq.* = hard luck. **hard luck** worse fortune than one deserves. **hard-nosed** *colloq.* realistic, uncompromising. **hard nut** *sl.* a tough, aggressive person. **a hard nut to crack** *colloq.* **1** a difficult problem. **2** a person or thing not easily understood or influenced. **hard of hearing** somewhat deaf. **hard on** (or **upon**) close to in pursuit etc. **hard-on** *n.* *coarse sl.* an erection of the penis. **hard pad** a form of distemper in dogs etc. **hard palate** the front part of the palate. **hard-pressed 1** closely pursued. **2** burdened with urgent business. **hard sell** aggressive salesmanship or advertising. **hard shoulder** *Brit.* a hardened strip alongside a motorway for stopping on in an emergency. **hard stuff** *sl.* strong alcoholic drink, esp. whisky. **hard tack** ship's biscuit. **hard up 1** short of money. **2** (foll. by *for*) at a loss for; lacking. **hard-wearing** able to stand much wear. **hard-wired** involving or achieved by permanently connected circuits designed to perform a specific function. **hard-working** diligent. **put the hard word on** *Austral.* & *NZ*

sl. ask a favour (esp. sexual or financial) of. □ **hardish** *adj.* **hardness** *n.* [OE *hard*, *heard* f. Gmc]

hardback /ˈhɑːdbæk/ *adj.* & *n.* —*adj.* (of a book) bound in stiff covers. —*n.* a hardback book.

hardball /ˈhɑːdbɔːl/ *n.* & *v.* *US* —*n.* **1** = BASEBALL. **2** *sl.* uncompromising methods or dealings, esp. in politics (*play hardball*). —*v.tr.* *sl.* pressure or coerce politically.

hardbitten /ˈhɑːdˌbɪt(ə)n/ *adj. colloq.* tough and cynical.

hardboard /ˈhɑːdbɔːd/ *n.* stiff board made of compressed and treated wood pulp.

harden /ˈhɑːd(ə)n/ *v.* **1** *tr.* & *intr.* make or become hard or harder. **2** *intr.* & *tr.* become, or make (one's attitude etc.), uncompromising or less sympathetic. **3** *intr.* (of prices etc.) cease to fall or fluctuate. □ **harden off** inure (a plant) to cold by gradual increase of its exposure. □ **hardener** *n.*

hardening /ˈhɑːdənɪŋ/ *n.* **1** the process or an instance of becoming hard. **2** (in full **hardening of the arteries**) *Med.* = ARTERIOSCLEROSIS.

hard-headed /hɑːˈdhedɪd/ *adj.* practical, realistic; not sentimental. □ **hard-headedly** *adv.* **hard-headedness** *n.*

hard-hearted /hɑːˈdhɑːtɪd/ *adj.* unfeeling, unsympathetic. □ **hard-heartedly** *adv.* **hard-heartedness** *n.*

hardihood /ˈhɑːdɪˌhʊd/ *n.* boldness, daring.

hardly /ˈhɑːdlɪ/ *adv.* **1** scarcely; only just (*we hardly knew them*). **2** only with difficulty (*could hardly speak*). **3** harshly.

hardship /ˈhɑːdʃɪp/ *n.* **1** severe suffering or privation. **2** the circumstance causing this.

hardware /ˈhɑːdweə(r)/ *n.* **1** tools and household articles of metal etc. **2** heavy machinery or armaments. **3** the mechanical and electronic components of a computer etc.

hardwood /ˈhɑːdwʊd/ *n.* the wood from a deciduous broad-leaved tree as distinguished from that of conifers.

hardy /ˈhɑːdɪ/ *adj.* (**hardier**, **hardiest**) **1** robust; capable of enduring difficult conditions. **2** (of a plant) able to grow in the open air all the year. □ **hardy annual 1** an annual plant that may be sown in the open. **2** *joc.* a subject that comes up at regular intervals. □ **hardily** *adv.* **hardiness** *n.* [ME f. OF *hardi* past part. of *hardir* become bold, f. Gmc, rel. to HARD]

hare /heə(r)/ *n.* & *v.* —*n.* **1** any of various mammals of the family Leporidae, esp. *Lepus europaeus*, like a large rabbit, inhabiting fields, hills, etc. **2** (in full **electric hare**) a dummy hare propelled by electricity, used in greyhound racing. —*v.intr.* run with great speed. □ **hare-brained** rash, wild. **start a hare** raise a topic of conversation. [OE *hara* f. Gmc]

harebell /ˈheəbel/ *n.* **1** a plant, *Campanula rotundifolia*, with slender stems and pale-blue bell-shaped flowers. **2** = BLUEBELL 2.

harelip /ˈheəlɪp/ *n.* *offens.* a cleft lip. □ **harelipped** *adj.*

harem /ˈhɑːriːm, hɑːˈriːm/ *n.* **1** the women of a Muslim household, living in a separate part of the house. **2** their quarters. [Arab. *ḥarām*, *ḥarīm*, orig. = prohibited, prohibited place, f. *ḥarama* prohibit]

haricot /ˈhærɪˌkəʊ/ *n.* **1** (in full **haricot bean**) a variety of French bean with small white seeds. **2** the dried seed of this used as a vegetable. [F]

hark *v.intr.* (usu. in *imper.*) *archaic* listen attentively. □ **hark back** revert to a topic discussed earlier. [ME *herkien* f. OE *heorcian* (unrecorded): cf. HEARKEN: *hark back* was orig. a hunting call to retrace steps]

harken var. of HEARKEN.

harlequin /ˈhɑːlɪkwɪn/ *n.* & *adj.* —*n.* (**Harlequin**) a mute character in pantomime, usu. masked and dressed in a diamond-patterned costume. —*adj.* in varied colours; variegated. [F f. earlier *Herlequin* leader of a legendary troup of demon horsemen]

harlequinade /ˌhɑːlɪkwɪˈneɪd/ *n.* 1 the part of a pantomime featuring Harlequin. 2 a piece of buffoonery. [F *arlequinade* (as HARLEQUIN)]

harlot /ˈhɑːlət/ *n.* *archaic* a prostitute. □ **harlotry** *n.* [ME f. OF *harlot, herlot* lad, knave, vagabond]

harm *n.* & *v.* —*n.* hurt, damage. —*v.tr.* cause harm to. □ **out of harm's way** in safety. [OE *hearm, hearmian* f. Gmc]

harmful /ˈhɑːmfʊl/ *adj.* causing or likely to cause harm. □ **harmfully** *adv.* **harmfulness** *n.*

harmless /ˈhɑːmlɪs/ *adj.* 1 not able or likely to cause harm. 2 inoffensive. □ **harmlessly** *adv.* **harmlessness** *n.*

harmonic /hɑːˈmɒnɪk/ *adj.* & *n.* —*adj.* 1 of or characterized by harmony; harmonious. 2 *Mus.* **a** of or relating to harmony. **b** (of a tone) produced by vibration of a string etc. in an exact fraction of its length. —*n.* *Mus.* an overtone accompanying at a fixed interval (and forming a note with) a fundamental. □ **harmonically** *adv.* [L *harmonicus* f. Gk *harmonikos* (as HARMONY)]

harmonica /hɑːˈmɒnɪkə/ *n.* a small rectangular wind instrument with a row of metal reeds along its length, held against the lips and moved from side to side to produce different notes by blowing or sucking. [L, fem. sing. or neut. pl. of *harmonicus*: see HARMONIC]

harmonious /hɑːˈməʊnɪəs/ *adj.* 1 sweet-sounding, tuneful. 2 forming a pleasing or consistent whole; concordant. 3 free from disagreement or dissent. □ **harmoniously** *adv.* **harmoniousness** *n.*

harmonist /ˈhɑːmənɪst/ *n.* a person skilled in musical harmony, a harmonizer. □ **harmonistic** /-ˈnɪstɪk/ *adj.*

harmonium /hɑːˈməʊnɪəm/ *n.* a keyboard instrument in which the notes are produced by air driven through metal reeds by bellows operated by the feet. [F f. L (as HARMONY)]

harmonize /ˈhɑːmənaɪz/ *v.* (also **-ise**) 1 *tr.* add notes to (a melody) to produce harmony. 2 *tr.* & *intr.* (often foll. by *with*) bring into or be in harmony. 3 *intr.* make or form a pleasing or consistent whole. □ **harmonization** /-ˈzeɪʃ(ə)n/ *n.* [F *harmoniser* (as HARMONY)]

harmony /ˈhɑːmənɪ/ *n.* (pl. **-ies**) 1 **a** a combination of simultaneously sounded musical notes to produce chords and chord progressions, esp. as having a pleasing effect. **b** the study of this. 2 **a** an apt or aesthetic arrangement of parts. **b** the pleasing effect of this. 3 agreement, concord. □ **in harmony 1** (of singing etc.) producing chords; not discordant. 2 (often foll. by *with*) in agreement. [ME f. OF *harmonie* f. L *harmonia* f. Gk *harmonia* joining, concord, f. *harmos* joint]

harness /ˈhɑːnɪs/ *n.* & *v.* —*n.* 1 the equipment of straps and fittings by which a horse is fastened to a cart etc. and controlled. 2 a similar arrangement for fastening a thing to a person's body, for restraining a young child, etc. —*v.tr.* 1 **a** put a harness on (esp. a horse). **b** (foll. by *to*) attach by a harness. 2 make use of (natural resources) esp. to produce energy. □ **in harness** in the routine of daily work. □ **harnesser** *n.* [ME f. OF *harneis* military equipment f. ON *hernest* (unrecorded) f. *herr* army + *nest* provisions]

harp /hɑːp/ *n.* & *v.* —*n.* a large upright roughly triangular musical instrument consisting of a frame housing a graduated series of vertical strings, played by plucking with the fingers. —*v.intr.* (foll. by *on, on about*) talk repeatedly and tediously about. □ **harper** *n.* **harpist** *n.* [OE *hearpe* f. Gmc]

harpoon /hɑːˈpuːn/ *n.* & *v.* —*n.* a barbed spear-like missile with a rope attached, for catching whales etc. —*v.tr.* spear with a harpoon. □ **harpoon-gun** a gun for firing a harpoon. □ **harpooner** *n.* [F *harpon* f. *harpe* clamp f. L *harpa* f. Gk *harpē* sickle]

harpsichord /ˈhɑːpsɪˌkɔːd/ *n.* a keyboard instrument with horizontal strings which are plucked mechanically. □ **harpsichordist** *n.* [obs. F *harpechorde* f. LL *harpa* harp, + *chorda* string, the *-s-* being unexplained]

harpy /ˈhɑːpɪ/ *n.* (pl. **-ies**) 1 (in Greek and Roman mythology) a monster with a woman's head and body and bird's wings and claws. 2 a grasping unscrupulous person. [F *harpie* or L *harpyia* f. Gk *harpuiai* snatchers (cf. *harpazō* snatch)]

harquebus /ˈhɑːkwɪbəs/ *n.* (also **arquebus** /ˈɑːk-/) *hist.* an early type of portable gun supported on a tripod or on a forked rest. [F (h)*arquebuse* ult. f. MLG *hakebusse* or MHG *hakenbühse*, f. *haken* hook + *busse* gun]

harridan /ˈhærɪd(ə)n/ *n.* a bad-tempered old woman. [17th-c. cant, perhaps f. F *haridelle* old horse]

harrier[1] /ˈhærɪə(r)/ *n.* a person who harries or lays waste.

harrier[2] /ˈhærɪə(r)/ *n.* 1 a hound used for hunting hares. 2 (in *pl.*) a group of cross-country runners. [HARE + -IER, assim. to HARRIER[1]]

harrier[3] /ˈhærɪə(r)/ *n.* any bird of prey of the genus *Circus*, with long wings. [*harrower* f. *harrow* harry, rob, assim. to HARRIER[1]]

harrow /ˈhærəʊ/ *n.* & *v.* —*n.* a heavy frame with iron teeth dragged over ploughed land to break up clods, remove weeds, cover seed, etc. —*v.tr.* 1 draw a harrow over (land). 2 (usu. as **harrowing** *adj.*) distress greatly. □ **harrower** *n.* **harrowingly** *adv.* [ME f. ON *hervi*]

harry /ˈhærɪ/ *v.tr.* (**-ies, -ied**) 1 ravage or despoil. 2 harass, worry. [OE *herian, hergian* f. Gmc, rel. to OE *here* army]

harsh *adj.* 1 unpleasantly rough or sharp, esp. to the senses. 2 severe, cruel. □ **harshen** *v.tr.* & *intr.* **harshly** *adv.* **harshness** *n.* [MLG *harsch* rough, lit. 'hairy', f. *haer* HAIR]

hart *n.* the male of the deer (esp. the red deer) usu. over five years old. [OE *heor(o)t* f. Gmc]

hartebeest /ˈhɑːtɪˌbiːst/ *n.* any large African antelope of the genus *Alcelaphus*, with ringed horns bent back at the tips. [Afrik. f. Du. *hert* HART + *beest* BEAST]

harum-scarum /ˌheərəmˈskeərəm/ *adj.* & *n.* *colloq.* —*adj.* wild and reckless. —*n.* such a person. [rhyming form. on HARE, SCARE]

harvest /ˈhɑːvɪst/ n. & v. —n. **1 a** the process of gathering in crops etc. **b** the season when this takes place. **2** the season's yield or crop. **3** the product or result of any action. —v.tr. **1** gather as a harvest, reap. **2** experience (consequences). □ **harvest festival** a thanksgiving festival in church for the harvest. **harvest home** the close of harvesting or the festival to mark this. **harvest moon** the full moon nearest to the autumn equinox (22 or 23 Sept.). **harvest mouse** a small rodent, *Micromys minutus*, that nests in the stalks of growing grain. □ **harvestable** adj. [OE *hærfest* f. Gmc]

harvester /ˈhɑːvɪstə(r)/ n. **1** a reaper. **2** a reaping-machine, esp. with sheaf-binding.

harvestman /ˈhɑːvɪstmən/ n. (pl. **-men**) any of various arachnids of the family Opilionidae, with very long thin legs.

has 3rd sing. present of HAVE.

has-been /ˈhæzbɪn/ n. colloq. a person or thing that has lost a former importance or usefulness.

hash[1] n. & v. —n. **1** a dish of cooked meat cut into small pieces and recooked. **2 a** a mixture; a jumble. **b** a mess. **3** re-used or recycled material. —v.tr. (often foll. by *up*) make (meat etc.) into a hash. **2** recycle (old material). □ **make a hash of** colloq. make a mess of; bungle. **settle a person's hash** colloq. deal with and subdue a person. [F *hacher* f. *hache* HATCHET]

hash[2] n. colloq. hashish. [abbr.]

hashish /ˈhæʃiːʃ/ n. a resinous product of the top leaves and tender parts of hemp, smoked or chewed for its narcotic effects. [f. Arab. *ḥašīš* dry herb; powdered hemp leaves]

haslet /ˈhæzlɪt/ n. (also **harslet** /ˈhɑː-/) pieces of (esp. pig's) offal cooked together and usu. compressed into a meat loaf. [ME f. OF *hastelet* dimin. of *haste* roast meat, spit, f. OLG, OHG *harst* roast]

hasn't /ˈhæz(ə)nt/ contr. has not.

hasp /hɑːsp/ n. & v. —n. a hinged metal clasp that fits over a staple and can be secured by a padlock. —v.tr. fasten with a hasp. [OE *hæpse*, *hæsp*]

hassle /ˈhæs(ə)l/ n. & v. colloq. —n. **1** a prolonged trouble or inconvenience. **2** an argument or involved struggle. —v. **1** tr. harass, annoy; cause trouble to. **2** intr. argue, quarrel. [20th c.: orig. dial.]

hassock /ˈhæsək/ n. **1** a thick firm cushion for kneeling on, esp. in church. **2** a tuft of matted grass etc. [OE *hassuc*]

haste /heist/ n. & v. —n. **1** urgency of movement or action. **2** excessive hurry. —v.intr. archaic = HASTEN. □ **in haste** quickly, hurriedly. **make haste** hurry; be quick. [ME f. OF *haste*, *haster* f. WG]

hasten /ˈheis(ə)n/ v. **1** intr. (often foll. by *to* + infin.) make haste; hurry. **2** tr. cause to occur or be ready or be done sooner.

hasty /ˈheisti/ adj. (**hastier**, **hastiest**) **1** hurried; acting too quickly or hurriedly. **2** said, made, or done too quickly or too soon; rash, unconsidered. **3** quick-tempered. □ **hastily** adv. **hastiness** n. [ME f. OF *hasti*, *hastif* (as HASTE, -IVE)]

hat n. **1** a covering for the head, often with a brim and worn out of doors. **2** colloq. a person's occupation or capacity, esp. one of several (*wearing his managerial hat*). □ **hat trick 1** Cricket the taking of three wickets by the same bowler with three successive balls. **2** the scoring of three goals, points, etc. in other sports. **keep it under one's hat** colloq. keep it secret. **out of a hat** by random selection. **pass the hat round** collect contributions of money. **take off one's hat to** colloq. acknowledge admiration for. **throw one's hat in the ring** take up a challenge. □ **hatful** n. (pl. **-fuls**). **hatless** adj. [OE *hætt* f. Gmc]

hatband /ˈhætbænd/ n. a band of ribbon etc. round a hat above the brim.

hatch[1] n. **1** an opening between two rooms, e.g. between a kitchen and a dining-room for serving food. **2** an opening or door in an aircraft, spacecraft, etc. **3** Naut. **a** = HATCHWAY. **b** a trapdoor or cover for this (often in pl.: *batten the hatches*). [OE *hæcc* f. Gmc]

hatch[2] v. & n. —v. **1** intr. **a** (often foll. by *out*) (of a young bird or fish etc.) emerge from the egg. **b** (of an egg) produce a young animal. **2** tr. incubate (an egg). **3** tr. (also foll. by *up*) devise (a plot etc.). —n. **1** the act or an instance of hatching. **2** a brood hatched. [ME *hacche*, of unkn. orig.]

hatch[3] v.tr. mark (a surface, e.g. a map or drawing) with close parallel lines. [ME f. F *hacher* f. *hache* HATCHET]

hatchback /ˈhætʃbæk/ n. a car with a sloping back hinged at the top to form a door.

hatchery /ˈhætʃəri/ n. (pl. **-ies**) a place for hatching eggs, esp. of fish or poultry.

hatchet /ˈhætʃɪt/ n. a light short-handled axe. □ **hatchet-faced** colloq. sharp-featured or grim-looking. **hatchet job** colloq. a fierce verbal attack on a person, esp. in print. **hatchet man** colloq. **1** a hired killer. **2** a person employed to carry out a hatchet job. [ME f. OF *hachette* dimin. of *hache* axe f. med.L *hapia* f. Gmc]

hatching /ˈhætʃɪŋ/ n. Art & Archit. close parallel lines forming shading esp. on a map or an architectural drawing.

hatchway /ˈhætʃwei/ n. an opening in a ship's deck for lowering cargo into the hold.

hate v. & n. —v.tr. **1** dislike intensely; feel hatred towards. **2** colloq. **a** dislike. **b** (foll. by verbal noun or *to* + infin.) be reluctant (to do something) (*I hate to disturb you*). —n. **1** hatred. **2** colloq. a hated person or thing. □ **hatable** adj. (also **hateable**). **hater** n. [OE *hatian* f. Gmc]

hateful /ˈheitfʊl/ adj. arousing hatred. □ **hatefully** adv. **hatefulness** n.

hatred /ˈheitrɪd/ n. intense dislike or ill will. [ME f. HATE + -red f. OE *ræden* condition]

hatstand /ˈhætstænd/ n. a stand with hooks on which to hang hats.

hatter /ˈhætə(r)/ n. a maker or seller of hats.

haughty /ˈhɔːti/ adj. (**haughtier**, **haughtiest**) arrogantly self-admiring and disdainful. □ **haughtily** adv. **haughtiness** n. [extension of *haught* (adj.), earlier *haut* f. OF *haut* f. L *altus* high]

haul v. & n. —v. **1** tr. pull or drag forcibly. **2** tr. transport by lorry, cart, etc. **3** intr. turn a ship's course. **4** tr. colloq. (usu. foll. by *up*) bring for reprimand or trial. —n. **1** the act or an instance of hauling. **2** an amount gained or acquired. **3** a distance to be traversed (*a short haul*). [var. of HALE[2]]

haulage /ˈhɔːlɪdʒ/ n. **1** the commercial transport of goods. **2** a charge for this.

hauler /ˈhɔːlə(r)/ n. **1** a person or thing that hauls. **2** a person or firm engaged in the transport of goods.

haulier /ˈhɔːlɪə(r)/ n. Brit. = HAULER.

haulm /hɔːm, hɑːm/ n. (also **halm**) **1** a stalk or stem. **2** the stalks or stems collectively of peas, beans, potatoes, etc. [OE h(e)alm f. Gmc]

haulyard var. of HALYARD.

haunch n. **1** the fleshy part of the buttock with the thigh, esp. in animals. **2** the leg and loin of a deer etc. as food. [ME f. OF hanche, of Gmc orig.: cf. LG hanke hind leg of a horse]

haunt v. & n. —v. **1** tr. (of a ghost) visit (a place) regularly, usu. reputedly giving signs of its presence. **2** tr. (of a person or animal) frequent or be persistently in (a place). **3** tr. (of a memory etc.) be persistently in the mind of. **4** intr. (foll. by with, in) stay habitually. —n. **1** (often in pl.) a place frequented by a person. **2** a place frequented by animals, esp. for food and drink. □ **haunter** n. [ME f. OF hanter f. Gmc]

haunting /ˈhɔːntɪŋ/ adj. (of a memory, melody, etc.) poignant, wistful, evocative. □ **hauntingly** adv.

haute couture /ˌəʊt kuːˈtjʊə(r)/ n. high fashion; the leading fashion houses or their products. [F, lit. = high dressmaking]

haute cuisine /ˌəʊt kwɪˈziːn/ n. cookery of a high standard, esp. of the French traditional school. [F, lit. = high cookery]

hauteur /əʊˈtɜː(r)/ n. haughtiness of manner. [F f. haut high]

Havana /həˈvænə/ n. a cigar made at Havana or elsewhere in Cuba.

have /hæv, həv/ v. & n. —v. (3rd sing. present **has** /hæz, həz/; past and past part. **had** /hæd/) —v.tr. **1** hold in possession as one's property or at one's disposal; be provided with (has a car; had no time to read; has nothing to wear). **2** hold in a certain relationship (has a sister; had no equals). **3** contain as a part or quality (house has two floors; has green eyes). **4 a** undergo, experience, enjoy, suffer (had a good time; had a shock; has a headache). **b** be subjected to a specified state (had my car stolen; the book has a page missing). **c** cause, instruct, or invite (a person or thing) to be in a particular state or take a particular action (had him dismissed; had my hair cut; had them to stay). **5 a** engage in (an activity) (had an argument; had sex). **b** hold (a meeting, party, etc.). **6** eat or drink (had a beer). **7** (usu. in neg.) accept or tolerate; permit to (I won't have it). **8 a** let (a feeling etc.) be present (have no doubt; has a lot of sympathy for me; have nothing against them). **b** show or feel (mercy, pity, etc.) towards another person (have mercy!). **c** (foll. by to + infin.) show by action that one is influenced by (a feeling, quality, etc.) (have the goodness to leave now). **9 a** give birth to (offspring). **b** conceive mentally (an idea etc.). **10** receive, obtain (had a letter from him; not a ticket to be had). **11** be burdened with or committed to (has a job to do; have my garden to attend to). **12 a** have obtained (a qualification) (has six O levels). **b** know (a language) (has no Latin). **13** sl. **a** get the better of (I had him there). **b** (usu. in passive) Brit. cheat, deceive (you were had). **14** coarse sl. have sexual intercourse with. —v.aux. (with past part. or ellipt., to form the perfect, pluperfect, and future perfect tenses, and the conditional mood) (have worked; had seen; will have been; had I known, I would have gone; have

you met her? yes, I have). —n. (usu. in pl.) colloq. a person who has wealth or resources. □ **had better** would find it prudent to. **have got to** colloq. = have to. **have had it** colloq. **1** have missed one's chance. **2** have passed one's prime. **3** have been killed, defeated, etc. **have it 1** (foll. by that + clause) express the view that. **2** win a decision in a vote etc. **3** colloq. have found the answer etc. **have it away** (or **off**) Brit. coarse sl. have sexual intercourse. **have it in for** colloq. be hostile or ill-disposed towards. **have it out** (often foll. by with) colloq. attempt to settle a dispute by discussion or argument. **have-not** (usu. in pl.) colloq. a person lacking wealth or resources. **have on 1** be wearing (clothes). **2** be committed to (an engagement). **3** colloq. tease, play a trick on. **have out** get (a tooth etc.) extracted (had her tonsils out). **have something** (or **nothing**) **on a person 1** know something (or nothing) discreditable or incriminating about a person. **2** have an (or no) advantage or superiority over a person. **have to** be obliged to, must. **have up** Brit. colloq. bring (a person) before a court of justice, interviewer, etc. [OE habban f. Gmc, prob. rel. to HEAVE]

haven /ˈheɪv(ə)n/ n. **1** a harbour or port. **2** a place of refuge. [OE hæfen f. ON höfn]

haven't /ˈhæv(ə)nt/ contr. have not.

haver /ˈheɪvə(r)/ v. & n. —v.intr. Brit. **1** talk foolishly; babble. **2** vacillate, hesitate. —n. (usu. in pl.) Sc. foolish talk; nonsense. [18th c.: orig. unkn.]

haversack /ˈhævəˌsæk/ n. a stout bag for provisions etc., carried on the back or over the shoulder. [F havresac f. G Habersack f. Haber oats + Sack SACK¹]

havoc /ˈhævək/ n. widespread destruction; great confusion or disorder. □ **play havoc with** colloq. cause great confusion or difficulty to. [ME f. AF havok f. OF havo(t), of unkn. orig.]

haw¹ n. the hawthorn or its fruit. [OE haga f. Gmc, rel. to HEDGE]

haw² /hɔː/ int. & v. —int. expressing hesitation. —v.intr. (in **hum and haw**: see HUM¹) [imit.: cf. HA]

hawfinch /ˈhɔːfɪntʃ/ n. any large stout finch of the genus Coccothraustes, with a thick beak for cracking seeds. [HAW¹ + FINCH]

hawk¹ n. & v. —n. **1** any of various diurnal birds of prey of the family Accipitridae, having a curved beak, rounded short wings, and a long tail. **2** Polit. a person who advocates an aggressive or warlike policy, esp. in foreign affairs. **3** a rapacious person. —v. intr. hunt game with a hawk. □ **hawk-eyed** keen-sighted. □ **hawkish** adj. **hawkishness** n. **hawklike** adj. [OE h(e)afoc, hæbuc f. Gmc]

hawk² v.tr. **1** carry about or offer around (goods) for sale. **2** (often foll. by about) relate (news, gossip, etc.) freely. [back-form. f. HAWKER]

hawk³ /hɔːk/ v. **1** intr. clear the throat noisily. **2** tr. (foll. by up) bring (phlegm etc.) up from the throat. [prob. imit.]

hawker /ˈhɔːkə(r)/ n. a person who travels about selling goods. [16th c.: prob. f. LG or Du.; cf. HUCKSTER]

hawser /ˈhɔːzə(r)/ n. Naut. a thick rope or cable for mooring or towing a ship. [ME f. AF haucer, hauceour f. OF haucier hoist ult. f. L altus high]

hawthorn /ˈhɔːθɔːn/ n. any thorny shrub or tree of the genus Crataegus, esp. C. monogyna, with white, red, or pink blossom and small dark-red fruit or haws. [OE *hagathorn* (as HAW[1], THORN)]

hay *n*. grass mown and dried for fodder. □ **hay fever** an allergy with catarrhal and other asthmatic symptoms, caused by pollen or dust. **make hay of** throw into confusion. **make hay (while the sun shines)** seize opportunities for profit or enjoyment. [OE *hēg, hīeg, hīg* f. Gmc]

hayfield /ˈheɪfiːld/ *n*. a field where hay is being or is to be made.

haymaker /ˈheɪˌmeɪkə(r)/ *n*. **1** a person who tosses and spreads hay to dry after mowing. **2** an apparatus for shaking and drying hay. **3** *sl*. a forceful blow or punch. □ **haymaking** *n*.

hayrick /ˈheɪrɪk/ *n*. = HAYSTACK.

hayseed /ˈheɪsiːd/ *n*. **1** grass seed obtained from hay. **2** *US colloq*. a rustic or yokel.

haystack /ˈheɪstæk/ *n*. a packed pile of hay with a pointed or ridged top.

haywire /ˈheɪˌwaɪə(r)/ *adj. colloq*. **1** badly disorganized, out of control. **2** (of a person) badly disturbed; erratic. [HAY + WIRE, from the use of hay-baling wire in makeshift repairs]

hazard /ˈhæzəd/ *n. & v.* —*n.* **1** a danger or risk. **2** a source of this. **3** chance. **4** *Golf* an obstruction in playing a shot, e.g. a bunker, water, etc. —*v.tr.* **1** venture on (*hazard a guess*). **2** run the risk of. **3** expose to hazard. [ME f. OF *hasard* f. Sp. *azar* f. Arab. *az-zahr* chance, luck]

hazardous /ˈhæzədəs/ *adj*. **1** risky, dangerous. **2** dependent on chance. □ **hazardously** *adv*. **hazardousness** *n*. [F *hasardeux* (as HAZARD)]

haze *n*. **1** obscuration of the atmosphere near the earth by fine particles of water, smoke, or dust. **2** mental obscurity or confusion. [prob. back-form. f. HAZY]

hazel /ˈheɪz(ə)l/ *n*. **1** any shrub or small tree of the genus *Corylus*, esp. *C. avellana* bearing round brown edible nuts. **2** wood from the hazel. **3** a reddish-brown or greenish-brown colour (esp. of the eyes). *Tetrastes bonasia*. [OE *hæsel* f. Gmc]

hazelnut /ˈheɪz(ə)lˌnʌt/ *n*. the fruit of the hazel.

hazy /ˈheɪzɪ/ *adj*. (**hazier, haziest**) **1** misty. **2** vague, indistinct. **3** confused, uncertain. □ **hazily** *adv*. **haziness** *n*. [17th c. in Naut. use: orig. unkn.]

HB *abbr*. hard black (pencil-lead).

H-bomb /ˈeɪtʃbɒm/ *n*. = *hydrogen bomb*. [H³ + BOMB]

HE *abbr*. **1** His or Her Excellency. **2** His Eminence. **3** high explosive.

He *symb. Chem*. the element helium.

he /hiː, hɪ/ *pron. & n.* —*pron.* (*obj.* **him** /hɪm/; *poss.* **his** /hɪz/; *pl.* **they** /ðeɪ/) **1** the man or boy or male animal previously named or in question. **2** a person etc. of unspecified sex, esp. referring to one already named or identified (*if anyone comes he will have to wait*). —*n.* **1** a male; a man. **2** (in *comb*.) male (*he-goat*). **3** a children's chasing game, with the chaser designated 'he'. □ **he-man** (*pl.* **-men**) a masterful or virile man. [OE f. Gmc]

head /hed/ *n., adj., & v.* —*n.* **1** the upper part of the human body, or the foremost or upper part of an animal's body, containing the brain, mouth, and sense-organs. **2 a** the head regarded as the seat of intellect or repository of comprehended information. **b** intelligence; imagination (*use your head*). **c** mental aptitude or tolerance (usu. foll. by *for*: *a good head for business*;

no head for heights). **3** *colloq*. a headache, esp. resulting from a blow or from intoxication. **4** a thing like a head in form or position, esp.: **a** the operative part of a tool. **b** the flattened top of a nail. **c** the ornamented top of a pillar. **d** a mass of leaves or flowers at the top of a stem. **e** the flat end of a drum. **f** the foam on top of a glass of beer etc. **g** the upper horizontal part of a window frame, door frame, etc. **5 a** a person in charge; a director or leader (esp. the principal teacher at a school or college). **b** a position of leadership or command. **6** the front or forward part of something, e.g. a queue. **7** the upper end of something, e.g. a table or bed. **8** the top or highest part of something, e.g. a page, stairs, etc. **9** a person or individual regarded as a numerical unit (*£10 per head*). **10** (*pl.* same) **a** an individual animal as a unit. **b** (as *pl.*) a number of cattle or game as specified (*20 head*). **11 a** the side of a coin bearing the image of a head. **b** (usu. in *pl.*) this side as a choice when tossing a coin. **12 a** the source of a river or stream etc. **b** the end of a lake at which a river enters it. **13** the height or length of a head as a measure. **14** the component of a machine that is in contact with or very close to what is being processed or worked on, esp.: **a** the component on a tape recorder that touches the moving tape in play and converts the signals. **b** the part of a record-player that holds the playing cartridge and stylus. **c** = PRINTHEAD. **15 a** a confined body of water or steam in an engine etc. **b** the pressure exerted by this. **16** a promontory (esp. in place-names) (*Beachy Head*). **17** *Naut*. **a** the bows of a ship. **b** (often in *pl.*) a ship's latrine. **18** a main topic or category for consideration or discussion. **19** a culmination, climax, or crisis. **20** the fully developed top of a boil etc. —*attrib.adj.* chief or principal (*head gardener; head office*). —*v.* **1** *tr.* be at the head or front of. **2** *tr.* be in charge of (*headed a small team*). **3** *tr.* **a** provide with a head or heading. **b** (of an inscription, title, etc.) be at the top of, serve as a heading for. **4 a** *intr.* face or move in a specified direction or towards a specified result (often foll. by *for*: *is heading for trouble*). **b** *tr.* direct in a specified direction. **5** *tr. Football* strike (the ball) with the head. **6 a** *tr.* (often foll. by *down*) cut the head off (a plant etc.). **b** *intr.* (of a plant etc.) form a head. □ **above** (or **over**) **one's head** beyond one's ability to understand. **come to a head** reach a crisis. **enter** (or **come into**) **one's head** *colloq*. occur to one. **from head to toe** (or **foot**) all over a person's body. **get one's head down** *sl.* **1** go to bed. **2** concentrate on the task in hand. **give a person his** or **her head** allow a person to act freely. **go out of one's head** go mad. **go to one's head 1** (of liquor) make one dizzy or slightly drunk. **2** (of success) make one conceited. **head and shoulders** *colloq*. by a considerable amount. **head back 1** get ahead of so as to intercept and turn back. **2** return home etc. **head-banger** *sl.* **1** a young person shaking violently to the rhythm of pop music. **2** a crazy or eccentric person. **head-butt** *n*. a forceful thrust with the top of the head into the chin or body of another person. —*v.tr.* attack (another person) with a head-butt. **head-dress** an ornamental covering or band for the head. **head first 1** with the head foremost. **2** precipitately. **head in the sand** refusal to acknowledge an obvious danger or difficulty.

head off 1 get ahead of so as to intercept and turn aside. **2** forestall. **a head of hair** the hair on a person's head, esp. as a distinctive feature. **head-on 1** with the front foremost (*a head-on crash*). **2** in direct confrontation. **head over heels 1** turning over completely in forward motion as in a somersault etc. **2** topsy-turvy. **3** utterly, completely (*head over heels in love*). **head-shrinker** *sl.* a psychiatrist. **head start** an advantage granted or gained at an early stage. **head wind** a wind blowing from directly in front. **hold up one's head** be confident or unashamed. **in one's head 1** in one's thoughts or imagination. **2** by mental process without use of physical aids. **keep one's head** remain calm. **keep one's head above water** *colloq.* **1** keep out of debt. **2** avoid succumbing to difficulties. **keep one's head down** *colloq.* remain inconspicuous in difficult or dangerous times. **lose one's head** lose self-control; panic. **make head or tail of** (usu. with *neg.* or *interrog.*) understand at all. **off one's head** *sl.* crazy. **off the top of one's head** *colloq.* impromptu; without careful thought or investigation. **on one's** (or **one's own**) **head** as one's sole responsibility. **out of one's head 1** *sl.* crazy. **2** from one's imagination or memory. **over one's head 1** beyond one's ability to understand. **2** without one's knowledge or involvement, esp. when one has a right to this. **3** with disregard for one's own (stronger) claim (*was promoted over their heads*). **put heads together** consult together. **put into a person's head** suggest to a person. **take** (or **get**) **it into one's head** (foll. by *that* + clause or *to* + infin.) form a definite idea or plan. **turn a person's head** make a person conceited. □ **headed** *adj.* (also in *comb.*). **headless** *adj.* **headward** *adj.* & *adv.* [OE *hēafod* f. Gmc]

-head /hed/ *suffix* = -HOOD (*godhead*; *maidenhead*). [ME *-hed*, *-hede* = -HOOD]

headache /ˈhedeɪk/ *n.* **1** a continuous pain in the head. **2** *colloq.* **a** a worrying problem. **b** a troublesome person. □ **headachy** *adj.*

headband /ˈhedbænd/ *n.* a band worn round the head as decoration or to keep the hair off the face.

headboard /ˈhedbɔːd/ *n.* an upright panel placed behind the head of a bed.

headcount /ˈhedkaʊnt/ *n.* **1** a counting of individual people. **2** a total number of people, esp. the number of people employed in a particular organization.

header /ˈhedə(r)/ *n.* **1** *Football* a shot or pass made with the head. **2** *colloq.* a headlong fall or dive. **3** a brick or stone laid at right angles to the face of a wall. **4** (in full **header-tank**) a tank of water etc. maintaining pressure in a plumbing system.

headgear /ˈhedgɪə(r)/ *n.* a hat or head-dress.

head-hunting /ˈhedˌhʌntɪŋ/ *n.* **1** the practice among some peoples of collecting the heads of dead enemies as trophies. **2** the practice of filling a (usu. senior) business position by approaching a suitable person employed elsewhere. □ **head-hunt** *v.tr.* (also *absol.*). **head-hunter** *n.*

heading /ˈhedɪŋ/ *n.* **1 a** a title at the head of a page or section of a book etc. **b** a division or section of a subject of discourse etc. **2 a**

horizontal passage made in preparation for building a tunnel.

headlamp /ˈhedlæmp/ *n.* = HEADLIGHT.

headland *n.* /ˈhedlənd/ a promontory.

headlight /ˈhedlaɪt/ *n.* **1** a strong light at the front of a motor vehicle or railway engine. **2** the beam from this.

headline /ˈhedlaɪn/ *n.* & *v.* —*n.* **1** a heading at the top of an article or page, esp. in a newspaper. **2** (in *pl.*) the most important items of news in a newspaper or broadcast news bulletin. —*v.tr.* give a headline to.

headlock /ˈhedlɒk/ *n. Wrestling* a hold with an arm round the opponent's head.

headlong /ˈhedlɒŋ/ *adv.* & *adj.* **1** with head foremost. **2** in a rush. [ME *headling* (as HEAD, -LING²), assim. to -LONG]

headman /ˈhedmən/ *n.* (*pl.* **-men**) the chief man of a tribe etc.

headmaster /hedˈmɑːstə(r)/ *n.* (*fem.* **headmistress** /-ˈmɪstrɪs/) the principal teacher in charge of a school.

headphone /ˈhedfəʊn/ *n.* (usu. in *pl.*) a pair of earphones joined by a band placed over the head, for listening to audio equipment etc.

headquarters /hedˈkwɔːtəz/ *n.* (as *sing.* or *pl.*) **1** the administrative centre of an organization. **2** the premises occupied by a military commander and the commander's staff.

headrest /ˈhedrest/ *n.* a support for the head, esp. on a seat or chair.

headroom /ˈhedruːm, -rʊm/ *n.* **1** the space or clearance between the top of a vehicle and the underside of a bridge etc. which it passes under. **2** the space above a driver's or passenger's head in a vehicle.

headscarf /ˈhedskɑːf/ *n.* a scarf worn round the head and tied under the chin, instead of a hat.

headset /ˈhedset/ *n.* a set of headphones, often with a microphone attached, used esp. in telephony and radio communication.

headship /ˈhedʃɪp/ *n.* the position of chief or leader, esp. of a headmaster or headmistress.

headsquare /ˈhedskweə(r)/ *n.* a rectangular scarf for wearing on the head.

headstall /ˈhedstɔːl/ *n.* the part of a halter or bridle that fits round a horse's head.

headstone /ˈhedstəʊn/ *n.* a (usu. inscribed) stone set up at the head of a grave.

headstrong /ˈhedstrɒŋ/ *adj.* self-willed and obstinate. □ **headstrongly** *adv.* **headstrongness** *n.*

headwater /ˈhedˌwɔːtə(r)/ *n.* (in *sing.* or *pl.*) streams flowing from the sources of a river.

headway /ˈhedweɪ/ *n.* **1** progress. **2** the rate of progress of a ship. **3** = HEADROOM 1.

headword /ˈhedwɜːd/ *n.* a word forming a heading, e.g. of an entry in a dictionary or encyclopedia.

heady /ˈhedɪ/ *adj.* (**headier**, **headiest**) **1** (of liquor) potent, intoxicating. **2** (of success etc.) likely to cause conceit. **3** (of a person, thing, or action) impetuous, violent. □ **headily** *adv.* **headiness** *n.*

heal /hiːl/ *v.* **1** *intr.* (often foll. by *up*) (of a wound or injury) become sound or healthy again. **2** *tr.* cause (a wound, disease, or person) to heal or be healed. **3** *tr.* put right (differences etc.). **4** *tr.* alleviate (sorrow etc.). □ **healable** *adj.* **healer** *n.* [OE *hǣlan* f. Gmc, rel. to WHOLE]

health /helθ/ n. 1 the state of being well in body or mind. 2 a person's mental or physical condition (has poor health). 3 soundness, esp. financial or moral (the health of the nation). 4 a toast drunk in someone's honour. □ **health centre** the headquarters of a group of local medical services. **health farm** a residential establishment where people seek improved health by a regime of dieting, exercise, etc. **health food** natural food thought to have health-giving qualities. **health service** a public service providing medical care. **health visitor** Brit. a trained nurse who visits those in need of medical attention in their homes. [OE hǣlth f. Gmc]

healthful /ˈhelθfʊl/ adj. conducive to good health; beneficial. □ **healthfully** adv. **healthfulness** n.

healthy /ˈhelθɪ/ adj. (**healthier, healthiest**) 1 having, showing, or promoting good health. 2 beneficial, helpful (a healthy respect for experience). □ **healthily** adv. **healthiness** n.

heap n. & v. —n. 1 a collection of things lying haphazardly one on another. 2 (esp. in pl.) colloq. a large number or amount (there's heaps of time; is heaps better). 3 sl. an old or dilapidated thing, esp. a motor vehicle or building. —v. 1 tr. & intr. (foll. by up, together, etc.) collect or be collected in a heap. 2 tr. (foll. by with) load copiously or to excess. 3 tr. (foll. by on, upon) accord or offer copiously to (heaped insults on them). 4 tr. (as **heaped** adj.) (of a spoonful etc.) with the contents piled above the brim. [OE hēap, hēapian f. Gmc]

hear v. (past and past part. **heard** /hɜːd/) 1 tr. (also absol.) perceive (sound etc.) with the ear. 2 tr. listen to (heard them on the radio). 3 tr. listen judicially to and judge (a case, plaintiff, etc.). 4 intr. (foll. by about, of, or that + clause) be told or informed. 5 intr. (foll. by from) be contacted by, esp. by letter or telephone. 6 tr. be ready to obey (an order). 7 tr. grant (a prayer). □ **have heard of** be aware of; know of the existence of. **hear! hear!** int. expressing agreement. **hear a person out** listen to all that a person says. **hear say** (or **tell**) (usu. foll. by of, or that + clause) be informed. **will not hear of** will not allow or agree to. □ **hearable** adj. **hearer** n. [OE hīeran f. Gmc]

hearing /ˈhɪərɪŋ/ n. 1 the faculty of perceiving sounds. 2 the range within which sounds may be heard; earshot (within hearing; in my hearing). 3 an opportunity to state one's case (give them a fair hearing). 4 the listening to evidence and pleadings in a law court. □ **hearing-aid** a small device to amplify sound, worn by a partially deaf person.

hearken /ˈhɑːkən/ v.intr. (also **harken**) archaic or literary (often foll. by to) listen. [OE heorcnian (as HARK)]

hearsay /ˈhɪəseɪ/ n. rumour, gossip.

hearse /hɜːs/ n. a vehicle for conveying the coffin at a funeral. [ME f. OF herse harrow f. med.L herpica ult. f. L hirpex -icis large rake]

heart /hɑːt/ n. 1 a hollow muscular organ maintaining the circulation of blood by rhythmic contraction and dilation. 2 the region of the heart; the breast. 3 a the heart regarded as the centre of thought, feeling, and emotion (esp. love). b a person's capacity for feeling emotion (has no heart). 4 a courage or enthusiasm (take

heart; lose heart). b one's mood or feeling (change of heart). 5 a the central or innermost part of something. b the vital part or essence (the heart of the matter). 6 the close compact head of a cabbage, lettuce, etc. 7 a a heart-shaped thing. b a conventional representation of a heart. 8 a a playing-card of a suit denoted by a red figure of a heart. b (in pl.) this suit. 9 condition of land as regards fertility (in good heart). □ **at heart** 1 in one's inmost feelings. 2 basically, essentially. **break a person's heart** overwhelm a person with sorrow. **by heart** in or from memory. **give** (or **lose**) **one's heart** (often foll. by to) fall in love (with). **have the heart** (usu. with neg.; foll. by to + infin.) be insensitive or hard-hearted enough (didn't have the heart to ask him). **heart attack** a sudden occurrence of coronary thrombosis usu. resulting in the death of part of a heart muscle. **heart failure** a gradual failure of the heart to function properly, resulting in breathlessness, oedema, etc. **heart-lung machine** a machine that temporarily takes over the functions of the heart and lungs, esp. in surgery. **heart-rending** very distressing. **heart-searching** thorough examination of one's own feelings and motives. **heart-to-heart** adj. (of a conversation etc.) candid, intimate. —n. a candid or personal conversation. **heart-warming** emotionally rewarding or uplifting. **in heart** in good spirits. **in one's heart of hearts** in one's inmost feelings. **take to heart** be much affected or distressed by. **wear one's heart on one's sleeve** make one's feelings apparent. **with all one's heart** sincerely; with all goodwill. □ **-hearted** adj. [OE heorte f. Gmc]

heartache /ˈhɑːteɪk/ n. mental anguish or grief.

heartbeat /ˈhɑːtbiːt/ n. a pulsation of the heart.

heartbreak /ˈhɑːtbreɪk/ n. overwhelming distress. □ **heartbreaker** n. **heartbreaking** adj. **heartbroken** adj.

heartburn /ˈhɑːtbɜːn/ n. a burning sensation in the chest resulting from indigestion; pyrosis.

hearten /ˈhɑːt(ə)n/ v.tr. & intr. make or become more cheerful. □ **hearteningly** adv.

heartfelt /ˈhɑːtfelt/ adj. sincere; deeply felt.

hearth /hɑːθ/ n. 1 a the floor of a fireplace. b the area in front of a fireplace. 2 this symbolizing the home. [OE heorth f. WG]

hearthrug /ˈhɑːθrʌg/ n. a rug laid before a fireplace.

heartily /ˈhɑːtɪlɪ/ adv. 1 in a hearty manner; with goodwill, appetite, or courage. 2 very; to a great degree (esp. with ref. to personal feelings) (am heartily sick of it; disliked him heartily).

heartland /ˈhɑːtlənd/ n. the central or most important part of an area.

heartless /ˈhɑːtlɪs/ adj. unfeeling, pitiless. □ **heartlessly** adv. **heartlessness** n.

heartsick /ˈhɑːtsɪk/ adj. very despondent. □ **heartsickness** n.

heartstrings /ˈhɑːtstrɪŋz/ n.pl. one's deepest feelings or emotions.

heartthrob /ˈhɑːtθrɒb/ n. 1 beating of the heart. 2 colloq. a person for whom one has (esp. immature) romantic feelings.

heartwood /ˈhɑːtwʊd/ n. the dense inner part of a tree-trunk yielding the hardest timber.

hearty /ˈhɑːtɪ/ adj. (**heartier, heartiest**) 1 strong, vigorous. 2 spirited. 3 (of a meal or appetite) large. **4** warm, friendly. □ **heartiness** *n.*

heat *n.* & *v.* —*n.* **1 a** the condition of being hot. **b** the sensation or perception of this. **c** high temperature of the body. **2** *Physics* a form of energy arising from the random motion of the molecules of bodies, which may be transferred by conduction, convection, or radiation. **3** hot weather (*succumbed to the heat*). **4 a** warmth of feeling. **b** anger or excitement. **5** (foll. by *of*) the most intense part or period of an activity (*in the heat of the battle*). **6 a** (usu. preliminary or trial) round in a race or contest. **7** the receptive period of the sexual cycle, esp. in female mammals. **8** redness of the skin with a sensation of heat (*prickly heat*). **9** pungency of flavour. —*v.* **1** *tr.* & *intr.* make or become hot or warm. **2** *tr.* inflame; excite or intensify. □ **heat-exchanger** a device for the transfer of heat from one medium to another. **heat pump** a device for the transfer of heat from a colder area to a hotter area by using mechanical energy. **heat treatment** the use of heat to modify the properties of a metal etc. **heat wave** a period of very hot weather. **in the heat of the moment** during or resulting from intense activity, without pause for thought. **on heat** (of mammals, esp. females) sexually receptive. **turn the heat on** *colloq.* concentrate an attack or criticism on (a person). [OE *hǣtu* f. Gmc]

heated /ˈhiːtɪd/ *adj.* **1** (of a person, discussions, etc.) angry; inflamed with passion or excitement. **2** made hot. □ **heatedly** *adv.*

heater /ˈhiːtə(r)/ *n.* **1** a device for supplying heat to its environment. **2** a container with an element etc. for heating the contents (*water-heater*). **3** *sl.* a gun.

heath /hiːθ/ *n.* **1** an area of flattish uncultivated land with low shrubs. **2** a plant growing on a heath, esp. heather. □ **heathless** *adj.* **heathlike** *adj.* **heathy** *adj.* [OE *hǣth* f. Gmc]

heathen /ˈhiːð(ə)n/ *n.* & *adj.* —*n.* **1** a person who does not belong to a widely-held religion (esp. who is not Christian, Jew, or Muslim) as regarded by those that do. **2** an unenlightened person; a person regarded as lacking culture or moral principles. **3** (**the heathen**) heathen people collectively. **4** *Bibl.* a Gentile. —*adj.* **1** of or relating to heathens. **2** having no religion. □ **heathendom** *n.* **heathenism** *n.* [OE *hǣthen* f. Gmc]

heather /ˈheðə(r)/ *n.* **1** an evergreen shrub, *Calluna vulgaris*, with purple bell-shaped flowers. **2** any of various shrubs of the genus *Erica* or *Daboecia*, growing esp. on moors and heaths. □ **heathery** *adj.* [ME, Sc., & N.Engl. *hathir* etc., of unkn. orig.: assim. to *heath*]

Heath Robinson /hiːθ ˈrɒbɪns(ə)n/ *adj.* absurdly ingenious and impracticable in design or construction. [W. *Heath Robinson*, Engl. cartoonist d. 1944 who drew such contrivances]

heating /ˈhiːtɪŋ/ *n.* **1** the imparting or generation of heat. **2** equipment or devices used to provide heat, esp. to a building.

heatproof /ˈhiːtpruːf/ *adj.* & *v.* —*adj.* able to resist great heat. —*v.tr.* make heatproof.

heatstroke /ˈhiːtstrəʊk/ *n.* a feverish condition caused by excessive exposure to high temperature.

heatwave /ˈhiːtweɪv/ *n.* a prolonged period of abnormally hot weather.

heave *v.* & *n.* —*v.* (*past* and *past part.* **heaved** or esp. *Naut.* **hove** /həʊv/) **1** *tr.* lift or haul (a heavy thing) with great effort. **2** *tr.* utter with effort or resignation (*heaved a sigh*). **3** *tr. colloq.* throw. **4** *intr.* rise and fall rhythmically or spasmodically. **5** *tr. Naut.* haul by rope. **6** *intr.* retch. —*n.* an instance of heaving. □ **heave in sight** *Naut.* or *colloq.* come into view. **heave to** esp. *Naut.* bring or be brought to a standstill. □ **heaver** *n.* [OE *hebban* f. Gmc, rel. to L *capere* take]

heaven /ˈhev(ə)n/ *n.* **1** a place regarded in some religions as the abode of God and the angels, and of the good after death, often characterized as above the sky. **2** a place or state of supreme bliss. **3** *colloq.* something delightful. **4** (usu. **Heaven**) God, Providence. **5** (**the heavens**) esp. *poet.* the sky as the abode of the sun, moon, and stars and regarded from earth. □ **heaven-sent** providential; wonderfully opportune. □ **heavenward** *adj.* & *adv.* **heavenwards** *adv.* [OE *heofon*]

heavenly /ˈhevənlɪ/ *adj.* **1** of heaven; divine. **2** of the heavens or sky. **3** *colloq.* very pleasing; wonderful. □ **heavenly bodies** the sun, stars, planets, etc. □ **heavenliness** *n.* [OE *heofonlic* (as HEAVEN)]

heavy /ˈhevɪ/ *adj.*, *n.*, & *adv.* —*adj.* (**heavier**, **heaviest**) **1** of great or exceptionally high weight; difficult to lift. **2** of great density. **3** abundant, considerable (*a heavy crop*). **4** severe, intense, extensive, excessive (*heavy fighting*; *a heavy sleep*). **5** doing something to excess (*a heavy drinker*). **6 a** striking or falling with force (*heavy blows*; *heavy rain*). **b** (of the sea) having large powerful waves. **7** (of machinery, artillery, etc.) very large of its kind; large in calibre etc. **8** causing a strong impact (*a heavy fall*). **9** needing much physical effort (*heavy work*). **10** (foll. by *with*) laden. **11** carrying heavy weapons (*the heavy brigade*). **12** (of a person, writing, music, etc.) serious or sombre in tone or attitude; dull, tedious. **13 a** (of food) hard to digest. **b** (of a literary work etc.) hard to read or understand. **14** (of bread etc.) too dense from not having risen. **15** (of ground) difficult to traverse or work. **16** oppressive; hard to endure (*a heavy fate*; *heavy demands*). **17 a** coarse, ungraceful (*heavy features*). **b** unwieldy. —*n.* (*pl.* **-ies**) **1** *colloq.* a large violent person; a thug. **2** a villainous or tragic role or actor in a play etc. (usu. in *pl.*). **3** *colloq.* a serious newspaper. —*adv.* heavily (esp. in *comb.*: *heavy-laden*). □ **heavier-than-air** (of an aircraft) weighing more than the air it displaces. **heavy-duty** *adj.* intended to withstand hard use. **heavy-footed** awkward, ponderous. **heavy going** slow or difficult progress. **heavy-hearted** sad, doleful. **heavy hydrogen** = DEUTERIUM. **heavy industry** industry producing metal, machinery, etc. **heavy metal 1** heavy guns. **2** metal of high density. **3** *colloq.* (often *attrib.*) a type of highly-amplified rock music with a strong beat. **heavy sleeper** a person who sleeps deeply. **heavy water** a substance composed entirely or mainly of deuterium oxide. □ **heavily** *adv.* **heaviness** *n.* **heavyish** *adj.* [OE *hefig* f. Gmc, rel. to HEAVE]

heavy-handed /hevɪˈhændɪd/ *adj.* **1** clumsy. **2** overbearing, oppressive. □ **heavy-handedly** *adv.* **heavy-handedness** *n.*

heavyweight /ˈhevɪweɪt/ *n.* **1 a** a weight in certain sports, in the amateur boxing scale over

81 kg but differing for professional boxers, wrestlers, and weightlifters. **b** a sportsman of this weight. **2** a person, animal, or thing of above average weight. **3** *colloq.* a person of influence or importance. □ **light heavyweight 1** the weight in some sports between middleweight and heavyweight. **2** a sportsman of this weight.

hebe /ˈhiːbɪ/ *n.* any flowering shrub of the genus *Hebe*, with usu. overlapping scale-like leaves. [mod.L after the Gk goddess *Hēbē*]

Hebraic /hɪˈbreɪɪk/ *adj.* of Hebrew or the Hebrews. □ **Hebraically** *adv.* [LL f. Gk *Hebraikos* (as HEBREW)]

Hebraist /ˈhiːbreɪɪst/ *n.* an expert in Hebrew.

Hebrew /ˈhiːbruː/ *n. & adj.* —*n.* **1** a member of a Semitic people orig. centred in ancient Palestine. **2 a** the language of this people. **b** a modern form of this used esp. in Israel. —*adj.* **1** of or in Hebrew. **2** of the Hebrews or the Jews. [ME f. OF *Ebreu* f. med.L *Ebreus* f. L *hebraeus* f. Gk *Hebraios* f. Aram. *ʿiḇray* f. Heb. *ʿiḇrî* one from the other side (of the river)]

heck *int. colloq.* a mild exclamation of surprise or dismay. [alt. f. HELL]

heckle /ˈhek(ə)l/ *v.tr.* interrupt and harass (a public speaker). □ **heckler** *n.* [ME, northern and eastern form of HACKLE]

hectare /ˈhekteə(r), -tɑː(r)/ *n.* a metric unit of square measure, equal to 100 ares (2.471 acres or 10,000 square metres). □ **hectarage** /ˈhektərɪdʒ/ *n.* [F (as HECTO-, ARE²)]

hectic /ˈhektɪk/ *adj.* **1** busy and confused; excited. **2** morbidly flushed. □ **hectically** *adv.* [ME *etik* f. OF *etique* f. LL *hecticus* f. Gk *hektikos* habitual f. *hexis* habit, assim. to F *hectique* or LL]

hecto- /ˈhektəʊ/ *comb. form* a hundred, esp. of a unit in the metric system. [F, irreg. f. Gk *hekaton* hundred]

hectogram /ˈhektəˌgræm/ *n.* (also **hectogramme**) a metric unit of mass, equal to one hundred grams.

hectolitre /ˈhektəˌliːtə(r)/ *n.* (*US* **hectoliter**) a metric unit of capacity, equal to one hundred litres.

hectometre /ˈhektəˌmiːtə(r)/ *n.* (*US* **hectometer**) a metric unit of length, equal to one hundred metres.

hector /ˈhektə(r)/ *v. & n.* —*v.tr.* bully, intimidate. —*n.* a bully. □ **hectoringly** *adv.* [*Hector*, L f. Gk *Hektōr*, Trojan hero and son of Priam in Homer's *Iliad*, f. its earlier use to mean 'swaggering fellow']

hedge *n. & v.* —*n.* **1** a fence or boundary formed by closely growing bushes or shrubs. **2** a protection against possible loss or diminution. —*v.* **1** *tr.* surround or bound with a hedge. **2** *tr.* (foll. by *in*) enclose. **3 a** *tr.* reduce one's risk of loss on (a bet or speculation) by compensating transactions on the other side. **b** *intr.* avoid a definite decision. **4** *intr.* make or trim hedges. □ **hedge-hop** fly at a very low altitude. **hedge sparrow** a common grey and brown bird, *Prunella modularis*; the dunnock. □ **hedger** *n.* [OE *hegg* f. Gmc]

hedgehog /ˈhedʒhɒg/ *n.* any small nocturnal insect-eating mammal of the genus *Erinaceus*, esp. *E. europaeus*, having a coat of spines, and rolling itself up into a ball for defence. □ **hedgehoggy** *adj.* [ME f. HEDGE (from its habitat) + HOG (from its snout)]

hedgerow /ˈhedʒrəʊ/ *n.* a row of bushes etc. forming a hedge.

hedonism /ˈhiːdəˌnɪz(ə)m, ˈhe-/ *n.* **1** belief in pleasure as the highest good and mankind's proper aim. **2** behaviour based on this. □ **hedonist** *n.* **hedonistic** /-ˈnɪstɪk/ *adj.* [Gk *hēdonē* pleasure]

-hedron /ˈhiːdrən, ˈhedrən/ *comb. form* (pl. **-hedra**) forming nouns denoting geometrical solids with various numbers or shapes of faces (*dodecahedron*; *rhombohedron*). □ **-hedral** *comb. form* forming adjectives. [Gk *hedra* seat]

heebie-jeebies /ˌhiːbɪˈdʒiːbɪz/ *n.pl.* (prec. by *the*) *sl.* a state of nervous depression or anxiety. [20th c.: orig. unkn.]

heed *v. & n.* —*v.tr.* attend to; take notice of. —*n.* careful attention. □ **heedful** *adj.* **heedfully** *adv.* **heedfulness** *n.* **heedless** *adj.* **heedlessly** *adv.* **heedlessness** *n.* [OE *hēdan* f. WG]

hee-haw /ˈhiːhɔː/ *n. & v.* —*n.* the bray of a donkey. —*v.intr.* (of or like a donkey) emit a braying sound. [imit.]

heel¹ *n. & v.* —*n.* **1** the back part of the foot below the ankle. **2** the corresponding part in vertebrate animals. **3 a** the part of a sock etc. covering the heel. **b** the part of a shoe or boot supporting the heel. **4** a thing like a heel in form or position, e.g. the part of the palm next to the wrist, or the end of a violin bow at which it is held. **5** the crust end of a loaf of bread. **6** *colloq.* a person regarded with contempt or disapproval. —*v.* **1** *tr.* fit or renew a heel on (a shoe or boot). **2** *intr.* touch the ground with the heel as in dancing. **3** *intr.* (foll. by *out*) Rugby Football pass the ball with the heel. □ **at heel 1** (of a dog) close behind. **2** (of a person etc.) under control. **at (or on) the heels of** following closely after (a person or event). **cool (or kick) one's heels** be kept waiting. **down at heel 1** (of a shoe) with the heel worn down. **2** (of a person) shabby. **take to one's heels** run away. **to heel 1** (of a dog) close behind. **2** (of a person etc.) under control. **turn on one's heel** turn sharply round. **well-heeled** *colloq.* wealthy. □ **heelless** *adj.* [OE *hēla*, *hǣla* f. Gmc]

heel² *v. & n.* —*v.* **1** *intr.* (of a ship etc.) lean over owing to the pressure of wind or an uneven load. **2** *tr.* cause (a ship etc.) to do this. —*n.* the act or amount of heeling. [prob. f. obs. *heeld*, *hield* incline, f. OE *hieldan*, OS *-heldian* f. Gmc]

heel³ var. of HELE.

heelball /ˈhiːlbɔːl/ *n.* **1** a mixture of hard wax and lampblack used by shoemakers for polishing. **2** this or a similar mixture used in brass-rubbing.

heft *v.tr.* lift (something heavy), esp. to judge its weight. [prob. f. HEAVE after *cleft*, *weft*]

hefty /ˈheftɪ/ *adj.* (**heftier**, **heftiest**) **1** (of a person) big and strong. **2** (of a thing) large, heavy, powerful. □ **heftily** *adv.* **heftiness** *n.*

hegemony /hɪˈdʒemənɪ, -ˈgemənɪ/ *n.* leadership esp. by one State of a confederacy. [Gk *hēgemonia* f. *hēgemōn* leader f. *hēgeomai* lead]

Hegira /ˈhedʒɪrə/ *n.* (also **hejira**, **hijra** /ˈhɪdʒrə/) **1** Muhammad's departure from Mecca to Medina in AD 622. **2** the Muslim era reckoned from this date. [med.L *hegira* f. Arab. *hijra* departure from one's country f. *hajara* separate]

heifer /ˈhefə(r)/ *n.* **1** a young cow, esp. one that has not had more than one calf. **2** a female calf. [OE *heahfore*]

heigh /heɪ/ int. expressing encouragement or enquiry. □ **heigh-ho** expressing boredom, resignation, etc. [imit.]

height /haɪt/ n. **1** the measurement from base to top or (of a standing person) from head to foot. **2** the elevation above ground or a recognized level (usu. sea level). **3** any considerable elevation (*situated at a height*). **4 a** a high place or area. **b** rising ground. **5** the top of something. **6 a** the most intense part or period of anything (*the battle was at its height*). **b** an extreme instance or example (*the height of fashion*). □ **height of land** US a watershed. [OE *hēhthu* f. Gmc]

heighten /ˈhaɪt(ə)n/ v.tr. & intr. make or become higher or more intense.

heinous /ˈheɪnəs, ˈhiːnəs/ adj. (of a crime or criminal) utterly odious or wicked. □ **heinously** adv. **heinousness** n. [ME f. OF *haïneus* ult. f. *haïr* to hate f. Frank.]

heir /eə(r)/ n. **1** a person entitled to property or rank as the legal successor of its former owner. **2** a person deriving or morally entitled to something, quality, etc., from a predecessor. □ **heir apparent** an heir whose claim cannot be set aside by the birth of another heir. **heir presumptive** an heir whose claim may be set aside in this way. □ **heirdom** n. **heirless** adj. **heirship** n. [ME f. OF *eir* f. LL *herem* f. L *heres -edis*]

heiress /ˈeərɪs/ n. a female heir, esp. to wealth or high title.

heirloom /ˈeəluːm/ n. **1** a piece of personal property that has been in a family for several generations. **2** a piece of property received as part of an inheritance. [HEIR + LOOM¹ in the sense 'tool']

heist /haɪst/ n. & v. US sl. —n. a robbery. —v.tr. rob. [repr. a local pronunc. of HOIST]

held past and past part. of HOLD.

hele /hiːl/ v.tr. (also **heel**) (foll. by *in*) set (a plant) in the ground and cover its roots. [OE *helian* f. Gmc]

heli- /ˈhelɪ/ comb. form helicopter (*heliport*).

helical /ˈhelɪk(ə)l/ adj. having the form of a helix. □ **helically** adv. **helicoid** adj. & n.

helices pl. of HELIX.

helicopter /ˈhelɪˌkɒptə(r)/ n. a type of aircraft without wings, obtaining lift and propulsion from horizontally revolving overhead blades or rotors. [F *hélicoptère* f. Gk *helix* (see HELIX) + *pteron* wing]

helio- /ˈhiːlɪəʊ/ comb. form the sun. [Gk *hēlios* sun]

heliocentric /ˌhiːlɪəˈsentrɪk/ adj. **1** regarding the sun as centre. **2** considered as viewed from the sun's centre. □ **heliocentrically** adv.

heliogram /ˈhiːlɪəˌɡræm/ n. a message sent by heliograph.

heliograph /ˈhiːlɪəˌɡrɑːf/ n. & v. —n. **1** a signalling apparatus reflecting sunlight in flashes from a movable mirror. **2** a message sent by means of this; a heliogram. —v.tr. send (a message) by heliograph. □ **heliography** /-ˈɒɡrəfɪ/ n.

heliotrope /ˈhiːlɪəˌtrəʊp, ˈhel-/ n. **1** any plant of the genus *Heliotropium*, with fragrant purple flowers. **2** a light purple colour. [L *heliotropium* f. Gk *hēliotropion* plant turning its flowers to the sun, f. *hēlios* sun + *-tropos* f. *trepō* turn]

heliport /ˈhelɪˌpɔːt/ n. a place where helicopters take off and land. [HELI-, after *airport*]

helium /ˈhiːlɪəm/ n. Chem. a colourless light inert gaseous element occurring in deposits of natural gas, used in airships and as a refrigerant. [Gk *hēlios* sun (having been first identified in the sun's atmosphere)]

helix /ˈhiːlɪks/ n. (pl. **helices** /ˈhiːlɪˌsiːz, ˈhel-/) a spiral curve (like a corkscrew) or a coiled curve (like a watch spring). [L *helix -icis* f. Gk *helix -ikos*]

hell n. **1** a place regarded in some religions as the abode of the dead, or of condemned sinners and devils. **2** a place or state of misery or wickedness. **3** colloq. used as an exclamation of surprise or annoyance (*who the hell are you?*; *a hell of a mess*). □ **beat** (or **knock** etc.) **the hell out of** colloq. beat etc. without restraint. **for the hell of it** colloq. for fun; on impulse. **get** (or **catch**) **hell** colloq. be severely scolded or punished. **give a person hell** colloq. scold or punish or make things difficult for a person. **hell-bent** (foll. by *on*) recklessly determined. **hell-cat** a spiteful violent woman. **hell-fire** the fire or fires regarded as existing in hell. **hell for leather** at full speed. **hell-hole** an oppressive or unbearable place. **hell-hound** a fiend. **hell's angel** a member of a gang of male motor-cycle enthusiasts notorious for outrageous and violent behaviour. **like hell** colloq. **1** not at all. **2** recklessly, exceedingly. **play hell** (or **merry hell**) **with** colloq. be upsetting or disruptive to. **what the hell** colloq. it is of no importance. □ **hell-like** adj. **hellward** adv. & adj. [OE *hel, hell* f. Gmc]

hellebore /ˈhelɪˌbɔː(r)/ n. any evergreen plant of the genus *Helleborus*, having large white, green, or purplish flowers, e.g. the Christmas rose. [ME f. OF *ellebre, elebore* or med.L *eleborus* f. L *elleborus* f. Gk *(h)elleboros*]

Hellene /ˈheliːn/ n. **1** a native of modern Greece. **2** an ancient Greek. □ **Hellenic** /heˈlenɪk, -ˈliːnɪk/ adj. [Gk *Hellēn* a Greek]

Hellenism /ˈhelɪˌnɪz(ə)m/ n. **1** Greek character or culture (esp. of ancient Greece). **2** the study or imitation of Greek culture. □ **Hellenize** v.tr. & intr. (also **-ise**). **Hellenization** /-naɪˈzeɪʃ(ə)n/ n. [Gk *hellēnismos* f. *hellēnizō* speak Greek, make Greek (as HELLENE)]

Hellenist /ˈhelɪnɪst/ n. an expert on or admirer of Greek language or culture. [Gk *Hellēnistēs* (as HELLENISM)]

Hellenistic /ˌhelɪˈnɪstɪk/ adj. of or relating to Greek history, language, and culture from the death of Alexander the Great to the time of Augustus (4th–1st c. BC).

hellion /ˈhelɪən/ n. US colloq. a mischievous or troublesome person, esp. a child. [perh. f. dial. *hallion* a worthless fellow, assim. to HELL]

hellish /ˈhelɪʃ/ adj. & adv. —adj. **1** of or like hell. **2** colloq. extremely difficult or unpleasant. —adv. Brit. colloq. (as an intensifier) extremely (*hellish expensive*). □ **hellishly** adv. **hellishness** n.

hello /həˈləʊ/ int., n., & v. (also **hallo, hullo**) —int. **1** an expression of informal greeting, or of surprise. **2** a cry used to call attention. —n. (pl. **-os**) a cry of 'hello'. —v.intr. (**-oes, -oed**) cry 'hello'. [var. of earlier *hollo* HOLLER]

helm n. a tiller or wheel by which a ship's rudder is controlled. □ **at the helm** in control;

at the head (of an organization etc.). [OE *helma*, prob. related to HELVE]

helmet /ˈhelmɪt/ *n.* any of various protective head-coverings worn by soldiers, policemen, firemen, divers, motor cyclists, etc. □ **helmeted** *adj.* [ME f. OF, dimin. of *helme* f. WG]

helmsman /ˈhelmzmən/ *n.* (*pl.* **-men**) a steersman.

helot /ˈhelət/ *n.* a serf (esp. **Helot**), of a class in ancient Sparta. □ **helotism** *n.* **helotry** *n.* [L *helotes* pl. f. Gk *heilōtes*, -ōtai, erron. taken as = inhabitants of *Helos*, a Laconian town]

help *v.* & *n.* —*v.tr.* **1** provide (a person etc.) with the means towards what is needed or sought (*helped me with my work*; *helped me (to) pay my debts*). **2** (foll. by *up*, *down*, etc.) assist or give support to (a person) in moving etc. as specified (*helped her into the chair*; *helped him on with his coat*). **3** (often *absol.*) be of use or service to (a person) (*does that help?*). **4** contribute to alleviating (a pain or difficulty). **5** prevent or remedy (*it can't be helped*). **6** (usu. with *neg.*) **a** *tr.* refrain from (*can't help it*; *could not help laughing*). **b** *refl.* refrain from acting (*couldn't help himself*). **7** *tr.* (often foll. by *to*) serve (a person with food) (*shall I help you to greens?*). —*n.* **1** the act of helping or being helped (*we need your help*; *came to our help*). **2** a person or thing that helps. **3** a domestic servant or employee, or several collectively. **4** a remedy or escape (*there is no help for it*). □ **helping hand** assistance. **help oneself** (often foll. by *to*) **1** serve oneself (with food). **2** take without seeking help or permission. **help a person out** give a person help, esp. in difficulty. **so help me** (or **help me God**) (as an invocation or oath) I am speaking the truth. □ **helper** *n.* [OE *helpan* f. Gmc]

helpful /ˈhelpfʊl/ *adj.* (of a person or thing) giving help; useful. □ **helpfully** *adv.* **helpfulness** *n.*

helping /ˈhelpɪŋ/ *n.* a portion of food esp. at a meal.

helpless /ˈhelplɪs/ *adj.* **1** lacking help or protection; defenceless. **2** unable to act without help. □ **helplessly** *adv.* **helplessness** *n.*

helpline /ˈhelplaɪn/ *n.* a telephone service providing help with problems.

helpmate /ˈhelpmeɪt/ *n.* a helpful companion or partner (usu. a husband or wife).

helter-skelter /ˌheltəˈskeltə(r)/ *adv.*, *adj.*, & *n.* —*adv.* & *adj.* in disorderly haste. —*n.* Brit. a tall spiral slide round a tower, at a fairground or funfair. [imit., orig. in a rhyming jingle, perh. f. ME *skelte* hasten]

helve /helv/ *n.* the handle of a weapon or a tool. [OE *helfe* f. WG]

hem[1] *n.* & *v.* —*n.* the border of a piece of cloth, esp. a cut edge turned under and sewn down. —*v.tr.* (**hemmed**, **hemming**) turn down and sew in the edge of (a piece of cloth etc.). □ **hem in** confine; restrict the movement of. [OE, perh. rel. to dial. *ham* enclosure]

hem[2] /hem, həm/ *int.*, *n.*, & *v.* —*int.* calling attention or expressing hesitation by a slight cough or clearing of the throat. —*n.* an utterance of this. —*v.intr.* (**hemmed**, **hemming**) say *hem*; hesitate in speech. □ **hem and haw** = *hum and haw* (see HUM[1]). [imit.]

hemal etc. *US* var. of HAEMAL etc.

hemato- etc. *US* var. of HAEMATO- etc.

hemi- /ˈhemɪ/ *comb. form* half. [Gk *hēmi-* = L *semi-*: see SEMI-]

hemiplegia /ˌhemɪˈpliːdʒɪə/ *n. Med.* paralysis of one side of the body. □ **hemiplegic** *n.* & *adj.* [mod.L f. Gk *hēmiplēgia* paralysis (as HEMI-, *plēgē* stroke)]

hemipterous /heˈmɪptərəs/ *adj.* of the insect order Hemiptera including aphids, bugs, and cicadas, with piercing or sucking mouthparts. [HEMI- + Gk *pteron* wing]

hemisphere /ˈhemɪsfɪə(r)/ *n.* **1** half of a sphere. **2** a half of the earth, esp. as divided by the equator (into *northern* and *southern hemisphere*) or by a line passing through the poles (into *eastern* and *western hemisphere*). □ **hemispheric** /-ˈsferɪk/ *adj.* **hemispherical** /-ˈsferɪk(ə)l/ *adj.* [OF *emisphere* & L *hemisphaerium* f. Gk *hēmisphaira* (as HEMI, SPHERE)]

hemline /ˈhemlaɪn/ *n.* the line or level of the lower edge of a skirt, dress, or coat.

hemlock /ˈhemlɒk/ *n.* **1 a** a poisonous umbelliferous plant, *Conium maculatum*, with fernlike leaves and small white flowers. **b** a poisonous potion obtained from this. **2** (in full **hemlock fir** or **spruce**) **a** any coniferous tree of the genus *Tsuga*, having foliage that smells like hemlock when crushed. **b** the timber or pitch of these trees. [OE *hymlic(e)*]

hemo- *comb. form US* var. of HAEMO-.

hemp *n.* **1** (in full **Indian hemp**) a herbaceous plant, *Cannabis sativa*, native to Asia. **2** its fibre extracted from the stem and used to make rope and stout fabrics. **3** any of several narcotic drugs made from the hemp plant. **4** any of several other plants yielding fibre, including Manila hemp and sunn hemp. [OE *henep*, *hænep* f. Gmc, rel. to Gk *kannabis*]

hempen /ˈhempən/ *adj.* made from hemp.

hemstitch /ˈhemstɪtʃ/ *n.* & *v.* —*n.* a decorative stitch used in sewing hems. —*v.tr.* hem with this stitch.

hen *n.* **1 a** a female bird, esp. of a domestic fowl. **b** (in *pl.*) domestic fowls of either sex. **2** a female lobster or crab or salmon. □ **hen-coop** a coop for keeping fowls in. **hen-party** *colloq. derog.* a social gathering of women. [OE *henn* f. WG]

henbane /ˈhenbeɪn/ *n.* a poisonous herbaceous plant, *Hyoscyamus niger*, with an unpleasant smell.

hence *adv.* **1** from this time (*two years hence*). **2** for this reason; as a result of inference (*hence we seem to be wrong*). **3** *archaic* from here; from this place. [ME *hens*, *hennes*, *henne* f. OE *heonan* f. the same root as HE]

henceforth /hensˈfɔːθ/ *adv.* (also **henceforward** /-ˈfɔːwəd/) from this time onwards.

henchman /ˈhentʃmən/ *n.* (*pl.* **-men**) a trusted supporter or attendant. [ME *henxman*, *hengstman* f. OE *hengst* male horse]

hendeca- /henˈdekə/ *comb. form* eleven. [Gk *hendeka* eleven]

hendecagon /henˈdekəˌgɒn/ *n.* a plane figure with eleven sides and angles.

henge /hendʒ/ *n.* a prehistoric monument consisting of a circle of massive stone or wood uprights. [back-form. f. *Stonehenge*, such a monument in S. England]

henna /ˈhenə/ *n.* **1** a tropical shrub, *Lawsonia inermis*, having small pink, red, or white flowers. **2** the reddish dye from its shoots and leaves esp. used to colour hair. [Arab. *ḥinnā*ʼ]

hennaed /ˈhenəd/ adj. treated with henna.

henpeck /ˈhenpek/ v.tr. (of a woman) constantly harass (a man, esp. her husband).

henry /ˈhenrɪ/ n. (pl. **-ies** or **henrys**) Electr. the SI unit of inductance. [J. Henry, Amer. physicist d. 1878]

hep[1] var. of HIP[3].

hep[2] var. of HIP[2].

hepatic /hɪˈpætɪk/ adj. **1** of or relating to the liver. **2** dark brownish-red; liver-coloured. [ME f. L hepaticus f. Gk hēpatikos f. hēpar -atos liver]

hepatitis /ˌhepəˈtaɪtɪs/ n. inflammation of the liver. [mod.L: see HEPATIC]

hepta- /ˈheptə/ comb. form seven. [Gk hepta seven]

heptad /ˈheptæd/ n. a group of seven. [Gk heptas -ados set of seven (hepta)]

heptagon /ˈheptəgən/ n. a plane figure with seven sides and angles. □ **heptagonal** /-ˈtægən(ə)l/ adj. [F heptagone or med.L heptagonum f. Gk (as HEPTA-, -GON)]

heptahedron /ˌheptəˈhiːdrən/ n. a solid figure with seven faces. □ **heptahedral** adj. [HEPTA- + -HEDRON after POLYHEDRON]

her /hɜː(r), hə(r)/ pron. & poss.pron. —pron. **1** objective case of SHE (I like her). **2** colloq. she (it's her all right; am older than her). —poss.pron. (attrib.) **1** of or belonging to her or herself (her house; her own business). **2** (**Her**) (in titles) that she is (Her Majesty). [OE hi(e)re dative & genit. of hio, hēo fem. of HE]

herald /ˈher(ə)ld/ n. & v. —n. **1** an official messenger bringing news. **2** a forerunner (spring is the herald of summer). **3 a** hist. an officer responsible for State ceremonial and etiquette. **b** Brit. official concerned with pedigrees and coats of arms. —v.tr. proclaim the approach of; usher in (the storm heralded trouble). [ME f. OF herau(l)t, herauder f. Gmc]

heraldic /heˈrældɪk/ adj. of or concerning heraldry. □ **heraldically** adv. [HERALD]

heraldry /ˈherəldrɪ/ n. **1** the science or art of a herald, esp. in dealing with armorial bearings. **2** heraldic pomp. **3** armorial bearings.

herb n. **1** any non-woody seed-bearing plant which dies down to the ground after flowering. **2** any plant with leaves, seeds, or flowers used for flavouring, food, medicine, scent, etc. □ **herb tea** an infusion of herbs. **herb tobacco** a mixture of herbs smoked as a substitute for tobacco. □ **herbiferous** /-ˈbɪfərəs/ adj. **herblike** adj. [ME f. OF erbe f. L herba grass, green crops, herb; herb bennet prob. f. med.L herba benedicta blessed herb (thought of as expelling the Devil)]

herbaceous /hɜːˈbeɪʃəs/ adj. of or like herbs (see HERB 1). □ **herbaceous border** a garden border containing esp. perennial flowering plants. **herbaceous perennial** a plant whose growth dies down annually but whose roots etc. survive. [L herbaceus grassy (as HERB)]

herbage /ˈhɜːbɪdʒ/ n. **1** herbs collectively. **2** the succulent part of herbs, esp. as pasture. [ME f. OF erbage f. med.L herbaticum, herbagium right of pasture, f. L herba herb]

herbal /ˈhɜːb(ə)l/ adj. & n. —adj. of herbs in medicinal and culinary use. —n. a book with descriptions and accounts of the properties of these. [med.L herbalis (as HERB)]

herbalist /ˈhɜːbəlɪst/ n. **1** a dealer in medicinal herbs. **2** a person skilled in herbs, esp. an early botanical writer.

herbarium /hɜːˈbeərɪəm/ n. (pl. **herbaria** /-rɪə/) **1** a systematically arranged collection of dried plants. **2** a book, room, or building for these. [LL (as HERB)]

herbicide /ˈhɜːbɪˌsaɪd/ n. a substance toxic to plants and used to destroy unwanted vegetation.

herbivore /ˈhɜːbɪˌvɔː(r)/ n. an animal that feeds on plants. □ **herbivorous** /-ˈbɪvərəs/ adj. [L herba herb + -VORE (see -VOROUS)]

herby /ˈhɜːbɪ/ adj. (**herbier**, **herbiest**) **1** abounding in herbs. **2** of the nature of a culinary or medicinal herb.

Herculean /ˌhɜːkjʊˈliːən, -ˈkjuːlɪən/ adj. having or requiring great strength or effort. [L Herculeus f. Hercules L name of Hēraklēs a hero noted for his strength]

herd n. & v. —n. **1** a large number of animals, esp. cattle, feeding or travelling or kept together. **2** (prec. by the) derog. a large number of people; a mob (prefers not to follow the herd). **3** (esp. in comb.) a keeper of herds; a herdsman (cowherd). —v. **1** intr. & tr. go or cause to go in a herd (herded together for warmth; herded the cattle into the field). **2** tr. tend (sheep, cattle, etc.) (he herds the goats). □ **herder** n. [OE heord, (in sense 3) hirdi, f. Gmc]

herdsman /ˈhɜːdzmən/ n. (pl. **-men**) the owner or keeper of herds (of domesticated animals).

here adv., n., & int. —adv. **1** in or at or to this place or position (put it here; has lived here for many years; comes here every day). **2** indicating a person's presence or a thing offered (here is your coat; my son here will show you). **3** at this point in the argument, situation, etc. (here I have a question). —n. this place (get out of here; lives near here; fill it up to here). —int. **1** calling attention: short for come here, look here, etc. (here, where are you going with that?). **2** indicating one's presence in a roll-call: short for I am here. □ **here and there** in various places. **here goes!** colloq. an expression indicating the start of a bold act. **here's to** I drink to the health of. **neither here nor there** of no importance or relevance. [OE hēr f. Gmc: cf. HE]

hereabouts /ˌhɪərəˈbaʊts/ adv. (also **hereabout**) near this place.

hereafter /hɪərˈɑːftə(r)/ adv. & n. —adv. **1** from now on; in the future. **2** in the world to come (after death). —n. **1** the future. **2** life after death.

hereby /hɪəˈbaɪ/ adv. by this means; as a result of this.

hereditable /hɪˈredɪtəb(ə)l/ adj. that can be inherited. [obs. F héréditable or med.L hereditabilis f. eccl.L hereditare f. L heres -edis heir]

hereditary /hɪˈredɪtərɪ/ adj. **1** (of disease, instinct, etc.) able to be passed down from one generation to another. **2 a** descending by inheritance. **b** holding a position by inheritance. □ **hereditarily** adv. **hereditariness** n. [L hereditarius (as HEREDITY)]

heredity /hɪˈredɪtɪ/ n. **1 a** the passing on of physical or mental characteristics genetically from one generation to another. **b** these characteristics. **2** the genetic constitution of an individual. [F hérédité or L hereditas heirship (as HEIR)]

Hereford /ˈherɪfəd/ n. **1** an animal of a breed of red and white beef cattle. **2** this breed. [Hereford in England, where it originated]

herein /hɪəˈrɪn/ adv. formal in this matter, book, etc.

hereinafter /ˌhɪərɪn'ɑːftə(r)/ *adv.* esp. *Law formal* in a later part of this document etc.

hereof /hɪər'ɒv/ *adv. formal* of this.

heresy /'herəsɪ/ *n.* (*pl.* -**ies**) **1 a** belief or practice contrary to the orthodox doctrine of the Christian Church. **b** an instance of this. **2 a** opinion contrary to what is normally accepted or maintained. **b** an instance of this. □ **heresiology** /ˌherɪsɪ'ɒlədʒɪ/ *n.* [ME f. OF (*h*)*eresie*, f. eccl.L *haeresis*, in L = school of thought, f. Gk *hairesis* choice, sect f. *haireomai* choose]

heretic /'herətɪk/ *n.* **1** the holder of an unorthodox opinion. **2** *hist.* a person believing in or practising religious heresy. □ **heretical** /hɪ'retɪk(ə)l/ *adj.* **heretically** /hɪ'retɪkəlɪ/ *adv.* [ME f. OF *heretique* f. eccl.L *haereticus* f. Gk *hairetikos* able to choose (as HERESY)]

hereto /hɪə'tuː/ *adv. formal* to this matter.

heretofore /ˌhɪətʊ'fɔː(r)/ *adv. formal* before this time.

hereupon /ˌhɪərə'pɒn/ *adv.* after this; in consequence of this.

herewith /hɪə'wɪð, -'wɪθ/ *adv.* with this (esp. of an enclosure in a letter etc.).

heritable /'herɪtəb(ə)l/ *adj.* **1** *Law* **a** (of property) capable of being inherited. **b** capable of inheriting. **2** *Biol.* (of a characteristic) transmissible from parent to offspring. □ **heritability** /-'bɪlɪtɪ/ *n.* **heritably** *adv.* [ME f. OF f. *heriter* f. eccl.L *hereditare*: see HEREDITABLE]

heritage /'herɪtɪdʒ/ *n.* **1** anything that is or may be inherited. **2** inherited circumstances, benefits, etc. (*a heritage of confusion*). **3** a nation's historic buildings, monuments, countryside, etc. [ME f. OF (as HERITABLE)]

hermaphrodite /hɜː'mæfrədaɪt/ *n. & adj.* —*n.* **1 a** *Zool.* an animal having both male and female sexual organs. **b** *Bot.* a plant having stamens and pistils in the same flower. **2** a human being in which both male and female sex organs are present. **3** a person or thing combining opposite qualities or characteristics. —*adj.* **1** combining both sexes. **2** combining opposite qualities or characteristics. □ **hermaphroditic** /-'dɪtɪk/ *adj.* **hermaphroditical** /-'dɪtɪk(ə)l/ *adj.* **hermaphroditism** *n.* [L *hermaphroditus* f. Gk *hermaphroditos*, orig. the name of a son of Hermes and Aphrodite in Greek mythology, who became joined in one body with the nymph Salmacis]

hermetic /hɜː'metɪk/ *adj.* (also **hermetical**) **1** with an airtight closure. **2** protected from outside agencies. □ **hermetic seal** an airtight seal. □ **hermetically** *adv.* **hermetism** /'hɜː-mɪˌtɪz(ə)m/ *n.* [mod.L *hermeticus* irreg. f. *Hermes Trismegistus* thrice-greatest Hermes (as the founder of alchemy)]

hermit /'hɜːmɪt/ *n.* **1** an early Christian recluse. **2** any person living in solitude. □ **hermit-crab** any crab of the family Paguridae that lives in a cast-off mollusc shell for protection. □ **hermitic** /-'mɪtɪk/ *adj.* [ME f. OF (*h*)*ermite* or f. LL *eremita* f. Gk *erēmitēs* f. *erēmia* desert f. *erēmos* solitary]

hermitage /'hɜːmɪtɪdʒ/ *n.* **1** a hermit's dwelling. **2** a monastery. **3** a solitary dwelling. [ME f. OF (*h*)*ermitage* (as HERMIT)]

hernia /'hɜːnɪə/ *n.* (*pl.* **hernias** or **herniae** /-nɪˌiː/) the displacement and protrusion of part of an organ through the wall of the cavity containing it, esp. of the abdomen. □ **hernial** *adj.* **herniary** *adj.* **herniated** *adj.* [L]

hero /'hɪərəʊ/ *n.* (*pl.* -**oes**) **1 a** a man noted or admired for nobility, courage, outstanding achievements, etc. (*Newton, a hero of science*). **b** a great warrior. **2** the chief male character in a poem, play, story, etc. □ **hero-worship** *n.* idealization of an admired man. —*v.tr.* (**-worshipped, -worshipping;** *US* **-worshiped, -worshiping**) worship as a hero; idolize. **hero-worshipper** a person engaging in hero-worship. [ME f. L *heros* f. Gk *hērōs*]

heroic /hɪ'rəʊɪk/ *adj. & n.* —*adj.* **1 a** (of an act or a quality) of or fit for a hero. **b** (of a person) like a hero. **2 a** (of language) grand, high-flown, dramatic. **b** (of a work of art) heroic in scale or subject. **3** (of poetry) dealing with the ancient heroes. —*n.* (in *pl.*) **1 a** high-flown language or sentiments. **b** unduly bold behaviour. **2** = *heroic verse*. □ **the heroic age** the period in Greek history before the return from Troy. **heroic couplet** two lines of rhyming iambic pentameters. **heroic verse** a type of verse used for heroic poetry, esp. the hexameter, the iambic pentameter, or the alexandrine. □ **heroically** *adv.* [F *héroïque* or L *heroicus* f. Gk *hērōikos* (as HERO)]

heroin /'herəʊɪn/ *n.* a highly addictive white crystalline analgesic drug derived from morphine, often used as a narcotic. [G (as HERO, from its effects on the user's self-esteem)]

heroine /'herəʊɪn/ *n.* **1** a woman noted or admired for nobility, courage, outstanding achievements, etc. **2** the chief female character in a poem, play, story, etc. [F *héroïne* or L *heroina* f. Gk *hērōinē*, fem. of *hērōs* HERO]

heroism /'herəʊˌɪz(ə)m/ *n.* heroic conduct or qualities. [F *héroïsme* f. *héros* HERO]

heron /'herən/ *n.* any of various large wading birds of the family Ardeidae, esp. *Ardea cinerea*, with long legs and a long S-shaped neck. □ **heronry** *n.* (*pl.* -**ies**). [ME f. OF *hairon* f. Gmc]

herpes /'hɜːpiːz/ *n.* a virus disease with outbreaks of blisters on the skin etc. □ **herpes simplex** a viral infection which may produce blisters or conjunctivitis. **herpes zoster** /'zɒstə(r)/ = SHINGLES. □ **herpetic** /-'petɪk/ *adj.* [ME f. L f. Gk *herpēs* -*ētos* shingles f. *herpō* creep: *zoster* f. Gk *zōstēr* belt, girdle]

herpetology /ˌhɜːpɪ'tɒlədʒɪ/ *n.* the study of reptiles. □ **herpetological** /-tə'lɒdʒɪk(ə)l/ *adj.* **herpetologist** *n.* [Gk *herpeton* reptile f. *herpō* creep]

Herr /heə(r)/ *n.* (*pl.* **Herren** /'herən/) **1** the title of a German man; Mr. **2** a German man. [G f. OHG *hērro* compar. of *hēr* exalted]

herring /'herɪŋ/ *n.* a N. Atlantic fish, *Clupea harengus*, coming near the coast in large shoals to spawn. □ **herring-gull** a large gull, *Larus argentatus*, with dark wing-tips. [OE *hæring*, *hēring* f. WG]

herring-bone /'herɪŋbəʊn/ *n. & v.* —*n.* **1** a stitch with a zigzag pattern, resembling the pattern of a herring's bones. **2** this pattern, or cloth woven in it. **3** any zigzag pattern, e.g. in building. —*v. tr.* a work with a herring-bone stitch. **b** mark with a herring-bone pattern.

hers /hɜːz/ *poss.pron.* the one or ones belonging to or associated with her (*it is hers; hers are over there*). □ **of hers** of or belonging to her (*a friend of hers*).

herself /hə'self/ *pron.* **1 a** *emphat. form* of SHE or HER (*she herself will do it*). **b** *refl. form* of HER (*she* has hurt herself). **2** in her normal state of body or mind (*does not feel quite herself today*). □ **be herself** act in her normal unconstrained manner. **by herself** see *by oneself*. [OE *hire self* (as HER, SELF)]

hertz /hɜːts/ n. (pl. same) the SI unit of frequency, equal to one cycle per second. [H. R. *Hertz*, Ger. physicist d. 1894]

hesitant /ˈhezɪt(ə)nt/ adj. hesitating; irresolute. □ **hesitance** n. **hesitancy** n. **hesitantly** adv.

hesitate /ˈhezɪˌteɪt/ v.intr. **1** (often foll. by *about*, *over*) show or feel indecision or uncertainty; pause in doubt (*hesitated over her choice*). **2** (often foll. by *to* + infin.) be deterred by scruples; be reluctant (*I hesitate to inform against him*). □ **hesitater** n. **hesitatingly** adv. **hesitation** /-ˈteɪʃ(ə)n/ n. **hesitative** adj. [L *haesitare* frequent. of *haerēre haes-* stick fast]

hessian /ˈhesɪən/ n. a strong coarse sacking made of hemp or jute. [*Hesse* in Germany]

hest /hest/ n. archaic behest. [OE *hǣs* f. *hātan* call, command, assim. to ME nouns in -*t*]

hetaera /hɪˈtɪərə/ n. (also **hetaira** /-ˈtaɪrə/) (pl. **-as**, **hetaerae** /-ˈtɪəriː/, or **hetairai** /-ˈtaɪraɪ/) a courtesan or mistress, esp. in ancient Greece. [Gk *hetaira*, fem. of *hetairos* companion]

hetero /ˈhetərəʊ/ n. (pl. **-os**) colloq. a heterosexual. [abbr.]

hetero- /ˈhetərəʊ/ comb. form other, different (often opp. HOMO-). [Gk *heteros* other]

heterodox /ˈhetərəʊˌdɒks/ adj. (of a person, opinion, etc.) not orthodox. □ **heterodoxy** n. [LL *heterodoxus* f. Gk (as HETERO-, *doxos* f. *doxa* opinion)]

heterodyne /ˈhetərəʊˌdaɪn/ adj. & v. Radio —adj. relating to the production of a lower frequency from the combination of two almost equal high frequencies. —v.intr. produce a lower frequency in this way.

heterogeneous /ˌhetərəʊˈdʒiːnɪəs/ adj. **1** diverse in character. **2** varied in content. □ **heterogeneity** /-dʒɪˈniːɪtɪ/ n. **heterogeneously** adv. **heterogeneousness** n. [med.L *heterogeneus* f. Gk *heterogenēs* (as HETERO-, *genos* kind)]

heterograft /ˈhetərəʊˌɡrɑːft/ n. living tissue grafted from one individual to another of a different species.

heterologous /ˌhetəˈrɒləɡəs/ adj. not homologous. □ **heterology** n.

heteromorphic /ˌhetərəʊˈmɔːfɪk/ adj. (also **heteromorphous** /-ˈmɔːfəs/) Biol. **1** of dissimilar forms. **2** (of insects) existing in different forms at different stages in their life cycle.

heteromorphism /ˌhetərəʊˈmɔːfɪz(ə)m/ n. existing in various forms.

heterosexual /ˌhetərəʊˈseksjʊəl/ adj. & n. —adj. **1** feeling or involving sexual attraction to persons of the opposite sex. **2** concerning heterosexual relations or people. **3** relating to the opposite sex. —n. a heterosexual person. □ **heterosexuality** /-ˈælɪtɪ/ n. **heterosexually** adv.

heterotransplant /ˌhetərəʊˈtrænsplɑːnt/ n. = HETEROGRAFT.

het up /het ˈʌp/ adj. colloq. excited, overwrought. [*het* dial. past part. of HEAT]

heuristic /hjʊəˈrɪstɪk/ adj. & n. —adj. **1** allowing or assisting to discover. **2** Computing proceeding to a solution by trial and error. —n. **1** the science of heuristic procedure. **2** a heuristic process or method. **3** (in pl., usu. treated as sing.) Computing the study and use of heuristic techniques in data processing. □ **heuristic method** a system of education under which pupils are trained to find out things for themselves. □ **heuristically** adv. [irreg. f. Gk *heuriskō* find]

hew v. (past part. **hewn** /hjuːn/ or **hewed**) **1** tr. **a** (often foll. by *down*, *away*, *off*) chop or cut (a thing) with an axe, a sword, etc. **b** cut (a block of wood etc.) into shape. **2** intr. (often foll. by *at*, *among*, etc.) strike cutting blows. **3** intr. US (usu. foll. by *to*) conform. □ **hew one's way** make a way for oneself by hewing. [OE *hēawan* f. Gmc]

hewer /ˈhjuːə(r)/ n. **1** a person who hews. **2** a person who cuts coal from a seam. □ **hewers of wood and drawers of water** menial drudges; labourers (Josh. 9:21).

hex v. & n. US —v. **1** intr. practise witchcraft. **2** tr. bewitch. —n. **1** a magic spell. **2** a witch. [Pennsylvanian G *hexe* (v.), *Hex* (n.), f. G *hexen*, *Hexe*]

hexa- /ˈheksə/ comb. form six. [Gk *hex* six]

hexad /ˈheksæd/ n. a group of six. [Gk *hexas -ados* f. *hex* six]

hexadecimal /ˌheksəˈdesɪm(ə)l/ adj. & n. esp. Computing. —adj. relating to or using a system of numerical notation that has 16 rather than 10 as a base. —n. the hexadecimal system; hexadecimal notation. □ **hexadecimally** adv.

hexagon /ˈheksəɡən/ n. a plane figure with six sides and angles. □ **hexagonal** /-ˈsæɡən(ə)l/ adj. [LL *hexagonum* f. Gk (as HEXA-, -GON)]

hexagram /ˈheksəˌɡræm/ n. **1** a figure formed by two intersecting equilateral triangles. **2** a figure of six lines. [HEXA- + Gk *gramma* line]

hexahedron /ˌheksəˈhiːdrən/ n. a solid figure with six faces. □ **hexahedral** adj. [Gk (as HEXA-, -HEDRON)]

hexameter /hekˈsæmɪtə(r)/ n. a line or verse of six metrical feet. □ **hexametric** /-səˈmetrɪk/ adj. **hexametrist** n. [ME f. L f. Gk *hexametros* (as HEXA-, *metron* measure)]

hexapod /ˈheksəˌpɒd/ n. & adj. —n. any arthropod with six legs; an insect. —adj. having six legs. [Gk *hexapous*, *hexapod-* (as HEXA-, *pous* pod-foot)]

hey /heɪ/ int. calling attention or expressing joy, surprise, inquiry, enthusiasm, etc. □ **hey presto!** a phrase of command, or indicating a successful trick, used by a conjuror etc. [ME: cf. OF *hay*, Du., G *hei*]

heyday /ˈheɪdeɪ/ n. the flush or full bloom of youth, vigour, prosperity, etc. [archaic *heyday* expression of joy, surprise, etc.: cf. LG *heidi*, *heida*, excl. denoting gaiety]

HF abbr. high frequency.

Hf symb. Chem. the element hafnium.

hf. abbr. half.

Hg symb. Chem. the element mercury. [mod.L *hydrargyrum*].

hg abbr. hectogram(s).

HGV abbr. Brit. heavy goods vehicle.

HH abbr. **1** Her or His Highness. **2** His Holiness. **3** double-hard (pencil-lead).

H-hour /ˈeɪtʃˌaʊə(r)/ n. the hour at which an operation is scheduled to begin. [*H* for *hour* + HOUR]

hi /haɪ/ int. calling attention or as a greeting. [parallel form to HEY]

hiatus /haɪˈeɪtəs/ n. (pl. **hiatuses**) **1** a break or gap, esp. in a series, account, or chain of proof. **2** *Prosody & Gram.* a break between two vowels coming together but not in the same syllable, as in *though oft the ear.* □ **hiatal** adj. [L, = gaping f. *hiare* gape]

hibernate /ˈhaɪbəˌneɪt/ v.intr. **1** (of some animals) spend the winter in a dormant state. **2** remain inactive. □ **hibernation** /-ˈneɪʃ(ə)n/ n. **hibernator** n. [L *hibernare* f. *hibernus* wintry]

Hibernian /haɪˈbɜːnɪən/ adj. & n. archaic poet. —adj. of or concerning Ireland. —n. a native of Ireland. [L *Hibernia, Iverna* f. Gk *Iernē* f. OCelt.]

Hibernicism /haɪˈbɜːnɪˌsɪz(ə)m/ n. an Irish idiom or expression; = BULL³ 1. [as HIBERNIAN after *Anglicism* etc.]

Hiberno- /haɪˈbɜːnəʊ/ comb. form Irish (*Hiberno-British*). [med.L *hibernus* Irish (as HIBERNIAN)]

hibiscus /hɪˈbɪskəs/ n. any tree or shrub of the genus *Hibiscus*, cultivated for its large bright-coloured flowers. [L f. Gk *hibiskos* marsh mallow]

hic int. expressing the sound of a hiccup, esp. a drunken hiccup. [imit.]

hiccup /ˈhɪkʌp/ n. & v. (also **hiccough**) —n. **1 a** an involuntary spasm of the diaphragm and respiratory organs, with sudden closure of the glottis and characteristic coughlike sound. **b** (in pl.) an attack of such spasms. **2** a temporary or minor stoppage or difficulty. —v. **1** intr. make a hiccup or series of hiccups. **2** tr. utter with a hiccup. □ **hiccupy** adj. [imit.]

hick n. esp. US colloq. a country dweller; a provincial. [pet-form of the name *Richard*: cf. DICK¹]

hickey /ˈhɪkɪ/ n. (pl. **-eys**) US colloq. a gadget (cf. DOOHICKEY). [20th c.: orig. unkn.]

hickory /ˈhɪkərɪ/ n. (pl. **-ies**) **1** any N. American tree of the genus *Carya*, yielding tough heavy wood and bearing nutlike edible fruits. **2** the wood of these trees. [native Virginian *pohickery*]

hid past of HIDE¹.

hidalgo /hɪˈdælgəʊ/ n. (pl. **-os**) a Spanish gentleman. [Sp. f. *hijo dalgo* son of something]

hidden past part. of HIDE¹. □ **hiddenness** n.

hide¹ v. & n. —v. (past **hid**; past part. **hidden** /ˈhɪd(ə)n/ or archaic **hid**) **1** tr. put or keep out of sight (*hid it under the cushion; hid her in the cupboard*). **2** intr. conceal oneself. **3** tr. (usu. foll. by *from*) keep (a fact) secret (*hid his real motive from her*). **4** tr. conceal (a thing) from sight intentionally or not (*trees hid the house*). —n. Brit. a camouflaged shelter used for observing wildlife or hunting animals. □ **hidden agenda** a secret motivation behind a policy, statement, etc.; an ulterior motive. **hidden reserves** extra profits, resources, etc. kept concealed in reserve. **hide-and-seek 1** a children's game in which one or more players seek a child or children hiding. **2** a process of attempting to find an evasive person or thing. **hide one's head** keep out of sight, esp. from shame. **hide one's light under a bushel** conceal one's merits (Matthew 5:15). **hide out** (or **up**) remain in concealment. **hide-out** colloq. a hiding-place. **hidey-** (or **hidy-**) **hole** colloq. a hiding-place. □ **hider** n. [OE *hȳdan* f. WG]

hide² /haɪd/ n. & v. —n. **1** the skin of an animal, esp. when tanned or dressed. **2** colloq. the human skin (*saved his own hide; I'll tan your hide*). —v.tr. colloq. flog. □ **hided** adj. (also in comb.). [OE *hȳd* f. Gmc]

hideaway /ˈhaɪdəˌweɪ/ n. a hiding-place or place of retreat.

hidebound /ˈhaɪdbaʊnd/ adj. **1** narrow-minded; bigoted. **2** (of the law, rules, etc.) constricted by tradition. [HIDE² + BOUND⁴]

hideosity /ˌhɪdɪˈɒsɪtɪ/ n. (pl. **-ies**) **1** a hideous object. **2** hideousness.

hideous /ˈhɪdɪəs/ adj. **1** frightful, repulsive, or revolting, to the senses or the mind (*a hideous monster; a hideous pattern*). **2** colloq. unpleasant. □ **hideously** adv. **hideousness** n. [ME *hidous* f. AF *hidous*, OF *hidos, -eus,* f. OF *hide, hisde* fear, of unkn. orig.]

hiding¹ /ˈhaɪdɪŋ/ n. colloq. a thrashing. □ **on a hiding to nothing** in a position from which there can be no successful outcome. [HIDE² + -ING¹]

hiding² /ˈhaɪdɪŋ/ n. **1** the act or an instance of hiding. **2** the state of remaining hidden (*go into hiding*). □ **hiding-place** a place of concealment. [ME, f. HIDE¹ + -ING¹]

hie v.intr. & refl. (**hies, hied, hieing** or **hying**) archaic or poet. go quickly (*hie to your chamber; hied him to the chase*). [OE *hīgian* strive, pant, of unkn. orig.]

hierarch /ˈhaɪəˌrɑːk/ n. **1** a chief priest. **2** an archbishop. □ **hierarchal** /-ˈrɑːk(ə)l/ adj. [med.L f. Gk *hierarkhēs* f. *hieros* sacred + *-arkhēs* ruler]

hierarchy /ˈhaɪəˌrɑːkɪ/ n. (pl. **-ies**) **1 a** a system in which grades or classes of status or authority are ranked one above the other (*ranks third in the hierarchy*). **b** the hierarchical system (of government, management, etc.). **2** priestly government. □ **hierarchic** /-ˈrɑːkɪk/ adj. **hierarchical** /-ˈrɑːkɪk(ə)l/ adj. **hierarchism** n. **hierarchize** v.tr. (also -**ise**). [ME f. OF *ierarchie* f. med.L *(h)ierarchia* f. Gk *hierarkhia* (as HIERARCH)]

hieratic /ˌhaɪəˈrætɪk/ adj. **1** of or concerning priests. **2** of the ancient Egyptian writing of abridged hieroglyphics as used by priests. **3** priestly. □ **hieratically** adv. [L f. Gk *hieratikos* f. *hieraomai* be a priest f. *hiereus* priest]

hiero- /ˈhaɪərəʊ/ comb. form sacred, holy. [Gk *hieros* sacred + -o-]

hierocracy /ˌhaɪəˈrɒkrəsɪ/ n. (pl. **-ies**) **1** priestly rule. **2** a body of ruling priests. [HIERO- + -CRACY]

hieroglyph /ˈhaɪərəˌglɪf/ n. **1 a** a picture of an object representing a word, syllable, or sound, as used in ancient Egyptian and other writing. **b** a writing consisting of characters of this kind. **2** a secret or enigmatic symbol. **3** (in pl.) joc. writing difficult to read. [back-form. f. HIEROGLYPHIC]

hieroglyphic /ˌhaɪərəˈglɪfɪk/ adj. & n. —adj. **1** of or written in hieroglyphs. **2** symbolical. —n. (in pl.) hieroglyphs; hieroglyphic writing. □ **hieroglyphical** adj. **hieroglyphically** adv. [F *hiéroglyphique* or LL *hieroglyphicus* f. Gk *hieroglyphikos* (as HIERO-, *gluphikos* f. *gluphē* carving)]

hi-fi /ˈhaɪfaɪ/ adj. & n. colloq. —adj. = high fidelity. —n. (pl. **hi-fis**) a set of equipment for high-fidelity sound reproduction. [abbr.]

higgle /ˈhɪg(ə)l/ v.intr. dispute about terms; haggle. [var. of HAGGLE]

higgledy-piggledy /ˌhɪgəldɪˈpɪgəldɪ/ adv., adj., & n. —adv. & adj. in confusion or disorder. —n. a state of disordered confusion. [rhyming jingle, prob. with ref. to the irregular herding together of pigs]

high /haɪ/ adj., n., & adv. —adj. **1 a** of great vertical extent (a high building). **b** (predic.; often in comb.) of a specified height (one inch high; water was waist-high). **2 a** far above ground or sea level etc. (a high altitude). **b** inland, esp. when raised (High Asia). **3** extending above the normal or average level (high boots; jersey with a high neck). **4** of exalted, esp. spiritual, quality (high principles; high art). **5** of exalted rank (in high society; is high in the Government). **6 a** great; intense; extreme; powerful (high praise; high temperature). **b** greater than normal (high prices). **c** extreme in religious or political opinion (high Tory). **7** (of physical action, esp. athletics) performed at, to, or from a considerable height (high diving; high flying). **8** colloq. (often foll. by on) intoxicated by alcohol or esp. drugs. **9** (of a sound or note) of high frequency; shrill; at the top end of the scale. **10** (of a period, an age, a time, etc.) at its peak (high summer; High Renaissance). **11 a** (of meat) beginning to go bad; off. **b** (of game) well-hung and slightly decomposed. —n. **1** a high, or the highest, level or figure. **2** an area of high barometric pressure; an anticyclone. **3** sl. a euphoric drug-induced state. **4** top gear in a motor vehicle. **5** US colloq. high school. —adv. **1** far up; aloft (flew the flag high). **2** in or to a high degree. **3** at a high price. **4** (of a sound) at or to a high pitch (sang high). □ **from on high** from heaven or a high place. **high altar** the chief altar of a church. **high and dry 1** out of the current of events; stranded. **2** (of a ship) out of the water. **high and low 1** everywhere (searched high and low). **2** (people of all conditions. **high and mighty** colloq. arrogant. **high chair** an infant's chair with long legs and a tray, for use at meals. **High Church** n. a section of the Church of England emphasizing ritual, priestly authority, and sacraments. —adj. of or relating to this section. **high-class** of high quality. **high colour** a flushed complexion. **high command** an army commander-in-chief and associated staff. **High Commission** an embassy from one Commonwealth country to another. **High Commissioner** the head of such an embassy. **High Court** (also in England **High Court of Justice**) a supreme court of justice for civil cases. **higher animal** (or **plant**) an animal or plant evolved to a high degree. **higher court** Law a court that can overrule the decision of another. **higher education** education at university etc., esp. to degree level. **higher mathematics** advanced mathematics as taught at university etc. **higher-up** colloq. a person of higher rank. **highest common factor** Math. the highest number that can be divided exactly into each of two or more numbers. **high explosive** an extremely explosive substance used in shells, bombs, etc. **high fashion** = HAUTE COUTURE. **high fidelity** the reproduction of sound with little distortion, giving a result very similar to the original. **high finance** financial transactions involving large sums. **high-flown** (of language etc.) extravagant, bombastic. **high-flyer** (or **-flier**) **1** an ambitious person. **2** a person or thing with great potential for achievement. **high-flying** reaching a great height; ambitious. **high frequency** a frequency,

esp. in radio, of 3 to 30 megahertz. **high-grade** of high quality. **high hat 1** a tall hat; a top hat. **2** foot-operated cymbals. **3** a snobbish or overbearing person. **high-hat** —adj. supercilious; snobbish. —v. (**-hatted, -hatting**) US **1** tr. treat superciliously. **2** intr. assume a superior attitude. **high jinks** boisterous joking or merrymaking. **high jump 1** an athletic event consisting of jumping as high as possible over a bar of adjustable height. **2** colloq. a drastic punishment (he's for the high jump). **high kick** a dancer's kick high in the air. **high-level 1** (of negotiations etc.) conducted by high-ranking people. **2** Computing (of a programming language) that is not machine-dependent and is usu. at a level of abstraction close to natural language. **high life** (or **living**) a luxurious existence ascribed to the upper classes. **high-octane** (of petrol etc.) having good antiknock properties. **high old** colloq. most enjoyable (had a high old time). **high opinion** of a favourable opinion of. **high-pitched 1** (of a sound) high. **2** (of a roof) steep. **3** (of style etc.) lofty. **high places** the upper ranks of an organization etc. **high point** the maximum or best state reached. **high-powered 1** having great power or energy. **2** important or influential. **high pressure 1** a high degree of activity or exertion. **2** a condition of the atmosphere with the pressure above average. **high priest 1** a chief priest, esp. Jewish. **2** the head of any cult. **high profile** exposure to attention or publicity. **high-profile** adj. (usu. attrib.) having a high profile. **high-ranking** of high rank, senior. **high-rise 1** (of a building) having many storeys. **2** such a building. **high-risk** (usu. attrib.) involving or exposed to danger (high-risk sports). **high road 1** a main road. **2** (usu. foll. by to) a direct route (on the high road to success). **high roller** US sl. a person who gambles large sums or spends freely. **high school 1** Brit. a grammar school. **2** US & Sc. a secondary school. **high sea** (or **seas**) open seas not within any country's jurisdiction. **high season** the period of the greatest number of visitors at a resort etc. **high sign** US colloq. a surreptitious gesture indicating that all is well or that the coast is clear. **high-sounding** pretentious, bombastic. **high-speed 1** operating at great speed. **2** (of steel) suitable for cutting-tools even when red-hot. **high-spirited** vivacious; cheerful. **high spirits** vivacity; energy; cheerfulness. **high spot** sl. an important place or feature. **high street** Brit. a main road, esp. the principal shopping street of a town. **high table** a table on a platform at a public dinner or for the fellows of a college. **high tea** Brit. a main evening meal usu. consisting of a cooked dish, bread and butter, tea, etc. **high tech** n. = high technology. —adj. **1** (of interior design etc.) imitating styles more usual in industry etc., esp. using steel, glass, or plastic in a functional way. **2** employing, requiring, or involved in high technology. **high technology** advanced technological development, esp. in electronics. **high-tensile** (of metal) having great tensile strength. **high tension** = high voltage. **high tide** the time or level of the tide at its flow. **high time** a time that is late or overdue (it is high time they arrived). **high-toned** stylish; dignified; superior. **high-up** colloq. a person of high rank. **high voltage** electrical potential causing some danger of injury or damage. **high**

water 1 the tide at its fullest. **2** the time of this.
high-water mark 1 the level reached at high water. **2** the maximum recorded value or highest point of excellence. **high wire** a high tightrope. **high words** angry talk. **on high** in or to heaven or a high place. **on one's high horse** *colloq.* behaving superciliously or arrogantly. **run high 1** (of the sea) have a strong current with high tide. **2** (of feelings) be strong. [OE *hēah* f. Gmc]

highball /ˈhaɪbɔːl/ *n. US* a drink of spirits and soda etc., served with ice in a tall glass.

highbrow /ˈhaɪbraʊ/ *adj. & n. colloq.* —*adj.* intellectual; cultural. —*n.* an intellectual or cultured person.

highfalutin /ˌhaɪfəˈluːtɪn/ *adj. & n.* (also **high-faluting** /-tɪŋ/) *colloq.* —*adj.* absurdly pompous or pretentious. —*n.* highfalutin speech or writing. [HIGH + *-falutin*, of unkn. orig.]

high-handed /haɪˈhændɪd/ *adj.* disregarding others' feelings; overbearing. □ **high-handedly** *adv.* **high-handedness** *n.*

highland /ˈhaɪlənd/ *n. & adj.* —*n.* (usu. in *pl.*) **1** an area of high land. **2** (**the Highlands**) the mountainous part of Scotland. —*adj.* of or in a highland or the Highlands. □ **Highland cattle 1** cattle of a shaggy-haired breed with long curved widely-spaced horns. **2** this breed. **Highland dress** the kilt etc. □ **highlander** *n.* (also **Highlander**). **Highlandman** *n.* (*pl.* **-men**). [OE *hēahlond* promontory (as HIGH, LAND)]

highlight /ˈhaɪlaɪt/ *n. & v.* —*n.* **1** (in a painting etc.) a light area, or one seeming to reflect light. **2** a moment or detail of vivid interest; an outstanding feature. **3** (usu. in *pl.*) a bright tint in the hair produced by bleaching. —*v.tr.* **1 a** bring into prominence; draw attention to. **b** mark with a highlighter. **2** create highlights in (the hair).

highlighter /ˈhaɪˌlaɪtə(r)/ *n.* a marker pen which overlays colour on a printed word etc., leaving it legible and emphasized.

highly /ˈhaɪlɪ/ *adv.* **1** in a high degree (*highly amusing*; *highly probable*; *commend it highly*). **2** honourably; favourably (*think highly of him*). □ **highly-strung** very sensitive or nervous. [OE *hēalīce* (as HIGH)]

high-minded /haɪˈmaɪndɪd/ *adj.* **1** having high moral principles. **2** *archaic* proud. □ **high-mindedly** *adv.* **high-mindedness** *n.*

highness /ˈhaɪnɪs/ *n.* **1** the state of being high (*highness of taxation*). **2** (**Highness**) a title used in addressing and referring to a prince or princess (*Her Highness*; *Your Royal Highness*). [OE *hēanes* (as HIGH)]

hightail /ˈhaɪteɪl/ *v.intr. US colloq.* move at high speed.

highway /ˈhaɪweɪ/ *n.* **1 a** a public road. **b** a main route (by land or water). **2** a direct course of action (*on the highway to success*). □ **Highway Code** *Brit.* the official booklet of guidance for road-users. **King's** (or **Queen's**) **highway** a public road, regarded as being under the sovereign's protection.

highwayman /ˈhaɪweɪmən/ *n.* (*pl.* **-men**) *hist.* a robber of passengers, travellers, etc., usu. mounted. [HIGHWAY]

hijack /ˈhaɪdʒæk/ *v. & n.* —*v.tr.* **1** seize control of (a loaded lorry, an aircraft in flight, etc.), esp. to force it to a different destination. **2** seize (goods) in transit. **3** take over (an organization etc.) by force or subterfuge in order to redirect

it. —*n.* an instance of hijacking. □ **hijacker** *n.* [20th c.: orig. unkn.]

hijra var. of HEGIRA.

hike *n. & v.* —*n.* **1** a long country walk, esp. with rucksacks etc. **2** esp. *US* an increase (of prices etc.). —*v.* **1** *intr.* walk, esp. across country, for a long distance, esp. with boots, rucksack, etc. **2** (usu. foll. by *up*) **a** *tr.* hitch up (clothing etc.); hoist; shove. **b** *intr.* work upwards out of place, become hitched up. **3** *tr.* esp. *US* increase (prices etc.). □ **hiker** *n.* [19th-c. dial.: orig. unkn.]

hilarious /hɪˈleərɪəs/ *adj.* **1** exceedingly funny. **2** boisterously merry. □ **hilariously** *adv.* **hilariousness** *n.* **hilarity** /-ˈlærɪtɪ/ *n.* [L *hilaris* f. Gk *hilaros* cheerful]

Hilary term /ˈhɪlərɪ/ *n. Brit.* the university term beginning in January, esp. at Oxford. [*Hilarius* bishop of Poitiers d. 367, with a festival on 13 Jan.]

hill *n. & v.* —*n.* **1 a** a naturally raised area of land, not as high as a mountain. **b** (as **the hills**) *Anglo-Ind.* = *hill-station*. **2** (often in *comb.*) a heap; a mound (*anthill*; *dunghill*). **3** a sloping piece of road. —*v.tr.* **1** form into a hill. **2** (usu. foll. by *up*) bank up (plants) with soil. □ **hill-billy** (*pl.* **-ies**) *US* **1** *colloq.*, often *derog.* a person from a remote rural area in a southern State. **2** folk music of or like that of the southern US. **hill climb** a race for vehicles up a steep hill. **hill-fort** a fort built on a hill. **hill-station** *Anglo-Ind.* a government settlement, esp. for holidays etc. during the hot season, in the low mountains of N. India. **old as the hills** very ancient. **over the hill** *colloq.* **1** past the prime of life; declining. **2** past the crisis. [OE *hyll*]

hillock /ˈhɪlək/ *n.* a small hill or mound. □ **hillocky** *adj.*

hillside /ˈhɪlsaɪd/ *n.* the sloping side of a hill.

hilltop /ˈhɪltɒp/ *n.* the summit of a hill.

hillwalking /ˈhɪlˌwɔːkɪŋ/ *n.* the pastime of walking in hilly country. □ **hillwalker** *n.*

hilly /ˈhɪlɪ/ *adj.* (**hillier, hilliest**) having many hills. □ **hilliness** *n.*

hilt *n. & v.* —*n.* **1** the handle of a sword, dagger, etc. **2** the handle of a tool. —*v.tr.* provide with a hilt. □ **up to the hilt** completely. [OE *hilt(e)* f. Gmc]

him *pron.* **1** *objective case* of HE (*I saw him*). **2** *colloq.* he (*it's him again*; *is taller than him*). **3** *archaic* himself (*fell and hurt him*). [OE, masc. and neut. dative sing. of HE, IT]

himself /hɪmˈself/ *pron.* **1 a** *emphat. form* of HE or HIM (*he himself will do it*). **b** *refl. form* of HIM (*he has hurt himself*). **2** in his normal state of body or mind (*does not feel quite himself today*). **3** esp. *Ir.* a third party of some importance; the master of the house. □ **be himself** act in his normal unconstrained manner. **by himself** see *by oneself*. [OE (as HIM, SELF)]

hind[1] /haɪnd/ *adj.* (esp. of parts of the body) situated at the back, posterior (*hind leg*) (opp. FORE). [ME, perh. shortened f. OE *bihindan* BEHIND]

hind[2] /haɪnd/ *n.* a female deer (usu. a red deer or sika), esp. in and after the third year. [OE f. Gmc]

hinder[1] /ˈhɪndə(r)/ *v.tr.* (also *absol.*) impede; delay; prevent (*you will hinder him*; *hindered me from working*). [OE *hindrian* f. Gmc]

hinder² /ˈhaɪndə(r)/ *adj.* rear, hind (*the hinder part*). [ME, perh. f. OE *hinderweard* backward: cf. HIND¹]

Hindi /ˈhɪndɪ/ *n. & adj.* —*n.* **1** a group of spoken dialects of N. India. **2** a literary form of Hindustani with a Sanskrit-based vocabulary, an official language of India. —*adj.* of or concerning Hindi. [Urdu *hindī* f. *Hind* India]

hindmost /ˈhaɪndməʊst/ *adj.* furthest behind; most remote.

hindquarters /haɪndˈkwɔːtəz/ *n.pl.* the hind legs and adjoining parts of a quadruped.

hindrance /ˈhɪndrəns/ *n.* **1** the act or an instance of hindering; the state of being hindered. **2** a thing that hinders; an obstacle.

hindsight /ˈhaɪndsaɪt/ *n.* **1** wisdom after the event (*realized with hindsight that they were wrong*). **2** the backsight of a gun.

Hindu /ˈhɪnduː, -ˈduː/ *n. & adj.* —*n.* a follower of Hinduism. —*adj.* of or concerning Hindus or Hinduism. [Urdu f. Pers. f. *Hind* India]

Hinduism /ˈhɪnduːˌɪz(ə)m/ *n.* the main religious and social system of India, including belief in reincarnation, the worship of several gods, and a caste system as the basis of society. □ **Hinduize** *v.tr.* (also **-ise**).

Hindustani /ˌhɪnduˈstɑːnɪ/ *n.* **1** a language based on Western Hindi, with elements of Arabic, Persian, etc., used as a lingua franca in much of India. **2** *archaic* Urdu. [Urdu f. Pers. *hindūstānī* (as HINDU, *stān* country)]

hinge *n. & v.* —*n.* **1 a** a movable, usu. metal, joint or mechanism such as that by which a door is hung on a side post. **b** *Biol.* a natural joint performing a similar function, e.g. that of a bivalve shell. **2** a central point or principle on which everything depends. —*v.* **1** *intr.* (foll. by *on*) **a** depend (on a principle, an event, etc.) (*all hinges on his acceptance*). **b** (of a door etc.) hang and turn (on a post etc.). **2** *tr.* attach with or as if with a hinge. □ **stamp-hinge** a small piece of gummed transparent paper used for fixing postage stamps in an album etc. □ **hinged** *adj.* **hingeless** *adj.* **hingewise** *adv.* [ME *heng* etc., rel. to HANG]

hinny /ˈhɪnɪ/ *n.* (*pl.* **-ies**) the offspring of a female donkey and a male horse. [L *hinnus* f. Gk *hinnos*]

hint *n. & v.* —*n.* **1** a slight or indirect indication or suggestion (*took the hint and left*). **2** a small piece of practical information (*handy hints on cooking*). **3** a very small trace; a suggestion (*a hint of perfume*). —*v.tr.* (often foll. by *that* + clause) suggest slightly (*hinted the contrary; hinted that they were wrong*). □ **hint at** give a hint of; refer indirectly to. [app. f. obs. *hent* grasp, lay hold of, f. OE *hentan*, f. Gmc, rel. to HUNT]

hinterland /ˈhɪntəˌlænd/ *n.* **1** the often deserted or uncharted areas beyond a coastal district or a river's banks. **2** an area served by a port or other centre. **3** a remote or fringe area. [G f. *hinter* behind + *Land* LAND]

hip¹ *n.* **1** a projection of the pelvis and upper thigh-bone on each side of the body in human beings and quadrupeds. **2** (often in *pl.*) the circumference of the body at the buttocks. □ **hip-bath** a portable bath in which a person sits. **hip-bone** a bone forming the hip, esp. the ilium. **hip-flask** a flask for spirits etc., carried in a hip-pocket. **hip-joint** the articulation of the head of the thigh-bone with the ilium. **hip- (or hipped-) roof** a roof with the sides and

the ends inclined. □ **on the hip** *archaic* at a disadvantage. □ **hipless** *adj.* **hipped** *adj.* (also in comb.). [OE *hype* f. Gmc, rel. to HOP¹]

hip² *n.* (also **hep** /hep/) the fruit of a rose, esp. a wild kind. [OE *hēope*, *hīope* f. WG]

hip³ *adj.* (also **hep** /hep/) (**hipper**, **hippest** or **hepper**, **heppest**) *sl.* **1** following the latest fashion in esp. jazz music, clothes, etc.; stylish. **2** (often foll. by *to*) understanding, aware. □ **hip-cat** a hip person; a devotee of jazz or swing. **hip hop** a style of Black rock music or the street subculture that surrounds it (typically including graffiti art, rap, and break-dancing). □ **hipness** *n.* [20th c.: orig. unkn.]

hip⁴ *int.* introducing a united cheer (*hip, hip, hooray*). [19th c.: orig. unkn.]

hipped /hɪpt/ *adj.* (usu. foll. by *on*) esp. *US sl.* obsessed, infatuated. [past part. of *hip* (v.) = make hip (HIP³)]

hippie /ˈhɪpɪ/ *n.* (also **hippy**) (*pl.* **-ies**) *colloq.* (esp. in the 1960s) a person of unconventional appearance, typically with long hair, jeans, beads, etc., often associated with hallucinogenic drugs and a rejection of conventional values. [HIP³]

hippo /ˈhɪpəʊ/ *n.* (*pl.* **-os**) *colloq.* a hippopotamus. [abbr.]

hippocampus /ˌhɪpəˈkæmpəs/ *n.* (*pl.* **hippocampi** /-paɪ/) **1** any marine fish of the genus *Hippocampus*, swimming vertically and with a head suggestive of a horse; a sea horse. **2** *Anat.* the elongated ridges on the floor of each lateral ventricle of the brain, thought to be the centre of emotion and the autonomic nervous system. [L f. Gk *hippokampos* f. *hippos* horse + *kampos* sea monster]

Hippocratic oath /ˌhɪpəˈkrætɪk/ *n.* an oath formerly taken by doctors affirming their obligations and proper conduct. [med.L *Hippocraticus* f. *Hippocrates*, Gk physician of the 5th c. BC]

hippodrome /ˈhɪpəˌdrəʊm/ *n.* **1** a music- or dance-hall. **2** (in classical antiquity) a course for chariot races etc. **3** a circus. [F *hippodrome* or L *hippodromus* f. Gk *hippodromos* f. *hippos* horse + *dromos* race, course]

hippopotamus /ˌhɪpəˈpɒtəməs/ *n.* (*pl.* **hippopotamuses** or **hippopotami** /-ˌmaɪ/) **1** a large thick-skinned four-legged mammal, *Hippopotamus amphibius*, native to Africa, inhabiting rivers, lakes, etc. **2** (in full **pigmy hippopotamus**) a smaller related mammal, *Choeropsis liberiensis*, native to Africa, inhabiting forests and swamps. [ME f. L f. Gk *hippopotamos* f. *hippos* horse + *potamos* river]

hippy¹ var. of HIPPIE.

hippy² /ˈhɪpɪ/ *adj.* having large hips.

hipster¹ /ˈhɪpstə(r)/ *adj. & n. Brit.* —*adj.* (of a garment) hanging from the hips rather than the waist. —*n.* (in *pl.*) trousers hanging from the hips.

hipster² /ˈhɪpstə(r)/ *n. sl.* a person who is hip; a hip-cat. □ **hipsterism** *n.*

hire *v. & n.* —*v.tr.* **1** (often foll. by *from*) procure the temporary use of (a thing) for an agreed payment (*hired a van from them*). **2** esp. *US* employ (a person) for wages or a fee. **3** *US* borrow (money). —*n.* **1** hiring or being hired. **2** payment for this. □ **for** (or **on**) **hire** ready to be hired. **hire-car** a car available for hire. **hired girl** (or **man**) *US* a domestic servant, esp. on a farm. **hire out** grant the temporary use of (a thing) for an agreed payment. **hire purchase** *Brit.* a system by which a person may purchase a thing by regular payments while having the use of it. □ **hireable** *adj.* (*US* **hirable**). **hirer** *n.* [OE *hȳrian*, *hȳr* f. WG]

hireling /ˈhaɪəlɪŋ/ *n.* usu. *derog.* a person who works for hire. [OE *hȳrling* (as HIRE, -LING¹)]

hirsute /ˈhɜːsjuːt/ *adj.* **1** hairy, shaggy. **2** untrimmed. □ **hirsuteness** *n.* [L *hirsutus*]

hirsutism /ˈhɜːsjuːˌtɪz(ə)m/ *n.* the excessive growth of hair on the face and body.

his /hɪz/ *poss.pron.* **1** (*attrib.*) of or belonging to him or himself (*his house*; *his own business*). **2** (**His**) (*attrib.*) (in titles) that he is (*His Majesty*). **3** the one or ones belonging to or associated with him (*it is his*; *his are over there*). □ **his and hers** *joc.* (of matching items) for husband and wife, or men and women. **of his** of or belonging to him (*a friend of his*). [OE, genit. of HE, IT¹]

Hispanic /hɪˈspænɪk/ *adj.* & *n.* —*adj.* **1** of or relating to Spain or to Spain and Portugal. **2** of Spain and other Spanish-speaking countries. —*n.* a Spanish-speaking person, esp. one of Latin-American descent, living in the US. □ **Hispanicize** /-ˌsaɪz/ *v.tr.* (also **-ise**). [L *Hispanicus* f. *Hispania* Spain]

Hispanist /ˈhɪspənɪst/ *n.* (also **Hispanicist** /hɪˈspænɪsɪst/) an expert in or student of the language, literature, and civilization of Spain.

Hispano- /hɪˈspænəʊ/ *comb. form* Spanish. [L *Hispanus* Spanish]

hiss *v.* & *n.* —*v.* **1** *intr.* (of a person, snake, goose, etc.) make a sharp sibilant sound, esp. as a sign of disapproval or derision (*audience booed and hissed*; *the water hissed on the hotplate*). **2** *tr.* express disapproval of (a person etc.) by hisses. **3** *tr.* whisper (a threat etc.) urgently or angrily ('*Where's the door?*' *he hissed*). —*n.* **1** a sharp sibilant sound as of the letter *s*. **2** *Electronics* unwanted interference at audio frequencies. [ME: imit.]

hist *int. archaic* used to call attention, enjoin silence, incite a dog, etc. [16th c.: natural excl.]

histamine /ˈhɪstəmɪn, ˈhɪstəˌmiːn/ *n. Biochem.* an organic compound occurring in injured body tissues etc., and also associated with allergic reactions. □ **histaminic** /-ˈmɪnɪk/ *adj.* [HISTO- + AMINE]

histo- /ˈhɪstəʊ/ *comb. form* (also **hist-** before a vowel) *Biol.* tissue. [Gk *histos* web]

histogram /ˈhɪstəˌɡræm/ *n. Statistics* a chart consisting of rectangles (usu. drawn vertically from a base line) whose areas and positions are proportional to the value or range of a number of variables. [Gk *histos* mast + -GRAM]

histology /hɪˈstɒlədʒɪ/ *n.* the study of the structure of tissues. □ **histological** /ˌhɪstəˈlɒdʒɪk(ə)l/ *adj.* **histologist** /hɪˈstɒlədʒɪst/ *n.*

historian /hɪˈstɔːrɪən/ *n.* **1** a writer of history, esp. a critical analyst, rather than a compiler. **2** a person learned in or studying history (*English historian*; *ancient historian*). [F *historien* f. L (as HISTORY)]

historic /hɪˈstɒrɪk/ *adj.* **1** famous or important in history or potentially so (*a historic moment*). **2** *Gram.* (of a tense) normally used in the narration of past events. **3** *archaic* or *disp.* = HISTORICAL. □ **historic present** the present tense used instead of the past in vivid narration. [L *historicus* f. Gk *historikos* (as HISTORY)]

historical /hɪˈstɒrɪk(ə)l/ *adj.* **1** of or concerning history (*historical evidence*). **2** belonging to history, not to prehistory or legend. **3** (of the study of a subject) based on an analysis of its development over a period. **4** belonging to the past, not the present. **5** (of a novel, a film, etc.) dealing or professing to deal with historical events. **6** in connection with history, from the historian's point of view (*of purely historical interest*). □ **historically** *adv.*

historicism /hɪˈstɒrɪˌsɪz(ə)m/ *n.* **1 a** the theory that social and cultural phenomena are determined by history. **b** the belief that historical events are governed by laws. **2** the tendency to regard historical development as the most basic aspect of human existence. **3** an excessive regard for past styles etc. □ **historicist** *n.* [HISTORIC after G *Historismus*]

historicity /ˌhɪstəˈrɪsɪtɪ/ *n.* the historical genuineness of an event etc.

historiographer /hɪˌstɔːrɪˈɒɡrəfə(r)/ *n.* **1** an expert in or student of historiography. **2** a writer of history, esp. an official historian. [ME f. F *historiographe* or f. LL *historiographus* f. Gk *historiographos* (as HISTORY, -GRAPHER)]

historiography /hɪˌstɔːrɪˈɒɡrəfɪ/ *n.* **1** the writing of history. **2** the study of history-writing. □ **historiographic** /-ˈɡræfɪk/ *adj.* **historiographical** /-ˈɡræfɪk(ə)l/ *adj.* [med.L *historiographia* f. Gk *historiographia* (as HISTORY, -GRAPHY)]

history /ˈhɪstərɪ/ *n.* (*pl.* **-ies**) **1** a continuous, usu. chronological, record of important or public events. **2 a** the study of past events, esp. human affairs. **b** the total accumulation of past events, esp. relating to human affairs or to the accumulation of developments connected with a particular nation, person, thing, etc. (*the history of astronomy*). **3** an eventful past (*this house has a history*). **4 a** a systematic or critical account of or research into a past event or events etc. **b** a similar record or account of natural phenomena. **5** a historical play. □ **make history 1** influence the course of history. **2** do something memorable. [ME f. L *historia* f. Gk *historia* finding out, narrative, history f. *histōr* learned, wise man, rel. to WIT²]

histrionic /ˌhɪstrɪˈɒnɪk/ *adj.* & *n.* —*adj.* **1** of or concerning actors or acting. **2** (of behaviour) theatrical, dramatic. —*n.* **1** (in *pl.*) insincere and dramatic behaviour designed to impress. **2** theatricals; theatrical art. □ **histrionically** *adv.* [LL *histrionicus* f. L *histrio -onis* actor]

hit *v.* & *n.* —*v.* (**hitting**; *past* and *past part.* **hit**) **1** *tr.* a strike with a blow or a missile. **b** (of a moving body) strike (*the plane hit the ground*). **c** reach (a target, a person, etc.) with a directed missile (*hit the window with the ball*). **2** *tr.* cause to suffer or affect adversely; wound (*the loss hit him hard*). **3** *intr.* (often foll. by *at*, *against*, *upon*) direct a blow. **4** *tr.* (often foll. by *against*, *on*) knock (a part of the body) (*hit his head on the door-frame*). **5** *tr.* light upon; get at (a thing aimed at) (*he's hit the truth at last*; *tried to hit the right tone in his apology*) (see *hit on*). **6** *tr. colloq.* a encounter (*hit a snag*). **b** arrive at (*hit an all-time low*; *hit the town*). **c** indulge in, esp. liquor etc. (*hit the bottle*). **7** *tr. esp. US sl.* rob or kill. **8** *tr.* occur forcefully to (*the seriousness of the situation only hit him later*). **9** *tr. Sport* **a** propel (a ball etc.) with a bat etc. to score runs or points. **b** score (runs etc.) in this way. **c** (usu. foll. by *for*) strike (a ball or a bowler) for so many runs (*hit him for six*). **10** *tr.* represent exactly. —*n.* **1 a** a blow; a stroke. **b** a collision. **2** a shot etc. that hits its target. **3** *colloq.* a popular success in entertainment. **4** a stroke of sarcasm, wit, etc. **5** a stroke of good luck. **6** esp. *US sl.* **a** a murder or other violent crime. **b** a drug injection etc. **7** a successful attempt. □ **hit and run** cause (accidental or wilful) damage and escape or leave the scene before being discovered. **hit back** retaliate. **hit below the belt 1** esp. *Boxing* give a foul blow. **2** treat or behave unfairly. **hit the hay** (or **sack**) *colloq.* go to bed. **hit home** make a salutary impression. **hit it off** (often foll. by *with*, *together*) agree or be congenial. **hit list** *sl.* a list of prospective victims. **hit man** (*pl.* **hit men**) *sl.* a hired assassin. **hit the nail on the head** state the truth exactly. **hit on** (or **upon**) find (what is sought); esp. by chance. **hit-or-miss** aimed or done carelessly. **hit out** deal vigorous physical or verbal blows (*hit out at her enemies*). **hit parade** *colloq.* a list of the current best-selling records of popular music. **hit the road** (*US* **trail**) *sl.* depart. **make a hit** (usu. foll. by *with*) be successful or popular. □ **hitter** *n.* [ME f. OE *hittan* f. ON *hitta* meet with, of unkn. orig.]

hitch *v.* & *n.* —*v.* **1 a** *tr.* fasten with a loop, hook, etc.; tether (*hitched the horse to the cart*). **b** *intr.* (often foll. by *in*, *on to*, etc.) become fastened in this way. **2** *tr.* move (a thing) with a jerk; shift slightly (*hitched the pillow to a comfortable position*). **3** *colloq.* **a** *intr.* = HITCHHIKE. **b** *tr.* obtain (a lift) by hitchhiking. —*n.* **1** an impediment; a temporary obstacle. **2** an abrupt pull or push; a jerk. **3** a noose or knot of various kinds. **4** *colloq.* a free ride in a vehicle. □ **get hitched** *colloq.* marry. **hitch up** lift (esp. clothing) with a jerk. □ **hitcher** *n.* [ME: orig. uncert.]

hitchhike /ˈhɪtʃhaɪk/ *v.* & *n.* —*v.intr.* travel by seeking free lifts in passing vehicles. —*n.* a journey made by hitchhiking. □ **hitchhiker** *n.*

hi-tech /ˈhaɪtek/ *n.* = *high tech.* [abbr.]

hither /ˈhɪðə(r)/ *adv.* & *adj.* formal —*adv.* to or towards this place. —*adj.* archaic situated on this side; the nearer (of two). □ **hither and thither** (or **yon**) in various directions; to and fro. [OE *hider*: cf. THITHER]

hitherto /ˌhɪðəˈtuː/ *adv.* until this time, up to now.

Hittite /ˈhɪtaɪt/ *n.* & *adj.* —*n.* **1** a member of an ancient people of Asia Minor and Syria. **2** the language of the Hittites. —*adj.* of or relating to the Hittites or their language. [Heb. *Ḥittīm*]

HIV *abbr.* human immunodeficiency virus, either of two retroviruses causing Aids.

hive /haɪv/ *n.* & *v.* —*n.* **1 a** a beehive. **b** the bees in a hive. **2** a busy swarming place. **3** a swarming multitude. **4** a thing shaped like a hive in being domed. —*v.* **1** *tr.* **a** place (bees) in a hive. **b** house (people etc.) snugly. **2** *intr.* **a** enter a hive. **b** live together like bees. □ **hive off 1** separate from a larger group. **2 a** form into or assign (work) to a subsidiary department or company. **b** denationalize or privatize (an industry etc.). [OE *hȳf* f. Gmc]

hives /haɪvz/ *n.pl.* **1** a skin-eruption, esp. nettle-rash. **2** inflammation of the larynx etc. [16th c. (orig. Sc.): orig. unkn.]

hiya /ˈhaɪjə/ *int. colloq.* a word used in greeting. [corrupt. of *how are you?*]

hl *abbr.* hectolitre(s).

HM *abbr.* Her (or His) Majesty('s).

hm *abbr.* hectometre(s).

h'm /hm/ *int.* & *n.* (also **hmm**) = HEM², HUM².

HMG *abbr.* Her or His Majesty's Government.

HMS *abbr.* Her or His Majesty's Ship.

HMSO *abbr.* Her or His Majesty's Stationery Office.

HNC *abbr.* (in the UK) Higher National Certificate.

HND *abbr.* (in the UK) Higher National Diploma.

Ho *symb. Chem.* the element holmium.

ho /həʊ/ *int.* **1 a** an expression of surprise, admiration, triumph, or (often repeated as **ho! ho!** etc.) derision. **b** (in *comb.*) (*heigh-ho*; *what ho*). **2** a call for attention. **3** (in *comb.*) *Naut.* an addition to the name of a destination etc. (*westward ho*). [ME, imit.: cf. ON *hó*]

hoar *adj.* & *n. literary* —*adj.* **1** grey-haired with age. **2** greyish-white. **3** (of a thing) grey with age. —*n.* **1** = *hoar-frost.* **2** hoariness. □ **hoar-frost** frozen water vapour deposited in clear still weather on vegetation etc. [OE *hār* f. Gmc]

hoard *n.* & *v.* —*n.* **1** a stock or store (esp. of money) laid by. **2** an amassed store of facts etc. **3** *Archaeol.* an ancient store of treasure etc. —*v.* **1** *tr.* (often *absol.*; often foll. by *up*) amass (money etc.) and put away; store. **2** *intr.* accumulate more than one's current requirements of food etc. in a time of scarcity. **3** *tr.* store in the mind. □ **hoarder** *n.* [OE *hord* f. Gmc]

hoarding /ˈhɔːdɪŋ/ *n.* **1** *Brit.* a large, usu. wooden, structure used to carry advertisements etc. **2** a board fence erected round a building site etc., often used for displaying posters etc. [obs. *hoard* f. AF *h(o)urdis* f. OF *hourd*, *hort*, rel. to HURDLE]

hoarhound var. of HOREHOUND.

hoarse *adj.* **1** (of the voice) rough and deep; husky; croaking. **2** having such a voice. □ **hoarsely** *adv.* **hoarsen** *v.tr.* & *intr.* **hoarseness** *n.* [ME f. ON *hārs* (unrecorded) f. Gmc]

hoary /ˈhɔːrɪ/ *adj.* (**hoarier**, **hoariest**) **1 a** (of hair) grey or white with age. **b** having such hair; aged. **2** old and trite (*a hoary joke*). □ **hoarily** *adv.* **hoariness** *n.*

hoax *n.* & *v.* —*n.* a humorous or malicious deception; a practical joke. —*v.tr.* deceive (a person) with a hoax. □ **hoaxer** *n.* [18th c.: prob. contr. f. HOCUS-POCUS]

hob *n.* **1 a** a flat heating surface for a pan on a cooker. **b** a flat metal shelf at the side of a fireplace, having its surface level with the top of the grate, used esp. for heating a pan etc. **2** = HOBNAIL. [perh. var. of HUB, orig. = lump]

hobbit /ˈhɒbɪt/ *n.* a member of an imaginary race of half-sized people in stories by Tolkien. □ **hobbitry** *n.* [invented by J. R. R. Tolkien, Engl. writer d. 1973, and said by him to mean 'hole-dweller']

hobble /ˈhɒb(ə)l/ *v.* & *n.* —*v.* **1** *intr.* **a** walk lamely; limp. **b** proceed haltingly in action or speech (*hobbled lamely to his conclusion*). **2** *tr.* **a** tie together the legs of (a horse etc.) to prevent it from straying. **b** tie (a horse's etc. legs). **3** *tr.* cause (a person etc.) to limp. —*n.* **1** an uneven or infirm gait. **2** a rope, clog, etc. used for hobbling a horse etc. □ **hobbler** *n.* [ME, prob. f. LG: cf. Du. *hobbelen* rock from side to side]

hobbledehoy /ˈhɒbəldɪhɔɪ/ *n. colloq.* **1** a clumsy or awkward youth. **2** a hooligan. [16th c.: orig. unkn.]

hobby[1] /ˈhɒbɪ/ n. (pl. -ies) a favourite leisure-time activity or occupation. □ **hobbyist** n. [ME *hobyn, hoby*, f. pet-forms of *Robin*]

hobby[2] /ˈhɒbɪ/ n. (pl. -ies) any of several small long-winged falcons, esp. *Falco subbuteo*, catching prey on the wing. [ME f. OF *hobé, hobet* dimin. of *hobe* small bird of prey]

hobby-horse /ˈhɒbɪˌhɔːs/ n. **1** a child's toy consisting of a stick with a horse's head. **2** a preoccupation; a favourite topic of conversation. **3** a model of a horse, esp. of wicker, used in morris dancing etc. **4** a rocking horse. **5** a horse on a merry-go-round.

hobgoblin /ˈhɒbˌgɒblɪn/ n. a mischievous imp; a bogy; a bugbear. [*hob*, short for *Robin* or *Robert* + GOBLIN]

hobnail /ˈhɒbneɪl/ n. a heavy-headed nail used for boot-soles. □ **hobnail** (or **hobnailed**) **liver** a liver having many small knobbly projections due to cirrhosis. □ **hobnailed** adj. [HOB + NAIL]

hobnob /ˈhɒbnɒb/ v.intr. (**hobnobbed, hobnobbing**) **1** (usu. foll. by *with*) mix socially or informally. **2** drink together. [*hob or nob* = give or take, of alternate drinking; earlier *hab nab*, = have or not have]

hobo /ˈhəʊbəʊ/ n. (pl. -**oes** or -**os**) US a wandering worker; a tramp. [19th c.: orig. unkn.]

Hobson's choice /ˈhɒbs(ə)nz/ n. a choice of taking the thing offered or nothing. [T. *Hobson*, Cambridge carrier d. 1631, who let out horses on the basis that customers must take the one nearest the door]

hock[1] n. **1** the joint of a quadruped's hind leg between the knee and the fetlock. **2** a knuckle of pork; the lower joint of a ham. [obs. *hockshin* f. OE *hōhsinu*: see HOUGH]

hock[2] n. Brit. a German white wine from the Rhineland. [abbr. of obs. *hockamore* f. G *Hochheimer*]

hock[3] v. & n. esp. US colloq. —v.tr. pawn; pledge. —n. a pawnbroker's pledge. □ **in hock 1** in pawn. **2** in debt. **3** in prison. [Du. *hok* hutch, prison, debt]

hockey[1] /ˈhɒkɪ/ n. **1** a game played between two teams on a field with curved sticks and a small hard ball. **2** US = ice hockey. □ **hockeyist** n. (in sense 2). [16th c.: orig. unkn.]

hockey[2] var. of OCHE.

hocus-pocus /ˌhəʊkəsˈpəʊkəs/ n. & v. —n. **1** deception; trickery. **2** a typical verbal formula used in conjuring. —v. (-**pocussed, -pocussing;** US -**pocused, -pocusing**) **1** intr. (often foll. by *with*) play tricks. **2** tr. play tricks on, deceive. [17th-c. sham L]

hod /hɒd/ n. **1** a V-shaped open trough on a pole used for carrying bricks, mortar, etc. **2** a portable receptacle for coal. [prob. = dial. *hot* f. OF *hotte* pannier, f. Gmc]

hodgepodge /ˈhɒdʒpɒdʒ/ n. = HOTCHPOTCH 1. [ME]

Hodgkin's disease /ˈhɒdʒkɪnz/ n. a malignant disease of lymphatic tissues usu. characterized by enlargement of the lymph nodes. [T. *Hodgkin*, Engl. physician d. 1866]

hodman /ˈhɒdmæn/ n. (pl. -**men**) a labourer who carries a hod.

hodometer /hɒˈdɒmɪtə(r)/ var. of ODOMETER.

hoe n. & v. —n. a long-handled tool with a thin metal blade, used for weeding etc. —v. (**hoes, hoed, hoeing**) **1** tr. weed (crops); loosen (earth);

dig up or cut down with a hoe. **2** intr. use a hoe. □ **hoe in** *Austral.* & *NZ sl.* eat eagerly. **hoe into** *Austral.* & *NZ sl.* attack (food, a person, a task). □ **hoer** n. [ME *howe* f. OF *houe* f. Gmc]

hoedown /ˈhəʊdaʊn/ n. US a lively dance or dance-party.

hog n. & v. —n. **1 a** a domesticated pig, esp. a castrated male reared for slaughter. **b** any of several other pigs of the family Suidae, e.g. a wart-hog. **2** colloq. a greedy person. —v. (**hogged, hogging**) tr. colloq. take greedily; hoard selfishly. □ **go the whole hog** colloq. do something completely or thoroughly. **hog-tie** US **1** secure by fastening the hands and feet or all four feet together. **2** restrain, impede. □ **hogger** n. **hoggery** n. **hoggish** adj. **hoggishly** adv. **hoggishness** n. **hoglike** adj. [OE *hogg, hocg*, perh. of Celt. orig.]

hogback /ˈhɒgbæk/ n. (also **hog's back**) a steep-sided ridge of a hill.

hogget /ˈhɒgɪt/ n. Brit. a yearling sheep. [HOG]

hoggin /ˈhɒgɪn/ n. **1** a mixture of sand and gravel. **2** sifted gravel. [19th c.: orig. unkn.]

hogmanay /ˈhɒgməˌneɪ, -ˈneɪ/ n. Sc. **1** New Year's Eve. **2** a celebration on this day. [17th c.: perh. f. Norman F *hoguinané* f. OF *aguillanneuf* (also = new year's gift)]

hog's back var. of HOGBACK.

hogshead /ˈhɒgzhed/ n. **1** a large cask. **2** a liquid or dry measure, usu. about 50 imperial gallons. [ME f. HOG, HEAD: reason for the name unkn.]

hogwash /ˈhɒgwɒʃ/ n. colloq. nonsense, rubbish.

hogweed /ˈhɒgwiːd/ n. any of various coarse weeds of the genus *Heracleum*, esp. *H. sphondylium*.

ho-ho /həʊˈhəʊ/ int. expressing surprise, triumph, or derision. [redupl. of HO]

ho-hum /ˈhəʊhʌm/ int. expressing boredom. [imit. of yawn]

hoick /hɔɪk/ v. & n. colloq. —v.tr. (often foll. by *out*) lift or pull, esp. with a jerk. —n. a jerky pull; a jerk. [perh. var. of HIKE]

hoi polloi /ˌhɔɪ pəˈlɔɪ/ n. (often prec. by *the*: see note below) (prec. by *the*) **1** the masses; the common people. **2** the majority. [Gk, = the many]

■ **Usage** This phrase is often preceded by *the*, which is strictly speaking unnecessary, since *hoi* means 'the'.

hoist /hɔɪst/ v. & n. —v.tr. **1** raise or haul up. **2** raise by means of ropes and pulleys etc. —n. **1** an act of hoisting, a lift. **2** an apparatus for hoisting. **3 a** the part of a flag nearest the staff. **b** a group of flags raised as a signal. □ **hoist the flag** stake one's claim to discovered territory by displaying a flag. □ **hoister** n. [16th c.: alt. of *hoise* f. (15th-c.) *hysse*, prob. of LG orig.: cf. LG *hissen*]

hoity-toity /ˌhɔɪtɪˈtɔɪtɪ/ adj. & int. —adj. haughty; petulant; snobbish. —int. expressing surprised at presumption etc. [obs. *hoit* indulge in riotous mirth, of unkn. orig.]

hokey /ˈhəʊkɪ/ adj. (also **hoky**) (**hokier, hokiest**) US sl. sentimental, melodramatic, artificial. □ **hokeyness** n. (also **hokiness**). **hokily** adv. [HOKUM + -Y²]

hokey-cokey /ˌhəʊkɪˈkəʊkɪ/ n. a communal dance performed in a circle with synchronized shaking of the limbs in turn. [perh. f. HOCUS-POCUS]

hokum /ˈhəʊkəm/ n. esp. US sl. **1** sentimental, popular, sensational, or unreal situations, dialogue, etc., in a film or play etc. **2** bunkum; rubbish. [20th c.: orig. unkn.]

Holarctic /hɒˈlɑːktɪk/ adj. of or relating to the geographical distribution of animals in the whole northern or arctic region. [HOLO- + ARCTIC]

hold[1] /həʊld/ v. & n. —v. (past and past part. **held** /held/) **1** tr. **a** keep fast; grasp (esp. in the hands or arms). **b** (also refl.) keep or sustain (a thing, oneself, one's head, etc.) in a particular position (hold it to the light; held himself erect). **c** grasp so as to control (hold the reins). **2** tr. (of a vessel etc.) contain or be capable of containing (the jug holds two pints; the hall holds 900). **3** tr. possess, gain, or have, esp.: **a** be the owner or tenant of (land, property, stocks, etc.) (holds the farm from the trust). **b** gain or have gained (a degree, record, etc.) (holds the long-jump record). **c** have the position of (a job or office). **d** have (a specified card) in one's hand. **e** keep possession of (a place, a person's thoughts, etc.) esp. against attack (held the fort against the enemy; held his place in her estimation). **4** intr. remain unbroken; not give way (the roof held under the storm). **5** tr. observe; celebrate; conduct (a meeting, festival, conversation, etc.). **6** tr. **a** keep (a person etc.) in a specified condition, place, etc. (held him prisoner; held him at arm's length). **b** detain, esp. in custody (hold him until I arrive). **7** tr. **a** engross (a person or a person's attention) (the book held him for hours). **b** dominate (held the stage). **8** tr. (foll. by to) make (a person etc.) adhere to (terms, a promise, etc.). **9** intr. (of weather) continue fine. **10** tr. (often foll. by to + infin., or that + clause) think; believe (held it to be self-evident). **11** tr. regard with a specified feeling (held him in contempt). **12** tr. **a** cease; restrain (hold your fire). **b** US colloq. withhold; not use (a burger please, and hold the onions!). **13** tr. keep or reserve (will you hold our seats please?). **14** tr. be able to drink (liquor) without effect (can't hold his drink). **15** tr. (usu. foll. by that + clause) (of a judge, a court, etc.) lay down; decide. **16** tr. Mus. sustain (a note). —n. **1** a grasp (catch hold of him; keep a hold on him). **2** (often in comb.) a thing to hold by (seized the handhold). **3** (foll. by on, over) influence over (has a strange hold over them). **4** a manner of holding in wrestling etc. □ **hold (a thing) against (a person)** resent or regard it as discreditable to (a person). **hold aloof** avoid communication with people etc. **hold back 1** impede the progress of; restrain. **2** keep (a thing) to or for oneself. **3** (often foll. by from) hesitate; refrain. **hold by** (or **to**) adhere to (a choice, purpose, etc.). **hold cheap** not value highly; despise. **hold the clock on** time (a sporting event etc.). **hold court** preside over one's admirers etc., like a sovereign. **hold dear** regard with affection. **hold down 1** repress. **2** colloq. be competent enough to keep (one's job etc.). **hold everything!** (or **it!**) cease action or movement. **hold the fort 1** act as a temporary substitute. **2** cope in an emergency. **hold forth 1** offer (an inducement etc.). **2** usu. derog. speak at length or tediously. **hold good** (or **true**) be valid; apply. **hold a person's hand** give a person guidance or moral support. **hold hands** grasp one another by the hand as a sign of affection or for support or guidance. **hold hard!**

stop!; wait! **hold one's head high** behave proudly and confidently. **hold one's horses** colloq. stop; slow down. **hold in** keep in check, confine. **hold the line 1** not yield. **2** maintain a telephone connection. **hold off 1** delay; not begin. **2** keep one's distance. **hold on 1** keep one's grasp on something. **2** wait a moment. **3** (when telephoning) not ring off. **hold out 1** stretch forth (a hand etc.). **2** offer (an inducement etc.). **3** maintain resistance. **4** persist or last. **hold out for** continue to demand. **hold out on** colloq. refuse something to (a person). **hold over** postpone. **hold something over** threaten (a person) constantly with something. **hold to a draw** manage to achieve a draw against (an opponent thought likely to win). **hold together 1** cohere. **2** cause to cohere. **hold one's tongue** colloq. be silent. **hold to ransom 1** keep (a person) prisoner until a ransom is paid. **2** demand concessions from by threats of damaging action. **hold up 1 a** support; sustain. **b** maintain (the head etc.) erect. **2** exhibit; display. **3** arrest the progress of; obstruct. **4** stop and rob by violence or threats. **hold-up 1** a stoppage or delay by traffic, fog, etc. **2** a robbery, esp. by the use of threats or violence. **hold water** (of reasoning) be sound; bear examination. **hold with** (usu. with neg.) colloq. approve of (don't hold with motor bikes). **take hold** (of a custom or habit) become established. **there is no holding him** (or **her** etc.) he (or she etc.) is restive, high-spirited, determined, etc. **with no holds barred** with no restrictions, all methods being permitted. □ **holdable** adj. [OE h(e)aldan, heald]

hold[2] /həʊld/ n. a cavity in the lower part of a ship or aircraft in which the cargo is stowed. [obs. holl f. OE hol (orig. adj. = hollow), rel. to HOLE, assim. to HOLD[1]]

holdall /ˈhəʊldɔːl/ n. a portable case for miscellaneous articles.

holder /ˈhəʊldə(r)/ n. **1** (often in comb.) a device or implement for holding something (cigarette-holder). **2 a** the possessor of a title etc. **b** the occupant of an office etc. **3** = SMALLHOLDER.

holdfast /ˈhəʊldfɑːst/ n. **1** a firm grasp. **2** a staple or clamp securing an object to a wall etc.

holding /ˈhəʊldɪŋ/ n. **1 a** land held by lease (cf. SMALLHOLDING). **b** the tenure of land. **2** stocks, property, etc. held. □ **holding company** a company created to hold the shares of other companies, which it then controls. **holding operation** a manoeuvre designed to maintain the status quo.

hole /həʊl/ n. & v. —n. **1 a** an empty space in a solid body. **b** an aperture in or through something. **2** an animal's burrow. **3** a cavity or receptacle for a ball in various sports or games. **4** colloq. a small, mean, or dingy abode. **5** colloq. an awkward situation. **6** Golf **a** a point scored by a player who gets the ball from tee to hole with the fewest strokes. **b** the terrain or distance from tee to hole. —v.tr. **1** make a hole or holes in. **2** pierce the side of (a ship). **3** put into a hole. **4** (also absol.; often foll. by out) send (a golf ball) into a hole. □ **hole-and-corner** secret; underhand. **hole in the heart** a congenital defect in the heart septum. **hole in one** Golf a shot that enters the hole from the tee. **hole in the wall** a small dingy place (esp. of business). **hole up** US colloq. hide oneself. **in holes** worn so much that holes have formed. **make a hole in** use a large amount of. □ **holey** adj. [OE *hol*, *holian* (as HOLD²)]

holibut var. of HALIBUT.

holiday /ˈhɒlɪˌdeɪ, -dɪ/ n. & v. —n. **1** esp. *Brit.* (often in *pl.*) an extended period of recreation, esp. away from home or in travelling; a break from work. **2** a day of festivity or recreation when no work is done, esp. a religious festival etc. —*v.intr.* esp. *Brit.* spend a holiday. □ **holiday camp** *Brit.* a camp for holiday-makers with accommodation, entertainment, and facilities on site. **holiday-maker** esp. *Brit.* a person on holiday. **on holiday** (or **one's holidays**) in the course of one's holiday. **take a** (or **make**) **holiday** have a break from work. [OE *hāligdæg* (HOLY, DAY)]

holily /ˈhəʊlɪlɪ/ adv. in a holy manner. [OE *hāliglīce* (as HOLY)]

holiness /ˈhəʊlɪnɪs/ n. **1** sanctity; the state of being holy. **2** (**Holiness**) a title used when referring to or addressing the Pope. [OE *hālignes* (as HOLY)]

holism /ˈhɒlɪz(ə)m, ˈhəʊ-/ n. (also **wholism**) **1** *Philos.* the theory that certain wholes are to be regarded as greater than the sum of their parts. **2** *Med.* the treating of the whole person including mental and social factors rather than just the symptoms of a disease. □ **holistic** /-ˈlɪstɪk/ adj. **holistically** /-ˈlɪstɪkəlɪ/ adv. [as HOLO- + -ISM]

holland /ˈhɒlənd/ n. a smooth, hard-wearing, linen fabric. □ **brown holland** unbleached holland. [*Holland* = Netherlands: Du., earlier *Holtlant* f. *holt* wood + *-lant* land, describing the Dordrecht district]

hollandaise sauce /ˌhɒlənˈdeɪz, ˈhɒl-/ n. a creamy sauce of melted butter, egg-yolks, vinegar, etc., served esp. with fish. [F, fem. of *hollandais* Dutch f. *Hollande* Holland]

holler /ˈhɒlə(r)/ v. & n. *US colloq.* —v. **1** intr. make a loud cry or noise. **2** tr. express with a loud cry or shout. —n. a loud cry, noise, or shout. [var. of HOLLO]

hollow /ˈhɒləʊ/ adj., n., v., & adv. —adj. **1 a** having a hole or cavity inside; not solid throughout. **b** having a depression; sunken (*hollow cheeks*). **2** (of a sound) echoing, as though made in or on a hollow container. **3** empty; hungry. **4** without significance; meaningless (*a hollow triumph*). **5** insincere; cynical; false (*a hollow laugh*; *hollow promises*). —n. **1** a hollow place; a hole. **2** a valley; a basin. —v.tr. (often foll. by *out*) make hollow; excavate. —adv. *colloq.* completely (*beaten hollow*). □ **hollow-eyed** with eyes deep sunk. **in the hollow of one's hand** entirely subservient to one. □ **hollowly** adv. **hollowness** n. [ME *holg, holu, hol(e)we* f. OE *holh* cave, rel. to HOLE]

hollowware /ˈhɒləʊˌweə(r)/ n. hollow articles of metal, china, etc., such as pots, kettles, jugs, etc.

holly /ˈhɒlɪ/ n. (pl. **-ies**) **1** an evergreen shrub, *Ilex aquifolium*, with prickly usu. dark-green leaves and red berries. **2** its branches and foliage used as decorations at Christmas. [OE *hole(g)n*]

hollyhock /ˈhɒlɪˌhɒk/ n. a tall plant, *Alcea rosea*, with large showy flowers of various colours. [ME (orig. = marsh mallow) f. HOLY + obs. *hock* mallow, OE *hoc*, of unkn. orig.]

Hollywood /ˈhɒlɪˌwʊd/ n. the American cinema industry or its products, with its principal centre at Hollywood in California.

holm /həʊm/ n. (in full **holm-oak**) an evergreen oak, *Quercus ilex*, with holly-like young leaves. [ME alt. of obs. *holin* (as HOLLY)]

holmium /ˈhəʊlmɪəm/ n. *Chem.* a soft silvery metallic element of the lanthanide series. [mod.L f. *Holmia* Stockholm]

holo- /ˈhɒləʊ/ comb. form whole (*Holocene*; *holocaust*). [Gk *holos* whole]

holocaust /ˈhɒləˌkɔːst/ n. **1** a case of large-scale destruction, esp. by fire or nuclear war. **2** (**the Holocaust**) the mass murder of the Jews by the Nazis 1939–45. [ME f. OF *holocauste* f. LL *holocaustum* f. Gk *holokauston* (as HOLO-, *kaustos* burnt f. *kaiō* burn)]

Holocene /ˈhɒləˌsiːn/ adj. & n. *Geol.* —adj. of or relating to the most recent epoch of the Quaternary period. —n. this period or system. [HOLO- + Gk *kainos* new]

hologram /ˈhɒləˌgræm/ n. *Physics* **1** a three-dimensional image formed by the interference of light beams from a coherent light source. **2** a photograph of the interference pattern, which when suitably illuminated produces a three-dimensional image.

holograph /ˈhɒləˌgrɑːf/ adj. & n. —adj. wholly written by hand by the person named as the author. —n. a holograph document. [F *holographe* or LL *holographus* f. Gk *holographos* (as HOLO-, -GRAPH)]

holography /həˈlɒgrəfɪ/ n. *Physics* the study or production of holograms. □ **holographic** /-ləˈgræfɪk/ adj. **holographically** /-ləˈgræfɪkəlɪ/ adv.

holothurian /ˌhɒləˈθjʊərɪən/ n. any echinoderm of the class Holothurioidea, with a wormlike body, e.g. a sea cucumber. [mod.L *Holothuria* (n.pl.) f. Gk *holothourion*, a zoophyte]

hols /hɒlz/ n.pl. *Brit. colloq.* holidays. [abbr.]

holster /ˈhəʊlstə(r)/ n. a leather case for a pistol or revolver, worn on a belt or under an arm or fixed to a saddle. [17th c., synonymous with Du. *holster*: orig. unkn.]

holt¹ /həʊlt/ n. an animal's (esp. an otter's) lair. [var. of HOLD¹]

holt² /həʊlt/ n. *archaic* or *dial.* **1** a wood or copse. **2** a wooded hill. [OE f. Gmc]

holy /ˈhəʊlɪ/ adj. (**holier, holiest**) **1** morally and spiritually excellent or perfect, and to be revered. **2** belonging to, devoted to, or empowered by, God. **3** consecrated; sacred. **4** used in trivial exclamations (*holy Moses!*; *holy smoke!*). □ **holier-than-thou** *colloq.* self-righteous. **Holy City 1** a city held sacred by the adherents of a religion, esp. Jerusalem. **2** Heaven. **holy day** a religious festival. **Holy Family** the young Jesus with his mother and St Joseph (often with St John the Baptist, St Anne, etc.) as grouped in pictures etc. **Holy Father** the Pope. **Holy Ghost** = Holy Spirit. **Holy Land 1** W. Palestine, esp. Judaea. **2** a region similarly revered in non-Christian religions. **holy of holies 1** the inner chamber of the sanctuary in the Jewish temple, separated by a veil from the outer chamber. **2** an innermost shrine. **3** a thing regarded as most sacred. **holy place 1** (in pl.) places to which religious pilgrimage is made. **2** the outer chamber of the sanctuary in the Jewish temple. **holy roller** sl.

a member of a religious group characterized by frenzied excitement or trances. **Holy Saturday** Saturday in Holy Week. **Holy Scripture** the Bible. **Holy See** the papacy or the papal court. **Holy Spirit** the Third Person of the Trinity, God as spiritually acting. **Holy Thursday 1** *Anglican Ch.* Ascension Day. **2** *RC Ch.* Maundy Thursday. **holy war** a war waged in support of a religious cause. **holy water** water dedicated to holy uses, or blessed by a priest. **Holy Week** the week before Easter. **Holy Writ** holy writings collectively, esp. the Bible. [OE *hālig* f. Gmc, rel. to WHOLE]

homage /ˈhɒmɪdʒ/ *n.* **1** acknowledgement of superiority, dutiful reverence (*pay homage to; do homage to*). **2** *hist.* formal public acknowledgement of feudal allegiance. [ME f. OF (*h*)*omage* f. med.L *hominaticum* f. L *homo -minis* man]

Homburg /ˈhɒmbɜːg/ *n.* a man's felt hat with a narrow curled brim and a lengthwise dent in the crown. [*Homburg* in Germany, where first worn]

home *n., adj., adv.,* & *v.* —*n.* **1 a** the place where one lives; the fixed residence of a family or household. **b** a dwelling-house. **2** the members of a family collectively; one's family background (*comes from a good home*). **3** the native land of a person or of a person's ancestors. **4** an institution for persons needing care, rest, or refuge (*nursing home*). **5** the place where a thing originates or is native or most common. **6** the finishing-point in a race. **7** *Sport* a home match or win. —*attrib.adj.* **1 a** of or connected with one's home. **b** carried on, done, or made, at home. **c** proceeding from home. **2 a** carried on or produced in one's own country (*home industries; the home market*). **b** dealing with the domestic affairs of a country. **3** *Sport* played on one's own ground etc. (*home match; home win*). **4** in the neighbourhood of home. —*adv.* **1 a** to one's home or country (*go home*). **b** arrived at home (*is he home yet?*). **c** *US* at home (*stay home*). **2 a** to the point aimed at (*the thrust went home*). **b** as far as possible (*drove the nail home; pressed his advantage home*). —*v.* **1** *intr.* (esp. of a trained pigeon) return home. **2** *intr.* (often foll. by *on, in on*) (of a vessel, missile, etc.) be guided towards a destination or target by a landmark, radio beam, etc. **3** *tr.* send or guide homewards. □ **at home 1** in one's own house or native land. **2** at ease as if in one's own home (*make yourself at home*). **3** (usu. foll. by *in, on, with*) familiar or well informed. **4** available to callers. **at-home** *n.* a social reception in a person's home. **come home to** become fully realized by. **home and dry** having achieved one's purpose. **home-bird** a person who likes to stay at home. **home-brew** beer or other alcoholic drink brewed at home. **home-coming** arrival at home. **Home Counties** the counties closest to London. **home economics** the study of household management. **home farm** *Brit.* a farm (one of several on an estate) set aside to provide produce for the owner. **home-felt** felt intimately. **home from home** a place other than one's home where one feels at home; a place providing homelike amenities. **home-grown** grown or produced at home. **Home Guard** *hist.* **1** the British citizen army organized in 1940 to defend the UK against invasion, and disbanded in 1957. **2** a member of this. **home help** *Brit.* a woman employed to help in a person's home, esp. one provided by a local authority. **home-made** made at home. **home-making** creation of a (pleasant) home. **home movie** a film made at home or of one's own activities. **Home Office 1** the British government department dealing with law and order, immigration, etc., in England and Wales. **2** the building used for this. **home-owner** a person who owns his or her own home. **home plate** *Baseball* a plate beside which the batter stands. **home port** the port from which a ship originates. **home rule** the government of a country or region by its own citizens. **home run** *Baseball* a hit that allows the batter to make a complete circuit of the bases. **Home Secretary** (in the UK) the Secretary of State in charge of the Home Office. **home signal** a signal indicating whether a train may proceed into a station or to the next section of the line. **home straight** (*US* **stretch**) the concluding stretch of a racecourse. **home town** the town of one's birth or early life or present fixed residence. **home trade** trade carried on within a country. **home truth** basic but unwelcome information concerning oneself. **home unit** *Austral.* a private residence, usu. occupied by the owner, as one of several in a building. **near home** affecting one closely. □ **homelike** *adj.* [OE *hām* f. Gmc]

homebody /ˈhəʊmˌbɒdɪ/ *n.* (*pl.* **-ies**) a person who likes to stay at home.

homeland /ˈhəʊmlænd/ *n.* **1** one's native land. **2** an area in S. Africa reserved for a particular African people (the official name for a Bantustan).

homeless /ˈhəʊmlɪs/ *adj.* lacking a home. □ **homelessness** *n.*

homely /ˈhəʊmlɪ/ *adj.* (**homelier, homeliest**) **1** a simple, plain. **b** unpretentious. **c** primitive. **2** *US* (of people or their features) not attractive in appearance, ugly. **3** comfortable in the manner of a home, cosy. **4** skilled at housekeeping. □ **homeliness** *n.*

homer /ˈhəʊmə(r)/ *n.* **1** a homing pigeon. **2** *Baseball* a home run.

Homeric /hɒˈmerɪk, həˈm-/ *adj.* **1** of, or in the style of, Homer or the epic poems ascribed to him. **2** of Bronze Age Greece as described in these poems. **3** epic, large-scale, titanic (*Homeric conflict*). [L *Homericus* f. Gk *Homērikos* f. *Homēros* Homer, traditional author of the *Iliad* and the *Odyssey*]

homesick /ˈhəʊmsɪk/ *adj.* depressed by longing for one's home during absence from it. □ **homesickness** *n.*

homespun /ˈhəʊmspʌn/ *adj.* & *n.* —*adj.* **1 a** (of cloth) made of yarn spun at home. **b** (of yarn) spun at home. **2** plain, simple, unsophisticated, homely. —*n.* **1** homespun cloth. **2** anything plain or homely.

homestead /ˈhəʊmsted, -stɪd/ *n.* **1** a house, esp. a farmhouse, and outbuildings. **2** *Austral.* & *NZ* the owner's residence on a sheep or cattle station. **3** *US* an area of land (usu. 160 acres) granted to a settler as a home. □ **homesteader** *n.* [OE *hāmstede* (as HOME, STEAD)]

homestyle /ˈhəʊmstaɪl/ *adj.* *US* (esp. of food) of a kind made or done at home, homely.

homeward /ˈhəʊmwəd/ *adv.* & *adj.* —*adv.* (also **homewards** /-wədz/) towards home. —*adj.*

going or leading towards home. □ **homeward-bound** (esp. of a ship) preparing to go, or on the way, home. [OE *hāmweard(es)* (as HOME, -WARD)]

homework /ˈhəʊmwɜːk/ n. **1** work to be done at home, esp. by a school pupil. **2** preparatory work or study.

homey /ˈhəʊmɪ/ adj. (also **homy**) (**homier**, **homiest**) suggesting home; cosy. □ **homeyness** n. (also **hominess**).

homicide /ˈhɒmɪˌsaɪd/ n. **1** the killing of a human being by another. **2** a person who kills a human being. □ **homicidal** /-ˈsaɪd(ə)l/ adj. [ME f. OF f. L *homicidium* (sense 1), *homicida* (sense 2) (HOMO man)]

homiletic /ˌhɒmɪˈletɪk/ adj. & n. —adj. of homilies. —n. (usu. in pl.) the art of preaching. [LL *homileticus* f. Gk *homilētikos* f. *homileō* hold converse, consort (as HOMILY)]

homily /ˈhɒmɪlɪ/ n. (pl. **-ies**) **1** a sermon. **2** a tedious moralizing discourse. □ **homilist** n. [ME f. OF *omelie* f. eccl.L *homilia* f. Gk *homilía* f. *homilos* crowd]

homing /ˈhəʊmɪŋ/ attrib.adj. **1** (of a pigeon) trained to fly home, bred for long-distance racing. **2** (of a device) for guiding to a target etc. **3** that goes home. □ **homing instinct** the instinct of certain animals to return to the territory from which they have been moved.

hominid /ˈhɒmɪnɪd/ n. & adj. —n. any member of the primate family Hominidae, including humans and their fossil ancestors. —adj. of or relating to this family. [mod.L *Hominidae* f. L *homo hominis* man]

hominoid /ˈhɒmɪˌnɔɪd/ adj. & n. —adj. like a human. —n. an animal resembling a human.

hominy /ˈhɒmɪnɪ/ n. esp. US coarsely ground maize kernels esp. boiled with water or milk. [Algonquian]

Homo /ˈhəʊməʊ, ˈhɒməʊ/ n. any primate of the genus *Homo*, including modern humans and various extinct species. [L, = man]

homo /ˈhəʊməʊ/ n. (pl. **-os**) colloq. a homosexual. [abbr.]

homo- /ˈhəʊməʊ, ˈhɒməʊ/ comb. form same (often opp. HETERO-). [Gk *homos* same]

homoeopath /ˈhəʊmɪəʊˌpæθ, ˈhɒmɪ-/ n. (US **homeopath**) a person who practises homoeopathy. [G *Homöopath* (as HOMOEOPATHY)]

homoeopathy /ˌhəʊmɪˈɒpəθɪ, ˌhɒmɪ-/ n. (US **homeopathy**) the treatment of disease by minute doses of drugs that in a healthy person would produce symptoms of the disease. □ **homoeopathic** /-ˈpæθɪk/ adj. **homoeopathist** n. [G *Homöopathie* f. Gk *homoios* like + *patheia* -PATHY]

homoeostasis /ˌhəʊmɪəʊˈsteɪsɪs, ˌhɒm-/ n. (US **homeostasis**) (pl. **-stases** /-siːz/) the tendency towards a relatively stable equilibrium between interdependent elements, esp. as maintained by physiological processes. □ **homoeostatic** adj. [mod.L f. Gk *homoios* like + *stasis* standing]

homoerotic /ˌhəʊməʊɪˈrɒtɪk, ˌhɒməʊ-/ adj. homosexual.

homogeneous /ˌhəʊməʊˈdʒiːnɪəs, ˌhɒməʊ-/ adj. **1** of the same kind. **2** consisting of parts all of the same kind; uniform. **3** Math. containing terms all of the same degree. □ **homogeneity** /-dʒɪˈniːɪtɪ/ n. **homogeneously** adv. **homogeneousness** n. [med.L f. Gk *homogenēs* (as HOMO-, *genēs* f. *genos* kind)]

■ **Usage** This word is often confused with *homogenous* which is a term in biology meaning 'similar owing to common descent'.

homogenize /həˈmɒdʒɪˌnaɪz/ v. (also **-ise**) **1** tr. & intr. make or become homogeneous. **2** tr. treat (milk) so that the fat droplets are emulsified and the cream does not separate. □ **homogenization** /-ˈzeɪʃ(ə)n/ n. **homogenizer** n.

homogeny /hɒˈmɒdʒɪnɪ/ n. Biol. similarity due to common descent. □ **homogenous** adj.

■ **Usage** See the note at *homogeneous*.

homograft /ˈhɒməˌɡrɑːft/ n. a graft of living tissue from one to another of the same species but different genotype.

homograph /ˈhɒməˌɡrɑːf/ n. a word spelt like another but of different meaning or origin (e.g. POLE[1], POLE[2]).

homologize /həˈmɒləˌdʒaɪz/ v. (also **-ise**) **1** intr. be homologous; correspond. **2** tr. make homologous.

homologous /həˈmɒləɡəs/ adj. **1 a** having the same relation, relative position, etc. **b** corresponding. **2** Biol. (of organs etc.) similar in position and structure but not necessarily in function. [med.L *homologus* f. Gk (as HOMO-, *logos* ratio, proportion)]

homologue /ˈhɒməˌlɒɡ/ n. (US **homolog**) a homologous thing. [F f. Gk *homologon* (neut. adj.) (as HOMOLOGOUS)]

homology /həˈmɒlədʒɪ/ n. a homologous state or relation; correspondence. □ **homological** /ˌhɒmə ˈlɒdʒɪk(ə)l/ adj.

homomorphic /ˌhəʊməʊˈmɔːfɪk, ˌhɒməʊ-/ adj. (also **homomorphous**) of the same or similar form. □ **homomorphically** adv. **homomorphism** n. **homomorphy** n.

homonym /ˈhɒmənɪm/ n. **1** a word of the same spelling or sound as another but of different meaning; a homograph or homophone. **2** a namesake. □ **homonymic** /-ˈnɪmɪk/ adj. **homonymous** /həˈmɒnɪməs/ adj. [L *homonymum* f. Gk *homōnumon* (neut. adj.) (as HOMO-, *onoma* name)]

homophobia /ˌhəʊməˈfəʊbɪə/ n. a hatred or fear of homosexuals. □ **homophobe** /ˈhəʊm-/ n. **homophobic** /-ˈfəʊbɪk/ adj.

homophone /ˈhɒməˌfəʊn/ n. **1** a word having the same sound as another but of different meaning or origin (e.g. *pair*, *pear*). **2** a symbol denoting the same sound as another.

homophonic /ˌhɒməʊˈfɒnɪk/ adj. Mus. in unison; characterized by movement of all parts to the same melody. □ **homophonically** adv.

homophonous /həˈmɒfənəs/ adj. **1** (of music) homophonic. **2** (of a word or symbol) that is a homophone. □ **homophony** n.

Homo sapiens /ˌhəʊməʊ ˈsæpɪenz/ n. modern humans regarded as a species. [L, = wise man]

homosexual /ˌhəʊməʊˈseksjʊəl, ˌhɒm-/ adj. & n. —adj. **1** feeling or involving sexual attraction only to persons of the same sex. **2** concerning homosexual relations or people. **3** relating to the same sex. —n. a homosexual person. □ **homosexuality** /-ˈælɪtɪ/ n. **homosexually** adv.

homunculus /həˈmʌŋkjʊləs/ n. (also **homuncule** /-kjuːl/) (pl. **homunculi** /-ˌlaɪ/ or **homuncules**) a little man, a manikin. [L *homunculus* f. *homo -minis* man]

homy var. of HOMEY.

Hon. *abbr.* **1** Honorary. **2** Honourable.

honcho /ˈhɒntʃəʊ/ *n.* (*pl.* **-os**) *US sl.* **1** a leader or manager, the person in charge. **2** an admirable man. [Jap. *han'chō* group leader]

hone *n. & v.* —*n.* **1** a whetstone, esp. for razors. **2** any of various stones used as material for this. —*v.tr.* sharpen on or as on a hone. [OE *hān* stone f. Gmc]

honest /ˈɒnɪst/ *adj. & adv.* —*adj.* **1** fair and just in character or behaviour, not cheating or stealing. **2** free of deceit and untruthfulness, sincere. **3** fairly earned (*an honest living*). **4** (of an act or feeling) showing fairness. **5** (of a thing) unadulterated, unsophisticated. —*adv. colloq.* genuinely, really. □ **honest broker** a mediator in international, industrial, etc. disputes (orig. of Bismarck). **honest-to-God** (or **-goodness**) *colloq. adj.* genuine, real. —*adv.* genuinely, really. **make an honest woman of** *colloq.* marry (esp. a pregnant woman). [ME f. OF (h)*oneste* f. L *honestus* f. *honos* HONOUR]

honestly /ˈɒnɪstlɪ/ *adv.* **1** in an honest way. **2** really (*honestly, the cheek of it!*).

honesty /ˈɒnɪstɪ/ *n.* **1** being honest. **2** truthfulness. **3** a plant of the genus *Lunaria* with purple or white flowers. [ME f. OF (h)*onesté* f. L *honestas -tatis* (as HONEST)]

honey /ˈhʌnɪ/ *n.* (*pl.* **-eys**) **1** a sweet sticky yellowish fluid made by bees and other insects from nectar collected from flowers. **2** the colour of this. **3 a** sweetness. **b** a sweet thing. **4** a person or thing excellent of its kind. **5** esp. *US* (usu. as a form of address) darling, sweetheart. □ **honey-bee** any of various bees of the genus *Apis*, esp. the common hive-bee (*A. mellifera*). **honey-fungus** a parasitic fungus, *Armillaria mellea*, with honey-coloured edible toadstools. **honey-pot 1** a pot for honey. **2** a posture with the hands clasped under the hams. **3** something very attractive or tempting. [OE *hunig* f. Gmc]

honeycomb /ˈhʌnɪkəʊm/ *n. & v.* —*n.* **1 a** structure of hexagonal cells of wax, made by bees to store honey and eggs. **2 a** a pattern arranged hexagonally. **b** fabric made with a pattern of raised hexagons etc. —*v.tr.* **1** fill with cavities or tunnels, undermine. **2** mark with a honeycomb pattern. [OE *hunigcamb* (as HONEY, COMB)]

honeydew /ˈhʌnɪdjuː/ *n.* **1** a sweet sticky substance found on leaves and stems, excreted by aphids. **2** a variety of melon with smooth pale skin and sweet green flesh. **3** an ideally sweet substance.

honeyed /ˈhʌnɪd/ *adj.* (also **honied**) **1** of or containing honey. **2** sweet.

honeymoon /ˈhʌnɪˌmuːn/ *n. & v.* —*n.* **1** a holiday spent together by a newly married couple. **2** an initial period of enthusiasm or goodwill. —*v.intr.* (usu. foll. by *in, at*) spend a honeymoon. □ **honeymooner** *n.* [HONEY + MOON, orig. with ref. to waning affection, not to a period of a month]

honeysuckle /ˈhʌnɪˌsʌk(ə)l/ *n.* any climbing shrub of the genus *Lonicera* with fragrant yellow and pink flowers. [ME *hunisuccle*, *-soukel*, extension of *hunisuce*, *-souke*, f. OE *hunigsūce*, *-sūge* (as HONEY, SUCK)]

honk *n. & v.* —*n.* **1** the cry of a wild goose. **2** the harsh sound of a car horn. —*v.* **1** *intr.* emit or give a honk. **2** *tr.* cause to do this. [imit.]

honky /ˈhɒŋkɪ/ *n.* (*pl.* **-ies**) *US Black sl. offens.* **1** a White person. **2** White people collectively. [20th c.: orig. unkn.]

honky-tonk /ˈhɒŋkɪˌtɒŋk/ *n. colloq.* **1** ragtime piano music. **2** a cheap or disreputable nightclub, dancehall, etc. [20th c.: orig. unkn.]

honorarium /ˌɒnəˈreərɪəm/ *n.* (*pl.* **honorariums** or **honoraria** /-rɪə/) a fee, esp. a voluntary payment for professional services rendered without the normal fee. [L, neut. of *honorarius*: see HONORARY]

honorary /ˈɒnərərɪ/ *adj.* **1 a** conferred as an honour, without the usual requirements, functions, etc. (*honorary degree*). **b** holding such a title or position (*honorary colonel*). **2** (of an office or its holder) unpaid (*honorary secretaryship*; *honorary treasurer*). **3** (of an obligation) depending on honour, not legally enforceable. [L *honorarius* (as HONOUR)]

honorific /ˌɒnəˈrɪfɪk/ *adj. & n.* —*adj.* **1** conferring honour. **2** (esp. of Oriental forms of speech) implying respect. —*n.* an honorific form of words. □ **honorifically** *adv.* [L *honorificus* (as HONOUR)]

honour /ˈɒnə(r)/ *n. & v.* (*US* **honor**) —*n.* **1** high respect; glory; credit, reputation, good name. **2** adherence to what is right or to a conventional standard of conduct. **3** nobleness of mind, magnanimity (*honour among thieves*). **4** a thing conferred as a distinction, esp. an official award for bravery or achievement. **5** (foll. by *of* + verbal noun, or *to* + infin.) privilege, special right (*had the honour of being invited*). **6 a** exalted position. **b** (**Honour**) (prec. by *your, his,* etc.) a title of a circuit judge, *US* a mayor, and *Ir.* or in rustic speech any person of rank. **7** (foll. by *to*) a person or thing that brings honour (*she is an honour to her profession*). **8 a** (of a woman) chastity. **b** the reputation for this. **9** (in *pl.*) a special distinction for proficiency in an examination. **b** a course of degree studies more specialized than for an ordinary pass. **10 a** *Bridge* the ace, king, queen, jack, and ten, esp. of trumps, or the four aces at no trumps. **b** *Whist* the ace, king, queen, and jack, esp. of trumps. **11** *Golf* the right of driving off first as having won the last hole (*it is my honour*). —*v.tr.* **1** respect highly. **2** confer honour on. **3** accept or pay (a bill or cheque) when due. **4** acknowledge. □ **do the honours** perform the duties of a host to guests etc. **honours are even** there is equality in the contest. **honours list** a list of persons awarded honours. **honours of war** privileges granted to a capitulating force, e.g. that of marching out with colours flying. **honour system** a system of examinations etc. without supervision, relying on the honour of those concerned. **in honour bound** = *on one's honour*. **in honour of** as a celebration of. **on one's honour** (usu. foll. by *to* + infin.) under a moral obligation. **on** (or **upon**) **my honour** an expression of sincerity. [ME f. OF (h)*onor* (n.), *onorer* (v.) f. L *honor, honorare*]

honourable /ˈɒnərəb(ə)l/ *adj.* (*US* **honorable**) **1 a** worthy of honour. **b** bringing honour to its possessor. **c** showing honour, not base. **d** consistent with honour. **e** *colloq.* (of the intentions of a man courting a woman) directed towards marriage. **2** (**Honourable**) a title indicating eminence or distinction, given to certain high officials, the children of certain ranks of the nobility, and MPs. □ **honourable mention** an award of merit to a candidate in an examination, a work of art, etc., not awarded a prize. □ **honourableness** n. **honourably** adv. [ME f. OF honorable f. L honorabilis (as HONOUR)]

hooch /huːtʃ/ n. (also **hootch**) US colloq. alcoholic liquor, esp. inferior or illicit whisky. [abbr. of Alaskan hoochinoo, name of a liquor-making tribe]

hood¹ /hʊd/ n. & v. —n. **1 a** a covering for the head and neck, whether part of a cloak etc. or separate. **b** a separate hoodlike garment worn over a university gown or a surplice to indicate the wearer's degree. **2** Brit. a folding waterproof top of a motor car, pram, etc. **3** US the bonnet of a motor vehicle. **4** a canopy to protect users of machinery or to remove fumes etc. **5** the hoodlike part of a cobra, seal, etc. **6** a leather covering for a hawk's head. —v.tr. cover with a hood. □ **hoodless** adj. **hoodlike** adj. [OE hōd f. WG, rel. to HAT]

hood² /hʊd, huːd/ n. US sl. a gangster or gunman. [abbr. of HOODLUM]

-hood /hʊd/ suffix forming nouns: **1** of condition or state (childhood; falsehood). **2** indicating a collection or group (sisterhood; neighbourhood). [OE -hād, orig. an independent noun, = person, condition, quality]

hooded /'hʊdɪd/ adj. having a hood; covered with a hood. □ **hooded crow** a piebald grey and black crow, Corvus cornix.

hoodlum /'huːdləm/ n. **1** a street hooligan, a young thug. **2** a gangster. [19th c.: orig. unkn.]

hoodoo /'huːduː/ n. & v. esp. US —n. **1 a** a bad luck. **b** a thing or person that brings or causes this. **2** voodoo. —v.tr. (**hoodoos, hoodooed**) **1** make unlucky. **2** bewitch. [alt. of VOODOO]

hoodwink /'hʊdwɪŋk/ v.tr. deceive, delude. [orig. 'blindfold', f. HOOD¹ n. + WINK]

hooey /'huːɪ/ n. & int. sl. nonsense, humbug. [20th c.: orig. unkn.]

hoof /huːf/ n. & v. —n. (pl. **hoofs** or **hooves** /-vz/) the horny part of the foot of a horse, antelope, and other ungulates. —v. **1** tr. strike with a hoof. **2** tr. sl. kick or shove. □ **hoof it** sl. **1** go on foot. **2** dance. **on the hoof** (of cattle) not yet slaughtered. □ **hoofed** adj. (also in comb.). [OE hōf f. Gmc]

hoofer /'huːfə(r)/ n. sl. a professional dancer.

hoo-ha /'huːhaː/ n. sl. a commotion, a row; uproar, trouble. [20th c.: orig. unkn.]

hook /hʊk/ n. & v. —n. **1 a** a piece of metal or other material bent back at an angle or with a round bend, for catching hold or for hanging things on. **b** (in full **fish-hook**) a bent piece of wire, usu. barbed and baited, for catching fish. **2** a curved cutting instrument (reaping-hook). **3 a** a sharp bend, e.g. in a river. **b** a projecting point of land (Hook of Holland). **4 a** Cricket & Golf a hooking stroke (see sense 5 of v.). **b** Boxing a short swinging blow with the elbow bent and rigid. **5** a trap, a snare. —v. **1** tr. **a** grasp with a hook. **b** secure with a hook or hooks. **2** (often foll. by on, up) **a** tr. attach with or as with a hook. **b** intr. be or become attached with a hook. **3** tr. catch with or as with a hook (he hooked a fish; she hooked a husband). **4** tr. sl. steal. **5** tr. **a** Cricket play (the ball) round from the off to the on side with an upward stroke. **b** (also absol.) Golf strike (the ball) so that it deviates towards the striker. **6** tr. Rugby Football secure (the ball)

and pass it backward with the foot in the scrum. **7** tr. Boxing strike (one's opponent) with the elbow bent and rigid. □ **be hooked on** sl. be addicted to or captivated by. **by hook or by crook** by one means or another, by fair means or foul. **hook and eye** a small metal hook and loop as a fastener on a garment. **hook it** sl. make off, run away. **hook, line, and sinker** entirely. **hook-nose** an aquiline nose. **hooknosed** having an aquiline nose. **hook-up** a connection, esp. an interconnection of broadcasting equipment for special transmissions. **off the hook 1** colloq. no longer in difficulty or trouble. **2** (of a telephone receiver) not on its rest, and so preventing incoming calls. **sling** (or **take**) **one's hook** sl. = hook it. □ **hookless** adj. **hooklet** n. **hooklike** adj. [OE hōc: sense 3 of n. prob. influenced by Du. hoek corner]

hookah /'hʊkə/ n. an oriental tobacco-pipe with a long tube passing through water for cooling the smoke as it is drawn through. [Urdu f. Arab. ḥuḳḳah casket]

hooked /hʊkt/ adj. **1** hook-shaped (hooked nose). **2** furnished with a hook or hooks. **3** in senses of HOOK v. **4** (of a rug or mat) made by pulling woollen yarn through canvas with a hook.

hooker /'hʊkə(r)/ n. **1** Rugby Football the player in the middle of the front row of the scrum who tries to hook the ball. **2** sl. a prostitute. **3** a person or thing that hooks.

hookey /'hʊkɪ/ n. (also **hooky**) US □ **play hookey** sl. play truant. [19th c.: orig. unkn.]

hookworm /'hʊkwɜːm/ n. **1** any of various nematode worms, with hooklike mouthparts for attachment and feeding, infesting humans and animals. **2** a disease caused by one of these, often resulting in severe anaemia.

hooligan /'huːlɪgən/ n. a young ruffian, esp. a member of a gang. □ **hooliganism** n. [19th c.: orig. unkn.]

hoop¹ /huːp/ n. & v. —n. **1** a circular band of metal, wood, etc., esp. for binding the staves of casks etc. or for forming part of a framework. **2 a** a ring bowled along by a child. **b** a large ring for circus performers to jump through. **3** an arch of iron etc. through which the balls are hit in croquet. **4 a** a band in contrasting colour on a jockey's blouse, sleeves, or cap. **b** Austral. colloq. a jockey. —v.tr. **1** bind with a hoop or hoops. **2** encircle with or as with a hoop. □ **be put** (or **go**) **through the hoop** (or **hoops**) undergo an ordeal. **hoop-la 1** Brit. a game in which rings are thrown in an attempt to encircle one of various prizes. **2** sl. commotion. **3** sl. pretentious nonsense. [OE hōp f. WG]

hoop² var. of WHOOP.

hoopoe /'huːpuː/ n. a salmon-pink bird, Upupa epops, with a large erectile crest, and a long bill. [alt. of ME hoop f. OF huppe f. L upupa, imit. of its cry]

hooray /hʊ'reɪ/ int. **1** = HURRAH. **2** Austral. & NZ goodbye. □ **Hooray Henry** /'hʊreɪ/ Brit. sl. a rich ineffectual young man. [var. of HURRAH]

hoot /huːt/ n. & v. —n. **1** an owl's cry. **2** the sound made by a motor horn or a steam whistle. **3** a shout expressing scorn or disapproval; an inarticulate shout. **4** colloq. **a** laughter. **b** a cause of this. **5** (also **two hoots**) sl. anything at all (don't care a hoot; don't give a hoot; doesn't matter two hoots). —v. **1** intr. **a** (of an owl) utter its cry. **b** (of a motor horn or steam whistle) make a

hoot. c (often foll. by *at*) make loud sounds, esp. of scorn or disapproval or *colloq.* merriment (*hooted with laughter*). **2** *tr.* **a** assail with scornful shouts. **b** (often foll. by *out, away*) drive away by hooting. **3** *tr.* sound (a motor horn or steam whistle). [ME *hūten* (v.), perh. imit.]

hootch var. of HOOCH.

hooter /ˈhuːtə(r)/ *n.* **1** *Brit.* a siren or steam whistle, esp. as a signal for work to begin or cease. **2** *Brit.* the horn of a motor vehicle. **3** *sl.* a nose. **4** a person or animal that hoots.

hoots /huːts/ *int. Sc.* & *N.Engl.* expressing dissatisfaction or impatience. [natural exclam.: cf. Sw. *hut* begone, Welsh *hwt* away, Ir. *ut* out, all in similar sense]

Hoover /ˈhuːvə(r)/ *n.* & *v.* —*n. propr.* a vacuum cleaner (properly that one made by the Hoover company). —*v.* (**hoover**) **1** *tr.* (also *absol.*) clean (a carpet etc.) with a vacuum cleaner. **2** (foll. by *up*) **a** suck up with or as with a vacuum cleaner (*hoovered up the crumbs*). **b** *absol.* clean a room etc. with a vacuum cleaner (*decided to hoover up before they arrived*). [W. H. *Hoover*, Amer. manufacturer d. 1932]

hooves pl. of HOOF.

hop[1] *v.* & *n.* —*v.* (**hopped, hopping**) **1** *intr.* (of a bird, frog, etc.) spring with two or all feet at once. **2** *intr.* (of a person) jump on one foot. **3** *tr.* cross (a ditch etc.) by hopping. **4** *intr. colloq.* **a** make a quick trip. **b** make a quick change of position or location. **5** *tr. colloq.* **a** jump into (a vehicle). **b** obtain (a ride) in this way. **6** *tr.* (usu. as **hopping** *n.*) (esp. of aircraft) pass quickly from one (place of a specified type) to another (*hedge-hopping*). —*n.* **1** a hopping movement. **2** *colloq.* an informal dance. **3** a short flight in an aircraft; the distance travelled by air without landing; a stage of a flight or journey. □ **hop in** (or **out**) *colloq.* get into (or out of) a car etc. **hop it** *Brit. sl.* go away. **hopping mad** *colloq.* very angry. **hop, skip** (or **step**)**, and jump** = *triple jump.* **on the hop** *colloq.* **1** unprepared (*caught on the hop*). **2** bustling about. [OE *hoppian*]

hop[2] *n.* & *v.* —*n.* **1** a climbing plant, *Humulus lupulus*, cultivated for the cones borne by the female. **2** (in *pl.*) **a** the ripe cones of this, used to give a bitter flavour to beer. **b** *Austral.* & *NZ colloq.* beer. —*v.* (**hopped, hopping**) **1** *tr.* flavour with hops. **2** *intr.* produce or pick hops. □ **hop-bind** (or **-bine**) the climbing stem of the hop. **hop-sack** (or **-sacking**) **1 a** a coarse material made from hemp etc. **b** sacking for hops made from this. **2** a coarse clothing fabric of a loose plain weave. [ME *hoppe* f. MLG, MDu. *hoppe*]

hope *n.* & *v.* —*n.* **1** (in *sing.* or *pl.*; often foll. by *of, that*) expectation and desire combined, e.g. for a certain thing to occur (*hope of getting the job*). **2 a** a person, thing, or circumstance that gives cause for hope. **b** ground of hope, promise. **3** what is hoped for. **4** *archaic* a feeling of trust. —*v.* **1** *intr.* (often foll. by *for*) feel hope. **2** *tr.* expect and desire. **3** *tr.* feel fairly confident. □ **hope against hope** cling to a mere possibility. **hope chest** *US* = *bottom drawer.* **not a** (or **some**) **hope!** *colloq.* no chance at all. □ **hoper** *n.* [OE *hopa*]

hopeful /ˈhəʊpfʊl/ *adj.* & *n.* —*adj.* **1** feeling hope. **2** causing or inspiring hope. **3** likely to succeed, promising. —*n.* (in full **young hopeful**) a person likely to succeed. □ **hopefulness** *n.*

hopefully /ˈhəʊpfʊlɪ/ *adv.* **1** in a hopeful manner. **2** *disp.* (qualifying a whole sentence) it is to be hoped (*hopefully, the car will be ready by then*).

■ **Usage** Sense 2 is common, but is considered incorrect by some people.

hopeless /ˈhəʊplɪs/ *adj.* **1** feeling no hope. **2** admitting no hope (*a hopeless case*). **3** inadequate, incompetent (*am hopeless at tennis*). □ **hopelessly** *adv.* **hopelessness** *n.*

hopper[1] /ˈhɒpə(r)/ *n.* **1** a person who hops. **2** a hopping arthropod, esp. a flea or cheese-maggot, or young locust. **3 a** a container tapering downward (orig. having a hopping motion) through which grain passes into a mill. **b** a similar contrivance in various machines.

hopper[2] /ˈhɒpə(r)/ *n.* a hop-picker.

hopscotch /ˈhɒpskɒtʃ/ *n.* a children's game of hopping over squares or oblongs marked on the ground to retrieve a flat stone etc. [HOP[1] + SCOTCH]

horde /hɔːd/ *n.* **1 a** usu. *derog.* a large group, a gang. **b** a moving swarm or pack (of insects, wolves, etc.). **2** a troop of Tartar or other nomads. [Pol. *horda* f. Turki *ordī, ordū* camp: cf. URDU]

horehound /ˈhɔːhaʊnd/ *n.* (also **hoarhound**) **1** a herbaceous plant, *Marrubium vulgare*, with a white cottony covering on its stem and leaves. **2** its bitter aromatic juice used against coughs etc. [OE *hāre hūne* f. *hār* HOAR + *hūne* a plant]

horizon /həˈraɪz(ə)n/ *n.* **1** the line at which the earth and sky appear to meet. **2** limit of mental perception, experience, interest, etc. **3** a geological stratum or set of strata, or layer of soil, with particular characteristics. □ **on the horizon** (of an event) just imminent or becoming apparent. [ME f. OF *orizon(te)* f. LL *horizon -ontis* f. Gk *horizōn (kuklos)* limiting (circle)]

horizontal /ˌhɒrɪˈzɒnt(ə)l/ *adj.* & *n.* —*adj.* **1 a** parallel to the plane of the horizon, at right angles to the vertical (*horizontal plane*). **b** (of machinery etc.) having its parts working in a horizontal direction. **2 a** combining firms engaged in the same stage of production (*horizontal integration*). **b** involving social groups of equal status etc. **3** of or at the horizon. —*n.* a horizontal line, plane, etc. □ **horizontality** /-ˈtælɪtɪ/ *n.* **horizontally** *adv.* **horizontalness** *n.* [F *horizontal* or mod.L *horizontalis* (as HORIZON)]

hormone /ˈhɔːməʊn/ *n.* **1** *Biochem.* a regulatory substance produced in an organism and transported in tissue fluids such as blood or sap to stimulate cells or tissues into action. **2** a synthetic substance with a similar effect. □ **hormonal** /-ˈməʊn(ə)l/ *adj.* [Gk *hormōn* part. of *hormaō* impel]

horn *n.* & *v.* —*n.* **1** a hard permanent outgrowth, often curved and pointed, on the head of cattle, rhinoceroses, giraffes, and other esp. hoofed mammals. **2** each of two deciduous branched appendages on the head of (esp. male) deer. **3** a hornlike projection on the head of other animals, e.g. a snail's tentacle. **4** the substance of which horns are composed. **5** anything resembling or compared to a horn in shape. **6** *Mus.* **a** = *French horn.* **b** a wind instrument played by lip vibration, orig. made of horn, now usu. of brass. **c** a horn player. **7** an instrument sounding a warning or other signal (*car horn; foghorn*). **8** a receptacle or instrument made of horn, e.g. a drinking-vessel or powder-flask etc. **9** a horn-shaped projection. **10** the extremity of the moon or other crescent. **11** an arm or branch of a river, bay, etc. —*v.tr.* **1** (esp. as **horned** *adj.*) provide with horns. **2** gore with the horns. □ **horn in** *sl.* **1** (usu. foll. by *on*) intrude. **2** interfere. **horn of plenty** a cornucopia. **horn-rimmed** (esp. of spectacles) having rims made of horn or a substance resembling it. **on the horns of a dilemma** faced with a decision involving equally unfavourable alternatives. □ **hornist** *n.* (in sense 6 of *n.*). **hornless** *adj.* **hornlike** *adj.* [OE f. Gmc, rel. to L *cornu*]

hornbeam /ˈhɔːnbiːm/ *n.* any tree of the genus *Carpinus*, with a smooth bark and a hard tough wood.

hornbill /ˈhɔːnbɪl/ *n.* any bird of the family Bucerotidae, with a hornlike excrescence on its bill.

hornblende /ˈhɔːnblend/ *n.* a dark-brown, black, or green mineral occurring in many igneous and metamorphic rocks. [G (as HORN, BLENDE)]

horned /hɔːnd/ *adj.* having a horn.

hornet /ˈhɔːnɪt/ *n.* a large wasp, *Vespa crabro*. □ **stir up a hornets' nest** provoke or cause trouble or opposition. [prob. f. MLG, MDu. *horn(e)te*, corresp. to OE *hyrnet*, perh. rel. to HORN]

hornpipe /ˈhɔːnpaɪp/ *n.* **1** a lively dance, usu. by one person (esp. associated with sailors). **2** the music for this. [name of an obs. wind instrument partly of horn: ME, f. HORN + PIPE]

horny /ˈhɔːnɪ/ *adj.* (**hornier, horniest**) **1** of or like horn. **2** hard like horn, callous (*horny-handed*). **3** *sl.* sexually excited. □ **horniness** *n.*

horology /həˈrɒlədʒɪ/ *n.* the art of measuring time or making clocks, watches, etc.; the study of this. □ **horologer** *n.* **horologic** /ˌhɒrəˈlɒdʒɪk/ *adj.* **horological** /ˌhɒrəˈlɒdʒɪk(ə)l/ *adj.* **horologist** *n.* [Gk *hōra* time + -LOGY]

horoscope /ˈhɒrəˌskəʊp/ *n.* Astrol. **1** a forecast of a person's future based on a diagram showing the relative positions of the stars and planets at that person's birth. **2** such a diagram (*cast a horoscope*). **3** observation of the sky and planets at a particular moment, esp. at a person's birth. □ **horoscopic** /-ˈskɒpɪk/ *adj.* **horoscopical** /-ˈskɒpɪk(ə)l/ *adj.* **horoscopy** /həˈrɒskəpɪ/ *n.* [F f. L *horoscopus* f. Gk *hōroskopos* f. *hōra* time + *skopos* observer]

horrendous /həˈrendəs/ *adj.* horrifying. □ **horrendously** *adv.* **horrendousness** *n.* [L *horrendus* gerundive of *horrēre*: see HORRID]

horrible /ˈhɒrɪb(ə)l/ *adj.* **1** causing or likely to cause horror; hideous, shocking. **2** *colloq.* unpleasant, excessive (*horrible weather; horrible noise*). □ **horribleness** *n.* **horribly** *adv.* [ME f. OF (h)orrible f. L horribilis f. horrēre: see HORRID]

horrid /ˈhɒrɪd/ *adj.* **1** horrible, revolting. **2** *colloq.* unpleasant, disagreeable (*horrid weather; horrid children*). □ **horridly** *adv.* **horridness** *n.* [L *horridus* f. *horrēre* bristle, shudder]

horrific /həˈrɪfɪk/ *adj.* horrifying. □ **horrifically** *adv.* [F *horrifique* or L *horrificus* f. *horrēre*: see HORRID]

horrify /ˈhɒrɪˌfaɪ/ *v.tr.* (**-ies, -ied**) arouse horror in; shock, scandalize. □ **horrification**

/-fɪˈkeɪʃ(ə)n/ *n.* **horrifiedly** /-ˌfaɪdlɪ/ *adv.* **horrifying** *adj.* **horrifyingly** *adv.* [L *horrificare* (as HORRIFIC)]

horror /ˈhɒrə(r)/ *n. & adj.* —*n.* **1** a painful feeling of loathing and fear. **2 a** (often foll. by *of*) intense dislike. **b** (often foll. by *at*) *colloq.* intense dismay. **3 a** a person or thing causing horror. **b** *colloq.* a bad or mischievous person etc. **4** (in *pl.*; prec. by *the*) **a** fit of horror, depression, or nervousness, esp. as in delirium tremens. **5** a terrified and revolted shuddering. **6** (in *pl.*) an exclamation of dismay. —*attrib. adj.* (of literature, films, etc.) designed to attract by arousing pleasurable feelings of horror. □ **Chamber of Horrors** a place full of horrors (orig. a room of criminals etc. in Madame Tussaud's waxworks). **horror-struck** (or **-stricken**) horrified, shocked. [ME f. OF (h)orrour f. L *horror -oris* (as HORRID)]

hors-d'œuvre /ɔːˈdɜːvr, -ˈdɜːv/ *n.* an appetizer served at the beginning of a meal or (occasionally) during a meal. [F, lit. 'outside the work']

horse /hɔːs/ *n. & v.* —*n.* **1 a** a solid-hoofed plant-eating quadruped, *Equus caballus*, with flowing mane and tail, used for riding and to carry and pull loads. **b** an adult male horse; a stallion or gelding. **c** any other four-legged mammal of the genus *Equus*, including asses and zebras. **d** (*collect.*; as *sing.*) cavalry. **e** a representation of a horse. **2** a vaulting-block. **3** a supporting frame esp. with legs (*clothes-horse*). **4** *sl.* heroin. **5** *colloq.* a unit of horsepower. —*v.* **1** *intr.* (foll. by *around*) fool about. **2** *tr.* provide (a person or vehicle) with a horse or horses. **3** *intr.* mount or go on horseback. □ **from the horse's mouth** (of information etc.) from the person directly concerned or another authoritative source. **horse chestnut** any large ornamental tree of the genus *Aesculus*, with upright conical clusters of white or pink or red flowers. **2** the dark brown fruit of this (like an edible chestnut, but with a coarse bitter taste). **Horse Guards 1** (in the UK) the cavalry brigade of the household troops. **2** the headquarters of such cavalry, esp. a building in Whitehall. **horse latitudes** a belt of calms in each hemisphere between the trade winds and the westerlies. **horse opera** *US sl.* a western film. **horse-race** a race between horses with riders. **horse-racing** the sport of conducting horse-races. **horse sense** *colloq.* plain common sense. **horses for courses** the matching of tasks and talents. **horse-trading 1** *US* dealing in horses. **2** shrewd bargaining. □ **horseless** *adj.* **horselike** *adj.* [OE *hors* f. Gmc]

horseback /ˈhɔːsbæk/ *n.* the back of a horse, esp. as sat on in riding. □ **on horseback** mounted on a horse.

horsebox /ˈhɔːsbɒks/ *n.* Brit. a closed vehicle for transporting a horse or horses.

horseflesh /ˈhɔːsfleʃ/ *n.* **1** the flesh of a horse, esp. as food. **2** horses collectively.

horsefly /ˈhɔːsflaɪ/ *n.* (*pl.* **-flies**) any of various biting dipterous insects of the family Tabanidae troublesome esp. to horses.

horsehair /ˈhɔːsheə(r)/ *n.* hair from the mane or tail of a horse, used for padding etc.

horseless /ˈhɔːslɪs/ *adj.* without a horse. □ **horseless carriage** *archaic* a motor car.

horseman /ˈhɔːsmən/ *n.* (*pl.* **-men**) **1** a rider on horseback. **2** a skilled rider.

horsemanship /ˈhɔːsmənʃɪp/ n. the art of riding on horseback; skill in doing this.

horseplay /ˈhɔːspleɪ/ n. boisterous play.

horsepower /ˈhɔːsˌpaʊə(r)/ n. (pl. same) 1 an imperial unit of power equal to 550 foot-pounds per second (about 750 watts). 2 the power of an engine etc. measured in terms of this.

horseradish /ˈhɔːsˌrædɪʃ/ n. 1 a cruciferous plant, Armoracia rusticana, with long lobed leaves. 2 the pungent root of this scraped or grated as a condiment, often made into a sauce.

horseshoe /ˈhɔːʃʃuː, ˈhɔːsʃuː/ n. 1 an iron shoe for a horse shaped like the outline of the hard part of the hoof. 2 a thing of this shape; an object shaped like C or U.

horsetail /ˈhɔːsteɪl/ n. 1 the tail of a horse. 2 any cryptogamous plant of the genus Equisetum, like a horse's tail, with a hollow jointed stem and scale-like leaves.

horsewhip /ˈhɔːswɪp/ n. & v. —n. a whip for driving horses. —v.tr. (-whipped, -whipping) beat with a horsewhip.

horsewoman /ˈhɔːsˌwʊmən/ n. (pl. -women) 1 a woman who rides on horseback. 2 a skilled woman rider.

horsy /ˈhɔːsɪ/ adj. (also **horsey**) (**horsier, horsiest**) 1 of or like a horse. 2 concerned with or devoted to horses or horse-racing. □ **horsily** adv. **horsiness** n.

hortative /ˈhɔːtətɪv/ adj. (also **hortatory** /ˈhɔːtətərɪ/) tending or serving to exhort. □ **hortation** /hɔːˈteɪʃ(ə)n/ n. [L hortativus f. hortari exhort]

horticulture /ˈhɔːtɪˌkʌltʃə(r)/ n. the art of garden cultivation. □ **horticultural** /-ˈkʌltʃər(ə)l/ adj. **horticulturist** /-ˈkʌltʃərɪst/ n. [L hortus garden, after AGRICULTURE]

hosanna /həʊˈzænə/ n. & int. a shout of adoration (Matt. 21:9, 15, etc.). [ME f. LL f. Gk hōsanna f. Heb. hôšaʿnâ for hôšîʿa-nnâ save now!]

hose /həʊz/ n. & v. —n. 1 (also **hose-pipe**) a flexible tube conveying water for watering plants etc., putting out fires, etc. 2 a (collect.; as pl.) stockings and socks (esp. in trade use). b hist. breeches (doublet and hose). —v.tr. 1 (often foll. by down) water or spray or drench with a hose. 2 provide with hose. □ **half-hose** socks. [OE f. Gmc]

hosier /ˈhəʊzɪə(r), ˈhəʊʒə(r)/ n. a dealer in hosiery.

hosiery /ˈhəʊzɪərɪ, ˈhəʊʒərɪ/ n. 1 stockings and socks. 2 Brit. knitted or woven underwear.

hospice /ˈhɒspɪs/ n. 1 Brit. a home for people who are ill (esp. terminally) or destitute. 2 a lodging for travellers, esp. one kept by a religious order. [F f. L hospitium (as HOST²)]

hospitable /ˈhɒspɪtəb(ə)l, hɒˈspɪt-/ adj. giving or disposed to give welcome and entertainment to strangers or guests. □ **hospitably** adv. [F f. hospiter f. med.L hospitare entertain (as HOST²)]

hospital /ˈhɒspɪt(ə)l/ n. 1 an institution providing medical and surgical treatment and nursing care for ill or injured people. 2 hist. a a hospice. b an establishment of the Knights Hospitallers. 3 Law a charitable institution (also in proper names, e.g. Christ's Hospital). [ME f. OF f. med.L hospitale neut. of L hospitalis (adj.) (as HOST²)]

hospitalism /ˈhɒspɪtəˌlɪz(ə)m/ n. the adverse effects of a prolonged stay in hospital.

hospitality /ˌhɒspɪˈtælɪtɪ/ n. the friendly and generous reception and entertainment of guests or strangers. [ME f. OF hospitalité f. L hospitalitas -tatis (as HOSPITAL)]

hospitalize /ˈhɒspɪtəˌlaɪz/ v.tr. (also **-ise**) send or admit (a patient) to hospital. □ **hospitalization** /-ˈzeɪʃ(ə)n/ n.

hospitaller /ˈhɒspɪtələ(r)/ n. (US **hospitaler**) 1 a member of a charitable religious order. 2 a chaplain (in some London hospitals). [ME f. OF hospitalier f. med.L hospitalarius (as HOSPITAL)]

host¹ /həʊst/ n. 1 (usu. foll. by of) a large number of people or things. 2 archaic an army. [ME f. OF f. L hostis stranger, enemy, in med.L 'army']

host² /həʊst/ n. & v. —n. 1 a person who receives or entertains another as a guest. 2 the landlord of an inn (mine host). 3 Biol. an animal or plant having a parasite or commensal. 4 an animal or person that has received a transplanted organ etc. 5 the compère of a show, esp. of a television or radio programme. —v.tr. act as host to (a person) or at (an event). [ME f. OF oste f. L hospes -pitis host, guest]

host³ /həʊst/ n. the bread consecrated in the Eucharist. [ME f. OF (h)oiste f. L hostia victim]

hosta /ˈhɒstə/ n. any perennial garden plant of the genus Hosta (formerly Funkia) with green or variegated ornamental leaves. [mod.L, f. N. T. Host, Austrian physician d. 1834]

hostage /ˈhɒstɪdʒ/ n. 1 a person seized or held as security for the fulfilment of a condition. 2 a pledge or security. □ **a hostage to fortune** an acquisition, commitment, etc., regarded as endangered by unforeseen circumstances. □ **hostageship** n. [ME f. OF (h)ostage ult. f. LL obsidatus hostageship f. L obses obsidis hostage]

hostel /ˈhɒst(ə)l/ n. 1 Brit. a house of residence or lodging for students, nurses, etc. 2 = youth hostel. 3 archaic an inn. [ME f. OF (h)ostel f. med.L (as HOSPITAL)]

hostelling /ˈhɒstəlɪŋ/ n. (US **hosteling**) the practice of staying in youth hostels, esp. while travelling. □ **hosteller** n.

hostelry /ˈhɒstəlrɪ/ n. (pl. -ies) archaic or literary an inn. [ME f. OF (h)ostelerie f. (h)ostelier innkeeper (as HOSTEL)]

hostess /ˈhəʊstɪs/ n. 1 a woman who receives or entertains a guest. 2 a woman employed to welcome and entertain customers at a nightclub etc. 3 a stewardess on an aircraft, train, etc. (air hostess). [ME f. OF (h)ostesse (as HOST²)]

hostile /ˈhɒstaɪl/ adj. 1 of an enemy. 2 (often foll. by to) unfriendly, opposed. □ **hostile witness** Law a witness who appears hostile to the party calling him or her and therefore untrustworthy. □ **hostilely** adv. [F hostile or L hostilis (as HOST¹)]

hostility /hɒˈstɪlɪtɪ/ n. (pl. -ies) 1 being hostile, enmity. 2 a state of warfare. 3 (in pl.) acts of warfare. 4 opposition (in thought etc.). [F hostilité or LL hostilitas (as HOSTILE)]

hot adj., v., & adv. —adj. (**hotter, hottest**) 1 a having a relatively or noticeably high temperature. b (of food or drink) prepared by heating and served without cooling. 2 producing the sensation of heat (hot fever; hot flush). 3 (of pepper, spices, etc.) pungent. 4 (of a person) feeling heat. 5 a ardent, passionate, excited. b (often foll. by for, on) eager, keen (in hot pursuit). c angry or upset. d lustful. e exciting. 6 (of news etc.) fresh, recent. 7 Hunting (of the scent) fresh and strong, indicating that the quarry has passed recently. **8 a** (of a player) very skilful. **b** (of a competitor in a race or other sporting event) strongly fancied to win (*a hot favourite*). **9** (of music, esp. jazz) strongly rhythmical and emotional. **10** *sl.* **a** (of goods) stolen, esp. easily identifiable and hence difficult to dispose of. **b** (of a person) wanted by the police. **11** *sl.* radioactive. **12** *colloq.* (of information) unusually reliable (*hot tip*). —*v.* (**hotted, hotting**) (usu. foll. by *up*) *Brit. colloq.* **1** *tr.* & *intr.* make or become hot. **2** *tr.* & *intr.* make or become active, lively, exciting, or dangerous. —*adv.* **1** angrily, severely (*give it him hot*). **2** eagerly. □ **have the hots for** *sl.* be sexually attracted to. **hot air** *sl.* empty, boastful, or excited talk. **hot-air balloon** a balloon (see BALLOON *n.* 2) consisting of a bag in which air is heated by burners located below it, causing it to rise. **hot dog** *n. colloq.* a hot sausage sandwiched in a soft roll. —*int. US sl.* expressing approval. **hot line** a direct exclusive line of communication, esp. for emergencies. **hot metal** *Printing* using type made from molten metal. **hot money** capital transferred at frequent intervals. **hot potato** *colloq.* a controversial or awkward matter or situation. **hot rod** a motor vehicle modified to have extra power and speed. **hot seat** *sl.* **1** a position of difficult responsibility. **2** the electric chair. **hot spot 1** a small region that is relatively hot. **2** a lively or dangerous place. **hot spring** a spring of naturally hot water. **hot stuff** *colloq.* **1** a formidably capable person. **2** an important person or thing. **3** a sexually attractive person. **4** a spirited, strong-willed, or passionate person. **5** a book, film, etc. with a strongly erotic content. **hot-tempered** impulsively angry. **hot under the collar** angry, resentful, or embarrassed. **hot war** an open war, with active hostilities. **hot water** *colloq.* difficulty, trouble, or disgrace (*be in hot water; get into hot water*). **hot-water bottle** (*US* **bag**) a container, usu. made of rubber, filled with hot water, esp. to warm a bed. **make it** (or **things**) **hot for a person** persecute a person. **not so hot** *colloq.* only mediocre. □ **hotly** *adv.* **hotness** *n.* **hottish** *adj.* [OE *hāt* f. Gmc: cf. HEAT]

hotbed /ˈhɒtbed/ *n.* **1** a bed of earth heated by fermenting manure. **2** (foll. by *of*) an environment promoting the growth of something, esp. something unwelcome (*hotbed of vice*).

hotchpotch /ˈhɒtʃpɒtʃ/ *n.* (also **hotchpot** /-pɒt/) **1** a confused mixture, a jumble. **2** a dish of many mixed ingredients, esp. a mutton broth or stew with vegetables. [ME f. AF & OF *hochepot* f. OF *hocher* shake + POT¹: -*potch* by assim.]

hotel /həʊˈtel/ *n.* **1** an establishment providing accommodation and meals for payment. **2** *Austral.* & *NZ* a public house. [F *hôtel*, later form of HOSTEL]

hotelier /həʊˈteliə(r)/ *n.* a hotel-keeper. [F *hôtelier* f. OF *hostelier*: see HOSTELRY]

hotfoot /ˈhɒtfʊt/ *adv., v.,* & *adj.* —*adv.* in eager haste. —*v.tr.* hurry eagerly (esp. *hotfoot it*). —*adj.* acting quickly.

hothead /ˈhɒthed/ *n.* an impetuous person.

hotheaded /hɒtˈhedɪd/ *adj.* impetuous, excitable. □ **hotheadedly** *adv.* **hotheadedness** *n.*

hothouse /ˈhɒthaʊs/ *n.* **1** a heated building, usu. largely of glass, for rearing plants out of season or in a climate colder than is natural for them.

2 an environment that encourages the rapid growth or development of something.

hotplate /ˈhɒtpleɪt/ *n.* a heated metal plate etc. (or a set of these) for cooking food or keeping it hot.

hotpot /ˈhɒtpɒt/ *n.* a casserole of meat and vegetables, usu. with a layer of potato on top.

hotshot /ˈhɒtʃɒt/ *n.* & *adj.* esp. *US colloq.* —*n.* an important or exceptionally able person. —*adj.* (*attrib.*) important, able, expert, suddenly prominent.

Hottentot /ˈhɒtən‚tɒt/ *n.* & *adj.* —*n.* **1** a member of a stocky Negroid people of SW Africa. **2** their language. —*adj.* of this people. [Afrik., perh. = stammerer, with ref. to their mode of pronunc.]

hough /hɒk/ *n.* & *v. Brit.* —*n.* **1** = HOCK¹. **2** a cut of beef etc. from this and the leg above it. —*v.tr.* hamstring. □ **hougher** *n.* [ME *ho(u)gh* = OE *hōh* (heel) in *hōhsinu* hamstring]

hoummos var. of HUMMUS.

hound /haʊnd/ *n.* & *v.* —*n.* **1 a** a dog used for hunting, esp. one able to track by scent. **b** (**the hounds**) *Brit.* a pack of foxhounds. **2** *colloq.* a despicable man. **3** a person keen in pursuit of something (usu. in *comb.*: *news-hound*). —*v.tr.* **1** harass or pursue relentlessly. **2** chase or pursue with a hound. **3** (foll. by *at*) set (a dog or person) on (a quarry). **4** urge on or nag (a person). □ **hound's-tooth** a check pattern with notched corners suggestive of a canine tooth. **ride to hounds** go fox-hunting on horseback. □ **hounder** *n.* **houndish** *adj.* [OE *hund* f. Gmc]

hour /aʊə(r)/ *n.* **1** a twenty-fourth part of a day and night, 60 minutes. **2** a time of day, a point in time (*a late hour; what is the hour?*). **3** (in *pl.* with preceding numerals in form 18.00, 20.30, etc.) this number of hours and minutes past midnight on the 24-hour clock (*will assemble at 20.00 hours*). **4 a** a period set aside for some purpose (*lunch hour; keep regular hours*). **b** (in *pl.*) a fixed period of time for work, use of a building, etc. (*office hours; opening hours*). **5** a short indefinite period of time (*an idle hour*). **6** the present time (*question of the hour*). **7** a time for action etc. (*the hour has come*). **8** the distance traversed in one hour by a means of transport stated or implied (*we are an hour from London*). **9** *RC Ch.* **a** prayers to be said at one of seven fixed times of the day (*book of hours*). **b** any of these times. **10** (*prec.* by *the*) each time o'clock of a whole number of hours (*buses leave on the hour; on the half hour; at quarter past the hour*). □ **after hours** after closing-time. **hour-hand** the hand on a clock or watch which shows the hour. [ME *ure* etc. f. AF *ure,* OF *ore, eure* f. L *hora* f. Gk *hōra* season, hour]

hourglass /ˈaʊəglɑːs/ *n.* a reversible device with two connected glass bulbs containing sand that takes an hour to pass from the upper to the lower bulb.

houri /ˈhʊərɪ/ *n.* a beautiful young woman, esp. in the Muslim Paradise. [F f. Pers. *ḥūrī* f. Arab. *ḥūr* pl. of *ḥawrā'* gazelle-like (in the eyes)]

hourly /ˈaʊəlɪ/ *adj.* & *adv.* —*adj.* **1** done or occurring every hour. **2** frequent, continual. **3** reckoned hour by hour (*hourly wage*). —*adv.* **1** every hour. **2** frequently, continually.

house *n.* & *v.* —*n.* /haʊs/ (*pl.* /ˈhaʊzɪz/) **1 a** a building for human habitation. **b** (*attrib.*) (of an animal) kept in, frequenting, or infesting houses (*house-cat; housefly*). **2** a building for a special purpose (*opera-house; summer-house*). **3** a building for keeping animals or goods (*hen-house*). **4 a** a religious community. **b** the buildings occupied by it. **5 a** a body of pupils living in the same building at a boarding-school. **b** such a building. **c** a division of a day-school for games, competitions, etc. **6** a family, esp. a royal family; a dynasty (*House of York*). **7 a** a firm or institution. **b** its place of business. **c** (**the House**) *Brit. colloq.* the Stock Exchange. **8 a** a legislative or deliberative assembly. **b** the building where it meets. **c** (**the House**) (in the UK) the House of Commons or Lords; (in the US) the House of Representatives. **9 a** an audience in a theatre, cinema, etc. **b** a performance in a theatre or cinema (*second house starts at 9 o'clock*). **c** a theatre. **10** *Astrol.* a twelfth part of the heavens. **11** (*attrib.*) living in a hospital as a member of staff (*house officer; house physician; house surgeon*). **12 a** a place of public refreshment, a restaurant or inn (*coffee-house; public house*). **b** (*attrib.*) (of wine) selected by the management of a restaurant, hotel, etc. to be offered at a special price. **13** *Sc.* a dwelling that is one of several in a building. —*v.tr.* /haʊz/ **1** provide (a person, a population, etc.) with a house or houses or other accommodation. **2** store (goods etc.). **3** enclose or encase (a part or fitting). **4** fix in a socket, mortise, etc. □ **house-agent** *Brit.* an agent for the sale and letting of houses. **house arrest** detention in one's own house etc., not in prison. **house-broken** = *house-trained*. **house-dog** a dog kept to guard a house. **house-father** a man in charge of a house, esp. of a home for children. **house guest** a guest staying for some days in a private house. **house-hunting** seeking a house to live in. **house-husband** a husband who carries out the household duties traditionally carried out by a housewife. **house lights** the lights in the auditorium of a theatre. **house magazine** a magazine published by a firm and dealing mainly with its own activities. **house-martin** a black and white swallow-like bird, *Delichon urbica*, which builds a mud nest on house walls etc. **house-mother** a woman in charge of a house, esp. of a home for children. **house music** a style of pop music typically using drum machines and synthesized bass lines with sparse repetitive vocals and a fast beat. **house of cards 1** an insecure scheme etc. **2** a structure built (usu. by a child) out of playing cards. **House of Commons** (in the UK) the elected chamber of Parliament. **house of God** a church, a place of worship. **house of ill fame** *archaic* a brothel. **House of Keys** (in the Isle of Man) the elected chamber of Tynwald. **House of Lords 1** (in the UK) the chamber of Parliament composed of peers and bishops. **2** a committee of specially qualified members of this appointed as the ultimate judicial appeal court. **House of Representatives** the lower house of the US Congress and other legislatures. **house-parent** a house-mother or house-father. **house party** a group of guests staying at a country house etc. **house-plant** a plant grown indoors. **house-proud** attentive to, or unduly preoccupied with, the care and appearance of the home. **Houses of Parliament 1** the Houses of Lords and Commons regarded together. **2** the buildings where they meet. **house sparrow** a common brown and grey sparrow, *Passer domesticus*, which nests in the eaves and roofs of houses. **house style** a particular printer's or publisher's etc. preferred way of presentation. **house-trained** *Brit.* **1** (of animals) trained to be clean in the house. **2** *colloq.* well-mannered. **house-warming** a party celebrating a move to a new home. **keep house** provide for or manage a household. **like a house on fire 1** vigorously, fast. **2** successfully, excellently. **on the house** at the management's expense, free. **play house** play at being a family in its home. **put** (or **set**) **one's house in order** make necessary reforms. **set up house** begin to live in a separate dwelling. □ **houseful** *n.* (*pl.* **-fuls**). **houseless** *adj.* [OE *hūs, hūsian*, f. Gmc]

houseboat /ˈhaʊsbəʊt/ *n.* a boat fitted up for living in.

housebound /ˈhaʊsbaʊnd/ *adj.* unable to leave one's house through illness etc.

houseboy /ˈhaʊsbɔɪ/ *n.* a boy or man as a servant in a house.

housebreaker /ˈhaʊsˌbreɪkə(r)/ *n.* **1** a person guilty of housebreaking. **2** *Brit.* a person who is employed to demolish houses.

housebreaking /ˈhaʊsˌbreɪkɪŋ/ *n.* the act of breaking into a building, esp. in daytime, to commit a crime.

■ **Usage** In 1968 housebreaking was replaced as a statutory crime in English law by *burglary*.

housecoat /ˈhaʊskəʊt/ *n.* a woman's garment for informal wear in the house.

housecraft /ˈhaʊskrɑːft/ *n. Brit.* skill in household management.

housefly /ˈhaʊsflaɪ/ *n.* any fly of the family Muscidae, esp. *Musca domestica*, breeding in decaying organic matter and often entering houses.

household /ˈhaʊshəʊld/ *n.* **1** the occupants of a house regarded as a unit. **2** a house and its affairs. **3** (prec. by *the*) (in the UK) the royal household. □ **household troops** (in the UK) troops nominally employed to guard the sovereign. **household word** (or **name**) **1** a familiar name or saying. **2** a familiar person or thing.

householder /ˈhaʊsˌhəʊldə(r)/ *n.* **1** a person who owns or rents a house. **2** the head of a household.

housekeep /ˈhaʊskiːp/ *v.intr.* (*past* and *past part.* **-kept**) *colloq.* keep house.

housekeeper /ˈhaʊsˌkiːpə(r)/ *n.* **1** a person, esp. a woman, employed to manage a household. **2** a person in charge of a house, office, etc.

housekeeping /ˈhaʊsˌkiːpɪŋ/ *n.* **1** the management of household affairs. **2** money allowed for this. **3** operations of maintenance, record-keeping, etc., in an organization.

houseleek /ˈhaʊsliːk/ *n.* a plant, *Sempervivum tectorum*, with pink flowers, growing on walls and roofs.

housemaid /ˈhaʊsmeɪd/ *n.* a female servant in a house, esp. in charge of reception rooms and bedrooms. □ **housemaid's knee** inflammation of the kneecap, often due to excessive kneeling.

houseman /ˈhaʊsmən/ *n.* (*pl.* **-men**) **1** *Brit.* a resident doctor at a hospital etc. **2** = HOUSEBOY.

housemaster /ˈhaʊsˌmɑːstə(r)/ *n.* (*fem.* **housemistress** /ˈhaʊsˌmɪstrɪs/) the teacher in charge of a house at a boarding-school.

houseroom /ˈhaʊsruːm, -rʊm/ *n.* space or accommodation in one's house. □ **not give houseroom to** not have in any circumstances.

housetop /ˈhaʊstɒp/ *n.* the roof of a house. □ **proclaim** (or **shout** etc.) **from the housetops** announce publicly.

housewife /ˈhaʊswaɪf/ *n.* (*pl.* **-wives**) **1** a woman (usu. married) managing a household. **2** /ˈhʌzɪf/ a case for needles, thread, etc. □ **housewifely** *adj.* **housewifeliness** *n.* [ME *hus(e)wif* f. HOUSE + WIFE]

housewifery /ˈhaʊsˌwɪfrɪ/ *n.* **1** housekeeping. **2** skill in this, housecraft.

housework /ˈhaʊswɜːk/ *n.* regular work done in housekeeping, e.g. cleaning and cooking.

housing /ˈhaʊzɪŋ/ *n.* **1 a** dwelling-houses collectively. **b** the provision of these. **2** shelter, lodging. **3** a rigid casing, esp. for moving or sensitive parts of a machine. **4** the hole or niche cut in one piece of wood to receive some part of another in order to join them. □ **housing estate** a residential area planned as a unit.

hove *past* of HEAVE.

hovel /ˈhɒv(ə)l/ *n.* a small miserable dwelling. [ME: orig. unkn.]

hover /ˈhɒvə(r)/ *v.* & *n.* —*v.intr.* **1** (of a bird, helicopter, etc.) remain in one place in the air. **2** (often foll. by *about, round*) wait close at hand, linger. **3** remain undecided. —*n.* **1** hovering. **2** a state of suspense. □ **hover-fly** (*pl.* **-flies**) any fly of the family Syrphidae which hovers with rapidly beating wings. □ **hoverer** *n.* [ME f. obs. *hove* hover, linger]

hovercraft /ˈhɒvəˌkrɑːft/ *n.* (*pl.* same) a vehicle or craft that travels over land or water on a cushion of air provided by a downward blast.

hoverport /ˈhɒvəˌpɔːt/ *n.* a terminal for hovercraft.

hovertrain /ˈhɒvəˌtreɪn/ *n.* a train that travels on a cushion of air like a hovercraft.

how /haʊ/ *adv.* & *n.* —*interrog. adv.* **1** by what means, in what way (*how do you do it?*; *tell me how you do it*; *but how to bridge the gap?*). **2** in what condition, esp. of health (*how is the patient?*; *how do things stand?*). **3 a** to what extent (*how far is it?*) **b** to what extent good or well, what . . . like (*how was the film?*; *how did they play?*). —*rel. adv.* in whatever way, as (*do it how you can*). —*n.* the way a thing is done (*the how and why of it*). □ **how about 1** would you like (*how about a game of chess?*). **2** what is to be done about. **3** what is the news about. **how are you? 1** what is your state of health? **2** = *how do you do?* **how do you do?** a formal greeting. **how-do-you-do** (or **how-d'ye-do**) *n.* (*pl.* **-dos**) an awkward situation. **how many** what number. **how much 1** what amount (*how much do I owe you?*; *did not know how much to take*). **2** what price (*how much is it?*). **how's that? 1** what is your opinion or explanation of that? **2** *Cricket* (said to an umpire) is the batsman out or not? [OE *hū* f. WG]

howbeit /haʊˈbiːɪt/ *adv. archaic* nevertheless.

howdah /ˈhaʊdə/ *n.* a seat for two or more, usu. with a canopy, for riding on the back of an elephant or camel. [Urdu *hawda* f. Arab. *hawdaj* litter]

howdy /ˈhaʊdɪ/ *int. US* = *how do you do?* [corrupt.]

however /haʊˈevə(r)/ *adv.* **1 a** in whatever way (*do it however you want*). **b** to whatever extent, no matter how (*must go however inconvenient*). **2** nevertheless. **3** *colloq.* (as an emphatic) in what way, by what means (*however did that happen?*).

howitzer /ˈhaʊɪtsə(r)/ *n.* a short gun for high-angle firing of shells at low velocities. [Du.

houwitser f. G Haubitze f. Czech houfnice catapult]

howl /haʊl/ *n.* & *v.* —*n.* **1** a long loud doleful cry uttered by a dog, wolf, etc. **2** a prolonged wailing noise, e.g. as made by a strong wind. **3** a loud cry of pain or rage. **4** a yell of derision or merriment. **5** *Electronics* a howling noise in a loudspeaker due to electrical or acoustic feedback. —*v.* **1** *intr.* make a howl. **2** *intr.* weep loudly. **3** *tr.* utter (words) with a howl. □ **howl down** prevent (a speaker) from being heard by howls of derision. [ME *houle* (v.), prob. imit.: cf. OWL]

howler /ˈhaʊlə(r)/ *n.* **1** *colloq.* a glaring mistake. **2** a person or animal that howls.

howling /ˈhaʊlɪŋ/ *adj.* **1** that howls. **2** *sl.* extreme (*a howling shame*). □ **howling dervish** see DERVISH.

howsoever /ˌhaʊsəʊˈevə(r)/ *adv.* (also *poet.* **howsoe'er** /-ˈeə(r)/) **1** in whatsoever way. **2** to whatsoever extent.

hoy *int.* used to call attention, drive animals, or *Naut.* hail or call aloft. [ME: natural cry]

hoyden /ˈhɔɪd(ə)n/ *n.* a boisterous girl. □ **hoydenish** *adj.* [orig. = rude fellow, prob. f. MDu. *heiden* (= HEATHEN)]

h.p. *abbr.* **1** horsepower. **2** hire purchase. **3** high pressure.

HQ *abbr.* headquarters.

hr. *abbr.* hour.

HRH *abbr.* Her or His Royal Highness.

hrs. *abbr.* hours.

HT *abbr.* high tension.

hub *n.* **1** the central part of a wheel, rotating on or with the axle, and from which the spokes radiate. **2** a central point of interest, activity, etc. □ **hub-cap** a cover for the hub of a vehicle's wheel. [16th c.: perh. = HOB]

hubble-bubble /ˈhʌb(ə)lˌbʌb(ə)l/ *n.* **1** a rudimentary form of hookah. **2** a bubbling sound. **3** confused talk. [redupl. of BUBBLE]

hubbub /ˈhʌbʌb/ *n.* **1** a confused din, esp. from a crowd of people. **2** a disturbance or riot. [perh. of Ir. orig.: cf. Gael. *ubub* int. of contempt, Ir. *abú*, used in battle-cries]

hubby /ˈhʌbɪ/ *n.* (*pl.* **-ies**) *colloq.* a husband. [abbr.]

hubris /ˈhjuːbrɪs/ *n.* arrogant pride or presumption. □ **hubristic** /-ˈbrɪstɪk/ *adj.* [Gk]

huckaback /ˈhʌkəˌbæk/ *n.* a stout linen or cotton fabric with a rough surface, used for towelling. [17th c.: orig. unkn.]

huckleberry /ˈhʌk(ə)lˌbərɪ/ *n.* (*pl.* **-ies**) **1** any low-growing N. American shrub of the genus *Gaylussacia*. **2** the blue or black soft fruit of this plant. [prob. alt. of *hurtleberry*, WHORTLEBERRY]

huckster /ˈhʌkstə(r)/ *n.* & *v.* —*n.* **1** a mercenary person. **2** *US* a publicity agent, esp. for broadcast material. **3** a pedlar or hawker. —*v.* **1** *intr.* bargain, haggle. **2** *tr.* carry on a petty traffic in. **3** *tr.* adulterate. [ME prob. f. LG: cf. dial. *huck* to bargain, HAWKER]

huddle /ˈhʌd(ə)l/ *v.* & *n.* —*v.* **1** *tr.* & *intr.* (often foll. by *up*) crowd together; nestle closely. **2** *intr.* & *refl.* (often foll. by *up*) coil one's body into a small space. —*n.* **1** a confused or crowded mass of people or things. **2** *colloq.* a close or secret conference (esp. in **go into a huddle**). [16th c.: perh. f. LG and ult. rel. to OE *hȳ(gi)d* f. *hīw-*, *hīg-* household]

hue n. **1** a colour or tint. **2** a variety or shade of colour caused by the admixture of another. □ **-hued** adj. **hueless** adj. [OE *hīew*, *hēw* form, beauty f. Gmc: cf. ON *hȳ* down on plants]

hue and cry n. **1** a loud clamour or outcry. **2** hist. a loud cry raised for the pursuit of a wrongdoer. [AF *hu e cri* f. OF *hu* outcry (f. *huer* shout) + *e* and + *cri* cry]

huff v. & n. —v. **1** intr. give out loud puffs of air, steam, etc. **2** intr. bluster loudly or threateningly (*huffing and puffing*). **3** intr. & tr. take or cause to take offence. **4** tr. Draughts remove (an opponent's man that could have made a capture) from the board as a forfeit. —n. a fit of petty annoyance. □ **in a huff** annoyed and offended. □ **huffish** adj. [imit. of the sound of blowing]

huffy /ˈhʌfɪ/ adj. (**huffier**, **huffiest**) **1** apt to take offence. **2** offended. □ **huffily** adv. **huffiness** n.

hug v. & n. —v.tr. (**hugged**, **hugging**) **1** squeeze tightly in one's arms, esp. with affection. **2** (of a bear) squeeze (a person) between its forelegs. **3** keep close to (the shore, kerb, etc.). **4** cherish or cling to (prejudices etc.). **5** refl. congratulate or be pleased with (oneself). —n. **1** a strong clasp with the arms. **2** a squeezing grip in wrestling. □ **huggable** adj. [16th c.: prob. f. Scand.: cf. ON *hugga* console]

huge /hjuːdʒ/ adj. **1** extremely large; enormous. **2** (of immaterial things) very great (*a huge success*). □ **hugeness** n. [ME *huge* f. OF *ahuge*, *ahoge*, of unkn. orig.]

hugely /ˈhjuːdʒlɪ/ adv. **1** enormously (*hugely successful*). **2** very much (*enjoyed it hugely*).

hugger-mugger /ˈhʌɡəˌmʌɡə(r)/ adj., adv., n., & v. —adj. & adv. **1** in secret. **2** confused; in confusion. —n. **1** secrecy. **2** confusion. —v.intr. proceed in a secret or muddled fashion. [prob. rel. to ME *hoder* huddle, *mokere* conceal: cf. 15th-c. *hoder moder*, 16th-c. *hucker mucker* in the same sense]

Huguenot /ˈhjuːɡəˌnəʊ, -ˌnɒt/ n. hist. a French Protestant. [F, assim. of *eiguenot* (f. Du. *eedgenot* f. Swiss G *Eidgenoss* confederate) to the name of a Geneva burgomaster *Hugues*]

huh /hə/ int. expressing disgust, surprise, etc. [imit.]

hula /ˈhuːlə/ n. (also **hula-hula**) a Polynesian dance performed by women, with flowing movements of the arms. □ **hula hoop** a large hoop for spinning round the body with hula-like movements. **hula skirt** a long grass skirt. [Hawaiian]

hulk n. **1 a** the body of a dismantled ship, used as a store vessel etc. **b** (in pl.) hist. this used as a prison. **2** an unwieldy vessel. **3** colloq. a large clumsy-looking person or thing. [OE *hulc* & MLG, MDu. *hulk*: cf. Gk *holkas* cargo ship]

hulking /ˈhʌlkɪŋ/ adj. colloq. bulky; large and clumsy.

hull[1] n. & v. —n. the body or frame of a ship, airship, flying boat, etc. —v.tr. pierce the hull of (a ship) with gunshot etc. [ME, perh. rel. to HOLD[2]]

hull[2] n. & v. —n. **1** the outer covering of a fruit, esp. the pod of peas and beans, the husk of grain, or the green calyx of a strawberry. **2** a covering. —v.tr. remove the hulls from (fruit etc.). [OE *hulu* ult. f. *helan* cover: cf. HELE]

hullabaloo /ˌhʌləbəˈluː/ n. (pl. **hullabaloos**) an uproar or clamour. [18th c.: redupl. of *hallo*, *hullo*, etc.]

hullo var. of HELLO.

hum[1] v. & n. —v. (**hummed**, **humming**) **1** intr. make a low steady continuous sound like that of a bee. **2** tr. (also absol.) sing (a wordless tune) with closed lips. **3** intr. utter a slight inarticulate sound. **4** intr. colloq. be in an active state (*really made things hum*). **5** intr. Brit. colloq. smell unpleasantly. —n. **1** a humming sound. **2** an unwanted low-frequency noise caused by variation of electric current. **3** Brit. colloq. a bad smell. □ **hum and haw** (or **ha**) hesitate, esp. in speaking. □ **hummable** adj. **hummer** n. [ME, imit.]

hum[2] /həm/ int. expressing hesitation or dissent. [imit.]

human /ˈhjuːmən/ adj. & n. —adj. **1** of or belonging to the genus Homo. **2** consisting of human beings (*the human race*). **3** of or characteristic of mankind as opposed to God or animals or machines, esp. susceptible to the weaknesses of mankind (*is only human*). **4** showing (esp. the better) qualities of man (*proved to be very human*). —n. a human being. □ **human being** any man or woman or child of the species *Homo sapiens*. **human chain** a line of people formed for passing things along, e.g. buckets of water to the site of a fire. **human rights** rights held to be justifiably belonging to any person. **human shield** a person or persons placed in the line of fire in order to discourage attack. □ **humanness** n. [ME *humain(e)* f. OF f. L *humanus* f. *homo* human being]

humane /hjuːˈmeɪn/ adj. **1** benevolent, compassionate. **2** inflicting the minimum of pain. **3** (of a branch of learning) tending to civilize or confer refinement. □ **humanely** adv. **humaneness** n. [var. of HUMAN, differentiated in sense in the 18th c.]

humanism /ˈhjuːməˌnɪz(ə)m/ n. **1** an outlook or system of thought concerned with human rather than divine or supernatural matters. **2** a belief or outlook emphasizing common human needs and seeking solely rational ways of solving human problems, and concerned with mankind as responsible and progressive intellectual beings. **3** (often **Humanism**) literary culture, esp. that of the Renaissance humanists.

humanist /ˈhjuːmənɪst/ n. **1** an adherent of humanism. **2** a humanitarian. □ **humanistic** /-ˈnɪstɪk/ adj. **humanistically** /-ˈnɪstɪkəlɪ/ adv. [F *humaniste* f. It. *umanista* (as HUMAN)]

humanitarian /hjuːˌmænɪˈteərɪən/ n. & adj. —n. **1** a person who seeks to promote human welfare. **2** a person who advocates or practises humane action; a philanthropist. —adj. relating to or holding the views of humanitarians. □ **humanitarianism** n.

humanity /hjuːˈmænɪtɪ/ n. (pl. **-ies**) **1 a** the human race. **b** human beings collectively. **c** the fact or condition of being human. **2** humaneness, benevolence. **3** (in pl.) human attributes. **4** (in pl.) learning or literature concerned with human culture, esp. the study of Latin and Greek literature and philosophy. [ME f. OF *humanité* f. L *humanitas -tatis* (as HUMAN)]

humanize /ˈhjuːməˌnaɪz/ v.tr. (also **-ise**) **1** make human; give a human character to. **2** make humane. □ **humanization** /-ˈzeɪʃ(ə)n/ n. [F *humaniser* (as HUMAN)]

humankind /ˈhjuːmənˌkaɪnd/ n. human beings collectively.

humanly /ˈhjuːmənlɪ/ adv. **1** by human means (*I will do it if it is humanly possible*). **2** in a human manner. **3** from a human point of view. **4** with human feelings.

humble /ˈhʌmb(ə)l/ adj. & v. —adj. **1 a** having or showing a low estimate of one's own importance. **b** offered with or affected by such an estimate (*if you want my humble opinion*). **2** of low social or political rank (*humble origins*). **3** (of a thing) of modest pretensions, dimensions, etc. —v.tr. **1** make humble; bring low; abase. **2** lower the rank or status of. □ **eat humble pie** make a humble apology; accept humiliation. □ **humbleness** n. **humbly** adv. [ME *umble*, *humble* f. OF *umble* f. L *humilis* lowly f. *humus* ground: *humble pie* f. UMBLES]

humble-bee /ˈhʌmb(ə)lˌbiː/ n. = BUMBLE-BEE. [ME prob. f. MLG *hummelbē*, MDu. *hommel*, OHG *humbal*]

humbug /ˈhʌmbʌɡ/ n. & v. —n. **1** deceptive or false talk or behaviour. **2** an impostor. **3** *Brit.* a hard boiled sweet usu. flavoured with peppermint. —v. (**humbugged**, **humbugging**) **1** intr. be or behave like an impostor. **2** tr. deceive, hoax. □ **humbuggery** n. [18th c.: orig. unkn.]

humdinger /ˈhʌmˌdɪŋə(r)/ n. sl. an excellent or remarkable person or thing. [20th c.: orig. unkn.]

humdrum /ˈhʌmdrʌm/ adj. & n. —adj. **1** commonplace, dull. **2** monotonous. —n. **1** commonplaceness, dullness. **2** a monotonous routine etc. [16th c.: prob. f. HUM¹ by redupl.]

humerus /ˈhjuːmərəs/ n. (pl. **humeri** /-ˌraɪ/) **1** the bone of the upper arm in man. **2** the corresponding bone in other vertebrates. **humeral** adj. [L, = shoulder]

humid /ˈhjuːmɪd/ adj. (of the air or climate) warm and damp. □ **humidly** adv. [F *humide* or L *humidus* f. *umēre* be moist]

humidifier /hjuːˈmɪdɪˌfaɪə(r)/ n. a device for keeping the atmosphere moist in a room etc.

humidify /hjuːˈmɪdɪˌfaɪ/ v.tr. (**-ies**, **-ied**) make (air etc.) humid or damp. □ **humidification** /-fɪˈkeɪʃ(ə)n/ n.

humidity /hjuːˈmɪdɪtɪ/ n. (pl. **-ies**) **1** a humid state. **2** moisture. **3** the degree of moisture esp. in the atmosphere. [ME f. OF *humidité* or L *humiditas* (as HUMID)]

humiliate /hjuːˈmɪlɪˌeɪt/ v.tr. make humble; injure the dignity or self-respect of. □ **humiliating** adj. **humiliatingly** adv. **humiliation** /-ˈeɪʃ(ə)n/ n. **humiliator** n. [LL *humiliare* (as HUMBLE)]

humility /hjuːˈmɪlɪtɪ/ n. **1** humbleness, meekness. **2** a humble condition. [ME f. OF *humilité* f. L *humilitas -tatis* (as HUMBLE)]

hummingbird /ˈhʌmɪŋˌbɜːd/ n. any small nectar-feeding tropical bird of the family Trochilidae that makes a humming sound by the vibration of its wings when it hovers.

hummock /ˈhʌmək/ n. **1** a hillock or knoll. **2** US a piece of rising ground, esp. in a marsh. □ **hummocky** adj. [16th c.: orig. unkn.]

hummus /ˈhʊməs/ n. (also **hoummos**) a thick sauce or spread made from ground chick-peas. [Turk. *humus* mashed chick-peas]

humoresque /ˌhjuːməˈresk/ n. a short lively piece of music. [G *Humoreske* f. *Humor* HUMOUR]

humorist /ˈhjuːmərɪst/ n. **1** a facetious person. **2** a humorous talker, actor, or writer. □ **humoristic** /-ˈrɪstɪk/ adj.

humorous /ˈhjuːmərəs/ adj. **1** showing humour or a sense of humour. **2** facetious, comic. □ **humorously** adv. **humorousness** n.

humour /ˈhjuːmə(r)/ n. & v. (US **humor**) —n. **1 a** the condition of being amusing or comic. **b** the expression of humour in literature, speech, etc. **2** (in full **sense of humour**) the ability to perceive or express humour or take a joke. **3** a mood or state of mind (*bad humour*). **4** an inclination or whim (*in the humour for fighting*). **5** (in full **cardinal humour**) hist. each of the four chief fluids of the body (blood, phlegm, choler, melancholy), thought to determine a person's physical and mental qualities. —v.tr. **1** gratify or indulge (a person or taste etc.). **2** adapt oneself to; make concessions to. □ **out of humour** displeased. □ **-humoured** adj. **humourless** adj. **humourlessly** adv. **humourlessness** n. [ME f. AF *umour*, *humour*, OF *umor*, *humor* f. L *humor* moisture (as HUMID)]

hump n. & v. —n. **1 a** a rounded protuberance on the back of a camel etc., or as an abnormality on a person's back. **2** a rounded raised mass of earth etc. **3** (prec. by *the*) *Brit. sl.* a fit of depression or vexation (*it gives me the hump*). —v.tr. **1 a** (often foll. by *about*) *colloq.* lift or carry (heavy objects etc.) with difficulty. **b** esp. *Austral.* hoist up, shoulder (one's pack etc.). **2** make hump-shaped. **3** *coarse sl.* have sexual intercourse with. □ **hump bridge** = *humpback bridge*. **over the hump** over the worst; well begun. □ **humped** adj. **humpless** adj. [17th c.: perh. rel. to LG *humpel* hump, LG *humpe*, Du. *homp* lump, hunk (of bread)]

humpback /ˈhʌmpbæk/ n. **1 a** a deformed back with a hump. **b** a person having this. **2** a whale, *Megaptera novaeangliae*, with a dorsal fin forming a hump. □ **humpback bridge** *Brit.* a small bridge with a steep ascent and descent. □ **humpbacked** adj.

humph /həmf/ int. & n. an inarticulate sound expressing doubt or dissatisfaction. [imit.]

humpy /ˈhʌmpɪ/ adj. (**humpier**, **humpiest**) **1** having a hump or humps. **2** humplike.

humus /ˈhjuːməs/ n. the organic constituent of soil, usu. formed by the decomposition of plants and leaves by soil bacteria. □ **humusify** v.tr. & intr. (**-ies**, **-ied**). [L, = soil]

Hun n. **1** a member of a warlike Asiatic nomadic people who invaded and ravaged Europe in the 4th–5th c. **2** *offens.* a German (esp. in military contexts). □ **Hunnish** adj. [OE *Hūne* pl. f. LL *Hunni* f. Gk *Hounnoi* f. Turki *Hun-yü*]

hunch v. & n. —v. **1** tr. bend or arch into a hump. **2** tr. thrust out or up to form a hump. **3** intr. (usu. foll. by *up*) US sit with the body hunched. —n. **1** an intuitive feeling or conjecture. **2** a hint. **3** a hump. **4** a thick piece. [16th c.: orig. unkn.]

hunchback /ˈhʌntʃbæk/ n. = HUMPBACK. □ **hunchbacked** adj.

hundred /ˈhʌndrəd/ n. & adj. —n. (pl. **hundreds** or (in sense 1) **hundred**) (in *sing.*, prec. by *a* or *one*) **1** the product of ten and ten. **2** a symbol for this (100, c, C). **3** a set of a hundred things. **4** (in *sing.* or *pl.*) *colloq.* a large number. **5** (in *pl.*) the years of a specified century (*the seventeen hundreds*). **6** *Brit. hist.* a subdivision of a county or shire, having its own court. —adj. **1** that amount to a hundred. **2** used to express whole hours in the 24-hour system (*thirteen hundred* *hours*). □ **a** (or **one**) **hundred per cent** *adv.* entirely, completely. —*adj.* **1** entire, complete. **2** (usu. with *neg.*) fully recovered. **hundreds and thousands** tiny coloured sweets used chiefly for decorating cakes etc. □ **hundredfold** *adj.* & *adv.* **hundredth** *adj.* & *n.* [OE f. Gmc]

hundredweight /ˈhʌndrədˌweɪt/ *n.* (*pl.* same or **-weights**) **1** (in full **long hundredweight**) *Brit.* a unit of weight equal to 112 lb. avoirdupois (about 50.8 kg). **2** (in full **metric hundredweight**) a unit of weight equal to 50 kg. **3** (in full **short hundredweight**) *US* a unit of weight equal to 100 lb. (about 45.4 kg).

hung *past* and *past part.* of HANG.

Hungarian /hʌnˈgeərɪən/ *n.* & *adj.* —*n.* **1 a** a native or national of Hungary in E. Europe. **b** a person of Hungarian descent. **2** the language of Hungary. —*adj.* of or relating to Hungary or its people or language. [med.L *Hungaria* f. *Hungari* Magyar nation]

hunger /ˈhʌŋgə(r)/ *n.* & *v.* —*n.* **1** a feeling of pain or discomfort, or (in extremes) an exhausted condition, caused by lack of food. **2** (often foll. by *for, after*) a strong desire. —*v.intr.* **1** (often foll. by *for, after*) have a craving or strong desire. **2** feel hunger. □ **hunger strike** the refusal of food as a form of protest, esp. by prisoners. [OE *hungor, hyngran* f. Gmc]

hungry /ˈhʌŋgrɪ/ *adj.* (**hungrier, hungriest**) **1** feeling or showing hunger; needing food. **2** inducing hunger (*a hungry air*). **3** eager, greedy, craving. □ **hungrily** *adv.* **hungriness** *n.* [OE *hungrig* (as HUNGER)]

hunk *n.* **1 a** a large piece cut off (*a hunk of bread*). **b** a thick or clumsy piece. **2** *colloq.* **a** a very large person. **b** esp. *US* a sexually attractive man. □ **hunky** *adj.* (**hunkier, hunkiest**). [19th c.: prob. f. Flem. *hunke*]

hunkers /ˈhʌŋkəz/ *n.pl.* the haunches. [orig. Sc., f. *hunker* crouch, squat]

hunky-dory /ˌhʌŋkɪˈdɔːrɪ/ *adj.* esp. *US colloq.* excellent. [19th c.: orig. unkn.]

hunt /hʌnt/ *v.* & *n.* —*v.* **1** *tr.* (also *absol.*) **a** pursue and kill (wild animals, esp. foxes, or game), esp. on horseback and with hounds, for sport or food. **b** (of an animal) chase (its prey). **2** *intr.* (foll. by *after, for*) seek, search (*hunting for a pen*). **3** *intr.* **a** oscillate. **b** (of an engine etc.) run alternately too fast and too slow. **4** *tr.* (foll. by *away* etc.) drive off by pursuit. **5** *tr.* scour (a district) in pursuit of game. **6** *tr.* (as **hunted** *adj.*) (of a look etc.) expressing alarm or terror as of one being hunted. —*n.* **1** the practice of hunting or an instance of this. **2 a** an association of people engaged in hunting with hounds. **b** an area where hunting takes place. □ **hunt down** pursue and capture. **hunt out** find by searching; track down. [OE *huntian*, weak grade of *hentan* seize]

hunter /ˈhʌntə(r)/ *n.* **1** a (*fem.* **huntress**) a person or animal that hunts. **b** a horse used in hunting. **2** a person who seeks something. **3** a watch with a hinged cover protecting the glass.

hunting /ˈhʌntɪŋ/ *n.* the practice of pursuing and killing wild animals, esp. for sport. □ **hunting-ground 1** a place suitable for hunting. **2** a source of information or object of exploitation likely to be fruitful. **hunting horn** a straight horn used in hunting. [OE *huntung* (as HUNT)]

huntsman /ˈhʌntsmən/ *n.* (*pl.* **-men**) **1** a hunter. **2** a hunt official in charge of hounds.

hurdle /ˈhɜːd(ə)l/ *n.* & *v.* —*n.* **1** *Athletics* **a** each of a series of light frames to be cleared by athletes in a race. **b** (in *pl.*) a hurdle-race. **2** an obstacle or difficulty. **3** a portable rectangular frame strengthened with withes or wooden bars, used as a temporary fence etc. —*v.* **1** *Athletics* **a** *intr.* run in a hurdle-race. **b** *tr.* clear (a hurdle). **2** *tr.* fence off etc. with hurdles. [OE *hyrdel* f. Gmc]

hurdler /ˈhɜːdlə(r)/ *n.* **1** *Athletics* a person who runs in hurdle-races. **2** a person who makes hurdles.

hurdy-gurdy /ˈhɜːdɪˌgɜːdɪ/ *n.* (*pl.* **-ies**) **1** a musical instrument with a droning sound, played by turning a handle. **2** *colloq.* a barrel-organ. [prob. imit.]

hurl *v.* & *n.* —*v.* **1** *tr.* throw with great force. **2** *tr.* utter (abuse etc.) vehemently. **3** *intr.* play hurling. —*n.* **1** a forceful throw. **2** the act of hurling. [ME, prob. imit., but corresp. in form and partly in sense with LG *hurreln*]

hurling /ˈhɜːlɪŋ/ *n.* (also **hurley** /ˈhɜːlɪ/) **1** an Irish game somewhat resembling hockey, played with broad sticks. **2** a stick used in this.

hurly-burly /ˈhɜːlɪˌbɜːlɪ/ *n.* boisterous activity; commotion. [redupl. f. HURL]

hurrah /hʊˈrɑː/ *int., n.,* & *v.* (also **hurray** /hʊˈreɪ/) —*int.* & *n.* an exclamation of joy or approval. —*v.intr.* cry or shout 'hurrah' or 'hurray'. [alt. of earlier *huzza*, perh. orig. a sailor's cry when hauling]

hurricane /ˈhʌrɪkən, -ˌkeɪn/ *n.* **1** a storm with a violent wind, esp. a W. Indian cyclone. **2** *Meteorol.* a wind of 65 knots (75 m.p.h.) or more, force 12 on the Beaufort scale. **hurricane-lamp** an oil-lamp designed to resist a high wind. [Sp. *huracan* & Port. *furacão* of Carib orig.]

hurry /ˈhʌrɪ/ *n.* & *v.* —*n.* (*pl.* **-ies**) **1 a** great haste. **b** (with *neg.* or *interrog.*) a need for haste (*there is no hurry; what's the hurry?*). **2** (often foll. by *for*, or *to* + infin.) eagerness to get a thing done quickly. —*v.* (**-ies, -ied**) **1** move or act with great or undue haste. **2** *tr.* (often foll. by *away, along*) cause to move or proceed in this way. **3** *tr.* (as **hurried** *adj.*) hasty; done rapidly owing to lack of time. □ **in a hurry** hurrying, rushed; in a rushed manner. **2** *colloq.* easily or readily (*you will not beat that in a hurry*; *shall not ask again in a hurry*). □ **hurriedly** *adv.* **hurriedness** *n.* [16th c.: imit.]

hurry-scurry /ˌhʌrɪˈskʌrɪ/ *n., adj.,* & *adv.* —*n.* disorderly haste. —*adj.* & *adv.* in confusion. [jingling redupl. of HURRY]

hurt *v.* & *n.* —*v.* (*past* and *past part.* **hurt**) **1** *tr.* (also *absol.*) cause pain or injury to. **2** *tr.* cause mental pain or distress to (a person, feelings, etc.). **3** *intr.* suffer pain or harm (*my arm hurts*). —*n.* **1** bodily or material injury. **2** harm, wrong. □ **hurtless** *adj.* [ME f. OF *hurter, hurt* ult. perh. f. Gmc]

hurtful /ˈhɜːtfʊl/ *adj.* causing (esp. mental) hurt. □ **hurtfully** *adv.* **hurtfulness** *n.*

hurtle /ˈhɜːt(ə)l/ *v.* **1** *intr.* & *tr.* move or hurl rapidly or with a clattering sound. **2** *intr.* come with a crash. [HURT in obs. sense 'strike forcibly']

husband /ˈhʌzbənd/ *n.* & *v.* —*n.* a married man esp. in relation to his wife. —*v.tr.* manage thriftily; use (resources) economically. □ **husbander** *n.* **husbandhood** *n.* **husbandless** *adj.*

husbandlike *adj.* **husbandly** *adj.* **husbandship** *n.* [OE *hūsbonda* house-dweller f. ON *húsbóndi* (as HOUSE, *bóndi* one who has a household)]

husbandry /ˈhʌzbəndrɪ/ *n.* 1 farming. 2 **a** management of resources. **b** careful management.

hush *v.*, *int.*, & *n.* —*v.tr.* & *intr.* make or become silent or quiet. —*int.* calling for silence. —*n.* an expectant stillness or silence. □ **hush money** money paid to prevent the disclosure of a discreditable matter. **hush up** suppress public mention of (an affair). [back-form. f. obs. *husht* *int.*, = quiet!, taken as a past part.]

hush-hush /hʌʃˈhʌʃ/ *adj.* *colloq.* (esp. of an official plan or enterprise etc.) highly secret or confidential.

husk *n.* & *v.* —*n.* 1 the dry outer covering of some fruits or seeds, esp. of a nut or *US* maize. 2 the worthless outside part of a thing. —*v.tr.* remove a husk or husks from. [ME, prob. f. LG *hüske* sheath, dimin. of *hūs* HOUSE]

husky[1] /ˈhʌskɪ/ *adj.* (**huskier**, **huskiest**) 1 (of a person or voice) dry in the throat; hoarse. 2 of or full of husks. 3 dry as a husk. 4 tough, strong, hefty. □ **huskily** *adv.* **huskiness** *n.*

husky[2] /ˈhʌskɪ/ *n.* (*pl.* -**ies**) 1 a dog of a powerful breed used in the Arctic for pulling sledges. 2 this breed. [perh. contr. f. ESKIMO]

huss *n.* dogfish as food. [ME *husk*, of unkn. orig.]

hussar /hʊˈzɑː(r)/ *n.* 1 a soldier of a light cavalry regiment. 2 a Hungarian light horseman of the 15th c. [Magyar *huszár* f. OSerb. *husar* f. It. *corsaro* CORSAIR]

hussy /ˈhʌsɪ/ *n.* (*pl.* -**ies**) *derog.* an impudent or immoral girl or woman. [phonetic reduction of HOUSEWIFE (the orig. sense)]

hustings /ˈhʌstɪŋz/ *n.* parliamentary election proceedings. [late OE *husting* f. ON *hústhing* house of assembly]

hustle /ˈhʌs(ə)l/ *v.* & *n.* —*v.* 1 *tr.* push roughly; jostle. 2 *tr.* **a** (foll. by *into*, *out of*, etc.) force, coerce, or deal with hurriedly or unceremoniously (*hustled them out of the room*). **b** (foll. by *into*) coerce hurriedly (*was hustled into agreeing*). 3 *intr.* push one's way; hurry, bustle. 4 *tr.* *sl.* **a** obtain by forceful action. **b** swindle. 5 *intr.* *sl.* engage in prostitution. —*n.* 1 an act or instance of hustling. 2 *colloq.* a fraud or swindle. [MDu. *husselen* shake, toss, frequent. of *hutsen*, orig. imit.]

hustler /ˈhʌslə(r)/ *n.* *sl.* 1 an active, enterprising, or unscrupulous individual. 2 a prostitute.

hut *n.* & *v.* —*n.* 1 a small simple or crude house or shelter. 2 *Mil.* a temporary wooden etc. house for troops. —*v.* (**hutted**, **hutting**) 1 *tr.* provide with huts. 2 *tr.* *Mil.* place (troops etc.) in huts. 3 *intr.* lodge in a hut. □ **hutlike** *adj.* [F *hutte* f. MHG *hütte*]

hutch *n.* a box or cage, usu. with a wire mesh front, for keeping small pet animals. [ME, = coffer, f. OF *huche* f. med.L *hutica*, of unkn. orig.]

hyacinth /ˈhaɪəsɪnθ/ *n.* 1 any bulbous plant of the genus *Hyacinthus* with racemes of bell-shaped fragrant flowers. 2 = grape hyacinth. 3 the purplish-blue colour of the hyacinth flower. 4 an orange variety of zircon used as a precious stone. □ **wild** (or **wood**) **hyacinth** = BLUEBELL 1. □ **hyacinthine** /-ˈsɪnθɪːn/ *adj.* [F *hyacinthe* f. L *hyacinthus* f. Gk *huakinthos*, flower and gem, also the name of a youth loved by Apollo]

hyaena var. of HYENA.

hyalite /ˈhaɪəˌlaɪt/ *n.* a colourless variety of opal. [Gk *hualos* glass]

hybrid /ˈhaɪbrɪd/ *n.* & *adj.* —*n.* 1 *Biol.* the offspring of two plants or animals of different species or varieties. 2 a thing composed of incongruous elements, e.g. a word with parts taken from different languages. —*adj.* 1 bred as a hybrid from different species or varieties. 2 *Biol.* heterogeneous. □ **hybrid vigour** heterosis. □ **hybridism** *n.* **hybridity** /-ˈbrɪdɪtɪ/ *n.* [L *hybrida*, (h)*ibrida* offspring of a tame sow and wild boar, child of a freeman and slave, etc.]

hybridize /ˈhaɪbrɪˌdaɪz/ *v.* (also -**ise**) 1 *tr.* subject (a species etc.) to cross-breeding. 2 *intr.* **a** produce hybrids. **b** (of an animal or plant) interbreed. □ **hybridizable** *adj.* **hybridization** /-ˈzeɪʃ(ə)n/ *n.*

hydra /ˈhaɪdrə/ *n.* 1 a freshwater polyp of the genus *Hydra* with tubular body and tentacles around the mouth. 2 any water-snake. 3 something which is hard to destroy. [ME f. L f. Gk *hudra* water-snake, esp. a fabulous one with many heads that grew again when cut off]

hydrangea /haɪˈdreɪndʒə/ *n.* any shrub of the genus *Hydrangea* with large white, pink, or blue flowers. [mod.L f. Gk *hudōr* water + *aggos* vessel (from the cup-shape of its seed-capsule)]

hydrant /ˈhaɪdrənt/ *n.* a pipe (esp. in a street) with a nozzle to which a hose can be attached for drawing water from the main. [irreg. f. HYDRO- + -ANT]

hydrate /ˈhaɪdreɪt/ *n.* & *v.* —*n.* *Chem.* a compound of water combined with another compound or with an element. —*v.tr.* 1 **a** combine chemically with water. **b** (as **hydrated** *adj.*) chemically bonded to water. 2 cause to absorb water. □ **hydratable** *adj.* **hydration** /-ˈdreɪʃ(ə)n/ *n.* **hydrator** *n.* [F f. Gk *hudōr* water]

hydraulic /haɪˈdrɔːlɪk, -ˈdrɒlɪk/ *adj.* 1 (of water, oil, etc.) conveyed through pipes or channels usu. by pressure. 2 (of a mechanism etc.) operated by liquid moving in this manner (*hydraulic brakes*). 3 of or concerned with hydraulics (*hydraulic engineer*). 4 hardening under water (*hydraulic cement*). □ **hydraulically** *adv.* **hydraulicity** /-ˈlɪsɪtɪ/ *n.* [L *hydraulicus* f. Gk *hudraulikos* f. *hudōr* water + *aulos* pipe]

hydraulics /haɪˈdrɔːlɪks, -ˈdrɒlɪks/ *n.pl.* (usu. treated as *sing.*) the science of the conveyance of liquids through pipes etc. esp. as motive power.

hydride /ˈhaɪdraɪd/ *n.* *Chem.* a binary compound of hydrogen with an element, esp. with a metal.

hydro /ˈhaɪdrəʊ/ *n.* (*pl.* -**os**) *colloq.* 1 a hotel or clinic etc. orig. providing hydropathic treatment. 2 a hydroelectric power plant. [abbr.]

hydro- /ˈhaɪdrəʊ/ *comb. form* (also **hydr-** before a vowel) 1 having to do with water (*hydroelectric*). 2 *Chem.* combined with hydrogen (*hydrochloric*). [Gk *hudro-* f. *hudōr* water]

hydrocarbon /ˌhaɪdrəʊˈkɑːbən/ *n.* *Chem.* a compound of hydrogen and carbon.

hydrocephalus /ˌhaɪdrəˈsefələs/ *n.* *Med.* an abnormal amount of fluid within the brain, esp. in young children, which makes the head enlarge and can cause mental deficiency. □ **hydrocephalic** /-sɪˈfælɪk/ *adj.*

hydrochloric acid /ˌhaɪdrəˈklɔːrɪk, -ˈklɒrɪk/ *n.* *Chem.* a solution of the colourless gas hydrogen chloride in water.

hydrochloride /ˌhaɪdrəˈklɔːraɪd/ n. Chem. a compound of an organic base with hydrochloric acid.

hydrocortisone /ˌhaɪdrəˈkɔːtɪˌzəʊn/ n. Biochem. a steroid hormone produced by the adrenal cortex, used medicinally to treat inflammation and rheumatism.

hydrocyanic acid /ˌhaɪdrəsaɪˈænɪk/ n. Chem. a highly poisonous volatile liquid with a characteristic odour of bitter almonds.

hydrodynamics /ˌhaɪdrəʊdaɪˈnæmɪks/ n. the science of forces acting on or exerted by fluids (esp. liquids). □ **hydrodynamic** adj. **hydrodynamical** adj. **hydrodynamicist** /-sɪst/ n. [mod.L hydrodynamicus (as HYDRO-, DYNAMIC)]

hydroelectric /ˌhaɪdrəʊɪˈlektrɪk/ adj. **1** generating electricity by utilization of water-power. **2** (of electricity) generated in this way. □ **hydroelectricity** /-ˈtrɪsɪtɪ/ n.

hydrofoil /ˈhaɪdrəˌfɔɪl/ n. **1** a boat equipped with a device consisting of planes for lifting its hull out of the water to increase its speed. **2** this device. [HYDRO-, after AEROFOIL]

hydrogen /ˈhaɪdrədʒ(ə)n/ n. Chem. a colourless gaseous element, without taste or odour, the lightest of the elements and occurring in water and all organic compounds. □ **hydrogen bomb** an immensely powerful bomb utilizing the explosive fusion of hydrogen nuclei. **hydrogen peroxide** a colourless viscous unstable liquid with strong oxidizing properties. **hydrogen sulphide** a colourless poisonous gas with a disagreeable smell, formed by rotting animal matter. □ **hydrogenous** /-ˈdrɒdʒɪnəs/ adj. [F hydrogène (as HYDRO-, -GEN)]

hydrogenate /haɪˈdrɒdʒɪˌneɪt, ˈhaɪdrədʒəˌneɪt/ v.tr. charge with or cause to combine with hydrogen. □ **hydrogenation** /-ˈneɪʃ(ə)n/ n.

hydrography /haɪˈdrɒgrəfɪ/ n. the science of surveying and charting seas, lakes, rivers, etc. □ **hydrographer** n. **hydrographic** /ˌhaɪdrəˈgræfɪk/ adj. **hydrographical** /ˌhaɪdrəˈgræfɪk(ə)l/ adj. **hydrographically** /ˌhaɪdrəˈgræfɪkəlɪ/ adv.

hydrology /haɪˈdrɒlədʒɪ/ n. the science of the properties of the earth's water, esp. of its movement in relation to land. □ **hydrologic** /ˌhaɪdrəˈlɒdʒɪk/ adj. **hydrological** /ˌhaɪdrəˈlɒdʒɪk(ə)l/ adj. **hydrologically** /ˌhaɪdrəˈlɒdʒɪkəlɪ/ adv. **hydrologist** n.

hydrolyse /ˈhaɪdrəˌlaɪz/ v.tr. & intr. (US **hydrolyze**) subject to or undergo the chemical action of water.

hydrolysis /haɪˈdrɒlɪsɪs/ n. the chemical reaction of a substance with water, usu. resulting in decomposition. □ **hydrolytic** /ˌhaɪdrəˈlɪtɪk/ adj.

hydromechanics /ˌhaɪdrəʊmɪˈkænɪks/ n. the mechanics of liquids; hydrodynamics.

hydrometer /haɪˈdrɒmɪtə(r)/ n. an instrument for measuring the density of liquids. □ **hydrometric** /ˌhaɪdrəˈmetrɪk/ adj. **hydrometry** n.

hydropathy /haɪˈdrɒpəθɪ/ n. the (medically unorthodox) treatment of disease by external and internal application of water. □ **hydropathic** /ˌhaɪdrəˈpæθɪk/ adj. **hydropathist** n. [HYDRO-, after HOMOEOPATHY etc.]

hydrophil /ˈhaɪdrəfɪl/ adj. (also **hydrophile** /-ˌfaɪl/) = HYDROPHILIC. [as HYDROPHILIC]

hydrophilic /ˌhaɪdrəˈfɪlɪk/ adj. **1** having an affinity for water. **2** wettable by water. [HYDRO- + Gk philos loving]

hydrophobia /ˌhaɪdrəˈfəʊbɪə/ n. **1** a morbid aversion to water, esp. as a symptom of rabies in man. **2** rabies, esp. in man. □ **hydrophobic** adj. [LL f. Gk hudrophobia (as HYDRO-, -PHOBIA)]

hydroplane /ˈhaɪdrəˌpleɪn/ n. & v. —n. **1** a light fast motor boat designed to skim over the surface of water. **2** a finlike attachment which enables a submarine to rise and fall in water. —v.intr. **1** (of a boat) skim over the surface of water with its hull lifted. **2** = AQUAPLANE v. 2.

hydroponics /ˌhaɪdrəˈpɒnɪks/ n. the process of growing plants in sand, gravel, or liquid, without soil and with added nutrients. □ **hydroponic** adj. **hydroponically** adv. [HYDRO- + Gk ponos labour]

hydrosphere /ˈhaɪdrəˌsfɪə(r)/ n. the waters of the earth's surface.

hydrostatic /ˌhaɪdrəˈstætɪk/ adj. of the equilibrium of liquids and the pressure exerted by liquid at rest. □ **hydrostatical** adj. **hydrostatically** adv. [prob. f. Gk hudrostatēs hydrostatic balance (as HYDRO-, STATIC)]

hydrostatics /ˌhaɪdrəˈstætɪks/ n.pl. (usu. treated as sing.) the branch of mechanics concerned with the hydrostatic properties of liquids.

hydrotherapy /ˌhaɪdrəˈθerəpɪ/ n. the use of water in the treatment of disorders, usu. exercises in swimming pools for arthritic or partially paralysed patients. □ **hydrotherapist** n. **hydrotherapic** adj.

hydrothermal /ˌhaɪdrəˈθɜːm(ə)l/ adj. of the action of heated water on the earth's crust. □ **hydrothermally** adv.

hydrous /ˈhaɪdrəs/ adj. Chem. & Mineral. containing water. [Gk hudōr hudro- water]

hydroxide /haɪˈdrɒksaɪd/ n. Chem. a metallic compound containing oxygen and hydrogen either in the form of the hydroxide ion or the hydroxyl group.

hydroxy- /haɪˈdrɒksɪ/ comb. form Chem. having a hydroxide ion (or ions) or a hydroxyl group (or groups). [HYDROGEN + OXYGEN]

hydroxyl /haɪˈdrɒksɪl/ n. Chem. the univalent group containing hydrogen and oxygen. [HYDROGEN + OXYGEN + -YL]

hyena /haɪˈiːnə/ n. (also **hyaena**) any flesh-eating mammal of the order Hyaenidae, with hind limbs shorter than forelimbs. □ **laughing hyena** n. a hyena, Crocuta crocuta, whose howl is compared to a fiendish laugh. [ME f. OF hyene & L hyaena f. Gk huaina fem. of hus pig]

hygiene /ˈhaɪdʒiːn/ n. **1 a** a study, or set of principles, of maintaining health. **b** conditions or practices conducive to maintaining health. **2** sanitary science. [F hygiène f. mod.L hygieina f. Gk hugieinē (tekhnē) (art) of health f. hugiēs healthy]

hygienic /haɪˈdʒiːnɪk/ adj. conducive to hygiene; clean and sanitary. □ **hygienically** adv.

hygienist /ˈhaɪdʒiːnɪst/ n. a specialist in the promotion and practice of cleanliness for the preservation of health.

hygro- /ˈhaɪɡrəʊ/ comb. form moisture. [Gk hugro- f. hugros wet, moist]

hygrometer /haɪˈɡrɒmɪtə(r)/ n. an instrument for measuring the humidity of the air or a gas. □ **hygrometric** /ˌhaɪɡrəˈmetrɪk/ adj. **hygrometry** n.

hygroscope /ˈhaɪgrəˌskəʊp/ n. an instrument which indicates the humidity of the air.

hygroscopic /ˌhaɪgrəˈskɒpɪk/ adj. 1 of the hygroscope. 2 (of a substance) tending to absorb moisture from the air. □ **hygroscopically** adv.

hying pres. part. of HIE.

hymen /ˈhaɪmen/ n. Anat. a membrane which partially closes the opening of the vagina and is usu. broken at the first occurrence of sexual intercourse. □ **hymenal** adj. [LL f. Gk humēn membrane]

hymenopteran /ˌhaɪməˈnɒptərən/ n. any insect of the order Hymenoptera having four transparent wings, including bees, wasps, and ants. □ **hymenopterous** adj. [mod.L hymenoptera f. Gk humenopteros membrane-winged f. humenion dimin. of humēn membrane, + pteron wing]

hymn /hɪm/ n. & v. —n. 1 a song of praise, esp. to God in Christian worship, usu. a metrical composition sung in a religious service. 2 a song of praise in honour of a god or other exalted being or thing. —v. 1 tr. praise or celebrate in hymns. 2 intr. sing hymns. □ **hymn-book** a book of hymns. □ **hymnic** /ˈhɪmnɪk/ adj. [ME ymne etc. f. OF ymne f. L hymnus f. Gk humnos]

hymnal /ˈhɪmn(ə)l/ n. & adj. —n. a hymn-book. —adj. of hymns. [ME f. med.L hymnale (as HYMN)]

hyoscine /ˈhaɪəˌsiːn/ n. a poisonous alkaloid found in plants of the nightshade family, esp. of the genus Scopolia, and used as an antiemetic in motion sickness and a preoperative medication for examination of the eye.

hyoscyamine /ˌhaɪəˈsaɪəˌmiːn/ n. a poisonous alkaloid obtained from henbane, having similar properties to hyoscine. [mod.L hyoscyamus f. Gk huoskuamos henbane f. hus huos pig + kuamos bean]

hype[1] n. & v. sl. —n. 1 extravagant or intensive publicity promotion. 2 cheating; a trick. —v.tr. 1 promote (a product) with extravagant publicity. 2 cheat, trick. [20th c.: orig. unkn.]

hype[2] n. sl. 1 a drug addict. 2 a hypodermic needle or injection. □ **hyped up** stimulated by or as if by a hypodermic injection. [abbr. of HYPODERMIC]

hyper- /ˈhaɪpə(r)/ prefix meaning: 1 over, beyond, above (hyperphysical). 2 exceeding (hypersonic). 3 excessively; above normal (hyperbole; hypersensitive). [Gk huper over, beyond]

hyperactive /ˌhaɪpəˈræktɪv/ adj. (of a person, esp. a child) abnormally active. □ **hyperactivity** /-ˈtɪvɪtɪ/ n.

hyperbola /haɪˈpɜːbələ/ n. (pl. **hyperbolas** or **hyperbolae** /-ˌliː/) Geom. the plane curve of two equal branches, produced when a cone is cut by a plane that makes a larger angle with the base than the side of the cone. □ **hyperbolic** /ˌhaɪpəˈbɒlɪk/ adj. [mod.L f. Gk huperbolē excess (as HYPER-, ballō to throw)]

hyperbole /haɪˈpɜːbəlɪ/ n. Rhet. an exaggerated statement not meant to be taken literally. □ **hyperbolical** /-ˈbɒlɪk(ə)l/ adj. **hyperbolically** /-ˈbɒlɪkəlɪ/ adv. **hyperbolism** n. [L (as HYPERBOLA)]

hyperconscious /ˌhaɪpəˈkɒnʃəs/ adj. (foll. by of) acutely or excessively aware.

hypercritical /ˌhaɪpəˈkrɪtɪk(ə)l/ adj. excessively critical, esp. of small faults. □ **hypercritically** adv.

hyperglycaemia /ˌhaɪpəglaɪˈsiːmɪə/ n. (US **hyperglycemia**) an excess of glucose in the bloodstream, often associated with diabetes mellitus. □ **hyperglycaemic** adj. [HYPER- + GLYCO- + -aemia mod.L f. Gk haima blood]

hypericum /haɪˈperɪkəm/ n. any shrub of the genus Hypericum with five-petalled yellow flowers. [L f. Gk hupereikon (as HYPER-, ereikē heath)]

hypermarket /ˈhaɪpəˌmɑːkɪt/ n. Brit. a very large self-service store with a wide range of goods and extensive car-parking facilities, usu. outside a town. [transl. F hypermarché (as HYPER-, MARKET)]

hypermetropia /ˌhaɪpəmɪˈtrəʊpɪə/ n. the condition of having long sight. □ **hypermetropic** /-ˈtrɒpɪk/ adj. [mod.L f. HYPER- + Gk metron measure, ōps eye]

hyperphysical /ˌhaɪpəˈfɪzɪk(ə)l/ adj. supernatural. □ **hyperphysically** adv.

hypersensitive /ˌhaɪpəˈsensɪtɪv/ adj. abnormally or excessively sensitive. □ **hypersensitiveness** n. **hypersensitivity** /-ˈtɪvɪtɪ/ n.

hypersonic /ˌhaɪpəˈsɒnɪk/ adj. 1 relating to speeds of more than five times the speed of sound (Mach 5). 2 relating to sound-frequencies above about a thousand million hertz. □ **hypersonically** adv. [HYPER-, after SUPERSONIC, ULTRASONIC]

hypertension /ˌhaɪpəˈtenʃ(ə)n/ n. 1 abnormally high blood pressure. 2 a state of great emotional tension. □ **hypertensive** /-sɪv/ adj.

hyperthermia /ˌhaɪpəˈθɜːmɪə/ n. Med. the condition of having a body-temperature greatly above normal. □ **hyperthermic** adj. [HYPER- + Gk thermē heat]

hyperthyroidism /ˌhaɪpəˈθaɪrɔɪˌdɪz(ə)m/ n. Med. overactivity of the thyroid gland, resulting in rapid heartbeat and an increased rate of metabolism. □ **hyperthyroid** n. & adj. **hyperthyroidic** adj.

hypertonic /ˌhaɪpəˈtɒnɪk/ adj. 1 (of muscles) having high tension. 2 (of a solution) having a greater osmotic pressure than another solution. □ **hypertonia** /-ˈtəʊnɪə/ n. (in sense 1). **hypertonicity** /-təˈnɪsɪtɪ/ n.

hypertrophy /haɪˈpɜːtrəfɪ/ n. the enlargement of an organ or tissue from the increase in size of its cells. □ **hypertrophic** /ˌhaɪpəˈtrɒfɪk/ adj. **hypertrophied** adj. [mod.L hypertrophia (as HYPER-, Gk -trophia nourishment)]

hyperventilation /ˌhaɪpəˌventɪˈleɪʃ(ə)n/ n. breathing at an abnormally rapid rate, resulting in an increased loss of carbon dioxide.

hyphen /ˈhaɪf(ə)n/ n. & v. —n. the sign (-) used to join words semantically or syntactically (as in fruit-tree, pick-me-up, rock-forming), to indicate the division of a word at the end of a line, or to indicate a missing or implied element (as in man- and womankind). —v.tr. 1 write (a compound word) with a hyphen. 2 join (words) with a hyphen. [LL f. Gk huphen together f. hupo under + hen one]

hyphenate /ˈhaɪfəˌneɪt/ v.tr. = HYPHEN v. □ **hyphenation** /-ˈneɪʃ(ə)n/ n.

hypno- /ˈhɪpnəʊ/ comb. form sleep, hypnosis. [Gk hupnos sleep]

hypnology /hɪpˈnɒlədʒɪ/ n. the science of the phenomena of sleep. □ **hypnologist** n.

hypnosis /hɪpˈnəʊsɪs/ n. 1 a state like sleep in which the subject acts only on external suggestion. **2** artificially produced sleep. [mod.L f. Gk *hupnos* sleep + -OSIS]

hypnotherapy /ˌhɪpnəʊˈθerəpɪ/ n. the treatment of disease by hypnosis.

hypnotic /hɪpˈnɒtɪk/ adj. & n. —adj. **1** of or producing hypnotism. **2** (of a drug) soporific. —n. **1** a thing, esp. a drug, that produces sleep. **2** a person under or open to the influence of hypnotism. □ **hypnotically** adv. [F *hypnotique* f. LL *hypnoticus* f. Gk *hupnōtikos* f. *hupnoō* put to sleep]

hypnotism /ˈhɪpnəˌtɪz(ə)m/ n. the study or practice of hypnosis. □ **hypnotist** n.

hypnotize /ˈhɪpnəˌtaɪz/ v.tr. (also -ise) **1** produce hypnosis in. **2** fascinate; capture the mind of (a person). □ **hypnotizable** adj. **hypnotizer** n.

hypo¹ /ˈhaɪpəʊ/ n. *Photog.* the chemical sodium thiosulphate (incorrectly called hyposulphite) used as a photographic fixer. [abbr.]

hypo² /ˈhaɪpəʊ/ n. (pl. -os) colloq. = HYPODERMIC n. [abbr.]

hypo- /ˈhaɪpəʊ/ prefix (usu. **hyp-** before a vowel or *h*) **1** under (*hypodermic*). **2** below normal (*hypoxia*). **3** slightly (*hypomania*). [Gk f. *hupo* under]

hypocaust /ˈhaɪpəˌkɔːst/ n. a hollow space under the floor in ancient Roman houses, into which hot air was sent for heating a room or bath. [L *hypocaustum* f. Gk *hupokauston* place heated from below (as HYPO-, *kaiō*, *kau-* burn)]

hypochondria /ˌhaɪpəˈkɒndrɪə/ n. **1** abnormal anxiety about one's health. **2** morbid depression without real cause. [LL f. Gk *hupokhondria* soft parts of the body below the ribs, where melancholy was thought to arise (as HYPO-, *khondros* sternal cartilage)]

hypochondriac /ˌhaɪpəˈkɒndrɪˌæk/ n. & adj. —n. a person suffering from hypochondria. —adj. (also **hypochondriacal** /-ˈdraɪək(ə)l/) of or affected by hypochondria. [F *hypocondriaque* f. Gk *hupokhondriakos* (as HYPOCHONDRIA)]

hypocrisy /hɪˈpɒkrɪsɪ/ n. (pl. -ies) **1** the assumption or postulation of moral standards to which one's own behaviour does not conform; dissimulation, pretence. **2** an instance of this. [ME f. OF *ypocrisie* f. eccl.L *hypocrisis* f. Gk *hupokrisis* acting of a part, pretence (as HYPO-, *krinō* decide, judge)]

hypocrite /ˈhɪpəkrɪt/ n. a person given to hypocrisy. □ **hypocritical** /-ˈkrɪtɪk(ə)l/ adj. **hypocritically** /-ˈkrɪtɪkəlɪ/ adv. [ME f. OF *ypocrite* f. eccl.L f. Gk *hupokritēs* actor (as HYPOCRISY)]

hypodermic /ˌhaɪpəˈdɜːmɪk/ adj. & n. —adj. *Med.* **1** of or relating to the area beneath the skin. **2 a** (of a drug etc. or its application) injected beneath the skin. **b** (of a needle, syringe, etc.) used to do this. —n. a hypodermic injection or syringe. □ **hypodermically** adv. [HYPO- + Gk *derma* skin]

hypoglycaemia /ˌhaɪpəʊɡlaɪˈsiːmɪə/ n. (*US* **hypoglycemia**) a deficiency of glucose in the bloodstream. □ **hypoglycaemic** adj. [HYPO- + GLYCO- + -aemia (see HYPERGLYCAEMIA)]

hypomania /ˌhaɪpəˈmeɪnɪə/ n. a minor form of mania. □ **hypomanic** /-ˈmænɪk/ adj. [mod.L f. G *Hypomanie* (as HYPO-, MANIA)]

hypotension /ˌhaɪpəˈtenʃ(ə)n/ n. abnormally low blood pressure. □ **hypotensive** adj.

hypotenuse /haɪˈpɒtəˌnjuːz/ n. the side opposite the right angle of a right-angled triangle. [L *hypotenusa* f. Gk *hupoteinousa* (*grammē*) subtending (line) fem. part. of *hupoteinō* (as HYPO-, *teinō* stretch)]

hypothalamus /ˌhaɪpəˈθæləməs/ n. (pl. **-mi** /-ˌmaɪ/) *Anat.* the region of the brain which controls body-temperature, thirst, hunger, etc. □ **hypothalamic** adj. [mod.L formed as HYPO-, THALAMUS]

hypothermia /ˌhaɪpəʊˈθɜːmɪə/ n. *Med.* the condition of having an abnormally low body-temperature. [HYPO- + Gk *thermē* heat]

hypothesis /haɪˈpɒθɪsɪs/ n. (pl. **hypotheses** /-ˌsiːz/) **1** a proposition made as a basis for reasoning, without the assumption of its truth. **2** a supposition made as a starting-point for further investigation from known facts. **3** a groundless assumption. [LL f. Gk *hupothesis* foundation (as HYPO-, THESIS)]

hypothesize /haɪˈpɒθɪˌsaɪz/ v. (also -ise) **1** intr. frame a hypothesis. **2** tr. assume a hypothesis. □ **hypothesist** /-sɪst/ n. **hypothesizer** n.

hypothetical /ˌhaɪpəˈθetɪk(ə)l/ adj. **1** of or based on or serving as a hypothesis. **2** supposed but not necessarily real or true. □ **hypothetically** adv.

hypothyroidism /ˌhaɪpəʊˈθaɪrɔɪˌdɪz(ə)m/ n. *Med.* subnormal activity of the thyroid gland, resulting in cretinism in children, and mental and physical slowing in adults. □ **hypothyroid** n. & adj. **hypothyroidic** /-ˈrɔɪdɪk/ adj.

hypoventilation /ˌhaɪpəʊˌventɪˈleɪʃ(ə)n/ n. breathing at an abnormally slow rate, resulting in an increased amount of carbon dioxide in the blood.

hyssop /ˈhɪsəp/ n. any small bushy aromatic herb of the genus *Hyssopus*, esp. *H. officinalis*, formerly used medicinally. [OE (h)ysope (reinforced in ME by OF *ysope*) f. L *hyssopus* f. Gk *hyssōpos*, of Semitic orig.]

hysterectomy /ˌhɪstəˈrektəmɪ/ n. (pl. -ies) the surgical removal of the womb. □ **hysterectomize** v.tr. (also -ise). [Gk *hustera* womb + -ECTOMY]

hysteria /hɪˈstɪərɪə/ n. **1** a wild uncontrollable emotion or excitement. **2** a functional disturbance of the nervous system, of psychoneurotic origin. [mod.L (as HYSTERIC)]

hysteric /hɪˈsterɪk/ n. & adj. —n. **1** (in pl.) **a** a fit of hysteria. **b** colloq. overwhelming mirth or laughter (*we were in hysterics*). **2** a hysterical person. —adj. = HYSTERICAL. [L f. Gk *husterikos* of the womb (*hustera*), hysteria being thought to occur more frequently in women than in men and to be associated with the womb]

hysterical /hɪˈsterɪk(ə)l/ adj. **1** of or affected with hysteria. **2** morbidly or uncontrolledly emotional. **3** colloq. extremely funny or amusing. □ **hysterically** adv.

Hz abbr. hertz.

Ii

I¹ /aɪ/ *n.* (also **i**) (*pl.* **Is** or **I's**) **1** the ninth letter of the alphabet. **2** (as a Roman numeral) 1. □ **I-beam** a girder of I-shaped section.

I² /aɪ/ *pron.* (*obj.* **me**; *poss.* **my**, **mine**; *pl.* **we**) used by a speaker or writer to refer to himself or herself. [OE f. Gmc]

I³ *symb. Chem.* the element iodine.

I⁴ *abbr.* (also **I.**) **1** Island(s). **2** Isle(s).

-i /ɪ/ *suffix* forming adjectives from names of countries or regions in the Near or Middle East (*Israeli*; *Pakistani*). [*adj.* suffix in Semitic and Indo-Iranian languages]

-ia /ɪə/ *suffix* **1** forming abstract nouns (*mania*; *utopia*), often in *Med.* (*anaemia*; *pneumonia*). **2** *Bot.* forming names of classes and genera (*dahlia*; *fuchsia*). **3** forming names of countries (*Australia*; *India*). [from or after L & Gk]

-ial /ɪəl/ *suffix* forming adjectives (*celestial*; *dictatorial*; *trivial*). [from or after F *-iel* or L *-ialis*: cf. -AL]

iambic /aɪˈæmbɪk/ *adj.* & *n. Prosody* —*adj.* of or using iambuses. —*n.* (usu. in *pl.*) iambic verse. [F *iambique* f. LL *iambicus* f. Gk *iambikos* (as IAMBUS)]

iambus /aɪˈæmbəs/ *n.* (*pl.* **iambuses** or **-bi** /-baɪ/) *Prosody* a foot consisting of one short (or unstressed) followed by one long (or stressed) syllable. [L f. Gk *iambos* iambus, lampoon, f. *iaptō* assail in words, from its use by Gk satirists]

-ian /ɪən/ *suffix* var. of -AN. [from or after F *-ien* or L *-ianus*]

Iberian /aɪˈbɪərɪən/ *adj.* & *n.* —*adj.* of ancient Iberia, the peninsula now comprising Spain and Portugal; of Spain and Portugal. —*n.* **1** a native of ancient Iberia. **2** any of the languages of ancient Iberia. [L *Iberia* f. Gk *Ibēres* Spaniards]

ibex /ˈaɪbeks/ *n.* (*pl.* **ibexes**) a wild goat, *Capra ibex*, esp. of mountainous areas of Europe, N. Africa, and Asia, with thick curved ridged horns. [L]

ibid. *abbr.* (also **ib.**) in the same book or passage etc. [L *ibidem* in the same place]

-ibility /ɪˈbɪlɪtɪ/ *suffix* forming nouns from, or corresponding to, adjectives in *-ible* (*possibility*; *credibility*). [F *-ibilité* or L *-ibilitas*]

ibis /ˈaɪbɪs/ *n.* (*pl.* **ibises**) any wading bird of the family Threskiornithidae with a curved bill. [ME f. L f. Gk]

-ible /ˈɪb(ə)l/ *suffix* forming adjectives meaning 'that may or may be' (see -ABLE) (*terrible*; *forcible*; *possible*). [F *-ible* or L *-ibilis*]

-ibly /ˈɪblɪ/ *suffix* forming adverbs corresponding to adjectives in *-ible*.

i/c *abbr.* **1** in charge. **2** in command.

-ic /ɪk/ *suffix* **1** forming adjectives (*Arabic*; *classic*; *public*) and nouns (*critic*; *epic*; *mechanic*; *music*). **2** denoting a particular form or instance of a noun in *-ics* (*aesthetic*; *tactic*). [from or after F *-ique* or L *-icus* or Gk *-ikos*: cf. -ATIC, -ETIC, -FIC, -OTIC]

-ical /ˈɪk(ə)l/ *suffix* **1** forming adjectives corresponding to nouns or adjectives, usu. in *-ic* (*classical*; *comical*; *farcical*; *musical*). **2** forming adjectives corresponding to nouns in *-y* (*pathological*).

-ically /ˈɪkəlɪ/ *suffix* forming adverbs corresponding to adjectives in *-ic* or *-ical* (*comically*; *musically*; *tragically*).

ice *n.* & *v.* —*n.* **1 a** frozen water, a brittle transparent crystalline solid. **b** a sheet of this on the surface of water (*fell through the ice*). **2** *Brit.* a portion of ice-cream or water-ice (*would you like an ice?*). **3** *sl.* diamonds. —*v.* **1** *tr.* mix with or cool in ice (*iced drinks*). **2** *tr.* & *intr.* (often foll. by *over*, *up*) **a** cover or become covered with ice. **b** freeze. **3** *tr.* cover (a cake etc.) with icing. □ **ice age** a glacial period, esp. in the Pleistocene epoch. **ice-axe** a tool used by mountain-climbers for cutting footholds. **ice-blue** a very pale blue. **ice-boat 1** a boat mounted on runners for travelling on ice. **2** a boat used for breaking ice on a river etc. **ice-bound** confined by ice. **ice-breaker 1** = *ice-boat* 2. **2** something that serves to relieve inhibitions, start a conversation, etc. **ice-cap** a permanent covering of ice e.g. in polar regions. **ice-cream** a sweet creamy frozen food, usu. flavoured. **ice-cube** a small block of ice made in a refrigerator. **ice hockey** a form of hockey played on ice with a puck. **ice (or iced) lolly** *Brit.* a piece of flavoured ice, often with chocolate or ice-cream, on a stick. **ice-pick** a needle-like implement with a handle for splitting up small pieces of ice. **ice-skate** *n.* a skate consisting of a boot with a blade beneath, for skating on ice. —*v.intr.* skate on ice. **ice-skater** a person who skates on ice. **ice station** a meteorological research centre in polar regions. **on ice 1** (of an entertainment, sport, etc.) performed by skaters. **2** *colloq.* held in reserve; awaiting further attention. **on thin ice** in a risky situation. [OE *īs* f. Gmc]

-ice /ɪs/ *suffix* forming (esp. abstract) nouns (*avarice*; *justice*; *service*) (cf. -ISE²).

iceberg /ˈaɪsbɜːg/ *n.* a large floating mass of ice detached from a glacier or ice-sheet and carried out to sea. □ **iceberg lettuce** any of various crisp lettuces with a freely blanching head. **the tip of the iceberg** a small perceptible part of something (esp. a difficulty) the greater part of which is hidden. [prob. f. Du. *ijsberg* f. *ijs* ice + *berg* hill]

iceblock /ˈaɪsblɒk/ *n.* *Austral.* & *NZ* = *ice lolly*.

icebox /ˈaɪsbɒks/ *n.* **1** a compartment in a refrigerator for making and storing ice. **2** *US* a refrigerator.

iceman /ˈaɪsmən/ *n.* (*pl.* **-men**) esp. *US* **1** a man skilled in crossing ice. **2** a man who sells or delivers ice.

I Ching /iː ˈtʃɪŋ/ *n.* an ancient Chinese manual of divination based on symbolic trigrams and hexagrams. [Chin. *yijing* book of changes]

ichneumon /ɪkˈnjuːmən/ n. **1** (in full **ichneumon wasp**) any small hymenopterous insect of the family Ichneumonidae, depositing eggs in or on the larva of another insect as food for its own larva. **2** a mongoose of N. Africa, *Herpestes ichneumon*, noted for destroying crocodile eggs. [L f. Gk *ikhneumōn* spider-hunting wasp f. *ikhneuō* trace f. *ikhnos* footstep]

ichthyo- /ˈɪkθɪəʊ/ comb. form fish. [Gk *ikhthus* fish]

ichthyoid /ˈɪkθɪˌɔɪd/ adj. & n. —adj. fishlike. —n. any fishlike vertebrate.

ichthyology /ˌɪkθɪˈɒlədʒɪ/ n. the study of fishes. □ **ichthyological** /-əˈlɒdʒɪk(ə)l/ adj. **ichthyologist** n.

ichthyosaurus /ˌɪkθɪəˈsɔːrəs/ n. (also **ichthyosaur** /ˈɪkθɪəˌsɔːr/) any extinct marine reptile of the order Ichthyosauria, with long head, tapering body, four flippers, and usu. a large tail. [ICHTHYO- + Gk *sauros* lizard]

-ician /ˈɪʃ(ə)n/ suffix forming nouns denoting persons skilled in or concerned with subjects having nouns (usu.) in -ic or -ics (*magician*; *politician*). [from or after F -icien (as -IC, -IAN)]

icicle /ˈaɪsɪk(ə)l/ n. a hanging tapering piece of ice, formed by the freezing of dripping water. [ME f. ICE + *ickle* (now dial.) icicle]

icing /ˈaɪsɪŋ/ n. **1** a coating of sugar etc. on a cake or biscuit. **2** the formation of ice on a ship or aircraft. □ **icing on the cake** an attractive though inessential addition or enhancement. **icing sugar** Brit. finely powdered sugar for making icing for cakes etc.

-icist /ɪsɪst/ suffix = -ICIAN (*classicist*). [-IC + -IST]

-icity /ˈɪsɪtɪ/ suffix forming abstract nouns esp. from adjectives in -ic (*authenticity*; *publicity*). [-IC + -ITY]

-icle /ˈɪk(ə)l/ suffix forming (orig. diminutive) nouns (*article*; *particle*). [formed as -CULE]

icon /ˈaɪkɒn/ n. (also **ikon**) **1** a devotional painting or carving, usu. on wood, of Christ or another holy figure, esp. in the Eastern Church. **2** an image or statue. **3** Computing a symbol or graphic representation on a VDU screen of a program, option, or window, esp. one of several for selection. [L f. Gk *eikōn* image]

iconic /aɪˈkɒnɪk/ adj. **1** of or having the nature of an image or portrait. **2** (of a statue) following a conventional type. □ **iconicity** /-kəˈnɪsɪtɪ/ n. [L *iconicus* f. Gk *eikonikos* (as ICON)]

icono- /aɪˈkɒnəʊ/ comb. form an image or likeness. [Gk *eikōn*]

iconoclasm /aɪˈkɒnəˌklæz(ə)m/ n. **1** the breaking of images. **2** the assailing of cherished beliefs. [ICONOCLAST after *enthusiasm* etc.]

iconoclast /aɪˈkɒnəˌklæst/ n. **1** a person who attacks cherished beliefs. **2** a person who destroys images used in religious worship. □ **iconoclastic** /-ˈklæstɪk/ adj. **iconoclastically** /-ˈklæstɪkəlɪ/ adv. [med.L *iconoclastes* f. eccl.Gk *eikonoklastēs* (as ICONO-, *klaō* break)]

iconography /ˌaɪkəˈnɒɡrəfɪ/ n. (pl. **-ies**) **1** the illustration of a subject by drawings or figures. **2 a** the study of portraits, esp. of an individual. **b** the study of artistic images or symbols. □ **iconographer** n. **iconographic** /-nəˈɡræfɪk/ adj. **iconographical** /-nəˈɡræfɪk(ə)l/ adj. **iconographically** /-nəˈɡræfɪkəlɪ/ adv. [Gk *eikonographia* sketch (as ICONO- + -GRAPHY)]

icosahedron /ˌaɪkɒsəˈhedrən, -ˈhiːdrən/ n. a solid figure with twenty faces. □ **icosahedral** adj. [LL *icosahedrum* f. Gk *eikosaedron* f. *eikosi* twenty + -HEDRON]

-ics /ɪks/ suffix (treated as sing. or pl.) forming nouns denoting arts or sciences or branches of study or action (*athletics*; *politics*) (cf. -IC 2). [from or after F pl. -iques or L pl. -ica or Gk pl. -ika]

ictus /ˈɪktəs/ n. (pl. same or **ictuses**) **1** Prosody rhythmical or metrical stress. **2** Med. a stroke or seizure; a fit. [L, = blow f. *icere* strike]

icy /ˈaɪsɪ/ adj. (**icier, iciest**) **1** very cold. **2** covered with or abounding in ice. **3** (of a tone or manner) unfriendly, hostile. □ **icily** adv. **iciness** n.

ID abbr. esp. US identification, identity (*ID card*).

id /ɪd/ n. Psychol. the inherited instinctive impulses of the individual as part of the unconscious. [L, = that, transl. G *es*]

-id[1] /ɪd/ suffix forming adjectives (*arid*; *rapid*). [F -ide f. L -idus]

-id[2] /ɪd/ suffix forming nouns: **1** general (*pyramid*). **2** Biol. of structural constituents (*plastid*). **3** Bot. of a plant belonging to a family with a name in -aceae (*orchid*). [from or after F -ide f. L -is -idis f. Gk -is -ida or -idos]

-id[3] /ɪd/ suffix forming nouns denoting: **1** Zool. an animal belonging to a family with a name in -idae or a class with a name in -ida (*canid*; *arachnid*). **2** a member of a person's family (*Seleucid* from Seleucus). **3** Astron. **a** a meteor in a group radiating from a specified constellation (*Leonid* from Leo). **b** a star of a class like one in a specified constellation (*cepheid*). [from or after L -ides, pl. -idae or -ida]

-ide /aɪd/ suffix (also esp. US **-id**) Chem. forming nouns denoting: **1** binary compounds of an element (*chloride*; *calcium carbide*). **2** various other compounds (*amide*; *anhydride*; *peptide*; *saccharide*). **3** elements of a series in the periodic table (*actinide*; *lanthanide*). [orig. in OXIDE]

idea /aɪˈdɪə/ n. **1** a conception or plan formed by mental effort (*have you any ideas?*; *had the idea of writing a book*). **2 a** a mental impression or notion; a concept. **b** a vague belief or fancy (*had an idea you were married*). **3** an intention, purpose, or essential feature (*the idea is to make money*). **4** an archetype or pattern as distinguished from its realization in individual cases. □ **have no idea** colloq. **1** not know at all. **2** be completely incompetent. □ **idea'd** adj. **ideaed** adj. **idealess** adj. [Gk idea form, pattern f. stem id- see]

ideal /aɪˈdiːəl/ adj. & n. —adj. **1 a** answering to one's highest conception. **b** perfect or supremely excellent. **2 a** existing only in idea. **b** visionary. **3** embodying an idea. **4** relating to or consisting of ideas; dependent on the mind. —n. **1** a perfect type, or a conception of this. **2** an actual thing as a standard for imitation. □ **ideally** adv. [ME f. F idéal f. LL idealis (as IDEA)]

idealism /aɪˈdɪəˌlɪz(ə)m/ n. **1** the practice of forming or following after ideals, esp. unrealistically. **2** the representation of things in ideal or idealized form. **3** imaginative treatment. □ **idealist** n. **idealistic** /-ˈlɪstɪk/ adj. **idealistically** /-ˈlɪstɪkəlɪ/ adv. [F idéalisme or G Idealismus (as IDEAL)]

idealize /aɪˈdɪəlaɪz/ v.tr. (also **-ise**) **1** regard or represent (a thing or person) in ideal form or character. **2** exalt in thought to ideal perfection or excellence. □ **idealization** /-ˈzeɪʃ(ə)n/ n. **idealizer** n.

idée fixe /ˌiːdeɪ ˈfiːks/ *n.* (*pl.* **idées fixes** *pronunc.* same) an idea that dominates the mind; an obsession. [F, lit. 'fixed idea']

identical /aɪˈdentɪk(ə)l/ *adj.* **1** (often foll. by *with*) (of different things) agreeing in every detail. **2** (of one thing viewed at different times) one and the same. **3** (of twins) developed from a single fertilized ovum, therefore of the same sex and usu. very similar in appearance. □ **identically** *adv.* **identicalness** *n.* [med.L *identicus* (as IDENTITY)]

identification /aɪˌdentɪfɪˈkeɪʃ(ə)n/ *n.* **1** the act or an instance of identifying. **2** a means of identifying a person. **3** (*attrib.*) serving to identify (esp. the bearer) (*identification card*). □ **identification parade** an assembly of persons from whom a suspect is to be identified.

identify /aɪˈdentɪˌfaɪ/ *v.* (**-ies, -ied**) **1** *tr.* establish the identity of; recognize. **2** *tr.* establish or select by consideration or analysis of the circumstances (*identify the best method of solving the problem*). **3** *tr.* (foll. by *with*) associate (a person or oneself) inseparably or very closely (with a party, policy, etc.). **4** *tr.* (often foll. by *with*) treat (a thing) as identical. **5** *intr.* (foll. by *with*) **a** regard oneself as sharing characteristics of (another person). **b** associate oneself. □ **identifiable** *adj.* **identifier** *n.* [med.L *identificare* (as IDENTITY)]

Identikit /aɪˈdentɪkɪt/ *n.* (often *attrib.*) *propr.* a reconstructed picture of a person (esp. one sought by the police) assembled from transparent strips showing typical facial features according to witnesses' descriptions. [IDENTITY + KIT[1]]

identity /aɪˈdentɪtɪ/ *n.* (*pl.* **-ies**) **1 a** the quality or condition of being a specified person or thing. **b** individuality, personality (*felt he had lost his identity*). **2** identification or the result of it (*a case of mistaken identity; identity card*). **3** the state of being the same in substance, nature, qualities, etc.; absolute sameness (*no identity of interests between them*). **4** *Algebra* **a** the equality of two expressions for all values of the quantities expressed by letters. **b** an equation expressing this. **5** *Math.* **a** (in full **identity element**) an element in a set, left unchanged by any operation to it. **b** a transformation that leaves an object unchanged. □ **identity crisis** a phase in which an individual feels a need to establish an identity in relation to society. **identity parade** = *identification parade*. [LL *identitas* f. L *idem* same]

ideogram /ˈɪdɪəˌɡræm/ *n.* a character symbolizing the idea of a thing without indicating the sequence of sounds in its name (e.g. a numeral, and many Chinese characters). [Gk *idea* form + -GRAM]

ideograph /ˈɪdɪəˌɡrɑːf/ *n.* = IDEOGRAM. □ **ideographic** /-ˈɡræfɪk/ *adj.* **ideography** /ˌɪdɪˈɒɡrəfɪ/ *n.* [Gk *idea* form + -GRAPH]

ideologue /ˈaɪdɪəˌlɒɡ/ *n.* **1** a theorist; a visionary. **2** an adherent of an ideology. [F *idéologue* f. Gk *idea* (see IDEA) + -LOGUE]

ideology /ˌaɪdɪˈɒlədʒɪ/ *n.* (*pl.* **-ies**) **1** the system of ideas at the basis of an economic or political theory (*Marxist ideology*). **2** the manner of thinking characteristic of a class or individual (*bourgeois ideology*). □ **ideological** /-əˈlɒdʒɪk(ə)l/ *adj.* **ideologically** /-əˈlɒdʒɪkəlɪ/ *adv.* **ideologist** *n.* [F *idéologie* (as IDEOLOGUE)]

ides /aɪdz/ *n.pl.* the eighth day after the nones in the ancient Roman calendar (the 15th day of March, May, July, October, the 13th of other months). [ME f. OF f. L *idus* (pl.), perh. f. Etruscan]

idiocy /ˈɪdɪəsɪ/ *n.* (*pl.* **-ies**) **1** utter foolishness; idiotic behaviour or an idiotic action. **2** extreme mental imbecility. [ME f. IDIOT, prob. after *lunacy*]

idiom /ˈɪdɪəm/ *n.* **1** a group of words established by usage and having a meaning not deducible from those of the individual words (as in *over the moon, see the light*). **2** a form of expression peculiar to a language, person, or group of people. **3 a** the language of a people or country. **b** the specific character of this. **4** a characteristic mode of expression in music, art, etc. [F *idiome* or LL *idioma* f. Gk *idiōma -matos* private property f. *idios* own, private]

idiomatic /ˌɪdɪəˈmætɪk/ *adj.* **1** relating to or conforming to idiom. **2** characteristic of a particular language. □ **idiomatically** *adv.* [Gk *idiōmatikos* peculiar (as IDIOM)]

idiosyncrasy /ˌɪdɪəʊˈsɪŋkrəsɪ/ *n.* (*pl.* **-ies**) **1** a mental constitution, view or feeling, or mode of behaviour, peculiar to a person. **2** anything highly individualized or eccentric. **3** a mode of expression peculiar to an author. □ **idiosyncratic** /-ˈkrætɪk/ *adj.* **idiosyncratically** /-ˈkrætɪkəlɪ/ *adv.* [Gk *idiosugkrasia* f. *idios* own + *sun* together + *krasis* mixture]

idiot /ˈɪdɪət/ *n.* **1** *colloq.* a stupid person; an utter fool. **2** a person deficient in mind and permanently incapable of rational action. □ **idiot board** (or **card**) *colloq.* a board displaying a television script to a speaker as an aid to memory. □ **idiotic** /-ˈɒtɪk/ *adj.* **idiotically** /-ˈɒtɪkəlɪ/ *adv.* [ME f. OF f. L *idiota* ignorant person f. Gk *idiōtēs* private person, layman, ignorant person f. *idios* own, private]

idle /ˈaɪd(ə)l/ *adj. & v.* —*adj.* (**idler, idlest**) **1** lazy, indolent. **2** not in use; not working; unemployed. **3** (of time etc.) unoccupied. **4** having no special basis or purpose (*idle rumour; idle curiosity*). **5** useless. **6** (of an action, thought, or word) ineffective, worthless, vain. —*v.* **1 a** *intr.* (of an engine) run slowly without doing any work. **b** *tr.* cause (an engine) to idle. **2** *intr.* be idle. **3** *tr.* (foll. by *away*) pass (time etc.) in idleness. □ **idleness** *n.* **idler** *n.* **idly** *adv.* [OE *īdel* empty, useless]

idol /ˈaɪd(ə)l/ *n.* **1** an image of a deity etc. used as an object of worship. **2** *Bibl.* a false god. **3** a person or thing that is the object of excessive or supreme adulation (*cinema idol*). [ME f. OF *idole* f. L *idolum* f. Gk *eidōlon* phantom f. *eidos* form]

idolater /aɪˈdɒlətə(r)/ *n.* (*fem.* **idolatress** /-trɪs/) **1** a worshipper of idols. **2** (often foll. by *of*) a devoted admirer. □ **idolatrous** *adj.* [ME *idolatrer* f. OF or f. *idolatry* or f. OF *idolâtre*, ult. f. Gk *eidōlolatrēs* (as IDOL, -LATER)]

idolatry /aɪˈdɒlətrɪ/ *n.* **1** the worship of idols. **2** great adulation. [OF *idolatrie* (as IDOLATER)]

idolize /ˈaɪdəˌlaɪz/ *v.tr.* (also **-ise**) **1** venerate or love extremely or excessively. **2** make an idol of. □ **idolization** /-ˈzeɪʃ(ə)n/ *n.* **idolizer** *n.*

idyll /ˈɪdɪl/ *n.* (also **idyl**) **1** a short description in verse or prose of a picturesque scene or incident, esp. in rustic life. **2** an episode suitable for such treatment, usu. a love-story. □ **idyllist** *n.*

idyllize v.tr. (also **-ise**). [L idyllium f. Gk eidullion, dimin. of eidos form]

idyllic /ɪˈdɪlɪk/ adj. **1** blissfully peaceful and happy. **2** of or like an idyll. □ **idyllically** adv.

i.e. abbr. that is to say. [L id est]

-ie /ɪ/ suffix var. of -Y² (dearie; nightie). [earlier form of -Y]

-ier /ɪə(r)/ suffix forming personal nouns denoting an occupation or interest: **1** with stress on the preceding element (grazier). **2** with stress on the suffix (cashier; brigadier). [sense 1 ME of various orig.; sense 2 F -ier f. L -arius]

if conj. & n. —conj. **1** introducing a conditional clause: **a** on the condition or supposition that; in the event that (if he comes I will tell him; if you are tired we will rest). **b** (with past tense) implying that the condition is not fulfilled (if I were you; if I knew I would say). **2** even though (I'll finish it, if it takes me all day). **3** whenever (if I am not sure I ask). **4** whether (see if you can find it). **5 a** expressing wish or surprise (if I could just try!; if it isn't my old hat!). **b** expressing a request (if you wouldn't mind opening the door?). **6** with implied reservation, = and perhaps not (very rarely if at all). **7** (with reduction of the protasis to its significant word) if there is or it is etc. (took little if any). **8** despite being (a useful if cumbersome device). —n. a condition or supposition (too many ifs about it). □ **if only 1** even if for no other reason than (I'll come if only to see her). **2** (often ellipt.) an expression of regret (if only I had thought of it; if only I could swim!). **if so** if that is the case. [OE gif]

iffy /ˈɪfɪ/ adj. (**iffier**, **iffiest**) colloq. uncertain, doubtful.

igloo /ˈɪɡluː/ n. an Eskimo dome-shaped dwelling, esp. one built of snow. [Eskimo, = house]

igneous /ˈɪɡnɪəs/ adj. **1** of fire; fiery. **2** Geol. (esp. of rocks) produced by volcanic or magmatic action. [L igneus f. ignis fire]

ignite /ɪɡˈnaɪt/ v. **1** tr. set fire to; cause to burn. **2** intr. catch fire. **3** tr. Chem. heat to the point of combustion or chemical change. **4** tr. provoke or excite (feelings etc.). □ **ignitability** /-təˈbɪlɪtɪ/ n. **ignitable** adj. **igniter** n. **ignitibility** /-tɪˈbɪlɪtɪ/ n. **ignitible** adj. [L ignire ignit- f. ignis fire]

ignition /ɪɡˈnɪʃ(ə)n/ n. **1** a mechanism for, or the action of, starting the combustion of mixture in the cylinder of an internal-combustion engine. **2** the act or an instance of igniting or being ignited. □ **ignition key** a key to operate the ignition of a motor vehicle. [F ignition or med.L ignitio (as IGNITE)]

ignoble /ɪɡˈnəʊb(ə)l/ adj. (**ignobler**, **ignoblest**) **1** dishonourable, mean, base. **2** of low birth, position, or reputation. □ **ignobility** /-nəˈbɪlɪtɪ/ n. **ignobly** adv. [F ignoble or L ignobilis (as IN-¹, nobilis noble)]

ignominious /ˌɪɡnəˈmɪnɪəs/ adj. **1** causing or deserving ignominy. **2** humiliating. □ **ignominiously** adv. **ignominiousness** n. [ME f. F ignominieux or L ignominiosus]

ignominy /ˈɪɡnəmɪnɪ/ n. dishonour, infamy. [F ignominie or L ignominia (as IN-¹, nomen name)]

ignoramus /ˌɪɡnəˈreɪməs/ n. (pl. **ignoramuses**) an ignorant person. [L, = we do not know: in legal use (formerly of a grand jury rejecting a bill) we take no notice of it; mod. sense perh. from a character in Ruggle's Ignoramus (1615) exposing lawyers' ignorance]

ignorance /ˈɪɡnərəns/ n. (often foll. by of) lack of knowledge (about a thing). [ME f. OF f. L ignorantia (as IGNORANT)]

ignorant /ˈɪɡnərənt/ adj. **1 a** lacking knowledge. **b** (foll. by of, in) uninformed (about a fact or subject). **2** colloq. ill-mannered, uncouth. □ **ignorantly** adv. [ME f. OF f. L ignorare ignorant- (as IGNORE)]

ignore /ɪɡˈnɔː(r)/ v.tr. **1** refuse to take notice of or accept. **2** intentionally disregard. □ **ignorer** n. [F ignorer or L ignorare not know, ignore (as IN-¹, gno- know)]

iguana /ɪˈɡwɑːnə/ n. any of various large lizards of the family Iguanidae, having a dorsal crest and throat appendages. [Sp. f. Carib iwana]

iguanodon /ɪˈɡwɑːnɪˌdɒn/ n. a large extinct plant-eating dinosaur of the genus Iguanodon, with forelimbs smaller than hind limbs. [IGUANA (from its resemblance to this), after mastodon etc.]

ikebana /ˌɪkɪˈbɑːnə/ n. the art of Japanese flower arrangement. [Jap., = living flowers]

ikon var. of ICON.

-il /ɪl/ suffix (also **-ile** /aɪl/) forming adjectives or nouns denoting relation (civil; utensil) or capability (agile; sessile). [OF f. L -ilis]

ilea pl. of ILEUM.

ileum /ˈɪlɪəm/ n. (pl. **ilea** /ˈɪlɪə/) Anat. the third and last portion of the small intestine. □ **ileac** adj. [var. of ILIUM]

ilex /ˈaɪleks/ n. **1** any tree or shrub of the genus Ilex, esp. the common holly. **2** the holm-oak. [ME f. L]

ilia pl. of ILIUM.

iliac /ˈɪlɪˌæk/ adj. of the lower body or ilium (iliac artery). [LL iliacus (as ILIUM)]

ilium /ˈɪlɪəm/ n. (pl. **ilia** /ˈɪlɪə/) **1** the bone forming the upper part of each half of the human pelvis. **2** the corresponding bone in animals. [ME f. L]

ilk /ɪlk/ n. **1** colloq. disp. a family, class, or set (not of the same ilk as you). **2** (in **of that ilk**) Sc. of the same (name) (Guthrie of that ilk = of Guthrie). [OE ilca same]

ill adj., adv., & n. —adj. **1** (usu. predic.; often foll. by with) out of health; sick (is ill; was taken ill with pneumonia; mentally ill people). **2** (of health) unsound, disordered. **3** wretched, unfavourable (ill fortune; ill luck). **4** harmful (ill effects). **5** hostile, unkind (ill feeling). **6** archaic morally bad. **7** faulty, unskilful (ill taste; ill management). **8** (of manners or conduct) improper. —adv. **1** badly, wrongly (ill-matched). **2 a** imperfectly (ill-provided). **b** scarcely (can ill afford to do it). **3** unfavourably (it would have gone ill with them). —n. **1** injury, harm. **2** evil; the opposite of good. □ **ill-advised 1** acting foolishly or imprudently. **2** (of a plan etc.) not well formed or considered. **ill-assorted** not well matched. **ill at ease** embarrassed, uneasy. **ill-bred** badly brought up; rude. **ill breeding** bad manners. **ill-considered** = ill-advised. **ill-defined** not clearly defined. **ill-disposed 1** (often foll. by towards) unfavourably disposed. **2** disposed to evil; malevolent. **ill-equipped** (often foll. by to + infin.) not adequately equipped or qualified. **ill-fated** destined to or bringing bad fortune. **ill-favoured** (US **-favored**) unattractive, displeasing, objectionable. **ill feeling** bad feeling; animosity. **ill-founded** (of an idea etc.) not well founded;

baseless. **ill-gotten** gained by wicked or unlawful means. **ill-humoured** bad-tempered. **ill-judged** unwise; badly considered. **ill-mannered** having bad manners; rude. **ill-natured** churlish, unkind. **ill-omened** attended by bad omens. **ill-starred** unlucky; destined to failure. **ill success** partial or complete failure. **ill-tempered** morose, irritable. **ill-timed** done or occurring at an inappropriate time. **ill-treat** (or **-use**) treat badly; abuse. **ill-treatment** (or **ill use**) abuse; bad treatment. **ill will** bad feeling; animosity. **speak ill of** say something unfavourable about. [ME f. ON *illr*, of unkn. orig.]

illegal /ɪˈliːg(ə)l/ *adj.* **1** not legal. **2** contrary to law. □ **illegality** /-ˈgælɪtɪ/ *n.* (*pl.* **-ies**). **illegally** *adv.* [F *illégal* or med.L *illegalis* (as IN-¹, LEGAL)]

illegible /ɪˈledʒɪb(ə)l/ *adj.* not legible. □ **illegibility** /-ˈbɪlɪtɪ/ *n.* **illegibly** *adv.*

illegitimate *adj.*, *n.*, & *v.* —*adj.* /ˌɪlɪˈdʒɪtɪmət/ **1** (of a child) born of parents not married to each other. **2** not authorized by law; unlawful. **3** improper. **4** wrongly inferred. —*n.* /ˌɪlɪˈdʒɪtɪmət/ a person whose position is illegitimate, esp. by birth. —*v.tr.* /ˌɪlɪˈdʒɪtɪˌmeɪt/ declare or pronounce illegitimate. □ **illegitimacy** *n.* **illegitimately** *adv.* [LL *illegitimus*, after LEGITIMATE]

illiberal /ɪˈlɪbər(ə)l/ *adj.* **1** intolerant, narrow-minded. **2** without liberal culture. **3** not generous; stingy. **4** vulgar, sordid. □ **illiberality** /-ˈrælɪtɪ/ *n.* (*pl.* **-ies**). **illiberally** *adv.* [F *illibéral* f. L *illiberalis* mean, sordid (as IN-¹, LIBERAL)]

illicit /ɪˈlɪsɪt/ *adj.* unlawful, forbidden (*illicit dealings*). □ **illicitly** *adv.* **illicitness** *n.*

illimitable /ɪˈlɪmɪtəb(ə)l/ *adj.* limitless. □ **illimitability** /-ˈbɪlɪtɪ/ *n.* **illimitableness** *n.* **illimitably** *adv.* [LL *illimitatus* f. L *limitatus* (as IN-¹, L *limitatus* past part. of *limitare* LIMIT)]

illiterate /ɪˈlɪtərət/ *adj.* & *n.* —*adj.* **1** unable to read. **2** uneducated. —*n.* an illiterate person. □ **illiteracy** *n.* **illiterately** *adv.* **illiterateness** *n.* [L *illitteratus* (as IN-¹, *litteratus* LITERATE)]

illness /ˈɪlnɪs/ *n.* **1** a disease, ailment, or malady. **2** the state of being ill.

illogical /ɪˈlɒdʒɪk(ə)l/ *adj.* devoid of or contrary to logic. □ **illogicality** /-ˈkælɪtɪ/ *n.* (*pl.* **-ies**). **illogically** *adv.*

illuminant /ɪˈluːmɪnənt, ɪˈljuː-/ *n.* & *adj.* —*n.* a means of illumination. —*adj.* serving to illuminate. □ **illuminance** *n.* [L *illuminant-* part. stem of *illuminare* ILLUMINATE]

illuminate /ɪˈluːmɪˌneɪt, ɪˈljuː-/ *v.tr.* **1** light up; make bright. **2** decorate (buildings etc.) with lights as a sign of festivity. **3** decorate (an initial letter, a manuscript, etc.) with gold, silver, or brilliant colours. **4** help to explain (a subject etc.). **5** enlighten spiritually or intellectually. **6** shed lustre on. □ **illuminating** *adj.* **illuminatingly** *adv.* **illumination** /-ˈneɪʃ(ə)n/ *n.* **illuminative** /-ˌneɪtɪv, -nətɪv/ *adj.* **illuminator** *n.* [L *illuminare* (as IN-², *lumen luminis* light)]

illumine /ɪˈljuːmɪn, ɪˈluː-/ *v.tr. literary* **1** light up; make bright. **2** enlighten spiritually. [ME f. OF *illuminer* f. L (as ILLUMINATE)]

illusion /ɪˈluːʒ(ə)n, ɪˈljuː-/ *n.* **1** deception, delusion. **2** a misapprehension of the true state of affairs. **3** a the faulty perception of an external object. **b** an instance of this. **4** a figment of the imagination. **5** = *optical illusion.* □ **be under the illusion** (foll. by *that* + clause) believe

mistakenly. □ **illusional** *adj.* [ME f. F f. L *illusio -onis* f. *illudere* mock (as IN-², *ludere lus-* play)]

illusionist /ɪˈluːʒənɪst, ɪˈljuː-/ *n.* a person who produces illusions; a conjuror. □ **illusionism** *n.* **illusionistic** /-ˈnɪstɪk/ *adj.*

illusive /ɪˈluːsɪv, ɪˈljuː-/ *adj.* = ILLUSORY. [med.L *illusivus* (as ILLUSION)]

illusory /ɪˈluːsərɪ, ɪˈljuː-/ *adj.* **1** deceptive (esp. as regards value or content). **2** having the character of an illusion. □ **illusorily** *adv.* **illusoriness** *n.* [eccl.L *illusorius* (as ILLUSION)]

illustrate /ˈɪləˌstreɪt/ *v.tr.* **1** a provide (a book, newspaper, etc.) with pictures. **b** elucidate (a description etc.) by drawings or pictures. **2** serve as an example of. **3** explain or make clear, esp. by examples. [L *illustrare* (as IN-², *lustrare* light up)]

illustration /ˌɪləˈstreɪʃ(ə)n/ *n.* **1** a drawing or picture illustrating a book, magazine article, etc. **2** an example serving to elucidate. **3** the act or an instance of illustrating. □ **illustrational** *adj.* [ME f. OF f. L *illustratio -onis* (as ILLUSTRATE)]

illustrative /ˈɪləstrətɪv/ *adj.* (often foll. by *of*) serving as an explanation or example. □ **illustratively** *adv.*

illustrator /ˈɪləˌstreɪtə(r)/ *n.* a person who makes illustrations, esp. for magazines, books, advertising copy, etc.

illustrious /ɪˈlʌstrɪəs/ *adj.* distinguished, renowned. □ **illustriously** *adv.* **illustriousness** *n.* [L *illustris* (as ILLUSTRATE)]

-ily /ɪlɪ/ *suffix* forming adverbs corresponding to adjectives in *-y* (see -Y¹, -LY²).

image /ˈɪmɪdʒ/ *n.* & *v.* —*n.* **1** a representation of the external form of an object, e.g. a statue (esp. of a saint etc. as an object of veneration). **2** the character or reputation of a person or thing as generally perceived. **3** an optical appearance or counterpart produced by light or other radiation from an object reflected in a mirror, refracted through a lens, etc. **4** semblance, likeness (*God created man in His own image*). **5** a person or thing that closely resembles another (*is the image of his father*). **6** a typical example. **7** a simile or metaphor. **8 a** a mental representation. **b** an idea or conception. **9** *Math.* a set formed by mapping from another set. —*v.tr.* **1** make an image of; portray. **2** reflect, mirror. **3** describe or imagine vividly. **4** typify. □ **imageable** *adj.* **imageless** *adj.* [ME f. OF f. L *imago -ginis*, rel. to IMITATE]

imagery /ˈɪmɪdʒərɪ/ *n.* **1** figurative illustration, esp. as used by an author for particular effects. **2** images collectively. **3** statuary, carving. **4** mental images collectively. [ME f. OF *imagerie* (as IMAGE)]

imaginable /ɪˈmædʒɪnəb(ə)l/ *adj.* that can be imagined (*the greatest difficulty imaginable*). □ **imaginably** *adv.* [ME f. LL *imaginabilis* (as IMAGINE)]

imaginary /ɪˈmædʒɪnərɪ/ *adj.* **1** existing only in the imagination. **2** *Math.* being the square root of a negative quantity. □ **imaginarily** *adv.* [ME f. L *imaginarius* (as IMAGE)]

imagination /ɪˌmædʒɪˈneɪʃ(ə)n/ *n.* **1** a mental faculty forming images or concepts of external objects not present to the senses. **2** the ability of the mind to be creative or resourceful. **3** the process of imagining. [ME f. OF f. L *imaginatio -onis* (as IMAGINE)]

imaginative /ɪˈmædʒɪnətɪv/ *adj.* **1** having or showing in a high degree the faculty of imagination. **2** given to using the imagination. □ **imaginatively** *adv.* **imaginativeness** *n.* [ME f. OF *imaginatif -ive* f. med.L *imaginativus* (as IMAGINE)]

imagine /ɪˈmædʒɪn/ *v.tr.* **1 a** form a mental image or concept of. **b** picture to oneself (something non-existent or not present to the senses). **2** (often foll. by *to* + infin.) think or conceive (*imagined them to be soldiers*). **3** guess (*cannot imagine what they are doing*). **4** (often foll. by *that* + clause) suppose; be of the opinion (*I imagine you will need help*). □ **imaginer** *n.* [ME f. OF *imaginer* f. L *imaginari* (as IMAGE)]

imagines *pl.* of IMAGO.

imaginings /ɪˈmædʒɪnɪŋz/ *n.pl.* fancies, fantasies.

imago /ɪˈmeɪɡəʊ/ *n.* (*pl.* **-os** or **imagines** /ɪˈmædʒɪˌniːz/) the final and fully developed stage of an insect after all metamorphoses, e.g. a butterfly or beetle. [mod.L sense of *imago* IMAGE]

imam /ɪˈmɑːm/ *n.* **1** a leader of prayers in a mosque. **2** a title of various Muslim leaders, esp. of one succeeding Muhammad as leader of Islam. □ **imamate** /-meɪt/ *n.* [Arab. *'imām* leader f. *'amma* precede]

imbalance /ɪmˈbæləns/ *n.* **1** lack of balance. **2** disproportion.

imbecile /ˈɪmbɪˌsiːl/ *n.* & *adj.* —*n.* **1** a person of abnormally weak intellect, esp. an adult with a mental age of about five. **2** *colloq.* a stupid person. —*adj.* mentally weak; idiotic. □ **imbecilely** *adv.* **imbecilic** /-ˈsɪlɪk/ *adj.* **imbecility** /-ˈsɪlɪtɪ/ *n.* (*pl.* **-ies**). [F *imbécil(l)e* f. L *imbecillus* (as IN-[1], *baculum* stick) orig. in sense 'without supporting staff']

imbed var. of EMBED.

imbibe /ɪmˈbaɪb/ *v.tr.* **1** (also *absol.*) drink (esp. alcoholic liquor). **2 a** absorb or assimilate (ideas etc.). **b** absorb (moisture etc.). **3** inhale (air etc.). □ **imbiber** *n.* **imbibition** /ˌɪmbɪˈbɪʃ(ə)n/ *n.* [ME f. L *imbibere* (as IN-[2], *bibere* drink)]

imbroglio /ɪmˈbrəʊlɪəʊ/ *n.* (*pl.* **-os**) **1** a confused or complicated situation. **2** a confused heap. [It. *imbrogliare* confuse (as EMBROIL)]

imbue /ɪmˈbjuː/ *v.tr.* (**imbues, imbued, imbuing**) (often foll. by *with*) **1** inspire or permeate (with feelings, opinions, or qualities). **2** saturate. **3** dye. [orig. as past part., f. F *imbu* or L *imbutus* f. *imbuere* moisten]

imitate /ˈɪmɪˌteɪt/ *v.tr.* **1** follow the example of; copy the action(s) of. **2** mimic. **3** make a copy of; reproduce. [L *imitari imitat-*, rel. to *imago* IMAGE]

imitation /ˌɪmɪˈteɪʃ(ə)n/ *n.* **1** the act or an instance of imitating or being imitated. **2** a copy. **3** counterfeit (often *attrib.*: *imitation leather*). [F *imitation* or L *imitatio* (as IMITATE)]

imitative /ˈɪmɪtətɪv/ *adj.* **1** (often foll. by *of*) imitating; following a model or example. **2** counterfeit. **3** of a word: **a** that reproduces a natural sound (e.g. *fizz*). **b** whose sound is thought to correspond to the appearance etc. of the object or action described (e.g. *blob*). □ **imitatively** *adv.* **imitativeness** *n.* [LL *imitativus* (as IMITATE)]

immaculate /ɪˈmækjʊlət/ *adj.* **1** pure, spotless; perfectly clean. **2** perfectly or extremely well executed (*an immaculate performance*). **3** free from fault; innocent. □ **Immaculate Conception** *RC Ch.* the doctrine that God preserved the Virgin Mary from the taint of original sin from the moment she was conceived. □ **immaculacy** *n.* **immaculately** *adv.* **immaculateness** *n.* [ME f. L *immaculatus* (as IN-[1], *maculatus* f. *macula* spot)]

immanent /ˈɪmənənt/ *adj.* **1** (often foll. by *in*) indwelling, inherent. **2** (of the supreme being) permanently pervading the universe. □ **immanence** *n.* **immanency** *n.* **immanentism** *n.* **immanentist** *n.* [LL *immanēre* (as IN-[2], *manēre* remain)]

immaterial /ˌɪməˈtɪərɪəl/ *adj.* **1** of no essential consequence; unimportant. **2** not material; incorporeal. □ **immateriality** /-ˈælɪtɪ/ *n.* **immaterialize** *v.tr.* (also **-ise**). **immaterially** *adv.* [ME f. LL *immaterialis* (as IN-[1], MATERIAL)]

immature /ˌɪməˈtjʊə(r)/ *adj.* **1** not mature or fully developed. **2** lacking emotional or intellectual development. **3** unripe. □ **immaturely** *adv.* **immaturity** *n.* [L *immaturus* (as IN-[1], MATURE)]

immeasurable /ɪˈmeʒərəb(ə)l/ *adj.* not measurable; immense. □ **immeasurability** /-ˈbɪlɪtɪ/ *n.* **immeasurableness** *n.* **immeasurably** *adv.*

immediate /ɪˈmiːdɪət/ *adj.* **1** occurring or done at once or without delay (*an immediate reply*). **2** nearest, next; not separated by others (*the immediate vicinity; the immediate future*). **3** most pressing or urgent (*our immediate concern was to get him to hospital*). **4** (of a relation or action) having direct effect; without an intervening medium or agency (*the immediate cause of death*). □ **immediacy** *n.* **immediateness** *n.* [ME f. F *immédiat* or LL *immediatus* (as IN-[1], MEDIATE)]

immediately /ɪˈmiːdɪətlɪ/ *adj.* & *conj.* —*adv.* **1** without pause or delay. **2** without intermediary. —*conj.* as soon as.

immemorial /ˌɪmɪˈmɔːrɪəl/ *adj.* **1** ancient beyond memory or record. **2** very old. □ **immemorially** *adv.* [med.L *immemorialis* (as IN-[1], MEMORIAL)]

immense /ɪˈmens/ *adj.* **1** immeasurably large or great; huge. **2** very great; considerable (*made an immense difference*). **3** *colloq.* very good. □ **immenseness** *n.* **immensity** *n.* [ME f. F f. L *immensus* immeasurable (as IN-[1], *mensus* past part. of *metiri* measure)]

immensely /ɪˈmenslɪ/ *adv.* **1** very much (*enjoyed myself immensely*). **2** to an immense degree.

immerse /ɪˈmɜːs/ *v.tr.* **1 a** (often foll. by *in*) dip, plunge. **b** cause (a person) to be completely under water. **2** (often *refl.* or in *passive*; often foll. by *in*) absorb or involve deeply. **3** (often foll. by *in*) bury, embed. [L *immergere* (as IN-[2], *mergere mers-* dip)]

immersion /ɪˈmɜːʃ(ə)n/ *n.* **1** the act or an instance of immersing; the process of being immersed. **2** baptism by immersing the whole person in water. **3** mental absorption. □ **immersion heater** an electric heater designed for direct immersion in a liquid to be heated, esp. as a fixture in a hot-water tank. [ME f. LL *immersio* (as IMMERSE)]

immigrant /ˈɪmɪɡrənt/ *n.* & *adj.* —*n.* a person who immigrates. —*adj.* **1** immigrating. **2** of or concerning immigrants.

immigrate /ˈɪmɪˌɡreɪt/ *v.* **1** *intr.* come as a permanent resident to a country other than one's native land. **2** *tr.* bring in (a person) as an immigrant. □ **immigration** /-ˈɡreɪʃ(ə)n/ *n.* **immigratory** *adj.* [L *immigrare* (as IN-[2], MIGRATE)]

imminent /ˈɪmɪnənt/ adj. (of an event, esp. danger) impending; about to happen. □ **imminence** n. **imminently** adv. [L imminēre imminent-overhang, project]

immiscible /ɪˈmɪsɪb(ə)l/ adj. (often foll. by with) that cannot be mixed. □ **immiscibility** /-ˈbɪlɪtɪ/ n. **immiscibly** adv. [LL immiscibilis (as IN-¹, MISCIBLE)]

immobile /ɪˈməʊbaɪl/ adj. 1 not moving. 2 not able to move or be moved. □ **immobility** /-ˈbɪlɪtɪ/ n. [ME f. OF f. L immobilis (as IN-¹, MOBILE)]

immobilize /ɪˈməʊbɪˌlaɪz/ v.tr. (also -**ise**) 1 make or keep immobile. 2 make (a vehicle or troops) incapable of being moved. 3 keep (a limb or patient) restricted in movement for healing purposes. 4 restrict the free movement of. □ **immobilization** /-ˈzeɪʃ(ə)n/ n. **immobilizer** n. [F immobiliser (as IMMOBILE)]

immoderate /ɪˈmɒdərət/ adj. excessive; lacking moderation. □ **immoderately** adv. **immoderateness** n. **immoderation** /-ˈreɪʃ(ə)n/ n. [ME f. L immoderatus (as IN-¹, MODERATE)]

immodest /ɪˈmɒdɪst/ adj. 1 lacking modesty; forward, impudent. 2 lacking due decency. □ **immodestly** adv. **immodesty** n. [F immodeste or L immodestus (as IN-¹, MODEST)]

immolate /ˈɪməˌleɪt/ v.tr. kill or offer as a sacrifice. □ **immolation** /-ˈleɪʃ(ə)n/ n. **immolator** n. [L immolare sprinkle with sacrificial meal (as IN-², mola MEAL²)]

immoral /ɪˈmɒr(ə)l/ adj. 1 not conforming to accepted standards of morality. 2 morally wrong (esp. in sexual matters). 3 depraved, dissolute. □ **immorality** /ˌɪməˈrælɪtɪ/ n. (pl. -**ies**). **immorally** adv.

immortal /ɪˈmɔːt(ə)l/ adj. & n. —adj. 1 **a** living for ever; not mortal. **b** divine. 2 unfading, incorruptible. 3 likely or worthy to be famous for all time. —n. 1 **a** an immortal being. **b** (in pl.) the gods of antiquity. 2 a person (esp. an author) of enduring fame. □ **immortality** /ˌɪmɔːˈtælɪtɪ/ n. **immortalization** /-ˈzeɪʃ(ə)n/ n. **immortalize** v.tr. (also -**ise**). **immortally** adv. [ME f. L immortalis (as IN-¹, MORTAL)]

immortelle /ˌɪmɔːˈtel/ n. a composite flower of papery texture retaining its shape and colour after being dried. [F, fem. of immortel IMMORTAL]

immovable /ɪˈmuːvəb(ə)l/ adj. & n. (also **immoveable**) —adj. 1 that cannot be moved. 2 steadfast, unyielding. 3 emotionless. 4 not subject to change (immovable law). 5 motionless. 6 Law (of property) consisting of land, houses, etc. —n. (in pl.) Law immovable property. □ **immovability** /-ˈbɪlɪtɪ/ n. **immovableness** n. **immovably** adv.

immune /ɪˈmjuːn/ adj. 1 **a** (often foll. by against, from, to) protected against an infection owing to the presence of specific antibodies, or through inoculation or inherited or acquired resistance. **b** relating to immunity (immune mechanism). 2 (foll. by from, to) free or exempt from or not subject to (some undesirable factor or circumstance). □ **immune response** the reaction of the body to the introduction into it of an antigen. [ME f. L immunis exempt from public service or charge (as IN-¹, munis ready for service): sense 1 f. F immun]

immunity /ɪˈmjuːnɪtɪ/ n. (pl. -**ies**) 1 Med. the ability of an organism to resist infection, by means of the presence of circulating antibodies and white blood cells. 2 freedom or exemption from an obligation, penalty, or unfavourable circumstance. [ME f. L immunitas (as IMMUNE): sense 1 f. F immunité]

immunize /ˈɪmjuːˌnaɪz/ v.tr. (also -**ise**) make immune, esp. to infection, usu. by inoculation. □ **immunization** /-ˈzeɪʃ(ə)n/ n. **immunizer** n.

immuno- /ˈɪmjuːnəʊ/ comb. form immunity to infection.

immunodeficiency /ˌɪmjuːˌnəʊdɪˈfɪʃənsɪ/ n. a reduction in a person's normal immune defences.

immunogenic /ˌɪmjuːnəʊˈdʒenɪk/ adj. Biochem. of, relating to, or possessing the ability to elicit an immune response.

immunology /ˌɪmjuːˈnɒlədʒɪ/ n. the scientific study of immunity. □ **immunologic** /-nəˈlɒdʒɪk/ adj. **immunological** /-nəˈlɒdʒɪk(ə)l/ adj. **immunologically** /-nəˈlɒdʒɪkəlɪ/ adv. **immunologist** n.

immunosuppression /ˌɪmjuːnəʊsəˈpreʃ(ə)n/ n. Biochem. the partial or complete suppression of the immune response of an individual, esp. to maintain the survival of an organ after a transplant operation. □ **immunosuppressant** n.

immunosuppressive /ˌɪmjuːnəʊsəˈpresɪv/ adj. & n. —adj. partially or completely suppressing the immune response of an individual. —n. an immunosuppressive drug.

immure /ɪˈmjʊə(r)/ v.tr. 1 enclose within walls; imprison. 2 refl. shut oneself away. □ **immurement** n. [F emmurer or med.L immurare (as IN-², murus wall)]

immutable /ɪˈmjuːtəb(ə)l/ adj. 1 unchangeable. 2 not subject to variation in different cases. □ **immutability** /-ˈbɪlɪtɪ/ n. **immutably** adv. [ME f. L immutabilis (as IN-¹, MUTABLE)]

imp n. 1 a mischievous child. 2 a small mischievous devil or sprite. [OE impa, impe young shoot, scion, impian graft: ult. f. Gk emphutos implanted, past part. of emphuō]

impact n. & v. —n. /ˈɪmpækt/ 1 (often foll. by on, against) the action of one body coming forcibly into contact with another. 2 an effect or influence, esp. when strong. —v.tr. /ɪmˈpækt/ 1 (often foll. by in, into) press or fix firmly. 2 (as **impacted** adj.) **a** (of a tooth) wedged between another tooth and the jaw. **b** (of a fractured bone) with the parts crushed together. □ **impaction** /ɪmˈpækʃ(ə)n/ n. [L impact- part. stem of impingere IMPINGE]

impair /ɪmˈpeə(r)/ v.tr. damage or weaken. □ **impairment** n. [ME empeire f. OF empeirier (as IN-², LL pejorare f. L pejor worse)]

impala /ɪmˈpɑːlə, -ˈpælə/ n. (pl. same) a small antelope, Aepyceros melampus, of S. and E. Africa, capable of long high jumps. [Zulu]

impale /ɪmˈpeɪl/ v.tr. (foll. by on, upon, with) transfix or pierce with a sharp instrument. □ **impalement** n. [F empaler or med.L impalare (as IN-², palus stake)]

impalpable /ɪmˈpælpəb(ə)l/ adj. 1 not easily grasped by the mind; intangible. 2 imperceptible to the touch. □ **impalpability** /-ˈbɪlɪtɪ/ n. **impalpably** adv. [F impalpable or LL impalpabilis (as IN-¹, PALPABLE)]

impanel var. of EMPANEL.

impart /ɪmˈpɑːt/ v.tr. (often foll. by to) 1 communicate (news etc.). 2 give a share of (a thing). □ **impartable** adj. **impartation**

/ˌɪmpɑːˈteɪʃ(ə)n/ n. **impartment** n. [ME f. OF *impartir* f. L *impartire* (as IN-², *pars* part)]

impartial /ɪmˈpɑːʃ(ə)l/ adj. treating all sides in a dispute etc. equally; unprejudiced, fair. □ **impartiality** /-ʃɪˈælɪtɪ/ n. **impartially** adv.

impassable /ɪmˈpɑːsəb(ə)l/ adj. that cannot be traversed. □ **impassability** /-ˈbɪlɪtɪ/ n. **impassableness** n. **impassably** adv.

impasse /ˈæmpæs, ˈɪm-/ n. a position from which progress is impossible; deadlock. [F (as IN-¹, *passer* PASS¹)]

impassible /ɪmˈpæsɪb(ə)l/ adj. **1** impassive. **2** incapable of feeling or emotion. **3** incapable of suffering injury. □ **impassibility** /-ˈbɪlɪtɪ/ n. **impassibleness** n. **impassibly** adv. [ME f. OF f. eccl.L *impassibilis*]

impassioned /ɪmˈpæʃ(ə)nd/ adj. deeply felt; ardent (*an impassioned plea*). [It. *impassionare* (as IN-², PASSION]

impassive /ɪmˈpæsɪv/ adj. **1** deficient in or incapable of feeling emotion. **2** undisturbed by passion; serene. □ **impassively** adv. **impassiveness** n. **impassivity** /-ˈsɪvɪtɪ/ n.

impasto /ɪmˈpæstəʊ/ n. Art **1** the process of laying on paint thickly. **2** this technique of painting. [It. *impastare* (as IN-², *pastare* paste)]

impatient /ɪmˈpeɪʃ(ə)nt/ adj. **1 a** (often foll. by *at, with*) lacking patience or tolerance. **b** (of an action) showing a lack of patience. **2** (often foll. by *for*, or *to* + infin.) restlessly eager. **3** (foll. by *of*) intolerant. □ **impatience** n. **impatiently** adv. [ME f. OF f. L *impatiens* (as IN-¹, PATIENT)]

impeach /ɪmˈpiːtʃ/ v.tr. **1** Brit. charge with a crime against the State, esp. treason. **2** US charge (the holder of a public office) with misconduct. **3** call in question, disparage (a person's integrity etc.). □ **impeachable** adj. **impeachment** n. [ME f. OF *empecher* impede f. LL *impedicare* entangle (as IN-², *pedica* fetter f. *pes pedis* foot)]

impeccable /ɪmˈpekəb(ə)l/ adj. **1** (of behaviour, performance, etc.) faultless, exemplary. **2** not liable to sin. □ **impeccability** /-ˈbɪlɪtɪ/ n. **impeccably** adv. [L *impeccabilis* (as IN-¹, *peccare* sin)]

impecunious /ˌɪmpɪˈkjuːnɪəs/ adj. having little or no money. □ **impecuniosity** /-ˈɒsɪtɪ/ n. **impecuniousness** n. [IN-¹ + obs. *pecunious* having money f. L *pecuniosus* f. *pecunia* money f. *pecu* cattle]

impedance /ɪmˈpiːd(ə)ns/ n. Electr. the total effective resistance of an electric circuit etc. to alternating current. [IMPEDE + -ANCE]

■ **Usage** This word is sometimes confused with *impediment*, which means 'a hindrance' or 'a speech defect'.

impede /ɪmˈpiːd/ v.tr. retard by obstructing; hinder. [L *impedire* shackle the feet of (as IN-², *pes* foot)]

impediment /ɪmˈpedɪmənt/ n. **1** a hindrance or obstruction. **2** a defect in speech, e.g. a lisp or stammer. □ **impedimental** /-ˈment(ə)l/ adj. [ME f. L *impedimentum* (as IMPEDE)]

■ **Usage** See note at *impedance*.

impedimenta /ɪmˌpedɪˈmentə/ n.pl. **1** encumbrances. **2** travelling equipment, esp. of an army. [L, pl. of *impedimentum*: see IMPEDIMENT]

impel /ɪmˈpel/ v.tr. (**impelled**, **impelling**) **1** drive, force, or urge into action. **2** drive forward;

propel. □ **impellent** adj. & n. **impeller** n. [ME f. L *impellere* (as IN-², *pellere puls-* drive)]

impend /ɪmˈpend/ v.intr. **1** be about to happen. **2** (often foll. by *over*) **a** (of a danger) be threatening. **b** hang; be suspended. □ **impending** adj. [L *impendere* (as IN-², *pendēre* hang)]

impenetrable /ɪmˈpenɪtrəb(ə)l/ adj. **1** that cannot be penetrated. **2** inscrutable, unfathomable. **3** inaccessible to ideas, influences, etc. □ **impenetrability** /-ˈbɪlɪtɪ/ n. **impenetrableness** n. **impenetrably** adv. [ME f. F *impénétrable* f. L *impenetrabilis* (as IN-¹, PENETRATE)]

impenitent /ɪmˈpenɪt(ə)nt/ adj. not repentant or penitent. □ **impenitence** n. **impenitency** n. **impenitently** adv. [eccl.L *impaenitens* (as IN-¹, PENITENT)]

imperative /ɪmˈperətɪv/ adj. & n. —adj. **1** urgent. **2** obligatory. **3** commanding, peremptory. **4** Gram. (of a mood) expressing a command (e.g. *come here!*). —n. **1** Gram. the imperative mood. **2** a command. □ **imperatival** /ɪmperəˈtaɪv(ə)l/ adj. **imperatively** adv. **imperativeness** n. [LL *imperativus* f. *imperare* command (as IN-², *parare* make ready)]

imperceptible /ˌɪmpəˈseptɪb(ə)l/ adj. **1** that cannot be perceived. **2** very slight, gradual, or subtle. □ **imperceptibility** /-ˈbɪlɪtɪ/ n. **imperceptibly** adv. [F *imperceptible* or med.L *imperceptibilis* (as IN-¹, PERCEPTIBLE)]

imperfect /ɪmˈpɜːfɪkt/ adj. & n. —adj. **1** not fully formed or done; faulty, incomplete. **2** Gram. (of a tense) denoting a (usu. past) action in progress but not completed at the time in question (e.g. *they were singing*). —n. the imperfect tense. □ **imperfectly** adv. [ME *imparfit* etc. f. OF *imparfait* f. L *imperfectus* (as IN-¹, PERFECT)]

imperfection /ˌɪmpəˈfekʃ(ə)n/ n. **1** incompleteness. **2** a faultiness. **b** a fault or blemish. [ME f. OF *imperfection* or LL *imperfectio* (as IMPERFECT)]

imperial /ɪmˈpɪərɪəl/ adj. **1** of or characteristic of an empire or comparable sovereign State. **2 a** of or characteristic of an emperor. **b** supreme in authority. **c** majestic, august. **d** magnificent. **3** (of non-metric weights and measures) used or formerly used by statute in the UK (*imperial gallon*). □ **imperially** adv. [ME f. OF f. L *imperialis* f. *imperium* command, authority]

imperialism /ɪmˈpɪərɪəlɪz(ə)m/ n. **1** an imperial rule or system. **2** usu. derog. a policy of acquiring dependent territories or extending a country's influence through trade, diplomacy, etc. □ **imperialistic** /-ˈlɪstɪk/ adj. **imperialistically** /-ˈlɪstɪkəlɪ/ adv. **imperialize** v.tr. (also **-ise**).

imperialist /ɪmˈpɪərɪəlɪst/ n. & adj. —n. usu. derog. an advocate or agent of imperial rule or of imperialism. —adj. of or relating to imperialism or imperialists.

imperil /ɪmˈperɪl/ v.tr. (**imperilled**, **imperilling**; US **imperiled**, **imperiling**) bring or put into danger.

imperious /ɪmˈpɪərɪəs/ adj. **1** overbearing, domineering. **2** urgent, imperative. □ **imperiously** adv. **imperiousness** n. [L *imperiosus* f. *imperium* command, authority]

imperishable /ɪmˈperɪʃəb(ə)l/ adj. that cannot perish. □ **imperishability** /-ˈbɪlɪtɪ/ n. **imperishableness** n. **imperishably** adv.

impermanent /ɪmˈpɜːmənənt/ adj. not permanent; transient. □ **impermanence** n. **impermanency** n. **impermanently** adv.

impermeable /ɪmˈpɜːmɪəb(ə)l/ *adj.* **1** that cannot be penetrated. **2** *Physics* that does not permit the passage of fluids. □ **impermeability** /-ˈbɪlɪtɪ/ *n.* [F *imperméable* or LL *impermeabilis* (as IN-¹, PERMEABLE)]

impermissible /ɪmpəˈmɪsɪb(ə)l/ *adj.* not allowable. □ **impermissibility** /-ˈbɪlɪtɪ/ *n.*

impersonal /ɪmˈpɜːsən(ə)l/ *adj.* **1** having no personality. **2** having no personal feeling or reference. **3** *Gram.* **a** (of a verb) used only with a formal subject (usu. *it*) and expressing an action not attributable to a definite subject (e.g. *it is snowing*). **b** (of a pronoun) = INDEFINITE. □ **impersonality** /-ˈnælɪtɪ/ *n.* **impersonally** *adv.* [LL *impersonalis* (as IN-¹, PERSONAL)]

impersonate /ɪmˈpɜːsəˌneɪt/ *v.tr.* **1** pretend to be (another person) for the purpose of entertainment or fraud. **2** act (a character). □ **impersonation** /-ˈneɪʃ(ə)n/ *n.* **impersonator** *n.* [IN-² + L *persona* PERSON]

impertinent /ɪmˈpɜːtɪnənt/ *adj.* **1** rude or insolent; lacking proper respect. **2** out of place; absurd. □ **impertinence** *n.* **impertinently** *adv.* [ME f. OF or LL *impertinens* (as IN-¹, PERTINENT)]

imperturbable /ɪmpəˈtɜːbəb(ə)l/ *adj.* not excitable; calm. □ **imperturbability** /-ˈbɪlɪtɪ/ *n.* **imperturbableness** *n.* **imperturbably** *adv.* [ME f. LL *imperturbabilis* (as IN-¹, PERTURB)]

impervious /ɪmˈpɜːvɪəs/ *adj.* (usu. foll. by *to*) **1** not responsive to an argument etc. **2** not affording passage to a fluid. □ **imperviously** *adv.* **imperviousness** *n.* [L *impervius* (as IN-¹, PERVIOUS)]

impetigo /ˌɪmpɪˈtaɪɡəʊ/ *n.* a contagious bacterial skin infection forming pustules and yellow crusty sores. □ **impetiginous** /ˌɪmpɪˈtɪdʒɪnəs/ *adj.* [ME f. L *impetigo -ginis* f. *impetere* assail]

impetuous /ɪmˈpetjʊəs/ *adj.* **1** acting or done rashly or with sudden energy. **2** moving forcefully or rapidly. □ **impetuosity** /-ˈɒsɪtɪ/ *n.* **impetuously** *adv.* **impetuousness** *n.* [ME f. OF *impetueux* f. LL *impetuosus* (as IMPETUS)]

impetus /ˈɪmpɪtəs/ *n.* **1** the force or energy with which a body moves. **2** a driving force or impulse. [L, = assault, force, f. *impetere* assail (as IN-², *petere* seek)]

impiety /ɪmˈpaɪətɪ/ *n.* (pl. **-ies**) **1** a lack of piety or reverence. **2** an act etc. showing this. [ME f. OF *impiété* or L *impietas* (as IN-¹, PIETY)]

impinge /ɪmˈpɪndʒ/ *v.tr.* (usu. foll. by *on, upon*) **1** make an impact; have an effect. **2** encroach. □ **impingement** *n.* **impinger** *n.* [L *impingere* drive (a thing) at (as IN-², *pangere* fix, drive)]

impious /ˈɪmpɪəs/ *adj.* **1** not pious. **2** wicked, profane. □ **impiously** *adv.* **impiousness** *n.* [L *impius* (as IN-¹, PIOUS)]

impish /ˈɪmpɪʃ/ *adj.* of or like an imp; mischievous. □ **impishly** *adv.* **impishness** *n.*

implacable /ɪmˈplækəb(ə)l/ *adj.* that cannot be appeased; inexorable. □ **implacability** /-ˈbɪlɪtɪ/ *n.* **implacably** *adv.* [ME f. F *implacable* or L *implacabilis* (as IN-¹, PLACABLE)]

implant *v. & n.* —*v.tr.* /ɪmˈplɑːnt/ **1** (often foll. by *in*) insert or fix. **2** (often foll. by *in*) instil (a principle, idea, etc.) in a person's mind. **3** plant. **4** *Med.* **a** insert (tissue etc.) in a living body. **b** (in *passive*) (of a fertilized ovum) become attached to the wall of the womb. —*n.* /ˈɪmplɑːnt/ *n.* **1** a thing implanted. **2** a thing implanted in the body, e.g. a piece of tissue or a capsule containing material for radium therapy. □

implantation /-ˈteɪʃ(ə)n/ *n.* [F *implanter* or LL *implantare* engraft (as IN-², PLANT)]

implausible /ɪmˈplɔːzɪb(ə)l/ *adj.* not plausible. □ **implausibility** /-ˈbɪlɪtɪ/ *n.* **implausibly** *adv.*

implement *n. & v.* —*n.* /ˈɪmplɪmənt/ **1** a tool, instrument, or utensil. **2** (in *pl.*) equipment; articles of furniture, dress, etc. —*v.tr.* /ˈɪmplɪˌment/ **1 a** put (a decision, plan, etc.) into effect. **b** fulfil (an undertaking). **2** complete (a contract etc.). □ **implementation** /ˌɪmplɪmenˈteɪʃ(ə)n/ *n.* [ME f. med.L *implementa* (pl.) f. *implēre* employ (as IN-², L *plēre plet-* fill)]

implicate *v. & n.* —*v.tr.* /ˈɪmplɪˌkeɪt/ **1** (often foll. by *in*) show (a person) to be concerned or involved (in a charge, crime, etc.). **2** (in *passive*; often foll. by *in*) be affected or involved. **3** lead to as a consequence or inference. —*n.* /ˈɪmplɪkət/ a thing implied. □ **implicative** /ɪmˈplɪkətɪv/ *adj.* **implicatively** /ɪmˈplɪkətɪvlɪ/ *adv.* [L *implicatus* past part. of *implicare* (as IN-², *plicare*, *plicat-* or *plicit-* fold)]

implication /ˌɪmplɪˈkeɪʃ(ə)n/ *n.* **1** what is involved in or implied by something else. **2** the act of implicating or implying. □ **by implication** by what is implied or suggested rather than by formal expression. [ME f. L *implicatio* (as IMPLICATE)]

implicit /ɪmˈplɪsɪt/ *adj.* **1** implied though not plainly expressed. **2** absolute, unquestioning, unreserved (*implicit obedience*). □ **implicitly** *adv.* **implicitness** *n.* [F *implicite* or L *implicitus* (as IMPLICATE)]

implode /ɪmˈpləʊd/ *v.intr. & tr.* burst or cause to burst inwards. □ **implosion** /ɪmˈpləʊʒ(ə)n/ *n.* **implosive** /-sɪv, -zɪv/ *adj.* [IN-² + L *-plodere*, after EXPLODE]

implore /ɪmˈplɔː(r)/ *v.tr.* **1** (often foll. by *to* + infin.) entreat (a person). **2** beg earnestly for. □ **imploringly** *adv.* [F *implorer* or L *implorare* invoke with tears (as IN-², *plorare* weep)]

imply /ɪmˈplaɪ/ *v.tr.* (**-ies, -ied**) **1** (often foll. by *that* + clause) strongly suggest the truth or existence of (a thing not expressly asserted). **2** insinuate, hint (*what are you implying?*). **3** signify. □ **implied** *adj.* **impliedly** *adv.* [ME f. OF *emplier* f. L *implicare* (as IMPLICATE)]

impolite /ˌɪmpəˈlaɪt/ *adj.* (**impolitest**) ill-mannered, uncivil, rude. □ **impolitely** *adv.* **impoliteness** *n.* [L *impolitus* (as IN-¹, POLITE)]

impolitic /ɪmˈpɒlɪtɪk/ *adj.* **1** inexpedient, unwise. **2** not politic. □ **impoliticly** *adv.*

imponderable /ɪmˈpɒndərəb(ə)l/ *adj. & n.* —*adj.* that cannot be estimated or assessed in any definite way. —*n.* (usu. in *pl.*) something difficult or impossible to assess. □ **imponderability** /-ˈbɪlɪtɪ/ *n.* **imponderably** *adv.*

import *v. & n.* —*v.tr.* /ɪmˈpɔːt, ˈɪm-/ **1** bring in (esp. foreign goods or services) to a country. **2** (often foll. by *that* + clause) **a** imply, indicate, signify. **b** express, make known. —*n.* /ˈɪmpɔːt/ **1** the process of importing. **2 a** an imported article or service. **b** (in *pl.*) an amount imported (*imports exceeded £50m.*). **3** what is implied; meaning. **4** importance. □ **importable** /ɪmˈpɔːtəb(ə)l/ *adj.* **importation** /ˌɪmpɔːˈteɪʃ(ə)n/ *n.* **importer** /ɪmˈpɔːtə(r)/ *n.* (all in sense 1 of *v.*). [ME f. L *importare* bring in, in med.L = imply, be of consequence (as IN-², *portare* carry)]

importance /ɪmˈpɔːt(ə)ns/ *n.* **1** the state of being important. **2** weight, significance. **3** personal consequence; dignity. [F f. med.L *importantia* (as IMPORT)]

important /ɪmˈpɔːt(ə)nt/ *adj.* **1** (often foll. by *to*) of great effect or consequence; momentous. **2** (of a person) having high rank or status, or great authority. **3** pretentious, pompous. □ **importantly** *adv.* [F f. med.L (as IMPORT)]

importunate /ɪmˈpɔːtjʊnət/ *adj.* **1** making persistent or pressing requests. **2** (of affairs) urgent. □ **importunately** *adv.* **importunity** /ˌɪmpɔːˈtjuːnɪtɪ/ *n.* [L *importunus* inconvenient (as IN-¹, *portunus* f. *portus* harbour)]

importune /ɪmˈpɔːtjuːn, -ˈtjuːn/ *v.tr.* **1** solicit (a person) pressingly. **2** solicit for an immoral purpose. [F *importuner* or med.L *importunari* (as IMPORTUNATE)]

impose /ɪmˈpəʊz/ *v.* **1** *tr.* (often foll. by *on*, *upon*) require (a tax, duty, charge, or obligation) to be paid or undertaken (by a person etc.). **2** *tr.* enforce compliance with. **3** *intr.* & *refl.* (foll. by *on*, *upon*, or *absol.*) demand the attention or commitment of (a person) (*I do not want to impose on you any longer*). **4** *tr.* (often foll. by *on*, *upon*) palm (a thing) off on (a person). **5** *intr.* (often foll. by *on*, *upon*) practise deception. [ME f. F *imposer* f. L *imponere imposit-* inflict, deceive (as IN-², *ponere* put)]

imposing /ɪmˈpəʊzɪŋ/ *adj.* impressive, esp. in appearance. □ **imposingly** *adv.* **imposingness** *n.*

imposition /ˌɪmpəˈzɪʃ(ə)n/ *n.* **1** the act or an instance of imposing; the process of being imposed. **2** an unfair or resented demand or burden. **3** a tax or duty. [ME f. OF *imposition* or L *impositio* f. *imponere*: see IMPOSE]

impossibility /ɪmˌpɒsɪˈbɪlɪtɪ/ *n.* (*pl.* -ies) **1** the fact or condition of being impossible. **2** an impossible thing or circumstance. [F *impossibilité* or L *impossibilitas* (as IMPOSSIBLE)]

impossible /ɪmˈpɒsɪb(ə)l/ *adj.* **1** not possible; that cannot occur, exist, or be done (*such a thing is impossible*; *it is impossible to alter them*). **2** (loosely) not easy; not convenient; not easily believable. **3** *colloq.* (of a person or thing) outrageous, intolerable. □ **impossibly** *adv.* [ME f. OF *impossible* or L *impossibilis* (as IN-¹, POSSIBLE)]

impost /ˈɪmpəʊst/ *n.* a tax, duty, or tribute. [F f. med.L *impost-* part. stem of L *imponere*: see IMPOSE]

impostor /ɪmˈpɒstə(r)/ *n.* (also **imposter**) **1** a person who assumes a false character or pretends to be someone else. **2** a swindler. □ **impostorous** *adj.* **impostrous** *adj.* [F *imposteur* f. LL *impostor* (as IMPOST)]

imposture /ɪmˈpɒstʃə(r)/ *n.* the act or an instance of fraudulent deception. [F f. LL *impostura* (as IMPOST)]

impotent /ˈɪmpət(ə)nt/ *adj.* **1 a** powerless; lacking all strength. **b** helpless, decrepit. **2** (esp. of a male) unable to achieve a sexual erection or orgasm. □ **impotence** *n.* **impotency** *n.* **impotently** *adv.* [ME f. OF f. L *impotens* (as IN-¹, POTENT)]

impound /ɪmˈpaʊnd/ *v.tr.* **1** confiscate. **2** take possession of. **3** shut up in a pound. □ **impoundable** *adj.* **impounder** *n.* **impoundment** *n.*

impoverish /ɪmˈpɒvərɪʃ/ *v.tr.* **1** make poor. **2** exhaust the strength or natural fertility of. □ **impoverishment** *n.* [ME f. OF *empoverir* (as EN-¹, *povre* POOR)]

impracticable /ɪmˈpræktɪkəb(ə)l/ *adj.* impossible in practice. □ **impracticability** /-ˈbɪlɪtɪ/ *n.* **impracticableness** *n.* **impracticably** *adv.*

impractical /ɪmˈpræktɪk(ə)l/ *adj.* **1** not practical. **2** esp. *US* not practicable. □ **impracticality** /-ˈkælɪtɪ/ *n.* **impractically** *adv.*

imprecate /ˈɪmprɪˌkeɪt/ *v.tr.* (often foll. by *upon*) invoke, call down (evil). □ **imprecatory** *adj.* [L *imprecari* (as IN-², *precari* pray)]

imprecation /ˌɪmprɪˈkeɪʃ(ə)n/ *n.* **1** a spoken curse; a malediction. **2** imprecating.

imprecise /ˌɪmprɪˈsaɪs/ *adj.* not precise. □ **imprecisely** *adv.* **impreciseness** *n.* **imprecision** /-ˈsɪʒ(ə)n/ *n.*

impregnable /ɪmˈpregnəb(ə)l/ *adj.* (of a fortified position) that cannot be taken by force. □ **impregnability** /-ˈbɪlɪtɪ/ *n.* **impregnably** *adv.* [ME f. OF *imprenable* (as IN-¹, *prendre* take)]

impregnate *v.tr.* /ˈɪmpregˌneɪt/ **1** (often foll. by *with*) fill or saturate. **2** (often foll. by *with*) imbue, fill (with feelings, moral qualities, etc.). **3** make (a female) pregnant. □ **impregnation** /ˌɪmpregˈneɪʃ(ə)n/ *n.* [LL *impregnare impregnat-* (as IN-², *pregnare* be pregnant)]

impresario /ˌɪmprɪˈsɑːrɪəʊ/ *n.* (*pl.* -os) an organizer of public entertainments. [It. f. *impresa* undertaking]

impress¹ *v.* & *n.* —*v.tr.* /ɪmˈpres/ **1** (often foll. by *with*) **a** affect or influence deeply. **b** evoke a favourable opinion or reaction from (a person) (*was most impressed with your efforts*). **2** (often foll. by *on*) emphasize (an idea etc.) (*must impress on you the need to be prompt*). **3** (often foll. by *on*) **a** imprint or stamp. **b** apply (a mark etc.) with pressure. **4** make a mark or design on (a thing) with a stamp, seal, etc. —*n.* /ˈɪmpres/ **1** the act or an instance of impressing. **2** a mark made by a seal, stamp, etc. **3** a characteristic mark or quality. **4** = IMPRESSION 1. □ **impressible** /ɪmˈpresɪb(ə)l/ *adj.* [ME f. OF *empresser* (as EN-¹, PRESS¹)]

impress² /ɪmˈpres/ *v.tr. hist.* force (men) to serve in the army or navy. □ **impressment** *n.* [IN-² + PRESS²]

impression /ɪmˈpreʃ(ə)n/ *n.* **1** an effect produced (esp. on the mind or feelings). **2** a notion or belief (esp. a vague or mistaken one) (*my impression is they are afraid*). **3** an imitation of a person or sound, esp. done to entertain. **4 a** the impressing of a mark. **b** a mark impressed. **5** an unaltered reprint from standing type or plates (esp. as distinct from *edition*). **6** the number of copies of a book, newspaper, etc., issued at one time. **7** *Dentistry* a negative copy of the teeth or mouth made by pressing them into a soft substance. □ **impressional** *adj.* [ME f. OF f. L *impressio -onis* f. *imprimere impress-* (as IN-², PRESS¹)]

impressionable /ɪmˈpreʃənəb(ə)l/ *adj.* easily influenced; susceptible to impressions. □ **impressionability** /-ˈbɪlɪtɪ/ *n.* **impressionably** *adv.* [F *impressionnable* f. *impressionner* (as IMPRESSION)]

impressionism /ɪmˈpreʃəˌnɪz(ə)m/ *n.* a style or movement in art, music, etc. concerned with expression of feeling, rather than accurate depiction or systematic structure. □ **impressionist** *n.* [F *impressionnisme* (after *Impression: Soleil levant*, title of a painting by Monet, 1872)]

impressionistic /ɪmˌpreʃəˈnɪstɪk/ *adj.* **1** in the style of impressionism. **2** subjective, unsystematic. □ **impressionistically** *adv.*

impressive /ɪmˈpresɪv/ *adj.* **1** impressing the mind or senses, esp. so as to cause approval or admiration. **2** (of language, a scene, etc.) tending to excite deep feeling. □ **impressively** *adv.* **impressiveness** *n.*

imprimatur /ˌɪmprɪˈmeɪtə(r), -ˈmɑːtə(r), -tʊə(r)/ *n.* **1** *RC Ch.* an official licence to print (an ecclesiastical or religious book etc.). **2** official approval. [L, = let it be printed]

■ **Usage** This word is sometimes confused with sense 2 of *imprint.*

imprint *v.* & *n.* —*v.tr.* /ɪmˈprɪnt/ **1** (often foll. by *on*) impress or establish firmly, esp. on the mind. **2 a** (often foll. by *on*) make a stamp or impression of (a figure etc.) on a thing. **b** make an impression on (a thing) with a stamp etc. —*n.* /ˈɪmprɪnt/ **1** an impression or stamp. **2** the printer's or publisher's name and other details printed in a book. [ME f. OF *empreinter empreint* f. L *imprimere*: see IMPRESSION]

■ **Usage** See note at *imprimatur.*

imprinting /ɪmˈprɪntɪŋ/ *n.* **1** in senses of IMPRINT *v.* **2** *Zool.* the development in a young animal of a pattern of recognition and trust for its own species.

imprison /ɪmˈprɪz(ə)n/ *v.tr.* **1** put into prison. **2** confine; shut up. □ **imprisonment** *n.* [ME f. OF *emprisoner* (as EN-¹, PRISON)]

impro /ˈɪmprəʊ/ *n. colloq.* improvisation, esp. as a form of live entertainment.

improbable /ɪmˈprɒbəb(ə)l/ *adj.* **1** not likely to be true or to happen. **2** difficult to believe. □ **improbability** /-ˈbɪlɪtɪ/ *n.* **improbably** *adv.* [F *improbable* or L *improbabilis* (as IN-¹, PROBABLE)]

improbity /ɪmˈprəʊbɪtɪ/ *n.* (pl. **-ies**) wickedness; dishonesty. [L *improbitas* (as IN-¹, PROBITY)]

impromptu /ɪmˈprɒmptjuː/ *adj., adv., & n.* —*adj. & adv.* extempore, unrehearsed. —*n.* **1** an extempore performance or speech. **2** a short piece of usu. solo instrumental music, often songlike. [F f. L *in promptu* in readiness: see PROMPT]

improper /ɪmˈprɒpə(r)/ *adj.* **1 a** unseemly; indecent. **b** not in accordance with accepted rules of behaviour. **2** inaccurate, wrong. **3** not properly so called. □ **improper fraction** a fraction in which the numerator is greater than or equal to the denominator. □ **improperly** *adv.* [F *impropre* or L *improprius* (as IN-¹, PROPER)]

impropriety /ˌɪmprəˈpraɪətɪ/ *n.* (pl. **-ies**) **1** lack of propriety; indecency. **2** an instance of improper conduct etc. [F *impropriété* or L *improprietas* (as IN-¹, *proprius* proper)]

improvable /ɪmˈpruːvəb(ə)l/ *adj.* **1** that can be improved. **2** suitable for cultivation. □ **improvability** /-ˈbɪlɪtɪ/ *n.*

improve /ɪmˈpruːv/ *v.* **1 a** *tr. & intr.* make or become better. **b** *intr.* (foll. by *on, upon*) produce something better than. **2** *absol.* (as **improving** *adj.*) giving moral benefit (*improving literature*). □ **improver** *n.* [orig. *emprowe, improwe* f. AF *emprower* f. OF *emprou* f. *prou* profit, infl. by PROVE]

improvement /ɪmˈpruːvmənt/ *n.* **1** the act or an instance of improving or being improved. **2** something that improves, esp. an addition or alteration that adds to value. **3** something that

has been improved. [ME f. AF *emprowement* (as IMPROVE)]

improvident /ɪmˈprɒvɪd(ə)nt/ *adj.* **1** lacking foresight or care for the future. **2** not frugal; thriftless. □ **improvidence** *n.* **improvidently** *adv.*

improvise /ˈɪmprəˌvaɪz/ *v.tr.* (also *absol.*) **1** compose or perform (music, verse, etc.) extempore. **2** provide or construct (a thing) extempore. □ **improvisation** /-ˈzeɪʃ(ə)n/ *n.* **improvisational** /-ˈzeɪʃən(ə)l/ *adj.* **improvisatorial** /-zəˈtɔːrɪəl/ *adj.* **improvisatory** /-ˈzeɪtərɪ/ *adj.* **improviser** *n.* [F *improviser* or It. *improvvisare* f. *improvviso* extempore, f. L *improvisus* past part. (as IN-¹, PROVIDE)]

imprudent /ɪmˈpruːd(ə)nt/ *adj.* rash, indiscreet. □ **imprudence** *n.* **imprudently** *adv.* [ME f. L *imprudens* (as IN-¹, PRUDENT)]

impudent /ˈɪmpjʊd(ə)nt/ *adj.* **1** insolently disrespectful; impertinent. **2** shamelessly presumptuous. **3** unblushing. □ **impudence** *n.* **impudently** *adv.* [ME f. L *impudens* (as IN-¹, *pudere* be ashamed)]

impugn /ɪmˈpjuːn/ *v.tr.* challenge or call in question (a statement, action, etc.). □ **impugnable** *adj.* **impugnment** *n.* [ME f. L *impugnare* assail (as IN-², *pugnare* fight)]

impulse /ˈɪmpʌls/ *n.* **1** the act or an instance of impelling; a push. **2** an impetus. **3** *Physics* an indefinitely large force acting for a very short time but producing a finite change of momentum (e.g. the blow of a hammer). **4** a wave of excitation in a nerve. **5** a sudden desire or tendency to act without reflection (*did it on impulse*). [L *impulsus* (as IMPEL)]

impulsion /ɪmˈpʌlʃ(ə)n/ *n.* **1** the act or an instance of impelling. **2** a mental impulse. **3** impetus. [ME f. OF f. L *impulsio -onis* (as IMPEL)]

impulsive /ɪmˈpʌlsɪv/ *adj.* **1** (of a person or conduct etc.) apt to be affected or determined by sudden impulse. **2** tending to impel. **3** *Physics* acting as an impulse. □ **impulsively** *adv.* **impulsiveness** *n.* [ME f. F *impulsif -ive* or LL *impulsivus* (as IMPULSION)]

impunity /ɪmˈpjuːnɪtɪ/ *n.* exemption from punishment or from the injurious consequences of an action. □ **with impunity** without having to suffer the normal injurious consequences (of an action). [L *impunitas* f. *impunis* (as IN-¹, *poena* penalty)]

impure /ɪmˈpjʊə(r)/ *adj.* **1** mixed with foreign matter; adulterated. **2** dirty. **3** unchaste. **4** (of a colour) mixed with another colour. □ **impurely** *adv.* **impureness** *n.* [ME f. L *impurus* (as IN-¹, *purus* pure)]

impurity /ɪmˈpjʊərɪtɪ/ *n.* (pl. **-ies**) **1** the quality or condition of being impure. **2** an impure thing or constituent. [F *impurité* or L *impuritas* (as IMPURE)]

impute /ɪmˈpjuːt/ *v.tr.* (foll. by *to*) regard (esp. something undesirable) as being done or caused or possessed by. □ **imputable** *adj.* **imputation** /-ˈteɪʃ(ə)n/ *n.* **imputative** /-tətɪv/ *adj.* [ME f. OF *imputer* f. L *imputare* enter in the account (as IN-², *putare* reckon)]

In *symb. Chem.* the element indium.

in *prep., adv., & adj.* —*prep.* **1** expressing inclusion or position within limits of space, time, circumstance, etc. (*in England; in bed; in the rain*). **2** during the time of (*in the night; in 1989*). **3** within the time of (*will be back in two hours*). **4 a** with respect to (*blind in one eye; good in parts*). **b** as a kind of (*the latest thing in luxury*). **5** as a proportionate part of (*one in three failed; a gradient of one in six*). **6** with the form or arrangement of (*packed in tens; falling in folds*). **7** as a member of (*in the army*). **8** concerned with (*is in politics*). **9** as or regarding the content of (*there is something in what you say*). **10** within the ability of (*does he have it in him?*). **11** having the condition of; affected by (*in bad health; in danger*). **12** having as a purpose (*in search of; in reply to*). **13** by means of or using as material (*drawn in pencil; modelled in bronze*). **14 a** using as the language of expression (*written in French*). **b** (of music) having as its key (*symphony in C*). **15** (of a word) having as a beginning or ending (*words in un-*). **16** wearing as dress (*in blue; in a suit*). **17** with the identity of (*found a friend in Mary*). **18** (of an animal) pregnant with (*in calf*). **19** into (with a verb of motion or change: *put it in the box; cut it in two*). **20** introducing an indirect object after a verb (*believe in; engage in; share in*). **21** forming adverbial phrases (*in any case; in reality; in short*). —*adv.* expressing position within limits, or motion to such a position: **1** into a room, house, etc. (*come in*). **2** at home, in one's office, etc. (*is not in*). **3** so as to be enclosed or confined (*locked in*). **4** in a publication (*is the advertisement in?*). **5** in or to the inward side (*rub it in*). **6 a** in fashion, season, or office (*long skirts are in; strawberries are not yet in*). **b** elected (*the Democrat got in*). **7** exerting favourable action or influence (*their luck was in*). **8** *Cricket* (of a player or side) batting. **9** (of transport) at the platform etc. (*the train is in*). **10** (of a season, harvest, order, etc.) having arrived or been received. **11** *Brit.* (of a fire) continuing to burn. **12** denoting effective action (*join in*). **13** (of the tide) at the highest point. **14** (*in comb.*) *colloq.* denoting prolonged or concerted action, esp. by large numbers (*sit-in; teach-in*). —*adj.* **1** internal; living in; inside (*in-patient*). **2** fashionable, esoteric (*the in thing to do*). **3** confined to or shared by a group of people (*in-joke*). □ **in at present at; contributing to** (*in at the kill*). **in for 1** about to undergo (esp. something unpleasant). **2** competing in or for. **3** involved in; committed to. **in on** sharing in; privy to (*a secret etc.*). **ins and outs** (often foll. by *of*) all the details (of a procedure etc.). **in that** because; in so far as. **in with** on good terms with. [OE *in, inn*, orig. as adv. with verbs of motion]

in. *abbr.* inch(es).

in-¹ /ɪn/ *prefix* (also **il-, im-, ir-**) added to: **1** adjectives, meaning 'not' (*inedible; insane*). **2** nouns, meaning 'without, lacking' (*inaction*). [L]

in-² /ɪn/ *prefix* (also **il-** before *l*, **im-** before *b, m, p*, **ir-** before *r*) in, on, into, towards, within (*induce; influx; insight; intrude*). [IN, or from or after L *in* in IN *prep.*]

-in /ɪn/ *suffix Chem.* forming names of: **1** neutral substances (*gelatin*). **2** antibiotics (*penicillin*). [-INE⁴]

inability /ˌɪnəˈbɪlɪtɪ/ *n.* **1** the state of being unable. **2** a lack of power or means.

inaccessible /ˌɪnækˈsesɪb(ə)l/ *adj.* **1** not accessible; that cannot be reached. **2** (of a person) not open to advances or influence; unapproachable. □ **inaccessibility** /-ˈbɪlɪtɪ/ *n.* **inaccessibleness** *n.* **inaccessibly** *adv.* [ME f. F *inaccessible* or LL *inaccessibilis* (as IN-¹, ACCESSIBLE)]

inaccurate /ɪnˈækjʊrət/ *adj.* not accurate. □ **inaccuracy** *n.* (*pl.* **-ies**). **inaccurately** *adv.*

inaction /ɪnˈækʃ(ə)n/ *n.* **1** lack of action. **2** sluggishness, inertness.

inactivate /ɪnˈæktɪˌveɪt/ *v.tr.* make inactive or inoperative. □ **inactivation** /-ˈveɪʃ(ə)n/ *n.*

inactive /ɪnˈæktɪv/ *adj.* **1** not active or inclined to act. **2** passive. **3** indolent. □ **inactively** *adv.* **inactivity** /-ˈtɪvɪtɪ/ *n.*

inadequate /ɪnˈædɪkwət/ *adj.* (often foll. by *to*) **1** not adequate; insufficient. **2** (of a person) incompetent; unable to deal with a situation. □ **inadequacy** *n.* (*pl.* **-ies**). **inadequately** *adv.*

inadmissible /ˌɪnədˈmɪsɪb(ə)l/ *adj.* that cannot be admitted or allowed. □ **inadmissibility** /-ˈbɪlɪtɪ/ *n.* **inadmissibly** *adv.*

inadvertent /ˌɪnədˈvɜːt(ə)nt/ *adj.* **1** (of an action) unintentional. **2 a** not properly attentive. **b** negligent. □ **inadvertence** *n.* **inadvertency** *n.* **inadvertently** *adv.* [IN-¹ + obs. *advertent* attentive (as ADVERT²)]

inadvisable /ˌɪnədˈvaɪzəb(ə)l/ *adj.* not advisable. □ **inadvisability** /-ˈbɪlɪtɪ/ *n.* [ADVISABLE]

inalienable /ɪnˈeɪlɪənəb(ə)l/ *adj.* that cannot be transferred to another; not alienable. □ **inalienability** /-ˈbɪlɪtɪ/ *n.* **inalienably** *adv.*

inane /ɪˈneɪn/ *adj.* **1** silly, senseless. **2** empty, void. □ **inanely** *adv.* **inaneness** *n.* **inanity** /-ˈænɪtɪ/ *n.* (*pl.* **-ies**). [L *inanis* empty, vain]

inanimate /ɪnˈænɪmət/ *adj.* **1** destitute of life. **2** not endowed with animal life. **3** spiritless, dull. □ **inanimately** *adv.* **inanimation** /-ˈmeɪʃ(ə)n/ *n.* [LL *inanimatus* (as IN-¹, ANIMATE)]

inanition /ˌɪnəˈnɪʃ(ə)n/ *n.* emptiness, esp. exhaustion from lack of nourishment. [ME f. LL *inanitio* f. L *inanire* make empty (as INANE)]

inapplicable /ɪnˈæplɪkəb(ə)l/, ˌɪnəˈplɪk-/ *adj.* (often foll. by *to*) not applicable; unsuitable. □ **inapplicability** /-ˈbɪlɪtɪ/ *n.* **inapplicably** *adv.*

inapposite /ɪnˈæpəzɪt/ *adj.* not apposite; out of place. □ **inappositely** *adv.* **inappositeness** *n.*

inappropriate /ˌɪnəˈprəʊprɪət/ *adj.* not appropriate. □ **inappropriately** *adv.* **inappropriateness** *n.*

inapt /ɪnˈæpt/ *adj.* **1** not apt or suitable. **2** unskilful. □ **inaptitude** *n.* **inaptly** *adv.* **inaptness** *n.*

inarticulate /ˌɪnɑːˈtɪkjʊlət/ *adj.* **1** unable to speak distinctly or express oneself clearly. **2** (of speech) not articulate; indistinctly pronounced. **3** dumb. **4** esp. *Anat.* not jointed. □ **inarticulately** *adv.* **inarticulateness** *n.* [LL *inarticulatus* (as IN-¹, ARTICULATE)]

inartistic /ˌɪnɑːˈtɪstɪk/ *adj.* **1** not following the principles of art. **2** lacking skill or talent in art; not appreciating art. □ **inartistically** *adv.*

inasmuch /ˌɪnəzˈmʌtʃ/ *adv.* (foll. by *as*) **1** since, because. **2** to the extent that. [ME, orig. *in as much*]

inattentive /ˌɪnəˈtentɪv/ *adj.* **1** not paying due attention; heedless. **2** neglecting to show courtesy. □ **inattention** *n.* **inattentively** *adv.* **inattentiveness** *n.*

inaudible /ɪnˈɔːdɪb(ə)l/ *adj.* that cannot be heard. □ **inaudibility** /-ˈbɪlɪtɪ/ *n.* **inaudibly** *adv.*

inaugural /ɪˈnɔːgjʊr(ə)l/ *adj.* & *n.* —*adj.* **1** of inauguration. **2** (of a lecture etc.) given by a person being inaugurated. —*n.* an inaugural speech etc. [F f. *inaugurer* (as INAUGURATE)]

inaugurate /ɪˈnɔːgjʊˌreɪt/ v.tr. **1** admit (a person) formally to office. **2** initiate the public use of (a building etc.). **3** begin, introduce. **4** enter with ceremony upon (an undertaking etc.). □ **inauguration** /-ˈreɪʃ(ə)n/ n. **inaugurator** n. **inauguratory** adj. [L inaugurare (as IN-², augurare take omens: see AUGUR)]

inauspicious /ˌɪnɔːˈspɪʃəs/ adj. **1** ill-omened, unpropitious. **2** unlucky. □ **inauspiciously** adv. **inauspiciousness** n.

inboard /ˈɪnbɔːd/ adv. & adj. —adv. within the sides of or towards the centre of a ship, aircraft, or vehicle. —adj. situated inboard.

inborn /ˈɪnbɔːn/ adj. existing from birth; implanted by nature.

inbred /ɪnˈbred, ˈɪn-/ adj. **1** inborn. **2** produced by inbreeding.

inbreeding /ɪnˈbriːdɪŋ/ n. breeding from closely related animals or persons. □ **inbreed** v.tr. & intr. (past and past part. **inbred**).

inbuilt /ˈɪnbɪlt/ adj. incorporated as part of a structure.

Inc. abbr. US Incorporated.

Inca /ˈɪŋkə/ n. a member of an American Indian people in Peru before the Spanish conquest. □ **Incaic** /ɪŋˈkeɪɪk/ adj. **Incan** adj. [Quechua, = lord, royal person]

incalculable /ɪnˈkælkjʊləb(ə)l/ adj. **1** too great for calculation. **2** that cannot be reckoned beforehand. **3** (of a person, character, etc.) uncertain. □ **incalculability** /-ˈbɪlɪtɪ/ n. **incalculably** adv.

incandesce /ˌɪnkænˈdes/ v.intr. & tr. glow or cause to glow with heat. [back-form. f. INCANDESCENT]

incandescent /ˌɪnkænˈdes(ə)nt/ adj. **1** glowing with heat. **2** shining brightly. **3** (of an electric or other light) produced by a glowing white-hot filament. □ **incandescence** n. **incandescently** adv. [F f. L incandescere (as IN-², candescere inceptive of candēre be white)]

incantation /ˌɪnkænˈteɪʃ(ə)n/ n. **1 a** a magical formula. **b** the use of this. **2** a spell or charm. □ **incantational** adj. **incantatory** adj. [ME f. OF f. LL incantatio -onis f. incantare chant, bewitch (as IN-², cantare sing)]

incapable /ɪnˈkeɪpəb(ə)l/ adj. **1** (often foll. by of) **a** not capable. **b** lacking the required quality or characteristic (favourable or adverse) (incapable of hurting anyone). **2** not capable of rational conduct or of managing one's own affairs (drunk and incapable). □ **incapability** /-ˈbɪlɪtɪ/ n. **incapably** adv. [F incapable or LL incapabilis (as IN-¹, capabilis CAPABLE)]

incapacitate /ˌɪnkəˈpæsɪˌteɪt/ v.tr. **1** render incapable or unfit. **2** disqualify. □ **incapacitant** n. **incapacitation** /-ˈteɪʃ(ə)n/ n.

incapacity /ˌɪnkəˈpæsɪtɪ/ n. (pl. **-ies**) **1** inability; lack of the necessary power or resources. **2** legal disqualification. **3** an instance of incapacity. [F incapacité or LL incapacitas (as IN-¹, CAPACITY)]

incarcerate /ɪnˈkɑːsəˌreɪt/ v.tr. imprison or confine. □ **incarceration** /-ˈreɪʃ(ə)n/ n. **incarcerator** n. [med.L incarcerare (as IN-², L carcer prison)]

incarnate adj. & v. —adj. /ɪnˈkɑːnət/ **1** (of a person, spirit, quality, etc.) embodied in flesh, esp. in human form (is the devil incarnate). **2** represented in a recognizable or typical form (folly incarnate). —v.tr. /ˈɪnkɑːˌneɪt, -ˈkɑːneɪt/ **1** embody in flesh. **2** put (an idea etc.) into concrete

form; realize. **3** (of a person etc.) be the living embodiment of (a quality). [ME f. eccl.L incarnare incarnat- make flesh (as IN-², L caro carnis flesh)]

incarnation /ˌɪnkɑːˈneɪʃ(ə)n/ n. **1 a** embodiment in (esp. human) flesh. **b** (**the Incarnation**) Theol. the embodiment of God the Son in human flesh as Jesus Christ. **2** (often foll. by of) a living type (of a quality etc.). [ME f. OF f. eccl.L incarnatio -onis (as INCARNATE)]

incase var. of ENCASE.

incautious /ɪnˈkɔːʃəs/ adj. heedless, rash. □ **incaution** n. **incautiously** adv. **incautiousness** n.

incendiary /ɪnˈsendɪərɪ/ adj. & n. —adj. **1** (of a substance or device, esp. a bomb) designed to cause fires. **2 a** of or relating to the malicious setting on fire of property. **b** guilty of this. **3** tending to stir up strife; inflammatory. —n. (pl. **-ies**) **1** an incendiary bomb or device. **2** an incendiary person. □ **incendiarism** n. [L incendiarius f. incendium conflagration f. incendere incens- set fire to]

incense¹ /ˈɪnsens/ n. & v. —n. **1** a gum or spice producing a sweet smell when burned. **2** the smoke of this, esp. in religious ceremonial. —v.tr. **1** treat or perfume (a person or thing) with incense. **2** burn incense to (a deity etc.). □ **incensation** /-ˈseɪʃ(ə)n/ n. [ME f. OF encens, encenser f. eccl.L incensum a thing burnt, incense: see INCENDIARY]

incense² /ɪnˈsens/ v.tr. (often foll. by at, with, against) enrage; make angry. [ME f. OF incenser (as INCENDIARY)]

incentive /ɪnˈsentɪv/ n. & adj. —n. **1** (often foll. by to) a motive or incitement, esp. to action. **2** a payment or concession to stimulate greater output by workers. —adj. serving to motivate or incite. [ME f. L incentivus setting the tune f. incinere incent- sing to (as IN-², canere sing)]

inception /ɪnˈsepʃ(ə)n/ n. a beginning. [ME f. OF inception or L inceptio f. incipere incept- begin (as IN-², capere take)]

incertitude /ɪnˈsɜːtɪˌtjuːd/ n. uncertainty, doubt. [F incertitude or LL incertitudo (as IN-¹, CERTITUDE)]

incessant /ɪnˈses(ə)nt/ adj. unceasing, continual, repeated. □ **incessancy** n. **incessantly** adv. **incessantness** n. [F incessant or LL incessans (as IN-¹, cessans pres. part. of L cessare CEASE)]

incest /ˈɪnsest/ n. sexual intercourse between persons regarded as too closely related to marry each other. [ME f. L incestus (as IN-¹, castus CHASTE)]

incestuous /ɪnˈsestjʊəs/ adj. **1** involving or guilty of incest. **2** (of human relations generally) excessively restricted. □ **incestuously** adv. **incestuousness** n. [LL incestuosus (as INCEST)]

inch n. & v. —n. **1** a unit of linear measure equal to one-twelfth of a foot (2.54 cm). **2** (as a unit of rainfall) a quantity that would cover a horizontal surface to a depth of 1 inch. **3** (as a unit of map-scale) so many inches representing 1 mile on the ground (a 4-inch map). —v.tr. & intr. move gradually in a specified way (inched forward). [OE ynce f. L uncia twelfth part: cf. OUNCE¹]

inchoate /ɪnˈkəʊeɪt, ˈɪn-/ adj. **1** just begun. **2** undeveloped, rudimentary, unformed. □ **inchoately** adv. **inchoateness** n. **inchoation** /-ˈeɪʃ(ə)n/ n. **inchoative** /-ˈkəʊətɪv/ adj. [L

inchoatus past part. of *inchoare* (as IN-², *choare* begin)]

■ **Usage** This word is sometimes used incorrectly to mean 'chaotic' or 'incoherent'.

incidence /ˈɪnsɪd(ə)ns/ n. **1** (often foll. by *of*) the fact, manner, or rate of occurrence or action. **2** the range, scope, or extent of influence of a thing. **3** *Physics* the falling of a line, or of a thing moving in a line, upon a surface. **4** the act or an instance of coming into contact with a thing. [ME f. OF *incidence* or med.L *incidentia* (as INCIDENT)]

incident /ˈɪnsɪd(ə)nt/ n. & adj. —n. **1 a** an event or occurrence. **b** a minor or detached event attracting general attention or noteworthy in some way. **2** a hostile clash, esp. of troops of countries at war (*a frontier incident*). **3** a distinct piece of action in a play or a poem. —adj. **1** (often foll. by *to*) apt or liable to happen; naturally attaching or dependent. **2** (often foll. by *on*, *upon*) (of light etc.) falling or striking. [ME f. F *incident* or L *incidere* (as IN-², *cadere* fall)]

incidental /ˌɪnsɪˈdent(ə)l/ adj. **1** (often foll. by *to*) **a** having a minor role in relation to a more important thing, event, etc. **b** not essential. **2** (foll. by *to*) liable to happen. **3** (foll. by *on*, *upon*) following as a subordinate event. □ **incidental music** music used as a background to the action of a film, etc.

incidentally /ˌɪnsɪˈdentəlɪ/ adv. **1** by the way; as an unconnected remark. **2** in an incidental way.

incinerate /ɪnˈsɪnəˌreɪt/ v.tr. **1** consume (a body etc.) by fire. **2** reduce to ashes. □ **incineration** /-ˈreɪʃ(ə)n/ n. [med.L *incinerare* (as IN-², *cinis -eris* ashes)]

incinerator /ɪnˈsɪnəˌreɪtə(r)/ n. a furnace or apparatus for burning esp. refuse to ashes.

incipient /ɪnˈsɪpɪənt/ adj. **1** beginning. **2** in an initial stage. □ **incipience** n. **incipiency** n. **incipiently** adv. [L *incipere incipient-* begin]

incise /ɪnˈsaɪz/ v.tr. **1** make a cut in. **2** engrave. [F *inciser* f. L *incidere incis-* (as IN-², *caedere* cut)]

incision /ɪnˈsɪʒ(ə)n/ n. **1** a cut; a division produced by cutting; a notch. **2** the act of cutting into a thing. [ME f. OF *incision* or LL *incisio* (as INCISE)]

incisive /ɪnˈsaɪsɪv/ adj. **1** mentally sharp; acute. **2** clear and effective. **3** cutting, penetrating. □ **incisively** adv. **incisiveness** n. [med.L *incisivus* (as INCISE)]

incisor /ɪnˈsaɪzə(r)/ n. a cutting-tooth, esp. at the front of the mouth. [med.L, = cutter (as INCISE)]

incite /ɪnˈsaɪt/ v.tr. (often foll. by *to*) urge or stir up. □ **incitation** /-ˈteɪʃ(ə)n/ n. **incitement** n. **inciter** n. [ME f. F *inciter* f. L *incitare* (as IN-², *citare* rouse)]

incivility /ˌɪnsɪˈvɪlɪtɪ/ n. (pl. **-ies**) **1** rudeness, discourtesy. **2** a rude or discourteous act. [F *incivilité* or LL *incivilitas* (as IN-¹, CIVILITY)]

inclement /ɪnˈklemənt/ adj. (of the weather or climate) severe, esp. cold or stormy. □ **inclemency** n. (pl. **-ies**). **inclemently** adv. [F *inclément* or L *inclemens* (as IN-¹, CLEMENT)]

inclination /ˌɪnklɪˈneɪʃ(ə)n/ n. **1** (often foll. by *to*) a disposition or propensity. **2** (often foll. by *for*) a liking or affection. **3** a leaning, slope, or slant. **4** the difference of direction of two lines or planes, esp. as measured by the angle between them. **5** the dip of a magnetic needle. [ME f. OF *inclination* or L *inclinatio* (as INCLINE)]

incline v. & n. —v. /ɪnˈklaɪn/ **1** tr. (usu. in *passive*; often foll. by *to*, *for*, or *to* + infin.) **a** make (a person, feelings, etc.) willing or favourably disposed (*am inclined to think so*; *does not incline me to agree*). **b** give a specified tendency to (a thing) (*the door is inclined to bang*). **2** intr. **a** be disposed (*I incline to think so*). **b** (often foll. by *to*, *towards*) tend. **3** intr. & tr. lean or turn away from a given direction, esp. the vertical. **4** tr. bend (the head, body, or oneself) forward or downward. —n. /ˈɪnklaɪn/ **1** a slope. **2** an inclined plane. □ **inclined plane** a sloping plane (esp. as a means of reducing the force needed to raise a load). □ **incliner** n. [ME *encline* f. OF *encliner* f. L *inclinare* (as IN-², *clinare* bend)]

inclose var. of ENCLOSE.

inclosure var. of ENCLOSURE.

include /ɪnˈkluːd/ v.tr. **1** comprise or reckon in as part of a whole. **2** (as **including** prep.) if we include (*six members, including the chairman*). **3** treat or regard as so comprised. **4** (as **included** adj.) shut in; enclosed. □ **includable** adj. **includible** adj. **inclusion** /-ˈʒ(ə)n/ n. [ME f. L *includere inclus-* (as IN-², *claudere* shut)]

inclusive /ɪnˈkluːsɪv/ adj. **1** (often foll. by *of*) including, comprising. **2** with the inclusion of the extreme limits stated (*pages 7 to 26 inclusive*). **3** including all the normal services etc. (*a hotel offering inclusive terms*). □ **inclusive language** language that is deliberately non-sexist, esp. avoiding the use of masculine pronouns to cover both men and women. □ **inclusively** adv. **inclusiveness** n. [med.L *inclusivus* (as INCLUDE)]

incognito /ˌɪnkɒgˈniːtəʊ/ adj., adv., & n. —adj. & adv. with one's name or identity kept secret (*was travelling incognito*). —n. (pl. **-os**) **1** a person who is incognito. **2** the pretended identity of such a person. [It., = unknown, f. L *incognitus* (as IN-¹, *cognitus* past part. of *cognoscere* know)]

incoherent /ˌɪnkəʊˈhɪərənt/ adj. **1** (of a person) unable to speak intelligibly. **2** (of speech etc.) lacking logic or consistency. □ **incoherence** n. **incoherency** n. (pl. **-ies**). **incoherently** adv.

incombustible /ˌɪnkəmˈbʌstɪb(ə)l/ adj. that cannot be burnt or consumed by fire. □ **incombustibility** /-ˈbɪlɪtɪ/ n. [ME f. med.L *incombustibilis* (as IN-¹, COMBUSTIBLE)]

income /ˈɪnkʌm, ˈɪŋkəm/ n. the money or other assets received, esp. periodically or in a year, from one's business, lands, work, investments, etc. □ **income tax** a tax levied on income. [ME (orig. = arrival), prob. f. ON *innkoma*: in later use f. *come in*]

incomer /ˈɪnˌkʌmə(r)/ n. **1** a person who comes in. **2** a person who arrives to settle in a place; an immigrant. **3** an intruder. **4** a successor.

incoming /ˈɪnˌkʌmɪŋ/ adj. & n. **1** coming in (*the incoming tide*; *incoming telephone calls*). **2** succeeding another person or persons (*the incoming tenant*). —n. (usu. in *pl.*) revenue, income.

incommensurable /ˌɪnkəˈmenʃərəb(ə)l, -sjərəb(ə)l/ adj. (often foll. by *with*) **1** not comparable in respect of magnitude. **2** incapable of being measured (in comparison with). **3** *Math.* (of a magnitude or magnitudes) having no common factor, integral or fractional. □ **incommensurability** /-ˈbɪlɪtɪ/ n. **incommensurably** adv. [LL *incommensurabilis* (as IN-¹, COMMENSURABLE)]

incommensurate /ˌɪnkə'menʃərət, -sjərət/ adj.
1 (often foll. by with, to) out of proportion;
inadequate. 2 = INCOMMENSURABLE. □ **incommensurately** adv. **incommensurateness** n.

incommode /ˌɪnkə'məʊd/ v.tr. 1 hinder, inconvenience. 2 trouble, annoy. [F incommoder or L incommodare (as IN-¹, commodus convenient)]

incommodious /ˌɪnkə'məʊdɪəs/ adj. not affording good accommodation; uncomfortable. □ **incommodiously** adv. **incommodiousness** n.

incommunicable /ˌɪnkə'mjuːnɪkəb(ə)l/ adj. 1 that cannot be communicated or shared. 2 that cannot be uttered or told. □ **incommunicability** /-'bɪlɪtɪ/ n. **incommunicableness** n. **incommunicably** adv. [LL incommunicabilis (as IN-¹, COMMUNICABLE)]

incommunicado /ˌɪnkəˌmjuːnɪ'kɑːdəʊ/ adj. 1 without or deprived of the means of communication with others. 2 (of a prisoner) in solitary confinement. [Sp. incomunicado past part. of incomunicar deprive of communication]

incommunicative /ˌɪnkə'mjuːnɪkətɪv/ adj. not communicative; taciturn. □ **incommunicatively** adv. **incommunicativeness** n.

incomparable /ɪn'kɒmpərəb(ə)l/ adj. 1 without an equal; matchless. 2 (often foll. by with, to) not to be compared. □ **incomparability** /-'bɪlɪtɪ/ n. **incomparableness** n. **incomparably** adv. [ME f. OF f. L incomparabilis (as IN-¹, COMPARABLE)]

incompatible /ˌɪnkəm'pætɪb(ə)l/ adj. 1 opposed in character; discordant. 2 (often foll. by with) inconsistent. 3 (of persons) unable to live, work, etc., together in harmony. 4 (of equipment, machinery, etc.) not capable of being used in combination. □ **incompatibility** /-'bɪlɪtɪ/ n. **incompatibleness** n. **incompatibly** adv. [med.L incompatibilis (as IN-¹, COMPATIBLE)]

incompetent /ɪn'kɒmpɪt(ə)nt/ adj. & n. —adj. 1 (often foll. by to + infin.) not qualified or able to perform a particular task or function (an incompetent builder). 2 showing a lack of skill (an incompetent performance). —n. an incompetent person. □ **incompetence** n. **incompetency** n. **incompetently** adv. [F incompétent or LL incompetens (as IN-¹, COMPETENT)]

incomplete /ˌɪnkəm'pliːt/ adj. not complete. □ **incompletely** adv. **incompleteness** n. [ME f. LL incompletus (as IN-¹, COMPLETE)]

incomprehensible /ɪnˌkɒmprɪ'hensɪb(ə)l/ adj. (often foll. by to) that cannot be understood. □ **incomprehensibility** /-'bɪlɪtɪ/ n. **incomprehensibleness** n. **incomprehensibly** adv. [ME f. L incomprehensibilis (as IN-¹, COMPREHENSIBLE)]

incomprehension /ɪnˌkɒmprɪ'henʃ(ə)n/ n. failure to understand.

inconceivable /ˌɪnkən'siːvəb(ə)l/ adj. that cannot be imagined. □ **inconceivability** /-'bɪlɪtɪ/ n. **inconceivableness** n. **inconceivably** adv.

inconclusive /ˌɪnkən'kluːsɪv/ adj. (of an argument, evidence, or action) not decisive or convincing. □ **inconclusively** adv. **inconclusiveness** n.

incongruous /ɪn'kɒŋgrʊəs/ adj. 1 out of place; absurd. 2 (often foll. by with) disagreeing; out of keeping. □ **incongruity** /-'gruːɪtɪ/ n. (pl. -ies). **incongruously** adv. **incongruousness** n. [L incongruus (as IN-¹, CONGRUOUS)]

inconsequent /ɪn'kɒnsɪkwənt/ adj. 1 not following naturally; irrelevant. 2 lacking logical sequence. □ **inconsequence** n. **inconsequently** adv. [L inconsequens (as IN-¹, CONSEQUENT)]

inconsequential /ɪnˌkɒnsɪ'kwenʃ(ə)l, ˌɪnkɒn-/ adj. 1 unimportant. 2 = INCONSEQUENT. □ **inconsequentiality** /-ʃɪ'ælɪtɪ/ n. (pl. -ies). **inconsequentially** adv. **inconsequentialness** n.

inconsiderable /ˌɪnkən'sɪdərəb(ə)l/ adj. 1 of small size, value, etc. 2 not worth considering. □ **inconsiderableness** n. **inconsiderably** adv. [obs. F inconsidérable or LL inconsiderabilis (as IN-¹, CONSIDERABLE)]

inconsiderate /ˌɪnkən'sɪdərət/ adj. 1 (of a person or action) thoughtless, rash. 2 lacking in regard for the feelings of others. □ **inconsiderately** adv. **inconsiderateness** n. **inconsideration** /-'reɪʃ(ə)n/ n. [L inconsideratus (as IN-¹, CONSIDERATE)]

inconsistent /ˌɪnkən'sɪst(ə)nt/ adj. 1 acting at variance with one's own principles or former conduct. 2 (often foll. by with) not in keeping; discordant, incompatible. □ **inconsistency** n. (pl. -ies). **inconsistently** adv.

inconsolable /ˌɪnkən'səʊləb(ə)l/ adj. (of a person, grief, etc.) that cannot be consoled or comforted. □ **inconsolability** /-'bɪlɪtɪ/ n. **inconsolableness** n. **inconsolably** adv. [F inconsolable or L inconsolabilis (as IN-¹, consolabilis f. consolari CONSOLE¹)]

inconsonant /ɪn'kɒnsənənt/ adj. (often foll. by with, to) not harmonious; not compatible. □ **inconsonance** n. **inconsonantly** adv.

inconspicuous /ˌɪnkən'spɪkjʊəs/ adj. not conspicuous; not easily noticed. □ **inconspicuously** adv. **inconspicuousness** n. [L inconspicuus (as IN-¹, CONSPICUOUS)]

inconstant /ɪn'kɒnst(ə)nt/ adj. 1 (of a person) fickle, changeable. 2 frequently changing; variable, irregular. □ **inconstancy** n. (pl. -ies). **inconstantly** adv. [ME f. OF f. L inconstans -antis (as IN-¹, CONSTANT)]

incontestable /ˌɪnkən'testəb(ə)l/ adj. that cannot be disputed. □ **incontestability** /-'bɪlɪtɪ/ n. **incontestably** adv. [F incontestable or med.L incontestabilis (as IN-¹, contestabilis f. L contestari CONTEST)]

incontinent /ɪn'kɒntɪnənt/ adj. 1 unable to control movements of the bowels or bladder or both. 2 lacking self-restraint (esp. in regard to sexual desire). □ **incontinence** n. **incontinently** adv. [ME f. OF or L incontinens (as IN-¹, CONTINENT²)]

incontrovertible /ˌɪnkɒntrə'vɜːtɪb(ə)l/ adj. indisputable, indubitable. □ **incontrovertibility** /-'bɪlɪtɪ/ n. **incontrovertibly** adv.

inconvenience /ˌɪnkən'viːnɪəns/ n. & v. —n. 1 lack of suitability to personal requirements or ease. 2 a cause or instance of this. —v.tr. cause inconvenience to. [ME f. OF f. LL inconvenientia (as INCONVENIENT)]

inconvenient /ˌɪnkən'viːnɪənt/ adj. 1 unfavourable to ease or comfort; not convenient. 2 awkward, troublesome. □ **inconveniently** adv. [ME f. OF f. L inconveniens -entis (as IN-¹, CONVENIENT)]

incorporate v. /ɪn'kɔːpəˌreɪt/ 1 tr. (often foll. by in, with) unite; form into one body or whole. 2 combine; become incorporated. 3 tr. combine (ingredients) into one substance. 4 tr. admit as a member of a company etc. 5 tr. **a** constitute as a legal corporation. **b** (as **incorporated** adj.)

forming a legal corporation. □ **incorporation** /-ˈreɪʃ(ə)n/ n. **incorporator** n. [ME f. LL *incorporare* (as IN-², L *corpus -oris* body)]

incorporeal /ˌɪnkɔːˈpɔːrɪəl/ adj. **1** not composed of matter. **2** of immaterial beings. □ **incorporeality** /-ˈælɪtɪ/ n. **incorporeally** adv. **incorporeity** /-pəˈriːɪtɪ/ n. [L *incorporeus* (as INCORPORATE)]

incorrect /ˌɪnkəˈrekt/ adj. **1** not in accordance with fact; wrong. **2** (of style etc.) improper, faulty. □ **incorrectly** adv. **incorrectness** n. [ME f. OF or L *incorrectus* (as IN-¹, CORRECT)]

incorrigible /ɪnˈkɒrɪdʒɪb(ə)l/ adj. **1** (of a person or habit) incurably bad or depraved. **2** not readily improved. □ **incorrigibility** /-ˈbɪlɪtɪ/ n. **incorrigibleness** n. **incorrigibly** adv. [ME f. OF *incorrigible* or L *incorrigibilis* (as IN-¹, CORRIGIBLE)]

incorruptible /ˌɪnkəˈrʌptɪb(ə)l/ adj. **1** that cannot be corrupted, esp. by bribery. **2** that cannot decay; everlasting. □ **incorruptibility** /-ˈbɪlɪtɪ/ n. **incorruptibly** adv. [ME f. OF *incorruptible* or eccl.L *incorruptibilis* (as IN-¹, CORRUPT)]

increase v. & n. —v. /ɪnˈkriːs/ **1** tr. & intr. make or become greater in size, amount, etc., or more numerous. **2** intr. advance (in quality, attainment, etc.). **3** tr. intensify (a quality). —n. /ˈɪnkriːs/ **1** the act or process of becoming greater or more numerous; growth, enlargement. **2** (of people, animals, or plants) growth in numbers; multiplication. **3** the amount or extent of an increase. □ **on the increase** increasing, esp. in frequency. □ **increasable** adj. **increaser** n. **increasingly** adv. [ME f. OF *encreiss*- stem of *encreistre* f. L *increscere* (as IN-², *crescere* grow)]

incredible /ɪnˈkredɪb(ə)l/ adj. **1** that cannot be believed. **2** colloq. hard to believe; amazing. □ **incredibility** /-ˈbɪlɪtɪ/ n. **incredibleness** n. **incredibly** adv. [ME f. L *incredibilis* (as IN-¹, CREDIBLE)]

incredulous /ɪnˈkredjʊləs/ adj. (often foll. by *of*) unwilling to believe. □ **incredulity** /ˌɪnkrɪˈdjuːlɪtɪ/ n. **incredulously** adv. **incredulousness** n. [L *incredulus* (as IN-¹, CREDULOUS)]

increment /ˈɪnkrɪmənt/ n. **1** an increase or addition, esp. one of a series on a fixed scale. □ **incremental** /-ˈment(ə)l/ adj. [ME f. L *incrementum* f. *increscere* INCREASE]

incriminate /ɪnˈkrɪmɪˌneɪt/ v.tr. **1** tend to prove the guilt of (*incriminating evidence*). **2** involve in an accusation. **3** charge with a crime. □ **incrimination** /-ˈneɪʃ(ə)n/ n. **incriminatory** adj. [LL *incriminare* (as IN-², L *crimen* offence)]

incrust var. of ENCRUST.

incrustation /ˌɪnkrʌˈsteɪʃ(ə)n/ n. **1** the process of encrusting or state of being encrusted. **2** a crust or hard coating, esp. of fine material. **3** a concretion or deposit on a surface. [F *incrustation* or LL *incrustatio* (as ENCRUST)]

incubate /ˈɪŋkjʊbeɪt/ v. **1** tr. sit on or artificially heat (eggs) in order to bring forth young birds etc. **2** tr. cause the development of (bacteria etc.) by creating suitable conditions. **3** intr. sit on eggs; brood. [L *incubare* (as IN-², *cubare* *cubit-* or *cubat-* lie)]

incubation /ˌɪŋkjʊˈbeɪʃ(ə)n/ n. **1 a** the act of incubating. **b** brooding. **2** Med. **a** a phase through which the germs causing a disease pass before the development of the first symptoms. **b** the period of this. □ **incubational** adj. **incubative** /ˈɪŋkjʊˌbeɪtɪv/ adj. **incubatory** /ˈɪŋkjʊˌbeɪtərɪ/ adj. [L *incubatio* (as INCUBATE)]

incubator /ˈɪŋkjʊˌbeɪtə(r)/ n. **1** an apparatus used to provide a suitable temperature and environment for a premature baby or one of low birth-weight. **2** an apparatus used to hatch eggs or grow micro-organisms.

incubus /ˈɪŋkjʊbəs/ n. (pl. **incubuses** or **incubi** /-ˌbaɪ/) **1** an evil spirit supposed to descend on sleeping persons. **2** a nightmare. **3** a person or thing that oppresses like a nightmare. [ME f. LL, = L *incubo* nightmare (as INCUBATE)]

inculcate /ˈɪnkʌlˌkeɪt/ v.tr. (often foll. by *upon*, *in*) urge or impress (a fact, habit, or idea) persistently. □ **inculcation** /-ˈkeɪʃ(ə)n/ n. **inculcator** n. [L *inculcare* (as IN-², *calcare* tread f. *calx calcis* heel)]

inculpate /ˈɪnkʌlˌpeɪt/ v.tr. **1** involve in a charge. **2** accuse, blame. □ **inculpation** /-ˈpeɪʃ(ə)n/ n. **inculpative** /ɪnˈkʌlpətɪv/ adj. **inculpatory** /ɪnˈkʌlpətərɪ/ adj. [LL *inculpare* (as IN-², *culpare* blame f. *culpa* fault)]

incumbency /ɪnˈkʌmbənsɪ/ n. (pl. **-ies**) the office, tenure, or sphere of an incumbent.

incumbent /ɪnˈkʌmbənt/ adj. & n. —adj. (foll. by *on*, *upon*) resting as a duty (*it is incumbent on you to warn them*). —n. the holder of an office or post. [ME f. AL *incumbens* pres. part. of L *incumbere* lie upon (as IN-², *cubare* lie)]

incunabulum /ˌɪnkjuːˈnæbjʊləm/ n. (pl. **incunabula** /-lə/) a book printed at an early date, esp. before 1501. [L *incunabula* swaddling-clothes, cradle (as IN-², *cunae* cradle)]

incur /ɪnˈkɜː(r)/ v.tr. (**incurred**, **incurring**) suffer, experience, or become subject to (something unpleasant) as a result of one's own behaviour etc. (*incurred huge debts*). □ **incurrable** adj. [ME f. L *incurrere* *incurs-* (as IN-², *currere* run)]

incurable /ɪnˈkjʊərəb(ə)l/ adj. & n. —adj. that cannot be cured. —n. a person who cannot be cured. □ **incurability** /-ˈbɪlɪtɪ/ n. **incurableness** n. **incurably** adv. [ME f. OF *incurable* or LL *incurabilis* (as IN-¹, CURABLE)]

incurious /ɪnˈkjʊərɪəs/ adj. **1** lacking curiosity. **2** heedless, careless. □ **incuriosity** /-ˈɒsɪtɪ/ n. **incuriously** adv. **incuriousness** n. [L *incuriosus* (as IN-¹, CURIOUS)]

incursion /ɪnˈkɜːʃ(ə)n/ n. an invasion or attack, esp. when sudden or brief. □ **incursive** /-sɪv/ adj. [ME f. L *incursio* (as INCUR)]

incurve /ɪnˈkɜːv/ v.tr. **1** bend into a curve. **2** (as **incurved** adj.) curved inwards. □ **incurvation** /-ˈveɪʃ(ə)n/ n. [L *incurvare* (as IN-², CURVE)]

indebted /ɪnˈdetɪd/ adj. (usu. foll. by *to*) **1** owing gratitude or obligation. **2** owing money. □ **indebtedness** n. [ME f. OF *endetté* past part. of *endetter* involve in debt (as EN-¹, *detter* f. *dette* DEBT)]

indecent /ɪnˈdiːs(ə)nt/ adj. **1** offending against recognized standards of decency. **2** unbecoming; highly unsuitable (*with indecent haste*). □ **indecent assault** a sexual attack not involving rape. **indecent exposure** the intentional act of publicly and indecently exposing one's body, esp. the genitals. □ **indecency** n. (pl. **-ies**). **indecently** adv. [F *indécent* or L *indecens* (as IN-¹, DECENT)]

indecipherable /ˌɪndɪˈsaɪfərəb(ə)l/ adj. that cannot be deciphered.

indecision /ˌɪndɪˈsɪʒ(ə)n/ n. lack of decision; hesitation. [F *indécision* (as IN-¹, DECISION)]

indecisive /ˌɪndɪˈsaɪsɪv/ adj. **1** not decisive. **2** undecided, hesitating. □ **indecisively** adv. **indecisiveness** n.

indeclinable /ˌɪndɪˈklaɪnəb(ə)l/ adj. Gram. **1** that cannot be declined. **2** having no inflections. [ME f. F indéclinable f. L indeclinabilis (as IN-¹, DECLINE)]

indecorous /ɪnˈdekərəs/ adj. **1** improper. **2** in bad taste. □ **indecorously** adv. **indecorousness** n. [L indecorus (as IN-¹, decorus seemly)]

indeed /ɪnˈdiːd/ adv. & int. —adv. **1** in truth; really (they are, indeed, a remarkable family). **2** expressing emphasis or intensification (I shall be very glad indeed; indeed it is). **3** admittedly (there are indeed exceptions). **4** in point of fact (if indeed such a thing is possible). —int. expressing irony, contempt, incredulity, etc.

indefatigable /ˌɪndɪˈfætɪɡəb(ə)l/ adj. (of a person, quality, etc.) that cannot be tired out; unwearying, unremitting. □ **indefatigability** /-ˈbɪlɪtɪ/ n. **indefatigably** adv. [obs. F indéfatigable or L indefatigabilis (as IN-¹, defatigare wear out)]

indefensible /ˌɪndɪˈfensɪb(ə)l/ adj. that cannot be defended or justified. □ **indefensibility** /-ˈbɪlɪtɪ/ n. **indefensibly** adv.

indefinable /ˌɪndɪˈfaɪnəb(ə)l/ adj. that cannot be defined or exactly described. □ **indefinably** adv.

indefinite /ɪnˈdefɪnɪt/ adj. **1** vague, undefined. **2** unlimited. **3** Gram. not determining the person, thing, time, etc., referred to. □ **indefinite pronoun** Gram. a pronoun indicating a person, amount, etc., without being definite or particular, e.g. any, some, anyone. □ **indefiniteness** n. [L indefinitus (as IN-¹, DEFINITE)]

indefinitely /ɪnˈdefɪnɪtlɪ/ adv. **1** for an unlimited time (was postponed indefinitely). **2** in an indefinite manner.

indelible /ɪnˈdelɪb(ə)l/ adj. **1** that cannot be rubbed out or (in abstract senses) removed. **2** (of ink etc.) that makes indelible marks. □ **indelibility** /-ˈbɪlɪtɪ/ n. **indelibly** adv. [F indélébile or L indelebilis (as IN-¹, delebilis f. delēre efface)]

indelicate /ɪnˈdelɪkət/ adj. **1** coarse, unrefined. **2** tactless. **3** tending to indecency. □ **indelicacy** n. (pl. -ies). **indelicately** adv.

indemnify /ɪnˈdemnɪˌfaɪ/ v.tr. (-ies, -ied) **1** (often foll. by from, against) protect or secure (a person) in respect of harm, a loss, etc. **2** (often foll. by for) secure (a person) against legal responsibility for actions. **3** (often foll. by for) compensate (a person) for a loss, expenses, etc. □ **indemnification** /-fɪˈkeɪʃ(ə)n/ n. **indemnifier** n. [L indemnis unhurt (as IN-¹, damnum loss, damage)]

indemnity /ɪnˈdemnɪtɪ/ n. (pl. -ies) **1 a** compensation for loss incurred. **b** a sum paid for this, esp. a sum exacted by a victor in war etc. as one condition of peace. **2** security against loss. **3** legal exemption from penalties etc. incurred. [ME f. F indemnité or LL indemnitas -tatis (as INDEMNIFY)]

indent¹ v. & n. —v. /ɪnˈdent/ **1** tr. start (a line of print or writing) further from the margin than other lines, e.g. to mark a new paragraph. **2** Brit. a intr. (often foll. by on, upon a person, for a thing) make a requisition (orig. a written order with a duplicate). **b** tr. order (goods) by requisition. **3** tr. make toothlike notches in. **4** tr. form deep recesses in. —n. /ˈɪndent/ **1** Brit. an order (esp. from abroad) for goods. **b** an official requisition for stores. **2** an indented line. **3**

indentation. **4** an indenture. □ **indenter** n. **indentor** n. [ME f. AF endenter f. AL indentare (as IN-², L dens dentis tooth)]

indent² /ɪnˈdent/ v.tr. **1** make a dent in. **2** impress (a mark etc.). [ME f. IN-² + DENT]

indentation /ˌɪndenˈteɪʃ(ə)n/ n. **1** the act or an instance of indenting; the process of being indented. **2** a cut or notch. **3** a zigzag. **4** a deep recess.

indention /ɪnˈdenʃ(ə)n/ n. **1** the indenting of a line in printing or writing. **2** = INDENTATION.

indenture /ɪnˈdentʃə(r)/ n. & v. —n. **1** a sealed agreement or contract (usu. in pl.). **2** a formal list, certificate, etc. —v.tr. hist. bind (a person) by indentures, esp. as an apprentice. □ **indentureship** n. [ME (orig. Sc.) f. AF endenture (as INDENT¹)]

independence /ˌɪndɪˈpend(ə)ns/ n. (often foll. by of, from) the state of being independent.

independent /ˌɪndɪˈpend(ə)nt/ adj. & n. —adj. **1 a** (often foll. by of) not depending on authority or control. **b** self-governing. **2 a** not depending on another person for one's opinion or livelihood. **b** (of income or resources) making it unnecessary to earn one's living. **3** unwilling to be under an obligation to others. **4** Polit. not belonging to or supported by a party. **5** not depending on something else for its validity, efficiency, value, etc. (independent proof). **6** (of broadcasting, a school, etc.) not supported by public funds. —n. a person who is politically independent. □ **independently** adv.

indescribable /ˌɪndɪˈskraɪbəb(ə)l/ adj. **1** too unusual or extreme to be described. **2** vague, indefinite. □ **indescribability** /-ˈbɪlɪtɪ/ n. **indescribably** adv.

indestructible /ˌɪndɪˈstrʌktɪb(ə)l/ adj. that cannot be destroyed. □ **indestructibility** /-ˈbɪlɪtɪ/ n. **indestructibly** adv.

indeterminable /ˌɪndɪˈtɜːmɪnəb(ə)l/ adj. **1** that cannot be ascertained. **2** (of a dispute etc.) that cannot be settled. □ **indeterminably** adv. [ME f. LL indeterminabilis (as IN-¹, L determinare DETERMINE)]

indeterminate /ˌɪndɪˈtɜːmɪnət/ adj. **1** not fixed in extent, character, etc. **2** left doubtful; vague. **3** Math. (of a quantity) not limited to a fixed value by the value of another quantity. □ **indeterminacy** n. **indeterminately** adv. **indeterminateness** n. [ME f. LL indeterminatus (as IN-¹, DETERMINATE)]

indetermination /ˌɪndɪˌtɜːmɪˈneɪʃ(ə)n/ n. **1** lack of determination. **2** the state of being indeterminate.

index /ˈɪndeks/ n. & v. —n. (pl. **indexes** or esp. in technical use **indices** /ˈɪndɪˌsiːz/) **1** an alphabetical list of names, subjects, etc., with references, usu. at the end of a book. **2** = **card index**. **3** (in full **index number**) a number showing the variation of prices or wages as compared with a chosen base period (retail price index; Dow-Jones index). **4** Math. a the exponent of a number. **b** the power to which it is raised. **5 a** a pointer, esp. on an instrument, showing a quantity, a position on a scale, etc. **b** an indicator of a trend, direction, tendency, etc. **c** (usu. foll. by of) a sign, token, or indication of something. —v.tr. **1** provide (a book etc.) with an index. **2** enter in an index. **3** relate (wages etc.) to the value of a price index. □ **index finger** the forefinger. **index-linked** related to the value of

a retail price index. □ **indexation** /-'seɪʃ(ə)n/ *n.*
indexer *n.* **indexible** /'ɪndeks-, ɪn'deks-/ *adj.*
indexical /ɪn'deksɪ-/ *adj.* **indexless** *adj.* [ME f. L *index indicis* forefinger, informer, sign]

Indian /'ɪndɪən/ *n.* & *adj.* —*n.* **1 a** a native or national of India. **b** a person of Indian descent. **2** (in full **American Indian**) a member of the aboriginal peoples of America or their descendants. —*adj.* **1** of or relating to India, or to the subcontinent comprising India, Pakistan, and Bangladesh. **2** of or relating to the aboriginal peoples of America. □ **Indian clubs** a pair of bottle-shaped clubs swung to exercise the arms in gymnastics. **Indian corn** maize. **Indian file** = *single file.* **Indian ink** *Brit.* **1** a black pigment made orig. in China and Japan. **2** a dark ink made from this, used esp. in drawing and technical graphics. **Indian summer 1** a period of unusually dry warm weather sometimes occurring in late autumn. **2** a late period of life characterized by comparative calm. [ME f. *India* ult. f. Gk *Indos* the River Indus f. Pers. *Hind:* cf. HINDU]

India paper /'ɪndɪə/ *n.* a very thin tough opaque printing-paper.

indiarubber /ˌɪndɪə'rʌbə(r)/ *n.* = RUBBER¹.

indicate /'ɪndɪˌkeɪt/ *v.tr.* (often foll. by *that* + clause) **1** point out; make known; show. **2** be a sign or symptom of; express the presence of. **3** (often in *passive*) suggest; call for; require or show to be necessary (*stronger measures are indicated*). **4** admit to or state briefly (*indicated his disapproval*). **5** (of a gauge etc.) give as a reading. [L *indicare* (as IN-², *dicare* make known)]

indication /ˌɪndɪ'keɪʃ(ə)n/ *n.* **1** the act or an instance of indicating. **2** something indicated or suggested. **3** a reading given by a gauge or instrument. [F f. L *indicatio* (as INDICATE)]

indicative /ɪn'dɪkətɪv/ *adj.* & *n.* —*adj.* **1** (foll. by *of*) suggestive; serving as an indication. **2** *Gram.* (of a mood) denoting simple statement of a fact. —*n. Gram.* **1** the indicative mood. **2** a verb in this mood. □ **indicatively** *adv.* [ME f. F *indicatif -ive* f. LL *indicativus* (as INDICATE)]

indicator /'ɪndɪˌkeɪtə(r)/ *n.* **1** a person or thing that indicates. **2** a device indicating the condition of a machine etc. **3** a board in a railway station etc. giving current information. **4** a device (esp. a flashing light) on a vehicle to show that it is about to change direction. **5** a substance which changes colour at a given stage in a chemical reaction.

indicatory /'ɪndɪkətərɪ, ɪn'dɪk-/ *adj.* = INDICATIVE *adj.* 1.

indices pl. of INDEX.

indict /ɪn'daɪt/ *v.tr.* accuse (a person) formally by legal process. □ **indictee** /-'tiː/ *n.* **indicter** *n.* [ME f. AF *enditer* indict f. OF *enditier* declare f. Rmc *indictare* (unrecorded: as IN-², DICTATE)]

indictable /ɪn'daɪtəb(ə)l/ *adj.* **1** (of an offence) rendering the person who commits it liable to be charged with a crime. **2** (of a person) so liable.

indictment /ɪn'daɪtmənt/ *n.* **1** the act of indicting. **2 a** a formal accusation. **b** a legal process in which this is made. **c** a document containing a charge. **3** something that serves to condemn or censure. [ME f. AF *enditement* (as INDICT)]

indie /'ɪndɪ/ *adj.* & *n. colloq.* —*adj.* (of a pop group or record label) independent, not belonging to

one of the major companies. —*n.* such a group or label; an independent film company.

indifference /ɪn'dɪfrəns/ *n.* **1** lack of interest or attention. **2** unimportance (*a matter of indifference*). **3** neutrality. [L *indifferentia* (as INDIFFERENT)]

indifferent /ɪn'dɪfrənt/ *adj.* **1** neither good nor bad; average, mediocre. **2 a** not especially good. **b** fairly bad. **3** (foll. by *to*) having no partiality for or against; having no interest in or sympathy for. □ **indifferently** *adv.* [ME f. OF *indifferent* or L *indifferens* (as IN-¹, DIFFERENT)]

indigenize /ɪn'dɪdʒɪˌnaɪz/ *v.tr.* (also **-ise**) **1** make indigenous; subject to native influence. **2** subject to increased employment of indigenous people in government etc. □ **indigenization** /-'zeɪʃ(ə)n/ *n.*

indigenous /ɪn'dɪdʒɪnəs/ *adj.* **1 a** (esp. of flora or fauna) originating naturally in a region. **b** (of people) born in a region. **2** (foll. by *to*) belonging naturally to a place. □ **indigenously** *adv.* **indigenousness** *n.* [L *indigena* f. *indi-* = IN-² + gen- be born]

indigent /'ɪndɪdʒ(ə)nt/ *adj.* needy, poor. □ **indigence** *n.* [ME f. OF f. LL *indigēre* f. *indi-* = IN-² + *egēre* need]

indigestible /ˌɪndɪ'dʒestɪb(ə)l/ *adj.* **1** difficult or impossible to digest. **2** too complex or awkward to read or comprehend easily. □ **indigestibility** /-'bɪlɪtɪ/ *n.* **indigestibly** *adv.* [F *indigestible* or LL *indigestibilis* (as IN-¹, DIGEST)]

indigestion /ˌɪndɪ'dʒestʃ(ə)n/ *n.* **1** difficulty in digesting food. **2** pain or discomfort caused by this. □ **indigestive** *adj.* [ME f. OF *indigestion* or LL *indigestio* (as IN-¹, DIGESTION)]

indignant /ɪn'dɪgnənt/ *adj.* feeling or showing scornful anger or a sense of injured innocence. □ **indignantly** *adv.* [L *indignari indignant-* regard as unworthy (as IN-¹, *dignus* worthy)]

indignation /ˌɪndɪg'neɪʃ(ə)n/ *n.* scornful anger at supposed unjust or unfair conduct or treatment. [ME f. OF *indignation* or L *indignatio* (as INDIGNANT)]

indignity /ɪn'dɪgnɪtɪ/ *n.* (pl. **-ies**) **1** unworthy treatment. **2** a slight or insult. **3** the humiliating quality of something (*the indignity of my position*). [F *indignité* or L *indignitas* (as INDIGNANT)]

indigo /'ɪndɪˌgəʊ/ *n.* (pl. **-os**) **1 a** a natural blue dye obtained from the indigo plant. **b** a synthetic form of this dye. **2** any plant of the genus *Indigofera.* **3** (in full **indigo blue**) a colour between blue and violet in the spectrum. □ **indigotic** /-'gɒtɪk/ *adj.* [16th-c. *indico* (f. Sp.), *indigo* (f. Port.) f. L *indicum* f. Gk *indikon* INDIAN (dye)]

indirect /ˌɪndaɪ'rekt/ *adj.* **1** not going straight to the point. **2** (of a route etc.) not straight. **3** not directly sought or aimed at (*an indirect result*). **4** (of lighting) from a concealed source and diffusely reflected. □ **indirect object** *Gram.* a person or thing affected by a verbal action but not primarily acted on (e.g. *him* in *give him the book*). **indirect question** *Gram.* a question in reported speech (e.g. *they asked who I was*). **indirect speech** = *reported speech.* **indirect tax** a tax levied on goods and services and not on income or profits. □ **indirectly** *adv.* **indirectness** *n.* [ME f. OF *indirect* or med.L *indirectus* (as IN-¹, DIRECT)]

indiscernible /ˌɪndɪ'sɜːnɪb(ə)l/ *adj.* that cannot be discerned or distinguished from another. □

indiscernibility /ˌɪndɪ-ˈbɪlɪtɪ/ n. **indiscernibly** adv.

indiscipline /ɪnˈdɪsɪplɪn/ n. lack of discipline.

indiscreet /ˌɪndɪˈskriːt/ adj. **1** not discreet; revealing secrets. **2** injudicious, unwary. □ **indiscreetly** adv. [ME f. LL *indiscretus* (as IN-¹, DISCREET)]

indiscrete /ˌɪndɪˈskriːt/ adj. not divided into distinct parts. [L *indiscretus* (as IN-¹, DISCRETE)]

indiscretion /ˌɪndɪˈskreʃ(ə)n/ n. **1** lack of discretion; indiscreet conduct. **2** an indiscreet action, remark, etc. [ME f. OF *indiscretion* or LL *indiscretio* (as IN-¹, DISCRETION)]

indiscriminate /ˌɪndɪˈskrɪmɪnət/ adj. **1** making no distinctions. **2** confused, promiscuous. □ **indiscriminately** adv. **indiscriminateness** n. **indiscrimination** /-ˈneɪʃ(ə)n/ n. **indiscriminative** adj. [IN-¹ + *discriminate* (adj.) f. L *discriminatus* past part. (as DISCRIMINATE)]

indispensable /ˌɪndɪˈspensəb(ə)l/ adj. (often foll. by *to*, *for*) that cannot be dispensed with; necessary. □ **indispensability** /-ˈbɪlɪtɪ/ n. **indispensableness** n. **indispensably** adv. [med.L *indispensabilis* (as IN-¹, DISPENSABLE)]

indisposed /ˌɪndɪˈspəʊzd/ adj. **1** slightly unwell. **2** averse or unwilling.

indisposition /ˌɪndɪspəˈzɪʃ(ə)n/ n. **1** ill health, a slight or temporary ailment. **2** disinclination. **3** aversion. [F *indisposition* or IN-¹ + DISPOSITION]

indisputable /ˌɪndɪˈspjuːtəb(ə)l/ adj. **1** that cannot be disputed. **2** unquestionable. □ **indisputability** /-ˈbɪlɪtɪ/ n. **indisputableness** n. **indisputably** adv. [LL *indisputabilis* (as IN-¹, DISPUTABLE)]

indissoluble /ˌɪndɪˈsɒljʊb(ə)l/ adj. **1** that cannot be dissolved or decomposed. **2** lasting, stable (*an indissoluble bond*). □ **indissolubility** /-ˈbɪlɪtɪ/ n. **indissolubly** adv. [L *indissolubilis* (as IN-¹, DISSOLUBLE)]

indistinct /ˌɪndɪˈstɪŋkt/ adj. **1** not distinct. **2** confused, obscure. □ **indistinctly** adv. **indistinctness** n. [ME f. L *indistinctus* (as IN-¹, DISTINCT)]

indistinguishable /ˌɪndɪˈstɪŋgwɪʃəb(ə)l/ adj. (often foll. by *from*) not distinguishable. □ **indistinguishableness** n. **indistinguishably** adv.

indite /ɪnˈdaɪt/ v.tr. formal or joc. **1** put (a speech etc.) into words. **2** write (a letter etc.). [ME f. OF *enditier*: see INDICT]

indium /ˈɪndɪəm/ n. Chem. a soft silvery-white metallic element used for electroplating and in semiconductors. [L *indicum* indigo with ref. to its characteristic spectral lines]

individual /ˌɪndɪˈvɪdjʊəl/ adj. & n. —adj. **1** single. **2** particular, special; not general. **3** having a distinct character. **4** characteristic of a particular person. **5** designed for use by one person. —n. **1** a single member of a class. **2** a single human being as distinct from a family or group. **3** colloq. a person (*a most unpleasant individual*). [ME, = indivisible, f. med.L *individualis*, f. *dividuus* f. *dividere* DIVIDE)]

individualism /ˌɪndɪˈvɪdjʊəˌlɪz(ə)m/ n. **1** the habit or principle of being self-reliant. **2** a social theory favouring the free action of individuals. □ **individualist** n. **individualistic** /-ˈlɪstɪk/ adj. **individualistically** /-ˈlɪstɪkəlɪ/ adv.

individuality /ˌɪndɪvɪdjʊˈælɪtɪ/ n. (pl. -ies) **1** individual character, esp. when strongly marked. **2** (in pl.) individual tastes etc. **3** separate existence.

individualize /ˌɪndɪˈvɪdjʊəˌlaɪz/ v.tr. (also -ise) **1** give an individual character to. **2** specify. □ **individualization** /-ˈzeɪʃ(ə)n/ n.

individually /ˌɪndɪˈvɪdjʊəlɪ/ adv. **1** personally; in an individual capacity. **2** in a distinctive manner. **3** one by one; not collectively.

indivisible /ˌɪndɪˈvɪzɪb(ə)l/ adj. **1** not divisible. **2** not distributable among a number. □ **indivisibility** /-ˈbɪlɪtɪ/ n. **indivisibly** adv. [ME f. LL *indivisibilis* (as IN-¹, DIVISIBLE)]

Indo- /ˈɪndəʊ/ comb. form Indian; Indian and. [L *Indus* f. Gk *Indos*]

indoctrinate /ɪnˈdɒktrɪˌneɪt/ v.tr. **1** teach (a person or group) systematically or for a long period to accept ideas uncritically. **2** teach, instruct. □ **indoctrination** /-ˈneɪʃ(ə)n/ n. **indoctrinator** n. [IN-² + DOCTRINE + -ATE³]

Indo-European /ˌɪndəʊˌjʊərəˈpɪən/ adj. & n. —adj. **1** of or relating to the family of languages spoken over the greater part of Europe and Asia as far as N. India. **2** of or relating to the hypothetical parent language of this family. —n. **1** the Indo-European family of languages. **2** the hypothetical parent language of all languages belonging to this family.

indolent /ˈɪndələnt/ adj. lazy; wishing to avoid activity or exertion. □ **indolence** n. **indolently** adv. [LL *indolens* (as IN-¹, *dolēre* suffer pain)]

indomitable /ɪnˈdɒmɪtəb(ə)l/ adj. **1** that cannot be subdued; unyielding. **2** stubbornly persistent. □ **indomitability** /-ˈbɪlɪtɪ/ n. **indomitableness** n. **indomitably** adv. [LL *indomitabilis*, L *domitare* tame)]

indoor /ˈɪndɔː(r)/ adj. situated, carried on, or used within a building or under cover (*indoor aerial*; *indoor games*). [earlier *within-door*: cf. INDOORS]

indoors /ɪnˈdɔːz/ adv. into or within a building. [earlier *within doors*]

indorse var. of ENDORSE.

indrawn /ˈɪndrɔːn/ adj. **1** (of breath etc.) drawn in. **2** aloof.

indubitable /ɪnˈdjuːbɪtəb(ə)l/ adj. that cannot be doubted. □ **indubitably** adv. [F *indubitable* or L *indubitabilis* (as IN-¹, *dubitare* to doubt)]

induce /ɪnˈdjuːs/ v.tr. **1** (often foll. by *to* + infin.) prevail on; persuade. **2** bring about; give rise to. **3** Med. bring on (labour) artificially, esp. by use of drugs. **4** Electr. produce (a current) by induction. **5** infer; derive as a deduction. □ **inducer** n. **inducible** adj. [ME f. L *inducere induct-* (as IN-², *ducere* lead)]

inducement /ɪnˈdjuːsmənt/ n. **1** (often foll. by *to*) an attraction that leads one on. **2** a thing that induces.

induct /ɪnˈdʌkt/ v.tr. (often foll. by *to*, *into*) **1** introduce formally into possession of a benefice. **2** install into a room, office, etc. **3** introduce, initiate. **4** US enlist (a person) for military service. □ **inductee** /ˌɪndʌkˈtiː/ n. [ME (as INDUCE)]

inductance /ɪnˈdʌkt(ə)ns/ n. Electr. the property of an electric circuit that causes an electromotive force to be generated by a change in the current flowing.

induction /ɪnˈdʌkʃ(ə)n/ n. **1** the act or an instance of inducting or inducing. **2** Med. the process of bringing on (esp. labour) by artificial means. **3** Logic the inference of a general law from particular instances. **4** (often attrib.) a formal introduction to a new job, position, etc. (attended an *induction course*). **5** *Electr.* **a** the production of an electric or magnetic state by the proximity (without contact) of an electrified or magnetized body. **b** the production of an electric current in a conductor by a change of magnetic field. **6** the drawing of a fuel mixture into the cylinders of an internal-combustion engine. **7** US enlistment for military service. [ME f. OF *induction* or L *inductio* (as INDUCE)]

inductive /ɪnˈdʌktɪv/ *adj.* **1** (of reasoning etc.) of or based on induction. **2** of electric or magnetic induction. □ **inductively** *adv.* **inductiveness** *n.* [LL *inductivus* (as INDUCE)]

indue var. of ENDUE.

indulge /ɪnˈdʌldʒ/ *v.* **1** *intr.* (often foll. by *in*) take pleasure freely. **2** *tr.* yield freely to (a desire etc.). **3** *tr.* gratify the wishes of; favour. □ **indulger** *n.* [L *indulgēre indult-* give free rein to]

indulgence /ɪnˈdʌldʒ(ə)ns/ *n.* **1 a** the act of indulging. **b** the state of being indulgent. **2** something indulged in. **3** *RC Ch.* the remission of temporal punishment in purgatory, still due for sins after absolution. [ME f. OF f. L *indulgentia* (as INDULGENT)]

indulgent /ɪnˈdʌldʒ(ə)nt/ *adj.* **1** ready or too ready to overlook faults etc. **2** indulging or tending to indulge. □ **indulgently** *adv.* [F *indulgent* or L *indulgere indulgent-* (as INDULGE)]

indurate /ˈɪndjʊəˌreɪt/ *v.* **1** *tr.* & *intr.* make or become hard. **2** *tr.* make callous or unfeeling. **3** *intr.* become inveterate. □ **induration** /-ˈreɪʃ(ə)n/ *n.* **indurative** *adj.* [L *indurare* (as IN-², *durus* hard)]

industrial /ɪnˈdʌstrɪəl/ *adj.* **1** of or relating to industry or industries. **2** designed or suitable for industrial use (*industrial alcohol*). **3** characterized by highly developed industries (*the industrial nations*). □ **industrial action** *Brit.* any action, esp. a strike or work to rule, taken by employees as a protest. **industrial relations** the relations between management and workers in industries. □ **industrially** *adv.* [INDUSTRY + -AL: in 19th c. partly f. F *industriel*]

industrialism /ɪnˈdʌstrɪəˌlɪz(ə)m/ *n.* a social or economic system in which manufacturing industries are prevalent.

industrialist /ɪnˈdʌstrɪəlɪst/ *n.* a person engaged in the management of industry.

industrialize /ɪnˈdʌstrɪəˌlaɪz/ *v.* (also **-ise**) **1** *tr.* introduce industries to (a country or region etc.). **2** *intr.* become industrialized. □ **industrialization** /-ˈzeɪʃ(ə)n/ *n.*

industrious /ɪnˈdʌstrɪəs/ *adj.* diligent, hardworking. □ **industriously** *adv.* **industriousness** *n.* [F *industrieux* or LL *industriosus* (as INDUSTRY)]

industry /ˈɪndəstrɪ/ *n.* (*pl.* **-ies**) **1 a** a branch of trade or manufacture. **b** trade and manufacture collectively (*incentives to industry*). **2** concerted or copious activity (*the building was a hive of industry*). **3** diligence. [ME, = skill, f. F *industrie* or L *industria* diligence]

-ine¹ /aɪn, ɪn/ *suffix* forming adjectives, meaning 'belonging to, of the nature of' (*Alpine*; *asinine*). [from or after F *-in* *-ine*, or f. L *-inus*]

-ine² /aɪn/ *suffix* forming adjectives esp. from names of minerals, plants, etc. (*crystalline*). [L *-inus* from or after Gk *-inos*]

-ine³ /ɪn, iːn/ *suffix* forming feminine nouns (*heroine*; *margravine*). [F f. L *-ina* f. Gk *-inē*, or f. G *-in*]

-ine⁴ *suffix* **1** /ɪn/ forming (esp. abstract) nouns (*discipline*; *medicine*). **2** /iːn, ɪn/ *Chem.* forming nouns denoting derived substances, esp. alkaloids, halogens, amines, and amino acids. [F f. L *-ina* (fem.) = -INE¹]

inebriate *v., adj.,* & *n.* —*v.tr.* /ɪˈniːbrɪˌeɪt/ **1** make drunk; intoxicate. **2** excite. —*adj.* /ɪˈniːbrɪət/ drunken. —*n.* /ɪˈniːbrɪət/ a drunken person, esp. a habitual drunkard. □ **inebriation** /-ˈeɪʃ(ə)n/ *n.* **inebriety** /-ˈbraɪətɪ/ *n.* [ME f. L *inebriatus* past part. of *inebriare* (as IN-², *ebrius* drunk)]

inedible /ɪnˈedɪb(ə)l/ *adj.* not edible, esp. not suitable for eating (cf. UNEATABLE). □ **inedibility** /-ˈbɪlɪtɪ/ *n.*

ineducable /ɪnˈedjʊkəb(ə)l/ *adj.* incapable of being educated, esp. through mental retardation. □ **ineducability** /-ˈbɪlɪtɪ/ *n.*

ineffable /ɪnˈefəb(ə)l/ *adj.* **1** unutterable; too great for description in words. **2** that must not be uttered. □ **ineffability** /-ˈbɪlɪtɪ/ *n.* **ineffably** *adv.* [ME f. OF *ineffable* or L *ineffabilis* (as IN-¹, *effari* speak out, utter)]

ineffaceable /ˌɪnɪˈfeɪsəb(ə)l/ *adj.* that cannot be effaced. □ **ineffaceability** /-ˈbɪlɪtɪ/ *n.* **ineffaceably** *adv.*

ineffective /ˌɪnɪˈfektɪv/ *adj.* **1** not producing any effect or the desired effect. **2** (of a person) inefficient; not achieving results. **3** lacking artistic effect. □ **ineffectively** *adv.* **ineffectiveness** *n.*

ineffectual /ˌɪnɪˈfektjʊəl, -ˈʃʊəl/ *adj.* **1 a** without effect. **b** not producing the desired or expected effect. **2** (of a person) lacking the ability to achieve results (*an ineffectual leader*). □ **ineffectuality** /-tjʊˈælɪtɪ/ *n.* **ineffectually** *adv.* **ineffectualness** *n.* [ME f. med.L *ineffectualis* (as IN-¹, EFFECTUAL)]

inefficacious /ˌɪnefɪˈkeɪʃəs/ *adj.* (of a remedy etc.) not producing the desired effect. □ **inefficaciously** *adv.* **inefficaciousness** *n.* **inefficacy** /ɪnˈefɪkəsɪ/ *n.*

inefficient /ˌɪnɪˈfɪʃ(ə)nt/ *adj.* **1** not efficient. **2** (of a person) not fully capable; not well qualified. □ **inefficiency** *n.* **inefficiently** *adv.*

inelastic /ˌɪnɪˈlæstɪk/ *adj.* **1** not elastic. **2** unadaptable, inflexible, unyielding. □ **inelastically** *adv.* **inelasticity** /-ˈtɪsɪtɪ/ *n.*

inelegant /ɪnˈelɪgənt/ *adj.* **1** ungraceful. **2 a** unrefined. **b** (of a style) unpolished. □ **inelegance** *n.* **inelegantly** *adv.* [F *inélégant* f. L *inelegans* (as IN-¹, ELEGANT)]

ineligible /ɪnˈelɪdʒɪb(ə)l/ *adj.* **1** not eligible. **2** undesirable. □ **ineligibility** /-ˈbɪlɪtɪ/ *n.* **ineligibly** *adv.*

ineluctable /ˌɪnɪˈlʌktəb(ə)l/ *adj.* **1** against which it is useless to struggle. **2** that cannot be escaped from. □ **ineluctability** /-ˈbɪlɪtɪ/ *n.* **ineluctably** *adv.* [L *ineluctabilis* (as IN-¹, *eluctari* struggle out)]

inept /ɪˈnept/ *adj.* **1** unskilful. **2** absurd, silly. **3** out of place. □ **ineptitude** *n.* **ineptly** *adv.* **ineptness** *n.* [L *ineptus* (as IN-¹, APT)]

inequable /ɪnˈekwəb(ə)l/ *adj.* **1** not fairly distributed. **2** not uniform. [L *inaequabilis* uneven (as IN-¹, EQUABLE)]

inequality /ˌɪnɪˈkwɒlɪtɪ/ *n.* (*pl.* **-ies**) **1 a** a lack of equality in any respect. **b** an instance of this. **2** the state of being variable. **3** (of a surface) irregularity. [ME f. OF *inequalité* or L *inaequalitas* (as IN-¹, EQUALITY)]

inequitable /ɪnˈekwɪtəb(ə)l/ *adj.* unfair, unjust. □ **inequitably** *adv.*

inequity /ɪnˈekwɪtɪ/ n. (pl. **-ies**) unfairness, bias.

ineradicable /ˌɪnɪˈrædɪkəb(ə)l/ adj. that cannot be rooted out. □ **ineradicably** adv.

inert /ɪˈnɜːt/ adj. **1** without inherent power of action, motion, or resistance. **2** without active chemical or other properties. **3** sluggish, slow. □ **inert gas** = noble gas. □ **inertly** adv. **inertness** n. [L iners inert- (as IN-¹, ars ART)]

inertia /ɪˈnɜːʃə, -ʃɪə/ n. **1** Physics a property of matter by which it continues in its existing state of rest or uniform motion in a straight line, unless that state is changed by an external force. **2** inertness, sloth. □ **inertia reel** a reel device which allows a vehicle seat-belt to unwind freely but which locks under force of impact or rapid deceleration. **inertia selling** the sending of unsolicited goods in the hope of making a sale. □ **inertial** adj. **inertialess** adj. [L (as INERT)]

inescapable /ˌɪnɪˈskeɪpəb(ə)l/ adj. that cannot be escaped or avoided. □ **inescapability** /-ˈbɪlɪtɪ/ n. **inescapably** adv.

-iness /ɪnɪs/ suffix forming nouns corresponding to adjectives in -y (see -Y¹, -LY²).

inessential /ˌɪnɪˈsenʃ(ə)l/ adj. & n. —adj. **1** not necessary. **2** dispensable. —n. an inessential thing.

inestimable /ɪnˈestɪməb(ə)l/ adj. too great, intense, precious, etc., to be estimated. □ **inestimably** adv. [ME f. OF f. L inaestimabilis (as IN-¹, ESTIMABLE)]

inevitable /ɪnˈevɪtəb(ə)l/ adj. **1 a** unavoidable; sure to happen. **b** that is bound to occur or appear. **2** colloq. that is tiresomely familiar. □ **inevitability** /-ˈbɪlɪtɪ/ n. **inevitableness** n. **inevitably** adv. [L inevitabilis (as IN-¹, evitare avoid)]

inexact /ˌɪnɪɡˈzækt/ adj. not exact. □ **inexactitude** n. **inexactly** adv. **inexactness** n.

inexcusable /ˌɪnɪkˈskjuːzəb(ə)l/ adj. that cannot be excused or justified. □ **inexcusably** adv. [ME f. L inexcusabilis (as IN-¹, EXCUSE)]

inexhaustible /ˌɪnɪɡˈzɔːstɪb(ə)l/ adj. that cannot be exhausted or used up. □ **inexhaustibility** /-ˈbɪlɪtɪ/ n. **inexhaustibly** adv.

inexorable /ɪnˈeksərəb(ə)l/ adj. **1** relentless. **2** that cannot be persuaded by request or entreaty. □ **inexorability** /-ˈbɪlɪtɪ/ n. **inexorably** adv. [F inexorable or L inexorabilis (as IN-¹, exorare entreat)]

inexpedient /ˌɪnɪkˈspiːdɪənt/ adj. not expedient. □ **inexpediency** n.

inexpensive /ˌɪnɪkˈspensɪv/ adj. **1** not expensive, cheap. **2** offering good value for the price. □ **inexpensively** adv. **inexpensiveness** n.

inexperience /ˌɪnɪkˈspɪərɪəns/ n. lack of experience, or of the resulting knowledge or skill. □ **inexperienced** adj. [F inexpérience f. LL inexperientia (as IN-¹, EXPERIENCE)]

inexpert /ɪnˈekspɜːt/ adj. unskilful; lacking expertise. □ **inexpertly** adv. **inexpertness** n. [OF f. L inexpertus (as IN-¹, EXPERT)]

inexpiable /ɪnˈekspɪəb(ə)l/ adj. (of an act or feeling) that cannot be expiated or appeased. □ **inexpiably** adv. [L inexpiabilis (as IN-¹, EXPIATE)]

inexplicable /ˌɪnɪkˈsplɪkəb(ə)l, ɪnˈeks-/ adj. that cannot be explained or accounted for. □ **inexplicability** /-ˈbɪlɪtɪ/ n. **inexplicably** adv. [F inexplicable or L inexplicabilis that cannot be unfolded (as IN-¹, EXPLICABLE)]

inexpressible /ˌɪnɪkˈspresɪb(ə)l/ adj. that cannot be expressed in words. □ **inexpressibly** adv.

inexpressive /ˌɪnɪkˈspresɪv/ adj. not expressive. □ **inexpressively** adv. **inexpressiveness** n.

inextinguishable /ˌɪnɪkˈstɪŋgwɪʃəb(ə)l/ adj. **1** not quenchable; indestructible. **2** (of laughter etc.) irrepressible.

in extremis /ˌɪn ekˈstriːmɪs/ adj. **1** at the point of death. **2** in great difficulties. [L]

inextricable /ɪnˈekstrɪkəb(ə)l, ˌɪnɪkˈstrɪk-/ adj. **1** (of a circumstance) that cannot be escaped from. **2** (of a knot, problem, etc.) that cannot be unravelled or solved. □ **inextricability** /-ˈbɪlɪtɪ/ n. **inextricably** adv. [ME f. L inextricabilis (as IN-¹, EXTRICATE)]

infallible /ɪnˈfælɪb(ə)l/ adj. **1** incapable of error. **2** (of a method, test, proof, etc.) unfailing; sure to succeed. □ **infallibility** /-ˈbɪlɪtɪ/ n. **infallibly** adv. [ME f. F infaillible or LL infallibilis (as IN-¹, FALLIBLE)]

infamous /ˈɪnfəməs/ adj. **1** notoriously bad; having a bad reputation. **2** abominable. □ **infamously** adv. **infamy** /ˈɪnfəmɪ/ n. (pl. **-ies**). [ME f. med.L infamosus f. L infamis (as IN-¹, FAME)]

infancy /ˈɪnfənsɪ/ n. (pl. **-ies**) **1** early childhood; babyhood. **2** an early state in the development of an idea, undertaking, etc. **3** Law the state of being a minor. [L infantia (as INFANT)]

infant /ˈɪnf(ə)nt/ n. **1 a** a child during the earliest period of its life. **b** Brit. a schoolchild below the age of seven years. **2** (esp. attrib.) a thing in an early stage of its development. **3** Law a minor; a person under 18. □ **infant mortality** death before the age of one. [ME f. OF enfant f. L infans unable to speak (as IN-¹, fans fantis pres. part. of fari speak)]

infanticide /ɪnˈfæntɪˌsaɪd/ n. **1** the killing of an infant soon after birth. **2** the practice of killing newborn infants. **3** a person who kills an infant. □ **infanticidal** /-ˈsaɪd(ə)l/ adj. [F f. LL infanticidium, -cida (as INFANT)]

infantile /ˈɪnfənˌtaɪl/ adj. **1 a** like or characteristic of a child. **b** childish, immature (infantile humour). **2** in its infancy. □ **infantile paralysis** poliomyelitis. □ **infantility** /-ˈtɪlɪtɪ/ n. (pl. **-ies**). [F infantile or L infantilis (as INFANT)]

infantilism /ɪnˈfæntɪˌlɪz(ə)m/ n. childish behaviour.

infantry /ˈɪnfəntrɪ/ n. (pl. **-ies**) a body of soldiers who march and fight on foot; foot-soldiers collectively. [F infanterie f. It. infanteria f. infante youth, infantryman (as INFANT)]

infantryman /ˈɪnfəntrɪmən/ n. (pl. **-men**) a soldier of an infantry regiment.

infatuate /ɪnˈfætjʊˌeɪt/ v.tr. **1** inspire with intense usu. transitory fondness or admiration. **2** affect with extreme folly. □ **infatuation** /-ˈeɪʃ(ə)n/ n. [L infatuare (as IN-², fatuus foolish)]

infatuated /ɪnˈfætjʊˌeɪtɪd/ adj. (often foll. by with) affected by an intense fondness or admiration.

infect /ɪnˈfekt/ v.tr. **1** contaminate (air, water, etc.) with harmful organisms or noxious matter. **2** affect (a person) with disease etc. **3** instil bad feeling or opinion into (a person). □ **infector** n. [ME f. L inficere infect- taint (as IN-², facere make)]

infection /ɪnˈfekʃ(ə)n/ n. **1 a** the process of infecting or state of being infected. **b** an instance of this; an infectious disease. **2** communication of disease, esp. by the agency of air or water etc. **3** moral contamination. [ME f. OF *infection* or LL *infectio* (as INFECT)]

infectious /ɪnˈfekʃəs/ *adj.* **1** infecting with disease. **2** (of a disease) liable to be transmitted by air, water, etc. **3** (of emotions etc.) apt to spread; quickly affecting others. □ **infectiously** *adv.* **infectiousness** *n.*

infelicitous /ˌɪnfɪˈlɪsɪtəs/ *adj.* not felicitous; unfortunate. □ **infelicitously** *adv.*

infelicity /ˌɪnfɪˈlɪsɪtɪ/ *n.* (*pl.* **-ies**) **1 a** inaptness of expression etc. **b** an instance of this. **2 a** unhappiness. **b** a misfortune. [ME f. L *infelicitas* (as IN-¹, FELICITY)]

infer /ɪnˈfɜː(r)/ *v.tr.* (**inferred, inferring**) (often foll. by *that* + clause) **1** deduce or conclude from facts and reasoning. **2** imply, suggest. □ **inferable** *adj.* (also **inferrable**). [L *inferre* (as IN-², *ferre* bring)]

■ **Usage** Use as in sense 2 is considered incorrect by some people.

inference /ˈɪnfərəns/ *n.* **1** the act or an instance of inferring. **2** *Logic* **a** the forming of a conclusion from premisses. **b** a thing inferred. □ **inferential** /-ˈrenʃ(ə)l/ *adj.* **inferentially** /-ˈrenʃəlɪ/ *adv.* [med.L *inferentia* (as INFER)]

inferior /ɪnˈfɪərɪə(r)/ *adj.* & *n.* —*adj.* **1** (often foll. by *to*) **a** lower; in a lower position. **b** of lower rank, quality, etc. **2** poor in quality. **3** (of figures or letters) written or printed below the line. —*n.* **1** a person inferior to another, esp. in rank. **2** an inferior letter or figure. □ **inferiorly** *adv.* [ME f. L, compar. of *inferus* that is below]

inferiority /ɪnˌfɪərɪˈɒrɪtɪ/ *n.* the state of being inferior. □ **inferiority complex** an unrealistic feeling of general inadequacy, sometimes marked by aggressive behaviour in compensation.

infernal /ɪnˈfɜːn(ə)l/ *adj.* **1 a** of hell or the underworld. **b** hellish, fiendish. **2** *colloq.* detestable, tiresome. □ **infernally** *adv.* [ME f. OF f. LL *infernalis* f. L *infernus* situated below]

inferno /ɪnˈfɜːnəʊ/ *n.* (*pl.* **-os**) **1** a raging fire. **2** a scene of horror or distress. **3** hell, esp. with ref. to Dante's *Divine Comedy*. [It. f. LL *infernus* (as INFERNAL)]

infertile /ɪnˈfɜːtaɪl/ *adj.* not fertile. □ **infertility** /-ˈtɪlɪtɪ/ *n.* [F *infertile* or LL *infertilis* (as IN-¹, FERTILE)]

infest /ɪnˈfest/ *v.tr.* (of harmful persons or things, esp. vermin or disease) overrun (a place) in large numbers. □ **infestation** /-ˈsteɪʃ(ə)n/ *n.* [ME f. F *infester* or L *infestare* assail f. *infestus* hostile]

infidel /ˈɪnfɪd(ə)l/ *n.* & *adj.* —*n.* a person who does not believe in religion or in a particular religion; an unbeliever. —*adj.* **1** that is an infidel. **2** of unbelievers. [ME f. F *infidèle* or L *infidelis* (as IN-¹, *fidelis* faithful)]

infidelity /ˌɪnfɪˈdelɪtɪ/ *n.* (*pl.* **-ies**) **1** disloyalty or unfaithfulness, esp. to a husband or wife. **2** an instance of this. [ME f. F *infidélité* or L *infidelitas* (as INFIDEL)]

infield /ˈɪnfiːld/ *n.* **1** *Cricket* **a** the part of the ground near the wicket. **b** the fielders stationed there. **2** *Baseball* **a** the area between the four bases. **b** the four fielders stationed on its boundaries. □ **infielder** *n.* (in sense 2).

infighting /ˈɪnˌfaɪtɪŋ/ *n.* **1** hidden conflict or competitiveness within an organization. **2** boxing at closer quarters than arm's length. □ **infighter** *n.*

infill /ˈɪnfɪl/ *n.* & *v.* —*n.* **1** material used to fill a hole, gap, etc. **2** the placing of buildings to occupy the space between existing ones. —*v.tr.* fill in (a cavity etc.).

infilling /ˈɪnˌfɪlɪŋ/ *n.* = INFILL *n.*

infiltrate /ˈɪnfɪlˌtreɪt/ *v.* **1** *tr.* **a** gain entrance or access to surreptitiously and by degrees (as spies etc.). **b** cause to do this. **2** *tr.* permeate by filtration. **3** *tr.* (often foll. by *into, through*) introduce (fluid) by filtration. □ **infiltration** /-ˈtreɪʃ(ə)n/ *n.* **infiltrator** *n.* [IN-² + FILTRATE]

infinite /ˈɪnfɪnɪt/ *adj.* & *n.* —*adj.* **1** boundless, endless. **2** very great. **3** (usu. with *pl.*) innumerable; very many (*infinite resources*). —*n.* **1** (**the Infinite**) God. **2** (**the infinite**) infinite space. □ **infinitely** *adv.* **infiniteness** *n.* [ME f. L *infinitus* (as IN-¹, FINITE)]

infinitesimal /ˌɪnfɪnɪˈtesɪm(ə)l/ *adj.* & *n.* —*adj.* infinitely or very small. —*n.* an infinitesimal amount. □ **infinitesimal calculus** the differential and integral calculuses regarded as one subject. □ **infinitesimally** *adv.* [mod.L *infinitesimus* f. INFINITE: cf. CENTESIMAL]

infinitive /ɪnˈfɪnɪtɪv/ *n.* a form of a verb expressing the verbal notion without reference to a particular subject, tense, etc. (e.g. *see* in *we came to see, let him see*). □ **infinitival** /-ˈtaɪv(ə)l/ *adj.* **infinitivally** /-ˈtaɪvəlɪ/ *adv.* [L *infinitivus* (as IN-¹, *finitivus* definite f. *finire finit-* define)]

infinitude /ɪnˈfɪnɪˌtjuːd/ *n.* **1** the state of being infinite; boundlessness. **2** (often foll. by *of*) a boundless number or extent. [L *infinitus*: see INFINITE, -TUDE]

infinity /ɪnˈfɪnɪtɪ/ *n.* (*pl.* **-ies**) **1** the state of being infinite. **2** an infinite number or extent. **3** infinite distance. **4** *Math.* infinite quantity. [ME f. OF *infinité* or L *infinitas* (as INFINITE)]

infirm /ɪnˈfɜːm/ *adj.* **1** physically weak, esp. through age. **2** (of a person, mind, judgement, etc.) weak, irresolute. □ **infirmity** *n.* (*pl.* **-ies**). **infirmly** *adv.* [ME f. L *infirmus* (as IN-¹, FIRM¹)]

infirmary /ɪnˈfɜːmərɪ/ *n.* (*pl.* **-ies**) **1** a hospital. **2** a place for those who are ill in a monastery, school, etc. [med.L *infirmaria* (as INFIRM)]

infix *v.tr.* /ɪnˈfɪks/ (often foll. by *in*) **1** fix (a thing in another). **2** impress (a fact etc. in the mind). □ **infixation** /-ˈseɪʃ(ə)n/ *n.* [L *infigere infix-* (as IN-², FIX): (n.) after *prefix, suffix*]

in flagrante delicto /ˌɪn fləˌɡræntɪ dɪˈlɪktəʊ/ *adj.* in the very act of committing an offence. [L, = in blazing crime]

inflame /ɪnˈfleɪm/ *v.* **1** *tr.* & *intr.* (often foll. by *with, by*) provoke or become provoked to strong feeling, esp. anger. **2** *Med.* **a** *intr.* become hot, reddened, and sore. **b** *tr.* cause inflammation or fever in (a body etc.); make hot. **3** *tr.* aggravate. **4** *intr.* & *tr.* catch or set on fire. **5** *tr.* light up with or as if with flames. □ **inflamer** *n.* [ME f. OF *enflamer* f. L *inflammare* (as IN-², *flamma* flame)]

inflammable /ɪnˈflæməb(ə)l/ *adj.* **1** easily set on fire; flammable. **2** easily excited. □ **inflammability** /-ˈbɪlɪtɪ/ *n.* **inflammableness** *n.* **inflammably** *adv.* [INFLAME after F *inflammable*]

■ **Usage** Where there is a danger of this word being understood to mean the opposite, i.e. 'not easily set on fire', *flammable* can be used to avoid confusion.

inflammation /ˌɪnfləˈmeɪʃ(ə)n/ *n.* **1** the act or an instance of inflaming. **2** *Med.* a localized physical condition with heat, swelling, redness, and usu. pain, esp. as a reaction to injury or infection. [L *inflammatio* (as INFLAME)]

inflammatory /ɪnˈflæmətərɪ/ *adj.* **1** (esp. of speeches, leaflets, etc.) tending to cause anger etc. **2** of or tending to inflammation of the body.

inflatable /ɪnˈfleɪtəb(ə)l/ *adj.* & *n.* —*adj.* that can be inflated. —*n.* an inflatable plastic or rubber object.

inflate /ɪnˈfleɪt/ *v.tr.* **1** distend (a balloon etc.) with air. **2** (usu. foll. by *with*; usu. in *passive*) puff up (a person with pride etc.). **3 a** (often *absol.*) bring about inflation (of the currency). **b** raise (prices) artificially. **4** (as **inflated** *adj.*) (esp. of language, sentiments, etc.) bombastic. □ **inflatedly** *adv.* **inflatedness** *n.* **inflater** *n.* **inflator** *n.* [L *inflare inflat-* (as IN-², *flare* blow)]

inflation /ɪnˈfleɪʃ(ə)n/ *n.* **1 a** the act or condition of inflating or being inflated. **b** an instance of this. **2** *Econ.* **a** a general increase in prices and fall in the purchasing value of money. **b** an increase in available currency regarded as causing this. □ **inflationary** *adj.* **inflationism** *n.* **inflationist** *n.* & *adj.* [ME f. L *inflatio* (as INFLATE)]

inflect /ɪnˈflekt/ *v.* **1** *tr.* change the pitch of (the voice, a musical note, etc.). **2** *Gram.* **a** *tr.* change the form of (a word) to express tense, gender, number, mood, etc. **b** *intr.* (of a word, language, etc.) undergo such change. **3** *tr.* bend inwards; curve. □ **inflective** *adj.* [ME f. L *inflectere inflex-* (as IN-², *flectere* bend)]

inflection /ɪnˈflekʃ(ə)n/ *n.* (also **inflexion**) **1 a** the act or condition of inflecting or being inflected. **b** an instance of this. **2** *Gram.* **a** the process or practice of inflecting words. **b** an inflected form of a word. **c** a suffix etc. used to inflect, e.g. *-ed*. **3** a modulation of the voice. □ **inflectional** *adj.* **inflectionally** *adv.* **inflectionless** *adj.* [F *inflection* or L *inflexio* (as INFLECT)]

inflexible /ɪnˈfleksɪb(ə)l/ *adj.* **1** unbendable. **2** stiff; immovable; obstinate. □ **inflexibility** /-ˈbɪlɪtɪ/ *n.* **inflexibly** *adv.* [L *inflexibilis* (as IN-¹, FLEXIBLE)]

inflict /ɪnˈflɪkt/ *v.tr.* (usu. foll. by *on*, *upon*) **1** administer, deal (a stroke, wound, defeat, etc.). **2** (also *refl.*) often *joc.* impose (suffering, a penalty, oneself, one's company, etc.) on (*shall not inflict myself on you any longer*). □ **inflictable** *adj.* **inflicter** *n.* **infliction** *n.* **inflictor** *n.* [L *infligere inflict-* (as IN-², *fligere* strike)]

inflight /ˈɪnflaɪt/ *attrib.adj.* occurring or provided during an aircraft flight.

inflorescence /ˌɪnfləˈres(ə)ns/ *n.* **1** *Bot.* **a** the complete flower-head of a plant including stems, stalks, bracts, and flowers. **b** the arrangement of this. **2** the process of flowering. [mod.L *inflorescentia* f. LL *inflorescere* (as IN-², FLORESCENCE)]

inflow /ˈɪnfləʊ/ *n.* **1** a flowing in. **2** something that flows in. □ **inflowing** *n.* & *adj.*

influence /ˈɪnfluəns/ *n.* & *v.* —*n.* **1** (usu. foll. by *on*, *upon*) the effect a person or thing has on another. **2** (usu. foll. by *over*, *with*) moral ascendancy or power. **3** a thing or person exercising such power (*is a good influence on them*). —*v.tr.* exert influence on; have an effect on. □ **under the influence** *colloq.* affected by alcoholic drink. □ **influenceable** *adj.* **influencer** *n.* [ME f. OF *influence* or med.L *influentia* inflow f. L *influere* flow in (as IN-², *fluere* flow)]

influential /ˌɪnfluˈenʃ(ə)l/ *adj.* having a great influence or power (*influential in the financial world*). □ **influentially** *adv.* [med.L *influentia* INFLUENCE]

influenza /ˌɪnfluˈenzə/ *n.* a highly contagious virus infection causing fever, severe aching, and catarrh. □ **influenzal** *adj.* [It. f. med.L *influentia* INFLUENCE]

influx /ˈɪnflʌks/ *n.* **1** a continual stream of people or things (*an influx of complaints*). **2** (usu. foll. by *into*) a flowing in, esp. of a stream etc. [F *influx* or LL *influxus* (as IN-², FLUX)]

info /ˈɪnfəʊ/ *n.* *colloq.* information. [abbr.]

infold var. of ENFOLD.

inform /ɪnˈfɔːm/ *v.* **1** *tr.* (usu. foll. by *of*, *about*, *on*, or *that*, *how* + clause) tell. **2** *intr.* (usu. foll. by *against*, *on*) make an accusation. **3** *tr.* (usu. foll. by *with*) *literary* inspire or imbue (a person, heart, or thing) with a feeling, principle, quality, etc. **4** *tr.* impart its quality to; permeate. □ **informant** *n.* [ME f. OF *enfo(u)rmer* f. L *informare* give shape to, fashion, describe (as IN-², *forma* form)]

informal /ɪnˈfɔːm(ə)l/ *adj.* **1** without ceremony or formality (*just an informal chat*). **2** (of language, clothing, etc.) everyday; normal. □ **informal vote** *NZ* & *Austral.* an invalid vote or voting paper. □ **informality** /-ˈmælɪtɪ/ *n.* (*pl.* **-ies**) **informally** *adv.*

information /ˌɪnfəˈmeɪʃ(ə)n/ *n.* **1 a** something told; knowledge. **b** (usu. foll. by *on*, *about*) items of knowledge; news (*the latest information on the crisis*). **2** *Law* (usu. foll. by *against*) a charge or complaint lodged with a court or magistrate. □ **information retrieval** the tracing of information stored in books, computers, etc. **information science** the study of the processes for storing and retrieving information. **information theory** *Math.* the quantitative study of the transmission of information by signals etc. □ **informational** *adj.* **informationally** *adv.* [ME f. OF f. L *informatio -onis* (as INFORM)]

informative /ɪnˈfɔːmətɪv/ *adj.* (also **informatory** /ɪnˈfɔːmətərɪ/) giving information; instructive. □ **informatively** *adv.* **informativeness** *n.* [med.L *informativus* (as INFORM)]

informed /ɪnˈfɔːmd/ *adj.* **1** knowing the facts; instructed (*his answers show that he is badly informed*). **2** educated; intelligent. □ **informedly** /also ɪnˈfɔːmɪdlɪ/ *adv.* **informedness** /also ɪnˈfɔːmɪdnɪs/ *n.*

informer /ɪnˈfɔːmə(r)/ *n.* **1** a person who informs against another. **2** a person who informs or advises.

infra- /ˈɪnfrə/ *comb. form* **1** below (opp. SUPRA-). **2** *Anat.* below or under a part of the body. [from or after L *infra* below, beneath]

infraction /ɪnˈfrækʃ(ə)n/ *n.* esp. *Law* a violation or infringement. □ **infract** *v.tr.* **infractor** *n.* [L *infractio* (as INFRINGE)]

infra dig /ˌɪnfrə ˈdɪɡ/ *predic.adj.* *colloq.* beneath one's dignity; unbecoming. [abbr. of L *infra dignitatem*]

infrared /ˌɪnfrəˈred/ *adj.* **1** having a wavelength just greater than the red end of the visible light spectrum. **2** of or using such radiation.

infrasonic /ˌɪnfrəˈsɒnɪk/ *adj.* of or relating to sound waves with a frequency below the lower limit of human audibility. □ **infrasonically** *adv.*

infrasound /ˈɪnfrəˌsaʊnd/ n. sound waves with frequencies below the lower limit of human audibility.

infrastructure /ˈɪnfrəˌstrʌktʃə(r)/ n. **1 a** the basic structural foundations of a society or enterprise; a substructure or foundation. **b** roads, bridges, sewers, etc., regarded as a country's economic foundation. **2** permanent installations as a basis for military etc. operations. [F (as INFRA-, STRUCTURE)]

infrequent /ɪnˈfriːkwənt/ adj. not frequent. □ **infrequency** n. **infrequently** adv. [L infrequens (as IN-1, FREQUENT)]

infringe /ɪnˈfrɪndʒ/ v. **1** tr. **a** act contrary to; violate (a law, an oath, etc.). **b** act in defiance of (another's rights etc.). **2** intr. (usu. foll. by on, upon) encroach; trespass. □ **infringement** n. **infringer** n. [L infringere infract- (as IN-2, frangere break)]

infuriate /ɪnˈfjʊərɪˌeɪt/ v.tr. fill with fury; enrage. □ **infuriating** /ɪnˈfjʊərɪˌeɪtɪŋ/ adj. **infuriatingly** /ɪnˈfjʊərɪˌeɪtɪŋlɪ/ adv. **infuriation** /-ˈeɪʃ(ə)n/ n. [med.L infuriare infuriat- (as IN-2, L furia FURY)]

infuse /ɪnˈfjuːz/ v. **1** tr. (usu. foll. by with) imbue; pervade (anger infused with resentment). **2** tr. steep (herbs, tea, etc.) in liquid to extract the content. **3** tr. (usu. foll. by into) instil (grace, spirit, life, etc.). **4** intr. undergo infusion (let it infuse for five minutes). **5** tr. (usu. foll. by into) pour (a thing). □ **infusable** adj. **infuser** n. **infusive** /-sɪv/ adj. [ME f. L infundere infus- (as IN-2, fundere pour)]

infusible /ɪnˈfjuːzɪb(ə)l/ adj. not able to be fused or melted. □ **infusibility** /-ˈbɪlɪtɪ/ n.

infusion /ɪnˈfjuːʒ(ə)n/ n. **1** a liquid obtained by infusing. **2** an infused element; an admixture. **3 a** the act of infusing. **b** an instance of this. [ME f. F infusion or L infusio (as INFUSE)]

-ing1 suffix forming gerunds and nouns from verbs (or occas. from nouns), denoting: **1 a** the verbal action or its result (asking; carving; fighting; learning). **b** the verbal action as described or classified in some way (tough going). **2** material used for or associated with a process etc. (piping; washing). **3** an occupation or event (banking; wedding). **4** a set or arrangement of (colouring; feathering). [OE -ung, -ing f. Gmc]

-ing2 suffix **1** forming the present participle of verbs (asking; fighting), often as adjectives (charming; strapping). **2** forming adjectives from nouns (hulking) and verbs (balding). [ME alt. of OE -ende, later -inde]

-ing3 suffix forming nouns meaning 'one belonging to' or 'one having the quality of', surviving esp. in names of coins and fractional parts (farthing; gelding; riding). [OE f. Gmc]

ingenious /ɪnˈdʒiːnɪəs/ adj. **1** clever at inventing, constructing, organizing, etc.; skilful; resourceful. **2** (of a machine, theory, etc.) cleverly contrived. □ **ingeniously** adv. **ingeniousness** n. [ME, = talented, f. F ingénieux or L ingeniosus f. ingenium cleverness: cf. ENGINE]

■ **Usage** This word is sometimes confused with ingenuous.

ingénue /ˈæʒeɪˈnjuː/ n. **1** an innocent or unsophisticated young woman. **2** Theatr. **a** such a part in a play. **b** the actress who plays this part. [F, fem. of ingénu INGENUOUS]

ingenuity /ˌɪndʒɪˈnjuːɪtɪ/ n. skill in devising or contriving; ingeniousness. [L ingenuitas ingenuousness (as INGENUOUS); Engl. meaning by confusion of INGENIOUS with INGENUOUS]

ingenuous /ɪnˈdʒenjʊəs/ adj. **1** innocent; artless. **2** open; frank. □ **ingenuously** adv. **ingenuousness** n. [L ingenuus free-born, frank (as IN-2, root of gignere beget)]

■ **Usage** This word is sometimes confused with ingenious.

ingest /ɪnˈdʒest/ v.tr. **1** take in (food etc.); eat. **2** absorb (facts, knowledge, etc.). □ **ingestion** /ɪnˈdʒestʃ(ə)n/ n. **ingestive** adj. [L ingerere ingest- (as IN-2, gerere carry)]

inglenook /ˈɪŋg(ə)lˌnʊk/ n. a space within the opening on either side of a large fireplace. [dial. (orig. Sc.) ingle fire burning on a hearth, perh. f. Gael. aingeal fire, light, + NOOK]

inglorious /ɪnˈglɔːrɪəs/ adj. **1** shameful; ignominious. **2** not famous. □ **ingloriously** adv. **ingloriousness** n.

ingoing /ˈɪnˌgəʊɪŋ/ adj. **1** going in; entering. **2** penetrating; thorough.

ingot /ˈɪŋgɒt, -gət/ n. a usu. oblong piece of cast metal, esp. of gold, silver, or steel. [ME: perh. f. IN1 + goten past part. of OE geotan cast]

ingraft var. of ENGRAFT.

ingrained /ɪnˈgreɪnd, attrib. ˈɪn-/ adj. **1** deeply rooted; inveterate. **2** thorough. **3** (of dirt etc.) deeply embedded. □ **ingrainedly** /-ˈgreɪnɪdlɪ/ adv. [var. of engrained f. OF engrainer dye in grain (en graine, a cochineal dye)]

ingratiate /ɪnˈgreɪʃɪˌeɪt/ v.refl. (usu. foll. by with) bring oneself into favour. □ **ingratiating** adj. **ingratiatingly** adv. **ingratiation** /-ˈeɪʃ(ə)n/ n. [L in gratiam into favour]

ingratitude /ɪnˈgrætɪˌtjuːd/ n. a lack of due gratitude. [ME f. OF ingratitude or LL ingratitudo f. ingratus (as IN-1, gratus grateful)]

ingredient /ɪnˈgriːdɪənt/ n. a component part or element in a recipe, mixture, or combination. [ME f. L ingredi ingress- enter (as IN-2, gradi step)]

ingress /ˈɪngres/ n. the act or right of going in or entering. □ **ingression** /ɪnˈgreʃ(ə)n/ n. [ME f. L ingressus (as INGREDIENT)]

ingrowing /ˈɪnˌgrəʊɪŋ/ adj. growing inwards, esp. (of a toenail) growing into the flesh. □ **ingrown** adj. **ingrowth** n.

inguinal /ˈɪŋgwɪn(ə)l/ adj. of the groin. □ **inguinally** adv. [L inguinalis f. inguen -inis groin]

ingulf var. of ENGULF.

inhabit /ɪnˈhæbɪt/ v.tr. (**inhabited, inhabiting**) (of a person or animal) dwell in; occupy (a region, town, house, etc.). □ **inhabitability** /-təˈbɪlɪtɪ/ n. **inhabitable** adj. **inhabitant** n. **inhabitation** /-ˈteɪʃ(ə)n/ n. [ME inhabite, enhabite f. OF enhabiter or L inhabitare (as IN-2, habitare dwell): see HABIT]

inhalant /ɪnˈheɪlənt/ n. a medicinal preparation for inhaling.

inhale /ɪnˈheɪl/ v.tr. (often absol.) breathe in (air, gas, tobacco-smoke, etc.). □ **inhalation** /-həˈleɪʃ(ə)n/ n. [L inhalare breathe in (as IN-2, halare breathe)]

inhaler /ɪnˈheɪlə(r)/ n. a portable device used for relieving esp. asthma by inhaling.

inharmonious /ˌɪnhɑːˈməʊnɪəs/ adj. esp. Mus. not harmonious. □ **inharmoniously** adv.

inhere /ɪnˈhɪə(r)/ v.intr. (often foll. by in) **1** exist essentially or permanently in (goodness inheres *in that child).* **2** (of rights etc.) be vested in (a person etc.). [L *inhaerēre inhaes-* (as IN-², *haerēre* to stick)]

inherent /ɪnˈhɪərənt, ɪnˈherənt/ *adj.* (often foll. by *in*) **1** existing in something, esp. as a permanent or characteristic attribute. **2** vested in (a person etc.) as a right or privilege. □ **inherence** *n.* **inherently** *adv.* [L *inhaerēre inhaerent-* (as INHERE)]

inherit /ɪnˈherɪt/ *v.* (**inherited, inheriting**) **1** *tr.* receive (property, rank, title, etc.) by legal descent or succession. **2** *tr.* derive (a quality or characteristic) genetically from one's ancestors. **3** *absol.* succeed as an heir (*a younger son rarely inherits*). □ **inheritability** *n.* **inheritable** *adj.* **inheritor** *n.* (*fem.* **inheritress** or **inheritrix**). [ME f. OF *enheriter* f. LL *inhereditare* (as IN-², L *heres heredis* heir)]

inheritance /ɪnˈherɪt(ə)ns/ *n.* **1** something that is inherited. **2 a** the act of inheriting. **b** an instance of this. □ **inheritance tax** a tax levied on property etc. acquired by gift or inheritance. [ME f. AF *inheritaunce* f. OF *enheriter*: see INHERIT]

■ **Usage** This tax was introduced in 1986 to replace *capital transfer tax.*

inhibit /ɪnˈhɪbɪt/ *v.tr.* (**inhibited, inhibiting**) **1** hinder, restrain, or prevent (an action or progress). **2** (as **inhibited** *adj.*) subject to inhibition. **3** (usu. foll. by *from* + verbal noun) forbid or prohibit (a person etc.). □ **inhibitive** *adj.* **inhibitor** *n.* **inhibitory** *adj.* [L *inhibēre* (as IN-², *habēre* hold)]

inhibition /ˌɪnhɪˈbɪʃ(ə)n/ *n.* **1** *Psychol.* a restraint on the direct expression of an instinct. **2** *colloq.* an emotional resistance to a thought, an action, etc. (*has inhibitions about singing in public*). **3 a** the act of inhibiting. **b** the process of being inhibited. [ME f. OF *inhibition* or L *inhibitio* (as INHIBIT)]

inhospitable /ˌɪnhɒˈspɪtəb(ə)l, ɪnˈhɒsp-/ *adj.* **1** not hospitable. **2** (of a region, coast, etc.) not affording shelter etc. □ **inhospitableness** *n.* **inhospitably** *adv.* [obs. F (as IN-¹, HOSPITABLE)]

in-house /ˈɪnhaʊs, -ˈhaʊs/ *adj.* & *adv.* —*adj.* done or existing within an institution, company, etc. (*an in-house project*). —*adv.* internally, without outside assistance.

inhuman /ɪnˈhjuːmən/ *adj.* **1** (of a person, conduct, etc.) brutal; unfeeling; barbarous. **2** not of a human type. □ **inhumanly** *adv.* [L *inhumanus* (as IN-¹, HUMAN)]

inhumane /ˌɪnhjuːˈmeɪn/ *adj.* not humane. □ **inhumanely** *adv.* [L *inhumanus* (see INHUMAN) & f. IN-¹ + HUMANE, orig. = INHUMAN]

inhumanity /ˌɪnhjuːˈmænɪtɪ/ *n.* (*pl.* **-ies**) **1** brutality; barbarousness; callousness. **2** an inhumane act.

inimical /ɪˈnɪmɪk(ə)l/ *adj.* (usu. foll. by *to*) **1** hostile. **2** harmful. □ **inimically** *adv.* [LL *inimicalis* f. L *inimicus* (as IN-¹, *amicus* friend)]

inimitable /ɪˈnɪmɪtəb(ə)l/ *adj.* impossible to imitate. □ **inimitability** /-ˈbɪlɪtɪ/ *n.* **inimitableness** *n.* **inimitably** *adv.* [F *inimitable* or L *inimitabilis* (as IN-¹, *imitabilis* imitable)]

iniquity /ɪˈnɪkwɪtɪ/ *n.* (*pl.* **-ies**) **1** wickedness; unrighteousness. **2** a gross injustice. □ **iniquitous** *adj.* **iniquitously** *adv.* **iniquitousness** *n.* [ME f. OF *iniquité* f. L *iniquitas -tatis* f. *iniquus* (as IN-¹, *aequus* just)]

initial /ɪˈnɪʃ(ə)l/ *adj., n.,* & *v.* —*adj.* of, existing, or occurring at the beginning (*initial stage; initial expenses*). —*n.* **1** = *initial letter.* **2** (usu. in *pl.*) the first letter or letters of the words of a (esp. a person's) name or names. —*v.tr.* (**initialled, initialling;** *US* **initialed, initialing**) mark or sign with one's initials. □ **initial letter** (or **consonant**) a letter or consonant at the beginning of a word. □ **initially** *adv.* [L *initialis* f. *initium* beginning f. *inire init-* go in]

initialism /ɪˈnɪʃəˌlɪz(ə)m/ *n.* a group of initial letters used as an abbreviation for a name or expression, each letter being pronounced separately (e.g. *BBC*).

initialize /ɪˈnɪʃəˌlaɪz/ *v.tr.* (also **-ise**) (often foll. by *to*) *Computing* set to the value or put in the condition appropriate to the start of an operation. □ **initialization** /-ˈzeɪʃ(ə)n/ *n.*

initiate *v., n.,* & *adj.* —*v.tr.* /ɪˈnɪʃɪˌeɪt/ **1** begin; set going; originate. **2 a** (usu. foll. by *into*) admit (a person) into a society, an office, a secret, etc., esp. with a ritual. **b** (usu. foll. by *in, into*) instruct (a person) in science, art, etc. —*n.* /ɪˈnɪʃɪət/ a person who has been newly initiated. —*adj.* /ɪˈnɪʃɪət/ (of a person) newly initiated (*an initiate member*). □ **initiation** /-ˈeɪʃ(ə)n/ *n.* **initiator** *n.* **initiatory** /ɪˈnɪʃɪətərɪ, ɪˈnɪʃətərɪ/ *adj.* [L *initiare* f. *initium:* see INITIAL]

initiative /ɪˈnɪʃɪətɪv, ɪˈnɪʃɪətɪv/ *n.* **1** the ability to initiate things; enterprise (*I'm afraid he lacks all initiative*). **2** a first step; origination (*a peace initiative*). **3** the power or right to begin something. □ **on one's own initiative** without being prompted by others. **take the initiative** (usu. foll. by *in* + verbal noun) be the first to take action. [F (as INITIATE)]

inject /ɪnˈdʒekt/ *v.tr.* **1** *Med.* **a** (usu. foll. by *into*) drive or force (a solution, medicine, etc.) by or as if by a syringe. **b** (usu. foll. by *with*) fill (a cavity etc.) by injecting. **c** administer medicine etc. to (a person) by injection. **2** place or insert (an object, a quality, etc.) into something (*may I inject a note of realism?*). □ **injectable** *adj.* & *n.* **injector** *n.* [L *injicere* (as IN-², *jacere* throw)]

injection /ɪnˈdʒekʃ(ə)n/ *n.* **1 a** the act of injecting. **b** an instance of this. **2** a liquid or solution (to be) injected (*prepare a morphine injection*). [F *injection* or L *injectio* (as INJECT)]

injudicious /ˌɪndʒuːˈdɪʃəs/ *adj.* unwise; ill-judged. □ **injudiciously** *adv.* **injudiciousness** *n.*

injunction /ɪnˈdʒʌŋkʃ(ə)n/ *n.* **1** an authoritative warning or order. **2** *Law* a judicial order restraining a person from an act or compelling redress to an injured party. □ **injunctive** *adj.* [LL *injunctio* f. L *injungere* ENJOIN]

injure /ˈɪndʒə(r)/ *v.tr.* **1** do physical harm or damage to; hurt (*was injured in a road accident*). **2** harm or impair (*illness might injure her chances*). **3** do wrong to. □ **injurer** *n.* [back-form. f. INJURY]

injured /ˈɪndʒəd/ *adj.* **1** harmed or hurt (*the injured passengers*). **2** offended; wronged (*in an injured tone*).

injurious /ɪnˈdʒʊərɪəs/ *adj.* **1** hurtful. **2** (of language) insulting; libellous. **3** wrongful. □ **injuriously** *adv.* **injuriousness** *n.* [ME f. F *injurieux* or L *injuriosus* (as INJURY)]

injury /ˈɪndʒərɪ/ *n.* (*pl.* **-ies**) **1 a** a physical harm or damage. **b** an instance of this (*suffered head injuries*). **2** esp. *Law* **a** a wrongful action or treatment. **b** an instance of this. **3** damage to one's good name etc. [ME f. AF *injurie* f. L *injuria* a wrong (as IN-¹, *jus juris* right)]

injustice /ɪnˈdʒʌstɪs/ *n.* **1** a lack of fairness or justice. **2** an unjust act. □ **do a person an injustice** judge a person unfairly. [ME f. OF f. L *injustitia* (as IN-¹, JUSTICE)]

ink *n.* & *v.* —*n.* **1 a** a coloured fluid used for writing with a pen, marking with a rubber stamp, etc. **b** a thick paste used in printing, duplicating, in ball-point pens, etc. **2** *Zool.* a black liquid ejected by a cuttlefish, octopus, etc. to confuse a predator. —*v.tr.* **1** (usu. foll. by *in*, *over*, etc.) mark with ink. **2** cover (type etc.) with ink before printing. **3** apply ink to. □ **ink out** obliterate with ink. **ink-pad** an ink-soaked pad, usu. in a box, used for inking a rubber stamp etc. **ink-well** a pot for ink usu. housed in a hole in a desk. □ **inker** *n.* [ME *enke*, *inke* f. OF *enque* f. LL *encau(s)tum* f. Gk *egkauston* purple ink used by Roman emperors for signature (as EN-², CAUSTIC)]

inkling /ˈɪŋklɪŋ/ *n.* (often foll. by *of*) a slight knowledge or suspicion; a hint. [ME *inkle* utter in an undertone, of unkn. orig.]

inkstand /ˈɪŋkstænd/ *n.* a stand for one or more ink bottles, often incorporating a pen tray etc.

inky /ˈɪŋkɪ/ *adj.* (**inkier**, **inkiest**) of, as black as, or stained with ink. □ **inkiness** *n.*

inlaid *past* and *past part.* of INLAY.

inland /ˈɪnlənd, ˈɪnlænd/ *adj.*, *n.*, & *adv.* —*adj.* **1** situated in the interior of a country. **2** *esp. Brit.* carried on within the limits of a country; domestic (*inland trade*). —*n.* the parts of a country remote from the sea or frontiers; the interior. —*adv.* /ɪnˈlænd/ in or towards the interior of a country. □ **Inland Revenue** (in the UK) the government department responsible for assessing and collecting taxes and duties on inland trade. □ **inlander** *n.* **inlandish** *adj.*

in-law /ˈɪnlɔː/ *n.* (often in *pl.*) a relative by marriage.

inlay *v.* & *n.* —*v.tr.* /ɪnˈleɪ/ (*past* and *past part.* **inlaid** /ɪnˈleɪd/) **1 a** (usu. foll. by *in*) embed (a thing in another) so that the surfaces are even. **b** (usu. foll. by *with*) ornament (a thing with inlaid work). **2** (as **inlaid** *adj.*) (of a piece of furniture etc.) ornamented by inlaying. —*n.* /ˈɪnleɪ/ **1** inlaid work. **2** material inlaid. □ **inlayer** *n.* [IN-² + LAY¹]

inlet /ˈɪnlet, -lɪt/ *n.* **1** a small arm of the sea, a lake, or a river. **2** a piece inserted, esp. in dressmaking etc. **3** a way of entry. [ME f. IN + LET¹ *v.*]

in loco parentis /ɪn ˌləʊkəʊ pəˈrentɪs/ *adv.* in the place or position of a parent (used of a teacher etc. responsible for children). [L]

inmate /ˈɪnmeɪt/ *n.* (usu. foll. by *of*) **1** an occupant of a hospital, prison, institution, etc. **2** an occupant of a house etc., esp. one of several. [prob. orig. INN + MATE¹, assoc. with IN]

in memoriam /ɪn mɪˈmɔːrɪˌæm/ *prep.* & *n.* —*prep.* in memory of (a dead person). —*n.* a written article etc. in memory of a dead person; an obituary. [L]

inmost /ˈɪnməʊst, -məst/ *adj.* **1** most inward. **2** most intimate; deepest. [OE *innemest* (as IN, -MOST)]

inn *n.* **1** a public house providing alcoholic liquor for consumption on the premises, and sometimes accommodation etc. **2** *hist.* a house providing accommodation, esp. for travellers. □

Inn of Court *Brit. Law* each of the four legal societies having the exclusive right of admitting people to the English bar. [OE *inn* (as IN)]

innards /ˈɪnədz/ *n.pl. colloq.* **1** entrails. **2** works (of an engine etc.). [dial. etc. pronunc. of *inwards*: see INWARD *n.*]

innate /ɪˈneɪt, ˈɪ-/ *adj.* inborn; natural. □ **innately** *adv.* **innateness** *n.* [ME f. L *innatus* (as IN-², *natus* past part. of *nasci* be born)]

inner /ˈɪnə(r)/ *adj.* & *n.* —*adj.* (usu. *attrib.*) **1** further in; inside; interior (*the inner compartment*). **2** (of thoughts, feelings, etc.) deeper; more secret. —*n.* *Archery* **1** a division of the target next to the bull's-eye. **2** a shot that strikes this. □ **inner city** the central most densely populated area of a city. **inner man** (or **woman**) **1** the soul or mind. **2** *joc.* the stomach. **inner space** the region between the earth and outer space, or below the surface of the sea. **inner tube** a separate inflatable tube inside the cover of a pneumatic tyre. □ **innerly** *adv.* **innermost** *adj.* **innerness** *n.* [OE *innera* (adj.), compar. of IN]

inning /ˈɪnɪŋ/ *n.* *US* an innings at baseball etc. [*in* (v.) go in (f. IN)]

innings /ˈɪnɪŋz/ *n.* (*pl.* same or *colloq.* **inningses**) **1** *esp. Cricket* **a** the part of a game during which a side is in or batting. **b** the play of or score achieved by a player during a turn at batting. **2** a period during which a government, party, cause, etc. is in office or effective.

innkeeper /ˈɪnˌkiːpə(r)/ *n.* a person who keeps an inn.

innocent /ˈɪnəs(ə)nt/ *adj.* & *n.* —*adj.* **1** free from moral wrong; sinless. **2** (usu. foll. by *of*) not guilty (of a crime etc.). **3 a** simple; guileless; naïve. **b** pretending to be guileless. **4** harmless. **5** (foll. by *of*) *colloq.* without, lacking (*appeared, innocent of shoes*). —*n.* an innocent person, esp. a young child. □ **innocence** *n.* **innocency** *n.* **innocently** *adv.* [ME f. OF *innocent* or L *innocens innocent-* (as IN-¹, *nocēre* hurt)]

innocuous /ɪˈnɒkjʊəs/ *adj.* **1** not injurious; harmless. **2** inoffensive. □ **innocuity** /ˌɪnəˈkjuːɪtɪ/ *n.* **innocuously** *adv.* **innocuousness** *n.* [L *innocuus* (as IN-¹, *nocuus* formed as INNOCENT)]

innovate /ˈɪnəˌveɪt/ *v.intr.* **1** bring in new methods, ideas, etc. **2** (often foll. by *in*) make changes. □ **innovation** /-ˈveɪʃ(ə)n/ *n.* **innovational** /-ˈveɪʃən(ə)l/ *adj.* **innovative** *adj.* **innovator** *n.* **innovatory** /-ˌveɪtərɪ/ *adj.* [L *innovare* make new, alter (as IN-², *novus* new)]

innuendo /ˌɪnjʊˈendəʊ/ *n.* & *v.* —*n.* (*pl.* **-oes** or **-os**) **1** an allusive or oblique remark or hint, usu. disparaging. **2** a remark with a double meaning, usu. suggestive. —*v.intr.* (**-oes**, **-oed**) make innuendoes. [L, = by nodding at, by pointing to: ablat. gerund of *innuere* nod at (as IN-², *nuere* nod)]

Innuit var. of INUIT.

innumerable /ɪˈnjuːmərəb(ə)l/ *adj.* too many to be counted. □ **innumerability** /-ˈbɪlɪtɪ/ *n.* **innumerably** *adv.* [ME f. L *innumerabilis* (as IN-¹, NUMERABLE)]

innumerate /ɪˈnjuːmərət/ *adj.* having no knowledge of or feeling for mathematical operations; not numerate. □ **innumeracy** /-əsɪ/ *n.* [IN-¹, NUMERATE]

inoculate /ɪˈnɒkjʊˌleɪt/ *v.tr.* **1 a** treat (a person or animal) with a small quantity of the agent of a disease, in the form of vaccine or serum, usu. by injection, to promote immunity against the disease. **b** implant (a disease) by means of vaccine. **2** instil (a person) with ideas or opinions. □ **inoculable** *adj.* **inoculation** /-ˈleɪʃ(ə)n/ *n.* **inoculative** /-lətɪv/ *adj.* **inoculator** *n.* [orig. in sense 'insert (a bud) into a plant': L *inoculare inoculat-* engraft (as IN-², *oculus* eye, bud)]

inoffensive /ˌɪnəˈfensɪv/ *adj.* not objectionable; harmless. □ **inoffensively** *adv.* **inoffensiveness** *n.*

inoperable /ɪnˈɒpərəb(ə)l/ *adj.* **1** *Surgery* that cannot suitably be operated on (*inoperable cancer*). **2** that cannot be operated; inoperative. □ **inoperability** /-ˈbɪlɪtɪ/ *n.* **inoperably** *adv.* [F *inopérable* (as IN-¹, OPERABLE)]

inoperative /ɪnˈɒpərətɪv/ *adj.* not working or taking effect.

inopportune /ɪnˈɒpətjuːn/ *adj.* not appropriate, esp. as regards time; unseasonable. □ **inopportunely** *adv.* **inopportuneness** *n.* [L *inopportunus* (as IN-¹, OPPORTUNE)]

inordinate /ɪnˈɔːdɪnət/ *adj.* **1** immoderate; excessive. **2** intemperate. **3** disorderly. □ **inordinately** *adv.* [ME f. L *inordinatus* (as IN-¹, *ordinatus* past part. of *ordinare* ORDAIN)]

inorganic /ˌɪnɔːˈgænɪk/ *adj.* **1** *Chem.* (of a compound) not organic, usu. of mineral origin (opp. ORGANIC). **2** without organized physical structure. **3** not arising by natural growth; extraneous. □ **inorganic chemistry** the chemistry of inorganic compounds. □ **inorganically** *adv.*

in-patient /ˈɪnˌpeɪʃ(ə)nt/ *n.* a patient who lives in hospital while under treatment.

input /ˈɪnpʊt/ *n.* & *v.* —*n.* **1** what is put in or taken in, or operated on by any process or system. **2** *Electronics* **a** a place where, or a device through which, energy, information, etc., enters a system (*a tape recorder with inputs for microphone and radio*). **b** energy supplied to a device or system; an electrical signal. **3** the information fed into a computer. **4** the action or process of putting in or feeding in. **5** a contribution of information etc. —*v.tr.* (**inputting**; *past* and *past part.* **input** or **inputted**) (often foll. by *into*) **1** put in. **2** *Computing* supply (data, programs, etc., to a computer, program, etc.). □ **inputter** *n.*

inquest /ˈɪnkwest, ˈɪŋ-/ *n.* **1** *Law* **a** an inquiry by a coroner's court into the cause of a death. **b** a judicial inquiry to ascertain the facts relating to an incident etc. **c** a coroner's jury. **2** *colloq.* a discussion analysing the outcome of a game, an election, etc. [ME f. OF *enqueste* (as ENQUIRE)]

inquietude /ɪnˈkwaɪɪˌtjuːd, ɪŋ-/ *n.* uneasiness of mind or body. [ME f. OF *inquietude* or LL *inquietudo* f. L *inquietus* (as IN-¹, *quietus* quiet)]

inquire /ɪnˈkwaɪə(r), ɪŋ-/ *v.* **1** *intr.* seek information formally; make a formal investigation. **2** *intr.* & *tr.* = ENQUIRE. □ **inquirer** *n.* [var. of ENQUIRE]

inquiry /ɪnˈkwaɪərɪ, ɪŋ-/ *n.* (pl. **-ies**) **1** an investigation, esp. an official one. **2** = ENQUIRY.

inquisition /ˌɪnkwɪˈzɪʃ(ə)n, ˌɪŋ-/ *n.* **1** usu. *derog.* an intensive search or investigation. **2** a judicial or official inquiry. **3** (**the Inquisition**) *RC Ch. hist.* an ecclesiastical tribunal for the suppression of heresy, esp. in Spain. □ **inquisitional** *adj.* [ME f. OF f. L *inquisitio -onis* examination (as INQUIRE)]

inquisitive /ɪnˈkwɪzɪtɪv, ɪŋ-/ *adj.* **1** unduly curious; prying. **2** seeking knowledge; inquiring. □

inquisitively *adv.* **inquisitiveness** *n.* [ME f. OF *inquisitif -ive* f. LL *inquisitivus* (as INQUISITION)]

inquisitor /ɪnˈkwɪzɪtə(r), ɪŋ-/ *n.* **1** an official investigator. **2** *hist.* an officer of the Inquisition. [F *inquisiteur* f. L *inquisitor -oris* (as INQUIRE)]

inquisitorial /ɪnˌkwɪzɪˈtɔːrɪəl, ɪŋ-/ *adj.* **1** of or like an inquisitor. **2** offensively prying. □ **inquisitorially** *adv.* [med.L *inquisitorius* (as INQUISITOR)]

inquorate /ɪnˈkwɔːreɪt, ɪŋ-/ *adj.* not constituting a quorum.

in re /ɪn ˈriː, ˈreɪ/ *prep.* = RE¹. [L, = in the matter of]

inroad /ˈɪnrəʊd/ *n.* **1** (often in *pl.*; usu. foll. by *on*, *into*) an encroachment; a using up of resources etc. (*makes inroads on my time*). **2** a hostile attack; a raid. [IN + ROAD in sense 'riding']

inrush /ˈɪnrʌʃ/ *n.* a rushing in; an influx. □ **inrushing** *adj.* & *n.*

insalubrious /ˌɪnsəˈluːbrɪəs, -ˈljuːbrɪəs/ *adj.* (of a climate or place) unhealthy. □ **insalubrity** *n.* [L *insalubris* (as IN-¹, SALUBRIOUS)]

insane /ɪnˈseɪn/ *adj.* **1** not of sound mind; mad. **2** *colloq.* extremely foolish; irrational. □ **insanely** *adv.* **insaneness** *n.* **insanity** /-ˈsænɪtɪ/ *n.* (pl. **-ies**). [L *insanus* (as IN-¹, *sanus* healthy)]

insanitary /ɪnˈsænɪtərɪ/ *adj.* not sanitary; dirty or germ-carrying.

insatiable /ɪnˈseɪʃəb(ə)l/ *adj.* **1** unable to be satisfied. **2** (usu. foll. by *of*) extremely greedy. □ **insatiability** /-ˈbɪlɪtɪ/ *n.* **insatiably** *adv.* [ME f. OF *insaciable* or L *insatiabilis* (as IN-¹, SATIATE)]

insatiate /ɪnˈseɪʃɪət/ *adj.* never satisfied. [L *insatiatus* (as IN-¹, SATIATE)]

inscribe /ɪnˈskraɪb/ *v.tr.* **1 a** (usu. foll. by *in*, *on*) write or carve (words etc.) on stone, metal, paper, a book, etc. **b** (usu. foll. by *with*) mark (a sheet, tablet, etc.) with characters. **2** (usu. foll. by *to*) write an informal dedication (to a person) in or on (a book etc.). **3** enter the name of (a person) on a list or in a book. **4** *Geom.* draw (a figure) within another so that some or all points of it lie on the boundary of the other. □ **inscribable** *adj.* **inscriber** *n.* [L *inscribere inscript-* (as IN-², *scribere* write)]

inscription /ɪnˈskrɪpʃ(ə)n/ *n.* **1** words inscribed, esp. on a monument, coin, stone, or in a book etc. **2 a** the act of inscribing, esp. the informal dedication of a book etc. **b** an instance of this. □ **inscriptional** *adj.* **inscriptive** *adj.* [ME f. L *inscriptio* (as INSCRIBE)]

inscrutable /ɪnˈskruːtəb(ə)l/ *adj.* wholly mysterious, impenetrable. □ **inscrutability** /-ˈbɪlɪtɪ/ *n.* **inscrutableness** *n.* **inscrutably** *adv.* [ME f. eccl.L *inscrutabilis* (as IN-¹, *scrutari* search: see SCRUTINY)]

insect /ˈɪnsekt/ *n.* **1 a** any arthropod of the class Insecta, having a head, thorax, abdomen, two antennae, three pairs of thoracic legs, and usu. one or two pairs of thoracic wings. **b** (loosely) any other small segmented invertebrate animal. **2** an insignificant or contemptible person or creature. □ **insectile** /-ˈsektaɪl/ *adj.* [L *insectum* (*animal*) notched (animal) f. *insecare insect-* (as IN-², *secare* cut)]

insecticide /ɪnˈsektɪˌsaɪd/ *n.* a substance used for killing insects. □ **insecticidal** /-ˈsaɪd(ə)l/ *adj.*

insectivore /ɪnˈsektɪˌvɔː(r)/ *n.* **1** any mammal of the order Insectivora feeding on insects etc., e.g. a hedgehog or mole. **2** any plant which captures and absorbs insects. □ **insectivorous**

/-'tɪvərəs/ adj. [F f. mod.L insectivorus (as INSECT, -VORE: see -VOROUS)]

insecure /ˌɪnsɪ'kjʊə(r)/ adj. **1** (of a person or state of mind) uncertain; lacking confidence. **2 a** unsafe; not firm or fixed. **b** (of ice, ground, etc.) liable to give way. □ **insecurely** adv. **insecurity** /-'kjʊrɪtɪ/ n.

inseminate /ɪn'semɪˌneɪt/ v.tr. **1** introduce semen into (a female) by natural or artificial means. **2** sow (seed etc.). □ **insemination** /-'neɪʃ(ə)n/ n. **inseminator** n. [L inseminare (as IN-², SEMEN)]

insensate /ɪn'senseɪt/ adj. **1** without physical sensation; unconscious. **2** without sensibility; unfeeling. **3** stupid. □ **insensately** adv. [eccl.L insensatus (as IN-¹, sensatus f. sensus SENSE)]

insensibility /ɪnˌsensɪ'bɪlɪtɪ/ n. **1** unconsciousness. **2** a lack of mental feeling or emotion; hardness. **3** (often foll. by to) indifference. [F insensibilité or LL insensibilitas (as INSENSIBLE)]

insensible /ɪn'sensɪb(ə)l/ adj. **1 a** without one's mental faculties; unconscious. **b** (of the extremities etc.) numb; without feeling. **2** (usu. foll. by of, to) unaware; indifferent (insensible of her needs). **3** without emotion; callous. **4** too small or gradual to be perceived; inappreciable. □ **insensibly** adv. [ME f. OF insensible or L insensibilis (as IN-¹, SENSIBLE)]

insensitive /ɪn'sensɪtɪv/ adj. (often foll. by to) **1** unfeeling; boorish; crass. **2** not sensitive to physical stimuli. □ **insensitively** adv. **insensitiveness** n. **insensitivity** /-'tɪvɪtɪ/ n.

insentient /ɪn'senʃ(ə)nt/ adj. not sentient; inanimate. □ **insentience** n.

inseparable /ɪn'sep(ə)rəb(ə)l/ adj. & n. —adj. unable or unwilling to be separated. —n. (usu. in pl.) an inseparable person or thing, esp. a friend. □ **inseparability** /-'bɪlɪtɪ/ n. **inseparably** adv. [ME f. L inseparabilis (as IN-¹, SEPARABLE)]

insert v. & n. —v.tr. /ɪn'sɜːt/ **1** (usu. foll. by in, into, between, etc.) place, fit, or thrust (a thing) into another. **2** (usu. foll. by in, into) introduce (a letter, word, article, advertisement, etc.) into a newspaper etc. —n. /'ɪnsɜːt/ something inserted, e.g. a loose page in a magazine, a piece of cloth in a garment, a shot in a cinema film. □ **insertable** adj. **inserter** n. [L inserere (as IN-², serere sert- join)]

insertion /ɪn'sɜː.ʃ(ə)n/ n. **1** the act or an instance of inserting. **2** an amendment etc. inserted in writing or printing. **3** each appearance of an advertisement in a newspaper etc. **4** an ornamental section of needlework inserted into plain material (lace insertions). [LL insertio (as INSERT)]

in-service /'ɪnˌsɜːvɪs/ adj. (of training) intended for those actively engaged in the profession or activity concerned.

inset n. & v. —n. /'ɪnset/ **1 a** an extra page or pages inserted in a folded sheet or in a book; an insert. **b** a small map, photograph, etc., inserted within the border of a larger one. **2 a** piece let into a dress etc. —v.tr. /ɪn'set/ (**insetting**; past and past part. **inset** or **insetted**) **1** put in as an inset. **2** decorate with an inset. □ **insetter** n.

inshore /ɪn'ʃɔː(r), 'ɪn-/ adv. & adj. at sea but close to the shore. □ **inshore of** nearer to shore than.

inside n., adj., adv., & prep. —n. /ɪn'saɪd/ **1 a** the inner side or surface of a thing. **b** the inner part; the interior. **2 a** (of a path) the side next to

the wall or away from the road. **b** (of a double-decker bus) the lower section. **3** (usu. in pl.) colloq. the stomach and bowels (something wrong with my insides). **4** colloq. a position affording inside information (knows someone on the inside). —adj. /'ɪnsaɪd/ **1** situated on or in, or derived from, the inside. **2** Football & Hockey nearer to the centre of the field (inside forward; inside left; inside right). —adv. /ɪn'saɪd/ **1** on, in, or to the inside. **2** sl. in prison. —prep. /ɪn'saɪd/ **1** on the inner side of; within (inside the house). **2** in less than (inside an hour). □ **inside information** information not accessible to outsiders. **inside job** colloq. a crime committed by a person living or working on the premises burgled etc. **inside of** colloq. **1** in less than (a week etc.). **2** Brit. the middle part of. **inside out** with the inner surface turned outwards. **inside track 1** the track which is shorter, because of the curve. **2** a position of advantage. [IN + SIDE]

insider /ɪn'saɪdə(r)/ n. **1** a person who is within a society, organization, etc. (cf. OUTSIDER). **2** a person privy to a secret, esp. when using it to gain advantage. □ **insider dealing** Stock Exch. the illegal practice of trading to one's own advantage through having access to confidential information.

insidious /ɪn'sɪdɪəs/ adj. **1** proceeding or progressing inconspicuously but harmfully (an insidious disease). **2** treacherous; crafty. □ **insidiously** adv. **insidiousness** n. [L insidiosus cunning f. insidiae ambush (as IN-², sedēre sit)]

insight /'ɪnsaɪt/ n. (usu. foll. by into) **1** the capacity of understanding hidden truths etc., esp. of character or situations. **2** an instance of this. □ **insightful** adj. **insightfully** adv. [ME, = 'discernment', prob. of Scand. & LG orig. (as IN-², SIGHT)]

insignia /ɪn'sɪgnɪə/ n. (treated as sing. or pl.; usu. foll. by of) **1** badges (wore his insignia of office). **2** distinguishing marks. [L, pl. of insigne neut. of insignis distinguished (as IN-², signis f. signum SIGN)]

insignificant /ˌɪnsɪg'nɪfɪkənt/ adj. **1** unimportant; trifling. **2** (of a person) undistinguished. **3** meaningless. □ **insignificance** n. **insignificancy** n. **insignificantly** adv.

insincere /ˌɪnsɪn'sɪə(r)/ adj. not sincere; not candid. □ **insincerely** adv. **insincerity** /-'serɪtɪ/ n. (pl. -ies). [L insincerus (as IN-¹, SINCERE)]

insinuate /ɪn'sɪnjʊ.eɪt/ v.tr. **1** (often foll. by that + clause) convey indirectly or obliquely; hint (insinuated that she was lying). **2** (often refl.; usu. foll. by into) **a** introduce (oneself, a person, etc.) into favour, office, etc., by subtle manipulation. **b** introduce (a thing, oneself, etc.) subtly or deviously into a place (insinuated himself into the Royal Box). □ **insinuation** /-'eɪʃ(ə)n/ n. **insinuative** adj. **insinuator** n. **insinuatory** /-jʊətərɪ/ adj. [L insinuare insinuat- (as IN-², sinuare to curve)]

insipid /ɪn'sɪpɪd/ adj. **1** lacking vigour or interest; dull. **2** lacking flavour; tasteless. □ **insipidity** /-'pɪdɪtɪ/ n. **insipidly** adv. **insipidness** n. [F insipide or LL insipidus (as IN-¹, sapidus SAPID)]

insist /ɪn'sɪst/ v.tr. (usu. foll. by that + clause; also absol.) maintain or demand positively and assertively (insisted that he was innocent; give me the bag! I insist!). □ **insist on** demand or maintain (I insist on being present). □ **insister** n. **insistingly** adv. [L insistere stand on, persist (as IN-², sistere stand)]

insistent /ɪnˈsɪst(ə)nt/ adj. 1 (often foll. by on) insisting; demanding positively or continually (is insistent on taking me with him). 2 obtruding itself on the attention (the insistent rattle of the window frame). □ **insistence** n. **insistency** n. **insistently** adv.

in situ /ɪn ˈsɪtjuː/ adv. 1 in its place. 2 in its original place. [L]

insobriety /ˌɪnsəˈbraɪɪtɪ/ n. intemperance, esp. in drinking.

insofar /ˌɪnsəʊˈfɑː(r)/ adv. = in so far (see FAR).

insole /ˈɪnsəʊl/ n. 1 a removable sole worn in a boot or shoe for warmth etc. 2 the fixed inner sole of a boot or shoe.

insolent /ˈɪnsələnt/ adj. offensively contemptuous or arrogant; insulting. □ **insolence** n. **insolently** adv. [ME, = 'arrogant', f. L insolens (as IN-1, solens pres. part. of solēre be accustomed)]

insoluble /ɪnˈsɒljʊb(ə)l/ adj. 1 incapable of being solved. 2 incapable of being dissolved. □ **insolubility** /-ˈbɪlɪtɪ/ n. **insolubilize** /-bɪˌlaɪz/ v.tr. (also **-ise**). **insolubleness** n. **insolubly** adv. [ME f. OF insoluble or L insolubilis (as IN-1, SOLUBLE)]

insolvent /ɪnˈsɒlv(ə)nt/ adj. & n. —adj. 1 unable to pay one's debts. 2 relating to insolvency (insolvent laws). —n. a debtor. □ **insolvency** n.

insomnia /ɪnˈsɒmnɪə/ n. habitual sleeplessness; inability to sleep. □ **insomniac** /-ɪˌæk/ n. & adj. [L f. insomnis sleepless (as IN-1, somnus sleep)]

insomuch /ˌɪnsəʊˈmʌtʃ/ adv. 1 (foll. by that + clause) to such an extent. 2 (foll. by as) inasmuch. [ME, orig. in so much]

insouciant /ɪnˈsuːsɪənt, æ̃ˈsusjɑ̃/ adj. carefree; unconcerned. □ **insouciance** n. **insouciantly** adv. [F (as IN-1, souciant pres. part. of soucier care)]

inspect /ɪnˈspekt/ v.tr. 1 look closely at or into. 2 examine (a document etc.) officially. □ **inspection** n. [L inspicere inspect- (as IN-2, specere look at), or its frequent. inspectare]

inspector /ɪnˈspektə(r)/ n. 1 a person who inspects. 2 an official employed to supervise a service, a machine, etc., and make reports. 3 Brit. a police officer below a superintendent and above a sergeant in rank. □ **inspectorate** /-rət/ n. **inspectorial** /-ˈtɔːrɪəl/ adj. **inspectorship** n. [L (as INSPECT)]

inspiration /ˌɪnspɪˈreɪʃ(ə)n/ n. 1 a a supposed creative force or influence on poets, artists, musicians, etc. b a person, principle, faith, etc. stimulating artistic or moral fervour and creativity. c a similar divine influence supposed to have led to the writing of Scripture etc. 2 a sudden brilliant, creative, or timely idea. 3 a drawing in of breath; inhalation. □ **inspirational** adj. **inspirationism** n. **inspirationist** n. [ME f. OF f. LL inspiratio -onis (as INSPIRE)]

inspire /ɪnˈspaɪə(r)/ v.tr. 1 stimulate or arouse (a person) to esp. creative activity, esp. by supposed divine or supernatural agency (your faith inspired him; inspired by God). 2 a (usu. foll. by with) animate (a person) with a feeling. b (usu. foll. by into) instil (a feeling) into a person etc. c (usu. foll. by in) create (a feeling) in a person. 3 prompt; give rise to (the poem was inspired by the autumn). 4 (as **inspired** adj.) a (of a work of art etc.) as if prompted by or emanating from a supernatural source; characterized by inspiration (an inspired speech). b (of a guess) intuitive but accurate. 5 (also absol.) breathe in (air etc.); inhale. □ **inspiratory** /ɪnˈspɪrətərɪ/ adj. **inspiredly** /-rɪdlɪ/ adv. **inspirer** n. **inspiring**

adj. **inspiringly** adv. [ME f. OF inspirer f. L inspirare breathe in (as IN-2, spirare breathe)]

inspirit /ɪnˈspɪrɪt/ v.tr. (**inspirited**, **inspiriting**) 1 put life into; animate. 2 (usu. foll. by to, or to + infin.) encourage (a person). □ **inspiriting** adj. **inspiritingly** adv.

inst. abbr. = INSTANT adj. 4 (the 6th inst.).

instability /ˌɪnstəˈbɪlɪtɪ/ n. (pl. **-ies**) 1 a lack of stability. 2 Psychol. unpredictability in behaviour etc. 3 an instance of instability. [ME f. F instabilité f. L instabilitas -tatis f. instabilis (as IN-1, STABLE1)]

install /ɪnˈstɔːl/ v.tr. (also **instal**) (**installed**, **installing**) 1 place (equipment, machinery, etc.) in position ready for use. 2 place (a person) in an office or rank with ceremony (installed in the office of chancellor). 3 establish (oneself, a person, etc.) in a place, condition, etc. (installed herself at the head of the table). □ **installant** adj. & n. **installer** n. [med.L installare (as IN-2, stallare f. stallum STALL1)]

installation /ˌɪnstəˈleɪʃ(ə)n/ n. 1 a the act or an instance of installing. b the process or an instance of being installed. 2 a piece of apparatus, a machine, etc. installed. [med.L installatio (as INSTALL)]

instalment /ɪnˈstɔːlmənt/ n. (US **installment**) 1 a sum of money due as one of several usu. equal payments for something, spread over an agreed period of time. 2 any of several parts, esp. of a television or radio serial or a magazine story, published or shown in sequence at intervals. [alt. f. obs. estallment f. AF estalement f. estaler fix: prob. assoc. with INSTALLATION]

instance /ˈɪnst(ə)ns/ n. & v. —n. 1 an example or illustration of (just another instance of his lack of determination). 2 a particular case (that's not true in this instance). —v.tr. cite (a fact, case, etc.) as an instance. □ **for instance** as an example. **in the first** (or **second** etc.) **instance** in the first (or second etc.) place; at the first (or second etc.) stage of a proceeding. [ME f. OF f. L instantia (as INSTANT)]

instant /ˈɪnst(ə)nt/ adj. & n. —adj. 1 occurring immediately (gives an instant result). 2 a (of food etc.) ready for immediate use, with little or no preparation. b prepared hastily and with little effort (I have no instant solution). 3 urgent; pressing. 4 Commerce of the current month (the 6th instant). —n. 1 a precise moment of time, esp. the present (come here this instant; told you the instant I heard). 2 a short space of time (was there in an instant). □ **instant replay** the immediate repetition of part of a filmed sports event, often in slow motion. [ME f. F f. L instare instant- be present, press upon (as IN-2, stare stand)]

instantaneous /ˌɪnstənˈteɪnɪəs/ adj. occurring or done in an instant or instantly. □ **instantaneity** /-təˈniːɪtɪ/ n. **instantaneously** adv. **instantaneousness** n. [med.L instantaneus f. L instans (as INSTANT) after eccl.L momentaneus]

instantly /ˈɪnstəntlɪ/ adv. immediately; at once.

instead /ɪnˈsted/ adv. 1 (foll. by of) as a substitute or alternative to; in place of (instead of this one; stayed instead of going). 2 as an alternative (took me instead) (cf. STEAD). [ME, f. IN + STEAD]

instep /ˈɪnstep/ n. 1 the inner arch of the foot between the toes and the ankle. 2 the part of a shoe etc. fitting over or under this. [16th c.: ult. formed as IN-2 + STEP, but immed. orig. uncert.]

instigate /ˈɪnstɪˌɡeɪt/ v.tr. **1** bring about by incitement or persuasion; provoke (who instigated the inquiry?). **2** (usu. foll. by to) urge on, incite (a person etc.) to esp. an evil act. □ **instigation** /-ˈɡeɪʃ(ə)n/ n. **instigative** /-ɡətɪv/ adj. **instigator** n. [L instigare instigat-]

instil /ɪnˈstɪl/ v.tr. (US **instill**) (**instilled**, **instilling**) (often foll. by into) **1** introduce (a feeling, idea, etc.) into a person's mind etc. gradually. **2** put (a liquid) into something in drops. □ **instillation** /-ˈleɪʃ(ə)n/ n. **instiller** n. **instilment** n. [L instillare (as IN-², stillare drop): cf. DISTIL]

instinct n. & adj. —n. /ˈɪnstɪŋkt/ **1 a** an innate, usu. fixed, pattern of behaviour in most animals in response to certain stimuli. **b** a similar propensity in human beings to act without conscious intention; innate impulsion. **2** (usu. foll. by for) unconscious skill; intuition. —predic.adj. /ɪnˈstɪŋkt/ (foll. by with) imbued, filled (with life, beauty, force, etc.). □ **instinctual** /-ˈstɪŋktjʊəl/ adj. **instinctually** /-ˈstɪŋktjʊəlɪ/ adv. [ME, = 'impulse', f. L instinctus f. instinguere incite (as IN-², stinguere stinct- prick)]

instinctive /ɪnˈstɪŋktɪv/ adj. **1** relating to or prompted by instinct. **2** apparently unconscious or automatic (an instinctive reaction). □ **instinctively** adv.

institute /ˈɪnstɪˌtjuːt/ n. & v. —n. **1** a society or organization for the promotion of science, education, etc. **2** a building used by an institute. —v.tr. **1** establish; found. **2 a** initiate (an inquiry etc.). **b** begin (proceedings) in a court. **3** (usu. foll. by to, into) appoint (a person) as a cleric in a church etc. [ME f. L institutum design, precept, neut. past part. of instituere establish, arrange, teach (as IN-², statuere set up)]

institution /ˌɪnstɪˈtjuːʃ(ə)n/ n. **1** the act or an instance of instituting. **2 a** a society or organization founded esp. for charitable, religious, educational, or social purposes. **b** a building used by an institution. **3** an established law, practice, or custom. **4** colloq. (of a person, a custom, etc.) a familiar object. **5** the establishment of a cleric etc. in a church. [ME f. OF f. L institutio -onis (as INSTITUTE)]

institutional /ˌɪnstɪˈtjuːʃən(ə)l/ adj. **1** of or like an institution. **2** typical of institutions, esp. in being regimented or unimaginative. **3** (of religion) expressed or organized through institutions (churches etc.). □ **institutionalism** n. **institutionally** adv.

institutionalize /ˌɪnstɪˈtjuːʃənəˌlaɪz/ v.tr. (also **-ise**) **1** (as **institutionalized** adj.) (of a prisoner, a long-term patient, etc.) made apathetic and dependent after a long period in an institution. **2** place or keep (a person) in an institution. **3** convert into an institution; make institutional. □ **institutionalization** /-ˈzeɪʃ(ə)n/ n.

instruct /ɪnˈstrʌkt/ v.tr. **1** (often foll. by in) teach (a person) a subject etc. (instructed her in French). **2** (usu. foll. by to + infin.) direct; command (instructed him to fill in the hole). **3** (often foll. by of, or that etc. + clause) inform (a person) of a fact etc. [ME f. L instruere instruct- build, teach (as IN-², struere pile up)]

instruction /ɪnˈstrʌkʃ(ə)n/ n. **1** (often in pl.) a direction; an order (gave him his instructions). **2** teaching; education (took a course of instruction). **3** Computing a direction in a computer program

defining and effecting an operation. □ **instructional** adj. [ME f. OF f. LL instructio -onis (as INSTRUCT)]

instructive /ɪnˈstrʌktɪv/ adj. tending to instruct; conveying a lesson; enlightening. □ **instructively** adv. **instructiveness** n.

instructor /ɪnˈstrʌktə(r)/ n. (fem. **instructress** /-ˈstrʌktrɪs/) **1** a person who instructs; a teacher, demonstrator, etc. **2** US a university teacher ranking below professor. □ **instructorship** n.

instrument /ˈɪnstrəmənt/ n. & v. —n. **1** a tool or implement, esp. for delicate or scientific work. **2** (in full **musical instrument**) a device for producing musical sounds by vibration, wind, percussion, etc. **3 a** a thing used in performing an action (the meeting was an instrument in his success). **b** a person made use of (is merely their instrument). **4** a measuring-device, esp. in an aeroplane, serving to determine its position in darkness etc. **5** a formal, esp. legal, document. —v.tr. **1** arrange (music) for instruments. **2** equip with instruments (for measuring, recording, controlling, etc.). [ME f. OF instrument or L instrumentum (as INSTRUCT)]

instrumental /ˌɪnstrəˈment(ə)l/ adj. & n. —adj. **1** (usu. foll. by to, in, or in + verbal noun) serving as an instrument or means (was instrumental in finding the money). **2** (of music) performed on instruments, without singing. **3** of, or arising from, an instrument (instrumental error). —n. a piece of music performed by instruments, not by the voice. □ **instrumentalist** /-ˈmentəlɪst/ n. **instrumentality** /-ˈtælɪtɪ/ n. **instrumentally** adv. [ME f. F f. med.L instrumentalis (as INSTRUMENT)]

instrumentation /ˌɪnstrəmenˈteɪʃ(ə)n/ n. **1 a** the arrangement or composition of music for a particular group of musical instruments. **b** the instruments used in any one piece of music. **2 a** the design, provision, or use of such instruments in industry, science, etc. **b** such instruments collectively. [F f. instrumenter (as INSTRUMENT)]

insubordinate /ˌɪnsəˈbɔːdɪnət/ adj. disobedient; rebellious. □ **insubordinately** adv. **insubordination** /-ˈneɪʃ(ə)n/ n.

insubstantial /ˌɪnsəbˈstænʃ(ə)l, -ˈstɑː:nʃ(ə)l/ adj. **1** lacking solidity or substance. **2** not real. □ **insubstantiality** /-ʃɪˈælɪtɪ/ n. **insubstantially** adv. [LL insubstantialis (as IN-¹, SUBSTANTIAL)]

insufferable /ɪnˈsʌfərəb(ə)l/ adj. **1** intolerable. **2** unbearably arrogant or conceited etc. □ **insufferableness** n. **insufferably** adv.

insufficient /ˌɪnsəˈfɪʃ(ə)nt/ adj. not sufficient; inadequate. □ **insufficiency** n. **insufficiently** adv. [ME f. OF f. LL insufficiens (as IN-¹, SUFFICIENT)]

insufflator /ˈɪnsəˌfleɪtə(r)/ n. a device for blowing powder on to a surface in order to make fingerprints visible. [LL insufflare insufflat- (as IN-², sufflare blow upon)]

insular /ˈɪnsjʊlə(r)/ adj. **1 a** of or like an island. **b** separated or remote, like an island. **2** ignorant of or indifferent to cultures, peoples, etc., outside one's own experience; narrow-minded. □ **insularism** n. **insularity** /-ˈlærɪtɪ/ n. **insularly** adv. [LL insularis (as INSULATE)]

insulate /ˈɪnsjʊˌleɪt/ v.tr. **1** prevent the passage of electricity, heat, or sound from (a thing, room, etc.) by interposing non-conductors. **2** detach (a person or thing) from its surroundings; isolate. □ **insulation** /-ˈleɪʃ(ə)n/ n. [L insula island + -ATE³]

insulator /ˈɪnsjʊˌleɪtə(r)/ n. **1** a thing or substance used for insulation against electricity, heat, or sound. **2** an insulating device to support telegraph wires etc. **3** a device preventing contact between electrical conductors.

insulin /ˈɪnsjʊlɪn/ n. Biochem. a hormone produced in the pancreas, regulating the amount of glucose in the blood and the lack of which causes diabetes. [L insula island + -IN]

insult v. & n. —v.tr. /ɪnˈsʌlt/ **1** speak to or treat with scornful abuse or indignity. **2** offend the self-respect or modesty of. —n. /ˈɪnsʌlt/ **1** an insulting remark or action. **2** colloq. something so worthless or contemptible as to be offensive. □ **insulter** n. **insulting** adj. **insultingly** adv. [F insulte or L insultare (as IN-², saltare frequent. of salire salt- leap)]

insuperable /ɪnˈsuːpərəb(ə)l, ɪnˈsjuː-/ adj. **1** (of a barrier) impossible to surmount. **2** (of a difficulty etc.) impossible to overcome. □ **insuperability** /-ˈbɪlɪtɪ/ n. **insuperably** adv. [ME f. OF insuperable or L insuperabilis]

insupportable /ˌɪnsəˈpɔːtəb(ə)l/ adj. **1** unable to be endured. **2** unjustifiable. □ **insupportableness** n. **insupportably** adv. [F (as IN-¹, SUPPORT)]

insurance /ɪnˈʃʊərəns/ n. **1** the act or an instance of insuring. **2 a** a sum paid for this; a premium. **b** a sum paid out as compensation for theft, damage, loss, etc. **3** a measure taken to provide for a possible contingency (take an umbrella as insurance). [earlier ensurance f. OF enseürance (as ENSURE)]

insure /ɪnˈʃʊə(r)/ v.tr. **1** (often foll. by against; also absol.) secure the payment of a sum of money in the event of loss or damage to (property, life, a person, etc.) by regular payments or premiums (insured the house for £100,000; we have insured against flood damage). **2** (usu. foll. by against) provide for (a possible contingency) (insured themselves against the rain by taking umbrellas). **3** US = ENSURE. □ **insurability** /-ˈbɪlɪtɪ/ n. **insurable** adj. [ME, var. of ENSURE]

insured /ɪnˈʃʊəd/ adj. & n. —adj. covered by insurance. —n. (usu. prec. by the) a person etc. covered by insurance.

insurer /ɪnˈʃʊərə(r)/ n. **1** a person or company offering insurance policies for premiums; an under-writer. **2** a person who takes out insurance.

insurgent /ɪnˈsɜːdʒ(ə)nt/ adj. & n. —adj. rising in active revolt. —n. a rebel; a revolutionary. □ **insurgence** n. **insurgency** n. (pl. -ies). [F f. L insurgere insurrect- (as IN-², surgere rise)]

insurmountable /ˌɪnsəˈmaʊntəb(ə)l/ adj. unable to be surmounted or overcome. □ **insurmountably** adv.

insurrection /ˌɪnsəˈrekʃ(ə)n/ n. a rising in open resistance to established authority; a rebellion. □ **insurrectional** adj. **insurrectionary** adj. **insurrectionist** n. [ME f. OF f. LL insurrectio -onis (as INSURGENT)]

insusceptible /ˌɪnsəˈseptɪb(ə)l/ adj. (usu. foll. by of, to) not susceptible (of treatment, to an influence, etc.). □ **insusceptibility** /-ˈbɪlɪtɪ/ n.

intact /ɪnˈtækt/ adj. **1** entire; unimpaired. **2** untouched. □ **intactness** n. [ME f. L intactus (as IN-¹, tactus past part. of tangere touch)]

intaglio /ɪnˈtælɪəʊ, -ˈtɑːlɪəʊ/ n. (pl. -os) **1** a gem with an incised design (cf. CAMEO). **2** an engraved design. **3** a carving, esp. incised, in hard material. [It. intagliare cut into]

intake /ˈɪnteɪk/ n. **1 a** the action of taking in. **b** an instance of this. **2** a number or the amount taken in or received. **3** a place where water is taken into a channel or pipe from a river, or fuel or air enters an engine etc.

intangible /ɪnˈtændʒɪb(ə)l/ adj. & n. —adj. **1** unable to be touched; not solid. **2** unable to be grasped mentally. —n. something that cannot be precisely measured or assessed. □ **intangibility** /-ˈbɪlɪtɪ/ n. **intangibly** adv. [F intangible or med.L intangibilis (as IN-¹, TANGIBLE)]

integer /ˈɪntɪdʒə(r)/ n. **1** a whole number. **2** a thing complete in itself. [L (adj.) = untouched, whole: see ENTIRE]

integral /ˈɪntɪɡr(ə)l/ adj. & n. —adj. /ˈɪntɪɡr(ə)l, ɪnˈteɡr(ə)l/ **1 a** of a whole or necessary to the completeness of a whole. **b** forming a whole (integral design). **c** whole, complete. **2** Math. **a** of or denoted by an integer. **b** involving only integers, esp. as coefficients of a function. —n. Math. a quantity of which a given function is the derivative. □ **integral calculus** mathematics concerned with finding integrals, their properties and application, etc. □ **integrality** /-ˈɡrælɪtɪ/ n. **integrally** adv. [LL integralis (as INTEGER)]

■ **Usage** The second pronunciation given for the adjective, stressed on the second syllable, is considered incorrect by some people.

integrate v. /ˈɪntɪˌɡreɪt/ **1** tr. **a** combine (parts) into a whole. **b** complete (an imperfect thing) by the addition of parts. **2** tr. & intr. bring or come into equal participation or membership of society, a school, etc. **3** tr. desegregate, esp. racially (a school etc.). **4** tr. Math. find the integral of. □ **integrated circuit** Electronics a small chip etc. of material replacing several separate components in a conventional electrical circuit. □ **integrable** /ˈɪntɪɡrəb(ə)l/ adj. **integrability** /ˌɪntɪɡrəˈbɪlɪtɪ/ n. **integrative** /ˈɪntɪɡrətɪv/ adj. **integrator** n. [L integrare integrat- make whole (as INTEGER)]

integration /ˌɪntɪˈɡreɪʃ(ə)n/ n. **1** the act or an instance of integrating. **2** the intermixing of persons previously segregated. □ **integrationist** n. [L integratio (as INTEGRATE)]

integrity /ɪnˈteɡrɪtɪ/ n. **1** moral uprightness; honesty. **2** wholeness; soundness. [ME f. F intégrité or L integritas (as INTEGER)]

integument /ɪnˈteɡjʊmənt/ n. a natural outer covering, as a skin, husk, rind, etc. □ **integumental** /-ˈment(ə)l/ adj. **integumentary** /-ˈmentərɪ/ adj. [L integumentum f. integere (as IN-², tegere cover)]

intellect /ˈɪntɪˌlekt/ n. **1 a** the faculty of reasoning, knowing, and thinking, as distinct from feeling. **b** the understanding or mental powers (of a particular person etc.) (his intellect is not great). **2** a clever or knowledgeable person. [ME f. OF intellect or L intellectus understanding (as INTELLIGENT)]

intellectual /ˌɪntɪˈlektjʊəl/ adj. & n. —adj. **1** of or appealing to the intellect. **2** possessing a high level of understanding or intelligence; cultured. **3** requiring, or given to the exercise of, the intellect. —n. a person possessing a highly developed intellect. □ **intellectuality** /-ˈælɪtɪ/ n. **intellectualize** /-ˈlektjʊəˌlaɪz/ v.tr. &

intr. (also **-ise**). **intellectually** *adv.* [ME f. L *intellectualis* (as INTELLECT)]

intellectualism /ˌɪntɪˈlektjʊəˌlɪz(ə)m/ *n.* the exercise, esp. when excessive, of the intellect at the expense of the emotions.

intelligence /ɪnˈtelɪdʒ(ə)ns/ *n.* **1 a** the intellect; the understanding. **b** (of a person or an animal) quickness of understanding; wisdom. **2 a** the collection of information, esp. of military or political value. **b** people employed in this. **3** an intelligent or rational being. □ **intelligence quotient** a number denoting the ratio of a person's intelligence to the normal or average. **intelligence test** a test designed to measure intelligence rather than acquired knowledge. □ **intelligential** /-ˈdʒenʃ(ə)l/ *adj.* [ME f. OF f. L *intelligentia* (as INTELLIGENT)]

intelligent /ɪnˈtelɪdʒ(ə)nt/ *adj.* **1** having or showing intelligence, esp. of a high level. **2** quick of mind; clever. **3 a** (of a device or machine) able to vary its behaviour in response to varying situations and requirements and past experience. **b** (esp. of a computer terminal) having its own data-processing capability; incorporating a microprocessor. □ **intelligently** *adv.* [L *intelligere intellect-* understand (as INTER-, *legere* gather, pick out, read)]

intelligentsia /ɪnˌtelɪˈdʒentsɪə/ *n.* **1** the class of intellectuals regarded as possessing culture and political initiative. **2** people doing intellectual work; intellectuals. [Russ. f. Pol. *inteligencja* f. L *intelligentia* (as INTELLIGENT)]

intelligible /ɪnˈtelɪdʒɪb(ə)l/ *adj.* (often foll. by *to*) able to be understood; comprehensible. □ **intelligibility** /-ˈbɪlɪtɪ/ *n.* **intelligibly** *adv.* [L *intelligibilis* (as INTELLIGENT)]

intemperate /ɪnˈtempərət/ *adj.* **1** (of a person, conduct, or speech) immoderate; unbridled; violent (*used intemperate language*). **2 a** given to excessive indulgence in alcohol. **b** excessively indulgent in one's appetites. □ **intemperance** *n.* **intemperately** *adv.* **intemperateness** *n.* [ME f. L *intemperatus* (as IN-¹, TEMPERATE)]

intend /ɪnˈtend/ *v.tr.* **1** have as one's purpose; propose (*we intend to go; we intend going; we intend that it shall be done*). **2** (usu. foll. by *for, as*) design or destine (a person or a thing) (*I intend him to go; I intend it as a warning*). **3** mean (*what does he intend by that?*). **4** (in *passive;* foll. by *for*) **a** be meant for a person to have or use etc. (*they are intended for the children*). **b** be meant to represent (*the picture is intended for you*). [ME *entende, intende* f. OF *entendre, intendre* f. L *intendere intent-* or *intens-* strain, direct, purpose (as IN-², *tendere* stretch, tend)]

intended /ɪnˈtendɪd/ *adj. & n.* —*adj.* **1** done on purpose; intentional. **2** designed, meant. —*n. colloq.* one's fiancé or fiancée. □ **intendedly** *adv.*

intense /ɪnˈtens/ *adj.* (**intenser, intensest**) **1** (of a quality etc.) existing in a high degree; violent; forceful (*intense cold*). **2** (of a person) feeling, or apt to feel, strong emotion (*very intense about her music*). **3** (of a feeling or action etc.) extreme (*intense joy; intense thought*). □ **intensely** *adv.* **intenseness** *n.* [ME f. OF *intens* or L *intensus* (as INTEND)]

■ **Usage** This word is sometimes confused with *intensive*, and wrongly used to describe a course of study etc.

intensifier /ɪnˈtensɪˌfaɪə(r)/ *n.* **1** a person or thing that intensifies. **2** *Gram.* = INTENSIVE *n.*

intensify /ɪnˈtensɪˌfaɪ/ *v.* (**-ies, -ied**) *tr. & intr.* make or become intense or more intense. □ **intensification** /-fɪˈkeɪʃ(ə)n/ *n.*

intensity /ɪnˈtensɪtɪ/ *n.* (*pl.* **-ies**) **1** the quality of or an instance of being intense. **2** esp. *Physics* the measurable amount of some quality, e.g. force, brightness, a magnetic field, etc.

intensive /ɪnˈtensɪv/ *adj. & n.* —*adj.* **1** thorough, vigorous; directed to a single point, area, or subject (*intensive study; intensive bombardment*). **2** of or relating to intensity as opp. to extent; producing intensity. **3** serving to increase production in relation to costs (*intensive farming methods*). **4** (usu. in *comb.*) *Econ.* making much use of (*a labour-intensive industry*). **5** *Gram.* (of an adjective, adverb, etc.) expressing intensity; giving force, as *really* in *my feet are really cold.* —*n. Gram.* an intensive adjective, adverb, etc. □ **intensive care** medical treatment with constant monitoring etc. of a dangerously ill patient. □ **intensively** *adv.* **intensiveness** *n.* [F *intensif -ive* or med.L *intensivus* (as INTEND)]

■ **Usage** See note at *intense*.

intent /ɪnˈtent/ *n. & adj.* —*n.* (usu. without article) intention; a purpose (*with intent to defraud; my intent to reach the top; with evil intent*). —*adj.* **1** (usu. foll. by *on*) **a** resolved; bent; determined (*was intent on succeeding*). **b** attentively occupied (*intent on his books*). **2** (esp. of a look) earnest; eager; meaningful. □ **to all intents and purposes** practically; virtually. □ **intently** *adv.* **intentness** *n.* [ME *entent* f. OF f. L *intentus* (as INTEND)]

intention /ɪnˈtenʃ(ə)n/ *n.* **1** (often foll. by *to* + infin., or *of* + verbal noun) a thing intended; an aim or purpose (*it was not his intention to interfere; have no intention of staying*). **2** the act of intending (*done without intention*). **3** *colloq.* (usu. in *pl.*) a person's, esp. a man's, designs in respect to marriage (*are his intentions strictly honourable?*). □ **intentioned** *adj.* (usu. in *comb.*). [ME *entencion* f. OF f. L *intentio* stretching, purpose (as INTEND)]

intentional /ɪnˈtenʃən(ə)l/ *adj.* done on purpose. □ **intentionality** /-ˈnælɪtɪ/ *n.* **intentionally** *adv.* [F *intentionnel* or med.L *intentionalis* (as INTENTION)]

inter /ɪnˈtɜː(r)/ *v.tr.* (**interred, interring**) deposit (a corpse etc.) in the earth, a tomb, etc.; bury. [ME f. OF *enterrer* f. Rmc (as IN-², L *terra* earth)]

inter- /ˈɪntə(r)/ *comb. form* **1** between, among (*intercontinental*). **2** mutually, reciprocally (*interbreed*). [OF *entre-* or L *inter* between, among]

interact /ˌɪntərˈækt/ *v.intr.* act reciprocally; act on each other. □ **interactant** *adj. & n.* **interaction** *n.*

interactive /ˌɪntərˈæktɪv/ *adj.* **1** reciprocally active; acting upon or influencing each other. **2** (of a computer or other electronic device) allowing a two-way flow of information between it and a user, responding to the user's input. □ **interactively** *adv.* [INTERACT, after *active*]

inter alia /ˌɪntər ˈeɪlɪə, ˈælɪə/ *adv.* among other things. [L]

interblend /ˌɪntəˈblend/ *v.* **1** *tr.* (usu. foll. by *with*) mingle (things) together. **2** *intr.* blend with each other.

interbreed /ˌɪntəˈbriːd/ *v.* (*past* and *past part.* **-bred** /-ˈbred/) **1** *intr. & tr.* breed or cause to breed with members of a different race or species to produce a hybrid. **2** *tr.* breed within one family etc. in order to produce desired characteristics.

intercalary /ɪnˈtɜːkələrɪ, -ˈkælərɪ/ *adj.* **1 a** (of a day or a month) inserted in the calendar to harmonize it with the solar year, e.g. 29 Feb. in leap years. **b** (of a year) having such an addition. **2** interpolated; intervening. [L *intercalari(u)s* (as INTERCALATE)]

intercalate /ɪnˈtɜːkəˌleɪt/ *v.tr.* **1** (also *absol.*) insert (an intercalary day etc.). **2** interpose (anything out of the ordinary course). **3** (as **intercalated** *adj.*) (of strata etc.) interposed. □ **intercalation** /-ˈleɪʃ(ə)n/ *n.* [L *intercalare intercalat-* (as INTER-, *calare* proclaim)]

intercede /ˌɪntəˈsiːd/ *v.intr.* (usu. foll. by *with*) interpose or intervene on behalf of another; plead (*they interceded with the king for his life*). □ **interceder** *n.* [F *intercéder* or L *intercedere intercess-* intervene (as INTER-, *cedere* go)]

intercellular /ˌɪntəˈseljʊlə(r)/ *adj.* Biol. located or occurring between cells.

intercept *v.tr.* /ˌɪntəˈsept/ **1** seize, catch, or stop (a person, message, vehicle, ball, etc.) going from one place to another. **2** (usu. foll. by *from*) cut off (light etc.). **3** check or stop (motion etc.). □ **interception** /-ˈsepʃ(ə)n/ *n.* **interceptive** /-ˈseptɪv/ *adj.* [L *intercipere intercept-* (as INTER-, *capere* take)]

interceptor /ˌɪntəˈseptə(r)/ *n.* **1** an aircraft used to intercept enemy raiders. **2** a person or thing that intercepts.

intercession /ˌɪntəˈseʃ(ə)n/ *n.* **1** the act of interceding, esp. by prayer. **2** an instance of this. **3** a prayer. □ **intercessional** *adj.* **intercessor** *n.* **intercessorial** /-seˈsɔːrɪəl/ *adj.* **intercessory** *adj.* [F *intercession* or L *intercessio* (as INTERCEDE)]

interchange *v.* & *n.* —*v.tr.* /ˌɪntəˈtʃeɪndʒ/ **1** (of two people) exchange (things) with each other. **2** put each of (two things) in the other's place; alternate. —*n.* /ˈɪntəˌtʃeɪndʒ/ **1** (often foll. by *of*) a reciprocal exchange between two people etc. **2** alternation (*the interchange of woods and fields*). **3** a road junction designed so that traffic streams do not intersect. □ **interchangeability** /-ˈbɪlɪtɪ/ *n.* **interchangeable** *adj.* **interchangeableness** *n.* **interchangeably** *adv.* [ME f. OF *entrechangier* (as INTER-, CHANGE)]

inter-city /ˌɪntəˈsɪtɪ/ *adj.* existing or travelling between cities.

intercom /ˈɪntəˌkɒm/ *n.* colloq. a system of intercommunication by radio or telephone between or within offices, aircraft, etc. [abbr.]

intercommunicate /ˌɪntəkəˈmjuːnɪˌkeɪt/ *v.intr.* **1** communicate reciprocally. **2** (of rooms etc.) have free passage into each other; have a connecting door. □ **intercommunication** /-ˈkeɪʃ(ə)n/ *n.* **intercommunicative** /-kətɪv/ *adj.*

intercommunion /ˌɪntəkəˈmjuːnɪən/ *n.* **1** mutual communion. **2** a mutual action or relationship, esp. between Christian denominations.

intercommunity /ˌɪntəkəˈmjuːnɪtɪ/ *n.* **1** the quality of being common to various groups etc. **2** having things in common.

interconnect /ˌɪntəkəˈnekt/ *v.tr.* & *intr.* connect with each other. □ **interconnection** /-ˈnekʃ(ə)n/ *n.*

intercontinental /ˌɪntəˌkɒntɪˈnent(ə)l/ *adj.* connecting or travelling between continents. □ **intercontinentally** *adv.*

intercorrelate /ˌɪntəˈkɒrəˌleɪt/ *v.tr.* & *intr.* correlate with one another. □ **intercorrelation** /-ˈleɪʃ(ə)n/ *n.*

intercourse /ˈɪntəˌkɔːs/ *n.* **1** communication or dealings between individuals, nations, etc. **2** = *sexual intercourse.* [ME f. OF *entrecours* exchange, commerce, f. L *intercursus* (as INTER-, *currere cursrun*)]

intercrop /ˌɪntəˈkrɒp/ *v.tr.* (also *absol.*) (**-cropped, -cropping**) raise (a crop) among plants of a different kind, usu. in the space between rows. □ **intercropping** *n.*

intercut /ˌɪntəˈkʌt/ *v.tr.* (**-cutting**; *past* and *past part.* **-cut**) Cinematog. alternate (shots) with contrasting shots by cutting.

interdenominational /ˌɪntədɪˌnɒmɪˈneɪʃn(ə)l/ *adj.* concerning more than one (religious) denomination. □ **interdenominationally** *adv.*

interdepartmental /ˌɪntəˌdiːpɑːtˈment(ə)l/ *adj.* concerning more than one department. □ **interdepartmentally** *adv.*

interdepend /ˌɪntədɪˈpend/ *v.intr.* depend on each other. □ **interdependence** *n.* **interdependency** *n.* **interdependent** *adj.*

interdict *n.* & *v.* /ˈɪntədɪkt/ **1** an authoritative prohibition. **2** RC Ch. a sentence debarring a person, or esp. a place, from ecclesiastical functions and privileges. —*v.tr.* /ˌɪntəˈdɪkt/ **1** prohibit (an action). **2** forbid the use of. **3** (usu. foll. by *from* + verbal noun) restrain (a person). **4** (usu. foll. by *to*) forbid (a thing) to a person. □ **interdiction** /-ˈdɪkʃ(ə)n/ *n.* **interdictory** /-ˈdɪktərɪ/ *adj.* [ME f. OF *entredit* f. L *interdictum* past part. of *interdicere* interpose, forbid by decree (as INTER-, *dicere* say)]

interdisciplinary /ˌɪntəˌdɪsɪˈplɪnərɪ/ *adj.* of or between more than one branch of learning.

interest /ˈɪntrəst, -trɪst/ *n.* & *v.* —*n.* **1 a** concern; curiosity (*have no interest in fishing*). **b** a quality exciting curiosity or holding the attention (*this magazine lacks interest*). **2** a subject, hobby, etc., in which one is concerned (*his interests are gardening and sport*). **3** advantage or profit, esp. when financial (*it is in your interest to go*). **4** money paid for the use of money lent, or for not requiring the repayment of a debt. **5** (usu. foll. by *in*) **a** a financial stake (in an undertaking etc.). **b** a legal concern, title, or right (in property). **6 a** a party or group having a common interest (*the brewing interest*). **b** a principle in which a party or group is concerned. **7** the selfish pursuit of one's own welfare, self-interest. —*v.tr.* **1** excite the curiosity or attention of (*your story interests me greatly*). **2** (usu. foll. by *in*) cause (a person) to take a personal interest or share (*can I interest you in a holiday abroad?*). **3** (as **interested** *adj.*) having a private interest; not impartial or disinterested (*an interested party*). □ **interestedly** *adv.* **interestedness** *n.* [ME, earlier *interesse* f. AF f. med.L, alt. app. after OF *interest*, both f. L *interest*, 3rd sing. pres. of *interesse* matter, make a difference (as INTER-, *esse* be)]

interesting /ˈɪntrəstɪŋ, -trɪstɪŋ/ *adj.* causing curiosity; holding the attention. □ **interestingly** *adv.* **interestingness** *n.*

interface /ˈɪntəˌfeɪs/ *n. & v.* —*n.* **1** esp. *Physics* a surface forming a common boundary between two regions. **2** a point where interaction occurs between two systems, processes, subjects, etc. (*the interface between psychology and education*). **3** esp. *Computing* an apparatus for connecting two pieces of equipment so that they can be operated jointly. —*v.tr. & intr.* (often foll. by *with*) **1** connect with (another piece of equipment etc.) by an interface. **2** interact.

■ **Usage** The use of the noun and verb in sense 2 is deplored by some people.

interfacing /ˈɪntəˌfeɪsɪŋ/ *n.* a stiffish material, esp. buckram, between two layers of fabric in collars etc.

interfere /ˌɪntəˈfɪə(r)/ *v.intr.* **1** (usu. foll. by *with*) **a** (of a person) meddle; obstruct a process etc. **b** (of a thing) be a hindrance; get in the way. **2** (usu. foll. by *in*) take part or intervene, esp. without invitation or necessity. **3** (foll. by *with*) *euphem.* molest or assault sexually. **4** *Physics* (of light or other waves) combine so as to cause interference. □ **interferer** *n.* **interfering** *adj.* **interferingly** *adv.* [OF *s'entreferir* strike each other (as INTER-, *ferir* f. L *ferire* strike)]

interference /ˌɪntəˈfɪərəns/ *n.* **1** (usu. foll. by *with*) **a** the act of interfering. **b** an instance of this. **2** the fading or disturbance of received radio signals by the interference of waves from different sources, or esp. by atmospherics or unwanted signals. **3** *Physics* the combination of two or more wave motions to form a resultant wave in which the displacement is reinforced or cancelled. □ **interferential** /-fəˈrenʃ(ə)l/ *adj.*

interferon /ˌɪntəˈfɪəˌrɒn/ *n. Biochem.* any of various proteins that can inhibit the development of a virus in a cell etc. [INTERFERE + -ON]

interfile /ˌɪntəˈfaɪl/ *v.tr.* **1** file (two sequences) together. **2** file (one or more items) into an existing sequence.

interfuse /ˌɪntəˈfjuːz/ *v.* **1** *tr.* **a** (usu. foll. by *with*) mix (a thing) with; intersperse. **b** blend (things) together. **2** *intr.* (of two things) blend with each other. □ **interfusion** /-ˈfjuːʒ(ə)n/ *n.* [L *interfundere interfus-* (as INTER-, *fundere* pour)]

intergalactic /ˌɪntəɡəˈlæktɪk/ *adj.* of or situated between two or more galaxies. □ **intergalactically** *adv.*

interglacial /ˌɪntəˈɡleɪʃ(ə)l, -sɪəl/ *adj.* between glacial periods.

intergovernmental /ˌɪntəˌɡʌvənˈment(ə)l/ *adj.* concerning or conducted between two or more governments. □ **intergovernmentally** *adv.*

interim /ˈɪntərɪm/ *n. & adj.* —*n.* the intervening time (*in the interim he had died*). —*adj.* intervening; provisional, temporary. [L, as INTER- + adv. suffix -*im*]

interior /ɪnˈtɪərɪə(r)/ *adj. & n.* —*adj.* **1** inner. **2** remote from the coast or frontier; inland. **3** internal; domestic. **4** (usu. foll. by *to*) situated further in or within. **5** existing in the mind or soul; inward. **6** drawn, photographed, etc. within a building. **7** coming from inside. —*n.* **1** the interior part; the inside. **2** the interior part of a country or region. **3** the home affairs of a country (*Minister of the Interior*). **4** a representation of the inside of a building or a room (*Dutch interior*). □ **interior monologue** a form of writing expressing a character's inner

thoughts. □ **interiorize** *v.tr.* (also -**ise**). **interiorly** *adv.* [L, compar. f. *inter* among]

interject /ˌɪntəˈdʒekt/ *v.tr.* **1** utter (words) abruptly or parenthetically. **2** interrupt with. □ **interjectory** *adj.* [L *interjicere* (as INTER-, *jacere* throw)]

interjection /ˌɪntəˈdʒekʃ(ə)n/ *n.* an exclamation, esp. as a part of speech (e.g. *ah!, dear me!*). □ **interjectional** *adj.* [ME f. OF f. L *interjectio -onis* (as INTERJECT)]

interknit /ˌɪntəˈnɪt/ *v.tr. & intr.* (-**knitting**; *past* and *past part.* -**knitted** or -**knit**) knit together; intertwine.

interlace /ˌɪntəˈleɪs/ *v.* **1** *tr.* bind intricately together; interweave. **2** *tr.* mingle, intersperse. **3** *intr.* cross each other intricately. □ **interlacement** *n.* [ME f. OF *entrelacier* (as INTER-, LACE *v.*)]

interlard /ˌɪntəˈlɑːd/ *v.tr.* (usu. foll. by *with*) mix (writing or speech) with unusual words or phrases. [F *entrelarder* (as INTER-, LARD *v.*)]

interleave /ˌɪntəˈliːv/ *v.tr.* insert (usu. blank) leaves between the leaves of (a book etc.).

interline /ˌɪntəˈlaɪn/ *v.tr.* put an extra lining between the ordinary lining and the fabric of (a garment).

interlinear /ˌɪntəˈlɪnɪə(r)/ *adj.* written or printed between the lines of a text. [ME f. med.L *interlinearis* (as INTER-, LINEAR)]

interlining /ˈɪntəˌlaɪnɪŋ/ *n.* material used to interline a garment.

interlink /ˌɪntəˈlɪŋk/ *v.tr. & intr.* link or be linked together.

interlock /ˌɪntəˈlɒk/ *v. & adj.* —*v.* **1** *intr.* engage with each other by overlapping or by the fitting together of projections and recesses. **2** *tr.* (usu. in *passive*) lock or clasp within each other. —*adj.* (of a fabric) knitted with closely interlocking stitches. □ **interlocker** *n.*

interlocutor /ˌɪntəˈlɒkjʊtə(r)/ *n.* (*fem.* **interlocutrix** /-trɪks/) a person who takes part in a dialogue or conversation. □ **interlocution** /-ləˈkjuːʃ(ə)n/ *n.* [mod.L f. L *interloqui interlocut-* interrupt in speaking (as INTER-, *loqui* speak)]

interlocutory /ˌɪntəˈlɒkjʊtərɪ/ *adj.* of dialogue or conversation. [med.L *interlocutorius* (as INTERLOCUTOR)]

interloper /ˈɪntəˌləʊpə(r)/ *n.* **1** an intruder. **2** a person who interferes in others' affairs, esp. for profit. □ **interlope** *v.intr.* [INTER- + *loper* as in *landlope* vagabond f. MDu. *landlooper*]

interlude /ˈɪntəˌluːd, -ˌljuːd/ *n.* **1 a** a pause between the acts of a play. **b** something performed or done during this pause. **2 a** an intervening time, space, or event that contrasts with what goes before or after. **b** a temporary amusement or entertaining episode. [ME, = a light dramatic item between the acts of a morality play, f. med.L *interludium* (as INTER-, *ludus* play)]

intermarriage /ˌɪntəˈmærɪdʒ/ *n.* **1** marriage between people of different races, castes, families, etc. **2** (loosely) marriage between near relations.

intermarry /ˌɪntəˈmærɪ/ *v.intr.* (-**ies**, -**ied**) (foll. by *with*) (of races, castes, families, etc.) become connected by marriage.

intermediary /ˌɪntəˈmiːdɪərɪ/ *n. & adj.* —*n.* (*pl.* -**ies**) an intermediate person or thing, esp. a mediator. —*adj.* acting as mediator; intermediate. [F *intermédiaire* f. It. *intermediario* f. L *intermedius* (as INTERMEDIATE)]

intermediate /ˌɪntəˈmiːdɪət/ *adj.* & *n.* —*adj.* coming between two things in time, place, order, character, etc. —*n.* an intermediate thing. □ **intermediacy** /-sɪ/ *n.* **intermediately** *adv.* **intermediateness** *n.* **intermediation** /-ˈeɪʃ(ə)n/ *n.* **intermediator** /-ˌeɪtə(r)/ *n.* [med.L *intermediatus* (as INTER-, *medius* middle)]

interment /ɪnˈtɜːmənt/ *n.* the burial of a corpse, esp. with ceremony.

■ **Usage** This word is sometimes confused with *internment*, which means 'confinement'.

intermezzo /ˌɪntəˈmetsəʊ/ *n.* (*pl.* **intermezzi** /-tsɪ/ or -**os**) **1 a** a short connecting instrumental movement in an opera or other musical work. **b** a similar piece performed independently. **c** a short piece for a solo instrument. **2** a short light dramatic or other performance inserted between the acts of a play. [It. f. L *intermedium* interval (as INTERMEDIATE)]

interminable /ɪnˈtɜːmɪnəb(ə)l/ *adj.* **1** endless. **2** tediously long or habitual. **3** with no prospect of an end. □ **interminableness** *n.* **interminably** *adv.* [ME f. OF *interminable* or LL *interminabilis* (as IN-[1], TERMINATE)]

intermingle /ˌɪntəˈmɪŋg(ə)l/ *v.tr.* & *intr.* (often foll. by *with*) mix together; mingle.

intermission /ˌɪntəˈmɪʃ(ə)n/ *n.* **1** a pause or cessation. **2** an interval between parts of a play, film, concert, etc. **3** a period of inactivity. [F *intermission* or L *intermissio* f. *intermittere intermiss-* (as INTER-, *mittere* let go)]

intermittent /ˌɪntəˈmɪt(ə)nt/ *adj.* occurring at intervals; not continuous or steady. □ **intermittence** /-t(ə)ns/ *n.* **intermittency** /-tənsɪ/ *n.* **intermittently** *adv.* [L *intermittere intermittent-* (as INTERMISSION)]

intermix /ˌɪntəˈmɪks/ *v.tr.* & *intr.* mix together. □ **intermixable** *adj.* **intermixture** *n.* [back-form. f. *intermixed*, *intermixt* f. L *intermixtus* past part. of *intermiscēre* mix together (as INTER-, *miscēre* mix)]

intermolecular /ˌɪntəməˈlekjʊlə(r)/ *adj.* between molecules.

intern *n.* & *v.* —*n.* /ˈɪntɜːn/ (also **interne**) US a recent graduate or advanced student living in a hospital and acting as an assistant physician or surgeon. —*v.tr.* /ɪnˈtɜːn/ confine; oblige (a prisoner, alien, etc.) to reside within prescribed limits. □ **internment** *n.* **internship** *n.* [F *interne* f. L *internus* internal]

■ **Usage** *Internment* is sometimes confused with *interment*, which means 'burial'.

internal /ɪnˈtɜːn(ə)l/ *adj.* & *n.* —*adj.* **1** of or situated in the inside or invisible part. **2** relating or applied to the inside of the body (*internal injuries*). **3** of a nation's domestic affairs. **4** (of a student) attending a university etc. as well as taking its examinations. **5** used or applying within an organization. **6 a** of the inner nature of a thing; intrinsic. **b** of the mind or soul. —*n.* (in *pl.*) intrinsic qualities. □ **internal-combustion engine** an engine with its motive power generated by the explosion of gases or vapour with air in a cylinder. □ **internally** /-ˈnælɪtɪ/ *n.* **internalization** /-ˈzeɪʃ(ə)n/ *n.*

internalize *v.tr.* (also **-ise**). **internally** *adv.* [mod.L *internalis* (as INTERN)]

international /ˌɪntəˈnæʃ(ə)n(ə)l/ *adj.* & *n.* —*adj.* **1** existing, involving, or carried on between two or more nations. **2** agreed on or used by all or many nations (*international driving licence*). —*n.* **1 a** a contest, esp. in sport, between teams representing different countries. **b** a member of such a team. **2** (**International**) any of four associations founded (1864–1936) to promote socialist or communist action. □ **internationality** /-ˈnælɪtɪ/ *n.* **internationally** *adv.*

internationalism /ˌɪntəˈnæʃənəˌlɪz(ə)m/ *n.* **1** the advocacy of a community of interests among nations. **2** (**Internationalism**) the principles of any of the Internationals. □ **internationalist** *n.*

internationalize /ˌɪntəˈnæʃənəˌlaɪz/ *v.tr.* (also **-ise**) **1** make international. **2** bring under the protection or control of two or more nations. □ **internationalization** /-ˈzeɪʃ(ə)n/ *n.*

internecine /ˌɪntəˈniːsaɪn/ *adj.* mutually destructive. [orig. = deadly, f. L *internecinus* f. *internecio* massacre f. *internecare* slaughter (as INTER-, *necare* kill)]

internee /ˌɪntɜːˈniː/ *n.* a person interned.

interpenetrate /ˌɪntəˈpenɪˌtreɪt/ *v.* **1** intr. (of two things) penetrate each other. **2** *tr.* pervade; penetrate thoroughly. □ **interpenetration** /-ˈtreɪʃ(ə)n/ *n.* **interpenetrative** /-trətɪv/ *adj.*

interpersonal /ˌɪntəˈpɜːsən(ə)l/ *adj.* (of relations) occurring between persons, esp. reciprocally. □ **interpersonally** *adv.*

interplanetary /ˌɪntəˈplænɪtərɪ/ *adj.* **1** between planets. **2** relating to travel between planets.

interplay /ˈɪntəˌpleɪ/ *n.* **1** reciprocal action. **2** the operation of two things on each other.

Interpol /ˈɪntəˌpɒl/ *n.* International Criminal Police Organization. [abbr.]

interpolate /ɪnˈtɜːpəˌleɪt/ *v.tr.* **1 a** insert (words) in a book etc., esp. to give false impressions as to its date etc. **b** make such insertions in (a book etc.). **2** interject (a remark) in a conversation. **3** estimate (values) from known ones in the same range. □ **interpolation** /-ˈleɪʃ(ə)n/ *n.* **interpolative** /-lətɪv/ *adj.* **interpolator** *n.* [L *interpolare* furbish up (as INTER-, *polire* POLISH[1])]

interpose /ˌɪntəˈpəʊz/ *v.* **1** *tr.* (often foll. by *between*) place or insert (a thing) between others. **2** *tr.* say (words) as an interruption. **3** *tr.* exercise or advance (a veto or objection) so as to interfere. **4** *intr.* (foll. by *between*) intervene (between parties). [F *interposer* f. L *interponere* put (as INTER-, POSE[1])]

interposition /ˌɪntəpəˈzɪʃ(ə)n/ *n.* **1** the act of interposing. **2** a thing interposed. **3** an interference. [ME f. OF *interposition* or L *interpositio* (as INTER-, POSITION)]

interpret /ɪnˈtɜːprɪt/ *v.* (**interpreted, interpreting**) **1** *tr.* explain the meaning of (foreign or abstruse words, a dream, etc.). **2** *tr.* make out or bring out the meaning of (creative work). **3** *intr.* act as an interpreter, esp. of foreign languages. **4** *tr.* explain or understand (behaviour etc.) in a specified manner (*interpreted his gesture as mocking*). □ **interpretable** *adj.* **interpretability** /-təˈbɪlɪtɪ/ *n.* **interpretation** /-ˈteɪʃ(ə)n/ *n.* **interpretational** /-ˈteɪʃən(ə)l/ *adj.* **interpretative** /-tətɪv/ *adj.* **interpretive** *adj.* **interpretively** *adv.* [ME f. OF *interpreter* or L *interpretari* explain, translate f. *interpres -pretis* explainer]

interpreter /ɪnˈtɜːprɪtə(r)/ *n.* a person who interprets, esp. one who translates speech orally. [ME f. AF *interpretour*, OF *interpreteur* f. LL *interpretator -oris* (as **INTERPRET**)]

interracial /ˌɪntəˈreɪʃ(ə)l/ *adj.* existing between or affecting different races. □ **interracially** *adv.*

interregnum /ˌɪntəˈregnəm/ *n.* (*pl.* **interregnums** or **interregna** /-nə/) **1** an interval when the normal government is suspended, esp. between successive reigns or regimes. **2** an interval or pause. [L (as **INTER-**, *regnum* reign)]

interrelate /ˌɪntərɪˈleɪt/ *v.tr.* relate (two or more things) to each other. □ **interrelation** *n.* **interrelationship** *n.*

interrogate /ɪnˈterəˌgeɪt/ *v.tr.* ask questions of (a person) esp. closely, thoroughly, or formally. □ **interrogator** *n.* [ME f. L *interrogare interrogat-* ask (as **INTER-**, *rogare* ask)]

interrogation /ɪnˌterəˈgeɪʃ(ə)n/ *n.* **1** the act or an instance of interrogating; the process of being interrogated. **2** a question or enquiry. □ **interrogational** *adj.* [ME f. F *interrogation* or L *interrogatio* (as **INTERROGATE**)]

interrogative /ˌɪntəˈrɒgətɪv/ *adj.* & *n.* —*adj.* **1 a** of or like a question; used in questions. **b** *Gram.* (of an adjective or pronoun) asking a question (e.g. *who?, which?*). **2** having the form or force of a question. **3** suggesting enquiry (*an interrogative tone*). —*n.* an interrogative word (e.g. *what?, why?*). □ **interrogatively** *adv.* [LL *interrogativus* (as **INTERROGATE**)]

interrogatory /ˌɪntəˈrɒgətərɪ/ *adj.* questioning; of or suggesting enquiry (*an interrogatory eyebrow*). [LL *interrogatorius* (as **INTERROGATE**)]

interrupt /ˌɪntəˈrʌpt/ *v.tr.* **1** act so as to break the continuous progress of (an action, speech, a person speaking, etc.). **2** obstruct (a person's view etc.). **3** break the continuity of. □ **interrupter** *n.* **interruptible** *adj.* **interruption** /-ˈrʌpʃ(ə)n/ *n.* **interruptive** *adj.* **interruptor** *n.* **interruptory** *adj.* [ME f. L *interrumpere interrupt-* (as **INTER-**, *rumpere* break)]

intersect /ˌɪntəˈsekt/ *v.* **1** *tr.* divide (a thing) by passing or lying across it. **2** *intr.* (of lines, roads, etc.) cross or cut each other. [L *intersecare intersect-* (as **INTER-**, *secare* cut)]

intersection /ˌɪntəˈsekʃ(ə)n/ *n.* **1** the act of intersecting. **2** a place where two roads intersect. **3** a point or line common to lines or planes that intersect. □ **intersectional** *adj.* [L *intersectio* (as **INTERSECT**)]

intersexual /ˌɪntəˈseksjʊəl/ *adj.* existing between the sexes. □ **intersexuality** /-ˈælɪtɪ/ *n.* **intersexually** *adv.*

interspace /ˈɪntəˌspeɪs/ *n.* & *v.* —*n.* an interval of space or time. —*v.tr.* put interspaces between.

interspecific /ˌɪntəspəˈsɪfɪk/ *adj.* formed from different species.

intersperse /ˌɪntəˈspɜːs/ *v.tr.* **1** (often foll. by *between, among*) scatter; place here and there. **2** (foll. by *with*) diversify (a thing or things with others so scattered). □ **interspersion** *n.* [L *interspergere interspers-* (as **INTER-**, *spargere* scatter)]

interstate /ˈɪntəˌsteɪt/ *adj.* & *n.* *US* —*adj.* existing or carried on between States, esp. of the US. —*n.* a motorway, esp. crossing a State boundary.

interstellar /ˌɪntəˈstelə(r)/ *adj.* occurring or situated between stars.

interstice /ɪnˈtɜːstɪs/ *n.* **1** an intervening space. **2** a chink or crevice. [L *interstitium* (as **INTER-**, *sistere stit-* stand)]

interstitial /ˌɪntəˈstɪʃ(ə)l/ *adj.* of, forming, or occupying interstices. □ **interstitially** *adv.*

intertwine /ˌɪntəˈtwaɪn/ *v.* **1** *tr.* (often foll. by *with*) entwine (together). **2** *intr.* become entwined. □ **intertwinement** *n.*

interval /ˈɪntəv(ə)l/ *n.* **1** an intervening time or space. **2** *Brit.* a pause or break, esp. between the parts of a theatrical or musical performance. **3** the difference in pitch between two sounds. **4** the distance between persons or things in respect of qualities. □ **at intervals** here and there; now and then. □ **intervallic** /-ˈvælɪk/ *adj.* [ME ult. f. L *intervallum* space between ramparts, interval (as **INTER-**, *vallum* rampart)]

intervene /ˌɪntəˈviːn/ *v.intr.* (often foll. by *between, in*) **1** occur in time between events. **2** interfere; come between so as to prevent or modify the result or course of events. **3** be situated between things. **4** come in as an extraneous factor or thing. □ **intervener** *n.* **intervenient** *adj.* **intervenor** *n.* [L *intervenire* (as **INTER-**, *venire* come)]

intervention /ˌɪntəˈvenʃ(ə)n/ *n.* **1** the act or an instance of intervening. **2** interference, esp. by a State in another's affairs. **3** mediation. [ME f. F *intervention* or L *interventio* (as **INTERVENE**)]

interventionist /ˌɪntəˈvenʃ(ə)nɪst/ *n.* a person who favours intervention.

interview /ˈɪntəˌvjuː/ *n.* & *v.* —*n.* **1** an oral examination of an applicant for employment, a college place, etc. **2** a conversation between a reporter etc. and a person of public interest, used as a basis of a broadcast or publication. **3** a meeting of persons face to face, esp. for consultation. —*v.tr.* **1** hold an interview with. **2** question to discover the opinions or experience of (a person). □ **interviewee** /-vjuːˈiː/ *n.* **interviewer** *n.* [F *entrevue* f. *s'entrevoir* see each other (as **INTER-**, *voir* f. L *vidēre* see: see **VIEW**)]

interwar /ˌɪntəˈwɔː(r)/ *adj.* existing in the period between two wars, esp. the two world wars.

interweave /ˌɪntəˈwiːv/ *v.tr.* (*past* **-wove** /-ˈwəʊv/; *past part.* **-woven** /-ˈwəʊv(ə)n/) **1** (often foll. by *with*) weave together. **2** blend intimately.

intestate /ɪnˈtestət/ *adj.* & *n.* —*adj.* (of a person) not having made a will before death. —*n.* a person who has died intestate. □ **intestacy** /-təsɪ/ *n.* [ME f. L *intestatus* (as **IN-¹**, *testari testat-* make a will f. *testis* witness)]

intestine /ɪnˈtestɪn/ *n.* (in *sing.* or *pl.*) the lower part of the alimentary canal from the end of the stomach to the anus. □ **intestinal** /also ˌɪnteˈstaɪn(ə)l/ *adj.* [L *intestinum* f. *intestinus* internal]

inthrall *US* var. of **ENTHRAL**.

intifada /ɪntɪˈfɑːdə/ *n.* a movement of Palestinian uprising in the Israeli-occupied West Bank and Gaza Strip, beginning in 1987. [Arab., = uprising]

intimacy /ˈɪntɪməsɪ/ *n.* (*pl.* **-ies**) **1** the state of being intimate. **2** an intimate act, esp. sexual intercourse. **3** an intimate remark; an endearment.

intimate¹ /ˈɪntɪmət/ *adj.* & *n.* —*adj.* **1** closely acquainted; familiar, close (*an intimate friend; an intimate relationship*). **2** private and personal (*intimate thoughts*). **3** (usu. foll. by *with*) having sexual relations. **4** (of knowledge) detailed, thorough. **5** (of a relationship between things) close. **6** (of mixing etc.) thorough. **7** (of a place etc.) friendly; promoting close personal relationships. —*n.* a very close friend. □ **intimately** *adv.* [L *intimus* inmost]

intimate² /ˈɪntɪˌmeɪt/ *v.tr.* **1** (often foll. by *that* + clause) state or make known. **2** imply, hint. □ **intimater** *n.* **intimation** /-ˈmeɪʃ(ə)n/ *n.* [LL *intimare* announce f. L *intimus* inmost]

intimidate /ɪnˈtɪmɪˌdeɪt/ *v.tr.* frighten or over-awe, esp. to subdue or influence. □ **intimidation** /-ˈdeɪʃ(ə)n/ *n.* **intimidator** *n.* [med.L *intimidare* (as IN-², *timidare* f. *timidus* TIMID)]

into /ˈɪntʊ, ˈɪntə/ *prep.* **1** expressing motion or direction to a point on or within (*walked into a tree; ran into the house*). **2** expressing direction of attention or concern (*will look into it*). **3** expressing a change of state (*turned into a dragon; separated into groups; forced into cooperation*). **4** *colloq.* interested in; knowledgeable about (*is really into art*). [OE *intō* (as IN, TO)]

intolerable /ɪnˈtɒlərəb(ə)l/ *adj.* that cannot be endured. □ **intolerableness** *n.* **intolerably** *adv.* [ME f. OF *intolerable* or L *intolerabilis* (as IN-¹, TOLERABLE)]

intolerant /ɪnˈtɒlərənt/ *adj.* not tolerant, esp. of views, beliefs, or behaviour differing from one's own. □ **intolerance** *n.* **intolerantly** *adv.* [L *intolerans* (as IN-¹, TOLERANT)]

intonation /ˌɪntəˈneɪʃ(ə)n/ *n.* **1** modulation of the voice; accent. **2** the act of intoning. **3** accuracy of pitch in playing or singing (*has good intonation*). □ **intonational** *adj.* [med.L *intonatio* (as INTONE)]

intone /ɪnˈtəʊn/ *v.tr.* **1** recite (prayers etc.) with prolonged sounds, esp. in a monotone. **2** utter with a particular tone. □ **intoner** *n.* [med.L *intonare* (as IN-², L *tonus* TONE)]

in toto /ɪn ˈtəʊtəʊ/ *adv.* completely. [L]

intoxicant /ɪnˈtɒksɪkənt/ *adj.* & *n.* —*adj.* intoxicating. —*n.* an intoxicating substance.

intoxicate /ɪnˈtɒksɪˌkeɪt/ *v.tr.* **1** make drunk. **2** excite or elate beyond self-control. □ **intoxicatingly** *adv.* **intoxication** /-ˈkeɪʃ(ə)n/ *n.* [med.L *intoxicare* (as IN-², *toxicare* poison f. L *toxicum*): see TOXIC]

intra- /ˈɪntrə/ *prefix* forming adjectives usu. from adjectives, meaning 'on the inside, within' (*intramural*). [L *intra* inside]

intractable /ɪnˈtræktəb(ə)l/ *adj.* **1** hard to control or deal with. **2** difficult, stubborn. □ **intractability** /-ˈbɪlɪtɪ/ *n.* **intractableness** *n.* **intractably** *adv.* [L *intractabilis* (as IN-¹, TRACTABLE)]

intramural /ˌɪntrəˈmjʊər(ə)l/ *adj.* **1** situated or done within walls. **2** forming part of normal university or college studies. □ **intramurally** *adv.*

intramuscular /ˌɪntrəˈmʌskjʊlə(r)/ *adj.* in or into a muscle or muscles.

intransigent /ɪnˈtrænsɪdʒ(ə)nt, -zɪdʒ(ə)nt/ *adj.* & *n.* —*adj.* uncompromising, stubborn. —*n.* an intransigent person. □ **intransigence** /-dʒ(ə)ns/ *n.* **intransigency** /-dʒənsɪ/ *n.* **intransigently** *adv.* [F *intransigeant* f. Sp. *los intransigentes* extreme republicans in Cortes, ult. formed as IN-¹ + L *transigere transigent-* come to an understanding (as TRANS-, *agere* act)]

intransitive /ɪnˈtrænsɪtɪv, ɪnˈtrɑːn:n-, -zɪtɪv/ *adj.* (of a verb or sense of a verb) that does not take or require a direct object (whether expressed or implied), e.g. *look* in *look at the sky*. □

intransitively *adv.* **intransitivity** /-ˈtɪvɪtɪ/ *n.* [LL *intransitivus* (as IN-¹, TRANSITIVE)]

intra-uterine /ˌɪntrəˈjuːtəˌraɪn, -rɪn/ *adj.* within the womb.

intravenous /ˌɪntrəˈviːnəs/ *adj.* in or into a vein or veins. □ **intravenously** *adv.* [INTRA- + L *vena* vein]

in-tray /ˈɪntreɪ/ *n.* a tray for incoming documents, letters, etc.

intrepid /ɪnˈtrepɪd/ *adj.* fearless; very brave. □ **intrepidity** /-trɪˈpɪdɪtɪ/ *n.* **intrepidly** *adv.* [F *intrépide* or L *intrepidus* (as IN-¹, *trepidus* alarmed)]

intricate /ˈɪntrɪkət/ *adj.* very complicated; perplexingly detailed. □ **intricacy** /-kəsɪ/ *n.* (pl. -ies). **intricately** *adv.* [ME f. L *intricare* intricat- (as IN-², *tricare* f. *tricae* tricks)]

intrigue *v.* & *n.* —*v.* /ɪnˈtriːg/ (**intrigues**, **intrigued**, **intriguing**) **1** *intr.* (foll. by *with*) **a** carry on an underhand plot. **b** use secret influence. **2** *tr.* arouse the curiosity of; fascinate. —*n.* /ɪnˈtriːg, ˈɪn-/ **1** an underhand plot or plotting. **2** *archaic* a secret love affair. □ **intriguer** /ɪnˈtriːgə(r)/ *n.* **intriguing** *adj.* (esp. in sense 2 of *v.*) **intriguingly** /ɪnˈtriːgɪŋ-/ *adv.* [F *intrigue* (n.), *intriguer* (v.) f. It. *intrigo*, *intrigare* f. L (as INTRICATE)]

intrinsic /ɪnˈtrɪnzɪk/ *adj.* inherent, essential; belonging naturally (*intrinsic value*). □ **intrinsically** *adv.* [ME, = interior, f. F *intrinsèque* f. LL *intrinsecus* f. L *intrinsecus* (adv.) inwardly]

intro /ˈɪntrəʊ/ *n.* (pl. -os) *colloq.* an introduction. [abbr.]

intro- /ˈɪntrəʊ/ *comb. form* into. [L *intro* to the inside]

introduce /ˌɪntrəˈdjuːs/ *v.tr.* **1** (foll. by *to*) make (a person or oneself) known by name to another, esp. formally. **2** announce or present to an audience. **3** bring (a custom, idea, etc.) into use. **4** bring (a piece of legislation) before a legislative assembly. **5** (foll. by *to*) draw the attention or extend the understanding of (a person) to a subject. **6** insert; place in. **7** bring in; usher in; bring forward. **8** begin; occur just before the start of. □ **introducer** *n.* **introducible** *adj.* [ME f. L *introducere introduct-* (as INTRO-, *ducere* lead)]

introduction /ˌɪntrəˈdʌkʃ(ə)n/ *n.* **1** the act or an instance of introducing; the process of being introduced. **2** a formal presentation of one person to another. **3** an explanatory section at the beginning of a book etc. **4** a preliminary section in a piece of music, often thematically different from the main section. **5** an introductory treatise on a subject. **6** a thing introduced. [ME f. OF *introduction* or L *introductio* (as INTRODUCE)]

introductory /ˌɪntrəˈdʌktərɪ/ *adj.* serving as an introduction; preliminary. [LL *introductorius* (as INTRODUCTION)]

introspection /ˌɪntrəˈspekʃ(ə)n/ *n.* the examination or observation of one's own mental and emotional processes etc. □ **introspective** *adj.* **introspectively** *adv.* **introspectiveness** *n.* [L *introspicere introspect-* look inwards (as INTRO-, *specere* look)]

introvert *n.* & *adj.* —*n.* /ˈɪntrəˌvɜːt/ **1** *Psychol.* a person predominantly concerned with his or her own thoughts and feelings rather than with external things. **2** a shy inwardly thoughtful person. —*adj.* /ˈɪntrəˌvɜːt/ (also **introverted** /-tɪd/) typical or characteristic of an introvert. □ **introversion** /-ˈvɜːʃ(ə)n/ *n.* **introversive** /-ˈvɜː-

sɪv/ *adj.* **introverted** *adj.* **introvertive** /-'vɜːtɪv/ *adj.* [INTRO- + *vert* as in INVERT]

intrude /ɪn'truːd/ *v.* (foll. by *on, upon, into*) **1** *intr.* come uninvited or unwanted; force oneself abruptly on others. **2** *tr.* thrust or force (something unwelcome) on a person. □ **intrudingly** *adv.* [L *intrudere intrus-* (as IN-², *trudere* thrust)]

intruder /ɪn'truːdə(r)/ *n.* a person who intrudes, esp. into a building with criminal intent.

intrusion /ɪn'truːʒ(ə)n/ *n.* **1** the act or an instance of intruding. **2** an unwanted interruption etc. **3** *Geol.* an influx of molten rock between or through strata etc. but not reaching the surface. [ME f. OF *intrusion* or med.L *intrusio* (as INTRUDE)]

intrusive /ɪn'truːsɪv/ *adj.* **1** that intrudes or tends to intrude. **2** characterized by intrusion. □ **intrusively** *adv.* **intrusiveness** *n.*

intrust var. of ENTRUST.

intuit /ɪn'tjuːɪt/ *v.* **1** *tr.* know by intuition. **2** *intr.* receive knowledge by direct perception. □ **intuitable** *adj.* [L *intueri intuit-* consider (as IN-², *tueri* look)]

intuition /ˌɪntjuː'ɪʃ(ə)n/ *n.* **1** immediate apprehension by the mind without reasoning. **2** immediate apprehension by a sense. **3** immediate insight. □ **intuitional** *adj.* [LL *intuitio* (as INTUIT)]

intuitive /ɪn'tjuːɪtɪv/ *adj.* **1** of, characterized by, or possessing intuition. **2** perceived by intuition. □ **intuitively** *adv.* **intuitiveness** *n.* [med.L *intuitivus* (as INTUIT)]

intwine var. of ENTWINE.

Inuit /'ɪnjuːɪt, 'ɪnʊɪt/ *n.* (also **Innuit**) (*pl.* same or **Inuits**) a N. American Eskimo. [Eskimo *inuit* people]

inundate /'ɪnənˌdeɪt/ *v.tr.* (often foll. by *with*) **1** flood. **2** overwhelm (*inundated with enquiries*). □ **inundation** /-'deɪʃ(ə)n/ *n.* [L *inundare* flow (as IN-², *unda* wave)]

inure /ɪ'njʊə(r)/ *v.* (often in *passive*; foll. by *to*) accustom (a person) to something esp. unpleasant. □ **inurement** *n.* [ME f. AF *eneurer* f. phr. *en eure* (both unrecorded) in use or practice, f. *en* in + OF *e(u)vre* work f. L *opera*]

in utero /ɪn 'juːtəˌrəʊ/ *adv.* in the womb. [L]

invade /ɪn'veɪd/ *v.tr.* (often *absol.*) **1** enter (a country etc.) under arms to control or subdue it. **2** swarm into. **3** (of a disease) attack (a body etc.). **4** encroach upon (a person's rights, esp. privacy). □ **invader** *n.* [L *invadere invas-* (as IN-², *vadere* go)]

invalid¹ *n.* & *v.* —*n.* /'ɪnvəˌliːd, -lɪd/ **1** a person enfeebled or disabled by illness or injury. **2** (*attrib.*) **a** of or for invalids (*invalid car; invalid diet*). **b** being an invalid (*caring for her invalid mother*). —*v.tr.* /'ɪnvəˌliːd/ (**invalided, invaliding**) **1** (often foll. by *out* etc.) remove from active service (one who has become an invalid). **2** (usu. in *passive*) disable (a person) by illness. □ **invalidism** *n.* [L *invalidus* weak, infirm (as IN-¹, VALID)]

invalid² /ɪn'vælɪd/ *adj.* not valid, esp. having no legal force. □ **invalidly** *adv.* [L *invalidus* (as INVALID¹)]

invalidate /ɪn'vælɪˌdeɪt/ *v.tr.* **1** make (esp. an argument etc.) invalid. **2** remove the validity or force of (a treaty, contract, etc.). □ **invalidation** /-'deɪʃ(ə)n/ *n.* [med.L *invalidare invalidat-* (as IN-¹, *validus* VALID)]

invalidity /ˌɪnvə'lɪdɪtɪ/ *n.* **1** lack of validity. **2** bodily infirmity. [F *invalidité* or med.L *invaliditas* (as INVALID¹)]

invaluable /ɪn'væljʊəb(ə)l/ *adj.* above valuation; inestimable. □ **invaluableness** *n.* **invaluably** *adv.*

invariable /ɪn'veərɪəb(ə)l/ *adj.* **1** unchangeable. **2** always the same. **3** *Math.* constant, fixed. □ **invariability** /-'bɪlɪtɪ/ *n.* **invariableness** *n.* **invariably** *adv.* [F *invariable* or LL *invariabilis* (as IN-¹, VARIABLE)]

invasion /ɪn'veɪʒ(ə)n/ *n.* **1** the act of invading or process of being invaded. **2** an entry of a hostile army into a country. □ **invasive** /-sɪv/ *adj.* [F *invasion* or LL *invasio* (as INVADE)]

invective /ɪn'vektɪv/ *n.* **1 a** strongly attacking words. **b** the use of these. **2** abusive rhetoric. [ME f. OF f. LL *invectivus* attacking (as INVEIGH)]

inveigh /ɪn'veɪ/ *v.intr.* (foll. by *against*) speak or write with strong hostility. [L *invehi* go into, assail (as IN-², *vehi* passive of *vehere vect-* carry)]

inveigle /ɪn'veɪg(ə)l, -'viːg(ə)l/ *v.tr.* (foll. by *into*, or *to* + infin.) entice; persuade by guile. □ **inveiglement** *n.* [earlier *enve(u)gle* f. AF *envegler*, OF *aveugler* to blind f. *aveugle* blind prob. f. Rmc *ab oculis* (unrecorded) without eyes]

invent /ɪn'vent/ *v.tr.* **1** create by thought, devise; originate (a new method, an instrument, etc.). **2** concoct (a false story etc.). □ **inventable** *adj.* [ME, = discover, f. L *invenire invent-* find, contrive (as IN-², *venire vent-* come)]

invention /ɪn'venʃ(ə)n/ *n.* **1** the process of inventing. **2** a thing invented; a contrivance, esp. one for which a patent is granted. **3** a fictitious story. **4** inventiveness. [ME f. L *inventio* (as INVENT)]

inventive /ɪn'ventɪv/ *adj.* **1** able or inclined to invent; original in devising. **2** showing ingenuity of devising. □ **inventively** *adv.* **inventiveness** *n.* [ME f. F *inventif -ive* or med.L *inventivus* (as INVENT)]

inventor /ɪn'ventə(r)/ *n.* (*fem.* **inventress** /-trɪs/) a person who invents, esp. as an occupation.

inventory /'ɪnvəntərɪ/ *n.* & *v.* —*n.* (*pl.* **-ies**) **1** a complete list of goods in stock, house contents, etc. **2** the goods listed in this. **3** *US* the total of a firm's commercial assets. —*v.tr.* (**-ies, -ied**) **1** make an inventory of. **2** enter (goods) in an inventory. [ME f. med.L *inventorium* f. LL *inventarium* (as INVENT)]

inverse /'ɪnvɜːs, -'vɜːs/ *adj.* & *n.* —*adj.* inverted in position, order, or relation. —*n.* **1** the state of being inverted. **2** (often foll. by *of*) a thing that is the opposite or reverse of another. □ **inverse proportion** (or **ratio**) a relation between two quantities such that one increases in proportion as the other decreases. □ **inversely** *adv.* [L *inversus* past part. of *invertere*: see INVERT]

inversion /ɪn'vɜːʃ(ə)n/ *n.* **1** the act of turning upside down or inside out. **2** the reversal of a normal order, position, or relation. **3** the reversal of the order of words, for rhetorical effect. **4** the process or result of inverting. □ **inversive** /-sɪv/ *adj.* [L *inversio* (as INVERT)]

invert *v.* & *n.* —*v.tr.* /ɪn'vɜːt/ **1** turn upside down. **2** reverse the position, order, or relation of. —*n.* /'ɪnvɜːt/ a homosexual. □ **inverted comma** = *quotation mark.* □ **inverter** /ɪn'vɜːtə(r)/ *n.* **invertible** /ɪn'vɜːtɪb(ə)l/ *adj.* **invertibility** /-'bɪlɪtɪ/ *n.* [L *invertere invers-* (as IN-², *vertere* turn)]

invertebrate /ɪnˈvɜːtɪbrət, -ˌbreɪt/ adj. & n. —adj. **1** (of an animal) not having a backbone. **2** lacking firmness of character. —n. an invertebrate animal. [mod.L *invertebrata* (pl.) (as IN-¹, VERTEBRA)]

invest /ɪnˈvest/ v. **1** tr. (often foll. by *in*) apply or use (money), esp. for profit. **2** intr. (foll. by *in*) **a** put money for profit (into stocks etc.). **b** colloq. buy (*invested in a new car*). **3** tr. **a** (foll. by *with*) provide, endue, or attribute (a person with qualities, insignia, or rank). **b** (foll. by *in*) attribute or entrust (qualities or feelings to a person). □ **investable** adj. **investible** adj. **investor** n. [ME f. F *investir* or L *investire investit-* (as IN-², *vestire* clothe f. *vestis* clothing): sense 1 f. It. *investire*]

investigate /ɪnˈvestɪˌɡeɪt/ v. **1** tr. **a** inquire into; examine; study carefully. **b** make an official inquiry into. **2** intr. make a systematic inquiry or search. □ **investigator** n. **investigatory** /-ɡətərɪ/ adj. [L *investigare investigat-* (as IN-², *vestigare* track)]

investigation /ɪnˌvestɪˈɡeɪʃ(ə)n/ n. **1** the process or an instance of investigating. **2** a formal examination or study.

investigative /ɪnˈvestɪɡətɪv/ adj. seeking or serving to investigate, esp. (of journalism) inquiring intensively into controversial issues.

investiture /ɪnˈvestɪˌtjʊə(r)/ n. **1** the formal investing of a person with honours or rank, esp. a ceremony at which a sovereign confers honours. **2** (often foll. by *with*) the act of enduing (with attributes). [ME f. med.L *investitura* (as INVEST)]

investment /ɪnˈvestmənt/ n. **1** the act or process of investing. **2** money invested. **3** property etc. in which money is invested.

inveterate /ɪnˈvetərət/ adj. **1** (of a person) confirmed in an (esp. undesirable) habit etc. **2 a** (of a habit etc.) long-established. **b** (of an activity, esp. an undesirable one) habitual. □ **inveteracy** /-rəsɪ/ n. **inveterately** adv. [L *inveterare inveterat-* make old (as IN-², *vetus veteris* old)]

invidious /ɪnˈvɪdɪəs/ adj. (of an action, conduct, attitude, etc.) likely to excite resentment or indignation against the person responsible, esp. by real or seeming injustice. □ **invidiously** adv. **invidiousness** n. [L *invidiosus* f. *invidia* ENVY]

invigilate /ɪnˈvɪdʒɪˌleɪt/ v.intr. Brit. supervise candidates at an examination. □ **invigilation** /-ˈleɪʃ(ə)n/ n. **invigilator** n. [orig. = keep watch, f. L *invigilare invigilat-* (as IN-², *vigilare* watch f. *vigil* watchful)]

invigorate /ɪnˈvɪɡəˌreɪt/ v.tr. give vigour or strength to. □ **invigorating** adj. **invigoratingly** adv. **invigoration** /-ˈreɪʃ(ə)n/ n. **invigorative** /-rətɪv/ adj. **invigorator** n. [IN-² + med.L *vigorare vigorat-* make strong]

invincible /ɪnˈvɪnsɪb(ə)l/ adj. unconquerable; that cannot be defeated. □ **invincibility** /-ˈbɪlɪtɪ/ n. **invincibleness** n. **invincibly** adv. [ME f. OF f. L *invincibilis*]

inviolable /ɪnˈvaɪələb(ə)l/ adj. not to be violated or profaned. □ **inviolability** /-ˈbɪlɪtɪ/ n. **inviolably** adv. [F *inviolable* or L *inviolabilis* (as IN-¹, VIOLATE)]

inviolate /ɪnˈvaɪələt/ adj. not violated or profaned. □ **inviolacy** /-ləsɪ/ n. **inviolately** adv. **inviolateness** n. [ME f. L *inviolatus* (as IN-¹, *violare, violat-* treat violently)]

invisible /ɪnˈvɪzɪb(ə)l/ adj. **1** not visible to the eye, either characteristically or because hidden. **2** too small to be seen or noticed. **3** artfully concealed (*invisible mending*). □ **invisible exports** (or **imports** etc.) items, esp. services, involving payment between countries but not constituting tangible commodities. □ **invisibility** /-ˈbɪlɪtɪ/ n. **invisibleness** n. **invisibly** adv. [ME f. OF *invisible* or L *invisibilis* (as IN-¹, VISIBLE)]

invitation /ˌɪnvɪˈteɪʃ(ə)n/ n. the process of inviting or fact of being invited, esp. to a social occasion.

invite /ɪnˈvaɪt/ v. & n. —v. **1** tr. (often foll. by *to*, or *to* + infin.) ask (a person) courteously to come, or to do something (*were invited to lunch*; *invited them to reply*). **2** tr. make a formal courteous request for (*invited comments*). **3** tr. tend to call forth unintentionally (something unwanted). **4 a** tr. attract. **b** intr. be attractive. —n. /ˈɪnvaɪt/ colloq. an invitation. □ **invitee** /-ˈtiː/ n. **inviter** n. [F *inviter* or L *invitare*]

inviting /ɪnˈvaɪtɪŋ/ adj. **1** attractive. **2** enticing; tempting. □ **invitingly** adv. **invitingness** n.

in vitro /ɪn ˈviːtrəʊ/ adv. Biol. (of processes or reactions) taking place in a test-tube or other laboratory environment. [L, = in glass]

invocation /ˌɪnvəˈkeɪʃ(ə)n/ n. **1** the act or an instance of invoking, esp. in prayer. **2** an appeal to a supernatural being or beings, e.g. the Muses, for psychological or spiritual inspiration. □ **invocatory** /ɪnˈvɒkətərɪ/ adj. [ME f. OF f. L *invocatio -onis* (as INVOKE)]

invoice /ˈɪnvɔɪs/ n. & v. —n. a list of goods shipped or sent, or services rendered, with prices and charges; a bill. —v.tr. **1** make an invoice of (goods and services). **2** send an invoice to (a person). [earlier *invoyes* pl. of *invoy* f. *envoyer* send]

invoke /ɪnˈvəʊk/ v.tr. **1** call on (a deity etc.) in prayer or as a witness. **2** appeal to (the law, a person's authority, etc.). **3** summon (a spirit) by charms. **4** ask earnestly for (vengeance, help, etc.). □ **invocable** adj. **invoker** n. [F *invoquer* f. L *invocare* (as IN-², *vocare* call)]

involuntary /ɪnˈvɒləntərɪ/ adj. **1** done without the exercise of the will; unintentional. **2** (of a limb, muscle, or movement) not under the control of the will. □ **involuntarily** adv. **involuntariness** n. [LL *involuntarius* (as IN-¹, VOLUNTARY)]

involute /ˈɪnvəˌluːt, -ˌljuːt/ adj. **1** involved, intricate. **2** curled spirally. **3** Bot. rolled inwards at the edges. [L *involutus* past part. of *involvere*: see INVOLVE]

involuted /ˈɪnvəˌluːtɪd, -ˌljuːtɪd/ adj. **1** complicated, abstruse. **2** = INVOLUTE 2.

involution /ˌɪnvəˈluːʃ(ə)n, -ˈljuːʃ(ə)n/ n. **1** the process of involving. **2** an entanglement. **3** intricacy. **4** curling inwards. **5** a part that curls upwards. □ **involutional** adj. [L *involutio* (as INVOLVE)]

involve /ɪnˈvɒlv/ v.tr. **1** (often foll. by *in*) cause (a person or thing) to participate, or share the experience or effect (in a situation, activity, etc.). **2** imply, entail, make necessary. **3** (foll. by *in*) implicate (a person in a charge, crime, etc.). **4** include or affect in its operations. **5** (as **involved** adj.) **a** (often foll. by *in*) concerned or interested. **b** complicated in thought or form. □

involvement n. [ME f. L *involvere involut-* (as IN-², *volvere* roll)]

invulnerable /ɪnˈvʌlnərəb(ə)l/ adj. that cannot be wounded or hurt, physically or mentally. □ **invulnerability** /-ˈbɪlɪtɪ/ n. **invulnerably** adv. [L *invulnerabilis* (as IN-¹, VULNERABLE)]

inward /ˈɪnwəd/ adj. & adv. —adj. **1** directed toward the inside; going in. **2** situated within. **3** mental, spiritual. —adv. (also **inwards**) **1** (of motion or position) towards the inside. **2** in the mind or soul. [OE *innanweard* (as IN, -WARD)]

inwardly /ˈɪnwədlɪ/ adv. **1** on the inside. **2** in the mind or soul. **3** (of speaking) not aloud; inaudibly. [OE *inweardlíce* (as INWARD)]

inwardness /ˈɪnwədnɪs/ n. **1** inner nature; essence. **2** the condition of being inward. **3** spirituality.

inwards var. of INWARD adv.

inwrap var. of ENWRAP.

inwrought /ɪnˈrɔːt, attrib. ˈɪnrɔːt/ adj. **1 a** (often foll. by *with*) (of a fabric) decorated (with a pattern). **b** (often foll. by *in, on*) (of a pattern) wrought (in or on a fabric). **2** closely blended.

iodide /ˈaɪəˌdaɪd/ n. *Chem.* any compound of iodine with another element or group.

iodine /ˈaɪəˌdiːn, -ɪn/ n. **1** *Chem.* a non-metallic element of the halogen group, used in medicine and photography. **2** a solution of this in alcohol used as a mild antiseptic. [F *iode* f. Gk *iōdēs* violet-like f. *ion* violet + -INE⁴]

iodize /ˈaɪəˌdaɪz/ v.tr. (also **-ise**) treat or impregnate with iodine. □ **iodization** /-ˈzeɪʃ(ə)n/ n.

iodoform /aɪˈɒdəˌfɔːm, -ˈɒdəˌfɔːm/ n. a pale yellow volatile sweet-smelling solid compound of iodine with antiseptic properties. [IODINE after *chloroform*]

ion /ˈaɪən/ n. an atom or group of atoms that has lost one or more electrons (= CATION), or gained one or more electrons (= ANION). [Gk, neut. pres. part. of *eimi* go]

-ion suffix (usu. as **-sion**, **-tion**, **-xion**; see -ATION, -ITION, -UTION) forming nouns denoting: **1** verbal action (*excision*). **2** an instance of this (*a suggestion*). **3** a resulting state or product (*vexation; concoction*). [from or after F *-ion* or L *-io -ionis*]

Ionic /aɪˈɒnɪk/ adj. & n. —adj. **1** of the order of Greek architecture characterized by a column with scroll-shapes on either side of the capital. **2** of the ancient Greek dialect used in Ionia. —n. the Ionic dialect. [L *Ionicus* f. Gk *Iōnikos*]

ionic /aɪˈɒnɪk/ adj. of, relating to, or using ions. □ **ionically** adv.

ionization /ˌaɪənaɪˈzeɪʃ(ə)n/ n. (also **-isation**) the process of producing ions as a result of heat, radiation, etc.

ionize /ˈaɪəˌnaɪz/ v.tr. & intr. (also **-ise**) convert or be converted into an ion or ions. □ **ionizing radiation** a radiation of sufficient energy to cause ionization in the medium through which it passes. □ **ionizable** adj.

ionizer /ˈaɪəˌnaɪzə(r)/ n. any thing which produces ionization, esp. a device used to improve the quality of the air in a room etc.

ionosphere /aɪˈɒnəˌsfɪə(r)/ n. an ionized region of the atmosphere above the stratosphere, able to reflect radio waves for long-distance transmission round the earth. □ **ionospheric** /-ˈsferɪk/ adj.

-ior¹ /ɪə(r)/ suffix forming adjectives of comparison (*senior; ulterior*). [L]

-ior² var. of -IOUR.

iota /aɪˈəʊtə/ n. **1** the ninth letter of the Greek alphabet (*I, ι*). **2** (usu. with *neg.*) the smallest possible amount. [Gk *iōta*]

IOU /ˌaɪəʊˈjuː/ n. a signed document acknowledging a debt. [= I owe you]

-iour /ɪə(r)/ suffix (also **-ior**) forming nouns (*saviour; warrior*). [-*i*- (as a stem element) + -OUR², -OR¹]

-ious /-ɪəs, -əs/ suffix forming adjectives meaning 'characterized by, full of', often corresponding to nouns in *-ion* (*cautious; curious; spacious*). [from or after F *-ieux* f. L *-iosus*]

IPA abbr. International Phonetic Alphabet (or Association).

ipecacuanha /ˌɪpɪˌkækjʊˈɑːnə/ n. the root of a S. American shrub, *Cephaelis ipecacuanha*, used as an emetic and purgative. [Port. f. Tupi-Guarani *ipekaaguéne* emetic creeper]

ipso facto /ˌɪpsəʊ ˈfæktəʊ/ adv. **1** by that very fact or act. **2** thereby. [L]

IQ abbr. intelligence quotient.

Ir symb. *Chem.* the element iridium.

IRA abbr. Irish Republican Army.

irascible /ɪˈræsɪb(ə)l/ adj. irritable; hot-tempered. □ **irascibility** /-ˈbɪlɪtɪ/ n. **irascibly** adv. [ME f. F f. LL *irascibilis* f. L *irasci* grow angry f. *ira* anger]

irate /aɪˈreɪt/ adj. angry, enraged. □ **irately** adv. **irateness** n. [L *iratus* f. *ira* anger]

ire /ˈaɪə(r)/ n. *literary* anger. □ **ireful** adj. [ME f. OF f. L *ira*]

iridaceous /ˌɪrɪˈdeɪʃəs/ adj. *Bot.* of or relating to the family Iridaceae of plants growing from bulbs, corms, or rhizomes, e.g. iris, crocus, and gladiolus. [mod.L *iridaceus* (as IRIS)]

iridescent /ˌɪrɪˈdes(ə)nt/ adj. **1** showing rainbow-like luminous or gleaming colours. **2** changing colour with position. □ **iridescence** n. **iridescently** adv. [L IRIS + *escent* pres. part. stem]

iridium /ɪˈrɪdɪəm/ n. *Chem.* a hard white metallic element of the transition series used esp. in alloys. [mod.L f. L IRIS + -IUM]

iris /ˈaɪərɪs/ n. **1** the flat circular coloured membrane behind the cornea of the eye, with a circular opening (pupil) in the centre. **2** any herbaceous plant of the genus *Iris*, usu. with tuberous roots, sword-shaped leaves, and showy flowers. **3** (in full **iris diaphragm**) an adjustable diaphragm of thin overlapping plates for regulating the size of a central hole esp. for the admission of light to a lens. [ME f. L *iris iridis* f. Gk *iris iridos* rainbow, iris]

Irish /ˈaɪərɪʃ/ adj. & n. —adj. of or relating to Ireland; of or like its people. —n. **1** the Celtic language of Ireland. **2** (prec. by *the*; treated as pl.) the people of Ireland. □ **Irish coffee** coffee mixed with a dash of whisky and served with cream on top. **Irish stew** a stew of mutton, potato, and onion. [ME f. OE *Iras* the Irish]

Irishman /ˈaɪərɪʃmən/ n. (pl. **-men**) a man who is Irish by birth or descent.

Irishwoman /ˈaɪərɪʃˌwʊmən/ n. (pl. **-women**) a woman who is Irish by birth or descent.

irk /ɜːk/ v.tr. (usu. *impers.*; often foll. by *that* + clause) irritate, bore, annoy. [ME: orig. unkn.]

irksome /ˈɜːksəm/ *adj.* tedious, annoying, tiresome. □ **irksomely** *adv.* **irksomeness** *n.* [ME, = tired etc., f. IRK + -SOME¹]

iron /ˈaɪən/ *n., adj., & v. —n.* **1** *Chem.* a silver-white ductile metallic element much used for tools and implements. **2** this as a type of unyieldingness or a symbol of firmness (*man of iron; will of iron*). **3** a tool or implement made of iron (*branding iron; curling iron*). **4** a household, now usu. electrical, implement with a flat base which is heated to smooth clothes etc. **5** a golf club with an iron or steel sloping face used for lofting the ball. **6** (usu. in *pl.*) a fetter (*clapped in irons*). **7** (usu. in *pl.*) a stirrup. **8** (often in *pl.*) an iron support for a malformed leg. **9** a preparation of iron as a tonic or dietary supplement (*iron tablets*). —*adj.* **1** made of iron. **2** very robust. **3** unyielding, merciless (*iron determination*). —*v.tr.* **1** smooth (clothes etc.) with an iron. **2** furnish or cover with iron. **3** shackle with irons. □ **Iron Age** *Archaeol.* the period when iron replaced bronze in the making of implements and weapons. **Iron Curtain** *hist.* a notional barrier to the passage of people and information between the former Soviet bloc and the West. **ironing-board** a flat surface usu. on legs and of adjustable height on which clothes etc. are ironed. **iron out** remove or smooth over (difficulties etc.). **iron ration** a small emergency supply of food. □ **ironer** *n.* **ironing** *n.* (in sense 1 of *v.*). **ironless** *adj.* **iron-like** *adj.* [OE *īren*, *īsern* f. Gmc, prob. f. Celt.]

ironclad *adj. & n. —adj.* /ˌaɪənˈklæd/ **1** clad or protected with iron. **2** impregnable; rigorous. —*n.* /ˈaɪənˌklæd/ *hist.* an early name for a 19th-c. warship built of iron or protected by iron plates.

ironic /aɪˈrɒnɪk/ *adj.* (also **ironical**) **1** using or displaying irony. **2** in the nature of irony. □ **ironically** *adv.* [F *ironique* or LL *ironicus* f. Gk *eirōnikos* dissembling (as IRONY)]

ironist /ˈaɪərənɪst/ *n.* a person who uses irony. □ **ironize** *v.intr.* (also **-ise**). [Gk *eirōn* dissembler + -IST]

ironmonger /ˈaɪənˌmʌŋɡə(r)/ *n. Brit.* a dealer in hardware etc. □ **ironmongery** *n.* (*pl.* **-ies**).

ironstone /ˈaɪənˌstəʊn/ *n.* **1** any rock containing a substantial proportion of an iron compound. **2** a kind of hard white opaque stoneware.

ironware /ˈaɪənˌweə(r)/ *n.* articles made of iron, esp. domestic implements.

ironwork /ˈaɪənˌwɜːk/ *n.* **1** things made of iron. **2** work in iron.

ironworks /ˈaɪənˌwɜːks/ *n.* (as *sing.* or *pl.*) a place where iron is smelted or iron goods are made.

irony /ˈaɪrənɪ/ *n.* (*pl.* **-ies**) **1** an expression of meaning, often humorous or sarcastic, by the use of language of a different or opposite tendency. **2** an ill-timed or perverse arrival of an event or circumstance that is in itself desirable. [L *ironia* f. Gk *eirōneia* simulated ignorance f. *eirōn* dissembler]

irradiate /ɪˈreɪdɪˌeɪt/ *v.tr.* **1** subject to (any form of) radiation. **2** shine upon; light up. **3** throw light on (a subject). □ **irradiative** /-dɪətɪv/ *adj.* [L *irradiare irradiat-* (as IN-², *radiare* f. *radius* RAY¹)]

irradiation /ɪˌreɪdɪˈeɪʃ(ə)n/ *n.* **1** the process of irradiating. **2** shining, illumination. [F *irradiation* or LL *irradiatio* (as IRRADIATE)]

irrational /ɪˈræʃən(ə)l/ *adj.* **1** illogical; unreasonable. **2** not endowed with reason. **3** *Math.* (of a root etc.) not rational; not commensurate with the natural numbers (e.g. a non-terminating decimal). □ **irrationality** /-ˈnælɪtɪ/ *n.* **irrationalize** *v.tr.* (also **-ise**). **irrationally** *adv.* [L *irrationalis* (as IN-¹, RATIONAL)]

irreclaimable /ˌɪrɪˈkleɪməb(ə)l/ *adj.* that cannot be reclaimed or reformed. □ **irreclaimably** *adv.*

irreconcilable /ɪˈrekənˌsaɪləb(ə)l/ *adj.* **1** implacably hostile. **2** (of ideas etc.) incompatible. □ **irreconcilability** /-ˈbɪlɪtɪ/ *n.* **irreconcilableness** *n.* **irreconcilably** *adv.*

irrecoverable /ˌɪrɪˈkʌvərəb(ə)l/ *adj.* that cannot be recovered or remedied. □ **irrecoverably** *adv.*

irredeemable /ˌɪrɪˈdiːməb(ə)l/ *adj.* **1** that cannot be redeemed. **2** hopeless, absolute. □ **irredeemably** /-ˈbɪlɪtɪ/ *n.* **irredeemably** *adv.*

irredentist /ˌɪrɪˈdentɪst/ *n.* a person advocating the restoration to his or her country of any territory formerly belonging to it. □ **irredentism** *n.* [It. *irredentista* f. (*Italia*) *irredenta* unredeemed (Italy)]

irreducible /ˌɪrɪˈdjuːsɪb(ə)l/ *adj.* **1** that cannot be reduced or simplified. **2** (often foll. by *to*) that cannot be brought to a desired condition. □ **irreducibility** /-ˈbɪlɪtɪ/ *n.* **irreducibly** *adv.*

irrefutable /ɪˈrefjʊtəb(ə)l, ˌɪrɪˈfjuː-/ *adj.* that cannot be refuted. □ **irrefutability** /-ˈbɪlɪtɪ/ *n.* **irrefutably** *adv.* [LL *irrefutabilis* (as IN-¹, REFUTE)]

irregular /ɪˈreɡjʊlə(r)/ *adj. & n. —adj.* **1** not regular; unsymmetrical, uneven; varying in form. **2** (of a surface) uneven. **3** contrary to a rule, moral principle, or custom; abnormal. **4** uneven in duration, order, etc. **5** (of troops) not belonging to the regular army. **6** *Gram.* (of a verb, noun, etc.) not inflected according to the usual rules. **7** disorderly. —*n.* (in *pl.*) irregular troops. □ **irregularity** /-ˈlærɪtɪ/ *n.* (*pl.* **-ies**). **irregularly** *adv.* [ME f. OF *irreguler* f. LL *irregularis* (as IN-¹, REGULAR)]

irrelevant /ɪˈrelɪv(ə)nt/ *adj.* (often foll. by *to*) not relevant; not applicable (to a matter in hand). □ **irrelevance** *n.* **irrelevancy** *n.* **irrelevantly** *adv.*

irreligion /ˌɪrɪˈlɪdʒ(ə)n/ *n.* disregard of or hostility to religion. □ **irreligionist** *n.* [F *irréligion* or L *irreligio* (as IN-¹, RELIGION)]

irreligious /ˌɪrɪˈlɪdʒəs/ *adj.* **1** indifferent or hostile to religion. **2** lacking a religion. □ **irreligiously** *adv.* **irreligiousness** *n.*

irremediable /ˌɪrɪˈmiːdɪəb(ə)l/ *adj.* that cannot be remedied. □ **irremediably** *adv.* [L *irremediabilis* (as IN-¹, REMEDY)]

irremovable /ˌɪrɪˈmuːvəb(ə)l/ *adj.* that cannot be removed, esp. from office. □ **irremovability** /-ˈbɪlɪtɪ/ *n.* **irremovably** *adv.*

irreparable /ɪˈrepərəb(ə)l/ *adj.* (of an injury, loss, etc.) that cannot be rectified or made good. □ **irreparability** /-ˈbɪlɪtɪ/ *n.* **irreparableness** *n.* **irreparably** *adv.* [ME f. OF f. L *irreparabilis* (as IN-¹, REPARABLE)]

irreplaceable /ˌɪrɪˈpleɪsəb(ə)l/ *adj.* **1** that cannot be replaced. **2** of which the loss cannot be made good. □ **irreplaceably** *adv.*

irrepressible /ˌɪrɪˈpresɪb(ə)l/ *adj.* that cannot be repressed or restrained. □ **irrepressibility** /-ˈbɪlɪtɪ/ *n.* **irrepressibleness** *n.* **irrepressibly** *adv.*

irreproachable /ˌɪrɪˈprəʊtʃəb(ə)l/ *adj.* faultless, blameless. □ **irreproachability** /-ˈbɪlɪtɪ/ *n.* **irreproachableness** *n.* **irreproachably** *adv.* [F *irréprochable* (as IN-¹, REPROACH)]

irresistible /ˌɪrɪˈzɪstɪb(ə)l/ *adj.* **1** too strong or convincing to be resisted. **2** delightful; alluring. □ **irresistibility** /-ˈbɪlɪtɪ/ *n.* **irresistibleness** *n.* **irresistibly** *adv.* [med.L *irresistibilis* (as IN-¹, RESIST)]

irresolute /ɪˈrezəˌluːt, -ˌljuːt/ *adj.* **1** hesitant, undecided. **2** lacking in resoluteness. □ **irresolutely** *adv.* **irresoluteness** *n.* **irresolution** /-ˈluːʃ(ə)n, -ˈljuːʃ(ə)n/ *n.*

irresolvable /ˌɪrɪˈzɒlvəb(ə)l/ *adj.* **1** that cannot be resolved into its components. **2** (of a problem) that cannot be solved.

irrespective /ˌɪrɪˈspektɪv/ *adj.* (foll. by *of*) not taking into account; regardless of. □ **irrespectively** *adv.*

irresponsible /ˌɪrɪˈspɒnsɪb(ə)l/ *adj.* **1** acting or done without due sense of responsibility. **2** not responsible for one's conduct. □ **irresponsibility** /-ˈbɪlɪtɪ/ *n.* **irresponsibly** *adv.*

irretrievable /ˌɪrɪˈtriːvəb(ə)l/ *adj.* that cannot be retrieved or restored. □ **irretrievability** /-ˈbɪlɪtɪ/ *n.* **irretrievably** *adv.*

irreverent /ɪˈrevərənt/ *adj.* lacking reverence. □ **irreverence** *n.* **irreverential** /-ˈrenʃ(ə)l/ *adj.* **irreverently** *adv.* [L *irreverens* (as IN-¹, REVERENT)]

irreversible /ˌɪrɪˈvɜːsɪb(ə)l/ *adj.* not reversible or alterable. □ **irreversibility** /-ˈbɪlɪtɪ/ *n.* **irreversibly** *adv.*

irrevocable /ɪˈrevəkəb(ə)l/ *adj.* **1** unalterable. **2** gone beyond recall. □ **irrevocability** /-ˈbɪlɪtɪ/ *n.* **irrevocably** *adv.* [ME f. L *irrevocabilis* (as IN-¹, REVOKE)]

irrigate /ˈɪrɪˌɡeɪt/ *v.tr.* **1 a** water (land) by means of channels. **b** (of a stream etc.) supply (land) with water. **2** *Med.* supply (a wound etc.) with a constant flow of liquid. □ **irrigable** *adj.* **irrigation** /-ˈɡeɪʃ(ə)n/ *n.* **irrigative** *adj.* **irrigator** *n.* [L *irrigare* (as IN-², *rigare* moisten)]

irritable /ˈɪrɪtəb(ə)l/ *adj.* **1** easily annoyed or angered. **2** (of an organ etc.) very sensitive to contact. □ **irritability** /-ˈbɪlɪtɪ/ *n.* **irritably** *adv.* [L *irritabilis* (as IRRITATE)]

irritant /ˈɪrɪt(ə)nt/ *adj.* & *n.* —*adj.* causing irritation. —*n.* an irritant substance. □ **irritancy** *n.*

irritate /ˈɪrɪˌteɪt/ *v.tr.* **1** excite to anger; annoy. **2** stimulate discomfort or pain in (a part of the body). **3** *Biol.* stimulate (an organ) to action. □ **irritatedly** *adv.* **irritating** *adj.* **irritatingly** *adv.* **irritation** /-ˈteɪʃ(ə)n/ *n.* **irritative** /-tətɪv/ *adj.* **irritator** *n.* [L *irritare irritat-*]

is *3rd sing. present* of BE.

ISBN *abbr.* international standard book number.

-ise¹ *suffix* var. of -IZE.

■ **Usage** See note at -*ize*.

-ise² /aɪz, iːz/ *suffix* forming nouns of quality, state, or function (*exercise*; *expertise*; *franchise*; *merchandise*). [from or after F or OF -*ise* f. L -*itia* etc.]

-ise³ *suffix* var. of -ISH².

-ish¹ *suffix* forming adjectives: **1** from nouns, meaning: **a** having the qualities or characteristics of (*boyish*). **b** of the nationality of (*Danish*). **2** from adjectives, meaning 'somewhat' (*thickish*). **3** *colloq.* denoting an approximate age or time of day (*fortyish*; *six-thirtyish*). [OE -*isc*]

-ish² *suffix* (also -**ise** /aɪz/) forming verbs (*vanish*; *advertise*). [from or after F -*iss*- (in extended stems of verbs in -*ir*) f. L -*isc*- incept. suffix]

isinglass /ˈaɪzɪŋˌɡlɑːs/ *n.* **1** a kind of gelatin obtained from fish, esp. sturgeon, and used in making jellies, glue, etc. **2** mica. [corrupt. of obs. Du. *huisenblas* sturgeon's bladder, assim. to GLASS]

Islam /ˈɪzlɑːm, -læm, -ˈlɑːm/ *n.* **1** the religion of the Muslims, a monotheistic faith regarded as revealed through Muhammad as the Prophet of Allah. **2** the Muslim world. □ **Islamic** /ɪzˈlæmɪk/ *adj.* **Islamism** *n.* **Islamist** *n.* **Islamize** *v.tr.* (also -**ise**). **Islamization** /-aɪˈzeɪʃ(ə)n/ *n.* [Arab. *islām* submission (to God) f. *aslama* resign oneself]

island /ˈaɪlənd/ *n.* **1** a piece of land surrounded by water. **2** anything compared to an island, esp. in being surrounded in some way. **3** = *traffic island*. **4** a detached or isolated thing. [OE *īgland* f. *īg* island + LAND: first syll. infl. by ISLE]

islander /ˈaɪləndə(r)/ *n.* a native or inhabitant of an island.

isle /aɪl/ *n.* *poet.* (and in place-names) an island or peninsula, esp. a small one. [ME *ile* f. OF *ile* f. L *insula*: later ME & OF *isle* after L]

islet /ˈaɪlɪt/ *n.* **1** a small island. **2** *Anat.* a portion of tissue structurally distinct from surrounding tissues. [OF, dimin. of *isle* ISLE]

-ism /ˈɪz(ə)m/ *suffix* forming nouns, esp. denoting: **1** an action or its result (*baptism*; *organism*). **2** a system, principle, or ideological movement (*Conservatism*; *jingoism*; *feminism*). **3** a state or quality (*heroism*; *barbarism*). **4** a basis of prejudice or discrimination (*racism*; *sexism*). **5** a peculiarity in language (*Americanism*). **6** a pathological condition (*alcoholism*; *Parkinsonism*). [from or after F -*isme* f. L -*ismus* f. Gk -*ismos* or -*isma* f. -*izō* -IZE]

isn't /ˈɪz(ə)nt/ *contr.* is not.

iso- /ˈaɪsəʊ/ *comb. form* **1** equal (*isometric*). **2** *Chem.* isomeric, esp. of a hydrocarbon with a branched chain of carbon atoms (*isobutane*). [Gk *isos* equal]

isobar /ˈaɪsəʊˌbɑː(r)/ *n.* a line on a map connecting positions having the same atmospheric pressure at a given time or over an average over a given period. □ **isobaric** /-ˈbærɪk/ *adj.* [Gk *isobarēs* of equal weight (as ISO-, *baros* weight)]

isochronous /aɪˈsɒkrənəs/ *adj.* **1** occurring at the same time. **2** occupying equal time. □ **isochronously** *adv.* [ISO- + Gk *khronos* time]

isolate /ˈaɪsəˌleɪt/ *v.tr.* **1 a** place apart or alone, cut off from society. **b** place (a patient thought to be contagious or infectious) in quarantine. **2 a** identify and separate for attention (*isolated the problem*). **b** *Chem.* separate (a substance) from a mixture. **3** insulate (electrical apparatus). □ **isolable** /ˈaɪsələb(ə)l/ *adj.* **isolatable** *adj.* **isolator** *n.* [orig. in past part., f. F *isolé* f. It. *isolato* f. LL *insulatus* f. L *insula* island]

isolated /ˈaɪsəˌleɪtɪd/ *adj.* **1** lonely; cut off from society or contact; remote (*feeling isolated*; *an isolated farmhouse*). **2** untypical, unique (*an isolated example*).

isolation /ˌaɪsəˈleɪʃ(ə)n/ *n.* the act or an instance of isolating; the state of being isolated or separated. □ **in isolation** considered singly and not relatively. **isolation hospital** (or **ward** etc.) a hospital, ward, etc., for patients with contagious or infectious diseases.

isolationism /ˌaɪsəˈleɪʃəˌnɪz(ə)m/ *n.* the policy of holding aloof from the affairs of other countries or groups esp. in politics. □ **isolationist** *n.*

isomer /ˈaɪsəmə(r)/ *n.* **1** *Chem.* one of two or more compounds with the same molecular formula but a different arrangement of atoms and different properties. **2** *Physics* one of two or more atomic nuclei that have the same atomic number and the same mass number but different energy states. □ **isomeric** /-ˈmerɪk/ *adj.* **isomerism** /aɪˈsɒmərɪz(ə)m/ *n.* **isomerize** /aɪˈsɒmərˌaɪz/ *v.* (also **-ise**). [G f. Gk *isomerēs* sharing equally (as ISO-, *meros* share)]

isometric /ˌaɪsəʊˈmetrɪk/ *adj.* **1** of equal measure. **2** *Physiol.* (of muscle action) developing tension while the muscle is prevented from contracting. **3** (of a drawing etc.) with the plane of projection at equal angles to the three principal axes of the object shown. **4** *Math.* (of a transformation) without change of shape or size. □ **isometrically** *adv.* **isometry** /aɪˈsɒmɪtrɪ/ *n.* (in sense 4). [Gk *isometria* equality of measure (as ISO-, -METRY)]

isometrics /ˌaɪsəʊˈmetrɪks/ *n.pl.* a system of physical exercises in which muscles are caused to act against each other or against a fixed object.

isomorph /ˈaɪsəʊˌmɔːf/ *n.* an isomorphic substance or organism. [ISO- + Gk *morphē* form]

isomorphic /ˌaɪsəʊˈmɔːfɪk/ *adj.* (also **isomorphous** /-fəs/) **1** exactly corresponding in form and relations. **2** *Crystallog.* having the same form. □ **isomorphism** *n.*

-ison /ˈɪs(ə)n/ *suffix* forming nouns, = -ATION (*comparison; garrison; jettison; venison*). [OF -*aison* etc. f. L -*atio* etc.: see -ATION]

isosceles /aɪˈsɒsɪˌliːz/ *adj.* (of a triangle) having two sides equal. [LL f. Gk *isoskelēs* (as ISO-, *skelos* leg)]

isotherm /ˈaɪsəʊˌθɜːm/ *n.* a line on a map connecting places having the same temperature at a given time or on average over a given period. □ **isothermal** /-ˈθɜːm(ə)l/ *adj.* **isothermally** /-ˈθɜːməlɪ/ *adv.* [F *isotherme* (as ISO-, Gk *thermē* heat)]

isotonic /ˌaɪsəʊˈtɒnɪk/ *adj.* **1** having the same osmotic pressure. **2** *Physiol.* (of muscle action) taking place with normal contraction. □ **isotonically** *adv.* **isotonicity** /-təˈnɪsɪtɪ/ *n.* [Gk *isotonos* (as ISO-, TONE)]

isotope /ˈaɪsəˌtəʊp/ *n. Chem.* one of two or more forms of an element differing from each other in relative atomic mass, and in nuclear but not chemical properties. □ **isotopic** /-ˈtɒpɪk/ *adj.* **isotopically** /-ˈtɒpɪkəlɪ/ *adv.* **isotopy** /aɪˈsɒtəpɪ/ *n.* [ISO- + Gk *topos* place (i.e. in the periodic table of elements)]

isotropic /ˌaɪsəʊˈtrɒpɪk/ *adj.* having the same physical properties in all directions. □ **isotropically** *adv.* **isotropy** /aɪˈsɒtrəpɪ/ *n.* [ISO- + Gk *tropos* turn]

issue /ˈɪʃuː, ˈɪsjuː/ *n. & v.* —*n.* **1 a** a giving out or circulation of shares, notes, stamps, etc. **b** a quantity of coins, supplies, copies of a newspaper or book etc., circulated or put on sale at one time. **c** an item or amount given out or distributed. **d** each of a regular series of a magazine etc. (*the May issue*). **2 a** an outgoing, an outflow. **b** a way out, an outlet esp. the place of the emergence of a stream etc. **3** a point in question; an important subject of debate or litigation. **4** a result; an outcome; a decision. **5** *Law* children, progeny (*without male issue*). —*v.* (**issues, issued, issuing**) **1** *intr.* (often foll. by *out, forth*) *literary* go or come out. **2** *tr.* **a** send forth; publish; put into circulation. **b** supply,

esp. officially or authoritatively (foll. by *to, with*: *issued passports to them; issued them with passports*). **3** *intr.* **a** (often foll. by *from*) be derived or result. **b** (foll. by *in*) end, result. **4** *intr.* (foll. by *from*) emerge from a condition. □ **at issue 1** under discussion; in dispute. **2** at variance. **join** (or **take**) **issue** (foll. by *with, on*) identify an issue for argument. □ **issuable** *adj.* **issuance** *n.* **issueless** *adj.* **issuer** *n.* [ME f. OF ult. f. L *exitus* past part. of *exire* EXIT]

-ist *suffix* forming personal nouns (and in some senses related adjectives) denoting: **1** an adherent of a system etc. in -*ism*: see -ISM 2 (*Marxist; fatalist*). **2 a** a member of a profession (*pathologist*). **b** a person concerned with something (*tobacconist*). **3** a person who uses a thing (*violinist; balloonist; motorist*). **4** a person who does something expressed by a verb in -*ize* (*plagiarist*). **5** a person who subscribes to a prejudice or practises discrimination (*racist; sexist*). [OF -*iste*, L -*ista* f. Gk -*istēs*]

isthmus /ˈɪsməs, ˈɪsθ-/ *n.* **1** a narrow piece of land connecting two larger bodies of land. **2** *Anat.* a narrow part connecting two larger parts. □ **isthmian** *adj.* [L f. Gk *isthmos*]

it *pron.* (*poss.* **its**; *pl.* **they**) **1** the thing (or occas. the animal or child) previously named or in question (*took a stone and threw it*). **2** the person in question (*Who is it? It is I; is it a boy or a girl?*). **3** as the subject of an impersonal verb (*it is raining; it is Tuesday; it is two miles to Bath*). **4** as a substitute for a deferred subject or object (*it is silly to talk like that; I take it that you agree*). **5** as a substitute for a vague object (*brazen it out; run for it!*). **6** as the antecedent to a relative word (*it was an owl I heard*). **7** exactly what is needed (*absolutely it*). **8** the extreme limit of achievement. **9** *colloq.* sexual intercourse; sex appeal. **10** (in children's games) a player who has to perform a required feat, esp. to catch the others. □ **that's it** *colloq.* that is: **1** what is required. **2** the difficulty. **3** the end, enough. [OE *hit* neut. of HE]

Italian /ɪˈtæljən/ *n. & adj.* —*n.* **1 a** a native or national of Italy. **b** a person of Italian descent. **2** the Romance language used in Italy and parts of Switzerland. —*adj.* of or relating to Italy or its people or language. □ **Italian vermouth** a sweet kind of vermouth. [ME f. It. *Italiano* f. *Italia* Italy]

Italianate /ɪˈtæljəˌneɪt/ *adj.* of Italian style or appearance. [It. *Italianato*]

italic /ɪˈtælɪk/ *adj. & n.* —*adj.* **1** *Printing* of the sloping kind of letters now used esp. for emphasis or distinction and in foreign words. **2** (of handwriting) compact and pointed like early Italian handwriting. —*n.* **1** a letter in italic type. **2** this type. [L *italicus* f. Gk *italikos* Italian (because introduced by Aldo Manuzio of Venice)]

italicize /ɪˈtælɪˌsaɪz/ *v.tr.* (also **-ise**) print in italics. □ **italicization** /-ˈzeɪʃ(ə)n/ *n.*

itch /ɪtʃ/ *n. & v.* —*n.* **1** an irritation in the skin. **2** an impatient desire; a hankering. —*v.intr.* **1** feel an irritation in the skin, causing a desire to scratch it. **2** (usu. foll. by *to* + infin.) (of a person) feel a desire to do something (*am itching to tell you the news*). [OE *gycce, gyccan* f. WG]

itchy /ˈɪtʃɪ/ *adj.* (**itchier, itchiest**) having or causing an itch. □ **itchiness** *n.*

-ite¹ /aɪt/ *suffix* forming nouns meaning 'a person or thing connected with': **1** in names of persons:

a as natives of a country (*Israelite*). **b** often *derog.* as followers of a movement etc. (*pre-Raphaelite*; *Trotskyite*). **2** in names of things: **a** fossil organisms (*ammonite*). **b** minerals (*graphite*). **c** explosives (*dynamite*). **d** commercial products (*ebonite*; *vulcanite*). **e** salts of acids having names in *-ous* (*nitrite*; *sulphite*). [from or after F *-ite* f. L *-ita* f. Gk *-itēs*]

-ite[2] /aɪt, ɪt/ *suffix* **1** forming adjectives (*erudite*; *favourite*). **2** forming nouns (*appetite*). **3** forming verbs (*expedite*; *unite*). [from or after L *-itus* past part. of verbs in *-ēre, -ere*, and *-ire*]

item /ˈaɪtəm/ *n.* **1 a** any of a number of enumerated or listed things. **b** an entry in an account. **2** an article, esp. one for sale (*household items*). **3** a separate or distinct piece of news, information, etc. [orig. as adv.: L, = in like manner, also]

itemize /ˈaɪtəˌmaɪz/ *v.tr.* (also **-ise**) state or list item by item. □ **itemization** /-ˈzeɪʃ(ə)n/ *n.* **itemizer** *n.*

iterate /ˈɪtəˌreɪt/ *v.tr.* repeat; state repeatedly. □ **iteration** /-ˈreɪʃ(ə)n/ *n.* [L *iterare iterat-* f. *iterum* again]

iterative /ˈɪtərətɪv/ *adj. Gram.* = FREQUENTATIVE. □ **iteratively** *adv.*

-itic /ˈɪtɪk/ *suffix* forming adjectives and nouns corresponding to nouns in *-ite*, *-itis*, etc. (*Semitic*; *arthritic*; *syphilitic*). [from or after F *-itique* f. L *-iticus* f. Gk *-itikos*: see *-IC*]

itinerant /aɪˈtɪnərənt, ɪ-/ *adj.* & *n.* —*adj.* travelling from place to place. —*n.* an itinerant person; a tramp. □ **itineracy** *n.* **itinerancy** *n.* [LL *itinerari* travel f. L *iter itiner-* journey]

itinerary /aɪˈtɪnərərɪ, ɪ-/ *n.* (*pl.* **-ies**) **1** a detailed route. **2** a record of travel. **3** a guidebook. [LL *itinerarius* (adj.), *-um* f. L *iter*: see *ITINERANT*]

-ition /ˈɪʃ(ə)n/ *suffix* forming nouns, = *-ATION* (*admonition*; *perdition*; *position*). [from or after F *-ition* or L *-itio -itionis*]

-itious[1] /ˈɪʃəs/ *suffix* forming adjectives corresponding to nouns in *-ition* (*ambitious*; *suppositious*). [L *-itio* etc. + *-OUS*]

-itious[2] /ˈɪʃəs/ *suffix* forming adjectives meaning 'related to, having the nature of' (*adventitious*; *supposititious*). [L *-icius* + *-OUS*, commonly written with *t* in med.L manuscripts]

-itis /ˈaɪtɪs/ *suffix* forming nouns, esp.: **1** names of inflammatory diseases (*appendicitis*; *bronchitis*). **2** *colloq.* in extended uses with ref. to conditions compared to diseases (*electionitis*). [Gk *-itis*, forming fem. of adjectives in *-itēs* (with *nosos* 'disease' implied)]

-itive /ˈɪtɪv/ *suffix* forming adjectives, = *-ATIVE* (*positive*; *transitive*). [from or after F *-itif -itive* or L *-itivus* f. participial stems in *-it-*: see *-IVE*]

-itor /ˈɪtə(r)/ *suffix* forming agent nouns, usu. from Latin words (sometimes via French) (*creditor*). See also *-OR*[1].

-itory /ˈɪtərɪ/ *suffix* forming adjectives meaning 'relating to or involving (a verbal action)' (*inhibitory*). See also *-ORY*[2]. [L *-itorius*]

-itous /ˈɪtəs/ *suffix* forming adjectives corresponding to nouns in *-ity* (*calamitous*; *felicitous*). [from or after F *-iteux* f. L *-itosus*]

its /ɪts/ *poss.pron.* of it; of itself (*can see its advantages*).

it's /ɪts/ *contr.* **1** it is. **2** it has.

itself /ɪtˈsɛlf/ *pron.* emphatic and refl. form of IT. □ **by itself** apart from its surroundings, automatically, spontaneously. **in itself** viewed in its essential qualities (*not in itself a bad thing*). [OE f. IT + SELF, but often treated as ITS + SELF (cf. *its own self*)]

ITV *abbr.* (in the UK) Independent Television.

-ity /ˈɪtɪ/ *suffix* forming nouns denoting: **1** quality or condition (*authority*; *humility*; *purity*). **2** an instance or degree of this (*a monstrosity*; *humidity*). [from or after F *-ité* f. L *-itas -itatis*]

IUD *abbr.* intra-uterine (contraceptive) device.

-ium /ɪəm/ *suffix* forming nouns denoting esp.: **1** (also **-um**) names of metallic elements (*uranium*; *tantalum*). **2** a region of the body (*pericardium*). **3** a biological structure (*mycelium*). [from or after L *-ium* f. Gk *-ion*]

IV *abbr.* intravenous.

-ive /ɪv/ *suffix* forming adjectives meaning 'tending to, having the nature of', and corresponding nouns (*suggestive*; *corrosive*; *palliative*; *coercive*; *talkative*). □ **-ively** *suffix* forming adverbs. **-iveness** *suffix* forming nouns. [from or after F *-if -ive* f. L *-ivus*]

IVF *abbr.* in vitro fertilization.

ivied /ˈaɪvɪd/ *adj.* overgrown with ivy.

ivory /ˈaɪvərɪ/ *n.* (*pl.* **-ies**) **1** a hard creamy-white substance composing the main part of the tusks of an elephant, hippopotamus, walrus, and narwhal. **2** the colour of this. **3** (usu. in *pl.*) **a** an article made of ivory. **b** *sl.* anything made of or resembling ivory, esp. a piano key or a tooth. □ **ivory tower** a state of seclusion or separation from the ordinary world and the harsh realities of life. □ **ivoried** *adj.* [ME f. OF *yvoire* ult. f. L *ebur eboris*]

ivy /ˈaɪvɪ/ *n.* (*pl.* **-ies**) **1** a climbing evergreen shrub, *Hedera helix*, with usu. dark-green shining five-angled leaves. **2** any of various other climbing plants including ground ivy and poison ivy. □ **Ivy League** a group of universities in the eastern US. [OE *īfig*]

-ize /aɪz/ *suffix* (also **-ise**) forming verbs, meaning: **1** make or become such (*Americanize*; *pulverize*; *realize*). **2** treat in such a way (*monopolize*; *pasteurize*). **3 a** follow a special practice (*economize*). **b** have a specified feeling (*sympathize*). **4** affect with, provide with, or subject to (*oxidize*; *hospitalize*). ¶ The form *-ize* has been in use in English since the 16th c.; it is widely used in American English, but is not an Americanism. The alternative spelling *-ise* (reflecting a French influence) is in common use, esp. in British English, and is obligatory in certain cases: (*a*) where it forms part of a larger word-element, such as *-mise* (= sending) in *compromise*, and *-prise* (= taking) in *surprise*; and (*b*) in verbs corresponding to a noun with *-s-* in the stem, such as *advertise* and *televise*. □ **-ization** /-ˈzeɪʃ(ə)n/ *suffix* forming nouns. **-izer** *suffix* forming agent nouns. [from or after F *-iser* f. LL *-izare* f. Gk *-izō*]

Jj

J[1] /dʒeɪ/ n. (also **j**) (pl. **Js** or **J's**) the tenth letter of the alphabet.

J[2] abbr. (also **J.**) joule(s).

jab v. & n. —v.tr. (**jabbed, jabbing**) **1** a poke roughly. **b** stab. **2** (foll. by into) thrust (a thing) hard or abruptly. —n. **1** an abrupt blow with one's fist or a pointed implement. **2** colloq. a hypodermic injection, esp. a vaccination. [orig. Sc. var. of job prod, stab]

jabber /ˈdʒæbə(r)/ v. & n. —v. **1** intr. chatter volubly and incoherently. **2** tr. utter (words) fast and indistinctly. —n. meaningless jabbering; a gabble. [imit.]

jabot /ˈʒæbəʊ/ n. an ornamental frill or ruffle of lace etc. on the front of a shirt or blouse. [F, orig. = crop of a bird]

jacaranda /ˌdʒækəˈrændə/ n. **1** any tropical American tree of the genus Jacaranda, with trumpet-shaped blue flowers. **2** any tropical American tree of the genus Dalbergia, with hard scented wood. [Tupi-Guarani jacarandá]

jacinth /ˈdʒæsɪnθ, ˈdʒeɪ-/ n. a reddish-orange variety of zircon used as a gem. [ME iacynt etc. f. OF iacinte or med.L jacint(h)us f. L hyacinthus HYACINTH]

jack n. & v. —n. **1** a device for lifting heavy objects, esp. the axle of a vehicle off the ground while changing a wheel etc. **2** a court-card with a picture of a man, esp. a soldier, page, or knave, etc. **3** a ship's flag, esp. one flown from the bow and showing nationality. **4** a device using a single plug to connect an electrical circuit. **5** a small white ball in bowls, at which the players aim. **6 a** = JACKSTONE. **b** (in pl.) a game of jackstones. **7** (**Jack**) the familiar form of John esp. typifying the common man or the male of a species (I'm all right, Jack). —v.tr. (usu. foll. by up) **1** raise with or as with a jack (in sense 1). **2** colloq. raise e.g. prices. □ **every man jack** each and every person. **Jack Frost** frost personified. **jack in** (or **up**) sl. abandon (an attempt etc.). **jack-in-the-box** a toy figure that springs out of a box when it is opened. **jack-in-office** a self-important minor official. **jack of all trades** a person who can do many different kinds of work. **jack-o'-lantern 1** a will-o'-the-wisp. **2** a lantern made esp. from a pumpkin with holes for facial features. **jack plug** a plug for use with a jack (see sense 4 of n.). **Jack tar** a sailor. **on one's jack** (or **Jack Jones**) sl. alone; on one's own. [ME Iakke, a pet-name for John, erron. assoc. with F Jacques James]

jackal /ˈdʒæk(ə)l/ n. **1** any of various wild doglike mammals of the genus Canis, esp. C. aureus, found in Africa and S. Asia, usu. hunting or scavenging for food in packs. **2** colloq. a person who does preliminary drudgery for another. [Turk. çakal f. Pers. šaǧāl]

jackanapes /ˈdʒækəˌneɪps/ n. archaic a pert or insolent fellow. [earliest as Jack Napes (1450):

supposed to refer to the Duke of Suffolk, whose badge was an ape's clog and chain]

jackaroo /ˌdʒækəˈruː/ n. (also **jackeroo**) Austral. colloq. a novice on a sheep-station or cattle-station. [JACK + KANGAROO]

jackass /ˈdʒækæs/ n. **1** a male ass. **2** a stupid person.

jackboot /ˈdʒækbuːt/ n. **1** a large boot reaching above the knee. **2** this as a symbol of fascism or military oppression. □ **jackbooted** adj.

jackdaw /ˈdʒækdɔː/ n. a small grey-headed crow, Corvus monedula.

jacket /ˈdʒækɪt/ n. & v. —n. **1 a** a sleeved short outer garment. **b** a thing worn esp. round the torso for protection or support (life-jacket). **2** a casing or covering, e.g. as insulation round a boiler. **3** = dust-jacket. **4** the skin of a potato, esp. when baked whole. **5** an animal's coat. —v.tr. (**jacketed, jacketing**) cover with a jacket. □ **jacket potato** a baked potato served with the skin on. [ME f. OF ja(c)quet dimin. of jaque of uncert. origin]

jackhammer /ˈdʒækˌhæmə(r)/ n. US a pneumatic hammer or drill.

jackknife /ˈdʒæknaɪf/ n. & v. —n. (pl. **-knives**) **1** a large clasp-knife. **2** a dive in which the body is first bent at the waist and then straightened. —v.intr. (**-knifed, -knifing**) (of an articulated vehicle) fold against itself in an accidental skidding movement.

jackpot /ˈdʒækpɒt/ n. a large prize or amount of winnings, esp. accumulated in a game or lottery etc. □ **hit the jackpot** colloq. **1** win a large prize. **2** have remarkable luck or success. [JACK n. 2 + POT[1]: orig. in a form of poker with two jacks as minimum to open the pool]

jackrabbit /ˈdʒækˌræbɪt/ n. US any of various large prairie hares of the genus Lepus with very long ears and hind legs.

jackstone /ˈdʒækstəʊn/ n. **1** a small piece of metal etc. used with others in tossing-games. **2** (in pl.) **a** a game with a ball and jackstones. **b** the game of jacks.

Jacobean /ˌdʒækəˈbiːən/ adj. & n. —adj. of or relating to the reign of James I of England. —n. a Jacobean person. [mod.L Jacobaeus f. eccl.L Jacobus James f. Gk Iakōbos Jacob]

Jacobite /ˈdʒækəbaɪt/ n. hist. a supporter of James II of England after his removal from the throne in 1688, or of the Stuarts. □ **Jacobitical** /-ˈbɪtɪk(ə)l/ adj. **Jacobitism** n. [L Jacobus James: see JACOBEAN]

Jacquard /ˈdʒækɑːd/ n. **1** an apparatus with perforated cards, fitted to a loom to facilitate the weaving of figured fabrics. **2** (in full **Jacquard loom**) a loom fitted with this. **3** a fabric or article made with this, with an intricate variegated pattern. [J. M. Jacquard, Fr. inventor d. 1834]

Jacuzzi /dʒəˈkuːzɪ/ n. (pl. **Jacuzzis**) propr. a large bath with underwater jets of water to massage the body. [name of the inventor and manufacturers]

jade[1] n. **1** a hard usu. green stone composed of silicates of calcium and magnesium, or of sodium and aluminium, used for ornaments and implements. **2** the green colour of jade. [F: *le jade* for *l'ejade* f. Sp. *piedra de ijada* stone of the flank, i.e. stone for colic (which it was believed to cure)]

jade[2] n. **1** an inferior or worn-out horse. **2** *derog.* a disreputable woman. [ME: orig. unkn.]

jaded /ˈdʒeɪdɪd/ adj. tired or worn out; surfeited. □ **jadedly** adv. **jadedness** n.

jadeite /ˈdʒeɪdaɪt/ n. a green, blue, or white sodium aluminium silicate form of jade.

jag[1] n. & v. —n. a sharp projection of rock etc. —v.tr. (**jagged, jagging**) **1** cut or tear unevenly. **2** make indentations in. □ **jagger** n. [ME, prob. imit.]

jag[2] n. sl. **1** a drinking bout; a spree. **2** a period of indulgence in an activity, emotion, etc. [orig. 16th c., = load for one horse: orig. unkn.]

jagged /ˈdʒægɪd/ adj. **1** with an unevenly cut or torn edge. **2** deeply indented; with sharp points. □ **jaggedly** adv. **jaggedness** n.

jaguar /ˈdʒægjʊə(r)/ n. a large flesh-eating spotted feline, *Panthera onca*, of Central and S. America. [Tupi-Guarani *jaguara*]

jail n. & v. (also **gaol**) —n. **1** a place to which persons are committed by a court for detention. **2** confinement in a jail. —v.tr. put in jail. [ME *gayole* f. OF *jaiole, jeole* & ONF *gaole* f. Rmc dimin. of L *cavea* CAGE]

jailbird /ˈdʒeɪlbɜːd/ n. (also **gaolbird**) a prisoner or habitual criminal.

jailbreak /ˈdʒeɪlbreɪk/ n. (also **gaolbreak**) an escape from jail.

jailer /ˈdʒeɪlə(r)/ n. (also **gaoler**) a person in charge of a jail or of the prisoners in it.

Jain /dʒaɪn/ n. & adj. —n. an adherent of a non-Brahminical Indian religion. —adj. of or relating to this religion. □ **Jainism** n. **Jainist** n. [Hindi f. Skr. *jainas* saint, victor f. *jīna* victorious]

jake adj. Austral. & NZ sl. all right; satisfactory. [20th c.: orig. uncert.]

jalopy /dʒəˈlɒpɪ/ n. (pl. **-ies**) colloq. a dilapidated old motor vehicle. [20th c.: orig. unkn.]

jalousie /ˈʒæluˌziː/ n. a blind or shutter made of a row of angled slats to keep out rain etc. and control the influx of light. [F (as JEALOUSY)]

jam[1] v. & n. —v.tr. & intr. (**jammed, jamming**) **1 a** tr. (usu. foll. by *into*) squeeze or wedge into a space. **b** intr. become wedged. **2 a** tr. cause (machinery or a component) to become wedged or immovable so that it cannot work. **b** intr. become jammed in this way. **3** tr. push or cram together in a compact mass. **4** intr. (foll. by *in, on to*) push or crowd (*they jammed on to the bus*). **5** tr. **a** block (a passage, road, etc.) by crowding or obstructing. **b** (foll. by *in*) obstruct the exit of (*we were jammed in*). **6** tr. (usu. foll. by *on*) apply (brakes etc.) forcefully or abruptly. **7** tr. make (a radio transmission) unintelligible by causing interference. **8** colloq. (in jazz etc.) extemporize with other musicians. —n. **1** a squeeze or crush. **2** a crowded mass (*traffic jam*). **3** colloq. an awkward situation or predicament. **4** a stoppage (of a machine etc.) due to jamming. **5** (in full **jam session**) colloq. improvised playing by a group of jazz musicians. □ **jam-packed** colloq. full to capacity. □ **jammer** n. [imit.]

jam[2] n. & v. —n. **1** a conserve of fruit and sugar boiled to a thick consistency. **2** Brit. colloq. something easy or pleasant (*money for jam*). —v.tr. (**jammed, jamming**) **1** spread jam on. **2** make (fruit etc.) into jam. □ **jam tomorrow** a pleasant thing often promised but usu. never forthcoming. [perh. = JAM[1]]

jamb /dʒæm/ n. Archit. a side post or surface of a doorway, window, or fireplace. [ME f. OF *jambe* ult. f. LL *gamba* hoof]

jamboree /ˌdʒæmbəˈriː/ n. **1** a celebration or merrymaking. **2** a large rally of Scouts. [19th c.: orig. unkn.]

jamjar /ˈdʒæmdʒɑː(r)/ n. a glass jar for containing jam.

jammy /ˈdʒæmɪ/ adj. (**jammier, jammiest**) **1** covered with jam. **2** Brit. colloq. **a** lucky. **b** profitable.

Jan. abbr. January.

jangle /ˈdʒæŋg(ə)l/ v. & n. —v. **1** intr. & tr. make, or cause (a bell etc.) to make, a harsh metallic sound. **2** tr. irritate (the nerves etc.) by discordant sound or speech etc. —n. a harsh metallic sound. [ME f. OF *jangler*, of uncert. orig.]

Janglish /ˈdʒæŋglɪʃ/ n. = JAPLISH. [Japanese + English]

janitor /ˈdʒænɪtə(r)/ n. **1** a doorkeeper. **2** a caretaker of a building. □ **janitorial** /-ˈtɔːrɪəl/ adj. [L f. *janua* door]

janizary /ˈdʒænɪzərɪ/ n. (also **janissary** /-sərɪ/) (pl. **-ies**) **1** hist. a member of the Turkish infantry forming the Sultan's guard in the 14th–19th c. **2** a devoted follower or supporter. [ult. f. Turk. *yeniçeri* f. *yeni* new + *çeri* troops]

January /ˈdʒænjʊərɪ/ n. (pl. **-ies**) the first month of the year. [ME f. AF *Jenever* f. L *Januarius* (*mensis*) (month) of Janus the guardian god of doors and beginnings]

Jap /dʒæp/ n. & adj. colloq. often offens. = JAPANESE. [abbr.]

japan /dʒəˈpæn/ n. & v. —n. a hard usu. black varnish, esp. of a kind brought orig. from Japan. —v.tr. (**japanned, japanning**) **1** varnish with japan. **2** make black and glossy as with japan. [*Japan* in E. Asia]

Japanese /ˌdʒæpəˈniːz/ n. & adj. —n. (pl. same) **1 a** a native or national of Japan. **b** a person of Japanese descent. **2** the language of Japan. —adj. of or relating to Japan, its people, or its language.

jape n. & v. —n. a practical joke. —v.intr. play a joke. □ **japery** n. [ME: orig. uncert.]

Japlish /ˈdʒæplɪʃ/ n. a blend of Japanese and English, used in Japan. [Japanese + English]

japonica /dʒəˈpɒnɪkə/ n. any flowering shrub of the genus *Chaenomeles*, esp. *C. speciosa*, with round edible fruits and bright red flowers. [mod.L, fem. of *japonicus* Japanese]

jar[1] n. **1 a** a container of glass, earthenware, plastic, etc., usu. cylindrical. **b** the contents of this. **2** Brit. colloq. a glass of beer. □ **jarful** n. (pl. **-fuls**). [F *jarre* f. Arab. *jarra*]

jar[2] v. & n. —v. (**jarred, jarring**) **1** intr. (often foll. by *on*) (of sound, words, manner, etc.) sound discordant or grating (on the nerves etc.). **2 a** tr. (foll. by *against, on*) strike or cause to strike with vibration or a grating sound. **b** intr. (of a body affected) vibrate gratingly. **3** tr. send a shock through (a part of the body) (*the fall jarred his* neck). **4** *intr.* (often foll. by *with*) (of an opinion, fact, etc.) be at variance; be in conflict or in dispute. —*n.* **1** a jarring sound or sensation. **2** a physical shock or jolt. **3** lack of harmony; disagreement. [16th c.: prob. imit.]

jar³ *n.* □ **on the jar** ajar. [late form of obs. *char* turn: see AJAR, CHAR²]

jardinière /ˌʒɑːdɪˈnjeə(r)/ *n.* **1** an ornamental pot or stand for the display of growing plants. **2** a dish of mixed vegetables. [F]

jargon /ˈdʒɑːɡən/ *n.* **1** words or expressions used by a particular group or profession (*medical jargon*). **2** barbarous or debased language. □ **jargonic** /-ˈɡɒnɪk/ *adj.* **jargonistic** /-ˈnɪstɪk/ *adj.* **jargonize** *v.tr.* & *intr.* (also **-ise**). [ME f. OF: orig. unkn.]

jasmine /ˈdʒæsmɪn, ˈdʒæz-/ *n.* (also **jasmin**, **jessamin** /ˈdʒesəmɪn/, **jessamine** /ˈdʒesəmɪn/) any of various ornamental shrubs of the genus *Jasminum* usu. with white or yellow flowers. □ **jasmine tea** a tea perfumed with dried jasmine blossom. [F *jasmin*, *jessemin* f. Arab. *yās(a)mīn* f. Pers. *yāsamīn*]

jasper /ˈdʒæspə(r)/ *n.* an opaque variety of quartz, usu. red, yellow, or brown in colour. [ME f. OF *jasp(r)e* f. L *iaspis* f. Gk, of oriental orig.]

jaundice /ˈdʒɔːndɪs/ *n.* & *v.* —*n.* **1** *Med.* a condition with yellowing of the skin or whites of the eyes, often caused by obstruction of the bile duct or by liver disease. **2** disordered (esp. mental) vision. **3** envy. —*v.tr.* **1** affect with jaundice. **2** (esp. as **jaundiced** *adj.*) affect (a person) with envy, resentment, or jealousy. [ME *iaunes* f. OF *iaunice* yellowness f. *jaune* yellow]

jaunt *n.* & *v.* —*n.* a short excursion for enjoyment. —*v.intr.* take a jaunt. [16th c.: orig. unkn.]

jaunty /ˈdʒɔːntɪ/ *adj.* (**jauntier**, **jauntiest**) **1** cheerful and self-confident. **2** sprightly. □ **jauntily** *adv.* **jauntiness** *n.* [earlier *jentee* f. F *gentil* GENTLE]

javelin /ˈdʒævəlɪn, -vlɪn/ *n.* **1** a light spear thrown in a competitive sport or as a weapon. **2** the athletic event or sport of throwing the javelin. [F *javeline*, *javelot* f. Gallo-Roman *gabalottus*]

jaw *n.* & *v.* —*n.* **1 a** each of the upper and lower bony structures in vertebrates forming the framework of the mouth and containing the teeth. **b** the parts of certain invertebrates used for the ingestion of food. **2 a** (in *pl.*) the mouth with its bones and teeth. **b** the narrow mouth of a valley, channel, etc. **c** the gripping parts of a tool or machine. **d** gripping-power (*jaws of death*). **3** *colloq.* **a** talkativeness. **b** a sermonizing talk; a lecture. —*v. colloq.* **1** *intr.* speak esp. at tedious length. **2** *tr.* **a** persuade by talking. **b** admonish or lecture. [ME f. OF *joe* cheek, jaw, of uncert. orig.]

jawbone /ˈdʒɔːbəʊn/ *n.* **1** each of the two bones forming the lower jaw in most mammals. **2** these two combined into one in other mammals.

jay *n.* **1 a** a noisy chattering European bird, *Garrulus glandarius*, with vivid plumage. **b** any other bird of the subfamily Garrulinae. **2** a person who chatters impertinently. [ME f. OF f. LL *gaius*, *gaia*, perh. f. L praenomen *Gaius*: cf. *jackdaw*, *robin*]

jaywalk /ˈdʒeɪwɔːk/ *v.intr.* cross or walk in the street or road without regard for traffic. □ **jaywalker** *n.*

jazz *n.* & *v.* —*n.* **1** music of US Negro origin characterized by improvisation, syncopation,

and usu. a regular or forceful rhythm. **2** *sl.* pretentious talk or behaviour, nonsensical stuff (*all that jazz*). —*v.intr.* play or dance to jazz. □ **jazz up** brighten or enliven. □ **jazzer** *n.* [20th c.: orig. uncert.]

jazzman /ˈdʒæzmæn/ *n.* (*pl.* **-men**) a jazz-player.

jazzy /ˈdʒæzɪ/ *adj.* (**jazzier**, **jazziest**) **1** of or like jazz. **2** vivid, unrestrained, showy. □ **jazzily** *adv.* **jazziness** *n.*

JCB /ˌdʒeɪsiːˈbiː/ *n. propr.* a type of mechanical excavator with a shovel at the front and a digging arm at the rear. [J. C. Bamford, the makers]

jealous /ˈdʒeləs/ *adj.* **1** (often foll. by *of*) fiercely protective (of rights etc.). **2** afraid, suspicious, or resentful of rivalry in love or affection. **3** (often foll. by *of*) envious or resentful (of a person or a person's advantages etc.). **4** (of God) intolerant of disloyalty. **5** (of inquiry, supervision, etc.) vigilant. □ **jealously** *adv.* [ME f. *gelos* f. med.L *zelosus* ZEALOUS]

jealousy /ˈdʒeləsɪ/ *n.* (*pl.* **-ies**) **1** a jealous state or feeling. **2** an instance of this. [ME f. OF *gelosie* (as JEALOUS)]

jean /dʒiːn/ *n.* twilled cotton cloth. [ME, attrib. use of *Jene* f. OF *Janne* f. med.L *Janua* Genoa]

jeans /dʒiːnz/ *n.pl.* trousers made of jean or (more usually) denim, for informal wear.

Jeep /dʒiːp/ *n. propr.* a small sturdy esp. military motor vehicle with four-wheel drive. [orig. US, f. *GP* = general purposes, infl. by 'Eugene the Jeep', an animal in a comic strip]

jeepers /ˈdʒiːpəz/ *int. US sl.* expressing surprise etc. [corrupt. of *Jesus*]

jeer /dʒɪə(r)/ *v.* & *n.* —*v.* **1** *intr.* (usu. foll. by *at*) scoff derisively. **2** *tr.* scoff at; deride. —*n.* a scoff or taunt. □ **jeeringly** *adv.* [16th c.: orig. unkn.]

jehad var. of JIHAD.

Jehovah /dʒɪˈhəʊvə/ *n.* the Hebrew name of God in the Old Testament. □ **Jehovah's Witness** a member of a millenarian Christian sect. [med.L *Iehoua(h)* f. Heb. *YHVH* (with the vowels of *adonai* 'my lord' included: see YAHWEH]

jejune /dʒɪˈdʒuːn/ *adj.* **1** intellectually unsatisfying; shallow. **2** puerile. **3** (of ideas, writings, etc.) meagre, scanty; dry and uninteresting. **4** (of the land) barren, poor. □ **jejunely** *adv.* **jejuneness** *n.* [orig. = fasting, f. L *jejunus*]

jejunum /dʒɪˈdʒuːnəm/ *n. Anat.* the part of the small intestine between the duodenum and ileum. [L, neut. of *jejunus* fasting]

Jekyll and Hyde /ˌdʒekɪl ənd ˈhaɪd/ *n.* a person alternately displaying opposing good and evil personalities. [R. L. Stevenson's story *The Strange Case of Dr Jekyll and Mr Hyde*]

jell /dʒel/ *v.intr. colloq.* **1 a** set as a jelly. **b** (of ideas etc.) take a definite form. **2** (of two different things) cohere. [back-form. f. JELLY]

jellify /ˈdʒelɪˌfaɪ/ *v.tr.* & *intr.* (**-ies**, **-ied**) turn into jelly; make or become like jelly. □ **jellification** /-fɪˈkeɪʃ(ə)n/ *n.*

jelly /ˈdʒelɪ/ *n.* & *v.* —*n.* (*pl.* **-ies**) **1 a** a soft stiffish semi-transparent preparation of boiled sugar and fruit-juice or milk etc., often cooled in a mould and eaten as a dessert. **b** a similar preparation of fruit-juice etc. for use as a jam or a condiment (*redcurrant jelly*). **c** a similar preparation derived from meat, bones, etc., and gelatin (*marrowbone jelly*). **2** any substance of a similar consistency. **3** *Brit. sl.* gelignite. —*v.*

(**-ies**, **-ied**) **1** *intr.* & *tr.* set or cause to set as a jelly, congeal. **2** *tr.* set (food) in a jelly (*jellied eels*). □ **jelly baby** *Brit.* a jelly-like sweet in the stylized shape of a baby. **jelly bag** a bag for straining juice for jelly. **jelly bean** a jelly-like sweet in the shape of a bean. □ **jelly-like** *adj.* [ME f. OF *gelee* frost, jelly, f. Rmc *gelata* f. L *gelare* freeze f. *gelu* frost]

jellyfish /ˈdʒelɪfɪʃ/ *n.* (*pl.* usu. **same**) **1** a marine coelenterate of the class Scyphozoa having an umbrella-shaped jelly-like body and stinging tentacles. **2** *colloq.* a feeble person.

jemmy /ˈdʒemɪ/ *n.* & *v.* (*US* **jimmi** /ˈdʒɪmɪ/) —*n.* (*pl.* **-ies** or **jimmis**) a burglar's short crowbar, usu. made in sections. —*v.tr.* (**-ies**, **-ied**) force open with a jemmy. [pet-form of the name *James*]

je ne sais quoi /ʒə nə seɪ ˈkwɑː/ *n.* an indefinable something. [F, = I do not know what]

jenny /ˈdʒenɪ/ *n.* (*pl.* **-ies**) **1** *hist.* = a machine for spinning with more than one spindle at a time. **2** a female donkey or ass. **3** a locomotive crane. □ **jenny-wren** a popular name for a female wren. [pet-form of the name *Janet*]

jeopardize /ˈdʒepədaɪz/ *v.tr.* (also **-ise**) endanger; put into jeopardy.

jeopardy /ˈdʒepədɪ/ *n.* danger, esp. of severe harm or loss. [ME *iuparti* f. OF *ieu parti* divided (i.e. even) game, f. L *jocus* game + *partitus* past part. of *partire* divide f. *pars partis* part]

jerbil var. of GERBIL.

jerboa /dʒɜːˈbəʊə/ *n.* any small desert rodent of the family Dipodidae with long hind legs and the ability to make large jumps. [mod.L f. Arab. *yarbū* flesh of loins, jerboa]

jeremiad /ˌdʒerɪˈmaɪæd/ *n.* a doleful complaint or lamentation; a list of woes. [F *jérémiade* f. *Jérémie* Jeremiah f. eccl.L *Jeremias*, with ref. to the Lamentations of Jeremiah in the Old Testament]

Jeremiah /ˌdʒerɪˈmaɪə/ *n.* a dismal prophet, a denouncer of the times. [with ref. to Jeremiah (as JEREMIAD)]

jerk[1] *n.* & *v.* —*n.* **1** a sharp sudden pull, twist, twitch, start, etc. **2** a spasmodic muscular twitch. **3** (in *pl.*) *Brit. colloq.* exercises (*physical jerks*). **4** *sl.* a fool; a stupid person. —*v.* **1** *intr.* move with a jerk. **2** *tr.* pull, thrust, twist, etc., with a jerk. **3** *tr.* throw with a suddenly arrested motion. **4** *tr. Weight-lifting* raise (a weight) from shoulder-level to above the head. □ **jerker** *n.* [16th c.: perh. imit.]

jerk[2] *v.tr.* cure (beef) by cutting it in long slices and drying it in the sun. [Amer. Sp. *charquear* f. *charqui* f. Quechua *echarqui* dried flesh]

jerkin /ˈdʒɜːkɪn/ *n.* **1** a sleeveless jacket. **2** *hist.* a man's close-fitting jacket, often of leather. [16th c.: orig. unkn.]

jerky /ˈdʒɜːkɪ/ *adj.* (**jerkier**, **jerkiest**) **1** having sudden abrupt movements. **2** spasmodic. □ **jerkily** *adv.* **jerkiness** *n.*

jeroboam /ˌdʒerəˈbəʊəm/ *n.* a wine bottle of 4–12 times the ordinary size. [*Jeroboam* king of Israel (1 Kings 11:28, 14:16)]

Jerry /ˈdʒerɪ/ *n.* (*pl.* **-ies**) *Brit. sl.* **1** a German (esp. in military contexts). **2** the Germans collectively. [prob. alt. of *German*]

jerry /ˈdʒerɪ/ *n.* (*pl.* **-ies**) *Brit. sl.* a chamber-pot.

jerry-builder /ˈdʒerɪˌbɪldə(r)/ *n.* a builder of unsubstantial houses with poor-quality materials. □ **jerry-building** *n.* **jerry-built** *adj.*

jerrycan /ˈdʒerɪˌkæn/ *n.* (also **jerrican**) a kind of (orig. German) petrol- or water-can. [JERRY + CAN[2]]

jerrymander var. of GERRYMANDER.

jersey /ˈdʒɜːzɪ/ *n.* (*pl.* **-eys**) **1 a** a knitted usu. woollen pullover or similar garment. **b** a plain-knitted (orig. woollen) fabric. **2** (**Jersey**) a light brown dairy cow from Jersey. [*Jersey*, largest of the Channel Islands]

Jerusalem artichoke /dʒəˈruːsələm/ *n.* **1** a species of sunflower, *Helianthus tuberosus*, with edible underground tubers. **2** this tuber used as a vegetable. [corrupt. of It. *girasole* sunflower]

jessamin (also **jessamine**) var. of JASMINE.

jest *n.* & *v.* —*n.* **1** a joke. **b** fun. **2 a** raillery, banter. **b** an object of derision (*a standing jest*). —*v.intr.* **1** joke; make jests. **2** fool about; play or act triflingly. □ **in jest** in fun. □ **jestful** *adj.* [orig. = exploit, f. OF *geste* f. L *gesta* neut. pl. past part. of *gerere* do]

jester /ˈdʒestə(r)/ *n.* a professional joker or 'fool' at a medieval court etc., traditionally wearing a cap and bells and carrying a 'sceptre'.

Jesuit /ˈdʒezjʊɪt/ *n.* a member of the Society of Jesus, a Roman Catholic order founded by St Ignatius Loyola and others in 1534. [F *jésuite* or mod.L *Jesuita* f. *Jesus* name of the founder of the Christian religion]

Jesuitical /ˌdʒezjʊˈɪtɪk(ə)l/ *adj.* **1** of or concerning the Jesuits. **2** often *offens.* dissembling or equivocating, in the manner once associated with Jesuits. □ **Jesuitically** *adv.*

jet[1] *n.* & *v.* —*n.* **1** a stream of water, steam, gas, flame, etc. shot out esp. from a small opening. **2** a spout or nozzle for emitting water etc. in this way. **3 a** a jet engine. **b** an aircraft powered by one or more jet engines. —*v.* (**jetted**, **jetting**) **1** *intr.* spurt out in jets. **2** *tr.* & *intr. colloq.* send or travel by jet plane. □ **jet engine** an engine using jet propulsion for forward thrust, esp. of an aircraft. **jet lag** extreme tiredness and other bodily effects felt after a long flight involving marked differences of local time. **jet-propelled** **1** having jet propulsion. **2** (of a person etc.) very fast. **jet propulsion** propulsion by the backward ejection of a high-speed jet of gas etc. **jet set** *colloq.* wealthy people frequently travelling by air, esp. for pleasure. **jet stream 1** a narrow current of very strong winds encircling the globe several miles above the earth. **2** the stream from a jet engine. [earlier as verb (in sense 1): F *jeter* throw ult. f. L *jacere jact-* throw]

jet[2] *n.* **1 a** a hard black variety of lignite capable of being carved and highly polished. **b** (*attrib.*) made of this. **2** (in full **jet-black**) a deep glossy black colour. [ME f. AF *geet*, OF *jaiet* f. L *gagates* f. Gk *gagatēs* f. *Gagai* in Asia Minor]

jetsam /ˈdʒetsəm/ *n.* discarded material washed ashore, esp. that thrown overboard to lighten a ship etc. (cf. FLOTSAM). [contr. of JETTISON]

jettison /ˈdʒetɪs(ə)n, -z(ə)n/ *v.* & *n.* —*v.tr.* **1 a** throw (esp. heavy material) overboard to lighten a ship, hot-air balloon, etc. **b** drop (goods) from an aircraft. **2** abandon; get rid of (something no longer wanted). —*n.* the act of jettisoning. [ME f. AF *getteson*, OF *getaison* f. L *jactatio -onis* f. *jactare* throw: see JET[1]]

jetty /ˈdʒetɪ/ *n.* (*pl.* **-ies**) **1** a pier or breakwater constructed to protect or defend a harbour, coast, etc. **2** a landing-pier. [ME f. OF *jetee*, fem. past part. of *jeter* throw: see JET[1]]

Jew *n.* **1** a person of Hebrew descent or whose religion is Judaism. **2** *sl. offens.* (as a stereotype) a person considered to be parsimonious or to drive a hard bargain in trading. □ **jew's harp** a small lyre-shaped musical instrument held between the teeth and struck with the finger. [ME f. OF *giu* f. L *judaeus* f. Gk *ioudaios* ult. f. Heb. *yᵉhûḏî* f. *yᵉhûḏâh* Judah]

■ **Usage** The stereotype conveyed in sense 2 is deeply offensive. It arose from historical associations of Jews as moneylenders in medieval England.

jewel /ˈdʒuːəl/ *n. & v.* —*n.* **1 a** a precious stone. **b** this as used for its hardness as a bearing in watchmaking. **2** a personal ornament containing a jewel or jewels. **3** a precious person or thing. —*v.tr.* (**jewelled, jewelling;** *US* **jeweled, jeweling**) **1** (esp. as **jewelled** *adj.*) adorn or set with jewels. **2** (in watchmaking) set with jewels. □ **jewelly** *adj.* [ME f. AF *juel, jeuel*, OF *joel*, of uncert. orig.]

jeweller /ˈdʒuːələ(r)/ *n.* (*US* **jeweler**) a maker of or dealer in jewels or jewellery. [ME f. AF *jueler*, OF *juelier* (as JEWEL)]

jewellery /ˈdʒuːəlrɪ/ *n.* (also **jewelry** /ˈdʒuːəlrɪ/) jewels or other ornamental objects, esp. for personal adornment, regarded collectively. [ME f. OF *juelerie* and f. JEWEL, JEWELLER]

Jewess /ˈdʒuːes/ *n.* a female Jew.

Jewish /ˈdʒuːɪʃ/ *adj.* **1** of or relating to Jews. **2** of Judaism. □ **Jewishly** *adv.* **Jewishness** *n.*

Jewry /ˈdʒʊərɪ/ *n.* (*pl.* **-ies**) **1** Jews collectively. **2** *hist.* a Jews' quarter in a town etc. [ME f. AF *juerie*, OF *juierie* (as JEW)]

Jezebel /ˈdʒezəˌbel/ *n.* a shameless or immoral woman. [*Jezebel*, wife of Ahab in the Old Testament (1 Kings 16, 19, 21)]

jib[1] *n. & v.* —*n.* **1** a triangular staysail from the outer end of the jib-boom to the top of the foremast or from the bowsprit to the masthead. **2** the projecting arm of a crane. —*v.tr. & intr.* (**jibbed, jibbing**) (of a sail etc.) pull or swing round from one side of the ship to the other; gybe. □ **jib-boom** a spar run out from the end of the bowsprit. [17th c.: orig. unkn.]

jib[2] *v.intr.* (**jibbed, jibbing**) **1 a** (of an animal, esp. a horse) stop and refuse to go on; move backwards or sideways instead of going on. **b** (of a person) refuse to continue. **2** (foll. by *at*) show aversion to (a person or course of action). □ **jibber** *n.* [19th c.: orig. unkn.]

jibe[1] var. of GIBE.

jibe[2] *US* var. of GYBE.

jibe[3] *v.intr.* (usu. foll. by *with*) *US colloq.* agree; be in accord. [19th c.: orig. unkn.]

jiff *n.* (also **jiffy**, *pl.* **-ies**) *colloq.* a short time; a moment (*in a jiffy; half a jiff*). [18th c.: orig. unkn.]

Jiffy bag /ˈdʒɪfɪ/ *n. propr.* a type of padded envelope for postal use.

jig *n. & v.* —*n.* **1 a** a lively dance with leaping movements. **b** the music for this, usu. in triple time. **2** a device that holds a piece of work and guides the tools operating on it. —*v.* (**jigged, jigging**) **1** *intr.* dance a jig. **2** *tr. & intr.* move quickly and jerkily up and down. **3** *tr.* work on or equip with a jig or jigs. □ **jig about** fidget. [16th c.: orig. unkn.]

jigger[1] /ˈdʒɪgə(r)/ *n.* **1 a** a measure of spirits etc. **b** a small glass holding this. **2** a person or thing that jigs.

jigger[2] /ˈdʒɪgə(r)/ *n.* **1** = CHIGOE. **2** *US* = CHIGGER 2. [corrupt.]

jiggered /ˈdʒɪgəd/ *adj. colloq.* (as a mild oath) confounded (*I'll be jiggered*). [euphem.]

jiggery-pokery /ˌdʒɪgərɪˈpəʊkərɪ/ *n. Brit. colloq.* deceitful or dishonest dealing, trickery. [cf. Sc. *joukery-pawkery* f. *jouk* dodge, skulk]

jiggle /ˈdʒɪg(ə)l/ *v.* (often foll. by *about* etc.) **1** *tr.* shake lightly; rock jerkily. **2** *intr.* fidget. □ **jiggly** *adj.* [JIG or JOGGLE]

jigsaw /ˈdʒɪgsɔː/ *n.* **1 a** (in full **jigsaw puzzle**) a puzzle consisting of a picture on board or wood etc. cut into irregular interlocking pieces to be reassembled. **b** a mental puzzle resolvable by assembling various pieces of information. **2** a machine saw with a fine blade enabling it to cut curved lines in a sheet of wood, metal, etc.

jihad /dʒɪˈhæd, -ˈhɑːd/ *n.* (also **jehad**) a holy war undertaken by Muslims against unbelievers. [Arab. *jihād*]

jilt *v. & n.* —*v.tr.* abruptly reject or abandon (a lover etc.). —*n.* a person (esp. a woman) who jilts a lover. [17th c.: orig. unkn.]

Jim Crow /dʒɪm ˈkrəʊ/ *n. US* **1** the practice of segregating Blacks. **2** *offens.* a Black. □ **Jim Crowism** *n.* (in sense 1). [nickname]

jim-jams /ˈdʒɪmdʒæmz/ *n.pl.* **1** *sl.* = *delirium tremens*. **2** *colloq.* a fit of depression or nervousness. [fanciful redupl.]

jimmy *US* var. of JEMMY.

jingle /ˈdʒɪŋg(ə)l/ *n. & v.* —*n.* **1** a mixed noise of bells or light metal objects being shaken together. **2 a** a repetition of the same sound in words, esp. as an aid to memory or to attract attention. **b** a short verse of this kind used in advertising etc. —*v.* **1** *intr. & tr.* make or cause to make a jingling sound. **2** *intr.* (of writing) be full of alliterations, rhymes, etc. □ **jingly** *adj.* (**jinglier, jingliest**). [ME: imit.]

jingo /ˈdʒɪŋgəʊ/ *n.* (*pl.* **-oes**) a supporter of policy favouring war; a blustering patriot. □ **by jingo!** a mild oath. □ **jingoism** *n.* **jingoist** *n.* **jingoistic** /-ˈɪstɪk/ *adj.* [17th c.: orig. a conjuror's word: polit. sense from use of *by jingo* in a popular song, then applied to patriots]

jink *v. & n.* —*v.* **1** *intr.* move elusively; dodge. **2** *tr.* elude by dodging. —*n.* an act of dodging or eluding. [orig. Sc.: prob. imit. of nimble motion]

jinnee /dʒɪˈniː/ *n.* (also **jinn, djinn**) (*pl.* **jinn** or **djinn**) (in Muslim mythology) an intelligent being, able to appear in human and animal forms, and having power over people. [Arab. *jinnī*, pl. *jinn*: cf. GENIE]

jinx *n. & v. colloq.* —*n.* a person or thing that seems to cause bad luck. —*v.tr.* (often in *passive*) subject (a person) to an unlucky force. [perh. var. of *jynx* wryneck, charm]

jitter /ˈdʒɪtə(r)/ *n. & v. colloq.* —*n.* (**the jitters**) extreme nervousness. —*v.intr.* be nervous; act nervously. □ **jittery** *adj.* **jitteriness** *n.* [20th c.: orig. unkn.]

jitterbug /ˈdʒɪtəˌbʌg/ *n. & v.* —*n.* **1** a nervous person. **2** *hist.* **a** a fast popular dance. **b** a person fond of dancing this. —*v.intr.* (**-bugged, -bugging**) dance the jitterbug.

jiu-jitsu var. of JU-JITSU.

jive /dʒaɪv/ n. & v. —n. **1** a jerky lively style of dance esp. popular in the 1950s. **2** music for this. —v.intr. **1** dance the jive. **2** play jive music. □ **jiver** n. [20th c.: orig. uncert.]

Jnr. abbr. Junior.

job n. & v. —n. **1** a piece of work, esp. one done for hire or profit. **2** a paid position of employment. **3** colloq. anything one has to do. **4** colloq. a difficult task (had a job to find them). **5** a product of work, esp. if well done. **6** Computing an item of work regarded separately. **7** sl. a crime, esp. a robbery. **8** a state of affairs or set of circumstances (is a bad job). —v. (**jobbed**, **jobbing**) **1** intr. do jobs; do piece-work. **2** a intr. deal in stocks. **b** tr. buy and sell (stocks or goods) as a middleman. **3** a intr. turn a position of trust to private advantage. **b** tr. deal corruptly with (a matter). □ **job lot** a miscellaneous group of articles, esp. bought together. **job-sharing** an arrangement by which a full-time job is done jointly by several part-time employees who share the remuneration. **just the job** colloq. exactly what is wanted. **make a job** (or **good job**) **of** do thoroughly or successfully. **out of a job** unemployed. [16th c.: orig. unkn.]

jobber /ˈdʒɒbə(r)/ n. **1** Brit. a principal or wholesaler dealing on the Stock Exchange. **2** US **a** a wholesaler. **b** derog. a broker (see BROKER 2). **3** a person who jobs. [JOB].

■ **Usage** Up to Oct. 1986 jobbers were permitted to deal only with brokers, not directly with the public. From Oct. 1986 the name ceased to be in official use (see BROKER 2).

jobbery /ˈdʒɒbərɪ/ n. corrupt dealing.

jobbing /ˈdʒɒbɪŋ/ adj. working on separate or occasional jobs (esp. of a computer, gardener, or printer).

jobcentre /ˈdʒɒb,sentə(r)/ n. Brit. any of several government offices displaying information about available jobs.

jobless /ˈdʒɒblɪs/ adj. without a job; unemployed. □ **joblessness** n.

Job's comforter /dʒəʊbz/ n. a person who under the guise of comforting aggravates distress. [the patriarch Job in the Old Testament (Job 16:2)]

Jock n. sl. a Scotsman. [Sc. form of the name Jack (see JACK)]

jock n. colloq. a jockey. [abbr.]

jockey /ˈdʒɒkɪ/ n. & v. —n. (pl. **-eys**) a rider in horse-races, esp. a professional one. —v. (**-eys**, **-eyed**) **1** tr. **a** trick or cheat (a person). **b** outwit. **2** tr. (foll. by away, out, in, etc.) draw (a person) by trickery. **3** intr. cheat. □ **jockey cap** a cap with a long peak, as worn by jockeys. **jockey for position** try to gain an advantageous position esp. by skilful manoeuvring or unfair action. □ **jockeydom** n. **jockeyship** n. [dimin. of JOCK]

jockstrap /ˈdʒɒkstræp/ n. a support or protection for the male genitals, worn esp. by sportsmen. [sl. jock genitals + STRAP]

jocose /dʒəˈkəʊs/ adj. **1** playful in style. **2** fond of joking, jocular. □ **jocosely** adv. **jocoseness** n. **jocosity** /-ˈkɒsɪtɪ/ n. (pl. **-ies**). [L jocosus f. jocus jest]

jocular /ˈdʒɒkjʊlə(r)/ adj. **1** merry; fond of joking. **2** of the nature of a joke; humorous. □ **jocularity** /-ˈlærɪtɪ/ n. (pl. **-ies**). **jocularly** adv. [L jocularis f. joculus dimin. of jocus jest]

jocund /ˈdʒɒkənd/ adj. literary merry, cheerful, sprightly. □ **jocundity** /dʒəˈkʌndɪtɪ/ n. (pl. **-ies**). **jocundly** adv. [ME f. OF f. L jocundus, jucundus f. juvare delight]

jodhpurs /ˈdʒɒdpəz/ n.pl. long breeches for riding esp., close-fitting from the knee to the ankle. [Jodhpur in India]

joey /ˈdʒəʊɪ/ n. (pl. **-eys**) Austral. **1** a young kangaroo. **2** a young animal. [Aboriginal joë]

jog v. & n. —v. (**jogged**, **jogging**) **1** intr. run at a slow pace, esp. as physical exercise. **2** intr. (of a horse) move at a jogtrot. **3** intr. (often foll. by on, along) proceed laboriously; trudge. **4** intr. go on one's way. **5** intr. proceed; get through the time (we must jog on somehow). **6** intr. move up and down with an unsteady motion. **7** tr. nudge (a person), esp. to arouse attention. **8** tr. shake with a push or jerk. **9** tr. stimulate (a person's or one's own memory). —n. **1** a shake, push, or nudge. **2** a slow walk or trot. [ME: app. imit.]

jogger /ˈdʒɒɡə(r)/ n. a person who jogs, esp. one who runs for physical exercise.

joggle /ˈdʒɒɡ(ə)l/ v. & n. —v.tr. & intr. shake or move by or as if by repeated jerks. —n. **1** a slight shake. **2** the act or action of joggling. [frequent. of JOG]

jogtrot /ˈdʒɒɡtrɒt/ n. **1** a slow regular trot. **2** a monotonous progression.

john /dʒɒn/ n. US sl. a lavatory. [the name John]

John Bull /dʒɒn ˈbʊl/ n. a personification of England or the typical Englishman. [the name of a character repr. the English nation in J. Arbuthnot's satire Law is a Bottomless Pit (1712)]

John Dory /dʒɒn ˈdɔːrɪ/ n. (pl. **-ies**) a European marine fish, Zeus faber, with a laterally flattened body and a black spot on each side.

johnny /ˈdʒɒnɪ/ n. (pl. **-ies**) Brit. colloq. a fellow; a man. □ **johnny-come-lately** colloq. a recently arrived person. [familiar form of the name John]

joie de vivre /ʒwɑː də ˈviːvrə/ n. a feeling of healthy and exuberant enjoyment of life. [F, = joy of living]

join v. & n. —v. **1** tr. (often foll. by to, together) put together; fasten, unite (one thing or person to another or several together). **2** tr. connect (points) by a line etc. **3** tr. become a member of (an association, society, organization, etc.). **4** tr. take one's place with or in (a company, group, procession, etc.). **5** tr. **a** come into the company of (a person). **b** (foll. by in) take part with (others) in an activity etc. (joined me in condemnation of the outrage). **c** (foll. by for) share the company of for a specified occasion (may I join you for lunch?). **6** intr. (often foll. by with, to) come together; be united. **7** intr. (often foll. by in) take part with others in an activity etc. **8** tr. be or become connected or continuous with (the Inn joins the Danube at Passau). —n. a point, line, or surface at which two or more things are joined. □ **join battle** begin fighting. **join forces** combine efforts. **join hands 1 a** clasp each other's hands. **b** clasp one's hands together. **2** combine in an action or enterprise. **join up 1** enlist for military service. **2** (often foll. by with) unite, connect. □ **joinable** adj. [ME f. OF joindre (stem joign-) f. L jungere junct- join: cf. YOKE]

joiner /ˈdʒɔɪnə(r)/ n. **1** a person who makes furniture and light woodwork. **2** colloq. a person who readily joins societies etc. □ **joinery** n. (in sense 1). [ME f. AF joignour, OF joigneor (as JOIN)]

joint *n., adj., & v.* —*n.* **1 a** a place at which two things are joined together. **b** a point at which, or a contrivance by which, two parts of an artificial structure are joined. **2** a structure in an animal body by which two bones are fitted together. **3 a** any of the parts into which an animal carcass is divided for food. **b** any of the parts of which a body is made up. **4** *sl.* a place of meeting for drinking etc. **5** *sl.* a marijuana cigarette. **6** *Geol.* a fissure in a mass of rock. —*adj.* **1** held or done by, or belonging to, two or more persons etc. in conjunction (*a joint mortgage; joint action*). **2** sharing with another in some action, state, etc. (*joint author; joint favourite*). —*v.tr.* **1** connect by joints. **2** divide (a body or member) at a joint or into joints. □ **joint stock** capital held jointly; a common fund. **joint-stock company** one formed on the basis of a joint stock. **out of joint 1** (of a bone) dislocated. **2** out of order. □ **jointless** *adj.* **jointly** *adv.* [ME f. OF, past part. of *joindre* JOIN]

jointress /ˈdʒɔɪntrɪs/ *n.* a widow who holds a jointure. [obs. *jointer* joint possessor]

jointure /ˈdʒɔɪntʃə(r)/ *n. & v.* —*n.* an estate settled on a wife for the period during which she survives her husband. —*v.tr.* provide (a wife) with a jointure. [ME f. OF f. L *junctura* (as JOIN)]

joist *n.* each of a series of parallel supporting beams of timber, steel, etc., used in floors, ceilings, etc. □ **joisted** *adj.* [ME f. OF *giste* ult. f. L *jacēre* lie]

jojoba /hoʊˈhoʊbə/ *n.* a plant, *Simmondsia chinensis*, with seeds yielding an oily extract used in cosmetics etc. [Mex. Sp.]

joke *n. & v.* —*n.* **1 a** a thing said or done to excite laughter. **b** a witticism or jest. **2** a ridiculous thing, person, or circumstance. —*v.* **1** *intr.* make jokes. **2** *tr.* poke fun at; banter. □ **jokingly** *adv.* **joky** *adj.* (also **jokey**). **jokily** *adv.* **jokiness** *n.* [17th c. (*joque*), orig. *sl.*: perh. f. L *jocus* jest]

joker /ˈdʒoʊkə(r)/ *n.* **1** a person who jokes. **2** *sl.* a fellow; a man. **3** a playing-card usu. with a figure of a jester, used in some games esp. as a wild card. □ **the joker in the pack** an unpredictable factor or participant.

jollify /ˈdʒɒlɪˌfaɪ/ *v.tr. & intr.* (**-ies**, **-ied**) make or be merry, esp. in drinking. □ **jollification** /-fɪˈkeɪʃ(ə)n/ *n.*

jollity /ˈdʒɒlɪtɪ/ *n.* (*pl.* **-ies**) **1** merrymaking; festiveness. **2** (in *pl.*) festivities. [ME f. OF *joliveté* (as JOLLY¹)]

jolly¹ /ˈdʒɒlɪ/ *adj., adv., v., & n.* —*adj.* (**jollier**, **jolliest**) **1** cheerful and good-humoured; merry. **2** festive, jovial. **3** slightly drunk. **4** *colloq.* (of a person or thing) very pleasant, delightful (often *iron.: a jolly shame*). —*adv. colloq.* very (*they were jolly unlucky*). —*v.tr.* (**-ies**, **-ied**) **1** (usu. foll. by *along*) *colloq.* coax or humour (a person) in a friendly way. **2** chaff, banter. —*n.* (*pl.* **-ies**) *colloq.* a party or celebration. □ **Jolly Roger** a pirates' black flag, usu. with the skull and crossbones. □ **jollily** *adv.* **jolliness** *n.* [ME f. OF *jolif* gay, pretty, perh. f. ON *jól* YULE]

jolly² /ˈdʒɒlɪ/ *n.* (*pl.* **-ies**) (in full **jolly boat**) a clinker-built ship's boat smaller than a cutter. [18th c.: orig. unkn.: perh. rel. to YAWL]

jolt /dʒoʊlt, dʒɒlt/ *v. & n.* —*v.* **1** *tr.* disturb or shake from the normal position (esp. in a moving vehicle) with a jerk. **2** *tr.* give a mental shock to; perturb. **3** *intr.* (of a vehicle) move

along with jerks, as on a rough road. —*n.* **1** such a jerk. **2** a surprise or shock. □ **jolty** *adj.* (**joltier**, **joltiest**). [16th c.: orig. unkn.]

Jonah /ˈdʒoʊnə/ *n.* a person who seems to bring bad luck. [*Jonah* in the Old Testament]

jonquil /ˈdʒɒnkwɪl/ *n.* a bulbous plant, *Narcissus jonquilla*, with clusters of small fragrant yellow flowers. [mod.L *jonquilla* or F *jonquille* f. Sp. *junquillo* dimin. of *junco* f. L *juncus* rush plant]

josh *n. & v. sl.* —*n.* a good-natured or teasing joke. —*v.* **1** *tr.* tease or banter. **2** *intr.* indulge in ridicule. □ **josher** *n.* [19th c.: orig. unkn.]

joss /dʒɒs/ *n.* a Chinese idol. □ **joss-house** a Chinese temple. **joss-stick** a stick of fragrant tinder mixed with clay, burnt as incense. [perh. ult. f. Port. *deos* f. L *deus* god]

jostle /ˈdʒɒs(ə)l/ *v. & n.* —*v.* **1** *tr.* push against; elbow. **2** *tr.* (often foll. by *away*, *from*, etc.) push (a person) abruptly or roughly. **3** *intr.* (foll. by *against*) knock or push, esp. in a crowd. **4** *intr.* (foll. by *with*) struggle; have a rough exchange. —*n.* **1** the act or an instance of jostling. **2** a collision. [ME: earlier *justle* f. JOUST + -LE⁴]

jot *v. & n.* —*v.tr.* (**jotted**, **jotting**) (usu. foll. by *down*) write briefly or hastily. —*n.* (usu. with *neg.* expressed or implied) a very small amount (*not one jot*). [earlier as noun: L f. Gk *iōta*: see IOTA]

jotter /ˈdʒɒtə(r)/ *n.* a small pad or notebook for making notes etc.

jotting /ˈdʒɒtɪŋ/ *n.* (usu. in *pl.*) a note; something jotted down.

joule /dʒuːl/ *n.* the SI unit of work or energy. [J. P. *Joule*, Engl. physicist d. 1889]

jounce /dʒaʊns/ *v.tr. & intr.* bump, bounce, jolt. [ME: orig. unkn.]

journal /ˈdʒɜːn(ə)l/ *n.* **1** a newspaper or periodical. **2** a daily record of events. **3** the part of a shaft or axle that rests on bearings. [ME f. OF *jurnal* f. LL *diurnalis* DIURNAL]

journalese /ˌdʒɜːnəˈliːz/ *n.* a hackneyed style of language characteristic of some newspaper writing.

journalism /ˈdʒɜːnəˌlɪz(ə)m/ *n.* the business or practice of writing and producing newspapers.

journalist /ˈdʒɜːnəlɪst/ *n.* a person employed to write for or edit a newspaper or journal. □ **journalistic** /-ˈlɪstɪk/ *adj.* **journalistically** /-ˈlɪstɪkəlɪ/ *adv.*

journey /ˈdʒɜːnɪ/ *n. & v.* —*n.* (*pl.* **-eys**) **1** an act of going from one place to another, esp. at a long distance. **2** the distance travelled in a specified time (*a day's journey*). **3** the travelling of a vehicle along a route at a stated time. —*v.intr.* (**-eys**, **-eyed**) make a journey. □ **journeyer** *n.* [ME f. OF *jornee* day, day's work or travel, ult. f. L *diurnus* daily]

journeyman /ˈdʒɜːnɪmən/ *n.* (*pl.* **-men**) **1** a qualified mechanic or artisan who works for another. **2** *derog.* **a** a reliable but not outstanding worker. **b** a mere hireling. [JOURNEY in obs. sense 'day's work' + MAN]

joust /dʒaʊst/ *n. & v. hist.* —*n.* a combat between two knights on horseback with lances. —*v.intr.* engage in a joust. □ **jouster** *n.* [ME f. OF *juster* bring together ult. f. L *juxta* near]

Jove /dʒoʊv/ *n.* (in Roman mythology) Jupiter. □ **by Jove!** an exclamation of surprise or approval. [ME f. L *Jovis* genit. of OL *Jovis* used as genit. of the name *Jupiter*]

jovial /'dʒəʊvɪəl/ adj. **1** merry. **2** convivial. **3** hearty and good-humoured. □ **joviality** /-'ælɪtɪ/ n. **jovially** adv. [F f. LL jovialis of Jupiter (as JOVE), with ref. to the supposed influence of the planet Jupiter on those born under it]

jowl¹ /dʒaʊl/ n. **1** the jaw or jawbone. **2** the cheek (cheek by jowl). □ **-jowled** adj. (in comb.). [ME chavel jaw f. OE ceafl]

jowl² /dʒaʊl/ n. **1** the external loose skin on the throat or neck when prominent. **2** the dewlap of oxen, wattle of a bird, etc. □ **jowly** adj. [ME cholle neck f. OE ceole]

joy n. **1** (often foll. by at, in) a vivid emotion of pleasure; extreme gladness. **2** a thing that causes joy. **3** Brit. colloq. satisfaction, success (got no joy). □ **wish a person joy of** iron. be gladly rid of (what that person has to deal with). □ **joyless** adj. **joylessly** adv. [ME f. OF joie ult. f. L gaudium f. gaudēre rejoice]

joyful /'dʒɔɪfʊl/ adj. full of, showing, or causing joy. □ **joyfully** adv. **joyfulness** n.

joyous /'dʒɔɪəs/ adj. (of an occasion, circumstance, etc.) characterized by pleasure or joy; joyful. □ **joyously** adv. **joyousness** n.

joyride /'dʒɔɪraɪd/ n. & v. colloq. —n. a ride for pleasure in a motor car, esp. without the owner's permission. —v.intr. (past **-rode** /-rəʊd/; past part. **-ridden** /-rɪd(ə)n/) go for a joyride. □ **joyrider** n.

joystick /'dʒɔɪstɪk/ n. **1** colloq. the control column of an aircraft. **2** a lever that can be moved in several directions to control the movement of an image on a VDU screen.

JP abbr. Justice of the Peace.

Jr. abbr. Junior.

jube /dʒuːb/ n. Austral. & NZ = JUJUBE. [abbr.]

jubilant /'dʒuːbɪlənt/ adj. exultant, rejoicing, joyful. □ **jubilance** n. **jubilantly** adv. **jubilation** n. [L jubilare jubilant- shout for joy]

jubilee /'dʒuːbɪˌliː/ n. **1** a time or season of rejoicing. **2** an anniversary, esp. the 25th or 50th. [ME f. OF jubilé f. LL jubilaeus (annus) (year) of jubilee ult. f. Heb. yōḇēl, orig. = ram, ram's-horn trumpet]

Judaeo- /dʒuːˈdiːəʊ/ comb. form (US **Judeo-**) Jewish; Jewish and. [L judaeus Jewish]

Judaic /dʒuːˈdeɪɪk/ adj. of or characteristic of the Jews or Judaism. [L Judaicus f. Gk Ioudaïkos f. Ioudaios JEW]

Judaism /'dʒuːdeɪˌɪz(ə)m/ n. **1** the religion of the Jews, with a belief in one God and a basis in Mosaic and rabbinical teachings. **2** the Jews collectively. □ **Judaist** n. [ME f. LL Judaismus f. Gk Ioudaïsmos (as JUDAIC)]

Judaize /'dʒuːdeɪˌaɪz/ v. (also **-ise**) **1** intr. follow Jewish customs or rites. **2** tr. a make Jewish. **b** convert to Judaism. □ **Judaization** /-'zeɪʃ(ə)n/ n. [LL judaizare f. Gk ioudaïzō (as JUDAIC)]

Judas /'dʒuːdəs/ n. a person who betrays a friend. [Judas Iscariot who betrayed Christ (Luke 22)]

judder /'dʒʌdə(r)/ v. & n. esp. Brit. —v.intr. **1** (esp. of a mechanism) vibrate noisily or violently. **2** (of a singer's voice) oscillate in intensity. —n. an instance of juddering. [imit.: cf. SHUDDER]

judge n. & v. —n. **1** a public officer appointed to hear and try causes in a court of justice. **2** a person appointed to decide a dispute or contest. **3 a** a person who decides a question. **b** a person regarded in terms of capacity to decide on the merits of a thing or question (am no judge of that; a good judge of art). —v. **1** tr. **a** try (a cause) in a court of justice. **b** pronounce sentence on (a person). **2** tr. form an opinion about; estimate, appraise. **3** tr. act as a judge of (a dispute or contest). **4** tr. (often foll. by to + infin. or that + clause) conclude, consider, or suppose. **5** intr. **a** form a judgement. **b** act as judge. □ **judgelike** adj. **judgeship** n. [ME f. OF juge (n.), juger (v.) f. L judex judicis f. jus law + -dicus speaking]

judgement /'dʒʌdʒmənt/ n. (also **judgment**) **1** the critical faculty; discernment (an error of judgement). **2** good sense. **3** an opinion or estimate (in my judgement). **4** the sentence of a court of justice; a decision by a judge. **5** often joc. a misfortune viewed as a deserved recompense (it is a judgement on you for getting up late). **6** criticism. □ **against one's better judgement** contrary to what one really feels to be advisable. **Judgement Day** the day on which the Last Judgement is believed to take place. **the Last Judgement** (in some beliefs) the judgement of mankind expected to take place at the end of the world. [ME f. OF jugement (as JUDGE)]

judgemental /dʒʌdʒˈment(ə)l/ adj. (also **judgmental**) **1** of or concerning or by way of judgement. **2** condemning, critical. □ **judgementally** adv.

judicature /'dʒuːdɪkətʃə(r), -'dɪkətʃə(r)/ n. **1** the administration of justice. **2** a judge's office or term of office. **3** judges collectively. **4** a court of justice. [med.L judicatura f. L judicare to judge]

judicial /dʒuːˈdɪʃ(ə)l/ adj. **1** of, done by, or proper to a court of law. **2** having the function of judgement (a judicial assembly). **3** of or proper to a judge. **4** expressing a judgement; critical. **5** impartial. □ **judicial separation** the separation of man and wife by decision of a court. □ **judicially** adv. [ME f. L judicialis f. judicium judgement f. judex JUDGE]

judiciary /dʒuːˈdɪʃɪərɪ/ n. (pl. **-ies**) the judges of a State collectively. [L judiciarius (as JUDICIAL)]

judicious /dʒuːˈdɪʃəs/ adj. **1** sensible, prudent. **2** sound in discernment and judgement. □ **judiciously** adv. **judiciousness** n. [F judicieux f. L judicium (as JUDICIAL)]

judo /'dʒuːdəʊ/ n. a sport of unarmed combat derived from ju-jitsu. □ **judoist** n. [Jap. f. jū gentle + dō way]

jug n. & v. —n. **1 a** a deep vessel for holding liquids, with a handle and often with a spout or lip shaped for pouring. **b** the contents of this; a jugful. **2** US a large jar with a narrow mouth. **3** sl. prison. —v.tr. (**jugged**, **jugging**) **1** (usu. as **jugged** adj.) stew or boil (a hare or rabbit) in a covered vessel. **2** sl. imprison. □ **jugful** n. (pl. **-fuls**). [perh. f. Jug, pet-form of the name Joan etc.]

juggernaut /'dʒʌgəˌnɔːt/ n. **1** esp. Brit. a large heavy motor vehicle, esp. an articulated lorry. **2** a huge or overwhelming force or object. **3** (**Juggernaut**) an institution or notion to which persons blindly sacrifice themselves or others. [Hindi Jagannath f. Skr. Jagannātha = lord of the world: name of an idol of Krishna in Hindu mythol., carried in procession on a huge cart under which devotees are said to have formerly thrown themselves]

juggins /'dʒʌgɪnz/ n. Brit. sl. a simpleton. [perh. f. proper name Juggins (as JUG): cf. MUGGINS]

juggle /'dʒʌg(ə)l/ v. & n. —v. **1 a** intr. (often foll. by with) perform feats of dexterity, esp. by tossing objects in the air and catching them, keeping several in the air at the same time. **b** tr. perform such feats with. **2** tr. continue to deal with (several activities) at once, esp. with ingenuity. **3** intr. (foll. by with) & tr. **a** deceive or cheat. **b** misrepresent (facts). **c** rearrange adroitly. —n. **1** a piece of juggling. **2** a fraud. [ME, back-form. f. JUGGLER or f. OF jogler, jugler f. L joculari jest f. joculus dimin. of jocus jest]

juggler /'dʒʌglə(r)/ n. **1 a** a person who juggles. **b** a conjuror. **2** a trickster or impostor. □ **jugglery** n. [ME f. OF jouglere -eor f. L joculator -oris (as JUGGLE)]

Jugoslav var. of YUGOSLAV.

jugular /'dʒʌgjʊlə(r)/ adj. & n. —adj. of the neck or throat. —n. = jugular vein. □ **jugular vein** any of several large veins of the neck which carry blood from the head. [LL jugularis f. L jugulum collar-bone, throat, dimin. of jugum YOKE]

juice /dʒuːs/ n. **1** the liquid part of vegetables or fruits. **2** the fluid part of an animal body or substance, esp. a secretion (gastric juice). **3** the essence or spirit of anything. **4** colloq. petrol or electricity as a source of power. □ **juiceless** adj. [ME f. OF jus f. L jus broth, juice]

juicy /'dʒuːsɪ/ adj. (**juicier**, **juiciest**) **1** full of juice; succulent. **2** colloq. substantial or interesting; racy, scandalous. □ **juicily** adv. **juiciness** n.

ju-jitsu /dʒuː'dʒɪtsuː/ n. (also **jiu-jitsu**, **ju-jutsu**) a Japanese system of unarmed combat and physical training. [Jap. jūjutsu f. jū gentle + jutsu skill]

ju-ju /'dʒuːdʒuː/ n. **1** a charm or fetish of some W. African peoples. **2** a supernatural power attributed to this. [perh. f. F joujou toy]

jujube /'dʒuːdʒuːb/ n. a lozenge of gelatin etc. flavoured with or imitating this. [F jujube or med.L jujuba ult. f. Gk zizuphon]

jukebox /'dʒuːkbɒks/ n. a machine that automatically plays a selected musical recording when a coin is inserted. [Gullah juke disorderly + BOX¹]

Jul. abbr. July.

julep /'dʒuːlep/ n. **1 a** a sweet drink, esp. as a vehicle for medicine. **b** a medicated drink as a mild stimulant etc. **2** US iced and flavoured spirits and water (mint julep). [ME f. OF f. Arab. julāb f. Pers. gulāb f. gul rose + āb water]

Julian /'dʒuːlɪən/ adj. of or associated with Julius Caesar. □ **Julian calendar** a calendar introduced by Julius Caesar, in which the year consisted of 365 days, every fourth year having 366. [L Julianus f. Julius]

julienne /ˌdʒuːlɪ'en/ n. & adj. —n. foodstuff, esp. vegetables, cut into short thin strips. —adj. cut into thin strips. [F f. the name Jules or Julien]

Juliet cap /'dʒuːlɪət/ n. a small network ornamental cap worn by brides etc. [the heroine of Shakesp. Romeo & Juliet]

July /dʒuː'laɪ/ n. (pl. **Julys**) the seventh month of the year. [ME f. AF julie f. L Julius (mensis month), named after Julius Caesar]

jumble /'dʒʌmb(ə)l/ v. & n. —v. **1** tr. (often foll. by up) confuse; mix up. **2** intr. move about in disorder. —n. **1** a confused state or heap; a muddle. **2** Brit. articles collected for a jumble sale. □ **jumble sale** Brit. a sale of secondhand articles, esp. for charity. □ **jumbly** adj. [prob. imit.]

jumbo /'dʒʌmbəʊ/ n. & adj. colloq. —n. (pl. **-os**) **1** a large animal (esp. an elephant), person, or thing. **2** (in full **jumbo jet**) a large airliner with capacity for several hundred passengers. —adj. **1** very large of its kind. **2** extra large (jumbo packet). [19th c. (orig. of a person): orig. unkn.: popularized as the name of a zoo elephant sold in 1882]

■ **Usage** In sense 2, this word is usu. applied specifically to the Boeing 747.

jump v. & n. —v. **1** intr. move off the ground or other surface (usu. upward, at least initially) by sudden muscular effort in the legs. **2** intr. (often foll. by up, from, in, out, etc.) move suddenly or hastily in a specified way (we jumped into the car). **3** intr. give a sudden bodily movement from shock or excitement etc. **4** intr. undergo a rapid change, esp. an advance in status. **5** intr. (often foll. by about) change or move rapidly from one idea or subject to another. **6 a** intr. rise or increase suddenly (prices jumped). **b** tr. cause to do this. **7** tr. **a** pass over (an obstacle, barrier, etc.) by jumping. **b** move or pass over (an intervening thing) to a point beyond. **8** tr. skip or pass over (a passage in a book etc.). **9** tr. cause (a thing, or an animal, esp. a horse) to jump. **10** intr. (foll. by to, at) reach a conclusion hastily. **11** tr. (of a train) leave (the rails) owing to a fault. **12** tr. ignore and pass (a red traffic-light etc.). **13** tr. pounce on or attack (a person) unexpectedly. —n. **1** the act or an instance of jumping. **2 a** a sudden bodily movement caused by shock or excitement. **b** (**the jumps**) colloq. extreme nervousness or anxiety. **3** an abrupt rise in amount, price, value, status, etc. **4** an obstacle to be jumped, esp. by a horse. **5 a** a sudden transition. **b** a gap in a series, logical sequence, etc. □ **jump at** accept eagerly. **jump down a person's throat** colloq. reprimand or contradict a person fiercely. **jumped-up** colloq. upstart; presumptuously arrogant. **jump-jet** a jet aircraft that can take off and land vertically. **jump-lead** a cable for conveying current from the battery of a motor vehicle to boost (or recharge) another. **jump-off** a deciding round in a showjumping competition. **jump on** colloq. attack or criticize severely and without warning. **jump the queue 1** push forward out of one's turn. **2** take unfair precedence over others. **jump-rope** US a skipping-rope. **jump ship** (of a seaman) desert. **jump-start** v.tr. start (a motor vehicle) by pushing it or with jump-leads. —n. the action of jump-starting. **jump suit** a one-piece garment for the whole body. **jump to it** colloq. act promptly and energetically. □ **jumpable** adj. [16th c.: prob. imit.]

jumper¹ /'dʒʌmpə(r)/ n. **1** a knitted pullover. **2** a loose outer jacket of canvas etc. worn by sailors. **3** US a pinafore dress. [prob. f. (17th-c., now dial.) jump short coat perh. f. F jupe f. Arab. jubba]

jumper² /'dʒʌmpə(r)/ n. **1** a person or animal that jumps. **2** Electr. a short wire used to make or break a circuit.

jumpy /'dʒʌmpɪ/ adj. (**jumpier**, **jumpiest**) **1** nervous; easily startled. **2** making sudden movements, esp. of nervous excitement. □ **jumpily** adv. **jumpiness** n.

Jun. *abbr.* **1** June. **2** Junior.

junction /ˈdʒʌŋkʃ(ə)n/ *n.* **1** a point at which two or more things are joined. **2** a place where two or more railway lines or roads meet, unite, or cross. **3** the act or an instance of joining. □ **junction box** a box containing a junction of electric cables etc. [L *junctio* (as JOIN)]

juncture /ˈdʒʌŋktʃə(r)/ *n.* **1** a critical convergence of events; a critical point of time (*at this juncture*). **2** a place where things join. **3** an act of joining. [ME f. L *junctura* (as JOIN)]

June /dʒuːn/ *n.* the sixth month of the year. [ME f. OF *juin* f. L *Junius* var. of *Junonius* sacred to Juno]

jungle /ˈdʒʌŋg(ə)l/ *n.* **1 a** land overgrown with underwood or tangled vegetation, esp. in the tropics. **b** an area of such land. **2** a wild tangled mass. **3** a place of bewildering complexity or confusion, or of a struggle for survival (*blackboard jungle*). □ **jungled** *adj.* **jungly** *adj.* [Hindi *jangal* f. Skr. *jangala* desert, forest]

junior /ˈdʒuːnɪə(r)/ *adj.* & *n.* —*adj.* **1** less advanced in age. **2** (foll. by *to*) inferior in age, standing, or position. **3** the younger (esp. appended to a name for distinction from an older person of the same name). **4** of less or least standing; of the lower or lowest position (*junior partner*). **5** *Brit.* (of a school) having pupils in a younger age-range, usu. 7–11. **6** *US* of the year before the final year at university, high school, etc. —*n.* **1** a junior person. **2** one's inferior in length of service etc. **3** a junior student. **4** a barrister who is not a QC. **5** *US colloq.* a young male child, esp. in relation to his family. □ **juniority** /-ˈɒrɪtɪ/ *n.* [L, compar. of *juvenis* young]

juniper /ˈdʒuːnɪpə(r)/ *n.* any evergreen shrub or tree of the genus *Juniperus*, esp. *J. communis* with prickly leaves and dark purple berry-like cones. [ME f. L *juniperus*]

junk¹ *n.* & *v.* —*n.* **1** discarded articles; rubbish. **2** anything regarded as of little value. **3** *sl.* a narcotic drug, esp. heroin. —*v.tr.* discard as junk. □ **junk bond** *Stock Exch.* a bond bearing high interest but deemed to be a risky investment. **junk food** food with low nutritional value. **junk mail** unsolicited advertising matter sent by post. **junk shop** a shop selling cheap second-hand goods or antiques. [ME: orig. unkn.]

junk² *n.* a flat-bottomed sailing vessel used in the China seas. [obs. F *juncque*, Port. *junco*, or Du. *jonk*, f. Jav. *djong*]

junket /ˈdʒʌŋkɪt/ *n.* & *v.* —*n.* **1** a dish of sweetened and flavoured curds, often served with fruit or cream. **2** a feast. **3** a pleasure outing. **4** *US* an official's tour at public expense. —*v.intr.* (**junketed**, **junketing**) feast, picnic. □ **junketing** *n.* [ME *jonket* f. OF *jonquette* rushbasket (used to carry junket) f. *jonc* rush f. L *juncus*]

junkie /ˈdʒʌŋkɪ/ *n.* *sl.* a drug addict.

Junr. *abbr.* Junior.

junta /ˈdʒʌntə/ *n.* a political or military clique or faction taking power after a revolution or *coup d'état*. [Sp. & Port. f. L *juncta*, fem. past part. (as JOIN)]

jural /ˈdʒʊər(ə)l/ *adj.* **1** of law. **2** of rights and obligations. [L *jus juris* law, right]

Jurassic /dʒʊəˈræsɪk/ *adj.* & *n.* *Geol.* —*adj.* of or relating to the second period of the Mesozoic era. —*n.* this era or system. [F *jurassique* f. Jura (Mountains): cf. *Triassic*]

juridical /dʒʊəˈrɪdɪk(ə)l/ *n.* **1** of judicial proceedings. **2** relating to the law. □ **juridically**

adv. [L *juridicus* f. *jus juris* law + *-dicus* saying f. *dicere* say]

jurisdiction /ˌdʒʊərɪsˈdɪkʃ(ə)n/ *n.* **1** (often foll. by *over*, *of*) the administration of justice. **2 a** legal or other authority. **b** the extent of this; the territory it extends over. □ **jurisdictional** *adj.* [ME *jurisdiccioun* f. OF *jurediction, juridiction*, L *jurisdictio* f. *jus juris* law + *dictio* DICTION]

jurisprudence /ˌdʒʊərɪsˈpruːd(ə)ns/ *n.* the science or philosophy of law. □ **jurisprudent** *adj.* & *n.* **jurisprudential** /-ˈdenʃ(ə)l/ *adj.* [LL *jurisprudentia* f. L *jus juris* law + *prudentia* knowledge: see PRUDENT]

jurist /ˈdʒʊərɪst/ *n.* **1** an expert in law. **2** a legal writer. **3** *US* a lawyer. □ **juristic** /-ˈrɪstɪk/ *adj.* **juristical** /-ˈrɪstɪk(ə)l/ *adj.* [F *juriste* or med.L *jurista* f. *jus juris* law]

juror /ˈdʒʊərə(r)/ *n.* **1** a member of a jury. **2** a person who takes an oath. [ME f. AF *jurour*, OF *jureor* f. L *jurator -oris* f. *jurare jurat-* swear]

jury /ˈdʒʊərɪ/ *n.* (*pl.* **-ies**) **1** a body of usu. twelve persons sworn to render a verdict on the basis of evidence submitted to them in a court of justice. **2** a body of persons selected to award prizes in a competition. □ **jury-box** the enclosure for the jury in a lawcourt. [ME f. AF & OF *juree* oath, inquiry, f. *jurata* fem. past part. of L *jurare* swear]

juryman /ˈdʒʊərɪmən/ *n.* (*pl.* **-men**) a member of a jury.

jury-rigged /ˈdʒʊərɪrɪgd/ *n.* *Naut.* having temporary makeshift rigging. [perh. ult. f. OF *ajurie* aid]

jurywoman /ˈdʒʊərɪˌwʊmən/ *n.* (*pl.* **-women**) a woman member of a jury.

just *adj.* & *adv.* —*adj.* **1** acting or done in accordance with what is morally right or fair. **2** (of treatment etc.) deserved (*a just reward*). **3** (of feelings, opinions, etc.) well-grounded (*just resentment*). **4** right in amount etc.; proper. —*adv.* **1** exactly (*just what I need*). **2** exactly or nearly at this or that moment; a little time ago (*I have just seen them*). **3** *colloq.* simply, merely (*we were just good friends; it just doesn't make sense*). **4** barely; no more than (*I just managed it; just a minute*). **5** *colloq.* positively (*it is just splendid*). **6** quite (*not just yet; it is just as well that I checked*). □ **just about** *colloq.* almost exactly; almost completely. **just in case** as a precaution. **just now 1** at this moment. **2** a little time ago. **just so 1** exactly arranged (*they like everything just so*). **2** it is exactly as you say. □ **justly** *adv.* **justness** *n.* [ME f. OF *juste* f. L *justus* f. *jus* right]

justice /ˈdʒʌstɪs/ *n.* **1** just conduct. **2** fairness. **3** the exercise of authority in the maintenance of right. **4** judicial proceedings (*was duly brought to justice; the Court of Justice*). **5 a** a magistrate. **b** a judge. □ **do justice to** treat fairly or appropriately; show due appreciation of. **do oneself justice** perform in a manner worthy of one's abilities. **Justice of the Peace** an unpaid lay magistrate appointed to preserve the peace in a county, town, etc., hear minor cases, grant licences, etc. **Mr** (or **Mrs**) **Justice** *Brit.* a form of address or reference to a Supreme Court Judge. □ **justiceship** *n.* (in sense 5). [ME f. OF f. L *justitia* (as JUST)]

justiciary /dʒʌˈstɪʃjərɪ/ *n.* & *adj.* —*n.* (*pl.* **-ies**) an administrator of justice. —*adj.* of the administration of justice. [med.L *justitiarius* f. L *justitia*: see JUSTICE]

justifiable /ˈdʒʌstɪˌfaɪəb(ə)l/ *adj.* that can be justified or defended. □ **justifiable homicide** killing regarded as lawful and without criminal guilt, esp. the execution of a death sentence.

□ **justifiability** /-'brlrtr/ *n.* **justifiableness** *n.* **justifiably** *adv.* [F f. *justifier*: see JUSTIFY]

justify /'dʒʌstɪˌfaɪ/ *v.tr.* (**-ies, -ied**) **1** show the justice or rightness of (a person, act, etc.). **2** demonstrate the correctness of (an assertion etc.). **3** adduce adequate grounds for (conduct, a claim, etc.). **4 a** (esp. in *passive*) (of circumstances) be such as to justify. **b** vindicate. **5** (as **justified** *adj.*) just, right (*am justified in assuming*). **6** *Printing* adjust (a line of type) to fill a space evenly. □ **justification** /-fɪ'keɪʃ(ə)n/ *n.* **justificatory** /-fɪˌkeɪtərɪ/ *adj.* **justifier** *n.* [ME f. F *justifier* f. LL *justificare* do justice to f. L *justus* JUST]

jut *v.* & *n.* —*v.intr.* (**jutted, jutting**) (often foll. by *out, forth*) protrude, project. —*n.* a projection; a protruding point. [var. of JET[1]]

jute *n.* a rough fibre made from the bark of E. Indian plants of the genus *Corchorus*, used for making twine and rope, and woven into sacking, mats, etc. [Bengali *jhōṭo* f. Skr. *jūṭa* = *jaṭā* braid of hair]

juvenile /'dʒuːvəˌnaɪl/ *adj.* & *n.* —*adj.* **1 a** young, youthful. **b** of or for young persons. **2** suited to or characteristic of youth. **3** often *derog.* immature (*behaving in a very juvenile way*). —*n.* **1** a young person. **2** an actor playing the part of a youthful person. □ **juvenile court** a court for the trial of children under 17. **juvenile delinquency** offences committed by a person or persons below the age of legal responsibility. **juvenile delinquent** such an offender. □ **juvenilely** *adv.* **juvenility** /-'nɪlɪtɪ/ *n.* [L *juvenilis* f. *juvenis* young]

juvenilia /ˌdʒuːvə'nɪlɪə/ *n.pl.* works produced by an author or artist in youth. [L, neut. pl. of *juvenilis* (as JUVENILE)]

juxtapose /ˌdʒʌkstə'pəʊz/ *v.tr.* **1** place (things) side by side. **2** (foll. by *to, with*) place (a thing) beside another. □ **juxtaposition** /-pə'zɪʃ(ə)n/ *n.* **juxtapositional** /-pə'zɪʃən(ə)l/ *adj.* [F *juxtaposer* f. L *juxta* next: see POSE[1]]

K¹ /keɪ/ *n.* (also **k**) (*pl.* **Ks** or **K's**) the eleventh letter of the alphabet.

K² *abbr.* (also **K.**) **1** kelvin(s). **2** King, King's. **3** Köchel (catalogue of Mozart's works). **4** (also **k**) (prec. by a numeral) **a** *Computing* a unit of 1,024 (i.e. 2¹⁰) bytes or bits, or loosely 1,000. **b** 1,000. [sense 4 as abbr. of KILO-]

K³ *symb. Chem.* the element potassium.

k *abbr.* **1** kilo-. **2** knot(s).

Kaaba /ˈkɑːəbə/ *n.* (also **Caaba**) a sacred building at Mecca, the Muslim Holy of Holies containing the sacred black stone. [Arab. *Kaʿba*]

kabbala var. of CABBALA.

kabuki /kəˈbuːkɪ/ *n.* a form of popular traditional Japanese drama with highly stylized song, acted by males only. [Jap. f. *ka* song + *bu* dance + *ki* art]

kadi var. of CADI.

Kaffir /ˈkæfə(r)/ *n.* **1 a** a member of the Xhosa-speaking peoples of S. Africa. **b** the language of these peoples. **2** *S.Afr. offens.* any Black African. [Arab. *kāfir* infidel f. *kafara* not believe]

kaffiyeh var. of KEFFIYEH.

Kafkaesque /ˌkæfkəˈesk/ *adj.* (of a situation, atmosphere, etc.) impenetrably oppressive, nightmarish, in a manner characteristic of the fictional world of Franz Kafka, German-speaking novelist (d. 1924).

kaftan var. of CAFTAN.

kaiser /ˈkaɪzə(r)/ *n. hist.* an emperor, esp. the German Emperor, the Emperor of Austria, or the head of the Holy Roman Empire. □ **kaisership** *n.* [in mod. Eng. f. G *Kaiser* and Du. *keizer*; in ME f. OE *cāsere* f. Gmc adoption (through Gk *kaisar*) of L *Caesar*: see CAESAR]

kaka /ˈkɑːkɑː/ *n.* (*pl.* **kakas**) a large New Zealand parrot, *Nestor meridionalis*, with olive-brown plumage. [Maori]

kakapo /ˈkɑːkəˌpəʊ/ *n.* (*pl.* **-os**) an owl-like flightless New Zealand parrot, *Strigops habroptilus*. [Maori, = night kaka]

kale /keɪl/ *n.* (also **kail**) a variety of cabbage, esp. one with wrinkled leaves and no compact head. [ME, northern form of COLE]

kaleidoscope /kəˈlaɪdəˌskəʊp/ *n.* **1** a tube containing mirrors and pieces of coloured glass or paper, whose reflections produce changing patterns when the tube is rotated. **2** a constantly changing group of bright or interesting objects. □ **kaleidoscopic** /-ˈskɒpɪk/ *adj.* **kaleidoscopical** /-ˈskɒpɪk(ə)l/ *adj.* [Gk *kalos* beautiful + *eidos* form + -SCOPE]

kalends var. of CALENDS.

kaleyard /ˈkeɪljɑːd/ *n.* (also **kailyard**) *Sc.* a kitchen garden. [KALE + YARD²]

Kama /ˈkɑːmə/ *n.* the Hindu god of love. □ **Kama Sutra** /ˈsuːtrə/ an ancient Sanskrit treatise on the art of erotic love. [Skr.]

kame /keɪm/ *n.* a short ridge of sand and gravel deposited from the water of a melted glacier. [Sc. form of COMB]

kamikaze /ˌkæmɪˈkɑːzɪ/ *n. & adj.* —*n. hist.* **1** a Japanese aircraft loaded with explosives and deliberately crashed by its pilot on its target. **2** the pilot of such an aircraft. —*adj.* **1** of or relating to a kamikaze. **2** reckless, dangerous, potentially self-destructive. [Jap. f. *kami* divinity + *kaze* wind]

kampong /ˈkæmpɒŋ/ *n.* a Malayan enclosure or village. [Malay: cf. COMPOUND²]

kana /ˈkɑːnə/ *n.* any of various Japanese syllabaries. [Jap.]

kangaroo /ˌkæŋgəˈruː/ *n.* a plant-eating marsupial of the genus *Macropus*, native to Australia and New Guinea, with a long tail and strongly developed hind quarters enabling it to travel by jumping. □ **kangaroo court** an improperly constituted or illegal court held by strikers etc. **kangaroo vine** an evergreen climbing plant, *Cissus antarctica*, with tooth-edged leaves. [Aboriginal name]

kaolin /ˈkeɪəlɪn/ *n.* a fine soft white clay produced by the decomposition of other clays or feldspar, used esp. for making porcelain and in medicines. □ **kaolinic** /-ˈlɪnɪk/ *adj.* **kaolinize** *v.tr.* (also **-ise**). [F f. Chin. *gaoling* the name of a mountain f. *gao* high + *ling* hill]

kaon /ˈkeɪɒn/ *n. Physics* a meson having a mass several times that of a pion. [*ka* repr. the letter *K* (as symbol for the particle) + -ON]

kapellmeister /kəˈpelˌmaɪstə(r)/ *n.* (*pl.* same) the conductor of an orchestra, opera, choir, etc., esp. in German contexts. [G f. *Kapelle* court orchestra f. It. *cappella* CHAPEL + *Meister* master]

kapok /ˈkeɪpɒk/ *n.* a fine fibrous cotton-like substance found surrounding the seeds of a tropical tree, *Ceiba pentandra*, used for stuffing cushions, soft toys, etc. [ult. f. Malay *kāpoq*]

kappa /ˈkæpə/ *n.* the tenth letter of the Greek alphabet (*Κ*, *κ*). [Gk]

kaput /kæˈpʊt/ *predic.adj. sl.* broken, ruined; done for. [G *kaputt*]

karabiner /ˌkærəˈbiːnə(r)/ *n.* a coupling link with safety closure, used by mountaineers. [G, lit. 'carbine']

karakul /ˈkærəˌkʊl/ *n.* (also **caracul**) **1** a variety of Asian sheep with a dark curled fleece when young. **2** fur made from or resembling this. Also called *Persian lamb*. [Russ.]

karaoke /ˌkærɪˈəʊkɪ/ *n.* a form of entertainment in which people sing popular songs as soloists against a pre-recorded backing. □ **karaoke bar** (or **club**) a bar or club with this form of entertainment. [Jap., = empty orchestra]

karat US var. of CARAT 2.

karate /kəˈrɑːtɪ/ *n.* a Japanese system of unarmed combat using the hands and feet as weapons. [Jap. f. *kara* empty + *te* hand]

karma /ˈkɑːmə/ *n. Buddhism & Hinduism* **1** the sum of a person's actions in previous states of existence, viewed as deciding his or her fate in future existences. **2** destiny. □ **karmic** adj. [Skr., = action, fate]

Karoo /kəˈruː/ n. (also **Karroo**) an elevated semi-desert plateau in S. Africa. [Afrik. f. Hottentot karo dry]

karst /kɑːst/ n. a limestone region with underground drainage and many cavities and passages caused by the dissolution of the rock. [the Karst, a limestone region in NW Yugoslavia]

karyo- /ˈkærɪəʊ/ comb. form Biol. denoting the nucleus of a cell. [Gk karuon kernel]

kasbah /ˈkæzbɑː/ n. (also **casbah**) **1** the citadel of a N. African city. **2** an Arab quarter near this. [F casbah f. Arab. kas(a)ba citadel]

katabolism var. of CATABOLISM.

kathode var. of CATHODE.

katydid /ˈkeɪtɪdɪd/ n. any of various green grasshoppers of the family Tettigoniidae, native to the US. [imit. of the sound it makes]

kauri /ˈkaʊrɪ/ n. (pl. **kauris**) a coniferous New Zealand tree, Agathis australis, which produces valuable timber and a resin. □ **kauri-gum** this resin. [Maori]

kava /ˈkɑːvə/ n. **1** a Polynesian shrub, Piper methysticum. **2** an intoxicating drink made from the crushed roots of this. [Polynesian]

kayak /ˈkaɪæk/ n. **1** an Eskimo one-man canoe consisting of a light wooden frame covered with sealskins. **2** a small covered canoe resembling this. [Eskimo]

kayo /keɪˈəʊ/ v. & n. colloq. —v.tr. (**-oes, -oed**) knock out; stun by a blow. —n. (pl. **-os**) a knockout. [repr. pronunc. of KO]

kazoo /kəˈzuː/ n. a toy musical instrument into which the player sings or hums. [19th c., app. with ref. to the sound produced]

KB abbr. (in the UK) King's Bench.

KBE abbr. (in the UK) Knight Commander of the Order of the British Empire.

KC abbr. King's Counsel.

kc abbr. kilocycle(s).

kc/s abbr. kilocycles per second.

kea /ˈkiːə, ˈkeɪə/ n. a parrot, Nestor notabilis, of New Zealand, with brownish-green and red plumage. [Maori, imit.]

kebab /kɪˈbæb/ n. (usu. in pl.) small pieces of meat, vegetables, etc., packed closely and cooked on a skewer. [Urdu f. Arab. kabāb]

kedge v. & n. —v. **1** tr. move (a ship) by means of a hawser attached to a small anchor. **2** intr. (of a ship) move in this way. —n. (in full **kedge-anchor**) a small anchor for this purpose. [perh. a specific use of obs. cagge, dial. cadge bind, tie]

kedgeree /ˈkedʒəri, -ˈriː/ n. **1** an Indian dish of rice, split pulse, onions, eggs, etc. **2** a European dish of fish, rice, hard-boiled eggs, etc. [Hindi khichṛī, Skr. k'rsara dish of rice and sesame]

keek v. & n. Sc. —v.intr. peep. —n. a peep. [ME kike: cf. MDu., MLG kīken]

keel[1] n. & v. —n. **1** the lengthwise timber or steel structure along the base of a ship, airship, or some aircraft, on which the framework of the whole is built up. **2** poet. a ship. —v. **1** (often foll. by over) **a** intr. turn over or fall down. **b** tr. cause to do this. **2** tr. & intr. turn keel upwards. □ **keelless** adj. [ME kele f. ON kjǫlr f. Gmc]

keelhaul /ˈkiːlhɔːl/ v.tr. **1** drag (a person) through the water under the keel of a ship as a punishment. **2** scold or rebuke severely.

keelson /ˈkiːls(ə)n/ n. (also **kelson** /ˈkels(ə)n/) a line of timber fastening a ship's floor-timbers to its keel. [ME kelswayn, perh. f. LG kielswīn f. kiel KEEL + (prob.) swīn SWINE used as the name of a timber]

keen[1] adj. **1** (of a person, desire, or interest) eager, ardent (a keen sportsman). **2** (foll. by on) much attracted by; fond of or enthusiastic about. **3** (of the senses) sharp; highly sensitive. **4** intellectually acute. **5 a** having a sharp edge or point. **b** (of an edge etc.) sharp. **6** (of a sound, light, etc.) penetrating, vivid, strong. **7** (of a wind, frost, etc.) piercingly cold. **8** (of a pain etc.) acute, bitter. **9** Brit. (of a price) competitive. **10** colloq. excellent. □ **keenly** adv. **keenness** n. [OE cēne f. Gmc]

keen[2] n. & v. —n. an Irish funeral song accompanied with wailing. —v. **1** intr. utter the keen. **2** tr. bewail (a person) in this way. **3** tr. utter in a wailing tone. □ **keener** n. [Ir. caoine f. caoinim wail]

keep v. & n. —v. (past and past part. **kept**) **1** tr. have continuous charge of; retain possession of. **2** tr. (foll. by for) retain or reserve for a future occasion or time (will keep it for tomorrow). **3** tr. & intr. retain or remain in a specified condition, position, course, etc. (keep cool; keep off the grass; keep them happy). **4** tr. put or store in a regular place (knives are kept in this drawer). **5** tr. (foll. by from) cause to avoid or abstain from something (will keep you from going too fast). **6** tr. detain; cause to be late (what kept you?). **7** tr. **a** observe or pay due regard to (a law, custom, etc.) (keep one's word). **b** honour or fulfil (a commitment, undertaking, etc.). **c** respect the commitment implied by (a secret etc.). **d** act fittingly on the occasion of (keep the sabbath). **8** tr. own and look after (animals) (keeps bees). **9** tr. **a** provide for the sustenance of (a person, family, etc.). **b** (foll. by in) maintain (a person) with a supply of. **10** tr. carry on; manage (a shop, business, etc.). **11 a** tr. maintain (accounts, a diary, etc.) by making the requisite entries. **b** tr. maintain (a house) in proper order. **12** tr. have (a commodity) regularly on sale (do you keep buttons?). **13** tr. guard or protect (a person or place, a goal in football, etc.). **14** tr. preserve in being; continue to have (keep order). **15** intr. (foll. by verbal noun) continue or do repeatedly or habitually (why do you keep saying that?). **16** tr. continue to follow (a way or course). **17** intr. **a** (esp. of perishable commodities) remain in good condition. **b** (of news or information etc.) admit of being withheld for a time. **18** tr. remain in (one's bed, room, house, etc.). **19** tr. retain one's place in (a seat or saddle, one's ground, etc.) against opposition or difficulty. **20** tr. maintain (a person) in return for sexual favours (a kept woman). —n. **1** maintenance or the essentials for this (esp. food) (hardly earn your keep). **2** charge or control (is in your keep). **3** hist. a tower or stronghold. □ **for keeps** colloq. (esp. of something received or won) permanently, indefinitely. **how are you keeping?** how are you? **keep at** persist or cause to persist with (often foll. by from) **1** avoid being near. **2** prevent from being near. **keep back 1** remain or keep at a distance. **2** retard the progress of. **3** conceal; decline to disclose. **4** retain, withhold (kept back £50). **keep one's balance 1** remain stable; avoid falling. **2** retain one's composure. **keep down 1** hold in subjection. **2** keep low in amount. **3** lie low; stay hidden. **4** manage not to vomit (food eaten). **keep one's feet** manage not to fall. **keep-fit** regular exercises to promote personal fitness and health. **keep in 1** confine or restrain (one's feelings etc.). **2** remain or confine indoors. **3** keep (a fire) burning. **keep in with** remain on good terms with. **keep off 1** stay or cause to stay away from. **2** ward off; avert. **3** abstain from. **4** avoid (a subject) (*let's keep off religion*). **keep on 1** continue to do something; do continually (*kept on laughing*). **2** continue to use or employ. **3** (foll. by *at*) pester or harass. **keep out 1** keep or remain outside. **2** exclude. **keep to 1** adhere to (a course, schedule, etc.). **2** observe (a promise). **3** confine oneself to. **keep to oneself 1** avoid contact with others. **2** refuse to disclose or share. **keep together** remain or keep in harmony. **keep under** hold in subjection. **keep up 1** maintain (progress etc.). **2** prevent (prices, one's spirits, etc.) from sinking. **3** keep in repair, in an efficient or proper state, etc. **4** carry on (a correspondence etc.). **5** prevent (a person) from going to bed, esp. when late. **6** (often foll. by *with*) manage not to fall behind. **keep up with the Joneses** strive to compete socially with one's neighbours. □ **keepable** adj. [OE *cēpan*, of unkn. orig.]

keeper /ˈkiːpə(r)/ n. **1** a person who keeps or looks after something or someone. **2** a custodian of a museum, art gallery, forest, etc. **3 a** = GAMEKEEPER. **b** a person in charge of animals in a zoo. **4 a** = *wicket-keeper*. **b** = GOALKEEPER. **5** a fruit etc. that remains in good condition. **6** a bar of soft iron across the poles of a horseshoe magnet to maintain its strength. **7 a** a plain ring to preserve a hole in a pierced ear lobe; a sleeper. **b** a ring worn to guard against the loss of a more valuable one.

keeping /ˈkiːpɪŋ/ n. **1** custody, charge (*in safe keeping*). **2** agreement, harmony (esp. *in* or *out of keeping*).

keepsake /ˈkiːpseɪk/ n. a thing kept for the sake of or in remembrance of the giver.

keffiyeh /keˈfiːjeɪ/ n. (also **kaffiyeh**) a Bedouin Arab's kerchief worn as a head-dress. [Arab. *keffiya, kūfiyya,* perh. f. LL *cofea* COIF]

keg n. a small barrel, usu. of less than 10 gallons or (in the US) 30 gallons. □ **keg beer** beer supplied from a sealed metal container. [ME *cag* f. ON *kaggi,* of unkn. orig.]

kelp n. **1** any of several large broad-fronded brown seaweeds esp. of the genus *Laminaria,* suitable for use as manure. **2** the calcined ashes of seaweed formerly used in glass-making and soap manufacture. [ME *cülp(e),* of unkn. orig.]

kelpie /ˈkelpɪ/ n. Sc. **1** a water-spirit, usu. in the form of a horse, reputed to delight in the drowning of travellers etc. **2** an Australian sheepdog orig. bred from a Scottish collie. [18th c.: orig. unkn.]

kelson var. of KEELSON.

Kelt var. of CELT.

kelt /kelt/ n. a salmon or sea trout after spawning. [ME: orig. unkn.]

kelter var. of KILTER.

kelvin /ˈkelvɪn/ n. the SI unit of thermodynamic temperature, equal in magnitude to the degree celsius. □ **Kelvin scale** a scale of temperature with absolute zero as zero. [Lord *Kelvin,* Brit. physicist d. 1907]

kempt adj. combed; neatly kept. [past part. of (now dial.) *kemb* COMB v. f. OE *cemban* f. Gmc]

ken n. & v. —n. range of sight or knowledge (*it's beyond my ken*). —v.tr. (**kenning;** past and past part. **kenned** or **kent**) Sc. & N.Engl. **1** recognize at sight. **2** know. [OE *cennan* f. Gmc]

kendo /ˈkendəʊ/ n. a Japanese form of fencing with two-handed bamboo swords. [Jap., = sword-way]

kennel /ˈken(ə)l/ n. & v. —n. **1** a small shelter for a dog. **2** (in pl.) a breeding or boarding establishment for dogs. **3** a mean dwelling. —v. (**kennelled, kennelling;** US **kenneled, kenneling**) **1** tr. put into or keep in a kennel. **2** intr. live in or go to a kennel. [ME f. OF *chenil* f. med.L *canile* (unrecorded) f. L *canis* dog]

kenspeckle /ˈkenˌspek(ə)l/ adj. Sc. conspicuous. [*kenspeck* of Scand. orig.: rel. to KEN]

kent past and past part. of KEN.

kepi /ˈkepɪ, ˈkeɪpɪ/ n. (pl. **kepis**) a French military cap with a horizontal peak. [F *képi* f. Swiss G *käppi* dimin. of *kappe* cap]

kept past and past part. of KEEP.

keratin /ˈkerətɪn/ n. a fibrous protein which occurs in hair, feathers, hooves, claws, horns, etc. [Gk *keras keratos* horn + -IN]

keratinize /ˈkerətɪˌnaɪz/ v.tr. & intr. (also **-ise**) cover or become covered with a deposit of keratin. □ **keratinization** /-ˈzeɪʃ(ə)n/ n.

kerb n. Brit. a stone edging to a pavement or raised path. □ **kerb-crawler** a person who indulges in kerb-crawling. **kerb-crawling** the practice of driving slowly along the edge of a road, soliciting passers-by. **kerb drill** precautions, esp. looking to right and left, before crossing a road. [var. of CURB]

kerbstone /ˈkɜːbstəʊn/ n. each of a series of stones forming a kerb.

kerchief /ˈkɜːtʃiːf, -tʃɪf/ n. **1** a cloth used to cover the head. **2** poet. a handkerchief. □ **kerchiefed** adj. [ME *curchef* f. AF *courchef,* OF *couvrechief* f. *couvrir* COVER + CHIEF head]

kerfuffle /kəˈfʌf(ə)l/ n. esp. Brit. colloq. a fuss or commotion. [Sc. *curfuffle* f. *fuffle* to disorder: imit.]

kermes /ˈkɜːmɪz/ n. **1** the female of a bug, *Kermes ilicis,* with a berry-like appearance. **2** (in full **kermes oak**) an evergreen oak, *Quercus coccifera,* of S. Europe and N. Africa, on which this insect feeds. **3** a red dye made from the dried bodies of these insects. [F *kermès* f. Arab. & Pers. *ḳirmiz:* rel. to CRIMSON]

kernel /ˈkɜːn(ə)l/ n. **1** a central, softer, usu. edible part within a hard shell of a nut, fruit stone, seed, etc. **2** the whole seed of a cereal. **3** the nucleus or essential part of anything. [OE *cyrnel,* dimin. of CORN¹]

kerosine /ˈkerəˌsiːn/ n. (also **kerosene**) esp. US a fuel oil suitable for use in jet engines and domestic heating boilers; paraffin oil. [Gk *kēros* wax + -ENE]

kersey /ˈkɜːzɪ/ n. (pl. **-eys**) **1** a kind of coarse narrow cloth woven from long wool, usu. ribbed. **2** a variety of this. [ME, prob. f. *Kersey* in Suffolk]

kerseymere /ˈkɜːzɪmɪə(r)/ n. a twilled fine woollen cloth. [alt. of *cassimere,* var. of CASHMERE, assim. to KERSEY]

kestrel /ˈkestr(ə)l/ n. any small falcon, esp. *Falco tinnunculus,* which hovers whilst searching for its prey. [ME *castrell*, perh. f. F dial. *casserelle*, F *créc(er)elle*, perh. imit. of its cry]

ketch /ketʃ/ *n.* a two-masted fore-and-aft rigged sailing-boat with a mizen-mast stepped forward of the rudder and smaller than its foremast. [ME *catche*, prob. f. CATCH]

ketchup /ˈketʃʌp/ *n.* (also **catchup** /ˈkætʃʌp/) a spicy sauce made from tomatoes, mushrooms, vinegar, etc., used as a condiment. [Chin. dial. *kōechiap* pickled-fish brine]

ketone /ˈkiːtəʊn/ *n.* any of a class of organic compounds including propanone (acetone). □ **ketonic** /kɪˈtɒnɪk/ *adj.* [G *Keton* alt. of *Aketon* ACETONE]

kettle /ˈket(ə)l/ *n.* a vessel, usu. of metal with a lid, spout, and handle, for boiling water in. □ **kettle hole** a depression in the ground in a glaciated area. **a pretty kettle of fish** an awkward state of affairs. □ **kettleful** *n.* (*pl.* -**fuls**). [ME f. ON *ketill* ult. f. L *catillus* dimin. of *catinus* deep food-vessel]

kettledrum /ˈket(ə)lˌdrʌm/ *n.* a large drum shaped like a bowl with a membrane adjustable for tension (and so pitch) stretched across. □ **kettledrummer** *n.*

keV *abbr.* kilo-electronvolt.

kewpie /ˈkjuːpɪ/ *n.* a small chubby doll with wings and a curl or topknot. [CUPID + -IE]

key[1] /kiː/ *n. & v.* —*n.* (*pl.* **keys**) **1** an instrument, usu. of metal, for moving the bolt of a lock forwards or backwards to lock or unlock. **2** a similar implement for operating a switch in the form of a lock. **3** an instrument for grasping screws, pegs, nuts, etc., esp. one for winding a clock etc. **4** a lever depressed by the finger in playing the organ, piano, flute, concertina, etc. **5** (often in *pl.*) each of several buttons for operating a typewriter, word processor, or computer terminal, etc. **6** what gives or precludes the opportunity for or access to something. **7** (*attrib.*) essential; of vital importance (*the key element in the problem*). **8** a place that by its position gives control of a sea, territory, etc. **9 a** a solution or explanation. **b** a word or system for solving a cipher or code. **c** an explanatory list of symbols used in a map, table, etc. **d** a book of solutions to mathematical problems etc. **e** a literal translation of a book written in a foreign language. **f** the first move in a chess-problem solution. **10** *Mus.* a system of notes definitely related to each other, based on a particular note, and predominating in a piece of music (*a study in the key of C major*). **11** a tone or style of thought or expression. **12** a piece of wood or metal inserted between others to secure them. **13** the part of a first coat of wall plaster that passes between the laths and so secures the rest. **14** the roughness of a surface, helping the adhesion of plaster etc. **15** the winged seed of a sycamore etc. **16** a mechanical device for making or breaking an electric circuit, e.g. in telegraphy. —*v.tr.* (**keys**, **keyed**) **1** (foll. by *in*, *on*, etc.) fasten with a pin, wedge, bolt, etc. **2** (often foll. by *in*) enter (data) by means of a keyboard. **3** roughen (a surface) to help the adhesion of plaster etc. **4** (foll. by *to*) align or link (one thing to another). **5** regulate the pitch of the strings of (a violin etc.). □ **key industry** an industry essential to the carrying on of others, e.g. coal-mining, dyeing. **key map** a map in bare outline, to simplify the use of a full map). **key money** *Brit.* a payment demanded from an incoming tenant for the provision of a key to the premises. **key-ring** a ring for keeping keys on. **key signature** *Mus.* any of several combinations of sharps or flats after the clef at the beginning of each staff indicating the key of a composition. **key up** (often foll. by *to*, or *to* + *infin.*) make (a person) nervous or tense; excite. □ **keyer** *n.* **keyless** *adj.* [OE *cǣg*, of unkn. orig.]

key[2] /kiː/ *n.* a low-lying island or reef, esp. in the W. Indies. [Sp. *cayo* shoal, reef, infl. by QUAY]

keyboard /ˈkiːbɔːd/ *n. & v.* —*n.* **1** a set of keys on a typewriter, computer, piano, etc. **2** an electronic musical instrument with keys arranged as on a piano. —*v.tr.* enter (data) by means of a keyboard. □ **keyboarder** *n.*

keyhole /ˈkiːhəʊl/ *n.* a hole by which a key is put into a lock. □ **keyhole surgery** *colloq.* minimally invasive surgery carried out through a very small incision.

Keynesian /ˈkeɪnzɪən/ *adj. & n.* —*adj.* of or relating to the economic theories of J. M. Keynes (d. 1946), esp. regarding State control of the economy through money and taxation. —*n.* an adherent of these theories. □ **Keynesianism** *n.*

keynote /ˈkiːnəʊt/ *n.* **1** a prevailing tone or idea (*the keynote of the whole occasion*). **2** (*attrib.*) intended to set the prevailing tone at a meeting or conference (*keynote address*). **3** *Mus.* the note on which a key is based.

keypad /ˈkiːpæd/ *n.* a miniature keyboard or set of buttons for operating a portable electronic device, telephone, etc.

keypunch /ˈkiːpʌntʃ/ *n. & v.* —*n.* a device for transferring data by means of punched holes or notches on a series of cards or paper tape. —*v.tr.* transfer (data) by means of a keypunch. □ **keypuncher** *n.*

keystone /ˈkiːstəʊn/ *n.* **1** the central principle of a system, policy, etc., on which all the rest depends. **2** a central stone at the summit of an arch locking the whole together.

keystroke /ˈkiːstrəʊk/ *n.* a single depression of a key on a keyboard, esp. as a measure of work.

keyword /ˈkiːwɜːd/ *n.* **1** the key to a cipher etc. **2 a** a word of great significance. **b** a significant word used in indexing.

KG *abbr.* (in the UK) Knight of the Order of the Garter.

kg *abbr.* kilogram(s).

KGB /ˌkeɪdʒiːˈbiː/ *n.* the State security police of the former USSR from 1954. [Russ., abbr. of *Komitet gosudarstvennoĭ bezopasnosti* committee of State security]

khaki /ˈkɑːkɪ/ *adj. & n.* —*adj.* dust-coloured; dull brownish-yellow. —*n.* (*pl.* **khakis**) **1** khaki fabric of twilled cotton or wool, used esp. in military dress. **2** the dull brownish-yellow colour of this. [Urdu *ḵākī* dust-coloured f. *ḵāk* dust]

khan[1] /kɑːn, kæn/ *n.* a title given to rulers and officials in Central Asia, Afghanistan, etc. □ **khanate** *n.* [Turki *ḵān* lord]

khan[2] /kɑːn, kæn/ *n.* a caravanserai. [Arab. *ḵān* inn]

kHz *abbr.* kilohertz.

kibble /ˈkɪb(ə)l/ *v.tr.* grind coarsely. [18th c.: orig. unkn.]

kibbutz /kɪˈbʊts/ *n.* (*pl.* **kibbutzim** /-ˈtsiːm/) a communal esp. farming settlement in Israel. [mod.Heb. *ḳibbūṣ* gathering]

kibbutznik /kɪˈbʊtsnɪk/ *n.* a member of a kibbutz. [Yiddish (as KIBBUTZ)]

kibe /kaɪb/ *n.* an ulcerated chilblain, esp. on the heel. [ME, prob. f. Welsh *cibi*]

kibitz /ˈkɪbɪts/ *v.intr. colloq.* act as a kibitzer. [Yiddish f. G *kiebitzen* (as KIBITZER)]

kibitzer /ˈkɪbɪtsə(r), kɪˈbɪtsə(r)/ *n. colloq.* **1** an onlooker at cards etc., esp. one who offers unwanted advice. **2** a busybody, a meddler. [Yiddish *kibitser* f. G *Kiebitz* lapwing, busybody]

kibosh /ˈkaɪbɒʃ/ *n.* (also **kybosh**) *sl.* nonsense. □ **put the kibosh on** put an end to; finally dispose of. [19th c.: orig. unkn.]

kick *v. & n.* —*v.* **1** *tr.* strike or propel forcibly with the foot or hoof etc. **2** *intr.* (usu. foll. by *at, against*) **a** strike out with the foot. **b** express annoyance at or dislike of (treatment, a proposal, etc.); rebel against. **3** *tr. sl.* give up (a habit). **4** *tr.* (often foll. by *out* etc.) expel or dismiss forcibly. **5** *refl.* be annoyed with oneself (*I'll kick myself if I'm wrong*). **6** *tr. Football* score (a goal) by a kick. **7** *intr. Cricket* (of a ball) rise sharply from the pitch. —*n.* **1 a** a blow with the foot or hoof etc. **b** the delivery of such a blow. **2** *colloq.* **a** a sharp stimulant effect, esp. of alcohol (*has some kick in it; a cocktail with a kick in it*). **b** (often in *pl.*) a pleasurable thrill (*did it just for kicks; got a kick out of flying*). **3** strength, resilience (*have no kick left*). **4** *colloq.* a specified temporary interest or enthusiasm (*on a jogging kick*). **5** the recoil of a gun when discharged. □ **kick about** (or **around**) *colloq.* **1 a** drift idly from place to place. **b** be unused or unwanted. **2 a** treat roughly or scornfully. **b** discuss (an idea) unsystematically. **kick the bucket** *sl.* die. **kick in 1** knock down (a door etc.) by kicking. **2** esp. *US sl.* contribute (esp. money); pay one's share. **kick in the pants** (or **teeth**) *colloq.* a humiliating punishment or set-back. **kick off 1** a *Football* begin or resume a match. **b** *colloq.* begin. **2** remove (shoes etc.) by kicking. **kick-off 1** *Football* the start or resumption of a match. **2** (in **for a kick-off**) *colloq.* for a start (*that's wrong for a kick-off*). **kick-pleat** a pleat in a narrow skirt to allow freedom of movement. **kick up** (or **kick up a fuss, dust,** etc.) create a disturbance; object or register strong disapproval. **kick up one's heels** frolic. **kick a person upstairs** shelve a person by giving him or her promotion or a title. □ **kickable** *adj.* **kicker** *n.* [ME *kike,* of unkn. orig.]

kickback /ˈkɪkbæk/ *n. colloq.* **1** the force of a recoil. **2** payment for collaboration, esp. collaboration for profit.

kickshaw /ˈkɪkʃɔː/ *n.* **1** *archaic,* usu. *derog.* a fancy dish in cookery. **2** something elegant but insubstantial; a toy or trinket. [F *quelque chose* something]

kickstand /ˈkɪkstænd/ *n.* a rod attached to a bicycle or motor cycle and kicked into a vertical position to support the vehicle when stationary.

kick-start /ˈkɪkstɑːt/ *n. & v.* —*n.* (also **kick-starter**) a device to start the engine of a motor cycle etc. by the downward thrust of a pedal. —*v.tr.* start (a motor cycle etc.) in this way.

kid[1] *n. & v.* —*n.* **1** a young goat. **2** the leather made from its skin. **3** *sl.* a child or young person. —*v.intr.* (**kidded, kidding**) (of a goat) give birth. □ **handle with kid gloves** handle in a gentle, delicate, or gingerly manner. **kid brother** (or **sister**) *sl.* a younger brother or sister. **kids'**

stuff *sl.* something very simple. [ME *kide* f. ON *kith* f. Gmc]

kid[2] *v.* (**kidded, kidding**) *colloq.* **1** *tr. & refl.* deceive, trick (*don't kid yourself; kidded his mother that he was ill*). **2** *tr. & intr.* tease (*only kidding*). □ **no kidding** (or **kid**) *sl.* that is the truth. □ **kidder** *n.* **kiddingly** *adv.* [perh. f. KID[1]]

kiddie /ˈkɪdɪ/ *n.* (also **kiddy**) (*pl.* **-ies**) *sl.* = KID[1] *n.* 3.

kiddo /ˈkɪdəʊ/ *n.* (*pl.* **-os**) *sl.* = KID[1] *n.* 3.

kidnap /ˈkɪdnæp/ *v.tr.* (**kidnapped, kidnapping;** *US* **kidnaped, kidnaping**) **1** carry off (a person etc.) by illegal force or fraud esp. to obtain a ransom. **2** steal (a child). □ **kidnapper** *n.* [back-form. f. *kidnapper* f. KID[1] + *nap* = NAB]

kidney /ˈkɪdnɪ/ *n.* (*pl.* **-eys**) **1** either of a pair of organs in the abdominal cavity of mammals, birds, and reptiles, which remove nitrogenous wastes from the blood and excrete urine. **2** the kidney of a sheep, ox, or pig as food. **3** temperament, nature, kind (*a man of that kidney; of the right kidney*). □ **kidney bean 1** a dwarf French bean. **2** a scarlet runner bean. **kidney dish** a kidney-shaped dish, esp. one used in surgery. **kidney machine** an apparatus that performs the functions of the human kidney. [ME *kidnei,* pl. *kidneiren,* app. partly f. *ei* EGG[1]]

kidskin /ˈkɪdskɪn/ *n.* = KID[1] *n.* 2.

kilderkin /ˈkɪldəkɪn/ *n.* **1** a cask for liquids etc., holding 16 or 18 gallons. **2** this measure. [ME, alt. of *kinderkin* f. MDu. *kinde(r)kin, kinneken,* dimin. of *kintal* a weight of about 100 lb.]

kill *v. & n.* —*v.tr.* **1 a** deprive of life or vitality; put to death; cause the death of. **b** (*absol.*) cause or bring about death (*must kill to survive*). **2** destroy; put an end to (feelings etc.) (*overwork killed my enthusiasm*). **3** *refl.* (often foll. by pres. part.) *colloq.* **a** overexert oneself (*don't kill yourself lifting them all at once*). **b** laugh heartily. **4** *colloq.* overwhelm (a person) with amusement, delight, etc. (*the things he says really kill me*). **5** switch off (a spotlight, engine, etc.). **6** *colloq.* delete (a line, paragraph, etc.) from a computer file. **7** *colloq.* cause pain or discomfort to (*my feet are killing me*). **8** pass (time, or a specified amount of it) usu. while waiting for a specific event (*had an hour to kill before the interview*). **9** defeat (a bill in Parliament). **10** *colloq.* consume the entire contents of (a bottle of wine etc.). **11 a** *Tennis* etc. hit (the ball) so skilfully that it cannot be returned. **b** stop (the ball) dead. **12** neutralize or render ineffective (taste, sound, colour, etc.) (*thick carpet killed the sound of footsteps*). —*n.* **1** an act of killing (esp. an animal). **2** an animal or animals killed, esp. by a sportsman. **3** *colloq.* the destruction or disablement of an enemy aircraft, submarine, etc. □ **dressed to kill** dressed showily, alluringly, or impressively. **in at the kill** present at or benefiting from the successful conclusion of an enterprise. **kill off 1** get rid of or destroy completely (esp. a number of persons or things). **2** (of an author) bring about the death of (a fictional character). **kill or cure** (usu. *attrib.*) (of a remedy etc.) drastic, extreme. **kill two birds with one stone** achieve two aims at once. **kill with kindness** spoil (a person) with overindulgence. [ME *cülle, kille,* perh. ult. rel. to QUELL]

killer /ˈkɪlə(r)/ *n.* **1 a** a person, animal, or thing that kills. **b** a murderer. **2** *colloq.* **a** an impressive, formidable, or excellent thing (*this one is quite* difficult, but the next one is a real killer). **b** a hilarious joke. **c** a decisive blow (his brilliant header proved to be the killer). □ **killer instinct 1** an innate tendency to kill. **2** a ruthless streak. **killer whale** a voracious cetacean, Orcinus orca, with a white belly and prominent dorsal fin.

killing /ˈkɪlɪŋ/ n. & adj. —n. **1 a** the causing of death. **b** an instance of this. **2** a great (esp. financial) success (make a killing). —adj. colloq. **1** overwhelmingly funny. **2** exhausting; very strenuous. □ **killing-bottle** a bottle containing poisonous vapour to kill insects collected as specimens. □ **killingly** adv.

killjoy /ˈkɪldʒɔɪ/ n. a person who throws gloom over or prevents other people's enjoyment.

kiln n. a furnace or oven for burning, baking, or drying, esp. for calcining lime or firing pottery etc. [OE cylene f. L culina kitchen]

kiln-dry /ˈkɪlndraɪ/ v.tr. (-ies, -ied) dry in a kiln.

kilo /ˈkiːləʊ/ n. (pl. -os) **1** a kilogram. **2** a kilometre. [F: abbr.]

kilo- /ˈkɪləʊ/ comb. form denoting a factor of 1,000 (esp. in metric units). [F f. Gk khilioi thousand]

kilobyte /ˈkɪləˌbaɪt/ n. Computing 1,024 (i.e. 2^{10}) bytes as a measure of memory size.

kilocalorie /ˈkɪləˌkælərɪ/ n. = CALORIE 2.

kilocycle /ˈkɪləˌsaɪk(ə)l/ n. a former measure of frequency, equivalent to 1 kilohertz.

kilogram /ˈkɪləˌɡræm/ n. (also **-gramme**) the SI unit of mass, equivalent to the international standard kept at Sèvres near Paris (approx. 2.205 lb.). [F kilogramme (as KILO, GRAM)]

kilohertz /ˈkɪləˌhɜːts/ n. a measure of frequency equivalent to 1,000 cycles per second.

kilojoule /ˈkɪləˌdʒuːl/ n. 1,000 joules, esp. as a measure of the energy value of foods.

kilolitre /ˈkɪləˌliːtə(r)/ n. (US **-liter**) 1,000 litres (equivalent to 220 imperial gallons).

kilometre /ˈkɪləˌmiːtə(r), disp. kɪˈlɒmɪtə(r)/ n. (US **kilometer**) a metric unit of measurement equal to 1,000 metres (approx. 0.62 miles). □ **kilometric** /ˌkɪləˈmetrɪk/ adj. [F kilomètre (as KILO-, METRE¹)]

■ **Usage** The second pronunciation given, with the stress on the second syllable, is considered incorrect by some people.

kiloton /ˈkɪləˌtʌn/ n. (also **kilotonne**) a unit of explosive power equivalent to 1,000 tons of TNT.

kilovolt /ˈkɪləˌvɒlt/ n. 1,000 volts.

kilowatt /ˈkɪləˌwɒt/ n. 1,000 watts.

kilowatt-hour /ˌkɪləwɒtˈaʊə(r)/ n. a measure of electrical energy equivalent to a power consumption of 1,000 watts for one hour.

kilt n. & v. —n. **1** a skirtlike garment, usu. of pleated tartan cloth and reaching to the knees, as traditionally worn by Highland men. **2** a similar garment worn by women and children. —v.tr. **1** tuck up (skirts) round the body. **2** (esp. as **kilted** adj.) gather in vertical pleats. □ **kilted** adj. [orig. as verb: ME, of Scand. orig.]

kilter /ˈkɪltə(r)/ n. (also **kelter** /ˈkel-/) good working order (esp. out of kilter). [17th c.: orig. unkn.]

kiltie /ˈkɪltɪ/ n. a wearer of a kilt, esp. a kilted Highland soldier.

kimono /kɪˈməʊnəʊ/ n. (pl. -os) **1** a long loose Japanese robe worn with a sash. **2** a European dressing-gown modelled on this. □ **kimonoed** adj. [Jap.]

kin n. & adj. —n. one's relatives or family. —predic.adj. (of a person) related (we are kin; he is kin to me). □ **near of kin** closely related by blood, or in character. □ **kinless** adj. [OE cynn f. Gmc]

-kin /kɪn/ suffix forming diminutive nouns (cat-kin; manikin). [from or after MDu. -kijn, -ken, OHG -chin]

kinaesthesia /ˌkɪnəsˈθiːzɪə/ n. (US **kinesthesia**) a sense of awareness of the position and movement of the voluntary muscles of the body. □ **kinaesthetic** /-ˈθetɪk/ adj. [Gk kineō move + aisthēsis sensation]

kind¹ /kaɪnd/ n. **1 a** a race or species (human kind). **b** a natural group of animals, plants, etc. (the wolf kind). **2** class, type, sort, variety (what kind of job are you looking for?). **3** each of the elements of the Eucharist (communion under (or in) both kinds). **4** the manner or fashion natural to a person etc. (act after their kind; true to kind). □ **kind of** colloq. to some extent (felt kind of sorry; I kind of expected it). **a kind of** used to imply looseness, vagueness, exaggeration, etc., in the term used (a kind of Jane Austen of our times; I suppose he's a kind of doctor). **in kind 1** in the same form, likewise (was insulted and replied in kind). **2** (of payment) in goods or labour as opposed to money (received their wages in kind). **3** character, quality (differ in degree but not in kind). **nothing of the kind 1** not at all like the thing in question. **2** (expressing denial) not at all. **of its kind** within the limitations of its own class (good of its kind). **of a kind 1** derog. scarcely deserving the name (a choir of a kind). **2** similar in some important respect (they're two of a kind). **one's own kind** those with whom one has much in common. **something of the kind** something like the thing in question. [OE cynd(e), gecynd(e) f. Gmc]

■ **Usage** In sense 2 of the noun, these kinds of is usually preferred to these kind of.

kind² /kaɪnd/ adj. **1** of a friendly, generous, benevolent, or gentle nature. **2** (usu. foll. by to) showing friendliness, affection, or consideration. **3** affectionate. [OE gecynde (as KIND¹); orig. = 'natural, native']

kindergarten /ˈkɪndəˌɡɑːt(ə)n/ n. an establishment for preschool learning. [G, = children's garden]

kind-hearted /kaɪndˈhɑːtɪd/ adj. of a kind disposition. □ **kind-heartedly** adv. **kind-heartedness** n.

kindle /ˈkɪnd(ə)l/ v. **1** tr. light or set on fire (a flame, fire, substance, etc.). **2** intr. catch fire, burst into flame. **3** tr. arouse or inspire (kindle enthusiasm for the project; kindle jealousy in a rival). **4** intr. (usu. foll. by to) respond, react (to a person, an action, etc.) (kindle to his courage). **5** intr. become animated, glow with passion etc. (her imagination kindled). **6** tr. & intr. make or become bright (kindle the embers to a glow). □ **kindler** n. [ME f. ON kynda, kindle: cf. ON kindill candle, torch]

kindling /ˈkɪndlɪŋ/ n. small sticks etc. for lighting fires.

kindly¹ /ˈkaɪndlɪ/ adv. **1** in a kind manner (spoke to the child kindly). **2** often iron. used in a polite request or demand (kindly acknowledge this letter; kindly leave me alone). □ **look kindly upon** regard sympathetically. **take a thing kindly** like or be pleased by it. **take kindly to** be pleased by or endeared to (a person or thing). **thank kindly** thank very much. [OE *gecyndelīce* (as KIND²)]

kindly² /ˈkaɪndlɪ/ *adj.* (**kindlier, kindliest**) **1** kind, kind-hearted. **2** (of climate etc.) pleasant, genial. □ **kindlily** *adv.* **kindliness** *n.* [OE *gecyndelic* (as KIND¹)]

kindness /ˈkaɪndnɪs/ *n.* **1** the state or quality of being kind. **2** a kind act.

kindred /ˈkɪndrɪd/ *n.* & *adj.* —*n.* **1** one's relations, referred to collectively. **2** a relationship by blood. **3** a resemblance or affinity in character. —*adj.* **1** related by blood or marriage. **2** allied or similar in character (*other kindred symptoms*). □ **kindred spirit** a person whose character and outlook have much in common with one's own. [ME f. KIN + -*red* f. OE *ræden* condition]

kine /kaɪn/ *archaic pl.* of COW¹.

kinematics /ˌkɪnɪˈmætɪks, ˌkaɪ-/ *n.pl.* (usu. treated as *sing.*) the branch of mechanics concerned with the motion of objects without reference to the forces which cause the motion. □ **kinematic** *adj.* **kinematically** *adv.* [Gk *kinēma -matos* motion f. *kineō* move + -ICS]

kinematograph var. of CINEMATOGRAPH.

kinesthesia US var. of KINAESTHESIA.

kinetic /kɪˈnetɪk, kaɪ-/ *adj.* of or due to motion. □ **kinetic art** a form of art that depends on movement for its effect. **kinetic energy** the energy of motion. **kinetic theory** a theory which explains the physical properties of matter in terms of the motions of its constituent particles. □ **kinetically** *adv.* [Gk *kinētikos* f. *kineō* move]

kinetics /kɪˈnetɪks, kaɪ-/ *n.pl.* **1** = DYNAMICS 1a. **2** (usu. treated as *sing.*) the branch of physical chemistry concerned with measuring and studying the rates of chemical reactions.

kinfolk US var. of KINSFOLK.

king /kɪŋ/ *n.* **1** (as a title usu. **King**) a male sovereign, esp. the hereditary ruler of an independent State. **2** a person or thing pre-eminent in a specified field or class (*railway king*). **3** a large (or the largest) kind of plant, animal, etc. (*king penguin*). **4** *Chess* the piece on each side which the opposing side has to checkmate to win. **5** a piece in draughts with extra capacity of moving, made by crowning an ordinary piece that has reached the opponent's baseline. **6** a court-card bearing a representation of a king and usu. ranking next below an ace. □ **king it** play or act the king. **2** (usu. foll. by *over*) govern, control. **King James Bible** (or **Version**) = *Authorized Version.* **king of beasts** the lion. **king of birds** the eagle. **King of the Castle** a children's game consisting of trying to displace a rival from a mound. **King of Kings 1** God. **2** the title assumed by many eastern kings. **king-post** an upright post from the tie-beam of a roof to the apex of a truss. **king's evil** *hist.* scrofula, formerly held to be curable by the royal touch. **king-size** (or **-sized**) larger than normal; very large. **king's ransom** a fortune. □ **kinghood** *n.* **kingless** *adj.* **kinglike** *adj.* **kingly** *adj.* **kingliness** *n.* **kingship** *n.* [OE *cyning, cyng* f. Gmc]

kingbolt /ˈkɪŋbəʊlt/ *n.* = KINGPIN.

kingcup /ˈkɪŋkʌp/ *n. Brit.* a marsh marigold.

kingdom /ˈkɪŋdəm/ *n.* **1** an organized community headed by a king. **2** the territory subject to a king. **3 a** the spiritual reign attributed to God (*Thy kingdom come*). **b** the sphere of this

(*kingdom of heaven*). **4** a domain belonging to a person, animal, etc. **5** a province of nature (*the vegetable kingdom*). **6** a specified mental or emotional province (*kingdom of the heart*; *kingdom of fantasy*). **7** *Biol.* the highest category in taxonomic classification. □ **kingdom come** *sl.* eternity; the next world. □ **kingdomed** *adj.* [OE *cyningdōm* (as KING)]

kingfisher /ˈkɪŋˌfɪʃə(r)/ *n.* any bird of the family Alcedinidae esp. *Alcedo atthis* with a long sharp beak and brightly coloured plumage, which dives for fish in rivers etc.

kingmaker /ˈkɪŋˌmeɪkə(r)/ *n.* a person who makes kings, leaders, etc., through the exercise of political influence, orig. with ref. to the Earl of Warwick in the reign of Henry VI of England.

kingpin /ˈkɪŋpɪn/ *n.* **1 a** a main or large bolt in a central position. **b** a vertical bolt used as a pivot. **2** an essential person or thing, esp. in a complex system.

kink *n.* & *v.* —*n.* **1 a** a short backward twist in wire or tubing etc. such as may cause an obstruction. **b** a tight wave in human or animal hair. **2** a mental twist or quirk. —*v.intr.* & *tr.* form or cause to form a kink. [MLG *kinke* (v.) prob. f. Du. *kinken*]

kinky /ˈkɪŋkɪ/ *adj.* (**kinkier, kinkiest**) **1** *colloq.* **a** given to or involving abnormal sexual behaviour. **b** (of clothing etc.) bizarre in a sexually provocative way. **2** strange, eccentric. **3** having kinks or twists. □ **kinkily** *adv.* **kinkiness** *n.* [KINK + -Y¹]

-kins /kɪnz/ *suffix* = -KIN, often with suggestions of endearment (*babykins*).

kinsfolk /ˈkɪnzfəʊk/ *n.pl.* (US **kinfolk**) one's relations by blood.

kinship /ˈkɪnʃɪp/ *n.* **1** blood relationship. **2** the sharing of characteristics or origins.

kinsman /ˈkɪnzmən/ *n.* (*pl.* **-men**; *fem.* **kinswoman**, *pl.* **-women**) **1** a blood relation or *disp.* a relation by marriage. **2** a member of one's own tribe or people.

■ **Usage** The use of this word to mean 'a relation by marriage' is considered incorrect by some people.

kiosk /ˈkiːɒsk/ *n.* **1** a light open-fronted booth or cubicle from which food, newspapers, tickets, etc. are sold. **2** a telephone box. **3** *Austral.* a building in which refreshments are served in a park, zoo, etc. [F *kiosque* f. Turk. *kiūshk* pavilion f. Pers. *guš*]

kip¹ *n.* & *v. Brit. sl.* —*n.* **1** a sleep or nap. **2** a bed or cheap lodging-house. —*v.intr.* (**kipped, kipping**) sleep, take a nap. [cf. Da. *kippe* mean hut]

kip² /kɪp/ *n. Austral. sl.* a small piece of wood from which coins are spun in the game of two-up. [perh. f. E dial.: cf. *keper* a flat piece of wood preventing a horse from eating the corn, or Ir. dial. *kippeen* f. Ir. *cipín* a little stick]

kipper /ˈkɪpə(r)/ *n.* & *v.* —*n.* **1** a kippered fish, esp. herring. **2** a male salmon in the spawning season. —*v.tr.* cure (a herring etc.) by splitting open, salting, and drying in the open air or smoke. [ME: orig. uncert.]

kir /kɜː(r)/ *n.* a drink made from dry white wine and blackcurrant liqueur. [Canon Felix *Kir* d. 1968, said to have invented the recipe]

kirby-grip /ˈkɜːbɪgrɪp/ *n.* (also **Kirbigrip** *propr.*) a type of sprung hairgrip. [*Kirby*, part of orig. manufacturer's name]

kirk /kɜːk/ n. Sc. & N.Engl. **1** a church. **2 (the Kirk** or **the Kirk of Scotland)** the Church of Scotland as distinct from the Church of England or from the Episcopal Church in Scotland. □ **Kirk-session** the lowest court in the Church of Scotland. [ME f. ON *kirkja* f. OE *cir(i)ce* CHURCH]

kirsch /kɪəʃ/ n. (also **kirschwasser** /ˈkɪəʃˌvasə(r)/) a brandy distilled from the fermented juice of cherries. [G *Kirsche* cherry, *Wasser* water]

kismet /ˈkɪsmet, ˈkɪz-/ n. destiny, fate. [Turk. f. Arab. *ḳisma(t)* f. *ḳasama* divide]

kiss v. & n. —v. **1** tr. touch with the lips, esp. as a sign of love, affection, greeting, or reverence. **2** tr. express (greeting or farewell) in this way. **3** absol. (of two persons) touch each others' lips in this way. **4** tr. (also absol.) (of a snooker ball etc. in motion) lightly touch (another ball). —n. **1** a touch with the lips in kissing. **2** the slight impact when one snooker ball etc. lightly touches another. **3** a small sweetmeat or piece of confectionery. □ **kiss and tell** recount one's sexual exploits. **kiss a person's arse** coarse sl. act obsequiously towards a person. **kiss away** remove (tears etc.) by kissing. **kiss-curl** a small curl of hair on the forehead, at the nape, or in front of the ear. **kiss the dust** submit abjectly; be overthrown. **kiss goodbye to** colloq. accept the loss of. **kiss the ground** prostrate oneself as a token of homage. **kissing cousin** (or **kin** or **kind**) a distant relative (given a formal kiss on occasional meetings). **kissing-gate** Brit. a gate hung in a V- or U-shaped enclosure, to let one person through at a time. **kiss of death** an apparently friendly act which causes ruin. **kiss off** sl. **1** dismiss, get rid of. **2** go away, die. **kiss of life** mouth-to-mouth resuscitation. **kiss of peace** Eccl. a ceremonial kiss, esp. during the Eucharist, as a sign of unity. **kiss the rod** accept chastisement submissively. □ **kissable** adj. [OE cyssan f. Gmc]

kisser /ˈkɪsə(r)/ n. **1** a person who kisses. **2** (orig. Boxing) sl. the mouth; the face.

kissogram /ˈkɪsəˌɡræm/ n. (also **Kissagram** propr.) a novelty telegram or greetings message delivered with a kiss.

kissy /ˈkɪsɪ/ adj. colloq. given to kissing (not the kissy type).

kit[1] n. & v. —n. **1** a set of articles, equipment, or clothing needed for a specific purpose (first-aid kit; bicycle-repair kit). **2** the clothing etc. needed for any activity, esp. sport (football kit). **3** a set of all the parts needed to assemble an item, e.g. a piece of furniture, a model, etc. —v.tr. (**kitted**, **kitting**) (often foll. by out, up) equip with the appropriate clothing or tools. [ME f. MDu. kitte wooden vessel, of unkn. orig.]

kit[2] n. **1** a kitten. **2** a young fox, badger, etc. [abbr.]

kitbag /ˈkɪtbæɡ/ n. a large, usu. cylindrical bag used for carrying a soldier's, traveller's, or sportsman's equipment.

kitchen /ˈkɪtʃɪn, -tʃ(ə)n/ n. **1** the room or area where food is prepared and cooked. **2** (attrib.) of or belonging to the kitchen (kitchen knife; kitchen table). □ **kitchen cabinet** a group of unofficial advisers thought to be unduly influential. **kitchen garden** a garden where vegetables and sometimes fruit or herbs are grown. **kitchen midden** a prehistoric refuse-heap which marks an ancient settlement, chiefly containing bones, seashells, etc. **kitchen-sink** (in art forms)

depicting extreme realism, esp. drabness or sordidness (kitchen-sink school of painting; kitchen-sink drama). **kitchen tea** Austral. & NZ a party held before a wedding to which female guests bring items of kitchen equipment as presents. [OE cycene f. L coquere cook]

kitchenette /ˌkɪtʃɪˈnet, -tʃəˈnet/ n. a small kitchen or part of a room fitted as a kitchen.

kitchenware /ˈkɪtʃɪnˌweə(r), ˈkɪtʃ(ə)n-/ n. the utensils used in the kitchen.

kite n. & v. —n. **1** a toy consisting of a light framework with thin material stretched over it, flown in the wind at the end of a long string. **2** any of various soaring birds of prey esp. of the genus Milvus with long wings and usu. a forked tail. **3** Brit. sl. an aeroplane. **4** sl. a fraudulent cheque, bill, or receipt. **5** Geom. a quadrilateral figure symmetrical about one diagonal. —v. **1** intr. soar like a kite. **2** tr. (also absol.) originate or pass (fraudulent cheques, bills, or receipts). **3** tr. (also absol.) raise (money by dishonest means) (kite a loan). □ **kite-flying** fraudulent practice. [OE cȳta, of unkn. orig.]

Kitemark /ˈkaɪtmɑːk/ n. (in the UK) the official kite-shaped mark on goods approved by the British Standards Institution.

kith /kɪθ/ n. □ **kith and kin** friends and relations. [OE cȳthth f. Gmc]

kitsch /kɪtʃ/ n. (often attrib.) garish, pretentious, or sentimental art, usu. vulgar and worthless. □ **kitschy** adj. (**kitschier**, **kitschiest**). **kitschiness** n. [G]

kitten /ˈkɪt(ə)n/ n. & v. —n. **1** a young cat. **2** a young ferret etc. —v.intr. & tr. (of a cat etc.) give birth or give birth to. □ **have kittens** Brit. colloq. be extremely upset, anxious, or nervous. [ME kito(u)n, ketoun f. OF chitoun, chetoun dimin. of chat CAT]

kittenish /ˈkɪtənɪʃ/ adj. **1** like a young cat; playful and lively. **2** flirtatious. □ **kittenishly** adv. **kittenishness** n. [KITTEN]

kittiwake /ˈkɪtɪˌweɪk/ n. either of two small gulls, Rissa tridactyla and R. brevirostris, nesting on sea cliffs. [imit. of its cry]

kittle /ˈkɪt(ə)l/ adj. (also **kittle-cattle** /ˈkɪt(ə)lˌkæt(ə)l/) **1** (of a person) capricious, rash, or erratic in behaviour. **2** difficult to deal with. [ME (now Sc. & dial.) kittle tickle, prob. f. ON kitla]

kitty[1] /ˈkɪtɪ/ n. (pl. -ies) **1** a fund of money for communal use. **2** the pool in some card-games. **3** the jack in bowls. [19th c.: orig. unkn.]

kitty[2] /ˈkɪtɪ/ n. (pl. -ies) a pet-name or a child's name for a kitten or cat.

kiwi /ˈkiːwiː/ n. (pl. kiwis) **1** a flightless New Zealand bird of the genus Apteryx with hairlike feathers and a long bill. **2** (**Kiwi**) colloq. a New Zealander, esp. a soldier or member of a national sports team. □ **kiwi fruit** (or **berry**) the fruit of a climbing plant, Actinidia chinensis, having a thin hairy skin, green flesh, and black seeds. [Maori]

kJ abbr. kilojoule(s).

KKK abbr. US Ku Klux Klan.

kl abbr. kilolitre(s).

Klaxon /ˈklæks(ə)n/ n. propr. a horn or warning hooter, orig. on a motor vehicle. [name of the manufacturing company]

Kleenex /ˈkliːneks/ n. (pl. same or **Kleenexes**) orig. US propr. an absorbent disposable paper tissue, used esp. as a handkerchief.

Klein bottle /ˈklaɪn/ n. Math. a closed surface with only one side, formed by passing the neck of a tube through the side of the tube to join the hole in the base. [F. Klein, Ger. mathematician d. 1925]

kleptomania /ˌkleptəʊˈmeɪnɪə/ n. a recurrent urge to steal, usu. without regard for need or profit. □ **kleptomaniac** /-nɪˌæk/ n. & adj. [Gk kleptēs thief + -MANIA]

Klondike /ˈklɒndaɪk/ n. a source of valuable material. [Klondike in Yukon, Canada, where gold was found in 1896]

km abbr. kilometre(s).

K-meson /keɪˈmezɒn, -ˈmiːzɒn/ n. = KAON. [K (see KAON) + MESON]

kn. abbr. Naut. knot(s).

knack /næk/ n. **1** an acquired or intuitive faculty of doing a thing adroitly. **2** a trick or habit of action or speech etc. (has a knack of offending people). [ME, prob. identical with knack sharp blow or sound f. LG, ult. imit.]

knacker /ˈnækə(r)/ n. & v. Brit. —n. **1** a buyer of useless horses for slaughter. **2** a buyer of old houses, ships, etc. for the materials. —v.tr. sl. **1** kill. **2** (esp. as **knackered** adj.) exhaust, wear out. [19th c.: orig. unkn.]

knap[1] /næp/ n. chiefly dial. the crest of a hill or of rising ground. [OE cnæp(p), perh. rel. to ON knappr knob]

knap[2] /næp/ v.tr. (**knapped**, **knapping**) **1** break (stones for roads or building, flints, or Austral. ore) with a hammer. **2** archaic knock, rap, snap asunder. □ **knapper** n. [ME, imit.]

knapsack /ˈnæpsæk/ n. a soldier's or hiker's bag with shoulder-straps, carried on the back, and usu. made of canvas or weatherproof material. [MLG, prob. f. knappen bite + SACK[1]]

knapweed /ˈnæpwiːd/ n. any of various plants of the genus Centaurea, having thistle-like purple flowers. [ME, orig. knopweed f. KNOP + WEED]

knave /neɪv/ n. **1** a rogue, a scoundrel. **2** = JACK n. 2. □ **knavery** n. (pl. -ies). **knavish** adj. **knavishly** adv. **knavishness** n. [OE cnafa boy, servant, f. WG]

knead /niːd/ v.tr. **1 a** work (a yeast mixture, clay, etc.) into dough, paste, etc. by pummelling. **b** make (bread, pottery, etc.) in this way. **2** blend or weld together (kneaded them into a unified group). **3** massage (muscles etc.) as if kneading. □ **kneadable** adj. **kneader** n. [OE cnedan f. Gmc]

knee /niː/ n. & v. —n. **1 a** (often attrib.) the joint between the thigh and the lower leg in humans. **b** the corresponding joint in other animals. **c** the area around this. **d** the upper surface of the thigh of a sitting person; the lap (held her on his knee). **2** the part of a garment covering the knee. **3** anything resembling a knee in shape or position, esp. a piece of wood or iron bent at an angle, a sharp turn in a graph, etc. —v.tr. (**knees, kneed, kneeing**) **1** touch or strike with the knee (kneed the ball past him; kneed him in the groin). **2** colloq. cause (trousers) to bulge at the knee. □ **bend** (or **bow**) **the knee** kneel, esp. in submission. **bring a person to his** or **her knees** reduce a person to submission. **knee-bend** the action of bending the knee, esp. as a physical exercise in which the body is raised and lowered without the use of the hands. **knee-breeches** close-fitting trousers reaching to or just below the knee. **knee-deep 1** (usu. foll. by in) **a** immersed up to the knees. **b** deeply involved. **2** so deep as to reach the knees. **knee-high** so high as to reach the knees. **knee-hole** a space for the knees, esp. under a desk. **knee-jerk 1** a sudden involuntary kick caused by a blow on the tendon just below the knee. **2** (attrib.) predictable, automatic, stereotyped. **knee-joint 1** = senses 1a, b of n. **2** a joint made of two pieces hinged together. **knee-length** reaching the knees. **knee-pan** the kneecap. **knees-up** Brit. colloq. a lively party or gathering. **on** (or **on one's**) **bended knee** (or **knees**) kneeling, esp. in supplication, submission, or worship. [OE cnēo(w)]

kneecap /ˈniːkæp/ n. & v. —n. **1** the convex bone in front of the knee-joint. **2** a protective covering for the knee. —v.tr. (**-capped, -capping**) colloq. shoot (a person) in the knee or leg as a punishment, esp. for betraying a terrorist group. □ **kneecapping** n.

kneel /niːl/ v.intr. (past and past part. **knelt** /nelt/ or esp. US **kneeled**) fall or rest on the knees or a knee. [OE cnēowlian (as KNEE)]

kneeler /ˈniːlə(r)/ n. **1** a hassock or cushion used for kneeling, esp. in church. **2** a person who kneels.

knell /nel/ n. & v. —n. **1** the sound of a bell, esp. when rung solemnly for a death or funeral. **2** an announcement, event, etc., regarded as a solemn warning of disaster. —v. **1** intr. **a** (of a bell) ring solemnly, esp. for a death or funeral. **b** make a doleful or ominous sound. **2** tr. proclaim by or as by a knell (knelled the death of all their hopes). □ **ring the knell of** announce or herald the end of. [OE cnyll, cnyllan: perh. infl. by bell]

knelt past and past part. of KNEEL.

knew past of KNOW.

knickerbocker /ˈnɪkəˌbɒkə(r)/ n. (in pl.) loose-fitting breeches gathered at the knee or calf. □ **Knickerbocker Glory** ice-cream served with other ingredients in a tall glass. [Diedrich Knicker-bocker, pretended author of W. Irving's History of New York (1809)]

knickers /ˈnɪkəz/ n.pl. Brit. **1** a woman's or girl's undergarment covering the body from the waist or hips to the top of the thighs and having leg-holes or separate legs. **2** esp. US **a** knickerbockers. **b** a boy's short trousers. [abbr. of KNICKERBOCKER]

knick-knack /ˈnɪknæk/ n. **1** a useless and usu. worthless ornament; a trinket. **2** a small, dainty article of furniture, dress, etc. □ **knick-knackery** n. **knick-knackish** adj. [redupl. of knack in obs. sense 'trinket']

knife /naɪf/ n. & v. —n. (pl. **knives** /naɪvz/) **1 a** a metal blade used as a cutting tool with usu. one long sharp edge fixed rigidly in a handle or hinged. **b** a similar tool used as a weapon. **2** a cutting-blade forming part of a machine. **3** (as **the knife**) a surgical operation or operations. —v.tr. **1** cut or stab with a knife. **2** sl. bring about the defeat of (a person) by underhand means. □ **at knife-point** threatened with a knife or an ultimatum etc. **before you can say knife** colloq. very quickly or suddenly. **get one's knife into** treat maliciously or vindictively, persecute. **knife-board** a board on which knives are cleaned. **knife-edge 1** the edge of a knife. **2** a position of extreme danger or uncertainty. **3** a steel wedge on which a pendulum etc. oscillates. **4** = ARÊTE. **knife-pleat** a narrow flat pleat on a skirt etc., usu. overlapping another. **knife-rest** a metal or glass support for a carving-knife or -fork at table. **knife-throwing** a circus etc. act in which knives are thrown at targets. **that one could cut with a knife** *colloq.* (of an accent, atmosphere, etc.) very obvious, oppressive, etc. □ **knifelike** *adj.* **knifer** *n.* [OE *cnif* f. ON *knifr* f. Gmc]

knight /naɪt/ *n. & v. —n.* **1** a man awarded a non-hereditary title (*Sir*) by a sovereign in recognition of merit or service. **2** *hist.* **a** a man, usu. noble, raised esp. by a sovereign to honourable military rank after service as a page and squire. **b** a military follower or attendant, esp. of a lady as her champion in a war or tournament. **3** *Chess* a piece usu. shaped like a horse's head. *—v.tr.* confer a knighthood on. □ **knight errant 1** a medieval knight wandering in search of chivalrous adventures. **2** a man of a chivalrous or quixotic nature. **knight-errantry** the practice or conduct of a knight errant. **Knight Hospitaller** (*pl.* **Knights Hospitaller**) a member of an order of monks with a military history, founded at Jerusalem *c*.1050. **Knight Templar** (*pl.* **Knights Templar**) a member of a religious and military order for the protection of pilgrims to the Holy Land, suppressed in 1312. □ **knighthood** *n.* **knightlike** *adj.* **knightly** *adj. & adv. poet.* **knightliness** *n.* [OE *cniht* boy, youth, hero f. WG]

knit /nɪt/ *v. & n. —v.* (**knitting**; *past and past part.* **knitted** or (esp. in senses 2–4) **knit**) **1** *tr.* (also *absol.*) **a** make (a garment, blanket, etc.) by interlocking loops of esp. wool with knitting-needles. **b** make (a garment etc.) with a knitting machine. **c** make (a plain stitch) in knitting (*knit one, purl one*). **2 a** *tr.* contract (the forehead) in vertical wrinkles. **b** *intr.* (of the forehead) contract; frown. **3** *tr. & intr.* (often foll. by *together*) make or become close or compact esp. by common interests etc. (*a close-knit group*). **4** *intr.* (often foll. by *together*) (of parts of a broken bone) become joined; heal. *—n.* knitted material or a knitted garment. □ **knit up 1** make or repair by knitting. **2** conclude, finish, or end. □ **knitter** *n.* [OE *cnyttan* f. WG: cf. KNOT¹]

knitting /ˈnɪtɪŋ/ *n.* **1** a garment etc. in the process of being knitted. **2 a** the act of knitting. **b** an instance of this. □ **knitting-machine** a machine used for mechanically knitting garments etc. **knitting-needle** a thin pointed rod of steel, wood, plastic, etc., used esp. in pairs for knitting.

knitwear /ˈnɪtweə(r)/ *n.* knitted garments.

knives *pl.* of KNIFE.

knob /nɒb/ *n. & v. —n.* **1 a** a rounded protuberance, esp. at the end or on the surface of a thing. **b** a handle of a door, drawer, etc., shaped like a knob. **c** a knob-shaped attachment for pulling, turning, etc. (*press the knob under the desk*). **2** a small, usu. round, piece (of butter, coal, sugar, etc.). *—v.* (**knobbed, knobbing**) **1** *tr.* provide with knobs. **2** *intr.* (usu. foll. by *out*) bulge. □ **with knobs on** *Brit. sl.* that and more (used as a retort to an insult, in emphatic agreement, etc.) (*and the same to you with knobs on*). □ **knobby** *adj.* **knoblike** *adj.* [ME f. MLG *knobbe* knot, knob, bud: cf. KNOP, NOB², NUB]

knobble /ˈnɒb(ə)l/ *n.* a small knob. □ **knobbly** *adj.* [ME, dimin. of KNOB: cf. Du. & LG *knobbel*]

knobkerrie /ˈnɒbˌkerɪ/ *n.* a short stick with a knobbed head used as a weapon esp. by S. African tribes. [after Afrik. *knopkierie*]

knock /nɒk/ *v. & n. —v.* **1 a** *tr.* strike (a hard surface) with an audible sharp blow (*knocked the table three times*). **b** *intr.* strike, esp. a door to gain admittance (*can you hear someone knocking?*; *knocked at the door*). **2** *tr.* make (a hole, a dent, etc.) by knocking (*knock a hole in the fence*). **3** *tr.* (usu. foll. by *in, out, off,* etc.) drive (a thing, a person, etc.) by striking (*knocked the ball into the hole*; *knocked those ideas out of his head*; *knocked her hand away*). **4** *tr. sl.* criticize. **5** *intr.* **a** (of a motor or other engine) make a thumping or rattling noise esp. as the result of a loose bearing. **b** = PINK³. **6** *tr. Brit. sl.* make a strong impression on, astonish. *—n.* **1** an act of knocking. **2** a sharp rap, esp. at a door. **3** an audible sharp blow. **4** the sound of knocking in esp. a motor engine. □ **knock about** (or **around**) **1** strike repeatedly; treat roughly (*knocked her about*). **2** lead a wandering adventurous life; wander aimlessly. **3** be present without design or volition (*there's a cup knocking about somewhere*). **4** (usu. foll. by *with*) be associated socially (*knocks about with his brother*). **knock against 1** collide with. **2** come across casually. **knock back 1** *Brit. sl.* eat or drink, esp. quickly. **2** *Brit. sl.* disconcert. **3** *Austral. & NZ colloq.* refuse, rebuff. **knock down 1** strike (esp. a person) to the ground with a blow. **2** demolish. **3** (usu. foll. by *to*) (at an auction) dispose of (an article) to a bidder by a knock with a hammer (*knocked the Picasso down to him for a million*). **4** *colloq.* lower the price of (an article). **5** take (machinery, furniture, etc.) to pieces for transportation. **knock-down** *attrib.adj.* **1** (of a blow, misfortune, argument, etc.) overwhelming. **2** *Brit.* (of a price) very low. **3** (of a price at auction) reserve. **4** (of furniture etc.) easily dismantled and reassembled. *—n. Austral. & NZ sl.* an introduction (to a person). **knock for knock agreement** an agreement between insurance companies by which each pays its own policyholder regardless of liability. **knock one's head against** come into collision with (unfavourable facts or conditions). **knocking-shop** *Brit. sl.* a brothel. **knock into the middle of next week** *colloq.* send (a person) flying, esp. with a blow. **knock-kneed** having knock knees. **knock knees** an abnormal condition with the legs curved inwards at the knee. **knock off 1** strike off with a blow. **2** *colloq.* **a** finish work (*knocked off at 5.30*). **b** finish (work) (*knocked off work early*). **3** *colloq.* dispatch (business). **4** *colloq.* rapidly produce (a work of art, verses, etc.). **5** (often foll. by *from*) deduct (a sum) from a price, bill, etc. **6** *sl.* steal. **7** *Brit. coarse sl. offens.* have sexual intercourse with (a woman). **8** *sl.* kill. **knock on** *Rugby Football* drive (a ball) with the hand or arm towards the opponents' goal-line. **knock-on** *n.* an act of knocking on. **knock-on effect** a secondary, indirect, or cumulative effect. **knock on the head 1** stun or kill (a person) by a blow on the head. **2** *colloq.* put an end to (a scheme etc.). **knock on** (or **knock**) **wood** *US* = touch wood. **knock out 1** make (a person) unconscious by a blow on the head. **2** knock down (a boxer) for a count of 10, thereby winning the contest. **3** defeat, esp. in a knockout competition. **4** *sl.* astonish. **5** (*refl.*) *colloq.* exhaust (*knocked themselves out swimming*). **6** *colloq.* make or write (a plan etc.) hastily. **7** empty (a tobacco-pipe) by tapping. **8** *Austral., NZ, & US sl.* earn. **knock sideways** *colloq.* disconcert; astonish. **knock spots off** defeat easily. **knock together** put together or assemble hastily or roughly. **knock under** submit. **knock up 1** make or arrange hastily. **2** drive upwards with a blow. **3** **a** become exhausted or ill. **b** exhaust or make ill. **4** *Brit.* arouse (a person) by a knock at the door. **5** *Cricket* score (runs) rapidly. **6** esp. *US sl.* make pregnant. **7** practise a ball game before formal play begins. **knock-up** *n.* a practice at tennis etc. **take a** (or **the**) **knock** be hard hit financially or emotionally. [ME f. OE *cnocian*: prob. imit.]

knockabout /ˈnɒkəˌbaʊt/ *adj. & n.* —*attrib.adj.* **1** (of comedy) boisterous; slapstick. **2** (of clothes) suitable for rough use. **3** *Austral.* of a farm or station handyman. —*n.* **1** *Austral.* a farm or station handyman. **2** a knockabout performer or performance.

knocker /ˈnɒkə(r)/ *n.* **1** a metal or wooden instrument hinged to a door for knocking to call attention. **2** a person or thing that knocks. **3** (in *pl.*) *coarse sl.* a woman's breasts. **4** a person who buys or sells door to door. □ **on the knocker 1 a** (buying or selling) from door to door. **b** (obtained) on credit. **2** *Austral. & NZ colloq.* promptly.

knockout /ˈnɒkaʊt/ *n.* **1** the act of making unconscious by a blow. **2** *Boxing* etc. a blow that knocks an opponent out. **3** a competition in which the loser in each round is eliminated (also *attrib.*: *a knockout round*). **4** *colloq.* an outstanding or irresistible person or thing. □ **knockout drops** a drug added to a drink to cause unconsciousness.

knoll /nəʊl/ *n.* a small hill or mound. [OE *cnoll* hilltop, rel. to MDu., MHG *knolle* clod, ON *knollr* hilltop]

knop /nɒp/ *n.* **1** a knob, esp. ornamental. **2** an ornamental loop or tuft in yarn. [ME f. MLG, MDu. *knoppe*]

knot[1] /nɒt/ *n. & v.* —*n.* **1 a** an intertwining of a rope, string, tress of hair, etc., with another, itself, or something else to join or fasten together. **b** a set method of tying a knot (*a reef knot*). **c** a ribbon etc. tied as an ornament and worn on a dress etc. **d** a tangle in hair, knitting, etc. **2 a** a unit of a ship's or aircraft's speed equivalent to one nautical mile per hour. **b** *colloq.* a nautical mile. **3** (usu. foll. by *of*) a group or cluster (*a small knot of journalists at the gate*). **4** something forming or maintaining a union; a bond or tie, esp. of wedlock. **5** a hard lump of tissue in an animal or human body. **6 a** a knob or protuberance in a stem, branch, or root. **b** a hard mass formed in a tree trunk at the intersection with a branch. **c** a round cross-grained piece in timber where a branch has been cut through. **d** a node on the stem of a plant. **7** a difficulty; a problem. **8** a central point in a problem or the plot of a story etc. —*v.* (**knotted, knotting**) **1** *tr.* tie (a string etc.) in a knot. **2** *tr.* entangle. **3** *tr.* knit (the brows). **4** *tr.* unite closely or intricately (*knotted together in intrigue*). **5 a** *intr.* make knots for fringing. **b** *tr.* make (a fringe) with knots. □ **at a rate of knots** *colloq.* very fast. **get knotted!** *sl.* an expression of disbelief, annoyance, etc. **knot-garden** an intricately designed formal garden. **knot-hole**

a hole in a piece of timber where a knot has fallen out (sense 6). **tie in knots** *colloq.* baffle or confuse completely. □ **knotless** *adj.* **knotter** *n.* **knotting** *n.* (esp. in sense 5 of *v.*). [ME *cnotta* f. WG]

knot[2] /nɒt/ *n.* a small sandpiper, *Calidris canutus*. [ME: orig. unkn.]

knotty /ˈnɒtɪ/ *adj.* (**knottier, knottiest**) **1** full of knots. **2** hard to explain; puzzling (*a knotty problem*). □ **knottily** *adv.* **knottiness** *n.*

knotwork /ˈnɒtwɜːk/ *n.* ornamental work representing or consisting of intertwined cords.

know /nəʊ/ *v. & n.* —*v.* (*past* **knew** /njuː/; *past part.* **known** /nəʊn/) **1** *tr.* (often foll. by *that, how, what,* etc.) **a** have in the mind; have learnt; be able to recall (*knows a lot about cars; knows what to do*). **b** (also *absol.*) be aware of (a fact) (*he knows I am waiting; I think he knows*). **c** have a good command of (a subject or language) (*knew German; knows his tables*). **2** *tr.* be acquainted or friendly with (a person or thing). **3** *tr.* **a** recognize; identify (*I knew him at once; knew him for an American*). **b** (foll. by *to* + infin.) be aware of (a person or thing) as being or doing what is specified (*knew them to be rogues*). **c** (foll. by *from*) be able to distinguish (one from another) (*did not know him from Adam*). **4** *tr.* be subject to (*her joy knew no bounds*). **5** *tr.* have personal experience of (fear etc.). **6** *tr.* (as **known** *adj.*) **a** publicly acknowledged (*a known thief; a known fact*). **b** *Math.* (of a quantity etc.) having a value that can be stated. **7** *intr.* have understanding or knowledge. **8** *tr. archaic* have sexual intercourse with. —*n.* (in phr. **in the know**) *colloq.* well-informed; having special knowledge. □ **be not to know 1** have no way of learning (*wasn't to know they'd arrive late*). **2** be not to be told (*she's not to know about the party*). **don't I know it!** *colloq.* an expression of rueful assent. **don't you know** *colloq.* or *joc.* an expression used for emphasis (*such a bore, don't you know*). **for all** (or **aught**) **I know** so far as my knowledge extends. **have been known to** be known to have done (*they have been known to not turn up*). **I knew it!** I was sure that this would happen. **I know what** I have a new idea, suggestion, etc. **know about** have information about. **know-all** *colloq.* a person who seems to know everything. **know best** be or claim to be better informed etc. than others. **know better than** (foll. by *that,* or *to* + infin.) be wise, well-informed, or well-mannered enough to avoid (specified behaviour etc.). **know by name 1** have heard the name of. **2** be able to give the name of. **know by sight** recognize the appearance (only) of. **know how** know the way to do something. **know-how** *n.* **1** practical knowledge; technique, expertise. **2** natural skill or invention. **know-it-all** = *know-all.* **know-nothing 1** an ignorant person. **2** an agnostic. **know of** be aware of; have heard of (*not that I know of*). **know one's own mind** be decisive, not vacillate. **know the ropes** (or **one's stuff**) be fully knowledgeable or experienced. **know a thing or two** be experienced or shrewd. **know what's what** have adequate knowledge of the world, life, etc. **know who's who** be aware of who or what each person is. **not if I know it** only against my will. **not know that . . .** *colloq.* be fairly sure that . . . not (*I don't know that I want to go*). **not want to know** refuse to take any notice of. **what do you know** (or **know**

about that)? *colloq.* an expression of surprise. **you know something** (or **what)?** I am going to tell you something. **you-know-what** (or **-who)** a thing or person unspecified but understood. **you never know** nothing in the future is certain. □ **knowable** *adj.* **knower** *n.* [OE *(ge)cnāwan*, rel. to CAN¹, KEN]

knowing /ˈnəʊɪŋ/ *n.* & *adj.* —*n.* the state of being aware or informed of any thing. —*adj.* **1** usu. *derog.* cunning; sly. **2** showing knowledge; shrewd. □ **there is no knowing** no one can tell. □ **knowingness** *n.*

knowingly /ˈnəʊɪŋlɪ/ *adv.* **1** consciously; intentionally (*had never knowingly injured him*). **2** in a knowing manner (*smiled knowingly*).

knowledge /ˈnɒlɪdʒ/ *n.* **1 a** (usu. foll. by *of*) awareness or familiarity gained by experience (of a person, fact, or thing) (*have no knowledge of that*). **b** a person's range of information (*is not within his knowledge*). **2 a** (usu. foll. by *of*) a theoretical or practical understanding of a subject, language, etc. (*has a good knowledge of Greek*). **b** the sum of what is known (*every branch of knowledge*). **3** *Philos.* true, justified belief; certain knowledge, as opp. to opinion. **4** = *carnal knowledge*. □ **come to one's knowledge** become known to one. **to my knowledge** **1** so far as I know. **2** as I know for certain. [ME *knaulege*, with earlier *knawlechen* (v.) formed as KNOW + OE -*lǣcan* f. *lāc* as in WEDLOCK]

knowledgeable /ˈnɒlɪdʒəb(ə)l/ *adj.* (also **knowledgable**) well-informed; intelligent. □ **knowledgeability** /-ˈbɪlɪtɪ/ *n.* **knowledgeableness** *n.* **knowledgeably** *adv.*

known *past part.* of KNOW.

knuckle /ˈnʌk(ə)l/ *n.* & *v.* —*n.* **1** the bone at a finger-joint, esp. that adjoining the hand. **2 a** a projection of the carpal or tarsal joint of a quadruped. **b** a joint of meat consisting of this with the adjoining parts, esp. of bacon or pork. —*v.tr.* strike, press, or rub with the knuckles. □ **knuckle-bone 1** bone forming a knuckle. **2** the bone of a sheep or other animal corresponding to or resembling a knuckle. **3** a knuckle of meat. **knuckle-bones 1** animal knuckle-bones used in the game of jacks. **2** the game of jacks. **knuckle down** (often foll. by *to*) **1** apply oneself seriously (to a task etc.). **2** (also **knuckle under**) give in; submit. □ **knuckly** *adj.* [ME *knokel* f. MLG, MDu. *knökel*, dimin. of *knoke* bone]

knuckleduster /ˈnʌk(ə)lˌdʌstə(r)/ *n.* a metal guard worn over the knuckles in fighting, esp. to increase the effect of the blows.

knurl /nɜːl/ *n.* a small projecting knob, ridge, etc. □ **knurled** /nɜːld/ *adj.* [rel. to MHG *knorre* knobbed protuberance]

KO *abbr.* **1** knockout. **2** kick-off.

koala /kəʊˈɑːlə/ *n.* (in full **koala bear**) an Australian bearlike marsupial, *Phascolarctos cinereus*, having thick grey fur and feeding on eucalyptus leaves. [Aboriginal *kūl(l)a*]

Köchel number /ˈkɜːx(ə)l/ *n.* *Mus.* a number given to each of Mozart's compositions in the complete catalogue of his works compiled by Köchel and his successors. [L. von Köchel, Austrian scientist d. 1877]

KO'd /keɪˈəʊd/ *adj.* knocked out. [abbr.]

kohl /kəʊl/ *n.* a black powder, usu. antimony sulphide or lead sulphide, used as eye make-up esp. in Eastern countries. [Arab. *kuḥl*]

kohlrabi /kəʊlˈrɑːbɪ/ *n.* (pl. **kohlrabies**) a variety of cabbage with an edible turnip-like swollen stem. [G f. It. *cavoli rape* (pl.) f. med.L *caulorapa* (as COLE, RAPE²)]

kola var. of COLA.

kook /kuːk/ *n.* & *adj.* *US sl.* —*n.* a crazy or eccentric person. —*adj.* crazy; eccentric. [20th c.: prob. f. CUCKOO]

kookaburra /ˈkʊkəˌbʌrə/ *n.* any Australian kingfisher of the genus *Dacelo*, esp. *D. novaeguineae*, which makes a strange laughing cry. [Aboriginal]

kooky /ˈkuːkɪ/ *adj.* (**kookier, kookiest**) *sl.* crazy. □ **kookily** *adv.* **kookiness** *n.*

kopek (also **kopeck**) var. of COPECK.

koppie /ˈkɒpɪ/ *n.* (also **kopje**) *S.Afr.* a small hill. [Afrik. *koppie*, Du. *kopje*, dimin. of *kop* head]

Koran /kɔːˈrɑːn, kə-/ *n.* (also **Qur'an** /kə-/) the Islamic sacred book, believed to be the word of God as dictated to Muhammad and written down in Arabic. □ **Koranic** /-ˈrænɪk, -ˈrɑːnɪk/ *adj.* [Arab. *ḳur'ān* recitation f. *ḳara'a* read]

korfball /ˈkɔːfbɔːl/ *n.* a game like basketball played by two teams consisting of 6 men and 6 women each. [Du. *korfbal* f. *korf* basket + *bal* ball]

kosher /ˈkəʊʃə(r), ˈkɒʃ-/ *adj.* & *n.* —*adj.* **1** (of food or premises in which food is sold, cooked, or eaten) fulfilling the requirements of Jewish law. **2** *colloq.* correct; genuine; legitimate. —*n.* **1** kosher food. **2** a kosher shop. [Heb. *kāšēr* proper]

kowhai /ˈkəʊwaɪ/ *n.* any of several trees or shrubs of the genus *Sophora*, esp. *S. microphylla* native to New Zealand, with pendant clusters of yellow flowers. [Maori]

kowtow /kaʊˈtaʊ/ *n.* & *v.* (also **kotow** /kəʊˈtaʊ/) —*n.* *hist.* the Chinese custom of kneeling and touching the ground with the forehead in worship or submission. —*v.intr.* **1** *hist.* perform the kowtow. **2** (usu. foll. by *to*) act obsequiously. [Chin. *ketou* f. *ke* knock + *tou* head]

KP *n.* *US Mil.* *colloq.* **1** enlisted men detailed to help the cooks. **2** kitchen duty. [abbr. of *kitchen police*]

k.p.h. *abbr.* kilometres per hour.

Kr *symb.* *Chem.* the element krypton.

kraal /krɑːl/ *n.* *S.Afr.* **1** a village of huts enclosed by a fence. **2** an enclosure for cattle or sheep. [Afrik. f. Port. *curral*, of Hottentot orig.]

kraft /krɑːft/ *n.* (in full **kraft paper**) a kind of strong smooth brown wrapping paper. [G f. Sw. = strength]

kraken /ˈkrɑːkən/ *n.* a large mythical sea-monster said to appear off the coast of Norway. [Norw.]

kremlin /ˈkremlɪn/ *n.* **1** a citadel within a Russian town. **2** (**the Kremlin**) **a** the citadel in Moscow. **b** the former USSR Government housed within it. [F, f. Russ. *Kreml'*, of Tartar orig.]

kriegspiel /ˈkriːɡspiːl/ *n.* **1** a war-game in which blocks representing armies etc. are moved about on maps. **2** a form of chess with an umpire, in which each player has only limited information about the opponent's moves. [G f. *Krieg* war + *Spiel* game]

krill /krɪl/ *n.* tiny planktonic crustaceans found in the seas around the Antarctic and eaten by baleen whales. [Norw.]

kris /kriːs/ *n.* a Malay or Indonesian dagger with a wavy blade. [ult. f. Malay *k(i)rīs*]

krona /ˈkrəʊnə/ n. **1** (pl. **kronor** /ˈkrəʊnə(r)/) the chief monetary unit of Sweden. **2** (pl. **kronur** /ˈkrəʊnə(r)/) the chief monetary unit of Iceland. [Sw. & Icel., = CROWN]

krone /ˈkrəʊnə/ n. (pl. **kroner** /ˈkrəʊnə(r)/) the chief monetary unit of Denmark and of Norway. [Da. & Norw., = CROWN]

krugerrand /ˈkruːgəˌrænd, -ˌrɑːnt/ n. a S. African gold coin depicting President Kruger. [S. J. P. *Kruger*, S. Afr. statesman d. 1904, + RAND]

krypton /ˈkrɪptɒn/ n. *Chem.* an inert gaseous element of the noble gas group, forming a small portion of the earth's atmosphere and used in fluorescent lamps etc. [Gk *krupton* hidden, neut. adj. f. *kruptō* hide]

Kt. *abbr.* Knight.

kt. *abbr.* knot.

Ku *symb. Chem.* the element kurchatovium.

kudos /ˈkjuːdɒs/ n. *colloq.* glory; renown. [Gk]

Kufic /ˈkjuːfɪk/ n. & adj. (also **Cufic**) —n. an early angular form of the Arabic alphabet found chiefly in decorative inscriptions. —adj. of or in this type of script. [*Cufa*, a city S. of Baghdad in Iraq]

Ku Klux Klan /ˌkuːklʌksˈklæn, ˌkjuː-/ n. a secret society of White people in the southern States of the US, orig. formed after the Civil War and dedicated to persecuting and terrorizing Blacks. □ **Ku Klux Klansman** n. (pl. **-men**). [perh. f. Gk *kuklos* circle + CLAN]

kukri /ˈkʊkrɪ/ n. (pl. **kukris**) a curved knife broadening towards the point, used by Gurkhas. [Hindi *kukrī*]

kumara /ˈkuːmərə/ n. *NZ* a sweet potato. [Maori]

kümmel /ˈkʊm(ə)l/ n. a sweet liqueur flavoured with caraway and cumin seeds. [G (as CUMIN)]

kumquat /ˈkʌmkwɒt/ n. (also **cumquat**) **1** an orange-like fruit with a sweet rind and acid pulp, used in preserves. **2** any shrub or small tree of the genus *Fortunella* yielding this. [Cantonese var. of Chin. *kin kü* golden orange]

kung fu /kʊŋ ˈfuː, kʌŋ/ n. the Chinese form of karate. [Chin. *gongfu* f. *gong* merit + *fu* master]

kurchatovium /ˌkɜːtʃəˈtəʊvɪəm/ n. *Chem.* = RUTHERFORDIUM. [I. V. *Kurchatov*, Russ. physicist d. 1960]

kursaal /ˈkʊəzɑːl/ n. **1** a building for the use of visitors at a health resort, esp. at a German spa. **2** a casino. [G f. *Kur* CURE + *Saal* room]

kurta /ˈkɜːtə/ n. (also **kurtha**) a loose shirt or tunic worn by esp. Hindu men and women. [Hind.]

kV *abbr.* kilovolt(s).

kW *abbr.* kilowatt(s).

KWAC /kwæk/ n. *Computing* etc. keyword and context. [abbr.]

kWh *abbr.* kilowatt-hour(s).

KWIC /kwɪk/ n. *Computing* etc. keyword in context. [abbr.]

KWOC /kwɒk/ n. *Computing* etc. keyword out of context. [abbr.]

kybosh var. of KIBOSH.

kyle /kaɪl/ n. (in Scotland) a narrow channel between islands or between an island and the mainland. [Gael. *caol* strait]

kylie /ˈkaɪlɪ/ n. *W. Austral.* a boomerang. [Aboriginal]

Ll

L¹ /el/ n. (also **l**) (pl. **Ls** or **L's**) **1** the twelfth letter of the alphabet. **2** (as a Roman numeral) 50. **3** a thing shaped like an L, esp. a joint connecting two pipes at right angles.

L² abbr. (also **L.**) **1** Lake. **2** Brit. learner driver (cf. L-PLATE). **3** Liberal. **4** Licentiate.

l abbr. (also **l.**) **1** left. **2** line. **3** litre(s). **4** length.

£ abbr. (preceding a numeral) pound or pounds (of money). [L libra]

La symb. Chem. the element lanthanum.

la var. of LAH.

laager /ˈlɑːɡə(r)/ n. & v. —n. **1** esp. S.Afr. a camp or encampment, esp. formed by a circle of wagons. **2** Mil. a park for armoured vehicles. —v. **1** tr. **a** form (vehicles) into a laager. **b** encamp (people) in a laager. **2** intr. encamp. [Afrik. f. Du. leger camp, rel. to LAIR¹]

Lab. abbr. Labour.

lab /læb/ n. colloq. a laboratory. [abbr.]

label /ˈleɪb(ə)l/ n. & v. —n. **1** a usu. small piece of paper, card, linen, metal, etc., for attaching to an object and giving its name, information about it, instructions for use, etc. **2** esp. derog. a short classifying phrase or name applied to a person, a work of art, etc. **3 a** a small fabric label sewn into a garment bearing the maker's name. **b** the logo, title, or trademark of esp. a fashion or recording company (brought it out under his own label). **c** the piece of paper in the centre of a gramophone record describing its contents etc. **4** an adhesive stamp on a parcel etc. **5** a word placed before, after, or in the course of a dictionary definition etc. to specify its subject, register, nationality, etc. —v.tr. (**labelled, labelling**) **1** attach a label to. **2** (usu. foll. by as) assign to a category (labelled them as irresponsible). **3 a** replace (an atom) by an atom of a usu. radioactive isotope as a means of identification. **b** replace an atom in (a molecule) or atoms in the molecules of (a substance). **4** (as **labelled** adj.) made identifiable by the replacement of atoms. □ **labeller** n. [ME f. OF, = ribbon, prob. f. Gmc (as LAP¹)]

labia pl. of LABIUM.

labial /ˈleɪbɪəl/ adj. & n. —adj. **1 a** of the lips. **b** Zool. of, like, or serving as a lip, a liplike part, or a labium. **2** Phonet. (of a sound) requiring partial or complete closure of the lips (e.g. p, b, f, v, m, w; and vowels in which lips are rounded, e.g. oo in moon). —n. Phonet. a labial sound. □ **labialism** n. **labialize** v.tr. (also **-ise**). **labially** adv. [med.L labialis f. L labia lips]

labiate /ˈleɪbɪət/ n. & adj. —n. any plant of the family Labiatae, including mint and rosemary. —adj. **1** Bot. of or relating to the Labiatae. **2** Bot. & Zool. like a lip or labium. [mod.L labiatus (as LABIUM)]

labium /ˈleɪbɪəm/ n. (pl. **labia** /-bɪə/) (usu. in pl.) Anat. each of the two pairs of skin folds that enclose the vulva. [L, = lip]

labor etc. US & Austral. var. of LABOUR etc.

laboratory /ləˈbɒrətərɪ/ n. (pl. **-ies**) a room or building fitted out for scientific experiments, research, teaching, or the manufacture of drugs and chemicals. [med.L laboratorium f. L laborare LABOUR]

laborious /ləˈbɔːrɪəs/ adj. **1** needing hard work or toil (a laborious task). **2** (esp. of literary style) showing signs of toil; pedestrian; not fluent. □ **laboriously** adv. **laboriousness** n. [ME f. OF laborieus f. L laboriosus (as LABOUR)]

labour /ˈleɪbə(r)/ n. & v. (US, Austral. **labor**) —n. **1 a** physical or mental work; exertion; toil. **b** such work considered as supplying the needs of a community. **2 a** workers, esp. manual, considered as a class or political force. **b** (**Labour**) the Labour Party. **3** the process of childbirth, esp. the period from the start of uterine contractions to delivery. **4** a particular task, esp. of a difficult nature. —v. **1** intr. work hard; exert oneself. **2** intr. (usu. foll. by for, or to + infin.) strive for a purpose (laboured to fulfil his promise). **3** tr. **a** treat at excessive length; elaborate needlessly (I will not labour the point). **b** (as **laboured** adj.) done with great effort; not spontaneous or fluent. **4** intr. (often foll. by under) suffer under (a disadvantage or delusion) (laboured under universal disapproval). **5** intr. proceed with trouble or difficulty (laboured slowly up the hill). □ **labour camp** a prison camp enforcing a regime of hard labour. **Labour Day** May 1 (or in the US and Canada the first Monday in September), celebrated in honour of working people. **Labour Exchange** Brit. colloq. or hist. an employment exchange; a jobcentre. **labour force** the body of workers employed, esp. at a single plant. **labour-intensive** (of a form of work) needing a large work force. **labour-market** the supply of labour with reference to the demand on it. **labour of love** a task done for pleasure, not reward. **Labour Party 1** a British political party formed to represent the interests of ordinary working people. **2** any similar political party in other countries. **labour-saving** (of an appliance etc.) designed to reduce or eliminate work. **labour union** US a trade union. [ME f. OF labo(u)r, labourer f. L labor, -oris, laborare]

labourer /ˈleɪbərə(r)/ n. (US **laborer**) **1** a person doing unskilled, usu. manual, work for wages. **2** a person who labours. [ME f. OF laboureur (as LABOUR)]

Labrador /ˈlæbrədɔː(r)/ n. (in full **Labrador dog** or **retriever**) **1** a retriever of a breed with a black or golden coat often used as a gun dog or as a guide for a blind person. **2** this breed. [Labrador in Canada]

laburnum /ləˈbɜːnəm/ n. any small tree of the genus Laburnum with racemes of golden flowers yielding poisonous seeds. [L]

labyrinth /ˈlæbərɪnθ/ n. **1** a complicated irregular network of passages or paths etc.; a maze. **2** an intricate or tangled arrangement. □ **labyrinthian** /-ˈrɪnθɪən/ adj. **labyrinthine** /-ˈrɪnθaɪn/ adj. [F labyrinthe or L labyrinthus f. Gk laburinthos]

LAC abbr. Leading Aircraftman.

lac[1] n. a resinous substance secreted as a protective covering by the lac insect, and used to make varnish and shellac. □ **lac insect** an Asian scale insect, Laccifer lacca, living in trees. [ult. f. Hind. lākh f. Prakrit lakkha f. Skr. lākṣā]

lac[2] var. of LAKH.

lace n. & v. —n. **1** a fine open fabric, esp. of cotton or silk, made by weaving thread in patterns and used esp. to trim blouses, underwear, etc. **2** a cord or leather strip passed through eyelets or hooks on opposite sides of a shoe, corsets, etc., pulled tight and fastened. **3** braid used for trimming esp. dress uniform (gold lace). —v. **1** tr. (usu. foll. by up) **a** fasten or tighten (a shoe, corsets, etc.) with a lace or laces. **b** compress the waist of (a person) with a laced corset. **2** tr. flavour or fortify (coffee, beer, etc.) with a dash of spirits. **3** tr. (usu. foll. by with) **a** streak (a sky etc.) with colour (cheek laced with blood). **b** interlace or embroider (fabric) with thread etc. **4** tr. (often foll. by through) pass (a shoelace etc.) through. □ **lace-up** —n. a shoe fastened with a lace. —attrib.adj. (of a shoe etc.) fastened by a lace or laces. [ME f. OF laz, las, lacier ult. f. L laqueus noose]

lacemaker /ˈleɪsˌmeɪkə(r)/ n. a person who makes lace, esp. professionally. □ **lacemaking** n.

lacerate /ˈlæsəˌreɪt/ v.tr. **1** mangle or tear (esp. flesh or tissue). **2** distress or cause pain to (the feelings, the heart, etc.). □ **lacerable** adj. **laceration** /-ˈreɪʃ(ə)n/ n. [L lacerare f. lacer torn]

lachrymal /ˈlækrɪm(ə)l/ adj. (also **lacrimal**, **lacrymal**) —adj. **1** literary of or for tears. **2** (usu. as **lacrimal**) Anat. concerned in the secretion of tears (lacrimal canal; lacrimal duct). [ME f. med.L lachrymalis f. L lacrima tear]

lachrymation /ˌlækrɪˈmeɪʃ(ə)n/ n. (also **lacrimation**, **lacrymation**) formal the flow of tears. [L lacrimatio f. lacrimare weep (as LACHRYMAL)]

lachrymatory /ˈlækrɪmətərɪ/ adj. formal of or causing tears.

lachrymose /ˈlækrɪˌməʊs/ adj. formal given to weeping; tearful. □ **lachrymosely** adv. [L lacrimosus f. lacrima tear]

lacing /ˈleɪsɪŋ/ n. **1** lace trimming, esp. on a uniform. **2** a laced fastening on a shoe or corsets. **3** a dash of spirits in a beverage.

lack n. & v. —n. (usu. foll. by of) an absence, want, or deficiency (a lack of talent; felt the lack of warmth). —v.tr. be without or deficient in (lacks courage). □ **for lack of** owing to the absence of (went hungry for lack of money). **lack for** lack. [ME lac, lacen, corresp. to MDu., MLG lak deficiency, MDu. laken to lack]

lackadaisical /ˌlækəˈdeɪzɪk(ə)l/ adj. **1** unenthusiastic; listless; idle. **2** feebly sentimental and affected. □ **lackadaisically** adv. **lackadaisicalness** n. [archaic lackaday, -daisy (int.): see ALACK]

lackey /ˈlækɪ/ n. (also **lacquey**) (pl. **-eys**) **1** derog. **a** a servile political follower. **b** an obsequious parasitical person. **2 a** a (usu. liveried) footman or manservant. **b** a servant. [F laquais, obs. alaquais f. Cat. alacay = Sp. ALCALDE]

lacking /ˈlækɪŋ/ adj. **1** absent or deficient (money was lacking; is lacking in determination). **2** colloq. deficient in intellect; mentally subnormal.

lacklustre /ˈlækˌlʌstə(r)/ adj. (US **lackluster**) **1** lacking in vitality, force, or conviction. **2** (of the eye) dull.

laconic /ləˈkɒnɪk/ adj. **1** (of a style of speech or writing) brief; concise; terse. **2** (of a person) laconic in speech etc. □ **laconically** adv. **laconicism** /-ɪˌsɪz(ə)m/ n. [L f. Gk Lakōnikos f. Lakōn Spartan, the Spartans being known for their terse speech]

laconism /ˈlækəˌnɪz(ə)m/ n. **1** brevity of speech. **2** a short pithy saying. [Gk lakōnismos f. lakōnizō behave like a Spartan: see LACONIC]

lacquer /ˈlækə(r)/ n. & v. (also **lacker**) —n. **1** a sometimes coloured liquid made of shellac dissolved in alcohol, or of synthetic substances, that dries to form a hard protective coating for wood, brass, etc. **2** a chemical substance sprayed on hair to keep it in place. **3** the sap of the lacquer-tree used to varnish wood etc. —v.tr. coat with lacquer. □ **lacquer-tree** an E. Asian tree, Rhus verniciflua, the sap of which is used as a hard-wearing varnish for wood. □ **lacquerer** n. [obs. F lacre sealing-wax, f. unexpl. var. of Port. laca LAC[1]]

lacrosse /ləˈkrɒs/ n. a game like hockey, but with a ball driven by, caught, and carried in a netted stick. [F f. la the + CROSSE]

lactate[1] /lækˈteɪt/ v.intr. (of mammals) secrete milk. [as LACTATION]

lactate[2] /ˈlækteɪt/ n. Chem. any salt or ester of lactic acid.

lactation /lækˈteɪʃ(ə)n/ n. **1** the secretion of milk by the mammary glands. **2** the suckling of young. [L lactare suckle f. lac lactis milk]

lacteal /ˈlæktɪəl/ adj. & n. —adj. **1** of milk. **2** conveying chyle or other milky fluid. —n. (in pl.) the lymphatic vessels of the small intestine which absorb digested fats. [L lacteus f. lac lactis milk]

lactescent /lækˈtes(ə)nt/ adj. **1** milky. **2** yielding a milky juice. [L latescere f. lactēre be milky (as LACTIC)]

lactic /ˈlæktɪk/ adj. Chem. of, relating to, or obtained from milk. □ **lactic acid** a clear odourless syrupy acid formed in sour milk, and produced in the muscle tissues during strenuous exercise. [L lac lactis milk]

lacto- /ˈlæktəʊ/ comb. form milk. [L lac lactis milk]

lactobacillus /ˌlæktəʊbəˈsɪləs/ n. (pl. **-bacilli** /-laɪ/) Biol. any Gram-positive rod-shaped bacterium of the genus Lactobacillus, producing lactic acid from the fermentation of carbohydrates.

lactose /ˈlæktəʊs, -təʊz/ n. Chem. a sugar that occurs in milk, and is less sweet than sucrose. [as LACTO-]

lacuna /ləˈkjuːnə/ n. (pl. **lacunae** /-niː/ or **lacunas**) **1** a hiatus, blank, or gap. **2** a missing portion or empty page, esp. in an ancient MS, book, etc. □ **lacunal** adj. **lacunar** adj. **lacunary** adj. **lacunose** adj. [L, = pool, f. lacus LAKE[1]]

LACW abbr. Leading Aircraftwoman.

lacy /ˈleɪsɪ/ adj (**lacier**, **laciest**) of or resembling lace fabric. □ **lacily** adv. **laciness** n.

lad /læd/ n. **1 a** a boy or youth. **b** a young son. **2** (esp. in pl.) colloq. a man; a fellow, esp. a workmate, drinking companion, etc. (he's one of the lads). **3** colloq. a high-spirited fellow; a rogue (he's a bit of a lad). **4** Brit. a stable-worker (regardless of age). [ME ladde, of unkn. orig.]

ladder /ˈlædə(r)/ n. & v. —n. **1** a set of horizontal bars of wood or metal fixed between two uprights and used for climbing up or down. **2** Brit. a vertical strip of unravelled fabric in a stocking etc. resembling a ladder. **3 a** a hierarchical structure. **b** such a structure as a means of advancement, promotion, etc. —v. Brit. **1** intr. (of a stocking etc.) develop a ladder. **2** tr. cause a ladder in (a stocking etc.). □ **ladder-back** an upright chair with a back resembling a ladder. **ladder tournament** a sporting contest with each participant listed and entitled to a higher place by defeating the one above. [OE hlǣd(d)er, ult. f. Gmc: cf. LEAN¹]

laddie /ˈlædɪ/ n. colloq. a young boy or lad.

lade /leɪd/ v. (past part. **laden** /ˈleɪd(ə)n/) **1** tr. **a** put cargo on board (a ship). **b** ship (goods) as cargo. **2** intr. (of a ship) take on cargo. **3** tr. (as **laden** adj.) (usu. foll. by **with**) **a** (of a vehicle, donkey, person, tree, table, etc.) heavily loaded. **b** (of the conscience, spirit, etc.) painfully burdened with sin, sorrow, etc. [OE hladan]

la-di-da /ˌlɑːdɪˈdɑː/ adj. & n. colloq. —adj. pretentious or snobbish, esp. in manner or speech. —n. **1** a la-di-da person. **2** la-di-da speech or manners. [imit. of an affected manner of speech]

ladies pl. of LADY.

lading /ˈleɪdɪŋ/ n. **1** a cargo. **2** the act or process of lading.

ladle /ˈleɪd(ə)l/ n. & v. —n. **1** a large long-handled spoon with a cup-shaped bowl used for serving esp. soups and gravy. **2** a vessel for transporting molten metal in a foundry. —v.tr. (often foll. by out) transfer (liquid) from one receptacle to another. □ **ladle out** distribute, esp. lavishly. □ **ladleful** n. (pl. **-fuls**). **ladler** n. [OE hlædel f. hladan LADE]

lady /ˈleɪdɪ/ n. (pl. **-ies**) **1 a** a woman regarded as being of superior social status or as having the refined manners associated with this. **b** (**Lady**) a title used by peeresses, female relatives of peers, the wives and widows of knights, etc. **2** (often attrib.) a woman; a female person or animal (ask that lady over there; lady butcher; lady dog). **3** colloq. **a** a wife. **b** a man's girlfriend. **4** a ruling woman (lady of the house; lady of the manor). □ **the Ladies** (or **Ladies'**) Brit. a women's public lavatory. **ladies' fingers** = OKRA. **ladies'** (or **lady's**) **man** a man fond of female company; a seducer. **ladies' night** a function at a men's club etc. to which women are invited. **ladies' room** a women's lavatory in a hotel, office, etc. **Lady chapel** a chapel in a large church or cathedral, usu. to the E. of the high altar, dedicated to the Virgin Mary. **Lady Day** the Feast of the Annunciation, 25 Mar. **lady-in-waiting** a lady attending a queen or princess. **lady-killer** a practised and habitual seducer. **lady's maid** a lady's personal maidservant. **my lady** a form of address used chiefly by servants etc. to holders of the title 'Lady'. **Our Lady** the Virgin Mary. □ **ladyhood** n. [OE hlǣfdige f. hlāf LOAF¹ + (unrecorded) dig- knead, rel. to DOUGH): in Lady Day etc. f. OE genit. hlǣfdigan (Our) Lady's]

ladybird /ˈleɪdɪˌbɜːd/ n. a coleopterous insect of the family Coccinellidae, with wing-covers usu. of a reddish-brown colour with black spots.

ladybug /ˈleɪdɪˌbʌg/ n. US = LADYBIRD.

ladyfinger /ˈleɪdɪˌfɪŋgə(r)/ n. US a finger-shaped sponge cake.

ladylike /ˈleɪdɪˌlaɪk/ adj. **1 a** with the modesty, manners, etc., of a lady. **b** befitting a lady. **2** (of a man) effeminate.

ladyship /ˈleɪdɪʃɪp/ n. archaic being a lady. □ **her** (or **your** or **their**) **ladyship** (or **ladyships**) a respectful form of reference or address to a Lady or Ladies.

laevo- /ˈliːvəʊ/ comb. form (also **levo-**) on or to the left. [L laevus left]

laevulose /ˈliːvjʊˌləʊs, -ˌləʊz/ n. (US **levulose**) = FRUCTOSE. [LAEVO- + -ULE + -OSE²]

lag¹ v. & n. —v.intr. (**lagged, lagging**) (often foll. by behind) fall behind; not keep pace. —n. a delay. □ **lagger** n. [orig. = hindmost person, hang back: perh. f. a fanciful distortion of LAST¹ in a children's game (fog, seg, lag, = 1st, 2nd, last, in dial.)]

lag² v. & n. —v.tr. (**lagged, lagging**) enclose or cover in lagging. —n. **1** the non-heat-conducting cover of a boiler etc.; lagging. **2** a piece of this. [prob. f. Scand.: cf. ON lögg barrel-rim, rel. to LAY¹]

lag³ n. & v. sl. —n. (esp. as **old lag**) a habitual convict. —v.tr. (**lagged, lagging**) **1** send to prison. **2** apprehend; arrest. [19th c.: orig. unkn.]

lager /ˈlɑːgə(r)/ n. a kind of beer, effervescent and light in colour and body. □ **lager lout** colloq. a youth who behaves badly as a result of excessive drinking. [G Lagerbier beer brewed for keeping f. Lager store]

laggard /ˈlægəd/ n. & adj. —n. a dawdler; a person who lags behind. —adj. dawdling; slow. □ **laggardly** adj. & adv. **laggardness** n. [LAG¹]

lagging /ˈlægɪŋ/ n. material providing heat insulation for a boiler, pipes, etc. [LAG²]

lagoon /ləˈguːn/ n. **1** a stretch of salt water separated from the sea by a low sandbank, coral reef, etc. **2** the enclosed water of an atoll. **3** US, Austral., & NZ a small freshwater lake near a larger lake or river. [F lagune or It. & Sp. laguna f. L lacuna f. lacus LAKE¹]

lah n. (also **la**) Mus. **1** (in tonic sol-fa) the sixth note of a major scale. **2** the note A in the fixed-doh system. [ME f. L labii: see GAMUT]

laic /ˈleɪɪk/ adj. & n. —adj. non-clerical; lay; secular; temporal. —n. formal a lay person; a non-cleric. □ **laical** adj. **laically** adv. [LL f. Gk laïkos f. laos people]

laicize /ˈleɪɪˌsaɪz/ v.tr. (also **-ise**) **1** make (an office etc.) tenable by lay people. **2** subject (a school or institution) to the control of lay people. **3** secularize. □ **laicization** /-ˈzeɪʃ(ə)n/ n.

laid past and past part. of LAY¹.

lain past part. of LIE¹.

lair¹ /leə(r)/ n. **1 a** a wild animal's resting-place. **b** a person's hiding-place; a den (tracked him to his lair). **2** a place where domestic animals lie down. **3** Brit. a shed or enclosure for cattle on the way to market. □ **lairage** n. [OE leger f. Gmc: cf. LIE¹]

lair² /leə(r)/ n. & v. Austral. sl. —n. a youth or man who dresses flashily and shows off. —v.intr. (often foll. by up or dress) behave or dress like a lair. □ **lairy** *adj.* [*lair* back-form. f. *lairy*, alt. f. LEERY]

laird /leəd/ *n. Sc.* a landed proprietor. □ **laird-ship** *n.* [Sc. form of LORD]

laissez-faire /ˌleseɪˈfeə(r)/ *n.* (also **laisser-faire**) the theory or practice of governmental abstention from interference in the workings of the market etc. [F, = let act]

laity /ˈleɪɪtɪ/ *n.* (usu. prec. by *the*; usu. treated as *pl.*) **1** lay people, as distinct from the clergy. **2** non-professionals. [ME f. LAY² + -ITY]

lake¹ *n.* **1** a large body of water surrounded by land. □ **the Great Lakes** the Lakes Superior, Huron, Michigan, Erie, and Ontario, along the boundary of the US and Canada. **Lake District** (or **the Lakes**) the region of the English lakes in Cumbria. **lake-dweller** a prehistoric inhabitant of lake-dwellings. **lake-dwellings** prehistoric huts built on piles driven into the bed or shore of a lake. □ **lakeless** *adj.* **lakelet** *n.* [ME f. OF *lac* f. L *lacus* basin, pool, lake]

lake² *n.* **1** a reddish colouring orig. made from lac (*crimson lake*). **2** a complex formed by the action of dye and mordants applied to fabric to fix colour. **3** any insoluble product of a soluble dye and mordant. [var. of LAC¹]

lakeside /ˈleɪksaɪd/ *attrib.adj.* beside a lake.

lakh /læk, lɑːk/ *n.* (also **lac**) *Ind.* (usu. foll. by *of*) a hundred thousand (rupees etc.). [Hind. *lākh* f. Skr. *lakṣa*]

Lallan /ˈlælən/ *n. & adj. Sc.* —*n.* (now usu. **Lallans**) a Lowland Scots dialect, esp. as a literary language. —*adj.* of or concerning the Lowlands of Scotland. [var. of LOWLAND]

lam¹ *v.* (**lammed, lamming**) *sl.* **1** *tr.* thrash; hit. **2** *intr.* (foll. by *into*) hit (a person etc.) hard with a stick etc. [perh. f. Scand.: cf. ON *lemja* beat so as to LAME]

lam² *n.* □ **on the lam** *US sl.* in flight, esp. from the police. [20th c.: orig. unkn.]

lama /ˈlɑːmə/ *n.* a Tibetan or Mongolian Buddhist monk. □ **Lamaism** *n.* **Lamaist** *n. & adj.* [Tibetan *blama* (with silent *b*)]

lamasery /ˈlɑːməsərɪ, ləˈmɑːsərɪ/ *n.* (*pl.* **-ies**) a monastery of lamas. [F *lamaserie* irreg. f. *lama* LAMA]

lamb /læm/ *n. & v.* —*n.* **1** a young sheep. **2** the flesh of a lamb as food. **3** a mild or gentle person, esp. a young child. —*v.* **1 a** *tr.* (in *passive*) (of a lamb) be born. **b** *intr.* (of a ewe) give birth to lambs. **2** *tr.* tend (lambing ewes). □ **The Lamb** (or **The Lamb of God**) a name for Christ. **lamb's lettuce** a plant, *Valerianella locusta*, used in salad. **like a lamb** meekly, obediently. □ **lamber** *n.* **lambhood** *n.* **lambkin** *n.* **lamblike** *adj.* [OE *lamb* f. Gmc]

lambada /læmˈbɑːdə/ *n.* a fast erotic Brazilian dance in which couples dance with their stomachs touching each other.

lambaste /læmˈbeɪst/ *v.tr.* (also **lambast** /-ˈbæst/) *colloq.* **1** thrash; beat. **2** criticize severely. [LAM¹ + BASTE³]

lambda /ˈlæmdə/ *n.* **1** the eleventh letter of the Greek alphabet (Λ, λ). **2** (as λ) the symbol for wavelength. [ME f. Gk *la(m)bda*]

lambent /ˈlæmbənt/ *adj.* **1** (of a flame or a light) playing on a surface with a soft radiance but without burning. **2** (of the eyes, sky, etc.) softly radiant. **3** (of wit etc.) lightly brilliant. □ **lambency** *n.* **lambently** *adv.* [L *lambere lambent-* lick]

lambskin /ˈlæmskɪn/ *n.* a prepared skin from a lamb with the wool on or as leather.

lambswool /ˈlæmzwʊl/ *n.* (also **lamb's-wool**) soft fine wool from a young sheep used in knitted garments etc.

lame *adj. & v.* —*adj.* **1** disabled, esp. in the foot or leg; limping; unable to walk normally (*lame in his right leg*). **2 a** (of an argument, story, excuse, etc.) unconvincing; unsatisfactory; weak. **b** (of verse etc.) halting. —*v.tr.* **1** make lame; disable. **2** harm permanently. □ **lame-brain** *US colloq.* a stupid person. **lame duck 1** a disabled or weak person. **2** a defaulter on the Stock Exchange. **3** a firm etc. in financial difficulties. **4** *US* an official (esp. the President) in the final period of office, after the election of a successor. □ **lamely** *adv.* **lameness** *n.* **lamish** *adj.* [OE *lama* f. Gmc]

lamé /ˈlɑːmeɪ/ *n. & adj.* —*n.* a fabric with gold or silver threads interwoven. —*adj.* (of fabric, a dress, etc.) having such threads. [F]

lament /ləˈment/ *n. & v.* —*n.* **1** a passionate expression of grief. **2** a song or poem of mourning or sorrow. —*v.tr.* (also *absol.*) **1** express or feel grief for or about; regret (*lamented the loss of his ticket*). **2** (as **lamented** *adj.*) a conventional expression referring to a recently dead person (*your late lamented father*). □ **lament for** (or **over**) mourn or regret. □ **lamenter** *n.* **lamentingly** *adv.* [L *lamentum*]

lamentable /ˈlæməntəb(ə)l/ *adj.* (of an event, fate, condition, character, etc.) deplorable; regrettable. □ **lamentably** *adv.* [ME f. OF *lamentable* or L *lamentabilis* (as LAMENT)]

lamentation /ˌlæmənˈteɪʃ(ə)n/ *n.* **1** the act or an instance of lamenting. **2** a lament. [ME f. OF *lamentation* or L *lamentatio* (as LAMENT)]

lamina /ˈlæmɪnə/ *n.* (*pl.* **laminae** /-ˌniː/) a thin plate or scale, e.g. of bone, stratified rock, or vegetable tissue. □ **laminar** *adj.* **laminose** *adj.* [L]

laminate *v., n., & adj.* —*v.* /ˈlæmɪˌneɪt/ **1** *tr.* beat or roll (metal) into thin plates. **2** *tr.* overlay with metal plates, a plastic layer, etc. **3** *tr.* manufacture by placing layer on layer. **4** *tr. & intr.* split or be split into layers or leaves. —*n.* /ˈlæmɪnət/ a laminated structure or material, esp. of layers fixed together to form rigid or flexible material. —*adj.* /ˈlæmɪnət/ in the form of lamina or laminae. □ **lamination** /-ˈneɪʃ(ə)n/ *n.* **laminator** *n.* [LAMINA + -ATE², -ATE³]

Lammas /ˈlæməs/ *n.* (in full **Lammas Day**) the first day of August, formerly observed as harvest festival. [OE *hlāfmæsse* (as LOAF¹, MASS²)]

lamp *n.* **1** a device for producing a steady light, esp.: **a** an electric bulb, and usu. its holder and shade or cover (*bedside lamp*; *bicycle lamp*). **b** an oil-lamp. **c** a usu. glass holder for a candle. **d** a gas-jet and mantle. **2** a source of spiritual or intellectual inspiration. **3** a device producing esp. ultraviolet or infrared radiation as a treatment for various complaints. □ **lamp-chimney** a glass cylinder enclosing and making a draught for an oil-lamp flame. **lamp-holder** a device for supporting a lamp, esp. an electric one. **lamp standard** = LAMPPOST. □ **lampless** *adj.* [ME f. OF *lampe* f. LL *lampada* f. accus. of L *lampas* torch f. Gk]

lampblack /ˈlæmpblæk/ *n.* a pigment made from soot.

lamplight /ˈlæmplaɪt/ n. light given by a lamp or lamps.

lamplighter /ˈlæmpˌlaɪtə(r)/ n. 1 hist. a person who lights street lamps. 2 US a spill for lighting lamps.

lampoon /læmˈpuːn/ n. & v. —n. a satirical attack on a person etc. —v.tr. satirize. □ **lampooner** n. **lampoonery** n. **lampoonist** n. [F lampon, conjectured to be f. lampons let us drink f. lamper gulp down f. laper LAP³]

lamppost /ˈlæmpəʊst/ n. a tall post supporting a street-light.

lamprey /ˈlæmprɪ/ n. (pl. **-eys**) any eel-like aquatic vertebrate of the family Petromyzonidae, having a sucker mouth with horny teeth. [ME f. OF lampreie f. med.L lampreda: cf. LL lampetra perh. f. L lambere lick + petra stone]

lampshade /ˈlæmpʃeɪd/ n. a translucent cover for a lamp used to soften or direct its light.

Lancastrian /læŋˈkæstrɪən/ n. & adj. —n. 1 a native of Lancashire or Lancaster in NW England. 2 hist. a follower of the House of Lancaster or of the Red Rose party supporting it in the Wars of the Roses. —adj. of or concerning Lancashire or Lancaster, or the House of Lancaster.

lance /lɑːns/ n. & v. —n. 1 a a long weapon with a wooden shaft and a pointed steel head, used by a horseman in charging. b a similar weapon used for spearing a fish, killing a harpooned whale, etc. 2 a metal pipe supplying oxygen to burn metal. 3 = LANCER. —v.tr. 1 Surgery prick or cut open with a lancet. 2 pierce with a lance. □ **break a lance** (usu. foll. by for, with) argue. **lance-bombardier** a rank in the Royal Artillery corresponding to lance-corporal in the infantry. **lance-corporal** the lowest rank of NCO in the Army. [ME f. OF lancier f. L lancea: lance-corporal on analogy of obs. lancepesade lowest grade of NCO ult. f. It. lancia spezzata broken lance]

lanceolate /ˈlɑːnsɪələt/ adj. shaped like a lance-head, tapering to each end. [LL lanceolatus f. lanceola dimin. of lancea lance]

lancer /ˈlɑːnsə(r)/ n. 1 hist. a soldier of a cavalry regiment armed with lances. 2 (in pl.) a a quadrille for 8 or 16 pairs. b the music for this. [F lancier (as LANCE)]

lancet /ˈlɑːnsɪt/ n. a small broad two-edged surgical knife with a sharp point. □ **lancet arch** (or **light** or **window**) a narrow arch or window with a pointed head. □ **lanceted** adj. [ME f. OF lancette (as LANCE)]

land n. & v. —n. 1 the solid part of the earth's surface. 2 a an expanse of country; ground; soil. b such land in relation to its use, quality, etc., or (often prec. by the) as a basis for agriculture (building land; this is good land; works on the land). 3 a country, nation, or State (land of hope and glory). 4 a landed property. b (in pl.) estates. —v. 1 a tr. & intr. set or go ashore. b intr. (often foll. by at) disembark (landed at the harbour). 2 tr. bring (an aircraft, its passengers, etc.) to the ground or the surface of water. 3 intr. (of an aircraft, bird, parachutist, etc.) alight on the ground or water. 4 tr. bring (a fish) to land. 5 tr. & intr. (also refl.; often foll. by up) colloq. bring to, reach, or find oneself in a certain situation, place, or state (landed himself in jail; landed up in France; landed her in trouble; landed up penniless). 6 tr. colloq. a deal (a person etc.) a blow etc. (landed him one in the eye). b (foll. by with) present (a person) with (a problem, job, etc.). 7 tr. set down (a person, cargo, etc.) from a vehicle, ship, etc. 8 tr. colloq. win or obtain (a prize, job, etc.) esp. against strong competition. □ **how the land lies** what is the state of affairs. **land-agent 1** the steward of an estate. 2 an agent for the sale of estates. **land-bank** a bank issuing banknotes on the securities of landed property. **land breeze** a breeze blowing towards the sea from the land, esp. at night. **land-bridge** a neck of land joining two large land masses. **land force** (or **forces**) armies, not naval or air forces. **land-form** a natural feature of the earth's surface. **land-girl** Brit. a woman doing farm work, esp. in wartime. **land-grabber** an illegal seizer of land. **land-line** a means of telecommunication over land. **land-locked** almost or entirely enclosed by land. **land mass** a large area of land. **land-mine 1** an explosive mine laid in or on the ground. 2 a parachute mine. **land office** US an office recording dealings in public land. **land-office business** US enormous trade. **land on one's feet** attain a good position, job, etc., by luck. **land-tax** hist. a tax assessed on landed property. **land-wind** a wind blowing seaward from the land. **land yacht** a vehicle with wheels and sails for recreational use on a beach etc. □ **lander** n. **landless** adj. **landward** adj. & adv. **landwards** adv. [OE f. Gmc]

landau /ˈlændɔː/ n. a four-wheeled enclosed carriage with a removable front cover and a back cover that can be raised and lowered. [Landau near Karlsruhe in Germany, where it was first made]

landed /ˈlændɪd/ adj. 1 owning land (landed gentry). 2 consisting of, including, or relating to land (landed property).

landfall /ˈlændfɔːl/ n. the approach to land, esp. for the first time on a sea or air journey.

landfill /ˈlændfɪl/ n. 1 waste material etc. used to landscape or reclaim areas of ground. 2 the process of disposing of rubbish in this way. □ **landfill site** a place where rubbish is disposed of by burying it in the ground.

landholder /ˈlændˌhəʊldə(r)/ n. the proprietor or, esp., the tenant of land.

landing /ˈlændɪŋ/ n. 1 a the act or process of coming to land. b an instance of this. c (also **landing-place**) a place where ships etc. land. 2 a a platform between two flights of stairs, or at the top or bottom of a flight. b a passage leading to upstairs rooms. □ **landing-craft** any of several types of craft esp. designed for putting troops and equipment ashore. **landing-gear** the undercarriage of an aircraft. **landing-net** a net for landing a large fish which has been hooked. **landing-stage** a platform, often floating, on which goods and passengers are disembarked. **landing-strip** an airstrip.

landlady /ˈlændˌleɪdɪ/ n. (pl. **-ies**) 1 a woman who lets land, a building, part of a building, etc., to a tenant. 2 a woman who keeps a public house, boarding-house, or lodgings.

landlord /ˈlændlɔːd/ n. 1 a man who lets land, a building, part of a building, etc., to a tenant. 2 a man who keeps a public house, boarding-house, or lodgings.

landlubber /ˈlændˌlʌbə(r)/ n. a person unfamiliar with the sea or sailing.

landmark /ˈlændmɑːk/ n. **1 a** a conspicuous object in a district etc. **b** an object marking the boundary of an estate, country, etc. **2** an event, change, etc. marking a stage or turning-point in history etc.

landowner /ˈlændˌəʊnə(r)/ n. an owner of land. □ **landowning** adj. & n.

landscape /ˌlændskeɪp, ˈlæns-/ n. & v. —n. **1** natural or imaginary scenery, as seen in a broad view. **2** (often attrib.) a picture representing this; the genre of landscape painting. **3** (in graphic design etc.) a format in which the width of an illustration etc. is greater than the height. —v.tr. (also absol.) improve (a piece of land) by landscape gardening. □ **landscape gardener** (or **architect**) a person who plans the layout of landscapes, esp. extensive grounds. **landscape gardening** (or **architecture**) the laying out of esp. extensive grounds to resemble natural scenery. **landscape-painter** an artist who paints landscapes. □ **landscapist** n. [MDu. landscap (as LAND, -SHIP)]

landslide /ˈlændslaɪd/ n. **1** the sliding down of a mass of land from a mountain, cliff, etc. **2** an overwhelming majority for one side in an election.

landslip /ˈlændslɪp/ n. = LANDSLIDE 1.

landsman /ˈlændzmən/ n. (pl. **-men**) a non-sailor.

lane /leɪn/ n. **1** a narrow, often rural, road, street, or path. **2** a division of a road for a stream of traffic (three-lane highway). **3** a strip of track or water for a runner, rower, or swimmer in a race. **4** a path or course prescribed for or regularly followed by a ship, aircraft, etc. (ocean lane). **5** a gangway between crowds of people, objects, etc. [OE: orig. unkn.]

langlauf /ˈlæŋlaʊf/ n. cross-country skiing; a cross-country skiing race. [G, = long run]

langouste /lɑ̃ˈguːst, ˈlɒŋguːst/ n. a crawfish or spiny lobster. [F]

langoustine /ˌlɑ̃guːˈstiːn, ˈlɒŋguˌstiːn/ n. = NORWAY LOBSTER. [F]

lang syne /læŋ ˈsaɪn/ adv. & n. Sc. —adv. in the distant past. —n. the old days (cf. AULD LANG SYNE). [= long since]

language /ˈlæŋgwɪdʒ/ n. **1** the method of human communication, either spoken or written, consisting of the use of words in an agreed way. **2** the language of a particular community or country etc. (speaks several languages). **3 a** the faculty of speech. **b** a style or the faculty of expression; the use of words, etc. (his language was poetic; hasn't the language to express it). **c** (also **bad language**) coarse, crude, or abusive speech (didn't like his language). **4** a system of symbols and rules for writing computer programs or algorithms. **5** any method of expression (the language of mime; sign language). **6** a professional or specialized vocabulary. **7** literary style. □ **language laboratory** a room equipped with tape recorders etc. for learning a foreign language. [ME f. OF langage ult. f. L lingua tongue]

languid /ˈlæŋgwɪd/ adj. **1** lacking vigour; idle; inert; apathetic. **2** (of ideas etc.) lacking force; uninteresting. **3** (of trade etc.) slow-moving; sluggish. **4** faint; weak. □ **languidly** adv. **languidness** n. [F languide or L languidus (as LANGUISH)]

languish /ˈlæŋgwɪʃ/ v.intr. **1** be or grow feeble; lose or lack vitality. **2** put on a sentimentally tender or languid look. □ **languish for** droop or pine for. **languish under** suffer under (esp. depression, confinement, etc.). □ **languisher** n. **languishingly** adv. **languishment** n. [ME f. OF languir, ult. f. L languēre, rel. to LAX]

languor /ˈlæŋgə(r)/ n. **1** lack of energy or alertness; inertia; idleness; dullness. **2** faintness; fatigue. **3** a soft or tender mood or effect. **4** an oppressive stillness (of the air etc.). □ **languorous** adj. **languorously** adv. [ME f. OF f. L languor -oris (as LANGUISH)]

lank adj. **1** (of hair, grass, etc.) long, limp, and straight. **2** thin and tall. **3** shrunken; spare. □ **lankly** adv. **lankness** n. [OE hlanc f. Gmc: cf. FLANK, LINK]

lanky /ˈlæŋkɪ/ adj. (**lankier**, **lankiest**) (of limbs, a person, etc.) ungracefully thin and long or tall. □ **lankily** adv. **lankiness** n.

lanolin /ˈlænəlɪn/ n. a fat found naturally on sheep's wool and used purified for cosmetics etc. [G f. L lana wool + oleum oil]

lantern /ˈlænt(ə)n/ n. **1 a** a lamp with a transparent usu. glass case protecting a candle flame etc. **b** a similar electric etc. lamp. **c** its case. **2 a** a raised structure on a dome, room, etc., glazed to admit light. **b** a similar structure for ventilation etc. **3** the light-chamber of a lighthouse. **4** = magic lantern. □ **lantern jaws** long thin jaws and chin, giving a hollow look to the face. **lantern-slide** a slide for projection by a magic lantern etc. (see SLIDE n. 5b). [ME f. OF lanterne f. L lanterna f. Gk lamptēr torch, lamp]

lanthanide /ˈlænθəˌnaɪd/ n. Chem. element of the lanthanide series. □ **lanthanide series** a series of 15 metallic elements from lanthanum to lutetium in the periodic table, having similar chemical properties. [G Lanthanid (as LANTHANUM)]

lanthanum /ˈlænθənəm/ n. Chem. a silvery metallic element of the lanthanide series which is used in the manufacture of alloys. [Gk lanthanō escape notice, from having remained undetected in cerium oxide]

lanyard /ˈlænjəd, -jɑːd/ n. **1** a cord hanging round the neck or looped round the shoulder, esp. of a Scout or sailor etc., to which a knife, a whistle, etc., may be attached. **2** Naut. a short rope or line used for securing, tightening, etc. **3** a cord attached to a breech mechanism for firing a gun. [ME f. OF laniere, lasniere: assim. to YARD¹]

Laodicean /ˌleɪəʊdɪˈsiːən/ adj. & n. —adj. lukewarm or half-hearted, esp. in religion or politics. —n. such a person. [L Laodicea in Asia Minor (with ref. to the early Christians there: see Rev. 3:16)]

lap¹ n. **1 a** the front of the body from the waist to the knees of a sitting person (sat on her lap; caught it in his lap). **b** the clothing, esp. a skirt, covering the lap. **c** the front of a skirt held up to catch or contain something. **2** a hollow among hills. **3** a hanging flap on a garment, a saddle, etc. □ **in** (or **on**) **a person's lap** as a person's responsibility. **in the lap of the gods** (of an event etc.) open to chance; beyond human control. **in the lap of luxury** in extremely luxurious surroundings. **lap-dog** a small pet dog. **lap robe** US a travelling-rug. □ **lapful** n. (pl. **-fuls**). [OE læppa fold, flap]

lap[2] *n. & v.* —*n.* **1 a** one circuit of a racetrack etc. **b** a section of a journey etc. (*finally we were on the last lap*). **2 a** an amount of overlapping. **b** an overlapping or projecting part. **3** a single turn of rope, silk, thread, etc., round a drum or reel. —*v.* (**lapped, lapping**) **1** *tr.* lead or overtake (a competitor in a race) by one or more laps. **2** *tr.* (often foll. by *about, round*) coil, fold, or wrap (a garment etc.) round esp. a person. **3** *tr.* (usu. foll. by *in*) enfold or swathe (a person) in wraps etc. **4** *tr.* (as **lapped** *adj.*) (usu. foll. by *in*) protectively encircled; enfolded caressingly. **5** *tr.* surround (a person) with an influence etc. **6** *intr.* (usu. foll. by *over*) project; overlap. **7** *tr.* cause to overlap. □ **lap of honour** a ceremonial circuit of a football pitch, a track, etc., by a winner or winners. [ME, prob. f. LAP¹]

lap[3] *v. & n.* —*v.* (**lapped, lapping**) **1** *tr.* **a** (also *absol.*) (usu. of an animal) drink (liquid) with the tongue. **b** (usu. foll. by *up, down*) consume (liquid) greedily. **c** (usu. foll. by *up*) consume (gossip, praise, etc.) greedily. **2 a** *tr.* (of water) move or beat upon (a shore) with a rippling sound as of lapping. **b** *intr.* (of waves etc.) move in ripples; make a lapping sound. —*n.* **1 a** the process or an act of lapping. **b** the amount of liquid taken up. **2** the sound of wavelets on a beach. [OE *lapian* f. Gmc]

laparoscope /ˈlæpərəˌskəʊp/ *n. Surgery* a fibre optic instrument inserted through the abdominal wall to give a view of the organs in the abdomen. □ **laparoscopy** /-ˈrɒskəpɪ/ *n.* (*pl.* **-ies**). [Gk *lapara* flank + -SCOPE]

lapel /ləˈpel/ *n.* the part of a coat, jacket, etc., folded back against the front round the neck opening. □ **lapelled** *adj.* [LAP¹ + -EL]

lapidary /ˈlæpɪdərɪ/ *adj. & n.* —*adj.* **1** concerned with stone or stones. **2** engraved upon stone. **3** (of writing style) dignified and concise, suitable for inscriptions. —*n.* (*pl.* **-ies**) a cutter, polisher, or engraver of gems. [ME f. L *lapidarius* f. *lapis -idis* stone]

lapis lazuli /ˌlæpɪs ˈlæzjuːlɪ, -ˌlaɪ/ *n.* **1** a blue mineral containing sodium aluminium silicate and sulphur, used as a gemstone. **2** a bright blue pigment formerly made from this. **3** its colour. [ME f. L *lapis* stone + med.L *lazuli* genit. of *lazulum* f. Pers. (as AZURE)]

lappet /ˈlæpɪt/ *n.* **1** a small flap or fold of a garment etc. **2** a hanging or loose piece of flesh, such as a lobe or wattle. □ **lappeted** *adj.* [LAP¹ + -ET¹]

lapse /læps/ *n. & v.* —*n.* **1** a slight error; a slip of memory etc. **2** a weak or careless decline into an inferior state. **3** (foll. by *of*) an interval or passage of time (*after a lapse of three years*). **4** *Law* the termination of a right or privilege through disuse or failure to follow appropriate procedures. —*v.intr.* **1** fail to maintain a position or standard. **2** (foll. by *into*) fall back into an inferior or previous state. **3** (of a right or privilege etc.) become invalid because it is not used or claimed or renewed. **4** (as **lapsed** *adj.*) (of a person or thing) that has lapsed. □ **lapser** *n.* [L *lapsus* f. *labi laps-* glide, slip, fall]

laptop /ˈlæptɒp/ *n.* (*attrib.*) (of a microcomputer) portable and suitable for use while travelling.

lapwing /ˈlæpwɪŋ/ *n.* a plover, *Vanellus vanellus*, with black and white plumage, crested head, and a shrill cry. [OE *hlēapewince* f. *hlēapan* LEAP + WINK: assim. to LAP¹, WING]

larboard /ˈlɑːbəd/ *n. & adj. Naut. archaic* = PORT³. [ME *lade-, ladde-, lathe-* (perh. = LADE + BOARD): later assim. to *starboard*]

larceny /ˈlɑːsənɪ/ *n.* (*pl.* **-ies**) the theft of personal property. □ **larcener** *n.* **larcenist** *n.* **larcenous** *adj.* [OF *larcin* f. L *latrocinium* f. *latro* robber, mercenary f. Gk *latreus*]

■ **Usage** In 1968 *larceny* was replaced as a statutory crime in English law by *theft*.

larch *n.* **1** a deciduous coniferous tree of the genus *Larix*, with bright foliage and producing tough timber. **2** (in full **larchwood**) its wood. [MHG *larche* ult. f. L *larix -icis*]

lard *n. & v.* —*n.* the internal fat of the abdomen of pigs, esp. when rendered and clarified for use in cooking and pharmacy. —*v.tr.* **1** insert strips of fat or bacon in (meat etc.) before cooking. **2** (foll. by *with*) embellish (talk or writing) with foreign or technical terms. [ME f. OF *lard* bacon f. L *lardum, laridum*, rel. to Gk *larinos* fat]

larder /ˈlɑːdə(r)/ *n.* **1** a room or cupboard for storing food. **2** a wild animal's store of food, esp. for winter. [ME f. OF *lardier* f. med.L *lardarium* (as LARD)]

lardon /ˈlɑːd(ə)n/ *n.* (also **lardoon** /-ˈduːn/) a strip of fat bacon used to lard meat. [ME f. F *lardon* (as LARD)]

lardy /ˈlɑːdɪ/ *adj.* like or with lard. □ **lardy-cake** *Brit.* a cake made with lard, currants, etc.

large *adj. & n.* —*adj.* **1** of considerable or relatively great size or extent. **2** of the larger kind (*the large intestine*). **3** of wide range; comprehensive. **4** pursuing an activity on a large scale (*large farmer*). —*n.* (**at large**) **1** at liberty. **2** as a body or whole (*popular with the people at large*). **3** (of a narration etc.) at full length and with all details. **4** without a specific target (*scatters insults at large*). **5** *US* representing a whole area and not merely a part of it (*congressman at large*). □ **in large** on a large scale. **large-minded** liberal; not narrow-minded. **large-scale** made or occurring on a large scale or in large amounts. □ **largeness** *n.* **largish** *adj.* [ME f. OF f. fem. of L *largus* copious]

largely /ˈlɑːdʒlɪ/ *adv.* to a great extent; principally (*is largely due to laziness*).

largesse /lɑːˈʒes/ *n.* (also **largess**) **1** money or gifts freely given, esp. on an occasion of rejoicing, by a person in high position. **2** generosity, beneficence. [ME f. OF *largesse* ult. f. L *largus* copious]

largo /ˈlɑːgəʊ/ *adv., adj., & n. Mus.* —*adv. & adj.* in a slow tempo and dignified in style. —*n.* (*pl.* **-os**) a largo passage or movement. [It., = broad]

lariat /ˈlærɪət/ *n.* **1** a lasso. **2** a tethering-rope, esp. used by cowboys. [Sp. *la reata* f. *reatar* tie again (as RE-, L *aptare* adjust f. *aptus* APT, fit)]

lark[1] *n.* **1** any small bird of the family Alaudidae with brown plumage, elongated hind claw, and tuneful song, esp. the skylark. **2** any of various similar birds. [OE *lāferce, lǽwerce*, of unkn. orig.]

lark[2] *n. & v. colloq.* —*n.* **1** a frolic or spree; an amusing incident; a joke. **2** *Brit.* a type of activity, affair, etc. (*fed up with this digging lark*). —*v.intr.* (foll. by *about*) play tricks; frolic. □ **larky** *adj.* **larkiness** *n.* [19th c.: orig. uncert.]

larkspur /ˈlɑːkspɜː(r)/ *n.* any of various plants of the genus *Consolida*, with a spur-shaped calyx.

larn /lɑːn/ v. colloq. or joc. **1** intr. = LEARN. **2** tr. teach (that'll larn you). [dial. form of LEARN]

larrikin /ˈlærɪkɪn/ n. Austral. a hooligan. [also Engl. dial.: perh. f. the name Larry (pet-form of Lawrence) + -KIN]

Larry /ˈlærɪ/ n. □ **as happy as Larry** colloq. extremely happy. [20th c.: orig. uncert.: cf. LARRIKIN]

larva /ˈlɑːvə/ n. (pl. **larvae** /-viː/) **1** the stage of development of an insect between egg and pupa, e.g. a caterpillar. **2** an immature form of other animals that undergo some metamorphosis, e.g. a tadpole. □ **larval** adj. **larvicide** /ˈlɑːvɪˌsaɪd/ n. [L, = ghost, mask]

laryngeal /ləˈrɪndʒɪəl/ adj. of or relating to the larynx.

laryngitis /ˌlærɪnˈdʒaɪtɪs/ n. inflammation of the larynx. □ **laryngitic** /-ˈdʒɪtɪk/ adj.

larynx /ˈlærɪŋks/ n. (pl. **larynges** /ləˈrɪndʒiːz/) the hollow muscular organ forming an air passage to the lungs and holding the vocal cords in humans and other mammals. [mod.L f. Gk larugx -ggos]

lasagne /ləˈsænjə, -ˈsɑːnjə/ n. pasta in the form of sheets or wide ribbons, esp. as cooked and served with minced meat and cheese sauce. [It., pl. of lasagna f. L lasanum cooking-pot]

Lascar /ˈlæskə(r)/ n. an E. Indian seaman. [ult. f. Urdu & Pers. laškar army]

lascivious /ləˈsɪvɪəs/ adj. **1** lustful. **2** inciting to or evoking lust. □ **lasciviously** adv. **lasciviousness** n. [ME f. LL lasciviosus f. L lascivia lustfulness f. lascivus sportive, wanton]

lase /leɪz/ v.intr. **1** function as or in a laser. **2** (of a substance) undergo the physical processes employed in a laser. [back-form. f. LASER]

laser /ˈleɪzə(r)/ n. a device that generates an intense beam of coherent monochromatic radiation in the infrared, visible, or ultraviolet region of the electromagnetic spectrum, by stimulated emission of photons from an excited source. [light amplification by stimulated emission of radiation: cf. MASER]

laservision /ˈleɪzəˌvɪʒ(ə)n/ n. a system for the reproduction of video signals recorded on a disc with a laser. [LASER + VISION, after TELEVISION]

lash v. & n. —v. **1** intr. make a sudden whiplike movement with a limb or flexible instrument. **2** tr. beat with a whip, rope, etc. **3** intr. pour or rush with great force. **4** intr. (foll. by at, against) strike violently. **5** tr. castigate in words. **6** tr. urge on as with a lash. **7** tr. (foll. by down, together, etc.) fasten with a cord, rope, etc. **8** tr. (of rain, wind, etc.) beat forcefully upon. —n. **1 a** a sharp blow made by a whip, rope, etc. **b** (prec. by the) punishment by beating with a whip etc. **2** the flexible end of a whip. **3** (usu. in pl.) an eyelash. □ **lash out 1** speak or hit out angrily. **2** spend money extravagantly, be lavish. **lash-up** a makeshift or improvised structure or arrangement. □ **lasher** n. **lashingly** adv. (esp. in senses 4–5 of v.). **lashless** adj. [ME: prob. imit.]

lashing /ˈlæʃɪŋ/ n. **1** a beating. **2** cord used for lashing.

lashings /ˈlæʃɪŋz/ n.pl. Brit. colloq. (foll. by of) plenty; an abundance.

lass n. esp. Sc. & N.Engl. or poet. a girl or young woman. [ME lasce ult. f. ON laskwa unmarried (fem.)]

Lassa fever /ˈlæsə/ n. an acute and often fatal febrile viral disease of tropical Africa. [Lassa in Nigeria, where first reported]

lassie /ˈlæsɪ/ n. colloq. = LASS.

lassitude /ˈlæsɪˌtjuːd/ n. **1** languor, weariness. **2** disinclination to exert or interest oneself. [F lassitude or L lassitudo f. lassus tired]

lasso /læˈsuː, ˈlæsəʊ/ n. & v. —n. (pl. **-os** or **-oes**) a rope with a noose at one end, used esp. in N. America for catching cattle etc. —v.tr. (**-oes**, **-oed**) catch with a lasso. □ **lassoer** n. [Sp. lazo LACE]

last[1] /lɑːst/ adj., adv., & n. —adj. **1** after all others; coming at or belonging to the end. **2 a** most recent; next before a specified time (last Christmas; last week). **b** preceding; previous in a sequence (got on at the last station). **3** only remaining (the last biscuit; our last chance). **4** (prec. by the) least likely or suitable (the last person I'd want; the last thing I'd have expected). **5** the lowest in rank (the last place). —adv. **1** after all others (esp. in comb.: last-mentioned). **2** on the last occasion before the present (when did you last see him?). **3** (esp. in enumerating) lastly. —n. **1** a person or thing that is last, last-mentioned, most recent, etc. **2** (prec. by the) the last mention or sight etc. (shall never hear the last of it). **3** the last performance of certain acts (breathed his last). **4** (prec. by the) **a** the end or last moment. **b** death. □ **at last** (or **long last**) in the end; after much delay. **last ditch** a place of final desperate defence (often with hyphen) attrib.). **last minute** (or **moment**) the time just before an important event (often with hyphen) attrib.). **last name** surname. **last rites** sacred rites for a person about to die. **the last straw** a slight addition to a burden or difficulty that makes it finally unbearable. **the Last Supper** that of Christ and his disciples on the eve of the Crucifixion, as recorded in the New Testament. **last thing** adv. very late, esp. as a final act before going to bed. **the last word 1** a final or definitive statement (always has the last word; is the last word on this subject). **2** (often foll. by in) the latest fashion. **to** (or **till**) **the last** till the end; esp. till death. [OE latost superl.: see LATE]

last[2] /lɑːst/ v.intr. **1** remain unexhausted or adequate or alive for a specified or considerable time; suffice (enough food to last us a week; the battery lasts and lasts). **2** continue for a specified time (the journey lasts an hour). □ **last out** remain adequate or in existence for the whole of a period previously stated or implied. [OE lǣstan f. Gmc]

last[3] /lɑːst/ n. a shoemaker's model for shaping or repairing a shoe or boot. □ **stick to one's last** not meddle with what one does not understand. [OE lǣste last, lǣst boot, lāst footprint f. Gmc]

lasting /ˈlɑːstɪŋ/ adj. **1** continuing, permanent. **2** durable. □ **lastingly** adv. **lastingness** n.

lastly /ˈlɑːstlɪ/ adv. finally; in the last place.

lat. abbr. latitude.

latch /lætʃ/ n. & v. —n. **1** a bar with a catch and lever used as a fastening for a gate etc. **2** a spring-lock preventing a door from being opened from the outside without a key after being shut. —v.tr. & intr. fasten or be fastened with a latch. □ **latch on** (often foll. by to) colloq. **1** attach oneself (to). **2** understand. **on the latch**

fastened by the latch only, not locked. [prob. f. (now dial.) *latch* (v.) seize f. OE *læccan* f. Gmc]

latchkey /ˈlætʃkiː/ *n.* (*pl.* **-eys**) a key of an outer door. □ **latchkey child** a child who is alone at home after school until a parent returns from work.

late *adj.* & *adv.* —*adj.* **1** after the due or usual time; occurring or done after the proper time (*late for dinner*; *a late milk delivery*). **2 a** far on in the day or night or in a specified time or period. **b** far on in development. **3** flowering or ripening towards the end of the season (*late strawberries*). **4** (prec. by *the* or *my*, *his*, etc.) no longer alive or having the specified status (*my late husband*; *the late president*). **5** of recent date (*the late storms*). — *adv.* **1** after the due or usual time (*arrived late*). **2** far on in time (*this happened later on*). **3** at or till a late hour. **4** at a late stage of development. **5** formerly but not now (*late of the Scillies*). □ **at the latest** as the latest time envisaged (*will have done it by six at the latest*). **late in the day** *colloq.* at a late stage in the proceedings, esp. too late to be useful. **the latest** the most recent news, fashion, etc. (*have you heard the latest?*). □ **lateness** *n.* [OE *læt* (adj.), *late* (adv.) f. Gmc]

latecomer /ˈleɪtˌkʌmə(r)/ *n.* a person who arrives late.

lateen /ləˈtiːn/ *adj.* (of a ship) rigged with a lateen sail. □ **lateen sail** a triangular sail on a long yard at an angle of 45° to the mast. [F (*voile*) *latine* Latin (sail), because common in the Mediterranean]

lately /ˈleɪtlɪ/ *adv.* not long ago; recently; in recent times. [OE *lætlīce* (as LATE, -LY²)]

latent /ˈleɪt(ə)nt/ *adj.* **1** concealed, dormant. **2** existing but not developed or manifest. □ **latent heat** *Physics* the heat required to convert a solid into a liquid or vapour, or a liquid into a vapour, without change of temperature. **latent image** *Photog.* an image not yet made visible by developing. □ **latency** *n.* **latently** *adv.* [L *latēre latent-* be hidden]

-later /lətə(r)/ *comb. form* denoting a person who worships a particular thing or person (*idolater*). [Gk: see -LATRY]

lateral /ˈlætər(ə)l/ *adj.* & *n.* —*adj.* **1** of, at, towards, or from the side or sides. **2** descended from a brother or sister of a person in direct line. —*n.* a side part etc., esp. a lateral shoot or branch. □ **lateral thinking** a method of solving problems indirectly or by apparently illogical methods. □ **laterally** *adv.* [L *lateralis* f. *latus lateris* side]

laterite /ˈlætəˌraɪt/ *n.* a red or yellow ferruginous clay, friable and hardening in air, used for making roads in the tropics. □ **lateritic** /-ˈrɪtɪk/ *adj.* [L *later* brick + -ITE¹]

latex /ˈleɪteks/ *n.* (*pl.* **latexes** or **latices** /-tɪˌsiːz/) **1** a milky fluid of mixed composition found in various plants and trees, esp. the rubber tree, and used for commercial purposes. **2** a synthetic product resembling this. [L, = liquid]

lath /lɑːθ/ *n.* (*pl.* **laths** /lɑːðs, lɑːðz/) a thin flat strip of wood, esp. each of a series forming a framework or support for plaster etc. □ **lath and plaster** a common material for interior walls and ceilings etc. [OE *lætt*]

lathe /leɪð/ *n.* a machine for shaping wood, metal, etc., by means of a rotating drive which

turns the piece being worked on against changeable cutting tools. [prob. rel. to ODa. *lad* structure, frame, f. ON *hlath*, rel. to *hlatha* LADE]

lather /ˈlɑːðə(r), ˈlæðə(r)/ *n.* & *v.* —*n.* **1** a froth produced by agitating soap etc. and water. **2** frothy sweat, esp. of a horse. **3** a state of agitation. —*v.* **1** *intr.* (of soap etc.) form a lather. **2** *tr.* cover with lather. **3** *intr.* (of a horse etc.) develop or become covered with lather. **4** *tr.* *colloq.* thrash. □ **lathery** *adj.* [OE *lēathor* (n.), *lēthran* (v.)]

latices *pl.* of LATEX.

Latin /ˈlætɪn/ *n.* & *adj.* —*n.* the Italic language of ancient Rome and its empire. —*adj.* **1** of or in Latin. **2** of the countries or peoples (e.g. France and Spain) using languages developed from Latin. **3** of the Roman Catholic Church. □ **Latin America** the parts of Central and S. America where Spanish or Portuguese is the main language. **Latin American** *n.* a native of Latin America. —*adj.* of or relating to Latin America. **Latin Church** the Western Church. □ **Latinism** *n.* **Latinist** *n.* [ME f. OF *Latin* or L *Latinus* f. *Latium* in Central Italy]

Latinate /ˈlætɪˌneɪt/ *adj.* having the character of Latin.

latish /ˈleɪtɪʃ/ *adj.* & *adv.* fairly late.

latitude /ˈlætɪˌtjuːd/ *n.* **1** *Geog.* **a** the angular distance on a meridian north or south of the equator, expressed in degrees and minutes. **b** (usu. in *pl.*) regions or climes, esp. with reference to temperature (*warm latitudes*). **2** freedom from narrowness; liberality of interpretation. **3** tolerated variety of action or opinion (*was allowed much latitude*). □ **high latitudes** regions near the poles. **low latitudes** regions near the equator. □ **latitudinal** /-ˈtjuːdɪn(ə)l/ *adj.* **latitudinally** /-ˈtjuːdɪnəlɪ/ *adv.* [ME, = breadth, f. L *latitudo -dinis* f. *latus* broad]

latitudinarian /ˌlætɪˌtjuːdɪˈneərɪən/ *adj.* & *n.* —*adj.* allowing latitude esp. in religion; showing no preference among varying creeds and forms of worship. —*n.* a person with a latitudinarian attitude. □ **latitudinarianism** *n.* [L *latitudo -dinis* breadth + -ARIAN]

latrine /ləˈtriːn/ *n.* a communal lavatory, esp. in a camp, barracks, etc. [F f. L *latrina*, shortening of *lavatrina* f. *lavare* wash]

-latry /lətrɪ/ *comb. form* denoting worship (*idolatry*). [Gk *latreia* worship f. *latreuō* serve]

latter /ˈlætə(r)/ *adj.* **1 a** denoting the second-mentioned of two, or *disp.* the last-mentioned of three or more. **b** (prec. by *the*; usu. *absol.*) the second- or last-mentioned person or thing. **2** nearer to the end (*the latter part of the year*). **3** recent. **4** belonging to the end of a period, of the world, etc. □ **latter-day** modern, newfangled. **Latter-day Saints** the Mormons' name for themselves. [OE *lætra*, compar. of *læt* LATE]

■ **Usage** The sense 'last mentioned of three or more' is considered incorrect by some people.

latterly /ˈlætəlɪ/ *adv.* **1** in the latter part of life or of a period. **2** recently.

lattice /ˈlætɪs/ *n.* **1 a** a structure of crossed laths or bars with spaces between, used as a screen, fence, etc. **b** (in full **lattice-work**) laths arranged in lattice formation. **2** *Crystallog.* a regular periodic arrangement of atoms, ions, or molecules in a crystalline solid. □ **lattice window** a window with small panes set in diagonally crossing strips of lead. □ **latticed** *adj*. **latticing** *n*. [ME f. OF *lattis* f. *latte* lath f. WG]

laud *v. & n.* —*v.tr.* praise or extol, esp. in hymns. —*n*. **1** *literary* praise; a hymn of praise. **2** (in *pl.*) the traditional morning prayer of the Roman Catholic Church. [ME: (n.) f. OF *laude*, (v.) f. L *laudare*, f. L *laus laudis* praise]

laudable /ˈlɔːdəb(ə)l/ *adj*. commendable, praiseworthy. □ **laudability** /-ˈbɪlɪtɪ/ *n*. **laudably** *adv*. [ME f. L *laudabilis* (as LAUD)]

■ **Usage** This word is sometimes confused with *laudatory*.

laudanum /ˈlɔːdnəm, ˈlɒd-/ *n*. a solution containing morphine and prepared from opium, formerly used as a narcotic painkiller. [mod.L, the name given by Paracelsus to a costly medicament, later applied to preparations containing opium: perh. var. of *ladanum* gum resin]

laudatory /ˈlɔːdətərɪ/ *adj*. (also **laudative** /-tɪv/) expressing praise.

■ **Usage** This word is sometimes confused with *laudable*.

laugh /lɑːf/ *v. & n.* —*v*. **1** *intr*. make the spontaneous sounds and movements usual in expressing lively amusement, scorn, derision, etc. **2** *tr*. express by laughing. **3** *tr*. bring (a person) into a certain state by laughing (*laughed them into agreeing*). **4** *intr*. (foll. by *at*) ridicule, make fun of (*laughed at us for going*). **5** *intr*. (**be laughing**) *colloq*. be in a fortunate or successful position. —*n*. **1** the sound or act or manner of laughing. **2** *colloq*. a comical or ridiculous thing. □ **have the last laugh** be ultimately the winner. **laugh off** get rid of (embarrassment or humiliation) with a jest. **laugh on the other side of one's face** change from enjoyment or amusement to displeasure, shame, apprehension, etc. **laugh out of court** deprive of a hearing by ridicule. **laugh up one's sleeve** be secretly or inwardly amused. □ **laugher** *n*. [OE *hlæhhan, hliehhan* f. Gmc]

laughable /ˈlɑːfəb(ə)l/ *adj*. ludicrous; highly amusing. □ **laughably** *adv*.

laughing /ˈlɑːfɪŋ/ *n. & adj.* —*n*. laughter. —*adj*. in senses of LAUGH *v*. □ **laughing-gas** nitrous oxide as an anaesthetic, formerly used without oxygen and causing an exhilarating effect when inhaled. **laughing jackass** = KOOKABURRA. **laughing-stock** a person or thing open to general ridicule. **no laughing matter** something serious. □ **laughingly** *adv*.

laughter /ˈlɑːftə(r)/ *n*. the act or sound of laughing. [OE *hleahtor* f. Gmc]

launch[1] *v. & n.* —*v*. **1** *tr*. set (a vessel) afloat. **2** *tr*. hurl or send forth (a weapon, rocket, etc.). **3** *tr*. start or set in motion (an enterprise, a person on a course of action, etc.). **4** *tr*. formally introduce (a new product) with publicity etc. **5** *intr*. (often foll. by *out, into*, etc.) **a** make a start, esp. on an ambitious enterprise. **b** burst into strong language etc. —*n*. the act or an instance of launching. □ **launch** (or **launching**) **pad** a platform with a supporting structure, from which rockets are launched. [ME f. AF *launcher*, ONF *lancher*, OF *lancier* LANCE *v*.]

launch[2] *n*. **1** a large motor boat, used esp. for pleasure. **2** a man-of-war's largest boat. [Sp.

lancha pinnace perh. f. Malay *lancharan* f. *lanchār* swift]

launcher /ˈlɔːntʃə(r)/ *n*. a structure or device to hold a rocket during launching.

launder /ˈlɔːndə(r)/ *v*. **1** wash and iron (clothes, linen, etc.). **2** *colloq*. transfer (funds) to conceal a dubious or illegal origin. □ **launderer** *n*. [ME *launder* (n.) washer of linen, contr. of *lavander* f. OF *lavandier* ult. f. L *lavanda* things to be washed, neut. pl. gerundive of *lavare* wash]

launderette /lɔːnˈdret/ *n*. (also **laundrette**) an establishment with coin-operated washing-machines and driers for public use.

laundress /ˈlɔːndrɪs/ *n*. a woman who launders clothes, linen, etc., esp. professionally.

laundry /ˈlɔːndrɪ/ *n*. (pl. -**ies**) **1** an establishment for washing clothes or linen. **2** clothes or linen for laundering or newly laundered. [contr. f. *lavendry* (f. OF *lavanderie*) after LAUNDER]

laureate /ˈlɒrɪət, ˈlɔː-/ *adj. & n.* —*adj*. **1** wreathed with laurel as a mark of honour. **2** consisting of laurel; laurel-like. —*n*. **1** a person who is honoured for outstanding creative or intellectual achievement (*Nobel laureate*). **2** = Poet Laureate. □ **laureateship** *n*. [L *laureatus* f. *laurea* laurel-wreath f. *laurus* laurel]

laurel /ˈlɒr(ə)l/ *n. & v.* —*n*. **1** = BAY[2]. **2 a** (in *sing*. or *pl*.) the foliage of the bay-tree used as an emblem of victory or distinction in poetry usu. formed into a wreath or crown. **b** (in *pl*.) honour or distinction. **3** any plant with dark-green glossy leaves like a bay-tree. —*v.tr*. (**laurelled**, **laurelling**; US **laureled**, **laureling**) wreathe with laurel. □ **look to one's laurels** beware of losing one's pre-eminence. **rest on one's laurels** be satisfied with what one has done and not seek further success. [ME *lorer* f. OF *lorier* f. Prov. *laurier* f. *laur* f. L *laurus*]

lav *n*. *Brit. colloq*. lavatory. [abbr.]

lava /ˈlɑːvə/ *n*. **1** the molten matter which flows from a volcano. **2** the solid substance which it forms on cooling. [It. f. *lavare* wash f. L]

lavatorial /ˌlævəˈtɔːrɪəl/ *adj*. (esp. of humour) relating to lavatories and their use.

lavatory /ˈlævətərɪ/ *n*. (pl. -**ies**) **1** a large receptacle for urine and faeces, usu. with running water and a flush mechanism as a means of disposal. **2** a room or compartment containing one or more of these. □ **lavatory paper** = *toilet paper*. [ME, = washing vessel, f. LL *lavatorium* f. L *lavare lavat-* wash]

lavender /ˈlævɪndə(r)/ *n. & v.* —*n*. **1 a** any small evergreen shrub of the genus *Lavandula*, with narrow leaves and blue, purple, or pink aromatic flowers. **b** its flowers and stalks dried and used to scent linen, clothes, etc. **2 a** pale blue colour with a trace of red. —*v.tr*. put lavender among (linen etc.). □ **lavender-water** a perfume made from distilled lavender, alcohol, and ambergris. [ME f. AF *lavendre*, ult. f. med.L *lavandula*]

laver /ˈleɪvə(r), ˈlɑːvə(r)/ *n*. any of various edible seaweeds, esp. *Porphyra umbilicalis*, having sheet-like fronds. □ **laver bread** a Welsh dish of laver which is boiled, dipped in oatmeal, and fried. [L]

lavish /ˈlævɪʃ/ *adj. & v.* —*adj*. **1** giving or producing in large quantities; profuse. **2** generous, unstinting. **3** excessive, over-abundant. —*v.tr*. (often foll. by *on*) bestow or spend (money, effort, praise, etc.) abundantly. □ **lavishly** *adv*.

lavishness *n.* [ME f. obs. *lavish, lavas* (n.) profusion f. OF *lavasse* deluge of rain f. *laver* wash]

law *n.* **1 a** a rule enacted or customary in a community and recognized as enjoining or prohibiting certain actions and enforced by the imposition of penalties. **b** a body of such rules (*the law of the land; forbidden under Scots law*). **2** the controlling influence of laws; a state of respect for laws (*law and order*). **3** laws collectively as a social system or subject of study (*was reading law*). **4** (with defining word) any of the specific branches or applications of law (*commercial law; law of contract*). **5** binding force or effect (*their word is law*). **6** (prec. by *the*) **a** the legal profession. **b** *colloq.* the police. **7** the statute and common law (opp. EQUITY). **8** (in *pl.*) jurisprudence. **9 a** the judicial remedy; litigation. **b** the lawcourts as providing this (*go to law*). **10** a rule of action or procedure, e.g. in a game, social context, form of art, etc. **11** a regularity in natural occurrences, esp. as formulated or propounded in particular instances (*the law of gravity; Parkinson's law*). **12** divine commandments as expressed in the Bible or other sources. □ **at** (or **in**) **law** according to the laws. **be a law unto oneself** do what one feels is right; disregard custom. **go to law** take legal action; make use of the lawcourts. **law-abiding** obedient to the laws. **law centre** *Brit.* an independent publicly-funded advisory service on legal matters. **Law Lord** a member of the House of Lords qualified to perform its legal work. **law of nature** = *natural law.* **laws of war** the limitations on belligerents' action recognized by civilized nations. **law term** a period appointed for the sitting of lawcourts. **lay down the law** be dogmatic or authoritarian. **take the law into one's own hands** redress a grievance by one's own means, esp. by force. [OE *lagu* f. ON *lag* something 'laid down' or fixed, rel. to LAY¹]

lawbreaker /ˈlɔːˌbreɪkə(r)/ *n.* a person who breaks the law. □ **lawbreaking** *n.* & *adj.*

lawcourt /ˈlɔːkɔːt/ *n.* a court of law.

lawful /ˈlɔːfʊl/ *adj.* conforming with, permitted by, or recognized by law; not illegal or (of a child) illegitimate. □ **lawfully** *adv.* **lawfulness** *n.*

lawgiver /ˈlɔːˌgɪvə(r)/ *n.* a person who lays down laws.

lawless /ˈlɔːlɪs/ *adj.* **1** having no laws or enforcement of them. **2** disregarding laws. **3** unbridled, uncontrolled. □ **lawlessly** *adv.* **lawlessness** *n.*

lawmaker /ˈlɔːˌmeɪkə(r)/ *n.* a legislator.

lawman /ˈlɔːmæn/ *n.* (*pl.* **-men**) *US* a law-enforcement officer, esp. a sheriff or policeman.

lawn¹ /lɔːn/ *n.* a piece of grass kept mown and smooth in a garden, park, etc. □ **lawn tennis** the usual form of tennis, played with a soft ball on outdoor grass or a hard court. [ME *laund* glade f. OF *launde* f. OCelt., rel. to LAND]

lawn² /lɔːn/ *n.* a fine linen or cotton fabric used for clothes. □ **lawny** *adj.* [ME, prob. f. *Laon* in France]

lawnmower /ˈlɔːnˌməʊə(r)/ *n.* a machine for cutting the grass on a lawn.

lawrencium /ləˈrensɪəm/ *n. Chem.* an artificially made transuranic radioactive metallic element. [E. O. *Lawrence*, Amer. physicist d. 1958]

lawsuit /ˈlɔːsuːt, -sjuːt/ *n.* the process or an instance of making a claim in a lawcourt.

lawyer /ˈlɔɪə(r), ˈlɔːjə(r)/ *n.* a member of the legal profession, esp. a solicitor. □ **lawyerly** *adj.* [ME *law(i)er* f. LAW]

lax *adj.* **1** lacking care, concern, or firmness. **2** loose, relaxed; not compact. □ **laxity** *n.* **laxly** *adv.* **laxness** *n.* [ME, = loose, f. L *laxus*: rel. to SLACK¹]

laxative /ˈlæksətɪv/ *adj.* & *n.* —*adj.* tending to stimulate or facilitate evacuation of the bowels. —*n.* a laxative medicine. [ME f. OF *laxatif -ive* or LL *laxativus* f. L *laxare* loosen (as LAX)]

lay¹ *v.* & *n.* —*v.* (*past* and *past part.* **laid** /leɪd/) **1** *tr.* place on a surface, esp. horizontally or in the proper or specified place. **2** *tr.* put or bring into a certain or the required position or state (*laid his hand on her arm; lay a carpet*). **3** *intr. dial.* or *erron.* lie. **4** *tr.* make by laying (*lay the foundations*). **5** *tr.* (often *absol.*) (of a hen bird) produce (an egg). **6** *tr.* **a** cause to subside or lie flat. **b** deal with to remove (a ghost, fear, etc.). **7** *tr.* place or present for consideration (a case, proposal, etc.). **8** *tr.* set down as a basis or starting-point. **9** *tr.* (usu. foll. by *on*) attribute or impute (blame etc.). **10** *tr.* locate (a scene etc.) in a certain place. **11** *tr.* prepare or make ready (a plan or a trap). **12** *tr.* prepare (a table) for a meal. **13** *tr.* place or arrange the material for (a fire). **14** *tr.* put down as a wager; stake. **15** *tr.* (foll. by *with*) coat or strew (a surface). **16** *tr. sl. offens.* have sexual intercourse with (esp. a woman). —*n.* **1** the way, position, or direction in which something lies. **2** *sl. offens.* a partner (esp. female) in sexual intercourse. □ **in lay** (of a hen) laying eggs regularly. **laid-back** *colloq.* relaxed, unbothered, easygoing. **laid paper** paper with the surface marked in fine ribs. **laid up** confined to bed or the house. **lay about one 1** hit out on all sides. **2** criticize indiscriminately. **lay aside 1** put to one side. **2** cease to practise or consider. **3** save (money etc.) for future needs. **lay back** cause to slope back from the vertical. **lay bare** expose, reveal. **lay a charge** make an accusation. **lay claim to** claim as one's own. **lay down 1** put on the ground. **2** relinquish; give up (an office). **3** formulate (a rule or principle). **4** pay or wager (money). **5** begin to construct (a ship or railway). **6** store (wine) in a cellar. **7** set down on paper. **8** sacrifice (one's life). **9** convert (land) into pasture. **10** record (esp. popular music). **lay one's hands on** obtain, acquire, locate. **lay hands on 1** seize or attack. **2** place one's hands on or over, esp. in confirmation, ordination, or spiritual healing. **lay hold of** seize or grasp. **lay in** provide oneself with a stock of. **lay into** *colloq.* punish or scold heavily. **lay it on thick** (or **with a trowel**) *colloq.* flatter or exaggerate grossly. **lay low** overthrow, kill, or humble. **lay off 1** discharge (workers) temporarily because of a shortage of work. **2** *colloq.* desist. **lay-off** *n.* **1** a temporary discharge of workers. **2** a period when this is in force. **lay on 1** provide (a facility, amenity, etc.). **2** impose (a penalty, obligation, etc.). **3** inflict (blows). **4** spread on (paint etc.). **lay open 1** break the skin of. **2** (foll. by *to*) expose (to criticism etc.). **lay out 1** spread out. **2** expose to view. **3** prepare (a corpse) for burial. **4** *colloq.* knock unconscious. **5** dispose (grounds etc.) according to a plan. **6** expend (money). **7** *refl.* (foll. by *to* + infin.) take pains (to do something) (*laid themselves out to help*). **lay to**

rest bury in a grave. **lay up 1** store, save. **2** put (a ship etc.) out of service. [OE *lecgan* f. Gmc]

■ **Usage** The intransitive use of *lay* in sense 3 as in *she was laying on the floor*, is incorrect in standard English.

lay² *adj.* **1 a** non-clerical. **b** not ordained into the clergy. **2 a** not professionally qualified, esp. in law or medicine. **b** of or done by such persons. □ **lay brother** (or **sister**) a person who has taken the vows of a religious order but is not ordained and is employed in ancillary or manual work. **lay reader** a lay person licensed to conduct some religious services. [ME f. OF *lai* f. eccl.L *laicus* f. Gk *laikos* LAIC]

lay³ *n.* **1** a short lyric or narrative poem meant to be sung. **2** a song. [ME f. OF *lai*, Prov. *lais*, of unkn. orig.]

lay⁴ *past of* LIE.

layabout /ˈleɪəˌbaʊt/ *n.* a habitual loafer or idler.

lay-by /ˈleɪbaɪ/ *n.* (*pl.* **lay-bys**) **1** *Brit.* an area at the side of an open road where vehicles may stop. **2** *Austral.* & *NZ* a system of paying a deposit to secure an article for later purchase.

layer /ˈleɪə(r)/ *n.* & *v.* —*n.* **1** a thickness of matter, esp. one of several, covering a surface. **2** a person or thing that lays. **3** a hen that lays eggs. **4** a shoot fastened down to take root while attached to the parent plant. —*v.tr.* **1 a** arrange in layers. **b** cut (hair) in layers. **2** propagate (a plant) as a layer. □ **layered** *adj.* [ME f. LAY¹ + -ER¹]

layette /leɪˈet/ *n.* a set of clothing, toilet articles, and bedclothes for a newborn child. [F, dimin. of OF *laie* drawer f. MDu. *laege*]

lay figure /leɪ/ *n.* **1** a dummy or jointed figure of a human body used by artists for arranging drapery on etc. **2** an unrealistic character in a novel etc. **3** a person lacking in individuality. [*lay* f. obs. *layman* f. Du. *leeman* f. obs. *led* joint]

layman /ˈleɪmən/ *n.* (*pl.* **-men**; *fem.* **laywoman**, *pl.* **-women**) **1** any non-ordained member of a Church. **2** a person without professional or specialized knowledge in a particular subject.

layout /ˈleɪaʊt/ *n.* **1** the disposing or arrangement of a site, ground, etc. **2** the way in which plans, printed matter, etc., are arranged or set out. **3** something arranged or set out in a particular way. **4** the make-up of a book, newspaper, etc.

laze *v.* & *n.* —*v.* **1** *intr.* spend time lazily or idly. **2** *tr.* (often foll. by *away*) pass (time) in this way. —*n.* a spell of lazing. [back-form. f. LAZY]

lazuli /ˈlæzjuːlɪ, -ˌlaɪ/ *n.* = LAPIS LAZULI. [abbr.]

lazy /ˈleɪzɪ/ *adj.* (**lazier**, **laziest**) **1** disinclined to work, doing little work. **2** of or inducing idleness. **3** (of a river) slow-moving. □ **lazily** *adv.* **laziness** *n.* [earlier *laysie*, *lasie*, *laesy*, perh. f. LG: cf. LG *lasich* idle]

lazybones /ˈleɪzɪˌbəʊnz/ *n.* (*pl.* same) *colloq.* a lazy person.

lb. *abbr.* a pound or pounds (weight). [L *libra*]

L/Bdr *abbr.* Lance-Bombardier.

l.b.w. *abbr.* *Cricket* leg before wicket.

l.c. *abbr.* **1** in the passage etc. cited. **2** lower case. [sense 1 f. L *loco citato*]

LCD *abbr.* **1** liquid crystal display. **2** lowest (or least) common denominator.

LCM *abbr.* lowest (or least) common multiple.

L/Cpl *abbr.* Lance-Corporal.

Ld. *abbr.* Lord.

-le¹ /(ə)l/ *suffix* forming nouns, esp.: **1** names of appliances or instruments (*handle*; *thimble*). **2** names of animals and plants (*beetle*; *thistle*). [ult. from or repr. OE *-el* etc. f. Gmc]

-le² /(ə)l/ *suffix* (also **-el**) forming nouns with (or orig. with) diminutive sense, or = -AL (*angle*; *castle*; *mantle*; *syllable*; *novel*; *tunnel*). [ME *-el*, *-elle* f. OF ult. f. L forms *-ellus*, *-ella*, etc.]

-le³ /(ə)l/ *suffix* forming adjectives, often with (or orig. with) the sense 'apt or liable to' (*brittle*; *fickle*; *little*; *nimble*). [ME f. OE *-el* etc. f. Gmc, corresp. to L *-ulus*]

-le⁴ /(ə)l/ *suffix* forming verbs, esp. expressing repeated action or movement or having diminutive sense (*bubble*; *crumple*; *wriggle*). [OE *-lian* f. Gmc]

LEA *abbr.* (in the UK) Local Education Authority.

lea *n.* *poet.* a piece of meadow or pasture or arable land. [OE *lēa(h)* f. Gmc]

leach *v.* **1** *tr.* make (a liquid) percolate through some material. **2** *tr.* subject (bark, ore, ash, or soil) to the action of percolating fluid. **3** *tr.* & *intr.* (foll. by *away*, *out*) remove (soluble matter) or be removed in this way. □ **leacher** *n.* [prob. repr. OE *leccan* to water, f. WG]

lead¹ /liːd/ *v.* & *n.* —*v.* (*past* and *past part.* **led**) **1** *tr.* cause to go with one, esp. by guiding or showing the way or by going in front and taking a person's hand or an animal's halter etc. **2** *tr.* **a** direct the actions or opinions of. **b** (often foll. by *to*, or *to* + *infin.*) guide by persuasion or example or argument (*what led you to that conclusion?*; *was led to think you may be right*). **3** *tr.* (also *absol.*) provide access to; bring to a certain position or destination (*this door leads you into a small room*; *the path leads uphill*). **4** *tr.* pass or go through (a life etc. of a specified kind) (*led a miserable existence*). **5** *tr.* **a** have the first place in (*lead the dance*; *leads the world in sugar production*). **b** (*absol.*) go first; be ahead in a race or game. **c** (*absol.*) be pre-eminent in some field. **6** *tr.* be in charge of (*leads a team of researchers*). **7** *tr.* **a** direct by example. **b** set (a fashion). **c** be the principal player of (a group of musicians). **8** *tr.* (also *absol.*) begin a round of play at cards by playing (a card) or a card of (a particular suit). **9** *intr.* (foll. by *to*) have as an end or outcome; result in (*what does all this lead to?*). **10** *intr.* (foll. by *with*) *Boxing* make an attack (with a particular blow). **11 a** *intr.* (foll. by *with*) (of a newspaper) use a particular item as the main story (*led with the Stock Market crash*). **b** *tr.* (of a story) be the main feature of (a newspaper or part of it) (*the royal wedding will lead the front page*). —*n.* **1** guidance given by going in front; example. **2 a** a leading place; the leadership (*is in the lead*; *take the lead*). **b** the amount by which a competitor is ahead of the others (*a lead of ten yards*). **3** a clue, esp. an early indication of the resolution of a problem (*is the first real lead in the case*). **4** a strap or cord for leading a dog etc. **5** a conductor (usu. a wire) conveying electric current from a source to an appliance. **6 a** the chief part in a play etc. **b** the person playing this. **7** (in full **lead story**) the item of news given the greatest prominence in a newspaper or magazine. **8 a** the act or right of playing first in a game or round of cards. **b** the card led. □ **lead by the nose** cajole (a person) into compliance. **lead-in 1** an introduction, opening, etc. **2** a wire leading in from outside,

esp. from an aerial to a receiver or transmitter.
lead off 1 begin; make a start. **2** *colloq.* lose
one's temper. **lead on 1** entice into going
further than was intended. **2** mislead or deceive.
lead time the time between the initiation and
completion of a production process. **lead up
the garden path** *colloq.* mislead. □ **leadable**
adj. [OE *lǣdan* f. Gmc]

lead[2] /led/ *n.* & *v.* —*n.* **1** *Chem.* a heavy bluish-grey
soft ductile metallic element used in building
and the manufacture of alloys. **2 a** graphite. **b** a
thin length of this for use in a pencil. **3** a lump
of lead used in sounding water. **4** (in *pl.*) *Brit.* a
strips of lead covering a roof. **b** a piece of
lead-covered roof. **5** (in *pl.*) *Brit.* lead frames
holding the glass of a lattice or stained-glass
window. **6** *Printing* a blank space between lines
of print (orig. with ref. to the metal strip used
to give this space). **7** (*attrib.*) made of lead.
—*v.tr.* **1** cover, weight, or frame (a roof or
window panes) with lead. **2** *Printing* separate
lines of (printed matter) with leads. **3** add a lead
compound to (petrol etc.). □ **lead acetate** a
white crystalline compound of lead that dissolves in water to form a sweet-tasting solution.
lead-free (of petrol) without added lead compounds. **lead pencil** a pencil of graphite
enclosed in wood. □ **leadless** *adj.* [OE *lēad* f.
WG]

leaden /ˈled(ə)n/ *adj.* **1** of or like lead. **2** heavy,
slow, burdensome (*leaden limbs*). **3** inert, depressing (*leaden rule*). **4** lead-coloured (*leaden skies*). □
leadenly *adv.* **leadenness** *n.* [OE *lēaden* (as
LEAD[2])]

leader /ˈliːdə(r)/ *n.* **1 a** a person or thing that
leads. **b** a person followed by others. **2 a** the
principal player in a music group or of the first
violins in an orchestra. **b** *US* a conductor of an
orchestra. **3** *Brit.* = *leading article.* **4** (in full
Leader of the House) *Brit.* a member of the
government officially responsible for initiating
business in Parliament. **5** a shoot of a plant at
the apex of a stem or of the main branch. □
leaderless *adj.* **leadership** *n.* [OE *lǣdere* (as
LEAD[1])]

leading[1] /ˈliːdɪŋ/ *adj.* & *n.* —*adj.* chief; most
important. —*n.* guidance, leadership. □ **leading
aircraftman** the rank above aircraftman in
the RAF. **leading article** a newspaper article
giving the editorial opinion. **leading counsel**
the senior barrister of two or more in a case.
leading edge 1 the foremost edge of an aerofoil,
esp. a wing or propeller blade. **2** *colloq.* the
forefront of development, esp. in technology.
leading lady the actress playing the principal
part. **leading light** a prominent and influential
person. **leading man** the actor playing the
principal part. **leading question** a question
that prompts the answer wanted. **leading
seaman** the rank next below NCO in the Royal
Navy. **leading-strings** (or **-reins**) **1** strings for
guiding children learning to walk. **2** oppressive
supervision or control.

■ **Usage** The phrase *leading question* does not
mean a 'principal' (or 'loaded' or 'searching')
question.

leading[2] /ˈledɪŋ/ *n. Printing* = LEAD[2] n. 6.

leaf *n.* & *v.* —*n.* (*pl.* **leaves** /liːvz/) **1 a** each of
several flattened usu. green structures of a
plant, usu. on the side of a stem or branch and
the main organ of photosynthesis. **b** other
similar plant structures, e.g. bracts, sepals,
and petals (*floral leaf*). **2 a** foliage regarded
collectively. **b** the state of having leaves out (*a
tree in leaf*). **3** the leaves of tobacco or tea. **4** a
single thickness of paper, esp. in a book with
each side forming a page. **5** a very thin sheet of
metal, esp. gold or silver. **6 a** the hinged part or
flap of a door, shutter, table, etc. **b** an extra
section inserted to extend a table. —*v.* **1** *intr.*
put forth leaves. **2** *tr.* (foll. by *through*) turn over
the pages of (a book etc.). □ **leaf-mould** soil
consisting chiefly of decayed leaves. □ **leafage**
n. **leafed** *adj.* (also in *comb.*). **leafless** *adj.*
leaflessness *n.* **leaflike** *adj.* [OE *lēaf* f. Gmc]

leaflet /ˈliːflɪt/ *n.* & *v.* —*n.* **1** a young leaf. **2** *Bot.*
any division of a compound leaf. **3** a sheet of
(usu. printed) paper (sometimes folded but
not stitched) giving information, esp. for free
distribution. —*v.tr.* (**leafleted, leafleting**) distribute leaflets to.

leafy /ˈliːfɪ/ *adj.* (**leafier, leafiest**) **1** having many
leaves. **2** resembling a leaf. □ **leafiness** *n.*

league[1] /liːg/ *n.* & *v.* —*n.* **1** a collection of
people, countries, groups, etc., combining for a
particular purpose, esp. mutual protection or
cooperation. **2** an agreement to combine in this
way. **3** a group of sports clubs which compete
over a period for a championship. **4** a class of
contestants. —*v.intr.* (**leagues, leagued,
leaguing**) (often foll. by *together*) join in a league.
□ **in league** allied, conspiring. **league table 1**
a listing of competitors as a league, showing
their ranking according to performance. **2** any
list of ranking order. [F *ligue* or It. *liga*, var. of
lega f. *legare* bind f. L *ligare*]

league[2] /liːg/ *n. archaic* a varying measure of
travelling-distance by land, usu. about three
miles. [ME, ult. f. LL *leuga, leuca*, of Gaulish orig.]

leak *n.* & *v.* —*n.* **1 a** a hole in a vessel, pipe, or
container etc. caused by wear or damage,
through which matter, esp. liquid or gas, passes
accidentally in or out. **b** the matter passing in
or out through this. **c** the act or an instance of
leaking. **2 a** a similar escape of electrical charge.
b the charge that escapes. **3** the intentional
disclosure of secret information. —*v.* **1 a** *intr.*
(of liquid, gas, etc.) pass in or out through a
leak. **b** *tr.* lose or admit (liquid, gas, etc.)
through a leak. **2** *tr.* intentionally disclose (secret
information). **3** *intr.* (often foll. by *out*) (of a
secret, secret information) become known. □
have (or **take**) **a leak** *sl.* urinate. □ **leaker** *n.*
[ME prob. f. LG]

leakage /ˈliːkɪdʒ/ *n.* **1** the action or result of
leaking. **2** what leaks in or out. **3** an intentional
disclosure of secret information.

leaky /ˈliːkɪ/ *adj.* (**leakier, leakiest**) **1** having a
leak or leaks. **2** given to letting out secrets. □
leakiness *n.*

lean[1] *v.* & *n.* —*v.* (*past* and *past part.* **leaned**
/liːnd, lent/ or **leant** /lent/) **1** *intr.* & *tr.* (often
foll. by *across, back, over,* etc.) be or place in a
sloping position; incline from the perpen-
dicular. **2** *intr.* & *tr.* (foll. by *against, on, upon*)
rest or cause to rest for support against etc. **3**
intr. (foll. by *on, upon*) rely on; derive support
from. **4** *intr.* (foll. by *to, towards*) be inclined or
partial to; have a tendency towards. —*n.* a
deviation from the perpendicular; an inclination
(*has a decided lean to the right*). □ **lean on** *colloq.*
put pressure on (a person) to act in a certain
way. **lean-to** (*pl.* **-tos**) a building with its roof

leaning against a larger building or a wall. [OE *hleonian, hlinian* f. Gmc]

lean[2] *adj.* & *n.* —*adj.* **1** (of a person or animal) thin; having no superfluous fat. **2** (of meat) containing little fat. **3 a** meagre; of poor quality (*lean crop*). **b** not nourishing (*lean diet*). **4** unremunerative. —*n.* the lean part of meat. □ **lean years** years of scarcity. □ **leanly** *adv.* **leanness** *n.* [OE *hlǽne* f. Gmc]

leaning /ˈliːnɪŋ/ *n.* a tendency or partiality.

leap *v.* & *n.* —*v.* (*past* and *past part.* **leaped** /liːpt, lept/ or **leapt** /lept/) **1** *intr.* jump or spring forcefully. **2** *tr.* jump across. **3** *intr.* (of prices etc.) increase dramatically. —*n.* a forceful jump. □ **by leaps and bounds** with startlingly rapid progress. **leap in the dark** a daring step or enterprise whose consequences are unpredictable. **leap to the eye** be immediately apparent. **leap year** a year, occurring once in four, with 366 days (including 29th Feb. as an intercalary day). □ **leaper** *n.* [OE *hlýp, hléapan* f. Gmc: *leap year* prob. refers to the fact that feast-days after Feb. in such a year fall two days later (instead of the normal one day later) than in the previous year]

leap-frog /ˈliːpfrɒg/ *n.* & *v.* —*n.* a game in which players in turn vault with parted legs over another who is bending down. —*v.* (**-frogged, -frogging**) **1** *intr.* (foll. by *over*) perform such a vault. **2** *tr.* vault over in this way. **3** *tr.* & *intr.* (of two or more people, vehicles, etc.) overtake alternately.

learn /lɜːn/ *v.* (*past* and *past part.* **learned** /lɜːnt, lɜːnd/ or **learnt** /lɜːnt/) **1** *tr.* gain knowledge of or skill in by study, experience, or being taught. **2** *tr.* (foll. by *to* + infin.) acquire or develop a particular ability (*learn to swim*). **3** *tr.* commit to memory (*will try to learn your names*). **4** *intr.* (foll. by *of*) be informed about. **5** *tr.* (foll. by *that, how,* etc. + clause) become aware of by information or from observation. **6** *intr.* receive instruction; acquire knowledge or skill. **7** *tr. archaic* or *sl.* teach. □ **learnable** *adj.* **learnability** /-nəˈbɪlɪtɪ/ *n.* [OE *leornian* f. Gmc: cf. LORE]

learned /ˈlɜːnɪd/ *adj.* **1** having much knowledge acquired by study. **2** showing or requiring learning (*a learned work*). **3** studied or pursued by learned persons. **4** concerned with the interests of learned persons; scholarly (*a learned journal*). **5** *Brit.* as a courteous description of a lawyer in certain formal contexts (*my learned friend*). □ **learnedly** *adv.* **learnedness** *n.* [ME f. LEARN in the sense 'teach']

learner /ˈlɜːnə(r)/ *n.* **1** a person who is learning a subject or skill. **2** (in full **learner driver**) a person who is learning to drive a motor vehicle and has not yet passed a driving test.

learning /ˈlɜːnɪŋ/ *n.* knowledge acquired by study. [OE *leornung* (as LEARN)]

lease /liːs/ *n.* & *v.* —*n.* an agreement by which the owner of a building or land allows another to use it for a specified time, usu. in return for payment. —*v.tr.* grant or take on lease. □ **a new lease of** (*US* **on**) **life** a substantially improved prospect of living, or of use after repair. □ **leasable** *adj.* **leaser** *n.* [ME f. AF *les*, OF *lais*, *leis* f. *lesser, laissier* leave f. L *laxare* make loose (*laxus*)]

leaseback /ˈliːsbæk/ *n.* the leasing of a property back to the vendor.

leasehold /ˈliːshəʊld/ *n.* & *adj.* —*n.* **1** the holding of property by lease. **2** property held by lease. —*adj.* held by lease. □ **leaseholder** *n.*

leash /liːʃ/ *n.* & *v.* —*n.* a thong for holding a dog; a dog's lead. —*v.tr.* **1** put a leash on. **2** restrain. □ **straining at the leash** eager to begin. [ME f. OF *lesse, laisse* f. specific use of *laisser* let run on a slack lead: see LEASE]

least /liːst/ *adj., n.,* & *adv.* —*adj.* **1** smallest, slightest, most insignificant. **2** (prec. by *the;* esp. with *neg.*) any at all (*it does not make the least difference*). **3** (of a species or variety) very small (*least tern*). —*n.* the least amount. —*adv.* in the least degree. □ **at least 1** at all events; anyway; even if there is doubt about a more extended statement. **2** (also **at the least**) not less than. **in the least** (or **the least**) (usu. with *neg.*) in the smallest degree; at all (*not in the least offended*). [OE *lǽst, lǽsest* f. Gmc]

leastways /ˈliːstweɪz/ *adv.* (also **leastwise** /-waɪz/) *dial.* or at least, or rather.

leather /ˈleðə(r)/ *n.* & *v.* —*n.* **1 a** material made from the skin of an animal by tanning or a similar process. **b** (*attrib.*) made of leather. **2** a piece of leather for polishing with. **3** the leather part or parts of something. **4** *sl.* a cricket-ball or football. **5** (in *pl.*) leather clothes, esp. leggings, breeches, or clothes for wearing on a motor cycle. —*v.tr.* **1** cover with leather. **2** polish or wipe with a leather. **3** beat, thrash (orig. with a leather thong). □ **leather-jacket** *Brit.* a crane-fly grub with a tough skin. [OE *lether* f. Gmc]

leatherback /ˈleðəbæk/ *n.* a large marine turtle, *Dermochelys coriacea*, having a thick leathery carapace.

leathercloth /ˈleðəklɒθ/ *n.* strong fabric coated to resemble leather.

leatherette /ˌleðəˈret/ *n.* imitation leather.

leathern /ˈleð(ə)n/ *adj. archaic* made of leather.

leathery /ˈleðərɪ/ *adj.* **1** like leather. **2** (esp. of meat etc.) tough. □ **leatheriness** *n.*

leave[1] /liːv/ *v.* (*past* and *past part.* **left** /left/) **1 a** *tr.* go away from; cease to remain in or on (*left him quite well an hour ago; leave the track; leave here*). **b** *intr.* (often foll. by *for*) depart (*we leave tomorrow; has just left for London*). **2** *tr.* cause to or let remain; depart without taking (*has left his gloves; left a slimy trail; left a bad impression; six from seven leaves one*). **3** *tr.* (also *absol.*) cease to reside at or attend or belong to or work for (*has left the school; I am leaving for another firm*). **4** *tr.* abandon, forsake, desert. **5** *tr.* have remaining after one's death (*leaves a wife and two children*). **6** *tr.* bequeath. **7** *tr.* (foll. by *to* + infin.) allow (a person or thing) to do something without interference or assistance (*leave the future to take care of itself*). **8** *tr.* (foll. by *to*) commit or refer to another person (*leave that to me; nothing was left to chance*). **9** *tr.* **a** abstain from consuming or dealing with. **b** (in *passive;* often foll. by *over*) remain over. **10** *tr.* **a** deposit or entrust (a thing) to be attended to, collected, delivered, etc., in one's absence (*left a message with his secretary*). **b** depute (a person) to perform a function in one's absence. **11** *tr.* allow to remain or cause to be in a specified state or position (*left the door open; the performance left them unmoved; left nothing that was necessary undone*). **12** *tr.* pass (an object) so that it is in a specified relative direction (*leave the church on the left*). □ **be left with 1** retain (a feeling etc.). **2** be burdened with (a responsibility etc.). **have left** have remaining (*has no friends left*). **leave alone 1** refrain from disturbing, not interfere with. **2** not have dealings with. **leave be** *colloq.* refrain from disturbing, not interfere with. **leave behind 1** go away without. **2** leave as a consequence or a visible sign of passage. **3** pass. **leave a person cold** (or **cool**) not impress or excite a person. **leave go** *colloq.* relax one's hold. **leave hold of** cease holding. **leave it at that** *colloq.* abstain from comment or further action. **leave much** (or **a lot** etc.) **to be desired** be highly unsatisfactory. **leave off 1** come to or make an end. **2** discontinue (*leave off work; leave off talking*). **3** cease to wear. **leave out** omit, not include. **leave over** *Brit.* leave to be considered, settled, or used later. **leave a person to himself** or **herself 1** not attempt to control a person. **2** leave a person solitary. **left for dead** abandoned as being beyond rescue. **left luggage** *Brit.* luggage deposited for later retrieval, esp. at a railway station. □ **leaver** *n.* [OE *lǣfan* f. Gmc]

leave² /liːv/ *n.* **1** (often foll. by *to* + infin.) permission. **2 a** (in full **leave of absence**) permission to be absent from duty. **b** the period for which this lasts. □ **by** (or **with**) **your leave** often *iron.* an expression of apology for taking a liberty or making an unwelcome statement. **on leave** legitimately absent from duty. **take one's leave** bid farewell. **take one's leave of** bid farewell to. **take leave to** venture or presume to. [OE *lēaf* f. WG: cf. LOVE]

leaved /liːvd/ *adj.* **1** having leaves. **2** (in *comb.*) having a leaf or leaves of a specified kind or number (*four-leaved clover*).

leaven /ˈlev(ə)n/ *n. & v.* —*n.* **1 a** substance added to dough to make it ferment and rise, esp. yeast, or fermenting dough reserved for the purpose. **2 a** pervasive transforming influence (cf. Matt. 13:33). **b** (foll. by *of*) a tinge or admixture of a specified quality. —*v.tr.* **1** ferment (dough) with leaven. **2 a** permeate and transform. **b** (foll. by *with*) modify with a tempering element. [ME f. OF *levain* f. Gallo-Roman spec. use of L *levamen* relief f. *levare* lift]

leaves pl. of LEAF.

leavings /ˈliːvɪŋz/ *n.pl.* things left over, esp. as worthless.

lech /letʃ/ *v. & n. colloq.* —*v.intr.* feel lecherous; behave lustfully. —*n.* **1** a strong desire, esp. sexual. **2** a lecher. [back-form. f. LECHER: (n.) perh. f. *letch* longing]

lecher /ˈletʃə(r)/ *n.* a lecherous man; a debauchee. [ME f. OF *lecheor* etc. f. *lechier* live in debauchery or gluttony f. Frank., rel. to LICK]

lecherous /ˈletʃərəs/ *adj.* lustful, having strong or excessive sexual desire. □ **lecherously** *adv.* **lecherousness** *n.* [ME f. OF *lecheros* etc. f. *lecheur* LECHER]

lechery /ˈletʃərɪ/ *n.* unrestrained indulgence of sexual desire. [ME f. OF *lecherie* f. *lecheur* LECHER]

lecithin /ˈlesɪθɪn/ *n.* **1** any of a group of phospholipids found naturally in animals, egg-yolk, and some higher plants. **2** a preparation of this used to emulsify foods etc. [Gk *lekithos* egg-yolk + -IN]

lectern /ˈlektɜːn, -t(ə)n/ *n.* **1** a stand for holding a book in a church or chapel, esp. for a bible from which lessons are to be read. **2** a similar stand for a lecturer etc. [ME *lettorne* f. OF *let(t)run*, med.L *lectrum* f. *legere lect-* read]

lecture /ˈlektʃə(r)/ *n. & v.* —*n.* **1** a discourse giving information about a subject to a class or other audience. **2** a long serious speech esp. as a scolding or reprimand. —*v.* **1** *intr.* (often foll. by *on*) deliver a lecture or lectures. **2** *tr.* talk seriously or reprovingly to (a person). **3** *tr.* instruct or entertain (a class or other audience) by a lecture. [ME f. OF *lecture* or med.L *lectura* f. *legere lect-* read]

lecturer /ˈlektʃərə(r)/ *n.* a person who lectures, esp. as a teacher in higher education.

lectureship /ˈlektʃəʃɪp/ *n.* the office of lecturer.

LED *abbr.* light-emitting diode.

led past and past part. of LEAD¹.

ledge *n.* **1** a narrow horizontal surface projecting from a wall etc. **2** a shelflike projection on the side of a rock or mountain. **3** a ridge of rocks, esp. below water. □ **ledged** *adj.* **ledgy** *adj.* [perh. f. ME *legge* LAY¹]

ledger /ˈledʒə(r)/ *n.* a tall narrow book in which a firm's accounts are kept, esp. one which is the principal book of a set and contains debtor-and-creditor accounts. [ME f. senses of Du. *ligger* and *legger* (f. *liggen* LIE¹, *leggen* LAY¹) & pronunc. of ME *ligge, legge*]

lee /liː/ *n.* **1** shelter given by a neighbouring object (*under the lee of*). **2** (in full **lee side**) the sheltered side, the side away from the wind (opp. *weather side*). □ **lee shore** the shore to leeward of a ship. [OE *hlēo* f. Gmc]

leech¹ *n.* **1** any freshwater or terrestrial annelid worm of the class *Hirudinea* with suckers at both ends, esp. *Hirudo medicinalis*, a bloodsucking parasite of vertebrates formerly much used medicinally. **2** a person who extorts profit from or sponges on others. [OE *lǣce*, assim. to LEECH²]

leech² /liːtʃ/ *n. archaic* or *joc.* a physician; a healer. [OE *lǣce* f. Gmc]

leek *n.* **1** an alliaceous plant, *Allium porrum*, with flat overlapping leaves forming an elongated cylindrical bulb, used as food. **2** this as a Welsh national emblem. [OE *lēac* f. Gmc]

leer *v. & n.* —*v.intr.* look slyly or lasciviously or maliciously. —*n.* a leering look. □ **leeringly** *adv.* [perh. f. obs. *leer* cheek f. OE *hlēor*, as though 'to glance over one's cheek']

leery /ˈlɪərɪ/ *adj.* (**leerier, leeriest**) *sl.* **1** knowing, sly. **2** (foll. by *of*) wary. □ **leeriness** *n.* [perh. f. obs. *leer* looking askance f. LEER + -Y¹]

lees /liːz/ *n.pl.* **1** the sediment of wine etc. (*drink to the lees*). **2** dregs, refuse. [pl. of ME *lie* f. OF *lie* f. med.L *lia* f. Gaulish]

leeward /ˈliːwəd, *Naut.* ˈluːəd/ *adj., adv., & n.* —*adj. & adv.* on or towards the side sheltered from the wind. —*n.* the leeward region, side, or direction (*to leeward; on the leeward of*).

leeway /ˈliːweɪ/ *n.* **1** the sideways drift of a ship to leeward of the desired course. **2** a allowable deviation or freedom of action. **3** *US* margin of safety. □ **make up leeway** struggle out of a bad position, recover lost time, etc.

left¹ *adj., adv., & n.* (opp. RIGHT). —*adj.* **1** on or towards the side of the human body which corresponds to the position of west if one regards oneself as facing north. **2** on or towards the part of an object which is analogous to a person's left side or (with opposite sense) which is nearer to an observer's left hand. **3** (also **Left**) *Polit.* of the Left. —*adv.* on or to the left side. —*n.* **1** the left-hand part or region or direction. **2** *Boxing* **a** the left hand. **b** a blow with this. **3 a**

(often **Left**) *Polit.* a group or section favouring radical socialism; such radicals collectively. **b** the more advanced or innovative section of any group. **4** the side of a stage which is to the left of a person facing the audience. **5** (esp. in marching) the left foot. **6** the left wing of an army. □ **have two left feet** be clumsy. **left bank** the bank of a river on the left facing downstream. **left field** *Baseball* the part of the outfield to the left of the batter as he or she faces the pitcher. **left hand 1** the hand of the left side. **2** (usu. prec. by *at, on, to*) the region or direction on the left side of a person. **left-hand** *adj.* **1** on or towards the left side of a person or thing (*left-hand drive*). **2** done with the left hand (*left-hand blow*). **left turn** a turn that brings one's front to face as one's left side did before. **left wing 1** the radical or socialist section of a political party. **2** the left side of a football etc. team on the field. **3** the left side of an army. **left-wing** *adj.* socialist, radical. **left-winger** a person on the left wing. □ **leftish** *adj.* [ME *lüft, lift, left,* f. OE, orig. sense 'weak, worthless']

left² past and past part. of LEAVE¹.

left-handed /ˈleftˈhændɪd/ *adj.* **1** using the left hand by preference as more serviceable than the right. **2** (of a tool etc.) made to be used with the left hand. **3** (of a blow) struck with the left hand. **4 a** turning to the left; towards the left. **b** (of a screw) advanced by turning to the left (anticlockwise). **5** awkward, clumsy. **6** (of a compliment) ambiguous. □ **left-handedly** *adv.* **left-handedness** *n.*

left-hander /leftˈhændə(r)/ *n.* **1** a left-handed person. **2** a left-handed blow.

leftie var. of LEFTY.

leftism /ˈleftɪz(ə)m/ *n. Polit.* the principles or policy of the left. □ **leftist** *n.* & *adj.*

leftmost /ˈleftməʊst/ *adj.* furthest to the left.

leftovers /ˈleftˌəʊvəz/ *n.pl.* items (esp. of food) remaining after the rest has been used.

leftward /ˈleftwəd/ *adv.* & *adj.* —*adv.* (also **leftwards** /-wədz/) towards the left. —*adj.* going towards or facing the left.

lefty /ˈleftɪ/ *n.* (also **leftie**) (*pl.* **-ies**) *colloq.* **1** *Polit.* a left-winger. **2** a left-handed person.

leg *n.* **1 a** each of the limbs on which a person or animal walks and stands. **b** the part of this from the hip to the ankle. **2 a** leg of an animal or bird as food. **3** an artificial leg (*wooden leg*). **4** a part of a garment covering a leg or part of a leg. **5 a** a support of a chair, table, bed, etc. **b** a long thin support or prop, esp. a pole. **6** *Cricket* the half of the field (as divided lengthways through the pitch) in which the striker's feet are placed. **7 a** a section of a journey. **b** a section of a relay race. **c** a stage in a competition. **d** one of two or more games constituting a round. **8** one branch of a forked object. □ **feel** (or **find**) **one's legs** become able to stand or walk. **give a person a leg up** help a person to mount a horse etc. or get over an obstacle or difficulty. **leg before wicket** *Cricket* (of a batsman) out because of illegally obstructing the ball with a part of the body other than the hand. **leg break** *Cricket* **1** a ball which deviates from the leg side after bouncing. **2** such deviation. **leg-iron** a shackle or fetter for the leg. **leg it** *colloq.* walk or run hard. **leg-of-mutton sleeve** a sleeve which is full and loose on the upper arm but close-fitting on the forearm. **leg-pull** *colloq.* a

hoax. **leg-room** space for the legs of a seated person. **leg warmer** either of a pair of tubular knitted garments covering the leg from ankle to thigh. **not have a leg to stand on** be unable to support one's argument by facts or sound reasons. **on one's last legs** near death or the end of one's usefulness etc. **on one's legs 1** (also **on one's hind legs**) standing esp. to make a speech. **2** well enough to walk about. **take to one's legs** run away. □ **legged** /legd, ˈlegɪd/ *adj.* (also in *comb.*). **legger** *n.* [ME f. ON *leggr* f. Gmc]

legacy /ˈlegəsɪ/ *n.* (*pl.* **-ies**) **1** a gift left in a will. **2** something handed down by a predecessor (*legacy of corruption*). [ME f. OF *legacie* legateship f. med.L *legatia* f. L *legare* bequeath]

legal /ˈliːg(ə)l/ *adj.* **1** of or based on law; concerned with law; falling within the province of law. **2** appointed or required by law. **3** permitted by law, lawful. **4** recognized by law, as distinct from equity. □ **legal aid** payment from public funds allowed, in cases of need, to help pay for legal advice or proceedings. **legal fiction** an assertion accepted as true (though probably fictitious) to achieve a useful purpose, esp. in legal matters. **legal holiday** *US* a public holiday established by law. **legal tender** currency that cannot legally be refused in payment of a debt (usu. up to a limited amount for coins not made of gold). □ **legally** *adv.* [F *légal* or L *legalis* f. *lex legis* law: cf. LOYAL]

legalese /ˌliːgəˈliːz/ *n. colloq.* the technical language of legal documents.

legalism /ˈliːgəlɪz(ə)m/ *n.* excessive adherence to law or formula. □ **legalist** *n.* **legalistic** /-ˈlɪstɪk/ *adj.* **legalistically** /-ˈlɪstɪkəlɪ/ *adv.*

legality /lɪˈgælɪtɪ, liːˈg-/ *n.* (*pl.* **-ies**) **1** lawfulness. **2** legalism. **3** (in *pl.*) obligations imposed by law. [F *légalité* or med.L *legalitas* (as LEGAL)]

legalize /ˈliːgəlaɪz/ *v.tr.* (also **-ise**) **1** make lawful. **2** bring into harmony with the law. □ **legalization** /-ˈzeɪʃ(ə)n/ *n.*

legate /ˈlegət/ *n.* **1** a member of the clergy representing the Pope. **2** *archaic* an ambassador or delegate. □ **legateship** *n.* **legatine** /-tɪn/ *adj.* [OE f. OF *legat* f. L *legatus* past part. of *legare* depute, delegate]

legatee /ˌlegəˈtiː/ *n.* the recipient of a legacy. [as LEGATOR + -EE]

legation /lɪˈgeɪʃ(ə)n/ *n.* **1** a body of deputies. **2 a** the office and staff of a diplomatic minister (esp. when not having ambassadorial rank). **b** the official residence of a diplomatic minister. **3** a legateship. **4** the sending of a legate or deputy. [ME f. OF *legation* or L *legatio* (as LEGATE)]

legato /lɪˈgɑːtəʊ/ *adv., adj.,* & *n. Mus.* —*adv.* & *adj.* in a smooth flowing manner, without breaks between notes. —*n.* (*pl.* **-os**) **1** a legato passage. **2** legato playing. [It., = bound, past part. of *legare* f. L *ligare* bind]

legend /ˈledʒ(ə)nd/ *n.* **1 a** a traditional story sometimes popularly regarded as historical but unauthenticated; a myth. **b** such stories collectively. **c** a popular but unfounded belief. **d** *colloq.* a subject of such beliefs (*became a legend in his own lifetime*). **2 a** an inscription, esp. on a coin or medal. **b** *Printing* a caption. **c** wording on a map etc. explaining the symbols used. □ **legendry** *n.* [ME f. OF *legende* f. med.L *legenda* what is to be read, neut. pl. gerundive of L *legere* read]

legendary /ˈledʒəndərɪ/ *adj.* **1** of or connected with legends. **2** described in a legend. **3** *colloq.* remarkable enough to be a subject of legend. **4** based on a legend. □ **legendarily** *adv.* [med.L *legendarius* (as LEGEND)]

legerdemain /ˌledʒədəˈmeɪn/ *n.* **1** sleight of hand; conjuring or juggling. **2** trickery, sophistry. [ME f. F *léger de main* light of hand, dextrous]

leger line /ˈledʒə(r)/ *n. Mus.* a short line added for notes above or below the range of a staff. [var. of LEDGER]

legging /ˈlegɪŋ/ *n.* (usu. in *pl.*) a stout protective outer covering for the leg from the knee to the ankle.

leggy /ˈlegɪ/ *adj.* (**leggier, leggiest**) **1 a** long-legged. **b** (of a woman) having attractively long legs. **2** long-stemmed. □ **legginess** *n.*

leghorn /ˈleghɔːn, lɪˈgɔːn/ *n.* **1 a** fine plaited straw. **b** a hat of this. **2** (**Leghorn**) **a** a bird of a small hardy breed of domestic fowl. **b** this breed. [*Leghorn* (Livorno) in Italy, from where the straw and fowls were imported]

legible /ˈledʒɪb(ə)l/ *adj.* (of handwriting, print, etc.) clear enough to read; readable. □ **legibility** /-ˈbɪlɪtɪ/ *n.* **legibly** *adv.* [ME f. LL *legibilis* f. *legere* read]

legion /ˈliːdʒ(ə)n/ *n.* & *adj.* —*n.* **1** a division of 3,000–6,000 men, including a complement of cavalry, in the ancient Roman army. **2** a large organized body. **3** a vast host, multitude, or number. —*predic.adj.* great in number (*his good works have been legion*). □ **American Legion** (in the US) an association of ex-servicemen formed in 1919. **foreign legion** a body of foreign volunteers in a modern, esp. French, army. **Royal British Legion** (in the UK) an association of ex-servicemen (and now women) formed in 1921. [ME f. OF f. L *legio -onis* f. *legere* choose]

legionary /ˈliːdʒənərɪ/ *adj.* & *n.* —*adj.* of a legion or legions. —*n.* (*pl.* **-ies**) a member of a legion. [L *legionarius* (as LEGION)]

legionnaire /ˌliːdʒəˈneə(r)/ *n.* **1** a member of a foreign legion. **2** a member of the American Legion or the Royal British Legion. □ **legionnaires' disease** a form of bacterial pneumonia first identified after an outbreak at an American Legion meeting in 1976. [F *légionnaire* (as LEGION)]

legislate /ˈledʒɪsˌleɪt/ *v.intr.* **1** make laws. **2** (foll. by *for*) make provision by law. [back-form. f. LEGISLATION]

legislation /ˌledʒɪsˈleɪʃ(ə)n/ *n.* **1** the process of making laws. **2** laws collectively. [LL *legis latio* f. *lex legis* law + *latio* proposing f. *lat-* past part. stem of *ferre* bring]

legislative /ˈledʒɪslətɪv/ *adj.* of or empowered to make legislation. □ **legislatively** *adv.*

legislator /ˈledʒɪsˌleɪtə(r)/ *n.* **1** a member of a legislative body. **2** a lawgiver. [L (as LEGISLATION)]

legislature /ˈledʒɪsˌleɪtʃə(r), -lətʃə(r)/ *n.* the legislative body of a State.

legit /lɪˈdʒɪt/ *adj.* & *n. colloq.* —*adj.* legitimate. —*n.* **1** legitimate drama. **2** an actor in legitimate drama. [abbr.]

legitimate *adj.* & *v.* —*adj.* /lɪˈdʒɪtɪmət/ **1 a** (of a child) born of parents lawfully married to each other. **b** (of a parent, birth, descent, etc.) with, of, through, etc., a legitimate child. **2** lawful, proper, regular, conforming to the standard

type. **3** logically admissible. **4** constituting or relating to serious drama as distinct from musical comedy, revue, etc. —*v.tr.* /lɪˈdʒɪtɪˌmeɪt/ **1** make legitimate by decree, enactment, or proof. **2** justify, serve as a justification for. □ **legitimacy** /-məsɪ/ *n.* **legitimately** /-mətlɪ/ *adv.* **legitimation** /-ˈmeɪʃ(ə)n/ *n.* [med.L *legitimare* f. L *legitimus* lawful f. *lex legis* law]

legitimatize /lɪˈdʒɪtɪməˌtaɪz/ *v.tr.* (also **-ise**) legitimize. □ **legitimatization** /-ˈzeɪʃ(ə)n/ *n.*

legitimize /lɪˈdʒɪtɪˌmaɪz/ *v.tr.* (also **-ise**) **1** make legitimate. **2** serve as a justification for. □ **legitimization** /-ˈzeɪʃ(ə)n/ *n.*

legless /ˈleglɪs/ *adj.* **1** having no legs. **2** *sl.* drunk, esp. too drunk to stand.

legman /ˈlegmæn/ *n.* (*pl.* **-men**) a person employed to go about gathering news or running errands etc.

Lego /ˈlegəʊ/ *n. propr.* a construction toy consisting of interlocking plastic building blocks. [Da. *legetøj* toys f. *lege* to play]

legume /ˈlegjuːm/ *n.* **1** the seed pod of a leguminous plant. **2** any seed, pod, or other edible part of a leguminous plant used as food. [F *légume* f. L *legumen -minis* f. *legere* pick, because pickable by hand]

leguminous /lɪˈgjuːmɪnəs/ *adj.* of or like the family Leguminosae, including peas and beans, having seeds in pods and usu. root nodules able to fix nitrogen. [mod.L *leguminosus* (as LEGUME)]

legwork /ˈlegwɜːk/ *n.* work which involves a lot of walking, travelling, or physical activity.

lei /ˈleiː, leɪ/ *n.* a Polynesian garland of flowers. [Hawaiian]

leisure /ˈleʒə(r)/ *n.* **1** free time; time at one's own disposal. **2** enjoyment of free time. **3** (usu. foll. by *for*, or *to* + infin.) opportunity afforded by free time. □ **at leisure 1** not occupied. **2** in an unhurried manner. **at one's leisure** when one has time. □ **leisureless** *adj.* [ME f. AF *leisour*, OF *leisir* ult. f. L *licēre* be allowed]

leisured /ˈleʒəd/ *adj.* having ample leisure.

leisurely /ˈleʒəlɪ/ *adj.* & *adv.* —*adj.* having leisure; acting or done at leisure; unhurried, relaxed. —*adv.* without hurry. □ **leisureliness** *n.*

leisurewear /ˈleʒəˌweə(r)/ *n.* informal clothes, especially tracksuits and other sportswear.

leitmotif /ˈlaɪtməʊˌtiːf/ *n.* (also **leitmotiv**) a recurrent theme associated throughout a musical, literary, etc. composition with a particular person, idea, or situation. [G *Leitmotiv* (as LEAD¹, MOTIVE)]

lemming /ˈlemɪŋ/ *n.* any small arctic rodent of the genus *Lemmus*, esp. *L. lemmus* of Norway which is reputed to rush headlong into the sea and drown during migration. [Norw. dial.]

lemon /ˈlemən/ *n.* **1 a** a pale-yellow thick-skinned oval citrus fruit with acidic juice. **b** a tree of the species *Citrus limon* which produces this fruit. **2** a pale-yellow colour. **3** *colloq.* a person or thing regarded as feeble or unsatisfactory or disappointing. □ **lemon balm** a bushy plant, *Melissa officinalis*, with leaves smelling and tasting of lemon. **lemon curd** (or **cheese**) a conserve made from lemons, butter, eggs, and sugar. **lemon drop** a boiled sweet flavoured with lemon. **lemon grass** any fragrant tropical grass of the genus *Cymbopogon*, yielding an oil smelling of lemon. **lemon squash** *Brit.* a soft drink made from lemons and other ingredients, often sold in concentrated form. **lemon-squeezer** a device for extracting the juice from a lemon. □ **lemony** adj. [ME f. OF limon f. Arab. līma: cf. LIME²]

lemonade /ˌleməˈneɪd/ n. **1** an effervescent or still drink made from lemon juice. **2** a synthetic substitute for this.

lemon sole /ˈlemən/ n. a flat-fish, Microstomus kitt, of the plaice family. [F limande]

lemur /ˈliːmə(r)/ n. any arboreal primate of the family Lemuridae native to Madagascar, with a pointed snout and long tail. [mod.L f. L lemures (pl.) spirits of the dead, from its spectre-like face]

lend v.tr. (past and past part. **lent** /lent/) **1** (usu. foll. by to) grant (to a person) the use of (a thing) on the understanding that it or its equivalent shall be returned. **2** allow the use of (money) at interest. **3** bestow or contribute (something temporary) (lend assistance; lends a certain charm). □ **lend an ear** (or **one's ears**) listen. **lending library** a library from which books may be temporarily taken away. **lend itself to** (of a thing) be suitable for. **lend oneself to** accommodate oneself to (a policy or purpose). □ **lendable** adj. **lender** n. **lending** n. [ME, earlier lēne(n) f. OE lǣnan f. lǣn LOAN]

length /leŋθ, leŋkθ/ n. **1** measurement or extent from end to end; the greater of two or the greatest of three dimensions of a body. **2** extent in, of, or with regard to, time (a stay of some length; the length of a speech). **3** the distance a thing extends (at arm's length; ships a cable's length apart). **4** the length of a horse, boat, etc., as a measure of the lead in a race. **5** a long stretch or extent (a length of hair). **6** a degree of thoroughness in action (went to great lengths; prepared to go to any length). **7** a piece of material of a certain length (a length of cloth). **8** Prosody the quantity of a vowel or syllable. **9** Cricket **a** the distance from the batsman at which the ball pitches (the bowler keeps a good length). **b** the proper amount of this. **10** the extent of a garment in a vertical direction when worn. **11** the full extent of one's body. □ **at length 1** (also **at full** or **great** etc. **length**) in detail, without curtailment. **2** after a long time, at last. [OE lengthu f. Gmc (as LONG¹)]

lengthen /ˈleŋθ(ə)n, ˈleŋkθ(ə)n/ v. **1** tr. & intr. make or become longer. **2** tr. make (a vowel) long. □ **lengthener** n.

lengthways /ˈleŋθweɪz, ˈleŋkθ-/ adv. in a direction parallel with a thing's length.

lengthwise /ˈleŋθwaɪz, ˈleŋkθ-/ adv. & adj. —adv. lengthways. —adj. lying or moving lengthways.

lengthy /ˈleŋθɪ, ˈleŋkθɪ/ adj. (**lengthier, lengthiest**) **1** of unusual length. **2** (of speech, writing, style, a speaker, etc.) tedious, prolix. □ **lengthily** adv. **lengthiness** n.

lenient /ˈliːnɪənt/ adj. **1** merciful, tolerant, not disposed to severity. **2** (of punishment etc.) mild. **3** archaic emollient. □ **lenience** n. **leniency** n. **leniently** adv. [L lenire lenit- soothe f. lenis gentle]

lenity /ˈlenɪtɪ/ n. (pl. **-ies**) literary **1** mercifulness, gentleness. **2** an act of mercy. [F lénité or L lenitas f. lenis gentle]

lens /lenz/ n. **1** a piece of a transparent substance with one or (usu.) both sides curved for concentrating or dispersing light-rays esp. in optical instruments. **2** a combination of lenses used in

photography. □ **lensed** adj. **lensless** adj. [L lens lentis lentil (from the similarity of shape)]

Lent n. Eccl. the period from Ash Wednesday to Holy Saturday, of which the 40 weekdays are devoted to fasting and penitence in commemoration of Christ's fasting in the wilderness. □ **Lent term** Brit. the term at a university etc. in which Lent falls. [ME f. LENTEN]

lent past and past part. of LEND.

-lent /lənt/ suffix forming adjectives (pestilent; violent) (cf. -ULENT). [L -lentus -ful]

Lenten /ˈlent(ə)n/ adj. of, in, or appropriate to, Lent. □ **Lenten fare** food without meat. [orig. as noun, = spring, f. OE lencten f. Gmc, rel. to LONG¹, perh. with ref. to lengthening of the day in spring: now regarded as adj. f. LENT + -EN²]

lentil /ˈlentɪl/ n. **1** a leguminous plant, Lens culinaris, yielding edible biconvex seeds. **2** this seed, esp. used as food with the husk removed. [ME f. OF lentille f. L lenticula (as LENS)]

lento /ˈlentəʊ/ adj. & adv. Mus. —adj. slow. —adv. slowly. [It.]

Leo /ˈliːəʊ/ n. (pl. **-os**) **1** a constellation, traditionally regarded as contained in the figure of a lion. **2 a** the fifth sign of the zodiac (the Lion). **b** a person born when the sun is in this sign. [OE f. L, = LION]

leonine /ˈliːənaɪn/ adj. **1** like a lion. **2** of or relating to lions. [ME f. OF leonin -ine or L leoninus f. leo leonis lion]

leopard /ˈlepəd/ n. (fem. **leopardess** /-dɪs/) any large African or Asian flesh-eating cat, Panthera pardus, with either a black-spotted yellowish-fawn or all black coat. [ME f. OF f. LL f. late Gk leopardos (as LION + pardos leopard)]

leotard /ˈliːətɑːd/ n. a close-fitting one-piece garment worn by ballet-dancers, acrobats, etc. [J. Léotard, French trapeze artist d. 1870]

leper /ˈlepə(r)/ n. **1** a person suffering from leprosy. **2** a person shunned on moral grounds. [ME, prob. attrib. use of leper leprosy f. OF lepre f. L lepra f. Gk, fem. of lepros scaly f. lepos scale]

lepidopterous /ˌlepɪˈdɒptərəs/ adj. of the order Lepidoptera of insects, with four scale-covered wings often brightly coloured, including butterflies and moths. □ **lepidopteran** adj. & n. **lepidopterist** n. [Gk lepis -idos scale + pteron wing]

leprechaun /ˈleprəkɔːn/ n. a small mischievous sprite in Irish folklore. [OIr. luchorpán f. lu small + corp body]

leprosy /ˈleprəsɪ/ n. **1** a contagious bacterial disease that affects the skin, mucous membranes, and nerves, causing disfigurement. **2** moral corruption or contagion. [LEPROUS + -Y³]

leprous /ˈleprəs/ adj. **1** suffering from leprosy. **2** like or relating to leprosy. [ME f. OF f. LL leprosus f. lepra: see LEPER]

lepton /ˈleptɒn/ n. (pl. **leptons**) Physics any of a class of elementary particles which do not undergo strong interaction, e.g. an electron, muon, or neutrino. [LEPTO- + -ON]

lesbian /ˈlezbɪən/ n. & adj. —n. a homosexual woman. —adj. **1** of homosexuality in women. **2** (**Lesbian**) of Lesbos. □ **lesbianism** n. [L Lesbius f. Gk Lesbios f. Lesbos, island in the Aegean Sea, home of Sappho (see SAPPHIC)]

lese-majesty /liːz ˈmædʒɪstɪ/ n. (also **lèse-majesté** /leɪz ˈmæʒeˌsteɪ/) **1** treason. **2** an insult to a sovereign or ruler. **3** presumptuous conduct. [F *lèse-majesté* f. L *laesa majestas* injured sovereignty f. *laedere* laes- injure + *majestas* MAJESTY]

lesion /ˈliːʒ(ə)n/ *n.* **1** damage. **2** injury. **3** *Med.* a morbid change in the functioning or texture of an organ etc. [ME f. OF f. L *laesio -onis* f. *laedere* laes- injure]

less *adj., adv., n.,* & *prep.* —*adj.* **1** smaller in extent, degree, duration, number, etc. (*of less importance; in a less degree*). **2** of smaller quantity, not so much (*find less difficulty; eat less meat*). **3** *disp.* fewer (*eat less biscuits*). **4** of lower rank etc. (*no less a person than; James the Less*). —*adv.* to a smaller extent, in a lower degree. —*n.* a smaller amount or quantity or number (*cannot take less; for less than £10; is little less than disgraceful*). —*prep.* minus (*made £1,000 less tax*). □ **much** (or **still**) **less** with even greater force of denial (*do not suspect him of negligence, much less of dishonesty*). [OE *lǣssa* (adj.), *lǣs* (adv.), f. Gmc]

■ **Usage** The use of *less* to mean 'fewer', as in sense 3, is regarded as incorrect in standard English.

-less /lɪs/ *suffix* forming adjectives and adverbs: **1** from nouns, meaning 'not having, without, free from' (*doubtless; powerless*). **2** from verbs, meaning 'not affected by or doing the action of the verb' (*fathomless; tireless*). □ **-lessly** *suffix* forming adverbs. **-lessness** *suffix* forming nouns. [OE *-lēas* f. *lēas* devoid of]

lessee /leˈsiː/ *n.* (often foll. by *of*) a person who holds a property by lease. □ **lesseeship** *n.* [ME f. AF past part., OF *lessé* (as LEASE)]

lessen /ˈles(ə)n/ *v.tr.* & *intr.* make or become less, diminish.

lesser /ˈlesə(r)/ *adj.* (usu. *attrib.*) not so great as the other or the rest (*the lesser evil; the lesser celandine*). [double compar., f. LESS + -ER³]

lesson /ˈles(ə)n/ *n.* **1 a** an amount of teaching given at one time. **b** the time assigned to this. **2** (in *pl.*; foll. by *in*) systematic instruction (*gives lessons in dancing; took lessons in French*). **3** a thing learnt or to be learnt by a pupil. **4 a** an occurrence, example, rebuke, or punishment, that serves or should serve to warn or encourage (*let that be a lesson to you*). **b** a thing inculcated by experience or study. **5** a passage from the Bible read aloud during a church service. □ **learn one's lesson** profit from or bear in mind a particular (usu. unpleasant) experience. **teach a person a lesson** punish a person, esp. as a deterrent. [ME f. OF *leçon* f. L *lectio -onis* reading]

lessor /leˈsɔː(r)/ *n.* a person who lets a property by lease. [AF f. *lesser*: see LEASE]

lest *conj.* **1** in order that not, for fear that (*lest we forget*). **2** that (*afraid lest we should be late*). [OE *thȳ lǣs the* whereby less that, later *the lǣste*, ME *lest(e)*]

■ **Usage** *Lest* is followed by *should* or the subjunctive (see examples above).

let¹ *v.* & *n.* —*v.* (**letting**; *past* and *past part.* **let**) **1** *tr.* **a** allow to, not prevent or forbid (*we let them go*). **b** cause to (*let me know; let it be known*). **2** *tr.* (foll. by *into*) **a** allow to enter. **b** make acquainted with (a secret etc.). **c** inlay in. **3** *tr. Brit.* grant the use of (rooms, land, etc.) for rent or hire (*was let to the new tenant for a year*). **4** *tr.* allow or cause (liquid or air) to escape (*let blood*). **5** *tr.* award (a contract for work). **6** *aux.* supplying the first and third persons of the imperative in exhortations (*let us pray*), commands (*let it be done at once; let there be light*), assumptions (*let AB be equal to CD*), and permission or challenge (*let him do his worst*). —*n. Brit.* the act or an instance of letting a house, room, etc. (*a long let*). □ **let alone 1** not to mention, far less or more (*hasn't got a television, let alone a video*). **2** = **let be. let be** not interfere with, attend to, or do. **let down 1** lower. **2** fail to support or satisfy, disappoint. **3** lengthen (a garment). **4** deflate (a tyre). **let-down** *n.* a disappointment. **let down gently** avoid humiliating abruptly. **let drop** (or **fall**) drop (esp. a word or hint) intentionally or by accident. **let fly 1** (often foll. by *at*) attack physically or verbally. **2** discharge (a missile). **let go 1** release, set at liberty. **2 a** (often foll. by *of*) lose or relinquish one's hold. **b** lose hold of. **3** cease to think or talk about. **let oneself go 1** give way to enthusiasm, impulse, etc. **2** cease to take trouble, neglect one's appearance or habits. **let in 1** allow to enter (*let the dog in; let in a flood of light; this would let in all sorts of evils*). **2** (usu. foll. by *for*) involve (a person, often oneself) in loss or difficulty. **3** (foll. by *on*) allow (a person) to share privileges, information, etc. **4** inlay (a thing) in another. **let oneself in** enter a building by means of a latchkey. **let loose** release or unchain (a dog, fury, a maniac, etc.). **let off 1 a** fire (a gun). **b** explode (a bomb or firework). **2** allow or cause (steam, liquid, etc.) to escape. **3** allow to alight from a vehicle etc. **4 a** not punish or compel. **b** (foll. by *with*) punish lightly. **5** *Brit.* let (part of a house etc.). **let-off** *n.* being allowed to escape something. **let on** *colloq.* **1** reveal a secret. **2** pretend (*let on that he had succeeded*). **let out 1** allow to go out, esp. through a doorway. **2** release from restraint. **3** (often foll. by *that* + clause) reveal (a secret etc.). **4** make (a garment) looser esp. by adjustment at a seam. **5** put out to rent esp. to several tenants, or to contract. **6** exculpate. **let-out** *n. colloq.* an opportunity to escape. **let through** allow to pass. **let up** *colloq.* **1** become less intense or severe. **2** relax one's efforts. **let-up** *n. colloq.* **1** a reduction in intensity. **2** a relaxation of effort. **to let** available for rent. [OE *lǣtan* f. Gmc, rel. to LATE]

let² /let/ *n.* & *v.* —*n.* **1** (in lawn tennis, squash, etc.) an obstruction of a ball or a player in certain ways, requiring the ball to be served again. **2** (*archaic* except in **without let** or **hindrance**) obstruction, hindrance. —*v.tr.* (**letting**; *past* and *past part.* **letted** or **let**) *archaic* hinder, obstruct. [OE *lettan* f. Gmc, rel. to LATE]

-let /lɪt, lət/ *suffix* forming nouns, usu. diminutives (*flatlet; leaflet*) or denoting articles of ornament or dress (*anklet*). [orig. corresp. (in *bracelet, crosslet*, etc.) to F *-ette* added to nouns in *-el*]

lethal /ˈliːθ(ə)l/ *adj.* causing or sufficient to cause death. □ **lethal chamber** a chamber in which animals may be killed painlessly with gas. **lethal dose** the amount of a toxic compound or drug that causes death in humans or animals. □ **lethality** /lɪˈθælɪtɪ/ *n.* **lethally** *adv.* [L *let(h)alis* f. *letum* death]

lethargy /ˈleθədʒɪ/ *n.* **1** lack of energy or vitality; a torpid, inert, or apathetic state. **2** *Med.* morbid drowsiness or prolonged and unnatural sleep. □ **lethargic** /lɪˈθɑːdʒɪk/ *adj.* **lethargically** /lɪˈθɑːdʒɪkəlɪ/ *adv.* [ME f. OF *litargie* f. LL *lethargia*

f. Gk *lēthargia* f. *lēthargos* forgetful f. *lēth-*, *lanthanomai* forget]

letter /ˈletə(r)/ *n.* & *v.* —*n.* **1 a** a character representing one or more of the simple or compound sounds used in speech, any of the alphabetic symbols. **b** (in *pl.*) *colloq.* the initials of a degree etc. after the holder's name. **2 a** a written, typed, or printed communication, usu. sent by post or messenger. **b** (in *pl.*) an addressed legal or formal document for any of various purposes. **3** the precise terms of a statement, the strict verbal interpretation (*according to the letter of the law*). **4** (in *pl.*) **a** literature. **b** acquaintance with books, erudition. **c** authorship (*the profession of letters*). —*v.tr.* **1 a** inscribe letters on. **b** impress a title etc. on (a book-cover). **2** classify with letters. □ **letter-bomb** a terrorist explosive device in the form of a postal packet. **letter-box** esp. *Brit.* a box or slot into which letters are posted or delivered. **letter-heading** = LETTERHEAD. **letter-quality** of the quality of printing suitable for a business letter; producing print of this quality. **man of letters** a scholar or author. **to the letter** with adherence to every detail. □ **letterer** *n.* **letterless** *adj.* [ME f. OF *lettre* f. L *litera*, *littera* letter of alphabet, (in *pl.*) epistle, literature]

lettered /ˈletəd/ *adj.* well read or educated.

letterhead /ˈletəˌhed/ *n.* **1** a printed heading on stationery. **2** stationery with this.

lettering /ˈletərɪŋ/ *n.* **1** the process of inscribing letters. **2** letters inscribed.

letterpress /ˈletəˌpres/ *n.* **1 a** the contents of an illustrated book other than the illustrations. **b** printed matter relating to illustrations. **2** printing from raised type, not from lithography etc.

lettuce /ˈletɪs/ *n.* **1** a composite plant, *Lactuca sativa*, with crisp edible leaves used in salads. **2** any of various plants resembling this. [ME *letus(e)*, rel. to OF *laitue* f. L *lactuca* f. *lac lactis* milk, with ref. to its milky juice]

leuco- /ˈluːkəʊ/ *comb. form* white. [Gk *leukos* white]

leucocyte /ˈluːkəˌsaɪt/ *n.* (also **leukocyte**) **1** a white blood cell. **2** any blood cell that contains a nucleus. □ **leucocytic** /-ˈsɪtɪk/ *adj.*

leucotomy /luːˈkɒtəmɪ/ *n.* (*pl.* **-ies**) the surgical lesions of white nerve fibres within the brain, formerly used in psychosurgery.

leukaemia /luːˈkiːmɪə/ *n.* (US **leukemia**) *Med.* any of a group of malignant diseases in which the bone-marrow and other blood-forming organs produce increased numbers of leucocytes. □ **leukaemic** *adj.* [mod.L f. G *Leukämie* f. Gk *leukos* white + *haima* blood]

Levant /lɪˈvænt/ *n.* (prec. by *the*) the eastern part of the Mediterranean with its islands and neighbouring countries. [F, pres. part. of *lever* rise, used as noun = point of sunrise, east]

levant /lɪˈvænt/ *v.intr. Brit.* abscond or bolt, esp. with betting or gaming losses unpaid. □ **levanter** *n.* [perh. f. LEVANT]

Levantine /lɪˈvæntaɪn, ˈlevən-/ *adj.* & *n.* —*adj.* of or trading to the Levant. —*n.* a native or inhabitant of the Levant.

levee[1] /ˈlevɪ/ *n.* **1** *archaic* or *US* an assembly of visitors or guests, esp. at a formal reception. **2** *hist.* (in the UK) an assembly held by the sovereign or sovereign's representative at which men only were received. **3** *hist.* a reception of visitors on rising from bed. [F *levé* var. of *lever* rising f. *lever* to rise: see LEVY]

levee[2] /ˈlevɪ, lɪˈviː/ *n.* *US* **1** an embankment against river floods. **2** a natural embankment built up by a river. **3** a landing-place, a quay. [F *levée* fem. past part. of *lever* raise: see LEVY]

level /ˈlev(ə)l/ *n., adj.,* & *v.* —*n.* **1** a horizontal line or plane. **2** a height or value reached, a position on a real or imaginary scale (*eye level; sugar level in the blood; danger level*). **3** a social, moral, or intellectual standard. **4** a plane of rank or authority (*discussions at Cabinet level*). **5** an instrument giving a line parallel to the plane of the horizon for testing whether things are horizontal. **6** a more or less level surface. **7** a flat tract of land. —*adj.* **1** having a flat and even surface; not bumpy. **2** horizontal; perpendicular to the plumb-line. **3** (often foll. by *with*) **a** on the same horizontal plane as something else. **b** having equality with something else. **c** (of a spoonful etc.) with the contents flat with the brim. **4** even, uniform, equable, or well-balanced in quality, style, temper, judgement, etc. **5** (of a race) having the leading competitors close together. —*v.* (**levelled, levelling**; US **leveled, leveling**) **1** *tr.* make level, even, or uniform. **2** *tr.* (often foll. by *to* (or *with*) *the ground, in the dust*) raze or demolish. **3** *tr.* (also *absol.*) aim (a missile or gun). **4** *tr.* (also *absol.*; foll. by *at, against*) direct (an accusation, criticism, or satire). **5** *tr.* abolish (distinctions). **6** *intr.* (usu. foll. by *with*) *sl.* be frank or honest. **7** *tr.* place on the same level. □ **do one's level best** *colloq.* do one's utmost; make all possible efforts. **level crossing** *Brit.* a crossing of a railway and a road, or two railways, at the same level. **level down** bring down to a standard. **level off** make or become level or smooth. **level out** make or become level, remove differences from. **level pegging** *Brit.* equality of scores or achievements. **level up** bring up to a standard. **on the level** *colloq. adv.* honestly, without deception. —*adj.* honest, truthful. **on a level with 1** in the same horizontal plane as. **2** equal with. □ **levelly** *adv.* **levelness** *n.* [ME f. OF *livel* ult. f. L *libella* dimin. of *libra* scales, balance]

level-headed /ˌlev(ə)lˈhedɪd/ *adj.* mentally well-balanced, cool, sensible. □ **level-headedly** *adv.* **level-headedness** *n.*

leveller /ˈlevələ(r)/ *n.* (US **leveler**) **1** a person who advocates the abolition of social distinctions. **2** a person or thing that levels.

lever /ˈliːvə(r)/ *n.* & *v.* —*n.* **1** a bar resting on a pivot, used to help lift a heavy or firmly fixed object. **2** *Mech.* a simple machine consisting of a rigid bar pivoted about a fulcrum (fixed point) which can be acted upon by a force (effort) in order to move a load. **3** a projecting handle moved to operate a mechanism. **4** a means of exerting moral pressure. —*v.* **1** *intr.* use a lever. **2** *tr.* (often foll. by *away, out, up,* etc.) lift, move, or act on with a lever. [ME f. OF *levier, leveor* f. *lever* raise: see LEVY]

leverage /ˈliːvərɪdʒ/ *n.* **1** the action of a lever; a way of applying a lever. **2** the power of a lever; the mechanical advantage gained by use of a lever. **3** a means of accomplishing a purpose; power, influence. □ **leveraged buyout**

/ˈlevərɪdʒd/ esp. *US* the buyout of a company by its management using outside capital.

■ **Usage** The pronunciation of *leveraged* in *leveraged buyout* is American because the practice takes place mainly in the US.

leveret /ˈlevərɪt/ *n.* a young hare, esp. one in its first year. [ME f. AF, dimin. of *levre*, OF *lievre* f. L *lepus leporis* hare]

leviathan /lɪˈvaɪəθ(ə)n/ *n.* **1** *Bibl.* a sea-monster. **2** anything very large or powerful. [ME f. LL f. Heb. *liwyāṯān*]

Levis /ˈliːvaɪz/ *n.pl. propr.* a type of (orig. blue) denim jeans or overalls reinforced with rivets. [*Levi* Strauss, orig. US manufacturer in 1860s]

levitate /ˈlevɪteɪt/ *v.* **1** *intr.* rise and float in the air (esp. with reference to spiritualism). **2** *tr.* cause to do this. □ **levitation** /-ˈteɪʃ(ə)n/ *n.* **levitator** *n.* [L *levis* light, after GRAVITATE]

levity /ˈlevɪtɪ/ *n.* **1** lack of serious thought, frivolity, unbecoming jocularity. **2** inconstancy. **3** undignified behaviour. [L *levitas* f. *levis* light]

levo- *US* var. of LAEVO-.

levulose *US* var. of LAEVULOSE.

levy /ˈlevɪ/ *v.* & *n.* —*v.tr.* (**-ies, -ied**) **1 a** impose (a rate or toll). **b** raise (contributions or taxes). **c** (also *absol.*) raise (a sum of money) by legal execution or process (*the debt was levied on the debtor's goods*). **d** seize (goods) in this way. **e** extort (*levy blackmail*). **2** enlist or enrol (troops etc.). **3** (usu. foll. by *upon, against*) wage, proceed to make (war). —*n.* (*pl.* **-ies**) **1 a** the collecting of a contribution, tax, etc., or of property to satisfy a legal judgement. **b** a contribution, tax, etc., levied. **2 a** the act or an instance of enrolling troops etc. **b** (*in pl.*) men enrolled. **c** a body of men enrolled. **d** the number of men enrolled. □ **leviable** *adj.* [ME f. OF *levee* fem. past part. of *lever* f. L *levare* raise f. *levis* light]

lewd /ljuːd/ *adj.* **1** lascivious. **2** indecent, obscene. □ **lewdly** *adv.* **lewdness** *n.* [OE *lǣwede* LAY², of unkn. orig.]

lexical /ˈleksɪk(ə)l/ *adj.* **1** of the words of a language. **2** of or as of a lexicon. □ **lexically** *adv.* [Gk *lexikos, lexikon*: see LEXICON]

lexicography /ˌleksɪˈkɒɡrəfɪ/ *n.* the compiling of dictionaries. □ **lexicographer** *n.* **lexicographic** /-kəˈɡræfɪk/ *adj.* **lexicographical** /-kəˈɡræfɪk(ə)l/ *adj.* **lexicographically** /-kəˈɡræfɪkəlɪ/ *adv.*

lexicology /ˌleksɪˈkɒlədʒɪ/ *n.* the study of the form, history, and meaning of words. □ **lexicological** /-kəˈlɒdʒɪk(ə)l/ *adj.* **lexicologically** /-kəˈlɒdʒɪkəlɪ/ *adv.* **lexicologist** *n.*

lexicon /ˈleksɪkən/ *n.* **1 a** dictionary, esp. of Greek, Hebrew, Syriac, or Arabic. **2** the vocabulary of a person, language, branch of knowledge, etc. [mod.L f. Gk *lexikon* (*biblion* book), neut. of *lexikos* f. *lexis* word f. *legō* speak]

lexis /ˈleksɪs/ *n.* **1** words, vocabulary. **2** the total stock of words in a language. [Gk: see LEXICON]

ley¹ /leɪ/ *n.* a field temporarily under grass. □ **ley farming** alternate growing of crops and grass. [ME (orig. adj.), perh. f. OE, rel. to LAY¹, LIE¹]

ley² /liː, leɪ/ *n.* the supposed straight line of a prehistoric track, usu. between hilltops. [var. of LEA]

LF *abbr.* low frequency.

l.h. *abbr.* left hand.

Li *symb. Chem.* the element lithium.

liability /ˌlaɪəˈbɪlɪtɪ/ *n.* (*pl.* **-ies**) **1** the state of being liable. **2** a person or thing that is troublesome as an unwelcome responsibility; a handicap. **3** what a person is liable for, esp. (in *pl.*) debts or pecuniary obligations.

liable /ˈlaɪəb(ə)l/ *predic.adj.* **1** legally bound. **2** (foll. by *to*) subject to (a tax or penalty). **3** (foll. by *to* + infin.) under an obligation. **4** (foll. by *to*) exposed or open to (something undesirable). **5** (foll. by *to* + infin.) *disp.* apt, likely (*it is liable to rain*). **6** (foll. by *for*) answerable. [ME perh. f. AF f. OF *lier* f. L *ligare* bind]

■ **Usage** Sense 5, though common, is considered incorrect by some people.

liaise /lɪˈeɪz/ *v.intr.* (foll. by *with, between*) *colloq.* establish cooperation, act as a link. [back-form. f. LIAISON]

liaison /lɪˈeɪzɒn/ *n.* **1** communication or cooperation, esp. between military forces or units. **2** an illicit sexual relationship. **3** the binding or thickening agent of a sauce. [F f. *lier* bind f. L *ligare*]

liana /lɪˈɑːnə/ *n.* (also **liane** /-ˈɑːn/) any of several climbing and twining plants of tropical forests. [F *liane, lierne* clematis, of uncert. orig.]

liar /ˈlaɪə(r)/ *n.* a person who tells a lie or lies, esp. habitually. □ [OE *lēogere* (as LIE², -AR⁴)]

lias /ˈlaɪəs/ *n.* **1** (**Lias**) *Geol.* the lower strata of the Jurassic system of rocks, consisting of shales and limestones rich in fossils. **2** a blue limestone rock found in SW England. □ **liassic** /laɪˈæsɪk/ *adj.* (in sense 1). [ME f. OF *liois* hard limestone, prob. f. Gmc]

Lib. *abbr.* Liberal.

lib /lɪb/ *n. colloq.* liberation (*women's lib*). [abbr.]

libation /laɪˈbeɪʃ(ə)n, lɪ-/ *n.* **1 a** the pouring out of a drink-offering to a god. **b** such a drink-offering. **2** *joc.* a potation. [ME f. L *libatio* f. *libare* pour as offering]

libber /ˈlɪbə(r)/ *n. colloq.* an advocate of women's liberation.

libel /ˈlaɪb(ə)l/ *n.* & *v.* —*n.* **1** *Law* **a** a published false statement damaging to a person's reputation. **b** the act of publishing this. **2 a** a false and defamatory written statement. **b** (foll. by *on*) a thing that brings discredit by misrepresentation etc. (*the portrait is a libel on him; the book is a libel on human nature*). —*v.tr.* (**libelled, libelling**; *US* **libeled, libeling**) **1** defame by libellous statements. **2** accuse falsely and maliciously. **3** *Law* publish a libel against. □ **libeller** *n.* [ME f. OF f. L *libellus* dimin. of *liber* book]

libellous /ˈlaɪbələs/ *adj.* containing or constituting a libel. □ **libellously** *adv.*

liberal /ˈlɪbər(ə)l/ *adj.* & *n.* —*adj.* **1** given freely; ample, abundant. **2** (often foll. by *of*) giving freely, generous, not sparing. **3** open-minded, not prejudiced. **4** not strict or rigorous; (of interpretation) not literal. **5** for general broadening of the mind, not professional or technical (*liberal studies*). **6 a** favouring individual liberty, free trade, and moderate political and social reform. **b** (**Liberal**) of or characteristic of Liberals or a Liberal Party. **7** *Theol.* regarding many traditional beliefs as dispensable, invalidated by modern thought, or liable to change (*liberal Protestant; liberal Judaism*). —*n.* **1** a person of liberal views. **2** (**Liberal**) a supporter or member of a Liberal Party. □ **liberal arts** *US* the arts as distinct from science and technology. **Liberal Democrat** (in the UK) a member of a party formed from the Liberal Party and members of the Social Democratic Party. **Liberal Party** a political party advocating liberal policies. □ **liberalism** *n.* **liberalist** *n.* **liberalistic** /-ˈlɪstɪk/ *adj.* **liberally** *adv.* **liberalness** *n.* [ME, orig. = befitting a free man, f. OF f. L *liberalis* f. *liber* free (man)]

■ **Usage** In the UK the name Liberal was discontinued in official political use in 1988, when the party regrouped with others to form the *Social and Liberal Democrats*. In 1989 this name was officially replaced by *Liberal Democrats*.

liberality /ˌlɪbəˈrælɪtɪ/ *n.* **1** free giving, munificence. **2** freedom from prejudice, breadth of mind. [ME f. OF *liberalite* or L *liberalitas* (as LIBERAL)]

liberalize /ˈlɪbərəˌlaɪz/ *v.tr.* & *intr.* (also **-ise**) make or become more liberal or less strict. □ **liberalization** /-ˈzeɪʃ(ə)n/ *n.* **liberalizer** *n.*

liberate /ˈlɪbəˌreɪt/ *v.tr.* **1** (often foll. by *from*) set at liberty, set free. **2** free (a country etc.) from an oppressor or an enemy occupation. **3** (often as **liberated** *adj.*) free (a person) from rigid social conventions, esp. in sexual behaviour. □ **liberator** *n.* [L *liberare liberat-* f. *liber* free]

liberation /ˌlɪbəˈreɪʃ(ə)n/ *n.* the act or an instance of liberating; the state of being liberated. □ **liberation theology** a theory which interprets liberation from social, political, and economic oppression as an anticipation of ultimate salvation. □ **liberationist** *n.* [ME f. L *liberatio* f. *liberare*: see LIBERATE]

libertarian /ˌlɪbəˈteərɪən/ *n.* an advocate of liberty. □ **libertarianism** *n.*

libertine /ˈlɪbəˌtiːn, -tɪn, -ˌtaɪn/ *n.* & *adj.* —*n.* a dissolute or licentious person. —*adj.* licentious, dissolute. □ **libertinage** *n.* **libertinism** *n.* [L *libertinus* freedman f. *libertus* made free f. *liber* free]

liberty /ˈlɪbətɪ/ *n.* (*pl.* **-ies**) **1 a** freedom from captivity, imprisonment, slavery, or despotic control. **b** a personification of this. **2 a** the right or power to do as one pleases. **b** (foll. by *to* + infin.) right, power, opportunity, permission. **3** (usu. in *pl.*) a right, privilege, or immunity, enjoyed by prescription or grant. **4** setting aside of rules or convention. □ **at liberty 1** free, not imprisoned (*set at liberty*). **2** (foll. by *to* + infin.) entitled, permitted. **3** available, disengaged. **Liberty Bell** (in the US) a bell in Philadelphia rung at the adoption of the Declaration of Independence. **liberty bodice** a close-fitting under-bodice. **liberty hall** a place where one may do as one likes. **liberty horse** a horse performing in a circus without a rider. **take liberties 1** (often foll. by *with*) behave in an unduly familiar manner. **2** (foll. by *with*) deal freely or superficially with rules or facts. **take the liberty** (foll. by *to* + infin., or *of* + verbal noun) presume, venture. [ME f. OF *liberté* f. L *libertas -tatis* f. *liber* free]

libidinous /lɪˈbɪdɪnəs/ *adj.* lustful. □ **libidinously** *adv.* **libidinousness** *n.* [ME f. L *libidinosus* f. *libido -dinis* lust]

libido /lɪˈbiːˌdəʊ, lɪˈbaɪdəʊ/ *n.* (*pl.* **-os**) *Psychol.* psychic drive or energy, esp. that associated with sexual desire. □ **libidinal** /lɪˈbɪdɪn(ə)l/ *adj.* **libidinally** *adv.* [L: see LIBIDINOUS]

Libra /ˈliːbrə, ˈlɪb-, ˈlaɪb-/ *n.* **1** a constellation, traditionally regarded as contained in the figure of scales. **2 a** the seventh sign of the zodiac (the Balance or Scales). **b** a person born when the sun is in this sign. □ **Libran** *n.* & *adj.* [ME f. L, orig. = pound weight]

librarian /laɪˈbreərɪən/ *n.* a person in charge of, or an assistant in, a library. □ **librarianship** *n.* [L *librarius*: see LIBRARY]

library /ˈlaɪbrərɪ/ *n.* (*pl.* **-ies**) **1 a** a collection of books etc. for use by the public or by members of a group. **b** a person's collection of books. **2** a room or building containing a collection of books (for reading or reference rather than for sale). **3 a** a similar collection of films, records, computer routines, etc. **b** the place where these are kept. [ME f. OF *librairie* f. L *libraria* (*taberna* shop), fem. of *librarius* bookseller's, of books, f. *liber libri* book]

libretto /lɪˈbretəʊ/ *n.* (*pl.* **libretti** /-tɪ/ or **-os**) the text of an opera or other long musical vocal work. □ **librettist** *n.* [It., dimin. of *libro* book f. L *liber libri*]

Librium /ˈlɪbrɪəm/ *n. propr.* a white crystalline drug used as a tranquillizer.

lice *pl.* of LOUSE.

licence /ˈlaɪs(ə)ns/ *n.* (*US* **license**) **1** a permit from an authority to own or use something (esp. a dog, gun, television set, or vehicle), do something (esp. marry, print something, preach, or drive on a public road), or carry on a trade (esp. in alcoholic liquor). **2** leave, permission (*have I your licence to remove the fence?*). **3 a** liberty of action, esp. when excessive; disregard of law or propriety, abuse of freedom. **b** licentiousness. **4** a writer's or artist's irregularity in grammar, metre, perspective, etc., or deviation from fact, esp. for effect (*poetic licence*). □ **license plate** *US* the number plate of a licensed vehicle. [ME f. OF f. L *licentia* f. *licēre* be lawful: *-se* by confusion with LICENSE]

license /ˈlaɪs(ə)ns/ *v.tr.* (also **licence**) **1** grant a licence to (a person). **2** authorize the use of (premises) for a certain purpose, esp. the sale and consumption of alcoholic liquor. **3** authorize the publication of (a book etc.) or the performance of (a play). □ **licensable** *adj.* **licenser** *n.* **licensor** *n.* [ME f. LICENCE: *-se* on analogy of the verbs PRACTISE, PROPHESY, perh. after ADVISE, where the sound differs from the corresp. noun]

licensee /ˌlaɪsənˈsiː/ *n.* the holder of a licence, esp. to sell alcoholic liquor.

licentiate /laɪˈsenʃɪət, -ʃət/ *n.* a holder of a certificate of competence to practise a certain profession. [ME f. med.L *licentiatus* past part. of *licentiare* f. L *licentia*: see LICENCE]

licentious /laɪˈsenʃəs/ *adj.* immoral in sexual relations. □ **licentiously** *adv.* **licentiousness** *n.* [L *licentiosus* f. *licentia*: see LICENCE]

lichee *var.* of LYCHEE.

lichen /ˈlaɪkən, ˈlɪtʃ(ə)n/ *n.* any plant organism of the group Lichenes, composed of a fungus and an alga in symbiotic association, usu. of green, grey, or yellow tint and growing on and colouring rocks, tree-trunks, roofs, walls, etc. □ **lichened** *adj.* **lichenology** /-ˈnɒlədʒɪ/ *n.* [L f. Gk *leikhēn*]

lich-gate /ˈlɪtʃɡeɪt/ *n.* (also **lych-gate**) a roofed gateway to a churchyard where a coffin awaits the clergyman's arrival. [ME f. OE līc corpse f. Gmc + GATE¹]

licit /ˈlɪsɪt/ adj. not forbidden; lawful. □ **licitly** adv. [L licitus past part. of licēre be lawful]

lick v. & n. —v.tr. & intr. **1** tr. pass the tongue over, esp. to taste, moisten, or (of animals) clean. **2** tr. bring into a specified condition or position by licking (licked it all up; licked it clean). **3** tr. (of a flame, waves, etc.) touch; play lightly over. **4** colloq. defeat, excel. **5** colloq. thrash. —n. **1** an act of licking with the tongue. **2** = salt-lick. **3** colloq. a fast pace (at a lick; at full lick). **4** colloq. **a** a small amount, quick treatment with (foll. by of: a lick of paint). **b** a quick wash. □ **lick a person's boots** (or **shoes**) toady; be servile. **lick one's lips** (or **chops**) **1** look forward with relish. **2** show one's satisfaction. **lick one's wounds** be in retirement after defeat. □ **licker** n. (also in comb.). [OE liccian f. WG]

licking /ˈlɪkɪŋ/ n. colloq. **1** a thrashing. **2** a defeat.

lickspittle /ˈlɪkˌspɪt(ə)l/ n. a toady.

licorice var. of LIQUORICE.

lictor /ˈlɪktɔː(r)/ n. (usu. in pl.) Rom.Hist. an officer attending the consul or other magistrate. [ME f. L, perh. rel. to ligare bind]

lid n. **1** a hinged or removable cover, esp. for the top of a container. **2** = EYELID. □ **take the lid off** colloq. expose (a scandal etc.). □ **lidded** adj. (also in comb.). **lidless** adj. [OE hlid f. Gmc]

lido /ˈliːdəʊ, ˈlaɪ-/ n. (pl. **-os**) a public open-air swimming-pool or bathing-beach. [It. f. Lido, the name of a bathing-beach near Venice, f. L litus shore]

lie¹ v. & n. —v.intr. (**lying** /ˈlaɪɪŋ/; past **lay**; past part. **lain**) **1** be in or assume a horizontal position on a supporting surface; be at rest on something. **2** (of a thing) rest flat on a surface (snow lay on the ground). **3** (of abstract things) remain undisturbed or undiscussed etc. (let matters lie). **4 a** be kept or remain or be in a specified, esp. concealed, state or place (lie in wait; malice lay behind those words; the books lay unread; the money is lying in the bank). **b** (of abstract things) exist, reside; be in a certain position or relation (foll. by in, with, etc.: the answer lies in education; my sympathies lie with the family). **5 a** be situated or stationed (the village lay to the east; the ships are lying off the coast). **b** (of a road, route, etc.) lead (the road lies over mountains). **c** be spread out to view (the desert lay before us). **6** (of the dead) be buried in a grave. **7** (foll. by with) archaic have sexual intercourse. **8** Law be admissible or sustainable (the objection will not lie). —n. **1** the way or direction or position in which a thing lies. □ **let lie** not raise (a controversial matter etc.) for discussion etc. **lie about** (or **around**) be left carelessly out of place. **lie ahead** be going to happen; be in store. **lie back** recline so as to rest. **lie down** assume a lying position; have a short rest. **lie-down** n. a short rest. **lie down under** accept (an insult etc.) without protest. **lie heavy** cause discomfort or anxiety. **lie in** remain in bed in the morning. **lie-in** n. a prolonged stay in bed in the morning. **lie in state** (of a deceased great personage) be laid in a public place of honour before burial. **lie low 1** keep quiet or unseen. **2** be discreet about one's intentions. **lie off** Naut. stand some distance from shore or from another ship. **the lie of the land** the current state of affairs. **lie over** be deferred.

lie with (often foll. by to + infin.) be the responsibility of (a person) (it lies with you to answer). **take lying down** (usu. with neg.) accept (defeat, rebuke, etc.) without resistance or protest etc. [OE licgan f. Gmc]

■ **Usage** The transitive use of lie, meaning lay, as in lie her on the bed, is incorrect in standard English.

lie² /laɪ/ n. & v. —n. **1** an intentionally false statement (tell a lie; pack of lies). **2** imposture; false belief (live a lie). —v.intr. & tr. (**lies**, **lied**, **lying** /ˈlaɪɪŋ/) **1** intr. **a** tell a lie or lies (they lied to me). **b** (of a thing) be deceptive (the camera cannot lie). **2** tr. (usu. refl.; foll. by into, out of) get (oneself) into or out of a situation by lying (lied themselves into trouble; lied my way out of danger). □ **give the lie to** serve to show the falsity of (a supposition etc.). **lie-detector** an instrument for determining whether a person is telling the truth by testing for physiological changes considered to be symptomatic of lying. [OE lyge lēogan f. Gmc]

lied /liːd, liːt/ n. (pl. **lieder** /ˈliːdə(r)/) a type of German song, esp. of the Romantic period, usu. for solo voice with piano accompaniment. [G]

liege /liːdʒ/ adj. & n. usu. hist. —adj. (of a superior) entitled to receive or (of a vassal) bound to give feudal service or allegiance. —n. **1** (in full **liege lord**) a feudal superior or sovereign. **2** (usu. in pl.) a vassal or subject. [ME f. OF lige, liege f. med.L laeticus, prob. f. Gmc]

liegeman /ˈliːdʒmæn/ n. (pl. **-men**) hist. a sworn vassal; a faithful follower.

lien /ˈliːən/ n. Law a right over another's property to protect a debt charged on that property. [F f. OF loien f. L ligamen bond f. ligare bind]

lieu /ljuː/ n. □ **in lieu 1** instead. **2** (foll. by of) in the place of. [ME f. F f. L locus place]

Lieut. abbr. Lieutenant.

lieutenant /lefˈtenənt/ n. **1** a deputy or substitute acting for a superior. **2 a** an army officer next in rank below captain. **b** a naval officer next in rank below lieutenant commander. **3** US a police officer next in rank below captain. □ **lieutenant colonel** (or **commander** or **general**) officers ranking next below colonel, commander, or general. **lieutenant-governor** the acting or deputy governor of a State, province, etc., under a governor or Governor-General. □ **lieutenancy** n. (pl. **-ies**). [ME f. OF (as LIEU, TENANT)]

life n. (pl. **lives** /laɪvz/) **1** the condition which distinguishes active animals and plants from inorganic matter, including the capacity for growth, functional activity, and continual change preceding death. **2 a** living things and their activity (insect life; is there life on Mars?). **b** human presence or activity (no sign of life). **3 a** the period during which life lasts, or the period from birth to the present time or from the present time to death (have done it all my life; will regret it all my life; life membership). **b** the duration of a thing's existence or of its ability to function; validity, efficacy, etc. (the battery has a life of two years). **4 a** a person's state of existence as a living individual (sacrificed their lives; took many lives). **b** a living person (many lives were lost). **5 a** an individual's occupation, actions, or fortunes; the manner of one's existence (that would make life easy; start a new life). **b** a particular aspect of this (love-life; private life). **6** the active part of existence; the business and pleasures of the world (*travel is the best way to see life*). **7** man's earthly or supposed future existence. **8 a** energy, liveliness, animation (*full of life*; *put some life into it!*). **b**. an animating influence (*was the life of the party*). **9** the living, esp. nude, form or model (*taken from the life*). **10** a written account of a person's life; a biography. **11** *colloq.* a sentence of imprisonment for life (*they were all serving life*). **12** a chance; a fresh start (*cats have nine lives*; *gave the player three lives*). □ **come to life 1** emerge from unconsciousness or inactivity; begin operating. **2** (of an inanimate object) assume an imaginary animation. **for dear** (or **one's**) **life** as if or in order to escape death; as a matter of extreme urgency (*hanging on for dear life*; *run for your life*). **for life** for the rest of one's life. **for the life of** (foll. by pers. pron.) even if (one's) life depended on it (*cannot for the life of me remember*). **give one's life 1** (foll. by *for*) die; sacrifice oneself. **2** (foll. by *to*) dedicate oneself. **large as life** *colloq.* in person, esp. prominently (*stood there large as life*). **larger than life 1** exaggerated. **2** (of a person) having an exuberant personality. **life cycle** the series of changes in the life of an organism including reproduction. **life expectancy** the average period that a person at a specified age may expect to live. **life-form** an organism. **Life Guards** (in the UK) a regiment of the royal household cavalry. **life insurance** insurance for a sum to be paid on the death of the insured person. **life-jacket** a buoyant or inflatable jacket for keeping a person afloat in water. **life peer** *Brit.* a peer whose title lapses on death. **life-preserver 1** a short stick with a heavily loaded end. **2** a life-jacket etc. **life-raft** an inflatable or timber etc. raft for use in an emergency instead of a boat. **life-saver** *colloq.* **1** a thing that saves one from serious difficulty. **2** *Austral.* & *NZ* = LIFEGUARD. **life sciences** biology and related subjects. **life sentence 1** a sentence of imprisonment for life. **2** an illness or commitment etc. perceived as a continuing threat to one's freedom. **life-size** (or **-sized**) of the same size as the person or thing represented. **life-support** *adj.* (of equipment) allowing vital functions to continue in an adverse environment or during severe disablement. **life-support machine** *Med.* a ventilator or respirator. **lose one's life** be killed. **a matter of life and death** a matter of vital importance. **not on your life** *colloq.* most certainly not. **save a person's life 1** prevent a person's death. **2** save a person from serious difficulty. **take one's life in one's hands** take a crucial personal risk. **to the life** true to the original. [OE *līf* f. Gmc]

lifebelt /ˈlaɪfbɛlt/ *n.* a belt of buoyant or inflatable material for keeping a person afloat in water.

lifeblood /ˈlaɪfblʌd/ *n.* **1** the blood, as being necessary to life. **2** the vital factor or influence.

lifeboat /ˈlaɪfbəʊt/ *n.* **1** a specially constructed boat launched from land to rescue those in distress at sea. **2** a ship's small boat for use in emergency.

lifebuoy /ˈlaɪfbɔɪ/ *n.* a buoyant support (usu. a ring) for keeping a person afloat in water.

lifeguard /ˈlaɪfɡɑːd/ *n.* an expert swimmer employed to rescue bathers from drowning.

lifeless /ˈlaɪflɪs/ *adj.* **1** lacking life; no longer living. **2** unconscious. **3** lacking movement or vitality. □ **lifelessly** *adv.* **lifelessness** *n.* [OE *līflēas* (as LIFE, -LESS)]

lifelike /ˈlaɪflaɪk/ *adj.* closely resembling the person or thing represented. □ **lifelikeness** *n.*

lifeline /ˈlaɪflaɪn/ *n.* **1 a** a rope etc. used for life-saving, e.g. that attached to a lifebuoy. **b** a diver's signalling line. **2** a sole means of communication or transport.

lifelong /ˈlaɪflɒŋ/ *adj.* lasting a lifetime.

lifer /ˈlaɪfə(r)/ *n. sl.* a person serving a life sentence.

lifestyle /ˈlaɪfstaɪl/ *n.* the particular way of life of a person or group.

lifetime /ˈlaɪftaɪm/ *n.* **1** the duration of a person's life. **2** the duration of a thing or its usefulness. **3** *colloq.* an exceptionally long time. □ **of a lifetime** such as does not occur more than once in a person's life (*the chance of a lifetime*; *the journey of a lifetime*).

lift *v.* & *n.* —*v.* **1** *tr.* (often foll. by *up, off, out,* etc.) raise or remove to a higher position. **2** *intr.* go up; be raised; yield to an upward force (*the window will not lift*). **3** *tr.* give an upward direction to (the eyes or face). **4** *tr.* **a** elevate to a higher plane of thought or feeling (*the news lifted their spirits*). **b** make less heavy or dull; add interest to (something esp. artistic). **c** enhance, improve (*lifted their game after half-time*). **5** *intr.* (of a cloud, fog, etc.) rise, disperse. **6** *tr.* remove (a barrier or restriction). **7** *tr.* transport supplies, troops, etc. by air. **8** *tr. colloq.* **a** steal. **b** plagiarize (a passage of writing etc.). **9** *tr.* hold or have on high (*the church lifts its spire*). **10** *tr.* hit (a cricket-ball) into the air. **11** *tr.* (usu. in *passive*) perform cosmetic surgery on (esp. the face or breasts) to reduce sagging. —*n.* **1** the act of lifting or process of being lifted. **2** a free ride in another person's vehicle (*gave them a lift*). **3 a** *Brit.* a platform or compartment housed in a shaft for raising and lowering persons or things to different floors of a building or different levels of a mine etc. **b** a similar apparatus for carrying persons up or down a mountain etc. **4 a** transport by air (see AIRLIFT *n.*). **b** a quantity of goods transported by air. **5** the upward pressure which air exerts on an aerofoil to counteract the force of gravity. **6** a supporting or elevating influence; a feeling of elation. **7** a layer of leather in the heel of a boot or shoe, esp. to correct shortening of a leg or increase height. □ **lift a finger** (or **hand** etc.) (in *neg.*) make the slightest effort (*didn't lift a finger to help*). **lift off** (of a spacecraft or rocket) rise from the launching pad. **lift-off** *n.* the vertical take-off of a spacecraft or rocket. **lift up one's voice** sing out. □ **liftable** *adj.* **lifter** *n.* [ME f. ON *lypta* f. Gmc]

ligament /ˈlɪɡəmənt/ *n. Anat.* **1** a short band of tough flexible fibrous connective tissue linking bones together. **2** any membranous fold keeping an organ in position. □ **ligamental** /-ˈment(ə)l/ *adj.* **ligamentary** /-ˈmentərɪ/ *adj.* **ligamentous** /-ˈmentəs/ *adj.* [ME f. L *ligamentum* bond f. *ligare* bind]

ligature /ˈlɪɡətʃə(r)/ *n.* & *v.* —*n.* **1** a tie or bandage, esp. in surgery for a bleeding artery etc. **2** *Mus.* a slur; a tie. **3** *Printing* two or more letters joined, e.g. æ. **4** a bond; a thing that unites. **5** the act of tying or binding. —*v.tr.* bind or connect with a ligature. [ME f. LL *ligatura* f. L *ligare ligat-* tie, bind]

■ **Usage** Sense 3 of this word is sometimes confused with *digraph*, which means two separate letters together representing one sound.

light[1] /laɪt/ n., v., & adj. —n. **1** the natural agent that stimulates sight and makes things visible. **2** the medium or condition of the space in which this is present. **3** an appearance of brightness (*saw a distant light*). **4 a** a source of light, e.g. the sun, or a lamp, fire, etc. **b** (in *pl.*) illuminations. **5** (often in *pl.*) a traffic-light (*went through a red light; stop at the lights*). **6 a** the amount or quality of illumination in a place (*bad light stopped play*). **b** one's fair or usual share of this (*you are standing in my light*). **7 a** a flame or spark serving to ignite (*struck a light*). **b** a device producing this (*have you got a light?*). **8** the aspect in which a thing is regarded or considered (*appeared in a new light*). **9 a** mental illumination; elucidation, enlightenment. **b** hope, happiness; a happy outcome. **c** spiritual illumination by divine truth. **10** vivacity, enthusiasm, or inspiration visible in a person's face, esp. in the eyes. **11** (in *pl.*) a person's mental powers or ability (*according to one's lights*). **12** an eminent person (*a leading light*). **13 a** the bright part of a thing; a highlight. **b** the bright parts of a picture etc. esp. suggesting illumination (*light and shade*). **14 a** a window or opening in a wall to let light in. **b** the perpendicular division of a mullioned window. **c** a pane of glass esp. in the side or roof of a greenhouse. **15** (in a crossword etc.) each of the items filling a space and to be deduced from the clues. —v. (*past* lit /lɪt/; *past part.* lit *or* (attrib) **lighted**) **1** tr. & intr. set burning or begin to burn; ignite. **2** tr. provide with light or lighting. **3** tr. show (a person) the way or surroundings with a light. **4** intr. (usu. foll. by *up*) (of the face or eyes) brighten with animation. —adj. **1** well provided with light; not dark. **2** (of a colour) pale (*light blue; a light-blue ribbon*). □ **bring** (or **come**) **to light** reveal or be revealed. **festival of lights 1** = HANUKKAH. **2** = DIWALI. **in a good** (or **bad**) **light** giving a favourable (or unfavourable) impression. **in the light of** having regard to; drawing information from. **light-bulb** a glass bulb containing an inert gas and a metal filament, providing light when an electric current is passed through. **lighting-up time** the time during or after which vehicles on the road must show the prescribed lights. **light of day 1** daylight, sunlight. **2** general notice; public attention. **light of one's life** usu. *joc.* a much-loved person. **light-pen** (or **-gun**) **1** a penlike or gunlike photosensitive device held to the screen of a computer terminal for passing information on to it. **2** a light-emitting device used for reading bar-codes. **light up 1** *colloq.* begin to smoke a cigarette etc. **2** switch on lights or lighting; illuminate a scene. **light-year** *Astron.* the distance light travels in one year, nearly 6 million million miles. **lit up** *colloq.* drunk. **throw** (or **shed**) **light on** help to explain. □ **lightish** adj. **lightless** adj. **lightness** n. [OE *lēoht, līht, līhtan* f. Gmc]

light[2] /laɪt/ adj., adv., & v. —adj. **1** of little weight; not heavy; easy to lift. **2 a** relatively low in weight, amount, density, intensity, etc. (*light arms; light traffic; light metal; light rain; a light

breeze*). **b** deficient in weight (*light coin*). **3 a** carrying or suitable for small loads (*light aircraft; light railway*). **b** (of a ship) unladen. **c** carrying only light arms, armaments, etc. (*light brigade; light infantry*). **4 a** (of food, a meal, etc.) small in amount; easy to digest (*had a light lunch*). **b** (of drink) not heavy on the stomach or strongly alcoholic. **5 a** (of entertainment, music, etc.) intended for amusement, rather than edification; not profound. **b** frivolous, thoughtless, trivial (*a light remark*). **6** (of sleep or a sleeper) easily disturbed. **7** easily borne or done (*light duties*). **8** nimble; quick-moving (*a light step; light of foot*). **9** (of a building etc.) graceful, elegant, delicate. **10** (of type) not heavy or bold. **11 a** free from sorrow; cheerful (*a light heart*). **b** giddy (*light in the head*). **12** (of soil) not dense; porous. **13** (of pastry, sponge, etc.) fluffy and well-aerated during cooking and with the fat fully absorbed. **14** (of a woman) unchaste or wanton; fickle. —adv. **1** in a light manner (*tread light; sleep light*). **2** with a minimum load or minimum luggage (*travel light*). —v.intr. (*past* and *past part.* lit /lɪt/ *or* **lighted**) **1** (foll. by *on, upon*) come upon or find by chance. **2** *archaic* a alight, descend. **b** (foll. by *on*) land on (shore etc.). □ **light-fingered** given to stealing. **light-footed** nimble. **light-headed** giddy, frivolous, delirious. **light-hearted 1** cheerful. **2** (unduly) casual, thoughtless. **light industry** the manufacture of small or light articles. **light into** *colloq.* attack. **light out** *colloq.* depart. **light touch** delicate or tactful treatment. **make light of** treat as unimportant. **make light work of** do a thing quickly and easily. □ **lightish** adj. **lightness** n. [OE *lēoht, līht, līhtan* f. Gmc, the verbal sense from the idea of relieving a horse etc. of weight]

lighten[1] /ˈlaɪt(ə)n/ v. **1 a** tr. & intr. make or become lighter in weight. **b** tr. reduce the weight or load of. **2** tr. bring relief to (the heart, mind, etc.). **3** tr. mitigate (a penalty).

lighten[2] /ˈlaɪt(ə)n/ v. **1 a** tr. shed light on. **b** tr. & intr. make or grow bright. **2** intr. **a** shine brightly; flash. **b** emit lightning (*it is lightening*).

lighter[1] /ˈlaɪtə(r)/ n. a device for lighting cigarettes etc.

lighter[2] /ˈlaɪtə(r)/ n. a boat, usu. flat-bottomed, for transferring goods from a ship to a wharf or another ship. [ME f. MDu. *lichter* (as LIGHT[2] in the sense 'unload')]

lighthouse /ˈlaɪthaʊs/ n. a tower or other structure containing a beacon light to warn or guide ships at sea.

lighting /ˈlaɪtɪŋ/ n. **1** equipment in a room or street etc. for producing light. **2** the arrangement or effect of lights.

lightly /ˈlaɪtlɪ/ adv. in a light (esp. frivolous or unserious) manner. □ **get off lightly** escape with little or no punishment. **take lightly** not be serious about (a thing).

lightning /ˈlaɪtnɪŋ/ n. & adj. —n. a flash of bright light produced by an electric discharge between clouds or between clouds and the ground. —attrib.adj. very quick (*with lightning speed*). □ **lightning-conductor** (or **-rod**) a metal rod or wire fixed to an exposed part of a building or to a mast to divert lightning into the earth or sea. **lightning strike** a strike by workers at short notice, esp. without official union backing. [ME, differentiated from *lightening*, verbal noun f. LIGHTEN²]

lightproof /ˈlaɪtpruːf/ *adj.* able to resist the harmful effects of (esp. excessive) light.

lights /laɪts/ *n.pl.* the lungs of sheep, pigs, bullocks, etc., used as a food esp. for pets. [ME, noun use of LIGHT²: cf. LUNG]

lightship /ˈlaɪtʃɪp/ *n.* a moored or anchored ship with a beacon light.

lightweight /ˈlaɪtweɪt/ *adj. & n.* —*adj.* **1** (of a person, animal, garment, etc.) of below average weight. **2** of little importance or influence. —*n.* **1** a lightweight person, animal, or thing. **2 a** a weight in certain sports intermediate between featherweight and welterweight. **b** a sportsman of this weight. □ **junior lightweight 1** a weight in professional boxing of 57.1–59 kg. **2** a professional boxer of this weight.

ligneous /ˈlɪɡnɪəs/ *adj.* **1** (of a plant) woody. **2** of the nature of wood. [L *ligneus* (as LIGNI-)]

ligni- /ˈlɪɡnɪ/ *comb. form* wood. [L *lignum* wood]

lignin /ˈlɪɡnɪn/ *n. Bot.* a complex organic polymer deposited in the cell-walls of many plants making them rigid and woody. [as LIGNI- + -IN]

lignite /ˈlɪɡnaɪt/ *n.* a soft brown coal showing traces of plant structure, intermediate between bituminous coal and peat. □ **lignitic** /-ˈnɪtɪk/ *adj.* [F (as LIGNI-, -ITE¹)]

like¹ *adj., prep., adv., conj., & n.* —*adj.* (often governing a noun as if a transitive participle such as *resembling*) (**more like, most like**) **1 a** having some or all of the qualities of another or each other or an original; alike (*in like manner*; *as like as two peas*; *is very like her brother*). **b** resembling in some way, such as; in the same class as (*good writers like Dickens*). **c** (usu. in pairs correlatively) as one is so will the other be (*like mother, like daughter*). **2** characteristic of (*it is not like them to be late*). **3** in a suitable state or mood for (doing or having something) (*felt like working*; *felt like a cup of tea*). —*prep.* in the manner of; to the same degree as (*drink like a fish*; *sell like hot cakes*; *acted like an idiot*). —*adv.* **1** *archaic* likely (*they will come, like enough*). **2** *sl.* so to speak (*did a quick getaway, like*; *as I said, like, I'm no Shakespeare*). **3** *colloq.* likely, probably (*as like as not*). —*conj. colloq. disp.* **1** as (*cannot do it like you do*). **2** as if (*ate like they were starving*). —*n.* **1** a counterpart; an equal; a similar person or thing (*shall not see its like again*; *compare like with like*). **2** (prec. by *the*) a thing or things of the same kind (*will never do the like again*). □ **and the like** and similar things; et cetera (*music, painting, and the like*). **be nothing like** (usu. with compl.) be in no way similar or comparable or adequate. **like** (or **as like**) **as not** probably. **like-minded** having the same tastes, opinions, etc. **like so** *colloq.* like this; in this manner. **the likes of** *colloq.* a person such as. [ME *līc, līk,* shortened form of OE *gelīc* ALIKE]

■ **Usage** The use of *like* as a conjunction is considered incorrect by some people.

like² *v. & n.* —*v.tr.* **1 a** find agreeable or enjoyable or satisfactory (*like reading*; *like the sea*; *like to dance*). **b** be fond of (a person). **2 a** choose to have; prefer (*like my coffee black*; *do not like such things discussed*). **b** wish for or be inclined to (*would like a cup of tea*; *should like to come*). **3** (usu. in *interrog.*; prec. by *how*) feel about; regard (*how would you like it if it happened to you?*). —*n.* (in pl.)

the things one likes or prefers. [OE *līcian* f. Gmc]

-like *comb. form* forming adjectives from nouns, meaning 'similar to, characteristic of' (*doglike*; *shell-like*; *tortoise-like*).

■ **Usage** In formations not generally current the hyphen should be used. It may be omitted when the first element is of one syllable, unless it ends in -l.

likeable /ˈlaɪkəb(ə)l/ *adj.* (also **likable**) pleasant; easy to like. □ **likeableness** *n.* **likeably** /-blɪ/ *adv.*

likelihood /ˈlaɪklɪˌhʊd/ *n.* probability; being likely. □ **in all likelihood** very probably.

likely /ˈlaɪklɪ/ *adj. & adv.* —*adj.* **1** probable; such as well might happen or be true (*it is not likely that they will come*; *the most likely place is London*; *a likely story*). **2** (foll. by *to* + infin.) to be reasonably expected (*he is not likely to come now*). **3** promising; apparently suitable (*this is a likely spot*; *three likely lads*). —*adv.* probably (*is very likely true*). □ **not likely!** *colloq.* certainly not, I refuse. □ **likeliness** *n.* [ME f. ON *líkligr* (as LIKE¹, -LY¹)]

liken /ˈlaɪkən/ *v.tr.* (foll. by *to*) point out the resemblance of (a person or thing to another). [ME f. LIKE¹ + -EN¹]

likeness /ˈlaɪknɪs/ *n.* **1** (foll. by *between, to*) resemblance. **2** (foll. by *of*) a semblance or guise (*in the likeness of a ghost*). **3** a portrait or representation (*is a good likeness*). [OE *gelīknes* (as LIKE¹, -NESS)]

likewise /ˈlaɪkwaɪz/ *adv.* **1** also, moreover, too. **2** similarly (*do likewise*). [for *in like wise*]

liking /ˈlaɪkɪŋ/ *n.* **1** what one likes; one's taste (*is it to your liking?*). **2** (foll. by *for*) regard or fondness; taste or fancy (*had a liking for toffee*). [OE *līcung* (as LIKE², -ING¹)]

lilac /ˈlaɪlək/ *n. & adj.* —*n.* **1** any shrub or small tree of the genus *Syringa,* esp. *S. vulgaris* with fragrant pale pinkish-violet or white blossoms. **2** a pale pinkish-violet colour. —*adj.* of this colour. [obs. F f. Sp. f. Arab. *līlāk* f. Pers. *līlak,* var. of *nīlak* bluish f. *nīl* blue]

liliaceous /ˌlɪlɪˈeɪʃəs/ *adj.* **1** of or relating to the family Liliaceae of plants with elongated leaves growing from a corm, bulb, or rhizome, e.g. tulip, lily, or onion. **2** lily-like. [LL *liliaceus* f. L *lilium* lily]

lilliputian /ˌlɪlɪˈpjuːʃ(ə)n/ *n. & adj.* —*n.* a diminutive person or thing. —*adj.* diminutive. [*Lilliput* in Swift's *Gulliver's Travels*]

Lilo /ˈlaɪləʊ/ *n.* (pl. **-os**) *propr.* a type of inflatable mattress. [f. *lie low*]

lilt /lɪlt/ *n. & v.* —*n.* **1 a** a light springing rhythm or gait. **b** a song or tune marked by this. **2** (of the voice) a characteristic cadence or inflection; a pleasant accent. —*v.intr.* (esp. as **lilting** *adj.*) move or speak etc. with a lilt (*a lilting step*; *a lilting melody*). [ME *lilte, lülte,* of unkn. orig.]

lily /ˈlɪlɪ/ *n.* (pl. **-ies**) **1 a** any bulbous plant of the genus *Lilium* with large trumpet-shaped flowers on a tall slender stem. **b** any of several other plants of the family Liliaceae with similar flowers. **c** the water lily. **2** a person or thing of special whiteness or purity. **3** a heraldic fleur-de-lis. **4** (*attrib.*) **a** delicately white (*a lily hand*). **b** pallid. □ **lily-livered** cowardly. **lily of the valley** any liliaceous plant of the genus *Convallaria,* with racemes of white bell-shaped fragrant flowers. **lily-pad** a floating leaf of a water lily. **lily-white 1** as white as a lily. **2** faultless. □ **lilied** adj. [OE lilie f. L lilium prob. f. Gk leirion]

lima bean /ˈliːmə/ n. **1** a tropical American bean plant, Phaseolus limensis, having large flat white edible seeds. **2** the seed of this plant. [Lima in Peru]

limb[1] /lɪm/ n. **1** any of the projecting parts of a person's or animal's body used for contact or movement. **2** a large branch of a tree. **3** a branch of a cross. **4** a spur of a mountain. □ **out on a limb 1** isolated, stranded. **2** at a disadvantage. □ **limbed** adj. (also in comb.). **limbless** adj. [OE lim f. Gmc]

limb[2] /lɪm/ n. Astron. a specified edge of the sun, moon, etc. (eastern limb; lower limb). [F limbe or L limbus hem, border]

limber[1] /ˈlɪmbə(r)/ adj. & v. —adj. **1** lithe, agile, nimble. **2** flexible. —v. (usu. foll. by up) **1** tr. make (oneself or a part of the body etc.) supple. **2** intr. warm up in preparation for athletic etc. activity. □ **limberness** n. [16th c.: orig. uncert.]

limber[2] /ˈlɪmbə(r)/ n. & v. —n. the detachable front part of a gun-carriage. —v. **1** tr. attach a limber to (a gun etc.). **2** intr. fasten together the two parts of a gun-carriage. [ME limo(u)r, app. rel. to med.L limonarius f. limo -onis shaft]

limbo[1] /ˈlɪmbəʊ/ n. (pl. -os) **1** (in some Christian beliefs) the supposed abode of the souls of unbaptized infants, and of the just who died before Christ. **2** an intermediate state or condition of awaiting a decision etc. **3** prison. **4** a state of neglect or oblivion. [ME f. med.L phr. in limbo, f. limbus: see LIMB[2]]

limbo[2] /ˈlɪmbəʊ/ n. (pl. -os) a W. Indian dance in which the dancer bends backwards to pass under a horizontal bar which is progressively lowered. [a W. Indian word, perh. = LIMBER[1]]

lime[1] n. & v. —n. **1** (in full **quicklime**) a white caustic alkaline substance (calcium oxide) obtained by heating limestone and used for making mortar or as a fertilizer or bleach etc. **2** = BIRDLIME. —v.tr. treat (wood, skins, land, etc.) with lime. □ **limeless** adj. **limy** adj. (**limier, limiest**). [OE lím f. Gmc, rel. to LOAM]

lime[2] n. **1 a** a round citrus fruit like a lemon but greener, smaller, and more acid. **b** the tree, Citrus aurantifolia, bearing this. **2** (in full **lime-juice**) the juice of limes as a drink. **3** (in full **lime-green**) a pale green colour like a lime. [F f. mod.Prov. limo, Sp. lima f. Arab. līma: cf. LEMON]

lime[3] n. **1** (in full **lime-tree**) any ornamental tree of the genus Tilia, esp. T. europaea with heart-shaped leaves and fragrant yellow blossom. **2** the wood of this. [alt. of line = OE lind = LINDEN]

limekiln /ˈlaɪmkɪln/ n. a kiln for heating limestone to produce quicklime.

limelight /ˈlaɪmlaɪt/ n. **1** an intense white light obtained by heating a cylinder of lime in an oxyhydrogen flame, used formerly in theatres. **2** (prec. by the) the full glare of publicity; the focus of attention.

limerick /ˈlɪmərɪk/ n. a humorous or comic form of five-line stanza. [said to be from the chorus 'will you come up to Limerick?' sung between improvised verses at a gathering: f. Limerick in Ireland]

limestone /ˈlaɪmstəʊn/ n. Geol. a sedimentary rock composed mainly of calcium carbonate,

used as building material and in the making of cement.

Limey /ˈlaɪmɪ/ n. (pl. -eys) US sl. offens. a British person (orig. a sailor) or ship. [LIME[2], because of the former enforced consumption of lime-juice in the British Navy to prevent scurvy]

limit /ˈlɪmɪt/ n. & v. —n. **1** a point, line, or level beyond which something does not or may not extend or pass. **2** (often in pl.) the boundary of an area. **3** the greatest or smallest amount permissible or possible (upper limit; lower limit). —v.tr. (**limited, limiting**) **1** set or serve as a limit to. **2** (foll. by to) restrict. □ **off limits** US out of bounds. **within limits** moderately; with some degree of freedom. □ **limitable** adj. **limitative** /-tətɪv/ adj. **limiter** n. [ME f. L limes limitis boundary, frontier]

limitation /ˌlɪmɪˈteɪʃ(ə)n/ n. **1** the act or an instance of limiting; the process of being limited. **2** a condition of limited ability (often in pl.: know one's limitations). **3** a limiting rule or circumstance (often in pl.: has its limitations). **4** a legally specified period beyond which an action cannot be brought, or a property right is not to continue. [ME f. L limitatio (as LIMIT)]

limited /ˈlɪmɪtɪd/ adj. **1** confined within limits. **2** not great in scope or talents (has limited experience). **3 a** few, scanty, restricted (limited accommodation). **b** restricted to a few examples (limited edition). □ **limited** (or **limited liability**) **company** a company whose owners are legally responsible only to a limited amount for its debts. **limited liability** Brit. the status of being legally responsible only to a limited amount for debts of a trading company. □ **limitedly** adv. **limitedness** n.

limitless /ˈlɪmɪtlɪs/ adj. **1** extending or going on indefinitely (a limitless expanse). **2** unlimited (limitless generosity). □ **limitlessly** adv. **limitlessness** n.

limnology /lɪmˈnɒlədʒɪ/ n. the study of the physical phenomena of lakes and other fresh waters. □ **limnological** /-nəˈlɒdʒɪk(ə)l/ adj. **limnologist** n. [Gk limnē lake + -LOGY]

limo /ˈlɪməʊ/ n. (pl. -os) US colloq. a limousine. [abbr.]

limousine /ˈlɪmʊˌziːn, ˌlɪmʊˈziːn, ˈlɪməˌziːn/ n. a large luxurious motor car, often with a partition behind the driver. [F, orig. a caped cloak worn in the former French province of Limousin]

limp[1] v. & n. —v.intr. **1** walk lamely. **2** (of a damaged ship, aircraft, etc.) proceed with difficulty. **3** (of verse) be defective. —n. a lame walk. □ **limper** n. **limpingly** adv. [rel. to obs. limphalt lame, OE lemp-healt]

limp[2] adj. **1** not stiff or firm; easily bent. **2** without energy or will. **3** (of a book) having a soft cover. □ **limply** adv. **limpness** n. [18th c.: orig. unkn.: perh. rel. to LIMP[1] in the sense 'hanging loose']

limpet /ˈlɪmpɪt/ n. **1** any of various marine gastropod molluscs, esp. the common limpet Patella vulgata, with a shallow conical shell and a broad muscular foot that sticks tightly to rocks. **2** a clinging person. □ **limpet mine** a mine designed to be attached to a ship's hull and set to explode after a certain time. [OE lempedu f. med.L lampreda limpet, LAMPREY]

limpid /ˈlɪmpɪd/ adj. **1** (of water, eyes, etc.) clear, transparent. **2** (of writing) clear and easily comprehended. □ **limpidity** /-'pɪdɪtɪ/ n. **limpidly** adv. **limpidness** n. [F limpide or L limpidus, perh. rel. to LYMPH]

linage /'laɪnɪdʒ/ n. **1** the number of lines in printed or written matter. **2** payment by the line.

linchpin /'lɪntʃpɪn/ n. **1** a pin passed through an axle-end to keep a wheel in position. **2** a person or thing vital to an enterprise, organization, etc. [ME linch f. OE lynis + PIN]

linctus /'lɪŋktəs/ n. a syrupy medicine, esp. a soothing cough mixture. [L f. lingere lick]

lindane /'lɪndeɪn/ n. Chem. a colourless crystalline chlorinated derivative of cyclohexane used as an insecticide. [T. van der Linden, Du. chemist b. 1884]

linden /'lɪnd(ə)n/ n. a lime-tree. [(orig. adj.) f. OE lind lime-tree: cf. LIME³]

line¹ n. & v. —n. **1** a continuous mark or band made on a surface (drew a line). **2** use of lines in art, esp. draughtsmanship or engraving (boldness of line). **3** a thing resembling such a mark esp. a furrow or wrinkle. **4** Mus. **a** each of (usu. five) horizontal marks forming a stave in musical notation. **b** a sequence of notes or tones forming an instrumental or vocal melody. **5 a** a straight or curved continuous extent of length without breadth. **b** the track of a moving point. **6 a** a contour or outline, esp. as a feature of design (admired the sculpture's clean lines; the ship's lines). **b** a facial feature (the cruel line of his mouth). **7 a** (on a map or graph) a curve connecting all points having a specified common property. **b** (the Line) the Equator. **8 a** a limit or boundary. **b** a mark limiting the area of play, the starting or finishing point in a race, etc. **9 a** a row of persons or things. **b** a direction as indicated by them (line of march). **c** US a queue. **10 a** a row of printed or written words. **b** a portion of verse written in one line. **11** (in pl.) **a** a piece of poetry. **b** the words of an actor's part. **c** a specified amount of text etc. to be written out as a school punishment. **12** a short letter or note (drop me a line). **13** (in pl.) = marriage lines. **14** a length of cord, rope, wire, etc., usu. serving a specified purpose, esp. a fishing-line or clothes-line. **15 a** a wire or cable for a telephone or telegraph. **b** a connection by means of this (am trying to get a line). **16 a** a single track of a railway. **b** one branch or route of a railway system, or the whole system under one management. **17 a** a regular succession of buses, ships, aircraft, etc., plying between certain places. **b** a company conducting this (shipping line). **18** a connected series of persons following one another in time (esp. several generations of a family); stock, succession (a long line of craftsmen; next in line to the throne). **19 a** a course or manner of procedure, conduct, thought, etc. (did it along these lines; don't take that line with me). **b** policy (the party line). **c** conformity (bring them into line). **20** a direction, course, or channel (lines of communication). **21** a department of activity; a province; a branch of business (not in my line). **22** a class of commercial goods (a new line in hats). **23** colloq. a false or exaggerated account or story; a dishonest approach (gave me a line about missing the bus). **24 a** a connected series of military fieldworks, defences, etc. (behind enemy lines). **b** an arrangement of soldiers or ships side by side; a line of battle (ship of the line). **c** (prec. by

the) regular army regiments (not auxiliary forces or Guards). **25** each of the very narrow horizontal sections forming a television picture. **26** the level of the base of most letters in printing and writing. **27** (as a measure) one twelfth of an inch. —v. **1** tr. mark with lines. **2** tr. cover with lines (a face lined with pain). **3** tr. & intr. position or stand at intervals along (crowds lined the route). □ **bring into line** make conform. **come into line** conform. **end of the line** the point at which further effort is unproductive or one can go no further. **get a line on** colloq. learn something about. **in line for** likely to receive. **in the line of** in the course of (esp. duty). **in** (or **out of**) **line with** in (or not in) accordance with. **lay** (or **put**) **it on the line** speak frankly. **line-drawing** a drawing in which images are produced from variations of lines. **line of fire** the expected path of gunfire, a missile, etc. **line of vision** the straight line along which an observer looks. **line-out** (in Rugby Football) parallel lines of opposing forwards at right angles to the touchline for the throwing in of the ball. **line printer** a machine that prints output from a computer a line at a time rather than character by character. **line up 1** arrange or be arranged in a line or lines. **2** have ready; organize (had a job lined up). **line-up** n. **1** a line of people for inspection. **2** an arrangement of persons in a team or nations etc. in an alliance. **on the line 1** at risk (put my reputation on the line). **2** speaking on the telephone. **out of line** not in alignment; discordant. [ME line, ligne f. OF ligne ult. f. L linea f. linum flax, & f. OE líne rope, series]

line² /laɪn/ v.tr. **1 a** cover the inside surface of (a garment, box, etc.) with a layer of usu. different material. **b** serve as a lining for. **2** cover as if with a lining (shelves lined with books). **3** colloq. fill, esp. plentifully. □ **line one's pocket** (or **purse**) make money, usu. by corrupt means. [ME f. obs. line flax, with ref. to the use of linen for linings]

lineage /'lɪnɪɪdʒ/ n. lineal descent; ancestry, pedigree. [ME f. OF linage, lignage f. Rmc f. L linea LINE¹]

lineal /'lɪnɪəl/ adj. **1** in the direct line of descent or ancestry. **2** linear; of or in lines. □ **lineally** adv. [ME f. OF f. LL linealis (as LINE¹)]

lineament /'lɪnɪəmənt/ n. (usu. in pl.) a distinctive feature or characteristic, esp. of the face. [ME f. L lineamentum f. lineare make straight f. linea LINE¹]

linear /'lɪnɪə(r)/ adj. **1 a** of or in lines; in lines rather than masses (linear development). **b** of length (linear extent). **2** long and narrow and of uniform breadth. **3** involving one dimension only. □ **Linear B** a form of Bronze Age writing found in Crete and parts of Greece and recording a form of Mycenaean Greek: an earlier undeciphered form (**Linear A**) also exists. □ **linearity** /-'ærɪtɪ/ n. **linearize** v.tr. (also **-ise**). **linearly** adv. [L linearis f. linea LINE¹]

lineation /ˌlɪnɪ'eɪʃ(ə)n/ n. **1** a marking with or drawing of lines. **2** a division into lines. [ME f. L lineatio f. lineare make straight]

lineman /'laɪnmən/ n. (pl. **-men**) **1 a** a person who repairs and maintains telephone or electrical etc. lines. **b** a person who tests the safety of railway lines. **2** US Football a player in the line formed before a scrimmage.

linen /ˈlɪnɪn/ n. & adj. —n. **1 a** cloth woven from flax. **b** a particular kind of this. **2** (collect.) articles made or orig. made of linen, calico, etc., as sheets, cloths, shirts, undergarments, etc. —adj. made of linen or flax (linen cloth). □ **linen basket** a basket for soiled clothes. [OE līnen f. WG, rel. to obs. line flax]

liner¹ /ˈlaɪnə(r)/ n. a ship or aircraft etc. carrying passengers on a regular line.

liner² /ˈlaɪnə(r)/ n. a removable lining.

linesman /ˈlaɪnzmən/ n. (pl. -men) **1** (in games played on a pitch or court) an umpire's or referee's assistant who decides whether a ball falls within the playing area or not. **2** Brit. = LINEMAN 1.

ling¹ /lɪŋ/ n. a long slender marine fish, Molva molva, of N. Europe, used as food. [ME leng(e), prob. f. MDu, rel. to LONG¹]

ling² /lɪŋ/ n. any of various heathers, esp. Calluna vulgaris. □ **lingy** adj. [ME f. ON lyng]

-ling¹ /lɪŋ/ suffix **1** denoting a person or thing: **a** connected with (hireling; sapling). **b** having the property of being (weakling; underling) or undergoing (starveling). **2** denoting a diminutive (duckling), often derogatory (lordling). [OE (as -LE¹ + -ING³): sense 2 f. ON]

-ling² /lɪŋ/ suffix forming adverbs and adjectives (darkling; grovelling) (cf. -LONG). [OE f. Gmc]

linger /ˈlɪŋgə(r)/ v.intr. **1 a** be slow or reluctant to depart. **b** stay about. **c** (foll. by over, on, etc.) dally (lingered over dinner; lingered on what they said). **2** (esp. of an illness) be protracted. **3** (foll. by on) (of a dying person or custom) be slow in dying; drag on feebly. □ **lingerer** n. **lingeringly** adv. [ME lenger, frequent. of leng f. OE lengan f. Gmc, rel. to LENGTHEN]

lingerie /ˈlæ̃ʒərɪ/ n. women's underwear and nightclothes. [F f. linge linen]

lingo /ˈlɪŋgəʊ/ n. (pl. -os or -oes) colloq. **1** a foreign language. **2** the vocabulary of a special subject or group of people. [prob. f. Port. lingoa f. L lingua tongue]

lingua franca /ˌlɪŋgwə ˈfræŋkə/ n. (pl. **lingua francas**) **1** a language adopted as a common language between speakers whose native languages are different. **2** a system for mutual understanding. [It., = Frankish tongue]

lingual /ˈlɪŋgw(ə)l/ adj. **1** of or formed by the tongue. **2** of speech or languages. □ **lingualize** v.tr. (also -ise). **lingually** adv. [med.L lingualis f. L lingua tongue, language]

linguist /ˈlɪŋgwɪst/ n. a person skilled in languages or linguistics. [L lingua language]

linguistic /lɪŋˈgwɪstɪk/ adj. of or relating to language or the study of languages. □ **linguistically** adv.

linguistics /lɪŋˈgwɪstɪks/ n. the scientific study of language and its structure. □ **linguistician** /-ˈstɪʃ(ə)n/ n. [F linguistique or G Linguistik (as LINGUIST)]

liniment /ˈlɪnɪmənt/ n. an embrocation, usu. made with oil. [LL linimentum f. L linire smear]

lining /ˈlaɪnɪŋ/ n. **1** a layer of material used to line a surface etc. **2** an inside layer or surface etc. (stomach lining).

link n. & v. —n. **1** one loop or ring of a chain etc. **2 a** a connecting part, esp. a thing or person that unites or provides continuity; one in a series. **b** a state or means of connection. **3** a means of contact by radio or telephone between two points. **4** a means of travel or transport between two places. **5** = cuff-link. —v. **1** tr. (foll. by together, to, with) connect or join (two things or one to another). **2** tr. clasp or intertwine (hands or arms). **3** intr. (foll. by on, to, in to) be joined; attach oneself to (a system, company, etc.). □ **link up** (foll. by with) connect or combine. [ME f. ON f. Gmc]

linkage /ˈlɪŋkɪdʒ/ n. **1** a connection. **2** a system of links; a linking or link.

linkman /ˈlɪŋkmæn/ n. (pl. -men) **1** a person providing continuity in a broadcast programme. **2** a player between the forwards and half-backs or strikers and backs in football etc.

links /lɪŋks/ n.pl. (treated as sing. or pl.) a golf-course, esp. one having undulating ground, coarse grass, etc. [pl. of link 'rising ground' f. OE hlinc]

Linnaean /lɪˈniːən, lɪˈneɪən/ adj. of or relating to the Swedish naturalist Linnaeus (Linné, d. 1778) or his system of binary nomenclature in the classification of plants and animals.

■ **Usage** This word is spelt Linnean in Linnean Society.

linnet /ˈlɪnɪt/ n. a finch, Acanthis cannabina, with brown and grey plumage. [OF linette f. lin flax (the bird feeding on flax-seeds)]

lino /ˈlaɪnəʊ/ n. (pl. -os) linoleum. [abbr.]

linocut /ˈlaɪnəʊˌkʌt/ n. **1** a design or form carved in relief on a block of linoleum. **2** a print made from this. □ **linocutting** n.

linoleum /lɪˈnəʊlɪəm/ n. a material consisting of a canvas backing thickly coated with a preparation of linseed oil and powdered cork etc., used esp. as a floor-covering. □ **linoleumed** adj. [L linum flax + oleum oil]

Linotype /ˈlaɪnəʊˌtaɪp/ n. Printing propr. a composing-machine producing lines of words as single strips of metal, used esp. for newspapers. [= line o' type]

linseed /ˈlɪnsiːd/ n. the seed of flax. □ **linseed oil** oil extracted from linseed and used in paint and varnish. [OE līnsǣd f. līn flax + sǣd seed]

linsey-woolsey /ˌlɪnzɪˈwʊlzɪ/ n. a fabric of coarse wool woven on a cotton warp. [ME f. linsey coarse linen, prob. f. Lindsey in Suffolk + WOOL, with jingling ending]

lint n. **1** a fabric, orig. of linen, with a raised nap on one side, used for dressing wounds. **2** fluff. □ **linty** adj. [ME lyn(n)et, perh. f. OF linette linseed f. lin flax]

lintel /ˈlɪnt(ə)l/ n. Archit. a horizontal supporting piece of timber, stone, etc., across the top of a door or window. □ **lintelled** adj. (US **linteled**). [ME f. OF lintel threshold f. Rmc limitale (unrecorded), infl. by LL liminare f. L limen threshold]

liny /ˈlaɪnɪ/ adj. (**linier**, **liniest**) marked with lines; wrinkled.

lion /ˈlaɪən/ n. **1** (fem. **lioness** /-nɪs/) a large flesh-eating cat, Panthera leo, of Africa and S. Asia, with a tawny coat and, in the male, a flowing shaggy mane. **2** (**the Lion**) the zodiacal sign or constellation Leo. **3** a brave or celebrated person. □ **lion-heart** a courageous person (esp. as a sobriquet of Richard I of England). **lion-hearted** brave and generous. **the lion's share** the largest or best part. □ **lionhood** n. **lion-like** adj. [ME f. AF liun f. L leo -onis f. Gk leōn leontos]

lionize /ˈlaɪəˌnaɪz/ v.tr. (also **-ise**) treat as a celebrity. □ **lionization** /-ˈzeɪʃ(ə)n/ n. **lionizer** n.

lip n. & v. —n. **1 a** either of the two fleshy parts forming the edges of the mouth-opening. **b** a thing resembling these. **c** = LABIUM. **2** the edge of a cup, vessel, etc., esp. the part shaped for pouring from. **3** colloq. impudent talk (that's enough of your lip!). —v.tr. (**lipped, lipping**) **1 a** touch with the lips; apply the lips to. **b** touch lightly. □ **hang on a person's lips** listen attentively to a person. **lip-read** (past and past part. **-read** /-red/) (esp. of a deaf person) understand (speech) entirely from observing a speaker's lip-movements. **lip-service** an insincere expression of support etc. **pass a person's lips** be eaten, drunk, spoken, etc. **smack one's lips** part the lips noisily in relish or anticipation, esp. of food. □ **lipless** adj. **liplike** adj. **lipped** adj. (also in comb.). [OE lippa f. Gmc]

lipase /ˈlaɪpeɪz, -peɪs/ n. Biochem. an enzyme that catalyses the decomposition of fats. [Gk lipos fat + ase suffix denoting an enzyme]

lipid /ˈlɪpɪd/ n. Chem. any of a group of organic compounds that are insoluble in water but soluble in organic solvents, including fatty acids, oils, waxes, and steroids. [F lipide (as LIPASE)]

liposuction /ˈlaɪpəʊˌsʌkʃ(ə)n/ n. a technique in cosmetic surgery for removing excess fat from under the skin by suction. [Gk lipos fat + SUCTION]

lippy /ˈlɪpɪ/ adj. (**lippier, lippiest**) colloq. **1** insolent, impertinent. **2** talkative.

lipsalve /ˈlɪpsælv/ n. **1** a preparation, usu. in stick form, to prevent or relieve sore lips. **2** flattery.

lipstick /ˈlɪpstɪk/ n. a small stick of cosmetic for colouring the lips.

liquefy /ˈlɪkwɪˌfaɪ/ v.tr. & intr. (also **liquify**) (**-ies, -ied**) Chem. make or become liquid. □ **liquefacient** /-ˈfeɪʃ(ə)nt/ adj. & n. **liquefaction** /-ˈfækʃ(ə)n/ n. **liquefactive** /-ˈfæktɪv/ adj. **liquefiable** adj. **liquefier** n. [F liquéfier f. L liquefacere f. liquēre be liquid]

liqueur /lɪˈkjʊə(r)/ n. any of several strong sweet alcoholic spirits, variously flavoured, usu. drunk after a meal. [F. = LIQUOR]

liquid /ˈlɪkwɪd/ adj. & n. —adj. **1** having a consistency like that of water or oil, flowing freely but of constant volume. **2** having the qualities of water in appearance; translucent (liquid blue; a liquid lustre). **3** (of a gas, e.g. air, hydrogen) reduced to a liquid state by intense cold. **4** (of sounds) clear and pure; harmonious, fluent. **5** (of assets) easily converted into cash. —n. **1** a liquid substance. **2** Phonet. the sound of l or r. □ **liquid crystal** a turbid liquid with some order in its molecular arrangement. **liquid crystal display** a form of visual display in electronic devices, in which the reflectivity of a matrix of liquid crystals changes as a signal is applied. **liquid measure** a unit for measuring the volume of liquids. **liquid paraffin** Pharm. a colourless odourless oily liquid obtained from petroleum and used as a laxative. □ **liquidly** adv. **liquidness** n. [ME f. L liquidus f. liquēre be liquid]

liquidate /ˈlɪkwɪˌdeɪt/ v. **1 a** tr. wind up the affairs of (a company or firm) by ascertaining liabilities and apportioning assets. **b** intr. (of a

company) be liquidated. **2** tr. clear or pay off (a debt). **3** tr. put an end to or get rid of (esp. by violent means). [med.L liquidare make clear (as LIQUID)]

liquidation /ˌlɪkwɪˈdeɪʃ(ə)n/ n. the process of liquidating a company etc. □ **go into liquidation** (of a company etc.) be wound up and have its assets apportioned.

liquidator /ˈlɪkwɪˌdeɪtə(r)/ n. a person called in to wind up the affairs of a company etc.

liquidity /lɪˈkwɪdɪtɪ/ n. (pl. **-ies**) **1** the state of being liquid. **2** availability of liquid assets. **b** (in pl.) liquid assets. [F liquidité or med.L liquiditas (as LIQUID)]

liquidize /ˈlɪkwɪˌdaɪz/ v.tr. (also **-ise**) reduce (esp. food) to a liquid or puréed state.

liquidizer /ˈlɪkwɪˌdaɪzə(r)/ n. a machine for liquidizing.

liquor /ˈlɪkə(r)/ n. **1** an alcoholic (esp. distilled) drink. **2** water used in brewing. **3** other liquid, esp. that produced in cooking. [ME f. OF lic(o)ur f. L liquor -oris (as LIQUID)]

liquorice /ˈlɪkərɪs, -rɪʃ/ n. (also **licorice**) **1** a black root extract used as a sweet and in medicine. **2** the leguminous plant Glycyrrhiza glabra from which it is obtained. [ME f. AF lycorys, OF licoresse f. LL liquiritia f. Gk glukurrhiza f. glukus sweet + rhiza root]

lira /ˈlɪərə/ n. (pl. **lire** /ˈlɪəre, ˈlɪərɪ/) **1** the chief monetary unit of Italy. **2** the chief monetary unit of Turkey. [It. f. Prov. liura f. L libra pound (weight etc.)]

lisle /laɪl/ n. (in full **lisle thread**) a fine smooth cotton thread for stockings etc. [Lisle, former spelling of Lille in France, where orig. made]

lisp n. & v. —n. a speech defect in which s is pronounced like th in thick and z is pronounced like th in this. —v.intr. & tr. speak or utter with a lisp. □ **lisper** n. **lispingly** adv. [OE wlispian (recorded in āwlyspian) f. wlisp (adj.) lisping, of uncert. orig.]

lissom /ˈlɪsəm/ adj. (also **lissome**) lithe, supple, agile. □ **lissomly** adv. **lissomness** n. [ult. f. LITHE + -SOME¹]

list¹ n. & v. —n. **1** a number of connected items, names, etc., written or printed together usu. consecutively to form a record or aid to memory (shopping list). **2** (in pl.) a palisades enclosing an area for a tournament. **b** the scene of a contest. **3** Brit. **a** a selvage or edge of cloth, usu. of different material from the main body. **b** such edges used as a material. —v. **1** tr. make a list of. **2** tr. enter in a list. **3** tr. (as **listed** adj.) **a** (of securities) approved for dealings on the Stock Exchange. **b** (of a building in the UK) officially designated as being of historical importance and having protection from demolition or major alterations. **4** tr. & intr. archaic enlist. □ **enter the lists** issue or accept a challenge. **list price** the price of something as shown in a published list. □ **listable** adj. [OE liste border, strip f. Gmc]

list² /lɪst/ v. & n. —v.intr. (of a ship etc.) lean over to one side, esp. owing to a leak or shifting cargo. —n. the process or an instance of listing. [17th c.: orig. unkn.]

listen /ˈlɪs(ə)n/ v.intr. **1 a** make an effort to hear something. **b** attentively hear a person speaking. **2** (foll. by to) give attention with the ear (listened to my story). **b** take notice of; respond to advice or a request or to the person expressing it. **3** (also **listen out**) (often foll. by for) seek to hear or be aware of by waiting alertly. □ **listen in 1** tap a telephonic communication. **2** use a radio receiving set. **listening-post 1** a point near an enemy's lines for detecting movements by sound. **2** a station for intercepting electronic communications. [OE *hlysnan* f. WG]

listenable /ˈlɪsənəb(ə)l/ *adj.* easy or pleasant to listen to. □ **listenability** /-əˈbɪlɪtɪ/ *n.*

listener /ˈlɪsnə(r)/ *n.* **1** a person who listens. **2** a person receiving broadcast radio programmes.

listeria /lɪˈstɪərɪə/ *n.* any motile rodlike bacterium of the genus *Listeria*, esp. *L. monocytogenes* infecting humans and animals eating contaminated food. [mod.L f. J. *Lister*, Engl. surgeon d. 1912]

listing /ˈlɪstɪŋ/ *n.* **1** a list or catalogue. **2** the drawing up of a list.

listless /ˈlɪstlɪs/ *adj.* lacking energy or enthusiasm; disinclined for exertion. □ **listlessly** *adv.* **listlessness** *n.* [ME f. obs. *list* inclination + -LESS]

lit *past* and *past part.* of LIGHT¹, LIGHT².

litany /ˈlɪtənɪ/ *n.* (*pl.* **-ies**) **1 a** a series of petitions for use in church services or processions, usu. recited by the clergy and responded to in a recurring formula by the people. **b** (**the Litany**) that contained in the Book of Common Prayer. **2** a tedious recital (*a litany of woes*). [ME f. OF *letanie* f. eccl.L *litania* f. Gk *litaneia* prayer f. *litē* supplication]

litchi var. of LYCHEE.

-lite /laɪt/ *suffix* forming names of minerals (*rhyolite*; *zeolite*). [F f. Gk *lithos* stone]

liter US var. of LITRE.

literacy /ˈlɪtərəsɪ/ *n.* the ability to read and write. [LITERATE + -ACY after *illiteracy*]

literal /ˈlɪtər(ə)l/ *adj.* & *n.* —*adj.* **1** taking words in their usual or primary sense without metaphor or allegory (*literal interpretation*). **2** following the letter, text, or exact or original words (*literal translation*; *a literal transcript*). **3** (in full **literal-minded**) (of a person) prosaic; matter of fact. **4 a** not exaggerated (*the literal truth*). **b** so called without exaggeration (*a literal extermination*). **5** *colloq. disp.* so called with some exaggeration or using metaphor (*a literal avalanche of mail*). **6** of, in, or expressed by a letter or the letters of the alphabet. —*n.* Printing a misprint of a letter. □ **literality** /-ˈrælɪtɪ/ *n.* **literalize** *v.tr.* (also **-ise**). **literally** *adv.* **literalness** *n.* [ME f. OF *literal* or LL *litteralis* f. L *littera* (as LETTER)]

literalism /ˈlɪtərəˌlɪz(ə)m/ *n.* insistence on a literal interpretation; adherence to the letter. □ **literalist** *n.* **literalistic** /-ˈlɪstɪk/ *adj.*

literary /ˈlɪtərərɪ/ *adj.* **1** of, constituting, or occupied with books or literature or written composition. esp. of the kind valued for quality of form. **2** well informed about literature. **3** (of a word or idiom) used chiefly in literary works or other formal writing. □ **literarily** *adv.* **literariness** *n.* [L *litterarius* (as LETTER)]

literate /ˈlɪtərət/ *adj.* & *n.* —*adj.* able to read and write. —*n.* a literate person. □ **literately** *adv.* [ME f. L *litteratus* (as LETTER)]

literati /ˌlɪtəˈrɑːtiː/ *n.pl.* **1** men of letters. **2** the learned class. [L, pl. of *literatus* (as LETTER)]

literature /ˈlɪtərətʃə(r), ˈlɪtrə-/ *n.* **1** written works, esp. those whose value lies in beauty of language or in emotional effect. **2** the realm of letters. **3** the writings of a country or period. **4** literary

production. **5** *colloq.* printed matter, leaflets, etc. **6** the material in print on a particular subject (*there is a considerable literature on geraniums*). [ME, = literary culture, f. L *litteratura* (as LITERATE)]

-lith /lɪθ/ *suffix* denoting types of stone (*laccolith*; *monolith*). [Gk *lithos* stone]

lithe /laɪð/ *adj.* flexible, supple. □ **lithely** *adv.* **litheness** *n.* **lithesome** *adj.* [OE *līthe* f. Gmc]

lithium /ˈlɪθɪəm/ *n. Chem.* a soft silver-white metallic element, the lightest metal, used in alloys and in batteries. [mod. L, f. Gk neut. of *litheios* f. *lithos* stone]

litho /ˈlaɪθəʊ/ *n.* & *v. colloq.* —*n.* = LITHOGRAPHY. —*v.tr.* (**-oes**, **-oed**) produce by lithography. [abbr.]

litho- /ˈlɪθəʊ, ˈlaɪθəʊ/ *comb. form* stone. [Gk *lithos* stone]

lithograph /ˈlɪθəˌgrɑːf, ˈlaɪθə-/ *n.* & *v.* —*n.* a lithographic print. —*v.tr.* **1** print by lithography. **2** write or engrave on stone. [back-form. f. LITHOGRAPHY]

lithography /lɪˈθɒɡrəfɪ/ *n.* a process of obtaining prints from a stone or metal surface so treated that what is to be printed can be inked but the remaining area rejects ink. □ **lithographer** *n.* **lithographic** /ˌlɪθəˈɡræfɪk/ *adj.* **lithographically** /ˌlɪθəˈɡræfɪkəlɪ/ *adv.* [G *Lithographie* (as LITHO-, -GRAPHY)]

lithosphere /ˈlɪθəˌsfɪə(r)/ *n.* **1** the layer including the earth's crust and upper mantle. **2** solid earth. □ **lithospheric** /-ˈsfɛrɪk/ *adj.*

litigant /ˈlɪtɪɡənt/ *n.* & *adj.* —*n.* a party to a lawsuit. —*adj.* engaged in a lawsuit. [F (as LITIGATE)]

litigate /ˈlɪtɪˌɡeɪt/ *v.* **1** *intr.* go to law; be a party to a lawsuit. **2** *tr.* contest (a point) in a lawsuit. □ **litigable** /ˈlɪtɪɡəb(ə)l/ *adj.* **litigation** /-ˈɡeɪʃ(ə)n/ *n.* **litigator** *n.* [L *litigare litigat-* f. *lis litis* lawsuit]

litigious /lɪˈtɪdʒəs/ *adj.* **1** given to litigation; unreasonably fond of going to law. **2** of lawsuits. □ **litigiously** *adv.* **litigiousness** *n.* [ME f. OF *litigieux* or L *litigiosus* f. *litigium* litigation: see LITIGATE]

litmus /ˈlɪtməs/ *n.* a dye obtained from lichens that is red under acid conditions and blue under alkaline conditions. □ **litmus paper** a paper stained with litmus to be used as a test for acids or alkalis. [ME f. ONorw. *litmosi* f. ON *litr* dye + *mosi* moss]

litotes /laɪˈtəʊtiːz/ *n.* ironical understatement, esp. the expressing of an affirmative by the negative of its contrary (e.g. *I shan't be sorry for I shall be glad*). [LL f. Gk *litotēs* f. *litos* plain, meagre]

litre /ˈliːtə(r)/ *n.* (US **liter**) a metric unit of capacity, equal to 1 cubic decimetre (about 1.75 pints). □ **litreage** /ˈliːtərɪdʒ/ *n.* [F f. *litron*, an obs. measure of capacity, f. med.L f. Gk *litra* a Sicilian monetary unit]

Litt.D. *abbr.* Doctor of Letters. [L *Litterarum Doctor*]

litter /ˈlɪtə(r)/ *n.* & *v.* —*n.* **1 a** refuse, esp. paper, discarded in an open or public place. **b** odds and ends lying about. **c** (*attrib.*) for disposing of litter (*litter-bin*). **2** a state of untidiness, disorderly accumulation of papers etc. **3** the young animals brought forth at a birth. **4** a vehicle containing a couch shut in by curtains and carried on men's shoulders or by beasts of burden. **5** a framework with a couch for transporting the sick and wounded. **6 a** straw, rushes, etc., as bedding, esp. for animals. **b** straw and dung in a farmyard. —*v.tr.* **1** make (a place) untidy with litter. **2** scatter untidily and leave lying about. **3** give birth to (whelps etc.). **4** (often foll. by *down*) **a** provide (a horse etc.) with litter as bedding. **b** spread litter or straw on (a floor) or in (a stable). □ **litter-lout** = LITTERBUG. □ **littery** *adj.* (in senses 1, 2 of *n.*). [ME f. AF *litere*, OF *litiere* f. med.L *lectaria* f. L *lectus* bed]

litterbug /ˈlɪtəˌbʌg/ *n.* a person who carelessly leaves litter in a public place.

little /ˈlɪt(ə)l/ *adj.*, *n.*, & *adv.* —*adj.* (**littler**, **littlest**; **less** or **lesser** /ˈlesə(r)/; **least**) **1** small in size, amount, degree, etc.; not great or big: often used to convey affectionate or emotional overtones, or condescension, not implied by *small* (*a friendly little chap; a silly little fool; a nice little car*). **2** a short in stature (*a little man*). **b** of short distance or duration (*will go a little way with you; wait a little while*). **3** (prec. by *a*) a certain though small amount of (*give me a little butter*). **4** trivial; relatively unimportant (*exaggerates every little difficulty*). **5** not much; inconsiderable (*gained little advantage from it*). **6** operating on a small scale (*the little shopkeeper*). **7** as a distinctive epithet: **a** of a smaller or the smallest size etc. (*little finger*). **b** that is the smaller or smallest of the name (*little auk; little grebe*). **8** young or younger (*a little boy; my little sister*). **9** as of a child, evoking tenderness, condescension, amusement, etc. (*we know their little ways*). **10** mean, paltry, contemptible (*you little sneak*). —*n.* **1** not much; only a small amount (*got very little out of it; did what little I could*). **2** (usu. prec. by *a*) **a** a certain but no great amount (*knows a little of everything; every little helps*). **b** a short time or distance (*after a little*). —*adv.* (**less, least**) **1** to a small extent only (*little-known authors; is little more than speculation*). **2** not at all; hardly (*they little thought*). **3** (prec. by *a*) somewhat (*is a little deaf*). □ **in little** on a small scale. **little by little** by degrees; gradually. **little end** the smaller end of a connecting-rod, attached to the piston. **little finger** the smallest finger, at the outer end of the hand. **little ones** young children or animals. **little or nothing** hardly anything. **the little people** fairies. **the little woman** *colloq.* often *derog.* one's wife. **no little** considerable, a good deal of (*took no little trouble over it*). **not a little** *n.* much; a great deal. —*adv.* extremely (*not a little concerned*). □ **littleness** *n.* [OE *lȳtel* f. Gmc]

littoral /ˈlɪtər(ə)l/ *adj.* & *n.* —*adj.* of or on the shore of the sea, a lake, etc. —*n.* a region lying along a shore. [L *littoralis* f. *litus litoris* shore]

liturgical /lɪˈtɜːdʒɪk(ə)l/ *adj.* of or related to liturgies or public worship. □ **liturgically** *adv.* **liturgist** /ˈlɪtədʒɪst/ *n.* [med.L f. Gk *leitourgikos* (as LITURGY)]

liturgy /ˈlɪtədʒɪ/ *n.* (pl. **-ies**) **1 a** a form of public worship. **b** a set of formularies for this. **c** public worship in accordance with a prescribed form. **2 (the Liturgy)** the Book of Common Prayer. [F *liturgie* or LL *liturgia* f. Gk *leitourgia* public worship f. *leitourgos* minister f. *leit-* public + *ergon* work]

live[1] /lɪv/ *v.* **1** *intr.* have (esp. animal) life; be or remain alive. **2** *intr.* (foll. by *on*) subsist or feed (*lives on fruit*). **3** *intr.* (foll. by *on, off*) depend for subsistence (*lives off the family; lives on income from investments*). **4** *intr.* (foll. by *on, by*) sustain one's position or repute (*live on their reputation;*

lives by his wits). **5** *tr.* **a** (with compl.) spend, pass, experience (*lived a happy life*). **b** express in one's life (*was living a lie*). **6** *intr.* conduct oneself in a specified way (*live quietly*). **7** *intr.* arrange one's habits, expenditure, feeding, etc. (*live modestly*). **8** *intr.* make or have one's abode. **9** *intr.* (foll. by *in*) spend the daytime (*the room does not seem to be lived in*). **10** *intr.* (of a person or thing) survive. □ **live and let live** condone others' failings so as to be similarly tolerated. **live down** (usu. with *neg.*) cause (past guilt, embarrassment, etc.) to be forgotten by different conduct over a period of time (*you'll never live that down!*). **live in** *Brit.* (of a domestic employee) reside on the premises of one's work. **live-in** *attrib.adj.* (of a sexual partner) cohabiting. **live it up** *colloq.* live gaily and extravagantly. **live out 1** survive (a danger, difficulty, etc.). **2** (of a domestic employee) reside away from one's place of work. **live together** (esp. of a man and woman not married to each other) share a home and have a sexual relationship. **live up to** honour or fulfil; put into practice (principles etc.). **live with 1** share a home with. **2** tolerate; find congenial. **long live . . . !** an exclamation of loyalty (to a person etc. specified). [OE *libban*, *lifian*, f. Gmc]

live[2] /laɪv/ *adj.* **1** (*attrib.*) that is alive; living. **2** (of a broadcast) heard or seen at the time of its performance, not from a recording. **3** full of power, energy, or importance; not obsolete or exhausted (*disarmament is still a live issue*). **4** expending or still able to expend energy in various forms, esp.: **a** (of coals) glowing, burning. **b** (of a shell) unexploded. **c** (of a match) unkindled. **d** (of a wire etc.) connected to a source of electrical power. **5** (of a wheel or axle etc. in machinery) moving or imparting motion. □ **live wire** an energetic and forceful person. [aphetic form of ALIVE]

liveable /ˈlɪvəb(ə)l/ *adj.* (also **livable**) **1** (of a house, room, climate, etc.) fit to live in. **2** (of a life) worth living. **3** (of a person) companionable; easy to live with. □ **liveability** /-ˈbɪlɪtɪ/ *n.* **liveableness** *n.*

livelihood /ˈlaɪvlɪˌhʊd/ *n.* a means of living; sustenance. [OE *līflād* f. *līf* LIFE + *lād* course (see LOAD): assim. to obs. *livelihood* liveliness]

livelong /ˈlɪvlɒŋ/ *adj.* poet. or *rhet.* in its entire length or apparently so (*the livelong day*). [ME *lefe longe* (as OE *lēof* dear, pleasant + LONG¹): assim. to LIVE¹]

lively /ˈlaɪvlɪ/ *adj.* (**livelier**, **liveliest**) **1** full of life; vigorous, energetic. **2** brisk (*a lively pace*). **3** vivid, stimulating. □ **livelily** *adv.* **liveliness** *n.* [OE *līflīc* (as LIFE, -LY¹)]

liven /ˈlaɪv(ə)n/ *v.tr.* & *intr.* (often foll. by *up*) *colloq.* brighten, cheer.

liver[1] /ˈlɪvə(r)/ *n.* **1 a** a large lobed glandular organ in the abdomen of vertebrates, functioning in many metabolic processes including the regulation of toxic materials in the blood, secreting bile, etc. **b** a similar organ in other animals. **2** the flesh of an animal's liver as food. **3** (in full **liver-colour**) a dark reddish-brown. □ **liver fluke** either of two types of fluke, esp. *Fasciola hepatica*, the adults of which live within the liver tissues of vertebrates, and the larvae within snails. **liver salts** *Brit.* salts to cure dyspepsia or biliousness. **liver sausage** a sausage containing cooked liver etc. □ **liverless** adj. [OE lifer f. Gmc]

liver[2] /ˈlɪvə(r)/ n. a person who lives in a specified way (a clean liver).

liverish /ˈlɪvərɪʃ/ adj. **1** suffering from a disorder of the liver. **2** peevish, glum. □ **liverishly** adv. **liverishness** n.

Liverpudlian /ˌlɪvəˈpʌdlɪən/ n. & adj. —n. a native of Liverpool in NW England. —adj. of or relating to Liverpool. [joc. f. Liverpool + PUDDLE]

liverwort /ˈlɪvəˌwɜːt/ n. any small leafy or thalloid bryophyte of the class Hepaticae, of which some have liver-shaped parts.

livery /ˈlɪvərɪ/ n. (pl. -ies) **1 a** distinctive clothing worn by a member of a City Company or by a servant. **b** membership of a City livery company. **2** a distinctive guise or marking or outward appearance (birds in their winter livery). **3** a distinctive colour scheme in which the vehicles, aircraft, etc., of a particular company or line are painted. **4** US a place where horses can be hired. □ **at livery** (of a horse) kept for the owner and fed and groomed for a fixed charge. **livery company** Brit. one of the London City Companies that formerly had a distinctive costume. **livery stable** a stable where horses are kept at livery or let out for hire. □ **liveried** adj. (esp. in senses 1, 2). [ME f. AF liveré, OF livrée, fem. past part. of livrer DELIVER]

lives pl. of LIFE.

livestock /ˈlaɪvstɒk/ n. (usu. treated as pl.) animals, esp. on a farm, regarded as an asset.

livid /ˈlɪvɪd/ adj. **1** colloq. furiously angry. **2 a** of a bluish leaden colour. **b** discoloured as by a bruise. □ **lividity** /lɪˈvɪdɪtɪ/ n. **lividly** adv. **lividness** n. [F livide or L lividus f. livēre be bluish]

living /ˈlɪvɪŋ/ n. & adj. —n. **1** a livelihood or means of maintenance (made my living as a journalist; what does she do for a living?). **2** Brit. Eccl. a position as a vicar or rector with an income or property. —adj. **1** contemporary; now existent (the greatest living poet). **2** (of a likeness or image of a person) exact. **3** (of a language) still in vernacular use. □ **living-room** a room for general day use. **living will** a written statement of a person's desire not to be kept alive by artificial means in the event of terminal illness or accident. **within living memory** within the memory of people still living.

lizard /ˈlɪzəd/ n. any reptile of the suborder Lacertilia, having usu. a long body and tail and a rough or scaly hide. [ME f. OF lesard(e) f. L lacertus]

LJ abbr. (pl. **L JJ**) (in the UK) Lord Justice.

'll v. (usu. after pronouns) shall, will (I'll; that'll). [abbr.]

llama /ˈlɑːmə/ n. **1** a S. American ruminant, Lama glama, kept as a beast of burden and for its soft woolly fleece. **2** the wool from this animal, or cloth made from it. [Sp., prob. f. Quechua]

LL B abbr. Bachelor of Laws. [L legum baccalaureus]

LL D abbr. Doctor of Laws. [L legum doctor]

LL M abbr. Master of Laws. [L legum magister]

Lloyd's /lɔɪdz/ n. an incorporated society of underwriters in London. □ **Lloyd's Register 1** an annual alphabetical list of ships assigned to various classes. **2** a society that produces this. [after the orig. meeting in a coffee-house established in 1688 by Edward Lloyd]

lm abbr. lumen(s).

lo int. archaic calling attention to an amazing sight. □ **lo and behold** joc. a formula introducing a surprising or unexpected fact. [OE lā int. of surprise etc., & ME lō = lōke LOOK]

loach n. any small edible freshwater fish of the family Cobitidae. [ME f. OF loche, of unkn. orig.]

load n. & v. —n. **1 a** what is carried or is to be carried; a burden. **b** an amount usu. or actually carried (often in comb.: a busload of tourists; a lorry-load of bricks). **2** a unit of measure or weight of certain substances. **3** a burden or commitment of work, responsibility, care, grief, etc. **4** (in pl.; often foll. by of) colloq. plenty; a lot. **5 a** Electr. the amount of power supplied by a generating system at any given time. **b** Electronics an impedance or circuit that receives or develops the output of a transistor or other device. **6** the weight or force borne by the supporting part of a structure. **7** a material object or force acting as a weight or clog. **8** the resistance of machinery to motive power. —v. **1** tr. **a** put a load on or aboard (a person, vehicle, ship, etc.). **b** place (a load or cargo) aboard a ship, on a vehicle, etc. **2** intr. (often foll. by up) (of a ship, vehicle, or person) take a load aboard, pick up a load. **3** tr. (often foll. by with) **a** add weight to; be a weight or burden upon. **b** oppress (a stomach loaded with food). **4** tr. strain the bearing-capacity of (a table loaded with food). **5** tr. (also **load up**) (foll. by with) **a** supply overwhelmingly (loaded us with work). **b** assail overwhelmingly (loaded us with abuse). **6** tr. charge (a firearm) with ammunition. **7** tr. insert (the required operating medium) in a device, e.g. film in a camera, magnetic tape in a tape recorder, a program into a computer, etc. **8** tr. add an extra charge to (an insurance premium) in the case of a poorer risk. □ **load line** a Plimsoll line. [OE lād way, journey, conveyance, f. Gmc: rel. to LEAD[1], LODE]

loaded /ˈləʊdɪd/ adj. **1** bearing or carrying a load. **2** sl. **a** wealthy. **b** drunk. **c** US drugged. **3** (of dice etc.) weighted or given a bias. **4** (of a question or statement) charged with some hidden or improper implication.

loader /ˈləʊdə(r)/ n. **1** a loading-machine. **2** (in comb.) a gun, machine, lorry, etc., loaded in a specified way (breech-loader). **3** an attendant who loads guns at a shoot. □ **-loading** adj. (in comb.) (in sense 2).

loadstar var. of LODESTAR.

loadstone var. of LODESTONE.

loaf[1] n. (pl. **loaves** /ləʊvz/) **1** a portion of baked bread, usu. of a standard size or shape. **2** a quantity of other food formed into a particular shape (sugar loaf; meat loaf). **3** sl. the head, esp. as a source of common sense (use your loaf). □ **loaf sugar** a sugar loaf as a whole or cut into lumps. [OE hlāf f. Gmc]

loaf[2] v. & n. —v. **1** intr. (often foll. by about, around) spend time idly; hang about. **2** tr. (foll. by away) waste (time) idly (loafed away the morning). **3** intr. saunter. —n. an act or spell of loafing. [prob. a back-form. f. LOAFER]

loafer /ˈləʊfə(r)/ n. **1** an idle person. **2** (**Loafer**) propr. a leather shoe shaped like a moccasin with a flat heel. [perh. f. G Landläufer vagabond]

loam n. **1** a fertile soil of clay and sand containing decayed vegetable matter. **2** a paste of clay and water with sand, chopped straw,

etc., used in making bricks, plastering, etc. □
loamy *adj.* **loaminess** *n.* [OE *lām* f. WG, rel. to
LIME[1]]

loan /ləʊn/ *n. & v.* —*n.* **1** something lent, esp. a
sum of money to be returned normally with
interest. **2** the act of lending or state of being
lent. —*v.tr.* lend (esp. money). □ **loan shark**
colloq. a person who lends money at exorbitant
rates of interest. **on loan** acquired or given as a
loan. □ **loanable** *adj.* **loanee** /ləʊˈniː/ *n.* **loaner**
n. [ME *lan* f. ON *lán* f. Gmc: cf. LEND]

loanword /ˈləʊnwɜːd/ *n.* a word adopted, usu.
with little modification, from a foreign
language.

loath /ləʊθ/ *predic.adj.* (also **loth**) (usu. foll. by *to*
+ infin.) disinclined, reluctant, unwilling (*was
loath to admit it*). □ **nothing loath** *adj.* quite
willing. [OE *lāth* f. Gmc]

loathe /ləʊð/ *v.tr.* regard with disgust; abominate, detest. □ **loather** *n.* **loathing** *n.* [OE *lāthian*
f. Gmc, rel. to LOATH]

loathsome /ˈləʊðsəm/ *adj.* arousing hatred or
disgust; offensive, repulsive. □ **loathsomely**
adv. **loathsomeness** *n.* [ME f. *loath* disgust f.
LOATHE]

loaves *pl.* of LOAF[1].

lob *v. & n.* —*v.tr.* (**lobbed, lobbing**) **1** hit or
throw (a ball or missile etc.) slowly or in a high
arc. **2** send (an opponent) a lobbed ball. —*n.* **1 a**
a ball struck in a high arc. **b** a stroke producing
this result. **2** *Cricket* a slow underarm ball.
[earlier as noun, prob. f. LG or Du.]

lobar /ˈləʊbə(r)/ *adj.* **1** of the lungs (*lobar pneumonia*). **2** of, relating to, or affecting a lobe.

lobate /ˈləʊbeɪt/ *adj. Biol.* having a lobe or lobes.
□ **lobation** /-ˈbeɪʃ(ə)n/ *n.*

lobby /ˈlɒbɪ/ *n. & v.* —*n.* (*pl.* -**ies**) **1** a porch,
ante-room, entrance-hall, or corridor. **2 a** (in
the House of Commons) a large hall used esp.
for interviews between MPs and members of
the public. **b** (also **division lobby**) each of two
corridors to which MPs retire to vote. **3 a** a
body of persons seeking to influence legislators
on behalf of a particular interest (*the anti-abortion
lobby*). **b** an organized attempt by members of
the public to influence legislators (*a lobby of
MPs*). **4** (prec. by *the*) (in the UK) a group of
journalists who receive unattributable briefings
from the government (*lobby correspondent*). —*v.*
(-**ies, -ied**) **1** *tr.* solicit the support of (an
influential person). **2** *tr.* (of members of the
public) seek to influence (the members of a
legislature). **3** *intr.* frequent a parliamentary
lobby. **4** *tr.* (foll. by *through*) get (a bill etc.)
through a legislature, by interviews etc. in the
lobby. □ **lobbyer** *n.* **lobbyism** *n.* **lobbyist** *n.*
[med.L *lobia, lobium* LODGE]

lobe *n.* **1** a roundish and flattish projecting or
pendulous part, often each of two or more such
parts divided by a fissure (*lobes of the brain*). **2** =
ear lobe. □ **lobed** *adj.* **lobeless** *adj.* [LL f. Gk *lobos*
lobe, pod]

lobelia /ləˈbiːlɪə/ *n.* any plant of the genus *Lobelia*,
with flowers having a deeply cleft corolla. [M.
de *Lobel*, Flemish botanist in England d. 1616]

lobotomy /ləˈbɒtəmɪ/ *n.* (*pl.* -**ies**) *Surgery* =
LEUCOTOMY. [LOBE + -TOMY]

lobscouse /ˈlɒbskaʊs/ *n.* a sailor's dish of meat
stewed with vegetables and ship's biscuit. [18th
c.: orig. unkn.: cf. Du. *lapskous*, Da. *labskovs*,
Norw. *lapskaus*, G *Lapskaus*]

lobster /ˈlɒbstə(r)/ *n.* **1** any large marine crustacean of the family Nephropidae, with two
pincer-like claws as the first pair of ten limbs. **2**
its flesh as food. □ **lobster-pot** a basket in
which lobsters are trapped. [OE *lopustre*, corrupt.
of L *locusta* crustacean, locust]

lobworm /ˈlɒbwɜːm/ *n.* **1** a large earthworm
used as fishing-bait. **2** = LUGWORM. [LOB in obs.
sense 'pendulous object']

local /ˈləʊk(ə)l/ *adj. & n.* —*adj.* **1** belonging to or
existing in a particular place or places. **2**
peculiar to or only encountered in a particular
place or places. **3** of or belonging to the
neighbourhood (*the local doctor*). **4** of or affecting
a part and not the whole, esp. of the body (*a
local anaesthetic*). **5** in regard to place. —*n.* a local
person or thing, esp.: **1** an inhabitant of a
particular place regarded with reference to that
place. **2** a local train, bus, etc. **3** (often prec. by
the) *Brit. colloq.* a local public house. **4** a local
anaesthetic. **5** *US* a local branch of a trade
union. □ **local authority** *Brit.* an administrative
body in local government. **local government**
a system of administration of a county, district,
parish, etc., by the elected representatives of
those who live there. **local time 1** time measured from the sun's transit over the meridian
of a place. **2** the time as reckoned in a particular
place, esp. with reference to an event recorded
there. □ **locally** *adv.* **localness** *n.* [ME f. OF f. LL
localis f. L *locus* place]

locale /ləʊˈkɑːl/ *n.* a scene or locality, esp. with
reference to an event or occurrence taking place
there. [F *local* (n.) (as LOCAL), respelt to indicate
stress: cf. MORALE]

locality /ləʊˈkælɪtɪ/ *n.* (*pl.* -**ies**) **1** a district or
neighbourhood. **2** the site or scene of something,
esp. in relation to its surroundings. **3** the
position of a thing; the place where it is. [F
localité or LL *localitas* (as LOCAL)]

localize /ˈləʊkəˌlaɪz/ *v.tr.* (also **-ise**) **1** restrict or
assign to a particular place. **2** invest with the
characteristics of a particular place. **3** attach
to districts; decentralize. □ **localizable** *adj.*
localization /-ˈzeɪʃ(ə)n/ *n.*

locate /ləʊˈkeɪt/ *v.* **1** *tr.* discover the exact place
or position of (*locate the enemy's camp*). **2** *tr.*
establish in a place or in its proper place. **3** *tr.*
state the locality of. **4** *tr.* (in *passive*) be situated.
□ **locatable** *adj.* **locator** *n.* [L *locare* locat- f. *locus*
place]

■ **Usage** This word should not be used to mean
merely 'find', as in *can't locate my key*.

location /ləʊˈkeɪʃ(ə)n/ *n.* **1** a particular place; the
place or position in which a person or thing is.
2 the act of locating or process of being located.
3 an actual place or natural setting featured in
a film or broadcast, as distinct from a simulation
in a studio (*filmed entirely on location*). **4** *S.Afr.* an
area where Blacks are obliged to live, usu. on
the outskirts of a town or city. [L *locatio* (as
LOCATE)]

locative /ˈlɒkətɪv/ *n. & adj. Gram.* —*n.* the case
of nouns, pronouns, and adjectives, expressing
location. —*adj.* of or in the locative. [formed as
LOCATE + -IVE, after *vocative*]

loc. cit. *abbr.* in the passage already cited. [L
loco citato]

loch /lɒx, lɒx/ n. Sc. **1** a lake. **2** an arm of the sea, esp. when narrow or partially land-locked. [ME f. Gael.]

loci pl. of LOCUS.

lock¹ n. & v. —n. **1** a mechanism for fastening a door, lid, etc., with a bolt that requires a key of a particular shape, or a combination of movements (see *combination lock*), to work it. **2** a confined section of a canal or river where the level can be changed for raising and lowering boats between adjacent sections. **3 a** the turning of the front wheels of a vehicle to change its direction of motion. **b** (in full **full lock**) the maximum extent of this. **4** an interlocked or jammed state. **5** *Wrestling* a hold that keeps an opponent's limb fixed. **6** (in full **lock forward**) *Rugby Football* a player in the second row of a scrum. **7** a mechanism for exploding the charge of a gun. **8** = AIRLOCK 2. —v. **1 a** tr. fasten with a lock. **b** tr. (foll. by *up*) shut and secure (esp. a building) by locking. **c** intr. (of a door, window, box, etc.) have the means of being locked. **2** tr. (foll. by *up*, *in*, *into*) enclose (a person or thing) by locking or as if by locking. **3** tr. (often foll. by *up*, *away*) store or allocate inaccessibly (*capital locked up in land*). **4** tr. & intr. make or become rigidly fixed or immovable. **5** intr. & tr. become or cause to become jammed or caught. **6** tr. (often in *passive*; foll. by *in*) entangle in an embrace or struggle. □ **lock-keeper** a keeper of a lock on a river or canal. **lock-knit** knitted with an interlocking stitch. **lock-nut** *Mech.* a nut screwed down on another to keep it tight. **lock on to** locate or cause to locate by radar etc. and then track. **lock out 1** keep (a person) out by locking the door. **2** (of an employer) submit (employees) to a lockout. **lock stitch** a stitch made by a sewing-machine by firmly locking together two threads or stitches. **lock, stock, and barrel** n. the whole of a thing. —adv. completely. **under lock and key** securely locked up. □ **lockable** adj. **lockless** adj. [OE *loc* f. Gmc]

lock² /lɒk/ n. **1** a portion of hair that coils or hangs together. **2** (in pl.) the hair of the head. □ **-locked** adj. (in comb.). [OE *locc* f. Gmc]

locker /ˈlɒkə(r)/ n. **1** a small lockable cupboard or compartment, esp. each of several for public use. **2** *Naut.* a chest or compartment for clothes, stores, ammunition, etc. **3** a person or thing that locks. □ **locker-room** a room containing lockers (in sense 1), esp. in a pavilion or sports centre.

locket /ˈlɒkɪt/ n. a small ornamental case holding a portrait, lock of hair, etc., and usu. hung from the neck. [OF *locquet* dimin. of *loc* latch, lock, f. WG (as LOCK¹)]

lockjaw /ˈlɒkdʒɔː/ n. = TRISMUS.

lockout /ˈlɒkaʊt/ n. the exclusion of employees by their employer from their place of work until certain terms are agreed to.

locksmith /ˈlɒksmɪθ/ n. a maker and mender of locks.

lock-up /ˈlɒkʌp/ n. & adj. —n. **1** a house or room for the temporary detention of prisoners. **2** *Brit.* non-residential premises etc. that can be locked up, esp. a small shop or storehouse. —attrib.adj. *Brit.* that can be locked up (*lock-up shop*).

loco¹ /ˈləʊkəʊ/ n. (pl. -os) colloq. a locomotive engine. [abbr.]

loco² /ˈləʊkəʊ/ adj. sl. crazy. [Sp., = insane]

locomotion /ˌləʊkəˈməʊʃ(ə)n/ n. **1** motion or the power of motion from one place to another. **2** travel; a means of travelling, esp. an artificial one. [L *loco* ablat. of *locus* place + *motio* MOTION]

locomotive /ˌləʊkəˈməʊtɪv/ n. & adj. —n. (in full **locomotive engine**) an engine powered by steam, diesel fuel, or electricity, used for pulling trains. —adj. **1** of or relating to or effecting locomotion (*locomotive power*). **2** having the power of or given to locomotion; not stationary.

locomotor /ˌləʊkəˈməʊtə(r)/ adj. of or relating to locomotion. [LOCOMOTION + MOTOR]

locum /ˈləʊkəm/ n. colloq. = LOCUM TENENS. [abbr.]

locum tenens /ˌləʊkəm ˈtiːnenz, ˈtenenz/ n. (pl. **locum tenentes** /ˌləʊkəm tɪˈnentiːz/) a deputy acting esp. for a cleric or doctor. [med.L, one holding a place: see LOCUS, TENANT]

locus /ˈləʊkəs, ˈlɒkəs/ n. (pl. **loci** /-saɪ, -kaɪ, -kiː/) **1** a position or point. **2** *Math.* a curve etc. formed by all the points satisfying a particular equation of the relation between coordinates, or by a point, line, or surface moving according to mathematically defined conditions. [L, = place]

locus classicus /ˌləʊkəs ˈklæsɪkəs, ˌlɒkəs/ n. (pl. **loci classici** /ˌləʊsaɪ ˈklæsɪsaɪ, ˌlɒkiː ˈklæsɪkiː/) the most authoritative passage on a subject. [L]

locust /ˈləʊkəst/ n. **1** any of various African and Asian grasshoppers of the family Acrididae, migrating in swarms and destroying vegetation. **2** *US* a cicada. **3** (in full **locust bean**) a carob. **4** (in full **locust tree**) **a** a carob tree. **b** = ACACIA 2. **c** = KOWHAI. [ME f. OF *locuste* f. L *locusta* lobster, locust]

locution /ləˈkjuːʃ(ə)n/ n. **1** a word or phrase in idiom. **2** style of speech. [ME f. OF *locution* or L *locutio* f. *loqui locut-* speak]

lode n. a vein of metal ore. [var. of LOAD]

lodestar /ˈləʊdstɑː(r)/ n. (also **loadstar**) **1** a star that a ship etc. is steered by, esp. the polestar. **2 a** a guiding principle. **b** an object of pursuit. [LODE in obs. sense 'way, journey' + STAR]

lodestone /ˈləʊdstəʊn/ n. (also **loadstone**) **1** magnetic oxide of iron, magnetite. **2 a** a piece of this used as a magnet. **b** a thing that attracts.

lodge n. & v. —n. **1** a small house at the gates of a park or in the grounds of a large house, occupied by a gatekeeper, gardener, etc. **2** any large house or hotel, esp. in a resort. **3** a house occupied in the hunting or shooting season. **4** a porter's room or quarters at the gate of a college or other large building. **5** the members or the meeting-place of a branch of a society such as the Freemasons. **6** a beaver's or otter's lair. —v. **1** tr. deposit in court or with an official a formal statement of (complaint or information). **2** tr. deposit (money etc.) for security. **3** tr. bring forward (an objection etc.). **4** tr. (foll. by *in*, *with*) place (power etc.) in a person or group. **5** tr. & intr. make or become fixed or caught without further movement (*the bullet lodged in his brain*). **6** tr. **a** provide with sleeping quarters. **b** receive as a guest or inmate. **7** intr. reside or live, esp. as a guest paying for accommodation. **8** tr. serve as a habitation for; contain. **9** tr. (in *passive*; foll. by *in*) be contained in. [ME *loge* f. OF *loge* arbour, hut, f. med.L *laubia*, *lobia* (see LOBBY) f. Gmc]

lodger /ˈlɒdʒə(r)/ n. a person receiving accommodation in another's house for payment.

lodging /ˈlɒdʒɪŋ/ n. **1** temporary accommodation (*a lodging for the night*). **2** (in pl.) a room or rooms (other than in a hotel) rented for lodging in. **3** a dwelling-place. □ **lodging-house** a house in which lodgings are let.

loess /ˈləʊɪs, lɜːs/ n. a deposit of fine light-coloured wind-blown dust found esp. in the basins of large rivers and very fertile when irrigated. □ **loessial** /ləʊˈesɪəl, ˈlɜːsɪəl/ adj. [G *Löss* f. Swiss G *lösch* loose f. *lösen* loosen]

loft n. & v. —n. **1** the space under the roof of a house, above the ceiling of the top floor; an attic. **2** a room over a stable, esp. for hay and straw. **3** a gallery in a church or hall (*organ-loft*). **4** US an upstairs room. **5** a pigeon-house. **6** *Golf* a backward slope in a club-head. —v.tr. **1** send (a ball etc.) high up. **2** clear (an obstacle) in this way. [OE f. ON *lopt* air, sky, upper room, f. Gmc (as LIFT)]

lofty /ˈlɒftɪ/ adj. (**loftier, loftiest**) **1** *literary* (of things) of imposing height, towering, soaring (*lofty heights*). **2** consciously haughty, aloof, or dignified (*lofty contempt*). **3** exalted or noble (*lofty ideals*). □ **loftily** adv. **loftiness** n. [ME f. LOFT as in *aloft*]

log¹ n. & v. —n. **1** an unhewn piece of a felled tree, or a similar rough mass of wood, esp. cut for firewood. **2 a** a float attached to a line wound on a reel for gauging the speed of a ship. **b** any other apparatus for the same purpose. **3** a record of events occurring during and affecting the voyage of a ship or aircraft. **4** any systematic record of things done, experienced, etc. **5** = LOGBOOK. —v.tr. (**logged, logging**) **1 a** enter (the distance made or other details) in a ship's logbook. **b** enter details about (a person or event) in a logbook. **c** (of a ship) achieve (a certain distance). **2 a** enter (information) in a regular record. **b** attain (a cumulative total of time etc. recorded in this way) (*logged 50 hours on the computer*). **3** cut into logs. □ **log cabin** a hut built of logs. **log in** = *log on*. **log-jam** **1** a crowded mass of logs in a river. **2** a deadlock. **log on** (or **off**) go through the procedures to begin (or conclude) use of a computer system. [ME: orig. unkn.]

log² /lɒg/ n. a logarithm (esp. prefixed to a number or algebraic symbol whose logarithm is to be indicated). [abbr.]

-log US var. of -LOGUE.

logan /ˈləʊgən/ n. (in full **logan-stone**) a poised heavy stone rocking at a touch. [= *logging* f. dial. *log* to rock + STONE]

loganberry /ˈləʊgənbərɪ/ n. (pl. **-ies**) **1** a hybrid, *Rubus loganobaccus*, between a blackberry and a raspberry with dull red acid fruits. **2** the fruit of this plant. [J. H. *Logan*, Amer. horticulturalist d. 1928 + BERRY]

logarithm /ˈlɒgəˌrɪð(ə)m/ n. one of a series of arithmetic exponents tabulated to simplify computation by making it possible to use addition and subtraction instead of multiplication and division. □ **logarithmic** /-ˈrɪðmɪk/ adj. **logarithmically** /-ˈrɪðmɪkəlɪ/ adv. [mod.L *logarithmus* f. Gk *logos* reckoning, ratio + *arithmos* number]

logbook /ˈlɒgbʊk/ n. **1** a book containing a detailed record or log. **2** *Brit.* a document recording the registration details of a motor vehicle.

-loger /ləʤə(r)/ comb. form forming nouns, = -LOGIST. [after *astrologer*]

logger /ˈlɒgə(r)/ n. US a lumberjack.

loggerhead /ˈlɒgəˌhed/ n. □ **at loggerheads** (often foll. by *with*) disagreeing or disputing. [prob. f. dial. *logger* block of wood for hobbling a horse + HEAD]

loggia /ˈləʊdʒə, ˈlɒ-/ n. **1** an open-sided gallery or arcade. **2** an open-sided extension of a house. [It., = LODGE]

logging /ˈlɒgɪŋ/ n. the work of cutting and preparing forest timber.

logic /ˈlɒdʒɪk/ n. **1 a** the science of reasoning, proof, thinking, or inference. **b** a particular scheme or treatise on this. **2 a** a chain of reasoning (*I don't follow your logic*). **b** the correct or incorrect use of reasoning (*your logic is flawed*). **c** ability in reasoning (*argues with great learning and logic*). **d** arguments (*is not governed by logic*). **3 a** the inexorable force or compulsion of a thing (*the logic of events*). **b** the necessary consequence of (an argument, decision, etc.). **4 a** a system or set of principles underlying the arrangements of elements in a computer or electronic device so as to perform a specified task. **b** logical operations collectively. □ **logician** /ləˈdʒɪʃ(ə)n/ n. [ME f. OF *logique* f. LL *logica* f. Gk *logikē* (*tekhnē*) (art) of reason]

-logic /ˈlɒdʒɪk/ comb. form (also **-logical**) forming adjectives corresponding esp. to nouns in -logy (*pathological; theological*). [from or after Gk -*logikos*: see -IC, -ICAL]

logical /ˈlɒdʒɪk(ə)l/ adj. **1** of logic or formal argument. **2** not contravening the laws of thought, correctly reasoned. **3** deducible or defensible on the ground of consistency; reasonably to be believed or done. **4** capable of correct reasoning. □ **logical positivism** (or **empiricism**) a form of positivism in which symbolic logic is used and linguistic problems of meaning are emphasized. □ **logicality** /-ˈkælɪtɪ/ n. **logically** adv. [med.L *logicalis* f. LL *logica* (as LOGIC)]

-logist /lədʒɪst/ comb. form forming nouns denoting a person skilled or involved in a branch of study etc. with a name in -logy (*archaeologist; etymologist*).

logistics /ləˈdʒɪstɪks/ n.pl. **1** the organization of moving, lodging, and supplying troops and equipment. **2** the detailed organization and implementation of a plan or operation. □ **logistic** adj. **logistical** adj. **logistically** adv. [F *logistique* f. *loger* lodge]

logo /ˈləʊgəʊ, ˈlɒgəʊ/ n. (pl. **-os**) *colloq.* = LOGOTYPE 2. [abbr.]

logotype /ˈlɒgəˌtaɪp/ n. **1** *Printing* a single piece of type that prints a word or group of separate letters. **2 a** an emblem or device used as the badge of an organization in display material. **b** *Printing* a single piece of type that prints this. [Gk *logos* word + TYPE]

logrolling /ˈlɒgˌrəʊlɪŋ/ n. US *colloq.* the practice of exchanging favours, esp. (in politics) of exchanging votes to mutual benefit. □ **logroll** v.intr. & tr. **logroller** n. [from phr. *you roll my log and I'll roll yours*]

-logue /lɒg/ comb. form (US **-log**) **1** forming nouns denoting talk (*dialogue*) or compilation (*catalogue*). **2** = -LOGIST (*ideologue*). [from or after F -*logue* f. Gk -*logos, -logon*]

-logy /lədʒɪ/ comb. form forming nouns denoting: **1** (usu. as **-ology**) a subject of study or interest (*archaeology; zoology*). **2** a characteristic of speech or language (*tautology*). **3** discourse (*trilogy*). [F -*logie* or med.L -*logia* f. Gk *logos* word, reason]

loin *n.* **1** (in *pl.*) the part of the body on both sides of the spine between the false ribs and the hip-bones. **2** a joint of meat that includes the loin vertebrae. [ME f. OF *loigne* ult. f. L *lumbus*]

loincloth /ˈlɔɪnklɒθ/ *n.* a cloth worn round the loins, esp. as a sole garment.

loiter /ˈlɔɪtə(r)/ *v.* **1** *intr.* hang about; linger idly. **2** *intr.* travel indolently and with long pauses. **3** *tr.* (foll. by *away*) pass (time etc.) in loitering. □ **loiter with intent** hang about in order to commit a felony. □ **loiterer** *n.* [ME f. MDu. *loteren* wag about]

loll *v.* **1** *intr.* stand, sit, or recline in a lazy attitude. **2** *intr.* (foll. by *out*) (of the tongue) hang out. **3** *tr.* (foll. by *out*) hang (one's tongue) out. **4** *tr.* let (one's head or limbs) rest lazily on something. □ **loller** *n.* [ME: prob. imit.]

lollipop /ˈlɒlɪˌpɒp/ *n.* a large usu. flat rounded boiled sweet on a small stick. □ **lollipop man** (or **lady** or **woman**) *Brit. colloq.* an official using a circular sign on a stick to stop traffic for children to cross the road. [perh. f. dial. *lolly* tongue + POP¹]

lollop /ˈlɒləp/ *v.intr.* (**lolloped**, **lolloping**) *colloq.* **1** flop about. **2** move or proceed in a lounging or ungainly way. [prob. f. LOLL, assoc. with TROLLOP]

lolly /ˈlɒlɪ/ *n.* (*pl.* -**ies**) **1** *colloq.* **a** a lollipop. **b** *Austral.* a sweet. **c** *Brit.* = *ice lolly.* **2** *Brit. sl.* money. [abbr. of LOLLIPOP]

London clay /ˈlʌnd(ə)n/ *n.* a geological formation in the lower division of Eocene in SE England. [*London*, capital of the UK]

Londoner /ˈlʌndənə(r)/ *n.* a native or inhabitant of London.

London pride /ˈlʌnd(ə)n/ *n.* a pink-flowered saxifrage, *Saxifraga urbium.*

lone *attrib.adj.* **1** (of a person) solitary; without a companion or supporter. **2** (of a place) unfrequented, uninhabited, lonely. □ **lone hand 1** a hand played or a player playing against the rest at quadrille and euchre. **2** a person or action without allies. **lone wolf** a person who prefers to act alone. [ME, f. ALONE]

lonely /ˈləʊnlɪ/ *adj.* (**lonelier**, **loneliest**) **1** solitary, companionless, isolated. **2** (of a place) unfrequented. **3** sad because without friends or company. □ **lonely heart** a lonely person (in sense 3). □ **loneliness** *n.*

loner /ˈləʊnə(r)/ *n.* a person or animal that prefers not to associate with others.

lonesome /ˈləʊnsəm/ *adj.* **1** solitary, lonely. **2** feeling lonely or forlorn. **3** causing such a feeling. □ **by** (or **on**) **one's lonesome** all alone. □ **lonesomely** *adv.* **lonesomeness** *n.*

long¹ *adj., n.,* & *adv.* —*adj.* (**longer** /ˈlɒŋgə(r)/; **longest** /ˈlɒŋgɪst/) **1** measuring much from end to end in space or time; not soon traversed or finished (*a long line; a long journey; a long time ago*). **2** (following a measurement) in length or duration (*2 metres long; the vacation is two months long*). **3** relatively great in extent or duration (*a long meeting*). **4 a** consisting of a large number of items (*a long list*). **b** seemingly more than the stated amount; tedious, lengthy (*ten long miles*). **5** of elongated shape. **6 a** lasting or reaching far back or forward in time (*a long friendship*). **b** (of a person's memory) retaining things for a

long time. **7** far-reaching; acting at a distance; involving a great interval or difference. **8** *Phonet.* & *Prosody* (of a vowel or syllable: **a** having the greater of the two recognized durations. **b** stressed. **9** (of odds or a chance) reflecting or representing a low level of probability. **10** *Stock Exch.* (of stocks) bought in large quantities in advance, with the expectation of a rise in price. **11** (of a cold drink) large and refreshing. **12** *colloq.* (of a person) tall. **13** (foll. by *on*) *colloq.* well supplied with. —*n.* **1** a long interval or period (*shall not be away for long; it will not take long*). **2** *Phonet.* a long syllable or vowel. **3** long-dated stock. —*adv.* (**longer** /ˈlɒŋgə(r)/; **longest** /ˈlɒŋgɪst/) **1** by or for a long time (*long before; long ago; long live the king!*). **2** (following nouns of duration) throughout a specified time (*all day long*). **3** (in *compar.*; with *neg.*) after an implied point of time (*shall not wait any longer*). □ **as** (or **so**) **long as 1** during the whole time that. **2** provided that; only if. **before long** fairly soon (*shall see you before long*). **be long** (often foll. by *pres. part.* or *in* + verbal noun) take a long time; be slow (*the chance was long in coming; I shan't be long*). **in the long run 1** over a long period. **2** eventually; finally. **long ago** in the distant past. **the long and the short of it 1** all that can or need be said. **2** the eventual outcome. **long-case clock** a grandfather clock. **long-distance 1** (of a telephone call, public transport, etc.) between distant places. **2** (of a weather forecast) long-range. **long division** division of numbers with details of the calculations written down. **long-drawn** (or -**drawn-out**) prolonged, esp. unduly. **long face** a dismal or disappointed expression. **long haul 1** the transport of goods or passengers over a long distance. **2** a prolonged effort or task. **long-headed** shrewd, far-seeing, sagacious. **long in the tooth** rather old (orig. of horses, from the recession of the gums with age). **long johns** *colloq.* underpants with full-length legs. **long-jump** an athletic contest of jumping as far as possible along the ground in one leap. **long-life** (of consumable goods) treated to preserve freshness. **long-lived** having a long life; durable. **long-player** a long-playing record. **long-playing** (of a gramophone record) playing for about 20–30 minutes on each side. **long-range 1** (of a missile etc.) having a long range. **2** of or relating to a period of time far into the future. **long-running** continuing for a long time. **long ship** *hist.* a long narrow warship with many rowers, used esp. by the Vikings. **long shot 1** a wild guess or venture. **2** a bet at long odds. **3** *Cinematog.* a shot including objects at a distance. **long sight** the ability to see clearly only what is comparatively distant. **long-standing** that has long existed; not recent. **long-suffering** bearing provocation patiently. **long suit 1** many cards of one suit in a hand (esp. more than 3 or 4 in a hand of 13). **2** a thing at which one excels. **long-term** occurring in or relating to a long period of time (*long-term plans*). **long vacation** *Brit.* the summer vacation of lawcourts and universities. **long waist** a low or deep waist of a dress or body. **long wave** a radio wave of frequency less than 300 kHz. **not by a long shot** by no means. □ **longish** *adj.* [OE *long, lang*]

long[2] /lɒŋ/ v.intr. (foll. by *for* or *to* + infin.) have a strong wish or desire for. [OE *langian* seem long to]

long. abbr. longitude.

-long /lɒŋ/ comb. form forming adjectives and adverbs: **1** for the duration of (*lifelong*). **2** = -LING[2] (*headlong*).

longboat /ˈlɒŋbəʊt/ n. a sailing ship's largest boat.

longbow /ˈlɒŋbəʊ/ n. a bow drawn by hand and shooting a long feathered arrow.

longeron /ˈlɒndʒərən/ n. a longitudinal member of a plane's fuselage. [F, = girder]

longevity /lɒnˈdʒevɪtɪ/ n. long life. [LL *longaevitas* f. L *longus* long + *aevum* age]

longhand /ˈlɒŋhænd/ n. ordinary handwriting (as opposed to shorthand or typing or printing).

longing /ˈlɒŋɪŋ/ n. & adj. —n. a feeling of intense desire. —adj. having or showing this feeling. □ **longingly** adv.

longitude /ˈlɒŋgɪˌtjuːd, ˈlɒndʒ-/ n. **1** Geog. the angular distance east or west from a standard meridian such as Greenwich to the meridian of any place. **2** Astron. the angular distance of a celestial body north or south of the ecliptic. [ME f. L *longitudo -dinis* f. *longus* long]

longitudinal /ˌlɒŋgɪˈtjuːdɪn(ə)l, ˌlɒndʒ-/ adj. **1** of or in length. **2** running lengthwise. **3** of longitude. □ **longitudinally** adv.

longshore /ˈlɒŋʃɔː(r)/ adj. **1** existing on or frequenting the shore. **2** directed along the shore. [*along shore*]

longshoreman /ˈlɒŋʃɔːmən/ n. (pl. **-men**) US a docker.

long-sighted /lɒŋˈsaɪtɪd, ˈlɒŋ-/ adj. **1** having long sight. **2** having imagination or foresight. □ **long-sightedly** adv. **long-sightedness** n.

longstop /ˈlɒŋstɒp/ n. **1** Cricket **a** a position directly behind the wicket-keeper. **b** a fielder in this position. **2** a last resort.

longueur /lɔ̃ˈgɜː(r)/ n. **1** a tedious passage in a book etc. **2** a tedious stretch of time. [F, = length]

longways /ˈlɒŋweɪz/ adv. (also **longwise** /ˈlɒŋwaɪz/) = LENGTHWAYS.

long-winded /lɒŋˈwɪndɪd/ adj. (of speech or writing) tediously lengthy. □ **long-windedly** adv. **long-windedness** n.

loo /luː/ n. Brit. colloq. a lavatory. [20th c.: orig. uncert.]

loof var. of LUFF.

loofah /ˈluːfə/ n. (also **luffa** /ˈlʌfə/) **1** a climbing gourdlike plant, *Luffa cylindrica*, native to Asia, producing edible marrow-like fruits. **2** the dried fibrous vascular system of this fruit used as a sponge. [Egypt. Arab. *lūfa*, the plant]

look /lʊk/ v., n., & int. —v. **1** a intr. (often foll. by *at*) use one's sight; turn one's eyes in some direction. **b** tr. turn one's eyes on; contemplate or examine (*looked me in the eyes*). **2** intr. **a** make a visual or mental search (*I'll look in the morning*). **b** (foll. by *at*) consider, examine (*we must look at the facts*). **3** intr. (foll. by *for*) **a** search for. **b** hope or be on the watch for. **c** expect. **4** intr. inquire (*when one looks deeper*). **5** intr. have a specified appearance; seem (*look a fool*; *look foolish*). **6** intr. (foll. by *to*) **a** consider; take care of; be careful about (*look to the future*). **b** rely on (a person or thing) (*you can look to me for support*). **c** expect; count on; aim at. **7** intr. (foll. by *into*) investigate or examine. **8** tr. (foll. by *what*, *where*, etc. + clause) ascertain or observe by sight (*look where we are*). **9** intr. (of a thing) face or be turned, or have or afford an outlook, in a specified direction. **10** tr. express, threaten, or show (an emotion etc.) by one's looks. **11** intr. (foll. by *that* + clause) take care; make sure. **12** intr. (foll. by *to* + infin.) expect (*am looking to finish this today*). —n. **1** an act of looking; the directing of the eyes to look at a thing or person; a glance (*a scornful look*). **2** (in sing. or pl.) the appearance of a face; a person's expression or personal aspect. **3** the (esp. characteristic) appearance of a thing (*the place has a European look*). —int. (also **look here!**) calling attention, expressing a protest, etc. □ **look after 1** attend to; take care of. **2** follow with the eye. **3** seek for. **look one's age** appear to be as old as one really is. **look-alike** a person or thing closely resembling another (*a Prince Charles look-alike*). **look alive** (or **lively**) colloq. be brisk and alert. **look as if** suggest by appearance the belief that (*it looks as if he's gone*). **look back 1** (foll. by *on*, *upon*, *to*) turn one's thoughts to (something past). **2** (usu. with *neg.*) cease to progress (*since then we have never looked back*). **3** Brit. make a further visit later. **look down on** (or **upon** or **look down one's nose at**) regard with contempt or a feeling of superiority. **look forward to** await (an expected event) eagerly or with specified feelings. **look in** make a short visit or call. **look-in** n. colloq. **1** an informal call or visit. **2** a chance of participation or success (*never gets a look-in*). **look a person in the eye** (or **eyes** or **face**) look directly and unashamedly at him or her. **look like 1** have the appearance of. **2** Brit. seem to be (*they look like winning*). **3** threaten or promise (*it looks like rain*). **4** indicate the presence of (*it looks like woodworm*). **look on 1** (often foll. by *as*) regard (*looks on you as a friend*; *looked on them with disfavour*). **2** be a spectator; avoid participation. **look out 1** direct one's sight or put one's head out of a window etc. **2** (often foll. by *for*) be vigilant or prepared. **3** (foll. by *on*, *over*, etc.) have or afford a specified outlook. **4** search for and produce (*shall look one out for you*). **look over 1** inspect or survey (*looked over the house*). **2** examine (a document etc.) esp. cursorily (*shall look it over*). **look round 1** look in every or another direction. **2** examine the objects of interest in a place (*you must come and look round sometime*). **3** examine the possibilities etc. with a view to deciding on a course of action. **look-see** colloq. a survey or inspection. **look sharp** act promptly; make haste (orig. = keep strict watch). **look through 1** examine the contents of, esp. cursorily. **2** penetrate (a pretence or pretender) with insight. **3** ignore by pretending not to see (*I waved, but you just looked through me*). **look up 1** search for (esp. information in a book). **2** colloq. go to visit (a person) (*had intended to look them up*). **3** raise one's eyes (*looked up when I went in*). **4** improve, esp. in price, prosperity, or well-being (*things are looking up all round*). **look up to** respect or venerate. **not like the look of** find alarming or suspicious. □ **-looking** adj. (in comb.). [OE *lōcian* f. WG]

looker /ˈlʊkə(r)/ n. **1** a person having a specified appearance (*a good-looker*). **2** colloq. an attractive woman. □ **looker-on** a person who is a mere spectator.

looking-glass /ˈlʊkɪŋˌglɑːs/ n. a mirror for looking at oneself.

lookout /ˈlʊkaʊt/ n. 1 a watch or looking out (on the lookout for bargains). 2 a a post of observation. b a person or party or boat stationed to keep watch. 3 a view over a landscape. 4 a prospect of luck (it's a bad lookout for them). 5 colloq. a person's own concern.

loom¹ n. an apparatus for weaving yarn or thread into fabric. [ME lōme f. OE gelōma tool]

loom² v.intr. (often foll. by up) 1 come into sight dimly, esp. as a vague and often threatening shape. 2 (of an event or prospect) be ominously close. [prob. f. LG or Du.: cf. E Fris. lōmen move slowly, MHG lüemen be weary]

loon n. 1 US any aquatic diving bird of the family Gaviidae, with a long slender body and a sharp bill; a diver. 2 colloq. a crazy person (cf. LOONY). [alt. f. loom f. ON lómr]

loony /ˈluːnɪ/ n. & adj. sl. —n. (pl. -ies) a mad or silly person; a lunatic. —adj. (loonier, looniest) crazy, silly. □ loony-bin sl. a mental home or hospital. □ looniness n. [abbr. of LUNATIC]

loop n. & v. —n. 1 a a figure produced by a curve, or a doubled thread etc., that crosses itself. b anything forming this figure. 2 a similarly shaped attachment or ornament formed of cord or thread etc. and fastened at the crossing. 3 a ring or curved piece of material as a handle etc. 4 a contraceptive coil. 5 (in full **loop-line**) a railway or telegraph line that diverges from a main line and joins it again. 6 a manoeuvre in which an aeroplane describes a vertical loop. 7 Skating a manoeuvre describing a curve that crosses itself, made on a single edge. 8 Electr. a complete circuit for a current. 9 an endless strip of tape or film allowing continuous repetition. 10 Computing a programmed sequence of instructions that is repeated until or while a particular condition is satisfied. —v. 1 tr. form (thread etc.) into a loop or loops. 2 tr. enclose with or as with a loop. 3 tr. (often foll. by up, back, together) fasten or join with a loop or loops. 4 intr. a form a loop. b move in looplike patterns. 5 intr. (also **loop the loop**) Aeron. perform an aerobatic loop. [ME: orig. unkn.]

loophole /ˈluːphəʊl/ n. 1 a means of evading a rule etc. without infringing the letter of it. 2 a narrow vertical slit in a wall for shooting or looking through or to admit light or air. [ME loop in the same sense + HOLE]

loopy /ˈluːpɪ/ adj. (loopier, loopiest) 1 sl. crazy. 2 having many loops.

loose /luːs/ adj., n., & v. —adj. 1 a not or no longer held by bonds or restraint. b (of an animal) not confined or tethered etc. 2 detached or detachable from its place (has come loose). 3 not held together or contained or fixed. 4 not specially fastened or packaged (loose papers; had her hair loose). 5 hanging partly free (a loose end). 6 slack, relaxed; not tense or tight. 7 not compact or dense (loose soil). 8 (of language, concepts, etc.) inexact; conveying only the general sense. 9 morally lax; dissolute (loose living). 10 (of the tongue) likely to speak indiscreetly. 11 (of the bowels) tending to diarrhoea. 12 (in comb.) loosely (loose-flowing; loose-fitting). —n. a state of freedom or unrestrainedness. —v.tr. 1 release; set free; free from constraint. 2 untie or undo (something that constrains). 3 detach

from moorings. 4 relax (loosed my hold on it). 5 discharge (a gun or arrow etc.). □ **at a loose end** (US **at loose ends**) (of a person) unoccupied, esp. temporarily. **loose box** a compartment for a horse, in a stable or vehicle, in which it can move about. **loose change** money as coins in the pocket etc. for casual use. **loose cover** Brit. a removable cover for a chair or sofa etc. **loose-leaf** adj. (of a notebook, manual, etc.) with each leaf separate and removable. —n. a loose-leaf notebook etc. **loose-limbed** having supple limbs. **on the loose** 1 escaped from captivity. 2 having a free enjoyable time. □ **loosely** adv. **looseness** n. **loosish** adj. [ME lōs f. ON lauss f. Gmc]

loosen /ˈluːs(ə)n/ v. 1 tr. & intr. make or become less tight or compact or firm. 2 tr. make (a regime etc.) less severe. 3 tr. release (the bowels) from constipation. 4 tr. relieve (a cough) from dryness. □ **loosen a person's tongue** make a person talk freely. **loosen up** = limber up (see LIMBER¹). □ **loosener** n.

loot n. & v. —n. 1 goods taken from an enemy; spoil. 2 booty; illicit gains made by an official. 3 sl. money. —v.tr. 1 rob (premises) or steal (goods) left unprotected, esp. after riots or other violent events. 2 plunder or sack (a city, building, etc.). 3 carry off as booty. □ **looter** n. [Hindi lūṭ]

lop¹ v. & n. —v. (**lopped, lopping**) 1 tr. a (often foll. by off, away) cut or remove (a part or parts) from a whole, esp. branches from a tree. b remove branches from (a tree). 2 tr. (often foll. by off, away) remove (items) as superfluous. 3 intr. (foll. by at) make lopping strokes on (a tree etc.). —n. parts lopped off, esp. branches and twigs of trees. □ **lopper** n. [ME f. OE loppian (unrecorded): cf. obs. lip to prune]

lop² v. (**lopped, lopping**) intr. & tr. hang limply. □ **lop-ears** drooping ears. **lop-eared** (of an animal) having drooping ears. □ **loppy** adj. [rel. to LOB]

lope v. & n. —v.intr. (esp. of animals) run with a long bounding stride. —n. a long bounding stride. [ME, var. of Sc. loup f. ON hlaupa LEAP]

lopsided /lɒpˈsaɪdɪd/ adj. with one side lower or smaller than the other; unevenly balanced. □ **lopsidedly** adv. **lopsidedness** n. [LOP² + SIDE]

loquacious /lɒˈkweɪʃəs/ adj. 1 talkative. 2 (of birds or water) chattering, babbling. □ **loquaciously** adv. **loquaciousness** n. **loquacity** /-ˈkwæsɪtɪ/ n. [L loquax -acis f. loqui talk]

loquat /ˈləʊkwɒt/ n. 1 a rosaceous tree, Eriobotrya japonica, bearing small yellow egg-shaped fruits. 2 this fruit. [Chin. dial. luh kwat rush orange]

lord n. & int. —n. 1 a master or ruler. 2 hist. a feudal superior, esp. of a manor. 3 a peer of the realm or a person entitled to the title Lord, esp. a marquess, earl, viscount, or baron. 4 (Lord) (often prec. by the) a name for God or Christ. 5 (Lord) a prefixed as the designation of a marquis, earl, viscount, or baron. b prefixed to the Christian name of the younger son of a duke or marquis. c (the Lords) = House of Lords. —int. (Lord) expressing surprise, dismay, etc. □ **Lord Advocate** the principal law-officer of the Crown in Scotland. **Lord** (or **Lord High**) **Chancellor** (in the UK) the highest officer of the Crown, presiding in the House of Lords etc. **Lord Chief Justice** (in the UK) the president of the Queen's Bench Division. **lord it over** domineer. **Lord Lieutenant** (in the UK) the chief executive authority and head of magistrates in each county. **Lord Mayor** the title of the mayor in London and some other large cities. **lord over** (usu. in *passive*) domineer, rule over. **Lord President of the Council** (in the UK) the cabinet minister presiding at the Privy Council. **Lord Privy Seal** (in the UK) a senior cabinet minister without official duties. **Lord's Day** Sunday. **Lord's Prayer** the Our Father, the prayer taught by Christ to his disciples. **Lords spiritual** the bishops in the House of Lords. **Lord's Supper** the Eucharist. **Lords temporal** the members of the House of Lords other than the bishops. **Our Lord** a name for Christ. **Sea Lord** a naval member of the Admiralty Board. □ **lordless** adj. **lordlike** adj. [OE *hlāford* f. *hlāfweard* = bread-keeper (as LOAF¹, WARD)]

lordly /ˈlɔːdlɪ/ adj. (**lordlier**, **lordliest**) **1** haughty, imperious. **2** suitable for a lord. □ **lordliness** n. [OE *hlāfordlic* (as LORD)]

lordship /ˈlɔːdʃɪp/ n. (usu. **Lordship**) a title used in addressing or referring to a man with the rank of Lord or a judge or a bishop (*Your Lordship; His Lordship*). [OE *hlāfordscipe* (as LORD, -SHIP)]

lore n. a body of traditions and knowledge on a subject or held by a particular group (*herbal lore; gypsy lore*). [OE *lār* f. Gmc, rel. to LEARN]

lorgnette /lɔːˈnjet/ n. (in *sing.* or *pl.*) a pair of eyeglasses or opera-glasses held by a long handle. [F f. *lorgner* to squint]

lorikeet /ˈlɒrɪˌkiːt/ n. any of various small brightly coloured parrots of the subfamily Loriinae, including the rainbow lorikeet. [dimin. of LORY, after *parakeet*]

lorn adj. *literary* desolate, forlorn, abandoned. [past part. of obs. *leese* f. OE *-lēosan* lose]

lorry /ˈlɒrɪ/ n. *Brit.* (pl. **-ies**) a large strong motor vehicle for transporting goods etc. [19th c.: orig. uncert.]

lory /ˈlɔːrɪ/ n. (pl. **-ies**) any of various brightly-coloured Australasian parrots of the subfamily Loriinae. [Malay *lūrī*]

lose /luːz/ v. (*past* and *past part.* **lost**) **1** tr. be deprived of or cease to have, esp. by negligence or misadventure. **2** tr. **a** be deprived of (a person, esp. a close relative) by death. **b** suffer the loss of (a baby) in childbirth. **3** tr. become unable to find; fail to keep in sight or follow or mentally grasp (*lose one's way*). **4** tr. let or have pass from one's control or reach (*lose one's chance; lose one's bearings*). **5** tr. be defeated in (a game, race, lawsuit, battle, etc.). **6** tr. evade; get rid of (*lost our pursuers*). **7** tr. fail to obtain, catch, or perceive (*lose a train; lose a word*). **8** tr. forfeit (a stake, deposit, right to a thing, etc.). **9** tr. spend (time, efforts, etc.) to no purpose (*lost no time in raising the alarm*). **10** intr. **a** suffer loss or detriment; incur a disadvantage. **b** be worse off, esp. financially. **11** tr. cause (a person) the loss of (*will lose you your job*). **12** intr. & tr. (of a timepiece) become slow; become slow by (a specified amount of time). **13** tr. (in *passive*) disappear, perish; be dead (*was lost in the war; is a lost art*). □ **be lost** (or **lose oneself**) **in** be engrossed in. **be lost on** be wasted on, or not noticed or appreciated by. **be lost to** be no longer affected by or accessible to (*is lost to pity; is lost to the world*). **get lost** *sl.* (usu. in *imper.*) go away. **lose one's balance 1** fail to remain stable; fall. **2** fail to retain one's composure. **lose one's**

cool *colloq.* lose one's composure. **lose face** be humiliated; lose one's credibility. **lose heart** be discouraged. **lose one's nerve** become timid or irresolute. **lose out** (often foll. by *on*) *colloq.* be unsuccessful; not get a fair chance or advantage (in). **lose one's temper** become angry. **lose time** allow time to pass with something unachieved etc. **lose the** (or **one's**) **way** become lost; fail to reach one's destination. **losing battle** a contest or effort in which failure seems certain. **lost cause 1** an enterprise etc. with no chance of success. **2** a person one can no longer hope to influence. □ **losable** adj. [OE *losian* perish, destroy f. *los* loss]

loser /ˈluːzə(r)/ n. **1** a person or thing that loses or has lost (esp. a contest or game) (*is a poor loser; the loser pays*). **2** *colloq.* a person who regularly fails.

loss n. **1** the act or an instance of losing; the state of being lost. **2** a person, thing, or amount lost. **3** the detriment or disadvantage resulting from losing (*that is no great loss*). □ **at a loss** (sold etc.) for less than was paid for it. **be at a loss** be puzzled or uncertain. **be at a loss for words** not know what to say. **loss adjuster** an insurance agent who assesses the amount of compensation arising from a loss. **loss-leader** an item sold at a loss to attract customers. [ME *los, loss* prob. back-form. f. *lost*, past part. of LOSE]

lost *past* and *past part.* of LOSE.

lot n. & v. —n. **1** *colloq.* (prec. by *a* or in *pl.*) **a** a large number or amount (*a lot of people; lots of chocolate*). **b** *colloq.* much (*a lot warmer; smiles a lot; is lots better*). **2 a** each of a set of objects used in making a chance selection. **b** this method of deciding (*chosen by lot*). **3** a share, or the responsibility resulting from it. **4** a person's destiny, fortune, or condition. **5** esp. *US* a plot; an allotment of land (*parking lot*). **6** an article or set of articles for sale at an auction etc. **7** a number or quantity of associated persons or things. —v.tr. (**lotted**, **lotting**) divide into lots. □ **bad lot** a person of bad character. **cast** (or **draw**) **lots** decide by means of lots. **throw in one's lot with** decide to share the fortunes of. **the** (or **the whole**) **lot** the whole number or quantity. **a whole lot** *colloq.* very much (*is a whole lot better*). [OE *hlot* portion, choice f. Gmc]

■ **Usage** In sense 1a, *a lot of* is somewhat informal, but is acceptable in serious writing, whereas *lots of* is not acceptable.

---

loth var. of LOATH.

lotion /ˈləʊʃ(ə)n/ n. a medicinal or cosmetic liquid preparation applied externally. [ME f. OF *lotion* or L *lotio* f. *lavare lot-* wash]

lottery /ˈlɒtərɪ/ n. (pl. **-ies**) **1** a means of raising money by selling numbered tickets and giving prizes to the holders of numbers drawn at random. **2** an enterprise, process, etc., whose success is governed by chance. [prob. f. Du. *loterij* (as LOT)]

lotto /ˈlɒtəʊ/ n. a game of chance like bingo, but with numbers drawn instead of called. [It.]

lotus /ˈləʊtəs/ n. **1** (in Greek mythology) a legendary plant inducing luxurious languor when eaten. **2 a** any water lily of the genus *Nelumbo*, esp. *N. nucifera* of India, with large pink flowers. **b** this flower used symbolically in Hinduism and Buddhism. **3** an Egyptian water lily, *Nymphaea lotus*, with white flowers. **4** any plant of the genus *Lotus*. □ **lotus-eater** a person given to indolent enjoyment. **lotus position** a cross-legged position of meditation with the feet resting on the thighs. [L f. Gk *lōtos*, of Semitic orig.]

louche /luːʃ/ *adj*. disreputable, shifty. [F, = squinting]

loud /laʊd/ *adj*. & *adv*. —*adj*. **1 a** strongly audible, esp. noisily or oppressively so. **b** able or liable to produce loud sounds (*a loud engine*). **c** clamorous, insistent (*loud complaints*). **2** (of colours, design, etc.) gaudy, obtrusive. **3** (of behaviour) aggressive and noisy. —*adv*. in a loud manner. □ **loud hailer** an electronic device for amplifying the sound of the voice so that it can be heard at a distance. **loud-mouth** *colloq*. a loud-mouthed person. **loud-mouthed** *colloq*. noisily self-assertive; vociferous. **out loud 1** aloud. **2** loudly (*laughed out loud*). □ **louden** *v.tr*. & *intr*. **loudish** *adj*. **loudly** *adv*. **loudness** *n*. [OE *hlūd* f. WG]

loudspeaker /laʊdˈspiːkə(r)/ *n*. an apparatus that converts electrical impulses into sound, esp. music and voice.

lough /lɒk, lɒx/ *n*. *Ir*. = LOCH. [Ir. *loch* LOCH, assim. to the related obs. ME form *lough*]

lounge /laʊndʒ/ *v*. & *n*. —*v.intr*. **1** recline comfortably and casually; loll. **2** stand or move about idly. —*n*. **1** a place for lounging, esp.: **a** a public room (e.g. in a hotel). **b** a place in an airport etc. with seats for waiting passengers. **c** a sitting-room in a house. **2** a spell of lounging. □ **lounge bar** *Brit*. a more comfortable room for drinking in a public house. **lounge suit** *Brit*. a man's formal suit for ordinary day wear. [perh. f. obs. *lungis* lout]

lounger /ˈlaʊndʒə(r)/ *n*. **1** a person who lounges. **2** a piece of furniture for relaxing on. **3** a casual garment for wearing when relaxing.

lour /ˈlaʊə(r)/ *v*. & *n*. (also **lower**) —*v.intr*. **1** frown; look sullen. **2** (of the sky etc.) look dark and threatening. —*n*. **1** a scowl. **2** a gloomy look (of the sky etc.). □ **louringly** *adv*. **loury** *adj*. [ME *loure*, of unkn. orig.]

louse /laʊs/ *n*. & *v*. —*n*. **1** (*pl*. **lice** /laɪs/) **a** a parasitic insect, *Pediculus humanus*, infesting the human hair and skin and transmitting various diseases. **b** any insect of the order Anoplura or Mallophaga parasitic on mammals, birds, fish, or plants. **2** *sl*. (*pl*. **louses**) a contemptible or unpleasant person. —*v.tr*. remove lice from. □ **louse up** *sl*. make a mess of. [OE *lūs*, pl. *lȳs*]

lousy /ˈlaʊzɪ/ *adj*. (**lousier**, **lousiest**) **1** infested with lice. **2** *colloq*. very bad; disgusting (also as a term of general disparagement). **3** *colloq*. (often foll. by *with*) well supplied, teeming. □ **lousily** *adv*. **lousiness** *n*.

lout /laʊt/ *n*. a rough, crude, or ill-mannered person (usu. a man). □ **loutish** *adj*. **loutishly** *adv*. **loutishness** *n*. [perh. f. archaic *lout* to bow]

louvre /ˈluːvə(r)/ *n*. (also **louver**) **1** each of a set of overlapping slats designed to admit air and some light and exclude rain. **2** a domed structure on a roof with side openings for ventilation etc. □ **louvred** *adj*. [ME f. OF *lover*, *lovier* skylight, prob. f. Gmc]

lovable /ˈlʌvəb(ə)l/ *adj*. (also **loveable**) inspiring or deserving love or affection. □ **lovability** /-ˈbɪlɪtɪ/ *n*. **lovableness** *n*. **lovably** *adv*.

lovage /ˈlʌvɪdʒ/ *n*. a S. European herb, *Levisticum officinale*, used for flavouring etc. [ME *loveache*

alt. f. OF *levesche* f. LL *levisticum* f. L *ligusticum* neut. of *ligusticus* Ligurian]

love /lʌv/ *n*. & *v*. —*n*. **1** an intense feeling of deep affection or fondness for a person or thing; great liking. **2** sexual passion. **3** sexual relations. **4 a** a beloved one; a sweetheart (often as a form of address). **b** *Brit*. *colloq*. a form of address regardless of affection. **5** *colloq*. a person of whom one is fond. **6** affectionate greetings (*give him my love*). **7** (often **Love**) a representation of Cupid. **8** (in some games) no score; nil. —*v.tr*. **1** (also *absol*.) feel love or deep fondness for. **2** delight in; admire; greatly cherish. **3** *colloq*. like very much (*loves books*). **4** (foll. by verbal noun, or *to* + infin.) be inclined, esp. as a habit; greatly enjoy; find pleasure in (*children love dressing up; loves to find fault*). □ **fall in love** (often foll. by *with*) develop a great (esp. sexual) love (for). **for love** for pleasure not profit. **for the love of** for the sake of. **in love** (often foll. by *with*) deeply enamoured (of). **love affair** a romantic or sexual relationship between two people in love. **love-bird** any of various African and Madagascan parrots, esp. *Agapornis personata*. **love-child** an illegitimate child. **love game** a game in which the loser makes no score. **love-match** a marriage made for love's sake. **love-nest** a place of intimate lovemaking. **love-seat** an armchair or small sofa for two. **make love** (often foll. by *to*) **1** have sexual intercourse (with). **2** *archaic* pay amorous attention (to). **out of love** no longer in love. □ **loveworthy** *adj*. [OE *lufu* f. Gmc]

loveless /ˈlʌvlɪs/ *adj*. without love; unloving or unloved or both. □ **lovelessly** *adv*. **lovelessness** *n*.

lovelorn /ˈlʌvlɔːn/ *adj*. pining from unrequited love.

lovely /ˈlʌvlɪ/ *adj*. & *n*. —*adj*. (**lovelier**, **loveliest**) **1** exquisitely beautiful. **2** *colloq*. pleasing, delightful. —*n*. (*pl*. **-ies**) *colloq*. a pretty woman. □ **lovely** and *colloq*. delightfully (*lovely and warm*). □ **lovelily** *adv*. **loveliness** *n*. [OE *luflic* (as LOVE)]

lovemaking /ˈlʌvˌmeɪkɪŋ/ *n*. **1** amorous sexual activity, esp. sexual intercourse. **2** *archaic* courtship.

lover /ˈlʌvə(r)/ *n*. **1** a person in love with another. **2** a person with whom another is having sexual relations. **3** (in *pl*.) a couple in love or having sexual relations. **4** a person who likes or enjoys something specified (*a music lover; a lover of words*). □ **lovers** *adj*.

lovesick /ˈlʌvsɪk/ *adj*. languishing with romantic love. □ **lovesickness** *n*.

lovesome /ˈlʌvsəm/ *adj*. *literary* lovely, lovable.

lovey-dovey /ˌlʌvɪˈdʌvɪ/ *adj*. fondly affectionate, esp. unduly sentimental.

loving /ˈlʌvɪŋ/ *adj*. & *n*. —*adj*. feeling or showing love; affectionate. —*n*. affection; active love. □ **loving-cup** a two-handled drinking-cup passed round at banquets. □ **lovingly** *adv*. **lovingness** *n*. [OE *lufiende* (as LOVE)]

low¹ /ləʊ/ *adj*., *n*., & *adv*. —*adj*. **1** of less than average height; not high or tall or reaching far up (*a low wall*). **2 a** situated close to ground or sea level etc.; not elevated in position (*low altitude*). **b** (of the sun) near the horizon. **c** (of latitude) near the equator. **3** of or in humble rank or position (*of low birth*). **4** of small or less than normal amount or extent or intensity (*low price; low temperature; low in calories*). **5** small or reduced in quantity (*stocks are low*). **6** coming below the normal level (*a dress with a low neck*). **7** dejected; lacking vigour (*feeling low; in low spirits*). **8** (of a sound) not shrill or loud or high-pitched. **9** not exalted or sublime; commonplace. **10** unfavourable (*a low opinion*). **11** abject, mean, vulgar (*low cunning; low slang*). **12** (in *compar.*) situated on less high land or to the south. **13** (of a geographical period) earlier. —*n.* **1** a low or the lowest level or number (*the dollar has reached a new low*). **2** an area of low pressure. —*adv.* **1** in or to a low position or state. **2** in a low tone (*speak low*). **3** (of a sound) at or to a low pitch. □ **low-born** of humble birth. **Low Church** the section of the Church of England giving a low place to ritual, priestly authority, and the sacraments. **low-class** of low quality or social class. **low comedy** that in which the subject and the treatment border on farce. **Low Countries** the Netherlands, Belgium, and Luxembourg. **low-cut** (of a dress etc.) made with a low neckline. **low-down** *adj.* abject, mean, dishonourable. —*n. colloq.* (usu. foll. by *on*) the relevant information (about). **low frequency** (in radio) 30–300 kilohertz. **low-grade** of low quality or strength. **low-key** lacking intensity or prominence; restrained. **low-level** *Computing* (of a programming language) close in form to machine language. **low-lying** at low altitude (above sea level etc.). **low-pitched 1** (of a sound) low. **2** (of a roof) having only a slight slope. **low pressure 1** little demand for activity or exertion. **2** an atmospheric condition with pressure below average. **low profile** avoidance of attention or publicity. **low-rise** (of a building) having few storeys. **low season** the period of fewest visitors at a resort etc. **low-spirited** dejected, dispirited. **low spirits** dejection, depression. **Low Sunday** the Sunday after Easter. **low tide** the time or level of the tide at its ebb. **low water** the tide at its lowest. **low-water mark 1** the level reached at low water. **2** a minimum recorded level or value etc. □ **lowish** *adj.* **lowness** *n.* [ME *lāh* f. ON *lágr* f. Gmc]

low² /ləʊ/ *n. & v.* —*n.* a sound made by cattle; a moo. —*v.intr.* utter this sound. [OE *hlōwan* f. Gmc]

lowbrow /ˈləʊbraʊ/ *adj. & n.* —*adj.* not highly intellectual or cultured. —*n.* a lowbrow person. □ **lowbrowed** *adj.*

lower¹ /ˈləʊə(r)/ *adj. & adv.* —*adj.* (*compar.* of LOW¹). **1** less high in position or status. **2** situated below another part (*lower lip; lower atmosphere*). **3 a** situated on less high land (*Lower Egypt*). **b** situated to the South (*Lower California*). **4** (of a mammal, plant, etc.) evolved to only a slight degree (e.g. a platypus or fungus). —*adv.* in or to a lower position, status, etc. □ **lower class** working-class people and their families. **lower-class** *adj.* of the lower class. **lower deck 1** the deck of a ship situated immediately over the hold. **2** the petty officers and men of a ship collectively. **Lower House** the larger and usu. elected body in a legislature, esp. the House of Commons. **lower regions** (or **world**) hell; the realm of the dead. □ **lowermost** *adj.*

lower² /ˈləʊə(r)/ *v.* **1** let or haul down. **2** *tr. & intr.* make or become lower. **3** *tr.* reduce the height or pitch or elevation of (*lower your voice;*

lower one's eyes). **4** *tr.* degrade. **5** *tr. & intr.* diminish.

lower³ var. of LOUR.

lowland /ˈləʊlənd/ *n. & adj.* —*n.* **1** (usu. in *pl.*) low-lying country. **2** (**Lowland**) (usu. in *pl.*) the region of Scotland lying south and east of the Highlands. —*adj.* of or in lowland or the Scottish Lowlands. □ **lowlander** *n.* (also **Lowlander**).

lowlight /ˈləʊlaɪt/ *n.* **1** a monotonous or dull period; a feature of little prominence (*one of the lowlights of the evening*). **2** (usu. in *pl.*) a dark tint in the hair produced by dyeing. [after HIGHLIGHT]

lowly /ˈləʊlɪ/ *adj.* (**lowlier, lowliest**) **1** humble in feeling, behaviour, or status. **2** modest, unpretentious. □ **lowlily** *adv.* **lowliness** *n.*

lox /lɒks/ *n. US* smoked salmon. [Yiddish *laks*]

loyal /ˈlɔɪəl/ *adj.* **1** (often foll. by *to*) true or faithful (to duty, love, or obligation). **2** steadfast in allegiance; devoted to the legitimate sovereign or government of one's country. **3** showing loyalty. □ **loyal toast** a toast to the sovereign. □ **loyally** *adv.* [F f. OF *loial* etc. f. L *legalis* LEGAL]

loyalist /ˈlɔɪəlɪst/ *n.* **1** a person who remains loyal to the legitimate sovereign etc., esp. in the face of rebellion or usurpation. **2** (**Loyalist**) a supporter of Parliamentary union between Great Britain and Northern Ireland. □ **loyalism** *n.*

loyalty /ˈlɔɪəltɪ/ *n.* (*pl.* **-ies**) **1** the state of being loyal. **2** (often in *pl.*) a feeling or application of loyalty.

lozenge /ˈlɒzɪndʒ/ *n.* **1** a rhombus or diamond figure. **2** a small sweet or medicinal tablet for dissolving in the mouth. □ **lozengy** *adj.* [ME f. OF *losenge*, ult. of Gaulish or Iberian orig.]

LP *abbr.* long-playing (gramophone record).

L-plate /ˈelpleɪt/ *n. Brit.* a sign bearing the letter L, attached to the front and rear of a motor vehicle to indicate that it is being driven by a learner.

LSD *abbr.* lysergic acid diethylamide.

l.s.d. /ˌeles'diː/ *n.* (also **£.s.d.**) *Brit.* **1** pounds, shillings, and pence (in former British currency). **2** money, riches. [L *librae, solidi, denarii*]

Lt. *abbr.* **1** Lieutenant. **2** light.

Ltd. *abbr.* Limited.

Lu *symb. Chem.* the element lutetium.

lubber /ˈlʌbə(r)/ *n.* a big clumsy fellow; a lout. □ **lubberlike** *adj.* **lubberly** *adj. & adv.* [ME, perh. f. OF *lobeor* swindler, parasite f. *lober* deceive]

lubricant /ˈluːbrɪkənt/ *n. & adj.* —*n.* a substance used to reduce friction. —*adj.* lubricating.

lubricate /ˈluːbrɪˌkeɪt/ *v.tr.* **1** reduce friction in (machinery etc.) by applying oil or grease etc. **2** make slippery or smooth with oil or grease. □ **lubrication** /-ˈkeɪʃ(ə)n/ *n.* **lubricative** /-kətɪv/ *adj.* **lubricator** *n.* [L *lubricare lubricat-* f. *lubricus* slippery]

lubricious /luːˈbrɪʃəs/ *adj.* (also **lubricous** /ˈluːbrɪkəs/) **1** slippery, smooth, oily. **2** lewd, prurient, evasive. □ **lubricity** *n.* [L *lubricus* slippery]

lucerne /luːˈsɜːn/ *n.* (also **lucern**) *Brit.* = ALFALFA. [F *luzerne* f. mod. Prov. *luzerno* glow-worm, with ref. to its shiny seeds]

lucid /ˈluːsɪd/ *adj.* **1** expressing or expressed clearly; easy to understand. **2** of or denoting intervals of sanity between periods of insanity or dementia. □ **lucidity** /-ˈsɪdɪtɪ/ *n.* **lucidly** *adv.*

634

lucidness *n.* [L *lucidus* (perh. through F *lucide* or It. *lucido*) f. *lucēre* shine (as LUX)]
Lucifer /ˈluːsɪfə(r)/ *n.* Satan. [OE f. L, = light-bringing, morning-star (as LUX, -*fer* f. *ferre* bring)]
luck *n.* **1** chance regarded as the bringer of good or bad fortune. **2** circumstances of life (beneficial or not) brought by this. **3** good fortune; success due to chance (*in luck; out of luck*). □ **for luck** to bring good fortune. **good luck 1** good fortune. **2** an omen of this. **hard luck** worse fortune than one deserves. **no such luck** *colloq.* unfortunately not. **try one's luck** make a venture. **with luck** if all goes well. **worse luck** *colloq.* unfortunately. [ME f. LG *luk* f. MLG *geluke*]
luckily /ˈlʌkɪlɪ/ *adv.* **1** (qualifying a whole sentence or clause) fortunately (*luckily there was enough food*). **2** in a lucky or fortunate manner.
luckless /ˈlʌklɪs/ *adj.* having no luck; unfortunate. □ **lucklessly** *adv.* **lucklessness** *n.*
lucky /ˈlʌkɪ/ *adj.* (**luckier, luckiest**) **1** having or resulting from good luck, esp. as distinct from skill or design or merit. **2** bringing good luck (*a lucky mascot*). **3** fortunate, appropriate (*a lucky guess*). □ **lucky dip** *Brit.* a tub containing different articles concealed in wrapping or bran etc., and chosen at random by participants. □ **luckiness** *n.*
lucrative /ˈluːkrətɪv/ *adj.* profitable, yielding financial gain. □ **lucratively** *adv.* **lucrativeness** *n.* [ME f. L *lucrativus* f. *lucrari* to gain]
lucre /ˈluːkə(r)/ *n. derog.* financial profit or gain. [ME f. F *lucre* or L *lucrum*]
lud /lʌd/ *n. Brit.* □ **m'lud** (or **my lud**) a form of address to a judge in a court of law. [corrupt. of LORD]
Luddite /ˈlʌdaɪt/ *n. & adj.* —*n.* **1** *hist.* a member of any of the bands of English artisans who rioted against mechanization and destroyed machinery (1811–16). **2** a person opposed to increased industrialization or new technology. —*adj.* of the Luddites or their beliefs. □ **Luddism** *n.* **Ludditism** *n.* [perh. f. Ned *Lud*, who destroyed machinery *c*.1779]
ludicrous /ˈluːdɪkrəs/ *adj.* absurd or ridiculous; laughable. □ **ludicrously** *adv.* **ludicrousness** *n.* [L *ludicrus* prob. f. *ludicrum* stage play]
ludo /ˈluːdəʊ/ *n. Brit.* a simple board game in which counters are moved round according to the throw of dice. [L, = I play]
luff *v.tr.* (also *absol.*) (also **loof** /luːf/) *Naut.* **1** steer (a ship) nearer the wind. **2** turn (the helm) so as to achieve this. **3** obstruct (an opponent in yacht-racing) by sailing closer to the wind. **4** raise or lower (the jib of a crane or derrick). [ME *lo(o)f* f. OF *lof*, prob. f. LG]
luffa var. of LOOFAH.
lug[1] *v. & n.* —*v.* (**lugged, lugging**) **1** *tr.* **a** drag or tug (a heavy object) with effort or violence. **b** (usu. foll. by *round, about*) carry (something heavy) around with one. **2** *intr.* (usu. foll. by *at*) pull hard. —*n.* **1** a hard or rough pull. **2** (in *pl.*) US affectation (*put on lugs*). [ME, prob. f. Scand.: cf. Sw. *lugga* pull a person's hair f. *lugg* forelock]
lug[2] *n.* **1** *Sc.* or *colloq.* an ear. **2** a projection on an object by which it may be carried, fixed in place, etc. **3** esp. *US sl.* a lout; a sponger; a stupid person. [prob. of Scand. orig.: cf. LUG[1]]
lug[3] *n.* = LUGWORM. [17th c.: orig. unkn.]
lug[4] *n.* = LUGSAIL. [abbr.]

luge /luːʒ/ *n. & v.* —*n.* a light toboggan for one or two people, ridden in the sitting position. —*v.intr.* ride on a luge. [Swiss F]
luggage /ˈlʌgɪdʒ/ *n.* suitcases, bags, etc. to hold a traveller's belongings. □ **luggage-van** *Brit.* a railway carriage for travellers' luggage. [LUG[1] + -AGE]
lugger /ˈlʌgə(r)/ *n.* a small ship carrying two or three masts with a lugsail on each. [LUGSAIL + -ER[1]]
lughole /ˈlʌghəʊl, ˈlʌgəʊl/ *n. sl.* the ear orifice. [LUG[2] + HOLE]
lugsail /ˈlʌgseɪl, -s(ə)l/ *n. Naut.* a quadrilateral sail which is bent on and hoisted from a yard. [prob. f. LUG[2]]
lugubrious /luːˈɡuːbrɪəs, lʊ-/ *adj.* doleful, mournful, dismal. □ **lugubriously** *adv.* **lugubriousness** *n.* [L *lugubris* f. *lugēre* mourn]
lugworm /ˈlʌgwɜːm/ *n.* any polychaete worm of the genus *Arenicola*, often used as bait by fishermen. [LUG[3]]
lukewarm /luːkˈwɔːm, ˈluːk-/ *adj.* **1** moderately warm; tepid. **2** unenthusiastic, indifferent. □ **lukewarmly** *adv.* **lukewarmness** *n.* [ME f. (now dial.) *luke, lew* f. OE]
lull /lʌl/ *v. & n.* —*v.* **1** *tr.* soothe or send to sleep gently. **2** *tr.* (usu. foll. by *into*) deceive (a person) into confidence (*lulled into a false sense of security*). **3** *tr.* allay (suspicions etc.) usu. by deception. **4** *intr.* (of noise, a storm, etc.) abate or fall quiet. —*n.* a temporary quiet period in a storm or in any activity. [ME, imit. of sounds used to quieten a child]
lullaby /ˈlʌləbaɪ/ *n. & v.* —*n.* (*pl.* -**ies**) **1** a soothing song to send a child to sleep. **2** the music for this. —*v.tr.* (-**ies, -ied**) sing to sleep. [as LULL + -*by* as in BYE-BYE[2]]
lumbago /lʌmˈbeɪgəʊ/ *n.* rheumatic pain in the muscles of the lower back. [L f. *lumbus* loin]
lumbar /ˈlʌmbə(r)/ *adj. Anat.* relating to the loin, esp. the lower back area. □ **lumbar puncture** the withdrawal of spinal fluid from the lower back with a hollow needle, usu. for diagnosis. [med.L *lumbaris* f. L *lumbus* loin]
lumber[1] /ˈlʌmbə(r)/ *v.intr.* (usu. foll. by *along, past, by*, etc.) move in a slow clumsy noisy way. □ **lumbering** *adj.* [ME *lomere*, perh. imit.]
lumber[2] /ˈlʌmbə(r)/ *n. & v.* —*n.* **1** disused articles of furniture etc. inconveniently taking up space. **2** useless or cumbersome objects. **3** *US* partly prepared timber. —*v.* **1** *tr.* **a** (usu. foll. by *with*) leave (a person etc.) with something unwanted or unpleasant (*always lumbering me with the cleaning*). **b** (as **lumbered** *adj.*) in an unwanted or inconvenient situation (*afraid of being lumbered*). **2** *tr.* (usu. foll. by *together*) heap or group together carelessly. **3** *tr.* (usu. foll. by *up*) obstruct. **4** *intr.* cut and prepare forest timber for transport. □ **lumber-jacket** a jacket, usu. of warm checked material, of the kind worn by lumberjacks. **lumber-room** a room where disused or cumbrous things are kept. □ **lumberer** *n.* (in sense 4 of v.). **lumbering** *n.* (in sense 4 of v.). [perh. f. LUMBER[1]: later assoc. with obs. *lumber* pawnbroker's shop]
lumberjack /ˈlʌmbədʒæk/ *n.* (also **lumberman** *pl.* -**men**) esp. *US* one who fells, prepares, or conveys lumber.
lumen /ˈluːmen/ *n. Physics* the SI unit of luminous flux. □ **luminal** /ˈluːmɪn(ə)l/ *adj.* [L *lumen luminis* a light, an opening]

luminary /'lu:mɪnərɪ/ n. (pl. **-ies**) **1** literary a natural light-giving body, esp. the sun or moon. **2** a person as a source of intellectual light or moral inspiration. **3** a prominent member of a group or gathering (a host of show-business luminaries). [ME f. OF luminarie or LL luminarium f. L LUMEN]

luminescence /ˌlu:mɪˈnes(ə)ns/ n. the emission of light by a substance other than as a result of incandescence. □ **luminescent** adj. [as LUMEN: see IRIDESCENT]

luminous /'lu:mɪnəs, 'lju:-/ adj. **1** full of or shedding light; radiant, bright, shining. **2** phosphorescent, visible in darkness (luminous paint). **3** (esp. of a writer or a writer's work) throwing light on a subject. **4** of visible radiation (luminous intensity). □ **luminosity** /-ˈnɒsɪtɪ/ n. **luminously** adj. **luminousness** n. [ME f. OF lumineux or L luminosus]

lump¹ n. & v. —n. **1** a compact shapeless or unshapely mass. **2** sl. a quantity or heap. **3** a tumour, swelling, or bruise. **4** a heavy, dull, or ungainly person. **5** (prec. by the) Brit. casual workers in the building and other trades. —v. **1** tr. (usu. foll. by together, with, in with, under, etc.) mass together or group indiscriminately. **2** tr. carry or throw carelessly (lumping crates round the yard). **3** intr. become lumpy. **4** intr. (usu. foll. by along) proceed heavily or awkwardly. **5** intr. (usu. foll. by down) sit down heavily. □ **in the lump** taking things as a whole; in a general manner. **lump in the throat** a feeling of pressure there, caused by emotion. **lump sugar** sugar shaped into lumps or cubes. **lump sum 1** a sum covering a number of items. **2** money paid down at once. □ **lumper** n. (in sense 2 of v.). [ME, perh. of Scand. orig.]

lump² /lʌmp/ v.tr. colloq. endure or suffer (a situation) ungraciously. □ **like it or lump it** put up with something whether one likes it or not. [imit.: cf. dump, grump, etc.]

lumpectomy /lʌmˈpektəmɪ/ n. (pl. **-ies**) the surgical removal of a usu. cancerous lump from the breast.

lumpfish /'lʌmpfɪʃ/ n. (pl. **-fishes** or **-fish**) a spiny-finned fish, Cyclopterus lumpus, of the N. Atlantic with modified pelvic fins for clinging to objects. [MLG lumpen, MDu. lumpe (perh. = LUMP¹) + FISH¹]

lumpish /'lʌmpɪʃ/ adj. **1** heavy and clumsy. **2** stupid, lethargic. □ **lumpishly** adv. **lumpishness** n.

lumpy /'lʌmpɪ/ adj. (**lumpier, lumpiest**) full of or covered with lumps. □ **lumpily** adv. **lumpiness** n.

lunacy /'lu:nəsɪ/ n. (pl. **-ies**) **1** insanity (orig. of the intermittent kind attributed to changes of the moon); the state of being a lunatic. **2** great folly or eccentricity; a foolish act.

lunar /'lu:nə(r), 'lju:-/ adj. **1** of, relating to, or determined by the moon. **2** concerned with travel to the moon and related research. □ **lunar module** a small craft used for travelling between the moon's surface and a spacecraft in orbit around the moon. **lunar month 1** the period of the moon's revolution, esp. the interval between new moons of about 29½ days. **2** (in general use) a period of four weeks. **lunar year** a period of 12 lunar months. [L lunaris f. luna moon]

lunate /'lu:neɪt, 'lju:-/ adj. crescent-shaped. [L lunatus f. luna moon]

lunatic /'lu:nətɪk/ n. & adj. —n. **1** an insane person. **2** someone foolish or eccentric. —adj. mad, foolish. □ **lunatic asylum** hist. a mental home or hospital. **lunatic fringe** an extreme or eccentric minority group. [ME f. OF lunatique f. LL lunaticus f. L luna moon]

lunation /lu:ˈneɪʃ(ə)n, lju:-/ n. the interval between new moons, about 29½ days. [ME f. med.L lunatio (as LUNATIC)]

lunch /lʌntʃ/ n. & v. —n. **1** the meal eaten in the middle of the day. **2** a light meal eaten at any time. —v. **1** intr. eat one's lunch. **2** tr. provide lunch for. □ **luncher** n. [LUNCHEON]

luncheon /'lʌntʃ(ə)n/ n. formal lunch. □ **luncheon meat** a usu. tinned block of ground meat ready to cut and eat. **luncheon voucher** Brit. a voucher or ticket issued to employees and exchangeable for food at many restaurants and shops. [17th c.: orig. unkn.]

lunette /lu:ˈnet/ n. **1** an arched aperture in a domed ceiling to admit light. **2** a crescent-shaped or semicircular space or alcove which contains a painting, statue, etc. **3** a ring through which a hook is placed to attach a vehicle to the vehicle towing it. [F, dimin. of lune (f. L luna moon)]

lung n. either of the pair of respiratory organs which bring air into contact with the blood in humans and many other vertebrates. □ **lung-power** the power of one's voice. □ **lunged** adj. **lungful** n. (pl. **-fuls**). **lungless** adj. [OE lungen f. Gmc, rel. to LIGHT²]

lunge n. & v. —n. **1** a sudden movement forward. **2** a thrust with a sword etc., esp. the basic attacking move in fencing. **3** a movement forward by bending the front leg at the knee while keeping the back leg straight. —v. **1** intr. make a lunge. **2** intr. (usu. foll. by at, out) deliver a blow from the shoulder in boxing. **3** tr. drive (a weapon etc.) violently in some direction. [earlier allonge f. F allonger lengthen f. à to + long LONG¹]

lungi /'lʊŋɡi:/ n. (pl. **lungis**) a length of cotton cloth, usu. worn as a loincloth in India, or as a skirt in Burma (now Myanmar) where it is the national dress for both sexes. [Urdu]

lupin /'lu:pɪn/ n. (also **lupine** /-pɪn/) any plant of the genus Lupinus, with long tapering spikes of flowers. [ME f. L lupinus]

lupine /'lu:paɪn/ adj. of or like a wolf or wolves. [L lupinus f. lupus wolf]

lupus /'lu:pəs/ n. any of various ulcerous skin diseases, esp. tuberculosis of the skin. □ **lupoid** adj. **lupous** adj. [L, = wolf]

lurch¹ /lɜ:tʃ/ n. & v. —n. a stagger, a sudden unsteady movement or leaning. —v.intr. stagger, move suddenly and unsteadily. [orig. Naut., lee-lurch alt. of lee-latch drifting to leeward]

lurch² /lɜ:tʃ/ n. □ **leave in the lurch** desert (a friend etc.) in difficulties. [orig. = a severe defeat in a game, f. F lourche (also the game itself, like backgammon)]

lurcher /'lɜ:tʃə(r)/ n. Brit. a cross-bred dog, usu. a retriever, collie, or sheepdog crossed with a greyhound, used esp. for hunting and by poachers. [f. obs. lurch (v.) var. of LURK]

lure /ljʊə(r), lʊə(r)/ v. & n. —v.tr. **1** (usu. foll. by away, into) entice (a person, an animal, etc.) usu. with some form of bait. **2** attract back again or recall (a person, animal, etc.) with the promise of a reward. —*n.* **1** a thing used to entice. **2** (usu. foll. by *of*) the attractive or compelling qualities (of a pursuit etc.). **3** a falconer's apparatus for recalling a hawk. □ **luring** *adj.* **luringly** *adv.* [ME f. OE *luere* f. Gmc]

Lurex /ˈljʊəreks/ *n. propr.* **1** a type of yarn which incorporates a glittering metallic thread. **2** fabric made from this yarn.

lurid /ˈljʊərɪd, ˈlʊə-/ *adj.* **1** vivid or glowing in colour (*lurid orange*). **2** of an unnatural glare (*lurid nocturnal brilliance*). **3** sensational, horrifying, or terrible (*lurid details*). **4** showy, gaudy (*paperbacks with lurid covers*). **5** ghastly, wan (*lurid complexion*). □ **luridly** *adv.* **luridness** *n.* [L *luridus* f. *luror* wan or yellow colour]

lurk *v.intr.* **1** linger furtively or unobtrusively. **2 a** lie in ambush. **b** (usu. foll. by *in, under, about,* etc.) hide, esp. for sinister purposes. **3** (as **lurking** *adj.*) latent, semi-conscious (*a lurking suspicion*). □ **lurker** *n.* [ME perh. f. LOUR with frequent. *-k* as in TALK]

luscious /ˈlʌʃəs/ *adj.* **1 a** richly sweet in taste or smell. **b** *colloq.* delicious. **2** (of literary style, music, etc.) over-rich in sound, imagery, or voluptuous suggestion. **3** voluptuously attractive. □ **lusciously** *adv.* **lusciousness** *n.* [ME perh. alt. of obs. *licious* f. DELICIOUS]

lush[1] /lʌʃ/ *adj.* **1** (of vegetation, esp. grass) luxuriant and succulent. **2** luxurious. □ **lushly** *adv.* **lushness** *n.* [ME, perh. var. of obs. *lash* soft, f. OF *lasche* lax: assoc. with LUSCIOUS]

lush[2] /lʌʃ/ *n. & v.* esp. *US sl.* —*n.* **1** alcohol, liquor. **2** an alcoholic, a drunkard. —*v.* **1** *tr. & intr.* drink (alcohol). **2** *tr.* ply with alcohol. [18th c.: perh. joc. use of LUSH[1]]

lust *n. & v.* —*n.* **1** strong sexual desire. **2 a** (usu. foll. by *for, of*) a passionate desire for (*a lust for power*). **b** (usu. foll. by *of*) a passionate enjoyment of (*the lust of battle*). **3** (usu. in *pl.*) a sensuous appetite regarded as sinful (*the lusts of the flesh*). —*v.intr.* (usu. foll. by *after, for*) have a strong or excessive (esp. sexual) desire. □ **lustful** *adj.* **lustfully** *adv.* **lustfulness** *n.* [OE f. Gmc]

lustre /ˈlʌstə(r)/ *n.* (*US* **luster**) **1** gloss, brilliance, or sheen. **2** a shining or reflective surface. **3** a thin metallic coating giving an iridescent glaze to ceramics. **4** a radiance or attractiveness; splendour, glory, distinction of achievements etc.) (*add lustre to; shed lustre on*). □ **lustreless** *adj.* (*US* **lusterless**). **lustrous** *adj.* **lustrously** *adv.* **lustrousness** *n.* [F f. It. *lustro* f. *lustrare* f. L *lustrare* illuminate]

lusty /ˈlʌstɪ/ *adj.* (**lustier, lustiest**) **1** healthy and strong. **2** vigorous or lively. □ **lustily** *adv.* **lustiness** *n.* [ME f. LUST + -Y[1]]

lute[1] /luːt, ljuːt/ *n.* a guitar-like instrument with a long neck and a pear-shaped body, much used in the 14th–17th c. [ME f. F *lut, leüt*, prob. f. Prov. *laüt* f. Arab. *al-'ūd*]

lute[2] /luːt, ljuːt/ *n. & v.* —*n.* clay or cement used to stop a hole, make a joint airtight, protect a graft, etc. —*v.tr.* apply lute to. [ME f. OF *lut* f. L *lutum* mud, clay]

lutenist /ˈluːtənɪst, ˈljuː-/ *n.* (also **lutanist**) a lute-player. [med.L *lutanista* f. *lutana* LUTE[1]]

lutetium /luːˈtiːʃəm, ljuː-/ *n.* (also **lutecium**) *Chem.* a silvery metallic element of the lanthanide series. [F *lutécium* f. L *Lutetia* the ancient name of Paris]

Lutheran /ˈluːθərən, ˈljuː-/ *n. & adj.* —*n.* **1** a follower of Martin Luther, Ger. religious reformer d. 1546. **2** a member of the Lutheran Church, with justification by faith alone as a cardinal doctrine. —*adj.* of or characterized by the theology of Martin Luther. □ **Lutheranism** *n.* **Lutheranize** *v.tr. & intr.* (also **-ise**).

luting /ˈluːtɪŋ/ *n.* = LUTE[2] *n.*

lux *n.* (*pl.* same) *Physics* the SI unit of illumination. [L *lux lucis* light]

luxe /lʊks, lʌks/ *n.* luxury (cf. DE LUXE). [F f. L *luxus*]

luxuriant /lʌgˈzjʊərɪənt, lʌkˈsj-, lʌgˈʒʊə-/ *adj.* **1** (of vegetation etc.) lush, profuse in growth. **2** prolific, exuberant, rank (*luxuriant imagination*). **3** (of literary or artistic style) florid, richly ornate. □ **luxuriance** *n.* **luxuriantly** *adv.* [L *luxuriare* grow rank f. *luxuria* LUXURY]

■ **Usage** This word is sometimes confused with *luxurious*.

luxuriate /lʌgˈzjʊərɪˌeɪt, lʌkˈsj-, lʌgˈʒʊə-/ *v.intr.* **1** (foll. by *in*) take self-indulgent delight in, enjoy in a luxurious manner. **2** take one's ease, relax in comfort.

luxurious /lʌgˈzjʊərɪəs, lʌkˈsj-, lʌgˈʒʊə-/ *adj.* **1** supplied with luxuries. **2** extremely comfortable. **3** fond of luxury, self-indulgent, voluptuous. □ **luxuriously** *adv.* **luxuriousness** *n.* [ME f. OF *luxurios* f. L *luxuriosus* (as LUXURY)]

■ **Usage** This word is sometimes confused with *luxuriant*.

luxury /ˈlʌkʃərɪ/ *n.* (*pl.* **-ies**) **1** choice or costly surroundings, possessions, food, etc.; luxuriousness (*a life of luxury*). **2** something desirable for comfort or enjoyment, but not indispensable. **3** (*attrib.*) providing great comfort, expensive (*a luxury flat; a luxury holiday*). [ME f. OF *luxurie, luxure* f. L *luxuria* f. *luxus* abundance]

LV *abbr. Brit.* luncheon voucher.

Lw *symb. Chem.* the element lawrencium.

lx *abbr.* lux.

-ly[1] /lɪ/ *suffix* forming adjectives esp. from nouns, meaning: **1** having the qualities of (*princely; manly*). **2** recurring at intervals of (*daily; hourly*). [from or after OE *-lic* f. Gmc, rel. to LIKE[1]]

-ly[2] /lɪ/ *suffix* forming adverbs from adjectives, denoting esp. manner or degree (*boldly; happily; miserably; deservedly; amusingly*). [from or after OE *-līce* f. Gmc (as -LY[1])]

lycanthropy /laɪˈkænθrəpɪ/ *n.* the mythical transformation of a person into a wolf. [mod.L *lycanthropia* f. Gk *lukanthrōpia* f. *lukos* wolf + *anthrōpos* man]

lychee /ˈlaɪtʃiː, ˈliː-/ *n.* (also **litchi, lichee**) **1** a sweet fleshy fruit with a thin spiny skin. **2** the tree, *Nephelium litchi*, orig. from China, bearing this. [Chin. *lizhi*]

lych-gate var. of LICH-GATE.

Lycra /ˈlaɪkrə/ *n. propr.* an elastic polyurethane fibre or fabric used esp. for close-fitting sports clothing.

lye /laɪ/ *n.* **1** water that has been made alkaline by lixiviation of vegetable ashes. **2** any strong alkaline solution, esp. of potassium hydroxide used for washing or cleansing. [OE *lēag* f. Gmc: cf. LATHER]

lying[1] /ˈlaɪɪŋ/ *pres. part.* of LIE[1]. —*n.* a place to lie (*a dry lying*).

lying[2] /ˈlaɪɪŋ/ *pres. part.* of LIE[2]. —*adj.* deceitful, false. □ **lyingly** *adv.*

lymph /lɪmf/ *n.* **1** *Physiol.* a colourless fluid containing white blood cells, drained from the tissues and conveyed through the body in the lymphatic system. **2** this fluid used as a vaccine. **3** exudation from a sore etc. □ **lymph gland** (or **node**) a small mass of tissue in the lymphatic system where lymph is purified and lymphocytes are formed. □ **lymphoid** *adj.* **lymphous** *adj.* [F *lymphe* or L *lympha, limpa* water]

lymphatic /lɪmˈfætɪk/ *adj.* & *n.* —*adj.* **1** of or secreting or conveying lymph (*lymphatic gland*). **2** (of a person) pale, flabby, or sluggish. —*n.* a veinlike vessel conveying lymph. □ **lymphatic system** a network of vessels conveying lymph. [orig. = frenzied, f. L *lymphaticus* mad f. Gk *numpholēptos* seized by nymphs: now assoc. with LYMPH (on the analogy of *spermatic* etc.)]

lymphocyte /ˈlɪmfəˌsaɪt/ *n.* a form of leucocyte occurring in the blood, in lymph, etc. □ **lymphocytic** /-ˈsɪtɪk/ *adj.*

lymphoma /lɪmˈfəʊmə/ *n.* (*pl.* **lymphomata** /-mətə/) any malignant tumour of the lymph nodes, excluding leukaemia.

lynch /lɪntʃ/ *v.tr.* (of a body of people) put (a person) to death for an alleged offence without a legal trial. □ **lynch law** the procedure of a self-constituted illegal court that punishes or executes. □ **lyncher** *n.* **lynching** *n.* [*Lynch's law*, after Capt. W. *Lynch* of Virginia *c.*1780]

lynchpin var. of LINCHPIN.

lynx /lɪŋks/ *n.* **1** a medium-sized cat, *Felis lynx*, with short tail, spotted fur, and tufted ear-tips. **2** its fur. □ **lynx-eyed** keen-sighted. □ **lynxlike** *adj.* [ME f. L f. Gk *lugx*]

lyre /ˈlaɪə(r)/ *n. Gk Antiq.* an ancient stringed instrument like a small U-shaped harp, usu. accompanying the voice. □ **lyre-bird** any Australian bird of the family Menuridae, the male of which has a lyre-shaped tail display. [ME f. OF *lire* f. L *lyra* f. Gk *lura*]

lyric /ˈlɪrɪk/ *adj.* & *n.* —*adj.* **1** (of poetry) expressing the writer's emotions, usu. briefly and in stanzas or recognized forms. **2** (of a poet) writing in this manner. **3** of or for the lyre. **4** meant to be sung, fit to be expressed in song, songlike (*lyric drama; lyric opera*). —*n.* **1** a lyric poem or verse. **2** (in *pl.*) lyric verses. **3** (usu. in *pl.*) the words of a song. [F *lyrique* or L *lyricus* f. Gk *lurikos* (as LYRE)]

lyrical /ˈlɪrɪk(ə)l/ *adj.* **1** = LYRIC. **2** resembling, couched in, or using language appropriate to, lyric poetry. **3** *colloq.* highly enthusiastic (*wax lyrical about*). □ **lyrically** *adv.* **lyricalness** *n.*

lyricism /ˈlɪrɪˌsɪz(ə)m/ *n.* **1** the character or quality of being lyric or lyrical. **2** a lyrical expression. **3** high-flown sentiments.

lyricist /ˈlɪrɪsɪst/ *n.* a person who writes the words to a song.

lysergic acid /laɪˈsɜːdʒɪk/ *n.* a crystalline acid extracted from ergot or prepared synthetically. □ **lysergic acid diethylamide** /ˌdaɪəˈθaɪləˌmaɪd/ a powerful hallucinogenic drug. [*hydrolysis* + *ergot* + -IC]

lysin /ˈlaɪsɪn/ *n.* a protein in the blood able to cause lysis. [G *Lysine*]

lysis /ˈlaɪsɪs/ *n.* (*pl.* **lyses** /-siːz/) the disintegration of a cell. [L f. Gk *lusis* loosening f. *luō* loosen]

-lysis /lɪsɪs/ *comb. form* forming nouns denoting disintegration or decomposition (*electrolysis; haemolysis*).

lytic /ˈlɪtɪk/ *adj.* of, relating to, or causing lysis.

-lytic /ˈlɪtɪk/ *comb. form* forming adjectives corresponding to nouns in *-lysis*. [Gk *lutikos* (as LYSIS)]

Mm

M¹ /em/ *n.* (*pl.* **Ms** or **M's**) **1** the thirteenth letter of the alphabet. **2** (as a Roman numeral) 1,000.

M² *abbr.* (also **M.**) **1** Master. **2** (in titles) Member of. **3** *Monsieur.* **4** (in the UK in road designations) motorway. **5** mega-.

m *abbr.* (also **m.**) **1 a** masculine. **b** male. **2** married. **3** mile(s). **4** metre(s). **5** million(s). **6** minute(s). **7** milli-.

MA *abbr.* Master of Arts.

ma *n. colloq.* mother. [abbr. of MAMMA¹]

ma'am /mæm, mɑːm, məm/ *n.* madam (used esp. in addressing royalty). [contr.]

Mac *n. colloq.* **1** a Scotsman. **2** *US* man (esp. as a form of address). [*Mac-* as a patronymic prefix in many Scottish and Irish surnames]

mac *n.* (also **mack**) *Brit. colloq.* mackintosh. [abbr.]

macabre /məˈkɑːbr/ *adj.* grim, gruesome. [ME f. OF *macabré* perh. f. *Macabé* a Maccabee, with ref. to a miracle play showing the slaughter of the Maccabees]

macadam /məˈkædəm/ *n.* **1** material for road-making with successive layers of compacted broken stone. **2** = TARMACADAM. □ **macadamize** *v.tr.* (also **-ise**). [J. L. *McAdam*, Brit. surveyor d. 1836, who advocated using this material]

macaque /məˈkæk/ *n.* any monkey of the genus *Macaca*, including the rhesus monkey and Barbary ape. [F f. Port. *macaco* f. Fiot *makaku* some monkeys f. *kaku* monkey]

macaroni /ˌmækəˈrəʊnɪ/ *n.* a tubular variety of pasta. [It. *maccaroni* f. late Gk *makaria* food made from barley]

macaroon /ˌmækəˈruːn/ *n.* a small light cake or biscuit made with white of egg, sugar, and ground almonds or coconut. [F *macaron* f. It. (as MACARONI)]

Macassar /məˈkæsə(r)/ *n.* (in full **Macassar oil**) a kind of oil formerly used as a dressing for the hair. [*Macassar*, now in Indonesia, from where its ingredients were said to come]

macaw /məˈkɔː/ *n.* any long-tailed brightly coloured parrot of the genus *Ara* or *Anodorhynchus*, native to S. and Central America. [Port. *macao*, of unkn. orig.]

McCarthyism /məˈkɑːθɪˌɪz(ə)m/ *n.* (esp. in the US) the policy of hunting out suspected or known Communists and removing them esp. from government departments. [J. R. *McCarthy*, US senator d. 1957]

McCoy /məˈkɔɪ/ *n. colloq.* □ **the** (or **the real**) **McCoy** the real thing; the genuine article. [19th c.: orig. uncert.]

mace¹ *n.* **1** a staff of office, esp. the symbol of the Speaker's authority in the House of Commons. **2** *hist.* a heavy club usu. having a metal head and spikes. [ME f. OF *mace*, *masse* f. Rmc *mattea* (unrecorded) club]

mace² *n.* the dried outer covering of the nutmeg, used as a spice. [ME *macis* (taken as pl.) f. OF *macis* f. L *macir* a red spicy bark]

macédoine /ˈmæsɪˌdwɑːn/ *n.* mixed vegetables or fruit, esp. cut up small or in jelly. [F, = Macedonia, with ref. to the mixture of peoples there]

macerate /ˈmæsəˌreɪt/ *v.* **1** *tr.* & *intr.* make or become soft by soaking. **2** *intr.* waste away by fasting. □ **maceration** /-ˈreɪʃ(ə)n/ *n.* **macerator** *n.* [L *macerare macerat-*]

Mach /mɑːk, mæk/ *n.* (in full **Mach number**) the ratio of the speed of a body to the speed of sound in the surrounding medium. □ **Mach one** (or **two** etc.) the speed (or twice the speed) of sound. [E. *Mach*, Austrian physicist d. 1916]

machete /məˈtʃetɪ, məˈʃetɪ/ *n.* (also **matchet** /ˈmætʃɪt/) a broad heavy knife used in Central America and the W. Indies as an implement and weapon. [Sp. f. *macho* hammer f. LL *marcus*]

machiavellian /ˌmækɪəˈvelɪən/ *adj.* elaborately cunning; scheming, unscrupulous. □ **machiavellianism** *n.* [N. dei *Machiavelli*, Florentine statesman and political writer d. 1527, who advocated resort to morally questionable methods in the interests of the State]

machinable /məˈʃiːnəb(ə)l/ *adj.* capable of being cut by machine tools. □ **machinability** /-ˈbɪlɪtɪ/ *n.*

machinate /ˈmækɪˌneɪt, ˈmæʃ-/ *v.intr.* lay plots; intrigue. □ **machination** /-ˈneɪʃ(ə)n/ *n.* **machinator** *n.* [L *machinari* contrive (as MACHINE)]

machine /məˈʃiːn/ *n.* & *v.* —*n.* **1** an apparatus using or applying mechanical power, having several parts each with a definite function and together performing certain kinds of work. **2** a particular kind of machine, esp. a vehicle, a piece of electrical or electronic apparatus, etc. **3** an instrument that transmits a force or directs its application. **4** the controlling system of an organization etc. (*the party machine*). **5** a person who acts mechanically and with apparent lack of emotion. —*v.tr.* make or operate on with a machine (esp. in sewing or printing). □ **machine code** (or **language**) a computer language that a particular computer can respond to directly. **machine-readable** in a form that a computer can process. **machine tool** a mechanically operated tool for working on metal, wood, or plastics. **machine-tooled 1** shaped by a machine tool. **2** (of artistic presentation etc.) precise, slick, esp. excessively so. [F f. L *machina* f. Gk *makhana* Doric form of *mēkhanē* f. *mēkhos* contrivance]

machine-gun /məˈʃiːngʌn/ *n.* & *v.* —*n.* an automatic gun giving continuous fire. —*v.tr.* (**-gunned, -gunning**) shoot at with a machine-gun. □ **machine-gunner** *n.*

machinery /məˈʃiːnərɪ/ *n.* (*pl.* **-ies**) **1** machines collectively. **2** the components of a machine; a mechanism. **3** (foll. by *of*) an organized system.

4 (foll. by *for*) the means devised or available (*the machinery for decision-making*).

machinist /məˈʃiːnɪst/ *n.* **1** a person who operates a machine, esp. a sewing-machine or a machine tool. **2** a person who makes machinery.

machismo /məˈtʃɪzməʊ, -ˈkɪzməʊ/ *n.* exaggeratedly assertive manliness; a show of masculinity. [Sp. f. *macho* MALE f. L *masculus*]

macho /ˈmætʃəʊ/ *adj.* & *n.* —*adj.* showily manly or virile. —*n.* (*pl.* -**os**) **1** a macho man. **2** = MACHISMO. [MACHISMO]

mack var. of MAC.

mackerel /ˈmækər(ə)l/ *n.* (*pl.* same or **mackerels**) a N. Atlantic marine fish, *Scomber scombrus*, with a greenish-blue body, used for food. □ **mackerel sky** a sky dappled with rows of small white fleecy clouds. [ME f. AF *makerel*, OF *maquerel*]

mackintosh /ˈmækɪnˌtɒʃ/ *n.* (also **macintosh**) **1** *Brit.* a waterproof coat or cloak. **2** cloth waterproofed with rubber. [C. *Macintosh*, Sc. inventor d. 1843, who orig. patented the cloth]

macramé /məˈkrɑːmɪ/ *n.* **1** the art of knotting cord or string in patterns to make decorative articles. **2** articles made in this way. [Turk. *makrama* bedspread f. Arab. *miḳrama*]

macro /ˈmækrəʊ/ *n.* (also **macro-instruction**) *Computing* a series of abbreviated instructions expanded automatically when required.

macro- /ˈmækrəʊ/ *comb. form* **1** long. **2** large, large-scale. [Gk *makro-* f. *makros* long, large]

macrobiotic /ˌmækrəʊbaɪˈɒtɪk/ *adj.* & *n.* —*adj.* relating to or following a diet intended to prolong life, comprising pure vegetable foods, brown rice, etc. —*n.* (in *pl.*; treated as *sing.*) the use or theory of such a dietary system.

macrocosm /ˈmækrəʊˌkɒz(ə)m/ *n.* **1** the universe. **2** the whole of a complex structure. □ **macrocosmic** /-ˈkɒzmɪk/ *adj.* **macrocosmically** /-ˈkɒzmɪkəlɪ/ *adv.*

macroeconomics /ˌmækrəʊˌiːkəˈnɒmɪks/ *n.* the study of large-scale or general economic factors, e.g. national productivity. □ **macroeconomic** *adj.*

macromolecule /ˌmækrəʊˈmɒlɪˌkjuːl/ *n. Chem.* a molecule containing a very large number of atoms. □ **macromolecular** /-məˈlekjʊlə(r)/ *adj.*

macron /ˈmækrɒn/ *n.* a written or printed mark (¯) over a long or stressed vowel. [Gk *makron* neut. of *makros* large]

macrophotography /ˌmækrəʊfəˈtɒgrəfɪ/ *n.* photography producing photographs larger than life.

macroscopic /ˌmækrəʊˈskɒpɪk/ *adj.* **1** visible to the naked eye. **2** regarded in terms of large units. □ **macroscopically** *adv.*

macula /ˈmækjʊlə/ *n.* (*pl.* **maculae** /-liː/) a dark spot, esp. a permanent one, in the skin. □ **macular** *adj.* **maculation** /-ˈleɪʃ(ə)n/ *n.* [L, = spot, mesh]

mad *adj.* & *v.* —*adj.* (**madder, maddest**) **1** insane; having a disordered mind. **2** (of a person, conduct, or an idea) wildly foolish. **3** (often foll. by *about, on*) wildly excited or infatuated (*mad about football; is chess-mad*). **4** *colloq.* angry. **5** (of an animal) rabid. **6** wildly light-hearted. —*v.* (**madded, madding**) **1** *tr. US* make angry. **2** *intr. archaic* be mad; act madly (*the madding crowd*). □ **like mad** *colloq.* with great energy, intensity, or enthusiasm. **mad cow disease** *colloq.* = BSE. **mad keen** *colloq.* extremely eager.

□ **madness** *n.* [OE *gemǣded* part. form f. *gemād* mad]

madam /ˈmædəm/ *n.* **1** a polite or respectful form of address or mode of reference to a woman. **2** *Brit. colloq.* a conceited or precocious girl or young woman. **3** a woman brothel-keeper. [ME f. OF *ma dame* my lady]

Madame /məˈdɑːm, ˈmædəm/ *n.* (*pl.* **Mesdames** /meɪˈdɑːm, -ˈdæm/) a title or form of address used of or to a French-speaking woman, corresponding to Mrs or madam. **2** (**madame**) = MADAM 1. [F (as MADAM)]

madcap /ˈmædkæp/ *adj.* & *n.* —*adj.* **1** wildly impulsive. **2** undertaken without forethought. —*n.* a wildly impulsive person.

madden /ˈmæd(ə)n/ *v.* **1** *tr.* & *intr.* make or become mad. **2** *tr.* irritate intensely. □ **maddening** *adj.* **maddeningly** *adv.*

madder /ˈmædə(r)/ *n.* **1** a herbaceous plant, *Rubia tinctorum*, with yellowish flowers. **2** a red dye obtained from the root of the madder, or its synthetic substitute. [OE *mædere*]

made 1 past and past part. of MAKE. **2** *adj.* (usu. in *comb.*) **a** (of a person or thing) built or formed (*well-made; strongly-made*). **b** successful (*a self-made man*).

Madeira /məˈdɪərə/ *n.* **1** a fortified white wine from the island of Madeira off the coast of N. Africa. **2** (in full **Madeira cake**) a kind of rich sponge cake.

madeleine /ˈmædəˌleɪn/ *n.* a small fancy sponge cake. [F]

Mademoiselle /ˌmædəmwəˈzel/ *n.* (*pl.* **Mesdemoiselles** /ˌmeɪdm-/) **1** a title or form of address used of or to an unmarried French-speaking woman, corresponding to Miss or madam. **2** (**mademoiselle**) **a** a young Frenchwoman. **b** a French governess. [F f. *ma* my + *demoiselle* DAMSEL]

madhouse /ˈmædhaʊs/ *n.* **1** *archaic* or *colloq.* a mental home or hospital. **2** *colloq.* a scene of extreme confusion or uproar.

madly /ˈmædlɪ/ *adv.* **1** in a mad manner. **2** *colloq.* **a** passionately. **b** extremely.

madman /ˈmædmən/ *n.* (*pl.* -**men**) a man who is mad.

Madonna /məˈdɒnə/ *n. Eccl.* **1** (prec. by *the*) a name for the Virgin Mary. **2** (usu. **madonna**) a picture or statue of the Madonna. [It. f. *ma* = *mia* my + *donna* lady f. L *domina*]

madras /məˈdræs/ *n.* a strong cotton fabric with coloured or white stripes, checks, etc. [*Madras* in India]

madrigal /ˈmædrɪg(ə)l/ *n.* a usu. 16th-c. or 17th-c. part-song for several voices, usu. arranged in elaborate counterpoint and without instrumental accompaniment. □ **madrigalian** /-ˈgeɪlɪən/ *adj.* **madrigalesque** /-gəˈlesk/ *adj.* **madrigalist** *n.* [It. *madrigale* f. med.L *matricalis* mother (church), formed as MATRIX]

madwoman /ˈmædˌwʊmən/ *n.* (*pl.* -**women**) a woman who is mad.

maelstrom /ˈmeɪlstrəm/ *n.* **1** a great whirlpool. **2** a state of confusion. [early mod. Du. f. *malen* grind, whirl + *stroom* STREAM]

maenad /ˈmiːnæd/ *n.* **1** a bacchante. **2** a frenzied woman. □ **maenadic** /-ˈnædɪk/ *adj.* [L *Maenas Maenad-* f. Gk *Mainas -ados* f. *mainomai* rave]

maestro /ˈmaɪstrəʊ/ *n.* (*pl.* **maestri** /-strɪ/ or -**os**) (often as a respectful form of address) **1** a distinguished musician, esp. a conductor or performer. **2** a great performer in any sphere, esp. artistic. [It., = master]

Mae West /meɪ ˈwest/ n. an inflatable life-jacket. [the name of an American film actress d. 1980, noted for her large bust]

Mafia /ˈmæfɪə, ˈmɑː-/ n. **1** an organized international body of criminals, orig. in Sicily, now also in Italy and the US. **2** (**mafia**) a group regarded as exerting a hidden sinister influence. [It. dial. (Sicilian), = bragging]

Mafioso /ˌmæfɪˈəʊsəʊ, ˌmɑː-/ n. (pl. **Mafiosi** /-sɪ/) a member of the Mafia. [It. (as MAFIA)]

mag n. colloq. a magazine (periodical). [abbr.]

magazine /ˌmægəˈziːn/ n. **1** a periodical publication containing articles, stories, etc., usu. with photographs, illustrations, etc. **2** a chamber for holding a supply of cartridges to be fed automatically to the breech of a gun. **3** a similar device feeding a camera, slide projector, etc. **4** a store for arms, ammunition, and provisions for use in war. **5** a store for explosives. [F magasin f. It. magazzino f. Arab. mak̲āzin pl. of mak̲zan storehouse f. k̲azana store up]

magenta /məˈdʒentə/ n. & adj. —n. **1** a brilliant mauvish-crimson shade. **2** an aniline dye of this colour. —adj. of or coloured with magenta. [Magenta in N. Italy, site of a battle (1859) fought shortly before the dye was discovered]

maggot /ˈmægət/ n. a larva, esp. of the cheese-fly or bluebottle. □ **maggoty** adj. [ME perh. alt. f. maddock, earlier mathek f. ON mathkr: cf. MAWKISH]

magi pl. of MAGUS.

magic /ˈmædʒɪk/ n., adj., & v. —n. **1 a** the supposed art of influencing the course of events by the occult control of nature or of the spirits. **b** witchcraft. **2** conjuring tricks. **3** an inexplicable or remarkable influence producing surprising results. **4** an enchanting quality or phenomenon. —adj. **1** of or resulting from magic. **2** producing surprising results. **3** colloq. wonderful, exciting. —v.tr. (**magicked**, **magicking**) change or create by magic, or apparently so. □ **like magic** very rapidly. **magic away** cause to disappear as if by magic. **magic carpet** a mythical carpet able to transport a person on it to any desired place. **magic eye 1** a photoelectric device used in equipment for detection, measurement, etc. **2** a small cathode-ray tube used to indicate the correct tuning of a radio receiver. **magic lantern** a simple form of image-projector using slides. **magic mushroom** a mushroom producing psilocybin. [ME f. OF magique f. L magicus adj., LL magica n., f. Gk magikos (as MAGUS)]

magical /ˈmædʒɪk(ə)l/ adj. **1** of or relating to magic. **2** resembling magic; produced as if by magic. **3** wonderful, enchanting. □ **magically** adv.

magician /məˈdʒɪʃ(ə)n/ n. **1** a person skilled in or practising magic. **2** a conjuror. **3** a person with exceptional skill. [ME f. OF magicien f. LL magica (as MAGIC)]

magisterial /ˌmædʒɪˈstɪərɪəl/ adj. **1** imperious. **2** invested with authority. **3** of or conducted by a magistrate. **4** (of a work, opinion, etc.) highly authoritative. □ **magisterially** adv. [med.L magisterialis f. LL magisterius f. L magister MASTER]

magistracy /ˈmædʒɪstrəsɪ/ n. (pl. **-ies**) **1** the office or authority of a magistrate. **2** magistrates collectively.

magistrate /ˈmædʒɪstrət, -ˌstreɪt/ n. **1** a civil officer administering the law. **2** an official conducting a court for minor cases and preliminary hearings (magistrates' court). □ **magistrateship** n. **magistrature** /-trəˌtjʊə(r)/ n. [ME f. L magistratus f. magister MASTER]

magma /ˈmægmə/ n. (pl. **magmata** /-mətə/ or **magmas**) fluid or semifluid material from which igneous rock is formed by cooling. □ **magmatic** /-ˈmætɪk/ adj. [ME, = a solid residue f. L f. Gk magma -atos f. the root of massō knead]

Magna Carta /ˌmægnə ˈkɑːtə/ n. (also **Magna Charta**) **1** a charter of liberty and political rights obtained from King John of England in 1215. **2** any similar document of rights. [med.L, = great charter]

magnanimous /mægˈnænɪməs/ adj. nobly generous; not petty in feelings or conduct. □ **magnanimity** /ˌmægnəˈnɪmɪtɪ/ n. **magnanimously** adv. [L magnanimus f. magnus great + animus soul]

magnate /ˈmægneɪt, -nɪt/ n. a wealthy and influential person, esp. in business (shipping magnate; financial magnate). [ME f. LL magnas -atis f. L magnus great]

magnesia /mægˈniːʒə, -ʃə, -zjə/ n. **1** Chem. magnesium oxide. **2** (in general use) hydrated magnesium carbonate, a white powder used as an antacid and laxative. □ **magnesian** adj. [ME f. med.L f. Gk Magnēsia (lithos) (stone) of Magnesia in Asia Minor, orig. referring to loadstone]

magnesite /ˈmægnɪˌsaɪt/ n. a white or grey mineral form of magnesium carbonate.

magnesium /mægˈniːzɪəm/ n. Chem. a silvery metallic element used for making light alloys and important as an essential element in living organisms. □ **magnesium flare** (or **light**) a blinding white light produced by burning magnesium wire.

magnet /ˈmægnɪt/ n. **1** a piece of iron, steel, alloy, ore, etc., usu. in the form of a bar or horseshoe, having properties of attracting or repelling iron. **2** a lodestone. **3** a person or thing that attracts. [ME f. L magnes magnetis f. Gk magnēs = Magnēs -ētos (lithos) (stone) of Magnesia: cf. MAGNESIA]

magnetic /mægˈnetɪk/ adj. **1 a** having the properties of a magnet. **b** producing, produced by, or acting by magnetism. **2** capable of being attracted by or acquiring the properties of a magnet. **3** very attractive or alluring (a magnetic personality). □ **magnetic field** a region of variable force around magnets, magnetic materials, or current-carrying conductors. **magnetic mine** a submarine mine detonated by the proximity of a magnetized body such as that of a ship. **magnetic needle** a piece of magnetized steel used as an indicator on the dial of a compass and in magnetic and electrical apparatus, esp. in telegraphy. **magnetic north** the point indicated by the north end of a compass needle. **magnetic pole 1** each of the points near the extremities of the axis of rotation of the earth or another body where a magnetic needle dips vertically. **2** each of the regions of an artificial or natural magnet, from which the magnetic forces appear to originate. **magnetic storm** a disturbance of the earth's magnetic field caused by charged particles from the sun etc. **magnetic tape** a tape coated with magnetic material for recording sound or pictures or for the storage of information. □ **magnetically** adv. [LL magneticus (as MAGNET)]

magnetism /ˈmægnɪˌtɪz(ə)m/ n. **1 a** magnetic phenomena and their study. **b** the property of producing these phenomena. **2** attraction; personal charm. [mod.L magnetismus (as MAGNET)]

magnetite /ˈmægnɪˌtaɪt/ n. magnetic iron oxide. [G Magnetit (as MAGNET)]

magnetize /ˈmægnɪˌtaɪz/ v.tr. (also **-ise**) **1** give magnetic properties to. **2** make into a magnet. **3** attract as or like a magnet. □ **magnetizable** adj. **magnetization** /-ˈzeɪʃ(ə)n/ n. **magnetizer** n.

magneto /mægˈniːtəʊ/ n. (pl. **-os**) an electric generator using permanent magnets and producing high voltage, esp. for the ignition of an internal-combustion engine. [abbr. of magneto-electric generator]

magnetosphere /mægˈniːtəˌsfɪə(r)/ n. the region surrounding a planet, star, etc. in which its magnetic field is effective.

magnification /ˌmægnɪfɪˈkeɪʃ(ə)n/ n. **1** the act or an instance of magnifying; the process of being magnified. **2** the amount or degree of magnification. **3** the apparent enlargement of an object by a lens.

magnificent /mægˈnɪfɪs(ə)nt/ adj. **1** splendid, stately. **2** sumptuously constructed or adorned. **3** splendidly lavish. **4** colloq. fine, excellent. □ **magnificence** n. **magnificently** adv. [F magnificent or L magnificus f. magnus great]

magnifico /mægˈnɪfɪˌkəʊ/ n. (pl. **-oes**) a magnate or grandee. [It., = MAGNIFICENT: orig. with ref. to Venice]

magnify /ˈmægnɪˌfaɪ/ v.tr. (**-ies, -ied**) **1** make (a thing) appear larger than it is, as with a lens. **2** exaggerate. **3** intensify. **4** archaic extol, glorify. □ **magnifying glass** a lens used to produce an enlarged image. □ **magnifiable** adj. **magnifier** n. [ME f. OF magnifier or L magnificare (as MAGNIFICENT)]

magnitude /ˈmægnɪˌtjuːd/ n. **1** largeness. **2** size. **3** importance. **4 a** the degree of brightness of a star. **b** a class of stars arranged according to this (of the third magnitude). □ **of the first magnitude** very important. [ME f. L magnitudo f. magnus great]

magnolia /mægˈnəʊlɪə/ n. **1** any tree or shrub of the genus Magnolia, cultivated for its dark-green foliage and large waxlike flowers in spring. **2** a pale creamy-pink colour. [mod.L f. P. Magnol, Fr. botanist d. 1715]

magnox /ˈmægnɒks/ n. any of various magnesium-based alloys used to enclose uranium fuel elements in a nuclear reactor. [magnesium no oxidation]

magnum /ˈmægnəm/ n. (pl. **magnums**) **1** a wine bottle of about twice the standard size. **2** a cartridge or shell that is especially powerful or large. [L, neut. of magnus great]

magnum opus /ˌmægnəm ˈəʊpəs/ n. **1** a great and usu. large work of art, literature, etc. **2** the most important work of an artist, writer, etc. [L, = great work: see OPUS]

magpie /ˈmægpaɪ/ n. **1 a** European and American crow, Pica pica, with a long pointed tail and black and white plumage. **2** any of various birds

with plumage like a magpie, esp. Gymnorhina tibicen of Australia. **3** an idle chatterer. **4** a person who collects things indiscriminately. [Mag, abbr. of Margaret + PIE²]

magus /ˈmeɪgəs/ n. (pl. **magi** /ˈmeɪdʒaɪ/) **1** a member of a priestly caste of ancient Persia. **2** a sorcerer. **3** (**the** (**three**) **Magi**) the 'wise men' from the East who brought gifts to the infant Christ (Matt. 2:1). [ME f. L f. Gk magos f. OPers. magus]

Magyar /ˈmægjɑː(r)/ n. & adj. —n. **1** a member of a Ural-Altaic people now predominant in Hungary. **2** the language of this people. —adj. of or relating to this people or language. [native name]

maharaja /ˌmɑːhəˈrɑːdʒə/ n. (also **maharajah**) hist. a title of some Indian princes. [Hindi mahārājā f. mahā great + RAJA]

maharanee /ˌmɑːhəˈrɑːnɪ/ n. (also **maharani**) hist. a maharaja's wife or widow. [Hindi mahārānī f. mahā great + RANEE]

maharishi /ˌmɑːhəˈrɪʃɪ/ n. a great Hindu sage or spiritual leader. [Hindi f. mahā great + RISHI]

mahatma /məˈhætmə/ n. **1 a** (in India etc.) a person regarded with reverence. **b** a sage. **2** each of a class of persons in India and Tibet supposed by some to have preternatural powers. [Skr. mahātman f. mahā great + ātman soul]

mah-jong /mɑːˈdʒɒŋ/ n. (also **mah-jongg**) a Chinese game for four resembling rummy and played with 136 or 144 pieces called tiles. [Chin. dial. ma-tsiang, lit. sparrows]

mahlstick var. of MAULSTICK.

mahogany /məˈhɒgənɪ/ n. (pl. **-ies**) **1 a** reddish-brown wood used for furniture. **b** the colour of this. **2** any tropical tree of the genus Swietenia, esp. S. mahagoni, yielding this wood. [17th c.: orig. unkn.]

mahout /məˈhaʊt/ n. (in India etc.) an elephant-driver or -keeper. [Hindi mahāut f. Skr. mahā-mātra high official, lit. 'great in measure']

maid n. **1** a female domestic servant. **2** archaic or poet. a girl or young woman. □ **maid of honour 1** an unmarried lady attending a queen or princess. **2** a kind of small custard tart. **3** esp. US a principal bridesmaid. □ **maidish** adj. [ME, abbr. of MAIDEN]

maiden /ˈmeɪd(ə)n/ n. **1 a** archaic or poet. a girl; a young unmarried woman. **b** (attrib.) unmarried (maiden aunt). **2** Cricket = maiden over. **3** (attrib.) (of a female animal) unmated. **4** (often attrib.) **a** a horse that has never won a race. **b** a race open only to such horses. **5** (attrib.) being or involving the first attempt or occurrence (maiden speech; maiden voyage). □ **maiden name** a wife's surname before marriage. **maiden over** Cricket an over in which no runs are scored off the bat. □ **maidenhood** n. **maidenish** adj. **maidenlike** adj. **maidenly** adj. [OE mægden, dimin. f. mægeth f. Gmc]

maidenhair /ˈmeɪd(ə)nˌheə(r)/ n. (in full **maidenhair fern**) a fern of the genus Adiantum, esp. A. capillus-veneris, with delicate fronds.

maidenhead /ˈmeɪd(ə)nˌhed/ n. **1** virginity. **2** the hymen.

maidservant /ˈmeɪdˌsɜːv(ə)nt/ n. a female domestic servant.

mail¹ n. & v. —n. **1 a** letters and parcels etc. conveyed by post. **b** the postal system. **c** one complete delivery or collection of mail. **d** one delivery of letters to one place, esp. to a business

on one occasion. **2** a vehicle carrying mail.
—*v.tr.* esp. *US* send (a letter etc.) by post. □ **mail
carrier** *US* a postman or postwoman. **mail
drop** *US* a receptacle for mail. **mailing list** a
list of people to whom advertising matter,
information, etc., is to be posted. **mail order**
an order for goods sent by post. **mail train** a
train carrying mail. [ME f. OF *male* wallet f. WG]

mail² *n. & v.* —*n.* armour made of rings, chains,
or plates, joined together flexibly. —*v.tr.* clothe
with or as if with mail. □ **coat of mail** a jacket
covered with mail or composed of mail. **mailed
fist** physical force. □ **mailed** *adj.* [ME f. OF
maille f. L *macula* spot, mesh]

mailable /ˈmeɪləb(ə)l/ *adj.* acceptable for conveyance by post.

mailbag /ˈmeɪlbæg/ *n.* a large sack or bag for
carrying mail.

mailbox /ˈmeɪlbɒks/ *n.* *US* a letter-box.

mailman /ˈmeɪlmən/ *n.* (*pl.* **-men**) *US* a postman.

maim *v.tr.* **1** cripple, disable, mutilate. **2** harm,
impair (*emotionally maimed by neglect*). [ME *maime*
etc. f. OF *mahaignier* etc., of unkn. orig.]

main *adj. & n.* —*adj.* **1** chief in size, importance,
extent, etc.; principal (*the main part*; *the main
point*). **2** exerted to the full (*by main force*). —*n.* **1**
a principal channel, duct, etc., for water, sewage,
etc. (*water main*). **2** (usu. in *pl.*; prec. by **the**) **a** the
central distribution network for electricity, gas,
water, etc. **b** a domestic electricity supply as
distinct from batteries. **3** *archaic* or *poet.* **a**
the ocean or oceans (*the Spanish Main*). **b** the
mainland. □ **in the main** for the most part.
main brace *Naut.* the brace attached to the
main yard. **the main chance** one's own interests. **main line 1** a chief railway line. **2** *sl.* a
principal vein, esp. as a site for a drug injection
(cf. MAINLINE). **3** *US* a chief road or street. **main
street** the principal street of a town. **main
yard** *Naut.* the yard on which the mainsail is
extended. **with might and main** with all one's
force. [ME, partly f. ON *megenn, megn* (adj.),
partly f. OE *mægen-* f. Gmc: (n.) orig. = physical
force]

mainframe /ˈmeɪnfreɪm/ *n.* **1** the central processing unit and primary memory of a
computer. **2** (often *attrib.*) a large computer
system.

mainland /ˈmeɪnlənd/ *n.* a large continuous
extent of land, excluding neighbouring islands
etc. □ **mainlander** *n.*

mainline /ˈmeɪnlaɪn/ *v.* *sl.* **1** *intr.* take drugs
intravenously. **2** *tr.* inject (drugs) intravenously.
□ **mainliner** *n.*

mainly /ˈmeɪnlɪ/ *adv.* for the most part; chiefly.

mainmast /ˈmeɪnmɑːst/ *n.* *Naut.* the principal
mast of a ship.

mainplane /ˈmeɪnpleɪn/ *n.* the principal supporting surface of an aircraft.

mainsail /ˈmeɪnseɪl, -s(ə)l/ *n.* *Naut.* **1** (in a
square-rigged vessel) the lowest sail on the
mainmast. **2** (in a fore-and-aft rigged vessel) a
sail set on the after part of the mainmast.

mainspring /ˈmeɪnsprɪŋ/ *n.* **1** the principal
spring of a mechanical watch, clock, etc. **2** a
chief motive power; an incentive.

mainstay /ˈmeɪnsteɪ/ *n.* **1** a chief support (*has
been his mainstay since his trouble*). **2** *Naut.* a stay
from the maintop to the foot of the foremast.

mainstream /ˈmeɪnstriːm/ *n.* **1** (often *attrib.*)
the prevailing trend in opinion, fashion, etc. **2** a

type of jazz based on the 1930s swing style. **3**
the principal current of a river.

maintain /meɪnˈteɪn/ *v.tr.* **1** cause to continue;
keep up, preserve (a state of affairs, an activity,
etc.) (*maintained friendly relations*). **2** (often foll.
by *in*; often *refl.*) support (life, a condition,
etc.) by work, nourishment, expenditure, etc.
(*maintained him in comfort*; *maintained themselves
by fishing*). **3** (often foll. by *that* + clause) assert
(an opinion, statement, etc.) as true (*maintained
that she was the best*; *his story was true, he
maintained*). **4** preserve or provide for the preservation of (a building, machine, road, etc.) in
good repair. **5** give aid to (a cause, party, etc.). **6**
provide means for (a garrison etc. to be
equipped). □ **maintained school** *Brit.* a school
supported from public funds. □ **maintainable**
adj. **maintainability** /-ˈbɪlɪtɪ/ *n.* [ME f. OF
maintenir ult. f. L *manu tenēre* hold in the hand]

maintenance /ˈmeɪntənəns/ *n.* **1** the process of
maintaining or being maintained. **2 a** the
provision of the means to support life, esp. by
work etc. **b** (also **separate maintenance**) a
husband's or wife's provision for a spouse after
separation or divorce; alimony. [ME f. OF f.
maintenir: see MAINTAIN]

maintop /ˈmeɪntɒp/ *n.* *Naut.* a platform above
the head of the lower mainmast.

maisonette /ˌmeɪzəˈnet/ *n.* (also **maisonnette**)
1 a part of a house, block of flats, etc., forming
separate living accommodation, usu. on two
floors and having a separate entrance. **2** a small
house. [F *maisonnette* dimin. of *maison* house]

maître d'hôtel /ˌmetrə dəʊˈtel, ˌmeɪt-/ *n.* **1** the
manager, head steward, etc., of a hotel. **2** a head
waiter. [F, = master of (the) house]

maize /meɪz/ *n.* a cereal plant, *Zea mays*, native
to N. America, yielding large grains set in rows
on a cob. [F *maïs* or Sp. *maíz*, of Carib orig.]

Maj. *abbr.* Major.

majestic /məˈdʒestɪk/ *adj.* showing majesty;
stately and dignified; grand, imposing. □
majestically *adv.*

majesty /ˈmædʒɪstɪ/ *n.* (*pl.* **-ies**) **1** impressive
stateliness, dignity, or authority, esp. of bearing,
language, the law, etc. **2 a** royal power. **b**
(**Majesty**) part of several titles given to a
sovereign or a sovereign's wife or widow or
used in addressing them (*Your Majesty*; *Her
Majesty the Queen Mother*). [ME f. OF *majesté* f. L
majestas -tatis (as MAJOR)]

majolica /məˈjɒlɪkə, məˈdʒɒl-/ *n.* (also **maiolica**
/məˈjɒl-/) a 19th-c. trade name for earthenware
with coloured decoration on an opaque white
glaze. [alt. f. It. *Maiolica*, f. former name of
Majorca.]

major /ˈmeɪdʒə(r)/ *adj., n., & v.* —*adj.* **1** important, large, serious, significant (*a major road*; *the
major consideration must be their health*). **2** (of an
operation) serious or life-threatening. **3** *Mus.* **a**
(of a scale) having intervals of a semitone
between the third and fourth, and seventh and
eighth degrees. **b** (of an interval) greater by a
semitone than a minor interval (*major third*). **c**
(of a key) based on a major scale. **4** of full age. **5**
Brit. (appended to a surname, esp. in public
schools) the elder of two brothers or the first to
enter the school (*Smith major*). —*n.* **1** *Mil.* **a** an
army officer next below lieutenant-colonel and
above captain. **b** an officer in charge of a section
of band instruments (*drum major*; *pipe major*). **2**

a person of full age. **3** *US* **a** a student's special subject or course. **b** a student specializing in a specified subject (*a philosophy major*). —*v.intr.* (foll. by *in*) *US* study or qualify in a subject (*majored in theology*). □ **major-general** an officer next below a lieutenant-general. **major league** *US* a league of major importance in baseball etc. □ **majorship** *n.* [ME f. L, compar. of *magnus* great]

major-domo /ˌmeɪdʒəˈdəʊməʊ/ *n.* (pl. **-os**) **1** the chief official of an Italian or Spanish princely household. **2** a house-steward; a butler. [orig. *mayordome* f. Sp. *mayordomo*, It. *maggiordomo* f. med.L *major domus* highest official of the household (as MAJOR, DOME)]

majority /məˈdʒɒrɪtɪ/ *n.* (pl. **-ies**) **1** (usu. foll. by *of*) the greater number or part. **2** *Polit.* **a** the number by which the votes cast for one party, candidate, etc. exceed those of the next in rank (*won by a majority of 151*). **b** a party etc. receiving the greater number of votes. **3** full legal age (*attained his majority*). **4** the rank of major. □ **majority rule** the principle that the greater number should exercise greater power. **majority verdict** a verdict given by more than half of the jury, but not unanimous. [F *majorité* f. med.L *majoritas -tatis* (as MAJOR)]

■ **Usage** In sense 1, this word is strictly used only with countable nouns, e.g. *the majority of people*, but not *the majority of the work*.

make *v.* & *n.* —*v.* (*past* and *past part.* **made** /meɪd/) **1** *tr.* construct; create; form from parts or other substances (*made a table; made it out of cardboard; made him a sweater*). **2** *tr.* (foll. by *to* + infin.) cause or compel (a person etc.) to do something (*make him repeat it; was made to confess*). **3** *tr.* **a** cause to exist; create; bring about (*made a noise; made an enemy*). **b** cause to become or seem (*made an exhibition of myself; made him angry*). **c** appoint; designate (*made him a Cardinal*). **4** *tr.* compose; prepare; draw up (*made her will; made a film about Japan*). **5** *tr.* constitute; amount to (*makes a difference; 2 and 2 make 4; this makes the tenth time*). **6** *tr.* **a** undertake or agree to (an aim or purpose) (*made a promise; make an effort*). **b** execute or perform (a bodily movement, a speech, etc.) (*made a face; made a bow*). **7** *tr.* gain; acquire, procure (money, a profit, etc.) (*made £20,000 on the deal*). **8** *tr.* prepare (tea, coffee, a dish, etc.) for consumption (*made egg and chips*). **9** *tr.* **a** arrange bedclothes tidily on (a bed) ready for use. **b** arrange and light materials for (a fire). **10** *intr.* **a** proceed (*made towards the river*). **b** (foll. by *to* + infin.) begin an action (*he made to go*). **11** *tr.* *colloq.* **a** arrive at (a place) or in time for (a train etc.) (*made the border before dark; made the six o'clock train*). **b** manage to attend; manage to attend on (a certain day) or at (a certain time) (*couldn't make the meeting last week*). **c** achieve a place in (*made the first eleven; made the six o'clock news*). **d** *US* achieve the rank of (*made colonel in three years*). **12** *tr.* establish or enact (a distinction, rule, law, etc.). **13** *tr.* consider to be; estimate as (*what do you make the time?*). **14** *tr.* secure the success or advancement of (*his mother made him; it made my day*). **15** *tr.* accomplish (a distance, speed, score, etc.) (*made 60 m.p.h. on the motorway*). **16** *tr.* **a** become by development or training (*made a great leader*). **b** serve as (*a log makes a useful seat*). **17** *tr.* (usu. foll. by *out*) represent as; cause to appear as (*makes him out a liar*). **18** *tr.*

form in the mind; feel (*I make no judgement*). **19** *tr.* (foll. by *it* + compl.) **a** determine, establish, or choose (*let's make it Tuesday; made it my business to know*). **b** bring to (a chosen value etc.) (*decided to make it a dozen*). **20** *tr.* *sl.* have sexual relations with. **21** *tr.* *Cards* **a** win (a trick). **b** win the number of tricks that fulfils (a contract). —*n.* **1** (esp. of a product) a type, origin, brand, etc. of manufacture (*different make of car; our own make*). **2** a kind of mental, moral, or physical structure or composition. □ **be made for** be ideally suited to. **be made of** consist of. **have it made** *colloq.* be sure of success. **made of money** *colloq.* very rich. **made road** a properly surfaced road of tarmac, concrete, etc. **made to measure** (of a suit etc.) made to a specific customer's measurements. **make as if** (or **though**) (foll. by *to* + infin. or conditional) act as if the specified circumstances applied (*made as if to leave; made as if he would hit me; made as if I had not noticed*). **make away** (or **off**) depart hastily. **make away with 1** get rid of; kill. **2** squander. **make-believe** (or **-belief**) **1** pretence. **2** pretended. **make believe** pretend. **make conversation** talk politely. **make a day** (or **night** etc.) **of it** devote a whole day (or night etc.) to an activity. **make do 1** manage with the limited or inadequate means available. **2** (foll. by *with*) manage with (something) as an inferior substitute. **make an example of** punish as a warning to others. **make for 1** tend to result in (happiness etc.). **2** proceed towards (a place). **3** assault; attack. **4** confirm (an opinion). **make friends** (often foll. by *with*) become friendly. **make it** *colloq.* **1** succeed in reaching, esp. in time. **2** be successful. **3** (usu. foll. by *with*) *sl.* have sexual intercourse (with). **make it up 1** be reconciled, esp. after a quarrel. **2** fill in a deficit. **make it up to** remedy negligence, an injury, etc. to (a person). **make money** acquire wealth or an income. **make much** (or **little** or **the best**) **of 1** derive much (or little etc.) advantage from. **2** give much (or little etc.) attention, importance, etc., to. **make nothing of 1** do without hesitation. **2** treat as a trifle. **3** be unable to understand, use, or deal with. **make of 1** construct from. **2** conclude to be the meaning or character of (*can you make anything of it?*). **make off** = *make away*. **make off with** carry away; steal. **make or break** (or **mar**) cause the success or ruin of. **make out 1 a** distinguish by sight or hearing. **b** decipher (handwriting etc.). **2** understand (*can't make him out*). **3** assert; pretend (*made out he liked it*). **4** *colloq.* make progress; fare (*how did you make out?*). **5** (usu. foll. by *to*, *in favour of*) draw up; write out (*made out a cheque to her*). **6** prove or try to prove (*how do you make that out?*). **make over 1** transfer the possession of (a thing) to a person. **2** refashion (a garment etc.). **make time** (usu. foll. by *for* or *to* + infin.) find an occasion when time is available. **make-up 1** cosmetics for the face etc., either generally or to create an actor's appearance or disguise. **2** the appearance of the face etc. when cosmetics have been applied (*his make-up was not convincing*). **3** a person's character, temperament, etc. **4** the composition or constitution (of a thing). **make up 1** serve or act to overcome (a deficiency). **2** complete (an amount, a party, etc.). **3** compensate. **4** be reconciled. **5** put together; compound; prepare (*made up the medicine*). **6** sew (parts of a garment etc.) together. **7** get (a sum of money, a company, etc.) together. **8** concoct (a story). **9** (of parts) compose (a whole). **10 a** apply cosmetics. **b** apply cosmetics to. **11** settle (a dispute). **12** prepare (a bed) for use with fresh sheets etc. **13** compile (a list, an account, a document, etc.). **make up one's mind** decide, resolve. **make up to** curry favour with; court. **make water 1** urinate. **2** (of a ship) take in water. **make way 1** (often foll. by *for*) allow room for others to proceed. **2** achieve progress. **make one's way** proceed. **make with** *US colloq.* supply; perform; proceed with (*made with the feet and left in a hurry*). **on the make** *colloq.* **1** intent on gain. **2** looking for sexual partners. **self-made man** etc. a man etc. who has succeeded by his own efforts. □ **makable** *adj.* [OE *macian* f. WG: rel. to MATCH¹]

makeover /ˈmeɪkəʊvə(r)/ n. a complete transformation or remodelling.

maker /ˈmeɪkə(r)/ n. **1** (often in *comb.*) a person or thing that makes. **2** (**our, the,** etc. **Maker**) God.

makeshift /ˈmeɪkʃɪft/ *adj. & n.* —*adj.* temporary; serving for the time being (*a makeshift arrangement*). —*n.* a temporary substitute or device.

makeweight /ˈmeɪkweɪt/ n. **1** a small quantity or thing added to make up the full weight. **2** an unimportant extra person. **3** an unimportant point added to make an argument seem stronger.

making /ˈmeɪkɪŋ/ n. **1** in senses of MAKE *v.* **2** (in *pl.*) **a** earnings; profit. **b** (foll. by *of*) essential qualities or ingredients (*has the makings of a general; we have the makings of a meal*). **c** *US & Austral. colloq.* paper and tobacco for rolling a cigarette. □ **be the making of** ensure the success or favourable development of. **in the making** in the course of being made or formed. [OE *macung* (as MAKE)]

mal- /mæl/ *comb. form* **1 a** bad, badly (*malpractice; maltreat*). **b** faulty, faultily (*malfunction*). **2** not (*maladroit*). [F *mal* badly f. L *male*]

malacca /məˈlækə/ n. (in full **malacca cane**) a rich-brown cane from the stem of the palm-tree *Calamus scipionum*, used for walking-sticks etc. [*Malacca* in Malaysia]

malachite /ˈmæləkaɪt/ n. a bright-green mineral of hydrous copper carbonate, taking a high polish and used for ornament. [OF *melochite* f. L *molochites* f. Gk *molokhitis* f. *molokhē* = *malakhē* mallow]

maladaptive /ˌmæləˈdæptɪv/ *adj.* (of an individual, species, etc.) failing to adjust adequately to the environment, and undergoing emotional, behavioural, physical, or mental repercussions. □ **maladaptation** /ˌmælædæpˈteɪʃ(ə)n/ n.

maladjusted /ˌmæləˈdʒʌstɪd/ *adj.* **1** not correctly adjusted. **2** (of a person) unable to adapt to or cope with the demands of a social environment. □ **maladjustment** n.

maladminister /ˌmælədˈmɪnɪstə(r)/ *v.tr.* manage or administer inefficiently, badly, or dishonestly. □ **maladministration** /-ˈstreɪʃ(ə)n/ n.

maladroit /ˌmælədˈrɔɪt, ˈmæl-/ *adj.* clumsy; bungling. □ **maladroitly** *adv.* **maladroitness** n. [F (as MAL-, ADROIT)]

malady /ˈmælədɪ/ n. (pl. **-ies**) **1** an ailment; a disease. **2** a morbid or depraved condition; something requiring a remedy. [ME f. OF *maladie* f. *malade* sick ult. f. L *male* ill + *habitus* past part. of *habēre* have]

malaise /məˈleɪz/ n. **1** a nonspecific bodily discomfort not associated with the development of a disease. **2** a feeling of uneasiness. [F f. OF *mal* bad + *aise* EASE]

malapropism /ˈmæləprɒˌpɪz(ə)m/ n. (also **malaprop** /ˈmæləˌprɒp/) the use of a word in mistake for one sounding similar, to comic effect, e.g. *allegory* for *alligator*. [Mrs *Malaprop* (f. MALAPROPOS) in Sheridan's *The Rivals* (1775)]

malapropos /ˌmæræprəˈpəʊ/ *adv., adj.,* & n. —*adv.* inopportunely; inappropriately. —*adj.* inopportune; inappropriate. —n. something inappropriately said, done, etc. [F *mal à propos* f. *mal* ill: see APROPOS]

malaria /məˈleərɪə/ n. an intermittent and remittent fever caused by a protozoan parasite of the genus *Plasmodium*, introduced by the bite of a mosquito. □ **malarial** *adj.* **malarian** *adj.* **malarious** *adj.* [It. *mal'aria* bad air]

malarkey /məˈlɑːkɪ/ n. *colloq.* humbug; nonsense. [20th c.: orig. unkn.]

malathion /ˌmæləˈθaɪɒn/ n. an insecticide containing phosphorus, with low toxicity to plants. [diethyl *maleate* + *thio-* acid + -ON]

Malay /məˈleɪ/ n. & *adj.* —n. **1 a** a member of a people predominating in Malaysia and Indonesia. **b** a person of Malay descent. **2** the language of this people, the official language of Malaysia. —*adj.* of or relating to this people or language. □ **Malayan** n. & *adj.* [Malay *malāyu*]

malcontent /ˈmælkənˌtent/ n. & *adj.* —n. a discontented person; a rebel. —*adj.* discontented or rebellious. [F (as MAL-, CONTENT¹)]

male *adj.* & n. —*adj.* **1** of the sex that can beget offspring by fertilization or insemination (*male child; male dog*). **2** of men or male animals, plants, etc.; masculine (*the male sex; a male-voice choir*). **3** (of plants or their parts) containing only fertilizing organs. **4** (of parts of machinery etc.) designed to enter or fill the corresponding female part (*a male screw*). —n. a male person or animal. □ **male chauvinist** a man who is prejudiced against women or regards women as inferior. **male menopause** a crisis of potency, confidence, etc., supposed to afflict men in middle life. □ **maleness** n. [ME f. OF *ma(s)le*, f. L *masculus* f. *mas* a male]

malediction /ˌmælɪˈdɪkʃ(ə)n/ n. **1** a curse. **2** the utterance of a curse. □ **maledictive** *adj.* **maledictory** *adj.* [ME f. L *maledictio* f. *maledicere* speak evil of f. *male* ill + *dicere dict-* speak]

malefactor /ˈmælɪˌfæktə(r)/ n. a criminal; an evil-doer. □ **malefaction** /-ˈfækʃ(ə)n/ n. [ME f. L *malefacere malefact-* f. *male* ill + *facere* do]

malevolent /məˈlevələnt/ *adj.* wishing evil to others. □ **malevolence** n. **malevolently** *adv.* [OF *malivolent* or f. L *malevolens* f. *male* ill + *volens* willing, part. of *velle*]

malfeasance /mælˈfiːz(ə)ns/ n. *Law* evil-doing. □ **malfeasant** n. & *adj.* [AF *malfaisance* f. OF *malfaisant* (as MAL-, *faisant* part. of *faire* do f. L *facere*)]

malformation /ˌmælfɔːˈmeɪʃ(ə)n/ n. faulty formation. □ **malformed** /-ˈfɔːmd/ *adj.*

malfunction /mælˈfʌŋkʃ(ə)n/ n. & v. —n. a failure to function in a normal or satisfactory manner. —*v.intr.* fail to function normally or satisfactorily.

malice /ˈmælɪs/ n. **1 a** the intention to do evil. **b** a desire to tease, esp. cruelly. **2** *Law* wrongful intention, esp. as increasing the guilt of certain offences. □ **malice aforethought** (or **prepense**) *Law* the intention to commit a crime, esp. murder. [ME f. OF f. L *malitia* f. *malus* bad]

malicious /məˈlɪʃəs/ *adj.* characterized by malice; intending or intended to do harm. □ **maliciously** *adv.* **maliciousness** *n.* [OF *malicius* f. L *malitiosus* (as MALICE)]

malign /məˈlaɪn/ *adj.* & *v.* —*adj.* **1** (of a thing) injurious. **2** (of a disease) malignant. **3** malevolent. —*v.tr.* speak ill of; slander. □ **maligner** *n.* **malignity** /məˈlɪgnɪtɪ/ *n.* (*pl.* -**ies**). **malignly** *adv.* [ME f. OF *malin maligne*, *malignier* f. LL *malignare* contrive maliciously f. L *malignus* f. *malus* bad: cf. BENIGN]

malignant /məˈlɪgnənt/ *adj.* **1 a** (of a disease) very virulent or infectious (*malignant cholera*). **b** (of a tumour) tending to invade normal tissue and recur after removal; cancerous. **2** harmful; feeling or showing intense ill will. □ **malignancy** *n.* (*pl.* -**ies**). **malignantly** *adv.* [LL *malignare* (as MALIGN)]

malinger /məˈlɪŋgə(r)/ *v.intr.* exaggerate or feign illness in order to escape duty, work, etc. □ **malingerer** *n.* [back-form. f. *malingerer* app. f. F *malingre*, perh. formed as MAL- + *haingre* weak]

mall /mæl, mɔːl/ *n.* **1** a sheltered walk or promenade. **2** an enclosed shopping precinct. [var. of MAUL: applied to *The Mall* in London]

mallard /ˈmælɑːd/ *n.* (*pl.* same or **mallards**) a wild duck or drake, *Anas platyrhynchos*, of the northern hemisphere. [ME f. OF prob. f. *maslart* (unrecorded, as MALE)]

malleable /ˈmælɪəb(ə)l/ *adj.* **1** (of metal etc.) able to be hammered or pressed permanently out of shape without breaking or cracking. **2** adaptable; pliable, flexible. □ **malleability** /-ˈbɪlɪtɪ/ *n.* **malleably** *adv.* [ME f. OF f. med.L *malleabilis* f. L *malleare* to hammer f. *malleus* hammer]

mallet /ˈmælɪt/ *n.* **1** a hammer, usu. of wood. **2** a long-handled wooden hammer for striking a croquet or polo ball. [ME f. OF *maillet* f. *mailler* to hammer f. *mail* hammer f. L *malleus*]

mallow /ˈmæləʊ/ *n.* **1** any plant of the genus *Malva*, esp. *M. sylvestris*, with hairy stems and leaves and pink or purple flowers. **2** any of several other plants of the family Malvaceae, including marsh mallow. [OE *meal(u)we* f. L *malva*]

malmsey /ˈmɑːmzɪ/ *n.* a strong sweet wine orig. from Greece, now chiefly from Madeira. [ME f. MDu., MLG *malmesie*, -*eye*, f. *Monemvasia* in S. Greece]

malnourished /mælˈnʌrɪʃt/ *adj.* suffering from malnutrition. □ **malnourishment** *n.*

malnourishment /mælˈnʌrɪʃmənt/ *n.* = MALNUTRITION.

malnutrition /ˌmælnjuːˈtrɪʃ(ə)n/ *n.* a dietary condition resulting from the absence of some foods or essential elements necessary for health; insufficient nutrition.

malodorous /mælˈəʊdərəs/ *adj.* evil-smelling.

malpractice /mælˈpræktɪs/ *n.* **1** improper or negligent professional treatment, esp. by a medical practitioner. **2 a** criminal wrongdoing; misconduct. **b** an instance of this.

malt /mɔːlt, mɒlt/ *n.* & *v.* —*n.* **1** barley or other grain that is steeped, germinated, and dried, esp. for brewing or distilling and vinegar-making. **2** *colloq.* malt whisky; malt liquor. —*v.* **1** *tr.* convert (grain) into malt. **2** *intr.* (of seeds) become malt when germination is checked by drought. □

malted milk 1 a hot drink made from dried milk and a malt preparation. **2** the powdered mixture from which this is made. **malt-house** a building used for preparing and storing malt.

malt liquor alcoholic liquor made from malt by fermentation, not distillation, e.g. beer, stout.

malt whisky whisky made from malted barley. [OE *m(e)alt* f. Gmc, rel. to MELT]

Maltese /mɔːlˈtiːz, mɒl-/ *n.* & *adj.* —*n.* **1** (*pl.* same) **a** a native or national of Malta, an island in the W. Mediterranean. **b** a person of Maltese descent. **2** the language of Malta. —*adj.* of or relating to Malta or its people or language. □ **Maltese cross** a cross with arms of equal length broadening from the centre, often indented at the ends.

Malthusian /mælˈθjuːzɪən/ *adj.* & *n.* —*adj.* of or relating to T. R. Malthus, English clergyman and economist (d. 1834) or his theories, esp. that sexual restraint should be exercised as a means of preventing an increase of the population beyond its means of subsistence. —*n.* a follower of Malthus. □ **Malthusianism** *n.*

malting /ˈmɔːltɪŋ, ˈmɒl-/ *n.* **1** the process or an instance of brewing or distilling with malt. **2** = *malt-house*.

maltreat /mælˈtriːt/ *v.tr.* ill-treat. □ **maltreater** *n.* **maltreatment** *n.* [F *maltraiter* (as MAL-, TREAT)]

malty /ˈmɔːltɪ, ˈmɒl-/ *adj.* (**maltier, maltiest**) of, containing, or resembling malt. □ **maltiness** *n.*

malversation /ˌmælvəˈseɪʃ(ə)n/ *n.* *formal* **1** corrupt behaviour in a position of trust. **2** (often foll. by *of*) corrupt administration (of public money etc.). [F f. *malverser* f. L *male* badly + *versari* behave]

mam *n.* *colloq.* mother. [formed as MAMA]

mama /ˈmæmə, məˈmɑː/ *n.* *colloq.* (esp. as a child's term) = MAMMA.

mamba /ˈmæmbə/ *n.* any venomous African snake of the genus *Dendroaspis*, esp. the green mamba (*D. angusticeps*) or black mamba (*D. polylepis*). [Zulu *imamba*]

mambo /ˈmæmbəʊ/ *n.* & *v.* —*n.* (*pl.* -**os**) **1** a Latin American dance like the rumba. **2** the music for this. —*v.intr.* (-**oes, -oed**) perform the mambo. [Amer. Sp. prob. f. Haitian]

mamma[1] /ˈmæmə/ *n.* (also **momma** /ˈmɒmə/) *colloq.* (esp. as a child's term) mother. [imit. of child's *ma*, *ma*]

mamma[2] /ˈmæmə/ *n.* (*pl.* **mammae** /-miː/) **1** a milk-secreting organ of female mammals. **2** a corresponding non-secretory structure in male mammals. □ **mammiform** *adj.* [OE f. L]

mammal /ˈmæm(ə)l/ *n.* any vertebrate of the class Mammalia, the females of which possess milk-secreting mammae for the nourishment of the young, and including human beings, dogs, whales, etc. □ **mammalian** /-ˈmeɪlɪən/ *adj.* & *n.* **mammalogy** /-ˈmælədʒɪ/ *n.* [mod.L *mammalia* neut. pl. of L *mammalis* (as MAMMA[2])]

mammary /ˈmæmərɪ/ *adj.* of the human female breasts or milk-secreting organs of other mammals. □ **mammary gland** the milk-producing gland of female mammals. [MAMMA[2] + -ARY[1]]

mammography /mæˈmɒgrəfɪ/ *n.* *Med.* an X-ray technique of diagnosing and locating abnormalities (esp. tumours) of the breasts. [MAMMA[2] + -GRAPHY]

Mammon /ˈmæmən/ n. **1** wealth regarded as a god or as an evil influence. **2** the worldly rich. □ **Mammonish** adj. **Mammonism** n. **Mammonist** n. **Mammonite** n. [ME f. LL Mam(m)ona f. Gk mamōnas f. Aram. māmōn riches: see Matt. 6:24, Luke 16:9–13]

mammoth /ˈmæməθ/ n. & adj. —n. any large extinct elephant of the genus Mammuthus, with a hairy coat and curved tusks. —adj. huge. [Russ. mamo(n)t]

mammy /ˈmæmɪ/ n. (pl. -ies) **1** a child's word for mother. **2** US a Black nursemaid or nanny in charge of White children. [formed as MAMMA¹]

man n. & v. —n. (pl. **men** /men/) **1** an adult human male, esp. as distinct from a woman or boy. **2 a** a human being; a person (no man is perfect). **b** human beings in general; the human race (man is mortal). **3 a** a worker; an employee (the manager spoke to the men). **b** a manservant or valet. **4** a (usu. in pl.) soldiers, sailors, etc., esp. non-officers (was in command of 200 men). **b** an individual, usu. male, person (fought to the last man). **c** (usu. prec. by the, or poss. pron.) a person regarded as suitable or appropriate in some way; a person fulfilling requirements (I'm your man; not the man for the job). **5 a** a husband (man and wife). **b** colloq. a boyfriend or lover. **6 a** a human being of a specified historical period or character (Renaissance man). **b** a type of prehistoric man named after the place where the remains were found (Peking man; Piltdown man). **7** any one of a set of pieces used in playing chess, draughts, etc. **8** (as second element in comb.) a man of a specified nationality, profession, skill, etc. (Dutchman; clergyman; horseman; gentleman). **9 a** an expression of impatience etc. used in addressing a male (nonsense, man!). **b** colloq. a general mode of address among hippies etc. (blew my mind, man!). **10** (prec. by a) a person; one (what can a man do?). **11** a person pursued; an opponent etc. (the police have so far not caught their man). **12** (**the Man**) US sl. **a** the police. **b** Black sl. White people. —v.tr. (**manned, manning**) **1** supply (a ship, fort, factory, etc.) with a person or people for work or defence etc. **2** work or service or defend (a specified piece of equipment, a fortification, etc.) (man the pumps). □ **as one man** in unison; in agreement. **be a man** be courageous; not show fear. **be one's own man 1** be free to act; be independent. **2** be in full possession of one's faculties etc. **man about town** a fashionable man of leisure. **man and boy** from childhood. **man-hour** (or **day** etc.) an hour (or day etc.) regarded in terms of the amount of work that could be done by one person within this period. **man in** (US **on**) **the street** an ordinary average person, as distinct from an expert. **man-made** (esp. of a textile fibre) made by man, artificial, synthetic. **man of God** a clergyman. **man of honour** a man whose word can be trusted. **man of the house** the male head of a household. **man of letters** a scholar; an author. **man of the moment** a man of importance at a particular time. **man of straw 1** an insubstantial person; an imaginary person set up as an opponent. **2** a stuffed effigy. **3** a sham argument set up to be defeated. **man-of-war** an armed ship, esp. of a specified country. **man-size** (or **-sized**) **1** of the size of a man; very large. **2** big enough for a man. **man to man** with candour; honestly. **men's** (or

men's room) a usu. public lavatory for men. **to a man** all without exception. □ **manless** adj. [OE man(n), pl. menn, mannian, f. Gmc]

manacle /ˈmænək(ə)l/ n. & v. —n. (usu. in pl.) **1** a fetter or shackle for the hand; a handcuff. **2** a restraint. —v.tr. fetter with manacles. [ME f. OF manicle handcuff f. L manicula dimin. of manus hand]

manage /ˈmænɪdʒ/ v. **1** tr. organize; regulate; be in charge of (a business, household, team, a person's career, etc.). **2** tr. (often foll. by to + infin.) succeed in achieving; contrive (managed to arrive on time; managed a smile). **3** intr. **a** (often foll. by with) succeed in one's aim, esp. against heavy odds (managed with one assistant). **b** meet one's needs with limited resources etc. (just about manages on a pension). **4** tr. gain influence with or maintain control over (a person etc.) (cannot manage their teenage son). **5** tr. (also absol.; often prec. by can, be able to) **a** cope with; make use of (couldn't manage another bite). **b** be free to attend on (a certain day) or at (a certain time) (can you manage Thursday?). **6** tr. handle or wield (a tool, weapon, etc.). **7** tr. take or have charge or control of (an animal or animals, esp. cattle). [It. maneggiare, maneggio ult. f. L manus hand]

manageable /ˈmænɪdʒəb(ə)l/ adj. able to be easily managed, controlled, or accomplished etc. □ **manageability** /-ˈbɪlɪtɪ/ n. **manageableness** n. **manageably** adv.

management /ˈmænɪdʒmənt/ n. **1** the process or an instance of managing or being managed. **2 a** the professional administration of business concerns, public undertakings, etc. **b** the people engaged in this. **c** (prec. by the) a governing body; a board of directors or the people in charge of running a business, regarded collectively. **3** (usu. foll. by of) Med. the technique of treating a disease etc.

manager /ˈmænɪdʒə(r)/ n. **1** a person controlling or administering a business or part of a business. **2** a person controlling the affairs, training, etc. of a person or team in sports, entertainment, etc. **3** Brit. Parl. a member of either House of Parliament appointed with others for some duty in which both Houses are concerned. **4** a person regarded in terms of skill in household or financial or other management (a good manager). □ **managerial** /ˌmænɪˈdʒɪərɪəl/ adj. **managerially** /-ˈdʒɪərɪəlɪ/ adv. **managership** n.

manageress /ˌmænɪdʒəˈres/ n. a woman manager, esp. of a shop, hotel, theatre, etc.

managing /ˈmænɪdʒɪŋ/ adj. **1** (in comb.) having executive control or authority (managing director). **2** (attrib.) fond of controlling affairs etc.

mañana /mænˈjɑːnə/ adv. & n. —adv. in the indefinite future (esp. to indicate procrastination). —n. an indefinite future time. [Sp., = tomorrow]

manatee /ˌmænəˈtiː/ n. any large aquatic plant-eating mammal of the genus Trichechus, with paddle-like forelimbs, no hind limbs, and a powerful tail. [Sp. manati f. Carib manattoui]

Mancunian /mænˈkjuːnɪən/ n. & adj. —n. a native of Manchester in NW England. —adj. of or relating to Manchester. [L Mancunium Manchester]

-mancy /mænsɪ/ comb. form forming nouns meaning 'divination by' (geomancy; necromancy).

□ **-mantic** *comb. form* forming adjectives. [OF *-mancie* f. LL *-mantia* f. Gk *manteia* divination]

mandala /ˈmændələ/ *n.* a symbolic circular figure representing the universe in various religions. [Skr. *māṇḍala* disc]

mandamus /mænˈdeɪməs/ *n. Law* a judicial writ issued as a command to an inferior court, or ordering a person to perform a public or statutory duty. [L, = we command]

mandarin[1] /ˈmændərɪn/ *n.* **1** (**Mandarin**) the most widely spoken form of Chinese and the official language of China. **2** *hist.* a Chinese official in any of nine grades of the pre-Communist civil service. **3 a** a party leader; a bureaucrat. **b** a powerful member of the establishment. □ **mandarin collar** a small close-fitting upright collar. **mandarin duck** a small Chinese duck, *Aix galericulata*, noted for its bright plumage. **mandarin sleeve** a wide loose sleeve. □ **mandarinate** *n.* [Port. *mandarim* f. Malay f. Hindi *mantrī* f. Skr. *mantrin* counsellor]

mandarin[2] /ˈmændərɪn/ *n.* (also **mandarine** /-ˌriːn/) (in full **mandarin orange**) **1** a small flattish deep-coloured orange with a loose skin. **2** the tree, *Citrus reticulata*, yielding this. [F *mandarine* (perh. as MANDARIN[1], with ref. to the official's yellow robes)]

mandate /ˈmændeɪt/ *n. & v.* —*n.* **1** an official command or instruction by an authority. **2** support for a policy or course of action, regarded by a victorious party, candidate, etc., as derived from the wishes of the people in an election. **3** a commission to act for another. —*v.tr.*instruct (a delegate) to act or vote in a certain way. □ **mandator** *n.* [L *mandatum*, neut. past part. of *mandare* command f. *manus* hand + *dare* give: sense 2 of n. after F *mandat*]

mandatory /ˈmændətərɪ/ *adj.* **1** of or conveying a command. **2** compulsory. □ **mandatorily** *adv.* [LL *mandatorius* f. L (as MANDATE)]

mandible /ˈmændɪb(ə)l/ *n.* **1** the jaw, esp. the lower jaw in mammals and fishes. **2** the upper or lower part of a bird's beak. **3** either half of the crushing organ in an arthropod's mouthparts. □ **mandibular** /-ˈdɪbjʊlə(r)/ *adj.* **mandibulate** /-ˈdɪbjʊlət/ *adj.* [ME f. OF *mandible* or LL *mandibula* f. *mandere* chew]

mandolin /ˌmændəˈlɪn/ *n.* (also **mandoline**) a musical instrument resembling a lute, having paired metal strings plucked with a plectrum. □ **mandolinist** *n.* [F *mandoline* f. It. *mandolino* dimin. of MANDOLA]

mandragora /mænˈdrægərə/ *n. hist.* the mandrake, esp. as a type of narcotic (Shakesp. *Othello* III. iii. 334). [OE f. med.L f. L f. Gk *mandragoras*]

mandrake /ˈmændreɪk/ *n.* a poisonous plant, *Mandragora officinarum*, having emetic and narcotic properties and possessing a root once thought to resemble the human form and to shriek when plucked. [ME *mandrag(g)e*, prob. f. MDu. *mandrag(r)e* f. med.L (as MANDRAGORA): assoc. with MAN + *drake* dragon (cf. DRAKE[1])]

mandrill /ˈmændrɪl/ *n.* a large W. African baboon, *Papio sphinx*, the adult of which has a brilliantly coloured face and blue-coloured buttocks. [prob. f. MAN + DRILL[3]]

mane *n.* long hair growing in a line on the neck of a horse, lion, etc. □ **maned** *adj.* (also in *comb.*). **maneless** *adj.* [OE *manu* f. Gmc]

manège /mæˈneɪʒ/ *n.* (also **manege**) **1** a riding-school. **2** the movements of a trained horse. **3** horsemanship. [F *manège* f. It. (as MANAGE)]

maneuver *US* var. of MANOEUVRE.

manful /ˈmænfʊl/ *adj.* brave; resolute. □ **manfully** *adv.* **manfulness** *n.*

manganese /ˈmæŋɡəˌniːz/ *n. Chem.* a grey brittle metallic transition element used with steel to make alloys. □ **manganic** /-ˈɡænɪk/ *adj.* **manganous** /ˈmæŋɡənəs/ *adj.* [F *manganèse* f. It. *manganese*, alt. f. MAGNESIA]

mange /meɪndʒ/ *n.* a skin disease in hairy and woolly animals, caused by an arachnid parasite and occasionally communicated to man. [ME *mangie*, *maniewe* f. OF *manjue*, *mangeue* itch f. *mangier manju-* eat f. L *manducare* chew]

mangel /ˈmæŋɡ(ə)l/ *n.* (also **mangold** /ˈmæŋɡ(ə)ld/) (in full **mangel-wurzel**, **mangold-wurzel** /-ˈwɜːz(ə)l/) a large kind of beet, *Beta vulgaris*, used as cattle food. [G *Mangoldwurzel* f. *Mangold* beet + *Wurzel* root]

manger /ˈmeɪndʒə(r)/ *n.* a long open box or trough in a stable etc., for horses or cattle to eat from. [ME f. OF *mangeoire*, *mangeure* ult. f. L *mandere* chew]

mange-tout /ˈmɑ̃ʒtuː, -ˈtuː/ *n.* the sugar-pea. [F, = eat-all]

mangle[1] /ˈmæŋɡ(ə)l/ *n. & v. esp. Brit. hist.* —*n.* a machine having two or more cylinders usu. turned by a handle, between which wet clothes etc. are squeezed and pressed. —*v.tr.* press (clothes etc.) in a mangle. [Du. *mangel(stok)* f. *mangelen* to mangle, ult. f. Gk *magganon* + *stok* staff, STOCK]

mangle[2] /ˈmæŋɡ(ə)l/ *v.tr.* **1** hack, cut about, or mutilate by blows etc. **2** spoil (a quotation, text, etc.) by misquoting, mispronouncing, etc. **3** cut roughly so as to disfigure. □ **mangler** *n.* [AF *ma(ha)ngler*, app. frequent. of *mahaignier* MAIM]

mango /ˈmæŋɡəʊ/ *n.* (*pl.* **-oes** or **-os**) **1** a fleshy yellowish-red fruit, eaten ripe or used green for pickles etc. **2** the Indian evergreen tree, *Mangifera indica*, bearing this. [Port. *manga* f. Malay *mangā* f. Tamil *mānkāy* f. *mān* mango-tree + *kāy* fruit]

mangosteen /ˈmæŋɡəˌstiːn/ *n.* **1** a white juicy-pulped fruit with a thick reddish-brown rind. **2** the E. Indian tree, *Garcinia mangostana*, bearing this. [Malay *manggustan*]

mangrove /ˈmæŋɡrəʊv/ *n.* any tropical tree or shrub of the genus *Rhizophora*, growing in shore-mud with many tangled roots above ground. [17th c.: orig. uncert.: assim. to GROVE]

mangy /ˈmeɪndʒɪ/ *adj.* (**mangier**, **mangiest**) **1** (esp. of a domestic animal) having mange. **2** squalid; shabby. □ **mangily** *adv.* **manginess** *n.*

manhandle /ˈmænˌhænd(ə)l/ *v.tr.* **1** move (heavy objects) by human effort. **2** *colloq.* handle (a person) roughly.

manhole /ˈmænhəʊl/ *n.* a covered opening in a floor, pavement, sewer, etc. for workmen to gain access.

manhood /ˈmænhʊd/ *n.* **1** the state of being a man rather than a child or woman. **2 a** manliness; courage. **b** a man's sexual potency. **3** the men of a country etc. **4** the state of being human.

manhunt /ˈmænhʌnt/ *n.* an organized search for a person, esp. a criminal.

mania /ˈmeɪnɪə/ *n.* **1** *Psychol.* mental illness marked by periods of great excitement and violence. **2** (often foll. by *for*) excessive enthusiasm; an obsession (*has a mania for jogging*). [ME f. LL f. Gk, = madness f. *mainomai* be mad, rel. to MIND]

-mania /ˈmeɪnɪə/ *comb. form* **1** *Psychol.* denoting a special type of mental abnormality or obsession (*megalomania*; *nymphomania*). **2** denoting extreme enthusiasm or admiration (*bibliomania*; *Anglomania*).

maniac /ˈmeɪnɪˌæk/ *n. & adj. —n.* **1** *colloq.* a person exhibiting extreme symptoms of wild behaviour etc.; a madman. **2** *colloq.* an obsessive enthusiast. *—adj.* of or behaving like a maniac. □ **maniacal** /məˈnaɪək(ə)l/ *adj.* **maniacally** /məˈnaɪəkəlɪ/ *adv.* [LL *maniacus* f. late Gk *maniakos* (as MANIA)]

-maniac /ˈmeɪnɪæk/ *comb. form* forming adjectives and nouns meaning 'affected with -mania' or 'a person affected with -mania' (*nymphomaniac*).

manic /ˈmænɪk/ *adj.* of or affected by mania. □ **manic-depressive** *Psychol. adj.* affected by or relating to a mental disorder with alternating periods of elation and depression. *—n.* a person having such a disorder. □ **manically** *adv.*

manicure /ˈmænɪˌkjʊə(r)/ *n. & v. —n.* a usu. professional cosmetic treatment of the hands and fingernails. *—v.tr.* apply a manicure to (the hands or a person). [F f. L *manus* hand + *cura* care]

manicurist /ˈmænɪˌkjʊərɪst/ *n.* a person who manicures hands and fingernails professionally.

manifest[1] /ˈmænɪˌfest/ *adj. & v. —adj.* clear or obvious to the eye or mind (*his distress was manifest*). *—v.* **1** *tr.* display or show (a quality, feeling, etc.) by one's acts etc. **2** *tr.* show plainly to the eye or mind. **3** *tr.* be evidence of; prove. **4** *refl.* (of a thing) reveal itself. **5** *intr.* (of a ghost) appear. □ **manifestation** /-ˈsteɪʃ(ə)n/ *n.* **manifestative** /-ˈfestətɪv/ *adj.* **manifestly** *adv.* [ME f. OF *manifeste* (adj.), *manifester* (v.) or L *manifestus*, *manifestare* f. *manus* hand + *festus* (unrecorded) struck]

manifest[2] /ˈmænɪˌfest/ *n.* **1** a cargo-list for the use of customs officers. **2** a list of passengers in an aircraft or of trucks etc. in a goods train. [It. *manifesto*: see MANIFESTO]

manifesto /ˌmænɪˈfestəʊ/ *n.* (*pl.* **-os**) a public declaration of policy and aims esp. issued before an election by a political party, candidate, government, etc. [It. f. *manifestare* f. L (as MANIFEST[1])]

manifold /ˈmænɪˌfəʊld/ *adj. & n. —adj. literary* **1** many and various (*manifold vexations*). **2** having various forms, parts, applications, etc. **3** performing several functions at once. *—n.* **1** a thing with many different forms, parts, applications, etc. **2** *Mech.* a pipe or chamber branching into several openings. □ **manifoldly** *adv.* **manifoldness** *n.* [OE *manigfeald* (as MANY, -FOLD)]

manikin /ˈmænɪkɪn/ *n.* (also **mannikin**) **1** a little man; a dwarf. **2** an artist's lay figure. **3** an anatomical model of the body. [Du. *manneken*, dimin. of *man* MAN]

Manila /məˈnɪlə/ *n.* (also **Manilla**) **1** (in full **Manila hemp**) the strong fibre of a Philippine tree, *Musa textilis*, used for rope etc. **2** (also **manila**) a strong brown paper made from Manila hemp or other material and used for wrapping paper, envelopes, etc. [*Manila* in the Philippines]

manioc /ˈmænɪˌɒk/ *n.* **1** cassava. **2** the flour made from it. [Tupi *mandioca*]

manipulate /məˈnɪpjʊˌleɪt/ *v.tr.* **1** handle, treat, or use, esp. skilfully (a tool, question, material, etc.). **2** manage (a person, situation, etc.) to one's own advantage, esp. unfairly or unscrupulously. **3** manually examine and treat (a part of the body). **4** *Computing* alter, edit, or move (text, data, etc.). **5** stimulate (the genitals). □ **manipulable** /-ləb(ə)l/ *adj.* **manipulability** /-ləˈbɪlɪtɪ/ *n.* **manipulatable** *adj.* **manipulation** /-ˈleɪʃ(ə)n/ *n.* **manipulator** *n.* **manipulatory** /-lətərɪ/ *adj.* [back-form. f. *manipulation* f. F *manipulation* f. mod.L *manipulatio* after F *manipuler*]

manipulative /məˈnɪpjʊlətɪv/ *adj.* **1** characterized by unscrupulous exploitation of a situation, person, etc., for one's own ends. **2** of or concerning manipulation. □ **manipulatively** *adv.* **manipulativeness** *n.*

mankind *n.* **1** /mænˈkaɪnd/ the human species. **2** /ˈmænkaɪnd/ male people, as distinct from female.

manky /ˈmæŋkɪ/ *adj.* (**mankier, mankiest**) *colloq.* **1** bad, inferior, defective. **2** dirty. [obs. *mank* mutilated, defective]

manlike /ˈmænlaɪk/ *adj.* **1** having the qualities of a man. **2** (of a woman) mannish. **3** (of an animal, shape, etc.) resembling a human being.

manly /ˈmænlɪ/ *adj.* (**manlier, manliest**) **1** having qualities regarded as admirable in a man, such as courage, frankness, etc. **2** (of a woman) mannish. **3** (of things, qualities, etc.) befitting a man. □ **manliness** *n.*

manna /ˈmænə/ *n.* **1** the substance miraculously supplied as food to the Israelites in the wilderness (Exod. 16). **2** an unexpected benefit (esp. *manna from heaven*). [OE f. LL f. Gk f. Aram. *mannā* f. Heb. *mān*, explained as = *mān hū?* what is it? but prob. = Arab. *mann* exudation of common tamarisk (*Tamarix gallica*)]

manned /mænd/ *adj.* (of an aircraft, spacecraft, etc.) having a human crew. [past part. of MAN]

mannequin /ˈmænɪkɪn/ *n.* **1** a model employed by a dressmaker etc. to show clothes to customers. **2** a window dummy. [F, = MANIKIN]

manner /ˈmænə(r)/ *n.* **1** a way a thing is done or happens (*always dresses in that manner*). **2** (in *pl.*) **a** social behaviour (*it is bad manners to stare*). **b** polite or well-bred behaviour (*he has no manners*). **c** modes of life; conditions of society. **3** a person's outward bearing, way of speaking, etc. (*has an imperious manner*). **4 a** a style in literature, art, etc. (*in the manner of Rembrandt*). **b** = MANNERISM 2a. **5** *archaic* a kind or sort (*what manner of man is he?*). □ **all manner of** many different kinds of. **comedy of manners** satirical portrayal of social behaviour, esp. of the upper classes. **in a manner of speaking** in some sense; to some extent; so to speak. **to the manner born** *colloq.* naturally at ease in a specified job, situation, etc. **2** destined by birth to follow a custom or way of life (Shakesp. *Hamlet* I. iv. 17). □ **mannerless** *adj.* (in sense 2b of *n.*). [ME f. AF *manere*, OF *maniere* ult. f. L *manuarius* of the hand (*manus*)]

mannered /ˈmænəd/ *adj.* **1** (in *comb.*) behaving in a specified way (*ill-mannered*; *well-mannered*). **2** (of a style, artist, writer, etc.) showing idiosyncratic mannerisms. **3** (of a person) eccentrically affected in behaviour.

mannerism /ˈmænəˌrɪz(ə)m/ n. **1 a** a habitual gesture or way of speaking etc.; an idiosyncrasy. **2 a** excessive addiction to a distinctive style in art or literature. **b** a stylistic trick. □ **mannerist** n. **manneristic** /-ˈrɪstɪk/ adj. **manneristical** /-ˈrɪstɪk(ə)l/ adj. **manneristically** /-ˈrɪstɪkəlɪ/ adv. [MANNER]

mannerly /ˈmænəlɪ/ adj. & adv. —adj. well-mannered; polite. —adv. politely. □ **mannerliness** n.

mannikin var. of MANIKIN.

mannish /ˈmænɪʃ/ adj. **1** usu. derog. (of a woman) masculine in appearance or manner. **2** characteristic of a man. □ **mannishly** adv. **mannishness** n. [OE mennisc f. (and assim. to) MAN]

manoeuvre /məˈnuːvə(r)/ n. & v. (US maneuver) —n. **1** a planned and controlled movement or series of moves. **2** (in pl.) a large-scale exercise of troops, warships, etc. **3 a** an often deceptive planned or controlled action designed to gain an objective. **b** a skilful plan. —v. **1** intr. & tr. perform or cause to perform a manoeuvre (manoeuvred the car into the space). **2** intr. & tr. perform or cause (troops etc.) to perform military manoeuvres. **3 a** tr. (usu. foll. by into, out, away) force, drive, or manipulate (a person, thing, etc.) by scheming or adroitness. **b** intr. use artifice. □ **manoeuvrable** adj. **manoeuvrability** /-vrəˈbɪlɪtɪ/ n. **manoeuvrer** n. [F manœuvre, manœuvrer f. med.L manuoperare f. L manus hand + operari to work]

manometer /məˈnɒmɪtə(r)/ n. a pressure gauge for gases and liquids. □ **manometric** /ˌmænəˈmetrɪk/ adj. [F manomètre f. Gk manos thin]

manor /ˈmænə(r)/ n. **1** (also **manor-house**) **a** a large country house with lands. **b** the house of the lord of the manor. **2** Brit. **a** a unit of land consisting of a lord's demesne and lands rented to tenants etc. **b** hist. a feudal lordship over lands. **3** Brit. colloq. the district covered by a police station. □ **manorial** /məˈnɔːrɪəl/ adj. [ME f. AF maner, OF maneir, f. L manēre remain]

manpower /ˈmænˌpaʊə(r)/ n. **1** the power generated by a man working. **2** the number of people available for work, service, etc.

manqué /ˈmɒŋkeɪ/ adj. (placed after noun) that might have been but is not; unfulfilled (a comic actor manqué). [F, past part. of manquer lack]

mansard /ˈmænsɑːd/ n. a roof which has four sloping sides, each of which becomes steeper halfway down. [F mansarde f. F. Mansard, Fr. architect d. 1666]

manse /mæns/ n. the house of a minister, esp. a Scottish Presbyterian. □ **son** (or **daughter**) **of the manse** the child of a Presbyterian etc. minister. [ME f. med.L mansus, -sa, -sum, house f. manēre mans- remain]

manservant /ˈmænˌsɜːv(ə)nt/ n. (pl. **menservants**) a male servant.

-manship /mənʃɪp/ suffix forming nouns denoting skill in a subject or activity (craftsmanship; gamesmanship).

mansion /ˈmænʃ(ə)n/ n. **1** a large house. **2** (usu. in pl.) Brit. a large building divided into flats. □ **mansion-house** Brit. the house of a lord mayor or a landed proprietor. **the Mansion House** the official residence of the Lord Mayor of London. [ME f. OF f. L mansio -onis a staying (as MANSE)]

manslaughter /ˈmænˌslɔːtə(r)/ n. **1** the killing of a human being. **2** Law the unlawful killing of a human being without malice aforethought.

mantel /ˈmænt(ə)l/ n. **1** = MANTELPIECE 1. **2** = MANTELSHELF. [var. of MANTLE]

mantelpiece /ˈmænt(ə)lˌpiːs/ n. **1** a structure of wood, marble, etc. above and around a fireplace. **2** = MANTELSHELF.

mantelshelf /ˈmænt(ə)lˌʃelf/ n. a shelf above a fireplace.

mantilla /mænˈtɪlə/ n. a lace scarf worn by Spanish women over the hair and shoulders. [Sp., dimin. of manta MANTLE]

mantis /ˈmæntɪs/ n. (pl. same or **mantises**) any insect of the family Mantidae, feeding on other insects etc. □ **praying mantis** a mantis, Mantis religiosa, that holds its forelegs in a position suggestive of hands folded in prayer. [Gk, = prophet]

mantle /ˈmænt(ə)l/ n. & v. —n. **1** a loose sleeveless cloak, esp. of a woman. **2** a covering (a mantle of snow). **3** a spiritual influence or authority (see 2 Kings 2:13). **4** a fragile lacelike tube fixed round a gas-jet to give an incandescent light. **5** the region between the crust and the core of the earth. —v.tr. clothe in or as if in a mantle; cover, conceal, envelop. [ME f. OF f. L mantellum cloak]

mantra /ˈmæntrə/ n. a word or sound repeated to aid concentration in meditation, orig. in Hinduism and Buddhism. [Skr., = instrument of thought f. man think]

mantrap /ˈmæntræp/ n. a trap for catching poachers, trespassers, etc.

manual /ˈmænjʊəl/ adj. & n. —adj. **1** of or done with the hands (manual labour). **2** (of a machine etc.) worked by hand, not automatically. —n. **1 a** a book of instructions, esp. for operating a machine or learning a subject; a handbook (a computer manual). **b** any small book. **2** an organ keyboard played with the hands not the feet. □ **manual alphabet** sign language. □ **manually** adv. [ME f. OF manuel, f. (and later assim. to) L manualis f. manus hand]

manufacture /ˌmænjʊˈfæktʃə(r)/ n. & v. —n. **1** the making of articles esp. in a factory etc. **2** a branch of an industry (woollen manufacture). —v.tr. **1** make (articles), esp. on an industrial scale. **2** invent or fabricate (evidence, a story, etc.). □ **manufacturable** adj. **manufacturability** /-tʃərəˈbɪlɪtɪ/ n. **manufacturer** n. [F f. It. manifattura & L manufactum made by hand]

manure /məˈnjʊə(r)/ n. & v. —n. **1** animal dung, esp. of horses, cattle, used for fertilizing land. **2** any compost or artificial fertilizer. —v.tr. (also absol.) apply manure to (land etc.). □ **manurial** adj. [ME f. AF mainoverer = OF manouvrer MANOEUVRE]

manuscript /ˈmænjʊskrɪpt/ n. & adj. —n. **1** a book, document, etc. written by hand. **2** an author's handwritten or typed text, submitted for publication. **3** handwritten form (produced in manuscript). —adj. written by hand. [med.L manuscriptus f. manu by hand + scriptus past part. of scribere write]

Manx /mæŋks/ adj. & n. —adj. of or relating to the Isle of Man. —n. **1** Language hist. the now extinct Celtic language formerly spoken in the Isle of Man. **2** (prec. by the; treated as pl.) the Manx people. □ **Manx cat** a tailless cat. [ON f. OIr. Manu Isle of Man]

Manxman /ˈmæŋksmən/ n. (pl. **-men**; fem. **Manxwoman**, pl. **-women**) a native of the Isle of Man.

many /ˈmenɪ/ adj. & n. —adj. (**more** /mɔː(r)/; **most** /məʊst/) great in number; numerous (many times; many people; many a person; his reasons were many). —n. (as pl.) 1 a large number (many like skiing; many went). 2 (prec. by the) the multitude of esp. working people. □ **as many again** the same number additionally (sixty here and as many again there). **be too** (or **one too**) **many for** outwit, baffle. **a good** (or **great**) **many** a large number. **many-sided** having many sides, aspects, interests, capabilities, etc. **many's the time** often (many's the time we saw it). **many a time** many times. [OE manig, ult. f. Gmc]

Maoism /ˈmaʊɪz(ə)m/ n. the Communist doctrines of Mao Zedong (d. 1976), Chinese statesman. □ **Maoist** n. & adj.

Maori /ˈmaʊrɪ/ n. & adj. —n. (pl. same or **Maoris**) 1 a member of the Polynesian aboriginal people of New Zealand. 2 the language of the Maori. —adj. of or concerning the Maori or their language. [native name]

map n. & v. —n. 1 **a** a usu. flat representation of the earth's surface, or part of it, showing physical features, cities, etc. **b** a diagrammatic representation of a route etc. (drew a map of the journey). 2 a two-dimensional representation of the stars, the heavens, etc., or of the surface of a planet, the moon, etc. 3 a diagram showing the arrangement or components of a thing. 4 sl. the face. —v.tr. (**mapped**, **mapping**) 1 represent (a country etc.) on a map. 2 Math. associate each element of (a set) with one element of another set. □ **map out** arrange in detail; plan (a course of conduct etc.). **off the map** colloq. 1 of no account; obsolete. 2 very distant. **on the map** colloq. prominent, important. □ **mapless** adj. **mappable** adj. **mapper** n. [L mappa napkin: in med.L mappa (mundi) map (of the world)]

maple /ˈmeɪp(ə)l/ n. 1 any tree or shrub of the genus Acer grown for shade, ornament, wood, or its sugar. 2 the wood of the maple. □ **maple-leaf** the leaf of the maple, used as an emblem of Canada. **maple sugar** a sugar produced by evaporating the sap of the sugar maple etc. **maple syrup** a syrup produced from the sap of the sugar maple etc. [ME mapul etc. f. OE mapeltrēow, mapulder]

maquette /məˈket/ n. 1 a sculptor's small preliminary model in wax, clay, etc. 2 a preliminary sketch. [F f. It. machietta dimin. of macchia spot]

Maquis /mæˈkiː/ n. 1 the French resistance movement during the German occupation (1940–45). 2 a member of this. [F, = brushwood, f. Corsican It. macchia thicket]

Mar. abbr. March.

mar v.tr. (**marred**, **marring**) 1 ruin. 2 impair the perfection of; spoil; disfigure. [OE merran hinder]

marabou /ˈmærəˌbuː/ n. (also **marabout**) 1 a large W. African stork, Leptoptilos crumeniferus. 2 a tuft of down from the wing or tail of the marabou used as a trimming for hats etc. [F f. Arab. murābiṭ holy man, the stork being regarded as holy]

maraca /məˈrækə/ n. a hollow clublike gourd or gourd-shaped container filled with beans etc. and usu. shaken in pairs as a percussion instrument in Latin American music. [Port. maracá, prob. f. Tupi]

maraschino /ˌmærəˈskiːnəʊ/ n. (pl. **-os**) a strong sweet liqueur made from a small black Dalmatian cherry. □ **maraschino cherry** a cherry preserved in maraschino and used to decorate cocktails etc. [It. f. marasca small black cherry, for amarasca f. amaro bitter f. L amarus]

marathon /ˈmærəθ(ə)n/ n. 1 a long-distance running race, usu. of 26 miles 385 yards (42.195 km). 2 a long-lasting or difficult task, operation, etc. (often attrib.: a marathon shopping expedition). □ **marathoner** n. [Marathon in Greece, scene of a victory over the Persians in 490 BC: a messenger was said to have run to Athens with the news, but the account has no authority]

maraud /məˈrɔːd/ v. 1 intr. **a** make a plundering raid. **b** pilfer systematically; plunder. 2 tr. plunder (a place). □ **marauder** n. [F marauder f. maraud rogue]

marble /ˈmɑːb(ə)l/ n. & v. —n. 1 limestone in a metamorphic crystalline (or granular) state, and capable of taking a polish, used in sculpture and architecture. 2 (often attrib.) anything made of marble (a marble clock). 3 **a** a small ball of marble, glass, clay, etc., used as a toy. **b** (in pl.; treated as sing.) a game using these. 4 (in pl.) sl. one's mental faculties (he's lost his marbles). 5 (in pl.) a collection of sculptures (Elgin Marbles). —v.tr. (esp. as **marbled** adj.) stain or colour (paper, the edges of a book, soap, etc.) to look like variegated marble. □ **marbly** adj. [ME f. OF marbre, marble, f. L marmor f. Gk marmaros shining stone]

marbling /ˈmɑːblɪŋ/ n. colouring or marking like marble.

marc n. 1 the refuse of pressed grapes etc. 2 a brandy made from this. [F f. marcher tread, MARCH[1]]

marcasite /ˈmɑːkəˌsaɪt/ n. 1 a yellowish crystalline iron sulphide mineral. 2 these bronze-yellow crystals used in jewellery. [ME f. med.L marcasita, f. Arab. markaṣīṭā f. Pers.]

March n. the third month of the year. □ **March hare** a hare in the breeding season, characterized by excessive leaping, strange behaviour, etc. (mad as a March hare). [ME f. OF march(e), dial. var. of marz, mars, f. L Martius (mensis) (month) of Mars]

march[1] v. & n. —v. 1 intr. (usu. foll. by away, off, out, etc.) walk in a military manner with a regular measured tread. 2 tr. (often foll. by away, on, off, etc.) cause (a person) to march or walk (marched the army to Moscow; marched him out of the room). 3 intr. **a** walk or proceed steadily, esp. across country. **b** (of events etc.) continue unrelentingly (time marches on). 4 intr. take part in a protest march. —n. 1 **a** the act or an instance of marching. **b** the uniform step of troops etc. (a slow march). 2 a long difficult walk. 3 a procession as a protest or demonstration. 4 (usu. foll. by of) progress or continuity (the march of events). 5 a piece of music composed to accompany a march. □ **marching order** Mil. equipment or a formation for marching. **marching orders** 1 Mil. the direction for troops to depart for war etc. 2 a dismissal (gave him his marching orders). **march on** 1 advance towards (a military objective). 2 proceed. **march past** n. the marching of troops past a saluting-point at a review. —v.intr. (of troops) carry out a march past. **on the**

march 1 marching. 2 in steady progress. □
marcher n. [F marche (n.), marcher (v.), f. LL
marcus hammer]

march² /mɑːtʃ/ n. & v. —n. hist. 1 (usu. in pl.) a
boundary, a frontier (esp. of the borderland
between England and Scotland or Wales). 2
a tract of often disputed land between two
countries. —v.intr. (foll. by upon, with) (of a
country, an estate, etc.) have a common frontier
with, border on. [ME f. OF marche, marchir ult. f.
Gmc: cf. MARK¹]

marchioness /ˌmɑːʃəˈnes, ˈmɑː-/ n. 1 the wife or
widow of a marquess. 2 a woman holding
the rank of marquess in her own right (cf.
MARQUISE). [med.L marchionissa f. marchio -onis
captain of the marches (as MARCH²)]

Mardi Gras /ˌmɑːdɪ ˈɡrɑː/ n. 1 a Shrove Tuesday
in some Catholic countries. b merrymaking on
this day. 2 the last day of a carnival etc. 3
Austral. a carnival or fair at any time. [F, = fat
Tuesday]

mare¹ /meə(r)/ n. 1 the female of any equine
animal, esp. the horse. 2 sl. derog. a woman. □
mare's nest an illusory discovery. **mare's tail**
1 a tall slender marsh plant, Hippuris vulgaris. 2
(in pl.) long straight streaks of cirrus cloud. [ME
f. OE mearh horse f. Gmc: cf. MARSHAL]

mare² /ˈmɑːreɪ/ n. (pl. **maria** /ˈmɑːrɪə/ or **mares**)
1 any of a number of large dark flat areas on
the surface of the moon, once thought to be
seas. 2 a similar area on Mars. [L, = sea]

margarine /ˌmɑːdʒəˈriːn, ˌmɑːɡə-, ˈmɑː-/ n. a
butter-substitute made from vegetable oils or
animal fats with milk etc. [F, misapplication of
a chem. term, f. margarique f. Gk margaron pearl]

marge /mɑːdʒ/ n. Brit. colloq. margarine. [abbr.]

margin /ˈmɑːdʒɪn/ n. & v. —n. 1 the edge or
border of a surface. 2 a the blank border on
each side of the print on a page etc. b a line
ruled esp. on exercise paper, marking off a
margin. 3 an amount (of time, money, etc.) by
which a thing exceeds, falls short, etc. (won by a
narrow margin; a margin of profit). 4 the lower
limit of possibility, success, etc. (his effort fell
below the margin). —v.tr. (**margined, mar-
gining**) provide with a margin or marginal
notes. □ **margin of error** a usu. small difference allowed for miscalculation, change of
circumstances, etc. [ME f. L margo -ginis]

marginal /ˈmɑːdʒɪn(ə)l/ adj. 1 a of or written in
a margin. b having marginal notes. 2 a of or at
the edge; not central. b not significant or
decisive (the work is of merely marginal interest). 3
Brit. (of a parliamentary seat or constituency)
having a small majority at risk in an election. 4
close to the limit, esp. of profitability. 5 (of land)
difficult to cultivate; unprofitable. 6 barely
adequate; unprovided for. □ **marginal cost** the
cost added by making one extra copy etc.
□ **marginality** /-ˈnælɪtɪ/ n. **marginally** adv.
[med.L marginalis (as MARGIN)]

marginalia /ˌmɑːdʒɪˈneɪlɪə/ n.pl. marginal notes.
[med.L, neut. pl. of marginalis]

marginalize /ˈmɑːdʒɪnəˌlaɪz/ v.tr. (also **-ise**)
make or treat as insignificant. □ **margin-
alization** /-ˈzeɪʃ(ə)n/ n.

marguerite /ˌmɑːɡəˈriːt/ n. an ox-eye daisy. [F f.
L margarita f. Gk margarītēs f. margaron pearl]

maria pl. of MARE².

Marian /ˈmeərɪən/ adj. RC Ch. of or relating to
the Virgin Mary (Marian vespers). [L Maria Mary]

marigold /ˈmærɪˌɡəʊld/ n. any plant of the
genus Calendula or Tagetes, with golden or bright
yellow flowers. [ME f. Mary (prob. the Virgin) +
dial. gold, OE golde, prob. rel. to GOLD]

marijuana /ˌmærɪˈhwɑːnə/ n. (also **marihuana**)
1 the dried leaves, flowering tops, and stems of
the hemp, used as a drug usu. smoked in
cigarettes. 2 the plant yielding these (cf. HEMP).
[Amer. Sp.]

marimba /məˈrɪmbə/ n. 1 a xylophone played
by natives of Africa and Central America. 2 a
modern orchestral instrument derived from
this. [Congo]

marina /məˈriːnə/ n. a specially designed harbour with moorings for pleasure-yachts etc. [It.
& Sp. fem. adj. f. marino f. L (as MARINE)]

marinade /ˌmærɪˈneɪd, ˈmæ-/ n. & v. —n. 1 a
mixture of wine, vinegar, oil, spices, etc., in
which meat, fish, etc., is soaked before cooking.
2 meat, fish, etc., soaked in this liquid. —v.tr.
soak (meat, fish, etc.) in a marinade. [F f. Sp.
marinada f. marinar pickle in brine f. marino (as
MARINE)]

marinate /ˈmærɪˌneɪt/ v.tr. = MARINADE. □
marination /-ˈneɪʃ(ə)n/ n. [It. marinare or F
mariner (as MARINE)]

marine /məˈriːn/ adj. & n. —adj. 1 of, found in,
or produced by the sea. 2 a of or relating to
shipping or naval matters (marine insurance). b
for use at sea. —n. 1 a country's shipping, fleet,
or navy (mercantile marine; merchant marine). 2 a
member of a body of troops trained to serve on
land or sea. [ME f. OF marin marine f. L marinus f.
mare sea]

mariner /ˈmærɪnə(r)/ n. a seaman. [ME f. AF
mariner, OF marinier f. med.L marinarius f. L (as
MARINE)]

marionette /ˌmærɪəˈnet/ n. a puppet worked by
strings. [F marionnette f. Marion dimin. of Marie
Mary]

marital /ˈmærɪt(ə)l/ adj. 1 of marriage or the
relations between husband and wife. 2 of or
relating to a husband. □ **maritally** adv. [L
maritalis f. maritus husband]

maritime /ˈmærɪˌtaɪm/ adj. 1 connected with
the sea or seafaring (maritime insurance). 2 living
or found near the sea. [L maritimus f. mare sea]

marjoram /ˈmɑːdʒərəm/ n. either of two aromatic herbs, Origanum vulgare (**wild marjoram**)
or Majorana hortensis (**sweet marjoram**), the
leaves of which are used as a flavouring in
cookery. [ME & OF majorane f. med.L majorana,
of unkn. orig.]

mark¹ n. & v. —n. 1 a trace, sign, stain, scar,
etc., on a surface, face, page, etc. 2 (esp. in comb.)
a a written or printed symbol (exclamation mark;
question mark). **b** a numerical or alphabetical
award denoting excellence, conduct, proficiency,
etc. (got a good mark for effort; gave him a black
mark; gained 46 marks out of 50). 3 (usu. foll. by of)
a sign or indication of quality, character, feeling,
etc. (took off his hat as a mark of respect). 4 **a** a sign,
seal, etc., used for distinction or identification. **b**
a cross etc. made in place of a signature by an
illiterate person. 5 **a** a target, object, goal, etc.
(missed the mark with his first play). **b** a standard
for attainment (his work falls below the mark). 6 a
line etc. indicating a position; a marker. 7 (usu.
Mark) (followed by a numeral) a particular
design, model, etc., of a car, aircraft, etc. (this is
the Mark 2 model). 8 a runner's starting-point in

a race. —*v.tr.* **1 a** make a mark on (a thing or person), esp. by writing, cutting, scraping, etc. **b** put a distinguishing or identifying mark, initials, name, etc., on (clothes etc.) (*marked the tree with their initials*). **2 a** allot marks to; correct (a student's work etc.). **b** record (the points gained in games etc.). **3** attach a price to (goods etc.) (*marked the doll at 50p*). **4** (often foll. by *by*) show or manifest (displeasure etc.) (*marked his anger by leaving early*). **5** notice or observe (*she marked his agitation*). **6 a** characterize or be a feature of (*the day was marked by storms*). **b** acknowledge, recognize, celebrate (*marked the occasion with a toast*). **7** name or indicate (a place on a map, the length of a syllable, etc.) by a sign or mark. **8** characterize (a person or a thing) as (*marked them as weak*). **9** *Brit.* keep close to so as to prevent the free movement of (an opponent in sport). **10** (as **marked** *adj.*) having natural marks (*is marked with silver spots*). **11** (of a graduated instrument) show, register (so many degrees etc.). □ **beside** (or **off** or **wide of**) **the mark 1** not to the point; irrelevant. **2** not accurate. **make one's mark** attain distinction. **mark down 1** mark (goods etc.) at a lower price. **2** make a written note of. **3** choose (a person) as one's victim. **mark-down** *n.* a reduction in price. **mark off** (often foll. by *from*) separate (one thing from another) by a boundary etc. (*marked off the subjects for discussion*). **mark out 1** plan (a course of action etc.). **2** destine (*marked out for success*). **3** trace out boundaries, a course, etc. **mark time 1** *Mil.* march on the spot, without moving forward. **2** act routinely; go through the motions. **3** await an opportunity to advance. **mark up 1** mark (goods etc.) at a higher price. **2** mark or correct (text etc.) for typesetting or alteration. **mark-up** *n.* **1** the amount added to the cost price of goods to cover overhead charges, profit, etc. **2** the corrections made in marking up text. **mark you** please note (*without obligation, mark you*). **off the mark** having made a start. **of mark** noteworthy. **on the mark** ready to start. **on your mark** (or **marks**) (as an instruction) get ready to start (esp. a race). **up to the mark** reaching the usual or normal standard, esp. of health. [OE *me(a)rc* (n.), *mearcian* (v.), f. Gmc]

mark² /maːk/ *n.* DEUTSCHE MARK. [OE *marc*, prob. rel. to med.L *marca, marcus*]

marked /maːkt/ *adj.* **1** having a visible mark. **2** clearly noticeable; evident (*a marked difference*). **3** (of playing-cards) having distinctive marks on their backs to assist cheating. □ **marked man 1** a person whose conduct is watched with suspicion or hostility. **2** a person destined to succeed. □ **markedly** /-kɪdlɪ/ *adv.* **markedness** /-kɪdnɪs/ *n.* [OE (past part. of MARK¹)]

marker /ˈmaːkə(r)/ *n.* **1** a stone, post, etc., used to mark a position, place reached, etc. **2** a person or thing that marks. **3** a felt-tipped pen with a broad tip. **4** a person who records a score, esp. in billiards. **5** *US sl.* a promissory note; an IOU.

market /ˈmaːkɪt/ *n. & v.* —*n.* **1 a** the gathering of people for the purchase and sale of provisions, livestock, etc., esp. with a number of different vendors. **b** the time of this. **2** an open space or covered building used for this. **3** (often foll. by *for*) a demand for a commodity or service (*goods find a ready market*). **4** a place or group providing

such a demand. **5** conditions as regards, or opportunity for, buying or selling. **6** the rate of purchase and sale, market value (*the market fell*). **7** (prec. by *the*) the trade in a specified commodity (*the corn market*). **8** (**the Market**) *Brit.* the European Economic Community. —*v.* (**marketed, marketing**) **1** *tr.* sell. **2** *tr.* offer for sale. **3** *intr.* buy or sell goods in a market. □ **be in the market for** wish to buy. **be on** (or **come into**) **the market** be offered for sale. **market garden** a place where vegetables and fruit are grown for the market etc. **market gardener** a person who owns or is employed in a market garden. **market-place 1** an open space where a market is held in a town. **2** the scene of actual dealings. **market price** the price in current dealings. **market research** the study of consumers' needs and preferences. **market town** *Brit.* a town where a market is held. **market value** value as a saleable thing. **put on the market** offer for sale. □ **marketer** *n.* **marketing** *n.* [ME ult. f. L *mercatus* f. *mercari* buy: see MERCHANT]

marketable /ˈmaːkɪtəb(ə)l/ *adj.* able or fit to be sold. □ **marketability** /-ˈbɪlɪtɪ/ *n.*

marketeer /ˌmaːkɪˈtɪə(r)/ *n.* **1** a supporter of the EC and British membership of it. **2** a marketer.

marking /ˈmaːkɪŋ/ *n.* (usu. in *pl.*) **1** an identification mark, esp. a symbol on an aircraft. **2** the colouring of an animal's fur, feathers, skin, etc. □ **marking-ink** indelible ink for marking linen etc.

marksman /ˈmaːksmən/ *n.* (*pl.* **-men**) a person skilled in shooting, esp. with a pistol or rifle. □ **marksmanship** *n.*

marl /maːl/ *n. & v.* —*n.* soil consisting of clay and lime, with fertilizing properties. —*v.tr.* apply marl to (the ground). □ **marly** *adj.* [ME f. OF *marle* f. med.L *margila* f. L *marga*]

marlin /ˈmaːlɪn/ *n.* *US* any of various large long-nosed marine fish of the family *Istophoridae*, esp. the blue marlin *Makaira nigricans*. [MARLINSPIKE, with ref. to its pointed snout]

marlinspike /ˈmaːlɪnˌspaɪk/ *n. Naut.* a pointed iron tool used to separate strands of rope or wire. [orig. app. *marling-spike* f. *marl* fasten (f. Du. *marlen* frequent. of MDu. *marren* bind) + -ING¹ + SPIKE¹]

marmalade /ˈmaːməˌleɪd/ *n.* a preserve of citrus fruit, usu. bitter oranges, made like jam. □ **marmalade cat** a cat with orange fur. [F *marmelade* f. Port. *marmelada* quince jam f. *marmelo* quince f. L *melimelum* f. Gk *melimēlon* f. *meli* honey + *mēlon* apple]

Marmite /ˈmaːmaɪt/ *n. Brit. propr.* a preparation made from yeast extract and vegetable extract, used in sandwiches and for flavouring. [F, = cooking-pot]

marmoreal /maːˈmɔːrɪəl/ *adj. poet.* of or like marble. □ **marmoreally** *adv.* [L *marmoreus* (as MARBLE)]

marmoset /ˈmaːməˌzet/ *n.* any of several small tropical American monkeys of the family Callitricidae, having a long bushy tail. [OF *marmouset* grotesque image, of unkn. orig.]

marmot /ˈmaːmət/ *n.* any burrowing rodent of the genus *Marmota*, with a heavy-set body and short bushy tail. [F *marmotte* prob. f. Romansh *murmont* f. L *murem* (nominative *mus*) *montis* mountain mouse]

marocain /ˈmærəˌkeɪn/ *n.* a dress-fabric of ribbed crêpe. [F, = Moroccan f. *Maroc* Morocco]

Maronite /ˈmærəˌnaɪt/ n. a member of a sect of Syrian Christians dwelling chiefly in Lebanon. [med.L *Maronita* f. *Maro* the 5th-c. Syrian founder]

maroon[1] /məˈruːn/ adj. & n. —adj. brownish-crimson. —n. **1** this colour. **2** an explosive device giving a loud report. [F *marron* chestnut f. It. *marrone* f. med.Gk *maraon*]

maroon[2] /məˈruːn/ v.tr. **1** leave (a person) isolated in a desolate place (esp. an island). **2** (of a person or a natural phenomenon) cause (a person) to be unable to leave a place. [F *marron* f. Sp. *cimarrón* wild f. *cima* peak]

marque /mɑːk/ n. a make of motor car, as distinct from a specific model (*the Jaguar marque*). [F, = MARK[1]]

marquee /mɑːˈkiː/ n. **1** a large tent used for social or commercial functions. **2** US a canopy over the entrance to a large building. [MARQUISE, taken as pl. & assim. to -EE]

marquess /ˈmɑːkwɪs/ n. a British nobleman ranking between a duke and an earl (cf. MARQUIS). □ **marquessate** /-sət/ n. [var. of MARQUIS]

marquetry /ˈmɑːkɪtrɪ/ n. (also **marqueterie**) inlaid work in wood, ivory, etc. [F *marqueterie* f. *marqueter* variegate f. MARQUE]

marquis /ˈmɑːkwɪs/ n. a foreign nobleman ranking between a duke and a count. □ **marquisate** /-sət/ n. [ME f. OF *marchis* f. Rmc (as MARCH[2], -ESE)]

marquise /mɑːˈkiːz/ n. **1** the wife or widow of a marquis. **2** a woman holding the rank of marquis in her own right. [F, fem. of MARQUIS]

marram /ˈmærəm/ n. a shore grass, *Ammophila arenaria*, that binds sand with its tough rhizomes. [ON *marálmr* f. *marr* sea + *hálmr* HAULM]

marriage /ˈmærɪdʒ/ n. **1** the legal union of a man and a woman in order to live together and often to have children. **2** an act or ceremony establishing this union. **3** one particular union of this kind (*by a previous marriage*). **4** an intimate union (*the marriage of true minds*). □ **by marriage** as a result of a marriage (*related by marriage*). **in marriage** as husband or wife (*give in marriage*; *take in marriage*). **marriage certificate** a certificate certifying the completion of a marriage ceremony. **marriage guidance** counselling of couples who have problems in married life. **marriage licence** a licence to marry. **marriage lines** Brit. a marriage certificate. **marriage of convenience** a marriage concluded to achieve some particular purpose, esp. financial or political. **marriage settlement** an arrangement securing property between spouses. [ME f. OF *mariage* f. *marier* MARRY]

marriageable /ˈmærɪdʒəb(ə)l/ adj. **1** fit for marriage, esp. old or rich enough to marry. **2** (of age) fit for marriage. □ **marriageability** /-ˈbɪlɪtɪ/ n.

married /ˈmærɪd/ adj. & n. —adj. **1** united in marriage. **2** of or relating to marriage (*married name*; *married life*). —n. (usu. in pl.) a married person (*young marrieds*).

marron glacé /ˌmærɒn ˈɡlɑːseɪ/ n. (pl. **marrons glacés** pronunc. same) a chestnut preserved in and coated with sugar. [F, = iced chestnut: cf. GLACÉ]

marrow /ˈmærəʊ/ n. **1** (in full **vegetable marrow**) a large usu. white-fleshed edible gourd

used as food. **2** a soft fatty substance in the cavities of bones, often taken as typifying vitality. **3** the essential part. □ **to the marrow** right through. □ **marrowless** adj. **marrowy** adj. [OE *mearg*, *mærg* f. Gmc]

marrowbone /ˈmærəʊˌbəʊn/ n. a bone containing edible marrow.

marrowfat /ˈmærəʊˌfæt/ n. a kind of large pea.

marry /ˈmærɪ/ v. (-ies, -ied) **1** tr. **a** take as one's wife or husband in marriage. **b** (often foll. by *to*) (of a priest etc.) join (persons) in marriage. **c** (of a parent or guardian) give (a son, daughter, etc.) in marriage. **2** intr. **a** enter into marriage. **b** (foll. by *into*) become a member of (a family) by marriage. **3** tr. **a** unite intimately. **b** correlate (things) as a pair. □ **marry off** find a wife or husband for. [ME f. OF *marier* f. L *maritare* f. *maritus* husband]

marrying /ˈmærɪɪŋ/ adj. likely or inclined to marry (*not a marrying man*).

Marsala /mɑːˈsɑːlə/ n. a dark sweet fortified dessert wine. [*Marsala* in Sicily, where orig. made]

Marseillaise /ˌmɑːseɪˈjeɪz, ˌmɑːsəˈleɪz/ n. the national anthem of France, first sung in Paris by Marseilles patriots. [F, fem. adj. f. *Marseille* Marseilles]

marsh n. **1** low land flooded in wet weather and usu. watery at all times. **2** (attrib.) of or inhabiting marshland. □ **marsh gas** methane.

marsh mallow a shrubby herbaceous plant, *Althaea officinalis*, the roots of which were formerly used to make marshmallow. **marsh marigold** a golden-flowered ranunculaceous plant, *Caltha palustris*, growing in moist meadows etc. □ **marshy** adj. (**marshier, marshiest**). **marshiness** n. [OE *mer(i)sc* f. WG]

marshal /ˈmɑːʃ(ə)l/ n. & v. —n. **1** (**Marshal**) **a** a high-ranking officer in the armed forces (*Air Marshal*; *Field Marshal*; *Marshal of France*). **b** a high-ranking officer of state (*Earl Marshal*). **2** an officer arranging ceremonies, controlling procedure at races, etc. **3** US the head of a police or fire department. —v. (**marshalled, marshalling**; US **marshaled, marshaling**) **1** tr. arrange (soldiers, facts, one's thoughts, etc.) in due order. **2** tr. (often foll. by *into, to*) conduct (a person) ceremoniously. □ **marshalling yard** a railway yard in which goods trains etc. are assembled. **Marshal of the Royal Air Force** an officer of the highest rank in the Royal Air Force. □ **marshaller** n. **marshalship** n. [ME f. OF *mareschal* f. LL *mariscalcus* f. Gmc, lit. 'horse-servant']

marshland /ˈmɑːʃlənd/ n. land consisting of marshes.

marshmallow /mɑːʃˈmæləʊ/ n. a soft sweet made of sugar, albumen, gelatin, etc.

marsupial /mɑːˈsuːpɪəl/ n. & adj. —n. any mammal of the order Marsupialia, characterized by being born incompletely developed and usu. carried and suckled in a pouch on the mother's belly. —adj. of or belonging to this order. [mod.L *marsupialis* f. L *marsupium* f. Gk *marsupion* pouch, dimin. of *marsipos* purse]

mart n. **1** a trade centre. **2** an auction-room. **3 a** a market. **b** a market-place. [ME f. obs. Du. *mart*, var. of *markt* MARKET]

Martello /mɑːˈteləʊ/ n. (pl. -os) (also **Martello tower**) a small circular fort, usu. on the coast to prevent a hostile landing. [alt. f. Cape *Mortella* in Corsica, where such a tower proved difficult to capture in 1794]

marten /ˈmɑːtɪn/ n. any weasel-like carnivore of the genus *Martes*, having valuable fur. [ME f. MDu. *martren* f. OF (*peau*) *martrine* marten (fur) f. *martre* f. WG]

martial /ˈmɑːʃ(ə)l/ adj. 1 of or appropriate to warfare. 2 warlike, brave; fond of fighting. □ **martial arts** fighting sports such as judo and karate. **martial law** military government, involving the suspension of ordinary law. □ **martially** adv. [ME f. OF *martial* or L *martialis* of the Roman god Mars: see MARTIAN]

Martian /ˈmɑːʃ(ə)n/ adj. & n. —adj. of the planet Mars. —n. a hypothetical inhabitant of Mars. [ME f. OF *martien* or L *Martianus* f. *Mars Martis* the Roman god of war.]

martin /ˈmɑːtɪn/ n. any of several swallows of the family Hirundinidae, esp. the house-martin and sand-martin. [prob. f. St *Martin*, bishop of Tours in the 4th c.]

martinet /ˌmɑːtɪˈnet/ n. a strict (esp. military or naval) disciplinarian. □ **martinettish** adj. (also **martinetish**). [J. *Martinet*, 17th-c. French drill-master]

Martini /mɑːˈtiːnɪ/ n. 1 propr. a type of vermouth. 2 a cocktail made of gin and French vermouth. [*Martini & Rossi*, Italian firm selling vermouth]

martyr /ˈmɑːtə(r)/ n. & v. —n. 1 a a person who is put to death for refusing to renounce a faith or belief. b a person who suffers for adhering to a principle, cause, etc. 2 (foll. by *to*) a constant sufferer from (an ailment). —v.tr. 1 put to death as a martyr. 2 torment. [OE *martir* f. eccl.L *martyr* f. Gk *martur*, *martus* -*uros* witness]

martyrdom /ˈmɑːtədəm/ n. 1 the sufferings and death of a martyr. 2 torment. [OE *martyrdōm* (as MARTYR, -DOM)]

marvel /ˈmɑːv(ə)l/ n. & v. —n. 1 a wonderful thing. 2 (foll. by *of*) a wonderful example of (a quality). —v.intr. (**marvelled, marvelling**; US **marveled, marveling**) *literary* 1 (foll. by *at*, or *that* + clause) feel surprise or wonder. 2 (foll. by *how, why*, etc. + clause) wonder. □ **marveller** n. [ME f. OF *merveille*, *merveiller* f. LL *mirabilia* neut. pl. of L *mirabilis* f. *mirari* wonder at: see MIRACLE]

marvellous /ˈmɑːvələs/ adj. (US **marvelous**) 1 astonishing. 2 excellent. 3 extremely improbable. □ **marvellously** adv. **marvellousness** n. [ME f. OF *merveillos*: see MARVEL]

Marxism /ˈmɑːksɪz(ə)m/ n. the political and economic theories of Karl Marx, German political philosopher (d. 1883), predicting the overthrow of capitalism and the eventual attainment of a classless society with the State controlling the means of production. □ **Marxist** n. & adj.

marzipan /ˈmɑːzɪˌpæn, -ˈpæn/ n. & v. —n. 1 a paste of ground almonds, sugar, etc., made up into small cakes etc., or used to coat large cakes. 2 a piece of marzipan. —v.tr. (**marzipanned, marzipanning**) cover with or as with marzipan. [G f. It. *marzapane*]

mascara /mæˈskɑːrə/ n. a cosmetic for darkening the eyelashes. [It. *mascara*, *maschera* MASK]

mascot /ˈmæskɒt/ n. a person, animal, or thing that is supposed to bring good luck. [F *mascotte* f. mod. Prov. *mascotto* fem. dimin. of *masco* witch]

masculine /ˈmæskjʊlɪn, ˈmɑːs-/ adj. & n. —adj. 1 of or characteristic of men. 2 manly, vigorous.

3 (of a woman) having qualities considered appropriate to a man. 4 *Gram.* of or denoting the gender proper to men's names. —n. *Gram.* the masculine gender; a masculine word. □ **masculinely** adv. **masculineness** n. **masculinity** /-ˈlɪnɪtɪ/ n. [ME f. OF *masculin* -*ine* f. L *masculinus* (as MALE)]

maser /ˈmeɪzə(r)/ n. a device using the stimulated emission of radiation by excited atoms to amplify or generate electromagnetic radiation in the microwave range (cf. LASER). [microwave amplification by the stimulated emission of radiation]

mash n. & v. —n. 1 a soft mixture. 2 a mixture of boiled grain, bran, etc., given warm to horses etc. 3 *Brit. colloq.* mashed potatoes (*sausage and mash*). 4 a mixture of malt and hot water used to form wort for brewing. 5 a soft pulp made by crushing, mixing with water, etc. —v.tr. 1 reduce (potatoes etc.) to a uniform mass by crushing. 2 crush or pound to a pulp. 3 mix (malt) with hot water to form wort. □ **masher** n. [OE *māsc* f. WG, perh. rel. to MIX]

mask /mɑːsk/ n. & v. —n. 1 a covering for all or part of the face: a worn as a disguise, or to appear grotesque and amuse or terrify. b made of wire, gauze, etc., and worn for protection (e.g. by a fencer) or by a surgeon to prevent infection of a patient. c worn to conceal the face at balls etc. and usu. made of velvet or silk. 2 a respirator used to filter inhaled air or to supply gas for inhalation. 3 a likeness of a person's face, esp. one made by taking a mould from the face (*death-mask*). 4 a disguise or pretence (*throw off the mask*). 5 *Photog.* a screen used to exclude part of an image. —v.tr. 1 cover (the face etc.) with a mask. 2 disguise or conceal (a taste, one's feelings, etc.). 3 protect from a process. □ **masking tape** adhesive tape used in painting to cover areas on which paint is not wanted. □ **masker** n. [F *masque* f. It. *maschera* f. Arab. *maskara* buffoon f. *sakira* to ridicule]

masked /mɑːskt/ adj. wearing or disguised with a mask. □ **masked ball** a ball at which masks are worn.

masochism /ˈmæsəˌkɪz(ə)m/ n. 1 a form of (esp. sexual) perversion characterized by gratification derived from one's own pain or humiliation. 2 *colloq.* the enjoyment of what appears to be painful or tiresome. □ **masochist** n. **masochistic** /-ˈkɪstɪk/ adj. **masochistically** /-ˈkɪstɪkəlɪ/ adv. [L. von Sacher-*Masoch*, Austrian novelist d. 1895, who described cases of it]

mason /ˈmeɪs(ə)n/ n. & v. —n. 1 a person who builds with stone. 2 (**Mason**) a Freemason. —v.tr. build or strengthen with masonry. [ME f. OF *masson*, *maçonner*, ONF *machun*, prob. ult. f. Gmc]

Masonic /məˈsɒnɪk/ adj. of or relating to Freemasons.

masonry /ˈmeɪsənrɪ/ n. 1 a the work of a mason. b stonework. 2 (**Masonry**) Freemasonry. [ME f. OF *maçonerie* (as MASON)]

masque /mɑːsk/ n. 1 a dramatic and musical entertainment esp. of the 16th and 17th c., orig. of pantomime, later with metrical dialogue. 2 a dramatic composition for this. □□ **masquer** n. [var. of MASK]

masquerade /ˌmɑːskəˈreɪd, ˌmæs-/ n. & v. —n. 1 a false show or pretence. 2 a masked ball. —v.intr. (often foll. by *as*) appear in disguise, assume a false appearance. □ **masquerader** n. [F *mascarade* f. Sp. *mascarada* f. *máscara* mask]

mass[1] n., v., & adj. —n. **1** a coherent body of matter of indefinite shape. **2** a dense aggregation of objects (*a mass of fibres*). **3** (in sing. or pl.; foll. by *of*) a large number or amount. **4** (usu. foll. by *of*) an unbroken expanse (of colour etc.). **5** (foll. by *of*) covered or abounding in (*was a mass of cuts and bruises*). **6** a main portion (of a painting etc.) as perceived by the eye. **7** (prec. by *the*) **a** the majority. **b** (in pl.) the ordinary people. **8** *Physics* the quantity of matter a body contains. **9** (attrib.) relating to, done by, or affecting large numbers of people or things; large-scale (*mass audience; mass action; mass murder*). —v.tr. & intr. **1** assemble into a mass or as one body (*massed bands*). **2** Mil. (with ref. to troops) concentrate or be concentrated. □ **centre of mass** a point representing the mean position of matter in a body or system. **in the mass** in the aggregate. **mass media** = MEDIA 2. **mass noun** *Gram.* a noun that is not countable and cannot be used with the indefinite article or in the plural (e.g. *bread*). **mass-produce** produce by mass production. **mass production** the production of large quantities of a standardized article by a standardized mechanical process. □ **massless** adj. [ME f. OF *masse, masser* f. L *massa* f. Gk *maza* barley-cake: perh. rel. to *massō* knead]

mass[2] /mæs, mɑːs/ n. (often **Mass**) **1** the Euchar- ist, esp. in the Roman Catholic Church. **2** a celebration of this. **3** the liturgy used in the mass. **4** a musical setting of parts of this. [OE *mæsse* f. eccl.L *missa* f. L *mittere miss-* dismiss, perh. f. the concluding dismissal *Ite, missa est* Go, it is the dismissal]

massacre /ˈmæsəkə(r)/ n. & v. —n. **1** a general slaughter (of persons, occasionally of animals). **2** an utter defeat or destruction. —v.tr. **1** make a massacre of. **2** murder (esp. a large number of people) cruelly or violently. [OF, of unkn. orig.]

massage /ˈmæsɑːʒ, -sɑːdʒ/ n. & v. —n. **1** the rubbing, kneading, etc., of muscles and joints of the body with the hands, to stimulate their action, cure strains, etc. **2** an instance of this. —v.tr. **1** apply massage to. **2** manipulate (statistics) to give an acceptable result. □ **mas- sage parlour 1** an establishment providing massage. **2** *euphem.* a brothel. □ **massager** n. [F f. *masser* treat with massage, perh. f. Port. *amassar* knead, f. *massa* dough: see MASS[1]]

masseur /mæˈsɜː(r)/ n. (*fem.* **masseuse** /mæˈsɜːz/) a person who provides massage professionally. [F f. *masser*: see MASSAGE]

massif /ˈmæsiːf, mæˈsiːf/ n. a compact group of mountain heights. [F *massif* used as noun: see MASSIVE]

massive /ˈmæsɪv/ adj. **1** large and heavy or solid. **2** (of the features, head, etc.) relatively large; of solid build. **3** exceptionally large (*took a massive overdose*). **4** substantial, impressive (*a massive reputation*). □ **massively** adv. **massiveness** n. [ME f. F *massif* -ive f. OF *massiz* ult. f. L *massa* MASS[1]]

mast[1] /mɑːst/ n. & v. —n. **1** a long upright post of timber, iron, etc., set up on a ship's keel, esp. to support sails. **2** a post or lattice-work upright for supporting a radio or television aerial. **3** a flag-pole (*half-mast*). **4** (in full **mooring-mast**) a strong steel tower to the top of which an airship can be moored. —v.tr. furnish (a ship) with

masts. □ **before the mast** serving as an ordinary seaman. □ **masted** adj. (also in comb.). **master** n. (also in comb.). [OE *mæst* f. WG]

mast[2] /mɑːst/ n. the fruit of the beech, oak, chestnut, and other forest-trees, esp. as food for pigs. [OE *mæst* f. WG, prob. rel. to MEAT]

mastectomy /mæsˈtektəmɪ/ n. (pl. -ies) *Surgery* the amputation of a breast. [Gk *mastos* breast + -ECTOMY]

master /ˈmɑːstə(r)/ n., adj., & v. —n. **1 a** a person having control of persons or things. **b** an employer. **c** a male head of a household (*master of the house*). **d** the owner of a dog, horse, etc. **e** the owner of a slave. **f** *Naut.* the captain of a merchant ship. **g** *Hunting* the person in control of a pack of hounds etc. **2 a** a male teacher or tutor, esp. a schoolmaster. **3 a** the head of a college, school, etc. **b** the presiding officer of a livery company, Masonic lodge, etc. **4** a person who has or gets the upper hand (*we shall see which of us is master*). **5** a person skilled in a particular trade and able to teach others (often attrib.: *master carpenter*). **6** a holder of a university degree orig. giving authority to teach in the university (*Master of Arts; Master of Science*). **7** a revered teacher in philosophy etc. **8** a great artist. **9** *Chess* etc. a player of proved ability at international level. **10** an original version (e.g. of a film or gramophone record) from which a series of copies can be made. **11** (**Master**) a title prefixed to the name of a boy not old enough to be called Mr (*Master T. Jones; Master Tom*). —adj. **1** commanding, superior (*a master spirit*). **2** main, principal (*master bedroom*). **3** controlling others (*master plan*). —v.tr. **1** overcome, defeat. **2** reduce to subjection. **3** acquire complete knowledge of (a subject) or facility in using (an instrument etc.). **4** rule as a master. □ **be master of 1** have at one's disposal. **2** know how to control. **be one's own master** be independent or free to do as one wishes. **make oneself master of** acquire a thorough knowledge of or facility in using. **Master Aircrew** an RAF rank equivalent to warrant-officer. **master-class** a class given by a person of distinguished skill, esp. in music. **master-key** a key that opens several locks, each of which also has its own key. **master mariner 1** the captain of a merchant ship. **2** a seaman certified competent to be captain. **master mason 1** a skilled mason, or one in business on his or her own account. **2** a fully qualified Freemason, who has passed the third degree. **Master of the Rolls** (in England and Wales) a judge who presides over the Court of Appeal and was formerly in charge of the Public Record Office. **master-stroke** an outstandingly skilful act of policy etc. **master-switch** a switch controlling the supply of electricity etc. to an entire system. □ **masterdom** n. **masterhood** n. **masterless** adj. [OE *mægester* (later also f. OF *maistre*) f. L *magister*, prob. rel. to *magis* more]

masterful /ˈmɑːstəfʊl/ adj. **1** imperious, dom- ineering. **2** masterly. □ **masterfully** adv. **masterfulness** n.

■ **Usage** This word is normally used of a person, whereas *masterly* is used of achievements, abil- ities, etc.

masterly /ˈmɑːstəlɪ/ adj. worthy of a master; very skilful (*a masterly piece of work*). □ **masterliness** n.

■ **Usage** See note at *masterful*.

mastermind /ˈmɑːstəˌmaɪnd/ n. & v. —n. **1 a** a person with an outstanding intellect. **b** such an intellect. **2** the person directing an intricate operation. —*v.tr.* plan and direct (a scheme or enterprise).

masterpiece /ˈmɑːstəˌpiːs/ *n.* **1** an outstanding piece of artistry or workmanship. **2** a person's best work.

mastership /ˈmɑːstəʃɪp/ *n.* **1** the position or function of a master, esp. a schoolmaster. **2** dominion, control.

mastery /ˈmɑːstərɪ/ *n.* **1** dominion, sway. **2** masterly skill. **3** (often foll. by *of*) comprehensive knowledge or use of a subject or instrument. **4** (prec. by *the*) the upper hand. [ME f. OF *maistrie* (as MASTER)]

masthead /ˈmɑːsthed/ *n.* **1** the highest part of a ship's mast, esp. that of a lower mast as a place of observation or punishment. **2** the title of a newspaper etc. at the head of the front or editorial page.

mastic /ˈmæstɪk/ *n.* **1** a gum or resin exuded from the bark of the mastic tree, used in making varnish. **2** (in full **mastic tree**) the evergreen tree, *Pistacia lentiscus*, yielding this. **3** a waterproof filler and sealant used in building. [ME f. OF f. LL *mastichum* f. L *mastiche* f. Gk *mastikhē*, perh. f. *mastikhaō* (see MASTICATE) with ref. to its use as chewing-gum]

masticate /ˈmæstɪˌkeɪt/ *v.tr.* grind or chew (food) with one's teeth. □ **mastication** /-ˈkeɪʃ(ə)n/ *n.* **masticator** *n.* **masticatory** *adj.* [LL *masticare masticat-* f. Gk *mastikhaō* gnash the teeth]

mastiff /ˈmæstɪf, ˈmɑːs-/ *n.* **1** a dog of a large strong breed with drooping ears and pendulous lips. **2** this breed of dog. [ME ult. f. OF *mastin* ult. f. L *mansuetus* tame]

mastitis /mæˈstaɪtɪs/ *n.* an inflammation of the mammary gland (the breast or udder). [Gk *mastos* breast + -ITIS]

mastodon /ˈmæstəˌdɒn/ *n.* a large extinct mammal of the genus *Mammut*, resembling the elephant but having nipple-shaped tubercles on the crowns of its molar teeth. □ **mastodontic** /-ˈdɒntɪk/ *adj.* [mod.L f. Gk *mastos* breast + *odous odontos* tooth]

mastoid /ˈmæstɔɪd/ *adj.* & *n.* —*adj.* shaped like a woman's breast. —*n.* = *mastoid process.* □ **mastoid process** a conical prominence on the temporal bone behind the ear. [F *mastoïde* or mod.L *mastoides* f. Gk *mastoeidēs* f. *mastos* breast]

mastoiditis /ˌmæstɔɪˈdaɪtɪs/ *n.* inflammation of the mastoid process.

masturbate /ˈmæstəˌbeɪt/ *v.intr.* & *tr.* arouse oneself sexually or cause (another person) to be aroused by manual stimulation of the genitals. □ **masturbation** /-ˈbeɪʃ(ə)n/ *n.* **masturbator** *n.* **masturbatory** *adj.* [L *masturbari masturbat-*]

mat¹ *n.* & *v.* —*n.* **1** a piece of coarse material for wiping shoes on, esp. a doormat. **2** a piece of cork, rubber, plastic, etc., to protect a surface from the heat or moisture of an object placed on it. **3** a piece of resilient material for landing on in gymnastics, wrestling, etc. **4** a piece of coarse fabric of plaited rushes, straw, etc., for lying on, packing furniture, etc. **5** a small rug. —*v.* (**matted, matting**) **1** *a tr.* (esp. as **matted** *adj.*) entangle in a thick mass (*matted hair*). **b** *intr.* become matted. **2** *tr.* cover or furnish with mats. □ **on the mat** *sl.* being reprimanded (orig. in the army, on the orderly-room mat before the commanding officer). [OE *m(e)att(e)* f. WG f. LL *matta*]

mat² var. of MATT.

matador /ˈmætəˌdɔː(r)/ *n.* a bullfighter whose task is to kill the bull. [Sp. f. *matar* kill f. Pers. *māt* dead]

match¹ *n.* & *v.* —*n.* **1** a contest or game of skill etc. in which persons or teams compete against each other. **2** *a* a person able to contend with another as an equal (*meet one's match; be more than a match for*). **b** a person equal to another in some quality (*we shall never see his match*). **c** a person or thing exactly like or corresponding to another. **3** a marriage. **4** a person viewed in regard to his or her eligibility for marriage, esp. as to rank or fortune (*an excellent match*). —*v.* **1** *a tr.* be equal to or harmonious with; correspond to in some essential respect (*the curtains match the wallpaper*). **b** *intr.* (often foll. by *with*) correspond; harmonize (*his socks do not match; does the ribbon match with your hat?*). **2** *tr.* (foll. by *against, with*) place (a person etc.) in conflict, contest, or competition with (another). **3** *tr.* find material etc. that matches (another) (*can you match this silk?*). **4** *tr.* find a person or thing suitable for another (*matching unemployed workers with vacant posts*). **5** *tr.* prove to be a match for. □ **make a match** bring about a marriage. **match play** Golf play in which the score is reckoned by counting the holes won by each side. **match point** Tennis etc. **a** the state of a game when one side needs only one more point to win the match. **b** this point. **to match** corresponding in some essential respect with what has been mentioned (*yellow dress with gloves to match*). **well-matched** fit to contend with each other, live together, etc., on equal terms. □ **matchable** *adj.* [OE *gemæcca* mate, companion, f. Gmc]

match² *n.* **1** a short thin piece of wood, wax, etc., tipped with a composition that can be ignited by friction. **2** a piece of wick, cord, etc., designed to burn at a uniform rate, for firing a cannon etc. [ME f. OF *mesche, meiche*, perh. f. L *myxa* lamp-nozzle]

matchboard /ˈmætʃbɔːd/ *n.* a board with a tongue cut along one edge and a groove along another, so as to fit with similar boards.

matchbox /ˈmætʃbɒks/ *n.* a box for holding matches.

matchet var. of MACHETE.

matchless /ˈmætʃlɪs/ *adj.* without an equal, incomparable. □ **matchlessly** *adv.*

matchmaker /ˈmætʃˌmeɪkə(r)/ *n.* a person fond of scheming to bring about marriages. □ **matchmaking** *n.*

matchstick /ˈmætʃstɪk/ *n.* the stem of a match.

matchwood /ˈmætʃwʊd/ *n.* **1** wood suitable for matches. **2** minute splinters. □ **make matchwood of** smash utterly.

mate¹ *n.* & *v.* —*n.* **1** a friend or fellow worker. **2** *colloq.* a general form of address, esp. to another man. **3** *a* each of a pair, esp. of birds. **b** *colloq.* a partner in marriage. **c** (in *comb.*) a fellow member or joint occupant of (*team-mate; room-mate*). **4** *Naut.* an officer on a merchant ship subordinate to the master. **5** an assistant to a skilled worker (*plumber's mate*). —*v.* (often foll. by *with*) **1** *a tr.* bring (animals or birds) together for breeding. **b** *intr.* (of animals or birds) come together for breeding. **2** *a tr.* join (persons) in marriage. **b** *intr.* (of persons) be joined in marriage. **3** *intr.* Mech. fit well. □ **mateless** *adj.*

[ME f. MLG *mate* f. *gemate* messmate f. WG, rel. to MEAT]

mate² *n.* & *v.tr. Chess* = CHECKMATE. [ME f. F *mat(er)*: see CHECKMATE]

matelot /ˈmætləʊ/ *n.* (also **matlow, matlo**) *Brit. sl.* a sailor. [F *matelot*]

mater /ˈmeɪtə(r)/ *n. Brit. sl.* mother. [L].

■ **Usage** This word is now only in jocular or affected use.

material /məˈtɪərɪəl/ *n.* & *adj.* —*n.* **1** the matter from which a thing is made. **2** cloth, fabric. **3** (in *pl.*) things needed for an activity (*building materials; cleaning materials; writing materials*). **4** a person or thing of a specified kind or suitable for a purpose (*officer material*). **5** (in *sing.* or *pl.*) information etc. to be used in writing a book etc. (*experimental material; materials for a biography*). **6** (in *sing.* or *pl.*, often foll. by *of*) the elements or constituent parts of a substance. —*adj.* **1** of matter; corporeal. **2** concerned with bodily comfort etc. (*material well-being*). **3** (of conduct, points of view, etc.) not spiritual. **4** (often foll. by *to*) important, essential, relevant (*at the material time*). **5** concerned with the matter, not the form, of reasoning. □ **materiality** /-ˈælɪtɪ/ *n.* [ME f. OF *materiel, -al*, f. LL *materialis* f. L (as MATTER)]

materialism /məˈtɪərɪəˌlɪz(ə)m/ *n.* a tendency to prefer material possessions and physical comfort to spiritual values. □ **materialist** *n.* **materialistic** /-ˈlɪstɪk/ *adj.* **materialistically** /-ˈlɪstɪkəlɪ/ *adv.*

materialize /məˈtɪərɪəˌlaɪz/ *v.* (also **-ise**) **1** *intr.* become actual fact. **2 a** *tr.* cause (a spirit) to appear in bodily form. **b** *intr.* (of a spirit) appear in this way. **3** *intr. colloq.* appear or be present when expected. **4** *tr.* represent or express in material form. **5** *tr.* make materialistic. □ **materialization** /-ˈzeɪʃ(ə)n/ *n.*

materially /məˈtɪərɪəlɪ/ *adv.* **1** substantially, considerably. **2** in respect of matter.

matériel /məˌtɪərɪˈel/ *n.* available means, esp. materials and equipment in warfare (opp. PERSONNEL). [F (as MATERIAL)]

maternal /məˈtɜːn(ə)l/ *adj.* **1** of or like a mother. **2** motherly. **3** related through the mother (*maternal uncle*). **4** of the mother in pregnancy and childbirth. □ **maternalism** *n.* **maternalistic** /-ˈlɪstɪk/ *adj.* **maternally** *adv.* [ME f. OF *maternel* or L *maternus* f. *mater* mother]

maternity /məˈtɜːnɪtɪ/ *n.* **1** motherhood. **2** motherliness. **3** (*attrib.*) **a** for women during and just after childbirth (*maternity hospital; maternity leave*). **b** suitable for a pregnant woman (*maternity dress*). [F *maternité* f. med.L *maternitas -tatis* f. L *maternus* f. *mater* mother]

mateship /ˈmeɪtʃɪp/ *n. Austral.* companionship, fellowship.

matey /ˈmeɪtɪ/ *adj.* & *n.* (also **maty**) —*adj.* (**matier, matiest**) (often foll. by *with*) sociable; familiar and friendly. —*n. Brit.* (*pl.* **-eys**) *colloq.* (usu. as a form of address) mate, companion. □ **mateyness** *n.* (also **matiness**). **matily** *adv.*

math /mæθ/ *n. US colloq.* mathematics (cf. MATHS). [abbr.]

mathematical /ˌmæθɪˈmætɪk(ə)l/ *adj.* **1** of or relating to mathematics. **2** (of a proof etc.) rigorously precise. □ **mathematically** *adv.* [F *mathématique* or L *mathematicus* f. Gk *mathēmatikos* f. *mathēma -matos* science f. *manthanō* learn]

mathematics /ˌmæθɪˈmætɪks/ *n.pl.* **1** (also treated as *sing.*) the abstract science of number, quantity, and space studied in its own right (**pure mathematics**), or as applied to other disciplines such as physics, engineering, etc. (**applied mathematics**). **2** (as *pl.*) the use of mathematics in calculation etc. □ **mathematician** /-məˈtɪʃ(ə)n/ *n.* [prob. f. F *mathématiques* pl. f. L *mathematica* f. Gk *mathēmatika*: see MATHEMATICAL]

maths /mæθs/ *n. Brit. colloq.* mathematics (cf. MATH). [abbr.]

matinée /ˈmætɪˌneɪ/ *n.* (*US* **matinee**) an afternoon performance in the theatre, cinema, etc. □ **matinée coat** (or **jacket**) a baby's short coat. **matinée idol** a handsome actor admired chiefly by women. [F, = what occupies a morning f. *matin* morning (as MATINS)]

matins /ˈmætɪnz/ *n.* (also **mattins**) (as *sing* or *pl.*) **1** a service of morning prayer in the Church of England. **2** the office of one of the canonical hours of prayer, properly a night office, but also recited with lauds at daybreak or on the previous evening. [ME f. OF *matines* f. eccl.L *matutinas*, accus. fem. pl. adj. f. L *matutinus* of the morning f. *Matuta* dawn-goddess]

matlo (also **matlow**) var. of MATELOT.

matriarch /ˈmeɪtrɪˌɑːk/ *n.* a woman who is the head of a family or tribe. □ **matriarchal** /-ˈɑːk(ə)l/ *adj.* [L *mater* mother, on the false analogy of PATRIARCH]

matriarchy /ˈmeɪtrɪˌɑːkɪ/ *n.* (*pl.* **-ies**) a form of social organization in which the mother is the head of the family and descent is reckoned through the female line.

matrices *pl.* of MATRIX.

matricide /ˈmeɪtrɪˌsaɪd/ *n.* **1** the killing of one's mother. **2** a person who does this. □ **matricidal** *adj.* [L *matricida, matricidium* f. *mater matris* mother]

matriculate /məˈtrɪkjʊˌleɪt/ *v.* **1** *intr.* be enrolled at a college or university. **2** *tr.* admit (a student) to membership of a college or university. □ **matriculation** *n.* **matriculatory** *adj.* [med.L *matriculare matriculat-* enrol f. LL *matricula* register, dimin. of L MATRIX]

matrimony /ˈmætrɪmənɪ/ *n.* (*pl.* **-ies**) **1** the rite of marriage. **2** the state of being married. □ **matrimonial** /-ˈməʊnɪəl/ *adj.* **matrimonially** /-ˈməʊnɪəlɪ/ *adv.* [ME f. AF *matrimonie*, OF *matremoi(g)ne* f. L *matrimonium* f. *mater matris* mother]

matrix /ˈmeɪtrɪks/ *n.* (*pl.* **matrices** /-ˌsiːz/ or **matrixes**) **1** a mould in which a thing is cast or shaped, such as a gramophone record, printing type, etc. **2 a** an environment or substance in which a thing is developed. **b** a womb. **3** a mass of fine-grained rock in which gems, fossils, etc., are embedded. **4** *Math.* a rectangular array of elements in rows and columns that is treated as a single element. **5** *Computing* a gridlike array of interconnected circuit elements. □ **matrix printer** = *dot matrix printer* (see DOT). [L, = breeding-female, womb, register f. *mater matris* mother]

matron /ˈmeɪtrən/ *n.* **1** a married woman, esp. a dignified and sober one. **2** a woman managing the domestic arrangements of a school etc. **3** *Brit.* a woman in charge of the nursing in a hospital. □ **matron of honour** a married woman attending the bride at a wedding. □

matronhood n. [ME f. OF *matrone* f. L *matrona* f. *mater matris* mother]

■ **Usage** In sense 3, *senior nursing officer* is now the official term.

matronly /ˈmeɪtrənlɪ/ adj. like or characteristic of a matron, esp. in respect of staidness or portliness.

matt adj. & n. (also **mat**) —adj. (of a colour, surface, etc.) dull, without lustre. —n. 1 a border of dull gold round a framed picture. 2 (in full **matt paint**) paint formulated to give a dull flat finish. [F *mat*, *mater*, identical with *mat* MATE²]

matte /mæt/ n. *Cinematog.* a mask to obscure part of an image and allow another image to be superimposed, giving a combined effect. [F]

matter /ˈmætə(r)/ n. & v. —n. 1 **a** physical substance in general, as distinct from mind and spirit. **b** that which has mass and occupies space. 2 a particular substance (*colouring matter*). 3 (prec. by *the*; often foll. by *with*) the thing that is amiss (*what is the matter?*; *there is something the matter with him*). 4 material for thought or expression. 5 the substance of a book, speech, etc., as distinct from its manner or form. 6 a thing or things of a specified kind (*printed matter*; *reading matter*). 7 an affair or situation being considered, esp. in a specified way (*a serious matter*; *a matter for concern*; *the matter of your overdraft*). 8 *Physiol.* **a** any substance in or discharged from the body (*faecal matter*; *grey matter*). **b** pus. 9 (foll. by *of*, *for*) what is or may be a good reason for (complaint, regret, etc.). —v.intr. (often foll. by *to*) be of importance; have significance (*it does not matter to me when it happened*). □ **as a matter of fact** in reality (esp. to correct a falsehood or misunderstanding). **for that matter** (or **for the matter of that**) 1 as far as that is concerned. 2 and indeed also. **in the matter of** as regards. **a matter of 1** approximately (*for a matter of 40 years*). 2 a thing that relates to, depends on, or is determined by (*a matter of habit*; *only a matter of time before they agree*). **a matter of fact** what belongs to the sphere of fact as distinct from opinion etc. **no matter 1** (foll. by *when*, *how*, etc.) regardless of (*will do it no matter what the consequences*). 2 it is of no importance. **what is the matter with** surely there is no objection to. **what matter?** that need not worry us. [ME f. AF *mater(i)e*, OF *matiere* f. L *materia* timber, substance, subject of discourse]

matter-of-fact /ˌmætərəˈfækt/ adj. 1 unimaginative, prosaic. 2 unemotional. □ **matter-of-factly** adv. **matter-of-factness** n.

matting /ˈmætɪŋ/ n. 1 fabric of hemp, bast, grass, etc., for mats (*coconut matting*). 2 in senses of MAT¹ v.

mattins var. of MATINS.

mattock /ˈmætək/ n. an agricultural tool shaped like a pickaxe, with an adze and a chisel edge as the ends of the head. [OE *mattuc*, of unkn. orig.]

mattress /ˈmætrɪs/ n. a fabric case stuffed with soft, firm, or springy material, or a similar case filled with air or water, used on or as a bed. [ME f. OF *materas* f. It. *materasso* f. Arab. *almaṭraḥ* the place, the cushion f. *ṭaraḥa* throw]

maturate /ˈmætjʊˌreɪt/ v.intr. Med. (of a boil etc.) come to maturation. [L *maturatus* (as MATURE v.)]

maturation /ˌmætjʊˈreɪʃ(ə)n/ n. 1 the act or an instance of maturing; the state of being matured. **b** the ripening of fruit. 2 *Med.* **a** the formation of purulent matter. **b** the causing of this. □ **maturative** /məˈtjʊərətɪv/ adj. [ME f. F *maturation* or med.L *maturatio* f. L (as MATURE v.)]

mature /məˈtjʊə(r)/ adj. & v. —adj. (**maturer**, **maturest**) 1 with fully developed powers of body and mind, adult. 2 complete in natural development, ripe. 3 (of thought, intentions, etc.) duly careful and adequate. 4 (of a bill etc.) due for payment. —v. 1 **a** tr. & intr. develop fully. **b** tr. & intr. ripen. **c** intr. come to maturity. 2 tr. perfect (a plan etc.). 3 intr. (of a bill etc.) become due for payment. □ **mature student** an adult student who is older than most students. □ **maturely** adv. **matureness** n. **maturity** n. [ME f. L *maturus* timely, early]

matutinal /ˌmætjuːˈtaɪn(ə)l, məˈtjuːtɪn(ə)l/ adj. 1 of or occurring in the morning. 2 early. [LL *matutinalis* f. L *matutinus*: see MATINS]

maty var. of MATEY.

matzo /ˈmɑːtsəʊ/ n. (pl. **-os** or **matzoth** /-əʊt/) 1 a wafer of unleavened bread for the Passover. 2 such bread collectively. [Yiddish f. Heb. *maṣṣāh*]

maudlin /ˈmɔːdlɪn/ adj. weakly or tearfully sentimental, esp. in a tearful and effusive stage of drunkenness. [ME f. OF *Madeleine* f. eccl.L *Magdalena*, with ref. to pictures of Mary Magdalen (Luke 8:2) weeping]

maul v. & n. —v.tr. 1 beat and bruise. 2 handle roughly or carelessly. 3 damage by criticism. —n. 1 *Rugby Football* a loose scrum with the ball off the ground. 2 a brawl. 3 a special heavy hammer, esp. for driving piles. □ **mauler** n. [ME f. OF *mail* f. L *malleus* hammer]

maulstick /ˈmɔːlstɪk/ n. (also **mahlstick**) a light stick with a padded leather ball at one end, held by a painter in one hand to support the other hand. [Du. *maalstok* f. *malen* to paint + *stok* stick]

maunder /ˈmɔːndə(r)/ v.intr. 1 talk in a dreamy or rambling manner. 2 move or act listlessly or idly. [perh. f. obs. *maunder* beggar, to beg]

Maundy /ˈmɔːndɪ/ n. (in the UK) the distribution of money on the Thursday before Easter (see below). □ **Maundy money** specially minted silver coins distributed by the British sovereign on Maundy Thursday. **Maundy Thursday** the Thursday before Easter. [ME f. OF *mandé* f. L *mandatum* MANDATE, commandment (see John 13:34)]

mausoleum /ˌmɔːsəˈliːəm/ n. a large and grand tomb. [L f. Gk *Mausōleion* f. *Mausōlos* Mausolus king of Caria (4th c. BC), to whose tomb the name was orig. applied]

mauve /məʊv/ adj. & n. —adj. pale purple. —n. 1 this colour. 2 a bright but delicate pale purple dye from coal-tar aniline. □ **mauvish** adj. [F, lit. = mallow, f. L *malva*]

maverick /ˈmævərɪk/ n. 1 *US* an unbranded calf or yearling. 2 an unorthodox or independent-minded person. [S. A. *Maverick*, Texas engineer and rancher d. 1870, who did not brand his cattle]

maw n. 1 **a** the stomach of an animal. **b** the jaws or throat of a voracious animal. 2 *colloq.* the stomach of a greedy person. [OE *maga* f. Gmc]

mawkish /ˈmɔːkɪʃ/ adj. 1 sentimental in a feeble or sickly way. 2 having a faint sickly flavour. □

mawkishly adv. **mawkishness** n. [obs. mawk maggot f. ON mathkr f. Gmc]

max. abbr. maximum.

maxi /ˈmæksɪ/ n. (pl. **maxis**) colloq. a maxi-coat, -skirt, etc. [abbr.]

maxi- /ˈmæksɪ/ comb. form very large or long (maxi-coat). [abbr. of MAXIMUM: cf. MINI-]

maxilla /mækˈsɪlə/ n. (pl. **maxillae** /-li:/) 1 the jaw or jawbone, esp. the upper jaw in most vertebrates. 2 the mouth-part of many arthropods used in chewing. □ **maxillary** adj. [L, = jaw]

maxim /ˈmæksɪm/ n. a general truth or rule of conduct expressed in a sentence. [ME f. F maxime or med.L maxima (propositio), fem. adj. (as MAXIMUM)]

maxima pl. of MAXIMUM.

maximal /ˈmæksɪm(ə)l/ adj. being or relating to a maximum; the greatest possible in size, duration, etc. □ **maximally** adv.

maximize /ˈmæksɪˌmaɪz/ v.tr. (also **-ise**) increase or enhance to the utmost. □ **maximization** /-ˈzeɪʃ(ə)n/ n. **maximizer** n. [L maximus: see MAXIMUM]

■ **Usage** This word should not be used to mean 'to make as good as possible' or 'to make the most of'.

maximum /ˈmæksɪməm/ n. & adj. —n. (pl. **maxima** /-mə/) the highest possible or attainable amount. —adj. that is a maximum. [mod.L, neut. of L maximus, superl. of magnus great]

May n. 1 the fifth month of the year. 2 (**may**) the hawthorn or its blossom. □ **May Day** 1 May esp. as a festival with dancing, or as an international holiday in honour of workers. **May queen** a girl chosen to preside over celebrations on May Day. **Queen of the May** = May queen. [ME f. OF mai f. L Maius (mensis) (month) of the goddess Maia]

may v.aux. (3rd sing. present **may**; past **might** /maɪt/) 1 (often foll. by well for emphasis) expressing possibility (it may be true; I may have been wrong; you may well lose your way). 2 expressing permission (you may not go; may I come in?). 3 expressing a wish (may he live to regret it). 4 expressing uncertainty or irony in questions (who may you be?; who are you, may I ask?). 5 in purpose clauses and after wish, fear, etc. (take such measures as may avert disaster; hope he may succeed). □ **be that as it may** (or **that is as may be**) that may or may not be so (implying that there are other factors) (be that as it may, I still want to go). [OE mæg f. Gmc, rel. to MAIN, MIGHT²]

■ **Usage** In sense 2, both can and may are used to express permission; in more formal contexts may is preferred since can also denotes capability (can I move? = am I physically able to move?; may I move? = am I allowed to move?).

Maya /ˈmɑːjə/ n. 1 (pl. same or **Mayas**) a member of an ancient Indian people of Central America. 2 the language of this people. □ **Mayan** adj. & n. [native name]

maybe /ˈmeɪbiː/ adv. perhaps, possibly. [ME f. it may be]

mayday /ˈmeɪdeɪ/ n. an international radio distress-signal used esp. by ships and aircraft. [repr. pronunc. of F m'aidez help me]

mayflower /ˈmeɪˌflaʊə(r)/ n. any of various flowers that bloom in May, esp. the trailing arbutus, Epigaea repens.

mayfly /ˈmeɪflaɪ/ n. (pl. **-flies**) 1 any insect of the order Ephemeroptera, living briefly in spring in the adult stage. 2 an imitation mayfly used by anglers.

mayhem /ˈmeɪhem/ n. 1 violent or damaging action. 2 hist. the crime of maiming a person so as to render him or her partly or wholly defenceless. [AF mahem, OF mayhem (as MAIM)]

maying /ˈmeɪɪŋ/ n. & adj. participation in May Day festivities. [ME f. MAY]

mayn't /ˈmeɪənt/ contr. may not.

mayonnaise /ˌmeɪəˈneɪz/ n. 1 a thick creamy dressing made of egg-yolks, oil, vinegar, etc. 2 a (usu. specified) dish dressed with this (chicken mayonnaise). [F, perh. f. mahonnais -aise of Port Mahon on Minorca]

mayor /meə(r)/ n. 1 the head of the municipal corporation of a city or borough. 2 (in England, Wales, and N. Ireland) the head of a district council with the status of a borough. □ **mayoral** adj. **mayorship** n. [ME f. OF maire f. L (as MAJOR)]

mayoralty /ˈmeərəltɪ/ n. (pl. **-ies**) 1 the office of mayor. 2 a mayor's period of office. [ME f. OF mairalté (as MAYOR)]

mayoress /ˈmeərɪs/ n. 1 a woman holding the office of mayor. 2 the wife of a mayor. 3 a woman fulfilling the ceremonial duties of a mayor's wife.

maypole /ˈmeɪpəʊl/ n. a pole painted and decked with flowers and ribbons, for dancing round on May Day.

mazarine /ˌmæzəˈriːn/ n. & adj. a rich deep blue. [17th c., perh. f. the name of Cardinal Mazarin, French statesman d. 1661, or Duchesse de Mazarin, French noblewoman d. 1699]

maze n. & v. —n. 1 a network of paths and hedges designed as a puzzle for those who try to penetrate it. 2 a complex network of paths or passages; a labyrinth. 3 confusion, a confused mass, etc. □ **mazy** adj. (**mazier**, **maziest**). [ME, orig. as mased (adj.): rel. to AMAZE]

mazer /ˈmeɪzə(r)/ n. hist. a hardwood drinking-bowl, usu. silver-mounted. [ME f. OF masere f. Gmc]

mazurka /məˈzɜːkə/ n. 1 a usu. lively Polish dance in triple time. 2 the music for this. [F mazurka or G Masurka, f. Pol. mazurka woman of the province Mazovia]

MB abbr. 1 Bachelor of Medicine. 2 Computing megabyte. [sense 1 f. L Medicinae Baccalaureus]

MBA abbr. Master of Business Administration.

MBE abbr. Member of the Order of the British Empire.

MC abbr. 1 Master of Ceremonies. 2 (in the UK) Military Cross. 3 (in the US) Member of Congress. 4 music cassette (of pre-recorded audiotape).

MCC abbr. Marylebone Cricket Club.

McCarthyism, McCoy see at MACC-.

M.Ch. abbr. (also **M.Chir.**) Master of Surgery. [L Magister Chirurgiae]

MD abbr. 1 Doctor of Medicine. 2 Managing Director. [sense 1 f. L Medicinae Doctor]

Md symb. Chem. the element mendelevium.

ME abbr. myalgic encephalomyelitis, an obscure disease with symptoms like those of influenza and prolonged periods of tiredness and depression.

me[1] /mi:, mɪ/ *pron.* **1** *objective case of* I[2] (*he saw me*). **2** *colloq.* = I[2] (*it's me all right; is taller than me*). **3** *US colloq.* myself, to or for myself (*I got me a gun*). **4** *colloq.* used in exclamations (*ah me!; dear me!; silly me!*). □ **me and mine** me and my relatives. [OE *me, mē* accus. & dative of I[2] f. Gmc]

me[2] /mi:/ *n.* (also **mi**) *Mus.* **1** (in tonic sol-fa) the third note of a major scale. **2** the note E in the fixed-doh system. [ME f. L *mira*: see GAMUT]

mead *n.* an alcoholic drink of fermented honey and water. [OE *me(o)du* f. Gmc]

meadow /ˈmedəʊ/ *n.* **1** a piece of grassland, esp. one used for hay. **2** a piece of low well-watered ground, esp. near a river. □ **meadowy** *adj.* [OE *mǣdwe*, oblique case of *mǣd* rel. to MOW]

meadowsweet /ˈmedəʊˌswi:t/ *n.* **1** a rosaceous plant, *Filipendula ulmaria*, with creamy-white fragrant flowers. **2** any of several rosaceous plants of the genus *Spiraea*, native to N. America.

meagre /ˈmi:gə(r)/ *adj.* (*US* **meager**) **1** lacking in amount or quality (*a meagre salary*). **2** (of literary composition, ideas, etc.) lacking fullness, unsatisfying. **3** (of a person or animal) lean, thin. □ **meagrely** *adv.* **meagreness** *n.* [ME f. AF *megre*, OF *maigre* f. L *macer*]

meal[1] *n.* **1** an occasion when food is eaten. **2** the food eaten on one occasion. □ **make a meal of 1** treat (a task etc.) too laboriously or fussily. **2** consume as a meal. **meals on wheels** *Brit.* a service by which meals are delivered to old people, invalids, etc. **meal-ticket 1** a ticket entitling one to a meal, esp. at a specified place with reduced cost. **2** a person or thing that is a source of food or income. [OE *mǣl* mark, fixed time, meal f. Gmc]

meal[2] /mi:l/ *n.* **1** the edible part of any grain or pulse (*us.* other than wheat) ground to powder. **2** *Sc.* oatmeal. **3** *US* maize flour. **4** any powdery substance made by grinding. [OE *melu* f. Gmc]

mealie /ˈmi:lɪ/ *n.* (also **mielie**) *S.Afr.* **1** (usu. in *pl.*) maize. **2** a corn-cob. [Afrik. *mielie* f. Port. *milho* maize, millet f. L *milium*]

mealtime /ˈmi:ltaɪm/ *n.* any of the usual times of eating.

mealy /ˈmi:lɪ/ *adj.* (**mealier, mealiest**) **1 a** of or like meal; soft and powdery. **b** containing meal. **2** (of a complexion) pale. **3** (in full **mealy-mouthed**) not outspoken; afraid to use plain expressions. □ **mealiness** *n.*

mean[1] *v.tr.* (*past and past part.* **meant** /ment/) **1 a** (often foll. by *to* + infin.) have as one's purpose or intention; have in mind (*they really mean mischief; I didn't mean to break it*). **b** (foll. by *by*) have as a motive in an explanation (*what do you mean by that?*). **2** (often in *passive*) design or destine for a purpose (*mean it to be used; mean it for a stopgap; is meant to be a gift*). **3** intend to convey or indicate or refer to (a particular thing or notion) (*I mean we cannot go; I mean Richmond in Surrey*). **4** entail, involve (*it means catching the early train*). **5** (often foll. by *that* + clause) portend, signify (*this means trouble; your refusal means that we must look elsewhere*). **6** (of a word) have as its explanation in the same language or its equivalent in another language. **7** (foll. by *to*) be of some specified importance to (a person), esp. as a source of benefit or object of affection etc. (*that means a lot to me*). □ **mean business** be in earnest. **mean it** not be joking or exaggerating. **mean to say** really admit (usu.

in interrog.: *do you mean to say you have lost it?*). **mean well** (often foll. by *to, towards, by*) have good intentions. [OE *mǣnan* f. WG, rel. to MIND]

mean[2] *adj.* **1** niggardly; not generous or liberal. **2** (of an action) ignoble, small-minded. **3** (of a person's capacity, understanding, etc.) inferior, poor. **4** (of housing) not imposing in appearance; shabby. **5 a** malicious, ill-tempered. **b** *US* vicious or aggressive in behaviour. **6** *colloq.* skilful, formidable (*is a mean fighter*). **7** *colloq.* ashamed (*feel mean*). □ **no mean** a very good (*that is no mean achievement*). □ **meanly** *adv.* **meanness** *n.* [OE *mǣne, gemǣne* f. Gmc]

mean[3] *n.* & *adj.* —*n.* **1** a condition, quality, virtue, or course of action equally removed from two opposite (usu. unsatisfactory) extremes. **2** *Math.* **a** the term or one of the terms midway between the first and last terms of an arithmetical or geometrical etc. progression (*2 and 8 have the arithmetic mean 5 and the geometric mean 4*). **b** the quotient of the sum of several quantities and their number, the average. —*adj.* **1** (of a quantity) equally far from two extremes. **2** calculated as a mean. □ **mean sea level** the sea level halfway between the mean levels of high and low water. **mean sun** an imaginary sun moving in the celestial equator at the mean rate of the real sun, used in calculating solar time. **mean time** the time based on the movement of the mean sun. [ME f. AF *meen* f. OF *meien, moien* f. L *medianus* MEDIAN]

meander /mɪˈændə(r)/ *v.* & *n.* —*v.intr.* **1** wander at random. **2** (of a stream) wind about. —*n.* **1** (in *pl.*) **a** the sinuous windings of a river. **b** winding paths. **2** a circuitous journey. **3** an ornamental pattern of lines winding in and out; a fret. [L *maeander* f. Gk *Maiandros*, the name of a winding river in Phrygia]

meanie /ˈmi:nɪ/ *n.* (also **meany**) (*pl.* **-ies**) *colloq.* a mean, niggardly, or small-minded person.

meaning /ˈmi:nɪŋ/ *n.* & *adj.* —*n.* **1** what is meant by a word, action, idea, etc. **2** significance. **3** importance. —*adj.* expressive, significant (*a meaning glance*). □ **meaningly** *adv.*

meaningful /ˈmi:nɪŋfʊl/ *adj.* **1** full of meaning; significant. **2** *Logic* able to be interpreted. □ **meaningfully** *adv.* **meaningfulness** *n.*

meaningless /ˈmi:nɪŋlɪs/ *adj.* having no meaning or significance. □ **meaninglessly** *adv.* **meaninglessness** *n.*

means /mi:nz/ *n.pl.* (often treated as *sing.*) that by which a result is brought about (*a means of quick travel*). **2 a** money resources (*live beyond one's means*). **b** wealth (*a man of means*). □ **by all means** (or **all manner of means**) **1** certainly. **2** in every possible way. **3** at any cost. **by means of** by the agency or instrumentality of (a thing or action). **by no means** (or **no manner of means**) not at all; certainly not. **means test** an official inquiry to establish need before financial assistance from public funds is given. [pl. of MEAN[3]]

meant *past and past part.* of MEAN[1].

meantime /ˈmi:ntaɪm/ *adv.* & *n.* —*adv.* = MEANWHILE. —*n.* the intervening period (esp. *in the meantime*). [MEAN[3] + TIME]

■ **Usage** As an adverb, *meantime* is less common then *meanwhile*.

meanwhile /ˈmi:nwaɪl/ *adv.* & *n.* —*adv.* **1** in the intervening period of time. **2** at the same time. —*n.* the intervening period (esp. *in the meanwhile*). [MEAN³ + WHILE]

measles /ˈmiːz(ə)lz/ *n.pl.* (also treated as *sing.*) **1** an acute infectious viral disease marked by red spots on the skin. **2** a tapeworm disease of pigs. [ME *masele(s)* prob. f. MLG *masele*, MDu. *masel* pustule (cf. Du. *mazelen* measles), OHG *masala*: change of form prob. due to assim. to ME *meser* leper]

measly /ˈmiːzlɪ/ *adj.* (**measlier, measliest**) **1** *colloq.* inferior, contemptible, worthless. **2** of or affected with measles. **3** (of pork) infested with tapeworms. [MEASLES + -Y¹]

measurable /ˈmeʒərəb(ə)l/ *adj.* that can be measured. □ **measurability** /-ˈbɪlɪtɪ/ *n.* **measurably** *adv.* [ME f. OF *mesurable* f. LL *mensurabilis* f. L *mensurare* (as MEASURE)]

measure /ˈmeʒə(r)/ *n.* & *v.* —*n.* **1** a size or quantity found by measuring. **2** a system of measuring (*liquid measure; linear measure*). **3** a rod or tape etc. for measuring. **4** a vessel of standard capacity for transferring or determining fixed quantities of liquids etc. (*a pint measure*). **5 a** the degree, extent, or amount of a thing. **b** (foll. by *of*) some degree of (*there was a measure of wit in her remark*). **6** a unit of capacity, e.g. a bushel (*20 measures of wheat*). **7** a factor by which a person or thing is reckoned or evaluated (*their success is a measure of their determination*). **8** (usu. in *pl.*) suitable action to achieve some end (*took measures to ensure a good profit*). **9** a legislative enactment. **10** a prescribed extent or quantity. **11** *Printing* the width of a page or column of type. **12** poetical rhythm; metre. **13** *US Mus.* a bar or the time-content of a bar. —*v.* **1** *tr.* ascertain the extent or quantity of (a thing) by comparison with a fixed unit or with an object of known size. **2** *intr.* be of a specified size (*it measures six inches*). **3** *tr.* ascertain the size and proportion of (a person) for clothes. **4** *tr.* estimate (a quality, person's character, etc.) by some standard or rule. **5** *tr.* (often foll. by *off*) mark (a line etc.) of a given length. **6** *tr.* (foll. by *out*) deal or distribute (a thing) in measured quantities. **7** *tr.* (foll. by *with, against*) bring (oneself or one's strength etc.) into competition with. □ **beyond measure** excessively. **for good measure** as something beyond the minimum; as a finishing touch. **in a** (or **some**) **measure** partly. **made to measure** *Brit.* (of clothes) made from measurements taken. **measure up 1 a** determine the size etc. of by measurement. **b** take comprehensive measurements. **2** (often foll. by *to*) have the necessary qualifications (for). **measuring-jug** (or **-cup**) a jug or cup marked to measure its contents. **measuring-tape** a tape marked to measure length. [ME f. OF *mesure* f. L *mensura* f. *metiri mens-* measure]

measured /ˈmeʒəd/ *adj.* **1** rhythmical; regular in movement (*a measured tread*). **2** (of language) carefully considered. □ **measuredly** *adv.*

measureless /ˈmeʒələs/ *adj.* not measurable; infinite. □ **measurelessly** *adv.*

measurement /ˈmeʒəmənt/ *n.* **1** the act or an instance of measuring. **2** an amount determined by measuring. **3** (in *pl.*) detailed dimensions.

meat *n.* **1** the flesh of animals (esp. mammals) as food. **2** (foll. by *of*) the essence or chief part of. **3** *US* the edible part of fruits, nuts, eggs, shellfish, etc. □ **meat and drink** a source of great pleasure. **meat loaf** minced or chopped

meat moulded into the shape of a loaf and baked. **meat safe** a cupboard for storing meat, usu. of wire gauze etc. □ **meatless** *adj.* [OE *mete* food f. Gmc]

meatball /ˈmiːtbɔːl/ *n.* minced meat compressed into a small round ball.

meaty /ˈmiːtɪ/ *adj.* (**meatier, meatiest**) **1** full of meat; fleshy. **2** of or like meat. **3** full of substance. □ **meatily** *adv.* **meatiness** *n.*

Mecca /ˈmekə/ *n.* **1** a place one aspires to visit. **2** the birthplace of a faith, policy, pursuit, etc. [*Mecca* in Arabia, birthplace of Muhammad and chief place of Muslim pilgrimage]

mechanic /mɪˈkænɪk/ *n.* a skilled worker, esp. one who makes or uses or repairs machinery. [ME (orig. as adj.) f. OF *mecanique* or L *mechanicus* f. Gk *mēkhanikos* (as MACHINE)]

mechanical /mɪˈkænɪk(ə)l/ *adj.* **1** of or relating to machines or mechanisms. **2** working or produced by machinery. **3** (of a person or action) like a machine; automatic; lacking originality. **4 a** (of an agency, principle, etc.) belonging to mechanics. **b** (of a theory etc.) explaining phenomena by the assumption of mechanical action. **5** of or relating to mechanics as a science. □ **mechanical drawing** a scale drawing of machinery etc. done with precision instruments. **mechanical engineer** a person skilled in the branch of engineering dealing with the design, construction, and repair of machines. □ **mechanicalism** *n.* (in sense 4). **mechanically** *adv.* **mechanicalness** *n.* [ME f. L *mechanicus* (as MECHANIC)]

mechanician /ˌmekəˈnɪʃ(ə)n/ *n.* a person skilled in constructing machinery.

mechanics /mɪˈkænɪks/ *n.pl.* (usu. treated as *sing.*) **1** the branch of applied mathematics dealing with motion and tendencies to motion. **2** the science of machinery. **3** the method of construction or routine operation of a thing.

mechanism /ˈmekənɪz(ə)m/ *n.* **1** the structure or adaptation of parts of a machine. **2** a system of mutually adapted parts working together in or as in a machine. **3** the mode of operation of a process. [mod.L *mechanismus* f. Gk (as MACHINE)]

mechanist /ˈmekənɪst/ *n.* **1** a mechanician. **2** an expert in mechanics. □ **mechanistic** /-ˈnɪstɪk/ *adj.* **mechanistically** /-ˈnɪstɪkəlɪ/ *adv.*

mechanize /ˈmekənaɪz/ *v.tr.* (also **-ise**) **1** give a mechanical character to. **2** introduce machines in. **3** *Mil.* equip with tanks, armoured cars, etc. (orig. as a substitute for horse-drawn vehicles and cavalry). □ **mechanization** /-ˈzeɪʃ(ə)n/ *n.* **mechanizer** *n.*

mechatronics /ˌmekəˈtrɒnɪks/ *n.* the science of the combination of electronics and mechanics in developing new manufacturing techniques. [*mechanics* + *electronics*]

M.Econ. *abbr.* Master of Economics.

Med /med/ *n. colloq.* the Mediterranean Sea. [abbr.]

M.Ed. *abbr.* Master of Education.

medal /ˈmed(ə)l/ *n.* a piece of metal, usu. in the form of a disc, struck or cast with an inscription or device to commemorate an event etc., or awarded as a distinction to a soldier, scholar, athlete, etc., for services rendered, for proficiency, etc. □ **medalled** *adj.* **medallic** /mɪˈdælɪk/ *adj.* [F *médaille* f. It. *medaglia* ult. f. L *metallum* METAL]

medallion /mɪˈdæljən/ n. **1** a large medal. **2** a thing shaped like this, e.g. a decorative panel or tablet, portrait, etc. [F *médaillon* f. It. *medaglione* augment. of *medaglia* (as MEDAL)]

medallist /ˈmedəlɪst/ n. (US **medalist**) a recipient of a (specified) medal (*gold medallist*).

meddle /ˈmed(ə)l/ v.intr. (often foll. by *with*, *in*) interfere in or busy oneself unduly with others' concerns. □ **meddler** n. [ME f. OF *medler*, var. of *mesler* ult. f. L *miscēre* mix]

meddlesome /ˈmedəlsəm/ adj. fond of meddling; interfering. □ **meddlesomely** adv. **meddlesomeness** n.

media /ˈmiːdɪə/ n.pl. **1** pl. of MEDIUM. **2** (usu. prec. by *the*) the main means of mass communication (esp. newspapers and broadcasting) regarded collectively. □ **media event** an event primarily intended to attract publicity.

■ **Usage** This word is commonly used with a singular verb (e.g. *the media is biased*), but this is not generally approved of (cf. DATA).

medial /ˈmiːdɪəl/ adj. **1** situated in the middle. **2** of average size. □ **medially** adv. [LL *medialis* f. L *medius* middle]

median /ˈmiːdɪən/ adj. & n. —adj. situated in the middle. —n. **1** Geom. a straight line drawn from any vertex of a triangle to the middle of the opposite side. **2** Math. the middle value of a series of values arranged in order of size. □ **medianly** adv. [F *médiane* or L *medianus* (as MEDIAL)]

mediate v. & adj. —v. /ˈmiːdɪeɪt/ **1** intr. (often foll. by *between*) intervene (between parties in a dispute) to produce agreement or reconciliation. **2** tr. be the medium for bringing about (a result) or for conveying (a gift etc.). **3** tr. form a connecting link between. —adj. /ˈmiːdɪət/ **1** connected not directly but through some other person or thing. **2** involving an intermediate agency. □ **mediately** /-ətlɪ/ adv. **mediation** /-ˈeɪʃ(ə)n/ n. **mediator** /ˈmiːdɪeɪtə(r)/ n. **mediatory** /ˈmiːdɪətərɪ/ adj. [LL *mediare mediat-* f. L *medius* middle]

medic /ˈmedɪk/ n. colloq. a medical practitioner or student. [L *medicus* physician f. *medēri* heal]

medicable /ˈmedɪkəb(ə)l/ adj. admitting of remedial treatment. [L *medicabilis* (as MEDICATE)]

Medicaid /ˈmedɪˌkeɪd/ n. (in the US) a Federal system of health insurance for those requiring financial assistance. [MEDICAL + AID]

medical /ˈmedɪk(ə)l/ adj. & n. —adj. **1** of or relating to the science of medicine in general. **2** of or relating to conditions requiring medical and not surgical treatment (*medical ward*). —n. colloq. a medical examination. □ **medical certificate** a certificate of fitness or unfitness to work etc. **medical examination** an examination to determine a person's physical fitness. **medical jurisprudence** the law relating to medicine. **medical officer** Brit. a person in charge of the health services of a local authority or other organization. **medical practitioner** a physician or surgeon. □ **medically** adv. [F *médical* or med.L *medicalis* f. L *medicus*: see MEDIC]

medicament /mɪˈdɪkəmənt, ˈmedɪkəmənt/ n. a substance used for medical treatment. [F *médicament* or L *medicamentum* (as MEDICATE)]

Medicare /ˈmedɪˌkeə(r)/ n. (in the US) a Federal system of health insurance for persons over 65 years of age. [MEDICAL + CARE]

medicate /ˈmedɪˌkeɪt/ v.tr. **1** treat medically. **2** impregnate with a medicinal substance. □ **medicative** /ˈmedɪkətɪv/ adj. [L *medicari medicat-* administer remedies to f. *medicus*: see MEDIC]

medication /ˌmedɪˈkeɪʃ(ə)n/ n. **1** a substance used for medical treatment. **2** treatment using drugs.

medicinal /mɪˈdɪsɪn(ə)l/ adj. & n. —adj. (of a substance) having healing properties. —n. a medicinal substance. □ **medicinally** adv. [ME f. OF f. L *medicinalis* (as MEDICINE)]

medicine /ˈmedsɪn, -dɪsɪn/ n. **1** the science or practice of the diagnosis, treatment, and prevention of disease. esp. as distinct from surgical methods. **2** any drug or preparation used for the treatment or prevention of disease, esp. one taken by mouth. □ **a dose** (or **taste**) **of one's own medicine** treatment such as one is accustomed to giving others. **medicine chest** a box containing medicines etc. **medicine man** a person believed to have magical powers of healing, esp. among N. American Indians. **take one's medicine** submit to something disagreeable. [ME f. OF *medecine* f. L *medicina* f. *medicus*: see MEDIC]

medico /ˈmedɪˌkəʊ/ n. (pl. **-os**) colloq. a medical practitioner or student. [It. f. L (as MEDIC)]

medico- /ˈmedɪkəʊ/ comb. form medical; medical and (*medico-legal*). [L *medicus* (as MEDIC)]

medieval /ˌmedɪˈiːv(ə)l/ adj. (also **mediaeval**) **1** of, or in the style of, the Middle Ages. **2** colloq. old-fashioned, archaic. □ **medievalism** n. **medievalist** n. **medievalize** v.tr. & intr. (also **-ise**). **medievally** adv. [mod.L *medium aevum* f. L *medius* middle + *aevum* age]

mediocre /ˌmiːdɪˈəʊkə(r)/ adj. **1** of middling quality, neither good nor bad. **2** second-rate. [F *médiocre* or f. L *mediocris* of middle height or degree f. *medius* middle + *ocris* rugged mountain]

mediocrity /ˌmiːdɪˈɒkrɪtɪ/ n. (pl. **-ies**) **1** the state of being mediocre. **2** a mediocre person or thing.

meditate /ˈmedɪˌteɪt/ v. **1** intr. **a** exercise the mind in (esp. religious) contemplation. **b** (usu. foll. by *on*, *upon*) focus on a subject in this manner. **2** tr. plan mentally; design. □ **meditation** /-ˈteɪʃ(ə)n/ n. **meditator** n. [L *meditari* contemplate]

meditative /ˈmedɪtətɪv/ adj. **1** inclined to meditate. **2** indicative of meditation. □ **meditatively** adv. **meditativeness** n.

Mediterranean /ˌmedɪtəˈreɪnɪən/ n. & adj. —n. **1** a large landlocked sea bordered by S. Europe, SW Asia, and N. Africa. **2** a native of a country bordering on the Mediterranean. —adj. of or characteristic of the Mediterranean or its surrounding region (*Mediterranean climate*; *Mediterranean cookery*). [L *mediterraneus* inland f. *medius* middle + *terra* land]

medium /ˈmiːdɪəm/ n. & adj. —n. (pl. **media** or **mediums**) **1** the middle quality, degree, etc. between extremes (*find a happy medium*). **2** the means by which something is communicated (*the medium of sound*; *the medium of television*). **3** the intervening substance through which impressions are conveyed to the senses etc. (*light passing from one medium into another*). **4** Biol. the physical environment or conditions of growth, storage, or transport of a living organism (*the shape of a fish is ideal for its fluid* *medium*; *growing mould on the surface of a medium*). **5** an agency or means of doing something (*the medium through which money is raised*). **6** the material or form used by an artist, composer, etc. (*language as an artistic medium*). **7** the liquid (e.g. oil or gel) with which pigments are mixed for use in painting. **8** (*pl.* **mediums**) a person claiming to be in contact with the spirits of the dead and to communicate between the dead and the living. —*adj.* **1** between two qualities, degrees, etc. **2** average; moderate (*of medium height*). □ **medium frequency** a radio frequency between 300 kHz and 3 MHz. **medium wave** a radio wave of medium frequency. □ **mediumism** *n.* (in sense 8 of *n.*). **mediumistic** /-ˈmɪstɪk/ *adj.* (in sense 8 of *n.*). **mediumship** *n.* (in sense 8 of *n.*). [L, = middle, neut. of *medius*]

medlar /ˈmedlə(r)/ *n.* **1** a rosaceous tree, *Mespilus germanica*, bearing small brown apple-like fruits. **2** the fruit of this tree which is eaten when decayed. [ME f. OF *medler* f. L *mespila* f. Gk *mespilē*, -*on*]

medley /ˈmedlɪ/ *n.* (*pl.* -**eys**) **1** a varied mixture; a miscellany. **2** a collection of musical items from one work or various sources arranged as a continuous whole. □ **medley relay** a relay race between teams in which each member runs a different distance, swims a different stroke, etc. [ME f. OF *medlee* var. of *meslee* f. Rmc (as MEDDLE)]

medulla /mɪˈdʌlə/ *n.* the inner region of certain organs or tissues usu. when it is distinguishable from the outer region or cortex, as in hair or a kidney. □ **medulla oblongata** /ˌɒblɒŋˈgɑːtə/ the continuation of the spinal cord within the skull, forming the lowest part of the brain stem. □ **medullary** *adj.* [L, = pith, marrow, prob. rel. to *medius* middle]

medusa /mɪˈdjuːsə/ *n.* (*pl.* **medusae** /-siː/ or **medusas**) **1** a jellyfish. **2** a free-swimming form of any coelenterate, having tentacles round the edge of a usu. umbrella-shaped jelly-like body, e.g. a jellyfish. □ **medusan** *adj.* [L f. Gk *Medousa*, name of a Gorgon with snakes instead of hair]

meek *adj.* **1** humble and submissive; suffering injury etc. tamely. **2** piously gentle in nature. □ **meekly** *adv.* **meekness** *n.* [ME *me(o)c* f. ON *mjúkr* soft, gentle]

meerkat /ˈmɪəkæt/ *n.* the suricate. [Du., = sea-cat]

meerschaum /ˈmɪəʃəm/ *n.* **1** a soft white form of hydrated magnesium silicate, chiefly found in Turkey, which resembles clay. **2** a tobacco-pipe with the bowl made from this. [G, = sea-foam f. *Meer* sea + *Schaum* foam, transl. Pers. *kef-i-daryā*, with ref. to its frothiness]

meet[1] *v.* & *n.* —*v.* (*past* and *past part.* **met** /met/) **1 a** *tr.* encounter (a person or persons) by accident or design; come face to face with. **b** *intr.* (of two or more people) come into each other's company by accident or design (*decided to meet on the bridge*). **2** *tr.* go to a place to be present at the arrival of (a person, train, etc.). **3 a** *tr.* (of a moving object, line, feature of landscape, etc.) come together or into contact with (*where the road meets the flyover*). **b** *intr.* come together or into contact (*where the sea and the sky meet*). **4 a** *tr.* make the acquaintance of (*delighted to meet you*). **b** *intr.* (of two or more people) make each other's acquaintance. **5** *intr.* & *tr.* come together or come into contact with for the

purposes of conference, business, worship, etc. (*the committee meets every week; the union met management yesterday*). **6** *tr.* **a** (of a person or a group) deal with or answer (a demand, objection, etc.) (*met the original proposal with hostility*). **b** satisfy or conform with (proposals, deadlines, a person, etc.) (*agreed to meet the new terms*). **7** *tr.* pay (a bill etc.); provide the funds required by (a cheque etc.) (*meet the cost of the move*). **8** *tr.* & (foll. by *with*) *intr.* experience, encounter, or receive (success, disaster, a difficulty, etc.) (*met their death; met with many problems*). **9** *tr.* oppose in battle, contest, or confrontation. **10** *intr.* (of clothes, curtains, etc.) join or fasten correctly (*my jacket won't meet*). —*n.* **1** the assembly of riders and hounds for a hunt. **2** the assembly of competitors for various sporting activities, esp. athletics. □ **meet the case** be adequate. **meet the eye** (or **the ear**) be visible (or audible). **meet a person's eye** check if another person is watching and look into his or her eyes in return. **meet a person half way** make a compromise, respond in a friendly way to the advances of another person. **meet up** *colloq.* happen to meet. **meet with 1** see sense 8 of *v.* **2** receive (a reaction) (*met with the committee's approval*). **3** esp. *US* = sense 1a of *v.* □ **meeter** *n.* [OE *mētan* f. Gmc: cf. MOOT]

meet[2] /miːt/ *adj.* *archaic* suitable, fit, proper. □ **meetly** *adv.* **meetness** *n.* [ME (i)*mete* repr. OE *gemǣte* f. Gmc, rel. to METE]

meeting /ˈmiːtɪŋ/ *n.* **1** in senses of MEET[1]. **2** an assembly of people, esp. the members of a society, committee, etc., for discussion or entertainment. **3** = *race meeting*. **4** an assembly (esp. of Quakers) for worship. **5** the persons assembled (*address the meeting*).

mega /ˈmegə/ *adj.* & *adv.* *sl.* —*adj.* **1** excellent. **2** enormous. —*adv.* extremely. [Gk f. as MEGA-]

mega- /ˈmegə/ *comb. form* **1** large. **2** denoting a factor of one million (10^6) in the metric system of measurement. [Gk f. *megas* great]

megabuck /ˈmegəˌbʌk/ *n.* *US* *colloq.* a million dollars.

megabyte /ˈmegəˌbaɪt/ *n.* *Computing* 1,048,576 (i.e. 2^{20}) bytes as a measure of data capacity, or loosely 1,000,000.

megadeath /ˈmegəˌdeθ/ *n.* the death of one million people (esp. as a unit in estimating the casualties of war).

megahertz /ˈmegəˌhɜːts/ *n.* one million hertz, esp. as a measure of frequency of radio transmissions.

megalith /ˈmegəlɪθ/ *n.* *Archaeol.* a large stone, esp. one placed upright as a monument or part of one. [MEGA- + Gk *lithos* stone]

megalithic /ˌmegəˈlɪθɪk/ *adj.* *Archaeol.* made of or marked by the use of large stones.

megalo- /ˈmegələʊ/ *comb. form* great (*megalomania*). [Gk f. *megas megal-* great]

megalomania /ˌmegələˈmeɪnɪə/ *n.* **1** a mental disorder producing delusions of grandeur. **2** a passion for grandiose schemes. □ **megalomaniac** *adj.* & *n.* **megalomaniacal** /-məˈnaɪək(ə)l/ *adj.* **megalomanic** /-ˈmænɪk/ *adj.*

megalopolis /ˌmegəˈlɒpəlɪs/ *n.* **1** a great city or its way of life. **2** an urban complex consisting of a city and its environs. □ **megalopolitan** /-ləˈpɒlɪt(ə)n/ *adj.* & *n.* [MEGA- + Gk *polis* city]

megalosaurus /ˌmegələˈsɔːrəs/ *n.* a large flesh-eating dinosaur of the genus *Megalosaurus*, with

stout hind legs and small forelimbs. [MEGALO-
+ Gk *sauros* lizard]

megaphone /ˈmegəˌfəʊn/ *n.* a large funnel-
shaped device for amplifying the sound of the
voice.

megastar /ˈmegəˌstɑː(r)/ *n.* a very famous
person, esp. in the world of entertainment.

megaton /ˈmegəˌtʌn/ *n.* (also **megatonne**) a
unit of explosive power equal to one million
tons of TNT.

megavolt /ˈmegəˌvəʊlt/ *n.* one million volts, esp.
as a unit of electromotive force.

megawatt /ˈmegəˌwɒt/ *n.* one million watts, esp.
as a measure of electrical power as generated
by power stations.

megohm /ˈmegəʊm/ *n. Electr.* one million ohms.
[MEGA- + OHM]

meiosis /maɪˈəʊsɪs/ *n.* **1** *Biol.* a type of cell
division that results in daughter cells with half
the chromosome number of the parent cell. **2**
= LITOTES. □ **meiotic** /-ˈɒtɪk/ *adj.* **meiotically**
/-ˈɒtɪkəlɪ/ *adv.* [mod.L f. Gk *meiōsis* f. *meioō* lessen
f. *meiōn* less]

melamine /ˈmeləˌmiːn/ *n.* **1** a white crystalline
compound used to make thermosetting resins.
2 (in full **melamine resin**) a plastic made from
melamine and used esp. for laminated coatings.
[*melam* (arbitrary) + AMINE]

melancholia /ˌmelənˈkəʊlɪə/ *n.* a mental illness
marked by depression and ill-founded fears. [LL:
see MELANCHOLY]

melancholy /ˈmelənkəlɪ/ *n. & adj.* —*n.* (*pl.* -**ies**)
1 a pensive sadness. **2 a** mental depression. **b** a
habitual or constitutional tendency to this. **3**
hist. one of the four humours; black bile. —*adj.*
(of a person) sad, gloomy; (of a thing) saddening,
depressing; (of words, a tune, etc.) expressing
sadness. □ **melancholic** /-ˈkɒlɪk/ *adj.* **mel-
ancholically** /-ˈkɒlɪkəlɪ/ *adv.* [ME f. OF *melancolie*
f. LL *melancholia* f. Gk *melagkholia* f. *melas melanos*
black + *kholē* bile]

mélange /meɪˈlɑ̃ʒ/ *n.* a mixture, a medley. [F f.
mêler mix (as MEDDLE)]

melanin /ˈmelənɪn/ *n.* a dark-brown to black
pigment occurring in the hair, skin, and iris of
the eye, that is responsible for tanning of the
skin when exposed to sunlight. [Gk *melas melanos*
black + -IN]

melanoma /ˌmeləˈnəʊmə/ *n.* a malignant
tumour of melanin-forming cells, usu. in the
skin. [MELANIN + -OMA]

Melba /ˈmelbə/ *n.* □ **do a Melba** *Austral. sl.* **1**
return from retirement. **2** make several farewell
appearances. **Melba sauce** a sauce made from
puréed raspberries thickened with icing sugar.
Melba toast very thin crisp toast. **peach
Melba** a dish of ice-cream and peaches with
liqueur or sauce. [Dame Nellie *Melba*, Austral.
operatic soprano d. 1931]

meld /meld/ *v.tr. & intr.* orig. *US* merge, blend,
combine. [perh. f. MELT + WELD]

mêlée /ˈmeleɪ/ *n.* (*US* **melee**) **1** a confused fight,
skirmish, or scuffle. **2** a muddle. [F (as MEDLEY)]

meliorate /ˈmiːlɪəˌreɪt/ *v.tr. & intr. literary*
improve. □ **melioration** /-ˈreɪʃ(ə)n/ *n.* **meli-
orative** /-rətɪv/ *adj.* [LL *meliorare* f. L *melior* better]

mellifluous /mɪˈlɪflʊəs/ *adj.* (of a voice or words)
pleasing, musical, flowing. □ **mellifluence** *n.*
mellifluent *adj.* **mellifluously** *adv.* **melli-
fluousness** *n.* [ME f. OF *melliflue* or LL *mellifluus*
f. *mel* honey + *fluere* flow]

mellow /ˈmeləʊ/ *adj. & v.* —*adj.* **1** (of sound,
colour, light) soft and rich, free from harshness.
2 (of character) softened or matured by age or
experience. **3** genial, jovial. **4** partly intoxicated.
5 (of fruit) soft, sweet, and juicy. **6** (of wine)
well-matured, smooth. **7** (of earth) rich, loamy.
—*v.tr. & intr.* make or become mellow. □
mellow out *v.intr. US sl.* relax, become laid-back.
□ **mellowly** *adv.* **mellowness** *n.* [ME, perh. f.
attrib. use of OE *melu, melw-* MEAL²]

melodeon /mɪˈləʊdɪən/ *n.* (also **melodion**) **1** a
small organ popular in the 19th c., similar to
the harmonium. **2** a small German accordion,
played esp. by folk musicians. [MELODY +
HARMONIUM with pseudo-Greek ending]

melodic /mɪˈlɒdɪk/ *adj.* **1** of or relating to
melody. **2** having or producing melody. □
melodically *adv.* [F *mélodique* f. LL *melodicus* f.
Gk *melōidikos* (as MELODY)]

melodious /mɪˈləʊdɪəs/ *adj.* **1** of, producing, or
having melody. **2** sweet-sounding. □ **melodiously** *adv.* **melodiousness** *n.* [ME f. OF *melodieus*
(as MELODY)]

melodist /ˈmelədɪst/ *n.* **1** a composer of melodies.
2 a singer.

melodize /ˈmeləˌdaɪz/ *v.* (also **-ise**) **1** *intr.* make
a melody or melodies; make sweet music. **2** *tr.*
make melodious. □ **melodizer** *n.*

melodrama /ˈmeləˌdrɑːmə/ *n.* **1** a sensational
dramatic piece with crude appeals to the emotions and usu. a happy ending. **2** the genre of
drama of this type. **3** language, behaviour, or an
occurrence suggestive of this. □ **melodramatic**
/-drəˈmætɪk/ *adj.* **melodramatically**
/-drəˈmætɪkəlɪ/ *adv.* **melodramatist**
/-ˈdræmətɪst/ *n.* **melodramatize** /-ˈdræməˌtaɪz/
v.tr. (also **-ise**). [earlier *melodrame* f. F *mélodrame*
f. Gk *melos* music + F *drame* DRAMA]

melodramatics /ˌmelədrəˈmætɪks/ *n.pl.* melodramatic behaviour, action, or writing.

melody /ˈmelədɪ/ *n.* (*pl.* -**ies**) **1** an arrangement
of single notes in a musically expressive succession. **2** the principal part in harmonized
music. **3** a musical arrangement of words. **4**
sweet music, tunefulness. [ME f. OF *melodie* f. LL
melodia f. Gk *melōidia* f. *melos* song]

melon /ˈmelən/ *n.* **1** the sweet fruit of various
gourds. **2** the gourd producing this (*honeydew
melon*; *water melon*). [ME f. OF f. LL *melo -onis*
abbr. of L *melopepo* f. Gk *mēlopepōn* f. *mēlon* apple
+ *pepōn* gourd f. *pepōn* ripe]

melt *v. & n.* —*v.* **1** *intr.* become liquefied by
heat. **2** *tr.* change to a liquid condition by heat.
3 *tr.* (as **molten** *adj.*) (usu. of materials that
require a great deal of heat to melt them)
liquefied by heat (*molten lava*; *molten lead*). **4 a**
intr. & tr. dissolve. **b** *intr.* (of food) be easily
dissolved in the mouth. **5** *intr.* **a** (of a person,
feelings, the heart, etc.) be softened as a result
of pity, love, etc. **b** dissolve into tears. **6** *tr.*
soften (a person, feelings, the heart, etc.) (*a look
to melt a heart of stone*). **7** *intr.* (usu. foll. by *into*)
change or merge imperceptibly into another
form or state (*night melted into dawn*). **8** *intr.*
(often foll. by *away*) (of a person) leave or
disappear unobtrusively (*melted into the background*; *melted away into the crowd*). **9** *intr.* (usu. as
melting *adj.*) (of sound) be soft and liquid
(*melting chords*). —*n.* **1** liquid metal etc. **2** an
amount melted at any one time. **3** the process

or an instance of melting. □ **melt away** disappear or make disappear by liquefaction. **melt down 1** melt (esp. metal articles) in order to reuse the raw material. **2** become liquid and lose structure (cf. MELTDOWN). **melting-point** the temperature at which any given solid will melt. **melting-pot 1** a pot in which metals etc. are melted and mixed. **2** a place where races, theories, etc. are mixed, or an imaginary pool where ideas are mixed together. **melt water** water formed by the melting of snow and ice, esp. from a glacier. □ **meltable** adj. & n. **melter** n. **meltingly** adv. [OE meltan, mieltan f. Gmc, rel. to MALT]

meltdown /ˈmeltdaʊn/ n. **1** the melting of (and consequent damage to) a structure, esp. the overheated core of a nuclear reactor. **2** a disastrous event, esp. a rapid fall in share prices.

member /ˈmembə(r)/ n. **1** a person belonging to a society, team, etc. **2 (Member)** a person formally elected to take part in the proceedings of certain organizations (Member of Parliament; Member of Congress). **3** (also attrib.) a part or branch of a political body (member State; a member of the EC). **4** a constituent portion of a complex structure. **5** a part of a sentence, equation, group of figures, mathematical set, etc. **6 a** any part or organ of the body, esp. a limb. **b** = PENIS. **7** used in the title awarded to a person admitted to (usu. the lowest grade of) certain honours (Member of the Order of the British Empire). □ **membered** adj. (also in comb.). **memberless** adj. [ME f. OF membre f. L membrum limb]

membership /ˈmembəʃɪp/ n. **1** being a member. **2** the number of members. **3** the body of members.

membrane /ˈmembreɪn/ n. **1** any pliable sheet-like structure acting as a boundary, lining, or partition in an organism. **2** a thin pliable sheet or skin of various kinds. □ **membranaceous** /ˌmembrəˈneɪʃəs/ adj. **membraneous** /memˈbreɪnɪəs/ adj. **membranous** /ˈmembrənəs/ adj. [L membrana skin of body, parchment (as MEMBER)]

memento /mɪˈmentəʊ/ n. (pl. **-oes** or **-os**) an object kept as a reminder or a souvenir of a person or an event. [L, imper. of meminisse remember]

memento mori /mɪˌmentəʊ ˈmɔːrɪ, -raɪ/ n. a warning or reminder of death (e.g. a skull). [L, = remember you must die]

memo /ˈmeməʊ/ n. (pl. **-os**) colloq. memorandum. [abbr.]

memoir /ˈmemwɑː(r)/ n. **1** a historical account or biography written from personal knowledge or special sources. **2** (in pl.) an autobiography or a written account of one's memory of certain events or people. **3** an essay on a learned subject specially studied by the writer. □ **memoirist** n. [F mémoire (masc.), special use of mémoire (fem.) MEMORY]

memorabilia /ˌmemərəˈbɪlɪə/ n.pl. **1** souvenirs of memorable events. **2** archaic memorable or noteworthy things. [L, neut. pl. (as MEMORABLE)]

memorable /ˈmemərəb(ə)l/ adj. **1** worth remembering, not to be forgotten. **2** easily remembered. □ **memorability** /-ˈbɪlɪtɪ/ n. **memorableness** n. **memorably** adv. [ME f. F mémorable or L memorabilis f. memorare bring to mind f. memor mindful]

memorandum /ˌmeməˈrændəm/ n. (pl. **memoranda** /-də/ or **memorandums**) **1** a note or record made for future use. **2** an informal written message, esp. in business, diplomacy, etc. [ME f. L neut. sing. gerundive of memorare: see MEMORABLE]

memorial /mɪˈmɔːrɪəl/ n. & adj. —n. **1** an object, institution, or custom established in memory of a person or event (the Albert Memorial). **2** (often in pl.) hist. a statement of facts as the basis of a petition etc.; a record; an informal diplomatic paper. —adj. intending to commemorate a person or thing (memorial service). □ **Memorial Day** US a day on which those who died on active service are remembered. □ **memorialist** n. [ME f. OF memorial or L memorialis (as MEMORY)]

memorialize /mɪˈmɔːrɪəlaɪz/ v.tr. (also **-ise**) **1** commemorate. **2** address a memorial to (a person or body).

memorize /ˈmeməraɪz/ v.tr. (also **-ise**) commit to memory. □ **memorizable** adj. **memorization** /-ˈzeɪʃ(ə)n/ n. **memorizer** n.

memory /ˈmemərɪ/ n. (pl. **-ies**) **1** the faculty by which things are recalled to or kept in the mind. **2 a** this faculty in an individual (my memory is beginning to fail). **b** one's store of things remembered (buried deep in my memory). **3** a recollection or remembrance (the memory of better times). **4** the storage capacity of a computer or other electronic machinery. **5** the remembrance of a person or thing (his mother's memory haunted him). **6** the reputation of a dead person (his memory lives on). **7** the length of time over which the memory or memories of any given person or group extends (within the memory of anyone still working here). □ **commit to memory** learn (a thing) so as to be able to recall it. **from memory** without verification in books etc. **in memory of** to keep alive the remembrance of. **memory bank** (or **board**) the memory device of a computer etc. **memory lane** (usu. prec. by down, along) an imaginary and sentimental journey into the past. [ME f. OF memorie, memoire f. L memoria f. memor mindful, remembering, rel. to MOURN]

memsahib /ˈmemˌsɑːɪb, -sɑːb/ n. Anglo-Ind. hist. a European married woman in India, as spoken of or to by Indians. [MA'AM + SAHIB]

men pl. of MAN.

menace /ˈmenɪs/ n. & v. —n. **1** a threat. **2** a dangerous or obnoxious thing or person. **3** joc. a pest, a nuisance. —v.tr. & intr. threaten, esp. in a malignant or hostile manner. □ **menacer** n. **menacingly** adv. [ME ult. f. L minax -acis threatening f. minari threaten]

ménage /meɪˈnɑːʒ/ n. the members of a household. [OF manaige ult. f. L (as MANSION)]

ménage à trois /meɪˌnɑːʒ ɑː ˈtrwɑː/ n. an arrangement in which three people live together, usu. a married couple and the lover of one of them. [F, = household of three (as MÉNAGE)]

menagerie /mɪˈnædʒərɪ/ n. **1** a collection of wild animals in captivity for exhibition etc. **2** the place where these are housed. [F ménagerie (as MÉNAGE)]

menaquinone /ˌmenəˈkwɪnəʊn/ n. one of the K vitamins, produced by bacteria found in the large intestine, essential for the blood-clotting process. [chem. deriv. of methyl- naphthoquinone]

menarche /meˈnɑːkɪ/ n. the onset of first menstruation. [mod.L formed as MENO- + Gk *arkhē* beginning]

mend v. & n. —v. **1** tr. restore to a sound condition; repair (a broken article, a damaged road, torn clothes, etc.). **2** intr. regain health. **3** tr. improve (*mend matters*). —n. a darn or repair in material etc. (*a mend in my shirt*). □ **mend one's fences** make peace with a person. **mend one's ways** reform, improve one's habits. **on the mend** improving in health or condition. □ **mendable** adj. **mender** n. [ME f. AF *mender* f. *amender* AMEND]

mendacious /menˈdeɪʃəs/ adj. lying, untruthful. □ **mendaciously** adv. **mendacity** /-ˈdæsɪtɪ/ n. (pl. **-ies**). [L *mendax -dacis* perh. f. *mendum* fault]

mendelevium /ˌmendəˈliːvɪəm/ n. Chem. an artificially made transuranic radioactive metallic element. [D. I. *Mendeleev*, Russ. chemist d. 1907]

Mendelism /ˈmendəˌlɪz(ə)m/ n. the theory of heredity based on the recurrence of certain inherited characteristics transmitted by genes. □ **Mendelian** /-ˈdiːlɪən/ adj. & n. [G. J. *Mendel*, Austrian botanist d. 1884 + -ISM]

mendicant /ˈmendɪkənt/ adj. & n. —adj. **1** begging. **2** (of a friar) living solely on alms. —n. **1** a beggar. **2** a mendicant friar. □ **mendicancy** n. **mendicity** /-ˈdɪsɪtɪ/ n. [L *mendicare* beg f. *mendicus* beggar f. *mendum* fault]

mending /ˈmendɪŋ/ n. **1** the action of a person who mends. **2** things, esp. clothes, to be mended.

menfolk /ˈmenfəʊk/ n.pl. **1** men in general. **2** the men of one's family.

menhir /ˈmenhɪə(r)/ n. Archaeol. a tall upright usu. prehistoric monumental stone. [Breton *men* stone + *hir* long]

menial /ˈmiːnɪəl/ adj. & n. —adj. **1** (esp. of unskilled domestic work) degrading, servile. **2** usu. derog. (of a servant) domestic. —n. **1** a menial servant. **2** a servile person. □ **menially** adv. [ME f. OF *meinee* household]

meningitis /ˌmenɪnˈdʒaɪtɪs/ n. an inflammation of the meninges due to infection by viruses or bacteria. □ **meningitic** /-ˈdʒɪtɪk/ adj.

meninx /ˈmiːnɪŋks/ n. (pl. **meninges** /mɪˈnɪndʒiːz/) (usu. in pl.) any of the three membranes that line the skull and vertebral canal and enclose the brain and spinal cord. □ **meningeal** /mɪˈnɪndʒɪəl/ adj. [mod.L f. Gk *mēnigx -iggos* membrane]

meniscus /mɪˈnɪskəs/ n. (pl. **menisci** /-saɪ/) **1** Physics the curved upper surface of a liquid in a tube. **2** a lens that is convex on one side and concave on the other. **3** Math. a crescent-shaped figure. □ **meniscoid** adj. [mod.L f. Gk *mēniskos* crescent, dimin. of *mēnē* moon]

meno- /ˈmenəʊ/ comb. form menstruation. [Gk *mēn mēnos* month]

menopause /ˈmenəˌpɔːz/ n. **1** the ceasing of menstruation. **2** the period in a woman's life (usu. between 45 and 50) when this occurs. □ **menopausal** /-ˈpɔːz(ə)l/ adj. [mod.L *menopausis* (as MENO-, PAUSE)]

menorah /mɪˈnɔːrə/ n. a seven-armed candelabrum used in Jewish worship, esp. as a symbol of Judaism. [Heb., = candlestick]

menorrhoea /ˌmenəˈrɪə/ n. ordinary flow of blood at menstruation. [MENO- + Gk *rhoia* f. *rheō* flow]

menses /ˈmensiːz/ n.pl. **1** blood and other materials discharged from the uterus at menstruation. **2** the time of menstruation. [L, pl. of *mensis* month]

menstrual /ˈmenstrʊəl/ adj. of or relating to the menses or menstruation. □ **menstrual cycle** the process of ovulation and menstruation in female primates. [ME f. L *menstrualis* f. *mensis* month]

menstruate /ˈmenstrʊˌeɪt/ v.intr. undergo menstruation. [LL *menstruare menstruat-* (as MENSTRUAL)]

menstruation /ˌmenstrʊˈeɪʃ(ə)n/ n. the process of discharging blood and other materials from the uterus in sexually mature non-pregnant women at intervals of about one lunar month until the menopause.

mensurable /ˈmensjʊrəb(ə)l/ adj. measurable, having fixed limits. [F *mensurable* or LL *mensurabilis* f. *mensurare* to measure f. L *mensura* MEASURE]

mensuration /ˌmensjʊəˈreɪʃ(ə)n/ n. **1** measuring. **2** Math. the measuring of geometric magnitudes such as the lengths of lines, areas of surfaces, and volumes of solids. [LL *mensuratio* (as MENSURABLE)]

menswear /ˈmenzweə(r)/ n. clothes for men.

-ment /mənt/ suffix **1** forming nouns expressing the means or result of the action of a verb (*abridgement*; *embankment*). **2** forming nouns from adjectives (*merriment*; *oddment*). [from or after F f. L *-mentum*]

mental /ˈment(ə)l/ adj. **1** of or in the mind. **2** done by the mind. **3** colloq. **a** insane. **b** crazy, wild, eccentric (*is mental about pop music*). □ **mental age** the degree of a person's mental development expressed as an age at which the same degree is attained by an average person. **mental arithmetic** arithmetic performed in the mind. **mental asylum** (or **home** or **hospital** or **institution**) an establishment for the care of mental patients. **mental cruelty** the infliction of suffering on another's mind, esp. *Law* as grounds for divorce. **mental defective** esp. *US* a person with impaired mental abilities. **mental illness** a disorder of the mind. **mental nurse** a nurse dealing with mentally ill patients. **mental patient** a sufferer from mental illness. **mental reservation** a qualification tacitly added in making a statement etc. □ **mentally** adv. [ME f. OF *mental* or LL *mentalis* f. L *mens -ntis* mind]

mentality /menˈtælɪtɪ/ n. (pl. **-ies**) **1** mental character or disposition. **2** kind or degree of intelligence. **3** what is in or of the mind.

menthol /ˈmenθɒl/ n. a mint-tasting organic alcohol found in oil of peppermint etc., used as a flavouring and to relieve local pain. [G f. L *mentha* MINT¹]

mentholated /ˈmenθəˌleɪtɪd/ adj. treated with or containing menthol.

mention /ˈmenʃ(ə)n/ v. & n. —v.tr. **1** refer to briefly. **2** specify by name. **3** reveal or disclose (*do not mention this to anyone*). **4** (in dispatches) award (a person) a minor honour for meritorious, usu. gallant, military service. —n. **1** a reference, esp. by name, to a person or thing. **2** (in dispatches) a military honour awarded for outstanding conduct. □ **not to mention** introducing a fact or thing of secondary or (as a rhetorical device) of primary importance. □

mentionable *adj.* [OF f. L *mentio -onis* f. the root of *mens* mind]

mentor /ˈmentɔː(r)/ *n.* an experienced and trusted adviser. [F f. L f. Gk *Mentōr* adviser of the young Telemachus in Homer's *Odyssey* and Fénelon's *Télémaque*]

menu /ˈmenjuː/ *n.* **1 a** a list of dishes available in a restaurant etc. **b** a list of items to be served at a meal. **2** *Computing* a list of options showing the commands or facilities available. □ **menu-driven** (of a program or computer) used by making selections from menus. [F, = detailed list, f. L *minutus* MINUTE²]

meow var. of MIAOW.

MEP *abbr.* Member of the European Parliament.

Mephistopheles /ˌmefɪˈstɒfɪˌliːz/ *n.* **1** an evil spirit to whom Faust, in the German legend, sold his soul. **2** a fiendish person. □ **Mephistophelean** /-ˈliːən/ *adj.* **Mephistophelian** /-ˈfiːlɪən/ *adj.* [G (16th c.), of unkn. orig.]

-mer /mə(r)/ *comb. form* denoting a substance of a specified class, esp. a polymer (*dimer; isomer; tautomer*). [Gk *meros* part, share]

mercantile /ˈmɜːkənˌtaɪl/ *adj.* **1** of trade, trading. **2** commercial. **3** mercenary, fond of bargaining. □ **mercantile marine** shipping employed in commerce not war. [F f. It. f. *mercante* MERCHANT]

mercenary /ˈmɜːsɪnərɪ/ *adj.* & *n.* —*adj.* primarily concerned with money or other reward (*mercenary motives*). —*n.* (*pl.* **-ies**) a hired soldier in foreign service. □ **mercenariness** *n.* [ME f. L *mercenarius* f. *merces -edis* reward]

mercer /ˈmɜːsə(r)/ *n.* *Brit.* a dealer in textile fabrics, esp. silk and other costly materials. □ **mercery** *n.* (*pl.* **-ies**). [ME f. AF *mercer*, OF *mercier* ult. f. L *merx mercis* goods]

mercerize /ˈmɜːsəˌraɪz/ *v.tr.* (also **-ise**) treat (cotton fabric or thread) under tension with caustic alkali to give greater strength and impart lustre. [J. *Mercer*, alleged inventor of the process d. 1866]

merchandise /ˈmɜːtʃənˌdaɪz/ *n.* & *v.* —*n.* goods for sale. —*v.* **1** *intr.* trade, traffic. **2** *tr.* trade or traffic in. **3** *tr.* **a** put on the market, promote the sale of (goods etc.). **b** advertise, publicize (an idea or person). □ **merchandisable** *adj.* **merchandiser** *n.* [ME f. OF *marchandise* f. *marchand:* see MERCHANT]

merchant /ˈmɜːtʃ(ə)nt/ *n.* **1** a wholesale trader, esp. with foreign countries. **2** esp. *US* & *Sc.* a retail trader. **3** *colloq.* usu. *derog.* a person showing a partiality for a specified activity or practice (*speed merchant*). □ **merchant bank** esp. *Brit.* a bank dealing in commercial loans and finance. **merchant banker** a member of a merchant bank. **merchant marine** *US* = *merchant navy*. **merchant navy** a nation's commercial shipping. **merchant prince** a wealthy merchant. **merchant ship** = MERCHANTMAN. [ME f. OF *marchand, marchant* ult. f. L *mercari* trade f. *merx mercis* merchandise]

merchantable /ˈmɜːtʃəntəb(ə)l/ *adj.* saleable, marketable. [ME f. *merchant* (v.) f. OF *marchander* f. *marchand:* see MERCHANT]

merchantman /ˈmɜːtʃəntmən/ *n.* (*pl.* **-men**) a ship conveying merchandise.

merciful /ˈmɜːsɪˌfʊl/ *adj.* having or showing or feeling mercy. □ **mercifulness** *n.*

mercifully /ˈmɜːsɪˌfʊlɪ/ *adv.* **1** in a merciful manner. **2** (qualifying a whole sentence) fortunately (*mercifully, the sun came out*).

merciless /ˈmɜːsɪləs/ *adj.* **1** pitiless. **2** showing no mercy. □ **mercilessly** *adv.* **mercilessness** *n.*

mercurial /mɜːˈkjʊərɪəl/ *adj.* **1** (of a person) sprightly, ready-witted, volatile. **2** of or containing mercury. □ **mercurialism** *n.* **mercuriality** /-ˈælɪtɪ/ *n.* **mercurially** *adv.* [ME f. OF *mercuriel* or L *mercurialis* (as MERCURY)]

mercury /ˈmɜːkjʊrɪ/ *n.* **1** *Chem.* a silvery-white heavy liquid metallic element used in barometers, thermometers, and amalgams; quicksilver. □ **mercuric** /-ˈkjʊərɪk/ *adj.* **mercurous** *adj.* [ME f. L *Mercurius* messenger of the gods and god of traders f. *merx mercis* merchandise]

mercy /ˈmɜːsɪ/ *n.* & *int.* —*n.* (*pl.* **-ies**) **1** compassion or forbearance shown to enemies or offenders in one's power. **2** the quality of compassion. **3** an act of mercy. **4** (*attrib.*) administered or performed out of mercy or pity for a suffering person (*mercy killing*). **5** something to be thankful for (*small mercies*). —*int.* expressing surprise or fear. □ **at the mercy of 1** wholly in the power of. **2** liable to danger or harm from. **have mercy on** (or **upon**) show mercy to. [ME f. OF *merci* f. L *merces -edis* reward, in LL pity, thanks]

mere¹ *attrib.adj.* (**merest**) that is solely or no more or better than what is specified (*a mere boy; no mere theory*). □ **merely** *adv.* [ME f. AF *meer*, OF *mier* f. L *merus* unmixed]

mere² *n.* archaic or poet. a lake or pond. [OE f. Gmc]

meretricious /ˌmerɪˈtrɪʃəs/ *adj.* (of decorations, literary style, etc.) showily but falsely attractive. □ **meretriciously** *adv.* **meretriciousness** *n.* [L *meretricius* f. *meretrix -tricis* prostitute f. *merēri* hired]

merganser /mɜːˈgænsə(r)/ *n.* any of various diving fish-eating northern ducks of the genus *Mergus*, with a long narrow serrated hooked bill. [mod.L f. L *mergus* diver f. *mergere* dive + *anser* goose]

merge *v.* **1** *tr.* & *intr.* (often foll. by *with*) **a** combine or be combined. **b** join or blend gradually. **2** *intr.* & *tr.* (foll. by *in*) lose or cause to lose character and identity in (something else). **3** *tr.* (foll. by *in*) embody (a title or estate) in (a larger one). □ **mergence** *n.* [L *mergere mers-* dip, plunge, partly through legal AF *merger*]

merger /ˈmɜːdʒə(r)/ *n.* **1** the combining of two commercial companies etc. into one. **2** a merging, esp. of one estate in another. [AF (as MERGE)]

meridian /məˈrɪdɪən/ *n.* & *adj.* —*n.* **1** a circle passing through the celestial poles and zenith of any place on the earth's surface. **2 a** a circle of constant longitude, passing through a given place and the terrestrial poles. **b** the corresponding line on a map. **3** prime; full splendour. —*adj.* **1** of noon. **2** of the period of greatest splendour, vigour, etc. [ME f. OF *meridien* or L *meridianus* (adj.) f. *meridies* midday f. *medius* middle + *dies* day]

meridional /məˈrɪdɪən(ə)l/ *adj.* & *n.* —*adj.* **1** of or in the south (esp. of Europe). **2** of or relating to a meridian. —*n.* an inhabitant of the south (esp. of France). [ME f. OF f. LL *meridionalis* irreg. f. L *meridies:* see MERIDIAN]

meringue /məˈræŋ/ *n.* **1** a confection of sugar, the white of eggs, etc., baked crisp. **2** a small cake or shell of this, usu. decorated or filled with whipped cream etc. [F, of unkn. orig.]

merino /məˈriːnəʊ/ n. (pl. **-os**) **1** (in full **merino sheep**) a variety of sheep with long fine wool. **2** a soft woollen or wool-and-cotton material like cashmere, orig. of merino wool. **3** a fine woollen yarn. [Sp., of uncert. orig.]

merit /ˈmerɪt/ n. & v. —n. **1** the quality of deserving well. **2** excellence, worth. **3** (usu. in pl.) **a** a thing that entitles one to reward or gratitude. **b** esp. Law intrinsic rights and wrongs (the merits of a case). —v.tr. (**merited, meriting**) deserve or be worthy of (reward, punishment, consideration, etc.). □ **on its merits** with regard only to its intrinsic worth. **Order of Merit** Brit. an order founded in 1902, for distinguished achievement. [ME f. OF merite f. L meritum price, value, = past part. of merēri earn, deserve]

meritocracy /ˌmerɪˈtɒkrəsɪ/ n. (pl. **-ies**) **1** government by persons selected competitively according to merit. **2** a group of persons selected in this way. **3** a society governed by meritocracy.

meritorious /ˌmerɪˈtɔːrɪəs/ adj. **1** (of a person or act) having merit; deserving reward, praise, or gratitude. **2** deserving commendation for thoroughness etc. □ **meritoriously** adv. **meritoriousness** n. [ME f. L meritorius f. merēri meritearn]

merlin /ˈmɜːlɪn/ n. a small European or N. American falcon, Falco columbarius, that hunts small birds. [ME f. AF merilun f. OF esmerillon augment. f. esmeril f. Frank.]

mermaid /ˈmɜːmeɪd/ n. an imaginary half-human sea creature, with the head and trunk of a woman and the tail of a fish. [ME f. MERE² in obs. sense 'sea' + MAID]

merman /ˈmɜːmæn/ n. (pl. **-men**) the male equivalent of a mermaid.

merriment /ˈmerɪmənt/ n. **1** exuberant enjoyment; being merry. **2** mirth, fun.

merry /ˈmerɪ/ adj. (**merrier, merriest**) **1 a** joyous. **b** full of laughter or gaiety. **2** Brit. colloq. slightly drunk. □ **make merry 1** be festive; enjoy oneself. **2** (foll. by over) make fun of. □ **merrily** adv. **merriness** n. [OE myrige f. Gmc]

merry-go-round /ˈmerɪgəʊˌraʊnd/ n. **1** a revolving machine with wooden horses or cars for riding on at a fair etc. **2** a cycle of bustling activities.

merrymaking /ˈmerɪˌmeɪkɪŋ/ n. festivity, fun. □ **merrymaker** n.

mesa /ˈmeɪsə/ n. US an isolated flat-topped hill with steep sides, found in landscapes with horizontal strata. [Sp., lit. table, f. L mensa]

mésalliance /meɪˈzælɪˌɑ̃s/ n. a marriage with a person of a lower social position. [F (as MIS-², ALLIANCE)]

mescal /ˈmeskæl/ n. a peyote cactus. □ **mescal buttons** disc-shaped dried tops from the peyote cactus, eaten or chewed as an intoxicant. [Sp. mezcal f. Nahuatl mexcalli]

mescaline /ˈmeskəˌliːn/ n. (also **mescalin** /-lɪn/) a hallucinogenic alkaloid present in mescal buttons.

Mesdames pl. of MADAME.

Mesdemoiselles pl. of MADEMOISELLE.

mesembryanthemum /mɪˌzembrɪˈænθɪməm/ n. any of various succulent plants of the genus Mesembryanthemum of S. Africa, having daisy-like flowers in a wide range of bright colours that fully open in sunlight. [mod.L f. Gk mesembria noon + anthemon flower]

mesh n. & v. —n. **1** a network fabric or structure. **2** each of the open spaces or interstices between the strands of a net or sieve etc. **3** (in pl.) **a** a network. **b** a snare. —v. **1** intr. (often foll. by with) (of the teeth of a wheel) be engaged (with others). **2** intr. be harmonious. **3** tr. catch in a net. □ **in mesh** (of the teeth of wheels) engaged. [earlier meish etc. f. MDu. maesche f. Gmc]

mesmerism /ˈmezməˌrɪz(ə)m/ n. **1** Psychol. **a** a hypnotic state produced in a person by another's influence over the will and nervous system. **b** a doctrine concerning this. **c** an influence producing this. **2** fascination. □ **mesmeric** /mezˈmerɪk/ adj. **mesmerically** /-ˈmerɪkəlɪ/ adv. **mesmerist** n. [F. A. Mesmer, Austrian physician d. 1815]

mesmerize /ˈmezməˌraɪz/ v.tr. (also **-ise**) **1** Psychol. hypnotize; exercise mesmerism on. **2** fascinate, spellbind. □ **mesmerization** /-ˈzeɪʃ(ə)n/ n. **mesmerizer** n. **mesmerizingly** adv.

meso- /ˈmesəʊ, ˈmez-/ comb. form middle, intermediate. [Gk mesos middle]

mesolithic /ˌmezəʊˈlɪθɪk/ adj. Archaeol. of or concerning the Stone Age between the palaeolithic and neolithic periods. [MESO- + Gk lithos stone]

mesomorph /ˈmesəʊˌmɔːf/ n. a person with a compact and muscular build of body. □ **mesomorphic** /-ˈmɔːfɪk/ adj. [MESO- + Gk morphē form]

meson /ˈmezɒn, ˈmiːzɒn/ n. Physics any of a class of elementary particles believed to participate in the forces that hold nucleons together in the atomic nucleus. □ **mesic** /ˈmezɪk, ˈmiːz-/ adj. **mesonic** /mɪˈzɒnɪk/ adj. [earlier mesotron: cf. MESO-, -ON]

mesosphere /ˈmesəʊˌsfɪə(r)/ n. the region of the atmosphere extending from the top of the stratosphere to an altitude of about 50 miles.

Mesozoic /ˌmesəʊˈzəʊɪk/ adj. & n. Geol. —adj. of or relating to an era of geological time marked by the development of dinosaurs. —n. this era (cf. CENOZOIC, PALAEOZOIC). [MESO- + Gk zōion animal]

mesquite /ˈmeskiːt/ n. (also **mesquit**) any N. American leguminous tree of the genus Prosopis, esp. P. juliflora. □ **mesquite bean** a pod from the mesquite, used as fodder. [Mex. Sp. mezquite]

mess n. & v. —n. **1** a dirty or untidy state of things (the room is a mess). **2** a state of confusion, embarrassment, or trouble. **3** something causing a mess, e.g. spilt liquid etc. **4** a domestic animal's excreta. **5 a** a company of persons who take meals together, esp. in the armed forces. **b** a place where such meals or recreation take place communally. **c** a meal taken there. **6** derog. a disagreeable concoction or medley. **7** a portion of liquid or pulpy food. —v. **1** tr. (often foll. by up) **a** make a mess of; dirty. **b** muddle; make into a state of confusion. **2** intr. (foll. by with) interfere with. **3** intr. take one's meals. **4** intr. colloq. defecate. □ **make a mess of** bungle (an undertaking). **mess about** (or **around**) **1** act desultorily. **2** colloq. make things awkward for; cause arbitrary inconvenience to (a person). **mess-jacket** a short close-fitting coat worn at the mess. **mess kit** a soldier's cooking and eating utensils. **mess tin** a small container as part of a mess kit. [ME f. OF *mes* portion of food f. LL *missus* course at dinner, past part. of *mittere* send]

message /ˈmesɪdʒ/ *n.* **1** an oral or written communication sent by one person to another. **2** an inspired or significant communication from a prophet, writer, or preacher. **3** a mission or errand. □ **get the message** *colloq.* understand what is meant. [ME f. OF ult. f. L *mittere miss-* send]

messenger /ˈmesɪndʒə(r)/ *n.* **1** a person who carries a message. **2** a person employed to carry messages. [ME & OF *messager* (as MESSAGE): *-n-* as in *harbinger, passenger*, etc.]

Messiah /mɪˈsaɪə/ *n.* **1** a liberator or would-be liberator of an oppressed people or country. **2 a** the promised deliverer of the Jews. **b** Christ regarded as this. □ **Messiahship** *n.* [ME f. OF *Messie* ult. f. Heb. *māšīaḥ* anointed]

Messianic /ˌmesɪˈænɪk/ *adj.* **1** of the Messiah. **2** inspired by hope or belief in a Messiah. □ **Messianism** /mɪˈsaɪəˌnɪz(ə)m/ *n.* [F *messianique* (as MESSIAH) after *rabbinique* rabbinical]

Messieurs *pl.* of MONSIEUR.

messmate /ˈmesmeɪt/ *n.* a person with whom one regularly takes meals, esp. in the armed forces.

Messrs /ˈmesəz/ *pl.* of MR. [abbr. of MESSIEURS]

messuage /ˈmeswɪdʒ/ *n.* *Law* a dwelling-house with outbuildings and land assigned to its use. [ME f. AF: perh. an alternative form of *mesnage* dwelling]

messy /ˈmesɪ/ *adj.* (**messier, messiest**) **1** untidy or dirty. **2** causing or accompanied by a mess. **3** difficult to deal with; full of awkward complications. □ **messily** *adv.* **messiness** *n.*

met[1] *past* and *past part.* of MEET[1].

met[2] *adj. colloq.* **1** meteorological. **2** metropolitan. **3** (**the Met**) **a** (in full **the Met Office**) (in the UK) the Meteorological Office. **b** the Metropolitan Police in London. **c** the Metropolitan Opera House in New York. [abbr.]

meta- /ˈmetə/ *comb. form* (usu. **met-** before a vowel or *h*) **1** denoting change of position or condition (*metabolism*). **2** denoting position: **a** behind. **b** after or beyond (*metaphysics*; *metacarpus*). **c** of a higher or second-order kind (*metalanguage*). [Gk *meta-, met-, meth-* f. *meta* with, after]

metabolism /mɪˈtæbəˌlɪz(ə)m/ *n.* all the chemical processes that occur within a living organism, resulting in energy production and growth. □ **metabolic** /ˌmetəˈbɒlɪk/ *adj.* **metabolically** /ˌmetəˈbɒlɪkəlɪ/ *adv.* [Gk *metabolē* change (as META-, *bolē* f. *ballō* throw)]

metabolite /mɪˈtæbəˌlaɪt/ *n.* *Physiol.* a substance formed in or necessary for metabolism.

metabolize /mɪˈtæbəˌlaɪz/ *v.tr.* & *intr.* (also **-ise**) process or be processed by metabolism. □ **metabolizable** *adj.*

metacarpus /ˌmetəˈkɑːpəs/ *n.* (*pl.* **metacarpi** /-paɪ/) **1** the set of five bones of the hand that connects the wrist to the fingers. **2** this part of the hand. □ **metacarpal** *adj.* [mod.L f. Gk *metakarpon* (as META-, CARPUS)]

metal /ˈmet(ə)l/ *n., adj.,* & *v.* —*n.* **1 a** any of a class of chemical elements such as gold, silver, iron, and tin, usu. lustrous ductile solids and good conductors of heat and electricity and forming basic oxides. **b** an alloy of any of these. **2** (in *pl.*) the rails of a railway line. **3** = *road-metal* (see ROAD). —*adj.* made of metal. —*v.tr.* (**metalled, metalling**; *US* **metaled, metaling**) **1** provide or fit with metal. **2** *Brit.* make or mend (a road) with road-metal. □ **metal detector** an electronic device giving a signal when it locates metal. **metal fatigue** fatigue (see FATIGUE n. 2) in metal. [ME f. OF *metal* or L *metallum* f. Gk *metallon* mine]

metalanguage /ˈmetəˌlæŋgwɪdʒ/ *n.* **1** a form of language used to discuss a language. **2** a system of propositions about propositions.

metallic /mɪˈtælɪk/ *adj.* **1** of, consisting of, or characteristic of metal or metals. **2** sounding sharp and ringing, like struck metal. **3** having the sheen or lustre of metals. □ **metallically** *adv.* [L *metallicus* f. Gk *metallikos* (as METAL)]

metalliferous /ˌmetəˈlɪfərəs/ *adj.* bearing or producing metal. [L *metallifer* (as METAL, -FEROUS)]

metallize /ˈmetəˌlaɪz/ *v.tr.* (also **-ise**; *US* **metalize**) **1** render metallic. **2** coat with a thin layer of metal. □ **metallization** /-ˈzeɪʃ(ə)n/ *n.*

metallography /ˌmetəˈlɒgrəfɪ/ *n.* the descriptive science of the structure and properties of metals. □ **metallographic** /mɪˌtæləˈgræfɪk/ *adj.* **metallographical** /mɪˌtæləˈgræfɪk(ə)l/ *adj.* **metallographically** /mɪˌtæləˈgræfɪkəlɪ/ *adv.*

metalloid /ˈmetəˌlɔɪd/ *adj.* & *n.* —*adj.* having the form or appearance of a metal. —*n.* any element intermediate in properties between metals and non-metals, e.g. boron, silicon, and germanium.

metallurgy /mɪˈtælədʒɪ, ˈmetəˌlɜːdʒɪ/ *n.* the science concerned with the production, purification, and properties of metals and their application. □ **metallurgic** /ˌmetəˈlɜːdʒɪk/ *adj.* **metallurgical** /ˌmetəˈlɜːdʒɪk(ə)l/ *adj.* **metallurgically** /ˌmetəˈlɜːdʒɪkəlɪ/ *adv.* **metallurgist** *n.* [Gk *metallon* metal + *-ourgia* working]

metalwork /ˈmet(ə)lwɜːk/ *n.* **1** the art of working in metal. **2** metal objects collectively. □ **metalworker** *n.*

metamorphic /ˌmetəˈmɔːfɪk/ *adj.* **1** of or marked by metamorphosis. **2** *Geol.* (of rock) that has undergone transformation by natural agencies such as heat and pressure. □ **metamorphism** *n.* [META- + Gk *morphē* form]

metamorphose /ˌmetəˈmɔːfəʊz/ *v.tr.* **1** change in form. **2** (foll. by *to, into*) **a** turn (into a new form). **b** change the nature of. [F *métamorphoser* f. *métamorphose* METAMORPHOSIS]

metamorphosis /ˌmetəˈmɔːfəsɪs, ˌmetəmɔːˈfəʊsɪs/ *n.* (*pl.* **metamorphoses** /-ˌsiːz/) **1** a change of form (by natural or supernatural means). **2** a changed form. **3** a change of character, conditions, etc. **4** *Zool.* the transformation between an immature form and an adult form, e.g. from a pupa to an insect, or from a tadpole to a frog. [L f. Gk *metamorphōsis* f. *metamorphoō* transform (as META-, *morphoō* f. *morphē* form)]

metaphor /ˈmetəˌfɔː(r)/ *n.* **1** the application of a name or descriptive term or phrase to an object or action to which it is imaginatively but not literally applicable (e.g. *a glaring error*). **2** an instance of this. □ **metaphoric** /-ˈfɒrɪk/ *adj.* **metaphorical** /-ˈfɒrɪk(ə)l/ *adj.* **metaphorically** /-ˈfɒrɪkəlɪ/ *adv.* [F *métaphore* or L *metaphora* f. Gk *metaphora* f. *metapherō* transfer]

metaphysic /ˌmetəˈfɪzɪk/ *n.* a system of metaphysics.

metaphysical /ˌmetə'fɪzɪk(ə)l/ *adj. & n. —adj.* **1** of or relating to metaphysics. **2** based on abstract general reasoning. **3** excessively subtle or theoretical. **4** incorporeal; supernatural. **5** visionary. **6** (of poetry, esp. in the 17th c. in England) characterized by subtlety of thought and complex imagery. *—n.* (**the Metaphysicals**) the metaphysical poets. □ **metaphysically** *adv.*

metaphysics /ˌmetə'fɪzɪks/ *n.pl.* (usu. treated as *sing.*) **1** the theoretical philosophy of being and knowing. **2** the philosophy of mind. **3** *colloq.* abstract or subtle talk; mere theory. □ **metaphysician** /-'zɪʃ(ə)n/ *n.* **metaphysicize** /-'fɪzɪˌsaɪz/ *v.intr.* [ME *metaphysic* f. OF *metaphysique* f. med.L *metaphysica* ult. f. Gk *ta meta ta phusika* the things after the Physics, from the sequence of Aristotle's works]

metapsychology /ˌmetəsaɪ'kɒlədʒɪ/ *n.* the study of the nature and functions of the mind beyond what can be studied experimentally. □ **metapsychological** /-kə'lɒdʒɪk(ə)l/ *adj.*

metastable /ˌmetə'steɪb(ə)l/ *adj.* **1** (of a state of equilibrium) stable only under small disturbances. **2** passing to another state so slowly as to seem stable. □ **metastability** /-stə'bɪlɪltɪ/ *n.*

metastasis /me'tæstəsɪs/ *n.* (*pl.* **metastases** /-ˌsiːz/) *Physiol.* **1** the transference of a bodily function, disease, etc., from one part or organ to another. **2** the transformation of chemical compounds into others in the process of assimilation by an organism. □ **metastasize** *v.intr.* (also **-ise**). **metastatic** /ˌmetə'stætɪk/ *adj.* [LL f. Gk f. *methistēmi* change]

metatarsus /ˌmetə'tɑːsəs/ *n.* (*pl.* **metatarsi** /-saɪ/) **1** the part of the foot between the ankle and the toes. **2** the set of bones in this. □ **metatarsal** *adj.* [mod.L (as META-, TARSUS)]

metathesis /mɪ'tæθɪsɪs/ *n.* (*pl.* **metatheses** /-ˌsiːz/) **1** *Gram.* the transposition of sounds or letters in a word. **2** *Chem.* the interchange of atoms or groups of atoms between two molecules. **3** an instance of either of these. □ **metathetic** /ˌmetə'θetɪk/ *adj.* **metathetical** /ˌmetə'θetɪk(ə)l/ *adj.* [LL f. Gk *metatithēmi* transpose]

mete /miːt/ *v.tr.* (usu. foll. by *out*) *literary* apportion or allot (a punishment or reward). [OE *metan* f. Gmc., rel. to MEET¹]

meteor /'miːtɪə(r)/ *n.* **1** a small body of matter from outer space that becomes incandescent as a result of friction with the earth's atmosphere. **2** a streak of light emanating from a meteor. □ **meteor shower** a group of meteors appearing to come from one point in the sky. [ME f. mod.L *meteorum* f. Gk *meteōron* neut. of *meteōros* lofty, (as META-, *aeirō* raise)]

meteoric /ˌmiːtɪ'ɒrɪk/ *adj.* **1 a** of or relating to the atmosphere. **b** dependent on atmospheric conditions. **2** of meteors. **3** rapid like a meteor; dazzling, transient (*meteoric rise to fame*). □ **meteorically** *adv.*

meteoric stone a meteorite. □ **meteorically** *adv.*

meteorite /'miːtɪəˌraɪt/ *n.* a fallen meteor, or fragment of natural rock or metal, that reaches the earth's surface from outer space. □ **meteoritic** /-'rɪtɪk/ *adj.*

meteoroid /'miːtɪəˌrɔɪd/ *n.* any small body moving in the solar system that becomes visible as it passes through the earth's atmosphere as a meteor. □ **meteoroidal** /-'rɔɪd(ə)l/ *adj.*

meteorology /ˌmiːtɪə'rɒlədʒɪ/ *n.* **1** the study of the processes and phenomena of the atmosphere, esp. as a means of forecasting the weather. **2** the atmospheric character of a region. □ **meteorological** /-rə'lɒdʒɪk(ə)l/ *adj.* **meteorologically** /-rə'lɒdʒɪkəlɪ/ *adv.* **meteorologist** *n.* [Gk *meteōrologia* (as METEOR)]

meter¹ /'miːtə(r)/ *n. & v. —n.* **1** a person or thing that measures, esp. an instrument for recording a quantity of gas, electricity, etc. supplied, present, or needed. **2** = *parking-meter* (see PARK). *—v.tr.* measure by means of a meter. [ME f. METE + -ER¹]

meter² *US* var. of METRE¹.

meter³ *US* var. of METRE².

-meter /mɪtə(r), miːtə(r)/ *comb. form* **1** forming nouns denoting measuring instruments (*barometer*). **2** *Prosody* forming nouns denoting lines of poetry with a specified number of measures (*pentameter*).

methadone /'meθəˌdəʊn/ *n.* a potent narcotic analgesic drug used to relieve severe pain, as a linctus to suppress coughs, and as a substitute for morphine or heroin. [6-dimethylamino-4,4-diphenyl-3-heptan*one*]

methamphetamine /ˌmeθæm'fetəmɪn, -ˌmiːn/ *n.* an amphetamine derivative with quicker and longer action, used as a stimulant. [METHYL + AMPHETAMINE]

methane /'miːθeɪn, 'miːθeɪn/ *n. Chem.* a colourless odourless inflammable gaseous hydrocarbon, the simplest in the alkane series, and the main constituent of natural gas. [METHYL + -ANE²]

methanol /'meθəˌnɒl/ *n. Chem.* a colourless volatile inflammable liquid, used as a solvent. [METHANE + ALCOHOL]

methinks /mɪ'θɪŋks/ *v.intr.* (past **methought** /mɪ'θɔːt/) *archaic* it seems to me. [OE *mē thyncth* f. *mē* dative of ME¹ + *thyncth* 3rd sing. of *thyncan* seem, THINK]

metho /'meθəʊ/ *n.* (*pl.* **-os**) *Austral. sl.* **1** methylated spirit. **2** a person addicted to drinking methylated spirit. [abbr.]

method /'meθəd/ *n.* **1** a special form of procedure esp. in any branch of mental activity. **2** orderliness; regular habits. **3** the orderly arrangement of ideas. **4** a scheme of classification. **5** *Theatr.* a technique of acting based on the actor's thorough emotional identification with the character. [F *méthode* or L *methodus* f. Gk *methodos* pursuit of knowledge (as META-, *hodos* way)]

methodical /mɪ'θɒdɪk(ə)l/ *adj.* (also **methodic**) characterized by method or order. □ **methodically** *adv.* [LL *methodicus* f. Gk *methodikos* (as METHOD)]

Methodist /'meθədɪst/ *n.* **1** a member of any of several Protestant religious bodies (now united) originating in the 18th-c. evangelistic movement of Charles and John Wesley and George Whitefield. **2** (**methodist**) a person who follows or advocates a particular method or system of procedure. □ **Methodism** *n.* **Methodistic** /-'dɪstɪk/ *adj.* **Methodistical** /-'dɪstɪk(ə)l/ *adj.* [mod.L *methodista* (as METHOD): sense 1 prob. from following a specified 'method' of devotional study]

methodize /ˈmeθəˌdaɪz/ v.tr. (also **-ise**) **1** reduce to order. **2** arrange in an orderly manner. □ **methodizer** n.

methodology /ˌmeθəˈdɒlədʒi/ n. (pl. **-ies**) **1** the science of method. **2** a body of methods used in a particular branch of activity. □ **methodological** /-dəˈlɒdʒɪk(ə)l/ adj. **methodologically** /-dəˈlɒdʒɪkəli/ adv. **methodologist** n. [mod.L methodologia or F méthodologie (as METHOD)]

methought past of METHINKS.

meths /meθs/ n. Brit. colloq. methylated spirit. [abbr.]

methyl /ˈmeθɪl, ˈmiːθaɪl/ n. Chem. a univalent hydrocarbon radical present in many organic compounds. □ **methyl alcohol** = METHANOL. **methyl benzene** = TOLUENE. □ **methylic** /mɪˈθɪlɪk/ adj. [G Methyl or F méthyle, ult. f. Gk methu wine + hulē wood]

methylate /ˈmeθɪˌleɪt/ v.tr. **1** mix or impregnate with methanol. **2** introduce a methyl group into (a molecule or compound). □ **methylated spirit** (or **spirits**) alcohol impregnated with methanol to make it unfit for drinking and exempt from duty. □ **methylation** /-ˈleɪʃ(ə)n/ n.

meticulous /məˈtɪkjʊləs/ adj. **1** giving great or excessive attention to details. **2** very careful and precise. □ **meticulously** adv. **meticulousness** n. [L meticulosus f. metus fear]

métier /ˈmetjeɪ/ n. **1** one's trade, profession, or department of activity. **2** one's forte. [F ult. f. L ministerium service]

metonym /ˈmetənɪm/ n. a word used in metonymy. [back-form. f. METONYMY, after synonym]

metonymy /mɪˈtɒnɪmɪ/ n. the substitution of the name of an attribute or adjunct for that of the thing meant (e.g. Crown for king, the turf for horse-racing). □ **metonymic** /ˌmetəˈnɪmɪk/ adj. **metonymical** /ˌmetəˈnɪmɪk(ə)l/ adj. [LL metonymia f. Gk metōnumia (as META-, onoma, onuma name)]

metre¹ /ˈmiːtə(r)/ n. (US **meter**) a metric unit and the base SI unit of linear measure, equal to about 39.4 inches. □ **metreage** /ˈmiːtərɪdʒ/ n. [F mètre f. Gk metron measure]

metre² /ˈmiːtə(r)/ n. (US **meter**) **1 a** any form of poetic rhythm, determined by the number and length of feet in a line. **b** a metrical group or measure. **2** the basic pulse and rhythm of a piece of music. [OF metre f. L metrum f. Gk metron MEASURE]

metric /ˈmetrɪk/ adj. of or based on the metre. □ **metric system** the decimal measuring system with the metre, litre, and gram (or kilogram) as units of length, volume, and mass (see also SI). **metric ton** (or **tonne**) 1,000 kilograms (2205 lb.). [F métrique (as METRE¹)]

-metric /ˈmetrɪk/ comb. form (also **-metrical** /-k(ə)l/) forming adjectives corresponding to nouns in -meter and -metry (thermometric; geometric). □ **-metrically** comb. form forming adverbs. [from or after F métrique f. L (as METRICAL)]

metrical /ˈmetrɪk(ə)l/ adj. **1** of, relating to, or composed in metre (metrical psalms). **2** of or involving measurement (metrical geometry). □ **metrically** adv. [ME f. L metricus f. Gk metrikos (as METRE²)]

metricate /ˈmetrɪˌkeɪt/ v.intr. & tr. change or adapt to a metric system of measurement. □ **metrication** /-ˈkeɪʃ(ə)n/ n. **metricize** /-ˌsaɪz/ v.tr. (also **-ise**).

metro /ˈmetrəʊ/ n. (pl. **-os**) an underground railway system in a city, esp. Paris. [F métro, abbr. of métropolitain METROPOLITAN]

metronome /ˈmetrəˌnəʊm/ n. Mus. an instrument marking time at a selected rate by giving a regular tick. □ **metronomic** /-ˈnɒmɪk/ adj. [Gk metron measure + nomos law]

metropolis /mɪˈtrɒpəlɪs/ n. **1** the chief city of a country; a capital city. **2** a metropolitan bishop's see. **3** a centre of activity. [LL f. Gk mētropolis parent State f. mētēr mētros mother + polis city]

metropolitan /ˌmetrəˈpɒlɪt(ə)n/ adj. & n. —adj. **1** of or relating to a metropolis, esp. as distinct from its environs (metropolitan New York). **2** belonging to, forming or forming part of, a mother country as distinct from its colonies etc. (metropolitan France). **3** of an ecclesiastical metropolis. —n. **1** (in full **metropolitan bishop**) a bishop having authority over the bishops of a province, in the Western Church equivalent to archbishop, in the Orthodox Church ranking above archbishop and below patriarch. **2** an inhabitant of a metropolis. □ **metropolitan county** hist. (in England) each of six units of local government centred on a large urban area (in existence 1974–86). **metropolitan magistrate** Brit. a paid professional magistrate in London. □ **metropolitanate** n. (in sense 1 of n.). **metropolitanism** n. [ME f. LL metropolitanus f. Gk mētropolitēs (as METROPOLIS)]

-metry /mɪtrɪ/ comb. form forming nouns denoting procedures and systems corresponding to instruments in -meter (calorimetry; thermometry). [after geometry etc. f. Gk -metria f. -metrēs measurer]

mettle /ˈmet(ə)l/ n. **1** the quality of a person's disposition or temperament (a chance to show your mettle). **2** natural ardour. **3** spirit, courage. □ **on one's mettle** incited to do one's best. □ **mettled** adj. (also in comb.). **mettlesome** adj. [var. of METAL n.]

meunière /mɜːˈnjeə(r)/ adj. (esp. of fish) cooked or served in lightly browned butter with lemon juice and parsley (sole meunière). [F (à la) meunière (in the manner of) a miller's wife]

MeV abbr. mega-electronvolt(s).

mew¹ v. & n. —v.intr. (of a cat, gull, etc.) utter its characteristic cry. —n. this sound, esp. of a cat. [ME: imit.]

mew² n. a gull, esp. the common gull, Larus canus. [OE mǣw f. Gmc]

mew³ n. & v. —n. a cage for hawks, esp. while moulting. —v.tr. **1'** put (a hawk) in a cage. **2** (often foll. by up) shut up; confine. [ME f. OF mue f. muer moult f. L mutare change]

mewl /mjuːl/ v.intr. (also **mule**) **1** cry feebly; whimper. **2** mew like a cat. [imit.: cf. MIAUL]

mews /mjuːz/ n. Brit. a set of stabling round an open yard or along a lane, now often converted into dwellings. [pl. (now used as sing.) of MEW³, orig. of the royal stables on the site of hawks' mews at Charing Cross]

mezzanine /ˈmetsəˌniːn, ˈmez-/ n. **1** a low storey between two others (usu. between the ground and first floors). **2** US Theatr. a dress circle. [F f. It. mezzanino dimin. of mezzano middle f. L medianus MEDIAN]

mezzo /ˈmetsəʊ/ adv. & n. Mus. —adv. half, moderately. —n. (in full **mezzo-soprano**) (pl. **-os**) **1 a** a female singing-voice between soprano and contralto. **b** a singer with this voice. **2** a part written for mezzo-soprano. □ **mezzo forte** fairly loud. **mezzo piano** fairly soft. [It., f. L *medius* middle]

mezzotint /ˈmetsəʊtɪnt/ n. & v. —n. **1** a method of printing or engraving in which the surface of a plate is roughened by scraping so that it produces tones and half-tones. **2** a print produced by this process. —v.tr. engrave in mezzotint. □ **mezzotinter** n. [It. *mezzotinto* f. *mezzo* half + *tinto* tint]

MF abbr. medium frequency.

mf abbr. mezzo forte.

Mg symb. Chem. the element magnesium.

mg abbr. milligram(s).

Mgr. abbr. **1** Manager. **2** *Monseigneur.* **3** Monsignor.

mho /məʊ/ n. (pl. **-os**) Electr. the reciprocal of an ohm, a former unit of conductance. [OHM reversed]

MHR abbr. (in the US and Australia) Member of the House of Representatives.

MHz abbr. megahertz.

MI abbr. Brit. hist. Military Intelligence.

mi var. of ME².

mi. abbr. US mile(s).

miaow /miˈaʊ/ n. & v. (also **meow**) —n. the characteristic cry of a cat. —v.intr. make this cry. [imit.]

miasma /miˈæzmə, maɪ-/ n. (pl. **miasmata** /-mətə/ or **miasmas**) archaic an infectious or noxious vapour. □ **miasmal** adj. **miasmatic** /-ˈmætɪk/ adj. **miasmic** adj. **miasmically** adv. [Gk, = defilement, f. *miainō* pollute]

miaul /miˈɔːl/ v.intr. cry like a cat; mew. [F *miauler*: imit.]

mica /ˈmaɪkə/ n. any of a group of silicate minerals with a layered structure. □ **micaceous** /-ˈkeɪʃəs/ adj. [L, = crumb]

mice pl. of MOUSE.

micelle /mɪˈsel, maɪˈsel/ n. Chem. an aggregate of molecules in a colloidal solution, as occurs e.g. when soap dissolves in water. [mod.L *micella* dimin. of L *mica* crumb]

Michaelmas /ˈmɪkəlməs/ n. the feast of St Michael, 29 September. □ **Michaelmas daisy** an autumn-flowering aster. **Michaelmas term** Brit. (in some universities) the autumn term. [OE *sancte Micheles mæsse* Saint Michael's mass: see MASS²]

mickey /ˈmɪkɪ/ n. (also **micky**) □ **take the mickey** (often foll. by out of) sl. tease, mock, ridicule. [20th c.: orig. uncert.]

Mickey Finn /ˌmɪkɪ ˈfɪn/ n. sl. **1** a strong alcoholic drink, esp. adulterated with a narcotic or laxative. **2** the adulterant itself. [20th c.: orig. uncert.]

mickle /ˈmɪk(ə)l/ adj. & n. (also **muckle** /ˈmʌk(ə)l/) archaic or Sc. —adj. much, great. —n. a large amount. □ **many a little makes a mickle** (orig. erron. **many a mickle makes a muckle**) many small amounts accumulate to make a large amount. [ME f. ON *mikell* f. Gmc]

micro /ˈmaɪkrəʊ/ n. (pl. **-os**) colloq. **1** = MICROCOMPUTER. **2** = MICROPROCESSOR.

micro- /ˈmaɪkrəʊ/ comb. form **1** small (*microchip*). **2** denoting a factor of one millionth (10^{-6}) (*microgram*). [Gk *mikro-* f. *mikros* small]

microanalysis /ˌmaɪkrəʊəˈnælɪsɪs/ n. the quantitative analysis of chemical compounds using a sample of a few milligrams.

microbe /ˈmaɪkrəʊb/ n. a minute living being; a micro-organism (esp. bacteria causing disease and fermentation). □ **microbial** /-ˈkrəʊbɪəl/ adj. **microbic** /-ˈkrəʊbɪk/ adj. [F f. Gk *mikros* small + *bios* life]

microbiology /ˌmaɪkrəʊbaɪˈɒlədʒɪ/ n. the scientific study of micro-organisms, e.g. bacteria, viruses, and fungi. □ **microbiological** /-ˌbaɪəˈlɒdʒɪk(ə)l/ adj. **microbiologically** /-ˌbaɪəˈlɒdʒɪkəlɪ/ adv. **microbiologist** n.

microchip /ˈmaɪkrəʊtʃɪp/ n. a small piece of semiconductor (usu. silicon) used to carry electronic circuits.

microcircuit /ˈmaɪkrəʊˌsɜːkɪt/ n. an integrated circuit on a microchip. □ **microcircuitry** n.

microclimate /ˈmaɪkrəʊˌklaɪmɪt/ n. the climate of a small local area, e.g. inside a greenhouse. □ **microclimatic** /-ˈmætɪk/ adj. **microclimatically** /-ˈmætɪkəlɪ/ adv.

microcode /ˈmaɪkrəʊˌkəʊd/ n. **1** = MICROINSTRUCTION. **2** = MICROPROGRAM.

microcomputer /ˈmaɪkrəʊkəmˌpjuːtə(r)/ n. a small computer that contains a microprocessor as its central processor.

microcosm /ˈmaɪkrəˌkɒz(ə)m/ n. **1** (often foll. by of) a miniature representation. **2** mankind viewed as the epitome of the universe. **3** any community or complex unity viewed in this way. □ **microcosmic** /-ˈkɒzmɪk/ adj. **microcosmically** /-ˈkɒzmɪkəlɪ/ adv. [ME f. F *microcosme* or med.L *microcosmus* f. Gk *mikros kosmos* little world]

microdot /ˈmaɪkrəʊˌdɒt/ n. a microphotograph of a document etc. reduced to the size of a dot.

micro-economics /ˌmaɪkrəʊˌiːkəˈnɒmɪks/ n. the branch of economics dealing with individual commodities, producers, etc.

micro-electronics /ˌmaɪkrəʊɪlekˈtrɒnɪks/ n. the design, manufacture, and use of microchips and microcircuits.

microfiche /ˈmaɪkrəʊˌfiːʃ/ n. (pl. same or **microfiches**) a flat rectangular piece of film bearing microphotographs of the pages of a printed text or document.

microfilm /ˈmaɪkrəʊfɪlm/ n. & v. —n. a length of film bearing microphotographs of documents etc. —v.tr. photograph (a document etc.) on microfilm.

microfloppy /ˈmaɪkrəʊˌflɒpɪ/ n. (pl. **-ies**) (in full **microfloppy disk**) Computing a floppy disk with a diameter of less than $5\frac{1}{4}$ inches (usu. $3\frac{1}{2}$ inches).

microform /ˈmaɪkrəʊˌfɔːm/ n. microphotographic reproduction on film or paper of a manuscript etc.

microgram /ˈmaɪkrəʊˌɡræm/ n. one-millionth of a gram.

micrograph /ˈmaɪkrəʊˌɡrɑːf/ n. a photograph taken by means of a microscope.

microgroove /ˈmaɪkrəʊˌɡruːv/ n. a very narrow groove on a long-playing gramophone record.

microinstruction /ˌmaɪkrəʊɪnˈstrʌkʃ(ə)n/ n. a machine-code instruction that effects a basic operation in a computer system.

microlight /ˈmaɪkrəʊˌlaɪt/ n. a kind of motorized hang-glider.

micromesh /ˈmaɪkrəʊˌmeʃ/ n. (often *attrib.*) material, esp. nylon, consisting of a very fine mesh.

micrometer /maɪˈkrɒmɪtə(r)/ n. a gauge for accurately measuring small distances, thicknesses, etc. □ **micrometry** n.

micrometre /ˈmaɪkrəʊˌmiːtə(r)/ n. one-millionth of a metre.

microminiaturization /ˌmaɪkrəʊˌmɪnɪtʃər aɪˈzeɪʃ(ə)n/ n. (also **-isation**) the manufacture of very small electronic devices by using integrated circuits.

micron /ˈmaɪkrɒn/ n. one-millionth of a metre. [Gk *mikron* neut. of *mikros* small: cf. MICRO-]

micro-organism /ˌmaɪkrəʊˈɔːɡəˌnɪz(ə)m/ n. any of various microscopic organisms, including algae, bacteria, fungi, protozoa, and viruses.

microphone /ˈmaɪkrəˌfəʊn/ n. an instrument for converting sound waves into electrical energy variations which may be reconverted into sound after transmission by wire or radio or after recording. □ **microphonic** /-ˈfɒnɪk/ adj.

microphotograph /ˌmaɪkrəʊˈfəʊtəˌɡrɑːf/ n. a photograph reduced to a very small size.

microprocessor /ˌmaɪkrəʊˈprəʊsesə(r)/ n. an integrated circuit that contains all the functions of a central processing unit of a computer.

microprogram /ˌmaɪkrəʊˈprəʊɡræm/ n. a microinstruction program that controls the functions of a central processing unit of a computer.

microscope /ˈmaɪkrəˌskəʊp/ n. an instrument magnifying small objects by means of a lens or lenses so as to reveal details invisible to the naked eye. [mod.L *microscopium* (as MICRO-, -SCOPE)]

microscopic /ˌmaɪkrəˈskɒpɪk/ adj. **1** so small as to be visible only with a microscope. **2** extremely small. **3** regarded in terms of small units. **4** of the microscope. □ **microscopical** adj. (in sense 4). **microscopically** adv.

microscopy /maɪˈkrɒskəpɪ/ n. the use of the microscope. □ **microscopist** n.

microsecond /ˈmaɪkrəʊˌsekənd/ n. one-millionth of a second.

Microsoft /ˈmaɪkrəʊˌsɒft/ n. propr. an operating system for microcomputers. [the name of the developing company]

microstructure /ˈmaɪkrəʊˌstrʌktʃə(r)/ n. (in a metal or other material) the arrangement of crystals etc. which can be made visible and examined with a microscope.

microsurgery /ˈmaɪkrəʊˌsɜːdʒərɪ/ n. intricate surgery performed using microscopes, enabling the tissue to be operated on with miniaturized precision instruments. □ **microsurgical** /-ˈsɜːdʒɪk(ə)l/ adj.

microswitch /ˈmaɪkrəʊswɪtʃ/ n. a switch that can be operated rapidly by a small movement.

microwave /ˈmaɪkrəʊˌweɪv/ n. & v. —n. **1** an electromagnetic wave with a wavelength in the range 0.001–0.3m. **2** (in full **microwave oven**) an oven that uses microwaves to cook or heat food quickly. —v.tr. (**-ving**) cook in a microwave oven.

micturition /ˌmɪktjʊəˈrɪʃ(ə)n/ n. *formal* urination. [L *micturire micturit-*, desiderative f. *mingere mict-* urinate]

mid[1] *attrib.adj.* **1** (usu. in *comb.*) that is the middle of (*in mid-air; from mid-June to mid-July*). **2** that is

in the middle; medium, half. [OE *midd* (recorded only in oblique cases), rel. to L *medius*, Gk *mesos*]

mid[2] *prep. poet.* = AMID. [abbr. f. AMID]

Midas touch /ˈmaɪdəs/ n. the ability to turn one's activities to financial advantage. [*Midas*, king of Phrygia, whose touch was said to turn all things to gold]

midday /ˈmɪddeɪ/ n. the middle of the day; noon. [OE *middæg* (as MID[1], DAY)]

midden /ˈmɪd(ə)n/ n. **1** a dunghill. **2** a refuse heap near a dwelling. **3** = *kitchen midden*. [ME *myddyng*, of Scand. orig.: cf. Da. *mødding* muck heap]

middle /ˈmɪd(ə)l/ adj., n., & v. —attrib.adj. **1** at an equal distance from the extremities of a thing. **2** (of a member of a group) so placed as to have the same number of members on each side. **3** intermediate in rank, quality, etc. **4** average (*of middle height*). **5** (of a language) of the period between the old and modern forms. —n. **1** (often foll. by *of*) the middle point or position or part. **2** a person's waist. —v.tr. **1** place in the middle. **2** *Football* return (the ball) from the wing to the midfield. **3** *Cricket* strike (the ball) with the middle of the bat. □ **in the middle of** (often foll. by *verbal noun*) in the process of; during. **middle age** the period between youth and old age, about 45 to 60. **middle-aged** in middle age. **the Middle Ages** the period of European history from the fall of the Roman Empire in the West (5th c.) to the fall of Constantinople (1453), or more narrowly from c.1000 to 1453. **middle-age** (or **-aged**) **spread** the increased bodily girth often associated with middle age. **Middle America 1** Mexico and Central America. **2** the middle class in the US, esp. as a conservative political force. **middle C** *Mus.* the C near the middle of the piano keyboard, the note between the treble and bass staves, at about 260 Hz. **middle class** the class of society between the upper and the lower, including professional and business workers and their families. **middle course** a compromise between two extremes. **middle distance 1** (in a painted or actual landscape) the part between the foreground and the background. **2** *Athletics* a race distance of esp. 400 or 800 metres. **middle ear** the cavity of the central part of the ear behind the drum. **the Middle East** the area covered by countries from Egypt to Iran inclusive. **Middle Eastern** of or in the Middle East. **Middle English** the English language from c.1150 to 1500. **middle finger** the finger next to the forefinger. **middle name 1** a person's name placed after the first name and before the surname. **2** a person's most characteristic quality (*sobriety is my middle name*). **middle-of-the-road** (of a person, course of action, etc.) moderate; avoiding extremes. **middle school** *Brit.* a school for children from about 9 to 13 years old. **middle-sized** of medium size. **middle way** = *middle course*. **Middle West** (in the US) the region adjoining the northern Mississippi. [OE *middel* f. Gmc]

middlebrow /ˈmɪd(ə)lˌbraʊ/ adj. & n. *colloq.* —adj. claiming to be or regarded as only moderately intellectual. —n. a middlebrow person.

middleman /ˈmɪd(ə)lˌmæn/ n. (pl. **-men**) **1** any of the traders who handle a commodity between its producer and its consumer. **2** an intermediary.

middleweight /ˈmɪd(ə)lˌweɪt/ n. **1** a weight in certain sports intermediate between welterweight and light heavyweight. **2** a sportsman of this weight. □ **junior middleweight 1** a weight in professional boxing of 66.7–69.8 kg. **2** a professional boxer of this weight. **light middleweight 1** a weight in amateur boxing of 67–71 kg. **2** an amateur boxer of this weight.

middling /ˈmɪdlɪŋ/ adj. & adv. —adj. **1** moderately good (esp. fair to middling). **2** colloq. (of a person's health) fairly well. **3** second-rate. —adv. fairly or moderately (middling good). □ **middlingly** adv. [ME, of Sc. orig.: prob. f. MID¹ + -LING²]

middy¹ /ˈmɪdɪ/ n. (pl. -ies) **1** colloq. a midshipman. **2** (in full **middy blouse**) a woman's or child's loose blouse with a collar like that worn by sailors.

middy² /ˈmɪdɪ/ n. (pl. -ies) Austral. sl. a measure of beer of varying size. [20th c.: orig. unkn.]

Mideast /ˈmɪdiːst/ n. US = Middle East.

midfield /ˈmɪdfiːld/ n. Football the central part of the pitch, away from the goals. □ **midfielder** n.

midge n. **1** colloq. **a** a gnatlike insect. **b** a small person. **2 a** any dipterous non-biting insect of the family Chironomidae. **b** any similar insect of the family Ceratopogonidae with piercing mouthparts for sucking blood or eating smaller insects. [OE mycg(e) f. Gmc]

midget /ˈmɪdʒɪt/ n. **1** an extremely small person or thing. **2** (attrib.) very small. [MIDGE + -ET¹]

MIDI /ˈmɪdɪ/ n. musical instrument digital interface. [abbr.]

midi /ˈmɪdɪ/ n. (pl. **midis**) a garment of medium length, usu. reaching to mid-calf. [MID¹ after MINI]

midibus /ˈmɪdɪˌbʌs/ n. a bus seating up to about 25 passengers.

midland /ˈmɪdlənd/ n. & adj. —n. **1** (**the Midlands**) the inland counties of central England. **2** the middle part of a country. —adj. **1** of or in the midland or Midlands. **2** Mediterranean. □ **midlander** n.

mid-life /ˈmɪdlaɪf/ n. middle age. □ **mid-life crisis** an emotional crisis of self-confidence that can occur in early middle age.

midline /ˈmɪdlaɪn/ n. a median line, or plane of bilateral symmetry.

midmost /ˈmɪdməʊst/ adj. & adv. in the very middle.

midnight /ˈmɪdnaɪt/ n. **1** the middle of the night; 12 o'clock at night. **2** intense darkness. □ **midnight blue** a very dark blue. **midnight sun** the sun visible at midnight during the summer in polar regions. [OE midniht (as MID¹, NIGHT)]

mid-off /mɪdˈɒf/ n. Cricket the position of the fielder near the bowler on the off side.

mid-on /mɪdˈɒn/ n. Cricket the position of the fielder near the bowler on the on side.

midrib /ˈmɪdrɪb/ n. the central rib of a leaf.

midriff /ˈmɪdrɪf/ n. **1 a** the region of the front of the body between the thorax and abdomen. **b** the diaphragm. **2** a garment or part of a garment covering the abdomen. [OE midhrif (as MID¹, hrif belly)]

midship /ˈmɪdʃɪp/ n. the middle part of a ship or boat.

midshipman /ˈmɪdʃɪpmən/ n. (pl. -men) **1** Brit. a naval officer of rank between naval cadet and sub-lieutenant. **2** US a naval cadet.

midships /ˈmɪdʃɪps/ adv. = AMIDSHIPS.

midst /mɪdst/ prep. & n. —prep. poet. amidst. —n. middle (now only in phrases as below). □ **in the midst of** among; in the middle of. **in our** (or **your** or **their**) **midst** among us (or you or them). [ME middest, middes f. in middes, in middan (as IN, MID¹)]

midsummer /mɪdˈsʌmə(r), ˈmɪd-/ n. the period of or near the summer solstice, about 21 June. □ **Midsummer** (or **Midsummer's**) **Day** 24 June. **midsummer madness** extreme folly. [OE midsumor (as MID¹, SUMMER)]

midtown /ˈmɪdtaʊn/ n. US the central part of a city between the downtown and uptown areas.

midway /ˈmɪdweɪ/ adv. in or towards the middle of the distance between two points.

Midwest /mɪdˈwest/ n. = Middle West.

midwicket /mɪdˈwɪkɪt/ n. Cricket the position of a fielder on the leg side opposite the middle of the pitch.

midwife /ˈmɪdwaɪf/ n. (pl. -wives /-waɪvz/) a person (usu. a woman) trained to assist women in childbirth. □ **midwifery** /-ˌwɪfrɪ/ n. [ME, prob. f. obs. prep. mid with + WIFE woman, in the sense of 'one who is with the mother']

midwinter /mɪdˈwɪntə(r)/ n. the period of or near the winter solstice, about 22 Dec. [OE (as MID¹, WINTER)]

mielie var. of MEALIE.

mien /miːn/ n. literary a person's look or bearing, as showing character or mood. [prob. f. obs. demean, assim. to F mine expression]

miff v. & n. colloq. —v.tr. (usu. in passive) put out of humour; offend. —n. **1** a petty quarrel. **2** a huff. [perh. imit.: cf. G muff, exclam. of disgust]

M.I.5 abbr. (in the UK) the department of Military Intelligence concerned with State security.

■ **Usage** This term is not in official use.

might¹ /maɪt/ past of MAY, used esp.: **1** in reported speech, expressing possibility (said he might come) or permission (asked if I might leave) (cf. MAY 1, 2). **2** (foll. by perfect infin.) expressing a possibility based on a condition not fulfilled (if you'd looked you might have found it; but for the radio we might not have known). **3** (foll. by present infin. or perfect infin.) expressing complaint that an obligation or expectation is not or has not been fulfilled (he might offer to help; they might have asked; you might have known they wouldn't come). **4** expressing a request (you might call in at the butcher's). **5** colloq. **a** = MAY 1 (it might be true). **b** (in tentative questions) = MAY 2 (might I have the pleasure of this dance?). **c** = MAY 4 (who might you be?). □ **might as well** expressing that it is probably at least as desirable to do a thing as not to do it (finished the work and decided they might as well go to lunch; won't win but might as well try). **might-have-been** colloq. **1** a past possibility that no longer applies. **2** a person who could have been more eminent.

might² /maɪt/ n. **1** great bodily or mental strength. **2** power to enforce one's will (usu. in contrast with right). □ **with all one's might** to the utmost of one's power. [OE miht, mieht f. Gmc, rel. to MAY¹]

mightn't /ˈmaɪt(ə)nt/ contr. might not.

mighty /ˈmaɪtɪ/ adj. & adv. —adj. (**mightier, mightiest**) **1** powerful or strong, in body, mind, or influence. **2** massive, bulky. **3** colloq. great, considerable. —adv. colloq. very (a mighty difficult task). □ **mightily** adv. **mightiness** n. [OE mihtig (as MIGHT²)]

mignonette /ˌmɪnjəˈnet/ n. **1 a** any of various plants of the genus Reseda, esp. R. odorata, with fragrant grey-green flowers. **b** the colour of these. **2** a light fine narrow pillow-lace. [F mignonnette dimin. of mignon small]

migraine /ˈmiːɡreɪn, ˈmaɪ-/ n. a recurrent throbbing headache that usually affects one side of the head, often accompanied by nausea and disturbance of vision. □ **migrainous** adj. [F f. LL hemicrania f. Gk hēmikrania (as HEMI-, CRANIUM): orig. of a headache confined to one side of the head]

migrant /ˈmaɪɡrənt/ adj. & n. —adj. that migrates. —n. a migrant person or animal, esp. a bird.

migrate /maɪˈɡreɪt/ v.intr. **1** (of people) move from one place of abode to another, esp. in a different country. **2** (of a bird or fish) change its area of habitation with the seasons. **3** move under natural forces. □ **migration** /-ˈɡreɪʃ(ə)n/ n. **migrational** /-ˈɡreɪʃən(ə)l/ adj. **migrator** n. **migratory** adj. [L migrare migrat-]

mihrab /ˈmiːrɑːb/ n. a niche or slab in a mosque, used to show the direction of Mecca. [Arab. miḥrāb praying-place]

mikado /mɪˈkɑːdəʊ/ n. (pl. **-os**) hist. the emperor of Japan. [Jap. f. mi august + kado door]

mike /maɪk/ n. colloq. a microphone. [abbr.]

milady /mɪˈleɪdɪ/ n. (pl. **-ies**) **1** an English noblewoman or great lady. **2** a form used in speaking of or to such a person. [F f. E my lady: cf. MILORD]

milch /mɪltʃ/ adj. (of a domestic mammal) giving or kept for milk. □ **milch cow** a source of easy profit, esp. a person. [ME m(i)elche repr. OE mielce (unrecorded) f. Gmc: see MILK]

mild /maɪld/ adj. **1** (esp. of a person) gentle and conciliatory. **2** (of a rule, punishment, illness, feeling, etc.) moderate; not severe. **3** (of the weather, esp. in winter) moderately warm. **4 a** (of food, tobacco, etc.) not sharp or strong in taste etc. **b** Brit. (of beer) not strongly flavoured with hops. **5** (of medicine) operating gently. **6** tame, feeble; lacking energy or vivacity. □ **mild steel** steel containing a small percentage of carbon, strong and tough but not readily tempered. □ **milden** v.tr. & intr. **mildish** adj. **mildness** n. [OE milde f. Gmc]

mildew /ˈmɪldjuː/ n. & v. —n. **1** a destructive growth of minute fungi on plants. **2** a similar growth on paper, leather, etc. exposed to damp. —v.tr. & intr. taint or be tainted with mildew. □ **mildewy** adj. [OE mildēaw f. Gmc]

mildly /ˈmaɪldlɪ/ adv. in a mild fashion. □ **to put it mildly** as an understatement (implying the reality is more extreme).

mile n. **1** (also **statute mile**) a unit of linear measure equal to 1,760 yards (approx. 1.609 kilometres). **2** (in pl.) colloq. a great distance or amount (miles better; beat them by miles). **3** a race extending over a mile. [OE mīl ult. f. L mil(l)ia pl. of mille thousand]

mileage /ˈmaɪlɪdʒ/ n. (also **milage**) **1 a** a number of miles travelled, used, etc. **b** the number of

miles travelled by a vehicle per unit of fuel. **2** travelling expenses (per mile). **3** colloq. benefit, profit, advantage.

milepost /ˈmaɪlpəʊst/ n. a post one mile from the finishing-post of a race etc.

miler /ˈmaɪlə(r)/ n. colloq. a person or horse qualified or trained specially to run a mile.

milestone /ˈmaɪlstəʊn/ n. **1** a stone set up beside a road to mark a distance in miles. **2** a significant event or stage in a life, history, project, etc.

milieu /mɪˈljɜː, ˈmiːljɜː/ n. (pl. **milieux** or **milieus** /-ljɜːz/) one's environment or social surroundings. [F f. mi MID¹ + lieu place]

militant /ˈmɪlɪt(ə)nt/ adj. & n. —adj. **1** combative; aggressively active esp. in support of a (usu. political) cause. **2** engaged in warfare. —n. a militant person, esp. a political activist. □ **militancy** n. **militantly** adv. [ME f. OF f. L (as MILITATE)]

militarism /ˈmɪlɪtəˌrɪz(ə)m/ n. **1** the spirit or tendencies of a professional soldier. **2** undue prevalence of the military spirit or ideals. □ **militaristic** /-ˈrɪstɪk/ adj. **militaristically** /-ˈrɪstɪkəlɪ/ adv. [F militarisme (as MILITARY)]

militarist /ˈmɪlɪtərɪst/ n. **1** a person dominated by militaristic ideas. **2** a student of military science.

militarize /ˈmɪlɪtəˌraɪz/ v.tr. (also **-ise**) **1** equip with military resources. **2** make military or warlike. **3** imbue with militarism. □ **militarization** /-ˈzeɪʃ(ə)n/ n.

military /ˈmɪlɪtərɪ/ adj. & n. —adj. of, relating to, or characteristic of soldiers or armed forces. —n. (as sing. or pl.; prec. by the) members of the armed forces, as distinct from civilians and the police. □ **military honours** marks of respect paid by troops at the burial of a soldier, to royalty, etc. **military police** a corps responsible for police and disciplinary duties in the army. □ **militarily** adv. **militariness** n. [F militaire or L militaris f. miles militis soldier]

militate /ˈmɪlɪˌteɪt/ v.intr. (usu. foll. by against) (of facts or evidence) have force or effect (what you say militates against our opinion). [L militare militat- f. miles militis soldier]

■ **Usage** This word is often confused with mitigate.

militia /mɪˈlɪʃə/ n. a military force, esp. one raised from the civil population and supplementing a regular army in an emergency. [L, = military service f. miles militis soldier]

militiaman /mɪˈlɪʃəmən/ n. (pl. **-men**) a member of a militia.

milk n. & v. —n. **1** an opaque white fluid secreted by female mammals for the nourishment of their young. **2** the milk of cows, goats, or sheep as food. **3** the milklike juice of plants, e.g. in the coconut. **4** a milklike preparation of herbs, drugs, etc. —v.tr. **1** draw milk from (a cow, ewe, goat, etc.). **2 a** exploit (a person) esp. financially. **b** get all possible advantage from (a situation). **3** extract sap, venom, etc. from. □ **in milk** secreting milk. **milk and honey** abundant means of prosperity. **milk and water** a feeble or insipid or mawkish discourse or sentiment. **milk bar** a snack bar selling milk drinks and other refreshments. **milk chocolate** chocolate for eating, made with milk. **milk float** Brit. a small usu. electric vehicle used in delivering milk. **milk-loaf** a loaf of bread made with milk.

milk of human kindness kindness regarded as natural to humanity. **Milk of Magnesia** *Brit. propr.* a white suspension of magnesium hydroxide usu. in water as an antacid or laxative. **milk-powder** milk dehydrated by evaporation. **milk pudding** a pudding of rice, sago, tapioca, etc., baked with milk in a dish. **milk round 1** a fixed route on which milk is delivered regularly. **2** a regular trip or tour involving calls at several places. **milk run** a routine expedition or service journey. **milk shake** a drink of milk, flavouring, etc., mixed by shaking or whisking. **milk sugar** lactose. **milk tooth** a temporary tooth in young mammals. □ **milker** *n.* [OE *milc, milcian* f. Gmc]

milkmaid /'mɪlkmeɪd/ *n.* a girl or woman who milks cows or works in a dairy.

milkman /'mɪlkmən/ *n.* (*pl.* **-men**) a person who sells or delivers milk.

milksop /'mɪlksɒp/ *n.* a spiritless man or youth.

milky /'mɪlkɪ/ *adj.* (**milkier, milkiest**) **1** of, like, or mixed with milk. **2** (of a gem or liquid) cloudy; not clear. **3** effeminate; weakly amiable. □ **Milky Way** a faintly luminous band of light emitted by countless stars encircling the heavens; the Galaxy. □ **milkiness** *n.*

mill *n. & v.* —*n.* **1 a** a building fitted with a mechanical apparatus for grinding corn. **b** such an apparatus. **2** an apparatus for grinding any solid substance to powder or pulp (*pepper-mill*). **3 a** a building fitted with machinery for manufacturing processes etc. (*cotton-mill*). **b** such machinery. —*v.* **1** *tr.* grind (corn), produce (flour), or hull (seeds) in a mill. **2** *tr.* produce regular ribbed markings on the edge of (a coin). **3** *tr.* cut or shape (metal) with a rotating tool. **4** *intr.* (often foll. by *about, around*) (of people or animals) move in an aimless manner, esp. in a confused mass. □ **go** (or **put**) **through the mill** undergo (or cause to undergo) intensive work or training etc. **mill-hand** a worker in a mill or factory. **mill-race** a current of water that drives a mill-wheel. **mill-wheel** a wheel used to drive a water-mill. □ **millable** *adj.* [OE *mylen* ult. f. LL *molinum* f. L *mola* grindstone, mill f. *molere* grind]

millboard /'mɪlbɔːd/ *n.* stout pasteboard for bookbinding etc.

millefeuille /miːˈlfɜːj/ *n.* a rich confection of puff pastry split and filled with jam, cream, etc. [F. = thousand-leaf]

millenarian /ˌmɪlɪˈneərɪən/ *adj. & n.* —*adj.* **1** of or related to the millennium. **2** believing in the millennium. —*n.* a person who believes in the millennium. [as MILLENARY]

millenary /mɪˈlenərɪ/ *n. & adj.* —*n.* (*pl.* **-ies**) **1** a period of 1,000 years. **2** the festival of the 1,000th anniversary of a person or thing. **3** a person who believes in the millennium. —*adj.* of or relating to a millenary. [LL *millenarius* consisting of a thousand f. *milleni* distrib. of *mille* thousand]

millennium /mɪˈlenɪəm/ *n.* (*pl.* **millenniums** or **millennia** /-nɪə/) **1** a period of 1,000 years, esp. that of Christ's prophesied reign in person on earth (Rev. 20:1–5). **2** a period of good government, great happiness, and prosperity. □ **millennial** *adj.* **millennialist** *n. & adj.* [mod.L f. L *mille* thousand after BIENNIUM]

miller /'mɪlə(r)/ *n.* **1** the proprietor or tenant of a corn-mill. **2** a person who works or owns a

mill. [ME *mylnere,* prob. f. MLG, MDu. *molner, mulner,* OS *mulineri* f. LL *molinarius* f. *molina* MILL]

millesimal /mɪˈlesɪm(ə)l/ *adj. & n.* —*adj.* **1** thousandth. **2** of or belonging to a thousandth. **3** of or dealing with thousandths. —*n.* a thousandth part. □ **millesimally** *adv.* [L *millesimus* f. *mille* thousand]

millet /'mɪlɪt/ *n.* **1** any of various cereal plants, esp. *Panicum miliaceum,* bearing a large crop of small nutritious seeds. **2** the seed of this. [ME f. F, dimin. of *mil* f. L *milium*]

milli- /'mɪlɪ/ *comb. form* a thousand, esp. denoting a factor of one thousandth. [L *mille* thousand]

milliard /'mɪljɑːd, -jɑːd/ *n. Brit.* one thousand million. [F f. *mille* thousand]

■ **Usage** This word is now largely superseded by *billion.*

millibar /'mɪlɪbɑː(r)/ *n.* one-thousandth of a bar, the cgs unit of atmospheric pressure equivalent to 100 pascals.

milligram /'mɪlɪˌgræm/ *n.* one-thousandth of a gram.

millilitre /'mɪlɪˌliːtə(r)/ *n.* one-thousandth of a litre (0.002 pint).

millimetre /'mɪlɪˌmiːtə(r)/ *n.* one-thousandth of a metre (0.039 in.).

milliner /'mɪlɪnə(r)/ *n.* a person who makes or sells women's hats. □ **millinery** *n.* [orig. = vendor of goods from *Milan*]

million /'mɪljən/ *n. & adj.* —*n.* (*pl.* same or (in sense 2) **millions**) (in *sing.* prec. by *a* or *one*) **1** a thousand thousand. **2** (in *pl.*) *colloq.* a very large number (*millions of years*). **3** (prec. by *the*) the bulk of the population. **4 a** *Brit.* a million pounds. **b** *US* a million dollars. —*adj.* that amount to a million. □ **gone a million** *Austral. sl.* completely defeated. □ **millionfold** *adj. & adv.* **millionth** *adj. & n.* [ME f. OF, prob. f. It. *millione* f. *mille* thousand + *-one* augment. suffix]

millionaire /ˌmɪljəˈneə(r)/ *n.* (*fem.* **millionairess** /-rɪs/) **1** a person whose assets are worth at least one million pounds, dollars, etc. **2** a person of great wealth. [F *millionnaire* (as MILLION)]

millipede /'mɪlɪˌpiːd/ *n.* (also **millepede**) any arthropod of the class Diplopoda, having a long segmented body with two pairs of legs on each segment. [L *millepeda* wood-louse f. *mille* thousand + *pes pedis* foot]

millisecond /'mɪlɪˌsekənd/ *n.* one-thousandth of a second.

millpond /'mɪlpɒnd/ *n.* a pool of water retained by a mill-dam for the operation of a mill. □ **like a millpond** (of a stretch of water) very calm.

millstone /'mɪlstəʊn/ *n.* **1** each of two circular stones used for grinding corn. **2** a heavy burden or responsibility (cf. Matt. 18:6).

milometer /maɪˈlɒmɪtə(r)/ *n.* an instrument for measuring the number of miles travelled by a vehicle.

milord /mɪˈlɔːd/ *n. hist.* an Englishman travelling in Europe in aristocratic style. [F f. E *my lord:* cf. MILADY]

milt *n.* **1** the spleen in mammals. **2** an analogous organ in other vertebrates. **3** a sperm-filled reproductive gland of a male fish. [OE *milt(e)* f. Gmc, perh. rel. to MELT]

mime *n. & v.* —*n.* **1** the theatrical technique of suggesting action, character, etc. by gesture and expression without using words. **2** a theatrical performance using this technique. **3** (also **mime artist**) a practitioner of mime. —*v.* **1** *tr.* (also *absol.*) convey (an idea or emotion) by gesture without words. **2** *intr.* (often foll. by *to*) (of singers etc.) mouth the words of a song etc. along with a soundtrack (*mime to a record*). □ **mimer** *n.* [L *mimus* f. Gk *mimos*]

mimeograph /ˈmɪmɪəˌɡrɑːf/ *n.* & *v.* —*n.* **1** (often *attrib.*) a duplicating machine which produces copies from a stencil. **2** a copy produced in this way. —*v.tr.* reproduce (text or diagrams) by this process. [irreg. f. Gk *mimeomai* imitate: see -GRAPH]

mimesis /mɪˈmiːsɪs, maɪ-/ *n.* *Biol.* a close external resemblance of an animal to another that is distasteful or harmful to predators of the first. [Gk *mimēsis* imitation]

mimetic /mɪˈmetɪk/ *adj.* **1** relating to or habitually practising imitation or mimicry. **2** *Biol.* or exhibiting mimesis. □ **mimetically** *adv.* [Gk *mimētikos* imitation (as MIMESIS)]

mimic /ˈmɪmɪk/ *v.* & *n.* —*v.tr.* (**mimicked**, **mimicking**) **1** imitate (a person, gesture, etc.) esp. to entertain or ridicule. **2** copy minutely or servilely. **3** (of a thing) resemble closely. —*n.* a person skilled in imitation. □ **mimicker** *n.* [L *mimicus* f. Gk *mimikos* (as MIME)]

mimicry /ˈmɪmɪkrɪ/ *n.* (*pl.* **-ies**) **1** the act or art of mimicking. **2** a thing that mimics another. **3** *Zool.* mimesis.

mimosa /mɪˈməʊzə/ *n.* **1** any leguminous shrub of the genus *Mimosa*, esp. *M. pudica*, having globular usu. yellow flowers and sensitive leaflets which droop when touched. **2** any of various acacia plants with showy yellow flowers. [mod.L, app. f. L (as MIME, from being as sensitive as animals) + -*osa* fem. suffix]

Min. *abbr.* **1** Minister. **2** Ministry.

min. *abbr.* **1** minute(s). **2** minimum.

mina var. of MYNA.

minaret /ˌmɪnəˈret/ *n.* a slender turret connected with a mosque and having a balcony from which the muezzin calls at hours of prayer. □ **minareted** *adj.* [F *minaret* or Sp. *minarete* f. Turk. *minare* f. Arab. *manār(a)* lighthouse, minaret f. *nār* fire, light]

minatory /ˈmɪnətərɪ/ *adj.* threatening, menacing. [LL *minatorius* f. *minari* *minat*-threaten]

mince *v.* & *n.* —*v.* **1** *tr.* cut up or grind (esp. meat) into very small pieces. **2** *tr.* (usu. with *neg.*) restrain (one's words etc.) within the bounds of politeness. **3** *intr.* (usu. as **mincing** *adj.*) speak or walk with an affected delicacy. —*n.* esp. *Brit.* minced meat. □ **mince matters** (usu. with *neg.*) use polite expressions etc. **mince pie** a usu. small round pie containing mincemeat. □ **mincer** *n.* **mincingly** *adv.* (in sense 3 of *v.*). [ME f. OF *mincier* ult. f. L (as MINUTIA)]

mincemeat /ˈmɪnsmiːt/ *n.* a mixture of currants, raisins, sugar, apples, candied peel, spices, and often suet. □ **make mincemeat of** utterly defeat (a person, argument, etc.).

mind /maɪnd/ *n.* & *v.* —*n.* **1 a** the seat of consciousness, thought, volition, and feeling. **b** attention, concentration (*my mind keeps wandering*). **2** the intellect; intellectual powers. **3** remembrance, memory (*it went out of my mind; I can't call it to mind*). **4** one's opinion (*we're of the same mind*). **5** a way of thinking or feeling

(*shocking to the Victorian mind*). **6** the focus of one's thoughts or desires (*put one's mind to it*). **7** the state of normal mental functioning (*lose one's mind; in one's right mind*). **8** a person as embodying mental faculties (*a great mind*). —*v.tr.* **1** (usu. with *neg.* or *interrog.*) object to (*do you mind if I smoke?; I don't mind your being late*). **2 a** remember; take care to (*mind you come on time*). **b** (often foll. by *out*) take care; be careful. **3** have charge of temporarily (*mind the house while I'm away*). **4** apply oneself to, concern oneself with (business, affairs, etc.) (*I try to mind my own business*). **5** give heed to; notice (*mind the step; don't mind the expense; mind how you go*). **6** *US* & *Ir.* be obedient to (*mind what your mother says*). □ **be in two minds** be undecided. **don't mind me** *iron.* do as you please. **do you mind!** *iron.* an expression of annoyance. **give a person a piece of one's mind** scold or reproach a person. **have a good** (or **great** or **half a**) **mind to** (often as a threat, usu. unfulfilled) feel tempted to (*I've a good mind to report you*). **have (it) in mind** intend. **have on one's mind** be troubled by the thought of. **in one's mind's eye** in one's imagination or mental view. **mind-bending** *colloq.* (esp. of a psychedelic drug) influencing or altering one's state of mind. **mind-blowing** *sl.* **1** confusing, shattering. **2** (esp. of drugs etc.) inducing hallucinations. **mind-boggling** *colloq.* overwhelming, startling. **mind out for** guard against, avoid. **mind-read** discern the thoughts of (another person). **mind-reader** a person capable of mind-reading. **mind-set** habits of mind formed by earlier events. **mind you** an expression used to qualify a previous statement (*I found it quite quickly; mind you, it wasn't easy*). **never mind 1** an expression used to comfort or console. **2** (also **never you mind**) an expression used to evade a question. **put a person in mind of** remind a person of. **put** (or **set**) **a person's mind at rest** reassure a person. **put a person or thing out of one's mind** deliberately forget. **read a person's mind** discern a person's thoughts. **to my mind** in my opinion. [ME *mynd* f. OE *gemynd* f. Gmc]

minded /ˈmaɪndɪd/ *adj.* **1** (in *comb.*) **a** inclined to think in some specified way (*mathematically minded; fair-minded*). **b** having a specified kind of mind (*high-minded*). **c** interested in or enthusiastic about a specified thing (*car-minded*). **2** (usu. foll. by *to* + infin.) disposed or inclined (to an action).

minder /ˈmaɪndə(r)/ *n.* **1 a** a person whose job it is to attend to a person or thing. **b** (in *comb.*) (*child-minder; machine-minder*). **2** *sl.* a bodyguard, esp. a person employed to protect a criminal.

mindful /ˈmaɪndfʊl/ *adj.* (often foll. by *of*) taking heed or care; being conscious. □ **mindfully** *adv.* **mindfulness** *n.*

mindless /ˈmaɪndlɪs/ *adj.* **1** lacking intelligence; stupid. **2** not requiring thought or skill (*totally mindless work*). **3** (usu. foll. by *of*) heedless of (advice etc.). □ **mindlessly** *adv.* **mindlessness** *n.*

mine[1] *poss.pron.* **1** the one or ones belonging to or associated with me (*it is mine; mine are over there*). **2** (*attrib.* before a vowel) *archaic* = MY (*mine eyes have seen; mine host*). □ **of mine** of or belonging to me (*a friend of mine*). [OE *mīn* f. Gmc]

mine[2] *n. & v. —n.* **1** an excavation in the earth for extracting metal, coal, salt, etc. **2** an abundant source (of information etc.). **3** a receptacle filled with explosive and placed in the ground or in the water for destroying enemy personnel, ships, etc. **4** a subterranean gallery in which explosive is placed to blow up fortifications. *—v.tr.* **1** obtain (metal, coal, etc.) from a mine. **2** (also *absol.*, often foll. by *for*) dig in (the earth etc.) for ore etc. **3 a** dig or burrow in (usu. the earth). **b** make (a hole, passage, etc.) underground. **4** lay explosive mines under or in. □ **mine-detector** an instrument for detecting the presence of mines. □ **mining** *n.* [ME f. OF *mine, miner,* perh. f. Celt.]

minefield /ˈmaɪnfiːld/ *n.* **1** an area planted with explosive mines. **2** a subject or situation presenting unseen hazards.

minelayer /ˈmaɪnˌleɪə(r)/ *n.* a ship or aircraft for laying mines.

miner /ˈmaɪnə(r)/ *n.* **1** a person who works in a mine. **2** any burrowing insect or grub. [ME f. OF *minëor, minour* (as MINE[2])]

mineral /ˈmɪnər(ə)l/ *n. & adj. —n.* **1** any of the species into which inorganic substances are classified. **2** a substance obtained by mining. **3** (often in *pl.*) *Brit.* an artificial mineral water or other effervescent drink. *—adj.* **1** of or containing a mineral or minerals. **2** obtained by mining. □ **mineral oil** petroleum or one of its distillation products. **mineral water 1** water found in nature with some dissolved salts present. **2** an artificial imitation of this, esp. soda water. **3** any effervescent non-alcoholic drink. **mineral wool** a wool-like substance made from inorganic material, used for packing etc. [ME f. OF *mineral* or med.L *mineralis* f. *minera* ore f. OF *miniere* mine]

mineralogy /ˌmɪnəˈrælədʒɪ/ *n.* the scientific study of minerals. □ **mineralogical** /-rəˈlɒdʒɪk(ə)l/ *adj.* **mineralogist** *n.*

minestrone /ˌmɪnɪˈstrəʊnɪ/ *n.* a soup containing vegetables and pasta, beans, or rice. [It.]

minesweeper /ˈmaɪnˌswiːpə(r)/ *n.* a ship for clearing away floating and submarine mines.

mineworker /ˈmaɪnˌwɜːkə(r)/ *n.* a person who works in a mine, esp. a coalmine.

Ming /mɪŋ/ *n.* **1** the dynasty ruling China 1368–1644. **2** Chinese porcelain made during the rule of this dynasty. [Chin.]

mingle /ˈmɪŋg(ə)l/ *v.tr. & intr.* mix, blend. □ **mingle with** go about among. □ **mingler** *n.* [ME *mengel* f. obs. *meng* f. OE *mengan,* rel. to AMONG]

mingy /ˈmɪndʒɪ/ *adj.* (**mingier, mingiest**) *Brit. colloq.* mean, stingy. □ **mingily** *adv.* [perh. f. MEAN[2] and STINGY]

mini /ˈmɪnɪ/ *n.* (*pl.* **minis**) **1** *colloq.* a miniskirt, minidress, etc. **2** (**Mini**) *propr.* a make of small car. [abbr.]

mini- /ˈmɪnɪ/ *comb. form* miniature; very small or minor of its kind (*minibus; mini-budget*). [abbr. of MINIATURE]

miniature /ˈmɪnɪtʃə(r)/ *adj. & n.* **1** much smaller than normal. **2** represented on a small scale. *—n.* **1** any object reduced in size. **2** a small-scale minutely finished portrait. **3** this branch of painting (*portrait in miniature*). □ **in miniature** on a small scale. □ **miniaturist** *n.* (in senses 2 and 3 of n.). [It. *miniatura* f. med.L *miniatura* f. L

miniare rubricate, illuminate f. L *minium* red lead, vermilion]

miniaturize /ˈmɪnɪtʃəˌraɪz/ *v.tr.* (also **-ise**) produce in a smaller version; make small. □ **miniaturization** /-ˈzeɪʃ(ə)n/ *n.*

minibus /ˈmɪnɪˌbʌs/ *n.* a small bus for about twelve passengers.

minicab /ˈmɪnɪˌkæb/ *n. Brit.* a car used as a taxi, but not licensed to ply for hire.

minicomputer /ˈmɪnɪkəmˌpjuːtə(r)/ *n.* a computer of medium power, more than a microcomputer but less than a mainframe.

minim /ˈmɪnɪm/ *n.* **1** *Mus.* a note having the time value of two crotchets or half a semibreve and represented by a hollow ring with a stem. **2** one-sixtieth of a fluid drachm, about a drop. [ME f. L *minimus* smallest]

minima *pl.* of MINIMUM.

minimal /ˈmɪnɪm(ə)l/ *adj.* **1** very minute or slight. **2** being or related to a minimum. **3** the least possible in size, duration, etc. **4** *Art* etc. characterized by the use of simple or primary forms or structures etc. □ **minimalism** *n.* **minimalist** *n.* **minimally** *adv.* (in senses 1–3). [L *minimus* smallest]

minimize /ˈmɪnɪˌmaɪz/ *v.* (also **-ise**) **1** *tr.* reduce to, or estimate at, the smallest possible amount or degree. **2** *tr.* estimate or represent at less than the true value or importance. □ **minimization** /-ˈzeɪʃ(ə)n/ *n.* **minimizer** *n.*

minimum /ˈmɪnɪməm/ *n. & adj.* (*pl.* **minima** /-mə/) *—n.* the least possible or attainable amount (*reduced to a minimum*). *—adj.* that is a minimum. □ **minimum wage** the lowest wage permitted by law or special agreement. [L, neut. of *minimus* least]

minion /ˈmɪnjən/ *n. derog.* a servile agent; a slave. [F *mignon,* OF *mignot,* of Gaulish orig.]

minipill /ˈmɪnɪpɪl/ *n.* a contraceptive pill containing a progestogen only (not oestrogen).

miniseries /ˈmɪnɪˌsɪərɪz/ *n.* a short series of television programmes on a common theme.

miniskirt /ˈmɪnɪˌskɜːt/ *n.* a very short skirt.

minister /ˈmɪnɪstə(r)/ *n. & v. —n.* **1** a head of a government department. **2** (in full **minister of religion**) a member of the clergy, esp. in the Presbyterian and Nonconformist Churches. **3** a diplomatic agent, usu. ranking below an ambassador. **4** (usu. foll. by *of*) a person employed in the execution of (a purpose, will, etc.) (*a minister of justice*). *—v.* **1** *intr.* (usu. foll. by *to*) render aid or service (to a person, cause, etc.). **2** *tr.* (usu. foll. by *with*) *archaic* furnish, supply, etc. □ **Minister of the Crown** *Brit. Parl.* a member of the Cabinet. **Minister of State** a government minister, in the UK usu. regarded as holding a rank below that of Head of Department. **Minister without Portfolio** a government minister who has Cabinet status, but is not in charge of a specific Department of State. □ **ministrable** *adj.* [ME f. OF *ministre* f. L *minister* servant f. *minus* less]

ministerial /ˌmɪnɪˈstɪərɪəl/ *adj.* **1** of a minister of religion or a minister's office. **2** of a government minister. **ministerially** *adv.* [F *ministériel* or LL *ministerialis* f. L (as MINISTRY)]

ministration /ˌmɪnɪˈstreɪʃ(ə)n/ *n.* **1** (usu. in *pl.*) aid or service (*the kind ministrations of his neighbours*). **2** ministering, esp. in religious matters. **3** (usu. foll. by *of*) the supplying (of help, justice, etc.). □ **ministrant** /ˈmɪnɪstrənt/ *adj. &*

n. **ministrative** /ˈmɪnɪstrətɪv/ *adj.* [ME f. OF *ministration* or L *ministratio* (as MINISTER)]

ministry /ˈmɪnɪstrɪ/ *n.* (*pl.* **-ies**) **1 a** a government department headed by a minister. **b** the building which it occupies (*the Ministry of Defence*). **2 a** (prec. by *the*) the vocation or profession of a religious minister (*called to the ministry*). **b** the office of a religious minister, priest, etc. **c** the period of tenure of this. **3** (prec. by *the*) the body of ministers of a government or of a religion. **4** a period of government under one Prime Minister. **5** ministering, ministration. [ME f. L *ministerium* (as MINISTER)]

mink *n.* **1** either of two small semi-aquatic stoatlike animals of the genus *Mustela, M. vison* of N. America and *M. intreola* of Europe. **2** the thick brown fur of these. **3** a coat made of this. [cf. Sw. *mänk*, *menk*]

minke /ˈmɪŋkə/ *n.* a small baleen whale, *Balaenoptera acutorostrata*, with a pointed snout. [prob. f. *Meincke*, the name of a Norw. whaler]

minnow /ˈmɪnəʊ/ *n.* any of various small freshwater fish of the carp family, esp. *Phoxinus phoxinus*. [late ME *menow*, perh. repr. OE *mynwe* (unrecorded), *myne*: infl. by ME *menuse, menise* f. OF *menuise*, ult. rel. to MINUTIA]

Minoan /mɪˈnəʊən/ *adj. & n. Archaeol.* —*adj.* of or relating to the Bronze Age civilization centred on Crete (*c.*3000–1100 BC). —*n.* an inhabitant of Minoan Crete or the Minoan world. [named after the legendary Cretan king *Minos* (Gk *Mīnōs*), to whom the palace excavated at Knossos was attributed]

minor /ˈmaɪnə(r)/ *adj., n., & v.* —*adj.* **1** lesser or comparatively small in size or importance (*minor poet; minor operation*). **2** *Mus.* **a** (of a scale) having intervals of a semitone between the second and third, fifth and sixth, and seventh and eighth degrees. **b** (of an interval) less by a semitone than a major interval. **c** (of a key) based on a minor scale. **3** *Brit.* (in schools) indicating the younger of two children from the same family or the second to enter the school (usu. put after the name). —*n.* **1** a person under the legal age limit or majority (*no unaccompanied minors*). **2** *Mus.* a minor key etc. **3** *US* a student's subsidiary subject or course. —*v.intr.* (foll. by *in*) *US* (of a student) undertake study in (a subject) as a subsidiary to a main subject. □ **minor canon** a cleric who is not a member of the chapter, who assists in daily cathedral services. **minor league** *US* (in baseball, football, etc.) a league of professional clubs other than the major leagues. [L, = smaller, less, rel. to *minuere* lessen]

minority /maɪˈnɒrɪtɪ/ *n.* (*pl.* **-ies**) **1** (often foll. by *of*) a smaller number or part, esp. within a political party or structure. **2** the number of votes cast for this (*a minority of two*). **3** the state of having less than half the votes or of being supported by less than half of the body of opinion (*in the minority*). **4** a relatively small group of people differing from others in the society of which they are a part in race, religion, language, political persuasion, etc. **5** (*attrib.*) relating to or done by the minority (*minority interests*). **6 a** the state of being under full legal age. **b** the period of this. [F *minorité* or med.L *minoritas* f. L *minor*: see MINOR]

minster /ˈmɪnstə(r)/ *n.* **1** a large or important church (*York Minster*). **2** the church of a monastery. [OE *mynster* f. eccl.L *monasterium* f. Gk *monastērion* MONASTERY]

minstrel /ˈmɪnstr(ə)l/ *n.* **1** a medieval singer or musician, esp. singing or reciting poetry. **2** (usu. in *pl.*) a member of a band of public entertainers with blackened faces etc., performing songs and music ostensibly of Negro origin. [ME f. OF *menestral* entertainer, servant, f. Prov. *menest(ai)ral* officer, employee, musician, f. LL *ministerialis* official, officer: see MINISTERIAL]

minstrelsy /ˈmɪnstr(ə)lsɪ/ *n.* (*pl.* **-ies**) **1** the minstrel's art. **2** minstrel poetry. [ME f. OF *menestralsie* (as MINSTREL)]

mint[1] *n.* **1** any aromatic plant of the genus *Mentha*. **2** a peppermint sweet or lozenge. □ **mint sauce** chopped mint in vinegar and sugar, usu. eaten with lamb. □ **minty** *adj.* (**mintier, mintiest**). [OE *minte* ult. f. L *ment(h)a* f. Gk *minthē*]

mint[2] /mɪnt/ *n. & v.* —*n.* **1** a place where money is coined, usu. under State authority. **2** a vast sum of money (*making a mint*). **3** a source of invention etc. (*a mint of ideas*). —*v.tr.* **1** make (coin) by stamping metal. **2** invent, coin (a word, phrase, etc.). □ **in mint condition** (or **state**) freshly minted; (of books etc.) as new. □ **mintage** *n.* [OE *mynet* f. WG f. L *moneta* MONEY]

minuet /ˌmɪnjʊˈet/ *n. & v.* —*n.* **1** a slow stately dance for two in triple time. **2** *Mus.* the music for this, or music in the same rhythm and style. —*v.intr.* (**minueted, minueting**) dance a minuet. [F *menuet*, orig. adj. = fine, delicate, dimin. of *menu*: see MENU]

minus /ˈmaɪnəs/ *prep., adj., & n.* —*prep.* **1** with the subtraction of (*7 minus 4 equals 3*). **2** (of temperature) below zero (*minus 2°*). **3** *colloq.* lacking; deprived of (*returned minus their dog*). —*adj.* **1** *Math.* negative. **2** *Electronics* having a negative charge. —*n.* **1** = minus sign. **2** *Math.* a negative quantity. **3** a disadvantage. □ **minus sign** the symbol –, indicating subtraction or a negative value. [L, neut. of *minor* less]

minuscule /ˈmɪnəˌskjuːl/ *adj.* **1** lower-case. **2** *colloq.* extremely small or unimportant. [F f. L *minuscula* (*littera* letter) dimin. of *minor*: see MINOR]

minute[1] /ˈmɪnɪt/ *n. & v.* —*n.* **1** the sixtieth part of an hour. **2** a distance covered in one minute (*twenty minutes from the station*). **3 a** a moment; an instant; a point of time (*expecting her any minute; the train leaves in a minute*). **b** (prec. by *the*) *colloq.* the present time (*what are you doing at the minute?*). **c** (foll. by *clause*) as soon as (*call me the minute you get back*). **4** the sixtieth part of an angular degree. **5** (in *pl.*) a brief summary of the proceedings at a meeting. **6** an official memorandum authorizing or recommending a course of action. —*v.tr.* **1** record (proceedings) in the minutes. **2** send the minutes to (a person). □ **minute-hand** the hand on a watch or clock which indicates minutes. **minute steak** a thin slice of steak to be cooked quickly. **up to the minute** completely up to date. [ME f. OF f. LL *minuta* (n.), f. fem. of *minutus* MINUTE[2]: senses 1 & 4 of noun f. med.L *pars minuta prima* first minute part (cf. SECOND[2]): senses 5 & 6 perh. f. med.L *minuta scriptura* draft in small writing]

minute[2] /maɪˈnjuːt/ *adj.* (**minutest**) **1** very small. **2** trifling, petty. **3** (of an inquiry, inquirer, etc.) accurate, detailed, precise. □ **minutely** *adv.* **minuteness** *n.* [ME f. L *minutus* past part. of *minuere* lessen]

minutia /maɪˈnjuːʃɪə, mɪ-/ n. (pl. -iae /-ʃɪ͵iː/) (usu. in pl.) a precise, trivial, or minor detail. [L, = smallness, in pl. trifles f. *minutus*: see MINUTE²]

minx /mɪŋks/ n. a pert, sly, or playful girl. □ **minxish** adj. **minxishly** adv. [16th c.: orig. unkn.]

Miocene /ˈmɪə͵siːn/ adj. & n. Geol. —adj. of or relating to the fourth epoch of the Tertiary period. —n. this epoch or system. [irreg. f. Gk *meiōn* less + *kainos* new]

mirabelle /͵mɪrəˈbel/ n. **1 a** a European variety of plum-tree, *Prunus insititia*, bearing small round yellow fruit. **b** a fruit from this tree. **2** a liqueur distilled from this fruit. [F]

miracle /ˈmɪrək(ə)l/ n. **1** an extraordinary event attributed to some supernatural agency. **2 a** any remarkable occurrence. **b** a remarkable development in some specified area (*an economic miracle*). **3** (usu. foll. by *of*) a remarkable or outstanding specimen (*the plan was a miracle of ingenuity*). □ **miracle play** a medieval play based on the Bible or the lives of the saints. [ME f. OF f. L *miraculum* object of wonder f. *mirari* wonder f. *mirus* wonderful]

miraculous /mɪˈrækjʊləs/ adj. **1** of the nature of a miracle. **2** supernatural. **3** remarkable, surprising. □ **miraculously** adv. **miraculousness** n. [F *miraculeux* or med.L *miraculosus* f. L (as MIRACLE)]

mirage /ˈmɪrɑːʒ/ n. **1** an optical illusion caused by atmospheric conditions, esp. the appearance of a sheet of water in a desert or on a hot road from the reflection of light. **2** an illusory thing. [F f. *se mirer* be reflected, f. L *mirare* look at]

mire n. & v. —n. **1** a stretch of swampy or boggy ground. **2** mud, dirt. —v. **1** tr. & intr. plunge or sink in a mire. **2** tr. involve in difficulties. □ **in the mire** in difficulties. [ME f. ON *mýrr* f. Gmc, rel. to MOSS]

mirk var. of MURK.

mirky var. of MURKY.

mirror /ˈmɪrə(r)/ n. & v. —n. **1** a polished surface, usu. of amalgam-coated glass or metal, which reflects an image; a looking-glass. **2** anything regarded as giving an accurate reflection or description of something else. —v.tr. reflect as in a mirror. □ **mirror finish** a reflective surface. **mirror image** an identical image, but with the structure reversed, as in a mirror. **mirror symmetry** symmetry as of an object and its reflection. **mirror writing** backwards writing, like ordinary writing reflected in a mirror. [ME f. OF *mirour* ult. f. L *mirare* look at]

mirth n. merriment, laughter. □ **mirthful** adj. **mirthfully** adv. **mirthfulness** n. **mirthless** adj. **mirthlessly** adv. **mirthlessness** n. [OE *myrgth* (as MERRY)]

mis-¹ /mɪs/ prefix added to verbs and verbal derivatives: meaning 'amiss', 'badly', 'wrongly', 'unfavourably' (*mislead*; *misshapen*; *mistrust*). [OE f. Gmc]

mis-² /mɪs/ prefix occurring in a few words adopted from French meaning 'badly', 'wrongly', 'amiss', 'ill-', or having a negative force (*misadventure*; *mischief*). [OF *mes-* ult. f. L *minus* (see MINUS): assim. to MIS-¹]

misaddress /͵mɪsəˈdres/ v.tr. **1** address (a letter etc.) wrongly. **2** address (a person) wrongly, esp. impertinently.

misadventure /͵mɪsədˈventʃə(r)/ n. **1** Law an accident without concomitant crime or negligence (*death by misadventure*). **2** bad luck. **3** a misfortune. [ME f. OF *mesaventure* f. *mesavenir* turn out badly (as MIS-², ADVENT: cf. ADVENTURE)]

misalign /͵mɪsəˈlaɪn/ v.tr. give the wrong alignment to. □ **misalignment** n.

misalliance /͵mɪsəˈlaɪəns/ n. an unsuitable alliance, esp. an unsuitable marriage. □ **misally** v.tr. (-ies, -ied). [MIS-¹ + ALLIANCE, after MÉSALLIANCE]

misanthrope /ˈmɪzən͵θrəʊp, ˈmɪs-/ n. (also **misanthropist** /mɪˈzænθrəpɪst/) **1** a person who hates mankind. **2** a person who avoids human society. □ **misanthropic** /-ˈθrɒpɪk/ adj. **misanthropical** /-ˈθrɒpɪk(ə)l/ adj. **misanthropically** /-ˈθrɒpɪkəlɪ/ adv. **misanthropy** /mɪˈzænθrəpɪ/ n. **misanthropize** /mɪˈzænθrə͵paɪz/ v.intr. (also -ise). [F f. Gk *misanthrōpos* f. *misos* hatred + *anthrōpos* man]

misapply /͵mɪsəˈplaɪ/ v.tr. (-ies, -ied) apply (esp. funds) wrongly. □ **misapplication** /mɪs͵æplɪˈkeɪʃ(ə)n/ n.

misapprehend /͵mɪsæprɪˈhend/ v.tr. misunderstand (words, a person). □ **misapprehension** /-ˈhenʃ(ə)n/ n. **misapprehensive** adj.

misappropriate /͵mɪsəˈprəʊprɪ͵eɪt/ v.tr. apply (usu. another's money) to one's own use, or to a wrong use. □ **misappropriation** /-prɪˈeɪʃ(ə)n/ n.

misbegotten /͵mɪsbɪˈgɒt(ə)n/ adj. **1** illegitimate, bastard. **2** contemptible, disreputable.

misbehave /͵mɪsbɪˈheɪv/ v.intr. & refl. (of a person or machine) behave badly. □ **misbehaver** n. **misbehaviour** n.

miscalculate /mɪsˈkælkjʊ͵leɪt/ v.tr. (also absol.) calculate (amounts, results, etc.) wrongly. □ **miscalculation** /-ˈleɪʃ(ə)n/ n.

miscall /mɪsˈkɔːl/ v.tr. call by a wrong or inappropriate name.

miscarriage /ˈmɪs͵kærɪdʒ, mɪsˈkærɪdʒ/ n. **1** a spontaneous abortion, esp. before the 28th week of pregnancy. **2** Brit. the failure (of a plan, letter, etc.) to reach completion or its destination. □ **miscarriage of justice** any failure of the judicial system to attain the ends of justice. [MISCARRY, after CARRIAGE]

miscarry /mɪsˈkærɪ/ v.intr. (-ies, -ied) **1** (of a woman) have a miscarriage. **2** Brit. (of a letter etc.) fail to reach its destination. **3** (of a business, plan, etc.) fail, be unsuccessful.

miscast /mɪsˈkɑːst/ v.tr. (past and past part. -cast) allot an unsuitable part to (an actor).

miscegenation /͵mɪsɪdʒɪˈneɪʃ(ə)n/ n. the interbreeding of races, esp. of Whites and non-Whites. [irreg. f. L *miscēre* mix + *genus* race]

miscellaneous /͵mɪsəˈleɪnɪəs/ adj. **1** of mixed composition or character. **2** (foll. by pl. noun) of various kinds. **3** (of a person) many-sided. □ **miscellaneously** adv. **miscellaneousness** n. [L *miscellaneus* f. *miscellus* mixed f. *miscēre* mix]

miscellany /mɪˈselənɪ/ n. (pl. -ies) **1** a mixture, a medley. **2** a book containing a collection of stories etc., or various literary compositions. □ **miscellanist** n. [F *miscellanées* (fem. pl.) or L *miscellanea*, neut. pl. of *miscellaneus* f. *miscellus* mixed]

mischance /mɪsˈtʃɑːns/ n. **1** bad luck. **2** an instance of this. [ME f. OF *mesch(e)ance* f. *mescheoir* (as MIS-², CHANCE)]

mischief /'mɪstʃɪf/ n. **1** conduct which is troublesome, but not malicious, esp. in children. **2** pranks, scrapes (*get into mischief*; *keep out of mischief*). **3** playful malice, satire (*eyes full of mischief*). **4** harm or injury caused by a person or thing. □ **do a person a mischief** wound or kill a person. **get up to** (or **make**) **mischief** create discord. [ME f. OF *meschief* f. *meschever* (as MIS-², *chever* come to an end f. *chef* head: see CHIEF)]

mischievous /'mɪstʃɪvəs/ adj. **1** (of a person) disposed to mischief. **2** (of conduct) playfully malicious. **3** (of a thing) having harmful effects. □ **mischievously** adv. **mischievousness** n. [ME f. AF *meschevous* f. OF *meschever*: see MISCHIEF]

miscible /'mɪsɪb(ə)l/ adj. (often foll. by *with*) capable of being mixed. □ **miscibility** /-'bɪlɪtɪ/ n. [med.L *miscibilis* f. L *miscēre* mix]

misconceive /ˌmɪskən'siːv/ v. **1** intr. (often foll. by *of*) have a wrong idea or conception. **2** tr. (as **misconceived** adj.) badly planned, organized, etc. **3** tr. misunderstand (a word, person, etc.). □ **misconceiver** n. **misconception** /-'sepʃ(ə)n/ n.

misconduct n. & v. —n. /mɪs'kɒndʌkt/ **1** improper or unprofessional behaviour. **2** bad management. —v. /ˌmɪskən'dʌkt/ **1** refl. misbehave. **2** tr. mismanage.

misconstrue /ˌmɪskən'struː/ v.tr. (**-construes**, **-construed**, **-construing**) **1** interpret (a word, action, etc.) wrongly. **2** mistake the meaning of (a person). □ **misconstruction** /-'strʌkʃ(ə)n/ n.

miscopy /mɪs'kɒpɪ/ v.tr. (**-ies**, **-ied**) copy (text etc.) incorrectly.

miscount /mɪs'kaʊnt/ v. & n. —v.tr. (also absol.) count wrongly. —n. a wrong count.

miscreant /'mɪskrɪənt/ n. & adj. —n. a vile wretch, a villain. —adj. depraved, villainous. [ME f. OF *mescreant* (as MIS-², *creant* part. of *croire* f. L *credere* believe)]

miscue /mɪs'kjuː/ n. & v. —n. (in snooker etc.) the failure to strike the ball properly with the cue. —v.intr. (**-cues**, **-cued**, **-cueing** or **-cuing**) make a miscue.

misdate /mɪs'deɪt/ v.tr. date (an event, a letter, etc.) wrongly.

misdeal /mɪs'diːl/ v. & n. —v.tr. (also absol.) (past and past part. **-dealt** /-'delt/) make a mistake in dealing (cards). —n. **1** a mistake in dealing cards. **2** a misdealt hand.

misdeed /mɪs'diːd/ n. an evil deed, a wrongdoing; a crime. [OE *misdǣd* (as MIS-¹, DEED)]

misdemeanour /ˌmɪsdɪ'miːnə(r)/ n. (US **misdemeanor**) **1** an offence, a misdeed. **2** Law an indictable offence, (in the UK formerly) less heinous than a felony.

misdiagnose /ˌmɪs'daɪəgˌnəʊz/ v.tr. diagnose incorrectly. □ **misdiagnosis** /-'nəʊsɪs/ n.

misdial /mɪs'daɪəl/ v.tr. (also absol.) (**-dialled**, **-dialling**; US **-dialed**, **-dialing**) dial (a telephone number etc.) incorrectly.

misdirect /ˌmɪsdaɪ'rekt, -dɪ'rekt/ v.tr. **1** direct (a person, letter, blow, etc.) wrongly. **2** (of a judge) instruct (the jury) wrongly. □ **misdirection** n.

misdoing /mɪs'duːɪŋ/ n. a misdeed.

mise en scène /ˌmiːz ɑ̃ 'sen/ n. **1** Theatr. the scenery and properties of a play. **2** the setting or surroundings of an event. [F]

misemploy /ˌmɪsɪm'plɔɪ/ v.tr. employ or use wrongly or improperly. □ **misemployment** n.

miser /'maɪzə(r)/ n. **1** a person who hoards wealth and lives miserably. **2** an avaricious person. [L, = wretched]

miserable /'mɪzərəb(ə)l/ adj. **1** wretchedly unhappy or uncomfortable (*felt miserable*; *a miserable hovel*). **2** contemptible, mean. **3** causing wretchedness or discomfort (*miserable weather*). **4** Sc., Austral., & NZ stingy, mean. □ **miserableness** n. **miserably** adv. [ME f. F *misérable* f. L *miserabilis* pitiable f. *miserari* to pity f. *miser* wretched]

misericord /mɪ'zerɪˌkɔːd/ n. a shelving projection on the under side of a hinged seat in a choir stall serving (when the seat is turned up) to help support a person standing. [ME f. OF *misericorde* f. L *misericordia* f. *misericors* compassionate f. stem of *miserēri* pity + *cor cordis* heart]

miserly /'maɪzəlɪ/ adj. like a miser, niggardly. □ **miserliness** n. [MISER]

misery /'mɪzərɪ/ n. (pl. **-ies**) **1** a wretched state of mind, or of outward circumstances. **2** a thing causing this. **3** colloq. a constantly depressed or discontented person. □ **put out of its** etc. **misery 1** release (a person, animal, etc.) from suffering or suspense. **2** kill (an animal) in pain. [ME f. OF *misere* or L *miseria* (as MISER)]

misfield /mɪs'fiːld/ v. & n. —v.tr. (also absol.) (in cricket, baseball, etc.) field (the ball) badly. —n. an instance of this.

misfire /mɪs'faɪə(r)/ v. & n. —v.intr. **1** (of a gun, motor engine, etc.) fail to go off or start or function regularly. **2** (of an action etc.) fail to have the intended effect. —n. a failure of function or intention.

misfit /'mɪsfɪt/ n. **1** a person unsuited to a particular kind of environment, occupation, etc. **2** a garment etc. that does not fit.

misfortune /mɪs'fɔːtʃuːn, -tjuːn/ n. **1** bad luck. **2** an instance of this.

misgive /mɪs'gɪv/ v.tr. (past **-gave** /-'geɪv/; past part. **-given** /-'gɪv(ə)n/) (often foll. by *about, that*) (of a person's mind, heart, etc.) fill (a person) with suspicion or foreboding.

misgiving /mɪs'gɪvɪŋ/ n. (usu. in pl.) a feeling of mistrust or apprehension.

misgovern /mɪs'gʌv(ə)n/ v.tr. govern (a State etc.) badly. □ **misgovernment** n.

misguide /mɪs'gaɪd/ v.tr. **1** (as **misguided** adj.) mistaken in thought or action. **2** mislead, misdirect. □ **misguidance** n. **misguidedly** adv. **misguidedness** n.

mishandle /mɪs'hænd(ə)l/ v.tr. **1** deal with incorrectly or ineffectively. **2** handle (a person or thing) roughly or rudely; ill-treat.

mishap /'mɪshæp/ n. an unlucky accident.

mishear /mɪs'hɪə(r)/ v.tr. (past and past part. **-heard** /-'hɜːd/) hear incorrectly or imperfectly.

mishit v. & n. —v.tr. /mɪs'hɪt/ (**-hitting**; past and past part. **-hit**) hit (a ball etc.) faultily. —n. /'mɪshɪt/ a faulty or bad hit.

mishmash /'mɪʃmæʃ/ n. a confused mixture. [ME, reduplication of MASH]

misidentify /ˌmɪsaɪ'dentɪˌfaɪ/ v.tr. (**-ies**, **-ied**) identify erroneously. □ **misidentification** /-fɪ'keɪʃ(ə)n/ n.

misinform /ˌmɪsɪn'fɔːm/ v.tr. give wrong information to, mislead. □ **misinformation** /-fə'meɪʃ(ə)n/ n.

misinterpret /ˌmɪsɪnˈtɜːprɪt/ v.tr. (-interpreted, -interpreting) 1 interpret wrongly. 2 draw a wrong inference from. □ **misinterpretation** /-ˈteɪʃ(ə)n/ n. **misinterpreter** n.

M.I.6 abbr. (in the UK) the department of Military Intelligence concerned with espionage.

■ **Usage** This term is not in official use.

misjudge /mɪsˈdʒʌdʒ/ v.tr. (also absol.) 1 judge wrongly. 2 have a wrong opinion of. □ **misjudgement** n. (also **misjudgment**).

miskey /mɪsˈkiː/ v.tr. (-keys, -keyed) key (data) wrongly.

miskick v. & n. —v.tr. /mɪsˈkɪk/ (also absol.) kick (a ball etc.) badly or wrongly. —n. /ˈmɪskɪk/ an instance of this.

mislay /mɪsˈleɪ/ v.tr. (past and past part. **-laid** /-leɪd/) 1 unintentionally put (a thing) where it cannot readily be found. 2 euphem. lose.

mislead /mɪsˈliːd/ v.tr. (past and past part. **-led** /-led/) 1 cause (a person) to go wrong, in conduct, belief, etc. 2 lead astray or in the wrong direction. □ **misleader** n.

misleading /mɪsˈliːdɪŋ/ adj. causing to err or go astray; imprecise, confusing. □ **misleadingly** adv. **misleadingness** n.

mismanage /mɪsˈmænɪdʒ/ v.tr. manage badly or wrongly. □ **mismanagement** n.

mismatch v. & n. —v.tr. /mɪsˈmætʃ/ match unsuitably or incorrectly, esp. in marriage. —n. /ˈmɪsmætʃ/ a bad match.

mismeasure /mɪsˈmeʒə(r)/ v.tr. measure or estimate incorrectly. □ **mismeasurement** n.

misname /mɪsˈneɪm/ v.tr. = MISCALL.

misnomer /mɪsˈnəʊmə(r)/ n. 1 a name or term used wrongly. 2 the wrong use of a name or term. [ME f. AF f. OF mesnom(m)er (as MIS-², nommer name f. L nominare formed as NOMINATE)]

misogyny /mɪˈsɒdʒɪnɪ/ n. the hatred of women. □ **misogynist** n. **misogynous** adj. [Gk misos hatred + gunē woman]

misplace /mɪsˈpleɪs/ v.tr. 1 put in the wrong place. 2 bestow (affections, confidence, etc.) on an inappropriate object. 3 time (words, actions, etc.) badly. □ **misplacement** n.

misplay /mɪsˈpleɪ/ v. & n. —v.tr. play (a ball, card, etc.) in a wrong or ineffective manner. —n. an instance of this.

misprint n. & v. —n. /ˈmɪsprɪnt/ a mistake in printing. —v.tr. /mɪsˈprɪnt/ print wrongly.

misprision /mɪsˈprɪʒ(ə)n/ n. Law 1 (in full **misprision of a felony** or **of treason**) the deliberate concealment of one's knowledge of a crime, treason, etc. 2 a wrong action or omission. [ME f. AF mesprisioun f. OF mesprison error f. mesprendre to mistake (as MIS-², prendre take)]

mispronounce /ˌmɪsprəˈnaʊns/ v.tr. pronounce (a word etc.) wrongly. □ **mispronunciation** /-ˌnʌnsɪˈeɪʃ(ə)n/ n.

misquote /mɪsˈkwəʊt/ v.tr. quote wrongly. □ **misquotation** /-ˈteɪʃ(ə)n/ n.

misread /mɪsˈriːd/ v.tr. (past and past part. **-read** /-red/) read or interpret (text, a situation, etc.) wrongly.

misremember /ˌmɪsrɪˈmembə(r)/ v.tr. remember imperfectly or incorrectly.

misreport /ˌmɪsrɪˈpɔːt/ v. & n. —v.tr. give a false or incorrect report of. —n. a false or incorrect report.

misrepresent /ˌmɪsreprɪˈzent/ v.tr. represent wrongly; give a false or misleading account or idea of. □ **misrepresentation** /-ˈteɪʃ(ə)n/ n. **misrepresentative** adj.

misrule /mɪsˈruːl/ n. & v. —n. bad government; disorder. —v.tr. govern badly.

miss¹ v. & n. —v. 1 tr. (also absol.) fail to hit, reach, find, catch, etc. (an object or goal). 2 tr. fail to catch (a bus, train, etc.). 3 tr. fail to experience, see, or attend (an occurrence or event). 4 tr. fail to meet (a person); fail to keep (an appointment). 5 tr. fail to seize (an opportunity etc.) (I missed my chance). 6 tr. fail to hear or understand (I'm sorry, I missed what you said). 7 tr. **a** regret the loss or absence of (a person or thing) (did you miss me while I was away?). **b** notice the loss or absence of (an object) (bound to miss the key if it isn't there). 8 tr. avoid (go early to miss the traffic). 9 tr. = miss out 1. 10 intr. (of an engine etc.) fail, misfire. —n. a failure to hit, reach, attain, connect, etc. □ **be missing** not have (see also MISSING adj.). **give (a person) a miss** avoid, leave alone (gave the party a miss). **miss fire** (of a gun) fail to go off or hit the mark (cf. MISFIRE). **miss out 1** omit, leave out (missed out my name from the list). 2 (usu. foll. by on) colloq. fail to get or experience (always misses out on the good times). □ **missable** adj. [OE missan f. Gmc]

miss² n. 1 a girl or unmarried woman. 2 (**Miss**) **a** the title of an unmarried woman or girl, or of a married woman retaining her maiden name for professional purposes. **b** the title of a beauty queen (Miss World). 3 usu. derog. or joc. a girl, esp. a schoolgirl, with implications of silliness etc. 4 the title used to address a female schoolteacher, shop assistant, etc. □ **missish** adj. (in sense 3). [abbr. of MISTRESS]

missal /ˈmɪs(ə)l/ n. RC Ch. 1 a book containing the texts used in the service of the Mass throughout the year. 2 a book of prayers, esp. an illuminated one. [ME f. med.L missale neut. of eccl.L missalis of the mass f. missa MASS²]

missel-thrush var. of MISTLE-THRUSH.

misshapen /mɪsˈʃeɪpən/ adj. ill-shaped, deformed, distorted. □ **misshapenly** adv. **misshapenness** n.

missile /ˈmɪsaɪl/ n. 1 an object or weapon suitable for throwing at a target or for discharge from a machine. 2 a weapon, esp. a nuclear weapon, directed by remote control or automatically. □ **missilery** /-lrɪ/ n. [L missilis f. mittere miss- send]

missing /ˈmɪsɪŋ/ adj. 1 not in its place; lost. 2 (of a person) not yet traced or confirmed as alive but not known to be dead. 3 not present. □ **missing link 1** a thing lacking to complete a series. 2 a hypothetical intermediate type, esp. between humans and apes.

mission /ˈmɪʃ(ə)n/ n. 1 **a** a particular task or goal assigned to a person or group. **b** a journey undertaken as part of this. **c** a person's vocation (mission in life). 2 a military or scientific operation or expedition for a particular purpose. 3 a body of persons sent, esp. to a foreign country, to conduct negotiations etc. 4 **a** a body sent to propagate a religious faith. **b** a field of missionary activity. **c** a missionary post or organization. [F mission or L missio f. mittere miss- send]

missionary /ˈmɪʃənərɪ/ adj. & n. —adj. of, concerned with, or characteristic of, religious missions. —n. (pl. **-ies**) a person doing missionary work. □ **missionary position** colloq. a position for sexual intercourse with the woman lying on her back and the man lying on top and facing her. [mod.L missionarius f. L (as MISSION)]

missis /ˈmɪsɪz/ n. (also **missus** /-səz/) sl. or joc. **1** a form of address to a woman. **2** a wife. □ **the missis** my or your wife. [corrupt. of MISTRESS: cf. MRS]

missive /ˈmɪsɪv/ n. **1** joc. a letter, esp. a long and serious one. **2** an official letter. [ME f. med.L missivus f. L (as MISSION)]

misspell /mɪsˈspel/ v.tr. (past and past part. **-spelt** or **-spelled**) spell wrongly.

misspelling /mɪsˈspelɪŋ/ n. a wrong spelling.

misspend /mɪsˈspend/ v.tr. (past and past part. **-spent** /-ˈspent/) (esp. as **misspent** adj.) spend amiss or wastefully.

misstate /mɪsˈsteɪt/ v.tr. state wrongly or inaccurately.

misstatement /mɪsˈsteɪtmənt/ n. a wrong or inaccurate statement.

missy /ˈmɪsɪ/ n. (pl. **-ies**) an affectionate or derogatory form of address to a young girl.

mist n. & v. —n. **1 a** water vapour near the ground in minute droplets limiting visibility. **b** condensed vapour settling on a surface and obscuring glass etc. **2** dimness or blurring of the sight caused by tears etc. **3** a cloud of particles resembling mist. —v.tr. & intr. (usu. foll. by up, over) cover or become covered with mist or as with mist. □ **mistful** adj. **mistlike** adj. [OE f. Gmc]

mistake /mɪˈsteɪk/ n. & v. —n. **1** an incorrect idea or opinion; a thing incorrectly done or thought. **2** an error of judgement. —v.tr. (past **mistook** /-ˈstʊk/; past part. **mistaken** /-ˈsteɪkən/) **1** misunderstand the meaning or intention of (a person, a statement, etc.). **2** (foll. by for) wrongly take or identify (mistook me for you). **3** choose wrongly (mistake one's vocation). □ **by mistake** accidentally; in error. □ **mistakable** adj. **mistakably** adv. [ME f. ON mistaka (as MIS-¹, TAKE)]

mistaken /mɪˈsteɪkən/ adj. **1** wrong in opinion or judgement. **2** based on or resulting from this (mistaken loyalty; mistaken identity). □ **mistakenly** adv. **mistakenness** n.

misteach /mɪsˈtiːtʃ/ v.tr. (past and past part. **-taught** /-ˈtɔːt/) teach wrongly or incorrectly.

mister /ˈmɪstə(r)/ n. **1** a man without a title of nobility etc. (a mere mister). **2** sl. or joc. a form of address to a man. [weakened form of MASTER in unstressed use before a name: cf. MR]

mistime /mɪsˈtaɪm/ v.tr. say or do at the wrong time. [OE mistīmian (as MIS-¹, TIME)]

mistitle /mɪsˈtaɪt(ə)l/ v.tr. give the wrong title or name to.

mistle thrush /ˈmɪs(ə)l/ n. (also **missel thrush**) a large thrush, Turdus viscivorus, with a spotted breast, that feeds on mistletoe berries. [OE mistel basil, mistletoe, of unkn. orig.]

mistletoe /ˈmɪs(ə)ltəʊ/ n. **1** a parasitic plant, Viscum album, growing on apple and other trees and bearing white glutinous berries in winter. **2** a similar plant, Phoradendron flavescens, native to N. America. [OE misteltān (as MISTLE (THRUSH), tān twig)]

mistook past of MISTAKE.

mistral /ˈmɪstrɑːl, mɪˈstrɑːl/ n. a cold northerly wind that blows down the Rhône valley and S. France into the Mediterranean. [F & Prov. f. L magistralis f. magister MASTER]

mistranslate /ˌmɪstrænzˈleɪt, ˌmɪstrɑː-, -sˈleɪt/ v.tr. translate incorrectly. □ **mistranslation** n.

mistreat /mɪsˈtriːt/ v.tr. treat badly. □ **mistreatment** n.

mistress /ˈmɪstrɪs/ n. **1** a female head of a household. **2 a** a woman in authority over others. **b** the female owner of a pet. **3** a woman with power to control etc. (often foll. by of: mistress of the situation). **4** Brit. a female teacher (music mistress). **b** a female head of a college etc. **5** a woman (other than his wife) with whom a married man has a sexual relationship. [ME f. OF maistresse f. maistre MASTER]

mistrial /mɪsˈtraɪəl/ n. **1** a trial rendered invalid through some error in the proceedings. **2** US a trial in which the jury cannot agree on a verdict.

mistrust /mɪsˈtrʌst/ v. & n. —v.tr. **1** be suspicious of. **2** feel no confidence in (a person, oneself, one's powers, etc.). —n. **1** suspicion. **2** lack of confidence.

mistrustful /mɪsˈtrʌstfʊl/ adj. **1** (foll. by of) suspicious. **2** lacking confidence or trust. □ **mistrustfully** adv. **mistrustfulness** n.

misty /ˈmɪstɪ/ adj. (**mistier**, **mistiest**) **1** of or covered with mist. **2** indistinct or dim in outline. **3** obscure, vague (a misty idea). □ **mistily** adv. **mistiness** n. [OE mistig (as MIST)]

mistype /mɪsˈtaɪp/ v.tr. type wrongly. [MIS-¹ + TYPE]

misunderstand /ˌmɪsʌndəˈstænd/ v.tr. (past and past part. **-understood** /-ˈstʊd/) **1** fail to understand correctly. **2** (usu. as **misunderstood** adj.) misinterpret the words or actions of (a person).

misunderstanding /ˌmɪsʌndəˈstændɪŋ/ n. **1** a failure to understand correctly. **2** a slight disagreement or quarrel.

misusage /mɪsˈjuːsɪdʒ/ n. **1** wrong or improper usage. **2** ill-treatment.

misuse v. & n. —v.tr. /mɪsˈjuːz/ **1** use wrongly; apply to the wrong purpose. **2** ill-treat. —n. /mɪsˈjuːs/ wrong or improper use or application. □ **misuser** n.

MIT abbr. Massachusetts Institute of Technology.

mite¹ n. any small arachnid of the order Acari, having four pairs of legs when adult. □ **mity** adj. [OE mīte f. Gmc]

mite² n. & adv. —n. **1** hist. a Flemish copper coin of small value. **2** any small monetary unit. **3** a small object or person, esp. a child. **4** a modest contribution; the best one can do (offered my mite of comfort). —adv. (usu. prec. by a) colloq. somewhat (is a mite shy). [ME f. MLG, MDu. mīte f. Gmc: prob. the same as MITE¹]

miter US var. of MITRE.

mitigate /ˈmɪtɪˌɡeɪt/ v.tr. make milder or less intense or severe; moderate (your offer certainly mitigated their hostility). □ **mitigating circumstances** Law circumstances permitting greater leniency. □ **mitigable** adj. **mitigation** /-ˈɡeɪʃ(ə)n/ n. **mitigator** n. **mitigatory** adj. [ME f. L mitigare mitigat- f. mitis mild]

mitosis /mɪˈtəʊsɪs, maɪ-/ n. Biol. a type of cell division that results in two daughter cells each having the same number and kind of chromosomes as the parent nucleus. □ **mitotic** /-ˈtɒtɪk/ adj. [mod.L f. Gk mitos thread]

mitre /ˈmaɪtə(r)/ n. & v. (US **miter**) —n. 1 a tall deeply-cleft head-dress worn by bishops and abbots, esp. as a symbol of office. 2 the joint of two pieces of wood or other material at an angle of 90°, such that the line of junction bisects this angle. 3 a diagonal join of two pieces of fabric that meet at a corner, made by folding. —v. 1 tr. bestow the mitre on. 2 tr. & intr. join with a mitre. □ **mitred** adj. [ME f. OF f. L mitra f. Gk mitra girdle, turban]

mitt /mɪt/ n. 1 = MITTEN. 2 a glove leaving the fingers and thumb-tip exposed. 3 sl. a hand or fist. 4 a baseball glove for catching the ball. [abbr. of MITTEN]

mitten /ˈmɪt(ə)n/ n. a glove with two sections, one for the thumb and the other for all four fingers. □ **mittened** adj. [ME f. OF mitaine ult. f. L medietas half: see MOIETY]

mix v. & n. —v. 1 tr. combine or put together (two or more substances or things) so that the constituents of each are diffused among those of the other(s). 2 tr. prepare (a compound, cocktail, etc.) by combining the ingredients. 3 tr. combine an activity etc. with another simultaneously (mix business and pleasure). 4 intr. a join, be mixed, or combine, esp. readily (oil and water will not mix). b be compatible. c be sociable (must learn to mix). 5 intr. a (foll. by with) (of a person) be harmonious or sociable with; have regular dealings with. b (foll. by in) participate in. 6 tr. drink different kinds of (alcoholic liquor) in close succession. —n. 1 a the act or an instance of mixing; a mixture. b the proportion of materials etc. in a mixture. 2 colloq. a group of persons of different types (social mix). 3 the ingredients prepared commercially for making a cake etc. or for a process such as making concrete. 4 the merging of film pictures or sound. □ **be mixed up** (or **with**) be involved in or with (esp. something undesirable). **mix in** be harmonious or sociable. **mix it** colloq. start fighting. **mix up** 1 mix thoroughly. 2 confuse; mistake the identity of. **mix-up** n. a confusion, misunderstanding, or mistake. □ **mixable** adj. [back-form. f. MIXED (taken as past part.)]

mixed /mɪkst/ adj. 1 of diverse qualities or elements. 2 containing persons from various backgrounds etc. 3 for or involving persons of both sexes (a mixed school; mixed bathing). □ **mixed bag** (or **bunch**) a diverse assortment of things or persons. **mixed blessing** a thing having advantages and disadvantages. **mixed doubles** Tennis a doubles game with a man and a woman as partners on each side. **mixed economy** an economic system combining private and State enterprise. **mixed farming** farming of both crops and livestock. **mixed feelings** a mixture of pleasure and dismay about something. **mixed grill** a dish of various grilled meats and vegetables etc. **mixed marriage** a marriage between persons of different races or religions. **mixed metaphor** a combination of inconsistent metaphors (e.g. this tower of strength will forge ahead). **mixed-up** colloq. mentally or emotionally confused; socially ill-adjusted. □ **mixedness** /-ɪdnɪs/ n. [ME mixt f. OF mixte f. L mixtus past part. of miscēre mix]

mixer /ˈmɪksə(r)/ n. 1 a device for mixing foods etc. or for processing other materials. 2 a person who manages socially in a specified way (a good mixer). 3 a (usu. soft) drink to be mixed with another. 4 Broadcasting & Cinematog. a a device for merging input signals to produce a combined output in the form of sound or pictures. b a person who operates this. □ **mixer tap** a tap through which mixed hot and cold water is drawn by means of separate controls.

mixture /ˈmɪkstʃə(r)/ n. 1 the process of mixing or being mixed. 2 the result of mixing; something mixed; a combination. 3 Chem. the product of the random distribution of one substance through another without any chemical reaction taking place between the components, as distinct from a chemical compound. 4 ingredients mixed together to produce a substance, esp. a medicine (cough mixture). 5 a person regarded as a combination of qualities and attributes. 6 gas or vaporized petrol or oil mixed with air, forming an explosive charge in an internal-combustion engine. [ME f. F mixture or L mixtura (as MIXED)]

mizen /ˈmɪz(ə)n/ n. (also **mizzen**) Naut. (in full **mizen-sail**) the lowest fore-and-aft sail of a fully rigged ship's mizen-mast. □ **mizen-mast** the mast next aft of the mainmast. [ME f. F misaine f. It. mezzana mizen-sail, fem. of mezzano middle: see MEZZANINE]

ml abbr. 1 millilitre(s). 2 mile(s).

M.Litt. abbr. Master of Letters. [L Magister Litterarum]

Mlle abbr. (pl. **Mlles**) Mademoiselle.

MM abbr. Messieurs.

mm abbr. millimetre(s).

Mme abbr. (pl. **Mmes**) Madame.

M.Mus. abbr. Master of Music.

Mn symb. Chem. the element manganese.

mnemonic /nɪˈmɒnɪk/ adj. & n. —adj. of or designed to aid the memory. —n. a mnemonic device. □ **mnemonically** adv. **mnemonist** /ˈniːmənɪst/ n. [med.L mnemonicus f. Gk mnēmonikos f. mnēmōn mindful]

mnemonics /nɪˈmɒnɪks/ n.pl. (usu. treated as sing.) 1 the art of improving memory. 2 a system for this.

MO abbr. 1 Medical Officer. 2 money order.

Mo symb. Chem. the element molybdenum.

mo n. (pl. **mos**) colloq. a moment (wait a mo). [abbr.]

moa /ˈməʊə/ n. (pl. **moas**) any extinct flightless New Zealand bird of the family Dinornithidae, resembling the ostrich. [Maori]

moan n. & v. —n. 1 a long murmur expressing physical or mental suffering. 2 a low plaintive sound of wind etc. 3 a complaint; a grievance. —v. 1 intr. make a moan or moans. 2 intr. colloq. complain or grumble. 3 tr. a utter with moans. b lament. □ **moaner** n. **moanful** adj. **moaningly** adv. [ME f. OE mān (unrecorded) f. Gmc]

moat n. & v. —n. a deep defensive ditch round a castle, town, etc., usu. filled with water. —v.tr. surround with or as with a moat. [ME mot(e) f. OF mote, motte mound]

mob n. & v. —n. 1 a disorderly crowd; a rabble. 2 (prec. by the) usu. derog. the populace. 3 colloq. a gang; an associated group of persons. 4 Austral. a flock or herd. —v.tr. & intr. (**mobbed**, **mobbing**) 1 tr. a crowd round in order to attack or admire. b (of a mob) attack. c US crowd into (a building). 2 intr. assemble in a mob. □ **mob law** (or **rule**) law or rule imposed and enforced by a mob. □ **mobber** n. & adj. [abbr. of mobile, short for L mobile vulgus excitable crowd: see MOBILE]

mob-cap /ˈmɒbkæp/ n. hist. a woman's large indoor cap covering all the hair, worn in the 18th and early 19th c. [obs. (18th-c.) mob, orig. = slut + CAP]

mobile /ˈməʊbaɪl/ adj. & n. —adj. 1 movable; not fixed; free or able to move or flow easily. 2 (of the face etc.) readily changing its expression. 3 (of a shop, library, etc.) accommodated in a vehicle so as to serve various places. 4 (of a person) able to change his or her social status. —n. a decorative structure that may be hung so as to turn freely. □ **mobile home** a large caravan permanently parked and used as a residence. **mobile sculpture** a sculpture having moving parts. □ **mobility** /məˈbɪlɪtɪ/ n. [ME f. F f. L mobilis f. movēre move]

mobilize /ˈməʊbɪˌlaɪz/ v. (also -ise) 1 a tr. organize for service or action (esp. troops in time of war). b intr. be organized in this way. 2 tr. render movable; bring into circulation. □ **mobilizable** adj. **mobilization** /-ˈzeɪʃ(ə)n/ n. **mobilizer** n. [F mobiliser (as MOBILE)]

Möbius strip /ˈmɜːbɪəs/ n. Math. a one-sided surface formed by joining the ends of a rectangle after twisting one end through 180°. [A. F. Möbius, Ger. mathematician d. 1868]

mobster /ˈmɒbstə(r)/ n. sl. a gangster.

moccasin /ˈmɒkəsɪn/ n. a type of soft leather slipper or shoe with combined sole and heel, as orig. worn by N. American Indians. [Amer. Ind. mockasin, makisin]

mocha /ˈmɒkə/ n. 1 a coffee of fine quality. 2 a beverage or flavouring made with this, often with chocolate added. [Mocha, a port on the Red Sea, from where the coffee first came]

mock v., adj., & n. —v. 1 a tr. ridicule; scoff at. b intr. (foll. by at) act with scorn or contempt for. 2 tr. mimic contemptuously. 3 tr. jeer, defy, or delude contemptuously. —attrib.adj. sham, imitation (esp. without intention to deceive); pretended (a mock battle; mock cream). —n. 1 a thing deserving scorn. 2 (in pl.) colloq. mock examinations. □ **make mock** (or a mock) **of** ridicule. **mock orange** a white-flowered heavy-scented shrub, Philadelphus coronarius. **mock turtle soup** soup made from a calf's head etc. to resemble turtle soup. **mock-up** an experimental model or replica of a proposed structure etc. □ **mockable** adj. **mockingly** adv. [ME mokke, mocque f. OF mo(c)quer deride f. Rmc]

mocker /ˈmɒkə(r)/ n. a person who mocks. □ **put the mockers on** sl. 1 bring bad luck to. 2 put a stop to.

mockery /ˈmɒkərɪ/ n. (pl. -ies) 1 a derision, ridicule. b a subject or occasion of this. 2 (often foll. by of) a counterfeit or absurdly inadequate representation. 3 a ludicrously or insultingly futile action etc. [ME f. OF moquerie (as MOCK)]

mockingbird /ˈmɒkɪŋˌbɜːd/ n. a bird that mimics the notes of other birds, esp. the American songbird Mimus polyglottos.

mod adj. & n. colloq. —adj. modern, esp. in style of dress. —n. Brit. a young person (esp. in the 1960s) of a group aiming at sophistication and smart modern dress. □ **mod cons** modern conveniences. [abbr.]

modal /ˈməʊd(ə)l/ adj. 1 of or relating to mode or form as opposed to substance. 2 Gram. a of

or denoting the mood of a verb. b (of an auxiliary verb, e.g. would) used to express the mood of another verb. □ **modality** /məˈdælɪtɪ/ n. **modally** adv. [med.L modalis f. L (as MODE)]

mode n. 1 a way or manner in which a thing is done; a method of procedure. 2 a prevailing fashion or custom. 3 Computing a way of operating or using a system (print mode). 4 Mus. a each of the scale systems that result when the white notes of the piano are played consecutively over an octave. b each of the two main modern scale systems, the major and minor (minor mode). 5 US Gram. = MOOD². [F mode and L modus measure]

model /ˈmɒd(ə)l/ n. & v. —n. 1 a representation in three dimensions of an existing person or thing or of a proposed structure, esp. on a smaller scale (often attrib.: a model train). 2 a simplified (often mathematical) description of a system etc., to assist calculations and predictions. 3 a figure in clay, wax, etc., to be reproduced in another material. 4 a particular design or style of a structure or commodity, esp. of a car. 5 a an exemplary person or thing (a model of self-discipline). b (attrib.) ideal, exemplary (a model student). 6 a person employed to pose for an artist or photographer or to display clothes etc. by wearing them. 7 a garment etc. by a well-known designer, or a copy of this. —v. (modelled, modelling; US modeled, modeling) 1 tr. a fashion or shape (a figure) in clay, wax, etc. b (foll. by after, on, etc.) form (a thing in imitation of). 2 a intr. act or pose as a model. b tr. (of a person acting as a model) display (a garment). 3 tr. devise a (usu. mathematical) model of (a phenomenon, system, etc.). □ **modeller** n. [F modelle f. It. modello ult. f. L modulus: see MODULUS]

modem /ˈməʊdem/ n. a combined device for modulation and demodulation, e.g. between a computer and a telephone line. [modulator + demodulator]

moderate adj., n., & v. —adj. /ˈmɒdərət/ 1 avoiding extremes; temperate in conduct or expression. 2 fairly or tolerably large or good. 3 (of the wind) of medium strength. 4 (of prices) fairly low. —n. /ˈmɒdərət/ a person who holds moderate views, esp. in politics. —v. /ˈmɒdəˌreɪt/ 1 tr. & intr. make or become less violent, intense, rigorous, etc. 2 tr. (also absol.) act as a moderator of or to. □ **moderately** /-rətlɪ/ adv. **moderateness** /-rətnəs/ n. **moderatism** /ˈmɒdərəˌtɪz(ə)m/ n. [ME f. L moderatus past part. of moderare reduce, control: rel. to MODEST]

moderation /ˌmɒdəˈreɪʃ(ə)n/ n. 1 the process or an instance of moderating. 2 the quality of being moderate. □ **in moderation** in a moderate manner or degree. [ME f. OF f. L moderatio -onis (as MODERATE)]

moderator /ˈmɒdəˌreɪtə(r)/ n. 1 an arbitrator or mediator. 2 a presiding officer. 3 Eccl. a Presbyterian minister presiding over an ecclesiastical body. □ **moderatorship** n. [ME f. L (as MODERATE)]

modern /ˈmɒd(ə)n/ adj. & n. —adj. 1 of the present and recent times. 2 in current fashion; not antiquated. —n. (usu. in pl.) a person living in modern times. □ **modern English** English from about 1500 onwards. **modern history** history from the end of the Middle Ages to the present day. □ **modernity** /-ˈdɜːnɪtɪ/ n.

modernly *adv.* **modernness** *n.* [F *moderne* or LL *modernus* f. L *modo* just now]

modernism /ˈmɒdəˌnɪz(ə)m/ *n.* **1 a** modern ideas or methods. **b** the tendency of religious belief to harmonize with modern ideas. **2 a** modern term or expression. □ **modernist** *n.* **modernistic** /-ˈnɪstɪk/ *adj.* **modernistically** /-ˈnɪstɪkəlɪ/ *adv.*

modernize /ˈmɒdəˌnaɪz/ *v.* (also **-ise**) **1** *tr.* make modern; adapt to modern needs or habits. **2** *intr.* adopt modern ways or views. □ **modernization** /-ˈzeɪʃ(ə)n/ *n.* **modernizer** *n.*

modest /ˈmɒdɪst/ *adj.* **1** having or expressing a humble or moderate estimate of one's own merits or achievements. **2** diffident, bashful, retiring. **3** decorous in manner and conduct. **4** moderate or restrained in amount, extent, severity, etc.; not excessive or exaggerated (*a modest sum*). **5** (of a thing) unpretentious in appearance etc. □ **modestly** *adv.* [F *modeste* f. L *modestus* keeping due measure]

modesty /ˈmɒdɪstɪ/ *n.* the quality of being modest.

modicum /ˈmɒdɪkəm/ *n.* (foll. by *of*) a small quantity. [L, = short distance or time, neut. of *modicus* moderate f. *modus* measure]

modification /ˌmɒdɪfɪˈkeɪʃ(ə)n/ *n.* **1** the act or an instance of modifying or being modified. **2** a change made. [F or f. L *modificatio* (as MODIFY)]

modifier /ˈmɒdɪˌfaɪə(r)/ *n.* **1** a person or thing that modifies. **2** *Gram.* a word, esp. an adjective or noun used attributively, that qualifies the sense of another word (e.g. *good* and *family* in *a good family house*).

modify /ˈmɒdɪˌfaɪ/ *v.tr.* (**-ies**, **-ied**) **1** make less severe or extreme; tone down (*modify one's demands*). **2** make partial changes in; make different. **3** *Gram.* qualify or expand the sense of (a word etc.). □ **modifiable** *adj.* **modificatory** /-fɪˌkeɪtərɪ/ *adj.* [ME f. OF *modifier* f. L *modificare* (as MODE)]

modish /ˈməʊdɪʃ/ *adj.* fashionable. □ **modishly** *adv.* **modishness** *n.*

modiste /mɒˈdiːst/ *n.* a milliner; a dressmaker. [F (as MODE)]

modular /ˈmɒdjʊlə(r)/ *adj.* of or consisting of modules or moduli. □ **modularity** /-ˈlærɪtɪ/ *n.* [mod.L *modularis* f. L *modulus*: see MODULUS]

modulate /ˈmɒdjʊˌleɪt/ *v.* **1** *tr.* **a** regulate or adjust. **b** moderate. **2** *tr.* adjust or vary the tone or pitch of (the speaking voice). **3** *tr.* alter the amplitude or frequency of (a wave) by a wave of a lower frequency to convey a signal. **4** *intr.* & *tr.* *Mus.* (often foll. by *from*, *to*) change or cause to change from one key to another. □ **modulation** /-ˈleɪʃ(ə)n/ *n.* **modulator** *n.* [L *modulari modulat-* to measure f. *modus* measure]

module /ˈmɒdjuːl/ *n.* **1** a standardized part or independent unit used in construction, esp. of furniture, a building, or an electronic system. **2** an independent self-contained unit of a spacecraft (*lunar module*). **3** a unit or period of training or education. [F *module* or L *modulus*: see MODULUS]

modulo /ˈmɒdjʊˌləʊ/ *prep.* & *adj.* *Math.* using, or with respect to, a modulus (see MODULUS 2). [L, ablat. of MODULUS]

modulus /ˈmɒdjʊləs/ *n.* (pl. **moduli** /-ˌlaɪ/) *Math.* **1** the magnitude of a real number without regard to its sign. **2** a constant factor or ratio. **3** (in number theory) a number used as a divisor

for considering numbers in sets giving the same remainder when divided by it. [L, = measure, dimin. of *modus*]

modus operandi /ˌmɒdəs ˌɒpəˈrændɪ/ *n.* (pl. **modi operandi** /ˌmɒdɪ/) **1** the particular way in which a person performs a task or action. **2** the way a thing operates. [L, = way of operating: see MODE]

modus vivendi /ˌmɒdəs vɪˈvendɪ/ *n.* (pl. **modi vivendi** /ˌmɒdɪ/) **1** a way of living or coping. **2** an arrangement whereby those in dispute can carry on pending a settlement. [L, = way of living: see MODE]

mog *n.* (also **moggie** /ˈmɒgɪ/) *Brit.* *sl.* a cat. [20th c.: of dial. orig.]

Mogadon /ˈmɒgəˌdɒn/ *n.* *propr.* a hypnotic drug used to treat insomnia.

mogul /ˈməʊg(ə)l/ *n.* **1** *colloq.* an important or influential person. **2** (**Mogul**) *hist.* any of the emperors of Delhi in the 16th–19th c. [Pers. *mugūl* MONGOL]

mohair /ˈməʊheə(r)/ *n.* **1** the hair of the angora goat. **2** a yarn or fabric from this, either pure or mixed with wool or cotton. [ult. f. Arab. *muḳayyar*, lit. choice, select]

Mohammedan *var.* of MUHAMMADAN.

moiety /ˈmɔɪətɪ/ *n.* (pl. **-ies**) *Law* or *literary* **1** a half. **2** each of the two parts into which a thing is divided. [ME f. OF *moité*, *moitié* f. L *medietas* *-tatis* middle f. *medius* (adj.) middle]

moil *v.* & *n.* *archaic* —*v.intr.* drudge (esp. *toil and moil*). —*n.* drudgery. [ME f. OF *moillier* moisten, paddle in mud, ult. f. L *mollis* soft]

moire /mwɑː(r)/ *n.* (in full **moire antique**) watered fabric, orig. mohair, now usu. silk. [F (earlier *mouaire*) f. MOHAIR]

moiré /ˈmwɑːreɪ/ *adj.* & *n.* —*adj.* **1** (of silk) watered. **2** (of metal) having a patterned appearance like watered silk. —*n.* **1** this patterned appearance. **2** = MOIRE. [F, past part. of *moirer* (as MOIRE)]

moist *adj.* **1** slightly wet; damp. □ **moistly** *adv.* **moistness** *n.* [ME f. OF *moiste*, ult. from or rel. to L *mucidus* (see MUCUS) and *musteus* fresh (see MUST²)]

moisten /ˈmɔɪs(ə)n/ *v.tr.* & *intr.* make or become moist.

moisture /ˈmɔɪstʃə(r)/ *n.* water or other liquid diffused in a small quantity as vapour, or within a solid, or condensed on a surface. □ **moistureless** *adj.* [ME f. OF *moistour* (as MOIST)]

moisturize /ˈmɔɪstʃəˌraɪz/ *v.tr.* (also **-ise**) make less dry (esp. the skin by use of a cosmetic). □ **moisturizer** *n.*

moke *n.* *sl.* **1** *Brit.* a donkey. **2** *Austral.* a very poor horse. [19th c.: orig. unkn.]

mol /məʊl/ *abbr.* = MOLE⁴.

molar¹ /ˈməʊlə(r)/ *adj.* & *n.* —*adj.* (usu. of a mammal's back teeth) serving to grind. —*n.* a molar tooth. [L *molaris* f. *mola* millstone]

molar² /ˈməʊlə(r)/ *adj.* *Chem.* **1** of a mass of substance usu. per mole (*molar latent heat*). **2** (of a solution) containing one mole of solute per litre of solvent. □ **molarity** /məˈlærɪtɪ/ *n.* [MOLE⁴ + -AR¹]

molasses /məˈlæsɪz/ *n.pl.* (treated as *sing.*) **1** uncrystallized syrup extracted from raw sugar during refining. **2** *US* treacle. [Port. *melaço* f. LL *mellaceum* MUST² f. *mel* honey]

mold *US* var. of MOULD¹, MOULD², MOULD³.

molder US var. of MOULDER.

molding US var. of MOULDING.

moldy US var. of MOULDY.

mole[1] *n*. **1** any small burrowing insect-eating mammal of the family Talpidae, esp. *Talpa europaea*, with dark velvety fur and very small eyes. **2** *colloq*. **a** a spy established deep within an organization and usu. dormant for a long period while attaining a position of trust. **b** a betrayer of confidential information. [ME *molle*, prob. f. MDu. *moll(e)*, *mol*, MLG *mol*, *mul*]

mole[2] *n*. a small often slightly raised dark blemish on the skin caused by a high concentration of melanin. [OE *māl* f. Gmc]

mole[3] /məʊl/ *n*. **1** a massive structure serving as a pier, breakwater, or causeway. **2** an artificial harbour. [F *môle* f. L *moles* mass]

mole[4] /məʊl/ *n*. *Chem*. the SI unit of amount of substance. [G *Mol* f. *Molekül* MOLECULE]

molecular /məˈlekjʊlə(r)/ *adj*. of, relating to, or consisting of molecules. □ **molecular biology** the study of the structure and function of large molecules associated with living organisms. **molecular weight** the ratio of the average mass of one molecule of an element or compound to one twelfth of the mass of an atom of carbon-12. □ **molecularity** /-ˈlærɪtɪ/ *n*. **molecularly** *adv*.

molecule /ˈmɒlɪˌkjuːl/ *n*. **1** *Chem*. the smallest fundamental unit (usu. a group of atoms) of a chemical compound that can take part in a chemical reaction. **2** (in general use) a small particle. [F *molécule* f. mod.L *molecula*]

molehill /ˈməʊlhɪl/ *n*. a small mound thrown up by a mole in burrowing. □ **make a mountain out of a molehill** exaggerate the importance of a minor difficulty.

molest /məˈlest/ *v.tr*. **1** annoy or pester (a person) in a hostile or injurious way. **2** attack or interfere with (a person), esp. sexually. □ **molestation** /ˌmɒleˈsteɪʃ(ə)n, ˌməʊl-/ *n*. **molester** *n*. [OF *molester* annoy f. L *molestus* troublesome]

moll *n*. *sl*. **1** a gangster's female companion. **2** a prostitute. [pet-form of the name *Mary*]

mollify /ˈmɒlɪˌfaɪ/ *v.tr*. (**-ies**, **-ied**) **1** appease, pacify. **2** reduce the severity of; soften. □ **mollification** /-fɪˈkeɪʃ(ə)n/ *n*. **mollifier** *n*. [ME f. F *mollifier* or L *mollificare* f. *mollis* soft]

mollusc /ˈmɒləsk/ *n*. (US **mollusk**) any invertebrate of the phylum Mollusca, with a soft body and usu. a hard shell, including limpets, snails, cuttlefish, oysters, mussels, etc. □ **molluscan** /məˈlʌskən/ *adj*. **molluscoid** /məˈlʌskɔɪd/ *adj*. **molluscous** /məˈlʌskəs/ *adj*. [mod.L *mollusca* neut. pl. of L *molluscus* f. *mollis* soft]

mollycoddle /ˈmɒlɪˌkɒd(ə)l/ *v. & n*. —*v.tr*. coddle, pamper. —*n*. an effeminate man or boy; a milksop. [formed as MOLL + CODDLE]

Molotov cocktail /ˈmɒləˌtɒf/ *n*. a crude incendiary device usu. consisting of a bottle filled with inflammable liquid. [V. M. *Molotov*, Russian statesman d. 1986]

molt US var. of MOULT.

molten /ˈməʊlt(ə)n/ *adj*. melted, esp. made liquid by heat. [past part. of MELT]

molto /ˈmɒltəʊ/ *adv*. *Mus*. very (*molto sostenuto*; *allegro molto*). [It. f. L *multus* much]

molybdenum /məˈlɪbdɪnəm/ *n*. *Chem*. a silver-white brittle metallic transition element used in steel to give strength and resistance to corrosion. [mod.L, earlier *molybdena*, orig. =

molybdenite, lead ore: L *molybdena* f. Gk *molubdaina* plummet f. *molubdos* lead]

mom *n*. US *colloq*. mother. [abbr. of MOMMA]

moment /ˈməʊmənt/ *n*. **1** a very brief portion of time; an instant. **2** a short period of time (*wait a moment*). **3** an exact or particular point of time (*at last the moment arrived; I came the moment you called*). **4** importance (*of no great moment*). **5** *Physics & Mech*. etc. **a** the turning effect produced by a force acting at a distance on an object. **b** this effect expressed as the product of the force and the distance from its line of action to a point. □ **at the moment** at this time; now. **in a moment 1** very soon. **2** instantly. **man (or woman** etc.) **of the moment** the one of importance at the time in question. **moment of truth** a time of crisis or test (orig. the final sword-thrust in a bullfight). **not for a** (or **one**) **moment** never; not at all. **this moment** immediately; at once (*come here this moment*). [ME f. OF f. L *momentum*: see MOMENTUM]

momenta pl. of MOMENTUM.

momentarily /ˈməʊməntərɪlɪ, -ˈterɪlɪ, -trɪlɪ/ *adv*. **1** for a moment. **2** US **a** at any moment. **b** instantly.

momentary /ˈməʊməntərɪ, -trɪ/ *adj*. **1** lasting only a moment. **2** short-lived; transitory. □ **momentariness** *n*. [L *momentarius* (as MOMENT)]

momentous /məˈmentəs/ *adj*. having great importance. □ **momentously** *adv*. **momentousness** *n*.

momentum /məˈmentəm/ *n*. (pl. **momenta** /-tə/) **1** *Physics* the quantity of motion of a moving body, measured as a product of its mass and velocity. **2** the impetus gained by movement. **3** strength or continuity derived from an initial effort. [L f. *movimentum* f. *movēre* move]

momma /ˈmɒmə/ *n*. var. of MAMMA[1].

mommy /ˈmɒmɪ/ *n*. (pl. **-ies**) esp. US = MUMMY[1].

Mon. abbr. Monday.

monad /ˈmɒnæd, ˈməʊ-/ *n*. **1** the number one; a unit. **2** *Biol*. a simple organism, e.g. one assumed as the first in the genealogy of living beings. □ **monadic** /məˈnædɪk/ *adj*. [F *monade* or LL *monas monad-* f. Gk *monas -ados* unit f. *monos* alone]

monandry /məˈnændrɪ/ *n*. the custom of having only one husband at a time. □ **monandrous** *adj*. [MONO- after *polyandry*]

monarch /ˈmɒnək/ *n*. **1** a sovereign with the title of king, queen, emperor, empress, or the equivalent. **2** a supreme ruler. **3** a powerful or pre-eminent person. □ **monarchal** /məˈnɑːk(ə)l/ *adj*. **monarchic** /məˈnɑːkɪk/ *adj*. **monarchical** /məˈnɑːkɪk(ə)l/ *adj*. **monarchically** /məˈnɑːkɪkəlɪ/ *adv*. [ME f. F *monarque* or LL *monarcha* f. Gk *monarkhēs, -os*, f. *monos* alone + *arkhō* to rule]

monarchism /ˈmɒnəˌkɪz(ə)m/ *n*. the advocacy of or the principles of monarchy. □ **monarchist** *n*. [F *monarchisme* (as MONARCHY)]

monarchy /ˈmɒnəkɪ/ *n*. (pl. **-ies**) **1** a form of government with a monarch at the head. **2** a State with this. □ **monarchial** /mɒˈnɑːkɪəl/ *adj*. [ME f. OF *monarchie* f. LL *monarchia* f. Gk *monarkhia* the rule of one (as MONARCH)]

monastery /ˈmɒnəstərɪ, -strɪ/ *n*. (pl. **-ies**) the residence of a religious community, esp. of monks living in seclusion. [ME f. eccl.L *monasterium* f. eccl.Gk *monastērion* f. *monazō* live alone f. *monos* alone]

monastic /mə'næstɪk/ *adj. & n.* —*adj.* **1** of or relating to monasteries or the religious communities living in them. **2** resembling these or their way of life; solitary and celibate. —*n.* a monk or other follower of a monastic rule. □ **monastically** *adv.* **monasticism** /-ˌsɪz(ə)m/ *n.* **monasticize** /-ˌsaɪz/ *v.tr.* (also **-ise**). [F *monastique* or LL *monasticus* f. Gk *monastikos* (as MONASTERY)]

monatomic /ˌmɒnə'tɒmɪk/ *adj.* *Chem.* **1** (esp. of a molecule) consisting of one atom. **2** having one replaceable atom or radical.

monaural /mɒ'nɔːr(ə)l/ *adj.* **1** = MONOPHONIC. **2** of or involving one ear. □ **monaurally** *adv.* [MONO- + AURAL]

Monday /'mʌndeɪ, -dɪ/ *n. & adv.* —*n.* the second day of the week, following Sunday. —*adv. colloq.* **1** on Monday. **2** (**Mondays**) on Mondays; each Monday. [OE *mōnandæg* day of the moon, transl. LL *lunae dies*]

monetarism /'mʌnɪtəˌrɪz(ə)m/ *n.* the theory or practice of controlling the supply of money as the chief method of stabilizing the economy.

monetarist /'mʌnɪtərɪst/ *n. & adj.* —*n.* an advocate of monetarism. —*adj.* in accordance with the principles of monetarism.

monetary /'mʌnɪtərɪ/ *adj.* **1** of the currency in use. **2** of or consisting of money. □ **monetarily** *adv.* [F *monétaire* or LL *monetarius* f. L (as MONEY)]

monetize /'mʌnɪˌtaɪz/ *v.tr.* (also **-ise**) **1** give a fixed value as currency. **2** put (a metal) into circulation as money. □ **monetization** /-'zeɪʃ(ə)n/ *n.* [F *monétiser* f. L (as MONEY)]

money /'mʌnɪ/ *n.* **1 a** a current medium of exchange in the form of coins and banknotes. **b** a particular form of this (*silver money*). **2** (*pl.* **-eys** or **-ies**) (in *pl.*) sums of money. **3 a** wealth; property viewed as convertible into money. **b** wealth as giving power or influence (*money speaks*). **c** a rich person or family (*has married into money*). **4 a** money as a resource (*time is money*). **b** profit, remuneration (*in it for the money*). □ **for my money** in my opinion or judgement; for my preference (*is too aggressive for my money*). **in the money** *colloq.* having or winning a lot of money. **money box** a box for saving money dropped through a slit. **money-changer** a person whose business it is to change money, esp. at an official rate. **money for jam** (or **old rope**) *colloq.* profit for little or no trouble. **money-grubber** *colloq.* a person greedily intent on amassing money. **money-grubbing** *n.* this practice. —*adj.* given to this. **money market** *Stock Exch.* trade in short-term stocks, loans, etc. **money order** an order for payment of a specified sum, issued by a bank or Post Office. **money spider** a small household spider supposed to bring financial luck. **money-spinner** a thing that brings in a profit. **money's-worth** good value for one's money. **put money into** invest in. □ **moneyless** *adj.* [ME f. OF *moneie* f. L *moneta* mint, money, orig. a title of Juno, in whose temple at Rome money was minted]

moneybags /'mʌnɪˌbægz/ *n.pl.* (treated as *sing.*) *colloq.* usu. *derog.* a wealthy person.

moneyed /'mʌnɪd/ *adj.* **1** having much money; wealthy. **2** consisting of money (*moneyed assistance*).

moneylender /'mʌnɪˌlendə(r)/ *n.* a person who lends money, esp. as a business, at interest. □ **moneylending** *n. & adj.*

moneymaker /'mʌnɪˌmeɪkə(r)/ *n.* **1** a person who earns much money. **2** a thing, idea, etc., that produces much money. □ **moneymaking** *n. & adj.*

monger /'mʌŋgə(r)/ *n.* (usu. in *comb.*) **1** a dealer or trader (*fishmonger; ironmonger*). **2** usu. *derog.* a person who promotes or deals in something specified (*warmonger; scaremonger*). [OE *mangere* f. *mangian* to traffic f. Gmc, ult. f. L *mango* dealer]

Mongol /'mɒŋg(ə)l/ *adj. & n.* —*adj.* **1** of or relating to the Asian people now inhabiting Mongolia in Central Asia. **2** resembling this people, esp. in appearance. **3** (**mongol**) often *offens.* suffering from Down's syndrome. —*n.* **1** a Mongolian. **2** (**mongol**) often *offens.* a person suffering from Down's syndrome. [native name: perh. f. *mong* brave]

Mongolian /mɒŋ'gəʊlɪən/ *n. & adj.* —*n.* a native or inhabitant of Mongolia; the language of Mongolia. —*adj.* of or relating to Mongolia or its people or language.

mongolism /'mɒŋgəˌlɪz(ə)m/ *n.* = DOWN'S SYNDROME. [MONGOL + -ISM, because its physical characteristics were thought to be reminiscent of Mongolians]

■ **Usage** The term *Down's syndrome* is now preferred.

Mongoloid /'mɒŋgəˌlɔɪd/ *adj. & n.* —*adj.* **1** characteristic of the Mongolians, esp. in having a broad flat yellowish face. **2** (**mongoloid**) often *offens.* having the characteristic symptoms of Down's syndrome. —*n.* a Mongoloid or mongoloid person.

mongoose /'mɒŋguːs/ *n.* (*pl.* **mongooses**) any of various small flesh-eating civet-like mammals of the family Viverridae, esp. of the genus *Herpestes*. [Marathi *mangūs*]

mongrel /'mʌŋgr(ə)l, 'mɒŋ-/ *n. & adj.* —*n.* **1** a dog of no definable type or breed. **2** any other animal or plant resulting from the crossing of different breeds or types. —*adj.* of mixed origin, nature, or character. □ **mongrelism** *n.* **mongrelize** *v.tr.* (also **-ise**). **mongrelization** /-'zeɪʃ(ə)n/ *n.* **mongrelly** *adj.* [earlier *meng-, mang-* f. Gmc: prob. rel. to MINGLE]

monies see MONEY 2.

moniker /'mɒnɪkə(r)/ *n.* (also **monicker, monniker**) *sl.* a name. [19th c.: orig. unkn.]

monism /'mɒnɪz(ə)m, 'məʊn-/ *n.* **1** any theory denying the duality of matter and mind. **2** the doctrine that only one ultimate principle or being exists. □ **monist** *n.* **monistic** /-'nɪstɪk/ *adj.* [mod.L *monismus* f. Gk *monos* single]

monitor /'mɒnɪt(ə)r/ *n. & v.* —*n.* **1** any of various persons or devices for checking or warning about a situation, operation, etc. **2** a school pupil with disciplinary or other special duties. **3 a** a television receiver used in a studio to select or verify the picture being broadcast. **b** = *visual display unit.* **4** a person who listens to and reports on foreign broadcasts etc. **5** a detector of radioactive contamination. **6** *Zool.* any tropical lizard of the genus *Varanus*, supposed to give warning of the approach of crocodiles. —*v.tr.* **1** act as a monitor of. **2** maintain regular surveillance over. **3** regulate the strength of (a recorded or transmitted signal). □ **monitorial** /-'tɔːrɪəl/ *adj.* **monitorship** *n.* [L f. *monēre monit-* warn]

monitory /ˈmɒnɪtərɪ/ *adj. literary* giving or serving as a warning. [L *monitorius* (as MONITOR)]

monk /mʌŋk/ *n.* a member of a religious community of men living under certain vows esp. of poverty, chastity, and obedience. □ **monkish** *adj.* [OE *munuc* ult. f. Gk *monakhos* solitary f. *monos* alone]

monkey /ˈmʌŋkɪ/ *n. & v.* —*n.* (*pl.* **-eys**) **1** any of various New World and Old World primates esp. of the families Cebidae (including capuchins), Callitrichidae (including marmosets and tamarins), and Cercopithecidae (including baboons and apes). **2** a mischievous person, esp. a child (*young monkey*). **3** *sl.* **a** *Brit.* £500. **b** *US* $500. —*v.* (**-eys, -eyed**) **1** *tr.* mimic or mock. **2** *intr.* (often foll. by *with*) tamper or play mischievous tricks. **3** *intr.* (foll. by *around, about*) fool around. □ **make a monkey of** humiliate by making appear ridiculous. **monkey business** *colloq.* mischief. **monkey-jacket** a short close-fitting jacket worn by sailors etc. or at a mess. **monkey-nut** a peanut. **monkey-puzzle** a coniferous tree, *Araucaria araucaria*, native to Chile, with downward-pointing branches and small close-set leaves. **monkey-suit** *colloq.* evening dress. **monkey tricks** *colloq.* mischief. **monkey wrench** a wrench with an adjustable jaw. □ **monkeyish** *adj.* [16th c.: orig. unkn. (perh. LG)]

monkeyshine /ˈmʌŋkɪˌʃaɪn/ *n.* (usu. in *pl.*) *US colloq.* = *monkey tricks.*

monkfish /ˈmʌŋkfɪʃ/ *n.* **1** an angler-fish, esp. *Lophius piscatorius*, often used as food. **2** a large cartilaginous fish, *Squatina squatina*, with a flattened body and large pectoral fins.

monkshood /ˈmʌŋkshʊd/ *n. Bot.* a poisonous garden plant *Aconitum napellus*, with hood-shaped blue or purple flowers.

mono /ˈmɒnəʊ/ *adj. & n. colloq.* —*adj.* monophonic. —*n.* (*pl.* **-os**) a monophonic record, reproduction, etc. [abbr.]

mono- /ˈmɒnəʊ/ *comb. form* (usu. **mon-** before a vowel) **1** one, alone, single. **2** *Chem.* (forming names of compounds) containing one atom or group of a specified kind. [Gk f. *monos* alone]

monoacid /ˌmɒnəʊˈæsɪd/ *adj. Chem.* (of a base) having one replaceable hydroxide ion.

monobasic /ˌmɒnəʊˈbeɪsɪk/ *adj. Chem.* (of an acid) having one replaceable hydrogen atom.

monocausal /ˌmɒnəʊˈkɔːz(ə)l/ *adj.* in terms of a sole cause.

monochromatic /ˌmɒnəkrəˈmætɪk/ *adj.* **1** *Physics* (of light or other radiation) of a single wavelength or frequency. **2** containing only one colour. □ **monochromatically** *adv.*

monochrome /ˈmɒnəˌkrəʊm/ *n. & adj.* —*n.* a photograph or picture done in one colour or different tones of this, or in black and white only. —*adj.* having or using only one colour or in black and white only. □ **monochromic** /-ˈkrəʊmɪk/ *adj.* [ult. f. Gk *monokhrōmatos* (as MONO-, *khrōmatos* f. *khrōma* colour)]

monocle /ˈmɒnək(ə)l/ *n.* a single eyeglass. □ **monocled** *adj.* [F, orig. adj. f. LL *monoculus* one-eyed (as MONO-, *oculus* eye)]

monocotyledon /ˌmɒnəˌkɒtɪˈliːd(ə)n/ *n. Bot.* any flowering plant with a single cotyledon. □ **monocotyledonous** *adj.*

monocular /məˈnɒkjʊlə(r)/ *adj.* with or for one eye. □ **monocularly** *adj.* [LL *monoculus* having one eye]

monoculture /ˈmɒnəʊˌkʌltʃə(r)/ *n.* the cultivation of a single crop.

monocycle /ˈmɒnəˌsaɪk(ə)l/ *n.* = UNICYCLE.

monody /ˈmɒnədɪ/ *n.* (*pl.* **-ies**) **1** an ode sung by a single actor in a Greek tragedy. **2** a poem lamenting a person's death. **3** *Mus.* a composition with only one melodic line. □ **monodic** /məˈnɒdɪk/ *adj.* **monodist** *n.* [LL *monodia* f. Gk *monōidia* f. *monōidos* singing alone (as MONO-, ODE)]

monoecious /məˈniːʃəs/ *adj.* **1** *Bot.* with unisexual male and female organs on the same plant. **2** *Zool.* hermaphrodite. [mod.L *Monoecia* the class of such plants (Linnaeus) f. Gk *monos* single + *oikos* house]

monogamy /məˈnɒɡəmɪ/ *n.* **1** the practice or state of being married to one person at a time. **2** *Zool.* the habit of having only one mate at a time. □ **monogamist** *n.* **monogamous** *adj.* **monogamously** *adv.* [F *monogamie* f. eccl.L f. Gk *monogamia* (as MONO-, *gamos* marriage)]

monoglot /ˈmɒnəˌɡlɒt/ *adj. & n.* —*adj.* using only one language. —*n.* a monoglot person.

monogram /ˈmɒnəˌɡræm/ *n.* two or more letters, esp. a person's initials, interwoven as a device. □ **monogrammatic** /-ɡrəˈmætɪk/ *adj.* **monogrammed** *adj.* [F *monogramme* f. LL *monogramma* f. Gk (as MONO-, -GRAM)]

monograph /ˈmɒnəˌɡrɑːf/ *n. & v.* —*n.* a separate treatise on a single subject or an aspect of it. —*v.tr.* write a monograph on. □ **monographer** /məˈnɒɡrəfə(r)/ *n.* **monographist** /məˈnɒɡrəfɪst/ *n.* **monographic** /ˌmɒnəˈɡræfɪk/ *adj.* [earlier *monography* f. mod.L *monographia* f. *monographus* writer on a single genus or species (as MONO-, -GRAPH, -GRAPHY)]

monogyny /məˈnɒdʒɪnɪ/ *n.* the custom of having only one wife at a time.

monohull /ˈmɒnəʊˌhʌl/ *n.* a boat with a single hull.

monohybrid /ˌmɒnəʊˈhaɪbrɪd/ *n.* a hybrid with respect to only one allele.

monokini /ˌmɒnəʊˈkiːnɪ/ *n.* a woman's one-piece beach-garment equivalent to the lower half of a bikini. [MONO- + BIKINI, by false assoc. with BI-]

monolingual /ˌmɒnəʊˈlɪŋɡw(ə)l/ *adj.* speaking or using only one language.

monolith /ˈmɒnəlɪθ/ *n.* **1** a single block of stone, esp. shaped into a pillar or monument. **2** a person or thing like a monolith in being massive, immovable, or solidly uniform. **3** a large block of concrete. □ **monolithic** /-ˈlɪθɪk/ *adj.* [F *monolithe* f. Gk *monolithos* (as MONO-, *lithos* stone)]

monologue /ˈmɒnəˌlɒɡ/ *n.* **1 a** a scene in a drama in which a person speaks alone. **b** a dramatic composition for one performer. **2** a long speech by one person in a conversation etc. □ **monologic** /-ˈlɒdʒɪk/ *adj.* **monological** /-ˈlɒdʒɪk(ə)l/ *adj.* **monologist** /məˈnɒlədʒɪst/ *n.* (also **-loguist**). **monologize** /məˈnɒləˌdʒaɪz/ *v.intr.* (also **-ise**). [F f. Gk *monologos* speaking alone (as MONO-, -LOGUE)]

monomania /ˌmɒnəˈmeɪnɪə/ *n.* obsession of the mind by one idea or interest. □ **monomaniac** *n. & adj.* **monomaniacal** /-məˈnaɪək(ə)l/ *adj.* [F *monomanie* (as MONO-, -MANIA)]

monomark /ˈmɒnəʊˌmɑːk/ *n. Brit.* a combination of letters, with or without figures, registered as an identification mark for goods, articles, addresses, etc.

monomer /ˈmɒnəmə(r)/ n. Chem. **1** a unit in a dimer, trimer, or polymer. **2** a molecule or compound that can be polymerized. □ **monomeric** /-ˈmerɪk/ adj.

mononucleosis /ˌmɒnəʊˌnjuːklɪˈəʊsɪs/ n. = glandular fever. [MONO- + NUCLEO- + -OSIS]

monophonic /ˌmɒnəˈfɒnɪk/ adj. **1** (of sound-reproduction) using only one channel of transmission (cf. STEREOPHONIC). **2** Mus. homophonic. □ **monophonically** adv. [MONO- + Gk phōnē sound]

monoplane /ˈmɒnəˌpleɪn/ n. an aeroplane with one set of wings (cf. BIPLANE).

monopolist /məˈnɒpəlɪst/ n. a person who has or advocates a monopoly. □ **monopolistic** /-ˈlɪstɪk/ adj.

monopolize /məˈnɒpəˌlaɪz/ v.tr. (also **-ise**) **1** obtain exclusive possession or control of (a trade or commodity etc.). **2** dominate or prevent others from sharing in (a conversation, person's attention, etc.). □ **monopolization** /-ˈzeɪʃ(ə)n/ n. **monopolizer** n.

monopoly /məˈnɒpəlɪ/ n. (pl. **-ies**) **1 a** the exclusive possession or control of the trade in a commodity or service. **b** this conferred as a privilege by the State. **2 a** a commodity or service that is subject to a monopoly. **b** a company etc. that possesses a monopoly. **3** (foll. by of, US on) exclusive possession, control, or exercise. [L monopolium f. Gk monopōlion (as MONO-, pōleō sell)]

monorail /ˈmɒnəʊˌreɪl/ n. a railway in which the track consists of a single rail, usu. elevated with the train units suspended from it.

monosaccharide /ˌmɒnəʊˈsækəˌraɪd/ n. Chem. a sugar that cannot be hydrolysed to give a simpler sugar, e.g. glucose.

monosodium glutamate /ˌmɒnəʊˈsəʊdɪəm ˈgluːtəˌmeɪt/ n. Chem. a sodium salt of glutamic acid used to flavour food (cf. GLUTAMATE).

monosyllabic /ˌmɒnəsɪˈlæbɪk/ adj. **1** (of a word) having one syllable. **2** (of a person or statement) using or expressed in monosyllables. □ **monosyllabically** adv.

monosyllable /ˈmɒnəˌsɪləb(ə)l/ n. a word of one syllable. □ **in monosyllables** in simple direct words.

monotheism /ˈmɒnəˌθiːɪz(ə)m/ n. the doctrine that there is only one God. □ **monotheist** n. **monotheistic** /-ˈɪstɪk/ adj. **monotheistically** /-ˈɪstɪkəlɪ/ adv. [MONO- + Gk theos god]

monotone /ˈmɒnəˌtəʊn/ n. & adj. —n. **1** a sound or utterance continuing or repeated on one note without change of pitch. **2** sameness of style in writing. —adj. without change of pitch. [mod.L monotonus f. late Gk monotonos (as MONO-, TONE)]

monotonous /məˈnɒtənəs/ adj. **1** lacking in variety; tedious through sameness. **2** (of a sound or utterance) without variation in tone or pitch. □ **monotonize** v.tr. (also **-ise**). **monotonously** adv. **monotonousness** n.

monotony /məˈnɒtənɪ/ n. **1** the state of being monotonous. **2** dull or tedious routine.

monotreme /ˈmɒnəˌtriːm/ n. any mammal of the order Monotremata, native to Australia and New Guinea, including the duckbill and spiny anteater, laying large yolky eggs through a common opening for urine, faeces, etc. [MONO- + Gk trēma -matos hole]

monovalent /ˌmɒnəˈveɪlənt/ adj. Chem. having a valency of one; univalent. □ **monovalence** n. **monovalency** n.

monoxide /məˈnɒksaɪd/ n. Chem. an oxide containing one oxygen atom (carbon monoxide). [MONO- + OXIDE]

Monseigneur /ˌmɒnsenˈjɜː(r)/ n. (pl. **Messeigneurs** /ˌmesenˈjɜː(r)/) a title given to an eminent French person, esp. a prince, cardinal, archbishop, or bishop. [F f. mon my + seigneur lord]

Monsieur /məˈsjɜː(r)/ n. (pl. **Messieurs** /meˈsjɜː(r)/) **1** the title or form of address used of or to a French-speaking man, corresponding to Mr or sir. **2** a Frenchman. [F f. mon my + sieur lord]

Monsignor /mɒnˈsiːnjə(r), -ˈnjɔː(r)/ n. (pl. **Monsignori** /-ˈnjɔːrɪ/) the title of various Roman Catholic prelates, officers of the papal court, etc. [It., after MONSEIGNEUR: see SIGNOR]

monsoon /mɒnˈsuːn/ n. **1** a wind in S. Asia, esp. in the Indian Ocean, blowing from the south west in summer (**wet monsoon**) and the north east in winter (**dry monsoon**). **2** a rainy season accompanying a wet monsoon. **3** any other wind with periodic alternations. □ **monsoonal** adj. [obs. Du. monssoen f. Port. monção f. Arab. mawsim fixed season f. wasama to mark]

monster /ˈmɒnstə(r)/ n. **1** an imaginary creature, usu. large and frightening, compounded of incongruous elements. **2** an inhumanly cruel or wicked person. **3** a misshapen animal or plant. **4** a large hideous animal or thing (e.g. a building). **5** (attrib.) huge; extremely large of its kind. [ME f. OF monstre f. L monstrum portent, monster f. monēre warn]

monstera /mɒnˈstɪərə/ n. any climbing plant of the genus Monstera, including Swiss cheese plant. [mod.L, perh. f. L monstrum monster (from the odd appearance of its leaves)]

monstrance /ˈmɒnstrəns/ n. RC Ch. a vessel in which the Host is exposed for veneration. [ME, = demonstration, f. med.L monstrantia f. L monstrare show]

monstrosity /mɒnˈstrɒsɪtɪ/ n. (pl. **-ies**) **1** a huge or outrageous thing. **2** monstrousness. **3** = MONSTER 3. [LL monstrositas (as MONSTROUS)]

monstrous /ˈmɒnstrəs/ adj. **1** like a monster; abnormally formed. **2** huge. **3 a** outrageously wrong or absurd. **b** atrocious. □ **monstrously** adv. **monstrousness** n. [ME f. OF monstreux or L monstrosus (as MONSTER)]

montage /mɒnˈtɑːʒ/ n. **1 a** a process of selecting, editing, and piecing together separate sections of cinema or television film to form a continuous whole. **b** a sequence of such film as a section of a longer film. **2 a** the technique of producing a new composite whole from fragments of pictures, words, music, etc. **b** a composition produced in this way. [F f. monter MOUNT[1]]

montane /ˈmɒnteɪn/ adj. of or inhabiting mountainous country. [L montanus (as MOUNT[2], -ANE[1])]

montbretia /mɒnˈbriːʃə/ n. a hybrid plant of the genus Crocosmia, with bright orange-yellow trumpet-shaped flowers. [mod.L f. A. F. E. Coquebert de Montbret, Fr. botanist d. 1801]

month /mʌnθ/ n. **1** (in full **calendar month**) **a** each of usu. twelve periods into which a year is divided. **b** a period of time between the same dates in successive calendar months. **2** a period

of 28 days or of four weeks. **3** = *lunar month.* □
month of Sundays a very long period. [OE
mōnath f. Gmc, rel. to MOON]

monthly /ˈmʌnθlɪ/ *adj.*, *adv.*, & *n.* —*adj.* done,
produced, or occurring once a month. —*adv.*
once a month; from month to month. —*n.* (*pl.*
-ies) **1** a monthly periodical. **2** (in *pl.*) *colloq.* a
menstrual period.

monument /ˈmɒnjʊmənt/ *n.* **1** anything enduring that serves to commemorate or make
celebrated, esp. a structure or building. **2** a
stone or other structure placed over a grave or
in a church etc. in memory of the dead. **3** an
ancient building or site etc. that has survived
or been preserved. **4** (foll. by *of*, *to*) a typical or
outstanding example (*a monument of indiscretion*).
[ME f. F f. L *monumentum* f. *monēre* remind]

monumental /ˌmɒnjʊˈment(ə)l/ *adj.* **1 a**
extremely great; stupendous (*a monumental
achievement*). **b** (of a literary work) massive and
permanent. **2** of or serving as a monument. □
monumental mason a maker of tombstones
etc. □ **monumentality** /-ˈtælɪtɪ/ *n.* **monu-
mentally** *adv.*

monumentalize /ˌmɒnjʊˈmentəˌlaɪz/ *v.tr.* (also
-ise) record or commemorate by or as by a
monument.

-mony /mənɪ/ *suffix* forming nouns esp. denoting an abstract state or quality (*acrimony*; *testimony*). [L -*monia*, -*monium*, rel. to -MENT]

moo *v.* & *n.* —*v.intr.* (**moos**, **mooed**) make the
characteristic vocal sound of cattle; low low². —*n.*
(*pl.* **moos**) this sound. □ **moo-cow** a childish
name for a cow. [imit.]

mooch /muːtʃ/ *v. colloq.* **1** *intr.* loiter or saunter
desultorily. **2** *tr.* esp. *US* **a** steal. **b** beg. □
moocher *n.* [ME, prob. f. OF *muchier* hide, skulk]

mood¹ /muːd/ *n.* **1** a state of mind or feeling. **2**
(in *pl.*) fits of melancholy or bad temper. **3**
(*attrib.*) inducing a particular mood (*mood music*).
□ **in the** (or **no**) **mood** (foll. by *for*, or to +
infin.) inclined (or disinclined) (*was in no mood to
agree*). [OE *mōd* mind, thought, f. Gmc]

mood² /muːd/ *n. Gram.* **1** a form or set of forms
of a verb serving to indicate whether it is to
express fact, command, wish, etc. (*subjunctive
mood*). **2** the distinction of meaning expressed
by different moods. [var. of MODE, assoc. with
MOOD¹]

moody /ˈmuːdɪ/ *adj.* & *n.* —*adj.* (**moodier**,
moodiest) given to changes of mood; gloomy,
sullen. —*n. colloq.* a bad mood; a tantrum. □
moodily *adv.* **moodiness** *n.* [OE *mōdig* brave
(as MOOD¹)]

moon /muːn/ *n.* & *v.* —*n.* **1 a** the natural satellite
of the earth, orbiting it monthly, illuminated
by the sun and reflecting some light to the
earth. **b** this regarded in terms of its waxing
and waning in a particular month (*new moon*). **c**
the moon when visible (*there is no moon tonight*).
2 a satellite of any planet. **3** *poet.* a month. —*v.*
1 *intr.* (often foll. by *about*, *around*, etc.) move or
look listlessly. **2** *tr.* (foll. by *away*) spend (time) in
a listless manner. **3** *intr.* (foll. by *over*) act
aimlessly or inattentively from infatuation for
(a person). □ **moon boot** a thickly-padded boot
designed for low temperatures. **moon-faced**
having a round face. **over the moon** extremely
happy or delighted. □ **moonless** *adj.* [OE *mōna*
f. Gmc, rel. to MONTH]

moonbeam /ˈmuːnbiːm/ *n.* a ray of moonlight.

Moonie /ˈmuːnɪ/ *n. sl.* a member of the Unification Church. [Sun Myung *Moon*, its founder]

moonlight /ˈmuːnlaɪt/ *n.* & *v.* —*n.* **1** the light of
the moon. **2** (*attrib.*) lighted by the moon. —*v.intr.*
(**-lighted**) *colloq.* have two paid occupations, esp.
one by day and one by night. □ **moonlight flit**
a hurried departure by night, esp. to avoid
paying a debt. □ **moonlighter** *n.*

moonlit /ˈmuːnlɪt/ *adj.* lighted by the moon.

moonquake /ˈmuːnkweɪk/ *n.* a tremor of the
moon's surface.

moonrise /ˈmuːnraɪz/ *n.* **1** the rising of the
moon. **2** the time of this.

moonscape /ˈmuːnskeɪp/ *n.* **1** the surface or
landscape of the moon. **2** an area resembling
this; a wasteland.

moonset /ˈmuːnset/ *n.* **1** the setting of the moon.
2 the time of this.

moonshine /ˈmuːnʃaɪn/ *n.* **1** foolish or unrealistic talk or ideas. **2** *sl.* illicitly distilled or
smuggled alcoholic liquor.

moonshiner /ˈmuːnˌʃaɪnə(r)/ *n. US sl.* an illicit
distiller or smuggler of alcoholic liquor.

moonshot /ˈmuːnʃɒt/ *n.* the launching of a
spacecraft to the moon.

moonstone /ˈmuːnstəʊn/ *n.* feldspar of pearly
appearance.

moonstruck   /ˈmuːnstrʌk/ *adj.* mentally
deranged.

moony /ˈmuːnɪ/ *adj.* (**moonier**, **mooniest**) **1**
listless; stupidly dreamy. **2** of or like the moon.

Moor /mʊə(r), mɔː(r)/ *n.* a member of a Muslim
people of mixed Berber and Arab descent,
inhabiting NW Africa. □ **Moorish** *adj.* [ME f. OF
More f. L *Maurus* f. Gk *Mauros* inhabitant of
Mauretania, a region of N. Africa]

moor¹ /mʊə(r), mɔː(r)/ *n.* **1** a tract of open
uncultivated upland, esp. when covered with
heather. **2** a tract of ground preserved for
shooting. **3** *US* a fen. □ **moorish** *adj.* **moory**
adj. [OE *mōr* waste land, marsh, mountain, f.
Gmc]

moor² /mʊə(r), mɔː(r)/ *v.* **1** *tr.* make fast (a boat,
buoy, etc.) by attaching a cable etc. to a fixed
object. **2** *intr.* (of a boat) be moored. □ **moorage**
n. [ME *more*, prob. f. LG or MLG *mōren*]

moorhen /ˈmʊəhen, ˈmɔː-/ *n.* a small aquatic
bird, *Gallinula chloropus*, with long legs and a
short red-yellow bill.

mooring /ˈmʊərɪŋ, ˈmɔːrɪŋ/ *n.* **1 a** a fixed object
to which a boat, buoy, etc., is moored. **b** (often
in *pl.*) a place where a boat etc. is moored. **2** (in
pl.) a set of permanent anchors and chains laid
down for ships to be moored in.

moorland /ˈmʊələnd, ˈmɔː-/ *n.* an extensive area
of moor.

moose /muːs/ *n.* (*pl.* same) a N. American deer;
an elk. [Narragansett *moos*]

moot /muːt/ *adj.*, *v.*, & *n.* —*adj.* (orig. the noun
used *attrib.*) debatable, undecided (*a moot point*).
—*v.tr.* raise (a question) for discussion. —*n.* **1**
hist. an assembly. **2** *Law* a discussion of a
hypothetical case as an academic exercise. [OE
mōt, and *mōtian* converse, f. Gmc, rel. to MEET¹]

mop *n.* & *v.* —*n.* **1** a wad or bundle of cotton or
synthetic material fastened to the end of a stick,
for cleaning floors etc. **2** a similarly-shaped
large or small implement for various purposes.
3 anything resembling a mop, esp. a thick mass
of hair. **4** an act of mopping or being mopped

(*gave it a mop*). —*v.tr.* (**mopped, mopping**) **1** wipe or clean with or as with a mop. **2 a** wipe tears or sweat etc. from (one's face or brow etc.). **b** wipe away (tears etc.). □ **mop up 1** wipe up with or as with a mop. **2** *colloq.* absorb (profits etc.). **3** dispatch; make an end of. **4** *Mil.* complete the occupation of (a district etc.) by capturing or killing enemy troops left there. □ **moppy** *adj.* [ME *mappe*, perh. ult. rel. to L *mappa* napkin]

mope *v. & n.* —*v.intr.* be gloomily depressed or listless; behave sulkily. —*n.* **1** a person who mopes. **2** (**the mopes**) low spirits. □ **moper** *n.* **mopy** *adj.* (**mopier, mopiest**). **mopily** *adv.* **mopiness** *n.* [16th c.: prob. rel. to *mope, mopp(e)* fool]

moped /ˈməʊped/ *n.* a motorized bicycle with an engine capacity below 50 cc. [Sw. (as MOTOR, PEDAL¹)]

mophead /ˈmɒphed/ *n.* a person with thick matted hair.

mopoke /ˈməʊpəʊk/ *n.* (also **morepork** /ˈmɔːpɔːk/) **1** a boobook. **2** an Australian nocturnal insect-eating bird, *Podargus strigoides*. [imit. of the bird's cry]

moppet /ˈmɒpɪt/ *n.* *colloq.* (esp. as a term of endearment) a baby or small child. [obs. *moppe* baby, doll]

moquette /mɒˈket/ *n.* a thick pile or looped material used for carpets and upholstery. [F, perh. f. obs. It. *mocaiardo* mohair]

moraine /məˈreɪn/ *n.* an area covered by rocks and debris carried down and deposited by a glacier. □ **morainal** *adj.* **morainic** *adj.* [F f. It. dial. *morena* f. F dial. *mor(re)* snout f. Rmc]

moral /ˈmɒr(ə)l/ *adj. & n.* —*adj.* **1 a** concerned with goodness or badness of human character or behaviour, or with the distinction between right and wrong. **b** concerned with accepted rules and standards of human behaviour. **2 a** conforming to accepted standards of general conduct. **b** capable of moral action (*man is a moral agent*). **3** (of rights or duties etc.) founded on moral law. **4 a** concerned with morals or ethics (*moral philosophy*). **b** (of a literary work etc.) dealing with moral conduct. **5** concerned with or leading to a psychological effect associated with confidence in a right action (*moral courage; moral support; moral victory*). —*n.* **1 a** a moral lesson (esp. at the end) of a fable, story, event, etc. **b** a moral maxim or principle. **2** (in *pl.*) moral behaviour, e.g. in sexual conduct. □ **moral certainty** probability so great as to allow no reasonable doubt. **moral law** the conditions to be satisfied by any right course of action. **moral philosophy** the branch of philosophy concerned with ethics. **moral pressure** persuasion by appealing to a person's moral sense. **moral sense** the ability to distinguish right and wrong. □ **morally** *adv.* [ME f. L *moralis* f. *mos moris* custom, pl. *mores* morals]

morale /məˈrɑːl/ *n.* the mental attitude or bearing of a person or group, esp. as regards confidence, discipline, etc. [F *moral* respelt to preserve the pronunciation]

moralism /ˈmɒrəlɪz(ə)m/ *n.* **1** a natural system of morality. **2** religion regarded as moral practice.

moralist /ˈmɒrəlɪst/ *n.* **1** a person who practises or teaches morality. **2** a person who follows a

natural system of ethics. □ **moralistic** /-ˈlɪstɪk/ *adj.* **moralistically** /-ˈlɪstɪkəlɪ/ *adv.*

morality /məˈrælɪtɪ/ *n.* (pl. **-ies**) **1** the degree of conformity of an idea, practice, etc., to moral principles. **2** right moral conduct. **3** a lesson in morals. **4** the science of morals. **5** a particular system of morals (*commercial morality*). **6** (in *pl.*) moral principles; points of ethics. **7** (in full **morality play**) *hist.* a kind of drama with personified abstract qualities as the main characters and inculcating a moral lesson, popular in the 16th c. [ME f. OF *moralité* or LL *moralitas* f. L (as MORAL)]

moralize /ˈmɒrəlaɪz/ *v.* (also **-ise**) **1** *intr.* (often foll. by *on*) indulge in moral reflection or talk. **2** *tr.* interpret morally; point the moral of. **3** *tr.* make moral or more moral. □ **moralization** /-ˈzeɪʃ(ə)n/ *n.* **moralizer** *n.* **moralizingly** *adv.* [F *moraliser* or med.L *moralizare* f. L (as MORAL)]

morass /məˈræs/ *n.* **1** an entanglement; a disordered situation, esp. one impeding progress. **2** *literary* a bog or marsh. [Du. *moeras* (assim. to *moer* MOOR¹) f. MDu. *marasch* f. OF *marais* marsh f. med.L *mariscus*]

moratorium /ˌmɒrəˈtɔːrɪəm/ *n.* (pl. **moratoriums** or **moratoria** /-rɪə/) **1** (often foll. by *on*) a temporary prohibition or suspension (of an activity). **2 a** a legal authorization to debtors to postpone payment. **b** the period of this postponement. [mod.L, neut. of LL *moratorius* delaying f. L *morari morat-* to delay f. *mora* delay]

morbid /ˈmɔːbɪd/ *adj.* **1 a** (of the mind, ideas, etc.) unwholesome, sickly. **b** given to morbid feelings. **2** *colloq.* melancholy. **3** *Med.* of the nature of or indicative of disease. □ **morbidity** /-ˈbɪdɪtɪ/ *n.* **morbidly** *adv.* **morbidness** *n.* [L *morbidus* f. *morbus* disease]

mordant /ˈmɔːd(ə)nt/ *adj. & n.* —*adj.* **1** (of sarcasm etc.) caustic, biting. **2** pungent, smarting. **3** corrosive or cleansing. **4** (of a substance) serving to fix colouring-matter or gold leaf on another substance. —*n.* a mordant substance (in senses 3, 4 of *adj.*). □ **mordancy** *n.* **mordantly** *adv.* [ME f. F, part. of *mordre* bite f. L *mordēre*]

more /mɔː(r)/ *adj., n., & adv.* —*adj.* **1** existing in a greater or additional quantity, amount, or degree (*more problems than last time; bring some more water*). **2** greater in degree (*more's the pity; the more fool you*). —*n.* a greater quantity, number, or amount (*more than three people; more to it than meets the eye*). —*adv.* **1** in a greater degree (*do it more carefully*). **2** to a greater extent (*people like to walk more these days*). **3** forming the comparative of adjectives and adverbs, esp. those of more than one syllable (*more absurd; more easily*). **4** again (*once more; never more*). **5** moreover. □ **more and more** in an increasing degree. **more of** to a greater extent (*more of a poet than a musician*). **more or less 1** in a greater or less degree. **2** approximately; as an estimate. **more so** of the same kind to a greater degree. [OE *māra* f. Gmc]

moreish /ˈmɔːrɪʃ/ *adj.* (also **morish**) *colloq.* pleasant to eat, causing a desire for more.

morel /məˈrel/ *n.* an edible fungus, *Morchella esculenta*, with ridged mushroom caps. [F *morille* f. Du. *morilje*]

morello /məˈreləʊ/ *n.* (pl. **-os**) a sour kind of dark cherry. [It. *morello* blackish f. med.L *morellus* f. L, ult. *Maurus* MOOR¹]

moreover /mɔːˈrəʊvə(r)/ *adj.* (introducing or accompanying a new statement) further, besides.

morepork var. of MOPOKE.

mores /ˈmɔːreɪz, -riːz/ *n.pl.* customs or conventions regarded as essential to or characteristic of a community. [L, pl. of *mos* custom]

morganatic /ˌmɔːɡəˈnætɪk/ *adj.* **1** (of a marriage) between a person of high rank and another of lower rank, the spouse and children having no claim to the possessions or title of the person of higher rank. **2** (of a wife) married in this way. □ **morganatically** *adv.* [F *morganatique* or G *morganatisch* f. med.L *matrimonium ad morganaticam* 'marriage with a morning gift', the husband's gift to the wife after consummation being his only obligation in such a marriage]

morgue /mɔːɡ/ *n.* **1** a mortuary. **2** (in a newspaper office) a room or file of miscellaneous information, esp. for future obituaries. [F, orig. the name of a Paris mortuary]

moribund /ˈmɒrɪˌbʌnd/ *adj.* **1** at the point of death. **2** lacking vitality. □ **moribundity** /-ˈbʌndɪtɪ/ *n.* [L *moribundus* f. *mori* die]

Mormon /ˈmɔːmən/ *n.* a member of the Church of Jesus Christ of Latter-Day Saints, a millenary religion based on revelations in the Book of Mormon. □ **Mormonism** *n.*

morn *n. poet.* morning. [OE *morgen* f. Gmc]

mornay /ˈmɔːneɪ/ *n.* a cheese-flavoured white sauce. [20th c.: orig. uncert.]

morning /ˈmɔːnɪŋ/ *n.* & *int.* —*n.* **1** the early part of the day, esp. from sunrise to noon (*this morning*; *during the morning*; *morning coffee*). **2** this time spent in a particular way (*had a busy morning*). **3** sunrise, daybreak. **4** a time compared with the morning, esp. the early part of one's life etc. —*int.* good morning. □ **in the morning 1** during or in the course of the morning. **2** *colloq.* tomorrow. **morning after** *colloq.* a hangover. **morning-after pill** a contraceptive pill effective when taken some hours after intercourse. **morning coat** a coat with tails, and with the front cut away below the waist. **morning dress** a man's morning coat and striped trousers. **morning glory** any of various twining plants of the genus *Ipomoea*, with trumpet-shaped flowers. **morning-room** a sitting-room for the morning. **morning sickness** nausea felt in the morning in pregnancy. **morning star** a planet or bright star, usu. Venus, seen in the east before sunrise. [ME *mor(we)ning* f. *morwen* MORN + -ING¹ after *evening*]

morocco /məˈrɒkəʊ/ *n.* (pl. **-os**) **1** a fine flexible leather made (orig. in Morocco) from goatskins tanned with sumac. **2** an imitation of this in grained calf etc.

moron /ˈmɔːrɒn/ *n.* **1** *colloq.* a very stupid or foolish person. **2** an adult with a mental age of about 8–12. □ **moronic** /məˈrɒnɪk/ *adj.* **moronically** /-ˈrɒnɪkəlɪ/ *adv.* **moronism** *n.* [Gk *mōron*, neut. of *mōros* foolish]

morose /məˈrəʊs/ *adj.* sullen and ill-tempered. □ **morosely** *adv.* **moroseness** *n.* [L *morosus* peevish etc. f. *mos moris* manner]

morpheme /ˈmɔːfiːm/ *n. Linguistics* a meaningful morphological unit of a language that cannot be further divided (e.g. *in*, *come*, *-ing*, forming *incoming*). □ **morphemic** /-ˈfiːmɪk/ *adj.* **morphemically** /-ˈfiːmɪkəlɪ/ *adv.* [F *morphème* f. Gk *morphē* form, after PHONEME]

morphia /ˈmɔːfɪə/ *n.* (in general use) = MORPHINE.

morphine /ˈmɔːfiːn/ *n.* an analgesic and narcotic drug obtained from opium and used medicinally to relieve pain. □ **morphinism** /-fɪˌnɪz(ə)m/ *n.* [G *Morphin* & mod.L *morphia* f. *Morpheus* god of sleep]

morphology /mɔːˈfɒlədʒɪ/ *n.* the study of the forms of things, esp.: **1** *Biol.* the study of the forms of organisms. **2** *Philol.* **a** the study of the forms of words. **b** the system of forms in a language. □ **morphological** /ˌmɔːfəˈlɒdʒɪk(ə)l/ *adj.* **morphologically** /-fəˈlɒdʒɪkəlɪ/ *adv.* **morphologist** *n.* [Gk *morphē* form + -LOGY]

morris dance /ˈmɒrɪs/ *n.* a traditional English dance by groups of people in fancy costume, with ribbons and bells. □ **morris dancer** *n.* **morris dancing** *n.* [*morys*, var. of *Moorish* (see MOOR)]

morrow /ˈmɒrəʊ/ *n.* (usu. prec. by *the*) *literary* **1** the following day. **2** the time following an event. [ME *morwe*, *moru* (as MORN)]

Morse /mɔːs/ *n.* & *v.* —*n.* (in full **Morse code**) an alphabet or code in which letters are represented by combinations of long and short light or sound signals. —*v.tr.* & *intr.* signal by Morse code. [S. F. B. *Morse*, Amer. electrician d. 1872, who devised it]

morsel /ˈmɔːs(ə)l/ *n.* a mouthful; a small piece (esp. of food). [ME f. OF, dimin. of *mors* a bite f. *mordēre mors-* to bite]

mortadella /ˌmɔːtəˈdelə/ *n.* (pl. **mortadelle** /-ˈdele/) a large spiced pork sausage. [It. dimin., irreg. f. L *murtatum* seasoned with myrtle berries]

mortal /ˈmɔːt(ə)l/ *adj.* & *n.* —*adj.* **1** (of a living being, esp. a human) subject to death. **2** (often foll. by *to*) causing death; fatal. **3** (of a battle) fought to the death. **4** associated with death (*mortal agony*). **5** (of an enemy) implacable. **6** (of pain, fear, an affront, etc.) intense, very serious. **7** *colloq.* **a** very great (*in a mortal hurry*). **b** long and tedious (*for two mortal hours*). **8** *colloq.* conceivable, imaginable (*every mortal thing*; *of no mortal use*). —*n.* a mortal being, esp. a human. □ **mortal sin** *Theol.* a grave sin that is regarded as depriving the soul of divine grace. □ **mortally** *adv.* [ME f. OF *mortal*, *mortel* or L *mortalis* f. *mors mortis* death]

mortality /mɔːˈtælɪtɪ/ *n.* (pl. **-ies**) **1** the state of being subject to death. **2** loss of life on a large scale. **3** **a** the number of deaths in a given period etc. **b** (in full **mortality rate**) a death rate. [ME f. OF *mortalité* f. L *mortalitas -tatis* (as MORTAL)]

mortar /ˈmɔːtə(r)/ *n.* & *v.* —*n.* **1** a mixture of lime with cement, sand, and water, used in building to bond bricks or stones. **2** a short large-bore cannon for firing shells at high angles. **3** a contrivance for firing a lifeline or firework. **4** a vessel made of hard material, in which ingredients are pounded with a pestle. —*v.tr.* **1** plaster or join with mortar. **2** attack or bombard with mortar shells. □ **mortarless** *adj.* (in sense 1). **mortary** *adj.* (in sense 1). [ME f. AF *morter*, OF *mortier* f. L *mortarium*: partly from LG]

mortarboard /ˈmɔːtəˌbɔːd/ *n.* **1** an academic cap with a stiff flat square top. **2** a flat board with a handle on the under-surface, for holding mortar in bricklaying etc.

mortgage /ˈmɔːgɪdʒ/ n. & v. —n. **1 a** a conveyance of property by a debtor to a creditor as security for a debt (esp. one incurred by the purchase of the property), on the condition that it shall be returned on payment of the debt within a certain period. **b** a deed effecting this. **2 a** a debt secured by a mortgage. **b** a loan resulting in such a debt. —v.tr. **1** convey (a property) by mortgage. **2** (often foll. by to) pledge (oneself, one's powers, etc.). □ **mortgage rate** the rate of interest charged by a mortgagee. □ **mortgageable** adj. [ME f. OF, = dead pledge f. mort f. L mortuus dead + gage GAGE¹]

mortgagee /ˌmɔːgɪˈdʒiː/ n. the creditor in a mortgage, usu. a bank or building society.

mortgager /ˈmɔːgɪdʒə(r)/ n. (also **mortgagor** /-ˈdʒɔː(r)/) the debtor in a mortgage.

mortician /mɔːˈtɪʃ(ə)n/ n. US an undertaker; a manager of funerals. [L mors mortis death + -ICIAN]

mortify /ˈmɔːtɪˌfaɪ/ v. (-ies, -ied) **1** tr. **a** cause (a person) to feel shamed or humiliated. **b** wound (a person's feelings). **2** tr. bring (the body, the flesh, the passions, etc.) into subjection by self-denial or discipline. **3** intr. (of flesh) be affected by gangrene or necrosis. □ **mortification** /-fɪˈkeɪʃ(ə)n/ n. **mortifying** adj. **mortifyingly** adv. [ME f. OF mortifier f. eccl.L mortificare kill, subdue f. mors mortis death]

mortise /ˈmɔːtɪs/ n. & v. (also **mortice**) —n. a hole in a framework designed to receive the end of another part, esp. a tenon. —v.tr. **1** join securely, esp. by mortise and tenon. **2** cut a mortise in. □ **mortise lock** a lock recessed into a mortise in the frame of a door or window etc. [ME f. OF mortoise f. Arab. murtazz fixed in]

mortuary /ˈmɔːtjʊərɪ/ n. & adj. —n. (pl. -ies) a room or building in which dead bodies may be kept until burial or cremation. —adj. of or concerning death or burial. [ME f. AF mortuarie f. med.L mortuarium f. L mortuarius f. mortuus dead]

Mosaic /məʊˈzeɪɪk/ adj. of or associated with Moses (in the Hebrew Bible). □ **Mosaic Law** the laws attributed to Moses and listed in the Pentateuch. [F mosaïque or mod.L Mosaicus f. Moses f. Heb. Mōšeh]

mosaic /məʊˈzeɪɪk/ n. & v. —n. **1 a** a picture or pattern produced by an arrangement of small variously coloured pieces of glass or stone etc. **b** work of this kind as an art form. **2** a diversified thing. **3** (in full **mosaic disease**) a virus disease causing leaf-mottling in plants, esp. tobacco, maize, and sugar cane. **4** (attrib.) **a** of or like a mosaic. **b** diversified. —v.tr. (**mosaicked**, **mosaicking**) **1** adorn with mosaics. **2** combine into or as into a mosaic. □ **mosaicist** /-ɪsɪst/ n. [ME f. F mosaïque f. It. mosaico f. med.L mosaicus, musaicus f. Gk mous(e)ion mosaic work f. mousa MUSE¹]

mosasaurus /ˌməʊsəˈsɔːrəs/ n. any large extinct marine reptile of the genus Mosasaurus, with a long slender body and flipper-like limbs. [mod.L f. Mosa river Meuse (near which it was first discovered) + Gk sauros lizard]

moselle /məʊˈzel/ n. a light medium-dry white wine produced in the valley of the river Moselle in Germany.

mosey /ˈməʊzɪ/ v.intr. (-eys, -eyed) (often foll. by along) sl. walk in a leisurely or aimless manner. [19th c.: orig. unkn.]

Moslem var. of MUSLIM.

mosque /mɒsk/ n. a Muslim place of worship. [F mosquée f. It. moschea f. Arab. masjid]

mosquito /mɒsˈkiːtəʊ/ n. (pl. -oes) any of various slender biting insects, esp. of the genus Culex, Anopheles, or Aedes, the female of which punctures the skin of humans and other animals with a long proboscis to suck their blood and transmits diseases such as filariasis and malaria. □ **mosquito-net** a net to keep off mosquitoes. [Sp. & Port., dimin. of mosca f. L musca fly]

moss n. & v. —n. **1** any small cryptogamous plant of the class Musci, growing in dense clusters on the surface of the ground, in bogs, on trees, stones, etc. —v.tr. cover with moss. □ **moss agate** agate with mosslike dendritic markings. **moss-grown** overgrown with moss. **moss-stitch** alternate plain and purl in knitting. □ **mosslike** adj. [OE mos bog, moss f. Gmc]

mossy /ˈmɒsɪ/ adj. (**mossier**, **mossiest**) **1** covered in or resembling moss. **2** US sl. antiquated, old-fashioned. □ **mossiness** n.

most /məʊst/ adj., n., & adv. —adj. **1** existing in the greatest quantity or degree (you have made most mistakes; see who can make the most noise). **2** the majority of; nearly all of (most people think so). —n. **1** the greatest quantity or number (this is the most I can do). **2** (**the most**) sl. the best of all. **3** the majority (most of them are missing). —adv. **1** in the highest degree (this is most interesting; what most annoys me). **2** forming the superlative of adjectives and adverbs, esp. those of more than one syllable (most certain; most easily). **3** US colloq. almost. □ **at most** no more or better than (this is at most a makeshift). **at the most 1** as the greatest amount. **2** not more than. **for the most part 1** as regards the greater part. **2** usually. **make the most of 1** employ to the best advantage. **2** represent at its best or worst. [OE māst f. Gmc]

-most /məʊst/ suffix forming superlative adjectives and adverbs from prepositions and other words indicating relative position (foremost; uttermost). [OE -mest f. Gmc]

mostly /ˈməʊstlɪ/ adv. **1** as regards the greater part. **2** usually.

MOT abbr. **1** (in the UK) Ministry of Transport. **2** (in full **MOT test**) a compulsory annual test of motor vehicles of more than a specified age.

mot /məʊ/ n. (pl. **mots** pronunc. same) a witty saying. □ **mot juste** /ˈʒuːst/ (pl. **mots justes** pronunc. same) the most appropriate expression. [F, = word, ult. f. L muttum uttered sound f. muttire murmur]

mote n. a speck of dust. [OE mot, corresp. to Du. mot dust, sawdust, of unkn. orig.]

motel /məʊˈtel/ n. a roadside hotel providing accommodation for motorists and parking for their vehicles. [portmanteau word f. MOTOR + HOTEL]

motet /məʊˈtet/ n. Mus. a short sacred choral composition. [ME f. OF, dimin. of mot: see MOT]

moth /mɒθ/ n. **1** any usu. nocturnal insect of the order Lepidoptera excluding butterflies, having a stout body and without clubbed antennae. **2** any small lepidopterous insect of the family Tineidae breeding in cloth etc., on which its larva feeds. □ **moth-eaten 1** damaged or destroyed by moths. **2** antiquated, time-worn. [OE moththe]

mothball /ˈmɒθbɔːl/ n. & v. —n. a ball of naphthalene etc. placed in stored clothes to keep away moths. —v.tr. **1** place in mothballs. **2** leave unused. □ **in mothballs** stored unused for a considerable time.

mother /ˈmʌðə(r)/ n. & v. —n. **1 a** a woman in relation to a child or children to whom she has given birth. **b** (in full **adoptive mother**) a woman who has continuous care of a child, esp. by adoption. **2** any female animal in relation to its offspring. **3** a quality or condition etc. that gives rise to another (*necessity is the mother of invention*). **4** (in full **Mother Superior**) the head of a female religious community. **5** (*attrib.*) **a** designating an institution etc. regarded as having maternal authority (*Mother Church; mother earth*). **b** designating the main ship, spacecraft, etc., in a convoy or mission (*the mother craft*). —v.tr. **1** give birth to; be the mother of. **2** protect as a mother. **3** give rise to; be the source of. □ **mother country** a country in relation to its colonies. **mother-figure** an older woman who is regarded as a source of nurture, support, etc. **Mother Goose rhyme** *US* a nursery rhyme. **mother-in-law** (*pl.* **mothers-in-law**) the mother of one's husband or wife. **mother-naked** stark naked. **mother-of-pearl** a smooth iridescent substance forming the inner layer of the shell of some molluscs. **Mother's Day 1** *Brit.* = MOTHERING SUNDAY. **2** *US* an equivalent day on the second Sunday in May. **mother's ruin** *colloq.* gin. **mother tongue 1** one's native language. **2** a language from which others have evolved. **mother wit** native wit; common sense. □ **motherhood** n. **motherless** adj. **motherlessness** n. **motherlike** adj. & adv. [OE *mōdor* f. Gmc]

mothercraft /ˈmʌðəkrɑːft/ n. skill in or knowledge of looking after children as a mother.

Mothering Sunday /ˈmʌðərɪŋ/ n. *Brit.* the fourth Sunday in Lent, traditionally a day for honouring mothers with gifts.

motherland /ˈmʌðəlænd/ n. one's native country.

motherly /ˈmʌðəlɪ/ adj. **1** like or characteristic of a mother in affection, care, etc. **2** of or relating to a mother. □ **motherliness** n. [OE *mōdorlic* (as MOTHER)]

mothproof /ˈmɒθpruːf/ adj. & v. —adj. (of clothes) treated so as to repel moths. —v.tr. treat (clothes) in this way.

mothy /ˈmɒθɪ/ adj. (**mothier, mothiest**) infested with moths.

motif /məʊˈtiːf/ n. **1** a distinctive feature or dominant idea in artistic or literary composition. **2** *Mus.* = FIGURE n. 10. **3** an ornament of lace etc. sewn separately on a garment. **4** an ornament on a vehicle identifying the maker, model, etc. [F (as MOTIVE)]

motion /ˈməʊʃ(ə)n/ n. & v. —n. **1** the act or process of moving or of changing position. **2** a particular manner of moving the body in walking etc. **3** a change of posture. **4** a gesture. **5** a formal proposal put to a committee, legislature, etc. **6** *Law* an application for a rule or order of court. **7 a** an evacuation of the bowels. **b** (in *sing.* or *pl.*) faeces. **8** a piece of moving mechanism. —v. (often foll. by *to* + infin.) **1** tr. direct (a person) by a sign or gesture. **2** intr. (often foll. by *to* a person) make a gesture directing (*motioned to me to leave*). □ **go through**

the motions 1 make a pretence; do something perfunctorily or superficially. **2** simulate an action by gestures. **in motion** moving; not at rest. **motion picture** (often (with hyphen) *attrib.*) a film (see FILM n. 3) with the illusion of movement. **put** (or **set**) **in motion** set going or working. □ **motional** adj. **motionless** adj. [ME f. OF f. L *motio -onis* (as MOVE)]

motivate /ˈməʊtɪveɪt/ v.tr. **1** supply a motive to; be the motive of. **2** cause (a person) to act in a particular way. **3** stimulate the interest of (a person in an activity). □ **motivation** /-ˈveɪʃ(ə)n/ n. **motivational** /-ˈveɪʃən(ə)l/ adj. **motivationally** /-ˈveɪʃənəlɪ/ adv.

motive /ˈməʊtɪv/ n. & adj. —n. **1** a factor or circumstance that induces a person to act in a particular way. **2** = MOTIF. —adj. **1** tending to initiate movement. **2** concerned with movement. □ **motive power** a moving or impelling power, esp. a source of energy used to drive machinery. □ **motiveless** adj. **motivelessly** adv. **motivelessness** n. **motivity** /-ˈtɪvɪtɪ/ n. [ME f. OF *motif* (adj. & n.) f. LL *motivus* (adj.) (as MOVE)]

motley /ˈmɒtlɪ/ adj. & n. —adj. (**motlier, motliest**) **1** diversified in colour. **2** of varied character (*a motley crew*). —n. *hist.* the particoloured costume of a jester. [ME *mottelay*, perh. ult. rel. to MOTE]

moto-cross /ˈməʊtəʊˌkrɒs/ n. cross-country racing on motor cycles. [MOTOR + CROSS-]

motor /ˈməʊtə(r)/ n. & v. —n. **1** a thing that imparts motion. **2** a machine (esp. one using electricity or internal combustion) supplying motive power for a vehicle etc. or for some other device with moving parts. **3** *Brit.* = *motor car*. **4** (*attrib.*) **a** giving, imparting, or producing motion. **b** driven by a motor (*motor-mower*). **c** of or for motor vehicles. **d** *Anat.* relating to muscular movement or the nerves activating it. —v.intr. & tr. *Brit.* go or convey in a motor vehicle. □ **motor bike** *colloq.* = *motor cycle.* **motor boat** a motor-driven boat. **motor cycle** a two-wheeled motor-driven road vehicle without pedal propulsion. **motor cyclist** a rider of a motor cycle. **motor mouth** *US sl.* a person who talks incessantly and trivially. **motor nerve** a nerve carrying impulses from the brain or spinal cord to a muscle. **motor vehicle** a road vehicle powered by an internal-combustion engine. □ **motorial** /məʊˈtɔːrɪəl/ adj. (in sense 4a of n.). **motory** adj. (in sense 4a of n.). [L, = mover (as MOVE)]

motorcade /ˈməʊtəkeɪd/ n. a procession of motor vehicles. [MOTOR, after *cavalcade*]

motorist /ˈməʊtərɪst/ n. the driver of a motor vehicle.

motorize /ˈməʊtəraɪz/ v.tr. (also **-ise**) **1** equip (troops etc.) with motor transport. **2** provide with a motor for propulsion etc. □ **motorization** /-ˈzeɪʃ(ə)n/ n.

motorman /ˈməʊtəmæn/ n. (*pl.* **-men**) the driver of an underground train, tram, etc.

motorway /ˈməʊtəweɪ/ n. *Brit.* a main road with separate carriageways and limited access, specially constructed and controlled for fast motor traffic.

Motown /ˈməʊtaʊn/ n. music with rhythm and blues elements, associated with Detroit. [shortening of *Motor Town*, a name for Detroit]

motte /mɒt/ n. a mound forming the site of a castle, camp, etc. [ME f. OF *mote* (as MOAT)]

mottle /ˈmɒt(ə)l/ v. & n. —v.tr. (esp. as **mottled** adj.) mark with spots or smears of colour. —n. 1 an irregular arrangement of spots or patches of colour. 2 any of these spots or patches. [prob. back-form. f. MOTLEY]

motto /ˈmɒtəʊ/ n. (pl. **-oes**) 1 a maxim adopted as a rule of conduct. 2 a phrase or sentence accompanying a coat of arms or crest. 3 a sentence inscribed on some object and expressing an appropriate sentiment. 4 verses etc. in a paper cracker. [It. (as MOT)]

mould¹ /məʊld/ n. & v. (US **mold**) —n. 1 a hollow container into which molten metal etc. is poured or soft material is pressed to harden into a required shape. 2 **a** a metal or earthenware vessel used to give shape to puddings etc. **b** a pudding etc. made in this way. 3 a form or shape, esp. of an animal body. 4 a frame or template for producing mouldings. 5 character or disposition (*in heroic mould*). —v.tr. 1 make (an object) in a required shape or from certain ingredients (*was moulded out of clay*). 2 give a shape to. 3 influence the formation or development of (*consultation helps to mould policies*). □ **mouldable** adj. **moulder** n. [ME *mold(e)*, app. f. OF *modle* f. L *modulus*: see MODULUS]

mould² /məʊld/ n. (US **mold**) a woolly or furry growth of minute fungi occurring esp. in moist warm conditions. [ME prob. f. obs. *mould* adj.; past part. of *moul* grow mouldy f. ON *mygla*]

mould³ /məʊld/ n. (US **mold**) 1 loose earth. 2 the upper soil of cultivated land, esp. when rich in organic matter. [OE *molde* f. Gmc., rel. to MEAL²]

moulder /ˈməʊldə(r)/ v.intr. (US **molder**) 1 decay to dust. 2 (foll. by *away*) rot or crumble. 3 deteriorate. [perh. f. MOULD³, but cf. Norw. dial. *muldra* crumble]

moulding /ˈməʊldɪŋ/ n. (US **molding**) 1 **a** an ornamentally shaped outline as an architectural feature, esp. in a cornice. **b** a strip of material in wood or stone etc. for use as moulding. 2 similar material in wood or plastic etc. used for other decorative purposes, e.g. in picture-framing.

mouldy /ˈməʊldɪ/ adj. (US **moldy**) (**-ier**, **-iest**) 1 covered with mould. 2 stale; out of date. 3 *colloq.* (as a general term of disparagement) dull, miserable, boring. □ **mouldiness** n.

moult /məʊlt/ v. & n. (US **molt**) —v. 1 intr. shed feathers, hair, a shell, etc., in the process of renewing plumage, a coat, etc. 2 tr. (of an animal) shed (feathers, hair, etc.). —n. the act or an instance of moulting (*is in moult once a year*). □ **moulter** n. [ME *moute* f. OE *mutian* (unrecorded) f. L *mutare* change: -l- after *fault* etc.]

mound /maʊnd/ n. & v. —n. 1 a raised mass of earth, stones, or other compacted material. 2 a heap or pile. —v.tr. heap up in a mound or mounds. [16th c. (orig. = hedge or fence): orig. unkn.]

mount¹ /maʊnt/ v. & n. —v. 1 tr. ascend or climb (a hill, stairs, etc.). 2 tr. **a** get up on (an animal, esp. a horse) to ride it. **b** set (a person) on horseback. **c** provide (a person) with a horse. **d** (as **mounted** adj.) serving on horseback (*mounted police*). 3 tr. go up or climb on to (a raised surface). 4 intr. **a** move upwards. **b** (often foll. by *up*) increase, accumulate. **c** (of a feeling) become stronger or more intense (*excitement was mounting*). **d** (of the blood) rise into the cheeks. 5 tr. (esp. of a male animal) get on to (a female) to copulate. 6 tr. (often foll. by *on*) place (an object) on an elevated support. 7 tr. **a** set in or attach to a backing, setting, or other support. **b** attach (a picture etc.) to a mount or frame. **c** fix (an object for viewing) on a microscope slide. 8 tr. **a** arrange (a play, exhibition, etc.) or present for public view or display. **b** take action to initiate (a programme, campaign, etc.). 9 tr. prepare (specimens) for preservation. 10 tr. bring into readiness for operation. —n. 1 a backing, setting, or other support on which a picture etc. is set for display. 2 the margin surrounding a picture or photograph. 3 **a** a horse available for riding. **b** an opportunity to ride a horse, esp. as a jockey. 4 = *stamp-hinge* (see HINGE). □ **mount guard** (often foll. by *over*) perform the duty of guarding; take up sentry duty. □ **mountable** adj. **mounter** n. [ME f. OF *munter*, *monter* ult. f. L (as MOUNT²)]

mount² /maʊnt/ n. archaic (except before a name): mountain, hill (*Mount Everest*; *Mount of Olives*). [ME f. OE *munt* & OF *mont* f. L *mons montis* mountain]

mountain /ˈmaʊntɪn/ n. 1 a large natural elevation of the earth's surface rising abruptly from the surrounding level; a large or high and steep hill. 2 a large heap or pile; a huge quantity (*a mountain of work*). 3 a large surplus stock of a commodity (*butter mountain*). □ **mountain ash** a tree, *Sorbus aucuparia*, with delicate pinnate leaves and scarlet berries. **mountain bike** a sturdy lightweight bike with many gears for riding over rough terrain. **mountain chain** a connected series of mountains. **mountain goat** a white goatlike animal, *Oreamnos americanus*, of the Rocky Mountains etc. **mountain lion** a puma. **mountain range** a line of mountains connected by high ground. **mountain sickness** a sickness caused by the rarefaction of the air at great heights. □ **mountainy** adj. [ME f. OF *montaigne* ult. f. L (as MOUNT²)]

mountaineer /ˌmaʊntɪˈnɪə(r)/ n. & v. —n. a person skilled in mountain-climbing. —v.intr. climb mountains as a sport. □ **mountaineering** n.

mountainous /ˈmaʊntɪnəs/ adj. 1 (of a region) having many mountains. 2 huge.

mountainside /ˈmaʊntɪnˌsaɪd/ n. the slope of a mountain below the summit.

mountebank /ˈmaʊntɪˌbæŋk/ n. 1 a swindler; a charlatan. 2 a clown. □ **mountebankery** n. [It. *montambanco* = *monta in banco* climb on bench: see MOUNT¹, BENCH]

Mountie /ˈmaʊntɪ/ n. colloq. a member of the Royal Canadian Mounted Police.

mounting /ˈmaʊntɪŋ/ n. 1 = MOUNT¹ n. 1. 2 in senses of MOUNT¹ v. □ **mounting-block** a block of stone placed to help a rider mount a horse.

mourn /mɔːn/ v. tr. & (foll. by *for*) intr. feel or show deep sorrow or regret for (a dead person, a lost thing, a past event, etc.). [OE *murnan*]

mourner /ˈmɔːnə(r)/ n. 1 a person who mourns, esp. at a funeral. 2 a person hired to attend a funeral.

mournful /ˈmɔːnfʊl/ adj. 1 doleful, sad, sorrowing. 2 expressing or suggestive of mourning. □ **mournfully** adv. **mournfulness** n.

mourning /ˈmɔːnɪŋ/ n. **1** the expression of deep sorrow, esp. for a dead person, by the wearing of solemn dress. **2** the clothes worn in mourning. □ **in mourning** assuming the signs of mourning, esp. in dress.

mouse /maʊs/ n. & v. —n. (pl. **mice** /maɪs/) **1 a** any of various small rodents of the family Muridae, esp. of the genus *Mus*. **b** any of several similar rodents such as a small shrew or vole. **2** a timid or feeble person. **3** Computing a small hand-held device which controls the cursor on a VDU screen. —v.intr. /also maʊz/ **1** (esp. of a cat, owl, etc.) hunt for or catch mice. **2** (foll. by *about*) search industriously; prowl about as if searching. □ **mouse-coloured 1** dark-grey with a yellow tinge. **2** nondescript light brown. □ **mouselike** adj. & adv. **mouser** n. [OE *mūs*, pl. *mȳs* f. Gmc]

mousetrap /ˈmaʊstræp/ n. **1** a sprung trap with bait for catching and usu. killing mice. **2** (often *attrib.*) cheese of poor quality.

moussaka /muːˈsɑːkə, ˌmuːsɑːˈkɑː/ n. (also **mousaka**) a Greek dish of minced meat, aubergine, etc. with a cheese sauce. [mod. Gk or Turk.]

mousse /muːs/ n. **1 a** a dessert of whipped cream, eggs, etc., usu. flavoured with fruit or chocolate. **b** a meat or fish purée made with whipped cream etc. **2** a preparation applied to the hair enabling it to be styled more easily. **3** a mixture of oil and sea-water which forms a froth on the surface of the water after an oil-spill. [F, = moss, froth]

mousseline /muːˈsliːn/ n. **1** a muslin-like fabric of silk etc. **2** a sauce of seasoned or sweet eggs and cream. [F: see MUSLIN]

moustache /məˈstɑːʃ/ n. (US **mustache**) **1** hair left to grow on a man's upper lip. **2** a similar growth round the mouth of some animals. □ **moustached** adj. [F f. It. *mostaccio* f. Gk *mustax -akos*]

mousy /ˈmaʊsɪ/ adj. (**mousier, mousiest**) **1** of or like a mouse. **2** (of a person) shy or timid; ineffectual. **3** = *mouse-coloured*. □ **mousily** adv. **mousiness** n.

mouth n. & v. —n. /maʊθ/ (pl. **mouths** /maʊðz/) **1 a** an external opening in the head, through which most animals admit food and emit communicative sounds. **b** (in humans and some animals) the cavity behind it containing the means of biting and chewing and the vocal organs. **2 a** the opening of a container such as a bag or sack. **b** the opening of a cave, volcano, etc. **c** the open end of a woodwind or brass instrument. **d** the muzzle of a gun. **3** the place where a river enters the sea. **4** colloq. **a** talkativeness. **b** impudent talk; cheek. **5 a** individual regarded as needing sustenance (*an extra mouth to feed*). —v. /maʊð/ **1** tr. & intr. utter or speak solemnly with affectations; rant, declaim (*mouthing platitudes*). **2** tr. utter very distinctly. **3** intr. move the lips silently. □ **keep one's mouth shut** colloq. not reveal a secret. **mouth-organ** = HARMONICA. **mouth-to-mouth** (of resuscitation) in which a person breathes into a subject's lungs through the mouth. **mouth-watering 1** (of food etc.) having a delicious smell or appearance. **2** tempting, alluring. **put words into a person's mouth** represent a person as having said something in a particular way. **take the words out of a person's mouth** say what another was about to say. □ **mouthed** /maʊðd/ adj. (also in *comb.*).

mouther /ˈmaʊðə(r)/ n. **mouthless** /ˈmaʊθlɪs/ adj. [OE *mūth* f. Gmc]

mouthful /ˈmaʊθfʊl/ n. (pl. **-fuls**) **1** a quantity, esp. of food, that fills the mouth. **2** a small quantity. **3** a long or complicated word or phrase. **4** US colloq. something important said.

mouthpiece /ˈmaʊθpiːs/ n. **1 a** the part of a musical instrument placed between or against the lips. **b** the part of a telephone for speaking into. **c** the part of a tobacco-pipe placed between the lips. **2** a person who speaks for another or others.

mouthwash /ˈmaʊθwɒʃ/ n. **1** a liquid antiseptic etc. for rinsing the mouth or gargling. **2** colloq. nonsense.

movable /ˈmuːvəb(ə)l/ adj. & n. (also **moveable**) —adj. **1** that can be moved. **2** Law (of property) of the nature of a chattel, as distinct from land or buildings. **3** (of a feast or festival) variable in date from year to year. —n. **1** an article of furniture that may be removed from a house, as distinct from a fixture. **2** (in pl.) personal property. □ **movable-doh** Mus. applied to a system of sight-singing in which doh is the keynote of any major scale (cf. *fixed-doh*). □ **movability** /-ˈbɪlɪtɪ/ n. **movableness** n. **movably** adv. [ME f. OF (as MOVE)]

move /muːv/ v. & n. —v. **1** intr. & tr. change one's position or posture, or cause to do this. **2** tr. & intr. put or keep in motion; rouse, stir. **3 a** intr. make a move in a board-game. **b** tr. change the position of (a piece) in a board-game. **4** intr. (often foll. by *about, away*, etc.) go or pass from place to place. **5** intr. take action, esp. promptly (*moved to reduce unemployment*). **6** intr. make progress (*the project is moving fast*). **7** intr. **a** change one's place of residence. **b** (of a business etc.) change to new premises (also tr.: *move house; move offices*). **8** intr. (foll. by *in*) live or be socially active in (a specified place or group etc.) (*moves in the best circles*). **9** tr. affect (a person) with (usu. tender or sympathetic) emotion. **10** tr. **a** (foll. by *in*) stimulate (laughter, anger, etc., in a person). **b** (foll. by *to*) provoke (a person to laughter etc.). **11** tr. (foll. by *to*, or *to* + infin.) prompt or incline (a person to a feeling or action). **12 a** tr. cause (the bowels) to be evacuated. **b** intr. (of the bowels) be evacuated. **13** tr. (often foll. by *that* + clause) propose in a meeting, deliberative assembly, etc. **14** intr. (foll. by *for*) make a formal request or application. **15** intr. (of merchandise) be sold. —n. **1** the act or an instance of moving. **2** a change of house, business premises, etc. **3** a step taken to secure some action or effect; an initiative. **4 a** the changing of the position of a piece in a board-game. **b** a player's turn to do this. □ **get a move on** colloq. **1** hurry up. **2** make a start. **move along** (or **on**) change to a new position, esp. to avoid crowding, getting in the way, etc. **move in 1** take possession of a new house. **2** get into a position of influence, interference, etc. **3** get into a position of readiness or proximity (for an offensive action etc.). **move out** **1** leave one's home; change one's place of residence. **2** leave a position, job, etc. **move over** (or **up**) adjust one's position to make room for another. **on the move 1** progressing. **2** moving about. [ME f. AF *mover*, OF *moveir* f. L *movēre mot-*]

movement /ˈmuːvmənt/ n. 1 the act or an instance of moving or being moved. 2 **a** the moving parts of a mechanism (esp. a clock or watch). **b** a particular group of these. 3 a body of persons with a common object (the peace movement). 4 (usu. in pl.) a person's activities and whereabouts, esp. at a particular time. 5 Mus. a principal division of a longer musical work, self-sufficient in terms of key, tempo, structure, etc. 6 motion of the bowels. 7 **a** an activity in a market for some commodity. **b** a rise or fall in price. [ME f. OF f. med.L movimentum (as MOVE)]

mover /ˈmuːvə(r)/ n. 1 a person or thing that moves. 2 a person who moves a proposition. 3 US a remover of furniture.

movie /ˈmuːvɪ/ n. esp. US colloq. 1 a motion-picture film. 2 (in full **movie-house**) a cinema.

moving /ˈmuːvɪŋ/ adj. 1 that moves or causes to move. 2 affecting with emotion. □ **moving pavement** a structure like a conveyor belt for pedestrians. **moving picture** a continuous picture of events obtained by projecting a sequence of photographs taken at very short intervals. **moving staircase** an escalator. □ **movingly** adv. (in sense 2).

mow /məʊ/ v.tr. (past part. **mowed** or **mown**) 1 cut down (grass, hay, etc.) with a scythe or machine. 2 cut down the produce of (a field) or the grass etc. of (a lawn) by mowing. □ **mow down** kill or destroy randomly or in great numbers. □ **mowable** adj. **mower** n. [OE māwan f. Gmc]

mozzarella /ˌmɒtsəˈrelə/ n. an Italian curd cheese orig. of buffalo milk. [It.]

MP abbr. 1 Member of Parliament. 2 **a** military police. **b** military policeman.

mp abbr. mezzo piano.

m.p.g. abbr. miles per gallon.

m.p.h. abbr. miles per hour.

M.Phil. abbr. Master of Philosophy.

Mr /ˈmɪstə(r)/ n. (pl. **Messrs**) 1 the title of a man without a higher title (Mr Jones). 2 a title prefixed to a designation of office etc. (Mr President; Mr Speaker). [abbr. of MISTER]

Mrs /ˈmɪsɪz/ n. (pl. same or **Mesdames**) the title of a married woman without a higher title (Mrs Jones). [abbr. of MISTRESS: cf. MISSIS]

MS abbr. 1 manuscript. 2 Master of Science. 3 Master of Surgery. 4 multiple sclerosis.

Ms /mɪz, məz/ n. the title of a woman without a higher title, used regardless of marital status. [combination of MRS, MISS²]

M.Sc. abbr. Master of Science.

MS-DOS /ˌemesˈdɒs/ abbr. Computing Microsoft disk operating system.

MSS /emˈesɪz/ abbr. manuscripts.

Mt. abbr. Mount.

M.Tech. abbr. Master of Technology.

mu /mjuː/ n. 1 the twelfth Greek letter (M, μ). 2 (μ, as a symbol) = MICRO- 2. □ **mu-meson** = MUON. [Gk]

much /mʌtʃ/ adj., n., & adv. —adj. 1 existing or occurring in a great quantity (much trouble; not much rain; too much noise). 2 (prec. by as, how, that, etc.) with relative rather than distinctive sense (I don't know how much money you want). —n. 1 a great quantity (much of that is true). 2 (prec. by as, how, that, etc.) with relative rather than distinctive sense (we do not need that much). 3 (usu. in neg.) a noteworthy or outstanding example (not much to look at; not much of a party). —adv. 1 **a** in a great degree (much to my surprise; is much the same). **b** (qualifying a verb or past participle) greatly (they much regret the mistake; I was much annoyed). **c** qualifying a comparative or superlative adjective (much better; much the most likely). 2 for a large part of one's time (is much away from home). □ **as much** the extent or quantity just specified; the idea just mentioned (I thought as much; as much as that?). **a bit much** colloq. somewhat excessive or immoderate. **much as** even though (cannot come, much as I would like to). **not much** colloq. 1 iron. very much. 2 certainly not. **too much** colloq. an intolerable situation etc. (that really is too much). **too much for** 1 more than a match for. 2 beyond what is endurable by. □ **muchly** adv. joc. [ME f. muchel MICKLE: for loss of el cf. BAD, WENCH]

muchness /ˈmʌtʃnɪs/ n. greatness in quantity or degree. □ **much of a muchness** very nearly the same or alike.

mucilage /ˈmjuːsɪlɪdʒ/ n. a viscous substance obtained from plant seeds etc. □ **mucilaginous** /-ˈlædʒɪnəs/ adj. [ME f. F f. LL mucilago -ginis musty juice (MUCUS)]

muck n. & v. —n. 1 farmyard manure. 2 colloq. dirt or filth; anything disgusting. 3 colloq. an untidy state; a mess. —v.tr. 1 (usu. foll. by up) Brit. colloq. bungle (a job). 2 (foll. by out) remove muck from. 3 make dirty. 4 manure with muck. □ **make a muck of** colloq. bungle. **muck about** (or **around**) Brit. colloq. 1 potter or fool about. 2 (foll. by with) fool or interfere with. **muck in** Brit. (often foll. by with) share tasks etc. equally. **muck sweat** Brit. colloq. a profuse sweat. [ME muk prob. f. Scand.: cf. ON myki dung, rel. to MEEK]

muckle var. of MICKLE.

muckrake /ˈmʌkreɪk/ v.intr. search out and reveal scandal, esp. among famous people. □ **muckraker** n. **muckraking** n.

mucky /ˈmʌkɪ/ adj. (**muckier**, **muckiest**) 1 covered with muck. 2 dirty. □ **muckiness** n.

mucous /ˈmjuːkəs/ adj. of or covered with mucus. □ **mucous membrane** a mucus-secreting epithelial tissue lining many body cavities and tubular organs. □ **mucosity** /-ˈkɒsɪtɪ/ n. [L mucosus (as MUCUS)]

mucus /ˈmjuːkəs/ n. 1 a slimy substance secreted by a mucous membrane. 2 a gummy substance found in all plants. 3 a slimy substance exuded by some animals, esp. fishes. [L]

mud n. 1 wet soft earthy matter. 2 hard ground from the drying of an area of this. □ **fling** (or **sling** or **throw**) **mud** speak disparagingly or slanderously. **mud-brick** a brick made from baked mud. **mud-flat** a stretch of muddy land left uncovered at low tide. **mud pack** a cosmetic paste applied thickly to the face. **mud pie** mud made into a pie shape by a child. **mud-slinging** colloq. abuse, disparagement. **one's name is mud** one is unpopular or in disgrace. [ME mode, mudde, prob. f. MLG mudde, MHG mot bog]

muddle /ˈmʌd(ə)l/ v. & n. —v. 1 tr. (often foll. by up, together) bring into disorder. 2 tr. bewilder, confuse. 3 tr. mismanage (an affair). —n. 1 disorder. 2 a muddled condition. □ **make a muddle of** 1 bring into disorder. 2 bungle. **muddle along** (or **on**) progress in a haphazard way. **muddle-headed** stupid, confused. **muddle through** succeed by perseverance rather than skill or efficiency. **muddle up** confuse (two or more things). □ **muddler** *n.* **muddlingly** *adv.* [perh. f. MDu. *moddelen*, frequent. of *modden* dabble in mud (as MUD)]

muddy /ˈmʌdɪ/ *adj.* & *v.* —*adj.* (**muddier, muddiest**) **1** like mud. **2** covered in or full of mud. **3** (of liquid) turbid. **4** mentally confused. **5** obscure. **6** (of light) dull. **7** (of colour) impure. —*v.tr.* (**-ies, -ied**) make muddy. □ **muddily** *adv.* **muddiness** *n.*

mudflap /ˈmʌdflæp/ *n.* a flap hanging behind the wheel of a vehicle, to catch mud and stones etc. thrown up from the road.

mudguard /ˈmʌdɡɑːd/ *n.* a curved strip or cover over a wheel of a bicycle or motor cycle to reduce the amount of mud etc. thrown up from the road.

muesli /ˈmuːzlɪ, ˈmjuː-/ *n.* a breakfast food of crushed cereals, dried fruits, nuts, etc., eaten with milk. [Swiss G]

muezzin /muːˈɛzɪn/ *n.* a Muslim crier who proclaims the hours of prayer usu. from a minaret. [Arab. *muʾaddin* part. of *ʾaddana* proclaim]

muff[1] *n.* a fur or other covering, usu. in the form of a tube with an opening at each end for the hands to be inserted for warmth. [Du. *mof*, MDu. *moffel*, *muffel* f. med.L *muff(u)la*, of unkn. orig.]

muff[2] *v.* & *n.* —*v.tr.* **1** bungle; deal clumsily with. **2** fail to catch or receive (a ball etc.). **3** blunder in (a theatrical part etc.). —*n.* **1** a person who is awkward or stupid, orig. in some athletic sport. **2** a failure, esp. to catch a ball at cricket etc. □ **muffish** *adj.* [19th c.: orig. unkn.]

muffin /ˈmʌfɪn/ *n.* **1** *Brit.* a light flat round spongy cake, eaten toasted and buttered. **2** *US* a similar round cake made from batter or dough. [18th c.: orig. unkn.]

muffle /ˈmʌf(ə)l/ *v.tr.* **1** (often foll. by *up*) wrap or cover for warmth. **2** cover or wrap up (a source of sound) to reduce its loudness. **3** (usu. as **muffled** *adj.*) stifle (an utterance, e.g. a curse). **4** prevent from speaking. [ME: (n.) f. OF *moufle* thick glove; (v.) perh. f. OF *enmoufler* f. *moufle*]

muffler /ˈmʌflə(r)/ *n.* **1** a wrap or scarf worn for warmth. **2** any of various devices used to deaden sound in musical instruments. **3** *US* the silencer of a motor vehicle.

mufti /ˈmʌftɪ/ *n.* plain clothes worn by a person who also wears (esp. military) uniform (*in mufti*). [19th c.: perh. f. Arab *muftī*, legal expert]

mug[1] *n.* & *v.* —*n.* **1 a** a drinking-vessel, usu. cylindrical and with a handle and used without a saucer. **b** its contents. **2** *sl.* the face or mouth of a person. **3** *Brit. sl.* **a** a simpleton. **b** a gullible person. **4** *US sl.* a hoodlum or thug. —*v.* (**mugged, mugging**) **1** *tr.* rob (a person) with violence esp. in a public place. **2** *tr.* thrash. **3** *tr.* strangle. **4** *intr. sl.* make faces, esp. before an audience, a camera, etc. □ **mug shot** *sl.* a photograph of a face, esp. for official purposes. □ **mugger** *n.* (esp. in sense 1 of *v.*). **mugful** *n.* (*pl.* **-fuls**). **mugging** *n.* (in sense 1 of *v.*). [prob. f. Scand.: sense 2 of *n.* prob. f. the representation of faces on mugs, and sense 3 prob. from this]

mug[2] /mʌɡ/ *v.tr.* (**mugged, mugging**) *Brit.* (usu. foll. by *up*) *sl.* learn (a subject) by concentrated study. [19th c.: orig. unkn.]

muggins /ˈmʌɡɪnz/ *n.* (*pl.* same or **mugginses**) *colloq.* **1** a simpleton. **2** a person who is easily outwitted (often with allusion to oneself: *so muggins had to pay*). [perh. the surname *Muggins*, with allusion to MUG[1]]

muggy /ˈmʌɡɪ/ *adj.* (**muggier, muggiest**) (of the weather, a day, etc.) oppressively damp and warm; humid. □ **mugginess** *n.* [dial. *mug* mist, drizzle f. ON *mugga*]

Muhammadan /məˈhæməd(ə)n/ *n.* & *adj.* (also **Mohammedan**) = MUSLIM. □ **Muhammadanism** *n.* [*Muhammad*, Arabian prophet d. 632]

■ **Usage** This word is not used by Muslims, and is often regarded as offensive.

---

mujahidin /ˌmuːdʒæhɪˈdiːn/ *n.pl.* (also **mujahedin, -deen**) guerrilla fighters in Islamic countries, esp. supporting Muslim fundamentalism. [Pers. & Arab. *mujāhidīn* pl. of *mujāhid* one who fights a JIHAD]

mulatto /mjuːˈlætəʊ/ *n.* (*pl.* **-os** or **-oes**) a person of mixed White and Black parentage. [Sp. *mulato* young mule, *mulatto*, irreg. f. *mulo* MULE[1]]

mulberry /ˈmʌlbərɪ/ *n.* (*pl.* **-ies**) **1** any deciduous tree of the genus *Morus*, grown originally for feeding silkworms, and now for its fruit and ornamental qualities. **2** its dark-red or white berry. **3** a dark-red or purple colour. [ME *mol-*, *mool-*, *mulberry*, dissim. f. *murberie* f. OE *mōrberie*, f. L *morum*: see BERRY]

mulch /mʌltʃ, mʌlʃ/ *n.* & *v.* —*n.* a mixture of wet straw, leaves, etc., spread around or over a plant to enrich or insulate the soil. —*v.tr.* treat with mulch. [prob. use as noun of *mulsh* soft: cf. dial. *melsh* mild f. OE *melsc*]

mulct *v.* & *n.* —*v.tr.* **1** extract money from by fine or taxation. **2 a** (often foll. by *of*) deprive by fraudulent means; swindle. **b** obtain by swindling. —*n.* a fine. [earlier *mult(e)* f. L *multa*, *mulcta*: (v.) through F *mulcter* & L *mulctare*]

mule[1] *n.* **1** the offspring (usu. sterile) of a male donkey and a female horse, or (in general use) of a female donkey and a male horse, used as a beast of burden. **2** a stupid or obstinate person. [ME f. OF *mul(e)* f. L *mulus mula*]

mule[2] /mjuːl/ *n.* a light shoe or slipper without a back. [F]

mule[3] var. of MEWL.

muleteer /ˌmjuːlɪˈtɪə(r)/ *n.* a mule-driver. [F *muletier* f. *mulet* dimin. of OF *mul* MULE[1]]

mulga /ˈmʌlɡə/ *n. Austral.* **1** a small spreading tree, *Acacia aneura*. **2** the wood of this tree. **3** scrub or bush. **4** *colloq.* the outback. [Aboriginal]

mulish /ˈmjuːlɪʃ/ *adj.* **1** like a mule. **2** stubborn. □ **mulishly** *adv.* **mulishness** *n.*

mull[1] /mʌl/ *v.tr.* & *intr.* (often foll. by *over*) ponder or consider. [perh. f. *mull* grind to powder, ME *mul* dust f. MDu.]

mull[2] /mʌl/ *v.tr.* warm (wine or beer) with added sugar, spices, etc. [17th c.: orig. unkn.]

mull[3] /mʌl/ *n. Sc.* a promontory. [ME: cf. Gael. *maol*, Icel. *múli*]

mullah /ˈmʌlə/ *n.* a Muslim learned in Islamic theology and sacred law. [Pers., Turk., Urdu *mullā* f. Arab. *mawlā*]

mullet /ˈmʌlɪt/ *n.* any fish of the family Mullidae (**red mullet**) or Mugilidae (**grey mullet**), usu. with a thick body and a large blunt-nosed head, commonly used as food. [ME f. OF *mulet* dimin. of L *mullus* red mullet f. Gk *mollos*]

mulligatawny /ˌmʌlɪɡəˈtɔːnɪ/ n. a highly seasoned soup orig. from India. [Tamil *milagutannir* pepper-water]

mullion /ˈmʌljən/ n. (also **munnion** /ˈmʌn-/) a vertical bar dividing the lights in a window. □ **mullioned** adj. [prob. an altered form of *monial*, ME f. OF *moinel* middle]

multangular /mʌlˈtæŋɡjʊlə(r)/ adj. having many angles. [med.L *multangularis* (as MULTI-, ANGULAR)]

multi- /ˈmʌltɪ/ comb. form many; more than one. [L f. *multus* much, many]

multi-access /ˌmʌltɪˈækses/ n. (often attrib.) the simultaneous connection to a computer of a number of terminals.

multicellular /ˌmʌltɪˈseljʊlə(r)/ adj. Biol. having many cells.

multichannel /ˌmʌltɪˈtʃæn(ə)l/ adj. employing or possessing many communication or television channels.

multicolour /ˈmʌltɪˌkʌl(ə)r/ adj. (also **multicoloured**) of many colours.

multicultural /ˌmʌltɪˈkʌltʃər(ə)l/ adj. of or relating to or constituting several cultural or ethnic groups within a society. □ **multiculturally** adv.

multidimensional /ˌmʌltɪdaɪˈmenʃən(ə)l/ adj. of or involving more than three dimensions. □ **multidimensionality** /-ˈnælɪtɪ/ n. **multidimensionally** adv.

multidirectional /ˌmʌltɪdaɪˈrekʃən(ə)l/ adj. of, involving, or operating in several directions.

multifaceted /ˌmʌltɪˈfæsɪtɪd/ adj. having several facets.

multifarious /ˌmʌltɪˈfeərɪəs/ adj. 1 (foll. by pl. noun) many and various. 2 having great variety. □ **multifariously** adv. **multifariousness** n. [L *multifarius*]

multiform /ˈmʌltɪˌfɔːm/ n. (usu. attrib.) 1 having many forms. 2 of many kinds. □ **multiformity** /-ˈfɔːmɪtɪ/ n.

multifunctional /ˌmʌltɪˈfʌŋkʃən(ə)l/ adj. having or fulfilling several functions.

multigrade /ˈmʌltɪˌɡreɪd/ n. (usu. attrib.) an engine oil etc. meeting the requirements of several standard grades.

multilateral /ˌmʌltɪˈlætər(ə)l/ adj. 1 a (of an agreement, treaty, conference, etc.) in which three or more parties participate. b performed by more than one party (*multilateral disarmament*). 2 having many sides. □ **multilaterally** adv.

multilingual /ˌmʌltɪˈlɪŋɡw(ə)l/ adj. in or using several languages. □ **multilingually** adv.

multimillion /ˈmʌltɪˌmɪljən/ attrib.adj. costing or involving several million (pounds, dollars, etc.) (*multimillion dollar fraud*).

multimillionaire /ˌmʌltɪˌmɪljəˈneə(r)/ n. a person with a fortune of several millions.

multinational /ˌmʌltɪˈnæʃən(ə)l/ adj. & n. —adj. 1 (of a business organization) operating in several countries. 2 relating to or including several nationalities or ethnic groups. —n. a multinational company. □ **multinationally** adv.

multiple /ˈmʌltɪp(ə)l/ adj. & n. —adj. 1 having several or many parts, elements, or individual components. 2 (foll. by pl. noun) many and various. 3 Bot. (of fruit) collective. —n. 1 a number that may be divided by another a certain number of times without a remainder

(*56 is a multiple of 7*). 2 a multiple shop or store. □ **least** (or **lowest**) **common multiple** the least quantity that is a multiple of two or more given quantities. **multiple-choice** (of a question in an examination) accompanied by several possible answers from which the correct one has to be chosen. **multiple shop** (or **store**) Brit. a shop or store with branches in several places. □ **multiply** adv. [F f. LL *multiplus* f. L (as MULTIPLEX)]

multiplex /ˈmʌltɪˌpleks/ adj. & v. —adj. 1 manifold; of many elements. 2 involving simultaneous transmission of several messages along a single channel of communication. —v.tr. incorporate into a multiplex signal or system. □ **multiplexer** n. (also **multiplexor**). [L (as MULTI-, *-plex -plicis* -fold)]

multipliable /ˈmʌltɪˌplaɪəb(ə)l/ adj. that can be multiplied.

multiplicand /ˌmʌltɪplɪˈkænd/ n. a quantity to be multiplied by a multiplier. [med.L *multiplicandus* gerundive of L *multiplicare* (as MULTIPLY)]

multiplication /ˌmʌltɪplɪˈkeɪʃ(ə)n/ n. 1 the arithmetical process of multiplying. 2 the act or an instance of multiplying. □ **multiplication sign** the sign (×) to indicate that one quantity is to be multiplied by another, as in $2 \times 3 = 6$. **multiplication table** a list of multiples of a particular number, usu. from 1 to 12. □ **multiplicative** /-ˈplɪkətɪv/ adj. [ME f. OF *multiplication* or L *multiplicatio* (as MULTIPLY)]

multiplicity /ˌmʌltɪˈplɪsɪtɪ/ n. (pl. **-ies**) 1 manifold variety. 2 (foll. by *of*) a great number. [LL *multiplicitas* (as MULTIPLEX)]

multiplier /ˈmʌltɪˌplaɪə(r)/ n. a quantity by which a given number is multiplied.

multiply /ˈmʌltɪˌplaɪ/ v. (**-ies, -ied**) 1 tr. (also absol.) obtain from (a number) another that is a specified number of times its value (*multiply 6 by 4 and you get 24*). 2 intr. increase in number esp. by procreation. 3 tr. produce a large number of (instances etc.). 4 tr. a breed (animals). b propagate (plants). [ME f. OF *multiplier* f. L *multiplicare* (as MULTIPLEX)]

multiprocessing /ˌmʌltɪˈprəʊsesɪŋ/ n. Computing processing by a number of processors sharing a common memory and common peripherals.

multiprogramming /ˌmʌltɪˈprəʊɡræmɪŋ/ n. Computing the execution of two or more independent programs concurrently.

multi-purpose /ˌmʌltɪˈpɜːpəs/ n. (attrib.) having several purposes.

multiracial /ˌmʌltɪˈreɪʃ(ə)l/ adj. relating to or made up of many human races. □ **multiracially** adv.

multi-storey /ˌmʌltɪˈstɔːrɪ/ n. (attrib.) (of a building) having several (esp. similarly designed) storeys.

multitude /ˈmʌltɪˌtjuːd/ n. 1 (often foll. by *of*) a great number. 2 a large gathering of people; a crowd. 3 (**the multitude**) the common people. 4 the state of being numerous. [ME f. OF f. L *multitudo -dinis* f. *multus* many]

multitudinous /ˌmʌltɪˈtjuːdɪnəs/ adj. 1 very numerous. 2 consisting of many individuals or elements. 3 (of an ocean etc.) vast. □ **multitudinously** adv. **multitudinousness** n. [L (as MULTITUDE)]

multi-user /ˌmʌltɪˈjuːzə(r)/ n. (attrib.) (of a computer system) having a number of simultaneous users (cf. MULTI-ACCESS).

multivalent /ˌmʌltɪˈveɪlənt/ adj. Chem. 1 having a valency of more than two. 2 having a variable valency. □ **multivalency** n.

multi-way /ˈmʌltɪˌweɪ/ n. (attrib.) having several paths of communication etc.

mum[1] n. Brit. colloq. mother. [abbr. of MUMMY[1]]

mum[2] adj. colloq. silent (keep mum). □ **mum's the word** say nothing. [ME: imit. of closed lips]

mum[3] v.intr. (**mummed**, **mumming**) act in a traditional masked mime. [cf. MUM[2] and MLG mummen]

mumble /ˈmʌmb(ə)l/ v. & n. —v. 1 intr. & tr. speak or utter indistinctly. 2 tr. bite or chew with or as with toothless gums. —n. an indistinct utterance. □ **mumbler** n. **mumblingly** adv. [ME momele, as MUM[2]: cf. LG mummelen]

mumbo-jumbo /ˌmʌmbəʊˈdʒʌmbəʊ/ n. (pl. -**jumbos**) 1 meaningless or ignorant ritual. 2 language or action intended to mystify or confuse. 3 an object of senseless veneration. [Mumbo Jumbo, a supposed African idol]

mummer /ˈmʌmə(r)/ n. an actor in a traditional masked mime. [ME f. OF momeur f. momer MUM[3]]

mummery /ˈmʌmərɪ/ n. (pl. -**ies**) 1 ridiculous (esp. religious) ceremonial. 2 a performance by mummers. [OF momerie (as MUMMER)]

mummify /ˈmʌmɪfaɪ/ v.tr. (-**ies**, -**ied**) 1 embalm and preserve (a body) in the form of a mummy. 2 (usu. as **mummified** adj.) shrivel or dry up (tissues etc.). □ **mummification** /-fɪˈkeɪʃ(ə)n/ n.

mummy[1] /ˈmʌmɪ/ n. (pl. -**ies**) Brit. colloq. mother. [imit. of a child's pronunc.: cf. MAMMA[1]]

mummy[2] /ˈmʌmɪ/ n. (pl. -**ies**) a body of a human being or animal embalmed for burial, esp. in ancient Egypt. [F momie f. med.L mumia f. Arab. mūmiyā f. Pers. mūm wax]

mumps /mʌmps/ n.pl. (treated as sing.) a contagious and infectious viral disease with swelling of the salivary glands in the face. [archaic mump be sullen]

munch /mʌntʃ/ v.tr. eat steadily with a marked action of the jaws. [ME, imit.: cf. CRUNCH]

mundane /mʌnˈdeɪn/ adj. 1 dull, routine. 2 of this world; worldly. □ **mundanely** adv. **mundaneness** n. **mundanity** /-ˈdænɪtɪ/ n. (pl. -**ies**). [ME f. OF mondain f. LL mundanus f. L mundus world]

mung /mʌŋ/ n. (in full **mung bean**) a leguminous plant, Phaseolus aureus, native to India and used as food. [Hindi mūng]

municipal /mjuːˈnɪsɪp(ə)l/ adj. of or concerning a municipality or its self-government. □ **municipalize** v.tr. (also -**ise**). **municipalization** /-ˈzeɪʃ(ə)n/ n. **municipally** adv. [L municipalis f. municipium free city f. municeps -cipis citizen with privileges f. munia civic offices + capere take]

municipality /mjuːˌnɪsɪˈpælɪtɪ/ n. (pl. -**ies**) 1 a town or district having local government. 2 the governing body of this area. [F municipalité f. municipal (as MUNICIPAL)]

munificent /mjuːˈnɪfɪs(ə)nt/ adj. (of a giver or a gift) splendidly generous, bountiful. □ **munificence** n. **munificently** adv. [L munificent-, var. stem of munificus f. munus gift]

muniment /ˈmjuːnɪmənt/ n. (usu. in pl.) 1 a document kept as evidence of rights or privileges etc. 2 an archive. [ME f. OF f. L munimentum

defence, in med.L title-deed f. munire munit-fortify]

munition /mjuːˈnɪʃ(ə)n/ n. & v. —n. (usu. in pl.) military weapons, ammunition, equipment, and stores. —v.tr. supply with munitions. [F f. L munitio -onis fortification (as MUNIMENT)]

munnion var. of MULLION.

muntjac /ˈmʌntdʒæk/ n. (also **muntjak**) any small deer of the genus Muntiacus native to SE Asia, the male having tusks and small antlers. [Sundanese minchek]

muon /ˈmjuːɒn/ n. Physics an unstable elementary particle like an electron, but with a much greater mass. [μ (MU), as the symbol for it]

mural /ˈmjʊər(ə)l/ n. & adj. —n. a painting executed directly on a wall. —adj. 1 of or like a wall. 2 on a wall. □ **muralist** n. [F f. L muralis f. murus wall]

murder /ˈmɜːdə(r)/ n. & v. —n. 1 the unlawful premeditated killing of a human being by another. 2 colloq. an unpleasant, troublesome, or dangerous state of affairs (it was murder here on Saturday). —v.tr. 1 kill (a human being) unlawfully, esp. wickedly or inhumanly. 2 Law kill (a human being) with a premeditated motive. 3 colloq. utterly defeat or spoil by a bad performance, mispronunciation etc. (murdered the soliloquy in the second act). □ **cry blue murder** sl. make an extravagant outcry. **get away with murder** colloq. do whatever one wishes and escape punishment. □ **murderer** n. **murderess** n. [OE morthor & OF murdre f. Gmc]

murderous /ˈmɜːdərəs/ adj. (of a person, weapon, action, etc.) capable of, intending, or involving murder or great harm. □ **murderously** adv. **murderousness** n.

murk n. (also **mirk**). 1 darkness, poor visibility. 2 air obscured by fog etc. [prob. f. Scand.: cf. ON myrkr]

murky /ˈmɜːkɪ/ adj. (also **mirky**) (-**ier**, -**iest**) 1 dark, gloomy. 2 (of darkness) thick, dirty. 3 suspiciously obscure (murky past). □ **murkily** adv. **murkiness** n.

murmur /ˈmɜːmə(r)/ n. & v. —n. 1 a subdued continuous sound, as made by waves, a brook, etc. 2 a softly spoken or nearly inarticulate utterance. 3 Med. a recurring sound heard in the auscultation of the heart and usu. indicating abnormality. 4 a subdued expression of discontent. —v. 1 intr. make a subdued continuous sound. 2 tr. utter (words) in a low voice. 3 intr. (usu. foll. by at, against) complain in low tones, grumble. □ **murmurer** n. **murmuringly** adv. **murmurous** adj. [ME f. OF murmurer f. L murmurare: cf. Gk mormurō (of water) roar, Skr. marmaras noisy]

murphy /ˈmɜːfɪ/ n. (pl. -**ies**) sl. a potato. [Ir. surname]

murrain /ˈmʌrɪn/ n. an infectious disease of cattle, carried by parasites. [ME f. AF moryn, OF morine f. morir f. L mori die]

Mus.B. abbr. (also **Mus. Bac.**) Bachelor of Music. [L Musicae Baccalaureus]

muscadine /ˈmʌskədɪn, -ˌdaɪn/ n. a variety of grape with a musk flavour, used chiefly in wine-making. [perh. Engl. form f. Prov. MUSCAT]

muscat /ˈmʌskət/ n. 1 a sweet fortified white wine made from muscadines. 2 a muscadine. [F f. Prov. muscat muscade (adj.) f. musc MUSK]

muscatel /ˌmʌskəˈtel/ n. (also **muscadel** /-ˈdel/)
1 = MUSCAT. 2 a raisin from a muscadine grape.
[ME f. OF f. Prov. dimin. of *muscat*: see MUSCAT]

muscle /ˈmʌs(ə)l/ n. & v. —n. 1 a fibrous
tissue with the ability to contract, producing
movement in or maintaining the position of an
animal body. 2 the part of an animal body that
is composed of muscles. 3 physical power or
strength. —v.intr. (usu. foll. by in) colloq. force
oneself on others; intrude by forceful means. □
muscle-bound with muscles stiff and inelastic
through excessive exercise or training.
muscle-man a man with highly developed
muscles, esp. one employed as an intimidator.
not move a muscle be completely motionless.
□ **muscled** adj. (usu. in comb.). **muscleless** adj.
muscly adj. [F f. L *musculus* dimin. of *mus* mouse,
from the fancied mouselike form of some
muscles]

muscovado /ˌmʌskəˈvɑːdəʊ/ n. (pl. **-os**) an unrefined sugar made from the juice of sugar cane
by evaporation and draining off the molasses.
[Sp. *mascabado* (sugar) of the lowest quality]

Muscovite /ˈmʌskəˌvaɪt/ n. & adj. —n. a native
or citizen of Moscow. —adj. of or relating
to Moscow. [mod.L *Muscovita* f. *Muscovia* =
MUSCOVY]

Muscovy /ˈmʌskəvɪ/ n. □ **Muscovy duck** a
tropical American duck, *Cairina moschata*, having
a small crest and red markings on its head.
[obs. F *Muscovie* f. mod.L *Moscovia* f. Russ. *Moskva*
Moscow]

muscular /ˈmʌskjʊlə(r)/ adj. 1 of or affecting
the muscles. 2 having well-developed muscles.
□ **muscularity** /-ˈlærɪtɪ/ n. **muscularly** adv.
[earlier *musculous* (as MUSCLE)]

musculature /ˈmʌskjʊlətʃə(r)/ n. the muscular
system of a body or organ. [F f. L (as MUSCLE)]

Mus.D. abbr. (also **Mus. Doc.**) Doctor of Music.
[L *Musicae Doctor*]

muse[1] /mjuːz/ n. 1 (as **the Muses**) (in Greek and
Roman mythology) nine goddesses, who inspire
poetry, music, drama, etc. 2 (usu. prec. by *the*) a
a poet's inspiring goddess. b a poet's genius.
[ME f. OF *muse* or L *musa* f. Gk *mousa*]

muse[2] /mjuːz/ v. literary. 1 intr. a (usu. foll. by *on*,
upon) ponder, reflect. b (usu. foll. by *on*) gaze
meditatively (on a scene etc.). 2 tr. say meditatively. [ME f. OF *muser* to waste time f. Rmc
perh. f. med.L *musum* muzzle]

museum /mjuːˈzɪəm/ n. a building used for
storing and exhibiting objects of historical,
scientific, or cultural interest. □ **museum piece**
1 a specimen of art etc. fit for a museum. 2
derog. an old-fashioned or quaint person or
object. □ **museology** /-ˈɒlədʒɪ/ n. [L f. Gk *mouseion*
seat of the Muses: see MUSE[1]]

mush[1] /mʌʃ/ n. 1 soft pulp. 2 feeble sentimentality. 3 US maize porridge. □ **mushy** adj.
(**mushier, mushiest**). **mushily** adv. **mush-
iness** n. [app. var. of MASH]

mush[2] /mʌʃ/ v. & n. US —v.intr. 1 (in imper.) used
as a command to dogs pulling a sledge to urge
them forward. 2 go on a journey across snow
with a dog-sledge. —n. a journey across snow
with a dog-sledge. [prob. corrupt. f. F *marchons*
imper. of *marcher* advance]

mushroom /ˈmʌʃrʊm, -ruːm/ n. & v. —n. 1 the
usu. edible spore-producing body of various
fungi, esp. *Agaricus campestris*, with a stem and
domed cap. 2 the pinkish-brown colour of this.

3 any item resembling a mushroom in shape
(*darning mushroom*). 4 (usu. attrib.) something
that appears or develops suddenly or is ephemeral; an upstart. —v.intr. 1 appear or develop
rapidly. 2 expand and flatten like a mushroom
cap. 3 gather mushrooms. □ **mushroom cloud**
a cloud suggesting the shape of a mushroom,
esp. from a nuclear explosion. **mushroom
growth** 1 a sudden development or expansion.
2 anything undergoing this. □ **mushroomy**
adj. [ME f. OF *mousseron* f. LL *mussirio -onis*]

music /ˈmjuːzɪk/ n. 1 the art of combining vocal
or instrumental sounds (or both) to produce
beauty of form, harmony, and expression of
emotion. 2 the sounds so produced. 3 musical
compositions. 4 the written or printed score
of a musical composition. 5 certain pleasant
sounds, e.g. birdsong, the sound of a stream,
etc. □ **music centre** equipment combining
radio, record-player, tape recorder, etc. **music-
hall** Brit. 1 variety entertainment, popular
c.1850–1914, consisting of singing, dancing, and
novelty acts. 2 a theatre where this took place.
music stool a stool for a pianist, usu. with
adjustable height. **music to one's ears** something very pleasant to hear. [ME f. OF *musique* f.
L *musica* f. Gk *mousikē* (*tekhnē* art) of the Muses
(*mousa* Muse: see MUSE[1])]

musical /ˈmjuːzɪk(ə)l/ adj. & n. —adj. 1 of or
relating to music. 2 (of sounds, a voice, etc.)
melodious, harmonious. 3 fond of or skilled in
music (*the musical one of the family*). 4 set to or
accompanied by music. —n. a musical film or
comedy. □ **musical box** Brit. a mechanical
instrument playing a tune by causing a toothed
cylinder to strike a comblike metal plate within
a box. **musical chairs** a party game in which
the players compete in successive rounds for a
decreasing number of chairs. **musical comedy**
a light dramatic entertainment of songs,
dialogue, and dancing, connected by a slender
plot. **musical film** a film in which music is an
important feature. □ **musicality** /-ˈkælɪtɪ/ n.
musicalize v.tr. (also **-ise**). **musically** adv.
musicalness n. [ME f. OF f. med.L *musicalis* f. L
musica: see MUSIC]

musician /mjuːˈzɪʃ(ə)n/ n. a person who plays a
musical instrument, esp. professionally, or is
otherwise musically gifted. □ **musicianly** adj.
musicianship n. [ME f. OF *musicien* f. *musique*
(as MUSIC, -ICIAN)]

musicology /ˌmjuːzɪˈkɒlədʒɪ/ n. the study of
music other than that directed to proficiency in
performance or composition. □ **musicologist**
n. **musicological** /-kəˈlɒdʒɪk(ə)l/ adj. [F *music-
ologie* or MUSIC + -LOGY]

musk /mʌsk/ n. 1 a strong-smelling reddish-
brown substance produced by a gland in the
male musk deer and used as an ingredient in
perfumes. 2 the plant, *Mimulus moschatus*, with
pale-green ovate leaves and yellow flowers.
musk deer any small Asian deer of the genus
Moschus, having no antlers. **musk melon** the
common yellow or green melon, *Cucumis melo*,
usu. with a raised network of markings on the
skin. **musk ox** a large goat-antelope, *Ovibos
moschatus*, native to N. America, with a thick
shaggy coat and small curved horns. **musk-
rose** a rambling rose, *Rosa moschata*, with large
white flowers smelling of musk. □ **musky** adj.
(**muskier, muskiest**). **muskiness** n. [ME f. LL

muscus f. Pers. *mušk*, perh. f. Skr. *muṣka* scrotum (from the shape of the musk deer's gland)]

musket /ˈmʌskɪt/ *n. hist.* an infantryman's (esp. smooth-bored) light gun, often supported on the shoulder. [F *mousquet* f. It. *moschetto* crossbow bolt f. *mosca* fly]

musketeer /ˌmʌskɪˈtɪə(r)/ *n. hist.* a soldier armed with a musket.

musketry /ˈmʌskɪtrɪ/ *n.* **1** muskets, or soldiers armed with muskets, referred to collectively. **2** the knowledge of handling muskets.

muskrat /ˈmʌskræt/ *n.* **1** a large aquatic rodent, *Ondatra zibethica*, native to N. America, having a musky smell. **2** the fur of this.

Muslim /ˈmʊzlɪm, ˈmʌ-/ *n.* & *adj.* (also **Moslem** /ˈmɒzləm/) —*n.* a follower of the Islamic religion. —*adj.* of or relating to the Muslims or their religion. [Arab. *muslim*, part. of *aslama*: see ISLAM]

muslin /ˈmʌzlɪn/ *n.* **1** a fine delicately woven cotton fabric. **2** *US* a cotton cloth in plain weave. □ **muslined** *adj.* [F *mousseline* f. It. *mussolina* f. *Mussolo* Mosul in Iraq, where it was made]

musquash /ˈmʌskwɒʃ/ *n.* = MUSKRAT. [Algonquian]

muss *v.* & *n. US colloq.* —*v.tr.* (often foll. by *up*) disarrange; throw into disorder. —*n.* a state of confusion; untidiness, mess. □ **mussy** *adj.* [app. var. of MESS]

mussel /ˈmʌs(ə)l/ *n.* **1** any bivalve mollusc of the genus *Mytilus*, living in sea water and often used for food. **2** any similar freshwater mollusc of the genus *Margaritifer* or *Anodonta*, forming pearls. [ME f. OE *mus(c)le* & MLG *mussel*, ult. rel. to L *musculus* (as MUSCLE)]

must[1] *v.* & *n.* —*v.aux.* (*3rd sing. present* **must**; *past* **had** to or in indirect speech **must**) (foll. by infin., or *absol.*) **1 a** be obliged to (*you must go to school; must we leave now?; said he must go; I must away*). **b** in ironic questions (*must you slam the door?*). **2** be certain to (*we must win in the end; you must be her sister; they must have left by now; seemed as if the roof must blow off*). **3** ought to (*we must see what can be done; it must be said that*). **4** expressing insistence (*I must ask you to leave*). **5** (foll. by *not* + infin.) **a** not be permitted to, be forbidden to (*you must not smoke*). **b** ought not; need not (*you mustn't think he's angry; you must not worry*). **c** expressing insistence that something should not be done (*they must not be told*). **6** (as past or historic present) expressing the perversity of destiny (*what must I do but break my leg*). —*n. colloq.* a thing that cannot or should not be overlooked or missed (*if you go to London St Paul's is a must*). □ **I must say** often *iron.* I cannot refrain from saying (*I must say he made a good attempt; a fine way to behave, I must say*). [OE *mōste* past of *mōt* may]

■ **Usage** In sense 1a, the negative (i.e. lack of obligation) is expressed by *not have to* or *need not*; *must not* denotes positive forbidding, as in *you must not smoke.*

must[2] *n.* grape-juice before fermentation is complete. [OE f. L *mustum* neut. of *mustus* new]

must[3] *n.* mustiness, mould. [back-form. f. MUSTY]

mustache *US* var. of MOUSTACHE.

mustachio /məˈstɑːʃɪəʊ/ *n.* (*pl.* **-os**) (often in *pl.*) archaic a moustache. □ **mustachioed** *adj.* [Sp. *mostacho* & It. *mostaccio* (as MOUSTACHE)]

mustang /ˈmʌstæŋ/ *n.* a small wild horse native to Mexico and California. [Sp. *mestengo* f. *mesta* company of graziers, & Sp. *mostrenco*]

mustard /ˈmʌstəd/ *n.* **1 a** any of various plants of the genus *Brassica* with slender pods and yellow flowers, esp. *B. nigra*. **b** any of various plants of the genus *Sinapis*, esp. *S. alba*, eaten at the seedling stage, often with cress. **2** the seeds of these which are crushed, made into a paste, and used as a spicy condiment. **3** the brownish-yellow colour of this condiment. □ **mustard gas** a colourless oily liquid, whose vapour is a powerful irritant and vesicant. **mustard plaster** a poultice made with mustard. **mustard seed 1** the seed of the mustard plant. **2** a small thing capable of great development (Matt. 13:31). [ME f. OF *mo(u)starde*: orig. the condiment as prepared with MUST[2]]

muster /ˈmʌstə(r)/ *v.* & *n.* —*v.* **1** *tr.* collect (orig. soldiers) for inspection, to check numbers, etc. **2** *tr.* & *intr.* collect, gather together. **3** *tr. Austral.* round up (livestock). —*n.* **1** the assembly of persons for inspection. **2** an assembly, a collection. **3** *Austral.* a rounding up of livestock. **4** *Austral. sl.* attendance (at a meeting, etc.) (*had a good muster*). □ **muster up** collect or summon (courage, strength, etc.). **pass muster** be accepted as adequate. □ **musterer** *n.* (in sense 3 of *n.* & *v.*). [ME f. OF *mo(u)stre* ult. f. L *monstrare* show]

mustn't /ˈmʌs(ə)nt/ *contr.* must not.

musty /ˈmʌstɪ/ *adj.* (**mustier**, **mustiest**) **1** mouldy. **2** of a mouldy or stale smell or taste. □ **mustily** *adv.* **mustiness** *n.* [perh. alt. f. *moisty* (MOIST) by assoc. with MUST[2]]

mutable /ˈmjuːtəb(ə)l/ *adj. literary* **1** liable to change. **2** fickle. □ **mutability** /-ˈbɪlɪtɪ/ *n.* [L *mutabilis* f. *mutare* change]

mutant /ˈmjuːt(ə)nt/ *adj.* & *n.* —*adj.* resulting from mutation. —*n.* a mutant form. [L *mutant-* part. f. *mutare* change]

mutate /mjuːˈteɪt/ *v.intr.* & *tr.* undergo or cause to undergo mutation. [back-form. f. MUTATION]

mutation /mjuːˈteɪʃ(ə)n/ *n.* **1** the process or an instance of change or alteration. **2** a genetic change which, when transmitted to offspring, gives rise to heritable variations. **3** a mutant. □ **mutational** *adj.* **mutationally** *adv.* [ME f. L *mutatio* f. *mutare* change]

mutatis mutandis /muːˌtɑːtɪs muːˈtændɪs, mjuː-, -iːs/ *adv.* (in comparing cases) making the necessary alterations. [L]

mute *adj., n.,* & *v.* —*adj.* **1** silent, refraining from or temporarily bereft of speech. **2** not emitting articulate sound. **3** (of a person or animal) dumb. **4** not expressed in speech (*mute protest*). **5** (of a letter) not pronounced. —*n.* **1** a dumb person (*a deaf mute*). **2** *Mus.* **a** a clamp for damping the resonance of the strings of a violin etc. **b** a pad or cone for damping the sound of a wind instrument. **3** an unsounded consonant. **4** an actor whose part is in a dumb show. —*v.tr.* **1** deaden, muffle, or soften the sound of (a thing, esp. a musical instrument). **2 a** tone down, make less intense. **b** (as **muted** *adj.*) (of colours etc.) subdued (*a muted green*). □ **mute button** a device on a telephone etc. to temporarily prevent the caller from hearing what is being said at the receiver's end. **mute swan** the common white swan. □ **mutely** *adv.* **muteness** *n.* [ME f. OF *muet*, dimin. of *mu* f. L *mutus*, assim. to L]

mutilate /ˈmjuːtɪˌleɪt/ v.tr. **1 a** deprive (a person or animal) of a limb or organ. **b** destroy the use of (a limb or organ). **2** render (a book etc.) imperfect by excision or some act of destruction. □ **mutilation** /-ˈleɪʃ(ə)n/ n. **mutilative** /-ˈlətɪv/ adj. **mutilator** n. [L mutilare f. mutilus maimed]

mutineer /ˌmjuːtɪˈnɪə(r)/ n. a person who mutinies. [F mutinier f. mutin rebellious f. muete movement ult. f. L movēre move]

mutinous /ˈmjuːtɪnəs/ adj. rebellious; tending to mutiny. □ **mutinously** adv. [obs. mutine rebellion f. F mutin: see MUTINEER]

mutiny /ˈmjuːtɪnɪ/ n. & v. —n. (pl. **-ies**) an open revolt against constituted authority, esp. by soldiers or sailors against their officers. —v.intr. (**-ies, -ied**) (often foll. by against) revolt; engage in mutiny. [obs. mutine (as MUTINOUS)]

mutt n. **1** sl. an ignorant, stupid, or blundering person. **2** derog. a dog. [abbr. of mutton-head]

mutter /ˈmʌtə(r)/ v. & n. —v. **1** intr. speak low in a barely audible manner. **2** intr. (often foll. by against, at) murmur or grumble about. **3** tr. utter (words etc.) in a low tone. **4** tr. say in secret. —n. **1** muttered words or sounds. **2** muttering. □ **mutterer** n. **mutteringly** adv. [ME, rel. to MUTE]

mutton /ˈmʌt(ə)n/ n. **1** the flesh of sheep used for food. **2** joc. a sheep. □ **mutton dressed as lamb** colloq. a usu. middle-aged or elderly woman dressed or made up to appear younger. □ **muttony** adj. [ME f. OF moton f. med.L multo -onis prob. f. Gaulish]

mutual /ˈmjuːtʃʊəl, -tjʊəl/ adj. **1** (of feelings, actions, etc.) experienced or done by each of two or more parties with reference to the other or others (mutual affection). **2** colloq. disp. common to two or more persons (a mutual friend; a mutual interest). **3** standing in (a specified) relation to each other (mutual well-wishers; mutual beneficiaries). □ **mutual fund** US a unit trust. **mutual insurance** insurance in which some or all of the profits are divided among the policyholders. □ **mutuality** /-ˈælɪtɪ/ n. **mutually** adv. [ME f. OF mutuel f. L mutuus mutual, borrowed, rel. to mutare change]

■ **Usage** The use of this word in sense 2, although often found, is considered incorrect by some people, for whom common is preferable.

muu-muu /ˈmuːmuː/ n. a woman's loose brightly-coloured dress. [Hawaiian]

Muzak /ˈmjuːzæk/ n. **1** propr. a system of music transmission for playing in public places. **2** (**muzak**) recorded light background music. [alt. f. MUSIC]

muzzle /ˈmʌz(ə)l/ n. & v. —n. **1** the projecting part of an animal's face, including the nose and mouth. **2** a guard, usu. made of straps or wire, fitted over an animal's nose and mouth to stop it biting or feeding. **3** the open end of a firearm. —v.tr. **1** put a muzzle on (an animal etc.). **2** impose silence upon. □ **muzzle-loader** a gun that is loaded through the muzzle. **muzzle velocity** the velocity with which a projectile leaves the muzzle of a gun. □ **muzzler** n. [ME f. OF musel ult. f. med.L musum: cf. MUSE²]

muzzy /ˈmʌzɪ/ adj. (**muzzier, muzziest**) **1 a** mentally hazy; dull, spiritless. **b** stupid from drinking alcohol. **2** blurred, indistinct. □ **muzzily** adv. **muzziness** n. [18th c.: orig. unkn.]

MW abbr. **1** megawatt(s). **2** medium wave.

my /maɪ/ poss.pron. (attrib.) **1** of or belonging to me or myself (my house; my own business). **2** as a form of address in affectionate, sympathetic, jocular, or patronizing contexts (my dear boy). **3** in various expressions of surprise (my God!; oh my!). [ME mī, reduced f. mīn MINE¹]

myalgia /maɪˈældʒə/ n. a pain in a muscle or group of muscles. □ **myalgic** adj. [mod.L f. Gk mus muscle]

myasthenia /ˌmaɪəsˈθiːnɪə/ n. a condition causing abnormal weakness of certain muscles. [mod.L f. Gk mus muscle + astheneia f. asthenēs weak]

mycelium /maɪˈsiːlɪəm/ n. (pl. **mycelia** /-lɪə/) the vegetative part of a fungus. □ **mycelial** adj. [mod.L f. Gk mukēs mushroom, after EPITHELIUM]

Mycenaean /ˌmaɪsɪˈniːən/ adj. & n. —adj. Archaeol. of or relating to the late Bronze Age civilization in Greece (c.1500–1100 BC). —n. an inhabitant of Mycenae or the Mycenaean world. [L Mycenaeus]

mycology /maɪˈkɒlədʒɪ/ n. **1** the study of fungi. **2** the fungi of a particular region. □ **mycological** /-kəˈlɒdʒɪk(ə)l/ adj. **mycologically** /-kəˈlɒdʒɪkəlɪ/ adv. **mycologist** n. [Gk mukēs mushroom + -LOGY]

myelin /ˈmaɪɪlɪn/ n. a white substance which forms a sheath around certain nerve-fibres. □ **myelination** /-ˈneɪʃ(ə)n/ n. [Gk muelos marrow + -IN]

myelitis /maɪɪˈlaɪtɪs/ n. inflammation of the spinal cord. [mod.L f. Gk muelos marrow]

myeloid /ˈmaɪɪˌlɔɪd/ adj. of or relating to bone marrow or the spinal cord. [Gk muelos marrow]

myeloma /ˌmaɪɪˈləʊmə/ n. (pl. **myelomas** or **myelomata** /-mətə/) a malignant tumour of the bone marrow. [mod.L, as MYELITIS + -OMA]

mylodon /ˈmaɪlədɒn/ n. an extinct gigantic ground sloth of the genus Mylodon, with cylindrical teeth and found in deposits formed during the ice age of the Pleistocene epoch in South America. [mod.L f. Gk mulē mill, molar + odous odontos tooth]

myna /ˈmaɪnə/ n. (also **mynah**, **mina**) any of various SE Asian starlings, esp. Gracula religiosa able to mimic the human voice. [Hindi mainā]

myope /ˈmaɪəʊp/ n. a short-sighted person. [F f. LL myops f. Gk muōps f. muō shut + ōps eye]

myopia /maɪˈəʊpɪə/ n. **1** short-sightedness. **2** lack of imagination or intellectual insight. □ **myopic** /-ˈɒpɪk/ adj. **myopically** /-ˈɒpɪkəlɪ/ adv. [mod.L (as MYOPE)]

myosotis /ˌmaɪəˈsəʊtɪs/ n. (also **myosote** /ˈmaɪəˌsəʊt/) any plant of the genus Myosotis with blue, pink, or white flowers, esp. a forget-me-not. [L f. Gk muosōtis f. mus muos mouse + ous ōtos ear]

myriad /ˈmɪrɪəd/ n. & adj. literary —n. **1** an indefinitely great number. **2** ten thousand. —adj. of an indefinitely great number. [LL mirias miriad- f. Gk murias -ados f. murioi 10,000]

myriapod /ˈmɪrɪəˌpɒd/ n. & adj. —n. any land-living arthropod of the group Myriapoda, with numerous leg-bearing segments, e.g. centipedes and millipedes. —adj. of or relating to this group. [mod.L Myriapoda (as MYRIAD, Gk pous podos foot)]

myrmidon /ˈmɜːmɪd(ə)n/ n. **1** a hired ruffian. **2** a base servant. [L Myrmidones (pl.) f. Gk Murmidones, warlike Thessalian people who went with Achilles to Troy]

myrrh /mɜ:(r)/ n. a gum resin from several trees of the genus *Commiphora* used, esp. in the Near East, in perfumery, medicine, incense, etc. □ **myrrhic** *adj.* **myrrhy** *adj.* [OE *myrra, myrre* f. L *myrr(h)a* f. Gk *murra*, of Semitic orig.]

myrtle /ˈmɜ:t(ə)l/ n. 1 an evergreen shrub of the genus *Myrtus* with aromatic foliage and white flowers, esp. M. *communis*, bearing purple-black ovoid berries. 2 US = PERIWINKLE[1]. [ME f. med.L *myrtilla, -us* dimin. of L *myrta, myrtus* f. Gk *murtos*]

myself /maɪˈself/ pron. 1 *emphat. form* of I[2] or ME[1] (*I saw it myself; I like to do it myself*). 2 *refl. form* of ME[1] (*I was angry with myself; able to dress myself; as bad as myself*). 3 in my normal state of body and mind (*I'm not myself today*). □ **by myself** see *by oneself*. **I myself** I for my part (*I myself am doubtful*). [ME[1] + SELF: my- partly after *herself* with *her* regarded as poss. pron.]

mysterious /mɪˈstɪərɪəs/ *adj.* 1 full of or wrapped in mystery. 2 (of a person) delighting in mystery. □ **mysteriously** *adv.* **mysteriousness** n. [F *mystérieux* f. *mystère* f. OF (as MYSTERY)]

mystery /ˈmɪstərɪ/ n. (pl. **-ies**) 1 a secret, hidden, or inexplicable matter (*the reason remains a mystery*). 2 secrecy or obscurity (*wrapped in mystery*). 3 (*attrib.*) secret, undisclosed (*mystery guest*). 4 the practice of making a secret of (esp. unimportant) things (*engaged in mystery and intrigue*). 5 (in full **mystery story**) a fictional work dealing with a puzzling event, esp. a crime (*a well-known mystery writer*). 6 a religious truth divinely revealed, esp. one beyond human reason. 7 (in *pl.*) the secret religious rites of the ancient Greeks, Romans, etc. **mystery play** a miracle play. **mystery tour** (or **trip**) a pleasure excursion to an unspecified destination. [ME f. OF *mistere* or L *mysterium* f. Gk *mustērion*, rel. to MYSTIC]

mystic /ˈmɪstɪk/ n. & *adj.* —n. a person who seeks by contemplation and self-surrender to obtain unity or identity with or absorption into the Deity or the ultimate reality, or who believes in the spiritual apprehension of truths that are beyond the understanding. —*adj.* 1 mysterious and awe-inspiring. 2 spiritually allegorical or symbolic. 3 occult, esoteric. 4 of hidden meaning. □ **mysticism** /-ˌsɪz(ə)m/ n. [ME f. OF *mystique* or L *mysticus* f. Gk *mustikos* f. *mustēs* initiated person f. *muō* close the eyes or lips, initiate]

mystical /ˈmɪstɪk(ə)l/ *adj.* of mystics or mysticism. □ **mystically** *adv.*

mystify /ˈmɪstɪˌfaɪ/ *v.tr.* (**-ies, -ied**) 1 bewilder, confuse. 2 wrap up in mystery. □ **mystification** /-fɪˈkeɪʃ(ə)n/ n. [F *mystifier* (irreg. formed as MYSTIC or MYSTERY)]

mystique /mɪˈstiːk/ n. 1 an atmosphere of mystery and veneration attending some activity or person. 2 any skill or technique impressive or mystifying to the layman. [F f. OF (as MYSTIC)]

myth /mɪθ/ n. 1 a traditional narrative usu. involving supernatural or imaginary persons and embodying popular ideas on natural or social phenomena etc. 2 such narratives collectively. 3 a widely held but false notion. 4 a fictitious person, thing, or idea. □ **mythic** *adj.* **mythical** *adj.* **mythically** *adv.* [mod.L *mythus* f. LL *mythos* f. Gk *muthos*]

mythicize /ˈmɪθɪˌsaɪz/ *v.tr.* (also **-ise**) treat (a story etc.) as a myth; interpret mythically. □ **mythicism** /-ˌsɪz(ə)m/ n. **mythicist** /-sɪst/ n.

mytho- /ˈmɪθəʊ/ *comb. form* myth.

mythology /mɪˈθɒlədʒɪ/ n. (pl. **-ies**) 1 a body of myths (*Greek mythology*). 2 the study of myths. □ **mythologer** n. **mythologic** /-θəˈlɒdʒɪk/ *adj.* **mythological** /-θəˈlɒdʒɪk(ə)l/ *adj.* **mythologically** /-θəˈlɒdʒɪkəlɪ/ *adv.* **mythologist** n. **mythologize** *v.tr.* & *intr.* (also **-ise**). **mythologizer** n. [ME f. F *mythologie* or LL *mythologia* f. Gk *muthologia* (as MYTHO-, -LOGY)]

myxomatosis /ˌmɪksəməˈtəʊsɪs/ n. an infectious usu. fatal viral disease in rabbits, causing swelling of the mucous membranes. [mod. L f. Gk *muxa* mucus + -OMA + -OSIS]

Nn

N¹ /en/ n. (also **n**) (pl. **Ns** or **N's**) **1** the fourteenth letter of the alphabet. **2** *Math.* an indefinite number. □ **to the nth** (or **nth degree**) **1** *Math.* to any required power. **2** to any extent; to the utmost.

N² abbr. (also **N.**) North; Northern.

N³ symb. Chem. the element nitrogen.

n abbr. (also **n.**) **1** name. **2** nano-. **3** neuter. **4** noun.

'n conj. (also **'n'**) colloq. and. [abbr.]

-n¹ suffix see -EN².

-n² suffix see -EN³.

Na symb. Chem. the element sodium.

na /nə/ adv. Sc. (in comb.; usu. with an auxiliary verb) = NOT (*I canna do it; they didna go*).

n/a abbr. **1** not applicable. **2** not available.

NAAFI /ˈnæfɪ/ abbr. Brit. **1** Navy, Army, and Air Force Institutes. **2** a canteen for servicemen run by the NAAFI.

nab v.tr. (**nabbed, nabbing**) sl. **1** arrest; catch in wrongdoing. **2** seize, grab. [17th c., also *napp*, as in KIDNAP: orig. unkn.]

nabob /ˈneɪbɒb/ n. **1** hist. a Muslim official or governor under the Mughal empire. **2** (formerly) a conspicuously wealthy person, esp. one returned from India with a fortune. [Port. *nababo* or Sp. *nabab*, f. Urdu (as NAWAB)]

nacho /ˈnætʃəʊ/ n. (pl. **-os**) (usu. in pl.) a tortilla chip, usu. topped with melted cheese and spices etc. [20th c.: orig. uncert.]

nacre /ˈneɪkə(r)/ n. mother-of-pearl from any shelled mollusc. □ **nacred** adj. **nacreous** /ˈneɪkrɪəs/ adj. **nacrous** /-krəs/ adj. [F]

nadir /ˈneɪdɪə(r), ˈnæd-/ n. **1** the part of the celestial sphere directly below an observer. **2** the lowest point in one's fortunes; a time of deep despair. [ME f. OF f. Arab. *naẓīr* (*as-samt*) opposite (to the zenith)]

naevus /ˈniːvəs/ n. (US **nevus**) (pl. **naevi** /-vaɪ/) **1** a birthmark in the form of a raised red patch on the skin. **2** = MOLE². □ **naevoid** adj. [L]

naff¹ v.intr. sl. **1** (in imper., foll. by off) go away. **2** (as **naffing** adj.) used as an intensive to express annoyance etc. [prob. euphem. for FUCK]

naff² adj. sl. **1** unfashionable; socially awkward. **2** worthless, rubbishy. [20th c.: orig. unkn.]

nag¹ v. & n. —v. (**nagged, nagging**) **1 a** tr. annoy or irritate (a person) with persistent fault-finding or continuous urging. **b** intr. (often foll. by at) find fault, complain, or urge, esp. persistently. **2** intr. (of a pain) ache dully but persistently. **3 a** tr. worry or preoccupy (a person, the mind, etc.) (*his mistake nagged him*). **b** intr. (often foll. by at) worry or gnaw. —n. a persistently nagging person. □ **nagger** n. **naggingly** adv. [of dial., perh. Scand. or LG, orig.: cf. Norw. *nage*, Sw. *nagga* gnaw, irritate, LG (g)*naggen* provoke]

nag² n. **1** colloq. a horse. **2** a small riding-horse or pony. [ME: orig. unkn.]

naiad /ˈnaɪæd/ n. (pl. **naiads** or **-des** /-əˌdiːz/) *Mythol.* a water-nymph. [L *Naïas Naïad-* f. Gk *Naïas -ados* f. *naō* flow]

nail n. & v. —n. **1** a small usu. sharpened metal spike with a broadened flat head, driven in with a hammer to join things together or to serve as a peg, protection, or decoration. **2 a** a horny covering on the upper surface of the tip of the human finger or toe. **b** a claw or talon. —v.tr. **1** fasten with a nail or nails (*nailed it to the beam; nailed the planks together*). **2** fix or keep (a person, attention, etc.) fixed. **3 a** secure, catch, or get hold of (a person or thing). **b** expose or discover (a lie or a liar). □ **nail one's colours to the mast** persist; refuse to give in. **nail down 1** bind (a person) to a promise etc. **2** define precisely. **3** fasten (a thing) with nails. **nail enamel** US = nail polish. **nail-file** a roughened metal or emery strip used for smoothing the nails. **nail in a person's coffin** something thought to increase the risk of death. **nail polish** a varnish applied to the nails to colour them or make them shiny. **nail-punch** (or **-set**) a tool for sinking the head of a nail below a surface. **nail up 1** close (a door etc.) with nails. **2** fix (a thing) at a height with nails. **nail varnish** Brit. = nail polish. **on the nail** (esp. of payment) without delay (*cash on the nail*). □ **nailed** adj. (also in comb.). **nailless** adj. [OE *nægel, næglan* f. Gmc]

nainsook /ˈneɪnsʊk/ n. a fine soft cotton fabric, orig. Indian. [Hindi *nainsukh* f. *nain* eye + *sukh* pleasure]

naïve /nɑːˈiːv, naɪˈiːv/ adj. (also **naive**) **1** artless; innocent; unaffected. **2** foolishly credulous; simple. □ **naïvely** adv. **naïveness** n. [F, fem. of *naif* f. L *nativus* NATIVE]

naïvety /nɑːˈiːvtɪ, naɪ-/ n. (also **naivety, naïveté** /nɑːˈiːvteɪ/) (pl. **-ies** or **naïvetés**) **1** the state or quality of being naïve. **2** a naïve action. [F *naïveté* (as NAÏVE)]

naked /ˈneɪkɪd/ adj. **1** without clothes; nude. **2** plain; undisguised; exposed (*the naked truth; his naked soul*). **3** (of a light, flame, etc.) unprotected from the wind etc.; unshaded. **4** defenceless. **5** without addition, comment, support, evidence, etc. (*his naked word; naked assertion*). **6 a** (of landscape) barren; treeless. **b** (of rock) exposed; without soil etc. **7** (of a sword etc.) unsheathed. **8** (usu. foll. by of) devoid; without. **9** without leaves, hairs, scales, shell, etc. □ **the naked eye** unassisted vision, e.g. without a telescope, microscope, etc. □ **nakedly** adv. **nakedness** n. [OE *nacod* f. Gmc]

namby-pamby /ˌnæmbɪˈpæmbɪ/ adj. & n. —adj. **1** lacking vigour or drive; weak. **2** insipidly pretty or sentimental. —n. (pl. **-ies**) a namby-pamby person. [fanciful formulation on name of *Ambrose Philips*, Engl. pastoral writer d. 1749]

name n. & v. —n. **1 a** the word by which an individual person, animal, place, or thing is known, spoken of, etc. (*mentioned him by name*; *her name is Joanna*). **b** all who go under one name; a family, clan, or people in terms of its name (*the Scottish name*). **2 a** a usu. abusive term used of a person etc. (*called him names*). **b** a word denoting an object or esp. a class of objects, ideas, etc. (*what is the name of that kind of vase?*). **3** a famous person (*many great names were there*). **4** a reputation, esp. a good one (*has a name for honesty*). —*v.tr.* **1** give a usu. specified name to (*named the dog Spot*). **2** call (a person or thing) by the right name (*named the man in the photograph*). **3** mention; specify; cite (*named his requirements*). **4** nominate; appoint, etc. (*was named the new chairman*). **5** specify as something desired (*named it as her dearest wish*). □ **by name** called (*Tom by name*). **have to one's name** possess. **in all but name** virtually. **in name** (or **name only**) as a mere formality; hardly at all (*is the leader in name only*). **in a person's name** = *in the name of*. **in the name of** calling to witness; invoking (*in the name of goodness*). **in one's own name** independently; without authority. **make a name for oneself** become famous. **name after** (US **for**) call (a person) by the name of (a specified person) (*named him after his uncle Roger*). **name-calling** abusive language. **name the day** arrange a date (esp. of a woman fixing the date for her wedding). **name-drop** (**-dropped**, **-dropping**) indulge in name-dropping. **name-dropping** the familiar mention of famous people as a form of boasting. **name names** mention specific names, esp. in accusation. **name of the game** *colloq.* the purpose or essence of an action etc. **name-part** the title role in a play etc. **name-plate** a plate or panel bearing the name of an occupant of a room etc. **name-tape** a tape fixed to a garment etc. and bearing the name of the owner. **of** (or **by**) **the name of** called. **put one's name down for 1** apply for. **2** promise to subscribe (a sum). **you name it** *colloq.* no matter what; whatever you like. □ **nameable** *adj.* [OE *nama, noma*, (*ge*)*namian* f. Gmc, rel. to L *nomen*, Gk *onoma*]

nameless /ˈneɪmlɪs/ *adj.* **1** having no name or name-inscription. **2** inexpressible; indefinable (*a nameless sensation*). **3** unnamed; anonymous, esp. deliberately (*our informant, who shall be nameless*). **4** too loathsome or horrific to be named (*nameless vices*). **5** obscure; inglorious. □ **namelessly** *adv.* **namelessness** *n.*

namely /ˈneɪmlɪ/ *adv.* that is to say; in other words.

namesake /ˈneɪmseɪk/ *n.* a person or thing having the same name as another (*was her aunt's namesake*). [prob. f. phr. *for the name's sake*]

nan *n.* (also **nana, nanna** /ˈnænə/) *Brit. colloq.* grandmother. [childish pronunc.]

nana /ˈnɑːnə/ *n. sl.* a silly person; a fool. [perh. f. BANANA]

nancy /ˈnænsɪ/ *n. & adj.* (also **nance** /næns/) *sl.* —*n.* (*pl.* **-ies**) (in full **nancy boy**) an effeminate man, esp. a homosexual. —*adj.* effeminate. [pet-form of the name *Ann*]

nankeen /næŋˈkiːn, næn-/ *n.* **1** a yellowish cotton cloth. **2** a yellowish buff colour. [*Nankin*(g) in China, where orig. made]

nanny /ˈnænɪ/ *n. & v.* —*n.* (*pl.* **-ies**) **1 a** a child's nurse. **b** an unduly protective person, institution, etc. (*the nanny State*). **2** = NAN. **3** (in full **nanny-goat**) a female goat. —*v.tr.* (**-ies**,

-ied) be unduly protective towards. [formed as NANCY]

nano- /ˈnænəʊ, ˈneɪnəʊ/ *comb. form* denoting a factor of 10^{-9} (*nanosecond*). [L f. Gk *nanos* dwarf]

nanometre /ˈnænəʊˌmiːt(ə)r/ *n.* one thousand-millionth of a metre.

nanosecond /ˈnænəʊˌsekənd/ *n.* one thousand-millionth of a second.

nap[1] *v. & n.* —*v.intr.* (**napped, napping**) sleep lightly or briefly. —*n.* a short sleep or doze, esp. by day (*took a nap*). □ **catch a person napping 1** find a person asleep or off guard. **2** detect in negligence or error. [OE *hnappian*, rel. to OHG (h)*naffezan* to slumber]

nap[2] *n.* **1** the raised pile on textiles, esp. velvet. **2** a soft downy surface. □ **napless** *adj.* [ME *noppe* f. MDu., MLG *noppe* nap, *noppen* trim nap from]

nap[3] *n. & v.* —*n.* **1** a form of whist in which players declare the number of tricks they expect to take, up to five. **2 a** the betting of all one's money on one horse etc. **b** a tipster's choice for this. —*v.tr.* (**napped, napping**) name (a horse etc.) as a probable winner. □ **go nap** risk everything in one attempt. [abbr. of *Napoléon*, name of Fr. emperors and orig. name of game]

napalm /ˈneɪpɑːm/ *n. & v.* —*n.* **1** a thickening agent produced from naphthalene. **2** a jellied petrol made from this, used in incendiary bombs. —*v.tr.* attack with napalm bombs. [NAPHTHA + *palmitic acid* in coconut oil]

nape *n.* the back of the neck. [ME: orig. unkn.]

napery /ˈneɪpərɪ/ *n. Sc.* or *archaic* household linen, esp. table linen. [ME f. OF *naperie* f. *nape* (as NAPKIN)]

naphtha /ˈnæfθə/ *n.* an inflammable oil obtained by the distillation of organic substances such as coal, shale, or petroleum. [L f. Gk, = inflammable volatile liquid issuing from the earth, of Oriental origin]

naphthalene /ˈnæfθəˌliːn/ *n.* a white crystalline aromatic substance produced by the distillation of coal tar and used in mothballs and the manufacture of dyes etc. □ **naphthalic** /-ˈθælɪk/ *adj.* [NAPHTHA + -ENE]

napkin /ˈnæpkɪn/ *n.* **1** (in full **table napkin**) a square piece of linen, paper, etc. used for wiping the lips, fingers, etc. at meals; a serviette. **2** *Brit.* a baby's nappy. **3** a small towel. □ **napkin-ring** a ring used to hold (and distinguish) a person's table napkin when not in use. [ME f. OF *nappe* f. L *mappa* (MAP)]

Napoleonic /nəˌpəʊlɪˈɒnɪk/ *adj.* of, relating to, or characteristic of Napoleon I or his time.

nappy /ˈnæpɪ/ *n.* (*pl.* **-ies**) *Brit.* a piece of towelling or other absorbent material wrapped round a baby to absorb or retain urine and faeces. □ **nappy rash** inflammation of a baby's skin, caused by prolonged contact with a damp nappy. [abbr. of NAPKIN]

narcissism /ˈnɑːsɪˌsɪz(ə)m, nɑːˈsɪs-/ *n. Psychol.* excessive or erotic interest in oneself, one's physical features, etc. □ **narcissist** *n.* **narcissistic** /-ˈsɪstɪk/ *adj.* **narcissistically** /-ˈsɪstɪkəlɪ/ *adv.* [*Narcissus* (Gk *Narkissos*), youth who fell in love with his reflection in water]

narcissus /nɑːˈsɪsəs/ *n.* (*pl.* **narcissi** /-saɪ/ or **narcissuses**) any bulbous plant of the genus *Narcissus*, esp. *N. poeticus* bearing a heavily scented single flower with an undivided corona edged with crimson and yellow. [L f. Gk *narkissos*, perh. f. *narkē* numbness, with ref. to its narcotic effects)

narcolepsy /ˈnɑːkəˌlepsɪ/ *n. Med.* a disease with fits of sleepiness and drowsiness. □ **narcoleptic** /-ˈleptɪk/ *adj.* & *n.* [Gk *narkoō* make numb, after EPILEPSY]

narcosis /nɑːˈkəʊsɪs/ *n.* **1** *Med.* the working or effects of soporific narcotics. **2** a state of insensibility. [Gk *narkōsis* f. *narkoō* make numb]

narcoterrorism /ˌnɑːkəʊˈterərɪz(ə)m/ *n.* violent crime associated with illicit drugs. □ **narcoterrorist** *adj.* & *n.* [NARCOTIC + TERRORISM]

narcotic /nɑːˈkɒtɪk/ *adj.* & *n.* —*adj.* **1** (of a substance) inducing drowsiness, sleep, stupor, or insensibility. **2** (of a drug) affecting the mind. **3** of or involving narcosis. **4** soporific. —*n.* a narcotic substance, drug, or influence. □ **narcotically** *adv.* **narcotism** /ˈnɑːkəˌtɪz(ə)m/ *n.* **narcotize** /ˈnɑːkəˌtaɪz/ *v.tr.* (also **-ise**). **narcotization** /ˌnɑːkətaɪˈzeɪʃ(ə)n/ *n.* [ME f. OF *narcotique* or med.L f. Gk *narkōtikos* (as NARCOSIS)]

nard *n.* **1** any of various plants yielding an aromatic balsam used by the ancients. **2** = SPIKENARD. [ME f. L *nardus* f. Gk *nardos* f. Semitic word]

nark *n.* & *v. Brit. sl.* —*n.* **1** a police informer or decoy. **2** *Austral.* an annoying person or thing. —*v.tr.* (usu. in *passive*) annoy; infuriate (*was narked by their attitude*). [Romany *nāk* nose]

narky /ˈnɑːkɪ/ *adj.* (**narkier**, **narkiest**) *sl.* bad-tempered, irritable. [NARK]

narrate /nəˈreɪt/ *v.tr.* (also *absol.*) **1** give a continuous story or account of. **2** provide a spoken commentary or accompaniment for (a film etc.). □ **narratable** *adj.* **narration** /nəˈreɪʃ(ə)n/ *n.* [L *narrare narrat-*]

narrative /ˈnærətɪv/ *n.* & *adj.* —*n.* **1** a spoken or written account of connected events in order of happening. **2** the practice or art of narration. —*adj.* in the form of, or concerned with, narration (*narrative verse*). □ **narratively** *adv.* [F *narratif -ive* f. LL *narrativus* (as NARRATE)]

narrator /nəˈreɪtə(r)/ *n.* **1** an actor, announcer, etc. who delivers a commentary in a film, broadcast, etc. **2** a person who narrates. [L (as NARRATE)]

narrow /ˈnærəʊ/ *adj.*, *n.*, & *v.* —*adj.* (**narrower**, **narrowest**) **1 a** of small width in proportion to length; lacking breadth. **b** confined or confining; constricted (*within narrow bounds*). **2** of limited scope; restricted (*in the narrowest sense*). **3** with little margin (*a narrow escape*). **4** searching; precise; exact (*a narrow examination*). **5** = NARROW-MINDED. —*n.* **1** (usu. in *pl.*) the narrow part of a strait, river, sound, etc. **2** a narrow pass or street. —*v.* **1** *intr.* become narrow; diminish; contract; lessen. **2** *tr.* make narrow; constrict; restrict. □ **narrow boat** *Brit.* a canal boat, esp. one less than 7 ft. (2.1 metres) wide. **narrow gauge** a railway track that has a smaller gauge than the standard one. **narrow squeak 1** a narrow escape. **2** a success barely attained. □ **narrowish** *adj.* **narrowly** *adv.* **narrowness** *n.* [OE *nearu nearw-* f. Gmc]

narrow-minded /ˌnærəʊˈmaɪndɪd/ *adj.* rigid or restricted in one's views, intolerant, prejudiced, illiberal. □ **narrow-mindedly** *adv.* **narrow-mindedness** *n.*

narwhal /ˈnɑːw(ə)l/ *n.* an Arctic white whale, *Monodon monoceros*, the male of which has a long straight tusk developed from one of its teeth.

[Du. *narwal* f. Da. *narhval* f. *hval* whale: cf. ON *náhvalr* (perh. f. *nár* corpse, with ref. to its skin-colour)]

nary /ˈneərɪ/ *adj. colloq.* or *dial.* not a; no (*nary a one*). [f. *ne'er a*]

NASA /ˈnæsə/ *abbr.* (in the US) National Aeronautics and Space Administration.

nasal /ˈneɪz(ə)l/ *adj.* & *n.* —*adj.* **1** of, for, or relating to the nose. **2** *Phonet.* (of a letter or a sound) pronounced with the breath passing through the nose, e.g. *m*, *n*, *ng*, or French *en*, *un*, etc. **3** (of the voice or speech) having an intonation caused by breathing through the nose. —*n. Phonet.* a nasal letter or sound. □ **nasality** /-ˈzælɪtɪ/ *n.* **nasalize** *v.intr.* & *tr.* (also **-ise**). **nasalization** /-ˈzeɪʃ(ə)n/ *n.* **nasally** *adv.* [F *nasal* or med.L *nasalis* f. L *nasus* nose]

nascent /ˈnæs(ə)nt, ˈneɪs-/ *adj.* **1** in the act of being born. **2** just beginning to be; not yet mature. □ **nascency** /ˈnæsənsɪ/ *n.* [L *nasci nascent-* be born]

naso- /ˈneɪzəʊ/ *comb. form* nose. [L *nasus* nose]

nasturtium /nəˈstɜːʃəm/ *n.* **1** (in general use) a trailing plant, *Tropaeolum majus*, with rounded edible leaves and bright orange, yellow, or red flowers. **2** any cruciferous plant of the genus *Nasturtium*, including watercress. [L]

nasty /ˈnɑːstɪ/ *adj.* & *n.* —*adj.* (**nastier**, **nastiest**) **1 a** highly unpleasant (*a nasty experience*). **b** annoying; objectionable (*the car has a nasty habit of breaking down*). **2** difficult to negotiate; dangerous, serious (*a nasty fence*; *a nasty question*; *a nasty illness*). **3** (of a person or animal) ill-natured, ill-tempered, spiteful; violent, offensive (*nasty to his mother*; *turns nasty when he's drunk*). **4** (of the weather) foul, wet, stormy. —*n.* (*pl.* **-ies**) *colloq.* a horror film, esp. one on video and depicting cruelty or killing. □ **a nasty bit** (or **piece**) **of work** *colloq.* an unpleasant or contemptible person. □ **nastily** *adv.* **nastiness** *n.* [ME: orig. unkn.]

Nat. *abbr.* **1** National. **2** Nationalist. **3** Natural.

natal /ˈneɪt(ə)l/ *adj.* of or from one's birth. [ME f. L *natalis* (as NATION)]

natch /nætʃ/ *adv. colloq.* = NATURALLY. [abbr.]

nates /ˈneɪtiːz/ *n.pl. Anat.* the buttocks. [L]

nation /ˈneɪʃ(ə)n/ *n.* **1** a community of people of mainly common descent, history, language, etc., forming a State or inhabiting a territory. **2** a tribe or confederation of tribes of N. American Indians. □ **law of nations** *Law* international law. □ **nationhood** *n.* [ME f. OF f. L *natio -onis* f. *nasci nat-* be born]

national /ˈnæʃən(ə)l/ *adj.* & *n.* —*adj.* **1** of or common to a nation or the nation. **2** peculiar to or characteristic of a particular nation. —*n.* **1** a citizen of a specified country, usu. entitled to hold that country's passport (*French nationals*). **2** a fellow countryman. **3** (**the National**) = *Grand National.* □ **national anthem** a song adopted by a nation, expressive of its identity etc. and intended to inspire patriotism. **national bank** *US* a bank chartered under the federal government. **national curriculum** *Education* a government-controlled common programme of study for pupils in the state schools of England and Wales. **national debt** the money owed by a State because of loans to it. **national football** *Austral.* Australian Rules football. **National Front** a UK political party with extreme reactionary views on immigration etc. **national**

grid *Brit.* **1** the network of high-voltage electric power lines between major power stations. **2** the metric system of geographical coordinates used in maps of the British Isles. **National Guard** (in the US) the primary reserve force partly maintained by the States but available for federal use. **National Health** (or **Health Service**) (in the UK) a system of national medical care paid for mainly by taxation and started in 1948. **National Insurance** (in the UK) the system of compulsory payments by employed persons (supplemented by employers) to provide State assistance in sickness, unemployment, retirement, etc. **national park** an area of natural beauty protected by the State for the use of the general public. **national service** *Brit. hist.* service in the army etc. under conscription. **National Socialism** *hist.* the doctrines of nationalism, racial purity, etc., adopted by the Nazis. **National Trust** (in the UK, Australia, etc.) an organization for maintaining and preserving historic buildings etc. □ **nationally** *adv.* [F (as NATION)]

nationalism /ˈnæʃənəˌlɪz(ə)m/ *n.* **1 a** patriotic feeling, principles, etc. **b** an extreme form of this; chauvinism. **2** a policy of national independence. □ **nationalist** *n.* & *adj.* **nationalistic** /-ˈlɪstɪk/ *adj.* **nationalistically** /-ˈlɪstɪkəlɪ/ *adv.*

nationality /ˌnæʃəˈnælɪtɪ/ *n.* (*pl.* **-ies**) **1 a** the status of belonging to a particular nation (*what is your nationality?*; *has British nationality*). **b** a nation (*people of all nationalities*). **2** the condition of being national; distinctive national qualities. **3** an ethnic group forming a part of one or more political nations. **4** existence as a nation; nationhood. **5** patriotic sentiment.

nationalize /ˈnæʃənəˌlaɪz/ *v.tr.* (also **-ise**) **1** take over (industry, land, etc.) from private ownership on behalf of the State. **2 a** make national. **b** make into a nation. □ **nationalization** /-ˈzeɪʃ(ə)n/ *n.* **nationalizer** *n.* [F *nationaliser* (as NATIONAL)]

nationwide /ˈneɪʃ(ə)nˌwaɪd/ *adj.* extending over the whole nation.

native /ˈneɪtɪv/ *n.* & *adj.* —*n.* **1 a** (usu. foll. by *of*) a person born in a specified place, or whose parents are domiciled in that place at the time of the birth (*a native of Bristol*). **b** a local inhabitant. **2** often *offens.* **a** a member of a non-White indigenous people, as regarded by the colonial settlers. **b** *S.Afr.* a Black person. **3** (usu. foll. by *of*) an indigenous animal or plant. **4** *Austral.* a White person born in Australia. —*adj.* **1** (usu. foll. by *to*) belonging to a person or thing by nature; inherent; innate (*spoke with the facility native to him*). **2** of one's birth or birthplace (*native dress*; *native country*). **3** belonging to one by right of birth. **4** (usu. foll. by *to*) belonging to a specified place (*the anteater is native to S. America*). **5 a** (esp. of a non-European) indigenous; born in a place. **b** of the natives of a place (*native customs*). **6** *Austral.* & *NZ* resembling an animal or plant familiar elsewhere (*native bear*). □ **go native** (of a settler) adopt the local way of life, esp. in a non-European country. **native bear** *Austral.* & *NZ* = KOALA. □ **natively** *adv.* **nativeness** *n.* [ME (earlier as adj.) f. OF *natif* *-ive* or L *nativus* f. *nasci* *nat-* be born]

nativity /nəˈtɪvɪtɪ/ *n.* (*pl.* **-ies**) **1** (esp. **the Nativity**) **a** the birth of Christ. **b** the festival of

Christ's birth; Christmas. **2** a picture of the Nativity. **3** birth. □ **nativity play** a play usu. performed by children at Christmas dealing with the birth of Christ. [ME f. OF *nativité* f. LL *nativitas* *-tatis* f. L (as NATIVE)]

NATO /ˈneɪtəʊ/ *abbr.* (also **Nato**) North Atlantic Treaty Organization.

natter /ˈnætə(r)/ *v.* & *n. colloq.* —*v.intr.* **1** chatter idly. **2** grumble; talk fretfully. —*n.* **1** aimless chatter. **2** grumbling talk. □ **natterer** *n.* [orig. Sc., imit.]

natterjack /ˈnætəˌdʒæk/ *n.* a toad, *Bufo calamita*, with a bright yellow stripe down its back. [perh. f. NATTER, from its loud croak, + JACK]

natty /ˈnætɪ/ *adj.* (**nattier, nattiest**) *colloq.* **1 a** smartly or neatly dressed, dapper. **b** spruce; trim; smart (*a natty blouse*). **2** deft. □ **nattily** *adv.* **nattiness** *n.* [orig. sl., perh. rel. to NEAT¹]

natural /ˈnætʃər(ə)l/ *adj.* & *n.* —*adj.* **1 a** existing in or caused by nature; not artificial (*natural landscape*). **b** uncultivated; wild (*existing in its natural state*). **2** in the course of nature; not exceptional or miraculous (*died of natural causes*; *a natural occurrence*). **3** (of human nature etc.) not surprising; to be expected (*natural for her to be upset*). **4 a** (of a person or a person's behaviour) unaffected, easy, spontaneous. **b** (foll. by *to*) spontaneous, easy (*friendliness is natural to him*). **5 a** (of qualities etc.) inherent; innate (*a natural talent for music*). **b** (of a person) having such qualities (*a natural linguist*). **6** not disguised or altered (as by make-up etc.). **7** lifelike; as if in nature (*the portrait looked very natural*). **8** likely by its or their nature to be such (*natural enemies*; *the natural antithesis*). **9** having a physical existence as opposed to what is spiritual, intellectual, etc. (*the natural world*). **10 a** related by nature, out of wedlock, esp. in a specified manner (*her natural son*). **b** illegitimate (*a natural child*). **11** based on the innate moral sense; instinctive (*natural justice*). **12** *Mus.* (of a note) not sharpened or flattened (*B natural*). —*n.* **1** *colloq.* (usu. foll. by *for*) a person or thing naturally suitable, adept, expert, etc. (*a natural for the championship*). **2** *Mus.* **a** a sign (♮) denoting a return to natural pitch after a sharp or a flat. **b** a natural note. **3** a pale fawn colour. □ **natural-born** having a character or position by birth. **natural childbirth** *Med.* childbirth with minimal medical or technological intervention. **natural death** death by age or disease, not by accident, poison, violence, etc. **natural gas** an inflammable mainly methane gas found in the earth's crust, not manufactured. **natural historian** a writer or expert on natural history. **natural history 1** the study of animals or plants esp. as set forth for popular use. **2** an aggregate of the facts concerning the flora and fauna etc. of a particular place or class (*a natural history of the Isle of Wight*). **natural law 1** *Philos.* unchanging moral principles common to all people by virtue of their nature as human beings. **2** a correct statement of an invariable sequence between specified conditions and a specified phenomenon. **3** the laws of nature; regularity in nature (*where they saw chance, we see natural law*). **natural life** the duration of one's life on earth. **natural note** *Mus.* a note that is neither sharp nor flat. **natural numbers** the integers 1, 2, 3, etc. **natural resources** materials or conditions occurring in nature and capable of economic exploitation. **natural science** the sciences used in the study of the physical world, e.g. physics, chemistry, geology, biology, botany. **natural selection** the Darwinian theory of the survival and propagation of organisms best adapted to their environment. □ **naturalness** n. [ME f. OF *naturel* f. L *naturalis* (as NATURE)]

naturalism /ˈnætʃərəˌlɪz(ə)m/ n. the theory or practice in art and literature of representing nature, character, etc. realistically and in great detail. [NATURAL, in Philos. after F *naturalisme*]

naturalist /ˈnætʃərəlɪst/ n. & adj. —n. 1 an expert in natural history. 2 a person who believes in or practises naturalism. —adj. = NATURALISTIC.

naturalistic /ˌnætʃərəˈlɪstɪk/ adj. 1 imitating nature closely; lifelike. 2 of or according to naturalism. 3 of natural history. □ **naturalistically** adv.

naturalize /ˈnætʃərəˌlaɪz/ v. (also **-ise**) 1 tr. admit (a foreigner) to the citizenship of a country. 2 tr. introduce (an animal, plant, etc.) into another region so that it flourishes in the wild. 3 tr. adopt (a foreign word, custom, etc.). 4 intr. become naturalized. 5 tr. free from conventions; make natural. 6 tr. cause to appear natural. □ **naturalization** /-ˈzeɪʃ(ə)n/ n. [F *naturaliser* (as NATURAL)]

naturally /ˈnætʃərəlɪ/ adv. 1 in a natural manner. 2 as a natural result. 3 (qualifying a whole sentence) as might be expected; of course.

nature /ˈneɪtʃə(r)/ n. 1 a thing's or person's innate or essential qualities or character (*not in their nature to be cruel*; *is the nature of iron to rust*). 2 (often **Nature**) a the physical power causing all the phenomena of the material world (*Nature is the best physician*). b these phenomena, including plants, animals, landscape, etc. (*nature gives him comfort*). 3 a kind, sort, or class (*things of this nature*). 4 = human nature. 5 a a specified element of human character (*the rational nature*; *our animal nature*). b a person of a specified character (*even strong natures quail*). 6 a an uncultivated or wild area, condition, community, etc. b the countryside, esp. when picturesque. 7 inherent impulses determining character or action. 8 heredity as an influence on or determinant of personality. □ **by nature** innately. **from nature** *Art* using natural objects as models. **human nature** general human characteristics, feelings, etc. **in nature** 1 actually existing. 2 anywhere; at all. **in** (or **of**) **the nature of** characteristically resembling or belonging to the class of (*the answer was in the nature of an excuse*). **in a state of nature** 1 in an uncivilized or uncultivated state. 2 totally naked. 3 in an unregenerate state. **law of nature** = *natural law* 2. **nature cure** = NATUROPATHY. **nature reserve** a tract of land managed so as to preserve its flora, fauna, physical features, etc. **nature study** the practical study of plant and animal life etc. as a school subject. **nature trail** a signposted path through the countryside designed to draw attention to natural phenomena. [ME f. OF f. L *natura* f. *nasci nat-* be born]

natured /ˈneɪtʃəd/ adj. (in *comb.*) having a specified disposition (*good-natured*; *ill-natured*).

naturism /ˈneɪtʃəˌrɪz(ə)m/ n. 1 nudism. 2 the worship of natural objects. □ **naturist** n.

naturopathy /ˌneɪtʃəˈrɒpəθɪ/ n. 1 the treatment of disease etc. without drugs, usu. involving diet, exercise, massage, etc. 2 this regimen used preventively. □ **naturopath** /ˈneɪtʃərəˌpæθ/ n. **naturopathic** /ˌneɪtʃərəˈpæθɪk/ adj.

naught /nɔːt/ n. & adj. —n. 1 archaic or literary nothing, nought. 2 US = NOUGHT. —adj. (usu. predic.) archaic or literary worthless; useless. □ **come to naught** be ruined or baffled. **set at naught** disregard; despise. [OE *nāwiht*, *-wuht* f. *nā* (see NO²) + *wiht* thing, creature]

naughty /ˈnɔːtɪ/ adj. (**naughtier, naughtiest**) 1 (esp. of children) disobedient; badly behaved. 2 *colloq. joc.* indecent. 3 archaic wicked. □ **naughtily** adv. **naughtiness** n. [ME f. NAUGHT + -Y¹]

nausea /ˈnɔːzɪə, -sɪə/ n. 1 a feeling of sickness with an inclination to vomit. 2 loathing; revulsion. [L f. Gk *nausia* f. *naus* ship]

nauseate /ˈnɔːzɪˌeɪt, -sɪˌeɪt/ v. 1 tr. affect with nausea (*was nauseated by the smell*). 2 intr. (usu. foll. by *at*) loathe food, an occupation, etc.; feel sick. □ **nauseating** adj. **nauseatingly** adv. [L *nauseare* (as NAUSEA)]

nauseous /ˈnɔːzɪəs, -sɪəs/ adj. 1 causing nausea. 2 offensive to the taste or smell. 3 disgusting; loathsome. □ **nauseously** adv. **nauseousness** n. [L *nauseosus* (as NAUSEA)]

nautch /nɔːtʃ/ n. a performance of professional Indian dancing-girls. □ **nautch-girl** a professional Indian dancing-girl. [Urdu (Hindi) *nāch* f. Prakrit *nachcha* f. Skr. *nṛitja* dancing]

nautical /ˈnɔːtɪk(ə)l/ adj. of or concerning sailors or navigation; naval; maritime. □ **nautical mile** a unit of approx. 2,025 yards (1,852 metres). □ **nautically** adv. [F *nautique* or f. L *nauticus* f. Gk *nautikos* f. *nautēs* sailor f. *naus* ship]

nautilus /ˈnɔːtɪləs/ n. (pl. **nautiluses** or **nautili** /-ˌlaɪ/) any cephalopod of the genus *Nautilus* with a light brittle spiral shell, esp. (**pearly nautilus**) one having a chambered shell with nacreous septa. [L f. Gk *nautilos*, lit. sailor (as NAUTICAL)]

naval /ˈneɪv(ə)l/ adj. 1 of, in, for, etc. the navy or a navy. 2 of or concerning ships (*a naval battle*). □ **naval academy** a college for training naval officers. **naval architect** a designer of ships. □ **navally** adv. [L *navalis* f. *navis* ship]

navarin /ˈnævəˌræ̃/ n. a casserole of mutton or lamb with vegetables. [F]

nave¹ n. the central part of a church, usu. from the west door to the chancel and excluding the side aisles. [med.L *navis* f. L *navis* ship]

nave² n. the hub of a wheel. [OE *nafu*, *nafa* f. Gmc, rel. to NAVEL]

navel /ˈneɪv(ə)l/ n. 1 a depression in the centre of the belly caused by the detachment of the umbilical cord. 2 a central point. □ **navel orange** a large seedless orange with a navel-like formation at the top. [OE *nafela* f. Gmc, rel. to NAVE²]

navigable /ˈnævɪgəb(ə)l/ adj. 1 (of a river, the sea, etc.) affording a passage for ships. 2 (of a ship etc.) seaworthy (*in navigable condition*). 3 (of a balloon, airship, etc.) steerable. □ **navigability** /-ˈbɪlɪtɪ/ n. [F *navigable* or L *navigabilis* (as NAVIGATE)]

navigate /ˈnævɪˌgeɪt/ v. 1 tr. manage or direct the course of (a ship, aircraft, etc.). 2 tr. a sail on (a sea, river, etc.). b travel or fly through (the air). 3 intr. (of a passenger in a vehicle) assist the driver by map-reading etc. 4 intr. sail a ship; sail in a ship. 5 tr. (often *refl.*) colloq. steer (oneself, a course, etc.) through a crowd etc. [L *navigare* f. *navis* ship + *agere* drive]

navigation /ˌnævɪˈɡeɪʃ(ə)n/ n. **1** the act or process of navigating. **2** any of several methods of determining or planning a ship's or aircraft's position and course by geometry, astronomy, etc. **3** a voyage. □ **navigational** adj. [F or f. L navigatio (as NAVIGATE)]

navigator /ˈnævɪˌɡeɪtə(r)/ n. **1** a person skilled or engaged in navigation. **2** an explorer by sea. [L (as NAVIGATE)]

navvy /ˈnævɪ/ n. & v. Brit. —n. (pl. **-ies**) a labourer employed in building or excavating roads, canals, etc. —v.intr. (**-ies, -ied**) work as a navvy. [abbr. of NAVIGATOR]

navy /ˈneɪvɪ/ n. (pl. **-ies**) **1** (often **the Navy**) **a** the whole body of a State's ships of war, including crews, maintenance systems, etc. **b** the officers and men of a navy. **2** (in full **navy blue**) a dark-blue colour as used in naval uniform. **3** poet. a fleet of ships. □ **Navy Department** US the government department in charge of the navy. **Navy List** Brit. an official list containing the names of all naval officers etc. [ME, = fleet f. OF navie ship, fleet f. Rmc & pop.L navia ship f. L navis]

nawab /nəˈwɑːb, -ˈwɔːb/ n. **1** the title of a distinguished Muslim in Pakistan. **2** hist. the title of a governor or nobleman in India. [Urdu nawwāb pl. f. Arab. nā'ib deputy: cf. NABOB]

nay adv. & n. —adv. **1** or rather; and even; and more than that (impressive, nay, magnificent). **2** archaic = NO² adv. 1. —n. **1** the word 'nay'. **2** a negative vote (counted 16 nays). [ME f. ON nei f. ne not + ei AYE²]

naysay /ˈneɪseɪ/ v. (3rd sing. present **-says**; past and past part. **-said**) esp. US **1** intr. utter a denial or refusal. **2** tr. refuse or contradict. □ **naysayer** n.

Nazarene /ˌnæzəˈriːn, ˈnæ-/ n. & adj. —n. **1** a (prec. by the) Christ. **b** (esp. in Jewish or Muslim use) a Christian. **2** a native or inhabitant of Nazareth. —adj. of or concerning Nazareth, the Nazarenes, etc. [ME f. LL Nazarenus f. Gk Nazarēnos f. Nazaret Nazareth]

Nazi /ˈnɑːtsɪ, ˈnɑːzɪ/ n. & adj. —n. (pl. **Nazis**) **1** hist. a member of the German National Socialist party. **2** derog. a person holding extreme racist or authoritarian views or behaving brutally. —adj. of or concerning the Nazis, Nazism, etc. □ **Nazidom** n. **Nazify** /-ˌfaɪ/ v.tr. (**-ies, -ied**). **Naziism** /-iːˌɪz(ə)m/ n. **Nazism** /ˈnɑːtsɪz(ə)m/ n. [repr. pronunc. of Nati- in G Nationalsozialist]

NB abbr. nota bene.

Nb symb. Chem. the element niobium.

NCB abbr. hist. (in the UK) National Coal Board.

■ **Usage** Since 1987 the official name has been British Coal.

NCO abbr. non-commissioned officer.

Nd symb. Chem. the element neodymium.

-nd¹ suffix forming nouns (fiend; friend). [OE -ond, orig. part. ending]

-nd² suffix see -AND, -END.

NE abbr. **1** north-east. **2** north-eastern.

Ne symb. Chem. the element neon.

né /neɪ/ adj. born (indicating a man's previous name) (Lord Beaconsfield, né Benjamin Disraeli). [F, past part. of naître be born: cf. NÉE]

Neanderthal /nɪˈændəˌtɑːl/ adj. of or belonging to the type of human widely distributed in palaeolithic Europe, with a retreating forehead and massive brow-ridges. [Neanderthal, a region in Germany where remains were found]

neap n. (in full **neap tide**) a tide just after the first and third quarters of the moon when there is least difference between high and low water. [OE nēpflōd (cf. FLOOD), of unkn. orig.]

Neapolitan /nɪəˈpɒlɪt(ə)n/ n. & adj. —n. a native or citizen of Naples in Italy. —adj. of or relating to Naples. □ **Neapolitan ice-cream** ice-cream made in layers of different colours. [ME f. L Neapolitanus f. L Neapolis Naples f. Gk f. neos new + polis city]

near adv., prep., adj., & v. —adv. **1** (often foll. by to) to or at a short distance in space or time; close by (the time drew near; dropped near to them). **2** closely (as near as one can guess). —prep. (compar. & superl. also used) **1** to or at a short distance (in space, time, condition, or resemblance) from (stood near the back; occurs nearer the end; the sun is near setting). **2** (in comb.) **a** that is almost (near-hysterical; a near-Communist). **b** intended as a substitute for; resembling (near-beer). —adj. **1** (usu. predic.) close at hand; close to, in place or time (the man nearest you; in the near future). **2 a** closely related (a near relation). **b** intimate (a near friend). **3** (of a part of a vehicle, animal, or road) left (the near fore leg; near side front wheel) (orig. of the side from which one mounted). **4** close; narrow (a near escape; a near guess). **5** (of a road or way) direct. **6** niggardly, mean. —v. **1** tr. approach; draw near to (neared the harbour). **2** intr. draw near (could distinguish them as they neared). □ **come** (or **go**) **near** (foll. by verbal noun, or to + verbal noun) be on the point of, almost succeed in (came near to falling). **go near** (foll. by to + infin.) narrowly fail. **near at hand 1** within easy reach. **2** in the immediate future. **the Near East** the region comprising the countries of the eastern Mediterranean. **Near Eastern** of the Near East. **near go** colloq. a narrow escape. **near the knuckle** colloq. verging on the indecent. **near miss 1** (of a bomb etc.) close to the target. **2** a situation in which a collision is narrowly avoided. **3** (of an attempt) almost but not quite successful. **near sight** esp. US = short sight. **near thing** a narrow escape. □ **nearish** adj. **nearness** n. [ME f. ON nær, orig. compar. of ná = OE nēah NIGH]

nearby adj. & adv. —adj. /ˈnɪəbaɪ/ situated in a near position (a nearby hotel). —adv. /nɪəˈbaɪ/ close; not far away.

nearly /ˈnɪəlɪ/ adv. **1** almost (we are nearly there). **2** closely (they are nearly related). □ **not nearly** nothing like; far from (not nearly enough).

nearside /ˈnɪəsaɪd/ n. (often attrib.) esp. Brit. the left side of a vehicle, animal, etc.

near-sighted /nɪəˈsaɪtɪd/ n. esp. US = SHORT-SIGHTED. □ **near-sightedly** adv. **near-sightedness** n.

neat¹ adj. **1** tidy and methodical. **2** elegantly simple in form etc.; well-proportioned. **3** (of language, style, etc.) brief, clear, and pointed; epigrammatic. **4 a** cleverly executed (a neat piece of work). **b** deft; dextrous. **5** (of esp. alcoholic liquor) undiluted. **6** US sl. (as a general term of approval) good, pleasing, excellent. □ **neatly** adv. **neatness** n. [F net f. L nitidus shining f. nitēre shine]

neat² /niːt/ n. archaic **1** a bovine animal. **2** (as pl.) cattle. □ **neat's-foot oil** oil made from boiled cow-heel and used to dress leather. [OE *nēat* f. Gmc]

neaten /ˈniːt(ə)n/ *v.tr.* make neat.

neath /niːθ/ *prep. poet.* beneath. [BENEATH]

nebula /ˈnebjʊlə/ *n.* (*pl.* **nebulae** /-ˌliː/ or **nebulas**) *Astron.* **1** a cloud of gas and dust, sometimes glowing and sometimes appearing as a dark silhouette against other glowing matter. **2** a bright area caused by a galaxy, or a large cloud of distant stars. □ **nebular** *adj.* [L, = mist]

nebulous /ˈnebjʊləs/ *adj.* **1** cloudlike. **2 a** formless, clouded. **b** hazy, indistinct, vague (*put forward a few nebulous ideas*). **3** *Astron.* of or like a nebula or nebulae. □ **nebulosity** /-ˈlɒsɪtɪ/ *n.* **nebulously** *adv.* **nebulousness** *n.* [ME f. F *nébuleux* or L *nebulosus* (as NEBULA)]

necessarily /ˈnesəsərɪlɪ, -ˈserɪlɪ/ *adv.* as a necessary result; inevitably.

necessary /ˈnesəsərɪ/ *adj.* & *n.* —*adj.* **1** requiring to be done, achieved, etc.; requisite, essential (*it is necessary to work; lacks the necessary documents*). **2** determined, existing, or happening by natural laws, predestination, etc., not by free will; inevitable (*a necessary evil*). —*n.* (*pl.* **-ies**) (usu. in *pl.*) any of the basic requirements of life, such as food, warmth, etc. □ **the necessary** *colloq.* **1** money. **2** an action, item, etc., needed for a purpose (*they will do the necessary*). [ME f. OF *necessaire* f. L *necessarius* f. *necesse* needful]

necessitate /nɪˈsesɪˌteɪt/ *v.tr.* make necessary (esp. as a result) (*will necessitate some sacrifice*). [med.L *necessitare* compel (as NECESSITY)]

necessitous /nɪˈsesɪtəs/ *adj.* poor; needy. [F *nécessiteux* or f. NECESSITY + -OUS]

necessity /nɪˈsesɪtɪ/ *n.* (*pl.* **-ies**) **1 a** an indispensible thing; a necessary (*central heating is a necessity*). **b** (usu. foll. by *of*) indispensability (*the necessity of a warm overcoat*). **2** a state of things or circumstances enforcing a certain course (*there was a necessity to hurry*). **3** imperative need (*necessity is the mother of invention*). **4** want; poverty; hardship (*stole because of necessity*). □ **of necessity** unavoidably. [ME f. OF *nécessité* f. L *necessitas -tatis* f. *necesse* needful]

neck *n.* & *v.* —*n.* **1 a** the part of the body connecting the head to the shoulders. **b** the part of a shirt, dress, etc. round or close to the neck. **2 a** something resembling a neck, such as the narrow part of a cavity or vessel, a passage, channel, pass, isthmus, etc. **b** the narrow part of a bottle near the mouth. **3** the part of a violin etc. bearing the finger-board. **4** the length of a horse's head and neck as a measure of its lead in a race. **5** the flesh of an animal's neck (*neck of lamb*). **6** *sl.* impudence (*you've got a neck, asking that*). —*v. intr.* & *tr. colloq.* kiss and caress amorously. □ **get it in the neck** *colloq.* **1** receive a severe reprimand or punishment. **2** suffer a fatal or severe blow. **neck and neck** running level in a race etc. **neck of the woods** *colloq.* a usu. remote locality. **up to one's neck** (often foll. by *in*) *colloq.* very deeply involved; very busy. □ **necked** *adj.* (also in *comb.*). **necker** *n.* (in sense 1 of *v.*). **neckless** *adj.* [OE *hnecca* ult. f. Gmc]

neckband /ˈnekbænd/ *n.* a strip of material round the neck of a garment.

neckerchief /ˈnekətʃɪf/ *n.* a square of cloth worn round the neck.

necklace /ˈnekləs, -lɪs/ *n.* & *v.* —*n.* **1** a chain or string of beads, precious stones, links, etc., worn as an ornament round the neck. **2** *S.Afr.* a tyre soaked or filled with petrol, placed round a victim's neck, and set alight. —*v.tr. S.Afr.* kill with a 'necklace'.

necklet /ˈneklɪt/ *n.* **1** = NECKLACE *n.* 1. **2** a strip of fur worn round the neck.

neckline /ˈneklaɪn/ *n.* the edge or shape of the opening of a garment at the neck (*a square neckline*).

necktie /ˈnektaɪ/ *n.* esp. *US* = TIE *n.* 2.

neckwear /ˈnekweə(r)/ *n.* collars, ties, etc.

necro- /ˈnekrəʊ/ *comb. form* corpse. [from or after Gk *nekro-* f. *nekros* corpse]

necromancy /ˈnekrəˌmænsɪ/ *n.* **1** the prediction of the future by the supposed communication with the dead. **2** witchcraft. □ **necromancer** *n.* **necromantic** /-ˈmæntɪk/ *adj.* [ME f. OF *nigromancie* f. med.L *nigromantia* changed (by assoc. with L *niger nigri* black) f. LL *necromantia* f. Gk *nekromanteia* (as NECRO-, -MANCY)]

necrophilia /ˌnekrəˈfɪlɪə/ *n.* (also **necrophily** /nɪˈkrɒfɪlɪ/) a morbid and esp. erotic attraction to corpses. □ **necrophil** /ˈnek-/ *n.* **necrophile** /ˈnekrəˌfaɪl/ *n.* **necrophiliac** /-ˈfɪlɪˌæk/ *n.* **necrophilic** *adj.* **necrophilism** /-ˈkrɒfɪˌlɪz(ə)m/ *n.* **necrophilist** /-ˈkrɒfɪlɪst/ *n.* [NECRO- + Gk -*philia* loving]

necropolis /neˈkrɒpəlɪs/ *n.* an ancient cemetery or burial place.

necrosis /neˈkrəʊsɪs/ *n.* *Med.* & *Physiol.* the death of tissue caused by disease or injury, esp. as one of the symptoms of gangrene or pulmonary tuberculosis. □ **necrose** /-ˈkrəʊs/ *v.intr.* **necrotic** /-ˈkrɒtɪk/ *adj.* **necrotize** /ˈnekrəˌtaɪz/ *v.intr.* (also **-ise**). [mod.L f. Gk *nekrōsis* (as NECRO-, -OSIS)]

nectar /ˈnektə(r)/ *n.* **1** a sugary substance produced by plants and made into honey by bees. **2** (in Greek and Roman mythology) the drink of the gods. **3** a drink compared to this. □ **nectarean** /-ˈteərɪən/ *adj.* **nectareous** /-ˈteərɪəs/ *adj.* **nectariferous** /-ˈrɪfərəs/ *adj.* **nectarous** *adj.* [L f. Gk *nektar*]

nectarine /ˈnektərɪn, -ˌriːn/ *n.* **1** a variety of peach with a thin brightly-coloured smooth skin and firm flesh. **2** the tree bearing this. [orig. as adj., = nectar-like, f. NECTAR + -INE⁴]

nectary /ˈnektərɪ/ *n.* (*pl.* **-ies**) the nectar-secreting organ of a flower or plant. [mod.L *nectarium* (as NECTAR)]

NEDC *abbr.* (in the UK) National Economic Development Council.

neddy /ˈnedɪ/ *n.* (*pl.* **-ies**) *colloq.* **1** a donkey. **2** (**Neddy**) = NEDC. [dimin. of *Ned*, pet-form of the name *Edward*]

née /neɪ/ *adj.* (US **nee**) (used in adding a married woman's maiden name after her surname) born (*Mrs Ann Smith, née Jones*). [F, fem. past part. of *naître* be born]

need *v.* & *n.* —*v.* **1** *tr.* stand in want of; require (*needs a new coat*). **2** *tr.* (foll. by *to* + infin.; *3rd sing. present neg.* or *interrog.* **need** without *to*) be under the necessity or obligation (*it needs to be done carefully; he need not come; need you ask?*). —*n.* **1 a** a want or requirement (*my needs are few; the need for greater freedom*). **b** a thing wanted (*my greatest need is a car*). **2** circumstances requiring some course of action; necessity (*there is no need to worry; let my need arise*). **3** destitution; poverty. **4** a crisis; an emergency (*failed them in their need*). □ **at need** in time of need. **have need of** require; want. **have need to** require to (*has need to be warned*). **in need** requiring help. **in need of** requiring. **need not have** did not need to (but did). [OE *nēodian*, *nēd* f. Gmc]

needful /ˈniːdfʊl/ *adj.* 1 requisite; necessary; indispensable. 2 (prec. by *the*) **a** what is necessary. **b** *colloq.* money or action needed for a purpose. □ **needfully** *adv.* **needfulness** *n.*

needle /ˈniːd(ə)l/ *n. & v.* —*n.* 1 **a** a very thin small piece of smooth steel etc. pointed at one end and with a slit (eye) for thread at the other, used in sewing. **b** a larger plastic, wooden, etc. slender stick without an eye, used in knitting. **c** a slender hooked stick used in crochet. 2 **a** pointer on a dial (see *magnetic needle*). 3 any of several small thin pointed instruments, esp.: **a** a surgical instrument for stitching. **b** the end of a hypodermic syringe. **c** = STYLUS. 4 **a** an obelisk (*Cleopatra's Needle*). **b** a pointed rock or peak. 5 the leaf of a fir or pine tree. 6 *Brit. sl.* a fit of bad temper or nervousness (*got the needle while waiting*). —*v.tr. colloq.* incite or irritate; provoke (*the silence needled him*). □ **needle game** (or **match** etc.) *Brit.* a contest that is very close or arouses personal grudges. **needle-lace** lace made with needles not bobbins. **needle-point** 1 a very sharp point. 2 = *needle-lace*. 3 = GROS OR PETIT POINT. **needle's eye** (or **eye of a needle**) the least possible aperture, esp. with ref. to Matt. 19:24. **needle time** an agreed maximum allowance of time for broadcasting music from records. [OE *nǽdl* f. Gmc]

needlecord /ˈniːd(ə)lˌkɔːd/ *n.* a fine-ribbed corduroy fabric.

needlecraft /ˈniːd(ə)lˌkrɑːft/ *n.* skill in needlework.

needleful /ˈniːd(ə)lˌfʊl/ *n.* (*pl.* **-fuls**) the length of thread etc. put into a needle at one time.

needless /ˈniːdlɪs/ *adj.* 1 unnecessary. 2 uncalled for; gratuitous. □ **needless to say** of course; it goes without saying. □ **needlessly** *adv.* **needlessness** *n.*

needlewoman /ˈniːd(ə)lˌwʊmən/ *n.* (*pl.* **-women**) 1 a seamstress. 2 a woman or girl with specified sewing skill (*a good needlewoman*).

needlework /ˈniːd(ə)lˌwɜːk/ *n.* sewing or embroidery.

needs /niːdz/ *adv.* archaic (usu. prec. or foll. by *must*) of necessity (*must needs decide*). [OE *nēdes* (as NEED, -S³)]

needy /ˈniːdɪ/ *adj.* (**needier, neediest**) 1 (of a person) poor; destitute. 2 (of circumstances) characterized by poverty. □ **neediness** *n.*

neep /niːp/ *n. Sc. & N.Engl.* a turnip. [OE *nǽp* f. L *napus*]

ne'er /neə(r)/ *adv. poet.* = NEVER. □ **ne'er-do-well** *n.* a good-for-nothing person. —*adj.* good-for-nothing. [ME contr. of NEVER]

nefarious /nɪˈfeərɪəs/ *adj.* wicked; iniquitous. □ **nefariously** *adv.* **nefariousness** *n.* [L *nefarius* f. *nefas* wrong f. *ne-* not + *fas* divine law]

neg. *abbr.* negative.

negate /nɪˈɡeɪt/ *v.tr.* 1 nullify; invalidate. 2 imply, involve, or assert the non-existence of. 3 be the negation of. □ **negator** *n.* [L *negare negat-* deny]

negation /nɪˈɡeɪʃ(ə)n/ *n.* 1 the absence or opposite of something actual or positive. 2 **a** the act of denying. **b** an instance of this. 3 (usu. foll. by *of*) a refusal, contradiction, or denial. 4 **a** negative statement or doctrine. 5 a negative or unreal thing; a nonentity. □ **negatory** /ˈnɛɡətərɪ/ *adj.* [F *negation* or L *negatio* (as NEGATE)]

negative /ˈnɛɡətɪv/ *adj., n. & v.* —*adj.* 1 expressing or implying denial, prohibition, or refusal (*a negative vote; a negative answer*). 2 (of a person or attitude): **a** lacking positive attributes; apathetic; pessimistic. **b** opposing or resisting; uncooperative. 3 marked by the absence of qualities (*a negative reaction; a negative result from the test*). 4 of the opposite nature to a thing regarded as positive (*debt is negative capital*). 5 *Algebra* (of a quantity) less than zero, to be subtracted from others or from zero. 6 *Electr.* **a** of the kind of charge carried by electrons. **b** containing or producing such a charge. —*n.* 1 **a** negative statement, reply, or word (*hard to prove a negative*). 2 *Photog.* **a** an image with black and white reversed or colours replaced by complementary ones, from which positive pictures are obtained. **b** a developed film or plate bearing such an image. 3 a negative quality; an absence of something. 4 (prec. by *the*) a position opposing the affirmative. —*v.tr.* 1 refuse to accept or countenance; veto; reject. 2 disprove (an inference or hypothesis). 3 contradict (a statement). 4 neutralize (an effect). □ **in the negative** with negative effect; so as to reject a proposal etc.; no (*the answer was in the negative*). **negative evidence** (or **instance**) evidence of the non-occurrence of something. **negative feedback** 1 the return of part of an output signal to the input, tending to decrease the amplification etc. 2 feedback that tends to diminish or counteract the process giving rise to it. **negative pole** the south-seeking pole of a magnet. **negative sign** a symbol (−) indicating subtraction or a value less than zero. □ **negatively** *adv.* **negativeness** *n.* **negativity** /-ˈtɪvɪtɪ/ *n.* [ME f. OF *negatif -ive* or LL *negativus* (as NEGATE)]

negativism /ˈnɛɡətɪˌvɪz(ə)m/ *n.* a negative position or attitude; extreme scepticism, criticism, etc. □ **negativist** *n.* **negativistic** /-ˈvɪstɪk/ *adj.*

neglect /nɪˈɡlɛkt/ *v. & n.* —*v.tr.* 1 fail to care for or to do; be remiss about (*neglected their duty; neglected his children*). 2 (foll. by verbal noun, or *to* + infin.) fail; overlook or forget the need to (*neglected to inform them; neglected telling them*). 3 not pay attention to; disregard (*neglected the obvious warning*). —*n.* 1 lack of caring; negligence (*the house suffered from neglect*). 2 **a** the act of neglecting. **b** the state of being neglected (*the house fell into neglect*). 3 (usu. foll. by *of*) disregard. □ **neglectful** *adj.* **neglectfully** *adv.* **neglectfulness** *n.* [L *neglegere neglect-* f. *neg-* not + *legere* choose, pick up]

negligée /ˈnɛɡlɪˌʒeɪ/ *n.* (also **negligee**, **négligé**) (usu. **negligee**) a woman's dressing-gown of thin fabric. [F, past part. of *négliger* NEGLECT]

negligence /ˈnɛɡlɪdʒ(ə)ns/ *n.* 1 a lack of proper care and attention; carelessness. 2 an act of carelessness. □ **negligent** *adj.* **negligently** *adv.* [ME f. OF *negligence* or L *negligentia* f. *negligere* = *neglegere*: see NEGLECT]

negligible /ˈnɛɡlɪdʒɪb(ə)l/ *adj.* not worth considering; insignificant. □ **negligibility** /-ˈbɪlɪtɪ/ *n.* **negligibly** *adv.* [obs. F f. *négliger* NEGLECT]

negotiable /nɪˈɡəʊʃəb(ə)l/ *adj.* 1 open to discussion or modification. 2 able to be negotiated. □ **negotiability** /-ˈbɪlɪtɪ/ *n.*

negotiate /nɪˈɡəʊʃɪˌeɪt/ *v.* 1 *intr.* (usu. foll. by *with*) confer with others in order to reach a compromise or agreement. 2 *tr.* arrange (an

affair) or bring about (a result) by negotiating
(*negotiated a settlement*). **3** *tr.* find a way over,
through, etc. (an obstacle, difficulty, fence, etc.).
4 *tr.* **a** transfer (a cheque etc.) to another for a
consideration. **b** convert (a cheque etc.) into
cash or notes. **c** get or give value for (a
cheque etc.) in money. □ **negotiant** /-ʃrənt/ *n.*
negotiation /-ʃɪˈeɪʃ(ə)n, -sɪˈeɪʃ(ə)n/ *n.* **negotiator**
n. [L *negotiari* f. *negotium* business f. *neg-* not +
otium leisure]

Negress /ˈniːgrɪs/ *n.* a female Negro.

■ **Usage** This word is often considered offensive;
the term *Black* is usually preferred.

Negritude /ˈniːgrɪˌtjuːd/ *n.* **1** the quality or
state of being a Negro. **2** the affirmation or
consciousness of the value of Negro culture. [F
négritude, ult. f. L *niger nigri* black]

Negro /ˈniːgrəʊ/ *n.* & *adj.* —*n.* (*pl.* **-oes**) a member
of a dark-skinned race orig. native to Africa.
—*adj.* of or concerning Negroes. □ **Negro
spiritual** a religious song derived from the
musical traditions of Black people in the southern US. [Sp. & Port., f. L *niger nigri* black]

■ **Usage** This word is often considered offensive;
the term *Black* is usually preferred.

Negroid /ˈniːgrɔɪd/ *adj.* & *n.* —*adj.* **1** (of features
etc.) characterizing a member of the Negro race,
esp. in having dark skin, tightly curled hair,
and a broad flattish nose. **2** of or concerning
Negroes. —*n.* a Negro. [NEGRO]

neigh /neɪ/ *n.* & *v.* —*n.* **1** the high whinnying
sound of a horse. **2** any similar sound, e.g. a
laugh. —*v.* **1** *intr.* make such a sound. **2** *tr.* say,
cry, etc. with such a sound. [OE *hnægan*, of imit.
orig.]

neighbour /ˈneɪbə(r)/ *n.* & *v.* (*US* **neighbor**) —*n.*
1 a person living next door to or near or nearest
another (*my next-door neighbour; his nearest neighbour is 12 miles away; they are neighbours*). **2 a** a
person regarded as having the duties or claims
of friendliness, consideration, etc., of a neighbour. **b** a fellow human being, esp. as having
claims on friendship. **3** a person or thing near
or next to another (*my neighbour at dinner*). **4**
(*attrib.*) neighbouring. —*v.* **1** *tr.* border on; adjoin.
2 *intr.* (often foll. by *on, upon*) border; adjoin. □
neighbouring *adj.* **neighbourless** *adj.* **neigh-
bourship** *n.* [OE *nēahgebūr* (as NIGH: *gebūr*, cf.
BOOR)]

neighbourhood /ˈneɪbəˌhʊd/ *n.* (*US* **neigh-
borhood**) **1 a** a district, esp. one forming a
community within a town or city. **b** the people
of a district; one's neighbours. **2** neighbourly
feeling or conduct. □ **in the neighbourhood
of** roughly; about (*paid in the neighbourhood of
£100*). **neighbourhood watch** systematic local
vigilance by householders to discourage crime,
esp. against property.

neighbourly /ˈneɪbəlɪ/ *adj.* (*US* **neighborly**)
characteristic of a good neighbour; friendly;
kind. □ **neighbourliness** *n.*

neither /ˈnaɪðə(r), ˈniːð-/ *adj.*, *pron.* & *adv.* —*adj.*
& *pron.* (foll. by sing. verb) **1** not the one nor the
other (of two things); not either (*neither of the
accusations is true; neither wish was granted; neither
went to the fair*). **2** *disp.* none of any number of
specified things. —*adv.* **1** not either; not on the
one hand (foll. by *nor*; introducing the first of
two or more things in the negative: *neither*

knowing nor caring; neither the teachers nor the
parents nor the children*). **2** not either; also not (*if
you do not, neither shall I*). **3** (with *neg.*) *disp.* either
(*I don't know that neither*). [ME *naither, neither* f.
OE *nōwther* contr. of *nōhwæther* (as NO², WHETHER):
assim. to EITHER]

nelly /ˈnelɪ/ *n.* (*pl.* **-ies**) a silly or effeminate
person. □ **not on your nelly** *Brit. sl.* certainly
not. [perh. f. the name *Nelly*: idiom f. rhyming
sl. *Nelly Duff* = puff = breath: cf. *not on your life*]

nelson /ˈnels(ə)n/ *n.* a wrestling-hold in which
one arm is passed under the opponent's arm
from behind and the hand is applied to the
neck (**half nelson**), or both arms and hands are
applied (**full nelson**). [app. f. the name *Nelson*]

nematode /ˈneməˌtəʊd/ *n.* any parasitic or free-
living worm of the phylum Nematoda, with a
slender unsegmented cylindrical shape. [Gk
nēma -matos thread + -ODE¹]

nem. con. *abbr.* with no one dissenting. [L
nemine contradicente]

nemesis /ˈnemɪsɪs/ *n.* (*pl.* **nemeses** /-ˌsiːz/) **1**
retributive justice. **2 a** a downfall caused by
this. **b** an agent of such a downfall. [Gk, =
righteous indignation, personified as goddess
of retribution f. *nemō* give what is due]

neo- /ˈniːəʊ/ *comb. form* **1** new, modern. **2** a new
or revived form of. [Gk f. *neos* new]

neoclassical /ˌniːəʊˈklæsɪk(ə)l/ *adj.* (also **neo-
classic** /-sɪk/) of or relating to a revival of a
classical style or treatment in art, literature,
music, etc. □ **neoclassicism** /-ˌsɪz(ə)m/ *n.* **neo-
classicist** /-sɪst/ *n.*

neocolonialism /ˌniːəʊkəˈləʊnɪəˌlɪz(ə)m/ *n.* the
use of economic, political, or other pressures to
control or influence other countries, esp. former
dependencies. □ **neocolonialist** *n.* & *adj.*

neodymium /ˌniːəˈdɪmɪəm/ *n.* *Chem.* a silver-grey
naturally-occurring metallic element of the
lanthanide series used in colouring glass etc.
[NEO- + Gk *didumos* twin]

neolithic /ˌniːəˈlɪθɪk/ *adj.* of or relating to the
later Stone Age, when ground or polished stone
weapons and implements prevailed. [NEO- +
Gk *lithos* stone]

neologism /niːˈɒlədʒ₁ɪz(ə)m/ *n.* **1** a new word or
expression. **2** the coining or use of new words.
□ **neologist** *n.* **neologize** /-ˌdʒaɪz/ *v.intr.* (also
-ise). [F *néologisme* (as NEO-, -LOGY, -ISM)]

neon /ˈniːɒn/ *n.* *Chem.* an inert gaseous element
occurring in traces in the atmosphere and
giving an orange glow when electricity is passed
through it in a sealed low-pressure tube, used
in lights and illuminated advertisements (*neon
light; neon sign*). [Gk, neut. of *neos* new]

neophyte /ˈniːəˌfaɪt/ *n.* **1** a new convert, esp. to a
religious faith. **2** *RC Ch.* **a** a novice of a religious
order. **b** a newly ordained priest. **3** a beginner; a
novice. [eccl.L *neophytus* f. NT Gk *neophutos* newly
planted (as NEO- *phuton* plant)]

neoprene /ˈniːəʊˌpriːn/ *n.* a synthetic rubber-like
polymer. [NEO- + *chloroprene* etc.]

neotropical /ˌniːəʊˈtrɒpɪk(ə)l/ *adj.* of or relating
to tropical and S. America in respect of the
distribution of plants and animals.

nephew /ˈnevjuː, ˈnef-/ *n.* a son of one's brother or
sister, or of one's brother-in-law or sister-in-law.
[ME f. OF *neveu* f. L *nepos nepotis* grandson,
nephew]

nephrite /ˈnefraɪt/ *n.* a green, yellow, or white
calcium magnesium silicate form of jade. [G

Nephrit f. Gk *nephros* kidney, with ref. to its supposed efficacy in treating kidney disease]

nephritic /nɪˈfrɪtɪk/ *adj.* **1** of or in the kidneys; renal. **2** of or relating to nephritis. [LL *nephriticus* f. Gk *nephritikos* (as NEPHRITIS)]

nephritis /nɪˈfraɪtɪs/ *n.* inflammation of the kidneys. [LL f. Gk *nephros* kidney]

nephro- /ˈnefrəʊ/ *comb. form* (usu. **nephr-** before a vowel) kidney. [Gk f. *nephros* kidney]

ne plus ultra /ˌneɪ plʊs ˈʊltrɑː/ *n.* **1** the furthest attainable point. **2** the culmination, acme, or perfection. [L, = not further beyond, the supposed inscription on the Pillars of Hercules (the Strait of Gibraltar) prohibiting passage by ships]

nepotism /ˈnepətɪz(ə)m/ *n.* favouritism shown to relatives in conferring offices or privileges. □ **nepotist** *n.* **nepotistic** /-ˈtɪstɪk/ *adj.* [F *népotisme* f. It. *nepotismo* f. *nepote* NEPHEW: orig. with ref. to popes with illegitimate sons called nephews]

neptunium /nepˈtjuːnɪəm/ *n. Chem.* a radioactive transuranic metallic element produced when uranium atoms absorb bombarding neutrons. [name of the planet *Neptune*, as the next planet beyond Uranus, + -IUM]

nerd /nɜːd/ *n.* (also **nurd**) esp. *US sl.* a foolish, feeble, or uninteresting person. □ **nerdy** *adj.* [20th c.: orig. uncert.]

nereid /ˈnɪərɪɪd/ *n. Mythol.* a sea-nymph. [L *Nereis Nereïd-* f. Gk *Nērēïs -idos* daughter of the sea-god Nereus]

nerve /nɜːv/ *n. & v.* —*n.* **1 a** a fibre or bundle of fibres that transmits impulses of sensation or motion between the brain or spinal cord and other parts of the body. **b** the material constituting these. **2 a** coolness in danger; bravery; assurance. **b** *colloq.* impudence, audacity (*they've got a nerve*). **3** (in *pl.*) **a** the bodily state in regard to physical sensitiveness and the interaction between the brain and other parts. **b** a state of heightened nervousness or sensitivity; a condition of mental or physical stress (*need to calm my nerves*). **4** a rib of a leaf, esp. the midrib. —*v.tr.* **1** (usu. *refl.*) brace (oneself) to face danger, suffering, etc. **2** give strength, vigour, or courage to. □ **get on a person's nerves** irritate or annoy a person. **have nerves of iron** (or **steel**) (of a person etc.) be not easily upset or frightened. **nerve-cell** an elongated branched cell transmitting impulses in nerve tissue. **nerve-centre 1** a group of closely connected nerve-cells associated in performing some function. **2** the centre of control of an organization etc. **nerve gas** a poisonous gas affecting the nervous system. **nerve-racking** stressful, frightening; straining the nerves. □ **nerved** *adj.* (also in *comb.*). [ME, = sinew, f. L *nervus*, rel. to Gk *neuron*]

nerveless /ˈnɜːvlɪs/ *adj.* **1** inert, lacking vigour or spirit. **2** confident; not nervous. **3** *Anat. & Zool.* without nerves. □ **nervelessly** *adv.* **nervelessness** *n.*

nervo- /ˈnɜːvəʊ/ *comb. form* (also **nerv-** before a vowel) a nerve or the nerves.

nervous /ˈnɜːvəs/ *adj.* **1** having delicate or disordered nerves. **2** timid or anxious. **3 a** excitable; highly strung; easily agitated. **b** resulting from this temperament (*nervous tension; a nervous headache*). **4** affecting or acting on the nerves. **5** (foll. by *of* + verbal noun) reluctant, afraid (*am nervous of meeting them*). □ **nervous breakdown** a period of mental illness, usu. resulting from severe depression or anxiety. **nervous system** the body's network of specialized cells which transmit nerve impulses between parts of the body. **nervous wreck** *colloq.* a person suffering from mental stress, exhaustion, etc. □ **nervously** *adv.* **nervousness** *n.* [ME f. L *nervosus* (as NERVE)]

nervy /ˈnɜːvɪ/ *adj.* (**nervier, nerviest**) **1** nervous; easily excited or disturbed. **2** *US* bold, impudent. □ **nervily** *adv.* **nerviness** *n.*

nescient /ˈnesɪənt/ *adj. literary* (foll. by *of*) lacking knowledge; ignorant. □ **nescience** *n.* [LL *nescientia* f. L *nescire* not know f. *ne-* not + *scire* know]

ness /nes/ *n.* a headland or promontory. [OE *næs*, rel. to OE *nasu* NOSE]

-ness /nɪs/ *suffix* forming nouns from adjectives, and occas. other words, expressing: **1** state or condition, or an instance of this (*bitterness; conceitedness; happiness; a kindness*). **2** something in a certain state (*wilderness*). [OE *-nes, -ness* f. Gmc]

nest *n. & v.* —*n.* **1** a structure or place where a bird lays eggs and shelters its young. **2** an animal's or insect's breeding-place or lair. **3** a snug or secluded retreat or shelter. **4** (often foll. by *of*) a place fostering something undesirable (*a nest of vice*). **5** a brood or swarm. **6** a group or set of similar objects, often of different sizes and fitting together for storage (*a nest of tables*). —*v.* **1** *intr.* use or build a nest. **2** *intr.* take wild birds' nests or eggs. **3** *intr.* (of objects) fit together or one inside another. □ **nest egg** a sum of money saved for the future. □ **nestful** *n.* (*pl.* **-fuls**). **nesting** *n.* (in sense 2 of *v.*). **nestlike** *adj.* [OE *nest*]

nestle /ˈnes(ə)l/ *v.* **1** *intr.* (often foll. by *down, in,* etc.) settle oneself comfortably. **2** *intr.* press oneself against another in affection etc. **3** *tr.* (foll. by *in, into,* etc.) push (a head or shoulder etc.) affectionately or snugly. **4** *intr.* lie half hidden or embedded. [OE *nestlian* (as NEST)]

nestling /ˈneslɪŋ, ˈnest-/ *n.* a bird that is too young to leave its nest.

net[1] *n. & v.* —*n.* **1** an open-meshed fabric of cord, rope, fibre, etc. **2** a piece of net used esp. to restrain, contain, or delimit, or to catch fish or other animals. **3** a structure with net to enclose an area of ground, esp. in sport. **4 a** a structure with net used in various games, esp. forming the goal in football, netball, etc., and dividing the court in tennis etc. **b** (often in *pl.*) a practice-ground in cricket, surrounded by nets. **5** a system or procedure for catching or entrapping a person or persons. **6** = NETWORK. —*v.* (**netted, netting**) **1** *tr.* **a** cover, confine, or catch with a net. **b** procure as with a net. **2** *tr.* hit (a ball) into the net, esp. of a goal. **3** *intr.* make netting. **4** *tr.* fish with nets, or set nets, in (a river). **5** *tr.* (usu. as **netted** *adj.*) mark with a netlike pattern; reticulate. □ **netful** *n.* (*pl.* **-fuls**). [OE *net, nett*]

net[2] /net/ *adj. & v.* (also **nett**) —*adj.* **1** (esp. of money) remaining after all necessary deductions, or free from deductions. **2** (of a price) to be paid in full; not reducible. **3** (of a weight) excluding that of the packaging or container etc. **4** (of an effect, result, etc.) ultimate, effective. —*v.tr.* (**netted, netting**) gain or yield (a sum) as net profit. □ **net profit** the effective profit; the actual gain after working expenses have been paid. [F *net* NEAT¹]

netball /ˈnetbɔːl/ *n.* a team game in which goals are scored by throwing a ball through a high horizontal ring with a net suspended from it.

nether /ˈneðə(r)/ *adj. archaic* = LOWER¹. □ **nether regions** (or **world**) hell; the underworld. □ **nethermost** *adj.* [OE *nithera* etc. f. Gmc]

netsuke /ˈnetsʊkɪ/ *n.* (*pl.* same or **netsukes**) (in Japan) a carved button-like ornament, esp. of ivory or wood. [Jap.]

netting /ˈnetɪŋ/ *n.* 1 netted fabric. 2 a piece of this.

nettle /ˈnet(ə)l/ *n. & v.* —*n.* 1 any plant of the genus *Urtica*, esp. *U. dioica*, with jagged leaves covered with stinging hairs. 2 any of various plants resembling this. —*v.tr.* 1 irritate, provoke, annoy. 2 sting with nettles. □ **nettle-rash** a skin eruption like nettle stings. [OE *netle, netele*]

network /ˈnetwɜːk/ *n. & v.* —*n.* 1 an arrangement of intersecting horizontal and vertical lines, like the structure of a net. 2 a complex system of railways, roads, canals, etc. 3 a group of people who exchange information, contacts, and experience for professional or social purposes. 4 a chain of interconnected computers, machines, or operations. 5 a system of connected electrical conductors. 6 a group of broadcasting stations connected for a simultaneous broadcast of a programme. —*v.* 1 *tr.* broadcast on a network. 2 *intr.* establish a network. 3 *tr.* link (machines, esp. computers) to operate interactively. 4 *intr.* be a member of a network (see sense 3 of *n.*).

networker /ˈnetˌwɜːkə(r)/ *n.* 1 *Computing* a member of an organization or computer network who operates from home or from an external office. 2 a member of a professional or social network.

neural /ˈnjʊər(ə)l/ *adj.* of or relating to a nerve or the central nervous system. □ **neural network** (or **neural net**) *Computing* a computer system modelled on the human brain and nervous system. □ **neurally** *adv.* [Gk *neuron* nerve]

neuralgia /njʊəˈrældʒə/ *n.* an intense intermittent pain along the course of a nerve, esp. in the head or face. □ **neuralgic** *adj.* [as NEURAL + -ALGIA]

neurasthenia /ˌnjʊərəsˈθiːnɪə/ *n.* a general term for fatigue, anxiety, listlessness, etc. □ **neurasthenic** /-ˈθenɪk/ *adj. & n.* [Gk *neuron* nerve + *astheneia* f. *asthenēs* weak]

neuritis /njʊəˈraɪtɪs/ *n.* inflammation of a nerve or nerves. □ **neuritic** /-ˈrɪtɪk/ *adj.* [formed as NEURO- + -ITIS]

neuro- /ˈnjʊərəʊ/ *comb. form* a nerve or the nerves. [Gk *neuron* nerve]

neurology /njʊəˈrɒlədʒɪ/ *n.* the scientific study of nerve systems. □ **neurological** /-rəˈlɒdʒɪk(ə)l/ *adj.* **neurologically** /-rəˈlɒdʒɪkəlɪ/ *adv.* **neurologist** *n.* [mod.L *neurologia* f. mod. Gk (as NEURO-, -LOGY)]

neuromuscular /ˌnjʊərəʊˈmʌskjʊlə(r)/ *adj.* of or relating to nerves and muscles.

neuron /ˈnjʊərɒn/ *n.* (also **neurone** /-rəʊn/) a specialized cell transmitting nerve impulses; a nerve-cell. □ **neuronal** /-ˈrəʊn(ə)l/ *adj.* **neuronic** /-ˈrɒnɪk/ *adj.* [Gk *neuron* nerve]

neuropathology /ˌnjʊərəʊpəˈθɒlədʒɪ/ *n.* the pathology of the nervous system. □ **neuropathologist** *n.*

neurophysiology /ˌnjʊərəʊˌfɪzɪˈɒlədʒɪ/ *n.* the physiology of the nervous system. □ **neurophysiological** /-zɪəˈlɒdʒɪk(ə)l/ *adj.* **neurophysiologist** *n.*

neurosis /njʊəˈrəʊsɪs/ *n.* (*pl.* **neuroses** /-siːz/) a mental illness characterized by irrational or depressive thought or behaviour, caused by a disorder of the nervous system usu. without organic change. [mod.L (as NEURO-, -OSIS)]

neurosurgery /ˌnjʊərəʊˈsɜːdʒərɪ/ *n.* surgery performed on the nervous system, esp. the brain and spinal cord. □ **neurosurgeon** *n.* **neurosurgical** *adj.*

neurotic /njʊəˈrɒtɪk/ *adj. & n.* —*adj.* 1 caused by or relating to neurosis. 2 (of a person) suffering from neurosis. 3 *colloq.* abnormally sensitive or obsessive. —*n.* a neurotic person. □ **neurotically** *adv.* **neuroticism** /-ˌsɪz(ə)m/ *n.*

neuter /ˈnjuːtə(r)/ *adj., n., & v.* —*adj.* 1 *Gram.* (of a noun etc.) neither masculine nor feminine. 2 (of a plant) having neither pistils nor stamen. 3 (of an insect) sexually undeveloped. —*n.* 1 *Gram.* a neuter word. 2 **a** a non-fertile insect, esp. a worker bee or ant. **b** a castrated animal. —*v.tr.* castrate or spay. [ME f. OF *neutre* or L *neuter* neither f. *ne-* not + *uter* either]

neutral /ˈnjuːtr(ə)l/ *adj. & n.* —*adj.* 1 not helping or supporting either of two opposing sides, esp. States at war or in dispute; impartial. 2 belonging to a neutral party, State, etc. (*neutral ships*). 3 indistinct, vague, indeterminate. 4 (of a gear) in which the engine is disconnected from the driven parts. 5 (of colours) not strong or positive; grey or beige. 6 *Chem.* neither acid nor alkaline. 7 *Electr.* neither positive nor negative. 8 *Biol.* sexually undeveloped; asexual. —*n.* 1 **a** a neutral State or person. **b** a subject of a neutral State. 2 a neutral gear. □ **neutrality** /-ˈtrælɪtɪ/ *n.* **neutrally** *adv.* [ME f. obs. F *neutral* or L *neutralis* of neuter gender (as NEUTER)]

neutralism /ˈnjuːtrəˌlɪz(ə)m/ *n.* a policy of political neutrality. □ **neutralist** *n.*

neutralize /ˈnjuːtrəlaɪz/ *v.tr.* (also **-ise**) 1 make neutral. 2 counterbalance; render ineffective by an opposite force or effect. 3 exempt or exclude (a place) from the sphere of hostilities. □ **neutralization** /-ˈzeɪʃ(ə)n/ *n.* **neutralizer** *n.* [F *neutraliser* f. med.L *neutralizare* (as NEUTRAL)]

neutrino /njuːˈtriːnəʊ/ *n.* (*pl.* **-os**) any of a group of stable elementary particles with zero electric charge and probably zero mass, which travel at the speed of light. [It., dimin. of *neutro* neutral (as NEUTER)]

neutron /ˈnjuːtrɒn/ *n.* an elementary particle of about the same mass as a proton but without an electric charge, present in all atomic nuclei except those of ordinary hydrogen. □ **neutron bomb** a bomb producing neutrons and little blast, causing damage to life but little destruction to property. [NEUTRAL + -ON]

never /ˈnevə(r)/ *adv.* 1 **a** at no time; on no occasion; not ever (*have never been to Paris; never saw them again*). **b** *colloq.* as an emphatic negative (*I never heard you come in*). 2 not at all (*never fear*). 3 *colloq.* (expressing surprise) surely not (*you never left the key in the lock!*). □ **never-never** (often prec. by *the*) *Brit. colloq.* hire purchase. **never-never land** an imaginary utopian place. **never a one** none. **well I never!** expressing great surprise. [OE *nǣfre* f. *ne* not + *ǣfre* EVER]

nevermore /ˌnevəˈmɔː(r)/ *adv.* at no future time.

nevertheless /ˌnevəðəˈles/ adv. in spite of that; notwithstanding; all the same.

nevus US var. of NAEVUS.

new adj. & adv. —adj. **1 a** of recent origin or arrival. **b** made, invented, discovered, acquired, or experienced recently or now for the first time (a new star; has many new ideas). **2** in original condition; not worn or used. **3 a** renewed or reformed (a new life; the new order). **b** reinvigorated (felt like a new person). **4** different from a recent previous one (has a new job). **5** in addition to others already existing (have you been to the new supermarket?). **6** (often foll. by to) unfamiliar or strange (a new sensation; the idea was new to me). **7** (often foll. by at) (of a person) inexperienced, unaccustomed (to doing something) (am new at this business). **8** (usu. prec. by the) often derog. **a** later, modern. **b** newfangled. **c** given to new or modern ideas (the new man). **d** recently affected by social change (the new rich). **9** (often prec. by the) advanced in method or theory (the new formula). **10** (in place-names) discovered or founded later than and named after (New York; New Zealand). —adv. (usu. in comb.) **1** newly, recently (new-found; new-baked). **2** anew, afresh. □ **New Age** a set of beliefs intended to replace traditional Western culture, with alternative approaches to religion, medicine, the environment, music, etc. **the new mathematics** (or **maths**) a system of teaching mathematics to children, with emphasis on investigation by them and on set theory. **new moon** **1** the moon when first seen as a crescent after conjunction with the sun. **2** the time of its appearance. **new potatoes** the earliest potatoes of a new crop. **new star** a nova. **New Testament** the part of the Bible concerned with the life and teachings of Christ and his earliest followers. **new town** Brit. a town established as a completely new settlement with government sponsorship. **new wave** a style of rock music popular in the 1970s. **New World** North and South America regarded collectively in relation to Europe. **new year** **1** the calendar year just begun or about to begin. **2** the first few days of a year. **New Year's Day** 1 January. **New Year's Eve** 31 December. □ **newish** adj. **newness** n. [OE nīwe f. Gmc]

newborn /njuːˈbɔːn, ˈnjuːbɔːn/ adj. (of a child etc.) recently born.

newcomer /ˈnjuːˌkʌmə(r)/ n. **1** a person who has recently arrived. **2** a beginner in some activity.

newel /ˈnjuːəl/ n. **1** the supporting central post of winding stairs. **2** the top or bottom supporting post of a stair-rail. [ME f. OF noel, nouel, knob f. med.L nodellus dimin. of L nodus knot]

newfangled /njuːˈfæŋg(ə)ld/ adj. derog. different from what one is used to; objectionably new. [ME newfangle (now dial.) liking what is new f. newe NEW adv. + -fangel f. OE fangol (unrecorded) inclined to take]

newly /ˈnjuːlɪ/ adv. **1** recently (a friend newly arrived; a newly-discovered country). **2** afresh, anew (newly painted). **3** in a new or different manner (newly arranged). □ **newly-wed** a recently married person.

news /njuːz/ n.pl. (usu. treated as sing.) **1** information about important or interesting recent events, esp. when published or broadcast. **2** (prec. by the) a broadcast report of news. **3** newly received or noteworthy information. **4** (foll. by to) colloq. information not previously known (to a person) (that's news to me). □ **news agency** an organization that collects and distributes news items. **news bulletin** a collection of items of news, esp. for broadcasting. **news conference** a press conference. **news room** a room in a newspaper or broadcasting office where news is processed. **news-sheet** a simple form of newspaper; a newsletter. **news-stand** a stall for the sale of newspapers. **news-vendor** a newspaper-seller. □ **newsless** adj. [ME, pl. of NEW after OF noveles or med.L nova neut. pl. of novus new]

newsagent /ˈnjuːzˌeɪdʒ(ə)nt/ n. Brit. a seller of or shop selling newspapers and usu. related items, e.g. stationery.

newsboy /ˈnjuːzbɔɪ/ n. a boy who sells or delivers newspapers.

newsbrief /ˈnjuːzbriːf/ n. a short item of news, esp. on television; a newsflash.

newscast /ˈnjuːzkɑːst/ n. a radio or television broadcast of news reports.

newscaster /ˈnjuːzˌkɑːstə(r)/ n. = NEWSREADER.

newsdealer /ˈnjuːzˌdiːlə(r)/ n. US = NEWSAGENT.

newsflash /ˈnjuːzflæʃ/ n. a single item of important news broadcast separately and often interrupting other programmes.

newsgirl /ˈnjuːzɡɜːl/ n. a girl who sells or delivers newspapers.

newsletter /ˈnjuːzˌletə(r)/ n. an informal printed report issued periodically to the members of a society, business, organization, etc.

newsman /ˈnjuːzmæn/ n. (pl. -men) a newspaper reporter; a journalist.

newspaper /ˈnjuːzˌpeɪpə(r)/ n. **1** a printed publication (usu. daily or weekly) containing news, advertisements, correspondence, etc. **2** the sheets of paper forming this (wrapped in newspaper).

newspaperman /ˈnjuːzpeɪpəˌmæn/ n. (pl. -men) a journalist.

Newspeak /ˈnjuːspiːk/ n. ambiguous euphemistic language used esp. in political propaganda. [an artificial official language in George Orwell's Nineteen Eighty-Four (1949)]

newsprint /ˈnjuːzprɪnt/ n. a type of low-quality paper on which newspapers are printed.

newsreader /ˈnjuːzˌriːdə(r)/ n. a person who reads out broadcast news bulletins.

newsreel /ˈnjuːzriːl/ n. a short cinema film of recent events.

newsworthy /ˈnjuːzˌwɜːðɪ/ adj. topical; noteworthy as news. □ **newsworthiness** n.

newsy /ˈnjuːzɪ/ adj. (**newsier, newsiest**) colloq. full of news.

newt /njuːt/ n. any of various small amphibians, esp. of the genus Triturus, having a well-developed tail. [ME f. ewt, with n from an (cf. NICKNAME): var. of evet EFT]

newton /ˈnjuːt(ə)n/ n. Physics the SI unit of force. [Sir Isaac Newton, Engl. scientist d. 1727]

New Zealander /ˈziːləndə(r)/ n. **1** a native or national of New Zealand, an island group in the Pacific. **2** a person of New Zealand descent.

next adj., adv., n., & prep. —adj. **1** (often foll. by to) being or positioned or living nearest (in the next house; the chair next to the fire). **2** the nearest in order of time; the first or soonest encountered or considered (next Friday; ask the next person you see). —adv. **1** (often foll. by to) in the nearest place or degree (*put it next to mine; came next to last*). **2** on the first or soonest occasion (*when we next meet*). —*n.* the next person or thing. —*prep. colloq.* next to. □ **next-best** the next in order of preference. **next of kin** the closest living relative or relatives. **next to** almost (*next to nothing left*). [OE *nēhsta* superl. (as NIGH)]

nexus /ˈneksəs/ *n.* (*pl.* same) **1** a connected group or series. **2** a bond; a connection. [L f. *nectere nex-* bind]

NGO *abbr.* non-governmental organization.

NHS *abbr.* (in the UK) National Health Service.

NI *abbr.* **1** (in the UK) National Insurance. **2** Northern Ireland.

Ni *symb. Chem.* the element nickel.

niacin /ˈnaɪəsɪn/ *n.* = NICOTINIC ACID. [*nicotinic* acid + -IN]

nib *n.* **1** the point of a pen, which touches the writing surface. **2** (in *pl.*) shelled and crushed coffee or cocoa beans. [prob. f. MDu. *nib* or MLG *nibbe*, var. of *nebbe* beak]

nibble /ˈnɪb(ə)l/ *v. & n.* —*v.* **1** *tr.* & (foll. by *at*) *intr.* **a** take small bites at. **b** eat in small amounts. **c** bite at gently or cautiously or playfully. **2** *intr.* (foll. by *at*) show cautious interest in. —*n.* **1** an instance of nibbling. **2** a very small amount of food. **3** *Computing* half a byte, i.e. 4 bits. □ **nibbler** *n.* [prob. of LG or Du. orig.: cf. LG *nibbeln* gnaw]

niblick /ˈnɪblɪk/ *n. Golf* an iron with a large round heavy head, used esp. for playing out of bunkers. [19th c.: orig. unkn.]

nibs /nɪbz/ *n.* □ **his nibs** *joc. colloq.* a mock title used with reference to an important or self-important person. [19th c.: orig. unkn. (cf. earlier *nabs*)]

nicad /ˈnaɪkæd/ *adj. & n.* —*adj.* nickel and cadmium. —*n.* a nickel and cadmium battery. [NICKEL + CADMIUM]

nice *adj.* **1** pleasant, agreeable, satisfactory. **2** (of a person) kind, good-natured. **3** *iron.* bad or awkward (*a nice mess you've made*). **4 a** fine or subtle (*a nice distinction*). **b** requiring careful thought or attention (*a nice problem*). **5** fastidious; delicately sensitive. **6** punctilious, scrupulous (*were not too nice about their methods*). **7** (foll. by an adj., often with *and*) satisfactory or adequate in terms of the quality described (*a nice long time; nice and warm*). □ **nice work** a task well done. □ **nicely** *adv.* **niceness** *n.* **nicish** *adj.* (also **niceish**). [ME, = stupid, wanton f. OF, = silly, simple f. L *nescius* ignorant (as *nescience*: see NESCIENT)]

nicety /ˈnaɪsɪtɪ/ *n.* (*pl.* **-ies**) **1** a subtle distinction or detail. **2** precision, accuracy. **3** intricate or subtle quality (*a point of great nicety*). **4** (in *pl.*) **a** minutiae; fine details. **b** refinements, trimmings. □ **to a nicety** with exactness. [ME f. OF *niceté* (as NICE)]

niche /nɪtʃ, niːʃ/ *n.* **1** a shallow recess, esp. in a wall to contain a statue etc. **2** a comfortable or suitable position in life or employment. **3** an appropriate combination of conditions for a species to thrive. [F f. *nicher* make a nest, ult. f. L *nidus* nest]

Nick *n.* □ **Old Nick** the Devil. [prob. f. a pet-form of the name *Nicholas*]

nick¹ *n. & v.* —*n.* **1** a small cut or notch. **2** *Brit. sl.* **a** a prison. **b** a police station. **3** (prec. by *in* with adj.) *Brit. colloq.* condition (*in reasonable nick*). —*v.tr.* **1** make a nick or nicks in. **2** *Brit. sl.*

a steal. **b** arrest, catch. □ **in the nick of time** only just in time; just at the right moment. [ME: orig. uncert.]

nick² *v.intr. Austral. sl.* (foll. by *off, in*, etc.) move quickly or furtively. [19th c.: orig. uncert. (cf. NIP¹ 4)]

nickel /ˈnɪk(ə)l/ *n. & v.* —*n.* **1** *Chem.* a malleable ductile silver-white metallic transition element, used in special steels, in magnetic alloys, and as a catalyst. **2** *colloq.* a US five-cent coin. —*v.tr.* (**nickelled, nickelling;** *US* **nickeled, nickeling**) coat with nickel. □ **nickel steel** a type of stainless steel with chromium and nickel. □ **nickelic** *adj.* **nickelous** *adj.* [abbr. of G *Kupfernickel* copper-coloured ore, from which nickel was first obtained, f. *Kupfer* copper + *Nickel* demon, because the ore failed to yield copper]

nickelodeon /ˌnɪkəˈləʊdɪən/ *n. US colloq.* a jukebox. [NICKEL + MELODEON]

nicker /ˈnɪkə(r)/ *n.* (*pl.* same) *Brit. sl.* a pound (in money). [20th c.: orig. unkn.]

nick-nack var. of KNICK-KNACK.

nickname /ˈnɪkneɪm/ *n. & v.* —*n.* a familiar or humorous name given to a person or thing instead of or as well as the real name. —*v.tr.* **1** give a nickname to. **2** call (a person or thing) by a nickname. [ME f. *eke-name*, with *n* from *an* (cf. NEWT): *eke* = addition, f. OE *ēaca* (as EKE)]

nicotine /ˈnɪkəˌtiːn/ *n.* a colourless poisonous alkaloid present in tobacco. □ **nicotinism** *n.* **nicotinize** *v.tr.* (also **-ise**). [F f. mod.L *nicotiana* (*herba*) tobacco-plant, f. J. *Nicot*, Fr. diplomat who introduced tobacco into France in the 16th c.]

nicotinic acid /ˌnɪkəˈtɪnɪk/ *n.* a vitamin of the B complex, found in milk, liver, and yeast.

nictitate /ˈnɪktɪˌteɪt/ *v.intr.* close and open the eyes; blink or wink. □ **nictitating membrane** a clear membrane forming a third eyelid in amphibians, birds, and some other animals. □ **nictitation** /-ˈteɪʃ(ə)n/ *n.* [med.L *nictitare* frequent. of L *nictare* blink]

niece /niːs/ *n.* a daughter of one's brother or sister, or of one's brother-in-law or sister-in-law. [ME f. OF ult. f. L *neptis* granddaughter]

niff *n. & v. Brit. colloq.* —*n.* a smell, esp. an unpleasant one. —*v.intr.* smell, stink. □ **niffy** *adj.* (**niffier, niffiest**). [orig. dial.]

nifty /ˈnɪftɪ/ *adj.* (**niftier, niftiest**) *colloq.* **1** clever, adroit. **2** smart, stylish. □ **niftily** *adv.* **niftiness** *n.* [19th c.: orig. uncert.]

niggard /ˈnɪgəd/ *n.* a mean or stingy person. [ME, alt. f. earlier (obs.) *nigon*, prob. of Scand. orig.: cf. NIGGLE]

niggardly /ˈnɪgədlɪ/ *adj. & adv.* —*adj.* **1** stingy, parsimonious. **2** meagre, scanty. —*adv.* in a stingy or meagre manner. □ **niggardliness** *n.*

nigger /ˈnɪgə(r)/ *n. offens.* **1** a Black person. **2** a dark-skinned person. □ **a nigger in the woodpile** a hidden cause of trouble or inconvenience. [earlier *neger* f. F *nègre* f. Sp. *negro* NEGRO]

niggle /ˈnɪg(ə)l/ *v. & n.* —*v.* **1** *intr.* be overattentive to details. **2** *intr.* find fault in a petty way. **3** *tr. colloq.* irritate; nag pettily. —*n.* a trifling complaint or criticism; a worry or annoyance. [app. of Scand. orig.: cf. Norw. *nigla* to be frugal]

niggling /ˈnɪglɪŋ/ *adj.* **1** troublesome or irritating in a petty way. **2** trifling or petty. □ **nigglingly** *adv.*

nigh /naɪ/ *adv., prep., & adj. archaic* or *dial.* near. [OE *nēh, nēah*]

night /naɪt/ n. **1** the period of darkness between one day and the next; the time from sunset to sunrise. **2** nightfall (*shall not reach home before night*). **3** the darkness of night (*as black as night*). **4** a night or evening appointed for some activity, or spent or regarded in a certain way (*last night of the Proms; a great night out*). □ **night-blindness** = NYCTALOPIA. **night-life** entertainment available at night in a town. **night-light** a dim light kept on in a bedroom at night. **night-long** throughout the night. **night-owl** *colloq.* a person active at night. **night safe** a safe with access from the outer wall of a bank for the deposit of money etc. when the bank is closed. **night school** an institution providing evening classes for those working by day. **night-time** the time of darkness. **night-watchman 1** a person whose job is to keep watch by night. **2** *Cricket* an inferior batsman sent in when a wicket falls near the close of a day's play. □ **nightless** adj. [OE *neaht, niht* f. Gmc]

nightbird /ˈnaɪtbɜːd/ n. a person who habitually goes about at night.

nightcap /ˈnaɪtkæp/ n. **1** *hist.* a cap worn in bed. **2** a hot or alcoholic drink taken at bedtime.

nightclothes /ˈnaɪtkləʊðz/ n. clothes worn in bed.

nightclub /ˈnaɪtklʌb/ n. a club that is open at night and provides refreshment and entertainment.

nightdress /ˈnaɪtdres/ n. a woman's or child's loose garment worn in bed.

nightfall /ˈnaɪtfɔːl/ n. the onset of night; the end of daylight.

nightgown /ˈnaɪtgaʊn/ n. **1** = NIGHTDRESS. **2** *hist.* a dressing-gown.

nightie /ˈnaɪtɪ/ n. *colloq.* a nightdress. [abbr.]

nightingale /ˈnaɪtɪŋˌgeɪl/ n. any small reddish-brown bird of the genus *Luscinia*, esp. *L. megarhynchos*, of which the male sings melodiously, esp. at night. [OE *nihtegala* (whence obs. *nightgale*) f. Gmc: for -n- cf. FARTHINGALE]

nightjar /ˈnaɪtdʒɑː(r)/ n. any nocturnal bird of the family Caprimulgidae, having a harsh cry.

nightly /ˈnaɪtlɪ/ adj. & adv. —adj. **1** happening, done, or existing in the night. **2** recurring every night. —adv. every night. [OE *nihtlic* (as NIGHT)]

nightmare /ˈnaɪtmeə(r)/ n. **1** a frightening or unpleasant dream. **2** *colloq.* a terrifying or very unpleasant experience or situation. **3** a haunting or obsessive fear. □ **nightmarish** adj. **nightmarishly** adv. [an evil spirit (incubus) once thought to lie on and suffocate sleepers: OE *mære* incubus]

nightshade /ˈnaɪtʃeɪd/ n. any of various poisonous plants, esp. of the genus *Solanum*, including *S. nigrum* (**black nightshade**) with black berries, and *S. dulcamara* (**woody nightshade**) with red berries. □ **deadly nightshade** = BELLADONNA. [OE *nihtscada* app. formed as NIGHT + SHADE, prob. with ref. to its poisonous properties]

nightshirt /ˈnaɪtʃɜːt/ n. a long shirt worn in bed.

nightspot /ˈnaɪtspɒt/ n. a nightclub.

nightstick /ˈnaɪtstɪk/ n. *US* a policeman's truncheon.

nihilism /ˈnaɪɪˌlɪz(ə)m, ˈnaɪhɪˌlɪz(ə)m/ n. **1** the rejection of all religious and moral principles. **2** an extreme form of scepticism maintaining that nothing has a real existence. □ **nihilist** n. **nihilistic** /-ˈlɪstɪk/ adj. [L *nihil* nothing]

-nik /nɪk/ *suffix* forming nouns denoting a person associated with a specified thing or quality (*beatnik; refusenik*). [Russ. (as SPUTNIK) and Yiddish]

nil /nɪl/ n. nothing; no number or amount (esp. as a score in games). [L, = *nihil* nothing]

nimble /ˈnɪmb(ə)l/ adj. (**nimbler, nimblest**) **1** quick and light in movement or action; agile. **2** (of the mind) quick to comprehend; clever, versatile. □ **nimbleness** n. **nimbly** adv. [OE *næmel* quick to seize f. *niman* take f. Gmc, with -b- as in THIMBLE]

nimbostratus /ˌnɪmbəʊˈstreɪtəs, -ˈstrɑːtəs/ n. (*pl.* **nimbostrati** /-taɪ/) *Meteorol.* a low dark-grey layer of cloud. [mod.L, f. NIMBUS + STRATUS]

nimbus /ˈnɪmbəs/ n. (*pl.* **nimbi** /-baɪ/ or **nimbuses**) **1 a** a bright cloud or halo investing a deity or person or thing. **b** the halo of a saint etc. **2** *Meteorol.* a rain-cloud. □ **nimbused** adj. [L, = cloud, aureole]

Nimby /ˈnɪmbɪ/ adj. & n. —adj. objecting to the siting of unpleasant developments in one's own locality. —n. a person who so objects. [not in my own back yard]

niminy-piminy /ˌnɪmɪnɪˈpɪmɪnɪ/ adj. feeble, affected; lacking in vigour. [cf. NAMBY-PAMBY]

nincompoop /ˈnɪŋkəmˌpuːp/ n. a simpleton; a fool. [17th c.: orig. unkn.]

nine n. & adj. —n. **1** one more than eight. **2** a symbol for this (9, ix, IX). **3** a size etc. denoted by nine. **4** a set or team of nine individuals. **5** the time of nine o'clock (*is it nine yet?*). **6** a card with nine pips. —adj. that amount to nine. □ **dressed up to the nines** dressed very elaborately. **nine days' wonder** a person or thing that is briefly famous. **nine times out of ten** nearly always. **nine to five** a designation of typical office hours. [OE *nigon* f. Gmc]

ninefold /ˈnaɪnfəʊld/ adj. & adv. **1** nine times as much or as many. **2** consisting of nine parts.

ninepin /ˈnaɪnpɪn/ n. **1** (in *pl.*; usu. treated as *sing.*) a game in which nine pins are set up at the end of an alley and bowled at in an attempt to knock them down. **2** a pin used in this game.

nineteen /naɪnˈtiːn/ n. & adj. —n. **1** one more than eighteen. **2** the symbol for this (19, xix, XIX). **3** a size etc. denoted by nineteen. —adj. that amount to nineteen. □ **nineteenth** adj. & n. [OE *nigontȳne*]

ninety /ˈnaɪntɪ/ n. & adj. —n. (*pl.* **-ies**) **1** the product of nine and ten. **2** a symbol for this (90, xc, XC). **3** (in *pl.*) the numbers from 90 to 99, esp. the years of a century or of a person's life. —adj. that amount to ninety. □ **ninetieth** adj. & n. **ninetyfold** adj. & adv. [OE *nigontig*]

ninja /ˈnɪndʒə/ n. a person skilled in ninjutsu. [Jap.]

ninjutsu /nɪnˈdʒʊtsuː/ n. one of the Japanese martial arts, characterized by stealthy movement and camouflage. [Jap.]

ninny /ˈnɪnɪ/ n. (*pl.* **-ies**) a foolish or simple-minded person. [perh. f. *innocent*]

ninth /naɪnθ/ n. & adj. —n. **1** the position in a sequence corresponding to the number 9 in the sequence 1–9. **2** something occupying this position. **3** each of nine equal parts of a thing. —adj. that is the ninth. □ **ninthly** adv.

niobium /naɪˈəʊbɪəm/ n. *Chem.* a rare grey-blue metallic transition element used in alloys for

superconductors. □ **niobic** adj. **niobous** adj.
[*Niobe* daughter of Tantalus: so called because
first found in the mineral tantalite]

nip¹ v. & n. —v. (**nipped, nipping**) **1** tr. pinch,
squeeze, or bite sharply. **2** tr. (often foll. by *off*)
remove by pinching etc. **3** tr. (of the cold, frost,
etc.) cause pain or harm to. **4** intr. (foll. by *in,
out*, etc.) *Brit. colloq.* go nimbly or quickly. **5** tr.
US sl. steal, snatch. —n. **1 a** a pinch, a sharp
squeeze. **b** a bite. **2** biting cold. □ **nip and tuck**
US neck and neck. **nip in the bud** suppress or
destroy (esp. an idea) at an early stage. □
nipping adj. [ME, prob. of LG or Du. orig.]

nip² n. a small quantity of spirits. [prob. abbr. of
nipperkin small measure: cf. LG, Du. *nippen* to
sip]

nipper /ˈnɪpə(r)/ n. **1** a person or thing that nips.
2 the claw of a crab, lobster, etc. **3** *Brit. colloq.* a
young child. **4** (in pl.) any tool for gripping or
cutting, e.g. forceps or pincers.

nipple /ˈnɪp(ə)l/ n. **1** a small projection in which
the mammary ducts of either sex of mammals
terminate and from which in females milk
is secreted for the young. **2** the teat of a
feeding-bottle. **3** a device like a nipple in
function, e.g. the tip of a grease-gun. **4** a
nipple-like protuberance. [16th c., also *neble,
nible*, perh. dimin. f. *neb*]

nippy /ˈnɪpɪ/ adj. (**nippier, nippiest**) *colloq.* **1**
quick, nimble, active. **2** chilly, cold. □ **nippily**
adv. [NIP¹ + -Y¹]

nirvana /nɜːˈvɑːnə, nɪə-/ n. (in Buddhism) perfect
bliss and release from karma, attained by the
extinction of individuality. [Skr. *nirvāṇa* f. *nirvā*
be extinguished f. *nis* out + *vā-* to blow]

Nissen hut /ˈnɪs(ə)n/ n. a tunnel-shaped hut of
corrugated iron with a cement floor. [P. N.
Nissen, British engineer d. 1930, its inventor]

nit n. **1** the egg or young form of a louse or
other parasitic insect esp. of human head-lice
or body-lice. **2** *Brit. sl.* a stupid person. □
nit-picking n. & adj. *colloq.* fault-finding in a
petty manner. [OE *hnitu* f. WG]

nitrate n. & v. —n. /ˈnaɪtreɪt/ **1** any salt or ester
of nitric acid. **2** potassium or sodium nitrate
when used as a fertilizer. —v.tr. /naɪˈtreɪt/ *Chem.*
treat, combine, or impregnate with nitric acid.
□ **nitration** /-ˈtreɪʃ(ə)n/ n. [F (as NITRE, -ATE¹)]

nitre /ˈnaɪtə(r)/ n. (*US* **niter**) saltpetre, potassium
nitrate. [ME f. OF f. L *nitrum* f. Gk *nitron*, of
Semitic orig.]

nitric /ˈnaɪtrɪk/ adj. of or containing nitrogen. □
nitric acid a colourless corrosive poisonous
liquid. [F *nitrique* (as NITRE)]

nitride /ˈnaɪtraɪd/ n. *Chem.* a binary compound
of nitrogen. [NITRE + -IDE]

nitrify /ˈnaɪtrɪfaɪ/ v.tr. (**-ies, -ied**) **1** impregnate
with nitrogen. **2** convert (nitrogen, usu. in the
form of ammonia) into nitrites or nitrates. □
nitrifiable adj. **nitrification** /-fɪˈkeɪʃ(ə)n/ n. [F
nitrifier (as NITRE)]

nitrite /ˈnaɪtraɪt/ n. any salt or ester of nitrous
acid.

nitro- /ˈnaɪtrəʊ/ comb. form **1** of or containing
nitric acid, nitre, or nitrogen. **2** made with or
by use of any of these. [Gk (as NITRE)]

nitrobenzene /ˌnaɪtrəʊˈbenziːn/ n. a yellow oily
liquid made by the nitration of benzene and
used to make aniline etc.

nitrocellulose /ˌnaɪtrəʊˈseljʊˌləʊz, -ˌləʊs/ n. a
highly flammable material made by treating

cellulose with concentrated nitric acid, used in
the manufacture of explosives and celluloid.

nitrogen /ˈnaɪtrədʒ(ə)n/ n. *Chem.* a colourless
tasteless odourless gaseous element that forms
four-fifths of the atmosphere and is an essential
constituent of proteins and nucleic acids. □
nitrogen cycle the interconversion of nitrogen
and its compounds, usu. in the form of nitrates,
in nature. **nitrogen fixation** a chemical process
in which atmospheric nitrogen is assimilated
into organic compounds in living organisms and
hence into the nitrogen cycle. □ **nitrogenous**
/-ˈtrɒdʒɪnəs/ adj. [F *nitrogène* (as NITRO-, -GEN)]

nitroglycerine /ˌnaɪtrəʊˈɡlɪsərɪn/ n. (also **nitro-
glycerin**) an explosive yellow liquid made by
reacting glycerol with a mixture of concentrated
sulphuric and nitric acids.

nitrous /ˈnaɪtrəs/ adj. of, like, or impregnated
with nitrogen. □ **nitrous acid** a weak acid
existing only in solution and in the gas phase.
nitrous oxide a colourless gas used as an
anaesthetic and as an aerosol propellant. [L
nitrosus (as NITRE), partly through F *nitreux*]

nitty-gritty /ˌnɪtɪˈɡrɪtɪ/ n. *sl.* the realities or
practical details of a matter. [20th c.: orig.
uncert.]

nitwit /ˈnɪtwɪt/ n. *colloq.* a stupid person. □
nitwittery /-ˈwɪtərɪ/ n. [perh. f. NIT + WIT¹]

nitwitted /ˈnɪtwɪtɪd/ adj. stupid. □ **nit-
wittedness** /-ˈwɪtɪdnɪs/ n.

nix n. & v. *sl.* —n. **1** nothing. **2** a denial or
refusal. —v.tr. **1** cancel. **2** reject. [G, colloq. var.
of *nichts* nothing]

NNE abbr. north-north-east.

NNW abbr. north-north-west.

No¹ symb. *Chem.* the element nobelium.

No² var. of NOH.

No. abbr. **1** number. **2** *US* North. [sense 1 f. L
numero, ablat. of *numerus* number]

no¹ adj. **1** not any (*there is no excuse; no circumstances
could justify it; no two of them are alike*). **2** not a,
quite other than (*is no fool; is no part of my plan;
caused no slight inconvenience*). **3** hardly any (*is no
distance; did it in no time*). **4** used elliptically as a
slogan, notice, etc., to forbid, reject, or deplore
the thing specified (*no parking; no surrender*). □
no-account unimportant, worthless. **no-ball**
Cricket n. an unlawfully delivered ball. **no-claim**
(or **-claims**) **bonus** a reduction of the insurance
premium charged when the insured has not
made a claim under the insurance during an
agreed preceding period. **no entry** (of a notice)
prohibiting vehicles or persons from entering a
road or place. **no-fault** *US* (of insurance) valid
regardless of the allocation of blame for an
accident etc. **no-frills** lacking ornament or
embellishment. **no go** impossible, hopeless.
no-go area an area forbidden to unauthorized
people. **no-hitter** *US Baseball* a game in which
a team does not get a player to first base.
no-hoper *Austral. sl.* a useless person. **no man**
no person, nobody. **no man's land 1** *Mil.* the
space between two opposing armies. **2** an area
not assigned to any owner. **3** an area not clearly
belonging to any one subject etc. **no-no** *colloq.*
a thing not possible or acceptable. **no-nonsense**
serious, without flippancy. **no place** *US*
nowhere. **no-show** a person who has reserved
a seat etc. but neither uses it nor cancels the
reservation. **no side** *Rugby Football* **1** the end of
a game. **2** the referee's announcement of this.

no sweat *colloq.* no bother, no trouble. **no thoroughfare** an indication that passage along a street, path, etc., is blocked or prohibited. **no way** *colloq.* **1** it is impossible. **2** I will not agree etc. **no-win** of or designating a situation in which success is impossible. **there is no . . .ing** it is impossible to . . . (*there is no accounting for tastes*). [ME f. *nān, nōn* NONE, orig. only before consonants]

no² *adv. & n.* —*adv.* **1** equivalent to a negative sentence: the answer to your question is negative, your request or command will not be complied with, the statement made or course of action intended or conclusion arrived at is not correct or satisfactory, the negative statement made is correct. **2** (foll. by *compar.*) by no amount; not at all (*no better than before*). **3** *Sc.* not (*will ye no come back again?*). —*n.* (*pl.* **noes**) **1** an utterance of the word *no.* **2** a denial or refusal. **3** a negative vote. □ **is no more** has died or ceased to exist. **no can do** *colloq.* I am unable to do it. **the noes have it** the negative voters are in the majority. **no less** (often foll. by *than*) **1** as much (*gave me £50, no less; gave me no less than £50; is no less than a scandal; a no less fatal victory*). **2** as important (*no less a person than the President*). **3** *disp.* no fewer (*no less than ten people have told me*). **no longer** not now or henceforth as formerly. **no more** *n.* nothing further (*have no more to say; want no more of it*). —*adj.* not any more (*no more wine?*). —*adv.* **1** no longer. **2** never again. **3** to no greater extent (*is no more a lord than I am; could no more do it than fly in the air*). **4** just as little, neither (*you did not come, and no more did he*). **not take no for an answer** persist in spite of refusals. **or no** or not (*pleasant or no, it is true*). **whether or no 1** in either case. **2** (as an indirect question) which of a case and its negative (*tell me whether or no*). [OE nō, nā f. *ne* not + ō, ā ever]

Noah's ark /ˈnəʊəz, nɔːz/ *n.* **1** the ship in which (according to the Bible) Noah, his family, and the animals were saved. **2** an imitation of this as a child's toy. [*Noah*, Hebrew patriarch in Gen. 6]

nob¹ *n. Brit. sl.* a person of wealth or high social position. [orig. *Sc. knabb, nab*; 18th c., of unkn. orig.]

nob² /nɒb/ *n. sl.* the head. [perh. var. of KNOB]

nobble /ˈnɒb(ə)l/ *v.tr. Brit. sl.* **1** try to influence (e.g. a judge), esp. unfairly. **2** tamper with (a racehorse) to prevent its winning. **3** get hold of (money etc.) dishonestly. **4** catch (a criminal). **5** secure the support of or weaken (a person) esp. by underhand means. **6** seize, grab. [prob. = dial. *knobble, knubble* knock, beat, f. KNOB]

nobbler /ˈnɒblə(r)/ *n. Austral. sl.* a glass or drink of liquor. [19th c.: orig. unkn.]

Nobelist /nəʊˈbelɪst/ *n.* US a winner of a Nobel prize.

nobelium /nəʊˈbiːlɪəm/ *n. Chem.* a radioactive transuranic metallic element. [*Nobel* (see NOBEL PRIZE) + -IUM]

Nobel prize /ˈnəʊbel, -ˈbel/ *n.* any of six international prizes awarded annually for physics, chemistry, physiology or medicine, literature, economics, and the promotion of peace. [Alfred *Nobel* (d. 1896), Swedish chemist and engineer, who endowed them]

nobility /nəʊˈbɪlɪtɪ/ *n.* (*pl.* **-ies**) **1** nobleness of character, mind, birth, or rank. **2** (prec. by *a,*

the) a class of nobles, an aristocracy. [ME f. OF *nobilité* or L *nobilitas* (as NOBLE)]

noble /ˈnəʊb(ə)l/ *adj. & n.* —*adj.* (**nobler, noblest**) **1** belonging by rank, title, or birth to the aristocracy. **2** of excellent character; having lofty ideals; free from pettiness and meanness, magnanimous. **3** of imposing appearance, splendid, magnificent, stately. **4** excellent, admirable (*noble horse; noble cellar*). —*n.* a nobleman or noblewoman. □ **noble gas** any gaseous element of a group that almost never combine with other elements. **noble metal** a metal (e.g. gold, silver, or platinum) that resists chemical action, does not corrode or tarnish in air or water, and is not easily attacked by acids. □ **nobleness** *n.* **nobly** *adv.* [ME f. OF f. L (g)*nobilis*, rel. to KNOW]

nobleman /ˈnəʊb(ə)lmən/ *n.* (*pl.* **-men**) a man of noble rank or birth, a peer.

noblesse /nəʊˈbles/ *n.* the class of nobles (esp. of a foreign country). □ **noblesse oblige** /əˈbliːʒ/ privilege entails responsibility. [ME = nobility, f. OF (as NOBLE)]

noblewoman /ˈnəʊb(ə)lˌwʊmən/ *n.* (*pl.* **-women**) a woman of noble rank or birth, a peeress.

nobody /ˈnəʊbədɪ/ *pron. & n.* —*pron.* no person. —*n.* (*pl.* **-ies**) a person of no importance, authority, or position. [ME f. NO¹ + BODY (= person)]

nock *n. & v.* —*n.* **1** a notch at either end of a bow for holding the string. **2** a notch at the butt-end of an arrow for receiving the bowstring. —*v.tr.* set (an arrow) on the string. [ME, perh. = *nock* forward upper corner of some sails, f. MDu. *nocke*]

noctambulist /nɒkˈtæmbjʊlɪst/ *n.* a sleepwalker. □ **noctambulism** *n.* [L *nox noctis* night + *ambulare* walk]

nocturnal /nɒkˈtɜːn(ə)l/ *adj.* of or in the night; done or active by night. □ **nocturnal emission** involuntary emission of semen during sleep. □ **nocturnally** *adv.* [LL *nocturnalis* f. L *nocturnus* of the night f. *nox noctis* night]

nocturne /ˈnɒktɜːn/ *n.* **1** *Mus.* a short composition of a romantic nature, usu. for piano. **2** a picture of a night scene. [F (as NOCTURNAL)]

nod *v. & n.* —*v.* (**nodded, nodding**) **1** *intr.* incline one's head slightly and briefly in greeting, assent, or command. **2** *intr.* let one's head fall forward in drowsiness; be drowsy. **3** *tr.* incline (one's head). **4** *tr.* signify (assent etc.) by a nod. **5** *intr.* (of flowers, plumes, etc.) bend downwards and sway, or move up and down. **6** *intr.* make a mistake due to a momentary lack of alertness or attention. —*n.* a nodding of the head. □ **get the nod** *US* be chosen or approved. **nodding acquaintance** (usu. foll. by *with*) a very slight acquaintance with a person or subject. **nod off** *colloq.* fall asleep. **on the nod** *colloq.* **1** with merely formal assent and no discussion. **2** on credit. □ **noddingly** *adv.* [ME *nodde*, of unkn. orig.]

noddle /ˈnɒd(ə)l/ *n. colloq.* the head. [ME *nodle*, of unkn. orig.]

noddy /ˈnɒdɪ/ *n.* (*pl.* **-ies**) **1** a simpleton. **2** any of various tropical sea birds of the genus *Anous.* [prob. f. obs. *noddy* foolish, which is perh. f. NOD]

node *n.* **1** *Bot.* **a** the part of a plant stem from which one or more leaves emerge. **b** a knob on a root or branch. **2** *Anat.* a natural swelling or bulge in an organ or part of the body. **3** *Astron.*

either of two points at which a planet's orbit intersects the plane of the ecliptic or the celestial equator. **4** *Physics* a point of minimum disturbance in a standing wave system. **5** *Electr.* a point of zero current or voltage. **6** *Math.* a point at which a curve intersects itself. **7** a component in a computer network. □ **nodal** *adj.* **nodical** *adj.* (in sense 3). [L *nodus* knot]

nodule /ˈnɒdjuːl/ *n.* **1** a small rounded lump of anything, e.g. flint in chalk, carbon in cast iron, or a mineral on the seabed. **2** a small swelling or aggregation of cells, e.g. a small tumour, node, or ganglion. □ **nodular** *adj.* **nodulated** *adj.* **nodulation** /-ˈleɪʃ(ə)n/ *n.* **nodulose** *adj.* **nodulous** *adj.* [L *nodulus* dimin. of *nodus* knot]

Noel /nəʊˈel/ *n.* Christmas (esp. as a refrain in carols). [F f. L (as NATAL)]

nog[1] *n.* a small block or peg of wood. [17th c.: orig. unkn.]

nog[2] *n.* **1** *Brit.* a strong beer brewed in East Anglia. **2** an egg-flip. [17th c.: orig. unkn.]

noggin /ˈnɒgɪn/ *n.* **1** a small mug. **2** a small measure, usu. ¼ pint, of spirits. **3** *sl.* the head. [17th c.: orig. unkn.]

nogging /ˈnɒgɪŋ/ *n.* brickwork or timber braces in a timber frame. [NOG[1] + -ING[1]]

Noh /nəʊ/ *n.* (also **No**) traditional Japanese drama with dance and song. [Jap. *nō*]

nohow /ˈnəʊhaʊ/ *adv.* **1** *US* in no way; by no means. **2** *dial.* out of order; out of sorts.

noise /nɔɪz/ *n. & v.* —*n.* **1** a sound, esp. a loud or unpleasant or undesired one. **2** a series of loud sounds, esp. shouts; a confused sound of voices and movements. **3** irregular fluctuations accompanying a transmitted signal but not relevant to it. **4** (in *pl.*) conventional remarks, or speechlike sounds without actual words (*made sympathetic noises*). —*v. tr.* (usu. in *passive*) make public; spread abroad (a person's fame or a fact). □ **make a noise 1** (usu. foll. by *about*) talk or complain much. **2** be much talked of; attain notoriety. **noise pollution** harmful or annoying noise. **noises off** sounds made off stage to be heard by the audience of a play. [ME f. OF, = outcry, disturbance, f. L *nausea*: see NAUSEA]

noiseless /ˈnɔɪzlɪs/ *adj.* **1** silent. **2** making no avoidable noise. □ **noiselessly** *adv.* **noiselessness** *n.*

noisette /nwaːˈzet/ *n.* a small round piece of meat etc. [F, dimin. of *noix* nut]

noisome /ˈnɔɪsəm/ *adj.* *literary* **1** harmful, noxious. **2** evil-smelling. **3** objectionable, offensive. □ **noisomeness** *n.* [ME f. obs. *noy* f. ANNOY]

noisy /ˈnɔɪzɪ/ *adj.* (**noisier, noisiest**) **1** full of or attended with noise. **2** making or given to making much noise. **3** clamorous, turbulent. **4** (of a colour, garment, etc.) loud, conspicuous. □ **noisily** *adv.* **noisiness** *n.*

nomad /ˈnəʊmæd/ *n. & adj.* —*n.* **1** a member of a tribe roaming from place to place for pasture. **2** a wanderer. —*adj.* **1** living as a nomad. **2** wandering. □ **nomadic** /-ˈmædɪk/ *adj.* **nomadically** /-ˈmædɪkəlɪ/ *adv.* **nomadism** *n.* **nomadize** *v.intr.* (also **-ise**). [F *nomade* f. L *nomas nomad-* f. Gk *nomas -ados* f. *nemō* to pasture]

nom de guerre /ˌnɒm də ˈgeə(r)/ *n.* (pl. ***noms de guerre*** *pronunc.* same) an assumed name under which a person fights, plays, writes, etc. [F, = war-name]

nom de plume /ˌnɒm də ˈpluːm/ *n.* (pl. ***noms de plume*** *pronunc.* same) an assumed name

under which a person writes. [formed in E of F words, = pen-name, after NOM DE GUERRE]

nomenclature /nəʊˈmenklətʃə(r), ˈnəʊmən‚kleɪtʃə(r)/ *n.* **1** a person's or community's system of names for things. **2** the terminology of a science etc. **3** systematic naming. **4** a catalogue or register. □ **nomenclative** *adj.* **nomenclatural** /-ˈklætʃər(ə)l/ *adj.* [F f. L *nomenclatura* f. *nomen* + *calare* call]

nominal /ˈnɒmɪn(ə)l/ *adj.* **1** existing in name only; not real or actual (*nominal and real prices*; *nominal ruler*). **2** (of a sum of money, rent, etc.) virtually nothing; much below the actual value of a thing. **3** of or in names (*nominal and essential distinctions*). **4** consisting of or giving the names (*nominal list of officers*). **5** of or as or like a noun. □ **nominal value** the face value (of a coin, shares, etc.). □ **nominally** *adv.* [ME f. F *nominal* or L *nominalis* f. *nomen -inis* name]

nominalize /ˈnɒmɪnə‚laɪz/ *v.tr.* (also **-ise**) form a noun from (a verb, adjective, etc.), e.g. *output*, *truth*, from *put out*, *true*. □ **nominalization** /-ˈzeɪʃ(ə)n/ *n.*

nominate /ˈnɒmɪ‚neɪt/ *v.tr.* **1** propose (a candidate) for election. **2** appoint to an office (*a board of six nominated and six elected members*). **3** name or appoint (a date or place). **4** mention by name. **5** call by the name of, designate. □ **nominator** *n.* [L *nominare nominat-* (as NOMINAL)]

nomination /ˌnɒmɪˈneɪʃ(ə)n/ *n.* **1** the act or an instance of nominating; the state of being nominated. **2** the right of nominating for an appointment (*have a nomination at your disposal*). [ME f. OF *nomination* or L *nominatio* (as NOMINATE)]

nominative /ˈnɒmɪnətɪv/ *n. & adj.* —*n. Gram.* **1** the case of nouns, pronouns, and adjectives, expressing the subject of a verb. **2** a word in this case. —*adj.* **1** *Gram.* of or in this case. **2** /-neɪtɪv/ of, or appointed by, nomination (as distinct from election). □ **nominatival** /-ˈtaɪv(ə)l/ *adj.* [ME f. OF *nominatif -ive* or L *nominativus* (as NOMINATE), transl. Gk *onomastikē* (*ptōsis* case)]

nominee /ˌnɒmɪˈniː/ *n.* **1** a person who is nominated. [NOMINATE]

-nomy /nəmɪ/ *comb. form* denoting an area of knowledge or the laws governing it (*aeronomy*; *economy*).

non- /nɒn/ *prefix* giving the negative sense of words with which it is combined, esp.: **1** not doing or having or involved with (*non-attendance*; *non-payment*; *non-productive*). **2 a** not of the kind or class described (*non-alcoholic*; *non-member*; *non-event*). **b** forming terms used adjectivally (*non-union*; *non-party*). **3** a lack of (*non-access*). **4** (with adverbs) not in the way described (*non-aggressively*). **5** forming adjectives from verbs, meaning 'that does not' or 'that is not meant to (or to be)' (*non-skid*; *non-iron*). **6** used to form a neutral negative sense when a form in *in-* or *un-* has a special sense or (usu. unfavourable) connotation (*non-controversial*; *non-effective*; *non-human*). [from or after ME *no(u)n-* f. AF *noun-*, OF *non-, nom-* f. L *non* not]

■ **Usage** The number of words that can be formed with this prefix is unlimited; consequently only the most current and noteworthy can be given here.

nona- /ˈnɒnə/ *comb. form* nine. [L f. *nonus* ninth]

non-abstainer /ˌnɒnəbˈsteɪnə(r)/ n. a person who does not abstain (esp. from alcohol).

non-acceptance /ˌnɒnəkˈsept(ə)ns/ n. a lack of acceptance.

non-access /nɒnˈækses/ n. a lack of access.

non-addictive /ˌnɒnəˈdɪktɪv/ adj. (of a drug, habit, etc.) not causing addiction.

nonage /ˈnəʊnɪdʒ, ˈnɒn-/ n. **1** hist. the state of being under full legal age, minority. **2** a period of immaturity. [ME f. AF nounage, OF nonage (as NON-, AGE)]

nonagenarian /ˌnəʊnədʒɪˈneərɪən, ˌnɒn-/ n. & adj. —n. a person from 90 to 99 years old. —adj. of this age. [L nonagenarius f. nonageni distributive of nonaginta ninety]

non-aggression /ˌnɒnəˈɡreʃ(ə)n/ n. lack of or restraint from aggression (often attrib.: non-aggression pact).

nonagon /ˈnɒnəɡən/ n. a plane figure with nine sides and angles. [L nonus ninth, after HEXAGON]

non-alcoholic /ˌnɒnælkəˈhɒlɪk/ adj. & n. (of a drink etc.) not containing alcohol.

non-aligned /ˌnɒnəˈlaɪnd/ adj. (of States etc.) not aligned with another (esp. major) power. □ **non-alignment** n.

non-allergic /ˌnɒnəˈlɜːdʒɪk/ adj. not causing allergy; not allergic.

non-ambiguous /ˌnɒnæmˈbɪɡjʊəs/ adj. not ambiguous.

non-appearance /ˌnɒnəˈpɪərəns/ n. failure to appear or be present.

non-attached /ˌnɒnəˈtætʃd/ adj. that is not attached.

non-attendance /ˌnɒnəˈtend(ə)ns/ n. failure to attend.

non-attributable /ˌnɒnəˈtrɪbjʊtəb(ə)l/ adj. that cannot or may not be attributed to a particular source etc. □ **non-attributably** adv.

non-availability /ˌnɒnəˌveɪləˈbɪlɪtɪ/ n. a state of not being available.

non-believer /ˌnɒnbɪˈliːvə(r)/ n. a person who does not believe or has no (esp. religious) faith.

non-belligerency /ˌnɒnbəˈlɪdʒərənsɪ/ n. a lack of belligerency.

non-belligerent /ˌnɒnbəˈlɪdʒərənt/ adj. & n. —adj. not engaged in hostilities. —n. a non-belligerent nation, State, etc.

non-biological /ˌnɒnbaɪəˈlɒdʒɪk(ə)l/ adj. not concerned with biology or living organisms.

non-Black /nɒnˈblæk/ adj. & n. —adj. **1** (of a person) not Black. **2** of or relating to non-Black people. —n. a non-Black person.

non-breakable /nɒnˈbreɪkəb(ə)l/ adj. not breakable.

non-capital /nɒnˈkæpɪt(ə)l/ adj. (of an offence) not punishable by death.

non-Catholic /nɒnˈkæθəlɪk, -ˈkæθlɪk/ adj. & n. —adj. not Roman Catholic. —n. a non-Catholic person.

nonce /nɒns/ n. □ **for the nonce** for the time being; for the present occasion. **nonce-word** a word coined for one occasion. [ME for than anes (unrecorded) = for the one, altered by wrong division (cf. NEWT)]

nonchalant /ˈnɒnʃələnt/ adj. calm and casual, unmoved, unexcited, indifferent. □ **nonchalance** n. **nonchalantly** adv. [F, part. of nonchaloir f. chaloir be concerned]

non-Christian /nɒnˈkrɪstjən, -ˈkrɪstʃ(ə)n/ adj. & n. —adj. not Christian. —n. a non-Christian person.

non-citizen /nɒnˈsɪtɪz(ə)n/ n. a person who is not a citizen (of a particular State, town, etc.).

non-classified /nɒnˈklæsɪˌfaɪd/ adj. (esp. of information) that is not classified.

non-clerical /nɒnˈklerɪk(ə)l/ adj. not doing or involving clerical work.

non-com /ˈnɒnkɒm/ n. colloq. a non-commissioned officer.

non-combatant /nɒnˈkɒmbət(ə)nt/ n. a person not fighting in a war, esp. a civilian, army chaplain, etc.

non-commissioned /ˌnɒnkəˈmɪʃ(ə)nd/ adj. Mil. (of an officer) not holding a commission.

noncommittal /ˌnɒnkəˈmɪt(ə)l/ adj. avoiding commitment to a definite opinion or course of action. □ **noncommittally** adv.

non-communicant /ˌnɒnkəˈmjuːnɪkənt/ n. a person who is not a communicant (esp. in the religious sense).

non-communicating /ˌnɒnkəˈmjuːnɪˌkeɪtɪŋ/ adj. that does not communicate.

non-communist /nɒnˈkɒmjʊnɪst/ adj. & n. (also **non-Communist** with ref. to a particular party) —adj. not advocating or practising communism. —n. a non-communist person.

non-compliance /ˌnɒnkəmˈplaɪəns/ n. failure to comply; a lack of compliance.

non compos mentis /ˌnɒn kɒmpɒs ˈmentɪs/ adj. (also **non compos**) not in one's right mind. [L, = not having control of one's mind]

non-conductor /ˌnɒnkənˈdʌktə(r)/ n. a substance that does not conduct heat or electricity. □ **non-conducting** adj.

non-confidential /ˌnɒnkɒnfɪˈdenʃ(ə)l/ adj. not confidential. □ **non-confidentially** adv.

nonconformist /ˌnɒnkənˈfɔːmɪst/ n. **1** a person who does not conform to the doctrine or discipline of an established Church, esp. (**Nonconformist**) a member of a (usu. Protestant) sect dissenting from the Anglican Church. **2** a person who does not conform to a prevailing principle. □ **nonconformism** n. **Nonconformism** n.

nonconformity /ˌnɒnkənˈfɔːmɪtɪ/ n. **1 a** nonconformists as a body, esp. (**Nonconformity**) Protestants dissenting from the Anglican Church. **b** the principles or practice of nonconformists, esp. (**Nonconformity**) Protestant dissent. **2** (usu. foll. by to) failure to conform to a rule etc. **3** lack of correspondence between things.

non-contagious /ˌnɒnkənˈteɪdʒəs/ adj. not contagious.

non-contentious /ˌnɒnkənˈtenʃəs/ adj. not contentious.

non-contributory /ˌnɒnkənˈtrɪbjʊtərɪ/ adj. not contributing or (esp. of a pension scheme) involving contributions.

non-controversial /nɒnˌkɒntrəˈvɜːʃ(ə)l/ adj. not controversial.

non-cooperation /ˌnɒnkəʊˌɒpəˈreɪʃ(ə)n/ n. failure to cooperate; a lack of cooperation.

non-delivery /ˌnɒndɪˈlɪvərɪ/ n. failure to deliver.

non-denominational /ˌnɒndɪˌnɒmɪˈneɪʃən(ə)l/ adj. not restricted as regards religious denomination.

nondescript /ˈnɒndɪskrɪpt/ adj. & n. —adj. lacking distinctive characteristics, not easily classified, neither one thing nor another. —n. a nondescript person or thing. □ **nondescriptly** adv. **nondescriptness** n. [NON- + descript described f. L descriptus (as DESCRIBE)]

non-destructive /ˌnɒndɪˈstrʌktɪv/ adj. that does not involve destruction or damage.

non-drinker /nɒnˈdrɪŋkə(r)/ n. a person who does not drink alcoholic liquor.

non-driver /nɒnˈdraɪvə(r)/ n. a person who does not drive a motor vehicle.

none /nʌn/ pron., adj., & adv. —pron. **1** (foll. by of) **a** not any of (none of this concerns me; none of them have found it; none of your impudence!). **b** not any one of (none of them has come). **2 a** no persons (none but fools have ever believed it). **b** no person (none can tell). —adj. (usu. with a preceding noun implied) **1** no; not any (you have money and I have none). **2** not to be counted in a specified class (if a linguist is wanted, I am none). —adv. (foll. by the + compar., or so, too) by no amount; not at all (am none the wiser). □ **none the less** nevertheless. **none other** (usu. foll. by than) no other person. [OE nān f. ne not + ān ONE]

■ **Usage** In sense 1b, the verb following none can be singular or plural according to the sense.

non-earning /nɒnˈɜːnɪŋ/ adj. not earning (esp. a regular wage or salary).

non-effective /ˌnɒnɪˈfektɪv/ adj. that does not have an effect.

nonentity /nɒˈnentɪtɪ/ n. (pl. -ies) **1** a person or thing of no importance. **2 a** non-existence. **b** a non-existent thing, a figment. [med.L nonentitas non-existence]

nones /nəʊnz/ n.pl. in the ancient Roman calendar, the ninth day before the ides by inclusive reckoning, i.e. the 7th day of March, May, July, October, the 5th of other months. [OF nones f. L nonae fem. pl. of nonus ninth]

non-essential /ˌnɒnɪˈsenʃ(ə)l/ adj. not essential.

■ **Usage** Neutral in sense: see NON- 6, INESSENTIAL.

nonesuch var. of NONSUCH.

nonet /nəʊˈnet/ n. **1** Mus. **a** a composition for nine voices or instruments. **b** the performers of such a piece. **2** a group of nine. [It. nonetto f. nono ninth f. L nonus]

nonetheless var. of none the less.

non-Euclidean /ˌnɒnjuːˈklɪdɪən/ adj. denying or going beyond Euclidean principles in geometry.

non-European /nɒnˌjʊərəˈpɪən/ adj. & n. —adj. not European. —n. a non-European person.

non-event /ˌnɒnɪˈvent/ n. an unimportant or anticlimactic occurrence.

non-existent /ˌnɒnɪgˈzɪst(ə)nt/ adj. not existing. □ **non-existence** n.

non-explosive /ˌnɒnɪkˈspləʊsɪv/ adj. (of a substance) that does not explode.

non-fattening /nɒnˈfætənɪŋ/ adj. (of food) that does not fatten.

non-ferrous /nɒnˈferəs/ adj. (of a metal) other than iron or steel.

non-fiction /nɒnˈfɪkʃ(ə)n/ n. literary work other than fiction. □ **non-fictional** adj.

non-flammable /nɒnˈflæməb(ə)l/ adj. not inflammable.

non-fulfilment /ˌnɒnfʊlˈfɪlmənt/ n. failure to fulfil (an obligation).

non-functional /nɒnˈfʌŋkʃən(ə)l/ adj. not having a function.

non-governmental /ˌnɒngʌvənˈment(ə)l/ adj. not belonging to or associated with a government.

non-human /nɒnˈhjuːmən/ adj. & n. —adj. (of a being) not human. —n. a non-human being.

non-infectious /ˌnɒnɪnˈfekʃəs/ adj. (of a disease) not infectious.

non-inflected /ˌnɒnɪnˈflektɪd/ adj. (of a language) not having inflections.

non-interference /ˌnɒnɪntəˈfɪərəns/ n. a lack of interference.

non-intervention /ˌnɒnɪntəˈvenʃ(ə)n/ n. the principle or practice of not becoming involved in others' affairs, esp. by one State in regard to another.

non-intoxicating /ˌnɒnɪnˈtɒksɪˌkeɪtɪŋ/ adj. (of drink) not causing intoxication.

non-iron /nɒnˈaɪən/ adj. (of a fabric) that needs no ironing.

non-linear /nɒnˈlɪnɪə(r)/ adj. not linear, esp. with regard to dimension.

non-literary /nɒnˈlɪtərərɪ/ adj. (of writing, a text, etc.) not literary in character.

non-logical /nɒnˈlɒdʒɪk(ə)l/ adj. not involving logic. □ **non-logically** adv.

non-magnetic /ˌnɒnmægˈnetɪk/ adj. (of a substance) not magnetic.

non-member /nɒnˈmembə(r)/ n. a person who is not a member (of a particular association, club, etc.). □ **non-membership** n.

non-metal /nɒnˈmet(ə)l/ adj. not made of metal. □ **non-metallic** /-mɪˈtælɪk/ adj.

non-militant /nɒnˈmɪlɪt(ə)nt/ adj. not militant.

non-military /nɒnˈmɪlɪtərɪ/ adj. not military; not involving armed forces, civilian.

non-ministerial /ˌnɒnmɪnɪˈstɪərɪəl/ adj. not ministerial (esp. in political senses).

non-moral /nɒnˈmɒr(ə)l/ adj. not concerned with morality. □ **non-morally** adv.

non-natural /nɒnˈnætʃər(ə)l/ adj. not involving natural means or processes.

non-negotiable /ˌnɒnnɪˈgəʊʃəb(ə)l/ adj. that cannot be negotiated (esp. in financial senses).

non-nuclear /nɒnˈnjuːklɪə(r)/ adj. **1** not involving nuclei or nuclear energy. **2** (of a State etc.) not having nuclear weapons.

non-observance /ˌnɒnəbˈzɜːv(ə)ns/ n. failure to observe (esp. an agreement, requirement, etc.).

non-operational /ˌnɒnɒpəˈreɪʃən(ə)l/ adj. **1** that does not operate. **2** out of order.

non-organic /ˌnɒnɔːˈgænɪk/ adj. not organic.

nonpareil /ˈnɒnpər(ə)l, ˌnɒnpəˈreɪl/ adj. & n. —adj. unrivalled or unique. —n. such a person or thing. [F f. pareil equal f. pop.L pariculus dimin. of L par]

non-participating /ˌnɒnpɑːˈtɪsɪˌpeɪtɪŋ/ adj. not taking part.

non-partisan /ˌnɒnpɑːtɪˈzæn/ adj. not partisan.

non-party /nɒnˈpɑːtɪ/ adj. independent of political parties.

non-payment /nɒnˈpeɪmənt/ n. failure to pay; a lack of payment.

non-person /ˈnɒnˌpɜːs(ə)n/ n. a person regarded as non-existent or insignificant (cf. UNPERSON).

non-personal /nɒnˈpɜːsən(ə)l/ adj. not personal.

non-physical /nɒnˈfɪzɪk(ə)l/ adj. not physical. □ **non-physically** adv.

non-playing /nɒnˈpleɪɪŋ/ adj. that does not play or take part (in a game etc.).

nonplus /nɒnˈplʌs/ v.tr. (**nonplussed, non-plussing**) completely perplex. [L non plus not more]

non-poisonous /nɒnˈpɔɪzənəs/ adj. (of a substance) not poisonous.

non-political /ˌnɒnpəˈlɪtɪk(ə)l/ adj. not political; not involved in politics.

non-porous /nɒnˈpɔːrəs/ adj. (of a substance) not porous.

non-productive /ˌnɒnprəˈdʌktɪv/ adj. not productive. □ **non-productively** adv.

non-professional /ˌnɒnprəˈfeʃən(ə)l/ adj. not professional (esp. in status).

non-profit /nɒnˈprɒfɪt/ adj. not involving or making a profit.

non-profit-making /nɒnˈprɒfɪtˌmeɪkɪŋ/ adj. (of an enterprise) not conducted primarily to make a profit.

non-proliferation /ˌnɒnprəˌlɪfəˈreɪʃ(ə)n/ n. the prevention of an increase in something, esp. possession of nuclear weapons.

non-racial /nɒnˈreɪʃ(ə)l/ adj. not involving race or racial factors.

non-reader /nɒnˈriːdə(r)/ n. a person who cannot read.

non-resident /nɒnˈrezɪd(ə)nt/ adj. & n. —adj. 1 not residing in a particular place, esp. (of a member of the clergy) not residing where his or her duties require. 2 (of a post) not requiring the holder to reside at the place of work. —n. a non-resident person, esp. a person using some of the facilities of a hotel. □ **non-residence** n. **non-residential** /-ˈdenʃ(ə)l/ adj.

non-resistance /ˌnɒnrɪˈzɪst(ə)ns/ n. failure to resist; a lack of resistance.

non-returnable /ˌnɒnrɪˈtɜːnəb(ə)l/ adj. that may or need not will not be returned.

non-rigid /nɒnˈrɪdʒɪd/ adj. (esp. of materials) not rigid.

non-scientific /ˌnɒnˌsaɪənˈtɪfɪk/ adj. not involving science or scientific methods. □ **non-scientist** /-ˈsaɪəntɪst/ n.

non-sectarian /ˌnɒnsekˈteərɪən/ adj. not sectarian.

nonsense /ˈnɒns(ə)ns/ n. 1 a (often as int.) absurd or meaningless words or ideas; foolish or extravagant conduct. b an instance of this. 2 a scheme, arrangement, etc., that one disapproves of. 3 (often attrib.) a form of literature meant to amuse by absurdity (nonsense verse). □ **non-sensical** /-ˈsensɪk(ə)l/ adj. **nonsensicality** /ˌnɒnsensɪˈkælɪtɪ/ n. (pl. **-ies**). **nonsensically** /-ˈsensɪkəlɪ/ adv.

non sequitur /nɒn ˈsekwɪtə(r)/ n. a conclusion that does not logically follow from the premises. [L. = it does not follow]

non-sexual /nɒnˈseksjʊəl, -ʃʊəl/ adj. not based on or involving sex. □ **non-sexually** adv.

non-skid /nɒnˈskɪd/ adj. 1 that does not skid. 2 that inhibits skidding.

non-slip /nɒnˈslɪp/ adj. 1 that does not slip. 2 that inhibits slipping.

non-smoker /nɒnˈsməʊkə(r)/ n. 1 a person who does not smoke. 2 a train compartment etc. in which smoking is forbidden. □ **non-smoking** adj. & n.

non-soluble /nɒnˈsɒljʊb(ə)l/ adj. (esp. of a substance) not soluble.

non-specialist /nɒnˈspeʃəlɪst/ n. a person who is not a specialist (in a particular subject).

non-specific /ˌnɒnspɪˈsɪfɪk/ adj. that cannot be specified.

non-standard /nɒnˈstændəd/ adj. not standard.

non-starter /nɒnˈstɑːtə(r)/ n. 1 a person or animal that does not start in a race. 2 colloq. a person or thing that is unlikely to succeed or be effective.

non-stick /nɒnˈstɪk/ adj. 1 that does not stick. 2 that does not allow things to stick to it.

non-stop /nɒnˈstɒp/ adj., adv., & n. —adj. 1 (of a train etc.) not stopping at intermediate places. 2 (of a journey, performance, etc.) done without a stop or intermission. —adv. without stopping or pausing. —n. a non-stop train etc.

non-subscriber /ˌnɒnsəbˈskraɪbə(r)/ n. a person who is not a subscriber.

nonsuch /ˈnʌnsʌtʃ/ n. (also **nonesuch**) a person or thing that is unrivalled, a paragon. [NONE + SUCH, usu. now assim. to NON-]

non-swimmer /nɒnˈswɪmə(r)/ n. a person who cannot swim.

non-technical /nɒnˈteknɪk(ə)l/ adj. 1 not technical. 2 without technical knowledge.

non-toxic /nɒnˈtɒksɪk/ adj. not toxic.

non-transferable /ˌnɒntrænsˈfɜːrəb(ə)l/ adj. that may not be transferred.

non-U /nɒnˈjuː/ adj. colloq. not characteristic of the upper class. [NON- + U²]

non-uniform /nɒnˈjuːnɪfɔːm/ adj. not uniform.

non-union /nɒnˈjuːnɪən/ adj. 1 not belonging to a trade union. 2 not done or produced by members of a trade union.

non-verbal /nɒnˈvɜːb(ə)l/ adj. not involving words or speech. □ **non-verbally** adv.

non-vintage /nɒnˈvɪntɪdʒ/ adj. (of wine etc.) not vintage.

non-violence /nɒnˈvaɪələns/ n. the avoidance of violence, esp. as a principle. □ **non-violent** adj.

non-volatile /nɒnˈvɒlətaɪl/ adj. (esp. of a substance) not volatile.

non-voting /nɒnˈvəʊtɪŋ/ adj. not having or using a vote. □ **non-voter** n.

non-White /nɒnˈwaɪt/ adj. & n. —adj. 1 (of a person) not White. 2 of or relating to non-White people. —n. a non-White person.

noodle¹ /ˈnuːd(ə)l/ n. a strip or ring of pasta. [G Nudel]

noodle² /ˈnuːd(ə)l/ n. 1 a simpleton. 2 sl. the head. [18th c.: orig. unkn.]

nook /nʊk/ n. a corner or recess; a secluded place. [ME nok(e) corner, of unkn. orig.]

nooky /ˈnʊkɪ/ n. (also **nookie**) sl. sexual intercourse. [20th c.: perh. f. NOOK]

noon /nuːn/ n. twelve o'clock in the day, midday. [OE nōn f. L nona (hora) ninth hour: orig. = 3 p.m.]

noonday /ˈnuːndeɪ/ n. midday.

no one /ˈnəʊ wʌn/ n. no person; nobody.

noose /nuːs/ n. & v. —n. 1 a loop with a running knot, tightening as the rope or wire is pulled, esp. in a snare, lasso, or hangman's halter. 2 a snare or bond. —v.tr. 1 catch with or enclose in a noose, ensnare. 2 a make a noose on (a cord). b (often foll. by round) arrange (a cord) in a noose. □ **put one's head in a noose** bring about one's own downfall. [ME nose, perh. f. OF no(u)s f. L nodus knot]

nor /nɔː(r), nə(r)/ *conj.* **1** and not; and not either (*neither one thing nor the other; not a man nor a child was to be seen; I said I had not seen it, nor had I; all that is true, nor must we forget ...; can neither read nor write*). **2** and no more; neither ('*I cannot go*'—'*Nor can I*'). [ME, contr. f. obs. *nother* f. OE *nawther*, *nāhwæther* (as NO², WHETHER)]

nor' /nɔː(r)/ *n.* & *adj.* & *adv.* (esp. in compounds) = NORTH (*nor'ward; nor'wester*). [abbr.]

Nordic /ˈnɔːdɪk/ *adj.* & *n.* —*adj.* **1** of or relating to the tall blond Germanic people found in N. Europe, esp. in Scandinavia. **2** of or relating to Scandinavia or Finland. —*n.* a Nordic person. [F *nordique* f. *nord* north]

Norfolk jacket /ˈnɔːfək/ *n.* a man's loose belted jacket, with box pleats. [*Norfolk* in S. England]

norm *n.* **1** a standard or pattern or type. **2** a standard quantity to be produced or amount of work to be done. **3** customary behaviour etc. [L *norma* carpenter's square]

normal /ˈnɔːm(ə)l/ *adj.* & *n.* —*adj.* **1** conforming to a standard; regular, usual, typical. **2** free from mental or emotional disorder. **3** *Geom.* (of a line) at right angles, perpendicular. —*n.* **1 a** the normal value of a temperature etc., esp. blood-heat. **b** the usual state, level, etc. **2** *Geom.* a line at right angles. □ **normal distribution** *Statistics* a function that represents the distribution of many random variables as a symmetrical bell-shaped graph. □ **normalcy** *n.* esp. US. **normality** /-ˈmælɪtɪ/ *n.* [F *normal* or L *normalis* (as NORM)]

normalize /ˈnɔːməlaɪz/ *v.* (also **-ise**) **1** *tr.* make normal. **2** *intr.* become normal. **3** *tr.* cause to conform. □ **normalization** /-ˈzeɪʃ(ə)n/ *n.* **normalizer** *n.*

normally /ˈnɔːməlɪ/ *adv.* **1** in a normal manner. **2** usually.

Norman /ˈnɔːmən/ *n.* & *adj.* —*n.* **1** a native or inhabitant of Normandy. **2** a descendant of the people of mixed Scandinavian and Frankish origin established there in the 10th c., who conquered England in 1066. **3** Norman French. —*adj.* **1** of or relating to the Normans. **2** of or relating to the Norman style of architecture. □ **Normanesque** /-ˈnesk/ *adj.* **Normanism** *n.* **Normanize** *v.tr.* & *intr.* (also **-ise**). [OF *Normans* pl. of *Normant* f. ON *Northmathr* (as NORTH, MAN)]

normative /ˈnɔːmətɪv/ *adj.* of or establishing a norm. □ **normatively** *adv.* **normativeness** *n.* [F *normatif -ive* f. L *norma* (see NORM)]

Norse /nɔːs/ *n.* & *adj.* —*n.* **1** the Norwegian language. **2** the Scandinavian language-group. —*adj.* of ancient Scandinavia, esp. Norway. □ **Old Norse** the Germanic language from which the Scandinavian languages are derived. □ **Norseman** *n.* (*pl.* **-men**). [Du. *noor(d)sch* f. *noord* north]

north *n.*, *adj.*, & *adv.* —*n.* **1 a** the point of the horizon 90° anticlockwise from east. **b** the compass point corresponding to this. **c** the direction in which this lies. **2** (usu. **the North**) **a** the part of the world or a country or a town lying to the north. **b** the Arctic. **c** the industrialized nations. —*adj.* **1** towards, at, near, or facing north. **2** coming from the north (*north wind*). —*adv.* **1** towards, at, or near the north. **2** (foll. by *of*) further north than. □ **North American** *adj.* of North America. —*n.* a native or inhabitant of North America, esp. a citizen of the US or Canada. **north country** the

northern part of England (north of the Humber). **North-countryman** (*pl.* **-men**) a native of the north country. **north-east** *n.* **1** the point of the horizon midway between north and east. **2** the compass point corresponding to this. **3** the direction in which this lies. —*adj.* of, towards, or coming from the north-east. —*adv.* towards, at, or near the north-east. **North-East** the part of a country or town lying to the north-east. **north-easterly** *adj.* & *adv.* = *north-east.* **north-eastern** lying on the north-east side. **north-north-east** the point or direction midway between north and north-east. **north-north-west** the point or direction midway between north and north-west. **North Pole 1** the northernmost point of the earth's axis of rotation. **2** the northernmost point about which the stars appear to revolve. **North Star** the pole-star. **north-west** *n.* **1** the point of the horizon midway between north and west. **2** the compass point corresponding to this. **3** the direction in which this lies. —*adj.* of, towards, or coming from the north-west. —*adv.* towards, at, or near the north-west. **North-West** the part of a country or town lying to the north-west. **north-westerly** *adj.* & *adv.* = *north-west.* **north-western** lying on the north-west side. **to the north** (often foll. by *of*) in a northerly direction. [OE f. Gmc]

northbound /ˈnɔːθbaʊnd/ *adj.* travelling or leading northwards.

northeaster /nɔːˈθiːstə(r)/ *n.* a north-east wind.

northerly /ˈnɔːðəlɪ/ *adj.*, *adv.*, & *n.* —*adj.* & *adv.* **1** in a northern position or direction. **2** (of wind) blowing from the north. —*n.* (*pl.* **-ies**) (usu. in *pl.*) a wind blowing from the north.

northern /ˈnɔːð(ə)n/ *adj.* **1** of or in the north; inhabiting the north. **2** lying or directed towards the north. □ **Northern hemisphere** the half of the earth north of the equator. **northern lights** the aurora borealis. **Northern States** the States in the north of the US. □ **northernmost** *adj.* [OE *northerne* (as NORTH, -ERN)]

northerner /ˈnɔːðənə(r)/ *n.* a native or inhabitant of the north.

Northman /ˈnɔːθmən/ *n.* (*pl.* **-men**) a native of Scandinavia, esp. of Norway. [OE]

northward /ˈnɔːθwəd/ *adj.*, *adv.*, & *n.* —*adj.* & *adv.* (also **northwards**) towards the north. —*n.* a northward direction or region.

northwester /nɔːˈθwestə(r)/ *n.* a north-west wind.

Norway lobster /ˈnɔːweɪ/ *n.* a small European lobster, *Nephrops norvegicus.* [*Norway* in N. Europe]

Norwegian /nɔːˈwiːdʒ(ə)n/ *n.* & *adj.* —*n.* **1 a** a native or national of Norway. **b** a person of Norwegian descent. **2** the language of Norway. —*adj.* of or relating to Norway or its people or language. [med.L *Norvegia* f. ON *Norvegr* (as NORTH, WAY), assim. to *Norway*]

Nos. *abbr.* numbers. [cf. No.]

nose /nəʊz/ *n.* & *v.* —*n.* **1** an organ above the mouth on the face or head of a human or animal, containing nostrils and used for smelling and breathing. **2 a** the sense of smell (*dogs have a good nose*). **b** the ability to detect a particular thing (*a nose for scandal*). **3** the odour or perfume of wine, tea, tobacco, hay, etc. **4** the open end or nozzle of a tube, pipe, pair of bellows, retort, etc. **5** the front end or projecting part of a thing, e.g. of a car or aircraft. **6** *sl.* an informer of the police. —*v.* **1** *tr.* (often foll. by *out*) **a** perceive the smell of, discover by smell. **b** detect. **2** *tr.* thrust or rub one's nose against or into, esp. in order to smell. **3** *intr.* (usu. foll. by *about, around,* etc.) pry or search. **4 a** *intr.* make one's way cautiously forward. **b** *tr.* make (one's or its way). □ **by a nose** by a very narrow margin (*won the race by a nose*). **get up a person's nose** *sl.* annoy a person. **keep one's nose clean** *sl.* stay out of trouble, behave properly. **nose-cone** the cone-shaped nose of a rocket etc. **nose-piece 1** = NOSEBAND. **2** the part of a helmet etc. protecting the nose. **3** the part of a microscope to which the object-glass is attached. **nose-wheel** a landing-wheel under the nose of an aircraft. **on the nose 1** *US sl.* precisely. **2** *Austral. sl.* annoying. **put a person's nose out of joint** *colloq.* embarrass, disconcert, frustrate, or supplant a person. **speak through one's nose** pronounce words with a nasal twang. **turn up one's nose** (usu. foll. by *at*) *colloq.* show disdain. **under a person's nose** *colloq.* right before a person (esp. of defiant or unnoticed actions). **with one's nose in the air** haughtily. □ **nosed** *adj.* (also in *comb.*). **noseless** *adj.* [OE *nosu*]

nosebag /'nəʊzbæg/ *n.* a bag containing fodder, hung on a horse's head.

noseband /'nəʊzbænd/ *n.* the lower band of a bridle, passing over the horse's nose.

nosebleed /'nəʊzbliːd/ *n.* an instance of bleeding from the nose.

nosedive /'nəʊzdaɪv/ *n.* & *v.* —*n.* **1** a steep downward plunge by an aeroplane. **2** a sudden plunge or drop. —*v.intr.* make a nosedive.

nosegay /'nəʊzgeɪ/ *n.* a bunch of flowers, esp. a sweet-scented posy. [NOSE + GAY in obs. use = ornament]

nosering /'nəʊzrɪŋ/ *n.* a ring fixed in the nose of an animal (esp. a bull) for leading it, or of a person for ornament.

nosh *v.* & *n. sl.* —*v.tr.* & *intr.* **1** eat or drink. **2** *US* eat between meals. —*n.* **1** food or drink. **2** *US* a snack. □ **nosh-up** *Brit.* a large meal. [Yiddish]

noshery /'nɒʃəri/ *n.* (*pl.* **-ies**) *sl.* a restaurant or snack bar.

nostalgia /nɒ'stældʒɪə, -dʒə/ *n.* **1** (often foll. by *for*) sentimental yearning for a period of the past. **2** regretful or wistful memory of an earlier time. **3** severe homesickness. □ **nostalgic** *adj.* **nostalgically** *adv.* [mod.L f. Gk *nostos* return home]

nostril /'nɒstrɪl/ *n.* either of two external openings of the nasal cavity in vertebrates that admit air to the lungs and smells to the olfactory nerves. □ **nostrilled** *adj.* (also in *comb.*). [OE *nosthyrl, nosterl* f. *nosu* NOSE + *thyr(e)l* hole: cf. THRILL]

nostrum /'nɒstrəm/ *n.* **1** a quack remedy, a patent medicine, esp. one prepared by the person recommending it. **2** a pet scheme, esp. for political or social reform. [L, neut. of *noster* our, used in sense 'of our own make']

nosy /'nəʊzɪ/ *adj.* & *n.* (also **nosey**) —*adj.* (**nosier, nosiest**) **1** *colloq.* inquisitive, prying. **2** having a large nose. **3** having a distinctive (good or bad) smell. —*n.* (*pl.* **-ies**) a person with a large nose. □ **Nosy Parker** esp. *Brit. colloq.* a busybody. □ **nosily** *adv.* **nosiness** *n.*

not *adv.* expressing negation, esp.: **1** (also **n't** joined to a preceding verb) following an auxiliary verb or *be* or (in a question) the subject of such a verb (*I cannot say; she isn't there; didn't you tell me?; am I not right?; aren't we smart?*). **2** used elliptically for a negative sentence or verb or phrase (*Is she coming?—I hope not; Do you want it?—Certainly not!*). **3** used to express the negative of other words (*not a single one was left; Are they pleased?—Not they; he is not my cousin, but my nephew*). □ **not at all** (in polite reply to thanks) there is no need for thanks. **not least** with considerable importance, notably. **not quite 1** almost (*am not quite there*). **2** noticeably not (*not quite proper*). **not that** (foll. by clause) it is not to be inferred that (*if he said so—not that he ever did—he lied*). **not a thing** nothing at all. [ME contr. of NOUGHT]

■ **Usage** The use of *not* with verbs other than auxiliaries or *be* is now *archaic*, except with participles and infinitives (*not knowing, I cannot say; we asked them not to come*).

nota bene /ˌnəʊtə 'beneɪ/ *v.tr.* (as *imper.*) observe what follows, take notice (usu. drawing attention to a following qualification of what has preceded). [L, = note well]

notability /ˌnəʊtə'bɪlɪtɪ/ *n.* (*pl.* **-ies**) **1** the state of being notable (*names of no historical notability*). **2** a prominent person. [ME f. OF *notabilité* or LL *notabilitas* (as NOTABLE)]

notable /'nəʊtəb(ə)l/ *adj.* & *n.* —*adj.* worthy of note; striking, remarkable, eminent. —*n.* an eminent person. □ **notableness** *n.* **notably** *adv.* [ME f. OF f. L *notabilis* (as NOTE)]

notarize /'nəʊtəˌraɪz/ *v.tr.* (also **-ise**) *US* certify (a document) as a notary.

notary /'nəʊtərɪ/ *n.* (*pl.* **-ies**) (in full **notary public**) a person authorized to perform certain legal formalities, esp. to draw up or certify contracts, deeds, etc. □ **notarial** /nəʊ'teərɪəl/ *adj.* **notarially** /nəʊ'teərɪəlɪ/ *adv.* [ME f. L *notarius* secretary (as NOTE)]

notate /nəʊ'teɪt/ *v.tr.* write in notation. [back-form. f. NOTATION]

notation /nəʊ'teɪʃ(ə)n/ *n.* **1 a** the representation of numbers, quantities, pitch and duration etc. of musical notes, etc. by symbols. **b** any set of such symbols. **2** a set of symbols used to represent chess moves, dance steps, etc. **3** *US* **a** a note or annotation. **b** a record. □ **notational** *adj.* [F *notation* or L *notatio* (as NOTE)]

notch *n.* & *v.* —*n.* **1** a V-shaped indentation on an edge or surface. **2** a nick made on a stick etc. in order to keep count. **3** *colloq.* a step or degree (*move up a notch*). —*v.tr.* **1** make notches in. **2** (foll. by *up*) record or score with or as with notches. **3** secure or insert by notches. □ **notched** *adj.* **notcher** *n.* **notchy** *adj.* (**notchier, notchiest**). [AF *noche* perh. f. a verbal form *nocher* (unrecorded), of uncert. orig.]

note *n.* & *v.* —*n.* **1** a brief record of facts, topics, thoughts, etc., as an aid to memory, for use in writing, public speaking, etc. (often in *pl.*: *make notes; spoke without notes*). **2** an observation, usu. unwritten, of experiences etc. (*compare notes*). **3** a short or informal letter. **4** a formal diplomatic or parliamentary communication. **5** a short annotation or additional explanation in a book etc.; a footnote. **6 a** *Brit.* = BANKNOTE (*a five-pound note*). **b** a written promise or notice of payment of various kinds. **7 a** notice, attention (*worthy of note*). **b** distinction, eminence (*a person of note*). **8 a** a written sign representing the pitch and duration of a musical sound. **b** a single tone of definite pitch made by a musical instrument, the human voice, etc. **c** a key of a piano etc. **9 a** bird's song or call. **10** a quality or tone of speaking, expressing mood or attitude etc. (*sound a note of warning; ended on a note of optimism*). —*v.tr.* **1** observe, notice; give or draw attention to. **2** (often foll. by *down*) record as a thing to be remembered or observed. **3** (in passive; often foll. by *for*) be famous or well known (for a quality, activity, etc.) (*were noted for their generosity*). □ **hit** (or **strike**) **the right note** speak or act in exactly the right manner. **of note** important, distinguished (*a person of note*). **take note** (often foll. by *of*) observe; pay attention (to). □ **noted** *adj.* (in sense 3 of v.). **noteless** *adj.* [ME f. OF *note* (n.), *noter* (v.) f. L *nota* mark]

notebook /ˈnəʊtbʊk/ *n.* a small book for making or taking notes.

notecase /ˈnəʊtkeɪs/ *n.* a wallet for holding banknotes.

notelet /ˈnəʊtlɪt/ *n.* a small folded sheet of paper, usu. with a decorative design, for an informal letter.

notepaper /ˈnəʊtˌpeɪpə(r)/ *n.* paper for writing letters.

noteworthy /ˈnəʊtˌwɜːðɪ/ *adj.* worthy of attention; remarkable. □ **noteworthiness** *n.*

nothing /ˈnʌθɪŋ/ *n. & adv.* —*n.* **1** not anything (*nothing has been done; have nothing to do*). **2** no thing (often foll. by compl.: *I see nothing that I want; can find nothing useful*). **3** a person or thing of no importance or concern; a trivial event or remark (*was nothing to me; the little nothings of life*). **4** non-existence; what does not exist. **5** (in calculations) no amount; nought (*a third of nothing is nothing*). —*adv.* not at all, in no way (*is nothing like enough*). □ **be nothing to 1** not concern. **2** not compare with. **be** (or **have**) **nothing to do with 1** have no connection with. **2** not be involved or associated with. **for nothing 1** at no cost; without payment. **2** to no purpose. **have nothing on 1** be naked. **2** have no engagements. **nothing doing** *colloq.* **1 a** there is no prospect of success or agreement. **b** I refuse. **2** nothing is happening. **nothing** (or **nothing else**) **for it** (often foll. by *but to* + infin.) no alternative (*nothing for it but to pay up*). **nothing** (or **not much**) **in it** (or **to it**) **1** untrue or unimportant. **2** simple to do. **3** no (or little) advantage to be seen in one possibility over another. **nothing less than** at least (*nothing less than a disaster*). **think nothing of it** do not apologize or feel bound to show gratitude. [OE *nān thing* (as NO[1], THING)]

nothingness /ˈnʌθɪŋnɪs/ *n.* **1** non-existence; the non-existent. **2** worthlessness, triviality.

notice /ˈnəʊtɪs/ *n. & v.* —*n.* **1** attention, observation (*it escaped my notice*). **2** a displayed sheet etc. bearing an announcement or other information. **3 a** an intimation or warning, esp. a formal one to allow preparations to be made (*give notice; at a moment's notice*). **b** (often foll. by *to* + infin.) a formal announcement or declaration of intention to end an agreement or leave employment at a specified time (*hand in one's notice; notice to quit*). **4** a short published review or comment about a new play, book, etc.

—*v.tr.* **1** (often foll. by *that, how,* etc. + clause) perceive, observe; take notice of. **2** remark upon; speak of. □ **at short** (or **a moment's**) **notice** with little warning. **notice-board** *Brit.* a board for displaying notices. **take notice** (or **no notice**) show signs (or no signs) of interest. **take notice of 1** observe; pay attention to. **2** act upon. **under notice** served with a formal notice. [ME f. OF f. L *notitia* being known f. *notus* past part. of *noscere* know]

noticeable /ˈnəʊtɪsəb(ə)l/ *adj.* **1** easily seen or noticed; perceptible. **2** noteworthy. □ **noticeably** *adv.*

notifiable /ˈnəʊtɪˌfaɪəb(ə)l/ *adj.* (of a disease) that must be notified to the health authorities.

notify /ˈnəʊtɪˌfaɪ/ *v.tr.* (**-ies, -ied**) **1** (often foll. by *of*, or *that* + clause) inform or give notice to (a person). **2** make known; announce or report (a thing). □ **notification** /-fɪˈkeɪʃ(ə)n/ *n.* [ME f. OF *notifier* f. L *notificare* f. *notus* known: see NOTICE]

notion /ˈnəʊʃ(ə)n/ *n.* **1 a** a concept or idea; a conception (*it was an absurd notion*). **b** an opinion (*has the notion that people are honest*). **c** a vague view or understanding (*have no notion what you mean*). **2** an inclination, impulse, or intention (*has no notion of conforming*). **3** (in pl.) small, useful articles, esp. haberdashery. [L *notio* idea f. *notus* past part. of *noscere* know]

notional /ˈnəʊʃən(ə)l/ *adj.* hypothetical, imaginary. □ **notionally** *adv.* [obs. F *notional* or med.L *notionalis* (as NOTION)]

notorious /nəʊˈtɔːrɪəs/ *adj.* well known, esp. unfavourably (*a notorious criminal; notorious for its climate*). □ **notoriety** /-təˈraɪətɪ/ *n.* **notoriously** *adv.* [med.L *notorius* f. L *notus* (as NOTION)]

notwithstanding /ˌnɒtwɪθˈstændɪŋ, -wɪð-/ *prep., adv., & conj.* —*prep.* in spite of; without prevention by (*notwithstanding your objections; this fact notwithstanding*). —*adv.* nevertheless; all the same. —*conj.* (usu. foll. by *that* + clause) although. [ME, orig. absol. part. f. NOT + WITHSTAND + -ING[2]]

nougat /ˈnuːgɑː/ *n.* a sweet made from sugar or honey, nuts, and egg-white. [F f. Prov. *nogat* f. *noga* nut]

nought /nɔːt/ *n.* **1** the digit 0; a cipher. **2** *poet.* or *archaic* (in certain phrases) nothing (cf. NAUGHT). □ **noughts and crosses** a paper–pencil game with a square grid of nine squares, in which players seek to complete a row of three noughts or three crosses entered alternately. [OE *nōwiht* f. *ne* not + *ōwiht* var. of *āwiht* AUGHT]

noun /naʊn/ *n. Gram.* a word (other than a pronoun) or group of words used to name or identify any of a class of persons, places, or things (**common noun**), or a particular one of these (**proper noun**). □ **nounal** *adj.* [ME f. AF f. L *nomen* name]

nourish /ˈnʌrɪʃ/ *v.tr.* **1 a** sustain with food. **b** enrich; promote the development of (the soil etc.). **c** provide with intellectual or emotional sustenance or enrichment. **2** foster or cherish (a feeling etc.). □ **nourisher** *n.* [ME f. OF *norir* f. L *nutrire*]

nourishing /ˈnʌrɪʃɪŋ/ *adj.* (esp. of food) containing much nourishment; sustaining. □ **nourishingly** *adv.*

nourishment /ˈnʌrɪʃmənt/ *n.* sustenance, food.

nous /naʊs/ *n.* **1** *colloq.* common sense; gumption. **2** *Philos.* the mind or intellect. [Gk]

nouveau riche /ˌnuːvəʊ ˈriːʃ/ *n.* (*pl.* **nouveaux riches** *pronunc.* same) a person who has recently acquired (usu. ostentatious) wealth. [F, = new rich]

nouvelle cuisine /ˌnuːvel kwiˈziːn/ *n.* a modern style of cookery avoiding heaviness and emphasizing presentation. [F, = new cookery]

Nov. *abbr.* November.

nova /ˈnəʊvə/ *n.* (*pl.* **novae** /-viː/ or **novas**) a star showing a sudden large increase of brightness and then subsiding. [L, fem. of *novus* new, because orig. thought to be a new star]

novel[1] /ˈnɒv(ə)l/ *n.* **1** a fictitious prose story of book length. **2** (prec. by *the*) this type of literature. [It. *novella* (*storia* story) fem. of *novello* new f. L *novellus* f. *novus*]

novel[2] /ˈnɒv(ə)l/ *adj.* of a new kind or nature; strange; previously unknown. □ **novelly** *adv.* [ME f. OF f. L *novellus* f. *novus* new]

novelette /ˌnɒvəˈlet/ *n.* **1** a short novel. **2** *Brit.* *derog.* a light romantic novel. □ **novelettish** /ˌnɒvəˈletɪʃ/ *adj.*

novelist /ˈnɒvəlɪst/ *n.* a writer of novels. □ **novelistic** /-ˈlɪstɪk/ *adj.*

novella /nəˈvelə/ *n.* (*pl.* **novellas**) a short novel or narrative story; a tale. [It.: see NOVEL[1]]

novelty /ˈnɒvəltɪ/ *n.* & *adj.* —*n.* (*pl.* **-ies**) **1 a** newness; new character. **b** originality. **2** a new or unusual thing or occurrence. **3** a small toy or decoration etc. of novel design. [ME f. OF *novelté* (as NOVEL[2])]

November /nəˈvembə(r)/ *n.* the eleventh month of the year. [ME f. OF *novembre* f. L *November* f. *novem* nine (orig. the ninth month of the Roman year)]

novena /nəˈviːnə/ *n.* *RC Ch.* a devotion consisting of special prayers or services on nine successive days. [med.L f. L *novem* nine]

novice /ˈnɒvɪs/ *n.* **1 a** a probationary member of a religious order, before the taking of vows. **b** a new convert. **2** a beginner; an inexperienced person. **3** an animal that has not won a major prize in a competition. [ME f. OF f. L *novicius* f. *novus* new]

noviciate /nəˈvɪʃɪət/ *n.* (also **novitiate**) **1** the period of being a novice. **2** a religious novice. **3** novices' quarters. [F *noviciat* or med.L *noviciatus* (as NOVICE)]

now /naʊ/ *adv.*, *conj.*, & *n.* —*adv.* **1** at the present or mentioned time. **2** immediately (*I must go now*). **3** by this or that time (*it was now clear*). **4** under the present circumstances (*I cannot now agree*). **5** on this further occasion (*what do you want now?*). **6** in the immediate past (*just now*). **7** (esp. in a narrative or discourse) then, next (*the police now arrived*; *now to consider the next point*). **8** (without reference to time, giving various tones to a sentence) surely, I insist, I wonder, etc. (*now what do you mean by that?*; *oh come now!*). —*conj.* (often foll. by *that* + clause) as a consequence of the fact (*now that I am older*; *now you mention it*). —*n.* this time; the present (*should be there by now*; *has happened before now*). □ **as of now** from or at this time. **for now** until a later time (*goodbye for now*). **now and again** (or **then**) from time to time; intermittently. [OE *nū*]

nowadays /ˈnaʊədeɪz/ *adv.* & *n.* —*adv.* at the present time or age; in these times. —*n.* the present time.

nowhere /ˈnəʊweə(r)/ *adv.* & *pron.* —*adv.* in or to no place. —*pron.* no place. □ **be** (or **come in**) **nowhere** be unplaced in a race or competition. **come from nowhere** be suddenly evident or successful. **get nowhere** make or cause to make no progress. **in the middle of nowhere** *colloq.* remote from urban life. **nowhere near** not nearly. [OE *nāhwǣr* (as NO[1], WHERE)]

nowt /naʊt/ *n.* *colloq.* or *dial.* nothing. [var. of NOUGHT]

noxious /ˈnɒkʃəs/ *adj.* harmful, unwholesome. □ **noxiously** *adv.* **noxiousness** *n.* [f. L *noxius* f. *noxa* harm]

nozzle /ˈnɒz(ə)l/ *n.* a spout on a hose etc. from which a jet issues. [NOSE + -LE[2]]

Np *symb. Chem.* the element neptunium.

nr. *abbr.* near.

NSPCC *abbr.* (in the UK) National Society for the Prevention of Cruelty to Children.

NSW *abbr.* New South Wales.

NT *abbr.* **1** New Testament. **2** Northern Territory (of Australia).

n't /ənt/ *adv.* (in comb.) = NOT (usu. with *is*, *are*, *have*, *must*, and the auxiliary verbs *can*, *do*, *should*, *would*: *isn't*; *mustn't*) (see also CAN'T, DON'T, WON'T). [contr.]

nth see N[1].

nu /njuː/ *n.* the thirteenth letter of the Greek alphabet (N, ν). [Gk]

nuance /ˈnjuːɑ̃s/ *n.* & *v.* —*n.* a subtle difference in or shade of meaning, feeling, colour, etc. —*v.tr.* give a nuance or nuances to. [F f. *nuer* to shade, ult. f. L *nubes* cloud]

nub *n.* **1** the point or gist (of a matter or story). **2** a small lump, esp. of coal. **3** a stub; a small residue. □ **nubby** *adj.* [app. var. of *knub*, f. MLG *knubbe*, *knobbe* KNOB]

nubile /ˈnjuːbaɪl/ *adj.* (of a woman) marriageable or sexually attractive. □ **nubility** /-ˈbɪlɪtɪ/ [L *nubilis* f. *nubere* become the wife of]

nuclear /ˈnjuːklɪə(r)/ *adj.* **1** of, relating to, or constituting a nucleus. **2** using nuclear energy (*nuclear reactor*). **3** having nuclear weapons. □ **nuclear bomb** a bomb involving the release of energy by nuclear fission or fusion or both. **nuclear disarmament** the renunciation of nuclear weapons. **nuclear energy** energy obtained by nuclear fission or fusion. **nuclear family** a couple and their children, regarded as a basic social unit. **nuclear fission** a nuclear reaction in which a heavy nucleus splits spontaneously or on impact with another particle, with the release of energy. **nuclear-free** free from nuclear weapons, power, etc. **nuclear fuel** a substance that will sustain a fission chain reaction so that it can be used as a source of nuclear energy. **nuclear fusion** a nuclear reaction in which atomic nuclei of low atomic number fuse to form a heavier nucleus with the release of energy. **nuclear physics** the physics of atomic nuclei and their interactions, esp. in the generation of nuclear energy. **nuclear power 1** electric or motive power generated by a nuclear reactor. **2** a country that has nuclear weapons. **nuclear reactor** a device in which a nuclear fission chain reaction is sustained and controlled in order to produce energy. **nuclear umbrella** supposed protection afforded by an alliance with a country possessing nuclear weapons. **nuclear warfare** warfare in which nuclear weapons are used. **nuclear waste** any radioactive waste material from the reprocessing of spent nuclear fuel.

nuclear winter obstruction of sunlight as a potential result of nuclear warfare, causing extreme cold. [NUCLEUS + -AR¹]

nucleate /ˈnjuːklɪˌeɪt/ adj. & v. —adj. having a nucleus. —v.intr. & tr. form or form into a nucleus. □ **nucleation** /-ˈeɪʃ(ə)n/ n. [LL nucleare nucleat- form a kernel (as NUCLEUS)]

nuclei pl. of NUCLEUS.

nucleic acid /njuːˈkliːɪk, -ˈkleɪɪk/ n. either of two complex organic molecules (DNA and RNA), consisting of many nucleotides linked in a long chain, and present in all living cells.

nucleo- /ˈnjuːklɪəʊ/ comb. form nucleus; nucleic acid (nucleo-protein).

nucleon /ˈnjuːklɪˌɒn/ n. Physics a proton or neutron.

nucleonics /ˌnjuːklɪˈɒnɪks/ n.pl. (treated as sing.) the branch of science and technology concerned with atomic nuclei and nucleons, esp. the exploitation of nuclear power. □ **nucleonic** adj. [NUCLEAR, after electronics]

nucleotide /ˈnjuːklɪəˌtaɪd/ n. Biochem. an organic compound consisting of a nucleoside linked to a phosphate group.

nucleus /ˈnjuːklɪəs/ n. (pl. **nuclei** /-lɪˌaɪ/) **1 a** the central part or thing round which others are collected. **b** the kernel of an aggregate or mass. **2** an initial part meant to receive additions. **3** Astron. the solid part of a comet's head. **4** Physics the positively charged central core of an atom that contains most of its mass. **5** Biol. a large dense organelle of cells, containing the genetic material. [L, = kernel, inner part, dimin. of nux nucis nut]

nude adj. & n. —adj. naked, bare, unclothed. —n. **1** a painting, sculpture, photograph, etc. of a nude human figure; such a figure. **2** a nude person. **3** (prec. by the) **a** an unclothed state. **b** the representation of an undraped human figure as a genre in art. [L nudus]

nudge v. & n. —v.tr. **1** prod gently with the elbow to attract attention. **2** push gently or gradually. **3** give a gentle reminder or encouragement to (a person). —n. the act or an instance of nudging; a gentle push. □ **nudger** n. [17th c.: orig. unkn.: cf. Norw. nugge to push, rub]

nudist /ˈnjuːdɪst/ n. a person who advocates or practises going unclothed. □ **nudism** n.

nudity /ˈnjuːdɪtɪ/ n. the state of being nude; nakedness.

nugatory /ˈnjuːgətərɪ/ adj. **1** futile, trifling, worthless. **2** inoperative; not valid. [L nugatorius f. nugari to trifle f. nugae jests]

nugget /ˈnʌgɪt/ n. **1 a** a lump of gold, platinum, etc., as found in the earth. **b** a lump of anything compared to this. **2** something valuable for its size (often abstract in sense: a little nugget of information). [app. f. dial. nug lump etc.]

nuisance /ˈnjuːs(ə)ns/ n. **1** a person, thing, or circumstance causing trouble or annoyance. **2** anything harmful or offensive to the community or a member of it and for which a legal remedy exists. □ **nuisance value** an advantage resulting from the capacity to harass or frustrate. [ME f. OF, = hurt, f. nuire nuis- f. L nocēre to hurt]

nuke n. & v. colloq. —n. a nuclear weapon. —v.tr. bomb or destroy with nuclear weapons. [abbr.]

null adj. **1** (esp. **null and void**) invalid; not binding. **2** non-existent; amounting to nothing. **3** having or associated with the value zero. **4** Computing **a** empty; having no elements (null list). **b** all the elements of which are zeros (null matrix). **5** without character or expression. □ **null character** Computing a character denoting nothing, usu. represented by a zero. **null hypothesis** a hypothesis suggesting that the difference between statistical samples does not imply a difference between populations. [F nul nulle or L nullus none f. ne not + ullus any]

nullify /ˈnʌlɪˌfaɪ/ v.tr. (-ies, -ied) make null; neutralize, invalidate, cancel. □ **nullification** /-fɪˈkeɪʃ(ə)n/ n. **nullifier** n.

nullity /ˈnʌlɪtɪ/ n. (pl. **-ies**) **1** Law **a** being null; invalidity, esp. of marriage. **b** an act, document, etc., that is null. **2 a** nothingness. **b** a mere nothing; a nonentity. [F nullité or med.L nullitas f. L nullus none]

numb /nʌm/ adj. & v. —adj. (often foll. by with) deprived of feeling or the power of motion (numb with cold). —v.tr. **1** make numb. **2** stupefy, paralyse. □ **numbly** adv. **numbness** n. [ME nome(n) past part. of nim take: for -b cf. THUMB]

number /ˈnʌmbə(r)/ n. & v. —n. **1 a** an arithmetical value representing a particular quantity and used in counting and making calculations. **b** a word, symbol, or figure representing this; a numeral. **c** an arithmetical value showing position in a series esp. for identification, reference, etc. (registration number). **2** (often foll. by of) the total count or aggregate (the number of accidents has decreased; twenty in number). **3 a** the study of the behaviour of numbers; numerical reckoning (the laws of number). **b** (in pl.) arithmetic (not good at numbers). **4 a** (in sing. or pl.) a quantity or amount; a total; a count (a large number of people; only in small numbers). **b** (in pl.) numerical preponderance (force of numbers; there is safety in numbers). **5 a** a person or thing having a place in a series, esp. a single issue of a magazine, an item in a programme, etc. **b** a song, dance, musical item, etc. **6** company, collection, group (among our number). **7** Gram. **a** the classification of words by their singular or plural forms. **b** a particular such form. **8** colloq. a person or thing regarded familiarly or affectionately (usu. qualified in some way: an attractive little number). —v.tr. **1** include (I number you among my friends). **2** assign a number or numbers to. **3** have or amount to (a specified number). **4 a** count. **b** include. □ **one's days are numbered** one does not have long to live. **have a person's number** colloq. understand a person's real motives, character, etc. **number cruncher** Computing & Math. sl. a machine capable of complex calculations etc. **number crunching** the act or process of making these calculations. **one's number is up** colloq. one is finished or doomed to die. **a number of** some, several. **number one** n. colloq. oneself (always takes care of number one). —adj. most important (the number one priority). **number-plate** a plate on a vehicle displaying its registration number. **Number Ten** 10 Downing Street, the official London home of the British Prime Minister. **number two** a second in command. **without number**

innumerable. [ME f. OF *nombre* (n.), *nombrer* (v.) f. L *numerus, numerare*]

■ **Usage** The expression *a number of* is normally used with a plural verb: *a number of problems remain.*

numberless /ˈnʌmbəlɪs/ *adj.* innumerable.

numerable /ˈnjuːmərəb(ə)l/ *adj.* that can be counted. □ **numerably** *adv.* [L *numerabilis* f. *numerare* NUMBER v.]

numeral /ˈnjuːmər(ə)l/ *n.* & *adj.* —*n.* a word, figure, or group of figures denoting a number. —*adj.* of or denoting a number. [LL *numeralis* f. L (as NUMBER)]

numerate /ˈnjuːmərət/ *adj.* acquainted with the basic principles of mathematics. □ **numeracy** *n.* [L *numerus* number + -ATE² after *literate*]

numeration /ˌnjuːməˈreɪʃ(ə)n/ *n.* 1 a method or process of numbering or computing. 2 calculation. [ME f. L *numeratio* payment, in LL numbering (as NUMBER)]

numerator /ˈnjuːməˌreɪtə(r)/ *n.* 1 the number above the line in a vulgar fraction showing how many of the parts indicated by the denominator are taken (e.g. 2 in ⅖). 2 a person or device that numbers. [F *numérateur* or LL *numerator* (as NUMBER)]

numerical /njuːˈmerɪk(ə)l/ *adj.* (also **numeric**) of or relating to a number or numbers (*numerical superiority*). □ **numerically** *adv.* [med.L *numericus* (as NUMBER)]

numerology /ˌnjuːməˈrɒlədʒɪ/ *n.* (*pl.* -ies) the study of the supposed occult significance of numbers. □ **numerological** /-rəˈlɒdʒɪk(ə)l/ *adj.* **numerologist** *n.* [L *numerus* number + -LOGY]

numerous /ˈnjuːmərəs/ *adj.* 1 (with *pl.*) great in number (*received numerous gifts*). 2 consisting of many (*a numerous family*). □ **numerously** *adv.* **numerousness** *n.* [L *numerosus* (as NUMBER)]

numinous /ˈnjuːmɪnəs/ *adj.* 1 indicating the presence of a divinity. 2 spiritual. 3 awe-inspiring. [L *numen* a presiding spirit]

numismatic /ˌnjuːmɪzˈmætɪk/ *adj.* of or relating to coins or medals. □ **numismatically** *adv.* [F *numismatique* f. L *numisma* f. Gk *nomisma -atos* current coin f. *nomizō* use currently]

numismatics /ˌnjuːmɪzˈmætɪks/ *n.pl.* (usu. treated as *sing.*) the study of coins or medals. □ **numismatist** /-ˈmɪzmətɪst/ *n.*

numismatology /njuːˌmɪzməˈtɒlədʒɪ/ *n.* = NUMISMATICS.

numskull /ˈnʌmskʌl/ *n.* (also **numbskull**) a stupid or foolish person. [NUMB + SKULL]

nun *n.* a member of a community of women living apart under religious vows. □ **nunhood** *n.* **nunlike** *adj.* **nunnish** *adj.* [ME f. OE *nunne* and OF *nonne* f. eccl.L *nonna* fem. of *nonnus* monk, orig. a title given to an elderly person]

nuncio /ˈnʌnʃɪəʊ, -sɪəʊ/ *n.* (*pl.* -os) *RC Ch.* a papal ambassador. [It. f. L *nuntius* messenger]

nunnery /ˈnʌnərɪ/ *n.* (*pl.* -ies) a religious house of nuns; a convent.

nuptial /ˈnʌpʃ(ə)l/ *adj.* & *n.* —*adj.* of or relating to marriage or weddings. —*n.* (usu. in *pl.*) a wedding. [F *nuptial* or L *nuptialis* f. *nuptiae* wedding f. *nubere nupt-* wed]

nurd var. of NERD.

nurse /nɜːs/ *n.* & *v.* —*n.* 1 a person trained to assist doctors in caring for the sick or infirm. 2 a person employed or trained to take charge of young children. —*v.* 1 a *intr.* work as a nurse. b *tr.* attend to (a sick person). c *tr.* give medical attention to (an illness or injury). 2 *tr.* & *intr.* feed or be fed at the breast. 3 *tr.* (in *passive*; foll. by *in*) be brought up in (a specified condition) (*nursed in poverty*). 4 *tr.* hold or treat carefully or caressingly. 5 *tr.* a foster; promote the development of (the arts, plants, etc.). b harbour or nurture (a grievance, hatred, etc.). c pay special attention to (*nursed the voters*). [reduced f. ME and OF *norice, nurice* f. LL *nutricia* fem. of L *nutricius* f. *nutrix -icis* f. *nutrire* NOURISH]

nursemaid /ˈnɜːsmeɪd/ *n.* 1 a woman in charge of a child or children. 2 a person who watches over or guides another carefully.

nursery /ˈnɜːsərɪ/ *n.* (*pl.* -ies) 1 a a room or place equipped for young children. b = *day nursery.* 2 a place where plants, trees, etc., are reared for sale or transplantation. 3 any sphere or place in or by which qualities or types of people are fostered or bred. □ **nursery nurse** a person trained to take charge of babies and young children. **nursery rhyme** a simple traditional song or story in rhyme for children. **nursery school** a school for children between the ages of three and five. **nursery slopes** *Skiing* gentle slopes suitable for beginners. **nursery stakes** a race for two-year-old horses.

nurseryman /ˈnɜːsərɪmən/ *n.* (*pl.* -men) an owner of or worker in a plant nursery.

nursing /ˈnɜːsɪŋ/ *n.* 1 the practice or profession of caring for the sick as a nurse. 2 (*attrib.*) concerned with or suitable for nursing the sick or elderly etc. (*nursing home; nursing sister*). □ **nursing officer** a senior nurse.

nursling /ˈnɜːslɪŋ/ *n.* (also **nurseling**) an infant that is being suckled.

nurture /ˈnɜːtʃə(r)/ *n.* & *v.* —*n.* 1 the process of bringing up or training (esp. children); fostering care. 2 nourishment. 3 sociological factors as an influence on or determinant of personality. —*v.tr.* 1 bring up; rear. 2 nourish. □ **nurturer** *n.* [ME f. OF *nour(e)ture* (as NOURISH)]

nut *n.* 1 a a fruit consisting of a hard or tough shell around an edible kernel. b this kernel. 2 a pod containing hard seeds. 3 a small usu. square or hexagonal flat piece of metal or other material with a threaded hole through it for screwing on the end of a bolt to secure it. 4 *sl.* a person's head. 5 *sl.* a a crazy or eccentric person. b an obsessive enthusiast or devotee (*a health-food nut*). 6 a small lump of coal, butter, etc. 7 (in *pl.*) *coarse sl.* the testicles. □ **do one's nut** *sl.* be extremely angry or agitated. **for nuts** *colloq.* even tolerably well (*cannot sing for nuts*). **nut cutlet** a cutlet-shaped portion of meat-substitute, made from nuts etc. **nut-house** *sl.* a mental home or hospital. **nut-oil** an oil obtained from hazelnuts and walnuts. **nuts and bolts** *colloq.* the practical details. **nut-tree** any tree bearing nuts, esp. a hazel. **off one's nut** *sl.* crazy. □ **nutlike** *adj.* [OE *hnutu* f. Gmc]

nutation /njuːˈteɪʃ(ə)n/ *n.* 1 the act or an instance of nodding. 2 *Astron.* a periodic oscillation of the earth's poles. [L *nutatio* f. *nutare* nod]

nutcase /ˈnʌtkeɪs/ *n.* *sl.* a crazy or foolish person.

nutcracker /ˈnʌtˌkrækə(r)/ *n.* (usu. in *pl.*) a device for cracking nuts.

nuthatch /ˈnʌthætʃ/ *n.* any small bird of the family Sittidae, climbing up and down tree-trunks and feeding on nuts, insects, etc. [NUT + *hatch* rel. to HATCH²]

nutmeg /'nʌtmeg/ n. **1** an evergreen E. Indian tree, *Myristica fragrans*, yielding a hard aromatic spheroidal seed. **2** the seed of this used as a spice and in medicine. [ME: partial transl. of OF *nois mug(u)ede* ult. f. L *nux* nut + LL *muscus* MUSK]

nutria /'nju:trɪə/ n. the skin or fur of a coypu. [Sp., = otter]

nutrient /'nju:trɪənt/ n. & adj. —n. any substance that provides essential nourishment for the maintenance of life. —adj. serving as or providing nourishment. [L *nutrire* nourish]

nutriment /'nju:trɪmənt/ n. **1** nourishing food. **2** an intellectual or artistic etc. nourishment or stimulus. □ **nutrimental** /-'ment(ə)l/ adj. [L *nutrimentum* (as NUTRIENT)]

nutrition /nju:'trɪʃ(ə)n/ n. **1 a** the process of providing or receiving nourishing substances. **b** food, nourishment. **2** the study of nutrients and nutrition. □ **nutritional** adj. [F *nutrition* or LL *nutritio* (as NUTRIENT)]

nutritionist /nju:'trɪʃənɪst/ n. a person who studies or is an expert on the processes of human nourishment.

nutritious /nju:'trɪʃəs/ adj. efficient as food; nourishing. □ **nutritiously** adv. **nutritiousness** n. [L *nutritius* (as NURSE)]

nutritive /'nju:trɪtɪv/ adj. & n. —adj. **1** of or concerned in nutrition. **2** serving as nutritious food. —n. a nutritious article of food. [ME f. F *nutritif -ive* f. med.L *nutritivus* (as NUTRIENT)]

nuts /nʌts/ adj. & int. —adj. sl. crazy, mad, eccentric. —int. sl. an expression of contempt or derision (*nuts to you*). □ **be nuts about** (or **on**) colloq. be enthusiastic about or very fond of.

nutshell /'nʌtʃel/ n. the hard exterior covering of a nut. □ **in a nutshell** in a few words.

nutter /'nʌtə(r)/ n. Brit. sl. a crazy or eccentric person.

nutty /'nʌtɪ/ adj. (**nuttier, nuttiest**) **1 a** full of nuts. **b** tasting like nuts. **2** sl. = NUTS adj. □ **nuttiness** n.

nux vomica /nʌks 'vɒmɪkə/ n. **1** an E. Indian tree, *Strychnos nux-vomica*, yielding a poisonous fruit. **2** the seeds of this tree, containing strychnine. [med.L f. L *nux* nut + *vomicus* f. *vomere* vomit]

nuzzle /'nʌz(ə)l/ v. **1** tr. prod or rub gently with the nose. **2** intr. (foll. by *into*, *against*, *up to*) press the nose gently. **3** tr. (also refl.) nestle; lie snug. [ME f. NOSE + -LE⁴]

NW abbr. **1** north-west. **2** north-western.

nyctalopia /ˌnɪktə'ləʊpɪə/ n. the inability to see in dim light or at night. Also called *night-blindness*. [LL f. Gk *nuktalōps* f. *nux nuktos* night + *alaos* blind + *ōps* eye]

nylon /'naɪlɒn/ n. **1** any of various synthetic polyamide fibres with tough, lightweight, elastic properties, used in industry and for textiles etc. **2** a nylon fabric. **3** (in pl.) stockings made of nylon. [invented word, after *cotton*, *rayon*]

nymph /nɪmf/ n. **1** any of various mythological semi-divine spirits regarded as maidens and associated with aspects of nature, esp. rivers and woods. **2** poet. a beautiful young woman. **3** an immature form of some insects. □ **nymphal** adj. **nymphean** /-'fiːən/ adj. **nymphlike** adj. [ME f. OF *nimphe* f. L *nympha* f. Gk *numphē*]

nymphet /'nɪmfet, -'fet/ n. **1** a young nymph. **2** colloq. a sexually attractive young woman.

nympho /'nɪmfəʊ/ n. (pl. **-os**) colloq. a nymphomaniac. [abbr.]

nymphomania /ˌnɪmfə'meɪnɪə/ n. excessive sexual desire in women. □ **nymphomaniac** n. & adj. [mod.L (as NYMPH, -MANIA)]

NZ abbr. New Zealand.

O[1] *n.* (also **o**) (*pl.* **Os** or **O's**) **1** the fifteenth letter of the alphabet. **2** (**o**) nought, zero (in a sequence of numerals esp. when spoken). **3** a human blood type.

O[2] *symb. Chem.* the element oxygen.

O[3] *int.* **1** var. of OH[1]. **2** prefixed to a name in the vocative (*O God*). [ME, natural excl.]

O' /əʊ, ə/ *prefix* of Irish patronymic names (*O'Connor*). [Ir. *ó, ua*, descendant]

o' /ə/ *prep.* of, on (esp. in phrases: *o'clock*; *will-o'-the-wisp*). [abbr.]

-o *suffix* forming usu. *sl.* or *colloq.* variants or derivatives (*beano*; *wino*). [perh. *-o* as joc. suffix]

-o- *suffix* the terminal vowel of combining forms (*spectro-*; *chemico-*; *Franco-*). [orig. Gk]

■ **Usage** This suffix is often elided before a vowel, as in *neuralgia*.

oaf *n.* (*pl.* **oafs**) **1** an awkward lout. **2** a stupid person. □ **oafish** *adj.* **oafishly** *adv.* **oafishness** *n.* [orig. = elf's child, var. of obs. *auf* f. ON *álfr* elf]

oak *n.* **1** any tree or shrub of the genus *Quercus* usu. having lobed leaves and bearing acorns. **2** the durable wood of this tree, used esp. for furniture and in building. **3** (*attrib.*) made of oak (*oak table*). **4** (**the Oaks**) (treated as *sing.*) an annual race at Epsom for three-year-old fillies. □ **oak-apple** (or **-gall**) an apple-like gall containing larvae of certain wasps, found on oak trees. □ **oaken** *adj.* [OE *āc* f. Gmc]

oakum /ˈəʊkəm/ *n.* a loose fibre obtained by picking old rope to pieces and used esp. in caulking. [OE *ǣcumbe, ācumbe*, lit. 'off-combings']

OAP *abbr. Brit.* old-age pensioner.

oar *n.* **1** a pole with a blade used for rowing or steering a boat by leverage against the water. **2** a rower. □ **put one's oar in** interfere, meddle. **rest** (*US* **lay**) **on one's oars** relax one's efforts. □ **oared** *adj.* (also in *comb.*). **oarless** *adj.* [OE *ār* f. Gmc, perh. rel. to Gk *eretmos* oar]

oarlock /ˈɔːlɒk/ *n. US* a rowlock.

oarsman /ˈɔːzmən/ *n.* (*pl.* **-men**; *fem.* **oarswoman**, *pl.* **-women**) a rower. □ **oarsmanship** *n.*

oasis /əʊˈeɪsɪs/ *n.* (*pl.* **oases** /-siːz/) **1** a fertile spot in a desert, where water is found. **2** an area or period of calm in the midst of turbulence. [LL f. Gk, app. of Egypt. orig.]

oast *n.* a kiln for drying hops. □ **oast-house** a building containing this. [OE *āst* f. Gmc]

oat *n.* **1 a** a cereal plant, *Avena sativa*, cultivated in cool climates. **b** (in *pl.*) the grain yielded by this, used as food. **2** any other cereal of the genus *Avena*, esp. the wild oat, *A. fatua*. **3** (in *pl.*) *sl.* sexual gratification. □ **feel one's oats** *colloq.* **1** be lively. **2** *US* feel self-important. **off one's oats** *colloq.* not hungry. **sow one's oats** (or **wild oats**) indulge in youthful excess or promiscuity. □ **oaten** *adj.* [OE *āte*, pl. *ātan*, of unkn. orig.]

oatcake /ˈəʊtkeɪk/ *n.* a thin unleavened biscuit-like food made of oatmeal, common in Scotland and N. England.

oath /əʊθ/ *n.* (*pl.* **oaths** /əʊðz/) **1** a solemn declaration or undertaking (often naming God) as to the truth of something or as a commitment to future action. **2** a statement or promise contained in an oath (*oath of allegiance*). **3** a profane or blasphemous utterance; a curse. □ **on** (or **under**) **oath** having sworn a solemn oath. **take** (or **swear**) **an oath** make such a declaration or undertaking. [OE *āth* f. Gmc]

oatmeal /ˈəʊtmiːl/ *n.* **1** meal made from ground oats used esp. in porridge and oatcakes. **2** a greyish-fawn colour flecked with brown.

ob. *abbr.* he or she died. [L *obiit*]

ob- /ɒb/ *prefix* (also **oc-** before *c*, **of-** before *f*, **op-** before *p*) occurring mainly in words of Latin origin, meaning: **1** exposure, openness (*object*; *obverse*). **2** meeting or facing (*occasion*; *obvious*). **3** direction (*oblong*; *offer*). **4** opposition, hostility, or resistance (*obstreperous*; *opponent*; *obstinate*). **5** hindrance, blocking, or concealment (*obese*; *obstacle*; *occult*). **6** finality or completeness (*obsolete*; *occupy*). [L f. *ob* towards, against, in the way of]

obbligato /ˌɒblɪˈɡɑːtəʊ/ *n.* (*pl.* **-os**) *Mus.* an accompaniment, usu. special and unusual in effect, forming an integral part of a composition (*with violin obbligato*). [It., = obligatory, f. L *obligatus* past part. (as OBLIGE)]

obdurate /ˈɒbdjʊrət/ *adj.* **1** stubborn. **2** hardened against persuasion or influence. □ **obduracy** *n.* **obdurately** *adv.* **obdurateness** *n.* [ME f. L *obduratus* past part. of *obdurare* (as OB-, *durare* harden f. *durus* hard)]

OBE *abbr.* (in the UK) Officer of the Order of the British Empire.

obeah /ˈəʊbɪə/ *n.* (also **obi** /ˈəʊbɪ/) a kind of sorcery practised esp. in the West Indies. [W. Afr.]

obedience /əʊˈbiːdɪəns/ *n.* **1** obeying as an act or practice or quality. **2** submission to another's rule or authority. **3** compliance with a law or command. □ **in obedience to** actuated by or in accordance with. [ME f. OF f. L *obedientia* (as OBEY)]

obedient /əʊˈbiːdɪənt/ *adj.* **1** obeying or ready to obey. **2** (often foll. by *to*) submissive to another's will; dutiful (*obedient to the law*). □ **obediently** *adv.* [ME f. OF f. L *obediens -entis* (as OBEY)]

obeisance /əʊˈbeɪs(ə)ns/ *n.* **1** a bow, curtsey, or other respectful or submissive gesture (*make an obeisance*). **2** homage, submission, deference (*pay obeisance*). □ **obeisant** *adj.* **obeisantly** *adv.* [ME f. OF *obeissance* (as OBEY)]

obeli *pl.* of OBELUS.

obelisk /ˈɒbəlɪsk/ *n.* **1** a tapering usu. four-sided stone pillar set up as a monument or landmark etc. **2** = OBELUS. [L *obeliscus* f. Gk *obeliskos* dimin. of *obelos* SPIT[2]]

obelus /ˈɒbələs/ n. (pl. **obeli** /-ˌlaɪ/) a dagger-shaped reference mark in printed matter. [L f. Gk obelos SPIT²]

obese /əʊˈbiːs/ adj. very fat; corpulent. □ **obeseness** n. **obesity** n. [L obesus (as OB-, edere eat)]

obey /əʊˈbeɪ/ v. **1** tr. **a** carry out the command of (you will obey me). **b** carry out (a command) (obey orders). **2** intr. do what one is told to do. **3** tr. be actuated by (a force or impulse). □ **obeyer** n. [ME f. OF obeir f. L obedire (as OB-, audire hear)]

obfuscate /ˈɒbfʌˌskeɪt/ v.tr. **1** obscure or confuse (a mind, topic, etc.). **2** stupefy, bewilder. □ **obfuscation** /-ˈkeɪʃ(ə)n/ n. **obfuscatory** adj. [LL obfuscare (as OB-, fuscus dark)]

obi var. of OBEAH.

obit /ˈɒbɪt, ˈəʊbɪt/ n. colloq. an obituary. [abbr.]

obituary /əˈbɪtjʊərɪ/ n. (pl. **-ies**) **1** a notice of a death or deaths esp. in a newspaper. **2** an account of the life of a deceased person. **3** (attrib.) of or serving as an obituary. □ **obituarial** /-tjʊˈeərɪəl/ adj. **obituarist** n. [med.L obituarius f. L obitus death f. obire obit- die (as OB-, ire go)]

object n. & v. —n. /ˈɒbdʒɪkt/ **1** a material thing that can be seen or touched. **2** (foll. by of) a person or thing to which action or feeling is directed (the object of attention; the object of our study). **3** a thing sought or aimed at; a purpose. **4** Gram. a noun or its equivalent governed by an active transitive verb or by a preposition. **5** Philos. a thing external to the thinking mind or subject. —v. /əbˈdʒekt/ **1** intr. (often foll. by to, against) express or feel opposition, disapproval, or reluctance; protest (I object to being treated like this; objecting against government policies). **2** tr. (foll. by that + clause) state as an objection (objected that they were kept waiting). **3** tr. (foll. by to, against, or that + clause) adduce (a quality or fact) as contrary or damaging (to a case). □ **no object** not forming an important or restricting factor (money no object). **object-glass** the lens in a telescope etc. nearest to the object observed. **object-lesson** a striking practical example of some principle. **object of the exercise** the main point of an activity. □ **objectless** /ˈɒbdʒɪktlɪs/ adj. **objector** /əbˈdʒektə(r)/ n. [ME f. med.L objectum thing presented to the mind, past part. of L objicere (as OB-, jacere ject- throw)]

objectify /ɒbˈdʒektɪˌfaɪ/ v.tr. (**-ies, -ied**) **1** make objective; embody. **2** present as an object of perception. □ **objectification** /-fɪˈkeɪʃ(ə)n/ n.

objection /əbˈdʒekʃ(ə)n/ n. **1** an expression or feeling of opposition or disapproval. **2** the act of objecting. **3** an adverse reason or statement. [ME f. OF objection or LL objectio (as OBJECT)]

objectionable /əbˈdʒekʃənəb(ə)l/ adj. **1** open to objection. **2** unpleasant, offensive. □ **objectionableness** n. **objectionably** /-blɪ/ adv.

objective /əbˈdʒektɪv/ adj. & n. —adj. **1** external to the mind; actually existing; real. **2** (of a person, writing, art, etc.) dealing with outward things or exhibiting facts uncoloured by feelings or opinions; not subjective. **3** Gram. (of a case or word) constructed as or appropriate to the object of a transitive verb or preposition. **4** aimed at (objective point). —n. **1** something sought or aimed at; an objective point. **2** Gram. the objective case. **3** = object-glass. □ **objectival** /ˌɒbdʒekˈtaɪv(ə)l/ adj. **objectively** adv. **objectiveness** n. **objectivity** /ˌɒbdʒekˈtɪvɪtɪ/ n. **objectivize** /əbˈdʒektɪˌvaɪz/ v.tr. (also **-ise**). **objectivization** /əbˌdʒektɪvaɪˈzeɪʃ(ə)n/ n. [med.L objectivus (as OBJECT)]

objet d'art /ˌɒbʒeɪ ˈdɑː/ n. (pl. **objets d'art** pronunc. same) a small decorative object. [F, lit. 'object of art']

objurgate /ˈɒbdʒəˌgeɪt/ v.tr. literary chide or scold. □ **objurgation** /-ˈgeɪʃ(ə)n/ n. **objurgatory** /ɒbˈdʒɜːgətərɪ/ adj. [L objurgare objurgat- (as OB-, jurgare quarrel f. jurgium strife)]

oblate¹ /ˈɒbleɪt/ n. a person dedicated to a monastic or religious life or work. [F f. med.L oblatus f. offere oblat- offer (as OB-, ferre bring)]

oblate² /ˈɒbleɪt/ adj. Geom. (of a spheroid) flattened at the poles. [mod.L oblatus (as OBLATE¹)]

oblation /əʊˈbleɪʃ(ə)n/ n. Relig. a thing offered to a divine being. □ **oblational** adj. **oblatory** /ˈɒblətərɪ/ adj. [ME f. OF oblation or LL oblatio (as OBLATE¹)]

obligate v.tr. /ˈɒblɪˌgeɪt/ (usu. in passive; foll. by to + infin.) bind (a person) legally or morally. □ **obligator** n. [L obligare obligat- (as OBLIGE)]

obligation /ˌɒblɪˈgeɪʃ(ə)n/ n. **1** the constraining power of a law, precept, duty, contract, etc. **2** a duty; a burdensome task. **3** a binding agreement, esp. one enforceable under legal penalty; a written contract or bond. **4 a** a service or benefit (repay an obligation). **b** indebtedness for this (be under an obligation). □ **obligational** adj. [ME f. OF f. L obligatio -onis (as OBLIGE)]

obligatory /əˈblɪgətərɪ/ adj. **1** legally or morally binding. **2** compulsory and not merely permissive. **3** constituting an obligation. □ **obligatorily** adv. [ME f. LL obligatorius (as OBLIGE)]

oblige /əˈblaɪdʒ/ v. **1** tr. (foll. by to + infin.) constrain, compel. **2** tr. be binding on. **3** tr. **a** make indebted by conferring a favour. **b** (foll. by with, or by + verbal noun) gratify (oblige me by leaving). **c** perform a service for (often absol.: will you oblige?). **4** tr. (in passive; foll. by to) be indebted (am obliged to you for your help). □ **much obliged** an expression of thanks. □ **obliger** n. [ME f. OF obliger f. L obligare (as OB-, ligare bind)]

obliging /əˈblaɪdʒɪŋ/ adj. courteous, accommodating; ready to do a service or kindness. □ **obligingly** adv. **obligingness** n.

oblique /əˈbliːk/ adj. & n. —adj. **1 a** slanting; declining from the vertical or horizontal. **b** diverging from a straight line or course. **2** not going straight to the point; roundabout, indirect. **3** Geom. **a** (of a line, plane figure, or surface) inclined at other than a right angle. **b** (of an angle) acute or obtuse. **4** Gram. denoting any case other than the nominative or vocative. —n. an oblique stroke (/). □ **obliquely** adv. **obliqueness** n. **obliquity** /əˈblɪkwɪtɪ/ n. [ME f. F f. L obliquus]

obliterate /əˈblɪtəˌreɪt/ v.tr. **1 a** blot out; efface, erase, destroy. **b** leave no clear traces of. **2** deface (a postage stamp etc.) to prevent further use. □ **obliteration** /-ˈreɪʃ(ə)n/ n. **obliterative** /-rətɪv/ adj. **obliterator** n. [L obliterare (as OB-, litera LETTER)]

oblivion /əˈblɪvɪən/ n. **1** the state of having or being forgotten. **2** disregard; an unregarded state. □ **fall into oblivion** be forgotten or disused. [ME f. OF f. L oblivio -onis f. oblivisci forget]

oblivious /əˈblɪvɪəs/ adj. **1** (often foll. by of) forgetful, unmindful. **2** (foll. by to, of) unaware or unconscious of. □ **obliviously** adv. **obliviousness** n. [ME f. L obliviosus (as OBLIVION)]

oblong /ˈɒblɒŋ/ adj. & n. —adj. **1** deviating from a square form by having one long axis, esp.

rectangular with adjacent sides unequal. **2** greater in breadth than in height. —*n.* an oblong figure or object. [ME f. L *oblongus* longish (as OB-, *longus* long)]

obloquy /ˈɒbləkwɪ/ *n.* **1** the state of being generally ill spoken of. **2** abuse, detraction. [ME f. LL *obloquium* contradiction f. L *obloqui* deny (as OB-, *loqui* speak)]

obnoxious /əbˈnɒkʃəs/ *adj.* offensive, objectionable, disliked. □ **obnoxiously** *adv.* **obnoxiousness** *n.* [orig. = vulnerable (to harm), f. L *obnoxiosus* or *obnoxius* (as OB-, *noxa* harm: assoc. with NOXIOUS)]

oboe /ˈəʊbəʊ/ *n.* **1** a woodwind double-reed instrument of treble pitch and plaintive incisive tone. **2** its player. □ **oboist** /ˈəʊbəʊɪst/ *n.* [It. *oboe* or F *hautbois* f. *haut* high + *bois* wood: *d'amore* = of love]

obscene /əbˈsiːn/ *adj.* **1** offensively or repulsively indecent, esp. by offending accepted sexual morality. **2** *colloq.* highly offensive or repugnant (*an obscene accumulation of wealth*). **3** *Brit. Law* (of a publication) tending to deprave or corrupt. □ **obscenely** *adv.* **obsceneness** *n.* [F *obscène* or L *obsc(a)enus* ill-omened, abominable]

obscenity /əbˈsenɪtɪ/ *n.* (*pl.* **-ies**) **1** the state or quality of being obscene. **2** an obscene action, word, etc. [L *obscaenitas* (as OBSCENE)]

obscurantism /ˌɒbskjʊəˈræntɪz(ə)m/ *n.* opposition to knowledge and enlightenment. □ **obscurant** /ɒbˈskjʊərənt/ *n.* **obscurantist** *n.* [*obscurant* f. G f. L *obscurans* f. *obscurare*: see OBSCURE]

obscure /əbˈskjʊə(r)/ *adj. & v.* —*adj.* **1** not clearly expressed or easily understood. **2** unexplained, doubtful. **3** dark, dim. **4** indistinct; not clear. **5** hidden; remote from observation. **6** a unnoticed. **b** (of a person) undistinguished, hardly known. **7** (of a colour) dingy, dull, indefinite. —*v.tr.* **1** make obscure, dark, indistinct, or unintelligible. **2** dim the glory of; outshine. **3** conceal from sight. □ **obscuration** /-ˈreɪʃ(ə)n/ *n.* **obscurely** *adv.* [ME f. OF *obscur* f. L *obscurus* dark]

obscurity /əbˈskjʊərɪtɪ/ *n.* (*pl.* **-ies**) **1** the state of being obscure. **2** an obscure person or thing. [F *obscurité* f. L *obscuritas* (as OBSCURE)]

obsequies /ˈɒbsɪkwɪz/ *n.pl.* **1** funeral rites. **2** a funeral. □ **obsequial** /əbˈsiːkwɪəl/ *adj.* [ME, pl. of obs. *obsequy* f. AF *obsequie*, OF *obseque* f. med.L *obsequiae* f. L *exsequiae* funeral rites (see EXEQUIES): assoc. with *obsequium* (see OBSEQUIOUS)]

obsequious /əbˈsiːkwɪəs/ *adj.* servilely obedient or attentive. □ **obsequiously** *adv.* **obsequiousness** *n.* [ME f. L *obsequiosus* f. *obsequium* compliance (as OB-, *sequi* follow)]

observance /əbˈzɜːv(ə)ns/ *n.* **1** the act or process of keeping or performing a law, duty, custom, ritual, etc. **2** an act of a religious or ceremonial character; a customary rite. [ME f. OF f. L *observantia* (as OBSERVE)]

observant /əbˈzɜːv(ə)nt/ *adj.* **1** acute or diligent in taking notice. **2** attentive in esp. religious observances (*an observant Jew*). □ **observantly** *adv.* [F (as OBSERVE)]

observation /ˌɒbzəˈveɪʃ(ə)n/ *n.* **1** the act or an instance of noticing; the condition of being noticed. **2** perception; the faculty of taking notice. **3** a remark or statement, esp. one that is of the nature of a comment. **4 a** the accurate watching and noting of phenomena as they occur in nature with regard to cause and effect or mutual relations. **b** the noting of the symptoms of a patient, the behaviour of a suspect, etc. □ **observation car** esp. *US* a carriage in a train built so as to afford good views. **observation post** *Mil.* a post for watching the effect of artillery fire etc. **under observation** being watched. □ **observational** *adj.* **observationally** *adv.* [ME f. L *observatio* (as OBSERVE)]

observatory /əbˈzɜːvətərɪ/ *n.* (*pl.* **-ies**) a room or building equipped for the observation of natural, esp. astronomical or meteorological, phenomena. [mod.L *observatorium* f. L *observare* (as OBSERVE)]

observe /əbˈzɜːv/ *v.* **1** *tr.* (often foll. by *that, how* + clause) perceive, note; take notice of; become conscious of. **2** *tr.* watch carefully. **3** *tr.* **a** follow or adhere to (a law, command, method, principle, etc.). **b** keep or adhere to (an appointed time). **c** maintain (silence). **d** duly perform (a rite). **e** celebrate (an anniversary). **4** *tr.* examine and note (phenomena) without the aid of experiment. **5** *tr.* (often foll. by *that* + clause) say, esp. by way of comment. **6** *intr.* (foll. by *on*) make a remark or remarks about. □ **observable** *adj.* **observably** *adv.* [ME f. OF *observer* f. L *observare* watch (as OB-, *servare* keep)]

observer /əbˈzɜːvə(r)/ *n.* **1** a person who observes. **2** an interested spectator. **3** a person who attends a conference etc. to note the proceedings but does not participate.

obsess /əbˈses/ *v.tr.* (often in *passive*) preoccupy, haunt; fill the mind of (a person) continually. □ **obsessive** *adj. & n.* **obsessively** *adv.* **obsessiveness** *n.* [L *obsidēre obsess-* (as OB-, *sedēre* sit)]

obsession /əbˈseʃ(ə)n/ *n.* **1** the act of obsessing or the state of being obsessed. **2** a persistent idea or thought dominating a person's mind. **3** a condition in which such ideas are present. □ **obsessional** *adj.* **obsessionalism** *n.* **obsessionally** *adv.* [L *obsessio* (as OBSESS)]

obsidian /əbˈsɪdɪən/ *n.* a dark glassy volcanic rock formed from hardened lava. [L *obsidianus*, error for *obsianus* f. *Obsius*, the name (in Pliny) of the discoverer of a similar stone]

obsolescent /ˌɒbsəˈles(ə)nt/ *adj.* becoming obsolete; going out of use or date. □ **obsolescence** *n.* [L *obsolescere obsolescent-* (as OB-, *solēre* be accustomed)]

obsolete /ˈɒbsəˌliːt/ *adj.* disused, discarded, antiquated. □ **obsoletely** *adv.* **obsoleteness** *n.* **obsoletism** *n.* [L *obsoletus* past part. (as OBSOLESCENT)]

obstacle /ˈɒbstək(ə)l/ *n.* a person or thing that obstructs progress. □ **obstacle-race** a race in which various obstacles have to be negotiated. [ME f. OF f. L *obstaculum* f. *obstare* impede (as OB-, *stare* stand)]

obstetric /əbˈstetrɪk/ *adj.* (also **obstetrical**) of or relating to childbirth and associated processes. □ **obstetrically** *adv.* **obstetrician** /-stəˈtrɪʃ(ə)n/ *n.* [mod.L *obstetricus* for L *obstetricius* f. *obstetrix* midwife f. *obstare* be present (as OB-, *stare* stand)]

obstetrics /əbˈstetrɪks/ *n.pl.* (treated as *sing.*) the branch of medicine and surgery concerned with childbirth and midwifery.

obstinate /ˈɒbstɪnət/ *adj.* **1** stubborn, intractable. **2** firmly adhering to one's chosen course of action or opinion despite dissuasion. **3** inflexible, self-willed. **4** unyielding; not readily responding to treatment etc. □ **obstinacy** n. **obstinately** adv. [ME f. L obstinatus past part. of obstinare persist (as OB-, stare stand)]

obstreperous /əbˈstrepərəs/ adj. **1** turbulent, unruly; noisily resisting control. **2** noisy, vociferous. □ **obstreperously** adv. **obstreperousness** n. [L obstreperus f. obstrepere (as OB-, strepere make a noise)]

obstruct /əbˈstrʌkt/ v.tr. **1** block up; make hard or impossible to pass. **2** prevent or retard the progress of; impede. □ **obstructor** n. [L obstruere obstruct- (as OB-, struere build)]

obstruction /əbˈstrʌkʃ(ə)n/ n. **1** the act or an instance of blocking; the state of being blocked. **2** the act of making or the state of becoming more or less impassable. **3** an obstacle or blockage. **4** the retarding of progress by deliberate delays, esp. of Parliamentary business. **5** Sport the act of unlawfully obstructing another player. **6** Med. a blockage in a bodily passage, esp. in an intestine. □ **obstructionism** n. (in sense 4). **obstructionist** n. (in sense 4). [L obstructio (as OBSTRUCT)]

obstructive /əbˈstrʌktɪv/ adj. & n. —adj. causing or intended to cause an obstruction. —n. an obstructive person or thing. □ **obstructively** adv. **obstructiveness** n.

obtain /əbˈteɪn/ v. **1** tr. acquire, secure; have granted to one. **2** intr. be prevalent or established or in vogue. □ **obtainable** adj. **obtainability** /-ˈbɪlɪtɪ/ n. **obtainer** n. **obtainment** n. **obtention** /əbˈtenʃ(ə)n/ n. [ME f. OF obtenir f. L obtinēre obtent- keep (as OB-, tenēre hold)]

obtrude /əbˈtruːd/ v. **1** intr. be or become obtrusive. **2** tr. (often foll. by on, upon) thrust forward (oneself, one's opinion, etc.) importunately. □ **obtruder** n. **obtrusion** /-ˈtruːʒ(ə)n/ n. [L obtrudere obtrus- (as OB-, trudere push)]

obtrusive /əbˈtruːsɪv/ adj. **1** unpleasantly or unduly noticeable. **2** obtruding oneself. □ **obtrusively** adv. **obtrusiveness** n. [as OBTRUDE]

obtuse /əbˈtjuːs/ adj. **1** dull-witted; slow to understand. **2** of blunt form; not sharp-pointed or sharp-edged. **3** (of an angle) more than 90° and less than 180°. **4** (of pain or the senses) dull; not acute. □ **obtusely** adv. **obtuseness** n. **obtusity** n. [L obtusus past part. obtundere obtus- (as OB-, tundere beat)]

obverse /ˈɒbvɜːs/ n. **1** the side of a coin or medal etc. bearing the head or principal design. **2** the front or proper or top side of a thing. **3** the counterpart of a fact or truth. □ **obversely** adv. [L obversus past part. obvertere obvers- (as OB-, vertere turn)]

obviate /ˈɒbvɪˌeɪt/ v.tr. get round or do away with (a need, inconvenience, etc.). □ **obviation** /-ˈeɪʃ(ə)n/ n. [LL obviare oppose (as OB-, via way)]

obvious /ˈɒbvɪəs/ adj. easily seen or recognized or understood; palpable, indubitable. □ **obviously** adv. **obviousness** n. [L obvius f. ob viam in the way]

OC abbr. Officer Commanding.

ocarina /ˌɒkəˈriːnə/ n. a small egg-shaped ceramic (usu. terracotta) or metal wind instrument. [It. f. oca goose (from its shape)]

occasion /əˈkeɪʒ(ə)n/ n. & v. —n. **1 a** a special or noteworthy event or happening (dressed for the occasion). **b** the time or occurrence of this (on the occasion of their marriage). **2** (often foll. by for, or to + infin.) a reason, ground, or justification (there is no occasion to be angry). **3** a juncture suitable for doing something; an opportunity. **4** an immediate but subordinate or incidental cause (the assassination was the occasion of the war). —v.tr. **1** be the occasion or cause of; bring about esp. incidentally. **2** (foll. by to + infin.) cause (a person or thing to do something). □ **on occasion** now and then; when the need arises. **rise to the occasion** produce the necessary will, energy, ability, etc., in unusually demanding circumstances. [ME f. OF occasion or L occasio juncture, reason, f. occidere occas- go down (as OB-, cadere fall)]

occasional /əˈkeɪʒən(ə)l/ adj. **1** happening irregularly and infrequently. **2** made or meant for, or associated with, a special occasion. **3** acting on a special occasion. □ **occasional table** a small table for irregular and varied use. □ **occasionality** /-ˈnælɪtɪ/ n. **occasionally** adv.

Occident /ˈɒksɪd(ə)nt/ n. poet. or rhet. **1** (prec. by the) the West. **2** western Europe. **3** Europe, America, or both, as distinct from the Orient. **4** European in contrast to Oriental civilization. [ME f. OF f. L occidens -entis setting, sunset, west (as OCCASION)]

occidental /ˌɒksɪˈdent(ə)l/ adj. & n. —adj. **1** of the Occident. **2** western. **3** of Western nations. —n. (**Occidental**) a native of the Occident. □ **occidentalism** n. **occidentalist** n. **occidentalize** v.tr. (also -ise). **occidentally** adv. [ME f. OF occidental or L occidentalis (as OCCIDENT)]

occiput /ˈɒksɪˌpʌt/ n. the back of the head. □ **occipital** /-ˈsɪpɪt(ə)l/ adj. [ME f. L occiput (as OB-, caput head)]

occlude /əˈkluːd/ v.tr. **1** stop up or close (pores or an orifice). **2** Chem. absorb and retain (gases or impurities). □ **occluded front** Meteorol. a front resulting from occlusion. [L occludere occlus- (as OB-, claudere shut)]

occlusion /əˈkluːʒ(ə)n/ n. **1** the act or process of occluding. **2** Meteorol. a phenomenon in which the cold front of a depression overtakes the warm front, causing upward displacement of warm air between them. □ **occlusive** adj.

occult adj. /ɒˈkʌlt, ˈɒkʌlt/ **1** involving the supernatural; mystical, magical. **2** kept secret; esoteric. **3** recondite, mysterious; beyond the range of ordinary knowledge. □ **the occult** occult phenomena generally. □ **occultation** /-ˈteɪʃ(ə)n/ n. **occultism** n. **occultist** n. **occultly** adv. **occultness** n. [L occulere occult- (as OB-, celare hide)]

occupant /ˈɒkjʊpənt/ n. **1** a person who occupies, resides in, or is in a place etc. (both occupants of the car were unhurt). **2** a person holding property, esp. land, in actual possession. **3** a person who establishes a title by taking possession of something previously without an established owner. □ **occupancy** n. (pl. -ies). [F occupant or L occupans -antis (as OCCUPY)]

occupation /ˌɒkjʊˈpeɪʃ(ə)n/ n. **1** what occupies one; a means of passing one's time. **2** a person's temporary or regular employment; a business, calling, or pursuit. **3** the act of occupying or state of being occupied. **4 a** the act of taking or holding possession of (a country, district, etc.) by military force. **b** the state or time of this. **5** tenure, occupancy. [ME f. AF ocupacioun, OF occupation f. L occupatio -onis (as OCCUPY)]

occupational /ˌɒkjʊˈpeɪʃən(ə)l/ *adj.* **1** of or in the nature of an occupation or occupations. **2** (of a disease, hazard, etc.) rendered more likely by one's occupation. □ **occupational therapy** mental or physical activity designed to assist recovery from disease or injury.

occupier /ˈɒkjʊˌpaɪə(r)/ *n. Brit.* a person residing in a property as its owner or tenant.

occupy /ˈɒkjʊˌpaɪ/ *v.tr.* (**-ies, -ied**) **1** reside in; be the tenant of. **2** take up or fill (space or time or a place). **3** hold (a position or office). **4** take military possession of (a country, region, town, strategic position). **5** place oneself in (a building etc.) forcibly or without authority. **6** (usu. in *passive*; often foll. by *in*, *with*) keep busy or engaged. [ME f. OF *occuper* f. L *occupare* seize (as OB-, *capere* take)]

occur /əˈkɜː(r)/ *v.intr.* (**occurred, occurring**) **1** come into being as an event or process at or during some time; happen. **2** exist or be encountered in some place or conditions. **3** (foll. by *to*; usu. foll. by *that* + clause) come into the mind of, esp. as an unexpected or casual thought (*it occurred to me that you were right*). [L *occurrere* go to meet, present itself (as OB-, *currere* run)]

occurrence /əˈkʌrəns/ *n.* **1** the act or an instance of occurring. **2** an incident or event. □ **of frequent occurrence** often occurring. [*occurrent* that occurs f. F f. L *occurrens -entis* (as OCCUR)]

ocean /ˈəʊʃ(ə)n/ *n.* **1 a** a large expanse of sea, esp. each of the main areas called the Atlantic, Pacific, Indian, Arctic, and Antarctic Oceans. **b** these regarded cumulatively as the body of water surrounding the land of the globe. **2** (usu. prec. by *the*) the sea. **3** (often in *pl.*) a very large expanse or quantity of anything (*oceans of time*). □ **ocean-going** (of a ship) able to cross oceans. □ **oceanward** *adv.* (also **-wards**). [ME f. OF *occean* f. L *oceanus* f. Gk *ōkeanos* stream encircling the earth's disc, Atlantic]

oceanic /ˌəʊʃɪˈænɪk, ˌəʊsɪ-/ *adj.* **1** of, like, or near the ocean. **2** (of a climate) governed by the ocean.

oceanography /ˌəʊʃəˈnɒgrəfɪ/ *n.* the study of the oceans. □ **oceanographer** *n.* **oceanographic** /-nəˈgræfɪk/ *adj.* **oceanographical** /-nəˈgræfɪk(ə)l/ *adj.*

ocelot /ˈɒsɪˌlɒt/ *n.* **1** a medium-sized cat, *Felis pardalis*, native to S. and Central America, having a deep yellow or orange coat with black striped and spotted markings. **2** its fur. [F f. Nahuatl *ocelotl* jaguar]

och /ɒx/ *int. Sc. & Ir.* expressing surprise or regret. [Gael. & Ir.]

oche /ˈɒkɪ/ *n.* (also **hockey** /ˈɒkɪ, ˈhɒkɪ/) *Darts* the line behind which the players stand when throwing. [20th c.: orig. uncert. (perh. connected with OF *ochen* cut a deep notch in)]

ochre /ˈəʊkə(r)/ *n.* (*US* **ocher**) **1** a mineral of clay and ferric oxide, used as a pigment varying from light yellow to brown or red. **2** a pale brownish yellow. □ **ochreish** *adj.* **ochreous** /ˈəʊkrɪəs/ *adj.* **ochrous** /ˈəʊkrəs/ *adj.* **ochry** /ˈəʊkrɪ/ *adj.* [ME f. OF *ocre* f. L *ochra* f. Gk *ōkhra* yellow ochre]

-ock /ək/ *suffix* forming nouns orig. with diminutive sense (*hillock*; *bullock*). [from or after OE *-uc, -oc*]

ocker /ˈɒkə(r)/ *n. Austral. sl.* a boorish or aggressive Australian (esp. as a stereotype). [20th c.: orig. uncert.]

o'clock /əˈklɒk/ *adv.* of the clock (used to specify the hour) (6 *o'clock*).

Oct. *abbr.* October.

oct. *abbr.* octavo.

octa- /ˈɒktə/ *comb. form* (also **oct-** before a vowel) eight. [Gk *okta-* f. *oktō* eight]

octad /ˈɒktæd/ *n.* a group of eight. [LL *octas octad-* f. Gk *oktas -ados* f. *oktō* eight]

octagon /ˈɒktəgən/ *n.* **1** a plane figure with eight sides and angles. **2** an object or building with this cross-section. □ **octagonal** /-ˈtægən(ə)l/ *adj.* **octagonally** /-ˈtægənəlɪ/ *adv.* [L *octagonos* f. Gk *octagōnos* (as OCTA-, -GON)]

octahedron /ˌɒktəˈhiːdrən, -ˈhedrən/ *n.* (*pl.* **octahedrons** or **octahedra** /-drə/) a solid figure contained by eight (esp. triangular) plane faces. □ **octahedral** *adj.* [Gk *oktaedron* (as OCTA-, -HEDRON)]

octal /ˈɒkt(ə)l/ *adj.* reckoning or proceeding by eights (*octal scale*).

octane /ˈɒkteɪn/ *n.* a colourless inflammable hydrocarbon of the alkane series. □ **high-octane** (of fuel used in internal-combustion engines) having good antiknock properties. [OCTA- + -ANE]

octave /ˈɒktɪv/ *n.* **1** *Mus.* **a** a series of eight notes occupying the interval between (and including) two notes, one having twice or half the frequency of vibration of the other. **b** this interval. **c** each of the two notes at the extremes of this interval. **d** these two notes sounding together. **2** a group or stanza of eight lines; an octet. [ME f. OF f. L *octava dies* eighth day (reckoned inclusively)]

octavo /ɒkˈteɪvəʊ, ɒkˈtɑːvəʊ/ *n.* (*pl.* **-os**) **1** a size of book or page given by folding a standard sheet three times to form a quire of eight leaves. **2** a book or sheet of this size. [L *in octavo* in an eighth f. *octavus* eighth]

octet /ɒkˈtet/ *n.* (also **octette**) **1** *Mus.* **a** a composition for eight voices or instruments. **b** the performers of such a piece. **2** a group of eight. **3** the first eight lines of a sonnet. [It. *ottetto* or G *Oktett*: assim. to OCTA-, DUET, QUARTET]

octo- /ˈɒktəʊ/ *comb. form* (also **oct-** before a vowel) eight. [L *octo* or Gk *oktō* eight]

October /ɒkˈtəʊbə(r)/ *n.* the tenth month of the year. [OE f. L (as OCTO-): cf. DECEMBER, SEPTEMBER]

octogenarian /ˌɒktəʊdʒɪˈneərɪən/ *n. & adj.* —*n.* a person from 80 to 89 years old. —*adj.* of this age. [L *octogenarius* f. *octogeni* distributive of *octoginta* eighty]

octopod /ˈɒktəˌpɒd/ *n.* any cephalopod of the order Octopoda, with eight arms usu. having suckers, and a round saclike body, including octopuses. [Gk *oktōpous -podos* f. *oktō* eight + *pous* foot]

octopus /ˈɒktəpəs/ *n.* (*pl.* **octopuses**) **1** any cephalopod mollusc of the genus *Octopus* having eight suckered arms, a soft saclike body, and strong beaklike jaws. **2** an organized and usu. harmful ramified power or influence. [Gk *oktōpous*: see OCTOPOD]

octuple /ˈɒktjʊp(ə)l/ *adj.*, *n.*, & *v.* —*adj.* eightfold. —*n.* an eightfold amount. —*v.tr. & intr.* multiply by eight. [F *octuple* or L *octuplus* (adj.) f. *octo* eight: cf. DOUBLE]

ocular /ˈɒkjʊlə(r)/ *adj. & n.* —*adj.* of or connected with the eyes or sight; visual. —*n.* the eyepiece of an optical instrument. □ **ocularly** adv. [F oculaire f. LL ocularis f. L oculus eye]

oculist /ˈɒkjʊlɪst/ n. a person who specializes in the medical treatment of eye disorders or defects. □ **oculistic** /-ˈlɪstɪk/ adj. [F oculiste f. L oculus eye]

oculo- /ˈɒkjʊləʊ/ comb. form eye (oculo-nasal). [L oculus eye]

OD /əʊˈdiː/ n. & v. esp. US sl. —n. an overdose, esp. of a narcotic drug. —v.intr. (**OD's, OD'd, OD'ing**) take an overdose. [abbr.]

odalisque /ˈɒʊdəlɪsk/ n. hist. an Eastern female slave or concubine. [F f. Turk. odalik f. oda chamber + lik function]

odd adj. **1** extraordinary, strange, queer, remarkable, eccentric. **2** casual, occasional, unconnected (odd jobs; odd moments). **3** not normally noticed or considered; unpredictable (in some odd corner; picks up odd bargains). **4** additional; beside the reckoning (earned the odd pound). **5 a** (of numbers such as 3 and 5) not integrally divisible by two. **b** (of things or persons numbered consecutively) bearing such a number (no parking on odd dates). **6** left over when the rest have been distributed or divided into pairs (have got an odd sock). **7** detached from a set or series (a few odd volumes). **8** (appended to a number, sum, weight, etc.) somewhat more than (forty odd; forty-odd people). **9** by which a round number, given sum, etc., is exceeded (we have 102—what shall we do with the odd 2?). □ **odd job** a casual isolated piece of work. **odd job man** (or **odd jobber**) Brit. a person who does odd jobs. **odd man out** a person or thing differing from all the others in a group in some respect. □ **oddish** adj. **oddly** adv. **oddness** n. [ME f. ON odda- in odda-mathr third man, odd man, f. oddi angle]

oddball /ˈɒdbɔːl/ n. colloq. **1** an odd or eccentric person. **2** (attrib.) strange, bizarre.

oddity /ˈɒdɪtɪ/ n. (pl. **-ies**) **1** a strange person, thing, or occurrence. **2** a peculiar trait. **3** the state of being odd.

oddment /ˈɒdmənt/ n. **1** an odd article; something left over. **2** (in pl.) miscellaneous articles.

odds n.pl. **1** the ratio between the amounts staked by the parties to a bet, based on the expected probability either way. **2** the chances or balance of probability in favour of or against some result (the odds are against it; the odds are that it will rain). **3** the balance of advantage (the odds are in your favour; won against all the odds). **4** a difference giving an advantage (it makes no odds). □ **at odds** (often foll. by with) in conflict or at variance. **lay** (or **give**) **odds** offer a bet with odds favourable to the other better. **odds and ends** miscellaneous articles or remnants. **odds-on** a state when success is more likely than failure, esp. as indicated by the betting odds. **over the odds** above a generally agreed price etc. **take odds** offer a bet with odds unfavourable to the other better. **what's the odds?** colloq. what does it matter? [app. pl. of odd n. (a handicap of one): cf. NEWS]

ode n. a lyric poem, usu. rhymed and in the form of an address, in varied or irregular metre. [F f. LL oda f. Gk ōidē Attic form of aoidē song f. aeidō sing]

-ode[1] /əʊd/ suffix forming nouns meaning 'thing of the nature of' (geode). [Gk -ōdēs adj. ending]

-ode[2] /əʊd/ comb. form Electr. forming names of electrodes, or devices having them (cathode; diode). [Gk hodos way]

odious /ˈəʊdɪəs/ adj. hateful, repulsive. □ **odiously** adv. **odiousness** n. [ME f. OF odieus f. L odiosus (as ODIUM)]

odium /ˈəʊdɪəm/ n. a general or widespread dislike or reprobation incurred by a person or associated with an action. [L, = hatred f. odi to hate]

odometer /əʊˈdɒmɪtə(r)/ n. (also **hodometer** /hɒ-/) an instrument for measuring the distance travelled by a wheeled vehicle. □ **odometry** n. [F odomètre f. Gk hodos way: see -METER]

odonto- /əʊˈdɒntəʊ/ comb. form tooth. [Gk odous odont- tooth]

odoriferous /ˌəʊdəˈrɪfərəs/ adj. diffusing a scent, esp. an agreeable one; fragrant. □ **odoriferously** adv. [ME f. L odorifer (as ODOUR)]

odorous /ˈəʊdərəs/ adj. **1** having a scent. **2** = ODORIFEROUS. □ **odorously** adv. [L odorus fragrant (as ODOUR)]

odour /ˈəʊdə(r)/ n. (US **odor**) **1** the property of a substance that has an effect on the nasal sense of smell. **2** a lasting quality or trace attaching to something (an odour of intolerance). **3** regard, repute (in bad odour). □ **odourless** adj. (in sense 1). [ME f. AF odour, OF odor f. L odor -oris smell, scent]

odyssey /ˈɒdɪsɪ/ n. (pl. **-eys**) a series of wanderings; a long adventurous journey. □ **Odyssean** adj. [L Odyssea f. Gk Odusseia, title of an epic poem attributed to Homer describing the adventures of Odysseus (Ulysses) on his journey home from Troy]

OECD abbr. Organization for Economic Cooperation and Development.

OED abbr. Oxford English Dictionary.

oedema /ɪˈdiːmə/ n. (US **edema**) a condition characterized by an excess of watery fluid collecting in the cavities or tissues of the body. □ **oedematose** adj. **oedematous** adj. [LL f. Gk oidēma -atos f. oideō swell]

Oedipus complex /ˈiːdɪpəs/ n. Psychol. (according to Freud etc.) the complex of emotions aroused in a young (esp. male) child by a subconscious sexual desire for the parent of the opposite sex and wish to exclude the parent of the same sex. □ **Oedipal** adj. [Gk Oidipous, legendary king of Thebes who unknowingly killed his father and married his mother]

oenology /iːˈnɒlədʒɪ/ n. (US **enology**) the study of wines. □ **oenological** /ˌiːnəˈlɒdʒɪk(ə)l/ adj. **oenologist** n. [Gk oinos wine]

oenophile /ˈiːnəfaɪl/ n. a connoisseur of wines. □ **oenophilist** /iːˈnɒfɪlɪst/ n. [as OENOLOGY]

o'er /ˈəʊə(r)/ adv. & prep. poet. = OVER. [contr.]

oesophagus /iːˈsɒfəgəs/ n. (US **esophagus**) (pl. **oesophagi** /-ˌdʒaɪ/ or **-guses**) the part of the alimentary canal from the mouth to the stomach; the gullet. □ **oesophageal** /iːˌsɒfəˈdʒiːəl, ˌiːsəˈfædʒɪəl/ adj. [ME f. Gk oisophagos]

oestrogen /ˈiːstrədʒ(ə)n/ n. (US **estrogen**) **1** any of various steroid hormones developing and maintaining female characteristics of the body. **2** this hormone produced artificially for use in oral contraceptives etc. □ **oestrogenic** /-ˈdʒenɪk/ adj. **oestrogenically** /-ˈdʒenɪkəlɪ/ adv. [OESTRUS + -GEN]

oestrus /ˈiːstrəs/ n. (also **oestrum**, US **estrus**, **estrum**) a recurring period of sexual receptivity in many female mammals; heat. □ **oestrous** *adj*. [Gk *oistros* gadfly, frenzy]

of /ɒv, əv/ *prep.* connecting a noun (often a verbal noun) or pronoun with a preceding noun, adjective, adverb, or verb, expressing a wide range of relations broadly describable as follows: **1** origin, cause, or authorship (*paintings of Turner; people of Rome; died of malnutrition*). **2** the material or substance constituting or identifying a thing (*a house of cards; was built of bricks*). **3** belonging, connection, or possession (*a thing of the past; articles of clothing; the tip of the iceberg*). **4** identity or close relation (*the city of Rome; a pound of apples; a fool of a man*). **5** removal, separation, or privation (*north of the city; got rid of them; robbed us of £1000*). **6** reference, direction, or respect (*beware of the dog; suspected of lying; very good of you; short of money; the selling of goods*). **7** objective relation (*love of music; in search of peace*). **8** partition, classification, or inclusion (*no more of that; part of the story; a friend of mine; this sort of book; some of us will stay*). **9** description, quality, or condition (*the hour of prayer; a girl of ten; on the point of leaving*). **10** *US* time in relation to the following hour (*a quarter of three*). □ **be of** possess intrinsically; give rise to (*is of great interest*). **of all** designating the (nominally) least likely or expected example (*you of all people!*). **of all the nerve** (or **cheek** etc.) an exclamation of indignation at a person's impudence etc. **of an evening** (or **morning** etc.) *colloq.* **1** on most evenings (or mornings etc.). **2** at some time in the evenings (or mornings etc.). **of late** recently. **of old** formerly; long ago. [OE, unaccented form of *æf*, f. Gmc]

Off. *abbr.* **1** Office. **2** Officer.

off *adv., prep., adj., & n.* —*adv.* **1** away; at or to a distance (*drove off; is three miles off*). **2** out of position; not on or touching or attached; loose, separate, gone (*has come off; take your coat off*). **3** so as to be rid of (*sleep it off*). **4** so as to break continuity or continuance; discontinued, stopped (*turn off the radio; take a day off; the game is off*). **5** not available as a choice, e.g. on a menu (*chips are off*). **6** to the end; entirely; so as to be clear (*clear off; finish off; pay off*). **7** situated as regards money, supplies, etc. (*is badly off; is not very well off*). **8** off-stage (*noises off*). **9** (of food etc.) beginning to decay. **10** (with preceding numeral) denoting a quantity produced or made at one time (esp. *one-off*). —*prep.* **1 a** from; away or down from (*fell off the chair; took something off the price*). **b** not on (*was already off the pitch*). **2 a** (temporarily) relieved of or abstaining from (*off duty; am off my diet*). **b** not attracted by for the time being (*off their food; off smoking*). **c** not achieving or doing one's best in (*off form; off one's game*). **3** using as a source or means of support (*live off the land*). **4** leading from; not far from (*a street off the Strand*). **5** at a short distance to sea from (*sank off Cape Horn*). —*adj.* **1** far, further (*the off side of the wall*). **2** (of a part of a vehicle, animal, or road) right (*the off front wheel*). **3** *Cricket* designating the half of the field (as divided lengthways through the pitch) to which the striker's feet are pointed. —*n.* **1** *Cricket* the off side. **2** the start of a race. □ **a bit off** *Brit. colloq.* **1** rather annoying or unfair. **2** somewhat unwell (*am feeling a bit off*). **off and on** intermittently; now and then. **off-centre** not quite coinciding with a central position. **off colour 1**

not in good health. **2** *US* somewhat indecent. **off-day** a day when one is not at one's best. **off-drive** *Cricket* drive (the ball) to the off side. **off-key 1** out of tune. **2** not quite suitable or fitting. **off-licence** *Brit.* **1** a shop selling alcoholic drink for consumption elsewhere. **2** a licence for this. **off-line** *Computing* (of a computer terminal or process) not directly controlled by or connected to a central processor. **off-peak** used or for use at times other than those of greatest demand. **off the point** *adj.* irrelevant. —*adv.* irrelevantly. **off-putting** *Brit.* disconcerting; repellent. **off-roading** driving on dirt tracks and other unmetalled surfaces as a sport or leisure activity. **off-season** a time when business etc. is slack. **off-stage** *adj. & adv.* not on the stage and so not visible or audible to the audience. **off-street** (esp. of parking vehicles) other than on a street. **off-time** a time when business etc. is slack. **off-the-wall** *sl.* crazy, absurd, outlandish. **off-white** white with a grey or yellowish tinge. [orig. var. of OF, to distinguish the sense]

■ **Usage** The use of *off of* for the preposition *off* (sense 1a), e.g. *picked it up off of the floor*, is non-standard and should be avoided.

offal /ˈɒf(ə)l/ *n.* **1** the less valuable edible parts of a carcass, esp. the entrails and internal organs. **2** refuse or waste stuff. [ME f. MDu. *afval* f. *af* OFF + *vallen* FALL]

offbeat *adj. & n.* —*adj.* /ˈɒfbiːt, ɒfˈbiːt/ **1** not coinciding with the beat. **2** eccentric, unconventional. —*n.* /ˈɒfbiːt/ any of the unaccented beats in a bar.

offcut /ˈɒfkʌt/ *n.* a remnant of timber, paper, etc., after cutting.

offence /əˈfens/ *n.* (*US* **offense**) **1** an illegal act; a transgression or misdemeanour. **2** a wounding of the feelings; resentment or umbrage (*no offence was meant*). **3** the act of attacking or taking the offensive; aggressive action. □ **give offence** cause hurt feelings. **take offence** suffer hurt feelings. □ **offenceless** *adj.* [orig. = stumbling, stumbling-block: ME & OF *offens* f. L *offensus* annoyance, and ME & F *offense* f. L *offensa* a striking against, hurt, displeasure, both f. *offendere* (as OB-, *fendere fens-* strike)]

offend /əˈfend/ *v.* **1** *tr.* cause offence to or resentment in; wound the feelings of. **2** *tr.* displease or anger. **3** *intr.* (often foll. by *against*) do wrong; transgress. □ **offendedly** *adv.* **offender** *n.* **offending** *adj.* [ME f. OF *offendre* f. L (as OFFENCE)]

offensive /əˈfensɪv/ *adj. & n.* —*adj.* **1** giving or meant or likely to give offence; insulting (*offensive language*). **2** disgusting, foul-smelling, nauseous, repulsive. **3 a** aggressive, attacking. **b** (of a weapon) meant for use in attack. —*n.* **1** an aggressive action or attitude (*take the offensive*). **2** an attack, an offensive campaign or stroke. **3** aggressive or forceful action in pursuit of a cause (*a peace offensive*). □ **offensively** *adv.* **offensiveness** *n.* [F *offensif -ive* or med.L *offensivus* (as OFFENCE)]

offer /ˈɒfə(r)/ *v. & n.* —*v.* **1** *tr.* present for acceptance or refusal or consideration (*offered me a drink; was offered a lift*). **2** *intr.* (foll. by *to* + infin.) express readiness or show intention (*offered to take the children*). **3** *tr.* provide; give an opportunity for. **4** *tr.* make available for sale. **5**

tr. (of a thing) present to one's attention or consideration (*each day offers new opportunities*). **6** *tr.* present (a sacrifice, prayer, etc.) to a deity. **7** *intr.* present itself; occur (*as opportunity offers*). **8** *tr.* give an opportunity for (battle) to an enemy. **9** *tr.* attempt, or try to show (violence, resistance, etc.). —*n.* **1** an expression of readiness to do or give if desired, or to buy or sell (for a certain amount). **2** an amount offered. **3** a proposal (esp. of marriage). **4** a bid. □ **on offer** for sale at a certain (esp. reduced) price. □ **offerer** *n.* **offeror** *n.* [OE *offrian* in religious sense, f. L *offerre* (as OB-, *ferre* bring)]

offering /ˈɒfərɪŋ/ *n.* **1** a contribution, esp. of money, to a Church. **2** a thing offered as a religious sacrifice or token of devotion. **3** anything, esp. money, contributed or offered.

offertory /ˈɒfətərɪ/ *n.* (*pl.* **-ies**) **1** *Eccl.* **a** the offering of the bread and wine at the Eucharist. **b** an anthem accompanying this. **2 a** the collection of money at a religious service. **b** the money collected. [ME f. eccl.L *offertorium* offering f. LL *offert-* for L *oblat-* past part. stem of *offerre* OFFER]

offhand *adj.* & *adv.* —*adj.* /ɒfˈhænd, ˈɒfhænd/ curt or casual in manner. —*adv.* /ɒfˈhænd/ **1** in an offhand manner. **2** without preparation or premeditation. □ **offhanded** *adj.* **offhandedly** *adv.* **offhandedness** *n.*

office /ˈɒfɪs/ *n.* **1** a room or building used as a place of business, esp. for clerical or administrative work. **2** a room or department or building for a particular kind of business (*ticket office; post office*). **3** the local centre of a large business (*our London office*). **4** US the consulting-room of a professional person. **5** a position with duties attached to it; a place of authority or trust or service, esp. of a public nature. **6** tenure of an official position, esp. that of a minister of State or of the party forming the Government (*hold office; out of office*). **7** (**Office**) the quarters or staff or collective authority of a Government department etc. (*Foreign Office*). **8** a duty attaching to one's position; a task or function. **9** (usu. in *pl.*) a piece of kindness or attention; a service (esp. *through the good offices of*). **10** *Eccl.* **a** an authorized form of worship (*Office for the Dead*). **b** in full **divine office**) the daily service of the Roman Catholic breviary (*say the office*). □ **office block** a large building designed to contain business offices. **office boy** (or **girl**) a young man (or woman) employed to do minor jobs in a business office. **office hours** the hours during which business is normally conducted. **office-worker** an employee in a business office. [ME f. OF f. L *officium* performance of a task (in med.L also office, divine service), f. *opus* work + *facere fic-* do]

officer /ˈɒfɪsə(r)/ *n.* & *v.* —*n.* **1** a person holding a position of authority or trust, esp. one with a commission in the armed services, in the mercantile marine, or on a passenger ship. **2** a policeman or policewoman. **3** a holder of a post in a society (e.g. the president or secretary). **4** a holder of a public, civil, or ecclesiastical office. —*v.tr.* **1** provide with officers. **2** act as the commander of. [ME f. AF *officer*, OF *officier* f. med.L *officiarius* f. L *officium*: see OFFICE]

official /əˈfɪʃ(ə)l/ *adj.* & *n.* —*adj.* **1** of or relating to an office (see OFFICE *n.* 5, 6) or its tenure or

duties. **2** characteristic of officials and bureaucracy. **3** emanating from or attributable to a person in office; properly authorized. **4** holding office; employed in a public capacity. —*n.* a person holding office or engaged in official duties. □ **official birthday** *Brit.* a day in June chosen for the observance of the sovereign's birthday. **official secrets** confidential information involving national security. □ **officialdom** *n.* **officialism** *n.* **officially** *adv.* [ME (as noun) f. OF f. L *officialis* (as OFFICE)]

officialese /əˌfɪʃəˈliːz/ *n.* *derog.* the formal precise language characteristic of official documents.

officiate /əˈfɪʃɪeɪt/ *v.intr.* **1** act in an official capacity, esp. on a particular occasion. **2** perform a divine service or ceremony. □ **officiation** *n.* **officiator** *n.* [med.L *officiare* perform a divine service (*officium*): see OFFICE]

officinal /ˌɒfɪˈsiːn(ə)l, əˈfɪsɪn(ə)l/ *adj.* (of a herb or drug) used in medicine. □ **officinally** *adv.* [med.L *officinalis* f. L *officina* workshop]

officious /əˈfɪʃəs/ *adj.* **1** asserting one's authority aggressively; domineering. **2** intrusive or excessively enthusiastic in offering help etc.; meddlesome. □ **officiously** *adv.* **officiousness** *n.* [L *officiosus* obliging f. *officium*: see OFFICE]

offing /ˈɒfɪŋ/ *n.* the more distant part of the sea in view. □ **in the offing** not far away; likely to appear or happen soon. [perh. f. OFF + -ING[1]]

offish /ˈɒfɪʃ/ *adj.* *colloq.* inclined to be aloof. □ **offishly** *adv.* **offishness** *n.* [OFF: cf. *uppish*]

offload /ˈɒfləʊd, ɒfˈləʊd/ *v.tr.* get rid of (esp. something unpleasant) by giving it to someone else.

offprint /ˈɒfprɪnt/ *n.* a printed copy of an article etc. originally forming part of a larger publication.

offscreen /ˈɒfskriːn/ *adj.* & *adv.* —*adj.* not appearing on a cinema, television, or VDU screen. —*adv.* outside the view presented by a cinema-film scene.

offset *n.* & *v.* —*n.* /ˈɒfset/ **1** a side-shoot from a plant serving for propagation. **2** an offshoot or scion. **3** a compensation; a consideration or amount diminishing or neutralizing the effect of a contrary one. **4** *Archit.* a sloping ledge in a wall etc. **5** a bend in a pipe etc. to carry it past an obstacle. **6** (often *attrib.*) a method of printing in which ink is transferred from a plate or stone to a uniform rubber surface and from there to paper etc. (*offset litho*). —*v.tr.* /ˈɒfset, ɒfˈset/ (**-setting**; *past* and *past part.* **-set**) **1** counterbalance, compensate. **2** place out of line. **3** print by the offset process.

offshoot /ˈɒfʃuːt/ *n.* **1** a side-shoot or branch. **2** something derivative.

offshore /ˈɒfʃɔː(r)/ *adj.* **1** situated at sea some distance from the shore. **2** (of the wind) blowing seawards. **3** (of goods, funds, etc.) made or registered abroad.

offside *adj.* & *n.* —*adj.* /ɒfˈsaɪd/ *Sport* (of a player in a field game) in a position, usu. ahead of the ball, that is not allowed if it affects play. —*n.* /ˈɒfsaɪd/ (often *attrib.*) esp. *Brit.* the right side of a vehicle, animal, etc.

offspring /ˈɒfsprɪŋ/ *n.* (*pl.* same) **1** a person's child or children or descendant(s). **2** an animal's young or descendant(s). **3** a result. [OE *ofspring* f. OF from + *springan* SPRING *v.*]

oft /ɒft/ *adv.* *archaic* or *literary* often (usu. in *comb.*: *oft-recurring*). □ **oft-times** often. [OE]

often /ˈɒf(ə)n, ˈɒft(ə)n/ *adv.* (**oftener, oftenest**) **1 a** frequently; many times. **b** at short intervals. **2** in many instances. □ **as often as not** in roughly half the instances. [ME: extended f. OFT, prob. after *selden* = SELDOM]

ogee /ˈəʊdʒiː, -ˈdʒiː/ *adj.* & *n. Archit.* —*adj.* showing in section a double continuous S-shaped curve. —*n.* an S-shaped line or moulding. □ **ogee arch** an arch with two ogee curves meeting at the apex. □ **ogee'd** *adj.* [app. f. OGIVE, as being the usu. moulding in groin-ribs]

ogive /ˈəʊdʒaɪv, -ˈdʒaɪv/ *n.* **1** a pointed or Gothic arch. **2** one of the diagonal groins or ribs of a vault. □ **ogival** *adj.* [ME f. F, of unkn. orig.]

ogle /ˈəʊg(ə)l/ *v.* & *n.* —*v.* **1** *tr.* eye amorously or lecherously. **2** *intr.* look amorously. —*n.* an amorous or lecherous look. □ **ogler** *n.* [prob. LG or Du.: cf. LG *oegeln*, frequent. of *oegen* look at]

ogre /ˈəʊgə(r)/ *n.* (*fem.* **ogress** /-grɪs/) **1** a man-eating giant in folklore etc. **2** a terrifying person. □ **ogreish** *adj.* (also **ogrish**). [F, first used by Perrault in 1697, of unkn. orig.]

oh[1] /əʊ/ *int.* (also **O**) expressing surprise, pain, entreaty, etc. (*oh, what a mess; oh for a holiday*). □ **oh boy** expressing surprise, excitement, etc. **oh well** expressing resignation. [var. of O[3]]

oh[2] /əʊ/ *n.* = O[1] 2.

ohm /əʊm/ *n. Electr.* the SI unit of resistance. □ **ohmage** *n.* [G. S. *Ohm*, Ger. physicist d. 1854]

OHMS *abbr.* on Her (or His) Majesty's Service.

oho /əʊˈhəʊ/ *int.* expressing surprise or exultation. [ME f. O[3] + HO]

OHP *abbr.* overhead projector.

oi /ɔɪ/ *int.* calling attention or expressing alarm etc. [var. of HOY[1]]

-oid *suffix* forming adjectives and nouns, denoting form or resemblance (*asteroid; rhomboid; thyroid*). □ **-oidal** *suffix* forming adjectives. **-oidally** *suffix* forming adverbs. [mod.L *-oides* f. Gk *-oeidēs* f. *eidos* form]

oil *n.* & *v.* —*n.* **1** any of various thick, viscous, usu. inflammable liquids insoluble in water but soluble in organic solvents. **2** *US* petroleum. **3** (in *comb.*) using oil as fuel (*oil-heater*). **4 a** (usu. in *pl.*) = *oil-paint.* **b** *colloq.* a picture painted in oil-paints. —*v.* **1** *tr.* apply oil to; lubricate. **2** *tr.* impregnate or treat with oil (*oiled silk*). **3** *tr.* & *intr.* supply with or take on oil as fuel. □ **oil drum** a metal drum used for transporting oil. **oiled silk** silk made waterproof with oil. **oil-fired** using oil as fuel. **oil a person's hand** (or **palm**) bribe a person. **oil-lamp** a lamp using oil as fuel. **oil-paint** (or **-colour**) a mix of ground colour pigment and oil. **oil-painting 1** the art of painting in oil-paints. **2** a picture painted in oil-paints. **oil rig** a structure with equipment for drilling an oil well. **oil-sand** a stratum of porous rock yielding petroleum. **oil-seed** any of various seeds from cultivated crops yielding oil, e.g. rape, peanut, or cotton. **oil-shale** a fine-grained rock from which oil can be extracted. **oil-slick** a smooth patch of oil, esp. one on the sea. **oil-tanker** a ship designed to carry oil in bulk. **oil well** a well from which mineral oil is drawn. **oil the wheels** help make things go smoothly. **well oiled** *colloq.* very drunk. □ **oilless** *adj.* [ME *oli, oile* f. AF, ONF *olie* = OF *oile* etc. f. L *oleum* (olive) oil f. *olea* olive]

oilcake /ˈɔɪlkeɪk/ *n.* a mass of compressed linseed etc. left after oil has been extracted, used as fodder or manure.

oilcan /ˈɔɪlkæn/ *n.* a can containing oil, esp. one with a long nozzle for oiling machinery.

oilcloth /ˈɔɪlklɒθ/ *n.* **1** a fabric waterproofed with oil. **2** an oilskin. **3** a canvas coated with linseed or other oil and used to cover a table or floor.

oiler /ˈɔɪlə(r)/ *n.* **1** an oilcan for oiling machinery. **2** an oil-tanker. **3** *US* **a** an oil well. **b** (in *pl.*) oilskin.

oilfield /ˈɔɪlfiːld/ *n.* an area yielding mineral oil.

oilman /ˈɔɪlmən/ *n.* (*pl.* **-men**) a person who deals in oil.

oilskin /ˈɔɪlskɪn/ *n.* **1** cloth waterproofed with oil. **2 a** a garment made of this. **b** (in *pl.*) a suit made of this.

oilstone /ˈɔɪlstəʊn/ *n.* a fine-grained flat stone used with oil for sharpening flat tools, e.g. chisels, planes, etc. (cf. WHETSTONE).

oily /ˈɔɪlɪ/ *adj.* (**oilier, oiliest**) **1** of, like, or containing much oil. **2** covered or soaked with oil. **3** (of a manner etc.) fawning, insinuating, unctuous. □ **oilily** *adv.* **oiliness** *n.*

oink /ɔɪŋk/ *v.intr.* (of a pig) make its characteristic grunt. [imit.]

ointment /ˈɔɪntmənt/ *n.* a smooth greasy healing or cosmetic preparation for the skin. [ME *oignement, ointment,* f. OF *oignement* ult. f. L (as UNGUENT): *oint-* after obs. *oint* anoint f. OF, past part. of *oindre* ANOINT]

OK /əʊˈkeɪ/ *adj., adv., n.,* & *v.* (also **okay**) *colloq.* —*adj.* (often as *int.* expressing agreement or acquiescence) all right; satisfactory. —*adv.* well, satisfactorily (*that worked out OK*). —*n.* (*pl.* **OKs**) approval, sanction. —*v.tr.* (**OK's, OK'd, OK'ing**) give an OK to; approve, sanction. [orig. US: prob. abbr. of *orl* (or *oll*) *korrect,* joc. form of 'all correct']

okey-dokey /ˌəʊkɪˈdəʊkɪ/ *adj.* & *adv.* (also **okey-doke** /-ˈdəʊk/) *sl.* = OK. [redupl.]

okra /ˈəʊkrə, ˈɒkrə/ *n.* **1** an African plant, *Abelmoschus esculentus,* yielding long ridged seed-pods. **2** the seed-pods eaten as a vegetable and used to thicken soups and stews. [W.Afr. native name]

-ol[1] /ɒl/ *suffix Chem.* the termination of *alcohol,* used in names of alcohols or analogous compounds (*methanol; phenol*).

-ol[2] /ɒl/ *comb. form* = -OLE. [L *oleum* oil]

old /əʊld/ *adj.* (**older, oldest**) (cf. ELDER, ELDEST). **1 a** advanced in age; far on in the natural period of existence. **b** not young or near its beginning. **2** made long ago. **3** long in use. **4** worn or dilapidated or shabby from the passage of time. **5** having the characteristics (experience, feebleness, etc.) of age (*the child has an old face*). **6** practised, inveterate (*an old offender; old in crime*). **7** belonging only or chiefly to the past; lingering on; former (*old times; haunted by old memories*). **8** dating from far back; long established or known; ancient, primeval (*old as the hills; old friends; an old family*). **9** (appended to a period of time) of age (*is four years old; a four-year-old boy; a four-year-old*). **10** (of language) used in former or earliest times. **11** *colloq.* as a term of affection or casual reference (*good old Charlie; old shipmate*). **12** the former or first of two or more similar things (*our old house; wants his old job back*). □ **old age** the later part of normal life. **old-age**

pension = *retirement pension*. **old-age pensioner** a person receiving this. **Old Bailey** the Central Criminal Court in London. **Old Bill** *Brit. sl.* the police. **old boy 1** a former male pupil of a school. **2** *colloq.* **a** an elderly man. **b** an affectionate form of address to a boy or man. **old boy network** *Brit. colloq.* preferment in employment of those from a similar social background, esp. fellow ex-pupils of public schools. **the old country** the native country of colonists etc. **Old English** the English language up to *c.*1150. **old-fashioned** in or according to a fashion or tastes no longer current; antiquated. **old girl 1** a former female pupil of a school. **2** *colloq.* **a** an elderly woman. **b** an affectionate term of address to a girl or woman. **Old Glory** *US* the US national flag. **old gold** a dull brownish-gold colour. **old guard** the original or past or conservative members of a group. **old hand** a person with much experience. **old hat** *colloq.* something tediously familiar or out of date. **old maid 1** *derog.* an elderly unmarried woman. **2** a prim and fussy person. **old-maidish** like an old maid. **old man** *colloq.* **1** one's husband or father. **2** one's employer or other person in authority over one. **3** an affectionate form of address to a boy or man. **old man's beard** a wild clematis, *Clematis vitalba*, with grey fluffy hairs round the seeds. **old master 1** a great artist of former times, esp. of the 13th–17th c. in Europe. **2** a painting by such a painter. **old moon** the moon in its last quarter, before the new moon. **Old Nick** *colloq.* the Devil. **old school 1** traditional attitudes. **2** people having such attitudes. **old school tie** *Brit.* **1** a necktie with a characteristic pattern worn by the pupils of a particular (usu. public) school. **2** the principle of excessive loyalty to traditional values. **old soldier** an experienced person, esp. in an arduous activity. **old stager** an experienced person, an old hand. **Old Testament** the part of the Christian Bible containing the scriptures of the Hebrews. **old-time** belonging to former times. **old-timer** *US* a person with long experience or standing. **old wives' tale** a foolish or unscientific tradition or belief. **old woman** *colloq.* **1** one's wife or mother. **2** a fussy or timid man. **old-womanish** fussy and timid. **Old World** Europe, Asia, and Africa. **old-world** belonging to or associated with old times. **old year** the year just ended or about to end. □ **oldish** *adj.* **oldness** *n.* [OE *ald* f. WG]

olden /ˈəʊld(ə)n/ *adj. archaic* of old; of a former age (esp. *in olden times*).

oldie /ˈəʊldɪ/ *n. colloq.* an old person or thing.

oldster /ˈəʊldstə(r)/ *n.* an old person. [OLD + -STER, after *youngster*]

-ole /əʊl/ *comb. form* forming names of esp. heterocyclic compounds (*indole*). [L *oleum* oil]

oleaginous /ˌəʊlɪˈædʒɪnəs/ *adj.* **1** having the properties of or producing oil. **2** oily, greasy. **3** obsequious. [F *oléagineux* f. L *oleaginus* f. *oleum* oil]

oleander /ˌəʊlɪˈændə(r)/ *n.* an evergreen poisonous shrub, *Nerium oleander*, native to the Mediterranean and bearing clusters of white, pink, or red flowers. [med.L]

olefin /ˈəʊlɪfɪn/ *n.* (also **olefine**) *Chem.* = ALKENE. [F *oléfiant* oil-forming (with ref. to oily ethylene dichloride)]

oleo- /ˈəʊlɪəʊ/ *comb. form* oil. [L *oleum* oil]

oleograph /ˈəʊlɪəˌɡrɑːf/ *n.* a print made to resemble an oil-painting.

O level /əʊ/ *n. Brit. hist.* = *ordinary level.* [abbr.]

olfaction /ɒlˈfækʃ(ə)n/ *n.* the act or capacity of smelling; the sense of smell. □ **olfactive** *adj.* [L *olfactus* a smell f. *olēre* to smell + *facere* fact-make]

olfactory /ɒlˈfæktərɪ/ *adj.* of or relating to the sense of smell (*olfactory nerves*). [L *olfactare* frequent. of *olfacere* (as OLFACTION)]

oligarch /ˈɒlɪˌɡɑːk/ *n.* a member of an oligarchy. [Gk *oligarkhēs* f. *oligoi* few + *arkhō* to rule]

oligarchy /ˈɒlɪˌɡɑːkɪ/ *n.* (pl. **-ies**) **1** government by a small group of people. **2** a State governed in this way. **3** the members of such a government. □ **oligarchic** /-ˈɡɑːkɪk/ *adj.* **oligarchical** /-ˈɡɑːkɪk(ə)l/ *adj.* **oligarchically** /-ˈɡɑːkɪkəlɪ/ *adv.* [F *oligarchie* or med.L *oligarchia* f. Gk *oligarkhia* (as OLIGARCH)]

oligo- /ˈɒlɪɡəʊ/ *comb. form* few, slight. [Gk *oligos* small, *oligoi* few]

Oligocene /ˈɒlɪɡəˌsiːn/ *adj. & n. Geol.* —*adj.* of or relating to the third epoch of the Tertiary period. —*n.* this epoch or system. [as OLIGO- + Gk *kainos* new]

olio /ˈəʊlɪəʊ/ *n.* (pl. **-os**) **1** a mixed dish; a stew of various meats and vegetables. **2** a hotchpotch or miscellany. [Sp. *olla* stew f. L *olla* cooking-pot]

olivaceous /ˌɒlɪˈveɪʃəs/ *adj.* olive-green; of a dusky yellowish green.

olive /ˈɒlɪv/ *n. & adj.* —*n.* **1** (in full **olive tree**) any evergreen tree of the genus *Olea*, having dark-green lance-shaped leathery leaves with silvery undersides, esp. *O. europaea* of the Mediterranean, and *O. africana* native to S. Africa. **2** the small oval fruit of this, having a hard stone and bitter flesh, green when unripe and bluish-black when ripe. **3** (in full **olive-green**) the greyish-green colour of an unripe olive. **4** the wood of the olive tree. **5** a slice of beef or veal made into a roll with stuffing inside and stewed. —*adj.* **1** coloured like an unripe olive. **2** (of the complexion) yellowish-brown, sallow. □ **olive branch 1** the branch of an olive tree as a symbol of peace. **2** a gesture of reconciliation or friendship. **olive drab** the dull olive colour of US army uniforms. **olive oil** an oil extracted from olives used esp. in cookery. [ME f. OF f. L *oliva* f. Gk *elaia* f. *elaion* oil]

olivine /ˈɒlɪˌviːn/ *n. Mineral.* a naturally occurring form of magnesium-iron silicate, usu. olive-green and found in igneous rocks.

-ology /ˈɒlədʒɪ/ *comb. form* see -LOGY.

Olympiad /əˈlɪmpɪˌæd/ *n.* **1 a** a period of four years between Olympic games, used by the ancient Greeks in dating events. **b** a four-yearly celebration of the ancient Olympic Games. **2** a celebration of the modern Olympic Games. **3** a regular international contest in chess etc. [ME f. F *Olympiade* f. L *Olympias Olympiad-* f. Gk *Olumpias Olumpiad-* f. *Olumpios*: see OLYMPIAN, OLYMPIC]

Olympian /əˈlɪmpɪən/ *adj. & n.* —*adj.* **1 a** of or associated with Mount Olympus in NE Greece, traditionally the home of the Greek gods. **b** celestial, godlike. **2** (of manners etc.) magnificent, condescending, superior. **3 a** of or relating to ancient Olympia in S. Greece. **b** = OLYMPIC. —*n.* **1** any of the pantheon of twelve gods regarded as living on Olympus. **2** a person of great attainments or of superhuman calm and detachment. [L *Olympus* or *Olympia*: see OLYMPIC]

Olympic /ə'lɪmpɪk/ *adj.* & *n.* —*adj.* of ancient Olympia or the Olympic games. —*n.* (**the Olympics**) the Olympic games. □ **Olympic games 1** an ancient Greek festival held at Olympia every four years, with athletic, literary, and musical competitions. **2** a modern international revival of this as a sports festival held every four years since 1896 in different venues. [L *Olympicus* f. Gk *Olumpikos* of Olympus or Olympia (the latter being named from the games in honour of Zeus of *Olympus*)]

OM *abbr.* (in the UK) Order of Merit.

-oma /'əʊmə/ *n.* forming nouns denoting tumours and other abnormal growths (*carcinoma*). [mod.L f. Gk -*ōma* suffix denoting the result of verbal action]

ombudsman /'ɒmbʊdzmən/ *n.* (*pl.* **-men**) an official appointed by a government to investigate individuals' complaints against public authorities etc. [Sw., = legal representative]

-ome /əʊm/ *suffix* forming nouns denoting objects or parts of a specified nature (*rhizome*). [var. of -OMA]

omega /'əʊmɪgə/ *n.* **1** the last (24th) letter of the Greek alphabet (Ω, ω). **2** the last of a series; the final development. [Gk, ō *mega* = great O]

omelette /'ɒmlɪt/ *n.* (also **omelet**) a dish of beaten eggs cooked in a frying-pan and served plain or with a savoury or sweet filling. [F *omelette*, obs. *amelette* by metathesis f. *alumette* var. of *alumelle* f. *lemele* knife-blade f. L *lamella* dimin. of *lamina*: see LAMINA]

omen /'əʊmən, -men/ *n.* **1** an occurrence or object regarded as portending good or evil. **2** prophetic significance (*of good omen*). □ **omened** *adj.* (also in *comb.*). [L *omen ominis*]

omicron /ə'maɪkrən/ *n.* the fifteenth letter of the Greek alphabet (O, o). [Gk, o *mikron* = small o]

ominous /'ɒmɪnəs/ *adj.* **1** threatening; indicating disaster or difficulty. **2** of evil omen; inauspicious. **3** giving or being an omen. □ **ominously** *adv.* **ominousness** *n.* [L *ominosus* (as OMEN)]

omission /ə'mɪʃ(ə)n/ *n.* **1** the act or an instance of omitting or being omitted. **2** something that has been omitted or overlooked. □ **omissive** *adj.* [ME f. OF *omission* or LL *omissio* (as OMIT)]

omit /ə'mɪt/ *v.tr.* (**omitted**, **omitting**) **1** leave out; not insert or include. **2** leave undone. **3** (foll. by verbal noun or *to* + infin.) fail or neglect (*omitted saying anything*; *omitted to say*). □ **omissible** *adj.* [ME f. L *omittere omiss-* (as OB-, *mittere* send)]

omni- /'ɒmnɪ/ *comb. form* **1** all; of all things. **2** in all ways or places. [L f. *omnis* all]

omnibus /'ɒmnɪbəs/ *n.* & *adj.* —*n.* **1** *formal* = BUS. **2** a volume containing several novels etc. previously published separately. —*adj.* **1** serving several purposes at once. **2** comprising several items. [F f. L (dative pl. of *omnis*), = for all]

omnicompetent /ˌɒmnɪ'kɒmpɪt(ə)nt/ *adj.* **1** able to deal with all matters. **2** having jurisdiction in all cases. □ **omnicompetence** *n.*

omnidirectional /ˌɒmnɪdɪ'rekʃ(ə)l/ *adj.* (of an aerial etc.) receiving or transmitting in all directions.

omnifarious /ˌɒmnɪ'feərɪəs/ *adj.* of all sorts or varieties. [LL *omnifarius* (as OMNI-): cf. MULTIFARIOUS]

omnipotent /ɒm'nɪpət(ə)nt/ *adj.* **1** having great or absolute power. **2** having great influence. □ **omnipotence** *n.* **omnipotently** *adv.* [ME f. OF f. L *omnipotens* (as OMNI-, POTENT)]

omnipresent /ˌɒmnɪ'prez(ə)nt/ *adj.* **1** present everywhere at the same time. **2** widely or constantly encountered. □ **omnipresence** *n.* [med.L *omnipraesens* (as OMNI-, PRESENT¹)]

omniscient /ɒm'nɪsɪənt, -ʃɪənt/ *adj.* knowing everything or much. □ **omniscience** *n.* **omnisciently** *adv.* [med.L *omnisciens -entis* (as OMNI-, *scire* know)]

omnivorous /ɒm'nɪvərəs/ *adj.* **1** feeding on many kinds of food, esp. on both plants and flesh. **2** making use of everything available. □ **omnivore** /'ɒmnɪˌvɔː(r)/ *n.* **omnivorously** *adv.* **omnivorousness** *n.* [L *omnivorus* (as OMNI-, -VOROUS)]

omphalos /'ɒmfəˌlɒs/ *n. Gk Antiq.* **1** a conical stone (esp. that at Delphi) representing the navel of the earth. **2** a boss on a shield. **3** a centre or hub. [Gk, = navel, boss, hub]

on *prep., adv., adj.,* & *n.* —*prep.* **1** (so as to be) supported by or attached to or covering or enclosing (*sat on a chair*; *stuck on the wall*; *rings on her fingers*; *leaned on his elbow*). **2** carried with; about the person of (*have you a pen on you?*). **3** (of time) exactly at; during; contemporaneously with (*on 29 May*; *on the hour*; *on schedule*; *working on Tuesday*). **4** immediately after or before (*I saw them on my return*). **5** as a result of (*on further examination I found this*). **6** (so as to be) having membership etc. of or residence at or in (*she is on the board of directors*; *lives on the continent*). **7** supported financially by (*lives on £50 a week*; *lives on his wits*). **8** close to; just by (*a house on the sea*; *lives on the main road*). **9** in the direction of; against. **10** so as to threaten; touching or striking (*advanced on him*; *pulled a knife on me*; *a punch on the nose*). **11** having as an axis or pivot (*turned on his heels*). **12** having as a basis or motive (*works on a ratchet*; *arrested on suspicion*). **13** having as a standard, confirmation, or guarantee (*had it on good authority*; *did it on purpose*; *I promise on my word*). **14** concerning or about (*writes on frogs*). **15** using or engaged with (*is on the pill*; *here on business*). **16** so as to affect (*walked out on her*). **17** at the expense of (*the drinks are on me*; *the joke is on him*). **18** added to (*disaster on disaster*; *ten pence on a pint of beer*). **19** in a specified manner or style (often foll. by *the* + adj. or noun: *on the cheap*; *on the run*). —*adv.* **1** (so as to be) covering or in contact with something, esp. of clothes (*put your boots on*). **2** in the appropriate direction; towards something (*look on*). **3** further forward; in an advanced position or state (*time is getting on*; *it happened later on*). **4** with continued movement or action (*went plodding on*; *keeps on complaining*). **5** in operation or activity (*the light is on*; *the chase was on*). **6** due to take place as planned (*is the party still on?*). **7** *colloq.* **a** (of a person) willing to participate or approve, or make a bet. **b** (of an idea, proposal, etc.) practicable or acceptable (*that's just not on*). **8** being shown or performed (*a good film on tonight*). **9** (of an actor) on stage. **10** (of an employee) on duty. **11** forward (*head on*). —*adj. Cricket* designating the part of the field on the striker's side and in front of the wicket. —n. Cricket the on side. □ **be on about** refer to or discuss esp. tediously or persistently (*what are they on about?*). **be on at** *colloq.* nag or grumble at. **be on to 1** realize the significance or intentions of. **2** get in touch with (esp. by telephone). **on and off** intermittently; now and then. **on and on** continually; at tedious length. **on-line** *Computing* (of equipment or a process) directly controlled by or connected to a central processor. **on-off 1** (of a switch) having two positions, 'on' and 'off'. **2** = *on and off*. **on-stage** *adj.* & *adv.* on the stage; visible to the audience. **on-street** (with ref. to parking vehicles) at the side of a street. **on time** punctual, punctually. **on to** to a position or state on or in contact with (cf. ONTO). [OE *on, an* f. Gmc]

-on /ɒn/ *suffix Physics, Biochem.,* & *Chem.* forming nouns denoting: **1** elementary particles (*meson; neutron*). **2** quanta (*photon*). **3** molecular units. **4** substances (*interferon*). [ION, orig. in *electron*]

onager /ˈɒnəgə(r)/ *n.* a wild ass, esp. *Equus hemionus* of Central Asia. [ME f. L f. Gk *onagros* f. *onos* ass + *agrios* wild] ↖

onanism /ˈɔʊnəˌnɪz(ə)m/ *n.* **1** masturbation. **2** coitus interruptus. □ **onanist** *n.* **onanistic** /-ˈnɪstɪk/ *adj.* [F *onanisme* or mod.L *onanismus* f. *Onan* (Gen. 38:9)]

ONC *abbr.* (in the UK) Ordinary National Certificate.

once /wʌns/ *adv., conj.,* & *n.* —*adv.* **1** on one occasion or for one time only (*did not once say please; have read it once*). **2** at some point or period in the past (*could once play chess*). **3** ever or at all (*if you once forget it*). **4** multiplied by one; by one degree. —*conj.* as soon as (*once they have gone we can relax*). —*n.* one time or occasion (*just the once*). □ **all at once 1** without warning; suddenly. **2** all together. **at once 1** immediately. **2** simultaneously. **for once** on this (or that) occasion, even if at no other. **once again** (or **more**) another time. **once and for all** (or **once for all**) (done) in a final or conclusive manner, esp. so as to end hesitation or uncertainty. **once** (or **every once**) **in a while** from time to time; occasionally. **once or twice** a few times. **once-over** *colloq.* a rapid preliminary inspection or piece of work. **once upon a time** at some vague time in the past. [ME *ānes, ōnes,* genit. of ONE]

oncer /ˈwʌnsə(r)/ *n.* **1** *Brit. hist. sl.* a one-pound note. **2** *colloq.* a thing that occurs only once.

oncoming /ˈɒnˌkʌmɪŋ/ *adj.* & *n.* —*adj.* approaching from the front. —*n.* an approach or onset.

oncost /ˈɒnkɒst/ *n. Brit.* an overhead expense.

OND *abbr.* (in the UK) Ordinary National Diploma.

one /wʌn/ *adj., n.,* & *pron.* —*adj.* **1** single and integral in number. **2** (with a noun implied) a single person or thing of the kind expressed or implied (*one of the best; a nasty one*). **3 a** particular but undefined, esp. as contrasted with another (*that is one view; one thing after another*). **b** *colloq.* (as an emphatic) a noteworthy example of (*that is one difficult question*). **4** only such (*the one man who can do it*). **5** forming a unity (*one and undivided*). **6** identical; the same (*of one opinion*). —*n.* **1 a** the lowest cardinal number. **b** a thing numbered with it. **2** unity; a unit (*one is half of two; came in ones and twos*). **3** a single thing or person or example (*often referring to a noun previously expressed or implied: the big dog and the small one*). **4** *colloq.* an alcoholic drink (*have a quick one; have one on me*). **5** a story or joke (*the one about the frog*). —*pron.* **1** a person of a specified kind (*loved ones; like one possessed*). **2** any person, as representing people in general (*one is bound to lose in the end*). **3** I, me (*one would like to help*). □ **all one** (often foll. by *to*) a matter of indifference. **at one** in agreement. **for one** being one, even if the only one (*I for one do not believe it*). **for one thing** as a single consideration, ignoring others. **one another** each the other or others (as a formula of reciprocity: *love one another*). **one-armed bandit** *colloq.* a fruit machine worked by a long handle at the side. **one by one** singly, successively. **one day 1** on an unspecified day. **2** at some unspecified future date. **one-horse 1** using a single horse. **2** *colloq.* small, poorly equipped. **one-liner** *colloq.* a single brief sentence, often witty or apposite. **one-man** involving, done, or operated by only one man. **one-night stand 1** a single performance of a play etc. in a place. **2** *colloq.* a sexual liaison lasting only one night. **one-off** *colloq.* made or done as the only one; not repeated. **one-piece** (of a bathing-suit etc.) made as a single garment. **one-sided 1** favouring one side in a dispute; unfair, partial. **2** having or occurring on one side only. **3** larger or more developed on one side. **one-time** former. **one-to-one** with one member of one group corresponding to one of another. **one-track mind** a mind preoccupied with one subject. **one-two** *colloq.* **1** *Boxing* the delivery of two punches in quick succession. **2** *Football* etc. a series of reciprocal passes between two advancing players. **one-up** *colloq.* having a particular advantage. **one-upmanship** *colloq.* the art of maintaining a psychological advantage. **one-way** allowing movement or travel in one direction only. [OE *ān* f. Gmc]

■ **Usage** The use of the pronoun *one* to mean 'I' or 'me' (e.g. *one would like to help*) is often regarded as an affectation.

-one /ɔʊn/ *suffix Chem.* forming nouns denoting various compounds, esp. ketones (*acetone*). [Gk -ōnē fem. patronymic]

oneness /ˈwʌnnɪs/ *n.* **1** the fact or state of being one; singleness. **2** uniqueness. **3** agreement; unity of opinion. **4** identity, sameness.

onerous /ˈɒnərəs, ˈɔʊn-/ *adj.* burdensome; causing or requiring trouble. □ **onerously** *adv.* **onerousness** *n.* [ME f. OF *onereus* f. L *onerosus* f. *onus oneris* burden]

oneself /wʌnˈself/ *pron.* the reflexive and (in apposition) emphatic form of *one* (*kill oneself; one has to do it oneself*).

ongoing /ˈɒnˌgɔʊɪŋ/ *adj.* **1** continuing to exist or be operative etc. **2** that is or are in progress (*ongoing discussions*). □ **ongoingness** *n.*

onion /ˈʌnjən/ *n.* **1** a liliaceous plant, *Allium cepa*, having a short stem and bearing greenish-white flowers. **2** the swollen bulb of this with many concentric skins used in cooking, pickling, etc. □ **know one's onions** be fully knowledgeable or experienced. **onion dome** a bulbous dome on a church, palace, etc. **onion-skin 1** the brown outermost skin or any outer skin of an onion. **2** thin smooth translucent paper. □ **oniony** *adj.* [ME f. AF *union*, OF *oignon* ult. f. L *unio -onis*]

onlooker /ˈɒnˌlʊkə(r)/ n. a non-participating observer; a spectator. □ **onlooking** adj.

only /ˈəʊnlɪ/ adv., adj., & conj. **1** solely, merely, exclusively; and no one or nothing more besides (I only want to sit down; will only make matters worse; needed six only; is only a child). **2** no longer ago than (saw them only yesterday). **3** not until (arrives only on Tuesday). **4** with no better result than (hurried home only to find her gone). —attrib.adj. **1** existing alone of its or their kind (their only son). **2** best or alone worth knowing (the only place to eat). —conj. colloq. **1** except that; but for the fact that (I would go, only I feel ill). **2** but then (as an extra consideration) (he always makes promises, only he never keeps them). □ **only too** extremely (is only too willing). [OE ānlic, ǣnlic, ME onliche (as ONE, -LY²)]

■ **Usage** In informal English only is usually placed between the subject and verb regardless of what it refers to (e.g. I only want to talk to you); in more formal English it is often placed more exactly, esp. to avoid ambiguity (e.g. I want to talk only to you). In speech, intonation usually serves to clarify the sense.

o.n.o. abbr. Brit. or near offer.

onomatopoeia /ˌɒnəˌmætəˈpiːə/ n. **1** the formation of a word from a sound associated with what is named (e.g. cuckoo, sizzle). **2** the use of such words. □ **onomatopoeic** adj. **onomatopoeically** adv. [LL f. Gk onomatopoiia word-making f. onoma -matos name + poieō make]

onrush /ˈɒnrʌʃ/ n. an onward rush.

onscreen /ˈɒnskriːn/ adj. & adv. —adj. appearing on a cinema, television, or VDU screen. —adv. **1** on or by means of a screen. **2** within the view presented by a cinema-film scene.

onset /ˈɒnset/ n. **1** an attack. **2** a beginning, esp. an energetic or determined one.

onshore /ˈɒnʃɔː(r)/ adj. **1** on the shore. **2** (of the wind) blowing from the sea towards the land.

onside /ˈɒnsaɪd, ɒnˈsaɪd/ adj. (of a player in a field game) in a lawful position; not offside.

onslaught /ˈɒnslɔːt/ n. a fierce attack. [earlier anslaight f. MDu. aenslag f. aen on + slag blow, with assim. to obs. slaught slaughter]

onto /ˈɒntuː/ prep. disp. to a position or state on or in contact with (cf. on to).

■ **Usage** The form onto is still not fully accepted in the way that into is, although it is in wide use. It is however useful in distinguishing sense as between we drove on to the beach (i.e. in that direction) and we drove onto the beach (i.e. in contact with it).

ontology /ɒnˈtɒlədʒɪ/ n. the branch of metaphysics dealing with the nature of being. □ **ontological** /-təˈlɒdʒɪk(ə)l/ adj. **ontologically** /-təˈlɒdʒɪkəlɪ/ adv. **ontologist** n. [mod.L ontologia f. Gk ōn ont- being + -LOGY]

onus /ˈəʊnəs/ n. (pl. **onuses**) a burden, duty, or responsibility. [L]

onward /ˈɒnwəd/ adv. & adj. —adv. (also **onwards**) **1** further on. **2** towards the front. **3** with advancing motion. —adj. directed onwards.

onyx /ˈɒnɪks/ n. a semiprecious variety of agate with different colours in layers. [ME f. OF oniche, onix f. L f. Gk onux fingernail, onyx]

oodles /ˈuːd(ə)lz/ n.pl. colloq. a very great amount. [19th-c. US: orig. unkn.]

ooh /uː/ int. expressing surprise, delight, pain, etc. [natural exclam.]

oolite /ˈəʊəˌlaɪt/ n. a sedimentary rock, usu. limestone, consisting of rounded grains made up of concentric layers. □ **oolitic** /-ˈlɪtɪk/ adj. [F oölite f. Gk ōion egg + -LITE)]

oomph /ʊmf/ n. sl. **1** energy, enthusiasm. **2** attractiveness, esp. sexual appeal. [20th c.: orig. uncert.]

-oon /uːn/ suffix forming nouns, orig. from French words in stressed -on (balloon; buffoon). [L -o -onis, sometimes via It. -one]

oops /uːps, ʊps/ int. colloq. expressing surprise or apology, esp. on making an obvious mistake. [natural exclam.]

ooze¹ /uːz/ v. & n. —v. **1** intr. (of fluid) pass slowly through the pores of a body. **2** intr. trickle or leak slowly out. **3** intr. (of a substance) exude moisture. **4** tr. exude or exhibit (a feeling) liberally (oozed sympathy). —n. a sluggish flow or exudation. □ **oozily** adv. **oozily** adv. **ooziness** n. [orig. as n. in sense 'oak-sap', f. OE wōs juice, sap]

ooze² /uːz/ n. **1** a deposit of wet mud or slime, esp. at the bottom of a river, lake, or estuary. **2** a bog or marsh; soft muddy ground. □ **oozy** adj. [OE wāse]

op /ɒp/ n. colloq. operation (in surgical and military senses).

op. /ɒp/ abbr. **1** Mus. opus. **2** operator.

opacify /əʊˈpæsɪˌfaɪ/ v.tr. & intr. (**-ies**, **-ied**) make or become opaque. □ **opacifier** n.

opacity /əˈpæsɪtɪ/ n. **1** the state of being opaque. **2** obscurity of meaning. **3** obtuseness of understanding. [F opacité f. L opacitas -tatis (as OPAQUE)]

opal /ˈəʊp(ə)l/ n. a quartzlike form of hydrated silica, usu. white or colourless and sometimes showing changing colours, often used as a gemstone. [F opale or L opalus prob. ult. f. Skr. upalas precious stone]

opalescent /ˌəʊpəˈles(ə)nt/ adj. showing changing colours like an opal. □ **opalesce** v.intr. **opalescence** n.

opaline /ˈəʊpəˌlaɪn/ adj. opal-like, opalescent, iridescent.

opaque /əʊˈpeɪk/ adj. & n. —adj. (**opaquer**, **opaquest**) **1** not transmitting light. **2** impenetrable to sight. **3** obscure; not lucid. **4** obtuse, dull-witted. □ **opaquely** adv. **opaqueness** n. [ME opak f. L opacus: spelling now assim. to F]

op art /ɒp/ n. colloq. = optical art. [abbr.]

op. cit. abbr. in the work already quoted. [L opere citato]

OPEC /ˈəʊpek/ abbr. Organization of Petroleum Exporting Countries.

open /ˈəʊpən/ adj., v., & n. —adj. **1** not closed or locked or blocked up; allowing entrance or passage or access. **2 a** (of a room, field, or other area) having its door or gate in a position allowing access, or part of its confining boundary removed. **b** (of a container) not fastened or sealed; in a position or with the lid etc. in a position allowing access to the inside part. **3** unenclosed, unconfined, unobstructed (the open road; open views). **4 a** uncovered, bare, exposed (open drain; open wound). **b** Sport (of a goal mouth or other object of attack) unprotected, vulnerable. **5** undisguised, public, manifest; not exclusive or limited (*open scandal*; *open hostilities*). **6** expanded, unfolded, or spread out (*had the map open on the table*). **7** (of a fabric) not close; with gaps or intervals. **8 a** (of a person) frank and communicative. **b** (of the mind) accessible to new ideas; unprejudiced or undecided. **9 a** (of an exhibition, shop, etc.) accessible to visitors or customers; ready for business. **b** (of a meeting) admitting all, not restricted to members etc. **10 a** (of a race, competition, scholarship, etc.) unrestricted as to who may compete. **b** (of a champion, scholar, etc.) having won such a contest. **11** (of government) conducted in an informative manner receptive to enquiry, criticism, etc., from the public. **12** (foll. by *to*) **a** willing to receive (*is open to offers*). **b** (of a choice, offer, or opportunity) still available (*there are three courses open to us*). **c** likely to suffer from or be affected by (*open to abuse*). **13 a** (of the mouth) with lips apart, esp. in surprise or incomprehension. **b** (of the ears or eyes) eagerly attentive. **14** *Mus.* **a** (of a string) allowed to vibrate along its whole length. **b** (of a pipe) unstopped at each end. **c** (of a note) sounded from an open string or pipe. **15** (of the bowels) not constipated. **16** (of a return ticket) not restricted as to day of travel. **17** (of a cheque) not crossed. **18** (of a boat) without a deck. —*v.* **1** *tr.* & *intr.* make or become open or more open. **2 a** *tr.* change from a closed or fastened position so as to allow access (*opened the door; opened the box*). **b** *intr.* (of a door, lid, etc.) have its position changed to allow access (*the door opened slowly*). **3** *tr.* remove the sealing or fastening element of (a container) to get access to the contents (*opened the envelope*). **4** *intr.* (foll. by *into, on to,* etc.) (of a door, room, etc.) afford access as specified (*opened on to a large garden*). **5 a** *tr.* start or establish or set going (a business, activity, etc.). **b** *intr.* be initiated; make a start (*the session opens tomorrow; the story opens with a murder*). **c** *tr.* (of a counsel in a lawcourt) make a preliminary statement in (a case) before calling witnesses. **6** *tr.* **a** spread out or unfold (a map, newspaper, etc.). **b** (often *absol.*) refer to the contents of (a book). **7** *intr.* (often foll. by *with*) (of a person) begin speaking, writing, etc. (*he opened with a warning*). **8** *tr.* ceremonially declare (a building etc.) to be completed and in use. **9** *tr.* cause evacuation of (the bowels). —*n.* **1** (prec. by *the*) **a** open space or country or air. **b** public notice or view; general attention (esp. *into the open*). **2** an open championship, competition, or scholarship. □ **be open with** speak frankly to. **open air** (usu. prec. by *the*) a free or unenclosed space outdoors. **open-air** (*attrib.*) out of doors. **open-and-shut** (of an argument, case, etc.) straightforward and conclusive. **open-armed** cordial; warmly receptive. **open book** a person who is easily understood. **Open College** a college offering training and vocational courses mainly by correspondence. **open day** a day when the public may visit a place normally closed to them. **open door** free admission of foreign trade and immigrants. **open-ended** having no predetermined limit or boundary. **open-faced** having a frank or ingenuous expression. **open-handed** generous. **open-hearted** frank and kindly. **open-heart surgery** surgery with the heart exposed and the blood made to bypass it. **open house** welcome or hospitality for all visitors. **open letter** a

letter, esp. of protest, addressed to an individual and published in a newspaper or journal. **open market** an unrestricted market with free competition of buyers and sellers. **open-minded** accessible to new ideas; unprejudiced. **open-mouthed** with the mouth open, esp. in surprise. **open out 1** unfold; spread out. **2** develop, expand. **3** become communicative. **4** accelerate. **open-plan** (usu. *attrib.*) (of a house, office, etc.) having large undivided rooms. **open prison** a prison with the minimum of physical restraints on prisoners. **open question** a matter on which differences of opinion are legitimate. **open-reel** (of a tape recorder) having reels of tape requiring individual threading, as distinct from a cassette. **open sandwich** a sandwich without a top slice of bread. **open sea** an expanse of sea away from land. **open season** the season when restrictions on the killing of game etc. are lifted. **open secret** a supposed secret that is known to many people. **Open University** (in the UK) a university that teaches mainly by broadcasting and correspondence, and is open to those without formal academic qualifications. **open up 1** unlock (premises). **2** make accessible. **3** reveal; bring to notice. **4** accelerate esp. a motor vehicle. **5** begin shooting or sounding. **open verdict** a verdict affirming that a crime has been committed but not specifying the criminal or (in case of violent death) the cause. □ **openable** *adj.* **openness** *n.* [OE *open*]

opencast /ˈəʊpənˌkɑːst/ *adj. Brit.* (of a mine or mining) with removal of the surface layers and working from above, not from shafts.

opener /ˈəʊpənə(r), ˈəʊpnə(r)/ *n.* **1** a device for opening tins, bottles, etc. **2** *colloq.* the first item on a programme etc. **3** *Cricket* an opening batsman.

opening /ˈəʊpənɪŋ, ˈəʊpnɪŋ/ *n.* & *adj.* —*n.* **1** an aperture or gap, esp. allowing access. **2** a favourable situation or opportunity. **3** a beginning; an initial part. **4** *Chess* a recognized sequence of moves at the beginning of a game. —*adj.* initial, first. □ **opening-time** *Brit.* the time at which public houses may legally open for custom.

openly /ˈəʊpənlɪ/ *adv.* **1** frankly, honestly. **2** publicly; without concealment. [OE *openlíce* (as OPEN, -LY²)]

openwork /ˈəʊpənˌwɜːk/ *n.* a pattern with intervening spaces in metal, leather, lace, etc.

opera¹ /ˈɒpərə, ˈɒprə/ *n.* **1 a** a dramatic work in one or more acts, set to music for singers (usu. in costume) and instrumentalists. **b** this as a genre. **2** a building for the performance of opera. □ **opera-glasses** small binoculars for use at the opera or theatre. **opera-hat** a man's tall collapsible hat. **opera-house** a theatre for the performance of opera. [It. f. L, = labour, work]

opera² *pl.* of OPUS.

operable /ˈɒpərəb(ə)l/ *adj.* **1** that can be operated. **2** suitable for treatment by surgical operation. □ **operability** /-ˈbɪlɪtɪ/ *n.* [LL *operabilis* f. L (as OPERATE)]

operand /ˈɒpəˌrænd/ *n. Math.* the quantity etc. on which an operation is to be done. [L *operandum* neut. gerundive of *operari*: see OPERATE]

operate /ˈɒpəˌreɪt/ *v.* **1** *tr.* manage, work, control; put or keep in a functional state. **2** *intr.* be in action; function. **3** *intr.* produce an effect;

exercise influence (*the tax operates to our disadvantage*). **4** *intr.* (often foll. by *on*) **a** perform a surgical operation. **b** conduct a military or naval action. **c** be active in business etc., esp. dealing in stocks and shares. **5** *intr.* (foll. by *on*) influence or affect (feelings etc.). **6** *tr.* bring about; accomplish. □ **operating system** the basic software that enables the running of a computer program. **operating theatre** (or **room**) a room for surgical operations. [L *operari* to work f. *opus operis* work]

operatic /ˌɒpəˈrætɪk/ *adj.* **1** of or relating to opera. **2** resembling or characteristic of opera. □ **operatically** *adv.* [irreg. f. OPERA¹, after *dramatic*]

operatics /ˌɒpəˈrætɪks/ *n.pl.* the production and performance of operas.

operation /ˌɒpəˈreɪʃ(ə)n/ *n.* **1 a** the action or process or method of working or operating. **b** the state of being active or functioning (*not yet in operation*). **c** the scope or range of effectiveness of a thing's activity. **2** an active process; a discharge of a function (*the operation of breathing*). **3** a piece of work, esp. one in a series (often in *pl.*: *begin operations*). **4** an act of surgery performed on a patient. **5 a** a strategic movement of troops, ships, etc. for military action. **b** preceding a code-name (*Operation Overlord*). **6** a financial transaction. **7** *Math.* the subjection of a number or quantity or function to a process affecting its value or form, e.g. multiplication, differentiation. [ME f. OF f. L *operatio -onis* (as OPERATE)]

operational /ˌɒpəˈreɪʃən(ə)l/ *adj.* **1 a** of or used for operations. **b** engaged or involved in operations. **2** able or ready to function. □ **operationally** *adv.*

operative /ˈɒpərətɪv/ *adj.* & *n.* —*adj.* **1** in operation; having effect. **2** having the principal relevance ('*may*' *is the operative word*). **3** of or by surgery. —*n.* **1** a worker, esp. a skilled one. **2** *US* a private detective. □ **operatively** *adv.* **operativeness** *n.* [LL *operativus* f. L (as OPERATE)]

operator /ˈɒpəˌreɪtə(r)/ *n.* **1** a person operating a machine etc., esp. making connections of lines in a telephone exchange. **2** a person operating or engaging in business. **3** *colloq.* a person acting in a specified way (*a smooth operator*). **4** *Math.* a symbol or function denoting an operation (e.g. ×, +). [LL f. L *operari* (as OPERATE)]

operculum /ɒˈpɜːkjʊləm, əʊˈp-/ *n.* (*pl.* **opercula** /-lə/) **1** *Zool.* **a** a flaplike structure covering the gills in a fish. **b** a platelike structure closing the aperture of a gastropod mollusc's shell when the organism is retracted. **c** any of various other parts covering or closing an aperture. **2** *Bot.* a lidlike structure of the spore-containing capsule of mosses. □ **opercular** *adj.* **operculate** /-lət/ *adj.* **operculi-** *comb. form.* [L f. *operire* cover]

operetta /ˌɒpəˈretə/ *n.* **1** a one-act or short opera. **2** a light opera. [It., dimin. of *opera*: see OPERA¹]

ophidian /əʊˈfɪdɪən/ *n.* & *adj.* —*n.* any reptile of the suborder Serpentes (formerly Ophidia), including snakes. —*adj.* **1** of or relating to this group. **2** snakelike. [mod.L *Ophidia* f. Gk *ophis* snake]

ophthalmia /ɒfˈθælmɪə/ *n.* an inflammation of the eye, esp. conjunctivitis. [LL f. Gk f. *ophthalmos* eye]

ophthalmic /ɒfˈθælmɪk/ *adj.* of or relating to the eye and its diseases. □ **ophthalmic optician**

an optician qualified to prescribe as well as dispense spectacles and contact lenses. [L *ophthalmicus* f. Gk *ophthalmikos* (as OPHTHALMIA)]

ophthalmo- /ɒfˈθælməʊ/ *comb. form* Optics denoting the eye. [Gk *ophthalmos* eye]

ophthalmology /ˌɒfθælˈmɒlədʒɪ/ *n.* the scientific study of the eye. □ **ophthalmological** /-məˈlɒdʒɪk(ə)l/ *adj.* **ophthalmologist** *n.*

ophthalmoscope /ɒfˈθælməˌskəʊp/ *n.* an instrument for inspecting the retina and other parts of the eye. □ **ophthalmoscopic** /-ˈskɒpɪk/ *adj.*

opiate /ˈəʊpɪət/ *adj.* & *n.* —*adj.* **1** containing opium. **2** narcotic, soporific. —*n.* **1** a drug containing opium, usu. to ease pain or induce sleep. **2** a thing which soothes or stupefies. [med.L *opiatus, -um, opiare* f. L *opium*: see OPIUM]

opine /əʊˈpaɪn/ *v.tr.* (often foll. by *that* + clause) hold or express as an opinion. [L *opinari* think, believe]

opinion /əˈpɪnjən/ *n.* **1** a belief or assessment based on grounds short of proof. **2** a view held as probable. **3** (often foll. by *on*) what one thinks about a particular topic or question (*my opinion on capital punishment*). **4** a formal statement of professional advice (*will get a second opinion*). **5** an estimation (*had a low opinion of it*). □ **be of the opinion that** believe or maintain that. **in one's opinion** according to one's view or belief. **a matter of opinion** a disputable point. **opinion poll** = GALLUP POLL. **public opinion** views generally prevalent, esp. on moral questions. [ME f. OF f. L *opinio -onis* (as OPINE)]

opinionated /əˈpɪnjəˌneɪtɪd/ *adj.* conceitedly assertive or dogmatic in one's opinions. □ **opinionatedly** *adv.* **opinionatedness** *n.* [obs. *opinionate* in the same sense f. OPINION]

opium /ˈəʊpɪəm/ *n.* **1** a reddish-brown heavy-scented addictive drug prepared from the juice of the opium poppy, used in medicine as an analgesic and narcotic. **2** anything regarded as soothing or stupefying. □ **opium den** a haunt of opium-smokers. **opium poppy** a poppy, *Papaver somniferum*, native to Europe and E. Asia, with white, red, pink, or purple flowers. [ME f. L f. Gk *opion* poppy-juice f. *opos* juice]

opossum /əˈpɒsəm/ *n.* **1** any mainly tree-living marsupial of the family Didelphidae, native to America, having a prehensile tail and hind feet with an opposable thumb. **2** *Austral.* & *NZ* = POSSUM 2. [Virginian Ind. *āpassūm*]

opp. *abbr.* opposite.

oppo /ˈɒpəʊ/ *n.* (*pl.* **-os**) *Brit. colloq.* a colleague or friend. [*opposite number*]

opponent /əˈpəʊnənt/ *n.* & *adj.* —*n.* a person who opposes or belongs to an opposing side. —*adj.* opposing, contrary, opposed. □ **opponency** *n.* [L *opponere opponent-* (as OB-, *ponere* place)]

opportune /ˈɒpəˌtjuːn/ *adj.* **1** (of a time) well-chosen or especially favourable or appropriate (*an opportune moment*). **2** (of an action or event) well-timed; done or occurring at a favourable or useful time. □ **opportunely** *adv.* **opportuneness** *n.* [ME f. OF *opportun -une* f. L *opportunus* (as OB-, *portus* harbour), orig. of the wind driving towards the harbour]

opportunism /ˌɒpəˈtjuːnɪz(ə)m, ˈɒpə-/ *n.* **1** the adaptation of policy or judgement to circumstances or opportunity, esp. regardless of principle. **2** the seizing of opportunities when they occur. □ **opportunist** n. **opportunistic** /-ˈnɪstɪk/ adj. **opportunistically** /-ˈnɪstɪkəlɪ/ adv. [OPPORTUNE after It. *opportunismo* and F *opportunisme* in political senses]

opportunity /ˌɒpəˈtjuːnɪtɪ/ n. (pl. **-ies**) **1** a good chance; a favourable occasion. **2** a chance or opening offered by circumstances. **3** good fortune. □ **opportunity knocks** an opportunity occurs. [ME f. OF *opportunité* f. L *opportunitas* -*tatis* (as OPPORTUNE)]

opposable /əˈpəʊzəb(ə)l/ adj. **1** able to be opposed. **2** Zool. (of the thumb in primates) capable of facing and touching the other digits on the same hand.

oppose /əˈpəʊz/ v.tr. (often absol.) **1** set oneself against; resist, argue against. **2** be hostile to. **3** take part in a game, sport, etc., against (another competitor or team). **4** (foll. by *to*) place in opposition or contrast. □ **as opposed to** in contrast with. □ **opposer** n. [ME f. OF *opposer* f. L *opponere*: see OPPONENT]

opposite /ˈɒpəzɪt/ adj., n., adv., & prep. —adj. **1** (often foll. by *to*) having a position on the other or further side, facing or back to back. **2** (often foll. by *to*, *from*) **a** of a contrary kind; diametrically different. **b** being the other of a contrasted pair. **3** (of angles) between opposite sides of the intersection of two lines. —n. an opposite thing or person or term. —adv. **1** in an opposite position (*the tree stands opposite*). **2** (of a leading theatrical etc. part) in a complementary role to (another performer). —prep. in a position opposite to (*opposite the house is a tree*). □ **opposite number** a person holding an equivalent position in another group or organization. **the opposite sex** women in relation to men or vice versa. □ **oppositely** adv. **oppositeness** n. [ME f. OF f. L *oppositus* past part. of *opponere*: see OPPONENT]

opposition /ˌɒpəˈzɪʃ(ə)n/ n. **1** resistance, antagonism. **2** the state of being hostile or in conflict or disagreement. **3** contrast or antithesis. **4 a** a group or party of opponents or competitors. **b** (**the Opposition**) Brit. the principal parliamentary party opposed to that in office. **5** the act of opposing or placing opposite. **6** diametrically opposite position. □ **oppositional** adj. [ME f. OF f. L *oppositio* (as OB-, POSITION)]

oppress /əˈpres/ v.tr. **1** keep in subservience by coercion. **2** govern or treat harshly or with cruel injustice. **3** weigh down (with cares or unhappiness). □ **oppressor** n. [ME f. OF *oppresser* f. med.L *oppressare* (as OB-, PRESS¹)]

oppression /əˈpreʃ(ə)n/ n. **1** the act or an instance of oppressing; the state of being oppressed. **2** prolonged harsh or cruel treatment or control. **3** mental distress. [OF f. L *oppressio* (as OPPRESS)]

oppressive /əˈpresɪv/ adj. **1** oppressing; harsh or cruel. **2** difficult to endure. **3** (of weather) close and sultry. □ **oppressively** adv. **oppressiveness** n. [F *oppressif* -*ive* f. med.L *oppressivus* (as OPPRESS)]

opprobrious /əˈprəʊbrɪəs/ adj. (of language) severely scornful; abusive. □ **opprobriously** adv. [ME f. LL *opprobriosus* (as OPPROBRIUM)]

opprobrium /əˈprəʊbrɪəm/ n. **1** disgrace or bad reputation attaching to some act or conduct. **2** a cause of this. [L f. *opprobrum* (as OB-, *probrum* disgraceful act)]

oppugn /əˈpjuːn/ v.tr. literary call into question; controvert. □ **oppugner** n. [ME f. L *oppugnare* attack, besiege (as OB-, L *pugnare* fight)]

opt v.intr. (usu. foll. by *for*, *between*) exercise an option; make a choice. □ **opt out** (often foll. by *of*) choose not to participate (*opted out of the race*). [F *opter* f. L *optare* choose, wish]

optative /ɒpˈteɪtɪv, ˈɒptətɪv/ adj. & n. Gram. —adj. expressing a wish. —n. the optative mood. □ **optative mood** a set of verb-forms expressing a wish etc. □ **optatively** adv. [F *optatif* -*ive* f. LL *optativus* (as OPT)]

optic /ˈɒptɪk/ adj. & n. —adj. of or relating to the eye or vision (*optic nerve*). —n. **1** a lens etc. in an optical instrument. **2** (**Optic**) Brit. propr. a device fastened to the neck of a bottle for measuring out spirits etc. [F *optique* or med.L *opticus* f. Gk *optikos* f. *optos* seen]

optical /ˈɒptɪk(ə)l/ adj. **1** of sight; visual. **2 a** of or concerning sight or light in relation to each other. **b** belonging to optics. **3** (esp. of a lens) constructed to assist sight or on the principles of optics. □ **optical art** a style of painting that gives the illusion of movement by the precise use of pattern and colour. **optical brightener** any fluorescent substance used to produce a whitening effect on laundry. **optical character recognition** the identification of printed characters using photoelectric devices. **optical fibre** thin glass fibre through which light can be transmitted. **optical glass** a very pure kind of glass used for lenses etc. **optical illusion 1** a thing having an appearance so resembling something else as to deceive the eye. **2** an instance of mental misapprehension caused by this. **optical microscope** a microscope using the direct perception of light (cf. *electron microscope*). □ **optically** adv.

optician /ɒpˈtɪʃ(ə)n/ n. **1** a maker or seller of optical instruments, esp. spectacles and contact lenses. **2** a person trained in the detection and correction of poor eyesight. [F *opticien* f. med.L *optica* (as OPTIC)]

optics /ˈɒptɪks/ n.pl. (treated as sing.) the scientific study of sight and the behaviour of light, or of other radiation or particles (*electron optics*).

optima pl. of OPTIMUM.

optimal /ˈɒptɪm(ə)l/ adj. best or most favourable, esp. under a particular set of circumstances. □ **optimally** adv. [L *optimus* best]

optimism /ˈɒptɪmɪz(ə)m/ n. **1** an inclination to hopefulness and confidence. **2** Philos. **a** the doctrine that this world is the best of all possible worlds. **b** the theory that good must ultimately prevail over evil in the universe. □ **optimist** n. **optimistic** /-ˈmɪstɪk/ adj. **optimistically** /-ˈmɪstɪkəlɪ/ adv. [F *optimisme* f. L OPTIMUM]

optimize /ˈɒptɪmaɪz/ v. (also **-ise**) **1** tr. make the best or most effective use of (a situation, an opportunity, etc.). **2** intr. be an optimist. □ **optimization** /-ˈzeɪʃ(ə)n/ n. [L *optimus* best]

optimum /ˈɒptɪməm/ n. & adj. —n. (pl. **optima** /-mə/ or **optimums**) **1 a** the most favourable conditions (for growth, reproduction, etc.). **b** the best or most favourable situation. **2** the best possible compromise between opposing tendencies. —adj. = OPTIMAL. [L, neut. (as n.) of *optimus* best]

option /ˈɒpʃ(ə)n/ n. **1 a** the act or an instance of choosing; a choice. **b** a thing that is or may be chosen (*those are the options*). **2** the liberty of choosing; freedom of choice. **3** *Stock Exch.* etc. the right, obtained by payment, to buy, sell, etc. specified stocks etc. at a specified price within a set time. □ **have no option but to** must. **keep** (or **leave**) **one's options open** not commit oneself. [F or f. L *optio*, stem of *optare* choose]

optional /ˈɒpʃən(ə)l/ *adj.* being an option only; not obligatory. □ **optionality** /-ˈnælɪtɪ/ *n.* **optionally** *adv.*

optometrist /ɒpˈtɒmɪtrɪst/ *n.* esp. *US* **1** a person who practises optometry. **2** = *ophthalmic optician.*

opulent /ˈɒpjʊlənt/ *adj.* **1** ostentatiously rich; wealthy. **2** luxurious (*opulent surroundings*). **3** abundant; profuse. □ **opulence** *n.* **opulently** *adv.* [L *opulens, opulent-* f. *opes* wealth]

opus /ˈəʊpəs, ˈɒp-/ *n.* (*pl.* **opuses** or **opera** /ˈɒpərə/) **1** *Mus.* **a** a separate musical composition or set of compositions of any kind. **b** (also **op.**) used before a number given to a composer's work, usu. indicating the order of publication (*Beethoven, op. 15*). **2** any artistic work. [L, = work]

or /ɔː(r), ə(r)/ *conj.* **1 a** introducing the second of two alternatives (*white or black*). **b** introducing all but the first, or only the last, of any number of alternatives (*white or grey or black; white, grey, or black*). **2** (often prec. by *either*) introducing the only remaining possibility or choice given (*take it or leave it; either come in or go out*). **3** (prec. by *whether*) introducing the second part of an indirect question or conditional clause (*ask him whether he was there or not*). **4** introducing a synonym or explanation of a preceding word etc. (*suffered from vertigo or giddiness*). **5** introducing a significant afterthought (*he must know—or is he bluffing?*). **6** = *or else* (*run or you'll be late*). □ **one or two** (or **two or three** etc.) *colloq.* a few. **or else 1** otherwise (*do it now, or else you'll have to do it tomorrow*). **2** *colloq.* expressing a warning or threat (*hand over the money or else*). **or rather** introducing a rephrasing or qualification of a preceding statement etc. (*he was there, or rather I heard that he was*). **or so** (after a quantity or a number) or thereabouts (*send me ten or so*). [reduced form of obs. *other* conj. (which superseded OE *oththe* or), of uncert. orig.]

-or[1] /ə(r)/ *suffix* forming nouns denoting a person or thing performing the action of a verb, or an agent more generally (*actor; escalator; tailor*). [L *-or, -ator,* etc., sometimes via AF *-eour,* OF *-ëor, -ëur*]

-or[2] /ə(r)/ *suffix* forming nouns denoting state or condition (*error; horror*). [L *-or -oris,* sometimes via (or after) OF *-or, -ur*]

-or[3] /ə(r)/ *suffix* forming adjectives with comparative sense (*major; senior*). [AF *-our* f. L *-or*]

-or[4] /ə(r)/ *suffix US* = -OUR[1].

oracle /ˈɒrək(ə)l/ *n.* **1 a** a place at which advice or prophecy was sought from the gods in classical antiquity. **b** the usu. ambiguous or obscure response given at an oracle. **c** a prophet or prophetess at an oracle. **2 a** a person or thing regarded as an infallible guide to future action etc. **b** a saying etc. regarded as infallible guidance. **3** divine inspiration or revelation. **4** (**Oracle**) *Brit. propr.* a teletext service provided by Independent Television. [ME f. OF f. L *oraculum* f. *orare* speak]

oracular /əˈrækjʊlə(r)/ *adj.* **1** of or concerning an oracle or oracles. **2** (esp. of advice etc.)

mysterious or ambiguous. **3** prophetic. □ **oracularity** /-ˈlærɪtɪ/ *n.* **oracularly** *adv.* [L (as ORACLE)]

oracy /ˈɔːrəsɪ/ *n.* the ability to express oneself fluently in speech. [L *os oris* mouth, after *literacy*]

oral /ˈɔːr(ə)l/ *adj.* & *n.* —*adj.* **1** by word of mouth; spoken; not written (*the oral tradition*). **2** done or taken by the mouth (*oral contraceptive*). **3** of the mouth. —*n. colloq.* a spoken examination, test, etc. □ **oral sex** sexual activity in which the genitals of one partner are stimulated by the mouth of the other. □ **orally** *adv.* [LL *oralis* f. L *os oris* mouth]

orange /ˈɒrɪndʒ/ *n.* & *adj.* —*n.* **1 a** a large roundish juicy citrus fruit with a bright reddish-yellow tough rind. **b** any of various trees or shrubs of the genus *Citrus,* esp. *C. sinensis* or *C. aurantium,* bearing fragrant white flowers and yielding this fruit. **2** a fruit or plant resembling this. **3 a** the reddish-yellow colour of an orange. **b** orange pigment. —*adj.* orange-coloured; reddish-yellow. □ **orange blossom** the flowers of the orange tree, traditionally worn by the bride at a wedding. **orange squash** *Brit.* a soft drink made from oranges and other ingredients, often sold in concentrated form. **orange-stick** a thin stick, pointed at one end and usu. of orange wood, for manicuring the fingernails. **orange-wood** the wood of the orange tree. [ME f. OF *orenge,* ult. f. Arab. *nāranj* f. Pers. *nārang*]

orangeade /ˌɒrɪndʒˈeɪd/ *n.* a usu. fizzy non-alcoholic drink flavoured with orange.

Orangeman /ˈɒrɪndʒmən/ *n.* (*pl.* **-men**) a member of a political society formed in 1795 to support Protestantism in Ireland. [after William of Orange (William III)]

orangery /ˈɒrɪndʒərɪ/ *n.* (*pl.* **-ies**) a place, esp. a special structure, where orange-trees are cultivated.

orang-utan /ɔːˌræŋuːˈtæn/ *n.* (also **orang-outang** /-uːˈtæŋ/) a large red long-haired tree-living ape, *Pongo pygmaeus,* native to Borneo and Sumatra, with characteristic long arms and hooked hands and feet. [Malay *ōrang ūtan* wild man]

orate /ɔːˈreɪt/ *v.intr.* esp. *joc.* or *derog.* make a speech or speak, esp. pompously or at length. [back-form. f. ORATION]

oration /ɔːˈreɪʃ(ə)n, ə-/ *n.* **1** a formal speech, discourse, etc., esp. when ceremonial. **2** *Gram.* a way of speaking; language. [ME f. L *oratio* discourse, prayer f. *orare* speak, pray]

orator /ˈɒrətə(r)/ *n.* **1** a person making a speech. **2** an eloquent public speaker. □ **oratorial** /-ˈtɔːrɪəl/ *adj.* [ME f. AF *oratour,* OF *orateur* f. L *orator -oris* speaker, pleader (as ORATION)]

oratorio /ˌɒrəˈtɔːrɪəʊ/ *n.* (*pl.* **-os**) a semi-dramatic work for orchestra and voices esp. on a sacred theme, performed without costume, scenery, or action. □ **oratorial** *adj.* [It. f. eccl.L *oratorium,* orig. of musical services at church of Oratory of St Philip Neri in Rome]

oratory /ˈɒrətərɪ/ *n.* (*pl.* **-ies**) **1** the art or practice of formal speaking, esp. in public. **2** exaggerated, eloquent, or highly coloured language. **3** a small chapel, esp. for private worship. □ **oratorian** /-ˈtɔːrɪən/ *adj.* & *n.* **oratorical** /-ˈtɒrɪk(ə)l/ *adj.* [senses 1 and 2 f. L *ars oratoria* art of speaking; sense 3 ME f. AF *oratorie,* OF *oratoire* f. eccl.L *oratorium:* both f. L *oratorius* f. *orare* pray, speak]

orb *n.* **1** a globe surmounted by a cross esp. carried by a sovereign at a coronation. **2** a sphere; a globe. [L *orbis* ring]

orbicular /ɔːˈbɪkjʊlə(r)/ *adj. formal* **1** circular and flat; disc-shaped; ring-shaped. **2** spherical; globular; rounded. □ **orbicularity** /-ˈlærɪtɪ/ *n.* **orbicularly** *adv.* [ME f. LL *orbicularis* f. L *orbiculus* dimin. of *orbis* ring]

orbit /ˈɔːbɪt/ *n. & v.* —*n.* **1 a** the curved, usu. closed course of a planet, satellite, etc. **b** (prec. by *in, into, out of*, etc.) the state of motion in an orbit. **c** one complete passage around an orbited body. **2** the path of an electron round an atomic nucleus. **3** a range or sphere of action. —*v.* (**orbited, orbiting**) **1** *intr.* (of a satellite etc.) go round in orbit. **2** *tr.* move in orbit round. **3** *tr.* put into orbit. □ **orbiter** *n.* [L *orbita* course, track (in med.L eye-cavity): fem. of *orbitus* circular f. *orbis* ring]

orbital /ˈɔːbɪt(ə)l/ *adj.* **1** Anat., Astron., & Physics of an orbit or orbits. **2** (of a road) passing round the outside of a town. □ **orbital sander** a sander having a circular and not oscillating motion.

orca /ˈɔːkə/ *n.* **1** any of various whales, esp. the killer whale. **2** any other large sea-animal or monster. [F *orque* or L *orca* a kind of whale]

Orcadian /ɔːˈkeɪdɪən/ *adj. & n.* —*adj.* of or relating to the Orkney Islands off the N. coast of Scotland. —*n.* a native of the Orkney Islands. [L *Orcades* Orkney Islands]

orchard /ˈɔːtʃəd/ *n.* a piece of enclosed land with fruit-trees. □ **orchardist** *n.* [OE *ortgeard* f. L *hortus* garden + YARD²]

orchestra /ˈɔːkɪstrə/ *n.* **1** a usu. large group of instrumentalists, esp. combining strings, woodwinds, brass, and percussion (*symphony orchestra*). **2 a** (in full **orchestra pit**) the part of a theatre, opera house, etc., where the orchestra plays, usu. in front of the stage. **b** *US* the stalls in a theatre. □ **orchestral** /-ˈkestr(ə)l/ *adj.* **orchestrally** /-ˈkestrəlɪ/ *adv.* [L f. Gk *orkhēstra* space where the chorus danced and sang f. *orkheomai* to dance]

orchestrate /ˈɔːkɪˌstreɪt/ *v.tr.* **1** arrange, score, or compose for orchestral performance. **2** combine, arrange, or build up (elements of a situation etc.) for maximum effect. □ **orchestration** /-ˈstreɪʃ(ə)n/ *n.* **orchestrator** *n.*

orchid /ˈɔːkɪd/ *n.* **1** any plant of the family Orchidaceae, bearing flowers in fantastic shapes and brilliant colours. **2** a flower of any of these plants. □ **orchidaceous** /-ˈdeɪʃəs/ *adj.* **orchidist** *n.* **orchidology** /-ˈdɒlədʒɪ/ *n.* [mod.L *Orchid(ac)eae* irreg. f. L *orchis* f. Gk *orkhis*, orig. = testicle (with ref. to the shape of its tuber)]

ordain /ɔːˈdeɪn/ *v.tr.* **1** confer holy orders on; appoint to the Christian ministry (*ordained him priest; was ordained in 1970*). **2 a** (often foll. by *that* + clause) decree (*ordained that he should go*). **b** (of God, fate, etc.) destine; appoint (*has ordained us to die*). □ **ordainer** *n.* **ordainment** *n.* [ME f. AF *ordeiner*, OF *ordein-* stressed stem of *ordener* f. L *ordinare* f. *ordo -inis* order]

ordeal /ɔːˈdiːl/ *n.* a painful or horrific experience; a severe trial. [OE *ordāl, ordēl* f. Gmc: cf. DEAL¹]

order /ˈɔːdə(r)/ *n. & v.* —*n.* **1 a** the condition in which every part, unit, etc. is in its right place; tidiness (*restored some semblance of order*). **b** a usu. specified sequence, succession, etc. (*alphabetical order; the order of events*). **2** (in *sing.* or *pl.*) an

authoritative command, direction, instruction, etc. (*only obeying orders; gave orders for it to be done; the judge made an order*). **3** a state of peaceful harmony under a constituted authority (*order was restored; law and order*). **4** (esp. in *pl.*) a social class, rank, etc., constituting a distinct group in society (*the lower orders; the order of baronets*). **5** a kind; a sort (*talents of a high order*). **6 a** a usu. written direction to a manufacturer, tradesman, waiter, etc. to supply something. **b** the quantity of goods etc. supplied. **7** the constitution or nature of the world, society, etc. (*the moral order; the order of things*). **8** *Biol.* a taxonomic rank below a class and above a family. **9** (esp. **Order**) a fraternity of monks and friars, or formerly of knights, bound by a common rule of life (*the Franciscan order; the order of Templars*). **10 a** any of the grades of the Christian ministry. **b** (in *pl.*) the status of a member of the clergy (*Anglican orders*). **11** any of the five classical styles of architecture (Doric, Ionic, Corinthian, Tuscan, and Composite) based on the proportions of columns, amount of decoration, etc. **12** (esp. **Order**) **a** a company of distinguished people instituted esp. by a sovereign to which appointments are made as an honour or reward (*Order of the Garter; Order of Merit*). **b** the insignia worn by members of an order. **13** the principles of procedure, etc., accepted by a meeting, legislative assembly, etc. or enforced by its president. **14** any of the nine grades of angelic beings (seraphim, cherubim, thrones, dominations, principalities, powers, virtues, archangels, angels). —*v.tr.* **1** (usu. foll. by *to* + infin., or *that* + clause) command; bid; prescribe (*ordered him to go; ordered that they should be sent*). **2** command or direct (a person) to a specified destination (*was ordered to Singapore; ordered them home*). **3** direct a manufacturer, waiter, tradesman, etc. to supply (*ordered a new suit; ordered dinner*). **4** put in order; regulate (*ordered her affairs*). **5** (of God, fate, etc.) ordain (*fate ordered it otherwise*). **6** *US* command (a thing) done or (a person) dealt with (*ordered it settled; ordered him expelled*). □ **by order** according to the proper authority. **holy orders** the status of a member of the clergy, esp. the grades of bishop, priest, and deacon. **in bad** (or **good** etc.) **order** not working (or working properly etc.). **in order 1** one after another according to some principle. **2** ready or fit for use. **3** according to the rules (of procedure at a meeting etc.). **in order that** with the intention; so that. **in order to** with the purpose of doing; with a view to. **keep order** enforce orderly behaviour. **made to order 1** made according to individual requirements, measurements, etc. (opp. *ready-made*). **2** exactly what is wanted. **not in order** not working properly. **of** (or **in** or **on**) **the order of 1** approximately. **2** having the order of magnitude specified by (*of the order of one in a million*). **on order** (of goods etc.) ordered but not yet received. **order about 1** dominate; command officiously. **2** send hither and thither. **order book 1** a book in which a tradesman enters orders. **2** the level of incoming orders. **order-form** a printed form in which details are entered by a customer. **Order in Council** *Brit.* a sovereign's order on an administrative matter given by the advice of the Privy Council. **Order of the Bath** (or **Garter** or **Merit**) each of several honours conferred by the sovereign for services etc. to the State. **order of the day 1** the prevailing state of things. **2** a principal topic of action or a procedure decided upon. **3** business set down for treatment; a programme. **order of magnitude** a class in a system of classification determined by size, usu. by powers of 10. **order-paper** esp. *Parl.* a written or printed order of the day; an agenda. **order to view** a house-agent's request for a client to be allowed to inspect premises. **out of order 1** not working properly. **2** not according to the rules (of a meeting, organization, etc.). **take orders 1** accept commissions. **2** accept and carry out commands. **3** (also **take holy orders**) be ordained. □ **orderer** n. [ME f. OF *ordre* f. L *ordo ordinis* row, array, degree, command, etc.]

orderly /ˈɔːdəlɪ/ adj. & n. —adj. **1** methodically arranged; regular. **2** obedient to discipline; well-behaved; not unruly. —n. (pl. **-ies**) **1** an esp. male cleaner in a hospital. **2** a soldier who carries orders for an officer etc. □ **orderly room** Brit. Mil. a room in a barracks used for company business. □ **orderliness** n.

ordinal /ˈɔːdɪn(ə)l/ n. & adj. —n. (in full **ordinal number**) a number defining a thing's position in a series, e.g. 'first', 'second', 'third', etc. —adj. **1 a** of or relating to an ordinal number. **b** defining a thing's position in a series etc. [ME f. LL *ordinalis* & med.L *ordinale* neut. f. L (as ORDER)]

ordinance /ˈɔːdɪnəns/ n. **1** an authoritative order; a decree. **2** an enactment by a local authority. **3** a religious rite. [ME f. OF *ordenance* f. med.L *ordinantia* f. L *ordinare*: see ORDAIN]

ordinand /ˈɔːdɪnænd/ n. Eccl. a candidate for ordination. [L *ordinandus*, gerundive of *ordinare* ORDAIN]

ordinary /ˈɔːdɪnərɪ/ adj. & n. —adj. **1** regular, normal, customary, usual (*in the ordinary course of events*). **2** boring; commonplace (*an ordinary little man*). —n. (pl. **-ies**) a rule or book laying down the order of divine service. □ **in the ordinary way** if the circumstances are or were not exceptional. **ordinary level** Brit. hist. the lowest of the three levels of the GCE examination. **ordinary seaman** a sailor of the lowest rank, that below able-bodied seaman. **ordinary shares** Brit. shares entitling holders to a dividend from net profits (cf. *preference shares*). **out of the ordinary** unusual. □ **ordinarily** adv. **ordinariness** n. [ME f. L *ordinarius* orderly (as ORDER)]

ordinate /ˈɔːdɪnɪt/ n. Math. a straight line from any point drawn parallel to one coordinate axis and meeting the other, usually a coordinate measured parallel to the vertical. [L *linea ordinata applicata* line applied parallel f. *ordinare*: see ORDAIN]

ordination /ˌɔːdɪˈneɪʃ(ə)n/ n. **1 a** the act of conferring holy orders esp. on a priest or deacon. **b** the admission of a priest etc. to church ministry. **2** the arrangement of things etc. in ranks; classification. **3** the act of decreeing or ordaining. [ME f. OF *ordination* or L *ordinatio* (as ORDAIN)]

ordnance /ˈɔːdnəns/ n. **1** mounted guns; cannon. **2** a branch of government service dealing esp. with military stores and materials. □ **Ordnance map** Brit. a map produced by Ordnance Survey. **Ordnance Survey** Brit. (in the UK) an official survey organization, orig. under the Master of the Ordnance, preparing large-scale detailed maps of the whole country. [ME var. of ORDINANCE]

Ordovician /ˌɔːdəˈvɪsɪən, ˌɔːdəʊˈvɪʃɪən/ adj. & n. Geol. —adj. of or relating to the second period of the Palaeozoic era. —n. this period or system. [L *Ordovices* ancient British tribe in N. Wales]

ordure /ˈɔːdjʊə(r)/ n. **1** excrement; dung. **2** obscenity; filth; foul language. [ME f. OF f. ord foul f. L *horridus*: see HORRID]

ore /ɔː(r)/ n. a naturally occurring solid material from which metal or other valuable minerals may be extracted. [OE *ōra* unwrought metal, *ār* bronze, rel. to L *aes* crude metal, bronze]

oregano /ˌɒrɪˈgɑːnəʊ/ n. the dried leaves of wild marjoram used as a culinary herb (cf. MARJORAM). [Sp., = ORIGANUM]

organ /ˈɔːgən/ n. **1 a** a usu. large musical instrument having pipes supplied with air from bellows, sounded by keys, and distributed into sets or stops which form partial organs, each with a separate keyboard (*choir organ*; *pedal organ*). **b** a smaller instrument without pipes, producing similar sounds electronically. **c** a smaller keyboard wind instrument with metal reeds; a harmonium. **d** = *barrel-organ*. **2 a** a usu. self-contained part of an organism having a special vital function (*vocal organs*; *digestive organs*). **b** esp. joc. the penis. **3** a medium of communication, esp. a newspaper, sectarian periodical, etc. □ **organ-grinder** the player of a barrel-organ. **organ-loft** a gallery in a church or concert-room for an organ. **organ-pipe** any of the pipes on an organ. **organ-screen** an ornamental screen usu. between the choir and the nave of a church, cathedral, etc., on which the organ is placed. **organ-stop 1** a set of pipes of a similar tone in an organ. **2** the handle of the mechanism that brings it into action. [ME f. OE *organa* & OF *organe*, f. L *organum* f. Gk *organon* tool]

organdie /ˈɔːgəndɪ, -ˈgændɪ/ n. (US **organdy**) (pl. **-ies**) a fine translucent cotton muslin, usu. stiffened. [F *organdi*, of unkn. orig.]

organelle /ˌɔːgəˈnel/ n. Biol. any of various organized or specialized structures which form part of a cell. [mod.L *organella* dimin.; see ORGAN, -LE]

organic /ɔːˈgænɪk/ adj. **1 a** Physiol. of or relating to a bodily organ or organs. **b** Med. (of a disease) affecting the structure of an organ. **2** (of a plant or animal) having organs or an organized physical structure. **3** Agriculture produced or involving production without the use of chemical fertilizers, pesticides, etc. (*organic crop*; *organic farming*). **4** Chem. (of a compound etc.) containing carbon. **5 a** structural, inherent. **b** constitutional, fundamental. **6** organized, systematic, coordinated (*an organic whole*). □ **organic chemistry** the chemistry of carbon compounds. □ **organically** adv. [F *organique* f. L *organicus* f. Gk *organikos* (as ORGAN)]

organism /ˈɔːgənɪz(ə)m/ n. **1** a living individual consisting of a single cell or of a group of interdependent parts sharing the life processes. **2 a** an individual live plant or animal. **b** the material structure of this. **3** a whole with interdependent parts compared to a living being. [F *organisme* (as ORGANIZE)]

organist /ˈɔːgənɪst/ n. the player of an organ.

organization /ˌɔːgənaɪˈzeɪʃ(ə)n/ n. (also **-isation**) **1** the act or an instance of organizing; the state of being organized. **2** an organized body, esp. a business, government department, charity, etc. **3** systematic arrangement; tidiness. □ **organizational** adj. **organizationally** adv.

organize /ˈɔːgəˌnaɪz/ v.tr. (also **-ise**) **1 a** give an orderly structure to, systematize. **b** bring the affairs of (another person or oneself) into order; make arrangements for (a person). **2 a** arrange for or initiate (a scheme etc.). **b** provide; take responsibility for (*organized some sandwiches*). **3** (often *absol.*) **a** enrol (new members) in a trade union, political party, etc. **b** form (a trade union or other political group). **4 a** form (different elements) into an organic whole. **b** form (an organic whole). **5** (esp. as **organized** adj.) make organic; make into a living being or tissue. □ **organizable** adj. **organizer** n. [ME f. OF *organiser* f. med.L *organizare* f. L (as ORGAN)]

organza /ɔːˈgænzə/ n. a thin stiff transparent silk or synthetic dress fabric. [prob. f. *Lorganza* (US trade name)]

orgasm /ˈɔːgæz(ə)m/ n. & v. —n. **1 a** the climax of sexual excitement, esp. during sexual intercourse. **b** an instance of this. **2** violent excitement; rage. —v.intr. experience a sexual orgasm. □ **orgasmic** /-ˈgæzmɪk/ adj. **orgasmically** /-ˈgæzmɪkəlɪ/ adv. **orgastic** /-ˈgæstɪk/ adj. **orgastically** /-ˈgæstɪkəlɪ/ adv. [F *orgasme* or mod.L f. Gk *orgasmos* f. *orgaō* swell, be excited]

orgiastic /ˌɔːdʒɪˈæstɪk/ adj. of or resembling an orgy. □ **orgiastically** adv. [Gk *orgiastikos* f. *orgiastēs* agent-noun f. *orgiazō* hold an orgy]

orgy /ˈɔːdʒɪ/ n. (pl. **-ies**) **1** a wild drunken festivity at which indiscriminate sexual activity takes place. **2** excessive indulgence in an activity. [orig. pl., f. F *orgies* f. L *orgia* f. Gk *orgia* secret rites]

oriel /ˈɔːrɪəl/ n. **1** a large polygonal recess built out usu. from an upper storey and supported from the ground or on corbels. **2** (in full **oriel window**) **a** any of the windows in an oriel. **b** the projecting window of an upper storey. [ME f. OF *oriol* gallery, of unkn. orig.]

orient /ˈɔːrɪənt/ n. & v. —n. **1** (**the Orient**) *poet.* the east. **2** the countries E. of the Mediterranean, esp. E. Asia. —v. /ˈɔːrɪˌent, ˈɒr-/ **1** tr. **a** place or exactly determine the position of with the aid of a compass; settle or find the bearings of. **b** (often foll. by *towards*) bring (oneself, different elements, etc.) into a clearly understood position or relationship; direct. **2** tr. place or build (a church, building, etc.) facing towards the East. **3** intr. turn eastward or in a specified direction. □ **orient oneself** determine how one stands in relation to one's surroundings. [ME f. OF *orient*, *orienter* f. L *oriens -entis* rising, sunrise, east, f. *oriri* rise]

oriental /ˌɔːrɪˈent(ə)l, ˌɒr-/ adj. & n. —adj. **1** (often **Oriental**) of or characteristic of Eastern civilization etc. **2** of or concerning the East, esp. E. Asia. —n. (esp. **Oriental**) a native of the Orient. □ **orientalism** n. **orientalist** n. **orientalize** v.intr. & tr. (also **-ise**). **orientally** adv. [ME f. OF *oriental* or L *orientalis* (as ORIENT)]

orientate /ˈɔːrɪenˌteɪt, ˈɔːr-/ v.tr. & intr. = ORIENT v. [prob. back-form. f. ORIENTATION]

orientation /ˌɔːrɪenˈteɪʃ(ə)n, ˌɔːr-/ n. **1** the act or an instance of orienting; the state of being oriented. **2 a** a relative position. **b** a person's attitude or adjustment in relation to circumstances, esp. politically or psychologically.

3 an introduction to a subject or situation; a briefing. **4** the faculty by which birds etc. find their way home from a distance. □ **orientation course** esp. US a course giving information to newcomers to a university etc. □ **orientational** adj. [app. f. ORIENT]

orienteering /ˌɔːrɪenˈtɪərɪŋ, ˌɒr-/ n. a competitive sport in which runners cross open country with a map, compass, etc. □ **orienteer** n. & v.intr. [Sw. *orientering*]

orifice /ˈɒrɪfɪs/ n. an opening, esp. the mouth of a cavity, a bodily aperture, etc. [F f. LL *orificium* f. *os oris* mouth + *facere* make]

origami /ˌɒrɪˈgɑːmɪ/ n. the Japanese art of folding paper into decorative shapes and figures. [Jap. f. *ori* fold + *kami* paper]

origan /ˈɒrɪgən/ n. (also **origanum** /əˈrɪgənəm/) any plant of the genus *Origanum*, esp. wild marjoram. [(ME f. OF *origan*) f. L *origanum* f. Gk *origanon*]

origin /ˈɒrɪdʒɪn/ n. **1** a beginning or starting-point; a derivation; a source (*a word of Latin origin*). **2** (often in pl.) a person's ancestry (*what are his origins?*). **3** *Math.* a fixed point from which coordinates are measured. [F *origine* or f. L *origo -ginis* f. *oriri* rise]

original /əˈrɪdʒɪn(ə)l/ adj. & n. —adj. **1** existing from the beginning; innate. **2** novel; inventive; creative (*has an original mind*). **3** serving as a pattern; not derivative or imitative; firsthand (*in the original Greek; has an original Rembrandt*). —n. **1** an original model, pattern, picture, etc. from which another is copied or translated (*kept the copy and destroyed the original*). **2** an eccentric or unusual person. **3 a** a garment specially designed for a fashion collection. **b** a copy of such a garment made to order. □ **original sin** the innate depravity of all mankind held to be a consequence of the Fall. □ **originally** adv. [ME f. OF *original* or L *originalis* (as ORIGIN)]

originality /əˌrɪdʒɪˈnælɪtɪ/ n. (pl. **-ies**) **1** the power of creating or thinking creatively. **2** newness or freshness (*this vase has originality*). **3** an original act, thing, trait, etc.

originate /əˈrɪdʒɪˌneɪt/ v. **1** tr. cause to begin; initiate. **2** intr. (usu. foll. by *from*, *in*, *with*) have as an origin; begin. □ **origination** /-ˈneɪʃ(ə)n/ n. **originative** /-nətɪv/ adj. **originator** n. [med. L *originare* (as ORIGIN)]

oriole /ˈɔːrɪəʊl/ n. **1** any Old World bird of the genus *Oriolus*, many of which have brightly coloured plumage. **2** any New World bird of the genus *Icterus*, with similar coloration. [med.L *oriolus* f. OF *oriol* f. L *aureolus* dimin. of *aureus* golden f. *aurum* gold]

-orium /ˈɔːrɪəm/ suffix forming nouns denoting a place for a particular function (*auditorium*; *crematorium*). [L, neut. of adjectives in -*orius*: see -ORY¹]

ormer /ˈɔːmə(r)/ n. an edible univalve mollusc, *Haliotis tuberculata*, having a flattened shell with a series of holes of increasing size along the outer margin. Also called *sea-ear*. [Channel Islands F f. F *ormier* f. L *auris maris* ear of sea]

ormolu /ˈɔːməluː/ n. **1** (often *attrib.*) **a** a gilded bronze or gold-coloured alloy of copper, zinc, and tin used to decorate furniture, make ornaments, etc. **b** articles made of or decorated with these. **2** showy trash. [F *or moulu* powdered gold (for use in gilding)]

ornament /ˈɔːnəmənt/ n. & v. —n. **1 a** a thing used or serving to adorn, esp. a small trinket, vase, figure, etc. (*a mantelpiece crowded with ornaments; her only ornament was a brooch*). **b** a quality or person conferring adornment, grace, or honour (*an ornament to her profession*). **2** decoration added to embellish esp. a building (*a tower rich in ornament*). —v.tr. /ˈɔːnəˌment/ adorn; beautify. □ **ornamentation** /-menˈteɪʃ(ə)n/ n. [ME f. AF *urnement*, OF *o(u)rnement* f. L *ornamentum* equipment f. *ornare* adorn]

ornamental /ˌɔːnəˈment(ə)l/ adj. & n. —adj. serving as an ornament; decorative. —n. a thing considered to be ornamental, esp. a cultivated plant. □ **ornamentalism** n. **ornamentalist** n. **ornamentally** adv.

ornate /ɔːˈneɪt/ adj. **1** elaborately adorned; highly decorated. **2** (of literary style) convoluted; flowery. □ **ornately** adv. **ornateness** n. [ME f. L *ornatus* past part. of *ornare* adorn]

ornery /ˈɔːnərɪ/ adj. US colloq. **1** cantankerous; unpleasant. **2** of poor quality. □ **orneriness** n. [var. of ORDINARY]

ornitho- /ˈɔːnɪθəʊ/ comb. form bird. [Gk f. *ornis ornithos* bird]

ornithology /ˌɔːnɪˈθɒlədʒɪ/ n. the scientific study of birds. □ **ornithological** /-θəˈlɒdʒɪk(ə)l/ adj. **ornithologically** /-θəˈlɒdʒɪkəlɪ/ adv. **ornithologist** n. [mod.L *ornithologia* f. Gk *ornithologos* treating of birds (as ORNITHO-, -LOGY)]

oro- /ˈɔːrəʊ/ comb. form mountain. [Gk *oros* mountain]

orogeny /ɔːˈrɒdʒɪnɪ/ n. (also **orogenesis** /ˌɒrəʊˈdʒenɪsɪs/) the process of the formation of mountains. □ **orogenetic** /ˌɔːrəʊdʒɪˈnetɪk/ adj. **orogenic** /ˌɒrəˈdʒenɪk/ adj.

orotund /ˈɒrəˌtʌnd, ˈɔːr-/ adj. **1** (of the voice or phrasing) full, round; imposing. **2** (of writing, style, expression, etc.) pompous; pretentious. [L *ore rotundo* with rounded mouth]

orphan /ˈɔːf(ə)n/ n. & v. —n. (often *attrib.*) **1** a child bereaved of a parent or usu. both parents. **2** a person bereft of previous protection, advantages, etc. —v.tr. bereave (a child) of its parents or a parent. □ **orphanhood** n. **orphanize** v.tr. (also **-ise**). [ME f. LL *orphanus* f. Gk *orphanos* bereaved]

orphanage /ˈɔːfənɪdʒ/ n. **1** a usu. residential institution for the care and education of orphans. **2** orphanhood.

Orphic /ˈɔːfɪk/ adj. of or concerning Orpheus, a legendary Greek poet and lyre-player, or the mysteries, doctrines, etc. associated with him; oracular; mysterious. □ **Orphism** n. [L *Orphicus* f. Gk *Orphikos* f. *Orpheus*]

orrery /ˈɒrərɪ/ n. (pl. **-ies**) a clockwork model of the solar system. [named after the fourth Earl of *Orrery*, for whom one was made]

orris /ˈɒrɪs/ n. **1** any plant of the genus *Iris*, esp. *I. florentina*. **2** = ORRISROOT. □ **orris-powder** powdered orrisroot. [16th c.: app. an unexpl. alt. of IRIS]

orrisroot /ˈɒrɪsˌruːt/ n. the fragrant rootstock of the orris, used in perfumery and formerly in medicine.

ortanique /ˈɔːtəˌniːk/ n. a citrus fruit produced by crossing an orange and a tangerine. [*orange* + *tangerine* + *unique*]

ortho- /ˈɔːθəʊ/ comb. form **1** straight, rectangular, upright. **2** right, correct. [Gk *orthos* straight]

orthodontics /ˌɔːθəˈdɒntɪks/ n.pl. (treated as *sing.*) (also **orthodontia** /-ˈdɒntɪə/) the treatment of irregularities in the teeth and jaws. □ **orthodontic** adj. **orthodontist** n. [ORTHO- + Gk *odous odont-* tooth]

orthodox /ˈɔːθəˌdɒks/ adj. **1 a** holding correct or currently accepted opinions, esp. on religious doctrine, morals, etc. **b** not independent-minded; unoriginal; unheretical. **2** (of religious doctrine, standards of morality, etc.) generally accepted as right or true; authoritatively established; conventional. **3** (also **Orthodox**) (of Judaism) strictly keeping to traditional doctrine and ritual. □ **Orthodox Church** the Eastern Church, having the Patriarch of Constantinople as its head, and including the national Churches of Russia, Romania, Greece, etc. □ **orthodoxly** adv. [eccl.L *orthodoxus* f. Gk *orthodoxos* f. *doxa* opinion]

orthodoxy /ˈɔːθəˌdɒksɪ/ n. (pl. **-ies**) **1** the state of being orthodox. **2 a** the orthodox practice of Judaism. **b** the body of orthodox Jews. **3** esp. *Relig.* an authorized or generally accepted theory, doctrine, etc. [LL *orthodoxia* f. late Gk *orthodoxia* sound doctrine (as ORTHODOX)]

orthogenesis /ˌɔːθəʊˈdʒenɪsɪs/ n. a theory of evolution which proposes that variations follow a defined direction and are not merely sporadic and fortuitous. □ **orthogenetic** /-dʒɪˈnetɪk/ adj. **orthogenetically** /-dʒɪˈnetɪkəlɪ/ adv.

orthogonal /ɔːˈθɒɡən(ə)l/ adj. of or involving right angles. [F f. *orthogone* (as ORTHO-, -GON)]

orthography /ɔːˈθɒɡrəfɪ/ n. (pl. **-ies**) **1** correct or conventional spelling. **2** spelling with reference to its correctness (*dreadful orthography*). **3** the study or science of spelling. □ **orthographer** n. **orthographic** /-ˈɡræfɪk/ adj. **orthographical** /-ˈɡræfɪk(ə)l/ adj. **orthographically** /-ˈɡræfɪkəlɪ/ adv. [ME f. OF *ortografie* f. L *orthographia* f. Gk *orthographia* (as ORTHO-, -GRAPHY)]

orthopaedics /ˌɔːθəˈpiːdɪks/ n.pl. (treated as *sing.*) (US **-pedics**) the branch of medicine dealing with the correction of deformities of bones or muscles, orig. in children. □ **orthopaedic** adj. **orthopaedist** n. [F *orthopédie* (as ORTHO-, *pédie* f. Gk *paideia* rearing of children)]

orthoptic /ɔːˈθɒptɪk/ adj. relating to the correct or normal use of the eyes. □ **orthoptist** n. [ORTHO- + Gk *optikos* of sight: see OPTIC]

orthoptics /ɔːˈθɒptɪks/ n. Med. the study or treatment of irregularities of the eyes, esp. with reference to the eye-muscles.

orthorhombic /ˌɔːθəʊˈrɒmbɪk/ adj. Crystallog. (of a crystal) characterized by three mutually perpendicular axes which are unequal in length, as in topaz and talc.

ortolan /ˈɔːtələn/ n. (in full **ortolan bunting**) Zool. a small European bird, *Emberiza hortulana*, eaten as a delicacy. [F f. Prov., lit. gardener, f. L *hortulanus* f. *hortulus* dimin. of *hortus* garden]

Orwellian /ɔːˈwelɪən/ adj. of or characteristic of the writings of George Orwell (E. A. Blair), English writer d. 1950, esp. with reference to the totalitarian development of the State as depicted in *1984* and *Animal Farm*.

-ory[1] /ərɪ/ suffix forming nouns denoting a place for a particular function (*dormitory; refectory*). □ **-orial** /ˈɔːrɪəl/ suffix forming adjectives. [L *-oria*, *-orium*, sometimes via ONF and AF *-orie*, OF *-oire*]

-ory[2] /ərɪ/ suffix forming adjectives (and occasionally nouns) relating to or involving a verbal action (accessory; compulsory; directory). [L -orius, sometimes via AF -ori(e), OF -oir(e)]

OS abbr. **1** ordinary seaman. **2** (in the UK) Ordnance Survey. **3** outsize.

Os symb. Chem. the element osmium.

Oscar /ˈɒskə(r)/ n. any of the statuettes awarded by the US Academy of Motion Picture Arts and Sciences for excellence in film acting, directing, etc. [the name Oscar]

oscillate /ˈɒsɪˌleɪt/ v. **1** intr. & tr. **a** swing to and fro like a pendulum. **b** move to and fro between points. **2** intr. vacillate; vary between extremes of opinion, action, etc. **3** intr. Physics move with periodic regularity. **4** intr. Electr. (of a current) undergo high-frequency alternations as across a spark-gap or in a valve-transmitter circuit. **5** intr. (of a radio receiver) radiate electromagnetic waves owing to faulty operation. □ **oscillation** /-ˈleɪʃ(ə)n/ n. **oscillator** n. **oscillatory** /ɒˈsɪlətərɪ, ˈɒsɪˌleɪtərɪ/ adj. [L oscillare oscillat- swing]

oscillo- /əˈsɪləʊ/ comb. form oscillation, esp. of electric current.

oscillogram /əˈsɪləˌgræm/ n. a record obtained from an oscillograph.

oscillograph /əˈsɪləˌɡrɑːf/ n. a device for recording oscillations. □ **oscillographic** /-ˈɡræfɪk/ adj. **oscillography** /-ˈlɒɡrəfɪ/ n.

oscilloscope /əˈsɪləˌskəʊp/ n. a device for viewing oscillations by a display on the screen of a cathode-ray tube. □ **oscilloscopic** /-ˈskɒpɪk/ adj.

oscular /ˈɒskjʊlə(r)/ adj. **1** of or relating to the mouth. **2** of or relating to kissing. [L osculum mouth, kiss, dimin. of os mouth]

-ose¹ /əʊs/ suffix forming adjectives denoting possession of a quality (grandiose; verbose). □ **-osely** suffix forming adverbs. **-oseness** suffix forming nouns (cf. -OSITY). [from or after L -osus]

-ose² /əʊs/ suffix Chem. forming names of carbohydrates (cellulose; sucrose). [after GLUCOSE]

osier /ˈəʊzɪə(r)/ n. **1** any of various willows, esp. Salix viminalis, with long flexible shoots used in basketwork. **2** a shoot of a willow. [ME f. OF: cf. med.L auseria osier-bed]

-osis /ˈəʊsɪs/ suffix (pl. **-oses** /ˈəʊsiːz/) denoting a process or condition (apotheosis; metamorphosis), esp. a pathological state (acidosis; neurosis; thrombosis). [L f. Gk -ōsis suffix of verbal nouns]

-osity /ˈɒsɪtɪ/ suffix forming nouns from adjectives in -ose (see -OSE¹) and -ous (verbosity; curiosity). [F -osité or L -ositas -ositatis: cf. -ITY]

osmic /ˈɒzmɪk/ adj. of or relating to odours or the sense of smell. □ **osmically** adv. [Gk osmē smell, odour]

osmium /ˈɒzmɪəm/ n. Chem. a hard bluish-white transition element, the heaviest known metal, used in certain alloys. [Gk osmē smell (from the pungent smell of its tetroxide)]

osmosis /ɒzˈməʊsɪs/ n. **1** Biochem. the passage of a solvent through a semi-permeable partition into a more concentrated solution. **2** any process by which something is acquired by absorption. □ **osmotic** /-ˈmɒtɪk/ adj. **osmotically** /-ˈmɒtɪkəlɪ/ adv. [orig. osmose, after F f. Gk ōsmos push]

osprey /ˈɒspreɪ, -prɪ/ n. (pl. **-eys**) **1** a large bird of prey, Pandion haliaetus, with a brown back and white markings, feeding on fish. **2** a plume on a woman's hat. [ME f. OF ospres app. ult. f. L ossifraga osprey f. os bone + frangere break]

osseous /ˈɒsɪəs/ adj. **1** consisting of bone. **2** having a bony skeleton. **3** ossified. [L osseus f. os ossis bone]

ossicle /ˈɒsɪk(ə)l/ n. **1** Anat. any small bone, esp. of the middle ear. **2** a small piece of bonelike substance. [L ossiculum dimin. (as OSSEOUS)]

Ossie var. of AUSSIE.

ossify /ˈɒsɪˌfaɪ/ v.tr. & intr. (-ies, -ied) **1** turn into bone; harden. **2** make or become rigid, callous, or unprogressive. □ **ossific** /ɒˈsɪfɪk/ adj. **ossification** /-fɪˈkeɪʃ(ə)n/ n. [F ossifier f. L os ossis bone]

osso bucco /ˌɒsəʊ ˈbʊkəʊ/ n. shin of veal containing marrowbone stewed in wine with vegetables. [It., = marrowbone]

ostensible /ɒˈstensɪb(ə)l/ adj. concealing the real; professed (his ostensible function was that of interpreter). □ **ostensibly** adv. [F f. med.L ostensibilis f. L ostendere ostens- stretch out to view (as OB-, tendere stretch)]

ostensive /ɒˈstensɪv/ adj. **1** directly demonstrative. **2** (of a definition) indicating by direct demonstration that which is signified by a term. □ **ostensively** adv. **ostensiveness** n. [LL ostensivus (as OSTENSIBLE)]

ostentation /ˌɒstenˈteɪʃ(ə)n/ n. **1** a pretentious and vulgar display esp. of wealth and luxury. **2** the attempt or intention to attract notice; showing off. □ **ostentatious** adj. **ostentatiously** adv. [ME f. OF f. L ostentatio -onis f. ostentare frequent. of ostendere: see OSTENSIBLE]

osteo- /ˈɒstɪəʊ/ comb. form bone. [Gk osteon]

osteoarthritis /ˌɒstɪəʊɑːˈθraɪtɪs/ n. a degenerative disease of joint cartilage, esp. in the elderly. □ **osteoarthritic** /-ˈθrɪtɪk/ adj.

osteology /ˌɒstɪˈɒlədʒɪ/ n. the study of the structure and function of the skeleton and bony structures. □ **osteological** /-əˈlɒdʒɪk(ə)l/ adj. **osteologically** /-əˈlɒdʒɪkəlɪ/ adv. **osteologist** n.

osteomyelitis /ˌɒstɪəʊmaɪˈlaɪtɪs/ n. inflammation of the bone or of bone marrow, usu. due to infection.

osteopathy /ˌɒstɪˈɒpəθɪ/ n. the treatment of disease through the manipulation of bones, esp. the spine, displacement of these being the supposed cause. □ **osteopath** /ˈɒstɪəˌpæθ/ n. **osteopathic** /ˌɒstɪəˈpæθɪk/ adj.

osteoporosis /ˌɒstɪəʊpəˈrəʊsɪs/ n. a condition of brittle and fragile bones caused by loss of bony tissue, esp. as a result of hormonal changes, or deficiency of calcium or vitamin D. [OSTEO- + Gk poros passage, pore]

ostler /ˈɒslə(r)/ n. Brit. hist. a stableman at an inn. [f. earlier hostler, hosteler f. AF hostiler, OF (h)ostelier (as HOSTEL)]

ostracize /ˈɒstrəˌsaɪz/ v.tr. (also **-ise**) **1** exclude (a person) from a society, favour, common privileges, etc.; refuse to associate with. **2** (esp. in ancient Athens) banish (a powerful or unpopular citizen) for five or ten years by popular vote. □ **ostracism** /-ˌsɪz(ə)m/ n. [Gk ostrakizō f. ostrakon shell, potsherd (used to write a name on in voting)]

ostrich /ˈɒstrɪtʃ/ n. **1** a large African swift-running flightless bird, Struthio camelus, with long legs and two toes on each foot. **2** a person who refuses to accept facts (from the belief that ostriches bury their heads in the sand when pursued). [ME f. OF ostric(h)e f. L avis bird + LL struthio f. Gk strouthiōn ostrich f. strouthos sparrow, ostrich]

OT abbr. Old Testament.

-ot¹ /ət/ suffix forming nouns, orig. diminutives (ballot; chariot; parrot). [F]

-ot² /ət/ *suffix* forming nouns for persons (*patriot*), e.g. natives of a place (*Cypriot*). [F *-ote*, L *-ota*, Gk *-ōtēs*]

other /ˈʌðə(r)/ *adj., n. or pron., & adv.* —*adj.* **1** not the same as one or some already mentioned or implied; separate in identity or distinct in kind (*other people; use other means; I assure you, my reason is quite other*). **2 a** further; additional (*a few other examples*). **b** alternative of two (*open your other eye*). **3** (*prec. by* the) that remains after all except the one or ones in question have been considered, eliminated, etc. (*must be in the other pocket; where are the other two?; the other three men left*). **4** (foll. by *than*) apart from; excepting (*any person other than you*). —*n. or pron.* (orig. an ellipt. use of the adj., now with pl. in *-s*) **1** an additional, different, or extra person, thing, example, etc. (*one or other of us will be there; some others have come*). **2** (in pl.; prec. by *the*) the ones remaining (*where are the others?*). —*adv.* (usu. foll. by *than*) *disp.* otherwise (*cannot react other than angrily*). □ **of all others** out of the many possible or likely (*on this night of all others*). **the other day** (or **night** or **week** etc.) a few days etc. ago (*heard from him the other day*). **other-directed** governed by external circumstances and trends. **other half** *colloq.* one's wife or husband. **other ranks** soldiers other than commissioned officers. **the other thing** esp. *joc.* an unexpressed alternative (*if you don't like it, do the other thing*). **other things being equal** if conditions are or were alike in all but the point in question. **the other woman** a married man's mistress. **someone** (or **something** or **somehow** etc.) **or other** some unspecified person, thing, manner, etc. [OE *ōther* f. Gmc]

■ **Usage** *Otherwise* is standard for the use of *other than* as an adverb except in less formal use.

otherness /ˈʌðənɪs/ *n.* **1** the state of being different; diversity. **2** a thing or existence other than the thing mentioned and the thinking subject.

otherwise /ˈʌðəˌwaɪz/ *adv. & adj.* —*adv.* **1** else; or else; in the circumstances other than those considered etc. (*bring your umbrella, otherwise you will get wet*). **2** in other respects (*he is untidy, but otherwise very suitable*). **3** (often foll. by *than*) in a different way (*could not have acted otherwise; cannot react otherwise than angrily*). **4** as an alternative (*otherwise known as Jack*). —*adj.* (*predic.*) in a different state (*the matter is quite otherwise*). □ **and** (or **or**) **otherwise** the negation or opposite (of a specified thing) (*the merits or otherwise of the Bill; experiences pleasant and otherwise*). [OE *on ōthre wisan* (as OTHER, WISE²)]

other-worldly /ˌʌðəˈwɜːldlɪ/ *adj.* **1** unworldly; impractical. **2** concerned with life after death etc. □ **other-worldliness** *n.*

otic /ˈəʊtɪk/ *adj.* of or relating to the ear. [Gk *ōtikos* f. *ous ōtos* ear]

-otic /ˈɒtɪk/ *suffix* forming adjectives and nouns corresponding to nouns in *-osis*, meaning 'affected with or producing or resembling a condition in *-osis*' or 'a person affected with this' (*narcotic; neurotic; osmotic*). □ **-otically** *suffix* forming adverbs. [from or after F *-otique* f. L f. Gk *-ōtikos* adj. suffix]

otiose /ˈəʊʃɪəʊs, ˈəʊt-, -əʊz/ *adj.* serving no practical purpose; not required; functionless. □ **otiosely** *adv.* **otioseness** *n.* [L *otiosus* f. *otium* leisure]

otitis /əˈtaɪtɪs/ *n.* inflammation of the ear. [mod.L (as OTO-)]

oto- /ˈəʊtəʊ/ *comb. form* ear. [Gk *ōto-* f. *ous ōtos* ear]

otology /əʊˈtɒlədʒɪ/ *n.* the study of the anatomy and diseases of the ear. □ **otological** /-təˈlɒdʒɪk(ə)l/ *adj.* **otologist** *n.*

otoscope /ˈəʊtəˌskəʊp/ *n.* an apparatus for examining the eardrum and the passage leading to it from the ear. □ **otoscopic** /-ˈskɒpɪk/ *adj.*

OTT *abbr. colloq.* over-the-top.

otter /ˈɒtə(r)/ *n.* **1 a** any of several aquatic fish-eating mammals of the family Mustelidae, esp. of the genus *Lutra*, having strong claws and webbed feet. **b** its fur or pelt. [OE *otr, ot(t)or* f. Gmc]

otto var. of ATTAR.

Ottoman /ˈɒtəmən/ *adj. & n.* —*adj. hist.* **1** of or concerning the dynasty of Osman or Othman I, the branch of the Turks to which he belonged, or the empire ruled by his descendants. **2** Turkish. —*n.* (pl. **Ottomans**) an Ottoman person; a Turk. [F f. Arab. *ʽutmānī* adj. of Othman (ʽutmān)]

ottoman /ˈɒtəmən/ *n.* (pl. **ottomans**) an upholstered seat, usu. square and without a back or arms, sometimes a box with a padded top. [F *ottomane* fem. (as OTTOMAN)]

OU *abbr. Brit.* **1** Open University. **2** Oxford University.

oubliette /ˌuːblɪˈet/ *n.* a secret dungeon with access only through a trapdoor. [F f. *oublier* forget]

ouch /aʊtʃ/ *int.* expressing pain or annoyance. [imit.: cf. G *autsch*]

ought¹ /ɔːt/ *v.aux.* (usu. foll. by *to* + infin.; present and past indicated by the following infin.) **1** expressing duty or rightness (*we ought to love our neighbours*). **2** expressing shortcoming (*it ought to have been done long ago*). **3** expressing advisability or prudence (*you ought to go for your own good*). **4** expressing esp. strong probability (*he ought to be there by now*). □ **ought not** the negative form of *ought* (*he ought not to have stolen it*). [OE *āhte*, past of *āgan* OWE]

ought² /ɔːt/ *n.* (also **aught**) *colloq.* a figure denoting nothing; nought. [perh. f. *an ought* for a NOUGHT; cf. ADDER]

ought³ var. of AUGHT.

Ouija /ˈwiːdʒə/ *n.* (in full **Ouija board**) *propr.* a board having letters or signs at its rim to which a planchette, movable pointer, or upturned glass points in answer to questions from attenders at a seance etc. [F *oui* yes + G *ja* yes]

ounce¹ /aʊns/ *n.* **1 a** a unit of weight of one-sixteenth of a pound avoirdupois (approx. 28 grams). **b** a unit of one-twelfth of a pound troy or apothecaries' measure, equal to 480 grains (approx. 31 grams). **2** a small quantity. □ **fluid ounce** *Brit.* **1** a unit of capacity equal to one-twentieth of a pint (approx. 0.028 litre). **2** *US* a unit of capacity equal to one-sixteenth of a pint (approx. 0.034 litre). [ME & OF *unce* f. L *uncia* twelfth part of pound or foot: cf. INCH]

ounce² /aʊns/ *n.* an Asian wild cat, *Panthera uncia*, with leopard-like markings on a cream-coloured coat. [ME f. OF *once* (earlier *lonce*) = It. *lonza* ult. f. L *lynx*: see LYNX]

OUP *abbr.* Oxford University Press.

our /ˈaʊə(r)/ *poss.pron.* (attrib.) **1** of or belonging to us or ourselves (*our house; our own business*). **2** of or belonging to all people (*our children's future*). **3** (esp. as **Our**) of Us the king or queen, emperor or empress, etc. (*given under Our seal*). **4** of us, the editorial staff of a newspaper etc. (*a foolish adventure in our view*). □ **Our Father 1** the Lord's Prayer. **2** God. **Our Lady** the Virgin Mary. **Our Lord 1** Jesus Christ. **2** God. **Our Saviour** Jesus Christ. [OE *ūre* orig. genit. pl. of 1st pers. pron. = of us, later treated as possessive adj.]

-our[1] /ə(r)/ *suffix* var. of -OR[2] surviving in some nouns (*ardour; colour; valour*).

-our[2] /ə(r)/ *suffix* var. of -OR[1] (*saviour*).

ours /ˈaʊəz/ *poss.pron.* the one or ones belonging to or associated with us (*it is ours; ours are over there*). □ **of ours** of or belonging to us (*a friend of ours*).

ourself /aʊəˈself/ *pron.* archaic a word formerly used instead of *myself* by a sovereign, newspaper editorial staff, etc. (cf. OUR 3, 4).

ourselves /aʊəˈselvz/ *pron.* **1 a** emphat. form of WE or US (*we ourselves did it; made it ourselves; for our friends and ourselves*). **b** refl. form of US (*are pleased with ourselves*). **2** in our normal state of body or mind (*not quite ourselves today*). □ **be ourselves** act in our normal unconstrained manner. **by ourselves** see *by oneself.*

-ous /əs/ *suffix* forming adjectives meaning 'abounding in, characterized by, of the nature of' (*envious; glorious; mountainous; poisonous*). □ **-ously** *suffix* forming adverbs. **-ousness** *suffix* forming nouns. [from or after AF *-ous*, OF *-eus*, f. L *-osus*]

ousel var. of OUZEL.

oust /aʊst/ *v.tr.* (usu. foll. by *from*) drive out or expel, esp. by forcing oneself into the place of. [AF *ouster*, OF *oster* take away, f. L *obstare* oppose, hinder (as OB-, *stare* stand)]

out /aʊt/ *adv., prep., n., adj., int., & v.* —*adv.* **1** away from or not in or at a place etc. (*keep him out; get out of here; my son is out in Canada*). **2** (forming part of phrasal verbs) **a** indicating dispersal away from a centre etc. (*hire out; share out; board out*). **b** indicating coming or bringing into the open for public attention etc. (*call out; send out; shine out; stand out*). **c** indicating a need for attentiveness (*watch out; look out; listen out*). **3** not in one's house, office, etc. (*went out for a walk*). **4** to or at an end; completely (*tired out; die out; out of bananas; fight it out; typed it out*). **5** (of a fire, candle, etc.) not burning. **6** in error (*was 3% out in my calculations*). **7** *colloq.* unconscious (*she was out for five minutes*). **8 a** (of a tooth) extracted. **b** (of a joint, bone, etc.) dislocated (*put his shoulder out*). **9** (of a party, politician, etc.) not in office. **10** (of a jury) considering its verdict in secrecy. **11** (of workers) on strike. **12** (of a secret) revealed. **13** (of a flower) blooming, open. **14** (of a book) published. **15** (of a star) visible after dark. **16** unfashionable (*turn-ups are out*). **17** (of a batsman, batter, etc.) no longer taking part as such, having been caught, stumped, etc. **18** not worth considering; rejected (*that idea is out*). **19** *colloq.* (prec. by *superl.*) known to exist (*the best game out*). **20** (of a stain, mark, etc.) not visible, removed (*painted out the sign*). **21** (of time) not spent working (*took five minutes out*). **22** (of a

rash, bruise, etc.) visible. **23** (of the tide) at the lowest point. **24** *Boxing* unable to rise from the floor (*out for the count*). **25** (in a radio conversation etc.) transmission ends (*over and out*). —*prep.* out of (*looked out the window*). —*n. colloq.* a way of escape; an excuse. —*adj.* **1** (of a match) played away. **2** (of an island) away from the mainland. —*int.* a peremptory dismissal, reproach, etc. (*out, you scoundrel!*). —*v.* **1** *tr.* **a** put out. **b** *colloq.* eject forcibly. **2** *intr.* come or go out; emerge (*murder will out*). **3** *tr. Boxing* knock out. **4** *tr. US colloq.* expose the homosexuality of (a prominent person). □ **out and about** (of a person, esp. after an illness) engaging in normal activity. **out and away** by far. **out and out 1** thorough; surpassing. **2** thoroughly; surpassingly. **out for** having one's interest or effort directed to; intent on. **out of 1** from within (*came out of the house*). **2** not within (*I was never out of England*). **3** from among (*nine people out of ten; must choose out of these*). **4** beyond the range of (*is out of reach*). **5** without or so as to be without (*was swindled out of his money; out of breath; out of sugar*). **6** from (*get money out of him*). **7** owing to; because of (*asked out of curiosity*). **8** by the use of (material) (*what did you make it out of?*). **9** at a specified distance from (a town, port, etc.) (*seven miles out of Liverpool*). **10** beyond (*something out of the ordinary*). **11** *Racing* (of an animal, esp. a horse) born of. **out of it** not included; forlorn. **out to** keenly striving to do. **out to lunch** *colloq.* crazy, mad. **out with** an exhortation to expel or dismiss (an unwanted person). **out with it** say what you are thinking. [OE *ūt*, OHG *ūz*, rel. to Skr. *ud-*]

■ **Usage** The use of *out* as a preposition, e.g. *he walked out the room*, is non-standard. *Out of* should be used.

out- /aʊt/ *prefix* added to verbs and nouns, meaning: **1** so as to surpass or exceed (*outdo; outnumber*). **2** external, separate (*outline; outhouse; outdoors*). **3** out of; away from; outward (*outspread; outgrowth*).

out-act /aʊtˈækt/ *v.tr.* surpass in acting or performing.

outage /ˈaʊtɪdʒ/ *n.* a period of time during which a power-supply etc. is not operating.

outback /ˈaʊtbæk/ *n.* esp. *Austral.* the remote and usu. uninhabited inland districts. □ **outbacker** *n.*

outbalance /aʊtˈbæləns/ *v.tr.* **1** count as more important than. **2** outweigh.

outbid /aʊtˈbɪd/ *v.tr.* (-**bidding**; past and past part. -**bid**) **1** bid higher than (another person) at an auction. **2** surpass in exaggeration etc.

outboard /ˈaʊtbɔːd/ *adj., adv., & n.* —*adj.* **1** (of a motor) portable and attachable to the outside of the stern of a boat. **2** (of a boat) having an outboard motor. —*adj. & adv.* on, towards, or near the outside of esp. a ship, an aircraft, etc. —*n.* **1** an outboard engine. **2** a boat with an outboard engine.

outbound /ˈaʊtbaʊnd/ *adj.* outward bound.

outbreak /ˈaʊtbreɪk/ *n.* **1** a usu. sudden eruption of anger, war, disease, rebellion, etc. **2** an outcrop.

outbreeding /ˈaʊtˌbriːdɪŋ/ *n.* the theory or practice of breeding from animals not closely related. □ **outbreed** *v.intr. & tr.* (past and past part. -**bred**).

outbuilding /ˈaʊtˌbɪldɪŋ/ n. a detached shed, barn, garage, etc. within the grounds of a main building; an outhouse.

outburst /ˈaʊtbɜːst/ n. 1 an explosion of anger etc., expressed in words. 2 an act or instance of bursting out. 3 an outcrop.

outcast /ˈaʊtkɑːst/ n. & adj. —n. 1 a person cast out from or rejected by his or her home, country, society, etc. 2 a tramp or vagabond. —adj. rejected; homeless; friendless.

outclass /aʊtˈklɑːs/ v.tr. 1 belong to a higher class than. 2 defeat easily.

outcome /ˈaʊtkʌm/ n. a result; a visible effect.

outcrop /ˈaʊtkrɒp/ n. & v. —n. 1 a the emergence of a stratum, vein, or rock, at the surface. b a stratum etc. emerging. 2 a noticeable manifestation or occurrence. —v.intr. (-cropped, -cropping) appear as an outcrop; crop out.

outcry /ˈaʊtkraɪ/ n. (pl. -ies) 1 the act or an instance of crying out. 2 an uproar. 3 a noisy or prolonged public protest.

outdance /aʊtˈdɑːns/ v.tr. surpass in dancing.

outdare /aʊtˈdeə(r)/ v.tr. 1 outdo in daring. 2 overcome by daring.

outdated /aʊtˈdeɪtɪd/ adj. out of date; obsolete.

outdistance /aʊtˈdɪst(ə)ns/ v.tr. leave (a competitor) behind completely.

outdo /aʊtˈduː/ v.tr. (3rd sing. present -does; past -did; past part. -done) exceed or excel in doing or performance; surpass.

outdoor /ˈaʊtdɔː(r)/ adj. done, existing, or used out of doors.

outdoors /aʊtˈdɔːz/ adv. & n. —adv. in or into the open air; out of doors. —n. the world outside buildings; the open air.

outer /ˈaʊtə(r)/ adj. & n. —adj. 1 outside; external (pierced the outer layer). 2 farther from the centre or inside; relatively far out. 3 objective or physical, not subjective or psychical. —n. 1 a the division of a target furthest from the bull's-eye. b a shot that strikes this. 2 Austral. sl. the part of a racecourse outside the enclosure. □ **outer garments** clothes worn over other clothes or outdoors. **outer space** the universe beyond the earth's atmosphere. **the outer world** people outside one's own circle. [ME f. OUT, replacing UTTER¹]

outermost /ˈaʊtəˌməʊst/ adj. furthest from the inside; the most far out.

outerwear /ˈaʊtəˌweə(r)/ n. = outer garments.

outface /aʊtˈfeɪs/ v.tr. disconcert or defeat by staring or by a display of confidence.

outfall /ˈaʊtfɔːl/ n. the mouth of a river, drain, etc., where it empties into the sea etc.

outfield /ˈaʊtfiːld/ n. 1 the outer part of a cricket or baseball field. 2 outlying land. □ **outfielder** n.

outfight /aʊtˈfaɪt/ v.tr. fight better than; beat in a fight.

outfit /ˈaʊtfɪt/ n. & v. —n. 1 a set of clothes worn or esp. designed to be worn together. 2 a complete set of equipment etc. for a specific purpose. 3 colloq. a group of people regarded as a unit, organization, etc.; a team. —v.tr. (also refl.) (-fitted, -fitting) provide with an outfit, esp. of clothes.

outfitter /ˈaʊtˌfɪtə(r)/ n. a supplier of equipment, esp. of men's clothing; a haberdasher.

outflank /aʊtˈflæŋk/ v.tr. 1 a extend one's flank beyond that of (an enemy). b outmanœuvre (an enemy) in this way. 2 get the better of; confound (an opponent).

outflow /ˈaʊtfləʊ/ n. 1 an outward flow. 2 the amount that flows out.

outfly /aʊtˈflaɪ/ v.tr. (-flies; past -flew; past part. -flown) 1 surpass in flying. 2 fly faster or farther than.

outfox /aʊtˈfɒks/ v.tr. colloq. outwit.

outgeneral /aʊtˈdʒenər(ə)l/ v.tr. (-generalled, -generalling; US -generaled, -generaling) 1 outdo in generalship. 2 get the better of by superior strategy or tactics.

outgoing /ˈaʊtˌɡəʊɪŋ/ adj. & n. —adj. 1 friendly; sociable; extrovert. 2 retiring from office. 3 going out or away. —n. 1 (in pl.) expenditure. 2 the act or an instance of going out.

outgrow /aʊtˈɡrəʊ/ v.tr. (past -grew; past part. -grown) 1 grow too big for (one's clothes). 2 leave behind (a childish habit, taste, ailment, etc.) as one matures. 3 grow faster or taller than (a person, plant, etc.). □ **outgrow one's strength** become lanky and weak through too rapid growth.

outgrowth /ˈaʊtɡrəʊθ/ n. 1 something that grows out. 2 an offshoot; a natural product. 3 the process of growing out.

outguess /aʊtˈɡes/ v.tr. guess correctly what is intended by (another person).

outgun /aʊtˈɡʌn/ v.tr. (-gunned, -gunning) 1 surpass in military or other power or strength. 2 shoot better than.

outhouse /ˈaʊthaʊs/ n. 1 a building, esp. a shed, lean-to, barn, etc. built next to or in the grounds of a house. 2 US an outdoor lavatory.

outing /ˈaʊtɪŋ/ n. 1 a short holiday away from home, esp. of one day or part of a day; a pleasure-trip, an excursion. 2 any brief journey from home. 3 an appearance in an outdoor match, race, etc. 4 US colloq. the practice or policy of exposing the homosexuality of a prominent person. [OUT v. + -ING¹]

outjump /aʊtˈdʒʌmp/ v.tr. surpass in jumping.

outlandish /aʊtˈlændɪʃ/ adj. 1 looking or sounding foreign. 2 bizarre, strange, unfamiliar. □ **outlandishly** adv. **outlandishness** n. [OE ūtlendisc f. ūtland foreign country f. OUT + LAND]

outlast /aʊtˈlɑːst/ v.tr. last longer than (a person, thing, or duration) (outlasted its usefulness).

outlaw /ˈaʊtlɔː/ n. & v. —n. 1 a fugitive from the law. 2 hist. a person deprived of the protection of the law. —v.tr. 1 declare (a person) an outlaw. 2 make illegal; proscribe (a practice etc.). □ **outlawry** n. [OE ūtlaga, ūtlagian f. ON útlagi f. útlagr outlawed, rel. to OUT, LAW]

outlay /ˈaʊtleɪ/ n. what is spent on something.

outlet /ˈaʊtlet, -lɪt/ n. 1 a means of exit or escape. 2 (usu. foll. by for) a means of expression (of a talent, emotion, etc.) (find an outlet for tension). 3 an agency, distributor, or market for goods (a new retail outlet in China). 4 US a power point. [ME f. OUT- + LET¹]

outline /ˈaʊtlaɪn/ n. & v. —n. 1 a rough draft of a diagram, plan, proposal, etc. 2 a a précis of a proposed novel, article, etc. b a verbal description of essential parts only; a summary. 3 a sketch containing only contour lines. 4 (in sing. or pl.) a lines enclosing or indicating an object (the outline of a shape under the blankets). b a contour. c an external boundary. 5 (in pl.) the main features or general principles (the outlines *of a plan).* —*v.tr.* **1** draw or describe in outline. **2** mark the outline of. □ **in outline** sketched or represented as an outline.

outlive /aʊtˈlɪv/ *v.tr.* **1** live longer than (another person). **2** live beyond (a specified date or time). **3** live through (an experience).

outlook /ˈaʊtlʊk/ *n.* **1** the prospect for the future (*the outlook is bleak*). **2** one's mental attitude or point of view (*narrow in their outlook*). **3** what is seen on looking out.

outlying /ˈaʊtˌlaɪɪŋ/ *adj.* situated far from a centre; remote.

outmanœuvre /ˌaʊtməˈnuːvə(r)/ *v.tr.* (*US* **-maneuver**) **1** use skill and cunning to secure an advantage over (a person). **2** outdo in manœuvring.

outmatch /aʊtˈmætʃ/ *v.tr.* be more than a match for (an opponent etc.); surpass.

outmoded /aʊtˈmoʊdɪd/ *adj.* **1** no longer in fashion. **2** obsolete. □ **outmodedly** *adv.* **outmodedness** *n.*

outnumber /aʊtˈnʌmbə(r)/ *v.tr.* exceed in number.

outpace /aʊtˈpeɪs/ *v.tr.* **1** go faster than. **2** outdo in a contest.

out-patient /ˈaʊtˌpeɪʃ(ə)nt/ *n.* a hospital patient who is resident at home but attends regular appointments at hospital.

outperform /ˌaʊtpəˈfɔːm/ *v.tr.* **1** perform better than. **2** surpass in a specified field or activity. □ **outperformance** *n.*

outplacement /ˈaʊtˌpleɪsmənt/ *n.* the act or process of finding new employment for esp. executive workers who have been dismissed or made redundant.

outplay /aʊtˈpleɪ/ *v.tr.* surpass in playing; play better than.

outpoint /aʊtˈpɔɪnt/ *v.tr.* (in various sports, esp. boxing) score more points than.

outpost /ˈaʊtpoʊst/ *n.* **1** a detachment set at a distance from the main body of an army, esp. to prevent surprise. **2** a distant branch or settlement. **3** the furthest territory of an (esp. the British) empire.

outpouring /ˈaʊtˌpɔːrɪŋ/ *n.* **1** (usu. in *pl.*) a copious spoken or written expression of emotion. **2** what is poured out.

output /ˈaʊtpʊt/ *n.* & *v.* —*n.* **1** the product of a process, esp. of manufacture, or of mental or artistic work. **2** the quantity or amount of this. **3** the printout, results, etc. supplied by a computer. **4** the power etc. delivered by an apparatus. **5** a place where energy, information, etc. leaves a system. —*v.tr.* (**-putting**; *past* and *past part.* **-put** or **-putted**) **1** put or send out. **2** (of a computer) supply (results etc.).

outrage /ˈaʊtreɪdʒ/ *n.* & *v.* —*n.* **1** an extreme or shocking violation of others' rights, sentiments, etc. **2** a gross offence or indignity. **3** fierce anger or resentment (*a feeling of outrage*). —*v.tr.* **1** subject to outrage. **2** injure, insult, etc. flagrantly. **3** shock and anger. [ME f. OF *outrage* f. *outrer* exceed f. *outre* f. L *ultra* beyond]

outrageous /aʊtˈreɪdʒəs/ *adj.* **1** immoderate. **2** shocking. **3** grossly cruel. **4** immoral, offensive. □ **outrageously** *adv.* **outrageousness** *n.* [ME f. OF *outrageus* (as OUTRAGE)]

outran *past of* OUTRUN.

outrank /aʊtˈræŋk/ *v.tr.* **1** be superior in rank to. **2** take priority over.

outré /ˈuːtreɪ/ *adj.* **1** outside the bounds of what is usual or proper. **2** eccentric or indecorous. [F, past part. of *outrer*: see OUTRAGE]

outreach *v.* & *n.* —*v.tr.* /aʊtˈriːtʃ/ **1** reach further than. **2** surpass. **3** *poet.* stretch out (one's arms etc.). —*n.* /ˈaʊtriːtʃ/ **1 a** any organization's involvement with or influence in the community, esp. in the context of social welfare. **b** the extent of this. **2** the extent or length of reaching out (*an outreach of 38 metres*).

outride /aʊtˈraɪd/ *v.tr.* (*past* **-rode**; *past part.* **-ridden**) **1** ride better, faster, or further than. **2** (of a ship) come safely through (a storm etc.).

outrider /ˈaʊtˌraɪdə(r)/ *n.* **1** a mounted attendant riding ahead of, or with, a carriage etc. **2** a motor cyclist acting as a guard in a similar manner. □ **outriding** *n.*

outrigger /ˈaʊtˌrɪɡə(r)/ *n.* **1** a beam, spar, or framework, rigged out and projecting from or over a ship's side for various purposes. **2** a similar projecting beam etc. in a building. **3** a log etc. fixed parallel to a canoe to stabilize it. **4 a** an iron bracket bearing a rowlock attached horizontally to a boat's side to increase the leverage of the oar. **b** a boat fitted with these. [OUT- + RIG¹: perh. partly after obs. (Naut.) *outligger*]

outright *adv.* & *adj.* —*adv.* /aʊtˈraɪt/ **1** altogether, entirely (*proved outright*). **2** not gradually, nor by degrees, nor by instalments (*bought it outright*). **3** without reservation, openly (*denied the charge outright*). —*adj.* /ˈaʊtraɪt/ **1** downright, direct, complete (*their resentment turned to outright anger*). **2** undisputed, clear (*the outright winner*). □ **outrightness** *n.*

outrode *past of* OUTRIDE.

outrun *v.tr.* /aʊtˈrʌn/ (**-running**; *past* **-ran**; *past part.* **-run**) **1 a** run faster or farther than. **b** escape from. **2** go beyond (a specified point or limit).

outrush /ˈaʊtrʌʃ/ *n.* **1** a rushing out. **2** a violent overflow.

outsail /aʊtˈseɪl/ *v.tr.* sail better or faster than.

outsell /aʊtˈsel/ *v.tr.* (*past* and *past part.* **-sold**) **1** sell more than. **2** be sold in greater quantities than.

outset /ˈaʊtset/ *n.* the start, beginning. □ **at** (or **from**) **the outset** from the beginning.

outshine /aʊtˈʃaɪn/ *v.tr.* (*past* and *past part.* **-shone**) shine brighter than; surpass in ability, excellence, etc.

outshoot /aʊtˈʃuːt/ *v.tr.* (*past* and *past part.* **-shot**) **1** shoot better or further than (another person). **2** esp. *US* score more goals, points, etc. than (another player or team).

outside *n.*, *adj.*, *adv.*, & *prep.* —*n.* /aʊtˈsaɪd, ˈaʊtsaɪd/ **1** the external side or surface; the outer parts (*painted blue on the outside*). **2** the external appearance; the outward aspect of a building etc. **3** (also *attrib.*) all that is without; the world as distinct from the thinking subject (*learn about the outside world*; *viewed from the outside the problem is simple*). **4** a position on the outer side (*the gate opens from the outside*). **5** *colloq.* the highest computation (*it is a mile at the outside*). **6** an outside player in football etc. —*adj.* /ˈaʊtsaɪd/ **1** of or on or nearer the outside; outer. **2** not of or belonging to some circle or institution (*outside help*; *outside work*). **3** (of a chance etc.) remote; very unlikely. **4** (of an estimate etc.) the greatest or highest possible (*the outside price*). **5** (of a player in football etc.) positioned nearest to the edge of the field. —*adv.* /aʊtˈsaɪd/ **1** on or to the outside. **2** in or to the open air. **3** not within or enclosed or included. **4** *sl.* not in prison. —*prep.* /aʊtˈsaɪd/ (also *disp.* foll. by *of*) **1** not in; to or at the exterior of (*meet me outside the post office*). **2** external to, not included in, beyond the limits of (*outside the law*). □ **at the outside** (of an estimate etc.) at the most. **outside broadcast** *Brit.* a broadcast made on location and not in a studio. **outside interest** a hobby; an interest not connected with one's work or normal way of life.

outsider /aʊtˈsaɪdə(r)/ *n.* **1 a** a non-member of some circle, party, profession, etc. **b** an uninitiated person, a layman. **2** a person without special knowledge, breeding, etc., or not fit to mix with good society. **3** a competitor, applicant, etc. thought to have little chance of success.

outsize /ˈaʊtsaɪz/ *adj. & n.* —*adj.* **1** unusually large. **2** (of garments etc.) of an exceptionally large size. —*n.* an exceptionally large person or thing, esp. a garment. □ **outsizeness** *n.*

outskirts /ˈaʊtskɜːts/ *n.pl.* the outer border or fringe of a town, district, subject, etc.

outsmart /aʊtˈsmɑːt/ *v.tr. colloq.* outwit, be cleverer than.

outsold past and past part. of OUTSELL.

outspan /ˈaʊtspæn/ *v.tr.* (also *absol.*) *S.Afr.* (**-spanned, -spanning**) unharness (animals) from a cart, plough, etc. [S.Afr. Du. *uitspannen* unyoke]

outspend /aʊtˈspend/ *v.tr.* (past and past part. **-spent**) spend more than (one's resources or another person).

outspoken /aʊtˈspəʊkən/ *adj.* given to or involving plain speaking; frank in stating one's opinions. □ **outspokenly** *adv.* **outspokenness** *n.*

outspread *adj. & v.* —*adj.* /aʊtˈspred, ˈaʊtspred/ spread out; fully extended or expanded. —*v.tr. & intr.* /aʊtˈspred/ (past and past part. **-spread**) spread out; expand.

outstanding /aʊtˈstændɪŋ/ *adj.* **1 a** conspicuous, eminent, esp. because of excellence. **b** (usu. foll. by *at, in*) remarkable in (a specified field). **2** (esp. of a debt) not yet settled (*£200 still outstanding*). □ **outstandingly** *adv.*

outstare /aʊtˈsteə(r)/ *v.tr.* **1** outdo in staring. **2** abash by staring.

outstation /ˈaʊtˌsteɪʃ(ə)n/ *n.* **1** a branch of an organization, enterprise, or business in a remote area or at a considerable distance from headquarters. **2** esp. *Austral. & NZ* part of a farming estate separate from the main estate.

outstay /aʊtˈsteɪ/ *v.tr.* **1** stay beyond the limit of (one's welcome, invitation, etc.). **2** stay or endure longer than (another person etc.).

outstep /aʊtˈstep/ *v.tr.* (**-stepped, -stepping**) step outside or beyond.

outstretch /ˈaʊtstretʃ, aʊtˈstretʃ/ *v.tr.* **1** (usu. as **outstretched** *adj.*) reach out or stretch out (esp. one's hands or arms). **2** reach or stretch further than.

outstrip /aʊtˈstrɪp/ *v.tr.* (**-stripped, -stripping**) **1** pass in running etc. **2** surpass in competition or relative progress or ability.

out-take /ˈaʊtteɪk/ *n.* a length of film or tape rejected in editing.

out-talk /aʊtˈtɔːk/ *v.tr.* outdo or overcome in talking.

out-think /aʊtˈθɪŋk/ *v.tr.* (past and past part. **-thought**) outwit; outdo in thinking.

out-thrust *adj., v., & n.* —*adj.* /ˈaʊtθrʌst/ extended; projected (*ran forward with out-thrust arms*). —*v.tr.* /aʊtˈθrʌst/ (past and past part. **-thrust**) thrust out. —*n.* /ˈaʊtθrʌst/ **1** the act or an instance of thrusting forcibly outward. **2** the act or an instance of becoming prominent or noticeable.

out-tray /ˈaʊttreɪ/ *n.* a tray for outgoing documents, letters, etc.

out-turn /ˈaʊttɜːn/ *n.* **1** the quantity produced. **2** the result of a process or sequence of events.

outvote /aʊtˈvəʊt/ *v.tr.* defeat by a majority of votes.

outwalk /aʊtˈwɔːk/ *v.tr.* **1** outdo in walking. **2** walk beyond.

outward /ˈaʊtwəd/ *adj., adv., & n.* —*adj.* **1** situated on or directed towards the outside. **2** going out (*on the outward voyage*). **3** bodily, external, apparent, superficial (*in all outward respects*). —*adv.* (also **outwards**) in an outward direction; towards the outside. —*n.* the outward appearance of something; the exterior. □ **outward bound 1** (of a ship, passenger, etc.) going away from home. **2** (**Outward Bound**) (in the UK) a movement to provide adventure training, naval training, and other outdoor activities for young people. □ **outwardly** *adv.* [OE *ūtweard* (as OUT, -WARD)]

outwardness /ˈaʊtwədnɪs/ *n.* external existence; objectivity.

outwards var. of OUTWARD *adv.*

outwash /ˈaʊtwɒʃ/ *n.* the material carried from a glacier by melt water and deposited beyond the moraine.

outwear *v. & n.* —*v.tr.* /aʊtˈweə(r)/ (past **-wore**; past part. **-worn**) **1** exhaust; wear out; wear away. **2** live or last beyond the duration of. **3** (as **outworn** *adj.*) out of date, obsolete. —*n.* /ˈaʊtweə(r)/ outer clothing.

outweigh /aʊtˈweɪ/ *v.tr.* exceed in weight, value, importance, or influence.

outwit /aʊtˈwɪt/ *v.tr.* (**-witted, -witting**) be too clever or crafty for; deceive by greater ingenuity.

outwith /aʊtˈwɪθ/ *prep. Sc.* outside, beyond.

outwore past of OUTWEAR.

outwork /ˈaʊtwɜːk/ *n.* **1** an advanced or detached part of a fortification. **2** work done outside the shop or factory which supplies it. □ **outworker** *n.* (in sense 2).

outworn past part. of OUTWEAR.

ouzel /ˈuːz(ə)l/ *n.* (also **ousel**) **1** = *ring ouzel*. **2** a diving bird, *Cinclus cinclus*. **3** *archaic* a blackbird. [OE *ōsle* blackbird, prob. f. Gmc]

ouzo /ˈuːzəʊ/ *n.* (pl. **-os**) a Greek aniseed-flavoured spirit. [mod.Gk]

ova pl. of OVUM.

oval /ˈəʊv(ə)l/ *adj. & n.* —*adj.* **1** egg-shaped, ellipsoidal. **2** having the outline of an egg, elliptical. —*n.* **1** an egg-shaped or elliptical closed curve. **2** any object with an oval outline. **3** *Austral.* a ground for Australian Rules football. □ **Oval Office** the office of the US President in the White House. □ **ovality** /-ˈvælɪtɪ/ *n.* **ovally** *adv.* **ovalness** *n.* [med.L *ovalis* (as OVUM)]

ovary /ˈəʊvərɪ/ *n.* (pl. **-ies**) **1** each of the female reproductive organs in which ova are produced. **2** the hollow base of the carpel of a flower, containing one or more ovules. □ **ovarian**

/ə'veərɪən/ adj. **ovariectomy** /-rɪ'ektəmɪ/ n. (pl. **-ies**) (in sense 1). **ovariotomy** /-rɪ'ɒtəmɪ/ n. (pl. **-ies**) (in sense 1). **ovaritis** /-'raɪtɪs/ n. (in sense 1). [mod.L *ovarium* (as OVUM)]

ovate /'əʊveɪt/ adj. Biol. egg-shaped as a solid or in outline; oval. [L *ovatus* (as OVUM)]

ovation /əʊ'veɪʃ(ə)n/ n. an enthusiastic reception, esp. spontaneous and sustained applause. □ **standing ovation** prolonged applause during which the crowd or audience rise to their feet. □ **ovational** adj. [L *ovatio* f. *ovare* exult]

oven /'ʌv(ə)n/ n. **1** an enclosed compartment of brick, stone, or metal for cooking food. **2** a chamber for heating or drying. □ **oven-ready** (of food) prepared before sale so as to be ready for immediate cooking in the oven. [OE *ofen* f. Gmc]

ovenproof /'ʌv(ə)n,pruːf/ adj. suitable for use in an oven; heat-resistant.

ovenware /'ʌv(ə)n,weə(r)/ n. dishes that can be used for cooking food in the oven.

over /'əʊvə(r)/ adv., prep., n., & adj. —adv. expressing movement or position or state above or beyond something stated or implied: **1** outward and downward from a brink or from any erect position (*knocked the man over*). **2** so as to cover or touch a whole surface (*paint it over*). **3** so as to produce a fold, or reverse a position; with the effect of being upside down. **4 a** across a street or other space (*decided to cross over; came over from America*). **b** for a visit etc. (*invited them over last night*). **5** with transference or change from one hand or part to another (*went over to the enemy; swapped them over*). **6** with motion above something; so as to pass across something (*climb over; fly over; boil over*). **7** from beginning to end with repetition or detailed concentration (*think it over; did it six times over*). **8** in excess; more than is right or required (*left over*). **9** for or until a later time (*hold it over*). **10** at an end; settled (*the crisis is over; all is over between us*). **11** (in full **over to you**) (as *int.*) (in radio conversations etc.) said to indicate that it is the other person's turn to speak. —prep. **1** above, in, or to a position higher than; upon. **2** out and down from; down from the edge of (*fell over the cliff*). **3** so as to cover (*a hat over his eyes*). **4** above and across; so as to clear (*flew over the North Pole; a bridge over the Thames*). **5** concerning; engaged with; as a result of; while occupied with (*laughed over a good joke; fell asleep over the newspaper*). **6 a** in superiority of; superior to; in charge of (*a victory over the enemy; reign over three kingdoms*). **b** in preference to. **7** divided by. **8 a** throughout; covering the extent of (*travelled over most of Africa; a blush spread over his face*). **b** so as to deal with completely (*went over the plans*). **9 a** for the duration of (*stay over Saturday night*). **b** at any point during the course of (*I'll do it over the weekend*). **10** beyond; more than (*bids of over £50; are you over 18?*). **11** transmitted by (*heard it over the radio*). **12** in comparison with (*gained 20% over last year*). **13** having recovered from (*am now over my cold; will get over it in time*). —n. Cricket **1** a sequence of balls (now usu. six), bowled from one end of the pitch. **2** play resulting from this (*a maiden over*). —adj. (see also OVER-). **1** upper, outer. **2** superior. **3** extra. □ **begin** (or **start** etc.) **over** US begin again. **get it over with** do or undergo something unpleasant etc. so as to be rid of it. **give over** (usu. as *int.*) *colloq.* stop

talking. **not over** not very; not at all (*not over friendly*). **over again** once again, again from the beginning. **over against** in an opposite situation to; adjacent to, in contrast with. **over-age** over a certain age limit. **over all** taken as a whole. **over and above** in addition to; not to mention (*£100 over and above the asking price*). **over and over** so that the same thing or the same point comes up again and again (*said it over and over; rolled it over and over*). **over-the-top** *colloq.* (esp. of behaviour, dress, etc.) outrageous, excessive. **over the way** (in a street etc.) facing or opposite. [OE *ofer* f. Gmc]

over- /'əʊvə(r)/ prefix added to verbs, nouns, adjectives, and adverbs, meaning: **1** excessively; to an unwanted degree (*overheat; overdue*). **2** upper, outer, extra (*overcoat; overtime*). **3** 'over' in various senses (*overhang; overshadow*). **4** completely, utterly (*overawe; overjoyed*).

over-abundant /,əʊvərə'bʌnd(ə)nt/ adj. in excessive quantity. □ **over-abound** /-'baʊnd/ v.intr. **over-abundance** n. **over-abundantly** adv.

overachieve /,əʊvərə'tʃiːv/ v. **1** intr. do more than might be expected (esp. scholastically). **2** tr. achieve more than (an expected goal or objective etc.). □ **overachievement** n. **overachiever** n.

overact /,əʊvər'ækt/ v.tr. & intr. act in an exaggerated manner.

over-active /,əʊvər'æktɪv/ adj. excessively active. □ **over-activity** /-'tɪvɪtɪ/ n.

overall adj., adv., & n. —adj. /'əʊvər,ɔːl/ **1** from end to end (*overall length*). **2** total, inclusive of all (*overall cost*). —adv. /,əʊvər'ɔːl/ in all parts; taken as a whole (*overall, the performance was excellent*). —n. /'əʊvər,ɔːl/ **1** Brit. an outer garment worn to keep out dirt, wet, etc. **2** (in pl.) protective trousers, dungarees, or a combination suit, worn by workmen etc. □ **overalled** /'əʊvər,ɔːld/ adj.

overambitious /,əʊvəræm'bɪʃəs/ adj. excessively ambitious. □ **overambition** n. **overambitiously** adv.

over-anxious /,əʊvər'æŋkʃəs/ adj. excessively anxious. □ **over-anxiety** /-æŋ'zaɪɪtɪ/ n. **over-anxiously** adv.

overarch /,əʊvər'ɑːtʃ/ v.tr. form an arch over. □ **overarching** adj.

overarm /'əʊvər,ɑːm/ adj. & adv. **1** Cricket & Tennis etc. with the hand above the shoulder (*bowl it overarm; an overarm service*). **2** Swimming with one or both arms lifted out of the water during a stroke.

overate past of OVEREAT.

overawe /,əʊvər'ɔː/ v.tr. **1** restrain by awe. **2** keep in awe.

overbalance /,əʊvə'bæləns/ v. **1** tr. cause (a person or thing) to lose its balance and fall. **2** intr. fall over, capsize. **3** tr. outweigh.

overbear /,əʊvə'beə(r)/ v.tr. (past **-bore**; past part. **-borne**) **1** (as **overbearing** adj.) a domineering, masterful. **b** overpowering. **2** bear down; upset by weight, force, or emotional pressure. **3** put down or repress by power or authority. □ **overbearingly** adv. **overbearingness** n.

overbid v. & n. —v. /,əʊvə'bɪd/ (**-bidding**; past and past part. **-bid**) **1** tr. make a higher bid than. **2** tr. (also absol.) Bridge bid more on (one's hand) than warranted. —n. /'əʊvəbɪd/ a bid that is higher than another, or higher than is justified. □ **overbidder** n.

overblouse /ˈəʊvəˌblaʊz/ n. a garment like a blouse, but worn without tucking it into a skirt or trousers.

overblown /ˌəʊvəˈbləʊn/ adj. **1** excessively inflated or pretentious. **2** (of a flower or a woman's beauty etc.) past its prime.

overboard /ˈəʊvəˌbɔːd/ adv. from on a ship into the water (fall overboard). □ **go overboard 1** be highly enthusiastic. **2** behave immoderately; go too far. **throw overboard** abandon, discard.

overbold /ˌəʊvəˈbəʊld/ adj. excessively bold.

overbook /ˌəʊvəˈbʊk/ v.tr. (also absol.) make too many bookings for (an aircraft, hotel, etc.).

overbore past of OVERBEAR.

overborne past part. of OVERBEAR.

overbought past and past part. of OVERBUY.

overburden /ˌəʊvəˈbɜːd(ə)n/ —v.tr. burden (a person, thing, etc.) to excess. □ **overburdensome** adj.

overbuy /ˌəʊvəˈbaɪ/ v.tr. & intr. (past and past part. **-bought**) buy (a commodity etc.) in excess of immediate need.

overcame past of OVERCOME.

overcapacity /ˌəʊvəkəˈpæsɪtɪ/ n. a state of saturation or an excess of productive capacity.

overcapitalize /ˌəʊvəˈkæpɪtəˌlaɪz/ v.tr. (also **-ise**) fix or estimate the capital of (a company etc.) too high.

overcareful /ˌəʊvəˈkeəfʊl/ adj. excessively careful. □ **overcarefully** adv.

overcast adj., v., & n. —adj. /ˈəʊvəˌkɑːst/ **1** (of the sky, weather, etc.) covered with cloud; dull and gloomy. **2** (in sewing) edged with stitching to prevent fraying. —v.tr. /ˌəʊvəˈkɑːst/ (past and past part. **-cast**) **1** cover (the sky etc.) with clouds or darkness. **2** stitch over (a raw edge etc.) to prevent fraying. —n. /ˈəʊvəˌkɑːst/ a cloud covering part of the sky.

overcautious /ˌəʊvəˈkɔːʃəs/ adj. excessively cautious. □ **overcaution** n. **overcautiously** adv. **overcautiousness** n.

overcharge /ˌəʊvəˈtʃɑːdʒ/ v.tr. **1** charge too high a price to (a person) or for (a thing). **2** put too much charge into (a battery, gun, etc.).

overcloud /ˌəʊvəˈklaʊd/ v.tr. **1** cover with cloud. **2** mar, spoil, or dim, esp. as the result of anxiety etc. (overclouded by uncertainties).

overcoat /ˈəʊvəˌkəʊt/ n. a heavy coat, esp. one worn over indoor clothes.

overcome /ˌəʊvəˈkʌm/ v. (past **-came**; past part. **-come**) **1** tr. prevail over, master, conquer. **2** tr. (as **overcome** adj.) **a** exhausted, made helpless. **b** (usu. foll. by with, by) affected by (emotion etc.). **3** intr. be victorious. [OE ofercuman (as OVER-, COME)]

overcompensate /ˌəʊvəˈkɒmpenˌseɪt/ v. **1** tr. (usu. foll. by for) compensate excessively for (something). **2** intr. Psychol. strive for power etc. in an exaggerated way, esp. to make allowance or amends for a real or fancied grievance, defect, handicap, etc. □ **overcompensation** /-penˈseɪʃ(ə)n/ n. **overcompensatory** /-ˈseɪtərɪ/ adj.

overconfident /ˌəʊvəˈkɒnfɪd(ə)nt/ adj. excessively confident. □ **overconfidence** n. **overconfidently** adv.

overcook /ˌəʊvəˈkʊk/ v.tr. cook too much or for too long. □ **overcooked** adj.

overcritical /ˌəʊvəˈkrɪtɪk(ə)l/ adj. excessively critical; quick to find fault.

overcrop /ˌəʊvəˈkrɒp/ v.tr. (**-cropped, -cropping**) exhaust (the land) by the continuous growing of crops.

overcrowd /ˌəʊvəˈkraʊd/ v.tr. fill (a space, object, etc.) beyond what is usual or comfortable. □ **overcrowding** n.

overdevelop /ˌəʊvədɪˈveləp/ v.tr. (**-developed, -developing**) **1** develop too much. **2** Photog. treat with developer for too long.

overdo /ˌəʊvəˈduː/ v.tr. (3rd sing. present **-does**; past **-did**; past part. **-done**) **1** carry to excess, go too far, exaggerate (I think you overdid the sarcasm). **2** (esp. as **overdone** adj.) overcook. □ **overdo it** (or **things**) exhaust oneself. [OE oferdōn (as OVER-, DO¹)]

overdose /ˈəʊvəˌdəʊs/ n. & v. —n. an excessive dose (of a drug etc.). —v.tr. give an excessive dose of (a drug etc.) or to (a person). □ **overdosage** /ˌəʊvəˈdəʊsɪdʒ/ n.

overdraft /ˈəʊvəˌdrɑːft/ n. **1** a deficit in a bank account caused by drawing more money than is credited to it. **2** the amount of this.

overdraw /ˌəʊvəˈdrɔː/ v. (past **-drew**; past part. **-drawn**) **1** tr. **a** draw a sum of money in excess of the amount credited to (one's bank account). **b** (as **overdrawn** adj.) having overdrawn one's account. **2** intr. overdraw one's account. **3** tr. exaggerate in describing or depicting. □ **overdrawer** n. (in senses 1 & 2).

overdress v. & n. —v. /ˌəʊvəˈdres/ **1** tr. dress with too much display or formality. **2** intr. overdress oneself. —n. /ˈəʊvəˌdres/ a dress worn over another dress or a blouse etc.

overdrive /ˈəʊvəˌdraɪv/ n. **1 a** a mechanism in a motor vehicle providing a gear ratio higher than that of the usual gear. **b** an additional speed-increasing gear. **2** (usu. prec. by in, into) a state of high or excessive activity.

overdub v. & n. —v. /ˌəʊvəˈdʌb/ (**-dubbed, -dubbing**) (also absol.) impose (additional sounds) on an existing recording. —n. /ˈəʊvəˌdʌb/ the act or an instance of overdubbing.

overdue /ˌəʊvəˈdjuː/ adj. **1** past the time when due or ready. **2** not yet paid, arrived, born, etc., though after the expected time.

overeager /ˌəʊvərˈiːɡə(r)/ adj. excessively eager. □ **overeagerly** adv. **overeagerness** n.

overeat /ˌəʊvərˈiːt/ v.intr. & refl. (past **-ate**; past part. **-eaten**) eat too much.

overelaborate /ˌəʊvərɪˈlæbərət/ adj. excessively elaborate. □ **overelaborately** adv.

over-emotional /ˌəʊvərɪˈməʊʃən(ə)l/ adj. excessively emotional. □ **over-emotionally** adv.

overemphasis /ˌəʊvərˈemfəsɪs/ n. excessive emphasis. □ **overemphasize** /-fəˌsaɪz/ v.tr. & intr. (also **-ise**).

overenthusiasm /ˌəʊvərɪnˈθjuːzɪˌæz(ə)m, -ˈθuː zɪˌæz(ə)m/ n. excessive enthusiasm. □ **overenthusiastic** /-ˈæstɪk/ adj. **overenthusiastically** /-ˈæstɪkəlɪ/ adv.

overestimate /ˌəʊvərˈestɪˌmeɪt/ v. & n. —v.tr. (also absol.) form too high an estimate of (a person, ability, cost, etc.). —n. too high an estimate. □ **overestimation** /-ˈmeɪʃ(ə)n/ n.

overexcite /ˌəʊvərɪkˈsaɪt/ v.tr. excite excessively. □ **overexcitement** n.

over-exercise /ˌəʊvərˈeksəˌsaɪz/ v. & n. —v. **1** tr. use or exert (a part of the body, one's authority, etc.) too much. **2** *intr.* take too much exercise; overexert oneself. —*n.* excessive exercise.

overexert /ˌəʊvərɪgˈzɜːt/ *v.tr.* & *refl.* exert too much. □ **overexertion** /-ɪgˈzɜːʃ(ə)n/ *n.*

overexpose /ˌəʊvərɪkˈspəʊz/ *v.tr.* (also *absol.*) expose too much, esp. to the public eye. **2** *Photog.* expose (film) for too long. □ **overexposure** *n.*

overextend /ˌəʊvərɪkˈstend/ *v.tr.* **1** extend (a thing) too far. **2** (also *refl.*) take on (oneself) or impose on (another person) an excessive burden of work.

overfamiliar /ˌəʊvəfəˈmɪlɪə(r)/ *adj.* excessively familiar.

overfeed /ˌəʊvəˈfiːd/ *v.tr.* (*past* and *past part.* **-fed**) feed excessively.

overfill /ˌəʊvəˈfɪl/ *v.tr.* & *intr.* fill to excess or to overflowing.

overfish /ˌəʊvəˈfɪʃ/ *v.tr.* deplete (a stream etc.) by too much fishing.

overflow *v.* & *n.* —*v.* /ˌəʊvəˈfləʊ/ **1** *tr.* **a** flow over (the brim, limits, etc.). **b** flow over the brim or limits of. **2** *intr.* **a** (of a receptacle etc.) be so full that the contents overflow it (*until the cup was overflowing*). **b** (of contents) overflow a container. **3** *tr.* (of a crowd etc.) extend beyond the limits of (a room etc.). **4** *tr.* flood (a surface or area). **5** *intr.* (foll. by *with*) be full of. **6** *intr.* (of kindness, a harvest, etc.) be very abundant. —*n.* /ˈəʊvəˌfləʊ/ (also *attrib.*) **1** what overflows or is superfluous (*mop up the overflow*; *put the overflow audience in another room*). **2** an instance of overflowing (*overflow occurs when both systems are run together*). **3** (esp. in a bath or sink) an outlet for excess water etc. **4** *Computing* the generation of a number having more digits than the assigned location. □ **overflow meeting** a meeting for those who cannot be accommodated at the main gathering. [OE *oferflōwan* (as OVER-, FLOW)]

overfly /ˌəʊvəˈflaɪ/ *v.tr.* (**-flies**; *past* **-flew**; *past part.* **-flown**) fly over or beyond (a place or territory). □ **overflight** /ˈəʊvəˌflaɪt/ *n.*

overfond /ˌəʊvəˈfɒnd/ *adj.* (often foll. by *of*) having too great an affection or liking (for a person or thing) (*overfond of chocolate*; *an overfond parent*). □ **overfondly** *adv.* **overfondness** *n.*

overfulfil /ˌəʊvəfʊlˈfɪl/ *v.tr.* (US **-fulfill**) (**-fulfilled**, **-fulfilling**) fulfil (a plan, quota, etc.) beyond expectation or before the appointed time. □ **overfulfilment** *n.*

overfull /ˌəʊvəˈfʊl/ *adj.* filled excessively or to overflowing.

overgenerous /ˌəʊvəˈdʒenərəs/ *adj.* excessively generous. □ **overgenerously** *adv.*

overground /ˈəʊvəˌɡraʊnd/ *adj.* **1** raised above the ground. **2** not underground.

overgrow /ˌəʊvəˈɡrəʊ/ *v.tr.* (*past* **-grew**; *past part.* **-grown**) **1** (as **overgrown** *adj.* /ˌəʊvəˈɡrəʊn, ˈəʊvəˌɡrəʊn/) **a** abnormally large (*a great overgrown child*). **b** wild; grown over with vegetation (*an overgrown pond*). **2** grow over, overspread, esp. so as to choke (*nettles have overgrown the pathway*). □ **overgrowth** *n.*

overhand /ˈəʊvəˌhænd/ *adj.* & *adv.* **1** (in cricket, tennis, baseball, etc.) thrown or played with the hand above the shoulder. **2** *Swimming* = OVERARM. □ **overhand knot** a simple knot made by forming a loop and passing the free end through it.

overhang *v.* & *n.* —*v.* /ˌəʊvəˈhæŋ/ (*past* and *past part.* **-hung**) **1** *tr.* & *intr.* project or jut over. **2** *tr.* menace, preoccupy, threaten. —*n.* /ˈəʊvəˌhæŋ/

1 the overhanging part of a structure or rock-formation. **2** the amount by which this projects.

overhaul *v.* & *n.* —*v.tr.* /ˌəʊvəˈhɔːl/ **1 a** take to pieces in order to examine. **b** examine the condition of (and repair if necessary). **2** overtake. —*n.* /ˈəʊvəˌhɔːl/ a thorough examination, with repairs if necessary. [orig. Naut., = release (rope-tackle) by slackening]

overhead *adv.*, *adj.*, & *n.* —*adv.* /ˌəʊvəˈhed/ **1** above one's head. **2** in the sky or in the storey above. —*adj.* /ˈəʊvəhed/ **1** (of a driving mechanism etc.) above the object driven. **2** (of expenses) arising from general running costs, as distinct from particular business transactions. —*n.* /ˈəʊvəˌhed/ (in *pl.* or *US* in *sing.*) overhead expenses. □ **overhead projector** a device that projects an enlarged image of a transparency on to a surface above and behind the user.

overhear /ˌəʊvəˈhɪə(r)/ *v.tr.* (*past* and *past part.* **-heard**) (also *absol.*) hear as an eavesdropper or as an unperceived or unintentional listener.

overheat /ˌəʊvəˈhiːt/ *v.* **1** *tr.* & *intr.* make or become too hot; heat to excess. **2** (as **over-heated** *adj.*) too passionate about a matter.

overindulge /ˌəʊvərɪnˈdʌldʒ/ *v.tr.* & *intr.* indulge to excess. □ **overindulgence** *n.* **overindulgent** *adj.*

overinsure /ˌəʊvərɪnˈʃʊə(r)/ *v.tr.* insure (property etc.) for more than its real value; insure excessively. □ **overinsurance** *n.*

overjoyed /ˌəʊvəˈdʒɔɪd/ *adj.* (often foll. by *at*, *to hear*, etc.) filled with great joy.

overkill *n.* & *v.* —*n.* /ˈəʊvəkɪl/ **1** the amount by which destruction or the capacity for destruction exceeds what is necessary for victory or annihilation. **2** excess; excessive behaviour. —*v.tr.* & *intr.* /ˈəʊvəkɪl, ˌəʊvəˈkɪl/ kill or destroy to a greater extent than necessary.

overladen /ˌəʊvəˈleɪd(ə)n/ *adj.* bearing or carrying too large a load.

overlaid *past* and *past part.* of OVERLAY[1].

overlain *past part.* of OVERLIE.

overland /ˈəʊvəˌlænd, ˌəʊvəˈlænd/ *adj.* & *adv.* **1** by land. **2** not by sea.

overlap *v.* & *n.* —*v.* /ˌəʊvəˈlæp/ (**-lapped**, **-lapping**) **1** *tr.* (of part of an object) partly cover (another object). **2** *tr.* cover and extend beyond. **3** *intr.* (of two things) partly coincide; not be completely separate. —*n.* /ˈəʊvəˌlæp/ **1** an instance of overlapping. **2** the amount of this.

over-large /ˌəʊvəˈlɑːdʒ/ *adj.* too large.

overlay[1] *v.* & *n.* —*v.tr.* /ˌəʊvəˈleɪ/ (*past* and *past part.* **-laid**) **1** lay over. **2** (foll. by *with*) cover the surface of (a thing) with (a coating etc.). **3** overlie. —*n.* /ˈəʊvəˌleɪ/ **1** a thing laid over another. **2** (in printing, mapreading, etc.) a transparent sheet to be superimposed on another sheet.

overlay[2] *past* of OVERLIE.

overleaf /ˌəʊvəˈliːf/ *adv.* on the other side of the leaf (of a book) (*see the diagram overleaf*).

overlie /ˌəʊvəˈlaɪ/ *v.tr.* (**-lying**; *past* **-lay**; *past part.* **-lain**) **1** lie on top of. **2** smother (a child etc.) by lying on top.

overload *v.* & *n.* —*v.tr.* /ˌəʊvəˈləʊd/ load excessively; force (a person, thing, etc.) beyond normal or reasonable capacity. —*n.* /ˈəʊvəˌləʊd/ an excessive quantity; a demand etc. which surpasses capability or capacity.

over-long /ˌəʊvəˈlɒŋ/ *adj.* & *adv.* too or excessively long.

overlook *v.* & *n.* —*v.tr.* /ˌəʊvəˈlʊk/ **1** fail to notice; ignore; condone (an offence etc.). **2** have a view from above, be higher than. **3** supervise, oversee. —*n.* /ˈəʊvəˌlʊk/ *US* a commanding position or view. □ **overlooker** /ˈəʊvəˌlʊkə(r)/ *n.*

overlord /ˈəʊvəˌlɔːd/ *n.* a supreme lord. □ **overlordship** *n.*

overly /ˈəʊvəli/ *adv.* esp. *US* & *Sc.* excessively; too.

overlying *pres. part.* of OVERLIE.

overman *v.tr.* /ˌəʊvəˈmæn/ (**-manned, -manning**) provide with too large a crew, staff, etc.

overmantel /ˈəʊvəˌmænt(ə)l/ *n.* ornamental shelves etc. over a mantelpiece.

overmaster /ˌəʊvəˈmɑːstə(r)/ *v.tr.* master completely, conquer. □ **overmastering** *adj.* **overmastery** *n.*

over-much /ˌəʊvəˈmʌtʃ/ *adv.* & *adj.* —*adv.* to too great an extent; excessively. —*adj.* excessive; superabundant.

over-nice /ˌəʊvəˈnaɪs/ *adj.* excessively fussy, punctilious, particular, etc. □ **over-niceness** *n.* **over-nicety** *n.*

overnight /ˌəʊvəˈnaɪt/ *adv.* & *adj.* —*adv.* **1** for the duration of a night (*stay overnight*). **2** during the course of a night. **3** suddenly, immediately (*the situation changed overnight*). —*adj.* **1** for use overnight (*an overnight bag*). **2** done etc. overnight (*an overnight stop*).

overpaid *past* and *past part.* of OVERPAY.

over-particular /ˌəʊvəpəˈtɪkjʊlə(r)/ *adj.* excessively particular or fussy.

overpass *n.* & *v.* —*n.* /ˈəʊvəˌpɑːs/ a road or railway line that passes over another by means of a bridge. —*v.tr.* /ˌəʊvəˈpɑːs/ **1** pass over or across or beyond. **2** get to the end of; surmount. **3** (as **overpassed** or **overpast** *adj.*) that has gone by, past.

overpay /ˌəʊvəˈpeɪ/ *v.tr.* (*past* and *past part.* **-paid**) recompense (a person, service, etc.) too highly. □ **overpayment** *n.*

overpitch /ˌəʊvəˈpɪtʃ/ *v.tr.* **1** *Cricket* bowl (a ball) so that it pitches or would pitch too near the stumps. **2** exaggerate.

overplay /ˌəʊvəˈpleɪ/ *v.tr.* play (a part) to excess; give undue importance to; overemphasize. □ **overplay one's hand 1** be unduly optimistic about one's capabilities. **2** spoil a good case by exaggerating its value.

overpopulated /ˌəʊvəˈpɒpjʊˌleɪtɪd/ *adj.* having too large a population. □ **overpopulation** /-ˈleɪʃ(ə)n/ *n.*

overpower /ˌəʊvəˈpaʊə(r)/ *v.tr.* **1** reduce to submission, subdue. **2** make (a thing) ineffective or imperceptible by greater intensity. **3** (of heat, emotion, etc.) be too intense for, overwhelm. □ **overpowering** *adj.* **overpoweringly** *adv.*

overprice /ˌəʊvəˈpraɪs/ *v.tr.* price (a thing) too highly.

overprint *v.* & *n.* —*v.tr.* /ˌəʊvəˈprɪnt/ **1** print further matter on (a surface already printed). **2** print (further matter) in this way. —*n.* /ˈəʊvəprɪnt/ the words etc. overprinted.

overproduce /ˌəʊvəprəˈdjuːs/ *tr.* (usu. *absol.*) **1** produce more of (a commodity) than is wanted. **2** produce to an excessive degree. □ **overproduction** *n.*

overqualified /ˌəʊvəˈkwɒlɪˌfaɪd/ *adj.* too highly qualified (esp. for a particular job etc.).

overran *past* of OVERRUN.

overrate /ˌəʊvəˈreɪt/ *v.tr.* assess too highly.

overreach /ˌəʊvəˈriːtʃ/ *v.tr.* circumvent, outwit; get the better of by cunning or artifice. □ **overreach oneself 1** strain oneself by reaching too far. **2** defeat one's object by going too far.

overreact /ˌəʊvərɪˈækt/ *v.intr.* respond more forcibly etc. than is justified. □ **overreaction** *n.*

overrefine /ˌəʊvərɪˈfaɪn/ *v.tr.* (also *absol.*) **1** refine too much. **2** make too subtle distinctions in (an argument etc.).

override *v.* & *n.* —*v.tr.* /ˌəʊvəˈraɪd/ (*past* **-rode**; *past part.* **-ridden**) **1** have or claim precedence or superiority over (*an overriding consideration*). **2 a** intervene and make ineffective. **b** interrupt the action of (an automatic device) esp. to take manual control. **3** supersede arrogantly. —*n.* /ˈəʊvəˌraɪd/ **1** the action or process of suspending an automatic function. **2** a device for this.

overripe /ˌəʊvəˈraɪp/ *adj.* (esp. of fruit etc.) past its best; excessively ripe; full-blown.

overrode *past* of OVERRIDE.

overrule /ˌəʊvəˈruːl/ *v.tr.* **1** set aside (a decision, argument, proposal, etc.) by exercising a superior authority. **2** annul a decision by or reject a proposal of (a person) in this way.

overrun *v.* & *n.* —*v.tr.* /ˌəʊvəˈrʌn/ (**-running**; *past* **-ran**; *past part.* **-run**) **1** (of vermin, weeds, etc.) swarm or spread over. **2** conquer or ravage (territory) by force. **3** (of time, expenditure, production, etc.) exceed (a fixed limit). **4** *Printing* carry over (a word etc.) to the next line or page. —*n.* /ˈəʊvəˌrʌn/ **1** an instance of overrunning. **2** the amount of this. [OE *oferyrnan* (as OVER-, RUN)]

oversaw *past* of OVERSEE.

overscrupulous /ˌəʊvəˈskruːpjʊləs/ *adj.* excessively scrupulous or particular.

overseas *adv.* & *adj.* —*adv.* /ˌəʊvəˈsiːz/ (also **oversea**) abroad (*was sent overseas for training; came back from overseas*). —*adj.* /ˈəʊvəˌsiːz/ (also **oversea**) **1** foreign; across or beyond the sea. **2** of or connected with movement or transport over the sea (*overseas postage rates*).

oversee /ˌəʊvəˈsiː/ *v.tr.* (**-sees**; *past* **-saw**; *past part.* **-seen**) officially supervise (workers, work, etc.). [OE *ofersēon* look at from above (as OVER-, SEE¹)]

overseer /ˈəʊvəˌsiːə(r)/ *n.* a person who supervises others, esp. workers. [OVERSEE]

oversell /ˌəʊvəˈsel/ *v.tr.* (*past* and *past part.* **-sold**) (also *absol.*) **1** sell more of (a commodity etc.) than one can deliver. **2** exaggerate the merits of.

over-sensitive /ˌəʊvəˈsensɪtɪv/ *adj.* excessively sensitive; easily hurt by, or too quick to react to, outside influences. □ **over-sensitiveness** *n.* **over-sensitivity** /-ˈtɪvɪtɪ/ *n.*

overset /ˌəʊvəˈset/ *v.tr.* (**-setting**; *past* and *past part.* **-set**) overturn, upset.

oversew /ˈəʊvəˌsəʊ/ *v.tr.* (*past part.* **-sewn** or **-sewed**) sew (two edges) with every stitch passing over the join.

oversexed /ˌəʊvəˈsekst/ *adj.* having unusually strong sexual desires.

overshadow /ˌəʊvəˈʃædəʊ/ *v.tr.* **1** appear much more prominent or important than. **2** cast into the shade; shelter from the sun. [OE *ofersceadwian* (as OVER-, SHADOW)]

overshoe /ˈəʊvəˌʃuː/ n. a shoe of rubber, felt, etc., worn over another as protection from wet, cold, etc.

overshoot v. & n. —v.tr. /ˌəʊvəˈʃuːt/ (past and past part. **-shot**) **1** pass or send beyond (a target or limit). **2** (of an aircraft) fly beyond or taxi too far along (the runway) when landing or taking off. —n. /ˈəʊvəˌʃuːt/ **1** the act of overshooting. **2** the amount of this. □ **overshoot the mark** go beyond what is intended or proper; go too far.

oversight /ˈəʊvəˌsaɪt/ n. **1** a failure to notice something. **2** an inadvertent mistake. **3** supervision.

oversimplify /ˌəʊvəˈsɪmplɪˌfaɪ/ v.tr. (**-ies, -ied**) (also absol.) distort (a problem etc.) by stating it in too simple terms. □ **oversimplification** /-fɪˈkeɪʃ(ə)n/ n.

oversize /ˈəʊvəˌsaɪz/ adj. (also **-sized** /-ˌsaɪzd/) of more than the usual size.

overskirt /ˈəʊvəˌskɜːt/ n. an outer or second skirt.

oversleep /ˌəʊvəˈsliːp/ v.intr. & refl. (past and past part. **-slept**) **1** continue sleeping beyond the intended time of waking. **2** sleep too long.

oversleeve /ˈəʊvəˌsliːv/ n. a protective sleeve covering an ordinary sleeve.

oversold past and past part. of OVERSELL.

oversolicitous /ˌəʊvəsəˈlɪsɪtəs/ adj. excessively worried, anxious, eager, etc. □ **oversolicitude** n.

overspecialize /ˌəʊvəˈspeʃəˌlaɪz/ v.intr. (also **-ise**) concentrate too much on one aspect or area. □ **overspecialization** /-ˈzeɪʃ(ə)n/ n.

overspend /ˌəʊvəˈspend/ v. (past and past part. **-spent**) **1** intr. & refl. spend too much. **2** tr. spend more than (a specified amount).

overspill /ˈəʊvəspɪl/ n. **1** what is spilt over or overflows. **2** the surplus population leaving a country or city to live elsewhere.

overspread /ˌəʊvəˈspred/ v.tr. (past and past part. **-spread**) **1** become spread or diffused over. **2** cover or occupy the surface of. [OE ofersprædan (as OVER-, SPREAD)]

overstaff /ˌəʊvəˈstɑːf/ v.tr. provide with too large a staff.

overstate /ˌəʊvəˈsteɪt/ v.tr. **1** state (esp. a case or argument) too strongly. **2** exaggerate. □ **overstatement** n.

overstay /ˌəʊvəˈsteɪ/ v.tr. stay longer than (one's welcome, a time limit, etc.).

oversteer /ˈəʊvəˌstɪə(r)/ v. & n. —v.intr. (of a motor vehicle) have a tendency to turn more sharply than was intended. —n. this tendency.

overstep /ˌəʊvəˈstep/ v.tr. (**-stepped, -stepping**) **1** pass beyond (a boundary or mark). **2** violate (certain standards of behaviour etc.).

overstock /ˌəʊvəˈstɒk/ v.tr. stock excessively.

overstrain /ˌəʊvəˈstreɪn/ v.tr. strain too much.

overstress /ˌəʊvəˈstres/ v. & n. —v.tr. stress too much. —n. an excessive degree of stress.

overstretch /ˌəʊvəˈstretʃ/ v.tr. **1** stretch too much. **2** (esp. as **overstretched** adj.) make excessive demands on (resources, a person, etc.).

overstrung adj. /ˌəʊvəˈstrʌŋ/ (of a person, disposition, etc.) intensely strained, highly strung.

overstuff /ˌəʊvəˈstʌf/ v.tr. **1** stuff more than is necessary. **2** (as **overstuffed** adj.) (of furniture) made soft and comfortable by thick upholstery.

oversubscribe /ˌəʊvəsəbˈskraɪb/ v.tr. (usu. as **oversubscribed** adj.) subscribe for more than the amount available of (a commodity offered for sale etc.) (the offer was oversubscribed).

oversubtle /ˌəʊvəˈsʌt(ə)l/ adj. excessively subtle; not plain or clear.

oversupply /ˌəʊvəsəˈplaɪ/ v. & n. —v.tr. (**-ies, -ied**) supply with too much. —n. an excessive supply.

oversusceptible /ˌəʊvəsəˈseptɪb(ə)l/ adj. too susceptible or vulnerable.

overt /əʊˈvɜːt, ˈəʊvɜːt/ adj. unconcealed; done openly. □ **overtly** adv. **overtness** n. [ME f. OF past part. of ovrir open f. L aperire]

overtake /ˌəʊvəˈteɪk/ v.tr. (past **-took**; past part. **-taken**) **1** (also absol.) catch up with and pass in the same direction. **2** (of a storm, misfortune, etc.) come suddenly or unexpectedly upon. **3** become level with and exceed (a compared value etc.).

overtask /ˌəʊvəˈtɑːsk/ v.tr. **1** give too heavy a task to. **2** be too heavy a task for.

overtax /ˌəʊvəˈtæks/ v.tr. **1** make excessive demands on (a person's strength etc.). **2** tax too heavily.

overthrow v. & n. —v.tr. /ˌəʊvəˈθrəʊ/ (past **-threw**; past part. **-thrown**) **1** remove forcibly from power. **2** put an end to (an institution etc.). **3** conquer, overcome. **4** knock down, upset. —n. /ˈəʊvəˌθrəʊ/ a defeat or downfall.

overtime /ˈəʊvəˌtaɪm/ n. & adv. —n. **1** the time during which a person works at a job in addition to the regular hours. **2** payment for this. **3** US Sport = extra time. —adv. in addition to regular hours.

overtire /ˌəʊvəˈtaɪə(r)/ v.tr. & refl. exhaust or wear out (esp. an invalid etc.).

overtone /ˈəʊvəˌtəʊn/ n. **1** Mus. any of the tones above the lowest in a harmonic series. **2** a subtle or elusive quality or implication (sinister overtones). [OVER- + TONE, after G Oberton]

overtop /ˌəʊvəˈtɒp/ v.tr. (**-topped, -topping**) **1** be or become higher than. **2** surpass.

overtrain /ˌəʊvəˈtreɪn/ v.tr. & intr. subject to or undergo too much (esp. athletic) training with a consequent loss of proficiency.

overture /ˈəʊvəˌtjʊə(r)/ n. **1** an orchestral piece opening an opera etc. **2** a one-movement composition in this style. **3** (usu. in pl.) **a** an opening of negotiations. **b** a formal proposal or offer (esp. make overtures to). **4** the beginning of a poem etc. [ME f. OF f. L apertura APERTURE]

overturn v. & n. —v. /ˌəʊvəˈtɜːn/ **1** tr. cause to fall down or over; upset. **2** tr. reverse; subvert; abolish; invalidate. **3** intr. fall down; fall over. —n. /ˈəʊvəˌtɜːn/ a subversion, an act of upsetting.

overuse v. & n. —v.tr. /ˌəʊvəˈjuːz/ use too much. —n. /ˌəʊvəˈjuːs/ excessive use.

overvalue /ˌəʊvəˈvæljuː/ v.tr. (**-values, -valued, -valuing**) value too highly; have too high an opinion of.

overview /ˈəʊvəˌvjuː/ n. a general survey.

overweening /ˌəʊvəˈwiːnɪŋ/ adj. arrogant, presumptuous, conceited, self-confident. □ **overweeningly** adv. **overweeningness** n.

overweight adj., n., & v. —adj. /ˌəʊvəˈweɪt/ beyond an allowed or suitable weight. —n. /ˈəʊvəˌweɪt/ excessive or extra weight; preponderance. —v.tr. /ˌəʊvəˈweɪt/ (usu. foll. by with) load unduly.

overwhelm /ˌəʊvəˈwelm/ v.tr. **1** overpower with emotion. **2** (usu. foll. by with) overpower with an excess of business etc. **3** bring to sudden ruin or destruction; crush. **4** bury or drown beneath a huge mass, submerge utterly.

overwhelming /ˌəʊvəˈwelmɪŋ/ *adj.* irresistible by force of numbers, influence, amount, etc. □ **overwhelmingly** *adv.* **overwhelmingness** *n.*

overwind *v. & n.* —*v.tr.* /ˌəʊvəˈwaɪnd/ (*past* and *past part.* **-wound**) wind (a mechanism, esp. a watch) beyond the proper stopping point. —*n.* /ˈəʊvəˌwaɪnd/ an instance of this.

overwinter /ˌəʊvəˈwɪntə(r)/ *v.* **1** *intr.* (usu. foll. by *at*, *in*) spend the winter. **2** *intr.* (of insects, fungi, etc.) live through the winter. **3** *tr.* keep (animals, plants, etc.) alive through the winter.

overwork /ˌəʊvəˈwɜːk/ *v. & n.* —*v.* **1** *intr.* work too hard. **2** *tr.* cause (another person) to work too hard. **3** *tr.* weary or exhaust with too much work. **4** *tr.* make excessive use of. —*n.* excessive work.

overwound *past* and *past part.* of OVERWIND.

overwrite /ˌəʊvəˈraɪt/ *v.* (*past* **-wrote**; *past part.* **-written**) **1** *tr.* write on top of (other writing). **2** *tr. Computing* destroy (data) in (a file etc.) by entering new data. **3** *intr.* (esp. as **overwritten** *adj.*) write too elaborately or too ornately. **4** *intr. & refl.* write too much; exhaust oneself by writing.

overwrought /ˌəʊvəˈrɔːt/ *adj.* **1** overexcited, nervous, distraught. **2** overdone; too elaborate.

overzealous /ˌəʊvəˈzeləs/ *adj.* too zealous in one's attitude, behaviour, etc.; excessively enthusiastic. □ **overzeal** /-ˈziːl/ *n.*

ovi- /ˈəʊvɪ/ *comb. form* egg, ovum. [L *ovum* egg]

oviduct /ˈəʊvɪˌdʌkt/ *n.* the tube through which an ovum passes from the ovary. □ **oviducal** /-ˈdjuːk(ə)l/ *adj.* **oviductal** /-ˈdʌkt(ə)l/ *adj.*

oviform /ˈəʊvɪˌfɔːm/ *adj.* egg-shaped.

ovine /ˈəʊvaɪn/ *adj.* of or like sheep. [LL *ovinus* f. L *ovis* sheep]

oviparous /əʊˈvɪpərəs/ *adj. Zool.* producing young by means of eggs expelled from the body before they are hatched. □ **oviparity** /-ˈpærɪtɪ/ *n.* **oviparously** *adv.*

ovipositor /ˌəʊvɪˈpɒzɪtə(r)/ *n.* a pointed tubular organ with which a female insect deposits her eggs. [mod.L f. OVI- + L *positor* f. *ponere posit-* to place]

ovoid /ˈəʊvɔɪd/ *adj. & n.* —*adj.* **1** (of a solid or of a surface) egg-shaped. **2** oval, with one end more pointed than the other. —*n.* an ovoid body or surface. [F *ovoïde* f. mod.L *ovoides* (as OVUM)]

ovulate /ˈɒvjʊˌleɪt/ *v.intr.* produce ova or ovules, or discharge them from the ovary. □ **ovulation** /-ˈleɪʃ(ə)n/ *n.* **ovulatory** *adj.* [mod.L *ovulum* (as OVULE)]

ovule /ˈəʊvjuːl/ *n.* the part of the ovary of seed plants that contains the germ cell; an unfertilized seed. □ **ovular** *adj.* [F f. med.L *ovulum*, dimin. of OVUM]

ovum /ˈəʊvəm/ *n.* (pl. **ova** /ˈəʊvə/) **1** a mature reproductive cell of female animals, produced by the ovary. **2** the egg cell of plants. [L, = egg]

ow /aʊ/ *int.* expressing sudden pain. [natural exclam.]

owe /əʊ/ *v.tr.* **1 a** be under obligation (to a person etc.) to pay or repay (money etc.) (*we owe you five pounds*; *owe more than I can pay*). **b** (*absol.*, usu. foll. by *for*) be in debt (*still owe for my car*). **2** (often foll. by *to*) render (gratitude etc., a person honour, gratitude, etc.) (*owe grateful thanks to*). **3**

(usu. foll. by *to*) be indebted to a person or thing for (*we owe to Newton the principle of gravitation*). □ **owe a person a grudge** cherish resentment against a person. [OE *āgan* (see OUGHT¹) f. Gmc]

owing /ˈəʊɪŋ/ *predic.adj.* **1** owed; yet to be paid (*the balance owing*). **2** (foll. by *to*) **a** caused by; attributable to (*the cancellation was owing to ill health*). **b** (as *prep.*) because of (*trains are delayed owing to bad weather*).

■ **Usage** The use of *owing to* as a preposition meaning 'because of' is entirely acceptable, unlike this use of *due to*.

owl /aʊl/ *n.* **1** any nocturnal bird of prey of the order Strigiformes, with large eyes and a hooked beak. **2** *colloq.* a person compared to an owl, esp. in looking solemn or wise. □ **owlery** *n.* (pl. **-ies**). **owlish** *adj.* **owlishly** *adv.* **owlishness** *n.* (in sense 2). **owl-like** *adj.* [OE *ūle* f. Gmc]

owlet /ˈaʊlɪt/ *n.* a small or young owl.

own /əʊn/ *adj. & v.* —*adj.* (prec. by possessive) **1 a** belonging to oneself or itself; not another's (*saw it with my own eyes*). **b** individual, peculiar, particular (*a charm all of its own*). **2** used to emphasize identity rather than possession (*cooks his own meals*). **3** (*absol.*) **a** private property (*is it your own?*). **b** kindred (*among my own*). —*v.* **1** *tr.* have as property; possess. **2 a** *tr.* confess; admit as valid, true, etc. (*own their faults*; *owns he did not know*). **b** *intr.* (foll. by *to*) confess to (*owned to a prejudice*). **3** *tr.* acknowledge paternity, authorship, or possession of. □ **come into one's own 1** receive one's due. **2** achieve recognition. **get one's own back** (often foll. by *on*) *colloq.* get revenge. **hold one's own** maintain one's position; not be defeated or lose strength. **of one's own** belonging to oneself alone. **on one's own 1** alone. **2** independently, without help. **own brand** (often *attrib.*) goods manufactured specially for a retailer and bearing the retailer's name. **own goal 1** a goal scored (usu. by mistake) against the scorer's own side. **2** an act or initiative that has the unintended effect of harming one's own interests. **own up** (often foll. by *to*) confess frankly. □ **-owned** *adj.* (in *comb.*). [OE *āgen*, *āgnian*: see OWE]

owner /ˈəʊnə(r)/ *n.* a person who owns something. □ **owner-occupier** a person who owns the house etc. he or she lives in. □ **ownerless** *adj.* **ownership** *n.*

owt /aʊt/ *n. colloq.* or *dial.* anything. [var. of AUGHT]

ox *n.* (pl. **oxen** /ˈɒks(ə)n/) **1** any bovine animal, esp. a large usu. horned domesticated ruminant used for draught, for supplying milk, and for eating as meat. **2** a castrated male of a domesticated species of cattle, *Bos taurus*. [OE *oxa* f. Gmc]

oxalic acid /ɒkˈsælɪk/ *n. Chem.* a very poisonous and sour acid found in sorrel and rhubarb leaves. □ **oxalate** /ˈɒksəˌleɪt/ *n.* [F *oxalique* f. L *oxalis* f. Gk *oxalis* wood sorrel]

oxbow /ˈɒksbəʊ/ *n.* **1** a U-shaped collar of an ox-yoke. **2 a** a loop formed by a horseshoe bend in a river. **b** a lake formed when the river cuts across the narrow end of the loop.

Oxbridge /ˈɒksbrɪdʒ/ *n. Brit.* **1** (also *attrib.*) Oxford and Cambridge universities regarded together, esp. in contrast to newer institutions. **2** (often *attrib.*) the characteristics of these universities. [portmanteau word f. Ox(ford) + (Cam)bridge]

oxen pl. of OX.

ox-eye /ˈɒksaɪ/ n. a plant with a flower like the eye of an ox. □ **ox-eye daisy** n. a daisy, Leucanthemum vulgare, having flowers with white petals and a yellow centre. □ **ox-eyed** adj.

Oxfam /ˈɒksfæm/ abbr. Oxford Committee for Famine Relief.

Oxford blue /ˈɒksfəd/ n. & adj. —n. a dark blue, sometimes with a purple tinge. —adj. of this colour.

oxherd /ˈɒkshɜːd/ n. a cowherd.

oxhide /ˈɒkshaɪd/ n. 1 the hide of an ox. 2 leather made from this.

oxidant /ˈɒksɪd(ə)nt/ n. an oxidizing agent. □ **oxidation** /-ˈdeɪʃ(ə)n/ n. **oxidational** /-ˈdeɪʃən(ə)l/ adj. **oxidative** /-ˌdeɪtɪv/ adj. [F, part. of oxider (as OXIDE)]

oxide /ˈɒksaɪd/ n. a binary compound of oxygen. [F f. oxygène OXYGEN + -ide after acide ACID]

oxidize /ˈɒksɪˌdaɪz/ v. (also **-ise**) 1 intr. & tr. combine or cause to combine with oxygen. 2 tr. & intr. cover (metal) or (of metal) become covered with a coating of oxide; make or become rusty. □ **oxidizable** adj. **oxidization** /-ˈzeɪʃ(ə)n/ n. **oxidizer** n.

Oxon. /ˈɒks(ə)n/ abbr. 1 Oxfordshire. 2 of Oxford University or the diocese of Oxford. [abbr. of med.L Oxoniensis f. Oxonia: see OXONIAN]

Oxonian /ɒkˈsəʊnɪən/ adj. & n. —adj. of or relating to Oxford or Oxford University. —n. 1 a member of Oxford University. 2 a native or inhabitant of Oxford. [Oxonia Latinized name of Ox(en)ford]

oxtail /ˈɒksteɪl/ n. the tail of an ox, often used in making soup.

oxtongue /ˈɒkstʌŋ/ n. the tongue of an ox, esp. cooked as food.

oxy- /ˈɒksɪ/ comb. form (also **ox-** /ɒks/) Chem. oxygen (oxyacetylene). [abbr.]

oxyacetylene /ˌɒksɪəˈsetɪˌliːn/ adj. of or using a mixture of oxygen and acetylene, esp. in cutting or welding metals (oxyacetylene burner).

oxygen /ˈɒksɪdʒ(ə)n/ n. Chem. a colourless tasteless odourless gaseous element, occurring naturally in air, water, and most minerals and organic substances, and essential to plant and animal life. □ **oxygen mask** a mask placed over the nose and mouth to supply oxygen for breathing. **oxygen tent** a tentlike enclosure supplying a patient with air rich in oxygen. □

oxygenous /ɒkˈsɪdʒɪnəs/ adj. [F oxygène acidifying principle f. Gk oxus sharp: it was at first held to be the essential principle in the formation of acids]

oxygenate /ˈɒksɪdʒəˌneɪt, ɒkˈsɪ-/ v.tr. 1 supply, treat, or mix with oxygen; oxidize. 2 charge (blood) with oxygen by respiration. □ **oxygenation** /-ˈneɪʃ(ə)n/ n. [F oxygéner (as OXYGEN)]

oxyhaemoglobin /ˌɒksɪˌhiːməˈgləʊbɪn/ n. Biochem. a bright red complex formed when haemoglobin combines with oxygen.

oxymoron /ˌɒksɪˈmɔːrɒn/ n. rhet. a figure of speech in which apparently contradictory terms appear in conjunction (e.g. faith unfaithful kept him falsely true). [Gk oxumōron neut. of oxumōros pointedly foolish f. oxus sharp + mōros foolish]

oyez /əʊˈjes, -ˈjez/ int. (also **oyes**) uttered, usu. three times, by a public crier or a court officer to command silence and attention. [ME f. AF, OF oiez, oyez, imper. pl. of oïr hear f. L audire]

oyster /ˈɔɪstə(r)/ n. 1 any of various bivalve molluscs of the family Ostreidae or Aviculidae, esp. an edible kind, Ostrea edulis, of European waters. 2 an oyster-shaped morsel of meat in a fowl's back. 3 something regarded as containing all that one desires (the world is my oyster). □ **oyster-bank** (or **-bed**) a part of the sea-bottom where oysters breed or are bred. [ME & OF oistre f. L ostrea, ostreum f. Gk ostreon]

Oz /ɒz/ n. Austral. sl. Australia. [abbr.]

oz. abbr. ounce(s). [It. f. onza ounce]

ozone /ˈəʊzəʊn/ n. 1 Chem. a colourless unstable gas with a pungent odour and powerful oxidizing properties, used for bleaching etc. 2 colloq. **a** invigorating air at the seaside etc. **b** exhilarating influence. □ **ozone depletion** a reduction of ozone concentration in the stratosphere, caused by atmospheric pollution. **ozone-friendly** (of manufactured articles) containing chemicals that are not destructive to the ozone layer. **ozone hole** an area of the ozone layer in which depletion has occurred. **ozone layer** a layer of ozone in the stratosphere that absorbs most of the sun's ultraviolet radiation. □ **ozonic** /əʊˈzɒnɪk/ adj. **ozonize** v.tr. (also **-ise**). **ozonization** /-ˈzeɪʃ(ə)n/ n. **ozonizer** n. [G Ozon f. Gk, neut. pres. part. of ozō smell]

Ozzie var. of AUSSIE.

P[1] /piː/ *n.* (also **p**) (*pl.* **Ps** or **P's**) the sixteenth letter of the alphabet.

P[2] *abbr.* (also **P.**) **1** (on road signs) parking. **2** *Chess* pawn. **3** (also Ⓟ) proprietary.

P[3] *symb. Chem.* the element phosphorus.

p *abbr.* (also **p.**) **1** *Brit.* penny, pence. **2** page. **3** pico-. **4** piano (softly).

PA *abbr.* **1** personal assistant. **2** public address (esp. *PA system*).

Pa *symb. Chem.* the element protactinium.

pa /pɑː/ *n. colloq.* father. [abbr. of PAPA]

pabulum /ˈpæbjʊləm/ *n.* food, esp. for the mind (*mental pabulum*). [L f. *pascere* feed]

PABX *abbr. Brit.* private automatic branch exchange.

pace[1] *n. & v.* —*n.* **1 a** a single step in walking or running. **b** the distance covered in this (about 75 cm or 30 in.). **c** the distance between two successive stationary positions of the same foot in walking. **2** speed in walking or running. **3** *Theatr. & Mus.* speed or tempo in theatrical or musical performance (*played with great pace*). **4** a rate of progression. **5 a** a manner of walking or running; a gait. **b** any of various gaits, esp. of a trained horse etc. (*rode at an ambling pace*). —*v.* **1** *intr.* **a** walk (esp. repeatedly or methodically) with a slow or regular pace (*pacing up and down*). **b** (of a horse) = AMBLE. **2** *tr.* traverse by pacing. **3** *tr.* set the pace for (a rider, runner, etc.). **4** *tr.* (foll. by *out*) measure (a distance) by pacing. □ **keep pace** (often foll. by *with*) advance at an equal rate (as). **pace-setter 1** a leader. **2** = PACEMAKER 1. **put a person through his** (or **her**) **paces** test a person's qualities in action etc. **set the pace** determine the speed, esp. by leading. **stand** (or **stay**) **the pace** be able to keep up with others. □ **-paced** *adj.* **pacer** *n.* [ME f. OF *pas* f. L *passus* f. *pandere pass-* stretch]

pace[2] /ˈpɑːtʃeɪ, ˈpeɪsɪ/ *prep.* (in stating a contrary opinion) with due deference to (the person named). [L, ablat. of *pax* peace]

pacemaker /ˈpeɪsˌmeɪkə(r)/ *n.* **1** a competitor who sets the pace in a race. **2** a natural or artificial device for stimulating the heart muscle and determining the rate of its contractions.

pacha var. of PASHA.

pachinko /pəˈtʃɪŋkəʊ/ *n.* a Japanese form of pinball. [Jap.]

pachyderm /ˈpækɪdɜːm/ *n.* any thick-skinned mammal, esp. an elephant or rhinoceros. □ **pachydermatous** /-ˈdɜːmətəs/ *adj.* [F *pachyderme* f. Gk *pakhudermos* f. *pakhus* thick + *derma -matos* skin]

pacific /pəˈsɪfɪk/ *adj. & n.* —*adj.* **1** characterized by or tending to peace; tranquil. **2** (**Pacific**) of or adjoining the Pacific. —*n.* (**the Pacific**) the generally placid expanse of ocean between America to the east and Asia to the west. □ **pacifically** *adv.* [F *pacifique* or L *pacificus* f. *pax pacis* peace]

pacification /ˌpæsɪfɪˈkeɪʃ(ə)n/ *n.* the act of pacifying or the process of being pacified. □ **pacificatory** /pəˈsɪfɪkətərɪ/ *adj.* [F f. L *pacificatio -onis* (as PACIFY)]

pacifier /ˈpæsɪˌfaɪə(r)/ *n.* **1** a person or thing that pacifies. **2** *US* a baby's dummy.

pacifism /ˈpæsɪˌfɪz(ə)m/ *n.* the belief that war and violence are morally unjustified and that all disputes can be settled by peaceful means. □ **pacifist** *n. & adj.* [F *pacifisme* f. *pacifier* PACIFY]

pacify /ˈpæsɪˌfaɪ/ *v.tr.* (**-ies, -ied**) **1** appease (a person, anger, etc.). **2** bring (a country etc.) to a state of peace. [ME f. OF *pacifier* or L *pacificare* (as PACIFIC)]

pack[1] *n. & v.* —*n.* **1 a** a collection of things wrapped up or tied together for carrying. **b** = BACKPACK. **2** a set of items packaged for use or disposal together. **3** usu. *derog.* a lot or set (of similar things or persons) (*a pack of lies; a pack of thieves*). **4** *Brit.* a set of playing cards. **5 a** a group of hounds esp. for foxhunting. **b** a group of wild animals, esp. wolves, hunting together. **6** an organized group of Cub Scouts or Brownies. **7** *Rugby Football* a team's forwards. **8** a medicinal or cosmetic substance applied to the skin. —*v.* **1** *tr.* (often foll. by *up*) **a** fill (a suitcase, bag, etc.) with clothes and other items. **b** put (things) together in a bag or suitcase, esp. for travelling. **2** *intr. & tr.* come or put closely together; crowd or cram (*packed a lot into a few hours; passengers packed like sardines*). **3** *tr.* (in *passive;* often foll. by *with*) be filled (with); contain extensively (*the restaurant was packed; the book is packed with information*). **4** *tr.* fill (a hall, theatre, etc.) with an audience etc. **5** *tr.* cover (a thing) with something pressed tightly round. **6** *intr.* be suitable for packing. **7** *tr. colloq.* **a** carry (a gun etc.). **b** be capable of delivering (a punch) with skill or force. **8** *intr.* (of animals or Rugby forwards) form a pack. □ **pack-animal** an animal for carrying packs. **pack-drill** a military punishment of marching up and down carrying full equipment. **packed lunch** a lunch carried in a bag, box, etc., esp. to work, school, etc. **packed out** *colloq.* full, crowded. **pack ice** an area of large crowded pieces of floating ice in the sea. **pack it in** (or **up**) *colloq.* end or stop it. **pack off** send (a person) away, esp. abruptly or promptly. **pack-saddle** a saddle adapted for supporting packs. **pack up** *colloq.* **1** (esp. of a machine) stop functioning; break down. **2** retire from an activity, contest, etc. **send packing** *colloq.* dismiss (a person) summarily. □ **packable** *adj.* [ME f. MDu., MLG *pak, pakken,* of unkn. orig.]

pack[2] /pæk/ *v.tr.* select (a jury etc.) or fill (a meeting) so as to secure a decision in one's favour. [prob. f. obs. verb *pact* f. PACT]

package /ˈpækɪdʒ/ *n. & v.* —*n.* **1 a** a bundle of things packed. **b** a parcel, box, etc., in which things are packed. **2** (in full **package deal**) a set of proposals or items offered or agreed to as a whole. **3** *Computing* a piece of software suitable for various applications rather than one which is custom-built. —*v.tr.* make up into or enclose in a package. □ **package holiday** (or **tour** etc.) a holiday or tour etc. with all arrangements made at an inclusive price. □ **packager** *n.* [PACK¹ + -AGE]

packaging /ˈpækɪdʒɪŋ/ *n.* **1** a wrapping or container for goods. **2** the process of packing goods.

packer /ˈpækə(r)/ *n.* a person or thing that packs, esp. a dealer who prepares and packs food for transportation and sale.

packet /ˈpækɪt/ *n.* **1** a small package. **2** *colloq.* a large sum of money won, lost, or spent. **3** (in full **packet-boat**) *hist.* a mail-boat or passenger ship. [PACK¹ + -ET¹]

packhorse /ˈpækhɔːs/ *n.* a horse for carrying loads.

packing /ˈpækɪŋ/ *n.* **1** the act or process of packing. **2** material used as padding to pack esp. fragile articles. □ **packing-case** a case (usu. wooden) or framework for packing goods in.

packthread /ˈpækθred/ *n.* stout thread for sewing or tying up packs.

pact *n.* an agreement or a treaty. [ME f. OF *pact(e)* f. L *pactum*, neut. past part. of *pacisci* agree]

pad¹ *n. & v.* —*n.* **1** a piece of soft material used to reduce friction or jarring, fill out hollows, hold or absorb liquid, etc. **2** a number of sheets of blank paper fastened together at one edge, for writing or drawing on. **3** = *ink-pad.* **4** the fleshy underpart of an animal's foot or of a human finger. **5** a guard for the leg and ankle in sports. **6** a flat surface for helicopter take-off or rocket-launching. **7** *colloq.* a lodging, esp. a bedsitter or flat. **8** the floating leaf of a water lily. —*v.tr.* (**padded, padding**) **1** provide with a pad or padding; stuff. **2** (foll. by *out*) lengthen or fill out (a book etc.) with unnecessary material. □ **padded cell** a room with padded walls in a mental hospital. [prob. of LG or Du. orig.]

pad² *v. & n.* —*v.* (**padded, padding**) **1** *intr.* walk with a soft steady step. **2 a** *tr.* tramp along (a road etc.) on foot. **b** *intr.* travel on foot. —*n.* the sound of soft steady steps. [LG *padden* tread, *pad* PATH]

padding /ˈpædɪŋ/ *n.* soft material used to pad or stuff with.

paddle¹ /ˈpæd(ə)l/ *n. & v.* —*n.* **1** a short broad-bladed oar used without a rowlock. **2** a paddle-shaped instrument. **3** *Zool.* a fin or flipper. **4** each of the boards fitted round the circumference of a paddle-wheel or mill-wheel. **5** the action or a spell of paddling. —*v.* **1** *intr. & tr.* move on water or propel a boat by means of paddles. **2** *intr. & tr.* row gently. **3** *tr.* esp. *US colloq.* spank. □ **paddle-boat** (or **-steamer** etc.) a boat, steamer, etc., propelled by a paddle-wheel. **paddle-wheel** a wheel for propelling a ship, with boards round the circumference so as to press backwards against the water. □ **paddler** *n.* [15th c.: orig. unkn.]

paddle² /ˈpæd(ə)l/ *v. & n.* —*v.intr.* walk barefoot or dabble the feet or hands in shallow water. —*n.* the action or a spell of paddling. □ **paddler** *n.* [prob. of LG or Du. orig.: cf. LG *paddeln* tramp about]

paddock /ˈpædək/ *n.* **1** a small field, esp. for keeping horses in. **2** a turf enclosure adjoining

a racecourse where horses or cars are assembled before a race. **3** *Austral. & NZ* a field; a plot of land. [app. var. of (now dial.) *parrock* (OE *pearruc*): see PARK]

Paddy /ˈpædɪ/ *n.* (*pl.* **-ies**) *colloq.* often *offens.* an Irishman. [pet-form of the Irish name *Padraig* (= Patrick)]

paddy¹ /ˈpædɪ/ *n.* (*pl.* **-ies**) **1** (in full **paddy-field**) a field where rice is grown. **2** rice before threshing or in the husk. [Malay *pādī*]

paddy² /ˈpædɪ/ *n.* (*pl.* **-ies**) *Brit. colloq.* a rage; a fit of temper. [PADDY]

padlock /ˈpædlɒk/ *n. & v.* —*n.* a detachable lock hanging by a pivoted hook on the object fastened. —*v.tr.* secure with a padlock. [ME f. LOCK¹: first element unexpl.]

padre /ˈpɑːdrɪ, -dreɪ/ *n.* a chaplain in any of the armed services. [It., Sp., & Port., = father, priest, f. L *pater patris* father]

paean /ˈpiːən/ *n.* (*US* **pean**) a song of praise or triumph. [L f. Doric Gk *paian* hymn of thanksgiving to Apollo (under the name of *Paian*)]

paederast var. of PEDERAST.

paederasty var. of PEDERASTY.

paediatrics /ˌpiːdɪˈætrɪks/ *n.pl.* (treated as *sing.*) (*US* **pediatrics**) the branch of medicine dealing with children and their diseases. □ **paediatric** *adj.* **paediatrician** /-əˈtrɪʃ(ə)n/ *n.* [PAEDO- + Gk *iatros* physician]

paedo- /ˈpiːdəʊ/ *comb. form* (*US* **pedo-**) child. [Gk *pais paid-* child]

paedophile /ˈpiːdəˌfaɪl/ *n.* (*US* **pedophile**) a person who displays paedophilia.

paedophilia /ˌpiːdəˈfɪlɪə/ *n.* (*US* **pedophilia**) sexual desire directed towards children.

paella /paɪˈelə, pɑː-/ *n.* a Spanish dish of rice, saffron, chicken, seafood, etc., cooked and served in a large shallow pan. [Catalan f. OF *paele* f. L *patella* pan]

paeony var. of PEONY.

pagan /ˈpeɪɡən/ *n. & adj.* —*n.* a person not subscribing to any of the main religions of the world, esp. formerly regarded by Christians as unenlightened or heathen. —*adj.* **1 a** of or relating to or associated with pagans. **b** irreligious. **2** identifying divinity or spirituality in nature; pantheistic. □ **paganish** *adj.* **paganism** *n.* **paganize** *v.tr. & intr.* (also **-ise**). [ME f. L *paganus* villager, rustic f. *pagus* country district: in Christian L = civilian, heathen]

page¹ *n. & v.* —*n.* **1 a** a leaf of a book, periodical, etc. **b** each side of this. **c** what is written or printed on this. **2** an episode that might fill a page in written history etc.; a record. —*v.tr.* paginate. [F f. L *pagina* f. *pangere* fasten]

page² *n. & v.* —*n.* **1** a boy or man, usu. in livery, employed to run errands, attend to a door, etc. **2** a boy employed as a personal attendant of a person of rank, a bride, etc. **3** *hist.* a boy in training for knighthood and attached to a knight's service. —*v.tr.* **1** (in hotels, airports, etc.) summon by making an announcement or by sending a messenger. **2** summon by means of a pager. [ME f. OF, perh. f. It. *paggio* f. Gk *paidion*, dimin. of *pais paidos* boy]

pageant /ˈpædʒ(ə)nt/ *n.* **1** a brilliant spectacle, esp. an elaborate parade. **2** a spectacular procession, or play performed in the open, illustrating historical events. **3** a tableau etc. on a fixed stage or moving vehicle. [ME *pagyn*, of unkn. orig.]

pageantry /ˈpædʒəntrɪ/ *n.* (*pl.* **-ies**) **1** elaborate or sumptuous show or display. **2** an instance of this.

pager /ˈpeɪdʒə(r)/ *n.* a radio device with a bleeper, activated from a central point to alert the person wearing it.

paginate /ˈpædʒɪˌneɪt/ *v.tr.* assign numbers to the pages of a book etc. □ **pagination** /-ˈneɪʃ(ə)n/ *n.* [F *paginer* f. L *pagina* PAGE¹]

pagoda /pəˈɡəʊdə/ *n.* **1** a Hindu or Buddhist temple or sacred building, esp. a many-tiered tower, in India and the Far East. **2** an ornamental imitation of this. [Port. *pagode*, prob. ult. f. Pers. *butkada* idol temple]

pah *int.* expressing disgust or contempt. [natural utterance]

paid *past* and *past part.* of PAY.

pail *n.* **1** a bucket. **2** an amount contained in this. □ **pailful** *n.* (*pl.* **-fuls**). [OE *pægel* gill (cf. MDu. *pegel* gauge), assoc. with OF *paelle*: see PAELLA]

paillasse var. of PALLIASSE.

pain *n.* & *v.* —*n.* **1 a** the range of unpleasant bodily sensations produced by illness or by harmful physical contact etc. **b** a particular kind or instance of this (often in *pl.*: *suffering from stomach pains*). **2** mental suffering or distress. **3** (in *pl.*) careful effort; trouble taken (*take pains; got nothing for my pains*). **4** (also **pain in the neck**) *colloq.* a troublesome person or thing; a nuisance. —*v.tr.* **1** cause pain to. **2** (as **pained** *adj.*) expressing pain (*a pained expression*). □ **in pain** suffering pain. **on** (or **under**) **pain of** with (death etc.) as the penalty. [ME f. OF *peine* f. L *poena* penalty]

painful /ˈpeɪnfʊl/ *adj.* **1** causing bodily or mental pain or distress. **2** (esp. of part of the body) suffering pain. **3** causing trouble or difficulty; laborious (*a painful climb*). □ **painfully** *adv.* **painfulness** *n.*

painkiller /ˈpeɪnˌkɪlə(r)/ *n.* a medicine or drug for alleviating pain. □ **painkilling** *adj.*

painless /ˈpeɪnlɪs/ *adj.* not causing or suffering pain. □ **painlessly** *adv.* **painlessness** *n.*

painstaking /ˈpeɪnzˌteɪkɪŋ/ *adj.* careful, industrious, thorough. □ **painstakingly** *adv.* **painstakingness** *n.*

paint /peɪnt/ *n.* & *v.* —*n.* **1 a** a colouring matter, esp. in liquid form for imparting colour to a surface. **b** this as a dried film or coating (*the paint peeled off*). **2** *joc.* or *archaic* cosmetic make-up, esp. rouge or nail varnish. —*v.tr.* **1 a** cover the surface of (a wall, object, etc.) with paint. **b** apply paint of a specified colour to (*paint the door green*). **2** depict (an object, scene, etc.) with paint; produce (a picture) by painting. **3** describe vividly as if by painting (*painted a gloomy picture of the future*). **4** *joc.* or *archaic* **a** apply liquid or cosmetic to (the face, skin, etc.). **b** apply (a liquid to the skin etc.). □ **paint out** efface with paint. **paint shop** the part of a factory where goods are painted, esp. by spraying. **paint-stick** a stick of water-soluble paint used like a crayon. **paint the town red** *colloq.* enjoy oneself flamboyantly. □ **paintable** *adj.* **painty** *adj.* [ME f. *peint* past part. of OF *peindre* f. L *pingere* pict- paint]

paintbox /ˈpeɪntbɒks/ *n.* a box holding dry paints for painting pictures.

paintbrush /ˈpeɪntbrʌʃ/ *n.* a brush for applying paint.

painter¹ /ˈpeɪntə(r)/ *n.* a person who paints, esp. an artist or decorator. [ME f. OF *peintour* ult. f. L *pictor* (as PAINT)]

painter² /ˈpeɪntə(r)/ *n.* a rope attached to the bow of a boat for tying it to a quay etc. [ME, prob. f. OF *penteur* rope from a masthead: cf. G *Pentertakel* f. *pentern* fish the anchor]

painterly /ˈpeɪntəlɪ/ *adj.* **1** using paint well; artistic. **2** characteristic of a painter or paintings.

painting /ˈpeɪntɪŋ/ *n.* **1** the process or art of using paint. **2** a painted picture.

paintwork /ˈpeɪntwɜːk/ *n.* **1** a painted surface or area in a building etc. **2** the work of painting.

pair *n.* & *v.* —*n.* **1** a set of two persons or things used together or regarded as a unit (*a pair of gloves; a pair of eyes*). **2** an article (e.g. scissors, trousers, or pyjamas) consisting of two joined or corresponding parts not used separately. **3 a** an engaged or married couple. **b** a mated couple of animals. **4** two horses harnessed side by side (*a coach and pair*). **5** the second member of a pair in relation to the first (*cannot find its pair*). **6** two playing cards of the same denomination. **7** *Parl.* either or both of two MPs etc. on opposite sides absenting themselves from voting by mutual arrangement. —*v.tr.* & *intr.* **1** (often foll. by *off*) arrange or be arranged in couples. **2 a** join or be joined in marriage. **b** (of animals) mate. **3** *Parl.* form a pair. □ **in pairs** in twos. [ME f. OF *paire* f. L *paria* neut. pl. of *par* equal]

Paisley /ˈpeɪzlɪ/ *n.* (often *attrib.*) **1** a distinctive detailed pattern of curved feather-shaped figures. **2** a soft woollen garment having this pattern. [*Paisley* in Scotland]

pajamas *US* var. of PYJAMAS.

pakeha /ˈpɑːkɪˌhɑː/ *n.* NZ a White person as opposed to a Maori. [Maori]

pal *n.* & *v.* —*n.* *colloq.* a friend, mate, or comrade. —*v.intr.* (**palled**, **palling**) (usu. foll. by *up*) associate; form a friendship. [Romany = brother, mate, ult. f. Skr. *bhrātr* BROTHER]

palace /ˈpælɪs/ *n.* **1** the official residence of a sovereign, president, archbishop, or bishop. **2** a splendid mansion; a spacious building. [ME f. OF *palais* f. L *Palatium* Palatine (hill) in Rome where the house of the emperor was situated]

paladin /ˈpælədɪn/ *n. hist.* **1** any of the twelve peers of Charlemagne's court, of whom the Count Palatine was the chief. **2** a knight errant; a champion. [F *paladin* f. It. *paladino* f. L *palatinus*: see PALATINE]

palaeo- /ˈpælɪəʊ, ˈpeɪlɪəʊ/ *comb. form* (*US* **paleo-**) ancient, old; of ancient (esp. prehistoric) times. [Gk *palaios* ancient]

Palaeocene /ˈpælɪəˌsiːn/ *adj.* & *n.* (*US* **Paleocene**) *Geol.* —*adj.* of or relating to the earliest epoch of the Tertiary period. —*n.* this epoch or system. [PALAEO- + Gk *kainos* new]

palaeography /ˌpælɪˈɒɡrəfɪ/ *n.* (*US* **paleography**) the study of writing and documents from the past. □ **palaeographer** *n.* **palaeographic** /-əˈɡræfɪk/ *adj.* **palaeographical** /-əˈɡræfɪk(ə)l/ *adj.* **palaeographically** /-əˈɡræfɪkəlɪ/ *adv.* [F *paléographie* f. mod.L *palaeographia* (as PALAEO-, -GRAPHY)]

palaeolithic /ˌpælɪəʊˈlɪθɪk/ *adj.* (*US* **paleolithic**) *Archaeol.* of or relating to the early part of the Stone Age. [PALAEO- + Gk *lithos* stone]

palaeontology /ˌpælɪɒnˈtɒlədʒɪ, ˌpeɪlɪ-/ *n.* (*US* **paleontology**) the study of life in the geological past. □ **palaeontological** /-təˈlɒdʒɪkəl/ *adj.* **palaeontologist** *n.* [PALAEO- + Gk *onta* neut. pl. of *ōn* being, part. of *eimi* be + -LOGY]

Palaeozoic /ˌpælɪəʊˈzəʊɪk/ *adj.* & *n.* (also **Paleozoic**) *Geol.* —*adj.* of or relating to an era of geological time marked by the appearance of marine and terrestrial plants and animals. —*n.* this era. [PALAEO- + Gk *zōē* life, *zōos* living]

palais /ˈpæleɪ/ *n. colloq.* a public hall for dancing. [F *palais* (*de danse*) (dancing) hall]

palanquin /ˌpælənˈkiːn/ *n.* (also **palankeen**) (in India and the East) a covered litter for one passenger. [Port. *palanquim*: cf. Hindi *pālkī* f. Skr. *palyanka* bed, couch]

palatable /ˈpælətəb(ə)l/ *adj.* **1** pleasant to taste. **2** (of an idea, suggestion, etc.) acceptable, satisfactory. □ **palatability** /-ˈbɪlɪtɪ/ *n.* **palatableness** *n.* **palatably** *adv.*

palatal /ˈpælət(ə)l/ *adj.* & *n.* —*adj.* **1** of the palate. **2** (of a sound) made by placing the surface of the tongue against the hard palate (e.g. *y* in *yes*). —*n.* a palatal sound. □ **palatalize** *v.tr.* (also **-ise**). **palatalization** /-ˈzeɪʃ(ə)n/ *n.* **palatally** *adv.* [F (as PALATE)]

palate /ˈpælət/ *n.* **1** a structure closing the upper part of the mouth cavity in vertebrates. **2** the sense of taste. **3** a mental taste or inclination; liking. [ME f. L *palatum*]

palatial /pəˈleɪʃ(ə)l/ *adj.* (of a building) like a palace, esp. spacious and splendid. □ **palatially** *adv.* [L (as PALACE)]

palatinate /pəˈlætɪˌneɪt/ *n.* territory under the jurisdiction of a Count Palatine.

palatine /ˈpæləˌtaɪn/ *adj.* (also **Palatine**) *hist.* **1** (of an official or feudal lord) having local authority that elsewhere belongs only to a sovereign (*Count Palatine*). **2** (of a territory) subject to this authority. [ME f. F *palatin -ine* f. L *palatinus* of the PALACE]

palaver /pəˈlɑːvə(r)/ *n.* & *v.* —*n.* **1** fuss and bother, esp. prolonged and tedious. **2** profuse or idle talk. **3** cajolery. **4** *colloq.* an affair or business. —*v.* **1** *intr.* talk profusely. **2** *tr.* flatter, wheedle. [Port. *palavra* word f. L (as PARABLE)]

pale[1] *adj.* & *v.* —*adj.* **1** (of a person or complexion) of a whitish or ashen appearance. **2 a** (of a colour) faint; not dark or deep. **b** faintly coloured. **3** of faint lustre; dim. —*v.* **1** *intr.* & *tr.* grow or make pale. **2** *intr.* (often foll. by *before*, *beside*) become feeble in comparison (with). □ **palely** *adv.* **paleness** *n.* **palish** *adj.* [ME f. OF *pale, palir* f. L *pallidus* f. *pallēre* be pale]

pale[2] *n.* **1** a pointed piece of wood for fencing etc.; a stake. **2** a boundary or enclosed area. □ **beyond the pale** outside the bounds of acceptable behaviour. [ME f. OF *pal* f. L *palus* stake]

paleface /ˈpeɪlfeɪs/ *n.* a name supposedly used by the N. American Indians for the White man.

palette /ˈpælɪt/ *n.* **1** a thin board or slab or other surface, usu. with a hole for the thumb, on which an artist lays and mixes colours. **2** the range of colours used by an artist. □ **palette-knife 1** a thin steel blade with a handle for mixing colours or applying or removing paint. **2** a kitchen knife with a long blunt round-ended flexible blade. [F, dimin. of *pale* shovel f. L *pala* spade]

palfrey /ˈpɔːlfrɪ/ *n.* (*pl.* **-eys**) *archaic* a horse for ordinary riding, esp. for women. [ME f. OF *palefrei* f. med.L *palefredus*, LL *paraveredus* f. Gk *para* beside, extra, + L *veredus* light horse, of Gaulish orig.]

palimony /ˈpælɪmənɪ/ *n.* esp. *US colloq.* an allowance made by one member of an unmarried couple to the other after separation. [PAL + ALIMONY]

palimpsest /ˈpælɪmpˌsest/ *n.* **1** a piece of writing-material or manuscript on which the original writing has been effaced to make room for other writing. **2** a monumental brass turned and re-engraved on the reverse side. [L *palimpsestus* f. Gk *palimpsēstos* f. *palin* again + *psēstos* rubbed smooth]

palindrome /ˈpælɪnˌdrəʊm/ *n.* a word or phrase that reads the same backwards as forwards (e.g. *rotator, nurses run*). □ **palindromic** /-ˈdrɒmɪk/ *adj.* **palindromist** *n.* [Gk *palindromos* running back again f. *palin* again + *drom-* run]

paling /ˈpeɪlɪŋ/ *n.* **1** a fence of pales. **2** a pale.

palisade /ˌpælɪˈseɪd/ *n.* & *v.* —*n.* **1 a** a fence of pales or iron railings. **b** a strong pointed wooden stake used in a close row for defence. **2** *US* (in *pl.*) a line of high cliffs. —*v.tr.* enclose or provide with a palisade. [F *palissade* f. Prov. *palissada* f. *palissa* paling ult. f. L *palus* stake]

pall[1] /pɔːl/ *n.* **1** a cloth spread over a coffin, hearse, or tomb. **2 a** shoulder-band with pendants, worn as an ecclesiastical vestment and sign of authority. **3** a dark covering (*a pall of darkness*; *a pall of smoke*). [OE *pæll*, f. L *pallium* cloak]

pall[2] /pɔːl/ *v.* **1** *intr.* (often foll. by *on*) become uninteresting (to). **2** *tr.* satiate, cloy. [ME, f. APPAL]

Palladian /pəˈleɪdɪən/ *adj. Archit.* in the neoclassical style of Palladio. □ **Palladianism** *n.* [A. *Palladio*, It. architect d. 1580]

palladium /pəˈleɪdɪəm/ *n. Chem.* a white ductile metallic element used in chemistry as a catalyst and for making jewellery. [mod.L f. *Pallas*, an asteroid discovered (1803) just before the element, + -IUM; cf. CERIUM]

pallbearer /ˈpɔːlˌbeərə(r)/ *n.* a person helping to carry or officially escorting a coffin at a funeral.

pallet[1] /ˈpælɪt/ *n.* **1** a straw mattress. **2** a mean or makeshift bed. [ME *pailet, paillet* f. AF *paillete* straw f. OF *paille* f. L *palea*]

pallet[2] /ˈpælɪt/ *n.* a portable platform for transporting and storing loads. □ **palletize** *v.tr.* (also **-ise**) (in sense 3). [F *palette*: see PALETTE]

palliasse /ˈpælɪˌæs/ *n.* (also **paillasse**) a straw mattress. [F *paillasse* f. It. *pagliaccio* ult. f. L *palea* straw]

palliate /ˈpælɪˌeɪt/ *v.tr.* **1** alleviate (disease) without curing it. **2** excuse, extenuate. □ **palliation** /-ˈeɪʃ(ə)n/ *n.* **palliator** *n.* [LL *palliare* to cloak f. *pallium* cloak]

palliative /ˈpælɪətɪv/ *n.* & *adj.* —*n.* anything used to alleviate pain, anxiety, etc. —*adj.* serving to alleviate. □ **palliatively** *adv.* [F *palliatif -ive* or med.L *palliativus* (as PALLIATE)]

pallid /ˈpælɪd/ *adj.* pale, esp. from illness. □ **pallidity** /-ˈlɪdɪtɪ/ *n.* **pallidly** *adv.* **pallidness** *n.* [L *pallidus* PALE[1]]

pallor /ˈpælə(r)/ *n.* pallidness, paleness. [L f. *pallēre* be pale]

pally /ˈpælɪ/ *adj.* (**pallier, palliest**) *colloq.* like a pal; friendly.

palm[1] /pɑːm/ *n.* **1** any usu. tropical tree of the family Palmae, with no branches and a mass of large pinnate or fan-shaped leaves at the top. **2** the leaf of this tree as a symbol of victory. **3 a** supreme excellence. **b** a prize for this. **4** a branch of various trees used instead of a palm in non-tropical countries, esp. in celebrating Palm Sunday. □ **palm oil** oil from the fruit of any of various palms. **Palm Sunday** the Sunday before Easter, celebrating Christ's entry into Jerusalem. □ **palmaceous** /pæl'meɪʃəs/ *adj.* [OE *palm*(a) f. Gmc f. L *palma* PALM², its leaf being likened to a spread hand]

palm[2] /pɑːm/ *n. & v.* —*n.* **1** the inner surface of the hand between the wrist and fingers. **2** the part of a glove that covers this. —*v.tr.* conceal in the hand. □ **in the palm of one's hand** under one's control or influence. **palm off 1** (often foll. by *on*) **a** impose or thrust fraudulently (on a person). **b** cause a person to accept unwillingly or unknowingly (*palmed my old car off on him*). **2** (often foll. by *with*) cause (a person) to accept unwillingly or unknowingly (*palmed him off with my old car*). □ **palmar** /'pælmə(r)/ *adj.* **palmed** *adj.* **palmful** *n.* (pl. **-fuls**). [ME *paume* f. OF *paume* f. L *palma*: later assim. to L]

palmate /'pælmeɪt/ *adj.* **1** shaped like an open hand. **2** having lobes etc. like spread fingers. [L *palmatus* (as PALM²)]

palmetto /pæl'metəʊ/ *n.* (pl. **-os**) a small palm tree, e.g. any of various fan palms of the genus *Sabal* or *Chamaerops*. [Sp. *palmito*, dimin. of *palma* PALM¹, assim. to It. words in *-etto*]

palmistry /'pɑːmɪstrɪ/ *n.* supposed divination from lines and other features on the palm of the hand. □ **palmist** *n.* [ME (orig. *palmestry*) f. PALM²: second element unexpl.]

palmy /'pɑːmɪ/ *adj.* (**palmier, palmiest**) **1** of or like or abounding in palms. **2** triumphant, flourishing (*palmy days*).

palomino /ˌpælə'miːnəʊ/ *n.* (pl. **-os**) a golden or cream-coloured horse with a light-coloured mane and tail, orig. bred in the south-western US. [Amer. Sp. f. Sp. *palomino* young pigeon f. *paloma* dove f. L *palumba*]

palp *n.* (also **palpus** /'pælpəs/) (pl. **palps** or **palpi** /-paɪ/) a segmented sense-organ at the mouth of an arthropod; a feeler. □ **palpal** *adj.* [L *palpus* f. *palpare* feel]

palpable /'pælpəb(ə)l/ *adj.* **1** that can be touched or felt. **2** readily perceived by the senses or mind. □ **palpability** /-'bɪlɪtɪ/ *n.* **palpably** *adv.* [ME f. LL *palpabilis* (as PALPATE)]

palpate /pæl'peɪt/ *v.tr.* examine (esp. medically) by touch. □ **palpation** /-'peɪʃ(ə)n/ *n.* [L *palpare palpat-* touch gently]

palpitate /'pælpɪteɪt/ *v.intr.* **1** pulsate, throb. **2** tremble. □ **palpitant** *adj.* [L *palpitare* frequent. of *palpare* touch gently]

palpitation /ˌpælpɪ'teɪʃ(ə)n/ *n.* **1** throbbing, trembling. **2** (often in *pl.*) increased activity of the heart due to exertion, agitation, or disease. [L *palpitatio* (as PALPITATE)]

palsy /'pɔːlzɪ/ *n. & v.* —*n.* (pl. **-ies**) **1** paralysis, esp. with involuntary tremors. **2 a** condition of utter helplessness. **b** a cause of this. —*v.tr.* (**-ies, -ied**) **1** affect with palsy. **2** render helpless. [ME *pa*(*r*)*lesi* f. OF *paralisie* ult. f. L *paralysis*: see PARALYSIS]

palter /'pɔːltə(r), 'pɒl-/ *v.intr.* **1** haggle or equivocate. **2** trifle. □ **palterer** *n.* [16th c.: orig. unkn.]

paltry /'pɔːltrɪ, 'pɒl-/ *adj.* (**paltrier, paltriest**) worthless, contemptible, trifling. □ **paltriness** *n.* [16th c.: f. *paltry* trash app. f. *palt*, *pelt* rubbish + -RY (cf. TRUMPERY): cf. LG *paltrig* ragged]

pampas /'pæmpəs/ *n.pl.* large treeless plains in S. America. □ **pampas-grass** a tall grass, *Cortaderia selloana*, from S. America, with silky flowering plumes. [Sp. f. Quechua *pampa* plain]

pamper /'pæmpə(r)/ *v.tr.* **1** overindulge (a person, taste, etc.), cosset. **2** spoil (a person) with luxury. □ **pamperer** *n.* [ME, prob. of LG or Du. orig.]

pamphlet /'pæmflɪt/ *n. & v.* —*n.* a small, usu. unbound booklet or leaflet containing information or a short treatise. —*v.tr.* (**pamphleted, pamphleting**) distribute pamphlets to. [ME f. *Pamphilet*, the familiar name of the 12th-c. Latin love poem *Pamphilus seu de Amore*]

pamphleteer /ˌpæmflɪ'tɪə(r)/ *n. & v.* —*n.* a writer of (esp. political) pamphlets. —*v.intr.* write pamphlets.

pan[1] *n. & v.* —*n.* **1 a** a vessel of metal, earthenware, or plastic, usu. broad and shallow, used for cooking and other domestic purposes. **b** the contents of this. **2** a panlike vessel in which substances are heated etc. **3** any similar shallow container such as the bowl of a pair of scales or that used for washing gravel etc. to separate gold. **4** *Brit.* the bowl of a lavatory. **5** part of the lock that held the priming in old guns. **6** a hollow in the ground (*salt-pan*). —*v.* (**panned, panning**) **1** *tr. colloq.* criticize severely. **2 a** *tr.* (foll. by *off, out*) wash (gold-bearing gravel) in a pan. **b** *intr.* search for gold by panning gravel. **c** *intr.* (foll. by *out*) (of gravel) yield gold. □ **pan out** (of an action etc.) turn out in a specified way. □ **panful** *n.* (pl. **-fuls**). **panlike** *adj.* [OE *panne*, perh. ult. f. L *patina* dish]

pan[2] /pæn/ *v. & n.* —*v.* (**panned, panning**) **1** *tr.* swing (a cine-camera) horizontally to give a panoramic effect or to follow a moving object. **2** *intr.* (of a cine-camera) be moved in this way. —*n.* a panning movement. [abbr. of PANORAMA]

pan- /pæn/ *comb. form* **1** all; the whole of. **2** relating to the whole or all the parts of a continent, racial group, religion, etc. (*pan-American*; *pan-African*; *pan-Hellenic*; *pan-Anglican*). [Gk f. *pan* neut. of *pas* all]

panacea /ˌpænə'siːə/ *n.* a universal remedy. □ **panacean** *adj.* [L f. Gk *panakeia* f. *panakēs* all-healing (as PAN-, *akos* remedy)]

panache /pə'næʃ/ *n.* assertiveness or flamboyant confidence of style or manner. [F f. It. *pennacchio* f. LL *pinnaculum* dimin. of *pinna* feather]

panama /'pænəˌmɑː/ *n.* a hat of strawlike material made from the leaves of a pine-tree. [*Panama* in Central America]

panatella /ˌpænə'telə/ *n.* a long thin cigar. [Amer. Sp. *panatela*, = long thin biscuit f. It. *panatella* dimin. of *panata* ult. f. L *panis* bread]

pancake /'pænkeɪk, 'pæŋ-/ *n. & v.* —*n.* **1** a thin flat cake of batter usu. fried and turned in a pan and rolled up with a filling. **2** a flat cake of make-up etc. —*v.* **1** *intr.* make a pancake landing. **2** *tr.* cause (an aircraft) to pancake. □ **flat as a pancake** completely flat. **Pancake Day** Shrove Tuesday (on which pancakes are traditionally eaten). **pancake landing** an emergency landing by an aircraft with its undercarriage still retracted, in which the pilot attempts to keep the aircraft in a horizontal position throughout. [ME f. PAN¹ + CAKE]

panchromatic /ˌpænkrəʊˈmætɪk/ adj. Photog. (of a film etc.) sensitive to all visible colours of the spectrum.

pancreas /ˈpæŋkrɪəs/ n. a gland near the stomach supplying the duodenum with digestive fluid and secreting insulin into the blood. □ **pancreatic** /-ˈætɪk/ adj. **pancreatitis** /-ˈtaɪtɪs/ n. [mod.L f. Gk *pagkreas* (as PAN-, *kreas* -*atos* flesh)]

panda /ˈpændə/ n. **1** (also **giant panda**) a large bearlike mammal, *Ailuropoda melanoleuca*, native to China and Tibet, having characteristic black and white markings. **2** (also **red panda**) a Himalayan racoon-like mammal, *Ailurus fulgens*, with reddish-brown fur and a long bushy tail. □ **panda car** Brit. a police patrol car (orig. white with black stripes on the doors). [Nepali name]

pandemic /pænˈdemɪk/ adj. & n. —adj. (of a disease) prevalent over a whole country or the world. —n. a pandemic disease. [Gk *pandēmos* (as PAN-, *dēmos* people)]

pandemonium /ˌpændɪˈməʊnɪəm/ n. **1** uproar; utter confusion. **2** a scene of this. [mod.L (place of all demons in Milton's *Paradise Lost*) f. PAN- + Gk *daimōn* DEMON]

pander /ˈpændə(r)/ v. & n. —v.intr. (foll. by *to*) gratify or indulge a person, a desire or weakness, etc. —n. **1 a** a go-between in illicit love affairs; a procurer. **2** a person who encourages coarse desires. [*Pandare*, a character in Boccaccio and in Chaucer's *Troilus and Criseyde*, f. L *Pandarus* f. Gk *Pandaros*]

pandit var. of PUNDIT 1.

Pandora's box /pænˈdɔːrəz/ n. a process that once activated will generate many unmanageable problems. [in Gk Mythol. the box from which the ills of mankind were released, Hope alone remaining: f. Gk *Pandōra* all-gifted (as PAN-, *dōron* gift)]

p. & p. abbr. Brit. postage and packing.

pane n. **1** a single sheet of glass in a window or door. **2** a rectangular division of a chequered pattern etc. [ME f. OF *pan* f. L *pannus* piece of cloth]

panegyric /ˌpænɪˈdʒɪrɪk/ n. a laudatory discourse; a eulogy. □ **panegyrical** adj. [F *panégyrique* f. L *panegyricus* f. Gk *panēgurikos* of public assembly (as PAN-, *ēguris* = *agora* assembly)]

panegyrize /ˈpænɪdʒɪˌraɪz/ v.tr. (also **-ise**) speak or write in praise of; eulogize. □ **panegyrist** /-ˈdʒɪrɪst/ n. [Gk *panēgurizō* (as PANEGYRIC)]

panel /ˈpæn(ə)l/ n. & v. —n. **1 a** a distinct, usu. rectangular, section of a surface (e.g. of a wall, door, or vehicle). **b** a board containing controls, instruments, dials, etc. **2** a strip of material as part of a garment. **3** a group of people forming a team in a broadcast game, discussion, etc. **4** Brit. hist. a list of medical practitioners registered in a district as accepting patients under the National Insurance Act. **5** a list of available jurors; a jury. —v.tr. (**panelled**, **panelling**; US **paneled**, **paneling**) **1** fit or provide with panels. **2** cover or decorate with panels. □ **panel-beater** one whose job is to beat out the metal panels of motor vehicles. **panel game** a broadcast quiz etc. played by a panel. **panel pin** a thin nail with a very small

head. [ME & OF, = piece of cloth, ult. f. L *pannus*: see PANE]

panelling /ˈpænəlɪŋ/ n. (US **paneling**) **1** panelled work. **2** wood for making panels.

panellist /ˈpænəlɪst/ n. (US **panelist**) a member of a panel (esp. in broadcasting).

pang n. (often in *pl.*) a sudden sharp pain or painful emotion. [16th c.: var. of earlier *prange* pinching f. Gmc]

pangolin /pæŋˈgəʊlɪn/ n. any scaly anteater of the genus *Manis*, native to Asia and Africa, having an elongated snout and tongue. [Malay *peng-gōling* roller (from its habit of rolling itself up)]

panhandle /ˈpænˌhænd(ə)l/ n. & v. US —n. a narrow strip of territory extending from one State into another. —v.tr. & intr. colloq. beg for money in the street. □ **panhandler** n.

panic /ˈpænɪk/ n. & v. —n. **1 a** sudden uncontrollable fear or alarm. **b** (attrib.) characterized or caused by panic (*panic buying*). **2** infectious apprehension or fright esp. in commercial dealings. —v.tr. & intr. (**panicked**, **panicking**) (often foll. by *into*) affect or be affected with panic (*was panicked into buying*). □ **panic button** a button for summoning help in an emergency. **panic stations** a state of emergency. **panic-stricken** (or **-struck**) affected with panic; very apprehensive. □ **panicky** adj. [F *panique* f. mod.L *panicus* f. Gk *panikos* f. *Pan* a rural god causing terror]

panicle /ˈpænɪk(ə)l/ n. Bot. a loose branching cluster of flowers, as in oats. □ **panicled** adj. [L *paniculum* dimin. of *panus* thread]

panjandrum /pænˈdʒændrəm/ n. **1** a mock title for an important person. **2** a pompous or pretentious official etc. [app. invented in nonsense verse by S. Foote 1755]

panne /pæn/ n. (in full **panne velvet**) a velvet-like fabric of silk or rayon with a flattened pile. [F]

pannier /ˈpænɪə(r)/ n. **1** a basket, esp. one of a pair carried by a beast of burden. **2** each of a pair of bags or boxes on either side of the rear wheel of a bicycle or motor cycle. **3** hist. **a** part of a skirt looped up round the hips. **b** a frame supporting this. [ME f. OF *panier* f. L *panarium* bread-basket f. *panis* bread]

panoply /ˈpænəplɪ/ n. (pl. **-ies**) **1** a complete or splendid array. **2** a complete suit of armour. □ **panoplied** adj. [F *panoplie* or mod.L *panoplia* full armour f. Gk (as PAN-, *oplia* f. *hopla* arms)]

panorama /ˌpænəˈrɑːmə/ n. **1** an unbroken view of a surrounding region. **2** a complete survey or presentation of a subject, sequence of events, etc. **3** a picture or photograph containing a wide view. **4** a continuous passing scene. □ **panoramic** /-ˈræmɪk/ adj. **panoramically** /-ˈræmɪkəlɪ/ adv. [PAN- + Gk *horama* view f. *horaō* see]

pan-pipes /ˈpænpaɪps/ n.pl. a musical instrument orig. associated with the Greek rural god Pan, made of a series of short pipes graduated in length and fixed together with the mouthpieces in line.

pansy /ˈpænzɪ/ n. (pl. **-ies**) **1** any garden plant of the genus *Viola*, with flowers of various rich colours. **2** colloq. derog. **a** an effeminate man. **b** a male homosexual. [F *pensée* thought, pansy f. *penser* think f. L *pensare* frequent. of *pendere* pens-weigh]

pant v. & n. —v. **1** intr. breathe with short quick breaths. **2** tr. (often foll. by *out*) utter breathlessly. **3** intr. (often foll. by *for*) yearn or crave. **4** intr. (of the heart etc.) throb violently. —n. **1** a panting breath. **2** a throb. □ **pantingly** adv. [ME f. OF *pantaisier* ult. f. Gk *phantasioō* cause to imagine]

pantalets /ˌpæntəˈlets/ n.pl. (also **pantalettes**) hist. **1** long underpants worn by women and girls in the 19th c., with a frill at the bottom of each leg. **2** women's cycling trousers. [dimin. of PANTALOONS]

pantaloons /ˌpæntəˈluːn/ n.pl. hist. **1** men's close-fitting breeches fastened below the calf or at the foot. **2** esp. US trousers. [F *pantalon* f. It. *pantalone*, a character in Italian comedy]

pantechnicon /pænˈteknɪkən/ n. Brit. a large van for transporting furniture. [PAN- + Gk *tekhnikon*, neut. of *tekhnikos* f. *tekhnē* art, used orig. as the name of a bazaar and then a furniture warehouse]

pantheism /ˈpænθɪˌɪz(ə)m/ n. **1** the belief that God is identifiable with the forces of nature and with natural substances. **2** worship that admits or tolerates all gods. □ **pantheist** n. **pantheistic** /-ˈɪstɪk/ adj. **pantheistical** /-ˈɪstɪk(ə)l/ adj. **pantheistically** /-ˈɪstɪkəlɪ/ adv. [PAN- + Gk *theos* god]

pantheon /ˈpænθɪən/ n. **1** a building in which illustrious dead are buried or have memorials. **2** the deities of a people collectively. **3** a temple dedicated to all the gods, esp. the circular one at Rome. [ME f. L f. Gk *pantheion* (as PAN-, *theion* holy f. *theos* god)]

panther /ˈpænθə(r)/ n. **1** a leopard, esp. with black fur. **2** US a puma. [ME f. OF *pantere* f. L *panthera* f. Gk *panthēr*]

pantie-girdle /ˈpæntɪˌgɜːd(ə)l/ n. a woman's girdle with a crotch shaped like pants.

panties /ˈpæntɪz/ n.pl. colloq. short-legged or legless underpants worn by women and girls. [dimin. of PANTS]

pantihose /ˈpæntɪˌhəʊz/ n. (US **panty hose**) (usu. treated as pl.) women's tights. [PANTIES + HOSE]

pantile /ˈpæntaɪl/ n. a roof-tile curved to form an S-shaped section, fitted to overlap. [PAN¹ + TILE]

panto /ˈpæntəʊ/ n. (pl. **-os**) Brit. colloq. = PANTOMIME 1. [abbr.]

panto- /ˈpæntəʊ/ comb. form all, universal. [Gk *pas pantos* all]

pantograph /ˈpæntəˌɡrɑːf/ n. **1** Art & Painting an instrument for copying a plan or drawing etc. on a different scale by a system of jointed rods. **2** a jointed framework conveying a current to an electric vehicle from overhead wires. □ **pantographic** /-ˈɡræfɪk/ adj. [PANTO- + Gk *-graphos* writing]

pantomime /ˈpæntəˌmaɪm/ n. **1** Brit. a theatrical entertainment based on a fairy tale, with music, topical jokes, etc., usu. produced about Christmas. **2** the use of gestures and facial expression to convey meaning, esp. in drama and dance. **3** colloq. an absurd or outrageous piece of behaviour. □ **pantomimic** /-ˈmɪmɪk/ adj. [F *pantomime* or L *pantomimus* f. Gk *pantomimos* (as PANTO-, MIME)]

pantothenic acid /ˌpæntəˈθenɪk/ n. a vitamin of the B complex, found in rice, bran, and many other foods, and essential for the oxidation of fats and carbohydrates. [Gk *pantothen* from every side]

pantry /ˈpæntrɪ/ n. (pl. **-ies**) **1** a small room or cupboard in which crockery, cutlery, table linen, etc., are kept. **2** a larder. [ME f. AF *panetrie*, OF *paneterie* f. *panetier* baker ult. f. LL *panarius* bread-seller f. L *panis* bread]

pants n.pl. **1** Brit. underpants or knickers. **2** US trousers or slacks. □ **bore** (or **scare** etc.) **the pants off** colloq. bore, scare, etc., to an intolerable degree. **pants** (or **pant**) **suit** esp. US a trouser suit. **with one's pants down** colloq. in an embarrassingly unprepared state. [abbr. of PANTALOONS]

panty hose US var. of PANTIHOSE.

panzer /ˈpæntsə(r), ˈpænz-/ n. **1** (in pl.) armoured troops. **2** (attrib.) heavily armoured (*panzer division*). [G, = coat of mail]

pap¹ n. **1 a** a soft or semi-liquid food for infants or invalids. **b** a mash or pulp. **2** light or trivial reading matter; nonsense. □ **pappy** adj. [ME prob. f. MLG, MDu. *pappe*, prob. ult. f. L *pappare* eat]

pap² /pæp/ n. archaic or dial. the nipple of a breast. [ME, of Scand. orig.: ult. imit. of sucking]

papa /pəˈpɑː/ n. archaic father (esp. as a child's word). [F f. LL f. Gk *papas*]

papacy /ˈpeɪpəsɪ/ n. (pl. **-ies**) **1** a pope's office or tenure. **2** the papal system. [ME f. med.L *papatia* f. *papa* pope]

papain /pəˈpeɪɪn/ n. an enzyme obtained from unripe pawpaws, used to tenderize meat and as a food supplement to aid digestion. [PAPAYA + -IN]

papal /ˈpeɪp(ə)l/ adj. of or relating to a pope or to the papacy. □ **papally** adv. [ME f. OF f. med.L *papalis* f. eccl.L *papa* POPE]

paparazzo /ˌpæpəˈrɑːtsəʊ/ n. (pl. **paparazzi** /-tsɪ/) a freelance photographer who pursues celebrities to get photographs of them. [It.]

papaw var. of PAWPAW.

papaya /pəˈpaɪjə/ n. = PAWPAW 1. [earlier form of PAWPAW]

paper /ˈpeɪpə(r)/ n. & v. —n. **1** a material manufactured in thin sheets from the pulp of wood or other fibrous substances, used for writing or drawing or printing on, or as wrapping material etc. **2** (attrib.) **a** made of or using paper. **b** flimsy like paper. **3** = NEWSPAPER. **4 a** a document printed on paper. **b** (in pl.) documents attesting identity or credentials. **c** (in pl.) documents belonging to a person or relating to a matter. **5** Commerce **a** negotiable documents, e.g. bills of exchange. **b** (attrib.) recorded on paper though not existing (*paper profits*). **6 a** a set of questions to be answered at one session in an examination. **b** the written answers to these. **7** = WALLPAPER. **8** an essay or dissertation, esp. one read to a learned society or published in a learned journal. **9** a piece of paper, esp. as a wrapper etc. —v.tr. **1** apply paper to, esp. decorate (a wall etc.) with wallpaper. **2** (foll. by *over*) **a** cover (a hole or blemish) with paper. **b** disguise or try to hide (a fault etc.). □ **on paper 1** in writing. **2** in theory; to judge from written or printed evidence. **paper-boy** (or **-girl**) a boy or girl who delivers or sells newspapers. **paper-chase** a cross-country run in which the runners follow a trail marked by torn-up paper. **paper-clip** a clip of bent wire or of plastic for holding several sheets of paper together.

paper-hanger a person who decorates with wallpaper, esp. professionally. **paper-knife** a blunt knife for opening letters etc. **paper-mill** a mill in which paper is made. **paper money** money in the form of banknotes. **paper round 1** a job of regularly delivering newspapers. **2** a route taken doing this. □ **paperer** n. **paperless** adj. [ME f. AF papir, = OF papier f. L papyrus: see PAPYRUS]

paperback /ˈpeɪpəˌbæk/ adj. & n. —adj. (of a book) bound in stiff paper not boards. —n. a paperback book.

paperweight /ˈpeɪpəˌweɪt/ n. a small heavy object for keeping loose papers in place.

paperwork /ˈpeɪpəˌwɜːk/ n. routine clerical or administrative work.

papery /ˈpeɪpərɪ/ adj. like paper in thinness or texture.

papier mâché /ˌpæpjeɪ ˈmæʃeɪ/ n. paper pulp used for moulding into boxes, trays, etc. [F, = chewed paper]

papilla /pəˈpɪlə/ n. (pl. **papillae** /-liː/) **1** a small nipple-like protuberance in a part or organ of the body. **2** Bot. a small fleshy projection on a plant. □ **papillary** adj. **papillate** /ˈpæpɪˌleɪt/ adj. **papillose** /ˈpæpɪˌləʊs/ adj. [L, = nipple, dimin. of papula: see PAPULA]

papilloma /ˌpæpɪˈləʊmə/ n. (pl. **papillomas** or **papillomata** /-mətə/) a wartlike usu. benign tumour.

papist /ˈpeɪpɪst/ n. & adj. often derog. —n. a Roman Catholic. —adj. of or relating to Roman Catholics. □ **papistic** /pəˈpɪstɪk/ adj. **papistical** /pəˈpɪstɪk(ə)l/ adj. **papistry** n. [F papiste or mod.L papista f. eccl.L papa POPE]

papoose /pəˈpuːs/ n. a N. American Indian young child. [Algonquin]

paprika /ˈpæprɪkə, pəˈpriːkə/ n. **1** Bot. a red pepper. **2** a condiment made from it. [Magyar]

papula /ˈpæpjʊlə/ n. (also **papule** /-pjuːl/) (pl. **papulae** /-ˌliː/) **1** a pimple. **2** a small fleshy projection on a plant. □ **papular** adj. **papulose** adj. **papulous** adj. [L]

papyrus /pəˈpaɪərəs/ n. (pl. **papyri** /-raɪ/) **1** an aquatic plant, Cyperus papyrus, with dark green stems topped with fluffy inflorescences. **2 a** a writing-material prepared in ancient Egypt from the pithy stem of this. **b** a document written on this. [ME f. L papyrus f. Gk papuros]

par[1] n. **1** the average or normal amount, degree, condition, etc. (feel below par; be up to par). **2** equality; an equal status or footing (on a par with). **3** Golf the number of strokes a first-class player should normally require for a hole or course. **4** Stock Exch. the face value of stocks and shares etc. (at par). **5** (in full **par of exchange**) the recognized value of one country's currency in terms of another's. □ **above** (or **below**) **par** Stock Exch. at a premium (or discount). **at par** Stock Exch. at face value. **par for the course** colloq. what is normal or expected in any given circumstances. [L (adj. & n.) = equal, equality]

par[2] /pɑː(r)/ n. Brit. esp. Journalism colloq. paragraph. [abbr.]

para /ˈpærə/ n. colloq. **1** a paratrooper. **2** a paragraph. [abbr.]

para-[1] /ˈpærə/ prefix (also **par-**) **1** beside (paramilitary). **2** beyond (paranormal). **3** Chem. modification of. [from or after Gk para- f. para beside, past, beyond]

para-[2] /ˈpærə/ comb. form protect, ward off (parachute; parasol). [F f. It. f. L parare defend]

parable /ˈpærəb(ə)l/ n. **1** a narrative of imagined events used to illustrate a moral or spiritual lesson. **2** an allegory. [ME f. OF parabole f. LL sense 'allegory, discourse' of L parabola comparison]

parabola /pəˈræbələ/ n. an open plane curve formed by the intersection of a cone with a plane parallel to its side. [mod.L f. Gk parabolē placing side by side, comparison (as PARA-[1], bolē a throw f. ballō)]

parabolic /ˌpærəˈbɒlɪk/ adj. **1** of or expressed in a parable. **2** of or like a parabola. □ **parabolically** adv. [LL parabolicus f. Gk parabolikos (as PARABOLA)]

parabolical /ˌpærəˈbɒlɪk(ə)l/ adj. = PARABOLIC 1.

paracetamol /ˌpærəˈsetəˌmɒl, -ˈsiːtəˌmɒl/ n. **1** a drug used to relieve pain and reduce fever. **2** a tablet of this. [para-acetylaminophenol]

parachute /ˈpærəˌʃuːt/ n. & v. —n. **1** a rectangular or umbrella-shaped apparatus allowing a person or heavy object attached to it to descend slowly from a height, esp. from an aircraft, or to retard motion in other ways. **2** (attrib.) dropped or to be dropped by parachute (parachute troops; parachute flare). —v.tr. & intr. convey or descend by parachute. [F (as PARA-[2], CHUTE[1])]

parachutist /ˈpærəˌʃuːtɪst/ n. **1** a person who uses a parachute. **2** (in pl.) parachute troops.

Paraclete /ˈpærəˌkliːt/ n. the Holy Spirit as advocate or counsellor (John 14:16, 26, etc.). [ME f. OF paraclet f. LL paracletus f. Gk paraklētos called in aid (as PARA-[1], klētos f. kaleō call)]

parade /pəˈreɪd/ n. & v. —n. **1 a** a formal or ceremonial muster of troops for inspection. **b** = parade-ground. **2** a public procession. **3** ostentatious display (made a parade of their wealth). **4** a public square, promenade, or row of shops. —v. **1** intr. assemble for parade. **2 a** tr. march through (streets etc.) in procession. **b** intr. march ceremonially. **3** tr. display ostentatiously. □ **on parade 1** taking part in a parade. **2** on display. **parade-ground** a place for the muster of troops. □ **parader** n. [F, = show, f. Sp. parada and It. parata ult. f. L parare prepare, furnish]

paradigm /ˈpærəˌdaɪm/ n. an example or pattern, esp. a representative set of the inflections of a noun, verb, etc. □ **paradigmatic** /-dɪɡˈmætɪk/ adj. **paradigmatically** /-dɪɡˈmætɪkəlɪ/ adv. [LL paradigma f. Gk paradeigma f. paradeiknumi show side by side (as PARA-[1], deiknumi show)]

paradise /ˈpærəˌdaɪs/ n. **1** (in some religions) heaven as the ultimate abode of the just. **2** a place or state of complete happiness. **3** (in full **earthly paradise**) the garden of Eden. □ **paradisaical** /-dɪˈseɪɪk(ə)l/ adj. **paradisal** /ˈpærəˌdaɪs(ə)l/ adj. **paradisiacal** /-dɪˈsaɪək(ə)l/ adj. **paradisical** /-ˈdɪsɪk(ə)l/ adj. [ME f. OF paradis f. LL paradisus f. Gk paradeisos f. Avestan pairidaēza park]

paradox /ˈpærəˌdɒks/ n. **1 a** a seemingly absurd or contradictory statement, even if actually well-founded. **b** a self-contradictory or essentially absurd statement. **2** a person or thing conflicting with a preconceived notion of what is reasonable or possible. **3** a paradoxical quality or character. [orig. = a statement contrary to accepted opinion, f. LL *paradoxum* f. Gk *paradoxon* neut. adj. (as PARA-¹, *doxa* opinion)]

paradoxical /ˌpærəˈdɒksɪk(ə)l/ *adj.* **1** of or like or involving paradox. **2** fond of paradox. □ **paradoxically** *adv.*

paraffin /ˈpærəfɪn/ *n.* **1** an inflammable waxy or oily substance obtained by distillation from petroleum or shale, used in liquid form (also **paraffin oil**) esp. as a fuel. **2** *Chem.* = ALKANE. □ **paraffin wax** paraffin in its solid form. [G (1830) f. L *parum* little + *affinis* related, from the small affinity it has for other substances]

paragon /ˈpærəgən/ *n.* **1 a** a model of excellence. **b** a supremely excellent person or thing. **2** (foll. by *of*) a model (of virtue etc.). [obs. F f. It. *paragone* touchstone, f. med.Gk *parakonē* whetstone]

paragraph /ˈpærəˌgrɑːf/ *n.* & *v.* —*n.* **1** a distinct section of a piece of writing, beginning on a new usu. indented line. **2** a symbol (usu. ¶) used to mark a new paragraph, and also as a reference mark. **3** a short item in a newspaper, news. of only one paragraph. —*v.tr.* arrange (a piece of writing) in paragraphs. □ **paragraphic** /-ˈgræfɪk/ *adj.* [F *paragraphe* or med.L *paragraphus* f. Gk *paragraphos* short stroke marking a break in sense (as PARA-¹, *graphō* write)]

parakeet /ˈpærəˌkiːt/ *n.* (*US* also **parrakeet**) any of various small usu. long-tailed parrots. [OF *paroquet*, It. *parrocchetto*, Sp. *periquito*, perh. ult. f. dimin. of *Pierre* etc. Peter: cf. PARROT]

paralegal /ˌpærəˈliːg(ə)l/ *adj.* & *n.* esp. *US* —*adj.* of or relating to auxiliary aspects of the law. —*n.* a person trained in subsidiary legal matters. [PARA-¹ + LEGAL]

parallax /ˈpærəˌlæks/ *n.* **1** the apparent difference in the position or direction of an object caused when the observer's position is changed. **2** the angular amount of this. □ **parallactic** /-ˈlæktɪk/ *adj.* [F *parallaxe* f. mod.L *parallaxis* f. Gk *parallaxis* change f. *parallassō* to alternate (as PARA-¹, *allassō* exchange f. *allos* other)]

parallel /ˈpærəˌlel/ *adj.*, *n.*, & *v.* —*adj.* **1 a** (of lines or planes) side by side and having the same distance continuously between them. **b** (foll. by *to*, *with*) (of a line or plane) having this relation (to another). **2** (of circumstances etc.) precisely similar, analogous, or corresponding. **3 a** (of processes etc.) occurring or performed simultaneously. **b** *Computing* involving the simultaneous performance of operations. —*n.* **1** a person or thing precisely analogous or equal to another. **2** a comparison (*drew a parallel between the two situations*). **3** (in full **parallel of latitude**) *Geog.* **a** each of the imaginary parallel circles of constant latitude on the earth's surface. **b** a corresponding line on a map (*the 49th parallel*). **4** *Printing* two parallel lines (||) as a reference mark. —*v.tr.* (**paralleled**, **paralleling**) **1** be parallel to; correspond to. **2** represent as similar; compare. **3** adduce as a parallel instance. □ **in parallel** (of electric circuits) arranged so as to join at common points at each end. **parallel bars** a pair of parallel rails on posts for gymnastics. □ **parallelism** *n.* [F *parallèle* f. L *parallelus* f. Gk *parallēlos* (as PARA-¹, *allēlos* one another)]

parallelepiped /ˌpærəlelˈepɪˌped, -ləˈpaɪpɪd/ *n.* *Geom.* a solid body of which each face is a

parallelogram. [Gk *parallēlepipedon* (as PARALLEL, *epipedon* plane surface)]

parallelogram /ˌpærəˈleləˌgræm/ *n.* *Geom.* a four-sided plane rectilinear figure with opposite sides parallel. [F *parallélogramme* f. LL *parallelogrammum* f. Gk *parallēlogrammon* (as PARALLEL, *grammē* line)]

paralyse /ˈpærəˌlaɪz/ *v.tr.* (*US* **paralyze**) **1** affect with paralysis. **2** render powerless; cripple. □ **paralysation** /-ˈzeɪʃ(ə)n/ *n.* **paralysingly** *adv.* [F *paralyser* f. *paralysie*: cf. PALSY]

paralysis /pəˈrælɪsɪs/ *n.* (*pl.* **paralyses** /-ˌsiːz/) **1** a nervous condition with impairment or loss of esp. the motor function of the nerves. **2** a state of utter powerlessness. [L f. Gk *paralusis* f. *paraluō* disable (as PARA-¹, *luō* loosen)]

paralytic /ˌpærəˈlɪtɪk/ *adj.* & *n.* —*adj.* **1** affected by paralysis. **2** *sl.* very drunk. —*n.* a person affected by paralysis. □ **paralytically** *adv.* [ME f. OF *paralytique* f. L *paralyticus* f. Gk *paralutikos* (as PARALYSIS)]

paramedic /ˌpærəˈmedɪk/ *n.* a paramedical worker.

paramedical /ˌpærəˈmedɪk(ə)l/ *adj.* (of services etc.) supplementing and supporting medical work.

parameter /pəˈræmɪtə(r)/ *n.* **1** *Math.* a quantity constant in the case considered but varying in different cases. **2 a** an (esp. measurable or quantifiable) characteristic or feature. **b** (loosely) a constant element or factor, esp. serving as a limit or boundary. □ **parametric** /ˌpærəˈmetrɪk/ *adj.* **parametrize** *v.tr.* (also **-ise**). [mod.L f. Gk *para* beside + *metron* measure]

paramilitary /ˌpærəˈmɪlɪtərɪ/ *adj.* (of forces) ancillary to and similarly organized to military forces.

paramount /ˈpærəˌmaʊnt/ *adj.* **1** supreme; requiring first consideration; pre-eminent (*of paramount importance*). **2** in supreme authority. □ **paramountcy** *n.* **paramountly** *adv.* [AF *paramont* f. OF *par* by + *amont* above: cf. AMOUNT]

paramour /ˈpærəˌmʊə(r)/ *n.* archaic or derog. an illicit lover of a married person. [ME f. OF *par amour* by love]

paranoia /ˌpærəˈnɔɪə/ *n.* **1** a mental disorder esp. characterized by delusions of persecution and self-importance. **2** an abnormal tendency to suspect and mistrust others. □ **paranoiac** *adj.* & *n.* **paranoiacally** *adv.* **paranoic** /-ˈnɔɪk, -ˈnɔɪɪk/ *adj.* **paranoically** /-ˈnɔɪkəlɪ, -ˈnɔɪɪkəlɪ/ *adv.* **paranoid** /ˈpærəˌnɔɪd/ *adj.* & *n.* [mod.L f. Gk f. *paranoos* distracted (as PARA-¹, *noos* mind)]

paranormal /ˌpærəˈnɔːm(ə)l/ *adj.* beyond the scope of normal objective investigation or explanation. □ **paranormally** *adv.*

parapet /ˈpærəpɪt/ *n.* **1** a low wall at the edge of a roof, balcony, etc., or along the sides of a bridge. **2** a defence of earth or stone to conceal and protect troops. □ **parapeted** *adj.* [F *parapet* or It. *parapetto* breast-high wall (as PARA-², *petto* breast f. L *pectus*)]

paraphernalia /ˌpærəfəˈneɪlɪə/ *n.pl.* (also treated as *sing.*) miscellaneous belongings, items of equipment, accessories, etc. [orig. = property owned by a married woman, f. med.L *paraphernalia* f. LL *parapherna* f. Gk *parapherna* property apart from a dowry (as PARA-¹, *pherna* f. *phernē* dower)]

paraphrase /ˈpærəˌfreɪz/ *n.* & *v.* —*n.* a free rendering or rewording of a passage. —*v.tr.*

express the meaning of (a passage) in other words. □ **paraphrastic** /-'fræstɪk/ *adj.* [F *paraphrase* or L *paraphrasis* f. Gk *paraphrasis* f. *paraphrazō* (as PARA-¹ *phrazō* tell)]

paraplegia /ˌpærə'pliːdʒə/ *n.* paralysis of the legs and part or the whole of the trunk. □ **paraplegic** *adj.* & *n.* [mod.L f. Gk *paraplēgia* f. *paraplēssō* (as PARA-¹, *plēssō* strike)]

parapsychology /ˌpærəsaɪ'kɒlədʒɪ/ *n.* the study of mental phenomena outside the sphere of ordinary psychology (hypnosis, telepathy, etc.). □ **parapsychological** /-ˌsaɪkə'lɒdʒɪk(ə)l/ *adj.* **parapsychologist** *n.*

paraquat /'pærəˌkwɒt/ *n.* a quick-acting herbicide, becoming inactive on contact with the soil. [PARA-¹ + QUATERNARY (from the position of the bond between the two parts of the molecule relative to quaternary nitrogen atom)]

parasailing /'pærəseɪlɪŋ/ *n.* a sport in which participants wearing open parachutes are towed behind a motor boat. □ **parasailer** *n.*, **parasailor** *n.*

parascending /'pærəˌsendɪŋ/ *n.* a sport in which participants wearing open parachutes are towed behind a vehicle or motor boat to gain height before release for a conventional descent, usu. towards a predetermined target. □ **parascender** *n.*

parasite /'pærəˌsaɪt/ *n.* **1** an organism living in or on another and benefiting at the expense of the other. **2** a person who lives off or exploits another or others. □ **parasitic** /-'sɪtɪk/ *adj.* **parasitical** /-'sɪtɪk(ə)l/ *adj.* **parasitically** /-'sɪtɪkəlɪ/ *adv.* **parasiticide** /-'sɪtɪˌsaɪd/ *n.* **parasitism** *n.* **parasitology** /-'tɒlədʒɪ/ *n.* **parasitologist** /-'tɒlədʒɪst/ *n.* [L *parasitus* f. Gk *parasitos* one who eats at another's table (as PARA-¹, *sitos* food)]

parasitize /'pærəsɪˌtaɪz/ *v.tr.* (also **-ise**) infest as a parasite. □ **parasitization** /-'zeɪʃ(ə)n/ *n.*

parasol /'pærəˌsɒl/ *n.* a light umbrella used to give shade from the sun. [F f. It. *parasole* (as PARA-², *sole* sun f. L *sol*)]

parathion /ˌpærə'θaɪən/ *n.* a highly toxic agricultural insecticide. [PARA-¹ + THIO- + -ON]

parathyroid /ˌpærə'θaɪrɔɪd/ *n.* & *adj. Anat.* —*n.* a gland next to the thyroid, secreting a hormone that regulates calcium levels in the body. —*adj.* of or associated with this gland.

paratroop /'pærəˌtruːp/ *n.* (*attrib.*) of or consisting of paratroops (*paratroop regiment*).

paratrooper /'pærəˌtruːpə(r)/ *n.* a member of a body of paratroops.

paratroops /'pærəˌtruːps/ *n.pl.* troops equipped to be dropped by parachute from aircraft. [contr. of PARACHUTE + TROOP]

paratyphoid /ˌpærə'taɪfɔɪd/ *n.* & *adj.* —*n.* a fever resembling typhoid but caused by various different though related bacteria. —*adj.* of, relating to, or caused by this fever.

parboil /'pɑːˌbɔɪl/ *v.tr.* partly cook by boiling. [ME f. OF *parbo(u)illir* f. LL *perbullire* boil thoroughly (as PER-, *bullire* boil: confused with PART)]

parcel /'pɑːs(ə)l/ *n.* & *v.* —*n.* **1 a** goods etc. wrapped up in a single package. **b** a bundle of things wrapped up, usu. in paper. **2** a piece of land, esp. as part of an estate. **3** a quantity dealt with in one commercial transaction. —*v.tr.* (**parcelled, parcelling**; US **parceled, parceling**) **1** (foll. by *up*) wrap as a parcel. **2** (foll. by *out*) divide into portions. □ **parcel post** the

branch of the postal service dealing with parcels. [ME f. OF *parcelle* ult. f. L *particula* (as PART)]

parch *v.* **1** *tr.* & *intr.* make or become hot and dry. **2** *tr.* roast (peas, corn, etc.) slightly. [ME *perch*, *parche*, of unkn. orig.]

parched /pɑːtʃt/ *adj.* **1** hot and dry; dried out with heat. **2** *colloq.* thirsty.

parchment /'pɑːtʃmənt/ *n.* **1 a** an animal skin, esp. that of a sheep or goat, prepared as a writing or painting surface. **b** a manuscript written on this. **2** (in full **vegetable parchment**) high-grade paper made to resemble parchment. [ME f. OF *parchemin*, ult. a blend of LL *pergamina* writing material from Pergamum (in Asia Minor) with *Parthica pellis* Parthian skin (leather)]

pardner /'pɑːdnə(r)/ *n.* US *colloq.* a partner or comrade. [corrupt.]

pardon /'pɑːd(ə)n/ *n.*, *v.*, & *int.* —*n.* **1** the act of excusing or forgiving an offence, error, etc. **2** (in full **free pardon**) a remission of the legal consequences of a crime or conviction. **3** *RC Ch.* an indulgence. —*v.tr.* **1** release from the consequences of an offence, error, etc. **2** forgive or excuse a person for (an offence etc.). **3** make (esp. courteous) allowances for; excuse. —*int.* (also **pardon me** or **I beg your pardon**) **1** a formula of apology or disagreement. **2** a request to repeat something said. □ **pardonable** *adj.* **pardonably** *adv.* [ME f. OF *pardun*, *pardoner* f. med.L *perdonare* concede, remit (as PER-, *donare* give)]

pare /peə(r)/ *v.tr.* **1 a** trim or shave (esp. fruit and vegetables) by cutting away the surface or edge. **b** (often foll. by *off*, *away*) cut off (the surface or edge). **2** (often foll. by *away*, *down*) diminish little by little. □ **parer** *n.* [ME f. OF *parer* adorn, peel (fruit), f. L *parare* prepare]

parent /'peərənt/ *n.* & *v.* —*n.* **1** a person who has begotten or borne offspring; a father or mother. **2** a person who has adopted a child. **3** a forefather. **4** an animal or plant from which others are derived. **5** a source or origin. **6** an initiating organization or enterprise. —*v.tr.* (also *absol.*) be a parent of. □ **parent company** a company of which other companies are subsidiaries. **parent–teacher association** a local organization of parents and teachers for promoting closer relations and improving educational facilities at a school. □ **parental** /pə'rent(ə)l/ *adj.* **parentally** /pə'rentəlɪ/ *adv.* **parenthood** *n.* [ME f. OF f. L *parens parentis* f. *parere* bring forth]

parentage /'peərəntɪdʒ/ *n.* lineage; descent from or through parents (*their parentage is unknown*). [ME f. OF (as PARENT)]

parenthesis /pə'renθəsɪs/ *n.* (*pl.* **parentheses** /-ˌsiːz/) **1 a** a word, clause, or sentence inserted as an explanation or afterthought into a passage which is grammatically complete without it, and usu. marked off by brackets or dashes or commas. **b** (in *pl.*) a pair of round brackets () used for this. **2** an interlude or interval. □ **in parenthesis** as a parenthesis or afterthought. [LL f. Gk *parenthesis* f. *parentithēmi* put in beside]

parenthetic /ˌpærən'θetɪk/ *adj.* **1** of or by way of a parenthesis. **2** interposed. □ **parenthetical** *adj.* **parenthetically** *adv.* [PARENTHESIS after *synthesis*, *synthetic*, etc.]

parenting /'peərəntɪŋ/ *n.* the occupation or concerns of parents.

par excellence /ˌpɑːr eksəˈlɑ̃s/ adv. as having special excellence; being the supreme example of its kind (*the short story par excellence*). [F, = by excellence]

parfait /ˈpɑːfeɪ/ n. **1** a rich iced pudding of whipped cream, eggs, etc. **2** layers of ice-cream, meringue, etc., served in a tall glass. [F *parfait* PERFECT *adj.*]

parget /ˈpɑːdʒɪt/ v. & n. —v.tr. (**targeted, targeting**) **1** plaster (a wall etc.) esp. with an ornamental pattern. **2** roughcast. —n. **1** plaster applied in this way; ornamental plasterwork. **2** roughcast. [ME f. OF *pargeter, parjeter* f. *par* all over + *jeter* throw]

pariah /pəˈraɪə, ˈpærɪə/ n. **1** a social outcast. **2** *hist.* a member of a low caste or of no caste in S. India. □ **pariah-dog** = PYE-DOG. [Tamil *paṟaiyar* pl. of *paṟaiyan* hereditary drummer f. *paṟai* drum]

parietal /pəˈraɪət(ə)l/ adj. **1** *Anat.* of the wall of the body or any of its cavities. **2** *Bot.* of the wall of a hollow structure etc. □ **parietal bone** either of a pair of bones forming the central part of the sides and top of the skull. [F *pariétal* or LL *parietalis* f. L *paries -etis* wall]

paring /ˈpeərɪŋ/ n. a strip or piece cut off.

parish /ˈpærɪʃ/ n. **1** an area having its own church and clergy. **2** (in full **civil parish**) a district constituted for purposes of local government. **3** the inhabitants of a parish. □ **parish clerk** an official performing various duties concerned with the church. **parish council** *Brit.* the administrative body in a civil parish. **parish pump** (often *attrib.*) a symbol of a parochial or restricted outlook. **parish register** a book recording christenings, marriages, and burials, at a parish church. [ME *paroche, parosse* f. OF *paroche, paroisse* f. eccl.L *parochia, paroechia* f. Gk *paroikia* sojourning f. *paroikos* (as PARA-¹, -oikos -dwelling f. *oikeō* dwell)]

parishioner /pəˈrɪʃ(ə)nə(r)/ n. an inhabitant of a parish. [obs. *parishen* f. ME f. OF *parossien*, formed as PARISH]

Parisian /pəˈrɪzɪən/ adj. & n. —adj. of or relating to Paris in France. —n. **1** a native or inhabitant of Paris. **2** the kind of French spoken in Paris. [F *parisien*]

parity /ˈpærɪtɪ/ n. **1** equality or equal status, esp. as regards status or pay. **2** parallelism or analogy (*parity of reasoning*). **3** equivalence of one currency with another; being at par. **4** (of a number) the fact of being even or odd. [F *parité* or LL *paritas* (as PAR¹)]

park n. & v. —n. **1** a large public garden in a town, for recreation. **2** a large enclosed piece of ground, usu. with woodland and pasture, attached to a country house etc. **3 a** a large area of land kept in its natural state for public recreational use. **b** a large enclosed area of land used to accommodate wild animals in captivity (*wildlife park*). **4** an area for motor vehicles etc. to be left in (*car park*). **5** an area devoted to a specified purpose (*industrial park*). **6 a** *US* a sports ground. **b** (usu. prec. by *the*) a football pitch. —v.tr. **1** (also *absol.*) leave (a vehicle) usu. temporarily, in a car park, by the side of the road, etc. **2** *colloq.* deposit and leave, usu. temporarily. □ **parking-lot** *US* an outdoor area for parking vehicles. **parking-meter** a coin-operated meter which receives fees for vehicles parked in the street and indicates the

time available. **parking-ticket** a notice, usu. attached to a vehicle, of a penalty imposed for parking illegally. **park oneself** *colloq.* sit down. [ME f. OF *parc* f. med.L *parricus* of Gmc orig., rel. to *pearruc*: see PADDOCK]

parka /ˈpɑːkə/ n. **1** a skin jacket with hood, worn by Eskimos. **2** a similar windproof fabric garment worn by mountaineers etc. [Aleutian]

parkin /ˈpɑːkɪn/ n. *Brit.* a cake or biscuit made with oatmeal, ginger, and treacle or molasses. [perh. f. the name *Parkin*, dimin. of *Peter*]

Parkinsonism /ˈpɑːkɪnsəˌnɪz(ə)m/ n. = PARKINSON'S DISEASE.

Parkinson's disease /ˈpɑːkɪns(ə)nz/ n. a progressive disease of the nervous system with tremor, muscular rigidity, and emaciation. Also called PARKINSONISM. [J. *Parkinson*, Engl. surgeon d. 1824]

Parkinson's law /ˈpɑːkɪns(ə)nz/ n. the notion that work expands so as to fill the time available for its completion. [C. N. *Parkinson*, Engl. writer b. 1909]

parkland /ˈpɑːklænd/ n. open grassland with clumps of trees etc.

parkway /ˈpɑːkweɪ/ n. **1** *US* an open landscaped highway. **2** *Brit.* a railway station with extensive parking facilities.

parky /ˈpɑːkɪ/ adj. (**parkier, parkiest**) *Brit. colloq.* chilly. [19th c.: orig. unkn.]

parlance /ˈpɑːləns/ n. a particular way of speaking, esp. as regards choice of words, idiom, etc. [OF f. *parler* speak, ult. f. L *parabola* (see PARABLE): in LL = 'speech']

parley /ˈpɑːlɪ/ n. & v. —n. (pl. **-eys**) a conference for debating points in a dispute, esp. a discussion of terms for an armistice etc. —v.intr. (**-leys, -leyed**) (often foll. by *with*) hold a parley. [perh. f. OF *parlee*, fem. past part. of *parler* speak: see PARLANCE]

parliament /ˈpɑːləmənt/ n. **1** (**Parliament**) **a** (in the UK) the highest legislature, consisting of the Sovereign, the House of Lords, and the House of Commons. **b** the members of this legislature for a particular period, esp. between one dissolution and the next. **2** a similar legislature in other nations and States. [ME f. OF *parlement* speaking (as PARLANCE)]

parliamentarian /ˌpɑːləmənˈteərɪən/ n. a member of a parliament, esp. one well-versed in its procedures.

parliamentary /ˌpɑːləˈmentərɪ/ adj. **1** of or relating to a parliament. **2** enacted or established by a parliament. **3** (of language) admissible in a parliament; polite. □ **Parliamentary Commissioner for Administration** the official name of the ombudsman in the UK. **parliamentary private secretary** a member of parliament assisting a government minister.

parlour /ˈpɑːlə(r)/ n. (*US* **parlor**) **1** a sitting-room in a private house. **2** a room in a hotel, convent, etc., for the private use of residents. **3** esp. *US* a shop providing specified goods or services (*beauty parlour; ice-cream parlour*). **4** a room or building equipped for milking cows. □ **parlour game** an indoor game, esp. a word game. **parlour-maid** *hist.* a maid who waits at table. [ME f. AF *parlur*, OF *parleor, parleur*: see PARLANCE]

parlous /ˈpɑːləs/ adj. & adv. archaic or joc. —adj. **1** dangerous or difficult. **2** hard to deal with. —adv. extremely. □ **parlously** adv. **parlousness** n. [ME, = PERILOUS]

Parma violet /ˈpɑːmə/ n. a variety of sweet violet with heavy scent and lavender-coloured flowers often crystallized for food decoration. [*Parma* in Italy]

Parmesan /ˌpɑːmɪˈzæn, ˈpɑː-/ n. a kind of hard dry cheese made orig. at Parma and used esp. in grated form. [F f. It. *parmegiano* of Parma in Italy]

parochial /pəˈrəʊkɪəl/ adj. **1** of or concerning a parish. **2** (of affairs, views, etc.) merely local, narrow or restricted in scope. □ **parochialism** n. **parochiality** /-ˈælɪtɪ/ n. **parochially** adv. [ME f. AF *parochiel*, OF *parochial* f. eccl.L *parochialis* (as PARISH)]

parody /ˈpærədɪ/ n. & v. —n. (pl. **-ies**) **1** a humorous exaggerated imitation of an author, literary work, style, etc. **2** a feeble imitation; a travesty. —v.tr. (**-ies**, **-ied**) **1** compose a parody of. **2** mimic humorously. □ **parodic** /pəˈrɒdɪk/ adj. **parodist** n. [LL *parodia* or Gk *parōidia* burlesque poem (as PARA-¹, *ōidē* ode)]

parole /pəˈrəʊl/ n. & v. —n. **1 a** the release of a prisoner temporarily for a special purpose or completely before the expiry of a sentence, on the promise of good behaviour. **b** such a promise. **2** a word of honour. —v.tr. put (a prisoner) on parole. □ **on parole** released on the terms of parole. □ **parolee** /-ˈliː/ n. [F, = word: see PARLANCE]

parotid /pəˈrɒtɪd/ adj. & n. —adj. situated near the ear. —n. (in full **parotid gland**) a salivary gland in front of the ear. [F *parotide* or L *parotis parotid*- f. Gk *parōtis -idos* (as PARA-¹, *ous ōtos* ear)]

-parous /pərəs/ comb. form bearing offspring of a specified number or kind (*multiparous*; *viviparous*). [L *-parus* -bearing f. *parere* bring forth]

paroxysm /ˈpærəkˌsɪz(ə)m/ n. **1** (often foll. by *of*) a sudden attack or outburst (of rage, laughter, etc.). **2** a fit of disease. □ **paroxysmal** /-ˈsɪzm(ə)l/ adj. [F *paroxysme* f. med.L *paroxysmus* f. Gk *paroxusmos* f. *paroxunō* exasperate (as PARA-¹, *oxunō* sharpen f. *oxus* sharp)]

parquet /ˈpɑːkɪ, -keɪ/ n. & v. —n. **1** a flooring of wooden blocks arranged in a pattern. **2** US the stalls of a theatre. —v.tr. (**parqueted** /-keɪd/; **parqueting** /-keɪɪŋ/) furnish (a room) with a parquet floor. [F, = small compartment, floor, dimin. of *parc* PARK]

parquetry /ˈpɑːkɪtrɪ/ n. the use of wooden blocks to make floors or inlay for furniture.

parr /pɑː(r)/ n. a young salmon with blue-grey finger-like markings on its sides, younger than a smolt. [18th c.: orig. unkn.]

parrakeet US var. of PARAKEET.

parricide /ˈpærɪˌsaɪd/ n. **1** the killing of a near relative, esp. of a parent. **2** an act of parricide. **3** a person who commits parricide. □ **parricidal** /-ˈsaɪd(ə)l/ adj. [F *parricide* or L *parricida* (= sense 3), *parricidium* (= sense 1), of uncert. orig., assoc. in L with *pater* father and *parens* parent]

parrot /ˈpærət/ n. & v. —n. **1** any of various mainly tropical birds of the order Psittaciformes, with a short hooked bill, often having vivid plumage and able to mimic the human voice. **2** a person who mechanically repeats the words or actions of another. —v.tr. (**parroted**, **parroting**) repeat mechanically. □ **parrot-fashion** (learning or repeating) mechanically without understanding. [prob. f. obs. or dial. F *perrot* parrot, dimin. of *Pierre* Peter: cf. PARAKEET]

parry /ˈpærɪ/ v. & n. —v.tr. (**-ies**, **-ied**) **1** avert or ward off (a weapon or attack), esp. with a counter-move. **2** deal skilfully with (an awkward question etc.). —n. (pl. **-ies**) an act of parrying. [prob. repr. F *parez* imper. of *parer* f. It. *parare* ward off]

parse /pɑːz/ v.tr. **1** describe (a word in context) grammatically, stating its inflection, relation to the sentence, etc. **2** resolve (a sentence) into its component parts and describe them grammatically. □ **parser** n. esp. *Computing* [perh. f. ME *pars* parts of speech f. OF *pars*, pl. of *part* PART, infl. by L *pars* part]

parsec /ˈpɑːsek/ n. a unit of stellar distance, equal to about 3.25 light years (3.08 × 10¹⁶ metres), the distance at which the mean radius of the earth's orbit subtends an angle of one second of arc. [PARALLAX + SECOND²]

Parsee /pɑːˈsiː/ n. **1** an adherent of Zoroastrianism. **2** a descendant of the Persians who fled to India from Muslim persecution in the 7th–8th c. □ **Parseeism** n. [Pers. *pārsī* Persian f. *pārs* Persia]

parsimony /ˈpɑːsɪmənɪ/ n. **1** carefulness in the use of money or other resources. **2** meanness, stinginess. □ **parsimonious** /-ˈməʊnɪəs/ adj. **parsimoniously** /-ˈməʊnɪəslɪ/ adv. **parsimoniousness** /-ˈməʊnɪəsnɪs/ n. [ME f. L *parsimonia, parcimonia* f. *parcere* pars- spare]

parsley /ˈpɑːslɪ/ n. a biennial herb, *Petroselinum crispum*, with white flowers and crinkly aromatic leaves, used for seasoning and garnishing food. [ME *percil, per(e)sil* f. OF *peresil*, and OE *petersilie* ult. f. L *petroselinum* f. Gk *petroselinon*]

parsnip /ˈpɑːsnɪp/ n. **1** a biennial umbelliferous plant, *Pastinaca sativa*, with a large pale-yellow tapering root. **2** this root eaten as a vegetable. [ME *pas(se)nep* (with assim. to *nep* turnip) f. OF *pasnaie* f. L *pastinaca*]

parson /ˈpɑːs(ə)n/ n. **1** a rector. **2** a vicar or any beneficed member of the clergy. **3** *colloq.* any (esp. Protestant) member of the clergy. □ **parson's nose** the piece of fatty flesh at the rump of a fowl. □ **parsonical** /-ˈsɒnɪk(ə)l/ adj. [ME *person(e), parson* f. OF *persone* f. L *persona* PERSON (in med.L rector)]

parsonage /ˈpɑːsənɪdʒ/ n. a church house provided for a parson.

part n., v., & adv. —n. **1** some but not all of a thing or number of things. **2** an essential member or constituent of anything (*part of the family; a large part of the job*). **3** a component of a machine etc. (*spare parts; needs a new part*). **4 a** a portion of a human or animal body. **b** (in pl.) = private parts. **5** a division of a book, broadcast serial, etc., esp. as much as is issued or broadcast at one time. **6** each of several equal portions of a whole (*the recipe has 3 parts sugar to 2 parts flour*). **7 a** a portion allotted; a share. **b** a person's share in an action or enterprise (*will have no part in it*). **c** one's duty (*was not my part to interfere*). **8 a** a character assigned to an actor on stage. **b** the words spoken by an actor on stage. **c** a copy of these. **9** *Mus.* a melody or other constituent of harmony assigned to a particular voice or instrument. **10** each of the sides in an agreement or dispute. **11** (in pl.) a region or district (*am not from these parts*). **12** (in pl.) abilities (*a man of many parts*). **13** US = PARTING 2. —v. **1** tr. & intr. divide or separate into parts (*the crowd parted to let them through*). **2** intr. **a** leave one another's company (*they parted the best of friends*). **b** (foll. by *from*) say goodbye to. **3** *tr.* cause to separate (*they fought hard and had to be parted*). **4** *intr.* (foll. by *with*) give up possession of; hand over. **5** *tr.* separate (the hair of the head on either side of the parting) with a comb. —*adv.* to some extent; partly (*is part iron and part wood*; *a lie that is part truth*). □ **for one's part** as far as one is concerned. **in part** (or **parts**) to some extent; partly. **look the part** appear suitable for a role. **on the part of** on the behalf or initiative of (*no objection on my part*). **part and parcel** (usu. foll. by *of*) an essential part. **part-exchange** *n.* a transaction in which goods are given as part of the payment for other goods, with the balance in money. —*v.tr.* give (goods) in such a transaction. **part of speech** *n.* each of the categories to which words are assigned in accordance with their grammatical and semantic functions. **part-song** a song with three or more voice-parts, often without accompaniment, and harmonic rather than contrapuntal in character. **part time** less than the full time required by an activity. **part-time** *adj.* occupying or using only part of one's working time. **part-timer** a person employed in part-time work. **part-work** *Brit.* a publication appearing in several parts over a period of time. **play a part 1** be significant or contributory. **2** act deceitfully. **3** perform a theatrical role. **take part** (often foll. by *in*) assist or have a share (in). **take the part of** support; back up. **three parts** three quarters. [ME f. OF f. L *pars partis* (n.), *partire, partiri* (v.)]

partake /pɑːˈteɪk/ *v.intr.* (*past* **partook** /-ˈtʊk/; *past part.* **partaken** /-ˈteɪkən/) **1** (foll. by *of, in*) take a share or part. **2** (foll. by *of*) eat or drink some or *colloq.* all (of a thing). **3** (foll. by *of*) have some (of a quality etc.) (*their manner partook of insolence*). □ **partakable** *adj.* **partaker** *n.* [16th c.: back-form. f. *partaker, partaking* = part-taker etc.]

parterre /pɑːˈteə(r)/ *n.* **1** a level space in a garden occupied by flower-beds arranged formally. **2** *US* the ground floor of a theatre auditorium, esp. the pit overhung by balconies. [F, = *par terre* on the ground]

parthenogenesis /ˌpɑːθɪnəʊˈdʒenɪsɪs/ *n.* *Biol.* reproduction by a male gamete without fertilization, esp. as a normal process in invertebrates and lower plants. □ **parthenogenetic** /-dʒɪˈnetɪk/ *adj.* **parthenogenetically** /-dʒɪˈnetɪkəlɪ/ *adv.* [mod.L f. Gk *parthenos* virgin + *genesis* as GENESIS]

Parthian shot /ˈpɑːθɪən/ *n.* a remark or glance etc. reserved for the moment of departure. [*Parthia*, an ancient kingdom in W. Asia: from the custom of a retreating Parthian horseman firing a shot at the enemy]

partial /ˈpɑːʃ(ə)l/ *adj.* **1** not complete; forming only part (*a partial success*). **2** biased, unfair. **3** (foll. by *to*) having a liking for. □ **partially** *adv.* **partialness** *n.* [ME f. OF *parcial* f. LL *partialis* (as PART)]

partiality /ˌpɑːʃɪˈælɪtɪ/ *n.* **1** bias, favouritism. **2** (foll. by *for*) fondness. [ME f. OF *parcialité* f. med.L *partialitas* (as PARTIAL)]

participant /pɑːˈtɪsɪpənt/ *n.* a participator.

participate /pɑːˈtɪsɪˌpeɪt/ *v.intr.* (foll. by *in*) take a part or share (in). □ **participation** /-ˈpeɪʃ(ə)n/

n. **participator** *n.* **participatory** *adj.* [L *participare* f. *particeps* -*cipis* taking part, formed as PART + -*cip*- = *cap*- stem of *capere* take]

participle /ˈpɑːtɪˌsɪp(ə)l/ *n.* *Gram.* a word formed from a verb (e.g. *going, gone, being, been*) and used in compound verb-forms (e.g. *is going, has been*) or as an adjective (e.g. *working woman, burnt toast*). □ **participial** /-ˈsɪpɪəl/ *adj.* **participially** /-ˈsɪpɪəlɪ/ *adv.* [ME f. OF, by-form of *participe* f. L *participium* (as PARTICIPATE)]

particle /ˈpɑːtɪk(ə)l/ *n.* **1** a minute portion of matter. **2** the least possible amount (*not a particle of sense*). **3** *Gram.* **a** a minor part of speech, esp. a short undeclinable one. **b** a common prefix or suffix such as *in-, -ness*. [ME f. L *particula* (as PART)]

particoloured /ˈpɑːtɪˌkʌləd/ *adj.* partly of one colour, partly of another or others. [PART + COLOURED]

particular /pəˈtɪkjʊlə(r)/ *adj.* & *n.* —*adj.* **1** relating to or considered as one thing or person as distinct from others; individual (*in this particular instance*). **2** more than is usual; special, noteworthy (*took particular trouble*). **3** scrupulously exact; fastidious. **4** detailed (*a full and particular account*). —*n.* **1** a detail; an item. **2** (in *pl.*) points of information; a detailed account. □ **in particular** especially, specifically. [ME f. OF *particuler* f. L *particularis* (as PARTICLE)]

particularity /pəˌtɪkjʊˈlærɪtɪ/ *n.* **1** the quality of being individual or particular. **2** fullness or minuteness of detail in a description.

particularize /pəˈtɪkjʊləˌraɪz/ *v.tr.* (also **-ise**) *tr.* (also *absol.*) **1** name specially or one by one. **2** specify (items). □ **particularization** /-ˈzeɪʃ(ə)n/ *n.* [F *particulariser* (as PARTICULAR)]

particularly /pəˈtɪkjʊləlɪ/ *adv.* **1** especially, very. **2** specifically (*they particularly asked for you*). **3** in a particular or fastidious manner.

particulate /pəˈtɪkjʊˌleɪt, -lət/ *adj.* & *n.* —*adj.* in the form of separate particles. —*n.* matter in this form. [L *particula* PARTICLE]

parting /ˈpɑːtɪŋ/ *n.* **1** a leave-taking or departure (often *attrib.*: *parting words*). **2** *Brit.* the dividing line of combed hair. **3** a division; an act of separating. □ **parting shot** = PARTHIAN SHOT.

partisan /ˈpɑːtɪˌzæn, -ˈzæn/ *n.* & *adj.* —*n.* (also **partizan**) **1** a strong, esp. unreasoning, supporter of a party, cause, etc. **2** *Mil.* a guerrilla in wartime. —*adj.* **1** of or characteristic of partisans. **2** loyal to a particular cause; biased. □ **partisanship** *n.* [F f. It. dial. *partigiano* etc. f. *parte* PART]

partition /pɑːˈtɪʃ(ə)n/ *n.* & *v.* —*n.* **1** division into parts, esp. *Polit.* of a country with separate areas of government. **2** a structure dividing a space into two parts, esp. a light interior wall. —*v.tr.* **1** divide into parts. **2** (foll. by *off*) separate (part of a room etc.) with a partition. □ **partitioned** *adj.* **partitioner** *n.* **partitionist** *n.* [ME f. OF f. L *partitio -onis* f. *partiri* PART v.]

partitive /ˈpɑːtɪtɪv/ *adj.* & *n.* *Gram.* —*adj.* (of a word, form, etc.) denoting part of a collective group or quantity. —*n.* a partitive word (e.g. *some, any*) or form. □ **partitively** *adv.* [F *partitif* -*ive* or med.L *partitivus* (as PARTITION)]

partly /ˈpɑːtlɪ/ *adv.* **1** with respect to a part or parts. **2** to some extent.

partner /ˈpɑːtnə(r)/ *n.* & *v.* —*n.* **1** a person who shares or takes part with another or others, esp. in a business firm with shared risks and profits. **2** a companion in dancing. **3** a player (esp. one of two) on the same side in a game. **4** either member of a married couple, or of an unmarried couple living together. —*v.tr.* **1** be the partner of. **2** associate as partners. □ **partnerless** *adj.* [ME, alt. of *parcener* joint heir, after PART]

partnership /ˈpɑːtnəʃɪp/ *n.* **1** the state of being a partner or partners. **2** a joint business. **3** a pair or group of partners.

partook *past of* PARTAKE.

partridge /ˈpɑːtrɪdʒ/ *n.* (*pl.* same or **partridges**) **1** any game-bird of the genus *Perdix*, esp. P. *perdix* of Europe and Asia. **2** any other of various similar birds of the family Phasianidae. [ME *partrich* etc. f. OF *perdriz* etc. f. L *perdix -dicis*: for *-dge* cf. CABBAGE]

parturient /pɑːˈtjʊərɪənt/ *adj.* about to give birth. [L *parturire* be in labour, incept. f. *parere* part-bring forth]

parturition /ˌpɑːtjʊˈrɪʃ(ə)n/ *n. formal* the act of bringing forth young; childbirth. [LL *parturitio* (as PARTURIENT)]

party /ˈpɑːtɪ/ *n.* & *v.* —*n.* (*pl.* **-ies**) **1** a social gathering, usu. of invited guests. **2** a body of persons engaged in an activity or travelling together (*fishing party; search party*). **3** a group of people united in a cause, opinion, etc., esp. a political group organized on a national basis. **4** a person or persons forming one side in an agreement or dispute. **5** (foll. by *to*) *Law* an accessory (to an action). **6** *colloq.* a person. —*v.tr.* & *intr.* (**-ies, -ied**) entertain at or attend a party. □ **party line 1** the policy adopted by a political party. **2** a telephone line shared by two or more subscribers. **party-wall** a wall common to two adjoining buildings or rooms. [ME f. OF *partie* ult. f. L *partire*: see PART]

parvenu /ˈpɑːvənuː/ *n.* & *adj.* —*n.* (*fem.* **parvenue**) **1** a person of obscure origin who has gained wealth or position. **2** an upstart. —*adj.* **1** associated with or characteristic of such a person. **2** upstart. [F, past part. of *parvenir* arrive f. L *pervenire* (as PER-, *venire* come)]

pas /pɑː/ *n.* (*pl.* same) a step in dancing, esp. in classical ballet. □ **pas de deux** /də ˈdɜː/ a dance for two persons. **pas seul** /ˈsɜːl/ a solo dance. [F, = step]

pascal *n.* **1** /ˈpæsk(ə)l/ the SI unit of pressure. **2** (**Pascal**) /pæsˈkɑːl/ *Computing* a programming language esp. used in education. [B. *Pascal*, Fr. scientist d. 1662: sense 2 so named because he built a calculating machine]

paschal /ˈpæsk(ə)l/ *adj.* **1** of or relating to the Jewish Passover. **2** of or relating to Easter. □ **paschal lamb 1** a lamb sacrificed at Passover. **2** Christ. [ME f. OF *pascal* f. eccl.L *paschalis* f. *pascha* f. Gk *paskha* f. Aram. *pasḥa*, rel. to Heb. *pesaḥ* PASSOVER]

pash *n. sl.* a brief infatuation. [abbr. of PASSION]

pasha /ˈpɑːʃə/ *n.* (also **pacha**) *hist.* the title (placed after the name) of a Turkish officer of high rank. [Turk. *paşa*, prob. = *başa* f. *baş* head, chief]

paso doble /ˌpæsəʊ ˈdəʊbleɪ/ *n.* **1** a ballroom dance based on a Latin American style of marching. **2** this style of marching. [Sp., = double step]

pasque-flower /ˈpæskˌflaʊə(r)/ *n.* a ranunculaceous plant, *Pulsatilla vulgaris*, with bell-shaped purple flowers and fernlike foliage.

[earlier *passe-flower* f. F *passe-fleur*: assim. to *pasque* = obs. *pasch* (as PASCHAL), Easter]

pass[1] /pɑːs/ *v.* & *n.* —*v.* (*past part.* **passed**) (see also PAST). **1** *intr.* (often foll. by *along, by, down, on,* etc.) move onward; proceed, esp. past some point of reference (*saw the procession passing*). **2** *tr.* a go past; leave (a thing etc.) on one side or behind in proceeding. **b** overtake, esp. in a vehicle. **c** go across (a frontier, mountain range, etc.). **3** *intr.* & *tr.* be transferred or cause to be transferred from one person or place to another (*pass the butter; the title passes to his son*). **4** *tr.* surpass; be too great for (*it passes my comprehension*). **5** *intr.* get through; effect a passage. **6** *intr.* **a** be accepted as adequate; go uncensured (*let the matter pass*). **b** (foll. by *as, for*) be accepted or currently known as. **7** *tr.* move; cause to go (*passed her hand over her face; passed a rope round it*). **8** **a** *intr.* (of a candidate in an examination) be successful. **b** *tr.* be successful in (an examination). **c** *tr.* (of an examiner) judge the performance of (a candidate) to be satisfactory. **9 a** *tr.* (of a bill) be examined and approved by (a parliamentary body or process). **b** *tr.* cause or allow (a bill) to proceed to further legislative processes. **c** *intr.* (of a bill or proposal) be approved. **10** *intr.* **a** occur, elapse (*the remark passed unnoticed; time passes slowly*). **b** happen; be done or said (*heard what passed between them*). **11 a** *intr.* circulate; be current. **b** *tr.* put into circulation (*was passing forged cheques*). **12** *tr.* spend or use up (a certain time or period) (*passed the afternoon reading*). **13** *tr.* (also *absol.*) (in field games) send (the ball) to another player of one's own side. **14** *intr.* forgo one's turn or chance in a game etc. **15** *intr.* (foll. by *to, into*) change from one form (to another). **16** *intr.* come to an end. **17** *tr.* discharge from the body as or with excreta. **18** *tr.* (foll. by *on, upon*) **a** utter (criticism) about. **b** pronounce (a judicial sentence) on. —*n.* **1** an act or instance of passing. **2 a** success in an examination. **b** *Brit.* the status of a university degree without honours. **3** written permission to pass into or out of a place, or to be absent from quarters. **4** a ticket or permit giving free entry or access etc. **5** (in field games) a transference of the ball to another player on the same side. **6** a thrust in fencing. **7** a juggling trick. **8** an act of passing the hands over anything, as in conjuring or hypnotism. **9** a critical position (*has come to a fine pass*). □ **in passing 1** by the way. **2** in the course of speech, conversation, etc. **make a pass at** *colloq.* make amorous or sexual advances to. **pass away 1** *euphem.* die. **2** cease to exist; come to an end. **pass by 1** go past. **2** disregard, omit. **pass one's eye over** read (a document etc.) cursorily. **pass off 1** (of feelings etc.) disappear gradually. **2** (of proceedings) be carried through (in a specified way). **3** (foll. by *as*) misrepresent (a person or thing) as something else. **4** evade or lightly dismiss (an awkward remark etc.). **pass on 1** proceed on one's way. **2** *euphem.* die. **3** transmit to the next person in a series. **pass out 1** become unconscious. **2** *Brit. Mil.* complete one's training as a cadet. **3** distribute. **pass over 1** omit, ignore, or disregard. **2** ignore the claims of (a person) to promotion or advancement. **3** *euphem.* die. **pass round 1** distribute. **2** send or give to each of a number in turn. **pass through** experience. **pass up** *colloq.* refuse or neglect (an opportunity etc.). **pass water** urinate. □ **passer** *n.* [ME f. OF *passer* ult. f. L *passus* PACE[1]]

pass[2] /pɑːs/ *n.* a narrow passage through mountains. □ **sell the pass** betray a cause. [ME, var. of PACE[1], infl. by F *pas* and by PASS[1]]

passable /ˈpɑːsəb(ə)l/ *adj.* **1** barely satisfactory; just adequate. **2** (of a road, pass, etc.) that can be passed. □ **passableness** *n.* **passably** *adv.* [ME f. OF (as PASS[1])]

passage /ˈpæsɪdʒ/ *n.* **1** the process or means of passing; transit. **2** = PASSAGEWAY. **3** the liberty or right to pass through. **4 a** the right of conveyance as a passenger by sea or air. **b** a journey by sea or air. **5** a transition from one state to another. **6 a** a short extract from a book etc. **b** a section of a piece of music. **7** the passing of a bill etc. into law. **8** (in *pl.*) an interchange of words etc. **9** *Anat.* a duct etc. in the body. □ **passage of** (or **at**) **arms** a fight or dispute. **work one's passage** earn a right (orig. of passage) by working for it. [ME f. OF (as PASS[1])]

passageway /ˈpæsɪdʒˌweɪ/ *n.* a narrow way for passing along, esp. with walls on either side; a corridor.

passbook /ˈpɑːsbʊk/ *n.* a book issued by a bank or building society etc. to an account-holder recording sums deposited and withdrawn.

passé /ˈpæseɪ/ *adj.* (*fem.* ***passée***) **1** behind the times; out of date. **2** past its prime. [F, past part. of *passer* PASS[1]]

passenger /ˈpæsɪndʒə(r)/ *n.* **1** a traveller in or on a public or private conveyance (other than the driver, pilot, crew, etc.). **2** *colloq.* a member of a team, crew, etc., who does no effective work. **3** (*attrib.*) for the use of passengers (*passenger seat*). □ **passenger-mile** one mile travelled by one passenger, as a unit of traffic. [ME f. OF *passager* f. OF *passager* (adj.) passing (as PASSAGE): -*n*- as in *messenger* etc.]

passer-by /ˌpɑːsəˈbaɪ/ *n.* (*pl.* **passers-by**) a person who goes past, esp. by chance.

passerine /ˈpæsəˌriːn/ *n.* & *adj.* —*n.* any perching bird of the order Passeriformes, including sparrows and most land birds. —*adj.* **1** of or relating to this order. **2** of the size of a sparrow. [L *passer* sparrow]

passim /ˈpæsɪm/ *adv.* (of allusions or references in a published work) to be found at various places throughout the text. [L f. *passus* scattered f. *pandere* spread]

passing /ˈpɑːsɪŋ/ *adj.* & *n.* —*adj.* **1** in senses of PASS *v.* **2** transient, fleeting (*a passing glance*). **3** cursory, incidental (*a passing reference*). —*n.* **1** in senses of PASS *v.* **2** *euphem.* the death of a person (*mourned his passing*). □ **passing shot** *Tennis* a shot aiming the ball beyond and out of reach of the other player. □ **passingly** *adv.*

passion /ˈpæʃ(ə)n/ *n.* **1** strong barely controllable emotion. **2** an outburst of anger (*flew into a passion*). **3** intense sexual love. **4** a strong enthusiasm (*has a passion for football*). **b** an object arousing this. **5** (**the Passion**) **a** *Relig.* the suffering of Christ during his last days. **b** a narrative of this from the Gospels. **c** a musical setting of any of these narratives. □ **passion-flower** any climbing plant of the genus *Passiflora*, with a flower that was supposed to suggest the instruments of the Crucifixion.

passion-fruit the edible fruit of some species of passion-flower, esp. *Passiflora edulis*. **passion-play** a miracle play representing Christ's Passion. **Passion Sunday** the fifth Sunday in Lent. □ **passionless** *adj.* [ME f. OF f. LL *passio -onis* f. L *pati pass-* suffer]

passionate /ˈpæʃənət/ *adj.* **1** dominated by or easily moved to strong feeling, esp. love or anger. **2** showing or caused by passion. □ **passionately** *adv.* **passionateness** *n.* [ME f. med.L *passionatus* (as PASSION)]

passive /ˈpæsɪv/ *adj.* **1** suffering action; acted upon. **2** offering no opposition; submissive. **3** not active; inert. **4** *Gram.* designating the voice in which the subject undergoes the action of the verb (e.g. in *they were killed*). □ **passive resistance** a non-violent refusal to cooperate. **passive smoking** the involuntary inhaling, esp. by a non-smoker, of smoke from others' cigarettes etc. □ **passively** *adv.* **passiveness** *n.* **passivity** /-ˈsɪvɪtɪ/ *n.* [ME f. OF *passif -ive* or L *passivus* (as PASSION)]

passkey /ˈpɑːskiː/ *n.* **1** a private key to a gate etc. for special purposes. **2** a master-key.

passmark /ˈpɑːsmɑːk/ *n.* the minimum mark needed to pass an examination.

Passover /ˈpɑːsˌəʊvə(r)/ *n.* the Jewish spring festival commemorating the liberation of the Israelites from Egyptian bondage, held from the 14th to the 21st day of the seventh month of the Jewish year. [*pass over* = pass without touching, with ref. to the exemption of the Israelites from the death of the first-born (Exod. 12)]

passport /ˈpɑːspɔːt/ *n.* **1** an official document issued by a government certifying the holder's identity and citizenship, and entitling the holder to travel under its protection to and from foreign countries. **2** (foll. by *to*) a thing that ensures admission or attainment (*a passport to success*). [F *passeport* (as PASS[1], PORT[1])]

password /ˈpɑːswɜːd/ *n.* a selected word or phrase securing recognition, admission, etc., when used by those to whom it is disclosed.

past /pɑːst/ *adj., n., prep.,* & *adv.* —*adj.* **1** gone by in time and no longer existing (*in past years*; *the time is past*). **2** recently completed or gone by (*the past month*; *for some time past*). **3** relating to a former time (*past president*). **4** *Gram.* expressing a past action or state. —*n.* **1** (prec. by *the*) **a** past time. **b** what has happened in past time (*cannot undo the past*). **2** a person's past life or career, esp. if discreditable (*a man with a past*). **3** a past tense or form. —*prep.* **1** beyond in time or place (*is past two o'clock*; *ran past the house*). **2** beyond the range, duration, or compass of (*past belief*; *past endurance*). —*adv.* so as to pass by (*hurried past*). □ **not put it past a person** believe it possible of a person. **past it** *colloq.* incompetent or unusable through age. **past master 1** a person who is especially adept or expert in an activity, subject, etc. **2** a person who has been a master in a guild, Freemason's lodge, etc. [past part. of PASS[1] *v.*]

pasta /ˈpæstə/ *n.* **1** a dried flour paste used in various shapes in cooking (e.g. lasagne, spaghetti). **2** a cooked dish made from this. [It., = PASTE]

paste /peɪst/ *n.* & *v.* —*n.* **1** any moist fairly stiff mixture, esp. of powder and liquid. **2 a** dough of flour with fat, water, etc., used in baking. **3** an adhesive of flour, water, etc., esp. for sticking paper and other light materials. **4** an easily spread preparation of ground meat, fish, etc. (*anchovy paste*). **5** a hard vitreous composition used in making imitation gems. —*v.tr.* **1** fasten or coat with paste. **2** *sl.* **a** beat or thrash. **b** bomb or bombard heavily. □ **paste-up** a document prepared for copying etc. by combining and pasting various sections on a backing. □ **pasting** *n.* (esp. in sense 2 of *v.*). [ME f. OF f. LL *pasta* small square medicinal lozenge f. Gk *pastē* f. *pastos* sprinkled]

pasteboard /ˈpeɪstbɔːd/ *n.* **1** a sheet of stiff material made by pasting together sheets of paper. **2** (*attrib.*) **a** flimsy, unsubstantial. **b** fake.

pastel /ˈpæst(ə)l/ *n.* **1** a crayon consisting of powdered pigments bound with a gum solution. **2** a work of art in pastel. **3** a light and subdued shade of a colour. □ **pastelist** *n.* **pastellist** *n.* [F *pastel* or It. *pastello*, dimin. of *pasta* PASTE]

pastern /ˈpæst(ə)n/ *n.* **1** the part of a horse's foot between the fetlock and the hoof. **2** a corresponding part in other animals. [ME *pastron* f. OF *pasturon* f. *pasture* hobble ult. f. L *pastorius* of a shepherd: see PASTOR]

pasteurize /ˈpɑːstjəˌraɪz, -tʃəˌraɪz, ˈpæst-/ *v.tr.* (also **-ise**) subject (milk etc.) to the process of partial sterilization by heating. □ **pasteurization** /-ˈzeɪʃ(ə)n/ *n.* **pasteurizer** *n.* [L. *Pasteur*, Fr. chemist d. 1895]

pastiche /pæˈstiːʃ/ *n.* **1** a medley, esp. a picture or a musical composition, made up from or imitating various sources. **2** a literary or other work of art composed in the style of a well-known author. [F f. It. *pasticcio* ult. f. LL *pasta* PASTE]

pastille /ˈpæstɪl/ *n.* **1** a small sweet or lozenge. **2** a small roll of aromatic paste burnt as a fumigator etc. [F f. L *pastillus* little loaf, lozenge f. *panis* loaf]

pastime /ˈpɑːstaɪm/ *n.* **1** a pleasant recreation or hobby. **2** a sport or game. [PASS¹ + TIME]

pastis /ˈpæstɪs/ *n.* an aniseed-flavoured aperitif. [F]

pastor /ˈpɑːstə(r)/ *n.* **1** a minister in charge of a church or a congregation. **2** a person exercising spiritual guidance. □ **pastorship** *n.* [ME f. AF & OF *pastour* f. L *pastor* -*oris* shepherd f. *pascere* *past*- feed, graze]

pastoral /ˈpɑːst(ə)l/ *adj.* & *n.* —*adj.* **1** of, relating to, or associated with shepherds or flocks and herds. **2** (of land) used for pasture. **3** (of a poem, picture, etc.) portraying country life, usu. in a romantic or idealized form. **4** of or appropriate to a pastor. —*n.* **1** a pastoral poem, play, picture, etc. **2** a letter from a pastor (esp. a bishop) to the clergy or people. □ **pastoralism** *n.* **pastorality** /-ˈrælɪtɪ/ *n.* **pastorally** *adv.* [ME f. L *pastoralis* (as PASTOR)]

pastoralist /ˈpɑːstərəlɪst/ *n.* *Austral.* a farmer of sheep or cattle.

pastorate /ˈpɑːstərət/ *n.* **1** the office or tenure of a pastor. **2** a body of pastors.

pastrami /pæˈstrɑːmɪ/ *n.* seasoned smoked beef. [Yiddish]

pastry /ˈpeɪstrɪ/ *n.* (*pl.* **-ies**) **1** a dough of flour, fat, and water baked and used as a base and covering for pies etc. **2** **a** food, esp. cake, made wholly or partly of this. **b** a piece or item of this food. □ **pastry-cook** a cook who specializes in pastry, esp. for public sale. [PASTE after OF *pastaierie*]

pasturage /ˈpɑːstʃərɪdʒ/ *n.* **1** land for pasture. **2** the process of pasturing cattle etc. [OF (as PASTURE)]

pasture /ˈpɑːstjə(r)/ *n.* & *v.* —*n.* **1** land covered with grass etc. suitable for grazing animals, esp. cattle or sheep. **2** herbage for animals. —*v.* **1** *tr.* put (animals) to graze in a pasture. **2** *intr.* & *tr.* (of animals) graze. [ME f. OF f. LL *pastura* (as PASTOR)]

pasty¹ /ˈpæstɪ/ *n.* (*pl.* **-ies**) a pastry case with a sweet or savoury filling, baked without a dish to shape it. [ME f. OF *pasté* ult. f. LL *pasta* PASTE]

pasty² /ˈpeɪstɪ/ *adj.* (**pastier, pastiest**) **1** of or like or covered with paste. **2** unhealthily pale (esp. in complexion)). □ **pastily** *adv.* **pastiness** *n.*

Pat. *abbr.* Patent.

pat¹ *v.* & *n.* —*v.* (**patted, patting**) **1** *tr.* strike gently with the hand or a flat surface. **2** *tr.* flatten or mould by patting. **3** *tr.* strike gently with the inner surface of the hand, esp. as a sign of affection, sympathy, or congratulation. **4** *intr.* (foll. by *on, upon*) beat lightly. —*n.* **1** a light stroke or tap, esp. with the hand in affection etc. **2** the sound made by this. **3** a small mass (esp. of butter) formed by patting. □ **pat on the back** a gesture of approval or congratulation. [ME, prob. imit.]

pat² /pæt/ *adj.* & *adv.* —*adj.* **1** known thoroughly and ready for any occasion. **2** apposite or opportune, esp. unconvincingly so (*gave a pat answer*). —*adv.* **1** in a pat manner. **2** appositely, opportunely. □ **have off pat** know or have memorized perfectly. **stand pat** esp. *US* **1** stick stubbornly to one's opinion or decision. **2** *Poker* retain one's hand as dealt; not draw other cards. □ **patly** *adv.* **patness** *n.* [16th c.: rel. to PAT¹]

patball /ˈpætbɔːl/ *n.* a simple game of ball played between two players.

patch /pætʃ/ *n.* & *v.* —*n.* **1** a piece of material or metal etc. used to mend a hole or as reinforcement. **2** a pad worn to protect an injured eye. **3** a dressing etc. put over a wound. **4** a large or irregular distinguishable area on a surface. **5** *colloq.* a period of time in terms of its characteristic quality (*went through a bad patch*). **6** a piece of ground. **7** *colloq.* an area assigned to or patrolled by an authorized person, esp. a police officer. **8** a number of plants growing in one place (*brier patch*). **9** a scrap or remnant. **10** a temporary electrical connection. —*v.tr.* **1** (often foll. by *up*) repair with a patch or patches; put a patch or patches on. **2** (of material) serve as a patch to. **3** (often foll. by *up*) put together, esp. hastily or in a makeshift way. **4** (foll. by *up*) settle (a quarrel etc.) esp. hastily or temporarily. □ **not a patch on** *colloq.* greatly inferior to. **patch pocket** one made of a piece of cloth sewn on a garment. **patch test** a test for allergy by applying to the skin patches containing allergenic substances. □ **patcher** *n.* [ME *pacche, patche*, perh. var. of *peche* f. OF *pieche* dial. var. of *piece* PIECE]

patchwork /ˈpætʃwɜːk/ *n.* **1** needlework using small pieces of cloth with different designs, forming a pattern. **2** a thing composed of various small pieces or fragments.

patchy /ˈpætʃɪ/ *adj.* (**patchier, patchiest**) **1** uneven in quality. **2** having or existing in patches. □ **patchily** *adv.* **patchiness** *n.*

pate /peɪt/ n. archaic or colloq. the head, esp. representing the seat of intellect. [ME: orig. unkn.]

pâté /ˈpæteɪ/ n. a rich paste or spread of mashed and spiced meat or fish etc. □ **pâté de foie gras** /də fwɑː ˈgrɑː/ a paste of fatted goose liver. [F f. OF pasté (as PASTY¹)]

patella /pəˈtelə/ n. (pl. **patellae** /-liː/) the kneecap. □ **patellar** adj. **patellate** /-lət/ adj. [L, dimin. of patina: see PATEN]

paten /ˈpæt(ə)n/ n. 1 a shallow dish used for the bread at the Eucharist. 2 a thin circular plate of metal. [ME ult. f. OF patene or L patena, patina shallow dish f. Gk patanē a plate]

patent /ˈpeɪt(ə)nt, ˈpæt-/ n., adj., & v. —n. 1 a government authority to an individual or organization conferring a right or title, esp. the sole right to make or use or sell some invention. 2 a document granting this authority. 3 an invention or process protected by it. —adj. 1 /ˈpeɪt(ə)nt/ obvious, plain. 2 conferred or protected by patent. 3 **a** made and marketed under a patent; proprietary. **b** to which one has a proprietary claim. 4 ingenious, well-contrived. 5 (of an opening etc.) allowing free passage. —v.tr. obtain a patent for (an invention). □ **patent leather** leather with a glossy varnished surface. **patent medicine** medicine made and marketed under a patent and available without prescription. **patent office** an office from which patents are issued. □ **patency** n. **patentable** adj. **patently** /ˈpeɪtəntlɪ/ adv. (in sense 1 of adj.). [ME f. OF patent and L patēre lie open]

patentee /ˌpeɪtənˈtiː/ n. 1 a person who takes out or holds a patent. 2 a person for the time being entitled to the benefit of a patent.

pater /ˈpeɪtə(r)/ n. Brit. colloq. father. [L]

■ **Usage** Now only in jocular or affected use.

paternal /pəˈtɜːn(ə)l/ adj. 1 of or like or appropriate to a father. 2 fatherly. 3 related through the father. 4 (of a government etc.) limiting freedom and responsibility by well-meant regulations. □ **paternally** adv. [LL paternalis f. L paternus f. pater father]

paternalism /pəˈtɜːnəˌlɪz(ə)m/ n. the policy of governing in a paternal way, or behaving paternally to one's associates or subordinates. □ **paternalist** n. **paternalistic** /-ˈlɪstɪk/ adj. **paternalistically** /-ˈlɪstɪkəlɪ/ adv.

paternity /pəˈtɜːnɪtɪ/ n. 1 fatherhood. 2 one's paternal origin. 3 the source or authorship of a thing. □ **paternity suit** a lawsuit held to determine whether a certain man is the father of a certain child. **paternity test** a blood test to determine whether a man may be or cannot be the father of a particular child. [ME f. OF paternité or LL paternitas]

paternoster /ˌpætəˈnɒstə(r)/ n. 1 **a** the Lord's Prayer, esp. in Latin. **b** a rosary bead indicating that this is to be said. 2 a lift consisting of a series of linked doorless compartments moving continuously on a circular belt. [OE f. L pater noster our father]

path /pɑːθ/ n. (pl. **paths** /pɑːðz/) 1 a way or track laid down for walking or made by continual treading. 2 the line along which a person or thing moves (flight path). 3 a course of action or conduct. 4 a sequence of movements or operations taken by a system. □ **pathless** adj. [OE pæth f. WG]

-path /pæθ/ comb. form forming nouns denoting: 1 a practitioner of curative treatment (homoeopath; osteopath). 2 a person who suffers from a disease (psychopath). [back-form. f. -PATHY, or f. Gk -pathēs -sufferer (as PATHOS)]

pathetic /pəˈθetɪk/ adj. 1 arousing pity or sadness or contempt. 2 Brit. colloq. miserably inadequate. □ **pathetic fallacy** the attribution of human feelings and responses to inanimate things, esp. in art and literature. □ **pathetically** adv. [F pathétique f. LL patheticus f. Gk pathētikos (as PATHOS)]

pathfinder /ˈpɑːθˌfaɪndə(r)/ n. 1 a person who explores new territory, investigates a new subject, etc. 2 an aircraft or its pilot sent ahead to locate and mark the target area for bombing.

patho- /ˈpæθəʊ/ comb. form disease. [Gk pathos suffering: see PATHOS]

pathogen /ˈpæθədʒ(ə)n/ n. an agent causing disease. □ **pathogenic** /-ˈdʒenɪk/ adj. **pathogenous** /-ˈθɒdʒənəs/ adj. [PATHO- + -GEN]

pathological /ˌpæθəˈlɒdʒɪk(ə)l/ adj. 1 of pathology. 2 of or caused by a physical or mental disorder (a pathological fear of spiders). □ **pathologically** adv.

pathology /pəˈθɒlədʒɪ/ n. 1 the science of bodily diseases. 2 the symptoms of a disease. □ **pathologist** n. [F pathologie or mod.L pathologia (as PATHO-, -LOGY)]

pathos /ˈpeɪθɒs/ n. a quality in speech, writing, events, etc., that excites pity or sadness. [Gk pathos suffering, rel. to paskhō suffer, penthos grief]

pathway /ˈpɑːθweɪ/ n. a path or its course.

-pathy /pəθɪ/ comb. form forming nouns denoting: 1 curative treatment (allopathy; homoeopathy). 2 feeling (telepathy). [Gk patheia suffering]

patience /ˈpeɪʃ(ə)ns/ n. 1 calm endurance of hardship, provocation, pain, delay, etc. 2 tolerant perseverance or forbearance. 3 the capacity for calm self-possessed waiting. 4 esp. Brit. a game for one player in which cards taken in random order have to be arranged in certain groups or sequences. [ME f. OF f. L patientia (as PATIENT)]

patient /ˈpeɪʃ(ə)nt/ adj. & n. —adj. having or showing patience. —n. a person receiving or registered to receive medical treatment. □ **patiently** adv. [ME f. OF f. L patiens -entis pres. part. of pati suffer]

patina /ˈpætɪnə/ n. (pl. **patinas**) 1 a film, usu. green, formed on the surface of old bronze. 2 a similar film on other surfaces. 3 a gloss produced by age on woodwork. □ **patinated** /-ˌneɪtɪd/ adj. **patination** /-ˈneɪʃ(ə)n/ n. [It. f. L patina dish]

patio /ˈpætɪəʊ/ n. (pl. **-os**) 1 a paved usu. roofless area adjoining and belonging to a house. 2 an inner court open to the sky in a Spanish or Spanish-American house. [Sp.]

patisserie /pəˈtiːsərɪ/ n. 1 a shop where pastries are made and sold. 2 pastries collectively. [F pâtisserie f. med.L pasticium pastry f. pasta PASTE]

Patna rice /ˈpætnə/ n. a variety of rice with long firm grains. [Patna in India, where it was orig. grown]

patois /ˈpætwɑː/ n. (pl. same /-wɑːz/) the dialect of the common people in a region, differing fundamentally from the literary language. [F, = rough speech, perh. f. OF patoier treat roughly f. patte paw]

patriarch /ˈpeɪtrɪˌɑːk/ n. **1** the male head of a family or tribe. **2** (often in pl.) Bibl. any of those regarded as fathers of the human race, esp. the sons of Jacob, or Abraham, Isaac, and Jacob, and their forefathers. **3** Eccl. the title of a chief bishop, esp. those presiding over the Churches of Antioch, Alexandria, Constantinople, and (formerly) Rome. **4 a** the founder of an order, science, etc. **b** a venerable old man. □ **patriarchal** /-ˈɑːk(ə)l/ adj. **patriarchally** /-ˈɑːkəlɪ/ adv. [ME f. OF patriarche f. eccl.L patriarcha f. Gk patriarkhēs f. patria family f. patēr father + -arkhēs -ruler]

patriarchate /ˈpeɪtrɪˌɑːkət/ n. **1** the office, see, or residence of an ecclesiastical patriarch. **2** the rank of a tribal patriarch. [med.L patriarchatus (as PATRIARCH)]

patriarchy /ˈpeɪtrɪˌɑːkɪ/ n. (pl. -ies) a system of society, government, etc., ruled by a man and with descent through the male line. □ **patriarchism** n. [med.L patriarchia f. Gk patriarkhia (as PATRIARCH)]

patrician /pəˈtrɪʃ(ə)n/ n. & adj. —n. **1** hist. a member of the ancient Roman nobility. **2** an aristocrat. —adj. **1** noble, aristocratic. **2** hist. of the ancient Roman nobility. [ME f. OF patricien f. L patricius having a noble father f. pater patris father]

patricide /ˈpætrɪˌsaɪd/ n. = PARRICIDE (esp. with reference to the killing of one's father). □ **patricidal** /-ˈsaɪd(ə)l/ adj. [LL patricida, patricidium, alt. of L parricida, parricidium (see PARRICIDE) after pater father]

patrimony /ˈpætrɪmənɪ/ n. (pl. -ies) **1** property inherited from one's father or ancestor. **2** a heritage. □ **patrimonial** /-ˈməʊnɪəl/ adj. [ME patrimoigne f. OF patrimoine f. L patrimonium f. pater patris father]

patriot /ˈpeɪtrɪət, ˈpæt-/ n. a person who is devoted to and ready to support or defend his or her country. □ **patriotic** /-ˈɒtɪk/ adj. **patriotically** /-ˈɒtɪklɪ/ adv. **patriotism** n. [F patriote f. LL patriota f. Gk patriōtēs f. patrios of one's fathers f. patēr patros father]

patrol /pəˈtrəʊl/ n. & v. —n. **1** the act of walking or travelling around an area, esp. at regular intervals, in order to protect or supervise it. **2** one or more persons or vehicles assigned or sent out on patrol. **3 a** a detachment of troops sent out to reconnoitre. **b** such reconnaissance. **4** a routine operational voyage of a ship or aircraft. **5** Brit. an official controlling traffic where children cross the road. **6** a unit of six to eight Scouts or Guides. —v. (**patrolled, patrolling**) **1** tr. carry out a patrol of. **2** intr. act as a patrol. □ **patrol car** a police car used in patrolling roads and streets. □ **patroller** n. [F patrouiller paddle in mud f. patte paw: (n.) f. G Patrolle f. F patrouille]

patrolman /pəˈtrəʊlmən/ n. (pl. -men) US a policeman of the lowest rank.

patron /ˈpeɪtrən/ n. (fem. **patroness**) **1** a person who gives financial or other support to a person, cause, work of art, etc., esp. one who buys works of art. **2** a usu. regular customer of a shop etc. □ **patron saint** the protecting or guiding saint of a person, place, etc. [ME f. OF f. L patronus protector of clients, defender f. pater patris father]

patronage /ˈpætrənɪdʒ/ n. **1** the support, promotion, or encouragement given by a patron. **2**

a patronizing or condescending manner. **3** a customer's support for a shop etc. [ME f. OF (as PATRON)]

patronize /ˈpætrəˌnaɪz/ v.tr. (also -ise) **1** treat condescendingly. **2** act as a patron towards (a person, cause, artist, etc.); support; encourage. **3** frequent (a shop etc.) as a customer. □ **patronization** /-ˈzeɪʃ(ə)n/ n. **patronizer** n. **patronizing** adj. **patronizingly** adv. [obs. F patroniser or med.L patronizare (as PATRON)]

patronymic /ˌpætrəˈnɪmɪk/ n. & adj. —n. a name derived from the name of a father or ancestor, e.g. Johnson, O'Brien, Ivanovich. —adj. (of a name) so derived. [LL patronymicus f. Gk patrōnumikos f. patrōnumos f. patēr patros father + onuma, onoma name]

patsy /ˈpætsɪ/ n. (pl. -ies) esp. US sl. a person who is deceived, ridiculed, tricked, etc. [20th c.: orig. unkn.]

patten /ˈpæt(ə)n/ n. hist. a shoe or clog with a raised sole or set on an iron ring, for walking in mud etc. [ME f. OF patin f. patte paw]

patter¹ /ˈpætə(r)/ v. & n. —v. **1** intr. make a rapid succession of taps, as of rain on a window-pane. **2** intr. run with quick short steps. **3** tr. cause (water etc.) to patter. —n. a rapid succession of taps, short light steps, etc. [PAT¹]

patter² /ˈpætə(r)/ n. & v. —n. **1 a** the rapid speech used by a comedian or introduced into a song. **b** the words of a comic song. **2** the words used by a person selling or promoting a product; a sales pitch. **3** the special language or jargon of a profession, class, etc. —v. **1** tr. repeat (prayers etc.) in a rapid mechanical way. **2** intr. talk glibly or mechanically. [ME f. pater = PATERNOSTER]

pattern /ˈpæt(ə)n/ n. & v. —n. **1** a repeated decorative design on wallpaper, cloth, a carpet, etc. **2** a regular or logical form, order, or arrangement of parts (behaviour pattern; the pattern of one's daily life). **3** a model or design, e.g. of a garment, from which copies can be made. **4** an example of excellence; an ideal; a model (a pattern of elegance). **5** a wooden or metal figure from which a mould is made for a casting. **6** a sample (of cloth, wallpaper, etc.). **7** a random combination of shapes or colours. —v.tr. **1** (usu. foll. by after, on) model (a thing) on a design etc. **2** decorate with a pattern. □ **pattern bombing** bombing over a large area, not on a single target. [ME patron (see PATRON): differentiated in sense and spelling since the 16th–17th c.]

patty /ˈpætɪ/ n. (pl. -ies) **1** a little pie or pastry. **2** US a small flat cake of minced meat etc. [F pâté f. PASTY¹]

paucity /ˈpɔːsɪtɪ/ n. smallness of number or quantity. [ME f. OF paucité f. L paucitas f. paucus few]

paunch /pɔːntʃ/ n. & v. —n. **1** the belly or stomach, esp. when protruding. **2** a ruminant's first stomach; the rumen. —v.tr. disembowel (an animal). □ **paunchy** adj. (**paunchier, paunchiest**). **paunchiness** n. [ME f. AF pa(u)nche, ONF panche ult. f. L pantex panticis bowels]

pauper /ˈpɔːpə(r)/ n. **1** a person without means; a beggar. **2** hist. a recipient of poor-law relief. □ **pauperdom** /-dəm/ n. **pauperism** /-ˌrɪz(ə)m/ n. **pauperize** v.tr. (also -ise). **pauperization** /-ˈzeɪʃ(ə)n/ n. [L, = poor]

pause /pɔːz/ n. & v. —n. **1** an interval of inaction, esp. when due to hesitation; a temporary stop.

2 a break in speaking or reading; a silence. **3** *Mus.* a mark (⌢) over a note or rest that is to be lengthened by an unspecified amount. —*v.intr.* **1** make a pause; wait. **2** (usu. foll. by *upon*) linger over (a word etc.). □ **give pause to** cause (a person) to hesitate. [ME f. OF *pause* or L *pausa* f. Gk *pausis* f. *pauō* stop]

pave *v.tr.* **1 a** cover (a street, floor, etc.) with paving etc. **b** cover or strew (a floor etc.) with anything (*paved with flowers*). **2** prepare (*paved the way for her arrival*). □ **paving-stone** a large flat usu. rectangular piece of stone etc. for paving. □ **paver** *n.* **paving** *n.* **pavior** /ˈpeɪvjə(r)/ *n.* (also **paviour**). [ME f. OF *paver*, back-form. (as PAVEMENT)]

pavement /ˈpeɪvmənt/ *n.* **1** *Brit.* a paved path for pedestrians at the side of and a little higher than a road. **2** the covering of a street, floor, etc., made of tiles, wooden blocks, asphalt, and esp. of rectangular stones. **3** *US* a roadway. [ME f. OF f. L *pavimentum* f. *pavire* beat, ram]

pavilion /pəˈvɪljən/ *n.* **1** *Brit.* a building at a cricket or other sports ground used for changing, refreshments, etc. **2** a summerhouse or other decorative building in a garden. **3** a tent, esp. a large one with crenellated decorations at a show, fair, etc. **4** a building used for entertainments. **5** a temporary stand at an exhibition. [ME f. OF *pavillon* f. L *papilio -onis* butterfly, tent]

pavior, paviour see PAVE.

pavlova /pævˈləʊvə/ *n.* a meringue cake with cream and fruit. [A. *Pavlova*, Russ. ballerina d. 1931]

paw *n. & v.* —*n.* **1** a foot of an animal having claws or nails. **2** *colloq.* a person's hand. —*v.* **1** *tr.* strike or scrape with a paw or foot. **2** *intr.* scrape the ground with a paw or hoof. **3** *tr. colloq.* fondle awkwardly or indecently. [ME *pawe*, *powe* f. OF *poue* etc. ult. f. Frank.]

pawky /ˈpɔːkɪ/ *adj.* (**pawkier, pawkiest**) *Sc. & dial.* **1** drily humorous. **2** shrewd. □ **pawkily** *adv.* **pawkiness** *n.* [Sc. & N.Engl. dial. *pawk* trick, of unkn. orig.]

pawl *n.* **1** a lever with a catch for the teeth of a wheel or bar. **2** *Naut.* a short bar used to lock a capstan, windlass, etc., to prevent it from recoiling. [perh. f. LG & Du. *pal*, rel. to *pal* fixed]

pawn¹ *n.* **1** *Chess* a piece of the smallest size and value. **2** a person used by others for their own purposes. [ME f. AF *poun*, OF *peon* f. med.L *pedo -onis* foot-soldier f. L *pes pedis* foot: cf. PEON]

pawn² *v. & n.* —*v.tr.* **1** deposit an object, esp. with a pawnbroker, as security for money lent. **2** pledge or wager (one's life, honour, word, etc.). —*n.* **1** an object left as security for money etc. lent. **2** anything or any person left with another as security etc. □ **in** (or **at**) **pawn** (of an object etc.) held as security. [ME f. OF *pan, pand, pant*, pledge, security f. WG]

pawnbroker /ˈpɔːnˌbrəʊkə(r)/ *n.* a person who lends money at interest on the security of personal property pawned. □ **pawnbroking** *n.*

pawnshop /ˈpɔːnʃɒp/ *n.* a shop where pawnbroking is conducted.

pawpaw /ˈpɔːpɔː/ *n.* (also **papaw** /pəˈpɔː/, **papaya** /pəˈpaɪə/) **1** an elongated melon-shaped fruit with edible orange flesh and small black seeds. **2** a tropical tree, *Carica papaya*, bearing this. [earlier *papay(a)* f. Sp. & Port. *papaya*, of Carib orig.]

pax *n.* **1** the kiss of peace. **2** (as *int.*) *Brit. sl.* a call for a truce (used esp. by schoolchildren). [ME f. L, = peace]

pay *v. & n.* —*v.tr.* (*past and past part.* **paid** /peɪd/) **1** (also *absol.*) give (a person etc.) what is due for services done, goods received, debts incurred, etc. (*paid him in full; I assure you I have paid*). **2 a** give a usu. specified amount for work done, a debt, a ransom, etc. (*they pay £6 an hour*). **b** (foll. by *to*) hand over the amount of (a debt, wages, recompense, etc.) to (*paid the money to the assistant*). **3 a** give, bestow, or express (attention, respect, a compliment, etc.) (*paid them no heed*). **b** make (a visit, a call, etc.) (*paid a visit to their uncle*). **4** (also *absol.*) (of a business, undertaking, attitude, etc.) be profitable or advantageous to (a person etc.). **5** reward or punish (*can never pay you for what you have done for us; I shall pay you for that*). **6** (usu. as **paid** *adj.*) recompense (work, time, etc.) (*paid holiday*). **7** (usu. foll. by *out, away*) let out (a rope) by slackening it. —*n.* wages; payment. □ **in the pay of** employed by. **pay-as-you-earn** *Brit.* the deduction of income tax from wages at source. **pay-bed** a hospital bed for private patients. **pay-claim** a demand for an increase in pay, esp. by a trade union. **pay-day** a day on which payment, esp. of wages, is made or expected to be made. **pay dearly** (usu. foll. by *for*) **1** obtain at a high cost, great effort, etc. **2** suffer for a wrongdoing etc. **pay dirt** (or **gravel**) *US* 1 *Mineral.* ground worth working for ore. **2** a financially promising situation. **pay envelope** *US* = *pay-packet*. **pay for 1** hand over the price of. **2** bear the cost of. **3** suffer or be punished for (a fault etc.). **pay in** pay (money) into a bank account. **paying guest** a boarder. **pay its** (or **one's**) **way** cover costs; not be indebted. **pay one's last respects** show respect towards a dead person by attending the funeral. **pay off 1** dismiss (workers) with a final payment. **2** *colloq.* yield good results; succeed. **3** pay (a debt) in full. **pay-off** *n. sl.* **1** an act of payment. **2** a climax. **3** a final reckoning. **pay out** (or **back**) punish or be revenged on. **pay-packet** *Brit.* a packet or envelope containing an employee's wages. **pay phone** a coin-box telephone. **pay one's respects** make a polite visit. **pay station** *US* = *pay phone*. **pay through the nose** *colloq.* pay much more than a fair price. **pay up** pay the full amount, or the full amount of. **put paid to** *colloq.* **1** deal effectively with (a person). **2** terminate (hopes etc.). □ **payee** /peɪˈiː/ *n.* **payer** *n.* [ME f. OF *paie, payer* f. L *pacare* appease f. *pax pacis* peace]

payable /ˈpeɪəb(ə)l/ *adj.* **1** that must be paid; due (*payable in April*). **2** that may be paid. **3** (of a mine etc.) profitable.

payback /ˈpeɪbæk/ *n.* **1** a financial return; a reward. **2** the profit from an investment etc., esp. one equal to the initial outlay.

PAYE *abbr. Brit.* pay-as-you-earn.

payload /ˈpeɪləʊd/ *n.* **1** the part of an aircraft's load from which revenue is derived. **2 a** the explosive warhead carried by an aircraft or rocket. **b** the instruments etc. carried by a spaceship.

paymaster /ˈpeɪˌmɑːstə(r)/ *n.* **1** an official who pays troops, workmen, etc. **2** a person, organization, etc., to whom another owes duty or loyalty because of payment given. **3** (in full **Paymaster General**) *Brit.* the minister at the head of the Treasury department responsible for payments.

payment /ˈpeɪmənt/ n. **1** the act or an instance of paying. **2** an amount paid. **3** reward, recompense. [ME f. OF *paiement* (as PAY)]

payola /peɪˈəʊlə/ n. esp. *US* **1** a bribe offered in return for unofficial promotion of a product etc. in the media. **2** the practice of such bribery. [PAY + -*ola* as in *Victrola*, make of gramophone]

payroll /ˈpeɪrəʊl/ n. a list of employees receiving regular pay.

Pb symb. Chem. the element lead. [L *plumbum*]

PBX abbr. private branch exchange (private telephone switchboard).

PC abbr. **1** (in the UK) police constable. **2** (in the UK) Privy Counsellor. **3** personal computer. **4** political correctness, politically correct.

p.c. abbr. **1** per cent. **2** postcard.

PCB abbr. **1** *Computing* printed circuit board. **2** *Chem.* polychlorinated biphenyl, any of several toxic aromatic compounds formed as waste in industrial processes.

pct. abbr. *US* per cent.

Pd symb. Chem. the element palladium.

pd. abbr. paid.

PE abbr. physical education.

pea n. **1 a** a hardy climbing plant, *Pisum sativum*, with seeds growing in pods and used for food. **b** its seed. **2** any of several similar plants (*sweet pea*; *chick-pea*). □ **pea-brain** colloq. a stupid or dim-witted person. **pea-green** bright green. **pea-souper** Brit. colloq. a thick yellowish fog. [back-form. f. PEASE (taken as pl.: cf. CHERRY)]

peace n. **1 a** quiet; tranquillity (*needs peace to work well*). **b** mental calm; serenity (*peace of mind*). **2 a** (often *attrib.*) freedom from or the cessation of war (*peace talks*). **b** (esp. **Peace**) a treaty of peace between two States etc. at war. **3** freedom from civil disorder. **4** *Eccl.* a ritual liturgical greeting. □ **at peace 1** in a state of friendliness. **2** serene. **hold one's peace** keep silence. **keep the peace** prevent, or refrain from, strife. **make one's peace** (often foll. by *with*) re-establish friendly relations. **make peace** bring about peace; reconcile. **the peace** (or **the queen's peace**) peace existing within a realm; civil order. **Peace Corps** *US* an organization sending young people to work as volunteers in developing countries. **peace dividend** public money which becomes available when defence spending is reduced. **peace-offering** a propitiatory or conciliatory gift. **peace-pipe** a tobacco-pipe as a token of peace among US Indians. [ME f. AF *pes*, OF *pais* f. L *pax pacis*]

peaceable /ˈpiːsəb(ə)l/ adj. **1** disposed to peace; unwarlike. **2** free from disturbance; peaceful. □ **peaceableness** n. **peaceably** adv. [ME f. OF *peisible*, *plaisible* f. LL *placibilis* pleasing f. L *placēre* please]

peaceful /ˈpiːsfʊl/ adj. **1** characterized by peace; tranquil. **2** not violating or infringing peace (*peaceful coexistence*). **3** belonging to a state of peace. □ **peacefully** adv. **peacefulness** n.

peacemaker /ˈpiːsˌmeɪkə(r)/ n. a person who brings about peace. □ **peacemaking** n. & adj.

peacetime /ˈpiːstaɪm/ n. a period when a country is not at war.

peach¹ n. **1 a** a round juicy stone-fruit with downy cream or yellow skin flushed with red. **b** the tree, *Prunus persica*, bearing it. **2** the yellowish-pink colour of a peach. **3** colloq. **a** a person or thing of superlative quality. **b** an attractive young woman. □ **peachy** adj. (**peachier, peachiest**). **peachiness** n. [ME f. OF *peche*, *pesche*, f. med.L *persica* f. L *persicum* (*malum*), lit. Persian apple]

peach² v. intr. (usu. foll. by *against*, *on*) colloq. turn informer; inform. [ME f. *appeach* f. AF *enpecher*, OF *empechier* IMPEACH]

peacock /ˈpiːkɒk/ n. **1** a male peafowl, having brilliant plumage and a tail (with eyelike markings) that can be expanded erect in display like a fan. **2** an ostentatious strutting person. □ **peacock blue** the lustrous greenish blue of a peacock's neck. [ME *pecock* f. OE *pēa* f. L *pavo* + COCK¹]

peafowl /ˈpiːfaʊl/ n. **1** a peacock or peahen. **2** a pheasant of the genus *Pavo*.

peahen /ˈpiːhen/ n. a female peafowl.

pea-jacket /ˈpiːˌdʒækɪt/ n. a sailor's short double-breasted overcoat of coarse woollen cloth. [prob. f. Du. *pijjakker* f. *pij* coat of coarse cloth + *jekker* jacket: assim. to JACKET]

peak¹ n. & v. —n. **1** a projecting usu. pointed part, esp.: **a** the pointed top of a mountain. **b** a mountain with a peak. **c** a stiff brim at the front of a cap. **2 a** the highest point in a curve (*on the peak of the wave*). **b** the time of greatest success (in a career etc.). **c** the highest point on a graph etc. —v.intr. reach the highest value, quality, etc. (*output peaked in September*). □ **peak hour** the time of the most intense traffic etc. □ **peaked** adj. **peaky** adj. **peakiness** n. [prob. back-form. f. *peaked* var. of dial. *picked* pointed (PICK²)]

peak² /piːk/ v.intr. **1** waste away. **2** (as **peaked** adj.) sharp-featured; pinched. [16th c.: orig. unkn.]

peaky /ˈpiːkɪ/ adj. (**peakier, peakiest**) **1** sickly; puny. **2** white-faced.

peal /piːl/ n. & v. —n. **1 a** the loud ringing of a bell or bells, esp. a series of changes. **b** a set of bells. **2** a loud repeated sound, esp. of thunder, laughter, etc. —v. **1** intr. sound forth in a peal. **2** tr. utter sonorously. **3** tr. ring (bells) in peals. [ME *pele* f. *apele* APPEAL]

pean *US* var. of PAEAN.

peanut /ˈpiːnʌt/ n. **1** a leguminous plant, *Arachis hypogaea*, bearing pods that ripen underground and contain seeds used as food and yielding oil. **2** the seed of this plant. **3** (in pl.) colloq. a paltry or trivial thing or amount, esp. of money. □ **peanut butter** a paste of ground roasted peanuts.

pear /peə(r)/ n. **1** a yellowish or brownish-green fleshy fruit, tapering towards the stalk. **2** any of various trees of the genus *Pyrus* bearing it, esp. *P. communis*. □ **pear-drop** a small sweet with the shape of a pear. [OE *pere*, *peru* ult. f. L *pirum*]

pearl¹ /pɜːl/ n. & v. —n. **1 a** (often *attrib.*) a usu. white or bluish-grey hard mass formed within the shell of a pearl-oyster or other bivalve mollusc, highly prized as a gem for its lustre (*pearl necklace*). **b** an imitation of this. **c** (in pl.) a necklace of pearls. **d** = *mother-of-pearl*. **2** a precious thing; the finest example. **3** anything resembling a pearl, e.g. a dewdrop, tear, etc. —v. **1** tr. poet. **a** sprinkle with pearly drops. **b** make pearly in colour etc. **2** tr. reduce (barley etc.) to small rounded grains. **3** intr. fish for pearl-oysters. **4** intr. poet. form pearl-like drops.

□ **pearl barley** barley reduced to small round grains by grinding. **pearl bulb** a translucent electric light bulb. **pearl button** a button made of mother-of-pearl or an imitation of it. **pearl-diver** a person who dives for pearl-oysters. **pearl onion** a very small onion used in pickles. **pearl-oyster** any of various marine bivalve molluscs of the genus *Pinctada*, bearing pearls. □ **pearler** *n.* [ME f. OF *perle* prob. f. L *perna* leg (applied to leg-of-mutton-shaped bivalve)]

pearl² /pɜːl/ *n. Brit.* = PICOT. [var. of PURL¹]

pearlized /ˈpɜːlaɪzd/ *adj.* treated so as to resemble mother-of-pearl.

pearly /ˈpɜːlɪ/ *adj. & n.* —*adj.* (**pearlier, pearliest**) **1** resembling a pearl; lustrous. **2** containing pearls or mother-of-pearl. **3** adorned with pearls. —*n.* (*pl.* **-ies**) (in *pl.*) *Brit.* **1** pearly kings and queens. **2** a pearly king's or queen's clothes or pearl buttons. □ **Pearly Gates** *colloq.* the gates of Heaven. **pearly king** (or **queen**) *Brit.* a London costermonger (or his wife) wearing clothes covered with pearl buttons. □ **pearliness** *n.*

pearmain /ˈpeəmeɪn, ˈpɜː-/ *n.* a variety of apple with firm white flesh. [ME, = warden pear, f. OF *parmain, permain*, prob. ult. f. L *parmensis* of *Parma* in Italy]

peasant /ˈpez(ə)nt/ *n.* **1** esp. *colloq.* a countryman or countrywoman; a rustic. **2 a** a worker on the land, esp. a labourer or smallholder. **b** *hist.* a member of an agricultural class dependent on subsistence farming. **3** *derog.* a lout; a boorish person. □ **peasantry** *n.* (*pl.* **-ies**). **peasanty** *adj.* [ME f. AF *paisant*, OF *païsent*, earlier *païsence* f. *païs* country ult. f. L *pagus* canton]

pease /piːz/ *n.pl. archaic* peas. □ **pease-pudding** boiled split peas (served esp. with boiled ham). [OE *pise* pea, pl. *pisan*, f. LL *pisa* f. L *pisum* f. Gk *pison*: cf. PEA]

peashooter /ˈpiːˌʃuːtə(r)/ *n.* a small tube for blowing dried peas through as a toy.

peat *n.* **1** vegetable matter decomposed in water and partly carbonized, used for fuel, in horticulture, etc. **2** a cut piece of this. □ **peaty** *adj.* [ME f. AL *peta*, perh. f. Celt.: cf. PIECE]

peatbog /ˈpiːtbɒg/ *n.* a bog composed of peat.

peatmoss /ˈpiːtmɒs/ *n.* **1** a peatbog. **2** any of various mosses of the genus *Sphagnum*, which grow in damp conditions and form peat as they decay.

pebble /ˈpeb(ə)l/ *n.* a small smooth stone worn by the action of water. □ **pebble-dash** mortar with pebbles in it used as a coating for external walls. □ **pebbly** *adj.* [OE *papel-stān* pebble-stone, *pyppelrīpig* pebble-stream, of unkn. orig.]

pecan /ˈpiːkən/ *n.* **1** a pinkish-brown smooth nut with an edible kernel. **2** a hickory, *Carya illinoensis*, of the southern US, producing this. [earlier *paccan*, of Algonquian orig.]

peccadillo /ˌpekəˈdɪləʊ/ *n.* (*pl.* **-oes** or **-os**) a trifling offence; a venial sin. [Sp. *pecadillo*, dimin. of *pecado* sin f. L *peccare* sin]

peccary /ˈpekərɪ/ *n.* (*pl.* **-ies**) any American wild pig of the family Tayassuidae, esp. *Tayassu tajacu* and *T. pecari*. [Carib *pakira*]

peck¹ *v. & n.* —*v.tr.* **1** strike or bite (something) with a beak. **2** kiss (esp. a person's cheek) hastily or perfunctorily. **3 a** make (a hole) by pecking. **b** (foll. by *out, off*) remove or pluck out by pecking. **4** *colloq.* (also *absol.*) eat (food) listlessly; nibble at. —*n.* **1 a** a stroke or bite with a beak. **b** a mark made by this. **2** a hasty or perfunctory kiss. □ **peck at 1** eat (food) listlessly; nibble. **2** carp at; nag. **3** strike (a thing) repeatedly with a beak. **pecking** (or **peck**) **order** a social hierarchy, orig. as observed among hens. [ME prob. f. MLG *pekken*, of unkn. orig.]

peck² *n.* **1** a measure of capacity for dry goods, equal to 2 gallons or 8 quarts. **2** a vessel used to contain this amount. □ **a peck of** a large number or amount of (troubles, dirt, etc.). [ME f. AF *pek*, of unkn. orig.]

pecker /ˈpekə(r)/ *n.* **1** a bird that pecks (*woodpecker*). **2** *US coarse sl.* the penis. □ **keep your pecker up** *Brit. colloq.* remain cheerful.

peckish /ˈpekɪʃ/ *adj. colloq.* **1** hungry. **2** *US* irritable.

pectin /ˈpektɪn/ *n. Biochem.* any of various soluble gelatinous polysaccharides found in ripe fruits etc. and used as a setting agent in jams and jellies. □ **pectic** *adj.* [Gk *pēktos* congealed f. *pēgnumi* make solid]

pectoral /ˈpektər(ə)l/ *adj. & n.* —*adj.* **1** of or relating to the breast or chest; thoracic (*pectoral fin; pectoral muscle*). **2** worn on the chest (*pectoral cross*). —*n.* **1** (esp. in *pl.*) a pectoral muscle. **2** a pectoral fin. [ME f. OF f. L *pectorale* (n.), *pectoralis* (adj.) f. *pectus pectoris* breast, chest]

peculate /ˈpekjʊˌleɪt/ *v.tr. & intr.* embezzle (money). □ **peculation** /-ˈleɪʃ(ə)n/ *n.* **peculator** *n.* [L *peculari* rel. to *peculium*: see PECULIAR]

peculiar /pɪˈkjuːlɪə(r)/ *adj. & n.* —*adj.* **1** strange; odd; unusual (*a peculiar flavour; is a little peculiar*). **2 a** (usu. foll. by *to*) belonging exclusively (*a fashion peculiar to the time*). **b** belonging to the individual (*in their own peculiar way*). **3** particular; special (*a point of peculiar interest*). —*n.* a peculiar property, privilege, etc. [ME f. L *peculiaris* of private property f. *peculium* f. *pecu* cattle]

peculiarity /pɪˌkjuːlɪˈærɪtɪ/ *n.* (*pl.* **-ies**) **1 a** idiosyncrasy; unusualness; oddity. **b** an instance of this. **2** a characteristic or habit (*meanness is his peculiarity*). **3** the state of being peculiar.

peculiarly /pɪˈkjuːlɪəlɪ/ *adv.* **1** more than usually; especially (*peculiarly annoying*). **2** oddly. **3** as regards oneself alone; individually (*does not affect him peculiarly*).

pecuniary /pɪˈkjuːnɪərɪ/ *adj.* **1** of, concerning, or consisting of, money (*pecuniary aid; pecuniary considerations*). **2** (of an offence) entailing a money penalty or fine. □ **pecuniarily** *adv.* [L *pecuniarius* f. *pecunia* money f. *pecu* cattle]

pedagogue /ˈpedəˌgɒg/ *n. archaic* or *derog.* a schoolmaster; a teacher. □ **pedagogic** /-ˈgɒgɪk, -ˈgɒdʒɪk/ *adj.* **pedagogical** /-ˈgɒgɪk(ə)l, -ˈgɒdʒɪk(ə)l/ *adj.* **pedagogically** /-ˈgɒgɪkəlɪ, -ˈgɒdʒɪkəlɪ/ *adv.* **pedagogism** *n.* (also **pedagoguism**). [ME f. L *paedagogus* f. Gk *paidagōgos* f. *pais paidos* boy + *agōgos* guide]

pedagogy /ˈpedəˌgɒdʒɪ, -ˌgɒgɪ/ *n.* the science of teaching. □ **pedagogics** /-ˈgɒdʒɪks, -ˈgɒgɪks/ *n.* [F *pédagogie* f. Gk *paidagōgia* (as PEDAGOGUE)]

pedal¹ /ˈped(ə)l/ *n. & v.* **1** any of several types of foot-operated levers or controls for mechanisms, esp.: **a** either of a pair of levers for transmitting power to a bicycle or tricycle wheel etc. **b** any of the foot-operated controls in a motor vehicle. **c** any of the foot-operated keys of an organ. **d** each of the foot-levers on a piano etc. for making the tone fuller or softer. **e** each of the foot-levers on a harp. —*v.*

(pedalled, pedalling; US **pedaled, pedaling) 1** *intr.* operate a cycle, organ, etc. by using the pedals. **2** *tr.* work (a bicycle etc.) with the pedals. □ **pedal cycle** a bicycle. [F *pédale* f. It. *pedale* f. L (as PEDAL²)]

pedal² /ˈped(ə)l, ˈpiːd(ə)l/ *adj. Zool.* of the foot or feet (esp. of a mollusc). [L *pedalis* f. *pes pedis* foot]

pedalo /ˈpedəˌləʊ/ *n.* (*pl.* **-os**) a pedal-operated pleasure-boat.

pedant /ˈped(ə)nt/ *n.* **1** a person who insists on strict adherence to formal rules or literal meaning at the expense of a wider view. **2** a person who rates academic learning or technical knowledge above everything. □ **pedantic** /pɪˈdæntɪk/ *adj.* **pedantically** /pɪˈdæntɪkəlɪ/ *adv.* **pedantize** *v.intr.* & *tr.* (also **-ise**). **pedantry** *n.* (*pl.* **-ies**). [F *pédant* f. It. *pedante*: app. formed as PEDAGOGUE]

peddle /ˈped(ə)l/ *v.* **1** *tr.* **a** sell (goods), esp. in small quantities, as a pedlar. **b** advocate or promote (ideas, a philosophy, a way of life, etc.). **2** *tr.* sell (drugs) illegally. **3** *intr.* engage in selling, esp. as a pedlar. [back-form. f. PEDLAR]

peddler /ˈpedlə(r)/ *n.* **1** a person who sells drugs illegally. **2** US var. of PEDLAR.

pederast /ˈpedəˌræst/ *n.* (also **paederast**) a man who performs pederasty.

pederasty /ˈpedəˌræstɪ/ *n.* (also **paederasty**) anal intercourse between a man and a boy. [mod.L *paederastia* f. Gk *paiderastia* f. *pais paidos* boy + *erastēs* lover]

pedestal /ˈpedɪst(ə)l/ *n.* & *v.* —*n.* **1** a base supporting a column or pillar. **2** the stone etc. base of a statue etc. **3** either of the two supports of a knee-hole desk or table, usu. containing drawers. —*v.tr.* (**pedestalled, pedestalling;** US **pedestaled, pedestaling**) set or support on a pedestal. □ **pedestal table** a table with a single central support. **put** (or **set**) **on a pedestal** regard as highly admirable, important, etc.; venerate. [F *piédestal* f. It. *piedestallo* f. *piè* foot f. L *pes pedis* + *di* of + *stallo* STALL¹]

pedestrian /pɪˈdestrɪən/ *n.* & *adj.* —*n.* **1** (often *attrib.*) a person who is walking, esp. in a town (*pedestrian crossing*). **2** a person who walks competitively. —*adj.* prosaic; dull; uninspired. □ **pedestrian crossing** Brit. a specified part of a road where pedestrians have right of way to cross. **pedestrian precinct** an area of a town restricted to pedestrians. □ **pedestrianism** *n.* **pedestrianize** *v.tr.* & *intr.* (also **-ise**). **pedestrianization** /-ˈzeɪʃ(ə)n/ *n.* [F *pédestre* or L *pedester -tris*]

pediatrics US var. of PAEDIATRICS.

pedicure /ˈpedɪˌkjʊə(r)/ *n.* **1** the care or treatment of the feet, esp. of the toenails. **2** a person practising this, esp. professionally. [F *pédicure* f. L *pes pedis* foot + *curare*: see CURE]

pedigree /ˈpedɪˌɡriː/ *n.* **1** (often *attrib.*) a recorded line of descent of a person or esp. a pure-bred domestic or pet animal. **2** the derivation of a word. **3** a genealogical table. □ **pedigreed** *adj.* [ME *pedegru* etc. f. AF f. OF *pie de grue* (unrecorded) crane's foot, a mark denoting succession in pedigrees]

pediment /ˈpedɪmənt/ *n.* **1** the triangular front part of a building in Grecian style, surmounting esp. a portico of columns. **2** a similar part of a building in Roman or Renaissance style. □ **pedimental** /-ˈment(ə)l/ *adj.* **pedimented** *adj.*

[earlier *pedament, periment,* perh. corrupt. of PYRAMID]

pedlar /ˈpedlə(r)/ *n.* (US **peddler**) **1** a travelling seller of small items esp. carried in a pack etc. **2** (usu. foll. by *of*) a retailer of gossip etc. □ **pedlary** *n.* [ME *pedlere* alt. of *pedder* f. *ped* pannier, of unkn. orig.]

pedo- *comb. form* US var. of PAEDO-.

pedometer /pɪˈdɒmɪtə(r)/ *n.* an instrument for estimating the distance travelled on foot by recording the number of steps taken. [F *pédomètre* f. L *pes pedis* foot]

peduncle /pɪˈdʌŋk(ə)l/ *n. Bot.* the stalk of a flower, fruit, or cluster, esp. a main stalk bearing a solitary flower or subordinate stalks. □ **peduncular** /-kjʊlə(r)/ *adj.* **pedunculate** /-kjʊlət/ *adj.* [mod.L *pedunculus* f. L *pes pedis* foot: see -UNCLE]

pee *v.* & *n. colloq.* —*v.* (**pees, peed**) **1** *intr.* urinate. **2** *tr.* pass (urine etc.) from the bladder. —*n.* **1** urination. **2** urine. [initial letter of PISS]

peek *v.* & *n.* —*v.intr.* (usu. foll. by *in, out, at*) look quickly or slyly; peep. —*n.* a quick or sly look. [ME *pike, pyke,* of unkn. orig.]

peel *v.* & *n.* —*v.* **1** *tr.* **a** strip the skin, rind, bark, wrapping, etc. from (a fruit, vegetable, tree, etc.). **b** (usu. foll. by *off*) strip (skin, peel, wrapping, etc.) from a fruit etc. **2** *intr.* **a** (of a tree, an animal's or person's body, a painted surface, etc.) become bare of bark, skin, paint, etc. **b** (often foll. by *off*) (of bark, a person's skin, paint, etc.) flake off. **3** *intr.* (often foll. by *off*) *colloq.* (of a person) strip for exercise etc. —*n.* the outer covering of a fruit, vegetable, prawn, etc.; rind. □ **peel off 1** veer away and detach oneself from a group of marchers, a formation of aircraft, etc. **2** *colloq.* strip off one's clothes. □ **peeler** *n.* (in sense 1 of *v.*). [earlier *pill, pele* (orig. = plunder) f. ME *pilien* etc. f. OE *pilian* (unrecorded) f. L *pilare* f. *pilus* hair]

peeling /ˈpiːlɪŋ/ *n.* a strip of the outer skin of a vegetable, fruit, etc. (*potato peelings*).

peen *n.* the wedge-shaped or thin or curved end of a hammer-head. [17th c.: also *pane,* app. f. F *panne* f. Du. *pen* f. L *pinna* point]

peep¹ *v.* & *n.* —*v.intr.* **1** (usu. foll. by *at, in, out, into*) look through a narrow opening; look furtively. **2** (usu. foll. by *out*) **a** (of daylight, a flower beginning to bloom, etc.) come slowly into view; emerge. **b** (of a quality etc.) show itself unconsciously. —*n.* **1** a furtive or peering glance. **2** the first appearance (*at peep of day*). □ **peep-hole** a small hole that may be looked through. **peeping Tom** a furtive voyeur. **peep-show** a small exhibition of pictures etc. viewed through a lens or hole set into a box etc. **peep-toe** (or **-toed**) (of a shoe) leaving the toes partly bare. [ME: cf. PEEK, PEER¹]

peep² *v.* & *n.* —*v.intr.* make a shrill feeble sound as of young birds, mice, etc.; squeak; chirp. —*n.* such a sound. [imit.: cf. CHEEP]

peeper /ˈpiːpə(r)/ *n.* **1** a person who peeps. **2** *colloq.* an eye. **3** US *sl.* a private detective.

peer¹ *v.intr.* **1** (usu. foll. by *into, at,* etc.) look keenly or with difficulty (*peered into the fog*). **2** appear; peep out. [var. of *pire,* LG *pīren;* perh. partly f. APPEAR]

peer² *n.* & *v.* —*n.* **1 a** (*fem.* **peeress**) a member of one of the degrees of the nobility in Britain, i.e. a duke, marquis, earl, viscount, or baron. **b** a noble of any country. **2 a** person who is equal in ability, standing, rank, or value; a contemporary (*tried by a jury of his peers*). —*v.intr.* & *tr.* (usu. foll. by *with*) rank or cause to rank equally. □ **peer group** a group of people of the same age, status, interests, etc. **peer of the realm** (or **the United Kingdom**) any of the class of peers whose adult members may all sit in the House of Lords. □ **peerless** *adj.* [ME f. AF & OF *pe(e)r, perer* f. LL *pariare* f. L *par* equal]

peerage /ˈpɪərɪdʒ/ *n.* **1** peers as a class; the nobility. **2** the rank of peer or peeress (*was given a life peerage*). **3** a book containing a list of peers with their genealogy etc.

peeve *v.* & *n.* *colloq.* —*v.tr.* (usu. as **peeved** *adj.*) annoy; vex; irritate. —*n.* **1** a cause of annoyance. **2** vexation. [back-form. f. PEEVISH]

peevish /ˈpiːvɪʃ/ *adj.* querulous; irritable. □ **peevishly** *adv.* **peevishness** *n.* [ME, = foolish, mad, spiteful, etc., of unkn. orig.]

peewit /ˈpiːwɪt/ *n.* (also **pewit**) **1** a lapwing. **2** its cry. [imit.]

peg *n.* & *v.* —*n.* **1 a** a usu. cylindrical pin or bolt of wood or metal, often tapered at one end, and used for holding esp. two things together. **b** such a peg attached to a wall etc. and used for hanging garments etc. on. **c** a peg driven into the ground and attached to a rope for holding up a tent. **d** a bung for stoppering a cask etc. **e** each of several pegs used to tighten or loosen the strings of a violin etc. **f** a small peg, matchstick, etc. stuck into holes in a board for calculating the scores at cribbage. **2** *Brit.* = *clothes-peg.* **3** *Brit.* a measure of spirits or wine. —*v.tr.* (**pegged, pegging**) **1** (usu. foll. by *down, in, out,* etc.) fix (a thing) with a peg. **2** *Econ.* a stabilize (prices, wages, exchange rates, etc.). **b** prevent the price of (stock etc.) from falling or rising by freely buying or selling at a given price. **3** mark (the score) with pegs on a cribbage-board. □ **off the peg** (of clothes) ready-made. **peg away** (often foll. by *at*) work consistently and esp. for a long period. **peg down** restrict (a person etc.) to rules, a commitment, etc. **peg-leg 1** an artificial leg. **2** a person with an artificial leg. **peg on** = *peg away.* **peg out 1** *sl.* die. **2** mark the boundaries of (land etc.). **take a person down a peg or two** humble a person. [ME, prob. of LG or Du. orig.: cf. MDu. *pegge,* Du. dial. *peg,* LG *pigge*]

pegboard /ˈpɛɡbɔːd/ *n.* a board having a regular pattern of small holes for pegs, used for commercial displays, games, etc.

pejorative /pɪˈdʒɒrətɪv, ˈpiːdʒə-/ *adj.* & *n.* —*adj.* (of a word, an expression, etc.) depreciatory. —*n.* a depreciatory word. □ **pejoratively** *adv.* [F *péjoratif -ive* f. LL *pejorare* make worse (*pejor*)]

peke *n. colloq.* a Pekingese dog. [abbr.]

Pekingese /ˌpiːkɪˈniːz/ *n.* & *adj.* (also **Pekinese**) —*n.* (*pl.* same) **1 a** a lap-dog of a short-legged breed with long hair and a snub nose. **b** this breed. **2** a citizen of Peking (Beijing) in China. **3** the form of the Chinese language used in Beijing. —*adj.* of or concerning Beijing or its language or citizens.

pelagian /pɪˈleɪdʒɪən/ *adj.* & *n.* —*adj.* inhabiting the open sea. —*n.* an inhabitant of the open sea. [L *pelagius* f. Gk *pelagios* of the sea (*pelagos*)]

pelagic /pɪˈlædʒɪk/ *adj.* **1** of or performed on the open sea (*pelagic whaling*). **2** (of marine life) belonging to the upper layers of the open sea. [L *pelagicus* f. Gk *pelagikos* (as PELAGIAN)]

pelargonium /ˌpɛləˈɡəʊnɪəm/ *n.* any plant of the genus *Pelargonium,* with red, pink, or white flowers and fragrant leaves. [mod.L f. Gk *pelargos* stork: cf. GERANIUM]

pelf *n. derog.* or *joc.* money; wealth. [ME f. ONF f. OF *pelfre, peufre* spoils, of unkn. orig.: cf. PILFER]

pelican /ˈpɛlɪkən/ *n.* any large waterfowl of the family Pelecanidae with a large bill and a pouch in the throat for storing fish. □ **pelican crossing** (in the UK) a pedestrian crossing with traffic lights operated by pedestrians. [OE *pellican* & OF *pelican* f. LL *pelicanus* f. Gk *pelekan* prob. f. *pelekus* axe, with ref. to its bill]

pelisse /pɛˈliːs/ *n. hist.* **1** a woman's cloak with armholes or sleeves, reaching to the ankles. **2** a fur-lined cloak, esp. as part of a hussar's uniform. [F f. med.L *pellicia (vestis)* (garment) of fur f. *pellis* skin]

pellagra /pɪˈlæɡrə, -ˈleɪɡrə/ *n.* a disease caused by deficiency of nicotinic acid, characterized by cracking of the skin and often resulting in insanity. □ **pellagrous** *adj.* [It. f. *pelle* skin, after PODAGRA]

pellet /ˈpɛlɪt/ *n.* & *v.* —*n.* **1** a small compressed ball of paper, bread, etc. **2** a pill. **3 a** a small mass of bones, feathers, etc. regurgitated by a bird of prey. **b** a small hard piece of animal, usu. rodent, excreta. **4 a** a piece of small shot. **b** an imitation bullet for a toy gun. —*v.tr.* (**pelleted, pelleting**) make into a pellet or pellets. □ **pelletize** *v.tr.* (also **-ise**). [ME f. OF *pelote* f. L *pila* ball]

pellicle /ˈpɛlɪk(ə)l/ *n.* a thin skin, membrane, or film. □ **pellicular** /-ˈlɪkjʊlə(r)/ *adj.* [F *pellicule* f. L *pellicula,* dimin. of *pellis* skin]

pell-mell /pɛlˈmɛl/ *adv.* & *adj.* —*adv.* **1** headlong, recklessly (*rushed pell-mell out of the room*). **2** in disorder or confusion (*stuffed the papers together pell-mell*). —*adj.* confused, tumultuous. [F *pêle-mêle,* OF *pesle mesle, mesle pesle,* etc., redupl. of *mesle* f. *mesler* mix]

pellucid /pɪˈluːsɪd, -ˈljuːsɪd/ *adj.* **1** (of water, light, etc.) transparent, clear. **2** (of style, speech, etc.) not confused; clear. **3** mentally clear. □ **pellucidity** /-ˈsɪdɪtɪ/ *n.* **pellucidly** *adv.* [L *pellucidus* f. *perlucēre* (as PER-, *lucēre* shine)]

pelmet /ˈpɛlmɪt/ *n.* a narrow border of cloth, wood, etc. above esp. a window, concealing the curtain rail. [prob. f. F *palmette,* dimin. of *palme* PALM]

pelota /pɪˈlɒtə, pɪˈləʊtə/ *n.* a Basque or Spanish game played in a walled court with a ball and basket-like rackets attached to the hand. [Sp., = ball, augment. of *pella* f. L *pila*]

pelt¹ *v.* & *n.* —*v.* **1** *tr.* (usu. foll. by *with*) **a** hurl many small missiles at. **b** strike repeatedly with missiles. **c** assail (a person etc.) with insults, abuse, etc. **2** *intr.* (usu. foll. by *down*) (of rain etc.) fall quickly and torrentially. **3** *intr.* run fast. —*n.* the act or an instance of pelting. □ **at full pelt** as fast as possible. [16th c.: orig. unkn.]

pelt² *n.* **1** the undressed skin of a fur-bearing mammal. **2** the skin of a sheep, goat, etc. with short wool, or stripped ready for tanning. **3** *joc.* the human skin. □ **peltry** *n.* [ME f. obs. *pelt* skin, dimin. of *pel* f. AF *pell,* OF *pel,* or back-form. f. *peltry,* AF *pelterie,* OF *peleterie* f. *peletier* furrier, ult. f. L *pellis* skin]

pelvic /ˈpɛlvɪk/ *adj.* of or relating to the pelvis. □ **pelvic girdle** the bony or cartilaginous structure in vertebrates to which the posterior limbs are attached.

pelvis /'pelvɪs/ n. (pl. **pelvises** or **pelves** /-viːz/) a basin-shaped cavity at the lower end of the torso of most vertebrates, formed from the bones of the haunch with the sacrum and other vertebrae. [L, = basin]

pemmican /'pemɪkən/ n. **1** a cake of dried pounded meat mixed with melted fat, orig. made by N. American Indians. **2** beef so treated and flavoured with currants etc. for use by Arctic travellers etc. [Cree *pimecan* f. *pime* fat]

pen[1] /pen/ n. & v. —n. **1** an instrument for writing or drawing with ink, orig. consisting of a shaft with a sharpened quill or metal nib, now more widely applied. **2 a** (usu. prec. by *the*) the occupation of writing. **b** a style of writing. **3** *Zool.* the internal feather-shaped cartilaginous shell of certain cuttlefish, esp. squid. —v.tr. (**penned, penning**) **1** write. **2** compose and write. □ **pen and ink** n. **1** the instruments of writing. **2** writing. **pen-and-ink** adj. drawn or written with ink. **pen-friend** a friend communicated with by letter only. **pen-light** a small electric torch shaped like a fountain-pen. **pen-name** a literary pseudonym. **pen-pal** *colloq.* = *pen-friend.* **pen-pusher** *colloq. derog.* a clerical worker. **pen-pushing** *colloq. derog.* clerical work. **put pen to paper** begin writing. [ME f. OF *penne* f. L *penna* feather]

pen[2] /pen/ n. & v. —n. **1** a small enclosure for cows, sheep, poultry, etc. **2** a place of confinement. —v.tr. (**penned, penning**) (often foll. by *in, up*) enclose or shut in a pen. [OE *penn*, of unkn. orig.]

pen[3] /pen/ n. a female swan. [16th c.: orig. unkn.]

pen[4] /pen/ n. US sl. = PENITENTIARY n. [abbr.]

penal /'piːn(ə)l/ adj. **1 a** of or concerning punishment or its infliction (*penal laws; a penal sentence; a penal colony*). **b** (of an offence) punishable, esp. by law. **2** extremely severe (*penal taxation*). □ **penal servitude** *hist.* imprisonment with compulsory labour. □ **penally** adv. [ME f. OF *penal* or L *poenalis* f. *poena* PAIN]

penalize /'piːnəlaɪz/ v.tr. (also **-ise**) **1** subject (a person) to a penalty or comparative disadvantage. **2** make or declare (an action) penal. □ **penalization** /-'zeɪʃ(ə)n/ n.

penalty /'pen(ə)ltɪ/ n. (pl. **-ies**) **1 a** a punishment, esp. a fine, for a breach of law, contract, etc. **b** a fine paid. **2** a disadvantage, loss, etc., esp. as a result of one's own actions (*paid the penalty for his carelessness*). **3 a** a disadvantage imposed on a competitor or side in a game etc. for a breach of the rules etc. **b** (*attrib.*) awarded against a side incurring a penalty (*penalty kick; penalty goal*). □ **penalty area** *Football* the ground in front of the goal in which a foul by defenders involves the award of a penalty kick. **penalty box** *Ice Hockey* an area reserved for penalized players and some officials. **the penalty of** a disadvantage resulting from (a quality etc.). **under** (or **on**) **penalty of** under the threat of (dismissal etc.). [AF *penalte* (unrecorded), F *pénalité* f. med.L *penalitas* (as PENAL)]

penance /'penəns/ n. & v. —n. **1** an act of self-punishment as reparation for guilt. **2 a** (in the RC and Orthodox Church) a sacrament including confession of and absolution for a sin. **b** a penalty imposed esp. by a priest for a sin. —v.tr. impose a penance on. □ **do penance** perform a penance. [ME f. OF f. L *paenitentia* (as PENITENT)]

pence pl. of PENNY.

penchant /'pãʃã/ n. an inclination or liking (*has a penchant for old films*). [F, pres. part. of *pencher* incline]

pencil /'pensɪl/ n. & v. —n. **1** (often *attrib.*) **a** an instrument for writing or drawing, usu. consisting of a thin rod of graphite etc. enclosed in a wooden cylinder (*a pencil sketch*). **b** a similar instrument with a metal or plastic cover and retractable lead. **c** a cosmetic in pencil form. **2** (*attrib.*) resembling a pencil in shape (*pencil skirt*). —v.tr. (**pencilled, pencilling;** US **penciled, penciling**) **1** tint or mark with or as if with a pencil. **2** (usu. foll. by *in*) **a** write, esp. tentatively or provisionally (*have pencilled in the 29th for our meeting*). **b** (esp. as **pencilled** adj.) fill (an area) with soft pencil strokes (*pencilled in her eyebrows*). □ **pencil-case** a container for pencils etc. **pencil-sharpener** a device for sharpening a pencil by rotating it against a cutting edge. □ **penciller** n. [ME f. OF *pincel* ult. f. L *penicillum* paintbrush, dimin. of *peniculus* brush, dimin. of *penis* tail]

pendant /'pend(ə)nt/ n. (also **pendent**) **1 a** hanging jewel etc., esp. one attached to a necklace, bracelet, etc. **2** a light fitting, ornament, etc., hanging from a ceiling. [ME f. OF f. *pendre* hang f. L *pendere*]

pendent /'pend(ə)nt/ adj. (also **pendant**) **1 a** hanging. **b** overhanging. **2** undecided; pending. □ **pendency** n. [ME (as PENDANT)]

pending /'pendɪŋ/ adj. & prep. —predic.adj. **1** awaiting decision or settlement, undecided (*a settlement was pending*). **2** about to come into existence (*patent pending*). —prep. **1** during (*pending these negotiations*). **2** until (*pending his return*). □ **pending-tray** a tray for documents, letters, etc., awaiting attention. [after F *pendant* (see PENDENT)]

pendulous /'pendjʊləs/ adj. **1** (of ears, breasts, flowers, bird's nests, etc.) hanging down; drooping and esp. swinging. **2** oscillating. □ **pendulously** adv. [L *pendulus* f. *pendēre* hang]

pendulum /'pendjʊləm/ n. a weight suspended so as to swing freely, esp. a rod with a weighted end regulating the movement of a clock's works. [L neut. adj. (as PENDULOUS)]

penetrate /'penɪtreɪt/ v. **1** tr. **a** find access into or through, esp. forcibly. **b** (usu. foll. by *with*) imbue (a person or thing) with; permeate. **2** tr. see into, find out, or discern (a person's mind, the truth, a meaning, etc.). **3** tr. see through (darkness, fog, etc.) (*could not penetrate the gloom*). **4** intr. be absorbed by the mind (*my hint did not penetrate*). **5** tr. (as **penetrating** adj.) **a** having or suggesting sensitivity or insight (*a penetrating remark*). **b** (of a voice etc.) easily heard through or above other sounds; piercing. **6** tr. (of a man) put the penis into the vagina of (a woman). **7** intr. (usu. foll. by *into, through, to*) make a way. □ **penetrable** /-trəb(ə)l/ adj. **penetrability** /-trə'bɪlɪtɪ/ n. **penetrant** adj. & n. **penetratingly** adv. **penetration** /-'treɪʃ(ə)n/ n. **penetrative** /-trətɪv/ adj. **penetrator** n. [L *penetrare* place or enter within f. *penitus* interior]

penguin /'peŋgwɪn/ n. any flightless sea bird of the family Spheniscidae of the southern hemisphere, with black upper-parts and white under-parts, and wings developed into scaly flippers for swimming underwater. [16th c., orig. = great auk: orig. unkn.]

penicillin /ˌpenɪˈsɪlɪn/ n. any of various antibiotics produced naturally by moulds of the genus *Penicillium*, or synthetically, and able to prevent the growth of certain disease-causing bacteria. [mod.L *Penicillium* genus name f. L *penicillum*: see PENCIL]

penile /ˈpiːnaɪl/ adj. of or concerning the penis. [mod.L *penilis*]

peninsula /pɪˈnɪnsjʊlə/ n. a piece of land almost surrounded by water or projecting far into a sea or lake etc. □ **peninsular** adj. [L *paeninsula* f. *paene* almost + *insula* island]

penis /ˈpiːnɪs/ n. (pl. **penises** or **penes** /-niːz/) 1 the male organ of copulation and (in mammals) urination. 2 the male copulatory organ in lower vertebrates. [L, = tail, penis]

penitent /ˈpenɪt(ə)nt/ adj. & n. —adj. regretting and wishing to atone for sins etc.; repentant. —n. 1 a repentant sinner. 2 a person doing penance under the direction of a confessor. □ **penitence** n. **penitently** adv. [ME f. OF f. L *paenitens* f. *paenitēre* repent]

penitential /ˌpenɪˈtenʃ(ə)l/ adj. of or concerning penitence or penance. □ **penitentially** adv. [OF *penitencial* f. LL *paenitentialis* f. *paenitentia* penitence (as PENITENT)]

penitentiary /ˌpenɪˈtenʃərɪ/ n. & adj. —n. (pl. **-ies**) US a reformatory prison. —adj. 1 of or concerning penance. 2 of or concerning reformatory treatment. [ME f. med.L *paenitentiarius* (adj. & n.) (as PENITENT)]

penknife /ˈpennaɪf/ n. a small folding knife, esp. for carrying in a pocket.

penman /ˈpenmən/ n. (pl. **-men**) 1 a person who writes by hand with a specified skill (a good penman). 2 an author. □ **penmanship** n.

pennant /ˈpenənt/ n. 1 Naut. a tapering flag, esp. that flown at the masthead of a vessel in commission. 2 = PENNON. 3 US a flag denoting a sports championship etc. [blend of PENDANT and PENNON]

penniless /ˈpenɪlɪs/ adj. having no money; destitute. □ **pennilessly** adv. **pennilessness** n.

pennon /ˈpenən/ n. 1 a long narrow flag, triangular or swallow-tailed, esp. as the military ensign of lancer regiments. 2 Naut. a long pointed streamer on a ship. 3 a flag. □ **pennoned** adj. [ME f. OF f. L *penna* feather]

penny /ˈpenɪ/ n. (pl. for separate coins **-ies**, for a sum of money **pence** /pens/) 1 a British coin and monetary unit equal to one-hundredth of a pound. 2 hist. a former British bronze coin and monetary unit equal to one-two-hundred-and-fortieth of a pound. 3 US colloq. a one-cent coin. □ **in for a penny, in for a pound** an exhortation to total commitment to an undertaking. **like a bad penny** continually returning when unwanted. **pennies from heaven** unexpected benefits. **penny black** the first adhesive postage stamp (1840, value one penny). **penny dreadful** Brit. a cheap sensational comic or story-book. **the penny drops** colloq. one begins to understand at last. **penny farthing** Brit. an early type of bicycle with one large and one small wheel. **penny-pinching** n. meanness. —adj. mean. **penny wise** too careful in saving small amounts. **penny wise and pound foolish** mean in small expenditures but wasteful of large amounts. **a pretty penny** a

large sum of money. **two a penny** almost worthless though easily obtained. [OE *penig, penning* f. Gmc, perh. rel. to PAWN²]

pennyroyal /ˌpenɪˈrɔɪəl/ n. 1 a creeping mint, *Mentha pulegium*, cultivated for its supposed medicinal properties. 2 US an aromatic plant, *Hedeoma pulegioides*. [app. f. earlier *puliol(e) ryall* f. AF *puliol*, OF *pouliol* ult. f. L *pulegium* + real ROYAL]

pennyweight /ˈpenɪˌweɪt/ n. a unit of weight, 24 grains or one-twentieth of an ounce troy.

pennywort /ˈpenɪˌwɜːt/ n. any of several wild plants with rounded leaves. [ME, f. PENNY + *wort* (OE *wyrt*), rel. to ROOT¹]

pennyworth /ˈpenɪˌwɜːθ/ n. (also **penn'orth** /ˈpenəθ/) 1 as much as can be bought for a penny. 2 a bargain of a specified kind (a bad pennyworth).

penology /piːˈnɒlədʒɪ/ n. the study of the punishment of crime and of prison management. □ **penological** /-nəˈlɒdʒɪk(ə)l/ adj. **penologist** n. [L *poena* penalty + -LOGY]

pensile /ˈpensaɪl/ adj. hanging down; pendulous. [L *pensilis* f. *pendēre pens-* hang]

pension¹ /ˈpenʃ(ə)n/ n. & v. —n. 1 a a regular payment made by a government to people above a specified age, to widows, or to the disabled. b similar payments made by an employer etc. on the retirement of an employee. 2 a pension paid to a scientist, artist, etc. for services to the state, or to fund work. —v.tr. grant a pension to. □ **pension off** 1 dismiss with a pension. 2 cease to employ or use. □ **pensionless** adj. [ME f. OF f. L *pensio -onis* payment f. *pendere pens-* pay]

pension² /pɑ̃ˈsjɔ̃/ n. a European, esp. French, boarding-house providing full or half board at a fixed rate. □ **en pension** /ɔ̃/ as a boarder. [F: see PENSION¹]

pensionable /ˈpenʃənəb(ə)l/ adj. 1 entitled to a pension. 2 (of a service, job, etc.) entitling an employee to a pension. □ **pensionability** /-ˈbɪlɪtɪ/ n.

pensionary /ˈpenʃənərɪ/ adj. & n. —adj. of or concerning a pension. —n. (pl. **-ies**) a pensioner. [med.L *pensionarius* (as PENSION¹)]

pensioner /ˈpenʃənə(r)/ n. a recipient of a pension, esp. the retirement pension. [ME f. AF *pensionner*, OF *pensionnier* (as PENSION¹)]

pensive /ˈpensɪv/ adj. 1 deep in thought. 2 sorrowfully thoughtful. □ **pensively** adv. **pensiveness** n. [ME f. OF *pensif, -ive* f. *penser* think f. L *pensare* frequent. of *pendere pens-* weigh]

pent adj. (often foll. by in, up) closely confined; shut in (pent up feelings). [past part. of *pend* var. of PEN² v.]

penta- /ˈpentə/ comb. form 1 five. 2 Chem. (forming the names of compounds) containing five atoms or groups of a specified kind (pentoxide). [Gk f. *pente* five]

pentacle /ˈpentək(ə)l/ n. a figure used as a symbol, esp. in magic, e.g. a pentagram. [med.L *pentaculum* (as PENTA-)]

pentad /ˈpentæd/ n. 1 the number five. 2 a group of five. [Gk *pentas -ados* f. *pente* five]

pentagon /ˈpentəgən/ n. 1 a plane figure with five sides and angles. 2 (**the Pentagon**) a the pentagonal Washington headquarters of the US defence forces. b the leaders of the US defence forces. □ **pentagonal** /-ˈtægən(ə)l/ adj. [F *pentagone* or f. LL *pentagonus* f. Gk *pentagōnon* (as PENTA-, -GON)]

pentagram /ˈpentəˌgræm/ *n.* a five-pointed star formed by extending the sides of a pentagon both ways until they intersect, formerly used as a mystic symbol. [Gk *pentagrammon* (as PENTA-, -GRAM)]

pentahedron /ˌpentəˈhiːdrən/ *n.* a solid figure with five faces. □ **pentahedral** *adj.*

pentameter /penˈtæmɪtə(r)/ *n.* **1** a verse of five feet. [L f. Gk *pentametros* (as PENTA-, -METER)]

pentangle /ˈpenˌtæŋg(ə)l/ *n.* = PENTAGRAM. [ME perh. f. med.L *pentaculum* PENTACLE, assim. to L *angulus* ANGLE]

Pentateuch /ˈpentəˌtjuːk/ *n.* the first five books of the Old Testament, traditionally ascribed to Moses. □ **pentateuchal** /-ˈtjuːk(ə)l/ *adj.* [eccl.L *pentateuchus* f. eccl.Gk *pentateukhos* (as PENTA-, *teukhos* implement, book)]

pentathlon /penˈtæθlən/ *n.* an athletic event comprising five different events for each competitor. □ **pentathlete** /-ˈtæθliːt/ *n.* [Gk f. *pente* five + *athlon* contest]

pentatonic /ˌpentəˈtɒnɪk/ *adj. Mus.* **1** consisting of five notes. **2** relating to such a scale.

Pentecost /ˈpentɪˌkɒst/ *n.* **1 a** Whit Sunday. **b** a festival celebrating the descent of the Holy Spirit on Whit Sunday. **2** the Jewish harvest festival, on the fiftieth day after the second day of Passover (Lev. 23:15–16). [OE *pentecosten* & OF *pentecoste*, f. eccl.L *pentecoste* f. Gk *pentēkostē* (*hēmera*) fiftieth (day)]

Pentecostal /ˌpentɪˈkɒst(ə)l/ *adj. & n.* —*adj.* (also **pentecostal**) **1** of or relating to Pentecost. **2** of or designating Christian sects and individuals who emphasize the gifts of the Holy Spirit, are often fundamentalist in outlook, and express religious feelings by clapping, shouting, dancing, etc. —*n.* a Pentecostalist. □ **Pentecostalism** *n.* **Pentecostalist** *n. & n.*

penthouse /ˈpenthaʊs/ *n.* **1** a house or flat on the roof or the top floor of a tall building. **2** a sloping roof, esp. of an outhouse built on to another building. [ME *pentis* f. OF *apentis*, *-dis*, f. med.L *appendicium*, in LL = appendage, f. L (as APPEND); infl. by HOUSE]

penult /pɪˈnʌlt, ˈpiːnʌlt/ *n. & adj.* —*n.* the last but one (esp. syllable). —*adj.* last but one. [abbr. of L *paenultimus* (see PENULTIMATE) or of PENULTIMATE]

penultimate /pɪˈnʌltɪmət/ *adj. & n.* —*adj.* last but one. —*n.* the last but one. [L *paenultimus* f. *paene* almost + *ultimus* last, after *ultimate*]

penumbra /pɪˈnʌmbrə/ *n.* (*pl.* **penumbrae** /-briː/ or **penumbras**) **1 a** the partly shaded region around the shadow of an opaque body, esp. that around the total shadow of the moon or earth in an eclipse. **b** the less dark outer part of a sunspot. **2** a partial shadow. □ **penumbral** *adj.* [mod.L f. L *paene* almost + UMBRA shadow]

penurious /pɪˈnjʊərɪəs/ *adj.* **1** poor; destitute. **2** stingy; grudging. **3** scanty. □ **penuriously** *adv.* **penuriousness** *n.* [med.L *penuriosus* (as PENURY)]

penury /ˈpenjʊrɪ/ *n.* (*pl.* **-ies**) **1** destitution; poverty. **2** a lack; scarcity. [ME f. L *penuria*, perh. rel. to *paene* almost]

peon /ˈpiːən/ *n.* **1 a** a Spanish American day labourer or farm-worker. **b** a poor or destitute South American. **2** /ˈpiːən, pjuːn/ an Indian office messenger, attendant, or orderly. □ **peonage** *n.* [Port. *peão* & Sp. *peon* f. med.L *pedo -onis* walker f. L *pes pedis* foot: cf. PAWN¹]

peony /ˈpiːənɪ/ *n.* (also **paeony**) (*pl.* **-ies**) any herbaceous plant of the genus *Paeonia*, with large globular red, pink, or white flowers, often double in cultivated varieties. [OE *peonie* f. L *peonia* f. Gk *paiōnia* f. *Paiōn*, physician of the gods]

people /ˈpiːp(ə)l/ *n. & v.* —*n.* **1** (usu. as *pl.*) **a** persons composing a community, tribe, race, nation, etc. (*a warlike people*; *the peoples of the Commonwealth*). **b** a group of persons of a usu. specified kind (*the chosen people*; *these people here*; *right-thinking people*). **2** (prec. by *the*; treated as *pl.*) **a** the mass of people in a country etc. not having special rank or position. **b** these considered as an electorate (*the people will reject it*). **3** parents or other relatives (*my people are French*). **4 a** subjects, armed followers, a retinue, etc. **b** a congregation of a parish priest etc. **5** persons in general (*people do not like rudeness*). —*v.tr.* (usu. foll. by *with*) **1** fill with people, animals, etc.; populate. **2** (esp. as **peopled** *adj.*) inhabit; occupy; fill (*thickly peopled*). [ME f. AF *poeple*, *people*, OF *pople*, *peuple*, f. L *populus*]

pep *n. & v. colloq.* —*n.* vigour; go; spirit. —*v.tr.* (**pepped**, **pepping**) (usu. foll. by *up*) fill with vigour. □ **pep pill** a pill containing a stimulant drug. **pep talk** a usu. short talk intended to enthuse, encourage, etc. [abbr. of PEPPER]

peplum /ˈpepləm/ *n.* **1** a short flounce etc. at waist level, esp. of a blouse or jacket over a skirt. **2** *Gk Antiq.* a woman's outer garment. [L f. Gk *peplos*]

pepper /ˈpepə(r)/ *n. & v.* —*n.* **1 a** a hot aromatic condiment from the dried berries of certain plants used whole or ground. **b** any climbing vine of the genus *Piper*, esp. *P. nigrum*, yielding these berries. **2** anything hot or pungent. **3 a** any plant of the genus *Capsicum*, esp. *C. annuum*. **b** the fruit of this used esp. as a vegetable or salad ingredient. **4** = CAYENNE. —*v.tr.* **1** sprinkle or treat with or as if with pepper. **2 a** pelt with missiles. **b** hurl abuse etc. at. **3** punish severely. □ **black pepper** the unripe ground or whole berries of *Piper nigrum* as a condiment. **green pepper** the unripe fruit of *Capsicum annuum*. **pepper-mill** a device for grinding pepper by hand. **pepper-pot** a small container with a perforated lid for sprinkling pepper. **red** (or **yellow**) **pepper** the ripe fruit of *Capsicum annuum*. **sweet pepper** a pepper with a relatively mild taste. **white pepper** the ripe or husked ground or whole berries of *Piper nigrum* as a condiment. [OE *piper*, *pipor* f. L *piper* f. Gk *peperi* f. Skr. *pippalī*- berry, peppercorn]

peppercorn /ˈpepəˌkɔːn/ *n.* **1** the dried berry of *Piper nigrum* as a condiment. **2** (in full **peppercorn rent**) a nominal rent.

peppermint /ˈpepəmɪnt/ *n.* **1 a** a mint plant, *Mentha piperita*, grown for the strong-flavoured oil obtained from its leaves. **b** the oil from this. **2** a sweet flavoured with peppermint. **3** *Austral.* any of various eucalyptuses yielding oil with a similar flavour. □ **pepperminty** *adj.*

pepperoni /ˌpepəˈrəʊnɪ/ *n.* (also **peperoni**) beef and pork sausage seasoned with pepper. [It. *peperone* chilli]

peppery /ˈpepərɪ/ *adj.* **1** of, like, or containing much, pepper. **2** hot-tempered. **3** pungent; stinging. □ **pepperiness** *n.*

peppy /ˈpepɪ/ adj. (**peppier, peppiest**) colloq. vigorous, energetic, bouncy. □ **peppily** adv. **peppiness** n.

pepsin /ˈpepsɪn/ n. an enzyme contained in the gastric juice, which hydrolyses proteins. [G f. Gk pepsis digestion]

peptic /ˈpeptɪk/ adj. concerning or promoting digestion. □ **peptic glands** glands secreting gastric juice. **peptic ulcer** an ulcer in the stomach or duodenum. [Gk peptikos able to digest f. peptos cooked]

peptide /ˈpeptaɪd/ n. Biochem. any of a group of organic compounds consisting of two or more amino acids bonded in sequence. [G Peptid (as PEPTIC)]

per prep. 1 for each; for every (two sweets per child; five miles per hour). 2 by means of; by; through (per rail). 3 (in full **as per**) in accordance with (as per instructions). □ **as per usual** colloq. as usual. [L]

per- /pɜː(r), pə(r)/ prefix 1 forming verbs, nouns, and adjectives meaning: **a** through; all over (perforate; perforation; pervade). **b** completely; very (perfervid; perturb). **c** to destruction; to the bad (pervert; perdition). 2 Chem. having the maximum of some element in combination, esp.: **a** in the names of binary compounds in -ide (peroxide). **b** in the names of oxides, acids, etc. in -ic (perchloric; permanganic). **c** in the names of salts of these acids (perchlorate; permanganate). [L per- (as PER)]

peradventure /pərədˈventʃə(r), ˌpɜː-/ adv. & n. archaic or joc. —adv. perhaps. —n. uncertainty; chance; conjecture; doubt (esp. beyond or without peradventure). [ME f. OF per or par auenture by chance (as PER, ADVENTURE)]

perambulate /pəˈræmbjʊˌleɪt/ v. 1 tr. walk through, over, or about (streets, the country, etc.). 2 intr. walk from place to place. □ **perambulation** /-ˈleɪʃ(ə)n/ n. **perambulatory** adj. [L perambulare perambulat- (as PER-, ambulare walk)]

perambulator /pəˈræmbjʊˌleɪtə(r)/ n. Brit. formal = PRAM. [PERAMBULATE]

per annum /pər ˈænəm/ adv. for each year. [L]

percale /pəˈkeɪl/ n. a closely woven cotton fabric like calico. [F, of uncert. orig.]

per capita /pə ˈkæpɪtə/ adv. & adj. (also **per caput** /ˈkæpʊt/) for each person. [L, = by heads]

perceive /pəˈsiːv/ v.tr. 1 apprehend, esp. through the sight; observe. 2 (usu. foll. by that, how, etc. + clause) apprehend with the mind; understand. 3 regard mentally in a specified manner (perceives the universe as infinite). □ **perceivable** adj. **perceiver** n. [ME f. OF perçoivre, f. L percipere (as PER-, capere take)]

per cent /pə ˈsent/ adv. & n. (US **percent**) —adv. in every hundred. —n. 1 percentage. 2 one part in every hundred (half a per cent).

percentage /pəˈsentɪdʒ/ n. 1 a rate or proportion per cent. 2 a proportion. 3 colloq. personal benefit or advantage.

percentile /pəˈsentaɪl/ n. Statistics one of 99 values of a variable dividing a population into 100 equal groups as regards the value of that variable.

perceptible /pəˈseptɪb(ə)l/ adj. capable of being perceived by the senses or intellect. □ **perceptibility** /-ˈbɪlɪtɪ/ n. **perceptibly** adv. [OF perceptible or LL perceptibilis f. L (as PERCEIVE)]

perception /pəˈsep(ə)n/ n. 1 **a** the faculty of perceiving. **b** an instance of this. 2 (often foll. by of) **a** the intuitive recognition of a truth, aesthetic quality, etc. **b** an instance of this (a sudden perception of the true position). □ **perceptional** adj. **perceptual** /pəˈseptjʊəl/ adj. **perceptually** /pəˈseptjʊəlɪ/ adv. [ME f. L perceptio (as PERCEIVE)]

perceptive /pəˈseptɪv/ adj. 1 capable of perceiving. 2 sensitive; discerning; observant (a perceptive remark). □ **perceptively** adv. **perceptiveness** n. **perceptivity** /-ˈtɪvɪtɪ/ n. [med.L perceptivus (as PERCEIVE)]

perch¹ n. & v. —n. 1 a usu. horizontal bar, branch, etc. used by a bird to rest on. 2 a usu. high or precarious place for a person or thing to rest on. 3 a measure of length, esp. for land, of 5½ yards. —v.intr. & tr. (usu. foll. by on) settle or rest, or cause to settle or rest on or as if on a perch etc. (the bird perched on a branch; a town perched on a hill). □ **knock a person off his perch 1** vanquish, destroy. **2** make less confident or secure. **square perch** 30¼ sq. yards. [ME f. OF perche, percher f. L pertica pole]

perch² /pɜːtʃ/ n. (pl. same or **perches**) any spiny-finned freshwater edible fish of the genus Perca, esp. P. fluviatilis of Europe. [ME f. OF perche f. L perca f. Gk perkē]

perchance /pəˈtʃɑːns/ adv. archaic or poet. 1 by chance. 2 possibly; maybe. [ME f. AF par chance f. par by, CHANCE]

percipient /pəˈsɪpɪənt/ adj. & n. —adj. 1 able to perceive; conscious. 2 discerning; observant. —n. a person who perceives, esp. something outside the range of the senses. □ **percipience** n. **percipiently** adv. [L (as PERCEIVE)]

percolate /ˈpɜːkəˌleɪt/ v. 1 intr. (often foll. by through) **a** (of liquid etc.) filter or ooze gradually (esp. through a porous surface). **b** (of an idea etc.) permeate gradually. 2 tr. prepare (coffee) by repeatedly passing boiling water through ground beans. 3 tr. ooze through; permeate. 4 tr. strain (a liquid, powder, etc.) through a fine mesh etc. □ **percolation** /-ˈleɪʃ(ə)n/ n. [L percolare (as PER-, colare strain f. colum strainer)]

percolator /ˈpɜːkəˌleɪtə(r)/ n. a machine for making coffee by circulating boiling water through ground beans.

percuss /pəˈkʌs/ v.tr. Med. tap (a part of the body) gently with a finger or an instrument as part of a diagnosis. [L percutere percuss- strike (as PER-, cutere = quatere shake)]

percussion /pəˈkʌʃ(ə)n/ n. 1 Mus. **a** (often attrib.) the playing of music by striking instruments with sticks etc. (a percussion band). **b** the section of such instruments in an orchestra (asked the percussion to stay behind). 2 Med. the act or an instance of percussing. 3 the forcible striking of one esp. solid body against another. □ **percussion cap** a small amount of explosive powder contained in metal or paper and exploded by striking, used esp. in toy guns and formerly in some firearms. □ **percussionist** n. **percussive** adj. **percussively** adv. **percussiveness** n. [F percussion or L percussio (as PERCUSS)]

percutaneous /ˌpɜːkjʊˈteɪnɪəs/ adj. esp. Med. made or done through the skin. [L per cutem through the skin]

per diem /pə ˈdiːem, ˈdaɪem/ adv., adj. & n. —adv. & adj. for each day. —n. an allowance or payment for each day. [L]

perdition /pəˈdɪʃ(ə)n/ *n.* eternal death; damnation. [ME f. OF *perdiciun* or eccl.L *perditio* f. L *perdere* destroy (as PER-, *dere dit-* = *dare* give)]

peregrine /ˈperɪgrɪn/ *n.* (in full **peregrine falcon**) a kind of falcon much used for hawking. [L *peregrinus* f. *peregre* abroad f. *per* through + *ager* field]

peremptory /pəˈremptərɪ, ˈperɪm-/ *adj.* **1** (of a statement or command) admitting no denial or refusal. **2** (of a person, a person's manner, etc.) dogmatic; imperious; dictatorial. □ **peremptorily** *adv.* **peremptoriness** *n.* [AF *peremptorie*, OF *peremptoire* f. L *peremptorius* deadly, decisive, f. *perimere perempt-* destroy, cut off (as PER-, *emere* take, buy)]

perennial /pəˈrenɪəl/ *adj.* & *n.* —*adj.* **1** lasting through a year or several years. **2** (of a plant) lasting several years. **3** lasting a long time or for ever. —*n.* a perennial plant (*a herbaceous perennial*). □ **perenniality** /-ˈælɪtɪ/ *n.* **perennially** *adv.* [L *perennis* (as PER-, *annus* year)]

perestroika /ˌpereˈstrɔɪkə/ *n.* (in the former Soviet Union) the policy or practice of restructuring or reforming the economic and political system. [Russ. *perestroĭka* = restructuring]

perfect /ˈpɜːfɪkt/ *adj.*, *v.*, & *n.* —*adj.* **1** complete; not deficient. **2** faultless (*a perfect diamond*). **3** very satisfactory (*a perfect evening*). **4** exact; precise (*a perfect circle*). **5** entire; unqualified (*a perfect stranger*). **6** *Gram.* (of a tense) denoting a completed action or event in the past, formed in English with *have* or *has* and the past participle, as in *they have eaten*. —*v.tr.* /pəˈfekt/ **1** make perfect; improve. **2** carry through; complete. —*n.* *Gram.* the perfect tense. □ **perfect interval** *Mus.* a fourth or fifth as it would occur in a major or minor scale starting on the lower note of the interval, or octave. **perfect pitch** = *absolute pitch* 1. □ **perfecter** *n.* **perfectible** /pəˈfektɪb(ə)l/ *adj.* **perfectibility** /pəˌfektɪˈbɪlɪtɪ/ *n.* **perfectness** *n.* [ME and OF *parfit*, *perfet* f. L *perfectus* past part. of *perficere* complete (as PER-, *facere* do)]

perfection /pəˈfekʃ(ə)n/ *n.* **1** the act or process of making perfect. **2** the state of being perfect; faultlessness, excellence. **3** a perfect person, thing, or example. **4** an accomplishment. **5** full development; completion. □ **to perfection** exactly; completely. [ME f. OF f. L *perfectio -onis* (as PERFECT)]

perfectionism /pəˈfekʃəˌnɪz(ə)m/ *n.* the uncompromising pursuit of excellence. □ **perfectionist** *n.* & *adj.* [PERFECT]

perfectly /ˈpɜːfɪktlɪ/ *adv.* **1** completely; absolutely (*I understand you perfectly*). **2** quite, completely (*is perfectly capable of doing it*). **3** in a perfect way.

perfidy /ˈpɜːfɪdɪ/ *n.* breach of faith; treachery. □ **perfidious** /-ˈfɪdɪəs/ *adj.* **perfidiously** /-ˈfɪdɪəslɪ/ *adv.* [L *perfidia* f. *perfidus* treacherous (as PER-, *fidus* f. *fides* faith)]

perforate *v.* & *adj.* —*v.* /ˈpɜːfəˌreɪt/ **1** *tr.* make a hole or holes through; pierce. **2** *tr.* make a row of small holes in (paper etc.) so that a part may be torn off easily. **3** *tr.* make an opening into; pass into or extend through. **4** *intr.* (usu. foll. by *into*, *through*, etc.) penetrate. —*adj.* /ˈpɜːfərət/ perforated. □ **perforation** /-ˈreɪʃ(ə)n/ *n.* **perforative** /ˈpɜːfərətɪv/ *adj.* **perforator** /ˈpɜːfəˌreɪtə(r)/ *n.* [L *perforare* (as PER-, *forare* pierce)]

perforce /pəˈfɔːs/ *adv.* *archaic* unavoidably; necessarily. [ME f. OF *par force* by FORCE]

perform /pəˈfɔːm/ *v.* **1** *tr.* (also *absol.*) carry into effect; be the agent of; do (a command, promise, task, etc.). **2** *tr.* (also *absol.*) go through, execute (a public function, play, piece of music, etc.). **3** *intr.* act in a play; play music, sing, etc. (*likes performing*). **4** *intr.* (of a trained animal) execute tricks etc. at a public show. □ **performable** *adj.* **performability** /-ˈbɪlɪtɪ/ *n.* **performatory** *adj.* & *n.* (*pl.* **-ies**). **performer** *n.* **performing** *adj.* [ME f. AF *parfourmer* f. OF *parfournir* (assim. to *forme* FORM) f. *par* PER- + *fournir* FURNISH]

performance /pəˈfɔːməns/ *n.* **1** (usu. foll. by *of*) **a** the act or process of performing or carrying out. **b** the execution or fulfilment (of a duty etc.). **2** a staging or production (of a drama, piece of music, etc.) (*the afternoon performance*). **3** a person's achievement under test conditions etc. (*put up a good performance*). **4** *colloq.* a fuss; a scene; a public exhibition (*made such a performance about leaving*). **5 a** the capabilities of a machine, esp. a car or aircraft. **b** (*attrib.*) of high capability (*a performance car*).

performing arts /pəˈfɔːmɪŋ/ *n.pl.* the arts, such as drama, music, and dance, that require performance for their realization.

perfume /ˈpɜːfjuːm/ *n.* & *v.* —*n.* **1** a sweet smell. **2** fluid containing the essence of flowers etc.; scent. —*v.tr.* /also pəˈfjuːm/ (usu. as **perfumed** *adj.*) impart a sweet scent to; impregnate with a sweet smell. □ **perfumy** *adj.* [F *parfum*, *parfumer* f. obs. It. *parfumare*, *perfumare* (as PER-, *fumare* smoke, FUME): orig. of smoke from a burning substance]

perfumer /pəˈfjuːmə(r)/ *n.* a maker or seller of perfumes. □ **perfumery** *n.* (*pl.* **-ies**).

perfunctory /pəˈfʌŋktərɪ/ *adj.* **1** done merely for the sake of getting through a duty. **2** super-ficial; mechanical. □ **perfunctorily** *adv.* **perfunctoriness** *n.* [LL *perfunctorius* careless f. L *perfungi perfunct-* (as PER-, *fungi* perform)]

pergola /ˈpɜːgələ/ *n.* an arbour or covered walk, formed of growing plants trained over trellis-work. [It. f. L *pergula* projecting roof f. *pergere* proceed]

perhaps /pəˈhæps/ *adv.* **1** it may be; possibly (*perhaps it is lost*). **2** introducing a polite request (*perhaps you would open the window?*). [PER + HAP]

peri- /ˈperɪ/ *prefix* **1** round, about. **2** *Astron.* the point nearest to (*perigee*; *perihelion*). [Gk *peri* around, about]

perianth /ˈperɪˌænθ/ *n.* the outer part of a flower. [F *périanthe* f. mod.L *perianthium* (as PERI- + Gk *anthos* flower)]

pericardium /ˌperɪˈkɑːdɪəm/ *n.* (*pl.* **pericardia** /-dɪə/) the membranous sac enclosing the heart. □ **pericardiac** /-dɪˌæk/ *adj.* **pericardial** *adj.* **pericarditis** /-ˈdaɪtɪs/ *n.* [mod.L f. Gk *perikardion* (as PERI- + *kardia* heart)]

pericarp /ˈperɪˌkɑːp/ *n.* the part of a fruit formed from the wall of the ripened ovary. [F *péricarpe* f. Gk *perikarpion* pod, shell (as PERI-, *karpos* fruit)]

perigee /ˈperɪˌdʒiː/ *n.* the point in a celestial body's orbit where it is nearest the earth (opp. APOGEE). □ **perigean** /ˌperɪˈdʒiːən/ *adj.* [F *périgée* f. mod.L f. Gk *perigeion* round the earth (as PERI-, *gē* earth)]

perihelion /ˌperɪˈhiːlɪən/ *n.* (*pl.* **perihelia** /-lɪə/) the point of a planet's or comet's orbit nearest to the sun's centre. [mod.L *perihelium* (as PERI-, Gk *hēlios* sun)]

peril /ˈperɪl/ n. & v. —n. serious and immediate danger. —v.tr. (**perilled, perilling**; US **periled, periling**) threaten; endanger. □ **at one's peril** at one's own risk. **in peril of** with great risk to (*in peril of your life*). [ME f. OF f. L *peric(u)lum*]

perilous /ˈperɪləs/ adj. **1** full of risk; dangerous; hazardous. **2** exposed to imminent risk of destruction etc. □ **perilously** adv. **perilousness** n. [ME f. OF *perillous* f. L *periculosus* f. *periculum*: see PERIL]

perilune /ˈperɪluːn, -ˌljuːn/ n. the point in a body's lunar orbit where it is closest to the moon's centre. [PERI- + L *luna* moon, after *perigee*]

perimeter /pəˈrɪmɪtə(r)/ n. **1 a** the circumference or outline of a closed figure. **b** the length of this. **2 a** the outer boundary of an enclosed area. **b** a defended boundary. □ **perimetric** /ˌperɪˈmetrɪk/ adj. [F *périmètre* or f. L *perimetrus* f. Gk *perimetros* (as PERI-, *metros* f. *metron* measure)]

perinatal /ˌperɪˈneɪt(ə)l/ adj. of or relating to the time immediately before and after birth.

perineum /ˌperɪˈniːəm/ n. the region of the body between the anus and the scrotum or vulva. □ **perineal** adj. [LL f. Gk *perinaion*]

period /ˈpɪərɪəd/ n. & adj. —n. **1** a length or portion of time (*showers and bright periods*). **2** a distinct portion of history, a person's life, etc. (*the Georgian period*; *Picasso's Blue Period*). **3** Geol. a time forming part of a geological era (*the Quaternary period*). **4** an interval between recurrences of an astronomical or other phenomenon. **5** the time allowed for a lesson in school. **6** an occurrence of menstruation. **7 a** a complete sentence, esp. one consisting of several clauses. **b** (in pl.) rhetorical language. **8** esp. US **a** = full stop. **b** used at the end of a sentence etc. to indicate finality, absoluteness, etc. (*we want the best, period*). —adj. belonging to or characteristic of some past period (*period furniture*). □ **of the period** of the era under discussion (*the custom of the period*). **period piece** an object or work whose main interest lies in its historical etc. associations. [ME f. OF *periode* f. L *periodus* f. Gk *periodos* (as PERI-, *odos* = *hodos* way)]

periodic /ˌpɪərɪˈɒdɪk/ adj. appearing or occurring at regular intervals. **periodic table** an arrangement of elements in order of increasing atomic number and in which elements of similar chemical properties appear at regular intervals. □ **periodicity** /-rɪəˈdɪsɪtɪ/ n. [F *périodique* or L *periodicus* f. Gk *periodikos* (as PERIOD)]

periodical /ˌpɪərɪˈɒdɪk(ə)l/ n. & adj. —n. a newspaper, magazine, etc. issued at regular intervals, usu. monthly or weekly. —adj. **1** published at regular intervals. **2** periodic, occasional. □ **periodically** adv.

peripatetic /ˌperɪpəˈtetɪk/ adj. & n. —adj. **1** (of a teacher) working in more than one school or college etc. **2** going from place to place; itinerant. **3** (**Peripatetic**) Aristotelian. —n. a peripatetic person, esp. a teacher. □ **peripatetically** adv. **peripateticism** /-ˌsɪz(ə)m/ n. [ME f. OF *peripatetique* or L *peripateticus* f. Gk *peripatētikos* f. *peripateō* (as PERI-, *pateō* walk)]

peripheral /pəˈrɪfər(ə)l/ adj. & n. —adj. **1** of minor importance; marginal. **2** of the periphery; on the fringe. **3** (of equipment) used with a

computer etc. but not an integral part of it. —n. a peripheral device or piece of equipment. □ **peripheral nervous system** Anat. the nervous system outside the brain and spinal cord. □ **peripherally** adv.

periphery /pəˈrɪfərɪ/ n. (pl. **-ies**) **1** the boundary of an area or surface. **2** an outer or surrounding region (*built on the periphery of the old town*). [LL *peripheria* f. Gk *peripereia* circumference (as PERI-, *phereia* f. *phero* bear)]

periphrasis /pəˈrɪfrəsɪs/ n. (pl. **periphrases** /-ˌsiːz/) **1** a roundabout way of speaking; circumlocution. **2** a roundabout phrase. □ **periphrastic** adj. **periphrastically** adv. [L f. Gk f. *periphrazō* (as PERI-, *phrazō* declare)]

periscope /ˈperɪskəʊp/ n. an apparatus with a tube and mirrors or prisms, by which an observer in a trench, submerged submarine, or at the rear of a crowd etc., can see things otherwise out of sight.

periscopic /ˌperɪˈskɒpɪk/ adj. of a periscope. □ **periscopic lens** a lens allowing distinct vision over a wide angle. □ **periscopically** adv.

perish /ˈperɪʃ/ v. **1** intr. be destroyed; suffer death or ruin. **2 a** intr. (esp. of rubber, a rubber object, etc.) lose its normal qualities; deteriorate, rot. **b** tr. cause to rot or deteriorate. **3** tr. (in passive) suffer from cold or exposure (*we were perished standing outside*). □ **perish the thought** an exclamation of horror against an unwelcome idea. □ **perishless** adj. [ME f. OF *perir* f. L *perire* pass away (as PER-, *ire* go)]

perishable /ˈperɪʃəb(ə)l/ adj. & n. —adj. liable to perish; subject to decay. —n. a thing, esp. a foodstuff, subject to speedy decay. □ **perishability** /-ˈbɪlɪtɪ/ n. **perishableness** n.

perisher /ˈperɪʃə(r)/ n. Brit. sl. an annoying person.

perishing /ˈperɪʃɪŋ/ adj. & adv. colloq. —adj. **1** confounded. **2** freezing cold, extremely chilly. —adv. confoundedly. □ **perishingly** adv.

peristalsis /ˌperɪˈstælsɪs/ n. an involuntary muscular wavelike movement by which the contents of the alimentary canal etc. are propelled along. □ **peristaltic** adj. **peristaltically** adv. [mod.L f. Gk *peristellō* wrap around (as PERI-, *stellō* place)]

peritoneum /ˌperɪtəˈniːəm/ n. (pl. **peritoneums** or **peritonea** /-ˈniːə/) the double serous membrane lining the cavity of the abdomen. □ **peritoneal** adj. [LL f. Gk *peritonaion* (as PERI-, *tonaion* f. *-tonos* stretched)]

peritonitis /ˌperɪtəˈnaɪtɪs/ n. an inflammatory disease of the peritoneum.

periwig /ˈperɪwɪg/ n. esp. hist. a wig. □ **periwigged** adj. [alt. of PERUKE, with *-wi-* for F *-u-* sound]

periwinkle[1] /ˈperɪˌwɪŋk(ə)l/ n. any plant of the genus *Vinca*, esp. an evergreen trailing plant with blue or white flowers. [ME f. AF *pervenke*, OF *pervenche* f. LL *pervinca*, assim. to PERIWINKLE[2]]

periwinkle[2] /ˈperɪˌwɪŋk(ə)l/ n. = WINKLE. [16th c.: orig. unkn.]

perjure /ˈpɜːdʒə/ v.refl. Law **1** wilfully tell an untruth when on oath. **2** (as **perjured** adj.) guilty of or involving perjury. □ **perjurer** n. [ME f. OF *parjurer* f. L *perjurare* (as PER-, *jurare* swear)]

perjury /ˈpɜːdʒərɪ/ n. (pl. **-ies**) Law **1** a breach of an oath, esp. the act of wilfully telling an untruth when on oath. **2** the practice of this. □

perjurious /-'dʒʊərɪəs/ adj. [ME f. AF perjurie f. OF parjurie f. L perjurium (as PERJURE)]

perk¹ v. & adj. —v.tr. raise (one's head etc.) briskly. —adj. perky; pert. □ **perk up 1** recover confidence, courage, life, or zest. **2** restore confidence or courage or liveliness in (esp. another person). **3** smarten up. [ME, perh. f. var. of PERCH¹]

perk² n. Brit. colloq. a perquisite. [abbr.]

perk³ v. colloq. **1** intr. (of coffee) percolate, make a bubbling sound in the percolator. **2** tr. percolate (coffee). [abbr. of PERCOLATE]

perky /'pɜːkɪ/ adj. (**perkier, perkiest**) **1** self-assertive; saucy; pert. **2** lively; cheerful. □ **perkily** adv. **perkiness** n.

perm¹ n. & v. —n. a permanent wave. —v.tr. give a permanent wave to (a person or a person's hair). [abbr.]

perm² n. & v. colloq. —n. a permutation. —v.tr. make a permutation of. [abbr.]

permafrost /'pɜːmə‚frɒst/ n. subsoil which remains below freezing-point throughout the year, as in polar regions. [PERMANENT + FROST]

permanent /'pɜːmənənt/ adj. lasting, or intended to last or function, indefinitely. □ **permanent magnet** a magnet retaining its magnetic properties without continued excitation. **permanent wave** an artificial wave in the hair, intended to last for some time. **permanent way** Brit. the finished roadbed of a railway. □ **permanence** n. **permanency** n. **permanentize** v.tr. (also **-ise**). **permanently** adv. [ME f. OF permanent or L permanēre (as PER-, manēre remain)]

permanganate /pə‚ˈmæŋgə‚neɪt, -nət/ n. Chem. any salt of permanganic acid, esp. potassium permanganate.

permanganic acid /‚pɜːmæŋˈgænɪk/ n. Chem. an acid containing manganese. [PER- + MANGANIC: see MANGANESE]

permeability /‚pɜːmɪəˈbɪlɪtɪ/ n. **1** the state or quality of being permeable. **2** a quantity measuring the influence of a substance on the magnetic flux in the region it occupies.

permeable /'pɜːmɪəb(ə)l/ adj. capable of being permeated. [L permeabilis (as PERMEATE)]

permeate /'pɜːmɪ‚eɪt/ v. **1** tr. penetrate throughout; pervade; saturate. **2** intr. (usu. foll. by through, among, etc.) diffuse itself. □ **permeance** n. **permeant** adj. **permeation** /-ˈeɪʃ(ə)n/ n. **permeator** n. [L permeare permeat- (as PER-, meare pass, go)]

Permian /'pɜːmɪən/ adj. & n. Geol. —adj. of or relating to the last period of the Palaeozoic era. —n. this period or system. [Perm in Russia]

permissible /pəˈmɪsɪb(ə)l/ adj. allowable. □ **permissibility** /-ˈbɪlɪtɪ/ n. **permissibly** adv. [ME f. F or f. med.L permissibilis (as PERMIT)]

permission /pəˈmɪʃ(ə)n/ n. (often foll. by to + infin.) consent; authorization. [ME f. OF or f. L permissio (as PERMIT)]

permissive /pəˈmɪsɪv/ adj. **1** tolerant; liberal, esp. in sexual matters (the permissive society). **2** giving permission. □ **permissive legislation** legislation giving powers but not enjoining their use. □ **permissively** adv. **permissiveness** n. [ME f. OF (-if -ive) or med.L permissivus (as PERMIT)]

permit v. & n. —v. /pəˈmɪt/ (**permitted, permitting**) **1** tr. give permission or consent to;

authorize (permit me to say). **2 a** tr. allow; give an opportunity to (permit the traffic to flow again). **b** intr. give an opportunity (circumstances permitting). **3** intr. (foll. by of) admit; allow for. —n. /'pɜːmɪt/ **1 a** a document giving permission to act in a specified way (was granted a work permit). **b** a document etc. which allows entry into a specified zone. **2** formal permission. □ **permittee** /‚pɜːmɪˈtiː/ n. **permitter** n. [L permittere (as PER-, mittere miss- let go)]

permittivity /‚pɜːmɪˈtɪvɪtɪ/ n. Electr. a quantity measuring the ability of a substance to store electrical energy in an electric field.

permutate /'pɜːmjʊ‚teɪt/ v.tr. change the order or arrangement of. [as PERMUTE, or back-form. f. PERMUTATION]

permutation /‚pɜːmjʊˈteɪʃ(ə)n/ n. **1 a** an ordered arrangement or grouping of a set of numbers, items, etc. **b** any one of the range of possible groupings. **2** any combination or selection of a specified number of things from a larger group, esp. Brit. matches in a football pool. □ **permutational** adj. [ME f. OF or f. L permutatio (as PERMUTE)]

permute /pəˈmjuːt/ v.tr. alter the sequence or arrangement of. [ME f. L permutare (as PER-, mutare change)]

pernicious /pəˈnɪʃəs/ adj. destructive; ruinous; fatal. □ **perniciously** adv. **perniciousness** n. [L perniciosus f. pernicies ruin f. nex necis death]

pernickety /pəˈnɪkɪtɪ/ adj. colloq. **1** fastidious. **2** precise or over-precise. **3** ticklish, requiring tact or careful handling. [19th-c. Sc.: orig. unkn.]

perorate /'perə‚reɪt/ v.intr. **1** sum up and conclude a speech. **2** speak at length. [L perorare perorat- (as PER-, orare speak)]

peroration /‚perəˈreɪʃ(ə)n/ n. the concluding part of a speech, forcefully summing up what has been said.

peroxide /pəˈrɒksaɪd/ n. & v. —n. Chem. **1 a** = hydrogen peroxide. **b** (often attrib.) a solution of hydrogen peroxide used to bleach the hair or as an antiseptic. **2** a compound of oxygen with another element containing the greatest possible proportion of oxygen. **3** any salt or ester of hydrogen peroxide. —v.tr. bleach (the hair) with peroxide. [PER- + OXIDE]

perpendicular /‚pɜːpənˈdɪkjʊlə(r)/ adj. & n. —adj. **1 a** at right angles to the plane of the horizon. **b** (usu. foll. by to) Geom. at right angles (to a given line, plane, or surface). **2** upright, vertical. **3** (of a slope etc.) very steep. **4** (**Perpendicular**) Archit. of the third stage of English Gothic (15th–16th c.) with vertical tracery in large windows. **5** joc. in a standing position. —n. **1** a perpendicular line. **2** a plumb-rule or a similar instrument. **3** (prec. by the) a perpendicular line or direction (is out of the perpendicular). □ **perpendicularity** /-ˈlærɪtɪ/ n. **perpendicularly** adv. [ME f. L perpendicularis f. perpendiculum plumb-line f. PER- + pendēre hang]

perpetrate /'pɜːpɪ‚treɪt/ v.tr. commit or perform (a crime, blunder, or anything outrageous). □ **perpetration** /-ˈtreɪʃ(ə)n/ n. **perpetrator** n. [L perpetrare perpetrat- (as PER-, patrare effect)]

perpetual /pəˈpetjʊəl/ adj. **1** eternal; lasting for ever or indefinitely. **2** continuous, uninterrupted. **3** colloq. frequent, much repeated (perpetual interruptions). **4** permanent during life (perpetual secretary). □ **perpetual motion** the motion of a hypothetical machine which once set in motion would run for ever unless subject to an external force or to wear. □ **perpetualism** *n.* **perpetually** *adv.* [ME f. OF *perpetuel* f. L *perpetualis* f. *perpetuus* f. *perpes -etis* continuous]

perpetuate /pə¹petjʊˌeɪt/ *v.tr.* **1** make perpetual. **2** preserve from oblivion. □ **perpetuance** *n.* **perpetuation** /-¹eɪʃ(ə)n/ *n.* **perpetuator** *n.* [L *perpetuare* (as PERPETUAL)]

perpetuity /ˌpɜːpɪ¹tjuːɪtɪ/ *n.* (*pl.* **-ies**) **1** the state or quality of being perpetual. **2** a perpetual annuity. **3** a perpetual possession or position. □ **in** (or **to** or **for**) **perpetuity** for ever. [ME f. OF *perpetuité* f. L *perpetuitas -tatis* (as PERPETUAL)]

perplex /pə¹pleks/ *v.tr.* **1** puzzle, bewilder, or disconcert (a person, a person's mind, etc.). **2** complicate or confuse (a matter). **3** (as **perplexed** *adj.*) *archaic* entangled, intertwined. □ **perplexedly** /-ɪdlɪ/ *adv.* **perplexingly** *adv.* [back-form. f. *perplexed* f. obs. *perplex* (adj.) f. OF *perplexe* or L *perplexus* (as PER-, *plexus* past part. of *plectere* plait)]

perplexity /pə¹pleksɪtɪ/ *n.* (*pl.* **-ies**) **1** bewilderment; the state of being perplexed. **2** a thing which perplexes. [ME f. OF *perplexité* or LL *perplexitas* (as PERPLEX)]

per pro. /pɜː ¹prəʊ/ *abbr.* through the agency of (used in signatures). [L *per procurationem*]

■ **Usage** The correct sequence is A *per pro.* B, where B is signing on behalf of A.

perquisite /¹pɜːkwɪzɪt/ *n.* **1** an extra profit or allowance additional to a main income etc. **2** a customary extra right or privilege. **3** an incidental benefit attached to employment etc. **4** a thing which has served its primary use and to which a subordinate or servant has a customary right. [ME f. med.L *perquisitum* f. L *perquirere* search diligently for (as PER-, *quaerere* seek)]

■ **Usage** This word is sometimes confused with prerequisite, which means 'thing required as a precondition'.

Perrier /¹perɪˌeɪ/ *n. propr.* an effervescent natural mineral water. [the name of a spring at Vergèze, France, its source]

perry /¹perɪ/ *n.* (*pl.* **-ies**) *Brit.* a drink like cider, made from the fermented juice of pears. [ME *pereye* etc. f. OF *peré*, ult. f. L *pirum* pear]

per se /pɜː ¹seɪ/ *adv.* by or in itself; intrinsically. [L]

persecute /¹pɜːsɪˌkjuːt/ *v.tr.* **1** subject (a person etc.) to hostility or ill-treatment, esp. on the grounds of political or religious belief. **2** harass; worry. **3** (often foll. by *with*) bombard (a person) with questions etc. □ **persecutor** *n.* **persecutory** *adj.* [ME f. OF *persecuter* back-form. f. *persecuteur* persecutor f. LL *persecutor* f. L *persequi* (as PER-, *sequi secut-* follow, pursue)]

persecution /ˌpɜːsɪ¹kjuːʃ(ə)n/ *n.* the act or an instance of persecuting; the state of being persecuted. □ **persecution complex** (or **mania**) an irrational obsessive fear that others are scheming against one.

perseverance /ˌpɜːsɪ¹vɪərəns/ *n.* **1** the steadfast pursuit of an objective. **2** (often foll. by *in*) constant persistence (in a belief etc.). [ME f. OF f. L *perseverantia* (as PERSEVERE)]

persevere /ˌpɜːsɪ¹vɪə(r)/ *v.intr.* (often foll. by *in, at, with*) continue steadfastly or determinedly; persist. [ME f. OF *perseverer* f. L *perseverare* persist f. *perseverus* very strict (as PER-, *severus* severe)]

Persian /¹pɜːʃ(ə)n/ *n. & adj.* —*n.* **1 a** a native or inhabitant of ancient or modern Persia (now Iran). **b** a person of Persian descent. **2** the language of ancient Persia or modern Iran. **3** (in full **Persian cat**) **a** a cat of a breed with long silky hair and a thick tail. **b** this breed. —*adj.* of or relating to Persia or its people or language. □ **Persian carpet** (or **rug**) a carpet or rug of a traditional pattern made in Persia. **Persian lamb** the silky tightly curled fur of a young karakul, used in clothing. [ME f. OF *persien* f. med.L]

■ **Usage** The preferred terms for the language (see sense 2 of the noun) are *Iranian* and *Farsi*.

persiflage /¹pɜːsɪˌflɑːʒ/ *n.* light raillery, banter. [F *persifler* banter, formed as PER- + *siffler* whistle]

persimmon /pɜː¹sɪmən/ *n.* **1** any usu. tropical evergreen tree of the genus *Diospyros* bearing edible tomato-like fruits. **2** the fruit of this. [corrupt. of an Algonquian word]

persist /pə¹sɪst/ *v.intr.* **1** (often foll. by *in*) continue firmly or obstinately (in an opinion or a course of action) esp. despite obstacles, remonstrance, etc. **2** (of an institution, custom, phenomenon, etc.) continue in existence; survive. [L *persistere* (as PER-, *sistere* stand)]

persistent /pə¹sɪst(ə)nt/ *adj.* **1** continuing obstinately; persisting. **2** enduring. **3** constantly repeated (*persistent nagging*). □ **persistence** *n.* **persistency** *n.* **persistently** *adv.*

person /¹pɜːs(ə)n/ *n.* **1** an individual human being (*a cheerful and forthright person*). **2** the living body of a human being (*hidden about your person*). **3** *Gram.* any of three classes of personal pronouns, verb-forms, etc.: the person speaking (**first person**); the person spoken to (**second person**); the person spoken of (**third person**). **4** (in *comb.*) used to replace -*man* in offices open to either sex (*salesperson*). **5** (in Christianity) God as Father, Son, or Holy Ghost (*three persons in one God*). **in person** physically present. **person-to-person 1** between individuals. **2** (of a phone call) booked through the operator to a specified person. [ME f. OF *persone* f. L *persona* actor's mask, character in a play, human being]

persona /pɜː¹səʊnə/ *n.* (*pl.* **personae** /-niː/) **1** an aspect of the personality as shown to or perceived by others. **2** *Literary criticism* an author's assumed character in his or her writing. □ ***persona grata*** /¹grɑːtə/ a person, esp. a diplomat, acceptable to certain others. ***persona non grata*** /nɒn, nəʊn ¹grɑːtə/ a person not acceptable. [L (as PERSON)]

personable /¹pɜːsənəb(ə)l/ *adj.* pleasing in appearance and behaviour. □ **personableness** *n.* **personably** *adv.*

personage /¹pɜːsənɪdʒ/ *n.* **1** a person, esp. of rank or importance. **2** a character in a play etc. [ME f. PERSON + -AGE, infl. by med.L *personagium* effigy & F *personnage*]

personal /¹pɜːsən(ə)l/ *adj.* **1** one's own; individual; private. **2** done or made in person (*made a personal appearance; my personal attention*). **3** directed to or concerning an individual (*a personal letter*). **4** referring (esp. in a hostile way) to an individual's private life or concerns (*making personal remarks; no need to be personal*). **5** of the body and clothing (*personal hygiene; personal appearance*). **6** existing as a person, not as an abstraction or thing (*a personal God*). **7** *Gram.* of or denoting one of the three persons (*personal pronoun*). □ **personal column** the part of a newspaper devoted to private advertisements or messages. **personal computer** a computer designed for use by a single individual, esp. in an office or business environment. **personal identification number** a number allocated to an individual, serving as a password esp. for a cash dispenser, computer, etc. **personal organizer 1** a loose-leaf notebook with sections for various kinds of information, including a diary etc. **2** a hand-held microcomputer serving the same purpose. **personal pronoun** a pronoun replacing the subject, object, etc., of a clause etc., e.g. *I, we, you, them, us*. **personal property** (or **estate**) *Law* all one's property except land and those interests in land that pass to one's heirs (cf. REAL¹ *adj.* 3). **personal stereo** a small portable audio cassette player, often with radio, or compact disc player, used with lightweight headphones. [ME f. OF f. L *personalis* (as PERSON)]

personality /ˌpɜːsəˈnælɪtɪ/ *n.* (*pl.* **-ies**) **1** the distinctive character or qualities of a person, often as distinct from others (*an attractive personality*). **2** a famous person; a celebrity (*a TV personality*). **3** a person who stands out from others by virtue of his or her character (*is a real personality*). **4** personal existence or identity; the condition of being a person. □ **have personality** have a lively character or noteworthy qualities. **personality cult** the extreme adulation of an individual. [ME f. OF *personalité* f. LL *personalitas -tatis* (as PERSONAL)]

personalize /ˈpɜːsənəˌlaɪz/ *v.tr.* (also **-ise**) **1** make personal, esp. by marking with one's name etc. **2** personify. □ **personalization** /-ˈzeɪʃ(ə)n/ *n.*

personally /ˈpɜːsənəlɪ/ *adv.* **1** in person (*see to it personally*). **2** for one's own part (*speaking personally*). **3** as a person (*a God existing personally*). **4** in a personal manner (*took the criticism personally*).

personate /ˈpɜːsəˌneɪt/ *v.tr.* **1** play the part of a character in a drama etc.; another type of person. **2** pretend to be (another person), esp. for fraudulent purposes; impersonate. □ **personation** /-ˈneɪʃ(ə)n/ *n.* **personator** *n.* [LL *personare personat-* (as PERSON)]

personhood /ˈpɜːsənˌhʊd/ *n.* the quality or condition of being an individual person.

personification /pəˌsɒnɪfɪˈkeɪʃ(ə)n/ *n.* **1** the act of personifying. **2** (foll. by *of*) a person or thing viewed as a striking example of a quality etc.) (*the personification of ugliness*).

personify /pəˈsɒnɪˌfaɪ/ *v.tr.* (**-ies, -ied**) **1** attribute a personal nature to (an abstraction or thing). **2** symbolize (a quality etc.) by a figure in human form. **3** (usu. as **personified** *adj.*) embody (a quality) in one's own person; exemplify typically (*has always been kindness personified*). □ **personifier** *n.* [F *personnifier* (as PERSON)]

personnel /ˌpɜːsəˈnel/ *n.* a body of employees, persons involved in a public undertaking, armed forces, etc. □ **personnel carrier** an armoured vehicle for transporting troops etc. **personnel department** etc. the part of an organization concerned with the appointment, training, and welfare of employees. [F, orig. adj. = personal]

perspective /pəˈspektɪv/ *n. & adj.* —*n.* **1 a** the art of drawing solid objects on a two-dimensional surface so as to give the right impression of

relative positions, size, etc. **b** a picture drawn in this way. **2** the apparent relation between visible objects as to position, distance, etc. **3** a mental view of the relative importance of things (*keep the right perspective*). **4** a geographical or imaginary prospect. —*adj.* of or in perspective. □ **in perspective 1** drawn or viewed according to the rules of perspective. **2** correctly regarded in terms of relative importance. □ **perspectival** /-ˈtaɪv(ə)l/ *adj.* **perspectively** *adv.* [ME f. med.L *perspectiva* (*ars art*) f. *perspicere* perspect- (as PER-, specere spect- look)]

Perspex /ˈpɜːspeks/ *n. propr.* a tough light transparent acrylic thermoplastic used instead of glass. [L *perspicere* look through (as PER-, specere look)]

perspicacious /ˌpɜːspɪˈkeɪʃəs/ *adj.* having mental penetration or discernment. □ **perspicaciously** *adv.* **perspicaciousness** *n.* **perspicacity** /-ˈkæsɪtɪ/ *n.* [L *perspicax -acis* (as PERSPEX)]

■ **Usage** This word is sometimes confused with *perspicuous.*

perspicuous /pəˈspɪkjʊəs/ *adj.* **1** easily understood; clearly expressed. **2** (of a person) expressing things clearly. □ **perspicuity** /-ˈkjuːɪtɪ/ *n.* **perspicuously** *adv.* **perspicuousness** *n.* [ME, = transparent f. L *perspicuus* (as PERSPECTIVE)]

■ **Usage** This word is sometimes confused with *perspicacious.*

perspiration /ˌpɜːspɪˈreɪʃ(ə)n/ *n.* **1** = SWEAT. **2** sweating. □ **perspiratory** /-ˈspɪrətərɪ/ *adj.* [F (as PERSPIRE)]

perspire /pəˈspaɪə(r)/ *v.* **1** *intr.* sweat or exude perspiration, esp. as the result of heat, exercise, anxiety, etc. **2** *tr.* sweat or exude (fluid etc.). [F *perspirer* f. L *perspirare* (as PER-, spirare breathe)]

persuade /pəˈsweɪd/ *v.tr. & refl.* **1** (often foll. by *of*, or *that* + clause) cause (another person or oneself) to believe; convince (*persuaded them that it would be helpful; tried to persuade me of its value*). **2 a** (often foll. by *to* + infin.) induce (another person or oneself) (*persuaded us to join them; managed to persuade them at last*). **b** (foll. by *away from, down to,* etc.) lure, attract, entice, etc. (*persuaded them away from the pub*). □ **persuadable** *adj.* **persuadability** /-dəˈbɪlɪtɪ/ *n.* **persuader** *n.* **persuasible** *adj.* [L *persuadēre* (as PER-, suadēre suas- advise)]

persuasion /pəˈsweɪʒ(ə)n/ *n.* **1** persuading (*yielded to persuasion*). **2** persuasiveness (*use all your persuasion*). **3** a belief or conviction (*my private persuasion*). **4** a religious belief, or the group or sect holding it (*of a different persuasion*). **5** *colloq.* any group or party (*the male persuasion*). [ME f. L *persuasio* (as PERSUADE)]

persuasive /pəˈsweɪsɪv/ *adj.* able to persuade. □ **persuasively** *adv.* **persuasiveness** *n.* [F *persuasif -ive* or med.L *persuasivus* (as PERSUADE)]

pert /pɜːt/ *adj.* **1** saucy or impudent, esp. in speech or conduct. **2** (of clothes etc.) neat and suggestive of jauntiness. □ **pertly** *adv.* **pertness** *n.* [ME f. OF *apert* f. L *apertus* past part. of *aperire* open & f. OF *aspert* f. L *expertus* EXPERT]

pertain /pəˈteɪn/ *v.intr.* **1** (foll. by *to*) **a** relate or have reference to. **b** belong to as a part or appendage or accessory. **2** (usu. foll. by *to*) be appropriate to. [ME f. OF *partenir* f. L *pertinēre* (as PER-, tenēre hold)]

pertinacious /ˌpɜːtɪˈneɪʃəs/ adj. stubborn; persistent; obstinate (in a course of action etc.). □ **pertinaciously** adv. **pertinaciousness** n. **pertinacity** /-ˈnæsɪtɪ/ n. [L pertinax (as PER-, tenax tenacious)]

pertinent /ˈpɜːtɪnənt/ adj. 1 (often foll. by to) relevant to the matter in hand; apposite. 2 to the point. □ **pertinence** n. **pertinency** n. **pertinently** adv. [ME f. OF pertinent or L pertinēre (as PERTAIN)]

perturb /pəˈtɜːb/ v.tr. 1 throw into confusion or disorder. 2 disturb mentally; agitate. □ **perturbable** adj. **perturbative** /pəˈtɜːbətɪv, ˈpɜːtəˌbeɪtɪv/ adj. **perturbingly** adv. [ME f. OF pertourber f. L (as PER-, turbare disturb)]

perturbation /ˌpɜːtəˈbeɪʃ(ə)n/ n. 1 the act or an instance of perturbing; the state of being perturbed. 2 a cause of disturbance or agitation.

peruke /pəˈruːk/ n. hist. a wig. [F perruque f. It. perrucca parrucca, of unkn. orig.]

peruse /pəˈruːz/ v.tr. 1 (also absol.) read or study, esp. thoroughly or carefully. 2 examine (a person's face etc.) carefully. □ **perusal** n. **peruser** n. [ME, orig. = use up, prob. f. AL f. Rmc (as PER-, USE)]

perv n. & v. (also **perve**) sl. —n. 1 a sexual pervert. 2 Austral. an erotic gaze. —v.intr. 1 act like a sexual pervert. 2 (foll. by at, on) Austral. gaze with erotic interest. [abbr.]

pervade /pəˈveɪd/ v.tr. 1 spread throughout, permeate. 2 (of influences etc.) become widespread among or in. 3 be rife among or through. □ **pervasion** /-ʒ(ə)n/ n. [L pervadere (as PER-, vadere vas- go)]

pervasive /pəˈveɪsɪv/ adj. 1 pervading. 2 able to pervade. □ **pervasively** adv. **pervasiveness** n.

perverse /pəˈvɜːs/ adj. 1 (of a person or action) deliberately or stubbornly departing from what is reasonable or required. 2 persistent in error. 3 wayward; intractable; peevish. 4 perverted; wicked. 5 (of a verdict etc.) against the weight of evidence or the judge's direction. □ **perversely** adv. **perverseness** n. **perversity** n. (pl. **-ies**). [ME f. OF pervers perverse f. L perversus (as PERVERT)]

perversion /pəˈvɜːʃ(ə)n/ n. 1 an act of perverting; the state of being perverted. 2 a perverted form of an act or thing. 3 **a** preference for an abnormal form of sexual activity. **b** such an activity. [ME f. L perversio (as PERVERT)]

pervert v. & n. —v.tr. /pəˈvɜːt/ 1 turn (a person or thing) aside from its proper use or nature. 2 misapply or misconstrue (words etc.). 3 lead astray (a person, a person's mind, etc.) from right opinion or conduct, or esp. religious belief. 4 (as **perverted** adj.) showing perversion. —n. /ˈpɜːvɜːt/ 1 a perverted person. 2 a person showing sexual perversion. □ **perversive** /pəˈvɜːsɪv/ adj. **pervertedly** /pəˈvɜːtɪdlɪ/ adv. **perverter** /-ˈvɜːtə(r)/ n. [ME f. OF pervertir or f. L pervertere (as PER-, vertere vers- turn): cf. CONVERT]

pervious /ˈpɜːvɪəs/ adj. 1 permeable. 2 (usu. foll. by to) **a** affording passage. **b** accessible (to reason etc.). □ **perviousness** n. [L pervius (as PER-, vius f. via way)]

peseta /pəˈseɪtə/ n. the chief monetary unit of Spain, orig. a silver coin. [Sp., dimin. of pesa weight f. L pensa pl. of pensum: see POISE]

pesky /ˈpeskɪ/ adj. (**peskier**, **peskiest**) esp. US colloq. troublesome; confounded; annoying. □ **peskily** adv. **peskiness** n. [18th c.: perh. f. PEST]

peso /ˈpeɪsəʊ/ n. (pl. **-os**) 1 the chief monetary unit of several Latin American countries and of the Philippines. 2 a note or coin worth one peso. [Sp., = weight, f. L pensum: see POISE]

pessary /ˈpesərɪ/ n. (pl. **-ies**) Med. 1 a device worn in the vagina to support the uterus or as a contraceptive. 2 a vaginal suppository. [ME f. LL pessarium, pessulum f. pessum, pessus f. Gk pessos oval stone]

pessimism /ˈpesɪˌmɪz(ə)m/ n. 1 a tendency to take the worst view or expect the worst outcome. 2 Philos. a belief that this world is as bad as it could be or that all things tend to evil. □ **pessimist** n. **pessimistic** /-ˈmɪstɪk/ adj. **pessimistically** /-ˈmɪstɪkəlɪ/ adv. [L pessimus worst, after OPTIMISM]

pest n. 1 a troublesome or annoying person or thing; a nuisance. 2 a destructive animal, esp. an insect which attacks crops, livestock, etc. [F peste or L pestis plague]

pester /ˈpestə(r)/ v.tr. trouble or annoy, esp. with frequent or persistent requests. □ **pesterer** n. [prob. f. impester f. F empestrer encumber: infl. by PEST]

pesticide /ˈpestɪˌsaɪd/ n. a substance used for destroying insects or other organisms harmful to cultivated plants or to animals. □ **pesticidal** /-ˈsaɪd(ə)l/ adj.

pestiferous /peˈstɪfərəs/ adj. 1 noxious; pestilent. 2 harmful; pernicious; bearing moral contagion. [L pestifer, -ferus (as PEST)]

pestilence /ˈpestɪləns/ n. a fatal epidemic disease, esp. bubonic plague. [ME f. OF f. L pestilentia (as PESTILENT)]

pestilent /ˈpestɪlənt/ adj. 1 destructive to life, deadly. 2 harmful or morally destructive. 3 colloq. troublesome; annoying. □ **pestilently** adv. [L pestilens, pestilentus f. pestis plague]

pestilential /ˌpestɪˈlenʃ(ə)l/ adj. 1 of or relating to pestilence. 2 dangerous; troublesome; pestilent. □ **pestilentially** adv. [ME f. med.L pestilentialis f. L pestilentia (as PESTILENT)]

pestle /ˈpes(ə)l/ n. a club-shaped instrument for pounding substances in a mortar. [ME f. OF pestel f. L pistillum f. pinsare pist- to pound]

pestology /peˈstɒlədʒɪ/ n. the scientific study of pests (esp. harmful insects) and of methods of dealing with them. □ **pestological** /-stəˈlɒdʒɪk(ə)l/ adj. **pestologist** n.

pet[1] n., adj., & v. —n. 1 **a** a domestic or tamed animal kept for pleasure or companionship. 2 a darling, a favourite (often as a term of endearment). —attrib.adj. 1 kept as a pet (pet lamb). 2 of or for pet animals (pet food). 3 often joc. favourite or particular (pet aversion). 4 expressing fondness or familiarity (pet name). —v.tr. (**petted**, **petting**) 1 treat as a pet. 2 (also absol.) fondle, esp. erotically. □ **petter** n. [16th-c. Sc. & N.Engl. dial.: orig. unkn.]

pet[2] n. a feeling of petty resentment or ill-humour (esp. be in a pet). [16th c.: orig. unkn.]

petal /ˈpet(ə)l/ n. each of the parts of the corolla of a flower. □ **petaline** /-ˌlaɪn, -lɪn/ adj. **petalled** adj. (also in comb.). **petal-like** adj. **petaloid** adj. [mod.L petalum, in LL metal plate f. Gk petalon leaf f. petalos outspread]

petard /pɪˈtɑːd/ n. hist. 1 a small bomb used to blast down a door etc. 2 a kind of firework or cracker. □ **hoist with one's own petard** affected oneself by one's schemes against others. [F pétard f. péter break wind]

peter /'piːtə(r)/ *v.intr.* (foll. by *out*) (orig. of a vein of ore etc.) diminish, come to an end. [19th c.: orig. unkn.]

Peter Pan /ˌpiːtə 'pæn/ *n.* a person who retains youthful features, or who is immature. [hero of J. M. Barrie's play of the same name (1904)]

petersham /'piːtəʃəm/ *n.* thick corded silk ribbon used for stiffening in dressmaking etc. [Lord *Petersham*, Engl. army officer d. 1851]

petiole /'petɪˌəʊl/ *n.* the slender stalk joining a leaf to a stem. □ **petiolar** *adj.* **petiolate** /-lət/ *adj.* [F *pétiole* f. L *petiolus* little foot, stalk]

petit bourgeois /ˌpetiː 'bʊəʒwɑː, ˌpətiː/ *n.* (*pl.* **petits bourgeois** *pronunc.* same) a member of the lower middle classes. [F]

petite /pə'tiːt/ *adj.* (of a woman) of small and dainty build. [F, fem. of *petit* small]

petit four /ˌpetiː 'fɔː(r), ˌpətiː/ *n.* (*pl.* **petits fours** /'fɔːz/) a very small fancy cake, biscuit, or sweet. [F, = little oven]

petition /pɪ'tɪʃ(ə)n/ *n.* & *v.* —*n.* **1** a supplication or request. **2** a formal written request, esp. one signed by many people, appealing to authority in some cause. **3** *Law* an application to a court for a writ etc. —*v.* **1** *tr.* make or address a petition to (*petition your MP*). **2** *intr.* (often foll. by *for, to*) appeal earnestly or humbly. □ **petitionable** *adj.* **petitionary** *adj.* **petitioner** *n.* [ME f. OF f. L *petitio -onis*]

petit mal /ˌpetiː 'mæl, ˌpətiː/ *n.* a mild form of epilepsy with only momentary loss of consciousness (cf. GRAND MAL). [F, = little sickness]

petit point /ˌpetiː 'pwæ̃, ˌpətiː 'pɔɪnt/ *n.* embroidery on canvas using small stitches. [F, = little point]

petits pois /ˌpetiː 'pwɑː, ˌpətiː/ *n.pl.* small green peas. [F]

petrel /'petr(ə)l/ *n.* any of various sea birds of the family Procellariidae or Hydrobatidae, usu. flying far from land. [17th c. (also *pitteral*), of uncert. orig.: later assoc. with St Peter (Matt. 14:30)]

Petri dish /'petrɪ, 'piːt-/ *n.* a shallow covered dish used for the culture of bacteria etc. [J. R. *Petri*, Ger. bacteriologist d. 1921]

petrifaction /ˌpetrɪ'fækʃ(ə)n/ *n.* **1** the process of fossilization whereby organic matter is turned into a stony substance. **2** a petrified substance or mass. **3** a state of extreme fear or terror. [PETRIFY after *stupefaction*]

petrify /'petrɪˌfaɪ/ *v.* (**-ies, -ied**) **1** *tr.* paralyse with fear, astonishment, etc. **2** *tr.* change (organic matter) into a stony substance. **3** *intr.* become like stone. [F *pétrifier* f. med.L *petrificare* f. L *petra* rock f. Gk]

petro- /'petrəʊ/ *comb. form* **1** rock. **2** petroleum (*petrochemistry*). [Gk *petros* stone or *petra* rock]

petrochemical /ˌpetrəʊ'kemɪk(ə)l/ *n.* & *adj.* —*n.* a substance industrially obtained from petroleum or natural gas. —*adj.* of or relating to petrochemistry or petrochemicals.

petrochemistry /ˌpetrəʊ'kemɪstrɪ/ *n.* **1** the chemistry of rocks. **2** the chemistry of petroleum.

petrodollar /'petrəʊˌdɒlə(r)/ *n.* a notional unit of currency earned by a petroleum-exporting country.

petrol /'petr(ə)l/ *n.* *Brit.* **1** refined petroleum used as a fuel in motor vehicles, aircraft, etc. **2** (*attrib.*) concerned with the supply of petrol (*petrol pump;*

petrol station). □ **petrol bomb** a simple bomb made of a petrol-filled bottle and a wick. [F *pétrole* f. med.L *petroleum*: see PETROLEUM]

petroleum /pɪ'trəʊlɪəm/ *n.* a hydrocarbon oil found in the upper strata of the earth, refined for use as a fuel for heating and in internal-combustion engines, for lighting, dry-cleaning, etc. □ **petroleum jelly** a translucent solid mixture of hydrocarbons used as a lubricant, ointment, etc. [med.L f. L *petra* rock f. Gk + L *oleum* oil]

petrology /pɪ'trɒlədʒɪ/ *n.* the study of the origin, structure, composition, etc., of rocks. □ **petrologic** /ˌpetrə'lɒdʒɪk/ *adj.* **petrological** /ˌpetrə'lɒdʒɪk(ə)l/ *adj.* **petrologist** *n.*

petticoat /'petɪˌkəʊt/ *n.* **1** a woman's or girl's skirted undergarment hanging from the waist or shoulders. **2** *sl.* **a** a woman or girl. **b** (in *pl.*) the female sex. **3** (*attrib.*) often *derog.* feminine; associated with women (*petticoat pedantry*). □ **petticoated** *adj.* **petticoatless** *adj.* [ME f. *petty coat*]

pettifog /'petɪˌfɒg/ *v.intr.* (**pettifogged, pettifogging**) **1** practise legal deception or trickery. **2** quibble or wrangle about petty points. [back-form. f. PETTIFOGGER]

pettifogger /'petɪˌfɒgə(r)/ *n.* **1** a rascally lawyer; an inferior legal practitioner. **2** a petty practitioner in any activity. □ **pettifoggery** *n.* **pettifogging** *adj.* [PETTY + *fogger* underhand dealer, prob. f. *Fugger* family of merchants in Augsburg in the 15th–16th c.]

pettish /'petɪʃ/ *adj.* peevish, petulant; easily put out. □ **pettishly** *adv.* **pettishness** *n.* [PET[2] + -ISH[1]]

petty /'petɪ/ *adj.* (**pettier, pettiest**) **1** unimportant; trivial. **2** mean, small-minded; contemptible. **3** minor; inferior; on a small scale (*petty princes*). **4** *Law* (of a crime) of lesser importance (*petty sessions*). □ **petty bourgeois** = PETIT BOURGEOIS. **petty cash** money from or for small items of receipt or expenditure. **petty officer** a naval NCO. □ **pettily** *adv.* **pettiness** *n.* [ME *pety* f. OF *petit* small]

petulant /'petjʊlənt/ *adj.* peevishly impatient or irritable. □ **petulance** *n.* **petulantly** *adv.* [F *pétulant* f. L *petulans -antis* f. *petere* seek]

petunia /pɪ'tjuːnɪə/ *n.* **1** any plant of the genus *Petunia* with white, purple, red, etc., funnel-shaped flowers. **2** a dark violet or purple colour. [mod.L f. F *petun* f. Guarani *petỹ* tobacco]

pew *n.* & *v.* —*n.* **1** (in a church) a long bench with a back; an enclosed compartment. **2** *Brit. colloq.* a seat (esp. *take a pew*). —*v.tr.* furnish with pews. □ **pewage** *n.* **pewless** *adj.* [ME *pywe, puwe* f. OF *puye* balcony f. L *podia* pl. of PODIUM]

pewit var. of PEEWIT.

pewter /'pjuːtə(r)/ *n.* **1** a grey alloy of tin with lead, copper, or antimony or various other metals. **2** utensils made of this. □ **pewterer** *n.* [ME f. OF *peutre, peualtre* f. Rmc, of unkn. orig.]

peyote /peɪ'əʊtɪ/ *n.* **1** any Mexican cactus of the genus *Lophophora*, esp. *L. williamsii* having no spines and button-like tops when dried. **2** a hallucinogenic drug containing mescaline prepared from this. [Amer. Sp. f. Nahuatl *peyotl*]

pfennig /'pfenɪg, 'fenɪg/ *n.* a small German coin, worth one-hundredth of a mark. [G, rel. to PENNY]

PG *abbr.* **1** (of films) classified as suitable for children subject to parental guidance. **2** paying guest.

pH /piːˈeɪtʃ/ *n. Chem.* a logarithm of the reciprocal of the hydrogen-ion concentration in moles per litre of a solution, giving a measure of its acidity or alkalinity. [G, f. *Potenz* power + *H* (symbol for hydrogen)]

phagocyte /ˈfæɡəˌsaɪt/ *n.* a type of cell capable of engulfing and absorbing foreign matter, esp. a leucocyte ingesting bacteria in the body. □ **phagocytic** /-ˈsɪtɪk/ *adj.* [Gk *phag-* eat + -CYTE]

-phagous /fəɡəs/ *comb. form* that eats (as specified) (*ichthyophagous*). [L -*phagus* f. Gk -*phagos* f. *phagein* eat]

-phagy /ˈfædʒɪ/ *comb. form* the eating of (specified food) (*ichthyophagy*). [Gk -*phagia* (as -PHAGOUS)]

phalanger /fəˈlændʒə(r)/ *n.* any of various marsupials of the family Phalangeridae, including possums. [F f. Gk *phalaggion* spider's web, f. the webbed toes of its hind feet]

phalanx /ˈfælæŋks/ *n.* (*pl.* **phalanxes** or **phalanges** /ˈfælænˌdʒiːz/) **1** *Gk Antiq.* a line of battle, esp. a body of infantry drawn up in close order. **2** a set of people etc. forming a compact mass, or banded for a common purpose. [L f. Gk *phalagx* -*ggos*]

phalli *pl.* of PHALLUS.

phallic /ˈfælɪk/ *adj.* of, relating to, or resembling a phallus. □ **phallically** *adv.* [F *phallique* & Gk *phallikos* (as PHALLUS)]

phallocentric /ˌfæləʊˈsentrɪk/ *adj.* centred on the phallus or on male attitudes. □ **phallocentricity** /-ˈtrɪsɪtɪ/ *n.* **phallocentrism** /-trɪz(ə)m/ *n.*

phallus /ˈfæləs/ *n.* (*pl.* **phalli** /-laɪ/ or **phalluses**) **1** the (esp. erect) penis. **2** an image of this as a symbol of generative power in nature. □ **phallicism** /-lɪˌsɪz(ə)m/ *n.* **phallism** *n.* [LL f. Gk *phallos*]

phantasize *var.* of FANTASIZE.

phantasm /ˈfænˌtæz(ə)m/ *n.* **1** an illusion, a phantom. **2** (usu. foll. by *of*) an illusory likeness. **3** a supposed vision of an absent (living or dead) person. □ **phantasmal** /-ˈtæzm(ə)l/ *adj.* **phantasmic** /-ˈtæzmɪk/ *adj.* [ME f. OF *fantasme* f. L f. Gk *phantasma* f. *phantazō* make visible f. *phainō* show]

phantasmagoria /ˌfæntæzməˈɡɔːrɪə/ *n.* a shifting series of real or imaginary figures as seen in a dream. □ **phantasmagoric** /-ˈɡɒrɪk/ *adj.* **phantasmagorical** /-ˈɡɒrɪk(ə)l/ *adj.* [prob. f. F *fantasmagorie* (as PHANTASM + fanciful ending)]

phantasy *var.* of FANTASY.

phantom /ˈfæntəm/ *n. & adj.* —*n.* **1** a ghost; an apparition; a spectre. **2** a form without substance or reality; a mental illusion. —*adj.* merely apparent; illusory. □ **phantom pregnancy** *Med.* the symptoms of pregnancy in a person not actually pregnant. [ME f. OF *fantosme* ult. f. Gk *phantasma* (as PHANTASM)]

Pharaoh /ˈfeərəʊ/ *n.* **1** the ruler of ancient Egypt. **2** the title of this ruler. □ **Pharaonic** /ˌfeəreɪˈɒnɪk/ *adj.* [OE f. eccl.L *Pharao* f. Gk *Pharaō* f. Heb. *par'ōh* f. Egypt. *pr-'o* great house]

Pharisee /ˈfærɪˌsiː/ *n.* **1** a member of an ancient Jewish sect, distinguished by strict observance of the traditional and written law, and commonly held to have pretensions to superior sanctity. **2** a self-righteous person; a hypocrite. □ **Pharisaic** /ˌfærɪˈseɪɪk/ *adj.* **Pharisaical** /ˌfærɪˈseɪɪk(ə)l/ *adj.* **Pharisaism** /ˈfærɪseɪˌɪz(ə)m/ *n.* [OE *fariseus* & OF *pharise* f. eccl.L *pharisaeus* f. Gk *Pharisaios* f. Aram. *p'rišayyâ* pl. f. Heb. *pārûš* separated] ˙

pharmaceutical /ˌfɑːməˈsjuːtɪk(ə)l/ *adj.* **1** of or engaged in pharmacy. **2** of the use or sale of medicinal drugs. □ **pharmaceutically** *adv.* **pharmaceutics** *n.* [LL *pharmaceuticus* f. Gk *pharmakeutikos* f. *pharmakeutēs* druggist f. *pharmakon* drug]

pharmacist /ˈfɑːməsɪst/ *n.* a person qualified to prepare and dispense drugs.

pharmacology /ˌfɑːməˈkɒlədʒɪ/ *n.* the science of the action of drugs on the body. □ **pharmacological** /-kəˈlɒdʒɪk(ə)l/ *adj.* **pharmacologically** /-kəˈlɒdʒɪkəlɪ/ *adv.* **pharmacologist** *n.* [mod.L *pharmacologia* f. Gk *pharmakon* drug]

pharmacopoeia /ˌfɑːməkəˈpiːə/ *n.* **1** a book, esp. one officially published, containing a list of drugs with directions for use. **2** a stock of drugs. □ **pharmacopoeial** *adj.* [mod.L f. Gk *pharmakopoiia* f. *pharmakopoios* drug-maker (as PHARMACOLOGY + -*poios* making)]

pharmacy /ˈfɑːməsɪ/ *n.* (*pl.* **-ies**) **1** the preparation and the (esp. medicinal) dispensing of drugs. **2** a pharmacist's shop, a dispensary. [ME f. OF *farmacie* f. med.L *pharmacia* f. Gk *pharmakeia* practice of the druggist f. *pharmakeus* f. *pharmakon* drug]

pharynx /ˈfærɪŋks/ *n.* (*pl.* **pharynges** /-rɪnˌdʒiːz/) a cavity, with enclosing muscles and mucous membrane, behind the nose and mouth, and connecting them to the oesophagus. □ **pharyngal** /-ˈrɪŋɡ(ə)l/ *adj.* **pharyngeal** /-ˈdʒiːəl/ *adj.* **pharyngitis** /-ˈdʒaɪtɪs/ *n.* [mod.L f. Gk *pharugx* -*ggos*]

phase /feɪz/ *n. & v.* —*n.* **1** a distinct period or stage in a process of change or development. **2** each of the aspects of the moon or a planet, according to the amount of its illumination, esp. the new moon, the first quarter, the last quarter, and the full moon. **3** *Physics* a stage in a periodically recurring sequence, esp. of alternating electric currents or light vibrations. —*v.tr.* carry out (a programme etc.) in phases or stages. □ **in phase** having the same phase at the same time. **out of phase** not in phase. **phase in** (or **out**) bring gradually into (or out of) use. □ **phasic** *adj.* [F *phase* & f. earlier *phasis* f. Gk *phasis* appearance f. *phainō* phan- show]

Ph.D. *abbr.* Doctor of Philosophy. [L *philosophiae doctor*]

pheasant /ˈfez(ə)nt/ *n.* any of several long-tailed game-birds of the family Phasianidae, orig. from Asia. □ **pheasantry** *n.* (*pl.* **-ies**). [ME f. AF *fesaunt* f. OF *faisan* f. L *phasianus* f. Gk *phasianos* (bird) of the river *Phasis* in Asia Minor]

phenacetin /fɪˈnæsɪtɪn/ *n.* an acetyl derivative of phenol used to treat fever etc. [PHENO- + ACETYL + -IN]

pheno- /ˈfiːnəʊ/ *comb. form* **1** *Chem.* derived from benzene (*phenol*). **2** showing (*phenotype*). [Gk *phainō* shine (with ref. to substances used for illumination), show]

phenobarbitone /ˌfiːnəʊˈbɑːbɪˌtəʊn/ *n.* (*US* **phenobarbital** /-t(ə)l/) a narcotic and sedative barbiturate drug used esp. to treat epilepsy.

phenol /ˈfiːnɒl/ n. *Chem.* **1** derivative of benzene used in dilute form as an antiseptic and disinfectant. **2** any hydroxyl derivative of an aromatic hydrocarbon. □ **phenolic** /fɪˈnɒlɪk/ adj. [F *phénole* f. *phène* benzene (formed as PHENO-)]

phenolphthalein /ˌfiːnɒlˈθeɪliːn/ n. *Chem.* a white crystalline solid used in solution as an acid-base indicator and medicinally as a laxative. [PHENOL + *phthal* f. NAPHTHALENE + -IN]

phenomena pl. of PHENOMENON.

phenomenal /fɪˈnɒmɪn(ə)l/ adj. **1** of the nature of a phenomenon. **2** extraordinary, remarkable, prodigious. □ **phenomenalize** v.tr. (also **-ise**). **phenomenally** adv.

phenomenology /fɪˌnɒmɪˈnɒlədʒɪ/ n. *Philos.* **1** the science of phenomena. **2** the description and classification of phenomena. □ **phenomenological** /-nəˈlɒdʒɪk(ə)l/ adj. **phenomenologically** /-nəˈlɒdʒɪkəlɪ/ adv.

phenomenon /fɪˈnɒmɪnən/ n. (pl. **phenomena** /-nə/) **1** a fact or occurrence that appears or is perceived, esp. one of which the cause is in question. **2** a remarkable person or thing. [LL f. Gk *phainomenon* neut. pres. part. of *phainomai* appear f. *phainō* show]

■ **Usage** The plural form of this word, *phenomena*, is often used mistakenly for the singular. This should be avoided.

phenotype /ˈfiːnəʊˌtaɪp/ n. *Biol.* a set of observable characteristics of an individual or group as determined by its genotype and environment. □ **phenotypic** /-ˈtɪpɪk/ adj. **phenotypical** /-ˈtɪpɪk(ə)l/ adj. **phenotypically** /-ˈtɪpɪkəlɪ/ adv. [G *Phaenotypus* (as PHENO-, TYPE)]

pheromone /ˈferəˌməʊn/ n. a chemical substance secreted and released by an animal for detection and response by another usu. of the same species. □ **pheromonal** /-ˈməʊn(ə)l/ adj. [Gk *pherō* convey + HORMONE]

phew /fjuː/ int. an expression of impatience, discomfort, relief, astonishment, or disgust. [imit. of puffing]

phi /faɪ/ n. the twenty-first letter of the Greek alphabet (Φ, φ). [Gk]

phial /ˈfaɪəl/ n. a small glass bottle, esp. for liquid medicine. [ME f. OF *fiole* f. L *phiola phiala* f. Gk *phialē*, a broad flat vessel: cf. VIAL]

phil- comb. form var. of PHILO-.

-phil comb. form var. of -PHILE.

philadelphus /ˌfɪləˈdelfəs/ n. any highly-scented deciduous flowering shrub of the genus *Philadelphus*, esp. the mock orange. [mod.L f. Gk *philadelphon*]

philander /fɪˈlændə(r)/ v.intr. (often foll. by *with*) flirt or have casual affairs with women; womanize. □ **philanderer** n. [*philander* (n.) used in Gk literature as the proper name of a lover, f. Gk *philandros* fond of men f. *anēr* male person: see PHIL-]

philanthrope /ˈfɪlənˌθrəʊp/ n. = PHILANTHROPIST (see PHILANTHROPY). [Gk *philanthrōpos* (as PHIL-, *anthrōpos* human being)]

philanthropic /ˌfɪlənˈθrɒpɪk/ adj. loving one's fellow men; benevolent. □ **philanthropically** adv. [F *philanthropique* (as PHILANTHROPE)]

philanthropy /fɪˈlænθrəpɪ/ n. **1** a love of mankind. **2** practical benevolence, esp. charity on a large scale. □ **philanthropism** n. **philanthropist** n. **philanthropize** v.tr. & intr. (also

-ise). [LL *philanthropia* f. Gk *philanthrōpia* (as PHILANTHROPE)]

philately /fɪˈlætəlɪ/ n. the collection and study of postage stamps. □ **philatelic** /ˌfɪləˈtelɪk/ adj. **philatelically** /ˌfɪləˈtelɪkəlɪ/ adv. **philatelist** n. [F *philatélie* f. Gk *ateleia* exemption from payment f. *a-* not + *telos* toll, tax]

-phile /faɪl/ comb. form (also **-phil** /fɪl/) forming nouns and adjectives denoting fondness for what is specified (*bibliophile*; *Francophile*). [Gk *philos* dear, loving]

philharmonic /ˌfɪlhɑːˈmɒnɪk/ adj. **1** fond of music. **2** used characteristically in the names of orchestras, choirs, etc. (*Royal Philharmonic Orchestra*). [F *philharmonique* f. It. *filarmonico* (as PHIL-, HARMONIC)]

-philia /ˈfɪlɪə/ comb. form **1** denoting (esp. abnormal) fondness or love for what is specified (*necrophilia*). **2** denoting undue inclination (*haemophilia*). □ **-philiac** /-lɪˌæk/ comb. form forming nouns and adjectives. **-philic** comb. form forming adjectives. **-philous** comb. form forming adjectives. [Gk f. *philos* loving]

philippic /fɪˈlɪpɪk/ n. a bitter verbal attack or denunciation. [L *philippicus* f. Gk *philippikos* the name of Demosthenes' speeches against Philip II of Macedon and Cicero's against Mark Antony]

Philistine /ˈfɪlɪˌstaɪn/ n. & adj. —n. **1** a member of a people opposing the Israelites in ancient Palestine. **2** (usu. **philistine**) a person who is hostile or indifferent to culture, or one whose interests or tastes are commonplace or material. —adj. hostile or indifferent to culture, commonplace, prosaic. □ **philistinism** /-stɪnɪz(ə)m/ n. [ME f. F *Philistin* or LL *Philistinus* f. Gk *Philistinos* = *Palaistinos* f. Heb. *pᵉlištî*]

Phillips /ˈfɪlɪps/ n. (usu. attrib.) propr. denoting a screw with a cross-shaped slot for turning, or a corresponding screwdriver. [name of the original US manufacturer]

philo- /ˈfɪləʊ/ comb. form (also **phil-** before a vowel or *h*) denoting a liking for what is specified.

philology /fɪˈlɒlədʒɪ/ n. **1** the science of language, esp. in its historical and comparative aspects. **2** the love of learning and literature. □ **philologian** /-ləˈʊdʒ(ə)n/ n. **philologist** n. **philological** /-ləˈlɒdʒɪk(ə)l/ adj. **philologically** /-ləˈlɒdʒɪkəlɪ/ adv. **philologize** v.intr. (also **-ise**). [F *philologie* f. L *philologia* love of learning f. Gk (as PHILO-, -LOGY)]

philosopher /fɪˈlɒsəfə(r)/ n. **1** a person engaged or learned in philosophy or a branch of it. **2** a person who lives by philosophy. **3** a person who shows philosophic calmness in trying circumstances. □ **philosophers'** (or **philosopher's**) **stone** the supreme object of alchemy, a substance supposed to change other metals into gold or silver. [ME f. AF *philosofre* var. of OF, *philosophe* f. L *philosophus* f. Gk *philosophos* (as PHILO-, *sophos* wise)]

philosophical /ˌfɪləˈsɒfɪk(ə)l/ adj. (also **philosophic**) **1** of or according to philosophy. **2** skilled in or devoted to philosophy or learning; learned (*philosophical society*). **3** wise; serene; temperate. **4** calm in adverse circumstances. □ **philosophically** adv. [LL *philosophicus* f. L *philosophia* (as PHILOSOPHY)]

philosophize /fɪˈlɒsəˌfaɪz/ v. (also **-ise**) **1** intr. reason like a philosopher. **2** intr. moralize. **3**

intr. speculate; theorize. **4** *tr.* render philosophic. □ **philosophizer** *n.* [app. f. F *philosopher*]

philosophy /fɪˈlɒsəfɪ/ *n.* (*pl.* **-ies**) **1** the use of reason and argument in seeking truth and knowledge of reality, esp. of the causes and nature of things and of the principles governing existence, the material universe, perception of physical phenomena, and human behaviour. **2 a** a particular system or set of beliefs reached by this. **b** a personal rule of life. **3** advanced learning in general (*doctor of philosophy*). **4** serenity; calmness; conduct governed by a particular philosophy. [ME f. OF *filosofie* f. L *philosophia* wisdom f. Gk (as PHILO-, *sophos* wise)]

philtre /ˈfɪltə(r)/ *n.* (*US* **philter**) a drink supposed to excite sexual love in the drinker. [F *philtre* f. L *philtrum* f. Gk *philtron* f. *phileō* to love]

-phily /ˈfɪlɪ/ *comb. form* = -PHILIA.

phlebitis /flɪˈbaɪtɪs/ *n.* inflammation of the walls of a vein. □ **phlebitic** /-ˈbɪtɪk/ *adj.* [mod.L f. Gk f. *phleps phlebos* vein]

phlegm /flem/ *n.* **1** the thick viscous substance secreted by the mucous membranes of the respiratory passages, discharged by coughing. **2 a** coolness and calmness of disposition. **b** sluggishness or apathy (supposed to result from too much phlegm in the constitution). **3** *archaic* phlegm regarded as one of the four bodily humours. □ **phlegmy** *adj.* [ME & OF *fleume* f. LL *phlegma* f. Gk *phlegma -atos* inflammation f. *phlegō* burn]

phlegmatic /fleɡˈmætɪk/ *adj.* stolidly calm; unexcitable, unemotional. □ **phlegmatically** *adv.*

phloem /ˈfləʊem/ *n. Bot.* the tissue conducting food material in plants. [Gk *phloos* bark]

phlogiston /fləˈdʒɪst(ə)n, -ˈɡɪst(ə)n/ *n.* a substance formerly supposed to exist in all combustible bodies, and to be released in combustion. [mod.L f. Gk *phlogizō* set on fire f. *phlox phlogos* flame]

phlox /flɒks/ *n.* any cultivated plant of the genus *Phlox*, with scented clusters of esp. white, blue, and red flowers. [L f. Gk *phlox*, the name of a plant (lit. flame)]

-phobe /fəʊb/ *comb. form* forming nouns and adjectives denoting fear or dislike of what is specified (*xenophobe*). [F f. L *-phobus* f. Gk *phobos* f. *phobos* fear]

phobia /ˈfəʊbɪə/ *n.* an abnormal or morbid fear or aversion. □ **phobic** *adj.* & *n.* [-PHOBIA used as a separate word]

-phobia /ˈfəʊbɪə/ *comb. form* forming abstract nouns denoting fear or aversion of what is specified (*agoraphobia*; *xenophobia*). □ **-phobic** *comb. form* forming adjectives. [L f. Gk]

phoenix /ˈfiːnɪks/ *n.* **1** a mythical bird, the only one of its kind, that burnt itself on a funeral pyre and rose from the ashes with renewed youth. **2** a unique person or thing. [OE & OF *fenix* f. L *phoenix* f. Gk *phoinix* Phoenician, purple, phoenix]

phon /fɒn/ *n.* a unit of the perceived loudness of sounds. [Gk *phōnē* sound]

phone /fəʊn/ *n.* & *v.tr.* & *intr. colloq.* = TELEPHONE. □ **phone book** = *telephone directory*. **phone-in** *n.* a broadcast programme during which the listeners or viewers telephone the studio etc. and participate. [abbr.]

-phone /fəʊn/ *comb. form* forming nouns and adjectives meaning: **1** an instrument using or connected with sound (*telephone*; *xylophone*). **2** a person who uses a specified language (*anglophone*). [Gk *phōnē* voice, sound]

phonecard /ˈfəʊnkɑːd/ *n.* a card containing prepaid units for use with a cardphone.

phoneme /ˈfəʊniːm/ *n.* any of the units of sound in a specified language that distinguish one word from another (e.g. *p*, *b*, *d*, *t* as in pad, pat, bad, bat, in English). □ **phonemic** /-ˈniːmɪk/ *adj.* **phonemics** /-ˈniːmɪks/ *n.* [F *phonème* f. Gk *phōnēma* sound, speech f. *phōneō* speak]

phonetic /fəˈnetɪk/ *adj.* **1** representing vocal sounds. **2** (of a system of spelling etc.) having a direct correspondence between symbols and sounds. **3** of or relating to phonetics. □ **phonetically** *adv.* **phoneticism** /-ˌsɪz(ə)m/ *n.* **phoneticist** /-sɪst/ *n.* **phoneticize** /-ˌsaɪz/ *v.tr.* (also **-ise**). [mod.L *phoneticus* f. Gk *phōnētikos* f. *phōneō* speak]

phonetics /fəˈnetɪks/ *n.pl.* (usu. treated as *sing.*) **1** vocal sounds and their classification. **2** the study of these. □ **phonetician** /ˌfəʊnɪˈtɪʃ(ə)n/ *n.*

phonetist /ˈfəʊnɪtɪst/ *n.* **1** a person skilled in phonetics. **2** an advocate of phonetic spelling.

phoney /ˈfəʊnɪ/ *adj.* & *n.* (also **phony**) *colloq.* —*adj.* (**phonier**, **phoniest**) **1** sham; counterfeit. **2** fictitious; fraudulent. —*n.* (*pl.* **-eys** or **-ies**) a phoney person or thing. □ **phonily** *adv.* **phoniness** *n.* [20th c.: orig. unkn.]

phonic /ˈfɒnɪk, ˈfəʊ-/ *adj.* & *n.* —*adj.* of sound; acoustic; of vocal sounds. —*n.* (in *pl.*) a method of teaching reading based on sounds. □ **phonically** *adv.* [Gk *phōnē* voice]

phono- /ˈfəʊnəʊ/ *comb. form* denoting sound. [Gk *phōnē* voice, sound]

phonograph /ˈfəʊnəˌɡrɑːf/ *n.* **1** *Brit.* an early form of gramophone using cylinders and able to record as well as reproduce sound. **2** *US* a gramophone.

phonology /fəˈnɒlədʒɪ/ *n.* the study of sounds in a language. □ **phonological** /ˌfəʊnəˈlɒdʒɪk(ə)l, ˌfɒn-/ *adj.* **phonologically** /ˌfəʊnəˈlɒdʒɪkəlɪ, ˌfɒn-/ *adv.* **phonologist** *n.*

phooey /ˈfuːɪ/ *int.* an expression of disgust or disbelief. [imit.]

-phore /fɔː(r)/ *comb. form* forming nouns meaning 'bearer' (*semaphore*). □ **-phorous** /fərəs/ *comb. form* forming adjectives. [mod.L f. Gk *-phoros -phoron* bearing, bearer f. *pherō* bear]

phormium /ˈfɔːmɪəm/ *n.* **1** a liliaceous plant, *Phormium tenax*, yielding a leaf-fibre that is used commercially. **2** New Zealand flax. [mod.L f. Gk *phormion* a species of plant]

phosgene /ˈfɒzdʒiːn/ *n.* a colourless poisonous gas (carbonyl chloride), formerly used in warfare. [Gk *phōs* light + -GEN, with ref. to its orig. production by the action of sunlight on chlorine and carbon monoxide]

phosphate /ˈfɒsfeɪt/ *n.* any salt or ester of phosphoric acid, esp. used as a fertilizer. □ **phosphatic** /-ˈfætɪk/ *adj.* [F f. *phosphore* PHOSPHORUS]

phosphite /ˈfɒsfaɪt/ *n. Chem.* any salt or ester of phosphorous acid. [F (as PHOSPHO-)]

phospho- /ˈfɒsfəʊ/ *comb. form* denoting phosphorus. [abbr.]

phospholipid /ˌfɒsfəˈlɪpɪd/ *n. Biochem.* any lipid consisting of a phosphate group and one or more fatty acids.

phosphor | phrase

phosphor /ˈfɒsfə(r)/ n. **1** = PHOSPHORUS. **2** a synthetic fluorescent or phosphorescent substance esp. used in cathode-ray tubes. [G f. L *phosphorus* PHOSPHORUS]

phosphorate /ˈfɒsfəˌreɪt/ v.tr. combine or impregnate with phosphorus.

phosphorescence /ˌfɒsfəˈres(ə)ns/ n. **1** radiation similar to fluorescence but detectable after excitation ceases. **2** the emission of light without combustion or perceptible heat. □ **phosphoresce** v.intr. **phosphorescent** adj.

phosphorus /ˈfɒsfərəs/ n. Chem. a non-metallic element existing in allotropic forms, esp. as a poisonous whitish waxy substance burning slowly at ordinary temperatures and so appearing luminous in the dark, and a reddish form used in matches, fertilizers, etc. □ **phosphoric** /-ˈfɒrɪk/ adj. **phosphorous** adj. [L, = morning star, f. Gk *phōsphoros* f. *phōs* light + *-phoros* -bringing]

phot /fɒt, fəʊt/ n. a unit of illumination. [Gk *phōs phōtos* light]

photic /ˈfəʊtɪk/ adj. **1** of or relating to light. **2** (of ocean layers) reached by sunlight.

photo /ˈfəʊtəʊ/ n. & v. —n. (pl. **-os**) = PHOTOGRAPH n. —v.tr. (**-oes, -oed**) = PHOTOGRAPH v. □ **photo-call** an occasion on which theatrical performers, famous personalities, etc., pose for photographers by arrangement. **photo finish** a close finish of a race or contest, esp. one where the winner is only distinguishable on a photograph. **photo opportunity** = photo call. [abbr.]

photo- /ˈfəʊtəʊ/ comb. form denoting: **1** light (*photosensitive*). **2** photography (*photocomposition*). [Gk *phōs phōtos* light, or as abbr. of PHOTOGRAPH]

photobiology /ˌfəʊtəʊbaɪˈɒlədʒɪ/ n. the study of the effects of light on living organisms.

photocell /ˈfəʊtəʊˌsel/ n. = photoelectric cell.

photochemistry /ˌfəʊtəʊˈkemɪstrɪ/ n. the study of the chemical effects of light. □ **photochemical** adj.

photocomposition /ˌfəʊtəʊˌkɒmpəˈzɪʃ(ə)n/ n. = FILMSETTING.

photocopier /ˈfəʊtəʊˌkɒpɪə(r)/ n. a machine for producing photocopies.

photocopy /ˈfəʊtəʊˌkɒpɪ/ n. & v. —n. (pl. **-ies**) a photographic copy of printed or written material produced by a process involving the action of light on a specially prepared surface. —v.tr. (**-ies, -ied**) make a photocopy of. □ **photocopiable** adj.

photoelectric /ˌfəʊtəʊɪˈlektrɪk/ adj. marked by or using emissions of electrons from substances exposed to light. □ **photoelectric cell** a device using this effect to generate current. □ **photoelectricity** /-ˈtrɪsɪtɪ/ n.

photofit /ˈfəʊtəʊfɪt/ n. a reconstructed picture of a person (esp. one sought by the police) made from composite photographs of facial features (cf. IDENTIKIT).

photogenic /ˌfəʊtəʊˈdʒenɪk, -ˈdʒiːnɪk/ adj. (esp. of a person) having an appearance that looks pleasing in photographs. □ **photogenically** adv.

photograph /ˈfəʊtəʊˌɡrɑːf/ n. & v. —n. a picture taken by means of the chemical action of light or other radiation on sensitive film. —v.tr. (also absol.) take a photograph of (a person etc.). □ **photographable** adj. **photographer** /fəˈtɒɡrəfə(r)/ n. **photographic** /-ˈɡræfɪk/ adj. **photographically** /-ˈɡræfɪkəlɪ/ adv.

photography /fəˈtɒɡrəfɪ/ n. the taking and processing of photographs.

photogravure /ˌfəʊtəʊɡrəˈvjʊə(r)/ n. **1** an image produced from a photographic negative transferred to a metal plate and etched in. **2** this process. [F (as PHOTO-, *gravure* engraving)]

photojournalism /ˌfəʊtəʊˈdʒɜːnəˌlɪz(ə)m/ n. the art or practice of relating news by photographs, with or without an accompanying text, esp. in magazines etc. □ **photojournalist** n.

photolithography /ˌfəʊtəʊlɪˈθɒɡrəfɪ/ n. (also **photolitho** /-ˈlaɪθəʊ/) lithography using plates made photographically. □ **photolithographer** n. **photolithographic** /-θəˈɡræfɪk/ adj. **photolithographically** /-θəˈɡræfɪkəlɪ/ adv.

photometer /fəʊˈtɒmɪtə(r)/ n. an instrument for measuring light. □ **photometric** /ˌfəʊtəʊˈmetrɪk/ adj. **photometry** /-ˈtɒmɪtrɪ/ n.

photomicrograph /ˌfəʊtəʊˈmaɪkrəˌɡrɑːf/ n. a photograph of an image produced by a microscope. □ **photomicrography** /-ˈkrɒɡrəfɪ/ n.

photomontage /ˌfəʊtəʊmɒnˈtɑːʒ/ n. **1** the technique of producing a montage using photographs. **2** a composite picture produced in this way.

photon /ˈfəʊtɒn/ n. a quantum of electromagnetic radiation energy, proportional to the frequency of radiation. [Gk *phōs phōtos* light, after *electron*]

photonovel /ˈfəʊtəʊˌnɒv(ə)l/ n. a novel told in a series of photographs with superimposed speech bubbles.

photo-offset /ˌfəʊtəʊˈɒfset/ n. offset printing with plates made photographically.

photophobia /ˌfəʊtəʊˈfəʊbɪə/ n. an abnormal fear of or aversion to light. □ **photophobic** adj.

photoreceptor /ˌfəʊtəʊrɪˈseptə(r)/ n. any living structure that responds to incident light.

photosensitive /ˌfəʊtəʊˈsensɪtɪv/ adj. reacting chemically, electrically, etc., to light. □ **photosensitivity** /-ˈtɪvɪtɪ/ n.

photosetting /ˈfəʊtəʊˌsetɪŋ/ n. = FILMSETTING. □ **photoset** v.tr. (past and past part. **-set**). **photosetter** n.

Photostat /ˈfəʊtəʊˌstæt/ n. & v. —n. propr. **1** a type of machine for making photocopies. **2** (**photostat**) a copy made by this means. —v.tr. (**photostat**) (**-statted, -statting**) make a photostat of. □ **photostatic** /-ˈstætɪk/ adj.

photosynthesis /ˌfəʊtəʊˈsɪnθɪsɪs/ n. the process in which the energy of sunlight is used by organisms, esp. green plants to synthesize carbohydrates from carbon dioxide and water. □ **photosynthesize** v.tr. & intr. (also **-ise**). **photosynthetic** /-ˈθetɪk/ adj. **photosynthetically** /-ˈθetɪkəlɪ/ adv.

phototropism /ˌfəʊtəʊˈtrəʊpɪz(ə)m, fəˈtɒtrəˌpɪz(ə)m/ n. the tendency of a plant etc. to bend or turn towards or away from a source of light. □ **phototropic** /-ˈtrɒpɪk/ adj.

phrasal /ˈfreɪz(ə)l/ adj. Gram. consisting of a phrase. □ **phrasal verb** an idiomatic phrase consisting of a verb and an adverb (e.g. *break down*) or a verb and a preposition (e.g. *see to*).

phrase /freɪz/ n. & v. —n. **1** a group of words forming a conceptual unit, but not a sentence. **2** an idiomatic or short pithy expression. **3** a manner or mode of expression (*a nice turn of phrase*). **4** Mus. a group of notes forming a distinct unit within a larger piece. —v.tr. **1**

express in words (*phrased the reply badly*). **2** (esp. when reading aloud or speaking) divide (sentences etc.) into units so as to convey the meaning of the whole. **3** *Mus.* divide (music) into phrases etc. in performance. □ **phrase book** a book for tourists etc. listing useful expressions with their equivalent in a foreign language. □ **phrasing** *n.* [earlier *phrasis* f. L f. Gk f. *phrazō* declare, tell]

phraseology /ˌfreɪzɪˈɒlədʒɪ/ *n.* (pl. **-ies**) **1** a choice or arrangement of words. **2** a mode of expression. □ **phraseological** /-zɪəˈlɒdʒɪk(ə)l/ *adj.* [mod.L *phraseologia* f. Gk *phraseōn* genit. pl. of *phrasis* PHRASE]

phrenetic /frɪˈnetɪk/ *adj.* **1** frantic. **2** fanatic. □ **phrenetically** *adv.* [ME, var. of FRENETIC]

phrenology /frɪˈnɒlədʒɪ/ *n. hist.* the study of the shape and size of the cranium as a supposed indication of character and mental faculties. □ **phrenological** /-nəˈlɒdʒɪk(ə)l/ *adj.* **phrenologist** *n.*

phthisis /ˈfθaɪsɪs, ˈθaɪ-/ *n.* any progressive wasting disease, esp. pulmonary tuberculosis. □ **phthisic** *adj.* **phthisical** *adj.* [L f. Gk f. *phthinō* to decay]

phut /fʌt/ *n.* a dull abrupt sound as of an impact or explosion. □ **go phut** *colloq.* (esp. of a scheme or plan) collapse, break down. [perh. f. Hindi *phaṭnā* to burst]

phyla *pl.* of PHYLUM.

phylactery /fɪˈlæktərɪ/ *n.* (pl. **-ies**) a small leather box containing Hebrew texts on vellum, worn by Jewish men at morning prayer as a reminder to keep the law. [ME f. OF f. LL *phylacterium* f. Gk *phulaktērion* amulet f. *phulassō* guard]

phylloquinone /ˌfaɪləʊˈkwɪnəʊn/ *n.* one of the K vitamins, found in leafy green vegetables, and essential for the blood clotting process.

phylo- /ˈfaɪləʊ/ *comb. form* Biol. denoting a race or tribe. [Gk *phulon*, *phulē*]

phylum /ˈfaɪləm/ *n.* (pl. **phyla** /-lə/) Biol. a taxonomic rank below kingdom comprising a class or classes and subordinate taxa. [mod.L f. Gk *phulon* race]

physalis /faɪˈsælɪs/ *n.* any plant of the genus *Physalis*, bearing fruit surrounded by lantern-like calyxes. [Gk *physallis* bladder, with ref. to the inflated calyx]

physic /ˈfɪzɪk/ *n.* & *v.* esp. *archaic.* —*n.* **1** a medicine (*a dose of physic*). **2** the art of healing. **3** the medical profession. —*v.tr.* (**physicked, physicking**) dose with physic. [ME f. OF *fisique* medicine f. L *physica* f. Gk *phusikē* (*epistēmē*) (knowledge) of nature]

physical /ˈfɪzɪk(ə)l/ *adj.* & *n.* —*adj.* **1** of or concerning the body (*physical exercise*; *physical education*). **2** of matter; material (*both mental and physical force*). **3 a** of, or according to, the laws of nature (*a physical impossibility*). **b** belonging to physics (*physical science*). —*n.* (in full **physical examination**) a medical examination to determine physical fitness. □ **physical chemistry** the application of physics to the study of chemical behaviour. **physical geography** geography dealing with natural features. **physical jerks** *colloq.* physical exercises. **physical science** the sciences used in the study of

inanimate natural objects, e.g. physics, chemistry, astronomy, etc. **physical training** exercises promoting bodily fitness and strength. □ **physicality** /-ˈkælɪtɪ/ *n.* **physically** *adv.* **physicalness** *n.* [ME f. med.L *physicalis* f. L *physica* (as PHYSIC)]

physician /fɪˈzɪʃ(ə)n/ *n.* **1 a** a person legally qualified to practise medicine and surgery. **b** a specialist in medical diagnosis and treatment. **c** any medical practitioner. **2** a healer (*work is the best physician*). [ME f. OF *fisicien* (as PHYSIC)]

physicist /ˈfɪzɪsɪst/ *n.* a person skilled or qualified in physics.

physics /ˈfɪzɪks/ *n.* the science dealing with the properties and interactions of matter and energy. [pl. of *physic* physical (thing), after L *physica*, Gk *phusika* natural things f. *phusis* nature]

physio /ˈfɪzɪəʊ/ *n.* (pl. **-os**) *colloq.* a physiotherapist. [abbr.]

physio- /ˈfɪzɪəʊ/ *comb. form* nature; what is natural. [Gk *phusis* nature]

physiognomy /ˌfɪzɪˈɒnəmɪ/ *n.* (pl. **-ies**) **1 a** the cast or form of a person's features, expression, body, etc. **b** the art of supposedly judging character from facial characteristics etc. **2** the external features of a landscape etc. **3** a characteristic, esp. moral, aspect. □ **physiognomic** /-zɪəˈnɒmɪk/ *adj.* **physiognomical** /-zɪəˈnɒmɪk(ə)l/ *adj.* **physiognomically** /-zɪəˈnɒmɪkəlɪ/ *adv.* **physiognomist** *n.* [ME *fisnomie* etc. f. OF *phisonomie* f. med.L *phisonomia* f. Gk *phusiognōmonia* judging of a man's nature (by his features) (as PHYSIO-, *gnōmōn* judge)]

physiography /ˌfɪzɪˈɒɡrəfɪ/ *n.* the description of nature, or natural phenomena, or of a class of objects; physical geography. □ **physiographer** *n.* **physiographic** /-zɪəˈɡræfɪk/ *adj.* **physiographical** /-zɪəˈɡræfɪk(ə)l/ *adj.* **physiographically** /-zɪəˈɡræfɪkəlɪ/ *adv.* [F *physiographie* (as PHYSIO-, -GRAPHY)]

physiological /ˌfɪzɪəˈlɒdʒɪk(ə)l/ *adj.* (also **physiologic**) of or concerning physiology. □ **physiologically** *adv.*

physiology /ˌfɪzɪˈɒlədʒɪ/ *n.* **1** the science of the functions of living organisms and their parts. **2** these functions. □ **physiologist** *n.* [F *physiologie* or L *physiologia* f. Gk *phusiologia* (as PHYSIO-, -LOGY)]

physiotherapy /ˌfɪzɪəʊˈθerəpɪ/ *n.* the treatment of disease, injury, deformity, etc., by physical methods including massage, remedial exercise, etc., not by drugs. □ **physiotherapist** *n.*

physique /fɪˈziːk/ *n.* the bodily structure, development, and organization of an individual (*an undernourished physique*). [F, orig. adj. (as PHYSIC)]

phyto- /ˈfaɪtəʊ/ *comb. form* denoting a plant.

phytochemistry /ˌfaɪtəʊˈkemɪstrɪ/ *n.* the chemistry of plant products. □ **phytochemical** *adj.* **phytochemist** *n.*

phytoplankton /ˌfaɪtəʊˈplæŋkt(ə)n/ *n.* plankton consisting of plants.

pi[1] /paɪ/ *n.* **1** the sixteenth letter of the Greek alphabet (Π, π). **2** (as π) the symbol of the ratio of the circumference of a circle to its diameter (approx. 3.14159). □ **pi-meson** = PION. [Gk: sense 2 f. Gk *periphereia* circumference]

pi[2] /paɪ/ *adj.* Brit. *sl.* pious. □ **pi jaw** a long moralizing lecture or reprimand. [abbr.]

pi[3] US var. of PIE[3].

piani *pl.* of PIANO[2].

pianissimo /ˌpɪəˈnɪsɪˌməʊ/ adj., adv., & n. Mus. —adj. performed very softly. —adv. very softly. —n. (pl. -os or **pianissimi** /-mɪ/) a passage to be performed very softly. [It., superl. of PIANO²]

pianist /ˈpɪənɪst/ n. the player of a piano. [F pianiste (as PIANO¹)]

piano¹ /pɪˈænəʊ/ n. (pl. -os) a large musical instrument played by pressing down keys on a keyboard and causing hammers to strike metal strings, the vibration from which is stopped by dampers when the keys are released. □ **piano-accordion** an accordion with the melody played on a small vertical keyboard like that of a piano. **piano roll** a roll of paper with perforations, used in a Pianola to reproduce music by allowing air to pass through the holes to depress the keys. [It., abbr. of PIANOFORTE]

piano² /ˈpjɑːnəʊ/ adj., adv., & n. —adj. 1 Mus. performed softly. 2 subdued. —adv. 1 Mus. softly. 2 in a subdued manner. —n. (pl. -os or **piani** /-nɪ/) Mus. a piano passage. [It. f. L planus flat, (of sound) soft]

pianoforte /ˌpjænəʊˈfɔːtɪ/ n. Mus. formal or archaic a piano. [It., earlier piano e forte soft and loud, expressing its gradation of tone]

Pianola /pɪəˈnəʊlə/ n. propr. a kind of automatic piano; a player-piano. [app. dimin. of PIANO¹]

piastre /pɪˈæstə(r)/ n. (US **piaster**) a small coin and monetary unit of several Middle Eastern countries. [F piastre f. It. piastra (d'argento) plate (of silver), formed as PLASTER]

piazza /pɪˈætsə/ n. 1 a public square or market-place esp. in an Italian town. 2 US the veranda of a house. [It., formed as PLACE]

pibroch /ˈpiːbrɒx, -brɒk/ n. a series of esp. martial or funerary variations on a theme for the bagpipes. [Gael. piobaireachd art of piping f. piobair piper f. piob f. E PIPE]

pic n. colloq. a picture, esp. a cinema film. [abbr.]

pica /ˈpaɪkə/ n. Printing 1 a unit of type-size ($\frac{1}{6}$ inch). 2 a size of letters in typewriting (10 per inch). [AL pica 15th-c. book of rules about church feasts, perh. formed as PIE²]

picador /ˈpɪkədɔː(r)/ n. a mounted man with a lance who goads the bull in a bullfight. [Sp. f. picar prick]

picaresque /ˌpɪkəˈresk/ adj. (of a style of fiction) dealing with the episodic adventures of rogues etc. [F f. Sp. picaresco f. pícaro rogue]

■ **Usage** This word does not mean 'transitory' or 'roaming'.

picayune /ˌpɪkəˈjuːn/ n. & adj. US —n. 1 colloq. a small coin of little value, esp. a 5-cent piece. 2 an insignificant person or thing. —adj. mean; contemptible; petty. [F picaillon Piedmontese coin, cash, f. Prov. picaioun, of unkn. orig.]

piccalilli /ˌpɪkəˈlɪlɪ/ n. (pl. **piccalillis**) a pickle of chopped vegetables, mustard, and hot spices. [18th c.: perh. f. PICKLE + CHILLI]

piccaninny /ˌpɪkəˈnɪnɪ/ n. (US **pickaninny**) —n. (pl. -ies) often offens. a small Black or Australian Aboriginal child. [W.Ind. Negro f. Sp. pequeño or Port. pequeno little]

piccolo /ˈpɪkələʊ/ n. (pl. -os) 1 a small flute sounding an octave higher than the ordinary one. 2 its player. [It., = small (flute)]

pick¹ v. & n. —v.tr. 1 (also absol.) choose carefully from a number of alternatives (picked the pink one; picked a team; picked the right moment to intervene). 2 detach or pluck (a flower, fruit, etc.) from a stem, tree, etc. 3 a probe (the teeth, nose, ears, a pimple, etc.) with the finger, an instrument, etc. to remove unwanted matter. b clear (a bone, carcass, etc.) of scraps of meat etc. 4 (also absol.) (of a person) eat (food, a meal, etc.) in small bits; nibble without appetite. 5 (also absol.) esp. US pluck the strings of (a banjo etc.). 6 a select (a route or path) carefully over difficult terrain by foot. b place (one's steps etc.) carefully. 7 pull apart (pick oakum). —n. 1 the act or an instance of picking. 2 a a selection or choice. b the right to select (had first pick of the prizes). 3 (usu. foll. by of) the best (the pick of the bunch). □ **pick and choose** select carefully or fastidiously. **pick at** 1 eat (food) without interest; nibble. 2 = pick on 1. **pick a person's brains** extract ideas, information, etc., from a person for one's own use. **pick holes** (or a **hole) in** 1 make holes in (material etc.) by plucking, poking, etc. 2 find fault with (an idea etc.). **pick a lock** open a lock with an instrument other than the proper key, esp. with intent to steal. **pick-me-up** 1 a tonic for the nerves etc. 2 a good experience, good news, etc. that cheers. **pick off** 1 pluck (leaves etc.) off. 2 shoot (people etc.) one by one without haste. 3 eliminate (opposition etc.) singly. **pick on** 1 find fault with; nag at. 2 select. **pick out** 1 take from a larger number (picked him out from the others). 2 distinguish from surrounding objects or at a distance (can just pick out the church spire). 3 play (a tune) by ear on the piano etc. 4 (often foll. by in, with) a highlight (a painting etc.) with touches of another colour. b accentuate (decoration, a painting, etc.) with a contrasting colour (picked out the handles in red). 5 make out (the meaning of a passage etc.). **pick over** select the best from. **pick a person's pockets** steal the contents of a person's pockets. **pick a quarrel** start an argument or a fight deliberately. **pick to pieces** = take to pieces. **pick up** 1 grasp and raise (from the ground etc.) (picked up his hat). 2 gain or acquire by chance or without effort (picked up a cold). 3 a fetch (a person, animal, or thing) left in another person's charge. b stop for and take along with one, esp. in a vehicle (pick me up on the corner). 4 make the acquaintance of (a person) casually, esp. as a sexual overture. 5 (of one's health, the weather, share prices, etc.) recover, prosper, improve. 6 (of a motor engine etc.) recover speed; accelerate. 7 (of the police etc.) take into charge; arrest. 8 detect by scrutiny or with a telescope, searchlight, radio, etc. (picked up most of the mistakes; picked up a distress signal). 9 (often foll. by with) form or renew a friendship. 10 accept the responsibility of paying (a bill etc.). 11 (refl.) raise (oneself etc.) after a fall etc. 12 raise (the feet etc.) clear of the ground. **pick-up** 1 sl. a person met casually, esp. for sexual purposes. 2 a small open motor truck. 3 **a** the part of a record-player carrying the stylus. **b** a detector of vibrations etc. 4 **a** the act of picking up. **b** something picked up. **pick-your-own** (usu. attrib.) (of commercially grown fruit and vegetables) dug or picked by the customer at the place of production. **take one's pick** make a choice. □ **pickable** adj. [ME, earlier pike, of unkn. orig.]

pick² /pɪk/ n. & v. —n. 1 a long-handled tool having a usu. curved iron bar pointed at one or both ends, used for breaking up hard ground, masonry, etc. **2** *colloq.* a plectrum. **3** any instrument for picking, such as a toothpick. —*v.tr.* **1** break the surface of (the ground etc.) with or as if with a pick. **2** make (holes etc.) in this way. [ME, app. var. of PIKE²]

pickaback var. of PIGGYBACK.

pickaxe /ˈpɪkæks/ *n.* & *v.* (US **pickax**) —*n.* = PICK² *n.* 1. —*v.* **1** *tr.* break (the ground etc.) with a pickaxe. **2** *intr.* work with a pickaxe. [ME *pikois* f. OF *picois*, rel. to PIKE²: assim. to AXE]

picker /ˈpɪkə(r)/ *n.* **1** a person or thing that picks. **2** (often in *comb.*) a person who gathers or collects (*hop-picker; rag-picker*).

picket /ˈpɪkɪt/ *n.* & *v.* —*n.* **1** a person or group of people outside a place of work, intending to persuade esp. workers not to enter during a strike etc. **2** a pointed stake or peg driven into the ground to form a fence or palisade, to tether a horse, etc. **3** (also **picquet, piquet**) *Mil.* **a** a small body of troops sent out to watch for the enemy, held in readiness, etc. **b** a party of sentries. **c** an outpost. **d** a camp-guard on police duty in a garrison town etc. —*v.* (**picketed, picketing**) **1** *tr.* & *intr.* station or act as a picket. **b** *tr.* beset or guard (a factory, workers, etc.) with a picket or pickets. **2** *tr.* secure (a place) with stakes. **3** *tr.* tether (an animal). □ **picket line** a boundary established by workers on strike, esp. at the entrance to the place of work, which others are asked not to cross. □ **picketer** *n.* [F *piquet* pointed stake f. *piquer* prick, f. *pic* PICK²]

pickings /ˈpɪkɪŋz/ *n.pl.* **1** perquisites; pilferings (*rich pickings*). **2** remaining scraps; gleanings.

pickle /ˈpɪk(ə)l/ *n.* & *v.* —*n.* **1 a** (often in *pl.*) food, esp. vegetables, preserved in brine, vinegar, mustard, etc. and used as a relish. **b** the brine, vinegar, etc. in which food is preserved. **2** *colloq.* a plight (*a fine pickle we are in!*). **3** *Brit. colloq.* a mischievous child. —*v.tr.* **1** preserve in pickle. **2** treat with pickle. **3** (as **pickled** *adj.*) *sl.* drunk. [ME *pekille, pykyl*, f. MDu., MLG *pekel*, of unkn. orig.]

pickler /ˈpɪklə(r)/ *n.* **1** a person who pickles vegetables etc. **2** a vegetable suitable for pickling.

picklock /ˈpɪklɒk/ *n.* **1** a person who picks locks. **2** an instrument for this.

pickpocket /ˈpɪkpɒkɪt/ *n.* a person who steals from the pockets of others.

picky /ˈpɪkɪ/ *adj.* (**pickier, pickiest**) *colloq.* excessively fastidious; choosy. □ **pickiness** *n.*

picnic /ˈpɪknɪk/ *n.* & *v.* —*n.* **1** an outing or excursion including a packed meal eaten out of doors. **2** any meal eaten out of doors or without preparation, tables, chairs, etc. **3** (usu. with *neg.*) *colloq.* something agreeable or easily accomplished etc. (*it was no picnic organizing the meeting*). —*v.intr.* (**picnicked, picnicking**) take part in a picnic. □ **picnicker** *n.* **picnicky** *adj. colloq.* [F *pique-nique*, of unkn. orig.]

picot /ˈpiːkəʊ/ *n.* a small loop of twisted thread in a lace edging etc. [F, dimin. of *pic* peak, point]

picquet var. of PICKET 3.

picric acid /ˈpɪkrɪk/ *n.* a very bitter yellow compound used in dyeing and surgery and in explosives. □ **picrate** /-reɪt/ *n.* [Gk *pikros* bitter]

Pict *n.* a member of an ancient people of N. Britain. □ **Pictish** *adj.* [ME f. LL *Picti* perh. f. *pingere pict-* paint, tattoo]

pictograph /ˈpɪktəˌɡrɑːf/ *n.* (also **pictogram** /ˈpɪktəˌɡræm/) **1 a** a pictorial symbol for a word or phrase. **b** an ancient record consisting of these. **2** a pictorial representation of statistics etc. on a chart, graph, etc. □ **pictographic** /-ˈɡræfɪk/ *adj.* **pictography** /-ˈtɒɡrəfɪ/ *n.* [L *pingere pict-* paint]

pictorial /pɪkˈtɔːrɪəl/ *adj.* & *n.* —*adj.* **1** of or expressed in a picture or pictures. **2** illustrated. **3** picturesque. —*n.* a journal, postage stamp, etc., with a picture or pictures as the main feature. □ **pictorially** *adv.* [LL *pictorius* f. L *pictor* painter (as PICTURE)]

picture /ˈpɪktʃə(r)/ *n.* & *v.* —*n.* **1 a** (often *attrib.*) a painting, drawing, photograph, etc., as a work of art (*picture frame*). **b** a portrait, esp. a photograph, of a person (*does not like to have her picture taken*). **c** a beautiful object (*her hat is a picture*). **2 a** a total visual or mental impression produced; a scene (*the picture looks bleak*). **b** a written or spoken description (*drew a vivid picture of moral decay*). **3 a** a film. **b** (in *pl.*) *Brit.* a showing of films at a cinema (*went to the pictures*). **c** (in *pl.*) films in general. **4** an image on a television screen. **5** *colloq.* **a** esp. *iron.* a person or thing exemplifying something (*he was the picture of innocence*). **b** a person or thing resembling another closely (*the picture of her aunt*). —*v.tr.* **1** represent in a picture. **2** (also *refl.*; often foll. by *to*) imagine, esp. visually or vividly (*pictured it to herself*). **3** describe graphically. □ **get the picture** *colloq.* grasp the tendency or drift of circumstances, information, etc. **in the picture** fully informed or noticed. **out of the picture** uninvolved, inactive; irrelevant. **picture-book** a book containing many illustrations. **picture-card** a court-card. **picture-gallery** a place containing an exhibition or collection of pictures. **picture-goer** a person who frequents the cinema. **picture hat** a woman's wide-brimmed highly decorated hat as in pictures by Reynolds and Gainsborough. **picture-moulding 1** woodwork etc. used for framing pictures. **2** a rail on a wall used for hanging pictures from. **picture-palace** (or **-theatre**) *Brit. archaic* a cinema. **picture postcard** a postcard with a picture on one side. **picture window** a very large window consisting of one pane of glass. [ME f. L *pictura* f. *pingere pict-* paint]

picturesque /ˌpɪktʃəˈresk/ *adj.* **1** (of landscape etc.) beautiful or striking, as in a picture. **2** (of language etc.) strikingly graphic; vivid. □ **picturesquely** *adv.* **picturesqueness** *n.* [F *pittoresque* f. It. *pittoresco* f. *pittore* painter f. L (as PICTORIAL): assim. to PICTURE]

piddle /ˈpɪd(ə)l/ *v.* & *n.* —*v.intr.* **1** *colloq.* urinate (used esp. to or by children). **2** work or act in a trifling way. **3** (as **piddling** *adj.*) *colloq.* trivial; trifling. —*n.* *colloq.* **1** urination. **2** urine (used esp. to or by children). □ **piddler** *n.* [sense 1 prob. f. PISS + PUDDLE: sense 2 perh. f. PEDDLE]

pidgin /ˈpɪdʒɪn/ *n.* a simplified language containing vocabulary from two or more languages, used for communication between people not having a common language. □ **pidgin English** a pidgin in which the chief language is English, used orig. between Chinese and Europeans. [corrupt. of *business*]

pi-dog var. of PYE-DOG.

pie[1] *n.* **1** a baked dish of meat, fish, fruit, etc., usu. with a top and base of pastry. **2** anything resembling a pie in form (*a mud pie*). □ **easy as pie** very easy. **pie chart** a circle divided into sectors to represent relative quantities. **pie-eyed** *sl.* drunk. **pie in the sky** an unrealistic prospect of future happiness after present suffering; a misleading promise. [ME, perh. = PIE[2] f. miscellaneous contents compared to objects collected by a magpie]

pie[2] *n. archaic* **1** a magpie. **2** a pied animal. [ME f. OF f. L *pica*]

pie[3] *n. & v.* (*US* **pi**) —*n.* **1** a confused mass of printers' type. **2** chaos. —*v.tr.* (**pieing**) muddle up (type). [perh. transl. F PÂTÉ = PIE[1]]

piebald /ˈpaɪbɔːld/ *adj. & n.* —*adj.* **1** (usu. of an animal, esp. a horse) having irregular patches of two colours, esp. black and white. **2** motley; mongrel. —*n.* a piebald animal, esp. a horse.

piece /piːs/ *n. & v.* —*n.* **1 a** (often foll. by *of*) one of the distinct portions forming part of or broken off from a larger object; a bit; a part (*a piece of string*). **b** each of the parts of which a set or category is composed (*a five-piece band; a piece of furniture*). **2** a coin of specified value (*50p piece*). **3 a** a usu. short literary or musical composition or a picture. **b** a theatrical play. **4** an item, instance, or example (*a piece of impudence; a piece of news*). **5 a** any of the objects used to make moves in board-games. **b** a chessman (strictly, other than a pawn). **6** a definite quantity in which a thing is sold. **7** (often foll. by *of*) an enclosed portion (of land etc.). **8** *derog. sl.* a woman. **9** *US* (foll. by *of*) *sl.* a financial share or investment in (*has a piece of the new production*). —*v.tr.* **1** (usu. foll. by *together*) form into a whole; put together; join (*finally pieced his story together*). **2** (usu. foll. by *out*) eke out. **b** form (a theory etc.) by combining parts etc. **3** (usu. foll. by *up*) patch. **4** join (threads) in spinning. □ **by the piece** (paid) according to the quantity of work done. **go to pieces** collapse emotionally; suffer a breakdown. **in one piece 1** unbroken. **2** unharmed. **in pieces** broken. **of a piece** (often foll. by *with*) uniform, consistent, in keeping. **piece-goods** fabrics woven in standard lengths. **piece of eight** *hist.* a Spanish dollar, equivalent to 8 reals. **a piece of one's mind** a sharp rebuke or lecture. **piece-rates** a rate paid according to the amount produced. **piece-work** work paid for by the amount produced. **say one's piece** give one's opinion or make a prepared statement. **take to pieces 1** break up or dismantle. **2** criticize harshly. □ **piecer** *n.* (in sense 4 of *v.*). [ME f. AF *pece*, OF *piece* f. Rmc, prob. of Gaulish orig.: cf. PEAT]

pièce de résistance /ˌpjɛs də reɪˈziːstɑ̃s/ *n.* (*pl.* **pièces de résistance** *pronunc.* same) **1** the most important or remarkable item. **2** the most substantial dish at a meal. [F]

piecemeal /ˈpiːsmiːl/ *adv. & adj.* —*adv.* piece by piece; gradually. —*adj.* partial; gradual; unsystematic. [ME f. PIECE + *-meal* f. OE *mǣlum* (instr. dative pl. of *mǣl* MEAL[1])]

piecrust /ˈpaɪkrʌst/ *n.* the baked pastry crust of a pie. □ **piecrust table** a table with an indented edge like a piecrust.

pied /paɪd/ *adj.* particoloured. □ **Pied Piper** a person enticing followers esp. to their doom. [ME f. PIE[2], orig. of friars]

pied-à-terre /ˌpjeɪdɑːˈteə(r)/ *n.* (*pl.* **pieds-à-terre** *pronunc.* same) a usu. small flat, house, etc. kept for occasional use. [F, lit. 'foot to earth']

pie-dog var. of PYE-DOG.

pier /pɪə(r)/ *n.* **1 a** a structure of iron or wood raised on piles and leading out to sea, a lake, etc., used as a promenade and landing-stage, and often with entertainment arcades etc. **b** a breakwater; a mole. **2 a** a support of an arch or of the span of a bridge; a pillar. **b** solid masonry between windows etc. □ **pier-glass** a large mirror, used orig. to fill wall-space between windows. [ME *per* f. AL *pera*, of unkn. orig.]

pierce /pɪəs/ *v.* **1** *tr.* **a** (of a sharp instrument etc.) penetrate the surface of. **b** (often foll. by *with*) prick with a sharp instrument, esp. to make a hole in. **c** make (a hole etc.) (*pierced a hole in the belt*). **d** (of cold, grief, etc.) affect keenly or sharply. **e** (of a light, glance, sound, etc.) penetrate keenly or sharply. **2** (as **piercing** *adj.*) (of a glance, intuition, high noise, bright light, etc.) keen, sharp, or unpleasantly penetrating. **3** *tr.* force (a way etc.) through or into (something) (*pierced their way through the jungle*). **4** *intr.* (usu. foll. by *through, into*) penetrate. □ **piercer** *n.* **piercingly** *adv.* [ME f. OF *percer* f. L *pertundere* bore through (as PER-, *tundere tus-* thrust)]

pierrot /ˈpɪərəʊ, ˈpjɛrəʊ/ *n.* (*fem.* **pierrette** /pɪəˈret, pjɛˈret/) *Theatr.* a white-faced entertainer in pier shows etc. with a loose white clown's costume. [F, dimin. of *Pierre* Peter]

pietà /ˌpɪeˈtɑː/ *n.* a picture or sculpture of the Virgin Mary holding the dead body of Christ on her lap or in her arms. [It. f. L (as PIETY)]

pietism /ˈpaɪətɪz(ə)m/ *n.* **1** pious sentiment. **2** an exaggerated or affected piety. □ **pietist** *n.* **pietistic** /-ˈtɪstɪk/ *adj.* **pietistical** /-ˈtɪstɪk(ə)l/ *adj.* [G *Pietismus* (as PIETY)]

piety /ˈpaɪətɪ/ *n.* (*pl.* **-ies**) **1** the quality of being pious. **2** a pious act. [ME f. OF *pieté* f. L *pietas -tatis* dutifulness (as PIOUS)]

piezoelectricity /paɪˌiːzəʊˌiːlekˈtrɪsɪtɪ/ *n.* electric polarization in a substance resulting from the application of mechanical stress, esp. in certain crystals. □ **piezoelectric** /-ɪˈlektrɪk/ *adj.* **piezoelectrically** /-ɪˈlektrɪkəlɪ/ *adv.* [Gk *piezō* press + ELECTRIC]

piffle /ˈpɪf(ə)l/ *n. & v. colloq.* —*n.* nonsense; empty speech. —*v.intr.* talk or act feebly; trifle. □ **piffler** *n.* [imit.]

piffling /ˈpɪflɪŋ/ *adj. colloq.* trivial; worthless.

pig *n. & v.* —*n.* **1 a** any omnivorous hoofed bristly mammal of the family Suidae, esp. a domesticated kind, *Sus scrofa*. **b** *US* a young pig; a piglet. **c** (often in *comb.*) any similar animal (*guinea-pig*). **2** the flesh of esp. a young or sucking pig as food (*roast pig*). **3** *colloq.* **a** a greedy, dirty, obstinate, sulky, or annoying person. **b** an unpleasant, awkward, or difficult thing, task, etc. **4** an oblong mass of metal (esp. iron or lead) from a smelting-furnace. **5** *sl. derog.* a policeman. —*v.* (**pigged, pigging**) **1** *tr.* (also *absol.*) (of a sow) bring forth (piglets). **2** *tr. colloq.* eat (food) greedily. □ **buy a pig in a poke** buy, accept, etc. something without knowing its value or esp. seeing it. **in pig** (of a sow) pregnant. **make a pig of oneself** overeat. **make a pig's ear of** *colloq.* make a mess of; bungle. **pig in the middle** a person who is placed in an awkward situation between two others (after a ball game for three with one in the middle). **pig-iron** crude iron from a smelting-furnace. **pig it** live in a disorderly, untidy, or filthy fashion. **pig-meat** *Brit.* pork, ham, or bacon. **pig out** (often foll. by *on*) esp. *US sl.* eat gluttonously. □ **piggish** *adj.* **piggishly** *adv.* **piggishness** *n.* **piglet** *n.* **piglike** *adj.* **pigling** *n.* [ME *pigge* f. OE *pigga* (unrecorded)]

pigeon[1] /ˈpɪdʒɪn, -dʒ(ə)n/ *n.* **1** any of several large usu. grey and white birds of the family Columbidae, esp. *Columba livia*, often domesticated and bred and trained to carry messages etc.; a dove. **2** a person easily swindled; a simpleton. □ **pigeon-breast** (or **-chest**) a deformed human chest with a projecting breastbone. **pigeon-fancier** a person who keeps and breeds fancy pigeons. **pigeon-hole** *n.* **1** each of a set of compartments in a cabinet or on a wall for papers, letters, etc. **2** a small recess for a pigeon to nest in. —*v.tr.* **1** deposit (a document) in a pigeon-hole. **2** put (a matter) aside for future consideration or to forget it. **3** assign (a person or thing) to a preconceived category. **pigeon-toed** (of a person) having the toes turned inwards. □ **pigeonry** *n.* (*pl.* **-ies**). [ME f. OF *pijon* f. LL *pipio -onis* (imit.)]

pigeon[2] /ˈpɪdʒɪn, -dʒ(ə)n/ *n.* **1** = PIDGIN. **2** *colloq.* a particular concern, job, or business (*that's not my pigeon*).

piggery /ˈpɪgərɪ/ *n.* (*pl.* **-ies**) **1** a pig-breeding farm etc. **2** = PIGSTY. **3** piggishness.

piggy /ˈpɪgɪ/ *n.* & *adj.* (also **piggie**) *colloq.* **1** a little pig. **2** a child's word for a pig. **b** a child's word for a toe. —*adj.* (**piggier**, **piggiest**) **1** like a pig. **2** (of features etc.) like those of a pig (*little piggy eyes*). □ **piggy bank** a pig-shaped money box. **piggy in the middle** = *pig in the middle*.

piggyback /ˈpɪgɪˌbæk/ *n.* & *adv.* (also **pickaback** /ˈpɪkəˌbæk/) —*n.* a ride on the back and shoulders of another person. —*adv.* **1** on the back and shoulders of another person. **2** on the back or top of a larger object. [16th c.: orig. unkn.]

pigheaded /pɪgˈhedɪd/ *adj.* obstinate. □ **pigheadedly** *adv.* **pigheadedness** *n.*

pigment /ˈpɪgmənt/ *n.* & *v.* —*n.* **1** colouring-matter used as paint or dye, usu. as an insoluble suspension. **2** the natural colouring-matter of animal or plant tissue, e.g. chlorophyll, haemoglobin. —*v.tr.* colour with or as if with pigment. □ **pigmental** /-ˈment(ə)l/ *adj.* **pigmentary** *adj.* [ME f. L *pigmentum* f. *pingere* paint]

pigmentation /ˌpɪgmənˈteɪʃ(ə)n/ *n.* **1** the natural colouring of plants, animals, etc. **2** the excessive colouring of tissue by the deposition of pigment.

pigmy var. of PYGMY.

pigpen /ˈpɪgpen/ *n.* *US* = PIGSTY.

pigskin /ˈpɪgskɪn/ *n.* **1** the hide of a pig. **2** leather made from this. **3** *US* a football.

pigsticking /ˈpɪgˌstɪkɪŋ/ *n.* **1** the hunting of wild boar with a spear on horseback. **2** the butchering of pigs.

pigsty /ˈpɪgstaɪ/ *n.* (*pl.* **-ies**) **1** a pen or enclosure for a pig or pigs. **2** a filthy house, room, etc.

pigswill /ˈpɪgswɪl/ *n.* kitchen refuse and scraps fed to pigs.

pigtail /ˈpɪgteɪl/ *n.* a plait of hair hanging from the back of the head, or either of a pair at the sides. □ **pigtailed** *adj.*

pike[1] *n.* (*pl.* same) **1** a large voracious freshwater fish, *Esox lucius*, with a long narrow snout and sharp teeth. **2** any other fish of the family Esocidae. [ME, = PIKE[2] (because of its pointed jaw)]

pike[2] *n.* **1** *hist.* an infantry weapon with a pointed steel or iron head on a long wooden shaft. **2** *N.Engl.* the peaked top of a hill, esp. in names of hills in the Lake District. [OE *pīc* point, prick: sense 2 perh. f. ON]

pike[3] *n.* **1** a toll-gate; a toll. **2** a turnpike road. [abbr. of TURNPIKE]

pike[4] *n.* a jackknife position in diving or gymnastics. [20th c.: orig. unkn.]

pikelet /ˈpaɪklɪt/ *n.* *N.Engl.* a thin kind of crumpet. [Welsh (*bara*) *pyglyd* pitchy (bread)]

pikestaff /ˈpaɪkstɑːf/ *n.* **1** the wooden shaft of a pike. **2** a walking-stick with a metal point. □ **plain as a pikestaff** quite plain or obvious (orig. *packstaff*, a smooth staff used by a pedlar).

pilaster /pɪˈlæstə(r)/ *n.* a rectangular column, esp. one projecting from a wall. □ **pilastered** *adj.* [F *pilastre* f. It. *pilastro* f. med.L *pilastrum* f. L *pila* pillar]

pilau /pɪˈlaʊ/ *n.* (also **pilaff** /pɪˈlæf/, **pilaw** /pɪˈlɔː/) a Middle Eastern or Indian dish of spiced rice or wheat with meat, fish, vegetables, etc. [Turk. *pilâv*]

pilchard /ˈpɪltʃəd/ *n.* a small marine fish, *Sardinia pilchardus* of the herring family (see SARDINE). [16th-c. *pilcher* etc.: orig. unkn.]

pile[1] *n.* & *v.* —*n.* **1** a heap of things laid or gathered upon one another (*a pile of leaves*). **2 a** a large imposing building (*a stately pile*). **b** a large group of tall buildings. **3** *colloq.* **a** a large quantity. **b** a large amount of money; a fortune (*made his pile*). **4 a** a series of plates of dissimilar metals laid one on another alternately to produce an electric current. **b** = *atomic pile*. **5** a funeral pyre. —*v.* **1** *tr.* **a** (often foll. by *up*, *on*) heap up (*piled the plates on the table*). **b** (foll. by *with*) load (*piled the bed with coats*). **2** *intr.* (usu. foll. by *in*, *into*, *on*, *out of*, etc.) crowd hurriedly or tightly (*all piled into the car; piled out of the restaurant*). □ **pile it on** *colloq.* exaggerate. **pile on the agony** *colloq.* exaggerate for effect or to gain sympathy etc. **pile up 1** accumulate; heap up. **2** *colloq.* run (a ship) aground or cause (a vehicle etc.) to crash. **pile-up** *n.* *colloq.* a multiple crash of road vehicles. [ME f. OF f. L *pila* pillar, pier, mole]

pile[2] *n.* & *v.* —*n.* **1** a heavy beam driven vertically into the bed of a river, soft ground, etc., to support the foundations of a superstructure. **2** a pointed stake or post. —*v.tr.* **1** provide with piles. **2** drive (piles) into the ground etc. □ **pile-driver** a machine for driving piles into the ground. [OE *pīl* f. L *pilum* javelin]

pile[3] *n.* **1** the soft projecting surface on velvet, plush, etc., or esp. on a carpet; nap. **2** soft hair or down, or wool of a sheep. [ME prob. f. AF *pyle*, *peile*, OF *poil* f. L *pilus* hair]

piles /paɪlz/ *n.pl.* *colloq.* haemorrhoids. [ME prob. f. L *pila* ball, f. the globular form of external piles]

pilfer /ˈpɪlfə(r)/ *v.tr.* (also *absol.*) steal (objects) esp. in small quantities. □ **pilferage** /-rɪdʒ/ *n.* **pilferer** *n.* [ME f. AF & OF *pelfrer* pillage, of unkn. orig.: assoc. with archaic *pill* plunder: PELF]

pilgrim /ˈpɪlgrɪm/ *n.* **1** a person who journeys to a sacred place for religious reasons. **2** a traveller. □ **Pilgrim Fathers** English Puritans who founded the colony of Plymouth, Massachusetts, in 1620. □ **pilgrimize** *v.intr.* (also **-ise**). [ME *pilegrim* f. Prov. *pelegrin* f. L *peregrinus* stranger: see PEREGRINE]

pilgrimage /ˈpɪlɡrɪmɪdʒ/ *n. & v.* —*n.* 1 a pilgrim's journey (*go on a pilgrimage*). 2 any journey taken for nostalgic or sentimental reasons. —*v.intr.* go on a pilgrimage. [ME f. Prov. *pilgrinatge* (as PILGRIM)]

pill *n.* 1 a a solid medicine formed into a ball or a flat disc for swallowing whole. b (usu. prec. by *the*) *colloq.* a contraceptive pill. 2 an unpleasant or painful necessity; a humiliation (*a bitter pill*; *must swallow the pill*). □ **sugar** (or **sweeten**) **the pill** make an unpleasant necessity acceptable. [MDu., MLG *pille* prob. f. L *pilula* dimin. of *pila* ball]

pillage /ˈpɪlɪdʒ/ *v. & n.* —*v.tr.* (also *absol.*) plunder; sack (a place or a person). —*n.* the act or an instance of pillaging, esp. in war. □ **pillager** *n.* [ME f. OF f. *piller* plunder]

pillar /ˈpɪlə(r)/ *n.* 1 a a usu. slender vertical structure of wood, metal, or esp. stone used as a support for a roof etc. b a similar structure used for ornament. c a post supporting a structure. 2 a person regarded as a mainstay or support (*a pillar of the faith*; *a pillar of strength*). 3 an upright mass of air, water, rock, etc. (*pillar of salt*). □ **from pillar to post** (driven etc.) from one place to another; to and fro. **pillar-box** *Brit.* a public postbox shaped like a pillar. **pillar-box red** a bright red colour, as of pillar-boxes. □ **pillared** *adj.* **pillaret** *n.* [ME & AF *piler*, OF *pilier* ult. f. L *pila* pillar]

pillbox /ˈpɪlbɒks/ *n.* 1 a small shallow cylindrical box for holding pills. 2 a hat of a similar shape. 3 *Mil.* a small partly underground enclosed concrete fort used as an outpost.

pillion /ˈpɪljən/ *n.* seating for a passenger behind a motor cyclist. □ **ride pillion** travel seated behind a motor cyclist etc. [Gael. *pillean*, *pillin* dimin. of *pell* cushion f. L *pellis* skin]

pillock /ˈpɪlək/ *n. Brit. sl.* a stupid person; a fool. [16th c., = penis (var. of *pillicock*): 20th c. in sense defined]

pillory /ˈpɪlərɪ/ *n. & v.* —*n.* (*pl.* **-ies**) *hist.* a wooden framework with holes for the head and hands, enabling the public to assault or ridicule a person so imprisoned. —*v.tr.* (**-ies**, **-ied**) expose (a person) to ridicule or public contempt. [ME f. AL *pillorium* f. OF *pilori* etc.: prob. f. Prov. *espilori* of uncert. orig.]

pillow /ˈpɪləʊ/ *n. & v.* —*n.* 1 a a usu. oblong support for the head, esp. in bed, with a cloth cover stuffed with feathers, flock, foam rubber, etc. b any pillow-shaped block or support. 2 = *lace-pillow*. —*v.tr.* 1 rest (the head etc.) on or as if on a pillow (*pillowed his head on his arms*). 2 serve as a pillow for (*moss pillowed her head*). **pillow-fight** a mock fight with pillows, esp. by children. **pillow-lace** lace made on a lace-pillow. **pillow talk** romantic or intimate conversation in bed. □ **pillowy** *adj.* [OE *pyle*, *pylu*, ult. f. L *pulvinus* cushion]

pillowcase /ˈpɪləʊkeɪs/ *n.* a washable cotton etc. cover for a pillow.

pillowslip /ˈpɪləʊslɪp/ *n.* = PILLOWCASE.

pilot /ˈpaɪlət/ *n. & v.* —*n.* 1 a person who operates the flying controls of an aircraft. 2 a person qualified to take charge of a ship entering or leaving harbour. 3 (usu. *attrib.*) an experimental undertaking or test, esp. in advance of a larger one (*a pilot project*). 4 a guide; a leader. 5 *archaic* a steersman. —*v.tr.* (**piloted**, **piloting**) 1 act as a pilot on (a ship) or of (an aircraft). 2 conduct, lead, or initiate as a pilot (*piloted the new scheme*). □ **pilot-house** = *wheel-house*. **pilot-light** 1 a small gas burner kept alight to light another. 2 an electric indicator light or control light. **pilot officer** *Brit.* the lowest commissioned rank in the RAF. □ **pilotage** *n.* **pilotless** *adj.* [F *pilote* f. med.L *pilotus*, *pedot(t)a* f. Gk *pēdon* oar]

Pilsner /ˈpɪlznə(r)/, -snə(r)/ *n.* (also **Pilsener**) a lager beer brewed at or like that brewed at *Pilsen* (Plzeň) in Czechoslovakia.

pilule /ˈpɪljuːl/ *n.* (also **pillule**) a small pill. □ **pilular** *adj.* **pilulous** *adj.* [F f. L *pilula*: see PILL]

pimento /pɪˈmentəʊ/ *n.* (*pl.* **-os**) 1 a small tropical tree, *Pimenta dioica*, native to Jamaica. 2 the unripe dried berries of this, usu. crushed for culinary use. 3 = PIMIENTO. [Sp. *pimiento* (as PIMIENTO)]

pimiento /ˌpɪmɪˈentəʊ, pɪmˈjentəʊ/ *n.* (*pl.* **-os**) = *sweet pepper* (see PEPPER). [Sp. f. L *pigmentum* PIGMENT, in med.L = spice]

pimp *n. & v.* —*n.* a man who lives off the earnings of a prostitute or a brothel; a pander; a ponce. —*v.intr.* act as a pimp. [17th c.: orig. unkn.]

pimpernel /ˈpɪmpənel/ *n.* any plant of the genus *Anagallis*, esp. = *scarlet pimpernel*. [ME f. OF *pimpernelle*, *piprenelle* ult. f. L *piper* PEPPER]

pimple /ˈpɪmp(ə)l/ *n.* 1 a small hard inflamed spot on the skin. 2 anything resembling a pimple, esp. in relative size. □ **pimpled** *adj.* **pimply** *adj.* [ME nasalized f. OE *piplian* break out in pustules]

PIN *n.* personal identification number (as issued by a bank etc. to validate electronic transactions). [abbr.]

pin *n. & v.* —*n.* 1 a a small thin pointed piece of esp. steel wire with a round or flattened head used (esp. in sewing) for holding things in place, attaching one thing to another, etc. b any of several types of pin (*drawing-pin*; *safety pin*; *hairpin*). c a small brooch (*diamond pin*). d a badge fastened with a pin. 2 a peg of wood or metal for various purposes, e.g. a wooden skittle in bowling. 3 something of small value (*don't care a pin*; *for two pins I'd resign*). 4 (in *pl.*) *colloq.* legs (*quick on his pins*). 5 *Med.* a steel rod used to join the ends of fractured bones while they heal. 6 *Golf* a stick with a flag placed in a hole to mark its position. 7 a half-firkin cask for beer. —*v.tr.* (**pinned**, **pinning**) 1 a (often foll. by *to*, *up*, *together*) fasten with a pin or pins (*pinned up the hem*; *pinned the papers together*). b transfix with a pin, lance, etc. 2 (usu. foll. by *on*) fix (blame, responsibility, etc.) on a person etc. (*pinned the blame on his friend*). 3 (often foll. by *against*, *on*, etc.) seize and hold fast. □ **on pins and needles** in an agitated state of suspense. **pin down 1** (often foll. by *to*) bind (a person etc.) to a promise, arrangement, etc. 2 force (a person) to declare his or her intentions. 3 restrict the actions or movement of (an enemy etc.). 4 specify (a thing) precisely (*could not pin down his unease to a particular cause*). 5 hold (a person etc.) down by force. **pin one's faith** (or **hopes** etc.) **on** rely implicitly on. **pin-money 1** *hist.* an allowance to a woman for dress etc. from her husband. 2 a very small sum of money, esp. for spending on inessentials (*only works for pin-money*). **pins and needles** a tingling sensation in a limb recovering from numbness. **pin-table** a table used in playing pinball. **pin-tuck** a very narrow ornamental tuck. **pin-up 1** a photograph of a popular or sexually attractive person, designed to be hung on the wall. **2** a person shown in such a photograph. **pin-wheel** a small Catherine wheel. **split pin** a metal cotter pin passed through a hole and held in place by its gaping split end. [OE *pinn* f. L *pinna* point etc., assoc. with *penna* PEN¹]

pina colada /ˌpiːnə kəˈlɑːdə/ *n.* a drink made from pineapple juice, rum, and coconut. [Sp., lit. 'strained pineapple']

pinafore /ˈpɪnəfɔː(r)/ *n.* esp. *Brit.* **1 a** an apron, esp. with a bib. **b** a woman's sleeveless wraparound washable covering for the clothes, tied at the back. **2** (in full **pinafore dress**) a collarless sleeveless dress worn over a blouse or jumper. [PIN + AFORE (because orig. pinned on the front of a dress)]

pinball /ˈpɪnbɔːl/ *n.* a game in which small metal balls are shot across a board and score points by striking pins with lights etc.

pince-nez /ˈpænsneɪ, pæsˈneɪ/ *n.* (*pl.* same) a pair of eyeglasses with a nose-clip instead of earpieces. [F, lit. = pinch-nose]

pincers /ˈpɪnsəz/ *n.pl.* **1** (also **pair of pincers**) a gripping-tool resembling scissors but with blunt usu. concave jaws to hold a nail etc. for extraction. **2** the front claws of lobsters and some other crustaceans. □ **pincer movement** *Mil.* a movement by two wings of an army converging on the enemy. [ME *pinsers, pinsours* f. AF f. OF *pincier* PINCH]

pinch *v. & n.* —*v.* **1** *tr.* **a** grip (esp. the skin of part of the body or of another person) tightly, esp. between finger and thumb (*pinched my finger in the door; stop pinching me*). **b** (often *absol.*) (of a shoe, garment, etc.) constrict (the flesh) painfully. **2** *tr.* (of cold, hunger, etc.) grip (a person) painfully (*she was pinched with cold*). **3** *tr. sl.* **a** steal; take without permission. **b** arrest (a person) (*pinched him for loitering*). **4** (as **pinched** *adj.*) (of the features) drawn, as with cold, hunger, worry, etc. **5 a** *tr.* (usu. foll. by *in, of, for,* etc.) stint (a person). **b** *intr.* be niggardly with money, food, etc. **6** *tr.* (usu. foll. by *out, back, down*) *Hort.* remove (leaves, buds, etc.) to encourage bushy growth. —*n.* **1** the act or an instance of pinching etc. the flesh. **2** an amount that can be taken up with fingers and thumb (*a pinch of snuff*). **3** the stress or pain caused by poverty, cold, hunger, etc. **4** *sl.* **a** an arrest. **b** a theft. □ **at** (or **in**) **a pinch** in an emergency; if necessary. **feel the pinch** experience the effects of poverty. **pinch-hitter** *US* **1** a baseball player who bats instead of another in an emergency. **2** a person acting as a substitute. [ME f. AF & ONF *pinchier* (unrecorded), OF *pincier,* ult. f. L *pungere* punct-prick]

pinchbeck /ˈpɪntʃbek/ *n. & adj.* —*n.* an alloy of copper and zinc resembling gold and used in cheap jewellery etc. —*adj.* **1** counterfeit; sham. **2** cheap; tawdry. [C. *Pinchbeck,* Engl. watchmaker d. 1732]

pinchpenny /ˈpɪntʃˌpeni/ *n.* (*pl.* -**ies**) (also *attrib.*) a miserly person.

pincushion /ˈpɪnˌkʊʃ(ə)n/ *n.* a small cushion for holding pins.

pine¹ *n.* **1** any evergreen tree of the genus *Pinus* native to northern temperate regions, with needle-shaped leaves growing in clusters. **2** the soft timber of this, often used to make furniture. **3** (*attrib.*) made of pine. □ **pine cone** the cone-shaped fruit of the pine tree. **pine marten** a weasel-like mammal, *Martes martes,* native to Europe and America, with a dark brown coat and white throat and stomach. **pine nut** the edible seed of various pine trees. □ **pinery** *n.* (*pl.* -**ies**). [ME f. OE *pīn* & OF *pin* f. L *pinus*]

pine² *v.intr.* **1** (often foll. by *away*) decline or waste away, esp. through grief, disease, etc. **2** (usu. foll. by *for, after,* or *to* + infin.) long eagerly; yearn. [OE *pīnian,* rel. to obs. E *pine* punishment, f. Gmc f. med.L *pena,* L *poena*]

pineal /ˈpɪnɪəl, ˈpaɪ-/ *adj.* shaped like a pine cone. □ **pineal body** (or **gland**) a pea-sized conical mass of tissue behind the third ventricle of the brain, secreting a hormone-like substance in some mammals. [F *pinéal* f. L *pinea* pine cone: see PINE¹]

pineapple /ˈpaɪnˌæp(ə)l/ *n.* **1** a tropical plant, *Ananas comosus,* with a spiral of sword-shaped leaves and a thick stem bearing a large fruit developed from many flowers. **2** the fruit of this, consisting of yellow flesh surrounded by a tough segmented skin and topped with a tuft of stiff leaves. [PINE¹, from the fruit's resemblance to a pine cone]

ping *n. & v.* —*n.* a single short high ringing sound. —*v.intr.* make a ping. [imit.]

pinger /ˈpɪŋə(r)/ *n.* **1** a device that transmits pings at short intervals for purposes of detection or measurement etc. **2** a device to ring a bell.

ping-pong /ˈpɪŋpɒŋ/ *n.* = table tennis. [imit. f. the sound of a bat striking a ball]

pinhead /ˈpɪnhed/ *n.* **1** the flattened head of a pin. **2** a very small thing. **3** *colloq.* a stupid or foolish person.

pinheaded /pɪnˈhedɪd/ *adj. colloq.* stupid, foolish. □ **pinheadedness** *n.*

pinhole /ˈpɪnhəʊl/ *n.* **1** a hole made by a pin. **2** a hole into which a peg fits. □ **pinhole camera** a camera with a pinhole aperture and no lens.

pinion¹ /ˈpɪnjən/ *n. & v.* —*n.* **1** the outer part of a bird's wing, usu. including the flight feathers. **2** *poet.* a wing; a flight-feather. —*v.tr.* **1** cut off the pinion of (a wing or bird) to prevent flight. **2 a** bind the arms of (a person). **b** (often foll. by *to*) bind (the arms, a person, etc.) esp. to a thing. [ME f. OF *pignon* ult. f. L *pinna:* see PIN]

pinion² /ˈpɪnjən/ *n.* **1** a small cog-wheel engaging with a larger one. **2** a cogged spindle engaging with a wheel. [F *pignon* alt. f. obs. *pignol* f. L *pinea* pine-cone (as PINE¹)]

pink¹ *n. & adj.* —*n.* **1** a pale red colour (*decorated in pink*). **2 a** any cultivated plant of the genus *Dianthus,* with sweet-smelling white, pink, crimson, etc. flowers. **b** the flower of this plant. **3** (prec. by *the*) the most perfect condition etc. (*the pink of elegance*). **4** (also **hunting pink**) a fox-hunter's red coat. —*adj.* **1** (often in *comb.*) of a pale red colour of any of various shades (*rose-pink; salmon-pink*). **2** esp. *derog.* tending to socialism. □ **in the pink** *colloq.* in very good health. **pink-collar** (usu. *attrib.*) (of a profession etc.) traditionally associated with women. □ **pinkish** *adj.* **pinkly** *adv.* **pinkness** *n.* **pinky** *adj.* [perh. f. dial. *pink-eyed* having small eyes]

pink² *v.tr.* **1** pierce slightly with a sword etc. **2** cut a scalloped or zigzag edge on. □ **pinking shears** (or **scissors**) a dressmaker's serrated shears for cutting a zigzag edge. [ME, perh. f. LG or Du.: cf. LG *pinken* strike, peck]

pink³ *v.intr.* (of a vehicle engine) emit a series of high-pitched explosive sounds caused by faulty combustion. [imit.]

pinkie /ˈpɪŋkɪ/ *n.* esp. *US & Sc.* the little finger. [cf. dial. *pink* small, half-shut (eye)]

pinnace /ˈpɪnɪs/ *n. Naut.* a ship's small boat. [F *pinnace, pinasse* ult. f. L *pinus* PINE¹]

pinnacle /ˈpɪnək(ə)l/ *n. & v.* —*n.* **1** the culmination or climax (of endeavour, success, etc.). **2** a natural peak. **3** a small ornamental turret usu. ending in a pyramid or cone, crowning a buttress, roof, etc. —*v.tr.* **1** set on or as if on a pinnacle. **2** form the pinnacle of. **3** provide with pinnacles. [ME *pinacle* f. OF *pin(n)acle* f. LL *pinnaculum* f. *pinna* wing, point (as PIN, -CULE)]

pinnate /ˈpɪneɪt/ *adj.* **1** (of a compound leaf) having leaflets arranged on either side of the stem, usu. in pairs opposite each other. **2** having branches, tentacles, etc., on each side of an axis. □ **pinnated** *adj.* **pinnately** *adv.* **pinnation** /-ˈneɪʃ(ə)n/ *n.* [L *pinnatus* feathered f. *penna* feather]

pinny /ˈpɪnɪ/ *n.* (pl. **-ies**) *colloq.* a pinafore. [abbr.]

pinochle /ˈpiːˌnʊk(ə)l/ *n. US* **1** a card-game with a double pack of 48 cards (nine to ace only). **2** the combination of queen of spades and jack of diamonds in this game. [19th c.: orig. unkn.]

piñon /pɪˈnjəʊn/ *n.* **1** a pine, *Pinus cembra*, bearing edible seeds. **2** the seed of this, a type of pine nut. [Sp. f. L *pinea* pine cone]

pinpoint /ˈpɪnpɔɪnt/ *n. & v.* —*n.* **1** the point of a pin. **2** something very small or sharp. **3** (*attrib.*) **a** very small. **b** precise, accurate. —*v.tr.* locate with precision (*pinpointed the target*).

pinprick /ˈpɪnprɪk/ *n.* **1** a prick caused by a pin. **2** a trifling irritation.

pinstripe /ˈpɪnstraɪp/ *n.* **1** a very narrow stripe in (esp. worsted or serge) cloth. **2** a fabric or garment with this.

pint /paɪnt/ *n.* **1** a measure of capacity for liquids etc., one-eighth of a gallon or 20 fluid oz. (0.568 litre). **2** *Brit.* **a** *colloq.* a pint of beer. **b** a pint of a liquid, esp. milk. **3** *Brit.* a measure of shellfish, being the amount containable in a pint mug (*bought a pint of whelks*). □ **pint-pot** a pot holding one pint, esp. of beer. **pint-sized** *colloq.* very small, esp. of a person. [ME f. OF *pinte*, of unkn. orig.]

pinta /ˈpaɪntə/ *n. Brit. colloq.* a pint of milk. [corrupt. of *pint of*]

pintail /ˈpɪnteɪl/ *n.* a duck, esp. *Anas acuta*, or grouse with a pointed tail.

pintle /ˈpɪnt(ə)l/ *n.* a pin or bolt, esp. one on which some other part turns. [OE *pintel* penis, of unkn. orig.: cf. OFris. etc. *pint*]

pinto /ˈpɪntəʊ, ˈpiː-/ *adj. & n. US* —*adj.* piebald. —*n.* (pl. **-os**) a piebald horse. [Sp., = mottled, ult. f. L *pictus* past part. of *pingere* paint]

piny /ˈpaɪnɪ/ *adj.* of, like, or full of pines.

Pinyin /pɪnˈjɪn/ *n.* a system of romanized spelling for transliterating Chinese. [Chin. *pīn-yīn*, lit. 'spell sound']

pion /ˈpaɪɒn/ *n. Physics* a meson having a mass approximately 270 times that of an electron. □

pionic /paɪˈɒnɪk/ *adj.* [PI¹ (the letter used as a symbol for the particle) + -ON]

pioneer /ˌpaɪəˈnɪə(r)/ *n. & v.* —*n.* **1** an initiator of a new enterprise, an inventor, etc. **2** an explorer or settler; a colonist. **3** *Mil.* a member of an infantry group preparing roads, terrain, etc. for the main body of troops. —*v.* **1** *tr.* initiate or originate (an enterprise etc.). **2** *intr.* act or prepare the way as a pioneer. [F *pionnier* foot-soldier, pioneer, OF *paonier, peon(n)ier* (as PEON)]

pious /ˈpaɪəs/ *adj.* **1** devout; religious. **2** hypocritically virtuous; sanctimonious. **3** dutiful. □ **pious fraud** a deception intended to benefit those deceived, esp. religiously. □ **piously** *adv.* **piousness** *n.* [L *pius* dutiful, pious]

pip¹ *n. & v.* —*n.* the seed of an apple, pear, orange, grape, etc. —*v.tr.* (**pipped**, **pipping**) remove the pips from (fruit etc.). □ **pipless** *adj.* [abbr. of PIPPIN]

pip² *n. Brit.* a short high-pitched sound, usu. mechanically produced, esp. as a time signal. [imit.]

pip³ *n.* **1** any of the spots on a playing-card, dice, or domino. **2** *Brit.* a star (1–3 according to rank) on the shoulder of an army officer's uniform. **3** an image of an object on a radar screen. [16th c. *peep*, of unkn. orig.]

pip⁴ *n.* **1** a disease of poultry etc. causing thick mucus in the throat and white scale on the tongue. **2** *colloq.* a fit of disgust or bad temper (esp. *give one the pip*). [ME f. MDu. *pippe*, MLG *pip* prob. ult. f. corrupt. of L *pituita* slime]

pip⁵ *v.tr.* (**pipped**, **pipping**) *Brit. colloq.* **1** hit with a shot. **2** defeat. **3** blackball. □ **pip at the post** defeat at the last moment. **pip out** die. [PIP² or PIP¹]

pipe *n. & v.* —*n.* **1** a tube of metal, plastic, wood, etc. used to convey water, gas, etc. **2** (also **tobacco-pipe**) **a** a narrow wooden or clay etc. tube with a bowl at one end containing burning tobacco, the smoke from which is drawn into the mouth. **b** the quantity of tobacco held by this. **3** *Mus.* **a** a wind instrument consisting of a single tube. **b** any of the tubes by which sound is produced in an organ. **c** (in *pl.*) = BAGPIPES. **d** (in *pl.*) a set of pipes joined together, e.g. pan-pipes. **4** a tubal organ, vessel, etc. in an animal's body. **5** a high note or song, esp. of a bird. **6** a boatswain's whistle. **b** the sounding of this. **7** a cask for wine, esp. as a measure of two hogsheads, usu. equivalent to 105 gallons (about 477 litres). —*v.tr.* **1** (also *absol.*) play (a tune etc.) on a pipe or pipes. **2** **a** convey (oil, water, gas, etc.) by pipes. **b** provide with pipes. **3** transmit (music, a radio programme, etc.) by wire or cable. **4** (usu. foll. by *up, on, to,* etc.) *Naut.* **a** summon (a crew) to a meal, work, etc. **b** signal the arrival of (an officer etc.) on board. **5** utter in a shrill voice; whistle. **6** **a** arrange (icing, cream, etc.) in decorative lines or twists on a cake etc. **b** ornament (a cake etc.) with piping. **7** trim (a dress etc.) with piping. **8** lead or bring (a person etc.) by the sound of a pipe. □ **pipe-cleaner** a piece of flexible covered wire for cleaning a tobacco-pipe. **pipe down** *colloq.* be quiet or less insistent. **pipe major** an NCO commanding regimental pipers. **pipe-organ** *Mus.* an organ using pipes instead of or as well as reeds. **pipe-rack** a rack for holding tobacco-pipes. **pipe-stem** the shaft of a tobacco-pipe. **pipe up** begin to play, sing, speak, etc. **put that in your pipe and smoke it** *colloq.* a challenge to another to accept something frank or unwelcome. □ **pipeful** *n.* (*pl.* **-fuls**). **pipeless** *adj.* **pipy** *adj.* [OE *pipe*, *pīpian* & OF *piper* f. Gmc ult. f. L *pipare* peep, chirp]

pipeclay /'paɪpkleɪ/ *n.* & *v.* **1** a fine white clay used for tobacco-pipes, whitening leather, etc. —*v.tr.* **1** whiten (leather etc.) with this. **2** put in order.

pipedream /'paɪpdriːm/ *n.* an unattainable or fanciful hope or scheme. [orig. as experienced when smoking an opium pipe]

pipeline /'paɪplaɪn/ *n.* **1** a long, usu. underground, pipe for conveying esp. oil. **2** a channel supplying goods, information, etc. □ **in the pipeline** awaiting completion or processing.

pip emma /pɪp 'emə/ *adv.* & *n. Brit. colloq.* = P.M. [formerly signallers' names for letters PM]

piper /'paɪpə(r)/ *n.* **1** a bagpipe-player. **2** a person who plays a pipe, esp. an itinerant musician. [OE *pipere* (as PIPE)]

pipette /pɪ'pet/ *n.* & *v.* —*n.* a slender tube for transferring or measuring small quantities of liquids esp. in chemistry. —*v.tr.* transfer or measure (a liquid) using a pipette. [F, dimin. of *pipe* PIPE]

piping /'paɪpɪŋ/ *n.* & *adj.* —*n.* **1** the act or an instance of piping, esp. whistling or singing. **2** a thin pipelike fold used to edge hems or frills on clothing, seams on upholstery, etc. **3** ornamental lines of icing, cream, potato, etc. on a cake or other dish. **4** lengths of pipe, or a system of pipes, esp. in domestic use. —*adj.* (of a noise) high; whistling. □ **piping hot** very or suitably hot (esp. as required of food, water, etc.).

pipistrelle /ˌpɪpɪ'strel/ *n.* any bat of the genus *Pipistrellus*, native to temperate regions and feeding on insects. [F f. It. *pipistrello*, *vip-*, f. L *vespertilio* bat f. *vesper* evening]

pipit /'pɪpɪt/ *n.* any of various birds of the family Motacillidae, esp. of the genus *Anthus*, found worldwide and having brown plumage often heavily streaked with a lighter colour. [prob. imit.]

pippin /'pɪpɪn/ *n.* **1 a** an apple grown from seed. **b** a red and yellow dessert apple. **2** *colloq.* an excellent person or thing; a beauty. [ME f. OF *pepin*, of unkn. orig.]

pipsqueak /'pɪpskwiːk/ *n. colloq.* an insignificant or contemptible person or thing. [imit.]

piquant /'piːkənt, -kɑːnt/ *adj.* **1** agreeably pungent, sharp, or appetizing. **2** pleasantly stimulating, or disquieting, to the mind. □ **piquancy** *n.* **piquantly** *adv.* [F, pres. part. of *piquer* (as PIQUE)]

pique /piːk/ *v.* & *n.* —*v.tr.* (**piques, piqued, piquing**) **1** wound the pride of, irritate. **2** arouse (curiosity, interest, etc.). **3** (*refl.*; usu. foll. by *on*) pride or congratulate oneself. —*n.* ill-feeling; enmity; resentment (*in a fit of pique*). [F *piquer* prick, irritate, f. Rmc]

piqué /'piːkeɪ/ *n.* a stiff ribbed cotton or other fabric. [F, past part. of *piquer*: see PIQUE]

piquet[1] /pɪ'ket/ *n.* a game for two players with a pack of 32 cards (seven to ace only). [F, of unkn. orig.]

piquet[2] var. of PICKET.

piracy /'paɪrəsɪ/ *n.* (*pl.* **-ies**) **1** the practice or an act of robbery of ships at sea. **2** a similar practice or act in other forms, esp. hijacking. **3** the infringement of copyright. [med.L *piratia* f. Gk *pirateia* (as PIRATE)]

piranha /pɪ'rɑːnə, -'rɑːnjə/ *n.* (also **piraya** /-'rɑːjə/) any of various freshwater predatory fish of the genera *Pygocentrus*, *Rooseveltiella*, or *Serrasalmus*, native to S. America and having sharp cutting teeth. [Port. f. Tupi, var. of *piraya* scissors]

pirate /'paɪrərət/ *n.* & *v.* —*n.* **1 a** a person who commits piracy. **b** a ship used by pirates. **2** a person who infringes another's copyright or other business rights; a plagiarist. **3** (often *attrib.*) a person, organization, etc., that broadcasts without official authorization (*pirate radio station*). —*v.tr.* **1** appropriate or reproduce (the work or ideas etc. of another) without permission, for one's own benefit. **2** plunder. □ **piratic** /-'rætɪk/ *adj.* **piratical** /-'rætɪk(ə)l/ *adj.* **piratically** /-'rætɪkəlɪ/ *adv.* [ME f. L *pirata* f. Gk *peiratēs* f. *peiraō* attempt, assault]

piraya var. of PIRANHA.

pirouette /ˌpɪrʊ'et/ *n.* & *v.* —*n.* a dancer's spin on one foot or the point of the toe. —*v.intr.* perform a pirouette. [F, = spinning-top]

piscatorial /ˌpɪskə'tɔːrɪəl/ *adj.* = PISCATORY 1. □ **piscatorially** *adv.*

piscatory /'pɪskətərɪ/ *adj.* **1** of or concerning fishermen or fishing. **2** addicted to fishing. [L *piscatorius* f. *piscator* fisherman f. *piscis* fish]

Pisces /'paɪsiːz, 'pɪskiːz/ *n.* (*pl.* same) **1** a constellation, traditionally regarded as contained in the figure of fishes. **2 a** the twelfth sign of the zodiac (the Fishes). **b** a person born when the sun is in this sign. □ **Piscean** /'paɪsɪən/ *n.* & *adj.* [ME f. L, pl. of *piscis* fish]

pisciculture /'pɪsɪˌkʌltʃə(r)/ *n.* the artificial rearing of fish. □ **piscicultural** /-'kʌltʃər(ə)l/ *adj.* **pisciculturist** /-'kʌltʃərɪst/ *n.* [L *piscis* fish, after *agriculture* etc.]

piscina /pɪ'siːnə, -'saɪnə/ *n.* (*pl.* **piscinae** /-niː/ or **piscinas**) **1** a stone basin near the altar in RC and pre-Reformation churches for draining water used in the Mass. **2** a fish-pond. [L f. *piscis* fish]

piscine /'pɪsaɪn/ *adj.* of or concerning fish. [L *piscis* fish]

piss *v.* & *n. coarse sl.* —*v.* **1** *intr.* urinate. **2** *tr.* **a** discharge (blood etc.) when urinating. **b** wet with urine. **3** *tr.* (as **pissed** *adj.*) *Brit.* drunk. —*n.* **1** urine. **2** an act of urinating. □ **piss about** fool or mess about. **piss artist 1** a drunkard. **2** a person who fools about. **3** a glib person. **piss down** rain heavily. **piss off** *Brit.* **1** go away. **2** (often as **pissed off** *adj.*) annoy; depress. **piss-taker** a person who mocks. **piss-taking** mockery. **piss-up** a drinking spree. **take the piss** (often foll. by *out of*) mock; deride. [ME f. OF *pisser* (imit.)]

pissoir /piː'swɑː(r)/ *n.* a public urinal. [F]

pistachio /pɪ'stɑːʃɪəʊ/ *n.* (*pl.* **-os**) **1** an evergreen tree, *Pistacia vera*, bearing small brownish-green flowers and ovoid reddish fruit. **2** (in full **pistachio nut**) the edible pale-green seed of this. **3** a pale green colour. [It. *pistaccio* and Sp. *pistacho* f. L *pistacium* f. Gk *pistakion* f. Pers. *pistah*]

piste /piːst/ *n.* a ski-run of compacted snow. [F, = racetrack]

pistil /'pɪstɪl/ *n.* the female organs of a flower, comprising the stigma, style, and ovary. □

pistillary *adj.* **pistilliferous** /-'lɪfərəs/ *adj.* **pis-
tilline** /-ˌlaɪn/ *adj.* [F *pistile* or L *pistillum* PESTLE]

pistol /'pɪst(ə)l/ *n. & v.* —*n.* **1** a small hand-held
firearm. **2** anything of a similar shape. —*v.tr.*
(**pistolled, pistolling**; US **pistoled, pistoling**)
shoot with a pistol. □ **hold a pistol to a
person's head** coerce a person by threats.
pistol-grip a handle shaped like a pistol-butt.
pistol-shot 1 the range of a pistol. **2** a shot
fired from a pistol. **pistol-whip (-whipped,
-whipping)** beat with a pistol. [obs. F f. G *Pistole*
f. Czech *pišt'al*]

piston /'pɪst(ə)n/ *n.* **1** a disc or short cylinder
fitting closely within a tube in which it moves
up and down against a liquid or gas, used in an
internal-combustion engine to impart motion,
or in a pump to receive motion. **2** a sliding
valve in a trumpet etc. □ **piston-ring** a ring on
a piston sealing the gap between the piston
and the cylinder wall. **piston-rod** a rod or
crankshaft attached to a piston to drive a wheel
or to impart motion. [F f. It. *pistone* var. of
pestone augment. of *pestello* PESTLE]

pit[1] *n. & v.* —*n.* **1 a** a usu. large deep hole in the
ground. **b** a hole made in digging for industrial
purposes, esp. for coal (*chalk pit; gravel pit*). **c** a
covered hole as a trap for esp. wild animals. **2 a**
an indentation left after smallpox, acne, etc. **b** a
hollow in a plant or animal body or on any
surface. **3** *Brit. Theatr.* **a** = *orchestra pit*. **b** usu.
hist. seating at the back of the stalls. **c** the
people in the pit. **4 a** (**the pit** or **bottomless
pit**) hell. **b** (**the pits**) *sl.* a wretched or the worst
imaginable place, situation, person, etc. **5 a** an
area at the side of a track where racing cars are
serviced and refuelled. **b** a sunken area in a
workshop floor for access to a car's underside.
—*v.* (**pitted, pitting**) **1** *tr.* (usu. foll. by *against*)
a set (one's wits, strength, etc.) in opposition or
rivalry. **b** set (a cock, dog, etc.) to fight, orig. in a
pit, against another. **2** *tr.* (usu. as **pitted** *adj.*)
make pits, esp. scars, in. □ **dig a pit for** try to
ensnare. **pit bull terrier** a small American dog
noted for its ferocity. **pit-head 1** the top of a
mineshaft. **2** the area surrounding this. **pit of
the stomach 1** the floor of the stomach. **2** the
depression below the bottom of the breastbone.
pit pony *hist.* a pony kept underground for
haulage in coal-mines. **pit-prop** a balk of wood
used to support the roof of a coal mine. [OE *pytt*
ult. f. L *puteus* well]

pit[2] *n. & v.* US —*n.* the stone of a fruit. —*v.tr.*
(**pitted, pitting**) remove pits from (fruit). [perh.
Du., rel. to PITH]

pita var. of PITTA.

pit-a-pat /'pɪtəˌpæt/ *adv. & n.* (also **pitter-
patter** /'pɪtəˌpætə(r)/) —*adv.* **1** with a sound like
quick light steps. **2** with a faltering sound (*heart
went pit-a-pat*). —*n.* such a sound. [imit.]

pitch[1] *v. & n.* —*v.* **1** *tr.* (also *absol.*) erect and fix
(a tent, camp, etc.). **2** *tr.* **a** a throw; fling. **b** (in
games) throw (a flat object) towards a mark. **3**
tr. fix or plant (a thing) in a definite position. **4**
tr. express in a particular style or at a particular
level (*pitched his argument at the most basic level*). **5**
intr. (often foll. by *against, into*, etc.) fall heavily,
esp. headlong. **6** *intr.* (of a ship etc.) plunge in a
longitudinal direction. **7** *tr. Mus.* set at a particular pitch. **8** *intr.* (of a roof etc.) slope
downwards. **9** *intr.* (often foll. by *about*) move
with a vigorous jogging motion, as in a train,

carriage, etc. **10** *Cricket* **a** *tr.* cause (a bowled
ball) to strike the ground at a specified point
etc. **b** *intr.* (of a bowled ball) strike the ground.
11 *tr. colloq.* tell (a yarn or a tale). —*n.* **1 a** the
area of play in a field-game. **b** *Cricket* the area
between the creases. **2** height, degree, intensity,
etc. (*the pitch of despair; nerves were strung to a
pitch*). **3 a** the steepness of a slope, esp. of a roof,
stratum, etc. **b** the degree of such a pitch. **4**
Mus. **a** that quality of a sound which is governed
by the rate of vibrations producing it; the degree
of highness or lowness of a tone. **b** = *concert
pitch*. **5** the pitching motion of a ship etc. **6**
Cricket the act or mode of delivery in bowling,
or the spot where the ball bounces. **7** *colloq.* a
salesman's advertising or selling approach. **8**
Brit. a place where a street vendor sells wares,
has a stall, etc. **9** the delivery of a baseball by a
pitcher. □ **pitch-and-toss** a gambling game in
which coins are pitched at a mark and then
tossed. **pitched battle 1** a vigorous argument
etc. **2** *Mil.* a battle planned beforehand and
fought on chosen ground. **pitched roof** a
sloping roof. **pitch in** *colloq.* set to work vigorously. **pitch into** *colloq.* **1** attack forcibly with
blows, words, etc. **2** assail (food, work, etc.)
vigorously. **pitch on** (or **upon**) happen to select.
pitch-pipe *Mus.* a small pipe blown to set the
pitch for singing or tuning. **pitch up** *Cricket*
bowl (a ball) to bounce near the batsman. **pitch
wickets** *Cricket* fix the stumps in the ground
and place the bails. [ME *pic(c)he*, perh. f. OE
picc(e)an (unrecorded: cf. *picung* stigmata)]

pitch[2] *n. & v.* —*n.* **1** a sticky resinous black or
dark-brown substance obtained by distilling tar
or turpentine, semi-liquid when hot, hard when
cold, and used for caulking the seams of ships
etc. **2** any of various bituminous substances
including asphalt. —*v.tr.* cover, coat, or smear
with pitch. □ **pitch-black** (or **-dark**) very or
completely dark. **pitch-pine** any of various
pine-trees, esp. *Pinus rigida* or *P. palustris*, yielding
much resin. [OE *pic* f. Gmc f. L *pix picis*]

pitchblende /'pɪtʃblend/ *n.* a mineral form of
uranium oxide occurring in pitchlike masses
and yielding radium. [G *Pechblende* (as PITCH[2],
BLENDE)]

pitcher[1] /'pɪtʃə(r)/ *n.* a large usu. earthenware
jug with a lip and a handle, for holding liquids.
□ **pitcher-plant** any of various plants, esp. of
the family Nepenthaceae or Sarraceniaceae,
with modified leaves that can hold liquids, trap
insects, etc. □ **pitcherful** *n.* (*pl.* **-fuls**). [ME f. OF
pichier, pechier, f. Frank.]

pitcher[2] /'pɪtʃə(r)/ *n.* **1** a person or thing that
pitches. **2** *Baseball* a player who delivers the ball
to the batter.

pitchfork /'pɪtʃfɔːk/ *n. & v.* —*n.* a long-handled
two-pronged fork for pitching hay etc. —*v.tr.* **1**
throw with or as if with a pitchfork. **2** (usu. foll.
by *into*) thrust (a person) forcibly into a position,
office, etc. [in ME *pickfork*, prob. f. PICK[1] + FORK,
assoc. with PITCH[1]]

pitchy /'pɪtʃɪ/ *adj.* (**pitchier, pitchiest**) of, like,
or dark as pitch.

piteous /'pɪtɪəs/ *adj.* deserving or causing pity;
wretched. □ **piteously** *adv.* **piteousness** *n.* [ME
pito(u)s etc. f. AF *pitous*, OF *pitos* f. Rmc (as PIETY)]

pitfall /'pɪtfɔːl/ *n.* **1** an unsuspected snare,
danger, or drawback. **2** a covered pit for trapping
animals etc.

pith /pɪθ/ n. & v. —n. **1** spongy white tissue lining the rind of an orange, lemon, etc. **2** the essential part; the quintessence (*came to the pith of his argument*). **3** *Bot.* the spongy cellular tissue in the stems and branches of dicotyledonous plants. **4 a** physical strength; vigour. **b** force; energy. □ **pith helmet** a lightweight sun-helmet made from the dried pith of the sola etc. □ **pithless** adj. [OE *pitha* f. WG]

pithecanthrope /ˌpɪθɪˈkænθrəʊp/ n. any prehistoric apelike human of the extinct genus *Pithecanthropus*, now considered to be part of the genus *Homo*. [Gk *pithēkos* ape + *anthrōpos* man]

pithy /ˈpɪθɪ/ adj. (**pithier, pithiest**) **1** (of style, speech, etc.) condensed, terse, and forcible. **2** of, like, or containing much pith. □ **pithily** adv. **pithiness** n.

pitiable /ˈpɪtɪəb(ə)l/ adj. **1** deserving or causing pity. **2** contemptible. □ **pitiableness** n. **pitiably** adv. [ME f. OF *piteable, pitoiable* (as PITY)]

pitiful /ˈpɪtɪˌfʊl/ adj. **1** causing pity. **2** contemptible. **3** *archaic* compassionate. □ **pitifully** adv. **pitifulness** n.

pitiless /ˈpɪtɪlɪs/ adj. showing no pity (*the pitiless heat of the desert*). □ **pitilessly** adv. **pitilessness** n.

pitman /ˈpɪtmən/ n. (pl. **-men**) a collier.

piton /ˈpiːtɒn/ n. a peg or spike driven into a rock or crack to support a climber or a rope. [F, = eye-bolt]

pitta /ˈpɪtə/ n. (also **pita**) a flat hollow unleavened bread which can be split and filled with salad etc. [mod.Gk, = a cake]

pittance /ˈpɪt(ə)ns/ n. a scanty or meagre allowance, remuneration, etc. (*paid him a mere pittance*). [ME f. OF *pitance* f. med.L *pi(e)tantia* f. L *pietas* PITY]

pitter-patter var. of PIT-A-PAT.

pittosporum /ˌpɪtəʊˈspɔːrəm/ n. any evergreen shrub of the family Pittosporaceae, chiefly native to Australasia with many species having fragrant foliage. [Gk *pitta* PITCH² + *sporos* seed]

pituitary /pɪˈtjuːɪtərɪ/ n. & adj. —n. (pl. **-ies**) (also **pituitary gland** or **body**) a small ductless gland at the base of the brain secreting various hormones essential for growth and other bodily functions. —adj. of or relating to this gland. [L *pituitarius* secreting phlegm f. *pituita* phlegm]

pity /ˈpɪtɪ/ n. & v. —n. (pl. **-ies**) **1** sorrow and compassion aroused by another's condition (*felt pity for the child*). **2** something to be regretted; grounds for regret (*what a pity!; the pity of it is that he didn't mean it*). —v.tr. (**-ies, -ied**) feel (often contemptuous) pity for (*they are to be pitied; I pity you if you think that*). □ **for pity's sake** an exclamation of urgent supplication, anger, etc. **more's the pity** so much the worse. **take pity on** feel or act compassionately towards. □ **pitying** adj. **pityingly** adv. [ME f. OF *pité* f. L *pietas* (as PIETY)]

pivot /ˈpɪvət/ n. & v. —n. **1** a short shaft or pin on which something turns or oscillates. **2** a crucial or essential person, point, etc., in a scheme or enterprise. **3** *Mil.* the man or men about whom a body of troops wheels. —v. (**pivoted, pivoting**) **1** *intr.* turn on or as if on a pivot. **2** *intr.* (foll. by *on, upon*) hinge on; depend on. **3** *tr.* provide with or attach by a pivot. □ **pivotable** adj. **pivotability** /-ˈbɪlɪtɪ/ n. **pivotal** adj. [F, of uncert. orig.]

pix¹ n.pl. *colloq.* pictures, esp. photographs. [abbr.: cf. PIC]

pix² var. of PYX.

pixel /ˈpɪks(ə)l/ n. *Electronics* any of the minute areas of uniform illumination of which an image on a display screen is composed. [abbr. of *picture element*: cf. PIX¹]

pixie /ˈpɪksɪ/ n. (also **pixy**) (pl. **-ies**) a being like a fairy; an elf. □ **pixie hat** (or **hood**) a child's hat with a pointed crown. [17th c.: orig. unkn.]

pixilated /ˈpɪksɪˌleɪtɪd/ adj. (also **pixillated**) **1** bewildered; crazy. **2** drunk. [var. of *pixie-led* (as PIXIE, LED)]

pizazz /pɪˈzæz/ n. (also **pizzazz, pzazz** etc.) *sl.* verve, energy, liveliness, sparkle.

pizza /ˈpiːtsə/ n. a flat round base of dough with a topping of tomatoes, cheese, onions, etc. [It., = pie]

pizzeria /ˌpiːtsəˈriːə/ n. a place where pizzas are made or sold. [It. (as PIZZA)]

pizzicato /ˌpɪtsɪˈkɑːtəʊ/ adv., adj., & n. *Mus.* —adv. plucking the strings of a violin etc. with the finger. —adj. (of a note, passage, etc.) performed pizzicato. —n. (pl. **pizzicatos** or **pizzicati** /-tɪ/) a note, passage, etc. played pizzicato. [It., past part. of *pizzicare* twitch f. *pizzare* f. *pizza* edge]

pl. abbr. **1** plural. **2** place. **3** plate.

placable /ˈplækəb(ə)l/ adj. easily placated; mild; forgiving. □ **placability** /-ˈbɪlɪtɪ/ n. **placably** adv. [ME f. OF *placable* or L *placabilis* f. *placare* appease]

placard /ˈplækɑːd/ n. & v. —n. a printed or handwritten poster esp. for advertising. —v.tr. /also plæˈkɑːd/ **1** set up placards on (a wall etc.). **2** advertise by placards. **3** display (a poster etc.) as a placard. [ME f. OF *placquart* f. *plaquier* to plaster f. MDu. *placken*]

placate /pləˈkeɪt, ˈplæ-, ˈpleɪ-/ v.tr. pacify; conciliate. □ **placatingly** adv. **placation** /pləˈkeɪʃ(ə)n/ n. **placatory** /pləˈkeɪtərɪ/ adj. [L *placare placat-*]

place n. & v. —n. **1 a** a particular portion of space. **b** a portion of space occupied by a person or thing (*it has changed its place*). **c** a proper or natural position (*he is out of his place; take your places*). **2** a city, town, village, etc. (*was born in this place*). **3** a residence; a dwelling (*has a place in the country; come round to my place*). **4 a** a group of houses in a town etc., esp. a square. **b** a country house with its surroundings. **5** a person's rank or status (*know their place; a place in history*). **6** a space, esp. a seat, for a person (*two places in the coach*). **7** a building or area for a specific purpose (*place of worship; bathing-place*). **8 a** a point reached in a book etc. (*lost my place*). **b** a passage in a book. **9** a particular spot on a surface, esp. of the skin (*a sore place on his wrist*). **10 a** employment or office, esp. government employment (*lost his place at the Ministry*). **b** the duties or entitlements of office etc. (*is his place to hire staff*). **11** a position as a member of a team, a student in a college, etc. **12** *Brit.* any of the first three or sometimes four positions in a race, esp. other than the winner (*backed it for a place*). **13** the position of a figure in a series indicated in decimal or similar notation (*calculated to 50 decimal places*). —v.tr. **1** put (a thing etc.) in a particular place or state; arrange. **2** identify, classify, or remember correctly (*cannot place him*). **3** assign to a particular place; locate.

4 a appoint (a person, esp. a member of the clergy) to a post. **b** find a situation, living, etc. for. **c** (usu. foll. by *with*) consign to a person's care etc. (*placed her with her aunt*). **5** assign rank, importance, or worth to (*place him among the best teachers*). **6 a** dispose of (goods) to a customer. **b** make (an order for goods etc.). **7** (often foll. by *in*, *on*, etc.) have (confidence etc.). **8** invest (money). **9** *Brit.* state the position of (any of the first three or sometimes four runners) in a race. **10** *tr.* (as **placed** *adj.*) **a** *Brit.* among the first three or sometimes four in a race. **b** *US* second in a race. **11** *Football* get (a goal) by a place-kick. □ **all over the place** in disorder; chaotic. **give place to 1** make room for. **2** yield precedence to. **3** be succeeded by. **go places** *colloq.* be successful. **in place** in the right position; suitable. **in place of** in exchange for; instead of. **in places** at some places or in some parts, but not others. **keep a person in his** or **her place** suppress a person's pretensions. **out of place 1** in the wrong position. **2** unsuitable. **place card** a card marking a person's place at a table etc. **place in the sun** a favourable situation, position, etc. **place-kick** *Football* a kick made when the ball is previously placed on the ground. **place-mat** a small mat on a table underneath a person's plate. **place-name** the name of a town, village, hill, field, lake, etc. **place-setting** a set of plates, cutlery, etc. for one person at a meal. **put oneself in another's place** imagine oneself in another's position. **put a person in his** or **her place** deflate or humiliate a person. **take place** occur. **take one's place** go to one's correct position, be seated, etc. **take the place of** be substituted for; replace. □ **placeless** *adj.* **placement** *n.* [ME f. OF f. L *platea* f. Gk *plateia* (*hodos*) broad (way)]

placebo /pləˈsiːbəʊ/ *n.* (pl. **-os**) **1** a pill, medicine, etc. prescribed for psychological reasons but having no physiological effect. **2** a placebo used as a control in testing new drugs etc. [L, = I shall be acceptable or pleasing f. *placēre* please, first word of Ps. 114:9]

placenta /pləˈsentə/ *n.* (pl. **placentae** /-tiː/ or **placentas**) a flattened circular organ in the uterus of pregnant mammals nourishing and maintaining the foetus through the umbilical cord and expelled after birth. □ **placental** *adj.* [L f. Gk *plakous -ountos* flat cake f. the root of *plax plakos* flat plate]

placer /ˈpleɪsə(r), ˈplæsə(r)/ *n.* a deposit of sand, gravel, etc., in the bed of a stream etc., containing valuable minerals in particles. [Amer. Sp., rel. to *placel* sandbank f. *plaza* PLACE]

placid /ˈplæsɪd/ *adj.* **1** (of a person) not easily aroused or disturbed; peaceful. **2** mild; calm; serene. □ **placidity** /pləˈsɪdɪtɪ/ *n.* **placidly** *adv.* **placidness** *n.* [F *placide* or L *placidus* f. *placēre* please]

placket /ˈplækɪt/ *n.* **1** an opening or slit in a garment, for fastenings or access to a pocket. **2** the flap of fabric under this. [var. of PLACARD]

plagiarism /ˈpleɪdʒəˌrɪz(ə)m/ *n.* **1** the act or an instance of plagiarizing. **2** something plagiarized. □ **plagiarist** *n.* **plagiaristic** /-ˈrɪstɪk/ *adj.*

plagiarize /ˈpleɪdʒəˌraɪz/ *v.tr.* (also **-ise**) (also *absol.*) **1** take and use (the thoughts, writings, inventions, etc. of another person) as one's own. **2** pass off the thoughts etc. of (another person)

as one's own. □ **plagiarizer** *n.* [L *plagiarius* kidnapper f. *plagium* a kidnapping f. Gk *plagion*]

plague /pleɪg/ *n.*, *v.*, & *int.* —*n.* **1** a deadly contagious disease spreading rapidly over a wide area. **2** (foll. by *of*) an unusual infestation of a pest etc. (*a plague of frogs*). **3 a** great trouble. **b** an affliction, esp. as regarded as divine punishment. **4** *colloq.* a nuisance. —*v.tr.* (**plagues**, **plagued**, **plaguing**) **1** affect with plague. **2** *colloq.* pester or harass continually. —*int.* *joc.* or *archaic* a curse etc. (*a plague on it!*). □ **plaguesome** *adj.* [ME f. L *plaga* stroke, wound prob. f. Gk *plaga*, *plēgē*]

plaice /pleɪs/ *n.* (pl. same) a European flatfish, *Pleuronectes platessa*, having a brown back with orange spots and a white underside, much used for food. **2** (in full **American plaice**) a N. Atlantic fish, *Hippoglossoides platessoides*. [ME f. OF *plaïz* f. LL *platessa* app. f. Gk *platus* broad]

plaid /plæd/ *n.* **1** (often *attrib.*) chequered or tartan, esp. woollen, twilled cloth (*a plaid skirt*). **2** a long piece of plaid worn over the shoulder as part of Highland Scottish costume. □ **plaided** *adj.* [Gael. *plaide*, of unkn. orig.]

plain *adj.*, *adv.*, & *n.* —*adj.* **1** clear; evident (*is plain to see*). **2** readily understood; simple (*in plain words*). **3 a** (of food, sewing, decoration, etc.) uncomplicated; not elaborate; unembellished; simple. **b** without a decorative pattern. **4** (esp. of a woman or girl) ugly. **5** outspoken; straightforward. **6** (of manners, dress, etc.) unsophisticated; homely (*a plain man*). —*adv.* **1** clearly; unequivocally (*to speak plain, I don't approve*). **2** simply (*that is plain stupid*). —*n.* **1** a level tract of esp. treeless country. **2** a basic knitting stitch made by putting the needle through the back of the stitch and passing the wool round the front of the needle. □ **plain chocolate** dark chocolate without added milk. **plain clothes** ordinary clothes worn esp. as a disguise by policemen etc. **plain-clothes** (*attrib.*) wearing plain clothes. **plain dealing** candour; straightforwardness. **plain flour** flour with no added raising agent. **plain sailing 1** sailing a straightforward course. **2** an uncomplicated situation or course of action. **plain-spoken** outspoken; blunt. □ **plainly** *adv.* **plainness** /ˈpleɪnnɪs/ *n.* [ME f. OF *plain* (adj. & n.) f. L *planus* (adj.), *planum* (n.)]

plainchant /ˈpleɪntʃɑːnt/ *n.* = PLAINSONG.

plainsman /ˈpleɪnzmən/ *n.* (pl. **-men**) a person who lives on a plain, esp. in N. America.

plainsong /ˈpleɪnsɒŋ/ *n.* unaccompanied church music sung in unison in medieval modes and in free rhythm corresponding to the accentuation of the words.

plaint *n.* **1** *Brit.* *Law* an accusation; a charge. **2** *literary* or *archaic* a complaint; a lamentation. [ME f. OF *plainte* fem. past part. of *plaindre*, and OF *plaint* f. L *planctus* f. *plangere planct-* lament]

plaintiff /ˈpleɪntɪf/ *n.* *Law* a person who brings a case against another into court (opp. DEFENDANT). [ME f. OF *plaintif* (adj.) (as PLAINTIVE)]

plaintive /ˈpleɪntɪv/ *adj.* **1** expressing sorrow; mournful. **2** mournful-sounding. □ **plaintively** *adv.* **plaintiveness** *n.* [ME f. OF (*-if*, *-ive*) f. *plainte* (as PLAINT)]

plait /plæt/ *n.* & *v.* —*n.* **1** a length of hair, straw, etc., in three or more interlaced strands. **2** = PLEAT. —*v.tr.* form (hair etc.) into a plait. [ME f. OF *pleit* fold ult. f. L *plicare* fold]

plan *n.* & *v.* —*n.* **1 a** a formulated and esp. detailed method by which a thing is to be done; a design or scheme. **b** an intention or proposed proceeding (*my plan was to distract them; plan of campaign*). **2** a drawing or diagram made by projection on a horizontal plane, esp. showing a building or one floor of a building (cf. ELEVATION). **3** a large-scale detailed map of a town or district. **4 a** a table etc. indicating times, places, etc. of intended proceedings. **b** a scheme or arrangement (*prepared the seating plan*). **5** an imaginary plane perpendicular to the line of vision and containing the objects shown in a picture. —*v.* (**planned, planning**) **1** *tr.* (often foll. by *that* + clause or *to* + infin.) arrange (a procedure etc.) beforehand; form a plan (*planned to catch the evening ferry*). **2** *tr.* **a** design (a building, new town, etc.). **b** make a plan of (an existing building, an area, etc.). **3** *tr.* (as **planned** *adj.*) in accordance with a plan (*his planned arrival; planned parenthood*). **4** *intr.* make plans. □ **planning permission** *Brit.* formal permission for building development etc., esp. from a local authority. **plan on** *colloq.* aim at doing; intend. □ **planning** *n.* [F f. earlier *plant*, f. It. *pianta* plan of building: cf. PLANT]

planar /ˈpleɪnə(r)/ *adj. Math.* of, relating to, or in the form of a plane.

planchette /plɑːnˈʃet/ *n.* a small usu. heart-shaped board on castors with a pencil that is supposedly caused to write spirit messages when a person's fingers rest lightly on it. [F, dimin. of *planche* PLANK]

plane[1] *n., adj.,* & *v.* —*n.* **1 a** a flat surface on which a straight line joining any two points on it would wholly lie. **b** an imaginary flat surface through or joining etc. material objects. **2** a level surface. **3** *colloq.* = AEROPLANE. **4** a flat surface producing lift by the action of air or water over and under it (usu. in *comb.*: *hydroplane*). —*adj.* **1** (of a surface etc.) perfectly level. **2** (of an angle, figure, etc.) lying in a plane. —*v.intr.* **1** (often foll. by *down*) travel or glide in an aeroplane. **2** (of a speedboat etc.) skim over water. **3** soar. □ **plane sailing 1** the practice of determining a ship's position on the theory that she is moving on a plane. **2** = *plain sailing* (see PLAIN). [L *planum* flat surface, neut. of *planus* PLAIN (different. f. PLAIN in 17th c.): adj. after F *plan, plane*]

plane[2] *n.* & *v.* —*n.* **1** a tool consisting of a wooden or metal block with a projecting steel blade, used to smooth a wooden surface by paring shavings from it. **2** a similar tool for smoothing metal. —*v.tr.* **1** smooth (wood, metal, etc.) with a plane. **2** (often foll. by *away, down*) pare (irregularities) with a plane. [ME f. OF var. of *plaine* f. LL *plana* f. L *planus* PLAIN]

plane[3] /pleɪn/ *n.* (in full **plane-tree**) any tree of the genus *Platanus* often growing to great heights, with bark which peels in uneven patches. [ME f. OF f. L *platanus* f. Gk *platanos* f. *platus* broad]

planet /ˈplænɪt/ *n.* a celestial body moving in an elliptical orbit round a star; the earth. □ **planetology** /-ˈtɒlədʒɪ/ *n.* [ME f. OF *planete* f. LL *planeta, planetes* f. Gk *planētēs* wanderer, planet f. *planaomai* wander]

planetarium /ˌplænɪˈteərɪəm/ *n.* (*pl.* **planetariums** or **planetaria** /-rɪə/) **1** a domed building in which images of stars, planets,

constellations, etc. are projected for public entertainment or education. **2** the device used for such projection. **3** = ORRERY. [mod.L (as PLANET)]

planetary /ˈplænɪtərɪ/ *adj.* **1** of or like planets (*planetary influence*). **2** terrestrial; mundane. **3** wandering; erratic. [LL *planetarius* (as PLANET)]

planetoid /ˈplænɪtɔɪd/ *n.* = ASTEROID.

plangent /ˈplændʒ(ə)nt/ *adj.* **1** (of a sound) loud and reverberating. **2** (of a sound) plaintive; sad. □ **plangency** *n.* [L *plangere plangent-* lament]

planisphere /ˈplænɪˌsfɪə(r)/ *n.* a map formed by the projection of a sphere or part of a sphere on a plane, esp. to show the appearance of the heavens at a specific time or place. □ **planispheric** /-ˈsferɪk/ *adj.* [ME f. med.L *planisphaerium* (as PLANE[1], SPHERE): infl. by F *planisphère*]

plank *n.* & *v.* —*n.* **1** a long flat piece of timber used esp. in building, flooring, etc. **2** an item of a political or other programme. —*v.tr.* **1** provide, cover, or floor, with planks. **2** (usu. foll. by *down*; also *absol.*) esp. *US colloq.* **a** put (a thing, person, etc.) down roughly or violently. **b** pay (money) on the spot or abruptly (*planked down £5*). □ **walk the plank** *hist.* (of a pirate's captive etc.) be made to walk blindfold along a plank over the side of a ship to one's death in the sea. [ME f. ONF *planke*, OF *planche* f. LL *planca* board f. *plancus* flat-footed]

planking /ˈplæŋkɪŋ/ *n.* planks as flooring etc.

plankton /ˈplæŋkt(ə)n/ *n.* the chiefly microscopic organisms drifting or floating in the sea or fresh water. □ **planktonic** /-ˈtɒnɪk/ *adj.* [G f. Gk *plagktos* wandering f. *plazomai* wander]

planner /ˈplænə(r)/ *n.* **1** a person who controls or plans the development of new towns, designs buildings, etc. **2** a person who makes plans. **3** a list, table, etc., with information helpful in planning.

plano- /ˈpleɪnəʊ/ *comb. form* level, flat. [L *planus* flat]

planoconcave /ˌpleɪnəʊˈkɒnkeɪv/ *adj.* (of a lens etc.) with one surface plane and the other concave.

planoconvex /ˌpleɪnəʊˈkɒnveks/ *adj.* (of a lens etc.) with one surface plane and the other convex.

plant /plɑːnt/ *n.* & *v.* —*n.* **1 a** any living organism of the kingdom Plantae, usu. containing chlorophyll enabling it to live wholly on inorganic substances and lacking specialized sense organs and the power of voluntary movement. **b** a small organism of this kind, as distinguished from a shrub or tree. **2 a** machinery, fixtures, etc., used in industrial processes. **b** a factory. **3** *colloq.* something, esp. incriminating or compromising, positioned or concealed so as to be discovered later. —*v.tr.* **1** place (a seed, bulb, or growing thing) in the ground so that it may take root and flourish. **2** (often foll. by *in, on,* etc.) put or fix in position. **3** station (a person etc.), esp. as a spy or source of information. **4** *refl.* take up a position (*planted myself by the door*). **5** cause (an idea etc.) to be established esp. in another person's mind. **6** deliver (a blow, kiss, etc.) with a deliberate aim. **7** *sl.* position or conceal (something incriminating or compromising) for later discovery. **8 a** settle or people (a colony etc.). **b** found or establish (a city, community, etc.). **9** bury. □ **plant-louse** a

small insect that infests plants, esp. an aphis.
plant out transfer (a plant) from a pot or frame
to the open ground; set out (seedlings) at
intervals. □ **plantable** adj. **plantlet** n. **plantlike**
adj. [OE plante & F plante f. L planta sprout, slip,
cutting]
Plantagenet /plænˈtædʒɪnɪt/ adj. & n. —adj. of
or relating to the kings of England from Henry
II to Richard II. —n. any of these kings. [=
sprig of broom (OF plant à genet f. L planta
genista) worn as a distinctive mark, the origin
of their surname]
plantain[1] /ˈplæntɪn/ n. any shrub of the genus
Plantago, with broad flat leaves spread out close
to the ground. [ME f. OF f. L plantago -ginis f.
planta sole of the foot (from its broad prostrate
leaves)]
plantain[2] /ˈplæntɪn/ n. 1 a banana plant, Musa
paradisiaca, widely grown for its fruit. 2 the
starchy fruit of this containing less sugar than
a dessert banana and chiefly used in cooking.
[earlier platan f. Sp. plá(n)tano plane-tree, prob.
assim. f. Galibi palatana etc.]
plantation /plænˈteɪʃ(ə)n, plɑːn-/ n. 1 an estate
on which cotton, tobacco, etc. is cultivated, esp.
in former colonies, formerly by slave labour. 2
an area planted with trees etc. 3 hist. a colony;
colonization. [ME f. OF plantation or L plantatio
(as PLANT)]
planter /ˈplɑːntə(r)/ n. 1 a person who cultivates
the soil. 2 the manager or occupier of a
coffee, cotton, tobacco, etc. plantation. 3 a large
container for decorative plants. 4 a machine for
planting seeds etc. (potato-planter).
plaque /plæk, plɑːk/ n. 1 an ornamental tablet
of metal, porcelain, etc., esp. affixed to a building
in commemoration. 2 a deposit on teeth where
bacteria proliferate. □ **plaquette** /plæˈket/ n. [F
f. Du. plak tablet f. plakken stick]
plash[1] n. & v. —n. 1 a splash; a plunge. 2 a a
marshy pool. b a puddle. —v. 1 tr. & intr. splash.
2 tr. strike the surface of (water). □ **plashy** adj.
[OE plæsc, prob. imit.]
plash[2] /plæʃ/ v.tr. 1 bend down and interweave
(branches, twigs, etc.) to form a hedge. 2 make
or renew (a hedge) in this way. [ME f. OF
pla(i)ssier ult. f. L plectere plait: cf. PLEACH]
plasma /ˈplæzmə/ n. (also **plasm** /ˈplæz(ə)m/) 1
the colourless fluid part of blood, lymph, or
milk, in which corpuscles or fat-globules are
suspended. 2 = PROTOPLASM. 3 a gas of positive
ions and free electrons with an approximately
equal positive and negative charge. □ **plasmatic**
/-ˈmætɪk/ adj. **plasmic** adj. [LL, = mould f. Gk
plasma -atos f. plassō to shape]
plaster /ˈplɑːstə(r)/ n. & v. —n. 1 a soft pliable
mixture esp. of lime putty with sand or Portland
cement etc. for spreading on walls, ceilings, etc.,
to form a smooth hard surface when dried. 2
Brit. = sticking-plaster. 3 hist. a curative or
protective substance spread on a bandage etc.
and applied to the body (mustard plaster). —v.tr.
1 cover (a wall etc.) with plaster or a similar substance. 2 (often foll. by with) coat thickly or to
excess; bedaub (plastered the bread with jam; the
wall was plastered with slogans). 3 stick or apply (a
thing) thickly like plaster (plastered glue all over
it). 4 (often foll. by down) make (esp. hair) smooth
with water, cream, etc.; fix flat. 5 (as **plastered**
adj.) sl. drunk. 6 apply a medical plaster or
plaster cast to. 7 sl. bomb or shell heavily. □

plaster cast 1 a bandage stiffened with plaster
of Paris and applied to a broken limb etc. 2 a
statue or mould made of plaster. **plaster of
Paris** fine white plaster made of gypsum and
used for making plaster casts etc. **plaster saint**
iron. a person regarded as being without moral
faults or human frailty. □ **plasterer** n. **plastery**
adj. [ME f. OE & OF plastre or F plastrer f. med.L
plastrum f. L emplastrum f. Gk emplastron]
plasterboard /ˈplɑːstəbɔːd/ n. two boards with
a filling of plaster used to form or line the inner
walls of houses etc.
plastic /ˈplæstɪk/ n. & adj. —n. 1 any of a
number of synthetic polymeric substances that
can be given any required shape. 2 (attrib.) made
of plastic (plastic bag). 3 colloq. = plastic money.
—adj. 1 capable of being moulded; pliant;
supple. 2 moulding or giving form to clay,
wax, etc. □ **plastic arts** art forms involving
modelling or moulding or the representation
of solid objects with three-dimensional effects.
plastic bomb a bomb containing plastic
explosive. **plastic explosive** a putty-like explosive capable of being moulded by hand. **plastic
money** colloq. a credit card, charge card, or
other plastic card that can be used in place of
money. **plastic surgeon** a practitioner of plastic surgery. **plastic surgery** the process of re-
constructing or repairing parts of the body by the
transfer of tissue, either in the treatment of injury
or for cosmetic reasons. □ **plastically** adv.
plasticity /-ˈtɪsɪtɪ/ n. **plasticize** /-ˌsaɪz/ v.tr. (also
-ise). **plasticization** /-saɪˈzeɪʃ(ə)n/ n. **plasticizer**
/-ˌsaɪzə(r)/ n. **plasticky** adj. [F plastique or L
plasticus f. Gk plastikos f. plassō mould]
Plasticine /ˈplæstɪˌsiːn/ n. propr. a soft plastic
material used, esp. by children, for modelling.
[PLASTIC + -INE[4]]
plate n. & v. —n. 1 a a shallow vessel, usu.
circular and of earthenware or china, from
which food is eaten or served. b the contents of
this (ate a plate of sandwiches). 2 a similar vessel
usu. of metal or wood, used esp. for making a
collection in a church etc. 3 US a main course
of a meal, served on one plate. 4 Austral. & NZ a
contribution of cakes, sandwiches, etc., to a
social gathering. 5 (collect.) a utensils of silver,
gold, or other metal. b objects of plated metal.
6 a piece of metal with a name or inscription
for affixing to a door, container, etc. 7 an
illustration on special paper in a book. 8 a thin
sheet of metal, glass, etc., coated with a sensitive
film for photography. 9 a flat thin usu. rigid
sheet of metal etc. with an even surface and
uniform thickness, often as part of a mechanism. 10 a a smooth piece of metal etc. for
engraving. b an impression made from this. 11
a a silver or gold cup as a prize for a horse-race
etc. b a race with this as a prize. 12 a a thin
piece of plastic material, moulded to the shape
of the mouth and gums, to which artificial teeth
or another orthodontic appliance are attached.
b colloq. a complete denture or orthodontic
appliance. 13 Geol. each of several rigid sheets
of rock thought to form the earth's outer crust.
14 a stereotype, electrotype, or plastic cast of a
page of composed movable types, or a metal or
plastic copy of filmset matter, from which
sheets are printed. 15 US Baseball a flat piece of
whitened rubber marking the station of a batter
or pitcher. 16 US the anode of a thermionic

valve. **17** a horizontal timber laid along the top of a wall to support the ends of joists or rafters (*window-plate*). —*v.tr.* **1** apply a thin coat esp. of silver, gold, or tin to (another metal). **2** cover (esp. a ship) with plates of metal, esp. for protection. **3** make a plate of (type etc.) for printing. □ **on a plate** *colloq.* available with little trouble to the recipient. **on one's plate** for one to deal with or consider. **plate armour** armour of metal plates, for a man, ship, etc. **plate glass** thick fine-quality glass for shop windows etc., orig. cast in plates. **plate-rack** *Brit.* a rack in which plates are placed to drain. **plate tectonics** *Geol.* the study of the earth's surface based on the concept of moving 'plates' (see sense 13 of *n.*) forming its structure. □ **plateful** *n.* (*pl.* **-fuls**). **plateless** *adj.* **plater** *n.* [ME f. OF f. med.L *plata* plate armour f. *platus* (adj.) ult. f. Gk *platus* flat]

plateau /ˈplætəʊ/ *n.* & *v.* —*n.* (*pl.* **plateaux** /-təʊz/ or **plateaus**) **1** an area of fairly level high ground. **2** a state of little variation after an increase. —*v.intr.* (**plateaus**, **plateaued**) (often foll. by *out*) reach a level or stable state after an increase. [F f. OF *platel* dimin. of *plat* flat surface]

platelet /ˈpleɪtlɪt/ *n.* a small colourless disc of protoplasm found in blood and involved in clotting.

platen /ˈplæt(ə)n/ *n.* **1** a plate in a printing-press which presses the paper against the type. **2** a cylindrical roller in a typewriter against which the paper is held. [OF *platine* a flat piece f. *plat* flat]

platform /ˈplætfɔːm/ *n.* **1** a raised level surface; a natural or artificial terrace. **2** a raised surface from which a speaker addresses an audience. **3** *Brit.* a raised elongated structure along the side of a track in a railway station. **4** the floor area at the entrance to a bus. **5** a thick sole of a shoe. **6** the declared policy of a political party. □ **platform ticket** a ticket allowing a non-traveller access to a station platform. [F *plate-forme* ground-plan f. *plate* flat + *forme* FORM]

plating /ˈpleɪtɪŋ/ *n.* a coating of gold, silver, etc.

platinize /ˈplætɪnaɪz/ *v.tr.* (also **-ise**) coat with platinum. □ **platinization** /-ˈzeɪʃ(ə)n/ *n.*

platinum /ˈplætɪnəm/ *n.* *Chem.* a ductile malleable silvery-white metallic element unaffected by simple acids and fusible only at a very high temperature, used in making jewellery and laboratory apparatus. □ **platinum blonde** (or **blond**) *adj.* silvery-blond. —*n.* a person with silvery-blond hair. [mod.L f. earlier *platina* f. Sp., dimin. of *plata* silver]

platitude /ˈplætɪˌtjuːd/ *n.* **1** a trite or commonplace remark, esp. one solemnly delivered. **2** the use of platitudes; dullness, insipidity. □ **platitudinize** /-ˈtjuːdɪˌnaɪz/ *v.intr.* (also **-ise**). **platitudinous** /-ˈtjuːdɪnəs/ *adj.* [F f. *plat* flat, after *certitude*, *multitudinous*, etc.]

Platonic /pləˈtɒnɪk/ *adj.* **1** of or associated with the Greek philosopher Plato (d. 347 BC) or his ideas. **2** (**platonic**) (of love or friendship) purely spiritual, not sexual. **3** (**platonic**) confined to words or theory; not leading to action; harmless. □ **Platonically** *adv.* [L *Platonicus* f. Gk *Platōnikos* f. *Platōn* Plato]

Platonism /ˈpleɪtəˌnɪz(ə)m/ *n.* the philosophy of Plato or his followers. □ **Platonist** *n.*

platoon /pləˈtuːn/ *n.* **1** *Mil.* a subdivision of a company, a tactical unit commanded by a

lieutenant and usu. divided into three sections. **2** a group of persons acting together. [F *peloton* small ball, dimin. of *pelote*: see PELLET, -OON]

platteland /ˈplɑːtəˌlɑːnt/ *n.* *S.Afr.* remote country districts. □ **plattelander** *n.* [Afrik., = flat land]

platter /ˈplætə(r)/ *n.* **1** a large flat dish or plate, esp. for food. **2** *colloq.* a gramophone record. □ **on a platter** = *on a plate*. [ME & AF *plater* f. AF *plat* PLATE]

platy- /ˈplætɪ/ *comb. form* broad, flat. [Gk *platu-* f. *platus* broad, flat]

platypus /ˈplætɪpəs/ *n.* an Australian aquatic egg-laying mammal, *Ornithorhynchus anatinus*, having a pliable ducklike bill, webbed feet, and sleek grey fur.

plaudit /ˈplɔːdɪt/ *n.* (usu. in *pl.*) **1** a round of applause. **2** an emphatic expression of approval. [shortened f. L *plaudite* applaud, imper. pl. of *plaudere plaus-* applaud, said by Roman actors at the end of a play]

plausible /ˈplɔːzɪb(ə)l/ *adj.* **1** (of an argument, statement, etc.) seeming reasonable or probable. **2** (of a person) persuasive but deceptive. □ **plausibility** /-ˈbɪlɪtɪ/ *n.* **plausibly** *adv.* [L *plausibilis* (as PLAUDIT)]

play *v.* & *n.* —*v.* **1** *intr.* (often foll. by *with*) occupy or amuse oneself pleasantly with some recreation, game, exercise, etc. **2** *intr.* (foll. by *with*) act light-heartedly or flippantly (with feelings etc.). **3** *tr.* **a** perform on or be able to perform on (a musical instrument). **b** perform (a piece of music etc.). **c** cause (a record, record-player, etc.) to produce sounds. **4 a** *intr.* (foll. by *in*) perform a role in (a drama etc.). **b** perform (a drama or role) on stage, or in a film or broadcast. **c** *tr.* give a dramatic performance at (a particular theatre or place). **5** *tr.* act in real life the part of (*play truant; play the fool*). **6** *tr.* (foll. by *on*) perform (a trick or joke etc.) on (a person). **7** *tr.* (foll. by *for*) regard (a person) as (something specified) (*played me for a fool*). **8** *intr. colloq.* participate, cooperate; do what is wanted (*they won't play*). **9** *intr.* gamble. **10** *tr.* gamble on. **11** *tr.* **a** take part in (a game or recreation). **b** compete with (another player or team) in a game. **c** occupy (a specified position) in a team for a game. **d** (foll. by *in, on, at*, etc.) assign (a player) to a position. **12** *tr.* move (a piece) or display (a playing-card) in one's turn in a game. **13** *tr.* (also *absol.*) strike (a ball etc.) or execute (a stroke) in a game. **14** *intr.* move about in a lively or unrestrained manner. **15** *intr.* (often foll. by *on*) **a** touch gently. **b** emit light, water, etc. (*fountains gently playing*). **16** *tr.* allow (a fish) to exhaust itself pulling against a line. **17** *intr.* (often foll. by *at*) **a** engage in a half-hearted way (in an activity). **b** pretend to be. **18** *intr. colloq.* act or behave (as specified) (*play fair*). **19** *tr.* (foll. by *in, out,* etc.) accompany (a person) with music (*were played out with bagpipes*). —*n.* **1** recreation, amusement, esp. the spontaneous activity of children and young animals. **2 a** the playing of a game. **b** the action or manner of this. **c** the status of the ball etc. in a game as being available to be played according to the rules (*in play; out of play*). **3** a dramatic piece for the stage etc. **4** activity or operation (*are in full play; brought into play*). **5 a** freedom of movement. **b** space or scope for this. **6** brisk, light, or fitful movement. **7** gambling. **8** an action or manoeuvre, esp. in or as in a game. □ **at play**

engaged in recreation. **in play** for amusement; not seriously. **make play** act effectively. **make a play for** *colloq.* make a conspicuous attempt to acquire. **make play with** use ostentatiously. **play about** (or **around**) behave irresponsibly. **play along** pretend to cooperate. **play back** play (sounds recently recorded), esp. to monitor recording quality etc. **play-back** *n.* a playing back of a sound or sounds. **play by ear 1** perform (music) without the aid of a score. **2** (also **play it by ear**) proceed instinctively or step by step according to results and circumstances. **play one's cards right** (or **well**) make good use of opportunities; act shrewdly. **play down** minimize the importance of. **played out** exhausted of energy or usefulness. **play false** act, or treat a (person), deceitfully or treacherously. **play fast and loose** act unreliably; ignore one's obligations. **play for time** seek to gain time by delaying. **play into a person's hands** act so as unwittingly to give a person an advantage. **play it cool** *colloq.* **1** affect indifference. **2** be relaxed or unemotional. **play the man** = *be a man* (see MAN). **play the market** speculate in stocks etc. **play off** (usu. foll. by *against*) **1** oppose (one person against another), esp. for one's own advantage. **2** play an extra match to decide a draw or tie. **play-off** *n.* a match played to decide a draw or tie. **play on 1** continue to play. **2** take advantage of (a person's feelings etc.). **play oneself in** become accustomed to the prevailing conditions in a game etc. **play on words** a pun. **play-pen** a portable enclosure for young children to play in. **play safe** (or **for safety**) avoid risks. **play-suit** a garment for a young child. **play up 1** behave mischievously. **2** cause trouble; be irritating (*my rheumatism is playing up again*). **3** obstruct or annoy in this way (*played the teacher up*). **4** put all one's energy into a game. **play up to** flatter, esp. to win favour. **play with fire** take foolish risks. □ **playable** *adj.* **playability** /-'bɪlɪtɪ/ *n.* [OE *plega* (n.), *pleg(i)an* (v.), orig. = (to) exercise]

play-act /'pleɪækt/ *v.* **1** *intr.* act in a play. **2** *intr.* behave affectedly or insincerely. **3** *tr.* act (a scene, part, etc.). □ **play-acting** *n.* **play-actor** *n.*

playbill /'pleɪbɪl/ *n.* **1** a poster announcing a theatrical performance. **2** *US* a theatre programme.

playboy /'pleɪbɔɪ/ *n.* an irresponsible pleasure-seeking man, esp. a wealthy one.

player /'pleɪə(r)/ *n.* **1** a person taking part in a sport or game. **2** a person playing a musical instrument. **3** a person who plays a part on the stage; an actor. **4** = *record-player.* □ **player-piano** a piano fitted with an apparatus enabling it to be played automatically. [OE *plegere* (as PLAY)]

playfellow /'pleɪˌfeləʊ/ *n.* a playmate.

playful /'pleɪfʊl/ *adj.* **1** fond of or inclined to play. **2** done in fun; humorous, jocular. □ **playfully** *adv.* **playfulness** *n.*

playgoer /'pleɪˌɡəʊə(r)/ *n.* a person who goes often to the theatre.

playground /'pleɪɡraʊnd/ *n.* an outdoor area for children to play on.

playgroup /'pleɪɡruːp/ *n.* a group of preschool children who play regularly together at a particular place under supervision.

playhouse /'pleɪhaʊs/ *n.* **1** a theatre. **2** a toy house for children to play in.

playing-card /'pleɪɪŋˌkɑːd/ *n.* each of a set of usu. 52 oblong pieces of card or other material with an identical pattern on one side and different values represented by numbers and symbols on the other, used to play various games.

playing-field /'pleɪɪŋˌfiːld/ *n.* a field used for outdoor team games.

playlet /'pleɪlɪt/ *n.* a short play or dramatic piece.

playmate /'pleɪmeɪt/ *n.* a child's companion in play.

playschool /'pleɪskuːl/ *n.* a nursery for preschool children.

plaything /'pleɪθɪŋ/ *n.* **1** a toy or other thing to play with. **2** a person treated as a toy.

playtime /'pleɪtaɪm/ *n.* time for play or recreation.

playwright /'pleɪraɪt/ *n.* a person who writes plays.

plaza /'plɑːzə/ *n.* a market-place or open square (esp. in a Spanish town). [Sp., = place]

plc *abbr.* (also **PLC**) Public Limited Company.

plea *n.* **1** an earnest appeal or entreaty. **2** *Law* a formal statement by or on behalf of a defendant. **3** an argument or excuse. □ **plea bargaining** *US* an arrangement between prosecutor and defendant whereby the defendant pleads guilty to a lesser charge in the expectations of leniency. [ME & AF *ple, plai,* OF *plait, plaid* agreement, discussion f. L *placitum* a decree, neut. past part. of *placēre* to please]

pleach *v.tr.* entwine or interlace (esp. branches to form a hedge). [ME *pleche* f. OF (as PLASH²)]

plead *v.* (*past* and *past part.* **pleaded** or esp. *US, Sc.,* & *dial.* **pled** /pled/) **1** *intr.* (foll. by *with*) make an earnest appeal to. **2** *intr. Law* address a lawcourt as an advocate on behalf of a party. **3** *tr.* maintain (a cause) esp. in a lawcourt. **4** *tr. Law* declare to be one's state as regards guilt in or responsibility for a crime (*plead guilty; plead insanity*). **5** *tr.* offer or allege as an excuse (*pleaded forgetfulness*). **6** *intr.* make an appeal or entreaty. □ **pleadable** *adj.* **pleader** *n.* **pleadingly** *adv.* [ME f. AF *pleder,* OF *plaidier* (as PLEA)]

pleading /'pliːdɪŋ/ *n.* (usu. in *pl.*) a formal statement of the cause of an action or defence.

pleasant /'plez(ə)nt/ *adj.* (**pleasanter**, **pleasantest**) pleasing to the mind, feelings, or senses. □ **pleasantly** *adv.* **pleasantness** *n.* [ME f. OF *plaisant* (as PLEASE)]

pleasantry /'plezəntrɪ/ *n.* (*pl.* **-ies**) **1** a pleasant or amusing remark, esp. made in casual conversation. **2** a humorous manner of speech. **3** jocularity. [F *plaisanterie* (as PLEASANT)]

please /pliːz/ *v.* **1** *tr.* (also *absol.*) be agreeable to; make glad; give pleasure to (*the gift will please them; anxious to please*). **2** *tr.* (in *passive*) **a** (foll. by *to* + *infin.*) be glad or willing to (*am pleased to help*). **b** (often foll. by *about, at, with*) derive pleasure or satisfaction (from). **3** *tr.* (with *it* as subject; usu. foll. by *to* + *infin.*) be the inclination or wish of (*it did not please them to attend*). **4** *intr.* think fit; have the will or desire (*take as many as you please*). **5** *tr.* (short for **may it please you**) used in polite requests (*come in, please*). □ **if you please** if you are willing, esp. *iron.* to indicate unreasonableness (*then, if you please, we had to pay*). **please oneself** do as one likes. □

pleased *adj.* **pleasing** *adj.* **pleasingly** *adv.* [ME *plaise* f. OF *plaisir* f. L *placēre*]

pleasurable /ˈpleʒərəb(ə)l/ *adj.* causing pleasure; agreeable. □ **pleasurableness** *n.* **pleasurably** *adv.* [PLEASURE + -ABLE, after *comfortable*]

pleasure /ˈpleʒə(r)/ *n.* & *v.* —*n.* **1** a feeling of satisfaction or joy. **2** enjoyment. **3** a source of pleasure or gratification (*painting was my chief pleasure; it is a pleasure to talk to them*). **4** *formal* a person's will or desire (*what is your pleasure?*). **5** sensual gratification or enjoyment (*a life of pleasure*). **6** (*attrib.*) done or used for pleasure (*pleasure-ground*). —*v.* **1** *tr.* give (esp. sexual) pleasure to. **2** *intr.* (often foll. by *in*) take pleasure. □ **take pleasure in** like doing. **with pleasure** gladly. [ME & OF *plesir, plaisir* PLEASE, used as a noun]

pleat *n.* & *v.* —*n.* a fold or crease, esp. a flattened fold in cloth doubled upon itself. —*v.tr.* make a pleat or pleats in. [ME, var. of PLAIT]

pleb *n. colloq.* usu. *derog.* an ordinary insignificant person. □ **plebby** *adj.* [abbr. of PLEBEIAN]

plebeian /plɪˈbiːən/ *n.* & *adj.* —*n.* a commoner, esp. in ancient Rome. —*adj.* **1** of low birth; of the common people. **2** uncultured. **3** coarse, ignoble. □ **plebeianism** *n.* [L *plebeius* f. *plebs plebis* the common people]

plebiscite /ˈplebɪsɪt, -ˌsaɪt/ *n.* the direct vote of all the electors of a State etc. on an important public question, e.g. a change in the constitution. □ **plebiscitary** /-ˈbɪsɪtərɪ/ *adj.* [F *plébiscite* f. L *plebiscitum* f. *plebs plebis* the common people + *scitum* decree f. *sciscere* vote for]

plectrum /ˈplektrəm/ *n.* (*pl.* **plectrums** or **plectra** /-trə/) a thin flat piece of plastic or horn etc. held in the hand and used to pluck a string, esp. of a guitar. [L f. Gk *plēktron* f. *plēssō* strike]

pled see PLEAD.

pledge *n.* & *v.* —*n.* **1** a solemn promise or undertaking. **2** a thing given as security for the fulfilment of a contract, the payment of a debt, etc., and liable to forfeiture in the event of failure. **3** a thing put in pawn. **4** a thing given as a token of love, favour, or something to come. **5** the drinking of a person's health; a toast. **6** a solemn undertaking to abstain from alcohol (*sign the pledge*). **7** the state of being pledged (*goods lying in pledge*). —*v.tr.* **1 a** deposit as security. **b** pawn. **2** promise solemnly by the pledge of (one's honour, word, etc.). **3** (often *refl.*) bind by a solemn promise. **4** drink to the health of. □ **pledgeable** *adj.* **pledger** *n.* **pledgor** *n.* [ME *plege* f. OF *plege* f. LL *plebium* f. *plebire* assure]

Pleiades /ˈplaɪəˌdiːz/ *n.pl.* a cluster of stars in the constellation Taurus, usu. known as 'the Seven Sisters'. [ME f. L *Pleïas* f. Gk *Plēïas -ados*]

Pleistocene /ˈplaɪstəˌsiːn/ *adj.* & *n.* *Geol.* —*adj.* of or relating to the first epoch of the Quaternary period. —*n.* this epoch or system. [Gk *pleistos* most + *kainos* new]

plenary /ˈpliːnərɪ/ *adj.* **1** entire, unqualified, absolute (*plenary indulgence*). **2** (of an assembly) to be attended by all members. [LL *plenarius* f. *plenus* full]

plenipotentiary /ˌplenɪpəˈtenʃərɪ/ *n.* & *adj.* —*n.* (*pl.* **-ies**) a person (esp. a diplomat) invested with the full power of independent action. —*adj.* **1** having this power. **2** (of power) absolute. [med.L *plenipotentiarius* f. *plenus* full + *potentia* power]

plenitude /ˈplenɪˌtjuːd/ *n.* *literary* **1** fullness, completeness. **2** abundance. [ME f. OF f. LL *plenitudo* f. *plenus* full]

plenteous /ˈplentɪəs/ *adj. poet.* plentiful. □ **plenteously** *adv.* **plenteousness** *n.* [ME f. OF *plentivous* f. *plentif -ive* f. *plenté* PLENTY: cf. *bounteous*]

plentiful /ˈplentɪˌfʊl/ *adj.* abundant, copious. □ **plentifully** *adv.* **plentifulness** *n.*

plenty /ˈplentɪ/ *n., adj.,* & *adv.* —*n.* (often foll. by *of*) a great or sufficient quantity or number (*we have plenty; plenty of time*). —*adj. colloq.* existing in an ample quantity. —*adv. colloq.* fully, entirely (*it is plenty large enough*). [ME *plenteth, plente* f. OF *plentet* f. L *plenitas -tatis* f. *plenus* full]

pleonasm /ˈpliːəˌnæz(ə)m/ *n.* the use of more words than are needed to give the sense (e.g. *see with one's eyes*). □ **pleonastic** /-ˈnæstɪk/ *adj.* **pleonastically** /-ˈnæstɪkəlɪ/ *adv.* [LL *pleonasmus* f. Gk *pleonasmos* f. *pleonazō* be superfluous]

plesiosaurus /ˌpliːsɪəˈsɔːrəs/ *n.* (also **plesiosaur** /ˈpliːsɪəˌsɔː(r)/) any of a group of extinct marine reptiles with a broad flat body, short tail, long flexible neck, and large paddle-like limbs. [mod.L f. Gk *plēsios* near + *sauros* lizard]

plethora /ˈpleθərə/ *n.* an oversupply, glut, or excess. □ **plethoric** /also plɪˈθɒrɪk/ *adj.* **plethorically** /plɪˈθɒrɪkəlɪ/ *adv.* [LL f. Gk *plēthōrē* f. *plēthō* be full]

pleura /ˈplʊərə/ *n.* (*pl.* **pleurae** /-riː/) each of a pair of serous membranes lining the thorax and enveloping the lungs in mammals. □ **pleural** *adj.* [med.L f. Gk, = side of the body, rib]

pleurisy /ˈplʊərɪsɪ/ *n.* inflammation of the pleura, marked by pain in the chest or side, fever, etc. □ **pleuritic** /-ˈrɪtɪk/ *adj.* [ME f. OF *pleurisie* f. LL *pleurisis* alt. f. L *pleuritis* f. Gk (as PLEURA)]

pleuro- /ˈplʊərəʊ/ *comb. form* denoting the pleura.

pleuropneumonia /ˌplʊərəʊnjuːˈməʊnɪə/ *n.* pneumonia complicated with pleurisy.

Plexiglas /ˈpleksɪˌglɑːs/ *n. propr.* = PERSPEX. [irreg. f. Gk *plēxis* percussion + GLASS]

plexus /ˈpleksəs/ *n.* (*pl.* same or **plexuses**) **1** *Anat.* a network of nerves or vessels in an animal body (*gastric plexus*). **2** any network or weblike formation. □ **plexiform** *adj.* [L f. *plectere* plexplait]

pliable /ˈplaɪəb(ə)l/ *adj.* **1** bending easily; supple. **2** yielding, compliant. □ **pliability** /-ˈbɪlɪtɪ/ *n.* **pliableness** *n.* **pliably** *adv.* [F f. *plier* bend: see PLY[1]]

pliant /ˈplaɪənt/ *adj.* = PLIABLE 1. □ **pliancy** *n.* **pliantly** *adv.* [ME f. OF (as PLIABLE)]

pliers /ˈplaɪəz/ *n.pl.* pincers with parallel flat usu. serrated surfaces for holding small objects, bending wire, etc. [(dial.) *ply* bend (as PLIABLE)]

plight[1] /plaɪt/ *n.* a condition or state, esp. an unfortunate one. [ME & AF *plit* = OF *pleit* fold: see PLAIT: *-gh-* by confusion with PLIGHT[2]]

plight[2] /plaɪt/ *v.tr. archaic.* **1** pledge or promise solemnly (one's faith, loyalty, etc.). **2** (foll. by *to*) engage, esp. in marriage. [orig. as noun, f. OE *pliht* danger f. Gmc]

plimsoll /ˈplɪms(ə)l/ *n.* (also **plimsole**) *Brit.* a rubber-soled canvas sports shoe. [prob. from the resemblance of the side of the sole to a PLIMSOLL LINE]

Plimsoll line /ˈplɪms(ə)l/ n. (also **Plimsoll mark**) a marking on a ship's side showing the limit of legal submersion under various conditions. [S. *Plimsoll*, Engl. politician d. 1898, promoter of the Merchant Shipping Act of 1876]

plinth /plɪnθ/ n. **1** the lower square slab at the base of a column. **2** a base supporting a vase or statue etc. [F *plinthe* or L *plinthus* f. Gk *plinthos* tile, brick, squared stone]

Pliocene /ˈplaɪəˌsiːn/ adj. & n. Geol. —adj. of or relating to the last epoch of the Tertiary period. —n. this epoch or system. [Gk *pleiōn* more + *kainos* new]

PLO abbr. Palestine Liberation Organization.

plod v. & n. —v. (**plodded**, **plodding**) **1** intr. (often foll. by *along*, *on*, etc.) walk doggedly or laboriously; trudge. **2** intr. (often foll. by *at*) work slowly and steadily. **3** tr. tread or make (one's way) laboriously. —n. the act or a spell of plodding. □ **plodder** n. **ploddingly** adv. [16th c.: prob. imit.]

-ploid /plɔɪd/ comb. form Biol. forming adjectives denoting the number of sets of chromosomes in a cell (*diploid*; *polyploid*). [after HAPLOID]

ploidy /ˈplɔɪdɪ/ n. the number of sets of chromosomes in a cell. [after DIPLOIDY, POLYPLOIDY, etc.]

plonk[1] v. & n. —v.tr. **1** set down hurriedly or clumsily. **2** (usu. foll. by *down*) set down firmly. —n. **1** an act of plonking. **2** a heavy thud. [imit.]

plonk[2] n. colloq. cheap or inferior wine. [orig. Austral.: prob. corrupt. of *blanc* in F *vin blanc* white wine]

plop n., v., & adv. —n. **1** a sound as of a smooth object dropping into water without a splash. **2** an act of falling with this sound. —v. (**plopped**, **plopping**) intr. & tr. fall or drop with a plop. —adv. with a plop. [19th c.: imit.]

plosive /ˈpləʊsɪv/ adj. & n. Phonet. —adj. pronounced with a sudden release of breath. —n. a plosive sound. [EXPLOSIVE]

plot n. & v. —n. **1** a defined and usu. small piece of ground. **2** the interrelationship of the main events in a play, novel, film, etc. **3** a conspiracy or secret plan, esp. to achieve an unlawful end. **4** esp. US a graph or diagram. —v. (**plotted**, **plotting**) tr. **1** make a plan or map of (an existing object, a place or thing to be laid out, constructed, etc.). **2** (also absol.) plan or contrive secretly (a crime, conspiracy, etc.). **3** mark (a point or course etc.) on a chart or diagram. **4 a** mark out or allocate (points) on a graph. **b** make (a curve etc.) by marking out a number of points. □ **plotless** adj. **plotlessness** n. **plotter** n. [OE and f. OF *complot* secret plan: both of unkn. orig.]

plough /plaʊ/ n. & v. (esp. US **plow**) —n. **1** an implement with a cutting blade fixed in a frame drawn by a tractor or by horses, for cutting furrows in the soil and turning it up. **2** an implement resembling this and having a comparable function (*snowplough*). **3** (**the Plough**) the constellation Ursa Major or its seven bright stars. —v. **1** tr. (also absol.) turn up (the earth) with a plough, esp. before sowing. **2** tr. (foll. by *out*, *up*, *down*, etc.) turn or extract (roots, weeds, etc.) with a plough. **3** tr. furrow or scratch (a surface) as if with a plough. **4** tr. produce (a furrow or line) in this way. **5** intr. (foll. by *through*) advance laboriously, esp. through work, a book, etc. **6** intr. (foll. by *through*, *into*) move

like a plough violently. **7** intr. & tr. Brit. colloq. fail in an examination. □ **plough back 1** plough (grass etc.) into the soil to enrich it. **2** reinvest (profits) in the business producing them. **put one's hand to the plough** undertake a task (Luke 9:62). □ **ploughable** adj. **plougher** n. [OE *plōh* f. ON *plógr* f. Gmc]

ploughman /ˈplaʊmən/ n. (pl. **-men**) a person who uses a plough. □ **ploughman's lunch** a meal of bread and cheese with pickle or salad.

ploughshare /ˈplaʊʃeə(r)/ n. the cutting blade of a plough.

plover /ˈplʌvə(r)/ n. any plump-breasted wading bird of the family Charadriidae, including the lapwing. [ME & AF f. OF *plo(u)vier* ult. f. L *pluvia* rain]

plow US var. of PLOUGH.

ploy n. colloq. a stratagem; a cunning manoeuvre to gain an advantage. [orig. Sc., 18th c.: orig. unkn.]

PLR abbr. (in the UK) Public Lending Right.

pluck v. & n. —v. **1** tr. (often foll. by *out*, *off*, etc.) remove by picking or pulling out or away. **2** tr. strip (a bird) of feathers. **3** tr. pull at, twitch. **4** intr. (foll. by *at*) tug or snatch at. **5** tr. sound (the string of a musical instrument) with the finger or plectrum etc. **6** tr. plunder. **7** tr. swindle. —n. **1** courage, spirit. **2** an act of plucking; a twitch. **3** the heart, liver, and lungs of an animal as food. □ **pluck up** summon up (one's courage, spirits, etc.). □ **plucker** n. **pluckless** adj. [OE *ploccian*, *pluccian*, f. Gmc]

plucky /ˈplʌkɪ/ adj. (**pluckier**, **pluckiest**) brave, spirited. □ **pluckily** adv. **pluckiness** n.

plug n. & v. —n. **1** a piece of solid material fitting tightly into a hole, used to fill a gap or cavity or act as a wedge or stopper. **2 a** a device of metal pins in an insulated casing fitting into holes in a socket for making an electrical connection, esp. between an appliance and the mains. **b** colloq. an electric socket. **3** = *sparking-plug*. **4** colloq. a piece of (often free) publicity for an idea, product, etc. **5** a mass of solidified lava filling the neck of a volcano. **6** a cake or stick of tobacco; a piece of this for chewing. —v. (**plugged**, **plugging**) **1** tr. (often foll. by *up*) stop (a hole etc.) with a plug. **2** tr. sl. shoot or hit (a person etc.). **3** tr. colloq. seek to popularize (an idea, product, etc.) by constant recommendation. **4** intr. colloq. (often foll. by *at*) work steadily away (at). □ **plug in** connect electrically by inserting a plug in a socket. **plug-in** adj. able to be connected by means of a plug. □ **plugger** n. [MDu. & MLG *plugge*, of unkn. orig.]

plum n. **1 a** an oval fleshy fruit, usu. purple or yellow when ripe, with sweet pulp and a flattish pointed stone. **b** any deciduous tree of the genus *Prunus* bearing this. **2** a reddish-purple colour. **3** a dried grape or raisin used in cooking. **4** colloq. the best of a collection; something especially prized (often attrib.: *a plum job*). □ **plum cake** a cake containing raisins, currants, etc. **plum pudding** a rich boiled suet pudding with raisins, currants, spices, etc. [OE *plūme* f. med.L *pruna* f. L *prunum*]

plumage /ˈpluːmɪdʒ/ n. a bird's feathers. □ **plumaged** adj. (usu. in comb.). [ME f. OF (as PLUME)]

plumb[1] /plʌm/ n., adv., adj., & v. —n. a ball of lead or other heavy material, esp. one attached to the end of a line for finding the depth of water or determining the vertical on an upright surface. —*adv.* **1** exactly (*plumb in the centre*). **2** vertically. **3** *US sl.* quite, utterly (*plumb crazy*). —*adj.* **1** vertical. **2** downright, sheer (*plumb nonsense*). —*v.tr.* **1 a** measure the depth of (water) with a plumb. **b** determine (a depth). **2** test (an upright surface) to determine the vertical. **3** reach or experience in extremes (*plumb the depths of fear*). **4** learn in detail the facts about (a matter). □ **out of plumb** not vertical. **plumb-line** a line with a plumb attached. [ME, prob. ult. f. L *plumbum* lead, assim. to OF *plomb* lead]

plumb² /plʌm/ *v.* **1** *tr.* provide (a building or room etc.) with plumbing. **2** *tr.* (often foll. by *in*) fit as part of a plumbing system. **3** *intr.* work as a plumber. [back-form. f. PLUMBER]

plumbago /plʌmˈbeɪɡəʊ/ *n.* = GRAPHITE. [L f. *plumbum* LEAD²]

plumber /ˈplʌmə(r)/ *n.* a person who fits and repairs the apparatus of a water-supply, heating, etc. [ME *plummer* etc. f. OF *plommier* f. L *plumbarius* f. *plumbum* LEAD²]

plumbing /ˈplʌmɪŋ/ *n.* **1** the system or apparatus of water-supply, heating, etc., in a building. **2** the work of a plumber.

plume *n. & v.* —*n.* **1** a feather, esp. a large one used for ornament. **2** an ornament of feathers etc. attached to a helmet or hat or worn in the hair. **3** something resembling this (*a plume of smoke*). —*v.* **1** *tr.* decorate or provide with a plume or plumes. **2** *refl.* (foll. by *on, upon*) pride (oneself on esp. something trivial). **3** *tr.* (of a bird) preen (itself or its feathers). □ **plumeless** *adj.* **plumelike** *adj.* **plumery** *n.* [ME f. OF f. L *pluma* down]

plummet /ˈplʌmɪt/ *n. & v.* —*n.* **1** a plumb or plumb-line. **2** a sounding-line. **3** a weight attached to a fishing-line to keep the float upright. —*v.intr.* (**plummeted, plummeting**) fall or plunge rapidly. [ME f. OF *plommet* dimin. (as PLUMB¹)]

plummy /ˈplʌmɪ/ *adj.* (**plummier, plummiest**) **1** abounding or rich in plums. **2** *colloq.* (of a voice) sounding affectedly rich or deep in tone. **3** *colloq.* good, desirable.

plump¹ *adj. & v.* —*adj.* (esp. of a person or animal or part of the body) having a full rounded shape; fleshy; filled out. —*v.tr. & intr.* (often foll. by *up, out*) make or become plump; fatten. □ **plumpish** *adj.* **plumply** *adv.* **plumpness** *n.* **plumpy** *adj.* [ME *plompe* f. MDu. *plomp* blunt, MLG *plump, plomp* shapeless etc.]

plump² *v., n., adv., & adj.* —*v.* **1** *intr. & tr.* (often foll. by *down*) drop or fall abruptly (*plumped down on the chair; plumped it on the floor*). **2** *intr.* (foll. by *for*) decide definitely in favour of (one of two or more possibilities). —*n.* an abrupt plunge; a heavy fall. —*adv. colloq.* **1** with a sudden or heavy fall. **2** directly, bluntly (*I told him plump*). —*adj. colloq.* direct, unqualified (*answered with a plump 'no'*). [ME f. MLG *plumpen*, MDu. *plompen*: orig. imit.]

plumy /ˈpluːmɪ/ *adj.* (**plumier, plumiest**) **1** plumelike, feathery. **2** adorned with plumes.

plunder /ˈplʌndə(r)/ *v. & n.* —*v.tr.* **1** rob (a place or person) forcibly of goods, e.g. as in war. **2** rob systematically. **3** (also *absol.*) steal or embezzle (goods). —*n.* **1** the violent or dishonest acquisition of property. **2** property acquired by plundering. **3** *colloq.* profit, gain. □ **plunderer** *n.* [LG *plündern* lit. 'rob of household goods' f. MHG *plunder* clothing etc.]

plunge *v. & n.* —*v.* **1** (usu. foll. by *in, into*) **a** *tr.* thrust forcefully or abruptly. **b** *intr.* dive; propel oneself forcibly. **c** *intr. & tr.* enter or cause to enter a certain condition or embark on a certain course abruptly or impetuously (*they plunged into a lively discussion; the room was plunged into darkness*). **2** *tr.* immerse completely. **3** *intr.* **a** move suddenly and dramatically downward. **b** (foll. by *down, into,* etc.) move with a rush (*plunged down the stairs*). **c** diminish rapidly (*share prices have plunged*). **4** *intr.* (of a horse) start violently forward. **5** *intr.* (of a ship) pitch. **6** *intr. colloq.* gamble heavily; run into debt. —*n.* a plunging action or movement; a dive. □ **plunging** (or **plunge**) **neckline** a low-cut neckline. **take the plunge** *colloq.* commit oneself to a (usu. risky) course of action. [ME f. OF *plungier* ult. f. L *plumbum* plummet]

plunger /ˈplʌndʒə(r)/ *n.* **1** a part of a mechanism that works with a plunging or thrusting movement. **2** a rubber cup on a handle for clearing blocked pipes by a plunging and sucking action.

plunk *n. & v.* —*n.* **1** the sound made by the sharply plucked string of a stringed instrument. **2** *US* a heavy blow. **3** *US* = PLONK¹ *n.* —*v.* **1** *intr. & tr.* sound or cause to sound with a plunk. **2** *tr. US* hit abruptly. **3** *tr. US* = PLONK¹ *v.* [imit.]

pluperfect /pluːˈpɜːfɪkt/ *adj. & n. Gram.* —*adj.* (of a tense) denoting an action completed prior to some past point of time specified or implied, as: *he had gone by then*. —*n.* the pluperfect tense. [mod.L *plusperfectum* f. L *plus quam perfectum* more than perfect]

plural /ˈplʊər(ə)l/ *adj. & n.* —*adj.* **1** more than one in number. **2** *Gram.* (of a word or form) denoting more than one, or (in languages with dual number) more than two. —*n. Gram.* **1** a plural word or form. **2** the plural number. □ **plurally** *adv.* [ME f. OF *plurel* f. L *pluralis* f. *plus pluris* more]

pluralism /ˈplʊərəˌlɪz(ə)m/ *n.* **1** holding more than one office, esp. an ecclesiastical office or benefice, at a time. **2** a form of society in which the members of minority groups maintain their independent cultural traditions. □ **pluralist** *n.* **pluralistic** /-ˈlɪstɪk/ *adj.* **pluralistically** /-ˈlɪstɪkəlɪ/ *adv.*

plurality /plʊəˈrælɪtɪ/ *n.* (*pl.* **-ies**) **1** the state of being plural. **2** = PLURALISM 1. **3** a large or the greater number. **4** *US* a majority that is not absolute. [ME f. OF *pluralité* f. LL *pluralitas* (as PLURAL)]

pluralize /ˈplʊərəˌlaɪz/ *v.* (also **-ise**) **1** *tr. & intr.* make or become plural. **2** *tr.* express in the plural.

plus /plʌs/ *prep., adj., n., & conj.* —*prep.* **1** *Math.* with the addition of (*3 plus 4 equals 7*). **2** (of temperature) above zero (*plus 2° C*). **3** *colloq.* with; having gained; newly possessing (*returned plus a new car*). —*adj.* **1** (after a number) at least (*fifteen plus*). **2** (after a grade etc.) rather better than (*beta plus*). **3** *Math.* positive. **4** having a positive electrical charge. —*n.* **1** = plus sign. **2** *Math.* an additional or positive quantity. **3** an advantage (*experience is a definite plus*). —*conj. colloq. disp.* also; and furthermore. □ **plus sign**

the symbol +, indicating addition or a positive value. [L, = more]

■ **Usage** The use of *plus* as a conjunction, as in *they arrived late, plus they wanted a meal*, is considered incorrect by some people.

plus-fours /plʌs'fɔːz/ *n.* long wide men's knickerbockers usu. worn for golf etc. [20th c.: so named because the overhang at the knee requires an extra four inches]

plush *n.* & *adj.* —*n.* cloth of silk or cotton etc., with a long soft nap. —*adj.* 1 made of plush. 2 plushy. □ **plushly** *adv.* **plushness** *n.* [obs. F *pluche* contr. f. *peluche* f. OF *peluchier* f. It. *peluzzo* dimin. of *pelo* f. L *pilus* hair]

plushy /'plʌʃɪ/ *adj.* (**plushier, plushiest**) *colloq.* stylish, luxurious. □ **plushiness** *n.*

plutocracy /pluːˈtɒkrəsɪ/ *n.* (*pl.* **-ies**) 1 a government by the wealthy. b a State governed in this way. 2 a wealthy élite or ruling class. □ **plutocratic** /ˌpluːtəˈkrætɪk/ *adj.* **plutocratically** /ˌpluːtəˈkrætɪkəlɪ/ *adv.* [Gk *ploutokratia* f. *ploutos* wealth + -CRACY]

plutocrat /'pluːtəˌkræt/ *n. derog.* or *joc.* 1 a member of a plutocracy or wealthy élite. 2 a wealthy and influential person.

plutonic /pluːˈtɒnɪk/ *adj.* *Geol.* (of rock) formed as igneous rock by solidification below the surface of the earth. [L *Plutonius* f. Gk *ploutōnios* f. *Ploutōn* god of the underworld]

plutonium /pluːˈtəʊnɪəm/ *n. Chem.* a dense silvery radioactive metallic transuranic element of the actinide series, used in some nuclear reactors and weapons. [formed as PLUTONIC]

pluvial /'pluːvɪəl/ *adj.* & *n.* —*adj.* 1 of rain; rainy. 2 *Geol.* caused by rain. —*n.* a period of prolonged rainfall. □ **pluvious** *adj.* (in sense 1). [L *pluvialis* f. *pluvia* rain]

ply¹ /plaɪ/ *n.* (*pl.* **-ies**) 1 a thickness or layer of certain materials, esp. wood or cloth (*three-ply*). 2 a strand of yarn or rope etc. [ME f. F *pli* f. *plier*, *pleier* f. L *plicare* fold]

ply² /plaɪ/ *v.* (**-ies, -ied**) 1 *tr.* use or wield vigorously (a tool, weapon, etc.). 2 *tr.* work steadily at (one's business or trade). 3 *tr.* (foll. by *with*) a supply (a person) continuously (with food, drink, etc.). b approach repeatedly (with questions, demands, etc.). 4 a *intr.* (often foll. by *between*) (of a vehicle etc.) travel regularly (to and fro between two points). b *tr.* work (a route) in this way. 5 *intr.* (of a taxi-driver, boatman, etc.) attend regularly for custom (*ply for trade*). [ME *plye*, f. APPLY]

Plymouth Brethren /'plɪməθ/ *n.pl.* a strict Calvinistic religious body formed at Plymouth in Devon *c.*1830.

plywood /'plaɪwʊd/ *n.* a strong thin board consisting of two or more layers glued and pressed together with the direction of the grain alternating.

PM *abbr.* 1 Prime Minister. 2 post-mortem.

Pm *symb. Chem.* the element promethium.

p.m. *abbr.* after noon. [L *post meridiem*]

PMS *abbr.* premenstrual syndrome.

PMT *abbr.* premenstrual tension.

pneumatic /njuːˈmætɪk/ *adj.* & *n.* —*adj.* 1 of or relating to air or wind. 2 containing or operated by compressed air. □ **pneumatic drill** a drill driven by compressed air, for breaking up a hard surface. □ **pneumatically** *adv.* **pneumaticity** /ˌnjuːməˈtɪsɪtɪ/ *n.* [F *pneumatique* or L *pneumaticus* f. Gk *pneumatikos* f. *pneuma* wind f. *pneō* breathe]

pneumato- /'njuːmətəʊ/ *comb. form* denoting: 1 air. 2 breath. 3 spirit. [Gk f. *pneuma* (as PNEUMATIC)]

pneumo- /'njuːməʊ/ *comb. form* denoting the lungs. [abbr. of *pneumono-* f. Gk *pneumōn* lung]

pneumoconiosis /ˌnjuːməʊˌkɒnɪ'əʊsɪs/ *n.* a lung disease caused by inhalation of dust or small particles. [PNEUMO- + Gk *konis* dust]

pneumonia /njuːˈməʊnɪə/ *n.* a bacterial inflammation of one lung (**single pneumonia**) or both lungs (**double pneumonia**) causing the air sacs to fill with pus and become solid. □ **pneumonic** /njuːˈmɒnɪk/ *adj.* [L f. Gk *pneumōn* lung]

PO *abbr.* 1 Post Office. 2 postal order. 3 Petty Officer. 4 Pilot Officer.

Po *symb. Chem.* the element polonium.

po /pəʊ/ *n.* (*pl.* **pos**) *Brit. colloq.* a chamber-pot.

poach¹ /pəʊtʃ/ *v.tr.* 1 cook (an egg) without its shell in or over boiling water. 2 cook (fish etc.) by simmering in a small amount of liquid. □ **poacher** *n.* [ME f. OF *pochier* f. *poche* POKE²]

poach² /pəʊtʃ/ *v.* 1 *tr.* (also *absol.*) catch (game or fish) illegally. 2 *intr.* (often foll. by *on*) trespass or encroach (on another's property, ideas, etc.). 3 *tr.* appropriate illicitly or unfairly (a person, thing, idea, etc.). □ **poacher** *n.* [earlier *poche*, perh. f. F *pocher* put in a pocket (as POACH¹)]

pochette /pɒ'ʃet/ *n.* a woman's envelope-shaped handbag. [F, dimin. of *poche* pocket: see POKE²]

pock *n.* (also **pock-mark**) 1 a small pus-filled spot on the skin, esp. caused by chickenpox or smallpox. 2 a mark resembling this. □ **pock-marked** bearing marks resembling or left by such spots. □ **pocky** *adj.* [OE *poc* f. Gmc]

pocket /'pɒkɪt/ *n.* & *v.* —*n.* 1 a small bag sewn into or on clothing, for carrying small articles. 2 a pouchlike compartment in a suitcase, car door, etc. 3 one's financial resources (*it is beyond my pocket*). 4 an isolated group or area. 5 a cavity in the earth containing ore, esp. gold. 6 a pouch at the corner or on the side of a billiard- or snooker-table into which balls are driven. 7 an apparent vacuum in the air causing an aircraft to drop suddenly. 8 (*attrib.*) a of a suitable size and shape for carrying in a pocket. b smaller than the usual size. —*v.tr.* (**pocketed, pocketing**) 1 put into one's pocket. 2 appropriate, esp. dishonestly. 3 confine as in a pocket. 4 submit to (an injury or affront). 5 conceal or suppress (one's feelings). 6 *Billiards* etc. drive (a ball) into a pocket. □ **in pocket** 1 having gained in a transaction. 2 (of money) available. **in a person's pocket** 1 under a person's control. 2 close to or intimate with a person. **out of pocket** having lost in a transaction. **out-of-pocket expenses** the actual outlay of cash incurred. **pocket knife** a knife with a folding blade or blades, for carrying in the pocket. **pocket money** 1 money for minor expenses. 2 *Brit.* an allowance of money made to a child. **put one's hand in one's pocket** spend or provide money. □ **pocketable** *adj.* **pocketless** *adj.* **pockety** *adj.* (in sense 5 of *n.*). [ME f. AF *poket(e)* dimin. of *poke* POKE²]

pocketbook /'pɒkɪtbʊk/ *n.* 1 a notebook. 2 a booklike case for papers or money carried in a pocket. 3 *US* a purse or handbag. 4 *US* a paperback or other small book.

pocketful /'pɒkɪtˌfʊl/ *n.* (*pl.* **-fuls**) as much as a pocket will hold.

pod *n.* & *v.* —*n.* **1** a long seed-vessel esp. of a leguminous plant, e.g. a pea. **2** a compartment suspended under an aircraft for equipment etc. —*v.* (**podded, podding**) **1** *intr.* bear or form pods. **2** *tr.* remove (peas etc.) from pods. □ **in pod** *colloq.* pregnant. [back-form. f. dial. *podware, podder* field crops, of unkn. orig.]

podagra /pə'dægrə, 'pɒdəgrə/ *n. Med.* gout of the foot, esp. the big toe. □ **podagral** *adj.* **podagric** *adj.* **podagrous** *adj.* [L f. Gk *pous podos* foot + *agra* seizure]

podgy /'pɒdʒɪ/ *adj.* (**podgier, podgiest**) **1** (of a person) short and fat. **2** (of a face etc.) plump, fleshy. □ **podginess** *n.* [19th c.: f. *podge* a short fat person]

podiatry /pə'daɪətrɪ/ *n. US* = CHIROPODY. □ **podiatrist** *n.* [Gk *pous podos* foot + *iatros* physician]

podium /'pəʊdɪəm/ *n.* (*pl.* **podiums** or **podia** /-dɪə/) **1** a continuous projecting base or pedestal round a room or house etc. **2** a raised platform round the arena of an amphitheatre. **3** a platform or rostrum. [L f. Gk *podion* dimin. of *pous pod-* foot]

poem /'pəʊɪm/ *n.* **1** a metrical composition, usu. concerned with feeling or imaginative description. **2** an elevated composition in verse or prose. **3** something with poetic qualities (*a poem in stone*). [F *poème* or L *poema* f. Gk *poēma* = *poiēma* f. *poieō* make]

poesy /'pəʊɪzɪ, -sɪ/ *n. archaic* **1** poetry. **2** the art or composition of poetry. [ME f. OF *poesie* ult. f. L *poesis* f. Gk *poēsis* = *poiēsis* making, poetry (as POEM)]

poet /'pəʊɪt/ *n.* (*fem.* **poetess**) **1** a writer of poems. **2** a person possessing high powers of imagination or expression etc. □ **Poet Laureate** (in the UK) a poet appointed to write poems for State occasions. **Poets' Corner** part of Westminster Abbey where several poets are buried or commemorated. [ME f. OF *poete* f. L *poeta* f. Gk *poētēs* = *poiētēs* maker, poet (as POEM)]

poetaster /ˌpəʊɪ'tæstə(r)/ *n.* a paltry or inferior poet. [mod.L (as POET): see -ASTER]

poetic /pəʊ'etɪk/ *adj.* (also **poetical** /-tɪk(ə)l/) **1** a of or like poetry or poets. **b** written in verse. **2** elevated or sublime in expression. □ **poetic justice** well-deserved unforeseen retribution or reward. **poetic licence** a writer's or artist's transgression of established rules for effect. □ **poetically** *adv.* [F *poétique* f. L *poeticus* f. Gk *poētikos* (as POET)]

poeticize /pəʊ'etɪˌsaɪz/ *v.tr.* (also **-ise**) make (a theme) poetic.

poetry /'pəʊɪtrɪ/ *n.* **1** the art or work of a poet. **2** poems collectively. **3** a poetic or tenderly pleasing quality. **4** anything compared to poetry. [ME f. med.L *poetria* f. L *poeta* POET, prob. after *geometry*]

po-faced /pəʊ'feɪsd/ *adj.* **1** solemn-faced, humourless. **2** smug. [20th c.: perh. f. PO, infl. by *poker-faced*]

pogo /'pəʊgəʊ/ *n.* (*pl.* **-os**) (also **pogo stick**) a toy consisting of a spring-loaded stick with rests for the feet, for springing about on. [20th c.: orig. uncert.]

pogrom /'pɒgrəm, -rɒm/ *n.* an organized massacre (orig. of Jews in Russia). [Russ., = devastation f. *gromit'* destroy]

poignant /'pɔɪnjənt/ *adj.* **1** painfully sharp to the emotions or senses; deeply moving. **2** arousing sympathy. **3** sharp or pungent in taste or smell. **4** pleasantly piquant. □ **poignance** *n.* **poignancy** *n.* **poignantly** *adv.* [ME f. OF, pres. part. of *poindre* prick f. L *pungere*]

poinsettia /pɔɪn'setɪə/ *n.* a shrub, *Euphorbia pulcherrima*, with large showy scarlet or pink bracts surrounding small yellow flowers. [mod.L f. J. R. Poinsett, Amer. diplomat d. 1851]

point *n.* & *v.* —*n.* **1** the sharp or tapered end of a tool, weapon, pencil, etc. **2** a tip or extreme end. **3** that which in geometry has position but not magnitude, e.g. the intersection of two lines. **4** a particular place or position (*Bombay and points east; point of contact*). **5** a a precise or particular moment (*at the point of death*). **b** the critical or decisive moment (*when it came to the point, he refused*). **6** a very small mark on a surface. **7** a dot or other punctuation mark, esp. = *full point*. **8** = *decimal point*. **9** a stage or degree in progress or increase (*abrupt to the point of rudeness; at that point we gave up*). **10** a level of temperature at which a change of state occurs (*freezing-point*). **11** a single item; a detail or particular (*we differ on these points; it is a point of principle*). **12** a a unit of scoring in games or of measuring value etc. **b** an advantage or success in less quantifiable contexts such as an argument or discussion. **13** a (usu. prec. by *the*) the significant or essential thing; what is actually intended or under discussion (*that was the point of the question*). **b** (usu. with *neg.* or *interrog.*; often foll. by *in*) sense or purpose; advantage or value (*saw no point in staying*). **c** (usu. prec. by *the*) a salient feature of a story, joke, remark, etc. (*don't see the point*). **14** a distinctive feature or characteristic (*it has its points; tact is not his good point*). **15** pungency, effectiveness (*their comments lacked point*). **16** a each of 32 directions marked at equal distances round a compass. **b** the corresponding direction towards the horizon. **17** (usu. in *pl.*) *Brit.* a junction of two railway lines, with a pair of linked tapering rails that can be moved laterally to allow a train to pass from one line to the other. **18** *Brit.* = *power point*. **19** (usu. in *pl.*) each of a set of electrical contacts in the distributor of a motor vehicle. **20** *Cricket* a a fielder on the off side near the batsman. **b** this position. **21** the tip of the toe in ballet. **22** a promontory. **23** *Printing* a unit of measurement for type bodies (in the UK and US 0.0138 in., in Europe 0.0148 in.). —*v.* **1** (usu. foll. by *to, at*) a *tr.* direct or aim (a finger, weapon, etc.). **b** *intr.* direct attention in a certain direction (*pointed to the house across the road*). **2** *intr.* (foll. by *at, towards*) a aim or be directed to. **b** tend towards. **3** *intr.* (foll. by *to*) indicate; be evidence of (*it all points to murder*). **4** *tr.* give point or force to (words or actions). **5** *tr.* fill in or repair the joints of (brickwork) with smoothly finished mortar or cement. **6** *tr.* punctuate. **7** *tr.* sharpen (a pencil, tool, etc.). **8** *tr.* (also *absol.*) (of a dog) indicate the presence of (game) by acting as pointer. □ **at all points** in every part or respect. **at the point of** (often foll. by verbal noun) on the verge of; about to do (the action specified). **beside the point** irrelevant or irrelevantly. **case in point** an instance that is relevant or (prec. by *the*) under consideration. **have a point** be correct or effective in one's contention. **in point** apposite, relevant. **make** (or **prove**) **a** (or **one's**) **point**

establish a proposition; prove one's contention. **make a point of** (often foll. by verbal noun) insist on; treat or regard as essential. **nine points** nine tenths, i.e. nearly the whole (esp. *possession is nine points of the law*). **on** (or **upon**) **the point of** (foll. by verbal noun) about to do (the action specified). **point-duty** the positioning of a police officer or traffic warden at a crossroad or other point to control traffic. **point of honour** an action or circumstance that affects one's reputation. **point of no return** a point in a journey or enterprise at which it becomes essential or more practical to continue to the end. **point of order** a query in a debate etc. as to whether correct procedure is being followed. **point-of-sale** (usu. *attrib.*) denoting publicity etc. associated with the place at which goods are retailed. **point of view 1** a position from which a thing is viewed. **2** a particular way of considering a matter. **point out** (often foll. by *that* + clause) indicate, show; draw attention to. **point-to-point** a steeplechase over a marked course for horses used regularly in hunting. **point up** emphasize; show as important. **score points off** get the better of in an argument etc. **take a person's point** concede that a person has made a valid contention. **to the point** relevant or relevantly. **up to a point** to some extent but not completely. **win on points** *Boxing* win by scoring more points, not by a knockout. [ME f. OF *point, pointer* f. L *punctum* f. *pungere punct-* prick]

point-blank /ˈpɔɪntˈblæŋk/ *adj. & adv.* —*adj.* **1 a** (of a shot) aimed or fired horizontally at a range very close to the target. **b** (of a distance or range) very close. **2** (of a remark, question, etc.) blunt, direct. —*adv.* **1** at very close range. **2** directly, bluntly. [prob. f. POINT + BLANK = white spot in the centre of a target]

pointed /ˈpɔɪntɪd/ *adj.* **1** sharpened or tapering to a point. **2** (of a remark etc.) having point; penetrating, cutting. **3** emphasized; made evident. □ **pointedly** *adv.* **pointedness** *n.*

pointer /ˈpɔɪntə(r)/ *n.* **1** a thing that points, e.g. the index hand of a gauge etc. **2** a rod for pointing to features on a map, chart, etc. **3** *colloq.* a hint, clue, or indication. **4 a** a dog of a breed that on scenting game stands rigid looking towards it. **b** this breed.

pointillism /ˈpwæntɪˌlɪz(ə)m/ *n. Art* a technique of impressionist painting using tiny dots of various pure colours, which become blended in the viewer's eye. □ **pointillist** *n. & adj.* **pointillistic** /-ˈlɪstɪk/ *adj.* [F *pointillisme* f. *pointiller* mark with dots]

pointing /ˈpɔɪntɪŋ/ *n.* **1** cement or mortar filling the joints of brickwork. **2** facing produced by this. **3** the process of producing this.

pointless /ˈpɔɪntlɪs/ *adj.* **1** without a point. **2** lacking force, purpose, or meaning. **3** (in games) without a point scored. □ **pointlessly** *adv.* **pointlessness** *n.*

pointy /ˈpɔɪntɪ/ *adj.* (**pointier, pointiest**) having a noticeably sharp end; pointed.

poise /pɔɪz/ *n. & v.* —*n.* **1** composure or self-possession of manner. **2** equilibrium; a stable state. **3** carriage (of the head etc.). —*v.* **1** *tr.* balance; hold suspended or supported. **2** *tr.* carry (one's head etc. in a specified way). **3** *intr.* be balanced; hover in the air etc. [ME f. OF *pois*,

peis, peser ult. f. L *pensum* weight f. *pendere pens-* weigh]

poised /pɔɪzd/ *adj.* **1** composed, self-assured. **2** (often foll. by *for*, or *to* + infin.) ready for action.

poison /ˈpɔɪz(ə)n/ *n. & v.* —*n.* **1 a** a substance that when introduced into or absorbed by a living organism causes death or injury, esp. one that kills by rapid action even in a small quantity. **2** *colloq.* a harmful influence or principle etc. —*v.tr.* **1** administer poison to (a person or animal). **2** kill or injure or infect with poison. **3** infect (air, water, etc.) with poison. **4** (esp. as **poisoned** *adj.*) treat (a weapon) with poison. **5** corrupt or pervert (a person or mind). **6** spoil or destroy (a person's pleasure etc.). **7** render (land etc.) foul and unfit for its purpose by a noxious application etc. □ **poison gas** = GAS *n.* 4. **poison ivy** a N. American climbing plant, *Rhus toxicodendron*, secreting an irritant oil from its leaves. **poison-pen letter** an anonymous libellous or abusive letter. □ **poisoner** *n.* **poisonous** *adj.* **poisonously** *adv.* [ME f. OF *poison, poisonner* (as POTION)]

poke[1] *v. & n.* —*v.* **1** (foll. by *in, up, down,* etc.) **a** thrust or push with the hand, point of a stick, etc. **b** *intr.* be thrust forward. **2** *intr.* (foll. by *at* etc.) make thrusts with a stick etc. **3** *tr.* thrust the end of a finger etc. against. **4** *tr.* (foll. by *in*) produce (a hole etc. in a thing) by poking. **5** *tr.* thrust forward, esp. obtrusively. **6** *tr.* stir (a fire) with a poker. **7** *intr.* **a** (often foll. by *about, around*) move or act desultorily; potter. **b** (foll. by *about, into*) pry; search casually. —*n.* **1** the act or an instance of poking. **2** a thrust or nudge. **3 a** a projecting brim or front of a woman's bonnet or hat. **b** (in full **poke-bonnet**) a bonnet having this. □ **poke fun at** ridicule, tease. **poke one's nose into** *colloq.* pry or intrude into (esp. a person's affairs). [ME f. MDu. and MLG *poken*, of unkn. orig.]

poke[2] *n. dial.* a bag or sack. [ME f. ONF *poke, poque* = OF *poche*: cf. POUCH]

poker[1] /ˈpəʊkə(r)/ *n.* a stiff metal rod with a handle for stirring an open fire. □ **poker-work** the technique of burning designs on white wood etc. with a heated metal rod.

poker[2] /ˈpəʊkə(r)/ *n.* a card-game in which bluff is used as players bet on the value of their hands. □ **poker-face 1** the impassive countenance appropriate to a poker-player. **2** a person with this. [19th c.: orig. unkn.: cf. G *pochen* to brag, *Pochspiel* bragging game]

poky /ˈpəʊkɪ/ *adj.* (**pokier, pokiest**) (of a room etc.) small and cramped. □ **pokily** *adv.* **pokiness** *n.* [POKE[1] (in colloq. sense 'confine') + -Y[1]]

polar /ˈpəʊlə(r)/ **1** *adj.* **a** of or near a pole of the earth or a celestial body, or of the celestial sphere. **b** (of a species or variety) living in the north polar region. **2** having magnetic polarity. **3 a** (of a molecule) having a positive charge at one end and a negative charge at the other. **b** (of a compound) having electric charges. **4** *Geom.* of or relating to a pole. **5** directly opposite in character or tendency. □ **polar bear** a white bear, *Ursus maritimus*, of the Arctic regions. **polar circle** each of the circles parallel to the equator at a distance of 23° 27′ from either pole. □ **polarly** *adv.* [F *polaire* or mod.L *polaris* (as POLE[2])]

polarity /pəˈlærɪtɪ/ *n.* (*pl.* **-ies**) **1** the tendency of a lodestone, magnetized bar, etc., to point with its extremities to the magnetic poles of the earth. **2** the condition of having two poles with contrary qualities. **3** the state of having two opposite tendencies, opinions, etc. **4** the electrical condition of a body (positive or negative).

polarize /ˈpəʊləˌraɪz/ v. (also **-ise**) **1** tr. restrict the vibrations of (a transverse wave, esp. light) to one direction. **2** tr. give magnetic or electric polarity to (a substance or body). **3** tr. & intr. divide into two groups of opposing opinion etc. □ **polarizable** adj. **polarization** /-ˈzeɪʃ(ə)n/ n. **polarizer** n.

Polaroid /ˈpəʊləˌrɔɪd/ n. propr. **1** material in thin plastic sheets that polarizes light passing through it. **2** a type of camera with internal processing that produces a finished print rapidly after each exposure. **3** (in pl.) sunglasses with lenses made from Polaroid. [POLAR + -OID]

polder /ˈpəʊldə(r)/ n. a piece of low-lying land reclaimed from the sea or a river, esp. in the Netherlands. [MDu. polre, Du. polder]

Pole n. **1** a native or national of Poland. **2** a person of Polish descent. [G f. Pol. Polanie, lit. field-dwellers f. pole field]

pole[1] n. & v. —n. **1** a long slender rounded piece of wood or metal, esp. with the end placed in the ground as a support etc. **2** a wooden shaft fitted to the front of a vehicle and attached to the yokes or collars of the draught animals. **3** = PERCH[1]. —v.tr. **1** provide with poles. **2** (usu. foll. by off) push off (a punt etc.) with a pole. □ **pole position** the most favourable position at the start of a motor race (orig. next to the inside boundary-fence). **pole-vault** (or **-jump**) n. the athletic sport of vaulting over a high bar with the aid of a long flexible pole held in the hands and giving extra spring. —v.intr. take part in this sport. **up the pole** sl. **1** crazy, eccentric. **2** in difficulty. [OE pāl ult. f. L palus stake]

pole[2] n. **1** (in full **north pole, south pole**) **a** each of the two points in the celestial sphere about which the stars appear to revolve. **b** each of the extremities of the axis of rotation of the earth or another body. **c** see magnetic pole. **2** each of the two opposite points on the surface of a magnet at which magnetic forces are strongest. **3** each of two terminals (positive and negative) of an electric cell or battery etc. **4** each of two opposed principles or ideas. □ **be poles apart** differ greatly, esp. in nature or opinion. □ **poleward** adj. **polewards** adj. & adv. [ME f. L polus f. Gk polos pivot, axis, sky]

■ **Usage** The spelling is North Pole and South Pole when used as geographical designations.

poleaxe /ˈpəʊlæks/ n. & v. —n. **1** a battleaxe. **2** a butcher's axe. —v.tr. hit or kill with or as if with a poleaxe. [ME pol(l)ax, -ex f. MDu. pol(l)aex, MLG pol(l)exe (as POLL, AXE)]

polecat /ˈpəʊlkæt/ n. **1** Brit. a small European brownish-black fetid flesh-eating mammal, Mustela putorius, of the weasel family. **2** US a skunk. [pole (unexplained) + CAT]

polemic /pəˈlemɪk/ n. & adj. —n. **1** a controversial discussion. **2** Polit. a verbal or written attack, esp. on a political opponent. —adj. (also **polemical**) involving dispute; controversial. □ **polemically** adv. **polemicist** /-sɪst/ n. **polemicize** v.tr. (also **-ise**). **polemize** /ˈpɒlɪˌmaɪz/ v.tr.

(also **-ise**). [med.L polemicus f. Gk polemikos f. polemos war]

polemics /pəˈlemɪks/ n.pl. the art or practice of controversial discussion.

polenta /pəˈlentə/ n. porridge made of maize meal etc. [It. f. L, = pearl barley]

polestar /ˈpəʊlstɑː(r)/ n. **1** Astron. a star in Ursa Minor now about 1° distant from the celestial north pole. **2** a thing or principle serving as a guide.

police /pəˈliːs/ n. & v. —n. **1** (usu. prec. by the) the civil force of a State, responsible for maintaining public order. **2** (as pl.) the members of a police force (several hundred police). **3** a force with similar functions of enforcing regulations (military police; railway police). —v.tr. **1** control (a country or area) by means of police. **2** provide with police. **3** keep order in; control. □ **police dog** a dog, esp. an Alsatian, used in police work. **police officer** a policeman or policewoman. **police State** a totalitarian State controlled by political police supervising the citizens' activities. **police station** the office of a local police force. [F f. med.L politia POLICY[1]]

policeman /pəˈliːsmən/ n. (pl. **-men**; fem. **policewoman**, pl. **-women**) a member of a police force.

policy[1] /ˈpɒlɪsɪ/ n. (pl. **-ies**) **1** a course or principle of action adopted or proposed by a government, party, business, or individual etc. **2** prudent conduct; sagacity. [ME f. OF policie f. L politia f. Gk politeia citizenship f. politēs citizen f. polis city]

policy[2] /ˈpɒlɪsɪ/ n. (pl. **-ies**) **1** a contract of insurance. **2** a document containing this. [F police bill of lading, contract of insurance, f. Prov. poliss(i)a prob. f. med.L apodissa, apodixa, f. L apodixis f. Gk apodeixis evidence, proof (as APO-, deiknumi show)]

■ **Usage** See note at polity.

polio /ˈpəʊlɪəʊ/ n. = POLIOMYELITIS. [abbr.]

poliomyelitis /ˌpəʊlɪəʊˌmaɪˈlaɪtɪs/ n. Med. an infectious viral disease that affects the central nervous system and which can cause temporary or permanent paralysis. [mod.L f. Gk polios grey + muelos marrow]

Polish /ˈpəʊlɪʃ/ adj. & n. —adj. **1** of or relating to Poland. **2** of the Poles or their language. —n. the language of Poland. [POLE + -ISH[1]]

polish /ˈpɒlɪʃ/ v. & n. —v. **1** tr. & intr. make or become smooth or glossy by rubbing. **2** (esp. as **polished** adj.) refine or improve; add finishing touches to. —n. **1** a substance used for polishing. **2** smoothness or glossiness produced by friction. **3** the act or an instance of polishing. **4** refinement or elegance of manner, conduct, etc. □ **polish off** finish (esp. food) quickly. **polish up** revise or improve (a skill etc.). □ **polishable** adj. **polisher** n. [ME f. OF polir f. L polire polit-]

polite /pəˈlaɪt/ adj. (**politer, politest**) **1** having good manners; courteous. **2** (of a person) refined, cultivated, cultured. **3** refined, elegant (polite letters). □ **politely** adv. **politeness** n. [L politus (as POLISH)]

politic /ˈpɒlɪtɪk/ adj. & v. —adj. **1** (of an action) judicious, expedient. **2** (of a person) prudent, sagacious. **3** political (now only in body politic). —v.intr. (**politicked, politicking**) engage in politics. □ **politicly** adv. [ME f. OF politique f. L politicus f. Gk politikos f. politēs citizen f. polis city]

political /pə'lɪtɪk(ə)l/ *adj.* **1 a** of or concerning the State or its government, or public affairs generally. **b** of, relating to, or engaged in politics. **c** belonging to or forming part of a civil administration. **2** having an organized form of society or government. **3** taking or belonging to a side in politics. **4** relating to or affecting interests of status or authority in an organization rather than matters of principle (*a political decision*). □ **political correctness** (esp. in the US) avoidance of forms of expression and action that exclude or marginalize racial and cultural minorities; explicit multiculturalism. **political economy** the study of the economic aspects of government. **political prisoner** a person imprisoned for political beliefs or actions. **political science** the study of the State and systems of government. **political scientist** a specialist in political science. □ **politically** *adv.* [L *politicus* (as POLITIC)]

politician /ˌpɒlɪ'tɪʃ(ə)n/ *n.* **1** a person engaged in or concerned with politics, esp. as a practitioner. **2** a person skilled in politics.

politicize /pə'lɪtɪˌsaɪz/ *v.* (also **-ise**) **1** *tr.* **a** give a political character to. **b** make politically aware. **2** *intr.* engage in or talk politics. □ **politicization** /-ˌzeɪʃ(ə)n/ *n.*

politico /pə'lɪtɪˌkəʊ/ *n.* (*pl.* **-os**) *colloq.* a politician or political enthusiast. [Sp. or It. (as POLITIC)]

politics /'pɒlɪtɪks/ *n.pl.* **1** (treated as *sing.* or *pl.*) **a** the art and science of government. **b** public life and affairs as involving authority and government. **2** (usu. treated as *pl.*) **a** a particular set of ideas, principles, or commitments in politics (*what are their politics?*). **b** activities concerned with the acquisition or exercise of authority or government. **c** an organizational process or principle affecting authority, status, etc. (*the politics of the decision*).

polity /'pɒlɪtɪ/ *n.* (*pl.* **-ies**) **1** a form or process of civil government or constitution. **2** an organized society; a State as a political entity. [L *politia* f. Gk *politeia* f. *politēs* citizen f. *polis* city]

■ **Usage** This word is sometimes confused with *policy*.

polka /'pɒlkə, 'pəʊlkə/ *n.* & *v.* —*n.* **1** a lively dance of Bohemian origin in duple time. **2** the music for this. —*v.intr.* (**polkas, polkaed** /-kəd/ or **polka'd, polkaing** /-kəɪŋ/) dance the polka. □ **polka dot** a round dot as one of many forming a regular pattern on a textile fabric etc. [F and G f. Czech *půlka* half-step f. *půl* half]

poll /pəʊl/ *n.* & *v.* —*n.* **1 a** the process of voting at an election. **b** the counting of votes at an election. **c** the result of voting. **d** the number of votes recorded (*a heavy poll*). **2** = GALLUP POLL, *opinion poll*. **3 a** a human head. **b** the part of this on which hair grows (*flaxen poll*). **4** a hornless animal, esp. one of a breed of hornless cattle. —*v.* **1** *tr.* **a** take the vote or votes of. **b** (in *passive*) have one's vote taken. **c** (of a candidate) receive (so many votes). **d** give (a vote). **2** *tr.* record the opinion of (a person or group) in an opinion poll. **3** *intr.* give one's vote. **4** *tr.* cut off the top of (a tree or plant), esp. make a pollard of. **5** *tr.* (esp. as **polled** *adj.*) cut the horns off (cattle). □ **poll tax 1** *hist.* a tax levied on every adult. **2** = *community charge.* □ **pollee** /pəʊ'liː/ *n.* (in sense 2 of *n.*). **pollster** *n.* [ME, perh. f. LG or Du.]

pollard /'pɒləd/ *n.* & *v.* —*n.* **1** an animal that has lost or cast its horns; an ox, sheep, or goat of a hornless breed. **2** a tree whose branches have been cut off to encourage the growth of new young branches, esp. a riverside willow. —*v.tr.* make (a tree) a pollard. [POLL + -ARD]

pollen /'pɒlən/ *n.* the fine dustlike grains discharged from the male part of a flower containing the gamete that fertilizes the female ovule. □ **pollen count** an index of the amount of pollen in the air, published esp. for the benefit of those allergic to it. □ **pollenless** *adj.* **pollinic** /pə'lɪnɪk/ *adj.* [L *pollen pollinis* fine flour, dust]

pollinate /'pɒlɪneɪt/ *v.tr.* (also *absol.*) sprinkle (a stigma) with pollen. □ **pollination** /-'neɪʃ(ə)n/ *n.* **pollinator** *n.*

polling /'pəʊlɪŋ/ *n.* the registering or casting of votes. □ **polling-booth** a compartment in which a voter stands to mark the ballot-paper. **polling-day** the day of a local or general election. **polling-station** a building where voting takes place during an election.

pollinic see POLLEN.

pollute /pə'luːt/ *v.tr.* **1** contaminate or defile (the environment). **2** make foul or filthy. **3** destroy the purity or sanctity of. □ **pollutant** *adj.* & *n.* **polluter** *n.* **pollution** *n.* [ME f. L *polluere pollut-*]

polly /'pɒlɪ/ *n.* (also **pollie**) (*pl.* **-ies**) *Austral.* & *US* a politician. [abbr.]

polo /'pəʊləʊ/ *n.* a game of Eastern origin like hockey played on horseback with a long-handled mallet. □ **polo-neck** a high round turned-over collar. **polo-stick** a mallet for playing polo. [Balti, = ball]

polonaise /ˌpɒlə'neɪz/ *n.* & *adj.* —*n.* **1** a dance of Polish origin in triple time. **2** the music for this. —*adj.* cooked in a Polish style. [F, fem. of *polonais* Polish f. med.L *Polonia* Poland]

polonium /pə'ləʊnɪəm/ *n.* *Chem.* a rare radioactive metallic element, occurring naturally in uranium ores. [F & mod.L f. med.L *Polonia* Poland (the discoverer's native country) + -IUM]

poltergeist /'pɒltəˌgaɪst/ *n.* a noisy mischievous ghost, esp. one manifesting itself by physical damage. [G f. *poltern* create a disturbance + *Geist* GHOST]

poltroon /pɒl'truːn/ *n.* a spiritless coward. □ **poltroonery** *n.* [F *poltron* f. It. *poltrone* perh. f. *poltro* sluggard]

poly /'pɒlɪ/ *n.* (*pl.* **polys**) *colloq.* polytechnic. [abbr.]

poly-¹ /'pɒlɪ/ *comb. form* denoting many or much. [Gk *polu-* f. *polus* much, *polloi* many]

poly-² /'pɒlɪ/ *comb. form* *Chem.* polymerized (*polyunsaturated*). [POLYMER]

polyamide /ˌpɒlɪ'æmaɪd/ *n.* *Chem.* any of a class of condensation polymers which includes many synthetic fibres such as nylon.

polyandry /'pɒlɪˌændrɪ/ *n.* polygamy in which a woman has more than one husband. □ **polyandrous** /-'ændrəs/ *adj.* [POLY-¹ + *andry* f. Gk *anēr andros* male]

polyanthus /ˌpɒlɪ'ænθəs/ *n.* (*pl.* **polyanthuses**) a flower cultivated from hybridized primulas. [mod.L, formed as POLY-¹ + Gk *anthos* flower]

polychaete /'pɒlɪˌkiːt/ *n.* any aquatic annelid worm of the class Polychaeta, including lugworms and ragworms. □ **polychaetan** /-'kiːt(ə)n/ *adj.* **polychaetous** /-'kiːtəs/ *adj.*

polychromatic /ˌpɒlɪkrəʊˈmætɪk/ adj. many-coloured. □ **polychromatism** /-ˈkrəʊməˌtɪz(ə)m/ n.

polychrome /ˈpɒlɪˌkrəʊm/ adj. & n. —adj. painted, printed, or decorated in many colours. —n. **1** a work of art in several colours, esp. a coloured statue. **2** varied colouring. □ **polychromic** /-ˈkrəʊmɪk/ adj. **polychromous** /-ˈkrəʊməs/ adj. [F f. Gk polukhrōmos as POLY-¹, khrōma colour]

polyester /ˌpɒlɪˈestə(r)/ n. any of a group of condensation polymers used to form synthetic fibres such as Terylene or to make resins.

polyethene /ˈpɒlɪˌeθiːn/ n. Chem. = POLYTHENE.

polyethylene /ˌpɒlɪˈeθɪliːn/ n. = POLYTHENE.

polygamous /pəˈlɪɡəməs/ adj. **1** having more than one wife or husband at the same time. **2** having more than one mate. □ **polygamic** /-ˈɡæmɪk/ adj. **polygamist** n. **polygamously** adv. **polygamy** n. [Gk polugamos (as POLY-¹, -gamos marrying)]

polyglot /ˈpɒlɪˌɡlɒt/ adj. & n. —adj. **1** of many languages. **2** (of a person) speaking or writing several languages. —n. a polyglot person. □ **polyglottal** /-ˈɡlɒt(ə)l/ adj. **polyglottic** /-ˈɡlɒtɪk/ adj. **polyglottism** n. [F polyglotte f. Gk poluglōttos (as POLY-¹, glōtta tongue)]

polygon /ˈpɒlɪɡən, -ɡɒn/ n. a plane figure with many (usu. a minimum of three) sides and angles. □ **polygonal** /pəˈlɪɡən(ə)l/ adj. [LL polygonum f. Gk polugōnon (neut. adj.) (as POLY-¹ + -gōnos angled)]

polygraph /ˈpɒlɪˌɡrɑːf/ n. a machine designed to detect and record changes in physiological characteristics (e.g. rates of pulse and breathing), used esp. as a lie-detector.

polygyny /pəˈlɪdʒɪnɪ/ n. polygamy in which a man has more than one wife. □ **polygynous** /pəˈlɪdʒɪnəs/ adj. [POLY-¹ + gyny f. Gk gunē woman]

polyhedron /ˌpɒlɪˈhiːdrən, -ˈhedrən/ n. (pl. **polyhedra** /-drə/) a solid figure with many (usu. more than six) faces. □ **polyhedral** adj. **polyhedric** adj. [Gk poluedron neut. of poluedros (as POLY-¹, hedra base)]

polymath /ˈpɒlɪˌmæθ/ n. **1** a person of much or varied learning. **2** a great scholar. □ **polymathic** /ˌpɒlɪˈmæθɪk/ adj. **polymathy** /pəˈlɪməθɪ/ n. [Gk polumathēs (as POLY-¹, math- stem manthanō learn)]

polymer /ˈpɒlɪmə(r)/ n. a compound composed of one or more large molecules that are formed from repeated units of smaller molecules. □ **polymeric** /-ˈmerɪk/ adj. **polymerism** n. **polymerize** v.intr. & tr. (also -ise). **polymerization** /-ˈzeɪʃ(ə)n/ n. [G f. Gk polumeros having many parts (as POLY-¹, meros share)]

polynomial /ˌpɒlɪˈnəʊmɪəl/ n. & adj. Math. —n. an expression of more than two algebraic terms, esp. the sum of several terms that contain different powers of the same variable(s). —adj. of or being a polynomial. [POLY-¹ after multinomial]

polyp /ˈpɒlɪp/ n. **1** Zool. an individual coelenterate. **2** Med. a small usu. benign growth protruding from a mucous membrane. [F polype (as POLYPUS)]

polyphonic /ˌpɒlɪˈfɒnɪk/ adj. Mus. (of vocal music etc.) in two or more relatively independent parts; contrapuntal. □ **polyphonically** adv. [Gk poluphōnos (as POLY-¹, phōnē voice, sound)]

polyphony /pəˈlɪfənɪ/ n. (pl. **-ies**) Mus. polyphonic style in musical composition; counterpoint. □ **polyphonous** adj.

polypi pl. of POLYPUS.

polyploid /ˈpɒlɪˌplɔɪd/ n. & adj. Biol. —n. a nucleus or organism that contains more than two sets of chromosomes. —adj. of or being a polyploid. □ **polyploidy** n. [G (as POLY-¹, -PLOID)]

polypropene /ˌpɒlɪˈprəʊpiːn/ n. = POLYPROPYLENE.

polypropylene /ˌpɒlɪˈprəʊpɪˌliːn/ n. Chem. any of various polymers of propylene including thermoplastic materials used for films, fibres, or moulding materials.

polypus /ˈpɒlɪpəs/ n. (pl. **polypi** /-ˌpaɪ/ or **polypuses**) Med. = POLYP 2. [ME f. L polypus f. Gk pōlupos, polupous cuttlefish, polyp (as POLY-¹, pous podos foot)]

polysaccharide /ˌpɒlɪˈsækəˌraɪd/ n. any of a group of carbohydrates whose molecules consist of long chains of monosaccharides.

polystyrene /ˌpɒlɪˈstaɪəˌriːn/ n. a thermoplastic polymer of styrene, usu. hard and colourless or expanded with a gas to produce a lightweight rigid white substance, used for insulation and in packaging.

polysyllabic /ˌpɒlɪsɪˈlæbɪk/ adj. **1** (of a word) having many syllables. **2** characterized by the use of words of many syllables. □ **polysyllabically** adv.

polysyllable /ˈpɒlɪˌsɪləb(ə)l/ n. a polysyllabic word.

polytechnic /ˌpɒlɪˈteknɪk/ n. & adj. —n. an institution of higher education offering courses in many (esp. vocational) subjects at degree level or below. —adj. dealing with or devoted to various vocational or technical subjects. [F polytechnique f. Gk polutekhnos (as POLY-¹ tekhnē art)]

polytetrafluoroethylene /ˌpɒlɪˌtetrəˌflʊərəʊˈeθɪˌliːn/ n. Chem. a tough translucent polymer resistant to chemicals and used to coat cooking utensils etc. [POLY-² + TETRA- + FLUORO- + ETHYLENE]

polytheism /ˈpɒlɪθiːˌɪz(ə)m/ n. the belief in or worship of more than one god. □ **polytheist** n. **polytheistic** /-ˈɪstɪk/ adj. [F polythéisme f. Gk polutheos of many gods (as POLY-¹, theos god)]

polythene /ˈpɒlɪˌθiːn/ n. Chem. a tough light thermoplastic polymer of ethylene, usu. translucent and flexible or opaque and rigid, used for packaging and insulating materials.

polyunsaturated /ˌpɒlɪʌnˈsætʃəˌreɪtɪd, -tjʊˌreɪtɪd/ adj. Chem. (of a compound, esp. a fat or oil molecule) containing several double or triple bonds and therefore capable of further reaction.

polyurethane /ˌpɒlɪˈjʊərəˌθeɪn/ n. any polymer containing the urethane group, used in adhesives, paints, plastics, rubbers, foams, etc.

polyvalent /ˌpɒlɪˈveɪlənt/ adj. Chem. having a valency of more than two, or several valencies. □ **polyvalence** n.

polyvinyl acetate /ˌpɒlɪˈvaɪnɪl/ n. Chem. a soft plastic polymer used in paints and adhesives.

polyvinyl chloride /ˌpɒlɪˈvaɪnɪl/ n. a tough transparent solid polymer of vinyl chloride, easily coloured and used for a wide variety of products including pipes, flooring, etc.

pom n. Austral. & NZ sl. offens. = POMMY. [abbr.]

pomace /ˈpʌmɪs/ n. 1 the mass of crushed apples in cider-making before or after the juice is pressed out. 2 the refuse of fish etc. after the oil has been extracted, generally used as a fertilizer. [ME f. med.L pomacium cider f. L pomum apple]

pomade /pəˈmɑːd/ n. & v. —n. scented dressing for the hair and the skin of the head. —v.tr. anoint with pomade. [F pommade f. It. pomata f. med.L f. L pomum apple (from which it was orig. made)]

pomander /pəˈmændə(r)/ n. 1 a ball of mixed aromatic substances placed in a cupboard etc. or hist. carried in a box, bag, etc. as a protection against infection. 2 a (usu. spherical) container for this. 3 a spiced orange etc. similarly used. [earlier pom(e)amber f. AF f. OF pome d'embre f. med.L pomum de ambra apple of ambergris]

pome /pəʊm/ n. a firm-fleshed fruit in which the carpels from the central core enclose the seeds, e.g. the apple, pear, and quince. □ **pomiferous** /pəˈmɪfərəs/ adj. [ME f. OF ult. f. poma pl. of L pomum fruit, apple]

pomegranate /ˈpɒmɪˌgrænɪt, ˈpɒmˌgrænɪt/ n. 1 an orange-sized fruit with a tough golden-orange outer skin containing many seeds in a red pulp. 2 the tree bearing this fruit, Punica granatum, native to N. Africa and W. Asia. [ME f. OF pome grenate (as POME, L granatum having many seeds f. granum seed)]

pomelo /ˈpʌməˌləʊ/ n. (pl. -os) 1 = SHADDOCK. 2 US = GRAPEFRUIT. [19th c.: orig. unkn.]

pomfret-cake /ˈpʌmfrɪt, ˈpɒ-/ n. (also **Pontefract-cake** /ˈpɒntɪˌfrækt/) Brit. a small round flat liquorice sweetmeat orig. made at Pontefract (earlier Pomfret) in Yorkshire.

pommel /ˈpʌm(ə)l/ n. & v. —n. 1 a knob, esp. at the end of a sword-hilt. 2 the upward projecting front part of a saddle. —v.tr. (**pommelled**, **pommelling**; US **pommeled**, **pommeling**) = PUMMEL. [ME f. OF pomel f. Rmc pomellum (unrecorded), dimin. of L pomum fruit, apple]

pommy /ˈpɒmɪ/ n. (also **pommie**) (pl. -ies) Austral. & NZ sl. offens. a British person, esp. a recent immigrant. [20th c.: orig. uncert.]

pomp n. a splendid display; splendour. [ME f. OF pompe f. L pompa f. Gk pompē procession, pomp f. pempō send]

pompadour /ˈpɒmpəˌdʊə(r)/ n. a woman's hair-style with the hair in a high turned-back roll round the face. [f. Marquise de Pompadour, the mistress of Louis XV of France d. 1764]

pom-pom /ˈpɒmpɒm/ n. an automatic quick-firing gun esp. on a ship. [imit.]

pompon /ˈpɒmpɒn/ n. (also **pompom**) 1 an ornamental ball or bobble made of wool, silk, or ribbons, usu. worn on women's or children's hats or clothing. 2 the round tuft on a soldier's cap, the front of a shako, etc. 3 (often attrib.) a dahlia or chrysanthemum with small tightly-clustered petals. [F, of unkn. orig.]

pompous /ˈpɒmpəs/ n. 1 self-important, affectedly grand or solemn. 2 (of language) pretentious; unduly grand in style. □ **pomposity** /pɒmˈpɒsɪtɪ/ n. (pl. -ies). **pompously** adv. **pompousness** n. [ME f. OF pompeux f. LL pomposus (as POMP)]

ponce n. & v. Brit. sl. —n. 1 a man who lives off a prostitute's earnings; a pimp. 2 offens. a homosexual; an effeminate man. —v.intr. act as a ponce. □ **ponce about** move about effeminately or ineffectually. □ **poncey** adj. (also **poncy**) (in sense 2 of n.). [perh. f. POUNCE]

poncho /ˈpɒntʃəʊ/ n. (pl. -os) 1 a S. American cloak made of a blanket-like piece of cloth with a slit in the middle for the head. 2 a garment in this style. [S.Amer. Sp., f. Araucan]

pond n. a fairly small body of still water formed naturally or by hollowing or embanking. □ **pond-life** animals (esp. invertebrates) that live in ponds. [ME var. of POUND³]

ponder /ˈpɒndə(r)/ v. 1 tr. weigh mentally; think over; consider. 2 intr. (usu. foll. by on, over) think; muse. [ME f. OF ponderer f. L ponderare f. pondus -eris weight]

ponderable /ˈpɒndərəb(ə)l/ adj. literary having appreciable weight or significance. □ **ponderability** /-ˈbɪlɪtɪ/ n. [LL ponderabilis (as PONDER)]

ponderosa /ˌpɒndəˈrəʊsə/ n. US 1 a N. American pine-tree, Pinus ponderosa. 2 the red timber of this tree. [mod.L, fem. of L ponderosus: see PONDEROUS]

ponderous /ˈpɒndərəs/ adj. 1 heavy; unwieldy. 2 laborious. 3 (of style etc.) dull; tedious. □ **ponderosity** /-ˈrɒsɪtɪ/ n. **ponderously** adv. **ponderousness** n. [ME f. L ponderosus f. pondus -eris weight]

pondweed /ˈpɒndwiːd/ n. any of various aquatic plants, esp. of the genus Potamogeton, growing in still or running water.

pong n. & v. Brit. colloq. —n. an unpleasant smell. —v.intr. stink. □ **pongy** /ˈpɒŋɪ/ adj. (**pongier**, **pongiest**). [20th c.: orig. unkn.]

pongee /pɒnˈdʒiː, pʌn-/ n. 1 a soft usu. unbleached type of Chinese silk fabric. 2 an imitation of this in cotton etc. [perh. f. Chin. dial. pun-chī own loom, i.e. home-made]

pont /pɒnt/ n. S.Afr. a flat-bottomed ferry-boat. [Du.]

Pontefract-cake var. of POMFRET-CAKE.

pontiff /ˈpɒntɪf/ n. RC Ch. (in full **sovereign** or **supreme pontiff**) the Pope. [F pontife f. L pontifex -ficis f. pons pontis bridge + -fex f. facere make]

pontifical /pɒnˈtɪfɪk(ə)l/ adj. 1 RC Ch. of or befitting a pontiff; papal. 2 pompously dogmatic; with an attitude of infallibility. □ **pontifically** adv. [ME f. F pontifical or L pontificalis as PONTIFF]

pontificate v. & n. —v.intr. 1 play the pontiff; pretend to be infallible. 2 be pompously dogmatic. —n. /pɒnˈtɪfɪkət/ 1 the office of pontifex, bishop, or pope. 2 the period of this. [L pontificatus (as PONTIFF)]

pontoon¹ /pɒnˈtuːn/ n. Brit. a card-game in which players try to acquire cards with a face value totalling 21 and no more. [prob. corrupt.]

pontoon² /pɒnˈtuːn/ n. 1 a flat-bottomed boat. 2 each of several boats, hollow metal cylinders, etc., used to support a temporary bridge. 3 = CAISSON 1,2. [F ponton f. L ponto -onis f. pons pontis bridge]

pony /ˈpəʊnɪ/ n. (pl. -ies) 1 a horse of any small breed. 2 a small drinking-glass. 3 (in pl.) sl. racehorses. 4 Brit. sl. £25. □ **pony-tail** a person's hair drawn back, tied, and hanging down like a pony's tail. **pony-trekker** a person who travels across country on a pony for pleasure. **pony-trekking** this as a hobby or activity. [perh. f. poulney (unrecorded) f. F poulenet dimin. of poulain foal]

pooch /puːtʃ/ *n. esp. US sl.* a dog. [20th c.: orig. unkn.]

poodle /ˈpuːd(ə)l/ *n.* **1 a** a dog of a breed with a curly coat that is usually clipped. **b** this breed. **2** a lackey or servile follower. [G *Pudel(hund)* f. LG *pud(d)eln* splash in water: cf. PUDDLE]

poof /puf, puːf/ *n.* (also **pouf**, **poove** /puːv/) *Brit. sl. derog.* **1** an effeminate man. **2** a male homosexual. □ **poofy** /ˈpufi/ *adj.* [19th c.: cf. PUFF in sense 'braggart']

poofter /ˈpuftə(r), ˈpuː-/ *n. sl. derog.* = POOF.

pooh /puː/ *int. & n.* —*int.* expressing impatience or contempt. —*n. sl.* excrement. [imit.]

pooh-pooh /puːˈpuː/ *v.tr.* express contempt for; ridicule; dismiss (an idea etc.) scornfully. [redupl. of POOH]

pooja var. of PUJA.

pool[1] /puːl/ *n. & v.* —*n.* **1** a small body of still water, usu. of natural formation. **2** a small shallow body of any liquid. **3** = *swimming-pool*. **4** a deep place in a river. —*v. tr.* form into a pool. [OE *pōl*, MLG, MDu. *pōl*, OHG *pfuol* f. WG]

pool[2] /puːl/ *n. & v.* —*n.* **1 a** (often *attrib.*) a common supply of persons, vehicles, commodities, etc. for sharing by a group of people (*a typing pool; a pool car*). **b** a group of persons sharing duties etc. **2 a** the collective amount of players' stakes in gambling etc. **b** a receptacle for this. **3 a** a joint commercial venture, esp. an arrangement between competing parties to fix prices and share business to eliminate competition. **b** the common funding for this. **4** *US* a game on a billiard-table with usu. 16 balls. —*v.tr.* **1** put (resources etc.) into a common fund. **2** share (things) in common. **3** (of transport or organizations etc.) share (traffic, receipts). **4** *Austral. sl.* **a** involve (a person) in a scheme etc., often by deception. **b** implicate, inform on. □ **the pools** *Brit.* = *football pool.* [F *poule* (= hen) in same sense: assoc. with POOL[1]]

poolroom /ˈpuːlruːm, -rʊm/ *n. US* **1** a betting shop. **2** a place for playing pool.

poop[1] *n.* the stern of a ship; the aftermost and highest deck. [ME f. OF *pupe, pope* ult. f. L *puppis*]

poop[2] *v.tr.* (esp. as **pooped** *adj.*) *US colloq.* exhaust; tire out. [20th c.: orig. unkn.]

poor /pʊə(r)/ *adj.* **1** lacking adequate money or means to live comfortably. **2** (foll. by *in*) deficient in (a possession or quality) (*the poor in spirit*). **3 a** scanty, inadequate (*a poor crop*). **b** less good than is usual or expected (*poor visibility; is a poor driver; in poor health*). **c** paltry; inferior (*poor condition; came a poor third*). **4 a** deserving pity or sympathy; unfortunate (*you poor thing*). **b** with reference to a dead person (*as my poor father used to say*). **5** spiritless; despicable (*is a poor creature*). □ **poor-box** a collection-box, esp. in church, for the relief of the poor. **poor law** *hist.* a law relating to the support of paupers. **poor man's** an inferior or cheaper substitute for. **poor relation** an inferior or subordinate member of a family or any other group. **poor-spirited** timid; cowardly. **poor White** *offens.* (esp. used by Blacks) a member of a socially inferior group of White people. **take a poor view of** regard with disfavour or pessimism. [ME & OF *pov(e)re, poure* f. L *pauper*]

poorhouse /ˈpʊəhaʊs/ *n. hist.* = WORKHOUSE 1.

poorly /ˈpʊəli/ *adv. & adj.* —*adv.* **1** scantily; defectively. **2** with no great success. **3** meanly; contemptibly. —*predic.adj.* unwell.

poorness /ˈpʊənɪs/ *n.* **1** defectiveness. **2** the lack of some good quality or constituent.

poove var. of POOF.

pop[1] /pɒp/ *n., v., & adv.* —*n.* **1** a sudden sharp explosive sound as of a cork when drawn. **2** *colloq.* an effervescent sweet drink. —*v.* (**popped**, **popping**) **1** *intr. & tr.* make or cause to make a pop. **2** *intr. & tr.* (foll. by *in, out, up, down,* etc.) go, move, come, or put unexpectedly or in a quick or hasty manner (*pop out to the shops; pop in for a visit; pop it on your head*). **3 a** *intr. & tr.* burst, making a popping sound. **b** *tr.* heat (popcorn etc.) until it pops. **4** *intr.* (often foll. by *at*) *colloq.* fire a gun (at birds etc.). **5** *tr. sl.* pawn. —*adv.* with the sound of a pop (*heard it go pop*). □ **pop off** *colloq.* **1** die. **2** quietly slip away (cf. sense 2 of *v.*). **pop the question** *colloq.* propose marriage. **pop-shop** *Brit. sl.* a pawnbroker's shop. **pop-up 1** (of a toaster etc.) operating so as to move the object (toast when ready etc.) quickly upwards. **2** (of a book, greetings card, etc.) containing three-dimensional figures, illustrations, etc., that rise up when the page is turned. **3** *Computing* (of a menu) able to be superimposed on the screen being worked on and suppressed rapidly. [ME: imit.]

pop[2] /pɒp/ *adj. & n. colloq.* —*adj.* **1** in a popular or modern style. **2** performing popular music etc. (*pop group; pop star*). —*n.* **1** pop music. **2** a pop record or song (*top of the pops*). □ **pop art** art based on modern popular culture and the mass media, esp. as a critical comment on traditional fine art values. **pop culture** commercial culture based on popular taste. **pop festival** a festival at which popular music etc. is performed. [abbr.]

pop[3] /pɒp/ *n. esp. US colloq.* father. [abbr. of POPPA]

popadam var. of POPPADAM.

popcorn /ˈpɒpkɔːn/ *n.* **1** Indian corn which bursts open when heated. **2** these kernels when popped.

pope *n.* (as title usu. **Pope**) the head of the Roman Catholic Church (also called the Bishop of Rome). □ **popedom** *n.* **popeless** *adj.* [OE f. eccl.L *pāpa* bishop, pope f. eccl.Gk *papas* = Gk *pappas* father: cf. PAPA]

popery /ˈpəʊpəri/ *n. derog.* the papal system; the Roman Catholic Church.

pop-eyed /ˈpɒpaɪd/ *adj. colloq.* **1** having bulging eyes. **2** wide-eyed (with surprise etc.).

popgun /ˈpɒpɡʌn/ *n.* a child's toy gun which shoots a pellet etc. by the compression of air with a piston.

popish /ˈpəʊpɪʃ/ *adj. derog.* Roman Catholic. □ **popishly** *adv.*

poplar /ˈpɒplə(r)/ *n.* **1** any tree of the genus *Populus*, with a usu. rapidly growing trunk and tremulous leaves. **2** *US* = *tulip-tree.* [ME f. AF *popler,* OF *poplier* f. *pople* f. L *populus*]

poplin /ˈpɒplɪn/ *n.* a plain-woven fabric usu. of cotton, with a corded surface. [obs. F *papeline* perh. f. It. *papalina* (fem.) PAPAL, f. the papal town Avignon where it was made]

poppa /ˈpɒpə/ *n. US colloq.* father (esp. as a child's word). [var. of PAPA]

poppadam /ˈpɒpədəm/ *n.* (also **poppadom**, **popadam**) *Ind.* a thin, crisp, spiced bread eaten with curry etc. [Tamil *pappaḍam*]

popper /ˈpɒpə(r)/ *n.* **1** *Brit. colloq.* a press-stud. **2** a person or thing that pops.

poppet /ˈpɒpɪt/ *n.* **1** *Brit. colloq.* (esp. as a term of endearment) a small or dainty person. **2** (in full **poppet-head**) the head of a lathe. □ **poppet-valve** *Engin.* a mushroom-shaped valve, lifted bodily from its seat rather than hinged. [ME *popet(te)*, ult. f. L *pup(p)a*: cf. PUPPET]

popping-crease /ˈpɒpɪŋˌkriːs/ *n. Cricket* a line four feet in front of and parallel to the wicket, within which the batsman must keep the bat or one foot grounded to avoid the risk of being stumped. [POP¹, perh. in obs. sense 'strike']

poppy /ˈpɒpɪ/ *n.* (*pl.* **-ies**) any plant of the genus *Papaver*, with showy often red flowers and a milky sap with narcotic properties. □ **Poppy Day** = *Remembrance Sunday*. **poppy-head 1** the seed capsule of the poppy. **2** an ornamental top on the end of a church pew. □ **poppied** *adj.* [OE *popig*, *papæg*, etc. f. med.L *papauum* f. L *papaver*]

poppycock /ˈpɒpɪˌkɒk/ *n. sl.* nonsense. [Du. dial. *pappekak*]

popsy /ˈpɒpsɪ/ *n.* (also **popsie**) (*pl.* **-ies**) *colloq.* (usu. as a term of endearment) a young woman. [shortening of POPPET]

populace /ˈpɒpjʊləs/ *n.* **1** the common people. **2** *derog.* the rabble. [F f. It. *popolaccio* f. *popolo* people + *-accio* pejorative suffix]

popular /ˈpɒpjʊlə(r)/ *adj.* **1** liked or admired by many people or by a specified group (*popular teachers*; *a popular hero*). **2 a** of or carried on by the general public (*popular meetings*). **b** prevalent among the general public (*popular discontent*). **3** adapted to the understanding, taste, or means of the people (*popular science*; *popular medicine*). □ **popular front** a party or coalition representing left-wing elements. **popular music** songs, folk tunes, etc., appealing to popular tastes. □ **popularism** *n.* **popularity** /-ˈlærɪtɪ/ *n.* **popularly** *adv.* [ME f. AF *populer*, OF *populeir* or L *popularis* f. *populus* people]

popularize /ˈpɒpjʊləˌraɪz/ *v.tr.* (also **-ise**) **1** make popular. **2** cause (a person, principle, etc.) to be generally known or liked. **3** present (a technical subject, specialized vocabulary, etc.) in a popular or readily understandable form. □ **popularization** /-ˈzeɪʃ(ə)n/ *n.* **popularizer** *n.*

populate /ˈpɒpjʊˌleɪt/ *v.tr.* **1** inhabit; form the population of (a town, country, etc.). **2** supply with inhabitants; people (*a densely populated district*). [med.L *populare populat-* (as PEOPLE)]

population /ˌpɒpjʊˈleɪʃ(ə)n/ *n.* **1 a** the inhabitants of a place, country, etc. referred to collectively. **b** any specified group within this (*the Irish population of Liverpool*). **2** the total number of any of these (*a population of eight million*; *the seal population*). **3** the act or process of supplying with inhabitants (*the population of forest areas*). **4** *Statistics* any finite or infinite collection of items under consideration. □ **population explosion** a sudden large increase of population. [LL *populatio* (as PEOPLE)]

populist /ˈpɒpjʊlɪst/ *n. & adj.* —*n.* a member or adherent of a political party seeking support mainly from the ordinary people. —*adj.* of or relating to such a political party. □ **populism** *n.* **populistic** /-ˈlɪstɪk/ *adj.* [L *populus* people]

populous /ˈpɒpjʊləs/ *adj.* thickly inhabited. □ **populously** *adv.* **populousness** *n.* [ME f. LL *populosus* (as PEOPLE)]

porbeagle /ˈpɔːˌbiːg(ə)l/ *n.* a large shark, *Lamna nasus*, having a pointed snout. [18th-c. Corn. dial., of unkn. orig.]

porcelain /ˈpɔːsəlɪn/ *n.* **1** a hard vitrified translucent ceramic. **2** objects made of this. □ **porcellaneous** /ˌpɔːsəˈleɪnɪəs/ *adj.* **porcellanous** /pɔːˈselənəs/ *adj.* [F *porcelaine* cowrie, porcelain f. It. *porcellana* f. *porcella* dimin. of *porca* sow (a cowrie being perh. likened to a sow's vulva) f. L *porca* fem. of *porcus* pig]

porch *n.* **1** a covered shelter for the entrance of a building. **2** *US* a veranda. □ **porched** *adj.* **porchless** *adj.* [ME f. OF *porche* f. L *porticus* (transl. Gk *stoa*) f. *porta* passage]

porcine /ˈpɔːsaɪn/ *adj.* of or like pigs. [F *porcin* or f. L *porcinus* f. *porcus* pig]

porcupine /ˈpɔːkjʊˌpaɪn/ *n.* any rodent of the family Hystricidae native to Africa, Asia, and SE Europe, or the family Erethizontidae native to America, having defensive spines or quills. □ **porcupinish** *adj.* **porcupiny** *adj.* [ME f. OF *porc espin* f. Prov. *porc espi(n)* ult. f. L *porcus* pig + *spina* thorn]

pore¹ *n. esp. Biol.* a minute opening in a surface through which gases, liquids, or fine solids may pass. [ME f. OF f. L *porus* f. Gk *poros* passage, pore]

pore² *v.intr.* (foll. by *over*) **1** be absorbed in studying (a book etc.). **2** meditate on, think intently about (a subject). [ME *pure* etc. perh. f. OE *purian* (unrecorded): cf. PEER¹]

pork *n.* the (esp. unsalted) flesh of a pig, used as food. □ **pork pie** a pie of minced pork etc. eaten cold. **pork pie hat** a hat with a flat crown and a brim turned up all round. [ME *porc* f. OF *porc* f. L *porcus* pig]

porker /ˈpɔːkə(r)/ *n.* **1** a pig raised for food. **2** a young fattened pig.

porky /ˈpɔːkɪ/ *adj.* (**porkier**, **porkiest**) **1** *colloq.* fleshy, fat. **2** of or like pork.

porn *n. colloq.* pornography. [abbr.]

porno /ˈpɔːnəʊ/ *n. & adj. colloq.* —*n.* pornography. —*adj.* pornographic. [abbr.]

pornography /pɔːˈnɒɡrəfɪ/ *n.* **1** the explicit description or exhibition of sexual activity in literature, films, etc., intended to stimulate erotic rather than aesthetic or emotional feelings. **2** literature etc. characterized by this. □ **pornographer** *n.* **pornographic** /-nəˈɡræfɪk/ *adj.* **pornographically** /-nəˈɡræfɪkəlɪ/ *adv.* [Gk *pornographos* writing of harlots f. *pornē* prostitute + *graphō* write]

porous /ˈpɔːrəs/ *adj.* **1** full of pores. **2** letting through air, water, etc. **3** (of an argument, security system, etc.) leaky, admitting infiltration. □ **porosity** /pɔːˈrɒsɪtɪ/ *n.* **porously** *adv.* **porousness** *n.* [ME f. OF *poreux* f. med.L *porosus* f. L *porus* PORE¹]

porphyry /ˈpɔːfɪrɪ/ *n.* (*pl.* **-ies**) **1** a hard rock quarried in ancient Egypt, composed of crystals of white or red feldspar in a red matrix. **2** *Geol.* an igneous rock with large crystals scattered in a matrix of much smaller crystals. □ **porphyritic** /-ˈrɪtɪk/ *adj.* [ME ult. f. med.L *porphyreum* f. Gk *porphuritēs* f. *porphura* purple]

porpoise /ˈpɔːpəs/ *n.* any of various small toothed whales of the family Phocaenidae, esp. of the genus *Phocaena*, with a low triangular dorsal fin and a blunt rounded snout. [ME *porpays* etc. f. OF *po(u)rpois* etc. ult. f. L *porcus* pig + *piscis* fish]

porridge /ˈpɒrɪdʒ/ n. **1** a dish consisting of oatmeal or another meal or cereal boiled in water or milk. **2** sl. imprisonment. □ **porridgy** adj. [16th c.: alt. of POTTAGE]

porringer /ˈpɒrɪndʒə(r)/ n. a small bowl, often with a handle, for soup, stew, etc. [earlier pottinger f. OF potager f. potage (see POTTAGE): -n- as in messenger etc.]

port[1] n. **1** a harbour. **2** a place of refuge. **3** a town or place possessing a harbour, esp. one where customs officers are stationed. □ **port of call** a place where a ship or a person stops on a journey. [OE f. L portus & ME prob. f. OF f. L portus]

port[2] n. (in full **port wine**) a strong, sweet, dark-red (occas. brown or white) fortified wine of Portugal. [shortened form of Oporto, city in Portugal from which port is shipped]

port[3] n. & v. —n. the left-hand side (looking forward) of a ship, boat, or aircraft (cf. STARBOARD). —v.tr. (also absol.) turn (the helm) to port. [prob. orig. the side turned towards PORT[1]]

port[4] n. **1 a** an opening in the side of a ship for entrance, loading, etc. **b** a porthole. **2** Electr. a socket or aperture in an electronic circuit, esp. in a computer network, where connections can be made with peripheral equipment. [ME & OF porte f. L porta]

port[5] v.tr. Mil. carry (a rifle, or other weapon) diagonally across and close to the body with the barrel etc. near the left shoulder (esp. port arms!). [ME f. OF port ult. f. L portare carry]

port[6] n. Austral. **1** a suitcase or travelling bag. **2** a shopping bag, sugar bag, etc. [abbr. of PORTMANTEAU]

portable /ˈpɔːtəb(ə)l/ adj. & n. —adj. **1** easily movable, convenient for carrying (portable TV; portable computer). **2** (of a right, privilege, etc.) capable of being transferred or adapted in altered circumstances (portable pension). —n. a portable object, e.g. a radio, typewriter, etc. (decided to buy a portable). □ **portability** /ˌpɔːtəˈbɪlɪtɪ/ n. **portableness** n. **portably** adv. [ME f. OF portable or LL portabilis f. L portare carry]

portage /ˈpɔːtɪdʒ/ n. & v. —n. **1** the carrying of boats or goods between two navigable waters. **2** a place at which this is necessary. —v.tr. convey (a boat or goods) between navigable waters. [ME f. OF f. porter: see PORT[5]]

Portakabin /ˈpɔːtəˌkæbɪn/ n. propr. a portable room or building designed for quick assembly. [PORTABLE + CABIN]

portal[1] /ˈpɔːt(ə)l/ n. a doorway or gate etc., esp. a large and elaborate one. [ME f. OF f. med.L portale (neut. adj.): see PORTAL[2]]

portal[2] /ˈpɔːt(ə)l/ adj. **1** of or relating to an aperture in an organ through which its associated vessels pass. **2** of or relating to the portal vein. □ **portal vein** a vein conveying blood to the liver from the spleen, stomach, pancreas, and intestines. [mod.L portalis f. L porta gate]

portcullis /pɔːtˈkʌlɪs/ n. a strong heavy grating sliding up and down in vertical grooves, lowered to block a gateway in a fortress etc. □ **portcullised** adj. [ME f. OF porte coleïce sliding door f. porte door f. L porta + col(e)ïce fem. of couleïs sliding ult. f. L colare filter]

portend /pɔːˈtend/ v.tr. **1** foreshadow as an omen. **2** give warning of. [ME f. L portendere portent- f. por- PRO-[1] + tendere stretch]

portent /ˈpɔːtent, -t(ə)nt/ n. **1** an omen, a significant sign of something to come. **2** a prodigy; a marvellous thing. [L portentum (as PORTEND)]

portentous /pɔːˈtentəs/ adj. **1** like or serving as a portent. **2** pompously solemn. □ **portentously** adv.

porter[1] /ˈpɔːtə(r)/ n. **1 a** a person employed to carry luggage etc., esp. a railway, airport, or hotel employee. **b** a hospital employee who moves equipment, trolleys, etc. **2** a dark-brown bitter beer brewed from charred or browned malt (app. orig. made esp. for porters). **3** US a sleeping-car attendant. □ **porterage** n. [ME f. OF port(e)our f. med.L portator -oris f. portare carry]

porter[2] /ˈpɔːtə(r)/ n. Brit. a gatekeeper or doorkeeper, esp. of a large building. [ME & AF, OF portier f. LL portarius f. porta door]

porterhouse /ˈpɔːtəˌhaʊs/ n. esp. US **1** hist. a house at which porter and other drinks were retailed. **2** a house where steaks, chops, etc. were served. □ **porterhouse steak** a thick steak cut from the thick end of a sirloin.

portfolio /pɔːtˈfəʊlɪəʊ/ n. (pl. **-os**) **1** a case for keeping loose sheets of paper, drawings, etc. **2** a range of investments held by a person, a company, etc. **3** the office of a minister of State. **4** samples of an artist's work. [It. portafogli f. portare carry + foglio leaf f. L folium]

porthole /ˈpɔːthəʊl/ n. an (esp. glazed) aperture in a ship's or aircraft's side for the admission of light.

portico /ˈpɔːtɪˌkəʊ/ n. (pl. **-oes** or **-os**) a colonnade; a roof supported by columns at regular intervals usu. attached as a porch to a building. [It. f. L porticus PORCH]

portière /ˌpɔːtɪˈeə(r)/ n. a curtain hung over a door or doorway. [F f. porte door f. L porta]

portion /ˈpɔːʃ(ə)n/ n. & v. —n. **1** a part or share. **2** the amount of food allotted to one person. **3** a specified or limited quantity. **4** one's destiny or lot. **5** a dowry. —v.tr. **1** divide (a thing) into portions. **2** (foll. by out) distribute. **3** give a dowry to. **4** (foll. by to) assign (a thing) to (a person). □ **portionless** adj. (in sense 5 of n.). [ME f. OF porcion portion f. L portio -onis]

Portland cement /ˈpɔːtlənd/ n. a cement manufactured from chalk and clay which when hard resembles Portland stone in colour.

Portland stone /ˈpɔːtlənd/ n. a limestone from the Isle of Portland in Dorset, used in building.

portly /ˈpɔːtlɪ/ adj. (**portlier**, **portliest**) **1** corpulent; stout. **2** archaic of a stately appearance. □ **portliness** n. [PORT[5] (in the sense 'bearing') + -LY[1]]

portmanteau /pɔːtˈmæntəʊ/ n. (pl. **portmanteaus** /-təʊz/ or **portmanteaux**) a leather trunk for clothes etc., opening into two equal parts. □ **portmanteau word** a word blending the sounds and combining the meanings of two others, as motel, Oxbridge. [F portmanteau f. porter carry f. L portare + manteau MANTLE]

portrait /ˈpɔːtrɪt/ n. **1** a representation of a person or animal, esp. of the face, made by drawing, painting, photography, etc. **2** a verbal picture; a graphic description. **3** a person etc. resembling or typifying another (is the portrait of his father). **4** (in graphic design etc.) a format in which the height of an illustration etc. is greater than the width. [F, past part. of OF portraire PORTRAY]

portraitist /ˈpɔːtrɪtɪst/ n. a person who takes or paints portraits.

portraiture /ˈpɔːtrɪtʃə(r)/ n. 1 the art of painting or taking portraits. 2 graphic description. 3 a portrait. [ME f. OF (as PORTRAIT)]

portray /pɔːˈtreɪ/ v.tr. 1 make a likeness of. 2 describe graphically. □ **portrayable** adj. **portrayal** n. **portrayer** n. [ME f. OF portraire f. por- = PRO-¹ + traire draw f. L trahere]

Portuguese /ˌpɔːtjʊˈgiːz, ˌpɔːtʃ-/ n. & adj. —n. (pl. same) 1 a a native or national of Portugal. b a person of Portuguese descent. 2 the language of Portugal. —adj. of or relating to Portugal or its people or language. □ **Portuguese man-of-war** a dangerous tropical or sub-tropical marine coelenterate of the genus Physalia with a large crest and a poisonous sting. [Port. portuguez f. med.L portugalensis]

pose¹ /pəʊz/ v. & n. —v. 1 intr. assume a certain attitude of body, esp. when being photographed or being painted for a portrait. 2 intr. (foll. by as) set oneself up as or pretend to be (another person etc.) (posing as a celebrity). 3 intr. behave affectedly in order to impress others. 4 tr. put forward or present (a question etc.). 5 tr. place (an artist's model etc.) in a certain attitude or position. —n. 1 an attitude of body or mind. 2 an attitude or pretence, esp. one assumed for effect (his generosity is a mere pose). [F poser (v.), pose (n.) f. LL pausare PAUSE: some senses by confusion with L ponere place (cf. COMPOSE)]

pose² /pəʊz/ v.tr. puzzle (a person) with a question or problem. [obs. appose f. OF aposer var. of oposer OPPOSE]

poser /ˈpəʊzə(r)/ n. 1 a person who poses (see POSE¹ v. 3). 2 a puzzling question or problem.

poseur /pəʊˈzɜː(r)/ n. (fem. **poseuse** /pəʊˈzɜːz/) a person who poses for effect or behaves affectedly. [F f. poser POSE¹]

posh adj. & adv. colloq. —adj. 1 smart; stylish. 2 of or associated with the upper classes (spoke with a posh accent). —adv. in a stylish or upper-class way (talk posh; act posh). □ **posh up** smarten up. □ **poshly** adv. **poshness** n. [20th c.: perh. f. sl. posh a dandy: port out starboard home (referring to the more comfortable accommodation on ships to and from the East) is a later association and not the true origin]

posit /ˈpɒzɪt/ v.tr. (**posited**, **positing**) 1 assume as a fact, postulate. 2 put in place or position. [L ponere posit- place]

position /pəˈzɪʃ(ə)n/ n. & v. —n. 1 a place occupied by a person or thing. 2 the way in which a thing or its parts are placed or arranged (sitting in an uncomfortable position). 3 the proper place (in position). 4 the state of being advantageously placed (jockeying for position). 5 a person's mental attitude; a way of looking at a question (changed their position on nuclear disarmament). 6 a person's situation in relation to others (puts one in an awkward position). 7 rank or status; high social standing. 8 paid employment. 9 a place where troops etc. are posted for strategical purposes (the position was stormed). 10 the configuration of chessmen etc. during a game. —v.tr. place in position. □ **in a position to** enabled by circumstances, resources, information, etc. to (do, state, etc.). □ **positional** adj. **positionally** adv. **positioner** n. [ME f. OF position or L positio -onis (as POSIT)]

positive /ˈpɒzɪtɪv/ adj. & n. —adj. 1 formally or explicitly stated; definite, unquestionable (positive proof). 2 (of a person) convinced, confident, or overconfident in his or her opinion (positive that I was not there). 3 a absolute; not relative. b Gram. (of an adjective or adverb) expressing a simple quality without comparison. 4 colloq. downright; complete (it would be a positive miracle). 5 constructive; directional (positive criticism; positive thinking). 6 marked by the presence rather than absence of qualities or Med. symptoms (a positive reaction to the plan; the test was positive). 7 greater than zero (positive and negative integers). 8 Electr. of, containing, or producing the kind of electrical charge produced by rubbing glass with silk; an absence of electrons. 9 (of a photographic image) showing lights and shades or colours true to the original. —n. a positive adjective, photograph, quantity, etc. □ **positive discrimination** the practice of making distinctions in favour of groups considered to be underprivileged. **positive feedback** 1 a constructive response to an experiment, questionnaire, etc. 2 Electronics the return of part of an output signal to the input, tending to increase the amplification etc. **positive pole** the north-seeking pole. **positive sign** = plus sign. **positive vetting** Brit. an exhaustive inquiry into the background and character of a candidate for a post in the Civil Service that involves access to secret material. □ **positively** adv. **positiveness** n. **positivity** /ˌpɒzɪˈtɪvɪtɪ/ n. [ME f. OF positif -ive or L positivus (as POSIT)]

positivism /ˈpɒzɪtɪˌvɪz(ə)m/ n. Philos. the philosophical system of Auguste Comte, recognizing only non-metaphysical facts and observable phenomena, and rejecting metaphysics and theism. □ **positivist** n. **positivistic** /-ˈvɪstɪk/ adj. **positivistically** /-ˈvɪstɪkəlɪ/ adv. [F positivisme (as POSITIVE)]

positron /ˈpɒzɪˌtrɒn/ n. Physics an elementary particle with a positive charge equal to the negative charge of an electron and having the same mass as an electron. [POSITIVE + -TRON]

posse /ˈpɒsɪ/ n. 1 a strong force or company or assemblage. 2 a a body of constables, law-enforcers, etc. b esp. US a body of men summoned by a sheriff etc. to enforce the law. [med.L, = power f. L posse be able]

possess /pəˈzes/ v.tr. 1 hold as property; own. 2 have a faculty, quality, etc. (they possess a special value for us). 3 (also refl.; foll. by in) maintain (oneself, one's soul, etc.) in a specified state (possess oneself in patience). 4 a (of a demon etc.) occupy; have power over (a person etc.) (possessed by the devil). b (of an emotion, infatuation, etc.) dominate, be an obsession of (possessed by fear). 5 have sexual intercourse with (esp. a woman). □ **be possessed of** own, have. **possess oneself of** take or get for one's own. **what possessed you?** an expression of incredulity. □ **possessor** n. **possessory** adj. [OF possesser f. L possidēre possess- f. potis able + sedēre sit]

possession /pəˈzeʃ(ə)n/ n. 1 the act or state of possessing or being possessed. 2 the thing possessed. 3 the act or state of actual holding or occupancy. 4 (in pl.) property, wealth, subject territory, etc. 5 Football etc. temporary control of the ball by a particular player. □ **in possession 1** (of a person) possessing. **2** (of a thing) possessed.

in possession of 1 having in one's possession. **2** maintaining control over (*in possession of one's wits*). **in the possession of** held or owned by. □ **possessionless** *adj.* [ME f. OF *possession* or L *possessio -onis* (as POSSESS)]

possessive /pə'zɛsɪv/ *adj. & n.* —*adj.* **1** showing a desire to possess or retain what one already owns. **2** showing jealous and domineering tendencies towards another person. **3** *Gram.* indicating possession. —*n.* (in full **possessive case**) *Gram.* the case of nouns and pronouns expressing possession. □ **possessive pronoun** each of the pronouns indicating possession (*my, your, his, their,* etc.) or the corresponding absolute forms (*mine, yours, his, theirs,* etc.). □ **possessively** *adv.* **possessiveness** *n.* [L *possessivus* (as POSSESS), transl. Gk *ktētikē* (*ptōsis* case)]

possibility /ˌpɒsɪ'bɪlɪtɪ/ *n.* (*pl.* **-ies**) **1** the state or fact of being possible, or an occurrence of this (*outside the range of possibility; saw no possibility of going away*). **2** a thing that may exist or happen (*there are three possibilities*). **3** (usu. in *pl.*) the capability of being used, improved, etc.; the potential of an object or situation (esp. *have possibilities*). [ME f. OF *possibilité* or LL *possibilitas -tatis* (as POSSIBLE)]

possible /'pɒsɪb(ə)l/ *adj. & n.* —*adj.* **1** capable of existing or happening; that may be managed, achieved, etc. (*came as early as possible; did as much as possible*). **2** that is likely to happen etc. (*few thought their victory possible*). **3** acceptable; potential (*a possible way of doing it*). —*n.* **1** a possible candidate, member of a team, etc. **2** (prec. by *the*) whatever is likely, manageable, etc. [ME f. OF *possible* or L *possibilis* f. *posse* be able]

possibly /'pɒsɪblɪ/ *adv.* **1** perhaps. **2** in accordance with possibility (*cannot possibly refuse*).

possum /'pɒsəm/ *n. colloq.* = OPOSSUM 1. **2** *Austral.* & *NZ colloq.* a phalanger resembling an American opossum. □ **play possum** pretend to be asleep or unconscious when threatened. [abbr.]

post¹ /pəʊst/ *n. & v.* —*n.* **1** a long stout piece of timber or metal set upright in the ground etc.: **a** to support something, esp. in building. **b** to mark a position, boundary, etc. **c** to carry notices. **2** a pole etc. marking the start or finish of a race. —*v.tr.* (often foll. by *up*) **1** attach (a paper etc.) in a prominent place; stick up (*post no bills*). **2** announce or advertise by placard or in a published text. [OE f. L *postis*: in ME also f. OF etc.]

post² /pəʊst/ *n. & v.* —*n.* **1** *Brit.* the official conveyance of parcels, letters, etc. (*send it by post*). **2** *Brit.* a single collection, dispatch, or delivery of these; the letters etc. dispatched (*has the post arrived yet?*). **3** *Brit.* a place where letters etc. are dealt with; a post office or postbox (*take it to the post*). —*v.* **1** *tr.* put (a letter etc.) in the post. **2** *tr.* (esp. as **posted** *adj.*) (often foll. by *up*) supply a person with information (*keep me posted*). **3** *tr.* **a** enter (an item) in a ledger. **b** (often foll. by *up*) complete (a ledger) in this way. □ **post-haste** with great speed. **Post Office 1** the public department or corporation responsible for postal services and (in some countries) telecommunication. **2** (**post office**) a room or building where postal business is carried on. **post-office box** a numbered place in a post office where letters are kept until called for. **post-paid** on which postage has been paid. **post room** the department of a company that deals with incoming and outgoing mail. **post-town** a town with a post office, esp. one that is not a sub-office of another. [F *poste* (fem.) f. It. *posta* ult. f. L *ponere posit-* place]

post³ /pəʊst/ *n. & v.* —*n.* **1** a place where a soldier is stationed or which he patrols. **2** a place of duty. **3 a** a position taken up by a body of soldiers. **b** a force occupying this. **c** a fort. **4** a situation, paid employment. **5** = *trading post.* —*v.tr.* **1** place or station (soldiers, an employee, etc.). **2** appoint to a post or command. □ **first** (or **last**) **post** *Brit.* a bugle-call giving notice of the hour of retiring at night. **last post** *Brit.* a bugle-call blown at military funerals etc. [F *poste* (masc.) f. It. *posto* f. Rmc *postum* (unrecorded) f. L *ponere posit-* place]

post- /pəʊst/ *prefix* after in time or order. [from or after L *post* (adv. & prep.)]

postage /'pəʊstɪdʒ/ *n.* the amount charged for sending a letter etc. by post, usu. prepaid in the form of a stamp (*£2 including postage & packing*). □ **postage meter** *US* a franking-machine. **postage stamp** an official stamp affixed to or imprinted on a letter etc. indicating the amount of postage paid.

postal /'pəʊst(ə)l/ *adj. & n.* —*adj.* **1** of the post. **2** by post (*postal vote*). —*n. US* a postcard. □ **postal card** *US* = POSTCARD. **postal code** = POSTCODE. **postal meter** a franking-machine. **postal note** *Austral.* & *NZ* = *postal order.* **postal order** a money order issued by the Post Office, payable to a specified person. □ **postally** *adv.* [F (*poste* POST²)]

postbag /'pəʊstbæg/ *n. Brit.* = MAILBAG.

postbox /'pəʊstbɒks/ *n. Brit.* a letter-box.

postcard /'pəʊstkɑːd/ *n.* a card, often with a photograph on one side, for sending a short message by post without an envelope.

postcode /'pəʊstkəʊd/ *n.* a group of letters or letters and figures which are added to a postal address to assist sorting.

post-coital /pəʊst'kɔɪt(ə)l/ *adj.* occurring or existing after sexual intercourse. □ **post-coitally** *adv.*

postdate *v. & n.* —*v.tr.* /pəʊst'deɪt/ affix or assign a date later than the actual one to (a document, event, etc.). —*n.* /'pəʊstdeɪt/ such a date.

poster /'pəʊstə(r)/ *n.* **1** a placard in a public place. **2** a large printed picture. **3** a billposter. □ **poster paint** a gummy opaque paint.

poste restante /ˌpəʊst re'stɑ̃t/ *n.* **1** a direction on a letter to indicate that it should be kept at a specified post office until collected by the addressee. **2** the department in a post office where such letters are kept. [F, = letter(s) remaining]

posterior /pɒ'stɪərɪə(r)/ *adj. & n.* —*adj.* **1** later; coming after in series, order, or time. **2** situated at the back. —*n.* (in *sing.* or *pl.*) the buttocks. □ **posteriority** /pɒˌstɪərɪ'ɒrɪtɪ/ *n.* **posteriorly** *adv.* [L, compar. of *posterus* following f. *post* after]

posterity /pɒ'sterɪtɪ/ *n.* **1** all succeeding generations. **2** the descendants of a person. [ME f. OF *posterité* f. L *posteritas -tatis* f. *posterus*: see POSTERIOR]

postern /'pɒst(ə)n, 'pəʊ-/ *n.* **1** a back door. **2** a side way or entrance. [ME f. OF *posterne, posterle,* f. LL *posterula* dimin. of *posterus*: see POSTERIOR]

postgraduate /pəʊstˈgrædjʊət/ *adj.* & *n.* —*adj.*
1 (of a course of study) carried on after taking a
first degree. **2** of or relating to students following this course of study. —*n.* a postgraduate
student.

posthumous /ˈpɒstjʊməs/ *adj.* **1** occurring after
death. **2** (of a child) born after the death of its
father. **3** (of a book etc.) published after the
author's death. □ **posthumously** *adv.* [L *post-
umus* last (superl. f. *post* after): in LL *posth-* by
assoc. with *humus* ground]

postilion /pɒˈstɪljən/ *n.* (also **postillion**) the
rider on the near (left-hand side) horse drawing
a coach etc. when there is no coachman. [F
postillon f. It. *postiglione* post-boy f. *posta* POST²]

post-impressionism /ˌpəʊstɪmˈprefəˌnɪz(ə)m/
n. artistic aims and methods developed as a
reaction against impressionism and intending
to express the individual artist's conception of
the objects represented rather than the ordinary
observer's view. □ **post-impressionist** *n.* &
adj. **post-impressionistic** /-ˈnɪstɪk/ *adj.*

postindustrial /ˌpəʊstɪnˈdʌstrɪəl/ *adj.* relating
to or characteristic of a society or economy
which no longer relies on heavy industry.

postlude /ˈpəʊstluːd/ *n. Mus.* a concluding voluntary. [POST-, after PRELUDE]

postman /ˈpəʊstmən/ *n.* (*pl.* **-men**; *fem.* **postwoman**, *pl.* **-women**) a person who is employed
to deliver and collect letters etc.

postmark /ˈpəʊstmɑːk/ *n.* & *v.* —*n.* an official
mark stamped on a letter, esp. one giving the
place, date, etc. of dispatch or arrival, and
serving to cancel the stamp. —*v.tr.* mark (an
envelope etc.) with this.

postmaster /ˈpəʊstˌmɑːstə(r)/ *n.* a man in charge
of a post office. □ **postmaster general** the
head of a country's postal service.

postmistress /ˈpəʊstˌmɪstrɪs/ *n.* a woman in
charge of a post office.

post-modern /pəʊstˈmɒd(ə)n/ *adj.* (in literature,
architecture, the arts, etc.) denoting a movement reacting against modern tendencies, esp.
by drawing attention to former conventions. □
post-modernism *n.* **post-modernist** *n.* & *adj.*

post-mortem /pəʊstˈmɔːtəm/ *n.*, *adv.*, & *adj.*
—*n.* **1** (in full **post-mortem examination**) an
examination made after death, esp. to determine its cause. **2** *colloq.* a discussion analysing
the course and result of a game, election, etc.
—*adv.* & *adj.* after death. [L]

postnatal /pəʊstˈneɪt(ə)l/ *adj.* characteristic of
or relating to the period after childbirth.

postoperative /pəʊstˈɒpərətɪv/ *adj.* relating to
or occurring in a period after a surgical
operation.

postpone /pəʊstˈpəʊn, pəˈspəʊn/ *v.tr.* cause or
arrange (an event etc.) to take place at a later
time. □ **postponable** *adj.* **postponement** *n.*
postponer *n.* [L *postponere* (as POST-, *ponere* posit-
place)]

postprandial /pəʊstˈprændɪəl/ *adj. formal* or *joc.*
after dinner or lunch. [POST- + L *prandium* a
meal]

postscript /ˈpəʊstskrɪpt, ˈpəʊskrɪpt/ *n.* **1** an
additional paragraph or remark, usu. at the end
of a letter after the signature and introduced
by 'PS'. **2** any additional information, action,
etc. [L *postscriptum* neut. past part. of *postscribere*
(as POST-, *scribere* write)]

postulant /ˈpɒstjʊlənt/ *n.* a candidate, esp. for
admission into a religious order. [F *postulant* or
L *postulans -antis* (as POSTULATE)]

postulate *v.* & *n.* —*v.tr.* /ˈpɒstjʊˌleɪt/ **1** (often
foll. by *that* + clause) assume as a necessary
condition, esp. as a basis for reasoning; take for
granted. **2** claim. —*n.* /ˈpɒstjʊlət/ **1** a thing
postulated. **2** a fundamental prerequisite or
condition. □ **postulation** /ˌpɒstjʊˈleɪʃ(ə)n/ *n.* [L
postulare postulat- demand]

posture /ˈpɒstʃə(r)/ *n.* & *v.* —*n.* **1** the relative
position of parts, esp. of the body (*in a reclining
posture*). **2** carriage or bearing (*improved by good
posture and balance*). **3** a mental or spiritual
attitude or condition. **4** the condition or state
(of affairs etc.) (*in more diplomatic postures*). —*v.* **1**
intr. assume a mental or physical attitude, esp.
for effect (*inclined to strut and posture*). **2** *tr.* pose
(a person). □ **postural** *adj.* **posturer** *n.* [F f. It.
postura f. L *positura* f. *ponere posit-* place]

postwar /pəʊstˈwɔː(r), ˈpəʊst-/ *adj.* occurring or
existing after a war (esp. the most recent major
war).

posy /ˈpəʊzɪ/ *n.* (*pl.* **-ies**) a small bunch of flowers.
[alt. f. POESY]

pot¹ *n.* & *v.* —*n.* **1** a vessel, usu. rounded, of
ceramic ware or metal or glass for holding
liquids or solids or for cooking in. **2 a** a
coffee-pot, flowerpot, glue-pot, jam-pot, teapot,
etc. **b** = *chimney-pot*. **c** = *lobster-pot*. **3** a drinking
vessel of pewter etc. **4** the contents of a pot (*ate
a whole pot of jam*). **5** the total amount of the bet
in a game etc. **6** *colloq.* a large sum (*pots of
money*). **7** *sl.* a vessel given as a prize in an
athletic contest, esp. a silver cup. **8** = *pot-belly*.
—*v.tr.* (**potted**, **potting**) **1** place in a pot. **2** (usu.
as **potted** *adj.*) preserve in a sealed pot (*potted
shrimps*). **3** sit (a young child) on a chamber pot.
4 pocket (a ball) in billiards etc. **5** shoot at, hit,
or kill (an animal) with a pot-shot. **6** seize or
secure. **7** abridge or epitomize (*in a potted version*;
potted wisdom). □ **go to pot** *colloq.* deteriorate; be
ruined. **pot-bellied** having a pot-belly. **pot-
belly** (*pl.* **-ies**) **1** a protruding stomach. **2** a
person with this. **pot-boiler** a work of literature or art done merely to make the writer
or artist a living. **pot-bound** (of a plant) having
roots which fill the flowerpot, leaving no room
to expand. **pot cheese** *US* cottage cheese.
pot-herb any herb grown in a kitchen garden.
pot luck whatever (hospitality etc.) is available.
pot plant a plant grown in a flowerpot. **pot
roast** a piece of meat cooked slowly in a covered
dish. **pot-roast** *v.tr.* cook (a piece of meat) in
this way. **pot-shot 1** a random shot. **2** a shot
aimed at an animal etc. within easy reach. □
potful *n.* (*pl.* **-fuls**). [OE *pott*, corresp. to OFris.,
MDu., MLG *pot*, f. pop.L]

pot² *n. sl.* marijuana. □ **pot-head** one who
smokes this. [prob. f. Mex. Sp. *potiguaya*]

potable /ˈpəʊtəb(ə)l/ *adj.* drinkable. □ **potability**
/-ˈbɪlɪtɪ/ *n.* [F *potable* or LL *potabilis* f. L *potare*
drink]

potage /pɒˈtɑːʒ/ *n.* thick soup. [F (as POTTAGE)]

potash /ˈpɒtæʃ/ *n.* an alkaline potassium compound, usu. potassium carbonate or hydroxide.
[17th-c. *pot-ashes* f. Du. *pot-asschen* (as POT¹, ASH¹):
orig. obtained by leaching vegetable ashes and
evaporating the solution in iron pots]

potassium /pəˈtæsɪəm/ *n. Chem.* a soft silver-
white metallic element, an essential element

for living organisms, and forming many useful compounds used industrially. □ **potassium chloride** a white crystalline solid used as a fertilizer and in photographic processing. **potassium cyanide** a highly toxic solid that can be hydrolysed to give poisonous hydrogen cyanide gas. **potassium iodide** a white crystalline solid used as an additive to table salt to prevent iodine deficiency. **potassium permanganate** a purple crystalline solid that is used in solution as an oxidizing agent and disinfectant. □ **potassic** adj. [POTASH + -IUM]

potation /pəˈteɪʃ(ə)n/ n. **1** a drink. **2** the act or an instance of drinking. **3** (usu. in pl.) the act or an instance of tippling. □ **potatory** /pəʊˈteɪtərɪ/ adj. [ME f. OF potation or L potatio f. potare drink]

potato /pəˈteɪtəʊ/ n. (pl. **-oes**) **1** a starchy plant tuber that is cooked and used for food. **2** the plant, *Solanum tuberosum*, bearing this. **3** colloq. a hole in (esp. the heel of) a sock or stocking. [Sp. *patata* var. of Taino *batata*]

poteen /pɒˈtiːn/ n. (also **potheen** /-ˈtʃiːn/) Ir. alcohol made illicitly, usu. from potatoes. [Ir. *poitín* dimin. of *pota* POT¹]

potent /ˈpəʊt(ə)nt/ adj. **1** powerful; strong. **2** (of a reason) cogent; forceful. **3** (of a male) capable of sexual erection or orgasm. **4** literary mighty. □ **potence** n. **potency** n. **potently** adv. [L *potens* -entis pres. part. of *posse* be able]

potentate /ˈpəʊtənˌteɪt/ n. a monarch or ruler. [ME f. OF *potentat* or L *potentatus* dominion f. *potentia* power (as POTENT)]

potential /pəˈtenʃ(ə)l/ adj. & n. —adj. capable of coming into being or action; latent. —n. **1** the capacity for use or development; possibility (*achieved its highest potential*). **2** usable resources. **3** Physics the quantity determining the energy of mass in a gravitational field or of charge in an electric field. □ **potential difference** the difference of electric potential between two points. **potential energy** a body's ability to do work by virtue of its position relative to others, stresses within itself, electric charge, etc. □ **potentiality** /-ʃɪˈælɪtɪ/ n. **potentialize** v.tr. (also **-ise**). **potentially** adv. [ME f. OF *potencial* or LL *potentialis* f. *potentia* (as POTENT)]

potentiate /pəˈtenʃɪˌeɪt/ v.tr. **1** make more powerful, esp. increase the effectiveness of (a drug). **2** make possible. [as POTENT after SUBSTANTIATE]

pother /ˈpɒðə(r)/ n. & v. literary —n. a noise; commotion; fuss. —v. **1** tr. fluster, worry. **2** intr. make a fuss. [16th c.: orig. unkn.]

pothole /ˈpɒthəʊl/ n. & v. **1** Geol. a deep hole or system of caves and underground river-beds formed by the erosion of rock esp. by the action of water. **2** a deep hole in the ground or a river-bed. **3** a hole in a road surface caused by wear or subsidence. —v.intr. Brit. explore potholes. □ **potholer** n. **potholing** n.

potion /ˈpəʊʃ(ə)n/ n. a dose or quantity of medicine, a drug, poison, etc. [ME f. OF f. L *potio* -onis f. *potus* having drunk]

pot-pourri /pəʊˈpʊərɪ, -ˈriː/ n. **1** a mixture of dried petals and spices used to perfume a room etc. **2** a musical or literary medley. [F, = rotten pot]

potsherd /ˈpɒtʃɜːd/ n. a broken piece of ceramic material, esp. one found on an archaeological site.

pottage /ˈpɒtɪdʒ/ n. archaic soup, stew. [ME f. OF *potage* (as POT¹)]

potter¹ /ˈpɒtə(r)/ v. (US **putter** /ˈpʌtə(r)/) **1** intr. **a** (often foll. by about, around) work or occupy oneself in a desultory but pleasant manner (*likes pottering about in the garden*). **b** (often foll. by at, in) dabble in a subject or occupation. **2** intr. go slowly, dawdle, loiter (*pottered up to the pub*). **3** tr. (foll. by away) fritter away (one's time etc.). □ **potterer** n. [frequent. of dial. *pote* push f. OE *potian*]

potter² /ˈpɒtə(r)/ n. a maker of ceramic vessels. □ **potter's wheel** a horizontal revolving disc to carry clay for making pots. [OE *pottere* (as POT¹)]

pottery /ˈpɒtərɪ/ n. (pl. **-ies**) **1** vessels etc. made of fired clay. **2** a potter's work. **3** a potter's workshop. [ME f. OF *poterie* f. *potier* POTTER²]

potting shed /ˈpɒtɪŋ/ n. a building in which plants are potted and tools etc. are stored.

potty¹ /ˈpɒtɪ/ adj. (**pottier, pottiest**) Brit. sl. **1** foolish or crazy. **2** insignificant, trivial (esp. *potty little*). □ **pottiness** n. [19th c.: orig. unkn.]

potty² /ˈpɒtɪ/ n. (pl. **-ies**) colloq. a chamber-pot, esp. for a child.

pouch /paʊtʃ/ n. & v. —n. **1** a small bag or detachable outside pocket. **2** a baggy area of skin underneath the eyes etc. **3 a** a pocket-like receptacle in which marsupials carry their young during lactation. **b** any of several similar structures in various animals, e.g. in the cheeks of rodents. —v.tr. put or make into a pouch. □ **pouched** adj. **pouchy** adj. [ME f. ONF *pouche*: cf. POKE²]

pouf var. of POOF.

pouffe /puːf/ n. (also **pouf**) a large firm cushion used as a low seat or footstool. [F *pouf*; ult. imit.]

poult /pəʊlt/ n. a young domestic fowl, turkey, pheasant, etc. [ME, contr. f. PULLET]

poulterer /ˈpəʊltərə(r)/ n. a dealer in poultry and usu. game. [ME *poulter* f. OF *pouletier* (as PULLET)]

poultice /ˈpəʊltɪs/ n. & v. —n. a soft medicated and usu. heated mass applied to the body and kept in place with muslin etc., for relieving soreness and inflammation. —v.tr. apply a poultice to. [orig. *pultes* (pl.) f. L *puls pultis* pottage, pap, etc.]

poultry /ˈpəʊltrɪ/ n. domestic fowls (ducks, geese, turkeys, chickens, etc.), esp. as a source of food. [ME f. OF *pouleterie* (as POULTERER)]

pounce /paʊns/ v. & n. —v.intr. **1** spring or swoop, esp. as in capturing prey. **2** (often foll. by on, upon) **a** make a sudden attack. **b** seize eagerly upon an object, remark, etc. (*pounced on what we said*). —n. the act or an instance of pouncing. □ **pouncer** n. [perh. f. *puncheon* f. OF *poinson*, *po(i)nchon*, ult. f. L *pungere punct-* prick]

pound¹ /paʊnd/ n. **1** a unit of weight equal to 16 oz. avoirdupois (0.4536 kg), or 12 oz. troy (0.3732 kg). **2** (in full **pound sterling**) (pl. same or **pounds**) the chief monetary unit of the UK and several other countries. □ **pound cake** a rich cake containing a pound (or equal weights) of each chief ingredient. **pound coin** (or **note**) a coin or note worth one pound sterling. **pound of flesh** any legitimate but crippling demand. **pound sign** the sign £, representing a pound. [OE *pund* ult. f. L *pondo* Roman pound weight of 12 ounces]

pound² /paʊnd/ v. **1** tr. **a** crush or beat with repeated heavy blows. **b** thump or pummel, esp. with the fists. **c** grind to a powder or pulp. **2** intr. (foll. by *at*, *on*) deliver heavy blows or gunfire. **3** intr. (foll. by *along* etc.) make one's way heavily or clumsily. **4** intr. (of the heart) beat heavily. □ **pound out** produce with or as if with heavy blows. □ **pounder** n. [OE *pūnian*, rel. to Du. *puin*, LG *pün* rubbish]

pound³ /paʊnd/ n. & v. —n. **1** an enclosure where stray animals or officially removed vehicles are kept until redeemed. **2** a place of confinement. —v.tr. enclose (cattle etc.) in a pound. [ME f. OE *pund-* in *pundfald* a pen for stray cattle]

poundage /ˈpaʊndɪdʒ/ n. **1** a commission or fee of so much per pound sterling or weight. **2** a percentage of the total earnings of a business, paid as wages. **3** a person's weight, esp. that which is regarded as excess.

-pounder /ˈpaʊndə(r)/ n. (usu. in *comb.*) **1** a thing or person weighing a specified number of pounds (*a five-pounder*). **2** a gun carrying a shell of a specified number of pounds. **3** a thing worth, or a person possessing, so many pounds sterling.

pour /pɔː(r)/ v. **1** intr. & tr. (usu. foll. by *down*, *out*, *over*, etc.) flow or cause to flow esp. downwards in a stream or shower. **2** tr. dispense (a drink, e.g. tea) by pouring. **3** intr. (of rain, or with it as subject) fall heavily. **4** intr. (usu. foll. by *in*, *out*, etc.) come or go in profusion or rapid succession (*the crowd poured out*; *letters poured in*). **5** tr. discharge or send freely (*poured forth arrows*). **6** tr. (often foll. by *out*) utter at length or in a rush (*poured out their story*; *poured scorn on my attempts*). □ **it never rains but it pours** misfortunes rarely come singly. **pour oil on the waters** (or **on troubled waters**) calm a disagreement or disturbance, esp. with conciliatory words. □ **pourable** adj. **pourer** n. [ME: orig. unkn.]

poussin /ˈpuːsæ̃/ n. a young chicken bred for eating. [F]

pout /paʊt/ v. & n. —v. **1** intr. **a** push the lips forward as an expression of displeasure or sulking. **b** (of the lips) be pushed forward. **2** tr. push (the lips) forward in pouting. —n. such an action or expression. □ **pouter** n. **poutingly** adv. **pouty** adj. [ME, perh. f. OE *putian* (unrecorded) be inflated]

pouter /ˈpaʊtə(r)/ n. **1** a person who pouts. **2** a kind of pigeon able to inflate its crop considerably.

poverty /ˈpɒvətɪ/ n. **1** the state of being poor; want of the necessities of life. **2** (often foll. by *of*, *in*) scarcity or lack. **3** inferiority, poorness, meanness. □ **poverty line** the minimum income level needed to secure the necessities of life. **poverty-stricken** extremely poor. **poverty trap** a situation in which an increase of income incurs a loss of State benefits. [ME f. OF *poverte*, *poverté* f. L *paupertas -tatis* f. *pauper* poor]

POW abbr. prisoner of war.

pow /paʊ/ int. expressing the sound of a blow or explosion. [imit.]

powder /ˈpaʊdə(r)/ n. & v. —n. **1** a substance in the form of fine dry particles. **2** a medicine or cosmetic in this form. **3** = GUNPOWDER. —v.tr. **1 a** apply powder to (*powder one's nose*). **b** sprinkle or decorate with or as with powder. **2** (esp. as **powdered** adj.) reduce to a fine powder (*powdered milk*). □ **keep one's powder dry** be

cautious and alert. **powder blue** pale blue. **powder-keg 1** a barrel of gunpowder. **2** a dangerous or volatile situation. **powder-puff** a soft pad for applying powder to the skin, esp. the face. **powder-room** a women's cloakroom or lavatory in a public building. **take a powder** sl. depart quickly. □ **powdery** adj. [ME f. OF *poudre* f. L *pulvis pulveris* dust]

power /ˈpaʊə(r)/ n. & v. —n. **1** the ability to do or act (*will do all in my power*; *has the power to change colour*). **2** a particular faculty of body or mind (*lost the power of speech*; *powers of persuasion*). **3 a** government, influence, or authority. **b** political or social ascendancy or control (*the party in power*; *Black Power*). **4** authorization; delegated authority (*power of attorney*; *police powers*). **5** (often foll. by *over*) personal ascendancy. **6** an influential person, group, or organization (*the press is a power in the land*). **7 a** military strength. **b** a state having international influence, esp. based on military strength (*the leading powers*). **8** vigour, energy. **9** an active property or function (*has a high heating power*). **10** colloq. a large number or amount (*has done me a power of good*). **11** the capacity for exerting mechanical force or doing work (*horsepower*). **12** mechanical or electrical energy as distinct from hand-labour (often *attrib.*: *power tools*; *power steering*). **13 a** a public supply of (esp. electrical) energy. **b** a particular source or form of energy (*hydroelectric power*). **14** a mechanical force applied e.g. by means of a lever. **15** the product obtained when a number is multiplied by itself a certain number of times (*2 to the power of 3 = 8*). **16** the magnifying capacity of a lens. —v.tr. **1** supply with mechanical or electrical energy. **2** (foll. by *up*, *down*) increase or decrease the power supplied to (a device); switch on or off. □ **in the power of** under the control of. **power behind the throne** a person who asserts authority or influence without having formal status. **power block** a group of nations constituting an international political force. **power cut** a temporary withdrawal or failure of an electric power supply. **power line** a conductor supplying electrical power, esp. one supported by pylons or poles. **power pack 1** a unit for supplying power. **2** the equipment for converting an alternating current (from the mains) to a direct current at a different (usu. lower) voltage. **power play 1** tactics involving the concentration of players at a particular point. **2** similar tactics in business, politics, etc., involving a concentration of resources, effort, etc. **power point** *Brit.* a socket in a wall etc. for connecting an electrical device to the mains. **power politics** political action based on power or influence. **power-sharing** a policy agreed between parties or within a coalition to share responsibility for decision-making and political action. **power station** a building where electrical power is generated for distribution. **the powers that be** those in authority (Rom. 13:1). □ **powered** adj. (also in *comb.*). [ME & AF *poer* etc., OF *poeir* ult. f. L *posse* be able]

powerboat /ˈpaʊəbəʊt/ n. a powerful motor boat.

powerful /ˈpaʊəfʊl/ adj. **1** having much power or strength. **2** politically or socially influential. □ **powerfully** adv. **powerfulness** n.

powerhouse /ˈpaʊəˌhaʊs/ n. **1** = power station. **2** a person or thing of great energy.

powerless /ˈpaʊəlɪs/ adj. **1** without power or strength. **2** (often foll. by to + infin.) wholly unable (powerless to help). □ **powerlessly** adv. **powerlessness** n.

powerplant /ˈpaʊəˌplɑːnt/ n. an apparatus or an installation which provides power for industry, a machine, etc.

powwow /ˈpaʊwaʊ/ n. & v. —n. a conference or meeting for discussion (orig. among N. American Indians). —v.tr. hold a powwow. [Algonquian powah, powwaw magician (lit. 'he dreams')]

pox n. **1** any virus disease producing a rash of pimples that become pus-filled and leave pock-marks on healing. **2** colloq. = SYPHILIS. [alt. spelling of pocks pl. of POCK]

poxy /ˈpɒksɪ/ adj. (**poxier**, **poxiest**) **1** infected by pox. **2** sl. of poor quality; worthless.

pp abbr. pianissimo.

pp. abbr. pages.

p.p. abbr. (also **pp**) per pro.

p.p.m. abbr. parts per million.

PPS abbr. Brit. **1** Parliamentary Private Secretary. **2** additional postscript.

PR abbr. **1** public relations. **2** proportional representation.

Pr symb. Chem. the element praseodymium.

pr. abbr. pair.

practicable /ˈpræktɪkəb(ə)l/ adj. **1** that can be done or used. **2** possible in practice. □ **practicability** /-ˈbɪlɪtɪ/ n. **practicableness** n. **practicably** adv. [F praticable f. pratiquer put into practice (as PRACTICAL)]

practical /ˈpræktɪk(ə)l/ adj. & n. —adj. **1** of or concerned with practice or use rather than theory. **2** suited to use or action; designed mainly to fulfil a function (practical shoes). **3** (of a person) inclined to action rather than speculation; able to make things function well. **4 a** that is such in effect though not nominally (for all practical purposes). **b** virtual (in practical control). **5** feasible; concerned with what is actually possible (practical politics). —n. a practical examination or lesson. □ **practical joke** a humorous trick played on a person. **practical joker** a person who plays practical jokes. □ **practicality** /-ˈkælɪtɪ/ n. (pl. -ies). **practicalness** n. [earlier practic f. obs. F practique or LL practicus f. Gk praktikos f. prassō do, act]

practically /ˈpræktɪkəlɪ/ adv. **1** virtually, almost (practically nothing). **2** in a practical way.

practice /ˈpræktɪs/ n. & v. —n. **1** habitual action or performance (the practice of teaching; makes a practice of saving). **2** a habit or custom (has been my regular practice). **3 a** repeated exercise in an activity requiring the development of skill. **b** a session of this. **4** action or execution as opposed to theory. **5** the professional work or business of a doctor, lawyer, etc. (has a practice in town). **6** procedure generally, esp. of a specified kind (bad practice). —v.tr. & intr. US var. of PRACTISE. □ **in practice 1** when actually applied; in reality. **2** skilful because of recent exercise in a particular pursuit. **out of practice** lacking a former skill from lack of recent practice. **put into practice** actually apply (an idea, method, etc.). [ME f. PRACTISE, after advice, device]

practise /ˈpræktɪs/ v. (US **practice**) **1** tr. perform habitually; carry out in action (practise the same method; practise what you preach). **2** tr. & (foll. by in, on) intr. do repeatedly as an exercise to improve a skill; exercise oneself in or on (an activity requiring skill) (had to practise in the art of speaking). **3** tr. (as **practised** adj.) experienced, expert (a practised liar). **4** tr. **a** pursue or be engaged in (a profession, religion, etc.). **b** (as **practising** adj.) currently active or engaged in (a profession or activity) (a practising Christian; a practising lawyer). **5** intr. (foll. by on, upon) take advantage of; impose upon. □ **practiser** n. [ME f. OF pra(c)tiser or med.L practizare alt. f. practicare (as PRACTICAL)]

practitioner /prækˈtɪʃənə(r)/ n. a person practising a profession, esp. medicine (general practitioner). [obs. practitian f. F practicien + -ER]

prae- /priː/ prefix = PRE- (esp. in words regarded as Latin or relating to Roman antiquity). [L: see PRE-]

praenomen /priːˈnəʊmen/ n. an ancient Roman's first or personal name (e.g. Marcus Tullius Cicero). [L f. prae before + nomen name]

praesidium var. of PRESIDIUM.

praetor /ˈpriːtə(r), -tɔː(r)/ n. (US **pretor**) Rom. Hist. each of two ancient Roman magistrates ranking below consul. □ **praetorial** /-ˈtɔːrɪəl/ adj. **praetorship** n. [ME f. F préteur or L praetor (perh. as PRAE-, ire it- go)]

praetorian /priːˈtɔːrɪən/ adj. & n. (US **pretorian**) Rom.Hist. —adj. of or having the powers of a praetor. —n. a man of praetorian rank. □ **praetorian guard** the bodyguard of the Roman emperor. [ME f. L praetorianus (as PRAETOR)]

pragmatic /prægˈmætɪk/ adj. **1** dealing with matters with regard to their practical requirements or consequences. **2** treating the facts of history with reference to their practical lessons. □ **pragmaticality** /-ˈkælɪtɪ/ n. **pragmatically** adv. [LL pragmaticus f. Gk pragmatikos f. pragma -matos deed]

pragmatism /ˈprægməˌtɪz(ə)m/ n. **1** a pragmatic attitude or procedure. **2** a philosophy that evaluates assertions solely by their practical consequences and bearing on human interests. □ **pragmatist** n. **pragmatistic** /-ˈtɪstɪk/ adj. [Gk pragma: see PRAGMATIC]

prairie /ˈpreərɪ/ n. a large area of usu. treeless grassland esp. in N. America. □ **prairie dog** any N. American rodent of the genus Cynomys, living in burrows and making a barking sound. **prairie oyster** a seasoned raw egg, swallowed without breaking the yolk. **prairie wolf** = COYOTE. [F f. OF praerie ult. f. L pratum meadow]

praise /preɪz/ v. & n. —v.tr. **1** express warm approval or admiration of. **2** glorify (God) in words. —n. the act or an instance of praising; commendation (won high praise; were loud in their praises). □ **praise be!** an exclamation of pious gratitude. **sing the praises of** commend (a person) highly. □ **praiseful** adj. **praiser** n. [ME f. OF preisier price, prize, praise, f. LL pretiare f. L pretium price: cf. PRIZE¹]

praiseworthy /ˈpreɪzˌwɜːðɪ/ adj. worthy of praise; commendable. □ **praiseworthily** adv. **praiseworthiness** n.

praline /ˈprɑːliːn/ n. a sweet made by browning nuts in boiling sugar. [F f. Marshal de Plessis-Praslin, Fr. soldier d. 1675, whose cook invented it]

pram /præm/ n. Brit. a four-wheeled carriage for a baby, pushed by a person on foot. [abbr. of PERAMBULATOR]

prance /prɑːns/ v. & n. —v.intr. **1** (of a horse) raise the forelegs and spring from the hind legs. **2** (often foll. by about) walk or behave in an elated or arrogant manner. —n. **1** the act of prancing. **2** a prancing movement. □ **prancer** n. [ME: orig. unkn.]

prandial /ˈprændɪəl/ adj. formal or joc. of dinner or lunch. [L prandium meal]

prang v. & n. Brit. sl. —v.tr. **1** crash or damage (an aircraft or vehicle). **2** bomb (a target) successfully. —n. the act or an instance of pranging. [imit.]

prank n. a practical joke; a piece of mischief. □ **prankful** adj. **prankish** adj. **pranksome** adj. [16th c.: orig. unkn.]

prankster /ˈpræŋkstə(r)/ n. a person fond of playing pranks.

praseodymium /ˌpreɪzɪəˈdɪmɪəm/ n. Chem. a soft silvery metallic element of the lanthanide series, used in catalyst mixtures. [G Praseodym f. Gk prasios leek-green f. prason leek (from its green salts), + G Didym f. Gk didumos twin]

prat n. sl. **1** Brit. a silly or foolish person. **2** the buttocks. [16th-c. cant (in sense 2): orig. unkn.]

prate v. & n. —v. **1** intr. chatter; talk too much. **2** intr. talk foolishly or irrelevantly. **3** tr. tell or say in a prating manner. —n. prating; idle talk. □ **prater** n. **prating** adj. [ME f. MDu., MLG praten, prob. imit.]

pratfall /ˈprætfɔːl/ n. US sl. **1** a fall on the buttocks. **2** a humiliating failure.

prattle /ˈpræt(ə)l/ v. & n. —v.intr. & tr. chatter or say in a childish way. —n. **1** childish chatter. **2** inconsequential talk. □ **prattler** n. **prattling** adj. [MLG pratelen (as PRATE)]

prawn /prɔːn/ n. & v. —n. any of various marine crustaceans, resembling a shrimp but usu. larger. —v.intr. fish for prawns. [ME pra(y)ne, of unkn. orig.]

pray v. (often foll. by for or to + infin. or that + clause) **1** intr. (often foll. by to) say prayers (to God etc.); make devout supplication. **2 a** tr. entreat, beseech. **b** tr. & intr. ask earnestly (prayed to be released). **3** tr. (as imper.) archaic & formal please (pray tell me). [ME f. OF preier f. LL precare f. L precari entreat]

prayer[1] /ˈpreə(r)/ n. **1 a** a solemn request or thanksgiving to God or an object of worship (say a prayer). **b** a formula or form of words used in praying (the Lord's prayer). **c** the act of praying (be at prayer). **d** a religious service consisting largely of prayers (morning prayers). **2 a** an entreaty to a person. **b** a thing entreated or prayed for. □ **not have a prayer** US colloq. have no chance (of success etc.). **prayer-book** a book containing the forms of prayer in regular use, esp. the Book of Common Prayer. **prayer-mat** a small carpet used by Muslims when praying. **prayer-wheel** a revolving cylindrical box inscribed with or containing prayers, used esp. by Tibetan Buddhists. □ **prayerless** adj. [ME f. OF preiere ult. f. L precarius obtained by entreaty f. prex precis prayer]

prayer[2] /ˈpreɪə(r)/ n. a person who prays.

prayerful /ˈpreəfʊl/ adj. **1** (of a person) given to praying; devout. **2** (of speech, actions, etc.) characterized by or expressive of prayer. □ **prayerfully** adv. **prayerfulness** n.

pre- /priː/ prefix before (in time, place, order, degree, or importance). [from or after L prae- f. prae (adv. & prep.)]

preach v. **1 a** intr. deliver a sermon or religious address. **b** tr. deliver (a sermon); proclaim or expound (the Gospel etc.). **2** intr. give moral advice in an obtrusive way. **3** tr. advocate or inculcate (a quality or practice etc.). □ **preachable** adj. [ME f. OF prechier f. L praedicare proclaim, in eccl.L preach (as PRAE-, dicare declare)]

preacher /ˈpriːtʃə(r)/ n. a person who preaches, esp. a minister of religion. [ME f. AF prech(o)ur, OF prech(e)or f. eccl.L praedicator (as PREACH)]

preachify /ˈpriːtʃɪfaɪ/ v.intr. (-ies, -ied) colloq. preach or moralize tediously.

preachy /ˈpriːtʃɪ/ adj. (**preachier, preachiest**) colloq. inclined to preach or moralize. □ **preachiness** n.

preadolescent /ˌpriːædəˈles(ə)nt/ adj. & n. —adj. **1** (of a child) having nearly reached adolescence. **2** of or relating to the two or three years preceding adolescence. —n. a preadolescent child. □ **preadolescence** n.

preamble /priːˈæmb(ə)l, ˈpriː-/ n. **1** a preliminary statement or introduction. **2** the introductory part of a statute or deed etc. □ **preambular** /-ˈæmbjʊlə(r)/ adj. [ME f. OF preambule f. med.L praeambulum f. LL praeambulus (adj.) going before (as PRE-, AMBLE)]

preamplifier /priːˈæmplɪfaɪə(r)/ n. an electronic device that amplifies a very weak signal (e.g. from a microphone or pickup) and transmits it to a main amplifier. □ **preamplified** adj.

prearrange /ˌpriːəˈreɪndʒ/ v.tr. arrange beforehand. □ **prearrangement** n.

preatomic /ˌpriːəˈtɒmɪk/ adj. existing or occurring before the use of atomic energy.

prebend /ˈprebənd/ n. **1** the stipend of a canon or member of chapter. **2** a portion of land or tithe from which this is drawn. □ **prebendal** adj. [ME f. OF prebende f. LL praebenda pension, neut.pl. gerundive of L praebēre grant f. prae forth + habēre hold]

prebendary /ˈprebəndərɪ/ n. (pl. **-ies**) **1** the holder of a prebend. **2** an honorary canon. □ **prebendaryship** n. [ME f. med.L praebendarius (as PREBEND)]

Precambrian /priːˈkæmbrɪən/ adj. & n. Geol. —adj. of or relating to the earliest era of geological time from the formation of the earth to the first forms of life. —n. this era.

precarious /prɪˈkeərɪəs/ adj. **1** uncertain; dependent on chance (makes a precarious living). **2** insecure, perilous (precarious health). □ **precariously** adv. **precariousness** n. [L precarius: see PRAYER[1]]

precast /priːˈkɑːst/ adj. (of concrete) cast in its final shape before positioning.

precaution /prɪˈkɔːʃ(ə)n/ n. **1** an action taken beforehand to avoid risk or ensure a good result. **2** (in pl.) colloq. the use of contraceptives. □ **precautionary** adj. [F précaution f. LL praecautio -onis f. L praecavēre (as PRAE-, cavēre caut- beware of)]

precede /prɪˈsiːd/ v.tr. **1 a** come or go before in time, order, importance, etc. (preceding generations; the preceding paragraph; sons of barons precede baronets). **b** walk etc. in front of (preceded by our guide). **2** (foll. by by) cause to be preceded (*must precede this measure by milder ones*). [OF *preceder* f. L *praecedere* (as PRAE-, *cedere* cess- go)]

precedence /ˈpresɪd(ə)ns/ n. (also **precedency**) **1** priority in time, order, or importance. **2** the right of preceding others on formal occasions. □ **take precedence** (often foll. by *over, of*) have priority (over).

precedent n. & adj. —n. /ˈpresɪd(ə)nt/ a previous case or legal decision etc. taken as a guide for subsequent cases or as a justification. —adj. /prɪˈsiːd(ə)nt, ˈpresɪ-/ preceding in time, order, importance, etc. □ **precedently** /ˈpriːsɪdəntlɪ, ˈpresɪ-/ adv. [ME f. OF (n. & adj.) (as PRECEDE)]

precedented /ˈpresɪˌdentɪd/ adj. having or supported by a precedent.

precentor /prɪˈsentə(r)/ n. **1** a person who leads the singing or (in a synagogue) the prayers of a congregation. **2** a minor canon who administers the musical life of a cathedral. □ **precentorship** n. [F *précenteur* or L *praecentor* f. *praecinere* (as PRAE-, *canere* sing)]

precept /ˈpriːsept/ n. **1** a command; a rule of conduct. **2** moral instruction (*example is better than precept*). **3** a writ or warrant. □ **preceptive** /prɪˈseptɪv/ adj. [ME f. L *praeceptum* neut. past part. of *praecipere* praecept- warn, instruct (as PRAE-, *capere* take)]

preceptor /prɪˈseptə(r)/ n. a teacher or instructor. □ **preceptorial** /ˌpriːsepˈtɔːrɪəl/ adj. **preceptorship** n. **preceptress** /-trɪs/ n. [L *praeceptor* (as PRECEPT)]

precession /prɪˈseʃ(ə)n/ n. the slow movement of the axis of a spinning body around another axis. □ **precession of the equinoxes 1** slow retrograde motion of equinoctial points along the ecliptic. **2** the resulting earlier occurrence of equinoxes in each successive sidereal year. □ **precessional** adj. [LL *praecessio* (as PRECEDE)]

pre-Christian /priːˈkrɪstɪən/ adj. before Christ or the advent of Christianity.

precinct /ˈpriːsɪŋkt/ n. **1** an enclosed or clearly defined area, e.g. around a cathedral, college, etc. **2** a specially designated area in a town, esp. with the exclusion of traffic (*shopping precinct*). **3** (in *pl.*) **a** the surrounding area or environs. **b** the boundaries. **4** US **a** a subdivision of a county, city, etc., for police or electoral purposes. **b** (in *pl.*) a neighbourhood. [ME f. med.L *praecinctum* neut. past part. of *praecingere* encircle (as PRAE-, *cingere* gird)]

preciosity /ˌpreʃɪˈɒsɪtɪ/ n. overrefinement in art or language, esp. in the choice of words. [OF *préciosité* f. L *pretiositas* f. *pretiosus* (as PRECIOUS)]

precious /ˈpreʃəs/ adj. & adv. —adj. **1** of great value or worth. **2** beloved; much prized (*precious memories*). **3** affectedly refined, esp. in language or manner. **4** colloq. often iron. **a** considerable (*a precious lot you know about it*). **b** expressing contempt or disdain (*you can keep your precious flowers*). —adv. colloq. extremely, very (*tried precious hard; had precious little left*). □ **precious metals** gold, silver, and platinum. **precious stone** a piece of mineral having great value esp. as used in jewellery. □ **preciously** adv. **preciousness** n. [ME f. OF *precios* f. L *pretiosus* f. *pretium* price]

precipice /ˈpresɪpɪs/ n. **1** a vertical or steep face of a rock, cliff, mountain, etc. **2** a dangerous situation. [F *précipice* or L *praecipitium* falling headlong, precipice (as PRECIPITOUS)]

precipitate v., adj., & n. —v.tr. /prɪˈsɪpɪˌteɪt/ **1** hasten the occurrence of; cause to occur prematurely. **2** (foll. by *into*) send rapidly into a certain state or condition (*were precipitated into war*). **3** throw down headlong. **4** Chem. cause (a substance) to be deposited in solid form from a solution. **5** Physics **a** cause (dust etc.) to be deposited from the air on a surface. **b** condense (vapour) into drops and so deposit it. —adj. /prɪˈsɪpɪtət/ **1** headlong; violently hurried (*precipitate departure*). **2** (of a person or act) hasty, rash, inconsiderate. —n. /prɪˈsɪpɪtət/ **1** Chem. a substance precipitated from a solution. **2** Physics moisture condensed from vapour by cooling and depositing, e.g. rain or dew. □ **precipitable** /prɪˈsɪpɪtəb(ə)l/ adj. **precipitability** /prɪˌsɪpɪtəˈbɪlɪtɪ/ n. **precipitately** /prɪˈsɪpɪtətlɪ/ adv. **precipitateness** /prɪˈsɪpɪtətnɪs/ n. **precipitator** /prɪˈsɪpɪˌteɪtə(r)/ n. [L *praecipitare* praecipitat- f. *praeceps* praecipitis headlong (as PRAE-, *caput* head)]

precipitation /prɪˌsɪpɪˈteɪʃ(ə)n/ n. **1** the act of precipitating or the process of being precipitated. **2** rash haste. **3 a** rain or snow etc. falling to the ground. **b** a quantity of this. [F *précipitation* or L *praecipitatio* (as PRECIPITATE)]

precipitous /prɪˈsɪpɪtəs/ adj. **1 a** of or like a precipice. **b** dangerously steep. **2** = PRECIPITATE adj. □ **precipitously** adv. **precipitousness** n. [obs. F *précipiteux* f. L *praeceps* (as PRECIPITATE)]

précis /ˈpreɪsiː/ n. & v. —n. (pl. same /-siːz/) a summary or abstract, esp. of a text or speech. —v.tr. (**précises** /-siːz/; **précised** /-siːd/; **précising** /-siːɪŋ/) make a précis of. [F, = PRECIS (as n.)]

precise /prɪˈsaɪs/ adj. **1 a** accurately expressed. **b** definite, exact. **2** punctilious; scrupulous in being exact, observing rules, etc. **3** identical, exact (*at that precise moment*). □ **preciseness** n. [F *précis* -ise f. L *praecidere* praecis- cut short (as PRAE-, *caedere* cut)]

precisely /prɪˈsaɪslɪ/ adv. **1** in a precise manner; exactly. **2** (as a reply) quite so; as you say.

precisian /prɪˈsɪʒ(ə)n/ n. a person who is rigidly precise or punctilious, esp. in religious observance. □ **precisianism** n.

precision /prɪˈsɪʒ(ə)n/ n. **1** the condition of being precise; accuracy. **2** the degree of refinement in measurement etc. **3** (attrib.) marked by or adapted for precision (*precision instruments; precision timing*). □ **precisionism** n. **precisionist** n. [F *précision* or L *praecisio* (as PRECISE)]

preclude /prɪˈkluːd/ v.tr. **1** (foll. by *from*) prevent, exclude (*precluded from taking part*). **2** make impossible; remove (*so as to preclude all doubt*). □ **preclusion** /-ˈkluːʒ(ə)n/ n. **preclusive** /-ˈkluːsɪv/ adj. [L *praecludere* praeclus- (as PRAE-, *claudere* shut)]

precocious /prɪˈkəʊʃəs/ adj. **1** often derog. (of a person, esp. a child) prematurely developed in some faculty or characteristic. **2** (of an action etc.) indicating such development. □ **precociously** adv. **precociousness** n. **precocity** /-ˈkɒsɪtɪ/ n. [L *praecox* -cocis f. *praecoquere* ripen fully (as PRAE-, *coquere* cook)]

precognition /ˌpriːkɒɡˈnɪʃ(ə)n/ n. (supposed) foreknowledge, esp. of a supernatural kind. □ **precognitive** /-ˈkɒɡnɪtɪv/ adj. [LL *praecognitio* (as PRE-, COGNITION)]

pre-Columbian /ˌpriːkəˈlʌmbɪən/ adj. before the discovery of America by Columbus.

preconceive /ˌpriːkənˈsiːv/ v.tr. form (an idea or opinion etc.) beforehand.

preconception /ˌpriːkənˈsepʃ(ə)n/ n. **1** a preconceived idea. **2** a prejudice.

precondition /ˌpriːkənˈdɪʃ(ə)n/ n. & v. —n. a prior condition, that must be fulfilled before other things can be done. —v.tr. bring into a required condition beforehand.

precook /priːˈkʊk/ v.tr. cook in advance.

precool /priːˈkuːl/ v.tr. cool in advance.

precursor /priːˈkɜːsə(r)/ n. **1 a** a forerunner. **b** a person who precedes in office etc. **2** a harbinger. [L *praecursor* f. *praecurrere praecurs-* (as PRAE-, *currere* run)]

precursory /priːˈkɜːsərɪ/ adj. (also **precursive** /-sɪv/) **1** preliminary, introductory. **2** (foll. by *of*) serving as a harbinger of. [L *praecursorius* (as PRECURSOR)]

precut /priːˈkʌt/ v.tr. (*past* and *past part.* **-cut**) cut in advance.

predacious /prɪˈdeɪʃəs/ adj. (also **predaceous**) **1** (of an animal) predatory. **2** relating to such animals (*predacious instincts*). □ **predaciousness** n. **predacity** /-ˈdæsɪtɪ/ n. [L *praeda* booty: cf. *audacious*]

predate /priːˈdeɪt/ v.tr. exist or occur at a date earlier than.

predation /prɪˈdeɪʃ(ə)n/ n. **1** (usu. in *pl.*) = DEPREDATION. **2** *Zool.* the natural preying of one animal on others. [L *praedatio -onis* taking of booty f. L *praeda* booty]

predator /ˈpredətə(r)/ n. **1** an animal naturally preying on others. **2** a person, State, etc., compared to this. [L *praedator* plunderer f. *praedari* seize as plunder f. *praeda* booty (as PREDACIOUS)]

predatory /ˈpredətərɪ/ adj. **1** (of an animal) preying naturally upon others. **2** (of a nation, State, or individual) plundering or exploiting others. □ **predatorily** adv. **predatoriness** n. [L *praedatorius* (as PREDATOR)]

predecease /ˌpriːdɪˈsiːs/ v. & n. —v.tr. die earlier than (another person). —n. a death preceding that of another.

predecessor /ˈpriːdɪˌsesə(r)/ n. **1** a former holder of an office or position with respect to a later holder (*my immediate predecessor*). **2** an ancestor. **3** a thing to which another has succeeded (*the new plan will share the fate of its predecessor*). [ME f. OF *predecesseur* f. LL *praedecessor* (as PRAE-, *decessor* retiring officer, as DECEASE)]

pre-decimal /ˌpriːˈdesɪm(ə)l/ adj. of or relating to a time before the introduction of a decimal system, esp. of coinage.

predestination /priːˌdestɪˈneɪʃ(ə)n/ n. *Theol.* (as a belief or doctrine) the divine foreordaining of all that will happen, esp. with regard to the salvation of some and not others. [ME f. eccl.L *praedestinatio* (as PREDESTINE)]

predestine /priːˈdestɪn/ v.tr. **1** determine beforehand. **2** ordain in advance by divine will or as if by fate. [ME f. OF *predestiner* or eccl.L *praedestinare praedestinat-* (as PRAE-, *destinare* establish)]

predetermine /ˌpriːdɪˈtɜːmɪn/ v.tr. **1** determine or decree beforehand. **2** predestine. □ **predeterminable** adj. **predeterminate** /-nət/ adj. **predetermination** /-ˈneɪʃ(ə)n/ n. [LL *praedeterminare* (as PRAE-, DETERMINE)]

predicable /ˈpredɪkəb(ə)l/ adj. that may be predicated or affirmed. □ **predicability** /-ˈbɪlɪtɪ/ n.

[med.L *praedicabilis* that may be affirmed (as PREDICATE)]

predicament /prɪˈdɪkəmənt/ n. **1** a difficult, unpleasant, or embarrassing situation. **2** *Philos.* a category in (esp. Aristotelian) logic. [ME (in sense 2) f. LL *praedicamentum* thing predicated: see PREDICATE]

predicate v. & n. —v.tr. /ˈpredɪˌkeɪt/ **1** assert or affirm as true or existent. **2** (foll. by *on*) found or base (a statement etc.) on. —n. /ˈpredɪkət/ **1** *Gram.* what is said about the subject of a sentence etc. (e.g. *went home* in *John went home*). **2** *Logic* **a** what is predicated. **b** what is affirmed or denied of the subject by means of the copula (e.g. *mortal* in *all men are mortal*). □ **predication** /-ˈkeɪʃ(ə)n/ n. [L *praedicare praedicat-* proclaim (as PRAE-, *dicare* declare)]

predicative /prɪˈdɪkətɪv/ adj. **1** *Gram.* (of an adjective or noun) forming or contained in the predicate, as *old* in *the dog is old* (but not in *the old dog*) and *house* in *there is a large house*. **2** that predicates. □ **predicatively** adv. [L *praedicativus* (as PREDICATE)]

predict /prɪˈdɪkt/ v.tr. (often foll. by *that* + clause) make a statement about the future; foretell, prophesy. □ **predictive** adj. **predictively** adv. **predictor** n. [L *praedicere praedict-* (as PRAE-, *dicere* say)]

predictable /prɪˈdɪktəb(ə)l/ adj. that can be predicted or is to be expected. □ **predictability** /-ˈbɪlɪtɪ/ n. **predictably** adv.

prediction /prɪˈdɪkʃ(ə)n/ n. **1** the art of predicting or the process of being predicted. **2** a thing predicted; a forecast. [L *praedictio -onis* (as PREDICT)]

predigest /ˌpriːdaɪˈdʒest/ v.tr. **1** render (food) easily digestible before being eaten. **2** make (reading matter) easier to read or understand. □ **predigestion** /-ˈdʒestʃ(ə)n/ n.

predilection /ˌpriːdɪˈlekʃ(ə)n/ n. (often foll. by *for*) a preference or special liking. [F *prédilection* ult. f. L *praediligere praedilect-* prefer (as PRAE-, *diligere* select): see DILIGENT]

predispose /ˌpriːdɪˈspəʊz/ v.tr. **1** influence favourably in advance. **2** (foll. by *to*, or *to* + infin.) render liable or inclined beforehand. □ **predisposition** /-pəˈzɪʃ(ə)n/ n.

predominant /prɪˈdɒmɪnənt/ adj. **1** predominating. **2** being the strongest or main element. □ **predominance** n. **predominantly** adv.

predominate /prɪˈdɒmɪˌneɪt/ v.intr. **1** (foll. by *over*) have or exert control. **2** be superior. **3** be the strongest or main element; preponderate (*a garden in which dahlias predominate*). [med.L *praedominari* (as PRAE-, DOMINATE)]

predominately /prɪˈdɒmɪnətlɪ/ adv. = PREDOMINANTLY (see PREDOMINANT). [rare *predominate* (adj.) = PREDOMINANT]

pre-echo /priːˈekəʊ/ n. (pl. **-oes**) **1** a faint copy heard just before an actual sound in a recording, caused by the accidental transfer of signals. **2** a foreshadowing.

pre-eclampsia /ˌpriːɪˈklæmpsɪə/ n. a condition of pregnancy characterized by high blood pressure and other symptoms associated with eclampsia. □ **pre-eclamptic** adj. & n.

pre-election /ˌpriːɪˈlekʃ(ə)n/ n. **1** an election held beforehand. **2** (*attrib.*) (esp. of an act or undertaking) done or given before an election.

pre-embryo /priːˈembrɪəʊ/ n. Med. a human embryo in the first fourteen days after fertilization. □ **pre-embryonic** /-ˈɒnɪk/ adj.

pre-eminent /priːˈemɪnənt/ adj. **1** excelling others. **2** outstanding; distinguished in some quality. □ **pre-eminence** n. **pre-eminently** adv. [ME f. L praeeminens (as PRAE-, EMINENT)]

pre-empt /priːˈempt/ v. **1** tr. **a** forestall. **b** acquire or appropriate in advance. **2** tr. prevent (an attack) by disabling the enemy. **3** tr. obtain by pre-emption. □ **preemptor** n. **preemptory** adj. [back-form. f. PRE-EMPTION]

■ **Usage** This word does not mean 'prevent'.

pre-emption /priːˈempʃ(ə)n/ n. **1 a** the purchase or appropriation by one person or party before the opportunity is offered to others. **b** the right to purchase (esp. public land) in this way. **2** prior appropriation or acquisition. [med.L praeemptio (as PRAE-, emere empt- buy)]

pre-emptive /priːˈemptɪv/ adj. **1** pre-empting; serving to pre-empt. **2** (of military action) intended to prevent attack by disabling the enemy (a pre-emptive strike).

preen v.tr. & refl. **1** (of a bird) tidy (the feathers or itself) with its beak. **2** (of a person) smarten or admire (oneself, one's hair, clothes, etc.). **3** (often foll. by on) congratulate or pride (oneself). □ **preener** n. [ME, app. var. of earlier prune (perh. rel. to PRUNE²): assoc. with Sc. & dial. preen pierce, pin]

pre-establish /ˌpriːɪˈstæblɪʃ/ v.tr. establish beforehand.

pre-exist /ˌpriːɪgˈzɪst/ v.intr. exist at an earlier time. □ **pre-existence** n. **pre-existent** adj.

prefab /ˈpriːfæb/ n. Brit. colloq. a prefabricated building, esp. a small house. [abbr.]

prefabricate /priːˈfæbrɪˌkeɪt/ v.tr. **1** manufacture sections of (a building etc.) prior to their assembly on a site. **2** produce in an artificially standardized way. □ **prefabrication** /-ˈkeɪʃ(ə)n/ n.

preface /ˈprefəs/ n. & v. —n. **1** an introduction to a book stating its subject, scope, etc. **2** the preliminary part of a speech. —v.tr. **1** (foll. by with) introduce or begin (a speech or event) (prefaced my remarks with a warning). **2** provide (a book etc.) with a preface. **3** (of an event etc.) lead up to (another). □ **prefatorial** /-ˈtɔːrɪəl/ adj. **prefatory** /-tərɪ/ adj. [ME f. OF f. med.L praefatia for L praefatio f. praefari (as PRAE-, fari speak)]

prefect /ˈpriːfekt/ n. **1** the chief administrative officer of certain departments, esp. in France. **2** esp. Brit. a senior pupil in a school etc. authorized to enforce discipline. □ **prefectoral** /-ˈfektər(ə)l/ adj. **prefectorial** /-ˈtɔːrɪəl/ adj. [ME f. OF f. L praefectus past part. of praeficere set in authority over (as PRAE-, facere make)]

prefecture /ˈpriːfektjʊə(r)/ n. **1** a district under the government of a prefect. **2 a** a prefect's office or tenure. **b** his official residence. □ **prefectural** /prɪˈfektʃər(ə)l/ adj. [F préfecture or L praefectura (as PREFECT)]

prefer /prɪˈfɜː(r)/ v.tr. (**preferred**, **preferring**) **1** (often foll. by to, or to + infin.) choose rather; like better (would prefer to stay; prefers coffee to tea). **2** submit (information, an accusation, etc.) for consideration. **3** promote or advance (a person). [ME f. OF preferer f. L praeferre (as PRAE-, ferre lat- bear)]

preferable /ˈprefərəb(ə)l/ adj. **1** to be preferred. **2** more desirable. □ **preferably** adv.

preference /ˈprefərəns/ n. **1** the act or an instance of preferring or being preferred. **2** a thing preferred. **3** the favouring of one person etc. before others. □ **in preference to** as a thing preferred over (another). **preference shares** (or **stock**) Brit. shares or stock whose entitlement to dividend takes priority over that of ordinary shares. [F préférence f. med.L praeferentia (as PREFER)]

preferential /ˌprefəˈrenʃ(ə)l/ adj. **1** of or involving preference (preferential treatment). **2** giving or receiving a favour. **3** Commerce (of a tariff etc.) favouring particular countries. **4** (of voting) in which the voter puts candidates in order of preference. □ **preferentially** adv. [as PREFERENCE, after differential]

preferment /prɪˈfɜːmənt/ n. promotion to office.

prefigure /priːˈfɪgə(r)/ v.tr. **1** represent beforehand by a figure or type. **2** imagine beforehand. □ **prefiguration** /-ˈreɪʃ(ə)n/ n. **prefigurative** /-rətɪv/ adj. **prefigurement** n. [ME f. eccl.L praefigurare (as PRAE-, FIGURE)]

prefix /ˈpriːfɪks/ n. & v. —n. **1** a verbal element placed at the beginning of a word to adjust or qualify its meaning (e.g. ex-, non-, re-) or (in some languages) as an inflectional formative. **2** a title placed before a name (e.g. Mr). —v.tr. (often foll. by to) **1** add as an introduction. **2** join (a word or element) as a prefix. □ **prefixation** /-ˈseɪʃ(ə)n/ n. **prefixion** /-ˈfɪkʃ(ə)n/ n. [earlier as verb: ME f. OF prefixer (as PRE-, FIX): (n.) f. L praefixum]

preform /priːˈfɔːm/ v.tr. form beforehand. □ **preformation** /-ˈmeɪʃ(ə)n/ n.

pregnable /ˈpregnəb(ə)l/ adj. able to be captured etc.; not impregnable. [ME f. OF prenable takable: see IMPREGNABLE]

pregnancy /ˈpregnənsɪ/ n. (pl. -ies) the condition or an instance of being pregnant.

pregnant /ˈpregnənt/ adj. **1** (of a woman or female animal) having a child or young developing in the uterus. **2** full of meaning; significant or suggestive (a pregnant pause). **3** (esp. of a person's mind) imaginative, inventive. **4** (foll. by with) plentifully provided (pregnant with danger). □ **pregnantly** adv. (in sense 2). [ME f. F prégnant or L praegnans -antis, earlier praegnas (prob. as PRAE-, (g)nasci be born)]

preheat /priːˈhiːt/ v.tr. heat beforehand.

prehensile /priːˈhensaɪl/ adj. Zool. (of a tail or limb) capable of grasping. □ **prehensility** /-ˈsɪlɪtɪ/ n. [F préhensile f. L prehendere prehens- (as PRE-, hendere grasp)]

prehistoric /ˌpriːhɪˈstɒrɪk/ adj. **1** of or relating to the period before written records. **2** colloq. utterly out of date. □ **prehistorian** /-ˈstɔːrɪən/ n. **prehistorically** adv. **prehistory** /-ˈhɪstərɪ/ n. [F préhistorique (as PRE-, HISTORIC)]

prehuman /priːˈhjuːmən/ adj. existing before the time of man.

pre-ignition /ˌpriːɪgˈnɪʃ(ə)n/ n. the premature firing of the explosive mixture in an internal-combustion engine.

prejudge /priːˈdʒʌdʒ/ v.tr. **1** form a premature judgement on (a person, issue, etc.). **2** pass judgement on (a person) before a trial or proper enquiry. □ **prejudgement** n. **prejudication** /-ˌdʒuːdɪˈkeɪʃ(ə)n/ n.

prejudice /ˈpredʒʊdɪs/ n. & v. —n. **1 a** a preconceived opinion. **b** (foll. by against, in favour *of*) bias or partiality. **2** harm or injury that results or may result from some action or judgement (*to the prejudice of*). —*v.tr.* **1** impair the validity or force of (a right, claim, statement, etc.). **2** (esp. as **prejudiced** *adj.*) cause (a person) to have a prejudice. □ **without prejudice** (often foll. by *to*) without detriment (to any existing right or claim). [ME f. OF *prejudice* f. L *praejudicium* (as PRAE-, *judicium* judgement)]

prejudicial /ˌpredʒʊˈdɪʃ(ə)l/ *adj.* causing prejudice; detrimental. □ **prejudicially** *adv.* [ME f. OF *prejudiciel* (as PREJUDICE)]

prelacy /ˈpreləsɪ/ *n.* (*pl.* **-ies**) **1** church government by prelates. **2** (prec. by *the*) prelates collectively. **3** the office or rank of prelate. [ME f. AF *prelacie* f. med.L *prelatia* (as PRELATE)]

prelate /ˈprelət/ *n.* a high ecclesiastical dignitary, e.g. a bishop. □ **prelatic** /prɪˈlætɪk/ *adj.* **prelatical** /prɪˈlætɪk(ə)l/ *adj.* [ME f. OF *prelat* f. med.L *praelatus* past part.: see PREFER]

prelim /ˈpriːlɪm, prɪˈlɪm/ *n. colloq.* **1** a preliminary examination, esp. at a university. **2** (in *pl.*) the pages preceding the text of a book. [abbr.]

preliminary /prɪˈlɪmɪnərɪ/ *adj., n.,* & *adv.* —*adj.* introductory, preparatory. —*n.* (*pl.* **-ies**) (usu. in *pl.*) **1** a preliminary action or arrangement (*dispense with the preliminaries*). **2** a preliminary trial or contest. —*adv.* (foll. by *to*) preparatory to; in advance of (*was completed preliminary to the main event*). □ **preliminarily** *adv.* [mod.L *praeliminaris* or F *préliminaire* (as PRE-, L *limen liminis* threshold)]

prelude /ˈpreljuːd/ *n.* & *v.* —*n.* (often foll. by *to*) **1** an action, event, or situation serving as an introduction. **2** the introductory part of a poem etc. **3 a** an introductory piece of music, often preceding a fugue or forming the first piece of a suite or beginning an act of an opera. **b** a short piece of music of a similar type, esp. for the piano. —*v.tr.* **1** serve as a prelude to. **2** introduce with a prelude. □ **preludial** /prɪˈljuːdɪəl/ *adj.* [F *prélude* or med.L *praeludium* f. L *praeludere praelus-* (as PRAE-, *ludere* play)]

premarital /priːˈmærɪt(ə)l/ *adj.* existing or (esp. of sexual relations) occurring before marriage. □ **premaritally** *adv.*

premature /ˈpreməˌtjʊə(r), -ˈtjʊə(r)/ *adj.* **1 a** occurring or done before the usual or proper time; too early (*a premature decision*). **b** too hasty (*must not be premature*). **2** (of a baby, esp. a viable one) born (esp. three or more weeks) before the end of the full term of gestation. □ **prematurely** *adv.* **prematureness** *n.* **prematurity** /-ˈtjʊərɪtɪ/ *n.* [L *praematurus* very early (as PRAE-, MATURE)]

premedication /ˌpriːmedɪˈkeɪʃ(ə)n/ *n.* medication to prepare for an operation or other treatment.

premeditate /priːˈmedɪˌteɪt/ *v.tr.* think out or plan (an action) beforehand (*premeditated murder*). □ **premeditation** /-ˈteɪʃ(ə)n/ *n.* [L *praemeditari* (as PRAE-, MEDITATE)]

premenstrual /priːˈmenstrʊəl/ *adj.* of, occurring, or experienced before menstruation (*premenstrual tension*). □ **premenstrual syndrome** any of a complex of symptoms (including tension, fluid retention, etc.) experienced by some women in the days immediately preceding menstruation. □ **premenstrually** *adv.*

premier /ˈpremɪə(r)/ *n.* & *adj.* —*n.* a prime minister or other head of government.

—*adj.* first in importance, order, or time. □ **premiership** *n.* [ME f. OF = first, f. L (as PRIMARY)]

première /ˈpremɪˌeə(r)/ *n.* & *v.* —*n.* the first performance or showing of a play or film. —*v.tr.* give a première of. [F, fem. of *premier* (adj.) (as PREMIER)]

premise *n.* & *v.* —*n.* /ˈpremɪs/ **1** *Logic* = PREMISS. **2** (in *pl.*) a house or building with its grounds and appurtenances. —*v.tr.* /prɪˈmaɪz/ say or write by way of introduction. □ **on the premises** in the building etc. concerned. [ME f. OF *premisse* f. med.L *praemissa* (*propositio*) (proposition) set in front f. L *praemittere praemiss-* (as PRAE-, *mittere* send)]

premiss /ˈpremɪs/ *n. Logic* a previous statement from which another is inferred. [var. of PREMISE]

premium /ˈpriːmɪəm/ *n.* **1** an amount to be paid for a contract of insurance. **2 a** a sum added to interest, wages, etc.; a bonus. **b** a sum added to ordinary charges. **3** a reward or prize. **4** (*attrib.*) (of a commodity) of best quality and therefore more expensive. □ **at a premium 1** highly valued; above the usual or nominal price. **2** scarce and in demand. **Premium Bond** (or **Savings Bond**) *Brit.* a government security without interest but with a draw for cash prizes. **put a premium on 1** provide or act as an incentive to. **2** attach special value to. [L *praemium* booty, reward (as PRAE-, *emere* buy, take)]

premolar /priːˈməʊlə(r)/ *adj.* & *n.* —*adj.* in front of a molar tooth. —*n.* (in an adult human) each of eight teeth situated in pairs between each of the four canine teeth and each first molar.

premonition /ˌpreməˈnɪʃ(ə)n, ˌpriː-/ *n.* a forewarning; a presentiment. □ **premonitor** /prɪˈmɒnɪtə(r)/ *n.* **premonitory** /prɪˈmɒnɪtərɪ/ *adj.* [F *prémonition* or LL *praemonitio* f. L *praemonēre praemonit-* (as PRAE-, *monēre* warn)]

prenatal /priːˈneɪt(ə)l/ *adj.* of or concerning the period before childbirth. □ **prenatally** *adv.*

preoccupation /priːˌɒkjʊˈpeɪʃ(ə)n/ *n.* **1** the state of being preoccupied. **2** a thing that engrosses the mind. [F *préoccupation* or L *praeoccupatio* (as PREOCCUPY)]

preoccupy /priːˈɒkjʊˌpaɪ/ *v.tr.* (**-ies**, **-ied**) **1** (of a thought etc.) dominate or engross the mind of (a person) to the exclusion of other thoughts. **2** (as **preoccupied** *adj.*) otherwise engrossed; mentally distracted. **3** occupy beforehand. [PRE- + OCCUPY, after L *praeoccupare* seize beforehand]

preordain /ˌpriːɔːˈdeɪn/ *v.tr.* ordain or determine beforehand.

prep *n. colloq.* **1** *Brit.* **a** the preparation of school work by a pupil. **b** the period when this is done. **2** *US* a student in a preparatory school. [abbr. of PREPARATION]

prep. *abbr.* preposition.

prepack /priːˈpæk/ *v.tr.* (also **pre-package** /-ˈpækɪdʒ/) pack (goods) on the site of production or before retail.

prepaid *past* and *past part.* of PREPAY.

preparation /ˌprepəˈreɪʃ(ə)n/ *n.* **1** the act or an instance of preparing; the process of being prepared. **2** (often in *pl.*) something done to make ready. **3** a specially prepared substance, esp. a food or medicine. **4** work done by school pupils to prepare for a lesson. [ME f. OF f. L *praeparatio -onis* (as PREPARE)]

preparatory /prɪˈpærətərɪ/ *adj. & adv.* —*adj.* (often foll. by *to*) serving to prepare; introductory. —*adv.* (often foll. by *to*) in a preparatory manner (*was packing preparatory to departure*). □ **preparatory school** a usu. private school preparing pupils for a higher school or *US* for college or university. □ **preparatorily** *adv.* [ME f. LL *praeparatorius* (as PREPARE)]

prepare /prɪˈpeə(r)/ *v.* **1** *tr.* make or get ready for use, consideration, etc. **2** *tr.* make ready or assemble (food, a meal, etc.) for eating. **3** *a tr.* make (a person or oneself) ready or disposed in some way (*prepares students for university*; *prepared them for a shock*). **b** *intr.* put oneself or things in readiness, get ready (*prepare to jump*). □ **be prepared** (often foll. by *for*, or *to* + infin.) be disposed or willing to. □ **preparer** *n.* [ME f. F *préparer* or L *praeparare* (as PRAE-, *parare* make ready)]

preparedness /prɪˈpeərɪdnɪs/ *n.* a state of readiness, esp. for war.

prepay /priːˈpeɪ/ *v.tr.* (*past* and *past part.* **prepaid**) **1** pay (a charge) in advance. **2** pay postage on (a letter or parcel etc.) before posting. □ **prepayable** *adj.* **prepayment** *n.*

prepense /prɪˈpens/ *adj.* (usu. placed after noun) esp. *Law* deliberate, intentional (*malice prepense*). □ **prepensely** *adv.* [earlier *prepensed* past part. of obs. *prepense* (v.) alt. f. earlier *purpense* f. AF & OF *purpenser* (as PUR-, *penser*): see PENSIVE]

preplan /priːˈplæn/ *v.tr.* (**preplanned, preplanning**) plan in advance.

preponderant /prɪˈpɒndərənt/ *adj.* surpassing in influence, power, number, or importance; predominant, preponderating. □ **preponderance** *n.* **preponderantly** *adv.*

preponderate /prɪˈpɒndəˌreɪt/ *v.intr.* (often foll. by *over*) **1 a** be greater in influence, quantity, or number. **b** predominate. **2 a** be of greater importance. **b** weigh more. [L *praeponderare* (as PRAE-, PONDER)]

preposition /ˌprepəˈzɪʃ(ə)n/ *n.* *Gram.* a word governing (and usu. preceding) a noun or pronoun and expressing a relation to another word or element, as in: 'the man *on* the platform', 'came *after* dinner', 'what did you do it *for*?' □ **prepositional** *adj.* **prepositionally** *adv.* [ME f. L *praepositio* f. *praeponere praeposit-* (as PRAE-, *ponere* place)]

prepossess /ˌpriːpəˈzes/ *v.tr.* **1** (usu. in *passive*) (of an idea, feeling, etc.) take possession of (a person); imbue. **2 a** prejudice (usu. favourably and spontaneously). **b** (as **prepossessing** *adj.*) attractive, appealing. □ **prepossession** /-ˈzeʃ(ə)n/ *n.*

preposterous /prɪˈpɒstərəs/ *adj.* **1** utterly absurd; outrageous. **2** contrary to nature, reason, or common sense. □ **preposterously** *adv.* **preposterousness** *n.* [L *praeposterus* reversed, absurd (as PRAE-, *posterus* coming after)]

preppy /ˈprepɪ/ *n. & adj. US colloq.* —*n.* (pl. **-ies**) a person attending an expensive private school or who looks like such a person (with short hair, blazer, etc.). —*adj.* (**preppier, preppiest**) **1** like a preppy. **2** neat and fashionable. [PREP (SCHOOL) + -Y²]

preprandial /priːˈprændɪəl/ *adj. formal or joc.* before dinner or lunch. [PRE- + L *prandium* a meal]

preprocessor /priːˈprəʊsesə(r)/ *n.* a computer program that modifies data to conform with the input requirements of another program.

prep school /prep/ *n.* = PREPARATORY SCHOOL. [abbr. of PREPARATORY]

prepublication /ˌpriːpʌblɪˈkeɪʃ(ə)n/ *adj. & n.* —*attrib.adj.* produced or occurring before publication. —*n.* publication in advance or beforehand.

prepuce /ˈpriːpjuːs/ *n.* **1** = FORESKIN. **2** the fold of skin surrounding the clitoris. □ **preputial** /priːˈpjuːʃ(ə)l/ *adj.* [ME f. L *praeputium*]

prequel /ˈpriːkw(ə)l/ *n.* a story, film, etc., whose events or concerns precede those of an existing work. [PRE- + SEQUEL]

Pre-Raphaelite /priːˈræfəˌlaɪt/ *n. & adj.* —*n.* a member of a group of English 19th-c. artists emulating the work of Italian artists before the time of Raphael. —*adj.* **1** of or relating to the Pre-Raphaelites. **2** (**pre-Raphaelite**) (esp. of a woman) like a type painted by a Pre-Raphaelite (e.g. with long thick curly auburn hair). □ **pre-Raphaelitism** *n.*

pre-record /ˌpriːrɪˈkɔːd/ *v.tr.* record (esp. material for broadcasting) in advance.

prerequisite /priːˈrekwɪzɪt/ *adj. & n.* —*adj.* required as a precondition. —*n.* a prerequisite thing.

■ **Usage** This word is sometimes confused with *perquisite*, which means 'an extra profit, allowance, or right'.

prerogative /prɪˈrɒgətɪv/ *n.* **1** a right or privilege exclusive to an individual or class. **2** (in full **royal prerogative**) *Brit.* the right of the sovereign, theoretically subject to no restriction. [ME f. OF *prerogative* or L *praerogativa* privilege (orig. to vote first) f. *praerogativus* asked first (as PRAE-, *rogare* ask)]

Pres. *abbr.* President.

presage *n. & v.* —*n.* /ˈpresɪdʒ/ **1** an omen or portent. **2** a presentiment or foreboding. —*v.tr.* /ˈpresɪdʒ, prɪˈseɪdʒ/ **1** portend, foreshadow. **2** give warning of (an event etc.) by natural means. **3** (of a person) predict or have a presentiment of. □ **presageful** /prɪˈseɪdʒfʊl/ *adj.* **presager** *n.* [ME f. F *présage*, *présager* f. L *praesagium* f. *praesagire* forebode (as PRAE-, *sagire* perceive keenly)]

presbyter /ˈprezbɪtə(r)/ *n.* **1** (in the Episcopal Church) a minister of the second order; a priest. **2** (in the Presbyterian Church) an elder. □ **presbyteral** /-ˈbɪtər(ə)l/ *adj.* **presbyterate** /-ˈbɪtərət/ *n.* **presbyterial** /-ˈtɪərɪəl/ *adj.* **presbytership** *n.* [eccl.L f. Gk *presbuteros* elder, compar. of *presbus* old]

Presbyterian /ˌprezbɪˈtɪərɪən/ *adj. & n.* —*adj.* (of a church) governed by elders all of equal rank, esp. with reference to the national Church of Scotland. —*n.* **1** a member of a Presbyterian Church. **2** an adherent of the Presbyterian system. □ **Presbyterianism** *n.* [eccl.L *presbyterium* (as PRESBYTERY)]

presbytery /ˈprezbɪtərɪ/ *n.* (pl. **-ies**) **1** the eastern part of a chancel beyond the choir; the sanctuary. **2 a** a body of presbyters, esp. a court next above a Kirk-session. **b** a district represented by this. **3** the house of a Roman Catholic priest. [ME f. OF *presbiterie* f. eccl.L f. Gk *presbuterion* (as PRESBYTER)]

preschool /ˈpriːskuːl, priːˈskuːl/ *adj.* of or relating to the time before a child is old enough to go to school. □ **preschooler** /-ˈskuːlə(r)/ *n.*

prescient /ˈpresɪənt/ *adj.* having foreknowledge or foresight. □ **prescience** *n.* **presciently** *adv.* [L *praescire praescient*- know beforehand (as PRAE-, *scire* know)]

prescribe /prɪˈskraɪb/ *v.* **1** *tr.* **a** advise the use of (a medicine etc.), esp. by an authorized prescription. **b** recommend, esp. as a benefit (*prescribed a change of scenery*). **2** *tr.* lay down or impose authoritatively. **3** *intr.* (foll. by *to, for*) assert a prescriptive right or claim. □ **prescriber** *n.* [L *praescribere praescript*- direct in writing (as PRAE-, *scribere* write)]

■ **Usage** This word is sometimes confused with *proscribe.*

prescript /ˈpriːskrɪpt/ *n.* an ordinance, law, or command. [L *praescriptum* neut. past part.: see PRESCRIBE]

prescription /prɪˈskrɪpʃ(ə)n/ *n.* **1** the act or instance of prescribing. **2 a** a doctor's (usu. written) instruction for the composition and use of a medicine. **b** a medicine prescribed. [ME f. OF f. L *praescriptio -onis* (as PRESCRIBE)]

prescriptive /prɪˈskrɪptɪv/ *adj.* **1** prescribing. **2** *Linguistics* concerned with or laying down rules of usage. □ **prescriptively** *adv.* **prescriptiveness** *n.* **prescriptivism** *n.* **prescriptivist** *n.* & *adj.* [LL *praescriptivus* (as PRESCRIBE)]

preselect /ˌpriːsɪˈlekt/ *v.tr.* select in advance. □ **preselection** *n.*

preselective /ˌpriːsɪˈlektɪv/ *adj.* that can be selected or set in advance.

preselector /ˌpriːsɪˈlektə(r)/ *n.* any of various devices for selecting a mechanical or electrical operation in advance of its execution, e.g. of a gear-change in a motor vehicle.

presence /ˈprez(ə)ns/ *n.* **1** the state or condition of being present (*your presence is requested*). **2** a place where a person is (*was admitted to their presence*). **3 a** a person's appearance or bearing, esp. when imposing (*an august presence*). **b** a person's force of personality (esp. *have presence*). **4** a person or thing that is present (*the royal presence; there was a presence in the room*). **5** representation for reasons of political influence (*maintained a presence*). □ **in the presence of** in front of; observed by. **presence of mind** calmness and self-command in sudden difficulty etc. [ME f. OF f. L *praesentia* (as PRESENT[1])]

present[1] /ˈprez(ə)nt/ *adj.* & *n.* —*adj.* **1** (usu. *predic.*) being in the place in question (*was present at the trial*). **2 a** now existing, occurring, or being such (*the present Duke; during the present season*). **b** now being considered or discussed etc. (*in the present case*). **3** *Gram.* expressing an action etc. now going on or habitually performed (*present participle; present tense*). —*n.* (prec. by *the*) **1** the time now passing (*no time like the present*). **2** *Gram.* the present tense. □ **at present** now. **for the present 1** just now. **2** as far as the present is concerned. **present-day** of this time; modern. [ME f. OF f. L *praesens -entis* part. of *praeesse* be at hand (as PRAE-, *esse* be)]

present[2] /prɪˈzent/ *v.tr.* **1** introduce, offer, or exhibit, esp. for public attention or consideration. **2 a** (with a thing as object, foll. by *to*) offer or give as a gift (to a person), esp. formally or ceremonially. **b** (with a person as object, foll. by *with*) make available to; cause to have (*presented them with a new car; that presents us with a problem*). **3 a** (of a company, producer, etc.) put (a form of entertainment) before the public. **b** (of a performer, compère, etc.) introduce or put before an audience. **4** introduce (a person) formally (*may I present my fiancé?*). **5** offer, give (compliments etc.) (*present my regards to your family*). **6 a** (of a circumstance) reveal (some quality etc.) (*this presents some difficulty*). **b** exhibit (an appearance etc.) (*presented a rough exterior*). **7** (of an idea etc.) offer or suggest itself. **8** deliver (a cheque, bill, etc.) for acceptance or payment. **9 a** (usu. foll. by *at*) aim (a weapon). **b** hold out (a weapon) in a position for aiming. □ **present arms** hold a rifle etc. vertically in front of the body as a salute. **present oneself 1** appear. **2** come forward for examination etc. □ **presenter** *n.* (in sense 3 of *v.*). [ME f. OF *presenter* f. L *praesentare* (as PRESENT[1])]

present[3] /ˈprez(ə)nt/ *n.* a gift; a thing given or presented. □ **make a present of** give as a gift. [ME f. OF (as PRESENT[1]), orig. in phr. *mettre une chose en present à quelqu'un* put a thing into the presence of a person]

presentable /prɪˈzentəb(ə)l/ *adj.* **1** of good appearance; fit to be presented to other people. **2** fit for presentation. □ **presentability** /-ˈbɪlɪtɪ/ *n.* **presentableness** *n.* **presentably** *adv.*

presentation /ˌprezənˈteɪʃ(ə)n/ *n.* **1 a** the act or an instance of presenting; the process of being presented. **b** a thing presented. **2** the manner or quality of presenting. **3** a demonstration or display of materials, information, etc.; a lecture. **4** an exhibition or theatrical performance. **5** a formal introduction. □ **presentational** *adj.* **presentationally** *adv.* [ME f. OF f. LL *praesentatio -onis* (as PRESENT[2])]

presentiment /prɪˈzentɪmənt, -ˈsentɪmənt/ *n.* a vague expectation; a foreboding (esp. of misfortune). [obs. F *présentiment* (as PRE-, SENTIMENT)]

presently /ˈprezəntlɪ/ *adv.* **1** soon; after a short time. **2** esp. *US* & *Sc.* at the present time; now.

preservation /ˌprezəˈveɪʃ(ə)n/ *n.* **1** the act of preserving or process of being preserved. **2** a state of being well or badly preserved (*in an excellent state of preservation*). [ME f. OF f. med.L *praeservatio -onis* (as PRESERVE)]

preservationist /ˌprezəˈveɪʃənɪst/ *n.* a supporter or advocate of preservation, esp. of antiquities and historic buildings.

preservative /prɪˈzɜːvətɪv/ *n.* & *adj.* —*n.* a substance for preserving perishable foodstuffs, wood, etc. —*adj.* tending to preserve. [ME f. OF *preservatifive* f. med.L *praeservativus -um* (as PRESERVE)]

preserve /prɪˈzɜːv/ *v.* & *n.* —*v.tr.* **1 a** keep safe or free from harm, decay, etc. **b** keep alive (a name, memory, etc.). **2** maintain (a thing) in its existing state. **3** retain (a quality or condition). **4 a** treat or refrigerate (food) to prevent decomposition or fermentation. **b** prepare (fruit) by boiling it with sugar, for long-term storage. **5** keep (game, a river, etc.) undisturbed for private use. —*n.* (in *sing.* or *pl.*) **1** preserved fruit; jam. **2** a place where game or fish etc. is preserved. **3** a sphere or area of activity regarded as a person's own. □ **well-preserved** (of an elderly person) showing little sign of ageing. □ **preservable**

adj. **preserver** *n.* [ME f. OF *preserver* f. LL *praeservare* (as PRAE-, *servare* keep)]

pre-set /priːˈset/ *v.tr.* (**-setting**; *past* and *past part.* **-set**) 1 set or fix (a device) in advance of its operation. 2 settle or decide beforehand.

preshrunk /priːˈʃrʌŋk/ *adj.* (of a fabric or garment) treated so that it shrinks during manufacture and not in use.

preside /prɪˈzaɪd/ *v.intr.* 1 (often foll. by *at*, *over*) be in a position of authority, esp. as the chairperson or president of a meeting. 2 exercise control or authority. [F *présider* f. L *praesidēre* (as PRAE-, *sedēre* sit)]

presidency /ˈprezɪdənsɪ/ *n.* (*pl.* **-ies**) 1 the office of president. 2 the period of this. [Sp. & Port. *presidencia*, It. *presidenza* f. med.L *praesidentia* (as PRESIDE)]

president /ˈprezɪd(ə)nt/ *n.* 1 the elected head of a republican State. 2 the head of a society or council etc. 3 the head of certain colleges. 4 *US* **a** the head of a university. **b** the head of a company, etc. 5 a person in charge of a meeting, council, etc. □ **presidential** /-ˈdenʃ(ə)l/ *adj.* **presidentially** /-ˈdenʃəlɪ/ *adv.* **presidentship** *n.* [ME f. OF f. L (as PRESIDE)]

presidium /prɪˈsɪdɪəm, -ˈzɪdɪəm/ *n.* (also **praesidium**) a standing executive committee in a Communist country. [Russ. *prezidium* f. L *praesidium* protection etc. (as PRESIDE)]

press[1] *v.* & *n.* —*v.* 1 *tr.* apply steady force to (a thing in contact) (*press a switch*; *pressed the two surfaces together*). 2 *tr.* **a** compress or apply pressure to a thing to flatten, shape, or smooth it, as by ironing (*got the curtains pressed*). **b** squeeze (a fruit etc.) to extract its juice. **c** manufacture (a gramophone record etc.) by moulding under pressure. 3 *tr.* (foll. by *out of*, *from*, etc.) squeeze (juice etc.). 4 *tr.* embrace or caress by squeezing (*pressed my hand*). 5 *intr.* (foll. by *on*, *against*, etc.) exert pressure. 6 *intr.* be urgent; demand immediate action (*time was pressing*). 7 *intr.* (foll. by *for*) make an insistent demand. 8 *intr.* (foll. by *up*, *round*, etc.) form a crowd. 9 *intr.* (foll. by *on*, *forward*, etc.) hasten insistently. 10 *tr.* (often in *passive*) (of an enemy etc.) bear heavily on. 11 *tr.* (often foll. by *for*, or *to* + infin.) urge or entreat (*pressed me to stay*; *pressed me for an answer*). 12 *tr.* (foll. by *on*, *upon*) **a** put forward or urge (an opinion, claim, or course of action). **b** insist on the acceptance of (an offer, a gift, etc.). 13 *tr.* insist on (*did not press the point*). 14 *intr.* (foll. by *on*) produce a strong mental or moral impression; oppress; weigh heavily. —*n.* 1 the act or an instance of pressing (*give it a slight press*). 2 a device for compressing, flattening, shaping, extracting juice, etc. (*trouser press*; *flower press*; *wine press*). 3 = *printing-press.* 4 (prec. by *the*) **a** the art or practice of printing. **b** newspapers, journalists, etc., generally or collectively (*read it in the press*; *pursued by the press*). 5 a notice or piece of publicity in newspapers etc. (*got a good press*). 6 (**Press**) **a** a printing house or establishment. **b** a publishing company. 7 **a** crowding. **b** a crowd (of people etc.). 8 the pressure of affairs. 9 esp. *Ir.* & *Sc.* a large usu. shelved cupboard for clothes, books, etc., esp. in a recess. □ **at** (or **in**) **press** (or **the press**) being printed. **be pressed for** have barely enough (time etc.). **go** (or **send**) **to press** go or send to be printed. **press agent** a person employed to attend to advertising and press publicity. **press-box** a reporters' enclosure esp. at a sports event. **press-button** *adj.* = *push-button.* **press conference** an interview given to journalists to make an announcement or answer questions. **press gallery** a gallery for reporters esp. in a legislative assembly. **press-on** (of a material) that can be pressed or ironed on. **press release** an official statement issued to newspapers for information. **press-stud** a small fastening device engaged by pressing its two halves together. **press-up** an exercise in which the prone downward-facing body is raised from the legs or trunk upwards by pressing down on the hands to straighten the arms. [ME f. OF *presser*, *presse* f. L *pressare* frequent. of *premere press-*]

press[2] *v.tr.* 1 *hist.* force to serve in the army or navy. 2 bring into use as a makeshift (*was pressed into service*). [alt. f. obs. *prest* (v. & n.) f. OF *prest* loan, advance pay f. *prester* f. L *praestare* furnish (as PRAE-, *stare* stand)]

press-gang /ˈpresgæŋ/ *n.* & *v.* —*n.* 1 *hist.* a body of men employed to press men into service in the army or navy. 2 any group using similar coercive methods. —*v.tr.* force into service.

pressie /ˈprezɪ/ *n.* (also **prezzie**) *colloq.* a present or gift. [abbr.]

pressing /ˈpresɪŋ/ *adj.* & *n.* —*adj.* 1 urgent (*pressing business*). 2 **a** urging strongly (*a pressing invitation*). **b** persistent, importunate (*since you are so pressing*). —*n.* 1 a thing made by pressing, esp. a gramophone record. 2 a series of these made at one time. 3 the act or an instance of pressing a thing, esp. a gramophone record or grapes etc. (*all at one pressing*). □ **pressingly** *adv.*

pressman /ˈpresmən/ *n.* (*pl.* **-men**) 1 a journalist. 2 an operator of a printing-press.

pressure /ˈpreʃə(r)/ *n.* & *v.* —*n.* 1 **a** the exertion of continuous force on or against a body by another in contact with it. **b** the force exerted. **c** the amount of this (expressed by the force on a unit area) (*atmospheric pressure*). 2 urgency; the need to meet a deadline etc. (*work under pressure*). 3 affliction or difficulty (*under financial pressure*). 4 constraining influence (*if pressure is brought to bear*). —*v.tr.* 1 apply (esp. moral) pressure to. 2 **a** coerce. **b** (often foll. by *into*) persuade (*was pressured into attending*). □ **pressure-cook** cook in a pressure-cooker. **pressure-cooker** an airtight pan for cooking quickly under steam pressure. **pressure gauge** a gauge showing the pressure of steam etc. **pressure group** a group or association formed to promote a particular interest or cause by influencing public policy. **pressure point 1** a point where an artery can be pressed against a bone to inhibit bleeding. **2** a point on the skin sensitive to pressure. **3** a target for political pressure or influence. **pressure suit** an inflatable suit for flying at a high altitude. [ME f. L *pressura* (as PRESS[1])]

pressurize /ˈpreʃəˌraɪz/ *v.tr.* (also **-ise**) 1 (esp. as **pressurized** *adj.*) maintain normal atmospheric pressure in (an aircraft cabin etc.) at a high altitude. 2 raise to a high pressure. 3 pressure (a person). □ **pressurized-water reactor** a nuclear reactor in which the coolant is water at high pressure. □ **pressurization** /-ˈzeɪʃ(ə)n/ *n.*

Prestel /ˈprestel/ *n. propr.* (in the UK) the computerized visual information system operated by British Telecom. [PRESS¹ + TELECOMMUNICATION]

prestidigitator /ˌprestɪˈdɪdʒɪˌteɪtə(r)/ *n. formal* a conjuror. □ **prestidigitation** /-ˈteɪʃ(ə)n/ *n.* [F *prestidigitateur* f. *preste* nimble (as PRESTO) + L *digitus* finger]

prestige /preˈstiːʒ/ *n.* **1** respect, reputation, or influence derived from achievements, power, associations, etc. **2** (*attrib.*) having or conferring prestige. □ **prestigeful** *adj.* [F, = illusion, glamour, f. LL *praestigium* (as PRESTIGIOUS)]

prestigious /preˈstɪdʒəs/ *adj.* having or showing prestige. □ **prestigiously** *adv.* **prestigiousness** *n.* [orig. = deceptive, f. L *praestigiosus* f. *praestigiae* juggler's tricks]

presto /ˈprestəʊ/ *adv. & n.* —*adv.* **1** *Mus.* in quick tempo. **2** (in a conjuror's formula in performing a trick) quickly (*hey presto!*). —*n.* (*pl.* **-os**) *Mus.* a movement to be played in a quick tempo. [It. f. LL *praestus* f. L *praesto* ready]

prestressed /priːˈstrest/ *adj.* strengthened by stressing in advance, esp. of concrete by means of stretched rods or wires put in during manufacture.

presumably /prɪˈzjuːməblɪ/ *adv.* as may reasonably be presumed.

presume /prɪˈzjuːm/ *v.* **1** *tr.* (often foll. by *that* + clause) suppose to be true; take for granted. **2** *tr.* (often foll. by *to* + infin.) **a** take the liberty; be impudent enough (*presumed to question their authority*). **b** dare, venture (*may I presume to ask?*). **3** *intr.* be presumptuous; take liberties. **4** *intr.* (foll. by *on*, *upon*) take advantage of or make unscrupulous use of (a person's good nature etc.). □ **presumable** *adj.* **presumedly** *adv.* [ME f. OF *presumer* f. L *praesumere praesumpt-* anticipate, venture (as PRAE-, *sumere* take)]

presumption /prɪˈzʌmpʃ(ə)n/ *n.* **1** arrogance; presumptuous behaviour. **2 a** the act of presuming a thing to be true. **b** a thing that is or may be presumed to be true. **3** a ground for presuming (*a strong presumption against their being guilty*). [ME f. OF *presumpcion* f. L *praesumptio -onis* (as PRESUME)]

presumptive /prɪˈzʌmptɪv/ *adj.* giving grounds for presumption (*presumptive evidence*). □ **presumptively** *adv.* [F *présomptif -ive* f. LL *praesumptivus* (as PRESUME)]

presumptuous /prɪˈzʌmptjʊəs/ *adj.* unduly or overbearingly confident and presuming. □ **presumptuously** *adv.* **presumptuousness** *n.* [ME f. OF *presumptueux* f. LL *praesumptuosus, -tiosus* (as PRESUME)]

presuppose /ˌpriːsəˈpəʊz/ *v.tr.* (often foll. by *that* + clause) **1** assume beforehand. **2** imply. [ME f. OF *presupposer*, after med.L *praesupponere* (as PRE-, SUPPOSE)]

presupposition /ˌpriːˌsʌpəˈzɪʃ(ə)n/ *n.* **1** the act or an instance of presupposing. **2 a** thing assumed beforehand as the basis of argument etc. [med.L *praesuppositio* (as PRAE-, *supponere* as SUPPOSE)]

pre-tax /priːˈtæks, ˈpriːtæks/ *adj.* (of income or profits) before the deduction of taxes.

pre-teen /priːˈtiːn/ *adj.* of or relating to a child before the age of thirteen.

pretence /prɪˈtens/ *n.* (US **pretense**) **1** pretending, make-believe. **2 a** a pretext or excuse (*on the slightest pretence*). **b** a false show of intentions or motives (*under the pretence of friendship*). **3** (foll. by *to*) a claim, esp. a false or ambitious one (*has

no pretence to any great talent*). **4 a** affectation, display. **b** pretentiousness, ostentation (*stripped of all pretence*). [ME f. AF *pretense* ult. f. med.L *pretensus* pretended (as PRETEND)]

pretend /prɪˈtend/ *v. & adj.* —*v.* **1** *tr.* claim or assert falsely so as to deceive (*pretend knowledge; pretended that they were foreigners*). **2** *tr.* imagine to oneself in play (*pretended to be monsters; pretended it was night*). **3** *tr.* **a** profess, esp. falsely or extravagantly (*does not pretend to be a scholar*). **b** (as **pretended** *adj.*) falsely claim to be such (*a pretended friend*). **4** *intr.* (foll. by *to*) **a** lay claim to (a right or title etc.). **b** profess to have (a quality etc.). —*adj. colloq.* pretended; in pretence (*pretend money*). [ME f. F *prétendre* or f. L (as PRAE-, *tendere tent-*, later *tens-* stretch)]

pretender /prɪˈtendə(r)/ *n.* **1** a person who claims a throne or title etc. **2** a person who pretends.

pretension /prɪˈtenʃ(ə)n/ *n.* **1** (often foll. by *to*) **a** an assertion of a claim. **b** a justifiable claim (*has no pretensions to the name; has some pretensions to be included*). **2** pretentiousness. [med.L *praetensio, -tio* (as PRETEND)]

pretentious /prɪˈtenʃəs/ *adj.* **1** making an excessive claim to great merit or importance. **2** ostentatious. □ **pretentiously** *adv.* **pretentiousness** *n.* [F *prétentieux* (as PRETENSION)]

preter- /ˈpriːtə(r)/ *comb. form* more than. [L *praeter* (adv. & prep.), = past, beyond]

preterite /ˈpretərɪt/ *adj. & n.* (US **preterit**) *Gram.* —*adj.* expressing a past action or state. —*n.* a preterite tense or form. [ME f. OF *preterite* or L *praeteritus* past part. of *praeterire* pass (as PRETER-, *ire it-* go)]

preterm /priːˈtɜːm/ *adj. & adv.* born or occurring prematurely.

preternatural /ˌpriːtəˈnætʃər(ə)l/ *adj.* outside the ordinary course of nature; supernatural. □ **preternaturalism** *n.* **preternaturally** *adv.*

pretext /ˈpriːtekst/ *n.* **1** an ostensible or alleged reason or intention. **2** an excuse offered. □ **on** (or **under**) **the pretext** (foll. by *of*, or *that* + clause) professing as one's object or intention. [L *praetextus* outward display f. *praetexere praetext-* (as PRAE-, *texere* weave)]

pretor US var. of PRAETOR.

pretorian US var. of PRAETORIAN.

prettify /ˈprɪtɪˌfaɪ/ *v.tr.* (**-ies, -ied**) make (a thing or person) pretty esp. in an affected way. □ **prettification** /-fɪˈkeɪʃ(ə)n/ *n.* **prettifier** *n.*

pretty /ˈprɪtɪ/ *adj., v. & adv.* —*adj.* (**prettier, prettiest**) **1** attractive in a delicate way without being truly beautiful or handsome (*a pretty child; a pretty dress; a pretty tune*). **2** fine or good of its kind (*a pretty wit*). **3** *iron.* considerable, fine (*a pretty penny; a pretty mess you have made*). —*adv. colloq.* fairly, moderately (*am pretty well; find it pretty difficult*). —*v.tr.* (**-ies, -ied**) (often foll. by *up*) make pretty or attractive. □ **pretty much** (or **nearly** or **well**) *colloq.* almost; very nearly. **pretty-pretty** too pretty. **sitting pretty** *colloq.* in a favourable or advantageous position. □ **prettily** *adv.* **prettiness** *n.* **prettyish** *adj.* **prettyism** *n.* [OE *prættig* f. WG]

pretzel /ˈprets(ə)l/ *n.* (also **bretzel** /ˈbret-/) a crisp knot-shaped or stick-shaped salted biscuit. [G]

prevail /prɪˈveɪl/ *v.intr.* **1** (often foll. by *against, over*) be victorious or gain mastery. **2** be the more usual or predominant. **3** exist or occur in general use or experience; be current. **4** (foll. by *on, upon*) persuade. □ **prevailing wind** the wind that most frequently occurs at a place. □ **prevailingly** *adv.* [ME f. L *praevalēre* (as PRAE-, *valēre* have power), infl. by AVAIL]

prevalent /ˈprevələnt/ *adj.* **1** generally existing or occurring. **2** predominant. □ **prevalence** *n.* **prevalently** *adv.* [as PREVAIL]

prevaricate /prɪˈværɪˌkeɪt/ *v.intr.* **1** speak or act evasively or misleadingly. **2** quibble, equivocate. □ **prevarication** /-ˈkeɪʃ(ə)n/ *n.* **prevaricator** *n.* [L *praevaricari* walk crookedly, practise collusion, in eccl.L transgress (as PRAE-, *varicari* straddle f. *varus* bent, knock-kneed)]

■ **Usage** This word is often confused with *procrastinate*, which means 'to defer or put off action'.

prevent /prɪˈvent/ *v.tr.* (often foll. by *from* + verbal noun) stop from happening or doing something; hinder; make impossible (*the weather prevented me from going*). □ **preventable** *adj.* (also **preventible**). **preventability** /-təˈbɪlɪti/ *n.* (also **preventibility**). **preventer** *n.* **prevention** *n.* [ME = anticipate, f. L *praevenire praevent*- come before, hinder (as PRAE-, *venire* come)]

■ **Usage** The use of *prevent* without 'from' as in *prevented me going* is informal. An acceptable alternative is *prevented my going*.

preventative /prɪˈventətɪv/ *adj.* & *n.* = PREVENTIVE. □ **preventatively** *adv.*

preventive /prɪˈventɪv/ *adj.* & *n.* —*adj.* serving to prevent, esp. preventing disease, breakdown, etc. (*preventive medicine*; *preventive maintenance*). —*n.* a preventive agent, measure, drug, etc. □ **preventively** *adv.*

preview /ˈpriːvjuː/ *n.* & *v.* —*n.* **1** the act of seeing in advance. **2 a** the showing of a film, play, exhibition, etc., before it is seen by the general public. **b** (*US* **prevue**) a film trailer. —*v.tr.* see or show in advance.

previous /ˈpriːvɪəs/ *adj.* & *adv.* —*adj.* **1** (often foll. by *to*) coming before in time or order. **2** done or acting hastily. —*adv.* (foll. by *to*) before (*had called previous to writing*). □ **previously** *adv.* **previousness** *n.* [L *praevius* (as PRAE-, *via* way)]

pre-war /priːˈwɔː(r), ˈpriːwɔː(r)/ *adj.* existing or occurring before a war (esp. the most recent major war).

prey /preɪ/ *n.* & *v.* —*n.* **1** an animal that is hunted or killed by another for food. **2** (often foll. by *to*) a person or thing that is influenced by or vulnerable to (something undesirable) (*became a prey to morbid fears*). —*v.intr.* (foll. by *on, upon*) **1** seek or take as prey. **2** make a victim of. **3** (of a disease, emotion, etc.) exert a harmful influence (*fear preyed on his mind*). □ **beast (or bird) of prey** an animal (or bird) which hunts animals for food. □ **preyer** *n.* [ME f. OF *preie* f. L *praeda* booty]

prezzie var. of PRESSIE.

price *n.* & *v.* —*n.* **1 a** the amount of money or goods for which a thing is bought or sold. **b** value or worth (*a pearl of great price*; *beyond price*). **2** what is or must be given, done, sacrificed, etc., to obtain or achieve something. **3** the odds in betting (*starting price*). —*v.tr.* **1** fix or find the price of (a thing for sale). **2** estimate the value of. □ **above** (or **beyond** or **without**) **price** so valuable that no price can be stated. **at any price** no matter what the cost, sacrifice, etc. (*peace at any price*). **at a price** at a high cost. **price on a person's head** a reward for a person's capture or death. **price oneself out of the market** lose to one's competitors by charging more than customers are willing to pay. **price-ring** a group of traders acting illegally to control certain prices. **price tag 1** the label on an item showing its price. **2** the cost of an enterprise or undertaking. **price war** fierce competition among traders cutting prices. **set a price on** declare the price of. **what price . . .?** (often foll. by verbal noun) *colloq.* **1** what is the chance of . . .? (*what price your finishing the course?*). **2** *iron.* the expected or much boasted . . . proves disappointing (*what price your friendship now?*). □ **priced** *adj.* (also in *comb.*). **pricer** *n.* [(n.) ME f. OF *pris* f. L *pretium*: (v.) var. of *prise* = PRIZE[1]]

priceless /ˈpraɪslɪs/ *adj.* **1** invaluable; beyond price. **2** *colloq.* very amusing or absurd. □ **pricelessly** *adv.* **pricelessness** *n.*

pricey /ˈpraɪsɪ/ *adj.* (also **pricy**) (**pricier, priciest**) *colloq.* expensive. □ **priciness** *n.*

prick *v.* & *n.* —*v.* **1** *tr.* pierce slightly; make a small hole in. **2** *tr.* (foll. by *off, out*) mark (esp. a pattern) with small holes or dots. **3** *tr.* trouble mentally (*my conscience is pricking me*). **4** *intr.* feel a pricking sensation. **5** *intr.* (foll. by *at, into,* etc.) make a thrust as if to prick. **6** *tr.* (foll. by *in, off, out*) plant (seedlings etc.) in small holes pricked in the earth. **7** *tr. Brit. archaic* mark off (a name in a list, esp. to select a sheriff) by pricking. **8** *tr. archaic* spur or urge on (a horse etc.). —*n.* **1** the act or an instance of pricking. **2** a small hole or mark made by pricking. **3** a pain caused as by pricking. **4** a mental pain (*felt the pricks of conscience*). **5** *coarse sl.* **a** the penis. **b** *derog.* (as a term of contempt) a person. **6** *archaic* a goad for oxen. □ **kick against the pricks** persist in futile resistance. **prick up one's ears 1** (of a dog etc.) make the ears erect when on the alert. **2** (of a person) become suddenly attentive. □ **pricker** *n.* [OE *prician* (v.), *pricca* (n.)]

■ **Usage** The noun in sense 5 is usually considered a taboo use.

prickle /ˈprɪk(ə)l/ *n.* & *v.* —*n.* **1 a** a small thorn. **b** *Bot.* a thornlike process developed from the epidermis of a plant. **2** a hard-pointed spine of a hedgehog etc. **3** a prickling sensation. —*v.tr.* & *intr.* affect or be affected with a sensation as of pricking. [OE *pricel* PRICK: (v.) also dimin. of PRICK]

prickly /ˈprɪklɪ/ *adj.* (**pricklier, prickliest**) **1** (esp. in the names of plants and animals) having prickles. **2** (of a person) ready to take offence. **3** tingling. □ **prickly heat** an itchy inflammation of the skin, causing a tingling sensation and common in hot countries. **prickly pear 1** any cactus of the genus *Opuntia*, native to arid regions of America, bearing large pear-shaped prickly fruits. **2** its fruit. □ **prickliness** *n.*

pride *n.* & *v.* —*n.* **1 a** a feeling of elation or satisfaction at achievements or qualities or possessions etc. that do one credit. **b** an object of this feeling. **2** a high or overbearing opinion of one's worth or importance. **3** (in full **proper pride**) a proper sense of what befits one's position; self-respect. **4** a group or company of animals, esp. lions. **5** the best condition; the prime. —*v.refl.* (foll. by *on, upon*) be proud of. □

my, his, etc. **pride and joy** a thing of which one is very proud. **pride of place** the most important or prominent position. **take pride** (or **a pride**) **in** 1 be proud of. 2 maintain in good condition or appearance. □ **prideful** adj. **pridefully** adv. **prideless** adj. [OE *prȳtu, prȳte, prȳde* f. *prūd* PROUD]

prie-dieu /priːˈdjəː/ n. (pl. **prie-dieux** pronunc. same) a kneeling-desk for prayer. [F, = pray God]

priest /priːst/ n. 1 an ordained minister of the Roman Catholic or Orthodox Church, or of the Anglican Church (above a deacon and below a bishop), authorized to perform certain rites and administer certain sacraments. 2 an official minister of a non-Christian religion. □ **priestless** adj. **priestlike** adj. **priestling** n. [OE *prēost*, ult. f. eccl.L *presbyter*: see PRESBYTER]

priestess /ˈpriːstɪs/ n. a female priest of a non-Christian religion.

priesthood /ˈpriːsthʊd/ n. (usu. prec. by *the*) 1 the office or position of priest. 2 priests in general.

priestly /ˈpriːstlɪ/ adj. of or associated with priests. □ **priestliness** n. [OE *prēostlic* (as PRIEST)]

prig n. a self-righteously correct or moralistic person. □ **priggery** n. **priggish** adj. **priggishly** adv. **priggishness** n. [16th-c. cant; = tinker: orig. unkn.]

prim adj. & v. —adj. (**primmer, primmest**) 1 (of a person or manner) stiffly formal and precise. 2 (of a woman or girl) demure. 3 prudish. —v.tr. (**primmed, primming**) 1 form (the face, lips, etc.) into a prim expression. 2 make prim. □ **primly** adv. **primness** n. [17th c.: prob. orig. cant f. OF *prin* prime excellent f. L *primus* first]

prima ballerina /ˌpriːmə ˌbæləˈriːnə/ n. the chief female dancer in a ballet or ballet company. [It.]

primacy /ˈpraɪməsɪ/ n. (pl. **-ies**) 1 pre-eminence. 2 the office of a primate. [ME f. OF *primatie* or med.L *primatia* (as PRIMATE)]

prima donna /ˌpriːmə ˈdɒnə/ n. (pl. **prima donnas**) 1 the chief female singer in an opera or opera company. 2 a temperamentally self-important person. □ **prima donna-ish** adj. [It.]

prima facie /ˌpraɪmə ˈfeɪʃiː/ adv. & adj. —adv. at first sight; from a first impression (*seems prima facie to be guilty*). —adj. (of evidence) based on the first impression (*can see a prima facie reason for it*). [ME f. L, fem. ablat. of *primus* first, *facies* FACE]

primal /ˈpraɪm(ə)l/ adj. 1 primitive, primeval. 2 chief, fundamental. □ **primally** adv. [med.L *primalis* f. L *primus* first]

primary /ˈpraɪmərɪ/ adj. & n. —adj. 1 a of the first importance; chief (*that is our primary concern*). b fundamental, basic. 2 earliest, original; first in a series. 3 of the first rank in a series; not derived (*the primary meaning of a word*). 4 designating any of the colours red, green, and blue, or for pigments red, blue, and yellow, from which all other colours can be obtained by mixing. 5 (of a battery or cell) generating electricity by irreversible chemical reaction. 6 (of education) for young children, esp. below the age of 11. 7 (**Primary**) Geol. of the lowest series of strata. 8 Biol. belonging to the first stage of development. 9 (of an industry

or source of production) concerned with obtaining or using raw materials. —n. (pl. **-ies**) 1 a thing that is primary. 2 (in full **primary election**) (in the US) a preliminary election to appoint delegates to a party conference or to select the candidates for a principal (esp. presidential) election. 3 (**Primary**) Geol. the Primary period. 4 = *primary feather*. □ **primary feather** a large flight-feather of a bird's wing. **primary school** a school where young children are taught, esp. below the age of 11. □ **primarily** /ˈpraɪmərɪlɪ, -ˈmeərɪlɪ/ adv. [ME f. L *primarius* f. *primus* first]

primate /ˈpraɪmeɪt/ n. 1 any animal of the order Primates, the highest order of mammals, including tarsiers, lemurs, apes, monkeys, and man. 2 an archbishop. □ **primatial** /-ˈmeɪʃ(ə)l/ adj. **primatology** /-məˈtɒlədʒɪ/ n. (in sense 1). [ME f. OF *primat* f. L *primas -atis* (adj.) of the first rank f. *primus* first, in med.L = primate]

prime[1] adj. & n. —adj. 1 chief, most important (*the prime agent; the prime motive*). 2 (esp. of cattle and provisions) first-rate, excellent. 3 primary, fundamental. 4 Math. (of a number) divisible only by itself and unity (e.g. 2, 3, 5, 7, 11). —n. 1 the state of the highest perfection of something (*in the prime of life*). 2 (prec. by *the*; foll. by *of*) the best part. 3 the beginning or first age of anything. 4 Eccl. the second canonical hour of prayer, appointed for the first hour of the day (i.e. 6 a.m.). 5 a prime number. □ **prime minister** the head of an elected government; the principal minister of a sovereign or State. **prime mover** 1 an initial natural or mechanical source of motive power. 2 the author of a fruitful idea. **prime time** the time at which a radio or television audience is expected to be at its highest. □ **primeness** n. [(n.) OE *prīm* f. L *prima (hora)* first (hour), & MF f. OF *prime*: (adj.) ME f. OF f. L *primus* first]

prime[2] v.tr. 1 prepare (a thing) for use or action. 2 prepare (a gun) for firing or (an explosive) for detonation. 3 a pour (a liquid) into a pump to prepare it for working. b inject petrol into (the cylinder or carburettor of an internal-combustion engine). 4 prepare (wood etc.) for painting by applying a substance that prevents paint from being absorbed. 5 equip (a person) with information etc. 6 ply (a person) with food or drink in preparation for something. [16th c.: orig. unkn.]

primer[1] /ˈpraɪmə(r)/ n. 1 a substance used to prime wood etc. 2 a cap, cylinder, etc., used to ignite the powder of a cartridge.

primer[2] /ˈpraɪmə(r)/ n. 1 an elementary textbook for teaching children to read. 2 an introductory book. [ME f. AF f. med.L *primarius -arium* f. L *primus* first]

primeval /praɪˈmiːv(ə)l/ adj. (also **primaeval**) 1 of or relating to the first age of the world. 2 ancient, primitive. □ **primevally** adv. [L *primaevus* f. *primus* first + *aevum* age]

primitive /ˈprɪmɪtɪv/ adj. & n. —adj. 1 early, ancient; at an early stage of civilization (*primitive man*). 2 undeveloped, crude, simple (*primitive methods*). 3 original, primary. —n. 1 a painter of the period before the Renaissance. 2 a modern imitator of such. 3 an untutored painter with a direct naïve style. □ **primitively** adv. **primitiveness** n. [ME f. OF *primitif -ive* or L *primitivus* first of its kind f. *primitus* in the first place f. *primus* first]

primitivism /ˈprɪmɪtɪˌvɪz(ə)m/ *n.* **1** primitive behaviour. **2** belief in the superiority of what is primitive. **3** the practice of primitive art. □ **primitivist** *n. & adj.*

primogeniture /ˌpraɪməʊˈdʒenɪtʃə(r)/ *n.* **1** the fact or condition of being the first-born child. **2** (in full **right of primogeniture**) the right of succession belonging to the first-born. □ **primogenital** *adj.* **primogenitary** *adj.* [med.L *primogenitura* f. L *primo* first + *genitura* f. *gignere genit-* beget]

primordial /praɪˈmɔːdɪəl/ *adj.* **1** existing at or from the beginning, primeval. **2** original, fundamental. □ **primordiality** /-ˈælɪtɪ/ *n.* **primordially** *adv.* [ME f. LL *primordialis* f. *primordius* original f. *primus* first + *ordiri* begin]

primp *v.tr.* **1** make (the hair, one's clothes, etc.) tidy. **2** *refl.* make (oneself) smart. [dial. var. of PRIM]

primrose /ˈprɪmrəʊz/ *n.* **1 a** any plant of the genus *Primula*, esp. *P. vulgaris*, bearing pale yellow flowers. **b** the flower of this. **2** a pale yellow colour. □ **primrose path** the pursuit of pleasure, esp. with disastrous consequences (with ref. to Shakesp. *Hamlet* I. iii. 50). [ME *primerose*, corresp. to OF *primerose* and med.L *prima rosa*, lit. first rose: reason for the name unkn.]

primula /ˈprɪmjʊlə/ *n.* any plant of the genus *Primula*, bearing primrose-like flowers in a wide variety of colours during the spring, including primroses, cowslips, and polyanthuses. [med.L, fem. of *primulus* dimin. of *primus* first]

Primus /ˈpraɪməs/ *n. propr.* a brand of portable stove burning vaporized oil for cooking etc. [L (as PRIMUS)]

prince *n.* **1** (as a title usu. **Prince**) a male member of a royal family other than a reigning king. **2** (in full **prince of the blood**) a son or grandson of a British monarch. **3** a ruler of a small State, actually or nominally subject to a king or emperor. **4** (as an English rendering of foreign titles) a noble usu. ranking next below a duke. **5** (often foll. by *of*) the chief or greatest (*the prince of novelists*). □ **Prince Charming** an idealized young hero or lover. **prince consort 1** the husband of a reigning female sovereign who is himself a prince. **2** the title conferred on him. **Prince of Darkness** Satan. **Prince of Peace** Christ. **Prince of Wales** the heir apparent to the British throne, as a title conferred by the monarch. **Prince Regent** a prince who acts as regent, esp. George (afterwards IV) as regent 1811–20. **prince royal** the eldest son of the reigning monarch. □ **princedom** *n.* **princelet** *n.* **princelike** *adj.* **princeship** *n.* [ME f. OF f. L *princeps principis* first, chief, sovereign f. *primus* first + *capere* take]

princeling /ˈprɪnslɪŋ/ *n.* a young or petty prince.

princely /ˈprɪnslɪ/ *adj.* (**princelier, princeliest**) **1 a** of or worthy of a prince. **b** held by a prince. **2** sumptuous, generous, splendid. □ **princeliness** *n.*

princess /prɪnˈses/ *n.* (as a title usu. **Princess** /ˈprɪnses/) **1** the wife of a prince. **2** a female member of a royal family other than a reigning queen. **3** (in full **princess of the blood**) a daughter or granddaughter of a British monarch. **4** a pre-eminent woman or thing personified as a woman. □ **Princess Royal** a monarch's eldest daughter, as a title conferred by the monarch. [ME f. OF *princesse* (as PRINCE)]

principal /ˈprɪnsɪp(ə)l/ *adj. & n.* —*adj.* **1** (usu. *attrib.*) first in rank or importance; chief (*the principal town of the district*). **2** main, leading (*a principal cause of my success*). **3** (of money) constituting the original sum invested or lent. —*n.* **1** a head, ruler, or superior. **2** the head of some schools, colleges, and universities. **3** the leading performer in a concert, play, etc. **4** a capital sum as distinguished from interest or income. **5** a person for whom another acts as agent etc. **6** (in the UK) a civil servant of the grade below Secretary. **7** the person actually responsible for a crime. □ **principal boy** (or **girl**) an actress who takes the leading male (or female) part in a pantomime. **principal parts** *Gram.* the parts of a verb from which all other parts can be deduced. □ **principalship** *n.* [ME f. OF f. L *principalis* first, original (as PRINCE)]

principality /ˌprɪnsɪˈpælɪtɪ/ *n.* (*pl.* **-ies**) **1** a State ruled by a prince. **2** the government of a prince. **3** (**the Principality**) *Brit.* Wales. [ME f. OF *principalité* f. LL *principalitas -tatis* (as PRINCIPAL)]

principally /ˈprɪnsɪpəlɪ/ *adv.* for the most part; chiefly.

principle /ˈprɪnsɪp(ə)l/ *n.* **1** a fundamental truth or law as the basis of reasoning or action (*arguing from first principles*; *moral principles*). **2 a** a personal code of conduct (*a person of high principle*). **b** (in *pl.*) such rules of conduct (*has no principles*). **3** a general law in physics etc. (*the uncertainty principle*). **4** a law of nature forming the basis for the construction or working of a machine etc. **5** a fundamental source; a primary element (*held water to be the first principle of all things*). **6** *Chem.* a constituent of a substance, esp. one giving rise to some quality, etc. □ **in principle** as regards fundamentals but not necessarily in detail. **on principle** on the basis of a moral attitude (*I refuse on principle*). [ME f. OF *principe* f. L *principium* source, (in *pl.*) foundations (as PRINCE)]

principled /ˈprɪnsɪp(ə)ld/ *adj.* based on or having (esp. praiseworthy) principles of behaviour.

prink *v.* **1** *tr.* (usu. *refl.*) **a** make (oneself etc.) smart. **b** (foll. by *up*) smarten (oneself) up. **c** (of a bird) preen. **2** *intr.* dress oneself up. [16th c.: prob. f. *prank* dress, adorn, rel. to MLG *prank* pomp, Du. *pronk* finery]

print /prɪnt/ *n. & v.* —*n.* **1** an indentation or mark on a surface left by the pressure of a thing in contact with it (*fingerprint*; *footprint*). **2 a** printed lettering or writing (*large print*). **b** words in printed form. **c** a printed publication, esp. a newspaper. **3** a picture or design printed from a block or plate. **4** *Photog.* a picture produced on paper from a negative. **5** a printed cotton fabric. —*v.tr.* **1 a** produce or reproduce (a book, picture, etc.) by applying inked types, blocks, or plates, to paper, vellum, etc. **b** (of an author, publisher, or editor) cause (a book or manuscript etc.) to be produced or reproduced in this way. **2** express or publish in print. **3 a** (often foll. by *on, in*) impress or stamp (a mark or figure on a surface). **b** (often foll. by *with*) impress or stamp (a soft surface, e.g. of butter or wax, with a seal, die, etc.). **4** (often *absol.*) write (words or letters) without joining, in imitation of typography. **5** (often foll. by *off, out*)

Photog. produce (a picture) by the transmission of light through a negative. **6** (usu. foll. by *out*) (of a computer etc.) produce output in printed form. **7** mark (a textile fabric) with a decorative design in colours. **8** (foll. by *on*) impress (an idea, scene, etc. on the mind or memory). □ **appear in print** have one's work published. **in print 1** (of a book etc.) available from the publisher. **2** in printed form. **out of print** no longer available from the publisher. **printed circuit** an electric circuit with thin strips of conductor on a flat insulating sheet, usu. made by a process like printing. □ **printable** *adj.* **printability** /-tə'bɪlɪtɪ/ *n.* **printless** *adj.* (in sense 1 of *n.*). [ME f. OF *priente, preinte,* fem. past part. of *preindre* press f. L *premere*]

printer /'prɪntə(r)/ *n.* **1** a person who prints books, magazines, advertising matter, etc. **2** the owner of a printing business. **3** a device that prints, esp. as part of a computer system.

printhead /'prɪnthed/ *n.* the component in a printer (see PRINTER 3) that assembles and prints the characters on the paper.

printing /'prɪntɪŋ/ *n.* **1** the production of printed books etc. **2** a single impression of a book. **3** printed letters or writing imitating them. □ **printing-press** a machine for printing from types or plates etc.

printmaker /'prɪnt‚meɪkə(r)/ *n.* a person who makes print. □ **printmaking** *n.*

printout /'prɪntaʊt/ *n.* computer output in printed form.

prior /'praɪə(r)/ *adj., adv.,* & *n.* —*adj.* **1** earlier. **2** (often foll. by *to*) coming before in time, order, or importance. —*adv.* (foll. by *to*) before (*decided prior to their arrival*). —*n.* **1** the superior officer of a religious house or order. **2** (in an abbey) the officer next under the abbot. □ **priorate** /-rət/ *n.* **prioress** *n.* **priorship** *n.* [L, = former, elder, compar. of OL *pri* = L *prae* before]

priority /praɪ'ɒrɪtɪ/ *n.* (pl. **-ies**) **1** the fact or condition of being earlier or antecedent. **2** precedence in rank etc. **3** an interest having prior claim to consideration. □ **prioritize** *v.tr.* (also **-ise**). **prioritization** /-taɪ'zeɪʃ(ə)n/ *n.* [ME f. OF *priorité* f. med.L *prioritas -tatis* f. L *prior* (as PRIOR)]

priory /'praɪərɪ/ *n.* (pl. **-ies**) a monastery governed by a prior or a nunnery governed by a prioress. [ME f. AF *priorie,* med.L *prioria* (as PRIOR)]

prise /praɪz/ *v.tr.* (also **prize**) force open or out by leverage (*prised up the lid; prised the box open*). [ME & OF *prise* levering instrument (as PRIZE[1])]

prism /'prɪz(ə)m/ *n.* **1** a solid geometric figure whose two ends are similar, equal, and parallel rectilinear figures, and whose sides are parallelograms. **2** a transparent body in this form, usu. triangular with refracting surfaces at an acute angle with each other, which separates white light into a spectrum of colours. □ **prismal** /'prɪzm(ə)l/ *adj.* [LL *prisma* f. Gk *prisma prismatos* thing sawn f. *prizō* to saw]

prismatic /prɪz'mætɪk/ *adj.* **1** of, like, or using a prism. **2 a** (of colours) distributed by or as if by a transparent prism. **b** (of light) displayed in the form of a spectrum. □ **prismatically** *adv.* [F *prismatique* f. Gk *prisma* (as PRISM)]

prison /'prɪz(ə)n/ *n.* **1** a place in which a person is kept in captivity, esp. a building to which persons are legally committed while awaiting trial or for punishment; a jail. **2** custody, confinement (*in prison*). □ **prison camp** a camp for prisoners of war or of State. [ME f. OF *prisun, -on* f. L *prensio -onis* f. *prehensio* f. *prehendere prehens-* lay hold of]

prisoner /'prɪznə(r)/ *n.* **1** a person kept in prison. **2** (in full **prisoner at the bar**) a person in custody on a criminal charge and on trial. **3** a person or thing confined by illness, another's grasp, etc. **4** (in full **prisoner of war**) a person who has been captured in war. □ **prisoner of State** (or **State prisoner**) a person confined for political reasons. **take prisoner** seize and hold as a prisoner. [ME f. AF *prisoner,* OF *prisonier* (as PRISON)]

prissy /'prɪsɪ/ *adj.* (**prissier, prissiest**) prim, prudish. □ **prissily** *adv.* **prissiness** *n.* [perh. f. PRIM + SISSY]

pristine /'prɪstiːn, 'prɪstaɪn/ *adj.* **1** in its original condition; unspoilt. **2** *disp.* spotless; fresh as if new. **3** ancient, primitive. [L *pristinus* former]

■ **Usage** The use of *pristine* in sense 2 is considered incorrect by some people.

privacy /'prɪvəsɪ, 'praɪ-/ *n.* **1 a** the state of being private and undisturbed. **b** a person's right to this. **2** freedom from intrusion or public attention. **3** avoidance of publicity.

private /'praɪvət, -vɪt/ *adj.* & *n.* —*adj.* **1** belonging to an individual; one's own; personal (*private property*). **2** confidential; not to be disclosed to others (*private talks*). **3** kept or removed from public knowledge or observation. **4 a** not open to the public. **b** for an individual's exclusive use (*private room*). **5** (of a place) secluded; affording privacy. **6** (of a person) not holding public office or an official position. **7** (of education or medical treatment) conducted outside the State system, at the individual's expense. —*n.* **1** a private soldier. **2** (in *pl.*) *colloq.* the genitals. □ **in private** privately; in private company or life. **private company** *Brit.* a company with restricted membership and no issue of shares. **private detective** a detective engaged privately, outside an official police force. **private enterprise 1** a business or businesses not under State control. **2** individual initiative. **private eye** *colloq.* a private detective. **private hotel** a hotel not obliged to take all comers. **private house** the dwelling-house of a private person, as distinct from a shop, office, or public building. **private life** life as a private person, not as an official, public performer, etc. **private means** income from investments etc., apart from earned income. **private member** a member of a legislative body not holding a government office. **private member's bill** a bill introduced by a private member, not part of government legislation. **private parts** the genitals. **private patient** *Brit.* a patient treated by a doctor other than under the National Health Service. **private practice** *Brit.* medical practice that is not part of the National Health Service. **private school 1** *Brit.* a school supported wholly by the payment of fees. **2** *US* a school not supported mainly by the State. **private secretary** a secretary dealing with the personal and confidential concerns of a businessman or businesswoman. **private sector** the part of the economy free of direct State control. **private soldier** an ordinary soldier other than the officers (and *US* other

privateer /ˌpraɪvəˈtɪə(r)/ n. **1** an armed vessel owned and officered by private individuals holding a government commission and authorized for war service. **2 a** a commander of such a vessel. **b** (in pl.) its crew. □ **privateering** n. [PRIVATE, after volunteer]

privation /praɪˈveɪʃ(ə)n/ n. **1** lack of the comforts or necessities of life (suffered many privations). **2** (often foll. by of) loss or absence (of a quality). [ME f. L privatio (as PRIVATE)]

privative /ˈprɪvətɪv/ adj. **1** consisting in or marked by the loss or removal or absence of some quality or attribute. **2** (of a term) denoting the privation or absence of a quality etc. □ **privatively** adv. [F privatif -ive or L privativus (as PRIVATION)]

privatize /ˈpraɪvəˌtaɪz, -vɪˌtaɪz/ v.tr. (also **-ise**) make private, esp. assign (a business etc.) to private as distinct from State control or ownership; denationalize. □ **privatization** /-ˈzeɪʃ(ə)n/ n.

privet /ˈprɪvɪt/ n. any evergreen shrub of the genus Ligustrum, esp. L. vulgare, much used for hedges. [16th c.: orig. unkn.]

privilege /ˈprɪvɪlɪdʒ/ n. & v. —n. **1 a** a right, advantage, or immunity, belonging to a person, class, or office. **b** the freedom of members of a legislative assembly when speaking at its meetings. **2** a special benefit or honour (it is a privilege to meet you). —v.tr. **1** invest with a privilege. **2** (foll. by to + infin.) allow (a person) as a privilege (to do something). □ **privileged** adj. [ME f. OF privilege f. L privilegium bill or law affecting an individual, f. privus private + lex legis law]

privy /ˈprɪvɪ/ adj. & n. —adj. **1** (foll. by to) sharing in the secret of (a person's plans etc.). **2** archaic hidden, secret. —n. (pl. **-ies**) US or archaic a lavatory. □ **Privy Council 1** (in the UK) a body of advisers appointed by the sovereign (now chiefly on an honorary basis). **privy counsellor** (or **councillor**) a private adviser, esp. a member of a Privy Council. **privy purse** Brit. **1** an allowance from the public revenue for the monarch's private expenses. **2** the keeper of this. □ **privily** adv. [ME f. OF privé f. L privatus PRIVATE]

prize¹ n. & v. —n. **1** something that can be won in a competition or lottery etc. **2** a reward given as a symbol of victory or superiority. **3** something striven for or worth striving for (missed all the great prizes of life). **4** (attrib.) **a** to which a prize is awarded (a prize bull; a prize poem). **b** supremely excellent or outstanding of its kind. —v.tr. value highly (a much prized possession). [(n.) ME, var. of PRICE: (v.) ME f. OF pris- stem of preisier PRAISE]

prize² n. a ship or property captured in naval warfare. [ME f. OF prise taking, booty, fem. past part. of prendre f. L prehendere prehens- seize: later identified with PRIZE¹]

prize³ var. of PRISE.

prizefight /ˈpraɪzfaɪt/ n. a boxing-match fought for prize-money. □ **prizefighter** n.

prizewinner /ˈpraɪzˌwɪnə(r)/ n. a winner of a prize. □ **prizewinning** adj.

PRO abbr. **1** Public Record Office. **2** public relations officer.

pro¹ /prəʊ/ n. & adj. colloq. —n. (pl. **-os**) a professional. —adj. professional. □ **pro-am** involving professionals and amateurs. [abbr.]

pro² /prəʊ/ adj., n., & prep. —adj. (of an argument or reason) for; in favour. —n. (pl. **-os**) a reason or argument for or in favour. —prep. in favour of. □ **pros and cons** reasons or considerations for and against a proposition etc. [L, = for, on behalf of]

pro-¹ /prəʊ/ prefix **1** favouring or supporting (pro-government). **2** acting as a substitute or deputy for (proconsul). **3** forwards (produce). **4** forwards and downwards (prostrate). **5** onwards (proceed; progress). **6** in front of (protect). [L pro in front (of), for, on behalf of, instead of, on account of]

pro-² /prəʊ/ prefix before in time, place, order, etc. (problem; proboscis; prophet). [Gk pro before]

proactive /prəʊˈæktɪv/ adj. **1** (of a person, policy, etc.) creating or controlling a situation by taking the initiative. **2** of or relating to mental conditioning or a habit etc. which has been learned. □ **proaction** /-ˈækʃ(ə)n/ n. **proactively** adv. **proactivity** /-ˈtɪvɪtɪ/ n. [PRO-², after REACTIVE]

probability /ˌprɒbəˈbɪlɪtɪ/ n. (pl. **-ies**) **1** the state or condition of being probable. **2** the likelihood of something happening. **3** a probable or most probable event (the probability is that they will come). **4** Math. the extent to which an event is likely to occur, measured by the ratio of the favourable cases to the whole number of cases possible. □ **in all probability** most probably. [F probabilité or L probabilitas (as PROBABLE)]

probable /ˈprɒbəb(ə)l/ adj. & n. —adj. (often foll. by that + clause) that may be expected to happen or prove true; likely (the probable explanation; it is probable that they forgot). —n. a probable candidate, member of a team, etc. □ **probably** adv. [ME f. OF f. L probabilis f. probare prove]

probate /ˈprəʊbeɪt, -bət/ n. & v. —n. **1** the official proving of a will. **2** a verified copy of a will with a certificate as handed to the executors. —v.tr. US establish the validity of (a will). [ME f. L probatum neut. past part. of probare PROVE]

probation /prəˈbeɪʃ(ə)n/ n. **1** Law a system of suspending the sentence on an offender subject to a period of good behaviour under supervision. **2** a process or period of testing the character or abilities of a person in a certain role, esp. of a new employee. □ **on probation** undergoing probation, esp. legal supervision. **probation officer** an official supervising offenders on probation. □ **probational** adj. **probationary** adj. [ME f. OF probation or L probatio (as PROVE)]

probationer /prəˈbeɪʃənə(r)/ n. **1** a person on probation, e.g. a newly appointed nurse, teacher, etc. **2** an offender on probation. □ **probationership** n.

probative /ˈprəʊbətɪv/ adj. affording proof; evidential. [L probativus (as PROVE)]

probe n. & v. —n. **1** a penetrating investigation. **2** any small device, esp. an electrode, for measuring, testing, etc. **3** a blunt-ended surgical instrument usu. of metal for exploring a wound etc. **4** (in full **space probe**) an unmanned exploratory spacecraft transmitting information about its environment. —v.tr. **1** examine or enquire into closely. **2** explore (a wound or part of the body) with a probe. **3** penetrate with a sharp instrument. □ **probeable** adj. **prober**

n. **probingly** *adv.* [LL *proba* proof, in med.L = examination, f. L *probare* test]

probity /ˈprəʊbɪti, ˈprɒ-/ *n.* uprightness, honesty. [F *probité* or L *probitas* f. *probus* good]

problem /ˈprɒbləm/ *n.* **1** a doubtful or difficult matter requiring a solution (*how to prevent it is a problem; the problem of ventilation*). **2** something hard to understand or accomplish or deal with. **3** (*attrib.*) causing problems; difficult to deal with (*problem child*). **4** *Physics & Math.* an inquiry starting from given conditions to investigate or demonstrate a fact, result, or law. **5 a** (in various games, esp. chess) an arrangement of men, cards, etc., in which the solver has to achieve a specified result. **b** a puzzle or question for solution. [ME f. OF *probleme* or L *problema* f. Gk *problēma -matos* f. *proballō* (as PRO-², *ballō* throw)]

problematic /ˌprɒbləˈmætɪk/ *adj.* (also **problematical**) **1** attended by difficulty. **2** doubtful or questionable. □ **problematically** *adv.* [F *problématique* or LL *problematicus* f. Gk *problēmatikos* (as PROBLEM)]

proboscis /prəʊˈbɒsɪs/ *n.* **1** the long flexible trunk or snout of some mammals, e.g. an elephant or tapir. **2** the elongated mouth parts of some insects. **3** the sucking organ in some worms. **4** *joc.* the human nose. [L *proboscis -cidis* f. Gk *proboskis* f. *proboskō* (as PRO-², *boskō* feed)]

procedure /prəˈsiːdjə(r), -dʒə(r)/ *n.* **1** a way of proceeding, esp. a mode of conducting business or a legal action. **2** a mode of performing a task. **3** a series of actions conducted in a certain order or manner. **4** a proceeding. **5** *Computing* = SUBROUTINE. □ **procedural** *adj.* **procedurally** *adv.* [F *procédure* (as PROCEED)]

proceed /prəˈsiːd, prəʊ-/ *v.intr.* **1** (often foll. by *to*) go forward or on further; make one's way. **2** (often foll. by *with*, or *to* + infin.) continue; go on with an activity (*proceeded with their work; proceeded to tell the whole story*). **3** (of an action) be carried on or continued (*the case will now proceed*). **4** adopt a course of action (*how shall we proceed?*). **5** go on to say. **6** (foll. by *against*) start a lawsuit (against a person). **7** (often foll. by *from*) come forth or originate (*shouts proceeded from the bedroom*). [ME f. OF *proceder* f. L *procedere process-* (as PRO-¹, *cedere* go)]

proceeding /prəˈsiːdɪŋ/ *n.* **1** an action or piece of conduct (*a high-handed proceeding*). **2** (in *pl.*) (in full **legal proceedings**) an action at law; a lawsuit. **3** (in *pl.*) a published report of discussions or a conference.

proceeds /ˈprəʊsiːdz/ *n.pl.* money produced by a transaction or other undertaking. [pl. of obs. *proceed* (n.) f. PROCEED]

process¹ /ˈprəʊses/ *n.* & *v.* —*n.* **1** a course of action or proceeding, esp. a series of stages in manufacture or some other operation. **2** the progress or course of something (*in process of construction*). **3** a natural or involuntary operation or series of changes (*the process of growing old*). **4** an action at law; a summons or writ. **5** *Anat., Zool., & Bot.* a natural appendage or outgrowth on an organism. —*v.tr.* **1** handle or deal with by a particular process. **2** treat (food, esp. to prevent decay) (*processed cheese*). **3** *Computing* operate on (data) by means of a program. □ **in process of time** as time goes on. **process server** a sheriff's officer who serves writs. □ **processable** *adj.* [ME f. OF *proces* f. L *processus* (as PROCEED)]

process² /prəˈses/ *v.intr.* walk in procession. [back-form. f. PROCESSION]

procession /prəˈseʃ(ə)n/ *n.* **1** a number of people or vehicles etc. moving forward in orderly succession, esp. at a ceremony, demonstration, or festivity. **2** the movement of such a group (*go in procession*). □ **processionist** *n.* [ME f. OF f. L *processio -onis* (as PROCEED)]

processional /prəˈseʃən(ə)l/ *adj.* **1** of processions. **2** used, carried, or sung in processions. [med.L *processionalis* (adj.), *-ale* (n.) (as PROCESSION)]

processor /ˈprəʊsesə(r)/ *n.* a machine that processes things, esp.: **1** = *central processor.* **2** = *food processor.*

proclaim /prəˈkleɪm/ *v.tr.* **1** (often foll. by *that* + clause) announce or declare publicly or officially. **2** declare (a person) to be (a king, traitor, etc.). **3** reveal as being (*an accent that proclaims you a Scot*). □ **proclaimer** *n.* **proclamation** /ˌprɒkləˈmeɪʃ(ə)n/ *n.* **proclamatory** /-ˈklæmətəri/ *adj.* [ME *proclame* f. L *proclamare* cry out (as PRO-¹, CLAIM)]

proclivity /prəˈklɪvɪti/ *n.* (*pl.* **-ies**) a tendency or inclination. [L *proclivitas* f. *proclivis* inclined (as PRO-¹, *clivus* slope)]

procrastinate /prəʊˈkræstɪˌneɪt/ *v.intr.* defer action; be dilatory. □ **procrastination** /-ˈneɪʃ(ə)n/ *n.* **procrastinative** /-nətɪv/ *adj.* **procrastinator** *n.* **procrastinatory** *adj.* [L *procrastinare procrastinat-* (as PRO-¹, *crastinus* of tomorrow f. *cras* tomorrow)]

■ **Usage** This word is often confused with *prevaricate* which means 'to be evasive, quibble'.

procreate /ˈprəʊkrɪˌeɪt/ *v.tr.* (often *absol.*) bring (offspring) into existence by the natural process of reproduction. □ **procreant** /ˈprəʊkrɪənt/ *adj.* **procreative** *adj.* **procreation** /-ˈeɪʃ(ə)n/ *n.* **procreator** *n.* [L *procreare procreat-* (as PRO-¹, *creare* create)]

Procrustean /prəʊˈkrʌstɪən/ *adj.* seeking to enforce uniformity by forceful or ruthless methods. [Gk *Prokroustēs*, lit. stretcher, f. *prokrouō* beat out: the name of a legendary robber who fitted victims to a bed by stretching them or cutting off parts of them]

proctor /ˈprɒktə(r)/ *n.* **1** *Brit.* an officer (usu. one of two) at certain universities, appointed annually and having mainly disciplinary functions. **2** *US* a supervisor of students in an examination etc. □ **proctorial** /-ˈtɔːrɪəl/ *adj.* **proctorship** *n.* [ME, syncopation of PROCURATOR]

procuration /ˌprɒkjʊˈreɪʃ(ə)n/ *n.* **1** *formal* the action of procuring, obtaining, or bringing about. **2** the function or an authorized action of an attorney. [ME f. OF *procuration* or L *procuratio* (as PROCURE)]

procurator /ˈprɒkjʊˌreɪtə(r)/ *n.* an agent or proxy, esp. one who has power of attorney. □ **procurator fiscal** (in Scotland) a local coroner and public prosecutor. □ **procuratorial** /-rəˈtɔːrɪəl/ *adj.* **procuratorship** *n.* [ME f. OF *procurateur* or L *procurator* administrator, finance-agent (as PROCURE)]

procure /prəˈkjʊə(r)/ *v.tr.* **1** obtain, esp. by care or effort; acquire (*managed to procure a copy*). **2** bring about (*procured their dismissal*). **3** (also *absol.*) obtain (women) for prostitution. □ **procurable** *adj.* **procural** *n.* **procurement** *n.* [ME f. OF *procurer* f. L *procurare* take care of, manage (as PRO-¹, *curare* see to)]

procurer /prəˈkjʊərə(r)/ *n.* (*fem.* **procuress** /-rɪs/) a person who obtains women for prostitution. [ME f. AF *procurour*, OF *procureur* f. L *procurator*: see PROCURATOR]

prod *v. & n.* —*v.* (**prodded, prodding**) 1 *tr.* poke with the finger or a pointed object. 2 *tr.* stimulate to action. 3 *intr.* (foll. by *at*) make a prodding motion. —*n.* 1 a poke or thrust. 2 a stimulus to action. 3 a pointed instrument. □ **prodder** *n.* [16th c.: perh. imit.]

prodigal /ˈprɒdɪg(ə)l/ *adj. & n.* —*adj.* 1 recklessly wasteful. 2 (foll. by *of*) lavish. —*n.* 1 a prodigal person. 2 (in full **prodigal son**) a repentant wastrel, returned wanderer, etc. (Luke 15:11–32). □ **prodigality** /-ˈɡælɪtɪ/ *n.* **prodigally** *adv.* [med.L *prodigalis* f. L *prodigus* lavish]

prodigious /prəˈdɪdʒəs/ *adj.* 1 marvellous or amazing. 2 enormous. 3 abnormal. □ **prodigiously** *adv.* **prodigiousness** *n.* [L *prodigiosus* (as PRODIGY)]

prodigy /ˈprɒdɪdʒɪ/ *n.* (*pl.* **-ies**) 1 a person endowed with exceptional qualities or abilities, esp. a precocious child. 2 a marvellous thing, esp. one out of the ordinary course of nature. 3 (foll. by *of*) a wonderful example (of a quality). [L *prodigium* portent]

produce *v. & n.* —*v.tr.* /prəˈdjuːs/ 1 bring forward for consideration, inspection, or use (*will produce evidence*). 2 manufacture (goods) from raw materials etc. 3 bear or yield (offspring, fruit, a harvest, etc.). 4 bring into existence. 5 cause or bring about (a reaction etc.). 6 *Geom.* extend or continue (a line). 7 **a** bring (a play, performer, book, etc.) before the public. **b** supervise the production of (a film, broadcast, etc.). —*n.* /ˈprɒdjuːs/ 1 **a** what is produced, esp. agricultural and natural products collectively (*dairy produce*). **b** an amount of this. 2 (often foll. by *of*) a result (of labour, efforts, etc.). □ **producible** /prəˈdjuːsɪb(ə)l/ *adj.* **producibility** /prədjuːsɪˈbɪlɪtɪ/ *n.* [ME f. L *producere* (as PRO-¹, *ducere duct-* lead)]

producer /prəˈdjuːsə(r)/ *n.* 1 *Econ.* a person who produces goods or commodities. 2 **a** a person generally responsible for the production of a film or play (apart from the direction of the acting). **b** *Brit.* the director of a play or broadcast programme.

product /ˈprɒdʌkt/ *n.* 1 a thing or substance produced by natural process or manufacture. 2 a result (*the product of their labours*). 3 *Math.* a quantity obtained by multiplying quantities together. [ME f. L *productum*, neut. past part. of *producere* PRODUCE]

production /prəˈdʌkʃ(ə)n/ *n.* 1 the act or an instance of producing; the process of being produced. 2 the process of being manufactured, esp. in large quantities (*go into production*). 3 a total yield. 4 a thing produced, esp. a literary or artistic work, a film, play, etc. □ **production line** a systematized sequence of mechanical or manual operations involved in producing a commodity. □ **productional** *n.* [ME f. OF f. L *productio -onis* (as PRODUCT)]

productive /prəˈdʌktɪv/ *adj.* 1 of or engaged in the production of goods. 2 producing much (*productive soil; a productive writer*). 3 (foll. by *of*) producing or giving rise to (*productive of great*

annoyance). □ **productively** *adv.* **productiveness** *n.* [F *productif -ive* or LL *productivus* (as PRODUCT)]

productivity /ˌprɒdʌkˈtɪvɪtɪ/ *n.* 1 the capacity to produce. 2 the quality or state of being productive. 3 the effectiveness of productive effort, esp. in industry. 4 production per unit of effort.

proem /ˈprəʊɪm/ *n.* 1 a preface or preamble to a book or speech. 2 a beginning or prelude. □ **proemial** /-ˈiːmɪəl/ *adj.* [ME f. OF *proeme* or L *prooemium* f. Gk *prooimion* prelude (as PRO-², *oimē* song)]

Prof. *abbr.* Professor.

prof /prɒf/ *n. colloq.* a professor. [abbr.]

profane /prəˈfeɪn/ *adj. & v.* —*adj.* 1 not belonging to what is sacred or biblical; secular. 2 irreverent, blasphemous. 3 (of a rite etc.) heathen. 4 not initiated into religious rites or any esoteric knowledge. —*v.tr.* 1 treat (a sacred thing) with irreverence or disregard. 2 violate or pollute (what is entitled to respect). □ **profanation** /ˌprɒfəˈneɪʃ(ə)n/ *n.* **profanely** *adv.* **profaneness** *n.* **profaner** *n.* [ME *prophane* f. OF *prophane* or med.L *prophanus* f. L *profanus* before (i.e. outside) the temple, not sacred (as PRO-¹, *fanum* temple)]

profanity /prəˈfænɪtɪ/ *n.* (*pl.* **-ies**) 1 a profane act. 2 profane language; blasphemy. [LL *profanitas* (as PROFANE)]

profess /prəˈfes/ *v.* 1 *tr.* claim openly to have (a quality or feeling). 2 *tr.* (foll. by *to* + infin.) pretend. 3 *tr.* declare (*profess ignorance*). 4 *tr.* affirm one's faith in or allegiance to. 5 *tr.* receive into a religious order under vows. 6 *tr.* have as one's profession or business. [ME f. L *profitēri profess-* declare publicly (as PRO-¹, *fatēri* confess)]

professed /prəˈfest/ *adj.* 1 self-acknowledged (*a professed Christian*). 2 alleged, ostensible. 3 claiming to be duly qualified. 4 (of a monk or nun) having taken the vows of a religious order. □ **professedly** /-sɪdlɪ/ *adv.* (in senses 1, 2).

profession /prəˈfeʃ(ə)n/ *n.* 1 a vocation or calling, esp. one that involves some branch of advanced learning or science (*the medical profession*). 2 a body of persons engaged in a profession. 3 a declaration or avowal. 4 a declaration of belief in a religion. 5 **a** the declaration or vows made on entering a religious order. **b** the ceremony or fact of being professed in a religious order. □ **professionless** *adj.* [ME f. OF f. L *professio -onis* (as PROFESS)]

professional /prəˈfeʃən(ə)l/ *adj. & n.* —*adj.* 1 of or belonging to or connected with a profession. 2 **a** having or showing the skill of a professional, competent. **b** worthy of a professional (*professional conduct*). 3 engaged in a specified activity as one's main paid occupation (*a professional boxer*). 4 *derog.* engaged in a specified activity regarded with disfavour (*a professional agitator*). —*n.* a professional person. □ **professional foul** a deliberate foul in football etc., esp. to prevent an opponent from scoring. □ **professionally** *adv.*

professionalism /prəˈfeʃənəˌlɪz(ə)m/ *n.* the qualities or typical features of a profession or of professionals. □ **professionalize** *v.tr.* (also **-ise**).

professor /prəˈfesə(r)/ *n.* 1 **a** (often as a title) a university academic of the highest rank; the holder of a university chair. **b** *US* a university teacher. 2 a person who professes a religion. □

professorate *n.* **professorial** /₁prɒfɪˈsɔːrɪəl/ *adj.* **professorially** /₁prɒfɪˈsɔːrɪəlɪ/ *adv.* **professoriate** /₁prɒfɪˈsɔːrɪət/ *n.* **professorship** *n.* [ME f. OF *professeur* or L *professor* (as PROFESS)]

proffer /ˈprɒfə(r)/ *v.tr.* (esp. as **proffered** *adj.*) offer (a gift, services, a hand, etc.). [ME f. AF & OF *proffrir* (as PRO-¹, *offrir* OFFER)]

proficient /prəˈfɪʃ(ə)nt/ *adj.* & *n.* —*adj.* (often foll. by *in*, *at*) adept, expert. —*n.* a person who is proficient. □ **proficiency** /-sɪ/ *n.* **proficiently** *adv.* [L *proficiens proficient-* (as PROFIT)]

profile /ˈprəʊfaɪl/ *n.* & *v.* —*n.* **1 a** an outline (esp. of a human face) as seen from one side. **b** a representation of this. **2** a short biographical or character sketch. **3** *Statistics* a representation by a graph or chart of information (esp. on certain characteristics) recorded in a quantified form. **4** a characteristic personal manner or attitude. —*v.tr.* **1** represent in profile. **2** give a profile to. □ **in profile** as seen from one side. **keep a low profile** remain inconspicuous. □ **profiler** *n.* **profilist** *n.* [obs. It. *profilo*, *profilare* (as PRO-¹, *filare* spin f. L *filare* f. *filum* thread)]

profit /ˈprɒfɪt/ *n.* & *v.* —*n.* **1** an advantage or benefit. **2** financial gain; excess of returns over outlay. —*v.* (**profited**, **profiting**) **1** *tr.* (also *absol.*) be beneficial to. **2** *intr.* obtain an advantage or benefit (*profited by the experience*). □ **at a profit** with financial gain. **profit margin** the profit remaining in a business after costs have been deducted. □ **profitless** *adj.* [ME f. OF f. L *profectus* progress, profit f. *proficere profect-* advance (as PRO-¹, *facere* do)]

profitable /ˈprɒfɪtəb(ə)l/ *adj.* **1** yielding profit; lucrative. **2** beneficial; useful. □ **profitability** /-ˈbɪlɪtɪ/ *n.* **profitableness** *n.* **profitably** *adv.* [ME f. OF (as PROFIT)]

profiteer /₁prɒfɪˈtɪə(r)/ *v.* & *n.* —*v.intr.* make or seek to make excessive profits, esp. illegally or in black market conditions. —*n.* a person who profiteers.

profiterole /prəˈfɪtə₁rəʊl/ *n.* a small hollow case of choux pastry usu. filled with cream and covered with chocolate sauce. [F, dimin. of *profit* PROFIT]

profligate /ˈprɒflɪgət/ *adj.* & *n.* —*adj.* **1** licentious; dissolute. **2** recklessly extravagant. —*n.* a profligate person. □ **profligacy** /-gəsɪ/ *n.* **profligately** *adv.* [L *profligatus* dissolute, past part. of *profligare* overthrow, ruin (as PRO-¹, *fligere* strike down)]

pro forma /prəʊ ˈfɔːmə/ *adv.*, *adj.*, & *n.* —*adv.* & *adj.* as or being a matter of form. —*n.* (in full **pro-forma invoice**) an invoice sent in advance of goods supplied. [L]

profound /prəˈfaʊnd/ *adj.* (**profounder**, **profoundest**) **1 a** having or showing great knowledge or insight (*a profound treatise*). **b** demanding deep study or thought (*profound doctrines*). **2** (of a state or quality) deep, intense, unqualified (*a profound sleep*; *profound indifference*). **3** at or extending to a great depth (*profound crevasses*). **4** (of a sigh) deep-drawn. □ **profoundly** *adv.* **profoundness** *n.* **profundity** /prəˈfʌndɪtɪ/ *n.* (*pl.* **-ies**). [ME f. AF & OF *profund*, *profond* f. L *profundus* deep (as PRO-¹, *fundus* bottom)]

profuse /prəˈfjuːs/ *adj.* **1** (often foll. by *in*, *of*) lavish; extravagant (*was profuse in her generosity*). **2** (of a thing) exuberantly plentiful; abundant (*profuse bleeding*; *a profuse variety*). □ **profusely** *adv.* **profuseness** *n.* **profusion** /prəˈfjuːʒ(ə)n/ *n.*

[ME f. L *profusus* past part. of *profundere profus-* (as PRO-¹, *fundere fus-* pour)]

progenitor /prəʊˈdʒenɪtə(r)/ *n.* **1** the ancestor of a person, animal, or plant. **2** a political or intellectual predecessor. □ **progenitorial** /-ˈtɔːrɪəl/ *adj.* **progenitorship** *n.* [ME f. OF *progeniteur* f. L *progenitor -oris* f. *progignere progenit-* (as PRO-¹, *gignere* beget)]

progeny /ˈprɒdʒɪnɪ/ *n.* **1** the offspring of a person or other organism. **2** a descendant or descendants. **3** an outcome or issue. [ME f. OF *progenie* f. L *progenies* f. *progignere* (as PROGENITOR)]

progesterone /prəʊˈdʒestə₁rəʊn/ *n.* a steroid hormone which stimulates the preparation of the uterus for pregnancy. [*progestin* (as PRO-², GESTATION) + *luteosterone* f. *corpus luteum* a body in the ovary + STEROL]

prognosis /prɒgˈnəʊsɪs/ *n.* (*pl.* **prognoses** /-siːz/) **1** a forecast; a prognostication. **2** a forecast of the course of a disease. [LL f. Gk *prognōsis* (as PRO-², *gignōskō* know)]

prognostic /prɒgˈnɒstɪk/ *n.* & *adj.* —*n.* **1** (often foll. by *of*) an advance indication or omen, esp. of the course of a disease etc. **2** a prediction; a forecast. *adj.* foretelling; predictive (*prognostic of a good result*). □ **prognostically** *adv.* [ME f. OF *pronostique* f. L *prognosticum* f. Gk *prognōstikon* neut. of *prognōstikos* (as PROGNOSIS)]

prognosticate /prɒgˈnɒstɪ₁keɪt/ *v.tr.* **1** (often foll. by *that* + clause) foretell; foresee; prophesy. **2** (of a thing) betoken; indicate (future events etc.). □ **prognosticable** /-kəb(ə)l/ *adj.* **prognostication** /-ˈkeɪʃ(ə)n/ *n.* **prognosticative** /-kətɪv/ *adj.* **prognosticator** *n.* **prognosticatory** *adj.* [med.L *prognosticare* (as PROGNOSTIC)]

programme /ˈprəʊgræm/ *n.* & *v.* (US **program**) —*n.* **1** a usu. printed list of a series of events, performers, etc. at a public function etc. **2** a radio or television broadcast. **3** a plan of future events (*the programme is dinner and an early night*). **4** a course or series of studies, lectures, etc.; a syllabus. **5** (usu. **program**) a series of coded instructions to control the operation of a computer or other machine. —*v.tr.* (**programmed**, **programming**; US **programed**, **programing**) **1** make a programme or definite plan of. **2** (usu. **program**) express (a problem) or instruct (a computer) by means of a program. □ **programmable** *adj.* **programmability** /-ˈbɪlɪtɪ/ *n.* **programmatic** /-grəˈmætɪk/ *adj.* **programmatically** /-grəˈmætɪkəlɪ/ *adv.* **programmer** *n.* [LL *programma* f. Gk *programma -atos* f. *prographō* write publicly (as PRO-², *graphō* write): spelling after F *programme*]

progress /ˈprəʊgres/ *n.* & *v.* —*n.* **1** forward or onward movement towards a destination. **2** advance or development towards completion, betterment, etc.; improvement (*has made little progress this term*; *the progress of civilization*). **3** *Brit. archaic* a State journey or official tour, esp. by royalty. —*v.* **1** *intr.* /prəˈgres/ move or be moved forward or onward; continue (*the argument is progressing*). **2** *intr.* /prəˈgres/ advance or develop towards completion, improvement, etc. (*science progresses*). **3** *tr.* cause (work etc.) to make regular progress. □ **in progress** in the course of developing; going on. **progress-chaser** a person employed to check the regular progress of manufacturing work. **progress report** an account of progress made. [ME f. L *progressus* f. *progredi* (as PRO-[1], *gradi* walk: (v.) readopted f. US after becoming obs. in Brit. use in the 17th c.]

progression /prəˈgreʃ(ə)n/ *n.* **1** the act or an instance of progressing (*a mode of progression*). **2** a succession; a series. **3** *Math.* **a** = *arithmetic progression*. **b** = *geometric progression*. **4** *Mus.* passing from one note or chord to another. □ **progressional** *adj.* [ME f. OF *progression* or L *progressio* (as PROGRESS)]

progressive /prəˈgresɪv/ *adj.* & *n.* —*adj.* **1** moving forward (*progressive motion*). **2** proceeding step by step; cumulative (*progressive drug use*). **3 a** (of a political party, government, etc.) favouring or implementing rapid progress or social reform. **b** modern; efficient (*this is a progressive company*). **4** (of disease, violence, etc.) increasing in severity or extent. **5** (of taxation) at rates increasing with the sum taxed. **6** (of a card-game, dance, etc.) with periodic changes of partners. **7** (of education) informal and without strict discipline, stressing individual needs. —*n.* (also **Progressive**) an advocate of progressive political policies. □ **progressively** *adv.* **progressiveness** *n.* **progressivism** *n.* **progressivist** *n.* & *adj.* [F *progressif -ive* or med.L *progressivus* (as PROGRESS)]

prohibit /prəˈhɪbɪt/ *v.tr.* (**prohibited, prohibiting**) (often foll. by *from* + verbal noun) **1** formally forbid, esp. by authority. **2** prevent; make impossible (*his accident prohibits him from playing football*). □ **prohibited degrees** degrees of blood relationship within which marriage is forbidden. □ **prohibiter** *n.* **prohibitor** *n.* [ME f. L *prohibēre* (as PRO-[1], *habēre* hold)]

prohibition /ˌprəʊhɪˈbɪʃ(ə)n, ˌprəʊɪˈb-/ *n.* **1** the act or an instance of forbidding; a state of being forbidden. **2** *Law* an edict or order that forbids. **3** (usu. **Prohibition**) the prevention by law of the manufacture and sale of alcohol, esp. in the US (1920–33). □ **prohibitionary** *adj.* **prohibitionist** *n.* [ME f. OF *prohibition* or L *prohibitio* (as PROHIBIT)]

prohibitive /prəʊˈhɪbɪtɪv/ *adj.* **1** prohibiting. **2** (of prices, taxes, etc.) so high as to prevent purchase, use, abuse, etc. □ **prohibitively** *adv.* **prohibitiveness** *n.* **prohibitory** *adj.* [F *prohibitif -ive* or L *prohibitivus* (as PROHIBIT)]

project *n.* & *v.* /ˈprɒdʒekt/ **1** a plan; a scheme. **2** a planned undertaking. **3** a usu. long-term task undertaken by a student to be submitted for assessment. —*v.* /prəˈdʒekt/ **1** *tr.* plan or contrive (a course of action, scheme, etc.). **2** *intr.* protrude; jut out. **3** *tr.* throw; cast; impel (*projected the stone into the water*). **4** *tr.* extrapolate (results etc.) to a future time; forecast (*I project that we shall produce two million next year*). **5** *tr.* cause (light, shadow, images, etc.) to fall on a surface, screen, etc. **6** *tr.* cause (a sound, esp. the voice) to be heard at a distance. **7** *tr.* (often *refl.* or *absol.*) express or promote (oneself or a positive image) forcefully or effectively. **8** *tr.* make a projection of (the earth, sky, etc.). **9** *tr.* *Psychol.* **a** (also *absol.*) attribute (an emotion etc.) to an external object or person, esp. unconsciously. **b** (*refl.*) project (oneself) into another's feelings, the future, etc. [ME f. L *projectum* neut. past part. of *projicere* (as PRO-[1], *jacēre* throw)]

projectile /ˈprɒdʒektaɪl/ *n.* & *adj.* —*n.* **1** a missile, esp. fired by a rocket. **2** a bullet, shell, etc. fired

from a gun. **3** any object thrown as a weapon. —*adj.* **1** capable of being projected by force, esp. from a gun. **2** projecting or impelling. [mod.L *projectilis* (adj.), *-ile* (n.) (as PROJECT)]

projection /prəˈdʒekʃ(ə)n/ *n.* **1** the act or an instance of projecting; the process of being projected. **2** a thing that projects or obtrudes. **3** the presentation of an image etc. on a surface or screen. **4 a** a forecast or estimate based on present trends (*a projection of next year's profits*). **b** this process. **5 a** a mental image or preoccupation viewed as an objective reality. **b** the unconscious transfer of one's own impressions or feelings to external objects or persons. **6** the representation on a plane surface of any part of the surface of the earth or a celestial sphere. □ **projectionist** *n.* (in sense 3). [L *projectio* (as PROJECT)]

projector /prəˈdʒektə(r)/ *n.* **1 a** an apparatus containing a source of light and a system of lenses for projecting slides or film on to a screen. **b** an apparatus for projecting rays of light. **2** a person who forms or promotes a project.

prolapse /ˈprəʊlæps/ *n.* & *v.* —*n.* (also **prolapsus** /-ˈlæpsəs/) **1** the forward or downward displacement of a part or organ. **2** the prolapsed part or organ, esp. the womb or rectum. —*v.intr.* undergo prolapse. [L *prolabi prolaps-* (as PRO-[1], *labi* slip)]

prolate /ˈprəʊleɪt/ *adj.* *Geom.* (of a spheroid) lengthened in the direction of a polar diameter. □ **prolately** *adv.* [L *prolatus* past part. of *proferre* prolong (as PRO-[1], *ferre* carry)]

prole /prəʊl/ *adj.* & *n.* *derog. colloq.* —*adj.* proletarian. —*n.* a proletarian. [abbr.]

prolegomenon /ˌprəʊlɪˈgɒmɪnən/ *n.* (*pl.* **prolegomena**) (usu. in *pl.*) an introduction or preface to a book etc., esp. when critical or discursive. □ **prolegomenary** *adj.* **prolegomenous** *adj.* [L f. Gk, neut. passive pres. part. of *prolegō* (as PRO-[2], *legō* say)]

proletarian /ˌprəʊlɪˈteərɪən/ *adj.* & *n.* —*adj.* of or concerning the proletariat. —*n.* a member of the proletariat. □ **proletarianism** *n.* **proletarianize** *v.tr.* (also **-ise**). [L *proletarius* one who served the State not with property but with offspring (*proles*)]

proletariat /ˌprəʊlɪˈteərɪət/ *n.* (also **proletariate**) **1** *Econ.* wage-earners collectively, esp. those without capital and dependent on selling their labour. **2** esp. *derog.* the lowest class of the community, esp. when considered as uncultured. [F *prolétariat* (as PROLETARIAN)]

pro-life /prəʊˈlaɪf/ *adj.* in favour of preserving life, esp. in opposing abortion.

proliferate /prəˈlɪfəˌreɪt/ *v.* **1** *intr.* reproduce; increase rapidly in numbers; grow by multiplication. **2** *tr.* produce (cells etc.) rapidly. □ **proliferation** /-ˈreɪʃ(ə)n/ *n.* **proliferative** /-rətɪv/ *adj.* [back-form. f. *proliferation* f. F *prolifération* f. *prolifère* f. L *proles* offspring]

prolific /prəˈlɪfɪk/ *adj.* **1** producing many offspring or much output. **2** (often foll. by *of*) abundantly productive. **3** (often foll. by *in*) abounding, copious. □ **prolificacy** *n.* **prolifically** *adv.* **prolificness** *n.* [med.L *prolificus* (as PROLIFERATE)]

prolix /ˈprəʊlɪks, prəˈlɪks/ *adj.* (of speech, writing, etc.) lengthy; tedious. □ **prolixity** /-ˈlɪksɪtɪ/ *n.* **prolixly** *adv.* [ME f. OF *prolixe* or L *prolixus* poured forth, extended (as PRO-¹, *liquĕre* be liquid)]

prologue /ˈprəʊlɒg/ n. & v. —n. **1 a** a preliminary speech, poem, etc., esp. introducing a play (cf. EPILOGUE). **b** the actor speaking the prologue. **2** (usu. foll. by *to*) any act or event serving as an introduction. —v.tr. (**prologues**, **prologued**, **prologuing**) introduce with or provide with a prologue. [ME *prolog* f. OF *prologue* f. L *prologus* f. Gk *prologos* (as PRO-², *logos* speech)]

prolong /prəˈlɒŋ/ v.tr. **1** extend (an action, condition, etc.) in time or space. **2** lengthen the pronunciation of (a syllable etc.). **3** (as **prolonged** *adj.*) lengthy, esp. tediously so. □ **prolongation** /ˌprəʊlɒŋˈgeɪʃ(ə)n/ n. **prolongedly** /-ɪdlɪ/ *adv.* **prolonger** n. [ME f. OF *prolonger* & f. LL *prolongare* (as PRO-¹, *longus* long)]

prom n. colloq. **1** Brit. = PROMENADE n. 1a. **2** Brit. = *promenade concert*. **3** US = PROMENADE n. 3. [abbr.]

promenade /ˌprɒməˈnɑːd/ n. & v. —n. **1 a** Brit. a paved public walk along the sea front at a resort. **b** any paved public walk. **2** a walk, or sometimes a ride or drive, taken esp. for display, social intercourse, etc. **3** US a school or university ball or dance. —v. **1** *intr.* make a promenade. **2** *tr.* lead (a person etc.) about a place esp. for display. **3** *tr.* make a promenade through (a place). □ **promenade concert** a concert at which the audience, or part of it, can stand, sit on the floor, or move about. **promenade deck** an upper deck on a passenger ship where passengers may promenade. [F f. *se promener* walk, refl. of *promener* take for a walk]

promenader /ˌprɒməˈnɑːdə(r)/ n. **1** a person who promenades. **2** Brit. a person who attends a promenade concert, esp. regularly.

promethium /prəˈmiːθɪəm/ n. Chem. a radioactive metallic element of the lanthanide series occurring in nuclear-waste material. [*Prometheus* a character in Gk myth]

prominence /ˈprɒmɪnəns/ n. **1** the state of being prominent. **2** a prominent thing, esp. a jutting outcrop, mountain, etc. [obs.F f. L *prominentia* jutting out (as PROMINENT)]

prominent /ˈprɒmɪnənt/ adj. **1** jutting out; projecting. **2** conspicuous. **3** distinguished; important. □ **prominency** n. **prominently** adv. [L *prominēre* jut out: cf. EMINENT]

promiscuous /prəˈmɪskjʊəs/ adj. **1 a** (of a person) having frequent and diverse sexual relationships, esp. transient ones. **b** (of sexual relationships) of this kind. **2** of mixed and indiscriminate composition or kinds; indiscriminate (*promiscuous hospitality*). **3** colloq. carelessly irregular; casual. □ **promiscuity** /-ˈskjuːɪtɪ/ n. **promiscuously** adv. **promiscuousness** n. [L *promiscuus* (as PRO-¹, *miscēre* mix)]

promise /ˈprɒmɪs/ n. & v. —n. **1** an assurance that one will or will not undertake a certain action, behaviour, etc. (*a promise of help*; *gave a promise to be generous*). **2** a sign or signs of future achievements, good results, etc. (*a writer of great promise*). —v.tr. **1** (usu. foll. by *to* + infin., or *that* + clause; also *absol.*) make (a person) a promise, esp. to do, give, or procure a thing (*I promise you a fair hearing*; *they promise not to be late*; *promised that he would be there*; *cannot positively promise*). **2 a** afford expectations of (*the discussions promise future problems*; *promises to be a good cook*). **b** (foll. by *to* + infin.) seem likely to (*is promising

to rain). **3** colloq. assure, confirm (*I promise you, it will not be easy*). □ **the promised land 1** Bibl. Canaan (Gen. 12:7 etc.). **2** any desired place, esp. heaven. **promise oneself** look forward to (a pleasant time etc.). **promise well** (or **ill** etc.) hold out good (or bad etc.) prospects. □ **promisee** /-ˈsiː/ n. esp. Law. **promiser** n. **promisor** n. esp. Law. [ME f. L *promissum* neut. past part. of *promittere* put forth, promise (as PRO-¹, *mittere* send)]

promising /ˈprɒmɪsɪŋ/ adj. likely to turn out well; hopeful; full of promise (*a promising start*). □ **promisingly** adv.

promissory /ˈprɒmɪsərɪ/ adj. **1** conveying or implying a promise. **2** (often foll. by *of*) full of promise. □ **promissory note** a signed document containing a written promise to pay a stated sum to a specified person or the bearer at a specified date or on demand. [med.L *promissorius* f. L *promissor* (as PROMISE)]

promo /ˈprəʊməʊ/ n. & adj. colloq. —n. (pl. **-os**) **1** publicity, advertising. **2** a trailer for a television programme. —adj. promotional. [abbr.]

promontory /ˈprɒməntərɪ/ n. (pl. **-ies**) a point of high land jutting out into the sea etc.; a headland. [med.L *promontorium* alt. (after *mons montis* mountain) f. L *promunturium* (perh. f. PRO-¹, *mons*)]

promote /prəˈməʊt/ v.tr. **1** (often foll. by *to*) advance or raise (a person) to a higher office, rank, etc. (*was promoted to captain*). **2** help forward; encourage; support actively (a cause, process, desired result, etc.) (*promoted women's suffrage*). **3** publicize and sell (a product). **4** attempt to ensure the passing of (a private act of parliament). □ **promotable** adj. **promotability** /-ˈbɪlɪtɪ/ n. **promotion** /-ˈməʊʃ(ə)n/ n. **promotional** /-ˈməʊʃ(ə)n/ adj. **promotive** adj. [ME f. L *promovēre promot-* (as PRO-¹, *movēre* move)]

promoter /prəˈməʊtə(r)/ n. **1** a person who promotes. **2** a person who finances, organizes, etc. a sporting event, theatrical production, etc. **3** (in full **company promoter**) a person who promotes the formation of a joint-stock company. [earlier *promotour* f. AF f. med.L *promotor* (as PROMOTE)]

prompt adj., adv., v., & n. —adj. **1 a** acting with alacrity; ready. **b** made, done, etc. readily or at once (*a prompt reply*). **2 a** (of a payment) made forthwith. **b** (of goods) for immediate delivery and payment. —adv. punctually (*at six o'clock prompt*). —v.tr. **1** (usu. foll. by *to*, or *to* + infin.) incite; urge (*prompted them to action*). **2 a** (also *absol.*) supply a forgotten word, sentence, etc., to (an actor, reciter, etc.). **b** assist (a hesitating speaker) with a suggestion. **3** give rise to; inspire (a feeling, thought, action, etc.). —n. **1** an act of prompting. **2** a thing said to help the memory of an actor etc. **3** = PROMPTER 2. **4** Computing an indication or sign on a VDU screen to show that the system is waiting for input. □ **prompting** n. **promptitude** n. **promptly** adv. **promptness** n. [ME f. OF *prompt* or L *promptus* past part. of *promere prompt-* produce (as PRO-¹, *emere* take)]

prompter /ˈprɒmptə(r)/ n. **1** a person who prompts. **2** Theatr. a person seated out of sight of the audience who prompts the actors.

promulgate /ˈprɒməlˌgeɪt/ v.tr. **1** make known to the public; disseminate; promote (a cause etc.). **2** proclaim (a decree, news. etc.). □ **promulgation** /-ˈgeɪʃ(ə)n/ n. **promulgator** n. [L *promulgare* (as PRO-¹, *mulgēre* milk, cause to come forth)]

prone adj. **1 a** lying face downwards. **b** lying flat; prostrate. **c** having the front part downwards, esp. the palm of the hand. **2** (usu. foll. by *to*, or *to* + infin.) disposed or liable, esp. to a bad action, condition, etc. (*is prone to bite his nails*). **3** (usu. in *comb.*) more than usually likely to suffer (*accident-prone*). □ **pronely** adv. **proneness** /ˈprəʊnnɪs/ n. [ME f. L *pronus* f. *pro* forwards]

prong n. & v. —n. each of two or more projecting pointed parts at the end of a fork etc. —v.tr. **1** pierce or stab with a fork. **2** turn up (soil) with a fork. □ **pronged** adj. (also in *comb.*). [ME (also *prang*, perh. rel. to MLG *prange* pinching instrument]

pronominal /prəʊˈnɒmɪn(ə)l/ adj. of, concerning, or being, a pronoun. □ **pronominalize** v.tr. (also -**ise**). **pronominally** adv. [LL *pronominalis* f. L *pronomen* (as PRO-¹, *nominis* noun)]

pronoun /ˈprəʊnaʊn/ n. a word used instead of and to indicate a noun already mentioned or known, esp. to avoid repetition (e.g. *we, their, this, ourselves*). [PRO-¹, + NOUN, after F *pronom*, L *pronomen* (as PRO-¹, *nomen* name)]

pronounce /prəˈnaʊns/ v. **1** tr. (also *absol.*) utter or speak (words, sounds, etc.) in a certain way. **2** tr. **a** utter or deliver (a judgement, sentence, curse, etc.) formally or solemnly. **b** proclaim or announce officially (*I pronounce you man and wife*). **3** tr. state or declare, as being one's opinion (*the apples were pronounced excellent*). **4** intr. (usu. foll. by *on, for, against, in favour of*) pass judgement; give one's opinion (*pronounced for the defendant*). □ **pronounceable** /-səb(ə)l/ adj. **pronouncement** n. **pronouncer** n. [ME f. OF *pronuncier* f. L *pronuntiare* (as PRO-¹, *nuntiare* announce f. *nuntius* messenger)]

pronounced /prəˈnaʊnst/ adj. **1** (of a word, sound, etc.) uttered. **2** strongly marked; decided (*a pronounced flavour; a pronounced limp*). □ **pronouncedly** /-ˈnaʊnsɪdlɪ/ adv.

pronto /ˈprɒntəʊ/ adv. colloq. promptly, quickly. [Sp. f. L (as PROMPT)]

pronunciation /prəˌnʌnsɪˈeɪʃ(ə)n/ n. **1** the way in which a word is pronounced, esp. with reference to a standard. **2** the act or an instance of pronouncing. **3** a person's way of pronouncing words etc. [ME f. OF *prononciation* or L *pronuntiatio* (as PRONOUNCE)]

proof /pruːf/ n., adj., & v. —n. **1** facts, evidence, argument, etc. establishing or helping to establish a fact (*proof of their honesty; no proof that he was there*). **2** a demonstration or act of proving (*not capable of proof; in proof of my assertion*). **3** a test or trial (*the proof of the pudding is in the eating*). **4** the standard of strength of distilled alcoholic liquors. **5** Printing a trial impression taken from type or film, used for making corrections before final printing. **6** a photographic print made for selection etc. —adj. **1** impervious to penetration, ill effects, etc. (*proof against the severest weather*). **2** (in *comb.*) able to withstand damage or destruction by a specified agent (*soundproof; childproof*). —v.tr. **1** make (something) proof, esp. make (fabric) waterproof. **2** make a proof of (a printed work, engraving, etc.). □

proof positive absolutely certain proof. **proof-sheet** a sheet of printer's proof. **proof spirit** a mixture of alcohol and water having proof strength. □ **proofless** adj. [ME *prof*, earlier *pref* etc. f. OF *proeve, prueve* f. LL *proba* f. L *probare* (see PROVE); adj. and sometimes v. formed app. by ellipsis f. phr. *of proof* = proved to be impenetrable]

proofread /ˈpruːfriːd/ v.tr. (past and past part. **-read** /-red/) read (printer's proofs) and mark any errors. □ **proofreader** n. **proofreading** n.

prop¹ n. & v. —n. **1** a rigid support, esp. one not an integral part of the thing supported. **2** a person who supplies support, assistance, comfort, etc. **3** Rugby Football a forward at either end of the front row of a scrum. —v. (**propped, propping**) tr. (often foll. by *against, up,* etc.) support with or as if with a prop (*propped him against the wall; propped it up with a brick*). [ME prob. f. MDu. *proppe*: cf. MLG, MDu. *proppen* (v.)]

prop² /prɒp/ n. Theatr. colloq. **1** = PROPERTY 3. **2** (in *pl.*) a property man or mistress. [abbr.]

prop³ /prɒp/ n. colloq. an aircraft propeller. □ **prop-jet** a turboprop. [abbr.]

propaganda /ˌprɒpəˈgændə/ n. **1** an organized programme of publicity, selected information, etc., used to propagate a doctrine, practice, etc. **2** usu. derog. the information, doctrines, etc., propagated in this way. [It. f. mod.L *congregatio de propaganda fide* congregation for propagation of the faith]

propagandist /ˌprɒpəˈgændɪst/ n. a member or agent of a propaganda organization; a person who spreads propaganda. □ **propagandism** n. **propagandistic** /-ˈdɪstɪk/ adj. **propagandistically** /-ˈdɪstɪkəlɪ/ adv. **propagandize** v.intr. & tr. (also -**ise**).

propagate /ˈprɒpəgeɪt/ v.tr. **1 a** breed specimens of (a plant, animal, etc.) by natural processes from the parent stock. **b** (*refl.* or *absol.*) (of a plant, animal, etc.) reproduce itself. **2** disseminate; spread (a statement, belief, theory, etc.). **3** hand down (a quality etc.) from one generation to another. **4** extend the operation of; transmit (a vibration, earthquake, etc.). □ **propagation** /-ˈgeɪʃ(ə)n/ n. **propagative** adj. [L *propagare propagat-* multiply plants from layers, f. *propago* (as PRO-¹, *pangere* fix, layer)]

propagator /ˈprɒpəgeɪtə(r)/ n. **1** a person or thing that propagates. **2** a small box that can be heated, used for germinating seeds or raising seedlings.

propane /ˈprəʊpeɪn/ n. a gaseous hydrocarbon of the alkane series used as bottled fuel. [*propionic* acid (f. F *propionique*) + -ANE]

propel /prəˈpel/ v.tr. (**propelled, propelling**) **1** drive or push forward. **2** urge on; encourage. □ **propelling pencil** a pencil with a replaceable lead moved upward by twisting the outer case. [ME, = expel, f. L *propellere* (as PRO-¹, *pellere puls-* drive)]

propellant /prəˈpelənt/ n. **1** a thing that propels. **2** an explosive that fires bullets etc. from a firearm. **3** a substance used as a reagent in a rocket engine etc. to provide thrust.

propellent /prəˈpelənt/ adj. propelling; capable of driving or pushing forward.

propeller /prəˈpelə(r)/ n. **1** a person or thing that propels. **2** a revolving shaft with blades, esp. for propelling a ship or aircraft.

propensity /prə'pensɪtɪ/ n. (pl. **-ies**) an inclination or tendency (has a propensity for wandering). [propense f. L propensus inclined, past part. of propendēre (as PRO-¹, pendēre hang)]

proper /'prɒpə(r)/ adj. & adv. —adj. **1 a** accurate, correct (in the proper sense of the word; gave him the proper amount). **b** fit, suitable, right (at the proper time; do it the proper way). **2** decent; respectable, esp. excessively so. **3** (usu. foll. by to) belonging or relating exclusively or distinctively (with the respect proper to them). **4** (usu. placed after noun) strictly so called; real; genuine (this is the crypt, not the cathedral proper). **5** colloq. thorough; complete (had a proper row about it). —adv. Brit. dial. or colloq. **1** completely; very (felt proper daft). **2** (with reference to speech) in a genteel manner (learn to talk proper). □ **proper fraction** a fraction that is less than unity, with the numerator less than the denominator. **proper noun** (or **name**) Gram. a name used for an individual person, place, animal, country, title, etc., and spelt with a capital letter, e.g. Jane, London, Everest. □ **properness** n. [ME f. OF propre f. L proprius one's own, special]

properly /'prɒpəlɪ/ adv. **1** fittingly; suitably (do it properly). **2** accurately; correctly (properly speaking). **3** rightly (he very properly refused). **4** with decency; respectably (behave properly). **5** colloq. thoroughly (they were properly ashamed).

propertied /'prɒpətɪd/ adj. having property, esp. land.

property /'prɒpətɪ/ n. (pl. **-ies**) **1 a** something owned; a possession, esp. a house, land, etc. **b** possessions collectively, esp. real estate (has money in property). **2** an attribute, quality, or characteristic (has the property of dissolving grease). **3** a moveable object used on a theatre stage, in a film, etc. □ **property man** (or **mistress**) a man (or woman) in charge of theatrical properties. **property tax** a tax levied directly on property. [ME through AF f. OF propriété f. L proprietas -tatis (as PROPER)]

prophecy /'prɒfɪsɪ/ n. (pl. **-ies**) **1 a** a prophetic utterance, esp. Biblical. **b** a prediction of future events (a prophecy of massive inflation). **2** the faculty, function, or practice of prophesying (the gift of prophecy). [ME f. OF profecie f. LL prophetia f. Gk prophēteia (as PROPHET)]

prophesy /'prɒfɪˌsaɪ/ v. (**-ies**, **-ied**) **1** tr. (usu. foll. by that, who, etc.) foretell (an event etc.). **2** intr. speak as a prophet; foretell future events. □ **prophesier** /-ˌsaɪə(r)/ n. [ME f. OF profecier (as PROPHECY)]

prophet /'prɒfɪt/ n. (fem. **prophetess** /-tɪs/) **1 a** teacher or interpreter of the supposed will of God, esp. any of the Old Testament or Hebrew prophets. **2 a** a person who foretells events. **b** a person who advocates and speaks innovatively for a cause (a prophet of the new order). **3** (**the Prophet**) **a** Muhammad. **b** Joseph Smith, founder of the Mormons, or one of his successors. **c** (in pl.) the prophetic writings of the Old Testament. □ **prophethood** n. **prophetism** n. **prophetship** n. [ME f. OF prophete f. L propheta, prophetes f. Gk prophētēs spokesman (as PRO-², phētēs speaker f. phēmi speak)]

prophetic /prə'fetɪk/ adj. **1** (often foll. by of) containing a prediction; predicting. **2** of or concerning a prophet. □ **prophetical** adj. **prophetically** adv. **propheticism** /-ˌsɪz(ə)m/ n.

[F prophétique or LL propheticus f. Gk prophētikos (as PROPHET)]

prophylactic /ˌprɒfɪ'læktɪk/ adj. & n. —adj. tending to prevent disease. —n. **1** a preventive medicine or course of action. **2** esp. US a condom. [F prophylactique f. Gk prophulaktikos f. prophulassō (as PRO-², phulassō guard)]

prophylaxis /ˌprɒfɪ'læksɪs/ n. (pl. **prophylaxes** /-siːz/) preventive treatment against disease. [mod.L f. PRO-² + Gk phulaxis act of guarding]

propinquity /prə'pɪŋkwɪtɪ/ n. **1** nearness in space; proximity. **2** close kinship. **3** similarity. [ME f. OF propinquité or L propinquitas f. propinquus near f. prope near to]

propitiate /prə'pɪʃɪˌeɪt/ v.tr. appease (an offended person etc.). □ **propitiation** n. **propitiator** n. [L propitiare (as PROPITIOUS)]

propitiatory /prə'pɪʃɪətərɪ/ adj. serving or intended to propitiate (a propitiatory smile). □ **propitiatorily** adv. [ME f. LL propitiatorius (as PROPITIATE)]

propitious /prə'pɪʃəs/ adj. **1** (of an omen etc.) favourable. **2** (often foll. by for, to) (of the weather, an occasion, etc.) suitable. **3** well-disposed (the fates were propitious). □ **propitiously** adv. **propitiousness** n. [ME f. OF propicieus or L propitius]

proponent /prə'pəʊnənt/ n. & adj. —n. a person advocating a motion, theory, or proposal. —adj. proposing or advocating a theory etc. [L proponere (as PROPOUND)]

proportion /prə'pɔːʃ(ə)n/ n. & v. —n. **1 a** a comparative part or share (a large proportion of the profits). **b** a comparative ratio (the proportion of births to deaths). **2** the correct or pleasing relation of things or parts of a thing (the house has fine proportions; exaggerated out of all proportion). **3** (in pl.) dimensions; size (large proportions). **4** Math. **a** an equality of ratios between two pairs of quantities, e.g. 3:5 and 9:15. **b** a set of such quantities. —v.tr. (usu. foll. by to) make (a thing etc.) proportionate (must proportion the punishment to the crime). □ **in proportion 1** by the same factor. **2** without exaggerating (importance etc.) (must get the facts in proportion). □ **proportioned** adj. (also in comb.). **proportionless** adj. **proportionment** n. [ME f. OF proportion or L proportio (as PRO-¹, PORTION)]

proportional /prə'pɔːʃən(ə)l/ adj. in due proportion; comparable (a proportional increase in the expense; resentment proportional to his injuries). □ **proportional representation** an electoral system in which all parties gain seats in proportion to the number of votes cast for them. □ **proportionality** /-'nælɪtɪ/ n. **proportionally** adv.

proportionate /prə'pɔːʃənət/ adj. = PROPORTIONAL. □ **proportionately** adv.

proposal /prə'pəʊz(ə)l/ n. **1 a** the act or an instance of proposing something. **b** a course of action etc. so proposed (the proposal was never carried out). **2** an offer of marriage.

propose /prə'pəʊz/ v. **1** tr. (also absol.) put forward for consideration or as a plan. **2** tr. (usu. foll. by to + infin., or verbal noun) intend; purpose (propose to open a restaurant). **3** intr. (usu. foll. by to) offer oneself in marriage. **4** tr. nominate (a person) as a member of a society, for an office, etc. **5** tr. offer (a person's health, a person, etc.) as a subject for a toast. □ **proposer** n. [ME f. OF proposer f. L proponere (as PROPOUND)]

proposition /ˌprɒpəˈzɪʃ(ə)n/ n. & v. —n. **1** a statement or assertion. **2** a scheme proposed; a proposal. **3** colloq. a problem, opponent, prospect, etc. that is to be dealt with (a difficult proposition). **4** Math. a formal statement of a theorem or problem, often including the demonstration. **5 a** an enterprise etc. with regard to its likelihood of commercial etc. success. **b** a person regarded similarly. **6** colloq. a sexual proposal. —v.tr. colloq. make a proposal (esp. of sexual intercourse) to (he propositioned her). □ **propositional** adj. [ME f. OF proposition or L propositio (as PROPOUND)]

propound /prəˈpaʊnd/ v.tr. offer for consideration; propose. □ **propounder** n. [earlier propoune, propone f. L proponere (as PRO-¹, ponere posit- place): cf. compound, expound]

proprietary /prəˈpraɪətərɪ/ adj. **1 a** of, holding, or concerning property (the proprietary classes). **b** of or relating to a proprietor (proprietary rights). **2** held in private ownership. □ **proprietary medicine** any of several drugs, medicines, etc. produced by private companies under brand names. **proprietary name** (or **term**) a name of a product etc. registered by its owner as a trade mark and not usable by another without permission. [LL proprietarius (as PROPERTY)]

proprietor /prəˈpraɪətə(r)/ n. (fem. **proprietress**) **1** a holder of property. **2** the owner of a business etc., esp. of a hotel. □ **proprietorial** /-ˈtɔːrɪəl/ adj. **proprietorially** /-ˈtɔːrɪəlɪ/ adv. **proprietorship** n.

propriety /prəˈpraɪətɪ/ n. (pl. **-ies**) **1** fitness; rightness (doubt the propriety of refusing him). **2** correctness of behaviour or morals (highest standards of propriety). **3** (in pl.) the details or rules of correct conduct (must observe the proprieties). [ME, = ownership, peculiarity f. OF propriété PROPERTY]

propulsion /prəˈpʌlʃ(ə)n/ n. **1** the act or an instance of driving or pushing forward. **2** an impelling influence. □ **propulsive** /-ˈpʌlsɪv/ adj. [med.L propulsio f. L propellere (as PROPEL)]

propylene /ˈprəʊpɪˌliːn/ n. Chem. a gaseous hydrocarbon of the alkene series used in the manufacture of chemicals.

pro rata /prəʊ ˈrɑːtə, ˈreɪtə/ adj. & adv. —adj. proportional. —adv. proportionally. [L, = according to the rate]

prorogue /prəˈrəʊg/ v. (**prorogues**, **prorogued**, **proroguing**) **1** tr. discontinue the meetings of (a parliament etc.) without dissolving it. **2** intr. (of a parliament etc.) be prorogued. □ **prorogation** /-rəˈgeɪʃ(ə)n/ n. [ME proroge f. OF proroger, -guer f. L prorogare prolong (as PRO-¹, rogare ask)]

pros- /prɒs/ prefix **1** to, towards. **2** in addition. [Gk f. pros (prep.)]

prosaic /prəˈzeɪɪk, prəʊ-/ adj. **1** like prose, lacking poetic beauty. **2** unromantic; dull; commonplace (took a prosaic view of life). □ **prosaically** adv. **prosaicness** n. [F prosaïque or LL prosaicus (as PROSE)]

proscenium /prəˈsiːnɪəm, prəʊ-/ n. (pl. **prosceniums** or **proscenia** /-nɪə/) the part of the stage in front of the drop or curtain, usu. with the enclosing arch. [L f. Gk proskēnion (as PRO-², skēnē stage)]

prosciutto /prəʊˈʃuːtəʊ/ n. (pl. **-os**) Italian ham. [It.]

proscribe /prəˈskraɪb/ v.tr. **1** banish, exile (proscribed from the club). **2** put (a person) outside the protection of the law. **3** reject or denounce (a practice etc.) as dangerous etc. □ **proscription** /-ˈskrɪpʃ(ə)n/ n. **proscriptive** /-ˈskrɪptɪv/ adj. [L proscribere (as PRO-¹, scribere script- write)]

prose /prəʊz/ n. & v. —n. **1** the ordinary form of the written or spoken language (opp. POETRY, VERSE) (Milton's prose works). **2** a tedious speech or conversation. **3** a plain matter-of-fact quality (the prose of existence). —v. intr. (usu. foll. by about, away, etc.) talk tediously (was prosing away about his dog). □ **prose poem** (or **poetry**) a piece of imaginative poetic writing in prose. □ **proser** n. [ME f. OF f. L prosa (oratio) straightforward (discourse), fem. of prosus, earlier prorsus direct]

prosecute /ˈprɒsɪˌkjuːt/ v.tr. **1** (also absol.) **a** institute legal proceedings against (a person). **b** institute a prosecution with reference to (a claim, crime, etc.) (decided not to prosecute). **2** follow up, pursue (an inquiry, studies, etc.). **3** carry on (a trade, pursuit, etc.). □ **prosecutable** adj. [ME f. L prosequi prosecut- (as PRO-¹, sequi follow)]

prosecution /ˌprɒsɪˈkjuːʃ(ə)n/ n. **1 a** the institution and carrying on of a criminal charge in a court. **b** the carrying on of legal proceedings against a person. **c** the prosecuting party in a court case (the prosecution denied this). **2** the act or an instance of prosecuting (met her in the prosecution of his hobby). [OF prosecution or LL prosecutio (as PROSECUTE)]

prosecutor /ˈprɒsɪˌkjuːtə(r)/ n. (fem. **prosecutrix** /-trɪks/) a person who prosecutes, esp. in a criminal court. □ **prosecutorial** /-ˈtɔːrɪəl/ adj.

proselyte /ˈprɒsɪˌlaɪt/ n. **1** a person converted, esp. recently, from one opinion, creed, party, etc., to another. **2** a Gentile convert to Judaism. □ **proselytism** /-lɪˌtɪz(ə)m/ n. [ME f. LL proselytus f. Gk prosēluthos stranger, convert (as PROS-, stem ēluth- of erkhomai come)]

proselytize /ˈprɒsɪlɪˌtaɪz/ v.tr. (also **-ise**) (also absol.) convert (a person or people) from one belief etc. to another, esp. habitually. □ **proselytizer** n.

prosody /ˈprɒsədɪ/ n. **1** the theory and practice of versification; the laws of metre. **2** the study of speech-rhythms. □ **prosodic** /prəˈsɒdɪk/ adj. **prosodist** n. [ME f. L prosodia accent f. Gk prosōidia (as PROS-, ODE)]

prospect /ˈprɒspekt/ n. & v. —n. **1 a** (often in pl.) an expectation, esp. of success in a career etc. (his prospects were brilliant; offers a gloomy prospect; no prospect of success). **b** something one has to look forward to (don't relish the prospect of meeting him). **2** an extensive view of landscape etc. (a striking prospect). **3** a mental picture (a new prospect in his mind). **4** a possible or probable customer, subscriber, etc. —v. /prəˈspekt/ **1** intr. (usu. foll. by for) **a** explore a region for gold etc. **b** look out for or search for something. **2** tr. explore (a region) for gold etc. □ **prospectless** adj. **prospector** /prəˈspektə(r)/ n. [ME f. L prospectus: see PROSPECTUS]

prospective /prəˈspektɪv/ adj. **1** concerned with or applying to the future (implies a prospective obligation). **2** some day to be; expected; future (prospective bridegroom). □ **prospectively** adv. **prospectiveness** n. [obs. F prospectif -ive or LL prospectivus (as PROSPECTUS)]

prospectus /prəˈspektəs/ n. a printed document advertising or describing a school, commercial enterprise, forthcoming book, etc. [L, = prospect f. *prospicere* (as PRO-¹, *specere* look)]

prosper /ˈprɒspə(r)/ v. intr. succeed; thrive (*nothing he touches prospers*). [ME f. OF *prosperer* or L *prosperare* (as PROSPEROUS)]

prosperity /prɒˈsperɪtɪ/ n. a state of being prosperous; wealth or success.

prosperous /ˈprɒspərəs/ adj. 1 successful; rich (*a prosperous merchant*). 2 flourishing; thriving (*a prosperous enterprise*). 3 auspicious (*a prosperous wind*). □ **prosperously** adv. **prosperousness** n. [ME f. obs. F *prospereus* f. L *prosper(us)*]

prostate /ˈprɒsteɪt/ n. (in full **prostate gland**) a gland surrounding the neck of the bladder in male mammals and releasing a fluid forming part of the semen. □ **prostatic** /-ˈstætɪk/ adj. [F f. mod.L *prostata* f. Gk *prostatēs* one that stands before (as PRO-², *statos* standing)]

prosthesis /ˈprɒsθɪsɪs, -ˈθiːsɪs/ n. (pl. **prostheses** /-ˌsiːz/) 1 an artificial part supplied to remedy a deficiency, e.g. a false breast, leg, tooth, etc. 2 the branch of surgery supplying and fitting prostheses. □ **prosthetic** /-ˈθetɪk/ adj. **prosthetically** /-ˈθetɪkəlɪ/ adv. [LL f. Gk *prosthesis* f. *prostithēmi* (as PROS-, *tithēmi* place)]

prosthetics /prɒsˈθetɪks/ n.pl. (usu. treated as *sing.*) = PROSTHESIS 2.

prostitute /ˈprɒstɪˌtjuːt/ n. & v. —n. 1 a a woman who engages in sexual activity for payment. b (usu. **male prostitute**) a man or boy who engages in sexual activity, esp. with homosexual men, for payment. 2 a person who debases himself or herself for personal gain. —v.tr. 1 (esp. *refl.*) make a prostitute of (esp. oneself). 2 a misuse (one's talents, skills, etc.) for money. b offer (oneself, one's honour, etc.) for unworthy ends, esp. for money. □ **prostitution** /-ˈtjuːʃ(ə)n/ n. **prostitutor** n. [L *prostituere prostitut-* offer for sale (as PRO-¹, *statuere* set up, place)]

prostrate adj. & v. —adj. /ˈprɒstreɪt/ 1 a lying face downwards, esp. in submission. b lying horizontally. 2 overcome, esp. by grief, exhaustion, etc. —v.tr. /prɒˈstreɪt, prə-/ 1 lay (a person etc.) flat on the ground. 2 (*refl.*) throw (oneself) down in submission etc. 3 (of fatigue, illness, etc.) overcome; reduce to extreme physical weakness. □ **prostration** /prɒˈstreɪʃ(ə)n, prə-/ n. [ME f. L *prostratus* past part. of *prosternere* (as PRO-¹, *sternere strat-* lay flat)]

prosy /ˈprəʊzɪ/ adj. (**prosier**, **prosiest**) tedious; commonplace; dull (*prosy talk*). □ **prosily** adv. **prosiness** n.

protactinium /ˌprəʊtækˈtɪnɪəm/ n. Chem. a radioactive metallic element whose chief isotope yields actinium by decay. [G (as PROTO-, ACTINIUM)]

protagonist /prəʊˈtæɡənɪst/ n. 1 the chief person in a drama, story, etc. 2 the leading person in a contest etc.; a principal performer. 3 (usu. foll. by *of, for*) *disp.* an advocate or champion of a cause, course of action, etc. (*a protagonist of women's rights*). [Gk *prōtagōnistēs* (as PROTO-, *agōnistēs* actor)]

■ **Usage** The use of this word in sense 3 is considered incorrect by some people.

protean /ˈprəʊtɪən, -ˈtiːən/ adj. 1 variable, taking many forms. 2 (of an artist, writer, etc.) versatile.

[f. Gk *Prōteus* a sea-god able to take various forms at will]

protect /prəˈtekt/ v.tr. 1 (often foll. by *from*, *against*) keep (a person, thing, etc.) safe; defend; guard (*goggles protected her eyes from dust*; *guards protected the queen*). 2 *Econ.* shield (home industry) from competition by imposing import duties on foreign goods. [L *protegere protect-* (as PRO-¹, *tegere* cover)]

protection /prəˈtekʃ(ə)n/ n. 1 a the act or an instance of protecting. b the state of being protected; defence (*affords protection against the weather*). c a thing, person, or animal that provides protection (*bought a dog as protection*). 2 (also **protectionism** /-ˌnɪz(ə)m/) *Econ.* the theory or practice of protecting home industries. 3 *colloq.* a immunity from molestation obtained by payment to gangsters etc. under threat of violence. b (in full **protection money**) the money so paid, esp. on a regular basis. 4 = *safe conduct*. □ **protectionist** n. [ME f. OF *protection* or LL *protectio* (as PROTECT)]

protective /prəˈtektɪv/ adj. & n. —adj. protecting; intended or intending to protect. —n. something that protects, esp. a condom. □ **protective clothing** clothing worn to shield the body from dangerous substances or a hostile environment. **protective colouring** colouring disguising or camouflaging a plant or animal. **protective custody** the detention of a person for his or her own protection. □ **protectively** adv. **protectiveness** n.

protector /prəˈtektə(r)/ n. (fem. **protectress** /-trɪs/) 1 a a person who protects. b a guardian or patron. 2 *hist.* a regent in charge of a kingdom during the minority, absence, etc. of the sovereign. 3 (often in *comb.*) a thing or device that protects. □ **protectoral** adj. **protectorship** n. [ME f. OF *protecteur* f. LL *protector* (as PROTECT)]

protectorate /prəˈtektərət/ n. 1 a a State that is controlled and protected by another. b such a relation of one State to another. 2 *hist.* the office of the protector of a kingdom or State.

protégé /ˈprɒtɪˌʒeɪ, -teɪˌʒeɪ, ˈprəʊ-/ n. (fem. **protégée** *pronunc.* same) a person under the protection, patronage, tutelage, etc. of another. [F, past part. of *protéger* f. L *protegere* PROTECT]

protein /ˈprəʊtiːn/ n. any of a group of organic compounds composed of one or more chains of amino acids and forming an essential part of all living organisms. □ **proteinaceous** /-ˈneɪʃəs/ adj. **proteinic** /-ˈtiːnɪk/ adj. **proteinous** /-ˈtiːnəs, -ˈtiːɪnəs/ adj. [F *protéine*, G Protein f. Gk *prōteios* primary]

pro tem /prəʊ ˈtem/ adj. & adv. *colloq.* = PRO TEMPORE. [abbr.]

pro tempore /prəʊ ˈtempərɪ/ adj. & adv. for the time being. [L]

Proterozoic /ˌprəʊtərəʊˈzəʊɪk/ adj. & n. *Geol.* —adj. of or relating to the later part of the Precambrian era. —n. this time. [Gk *proteros* former + *zōē* life, *zōos* living]

protest n. & v. —n. /ˈprəʊtest/ 1 a statement of dissent or disapproval; a remonstrance (*made a protest*). 2 (often *attrib.*) a usu. public demonstration of objection to government etc. policy (*marched in protest*; *protest demonstration*). —v. /prəˈtest/ 1 *intr.* (usu. foll. by *against*, *at*, *about*, etc.) make a protest against an action, proposal, etc. 2 *tr.* (often foll. by *that* + clause; also *absol.*) affirm (one's innocence etc.) solemnly, esp. in reply to an accusation etc. **3** *tr. US* object to (a decision etc.). □ **under protest** unwillingly. □ **protester** *n.* **protestingly** *adv.* **protestor** *n.* [ME f. OF *protest* (n.), *protester* (v.), f. L *protestari* (as PRO-¹, *testari* assert f. *testis* witness)]

Protestant /ˈprɒtɪst(ə)nt/ *n. & adj.* —*n.* **1** a member or follower of any of the western Christian Churches that are separate from the Roman Catholic Church in accordance with the principles of the Reformation. **2** (**protestant**) /ˈprɒtɪst(ə)nt, prəˈtest(ə)nt/ a protesting person. —*adj.* **1** of or relating to any of the Protestant Churches or their members etc. **2** (**protestant**) /also prəˈtestənt/ protesting. □ **Protestantism** *n.* **Protestantize** *v.tr. & intr.* (also **-ise**). [mod.L *protestans*, part. of L *protestari* (see PROTEST)]

protestation /ˌprɒtɪˈsteɪʃ(ə)n/ *n.* **1** a strong affirmation. **2** a protest. [ME f. OF *protestation* or LL *protestatio* (as PROTESTANT)]

protium /ˈprəʊtɪəm/ *n.* the ordinary isotope of hydrogen as distinct from heavy hydrogen. [mod.L f. PROTO- + -IUM]

proto- /ˈprəʊtəʊ/ *comb. form* **1** original, primitive (*proto-Germanic*; *proto-Slavic*). **2** first, original (*prototype*). [Gk *prōto-* f. *prōtos* first]

protocol /ˈprəʊtəˌkɒl/ *n. & v.* —*n.* **1 a** official, esp. diplomatic, formality and etiquette observed on State occasions etc. **b** the rules, formalities, etc. of any procedure, group, etc. **2** the original draft of a diplomatic document, esp. of the terms of a treaty agreed to in conference and signed by the parties. **3** the official formulae at the beginning and end of a charter, etc. —*v.* (**protocolled, protocolling**) **1** *intr.* draw up a protocol or protocols. **2** *tr.* record in a protocol. [orig. Sc. *prothocoll* f. OF *prothocole* f. med.L *protocollum* f. Gk *protokollon* flyleaf (as PROTO-, *kolla* glue)]

proton /ˈprəʊtɒn/ *n. Physics* a stable elementary particle with a positive electric charge, equal in magnitude to that of an electron, and occurring in all atomic nuclei. □ **protonic** /prəˈtɒnɪk/ *adj.* [Gk, neut. of *prōtos* first]

protoplasm /ˈprəʊtəˌplæz(ə)m/ *n.* the material comprising the living part of a cell, consisting of a nucleus embedded in membrane-enclosed cytoplasm. □ **protoplasmal** /-ˈplæzm(ə)l/ *adj.* **protoplasmatic** /-ˈmætɪk/ *adj.* **protoplasmic** /-ˈplæzmɪk/ *adj.* [Gk *protoplasma* (as PROTO-, PLASMA)]

prototype /ˈprəʊtəˌtaɪp/ *n.* **1** an original thing or person of which or whom copies, imitations, improved forms, representations, etc. are made. **2** a trial model or preliminary version of a vehicle, machine, etc. □ **prototypal** *adj.* **prototypic** /-ˈtɪpɪk/ *adj.* **prototypical** /-ˈtɪpɪk(ə)l/ *adj.* **prototypically** /-ˈtɪpɪkəlɪ/ *adv.* [F *prototype* or LL *prototypus* f. Gk *prototupos* (as PROTO-, TYPE)]

protozoan /ˌprəʊtəˈzəʊən/ *n. & adj.* —*n.* (also **protozoon** /-ˈzəʊɒn/) (*pl.* **protozoa** /-ˈzəʊə/ or **protozoans**) any usu. unicellular and microscopic organism of the subkingdom Protozoa, including amoebae and ciliates. —*adj.* (also **protozoic** /-ˈzəʊɪk/) of or relating to this phylum. □ **protozoal** *adj.* [mod.L (as PROTO-, Gk *zōion* animal)]

protract /prəˈtrækt/ *v.tr.* **1** prolong or lengthen in space or esp. time (*protracted their stay for some weeks*). **2** draw (a plan of ground etc.) to scale.

□ **protractedly** *adv.* **protractedness** *n.* [L *protrahere protract-* (as PRO-¹, *trahere* draw)]

protraction /prəˈtrækʃ(ə)n/ *n.* **1** the act or an instance of protracting; the state of being protracted. **2** a drawing to scale. **3** the action of a protractor muscle. [F *protraction* or LL *protractio* (as PROTRACT)]

protractor /prəˈtræktə(r)/ *n.* **1** an instrument for measuring angles, usu. in the form of a graduated semicircle. **2** a muscle serving to extend a limb etc.

protrude /prəˈtruːd/ *v.* **1** *intr.* extend beyond or above a surface; project. **2** *tr.* thrust or cause to thrust forth. □ **protrudent** *adj.* **protrusible** *adj.* **protrusion** /-ʒ(ə)n/ *n.* **protrusive** *adj.* [L *protrudere* (as PRO-¹, *trudere trus-* thrust)]

protuberant /prəˈtjuːbərənt/ *adj.* bulging out; prominent (*protuberant eyes*). □ **protuberance** *n.* [LL *protuberare* (as PRO-¹, *tuber* bump)]

proud /praʊd/ *adj.* **1** feeling greatly honoured or pleased (*am proud to know him*; *proud of his friendship*). **2 a** (often foll. by *of*) valuing oneself, one's possessions, etc. highly, or esp. too highly; haughty; arrogant (*proud of his ancient name*). **b** (often in *comb.*) having a proper pride; satisfied (*house-proud*; *proud of a job well done*). **3 a** (of an occasion etc.) justly arousing pride (*a proud day for us*; *a proud sight*). **b** (of an action etc.) showing pride (*a proud wave of the hand*). **4** (of a thing) imposing; splendid. **5** slightly projecting from a surface etc. (*the nail stood proud of the plank*). **6** (of flesh) overgrown round a healing wound. □ **do proud** *colloq.* **1** treat (a person) with lavish generosity or honour (*they did us proud on our anniversary*). **2** (*refl.*) act honourably or worthily. □ **proudly** *adv.* **proudness** *n.* [OE *prūt, prūd* f. OF *prud, prod* oblique case of *pruz* etc. valiant, ult. f. LL *prode* f. L *prodesse* be of value (as PRO-¹, *esse* be)]

prove /pruːv/ *v.* (*past part.* **proved** or **proven** /ˈpruːv(ə)n, ˈprəʊ-/) **1** *tr.* (often foll. by *that* + clause) demonstrate the truth of by evidence or argument. **2** *intr.* **a** (usu. foll. by *to* + infin.) be found (*it proved to be untrue*). **b** emerge incontrovertibly as (*will prove the winner*). **3** *tr.* establish the genuineness and validity of (a will). **4** *intr.* (of dough) rise in bread-making. **5** *tr. archaic* test the qualities of; try. □ **not proven** (in Scottish Law) a verdict that there is insufficient evidence to establish guilt or innocence. **prove oneself** show one's abilities, courage, etc. □ **provable** *adj.* **provability** /-ˈbɪlɪtɪ/ *n.* **provably** *adv.* [ME f. OF *prover* f. L *probare* test, approve, demonstrate f. *probus* good]

■ **Usage** In British English it is not standard to use *proven* as the past participle (it is standard Scots and American English). It is, however, common in certain expressions, such as *of proven ability*.

provenance /ˈprɒvɪnəns/ *n.* **1** the place of origin or history, esp. of a work of art etc. **2** origin. [F f. *provenir* f. L *provenire* (as PRO-¹, *venire* come)]

provender /ˈprɒvɪndə(r)/ *n.* **1** animal fodder. **2** *joc.* food for human beings. [ME f. OF *provendre*, *provende* ult. f. L *praebenda* (see PREBEND)]

proverb /ˈprɒvɜːb/ *n.* **1** a short pithy saying in general use, held to embody a general truth. **2** a person or thing that is notorious (*he is a proverb* *for inaccuracy*). [ME f. OF *proverbe* or L *proverbium* (as PRO-[1], *verbum* word)]

proverbial /prə'vɜːbɪəl/ *adj.* **1** (esp. of a specific characteristic etc.) as well-known as a proverb; notorious (*his proverbial honesty*). **2** of or referred to in a proverb (*the proverbial ill wind*). □ **proverbiality** /-bɪ'ælɪtɪ/ *n.* **proverbially** *adv.* [ME f. L *proverbialis* (as PROVERB)]

provide /prə'vaɪd/ *v.* **1** *tr.* supply; furnish (*provided them with food; provided food for them; provided a chance for escape*). **2** *intr.* **a** (usu. foll. by *for, against*) make due preparation (*provided for any eventuality; provided against invasion*). **b** (usu. foll. by *for*) prepare for the maintenance of a person etc. **3** *tr.* (also *refl.*) equip with necessities (*they had to provide themselves*). **4** *tr.* (usu. foll. by *that*) stipulate in a will, statute, etc. [ME f. L *providēre* (as PRO-[1], *vidēre* vis- see)]

provided /prə'vaɪdɪd/ *adj. & conj.* —*adj.* supplied, furnished. —*conj.* (often foll. by *that*) on the condition or understanding (that).

providence /'prɒvɪd(ə)ns/ *n.* **1** the protective care of God or nature. **2** (**Providence**) God in this aspect. **3** timely care or preparation; foresight; thrift. [ME f. OF *providence* or L *providentia* (as PROVIDE)]

provident /'prɒvɪd(ə)nt/ *adj.* having or showing foresight; thrifty. □ **providently** *adv.* [ME f. L (as PROVIDE)]

providential /ˌprɒvɪ'denʃ(ə)l/ *adj.* **1** of or by divine foresight or interposition. **2** opportune, lucky. □ **providentially** *adv.* [PROVIDENCE + -IAL, after *evidential* etc.]

provider /prə'vaɪdə(r)/ *n.* **1** a person or thing that provides. **2** the breadwinner of a family etc.

providing /prə'vaɪdɪŋ/ *conj.* = PROVIDED *conj.*

province /'prɒvɪns/ *n.* **1** a principal administrative division of a country etc. **2** (**the provinces**) the whole of a country outside the capital, esp. regarded as uncultured, unsophisticated, etc. **3** a sphere of action; business (*outside my province as a teacher*). **4** a branch of learning etc. (*in the province of aesthetics*). [ME f. OF f. L *provincia* charge, province]

provincial /prə'vɪnʃ(ə)l/ *adj. & n.* —*adj.* **1 a** of or concerning a province. **b** of or concerning the provinces. **2** unsophisticated or uncultured in manner, speech, opinion, etc. —*n.* **1** an inhabitant of a province or the provinces. **2** an unsophisticated or uncultured person. □ **provinciality** /-ʃɪ'ælɪtɪ/ *n.* **provincialize** *v.tr.* (also **-ise**). **provincially** *adv.* [ME f. OF f. L *provincialis* (as PROVINCE)]

provincialism /prə'vɪnʃəˌlɪz(ə)m/ *n.* **1** provincial manners, fashion, mode of thought, etc., esp. regarded as restricting or narrow. **2** a word or phrase peculiar to a provincial region. **3** concern for one's local area rather than one's country. □ **provincialist** *n.*

provision /prə'vɪʒ(ə)n/ *n. & v.* —*n.* **1 a** the act or an instance of providing (*made no provision for his future*). **b** something provided (*a provision of bread*). **2** (in *pl.*) food, drink, etc., esp. for an expedition. **3 a** a legal or formal statement providing for something. **b** a clause of this. —*v.tr.* supply (an expedition etc.) with provisions. □ **provisioner** *n.* **provisionless** *adj.* **provisionment** *n.* [ME f. OF f. L *provisio -onis* (as PROVIDE)]

provisional /prə'vɪʒən(ə)l/ *adj.* providing for immediate needs only; temporary. □ **provisionality** /-'nælɪtɪ/ *n.* **provisionally** *adv.* **provisionalness** *n.*

proviso /prə'vaɪzəʊ/ *n.* (*pl.* **-os**) **1** a stipulation. **2** a clause of stipulation or limitation in a document. [L, neut. ablat. past part. of *providēre* PROVIDE, in med.L phr. *proviso quod* it being provided that]

provisory /prə'vaɪzərɪ/ *adj.* **1** conditional; having a proviso. **2** making provision (*provisory care*). □ **provisorily** *adv.* [F *provisoire* or med.L *provisorius* (as PROVIDE)]

provocation /ˌprɒvə'keɪʃ(ə)n/ *n.* **1** the act or an instance of provoking; a state of being provoked (*did it under severe provocation*). **2** a cause of annoyance. [ME f. OF *provocation* or L *provocatio* (as PROVOKE)]

provocative /prə'vɒkətɪv/ *adj.* **1** (usu. foll. by *of*) tending to provoke, esp. anger or sexual desire. **2** intentionally annoying. □ **provocatively** *adv.* **provocativeness** *n.* [ME f. obs. F *provocatif -ive* f. LL *provocativus* (as PROVOKE)]

provoke /prə'vəʊk/ *v.tr.* **1 a** (often foll. by *to*, or *to* + infin.) rouse or incite (*provoked him to fury*). **b** (as **provoking** *adj.*) exasperating; irritating. **2** call forth; instigate (indignation, an inquiry, a storm, etc.). **3** (usu. foll. by *into* + verbal noun) irritate or stimulate (a person) (*the itch provoked him into scratching*). **4** tempt; allure. **5** cause, give rise to (*will provoke fermentation*). □ **provokable** *adj.* **provokingly** *adv.* [ME f. OF *provoquer* f. L *provocare* (as PRO-[1], *vocare* call)]

provost /'prɒvəst/ *n.* **1** *Brit.* the head of some colleges esp. at Oxford or Cambridge. **2** *Sc.* the head of a municipal corporation or burgh. **3** *US* a high administrative officer in a university. **4** = *provost marshal*. □ **provost marshal** /prə'vəʊ/ **1** the head of military police in camp or on active service. **2** the master-at-arms of a ship in which a court-martial is to be held. □ **provost-ship** *n.* [ME f. OE *profost* & AF *provost*, *prevost* f. med.L *propositus* for *praepositus* past part. of *praeponere* set over (as PRAE-, *ponere* posit- place)]

prow /praʊ/ *n.* **1** the fore-part or bow of a ship adjoining the stern. **2** a pointed or projecting front part. [F *proue* f. Prov. *proa* or It. dial. *prua* f. L *prora* f. Gk *prōira*]

prowess /'praʊɪs/ *n.* **1** skill; expertise. **2** valour; gallantry. [ME f. OF *proesce* f. *prou* valiant]

prowl /praʊl/ *v. & n.* —*v.* **1** *tr.* roam (a place) in search or as if in search of prey, plunder, etc. **2** *intr.* (often foll. by *about*, *around*) move about like a hunter. —*n.* the act or an instance of prowling. □ **on the prowl** moving about secretively or rapaciously, esp. in search of sexual contact etc. **prowl car** *US* a police squad car. □ **prowler** *n.* [ME *prolle*, of unkn. orig.]

prox. *abbr.* proximo.

proximate /'prɒksɪmət/ *adj.* **1** nearest or next before or after (in place, order, time, causation, thought process, etc.). **2** approximate. □ **proximately** *adv.* [L *proximatus* past part. of *proximare* draw near f. *proximus* nearest]

proximity /prɒk'sɪmɪtɪ/ *n.* nearness in space, time, etc. (*sat in close proximity to them*). [ME f. F *proximité* or L *proximitas* (as PROXIMATE)]

proximo /'prɒksɪˌməʊ/ *adj. Commerce* of next month (*the third proximo*). [L *proximo mense* in the next month]

proxy /'prɒksɪ/ n. (pl. **-ies**) (also attrib.) **1** the authorization given to a substitute or deputy (a proxy vote; was married by proxy). **2** a person authorized to act as a substitute etc. **3 a** a document giving the power to act as a proxy, esp. in voting. **b** a vote given by this. [ME f. obs. procuracy f. med.L procuratia (as PROCURATION)]

prude n. a person having or affecting an attitude of extreme propriety or modesty esp. in sexual matters. □ **prudery** n. (pl. **-ies**). **prudish** adj. **prudishly** adv. **prudishness** n. [F, back form. f. prudefemme fem. of prud'homme good man and true f. prou worthy]

prudent /'pruːd(ə)nt/ adj. **1** (of a person or conduct) careful to avoid undesired consequences; circumspect. **2** discreet. □ **prudence** n. **prudently** adv. [ME f. OF prudent or L prudens = providens PROVIDENT]

prudential /pruː'denʃ(ə)l/ adj. of, involving, or marked by prudence (prudential motives). □ **prudentialism** n. **prudentialist** n. **prudentially** adv. [PRUDENT + -IAL, after evidential etc.]

prune[1] n. **1** a dried plum. **2** colloq. a silly or disliked person. [ME f. OF ult. f. L prunum f. Gk prou(m)non plum]

prune[2] v.tr. **1 a** (often foll. by down) trim (a tree etc.) by cutting away dead or overgrown branches etc. **b** (usu. foll. by off, away) lop (branches etc.) from a tree. **2** reduce (costs etc.) (must try to prune expenses). **3 a** (often foll. by of) clear (a book etc.) of superfluities. **b** remove (superfluities). □ **pruning-hook** a long-handled hooked cutting tool used for pruning. □ **pruner** n. [ME prouyne f. OF pro(o)ignier ult. f. L rotundus ROUND]

prurient /'prʊərɪənt/ adj. **1** having an unhealthy obsession with sexual matters. **2** encouraging such an obsession. □ **prurience** n. **pruriency** n. **pruriently** adv. [L prurire itch, be wanton]

Prussian /'prʌʃ(ə)n/ adj. & n. —adj. of or relating to Prussia, a former German State, or relating to its rigidly militaristic tradition. —n. a native of Prussia. □ **Prussian blue** a deep blue pigment used in painting and dyeing.

prussic /'prʌsɪk/ adj. of or obtained from Prussian blue. □ **prussic acid** hydrocyanic acid. [F prussique f. Prusse Prussia]

pry[1] /praɪ/ v.intr. (**pries**, **pried**) **1** (usu. foll. by into) inquire impertinently (into a person's private affairs etc.). **2** (usu. foll. by into, about, etc.) look or peer inquisitively. □ **prying** adj. **pryingly** adv. [ME prie, of unkn. orig.]

pry[2] /praɪ/ v.tr. (**pries**, **pried**) US (often foll. by out of, open, etc.) = PRISE. [PRISE taken as pries 3rd sing. pres.]

PS abbr. **1** Police Sergeant. **2** postscript.

psalm /sɑːm/ n. **1 a** (also **Psalm**) any of the sacred songs contained in the Book of Psalms. **b** (**the Psalms** or **the Book of Psalms**) the book of the Old Testament containing the Psalms. **2** a sacred song or hymn. □ **psalm-book** a book containing the Psalms, esp. with metrical settings for worship. □ **psalmic** adj. [OE (p)sealm f. LL psalmus f. Gk psalmos song sung to a harp f. psallō pluck]

psalmist /'sɑːmɪst/ n. **1** the author or composer of a psalm. **2** (**the Psalmist**) David or the author of any of the Psalms. [LL psalmista (as PSALM)]

psalmody /'sɑːmədɪ, 'sæl-/ n. **1** the practice or art of singing psalms, hymns, etc., esp. in public worship. □ **psalmodic** /sæl'mɒdɪk/ adj. **psalmodist** n. **psalmodize** v.intr. (also **-ise**). [ME f. LL psalmodia f. Gk psalmōidia singing to a harp (as PSALM, ōidē song)]

psalter /'sɔːltə(r), 'sɒl-/ n. **1 a** the Book of Psalms. **b** a version of this (the English Psalter; Prayer-Book Psalter). **2** a copy of the Psalms, esp. for liturgical use. [ME f. AF sauter, OF sautier, & OE (p)saltere f. LL psalterium f. Gk psaltērion stringed instrument (psallō pluck), in eccl.L Book of Psalms]

psaltery /'sɔːltərɪ, 'sɒl-/ n. (pl. **-ies**) an ancient and medieval instrument like a dulcimer but played by plucking the strings with the fingers or a plectrum. [ME f. OF sauterie etc. f. L (as PSALTER)]

PSBR abbr. Brit. public sector borrowing requirement.

psephology /se'fɒlədʒɪ, pse-/ n. the statistical study of elections, voting, etc. □ **psephological** /-fə'lɒdʒɪk(ə)l/ adj. **psephologically** /-fə'lɒdʒɪkəlɪ/ adv. **psephologist** n. [Gk psēphos pebble, vote + -LOGY]

pseud /sjuːd/ adj. & n. colloq. —adj. intellectually or socially pretentious; not genuine. —n. such a person; a poseur. [abbr. of PSEUDO]

pseudo /'sjuːdəʊ/ adj. & n. —adj. **1** sham; spurious. **2** insincere. —n. (pl. **-os**) a pretentious or insincere person. [see PSEUDO-]

pseudo- /'sjuːdəʊ/ comb. form (also **pseud-** before a vowel) **1** supposed or purporting to be but not really so; false; not genuine (pseudo-intellectual). **2** resembling or imitating (often in technical applications) (pseudo-language; pseudo-acid). [Gk f. pseudēs false, pseudos falsehood]

pseudonym /'sjuːdənɪm/ n. a fictitious name, esp. one assumed by an author. [F pseudonyme f. Gk pseudōnymos (as PSEUDO-, -ōnumos f. onoma name)]

pseudonymous /sjuː'dɒnɪməs/ adj. writing or written under a false name. □ **pseudonymity** /-'nɪmɪtɪ/ n. **pseudonymously** adv.

pseudo-science /'sjuːdəʊˌsaɪəns/ n. a pretended or spurious science. □ **pseudo-scientific** /-'tɪfɪk/ adj.

psi /psaɪ/ n. **1** the twenty-third letter of the Greek alphabet (Ψ, ψ). **2** supposed parapsychological faculties, phenomena, etc. regarded collectively. [Gk]

psilocybin /ˌsɪlə'saɪbɪn/ n. a hallucinogenic alkaloid found in Mexican mushrooms of the genus Psilocybe. [Psilocybe f. Gk psilos bald + kubē head]

psittacosis /ˌsɪtə'kəʊsɪs/ n. a contagious viral disease of birds transmissible (esp. from parrots) to human beings as a form of pneumonia. [mod.L f. L psittacus f. Gk psittakos parrot + -OSIS]

psoriasis /sə'raɪəsɪs/ n. a skin disease marked by red scaly patches. □ **psoriatic** /ˌsɔːrɪ'ætɪk/ adj. [mod.L f. Gk psōriasis f. psōriaō have an itch f. psōra itch]

psst /pst/ int. (also **pst**) a whispered exclamation seeking to attract a person's attention surreptitiously. [imit.]

PSV abbr. Brit. public service vehicle.

psych /saɪk/ v.tr. colloq. **1** (usu. foll. by up; often refl.) prepare (oneself or another person) mentally for an ordeal etc. **2 a** (usu. foll. by out) analyse (a person's motivation etc.) for one's own advantage (can't psych him out). **b** subject to psychoanalysis. **3** (often foll. by out) influence a person psychologically, esp. negatively; intimidate, frighten. □ **psych out** break down mentally; become confused or deranged. [abbr.]

psyche /ˈsaɪkɪ/ *n.* **1** the soul; the spirit. **2** the mind. [L f. Gk *psukhē* breath, life, soul]

psychedelia /ˌsaɪkɪˈdiːlɪə/ *n.pl.* **1** psychedelic articles, esp. posters, paintings, etc. **2** psychedelic drugs.

psychedelic /ˌsaɪkɪˈdelɪk/ *adj. & n.* —*adj.* **1 a** expanding the mind's awareness etc., esp. through the use of hallucinogenic drugs. **b** (of an experience) hallucinatory; bizarre. **c** (of a drug) producing hallucinations. **2** *colloq.* **a** producing an effect resembling that of a psychedelic drug; having vivid colours or designs etc. **b** (of colours, patterns, etc.) bright, bold and often abstract. —*n.* a hallucinogenic drug. □ **psychedelically** *adv.* [irreg. f. Gk (as PSYCHE, *dēlos* clear, manifest)]

psychiatry /saɪˈkaɪətrɪ/ *n.* the study and treatment of mental disease. □ **psychiatric** /-kɪˈætrɪk/ *adj.* **psychiatrical** /-kɪˈætrɪk(ə)l/ *adj.* **psychiatrically** /-kɪˈætrɪkəlɪ/ *adv.* **psychiatrist** *n.* [as PSYCHE + *iatreia* healing f. *iatros* healer]

psychic /ˈsaɪkɪk/ *adj. & n.* —*adj.* **1 a** (of a person) considered to have occult powers, such as telepathy, clairvoyance, etc. **b** (of a faculty, phenomenon, etc.) inexplicable by natural laws. **2** of the soul or mind. —*n.* **1** a person considered to have psychic powers; a medium. **2** (in *pl.*) the study of psychic phenomena. [Gk *psukhikos* (as PSYCHE)]

psychical /ˈsaɪkɪk(ə)l/ *adj.* **1** concerning psychic phenomena or faculties (*psychical research*). **2** of the soul or mind. □ **psychically** *adv.* **psychicism** /-ɪˌsɪz(ə)m/ *n.* **psychicist** /-ɪˌsɪst/ *n.*

psycho /ˈsaɪkəʊ/ *n. & adj. colloq.* —*n.* (pl. **-os**) a psychopath. —*adj.* psychopathic. [abbr.]

psycho- /ˈsaɪkəʊ/ *comb. form* relating to the mind or psychology. [Gk *psukho-* (as PSYCHE)]

psychoactive /ˌsaɪkəʊˈæktɪv/ *adj.* affecting the mind.

psychoanalysis /ˌsaɪkəʊəˈnælɪsɪs/ *n.* a therapeutic method of treating mental disorders by investigating the interaction of conscious and unconscious elements in the mind and bringing repressed fears and conflicts into the conscious mind. □ **psychoanalyse** /-ˈænəˌlaɪz/ *v.tr.* **psychoanalyst** /-ˈænəlɪst/ *n.* **psychoanalytic** /-ˌænəˈlɪtɪk/ *adj.* **psychoanalytical** /-ˌænəˈlɪtɪk(ə)l/ *adj.* **psychoanalytically** /-ˌænəˈlɪtɪkəlɪ/ *adv.*

psychobabble /ˈsaɪkəʊˌbæb(ə)l/ *n.* *US colloq. derog.* jargon used in popular psychology.

psychodrama /ˈsaɪkəʊˌdrɑːmə/ *n.* **1** a form of psychotherapy in which patients act out events from their past. **2** a play or film etc. in which psychological elements are the main interest.

psychological /ˌsaɪkəˈlɒdʒɪk(ə)l/ *adj.* **1** of, relating to, or arising in the mind. **2** of or relating to psychology. **3** *colloq.* (of an ailment etc.) having a basis in the mind; imaginary (*her cold is psychological*). □ **psychological block** a mental inability or inhibition caused by emotional factors. **psychological moment** the most appropriate time for achieving a particular effect or purpose. **psychological warfare** a campaign directed at reducing an opponent's morale. □ **psychologically** *adv.*

psychology /saɪˈkɒlədʒɪ/ *n.* (pl. **-ies**) **1** the scientific study of the human mind and its functions, esp. those affecting behaviour in a given context. **2** a treatise on or theory of this. **3 a** the mental characteristics or attitude of a person or group. **b** the mental factors governing a situation or activity (*the psychology of crime*). □ **psychologist** *n.* **psychologize** *v.tr. & intr.* (also **-ise**). [mod.L *psychologia* (as PSYCHO-, -LOGY)]

psychopath /ˈsaɪkəˌpæθ/ *n.* **1** a person suffering from chronic mental disorder esp. with abnormal or violent social behaviour. **2** a mentally or emotionally unstable person. □ **psychopathic** /-ˈpæθɪk/ *adj.* **psychopathically** /-ˈpæθɪkəlɪ/ *adv.*

psychopathology /ˌsaɪkəʊpəˈθɒlədʒɪ/ *n.* **1** the scientific study of mental disorders. **2** a mentally or behaviourally disordered state. □ **psychopathological** /-ˌpæθəʊˈlɒdʒɪk(ə)l/ *adj.*

psychopathy /saɪˈkɒpəθɪ/ *n.* psychopathic or psychologically abnormal behaviour.

psychosexual /ˌsaɪkəʊˈseksjʊəl, -ˈsekʃʊəl/ *adj.* of or involving the psychological aspects of the sexual impulse. □ **psychosexually** *adv.*

psychosis /saɪˈkəʊsɪs/ *n.* (pl. **psychoses** /-siːz/) a severe mental derangement, esp. when resulting in delusions and loss of contact with external reality. [Gk *psukhōsis* f. *psukhoō* give life to (as PSYCHE)]

psychosocial /ˌsaɪkəʊˈsəʊʃ(ə)l/ *adj.* of or involving the influence of social factors or human interactive behaviour. □ **psychosocially** *adv.*

psychosomatic /ˌsaɪkəʊsəˈmætɪk/ *adj.* **1** (of an illness etc.) caused or aggravated by mental conflict, stress, etc. **2** of the mind and body together. □ **psychosomatically** *adv.*

psychosurgery /ˌsaɪkəʊˈsɜːdʒərɪ/ *n.* brain surgery as a means of treating mental disorder. □ **psychosurgical** *adj.*

psychotherapy /ˌsaɪkəʊˈθerəpɪ/ *n.* the treatment of mental disorder by psychological means. □ **psychotherapeutic** /-ˈpjuːtɪk/ *adj.* **psychotherapist** *n.*

psychotic /saɪˈkɒtɪk/ *adj. & n.* —*adj.* of or characterized by a psychosis. —*n.* a person suffering from a psychosis. □ **psychotically** *adv.*

psychotropic /ˌsaɪkəʊˈtrɒpɪk/ *n.* (of a drug) acting on the mind. [PSYCHO- + Gk *tropē* turning: see TROPIC]

PT *abbr.* physical training.

Pt *symb. Chem.* the element platinum.

pt. *abbr.* **1** part. **2** pint. **3** point. **4** port.

PTA *abbr.* parent-teacher association.

ptarmigan /ˈtɑːmɪɡən/ *n.* any of various gamebirds of the genus *Lagopus*, esp. *L. mutus*, with grouselike appearance and black or grey plumage in the summer and white in the winter. [Gael. *tàrmachan*: p- after Gk words in *pt-*]

Pte. *abbr.* Private (soldier).

ptero- /ˈterəʊ/ *comb. form* wing. [Gk *pteron* wing]

pterodactyl /ˌterəˈdæktɪl/ *n.* a large extinct flying birdlike reptile with a long slender head and neck.

pterosaur /ˈterəˌsɔː(r)/ *n.* any of a group of extinct flying reptiles with large bat-like wings, including pterodactyls. [PTERO- + Gk *saura* lizard]

PTO *abbr.* please turn over.

Ptolemaic /ˌtɒlɪˈmeɪɪk/ *adj. hist.* of or relating to Ptolemy, a 2nd-c. Alexandrian astronomer, or his theories. □ **Ptolemaic system** the theory that the earth is the stationary centre of the Universe. [L *Ptolemaeus* f. Gk *Ptolemaios*]

ptomaine /ˈtəʊmeɪn/ *n.* any of various amine compounds, some toxic, in putrefying animal and vegetable matter. □ **ptomaine poisoning** *archaic* food poisoning. [F *ptomaïne* f. It. *ptomaina* irreg. f. Gk *ptōma* corpse]

Pty. *abbr. Austral.*, *NZ*, & *S.Afr.* proprietary.

Pu *symb. Chem.* the element plutonium.

pub *n. colloq.* **1** *Brit.* a public house. **2** *Austral.* a hotel. □ **pub-crawl** *Brit. colloq.* a drinking tour of several pubs. [abbr.]

puberty /ˈpjuːbətɪ/ *n.* the period during which adolescents reach sexual maturity and become capable of reproduction. □ **pubertal** *adj.* [ME f. F *puberté* or L *pubertas* f. *puber* adult]

pubes[1] /ˈpjuːbiːz/ *n.* (*pl.* same) the lower part of the abdomen at the front of the pelvis, covered with hair from puberty. [L]

pubes[2] *pl.* of PUBIS.

pubescence /pjuːˈbes(ə)ns/ *n.* **1** the time when puberty begins. **2** *Bot.* soft down on the leaves and stems of plants. **3** *Zool.* soft down on various parts of animals, esp. insects. □ **pubescent** *adj.* [F *pubescence* or med.L *pubescentia* f. L *pubescere* reach puberty]

pubic /ˈpjuːbɪk/ *adj.* of or relating to the pubes or pubis.

pubis /ˈpjuːbɪs/ *n.* (*pl.* **pubes** /-biːz/) either of a pair of bones forming the two sides of the pelvis. [L *os pubis* bone of the PUBES]

public /ˈpʌblɪk/ *adj.* & *n.* **1** of or concerning the people as a whole (*a public holiday; the public interest*). **2** open to or shared by all the people (*public baths; public library; public meeting*). **3** done or existing openly (*made his views public; a public protest*). **4 a** (of a service, funds, etc.) provided by or concerning local or central government (*public money; public records; public expenditure*). **b** (of a person) in government (*had a distinguished public career*). **5** well-known; famous (*a public institution*). **6** *Brit.* of, for, or acting for, a university (*public examination*). —*n.* **1** (as *sing.* or *pl.*) the community in general, or members of the community. **2** a section of the community having a particular interest or in some special connection (*the reading public; my public demands my loyalty*). **3** *Brit. colloq.* **a** = *public bar.* **b** = *public house.* □ **go public** become a public company. **in public** openly, publicly. **in the public domain** belonging to the public as a whole, esp. not subject to copyright. **in the public eye** famous or notorious. **public-address system** loudspeakers, microphones, amplifiers, etc., used in addressing large audiences. **public bar** *Brit.* the least expensive bar in a public house. **public company** *Brit.* a company that sells shares to all buyers on the open market. **public enemy** a notorious wanted criminal. **public figure** a famous person. **public health** the provision of adequate sanitation, drainage, etc. by government. **public house 1** *Brit.* an inn providing alcoholic drinks for consumption on the premises. **2** an inn. **public lending right** the right of authors to payment when their books etc. are lent by public libraries. **public opinion** views, prevalent among the general public. **public ownership** the State ownership of the means of production, distribution, and

exchange. **public prosecutor** a law officer conducting criminal proceedings on behalf of the State or in the public interest. **Public Record Office** an institution keeping official archives, esp. birth, marriage, and death certificates, for public inspection. **public relations** the professional maintenance of a favourable public image, esp. by a company, famous person, etc. **public relations officer** a person employed by a company etc. to promote a favourable public image. **public school 1** *Brit.* a private fee-paying secondary school, esp. for boarders. **2** *US*, *Austral.*, & *Sc.* etc. any non-fee-paying school. **public sector** that part of an economy, industry, etc., that is controlled by the State. **public servant** a State official. **public spirit** a willingness to engage in community action. **public-spirited** having a public spirit. **public transport** buses, trains, etc., charging set fares and running on fixed routes, esp. when State-owned. **public utility** an organization supplying water, gas, etc. to the community. **public works** building operations etc. done by or for the State on behalf of the community. □ **publicly** *adv.* [ME f. OF *public* or L *publicus* f. *pubes* adult]

publican /ˈpʌblɪkən/ *n.* **1 a** *Brit.* the keeper of a public house. **b** *Austral.* the keeper of a hotel. **2** *Rom.Hist.* & *Bibl.* a tax-collector or tax-farmer. [ME f. OF *publicain* f. L *publicanus* f. *publicum* public revenue (as PUBLIC)]

publication /ˌpʌblɪˈkeɪʃ(ə)n/ *n.* **1 a** the preparation and issuing of a book, newspaper, engraving, music, etc. to the public. **b** a book etc. so issued. **2** the act or an instance of making something publicly known. [ME f. OF f. L *publicatio -onis* (as PUBLISH)]

publicist /ˈpʌblɪsɪst/ *n.* a publicity agent or public relations officer. □ **publicism** *n.* **publicistic** /-ˈsɪstɪk/ *adj.* [F *publiciste* f. L (*jus*) *publicum* public law]

publicity /pʌbˈlɪsɪtɪ/ *n.* **1 a** the professional exploitation of a product, company, person, etc., by advertising or popularizing. **b** material or information used for this. **2** public exposure; notoriety. □ **publicity agent** a person employed to produce or heighten public exposure. [F *publicité* (as PUBLIC)]

publicize /ˈpʌblɪˌsaɪz/ *v.tr.* (also **-ise**) advertise; make publicly known.

publish /ˈpʌblɪʃ/ *v.tr.* **1** (also *absol.*) (of an author, publisher, etc.) prepare and issue (a book, newspaper, engraving, etc.) for public sale. **2** make generally known. **3** announce (an edict etc.) formally; read (marriage banns). □ **publishable** *adj.* [ME *puplise* etc. f. OF *puplier, puplier* f. L *publicare* (as PUBLIC)]

publisher /ˈpʌblɪʃə(r)/ *n.* a person or esp. a company that produces and distributes copies of a book, newspaper, etc. for sale.

puce *adj.* & *n.* dark red or purple-brown. [F, = flea(-colour) f. L *pulex -icis*]

puck[1] *n.* a rubber disc used as a ball in ice hockey. [19th c.: orig. unkn.]

puck[2] *n.* **1** a mischievous or evil sprite. **2** a mischievous child. □ **puckish** *adj.* **puckishly** *adv.* **puckishness** *n.* **pucklike** *adj.* [OE *pūca*: cf. Welsh *pwca*, Ir. *púca*]

pucka var. of PUKKA.

pucker /ˈpʌkə(r)/ *v.* & *n.* —*v.tr.* & *intr.* (often foll. by *up*) gather or cause to gather into wrinkles, folds, or bulges (*puckered her eyebrows*; *this seam is puckered up*). —*n.* such a wrinkle, bulge, fold, etc. □ **puckery** *adj.* [prob. frequent., formed as POKE², POCKET (cf. PURSE)]

pud /pʊd/ *n. colloq.* = PUDDING. [abbr.]

pudding /ˈpʊdɪŋ/ *n.* **1 a** any of various sweet cooked dishes (*plum pudding*; *rice pudding*). **b** a savoury dish containing flour, suet, etc. (*Yorkshire pudding*; *steak and kidney pudding*). **c** the sweet course of a meal. **d** the intestines of a pig etc. stuffed with oatmeal, spices, blood, etc. (*black pudding*). **2** *colloq.* a person or thing resembling a pudding. □ **puddingy** *adj.* [ME *poding* f. OF *boudin* black pudding ult. f. L *botellus* sausage: see BOWEL]

puddle /ˈpʌd(ə)l/ *n. & v.* —*n.* **1** a small pool, esp. of rainwater on a road etc. **2** clay and sand mixed with water and used as a watertight covering for embankments etc. —*v.* **1** *tr.* **a** knead (clay and sand) into puddle. **b** line (a canal etc.) with puddle. **2** *intr.* make puddle from clay etc. **3** *tr.* stir (molten iron) to produce wrought iron by expelling carbon. □ **puddler** *n.* **puddly** *adj.* [ME *podel*, *puddel*, dimin. of OE *pudd* ditch]

pudendum /pjuːˈdendəm/ *n.* (*pl.* **pudenda** /-də/) (usu. in *pl.*) the genitals, esp. of a woman. □ **pudendal** *adj.* **pudic** /ˈpjuːdɪk/ *adj.* [L *pudenda* (*membra* parts), neut. pl. of gerundive of *pudēre* be ashamed]

pueblo /ˈpwebləʊ/ *n.* (*pl.* **-os**) a town or village in Latin America, esp. an Indian settlement. [Sp., = people, f. L *populus*]

puerile /ˈpjʊəraɪl/ *adj.* **1** trivial, childish, immature. **2** of or like a child. □ **puerilely** *adv.* **puerility** /-ˈrɪlɪtɪ/ *n.* (*pl.* **-ies**). [F *puéril* or L *puerilis* f. *puer* boy]

puerperal /pjuːˈɜːpər(ə)l/ *adj.* of or caused by childbirth. □ **puerperal fever** fever following childbirth and caused by uterine infection. [L *puerperus* f. *puer* child + *-parus* bearing]

puff *n. & v.* —*n.* **1 a** a short quick blast of breath or wind. **b** the sound of this; a similar sound. **c** a small quantity of vapour, smoke, etc., emitted in one blast (*went up in a puff of smoke*). **2** a cake etc. containing jam, cream, etc., and made of light esp. puff pastry. **3** a gathered mass of material in a dress etc. (*puff sleeve*). **4 a** an extravagantly enthusiastic review of a book etc., esp. in a newspaper. **b** an advertisement for goods etc., esp. in a newspaper. **5** = *powder-puff*. —*v.* **1** *intr.* emit a puff of air or breath; blow with short blasts. **2** *intr.* (usu. foll. by *away*, *out*, etc.) (of a person smoking, a steam engine, etc.) emit or move with puffs (*puffing away at his cigar*; *a train puffed out of the station*). **3** *tr.* (usu. in passive; often foll. by *out*) put out of breath (*arrived somewhat puffed*; *completely puffed him out*). **4** *intr.* breathe hard; pant. **5** *intr. & tr.* (usu. foll. by *up*, *out*) become or cause to become inflated; swell. **6** *tr.* (usu. foll. by *out*, *up*, *away*) blow or emit (dust, smoke, a light object, etc.) with a puff. **7** *tr.* smoke (a pipe etc.) in puffs. **8** *tr.* (usu. as **puffed up** *adj.*) elate; make proud or boastful. **9** *tr.* advertise or promote (goods, a book, etc.) with exaggerated or false praise. □ **puff-adder** a large venomous African viper, *Bitis arietans*, which inflates the upper part of its body and hisses when excited. **puff-ball** any of various fungi having a ball-shaped spore case. **puff pastry** light flaky pastry. □ **puffer** *n.* [ME *puf*, *puffe*, perh. f. OE, imit. of the sound of breath]

puffin /ˈpʌfɪn/ *n.* any of various sea birds of the family Alcidae native to the N. Atlantic and N. Pacific, esp. *Fratercula arctica*, having a large head with a brightly coloured triangular bill, and black and white plumage. [ME *poffin*, *pophyn*, of unkn. orig.]

puffy /ˈpʌfɪ/ *adj.* (**puffier**, **puffiest**) **1** swollen, esp. of the face etc. **2** fat. **3** short-winded. □ **puffily** *adv.* **puffiness** *n.*

pug *n.* (in full **pug-dog**) **1** a dwarf breed of dog like a bulldog with a broad flat nose and deeply wrinkled face. **2** a dog of this breed. □ **pug-nose** a short squat or snub nose. **pug-nosed** having such a nose. □ **puggish** *adj.* **puggy** *adj.* [16th c.: perh. f. LG or Du.]

pugilist /ˈpjuːdʒɪlɪst/ *n.* a boxer, esp. a professional. □ **pugilism** *n.* **pugilistic** /-ˈlɪstɪk/ *adj.* [L *pugil* boxer]

pugnacious /pʌgˈneɪʃəs/ *adj.* quarrelsome; disposed to fight. □ **pugnaciously** *adv.* **pugnaciousness** *n.* **pugnacity** /-ˈnæsɪtɪ/ *n.* [L *pugnax -acis* f. *pugnare* fight f. *pugnus* fist]

puisne /ˈpjuːnɪ/ *adj. Law* denoting a judge of a superior court inferior in rank to chief justices. [OF f. *puis* f. L *postea* afterwards + *né* born f. L *natus*: cf. PUNY]

puissance /ˈpjuːɪs(ə)ns, ˈpwɪs-, pwiːˈsãs/ *n.* a test of a horse's ability to jump large obstacles in showjumping. [ME f. OF (as PUISSANT)]

puissant /ˈpjuːɪs(ə)nt, ˈpwiːs-, ˈpwɪs-/ *adj. literary* or *archaic* having great power or influence; mighty. □ **puissantly** *adv.* [ME f. OF f. L *posse* be able: cf. POTENT]

puja /ˈpuːdʒə/ *n.* (also **pooja**) a Hindu rite of worship; a prayer. [Skr.]

puke /pjuːk/ *v. & n. sl.* —*v.tr. & intr.* vomit. —*n.* vomit. □ **pukey** *adj.* [16th c.: prob. imit.]

pukka /ˈpʌkə/ *adj.* (also **pukkah**, **pucka**) *Anglo-Ind.* **1** genuine. **2** of good quality; reliable (*did a pukka job*). [Hindi *pakkā* cooked, ripe, substantial]

pulchritude /ˈpʌlkrɪˌtjuːd/ *n. literary* beauty. □ **pulchritudinous** /-ˈtjuːdɪnəs/ *adj.* [ME f. L *pulchritudo -dinis* f. *pulcher -chri* beautiful]

pull /pʊl/ *v. & n.* —*v.* **1** *tr.* exert force upon a thing) tending to move it to oneself or the origin of the force (*stop pulling my hair*). **2** *tr.* cause to move in this way (*pulled it nearer*; *pulled me into the room*). **3** *intr.* exert a pulling force (*the horse pulls well*; *the engine will not pull*). **4** *tr.* extract (a cork or tooth) by pulling. **5** *tr.* damage (a muscle etc.) by abnormal strain. **6 a** *tr.* move (a boat) by pulling on the oars. **b** *intr.* (of a boat etc.) be caused to move, esp. in a specified direction. **7** *intr.* (often foll. by *up*) proceed with effort (up a hill etc.). **8** *tr.* (foll. by *on*) bring out (a weapon) for use against (a person). **9 a** *tr.* check the speed of (a horse), esp. so as to make it lose the race. **b** *intr.* (of a horse) strain against the bit. **10** *tr.* attract or secure (custom or support). **11** *tr.* draw (liquor) from a barrel etc. **12** *intr.* (foll. by *at*) tear or pluck at. **13** *intr.* (often foll. by *on*, *at*) inhale deeply; draw or suck (on a pipe etc.). **14** *tr.* (often foll. by *up*) remove (a plant) by the root. **15** *tr.* **a** *Cricket* strike (the ball) to the leg side. **b** *Golf* strike (the ball) widely to the left. **16** *tr.* print (a proof etc.). **17** *tr. colloq.* achieve or accomplish (esp. something illicit). —*n.* **1** the act of pulling. **2** the force exerted by this. **3** a means of exerting influence; an advantage. **4** something that attracts or draws attention. **5** a deep draught of liquor. **6** a prolonged effort, e.g. in going up a hill. **7** a handle etc. for applying a pull. **8** a spell of rowing. **9** a printer's rough proof. **10** *Cricket & Golf* a pulling stroke. **11** a suck at a cigarette. □ **pull about 1** treat roughly. **2** pull from side to side. **pull apart** (or **to pieces**) = take to pieces. **pull back** retreat or cause to retreat. **pull down 1** demolish (esp. a building). **2** humiliate. **3** *colloq.* earn (a sum of money) as wages etc. **pull a face** assume a distinctive or specified (e.g. sad or angry) expression. **pull in 1** (of a bus, train, etc.) arrive to take passengers. **2** (of a vehicle) move to the side of or off the road. **3** earn or acquire. **4** *colloq.* arrest. **pull-in** *n. Brit.* a roadside café or other stopping-place. **pull a person's leg** deceive a person playfully. **pull off 1** remove by pulling. **2** succeed in achieving or winning. **pull oneself together** recover control of oneself. **pull the other one** *colloq.* expressing disbelief (with ref. to *pull a person's leg*). **pull out 1** take out by pulling. **2** depart. **3** withdraw from an undertaking. **4** (of a bus, train, etc.) leave with its passengers. **5** (of a vehicle) move out from the side of the road, or from its normal position to overtake. **pull-out** *n.* something that can be pulled out, esp. a section of a magazine. **pull over** (of a vehicle) pull in. **pull the plug on** *colloq.* defeat, discomfit. **pull one's punches** avoid using one's full force. **pull rank** take unfair advantage of one's seniority. **pull round** (or **through**) recover or cause to recover from an illness. **pull strings** exert (esp. clandestine) influence. **pull the strings** be the real actuator of what another does. **pull together** work in harmony. **pull up 1** stop or cause to stop moving. **2** pull out of the ground. **3** reprimand. **4** check oneself. **pull one's weight** do one's fair share of work. **pull wires** esp. *US* = *pull strings*. □ **puller** *n.* [OE (ā)*pullian*, perh. rel. to LG *pūlen*, MDu. *polen* to shell]

pullet /ˈpʊlɪt/ *n.* a young hen, esp. one less than one year old. [ME f. OF *poulet* dimin. of *poule* ult. fem. of L *pullus* chicken]

pulley /ˈpʊlɪ/ *n.* (*pl.* **-eys**) **1** a grooved wheel or set of wheels for a cord etc. to pass over, set in a block and used for changing the direction of a force. **2** a wheel or drum fixed on a shaft and turned by a belt, used esp. to increase speed or power. [ME f. OF *polie* prob. ult. f. med. Gk *polidion* (unrecorded) pivot, dimin. of *polos* POLE²]

Pullman /ˈpʊlmən/ *n.* **1** a railway carriage or motor coach affording special comfort. **2** a sleeping-car. [G. M. *Pullman*, Amer. designer d. 1897]

pullover /ˈpʊlˌəʊvə(r)/ *n.* a knitted garment put on over the head and covering the top half of the body.

pullulate /ˈpʌljʊˌleɪt/ *v.intr.* **1** (of a seed, shoot, etc.) bud, sprout, germinate. **2** (esp. of an animal) swarm, multiply; breed prolifically. **3** develop; spring up; come to life. **4** (foll. by *with*) abound. □ **pullulant** *adj.* **pullulation** /-ˈleɪʃ(ə)n/ *n.* [L *pullulare* sprout f. *pullulus* dimin. of *pullus* young of an animal]

pulmonary /ˈpʌlmənərɪ/ *adj.* **1** of or relating to the lungs. **2** having lungs or lunglike organs. **3** affected with or susceptible to lung disease. □ **pulmonate** /-nət/ *adj.* [L *pulmonarius* f. *pulmo -onis* lung]

pulp *n. & v.* —*n.* **1** the soft fleshy part of fruit etc. **2** any soft thick wet mass. **3** a soft shapeless mass derived from rags, wood, etc., used in paper-making. **4** (often *attrib.*) poor quality (often sensational) writing orig. printed on rough paper (*pulp fiction*). —*v.* **1** *tr.* reduce to pulp. **2** *tr.* withdraw (a publication) from the market, usu. recycling the paper. **3** *tr.* remove pulp from. **4** *intr.* become pulp. □ **pulper** *n.* **pulpless** *adj.* **pulpy** *adj.* **pulpiness** *n.* [L *pulpa*]

pulpit /ˈpʊlpɪt/ *n.* **1** a raised enclosed platform in a church etc. from which the preacher delivers a sermon. **2** (prec. by *the*) preachers or preaching collectively. [ME f. L *pulpitum* scaffold, platform]

pulpwood /ˈpʌlpwʊd/ *n.* timber suitable for making pulp.

pulsar /ˈpʌlsɑː(r)/ *n. Astron.* a cosmic source of regular and rapid pulses of radiation usu. at radio frequencies. [*pulsating star*, after *quasar*]

pulsate /pʌlˈseɪt, ˈpʌl-/ *v.intr.* **1** expand and contract rhythmically; throb. **2** vibrate, quiver, thrill. □ **pulsation** /-ˈseɪʃ(ə)n/ *n.* **pulsator** /-ˈseɪtə(r)/ *n.* **pulsatory** /ˈpʌlsətərɪ/ *adj.* [L *pulsare* frequent. of *pellere puls-* drive, beat]

pulse¹ /pʌls/ *n. & v.* —*n.* **1 a** a rhythmical throbbing of the arteries as blood is propelled through them, esp. as felt in the wrists, temples, etc. **b** each successive beat of the arteries or heart. **2** a throb or thrill of life or emotion. **3** a latent feeling. **4** a single vibration of sound, electric current, light, etc., esp. as a signal. **5** a musical beat. **6** any regular or recurrent rhythm. —*v.intr.* **1** pulsate. **2** (foll. by *out*, *in*, etc.) transmit etc. by rhythmical beats. □ **pulseless** *adj.* [ME f. OF *pous* f. L *pulsus* f. *pellere puls-* drive, beat]

pulse² /pʌls/ *n.* (as *sing.* or *pl.*) **1** the edible seeds of various leguminous plants, e.g. chick-peas, lentils, beans, etc. **2** the plant or plants producing this. [ME f. OF *pols* f. L *puls pultis* porridge of meal etc.]

pulverize /ˈpʌlvəˌraɪz/ *v.* (also **-ise**) **1** *tr.* reduce to fine particles. **2** *tr. & intr.* crumble to dust. **3** *colloq. tr.* **a** demolish. **b** defeat utterly. □ **pulverizable** *adj.* **pulverization** /-ˈzeɪʃ(ə)n/ *n.* **pulverizer** *n.* [ME f. LL *pulverizare* f. *pulvis pulveris* dust]

puma /ˈpjuːmə/ *n.* a wild American cat, *Felis concolor*, usu. with a plain greyish-black coat. [Sp. f. Quechua]

pumice /ˈpʌmɪs/ *n. & v.* —*n.* (in full **pumice-stone**) **1** a light porous volcanic rock often used as an abrasive in cleaning or polishing substances. **2** a piece of this used for removing hard skin etc. —*v.tr.* rub or clean with a pumice. □ **pumiceous** /pjuːˈmɪʃəs/ *adj.* [ME f. OF *pomis* f. L *pumex pumicis* (dial. *pom-*)]

pummel /ˈpʌm(ə)l/ *v.tr.* (**pummelled**, **pummelling**; *US* **pummeled**, **pummeling**) strike repeatedly esp. with the fist. [alt. f. POMMEL]

pump¹ *n. & v.* —*n.* **1** a machine, usu. with rotary action or the reciprocal action of a piston, for raising or moving liquids, compressing gases, inflating tyres, etc. **2** an instance of pumping; a stroke of a pump. —*v.* **1** *tr.* (often foll. by *in*, *out*, *into*, *up*, etc.) raise or remove (liquid, gas, etc.) with a pump. **2** *tr.* (often foll. by *up*) fill (a tyre etc.) with air. **3** *tr.* remove (water etc.) with a pump. **4** *intr.* work a pump. **5** *tr.* (often foll. by *out*) cause to move, pour forth, etc., as if by pumping. **6** *tr.* elicit information from (a person) by persistent questioning. **7** *tr.* **a** move vigorously up and down. **b** shake (a person's hand) effusively. □ **pump iron** *colloq.* exercise with weights. **pump-priming 1** introduce fluid etc. into a pump to prepare it for working. **2** *esp. US* the stimulation of commerce etc. by investment.

pump room 1 a room where fuel pumps etc. are stored or controlled. **2** a room at a spa etc. where medicinal water is dispensed. [ME *pumpe*, *pompe* (orig. Naut.): prob. imit.]

pump² /pʌmp/ *n.* **1** a plimsoll. **2** a light shoe for dancing etc. **3** *US* a court shoe. [16th c.: orig. unkn.]

pumpernickel /ˈpʌmpəˌnɪk(ə)l, ˈpʊ-/ *n.* German wholemeal rye bread. [G, earlier = lout, bumpkin, of uncert. orig.]

pumpkin /ˈpʌmpkɪn/ *n.* **1** any of various plants of the genus *Cucurbita*, esp. *C. maxima*, with large lobed leaves and tendrils. **2** the large rounded yellow fruit of this with a thick rind and edible flesh. [alt. f. earlier *pompon, pumpion* f. obs. F *po(m)pon* f. L *pepo -onis* f. Gk *pepōn* large melon]

pun *n. & v.* —*n.* the humorous use of a word to suggest different meanings, or of words of the same sound and different meanings. —*v.intr.* (**punned, punning**) (foll. by *on*) make a pun or puns with (words). □ **punningly** *adv.* [17th c.: perh. f. obs. *pundigrion*, a fanciful formation]

punch¹ *v. & n.* —*v.* & *tr.* **1** strike bluntly, esp. with a closed fist. **2** prod or poke with a blunt object. **3 a** pierce a hole in (metal, paper, a ticket, etc.) as or with a punch. **b** pierce (a hole) by punching. **4** *US* drive (cattle) by prodding with a stick etc. —*n.* **1** a blow with a fist. **2** the ability to deliver this. **3** *colloq.* vigour, momentum; effective force. □ **punch-drunk** stupefied from or as though from a series of heavy blows. **punching-bag** *US* a suspended stuffed bag used as a punchball. **punch-line** words giving the point of a joke or story. **punch-up** *Brit. colloq.* a fist-fight; a brawl. □ **puncher** *n.* [ME, var. of POUNCE]

punch² *n.* **1** any of various devices or machines for punching holes in materials (e.g. paper, leather, metal, plaster). **2** a tool or machine for impressing a design or stamping a die on a material. [perh. f. PUNCH¹]

punch³ *n.* a drink of wine or spirits mixed with water, fruit juices, spices, etc., and usu. served hot. □ **punch-bowl 1** a bowl in which punch is mixed. **2** a deep round hollow in a hill. [17th c.: orig. unkn.]

punch⁴ *n.* **1** (**Punch**) a grotesque humpbacked figure in a puppet-show called *Punch and Judy*. **2** (in full **Suffolk punch**) a short-legged thickset draught horse. □ **as pleased as Punch** showing great pleasure. [abbr. of *Punchinello* the chief character in a traditional Italian puppet show.]

punchball /ˈpʌntʃbɔːl/ *n.* a stuffed or inflated ball suspended or mounted on a stand, for punching as a form of exercise.

punchy /ˈpʌntʃɪ/ *adj.* (**punchier, punchiest**) having punch or vigour; forceful. □ **punchily** *adv.* **punchiness** *n.*

punctilio /pʌŋkˈtɪlɪəʊ/ *n.* (*pl.* **-os**) **1** a delicate point of ceremony or honour. **2** the etiquette of such points. **3** petty formality. [It. *puntiglio* & Sp. *puntillo* dimin. of *punto* POINT]

punctilious /pʌŋkˈtɪlɪəs/ *adj.* **1** attentive to formality or etiquette. **2** precise in behaviour.

□ **punctiliously** *adv.* **punctiliousness** *n.* [F *pointilleux* f. *pointille* f. It. (as PUNCTILIO)]

punctual /ˈpʌŋktjʊəl/ *adj.* **1** observant of the appointed time. **2** neither early nor late. □ **punctuality** /-ˈælɪtɪ/ *n.* **punctually** *adv.* [ME f. med.L *punctualis* f. L *punctum* POINT]

punctuate /ˈpʌŋktjʊˌeɪt/ *v.tr.* **1** insert punctuation marks in. **2** interrupt at intervals (*punctuated his tale with heavy sighs*). [med.L *punctuare punctuat-* (as PUNCTUAL)]

punctuation /ˌpʌŋktjʊˈeɪʃ(ə)n/ *n.* **1** the system or arrangement of marks used to punctuate a written passage. **2** the practice or skill of punctuating. □ **punctuation mark** any of the marks (e.g. full stop and comma) used in writing to separate sentences and phrases etc. and to clarify meaning. [med.L *punctuatio* (as PUNCTUATE)]

puncture /ˈpʌŋktʃə(r)/ *n. & v.* —*n.* **1** a prick or pricking, esp. the accidental piercing of a pneumatic tyre. **2** a hole made in this way. —*v.* **1** *tr.* make a puncture in. **2** *intr.* undergo puncture. **3** *tr.* prick or pierce. [ME f. L *punctura* f. *pungere punct-* prick]

pundit /ˈpʌndɪt/ *n.* **1** (also **pandit**) a learned Hindu. **2** *often iron.* a learned expert or teacher. □ **punditry** *n.* [Hind. *paṇḍit* f. Skr. *paṇḍita* learned]

pungent /ˈpʌndʒ(ə)nt/ *adj.* **1** having a sharp or strong taste or smell, esp. so as to produce a pricking sensation. **2** (of remarks) penetrating, biting, caustic. **3** mentally stimulating. □ **pungency** *n.* **pungently** *adv.* [L *pungent-* pres. part. of *pungere* prick]

punish /ˈpʌnɪʃ/ *v.tr.* **1** cause (an offender) to suffer for an offence. **2** inflict a penalty for (an offence). **3** *colloq.* inflict severe blows on (an opponent). **4 a** tax severely; subject to severe treatment. **b** abuse or treat improperly. □ **punishable** *adj.* **punisher** *n.* **punishing** *adj.* (in sense 4a). **punishingly** *adv.* [ME f. OF *punir* f. L *punire* = *poenire* f. *poena* penalty]

punishment /ˈpʌnɪʃmənt/ *n.* **1** the act or an instance of punishing; the condition of being punished. **2** the loss or suffering inflicted in this. **3** *colloq.* severe treatment or suffering. [ME f. AF & OF *punissement* f. *punir*]

punitive /ˈpjuːnɪtɪv/ *adj.* (also **punitory** /-tərɪ/) **1** inflicting or intended to inflict punishment. **2** (of taxation etc.) extremely severe. □ **punitively** *adv.* [F *punitif -ive* or med.L *punitivus* (as PUNISHMENT)]

punk *n. & adj.* —*n.* **1 a** a worthless person or thing (often as a general term of abuse). **b** nonsense. **2 a** (in full **punk rock**) a loud fast-moving form of rock music with crude and aggressive effects. **b** (in full **punk rocker**) a devotee of this. **3** *US* a hoodlum or ruffian. —*adj.* **1** worthless, rotten. **2** denoting punk rock and its associations. □ **punky** *adj.* [18th c.: orig. unkn.: cf. SPUNK]

punkah /ˈpʌŋkə/ *n.* a large swinging cloth fan on a frame worked by a cord or electrically. □ **punkah-wallah** a person who works a punkah. [Hindi *pankhā* fan f. Skr. *pakṣaka* f. *pakṣa* wing]

punnet /ˈpʌnɪt/ *n. Brit.* a small light basket or container for fruit or vegetables. [19th c.: perh. dimin. of dial. *pun* POUND¹]

punster /ˈpʌnstə(r)/ *n.* a person who makes puns, esp. habitually.

punt[1] *n. & v.* —*n.* a long narrow flat-bottomed boat, square at both ends, propelled by a long pole. —*v.* **1** *tr.* propel (a punt) with a pole. **2** *intr. & tr.* travel or convey in a punt. □ **punter** *n.* [ME f. MLG *punte*, *punto* & MDu. *ponte* ferry-boat f. L *ponto* Gaulish transport vessel]

punt[2] *v. & n.* —*v.tr.* kick (a ball, esp. in rugby) after it has dropped from the hands and before it reaches the ground. —*n.* such a kick. □ **punter** *n.* [prob. f. dial. *punt* push forcibly]

punt[3] *v. & n.* —*v.intr.* **1** (in some card-games) lay a stake against the bank. **2** *Brit. colloq.* **a** bet on a horse etc. **b** speculate in shares etc. —*n.* **1** a bet. **2** a point in faro. [F *ponter* f. *ponte* player against the bank f. Sp. *punto* POINT]

punt[4] *n.* the chief monetary unit of the Republic of Ireland. [Ir., = pound]

punter /ˈpʌntə(r)/ *n.* **1** a person who gambles or lays a bet. **2 a** *colloq.* a customer or client; a member of an audience. **b** *sl.* a prostitute's client.

puny /ˈpjuːnɪ/ *adj.* (**punier**, **puniest**) **1** undersized. **2** weak, feeble. **3** petty. □ **punily** *adv.* **puniness** *n.* [phonetic spelling of PUISNE]

pup *n. & v.* —*n.* **1** a young dog. **2** a young wolf, rat, seal, etc. **3** *Brit.* an unpleasant or arrogant young man. —*v.tr.* (**pupped**, **pupping**) (also *absol.*) (of a bitch etc.) bring forth (young). □ **in pup** (of a bitch) pregnant. **sell a person a pup** swindle a person, esp. by selling something worthless. [back-form. f. PUPPY as if a dimin. in -Y[2]]

pupa /ˈpjuːpə/ *n.* (*pl.* **pupae** /-piː/) an insect in the stage of development between larva and imago. □ **pupal** *adj.* [mod.L f. L *pupa* girl, doll]

pupate /pjuːˈpeɪt/ *v.intr.* become a pupa. □ **pupation** *n.*

pupil[1] /ˈpjuːpɪl, -p(ə)l/ *n.* a person who is taught by another, esp. a schoolchild or student in relation to a teacher. □ **pupillage** *n.* (also **pupilage**). **pupillary** *adj.* (also **pupilary**). [ME, orig. = orphan, ward f. OF *pupille* or L *pupillus*, *-illa*, dimin. of *pupus* boy, *pupa* girl]

pupil[2] /ˈpjuːpɪl, -p(ə)l/ *n.* the dark circular opening in the centre of the iris of the eye, varying in size to regulate the passage of light to the retina. □ **pupillar** *adj.* (also **pupilar**). **pupillary** *adj.* (also **pupilary**). [OF *pupille* or L *pupilla*, dimin. of *pūpa* doll (as PUPIL[1]): so called from the tiny images visible in the eye]

puppet /ˈpʌpɪt/ *n.* **1** a small figure representing a human being or animal and moved by various means as entertainment. **2** a person whose actions are controlled by another. □ **puppet State** a country that is nominally independent but actually under the control of another power. □ **puppetry** *n.* [later form of POPPET]

puppeteer /ˌpʌpɪˈtɪə(r)/ *n.* a person who works puppets.

puppy /ˈpʌpɪ/ *n.* (*pl.* **-ies**) **1** a young dog. **2** a conceited or arrogant young man. □ **puppy-fat** temporary fatness of a child or adolescent. **puppy love** = calf-love. □ **puppyhood** *n.* **puppyish** *adj.* [ME perh. f. OF *po(u)pee* doll, plaything, toy f. Rmc (as POPPET)]

pur- /pɜː(r)/ *prefix* = PRO-[1] (*purchase*; *pursue*). [AF f. OF *pur-*, *pur-*, *pour-* f. L *por-*, *pro-*]

purblind /ˈpɜːblaɪnd/ *adj.* **1** partly blind; dim-sighted. **2** obtuse, dim-witted. □ **purblindness**

n. [ME *pur(e)* blind f. PURE orig. in sense 'utterly', with assim. to PUR-]

purchase /ˈpɜːtʃɪs, -tʃəs/ *v. & n.* —*v.tr.* **1** acquire by payment; buy. **2** obtain or achieve at some cost. —*n.* **1** the act or an instance of buying. **2** something bought. **3** a firm hold on a thing to move it or to prevent it from slipping; leverage. □ **purchase tax** *Brit. hist.* a tax on goods bought, levied at higher rates for non-essential or luxury goods. □ **purchasable** *adj.* **purchaser** *n.* [ME f. AF *purchacer*, OF *pourchacier* seek to obtain (as PUR-, CHASE[1])]

purdah /ˈpɜːdə/ *n. Ind.* **1** a system in certain Muslim and Hindu societies of screening women from strangers by means of a veil or curtain. **2** a curtain in a house, used for this purpose. [Urdu & Pers. *pardah* veil, curtain]

pure /pjʊə(r)/ *adj.* **1** unmixed, unadulterated (*pure white*; *pure alcohol*). **2** of unmixed origin or descent (*pure-blooded*). **3** chaste. **4** morally or sexually undefiled; not corrupt. **5** guiltless. **6** sincere. **7** mere, simple, nothing but, sheer (*it was pure malice*). **8** (of a sound) not discordant, perfectly in tune. **9** (of a subject of study) dealing with abstract concepts and not practical application. □ **pureness** *n.* [ME f. OF *pur* pure f. L *purus*]

purée /ˈpjʊəreɪ/ *n. & v.* —*n.* a pulp of vegetables or fruit etc. reduced to a smooth cream. —*v.tr.* (**purées**, **puréed**) make a purée of. [F]

purely /ˈpjʊəlɪ/ *adv.* **1** in a pure manner. **2** merely, solely, exclusively.

purgation /pɜːˈgeɪʃ(ə)n/ *n.* **1** purification. **2** purging of the bowels. [ME f. OF *purgation* or L *purgatio* (as PURGE)]

purgative /ˈpɜːgətɪv/ *adj. & n.* —*adj.* **1** serving to purify. **2** strongly laxative. —*n.* **1** a purgative thing. **2** a laxative. [ME f. OF *purgatif -ive* or LL *purgativus* (as PURGE)]

purgatory /ˈpɜːgətərɪ/ *n. & adj.* —*n.* (*pl.* **-ies**) **1** the condition or supposed place of spiritual cleansing, esp. (*RC Ch.*) of those dying in the grace of God but having to expiate venial sins etc. **2** a place or state of temporary suffering or expiation. —*adj.* purifying. □ **purgatorial** /-ˈtɔːrɪəl/ *adj.* [ME f. AF *purgatorie*, OF *-oire* f. med.L *purgatorium*, neut. of LL *purgatorius* (as PURGE)]

purge /pɜːdʒ/ *v. & n.* —*v.tr.* **1** (often foll. by *of*, *from*) make physically or spiritually clean. **2** remove by a cleansing process. **3** rid (an organization, party, etc.) of persons regarded as undesirable. **4 a** empty (the bowels). **b** empty the bowels of. **5** *Law* atone for or wipe out (an offence, esp. contempt of court). —*n.* **1** the act or an instance of purging. **2** a purgative. □ **purger** *n.* [ME f. OF *purg(i)er* f. L *purgare* purify f. *purus* pure]

purify /ˈpjʊərɪfaɪ/ *v.tr.* (**-ies**, **-ied**) **1** (often foll. by *of*, *from*) cleanse or make pure. **2** make ceremonially clean. **3** clear of extraneous elements. □ **purification** /-fɪˈkeɪʃ(ə)n/ *n.* **purificatory** /-fɪˌkeɪtərɪ/ *adj.* **purifier** *n.* [ME f. OF *purifier* f. L *purificare* (as PURE)]

purist /ˈpjʊərɪst/ *n.* a stickler for or advocate of scrupulous purity, esp. in language or art. □ **purism** *n.* **puristic** /-ˈrɪstɪk/ *adj.* [F *puriste* f. *pur* PURE]

puritan /ˈpjʊərɪt(ə)n/ *n. & adj.* —*n.* **1** (**Puritan**) *hist.* a member of a group of English Protestants who regarded the Reformation of the Church under Elizabeth as incomplete and sought to simplify and regulate forms of worship. **2** a purist member of any party. **3** a person practising or affecting extreme strictness in religion or morals. —*adj.* **1** *hist.* of or relating to the Puritans. **2** scrupulous and austere in religion or morals. □ **puritanism** *n.* [LL *puritas* (as PURITY) after earlier *Catharan* f. Gk *katharoi* pure]

puritanical /ˌpjʊərɪˈtænɪk(ə)l/ *adj.* often *derog.* practising or affecting strict religious or moral behaviour. □ **puritanically** *adv.*

purity /ˈpjʊərɪtɪ/ *n.* **1** pureness, cleanness. **2** freedom from physical or moral pollution. [ME f. OF *pureté*, with assim. to LL *puritas -tatis* f. L *purus* pure]

purl[1] *n. & v.* —*n.* **1** a knitting stitch made by putting the needle through the front of the previous stitch and passing the yarn round the back of the needle. **2** a chain of minute loops; a picot. —*v.tr.* (also *absol.*) knit with a purl stitch. [orig. *pyrle*, *pirle* f. Sc. *pirl* twist: the knitting sense may be f. a different word]

purl[2] *v. & n.* —*v.intr.* (of a brook etc.) flow with a swirling motion and babbling sound. —*n.* this motion or sound. [16th c.: prob. imit.: cf. Norw. *purle* babble]

purler /ˈpɜːlə(r)/ *n. Brit. colloq.* a headlong fall. [*purl* upset, rel. to PURL[1]]

purlieu /ˈpɜːljuː/ *n.* (*pl.* **purlieus**) **1** a person's bounds or limits. **2** a person's usual haunts. **3** *Brit. hist.* a tract on the border of a forest. **4** (in *pl.*) the outskirts; an outlying region. [ME *purlew*, prob. alt. after F *lieu* place f. AF *purale(e)*, OF *pourallee* a going round to settle the boundaries f. *po(u)raler* traverse]

purlin /ˈpɜːlɪn/ *n.* a horizontal beam along the length of a roof. [ME: orig. uncert.]

purloin /pəˈlɔɪn/ *v.tr. formal or joc.* steal, pilfer. □ **purloiner** *n.* [ME f. AF *purloigner* put away, do away with (as PUR-, *loign* far f. L *longe*)]

purple /ˈpɜːp(ə)l/ *n., adj., & v.* —*n.* **1** a colour intermediate between red and blue. **2** (in full **Tyrian purple**) a crimson dye obtained from some molluscs. **3** a purple robe, esp. as the dress of an emperor or senior magistrate. **4** the scarlet official dress of a cardinal. —*adj.* of a purple colour. —*v.tr. & intr.* make or become purple. □ **born in the purple 1** born into a reigning family. **2** belonging to the most privileged class. **purple heart** *Brit. colloq.* a heart-shaped stimulant tablet, esp. of amphetamine. **Purple Heart** (in the US) a decoration for those wounded in action. **purple passage** (or **patch**) **1** an ornate or elaborate passage in a literary composition. **2** *Austral. colloq.* a piece of luck or success. □ **purpleness** *n.* **purplish** *adj.* **purply** *adj.* [OE alt. f. *purpure* purpuran f. L *purpura* f. Gk *porphura*]

purport *v. & n.* —*v.tr.* /pəˈpɔːt/ **1** profess; be intended to seem (*purports to be the royal seal*). **2** (often foll. by *that* + clause) (of a document or speech) have as its meaning; state. —*n.* /ˈpɜː-pɔːt/ **1** the ostensible meaning of something. **2** the sense or tenor (of a document or statement). □ **purportedly** /pəˈpɔːtɪdlɪ/ *adv.* [ME f. AF & OF *purport*, *porport* f. *purporter* f. med.L *proportare* (as PRO-[1], *portare* carry)]

purpose /ˈpɜːpəs/ *n. & v.* —*n.* **1** an object to be attained; a thing intended. **2** the intention to act. **3** resolution, determination. —*v.tr.* have as one's purpose; design, intend. □ **on purpose** intentionally. **purpose-built** (or **-made**) built

or made for a specific purpose. **to no purpose** with no result or effect. **to the purpose 1** relevant. **2** useful. [ME f. OF *porpos*, *purpos* f. L *proponere* (as PROPOUND)]

purposeful /ˈpɜːpəsˌfʊl/ *adj.* **1** having or indicating purpose. **2** intentional. **3** resolute. □ **purposefully** *adv.* **purposefulness** *n.*

purposeless /ˈpɜːpəslɪs/ *adj.* having no aim or plan. □ **purposelessly** *adv.* **purposelessness** *n.*

purposely /ˈpɜːpəslɪ/ *adv.* on purpose; intentionally.

purposive /ˈpɜːpəsɪv/ *adj.* **1** having or serving a purpose. **2** done with a purpose. **3** (of a person or conduct) having purpose or resolution; purposeful. □ **purposively** *adv.* **purposiveness** *n.*

purr *v. & n.* —*v.* **1** *intr.* (of a cat) make a low vibratory sound expressing contentment. **2** *intr.* (of machinery etc.) make a similar sound. **3** *intr.* (of a person) express pleasure. **4** *tr.* utter or express (words or contentment) in this way. —*n.* a purring sound. [imit.]

purse /pɜːs/ *n. & v.* —*n.* **1** a small pouch of leather etc. for carrying money on the person. **2** *US* a handbag. **3** a receptacle resembling a purse in form or purpose. **4** money, funds. **5** a sum collected as a present or given as a prize in a contest. —*v.* **1** *tr.* (often foll. by *up*) pucker or contract (the lips). **2** *intr.* become contracted and wrinkled. □ **hold the purse-strings** have control of expenditure. **the public purse** the national treasury. [OE *purs* f. med.L *bursa*, *byrsa* purse f. Gk *bursa* hide, leather]

purser /ˈpɜːsə(r)/ *n.* an officer on a ship who keeps the accounts, esp. the head steward in a passenger vessel. □ **pursership** *n.*

pursuance /pəˈsjuːəns/ *n.* (foll. by *of*) the carrying out or observance (of a plan, idea, etc.).

pursuant /pəˈsjuːənt/ *adj. & adv.* —*adj.* pursuing. —*adv.* (foll. by *to*) conforming to or in accordance with. □ **pursuantly** *adv.* [ME, = prosecuting, f. OF *po(u)rsuiant* part. of *po(u)rsu(iv)ir* (as PURSUE): assim. to AF *pursuer* and PURSUE]

pursue /pəˈsjuː/ *v.* (**pursues**, **pursued**, **pursuing**) **1** *tr.* follow with intent to overtake or capture or do harm to. **2** *tr.* continue or proceed along (a route or course of action). **3** *tr.* follow or engage in (study or other activity). **4** *tr.* proceed in compliance with (a plan etc.). **5** *tr.* seek after, aim at. **6** *tr.* continue to investigate or discuss (a topic). **7** *tr.* seek the attention or acquaintance of (a person) persistently. **8** *tr.* (of misfortune etc.) persistently assail. **9** *tr.* persistently attend, stick to. **10** *intr.* go in pursuit. □ **pursuable** *adj.* **pursuer** *n.* [ME f. AF *pursiwer*, *-suer* = OF *porsivre* etc. ult. f. L *prosequi* follow after]

pursuit /pəˈsjuːt/ *n.* **1** the act or an instance of pursuing. **2** an occupation or activity pursued. □ **in pursuit of** pursuing. [ME f. OF *poursuite* (as PUR-, SUIT)]

pursy /ˈpɜːsɪ/ *adj.* **1** short-winded; puffy. **2** corpulent. □ **pursiness** *n.* [ME, earlier *pursive* f. AF *porsif* f. OF *polsif* f. *polser* breathe with difficulty f. L *pulsare* (as PULSATE)]

purulent /ˈpjʊərʊlənt/ *adj.* **1** consisting of or containing pus. **2** discharging pus. □ **purulence** *n.* **purulency** *n.* **purulently** *adv.* [F *purulent* or L *purulentus* (as PUS)]

purvey /pəˈveɪ/ *v.* **1** *tr.* provide or supply (articles of food) as one's business. **2** *intr.* (often foll. by *for*) **a** make provision. **b** act as supplier. □ **purveyor** *n*. [ME f. AF *purveier*, OF *porveïr* f. L *providēre* PROVIDE]

purview /ˈpɜːvjuː/ *n*. **1** the scope or range of a document, scheme, etc. **2** the range of physical or mental vision. [ME f. AF *purveü*, OF *porveü* past part. of *porveïr* (as PURVEY)]

pus /pʌs/ *n*. a thick yellowish or greenish liquid produced from infected tissue. [L *pus puris*]

push /pʊʃ/ *v*. & *n*. —*v*. **1** *tr*. exert a force on (a thing) to move it away from oneself or from the origin of the force. **2** *tr*. cause to move in this direction. **3** *intr*. exert such a force (*do not push against the door*). **4** *intr*. & *tr*. **a** thrust forward or upward. **b** project or cause to project (*pushes out new roots; the cape pushes out into the sea*). **5** *intr*. move forward by force or persistence. **6** *tr*. make (one's way) by pushing. **7** *intr*. exert oneself, esp. to surpass others. **8** *tr*. (often foll. by *to*, *into*, or *to* + infin.) urge or impel. **9** *tr*. tax the abilities or tolerance of; press (a person) hard. **10** *tr*. pursue (a claim etc.). **11** *tr*. promote the use or sale or adoption of, e.g. by advertising. **12** *intr*. (foll. by *for*) demand persistently (*pushed hard for reform*). **13** *tr. colloq*. sell (a drug) illegally. —*n*. **1** the act or an instance of pushing; a shove or thrust. **2** the force exerted in this. **3** a vigorous effort. **4** a military attack in force. **5** enterprise, determination to succeed. **6** the use of influence to advance a person. **7** the pressure of affairs. **8** a crisis. □ **be pushed for** *colloq*. have very little of (esp. time). **get the push** *colloq*. be dismissed or sent away. **give a person the push** *colloq*. dismiss or send away a person. **push along** (often in *imper*.) *colloq*. depart, leave. **push around** *colloq*. bully. **push-bike** *Brit. colloq*. a bicycle worked by pedals. **push-button 1** a button to be pushed esp. to operate an electrical device. **2** (*attrib*.) operated in this way. **push one's luck 1** take undue risks. **2** act presumptuously. **push off 1** push with an oar etc. to get a boat out into a river etc. **2** (often in *imper*.) *colloq*. go away. **push-start** *n*. the starting of a motor vehicle by pushing it to turn the engine. —*v.tr*. start (a vehicle) in this way. **push through** get (a scheme, proposal, etc.) completed or accepted quickly. **push-up** = *press-up*. [ME f. OF *pousser*, *pou(l)ser* f. L *pulsare* (as PULSATE)]

pushcart /ˈpʊʃkɑːt/ *n*. a handcart or barrow.

pushchair /ˈpʊʃtʃeə(r)/ *n*. *Brit*. a folding chair on wheels, for pushing a child in.

pusher /ˈpʊʃə(r)/ *n*. **1** *colloq*. an illegal seller of drugs. **2** *colloq*. a pushing or pushy person. **3** a child's utensil for pushing food onto a spoon etc.

pushful /ˈpʊʃfʊl/ *adj*. pushy; arrogantly self-assertive. □ **pushfully** *adv*.

pushing /ˈpʊʃɪŋ/ *adj*. **1** pushy; aggressively ambitious. **2** *colloq*. having nearly reached (a specified age). □ **pushingly** *adv*.

pushover /ˈpʊʃˌəʊvə(r)/ *n*. *colloq*. **1** something that is easily done. **2** a person who can easily be overcome, persuaded, etc.

pushy /ˈpʊʃɪ/ *adj*. (**pushier**, **pushiest**) *colloq*. **1** excessively or unpleasantly self-assertive. **2** selfishly determined to succeed. □ **pushily** *adv*. **pushiness** *n*.

pusillanimous /ˌpjuːsɪˈlænɪməs/ *adj*. lacking courage; timid. □ **pusillanimity** /-ləˈnɪmɪtɪ/

n. **pusillanimously** *adv*. [eccl.L *pusillanimis* f. *pusillus* very small + *animus* mind]

puss /pʊs/ *n. colloq*. **1** a cat (esp. as a form of address). **2** a playful or coquettish girl. [prob. f. MLG *pūs*, Du. *poes*, of unkn. orig.]

pussy /ˈpʊsɪ/ *n*. (*pl*. **-ies**) **1** (also **pussy-cat**) *colloq*. a cat. **2** *coarse sl*. the vulva. □ **pussy willow** any of various willows, esp. *Salix discolor*, with furry catkins.

pussyfoot /ˈpʊsɪfʊt/ *v.intr*. **1** move stealthily or warily. **2** act cautiously or noncommittally. □ **pussyfooter** *n*.

pustulate *v*. & *adj*. —*v.tr*. & *intr*. /ˈpʌstjʊˌleɪt/ form into pustules. —*adj*. /-lət/ of or relating to a pustule or pustules. □ **pustulation** /-ˈleɪʃ(ə)n/ *n*. [LL *pustulare* f. *pustula*: see PUSTULE]

pustule /ˈpʌstjuːl/ *n*. a pimple containing pus. □ **pustular** *adj*. **pustulous** *adj*. [ME f. OF *pustule* or L *pustula*]

put[1] /pʊt/ *v*. & *n*. —*v*. (**putting**; *past and past part*. **put**) **1** *tr*. move to or cause to be in a specified place or position (*put it in your pocket; put the children to bed; put your signature here*). **2** *tr*. bring into a specified condition, relation, or state (*puts me in great difficulty; an accident put the car out of action*). **3** *tr*. **a** (often foll. by *on*) impose or assign (*put a tax on beer; where do you put the blame?*). **b** (foll. by *on*, *to*) impose or enforce the existence of (*put a veto on it; put a stop to it*). **4** *tr*. **a** cause (a person) to go or be, habitually or temporarily (*put them at their ease; put them on the right track*). **b** *refl*. imagine (oneself) in a specified situation (*put yourself in my shoes*). **5** *tr*. (foll. by *for*) substitute (one thing for another). **6** *intr*. express (a thought or idea) in a specified way (*to put it mildly*). **7** *tr*. (foll. by *at*) estimate (an amount etc. at a specified amount) (*put the cost at £50*). **8** *tr*. (foll. by *into*) express or translate in (words, or another language). **9** *tr*. (foll. by *into*) invest (money in an asset, e.g. land). **10** *tr*. (foll. by *on*) stake (money) on (a horse etc.). **11** *tr*. (foll. by *to*) apply or devote to a use or purpose (*put it to good use*). **12** *tr*. (foll. by *to*) submit for consideration or attention (*let me put it to you another way; shall now put it to a vote*). **13** *tr*. (foll. by *to*) subject (a person) to (death, suffering, etc.). **14** *tr*. throw (esp. a shot or weight) as an athletic sport or exercise. **15** *intr*. (foll. by *back*, *off*, *out*, etc.) (of a ship etc.) proceed or follow a course in a specified direction. —*n*. a throw of the shot or weight. □ **put about 1** spread (information, rumour, etc.). **2** *Naut*. turn round; put (a ship) on the opposite tack. **3** trouble, distress. **put across 1** make acceptable or effective. **2** express in an understandable way. **3** (often in **put it** (**or one**) **across**) achieve by deceit. **put away 1** put (a thing) back in the place where it is normally kept. **2** lay (money etc.) aside for future use. **3 a** confine or imprison. **b** commit to a home or mental institution. **4** consume (food and drink), esp. in large quantities. **put back 1** restore to its proper or former place. **2** change (a planned event) to a later date or time. **3** move back the hands of (a clock or watch). **4** check the advance of. **put by** lay (money etc.) aside for future use. **put down 1** suppress by force or authority. **2** *colloq*. snub or humiliate. **3** record or enter in writing. **4** enter the name of (a person) on a list, esp. as a member or subscriber. **5** (foll. by *as*, *for*) account or reckon. **6** (foll. by *to*) attribute (*put it down to* *bad planning*). **7** put (an old or sick animal) to death. **8** pay (a specified sum) as a deposit. **9** put (a baby) to bed. **put-down** *n. colloq.* a snub or humiliating criticism. **put forward 1** suggest or propose. **2** advance the hands of (a clock or watch). **3** (often *refl.*) put into a prominent position; draw attention to. **put in 1 a** enter or submit (a claim etc.). **b** (foll. by *for*) submit a claim for (a specified thing). **2** (foll. by *for*) be a candidate for (an appointment, election, etc.). **3** spend (time). **put off 1 a** postpone. **b** postpone an engagement with (a person). **2** (often foll. by *with*) evade (a person) with an excuse etc. **3** hinder or dissuade. **4** offend, disconcert; cause (a person) to lose interest in something. **put on 1** clothe oneself with. **2** cause (an electrical device, light, etc.) to function. **3** cause (transport) to be available. **4** stage (a play, show, etc.). **5** advance the hands of (a clock or watch). **6 a** pretend to be affected by (an emotion). **b** assume, take on (a character or appearance). **c** (**put it on**) exaggerate one's feelings etc. **7** increase one's weight by (a specified amount). **put-on** *n. colloq.* a deception or hoax. **put out 1 a** (often as **put out** *adj.*) disconcert or annoy. **b** (often *refl.*) inconvenience (*don't put yourself out*). **2** extinguish (a fire or light). **3** dislocate (a joint). **4** exert (strength etc.). **put over 1** make acceptable or effective. **2** express in an understandable way. **3** *US* postpone. **4** *US* achieve by deceit. **put through 1** carry out or complete (a task or transaction). **2** (often foll. by *to*) connect (a person) by telephone to another subscriber. **put together 1** assemble (a whole) from parts. **2** combine (parts) to form a whole. **put under** render unconscious by anaesthetic etc. **put up 1** build or erect. **2** raise (a price etc.). **3** take or provide accommodation (*friends put me up for the night*). **4** engage in (a fight, struggle, etc.) as a form of resistance. **5** present (a proposal). **6 a** present oneself for election. **b** propose for election. **7** provide (money) as a backer in an enterprise. **8** display (a notice). **9** publish (banns). **10** offer for sale or competition. **put-up** *adj.* fraudulently presented or devised. **put upon** *colloq.* make unfair or excessive demands on; take advantage of (a person). **put a person up to 1** inform or instruct a person about. **2** (usu. foll. by verbal noun) instigate a person in (*put them up to stealing the money*). **put up with** endure, tolerate; submit to. □ **putter** *n.* [ME f. an unrecorded OE form *putian*, of unkn. orig.]

put² var. of PUTT.

putative /ˈpjuːtətɪv/ *adj.* reputed, supposed (*his putative father*). □ **putatively** *adv.* [ME f. OF *putatif -ive* or LL *putativus* f. L *putare* think]

putrefy /ˈpjuːtrɪˌfaɪ/ *v.* (**-ies, -ied**) **1** *intr.* & *tr.* become or make putrid; go bad. **2** *intr.* fester, suppurate. **3** *intr.* become morally corrupt. □ **putrefacient** /-ˈfeɪʃ(ə)nt/ *adj.* **putrefaction** /-ˈfækʃ(ə)n/ *n.* **putrefactive** /-ˈfæktɪv/ *adj.* [ME f. L *putrefacere* f. *puter putris* rotten]

putrescent /pjuːˈtres(ə)nt/ *adj.* **1** in the process of rotting. **2** of or accompanying this process. □ **putrescence** *n.* [L *putrescere* incept. of *putrēre* (as PUTRID)]

putrid /ˈpjuːtrɪd/ *adj.* **1** decomposed, rotten. **2** foul, noxious. **3** corrupt. **4** *sl.* of poor quality; contemptible; very unpleasant. □ **putridity** /-ˈrɪdɪtɪ/ *n.* **putridly** *adv.* **putridness** *n.* [L *putridus* f. *putrēre* to rot f. *puter putris* rotten]

putsch /pʊtʃ/ *n.* an attempt at political revolution; a violent uprising. [Swiss G, = thrust, blow]

putt /pʌt/ *v.* & *n.* (also **put**) —*v.tr.* (**putted, putting**) strike (a golf ball) gently to get it into or nearer to a hole on a putting-green. —*n.* a putting stroke. □ **putting-green** (in golf) the smooth area of grass round a hole. [differentiated f. PUT¹]

puttee /ˈpʌtɪ/ *n.* **1** a long strip of cloth wound spirally round the leg from ankle to knee for protection and support. **2** *US* a leather legging. [Hindi *paṭṭī* band, bandage]

putter¹ /ˈpʌtə(r)/ *n.* **1** a golf club used in putting. **2** a golfer who putts.

putter² *US* var. of POTTER¹.

putty /ˈpʌtɪ/ *n.* & *v.* —*n.* (*pl.* **-ies**) a cement made from whiting and raw linseed oil, used for fixing panes of glass, filling holes in woodwork, etc. —*v.tr.* (**-ies, -ied**) fix or fill up with putty. [F *potée*, lit. potful]

puzzle /ˈpʌz(ə)l/ *n.* & *v.* —*n.* **1** a difficult or confusing problem; an enigma. **2** a problem or toy designed to test knowledge or ingenuity. —*v.* **1** *tr.* confound or disconcert mentally. **2** *intr.* (usu. foll. by *over* etc.) be perplexed (about). **3** *tr.* (usu. as **puzzling** *adj.*) require much thought to comprehend (*a puzzling situation*). **4** *tr.* (foll. by *out*) solve or understand by hard thought. □ **puzzlement** *n.* **puzzlingly** *adv.* [16th c.: orig. unkn.]

puzzler /ˈpʌzlə(r)/ *n.* a difficult question or problem.

PVA *abbr.* polyvinyl acetate.

PVC *abbr.* polyvinyl chloride.

Pvt. *abbr.* **1** private. **2** *US* private soldier.

PW *abbr.* policewoman.

PWA *abbr.* *US* person with Aids.

PWR *abbr.* pressurized-water reactor.

pyaemia /paɪˈiːmɪə/ *n.* (*US* **pyemia**) blood-poisoning caused by the spread of pus-forming bacteria in the bloodstream from a source of infection. □ **pyaemic** *adj.* [mod.L f. Gk *puon* pus + *haima* blood]

pye-dog /ˈpaɪdɒg/ *n.* (also **pie-dog, pi-dog**) a vagrant mongrel, esp. in Asia. [Anglo-Ind. *pye*, *paē*, Hindi *pāhī* outsider + DOG]

pygmy /ˈpɪgmɪ/ *n.* (also **pigmy**) (*pl.* **-ies**) **1** a member of a dwarf people of equatorial Africa and parts of SE Asia. **2** a very small person, animal, or thing. **3** an insignificant person. **4** (*attrib.*) **a** of or relating to pygmies. **b** (of a person, animal, etc.) dwarf. □ **pygmaean** /-ˈmiːən/ *adj.* **pygmean** /-ˈmiːən/ *adj.* [ME f. L *pygmaeus* f. Gk *pugmaios* dwarf f. *pugmē* the length from elbow to knuckles, fist]

pyjamas /pɪˈdʒɑːməz, pə-/ *n.pl.* (*US* **pajamas**) **1** a suit of loose trousers and jacket for sleeping in. **2** loose trousers tied round the waist, worn by both sexes in some Asian countries. **3** (**pyjama**) (*attrib.*) designating parts of a suit of pyjamas (*pyjama jacket; pyjama trousers*). [Urdu *pā(ē)jāma* f. Pers. *pae, pay* leg + Hindi *jāma* clothing]

pylon /ˈpaɪlən, -lɒn/ *n.* a tall structure erected as a support (esp. for electric-power cables) or boundary or decoration. [Gk *pulōn* f. *pulē* gate]

pyorrhoea /ˌpaɪəˈriːə/ *n.* (*US* **pyorrhea**) **1** a disease causing shrinkage of the gums and loosening of the teeth. **2** any discharge of pus. [Gk *puo-* f. *puon* pus + *rhoia* flux f. *rheō* flow]

pyramid /ˈpɪrəmɪd/ *n.* **1** a monumental structure, usu. of stone, with a square base and sloping sides meeting centrally at an apex, esp. an ancient Egyptian royal tomb. **2** a solid of this type with a base of three or more sides. **3** a pyramid-shaped thing or pile of things. □ **pyramid selling** a system of selling goods in which agency rights are sold to an increasing number of distributors at successively lower levels. □ **pyramidal** /-ˈræmɪd(ə)l/ *adj.* **pyramidally** /-ˈræmɪdəlɪ/ *adv.* **pyramidic** /-ˈmɪdɪk/ *adj.* (also **pyramidical** /-ˈmɪdɪk(ə)l/). **pyramidically** /-ˈmɪdɪkəlɪ/ *adv.* **pyramidwise** *adj.* [ME f. L *pyramis* f. Gk *puramis -idos*]

pyre /ˈpaɪə(r)/ *n.* a heap of combustible material esp. a funeral pile for burning a corpse. [L *pyra* f. Gk *pura* f. *pur* fire]

pyrethrum /paɪˈriːθrəm/ *n.* **1** any of several aromatic chrysanthemums of the genus *Tanacetum*, esp. *T. coccineum*. **2** an insecticide made from the dried flowers of these plants, esp. *Tanacetum cinerariifolium*. [L f. Gk *purethron* feverfew]

pyretic /paɪˈretɪk, pɪ-/ *adj.* of, for, or producing fever. [mod.L *pyreticus* f. Gk *puretos* fever]

Pyrex /ˈpaɪəreks/ *n. propr.* a hard heat-resistant type of glass, often used for cookware. [invented word]

pyridoxine /ˌpɪrɪˈdɒksɪn/ *n.* a vitamin of the B complex found in yeast, and important in the body's use of unsaturated fatty acids. [PYRO + -OX- + -INE⁴]

pyrites /paɪˈraɪtiːz/ *n.* (in full **iron pyrites**) a yellow lustrous form of iron disulphide. □ **pyritic** /-ˈrɪtɪk/ *adj.* **pyritiferous** /-rɪˈtɪfərəs/ *adj.* **pyritize** /ˈpaɪrɪˌtaɪz/ *v.tr.* (also **-ise**). **pyritous** /ˈpaɪrɪtəs/ *adj.* [L f. Gk *puritēs* of fire (*pur*)]

pyro- /ˈpaɪərəʊ/ *comb. form* **1** denoting fire. **2** *Chem.* denoting a new substance formed from another by elimination of water (*pyrophosphate*).

pyromania /ˌpaɪərəʊˈmeɪnɪə/ *n.* an obsessive desire to set fire to things. □ **pyromaniac** *n.*

pyrotechnic /ˌpaɪərəʊˈteknɪk/ *adj.* **1** of or relating to fireworks. **2** (of wit etc.) brilliant or sensational. □ **pyrotechnical** *adj.* **pyrotechnist** *n.* **pyrotechny** /ˈpaɪərəʊ-/ *n.* [PYRO- + Gk *tekhnē* art]

pyrotechnics /ˌpaɪərəʊˈteknɪks/ *n.pl.* **1** the art of making fireworks. **2** a display of fireworks. **3** any brilliant display.

pyrrhic /ˈpɪrɪk/ *adj.* (of a victory) won at too great a cost to be of use to the victor. [*Pyrrhus* of Epirus, who defeated the Romans at Asculum in 279 BC, but sustained heavy losses]

Pythagoras' theorem /paɪˈθægərəs/ *n.* the theorem attributed to Pythagoras (see PYTHAGOREAN) that the square on the hypotenuse of a right-angled triangle is equal to the sum of the squares on the other two sides.

Pythagorean /paɪˌθægəˈriːən/ *adj. & n.* —*adj.* of or relating to the Greek philosopher Pythagoras (6th c. BC) or his philosophy, esp. regarding the transmigration of souls. —*n.* a follower of Pythagoras.

python /ˈpaɪθ(ə)n/ *n.* any constricting snake of the family Pythonidae, esp. of the genus *Python*, found throughout the tropics in the Old World. □ **pythonic** /-ˈθɒnɪk/ *adj.* [L f. Gk *Puthōn* a huge serpent or monster killed by Apollo]

pyx /pɪks/ *n.* (also **pix**) **1** *Eccl.* the vessel in which the consecrated bread of the Eucharist is kept. **2** (in the UK) a box at the Royal Mint in which specimen gold and silver coins are deposited to be tested annually. [ME f. L f. Gk *puxis* f. *puxos* box]

pzazz var. of PIZAZZ.

Qq

Q¹ /kjuː/ n. (also **q**) (pl. **Qs** or **Q's**) the seventeenth letter of the alphabet.

Q² abbr. (also **Q.**) **1** Queen, Queen's. **2** question.

QC abbr. Law Queen's Counsel.

QED abbr. quod erat demonstrandum.

qr. abbr. quarter(s).

QSO abbr. quasi-stellar object, quasar.

qt. abbr. quart(s).

q.t. n. colloq. quiet (esp. on the q.t.). [abbr.]

qu. abbr. **1** query. **2** question.

qua /kwɑː/ conj. in the capacity of; as being (Napoleon qua general). [L, ablat. fem. sing. of qui who (rel. pron.)]

quack¹ /kwæk/ n. & v. —n. the harsh sound made by ducks. —v.intr. **1** utter this sound. **2** colloq. talk loudly and foolishly. [imit.: cf. Du. kwakken, G quacken croak, quack]

quack² /kwæk/ n. **1 a** an unqualified practiser of medicine. **b** (attrib.) of or characteristic of unskilled medical practice (quack cure). **2** a charlatan. **3** sl. any doctor or medical officer. □ **quackery** n. **quackish** adj. [abbr. of quacksalver f. Du. (prob. f. obs. quacken prattle + salf SALVE¹)]

quad¹ /kwɒd/ n. colloq. a quadrangle. [abbr.]

quad² /kwɒd/ n. colloq. = QUADRUPLET. [abbr.]

quad³ /kwɒd/ n. & adj. —n. quadraphony. —adj. quadraphonic. [abbr.]

Quadragesima /ˌkwɒdrəˈdʒesɪmə/ n. the first Sunday in Lent. [LL, fem. of L quadragesimus fortieth f. quadraginta forty, Lent having 40 days]

quadrangle /ˈkwɒdˌræŋg(ə)l/ n. **1** a four-sided plane figure, esp. a square or rectangle. **2 a** a four-sided court, esp. enclosed by buildings, as in some colleges. **b** such a court with the buildings round it. □ **quadrangular** /-ˈræŋɡjʊlə(r)/ adj. [ME f. OF f. LL quadrangulum square, neut. of quadrangulus (as QUADRI-, ANGLE¹)]

quadrant /ˈkwɒdrənt/ n. **1** a quarter of a circle's circumference. **2** a plane figure enclosed by two radii of a circle at right angles and the arc cut off by them. **3** a quarter of a sphere etc. **4 a** a thing, esp. a graduated strip of metal, shaped like a quarter-circle. **b** an instrument graduated (esp. through an arc of 90°) for taking angular measurements. □ **quadrantal** /-ˈdrænt(ə)l/ adj. [ME f. L quadrant -antis quarter f. quattuor four]

quadraphonic /ˌkwɒdrəˈfɒnɪk/ adj. (also **quadrophonic**) (of sound reproduction) using four transmission channels. □ **quadraphonically** adv. **quadraphonics** n.pl. **quadraphony** /-ˈrɒfəni/ n. [QUADRI- + STEREOPHONIC]

quadrat /ˈkwɒdrət/ n. Ecol. a small area marked out for study. [var. of QUADRATE]

quadrate adj., n., & v. —adj. /ˈkwɒdrət/ esp. Anat. & Zool. square or rectangular (quadrate bone; quadrate muscle). —n. /ˈkwɒdrət/ **1** a quadrate bone or muscle. **2** a rectangular object. —v. /kwɒˈdreɪt/ **1** tr. make square. **2** intr. & tr. (often foll. by with) conform or make conform.

[ME f. L quadrare quadrat- make square f. quattuor four]

quadratic /kwɒˈdrætɪk/ adj. & n. Math. —adj. **1** involving the second and no higher power of an unknown quantity or variable (quadratic equation). **2** square. —n. **1** a quadratic equation. **2** (in pl.) the branch of algebra dealing with these. [F quadratique or mod.L quadraticus (as QUADRATE)]

quadrennial /kwɒˈdrenɪəl/ adj. **1** lasting four years. **2** recurring every four years. □ **quadrennially** adv. [as QUADRENNIUM]

quadrennium /kwɒˈdrenɪəm/ n. (pl. **quadrenniums** or **quadrennia** /-nɪə/) a period of four years. [L quadriennium (as QUADRI-, annus year)]

quadri- /ˈkwɒdrɪ/ comb. form denoting four. [L f. quattuor four]

quadrilateral /ˌkwɒdrɪˈlætər(ə)l/ adj. & n. —adj. having four sides. —n. a four-sided figure. [LL quadrilaterus (as QUADRI-, latus lateris side)]

quadrille /kwɒˈdrɪl/ n. **1** a square dance containing usu. five figures. **2** the music for this. [F f. Sp. cuadrilla troop, company f. cuadra square or It. quadriglia f. quadra square]

quadripartite /ˌkwɒdrɪˈpɑːtaɪt/ adj. **1** consisting of four parts. **2** shared by or involving four parties.

quadriplegia /ˌkwɒdrɪˈpliːdʒɪə, -dʒə/ n. Med. paralysis of all four limbs. □ **quadriplegic** adj. & n. [mod.L (as QUADRI-, Gk plēgē blow, strike)]

quadroon /kwɒˈdruːn/ n. the offspring of a White person and a mulatto; a person of one quarter Negro blood. [Sp. cuarterón f. cuarto fourth, assim. to QUADRI-]

quadruped /ˈkwɒdrʊˌped/ n. & adj. —n. a four-footed animal, esp. a four-footed mammal. —adj. four-footed. □ **quadrupedal** /-ˈruːpɪd(ə)l/ adj. [F quadrupède or L quadrupes -pedis f. quadru- var. of QUADRI- + L pes ped- foot]

quadruple /ˈkwɒdrʊp(ə)l/ adj., n., & v. —adj. **1** fourfold. **2 a** having four parts. **b** involving four participants (quadruple alliance). **3** being four times as many or as much. **4** (of time in music) having four beats in a bar. —n. a fourfold number or amount. —v.tr. & intr. multiply by four; increase fourfold. □ **quadruply** adv. [F f. L quadruplus (as QUADRI-, -plus as in duplus DUPLE)]

quadruplet /ˈkwɒdrʊplɪt, -ˈdruːplɪt/ n. each of four children born at one birth. [QUADRUPLE, after triplet]

quadruplicate adj. & v. —adj. /kwɒˈdruːplɪkət/ **1** fourfold. **2** of which four copies are made. —v.tr. /kwɒˈdruːplɪˌkeɪt/ **1** multiply by four. **2** make four identical copies of. □ **in quadruplicate** in four identical copies. □ **quadruplication** /-ˈkeɪʃ(ə)n/ n. [L quadruplicare f. quadruplex -plicis fourfold: cf. QUADRUPED, DUPLEX]

quaff /kwɒf, kwɑːf/ v. literary **1** tr. & intr. drink deeply. **2** tr. drain (a cup etc.) in long draughts.

□ **quaffable** *adj.* **quaffer** *n.* [16th c.: perh. imit.]

quag /kwæg, kwɒg/ *n.* a marshy or boggy place. □ **quaggy** *adj.* [rel. to dial. *quag* (v.) = shake: prob. imit.]

quagmire /ˈkwɒgˌmaɪə(r), ˈkwæg-/ *n.* **1** a soft boggy or marshy area that gives way underfoot. **2** a hazardous or awkward situation. [QUAG + MIRE]

quail[1] /kweɪl/ *n.* (*pl.* same or **quails**) any small migratory bird of the genus *Coturnix*, with a short tail and allied to the partridge. [ME f. OF *quaille* f. med.L *coacula* (prob. imit.)]

quail[2] /kweɪl/ *v.intr.* flinch; be apprehensive with fear. [ME, of unkn. orig.]

quaint /kweɪnt/ *adj.* **1** piquantly or attractively unfamiliar or old-fashioned. **2** daintily odd. □ **quaintly** *adv.* **quaintness** *n.* [earlier senses 'wise, cunning': ME f. OF *cointe* f. L *cognitus* past part. of *cognoscere* ascertain]

quake *v.* & *n.* —*v.intr.* **1** shake, tremble. **2** rock to and fro. **3** (of a person) shake or shudder (*was quaking with fear*). —*n.* **1** *colloq.* an earthquake. **2** an act of quaking. □ **quaky** *adj.* (**quakier, quakiest**). [OE *cwacian*]

Quaker /ˈkweɪkə(r)/ *n.* a member of the Society of Friends, a Christian movement devoted to peaceful principles and eschewing formal doctrine, sacraments, and ordained ministers. □ **Quakerish** *adj.* **Quakerism** *n.* [QUAKE + -ER[1]]

qualification /ˌkwɒlɪfɪˈkeɪʃ(ə)n/ *n.* **1** the act or an instance of qualifying. **2** an accomplishment fitting a person for a position or purpose. **3 a** a circumstance, condition, etc. that modifies or limits (*the statement had many qualifications*). **b** a thing that detracts from completeness or absoluteness (*their relief had one qualification*). **4** a condition that must be fulfilled before a right can be acquired etc. **5** an attribution of a quality (*the qualification of our policy as opportunist is unfair*). □ **qualificatory** /ˈkwɒlɪfɪˌkeɪtərɪ/ *adj.* [F *qualification* or med.L *qualificatio* (as QUALIFY)]

qualify /ˈkwɒlɪˌfaɪ/ *v.* (**-ies, -ied**) **1** *tr.* make competent or fit for a position or purpose. **2** *tr.* make legally entitled. **3** *intr.* (foll. by *for*) (of a person) satisfy the conditions or requirements (for a position, award, competition, etc.). **4** *tr.* add reservations to; modify or make less absolute (a statement or assertion). **5** *tr. Gram.* (of a word, esp. an adjective) attribute a quality to another word, esp. a noun. **6** *tr.* moderate, mitigate; make less severe or extreme. **7** *tr.* alter the strength or flavour of. **8** *tr.* (foll. by *as*) attribute a specified quality to, describe as (*the idea was qualified as absurd*). **9** *tr.* (as **qualifying** *adj.*) serving to determine those that qualify (*qualifying examination*). □ **qualifiable** *adj.* **qualifier** *n.* [F *qualifier* f. med.L *qualificare* f. L *qualis* such as]

qualitative /ˈkwɒlɪtətɪv, -ˌteɪtɪv/ *adj.* concerned with or depending on quality (*led to a qualitative change in society*). □ **qualitative analysis** *Chem.* detection of the constituents, as elements, functional groups, etc., present in a substance. □ **qualitatively** *adv.* [LL *qualitativus* (as QUALITY)]

quality /ˈkwɒlɪtɪ/ *n.* (*pl.* **-ies**) **1** the degree of excellence of a thing (*of good quality; poor in quality*). **2 a** general excellence (*their work has quality*). **b** (*attrib.*) of high quality (*a quality product*). **3** a distinctive attribute or faculty; a characteristic trait. **4** the relative nature or kind or character of a thing (*is made in three qualities*).

5 the distinctive timbre of a voice or sound. **6** *archaic* high social standing (*people of quality*). □ **quality control** a system of maintaining standards in manufactured products by testing a sample of the output against the specification. [ME f. OF *qualité* f. L *qualitas -tatis* f. *qualis* of what kind]

qualm /kwɑːm, kwɔːm/ *n.* **1** a misgiving; an uneasy doubt esp. about one's own conduct. **2** a scruple of conscience. **3** a momentary faint or sick feeling. □ **qualmish** *adj.* [16th c.: orig. uncert.]

quandary /ˈkwɒndərɪ/ *n.* (*pl.* **-ies**) **1** a state of perplexity. **2** a difficult situation; a practical dilemma. [16th c.: orig. uncert.]

quango /ˈkwæŋgəʊ/ *n.* (*pl.* **-os**) a semi-public body with financial support from and senior appointments made by the government. [abbr. of *quasi* (or *quasi-autonomous*) non-government(al) organization]

quanta *pl.* of QUANTUM.

quantal /ˈkwɒnt(ə)l/ *adj.* **1** composed of discrete units; varying in steps, not continuously. **2** of or relating to a quantum or quantum theory. □ **quantally** *adv.* [L *quantus* how much]

quantify /ˈkwɒntɪˌfaɪ/ *v.tr.* (**-ies, -ied**) **1** determine the quantity of. **2** measure or express as a quantity. □ **quantifiability** /-əˈbɪlɪtɪ/ *n.* **quantifiable** *adj.* **quantification** /ˌkwɒntɪfɪˈkeɪʃ(ə)n/ *n.* **quantifier** *n.* [med.L *quantificare* (as QUANTAL)]

quantitative /ˈkwɒntɪtətɪv, -ˌteɪtɪv/ *adj.* **1 a** concerned with quantity. **b** measured or measurable by quantity. **2** of or based on the quantity of syllables. □ **quantitative analysis** *Chem.* measurement of the amounts of the constituents of a substance. □ **quantitatively** *adv.* [med.L *quantitativus* (as QUANTITY)]

quantitive /ˈkwɒntɪtɪv/ *adj.* = QUANTITATIVE. □ **quantitively** *adv.*

quantity /ˈkwɒntɪtɪ/ *n.* (*pl.* **-ies**) **1** the property of things that is measurable. **2** the size, extent, weight, amount, or number. **3** a specified or considerable portion, number, or amount (*buys in quantity; the quantity of heat in a body*). **4** (in *pl.*) large amounts or numbers; an abundance (*quantities of food; is found in quantities on the shore*). **5** the length or shortness of vowel sounds or syllables. **6** *Math.* **a** a value, component, etc. that may be expressed in numbers. **b** the figure or symbol representing this. □ **quantity surveyor** a person who measures and prices building work. [ME f. OF *quantité* f. L *quantitas -tatis* f. *quantus* how much]

quantum /ˈkwɒntəm/ *n.* (*pl.* **quanta** /-tə/) **1** *Physics* **a** a discrete quantity of energy proportional in magnitude to the frequency of radiation it represents. **b** an analogous discrete amount of any other physical quantity. **2 a** a required or allowed amount. **b** a share or portion. □ **quantum jump** (or **leap**) **1** a sudden large increase or advance. **2** *Physics* an abrupt transition in an atom or molecule from one quantum state to another. **quantum mechanics** (or **theory**) *Physics* a system or theory using the assumption that energy exists in discrete units. [L, neut. of *quantus* how much]

quarantine /ˈkwɒrənˌtiːn/ *n.* & *v.* —*n.* **1** isolation imposed on persons or animals that have arrived from elsewhere or been exposed to, and might spread, infectious or contagious disease. **2** the period of this isolation. —*v.tr.* impose such isolation on, put in quarantine. [It. *quarantina* forty days f. *quaranta* forty]

quark[1] /kwɑːk/ *n. Physics* any of several postulated components of elementary particles. [invented word, assoc. with 'Three quarks for Muster Mark' in Joyce's *Finnegans Wake* (1939)]

quark[2] /kwɑːk/ *n.* a type of low-fat curd cheese. [G]

quarrel /ˈkwɒr(ə)l/ *n. & v. —n.* **1** a violent contention or altercation between individuals or with others. **2** a rupture of friendly relations. **3** an occasion of complaint against a person, a person's actions, etc. *—v.intr.* (**quarrelled**, **quarrelling**; US **quarreled**, **quarreling**) **1** (often foll. by *with*) take exception; find fault. **2** fall out; have a dispute; break off friendly relations. □ **quarreller** *n.* [ME f. OF *querele* f. L *querel(l)a* complaint f. *queri* complain]

quarrelsome /ˈkwɒrəlsəm/ *adj.* given to or characterized by quarrelling. □ **quarrelsomely** *adv.* **quarrelsomeness** *n.*

quarry[1] /ˈkwɒrɪ/ *n. & v. —n.* (*pl.* **-ies**) **1** an excavation made by taking stone etc. for building etc. from its bed. **2** a place from which stone etc. may be extracted. **3** a source of information, knowledge, etc. *—v.* (**-ies**, **-ied**) **1** *tr.* extract (stone) from a quarry. **2** *tr.* extract (facts etc.) laboriously from books etc. **3** *intr.* laboriously search documents etc. [ME f. med.L *quare(r)ia* f. OF *quarriere* f. L *quadrum* square]

quarry[2] /ˈkwɒrɪ/ *n.* (*pl.* **-ies**) **1** the object of pursuit by a bird of prey, hounds, hunters, etc. **2** an intended victim or prey. [ME f. AF f. OF *cuiree*, *couree* (assim. to *cuir* leather and *curer* disembowel) ult. f. L *cor* heart: orig. = parts of deer placed on hide and given to hounds]

quarry[3] /ˈkwɒrɪ/ *n.* (*pl.* **-ies**) **1** a diamond-shaped pane of glass as used in lattice windows. **2** (in full **quarry tile**) an unglazed floor-tile. [f. earlier *quarrel* square-headed arrow, ult. f. LL *quadrus* square]

quarryman /ˈkwɒrɪmən/ *n.* (*pl.* **-men**) a worker in a quarry.

quart /kwɔːt/ *n.* **1** a liquid measure equal to a quarter of a gallon; two pints. **2** a vessel containing this amount. **3** *US* a unit of dry measure, equivalent to one-thirty-second of a bushel (1.1 litre). □ **a quart into a pint pot 1** a large amount etc. fitted into a small space. **2** something difficult or impossible to achieve. [ME f. OF *quarte* f. L *quarta* fem. of *quartus* fourth]

quarter /ˈkwɔːtə(r)/ *n. & v. —n.* **1** each of four equal parts into which a thing is or might be divided. **2** a period of three months, usu. for which payments become due on the quarter day. **3** a point of time 15 minutes before or after any hour. **4** a school or *US* university term. **5 a** 25 US or Canadian cents. **b** a coin of this denomination. **6** a part of a town, esp. as occupied by a particular class or group (*residential quarter*). **7 a** a point of the compass. **b** a region at such a point. **8** the direction, district, or source of supply etc. (*help from any quarter*; *came from all quarters*). **9** (in *pl.*) **a** lodgings; an abode. **b** Mil. the living accommodation of troops etc. **10 a** one fourth of a lunar month. **b** the moon's position between the first and second (**first quarter**) or third and fourth (**last quarter**) of these. **11 a** each of the four parts into which an animal's or bird's carcass is divided, each including a leg or wing. **b** (in *pl.*) = HINDQUARTERS. **12** mercy offered or granted to an enemy in battle etc. on condition of surrender. **13 a** *Brit.* a grain measure equivalent to 8 bushels. **b** one-fourth of a hundredweight (28 lb. or *US* 25 lb.). **14** each of four divisions on a shield. **15** (in American and Australian football) each of four equal periods into which a match is divided. *—v.tr.* **1** divide into quarters. **2** *hist.* divide (the body of an executed person) in this way. **3 a** put (troops etc.) into quarters. **b** station or lodge in a specified place. **4** (foll. by *on*) impose (a person) on another as a lodger. **5** *Heraldry* place or bear (charges or coats of arms) on the four quarters of a shield's surface. □ **quarter day** one of four days on which quarterly payments are due, tenancies begin and end, etc. **quarter-final** a match or round preceding the semifinal. **quarter-hour 1** a period of 15 minutes. **2** = sense 3 of *n.* **quarter-light** *Brit.* a window in the side of a motor vehicle, closed carriage, etc. other than the main door-window. **quarter-line** *Rugby Football* a space enclosed by a line across the ground 22 metres from the goal-line. **quarter note** esp. *US Mus.* a crotchet. **quarter sessions** *hist.* (in the UK) a court of limited criminal and civil jurisdiction and of appeal, usu. held quarterly. **quarter-tone** *Mus.* half a semitone. [ME f. AF *quarter*, OF *quartier* f. L *quartarius* fourth part (of a measure) f. *quartus* fourth]

quarterback /ˈkwɔːtəˌbæk/ *n.* a player in American football who directs attacking play.

quarterdeck /ˈkwɔːtəˌdek/ *n.* **1** part of a ship's upper deck near the stern, usu. reserved for officers. **2** the officers of a ship or the navy.

quartering /ˈkwɔːtərɪŋ/ *n.* **1** (in *pl.*) the coats of arms marshalled on a shield to denote the alliances of a family with the heiresses of others. **2** the provision of quarters for soldiers. **3** the act or an instance of dividing, esp. into four equal parts.

quarterly /ˈkwɔːtəlɪ/ *adj., adv., & n. —adj.* produced or occurring once every quarter of a year. *—adv.* once every quarter of a year. *—n.* (*pl.* **-ies**) a quarterly review or magazine.

quartermaster /ˈkwɔːtəˌmɑːstə(r)/ *n.* **1** a regimental officer in charge of quartering, rations, etc. **2** a naval petty officer in charge of steering, signals, etc.

quartet /kwɔːˈtet/ *n.* (also **quartette**) **1** *Mus.* **a** a composition for four voices or instruments. **b** the performers of such a piece. **2** any group of four. [F *quartette* f. It. *quartetto* f. *quarto* fourth f. L *quartus*]

quarto /ˈkwɔːtəʊ/ *n.* (*pl.* **-os**) *Printing* **1** the size given by folding a (usu. specified) sheet of paper twice. **2** a book consisting of sheets folded in this way. [L (*in*) *quarto* (in) the fourth (of a sheet), ablat. of *quartus* fourth]

quartz /kwɔːts/ *n.* a mineral form of silica that crystallizes as hexagonal prisms. □ **quartz clock** a clock operated by vibrations of an electrically driven quartz crystal. **quartz lamp** a quartz tube containing mercury vapour and used as a light source. [G *Quarz* f. WSlav. *kwardy*]

quartzite /ˈkwɔːtsaɪt/ *n.* a metamorphic rock consisting mainly of quartz.

quasar /ˈkweɪzɑː(r), -sɑː(r)/ *n. Astron.* any of a class of starlike celestial objects having a spectrum with a large red-shift. [*quasi-stellar*]

quash /kwɒʃ/ v.tr. **1** annul; reject as not valid, esp. by a legal procedure. **2** suppress; crush (a rebellion etc.). [ME f. OF *quasser, casser* annul f. LL *cassare* f. *cassus* null, void or f. L *cassare* frequent. of *quatere* shake]

quasi- /ˈkweɪzaɪ, ˈkwɑːzɪ/ comb. form **1** seemingly; apparently but not really (*quasi-scientific*). **2** being partly or almost (*quasi-independent*). [L *quasi* as if, almost]

quassia /ˈkwɒʃə/ n. **1** an evergreen tree, *Quassia amara*, native to S. America. **2** the wood, bark, or root of this tree, yielding a bitter medicinal tonic and insecticide. [G. *Quassi*, 18th-c. Surinam slave, who discovered its medicinal properties]

quatercentenary /ˌkwætəsenˈtiːnərɪ/ n. & adj. —n. (pl. **-ies**) **1** a four-hundredth anniversary. **2** a festival marking this. —adj. of this anniversary. [L *quater* four times + CENTENARY]

quaternary /kwəˈtɜːnərɪ/ adj. & n. —adj. **1** having four parts. **2** (**Quaternary**) *Geol.* of or relating to the most recent period in the Cenozoic era. —n. (pl. **-ies**) **1** a set of four things. **2** (**Quaternary**) *Geol.* the Quaternary period or system. [ME f. L *quaternarius* f. *quaterni* distrib. of *quattuor* four]

quatrain /ˈkwɒtreɪn/ n. a stanza of four lines, usu. with alternate rhymes. [F f. *quatre* four f. L *quattuor*]

quatrefoil /ˈkætrəfɔɪl/ n. a four-pointed or four-leafed figure, esp. as an ornament in architectural tracery, resembling a flower or clover leaf. [ME f. AF f. *quatre* four: see FOIL²]

quattrocento /ˌkwætrəʊˈtʃentəʊ/ n. the style of Italian art of the 15th c. □ **quattrocentist** n. [It., = 400 used with reference to the years 1400–99]

quaver /ˈkweɪvə(r)/ v. & n. —v. **1** intr. **a** (esp. of a voice or musical sound) vibrate, shake, tremble. **b** use trills or shakes in singing. **2** tr. **a** sing (a note or song) with quavering. **b** (often foll. by *out*) say in a trembling voice. —n. **1** *Mus.* a note having the time value of an eighth of a semibreve or half a crotchet and represented by a large dot with a hooked stem. **2** a trill in singing. **3** a tremble in speech. □ **quaveringly** adv. [ME f. *quave*, perh. f. OE *cwafian* (unrecorded: cf. *cwacian* QUAKE)]

quavery /ˈkweɪvərɪ/ adj. (of a voice etc.) tremulous. □ **quaveriness** n.

quay /kiː/ n. a solid stationary artificial landing-place lying alongside or projecting into water for loading and unloading ships. □ **quayage** n. [ME *key(e), kay* f. OF *kay* f. Gaulish *caio* f. OCelt.]

quayside /ˈkiːsaɪd/ n. the land forming or near a quay.

queasy /ˈkwiːzɪ/ adj. (**-ier, -iest**) **1 a** (of a person) feeling nausea. **b** (of a person's stomach) easily upset, weak of digestion. **2** (of the conscience etc.) overscrupulous, tender. □ **queasily** adv. **queasiness** n. [ME *queysy, coisy* perh. f. AF & OF, rel. to OF *coisir* hurt]

queen n. & v. —n. **1** (as a title usu. **Queen**) a female sovereign etc., esp. the hereditary ruler of an independent State. **2** (in full **queen consort**) a king's wife. **3** a woman, country, or thing pre-eminent or supreme in a specified area or of its kind (*tennis queen; the queen of roses*). **4** the fertile female among ants, bees, etc. **5** the most powerful piece in chess. **6** a court card with a picture of a queen. **7** *sl.* a male homosexual, esp. an effeminate one. **8 a** an honoured

female, e.g. the Virgin Mary (*Queen of Heaven*). **b** an ancient goddess (*Venus, Queen of love*). **9** a belle or mock sovereign on some occasion (*beauty queen; queen of the May*). **10** (**the Queen**) (in the UK) the national anthem when there is a female sovereign. —v.tr. **1** make (a woman) queen. **2** *Chess* convert (a pawn) into a queen when it reaches the opponent's side of the board. □ **queen bee 1** the fertile female in a hive. **2** the chief or controlling woman in an organization or social group. **queen dowager** the widow of a king. **queen it** play the queen. **queen mother** the dowager who is mother of the sovereign. **queen of puddings** a pudding made with bread, jam, and meringue. **queen-post** one of two upright timbers between the tie-beam and principal rafters of a roof-truss. **queen-size** (or **-sized**) of an extra-large size, usu. smaller than king-size. □ **queendom** n. **queenhood** n. **queenless** adj. **queenlike** adj. **queenship** n. [OE *cwēn* f. Gmc]

queenly /ˈkwiːnlɪ/ adj. (**queenlier, queenliest**) **1** fit for or appropriate to a queen. **2** majestic; queenlike. □ **queenliness** n.

Queensberry Rules /ˈkwiːnzbərɪ/ n.pl. the standard rules, esp. of boxing. [the 8th Marquis of Queensberry, Engl. nobleman d. 1900, who supervised the preparation of boxing laws in 1867]

queer adj., n., & v. —adj. **1** strange; odd; eccentric. **2** shady; suspect; of questionable character. **3 a** slightly ill; giddy; faint. **b** *Brit. sl.* drunk. **4** *derog. sl.* (esp. of a man) homosexual. —n. *derog. sl.* a homosexual. —v.tr. *sl.* spoil; put out of order. □ **in Queer Street** *sl.* in a difficulty, in debt or trouble or disrepute. **queer a person's pitch** spoil a person's chances, esp. secretly or maliciously. □ **queerish** adj. **queerly** adv. **queerness** n. [perh. f. G *quer* oblique (as THWART)]

quell v.tr. **1 a** crush or put down (a rebellion etc.). **b** reduce (rebels etc.) to submission. **2** suppress (fear, anger, etc.). □ **queller** n. (also in comb.). [OE *cwellan* kill f. Gmc]

quench v.tr. **1** satisfy (thirst) by drinking. **2** extinguish (a fire or light etc.). **3** cool, esp. with water (heat, a heated thing). **4** esp. *Metallurgy* cool (a hot substance) in cold water, air, oil, etc. **5 a** stifle or suppress (desire etc.). **b** *Physics & Electronics* inhibit or prevent (oscillation, luminescence, etc.) by counteractive means. **6** *sl.* reduce (an opponent) to silence. □ **quenchable** adj. **quencher** n. **quenchless** adj. [ME f. OE *-cwencan* causative f. *-cwincan* be extinguished]

quern /kwɜːn/ n. **1** a hand-mill for grinding corn. **2** a small hand-mill for pepper etc. □ **quern-stone** a millstone. [OE *cweorn(e)* f. Gmc]

querulous /ˈkwerʊləs/ adj. complaining, peevish. □ **querulously** adv. **querulousness** n. [LL *querulosus* or L *querulus* f. *queri* complain]

query /ˈkwɪərɪ/ n. & v. —n. (pl. **-ies**) **1** a question, esp. expressing doubt or objection. **2** a question mark, or the word *query* spoken or written to question accuracy or as a mark of interrogation. —v. (**-ies, -ied**) **1** tr. (often foll. by *whether, if,* etc. + clause) ask or inquire. **2** tr. call (a thing) in question in speech or writing. **3** tr. dispute the accuracy of. **4** intr. put a question. [Anglicized form of *quaere* f. L *quaerere* ask, after INQUIRY]

quest /kwest/ *n. & v.* —*n.* **1** a search or the act of seeking. **2** the thing sought, esp. the object of a medieval knight's pursuit. —*v.* **1** *intr.* (often foll. by *about*) **a** (often foll. by *for*) go about in search of something. **b** (of a dog etc.) search about for game. **2** *tr. poet.* search for, seek out. □ **in quest of** seeking. □ **quester** *n.* **questingly** *adv.* [ME f. OF *queste, quester* ult. f. L *quaerere quaest-* seek]

question /'kwestʃ(ə)n/ *n. & v.* —*n.* **1** a sentence worded or expressed so as to seek information. **2 a** doubt about or objection to a thing's truth, credibility, advisability, etc. (*allowed it without question*). **b** the raising of such doubt etc. **3** a matter to be discussed or decided or voted on. **4** a problem requiring an answer or solution. **5** (foll. by *of*) a matter or concern depending on conditions (*it's a question of money*). —*v.tr.* **1** ask questions of; interrogate. **2** subject (a person) to examination. **3** throw doubt upon; raise objections to. **4** seek information from the study of (phenomena, facts). □ **be a question of time** be certain to happen sooner or later. **beyond all question** undoubtedly. **come into question** be discussed; become of practical importance. **in question** that is being discussed or referred to (*the person in question*). **is not the question** is irrelevant. **out of the question** too impracticable etc. to be worth discussing; impossible. **put the question** require supporters and opponents of a proposal to record their votes, divide a meeting. **question mark** a punctuation mark (?) indicating a question. **questionmaster** *Brit.* a person who presides over a quiz game etc. **question time** *Parl.* a period during parliamentary proceedings when MPs may question ministers. □ **questioner** *n.* **questioningly** *adv.* **questionless** *adj.* [ME f. AF *questiun,* OF *question, questionner* f. L *quaestio -onis* f. *quaerere quaest-* seek]

questionable /'kwestʃənəb(ə)l/ *adj.* **1** doubtful as regards truth or quality. **2** not clearly in accordance with honesty, honour, wisdom, etc. □ **questionability** /ˌkwestʃənə'bɪlɪtɪ/ *n.* **questionableness** *n.* **questionably** *adv.*

questionnaire /ˌkwestʃə'neə(r), ˌkestjə-/ *n.* **1** a formulated series of questions, esp. for statistical study. **2** a document containing these. [F f. *questionner* QUESTION + *-aire* -ARY[1]]

queue /kjuː/ *n. & v. esp. Brit.* —*n.* **1** a line or sequence of persons, vehicles, etc., awaiting their turn to be attended to or to proceed. **2** a pigtail or plait of hair. —*v.intr.* (**queues, queued, queuing** or **queueing**) (often foll. by *up*) (of persons etc.) form a queue; take one's place in a queue. □ **queue-jump** *Brit.* push forward out of turn in a queue. [F f. L *cauda* tail]

quibble /'kwɪb(ə)l/ *n. & v.* —*n.* **1** a petty objection; a trivial point of criticism. **2** a play on words; a pun. **3** an evasion; an insubstantial argument which relies on an ambiguity etc. —*v.intr.* use quibbles. □ **quibbler** *n.* **quibbling** *adj.* **quibblingly** *adv.* [dimin. of obs. *quib* prob. f. L *quibus* dative & ablat. pl. of *qui* who (familiar from use in legal documents)]

quiche /kiːʃ/ *n.* an open flan or tart with a savoury filling. [F]

quick *adj., adv., & n.* —*adj.* **1** taking only a short time (*a quick worker*). **2** arriving after a short time, prompt (*quick action; quick results*). **3** with only a short interval (*in quick succession*). **4** lively, intelligent. **5** acute, alert (*has a quick ear*). **6** (of a

temper) easily roused. **7** *archaic* living, alive (*the quick and the dead*). —*adv.* **1** quickly, at a rapid rate. **2** (as *int.*) come, go, etc., quickly. —*n.* **1** the soft flesh below the nails, or the skin, or a sore. **2** the seat of feeling or emotion (*cut to the quick*). □ **be quick** act quickly. **quick-fire 1** (of repartee etc.) rapid. **2** firing shots in quick succession.

quick-freeze 1 freeze (food) rapidly so as to preserve its natural qualities. **2** this process.

quick march *Mil.* **1** a march in quick time. **2** the command to begin this. **quick one** *colloq.* a drink taken quickly. □ **quickly** *adv.* **quickness** *n.* [OE *cwic(u)* alive f. Gmc]

quicken /'kwɪkən/ *v.* **1** *tr. & intr.* make or become quicker; accelerate. **2** *tr.* give life or vigour to; rouse; animate; stimulate. **3** *intr.* **a** (of a woman) reach a stage in pregnancy when movements of the foetus can be felt. **b** (of a foetus) begin to show signs of life. **4** *intr.* come to life.

quickie /'kwɪkɪ/ *n. colloq.* **1** a thing done or made quickly or hastily. **2** a drink taken quickly.

quicklime /'kwɪklaɪm/ *n.* = LIME[1] *n.* 1.

quicksand /'kwɪksænd/ *n.* **1** loose wet sand that sucks in anything placed or falling into it. **2** a bed of this.

quickset /'kwɪkset/ *adj. & n.* —*adj.* (of a hedge) formed of slips of plants, esp. hawthorn set in the ground to grow. —*n.* **1** such slips. **2** a hedge formed in this way.

quicksilver /'kwɪkˌsɪlvə(r)/ *n. & v.* —*n.* **1** mercury. **2** mobility of temperament or mood. —*v.tr.* coat (a mirror-glass) with an amalgam of tin.

quickstep /'kwɪkstep/ *n. & v.* —*n.* a fast foxtrot. —*v.intr.* (**-stepped, -stepping**) dance the quickstep.

quick-witted /kwɪk'wɪtɪd/ *adj.* quick to grasp a situation, make repartee, etc. □ **quick-wittedness** *n.*

quid[1] *n.* (*pl.* same) *Brit. sl.* one pound sterling. □ **not the full quid** *Austral. sl.* mentally deficient. **quids in** *sl.* in a position of profit. [prob. f. *quid* the nature of a thing f. L *quid* what, something]

quid[2] *n.* a lump of tobacco for chewing. [dial. var. of CUD]

quiddity /'kwɪdɪtɪ/ *n.* (*pl.* **-ies**) **1** *Philos.* the essence of a person or thing; what makes a thing what it is. **2** a quibble; a trivial objection. [med.L *quidditas* f. L *quid* what]

quid pro quo /ˌkwɪd prəʊ 'kwəʊ/ *n.* **1** a thing given as compensation. **2** return made (for a gift, favour, etc.). [L, = something for something]

quiescent /kwɪ'es(ə)nt/ *adj.* **1** motionless, inert. **2** silent, dormant. □ **quiescence** *n.* **quiescency** *n.* **quiescently** *adv.* [L *quiescere* f. *quies* QUIET]

quiet /'kwaɪət/ *adj., n., & v.* —*adj.* (**quieter, quietest**) **1** with little or no sound or motion. **2** of gentle or peaceful disposition. **3** (of a colour, piece of clothing, etc.) unobtrusive; not showy. **4** not overt; private; disguised (*quiet resentment*). **5** undisturbed; uninterrupted; free or far from vigorous action (*a quiet time for prayer*). **6** informal; simple (*just a quiet wedding*). **7** enjoyed in quiet (*a quiet smoke*). **8** tranquil; not anxious or remorseful. —*n.* **1** silence; stillness. **2** an undisturbed state; tranquillity. **3** a state of being free from urgent tasks or agitation. **4** a peaceful state of affairs. —*v.* **1** *tr.* soothe, make quiet. **2** *intr.* (often foll. by *down*) become quiet or calm. □ **be quiet** (esp. in *imper.*) cease talking etc. **keep quiet 1** refrain from making a noise. **2**

(often foll. by *about*) suppress or refrain from disclosing information etc. **on the quiet** unobtrusively; secretly. □ **quietly** *adv.* **quietness** *n.* [ME f. AF *quiete* f. OF *quiet(e)*, *quieté* f. L *quietus* past part. of *quiescere*: see QUIESCENT]

quieten /ˈkwaɪət(ə)n/ *v.tr. & intr.* Brit. (often foll. by *down*) = QUIET *v.*

quietism /ˈkwaɪəˌtɪz(ə)m/ *n.* **1** a passive attitude towards life, with devotional contemplation and abandonment of the will, as a form of religious mysticism. **2** the principle of non-resistance. □ **quietist** *n. & adj.* **quietistic** /-ˈtɪstɪk/ *adj.* [It. *quietismo* (as QUIET)]

quietude /ˈkwaɪɪˌtjuːd/ *n.* a state of quiet.

quietus /kwaɪˈiːtəs/ *n.* **1** something which quiets or represses. **2** discharge or release from life; death, final riddance. [med.L *quietus est* he is quit (QUIET) used as a form of receipt]

quiff *n.* Brit. **1** a man's tuft of hair, brushed upward over the forehead. **2** a curl plastered down on the forehead. [20th c.: orig. unkn.]

quill *n.* **1** (in full **quill-feather**) a large feather in a wing or tail. **2** the hollow stem of this. **3** (in full **quill pen**) a pen made of a quill. **4** (usu. in *pl.*) the spines of a porcupine. [ME prob. f. (M)LG *quiele*]

quilling /ˈkwɪlɪŋ/ *n.* the art or craft of paper filigree. [QUILL]

quilt *n. & v.* —*n.* **1** a bed-covering made of padding enclosed between layers of cloth etc. and kept in place by cross lines of stitching. **2** a bedspread of similar design (*patchwork quilt*). —*v.tr.* **1** cover or line with padded material. **2** make or join together (pieces of cloth with padding between) after the manner of a quilt. □ **quilter** *n.* **quilting** *n.* [ME f. OF *coilte*, *cuilte* f. L *culcita* mattress, cushion]

quim *n.* *coarse sl.* the female genitals. [18th c.: orig. unkn.]

quin *n.* esp. Brit. *colloq.* a quintuplet. [abbr.]

quince *n.* **1** a hard acid pear-shaped fruit used as a preserve or flavouring. **2** any shrub or small tree of the genus *Cydonia*, esp. *C. oblonga*, bearing this fruit. [ME, orig. collect. pl. of obs. *quoyn*, *coyn*, f. OF *cooin* f. L *cotoneum* var. of *cydoneum* (apple) of *Cydonia* in Crete]

quincentenary /ˌkwɪnsenˈtiːnəri/ *n. & adj.* —*n.* (*pl.* **-ies**) **1** a five-hundredth anniversary. **2** a festival marking this. —*adj.* of this anniversary. □ **quincentennial** /-ˈtenɪəl/ *adj. & n.* [irreg. f. L *quinque* five + CENTENARY]

quincunx /ˈkwɪŋkʌŋks/ *n.* **1** five objects set so that four are at the corners of a square or rectangle and the fifth is at its centre, e.g. the five on dice or cards. **2** this arrangement, esp. in planting trees. □ **quincuncial** /kwɪnˈkʌnʃ(ə)l/ *adj.* **quincuncially** /-ˈkʌnʃəlɪ/ *adv.* [L, = fivetwelfths f. *quinque* five, *uncia* twelfth]

quinine /ˈkwɪniːn, -ˈniːn/ *n.* **1** an alkaloid found esp. in cinchona bark. **2** a bitter drug containing this, used as a tonic and to reduce fever. [*quina* cinchona bark f. Sp. *quina* f. Quechua *kina* bark]

Quinquagesima /ˌkwɪŋkwəˈdʒesɪmə/ *n.* (in full **Quinquagesima Sunday**) the Sunday before the beginning of Lent. [med.L, fem. of L *quinquagesimus* fiftieth f. *quinquaginta* fifty, after QUADRAGESIMA]

quinque- /ˈkwɪŋkwɪ/ *comb. form* five. [L f. *quinque* five]

quinquennial /kwɪnˈkwenɪəl/ *adj.* **1** lasting five years. **2** recurring every five years. □ **quinquennially** *adv.* [L *quinquennis* (as QUINQUENNIUM)]

quinquennium /kwɪnˈkwenɪəm/ *n.* (*pl.* **quinquenniums** or **quinquennia** /-nɪə/) a period of five years. [L f. *quinque* five + *annus* year]

quinsy /ˈkwɪnzɪ/ *n.* an inflammation of the throat, esp. an abscess in the region around the tonsils. □ **quinsied** *adj.* [ME f. OF *quinencie* f. med.L *quinancia* f. Gk *kunagkhē* f. *kun-* dog + *agkhō* throttle]

quintessence /kwɪnˈtes(ə)ns/ *n.* **1** the most essential part of any substance; a refined extract. **2** (usu. foll. by *of*) the purest and most perfect, or most typical, form, manifestation, or embodiment of some quality or class. □ **quintessential** /ˌkwɪntɪˈsenʃ(ə)l/ *adj.* **quintessentially** /ˌkwɪntɪˈsenʃəlɪ/ *adv.* [ME f. F f. med.L *quinta essentia* fifth ESSENCE]

quintet /kwɪnˈtet/ *n.* (also **quintette**) **1** *Mus.* **a** a composition for five voices or instruments. **b** the performers of such a piece. **2** any group of five. [F *quintette* f. It. *quintetto* f. *quinto* fifth f. L *quintus*]

quintuple /ˈkwɪntjʊp(ə)l/ *adj., n., & v.* —*adj.* **1** fivefold; consisting of five parts. **2** involving five parties. **3** (of time in music) having five beats in a bar. —*n.* a fivefold number or amount. —*v.tr. & intr.* multiply by five; increase fivefold. □ **quintuply** *adv.* [F *quintuple* f. L *quintus* fifth, after QUADRUPLE]

quintuplet /ˈkwɪntjʊplɪt, -ˈtjuːplɪt/ *n.* each of five children born at one birth. [QUINTUPLE, after QUADRUPLET, TRIPLET]

quintuplicate *adj. & v.* —*adj.* /kwɪnˈtjuːplɪkət/ **1** fivefold. **2** of which five copies are made. —*v.tr. & intr.* /kwɪnˈtjuːplɪˌkeɪt/ multiply by five. □ **in quintuplicate 1** in five identical copies. **2** in groups of five. [F *quintuple* f. L *quintus* fifth, after QUADRUPLICATE]

quip *n. & v.* —*n.* **1** a clever saying; an epigram; a sarcastic remark etc. **2** a quibble; an equivocation. —*v.intr.* (**quipped, quipping**) make quips. □ **quipster** *n.* [abbr. of obs. *quippy* perh. f. L *quippe* forsooth]

quire *n.* **1** four sheets of paper etc. folded to form eight leaves, as often in medieval manuscripts. **2** any collection of leaves, one within another, in a manuscript or book. **3** 25 (also 24) sheets of paper. □ **in quires** unbound; in sheets. [ME f. OF *qua(i)er* ult. f. L *quaterni* set of four (as QUATERNARY)]

quirk *n.* **1** a peculiarity of behaviour. **2** a trick of fate; a freak. **3** a flourish in writing. □ **quirkily** *adv.* **quirkiness** *n.* **quirkish** *adj.* **quirky** *adj.* (**quirkier, quirkiest**). [16th c.: orig. unkn.]

quirt *n. & v.* —*n.* a short-handled riding-whip with a braided leather lash. —*v.tr.* strike with this. [Sp. *cuerda* CORD]

quisling /ˈkwɪzlɪŋ/ *n.* **1** a person cooperating with an occupying enemy; a collaborator or fifth-columnist. **2** a traitor. □ **quislingite** *adj. & n.* [V. *Quisling*, renegade Norwegian Army officer d. 1945]

quit *v. & adj.* —*v.tr.* (**quitting**; *past* and *past part.* **quitted** or **quit**) **1** (also *absol.*) give up; let go; abandon (a task etc.). **2** US cease; stop (*quit grumbling*). **3 a** leave or depart from (a place, person, etc.). **b** (*absol.*) (of a tenant) leave occupied premises (esp. *notice to quit*). **4** (*refl.*) acquit;

behave (*quit oneself well*). —*predic.adj.* (foll. by *of*) rid (*glad to be quit of the problem*). □ **quit hold of** loose. [ME f. OF *quitte, quitter* f. med.L *quittus* f. L *quietus* QUIET]

quitch *n.* (in full **quitch-grass**) = COUCH². [OE *cwice*, perh. rel. to QUICK]

quite *adv.* **1** completely; entirely; wholly; to the utmost extent; in the fullest sense. **2** somewhat; rather; to some extent. **3** (often foll. by *so*) said to indicate agreement. □ **quite another** (or **other**) very different (*that's quite another matter*). **quite a few** *colloq.* a fairly large number of. **quite something** a remarkable thing. [ME f. obs. *quite* (adj.) = QUIT]

quits *predic.adj.* on even terms by retaliation or repayment (*then we'll be quits*). □ **call it** (or **cry**) **quits** acknowledge that things are now even; agree not to proceed further in a quarrel etc. [perh. colloq. abbr. of med.L *quittus*: see QUIT]

quittance /ˈkwɪt(ə)ns/ *n. archaic* or *poet.* **1** (foll. by *from*) a release. **2** an acknowledgement of payment; a receipt. [ME f. OF *quitance* f. *quiter* QUIT]

quitter /ˈkwɪtə(r)/ *n.* **1** a person who gives up easily. **2** a shirker.

quiver¹ /ˈkwɪvə(r)/ *v. & n.* —*v.* **1** *intr.* tremble or vibrate with a slight rapid motion, esp.: **a** (usu. foll. by *with*) as the result of emotion (*quiver with anger*). **b** (usu. foll. by *in*) as the result of air currents etc. (*quiver in the breeze*). **2** *tr.* (of a bird, esp. a skylark) make (its wings) quiver. —*n.* a quivering motion or sound. □ **quiveringly** *adv.* **quivery** *adj.* [ME f. obs. *quiver* nimble: cf. QUAVER]

quiver² /ˈkwɪvə(r)/ *n.* a case for holding arrows. [ME f. OF *quivre* f. WG (cf. OE *cocor*)]

quiverful /ˈkwɪvəfʊl/ *n.* (pl. **-fuls**) **1** as much as a quiver can hold. **2** many children of one parent (Ps. 127:5). [QUIVER²]

qui vive /kiː ˈviːv/ *n.* □ **on the qui vive** on the alert; watching for something to happen. [F, = lit. '(long) live who?', i.e. on whose side are you?, as a sentry's challenge]

quixotic /kwɪkˈsɒtɪk/ *adj.* **1** extravagantly and romantically chivalrous; regardless of material interests in comparison with honour or devotion. **2** visionary; pursuing lofty but unattainable ideals. □ **quixotically** *adv.* **quixotism** /ˈkwɪksətɪz(ə)m/ *n.* **quixotry** /ˈkwɪksətrɪ/ *n.* [Don *Quixote*, hero of Cervantes' romance f. Sp. *quixote* thigh armour]

quiz¹ *n. & v.* —*n.* (pl. **quizzes**) **1** a test of knowledge, esp. between individuals or teams as a form of entertainment. **2** an interrogation, examination, or questionnaire. —*v.tr.* (**quizzed**, **quizzing**) examine by questioning. □ **quizmaster** a person who presides over a quiz. [19th-c. dial.: orig. unkn.]

quiz² *v. & n. archaic* —*v.tr.* (**quizzed, quizzing**) **1** look curiously at; observe the ways or oddities of; survey through an eyeglass. **2** make sport of; regard with a mocking air. —*n.* (pl. **quizzes**) **1** a hoax, a thing done to burlesque or expose another's oddities. **2 a** an odd or eccentric person; a person of ridiculous appearance. **b** a person given to quizzing. □ **quizzer** *n.* [18th c.: orig. unkn.]

quizzical /ˈkwɪzɪk(ə)l/ *adj.* **1** expressing or done with mild or amused perplexity. **2** strange; comical. □ **quizzicality** /-ˈkælɪtɪ/ *n.* **quizzically** *adv.* **quizzicalness** *n.*

quod *n. Brit. sl.* prison. [17th c.: orig. unkn.]

quod erat demonstrandum /kwɒd ˌeræt ˌdemɒnˈstrændəm/ (esp. at the conclusion of a proof etc.) which was the thing to be proved. [L]

quod vide /kwɒd ˈviːdeɪ/ which see (in cross-references etc.). [L]

quoin /kɔɪn/ *n. & v.* **1** an external angle of a building. **2** a stone or brick forming an angle; a cornerstone. □ **quoining** *n.* [var. of COIN]

quoit *n. & v.* **1** a heavy flattish sharp-edged iron ring thrown to encircle an iron peg or to land as near as possible to the peg. **2** (in *pl.*) a game consisting of aiming and throwing these. **3** a ring of rope, rubber, etc. for use in a similar game. **4 a** the flat stone of a dolmen. **b** the dolmen itself. —*v.tr.* fling like a quoit. [ME: orig. unkn.]

quondam /ˈkwɒndæm/ *attrib.adj.* that once was; sometime; former. [L (adv.), = formerly]

Quonset /ˈkwɒnsɪt/ *n. US propr.* a prefabricated metal building with a semicylindrical corrugated roof. [*Quonset* Point, Rhode Island, where it was first made]

quorate /ˈkwɔːrət, -reɪt/ *adj. Brit.* (of a meeting) attended by a quorum. [QUORUM]

quorum /ˈkwɔːrəm/ *n.* the fixed minimum number of members that must be present to make the proceedings of an assembly or society valid. [L, = of whom (we wish that you be two, three, etc.), in the wording of commissions]

quota /ˈkwəʊtə/ *n.* **1** the share that an individual person or company is bound to contribute to or entitled to receive from a total. **2** a quantity of goods etc. which under official controls must be manufactured, exported, imported, etc. **3** the number of yearly immigrants allowed to enter a country, students allowed to enrol for a course, etc. [med.L *quota* (*pars*) how great (a part), fem. of *quotus* f. *quot* how many]

quotable /ˈkwəʊtəb(ə)l/ *adj.* worth or suitable for quoting. □ **quotability** /-ˈbɪlɪtɪ/ *n.*

quotation /kwəʊˈteɪʃ(ə)n/ *n.* **1** the act or an instance of quoting or being quoted. **2** a passage or remark quoted. **3** *Mus.* a short passage or tune taken from one piece of music to another. **4** *Stock Exch.* an amount stated as the current price of stocks or commodities. **5** a contractor's estimate. □ **quotation mark** each of a set of punctuation marks, single (' ') or double (" "), used to mark the beginning and end of a quoted passage, a book title, etc., or words regarded as slang or jargon. [med.L *quotatio* (as QUOTE)]

quote *v. & n.* —*v.tr.* **1** cite or appeal to (an author, book, etc.) in confirmation of some view. **2** repeat a statement by (another person) or copy out a passage from (*don't quote me*). **3** (often *absol.*) **a** repeat or copy out (a passage) usu. with an indication that it is borrowed. **b** (foll. by *from*) cite (an author, book, etc.). **4** (foll. by *as*) cite (an author etc.) as proof, evidence, etc. **5 a** enclose (words) in quotation marks. **b** (as *int.*) (in dictation, reading aloud, etc.) indicate the presence of opening quotation marks (*he said, quote, 'I shall stay'*). **6** (often foll. by *at*) state the price of (a commodity, bet, etc.) (*quoted at 200 to 1*). **7** *Stock Exch.* regularly list the price of. —*n. colloq.* **1** a passage quoted. **2** a price quoted. **3** (usu. in *pl.*) quotation marks. [ME, earlier 'mark with numbers', f. med.L *quotare* f. *quot* how many, or as QUOTA]

quoth /kwəʊθ/ *v.tr.* (only in 1st and 3rd person) *archaic* said. [OE *cwæth* past of *cwethan* say f. Gmc]

quotidian /kwɒˈtɪdɪən/ *adj.* **1** daily, of every day. **2** commonplace, trivial. [ME f. OF *cotidien* & L *cotidianus* f. *cotidie* daily]

quotient /ˈkwəʊʃ(ə)nt/ *n.* a result obtained by dividing one quantity by another. [ME f. L *quotiens* how many times f. *quot* how many, by confusion with -ENT]

Qur'an var. of KORAN.

q.v. *abbr.* *quod vide.*

qwerty /ˈkwɜːtɪ/ *attrib.adj.* denoting the standard keyboard on English-language typewriters, word processors, etc., with *q*, *w*, *e*, *r*, *t*, and *y* as the first keys on the top row of letters.

qy. *abbr.* query.

Rr

R[1] /ɑː(r)/ n. (also **r**) (pl. **Rs** or **R's**) the eighteenth letter of the alphabet.

R[2] abbr. (also **R.**) **1** Regina (Elizabeth R). **2** Rex. **3** River. **4** (also ®) registered as a trademark. **5** (in names of societies etc.) Royal. **6** Chess rook. **7** Railway.

r. abbr. (also **r**) **1** right. **2** run(s).

RA abbr. **1** (in the UK) Royal Academy. **2** (in the UK) Royal Artillery.

Ra symb. Chem. the element radium.

RAAF abbr. Royal Australian Air Force.

rabbet /ˈræbɪt/ n. & v. —n. a step-shaped channel etc. cut along the edge or face or projecting angle of a length of wood etc., usu. to receive the edge or tongue of another piece. —v.tr. (**rabbeted**, **rabbeting**) **1** join or fix with a rabbet. **2** make a rabbet in. [ME f. OF rab(b)at abatement, recess f. rabattre REBATE[1]]

rabbi /ˈræbaɪ/ n. (pl. **rabbis**) **1** a Jewish scholar or teacher, esp. of the law. **2** a person appointed as a Jewish religious leader. □ **rabbinate** /ˈræbɪnət/ n. [ME & OE f. eccl.L f. Gk rhabbi f. Heb. rabbî my master f. raḇ master + pronominal suffix]

rabbinical /rəˈbɪnɪk(ə)l/ adj. (also **rabbinic**) of or relating to rabbis, or to Jewish law or teaching. □ **rabbinically** adv.

rabbit /ˈræbɪt/ n. & v. —n. **1 a** any of various burrowing gregarious plant-eating mammals of the hare family, esp. Oryctolagus cuniculus, with long ears and a short tail, and kept as a pet or for meat. **b** US a hare. **c** the fur of the rabbit. **2** Brit. colloq. a poor performer in any sport or game. —v. intr. (**rabbited**, **rabbiting**) **1** hunt rabbits. **2** (often foll. by on, away) Brit. colloq. talk excessively or pointlessly; chatter (rabbiting on about his holiday). □ **rabbit punch** a short chop with the edge of the hand to the nape of the neck. □ **rabbity** adj. [ME perh. f. OF: cf. F dial. rabotte, Walloon robète, Flem. robbe]

rabble[1] /ˈræb(ə)l/ n. **1** a disorderly crowd; a mob. **2** a contemptible or inferior set of people. **3** (prec. by the) the lower or disorderly classes of the populace. □ **rabble-rouser** a person who stirs up the rabble or a crowd of people in agitation for social or political change. [ME: orig. uncert.]

Rabelaisian /ˌræbəˈleɪzɪən/ adj. **1** of or like Rabelais or his writings. **2** marked by exuberant imagination and language, coarse humour, and satire. [F. Rabelais, Fr. satirist d. 1553]

rabid /ˈræbɪd, ˈreɪ-/ adj. **1** furious, violent (rabid hate). **2** unreasoning; headstrong; fanatical (a rabid anarchist). **3** (esp. of a dog) affected with rabies; mad. **4** of or connected with rabies. □ **rabidity** /rəˈbɪdɪtɪ/ n. **rabidly** adv. **rabidness** n. [L rabidus f. rabere rave]

rabies /ˈreɪbiːz/ n. a contagious and fatal viral disease esp. of dogs, transmissible through the saliva to humans etc. and causing madness and convulsions; hydrophobia. [L f. rabere rave]

RAC abbr. **1** (in the UK) Royal Automobile Club. **2** (in the UK) Royal Armoured Corps.

raccoon var. of RACOON.

race[1] n. & v. —n. **1** a contest of speed between runners, horses, vehicles, ships, etc. **2** (in pl.) a series of these for horses, dogs, etc. at a fixed time on a regular course. **3** a contest between persons to be first to achieve something. **4 a** a strong or rapid current flowing through a narrow channel in the sea or a river (a tide race). **b** the channel of a stream etc. (a mill-race). —v. **1** intr. take part in a race. **2** tr. have a race with. **3** tr. try to surpass in speed. **4** intr. (foll. by with) compete in speed with. **5** tr. cause (a horse, car, etc.) to race. **6 a** intr. go at full or (of an engine, propeller, the pulse, etc.) excessive speed. **b** tr. cause (a person or thing) to do this (raced the bill through the House). **7** intr. (usu. as **racing** adj.) follow or take part in horse-racing (a racing man). □ **race meeting** a sequence of horse-races at one place. **racing car** a motor car built for racing on a prepared track. [ME, = running, f. ON rás]

race[2] n. **1** each of the major divisions of humankind, having distinct physical characteristics. **2** a tribe, nation, etc., regarded as of a distinct ethnic stock. **3** the fact or concept of division into races (discrimination based on race). **4** a genus, species, breed, or variety of animals, plants, or micro-organisms. **5** a group of persons, animals, or plants connected by common descent. **6** descent; kindred (of noble race; separate in language and race). □ **race relations** relations between members of different races usu. in the same country. **race riot** an outbreak of violence due to racial antagonism. [F f. It. razza, of unkn. orig.]

racecard /ˈreɪskɑːd/ n. a programme of races.

racecourse /ˈreɪskɔːs/ n. a ground or track for horse-racing.

racegoer /ˈreɪsˌɡəʊə(r)/ n. a person who frequents horse-races.

racehorse /ˈreɪshɔːs/ n. a horse bred or kept for racing.

raceme /rəˈsiːm/ n. Bot. a flower cluster with the separate flowers attached by short equal stalks at equal distances along a central stem. [L racemus grape-bunch]

racer /ˈreɪsə(r)/ n. **1** a horse, yacht, bicycle, etc., of a kind used for racing. **2** a person or thing that races.

racetrack /ˈreɪstræk/ n. **1** = RACECOURSE. **2** a track for motor-racing.

rachitis /rəˈkaɪtɪs/ n. rickets. □ **rachitic** /-ˈkɪtɪk/ adj. [mod.L f. Gk rhakhitis f. rhakhis spine]

Rachmanism /ˈrækmə(r)nɪz(ə)m/ n. Brit. the exploitation and intimidation of slum tenants by unscrupulous landlords. [P. Rachman, London landlord of the early 1960s]

racial /ˈreɪʃ(ə)l/ adj. **1** of or concerning race (racial diversities; racial minority). **2** on the grounds of or connected with difference in race (*racial discrimination; racial tension*). □ **racially** *adv.*

racialism /ˈreɪʃəˌlɪz(ə)m/ *n.* = RACISM 1. □ **racialist** *n.* & *adj.*

racism /ˈreɪsɪz(ə)m/ *n.* **1 a** a belief in the superiority of a particular race; prejudice based on this. **b** antagonism towards other races, esp. as a result of this. **2** the theory that human abilities etc. are determined by race. □ **racist** *n.* & *adj.*

rack¹ *n.* & *v.* —*n.* **1 a** a framework usu. with rails, bars, hooks, etc., for holding or storing things. **b** a frame for holding animal fodder. **2** a cogged or toothed bar or rail engaging with a wheel or pinion etc. **3** *hist.* an instrument of torture stretching the victim's joints by the turning of rollers to which the wrists and ankles were tied. —*v.tr.* **1** (of disease or pain) inflict suffering on. **2** *hist.* torture (a person) on the rack. **3** place in or on a rack. **4** shake violently. **5** injure by straining. □ **on the rack** in distress or under strain. **rack one's brains** make a great mental effort (*racked my brains for something to say*). **rack-railway** a railway with a cogged rail between the bearing rails. [ME *rakke* f. MDu., MLG *rak*, *rek*, prob. f. *recken* stretch]

rack² *n.* destruction (esp. *rack and ruin*). [var. of WRACK, WRECK]

rack³ *n.* a joint of lamb etc. including the front ribs. [perh. f. RACK¹]

rack⁴ *v.tr.* (often foll. by *off*) draw off (wine, beer, etc.) from the lees. [ME f. Prov. *arracar* f. *raca* stems and husks of grapes, dregs]

racket¹ /ˈrækɪt/ *n.* (also **racquet**) **1** a bat with a round or oval frame strung with catgut, nylon, etc., used in tennis, squash, etc. **2** (in *pl.*) a ball game for two or four persons played with rackets in a plain four-walled court. [F *racquette* f. It. *racchetta* f. Arab. *rāḥa* palm of the hand]

racket² /ˈrækɪt/ *n.* **1 a** a disturbance; an uproar; a din. **b** social excitement; gaiety. **2** *sl.* **a** a scheme for obtaining money or attaining other ends by fraudulent and often violent means. **b** a dodge; a sly game. **3** *colloq.* an activity; a way of life; a line of business (*starting up a new racket*). □ **rackety** *adj.* [16th c.: perh. imit.]

racketeer /ˌrækɪˈtɪə(r)/ *n.* a person who operates a dishonest business. □ **racketeering** *n.*

raconteur /ˌrækɒnˈtɜː(r)/ *n.* (*fem.* **raconteuse** /-ˈtɜːz/) a teller of anecdotes. [F f. *raconter* relate, RECOUNT]

racoon /rəˈkuːn/ *n.* (also **raccoon**) **1** any greyish-brown furry N. American mammal of the genus *Procyon*, with a bushy tail and sharp snout. **2** the fur of the racoon. [Algonquian dial.]

racy /ˈreɪsɪ/ *adj.* (**racier**, **raciest**) **1** lively and vigorous in style. **2** risqué, suggestive. □ **racily** *adv.* **raciness** *n.* [RACE² + -Y¹]

rad *n.* *Physics* a unit of absorbed dose of ionizing radiation. [radiation *absorbed dose*]

RADA /ˈrɑːdə/ *abbr.* (in the UK) Royal Academy of Dramatic Art.

radar /ˈreɪdɑː(r)/ *n.* **1** a system for detecting the direction, range, or presence of aircraft, ships, and other (usu. moving) objects, by sending out pulses of high frequency electromagnetic waves. **2** the apparatus used for this. □ **radar trap** the use of radar to detect vehicles exceeding a speed limit. [radio detection and ranging]

RADC *abbr.* (in the UK) Royal Army Dental Corps.

raddle /ˈræd(ə)l/ *n.* & *v.* —*n.* red ochre (often used to mark sheep). —*v.tr.* **1** colour with raddle or too much rouge. **2** (as **raddled** *adj.*) worn out; untidy, unkempt. [var. of RUDDLE]

radial /ˈreɪdɪəl/ *adj.* & *n.* —*adj.* **1** of, concerning, or in rays. **2 a** arranged like rays or radii; having the position or direction of a radius. **b** having spokes or radiating lines. **c** acting or moving along lines diverging from a centre. **3** (in full **radial-ply**) (of a vehicle tyre) having the core fabric layers arranged radially at right angles to the circumference and the tread strengthened. —*n.* a radial-ply tyre. □ **radially** *adv.* [med.L *radialis* (as RADIUS)]

radian /ˈreɪdɪən/ *n.* *Geom.* a unit of angle, equal to an angle at the centre of a circle the arc of which is equal in length to the radius. [RADIUS + -AN]

radiant /ˈreɪdɪənt/ *adj.* & *n.* —*adj.* **1** emitting rays of light. **2** (of eyes or looks) beaming with joy or hope or love. **3** (of beauty) splendid or dazzling. **4** (of light) issuing in rays. **5** operating radially. **6** extending radially; radiating. —*n.* the point or object from which light or heat radiates, esp. in an electric or gas heater. □ **radiant heat** heat transmitted by radiation, not by conduction or convection. **radiant heater** a heater that works by this method. □ **radiance** *n.* **radiancy** *n.* **radiantly** *adv.* [ME f. L *radiare* (as RADIUS)]

radiate *v.* & *adj.* —*v.* /ˈreɪdɪeɪt/ **1** *intr.* **a** emit rays of light, heat, or other electromagnetic waves. **b** (of light or heat) be emitted in rays. **2** *tr.* emit (light, heat, or sound) from a centre. **3** *tr.* transmit or demonstrate (life, love, joy, etc.) (*radiates happiness*). **4** *intr.* & *tr.* diverge or cause to diverge or spread from a centre. **5** *tr.* (as **radiated** *adj.*) with parts arranged in rays. —*adj.* /ˈreɪdɪət/ having divergent rays or parts radially arranged. □ **radiately** /-ətlɪ/ *adv.* **radiative** /-ətɪv/ *adj.* [L *radiare radiat-* (as RADIUS)]

radiation /ˌreɪdɪˈeɪʃ(ə)n/ *n.* **1** the act or an instance of radiating; the process of being radiated. **2** *Physics* **a** the emission of energy as electromagnetic waves or as moving particles. **b** the energy transmitted in this way, esp. invisibly. **3** (in full **radiation therapy**) treatment of cancer and other diseases using radiation, such as X-rays or ultraviolet light. □ **radiation sickness** sickness caused by exposure to radiation, such as X-rays or gamma rays. □ **radiational** *adj.* **radiationally** *adv.* [L *radiatio* (as RADIATE)]

radiator /ˈreɪdɪˌeɪtə(r)/ *n.* **1** a person or thing that radiates. **2 a** a device for heating a room etc., consisting of a metal case through which hot water or steam circulates. **b** a usu. portable oil or electric heater resembling this. **3** an engine-cooling device in a motor vehicle or aircraft with a large surface for cooling circulating water. □ **radiator grille** a grille at the front of a motor vehicle allowing air to circulate to the radiator.

radical /ˈrædɪk(ə)l/ *adj.* & *n.* —*adj.* **1** of the root or roots; fundamental (*a radical error*). **2** far-reaching; thorough; going to the root (*radical change*). **3 a** advocating thorough reform; holding extreme political views; revolutionary. **b** (of a measure etc.) advanced by or according to principles of this kind. **4** forming the basis; primary (*the radical idea*). **5** *Math.* of the root of a number or quantity. **6** (of surgery etc.) seeking to ensure the removal of all diseased tissue. **7** of the roots of others. —*n.* **1** a person holding radical views or belonging to a radical party. **2** *Chem.* **a** a free radical. **b** an element or atom or a group of these normally forming part of a compound and remaining unaltered during the compound's ordinary chemical changes. **3** the root of a word. **4** a fundamental principle; a basis. **5** *Math.* a quantity forming or expressed as the root of another. □ **radicalism** *n.* **radicalize** *v.tr.* & *intr.* (also -**ise**). **radicalization** /-'zeɪ∫(ə)n/ *n.* **radically** *adv.* **radicalness** *n.* [ME f. LL *radicalis* f. L *radix radicis* root]

radicchio /ra'diːkɪəʊ/ *n.* (*pl.* -**os**) a variety of chicory with dark red-coloured leaves. [It., = chicory]

radices *pl.* of RADIX.

radicle /'rædɪk(ə)l/ *n.* the part of a plant embryo that develops into the primary root; a rootlet. □ **radicular** /rə'dɪkjʊlə(r)/ *adj.* [L *radicula* (as RADIX)]

radii *pl.* of RADIUS.

radio /'reɪdɪəʊ/ *n.* & *v.* —*n.* (*pl.* -**os**) **1** (often *attrib.*) **a** the transmission and reception of sound messages etc. by electromagnetic waves of radio-frequency (cf. WIRELESS). **b** an apparatus for receiving, broadcasting, or transmitting radio signals. **c** a message sent or received by radio. **2 a** sound broadcasting in general (*prefers the radio*). **b** a broadcasting station or channel (*Radio One*). —*v.* (-**oes**, -**oed**) **1** *tr.* **a** send (a message) by radio. **b** send a message to (a person) by radio. **2** *intr.* communicate or broadcast by radio. □ **radio cab** (or **car**) a cab or car equipped with a two-way radio. **radio star** a small star etc. emitting strong radio waves. **radio telescope** a directional aerial system for collecting and analysing radiation in the radio-frequency range from stars etc. [short for *radio-telegraphy* etc.]

radio- /'reɪdɪəʊ/ *comb. form* **1** denoting radio or broadcasting. **2** connected with radioactivity. **3** connected with rays or radiation. **4** *Anat.* belonging to the radius in conjunction with some other part (*radio-carpal*). [RADIUS + -o- or f. RADIO]

radioactive /ˌreɪdɪəʊ'æktɪv/ *adj.* of or exhibiting radioactivity. □ **radioactively** *adv.*

radioactivity /ˌreɪdɪəʊæk'tɪvɪtɪ/ *n.* the spontaneous disintegration of atomic nuclei, with the emission of usu. penetrating radiation or particles.

radiocarbon /ˌreɪdɪəʊ'kɑːbən/ *n.* a radioactive isotope of carbon. □ **radiocarbon dating** = *carbon dating.*

radio-controlled /ˌreɪdɪəʊkən'trəʊld/ *adj.* (of a model aircraft etc.) controlled from a distance by radio.

radio-element /ˌreɪdɪəʊ'elɪmənt/ *n.* a natural or artificial radioactive element or isotope.

radio-frequency /'reɪdɪəʊˌfriːkwənsɪ/ *n.* (*pl.* -**ies**) the frequency band of telecommunication, ranging from 10⁴ to 10¹¹ or 10¹² Hz.

radiogenic /ˌreɪdɪəʊ'dʒenɪk/ *adj.* **1** produced by radioactivity. **2** suitable for broadcasting by radio. □ **radiogenically** *adv.*

radiogram /'reɪdɪəʊˌgræm/ *n.* **1** *Brit.* a combined radio and record-player. **2** a picture obtained by X-rays, gamma rays, etc. **3** a radio-telegram. [RADIO- + -GRAM, GRAMOPHONE]

radiograph /'reɪdɪəʊˌgrɑːf/ *n.* & *v.* —*n.* **1** an instrument recording the intensity of radiation. **2** = RADIOGRAM 2. —*v.tr.* obtain a picture of by X-ray, gamma ray, etc. □ **radiographer** /-'ɒgrəfə(r)/ *n.* **radiographic** /-dɪə'græfɪk/ *adj.* **radiographically** /-dɪə'græfɪkəlɪ/ *adv.* **radiography** /-'ɒgrəfɪ/ *n.*

radioisotope /ˌreɪdɪəʊ'aɪsəˌtəʊp/ *n.* a radioactive isotope. □ **radioisotopic** /-'tɒpɪk/ *adj.* **radioisotopically** /-'tɒpɪkəlɪ/ *adv.*

radiology /ˌreɪdɪ'ɒlədʒɪ/ *n.* the scientific study of X-rays and other high-energy radiation, esp. as used in medicine. □ **radiologic** /-ə'lɒdʒɪk/ *adj.* **radiological** /-ə'lɒdʒɪk(ə)l/ *adj.* **radiologist** *n.*

radiometer /ˌreɪdɪ'ɒmɪtə(r)/ *n.* an instrument for measuring the intensity or force of radiation. □ **radiometry** *n.*

radiometric /ˌreɪdɪəʊ'metrɪk/ *adj.* of or relating to the measurement of radioactivity. □ **radiometric dating** a method of dating geological specimens by determining the relative proportions of the isotopes of a radioactive element present in a sample.

radiophonic /ˌreɪdɪəʊ'fɒnɪk/ *adj.* of or relating to synthetic sound, esp. music, produced electronically.

radioscopy /ˌreɪdɪ'ɒskəpɪ/ *n.* the examination by X-rays etc. of objects opaque to light. □ **radioscopic** /-ə'skɒpɪk/ *adj.*

radiosonde /'reɪdɪəʊˌsɒnd/ *n.* a miniature radio transmitter broadcasting information about pressure, temperature, etc., from various levels of the atmosphere, carried esp. by balloon. [RADIO- + G *Sonde* probe]

radio-telegram /ˌreɪdɪəʊ'telɪˌgræm/ *n.* a telegram sent by radio, usu. from a ship to land.

radio-telegraphy /ˌreɪdɪəʊtɪ'legrəfɪ/ *n.* telegraphy using radio transmission. □ **radio-telegraph** /-'telɪˌgrɑːf/ *n.*

radio-telephony /ˌreɪdɪəʊtɪ'lefənɪ/ *n.* telephony using radio transmission. □ **radio-telephone** /-'telɪˌfəʊn/ *n.* **radio-telephonic** /-ˌtelɪ'fɒnɪk/ *adj.*

radiotelex /ˌreɪdɪəʊ'teleks/ *n.* a telex sent usu. from a ship to land.

radiotherapy /ˌreɪdɪəʊ'θerəpɪ/ *n.* the treatment of disease by X-rays or other forms of radiation. □ **radiotherapeutic** /-'pjuːtɪk/ *adj.* **radiotherapist** *n.*

radish /'rædɪ∫/ *n.* **1** a cruciferous plant, *Raphanus sativus*, with a fleshy pungent root. **2** this root, eaten esp. raw in salads etc. [OE *rædic* f. L *radix radicis* root]

radium /'reɪdɪəm/ *n. Chem.* a radioactive metallic element orig. obtained from pitchblende etc., used esp. in luminous materials and in radiotherapy. [L *radius* ray]

radius /'reɪdɪəs/ *n.* & *v.* —*n.* (*pl.* **radii** /-dɪˌaɪ/ or **radiuses**) **1** *Math.* **a** a straight line from the centre to the circumference of a circle or sphere. **b** a radial line from the focus to any point of a curve. **c** the length of the radius of a circle etc. **2** a usu. specified distance from a centre in all directions (*within a radius of 20 miles*). **3 a** the thicker and shorter of the two bones in the human forearm. **b** the corresponding bone in a vertebrate's foreleg or a bird's wing. **4** any of the five arm-like structures of a starfish. **5 a** any of a set of lines diverging from a point like the radii of a circle. **b** an object of this kind, e.g.

a spoke. **6** the outer rim of a composite flower-head, e.g. a daisy. [L, = staff, spoke, ray]

radix /ˈreɪdɪks/ n. (pl. **radices** /-dɪˌsiːz/) **1** Math. a number or symbol used as the basis of a numeration scale (e.g. ten in the decimal system). **2** (usu. foll. by of) a source or origin. [L, = root]

radon /ˈreɪdɒn/ n. Chem. a gaseous radioactive inert element arising from the disintegration of radium, and used in radiotherapy. [RADIUM after argon etc.]

RAF abbr. /colloq. ræf/ (in the UK) Royal Air Force.

raffia /ˈræfɪə/ n. (also **raphia**) **1** a palm-tree, Raphia ruffia, native to Madagascar, having very long leaves. **2** the fibre from its leaves used for making hats, baskets, etc., and for tying plants etc. [Malagasy]

raffish /ˈræfɪʃ/ adj. **1** disreputable; rakish. **2** tawdry. □ **raffishly** adv. **raffishness** n. [as RAFT² + -ISH¹]

raffle /ˈræf(ə)l/ n. & v. —n. a fund-raising lottery with goods as prizes. —v.tr. (often foll. by off) dispose of by means of a raffle. [ME, a kind of dice-game, f. OF raffl(l)e, of unkn. orig.]

raft¹ /rɑːft/ n. **1** a flat floating structure of timber or other materials for conveying persons or things. **2** a lifeboat or small (often inflatable) boat, esp. for use in emergencies. **3** a floating accumulation of trees, ice, etc. [ME f. ON raptr RAFTER]

raft² /rɑːft/ n. colloq. **1** a large collection. **2** (foll. by of) a crowd. [raff rubbish, perh. of Scand. orig.]

rafter /ˈrɑːftə(r)/ n. each of the sloping beams forming the framework of a roof. □ **raftered** adj. [OE ræfter, rel. to RAFT¹]

rag¹ n. **1 a** a torn, frayed, or worn piece of woven material. **b** one of the irregular scraps to which cloth etc. is reduced by wear and tear. **2** (in pl.) old or worn clothes. **3** (collect.) scraps of cloth used as material for paper, stuffing, etc. **4** derog. **a** a newspaper. **b** a flag, handkerchief, curtain, etc. □ **in rags 1** much torn. **2** in old torn clothes. **rag-and-bone man** Brit. an itinerant dealer in old clothes, furniture, etc. **rag-bag 1** a bag in which scraps of fabric etc. are kept for use. **2** a miscellaneous collection. **3** sl. a sloppily-dressed woman. **rag book** a children's book made of untearable cloth. **rag doll** a stuffed doll made of cloth. **rags to riches** poverty to affluence. **rag trade** colloq. the business of designing, making, and selling women's clothes. [ME, prob. back-form. f. RAGGED]

rag² n. & v. sl. Brit. **1** a fund-raising programme of stunts, parades, and entertainment organized by students. **2** colloq. a prank. **3 a** a rowdy celebration. **b** a noisy disorderly scene. —v. (**ragged**, **ragging**) **1** tr. tease; torment; play rough jokes on. **2** intr. Brit. engage in rough play; be noisy and riotous. [18th c.: orig. unkn.]

rag³ n. **1** a large coarse roofing-slate. **2** any of various kinds of hard coarse sedimentary stone that break into thick slabs. [ME: orig. unkn., but assoc. with RAG¹]

rag⁴ n. Mus. a ragtime composition or tune. [perh. f. RAGGED: see RAGTIME]

raga /ˈrɑːɡə/ n. (also **rag** /rɑːɡ/) Ind. Mus. **1** a pattern of notes used as a basis for improvisation. **2** a piece using a particular raga. [Skr., = colour, musical tone]

ragamuffin /ˈræɡəˌmʌfɪn/ n. a person in ragged dirty clothes, esp. a child. [prob. based on RAG¹: cf. 14th-c. ragamoffyn the name of a demon]

rage n. & v. —n. **1** fierce or violent anger. **2** a fit of this (flew into a rage). **3** the violent action of a natural force (the rage of the storm). **4** (foll. by for) **a** a vehement desire or passion. **b** a widespread temporary enthusiasm or fashion. —v.intr. **1** be full of anger. **2** (often foll. by at, against) speak furiously or madly; rave. **3** (of wind, battle, fever, etc.) be violent; be at its height; continue unchecked. **4** Austral. sl. seek enjoyment; go on a spree. □ **all the rage** popular, fashionable. [ME f. OF rager ult. f. L RABIES]

ragged /ˈræɡɪd/ adj. **1** (of clothes etc.) torn; frayed. **2** rough; shaggy; hanging in tufts. **3** (of a person) in ragged clothes. **4** with a broken or jagged outline or surface. **5** faulty; imperfect. **6** lacking finish, smoothness, or uniformity (ragged rhymes). **7** exhausted (esp. be run ragged). □ **raggedly** adv. **raggedness** n. **raggedy** adj. [ME f. ON roggvathr tufted]

raggle-taggle /ˈræɡəlˌtæɡ(ə)l/ adj. (also **wraggle-taggle**) ragged; rambling, straggling. [app. fanciful var. of RAGTAG]

raglan /ˈræɡlən/ n. (often attrib.) an overcoat without shoulder seams, the sleeves running up to the neck. □ **raglan sleeve** a sleeve of this kind. [Lord Raglan, Brit. commander d. 1855]

ragout /ræˈɡuː/ n. & v. —n. meat in small pieces stewed with vegetables and highly seasoned. —v.tr. cook (food) in this way. [F ragoût f. ragoûter revive the taste of]

ragstone /ˈræɡstəʊn/ n. = RAG³ 2.

ragtag /ˈræɡtæɡ/ n. (in full **ragtag and bobtail**) derog. the rabble or common people. [earlier tag-rag, tag and rag, f. RAG¹ + TAG¹]

ragtime /ˈræɡtaɪm/ n. music characterized by a syncopated melodic line and regularly-accented accompaniment, evolved by American Black musicians in the 1890s and played esp. on the piano. [prob. f. RAG⁴]

ragwort /ˈræɡwɜːt/ n. any yellow-flowered ragged-leaved plant of the genus Senecio.

rah int. esp. US colloq. an expression of encouragement, approval, etc. [shortening of HURRAH]

rai /raɪ/ n. a style of rock music which fuses Arabic and Algerian folk elements with Western rock styles. [Algerian or Moroccan Arab.]

raid n. & v. —n. **1** a rapid surprise attack, esp.: **a** by troops, aircraft, etc. in warfare. **b** to commit a crime or do harm. **2** a surprise attack by police etc. to arrest suspected persons or seize illicit goods. —v.tr. **1** make a raid on (a person, place, or thing). **2** plunder, deplete. □ **raider** n. [ME, Sc. form of OE rād ROAD]

rail¹ n. & v. —n. **1** a level or sloping bar or series of bars: **a** used to hang things on. **b** running along the top of a set of banisters. **c** forming part of a fence or barrier as protection against contact, falling over, etc. **2** a steel bar or continuous line of bars laid on the ground, usu. as one of a pair forming a railway track. **3** (often attrib.) a railway (send it by rail; rail fares). **4** (in pl.) the inside boundary fence of a racecourse. —v.tr. **1** furnish with a rail or rails. **2** (usu. foll. by in, off) enclose with rails (a small space was railed *off*). **3** convey (goods) by rail. □ **off the rails** disorganized; out of order; deranged. **rail fence** esp. *US* a fence made of posts and rails. □ **railage** *n.* **railless** *adj.* [ME f. OF *reille* iron rod f. L *regula* RULE]

rail[2] *v.intr.* (often foll. by *at*, *against*) complain using abusive language; rant. □ **railer** *n.* **railing** *n.* & *adj.* [ME f. F *railler* f. Prov. *ralhar* jest, ult. f. L *rugire* bellow]

rail[3] *n.* any bird of the family Rallidae, often inhabiting marshes. [ME f. ONF *raille* f. Rmc, perh. imit.]

railcar /ˈreɪlkɑː(r)/ *n.* a railway vehicle consisting of a single powered coach.

railcard /ˈreɪlkɑːd/ *n. Brit.* a pass entitling the holder to reduced rail fares.

railhead /ˈreɪlhed/ *n.* **1** the furthest point reached by a railway under construction. **2** the point on a railway at which road transport of goods begins.

railing /ˈreɪlɪŋ/ *n.* **1** (usu. in *pl.*) a fence or barrier made of rails. **2** the material for these.

raillery /ˈreɪlərɪ/ *n.* (*pl.* **-ies**) **1** good-humoured ridicule; rallying. **2** an instance of this. [F *raillerie* (as RAIL[2])]

railman /ˈreɪlmən/ *n.* (*pl.* **-men**) = RAILWAYMAN.

railroad /ˈreɪlrəʊd/ *n.* & *v.* —*n.* esp. *US* = RAILWAY. —*v.tr.* (often foll. by *to*, *into*, *through*, etc.) rush or coerce (a person or thing) (*railroaded me into going too*).

railway /ˈreɪlweɪ/ *n.* **1** a track or set of tracks made of steel rails upon which goods trucks and passenger trains run. **2** such a system worked by a single company (*Great Western Railway*). **3** the organization and personnel required for its working.

railwayman /ˈreɪlweɪmən/ *n.* (*pl.* **-men**) a railway employee.

raiment /ˈreɪmənt/ *n. archaic* clothing. [ME f. obs. *arrayment* (as ARRAY)]

rain *n.* & *v.* —*n.* **1 a** the condensed moisture of the atmosphere falling visibly in separate drops. **b** the fall of such drops. **2** (in *pl.*) **a** rainfalls. **b** (prec. by *the*) the rainy season in tropical countries. **3 a** falling liquid or solid particles or objects. **b** the rainlike descent of these. —*v.* **1** *intr.* (prec. by *it* as subject) rain falls (*it is raining*; *if it rains*). **2 a** *intr.* fall in showers or like rain (*tears rained down their cheeks*; *blows rain upon him*). **b** *tr.* (prec. by *it* as subject) send in large quantities (*it rained blood*; *it is raining invitations*). **3** *tr.* send down like rain; lavishly bestow (*rained benefits on us*; *rained blows upon him*). **4** *intr.* (of the sky, the clouds, etc.) send down rain. □ **rain check** *US* **1** a ticket given for later use when a sporting fixture or other outdoor event is interrupted or postponed by rain. **2** a promise that an offer will be maintained though deferred. **rain forest** luxuriant tropical forest with heavy rainfall. **rain-gauge** an instrument measuring rainfall. **rain off** (or *US* **out**) (esp. in *passive*) cause (an event etc.) to be terminated or cancelled because of rain. □ **rainless** *adj.* **raintight** *adj.* [OE *regn*, *rēn*, *regnian* f. Gmc]

rainbow /ˈreɪnbəʊ/ *n.* & *adj.* —*n.* **1** an arch of colours (conventionally red, orange, yellow, green, blue, indigo, violet) formed in the sky (or across a cataract etc.) opposite the sun by reflection, twofold refraction, and dispersion of the sun's rays in falling rain or in spray or mist. **2** a similar effect formed by the moon's rays.

—*adj.* many-coloured. □ **rainbow trout** a large trout, *Salmo gairdneri*, orig. of the Pacific coast of N. America. [OE *regnboga* (as RAIN, BOW[1])]

raincoat /ˈreɪnkəʊt/ *n.* a waterproof or water-resistant coat.

raindrop /ˈreɪndrɒp/ *n.* a single drop of rain. [OE *regndropa*]

rainfall /ˈreɪnfɔːl/ *n.* **1** a fall of rain. **2** the quantity of rain falling within a given area in a given time.

rainproof /ˈreɪnpruːf/ *adj.* (esp. of a building, garment, etc.) resistant to rainwater.

rainstorm /ˈreɪnstɔːm/ *n.* a storm with heavy rain.

rainwater /ˈreɪnwɔːtə(r)/ *n.* water obtained from collected rain, as distinct from a well etc.

rainy /ˈreɪnɪ/ *adj.* (**rainier**, **rainiest**) **1** (of weather, a climate, day, region, etc.) in or on which rain is falling or much rain usually falls. **2** (of cloud, wind, etc.) laden with or bringing rain. □ **rainy day** a time of special need in the future. □ **rainily** *adv.* **raininess** *n.* [OE *rēnig* (as RAIN)]

raise /reɪz/ *v.* & *n.* —*v.tr.* **1** put or take into a higher position. **2** (often foll. by *up*) cause to rise or stand up or be vertical; set upright. **3** increase the amount or value or strength of (*raised their prices*). **4** (often foll. by *up*) construct or build up. **5** levy or collect or bring together (*raise money; raise an army*). **6** cause to be heard or considered (*raise a shout; raise an objection*). **7** set going or bring into being; rouse (*raise a protest; raise hopes*). **8** bring up; educate. **9** breed or grow (*raise one's own vegetables*). **10** promote to a higher rank. **11** (foll. by *to*) *Math.* multiply a quantity to a specified power. **12** cause (bread) to rise with yeast. **13** *Cards* **a** bet more than (another player). **b** increase (a stake). **c** *Bridge* make a bid contracting for more tricks in the same suit as (one's partner); increase (a bid) in this way. **14** abandon or force an enemy to abandon (a siege or blockade). **15** remove (a barrier or embargo). **16** cause (a ghost etc.) to appear. **17** *colloq.* find (a person etc. wanted). **18** establish contact with (a person etc.) by radio or telephone. **19** (usu. as **raised** *adj.*) cause (pastry etc.) to stand without support (*a raised pie*). —*n.* **1** *Cards* an increase in a stake or bid. **2** esp. *US* an increase in salary. □ **raise from the dead** restore to life. **raise one's glass to** drink the health of. **raise one's hand to** make as if to strike (a person). **raise hell** *colloq.* make a disturbance. **raise a laugh** cause others to laugh. **raise a person's spirits** give him or her new courage or cheerfulness. **raise one's voice** speak, esp. louder. □ **raisable** *adj.* [ME f. ON *reisa*, rel. to REAR[2]]

raisin /ˈreɪz(ə)n/ *n.* a partially dried grape. □ **raisiny** *adj.* [ME f. OF ult. f. L *racemus* grape-bunch]

raison d'être /ˌreɪzɔ̃ ˈdetr/ *n.* (*pl.* *raisons d'être* *pronunc.* same) a purpose or reason that accounts for or justifies or originally caused a thing's existence. [F, = reason for being]

raj /rɑːdʒ/ *n.* (prec. by *the*) *hist.* British sovereignty in India. [Hindi *rāj* reign]

raja /ˈrɑːdʒə/ *n.* (also **rajah**) *hist.* **1** an Indian king or prince. **2** a petty dignitary or noble in India. □ **rajaship** *n.* [Hindi *rājā* f. Skr. *rājan* king]

rake[1] *n.* & *v.* —*n.* **1** an implement consisting of a pole with a crossbar toothed like a comb at the end, or with several tines held together by a crosspiece, for drawing together hay etc. or smoothing loose soil or gravel. **2** a similar implement used for other purposes, e.g. by a croupier drawing in money at a gaming-table. —*v.* **1** *tr.* collect or gather or remove with or as with a rake. **2** *tr.* make tidy or smooth with a rake (*raked it level*). **3** *intr.* use a rake. **4** *tr.* & *intr.* search with or as with a rake, search thoroughly, ransack. **5** *tr.* **a** direct gunfire along (a line) from end to end. **b** sweep with the eyes. **c** (of a window etc.) have a commanding view of. **6** *tr.* scratch or scrape. □ **rake in** *colloq.* amass (profits etc.). **rake-off** *colloq.* a commission or share, esp. in a disreputable deal. **rake up** (or **over**) revive the memory of (past quarrels, grievances, etc.). □ **raker** *n.* [OE *raca, racu* f. Gmc, partly f. ON *raka* scrape, rake]

rake² *n.* a dissolute man of fashion. [short for archaic *rakehell* in the same sense]

rake³ *v.* & *n.* —*v.* **1** *tr.* & *intr.* set or be set at a sloping angle. **2** *intr.* (of a mast or funnel) incline from the perpendicular towards the stern. —*n.* **1** a raking position or build. **2** the amount by which a thing rakes. **3** the slope of the stage or the auditorium in a theatre. **4** the slope of a seat-back etc. [17th c.: prob. rel. to G *ragen* project, of unkn. orig.]

rakish¹ /ˈreɪkɪʃ/ *adj.* of or like a rake (see RAKE²); dashing; jaunty. □ **rakishly** *adv.* **rakishness** *n.*

rakish² /ˈreɪkɪʃ/ *adj.* (of a ship) smart and fast-looking, seemingly built for speed and therefore open to suspicion of piracy. [RAKE³, assoc. with RAKE²]

rallentando /ˌrælənˈtændəʊ/ *adv., adj.,* & *n. Mus.* —*adv.* & *adj.* with a gradual decrease of speed. —*n.* (pl. **-os** or **rallentandi** /-dɪ/) a passage to be performed in this way. [It.]

rally¹ /ˈrælɪ/ *v.* & *n.* —*v.* (**-ies, -ied**) **1** *tr.* & *intr.* (often foll. by *round, behind, to*) bring or come together as support or for concentrated action. **2** *tr.* & *intr.* bring or come together again after a rout or dispersion. **3 a** *intr.* renew a conflict. **b** *tr.* cause to do this. **4 a** *tr.* revive (courage etc.) by an effort of will. **b** *tr.* rouse (a person or animal) to fresh energy. **c** *intr.* pull oneself together. **5** *intr.* recover after illness or prostration or fear, regain health or consciousness, revive. **6** *intr.* (of share-prices etc.) increase after a fall. —*n.* (pl. **-ies**) **1** an act of reassembling forces or renewing conflict; a reunion for fresh effort. **2** a recovery of energy after or in the middle of exhaustion or illness. **3** a mass meeting of supporters or persons having a common interest. **4** a competition for motor vehicles, usu. over public roads. **5** (in lawn tennis etc.) an extended exchange of strokes between players. □ **rallier** *n.* [F *rallier* (as RE-, ALLY)]

rally² /ˈrælɪ/ *v.tr.* (**-ies, -ied**) subject to good-humoured ridicule. [F *railler*: see RAIL²]

RAM *abbr.* **1** (in the UK) Royal Academy of Music. **2** *Computing* random-access memory.

ram *n.* & *v.* —*n.* **1** an uncastrated male sheep. **2** (**the Ram**) the zodiacal sign or constellation Aries. **3** *hist.* = *battering ram* (see BATTER¹). **4** the falling weight of a pile-driving machine. **5** a hydraulic water-raising or lifting machine. —*v.tr.* (**rammed, ramming**) **1** force or squeeze into place by pressure. **2** (usu. foll. by *down, in, into*) beat down or drive in by heavy blows. **3** (of

a ship, vehicle, etc.) strike violently, crash against. **4** (foll. by *against, at, on, into*) dash or violently impel. □ **ram home** stress forcefully (an argument, lesson, etc.). **ram-raid** a form of robbery in which the front of a shop is rammed using a large vehicle, and the occupants of the vehicle then loot the shop and escape in the vehicle. □ **rammer** *n.* [OE *ram(m)*, perh. rel. to ON *rammr* strong]

Ramadan /ˈræməˌdæn/ *n.* (also **Ramadhan** /-ˌzæn/) the ninth month of the Muslim year, during which strict fasting is observed from sunrise to sunset. [Arab. *ramaḍān* f. *ramaḍa* be hot; reason for name uncert.]

ramble /ˈræmb(ə)l/ *v.* & *n.* —*v.intr.* **1** walk for pleasure, with or without a definite route. **2** wander in discourse, talk or write disconnectedly. —*n.* a walk taken for pleasure. [prob. f. MDu. *rammelen* (of an animal) wander about in sexual excitement, frequent. of *rammen* copulate with, rel. to RAM]

rambler /ˈræmblə(r)/ *n.* **1** a person who rambles. **2** a straggling or climbing rose (*crimson rambler*).

rambling /ˈræmblɪŋ/ *adj.* **1** peripatetic, wandering. **2** disconnected, desultory, incoherent. **3** (of a house, street, etc.) irregularly arranged. **4** (of a plant) straggling, climbing. □ **ramblingly** *adv.*

rambunctious /ræmˈbʌŋkʃəs/ *adj. US colloq.* **1** uncontrollably exuberant. **2** unruly. □ **rambunctiously** *adv.* **rambunctiousness** *n.* [19th c.: orig. unkn.]

rambutan /ræmˈbuːt(ə)n/ *n.* **1** a red plum-sized prickly fruit. **2** an East Indian tree, *Nephelium lappaceum,* that bears this. [Malay *rambūtan* f. *rambut* hair, in allusion to its spines]

RAMC *abbr.* (in the UK) Royal Army Medical Corps.

ramekin /ˈræmɪkɪn/ *n.* **1** (in full **ramekin case** or **dish**) a small dish for baking and serving an individual portion of food. **2** food served in such a dish. [F *ramequin*, of LG or Du. orig.]

ramification /ˌræmɪfɪˈkeɪʃ(ə)n/ *n.* **1** the act or an instance of ramifying; the state of being ramified. **2** a subdivision of a complex structure or process comparable to a tree's branches. [F f. *ramifier*: see RAMIFY]

ramify /ˈræmɪˌfaɪ/ *v.* (**-ies, -ied**) **1** *intr.* form branches or subdivisions or offshoots, branch out. **2** *tr.* (usu. in *passive*) cause to branch out; arrange in a branching manner. [F *ramifier* f. med.L *ramificare* f. L *ramus* branch]

ramjet /ˈræmdʒet/ *n.* a type of jet engine in which air is drawn in and compressed by the forward motion of the engine.

rammer see RAM.

ramp¹ *n.* & *v.* —*n.* **1** a slope or inclined plane, esp. for joining two levels of ground, floor, etc. **2** movable stairs for entering or leaving an aircraft. **3** *Brit.* a transverse ridge in a road to control the speed of vehicles. —*v.* **1** *tr.* furnish or build with a ramp. **2** *intr.* **a** assume or be in a threatening posture. **b** (often foll. by *about*) storm, rage, rush. [ME (as verb in heraldic sense) f. F *rampe* f. OF *ramper* creep, crawl]

ramp² *n.* & *v. Brit. sl.* —*n.* a swindle or racket, esp. one conducted by the levying of exorbitant prices. —*v.* **1** *intr.* engage in a ramp. **2** *tr.* subject (a person etc.) to a ramp. [16th c.: orig. unkn.]

rampage /ræmˈpeɪdʒ/ *v.* & *n.* —*v.intr.* **1** (often foll. by *about*) rush wildly or violently about. **2**

rage, storm. —*n.* /often ˈræm-/ wild or violent behaviour. □ **on the rampage** rampaging. □ **rampageous** *adj.* **rampager** *n.* [18th c., perh. f. RAMP[1]]

rampant /ˈræmpənt/ *adj.* **1** (placed after noun) *Heraldry* (of an animal) standing on its left hind foot with its forepaws in the air (*lion rampant*). **2** unchecked, flourishing excessively (*rampant violence*). **3** violent or extravagant in action or opinion (*rampant theorists*). **4** rank, luxuriant. □ **rampancy** *n.* **rampantly** *adv.* [ME f. OF, part. of *ramper*: see RAMP[1]]

rampart /ˈræmpɑːt/ *n.* & *v.* —*n.* **1 a** a defensive wall with a broad top and usu. a stone parapet. **b** a walkway on top of such a wall. **2** a defence or protection. —*v.tr.* fortify or protect with or as with a rampart. [F *rempart*, *rempar* f. *remparer* fortify f. *emparer* take possession of, ult. f. L *ante* before + *parare* prepare]

ramrod /ˈræmrɒd/ *n.* **1** a rod for ramming down the charge of a muzzle-loading firearm. **2** a thing that is very straight or rigid.

ramshackle /ˈræmˌʃæk(ə)l/ *adj.* (usu. of a house or vehicle) tumbledown, rickety. [earlier *ramshackled* past part. of obs. *ransackle* RANSACK]

RAN *abbr.* Royal Australian Navy.

ran past of RUN.

ranch /rɑːntʃ/ *n.* & *v.* —*n.* **1 a** a cattle-breeding establishment esp. in the US and Canada. **b** a farm where other animals are bred (*mink ranch*). **2** *US* a single-storey or split-level house. —*v.intr.* farm on a ranch. [Sp. *rancho* group of persons eating together]

rancher /ˈrɑːntʃə(r)/ *n.* **1** a person who farms on a ranch. **2** *US* a modern single-storey house.

rancid /ˈrænsɪd/ *adj.* smelling or tasting like rank stale fat. □ **rancidity** /-ˈsɪdɪtɪ/ *n.* **rancidness** *n.* [L *rancidus* stinking]

rancour /ˈræŋkə(r)/ *n.* (*US* **rancor**) inveterate bitterness, malignant hate, spitefulness. □ **rancorous** *adj.* **rancorously** *adv.* [ME f. OF f. LL *rancor -oris* (as RANCID)]

rand /rænd, rɑːnt/ *n.* the chief monetary unit of South Africa and some neighbouring countries. [Afrik., = edge, f. *the Rand*, gold-field district near Johannesburg]

R & B *abbr.* (also **R. & B.**) rhythm and blues.

R & D *abbr.* (also **R. & D.**) research and development.

random /ˈrændəm/ *adj.* **1** made, done, etc., without method or conscious choice (*random selection*). **2** *Statistics* **a** with equal chances for each item. **b** given by a random process. □ **at random** without aim or purpose or principle. **random-access** *Computing* (of a memory or file) having all parts directly accessible, so that it need not read sequentially. □ **randomize** *v.tr.* (also **-ise**). **randomization** /-ˈzeɪʃ(ə)n/ *n.* **randomly** *adv.* **randomness** *n.* [ME f. OF *randon* great speed f. *randir* gallop]

R and R *abbr.* (also **R. and R.**) **1** rescue and resuscitation. **2** rest and recreation.

randy /ˈrændɪ/ *adj.* (**randier**, **randiest**) **1** lustful; eager for sexual gratification. **2** *Sc.* loud-tongued, boisterous, lusty. □ **randily** *adv.* **randiness** *n.* [perh. f. obs. *rand* f. obs. Du. *randen*, *ranten* RANT]

ranee /ˈrɑːnɪ/ *n.* (also **rani**) *hist.* a raja's wife or widow; a Hindu queen. [Hindi *rānī* = Skr. *rājñī* fem. of *rājan* king]

rang past of RING[2].

range /reɪndʒ/ *n.* & *v.* —*n.* **1 a** the region between limits of variation, esp. as representing a scope of effective operation (*a voice of astonishing range; the whole range of politics*). **b** such limits. **c** a limited scale or series (*the range of the thermometer readings is about 10 degrees*). **2** the area included in or concerned with something. **3 a** the distance attainable by a gun or projectile (*the enemy are out of range*). **b** the distance between a gun or projectile and its objective. **4** a row, series, line, or tier, esp. of mountains or buildings. **5 a** an open or enclosed area with targets for shooting. **b** a testing-ground for military equipment. **6 a** a fireplace with ovens and hotplates for cooking. **b** *US* an electric or gas cooker. **7** the area over which a thing, esp. a plant or animal, is distributed (*gives the ranges of all species*). **8** the distance that can be covered by a vehicle or aircraft without refuelling. **9** the distance between a camera and the subject to be photographed. **10** the extent of time covered by a forecast etc. **11 a** a large area of open land for grazing or hunting. **b** a tract over which one wanders. —*v.* **1** *intr.* **a** reach; lie spread out; extend; be found or occur over a specified district; vary between limits (*ages ranging from twenty to sixty*). **b** run in a line (*ranges north and south*). **2** *tr.* (usu. in *passive* or *refl.*) place or arrange in a row or ranks or in a specified situation or order or company (*ranged their troops; ranged themselves with the majority party; trees ranged in ascending order of height*). **3** *intr.* rove, wander (*ranged through the woods; his thoughts range over past, present, and future*). **4** *tr.* traverse in all directions (*ranging the woods*). **5** *intr.* **a** (often foll. by *with*) be level. **b** (foll. by *with*, *among*) rank; find one's right place (*ranges with the great writers*). **6** *intr.* **a** (of a gun) send a projectile over a specified distance (*ranges over a mile*). **b** (of a projectile) cover a specified distance. **c** obtain the range of a target by adjustment after firing past it or short of it. [ME f. OF *range* row, rank f. *ranger* f. *rang* RANK[1]]

rangefinder /ˈreɪndʒˌfaɪndə(r)/ *n.* an instrument for estimating the distance of an object, esp. one to be shot at or photographed.

ranger /ˈreɪndʒə(r)/ *n.* **1** a keeper of a royal or national park, or of a forest. **2** a member of a body of armed men, esp.: **a** a mounted soldier. **b** *US* a commando. **3** (**Ranger**) *Brit.* a senior Guide. □ **rangership** *n.*

rangy /ˈreɪndʒɪ/ *adj.* (**rangier**, **rangiest**) (of a person) tall and slim.

rank[1] *n.* & *v.* —*n.* **1 a** a position in a hierarchy, a grade of advancement. **b** a distinct social class, a grade of dignity or achievement (*people of all ranks; in the top rank of performers*). **c** high social position (*persons of rank*). **d** a place in a scale. **2 a** row or line. **3** a single line of soldiers drawn up abreast. **4** *Brit.* a place where taxis stand to await customers. —*v.* **1** *intr.* have rank or place (*ranks next to the king*). **2** *tr.* classify, give a certain grade to. **3** *tr.* arrange (esp. soldiers) in a rank or ranks. **4** *US* **a** *tr.* take precedence of (a person) in respect to rank. **b** *intr.* have the senior position among the members of a hierarchy etc. □ **break rank** fail to remain in line. **close ranks** maintain solidarity. **keep rank** remain in line. **other ranks** soldiers other than commissioned officers. **rank and file** ordinary undistinguished people (orig. = *the ranks*). **the**

ranks the common soldiers, i.e. privates and corporals. [OF *ranc, renc,* f. Gmc, rel. to RING¹]

rank² *adj.* **1** too luxuriant, coarse; choked with or apt to produce weeds or excessive foliage. **2 a** foul-smelling, offensive. **b** loathsome, indecent, corrupt. **3** flagrant, virulent, gross, complete, unmistakable, strongly marked (*rank outsider*). □ **rankly** *adv.* **rankness** *n.* [OE *ranc* f. Gmc]

ranking /ˈræŋkɪŋ/ *n. & adj.* —*n.* ordering by rank; classification. —*adj. US* having a high rank or position.

rankle /ˈræŋk(ə)l/ *v.intr.* (of envy, disappointment, etc., or their cause) cause persistent annoyance or resentment. [ME f. OF *rancler, rancle, draoncle* festering sore f. med.L *dranculus, dracunculus* dimin. of *draco* serpent]

ransack /ˈrænsæk/ *v.tr.* **1** pillage or plunder (a house, country, etc.). **2** thoroughly search (a place, a receptacle, a person's pockets, one's conscience, etc.). □ **ransacker** *n.* [ME f. ON *rannsaka* f. *rann* house + *-saka* f. *sœkja* seek]

ransom /ˈrænsəm/ *n. & v.* —*n.* **1** a sum of money or other payment demanded or paid for the release of a prisoner. **2** the liberation of a prisoner in return for this. —*v.tr.* **1** buy the freedom or restoration of; redeem. **2** hold to ransom. **3** release for a ransom. □ **ransomer** *n.* (in sense 1 of *v.*). [ME f. OF *ransoun(er)* f. L *redemptio -onis* REDEMPTION]

rant *v. & n.* —*v.* **1** *intr.* use bombastic language. **2** *tr. & intr.* declaim, recite theatrically. **3** *tr. & intr.* preach noisily. —*n.* **1** a piece of ranting, a tirade. **2** empty turgid talk. □ **ranter** *n.* **rantingly** *n.* [Du. *ranten* rave]

ranunculus /rəˈnʌŋkjʊləs/ *n.* (*pl.* **ranunculuses** or **ranunculi** /-ˌlaɪ/) any plant of the genus *Ranunculus,* including buttercups and crowfoots. [L, orig. dimin. of *rana* frog]

RAOC *abbr.* (in the UK) Royal Army Ordnance Corps.

rap¹ *n. & v.* —*n.* **1** a smart slight blow. **2** a knock, a sharp tapping sound. **3** *sl.* blame, censure, or punishment. **4** *sl.* a conversation. **5 a** a rhyming monologue recited rhythmically to prerecorded music. **b** (in full **rap music**) a style of rock music with a pronounced beat and words recited rather than sung. —*v.* (**rapped, rapping**) **1** *tr.* strike smartly. **2** *intr.* knock; make a sharp tapping sound (*rapped on the table*). **3** *tr.* criticize adversely. **4** *intr. sl.* talk. □ **beat the rap** *US* escape punishment. **rap on** (or **over**) **the knuckles** a reprimand or reproof. **rap out 1** utter (an oath, order, pun, etc.) abruptly or on the spur of the moment. **2** *Spiritualism* express (a message or word) by raps. **take the rap** suffer the consequences. □ **rapper** *n.* [ME, prob. imit.]

rap² *n.* a small amount, the least bit (*don't care a rap*). [Ir. *ropaire* Irish counterfeit coin]

rapacious /rəˈpeɪʃəs/ *adj.* grasping, extortionate, predatory. □ **rapaciously** *adv.* **rapaciousness** *n.* **rapacity** /rəˈpæsɪti/ *n.* [L *rapax -acis* f. *rapere* snatch]

RAPC *abbr.* (in the UK) Royal Army Pay Corps.

rape¹ *n. & v.* —*n.* **1 a** the act of forcing a woman to have sexual intercourse against her will. **b** forcible sodomy. **2** (often foll. by *of*) violent assault, forcible interference, violation. **3** an instance of rape. —*v.tr.* **1** commit rape on (a person, usu. a woman). **2** violate, assault, pillage. [ME f. AF *rap(er)* f. L *rapere* seize]

rape² *n.* a plant, *Brassica napus,* grown as food for sheep and for its seed, from which oil is made. □ **rape-oil** an oil made from rape-seed and used as a lubricant and in foodstuffs. [ME f. L *rapum, rapa* turnip]

raphia var. of RAFFIA.

rapid /ˈræpɪd/ *adj. & n.* —*adj.* (**rapider, rapidest**) **1** quick, swift. **2** acting or completed in a short time. **3** (of a slope) descending steeply. —*n.* (usu. in *pl.*) a steep descent in a river-bed, with a swift current. □ **rapid eye-movement** a type of jerky movement of the eyes during periods of dreaming. **rapid-fire** (*attrib.*) fired, asked, etc., in quick succession. □ **rapidity** /rəˈpɪdɪti/ *n.* **rapidly** *adv.* **rapidness** *n.* [L *rapidus* f. *rapere* seize]

rapier /ˈreɪpɪə(r)/ *n.* a light slender sword used for thrusting. [prob. f. Du. *rapier* or LG *rappir,* f. F *rapière,* of unkn. orig.]

rapine /ˈræpaɪn, -pɪn/ *n. rhet.* plundering, robbery. [ME f. OF or f. L *rapina* f. *rapere* seize]

rapist /ˈreɪpɪst/ *n.* a person who commits rape.

rapport /ræˈpɔː(r)/ *n.* relationship or communication, esp. when useful and harmonious (*in rapport with; establish a rapport*). [F f. *rapporter* (as RE-, AD-, *porter* f. L *portare* carry)]

rapprochement /ræˈprɒʃmɑ̃/ *n.* the resumption of harmonious relations, esp. between States. [F f. *rapprocher* (as RE-, APPROACH)]

rapscallion /ræpˈskæljən/ *n.* archaic or *joc.* a rascal, scamp, or rogue. [earlier *rascallion,* perh. f. RASCAL]

rapt *adj.* **1** fully absorbed or intent, enraptured (*listen with rapt attention*). **2** carried away with feeling or lofty thought. □ **raptly** *adv.* **raptness** *n.* [ME f. L *raptus* past part. of *rapere* seize]

raptor /ˈræptə(r)/ *n.* any bird of prey, e.g. an owl, falcon, etc. [L, = ravisher, plunderer f. *rapere* rapt- seize]

raptorial /ræpˈtɔːrɪəl/ *adj. & n.* —*adj.* (of a bird or animal) adapted for seizing prey; predatory. —*n.* **1** = RAPTOR. **2** a predatory animal. [L *raptor:* see RAPTOR]

rapture /ˈræptʃə(r)/ *n.* **1** ecstatic delight, mental transport. **2** (in *pl.*) great pleasure or enthusiasm or the expression of it. □ **go into** (or **be in**) **raptures** be enthusiastic; talk enthusiastically. □ **rapturous** *adj.* **rapturously** *adv.* **rapturousness** *n.* [obs. F *rapture* or med.L *raptura* (as RAPT)]

rare¹ /reə(r)/ *adj.* (**rarer, rarest**) **1** seldom done or found or occurring, uncommon, unusual, few and far between. **2** exceptionally good (*had a rare time*). **3** of less than the usual density, with only loosely packed substance (*the rare atmosphere of the mountain tops*). □ **rare earth 1** a lanthanide element. **2** an oxide of such an element. **rare gas** = *noble gas.* □ **rareness** *n.* [ME f. L *rarus*]

rare² /reə(r)/ *adj.* (**rarer, rarest**) (of meat) underdone. [var. of obs. *rear* half-cooked (of eggs), f. OE *hrēr*]

rarebit /ˈreəbɪt/ *n.* = *Welsh rabbit.* [RARE¹ + BIT¹]

rarefy /ˈreərɪˌfaɪ/ *v.* (**-ies, -ied**) **1** *tr. & intr.* make or become less dense or solid (*rarefied air*). **2** *tr.* purify or refine (a person's nature etc.). **3** *tr.* make (an idea etc.) subtle. □ **rarefaction** /-ˈfækʃ(ə)n/ *n.* **rarefactive** /-ˈfæktɪv/ *adj.* **rarefication** /-fɪˈkeɪʃ(ə)n/ *n.* [ME f. OF *rarefier* or med.L *rarificare* f. L *rarefacere* f. *rarus* rare + *facere* make]

rarely /'reəlı/ *adv.* **1** seldom; not often. **2** in an unusual degree; exceptionally. **3** exceptionally well.

raring /'reərıŋ/ *adj.* (foll. by *to* + infin.) *colloq.* enthusiastic, eager (*raring to go*). [part. of RARE, dial. var. of ROAR or REAR²]

rarity /'reərıtı/ *n.* (pl. **-ies**) **1** rareness. **2** an uncommon thing, esp. one valued for being rare. [F *rareté* or L *raritas* (as RARE¹)]

rascal /'rɑːsk(ə)l/ *n.* often *joc.* a dishonest or mischievous person, esp. a child. □ **rascaldom** *n.* **rascalism** *n.* **rascality** /-'skælıtı/ *n.* (pl. **-ies**). **rascally** *adj.* [ME f. OF *rascaille* rabble, prob. ult. f. L *radere ras-* scrape]

rase var. of RAZE.

rash¹ *adj.* reckless, impetuous, hasty; acting or done without due consideration. □ **rashly** *adv.* **rashness** *n.* [ME, prob. f. OE *ræsc* (unrecorded) f. Gmc]

rash² *n.* **1** an eruption of the skin in spots or patches. **2** (usu. foll. by *of*) a sudden widespread phenomenon, esp. of something unwelcome (*a rash of strikes*). [18th c.: prob. rel. to OF *ra(s)che* eruptive sores, = It. *raschia* itch]

rasher /'ræʃə(r)/ *n.* a thin slice of bacon or ham. [16th c.: orig. unkn.]

rasp /rɑːsp/ *n.* & *v.* —*n.* a coarse kind of file having separate teeth. —*v.* **1** *tr.* **a** scrape with a rasp. **b** scrape roughly. **c** (foll. by *off*, *away*) remove by scraping. **2 a** *intr.* make a grating sound. **b** *tr.* say gratingly or hoarsely. **3** *tr.* grate upon (a person or a person's feelings), irritate. □ **raspingly** *adv.* **raspy** *adj.* [ME f. OF *raspe(r)* ult. f. WG]

raspberry /'rɑːzbərı/ *n.* (pl. **-ies**) **1 a** a bramble, *Rubus idaeus*, having usu. red berries. **b** this berry. **2** any of various red colours. **3** *colloq.* **a** a sound made with the lips expressing dislike, derision, or disapproval (orig. *raspberry tart*, rhyming sl. = *fart*). **b** a show of strong disapproval (*got a raspberry from the audience*). □ **raspberry-cane** a raspberry plant. **raspberry vinegar** a kind of syrup made from raspberries. [16th-c. *rasp* (now dial.) f. obs. *raspis*, of unkn. orig., + BERRY]

Rasta /'ræstə/ *n.* & *adj.* = RASTAFARIAN. [abbr.]

Rastafarian /ˌræstə'feərɪən/ *n.* & *adj.* —*n.* a member of a sect of Jamaican origin regarding Blacks as a chosen people and the former Emperor Haile Selassie of Ethiopia (d. 1975, entitled *Ras Tafari*) as God. —*adj.* of or relating to this sect. □ **Rastafarianism** *n.*

rat *n.* & *v.* —*n.* **1 a** any of several rodents of the genus *Rattus* (*brown rat*). **b** any similar rodent (*muskrat*; *water-rat*). **2** a deserter from a party, cause, difficult situation, etc.; a turncoat. **3** *colloq.* an unpleasant person. **4** (in *pl.*) *sl.* an exclamation of contempt, annoyance, etc. —*v.intr.* (**ratted**, **ratting**) **1** (of a person or dog) hunt or kill rats. **2** *colloq.* desert a cause, party, etc. **3** (foll. by *on*) **a** betray; let down. **b** inform on. □ **rat-catcher** a person who rids buildings of rats etc. **rat race** a fiercely competitive struggle for position, power, etc. **rat's tail** a thing shaped like a rat's tail, e.g. a tapering cylindrical file. [OE *ræt* & OF *rat*]

ratafia /ˌrætə'fiːə/ *n.* **1** a liqueur flavoured with almonds or kernels of peach, apricot, or cherry. **2** a kind of biscuit similarly flavoured. [F, perh. rel. to TAFIA]

ratatouille /ˌrætə'tuːı, -'twiː/ *n.* a vegetable dish made of stewed onions, courgettes, tomatoes, aubergines, and peppers. [F dial.]

ratbag /'rætbæg/ *n. sl.* an unpleasant person.

ratchet /'rætʃıt/ *n.* & *v.* —*n.* **1** a set of teeth on the edge of a bar or wheel in which a device engages to ensure motion in one direction only. **2** (in full **ratchet-wheel**) a wheel with a rim so toothed. —*v.* (**ratcheted**, **ratcheting**) **1** *tr.* **a** provide with a ratchet. **b** make into a ratchet. **2** *tr.* & *intr.* move as under the control of a ratchet. [F *rochet* blunt lance-head, bobbin, ratchet, etc., prob. ult. f. Gmc]

rate¹ *n.* & *v.* —*n.* **1** a stated numerical proportion between two sets of things (the second usu. expressed as unity), esp. as a measure of amount or degree (*moving at a rate of 50 miles per hour*) or as the basis of calculating an amount or value (*rate of taxation*). **2** a fixed or appropriate charge or cost or value; a measure of this (*postal rates*; *the rate for the job*). **3** rapidity of movement or change (*travelling at a great rate*; *prices increasing at a dreadful rate*). **4** class or rank (*first-rate*). **5** *Brit.* **a** an assessment levied by local authorities at so much per pound of the assessed value of buildings and land owned or leased. **b** (in *pl.*) the amount payable by this. —*v.* **1** *tr.* **a** estimate the worth or value of (*I do not rate him very highly*). **b** assign a fixed value to (a coin or metal) in relation to a monetary standard. **2** *tr.* consider; regard as (*I rate them among my benefactors*). **3** *intr.* (foll. by *as*) rank or be rated. **4** *tr. Brit.* **a** subject to the payment of a local rate. **b** value for the purpose of assessing rates. **5** *tr.* be worthy of, deserve. □ **at any rate** in any case, whatever happens. **at this** (or *that*) **rate** if this example is typical or this assumption is true. [ME f. OF f. med.L *rata* f. L *pro rata parte* or *portione* according to the proportional share f. *ratus* past part. of *rēri* reckon]

rate² *v.tr.* scold angrily. [ME: orig. unkn.]

rateable /'reɪtəb(ə)l/ *adj.* (also **ratable**) **1** *Brit.* liable to payment of rates. **2** able to be rated or estimated. □ **rateable value** the value at which a house etc. is assessed for payment of rates. □ **rateability** /-'bɪlɪtɪ/ *n.* **rateably** *adv.*

ratepayer /'reɪtˌpeɪə(r)/ *n. Brit.* a person liable to pay rates.

rather /'rɑːðə(r)/ *adv.* **1** (often foll. by *than*) by preference; for choice (*would rather not go*; *would rather stay than go*). **2** (usu. foll. by *than*) more truly; as a more likely alternative (*is stupid rather than honest*). **3** more precisely (*a book, or rather, a pamphlet*). **4** slightly; to some extent; somewhat (*became rather drunk*; *I rather think you know him*). **5** /rɑː'ðɜː(r)/ *Brit.* (as an emphatic response) indeed, assuredly (*Did you like it?—Rather!*). □ **had rather** would rather. [ME f. OE *hrathor*, compar. of *hræthe* (adv.) f. *hræth* (adj.) early-blooming]

ratify /'rætɪˌfaɪ/ *v.tr.* (**-ies**, **-ied**) confirm or accept (an agreement made in one's name) by formal consent, signature, etc. □ **ratifiable** *adj.* **ratification** /-fɪ'keɪʃ(ə)n/ *n.* **ratifier** *n.* [ME f. OF *ratifier* f. med.L *ratificare* (as RATE¹)]

rating¹ /'reɪtɪŋ/ *n.* **1** the act or an instance of placing in a rank or class or assigning a value to. **2** the estimated standing of a person as regards credit etc. **3** *Naut. Brit.* a non-commissioned sailor. **4** *Brit.* an amount fixed as a local rate. **5** the relative popularity of a broadcast programme as determined by the estimated size of the audience.

rating[2] /ˈreɪtɪŋ/ n. an angry reprimand.

ratio /ˈreɪʃɪəʊ/ n. (pl. **-os**) the quantitative relation between two similar magnitudes determined by the number of times one contains the other integrally or fractionally (*in the ratio of three to two; the ratios 1:5 and 20:100 are the same*). [L (as RATE[1])]

ratiocinate /ˌrætɪˈɒsɪˌneɪt, ˌræʃɪ-/ v.intr. literary go through logical processes, reason, esp. using syllogisms. □ **ratiocination** /-ˈneɪʃ(ə)n/ n. **ratiocinative** /-nətɪv/ adj. **ratiocinator** n. [L ratiocinari (as RATIO)]

ration /ˈræʃ(ə)n/ n. & v. —n. **1** a fixed official allowance of food, clothing, etc., in a time of shortage. **2** (foll. by *of*) a single portion of provisions, fuel, clothing, etc. **3** (usu. in *pl.*) a fixed daily allowance of food, esp. in the armed forces. **4** (in *pl.*) provisions. —v.tr. **1** limit (persons or provisions) to a fixed ration. **2** (usu. foll. by *out*) share out (food etc.) in fixed quantities. □ **ration book** (or **card**) a document entitling the holder to a ration. [F f. It. *razione* or Sp. *ración* f. L *ratio -onis* reckoning, RATIO]

rational /ˈræʃən(ə)l/ adj. **1** of or based on reasoning or reason. **2** sensible, sane, moderate; not foolish or absurd or extreme. **3** endowed with reason, reasoning. **4** rejecting what is unreasonable or cannot be tested by reason in religion or custom. **5** Math. (of a quantity or ratio) expressible as a ratio of whole numbers. □ **rationality** /-ˈnælɪtɪ/ n. **rationally** adv. [ME f. L rationalis (as RATION)]

rationale /ˌræʃəˈnɑːl/ n. **1** (often foll. by *of*) the fundamental reason or logical basis of anything. **2** a reasoned exposition; a statement of reasons. [mod.L, neut. of L rationalis: see RATIONAL]

rationalism /ˈræʃənəˌlɪz(ə)m/ n. **1** Philos. the theory that reason is the foundation of certainty in knowledge. **2** Theol. the practice of treating reason as the ultimate authority in religion. **3** a belief in reason rather than religion as a guiding principle in life. □ **rationalist** n. **rationalistic** /-ˈlɪstɪk/ adj. **rationalistically** /-ˈlɪstɪkəlɪ/ adv.

rationalize /ˈræʃənəˌlaɪz/ v. (also **-ise**) **1 a** tr. offer or subconsciously adopt a rational but specious explanation of (one's behaviour or attitude). **b** intr. explain one's behaviour or attitude in this way. **2** tr. make logical and consistent. **3** tr. make (a business etc.) more efficient by reorganizing it to reduce or eliminate waste of labour, time, or materials. **4** tr. (often foll. by *away*) explain or explain away rationally. □ **rationalization** /-ˈzeɪʃ(ə)n/ n. **rationalizer** n.

ratline /ˈrætlɪn/ n. (also **ratlin**) (usu. in *pl.*) any of the small lines fastened across a sailing-ship's shrouds like ladder-rungs. [ME: orig. unkn.]

rattan /rəˈtæn/ n. (also **ratan**) **1** any East Indian climbing palm of the genus *Calamus* etc. with long thin jointed pliable stems. **2** a piece of rattan stem used as a walking stick etc. [earlier rot(t)ang f. Malay rōtan prob. f. raut pare]

rat-tat /rætˈtæt/ n. (also **rat-tat-tat** /ˌrættætˈtæt/, **ratatat**, **rat-a-tat** /ˌrætəˈtæt/) a rapping sound, esp. of a knocker. [imit.]

rattle /ˈræt(ə)l/ v. & n. —v. **1 a** intr. give out a rapid succession of short sharp hard sounds. **b** tr. make (a chair, window, crockery, etc.) do this. **c** intr. cause such sounds by shaking something

(*rattled at the door*). **2 a** intr. move with a rattling noise. **b** intr. drive a vehicle or ride or run briskly. **c** tr. cause to move quickly (*the bill was rattled through Parliament*). **3 a** tr. (usu. foll. by *off*) say or recite rapidly. **b** intr. (usu. foll. by *on*) talk in a lively thoughtless way. **4** tr. colloq. disconcert, alarm, fluster, make nervous, frighten. —n. **1** a rattling sound. **2** an instrument or plaything made to rattle esp. in order to amuse babies or to give an alarm. **3** the set of horny rings in a rattlesnake's tail. **4 a** a noisy flow of words. **b** empty chatter, trivial talk. □ **rattle the sabre** threaten war. □ **rattly** adj. [ME, prob. f. MDu. & LG ratelen (imit.)]

rattler /ˈrætlə(r)/ n. **1** a thing that rattles, esp. an old or rickety vehicle. **2** colloq. a rattlesnake. **3** sl. a remarkably good specimen of anything.

rattlesnake /ˈræt(ə)lˌsneɪk/ n. any of various poisonous American snakes of the family Viperidae, esp. of the genus *Crotalus* or *Sistrurus*, with a rattling structure of horny rings in its tail.

rattletrap /ˈræt(ə)lˌtræp/ n. & adj. colloq. —n. a rickety old vehicle etc. —adj. rickety.

rattling /ˈrætlɪŋ/ adj. & adv. —adj. **1** that rattles. **2** brisk, vigorous (*a rattling pace*). —adv. remarkably (*a rattling good story*).

ratty adj. (**rattier**, **rattiest**) **1** relating to or infested with rats. **2** colloq. irritable or angry. **3** colloq. wretched, nasty. □ **rattily** adv. **rattiness** n.

raucous /ˈrɔːkəs/ adj. harsh-sounding, loud and hoarse. □ **raucously** adv. **raucousness** n. [L raucus]

raunchy /ˈrɔːntʃɪ/ adj. (**raunchier**, **raunchiest**) colloq. coarse, boisterous; sexually provocative. □ **raunchily** adv. **raunchiness** n. [20th c.: orig. unkn.]

ravage /ˈrævɪdʒ/ v. & n. —v.tr. & intr. devastate, plunder. —n. **1** the act or an instance of ravaging; devastation, damage. **2** (usu. in *pl.*; foll. by *of*) destructive effect (*survived the ravages of winter*). □ **ravager** n. [F ravage(r) alt. f. ravine rush of water]

rave v. & n. —v. **1** intr. talk wildly or furiously in or as in delirium. **2** intr. (usu. foll. by *about*, *of*, *over*) speak with rapturous admiration; go into raptures. **3** intr. colloq. enjoy oneself freely (esp. *rave it up*). —n. **1** (usu. *attrib.*) colloq. a highly enthusiastic review of a film, play, etc. (*a rave review*). **2** sl. an infatuation. **3** (also **rave-up**) colloq. a lively party. [ME, prob. f. ONF raver, rel. to (M)LG reven be senseless, rave]

ravel /ˈræv(ə)l/ v. & n. —v. (**ravelled, ravelling**; US **raveled, raveling**) **1** tr. & intr. entangle or become entangled or knotted. **2** tr. confuse or complicate (a question or problem). **3** intr. fray out. **4** tr. (often foll. by *out*) disentangle, unravel, distinguish the separate threads or subdivisions of. —n. **1** a tangle or knot. **2** a complication. **3** a frayed or loose end. [prob. f. Du. ravelen tangle, fray out, unweave]

raven[1] /ˈreɪv(ə)n/ n. & adj. —n. a large glossy blue-black crow, *Corvus corax*, feeding chiefly on carrion etc., having a hoarse cry. —adj. glossy black (*raven tresses*). [OE hræfn f. Gmc]

raven[2] /ˈræv(ə)n/ v. **1** intr. **a** plunder. **b** (foll. by *after*) seek prey or booty. **c** (foll. by *about*) go plundering. **d** prowl for prey (*ravening beast*). **2 a** tr. devour voraciously. **b** intr. (usu. foll. by *for*) have a ravenous appetite. **c** intr. (often foll. by *on*) feed voraciously. [OF raviner ravage ult. f. L rapina RAPINE]

ravenous /ˈrævənəs/ adj. **1** very hungry, famished. **2** (of hunger, eagerness, etc., or of an animal) voracious. **3** rapacious. □ **ravenously** adv. **ravenousness** n. [ME f. OF ravineus (as RAVEN²)]

raver /ˈreɪvə(r)/ n. **1** colloq. an uninhibited pleasure-loving person. **2** a person who raves.

ravine /rəˈviːn/ n. a deep narrow gorge or cleft. □ **ravined** adj. [F f. L rapina RAPINE]

raving /ˈreɪvɪŋ/ n., adj., & adv. —n. (usu. in pl.) wild or delirious talk. —adj. delirious, frenzied. —adj. & adv. colloq. as an intensive (a raving beauty; raving mad). □ **ravingly** adv.

ravioli /ˌrævɪˈəʊlɪ/ n. small pasta envelopes containing minced meat etc. [It.].

ravish /ˈrævɪʃ/ v.tr. **1** commit rape on (a woman). **2** enrapture; fill with delight. □ **ravisher** n. **ravishment** n. [ME f. OF ravir ult. f. L rapere seize]

ravishing /ˈrævɪʃɪŋ/ adj. entrancing, delightful. □ **ravishingly** adv.

raw adj. & n. —adj. **1** (of food) uncooked. **2** in the natural state; not processed or manufactured (raw sewage). **3** (of alcoholic spirit) undiluted. **4** (of statistics etc.) not analysed or processed. **5** (of a person) inexperienced, untrained; new to an activity (raw recruits). **6 a** stripped of skin; having the flesh exposed. **b** sensitive to the touch from having the flesh exposed. **7** (of the atmosphere, day, etc.) chilly and damp. **8** crude in artistic quality; lacking finish. **9** (of the edge of cloth) without hem or selvage. —n. a raw place on a person's or horse's body. □ **in the raw 1** in its natural state without mitigation (life in the raw). **2** naked. **raw-boned** gaunt and bony. **raw deal** harsh or unfair treatment. **raw material** that from which the process of manufacture makes products. **touch on the raw** upset (a person) on a sensitive matter. □ **rawish** adj. **rawly** adv. **rawness** n. [OE hrēaw f. Gmc]

rawhide /ˈrɔːhaɪd/ n. **1** untanned hide. **2** a rope or whip of this.

Rawlplug /ˈrɔːlplʌg/ n. propr. a thin cylindrical plug for holding a screw or nail in masonry. [Rawlings, name of the engineers who introduced it]

ray¹ n. **1** a single line or narrow beam of light from a small or distant source. **2** a straight line in which radiation travels to a given point. **3** (in pl.) radiation of a specified type (gamma rays; X-rays). **4** a trace or beginning of an enlightening or cheering influence (a ray of hope). **5 a** any of a set of radiating lines or parts of things. **b** any of a set of straight lines passing through one point. **6** the marginal portion of a composite flower, e.g. a daisy. □ **ray gun** (esp. in science fiction) a gun causing injury or damage by the emission of rays. □ **rayed** adj. **rayless** adj. **raylet** n. [ME f. OF rai f. L radius: see RADIUS]

ray² n. a large cartilaginous fish of the order Batoidea, with a broad flat body, winglike pectoral fins and a long slender tail, used as food. [ME f. OF raie f. L raia]

ray³ n. (also **re**) Mus. **1** (in tonic sol-fa) the second note of a major scale. **2** the note D in the fixed-doh system. [ME re f. L resonare: see GAMUT]

rayon /ˈreɪɒn/ n. any of various textile fibres or fabrics made from cellulose. [arbitrary f. RAY¹]

raze v.tr. (also **rase**) **1** completely destroy; tear down (esp. raze to the ground). **2** erase; scratch out (esp. in abstract senses). [ME rase = wound slightly f. OF raser shave close ult. f. L radere rasscrape]

razor /ˈreɪzə(r)/ n. & v. —n. an instrument with a sharp blade used in cutting hair esp. from the skin. —v.tr. **1** use a razor on. **2** shave; cut down close. □ **razor-bill** an auk, Alca torda, with a sharp-edged bill. **razor-blade** a blade used in a razor, esp. a flat piece of metal with a sharp edge or edges used in a safety razor. **razor-cut** a haircut made with a razor. **razor-** (or **razor's**) **edge 1** a keen edge. **2** a sharp mountain-ridge. **3** a critical situation (found themselves on a razor-edge). **4** a sharp line of division. **razor-fish** (or **-shell**) any of various bivalve molluscs of the family Solenidae, with a shell like the handle of a cutthroat razor. [ME f. OF rasor (as RAZE)]

razzle-dazzle /ˈræzəlˌdæz(ə)l/ n. (also **razzle**) sl. **1 a** glamorous excitement; bustle. **b** a spree. **2** extravagant publicity. [redupl. of DAZZLE]

razzmatazz /ˌræzməˈtæz/ n. (also **razzamatazz** /ˌræzəmə-/) colloq. **1** = RAZZLE-DAZZLE. **2** insincere actions; humbug. [prob. alt. f. RAZZLE-DAZZLE]

Rb symb. Chem. the element rubidium.

RC abbr. **1** Roman Catholic. **2** Red Cross.

RCA abbr. (in the UK) Royal College of Art.

RCAF abbr. Royal Canadian Air Force.

RCM abbr. (in the UK) Royal College of Music.

RCMP abbr. Royal Canadian Mounted Police.

RCN abbr. **1** (in the UK) Royal College of Nursing. **2** Royal Canadian Navy.

RCP abbr. (in the UK) Royal College of Physicians.

RCS abbr. (in the UK): **1** Royal College of Scientists. **2** Royal College of Surgeons. **3** Royal Corps of Signals.

RCVS abbr. (in the UK) Royal College of Veterinary Surgeons.

Rd. abbr. Road (in names).

RE abbr. **1** (in the UK) Royal Engineers. **2** religious education.

Re symb. Chem. the element rhenium.

re¹ /reɪ, riː/ prep. **1** in the matter of (as the first word in a heading, esp. of a legal document). **2** colloq. about, concerning. [L, ablat. of res thing]

re² var. of RAY³.

re- /riː, rɪ, rɛ/ prefix **1** attachable to almost any verb or its derivative, meaning: **a** once more; afresh, anew (readjust; renumber). **b** back; with return to a previous state (reassemble; reverse). **2** (also **red-** before a vowel, as in redolent) in verbs and verbal derivatives denoting: **a** in return; mutually (react; resemble). **b** opposition (repel; resist). **c** behind or after (relic; remain). **d** retirement or secrecy (recluse; reticence). **e** off, away, down (recede; relegate; repress). **f** frequentative or intensive force (redouble; resplendent). **g** negative force (recant; reveal). [L re-, red-, again, back, etc.]

■ **Usage** In sense 1, a hyphen is normally used when the word begins with e (re-enact), or to distinguish the compound from a more familiar one-word form (re-form = form again).

reabsorb /ˌriːəbˈsɔːb, -ˈzɔːb/ v.tr. absorb again. □ **reabsorption** n.

reach /riːtʃ/ v. & n. —v. **1** intr. & tr. (often foll. by out) stretch out; extend. **2** intr. stretch out a limb, the hand, etc.; make a reaching motion or effort. **3** intr. (often foll. by for) make a motion or effort to touch or get hold of, or to attain (*reached for his pipe*). **4** *tr.* get as far as; arrive at (*reached Lincoln at lunch-time; your letter reached me today*). **5** *tr.* get to or attain (a specified point) on a scale (*the number of applications reached 100*). **6** *intr.* (foll. by *to*) attain to; be adequate for (*my income will not reach to it*). **7** *tr.* succeed in achieving; attain (*have reached agreement*). **8** *tr.* make contact with the hand etc., or by telephone etc. (*was out all day and could not be reached*). **9** *tr.* succeed in influencing or having the required effect on (*could not manage to reach their audience*). **10** *tr.* hand, pass (*reach me that book*). **11** *tr.* take with an outstretched hand. **12** *intr. Naut.* sail with the wind abeam or abaft the beam. —*n.* **1** the extent to which a hand etc. can be reached out, influence exerted, motion carried out, or mental powers used. **2** an act of reaching out. **3** a continuous extent, esp. a stretch of river between two bends, or the part of a canal between locks. **4** *Naut.* a distance traversed in reaching. □ **out of reach** not able to be reached or attained. **reach-me-down** ready-made. □ **reachable** *adj.* **reacher** *n.* [OE *rǣcan* f. WG]

reacquaint /ˌriːəˈkweɪnt/ *v.tr.* & *refl.* (usu. foll. by *with*) make (a person or oneself) acquainted again. □ **reacquaintance** *n.*

react /rɪˈækt/ *v.* **1** *intr.* (foll. by *to*) respond to a stimulus; undergo a change or show behaviour due to some influence (*how did they react to the news?*). **2** *intr.* (often foll. by *against*) be actuated by repulsion to; tend in a reverse or contrary direction. **3** *intr.* (often foll. by *upon*) produce a reciprocal or responsive effect; act upon the agent (*they react upon each other*). **4** *intr.* (foll. by *with*) *Chem.* & *Physics* (of a substance or particle) be the cause of activity or interaction with another (*nitrous oxide reacts with the metal*). **5** *tr.* (foll. by *with*) *Chem.* cause (a substance) to react with another. [RE- + ACT or med.L *reagere react-* (as RE-, L *agere* do, act)]

reaction /rɪˈækʃ(ə)n/ *n.* **1** the act or an instance of reacting; a responsive or reciprocal action. **2 a** a responsive feeling (*what was your reaction to the news?*). **b** an immediate or first impression. **3** the occurrence of a (physical or emotional) condition after a period of its opposite. **4** a bodily response to an external stimulus, e.g. a drug. **5** a tendency to oppose change or to advocate return to a former system, esp. in politics. **6** the interaction of substances undergoing chemical change. □ **reactionist** *n.* & *adj.* [REACT + -ION or med.L *reactio* (as RE-, ACTION)]

reactionary /rɪˈækʃ(ə)nərɪ/ *adj.* & *n.* —*adj.* tending to oppose (esp. political) change. —*n.* (pl. **-ies**) a reactionary person.

reactivate /rɪˈæktɪˌveɪt/ *v.tr.* restore to a state of activity; bring into action again. □ **reactivation** /-ˈveɪʃ(ə)n/ *n.*

reactive /rɪˈæktɪv/ *adj.* showing reaction. □ **reactivity** /-ˈtɪvɪtɪ/ *n.*

reactor /rɪˈæktə(r)/ *n.* **1** a person or thing that reacts. **2** (in full **nuclear reactor**) an apparatus or structure in which a controlled nuclear chain reaction releases energy.

read /riːd/ *v.* & *n.* —*v.* (*past* and *past part.* **read** /red/) **1** *tr.* (also *absol.*) reproduce mentally or (often foll. by *aloud*, *out*, *off*, etc.) vocally the written or printed words of (a book, author, etc.) by following the symbols with the eyes or fingers. **2** *tr.* convert into or be able to convert into the intended words or meaning (written or

other symbols or the things expressed in this way). **3** *tr.* interpret mentally. **4** *tr.* deduce or declare an (esp. accurate) interpretation of (*read the expression on my face*). **5** *tr.* (often foll. by *that* + clause) find (a thing) recorded or stated in print etc. (*I read somewhere that you are leaving*). **6** *tr.* interpret (a statement or action) in a certain sense (*my silence is not to be read as consent*). **7** *tr.* (often foll. by *into*) assume as intended or deducible from a writer's words; find (implications) (*you read too much into my letter*). **8** *tr.* bring into a specified state by reading (*read myself to sleep*). **9** *tr.* (of a meter or other recording instrument) show (a specified figure etc.) (*the thermometer reads 20°*). **10** *intr.* convey meaning in a specified manner when read (*it reads persuasively*). **11 a** *tr.* study by reading (esp. a subject at university). **b** *intr.* carry out a course of study by reading (*is reading for the Bar*). **12** *tr.* (as **read** /red/ *adj.*) versed in a subject (esp. literature) by reading (*a well-read person*). **13** *tr.* **a** (of a computer) copy or transfer (data). **b** (foll. by *in*, *out*) enter or extract (data) in an electronic storage device. **14** *tr.* understand or interpret by hearing words or seeing signs, gestures, etc. as words probably used or intended by an author. —*n.* **1** a spell of reading. **2** *colloq.* a book etc. as regards its readability (*is a really good read*). □ **read between the lines** look for or find hidden meaning (in a document etc.). **read-only memory** *Computing* a memory read at high speed but not capable of being changed by program instructions. **read up** make a special study of (a subject). **read-write** *Computing* capable of reading existing data and accepting alterations or further input. [OE *rǣdan* advise, consider, discern f. Gmc]

readable /ˈriːdəb(ə)l/ *adj.* **1** able to be read; legible. **2** interesting or pleasant to read. □ **readability** /-ˈbɪlɪtɪ/ *n.* **readableness** *n.* **readably** *adv.*

readdress /ˌriːəˈdres/ *v.tr.* **1** change the address of (a letter or parcel). **2** address (a problem etc.) anew. **3** speak or write to anew.

reader /ˈriːdə(r)/ *n.* **1** a person who reads or is reading. **2** a book of extracts for learning, esp. a language. **3** a device for producing an image that can be read from microfilm etc. **4** *Brit.* a university lecturer of the highest grade below professor. **5** a publisher's employee who reports on submitted manuscripts. **6** a printer's proof-corrector. [OE (as READ)]

readership /ˈriːdəʃɪp/ *n.* **1** the readers of a newspaper etc. **2** the number or extent of these.

readily /ˈredɪlɪ/ *adv.* **1** without showing reluctance; willingly. **2** without difficulty.

reading /ˈriːdɪŋ/ *n.* **1 a** the act or an instance of reading or perusing (*the reading of the will*). **b** matter to be read (*have plenty of reading with me*). **c** the specified quality of this (*it made exciting reading*). **2** (in *comb.*) used for reading (*reading-lamp; reading-room*). **3** literary knowledge (*a person of wide reading*). **4** an entertainment at which a play, poems, etc., are read (*poetry reading*). **5** a figure etc. shown by a meter or other recording instrument. **6** an interpretation or view taken (*what is your reading of the facts?*). **7** an interpretation made (of drama, music, etc.). **8** each of the successive occasions on which a bill must be presented to a legislature for acceptance. [OE (as READ)]

readjust /ˌriːəˈdʒʌst/ v.tr. adjust again or to a former state. □ **readjustment** n.

readmit /ˌriːədˈmɪt/ v.tr. (**readmitted, readmitting**) admit again. □ **readmission** n.

readopt /ˌriːəˈdɒpt/ v.tr. adopt again. □ **readoption** n.

ready /ˈrɛdɪ/ adj., adv., n., & v. —adj. (**readier, readiest**) (usu. predic.) **1** with preparations complete (dinner is ready). **2** in a fit state (are you ready to go?). **3** willing, inclined, or resolved (he is always ready to complain; I am ready for anything). **4** within reach; easily secured (a ready source of income). **5** fit for immediate use (was ready to hand). **6** immediate, unqualified (found ready acceptance). **7** prompt, quick, facile (is always ready with excuses; has a ready wit). **8** (foll. by to + infin.) about to do something (a bud just ready to burst). **9** provided beforehand. —adv. **1** beforehand. **2** so as not to require doing when the time comes for use (the cases are ready packed). —n. (pl. **-ies**) sl. **1** (prec. by the) = ready money. **2** (in pl.) bank notes. —v.tr. (**-ies, -ied**) make ready; prepare. □ **at the ready** ready for action. **make ready** prepare. **ready-made** (or **-to-wear**) (esp. of clothes) made in a standard size, not to measure. **ready-mix** (or **-mixed**) (of concrete, paint, food, etc.) having some or all of the constituents already mixed together. **ready money 1** actual coin or notes. **2** payment on the spot. **ready reckoner** a book or table listing standard numerical calculations as used esp. in commerce. **ready, steady** (or **get set**), **go** the usual formula for starting a race. □ **readiness** n. [ME rædi(g), re(a)di, f. OE ræde f. Gmc]

reaffirm /ˌriːəˈfɜːm/ v.tr. affirm again. □ **reaffirmation** /-ˌæfəˈmeɪʃ(ə)n/ n.

reafforest /ˌriːəˈfɒrɪst/ v.tr. replant (former forest land) with trees. □ **reafforestation** /-ˈsteɪʃ(ə)n/ n.

reagent /riːˈeɪdʒ(ə)nt/ n. Chem. **1** a substance used to cause a reaction, esp. to detect another substance. **2** a reactive substance or force. [RE- + AGENT: cf. REACT]

real[1] /rɪl/ adj. & adv. —adj. **1** actually existing as a thing or occurring in fact. **2** genuine; rightly so called; not artificial or merely apparent. **3** Law consisting of or relating to immovable property such as land or houses (real estate) (cf. personal property). **4** appraised by purchasing power; adjusted for changes in the value of money (real value; income in real terms). —adv. Sc. & US colloq. really, very. □ **for real** colloq. as a serious or actual concern; in earnest. **real ale** beer regarded as brewed in a traditional way, with secondary fermentation in the cask. **real life** that lived by actual people, as distinct from fiction, drama, etc. **real live** (attrib.) often joc. actual; not pretended or simulated (a real live burglar). **real money** current coin or notes; cash. **real tennis** the original form of tennis played on an indoor court. **the real thing** (of an object or emotion) genuine, not inferior. **real time** the actual time during which a process or event occurs. **real-time** (attrib.) Computing (of a system) in which the response time is of the order of milliseconds, e.g. in an airline booking system. □ **realness** n. [AF = OF reel, LL realis f. L res thing]

real[2] /reɪˈɑːl/ n. hist. a former coin and monetary unit of various Spanish-speaking countries. [Sp., noun use of real (adj.) (as ROYAL)]

realign /ˌriːəˈlaɪn/ v.tr. **1** align again. **2** regroup in politics etc. □ **realignment** n.

realism /ˈrɪəlɪz(ə)m/ n. **1** the practice of regarding things in their true nature and dealing with them as they are. **2** fidelity to nature in representation; the showing of life etc. as it is in fact. □ **realist** n.

realistic /rɪəˈlɪstɪk/ adj. **1** regarding things as they are; following a policy of realism. **2** based on facts rather than ideals. □ **realistically** adv.

reality /rɪˈælɪtɪ/ n. (pl. **-ies**) **1** what is real or existent or underlies appearances. **2** (foll. by of) the real nature of (a thing). **3** real existence; the state of being real. **4** resemblance to an original (the model was impressive in its reality). □ **in reality** in fact. [med.L realitas or F réalité (as REAL[1])]

realize /ˈrɪəlaɪz/ v.tr. (also **-ise**) **1** (often foll. by that + clause) be fully aware of; conceive as real. **2** understand clearly. **3** present as real; make realistic; give apparent reality to (the story was powerfully realized on stage). **4** convert into actuality; achieve (realized a childhood dream). **5 a** convert into money. **b** acquire (profit). **c** be sold for (a specified price). □ **realizable** adj. **realizability** /-ˈbɪlɪtɪ/ n. **realization** /-ˈzeɪʃ(ə)n/ n. **realizer** n.

reallocate /riːˈæləˌkeɪt/ v.tr. allocate again or differently. □ **reallocation** /-ˈkeɪʃ(ə)n/ n.

really /ˈrɪəlɪ/ adv. **1** in reality; in fact. **2** positively, assuredly (really useful). **3** (as a strong affirmative) indeed, I assure you. **4** an expression of mild protest or surprise. **5** (in interrog.) (expressing disbelief) is that so? (They're musicians.—Really?).

realm /rɛlm/ n. **1** formal esp. Law a kingdom. **2** a sphere or domain (the realm of imagination). [ME f. OF realme, reaume, f. L regimen -minis (see REGIMEN): infl. by OF reiel ROYAL]

realtor /ˈriːəltə(r)/ n. US a real-estate agent, esp. (**Realtor**) a member of the National Association of Realtors.

ream[1] n. **1** twenty quires or 500 (formerly 480) sheets of paper (or a larger number, to allow for waste). **2** (in pl.) a large quantity of paper or writing (wrote reams about it). [ME rēm, rīm f. OF raime etc., ult. f. Arab. rīzma bundle]

ream[2] v.tr. widen (a hole in metal etc.) with a borer. □ **reamer** n. [19th c.: orig. uncert.]

reanimate /riːˈænɪˌmeɪt/ v.tr. **1** restore to life. **2** restore to activity or liveliness. □ **reanimation** /-ˈmeɪʃ(ə)n/ n.

reap v.tr. **1** cut or gather (a crop, esp. grain) as a harvest. **2** harvest the crop of (a field etc.). **3** receive as the consequence of one's own or others' actions. [OE ripan, reopan, of unkn. orig.]

reaper /ˈriːpə(r)/ n. **1** a person who reaps. **2** a machine for reaping. □ **the Reaper** (or **grim Reaper**) death personified.

reappear /ˌriːəˈpɪə(r)/ v.intr. appear again or as previously. □ **reappearance** n.

reapply /ˌriːəˈplaɪ/ v.tr. & intr. (**-ies, -ied**) apply again, esp. submit a further application (for a position etc.). □ **reapplication** /ˌriːæplɪˈkeɪʃ(ə)n/ n.

reappoint /ˌriːəˈpɔɪnt/ v.tr. appoint again to a position previously held. □ **reappointment** n.

reapportion /ˌriːəˈpɔːʃ(ə)n/ v.tr. apportion again or differently. □ **reapportionment** n.

reappraise /ˌriːəˈpreɪz/ v.tr. appraise or assess again. □ **reappraisal** n.

rear[1] n. & adj. —n. **1** the back part of anything. **2** the space behind, or position at the back of, anything (a large house with a terrace at the rear). **3** the hindmost part of an army or fleet. **4** colloq. the buttocks. —adj. at the back. □ **bring up the rear** come last. **in the rear** behind; at the back. **rear admiral** a naval officer ranking below vice admiral. **rear-lamp** (or **-light**) a usu. red light at the rear of a vehicle. **rear sight** the sight nearest to the stock on a firearm. **rear-view mirror** a mirror fixed inside the windscreen of a motor vehicle enabling the driver to see traffic etc. behind. [prob. f. (in the) REARWARD or REARGUARD]

rear[2] v. **1** tr. **a** bring up and educate (children). **b** breed and care for (animals). **c** cultivate (crops). **2** intr. (of a horse etc.) raise itself on its hind legs. **3** tr. **a** set upright. **b** build. **c** hold upwards (rear one's head). **4** intr. extend to a great height. □ **rearer** n. [OE rēran f. Gmc]

rearguard /ˈrɪəɡɑːd/ n. **1** a body of troops detached to protect the rear, esp. in retreats. **2** a defensive or conservative element in an organization etc. □ **rearguard action 1** Mil. an engagement undertaken by a rearguard. **2** a defensive stand in argument etc., esp. when losing. [OF rereguarde (as RETRO-, GUARD)]

rearm /riːˈɑːm/ v.tr. (also absol.) arm again, esp. with improved weapons. □ **rearmament** n.

rearmost /ˈrɪəməʊst/ adj. furthest back.

rearrange /ˌriːəˈreɪndʒ/ v.tr. arrange again in a different way. □ **rearrangement** n.

rearrest /ˌriːəˈrest/ v. & n. —v.tr. arrest again. —n. an instance of rearresting or being rearrested.

rearward /ˈrɪəwəd/ n., adj., & adv. —n. rear, esp. in prepositional phrases (to the rearward of; in the rearward). —adj. to the rear. —adv. (also **rearwards**) towards the rear. [AF rerewarde = REARWARD]

reason /ˈriːz(ə)n/ n. & v. —n. **1** a motive, cause, or justification (has good reasons for doing this; there is no reason to be angry). **2** a fact adduced or serving as this (I can give you my reasons). **3** the intellectual faculty by which conclusions are drawn from premisses. **4** sanity (has lost his reason). **5** a faculty transcending the understanding and providing a priori principles; intuition. **6** sense; sensible conduct; what is right or practical or practicable; moderation. —v. **1** intr. form or try to reach conclusions by connected thought. **2** intr. (foll. by with) use an argument (with a person) by way of persuasion. **3** tr. (foll. by that + clause) conclude or assert in argument. **4** tr. (foll. by why, whether, what + clause) discuss; ask oneself. **5** tr. (foll. by into, out of) persuade or move by argument (I reasoned them out of their fears). **6** tr. (foll. by out) think or work out (consequences etc.). **7** tr. (often as **reasoned** adj.) express in logical or argumentative form. **8** tr. embody reason in (an amendment etc.). □ **by reason of** owing to. **in** (or **within**) **reason** within the bounds of sense or moderation. **it stands to reason** (often foll. by that + clause) it is evident or logical. **listen to reason** be persuaded to act sensibly. **see reason** acknowledge the force of an argument. **with reason** justifiably. □ **reasoner** n. **reasoning** n. **reasonless** adj. [ME f. OF reisun,

res(o)un, raisoner, ult. f. L ratio -onis f. rēri rat-consider]

reasonable /ˈriːzənəb(ə)l/ adj. **1** having sound judgement; moderate; ready to listen to reason. **2** in accordance with reason; not absurd. **3 a** within the limits of reason; not greatly less or more than might be expected. **b** inexpensive; not extortionate. **c** tolerable, fair. □ **reasonableness** n. **reasonably** adv. [ME f. OF raisonable (as REASON) after L rationabilis]

reassemble /ˌriːəˈsemb(ə)l/ v.intr. & tr. assemble again or into a former state. □ **reassembly** n.

reassert /ˌriːəˈsɜːt/ v.tr. assert again. □ **reassertion** n.

reassess /ˌriːəˈses/ v.tr. assess again, esp. differently. □ **reassessment** n.

reassign /ˌriːəˈsaɪn/ v.tr. assign again or differently. □ **reassignment** n.

reassure /ˌriːəˈʃʊə(r)/ v.tr. **1** restore confidence to; dispel the apprehensions of. **2** confirm in an opinion or impression. □ **reassurance** n. **reassurer** n. **reassuring** adj. **reassuringly** adv.

reattach /ˌriːəˈtætʃ/ v.tr. attach again or in a former position. □ **reattachment** n.

reattain /ˌriːəˈteɪn/ v.tr. attain again. □ **reattainment** n.

reattempt /ˌriːəˈtempt/ v.tr. attempt again, esp. after failure.

reave /riːv/ v. (past and past part. **reft** /reft/) archaic **1** tr. **a** (foll. by of) forcibly deprive of. **b** (foll. by away, from) take by force or carry off. **2** intr. make raids; plunder. [OE rēafian f. Gmc: cf. ROB]

reawaken /ˌriːəˈweɪkən/ v.tr. & intr. awaken again.

rebate[1] /ˈriːbeɪt/ n. & v. —n. **1** a partial refund of money paid. **2** a deduction from a sum to be paid; a discount. —v.tr. pay back as a rebate. □ **rebatable** adj. **rebater** n. [earlier = diminish: ME f. OF rabattre (as RE-, ABATE)]

rebate[2] /ˈriːbeɪt/ n. & v.tr. = RABBET. [respelling of RABBET, after REBATE[1]]

rebel n., adj., & v. —n. /ˈreb(ə)l/ **1** a person who fights against, resists, or refuses allegiance to, the established government. **2** a person or thing that resists authority or control. —adj. /ˈreb(ə)l/ (attrib.) **1** rebellious. **2** of or concerning rebels. **3** in rebellion. —v.intr. /rɪˈbel/ (**rebelled, rebelling**; US **rebeled, rebeling**) (usu. foll. by against) **1** act as a rebel; revolt. **2** feel or display repugnance. [ME f. OF rebelle, rebeller f. L rebellis (as RE-, bellum war)]

rebellion /rɪˈbeljən/ n. open resistance to authority, esp. organized armed resistance to an established government. [ME f. OF f. L rebellio -onis (as REBEL)]

rebellious /rɪˈbeljəs/ adj. **1** tending to rebel, insubordinate. **2** in rebellion. **3** defying lawful authority. **4** (of a thing) unmanageable, refractory. □ **rebelliously** adv. **rebelliousness** n. [ME f. REBELLION + -OUS or f. earlier rebellous + -IOUS]

rebind /riːˈbaɪnd/ v.tr. (past and past part. **rebound**) bind (esp. a book) again or differently.

rebirth /riːˈbɜːθ, ˈriː-/ n. **1** a new incarnation. **2** spiritual enlightenment. **3** a revival (the rebirth of learning). □ **reborn** /riːˈbɔːn/ adj.

reboot /riːˈbuːt/ v.tr. (often absol.) Computing boot up (a system) again.

rebore v. & n. —v.tr. /riː'bɔː(r)/ make a new boring in, esp. widen the bore of (the cylinder in an internal-combustion engine). —n. /'riːbɔː(r)/ **1** the process of doing this. **2** a rebored engine.

rebound[1] v. & n. —v.intr. /rɪ'baʊnd/ **1** spring back after action or impact. **2** (foll. by upon) (of an action) have an adverse effect upon (the doer). —n. /'riːbaʊnd/ **1** the act or an instance of rebounding; recoil. **2** a reaction after a strong emotion. □ **on the rebound** while still recovering from an emotional shock, esp. rejection by a lover. □ **rebounder** n. [ME f. OF rebonder, rebondir (as RE-, BOUND[1])]

rebound[2] /riː'baʊnd/ past and past part. of REBIND.

rebuff /rɪ'bʌf/ n. & v. —n. **1** a rejection of one who makes advances, proffers help or sympathy, shows interest or curiosity, makes a request, etc. **2** a repulse; a snub. —v.tr. give a rebuff to. [obs. F rebuffe(r) f. It. ribuffo, ribuffare, rabbuffo, rabbuffare (as RE-, buffo puff)]

rebuild /riː'bɪld/ v.tr. (past and past part. **rebuilt**) build again or differently.

rebuke /rɪ'bjuːk/ v. & n. —v.tr. reprove sharply; subject to protest or censure. —n. **1** the act of rebuking. **2** the process of being rebuked. **3** a reproof. □ **rebuker** n. **rebukingly** adv. [ME f. AF & ONF rebuker (as RE-, OF buchier beat, orig. cut down wood f. busche log)]

rebus /'riːbəs/ n. an enigmatic representation of a word (esp. a name), by pictures etc. suggesting its parts. [F rébus f. L rebus, ablat. pl. of res thing]

rebut /rɪ'bʌt/ v.tr. (**rebutted**, **rebutting**) **1** refute or disprove (evidence or a charge). **2** force or turn back; check. □ **rebutment** n. **rebuttable** adj. **rebuttal** n. [ME f. AF rebuter, OF rebo(u)ter (as RE-, BUTT[1])]

recalcitrant /rɪ'kælsɪtrənt/ adj. & n. —adj. **1** obstinately disobedient. **2** objecting to restraint. —n. a recalcitrant person. □ **recalcitrance** n. **recalcitrantly** adv. [L recalcitrare (as RE-, calcitrare kick out with the heels f. calx calcis heel)]

recall /rɪ'kɔːl/ v. & n. —v.tr. **1** summon to return from a place or from a different occupation, inattention, a digression, etc. **2** recollect, remember. **3** bring back to memory; serve as a reminder of. **4** revoke or annul (an action or decision). —n. /also 'riːkɔl/ **1** the act or an instance of recalling, esp. a summons to come back. **2** the act of remembering. **3** the ability to remember. **4** the possibility of recalling, esp. in the sense of revoking (beyond recall). □ **recallable** adj.

recant /rɪ'kænt/ v. **1** tr. withdraw and renounce (a former belief or statement) as erroneous or heretical. **2** intr. disavow a former opinion, esp. with a public confession of error. □ **recantation** /ˌriːkæn'teɪʃ(ə)n/ n. **recanter** n. [L recantare revoke (as RE-, cantare sing, chant)]

recap /'riːkæp/ v. & n. colloq. —v.tr. & intr. (**recapped**, **recapping**) recapitulate. —n. recapitulation. [abbr.]

recapitulate /ˌriːkə'pɪtjʊˌleɪt/ v.tr. **1** go briefly through again; summarize. **2** go over the main points or headings of. □ **recapitulation** /-'leɪʃ(ə)n/ n. **recapitulative** /-lətɪv/ adj. **recapitulatory** /-lətərɪ/ adj. [L recapitulare (as RE-, capitulum CHAPTER)]

recapture /riː'kæptʃə(r)/ v. & n. —v.tr. **1** capture again; recover by capture. **2** re-experience (a past emotion etc.). —n. the act or an instance of recapturing.

recast /riː'kɑːst/ v. & n. —v.tr. (past and past part. **recast**) **1** put into a new form. **2** improve the arrangement of. **3** change the cast of (a play etc.). —n. **1** the act or an instance of recasting. **2** a recast form.

recce /'rekɪ/ n. & v. colloq. —n. a reconnaisance. —v.tr. & intr. (**recced**, **recceing**) reconnoitre. [abbr.]

recede /rɪ'siːd/ v.intr. **1** go or shrink back or further off. **2** be left at an increasing distance by an observer's motion. **3** slope backwards (a receding chin). **4** decline in force or value. **5** (of a man's hair) cease to grow at the front, sides, etc. [ME f. L recedere (as RE-, cedere cess- go)]

receipt /rɪ'siːt/ n. & v. —n. **1** the act or an instance of receiving or being received into one's possession (will pay on receipt of the goods). **2** a written acknowledgement of this, esp. of the payment of money. **3** (usu. in pl.) an amount of money etc. received. **4** archaic a recipe. —v.tr. place a written or printed receipt on (a bill). [ME receit(e) f. AF & ONF receite, OF reçoite, recete f. med.L recepta fem. past part. of L recipere RECEIVE: -p- inserted after L]

receive /rɪ'siːv/ v.tr. **1** take or accept (something offered or given) into one's hands or possession. **2** acquire; be provided with or given (have received no news; will receive a small fee). **3** accept delivery of (something sent). **4** have conferred or inflicted on one (received many honours; received a heavy blow on the head). **5 a** stand the force or weight of. **b** bear up against; encounter with opposition. **6** consent to hear (a confession or oath) or consider (a petition). **7** (also absol.) accept or have dealings with (stolen property knowing of the theft). **8** admit; consent or prove able to hold; provide accommodation for (received many visitors). **9** (of a receptacle) be able to hold (a specified amount or contents). **10** greet or welcome, esp. in a specified manner (how did they receive your offer?). **11** entertain as a guest etc. **12** admit to membership of a society, organization, etc. **13** be marked more or less permanently with (an impression etc.). **14** convert (broadcast signals) into sound or pictures. **15** Tennis be the player to whom the server serves (the ball). **16** (often as **received** adj.) give credit to; accept as authoritative or true (received opinion). □ **be at** (or **on**) **the receiving end** colloq. bear the brunt of something unpleasant. **received pronunciation** (or **Received Standard**) the form of spoken English based on educated speech in southern England. **receiving-order** Brit. an order of a court authorizing a receiver (see RECEIVER 3) to act. □ **receivable** adj. [ME f. OF receivre, reçoivre f. L recipere recept- (as RE-, capere take)]

receiver /rɪ'siːvə(r)/ n. **1** a person or thing that receives. **2** the part of a machine or instrument that receives sound, signals, etc. (esp. the part of a telephone that contains the earpiece). **3** (in full **official receiver**) a person appointed by a court to administer the property of a bankrupt or insane person, or property under litigation. **4** a radio or television receiving apparatus. **5** a person who receives stolen goods.

receivership /rɪ'siːvəʃɪp/ n. **1** the office of official receiver. **2** the state of being dealt with by a receiver (esp. in receivership).

recent /ˈriːs(ə)nt/ adj. & n. —adj. **1** not long past; that happened, appeared, began to exist, or existed lately. **2** not long established; lately begun; modern. **3** (**Recent**) Geol. = HOLOCENE. —n. Geol. = HOLOCENE. □ **recency** n. **recently** adv. **recentness** n. [L recens recentis or F récent]

receptacle /rɪˈsɛptək(ə)l/ n. **1** a containing vessel, place, or space. **2** Bot. the common base of floral organs. [ME f. OF receptacle or L receptaculum (as RECEPTION)]

reception /rɪˈsɛpʃ(ə)n/ n. **1** the act or an instance of receiving or the process of being received, esp. of a person into a place or group. **2** the manner in which a person or thing is received (got a cool reception). **3** a social occasion for receiving guests, esp. after a wedding. **4** a formal or ceremonious welcome. **5** a place where guests or clients etc. report on arrival at a hotel, office, etc. **6 a** the receiving of broadcast signals. **b** the quality of this (we have excellent reception). □ **reception room** a room available or suitable for receiving company or visitors. [ME f. OF reception or L receptio (as RECEIVE)]

receptionist /rɪˈsɛpʃənɪst/ n. a person employed in a hotel, office, etc., to receive guests, clients, etc.

receptive /rɪˈsɛptɪv/ adj. **1** able or quick to receive impressions or ideas. **2** concerned with receiving stimuli etc. □ **receptively** adv. **receptiveness** n. **receptivity** /ˌriːsɛpˈtɪvɪtɪ/ n. [F réceptif -ive or med.L receptivus (as RECEPTION)]

receptor /rɪˈsɛptə(r)/ n. (often attrib.) Biol. an organ able to respond to an external stimulus such as light, heat, or a drug, and transmit a signal to a sensory nerve. [OF receptour or L receptor (as RECEPTIVE)]

recess /rɪˈsɛs, ˈriːsɛs/ n. & v. —n. **1** a space set back in a wall; a niche. **2** (often in pl.) a remote or secret place (the innermost recesses). **3** a temporary cessation from work, esp. of Parliament, or US of a lawcourt or during a school day. —v. **1** tr. make a recess in. **2** tr. place in a recess; set back. **3** US **a** intr. take a recess; adjourn. **b** tr. order a temporary cessation from the work of (a court etc.). [L recessus (as RECEDE)]

recession /rɪˈsɛʃ(ə)n/ n. **1** a temporary decline in economic activity or prosperity. **2** a receding or withdrawal from a place or point. □ **recessionary** adj. [L recessio (as RECESS)]

recessional /rɪˈsɛʃən(ə)l/ adj. sung while the clergy and choir withdraw after a service.

recessive /rɪˈsɛsɪv/ adj. **1** tending to recede. **2** Genetics (of an inherited characteristic) appearing in offspring only when not masked by a dominant characteristic inherited from one parent. □ **recessively** adv. **recessiveness** n. [RECESS after excessive]

recharge v.tr. /riːˈtʃɑːdʒ/ **1** charge again. **2** reload. □ **rechargeable** /riːˈtʃɑːdʒəb(ə)l/ adj.

recheck v. & n. —v.tr. & intr. /riːˈtʃɛk/ check again. —n. /ˈriːtʃɛk/ a second or further check or inspection.

recherché /rəˈʃɛəʃeɪ/ adj. **1** carefully sought out; rare or exotic. **2** far-fetched, obscure. [F, past part. of rechercher (as RE-, chercher seek)]

rechristen /riːˈkrɪs(ə)n/ v.tr. **1** christen again. **2** give a new name to.

recidivist /rɪˈsɪdɪvɪst/ n. a person who relapses into crime. □ **recidivism** n. **recidivistic** /-ˈvɪstɪk/ adj. [F récidiviste f. récidiver f. med.L recidivare f. L recidivus f. recidere (as RE-, cadere fall)]

recipe /ˈrɛsɪpɪ/ n. **1** a statement of the ingredients and procedure required for preparing cooked food. **2** an expedient; a device for achieving something. **3** a medical prescription. [2nd sing. imper. (as used in prescriptions) of L recipere take, RECEIVE]

recipient /rɪˈsɪpɪənt/ n. & adj. —n. a person who receives something. —adj. **1** receiving. **2** receptive. □ **recipiency** n. [F récipient f. It. recipiente or L recipiens f. recipere RECEIVE]

reciprocal /rɪˈsɪprək(ə)l/ adj. & n. —adj. **1** in return (offered a reciprocal greeting). **2** mutual (their feelings are reciprocal). **3** Gram. (of a pronoun) expressing mutual action or relation (as in each other). —n. Math. an expression or function so related to another that their product is unity ($\frac{1}{3}$ is the reciprocal of 2). □ **reciprocality** /-ˈkælɪtɪ/ n. **reciprocally** adv. [L reciprocus ult. f. re- back + pro forward]

reciprocate /rɪˈsɪprəˌkeɪt/ v. **1** tr. return or requite (affection etc.). **2** intr. (foll. by with) offer or give something in return (reciprocated with an invitation to lunch). **3** tr. give and receive mutually; interchange. **4 a** intr. (of a part of a machine) move backwards and forwards. **b** tr. cause to do this. □ **reciprocation** /-ˈkeɪʃ(ə)n/ n. **reciprocator** n. [L reciprocare reciprocat- (as RECIPROCAL)]

reciprocity /ˌrɛsɪˈprɒsɪtɪ/ n. **1** the condition of being reciprocal. **2** mutual action. **3** give and take, esp. the interchange of privileges. [F réciprocité f. réciproque f. L reciprocus (as RECIPROCAL)]

recital /rɪˈsaɪt(ə)l/ n. **1** the act or an instance of reciting or being recited. **2** the performance of a programme of music by a solo instrumentalist or singer or by a small group. **3** (foll. by of) a detailed account of (connected things or facts); a narrative. □ **recitalist** n.

recitation /ˌrɛsɪˈteɪʃ(ə)n/ n. **1** the act or an instance of reciting. **2** a thing recited. [OF recitation or L recitatio (as RECITE)]

recitative /ˌrɛsɪtəˈtiːv/ n. **1** musical declamation of the kind usual in the narrative and dialogue parts of opera and oratorio. **2** the words or part given in this form. [It. recitativo (as RECITE)]

recite /rɪˈsaɪt/ v. **1** tr. repeat aloud or declaim (a poem or passage) from memory, esp. before an audience. **2** intr. give a recitation. **3** tr. mention in order; enumerate. □ **reciter** n. [ME f. OF reciter or L recitare (as RE-, CITE)]

reck v. archaic or poet. (only in neg. or interrog.) **1** tr. (foll. by of) pay heed to; take account of; care about. **2** tr. pay heed to. [OE reccan, rel. to OHG ruohhen]

reckless /ˈrɛklɪs/ adj. disregarding the consequences or danger etc.; lacking caution; rash. □ **recklessly** adv. **recklessness** n. [OE recceléas (as RECK)]

reckon /ˈrɛkən/ v. **1** tr. count or compute by calculation. **2** tr. (foll. by in) count in or include in computation. **3** tr. (often foll. by as or to be) consider or regard (reckon him wise; reckon them to be beyond hope). **4** tr. **a** (foll. by that + clause) conclude after calculation; be of the considered opinion. **b** colloq. (foll. by to + infin.) expect (reckons to finish by Friday). **5** intr. make calculations; add up an account or sum. **6** intr. (foll. by on, upon) rely on, count on, or base plans on. **7** *intr.* (foll. by *with*) **a** take into account. **b** settle accounts with. □ **reckon up 1** count up; find the total of. **2** settle accounts. **to be reckoned with** of considerable importance; not to be ignored. [OE *(ge)recenian* f. WG]

reckoner /ˈrekənə(r)/ *n.* = *ready reckoner*.

reckoning /ˈrekənɪŋ/ *n.* **1** the act or an instance of counting or calculating. **2** a consideration or opinion. **3 a** the settlement of an account. **b** account. □ **day of reckoning** the time when something must be atoned for or avenged.

reclaim /rɪˈkleɪm/ *v.* & *n.* —*v.tr.* **1** seek the return of (one's property). **2** claim in return or as a rebate etc. **3** bring under cultivation, esp. from a state of being under water. **4** win back or away from vice or error or a waste condition; reform. —*n.* the act or an instance of reclaiming; the process of being reclaimed. □ **reclaimable** *adj.* **reclamation** /ˌrekləˈmeɪʃ(ə)n/ *n.* [ME f. OF *reclamer reclaim-* f. L *reclamare* cry out against (as RE-, *clamare* shout)]

reclassify /riːˈklæsɪˌfaɪ/ *v.tr.* (**-ies**, **-ied**) classify again or differently. □ **reclassification** /-fɪˈkeɪʃ(ə)n/ *n.*

recline /rɪˈklaɪn/ *v.* **1** *intr.* assume or be in a horizontal or leaning position, esp. in resting. **2** *tr.* cause to recline or move from the vertical. □ **reclinable** *adj.* [ME f. OF *recliner* or L *reclinare* bend back, recline (as RE-, *clinare* bend)]

recliner /rɪˈklaɪnə(r)/ *n.* **1** a comfortable chair for reclining in. **2** a person who reclines.

reclothe /riːˈkləʊð/ *v.tr.* clothe again or differently.

recluse /rɪˈkluːs/ *n.* & *adj.* —*n.* a person given to or living in seclusion or isolation, esp. as a religious discipline; a hermit. —*adj.* favouring seclusion; solitary. □ **reclusion** /rɪˈkluːʒ(ə)n/ *n.* **reclusive** *adj.* [ME f. OF *reclus recluse* past part. of *reclure* f. L *recludere reclus-* (as RE-, *claudere* shut)]

recognition /ˌrekəgˈnɪʃ(ə)n/ *n.* the act or an instance of recognizing or being recognized. □ **recognitory** /rɪˈkɒgnɪtəri/ *adj.* [L *recognitio* (as RECOGNIZE)]

recognizance /rɪˈkɒgnɪz(ə)ns/ *n.* **1** a bond by which a person undertakes before a court or magistrate to observe some condition, e.g. to appear when summoned. **2** a sum pledged as surety for this. [ME f. OF *recon(n)issance* (as RE-, COGNIZANCE)]

recognizant /rɪˈkɒgnɪz(ə)nt/ *adj.* (usu. foll. by *of*) **1** showing recognition (of a favour etc.). **2** conscious or showing consciousness (of something).

recognize /ˈrekəgˌnaɪz/ *v.tr.* (also **-ise**) **1** identify (a person or thing) as already known; know again. **2** realize or discover the nature of. **3** (foll. by *that*) realize or admit. **4** acknowledge the existence, validity, character, or claims of. **5** show appreciation of; reward. **6** (foll. by *as*, *for*) treat or acknowledge. □ **recognizable** *n.* **recognizability** /-əˈbɪlɪtɪ/ *n.* **recognizably** *adv.* **recognizer** *n.* [OF *recon(n)iss-* stem of *reconnaistre* f. L *recognoscere recognit-* (as RE-, *cognoscere* learn)]

recoil /rɪˈkɔɪl/ *v.* & *n.* —*v.intr.* **1** suddenly move or spring back in fear, horror, or disgust. **2** shrink mentally in this way. **3** rebound after an impact. **4** (foll. by *on*, *upon*) have an adverse reactive effect on (the originator). **5** (of a gun) be driven backwards by its discharge. **6** retreat under an enemy's attack. —*n.* /also ˈriːkɔɪl/ **1** the act or an instance of recoiling. **2** the sensation of recoiling. [ME f. OF *reculer* (as RE-, L *culus* buttocks)]

recollect /ˌrekəˈlekt/ *v.tr.* **1** remember. **2** succeed in remembering; call to mind. [L *recolligere recollect-* (as RE-, COLLECT[1])]

recollection /ˌrekəˈlekʃ(ə)n/ *n.* **1** the act or power of recollecting. **2** a thing recollected. **3 a** a person's memory (*to the best of my recollection*). **b** the time over which memory extends (*happened within my recollection*). □ **recollective** *adj.* [F *recollection* or med.L *recollectio* (as RECOLLECT)]

recombine /ˌriːkəmˈbaɪn/ *v.tr.* & *intr.* combine again or differently. □ **recombination** /-kɒmbɪˈneɪʃ(ə)n/ *n.*

recommence /ˌriːkəˈmens/ *v.tr.* & *intr.* begin again. □ **recommencement** *n.*

recommend /ˌrekəˈmend/ *v.tr.* **1** suggest as fit for some purpose or use. **2** (often foll. by *that* + clause or *to* + infin.) advise as a course of action etc. (*I recommend that you stay where you are*). **3** (of qualities, conduct, etc.) make acceptable or desirable. **4** (foll. by *to*) commend or entrust (to a person or a person's care). □ **recommendable** *adj.* **recommendation** /-ˈdeɪʃ(ə)n/ *n.* **recommendatory** /-dətəri/ *adj.* **recommender** *n.* [ME (in sense 4) f. med.L *recommendare* (as RE-, COMMEND)]

recompense /ˈrekəmˌpens/ *v.* & *n.* —*v.tr.* **1** make amends to (a person) or for (a loss etc.). **2** requite; reward or punish (a person or action). —*n.* **1** a reward; requital. **2** retribution; satisfaction given for an injury. [ME f. OF *recompense(r)* f. LL *recompensare* (as RE-, COMPENSATE)]

reconcile /ˈrekənˌsaɪl/ *v.tr.* **1** make friendly again after an estrangement. **2** (usu. in *refl.* or *passive*; foll. by *to*) make acquiescent or contentedly submissive to (something disagreeable or unwelcome) (*was reconciled to failure*). **3** settle (a quarrel etc.). **4** harmonize; make compatible. □ **reconcilable** *adj.* **reconcilability** /-əˈbɪlɪtɪ/ *n.* **reconcilement** *n.* **reconciler** *n.* **reconciliation** /-ˌsɪlɪˈeɪʃ(ə)n/ *n.* **reconciliatory** /-kənˈsɪlɪətəri/ *adj.* [ME f. OF *reconcilier* or L *reconciliare* (as RE-, *conciliare* CONCILIATE)]

recondite /ˈrekənˌdaɪt, rɪˈkɒn-/ *adj.* **1** (of a subject or knowledge) abstruse; out of the way; little known. **2** (of an author or style) dealing in abstruse knowledge or allusions; obscure. □ **reconditely** *adv.* **reconditeness** *n.* [L *reconditus* (as RE-, *conditus* past part. of *condere* hide)]

recondition /ˌriːkənˈdɪʃ(ə)n/ *v.tr.* **1** overhaul, refit, renovate. **2** make usable again. □ **reconditioner** *n.*

reconfigure /ˌriːkənˈfɪgə(r)/ *v.tr.* configure again or differently. □ **reconfiguration** /-gəˈreɪʃ(ə)n/ *n.*

reconnaissance /rɪˈkɒnɪs(ə)ns/ *n.* **1** a survey of a region, esp. a military examination to locate an enemy or ascertain strategic features. **2** a preliminary survey or inspection. [F (earlier *-oissance*) f. stem of *reconnaître* (as RECONNOITRE)]

reconnect /ˌriːkəˈnekt/ *v.tr.* connect again. □ **reconnection** *n.*

reconnoitre /ˌrekəˈnɔɪtə(r)/ *v.* & *n.* (US **reconnoiter**) —*v.* **1** *tr.* make a reconnaissance of (an area, enemy position, etc.). **2** *intr.* make a reconnaissance. —*n.* a reconnaissance. [obs. F *reconnoître* f. L *recognoscere* RECOGNIZE]

reconquer /riːˈkɒŋkə(r)/ *v.tr.* conquer again. □ **reconquest** *n.*

reconsider /ˌriːkənˈsɪdə(r)/ v.tr. & intr. consider again, esp. for a possible change of decision. □ **reconsideration** /-ˈreɪʃ(ə)n/ n.

reconstitute /riːˈkɒnstɪˌtjuːt/ v. & tr. 1 build up again from parts; reconstruct. 2 reorganize. 3 restore the previous constitution of (dried food etc.) by adding water. □ **reconstitution** /-ˈtjuːʃ(ə)n/ n.

reconstruct /ˌriːkənˈstrʌkt/ v.tr. 1 build or form again. 2 a form a mental or visual impression of (past events) by assembling the evidence for them. b re-enact (a crime). 3 reorganize. □ **reconstructable** adj. (also **reconstructible**). **reconstruction** n. **reconstructive** adj. **reconstructor** n.

reconvene /ˌriːkənˈviːn/ v.tr. & intr. convene again, esp. (of a meeting etc.) after a pause in proceedings.

reconvert /ˌriːkənˈvɜːt/ v.tr. convert back to a former state. □ **reconversion** n.

record n. & v. —n. /ˈrekɔːd/ 1 a a piece of evidence or information constituting an (esp. official) account of something that has occurred, been said, etc. b a document preserving this. 2 the state of being set down or preserved in writing or some other permanent form (is a matter of record). 3 (in full **gramophone record**) a thin plastic disc carrying recorded sound in grooves on each surface, for reproduction by a record-player. 4 an official report of the proceedings and judgement in a court of justice. 5 a the facts known about a person's past (has an honourable record of service). b a list of a person's previous criminal convictions. 6 the best performance (esp. in sport) or most remarkable event of its kind on record (often attrib.: a record attempt). 7 an object serving as a memorial of a person or thing; a portrait. 8 Computing a number of related items of information which are handled as a unit. —v.tr. /rɪˈkɔːd/ 1 set down in writing or some other permanent form for later reference, esp. as an official record. 2 convert (sound, a broadcast, etc.) into permanent form for later reproduction. 3 establish or constitute a historical or other record of. □ **break** (or **beat**) **the record** outdo all previous performances etc. **for the record** as an official statement etc. **go on record** state one's opinion or judgement openly or officially, so that it is recorded. **have a record** be known as a criminal. **a matter of record** a thing established as a fact by being recorded. **off the record** as an unofficial or confidential statement etc. **on record** officially recorded; publicly known. **recorded delivery** a Post Office service in which the dispatch and receipt of a letter or parcel are reproduced. **record-player** an apparatus for reproducing sound from gramophone records. □ **recordable** adj. [ME f. OF record remembrance, recorder record, f. L recordari remember (as RE-, cor cordis heart)]

recorder /rɪˈkɔːdə(r)/ n. 1 an apparatus for recording, esp. a tape recorder. 2 a a keeper of records. b a person who makes an official record. 3 Brit. a barrister or solicitor of at least ten years' standing, appointed to serve as a part-time judge. 4 Mus. a woodwind instrument like a flute but blown through the end and having a more hollow tone. □ **recordership** n. (in sense 3). [ME f. AF recordour, OF recordeur f. RECORD (in obs. sense 'practise a tune')]

recording /rɪˈkɔːdɪŋ/ n. 1 the process by which audio or video signals are recorded for later reproduction. 2 material or a programme recorded.

recordist /rɪˈkɔːdɪst/ n. a person who records sound.

recount /rɪˈkaʊnt/ v.tr. 1 narrate. 2 tell in detail. [ONF & AF reconter (as RE-, COUNT¹)]

re-count v. & n. —v. /riːˈkaʊnt/ tr. count again. —n. /ˈriːkaʊnt/ a re-counting, esp. of votes in an election.

recoup /rɪˈkuːp/ v.tr. 1 recover or regain (a loss). 2 compensate or reimburse for a loss. 3 Law deduct or keep back (part of a sum due). □ **recoup oneself** recover a loss. □ **recoupable** adj. **recoupment** n. [F recouper (as RE-, couper cut)]

recourse /rɪˈkɔːs/ n. 1 resorting to a possible source of help. 2 a person or thing resorted to. □ **have recourse to** turn to (a person or thing) for help. [ME f. OF recours f. L recursus (as RE-, COURSE)]

recover /rɪˈkʌvə(r)/ v. 1 tr. regain possession or use or control of, reclaim. 2 intr. return to health or consciousness or to a normal state or position (have recovered from my illness; the country never recovered from the war). 3 tr. obtain or secure (compensation etc.) by legal process. 4 tr. retrieve or make up for (a loss, setback, etc.). 5 refl. regain composure or consciousness or control of one's limbs. 6 tr. retrieve (reusable substances) from industrial waste. □ **recoverable** adj. **recoverability** /-ˈbɪlɪtɪ/ n. **recoverer** n. [ME f. AF recoverer, OF recovrer f. L recuperare RECUPERATE]

re-cover /riːˈkʌvə(r)/ v.tr. 1 cover again. 2 provide (a chair etc.) with a new cover.

recovery /rɪˈkʌvərɪ/ n. (pl. **-ies**) the act or an instance of recovering; the process of being recovered. [ME f. AF recoverie, OF reco(u)vree (as RECOVER)]

re-create /ˌriːkrɪˈeɪt/ v.tr. create over again. □ **re-creation** n.

recreation /ˌrekrɪˈeɪʃ(ə)n/ n. 1 the process or means of refreshing or entertaining oneself. 2 a pleasurable activity. □ **recreation-ground** public land for games etc. □ **recreational** adj. **recreationally** adv. **recreative** /ˈrekrɪˌeɪtɪv/ adj. [ME f. OF f. L recreatio -onis f. recreare create again, renew]

recriminate /rɪˈkrɪmɪˌneɪt/ v.intr. make mutual or counter accusations. □ **recrimination** /-ˈneɪʃ(ə)n/ n. **recriminative** /-nətɪv/ adj. **recriminatory** /-nətərɪ/ adj. [med.L recriminare (as RE-, criminare accuse f. crimen CRIME)]

recross /riːˈkrɒs/ v.tr. & intr. cross or pass over again.

recrudesce /ˌriːkruːˈdes, ˌrek-/ v.intr. (of a disease or difficulty etc.) break out again, esp. after a dormant period. □ **recrudescence** n. **recrudescent** adj. [back-form. f. recrudescent, -ence f. L recrudescere (as RE-, crudus raw)]

recruit /rɪˈkruːt/ n. & v. —n. 1 a serviceman or servicewoman newly enlisted and not yet fully trained. 2 a new member of a society or organization. 3 a beginner. —v. 1 tr. enlist (a person) as a recruit. 2 tr. form (an army etc.) by enlisting recruits. 3 intr. get or seek recruits. 4 tr. replenish or reinvigorate (numbers, strength, etc.). □ **recruitable** adj. **recruiter** n. **recruitment** n. [earlier = reinforcement, f. obs. F dial.

recrute ult. f. F *recroître* increase again f. L *recrescere*]

recta *pl.* of RECTUM.

rectal /ˈrekt(ə)l/ *adj.* of or by means of the rectum. □ **rectally** *adv.*

rectangle /ˈrekˌtæŋg(ə)l/ *n.* a plane figure with four straight sides and four right angles, esp. one with the adjacent sides unequal. [F *rectangle* or med.L *rectangulum* f. LL *rectiangulum* f. L *rectus* straight + *angulus* ANGLE¹]

rectangular /rekˈtæŋgʊlə(r)/ *adj.* **1 a** shaped like a rectangle. **b** having the base or sides or section shaped like a rectangle. **2 a** placed at right angles. **b** having parts or lines placed at right angles. □ **rectangularity** /-ˈlærɪtɪ/ *n.* **rectangularly** *adv.*

rectify /ˈrektɪˌfaɪ/ *v.tr.* (**-ies, -ied**) **1** adjust or make right; correct, amend. **2** purify or refine, esp. by repeated distillation. **3** convert (alternating current) to direct current. □ **rectifiable** *adj.* **rectification** /-fɪˈkeɪʃ(ə)n/ *n.* **rectifier** *n.* [ME f. OF *rectifier* f. med.L *rectificare* f. L *rectus* right]

rectilinear /ˌrektɪˈlɪnɪə(r)/ *adj.* (also **rectilineal** /-nɪəl/) **1** bounded or characterized by straight lines. **2** in or forming a straight line. □ **rectilinearity** /-ˈærɪtɪ/ *n.* **rectilinearly** *adv.* [LL *rectilineus* f. L *rectus* straight + *linea* LINE¹]

rectitude /ˈrektɪˌtjuːd/ *n.* **1** moral uprightness. **2** righteousness. **3** correctness. [ME f. OF *rectitude* or LL *rectitudo* f. L *rectus* right]

recto /ˈrektəʊ/ *n.* (*pl.* **-os**) **1** the right-hand page of an open book. **2** the front of a printed leaf of paper or manuscript. [L *recto (folio)* on the right (leaf)]

rector /ˈrektə(r)/ *n.* **1** (in the Church of England) the incumbent of a parish where all tithes formerly passed to the incumbent. **2** *RC Ch.* a priest in charge of a church or religious institution. **3 a** the head of some schools, universities, and colleges. **b** (in Scotland) an elected representative of students on a university's governing body. □ **rectorate** /-rət/ *n.* **rectorial** /-ˈtɔːrɪəl/ *adj.* **rectorship** *n.* [ME f. OF *rectour* or L *rector* ruler f. *regere rect-* rule]

rectory /ˈrektərɪ/ *n.* (*pl.* **-ies**) **1** a rector's house. **2** (in the Church of England) a rector's benefice. [AF & OF *rectorie* or med.L *rectoria* (as RECTOR)]

rectum /ˈrektəm/ *n.* (*pl.* **rectums** or **recta** /-tə/) the final section of the large intestine, terminating at the anus. [L *rectum (intestinum)* straight (intestine)]

recumbent /rɪˈkʌmbənt/ *adj.* lying down; reclining. □ **recumbency** *n.* **recumbently** *adv.* [L *recumbere* recline (as RE-, *cumbere* lie)]

recuperate /rɪˈkuːpəˌreɪt/ *v.* **1** *intr.* recover from illness, exhaustion, loss, etc. **2** *tr.* regain (health, something lost, etc.). □ **recuperable** *adj.* **recuperation** /-ˈreɪʃ(ə)n/ *n.* **recuperative** /-rətɪv/ *adj.* **recuperator** *n.* [L *recuperare recuperat-* recover]

recur /rɪˈkɜː(r)/ *v.intr.* (**recurred, recurring**) **1** occur again; be repeated. **2** (of a thought, idea, etc.) come back to one's mind. **3** (foll. by *to*) go back in thought or speech. □ **recurring decimal** a decimal fraction in which the same figures are repeated indefinitely. [L *recurrere recurs-* (as RE-, *currere* run)]

recurrent /rɪˈkʌrənt/ *adj.* recurring; happening repeatedly. □ **recurrence** *n.* **recurrently** *adv.*

recusant /ˈrekjʊz(ə)nt/ *n.* a person who refuses submission to an authority or compliance with a regulation, esp. *hist.* one who refused to attend services of the Church of England. □ **recusance** *n.* **recusancy** *n.* [L *recusare* refuse]

recycle /riːˈsaɪk(ə)l/ *v.tr.* return (material) to a previous stage of a cyclic process, esp. convert (waste) to reusable material. □ **recyclable** *adj.*

red *adj.* & *n.* —*adj.* **1** of or near the colour seen at the least-refracted end of the visible spectrum, of shades ranging from that of blood to pink or deep orange. **2** flushed in the face with shame, anger, etc. **3** (of the eyes) bloodshot or red-rimmed with weeping. **4** (of the hair) reddish-brown, orange, tawny. **5** involving or having to do with bloodshed, burning, violence, or revolution. **6** *colloq.* communist or socialist. **7** *hist.* (**Red**) Russian, Soviet (*the Red Army*). **8** (of wine) made from dark grapes and coloured by their skins. —*n.* **1** a red colour or pigment. **2** red clothes or material (*dressed in red*). **3** *colloq.* a communist or socialist. **4 a** a red ball, piece, etc., in a game or sport. **b** the player using such pieces. **5** the debit side of an account (*in the red*). **6** a red light. □ **red admiral** a butterfly, *Vanessa atalanta*, with red bands on each pair of wings. **red-blooded** virile, vigorous. **red card** *Football* a card shown by the referee to a player being sent off the field. **red carpet** privileged treatment of an eminent visitor. **red cell** (or **corpuscle**) an erythrocyte. **red cent** *US* the smallest (*orig.* copper) coin; a trivial sum. **Red Crescent** an organization like the Red Cross in Muslim countries. **Red Cross 1** an international organization (originally medical) bringing relief to victims of war or natural disaster. **2** the emblem of this organization. **red dwarf** an old relatively cool star. **red-faced** embarrassed, ashamed. **red flag 1** the symbol of socialist revolution. **2** a warning of danger. **red giant** a relatively cool giant star. **red-handed** in or just after the act of committing a crime, doing wrong, etc. **red hat 1** a cardinal's hat. **2** the symbol of a cardinal's office. **red-headed** (of a person) having red hair. **red heat 1** the temperature or state of something so hot as to emit red light. **2** great excitement. **red herring 1** dried smoked herring. **2** a misleading clue or distraction. **red-hot 1** heated until red. **2** highly exciting. **3** (of news) fresh; completely new. **4** intensely excited. **5** enraged. **red-hot poker** any plant of the genus *Kniphofia*, with spikes of usually red or yellow flowers. **Red Indian** *offens.* an American Indian. **red lead** a red form of lead oxide used as a pigment. **red-letter day** a day that is pleasantly noteworthy or memorable (*orig.* a festival marked in red on the calendar). **red light 1** a signal to stop on a road, railway, etc. **2** a warning or refusal. **red-light district** a district containing many brothels. **red meat** meat that is red when raw (e.g. beef or lamb). **red pepper 1** cayenne pepper. **2** the ripe fruit of the capsicum plant, *Capsicum annuum*. **red rag** something that excites a person's rage (so called because red is supposed to provoke bulls). **red rose** the emblem of Lancashire or the Lancastrians. **red shift** the displacement of the spectrum to longer wavelengths in the light coming from distant galaxies etc. in recession. **red squirrel** a native British squirrel, *Sciurus vulgaris*, with reddish fur. **red tape** excessive bureaucracy or adherence to formalities esp. in

public business. □ **reddish** adj. **reddy** adj. **redly**
adv. **redness** n. [OE *rēad* f. Gmc]

redbreast /'redbrest/ n. colloq. a robin.

redbrick /'redbrɪk/ adj. esp. Brit. (of a university)
founded relatively recently.

redcap /'redkæp/ n. **1** Brit. a member of the
military police. **2** US a railway porter.

redcoat /'redkəʊt/ n. hist. a British soldier (so
called from the scarlet uniform of most
regiments).

redcurrant /'red,kʌrənt/ n. **1** a widely cultivated
shrub, *Ribes rubrum*. **2** a small red edible berry
of this plant.

redden /'red(ə)n/ v.tr. & intr. make or become
red.

reddle /'red(ə)l/ n. red ochre; ruddle. [var. of
RUDDLE]

redecorate /riː'dekə,reɪt/ v.tr. decorate again or
differently. □ **redecoration** /-'reɪʃ(ə)n/ n.

redeem /rɪ'diːm/ v.tr. **1** buy back; recover by
expenditure of effort or by a stipulated payment.
2 make a single payment to discharge (a regular
charge or obligation). **3** convert (tokens or bonds
etc.) into goods or cash. **4** (of God or Christ)
deliver from sin and damnation. **5** make up for;
be a compensating factor in (*has one redeeming
feature*). **6** (foll. by *from*) save from (a defect). **7**
refl. save (oneself) from blame. **8** purchase the
freedom of (a person). **9** save (a person's life) by
ransom. **10** save or rescue or reclaim. **11** fulfil (a
promise). □ **redeemable** adj. [ME f. OF *redimer*
or L *redimere* redempt- (as RE-, *emere* buy)]

redeemer /rɪ'diːmə(r)/ n. a person who redeems.
□ **the Redeemer** Christ.

redefine /,riːdɪ'faɪn/ v.tr. define again or differently. □ **redefinition** /-defɪ'nɪʃ(ə)n/ n.

redemption /rɪ'dempʃ(ə)n/ n. **1** the act or an
instance of redeeming; the process of being
redeemed. **2** man's deliverance from sin and
damnation. **3** a thing that redeems. □ **redempt-
ive** adj. [ME f. OF f. L *redemptio* (as REDEEM)]

redeploy /,riːdɪ'plɔɪ/ v.tr. send (troops, workers,
etc.) to a new place or task. □ **redeployment** n.

redesign /,riːdɪ'zaɪn/ v.tr. design again or
differently.

redevelop /,riːdɪ'veləp/ v.tr. develop anew (esp.
an urban area, with new buildings). □ **re-
developer** n. **redevelopment** n.

redhead /'redhed/ n. a person with red hair.

redial /riː'daɪəl/ v.tr. & intr. (**redialled, redi-
alling**; US **redialed, redialing**) dial again.

redid past of REDO.

rediffusion /,riːdɪ'fjuːʒ(ə)n/ n. the relaying of
broadcast programmes esp. by cable from a
central receiver.

redirect /,riːdaɪ'rekt, -dɪ'rekt/ v.tr. direct again,
esp. change the address of (a letter). □ **redir-
ection** n.

rediscover /,riːdɪ'skʌvə(r)/ v.tr. discover again. □
rediscovery n. (pl. **-ies**)

redistribute /,riːdɪ'strɪbjuːt, disp. riː'dɪs-/ v.tr.
distribute again or differently. □ **redis-
tribution** /-'bjuːʃ(ə)n/ n. **redistributive**
/-'trɪbjʊtɪv/ adj.

■ **Usage** The second pronunciation given, with
the stress on the second syllable, is considered
incorrect by some people.

---

redivide /,riːdɪ'vaɪd/ v.tr. divide again or differently. □ **redivision** /-'vɪʒ(ə)n/ n.

redneck /'rednek/ n. US often derog. a working-
class White in the southern US, esp. a politically
conservative one.

redo /riː'duː/ v.tr. (3rd sing. present **redoes**; past
redid; past part. **redone**) **1** do again or differently. **2** redecorate.

redolent /'redələnt/ adj. **1** (foll. by of, with)
strongly reminiscent or suggestive or mentally
associated. **2** fragrant. **3** having a strong smell;
odorous. □ **redolence** n. **redolently** adv. [ME f.
OF *redolent* or L *redolēre* (as RE-, *olēre* smell)]

redouble /riː'dʌb(ə)l/ v., tr. & intr. make or grow
greater or more intense or numerous; intensify,
increase. [F *redoubler* (as RE-, DOUBLE)]

redoubt /rɪ'daʊt/ n. Mil. an outwork or fieldwork
usu. square or polygonal and without flanking
defences. [F *redoute* f. obs. It. *ridotta* f. med.L
reductus refuge f. past part. of L *reducere* withdraw
(see REDUCE): -b- after DOUBT (cf. REDOUBTABLE)]

redoubtable /rɪ'daʊtəb(ə)l/ adj. formidable, esp.
as an opponent. □ **redoubtably** adv. [ME f. OF
redoutable f. *redouter* fear (as RE-, DOUBT)]

redound /rɪ'daʊnd/ v.intr. **1** (foll. by to) (of an
action etc.) make a great contribution to (one's
credit or advantage etc.). **2** (foll. by upon, on)
come as the final result to; come back or recoil
upon. [ME, orig. = overflow, f. OF *redonder* f. L
redundare surge (as RE-, *unda* wave)]

redraft /riː'drɑːft/ v.tr. draft (a writing or document) again.

redraw /riː'drɔː/ v.tr. (past **redrew**; past part.
redrawn) draw again or differently.

redress /rɪ'dres/ v. & n. —v.tr. **1** remedy or
rectify (a wrong or grievance etc.). **2** readjust;
set straight again. —n. **1** reparation for a wrong.
2 (foll. by of) the act or process of redressing (a
grievance etc.). □ **redress the balance** restore
equality. □ **redressable** adj. **redressal** n.
redresser n. (also **redressor**). [ME f. OF
redresse(r), *redrecier* (as RE-, DRESS)]

redshank /'redʃæŋk/ n. either of two sandpipers,
Tringa totanus and *T. erythropus*, with bright-red
legs.

redskin /'redskɪn/ n. colloq. offens. an American
Indian.

redstart /'redstɑːt/ n. **1** any European red-tailed
songbird of the genus *Phoenicurus*. **2** any of
various similar American warblers of the family
Parulidae. [RED + OE *steort* tail]

reduce /rɪ'djuːs/ v. **1** tr. & intr. make or become
smaller or less. **2** tr. (foll. by to) bring by force or
necessity (to some undesirable state or action)
(*reduced them to tears*; *were reduced to begging*). **3**
tr. convert to another (esp. simpler) form (*reduced
it to a powder*). **4** tr. convert (a fraction) to the
form with the lowest terms. **5** tr. (foll. by to)
bring or simplify or adapt by classification or
analysis (*the dispute may be reduced to three issues*).
6 tr. make lower in status or rank. **7** tr. lower
the price of. **8** intr. lessen one's weight or size. **9**
tr. weaken (*is in a very reduced state*). **10** tr.
impoverish. **11** tr. subdue; bring back to obedience. **12** intr. & tr. Chem. **a** combine or cause to
combine with hydrogen. **b** undergo or cause to
undergo addition of electrons. **13** tr. Chem.
convert (oxide etc.) to metal. **14** tr. **a** (in surgery)
restore (a dislocated etc. part) to its proper
position. **b** remedy (a dislocation etc.) in this
way. **15** tr. Cookery boil off excess liquid from. □
reduced circumstances poverty after relative
prosperity. **reduce to the ranks** demote (an

NCO) to the rank of private. **reducing agent** *Chem.* a substance that brings about reduction by oxidation and losing electrons. □ **reducer** *n.* **reducible** *adj.* **reducibility** /-ˈbɪlɪtɪ/ *n.* [ME in sense 'restore to original or proper position', f. L *reducere* *reduct-* (as RE-, *ducere* bring)]

reductio ad absurdum /rɪˌdʌktɪəʊ æd æbˈzɜːdəm/ *n.* a method of proving the falsity of a premiss by showing that the logical consequence is absurd; an instance of this. [L, = reduction to the absurd]

reduction /rɪˈdʌkʃ(ə)n/ *n.* **1** the act or an instance of reducing; the process of being reduced. **2** an amount by which prices etc. are reduced. **3** a reduced copy of a picture etc. □ **reductive** *adj.* [ME f. OF *reduction* or L *reductio* (as REDUCE)]

reductionism /rɪˈdʌkʃə,nɪz(ə)m/ *n.* **1** the tendency to or principle of analysing complex things into simple constituents. **2** *often derog.* the doctrine that a system can be fully understood in terms of its isolated parts, or an idea in terms of simple concepts. □ **reductionist** *n.* **reductionistic** /-ˈnɪstɪk/ *adj.*

redundant /rɪˈdʌnd(ə)nt/ *adj.* **1** superfluous; not needed. **2** that can be omitted without any loss of significance. **3** (of a person) no longer needed at work and therefore unemployed. □ **redundancy** *n.* (pl. **-ies**). **redundantly** *adv.* [L *redundare* *redundant-* (as REDOUND)]

reduplicate /rɪˈdjuːplɪ,keɪt/ *v.tr.* **1** make double. **2** repeat. **3** repeat (a letter or syllable or word) exactly or with a slight change (e.g. hurly-burly, see-saw). □ **reduplication** /-ˈkeɪʃ(ə)n/ *n.* **reduplicative** /-kətɪv/ *adj.* [LL *reduplicare* (as RE-, DUPLICATE)]

redwing /ˈredwɪŋ/ *n.* a thrush, *Turdus iliacus*, with red underwings showing in flight.

redwood /ˈredwʊd/ *n.* **1** an exceptionally large Californian conifer, *Sequoia sempervirens*, yielding red wood. **2** any tree yielding red wood.

reebok /ˈriːbɒk/ *n.* (also **rhebok**) a small S. African antelope, *Pelea capreolus*, with sharp horns. [Du., = roebuck]

re-echo /riːˈekəʊ/ *v.intr.* & *tr.* (**-oes, -oed**) **1** echo. **2** echo repeatedly; resound.

reed *n.* & *v.* —*n.* **1 a** any of various water or marsh plants with a firm stem, esp. of the genus *Phragmites*. **b** a tall straight stalk of this. **2** (*collect.*) reeds growing in a mass or used as material esp. for thatching. **3 a** the vibrating part of the mouthpiece of some wind instruments, e.g. the oboe and clarinet, made of reed or other material and producing the sound. **b** (esp. in *pl.*) a reed instrument. —*v.tr.* **1** thatch with reed. **2** fit (a musical instrument) with a reed. □ **reed-mace** a tall reedlike water-plant, *Typha latifolia*, with straplike leaves and a head of numerous tiny red-brown flowers. [OE *hrēod* f. WG]

reeded /ˈriːdɪd/ *adj.* *Mus.* (of an instrument) having a vibrating reed.

re-educate /riːˈedjʊ,keɪt/ *v.tr.* educate again, esp. to change a person's views or beliefs. □ **re-education** /-ˈkeɪʃ(ə)n/ *n.*

reedy /ˈriːdɪ/ *adj.* (**reedier, reediest**) **1** full of reeds. **2** like a reed, esp. in weakness or slenderness. **3** (of a voice) like a reed instrument in tone; not full. □ **reediness** *n.*

reef¹ *n.* a ridge of rock or coral etc. at or near the surface of the sea. [earlier *riff(e)* f. MDu., MLG *rif, ref,* f. ON *rif* RIB]

reef² *n.* & *v.* *Naut.* —*n.* each of several strips across a sail, for taking it in or rolling it up to reduce the surface area in a high wind. —*v.tr.* **1** take in a reef or reefs of (a sail). **2** shorten (a topmast or a bowsprit). □ **reefing-jacket** a thick close-fitting double-breasted jacket. **reef-knot** a double knot made symmetrically to hold securely and cast off easily. [ME *riff, refe* f. Du. *reef, rif* f. ON *rif* RIB, in the same sense: cf. REEF¹]

reefer /ˈriːfə(r)/ *n.* **1** *sl.* a marijuana cigarette. **2** = *reefing-jacket* (see REEF²). [REEF² (in sense 1, = a thing rolled) + -ER¹]

reek *v.* & *n.* —*v.intr.* (often foll. by *of*) **1** smell strongly and unpleasantly. **2** have unpleasant or suspicious associations (*this reeks of corruption*). **3** give off smoke or fumes. —*n.* **1** a foul or stale smell. **2** esp. *Sc.* smoke. **3** vapour; a visible exhalation. □ **reeky** *adj.* [OE *rēocan* (v.), *rēc* (n.), f. Gmc]

reel *n.* & *v.* —*n.* **1** a cylindrical device on which thread, silk, yarn, paper, film, wire, etc., are wound. **2** a quantity of thread etc. wound on a reel. **3** a device for winding and unwinding a line as required, esp. in fishing. **4** a revolving part in various machines. **5 a** a lively folk or Scottish dance, of two or more couples facing each other. **b** a piece of music for this. —*v.* **1** *tr.* wind (thread, a fishing-line, etc.) on a reel. **2** *tr.* (foll. by *in, up*) draw (fish etc.) in or up by the use of a reel. **3** *intr.* stand or walk or run unsteadily. **4** *intr.* be shaken mentally or physically. **5** *intr.* rock from side to side, or swing violently. **6** *intr.* dance a reel. □ **reel off** say or recite very rapidly and without apparent effort. □ **reeler** *n.* [OE *hrēol,* of unkn. orig.]

re-elect /ˌriːɪˈlekt/ *v.tr.* elect again, esp. to a further term of office. □ **re-election** /-ɪˈlekʃ(ə)n/ *n.* **re-eligible** /-ˈelɪdʒɪb(ə)l/ *adj.*

re-emerge /ˌriːɪˈmɜːdʒ/ *v.intr.* emerge again; come back out. □ **re-emergence** *n.* **re-emergent** *adj.*

re-emphasize /riːˈemfə,saɪz/ *v.tr.* place renewed emphasis on. □ **re-emphasis** /-ˈemfəsɪs/ *n.*

re-employ /ˌriːɪmˈplɔɪ/ *v.tr.* employ again. □ **re-employment** *n.*

re-enact /ˌriːɪˈnækt/ *v.tr.* act out (a past event). □ **re-enactment** *n.*

re-enlist /ˌriːɪnˈlɪst/ *v.intr.* enlist again, esp. in the armed services. □ **re-enlister** *n.*

re-enter /riːˈentə(r)/ *v.tr.* & *intr.* enter again; go back in. □ **re-entrance** /-ˈentrəns/ *n.*

re-entrant /riːˈentrənt/ *adj.* **1** esp. *Fortification* (of an angle) pointing inwards (opp. SALIENT). **2** *Geom.* reflex.

re-entry /riːˈentrɪ/ *n.* (pl. **-ies**) the act of entering again, esp. (of a spacecraft, missile, etc.) re-entering the earth's atmosphere.

re-equip /ˌriːɪˈkwɪp/ *v.tr.* & *intr.* (**-equipped, -equipping**) provide or be provided with new equipment.

re-establish /ˌriːɪˈstæblɪʃ/ *v.tr.* establish again or anew. □ **re-establishment** *n.*

re-evaluate /ˌriːɪˈvæljʊ,eɪt/ *v.tr.* evaluate again or differently. □ **re-evaluation** /-ˈeɪʃ(ə)n/ *n.*

reeve¹ /riːv/ *n.* *hist.* **1** the chief magistrate of a town or district. **2** an official supervising a landowner's estate. **3** any of various minor local officials. [OE (ge)*rēfa, girēfa*]

reeve² /riːv/ *v.tr.* (*past* **rove** /rəʊv/ *or* **reeved**) *Naut.* **1** (usu. foll. by *through*) thread (a rope or rod etc.) through a ring or other aperture. **2**

pass a rope through (a block etc.). **3** fasten (a rope or block) in this way. [prob. f. Du. *rēven* REEF²]

reeve³ /riːv/ *n.* a female ruff (see RUFF¹). [17th c.: orig. unkn.]

re-examine /ˌriːɪgˈzæmɪn/ *v.tr.* examine again or further (esp. a witness after cross-examination). □ **re-examination** /-ˈneɪʃ(ə)n/ *n.*

re-export *v. & n.* —*v.tr.* /ˌriːɪkˈspɔːt/ export again (esp. imported goods after further processing or manufacture). —*n.* /riːˈekspɔːt/ **1** the process of re-exporting. **2** something re-exported. □ **re-exportation** /-ˈteɪʃ(ə)n/ *n.* **re-exporter** /ˌriːɪkˈspɔːtə(r)/ *n.*

ref /ref/ *n. colloq.* a referee in sports. [abbr.]

reface /riːˈfeɪs/ *v.tr.* put a new facing on (a building).

refashion /riːˈfæʃ(ə)n/ *v.tr.* fashion again or differently.

refectory /rɪˈfektərɪ, ˈrefɪktərɪ/ *n.* (*pl.* **-ies**) a room used for communal meals, esp. in a monastery or college. □ **refectory table** a long narrow table. [LL *refectorium* f. L *reficere* refresh (as RE-, *facere* make)]

refer /rɪˈfɜː(r)/ *v.* (**referred, referring**) (usu. foll. by *to*) **1** *tr.* trace or ascribe (to a person or thing as a cause or source) (*referred their success to their popularity*). **2** *tr.* consider as belonging (to a certain date or place or class). **3** *tr.* send on or direct (a person, or a question for decision) (*the matter was referred to arbitration; referred him to her previous answer*). **4** *intr.* make an appeal or have recourse to (some authority or source of information) (*referred to his notes*). **5** *tr.* send (a person) to a medical specialist etc. **6** *tr.* (foll. by *back to*) send (a proposal etc.) back to (a lower body, court, etc.). **7** *intr.* (foll. by *to*) (of a person speaking) make an allusion or direct the hearer's attention (*decided not to refer to our other problems*). **8** *intr.* (foll. by *to*) (of a statement etc.) have a particular relation; be directed (*this paragraph refers to the events of last year*). **9** *tr.* (foll. by *to*) interpret (a statement) as being directed to (a particular context etc.). **10** *tr.* fail (a candidate in an examination). □ **referred pain** pain felt in a part of the body other than its actual source. □ **referable** /rɪˈfɜːrəb(ə)l, ˈrefər-/ *adj.* **referrer** *n.* [ME f. OF *referer* f. L *referre* carry back (as RE-, *ferre* bring)]

referee /ˌrefəˈriː/ *n. & v.* —*n.* **1** an umpire esp. in football or boxing. **2** a person whose opinion or judgement is sought in some connection, or who is referred to for a decision in a dispute etc. **3** a person willing to testify to the character of an applicant for employment etc. —*v.* (**referees, refereed**) **1** *intr.* act as referee. **2** *tr.* be the referee of (a game etc.).

reference /ˈrefərəns/ *n. & v.* —*n.* **1** the referring of a matter for decision or settlement or consideration to some authority. **2** the scope given to this authority. **3** (foll. by *to*) **a** a relation or respect or correspondence (*success seems to have little reference to merit*). **b** an allusion (*made no reference to our problems*). **c** a direction to a book etc. (or a passage in it) where information may be found. **d** a book or passage so cited. **4 a** the act of looking up a passage etc. or looking in a book for information. **b** the act of referring to a person etc. for information. **5 a** a written testimonial supporting an applicant for employment etc. **b** a person giving this. —*v.tr.* provide (a book etc.) with references to authorities. □ **reference book** a book intended to be consulted for information on individual matters rather than read continuously. **reference library** a library in which the books are for consultation not loan. **with** (or **in**) **reference to** regarding; as regards; about. **without reference to** not taking account of. □ **referential** /-ˈrenʃ(ə)l/ *adj.*

referendum /ˌrefəˈrendəm/ *n.* (*pl.* **referendums** or **referenda** /-də/) **1** the process of referring a political question to the electorate for a direct decision by general vote. **2** a vote taken by referendum. [L, gerund or neut. gerundive of *referre*: see REFER]

referral /rɪˈfɜːr(ə)l/ *n.* the referring of an individual to an expert or specialist for advice, esp. the directing of a patient by a GP to a medical specialist.

refill *v. & n.* —*v.tr.* /riːˈfɪl/ **1** fill again. **2** provide a new filling for. —*n.* /ˈriːfɪl/ **1** a new filling. **2** the material for this. □ **refillable** /-ˈfɪləb(ə)l/ *adj.*

refine /rɪˈfaɪn/ *v.* **1** free from impurities or defects; purify, clarify. **2** *tr. & intr.* make or become more polished or elegant or cultured. **3** *tr. & intr.* make or become more subtle or delicate in thought, feelings, etc. □ **refinable** *adj.* [RE- + FINE¹ *v.*]

refined /rɪˈfaɪnd/ *adj.* characterized by polish or elegance or subtlety.

refinement /rɪˈfaɪnmənt/ *n.* **1** the act of refining or the process of being refined. **2** fineness of feeling or taste. **3** polish or elegance in behaviour or manner. **4** an added development or improvement (*a car with several refinements*). **5** a piece of subtle reasoning. **6** a fine distinction. **7** a subtle or ingenious example or display (*all the refinements of reasoning*). [REFINE + -MENT, after F *raffinement*]

refiner /rɪˈfaɪnə(r)/ *n.* a person or firm whose business it is to refine crude oil, metal, sugar, etc.

refinery /rɪˈfaɪnərɪ/ *n.* (*pl.* **-ies**) a place where oil etc. is refined.

refit *v. & n.* —*v.tr. & intr.* /riːˈfɪt/ (**refitted, refitting**) make or become fit or serviceable again (esp. of a ship undergoing renewal and repairs). —*n.* /ˈriːfɪt/ the act or an instance of refitting; the process of being refitted. □ **refitment** *n.*

reflate /riːˈfleɪt/ *v.tr.* cause reflation of (a currency or economy etc.). [RE- after *inflate, deflate*]

reflation /riːˈfleɪʃ(ə)n/ *n.* the inflation of a financial system to restore its previous condition after deflation. □ **reflationary** *adj.* [RE- after *inflation, deflation*]

reflect /rɪˈflekt/ *v.* **1** *tr.* **a** (of a surface or body) throw back (heat, light, sound, etc.). **b** cause to rebound (*reflected light*). **2** *tr.* (of a mirror) show an image of; reproduce to the eye or mind. **3** *tr.* correspond in appearance or effect to; have as a cause or source (*their behaviour reflects a wish to succeed*). **4** *tr.* **a** (of an action, result, etc.) show or bring (credit, discredit, etc.). **b** (*absol.*; usu. foll. by *on, upon*) bring discredit on. **5 a** *intr.* (often foll. by *on, upon*) meditate on; think about. **b** *tr.* (foll. by *that, how*, etc. + clause) consider; remind oneself. [ME f. OF *reflecter* or L *reflectere* (as RE-, *flectere flex-* bend)]

reflection /rɪˈflekʃ(ə)n/ *n.* (also **reflexion**) **1** the act or an instance of reflecting; the process of being reflected. **2 a** reflected light, heat, or colour. **b** a reflected image. **3** reconsideration (*on reflection*). **4** (often foll. by *on*) discredit or a thing bringing discredit. **5** (often foll. by *on, upon*) an idea arising in the mind; a comment or apophthegm. □ **reflectional** *adj.* [ME f. OF *reflexion* or LL *reflexio* (as REFLECT), with assim. to *reflect*]

reflective /rɪˈflektɪv/ *adj.* **1** (of a surface etc.) giving a reflection or image. **2** (of mental faculties) concerned in reflection or thought. **3** (of a person or mood etc.) thoughtful; given to meditation. □ **reflectively** *adv.* **reflectiveness** *n.*

reflector /rɪˈflektə(r)/ *n.* **1** a piece of glass or metal etc. for reflecting light in a required direction, e.g. a red one on the back of a motor vehicle or bicycle. **2 a** a telescope etc. using a mirror to produce images. **b** the mirror itself.

reflex /ˈriːfleks/ *adj.* & *n.* —*adj.* **1** (of an action) independent of the will, as an automatic response to the stimulation of a nerve (e.g. a sneeze). **2** (of an angle) exceeding 180°. **3** bent backwards. —*n.* **1** a reflex action. **2** a sign or secondary manifestation (*law is a reflex of public opinion*). **3** reflected light or a reflected image. □ **reflex camera** a camera with a ground-glass focusing screen on which the image is formed by a combination of lens and mirror. □ **reflexly** *adv.* [L *reflexus* (as REFLECT)]

reflexible /rɪˈfleksɪb(ə)l/ *adj.* capable of being reflected. □ **reflexibility** /-ˈbɪlɪtɪ/ *n.*

reflexive /rɪˈfleksɪv/ *adj.* & *n. Gram.* —*adj.* **1** (of a word or form) referring back to the subject of a sentence (esp. of a pronoun, e.g. *myself*). **2** (of a verb) having a reflexive pronoun as its object (as in *to wash oneself*). —*n.* a reflexive word or form, esp. a pronoun. □ **reflexively** *adv.* **reflexiveness** *n.* **reflexivity** /-ˈsɪvɪtɪ/ *n.*

reflexology /ˌriːflekˈsɒlədʒɪ/ *n.* a therapy based on the application of pressure to reflex points on the feet, hands, and head, used to relieve tension and treat illness. □ **reflexologist** *n.*

refloat /riːˈfləʊt/ *v.tr.* set (a stranded ship) afloat again.

refocus /riːˈfəʊkəs/ *v.tr.* (**refocused, refocusing** or **refocussed, refocussing**) adjust the focus of (esp. a lens).

reforest /riːˈfɒrɪst/ *v.tr.* = REAFFOREST. □ **reforestation** /-ˈsteɪʃ(ə)n/ *n.*

reform /rɪˈfɔːm/ *v.* & *n.* —*v.* **1** *tr.* & *intr.* make or become better by the removal of faults and errors. **2** *tr.* abolish or cure (an abuse or malpractice). —*n.* **1** the removal of faults or abuses, esp. of a moral or political or social kind. **2** an improvement made or suggested. □ **Reformed Church** a Church that has accepted the principles of the Reformation, esp. a Calvinist Church (as distinct from Lutheran). **Reform Judaism** a simplified and rationalized form of Judaism. □ **reformable** *adj.* [ME f. OF *reformer* or L *reformare* (as RE-, FORM)]

re-form /riːˈfɔːm/ *v.tr.* & *intr.* form again. □ **re-formation** /-ˈmeɪʃ(ə)n/ *n.*

reformat /riːˈfɔːmæt/ *v.tr.* (**reformatted, reformatting**) format anew.

reformation /ˌrefəˈmeɪʃ(ə)n/ *n.* the act of reforming or process of being reformed, esp. a radical change for the better in political or religious or social affairs. □ **the Reformation** *hist.* a 16th-c. movement for the reform of abuses in the Roman Church ending in the

establishment of the Reformed and Protestant Churches. □ **Reformational** *adj.* [ME f. OF *reformation* or L *reformatio* (as REFORM)]

reformative /rɪˈfɔːmətɪv/ *adj.* tending or intended to produce reform. [OF *reformatif -ive* or med.L *reformativus* (as REFORM)]

reformatory /rɪˈfɔːmətərɪ/ *n.* & *adj.* —*n.* (*pl.* **-ies**) *US* & *hist.* an institution in which young offenders are reformed. —*adj.* reformative.

reformer /rɪˈfɔːmə(r)/ *n.* a person who advocates or brings about (esp. political or social) reform.

reformism /rɪˈfɔːmɪz(ə)m/ *n.* a policy of reform rather than abolition or revolution. □ **reformist** *n.*

refract /rɪˈfrækt/ *v.tr.* (of water, air, glass, etc.) deflect (a ray of light etc.) at a certain angle when it enters obliquely from another medium. [L *refringere refract-* (as RE-, *frangere* break)]

refraction /rɪˈfrækʃ(ə)n/ *n.* the process by which or the extent to which light is refracted. [F *réfraction* or LL *refractio* (as REFRACT)]

refractive /rɪˈfræktɪv/ *adj.* of or involving refraction.

refractor /rɪˈfræktə(r)/ *n.* **1** a refracting medium or lens. **2** a telescope using a lens to produce an image.

refractory /rɪˈfræktərɪ/ *adj.* **1** stubborn, unmanageable, rebellious. **2** (of a wound, disease, etc.) not yielding to treatment. **3** (of a substance) hard to fuse or work. □ **refractorily** *adv.* **refractoriness** *n.* [alt. of obs. *refractary* f. L *refractarius* (as REFRACT)]

refrain[1] /rɪˈfreɪn/ *v.intr.* (foll. by *from*) avoid doing (an action) (*refrain from smoking*). □ **refrainment** *n.* [ME f. OF *refrener* f. L *refrenare* (as RE-, *frenum* bridle)]

refrain[2] /rɪˈfreɪn/ *n.* **1** a recurring phrase or number of lines, esp. at the ends of stanzas. **2** the music accompanying this. [ME f. OF *refrain* (earlier *refrait*) ult. f. L *refringere* (as RE-, *frangere* break), because the refrain 'broke' the sequence]

refrangible /rɪˈfrændʒɪb(ə)l/ *adj.* that can be refracted. □ **refrangibility** /-ˈbɪlɪtɪ/ *n.* [mod.L *refrangibilis* f. *refrangere* = L *refringere*: see REFRACT]

refreeze /riːˈfriːz/ *v.tr.* & *intr.* (*past* **refroze**; *past part.* **refrozen**) freeze again.

refresh /rɪˈfreʃ/ *v.tr.* **1 a** (of food, rest, amusement, etc.) give fresh spirit or vigour to. **b** (esp. *refl.*) revive with food, rest, etc. (*refreshed myself with a short sleep*). **2** revive or stimulate (the memory), esp. by consulting the source of one's information. **3** make cool. [ME f. OF *refreschi(e)r* f. *fres fresche* FRESH]

refresher /rɪˈfreʃə(r)/ *n.* **1** something that refreshes, esp. a drink. **2** *Law* an extra fee payable to counsel in a prolonged case. □ **refresher course** a course reviewing or updating previous studies.

refreshing /rɪˈfreʃɪŋ/ *adj.* **1** serving to refresh. **2** welcome or stimulating. □ **refreshingly** *adv.*

refreshment /rɪˈfreʃmənt/ *n.* **1** the act of refreshing or the process of being refreshed in mind or body. **2** (usu. in *pl.*) food or drink that refreshes. **3** something that refreshes or stimulates the mind. [ME f. OF *refreschement* (as REFRESH)]

refrigerant /rɪˈfrɪdʒərənt/ *n.* & *adj.* —*n.* a substance used for refrigeration. —*adj.* cooling. [F *réfrigérant* or L *refrigerant-* (as REFRIGERATE)]

refrigerate /rɪˈfrɪdʒəˌreɪt/ v. 1 tr. & intr. make or become cool or cold. 2 tr. subject (food etc.) to cold in order to freeze or preserve it. □ **refrigeration** /-ˈreɪʃ(ə)n/ n. **refrigerative** /-rətɪv/ adj. [L refrigerare (as RE-, frigus frigoris cold)]

refrigerator /rɪˈfrɪdʒəˌreɪtə(r)/ n. a cabinet or room in which food etc. is kept cold.

refroze past of REFREEZE.

refrozen past part. of REFREEZE.

reft past part. of REAVE.

refuel /riːˈfjuːəl/ v. (**refuelled**, **refuelling**; US **refueled**, **refueling**) 1 intr. replenish a fuel supply. 2 tr. supply with more fuel.

refuge /ˈrefjuːdʒ/ n. 1 a shelter from pursuit or danger or trouble. 2 a person or place etc. offering this. 3 a person, thing, or course resorted to in difficulties. 4 a traffic island. [ME f. OF f. L refugium (as RE-, fugere flee)]

refugee /ˌrefjuˈdʒiː/ n. a person taking refuge, esp. in a foreign country from war or persecution or natural disaster. [F réfugié past part. of (se) réfugier (as REFUGE)]

refulgent /rɪˈfʌldʒ(ə)nt/ adj. literary shining; gloriously bright. □ **refulgence** n. **refulgently** adv. [L refulgēre (as RE-, fulgēre shine)]

refund v. & n. —v. /rɪˈfʌnd/ tr. (also absol.) 1 pay back (money or expenses). 2 reimburse (a person). —n. /ˈriːfʌnd/ 1 an act of refunding. 2 a sum refunded; a repayment. □ **refundable** /rɪˈfʌndəb(ə)l/ adj. **refunder** /rɪˈfʌndə(r)/ n. [ME in sense 'pay back', f. OF refonder or L refundere (as RE-, fundere pour), later assoc. with FUND]

refurbish /riːˈfɜːbɪʃ/ v.tr. 1 brighten up. 2 restore and redecorate. □ **refurbishment** n.

refurnish /riːˈfɜːnɪʃ/ v.tr. furnish again or differently.

refusal /rɪˈfjuːz(ə)l/ n. 1 the act or an instance of refusing; the state of being refused. 2 (in full **first refusal**) the right or privilege of deciding to take or leave a thing before it is offered to others.

refuse[1] /rɪˈfjuːz/ v. 1 tr. withhold acceptance of or consent to (refuse an offer; refuse orders). 2 tr. (often foll. by to + infin.) indicate unwillingness (I refuse to go; the car refuses to start; I refuse!). 3 tr. (often with double object) not grant (a request) made by (a person) (refused me a day off; I could not refuse them). 4 tr. (also absol.) (of a horse) be unwilling to jump (a fence etc.). □ **refusable** adj. **refuser** n. [ME f. OF refuser prob. ult. f. L recusare (see RECUSANT) after refutare REFUTE]

refuse[2] /ˈrefjuːs/ n. items rejected as worthless; waste. [ME, perh. f. OF refusé past part. (as REFUSE[1])]

refusenik /rɪˈfjuːznɪk/ n. hist. a Jew in the former Soviet Union who was refused permission to emigrate to Israel. [REFUSE[1] + -NIK]

refute /rɪˈfjuːt/ v.tr. 1 prove the falsity or error of (a statement etc. or the person advancing it). 2 rebut or repel by argument. 3 disp. deny or contradict (without argument). □ **refutable** adj. **refutal** n. **refutation** /ˌrefjuˈteɪʃ(ə)n/ n. **refuter** n. [L refutare (as RE-: cf. CONFUTE)]

■ **Usage** The use of this word in sense 3 is considered incorrect by some people. It is often confused in this sense with repudiate.

regain /rɪˈɡeɪn/ v.tr. obtain possession or use of after loss (regain consciousness). [F regagner (as RE-, GAIN)]

regal /ˈriːɡ(ə)l/ adj. 1 royal; of or by a monarch or monarchs. 2 fit for a monarch; magnificent. □ **regally** adv. [ME f. OF regal or L regalis f. rex regis king]

regality /rɪˈɡælɪtɪ/ n. royalty. [ME f. OF regal or L regalis f. rex regis king]

regale /rɪˈɡeɪl/ v.tr. 1 entertain lavishly with feasting. 2 (foll. by with) entertain or divert with (talk etc.). 3 (of beauty, flowers, etc.) give delight to. □ **regalement** n. [F régaler f. OF gale pleasure]

regalia /rɪˈɡeɪlɪə/ n.pl. 1 the insignia of royalty used at coronations. 2 the insignia of an order or of civic dignity. [med.L, = royal privileges, f. L neut. pl. of regalis REGAL]

regard /rɪˈɡɑːd/ v. & n. —v.tr. 1 gaze on steadily (usu. in a specified way) (regarded them suspiciously). 2 give heed to; take into account; let one's course be affected by. 3 look upon or contemplate mentally in a specified way (I regard them kindly; I regard it as an insult). 4 (of a thing) have relation to; have some connection with. —n. 1 a gaze; a steady or significant look. 2 (foll. by to, for) attention or care. 3 (foll. by for) esteem; kindly feeling; respectful opinion. 4 a respect; a point attended to (in this regard). 5 (in pl.) an expression of friendliness in a letter etc.; compliments (sent my best regards). □ **as regards** about, concerning; in respect of. **in** (or **with**) **regard to** as concerns; in respect of. [ME f. OF regard f. regarder (as RE-, garder GUARD)]

regardful /rɪˈɡɑːdfʊl/ adj. (foll. by of) mindful of; paying attention to.

regarding /rɪˈɡɑːdɪŋ/ prep. about, concerning; in respect of.

regardless /rɪˈɡɑːdlɪs/ adj. & adv. —adj. (foll. by of) without regard or consideration for (regardless of the expense). —adv. without paying attention (carried on regardless). □ **regardlessly** adv. **regardlessness** n.

regatta /rɪˈɡætə/ n. a sporting event consisting of a series of boat or yacht races. [It. (Venetian)]

regency /ˈriːdʒənsɪ/ n. (pl. **-ies**) 1 the office of regent. 2 a commission acting as regent. 3 a the period of office of a regent or regency commission. b (**Regency**) a particular period of a regency, esp. (in Britain) from 1811 to 1820, and (in France) from 1715 to 1723. [ME f. med.L regentia (as REGENT)]

regenerate v. & adj. —v. /rɪˈdʒenəˌreɪt/ 1 tr. & intr. bring or come into renewed existence; generate again. 2 tr. improve the moral condition of. 3 tr. impart new, more vigorous, and spiritually greater life to (a person or institution etc.). 4 intr. reform oneself. 5 tr. invest with a new and higher spiritual nature. 6 intr. & tr. Biol. regrow or cause (new tissue) to regrow to replace lost or injured tissue. —adj. /rɪˈdʒenərət/ 1 spiritually born again. 2 reformed. □ **regeneration** /-ˈreɪʃ(ə)n/ n. **regenerative** /-rətɪv/ adj. **regeneratively** /-rəˌtɪvlɪ/ adv. **regenerator** n. [L regenerare (as RE-, GENERATE)]

regent /ˈriːdʒ(ə)nt/ n. & adj. —n. 1 a person appointed to administer a State because the monarch is a minor or is absent or incapacitated. 2 US a member of the governing body of a State university. —adj. (placed after noun) acting as regent (Prince Regent). [ME f. OF regent or L regere rule]

reggae /ˈreɡeɪ/ n. a W. Indian style of music with a strongly accented subsidiary beat. [W.Ind.]

regicide /ˈredʒɪˌsaɪd/ n. 1 a person who kills or takes part in killing a king. 2 the act of killing a king. □ **regicidal** /-ˈsaɪd(ə)l/ adj. [L rex regis king + -CIDE]

regime /reɪˈʒiːm/ n. (also **régime**) **1 a** a method or system of government. **b** derog. a particular government. **2** a prevailing order or system of things. **3** the conditions under which a scientific or industrial process occurs. [F régime (as REGIMEN)]

regimen /ˈredʒɪˌmen/ n. esp. Med. a prescribed course of exercise, way of life, and diet. [L f. regere rule]

regiment n. & v. —n. /ˈredʒɪmənt/ **1 a** a permanent unit of an army usu. commanded by a colonel and divided into several companies or troops or batteries and often into two battalions. **b** an operational unit of artillery etc. **2** (usu. foll. by of) a large array or number. **3** archaic rule, government. —v.tr. /ˈredʒɪˌment/ **1** organize (esp. oppressively) in groups or according to a system. **2** form into a regiment or regiments. □ **regimentation** /-ˈteɪʃ(ə)n/ n. [ME (in sense 3) f. OF f. LL regimentum (as REGIMEN)]

regimental /ˌredʒɪˈment(ə)l/ adj. & n. —adj. of or relating to a regiment. —n. (in pl.) military uniform, esp. of a particular regiment. □ **regimentally** adv.

Regina /rɪˈdʒaɪnə/ n. the reigning queen (following a name or in the titles of lawsuits, e.g. Regina v. Jones the Crown versus Jones). [L, = queen f. rex regis king]

region /ˈriːdʒ(ə)n/ n. **1** an area of land, or division of the earth's surface, having definable boundaries or characteristics (a mountainous region; the region between London and the coast). **2** an administrative district esp. in Scotland. **3** a part of the body round or near some organ etc. (the lumbar region). **4** a sphere or realm (the region of metaphysics). □ **in the region of** approximately. □ **regional** adj. **regionalism** n. **regionalist** n. & adj. **regionalize** v.tr. (also **-ise**). **regionally** adv. [ME f. OF f. L regio -onis direction, district f. regere direct]

register /ˈredʒɪstə(r)/ n. & v. —n. **1** an official list e.g. of births, marriages, and deaths, of shipping, of professionally qualified persons, or of qualified voters in a constituency. **2** a book in which items are recorded for reference. **3** a device recording speed, force, etc. **4** (in electronic devices) a location in a store of data, used for a specific purpose and with quick access time. **5 a** the compass of a voice or instrument. **b** a part of this compass (lower register). **6** an adjustable plate for widening or narrowing an opening and regulating a draught, esp. in a fire-grate. **7 a** a set of organ pipes. **b** a sliding device controlling this. **8** = cash register (see CASH¹). —v. **1** tr. set down (a name, fact, etc.) formally; record in writing. **2** tr. make a mental note of; notice. **3** tr. enter or cause to be entered in a particular register. **4** tr. entrust (a letter etc.) to a post office for transmission by registered post. **5** intr. & refl. put one's name on a register, esp. as an eligible voter or as a guest in a register kept by a hotel etc. **6** tr. (of an instrument) record automatically; indicate. **7 a** tr. express (an emotion) facially or by gesture (registered surprise). **b** intr. (of an emotion) show in a person's face or gestures. **8** intr. make an impression on a person's mind (did not register at all). □ **registered nurse** a nurse with a State

certificate of competence. **registered post** a postal procedure with special precautions for safety and for compensation in case of loss. **register office** Brit. a State office where civil marriages are conducted and births, marriages, and deaths are recorded with the issue of certificates. □ **registrable** adj. [ME & OF registre, registre or med.L regestrum, registrum, alt. of regestum f. LL regesta things recorded (as RE-, L gerere gest- carry)]

■ **Usage** Register office is the official name, although registry office is often heard in colloquial usage.

registrar /ˌredʒɪˈstrɑː(r), ˈredʒ-/ n. **1** an official responsible for keeping a register or official records. **2** the chief administrative officer in a university. **3** a middle-ranking hospital doctor undergoing training as a specialist. □ **registrarship** n. [med.L registrarius f. registrum REGISTER]

registration /ˌredʒɪˈstreɪʃ(ə)n/ n. the act or instance of registering; the process of being registered. □ **registration mark** (or **number**) a combination of letters and figures identifying a motor vehicle etc. [obs. F régistration or med.L registratio (as REGISTRAR)]

registry /ˈredʒɪstrɪ/ n. (pl. **-ies**) **1** a place or office where registers or records are kept. **2** registration. □ **registry office** = register office. [obs. registery f. med.L registerium (as REGISTER)]

Regius professor /ˈriːdʒɪəs/ n. Brit. the holder of a chair founded by a sovereign or filled by Crown appointment. [L, = royal, f. rex regis king]

regrade /riːˈɡreɪd/ v.tr. grade again or differently.

regress v. & n. —v. /rɪˈɡres/ **1** intr. move backwards, esp. (in abstract senses) return to a former state. **2** intr. & tr. Psychol. return or cause to return mentally to a former stage of life, esp. through hypnosis or mental illness. —n. /ˈriːɡres/ the act or an instance of going back. [ME (as n.) f. L regressus f. regredi regress- (as RE-, gradi step)]

regression /rɪˈɡreʃ(ə)n/ n. **1** a backward movement, esp. a return to a former state. **2** a relapse or reversion. **3** Psychol. a return to an earlier stage of development, esp. through hypnosis or mental illness. [L regressio (as REGRESS)]

regressive /rɪˈɡresɪv/ adj. **1** regressing; characterized by regression. **2** (of a tax) proportionally greater on lower incomes. □ **regressively** adv. **regressiveness** n.

regret /rɪˈɡret/ v. & n. —v.tr. (**regretted**, **regretting**) (often foll. by that + clause) **1** feel or express sorrow or repentance or distress over (an action or loss etc.) (I regret that I forgot; regretted your absence). **2** (often foll. by to + infin. or that + clause) acknowledge with sorrow or remorse (I regret to say that you are wrong). —n. **1** a feeling of sorrow, repentance, disappointment, etc., over an action or loss etc. **2** (often in pl.) an (esp. polite or formal) expression of disappointment or sorrow at an occurrence, inability to comply, etc. (refused with many regrets). □ **give** (or **send**) **one's regrets** formally decline an invitation. [ME f. OF regreter bewail]

regretful /rɪˈɡretfʊl/ adj. feeling or showing regret. □ **regretfully** adv. **regretfulness** n.

regrettable /rɪˈɡretəb(ə)l/ adj. (of events or conduct) undesirable, unwelcome; deserving censure. □ **regrettably** adv.

regroup /riːˈgruːp/ v.tr. & intr. group or arrange again or differently. □ **regroupment** n.

regrow /riːˈɡrəʊ/ v.intr. & tr. grow again, esp. after an interval. □ **regrowth** n.

regulable /ˈreɡjʊləb(ə)l/ adj. able to be regulated.

regular /ˈreɡjʊlə(r)/ adj. & n. —adj. **1** conforming to a rule or principle; systematic. **2** (of a structure or arrangement) harmonious, symmetrical (*regular features*). **3** acting or done or recurring uniformly or calculably in time or manner; habitual, constant, orderly. **4** conforming to a standard of etiquette or procedure; correct; according to convention. **5** properly constituted or qualified; not defective or amateur; pursuing an occupation as one's main pursuit (*cooks as well as a regular cook*; *has no regular profession*). **6** Gram. (of a noun, verb, etc.) following the normal type of inflection. **7** colloq. complete, thorough, absolute (*a regular hero*). **8** Geom. **a** (of a figure) having all sides and all angles equal. **b** (of a solid) bounded by a number of equal figures. **9** Eccl. (placed before or after noun) **a** bound by religious rule. **b** belonging to a religious or monastic order (*canon regular*). **10** (of forces or troops etc.) relating to or constituting a permanent professional body (*regular soldiers*; *regular police force*). —n. **1** a regular soldier. **2** colloq. a regular customer, visitor, etc. **3** Eccl. one of the regular clergy. □ **regularity** /-ˈlærɪtɪ/ n. **regularize** v.tr. (also **-ise**). **regularization** /-ˈzeɪʃ(ə)n/ n. **regularly** adv. [ME reguler, regular f. OF reguler f. L regularis f. regula RULE]

regulate /ˈreɡjʊˌleɪt/ v.tr. **1** control by rule. **2** subject to restrictions. **3** adapt to requirements. **4** alter the speed of (a machine or clock) so that it may work accurately. □ **regulative** /-lətɪv/ adj. **regulator** n. **regulatory** /-lətərɪ/ adj. [LL regulare regulat- f. L regula RULE]

regulation /ˌreɡjʊˈleɪʃ(ə)n/ n. **1** the act or an instance of regulating; the process of being regulated. **2** a prescribed rule; an authoritative direction. **3** (*attrib.*) in accordance with regulations; of the correct type etc. (*the regulation speed*; *a regulation tie*).

regulo /ˈreɡjʊˌləʊ/ n. (usu. foll. by a numeral) each of the numbers of a scale denoting temperature in a gas oven (*cook at regulo 6*). [Regulo, propr. term for a thermostatic gas oven control]

regurgitate /rɪˈɡɜːdʒɪˌteɪt/ v. tr. **1** bring (swallowed food) up again to the mouth. **2** cast or pour out again (*required by the exam to regurgitate facts*). □ **regurgitation** /-ˈteɪʃ(ə)n/ n. [med.L regurgitare (as RE-, L gurges gurgitis whirlpool)]

rehabilitate /ˌriːhəˈbɪlɪˌteɪt/ v.tr. **1** restore to effectiveness or normal life by training etc., esp. after imprisonment or illness. **2** restore to former privileges or reputation or a proper condition. □ **rehabilitation** /-ˈteɪʃ(ə)n/ n. **rehabilitative** /-tətɪv/ adj. [med.L rehabilitare]

rehang /riːˈhæŋ/ v.tr. (*past* and *past part.* **rehung**) hang (esp. a picture or a curtain) again or differently.

rehash v. & n. —v.tr. /riːˈhæʃ/ put (old material) into a new form without significant change or improvement. —n. /ˈriːhæʃ/ **1** material rehashed. **2** the act or an instance of rehashing.

rehear /riːˈhɪə(r)/ v.tr. (*past* and *past part.* **reheard** /riːˈhɜːd/) hear again.

rehearsal /rɪˈhɜːs(ə)l/ n. **1** the act or an instance of rehearsing. **2** a trial performance or practice of a play, recital, etc.

rehearse /rɪˈhɜːs/ v. **1** tr. practise (a play, recital, etc.) for later public performance. **2** intr. hold a rehearsal. **3** tr. train (a person) by rehearsal. **4** tr. recite or say over. **5** tr. give a list of; enumerate. □ **rehearser** n. [ME f. AF rehearser, OF reherc(i)er, perh. formed as RE- + hercer to harrow f. herse harrow: see HEARSE]

reheat /riːˈhiːt/ v.tr. heat again. □ **reheater** /-ˈhiːtə(r)/ n.

reheel /riːˈhiːl/ v.tr. fit (a shoe etc.) with a new heel.

rehouse /riːˈhaʊz/ v.tr. provide with new housing.

rehung past and past part. of REHANG.

rehydrate /ˌriːhaɪˈdreɪt/ v. **1** intr. absorb water again after dehydration. **2** tr. add water to (esp. food) again to restore to a palatable state. □ **rehydratable** adj. **rehydration** /-ˈdreɪʃ(ə)n/ n.

Reich /raɪx/ n. the former German State, esp. the Third Reich. □ **Third Reich** the Nazi regime, 1933–45. [G, = empire]

reign /reɪn/ v. & n. —v.intr. **1** hold royal office; be king or queen. **2** prevail; hold sway (*confusion reigns*). **3** (as **reigning** adj.) (of a winner, champion, etc.) currently holding the title etc. —n. **1** sovereignty, rule. **2** the period during which a sovereign rules. [ME f. OF reigne kingdom f. L regnare f. rex regis king]

reignite /ˌriːɪɡˈnaɪt/ v.tr. & intr. ignite again.

Reilly var. of RILEY.

reimburse /ˌriːɪmˈbɜːs/ v.tr. **1** repay (a person who has expended money). **2** repay (a person's expenses). □ **reimbursable** adj. **reimbursement** n. **reimburser** n. [RE- + obs. imburse put in a purse f. med.L imbursare]

reimport v. & n. —v.tr. /ˌriːɪmˈpɔːt/ import (goods processed from exported materials). —n. /riːˈɪmpɔːt/ **1** the act or an instance of reimporting. **2** a reimported item. □ **reimportation** /-ˈteɪʃ(ə)n/ n.

reimpose /ˌriːɪmˈpəʊz/ v.tr. impose again, esp. after a lapse. □ **reimposition** /-pəˈzɪʃ(ə)n/ n.

rein /reɪn/ n. & v. —n. (in sing. or pl.) **1** a long narrow strap with each end attached to the bit, used to guide or check a horse etc. in riding or driving. **2** a similar device used to restrain a young child. **3** a means of control. —v.tr. **1** check or manage with reins. **2** (foll. by up, back) pull up or back with reins. **3** (foll. by in) hold in as with reins; restrain. **4** govern, restrain, control. □ **give free rein to** remove constraints from; allow full scope to. **keep a tight rein on** allow little freedom to. □ **reinless** adj. [ME f. OF rene, reigne, earlier resne, ult. f. L retinēre RETAIN]

reincarnation /ˌriːɪnkɑːˈneɪʃ(ə)n/ n. (in some beliefs) the rebirth of a soul in a new body. □ **reincarnate** /-ˈkɑːneɪt/ v.tr. **reincarnate** /-ˈkɑːnət/ adj.

reincorporate /ˌriːɪnˈkɔːpəˌreɪt/ v.tr. incorporate afresh. □ **reincorporation** /-ˈreɪʃ(ə)n/ n.

reindeer /ˈreɪndɪə(r)/ n. (pl. same or **reindeers**) a subarctic deer, *Rangifer tarandus*, of which both sexes have large antlers. [ME f. ON hreindýri f. hreinn reindeer + dýr DEER]

reinfect /ˌriːɪnˈfekt/ v.tr. infect again. □ **reinfection** /ˌriːɪnˈfekʃ(ə)n/ n.

reinforce /ˌriːɪnˈfɔːs/ v.tr. strengthen or support, esp. with additional personnel or material or by an increase of numbers or quantity or size etc. □ **reinforced concrete** concrete with metal bars or wire etc. embedded to increase its tensile strength. □ **reinforcer** n. [earlier *reinforce* f. F *renforcer*]

reinforcement /ˌriːɪnˈfɔːsmənt/ n. **1** the act or an instance of reinforcing; the process of being reinforced. **2** a thing that reinforces. **3** (in *pl.*) reinforcing personnel or equipment etc.

reinstate /ˌriːɪnˈsteɪt/ v.tr. **1** replace in a former position. **2** restore (a person etc.) to former privileges. □ **reinstatement** n.

reinsure /ˌriːɪnˈʃʊə(r)/ v.tr. & intr. insure again (esp. of an insurer securing himself by transferring some or all of the risk to another insurer). □ **reinsurance** n. **reinsurer** n.

reinterpret /ˌriːɪnˈtɜːprɪt/ v.tr. (**reinterpreted, reinterpreting**) interpret again or differently. □ **reinterpretation** /-ˈteɪʃ(ə)n/ n.

reintroduce /ˌriːɪntrəˈdjuːs/ v.tr. introduce again. □ **reintroduction** /-ˈdʌkʃ(ə)n/ n.

reinvest /ˌriːɪnˈvest/ v.tr. invest again (esp. money in other property etc.). □ **reinvestment** n.

reinvigorate /ˌriːɪnˈvɪɡəˌreɪt/ v.tr. impart fresh vigour to. □ **reinvigoration** /-ˈreɪʃ(ə)n/ n.

reissue /riːˈɪʃuː, -sjuː/ v. & n. —v.tr. (**reissues, reissued, reissuing**) issue again or in a different form. —n. a new issue, esp. of a previously published book.

reiterate /riːˈɪtəˌreɪt/ v.tr. say or do again or repeatedly. □ **reiteration** /-ˈreɪʃ(ə)n/ n. **reiterative** /-rətɪv/ adj. [L *reiterare* (as RE-, ITERATE)]

reject v. & n. —v.tr. /rɪˈdʒekt/ **1** put aside or send back as not to be used or done or complied with etc. **2** refuse to accept or believe in. **3** rebuff or snub (a person). **4** (of a body or digestive system) cast up again; vomit, evacuate. **5** *Med.* show an immune response to (a transplanted organ or tissue) so that it fails to survive. —n. /ˈriːdʒekt/ a thing or person rejected as unfit or below standard. □ **rejectable** /rɪˈdʒektəb(ə)l/ adj. **rejecter** /rɪˈdʒektə(r)/ n. (also **rejector**). **rejection** /rɪˈdʒekʃ(ə)n/ n. **rejective** adj. [ME f. L *rejicere reject-* (as RE-, *jacere* throw)]

rejig /riːˈdʒɪɡ/ v.tr. (**rejigged, rejigging**) **1** re-equip (a factory etc.) for a new kind of work. **2** rearrange.

rejoice /rɪˈdʒɔɪs/ v. **1** intr. feel great joy. **2** intr. (foll. by *that* + clause or *to* + infin.) be glad. **3** intr. (foll. by *in, at*) take delight. **4** intr. celebrate some event. **5** tr. cause joy to. □ **rejoicer** n. **rejoicingly** adv. [ME f. OF *rejoir rejoiss-* (as RE-, JOY)]

rejoin[1] /riːˈdʒɔɪn/ v. **1** tr. & intr. join together again; reunite. **2** tr. join (a companion etc.) again.

rejoin[2] /rɪˈdʒɔɪn/ v. **1** tr. say in answer, retort. **2** intr. *Law* reply to a charge or pleading in a lawsuit. [ME f. OF *rejoindre rejoign-* (as RE-, JOIN)]

rejoinder /rɪˈdʒɔɪndə(r)/ n. **1** what is said in reply. **2** a retort. [AF *rejoinder* (unrecorded: as REJOIN[2])]

rejuvenate /rɪˈdʒuːvɪˌneɪt/ v.tr. make young or as if young again. □ **rejuvenation** /-ˈneɪʃ(ə)n/ n. **rejuvenator** n. [RE- + L *juvenis* young]

rekindle /riːˈkɪnd(ə)l/ v.tr. & intr. kindle again.

relabel /riːˈleɪb(ə)l/ v.tr. (**relabelled, relabelling**; US **relabeled, relabeling**) label (esp. a commodity) again or differently.

relapse /rɪˈlæps/ v. & n. —v.intr. (usu. foll. by *into*) fall back or sink again (into a worse state after an improvement). —n. /also ˈriː-/ the act or an instance of relapsing, esp. a deterioration in a patient's condition after a partial recovery. □ **relapser** n. [L *relabi relaps-* (as RE-, *labi* slip)]

relate /rɪˈleɪt/ v. **1** tr. narrate or recount (incidents, a story, etc.). **2** tr. (in *passive*; often foll. by *to*) be connected by blood or marriage. **3** tr. (usu. foll. by *to, with*) bring into relation (with one another); establish a connection between (*cannot relate your opinion to my own experience*). **4** intr. (foll. by *to*) have reference to; concern (*see only what relates to themselves*). **5** intr. (foll. by *to*) bring oneself into relation to; associate with. □ **relatable** adj. [L *referre relat-* bring back: see REFER]

related /rɪˈleɪtɪd/ adj. connected, esp. by blood or marriage. □ **relatedness** n.

relation /rɪˈleɪʃ(ə)n/ n. **1 a** what one person or thing has to do with another. **b** the way in which one person stands or is related to another. **c** the existence or effect of a connection, correspondence, contrast, or feeling prevailing between persons or things, esp. when qualified in some way (*bears no relation to the facts; enjoyed good relations for many years*). **2** a relative; a kinsman or kinswoman. **3** (in *pl.*) **a** (foll. by *with*) dealings (with others). **b** sexual intercourse. **4** = RELATIONSHIP. **5 a** narration (*his relation of the events*). **b** a narrative. □ **in relation to** as regards. [ME f. OF *relation* or L *relatio* (as RELATE)]

relational /rɪˈleɪʃən(ə)l/ adj. **1** of, belonging to, or characterized by relation. **2** having relation. □ **relational database** *Computing* a database structured to recognize the relation of stored items of information.

relationship /rɪˈleɪʃ(ə)nʃɪp/ n. **1** the fact or state of being related. **2** *colloq.* **a** a connection or association (*enjoyed a good working relationship*). **b** an emotional (esp. sexual) association between two people. **3** a condition or character due to being related. **4** kinship.

relative /ˈrelətɪv/ adj. & n. —adj. **1** considered or having significance in relation to something else (*relative velocity*). **2** (foll. by *to*) having existence only as perceived or considered by. **3** (foll. by *to*) proportioned to (something else) (*growth is relative to input*). **4** implying comparison or contextual relation (*'heat' is a relative word*). **5** comparative; compared one with another (*their relative advantages*). **6** having mutual relations; corresponding in some way; related to each other. **7** (foll. by *to*) having reference or relating (*the facts relative to the issue*). **8** involving a different but corresponding idea (*the concepts of husband and wife are relative to each other*). **9** *Gram.* **a** (of a word, esp. a pronoun) referring to an expressed or implied antecedent and attaching a subordinate clause to it, e.g. *which, who.* **b** (of a clause) attached to an antecedent by a relative word. —n. **1** a person connected by blood or marriage. **2** a species related to another by common origin (*the apes, man's closest relatives*). **3** *Gram.* a relative word, esp. a pronoun. □ **relatival** /-ˈtaɪv(ə)l/ adj. (in sense 3 of n.). **relatively** adv. **relativeness** n. [ME f. OF *relatif -ive* or LL *relativus* having reference or relation (as RELATE)]

relativism /ˈrelətɪˌvɪz(ə)m/ n. the doctrine that knowledge is relative, not absolute. □ **relativist** n.

relativistic /ˌrelətɪˈvɪstɪk/ adj. Physics (of phenomena etc.) accurately described only by the theory of relativity. □ **relativistically** adv.

relativity /ˌreləˈtɪvɪtɪ/ n. **1** the fact or state of being relative. **2** Physics **a** (**special theory of relativity**) a theory based on the principle that all motion is relative and that light has constant velocity. **b** (**general theory of relativity**) a theory extending this to gravitation and accelerated motion.

relax /rɪˈlæks/ v. **1** tr. & intr. make or become less stiff or rigid or tense. **2** tr. & intr. make or become less formal or strict (rules were relaxed). **3** tr. reduce or abate (one's attention, efforts, etc.). **4** intr. cease work or effort. **5** tr. (as **relaxed** adj.) at ease; unperturbed. □ **relaxedly** adv. **relaxedness** n. **relaxer** n. [ME f. L relaxare (as RE-, LAX)]

relaxant /rɪˈlæks(ə)nt/ n. & adj. —n. a drug etc. that relaxes and reduces tension. —adj. causing relaxation.

relaxation /ˌriːlækˈseɪʃ(ə)n/ n. **1** the act of relaxing or state of being relaxed. **2** recreation or rest, esp. after a period of work. **3** a partial remission or relaxing of a penalty, duty, etc. **4** a lessening of severity, precision, etc. [L relaxatio (as RELAX)]

relay /ˈriːleɪ/ n. & v. —n. **1** a fresh set of people or horses substituted for tired ones. **2** a gang of workers, supply of material, etc., deployed on the same basis (operated in relays). **3** = relay race. **4** a device activating changes in an electric circuit etc. in response to other changes affecting itself. **5 a** a device to receive, reinforce, and transmit a telegraph message, broadcast programme, etc. **b** a relayed message or transmission. —v.tr. /ˈriːleɪ, rɪˈleɪ/ **1** receive (a message, broadcast, etc.) and transmit it to others. **2** arrange in relays. **b** provide with or replace by relays. □ **relay race** a race between teams of which each member in turn covers part of the distance. [ME f. OF relai (n.), relayer (v.) (as RE-, laier ult. f. L laxare; cf. RELAX]

re-lay /riːˈleɪ/ v.tr. (past and past part. **re-laid**) lay again or differently.

release /rɪˈliːs/ v. & n. —v.tr. **1** (often foll. by from) set free; liberate, unfasten. **2** allow to move from a fixed position. **3 a** make (information, a recording, etc.) publicly or generally available. **b** issue (a film etc.) for general exhibition. **4** Law make over (property or money) to another. —n. **1** deliverance or liberation from a restriction, duty, or difficulty. **2** a handle or catch that releases part of a mechanism. **3** a document or item of information made available for publication (press release). **4 a** a film or record etc. that is released. **b** the act or an instance of releasing or the process of being released in this way. **5** Law the act of releasing (property, money, or a right) to another. □ **releasable** adj. **releasee** /-ˈsiː/ n. (in sense 4 of v.). **releaser** n. **releasor** n. (in sense 4 of v.). [ME f. OF reles (n.), relesser (v.), relaiss(i)er f. L relaxare: see RELAX]

relegate /ˈrelɪˌgeɪt/ v.tr. **1** consign or dismiss to an inferior or less important position; demote. **2** transfer (a sports team) to a lower division of a league etc. □ **relegable** adj. **relegation** /-ˈgeɪʃ(ə)n/ n. [L relegare relegat- (as RE-, legare send)]

relent /rɪˈlent/ v.intr. **1** abandon a harsh intention. **2** yield to compassion. **3** relax one's

severity; become less stern. [ME f. med.L relentare (unrecorded), formed as RE- + L lentāre bend f. lentus flexible]

relentless /rɪˈlentlɪs/ adj. **1** unrelenting; insistent and uncompromising. **2** continuous; oppressively constant. □ **relentlessly** adv. **relentlessness** n.

re-let /riːˈlet/ v.tr. (**-letting**; past and past part. **-let**) let (a property) for a further period or to a new tenant.

relevant /ˈrelɪv(ə)nt/ adj. (often foll. by to) bearing on or having reference to the matter in hand. □ **relevance** n. **relevancy** n. **relevantly** adv. [med.L relevans, part. of L relevare RELIEVE]

reliable /rɪˈlaɪəb(ə)l/ adj. **1** that may be relied on. **2** of sound and consistent character or quality. □ **reliability** /-ˈbɪlɪtɪ/ n. **reliableness** n. **reliably** adv.

reliance /rɪˈlaɪəns/ n. **1** (foll. by in, on) trust, confidence (put full reliance in you). **2** a thing relied upon. □ **reliant** adj.

relic /ˈrelɪk/ n. **1** an object interesting because of its age or association. **2** a part of a deceased holy person's body or belongings kept as an object of reverence. **3** a surviving custom or belief etc. from a past age. **4** a memento or souvenir. [ME relike, relique, etc. f. OF relique f. L reliquiae (as RE-, linquere liq- leave)]

relict /ˈrelɪkt/ n. a geological or other object surviving in its primitive form. [L relinquere relict- leave behind (as RE-, linquere leave)]

relief /rɪˈliːf/ n. **1 a** the alleviation of or deliverance from pain, distress, anxiety, etc. **b** the feeling accompanying such deliverance. **2** a feature etc. that diversifies monotony or relaxes tension. **3** assistance (esp. financial) given to those in special need or difficulty (rent relief). **4 a** the replacing of a person or persons on duty by another or others. **b** a person or persons replacing others in this way. **5** (usu. attrib.) a thing supplementing another in some service, esp. an extra vehicle providing public transport at peak times. **6** a method of moulding or carving or stamping in which the design stands out from the surface, with projections proportioned and more (**high relief**) or less (**low relief**) closely approximating to those of the objects depicted. **7** vividness, distinctness (brings the facts out in sharp relief). **8** (foll. by of) the reinforcement (esp. the raising of a siege) of a place. □ **relief map** a map indicating hills and valleys by shading etc. rather than by contour lines alone. **relief road** a road taking traffic around a congested (esp. urban) area. [ME f. AF relef, OF relief (in sense 6 F relief f. It. rilievo) f. relever: see RELIEVE]

relieve /rɪˈliːv/ v.tr. **1** bring or provide aid or assistance to. **2** alleviate or reduce (pain, suffering, etc.). **3** mitigate the tedium or monotony of. **4** bring military support for (a besieged place). **5** release (a person) from a duty by acting as or providing a substitute. **6** (foll. by of) take (a burden or responsibility) away from (a person). **7** bring into relief; cause to appear solid or detached. □ **relieve one's feelings** use strong language or vigorous behaviour when annoyed. **relieve oneself** urinate or defecate. □ **relievable** adj. **reliever** n. [ME f. OF relever f. L relevare (as RE-, levis light)]

relieved /rɪˈliːvd/ predic.adj. freed from anxiety or distress (am very relieved to hear it). □ **relievedly** adv.

relievo /rɪˈliːvəʊ/ n. (also **rilievo** /riːˈljeɪvəʊ/) (pl. **-os**) = RELIEF 6. [It. rilievo RELIEF 6]

religio- /rɪˈlɪgɪəʊ, rɪˈlɪdʒɪəʊ/ comb. form 1 religion. 2 religious.

religion /rɪˈlɪdʒ(ə)n/ n. 1 the belief in a superhuman controlling power, esp. in a personal God or gods entitled to obedience and worship. 2 the expression of this in worship. 3 a particular system of faith and worship. 4 life under monastic vows (the way of religion). □ **religionless** adj. [ME f. AF religiun, OF religion f. L religio -onis obligation, bond, reverence]

religiose /rɪˈlɪdʒɪəʊs/ adj. excessively religious. [L religiosus (as RELIGIOUS)]

religiosity /rɪˌlɪdʒɪˈɒsɪtɪ/ n. the condition of being religious or religiose. [ME f. L religiositas (as RELIGIOUS)]

religious /rɪˈlɪdʒəs/ adj. & n. —adj. 1 devoted to religion; pious, devout. 2 of or concerned with religion. 3 of or belonging to a monastic order. 4 scrupulous, conscientious (a religious attention to detail). —n. (pl. same) a person bound by monastic vows. □ **religiously** adv. **religiousness** n. [ME f. AF religius, OF religious f. L religiosus (as RELIGION)]

reline /riːˈlaɪn/ v.tr. renew the lining of (a garment etc.).

relinquish /rɪˈlɪŋkwɪʃ/ v.tr. 1 surrender or resign (a right or possession). 2 give up or cease from (a habit, plan, belief, etc.). 3 relax hold of (an object held). □ **relinquishment** n. [ME f. OF relinquir f. L relinquere (as RE-, linquere leave)]

reliquary /ˈrelɪkwərɪ/ n. (pl. **-ies**) esp. Relig. a receptacle for relics. [F reliquaire (as RELIC)]

relish /ˈrelɪʃ/ n. & v. —n. 1 (often foll. by for) a great liking or enjoyment. 2 keen or pleasurable longing (had no relish for travelling). 2 **a** an appetizing flavour. **b** an attractive quality (fishing loses its relish in winter). 3 a condiment eaten with plainer food to add flavour, esp. a piquant sauce, pickle, etc. —v.tr. 1 **a** get pleasure out of; enjoy greatly. **b** look forward to, anticipate with pleasure (did not relish what lay before her). 2 add relish to. □ **relishable** adj. [alt. (with assim. to -ISH²) of obs. reles f. OF reles, relais remainder f. relaisser: see RELEASE]

relive /riːˈlɪv/ v.tr. live (an experience etc.) over again, esp. in the imagination.

reload /riːˈləʊd/ v.tr. (also absol.) load (esp. a gun) again.

relocate /ˌriːləʊˈkeɪt/ v. 1 tr. locate in a new place. 2 tr. & intr. move to a new place (esp. to live or work). □ **relocation** /-ˈkeɪʃən/ n.

reluctant /rɪˈlʌkt(ə)nt/ adj. (often foll. by to + infin.) unwilling or disinclined (most reluctant to agree). □ **reluctance** n. **reluctantly** adv. [L reluctari (as RE-, luctari struggle)]

rely /rɪˈlaɪ/ v.intr. (**-ies**, **-ied**) (foll. by on, upon) 1 depend on with confidence or assurance (am relying on your judgement). 2 be dependent on (relies on her for everything). [ME (earlier senses 'rally, be a vassal of') f. OF relier bind together f. L religare (as RE-, ligare bind)]

REM abbr. rapid eye-movement.

rem /rem/ n. (pl. same) a unit of effective absorbed dose of ionizing radiation in human tissue. [roentgen equivalent man]

remade past and past part. of REMAKE.

remain /rɪˈmeɪn/ v.intr. 1 be left over after others or other parts have been removed or used or dealt with. 2 be in the same place or condition during further time; continue to exist or stay; be left behind (remained at home; it will remain cold). 3 (foll. by compl.) continue to be (remained calm; remains President). [ME f. OF remain- stressed stem of remanoir or f. OF remaindre ult. f. L remanēre (as RE-, manēre stay)]

remainder /rɪˈmeɪndə(r)/ n. & v. —n. 1 a part remaining or left over. 2 remaining persons or things. 3 a number left after division or subtraction. 4 the copies of a book left unsold when demand has fallen. —v.tr. dispose of (a remainder of books) at a reduced price. [ME f. AF, = OF remaindre: see REMAIN]

remains /rɪˈmeɪnz/ n.pl. 1 what remains after other parts have been removed or used etc. 2 relics of antiquity, esp. of buildings (Roman remains). 3 a person's body after death.

remake v. & n. —v.tr. /riːˈmeɪk/ (past and past part. **remade**) make again or differently. —n. /ˈriːmeɪk/ a thing that has been remade, esp. a cinema film.

remand /rɪˈmɑːnd/ v. & n. —v.tr. return (a prisoner) to custody, esp. to allow further inquiries to be made. —n. a recommittal to custody. □ **on remand** in custody pending trial. [ME f. LL remandare (as RE-, mandare commit)]

remark /rɪˈmɑːk/ v. & n. —v. 1 tr. (often foll. by that + clause) **a** say by way of comment. **b** take notice of; regard with attention. 2 intr. (usu. foll. by on, upon) make a comment. —n. 1 a written or spoken comment; anything said. 2 **a** the act of noticing or observing (worthy of remark). **b** the act of commenting (let it pass without remark). [F remarque, remarquer (as RE-, MARK¹)]

remarkable /rɪˈmɑːkəb(ə)l/ adj. 1 worth notice; exceptional. 2 striking, conspicuous. □ **remarkableness** n. **remarkably** adv. [F remarquable (as REMARK)]

remarry /riːˈmærɪ/ v.intr. & tr. (**-ies**, **-ied**) marry again. □ **remarriage** n.

remaster /riːˈmɑːstə(r)/ v.tr. make a new master of (a recording), esp. to improve the sound quality.

rematch /ˈriːmætʃ/ n. a return match or game.

REME /ˈriːmiː/ abbr. (in the UK) Royal Electrical and Mechanical Engineers.

remedial /rɪˈmiːdɪəl/ adj. 1 affording or intended as a remedy (remedial therapy). 2 (of teaching) for slow or backward children. □ **remedially** adv. [LL remedialis f. L remedium (as REMEDY)]

remedy /ˈremɪdɪ/ n. & v. —n. (pl. **-ies**) (often foll. by for, against) 1 a medicine or treatment (for a disease etc.). 2 a means of counteracting or removing anything undesirable. 3 redress; legal or other reparation. —v.tr. (**-ies**, **-ied**) rectify; make good. □ **remediable** /rɪˈmiːdɪəb(ə)l/ adj. [ME f. AF remedie, OF remede or L remedium (as RE-, medēri heal)]

remember /rɪˈmembə(r)/ v.tr. 1 keep in the memory; not forget. 2 **a** (also absol.) bring back into one's thoughts, call to mind (knowledge or experience etc.). **b** (often foll. by to + infin. or that + clause) have in mind (a duty, commitment, etc.) (will you remember to lock the door?). 3 think of or acknowledge (a person) in some connection, esp. in making a gift etc. 4 (foll. by to) convey greetings from (one person) to (another) (*remember me to your mother*). **5** mention (in prayer). □ **rememberer** *n*. [ME f. OF *remembrer* f. LL *rememorari* (as RE-, L *memor* mindful)]

remembrance /rɪˈmembrəns/ *n*. **1** the act of remembering or process of being remembered. **2** a memory or recollection. **3** a keepsake or souvenir. **4** (in *pl*.) greetings conveyed through a third person. □ **Remembrance Day 1** = *Remembrance Sunday*. **2** *hist*. Armistice Day. **Remembrance Sunday** (in the UK) the Sunday nearest 11 Nov., when those who were killed in the wars of 1914–18 and 1939–45 are commemorated. [ME f. OF (as REMEMBER)]

remind /rɪˈmaɪnd/ *v.tr*. **1** (foll. by *of*) cause (a person) to remember or think of. **2** (foll. by *to* + infin. or *that* + clause) cause (a person) to remember (a commitment etc.).

reminder /rɪˈmaɪndə(r)/ *n*. **1** a thing that reminds, esp. a letter or bill. **2** (often foll. by *of*) a memento or souvenir.

reminisce /ˌremɪˈnɪs/ *v.intr*. indulge in reminiscence. □ **reminiscer** *n*. [back-form. f. REMINISCENCE]

reminiscence /ˌremɪˈnɪs(ə)ns/ *n*. **1** the act of remembering things past; the recovery of knowledge by mental effort. **2 a** a past fact or experience that is remembered. **b** the process of narrating this. **3** (in *pl*.) a collection in literary form of incidents and experiences that a person remembers. □ **reminiscential** /-ˈsenʃ(ə)l/ *adj*. [LL *reminiscentia* f. L *reminisci* remember]

reminiscent /ˌremɪˈnɪs(ə)nt/ *adj*. **1** (foll. by *of*) tending to remind one of or suggest. **2** concerned with reminiscence. **3** (of a person) given to reminiscing. □ **reminiscently** *adv*.

remiss /rɪˈmɪs/ *adj*. careless of duty; lax, negligent. □ **remissly** *adv*. **remissness** *n*. [ME f. L *remissus* past part. of *remittere* slacken: see REMIT]

remission /rɪˈmɪʃ(ə)n/ *n*. **1** the reduction of a prison sentence on account of good behaviour. **2** the remitting of a debt or penalty etc. **3** a diminution of force, effect, or degree (esp. of disease or pain). **4** (often foll. by *of*) forgiveness (of sins etc.). □ **remissive** *adj*. [ME f. OF *remission* or L *remissio* (as REMIT)]

remit *v*. & *n*. —*v*. /rɪˈmɪt/ (**remitted, remitting**) **1** *tr*. cancel or refrain from exacting or inflicting (a debt or punishment etc.). **2** *intr*. & *tr*. abate or slacken; cease or cease from partly or entirely. **3** *tr*. send (money etc.) in payment. **4** *tr*. **a** (foll. by *to*) refer (a matter for decision etc.) to some authority. **b** *Law* send back (a case) to a lower court. **5** *tr*. (often foll. by *to*) postpone or defer. **6** *tr*. *Theol*. (usu. of God) pardon (sins etc.). —*n*. /ˈriːmɪt, rɪˈmɪt/ **1** the terms of reference of a committee etc. **2** an item remitted for consideration. □ **remittable** /rɪˈmɪtəb(ə)l/ *adj*. **remittal** /rɪˈmɪt(ə)l/ *n*. **remittee** /rɪmɪˈtiː/ *n*. **remitter** /rɪˈmɪtə(r)/ *n*. [ME f. L *remittere remiss-* (as RE-, *mittere* send)]

remittance /rɪˈmɪt(ə)ns/ *n*. **1** money sent, esp. by post, for goods or services or as an allowance. **2** the act of sending money.

remix *v*. & *n*. —*v.tr*. /riːˈmɪks/ mix again. —*n*. /ˈriːmɪks/ a sound recording that has been remixed.

remnant /ˈremnənt/ *n*. **1** a small remaining quantity. **2** a piece of cloth etc. left when the greater part has been used or sold. **3** (foll. by *of*) a surviving trace (*a remnant of empire*). [ME

(earlier *remenant*) f. OF *remenant* f. *remenoir* REMAIN]

remodel /riːˈmɒd(ə)l/ *v.tr*. (**remodelled, remodelling**; *US* **remodeled, remodeling**) **1** model again or differently. **2** reconstruct.

remonstrance /rɪˈmɒnstrəns/ *n*. **1** the act or an instance of remonstrating. **2** an expostulation or protest. [ME f. obs. F *remonstrance* or med.L *remonstrantia* (as REMONSTRATE)]

remonstrate /ˈremənˌstreɪt/ *v*. **1** *intr*. (foll. by *with*) make a protest; argue forcibly (*remonstrated with them over the delays*). **2** *tr*. (often foll. by *that* + clause) urge protestingly. □ **remonstrant** /rɪˈmɒnstrənt/ *adj*. **remonstration** /-ˈstreɪʃ(ə)n/ *n*. **remonstrative** /rɪˈmɒnstrətɪv/ *adj*. **remonstrator** *n*. [med.L *remonstrare* (as RE-, *monstrare* show)]

remorse /rɪˈmɔːs/ *n*. **1** deep regret for a wrong committed. **2** compunction; a compassionate reluctance to inflict pain (esp. in *without remorse*). [ME f. OF *remors* f. med.L *remorsus* f. L *remordēre remors-* vex (as RE-, *mordēre* bite)]

remorseful /rɪˈmɔːsfʊl/ *adj*. filled with repentance. □ **remorsefully** *adv*.

remorseless /rɪˈmɔːslɪs/ *adj*. without compassion or compunction. □ **remorselessly** *adv*. **remorselessness** *n*.

remortgage /riːˈmɔːɡɪdʒ/ *v*. & *n*. —*v.tr*. (also *absol*.) mortgage again; revise the terms of an existing mortgage on (a property). —*n*. a different or altered mortgage.

remote /rɪˈməʊt/ *adj*. (**remoter, remotest**) **1** far away in place or time. **2** out of the way; situated away from the main centres of population, society, etc. **3** distantly related (*a remote ancestor*). **4** slight, faint (esp. in *not the remotest chance, idea,* etc.). **5** (of a person) aloof; not friendly. **6** (foll. by *from*) widely different; separate by nature (*ideas remote from the subject*). □ **remote control** control of a machine or apparatus from a distance by means of signals transmitted from a radio or electronic device. **remote-controlled** (of a machine etc.) controlled at a distance. □ **remotely** *adv*. **remoteness** *n*. [ME f. L *remotus* (as REMOVE)]

remould *v*. & *n*. (*US* **remold**) —*v.tr*. /riːˈməʊld/ **1** mould again; refashion. **2** re-form the tread of (a tyre). —*n*. /ˈriːməʊld/ a remoulded tyre.

remount *v*. & *n*. —*v*. /riːˈmaʊnt/ **1 a** *tr*. mount (a horse etc.) again. **b** *intr*. get on horseback again. **2** *tr*. get on to or ascend (a ladder, hill, etc.) again. **3** *tr*. provide (a person) with a fresh horse etc. **4** *tr*. put (a picture) on a fresh mount. —*n*. /ˈriːmaʊnt/ **1** a fresh horse for a rider. **2** a supply of fresh horses for a regiment.

removal /rɪˈmuːv(ə)l/ *n*. **1** the act or an instance of removing; the process of being removed. **2** the transfer of furniture and other contents on moving house.

remove /rɪˈmuːv/ *v*. & *n*. —*v*. **1** *tr*. take off or away from the place or position occupied (*remove the top carefully*). **2** *tr*. **a** move or take to another place; change the situation of (*will you remove the tea things?*). **b** get rid of; eliminate (*will remove all doubts*). **3** *tr*. cause to be no longer present or available; take away (*all privileges were removed*). **4** *tr*. (often foll. by *from*) dismiss (from office). **5** *tr*. (in *passive*; foll. by *from*) distant or remote in condition (*the country is not far removed from anarchy*). **6** *tr*. (as **removed** *adj*.) (esp. of cousins) separated by a specified number of steps of descent (a first cousin twice removed = a grand-child of a first cousin). —n. 1 a degree or remoteness; a distance. 2 a stage in a gradation; a degree (is several removes from what I expected). 3 Brit. a form or division in some schools. □ **removable** adj. **removability** /-'bɪlɪtɪ/ n. **remover** n. [ME f. OF removeir f. L removēre remot- (as RE-, movēre move)]

remunerate /rɪ'mjuːnəˌreɪt/ v.tr. 1 reward; pay for services rendered. 2 serve as or provide recompense for (toil etc.) or to (a person). □ **remuneration** /-'reɪʃ(ə)n/ n. **remunerative** /-rətɪv/ adj. **remuneratory** /-rətərɪ/ adj. [L remunerari (as RE-, munus muneris gift)]

Renaissance /rɪ'neɪs(ə)ns, rə'n-, -sɑ̃s/ n. 1 the revival of art and literature under the influence of classical models in the 14th–16th c. 2 the period of this. 3 the culture and style of art, architecture, etc. developed during this era. 4 (**renaissance**) any similar revival. [F renaissance (as RE-, F naissance birth f. L nascentia or F naître naiss- be born f. Rmc: cf. NASCENT)]

renal /'riːn(ə)l/ adj. of or concerning the kidneys. [F rénal f. LL renalis f. L renes kidneys]

rename /riː'neɪm/ v.tr. name again; give a new name to.

renascence /rɪ'næs(ə)ns/ n. 1 rebirth; renewal. 2 = RENAISSANCE. [RENASCENT]

renascent /rɪ'næs(ə)nt/ adj. springing up anew; being reborn. [L renasci (as RE-, nasci be born)]

rend v. (past and past part. **rent**) archaic or rhet. 1 tr. (foll. by off, from, away, etc.; also absol.) tear or wrench forcibly. 2 tr. & intr. split or divide in pieces or into factions (a country rent by civil war). 3 tr. cause emotional pain to (the heart etc.). [OE rendan, rel. to MLG rende]

render /'rendə(r)/ v.tr. 1 cause to be or become; make (rendered us helpless). 2 give or pay (money, service, etc.), esp. in return for or as a thing due (render thanks; rendered good for evil). 3 (often foll. by to) **a** give (assistance) (rendered aid to the injured man). **b** show (obedience etc.). **c** do (a service etc.). 4 submit; send in; present (an account, reason, etc.). 5 **a** represent or portray artistically, musically, etc. **b** act (a role); represent (a character, idea, etc.) (the dramatist's conception was well rendered). **c** Mus. perform; execute. 6 translate (rendered the poem into French). 7 (often foll. by down) melt down (fat etc.) esp. to clarify; extract by melting. 8 cover (stone or brick) with a coat of plaster. 9 archaic **a** give back; hand over; deliver, give up, surrender (render to Caesar the things that are Caesar's). **b** show (obedience). □ **renderer** n. [ME f. OF rendre ult. f. L reddere reddit- (as RE-, dare give)]

rendering /'rendərɪŋ/ n. 1 **a** the act or an instance of performing music, drama, etc.; an interpretation or performance (an excellent rendering of the part). **b** a translation. 2 **a** the act or an instance of plastering stone, brick, etc. **b** this coating.

rendezvous /'rɒndɪˌvuː, -deɪˌvuː/ n. & v. —n. (pl. same /-ˌvuːz/) 1 an agreed or regular meeting-place. 2 a meeting by arrangement. 3 a place appointed for assembling troops, ships, etc. —v.intr. (**rendezvouses** /-ˌvuːz/; **rendezvoused** /-ˌvuːd/; **rendezvousing** /-ˌvuːɪŋ/) meet at a rendezvous. [F rendez-vous present yourselves f. rendre: see RENDER]

rendition /ren'dɪʃ(ə)n/ n. (often foll. by of) an interpretation or rendering of a dramatic role, piece of music, etc. [obs. F f. rendre RENDER]

renegade /'renɪˌgeɪd/ n. a person who deserts a party or principles. [Sp. renegado f. med.L renegatus (as RE-, L negare deny)]

renege /rɪ'niːg, -'neg, -'neɪg/ v. (also **renegue**) 1 intr. **a** go back on one's word; change one's mind; recant. **b** (foll. by on) go back on (a promise or undertaking or contract). 2 tr. deny, renounce, abandon (a person, faith, etc.). 3 intr. Cards revoke. □ **reneger** n. **reneguer** n. [med.L renegare (as RE-, L negare deny)]

renegotiate /ˌriːnɪ'gəʊʃɪˌeɪt/ v.tr. (also absol.) negotiate again or on different terms. □ **renegotiable** adj. **renegotiation** /-'eɪʃ(ə)n/ n.

renew /rɪ'njuː/ v.tr. 1 revive; regenerate; make new again; restore to the original state. 2 reinforce; resupply; replace. 3 repeat or re-establish; resume after an interruption (renewed our acquaintance; a renewed attack). 4 get, begin, make, say, give, etc. anew. 5 (also absol.) grant or be granted a continuation of or continued validity of (a licence, subscription, lease, etc.). 6 recover (one's youth, strength, etc.). □ **renewable** adj. **renewability** /-ə'bɪlɪtɪ/ n. **renewal** n. **renewer** n.

rennet /'renɪt/ n. 1 curdled milk found in the stomach of an unweaned calf, used in curdling milk for cheese, junket, etc. 2 a preparation made from the stomach-membrane of a calf or from certain fungi, used for the same purpose. [ME, prob. f. an OE form rynet (unrecorded), rel. to RUN]

renounce /rɪ'naʊns/ v. 1 tr. consent formally to abandon; surrender; give up (a claim, right, possession, etc.). 2 tr. repudiate; refuse to recognize any longer (renouncing their father's authority). 3 tr. **a** decline further association or disclaim relationship with (renounced my former friends). **b** withdraw from; discontinue; forsake. □ **renounceable** adj. **renouncement** n. **renouncer** n. [ME f. OF renoncer f. L renuntiare (as RE-, nuntiare announce)]

renovate /'renəˌveɪt/ v.tr. 1 restore to good condition; repair. 2 make new again. □ **renovation** /-'veɪʃ(ə)n/ n. **renovative** adj. **renovator** n. [L renovare (as RE-, novus new)]

renown /rɪ'naʊn/ n. fame; high distinction; celebrity (a city of great renown). [ME f. AF ren(o)un, OF renon, renom f. renomer make famous (as RE-, L nominare NOMINATE)]

renowned /rɪ'naʊnd/ adj. famous; celebrated.

rent[1] n. & v. —n. 1 a tenant's periodical payment to an owner or landlord for the use of land or premises. 2 payment for the use of a service, equipment, etc. —v. 1 tr. (often foll. by from) take, occupy, or use at a rent (rented a cottage from the local farmer). 2 tr. (often foll. by out) let or hire (a thing) for rent. 3 intr. (foll. by at) be let or hired out at a specified rate (the land rents at £100 per month). □ **rent-boy** a young male prostitute. [ME f. OF rente f. Rmc (as RENDER)]

rent[2] n. 1 a large tear in a garment etc. 2 an opening in clouds etc. [obs. rent var. of REND]

rent[3] past and past part. of REND.

rental /'rent(ə)l/ n. 1 the amount paid or received as rent. 2 the act of renting. 3 an income from rents. 4 US a rented house etc. [ME f. AF rental or AL rentale (as RENT[1])]

renumber /riːˈnʌmbə(r)/ v.tr. change the number or numbers given or allocated to.

renunciation /rɪˌnʌnsɪˈeɪʃ(ə)n/ n. **1** the act or an instance of renouncing or giving up. **2** self-denial. **3** a document expressing renunciation. □ **renunciant** /rɪˈnʌnsɪənt/ n. & adj. **renunciative** /rɪˈnʌnsɪətɪv/ adj. **renunciatory** /rɪˈnʌnʃətərɪ/ adj. [ME f. OF renonciation or LL renuntiatio (as RENOUNCE)]

reoccupy /riːˈɒkjʊˌpaɪ/ v.tr. (-ies, -ied) occupy again. □ **reoccupation** /-ˈpeɪʃ(ə)n/ n.

reoccur /ˌriːəˈkɜː(r)/ v.intr. (**reoccurred, reoccurring**) occur again or habitually. □ **reoccurrence** /-ˈkʌrəns/ n.

reopen /riːˈəʊpən/ v.tr. & intr. open again.

reorder /riːˈɔːdə(r)/ v. & n. —v.tr. order again. —n. a renewed or repeated order for goods.

reorganize /riːˈɔːgəˌnaɪz/ v.tr. (also **-ise**) organize differently. □ **reorganization** /-ˈzeɪʃ(ə)n/ n. **reorganizer** n.

reorient /riːˈɔːrɪˌent, -ˈɒrɪˌent/ v.tr. **1** give a new direction to (ideas etc.); redirect (a thing). **2** help (a person) find his or her bearings again. **3** change the outlook of (a person). **4** (refl., often foll. by to) adjust oneself to or come to terms with something.

reorientate /riːˈɔːrɪənˌteɪt/ v.tr. = REORIENT. □ **reorientation** /-ˈteɪʃ(ə)n/ n.

rep[1] n. colloq. a representative, esp. a commercial traveller. [abbr.]

rep[2] n. colloq. **1** repertory. **2** a repertory theatre or company. [abbr.]

rep[3] n. (also **repp**) a textile fabric with a corded surface, used in curtains and upholstery. [F reps, of unkn. orig.]

repack /riːˈpæk/ v.tr. pack again.

repackage /riːˈpækɪdʒ/ v.tr. **1** package again or differently. **2** present in a new form. □ **repackaging** n.

repaginate /riːˈpædʒɪˌneɪt/ v.tr. paginate again; renumber the pages of. □ **repagination** /-ˈneɪʃ(ə)n/ n.

repaid past and past part. of REPAY.

repaint v. & n. —v.tr. /riːˈpeɪnt/ **1** paint again or differently. **2** restore the paint or colouring of. —n. /ˈriːpeɪnt/ **1** the act of repainting. **2** a repainted thing.

repair[1] /rɪˈpeə(r)/ v. & n. —v.tr. **1** restore to good condition after damage or wear. **2** renovate or mend by replacing or fixing parts or by compensating for loss or exhaustion. **3** set right or make amends for (loss, wrong, error, etc.). —n. **1** the act or an instance of restoring to sound condition (in need of repair; closed during repair). **2** the result of this (the repair is hardly visible). **3** good or relative condition for working or using (must be kept in repair; in good repair). □ **repairable** adj. **repairer** n. [ME f. OF reparer f. L reparare (as RE-, parare make ready)]

repair[2] /rɪˈpeə(r)/ v.intr. (foll. by to) resort; have recourse; go often or in great numbers or for a specific purpose (repaired to Spain). [ME f. OF repaire(r) f. LL repatriare REPATRIATE]

repairman /rɪˈpeəmən/ n. (pl. **-men**) a man who repairs machinery etc.

repaper /riːˈpeɪpə(r)/ v.tr. paper (a wall etc.) again.

reparable /ˈrepərəb(ə)l/ adj. (of a loss etc.) that can be made good. □ **reparability** /-ˈbɪlɪtɪ/ n. **reparably** adv. [F f. L reparabilis (as REPAIR[1])]

reparation /ˌrepəˈreɪʃ(ə)n/ n. **1** the act or an instance of making amends. **2 a** compensation. **b** (esp. in pl.) compensation for war damage paid by the defeated State. **3** the act or an instance of repairing or being repaired. □ **reparative** /ˈrepərətɪv, rɪˈpærətɪv/ adj. [ME f. OF f. LL reparatio -onis (as REPAIR[1])]

repartee /ˌrepɑːˈtiː/ n. **1** the practice or faculty of making witty retorts; sharpness or wit in quick reply. **2 a** a witty retort. **b** witty retorts collectively. [F repartie fem. past part. of repartir start again, reply promptly (as RE-, partir PART)]

repast /rɪˈpɑːst/ n. formal **1** a meal, esp. of a specified kind (a light repast). **2** food and drink supplied for or eaten at a meal. [ME f. OF repaistre f. L repascere repast- feed]

repatriate /riːˈpætrɪˌeɪt/ v. & n. —v. **1** tr. restore (a person) to his or her native land. **2** intr. return to one's own native land. —n. a person who has been repatriated. □ **repatriation** /-ˈeɪʃ(ə)n/ n. [LL repatriare (as RE-, L patria native land)]

repay /riːˈpeɪ/ v. (past and past part. **repaid**) **1** tr. pay back (money). **2** tr. return (a blow, visit, etc.). **3** tr. make repayment to (a person). **4** tr. make return for; requite (a service, action, etc.) (must repay their kindness; the book repays close study). **5** tr. (often foll. by for) give in recompense. **6** intr. make repayment. □ **repayable** adj. **repayment** n. [OF repaier (as RE-, PAY)]

repeal /rɪˈpiːl/ v. & n. —v.tr. revoke, rescind, or annul (a law, act of parliament, etc.). —n. the act or an instance of repealing. □ **repealable** adj. [ME f. AF repeler, OF rapeler (as RE-, APPEAL)]

repeat /rɪˈpiːt/ v. & n. —v. **1** tr. say or do over again. **2** tr. recite, rehearse, report, or reproduce (something from memory) (repeated a poem). **3** tr. imitate (an action etc.). **4** intr. recur; appear again, perhaps several times (a repeating pattern). **5** tr. used for emphasis (am not, repeat not, going). **6** intr. (of food) be tasted intermittently for some time after being swallowed as a result of belching or indigestion. —n. **1 a** the act or an instance of repeating. **b** a thing repeated (often attrib.: repeat prescription). **2** a repeated broadcast. **3** Mus. **a** a passage intended to be repeated. **b** a mark indicating this. **4** a pattern repeated in wallpaper etc. □ **repeat itself** recur in the same form. **repeat oneself** say or do the same thing over again. □ **repeatable** adj. **repeatability** /-ˈbɪlɪtɪ/ n. **repeatedly** adv. [ME f. OF repeter f. L repetere (as RE-, petere seek)]

repeater /rɪˈpiːtə(r)/ n. **1** a person or thing that repeats. **2** a firearm which fires several shots without reloading. **3** a watch or clock which repeats its last strike when required. **4** a device for the automatic re-transmission or amplification of an electrically transmitted message.

repel /rɪˈpel/ v.tr. (**repelled, repelling**) **1** drive back; ward off; repulse. **2** refuse admission or approach or acceptance to (repel an assailant). **3** be repulsive or distasteful to. □ **repeller** n. [ME f. L repellere (as RE-, pellere puls- drive)]

repellent /rɪˈpelənt/ adj. & n. —adj. **1** that repels. **2** disgusting, repulsive. —n. a substance that repels esp. insects etc. □ **repellence** n. **repellency** n. **repellently** adv. [L repellere (as REPEL)]

repent /rɪˈpent/ v. **1** intr. (often foll. by of) feel deep sorrow about one's actions etc. **2** tr. (also absol.) wish one had not done, regret (one's wrong, omission, etc.); resolve not to continue (a wrongdoing etc.). □ **repentance** *n.* **repentant** *adj.* **repenter** *n.* [ME f. OF *repentir* (as RE-, *pentir* ult. f. L *paenitēre*)]

repercussion /ˌriːpəˈkʌʃ(ə)n/ *n.* **1** (often foll. by *of*) an indirect effect or reaction following an event or action (*consider the repercussions of moving*). **2** the recoil after impact. **3** an echo or reverberation. □ **repercussive** /-ˈkʌsɪv/ *adj.* [ME f. OF *repercussion* or L *repercussio* (as RE-, PERCUSSION)]

repertoire /ˈrepətwɑː(r)/ *n.* **1** a stock of pieces etc. that a company or a performer knows or is prepared to give. **2** a stock of regularly performed pieces, regularly used techniques, etc. (*went through his repertoire of excuses*). [F *répertoire* f. LL (as REPERTORY)]

repertory /ˈrepətərɪ/ *n.* (*pl.* **-ies**) **1** = REPERTOIRE. **2** the theatrical performance of various plays for short periods by one company. **3 a** a repertory company. **b** repertory theatres regarded collectively. **4** a store or collection, esp. of information, instances, etc. □ **repertory company** a theatrical company that performs plays from a repertoire. [LL *repertorium* f. L *reperire repert-* find]

repetition /ˌrepɪˈtɪʃ(ə)n/ *n.* **1 a** the act or an instance of repeating or being repeated. **b** the thing repeated. **2** a copy or replica. □ **repetitional** *adj.* **repetitionary** *adj.* [F *répétition* or L *repetitio* (as REPEAT)]

repetitious /ˌrepɪˈtɪʃəs/ *adj.* characterized by repetition, esp. when unnecessary or tiresome. □ **repetitiously** *adv.* **repetitiousness** *n.*

repetitive /rɪˈpetɪtɪv/ *adj.* = REPETITIOUS. □ **repetitively** *adv.* **repetitiveness** *n.*

rephrase /riːˈfreɪz/ *v.tr.* express in an alternative way.

repine /rɪˈpaɪn/ *v.intr.* (often foll. by *at, against*) fret; be discontented. [RE- + PINE[2], after *repent*]

replace /rɪˈpleɪs/ *v.tr.* **1** put back in place. **2** take the place of; succeed; be substituted for. **3** find or provide a substitute for. **4** (often foll. by *with, by*) fill up the place of. **5** (in *passive*, often foll. by *by*) be succeeded or have one's place filled by another; be superseded. □ **replaceable** *adj.* **replacer** *n.*

replacement /rɪˈpleɪsmənt/ *n.* **1** the act or an instance of replacing or being replaced. **2** a person or thing that takes the place of another.

replan /riːˈplæn/ *v.tr.* (**replanned, replanning**) plan again or differently.

replant /riːˈplɑːnt/ *v.tr.* **1** transfer (a plant etc.) to a larger pot, a new site, etc. **2** plant (ground) again; provide with new plants.

replay *v.* & *n.* —*v.tr.* /riːˈpleɪ/ play (a match, recording, etc.) again. —*n.* /ˈriːpleɪ/ the act or an instance of replaying a match, a recording, or a recorded incident in a game etc.

replenish /rɪˈplenɪʃ/ *v.tr.* **1** (often foll. by *with*) fill up again. **2** renew (a supply etc.). **3** (as **replenished** *adj.*) filled; fully stored or stocked; full. □ **replenisher** *n.* **replenishment** *n.* [ME f. OF *replenir* (as RE-, *plenir* f. *plein* full f. L *plenus*)]

replete /rɪˈpliːt/ *adj.* (often foll. by *with*) **1** filled or well-supplied with. **2** gorged; sated. □ **repleteness** *n.* **repletion** *n.* [ME f. OF *replet* *replete* or L *repletus* past part. of *replēre* (as RE-, *plēre plet-* fill)]

replica /ˈreplɪkə/ *n.* **1** a duplicate of a work made by the original artist. **2** a facsimile, an exact copy. **3** a copy or model, esp. on a smaller scale. [It. f. *replicare* REPLY]

replicate /ˈreplɪˌkeɪt/ *v.tr.* **1** repeat (an experiment etc.). **2** make a replica of. □ **replicable** /ˈreplɪkəb(ə)l/ *adj.* (in sense 1 of *v.*). **replicability** /ˌreplɪkəˈbɪlɪtɪ/ *n.* (in sense 1 of *v.*). **replicative** /ˈreplɪkətɪv/ *adj.* [L *replicare* (as RE-, *plicare* fold)]

replication /ˌreplɪˈkeɪʃ(ə)n/ *n.* **1** the act or an instance of copying. **2** a copy. **3** the process by which genetic material or a living organism gives rise to a copy of itself. [ME f. OF *replicacion* f. L *replicatio -onis* (as REPLICATE)]

reply /rɪˈplaɪ/ *v.* & *n.* —*v.* (**-ies, -ied**) **1** *intr.* (often foll. by *to*) make an answer, respond in word or action. **2** *tr.* say in answer (*he replied, 'Please yourself'*). —*n.* (*pl.* **-ies**) **1** the act of replying (*what did they say in reply?*). **2** what is replied; a response. □ **replier** *n.* [ME f. OF *replier* f. L (as REPLICATE)]

repoint /riːˈpɔɪnt/ *v.tr.* point (esp. brickwork) again.

repopulate /riːˈpɒpjʊˌleɪt/ *v.tr.* populate again or increase the population of. □ **repopulation** /-ˈleɪʃ(ə)n/ *n.*

report /rɪˈpɔːt/ *v.* & *n.* —*v.* **1** *tr.* **a** bring back or give an account of. **b** state as fact or news, narrate or describe or repeat, esp. as an eye-witness or hearer etc. **c** relate as spoken by another. **2** *tr.* make an official or formal statement about. **3** *tr.* (often foll. by *to*) name or specify (an offender or offence) (*shall report you for insubordination; reported them to the police*). **4** *intr.* (often foll. by *to*) present oneself to a person as having returned or arrived (*report to the manager on arrival*). **5** *tr.* (also *absol.*) take down word for word or summarize or write a description of for publication. **6** *intr.* make or draw up or send in a report. **7** *intr.* (often foll. by *to*) be responsible (to a superior, supervisor, etc.) (*reports directly to the managing director*). —*n.* **1** an account given or opinion formally expressed after investigation or consideration. **2** a description, summary, or reproduction of a scene or speech or law case, esp. for newspaper publication or broadcast. **3** common talk; rumour. **4** the way a person or thing is spoken of (*I hear a good report of you*). **5** a periodical statement on (esp. a school pupil's) work, conduct, etc. **6** the sound of an explosion. □ **report back** deliver a report to the person, organization, etc. for whom one acts etc. **reported speech** the speaker's words with the changes of person, tense, etc. usual in reports, e.g. *he said that he would go*. **report progress** state what has been done so far. □ **reportable** *adj.* **reportedly** *adv.* [ME f. OF *reporter* f. L *reportare* (as RE-, *portare* bring)]

reportage /ˌrepɔːˈtɑːʒ/ *n.* **1** the describing of events, esp. the reporting of news etc. for the press and for broadcasting. **2** the typical style of this. **3** factual presentation in a book etc. [REPORT, after F]

reporter /rɪˈpɔːtə(r)/ *n.* **1** a person employed to report news etc. for newspapers or broadcasts. **2** a person who reports.

repose[1] /rɪˈpəʊz/ *n.* & *v.* —*n.* **1** the cessation of activity or excitement or toil. **2** sleep. **3** a peaceful or quiescent state; stillness; tranquillity. —*v.* **1** *intr.* & *refl.* lie down in rest (*reposed on a sofa*). **2** *tr.* (often foll. by *on*) lay (one's head etc.) to rest (on a pillow etc.). **3** *intr.* (often foll. by *in,* *on*) lie, be lying or laid, esp. in sleep or death. **4** *tr.* give rest to; refresh with rest. **5** *intr.* (foll. by *on*, *upon*) be supported or based on. □ **reposal** *n.* **reposeful** *adj.* **reposefully** *adv.* **reposefulness** *n.* [ME f. OF *repos(er)* f. LL *repausare* (as RE-, *pausare* PAUSE)]

repose² /rɪˈpəʊz/ *v.tr.* (foll. by *in*) place (trust etc.) in. □ **reposal** *n.* [RE- + POSE¹ after L *reponere reposit-*]

reposition /ˌriːpəˈzɪʃ(ə)n/ *v.* **1** *tr.* move or place in a different position. **2** *intr.* adjust or alter one's position.

repository /rɪˈpɒzɪtərɪ/ *n.* (*pl.* **-ies**) **1** a place where things are stored or may be found, esp. a warehouse or museum. **2** a receptacle. **3** (often foll. by *of*) **a** a book, person, etc. regarded as a store of information etc. **b** the recipient of confidences or secrets. [obs. F *repositoire* or L *repositorium* (as REPOSE²)]

repossess /ˌriːpəˈzes/ *v.tr.* regain possession of (esp. property or goods on which repayment of a debt is in arrears). □ **repossession** *n.* **repossessor** *n.*

repot /riːˈpɒt/ *v.tr.* (**repotted**, **repotting**) put a plant) in another, esp. larger, pot.

repp var. of REP³.

reprehend /ˌreprɪˈhend/ *v.tr.* rebuke; blame; find fault with. □ **reprehension** *n.* [ME f. L *reprehendere* (as RE-, *prehendere* seize)]

reprehensible /ˌreprɪˈhensɪb(ə)l/ *adj.* deserving censure or rebuke; blameworthy. □ **reprehensibility** /-ˈbɪlɪtɪ/ *n.* **reprehensibly** *adv.* [LL *reprehensibilis* (as REPREHEND)]

represent /ˌreprɪˈzent/ *v.tr.* **1** stand for or correspond to (*the comment does not represent all our views*). **2** (often in *passive*) be a specimen or example of; exemplify (*all types of people were represented in the audience*). **3** act as an embodiment of; symbolize (*the sovereign represents the majesty of the State; numbers are represented by letters*). **4** call up in the mind by description or portrayal or imagination; place a likeness of before the mind or senses. **5** serve or be meant as a likeness of. **6 a** state by way of expostulation or persuasion (*represented the rashness of it*). **b** (foll. by *to*) try to bring the facts influencing conduct) home to (*represented the risks to his client*). **7** (often foll. by *as, to be*) describe or depict as; declare or make out (*represented them as martyrs; not what you represent it to be*). **8** (foll. by *that* + clause) allege. **9** show, or play the part of, on stage. **10** fill the place of; be a substitute or deputy for; be entitled to act or speak for (*the Queen was represented by the Princess of Wales*). **11** be elected as a member of Parliament, a legislature, etc. by (*represents a rural constituency*). □ **representable** *adj.* **representability** /-ˈbɪlɪtɪ/ *n.* [ME f. OF *representer* or f. L *repraesentare* (as RE-, PRESENT²)]

representation /ˌreprɪzenˈteɪʃ(ə)n/ *n.* **1** the act or an instance of representing or being represented. **2** a thing (esp. a painting etc.) that represents another. **3** (esp. in *pl.*) a statement made by way of allegation or to convey opinion. □ **representational** *adj.* [ME f. OF *representation* or L *repraesentatio* (as REPRESENT)]

representative /ˌreprɪˈzentətɪv/ *adj. & n.* —*adj.* **1** typical of a class or category. **2** containing typical specimens of all or many classes (*a representative sample*). **3 a** consisting of elected deputies etc. **b** based on the representation of

a nation etc. by such deputies (*representative government*). **4** (foll. by *of*) serving as a portrayal or symbol of (*representative of their attitude to work*). —*n.* **1** (foll. by *of*) a sample, specimen, or typical embodiment or analogue of. **2 a** the agent of a person or society. **b** a commercial traveller. **3** a delegate; a substitute. **4** a deputy in a representative assembly. □ **representatively** *adv.* **representativeness** *n.* [ME f. OF *representatif -ive* or med.L *repraesentativus* (as REPRESENT)]

repress /rɪˈpres/ *v.tr.* **1 a** check; restrain; keep under; quell. **b** suppress; prevent from sounding, rioting, or bursting out. **2** *Psychol.* actively exclude (an unwelcome thought) from conscious awareness. **3** (usu. as **repressed** *adj.*) subject (a person) to the suppression of his or her thoughts or impulses. □ **represser** *n.* **repressible** *adj.* **repression** /-ˈpreʃ(ə)n/ *n.* **repressive** *adj.* **repressively** *adv.* **repressiveness** *n.* **repressor** *n.* [ME f. L *reprimere* (as RE-, *premere* PRESS¹)]

reprieve /rɪˈpriːv/ *v. & n.* —*v.tr.* **1** remit, commute, or postpone the execution of (a condemned person). **2** give respite to. —*n.* **1 a** the act or an instance of reprieving or being reprieved. **b** a warrant for this. **2** respite; a respite or temporary escape. [ME as past part. *repryed* f. AF & OF *repris* past part. of *reprendre* (as RE-, *prendre* f. L *prehendere* take): 16th-c. -*v*- unexpl.]

reprimand /ˈreprɪˌmɑːnd/ *n. & v.* —*n.* (often foll. by *for*) an official or sharp rebuke (for a fault etc.). —*v.tr.* administer this to. [F *réprimande(r)* f. Sp. *reprimenda* f. L *reprimenda* neut. pl. gerundive of *reprimere* REPRESS]

reprint *v. & n.* —*v.tr.* /riːˈprɪnt/ print again. —*n.* /ˈriːprɪnt/ **1** the act or an instance of reprinting a book etc. **2** the book etc. reprinted. **3** the quantity reprinted. □ **reprinter** *n.*

reprisal /rɪˈpraɪz(ə)l/ *n.* an act of retaliation. [ME f. AF *reprisaille* f. med.L *reprisalia* f. *repraehensalia* (as REPREHEND)]

reprise /rɪˈpriːz/ *n.* **1** a repeated passage in music. **2** a repeated item in a musical programme. [F, fem. past part. of *reprendre* (see REPRIEVE)]

repro /ˈriːprəʊ/ *n.* (*pl.* **-os**) (often *attrib.*) a reproduction or copy. [abbr.]

reproach /rɪˈprəʊtʃ/ *v. & n.* —*v.tr.* **1** express disapproval to (a person) for a fault etc. **2** scold; rebuke; censure. —*n.* **1** a rebuke or censure (*heaped reproaches on them*). **2** (often foll. by *to*) a thing that brings disgrace or discredit (*their behaviour is a reproach to us all*). **3** a disgraced or discredited state (*live in reproach and ignominy*). □ **above** (or **beyond**) **reproach** perfect. □ **reproachable** *adj.* **reproacher** *n.* **reproachingly** *adv.* [ME f. OF *reproche(r)* f. Rmc (as RE-, L *prope* near)]

reproachful /rɪˈprəʊtʃfʊl/ *adj.* full of or expressing reproach. □ **reproachfully** *adv.* **reproachfulness** *n.*

reprobate /ˈreprəˌbeɪt/ *n. & v.* —*n.* an unprincipled person; a person of highly immoral character. —*v.tr.* express or feel disapproval of; censure. □ **reprobation** /-ˈbeɪʃ(ə)n/ *n.* [ME f. L *reprobare reprobat-* disapprove (as RE-, *probare* approve)]

reproduce /ˌriːprəˈdjuːs/ *v.* **1** *tr.* produce a copy or representation of. **2** *tr.* cause to be seen or heard etc. again (*tried to reproduce the sound* *exactly*). **3** *intr.* produce further members of the same species by natural means. **4** *refl.* produce offspring (*reproduced itself several times*). □ **reproducer** *n.* **reproducible** *adj.* **reproducibility** /-ˈbɪlɪtɪ/ *n.* **reproducibly** *adv.*

reproduction /ˌriːprəˈdʌkʃ(ə)n/ *n.* **1** the act or an instance of reproducing. **2** a copy of a work of art, esp. a print or photograph of a painting. **3** (*attrib.*) (of furniture etc.) made in imitation of a certain style or of an earlier period. □ **reproductive** *adj.* **reproductively** *adv.* **reproductiveness** *n.*

reprogram /riːˈprəʊɡræm/ *v.tr.* (also **reprogramme**) (**reprogrammed**, **reprogramming**; *US* **reprogramed**, **reprograming**) program (esp. a computer) again or differently. □ **reprogrammable** *adj.* (also **reprogramable**).

reprography /rɪˈprɒɡrəfɪ/ *n.* the science and practice of copying documents by photography, xerography, etc. □ **reprographer** *n.* **reprographic** /ˌriːprəˈɡræfɪk/ *adj.* **reprographically** /ˌriːprəˈɡræfɪkəlɪ/ *adv.* [REPRODUCE + -GRAPHY]

reproof /rɪˈpruːf/ *n.* **1** blame (*a glance of reproof*). **2** a rebuke; words expressing blame. [ME f. OF *reprove* f. *reprover* REPROVE]

reprove /rɪˈpruːv/ *v.tr.* rebuke (a person, a person's conduct, etc.). □ **reprovable** *adj.* **reprover** *n.* **reprovingly** *adv.* [ME f. OF *reprover* f. LL *reprobare* disapprove: see REPROBATE]

reptile /ˈreptaɪl/ *n.* **1** any cold-blooded scaly animal of the class Reptilia, including snakes, lizards, tortoises, etc. **2** a mean, grovelling, or repulsive person. □ **reptilian** /-ˈtɪlɪən/ *adj.* & *n.* [ME f. LL *reptilis* f. L *repere rept-* crawl]

republic /rɪˈpʌblɪk/ *n.* a State in which supreme power is held by the people or their elected representatives or by an elected or nominated president, not by a monarch etc. [F *république* f. L *respublica* f. *res* concern + *publicus* PUBLIC]

republican /rɪˈpʌblɪkən/ *adj.* & *n.* —*adj.* **1** of or constituted as a republic. **2** characteristic of a republic. **3** advocating or supporting republican government. —*n.* **1** a person advocating or supporting republican government. **2** (**Republican**) (in the US) a member or supporter of the Republican Party. **3** an advocate of a united Ireland. □ **republicanism** *n.*

republish /riːˈpʌblɪʃ/ *v.tr.* (also *absol.*) publish again or in a new edition etc. □ **republication** /-ˈkeɪʃ(ə)n/ *n.*

repudiate /rɪˈpjuːdɪˌeɪt/ *v.tr.* **1 a** disown; disavow; reject. **b** refuse dealings with. **c** deny. **2** refuse to recognize or obey (authority or a treaty). **3** refuse to discharge (an obligation or debt). □ **repudiable** *adj.* **repudiation** /-ˈeɪʃ(ə)n/ *n.* **repudiator** *n.* [L *repudiare* f. *repudium* divorce]

■ **Usage** See note at *refute*.

repugnance /rɪˈpʌɡnəns/ *n.* (also **repugnancy**) **1** (usu. foll. by *to*, *against*) antipathy; aversion. **2** (usu. foll. by *of*, *between*, *to*, *with*) inconsistency or incompatibility of ideas, statements, etc. [ME (in sense 2) f. F *répugnance* or L *repugnantia* f. *repugnare* oppose (as RE-, *pugnare* fight)]

repugnant /rɪˈpʌɡnənt/ *adj.* **1** (often foll. by *to*) extremely distasteful. **2** (often foll. by *to*) contradictory. **3** (often foll. by *with*) incompatible. **4** *poet.* refractory; resisting. □ **repugnantly** *adv.* [ME f. F *répugnant* or L (as REPUGNANCE)]

repulse /rɪˈpʌls/ *v.* & *n.* —*v.tr.* **1** drive back (an attack or attacking enemy) by force of arms. **2 a** rebuff (friendly advances or their maker). **b** refuse (a request or offer or its maker). **3** be repulsive to, repel. —*n.* **1** the act or an instance of repulsing or being repulsed. **2** a rebuff. [L *repellere repuls-* drive back (as REPEL)]

repulsion /rɪˈpʌlʃ(ə)n/ *n.* **1** aversion; disgust. **2** esp. *Physics* the force by which bodies tend to repel each other or increase their mutual distance. [LL *repulsio* (as REPEL)]

repulsive /rɪˈpʌlsɪv/ *adj.* causing aversion or loathing; loathsome, disgusting. □ **repulsively** *adv.* **repulsiveness** *n.* [F *répulsif -ive* or f. REPULSE]

reputable /ˈrepjʊtəb(ə)l/ *adj.* of good repute; respectable. □ **reputably** *adv.* [obs. F or f. med.L *reputabilis* (as REPUTE)]

reputation /ˌrepjʊˈteɪʃ(ə)n/ *n.* **1** what is generally said or believed about a person's or thing's character or standing (*has a reputation for dishonesty*). **2** the state of being well thought of; distinction; respectability (*have my reputation to think of*). **3** (foll. by *of*, *for* + verbal noun) credit or discredit (*has the reputation of driving hard bargains*). [ME f. L *reputatio* (as REPUTE)]

repute /rɪˈpjuːt/ *n.* & *v.* —*n.* reputation (*known by repute*). —*v.tr.* **1** (as **reputed** *adj.*) (often foll. by *to* + infin.) be generally considered or reckoned (*is reputed to be the best*). **2** (as **reputed** *adj.*) passing as being, but probably not being (*his reputed father*). □ **reputedly** *adv.* [ME f. OF *reputer* or L *reputare* (as RE-, *putare* think)]

request /rɪˈkwest/ *n.* & *v.* —*n.* **1** the act or an instance of asking for something; a petition (*came at his request*). **2** a thing asked for. **3** the state of being sought after; demand (*in great request*). **4** a letter etc. asking for a particular record etc. to be played on a radio programme, often with a personal message. —*v.tr.* **1** ask to be given or allowed or favoured with (*request a hearing; requests your presence*). **2** (foll. by *to* + infin.) ask a person to do something (*requested her to answer*). **3** (foll. by *that* + clause) ask that. □ **by** (or **on**) **request** in response to an expressed wish. **request stop** a bus-stop at which a bus stops only on a passenger's request. □ **requester** *n.* [ME f. OF *requeste(r)* ult. f. L *requaerere* (as REQUIRE)]

requiem /ˈrekwɪˌem/ *n.* **1** (**Requiem**) (also *attrib.*) chiefly *RC Ch.* a mass for the repose of the souls of the dead. **2** *Mus.* the musical setting for this. [ME f. accus. of L *requies* rest, the initial word of the mass]

require /rɪˈkwaɪə(r)/ *v.tr.* **1** need; depend on for success or fulfilment (*the work requires much patience*). **2** lay down as an imperative (*did all that was required by law*). **3** command; instruct (a person etc.). **4** order; insist on (an action or measure). **5** (often foll. by *of*, *from*, or *that* + clause) demand (of or from a person) as a right. **6** wish to have (*is there anything else you require?*). □ **requirer** *n.* **requirement** *n.* [ME f. OF *requere* ult. f. L *requirere* (as RE-, *quaerere* seek)]

requisite /ˈrekwɪzɪt/ *adj.* & *n.* —*adj.* required by circumstances; necessary to success etc. —*n.* (often foll. by *for*) a thing needed (for some purpose). □ **requisitely** *adv.* [ME f. L *requisitus* past part. (as REQUIRE)]

requisition /ˌrekwɪˈzɪʃ(ə)n/ *n.* & *v.* —*n.* **1** an official order laying claim to the use of property or materials. **2** a formal written demand that some duty should be performed. **3** being called or put into service. —*v.tr.* demand the use or supply of, esp. by requisition order. □ **requisitioner** *n.* **requisitionist** *n.* [F *réquisition* or L *requisitio* (as REQUIRE)]

requite /rɪ'kwaɪt/ *v.tr.* **1** make return for (a service). **2** (often foll. by *with*) reward or avenge (a favour or injury). **3** (often foll. by *for*) make return to (a person). **4** (often foll. by *for*, *with*) repay with good or evil (*requite like for like*; *requite hate with love*). □ **requital** *n.* [RE- + *quite* var. of QUIT]

reran *past* of RERUN.

reread /riː'riːd/ *v. & n.* —*v.tr.* (*past* and *past part.* **reread** /-'red/) read again. —*n.* an instance of reading again. □ **re-readable** *adj.*

re-release /ˌriːrɪ'liːs/ *v. & n.* —*v.tr.* release (a record, film, etc.) again. —*n.* a re-released record, film, etc.

re-route /riː'ruːt/ *v.tr.* (**-routeing**) send or carry by a different route.

rerun /riː'rʌn/ *v. & n.* —*v.tr.* (**rerunning**; *past* **reran**; *past part.* **rerun**) run (a race, film, etc.) again. —*n.* /'riːrʌn/ **1** the act or an instance of rerunning. **2** a film etc. shown again.

resale /riː'seɪl/ *n.* the sale of a thing previously bought. □ **resalable** *adj.*

resat *past* and *past part.* of RESIT.

reschedule /riː'ʃedjuːl, -'skedʒʊəl/ *v.tr.* alter the schedule of; replan.

rescind /rɪ'sɪnd/ *v.tr.* abrogate, revoke, cancel. □ **rescindable** *adj.* **rescindment** *n.* **rescission** /-'sɪʒ(ə)n/ *n.* [L *rescindere resciss-* (as RE-, *scindere* cut)]

rescue /'reskjuː/ *v. & n.* —*v.tr.* (**rescues, rescued, rescuing**) (often foll. by *from*) save or set free or bring away from attack, custody, danger, or harm. —*n.* the act or an instance of rescuing or being rescued; deliverance. □ **rescuable** *adj.* **rescuer** *n.* [ME *rescowe* f. OF *rescoure* f. Rmc, formed as RE- + L *excutere* (as EX-[1], *quatere* shake)]

reseal /riː'siːl/ *v.tr.* seal again. □ **resealable** *adj.*

research /rɪ'sɜːtʃ, *disp.* 'riːsɜːtʃ/ *n. & v.* —*n.* **1 a** the systematic investigation into and study of materials, sources, etc., in order to establish facts and reach new conclusions. **b** (usu. in *pl.*) an endeavour to discover new or collate old facts etc. by the scientific study of a subject or by a course of critical investigation. **2** (*attrib.*) engaged in or intended for research (*research assistant*). —*v.* **1** *tr.* do research into or for. **2** *intr.* make researches. □ **research and development** (in industry etc.) work directed towards the innovation, introduction, and improvement of products and processes. □ **researchable** *adj.* **researcher** *n.* [obs. F *recerche* (as RE-, SEARCH)]

■ **Usage** The second pronunciation, with the stress on the first syllable, is considered incorrect by some people.

reselect /ˌriːsɪ'lekt/ *v.tr.* select again or differently. □ **reselection** *n.*

resell /riː'sel/ *v.tr.* (*past* and *past part.* **resold**) sell (an object etc.) after buying it.

resemblance /rɪ'zembləns/ *n.* (often foll. by *to*, *between*, *of*) a likeness or similarity. □ **resemblant** *adj.* [ME f. AF (as RESEMBLE)]

resemble /rɪ'zemb(ə)l/ *v.tr.* be like; have a similarity to, or features in common with, or the same appearance as. □ **resembler** *n.* [ME f. OF *resembler* (as RE-, *sembler* f. L *similare* f. *similis* like)]

resent /rɪ'zent/ *v.tr.* show or feel indignation at; be aggrieved by (*we resent being patronized*). [obs. F *resentir* (as RE-, L *sentire* feel)]

resentful /rɪ'zentfʊl/ *adj.* feeling resentment. □ **resentfully** *adv.* **resentfulness** *n.*

resentment /rɪ'zentmənt/ *n.* (often foll. by *at*, *of*) indignant or bitter feelings; anger. [It. *risentimento* or F *ressentiment* (as RESENT)]

reservation /ˌrezə'veɪʃ(ə)n/ *n.* **1** the act or an instance of reserving or being reserved. **2** a booking (of a room, berth, seat, etc.). **3** the thing booked, e.g. a room in a hotel. **4** an express or tacit limitation or exception to an agreement etc. (*had reservations about the plan*). **5** *Brit.* a strip of land between the carriageways of a road. **6** an area of land reserved for occupation by American Indians, African Blacks, or Australian Aboriginals, etc. [ME f. OF *reservation* or LL *reservatio* (as RESERVE)]

reserve /rɪ'zɜːv/ *v. & n.* —*v.tr.* **1** postpone, put aside, keep back for a later occasion or special use. **2** order to be specially retained or allocated for a particular person or at a particular time. **3** retain or secure, esp. by formal or legal stipulation (*reserve the right to*). **4** postpone delivery of (judgement etc.) (*reserved my comments until the end*). —*n.* **1** a thing reserved for future use; an extra stock or amount (*a great reserve of strength*; *huge energy reserves*). **2** a limitation, qualification, or exception attached to something (*accept your offer without reserve*). **3** self-restraint; reticence; lack of cordiality (*difficult to overcome his reserve*). **4** a company's profit added to capital. **5** (in *sing.* or *pl.*) assets kept readily available as cash or at a central bank, or as gold or foreign exchange (*reserve currency*). **6** (in *sing.* or *pl.*) **a** troops withheld from action to reinforce or protect others. **b** forces in addition to the regular army, navy, airforce, etc., but available in an emergency. **7** a member of the military reserve. **8** an extra player chosen to be a possible substitute in a team. **9** a place reserved for special use, esp. as a habitat for a native tribe or for wildlife (*game reserve*; *nature reserve*). □ **in reserve** unused and available if required. **reserve price** the lowest acceptable price stipulated for an item sold at an auction. □ **reservable** *adj.* **reserver** *n.* [ME f. OF *reserver* f. L *reservare* (as RE-, *servare* keep)]

reserved /rɪ'zɜːvd/ *adj.* **1** reticent; slow to reveal emotion or opinions; uncommunicative. **2 a** set apart, destined for some use or fate. **b** (often foll. by *for*, *to*) left by fate for; falling first or only to. □ **reservedly** /-vɪdlɪ/ *adv.* **reservedness** *n.*

reservist /rɪ'zɜːvɪst/ *n.* a member of the reserve forces.

reservoir /'rezə.vwɑː(r)/ *n.* **1** a large natural or artificial lake used as a source of water supply. **2 a** any natural or artificial receptacle esp. for or of fluid. **b** a place where fluid etc. collects. **3** a part of a machine etc. holding fluid. **4** (usu. foll. by *of*) a reserve or supply esp. of information. [F *réservoir* f. *réserver* RESERVE]

reset /riː'set/ *v.tr.* (**resetting**; *past* and *past part.* **reset**) set (a broken bone, gems, a mechanical device, etc.) again or differently. □ **resettable** *adj.* **resettability** /-'bɪlɪtɪ/ *n.*

resettle /riːˈset(ə)l/ v.tr. & intr. settle again. □ **resettlement** n.

reshape /riːˈʃeɪp/ v.tr. shape or form again or differently.

reshuffle /riːˈʃʌf(ə)l/ v. & n. —v.tr. **1** shuffle (cards) again. **2** interchange the posts of (government ministers etc.). —n. the act or an instance of reshuffling.

reside /rɪˈzaɪd/ v.intr. **1** (often foll. by at, in, abroad, etc.) (of a person) have one's home, dwell permanently. **2** (of power, a right, etc.) rest or be vested in. **3** (of an incumbent official) be in residence. **4** (foll. by in) (of a quality) be present or inherent in. [ME, prob. back-form. f. RESIDENT infl. by F résider or L residēre (as RE-, sedēre sit)]

residence /ˈrezɪd(ə)ns/ n. **1** the act or an instance of residing. **2 a** the place where a person resides; an abode. **b** a mansion; the official house of a government minister etc. **c** a house, esp. one of considerable pretension. □ **in residence** dwelling at a specified place, esp. for the performance of duties or work. [ME f. OF residence or med.L residentia f. L residēre: see RESIDE]

residency /ˈrezɪdənsɪ/ n. (pl. **-ies**) **1** = RESIDENCE 1, 2a. **2** US a period of specialized medical training; the position of a resident.

resident /ˈrezɪd(ə)nt/ n. & adj. —n. **1** (often foll. by of) **a** a permanent inhabitant (of a town or neighbourhood). **b** a bird belonging to a species that does not migrate. **2** a guest in a hotel etc. staying overnight. **3** US a medical graduate engaged in specialized practice under supervision in a hospital. —adj. **1** residing; in residence. **2 a** having quarters on the premises of one's work etc. (resident housekeeper; resident doctor). **b** working regularly in a particular place. **3** located in; inherent (powers of feeling are resident in the nerves). **4** (of birds etc.) non-migratory. □ **residentship** n. (in sense 3 of n.). [ME f. OF resident or L: see RESIDE]

residential /ˌrezɪˈdenʃ(ə)l/ adj. **1** suitable for or occupied by private houses (residential area). **2** used as a residence (residential hotel). **3** based on or connected with residence (the residential qualification for voters). □ **residentially** adv.

residua pl. of RESIDUUM.

residual /rɪˈzɪdjʊəl/ adj. remaining; left as a residue or residuum. □ **residually** adv.

residuary /rɪˈzɪdjʊərɪ/ adj. **1** of the residue of an estate (residuary bequest). **2** of or being a residuum; residual; still remaining.

residue /ˈrezɪˌdjuː/ n. **1** what is left over or remains; a remainder; the rest. **2** Law what remains of an estate after the payment of charges, debts, and bequests. **3** esp. Chem. a residuum. [ME f. OF residu f. L residuum: see RESIDUUM]

residuum /rɪˈzɪdjʊəm/ n. (pl. **residua** /-djʊə/) **1** Chem. a substance left after combustion or evaporation. **2** a remainder or residue. [L, neut. of residuus remaining f. residēre: see RESIDE]

resign /rɪˈzaɪn/ v. **1** intr. **a** (often foll. by from) give up office, one's employment, etc. (resigned from the Home Office). **b** (often foll. by as) retire (resigned as chief executive). **2** tr. (often foll. by to, into) relinquish; surrender; hand over (a right, charge, task, etc.). **3** tr. give up (hope etc.). **4** refl. (usu. foll. by to) reconcile (oneself, one's mind, etc.) to the inevitable (have resigned myself to the idea). □ **resigner** n. [ME f. OF resigner f. L resignare unseal, cancel (as RE-, signare sign, seal)]

resignation /ˌrezɪɡˈneɪʃ(ə)n/ n. **1** the act or an instance of resigning, esp. from one's job or office. **2** the state of being resigned; the uncomplaining endurance of a sorrow or difficulty. [ME f. OF f. med.L resignatio (as RESIGN)]

resigned /rɪˈzaɪnd/ adj. (often foll. by to) having resigned oneself; submissive, acquiescent. □ **resignedly** /-nɪdlɪ/ adv. **resignedness** n.

resilient /rɪˈzɪlɪənt/ adj. **1** (of a substance etc.) recoiling; springing back; resuming its original shape after bending, stretching, compression, etc. **2** (of a person) readily recovering from shock, depression, etc. □ **resilience** n. **resiliency** n. **resiliently** adv. [L resiliens resilient- f. resilire (as RE-, salire jump)]

resin /ˈrezɪn/ n. & v. —n. **1** an adhesive inflammable substance secreted by some plants. **2** (in full **synthetic resin**) a solid or liquid organic compound made by polymerization etc. and used in plastics etc. —v.tr. (**resined**, **resining**) rub or treat with resin. □ **resinate** /-nət/ n. **resinate** /-ˌneɪt/ v.tr. **resinoid** adj. & n. **resinous** adj. [ME resyn, rosyn f. L resina & med.L rosina, rosinum]

resist /rɪˈzɪst/ v. **1** tr. withstand the action or effect of; repel. **2** tr. stop the course or progress of; prevent from reaching, penetrating, etc. **3** tr. abstain from (pleasure, temptation, etc.). **4** tr. strive against; try to impede; refuse to comply with (resist arrest). **5** intr. offer opposition; refuse to comply. □ **cannot** (or **could not** etc.) **resist 1** (foll. by verbal noun) feel obliged or strongly inclined to (cannot resist teasing me about it). **2** is certain to be amused, attracted, etc., by (can't resist children's clothes). □ **resistant** adj. **resister** n. **resistible** adj. **resistibility** /-ˈbɪlɪtɪ/ n. [ME f. OF resister or L resistere (as RE-, sistere stop, redupl. of stare stand)]

resistance /rɪˈzɪst(ə)ns/ n. **1** the act or an instance of resisting; refusal to comply. **2** the power of resisting (showed resistance to wear and tear). **3** the impeding, slowing, or stopping effect exerted by one material thing on another. **4** Physics **a** the property of hindering the conduction of electricity, heat, etc. **b** the measure of this in a body. **5** a resistor. **6** (in full **resistance movement**) a secret organization resisting authority, esp. in an occupied country. [ME f. F résistance, résistence f. LL resistentia (as RESIST)]

resistor /rɪˈzɪstə(r)/ n. Electr. a device having resistance to the passage of an electrical current.

resit v. & n. —v.tr. /riːˈsɪt/ (**resitting**; past and past part. **resat**) sit (an examination) again after failing. —n. /ˈriːsɪt/ the act or an instance of resitting an examination.

resold past and past part. of RESELL.

resoluble /rɪˈzɒljʊb(ə)l/ adj. **1** that can be resolved. **2** (foll. by into) analysable. [F résoluble or L resolubilis (as RESOLVE, after soluble)]

resolute /ˈrezəˌluːt, -ˌljuːt/ adj. (of a person or a person's mind or action) determined; decided; firm of purpose; not vacillating. □ **resolutely** adv. **resoluteness** n. [L resolutus past part. of resolvere (see RESOLVE)]

resolution /ˌrezəˈluːʃ(ə)n, -ˈljuːʃ(ə)n/ n. **1** a resolute temper or character; boldness and firmness of purpose. **2** a thing resolved on; an intention (New Year's resolutions). **3 a** a formal expression of opinion or intention by a legislative body or public meeting. **b** the formulation of this (*passed a resolution*). **4** (usu. foll. by *of*) the act or an instance of solving doubt or a problem or question (*towards a resolution of the difficulty*). **5** separation into components; decomposition. **6** (foll. by *into*) analysis; conversion into another form. **7** *Mus.* the act or an instance of causing discord to pass into concord. **8** *Physics* etc. the smallest interval measurable by a scientific instrument; the resolving power. [ME f. L *resolutio* (as RESOLVE)]

resolve /rɪˈzɒlv/ v. & n. —v. **1** *intr.* make up one's mind; decide firmly (*resolve to do better*). **2** *tr.* (of circumstances etc.) cause (a person) to do this (*events resolved him to leave*). **3** *tr.* (foll. by *that* + clause) (of an assembly or meeting) pass a resolution by vote. **4** *intr.* & *tr.* (often foll. by *into*) separate or cause to separate into constituent parts; disintegrate; analyse; dissolve. **5** *tr.* solve; explain; clear up; settle (doubt, argument, etc.). **6** *tr.* & *intr. Mus.* convert or be converted into concord. —n. **1 a** a firm mental decision or intention; a resolution (*made a resolve not to go*). **b** US a formal resolution by a legislative body or public meeting. **2** resoluteness; steadfastness. □ **resolvable** *adj.* **resolvability** /-ˈbɪlɪtɪ/ n. **resolver** n. [ME f. L *resolvere resolut-* (as RE-, SOLVE)]

resolved /rɪˈzɒlvd/ *adj.* resolute, determined. □ **resolvedly** /-vɪdlɪ/ *adv.* **resolvedness** n.

resonant /ˈrezənənt/ *adj.* **1** (of sound) echoing, resounding; continuing to sound; reinforced or prolonged by reflection or synchronous vibration. **2** (of a body, room, etc.) tending to reinforce or prolong sounds esp. by synchronous vibration. **3** (often foll. by *with*) (of a place) resounding. **4** of or relating to resonance. □ **resonance** n. **resonantly** *adv.* [F *résonnant* or L *resonare resonant-* (as RE-, *sonare* sound)]

resonate /ˈrezəneɪt/ *v.intr.* produce or show resonance; resound. □ **resonator** n. [L *resonare resonat-* (as RESONANT)]

resort /rɪˈzɔːt/ n. & v. —n. **1** a place frequented esp. for holidays or for a specified purpose or quality (*seaside resort; health resort*). **2 a** a thing to which one has recourse; an expedient or measure (*a taxi was our best resort*). **b** (foll. by *to*) recourse; use of (*without resort to violence*). **3** a tendency to frequent or be frequented (*places of great resort*). —v.intr. **1** (foll. by *to*) turn to as an expedient (*resorted to threats*). **2** (foll. by *to*) go often or in large numbers to. □ **in the** (or **as a**) **last resort** when all else has failed. □ **resorter** n. [ME f. OF *resortir* (as RE-, *sortir* come or go out)]

resound /rɪˈzaʊnd/ *v.intr.* **1** (often foll. by *with*) (of a place) ring or echo (*the hall resounded with laughter*). **2** (of a voice, instrument, sound, etc.) produce echoes; go on sounding; fill the place with sound. **3 a** (of fame, a reputation, etc.) be much talked of. **b** (foll. by *through*) produce a sensation (*the call resounded through Europe*). [ME f. RE- + SOUND¹ v., after OF *resoner* or L *resonare*: see RESONANT]

resounding /rɪˈzaʊndɪŋ/ *adj.* **1** in senses of RESOUND. **2** unmistakable; emphatic (*was a resounding success*). □ **resoundingly** *adv.*

resource /rɪˈsɔːs, -ˈzɔːs/ n. **1** an expedient or device (*escape was their only resource*). **2** (usu. in pl.) **a** the means available to achieve an end,

fulfil a function, etc. **b** a stock or supply that can be drawn on. **3** (in *pl.*) a country's collective wealth or means of defence. **4** a leisure occupation (*reading is a great resource*). **5** skill in devising expedients (*a person of great resource*). □ **one's own resources** one's own abilities, ingenuity, etc. □ **resourceful** *adj.* **resourcefully** *adv.* **resourcefulness** n. **resourceless** *adj.* **resourcelessness** n. [F *ressource, ressourse*, fem. past part. of OF dial. *resourdre* (as RE-, L *surgere* rise)]

respect /rɪˈspekt/ n. & v. —n. **1** deferential esteem felt or shown towards a person or quality. **2 a** (foll. by *of, for*) heed or regard. **b** (foll. by *to*) attention to or consideration of (*without respect to the results*). **3** an aspect, detail, particular, etc. (*correct except in this one respect*). **4** reference, relation (*a morality that has no respect to religion*). **5** (in *pl.*) a person's polite messages or attentions (*give my respects to your mother*). —*v.tr.* **1** regard with deference, esteem, or honour. **2 a** avoid interfering with, harming, degrading, insulting, injuring, or interrupting. **b** treat with consideration. □ **in respect of** as concerns; with reference to. □ **respecter** n. [ME f. OF *respect* or L *respectus* f. *respicere* (as RE-, *specere* look at) or f. *respectare* frequent. of *respicere*]

respectability /rɪˌspektəˈbɪlɪtɪ/ n. **1** the state of being respectable. **2** those who are respectable.

respectable /rɪˈspektəb(ə)l/ *adj.* **1** deserving respect. **2 a** of fair social standing. **b** having the qualities necessary for such standing. **3** honest and decent in conduct etc. **4** of some merit or importance. **5** tolerable, passable, fairly good or competent (*a respectable try*). **6** (of activities, clothes, etc.) presentable; befitting a respectable person. **7** reasonably good in condition or appearance. **8** appreciable in number, size, amount, etc. □ **respectably** *adv.*

respectful /rɪˈspektfʊl/ *adj.* showing deference (*stood at a respectful distance*). □ **respectfully** *adv.* **respectfulness** n.

respecting /rɪˈspektɪŋ/ *prep.* with reference or regard to; concerning.

respective /rɪˈspektɪv/ *adj.* concerning or appropriate to each of several individually; proper to each (*go to your respective places*). [F *respectif -ive* f. med.L *respectivus* (as RESPECT)]

respectively /rɪˈspektɪvlɪ/ *adv.* for each separately or in turn, and in the order mentioned (*she and I gave £10 and £1 respectively*).

respell /riːˈspel/ *v.tr.* (past and *past part.* **respelt** or **respelled**) spell again or differently, esp. phonetically.

respiration /ˌrespɪˈreɪʃ(ə)n/ n. **1 a** the act or an instance of breathing. **b** a single inspiration or expiration; a breath. **2** *Biol.* in living organisms, the process involving the release of energy and carbon dioxide from the oxidation of complex organic substances. [ME f. F *respiration* or L *respiratio* (as RESPIRE)]

respirator /ˈrespɪˌreɪtə(r)/ n. **1** an apparatus worn over the face to prevent poison gas, cold air, dust particles, etc., from being inhaled. **2** *Med.* an apparatus for maintaining artificial respiration.

respire /rɪˈspaɪə(r)/ v. **1** *intr.* breathe air. **2** *intr.* inhale and exhale air. **3** *intr.* (of a plant) carry out respiration. **4** *tr.* breathe (air etc.). □ **respiratory** /rɪˈspɪrətərɪ, ˈrespəˌreɪtərɪ/ *adj.* [ME

f. OF *respirer* or f. L *respirare* (as RE-, *spirare* breathe)]

respite /ˈrespaɪt, -pɪt/ *n. & v.* —*n.* **1** an interval of rest or relief. **2** a delay permitted before the discharge of an obligation or the suffering of a penalty. —*v.tr.* grant respite to; reprieve. [ME f. OF *respit* f. L *respectus* RESPECT]

resplendent /rɪˈsplend(ə)nt/ *adj.* brilliant, dazzlingly or gloriously bright. □ **resplendence** *n.* **resplendency** *n.* **resplendently** *adv.* [ME f. L *resplendēre* (as RE-, *splendēre* glitter)]

respond /rɪˈspɒnd/ *v.intr.* **1** answer, give a reply. **2** act or behave in an answering or corresponding manner. **3** (usu. foll. by *to*) show sensitiveness to by behaviour or change (*does not respond to kindness*). **4** (of a congregation) make answers to a priest etc. □ **respondence** *n.* **respondency** *n.* **responder** *n.* [ME f. OF *respondre* answer ult. f. L *respondēre* respons- answer (as RE-, *spondēre* pledge)]

respondent /rɪˈspɒnd(ə)nt/ *n. & adj.* —*n.* **1** a defendant, esp. in an appeal or divorce case. **2** a person who makes an answer or defends an argument etc. —*adj.* **1** making answer. **2** (foll. by *to*) responsive. **3** in the position of defendant.

response /rɪˈspɒns/ *n.* **1** an answer given in word or act; a reply. **2** a feeling, movement, change, etc., caused by a stimulus or influence. **3** (often in *pl.*) *Eccl.* any part of the liturgy said or sung in answer to the priest. [ME f. OF *respons(e)* or L *responsum* neut. past part. of *respondēre* RESPOND]

responsibility /rɪˌspɒnsɪˈbɪlɪtɪ/ *n.* (*pl.* **-ies**) **1 a** (often foll. by *for*, *of*) the state or fact of being responsible (*refuses all responsibility for it; will take the responsibility of doing it*). **b** authority; the ability to act independently and make decisions (*a job with more responsibility*). **2** the person or thing for which one is responsible (*the food is my responsibility*).

responsible /rɪˈspɒnsɪb(ə)l/ *adj.* **1** (often foll. by *to*, *for*) liable to be called to account (to a person or for a thing). **2** morally accountable for one's actions; capable of rational conduct. **3** of good credit, position, or repute; respectable; evidently trustworthy. **4** (often foll. by *for*) being the primary cause (*a short circuit was responsible for the power failure*). **5** involving responsibility (*a responsible job*). □ **responsibleness** *n.* **responsibly** *adv.* [obs. F f. L *respondēre*: see RESPOND]

responsive /rɪˈspɒnsɪv/ *adj.* **1** (often foll. by *to*) responding readily (to some influence). **2** sympathetic; impressionable. □ **responsively** *adv.* **responsiveness** *n.* [F *responsif -ive* or LL *responsivus* (as RESPOND)]

respray *v. & n.* —*v.tr.* /riːˈspreɪ/ spray again (esp. to change the colour of the paint on a vehicle). —*n.* /ˈriːspreɪ/ the act or an instance of respraying.

rest[1] *v. & n.* —*v.* **1** *intr.* cease, abstain, or be relieved from exertion, action, movement, or employment; be tranquil. **2** *intr.* be still or asleep, esp. to refresh oneself or recover strength. **3** *tr.* give relief or repose to; allow to rest (*a chair to rest my legs*). **4** *intr.* (foll. by *on, upon, against*) lie on; be supported by; be spread out on; be propped against. **5** *intr.* (foll. by *on, upon*) depend, be based, or rely on. **6** *intr.* (foll. by *on, upon*) (of a look) alight or be steadily directed on. **7** *tr.* (foll. by *on, upon*) place for support or foundation. **8** *intr.* (of a problem or subject) be left without

further investigation or discussion (*let the matter rest*). **9** *intr.* **a** lie in death. **b** (foll. by *in*) lie buried in (a churchyard etc.). **10** *tr.* (as **rested** *adj.*) refreshed or reinvigorated by resting. **11** *intr.* US conclude the calling of witnesses in a law case (*the prosecution rests*). —*n.* **1** repose or sleep, esp. in bed at night (*get a good night's rest*). **2** freedom from or the cessation of exertion, worry, activity, etc. (*give the subject a rest*). **3** a period of resting (*take a 15-minute rest*). **4** a support or prop for holding or steadying something. **5** *Mus.* **a** an interval of silence of a specified duration. **b** the sign denoting this. □ **at rest** not moving; not agitated or troubled; dead. **be resting** *Brit. euphem.* (of an actor) be out of work. **rest one's case** conclude one's argument etc. **rest-cure** a rest usu. of some weeks as a medical treatment. **rest-day** **1** a day spent in rest. **2** = *day of rest*. **rest-home** a place where old or frail people can be cared for. **rest room** esp. US a public lavatory in a factory, shop, etc. **rest up** US rest oneself thoroughly. **set at rest** settle or relieve (a question, a person's mind, etc.). □ **rester** *n.* [OE *ræst, rest* (n.), *ræstan, restan* (v.)]

rest[2] *n. & v.* —*n.* (prec. by *the*) the remaining part or parts; the others; the remainder of some quantity or number (*finish what you can and leave the rest*). —*v.intr.* **1** remain in a specified state (*rest assured*). **2** (foll. by *with*) be left in the hands or charge of (*the final arrangements rest with you*). □ **and all the rest** (or **the rest of it**) and all else that might be mentioned; etcetera. **for the rest** as regards anything else. [ME f. OF *reste* *rester* f. L *restare* (as RE-, *stare* stand)]

restart *v. & n.* —*v.tr. & intr.* /riːˈstɑːt/ begin again. —*n.* /ˈriːstɑːt/ a new beginning.

restate /riːˈsteɪt/ *v.tr.* express again or differently, esp. more clearly or convincingly. □ **restatement** *n.*

restaurant /ˈrestəˌrɒnt, -ˌrɔ̃/ *n.* public premises where meals or refreshments may be had. □ **restaurant car** *Brit.* a dining-car on a train. [F f. *restaurer* RESTORE]

restaurateur /ˌrestərəˈtɜː(r)/ *n.* a restaurant-keeper. [F (as RESTAURANT)]

restful /ˈrestfʊl/ *adj.* **1** favourable to quiet or repose. **2** free from disturbing influences. **3** soothing. □ **restfully** *adv.* **restfulness** *n.*

restitution /ˌrestɪˈtjuːʃ(ə)n/ *n.* **1** (often foll. by *of*) the act or an instance of restoring a thing to its proper owner. **2** reparation for an injury (esp. *make restitution*). □ **restitutive** /ˈrestɪˌtjuːtɪv/ *adj.* [ME f. OF *restitution* or L *restitutio* f. *restituere* *restitut- restore* (as RE-, *statuere* establish)]

restive /ˈrestɪv/ *adj.* **1** fidgety; restless. **2** (of a horse) refusing to advance. □ **restively** *adv.* **restiveness** *n.* [ME f. OF *restif -ive* f. Rmc (as REST[2])]

restless /ˈrestlɪs/ *adj.* **1** finding or affording no rest. **2** uneasy; agitated. **3** constantly in motion, fidgeting, etc. □ **restlessly** *adv.* **restlessness** *n.* [OE *restlēas* (as REST[1], -LESS)]

restock /riːˈstɒk/ *v.tr.* (also *absol.*) stock again or differently.

restoration /ˌrestəˈreɪʃ(ə)n/ *n.* **1** the act or an instance of restoring or being restored. **2** a model or drawing representing the supposed original form of an extinct animal, ruined building, etc. **3** (**Restoration**) *hist.* (prec. by *the*) the re-establishment of Charles II as king of

England in 1660. [17th-c. alt. (after RESTORE) of *restauration*, ME f. OF *restauration* or LL *restauratio* (as RESTORE)]

restorative /rɪˈstɒrətɪv/ *adj. & n. —adj.* tending to restore health or strength. —*n.* a restorative medicine, food, etc. (*needs a restorative*). □ **restoratively** *adv.* [ME var. of obs. *restaurative* f. OF *restauratif -ive* (as RESTORE)]

restore /rɪˈstɔː(r)/ *v.tr.* **1** bring back or attempt to bring back to the original state by rebuilding, repairing, etc. **2** bring back to health etc.; cure. **3** give back to the original owner etc.; make restitution of. **4** reinstate; bring back to dignity or right. **5** replace; put back; bring back to a former condition. □ **restorable** *adj.* **restorer** *n.* [ME f. OF *restorer* f. L *restaurare*]

restrain /rɪˈstreɪn/ *v.tr.* **1** (often *refl.*, usu. foll. by *from*) check or hold in; keep in check or under control or within bounds. **2** repress; keep down. **3** confine; imprison. □ **restrainable** *adj.* **restrainer** *n.* [ME f. OF *restrei(g)n-* stem of *restreindre* f. L *restringere* restrict- (as RE-, *stringere* tie)]

restrainedly /rɪˈstreɪnɪdlɪ/ *adv.* with self-restraint.

restraint /rɪˈstreɪnt/ *n.* **1** the act or an instance of restraining or being restrained. **2** a stoppage; a check; a controlling agency or influence. **3 a** self-control; avoidance of excess or exaggeration. **b** austerity of literary expression. **4** reserve of manner. **5** confinement, esp. because of insanity. **6** something which restrains or holds in check. [ME f. OF *restreinte* fem. past part. of *restreindre*: see RESTRAIN]

restrict /rɪˈstrɪkt/ *v.tr.* (often foll. by *to, within*) **1** confine, bound, limit (*restricted parking; restricted them to five days a week*). **2** subject to limitation. □ **restrictedly** *adv.* **restrictedness** *n.* [L *restringere*: see RESTRAIN]

restriction /rɪˈstrɪkʃ(ə)n/ *n.* **1** the act or an instance of restricting; the state of being restricted. **2** a thing that restricts. **3** a limitation placed on action. □ **restrictionist** *adj. & n.* [ME f. OF *restriction* or L *restrictio* (as RESTRICT)]

restrictive /rɪˈstrɪktɪv/ *adj.* imposing restrictions. □ **restrictive practice** *Brit.* an agreement to limit competition or output in industry. □ **restrictively** *adv.* **restrictiveness** *n.* [ME f. OF *restrictif -ive* or med.L *restrictivus* (as RESTRICT)]

restring /riːˈstrɪŋ/ *v.tr.* (*past* and *past part.* **restrung**) **1** fit (a musical instrument) with new strings. **2** thread (beads etc.) on a new string.

restructure /riːˈstrʌktʃə(r)/ *v.tr.* give a new structure to; rebuild; rearrange.

restyle /riːˈstaɪl/ *v.tr.* **1** reshape; remake in a new style. **2** give a new designation to (a person or thing).

result /rɪˈzʌlt/ *n. & v. —n.* **1** a consequence, issue, or outcome of something. **2** a satisfactory outcome; a favourable result (*gets results*). **3** a quantity, formula, etc., obtained by calculation. **4** (in *pl.*) a list of scores or winners etc. in an examination or sporting event. —*v.intr.* **1** (often foll. by *from*) arise as the actual consequence or follow as a logical consequence (from conditions, causes, etc.). **2** (often foll. by *in*) have a specified end or outcome (*resulted in a large profit*). □ **resultful** *adj.* **resultless** *adj.* [ME f. med.L *resultare* f. L (as RE-, *saltare* frequent. of *salire* jump)]

resultant /rɪˈzʌlt(ə)nt/ *adj.* resulting, esp. as the total outcome of more or less opposed forces.

resume /rɪˈzjuːm/ *v.* **1** *tr. & intr.* begin again or continue after an interruption. **2** *tr. & intr.* begin to speak, work, or use again; recommence. **3** *tr.* get back; take back; recover; reoccupy (*resume one's seat*). □ **resumable** *adj.* [ME f. OF *resumer* or L *resumere* resumpt- (as RE-, *sumere* take)]

résumé /ˈrezjʊˌmeɪ/ *n.* **1** a summary. **2** *US* a curriculum vitae. [F past part. of *résumer* (as RESUME)]

resumption /rɪˈzʌmpʃ(ə)n/ *n.* the act or an instance of resuming (*ready for the resumption of negotiations*). □ **resumptive** *adj.* [ME f. OF *resumption* or LL *resumptio* (as RESUME)]

resurface /riːˈsɜːfɪs/ *v.* **1** *tr.* lay a new surface on (a road etc.). **2** *intr.* rise or arise again; turn up again.

resurgent /rɪˈsɜːdʒ(ə)nt/ *adj.* **1** rising or arising again. **2** tending to rise again. □ **resurgence** *n.* [L *resurgere* resurrect- (as RE-, *surgere* rise)]

resurrect /ˌrezəˈrekt/ *v.* **1** *tr.* *colloq.* revive the practice, use, or memory of. **2** *tr.* take from the grave; exhume. **3** *tr.* dig up. **4** *tr. & intr.* raise or rise from the dead. [back-form. f. RESURRECTION]

resurrection /ˌrezəˈrekʃ(ə)n/ *n.* **1** the act or an instance of rising from the dead. **2** (**Resurrection**) **a** Christ's rising from the dead. **b** the rising of the dead at the Last Judgement. **3** a revival after disuse, inactivity, or decay. **4** exhumation. **5** the unearthing of a lost or forgotten thing; restoration to vogue or memory. □ **resurrectional** *adj.* [ME f. OF f. LL *resurrectio -onis* (as RESURGENT)]

resurvey *v. & n. —v.tr.* /ˌriːsɜːˈveɪ/ survey again; reconsider. —*n.* /riːˈsɜːveɪ/ the act or an instance of resurveying.

resuscitate /rɪˈsʌsɪˌteɪt/ *v.tr. & intr.* **1** revive from unconsciousness or apparent death. **2** return or restore to vogue, vigour, or vividness. □ **resuscitation** /-ˈteɪʃ(ə)n/ *n.* **resuscitative** *adj.* **resuscitator** *n.* [L *resuscitare* (as RE-, *suscitare* raise)]

retail /ˈriːteɪl/ *n., adj., adv., & v. —n.* the sale of goods in relatively small quantities to the public, and usu. not for resale (cf. WHOLESALE). —*adj. & adv.* by retail; at a retail price (*do you buy wholesale or retail?*). —*v.* /also rɪˈteɪl/ **1** *tr.* sell (goods) in retail trade. **2** *intr.* (often foll. by *at, of*) (of goods) be sold in this way (esp. for a specified price) (*retails at £4.95*). **3** *tr.* recount; relate details of. □ **retail price index** an index of the variation in the prices of retail goods. □ **retailer** *n.* [ME f. OF *retaille* a piece cut off f. *retaillier* (as RE-, TAIL²)]

retain /rɪˈteɪn/ *v.tr.* **1 a** keep possession of; not lose; continue to have, practise, or recognize. **b** not abolish, discard, or alter. **2** keep in one's memory. **3** keep in place; hold fixed. **4** secure the services of (a person, esp. a barrister) with a preliminary payment. □ **retainable** *adj.* **retainability** /-ˈbɪlɪtɪ/ *n.* **retainment** *n.* [ME f. AF *retei(g)n-* f. stem of OF *retenir* ult. f. L *retinēre* retent- (as RE-, *tenēre* hold)]

retainer /rɪˈteɪnə(r)/ *n.* **1** a person or thing that retains. **2** *Law* a fee for retaining a barrister etc. **3 a** *hist.* a dependant or follower of a person of rank. **b** *joc.* an old and faithful friend or servant (esp. *old retainer*). **4** *Brit.* a reduced rent paid to retain accommodation during a period of non-occupancy.

retake v. & n. —v.tr. /riːˈteɪk/ (past **retook**; past part. **retaken**) 1 take again. 2 recapture. —n. /ˈriːteɪk/ 1 a the act or an instance of retaking. b a thing retaken, e.g. an examination. 2 a the act or an instance of filming a scene or recording music etc. again. b the scene or recording obtained in this way.

retaliate /riˈtælɪˌeɪt/ v. 1 intr. repay an injury, insult, etc., in kind; attack in return; make reprisals. 2 tr. repay (an injury or insult) in kind. □ **retaliation** /-ˈeɪʃ(ə)n/ n. **retaliative** /-ˈtæljətɪv/ adj. **retaliator** n. **retaliatory** /-ˈtæljətərɪ/ adj. [L retaliare (as RE-, talis such)]

retard /riˈtɑːd/ v.tr. 1 make slow or late. 2 delay the progress, development, arrival, or accomplishment of. □ **retardant** adj. & n. **retardation** /ˌriːtɑːˈdeɪʃ(ə)n/ n. **retardative** adj. **retardatory** adj. **retarder** n. **retardment** n. [F retarder f. L retardare (as RE-, tardus slow)]

retarded /riˈtɑːdɪd/ adj. backward in mental or physical development.

retch /retʃ, riːtʃ/ v. & n. —v.intr. make a motion of vomiting esp. involuntarily and without effect. —n. such a motion or the sound of it. [var. of (now dial.) reach f. OE hrǣcan spit, ON hrækja f. Gmc, of imit. orig.]

retell /riːˈtel/ v.tr. (past and past part. **retold**) tell again or in a different version.

retention /riˈtenʃ(ə)n/ n. 1 the act or an instance of retaining; the state of being retained. 2 the ability to retain things experienced or learned; memory. [ME f. OF retention or L retentio (as RETAIN)]

retentive /riˈtentɪv/ adj. 1 (often foll. by of) tending to retain (moisture etc.). 2 (of memory or a person) not forgetful. □ **retentively** adv. **retentiveness** n. [ME f. OF retentif -ive or med.L retentivus (as RETAIN)]

retexture /riːˈtekstʃə(r)/ v.tr. treat (material, a garment, etc.) so as to restore its original texture.

rethink v. & n. —v.tr. /riːˈθɪŋk/ (past and past part. **rethought**) think about (something) again, esp. with a view to making changes. —n. /ˈriːθɪŋk/ a reassessment; a period of rethinking.

reticence /ˈretɪs(ə)ns/ n. 1 the avoidance of saying all one knows or feels, or of saying more than is necessary; reserve in speech. 2 a disposition to silence; taciturnity. 3 the act or an instance of holding back some fact. □ **reticent** adj. **reticently** adv. [L reticentia f. reticēre (as RE-, tacēre be silent)]

reticulate v. & adj. —v.tr. & intr. /riˈtɪkjʊˌleɪt/ 1 divide or be divided in fact or appearance into a network. 2 arrange or be arranged in small squares or with intersecting lines. —adj. /riˈtɪkjʊlət/ reticulated. □ **reticulately** /riˈtɪkjʊlətlɪ/ adv. **reticulation** /-ˈleɪʃ(ə)n/ n. [L reticulatus reticulated f reticulum, dimin. of rete net]

retie /riːˈtaɪ/ v.tr. (**retying**) tie again.

retina /ˈretɪnə/ n. (pl. **retinas**, **retinae** /-ˌniː/) a layer at the back of the eyeball sensitive to light. □ **retinal** adj. [ME f. med.L f. L rete net]

retinol /ˈretɪˌnɒl/ n. a vitamin found in green and yellow vegetables, egg-yolk, and fish-liver oil, essential for growth and vision in dim light. Also called vitamin A. [RETINA + -OL¹]

retinue /ˈretɪˌnjuː/ n. a body of attendants accompanying an important person. [ME f. OF retenue fem. past part. of retenir RETAIN]

retire /riˈtaɪə(r)/ v. 1 a intr. leave office or employment, esp. because of age (retire from the army; retire on a pension). b tr. cause (a person) to retire from work. 2 intr. withdraw; go away; retreat. 3 intr. seek seclusion or shelter. 4 intr. go to bed. 5 tr. withdraw (troops). 6 intr. & tr. Cricket (of a batsman) voluntarily end or be compelled to suspend one's innings (retired hurt). □ **retirer** n. [F retirer (as RE-, tirer draw)]

retired /riˈtaɪəd/ adj. 1 a having retired from employment (a retired teacher). b relating to a retired person (received retired pay). 2 withdrawn from society or observation; secluded (lives a retired life). □ **retiredness** n.

retirement /riˈtaɪəmənt/ n. 1 a the act or an instance of retiring. b the condition of having retired. 2 a seclusion or privacy. b a secluded place. □ **retirement pension** Brit. a pension paid by the State to retired people above a certain age.

retiring /riˈtaɪərɪŋ/ adj. shy; fond of seclusion. □ **retiringly** adv.

retold past and past part. of RETELL.

retook past of RETAKE.

retort¹ /riˈtɔːt/ n. & v. —n. 1 an incisive or witty or angry reply. 2 the turning of a charge or argument against its originator. 3 a piece of retaliation. —v. 1 a tr. say by way of a retort. b intr. make a retort. 2 tr. repay (an insult or attack) in kind. [L retorquēre retort- (as RE-, torquēre twist)]

retort² /riˈtɔːt/ n. & v. —n. 1 a vessel usu. of glass with a long recurved neck used in distilling liquids. 2 a vessel for heating coal to generate gas, or iron and carbon to make steel. —v.tr. purify (mercury) by heating in a retort. [F retorte f. med.L retorta fem. past part. of retorquēre: see RETORT¹]

retouch /riːˈtʌtʃ/ v. & n. —v.tr. improve or repair (a composition, picture, photographic negative or print, etc.) by fresh touches or alterations. —n. the act or an instance of retouching. □ **retoucher** n. [prob. f. F retoucher (as RE-, TOUCH)]

retrace /riˈtreɪs/ v.tr. 1 go back over (one's steps etc.). 2 trace back to a source or beginning. 3 recall the course of in one's memory. [F retracer (as RE-, TRACE¹)]

retract /riˈtrækt/ v. 1 tr. (also absol.) withdraw or revoke (a statement or undertaking). 2 a tr. & intr. (esp. with ref. to part of the body) draw or be drawn back or in. b tr. draw (an undercarriage etc.) into the body of an aircraft. □ **retractable** adj. **retraction** n. **retractive** adj. [L retrahere or (in sense 1) retractare (as RE-, trahere tract- draw)]

retractile /riˈtræktaɪl/ adj. capable of being retracted. □ **retractility** /-ˈtɪlɪtɪ/ n. [RETRACT, after contractile]

retractor /riˈtræktə(r)/ n. 1 a muscle used for retracting. 2 a device for retracting.

retrain /riːˈtreɪn/ v.tr. & intr. train again or further, esp. for new work.

retranslate /ˌriːtrænzˈleɪt, -sˈleɪt, ˌriːtrɑːn-/ v.tr. translate again, esp. back into the original language. □ **retranslation** n.

retransmit /ˌriːtrænzˈmɪt, -sˈmɪt, ˌriːtrɑːn-/ v.tr. (**retransmitted**, **retransmitting**) transmit (esp. radio signals or broadcast programmes) back again or to a further distance. □ **retransmission** /-ˈmɪʃ(ə)n/ n.

retread *v. & n.* —*v.tr.* /riːˈtred/ (*past* **retrod**; *past part.* **retrodden** or (in sense 2) **retreaded**) **1** tread (a path etc.) again. **2** put a fresh tread on (a tyre). —*n.* /ˈriːtred/ a retreaded tyre.

retreat /rɪˈtriːt/ *v. & n.* —*v.* **1 a** *intr.* (esp. of military forces) go back, retire; relinquish a position. **b** *tr.* cause to retreat; move back. **2** *intr.* (esp. of features) recede; slope back. —*n.* **1 a** the act or an instance of retreating. **b** *Mil.* a signal for this. **2** withdrawal into privacy or security. **3** a place of shelter or seclusion. **4** a period of seclusion for prayer and meditation. **5** *Mil.* a bugle-call at sunset. [ME f. OF *retret* (n.), *retraiter* (v.) f. L *retrahere*: see RETRACT]

retrench /rɪˈtrentʃ/ *v.* **1** *tr.* reduce the amount (of costs). **2** *intr.* cut down expenses; introduce economies. □ **retrenchment** *n.* [obs. F *retrencher* (as RE-, TRENCH)]

retrial /riːˈtraɪəl/ *n.* a second or further (judicial) trial.

retribution /ˌretrɪˈbjuːʃ(ə)n/ *n.* requital usu. for evil done; vengeance. □ **retributive** /rɪˈtrɪbjʊtɪv/ *adj.* **retributory** /rɪˈtrɪbjʊtərɪ/ *adj.* [ME f. LL *retributio* (as RE-, *tribuere tribut-* assign)]

retrieve /rɪˈtriːv/ *v.tr.* **1 a** regain possession of. **b** recover by investigation or effort of memory. **2 a** restore to knowledge or recall to mind. **b** obtain (information stored in a computer etc.). **3** (of a dog) find and bring in (killed or wounded game etc.). **4** (foll. by *from*) recover or rescue (esp. from a bad state). **5** repair or set right (a loss or error etc.) (*managed to retrieve the situation*). □ **retrievable** *adj.* **retrieval** *n.* [ME f. OF *retroeve*-stressed stem of *retrover* (as RE-, *trover* find)]

retriever /rɪˈtriːvə(r)/ *n.* **1 a** a dog of a breed used for retrieving game. **b** this breed. **2** a person who retrieves something.

retro /ˈretrəʊ/ *adj. & n. sl.* —*adj.* reviving or harking back to the past. —*n.* a retro fashion or style.

retro- /ˈretrəʊ/ *comb. form* **1** denoting action back or in return (retroact; retroflex). **2** *Anat. & Med.* denoting location behind. [L *retro* backwards]

retroactive /ˌretrəʊˈæktɪv/ *adj.* (esp. of legislation) having retrospective effect. □ **retroactively** *adv.* **retroactivity** /-ˈtɪvɪtɪ/ *n.*

retrod *past* of RETREAD.

retrodden *past part.* of RETREAD.

retrofit /ˈretrəʊfɪt/ *v.tr.* (-**fitted**, -**fitting**) modify (machinery, vehicles, etc.) to incorporate changes and developments introduced after manufacture. [RETROACTIVE + REFIT]

retrograde /ˈretrəˌɡreɪd/ *adj. & v.* —*adj.* **1** directed backwards; retreating. **2** reverting esp. to an inferior state; declining. **3** inverse, reversed (*in retrograde order*). —*v.intr.* **1** move backwards; recede, retire. **2** decline, revert. □ **retrogradely** *adv.* [ME f. L *retrogradus* (as RETRO-, *gradus* step, *gradi* walk)]

retrogress /ˌretrəˈɡres/ *v.intr.* **1** go back; move backwards. **2** deteriorate. □ **retrogressive** *adj.* [RETRO-, after PROGRESS v.]

retrogression /ˌretrəˈɡreʃ(ə)n/ *n.* **1** backward or reversed movement. **2** a return to a less advanced state; a reversal of development; a decline or deterioration. □ **retrogressive** /-sɪv/ *adj.* [RETRO-, after *progression*]

retro-rocket /ˈretrəʊˌrɒkɪt/ *n.* an auxiliary rocket for slowing down a spacecraft etc., e.g. when re-entering the earth's atmosphere.

retrospect /ˈretrəˌspekt/ *n.* **1** (foll. by *to*) regard or reference to precedent or authority, or to previous conditions. **2** a survey of past time or events. □ **in retrospect** when looked back on. [RETRO-, after PROSPECT n.]

retrospection /ˌretrəˈspekʃ(ə)n/ *n.* the action of looking back esp. into the past. [prob. f. *retrospect* (v.) (as RETROSPECT)]

retrospective /ˌretrəˈspektɪv/ *adj. & n.* —*adj.* **1** looking back on or dealing with the past. **2** (of an exhibition, recital, etc.) showing an artist's development over his or her lifetime. **3** (of a statute etc.) applying to the past as well as the future; retroactive. —*n.* a retrospective exhibition, recital, etc. □ **retrospectively** *adv.*

retroussé /rəˈtruːseɪ/ *adj.* (of the nose) turned up at the tip. [F, past part. of *retrousser* tuck up (as RE-, TRUSS)]

retrovert /ˈretrəʊvɜːt/ *v.tr.* **1** turn backwards. **2** *Med.* (as **retroverted** *adj.*) (of the womb) having a backward inclination. □ **retroversion** /-ˈvɜːʃ(ə)n/ *n.* [LL *retrovertere* (as RETRO-, *vertere* vers-turn)]

retry /riːˈtraɪ/ *v.tr.* (-**ies**, -**ied**) try (a defendant or lawsuit) a second or further time. □ **retrial** *n.*

retsina /retˈsiːnə/ *n.* a Greek white wine flavoured with resin. [mod. Gk]

retune /riːˈtjuːn/ *v.tr.* **1** tune (a musical instrument) again or differently. **2** tune (a radio etc.) to a different frequency.

returf /riːˈtɜːf/ *v.tr.* provide with new turf.

return /rɪˈtɜːn/ *v. & n.* —*v.* **1** *intr.* come or go back. **2** *tr.* bring or put or send back to the person or place etc. where originally belonging or obtained (*returned the fish to the river*; *have you returned my scissors?*). **3** *tr.* pay back or reciprocate; give in response (*decided not to return the compliment*). **4** *tr.* yield (a profit). **5** *tr.* say in reply; retort. **6** *tr.* (in cricket or tennis etc.) hit or send (the ball) back after receiving it. **7** *tr.* state or mention or describe officially, esp. in answer to a writ or formal demand. **8** *tr.* (of an electorate) elect as an MP, government, etc. —*n.* **1** the act or an instance of coming or going back. **2 a** the act or an instance of giving or sending or putting or paying back. **b** a thing given or sent back. **3** (in full **return ticket**) esp. *Brit.* a ticket for a journey to a place and back to the starting-point. **4** (in *sing.* or *pl.*) **a** the proceeds or profit of an undertaking. **b** the acquisition of these. **5** a formal report or statement compiled or submitted by order (*an income-tax return*). **6** (in full **return match** or **game**) a second match etc. between the same opponents. □ **by return** (**of post**) by the next available post in the return direction. **in return** as an exchange or reciprocal action. **many happy returns** (**of the day**) a greeting on a birthday. **returning officer** *Brit.* an official conducting an election in a constituency and announcing the results. □ **returnable** *adj.* **returner** *n.* **returnless** *adj.* [ME f. OF *returner* (as RE-, TURN)]

returnee /rɪtɜːˈniː/ *n.* a person who returns home from abroad, esp. after war service.

retying *pres. part.* of RETIE.

retype /riːˈtaɪp/ *v.tr.* type again, esp. to correct errors.

reunify /riːˈjuːnɪˌfaɪ/ *v.tr.* (-**ies**, -**ied**) restore (esp. separated territories) to a political unity. □ **reunification** /-fɪˈkeɪʃ(ə)n/ *n.*

reunion / riːˈjuːnjən, -nɪən/ n. **1 a** the act or an instance of reuniting. **b** the condition of being reunited. **2** a social gathering esp. of people formerly associated. [F réunion or AL reunio f. L reunire unite (as RE-, UNION)]

reunite /ˌriːjuːˈnaɪt/ v.tr. & intr. bring or come back together.

reupholster /ˌriːʌpˈhəʊlstə(r)/ v.tr. upholster anew. □ **reupholstery** n.

reuse v. & n. —v.tr. /riːˈjuːz/ use again or more than once. —n. /riːˈjuːs/ a second or further use. □ **reusable** /-ˈjuːzəb(ə)l/ adj.

reutilize /riːˈjuːtɪˌlaɪz/ v.tr. (also **-ise**) utilize again or for a different purpose. □ **reutilization** /-ˈzeɪʃ(ə)n/ n.

Rev. abbr. Reverend.

rev /rev/ n. & v. colloq. —n. (in pl.) the number of revolutions of an engine per minute (running at 3,000 revs). —v. (**revved**, **revving**) **1** intr. (of an engine) revolve; turn over. **2** tr. (also absol.; often foll. by up) cause (an engine) to run quickly. [abbr.]

revalue /riːˈvæljuː/ v.tr. (**revalues**, **revalued**, **revaluing**) Econ. give a different value to, esp. give a higher value to, (a currency) in relation to other currencies or gold. □ **revaluation** /-ˈeɪʃ(ə)n/ n.

revamp /riːˈvæmp/ v.tr. **1** renovate, revise, improve. **2** patch up. [RE- + VAMP¹]

Revd abbr. Reverend.

reveal /rɪˈviːl/ v.tr. **1** display or show; allow to appear. **2** (often as **revealing** adj.) disclose, divulge, betray (revealed his plans; a revealing remark). **3** tr. (in refl. or passive) come to sight or knowledge. □ **revealable** adj. **revealer** n. **revealingly** adv. [ME f. OF reveler or L revelare (as RE-, velum veil)]

reveille /rɪˈvælɪ, rɪˈvelɪ/ n. a military waking-signal sounded in the morning on a bugle or drums etc. [F réveillez imper. pl. of réveiller awaken (as RE-, veiller f. L vigilare keep watch)]

revel /ˈrev(ə)l/ v. & n. —v.intr. (**revelled**, **revelling**; US **reveled**, **reveling**) **1** have a good time; be extravagantly festive. **2** (foll. by in) take keen delight in. —n. (in sing. or pl.) the act or an instance of revelling. □ **reveller** n. **revelry** n. (pl. **-ies**). [ME f. OF reveler riot f. L rebellare REBEL v.]

revelation /ˌrevəˈleɪʃ(ə)n/ n. **1 a** the act or an instance of revealing, esp. the supposed disclosure of knowledge to humankind by a divine or supernatural agency. **b** knowledge disclosed in this way. **2** a striking disclosure (it was a revelation to me). **3** (**Revelation** or colloq. **Revelations**) (in full the **Revelation of St John the Divine**) the last book of the New Testament, describing visions of heaven. □ **revelational** adj. [ME f. OF revelation or LL revelatio (as REVEAL)]

revelatory /ˌrevəˈleɪtərɪ/ adj. serving to reveal, esp. something significant. [L revelare: see REVEAL]

revenant /ˈrevənɒnt/ n. a person who has returned, esp. supposedly from the dead. [F, pres. part. of revenir: see REVENUE]

revenge /rɪˈvendʒ/ n. & v. —n. **1** retaliation for an offence or injury. **2** an act of retaliation. **3** the desire for this; a vindictive feeling. **4** (in games) a chance to win after an earlier defeat. —v. **1** tr. (in refl. or passive; often foll. by on, upon) inflict retaliation for an offence on. **2** tr. take

revenge for (an offence). **3** tr. avenge (a person). □ **revenger** n. [ME f. OF revenger, revencher f. LL revindicare (as RE-, vindicare lay claim to)]

revengeful /rɪˈvendʒfʊl/ adj. eager for revenge. □ **revengefully** adv. **revengefulness** n.

revenue /ˈrevəˌnjuː/ n. **1 a** income, esp. of a large amount, from any source. **b** (in pl.) items constituting this. **2** a State's annual income from which public expenses are met. **3** the department of the civil service collecting this. [ME f. OF revenu(e) past part. of revenir f. L revenire return (as RE-, venire come)]

reverberate /rɪˈvɜːbəˌreɪt/ v. **1 a** intr. (of sound, light, or heat) be returned or echoed or reflected repeatedly. **b** tr. return (a sound etc.) in this way. **2** intr. (of a story, rumour, etc.) be heard much or repeatedly. □ **reverberant** adj. **reverberantly** adv. **reverberation** /-ˈreɪʃ(ə)n/ n. **reverberative** /-rətɪv/ adj. **reverberator** n. **reverberatory** /-rətərɪ/ adj. [L reverberare (as RE-, verberare lash f. verbera (pl.) scourge]

revere /rɪˈvɪə(r)/ v.tr. hold in deep and usu. affectionate or religious respect; venerate. [F révérer or L reverēri (as RE-, verēri fear)]

reverence /ˈrevərəns/ n. & v. —n. **1** the act of revering or the state of being revered (hold in reverence; feel reverence for). **2** the capacity for revering (lacks reverence). —v.tr. regard or treat with reverence. [ME f. OF f. L reverentia (as REVERE)]

reverend /ˈrevərənd/ adj. & n. —adj. (esp. as the title of a clergyman) deserving reverence. —n. colloq. a clergyman. □ **Reverend Mother** the title of the Mother Superior of a convent. [ME f. OF reverend or L reverendus gerundive of reverēri: see REVERE]

reverent /ˈrevərənt/ adj. feeling or showing reverence. □ **reverently** adv. [ME f. L reverens (as REVERE)]

reverential /ˌrevəˈrenʃ(ə)l/ n. of the nature of, due to, or characterized by reverence. □ **reverentially** adv. [med.L reverentialis (as REVERE)]

reverie /ˈrevərɪ/ n. a fit of abstracted musing (was lost in a reverie). [obs. F resverie f. OF reverie rejoicing, revelry f. rever be delirious, of unkn. orig.]

revers /rɪˈvɪə(r)/ n. (pl. same /-ˈvɪəz/) **1** the turned-back edge of a garment revealing the under-surface. **2** the material on this surface. [F, = REVERSE]

reverse /rɪˈvɜːs/ v., adj., & n. —v. **1** tr. turn the other way round or up or inside out. **2** tr. change to the opposite character or effect (reversed the decision). **3** intr. & tr. travel or cause to travel backwards. **4** tr. make (an engine etc.) work in a contrary direction. **5** tr. revoke or annul (a decree, act, etc.). **6** intr. (of a dancer, esp. in a waltz) revolve in the opposite direction. —adj. **1** placed or turned in an opposite direction or position. **2** opposite or contrary in character or order; inverted. —n. **1** the opposite or contrary (the reverse is the case; is the reverse of the truth). **2** the contrary of the usual manner. **3** an occurrence of misfortune; a disaster, esp. a defeat in battle (suffered a reverse). **4** reverse gear or motion. **5** the reverse side of something. **6** the side of a coin or medal etc. bearing the secondary design. □ **reverse arms** hold a rifle with the butt upwards. **reverse the charges** Brit. make the recipient of a telephone call responsible for payment. **reverse gear** a gear used to make a vehicle etc. travel backwards. **reversing light** a white light at the rear of a vehicle operated when the vehicle is in reverse gear. □ **reversal** *n.* **reversely** *adv.* **reverser** *n.* **reversible** *adj.* **reversibility** /-'bɪlɪtɪ/ *n.* **reversibly** *adv.* [ME f. OF *revers* (n.), *reverser* (v.), f. L *revertere revers-* (as RE-, *vertere* turn)]

reversion /rɪ'vɜːʃ(ə)n/ *n.* **1** the legal right (esp. of the original owner, or his or her heirs) to possess or succeed to property on the death of the present possessor. **2** *Biol.* a return to ancestral type. **3** a return to a previous state, habit, etc. **4** a sum payable on a person's death, esp. by way of life insurance. □ **reversional** *adj.* **reversionary** *adj.* [ME f. OF *reversion* or L *reversio* (as REVERSE)]

revert /rɪ'vɜːt/ *v.* **1** *intr.* (foll. by *to*) return to a former state, practice, opinion, etc. **2** *intr.* (of property, an office, etc.) return by reversion. □ **reverter** *n.* (in sense 2). [ME f. OF *revertir* or L *revertere* (as REVERSE)]

revertible /rɪ'vɜːtɪb(ə)l/ *adj.* (of property) subject to reversion.

revetment /rɪ'vetmənt/ *n.* a retaining wall or facing. [F *revêtement* f. *revêtir* f. OF *revestir* f. LL *revestire* (as RE- *vestire* clothe f. *vestis*)]

review /rɪ'vjuː/ *n.* & *v.* —*n.* **1** a general survey or assessment of a subject or thing. **2** a retrospect or survey of the past. **3** revision or reconsideration (*is under review*). **4** a display and formal inspection of troops etc. **5** a published account or criticism of a book, play, etc. **6** a periodical publication with critical articles on current events, the arts, etc. —*v.tr.* **1** survey or look back on. **2** reconsider or revise. **3** hold a review of (troops etc.). **4** write a review of (a book, play, etc.). □ **reviewable** *adj.* **reviewal** *n.* **reviewer** *n.* [obs. F *reveue* f. *revoir* (as RE-, *voir* see)]

revile /rɪ'vaɪl/ *v.* **1** *tr.* abuse; criticize abusively. **2** *intr.* talk abusively; rail. □ **revilement** *n.* **reviler** *n.* **reviling** *n.* [ME f. OF *reviler* (as RE-, VILE)]

revise /rɪ'vaɪz/ *v.* & *n.* —*v.tr.* **1** examine or reexamine and improve or amend (esp. written or printed matter). **2** consider and alter (an opinion etc.). **3** (also *absol.*) *Brit.* read again (work learnt or done) to improve one's knowledge, esp. for an examination. —*n.* *Printing* a proof-sheet including corrections made in an earlier proof. □ **Revised Standard Version** a revision in 1946–52 of the Authorized Version of the Bible. **Revised Version** a revision in 1881–5 of the Authorized Version of the Bible. □ **revisable** *adj.* **revisal** *n.* **reviser** *n.* **revisory** *adj.* [F *réviser* look at, or L *revisere* (as RE-, *visere* intensive of *vidēre vis-* see)]

revision /rɪ'vɪʒ(ə)n/ *n.* **1** the act or an instance of revising; the process of being revised. **2** a revised edition or form. □ **revisionary** *adj.* [OF *revision* or LL *revisio* (as REVISE)]

revisionism /rɪ'vɪʒə,nɪz(ə)m/ *n.* often *derog.* a policy of revision or modification, esp. of Marxism on evolutionary socialist (rather than revolutionary) or pluralist principles. □ **revisionist** *n.* & *adj.*

revisit /riː'vɪzɪt/ *v.tr.* (**revisited**, **revisiting**) visit again.

revitalize /riː'vaɪtə,laɪz/ *v.tr.* (also **-ise**) imbue with new life and vitality. □ **revitalization** /-'zeɪʃ(ə)n/ *n.*

revival /rɪ'vaɪv(ə)l/ *n.* **1** the act or an instance of reviving; the process of being revived. **2** a new production of an old play etc. **3** a revived use of an old practice, custom, etc. **4 a** a reawakening of religious fervour. **b** a series of evangelistic meetings to promote this. **5** restoration to bodily or mental vigour or to life or consciousness.

revivalism /rɪ'vaɪvə,lɪz(ə)m/ *n.* belief in or the promotion of a revival, esp. of religious fervour. □ **revivalist** *n.* **revivalistic** /-'lɪstɪk/ *adj.*

revive /rɪ'vaɪv/ *v.intr.* & *tr.* **1** come or bring back to consciousness or life or strength. **2** come or bring back to existence, use, notice, etc. □ **revivable** *adj.* □ **reviver** *n.* [ME f. OF *revivre* or LL *revivere* (as RE-, L *vivere* live)]

revivify /rɪ'vɪvɪ,faɪ/ *v.tr.* (**-ies**, **-ied**) restore to animation, activity, vigour, or life. □ **revivification** /-fɪ'keɪʃ(ə)n/ *n.* [F *revivifier* or LL *revivificare* (as RE-, VIVIFY)]

revoke /rɪ'vəʊk/ *v.* & *n.* —*v.* **1** *tr.* rescind, withdraw, or cancel (a decree or promise etc.). **2** *intr.* *Cards* fail to follow suit when able to do so. —*n.* *Cards* the act of revoking. □ **revocable** /'revəkəb(ə)l/ *adj.* **revocability** /,revəkə'bɪlɪtɪ/ *n.* **revocation** /,revə'keɪʃ(ə)n/ *n.* **revocatory** /'revəkətərɪ/ *adj.* **revoker** *n.* [ME f. OF *revoquer* or L *revocare* (as RE-, *vocare* call)]

revolt /rɪ'vəʊlt/ *v.* & *n.* —*v.* **1** *intr.* **a** rise in rebellion against authority. **b** (as **revolted** *adj.*) having revolted. **2** *tr.* (often in *passive*) affect with strong disgust; nauseate (*was revolted by the thought of it*). **b** *intr.* (often foll. by *at*, *against*) feel strong disgust. —*n.* **1** an act of rebelling. **2** a state of insurrection (*in revolt*). **3** a sense of loathing. **4** a mood of protest or defiance. [F *révolter* f. It. *rivoltare* ult. f. L *revolvere* (as REVOLVE)]

revolting /rɪ'vəʊltɪŋ/ *adj.* disgusting, horrible. □ **revoltingly** *adv.*

revolution /,revə'luːʃ(ə)n/ *n.* **1** the forcible overthrow of a government or social order, in favour of a new system. **2** any fundamental change or reversal of conditions. **3** the act or an instance of revolving. **4 a** motion in orbit or a circular course or round an axis or centre; rotation. **b** the single completion of an orbit or rotation. **c** the time taken for this. **5** a cyclic recurrence. □ **revolutionism** *n.* **revolutionist** *n.* [ME f. OF *revolution* or LL *revolutio* (as REVOLVE)]

revolutionary /,revə'luːʃənərɪ/ *adj.* & *n.* —*adj.* **1** involving great and often violent change. **2** of or causing political revolution. —*n.* (*pl.* **-ies**) an instigator or supporter of political revolution.

revolutionize /,revə'luːʃə,naɪz/ *v.tr.* (also **-ise**) introduce fundamental change to.

revolve /rɪ'vɒlv/ *v.* **1** *intr.* & *tr.* turn or cause to turn round, esp. on an axis; rotate. **2** *intr.* move in a circular orbit. **3** *tr.* ponder (a problem etc.) in the mind. □ **revolving door** a door with usu. four partitions turning round a central axis. □ **revolvable** *adj.* [ME f. L *revolvere* (as RE-, *volvere* roll)]

revolver /rɪ'vɒlvə(r)/ *n.* a pistol with revolving chambers enabling several shots to be fired without reloading.

revue /rɪ'vjuː/ *n.* a theatrical entertainment of a series of short usu. satirical sketches and songs. [F, = REVIEW *n.*]

revulsion /rɪ'vʌlʃ(ə)n/ *n.* **1** abhorrence; a sense of loathing. **2** a sudden violent change of feeling. **3** a sudden reaction in taste, fortune, trade, etc. [F *revulsion* or L *revulsio* (as RE-, *vellere vuls-* pull)]

reward /rɪ'wɔːd/ *n.* & *v.* **1 a** a return or recompense for service or merit. **b** requital for good or evil; retribution. **2** a sum offered for the detection of a criminal, the restoration of lost property, etc. —*v.tr.* give a reward to (a person) or for (a service etc.). □ **rewardless** *adj.* [ME f. AF, ONF *reward* = OF *reguard* REGARD]

rewarding /rɪˈwɔːdɪŋ/ *adj.* (of an activity etc.) worth doing; providing satisfaction. □ **rewardingly** *adv.*

rewind /riːˈwaɪnd/ *v.tr.* (*past* and *past part.* **rewound**) wind (a film or tape etc.) back to the beginning. □ **rewinder** *n.*

rewire /riːˈwaɪə(r)/ *v.tr.* provide (a building etc.) with new wiring. □ **rewirable** *adj.*

reword /riːˈwɜːd/ *v.tr.* change the wording of.

rework /riːˈwɜːk/ *v.tr.* revise; refashion, remake.

rewound *v. past* and *past part.* of REWIND.

rewrite *v.* & *n.* —*v.tr.* /riːˈraɪt/ (*past* **rewrote**; *past part.* **rewritten**) write again or differently. —*n.* /ˈriːraɪt/ **1** the act or an instance of rewriting. **2** a thing rewritten.

Rex /reks/ *n.* the reigning king (following a name or in the titles of lawsuits, e.g. *Rex v. Jones* the Crown versus Jones). [L]

Rf *symb. Chem.* the element rutherfordium.

r.f. *abbr.* radio frequency.

Rh[1] *symb. Chem.* the element rhodium.

Rh[2] *abbr.* **1** Rhesus. **2** Rhesus factor.

r.h. *abbr.* right hand.

rhapsodize /ˈræpsədaɪz/ *v.intr.* (also **-ise**) talk or write rhapsodies.

rhapsody /ˈræpsədɪ/ *n.* (*pl.* **-ies**) **1** an enthusiastic or extravagant utterance or composition. **2** *Mus.* a piece of music in one extended movement, usu. emotional in character. □ **rhapsodic** /ræpˈsɒdɪk/ *adj.* **rhapsodical** /ræpˈsɒdɪk(ə)l/ *adj.* (in senses 1, 2). **rhapsodist** *n.* f. *rhaptō* stitch + *ōidē* song, ODE [L *rhapsodia* f. Gk *rhapsōidia*]

rhea /ˈriːə/ *n.* any of several S. American flightless birds of the family Rheidae, like but smaller than an ostrich. [mod.L genus name f. L f. Gk *Rhea* mother of Zeus]

rhebok var. of REEBOK.

rhenium /ˈriːnɪəm/ *n. Chem.* a rare metallic element of the manganese group, used in the manufacture of superconducting alloys. [mod.L f. L *Rhenus* Rhine]

rheostat /ˈriːəstæt/ *n. Electr.* an instrument used to control a current by varying the resistance. □ **rheostatic** /-ˈstætɪk/ *adj.* [Gk *rheos* stream + -STAT]

rhesus /ˈriːsəs/ *n.* (in full **rhesus monkey**) a small monkey, *Macaca mulatta*, common in N. India. □ **rhesus factor** an antigen occurring on the red blood cells of most humans and some other primates. **rhesus negative** lacking the rhesus factor. **rhesus positive** having the rhesus factor. [mod.L, arbitrary use of L *Rhesus* f. Gk *Rhēsos*, mythical King of Thrace]

rhetoric /ˈretərɪk/ *n.* **1** the art of effective or persuasive speaking or writing. **2** language designed to persuade or impress (often with an implication of insincerity or exaggeration etc.). [ME f. OF *rethorique* f. L *rhetorica*, -*ice* f. Gk *rhētorikē* (*tekhnē*) (art) of rhetoric f. *rhētōr* Gk or Roman teacher of rhetoric]

rhetorical /rɪˈtɒrɪk(ə)l/ *adj.* **1** expressed with a view to persuasive or impressive effect. **2** of the nature of rhetoric. □ **rhetorical question** a question asked not for information but to produce an effect, e.g. *who cares?* for *nobody cares.*

□ **rhetorically** *adv.* [ME f. L *rhetoricus* f. Gk *rhētorikos* (as RHETORIC)]

rheum /ruːm/ *n.* a watery discharge from a mucous membrane, esp. of the eyes or nose. [ME f. OF *reume* ult. f. Gk *rheuma -atos* stream f. *rheō* flow]

rheumatic /ruːˈmætɪk/ *adj.* & *n.* —*adj.* **1** of, relating to, or suffering from rheumatism. **2** producing or produced by rheumatism. —*n.* a person suffering from rheumatism. □ **rheumatic fever** a non-infectious fever with inflammation and pain in the joints. □ **rheumatically** *adv.* **rheumaticky** *adj. colloq.* [ME f. OF *reumatique* or L *rheumaticus* f. Gk *rheumatikos* (as RHEUM)]

rheumatics /ruːˈmætɪks/ *n.pl.* (treated as *sing.*; often prec. by *the*) *colloq.* rheumatism.

rheumatism /ˈruːmətɪz(ə)m/ *n.* any disease marked by inflammation and pain in the joints, muscles, or fibrous tissue, esp. rheumatoid arthritis. [F *rhumatisme* or L *rheumatismus* f. Gk *rheumatismos* f. *rheumatizō* f. *rheuma* stream]

rheumatoid /ˈruːmətɔɪd/ *adj.* having the character of rheumatism. □ **rheumatoid arthritis** a chronic progressive disease causing inflammation and stiffening of the joints.

rheumatology /ˌruːməˈtɒlədʒɪ/ *n.* the study of rheumatic diseases. □ **rheumatological** /-təˈlɒdʒɪk(ə)l/ *adj.* **rheumatologist** *n.*

rhinestone /ˈraɪnstəʊn/ *n.* an imitation diamond. [*Rhine*, river and region in Germany + STONE]

rhino /ˈraɪnəʊ/ *n.* (*pl.* same or **-os**) *colloq.* a rhinoceros. [abbr.]

rhino- /ˈraɪnəʊ/ *comb. form Anat.* the nose. [Gk *rhis rhinos* nostril, nose]

rhinoceros /raɪˈnɒsərəs/ *n.* (*pl.* same or **rhinoceroses**) any of various large thick-skinned plant-eating ungulates of the family Rhinocerotidae of Africa and S. Asia, with one horn or in some cases two horns on the nose and plated or folded skin. □ **rhinoceros horn** a mass of keratinized fibres, reputed to have medicinal or aphrodisiac powers. □ **rhinocerotic** /raɪˌnɒsəˈrɒtɪk/ *adj.* [ME f. L f. Gk *rhinokerōs* (as RHINO-, *keras* horn)]

rhinoplasty /ˈraɪnəʊˌplæstɪ/ *n.* plastic surgery of the nose. □ **rhinoplastic** *adj.*

rhizome /ˈraɪzəʊm/ *n.* an underground rootlike stem bearing both roots and shoots. [Gk *rhizōma* f. *rhizoō* take root]

rho /rəʊ/ *n.* the seventeenth letter of the Greek alphabet (*P*, ρ). [Gk]

rhodium /ˈrəʊdɪəm/ *n. Chem.* a hard white metallic element of the platinum group, used in making alloys and plating jewellery. [Gk *rhodon* rose (from the colour of the solution of its salts)]

rhodo- /ˈrəʊdəʊ/ *comb. form esp. Mineral.* & *Chem.* rose-coloured. [Gk *rhodon* rose]

rhododendron /ˌrəʊdəˈdendrən/ *n.* any evergreen shrub of the genus *Rhododendron*, with large clusters of trumpet-shaped flowers. [L, = oleander, f. Gk (as RHODO-, *dendron* tree)]

rhomb /rɒm/ *n.* = RHOMBUS. □ **rhombic** *adj.* [F *rhombe* or L *rhombus*]

rhombi *pl.* of RHOMBUS.

rhombohedron /ˌrɒmbəˈhiːdrən/ *n.* (*pl.* **-hedrons** or **-hedra** /-drə/) **1** a solid bounded by six equal rhombuses. **2** a crystal in this form. □

rhombohedral *adj.* [RHOMBUS, after *polyhedron* etc.]

rhomboid /ˈrɒmbɔɪd/ *adj.* & *n.* —*adj.* (also **rhomboidal** /-ˈbɔɪd(ə)l/) having or nearly having the shape of a rhombus. —*n.* a quadrilateral of which only the opposite sides and angles are equal. [F *rhomboïde* or LL *rhomboides* f. Gk *rhomboeidēs* (as RHOMB)]

rhombus /ˈrɒmbəs/ *n.* (pl. **rhombuses** or **rhombi** /-baɪ/) *Geom.* a parallelogram with oblique angles and equal sides. [L f. Gk *rhombos*]

rhubarb /ˈruːbɑːb/ *n.* **1 a** any of various plants of the genus *Rheum*, esp. *R. rhaponticum*, producing long fleshy dark-red leaf-stalks used cooked as food. **b** the leaf-stalks of this. **2 a** a root of a Chinese and Tibetan plant of the genus *Rheum*. **b** a purgative made from this. **3 a** *colloq.* a murmurous conversation or noise, esp. the repetition of the word 'rhubarb' by crowd actors. **b** *sl.* nonsense; worthless stuff. [ME f. OF *r(e)ubarbe*, shortening of med.L *r(h)eubarbarum*, alt. assoc. with Gk *rhēon* rhubarb) of *rhabarbarum* foreign 'rha', ult. f. Gk *rha* + *barbaros* foreign]

rhumba var. of RUMBA.

rhyme /raɪm/ *n.* & *v.* —*n.* **1** identity of sound between words or the endings of words, esp. in verse. **2** (in *sing.* or *pl.*) verse having rhymes. **3 a** the use of rhyme. **b** a poem having rhymes. **4** a word providing a rhyme. —*v.* **1** *intr.* **a** (of words or lines) produce a rhyme. **b** (foll. by *with*) act as a rhyme (with another). **2** *intr.* make or write rhymes; versify. **3** *tr.* put or make (a story etc.) into rhyme. **4** *tr.* (foll. by *with*) treat (a word) as rhyming with another. □ **rhyming slang** slang that replaces words by rhyming words or phrases, e.g. *stairs* by *apples and pears*, often with the rhyming element omitted (as in TITFER). **without rhyme or reason** lacking discernible sense or logic. □ **rhymeless** *adj.* **rhymer** *n.* **rhymist** *n.* [ME *rime* f. OF *rime* f. med.L *rithmus*, *rythmus* f. L f. Gk *rhuthmos* RHYTHM]

rhymester /ˈraɪmstə(r)/ *n.* a writer of (esp. simple) rhymes.

rhythm /ˈrɪð(ə)m/ *n.* **1** a measured flow of words and phrases in verse or prose determined by various relations of long and short or accented and unaccented syllables. **2** the aspect of musical composition concerned with periodical accent and the duration of notes. **3** *Physiol.* movement with a regular succession of strong and weak elements. **4** a regularly recurring sequence of events. □ **rhythm and blues** popular music with a blues theme and a strong rhythm. **rhythm method** birth control by avoiding sexual intercourse when ovulation is likely to occur. **rhythm section** the part of a dance band or jazz band mainly supplying rhythm, usu. consisting of piano, bass, and drums. □ **rhythmless** *adj.* [F *rhythme* or L *rhythmus* f. Gk *rhuthmos*, rel. to *rhēo* flow]

rhythmic /ˈrɪðmɪk/ *adj.* (also **rhythmical**) **1** relating to or characterized by rhythm. **2** regularly occurring. □ **rhythmically** *adv.* [F *rhythmique* or L *rhythmicus* f. Gk *rhythmicus* (as RHYTHM)]

rhythmicity /rɪðˈmɪsɪtɪ/ *n.* **1** rhythmical quality or character. **2** the capacity for maintaining a rhythm.

rib *n.* & *v.* —*n.* **1** each of the curved bones articulated in pairs to the spine and protecting the thoracic cavity and its organs. **2** a joint of meat from this part of an animal. **3** a ridge or long raised piece often of stronger or thicker material across a surface or through a structure serving to support or strengthen it. **4** any of a ship's transverse curved timbers forming the framework of the hull. **5** *Knitting* a combination of plain and purl stitches producing a ribbed somewhat elastic fabric. **6** each of the hinged rods supporting the fabric of an umbrella. **7** a vein of a leaf or an insect's wing. —*v.tr.* (**ribbed**, **ribbing**) **1** provide with ribs; act as the ribs of. **2** *colloq.* make fun of; tease. **3** mark with ridges. □ **ribless** *adj.* [OE *rib*, *ribb* f. Gmc]

ribald /ˈrɪb(ə)ld/ *adj.* (of language or its user) coarsely or disrespectfully humorous. [ME (earlier sense 'low-born retainer') f. OF *ribau(l)d* f. *riber* pursue licentious pleasures f. Gmc]

ribaldry /ˈrɪbəldrɪ/ *n.* ribald talk or behaviour.

riband /ˈrɪbənd/ *n.* a ribbon. [ME f. OF *riban*, prob. f. a Gmc compound of BAND[1]]

ribbed /rɪbd/ *adj.* having ribs or riblike markings.

ribbing /ˈrɪbɪŋ/ *n.* **1** ribs or a riblike structure. **2** *colloq.* the act or an instance of teasing.

ribbon /ˈrɪbən/ *n.* **1 a** a narrow strip or band of fabric, used esp. for trimming or decoration. **b** material in this form. **2** a ribbon of a special colour etc. worn to indicate some honour or membership of a sports team etc. **3** a long narrow strip of anything, e.g. impregnated material forming the inking agent in a typewriter. **4** (in *pl.*) ragged strips (*torn to ribbons*). □ **ribbon development** the building of houses along a main road, usu. one leading out of a town or village. □ **ribboned** *adj.* [var. of RIBAND]

ribcage /ˈrɪbkeɪdʒ/ *n.* the wall of bones formed by the ribs round the chest.

riboflavin /ˌraɪbəʊˈfleɪvɪn/ *n.* (also **riboflavine** /-viːn/) a vitamin of the B complex, found in liver, milk, and eggs, essential for energy production. [RIBOSE + L *flavus* yellow]

ribonucleic acid /ˌraɪbənjuːˈkliːɪk/ *n.* a nucleic acid present in living cells, and involved in protein synthesis. [RIBOSE + NUCLEIC ACID]

ribose /ˈraɪbəʊs/ *n.* a sugar found in several vitamins and enzymes. [G, alt. f. *Arabinose* a related sugar]

rice *n.* & *v.* *n.* **1** a swamp grass, *Oryza sativa*, cultivated in marshes, esp. in Asia. **2** the grains of this, used as cereal food. —*v.tr.* US sieve (cooked potatoes etc.) into thin strings. □ **rice-paper** edible paper made from the pith of an oriental tree and used for painting and in cookery. □ **ricer** *n.* [ME *rys* f. OF *ris* f. It. *riso*, ult. f. Gk *oruza*, of oriental orig.]

rich /rɪtʃ/ *adj.* **1** having much wealth. **2** (often foll. by *in*, *with*) splendid, costly, elaborate (*rich tapestries*; *rich with lace*). **3** valuable (*rich offerings*). **4** copious, abundant, ample (*a rich harvest*; *a rich supply of ideas*). **5** (often foll. by *in*, *with*) (of soil or a region etc.) abounding in natural resources or means of production; fertile (*rich in nutrients*; *rich with vines*). **6** (of food or diet) containing much fat or spice etc. **7** (of the mixture in an internal-combustion engine) containing a high proportion of fuel. **8** (of colour or sound or smell) mellow and deep, strong and full. **9 a** (of an incident or assertion etc.) highly amusing or ludicrous; outrageous. **b** (of humour) earthy. □ **richen** *v.intr.* & *tr.* **richness** *n.* [OE *rīce* f. Gmc f.

Celt., rel. to L *rex* king: reinforced in ME f. OF *riche* rich, powerful, of Gmc orig.]

riches /ˈrɪtʃɪz/ *n.pl.* abundant means; valuable possessions. [ME *richesse* f. OF *richeise* f. *riche* RICH, taken as pl.]

richly /ˈrɪtʃlɪ/ *adv.* **1** in a rich way. **2** fully, thoroughly (*richly deserves success*).

Richter scale /ˈrɪktə/ *n.* a scale of 0 to 10 for representing the strength of an earthquake. [C. F. *Richter*, Amer. seismologist d. 1985]

rick[1] *n.* & *v.* —*n.* a stack of hay, corn, etc., built into a regular shape and usu. thatched. —*v.tr.* form into a rick or ricks. [OE *hrēac*, of unkn. orig.]

rick[2] *n.* & *v.* (also **wrick**) —*n.* a slight sprain or strain. —*v.tr.* sprain or strain slightly. [ME *wricke* f. MLG *wricken* move about, sprain]

rickets /ˈrɪkɪts/ *n.* (treated as *sing.* or *pl.*) a disease of children with softening of the bones, caused by a deficiency of vitamin D. [17th c.: orig. uncert., but assoc. by medical writers with Gk *rhakhitis* RACHITIS]

rickety /ˈrɪkɪtɪ/ *adj.* **1 a** insecure or shaky in construction; likely to collapse. **b** feeble. **2 a** suffering from rickets. **b** resembling or of the nature of rickets. □ **ricketiness** *n.* [RICKETS + -Y[1]]

rickshaw /ˈrɪkʃɔː/ *n.* (also **ricksha** /-ʃə/) a light two-wheeled hooded vehicle drawn by one or more persons. [abbr. of *jinricksha*, *jinrikshaw* f. Jap. *jinrikisha* f. *jin* person + *riki* power + *sha* vehicle]

ricochet /ˈrɪkəˌʃeɪ, -ˌʃet/ *n.* & *v.* —*n.* **1** the action of a projectile, esp. a shell or bullet, in rebounding off a surface. **2** a hit made after this. —*v.intr.* (**ricocheted** /-ˌʃeɪd/; **ricocheting** /-ˌʃeɪɪŋ/ or **ricochetted** /-ˌʃetɪd/; **ricochetting** /-ˌʃetɪŋ/) (of a projectile) rebound one or more times from a surface. [F, of unkn. orig.]

ricotta /rɪˈkɒtə/ *n.* a soft Italian cheese. [It., = recooked, f. L *recoquere* (as RE-, *coquere* cook)]

ricrac /ˈrɪkræk/ *n.* (also **rickrack**) a zigzag braided trimming for garments. [redupl. of RACK[1]]

rictus /ˈrɪktəs/ *n.* Anat. & Zool. the expanse or gape of a mouth or beak. □ **rictal** *adj.* [L, = open mouth f. *ringi rict-* to gape]

rid *v.tr.* (**ridding**; *past* and *past part.* **rid** (foll. by *of*) make (a person or place) free of something unwanted. □ **be** (or **get**) **rid of** be freed or relieved of (something unwanted); dispose of. [ME, earlier = 'clear (land etc.)' f. ON *rythja*]

riddance /ˈrɪd(ə)ns/ *n.* the act of getting rid of something. □ **good riddance** welcome relief from an unwanted person or thing.

ridden *past part.* of RIDE.

riddle[1] /ˈrɪd(ə)l/ *n.* & *v.* —*n.* **1** a question or statement testing ingenuity in divining its answer or meaning. **2** a puzzling fact or thing or person. —*v.* **1** *intr.* speak in or propound riddles. **2** *tr.* solve or explain (a riddle). □ **riddler** *n.* [OE *rædels*, *rædelse* opinion, riddle, rel. to READ]

riddle[2] /ˈrɪd(ə)l/ *v.* & *n.* —*v.tr.* (usu. foll. by *with*) **1** make many holes in, esp. with gunshot. **2** (in *passive*) fill; spread through; permeate (*was riddled with errors*). **3** pass through a riddle. —*n.* a coarse sieve. [OE *hriddel*, earlier *hrīder*: cf. *hrīdrian* sift]

ride *v.* & *n.* —*v.* (*past* **rode**; *past part.* **ridden** /ˈrɪd(ə)n/) **1** *tr.* travel or be carried on (a bicycle

etc.) or esp. *US* in (a vehicle). **2** *intr.* (often foll. by *on, in*) travel or be conveyed (on a bicycle or in a vehicle). **3** *tr.* sit on and control or be carried by (a horse etc.). **4** *intr.* (often foll. by *on*) be carried (on a horse etc.). **5** *tr.* be carried or supported by (*the ship rides the waves*). **6** *tr.* **a** traverse on horseback etc., ride over or through (*ride 50 miles*; *rode the prairie*). **b** compete or take part in on horseback etc. (*rode a good race*). **7** *intr.* **a** lie at anchor; float buoyantly. **b** (of the moon) seem to float. **8** *intr.* (foll. by *in, on*) rest in or on while moving. **9** *tr.* yield to (a blow) so as to reduce its impact. **10** *tr.* give a ride to; cause to ride (*rode the child on his back*). **11** *tr.* (of a rider) cause (a horse etc.) to move forward (*rode their horses at the fence*). **12** *tr.* **a** (in *passive*; foll. by *by, with*) be oppressed or dominated by; be infested with (*was ridden with guilt*). **b** (as **ridden** *adj.*) infested or afflicted with (usu. in *comb.*: *a rat-ridden cellar*). —*n.* **1** an act or period of travel in a vehicle. **2** a spell of riding on a horse, bicycle, person's back, etc. **3** a path (esp. through woods) for riding on. **4** the quality of sensations when riding (*gives a bumpy ride*). □ **ride down** overtake or trample on horseback. **ride for a fall** act recklessly risking defeat or failure. **ride high** be elated or successful. **ride out** come safely through (a storm etc., or a danger or difficulty). **ride up** (of a garment, carpet, etc.) work or move out of its proper position. **take for a ride** *colloq.* hoax or deceive. □ **ridable** *adj.* [OE *rīdan*]

rider /ˈraɪdə(r)/ *n.* **1** a person who rides (esp. a horse). **2** an additional clause amending or supplementing a document etc. **3** Math. a problem arising as a corollary of a theorem etc. □ **riderless** *adj.* [OE *rīdere* (as RIDE)]

ridge *n.* & *v.* —*n.* **1** the line of the junction of two surfaces sloping upwards towards each other (*the ridge of a roof*). **2** a long narrow hilltop, mountain range, or watershed. **3** any narrow elevation across a surface. **4** Meteorol. an elongated region of high barometric pressure. **5** Agriculture a raised strip of arable land, usu. one of a set separated by furrows. —*v.* **1** *tr.* mark with ridges. **2** *tr.* Agriculture break up (land) into ridges. □ **ridge-piece** (or **-tree**) a beam along the ridge of a roof. **ridge-pole 1** the horizontal pole of a long tent. **2** = *ridge-piece*. **ridge-tile** a tile used in making a roof-ridge. □ **ridgy** *adj.* [OE *hrycg* f. Gmc]

ridgeway /ˈrɪdʒweɪ/ *n.* a road or track along a ridge.

ridicule /ˈrɪdɪˌkjuːl/ *n.* & *v.* —*n.* subjection to derision or mockery. —*v.tr.* make fun of; subject to ridicule; laugh at. [F or f. L *ridiculum* neut. of *ridiculus* laughable f. *ridēre* laugh]

ridiculous /rɪˈdɪkjʊləs/ *adj.* **1** deserving or inviting ridicule. **2** unreasonable, absurd. □ **ridiculously** *adv.* **ridiculousness** *n.* [L *ridiculosus* (as RIDICULE)]

riding[1] /ˈraɪdɪŋ/ *n.* **1** in senses of RIDE *v.* **2** the practice or skill of riders of horses. **3** = RIDE *n.* 3.

riding[2] /ˈraɪdɪŋ/ *n.* **1** each of three former administrative divisions (**East Riding**, **North Riding**, **West Riding**) of Yorkshire. **2** an electoral division of Canada. [OE *thriding* (unrecorded) f. ON *thrithjungr* third part f. *thrithi* THIRD: *th*- was lost owing to the preceding *-t* or *-th* of *east* etc.]

Riesling /ˈriːzlɪŋ, -slɪŋ/ *n.* **1** a kind of dry white wine produced in Germany, Austria, and elsewhere. **2** the variety of grape from which this is produced. [G]

rife *predic.adj.* **1** of common occurrence; widespread. **2** (foll. by *with*) abounding in; teeming with. □ **rifeness** *n.* [OE *rȳfe* prob. f. ON *rífr* acceptable f. *reifa* enrich, *reifr* cheerful]

riff *n.* & *v.* —*n.* a short repeated phrase in jazz etc. —*v.intr.* play riffs. [20th c.: abbr. of RIFFLE *n.*]

riffle /ˈrɪf(ə)l/ *v.* & *n.* —*v.* **1** *tr.* a turn (pages) in quick succession. **b** shuffle (playing-cards) esp. by flexing and combining the two halves of a pack. **2** *intr.* (often foll. by *through*) leaf quickly (through pages). —*n.* the act or an instance of riffling. [perh. var. of RUFFLE]

riff-raff /ˈrɪfræf/ *n.* (often prec. by *the*) rabble; disreputable or undesirable persons. [ME *riff and raff* f. OF *rif et raf*]

rifle[1] /ˈraɪf(ə)l/ *n.* & *v.* —*n.* **1** a gun with a long rifled barrel, esp. one fired from shoulder-level. **2** (in *pl.*) riflemen. —*v.tr.* make spiral grooves in (a gun or its barrel or bore) to make a bullet spin. □ **rifle-range** a place for rifle-practice. **rifle-shot 1** the distance coverable by a shot from a rifle. **2** a shot fired with a rifle. [OF *rifler* graze, scratch f. Gmc]

rifle[2] /ˈraɪf(ə)l/ *v.tr.* & (foll. by *through*) *intr.* search and rob, esp. of all that can be found. [ME f. OF *rifler* graze, scratch, plunder f. ODu. *riffelen*]

rifleman /ˈraɪf(ə)lmən/ *n.* (*pl.* **-men**) a soldier armed with a rifle.

rifling /ˈraɪflɪŋ/ *n.* the arrangement of grooves on the inside of a gun's barrel.

rift *n.* & *v.* —*n.* **1 a** a crack or split in an object. **b** an opening in a cloud etc. **2** a cleft or fissure in earth or rock. **3** a disagreement; a breach in friendly relations. —*v.tr.* tear or burst apart. □ **rift-valley** a steep-sided valley formed by subsidence of the earth's crust between nearly parallel faults. □ **riftless** *adj.* **rifty** *adj.* [ME, of Scand. orig.]

rig[1] /rɪg/ *v.* & *n.* —*v.tr.* (**rigged**, **rigging**) **1 a** provide (a sailing ship) with sails, rigging, etc. **b** prepare ready for sailing. **2** (often foll. by *out*, *up*) fit with clothes or other equipment. **3** (foll. by *up*) set up hastily or as a makeshift. **4** assemble and adjust the parts of (an aircraft). —*n.* **1** the arrangement of masts, sails, rigging, etc., of a sailing ship. **2** equipment for a special purpose, e.g. a radio transmitter. **3** = *oil rig.* □ **rig-out** *Brit. colloq.* an outfit of clothes. □ **rigged** *adj.* (also in *comb.*). **rigger** *n.* [ME, perh. of Scand. orig.: cf. Norw. *rigge*]

rig[2] *v.tr.* (**rigged**, **rigging**) manage or conduct fraudulently (*they rigged the election*). □ **rigger** *n.* [19th c.: orig. unkn.]

rigging /ˈrɪgɪŋ/ *n.* a ship's spars, ropes, etc., supporting and controlling the sails.

right /raɪt/ *adj.*, *n.*, *v.*, *adv.*, & *int.* —*adj.* **1** (of conduct etc.) just, morally or socially correct (*it is only right to tell you*; *I want to do the right thing*). **2** true, correct; not mistaken (*the right time*; *you were right about the weather*). **3** less wrong or not wrong (*which is the right way to town?*). **4** more or most suitable or preferable (*the right person for the job*; *along the right lines*). **5** in a sound or normal condition; physically or mentally healthy; satisfactory (*the engine doesn't sound right*). **6 a** on or towards the side of the human

body which corresponds to the position of east if one regards oneself as facing north. **b** on or towards that part of an object which is analogous to a person's right side or (with opposite sense) which is nearer to a spectator's right hand. **7** (of a side of fabric etc.) meant for display or use (*turn it right side up*). **8** *colloq.* or *archaic* real; properly so called (*made a right mess of it*; *a right royal welcome*). —*n.* **1** that which is morally or socially correct or just; fair treatment (often in *pl.*: *the rights and wrongs of the case*). **2** (often foll. by *to*, or *to* + *infin.*) a justification or fair claim (*has no right to speak like that*). **3** a thing one may legally or morally claim; the state of being entitled to a privilege or immunity or authority to act (*a right of reply*; *human rights*). **4** the right-hand part or region or direction. **5** *Boxing* **a** the right hand. **b** a blow with this. **6** (often **Right**) *Polit.* **a** a group or section favouring conservatism. **b** such conservatives collectively. **7** the side of a stage which is to the right of a person facing the audience. **8** (esp. in marching) the right foot. **9** the right wing of an army. —*v.tr.* **1** (often *refl.*) restore to a proper or straight or vertical position. **2 a** correct (mistakes etc.); set in order. **b** avenge (a wrong or a wronged person); make reparation for or to. —*adv.* **1** straight (*go right on*). **2** *colloq.* immediately; without delay (*I'll be right back*; *do it right now*). **3 a** (foll. by *to*, *round*, *through*, etc.) all the way (*sank right to the bottom*; *ran right round the block*). **b** (foll. by *off*, *out*, etc.) completely (*came right off its hinges*; *am right out of butter*). **4** exactly, quite (*right in the middle*). **5** justly, properly, correctly, truly, satisfactorily (*not holding it right*; *if I remember right*). **6** on or to the right side. **7** *archaic* very; to the full (*am right glad to hear it*; *dined right royally*). —*int.* *colloq.* expressing agreement or assent. □ **at right angles** placed to form a right angle. **by right** (or **rights**) if right were done. **do right by** act dutifully towards (a person). **in one's own right** through one's own position or effort etc. **in the right** having justice or truth on one's side. **in one's right mind** sane; competent to think and act. **of** (or **as of**) **right** having legal or moral etc. entitlement. **on the right side of 1** in the favour of (a person etc.). **2** somewhat less than (a specified age). **put** (or **set**) **right 1** restore to order, health, etc. **2** correct the mistaken impression etc. of (a person). **put** (or **set**) **to rights** make correct or well ordered. **right about** (or **about-turn** or **about-face**) **1** a right turn continued to face the rear. **2** a reversal of policy. **3** a hasty retreat. **right and left** (or **right, left, and centre**) on all sides. **right angle** an angle of 90°, made by lines meeting with equal angles on either side. **right-angled 1** containing or making a right angle. **2** involving right angles, not oblique. **right arm** one's most reliable helper. **right away** (or **off**) immediately. **right bank** the bank of a river on the right facing downstream. **right field** *Baseball* the part of the outfield to the right of the batter as he faces the pitcher. **right hand 1** = *right-hand man*. **2** the most important position next to a person (*stand at God's right hand*). **right-hand** *adj.* **1** on or towards the right side of a person or thing (*right-hand drive*). **2** done with the right hand (*right-hand blow*). **3** (of a screw) = RIGHT-HANDED 4b. **right-hand man** an indispensable or chief assistant. **Right Honourable** *Brit.* a title given to certain high officials, e.g. Privy Councillors. **right-minded** (or **-thinking**) having sound views and principles. **right of way 1** a right established by usage to pass over another's ground. **2** a path subject to such a right. **3** the right of one vehicle to proceed before another. **right oh!** (or **ho!**) = RIGHTO. **right on!** *colloq.* an expression of strong approval or encouragement. **right turn** a turn that brings one's front to face as one's right side did before. **right whale** any large-headed whale of the family Balaenidae, rich in whalebone and easily captured. **right wing 1** the right side of a football etc. team on the field. **2** the conservative section of a political party or system. **right-wing** *adj.* conservative or reactionary. **right-winger** a person on the right wing. **right you are!** *colloq.* an exclamation of assent. **she's** (or **she'll be**) **right** *Austral. colloq.* that will be all right. **too right** *sl.* an expression of agreement. **within one's rights** not exceeding one's authority or entitlement. □ **rightable** *adj.* **righter** *n.* **rightish** *adj.* **rightless** *adj.* **rightlessness** *n.* **rightness** *n.* [OE *riht* (adj.), *rihtan* (v.), *rihte* (adv.)]

righteous /ˈraɪtʃəs/ *adj.* (of a person or conduct) morally right; law-abiding. □ **righteously** *adv.* **righteousness** *n.* [OE *rihtwīs* (as RIGHT *n.* + -WISE or RIGHT *adj.* + WISE²), assim. to *bounteous* etc.]

rightful /ˈraɪtfʊl/ *adj.* **1 a** (of a person) legitimately entitled to (a position etc.) (*the rightful heir*). **b** (of status or property etc.) that one is entitled to. **2** (of an action etc.) equitable, fair. □ **rightfully** *adv.* **rightfulness** *n.* [OE *rihtful* (as RIGHT *n.*)]

right-handed /raɪtˈhændɪd/ *adj.* **1** using the right hand by preference as more serviceable than the left. **2** (of a tool etc.) made to be used with the right hand. **3** (of a blow) struck with the right hand. **4 a** turning to the right; towards the right. **b** (of a screw) advanced by turning to the right (clockwise). □ **right-handedly** *adv.* **right-handedness** *n.*

right-hander /raɪtˈhændə(r)/ *n.* **1** a right-handed person. **2** a right-handed blow.

rightism /ˈraɪtɪz(ə)m/ *n. Polit.* the principles or policy of the right. □ **rightist** *n. & adj.*

rightly /ˈraɪtlɪ/ *adv.* justly, properly, correctly, justifiably.

rightmost /ˈraɪtməʊst/ *adj.* furthest to the right.

righto /ˈraɪtəʊ, raɪˈtəʊ/ *intr. Brit. colloq.* expressing agreement or assent.

rightward /ˈraɪtwəd/ *adv. & adj.* —*adv.* (also **rightwards** /-wədz/) towards the right. —*adj.* going towards or facing the right.

rigid /ˈrɪdʒɪd/ *adj.* **1** not flexible; that cannot be bent (*a rigid frame*). **2** (of a person, conduct, etc.) inflexible, unbending, strict, harsh, punctilious (*a rigid disciplinarian*; *rigid economy*). □ **rigidity** /-ˈdʒɪdɪtɪ/ *n.* **rigidly** *adv.* **rigidness** *n.* [F *rigide* or L *rigidus* f. *rigēre* be stiff]

rigidify /rɪˈdʒɪdɪˌfaɪ/ *v.tr. & intr.* (**-ies**, **-ied**) make or become rigid.

rigmarole /ˈrɪgməˌrəʊl/ *n.* **1** a lengthy and complicated procedure. **2 a** a rambling or meaningless account or tale. **b** such talk. [orig. *ragman roll* = a catalogue, of unkn. orig.]

rigor /ˈrɪgə(r), ˈraɪgɔː(r)/ *n. Med.* **1** a sudden feeling of cold with shivering accompanied by a rise in

temperature, preceding a fever etc. **2** rigidity of the body caused by shock or poisoning etc. [ME f. L f. *rigēre* be stiff]

rigor mortis /ˌrɪgə ˈmɔːtɪs/ *n.* stiffening of the body after death. [L, = stiffness of death]

rigorous /ˈrɪgərəs/ *adj.* **1** characterized by or showing rigour; strict, severe. **2** strictly exact or accurate. □ **rigorously** *adv.* **rigorousness** *n.* [OF *rigorous* or LL *rigorosus* (as RIGOUR)]

rigour /ˈrɪgə(r)/ *n.* (*US* **rigor**) **1 a** severity, strictness, harshness. **b** (in *pl.*) harsh measures or conditions. **2** logical exactitude. **3** strict enforcement of rules etc. (*the utmost rigour of the law*). [ME f. OF *rigour* f. L *rigor* (as RIGOR)]

rile *v.tr. colloq.* anger, irritate. [perh. f. OF *ruiler* mix mortar f. LL *regulare* regulate]

Riley /ˈraɪlɪ/ *n.* (also **Reilly**) □ **the life of Riley** *colloq.* a carefree existence. [20th c.: orig. unkn.]

rilievo var. of RELIEVO.

rill *n.* a small stream. [LG *ril*, *rille*]

rim *n. & v.* —*n.* **1 a** a raised edge or border. **b** a margin or verge, esp. of something circular. **2** the part of a pair of spectacles surrounding the lenses. **3** the outer edge of a wheel, on which the tyre is fitted. —*v.tr.* (**rimmed**, **rimming**) **1** provide with a rim. **b** be a rim for or to. **2** edge, border. □ **rimless** *adj.* **rimmed** *adj.* (also in *comb.*). [OE *rima* edge: cf. ON *rimi* ridge (the only known cognate)]

rime *n. & v.* —*n.* **1** frost, esp. formed from cloud or fog. **2** *poet.* hoar-frost. —*v.tr.* cover with rime. □ **rimy** *adj.* [OE *hrīm*]

rind /raɪnd/ *n. & v.* —*n.* **1** the tough outer layer or covering of fruit and vegetables, cheese, bacon, etc. **2** the bark of a tree or plant. —*v.tr.* strip the bark from. □ **rinded** *adj.* (also in *comb.*). **rindless** *adj.* [OE *rind(e)*]

rinderpest /ˈrɪndəˌpest/ *n.* a virulent infectious disease of ruminants (esp. cattle). [G f. *Rinder* cattle + *Pest* PEST]

ring¹ *n. & v.* —*n.* **1** a circular band, usu. of precious metal, worn on a finger as an ornament or a token of marriage or betrothal. **2** a circular band of any material. **3** the rim of a cylindrical or circular object, or a line or band round it. **4** a mark or part having the form of a circular band (*had rings round his eyes*; *smoke rings*). **5** = *annual ring*. **6 a** an enclosure for a circus performance, betting at races, the showing of cattle, etc. **b** (prec. by *the*) bookmakers collectively. **c** a roped enclosure for boxing or wrestling. **7 a** a group of people or things arranged in a circle. **b** such an arrangement. **8** a combination of traders, bookmakers, spies, politicians, etc. acting together usu. illicitly for the control of operations or profit. **9** a circular or spiral course. **10** = *gas ring*. —*v.tr.* **1** make or draw a circle round. **2** (often foll. by *round*, *about*, *in*) encircle or hem in (game or cattle). **3** put a ring on (a bird etc.) or through the nose of (a pig, bull, etc.). □ **ring-binder** a loose-leaf binder with ring-shaped clasps that can be opened to pass through holes in the paper. **ring circuit** an electrical circuit serving a number of power points with one fuse in the supply to the circuit. **ring finger** the finger next to the little finger, esp. of the left hand, on which the wedding ring is usu. worn. **ring main 1** an electrical supply serving a series of consumers and returning to the original source. **2** = *ring circuit*. **ring ouzel** a thrush, *Turdus torquatus*, with a white crescent across its breast. **ring-pull** (of a tin) having a ring for pulling to break its seal. **ring road** a bypass encircling a town. **run** (or **make**) **rings round** *colloq.* outclass or outwit (another person). □ **ringed** *adj.* (also in *comb.*). **ringless** *adj.* [OE *hring* f. Gmc]

ring² *v. & n.* —*v.* (*past* **rang**; *past part.* **rung**) **1** *intr.* (often foll. by *out* etc.) give a clear resonant or vibrating sound of or as of a bell (*a shot rang out; a ringing laugh; the telephone rang*). **2** *tr.* make (esp. a bell) ring. **b** (*absol.*) call for service or attention by ringing a bell (*you rang, madam?*). **3** *tr.* (also *absol.*; often foll. by *up*) *Brit.* call by telephone (*will ring you on Monday; did you ring?*). **4** *intr.* (usu. foll. by *with, to*) (of a place) resound or be permeated with a sound, or an attribute, e.g. fame (*the theatre rang with applause*). **5** *intr.* (of the ears) be filled with a sensation of ringing. **6** *tr.* **a** sound (a peal etc.) on bells. **b** (of a bell) sound (the hour etc.). **7** *tr.* (foll. by *in, out*) usher in or out with bell-ringing (*ring in the May; rang out the Old Year*). **8** *intr.* (of sentiments etc.) convey a specified impression (*words rang hollow*). —*n.* **1** a ringing sound or tone. **2** the act of ringing a bell. **b** the sound caused by this. **3** *colloq.* a telephone call (*give me a ring*). **4** a specified feeling conveyed by an utterance (*had a melancholy ring*). **5** a set of esp. church bells. □ **ring back** make a return telephone call to (a person who has telephoned earlier). **ring down** (or **up**) **the curtain 1** cause the curtain to be lowered or raised. **2** (foll. by *on*) mark the end or the beginning of (an enterprise etc.). **ring in 1** report or make contact by telephone. **2** *Austral. & NZ sl.* substitute fraudulently. **ring in one's ears** (or **heart** etc.) linger in the memory. **ringing tone** a sound heard by a telephone caller when the number dialled is being rung. **ring off** *Brit.* end a telephone call by replacing the receiver. **ring true** (or **false**) convey an impression of truth or falsehood. **ring up 1** *Brit.* call by telephone. **2** record (an amount etc.) on a cash register. □ **ringed** *adj.* (also in *comb.*). **ringer** *n.* **ringing** *adj.* **ringingly** *adv.* [OE *hringan*]

ringer /ˈrɪŋə(r)/ *n. sl.* **1 a** esp. *US* an athlete or horse entered in a competition by fraudulent means, esp. as a substitute. **b** a person's double, esp. an imposter. **2** a person who rings, esp. a bell-ringer. □ **be a ringer** (or **dead ringer**) **for** resemble (a person) exactly. [RING² + -ER¹]

ringleader /ˈrɪŋˌliːdə(r)/ *n.* a leading instigator in an illicit or illegal activity.

ringlet /ˈrɪŋlɪt/ *n.* a curly lock of hair, esp. a long one. □ **ringleted** *adj.* **ringlety** *adj.*

ringmaster /ˈrɪŋˌmɑːstə(r)/ *n.* the person directing a circus performance.

ringside /ˈrɪŋsaɪd/ *n.* the area immediately beside a boxing ring or circus ring etc. (often *attrib.: a ringside seat; a ringside view*). □ **ringsider** *n.*

ringworm /ˈrɪŋwɜːm/ *n.* any of various fungous infections of the skin causing circular inflamed patches, esp. on a child's scalp.

rink *n.* **1** an area of natural or artificial ice for skating or the game of curling etc. **2** an enclosed area for roller-skating. **3** a building containing either of these. **4** *Bowls* a strip of the green used for playing a match. [ME (orig. Sc.), = jousting-ground: perh. orig. f. OF *renc* RANK¹]

rinse /rɪns/ *v. & n.* —*v.tr.* (often foll. by *through, out*) **1** wash with clean water. **2** apply liquid to. **3** wash lightly. **4** put (clothes etc.) through clean water to remove soap or detergent. **5** (foll. by *out, away*) clear (impurities) by rinsing. —*n.* **1** the act or an instance of rinsing (*give it a rinse*). **2** a solution for cleansing the mouth. **3** a dye for the temporary tinting of hair (*a blue rinse*). □ **rinser** *n.* [ME f. OF *rincer, raincier*, of unkn. orig.]

riot /ˈraɪət/ *n. & v.* —*n.* **1 a** a disturbance of the peace by a crowd; an occurrence of public disorder. **b** (*attrib.*) involved in suppressing riots (*riot police; riot shield*). **2** uncontrolled revelry; noisy behaviour. **3** (foll. by *of*) a lavish display or enjoyment (*a riot of colour and sound*). **4** *colloq.* a very amusing thing or person. —*v.intr.* **1** make or engage in a riot. **2** live wantonly; revel. □ **read the Riot Act** put a firm stop to insubordination etc.; give a severe warning. **run riot 1** throw off all restraint. **2** (of plants) grow or spread uncontrolled. □ **rioter** *n.* **riotless** *adj.* [ME f. OF *riote, rioter, rihoter*, of unkn. orig.]

riotous /ˈraɪətəs/ *adj.* **1** marked by or involving rioting. **2** characterized by wanton conduct. **3** wildly profuse. □ **riotously** *adv.* **riotousness** *n.* [ME f. OF (as RIOT)]

RIP *abbr.* may he or she or they rest in peace. [L *requiescat* (pl. *requiescant*) *in pace*]

rip¹ *v. & n.* —*v.tr. & intr.* (**ripped, ripping**) **1** *tr.* tear or cut (a thing) quickly or forcibly away or apart (*ripped out the lining; ripped the book up*). **2** *tr.* **a** make (a hole etc.) by ripping. **b** make a long tear or cut in. **3** *intr.* come violently apart; split. **4** *intr.* rush along. —*n.* **1** a long tear or cut. **2** an act of ripping. □ **let rip** *colloq.* **1** act or proceed without restraint. **2** speak violently. **3** not check the speed of or interfere with (a person or thing). **rip-cord** a cord for releasing a parachute from its pack. **rip into** attack (a person) verbally. **rip off** *colloq.* defraud, steal. **rip-off** *n. colloq.* **1** a fraud or swindle. **2** financial exploitation. [ME: orig. unkn.]

rip² /rɪp/ *n.* **1** a dissolute person. **2** a rascal. **3** a worthless horse. [perh. f. *rep*, abbr. of REPROBATE]

riparian /raɪˈpeərɪən/ *adj.* esp. *Law* of or on a river-bank (*riparian rights*). [L *riparius* f. *ripa* bank]

ripe *adj.* **1** (of grain, fruit, cheese, etc.) ready to be reaped or picked or eaten. **2** mature; fully developed (*ripe in judgement; a ripe beauty*). **3** (of a person's age) advanced. **4** (often foll. by *for*) fit or ready (*when the time is ripe; land ripe for development*). □ **ripely** *adv.* **ripeness** *n.* [OE *rīpe* f. WG]

ripen /ˈraɪpən/ *v.tr. & intr.* make or become ripe.

riposte /rɪˈpɒst/ *n. & v.* —*n.* **1** a quick sharp reply or retort. **2** a quick return thrust in fencing. —*v.intr.* deliver a riposte. [F *ri(s)poste, ri(s)poster* f. It. *risposta* RESPONSE]

ripper /ˈrɪpə(r)/ *n.* **1** a person or thing that rips. **2** a murderer who rips the victims' bodies.

ripple /ˈrɪp(ə)l/ *n. & v.* —*n.* **1** a ruffling of the water's surface, a small wave or series of waves. **2** a gentle lively sound that rises and falls, e.g. of laughter or applause. **3** a wavy appearance in hair, material, etc. —*v.* **1 a** *intr.* form ripples; flow in ripples. **b** *tr.* cause to do this. **2** *intr.* show or sound like ripples. □ **ripplet** *n.* **ripply** *adj.* [17th c.: orig. unkn.]

rip-roaring /ˈrɪpˌrɔːrɪŋ/ *adj.* **1** wildly noisy or boisterous. **2** excellent, first-rate. □ **rip-roaringly** *adv.*

ripsaw /ˈrɪpsɔː/ *n.* a coarse saw for sawing wood along the grain.

ripsnorter /ˈrɪpˌsnɔːtə(r)/ *n. colloq.* an energetic, remarkable, or excellent person or thing. □ **ripsnorting** *adj.* **ripsnortingly** *adv.*

rise /raɪz/ *v. & n.* —*v.intr.* (*past* **rose** /rəʊz/; *past part.* **risen** /ˈrɪz(ə)n/) **1** move from a lower position to a higher one; come or go up. **2** grow, project, expand, or incline upwards; become higher. **3** (of the sun, moon, or stars) appear above the horizon. **4 a** get up from lying or sitting or kneeling (*rose to their feet; rose from the table*). **b** get out of bed, esp. in the morning. **5** recover a standing or vertical position; become erect (*rose to my full height*). **6** (of a meeting etc.) cease to sit for business; adjourn (*the court will rise*). **7** reach a higher position or level or amount (*the flood has risen; prices are rising*). **8** develop greater intensity, strength, volume, or pitch (*the colour rose in her cheeks; the wind is rising; their voices rose with excitement*). **9** make progress; reach a higher social position (*rose from the ranks*). **10 a** come to the surface of liquid (*waited for the fish to rise*). **b** (of a person) react to provocation (*rise to the bait*). **11** become or be visible above the surroundings etc., stand prominently (*mountains rose to our right*). **12 a** (of buildings etc.) undergo construction from the foundations (*office blocks were rising all around*). **b** (of a tree etc.) grow to a (usu. specified) height. **13** come to life again (*rise from the ashes; risen from the dead*). **14** (of dough) swell by the action of yeast etc. **15** (often foll. by *up*) cease to be quiet or submissive; rebel (*rise in arms*). **16** originate; have as its source (*the river rises in the mountains*). **17** (of wind) start to blow. **18** (of a person's spirits) become cheerful. **19** (of a barometer) show a higher atmospheric pressure. —*n.* **1** an act or manner or amount of rising. **2** an upward slope or hill or movement (*the house stood on a rise; the rise and fall of the waves*). **3** an increase in sound or pitch. **4 a** an increase in amount, extent, etc. (*a rise in unemployment*). **b** *Brit.* an increase in salary, wages, etc. **5** an increase in status or power. **6** social, commercial, or political advancement; upward progress. **7** the movement of fish to the surface. **8** origin. **9 a** the vertical height of a step, arch, incline, etc. **b** = RISER 2. □ **get** (or **take**) **a rise out of** *colloq.* provoke an emotional reaction from (a person), esp. by teasing. **on the rise** on the increase. **rise above 1** superior to (petty feelings etc.). **2** show dignity or strength in the face of (difficulty, poor conditions, etc.). **rise to** develop powers equal to (an occasion). [OE *rīsan* f. Gmc]

riser /ˈraɪzə(r)/ *n.* **1** a person who rises esp. from bed (*an early riser*). **2** a vertical section between the treads of a staircase. **3** a vertical pipe for the flow of liquid or gas.

rishi /ˈrɪʃɪ/ *n.* (*pl.* **rishis**) a Hindu sage or saint. [Skr. *ṛṣi*]

risible /ˈrɪzɪb(ə)l/ *adj.* **1** laughable, ludicrous. **2** inclined to laugh. □ **risibility** /-ˈbɪlɪtɪ/ *n.* **risibly** *adv.* [LL *risibilis* f. L *rīdēre rīs-* laugh]

rising /ˈraɪzɪŋ/ *adj. & n.* —*adj.* **1** going up; getting higher. **2** increasing (*rising costs*). **3** advancing to maturity or high standing (*the rising generation; a rising young lawyer*). **4** approaching a specified age (*the rising fives*). **5** (of ground) sloping upwards. —*n.* a revolt or insurrection. □ **rising damp** moisture absorbed from the ground into a wall.

risk *n. & v.* —*n.* **1** a chance or possibility of danger, loss, injury, or other adverse consequences (*a health risk; a risk of fire*). **2** a person or thing causing a risk or regarded in relation to risk (*is a poor risk*). —*v.tr.* **1** expose to risk. **2** accept the chance of (*could not risk getting wet*). **3** venture on. □ **at risk** exposed to danger. **at one's** (**own**) **risk** accepting responsibility, agreeing to make no claims. **at the risk of** with the possibility of (an adverse consequence). **put at risk** expose to danger. **risk one's neck** put one's own life in danger. **run a** (or **the**) **risk** (often foll. by *of*) expose oneself to danger or loss etc. **take** (or **run**) **a risk** chance the possibility of danger etc. [F *risque, risquer* f. It. *risco* danger, *riscare* run into danger]

risky /ˈrɪskɪ/ *adj.* (**riskier, riskiest**) **1** involving risk. **2** = RISQUÉ. □ **riskily** *adv.* **riskiness** *n.*

risotto /rɪˈzɒtəʊ/ *n.* (*pl.* **-os**) an Italian dish of rice cooked in stock with meat, onions, etc. [It.]

risqué /ˈrɪskeɪ, -ˈkeɪ/ *adj.* (of a story etc.) slightly indecent. [F, past part. of *risquer* RISK]

rissole /ˈrɪsəʊl/ *n.* a compressed mixture of meat and spices, coated in breadcrumbs and fried. [F f. OF *ruissole, roussole* ult. f. LL *russeolus* reddish f. L *russus* red]

ritardando /ˌriːtaːˈdændəʊ/ *adv. & n. Mus.* (*pl.* **-os** or **ritardandi** /-dɪ/) = RALLENTANDO. [It.]

rite *n.* **1** a religious or solemn observance or act (*burial rites*). **2** an action or procedure required or usual in this. **3** a body of customary observances characteristic of a Church or a part of it (*the Latin rite*). □ **rite of passage** (often in *pl.*) a ritual or event marking a stage of a person's advance through life, e.g. marriage. □ **riteless** *adj.* [ME f. OF *rit, rite* or L *ritus* (esp. religious) usage]

ritual /ˈrɪtjʊəl/ *n. & adj.* —*n.* **1** a prescribed order of performing rites. **2** a procedure regularly followed. —*adj.* of or done as a ritual or rites. □ **ritualize** *v.tr. & intr.* (also **-ise**). **ritualization** /-ˈzeɪʃ(ə)n/ *n.* (also **-isation**). **ritually** *adv.* [L *ritualis* (as RITE)]

ritualism /ˈrɪtjʊəˌlɪz(ə)m/ *n.* the regular or excessive practice of ritual. □ **ritualist** *n.* **ritualistic** /-ˈlɪstɪk/ *adj.* **ritualistically** /-ˈlɪstɪkəlɪ/ *adv.*

ritzy /ˈrɪtsɪ/ *adj.* (**ritzier, ritziest**) *colloq.* **1** high-class, luxurious. **2** ostentatiously smart. □ **ritzily** *adv.* **ritziness** *n.* [*Ritz,* the name of luxury hotels f. C. Ritz, Swiss hotel-owner d. 1918]

rival /ˈraɪv(ə)l/ *n. & v.* —*n.* **1** a person competing with another for the same objective. **2** a person or thing that equals another in quality. —*v.tr.* (**rivalled, rivalling**; *US* **rivaled, rivaling**) **1** be the rival of or comparable to. **2** seem or claim to be as good as. [L *rivalis,* orig. = using the same stream, f. *rivus* stream]

rivalry /ˈraɪvəlrɪ/ *n.* (*pl.* **-ies**) the state or an instance of being rivals; competition.

river /ˈrɪvə(r)/ *n.* **1** a copious natural stream of water flowing in a channel to the sea or a lake etc. **2** a copious flow (*a river of lava; rivers of blood*). **3** (*attrib.*) (in the names of animals, plants, etc.) living in or associated with the river. □

rivered *adj.* (also in comb.). **riverless** *adj.* [ME f. AF *river, rivere,* OF *riviere* river or river-bank ult. f. L *riparius* f. *ripa* bank]

riverside /ˈrɪvəˌsaɪd/ *n.* the ground along a river-bank.

rivet /ˈrɪvɪt/ *n.* & *v.* —*n.* a nail or bolt for holding together metal plates etc., its headless end being beaten out or pressed down when in place. —*v.tr.* (**riveted, riveting**) **1 a** join or fasten with rivets. **b** beat out or press down the end of (a nail or bolt). **c** fix; make immovable. **2 a** (foll. by *on, upon*) direct intently (one's eyes or attention etc.). **b** (esp. as **riveting** *adj.*) engross (a person or the attention). □ **riveter** *n.* [ME f. OF f. *river* clench, of unkn. orig.]

riviera /ˌrɪviˈeərə/ *n.* a coastal region with a subtropical climate, vegetation, etc., esp. that of SE France and NW Italy. [It., = sea-shore]

rivulet /ˈrɪvjʊlɪt/ *n.* a small stream. [obs. *riveret* f. F, dimin. of *rivière* RIVER, perh. after It. *rivoletto* dimin. of *rivolo* dimin. of *rivo* f. L *rivus* stream]

RM *abbr.* (in the UK) Royal Marines.

RN *abbr.* (in the UK) Royal Navy.

Rn *symb. Chem.* the element radon.

RNA *abbr.* ribonucleic acid.

RNZAF *abbr.* Royal New Zealand Air Force.

RNZN *abbr.* Royal New Zealand Navy.

roach[1] *n.* (*pl.* same) a small freshwater fish, esp. *Rutilus rutilus,* allied to the carp. [ME f. OF *roc(h)e,* of unkn. orig.]

roach[2] *n.* **1** *US colloq.* a cockroach. **2** *sl.* the butt of a marijuana cigarette. [abbr.]

road *n.* **1 a** a path or way with a specially prepared surface, used by vehicles, pedestrians, etc. **b** the part of this used by vehicles (*don't step in the road*). **2** one's way or route (*our road took us through unexplored territory*). **3** (usu. in *pl.*) a partly sheltered piece of water near the shore in which ships can ride at anchor. □ **by road** using transport along roads. **get out of the** (or **my** etc.) **road** *colloq.* cease to obstruct a person. **in the** (or **my** etc.) **road** *colloq.* obstructing a person or thing. **on the road** travelling, esp. as a firm's representative, itinerant performer, or vagrant. **road fund licence** *Brit.* a disc displayed on a vehicle certifying payment of road tax. **road-hog** *colloq.* a reckless or inconsiderate road-user, esp. a motorist. **road-holding** the capacity of a moving vehicle to remain stable when cornering at high speeds etc. **road-house** an inn or club on a major road. **road hump** = *sleeping policeman.* **road-manager** the organizer and supervisor of a musicians' tour. **road-map** a map showing the roads of a country or area. **road-metal** broken stone used in road-making or for railway ballast. **road sense** a person's capacity for safe behaviour on the road, esp. in traffic. **road show 1 a** a performance given by a touring company, esp. a group of pop musicians. **b** a company giving such performances. **2** a radio or television programme done on location. **road sign** a sign giving information or instructions to road users. **road tax** a periodic tax payable on road vehicles. **road test** a test of the performance of a vehicle on the road. **road-test** *v.tr.* test (a vehicle) on the road. □ **roadless** *adj.* [OE *rād* f. *rīdan* RIDE]

roadblock /ˈrəʊdblɒk/ *n.* a barrier or barricade on a road, esp. one set up by the authorities to stop and examine traffic.

roadie /ˈrəʊdɪ/ *n. colloq.* an assistant employed by a touring band of musicians to erect and maintain equipment.

roadroller /ˈrəʊdˌrəʊlə(r)/ *n.* a motor vehicle with a heavy roller, used in road-making.

roadrunner /ˈrəʊdˌrʌnə(r)/ *n.* a bird of Mexican and US deserts, *Geococcyx californianus,* related to the cuckoo, and a poor flier but fast runner.

roadside /ˈrəʊdsaɪd/ *n.* the strip of land beside a road.

roadstead /ˈrəʊdstɛd/ *n.* = ROAD 3. [ROAD + *stead* in obs. sense 'place']

roadster /ˈrəʊdstə(r)/ *n.* **1** an open car without rear seats. **2** a horse or bicycle for use on the road.

roadway /ˈrəʊdweɪ/ *n.* **1** a road. **2** = ROAD 1b. **3** the part of a bridge or railway used for traffic.

roadwork /ˈrəʊdwɜːk/ *n.* **1** (in *pl.*) the construction or repair of roads, or other work involving digging up a road surface. **2** athletic exercise or training involving running on roads.

roadworthy /ˈrəʊdˌwɜːðɪ/ *adj.* fit to be used on the road. □ **roadworthiness** *n.*

roam *v.* & *n.* —*v.* **1** *intr.* ramble, wander. **2** *tr.* travel unsystematically over, through, or about. —*n.* an act of roaming; a ramble. □ **roamer** *n.* [ME: orig. unkn.]

roan *adj.* & *n.* —*adj.* (of an animal, esp. a horse or cow) having a coat of which the prevailing colour is thickly interspersed with hairs of another colour, esp. bay or sorrel or chestnut mixed with white or grey. —*n.* a roan animal. [OF, of unkn. orig.]

roar *n.* & *v.* —*n.* **1** a loud deep hoarse sound, as made by a lion, a person in pain or rage or excitement, thunder, a loud engine, etc. **2** a loud laugh. —*v.* **1** *intr.* **a** utter or make a roar. **b** utter loud laughter. **2** *intr.* travel in a vehicle at high speed, esp. with the engine roaring. **3** *tr.* (often foll. by *out*) say, sing, or utter (words, an oath, etc.) in a loud tone. □ **roarer** *n.* [OE *rārian,* of imit. orig.]

roaring /ˈrɔːrɪŋ/ *adj.* in senses of ROAR *v.* □ **roaring drunk** very drunk and noisy. **roaring trade** (or **business**) very brisk trade or business. □ **roaringly** *adv.*

roast *v., adj.,* & *n.* —*v.* **1** *tr.* **a** cook (food, esp. meat) in an oven or by exposure to open heat. **b** heat (coffee beans) before grinding. **2** *tr.* **a** expose to fire or great heat. **b** *tr.* & *refl.* expose (oneself or part of oneself) to warmth. **4** *tr.* criticize severely, denounce. **5** *intr.* undergo roasting. —*attrib.adj.* (of meat or a potato, chestnut, etc.) roasted. —*n.* **1 a** a roast meat. **b** a dish of this. **c** a piece of meat for roasting. **2** the process of roasting. **3** *US* a party where roasted food is eaten. [ME f. OF *rost, rostir,* f. Gmc]

roaster /ˈrəʊstə(r)/ *n.* **1** a person or thing that roasts. **2** an oven or dish for roasting food in. **b** a coffee-roasting apparatus. **3** something fit for roasting, e.g. a fowl, a potato, etc.

roasting /ˈrəʊstɪŋ/ *adj.* & *n.* —*adj.* very hot. —*n.* **1** in senses of ROAST *v.* **2** a severe criticism or denunciation.

rob *v.tr.* (**robbed, robbing**) (often foll. by *of*) **1** take unlawfully from, esp. by force or threat of force (*robbed the safe; robbed her of her jewels*). **2** deprive of what is due or normal (*was robbed of my sleep*). **3** (*absol.*) commit robbery. □ **robber** *n.* [ME f. OF *rob(b)er* f. Gmc: cf. REAVE]

robbery /ˈrɒbərɪ/ n. (pl. **-ies**) **1 a** the act or process of robbing, esp. with force or threat of force. **b** an instance of this. **2** excessive financial demand or cost. [ME f. OF *roberie* (as ROB)]

robe n. & v. —n. **1** a long loose outer garment. **2** esp. *US* a dressing-gown. **3** a baby's outer garment esp. at a christening. **4** (often in *pl.*) a long outer garment worn as an indication of the wearer's rank, office, profession, etc.; a gown or vestment. **5** *US* a blanket or wrap of fur. —v. **1** *tr.* clothe (a person) in a robe; dress. **2** *intr.* put on one's robes or vestments. [ME f. OF f. Gmc (as ROB, orig. sense 'booty')]

robin /ˈrɒbɪn/ n. **1** (also **robin redbreast**) a small brown European bird, *Erithacus rubecula*, the adult of which has a red throat and breast. **2** *US* a red-breasted thrush, *Turdus migratorius*. [ME f. OF, familiar var. of the name *Robert*]

robot /ˈrəʊbɒt/ n. **1** a machine with a human appearance or functioning like a human. **2** a machine capable of carrying out a complex series of actions automatically. **3** a person who works mechanically and efficiently but insensitively. **4** *S.Afr.* an automatic traffic-signal. □ **robotic** /-ˈbɒtɪk/ *adj.* **robotize** *v.tr.* (also **-ise**). [Czech (in K. Čapek's play *R.U.R.* (*Rossum's Universal Robots*) 1920), f. *robota* forced labour]

robotics /rəʊˈbɒtɪks/ n.pl. the study of robots; the art or science of their design and operation.

robust /rəʊˈbʌst/ adj. (**robuster**, **robustest**) **1** (of a person, animal, or thing) strong and sturdy, esp. in physique or construction. **2** (of exercise, discipline, etc.) vigorous, requiring strength. **3** (of intellect or mental attitude) straightforward, not given to nor confused by subtleties. **4** (of a statement, reply, etc.) bold, firm, unyielding. **5** (of wine etc.) full-bodied. □ **robustly** *adv.* **robustness** n. [F *robuste* or L *robustus* firm and hard f. *robus*, *robur* oak, strength]

ROC abbr. (in the UK) Royal Observer Corps.

roc n. a gigantic bird of Eastern legend. [Sp. *rocho* ult. f. Arab *ruḳ*]

rock[1] n. **1 a** the hard material of the earth's crust, exposed on the surface or underlying the soil. **b** a similar material on other planets. **2** a mass of rock projecting and forming a hill, cliff, reef, etc. **3** a large detached stone. **4** *US* a stone of any size. **5** a firm and dependable support or protection. **6** *Brit.* a hard usu. cylindrical stick of confectionery made from sugar with flavouring esp. of peppermint. **7** *sl.* a precious stone, esp. a diamond. □ **on the rocks** *colloq.* **1** short of money. **2** broken down. **3** (of a drink) served undiluted with ice-cubes. **rock-bottom** *adj.* (of prices etc.) the very lowest. —n. the very lowest level. **rock-bound** (of a coast) rocky and inaccessible. **rock-cake** a small currant cake with a hard rough surface. **rock-candy** *US* = sense 6 of n. **rock-crystal** transparent colourless quartz usu. in hexagonal prisms. **rock-face** a vertical surface of natural rock. **rock-garden** an artifical mound or bank of earth and stones planted with rock-plants etc.; a garden in which rockeries are the chief feature. **rock-plant** any plant growing on or among rocks. **rock rose** any plant of the genus *Cistus*, *Helianthemum*, etc., with rose-like flowers. **rock-salmon** any of several fishes, esp. *Brit.* (as a commercial name) the catfish and dogfish. **rock-salt** common salt as a solid mineral.

rock-wool inorganic material made into matted fibre esp. for insulation or soundproofing. □ **rockless** *adj.* **rocklet** n. **rocklike** *adj.* [ME f. OF *ro(c)que*, *roche*, med.L *rocca*, of unkn. orig.]

rock[2] v. & n. —v. **1** *tr.* move gently to and fro in or as if in a cradle; set or maintain such motion (*rock him to sleep; the ship was rocked by the waves*). **2** *intr.* be or continue in such motion (*sat rocking in his chair; the ship was rocking on the waves*). **3 a** *intr.* sway from side to side; shake, oscillate, reel (*the house rocks*). **b** *tr.* cause to do this (*an earthquake rocked the house*). **4** *tr.* distress, perturb. **5** *intr.* dance to or play rock music. —n. **1 a** rocking movement (*gave the chair a rock*). **2** a spell of rocking (*had a rock in his chair*). **3 a** = **rock and roll**. **b** any of a variety of types of modern popular music with a rocking or swinging beat, derived from rock and roll. □ **rock and** (or **rock 'n'**) **roll** a type of popular dance-music originating in the 1950s, characterized by a heavy beat and simple melodies, often with a blues element. **rock the boat** *colloq.* disturb the equilibrium of a situation. **rocking-chair** a chair mounted on rockers or springs for gently rocking in. **rocking-horse** a model of a horse on rockers or springs for a child to rock on. **rocking-stone** a poised boulder easily rocked. [OE *roccian*, prob. f. Gmc]

rockabilly /ˈrɒkəbɪlɪ/ n. a type of popular music combining elements of rock and roll and hill-billy music. [blend of *rock and roll* and *hill-billy*]

rocker /ˈrɒkə(r)/ n. **1** a person or thing that rocks. **2** a curved bar or similar support, on which something can rock. **3** a rocking-chair. **4** *Brit.* a young devotee of rock music, characteristically associated with leather clothing and motor cycles. **5** any rocking device forming part of a mechanism. □ **off one's rocker** *sl.* crazy.

rockery /ˈrɒkərɪ/ n. (pl. **-ies**) a heaped arrangement of rough stones with soil between them for growing rock-plants on.

rocket[1] /ˈrɒkɪt/ n. & v. —n. **1** a cylindrical projectile that can be propelled to a great height or distance by combustion of its contents, used esp. as a firework or signal. **2** an engine using a similar principle but not dependent on air intake for its operation. **3** a rocket-propelled missile, spacecraft, etc. **4** *Brit.* *sl.* a severe reprimand. —v. (**rocketed**, **rocketing**) **1** *tr.* bombard with rockets. **2** *intr.* **a** move rapidly upwards or away. **b** increase rapidly (*prices rocketed*). [F *roquette* f. It. *rochetto* dimin. of *rocca* ROCK[2], with ref. to its cylindrical shape]

rocket[2] /ˈrɒkɪt/ n. a cruciferous annual plant, *Eruca sativa*, grown for salad. [F *roquette* f. It. *rochetta*, *ruchetta* dimin. of *ruca* f. L *eruca* downy-stemmed plant]

rocketry /ˈrɒkɪtrɪ/ n. the science or practice of rocket propulsion.

rockfall /ˈrɒkfɔːl/ n. **1** a descent of loose rocks. **2** a mass of fallen rock.

rockhopper /ˈrɒkˌhɒpə(r)/ n. a small penguin, *Eudyptes crestatus*, of the Antarctic and New Zealand, with a crest of feathers on the forehead.

rocky[1] /ˈrɒkɪ/ adj. (**rockier**, **rockiest**) **1** of or like rock. **2** full of or abounding in rock or rocks (*a rocky shore*). □ **rockiness** n.

rocky² /ˈrɒkɪ/ adj. (**rockier, rockiest**) colloq. unsteady, tottering. □ **rockily** adv. **rockiness** n. [ROCK²]

rococo /rəˈkəʊkəʊ/ adj. & n. —adj. of a late baroque style of decoration prevalent in 18th-c. continental Europe, with asymmetrical patterns. —n. the rococo style. [F, joc. alt. f. rocaille f. roc. (as ROCK¹)]

rod n. **1** a slender straight bar esp. of wood or metal. **2** this as a symbol of office. **3 a** a stick or bundle of twigs used in caning or flogging. **b** (prec. by the) the use of this. **4 a** = fishing-rod. **b** an angler using a rod. **5** (as a measure) a perch or square perch (see PERCH¹). **6** US sl. = hot rod. **7** US sl. a pistol or revolver. **8** Anat. any of numerous rod-shaped structures in the eye, detecting dim light. □ **rodless** adj. **rodlet** n. **rodlike** adj. [OE rodd, prob. rel. to ON rudda club]

rode past of RIDE.

rodent /ˈrəʊd(ə)nt/ n. any mammal of the order Rodentia with strong incisors and no canine teeth, e.g. rat, mouse, squirrel, beaver, porcupine. □ **rodential** /-ˈdenʃ(ə)l/ adj. [L rodere rosgnaw]

rodenticide /rəˈdentɪˌsaɪd/ n. a poison used to kill rodents.

rodeo /ˈrəʊdɪəʊ, rəˈdeɪəʊ/ n. (pl. **-os**) **1** an exhibition or entertainment involving cowboys' skills in handling animals. **2** an exhibition of other skills, e.g. in motor cycling. **3 a** a round-up of cattle on a ranch for branding etc. **b** an enclosure for this. [Sp. f. rodear go round ult. f. L rotare ROTATE]

roe¹ n. **1** (also **hard roe**) the mass of eggs in a female fish's ovary. **2** (also **soft roe**) the milt of a male fish. □ **roed** adj. (also in comb.). [ME row(e), rough, f. MLG, MDu. roge(n), OHG rogo, rogan, ON hrogn]

roe² n. (pl. same or **roes**) (also **roe-deer**) a small European and Asian deer, Capreolus capreolus. [OE rā(ha)]

roebuck /ˈrəʊbʌk/ n. a male roe.

roentgen /ˈrʌntjən/ n. a unit of ionizing radiation. □ **roentgen rays** X-rays. [W. C. Röntgen, Ger. physicist d. 1923, discoverer of X-rays]

rogation /rəʊˈgeɪʃ(ə)n/ n. (usu. in pl.) Eccl. a solemn supplication consisting of the litany of the saints chanted on the three days before Ascension day. □ **Rogation Days** the three days before Ascension Day. **Rogation Sunday** the Sunday preceding these. □ **rogational** adj. [ME f. L rogatio f. rogare ask]

roger /ˈrɒdʒə(r)/ int. & v. —int. **1** your message has been received and understood (used in radio communication etc.). **2** sl. I agree. —v. coarse sl. **1** intr. have sexual intercourse. **2** tr. have sexual intercourse with (a woman). [the name Roger, code for R]

rogue /rəʊg/ n. **1** a dishonest or unprincipled person. **2** joc. a mischievous person, esp. a child. **3** (usu. attrib.) **a** a wild animal driven away or living apart from the herd and of fierce temper (rogue elephant). **b** a stray, irresponsible, or undisciplined person or thing (rogue trader). **4** an inferior or defective specimen among many acceptable ones. □ **rogues' gallery** a collection of photographs of known criminals etc., used for identification of suspects. [16th-c. cant word: orig. unkn.]

roguery /ˈrəʊgərɪ/ n. (pl. **-ies**) conduct or an action characteristic of rogues.

roguish /ˈrəʊgɪʃ/ adj. **1** playfully mischievous. **2** characteristic of rogues. □ **roguishly** adv. **roguishness** n.

roister /ˈrɔɪstə(r)/ v.intr. (esp. as **roistering** adj.) revel noisily; be uproarious. □ **roisterer** n. **roistering** n. **roisterous** adj. [obs. roister roisterer f. F rustre ruffian var. of ruste f. L rusticus RUSTIC]

role n. (also **rôle**) **1** an actor's part in a play, film, etc. **2** a person's or thing's characteristic or expected function (the role of the tape recorder in language-learning). □ **role model** a person looked to by others as an example in a particular role. **role-playing** an exercise in which participants take the part of another character, used in psychotherapy, language-teaching, etc. [F rôle and obs. F roule, rolle, = ROLL n.]

roll /rəʊl/ v. & n. —v. **1 a** intr. move or go in some direction by turning over and over on an axis (the ball rolled under the table; a barrel started rolling). **b** tr. cause to do this (rolled the barrel into the cellar). **2** tr. make revolve between two surfaces (rolled the clay between his palms). **3 a** intr. (foll. by along, by, etc.) move or advance on or (of time etc.) as if on wheels etc. (the bus rolled past; the years rolled by). **b** tr. cause to do this (rolled the tea trolley into the kitchen). **c** intr. (of a person) be conveyed in a vehicle. **4 a** tr. turn over and over on itself to form a more or less cylindrical or spherical shape (rolled a newspaper). **b** tr. make by forming material into a roll or ball (rolled a cigarette; rolled a huge snowball). **c** tr. accumulate into a mass (rolled the dough into a ball). **d** intr. (foll. by into) make a specified shape of itself (the hedgehog rolled into a ball). **5** tr. flatten or form by passing a roller etc. over or by passing between rollers (roll the lawn; roll pastry; roll thin foil). **6** intr. & tr. change or cause to change direction by rotatory movement (his eyes rolled; he rolled his eyes). **7** intr. wallow, turn about in a fluid or a loose medium (the dog rolled in the dust). **8** intr. **a** (of a moving ship, aircraft, or vehicle) sway to and fro on an axis parallel to the direction of motion. **b** walk with an unsteady swaying gait (they rolled out of the pub). **9 a** intr. undulate, show or go with an undulating surface or motion (rolling hills; the waves roll in). **b** tr. carry or propel with such motion (the river rolls its waters to the sea). **10 a** intr. (of machinery) start functioning or moving (the cameras rolled). **b** tr. cause (machinery) to do this. **11** intr. & tr. sound or utter with a vibratory or trilling effect (words rolled off his tongue; he rolls his rs). —n. **1** a rolling motion or gait; undulation (the roll of the hills). **2** a spell of rolling (a roll in the mud). **b** a gymnastic exercise in which the body is rolled into a tucked position and turned in a forward or backward circle. **3** the continuous rhythmic sound of thunder or a drum. **4** Aeron. a complete revolution of an aircraft about its longitudinal axis. **5 a** a cylinder formed by turning flexible material over and over on itself without folding (a roll of carpet; a roll of wallpaper). **b** a filled cake or pastry of similar form (fig roll; sausage roll). **6 a** a small portion of bread individually baked. **b** this with a specified filling (ham roll). **7** a more or less cylindrical or semicylindrical straight or curved mass of something (rolls of fat; a roll of hair). **8 a** an official list or register (the electoral roll). **b** the total numbers on this (*the schools' rolls have fallen*). **c** a document, esp. an official record, in scroll form. **9** a cylinder or roller, esp. to shape metal in a rolling-mill. □ **be rolling** *colloq.* be very rich. **be rolling in** *colloq.* have plenty of (esp. money). **on a roll** *US sl.* experiencing a bout of success or progress; engaged in a period of intense activity. **roll-call** a process of calling out a list of names to establish who is present. **rolled gold** gold in the form of a thin coating applied to a baser metal by rolling. **rolled into one** combined in one person or thing. **rolled oats** oats that have been husked and crushed. **roll in** arrive in great numbers or quantity. **rolling drunk** swaying or staggering from drunkenness. **rolling-mill** a machine or factory for rolling metal into shape. **rolling-pin** a cylinder for rolling out pastry, dough, etc. **rolling-stock 1** the locomotives, carriages, or other vehicles, used on a railway. **2** *US* the road vehicles of a company. **rolling stone** a person who is unwilling to settle for long in one place. **roll-neck** (of a garment) having a high loosely turned-over neck. **roll of honour** a list of those honoured, esp. the dead in war. **roll on** *v.tr.* **1** put on or apply by rolling. **2** (in *imper.*) *colloq.* (of a time, in eager expectation) come quickly (*roll on Friday!*). **roll-on** (*attrib.*) (of deodorant etc.) applied by means of a rotating ball in the neck of the container. —*n.* a light elastic corset. **roll-on roll-off** (of a ship, a method of transport, etc.) in which vehicles are driven directly on at the start of the voyage and off at the end of it. **roll over 1** send (a person) sprawling or rolling. **2** *Econ.* finance the repayment of (maturing stock etc.) by an issue of new stock. **roll-top desk** a desk with a flexible cover sliding in curved grooves. **roll up 1** *colloq.* arrive in a vehicle; appear on the scene. **2** make into or form a roll. **roll-up** (or **roll-your-own**) *n.* a hand-rolled cigarette. **strike off the rolls** debar (esp. a solicitor) from practising after dishonesty etc. □ **rollable** *adj.* [ME f. OF rol(l)er, rouler, ro(u)lle f. L *rotulus* dimin. of *rota* wheel]

roller /ˈrəʊlə(r)/ *n.* **1** a hard revolving cylinder for smoothing the ground, spreading ink or paint, crushing or stamping, rolling up cloth on, hanging a towel on, etc., used alone or as a rotating part of a machine. **2** a small cylinder on which hair is rolled for setting. **3** a long swelling wave. □ **roller-coaster** *n.* a switchback at a fair etc. **roller towel** a towel with the ends joined, hung on a roller.

rollick /ˈrɒlɪk/ *v.intr.* (esp. as **rollicking** *adj.*) be jovial or exuberant, indulge in high spirits, revel. [19th-c., prob. dial.: perh. f. ROMP + FROLIC]

rollmop /ˈrəʊlmɒp/ *n.* a rolled uncooked pickled herring fillet. [G *Rollmops*]

roly-poly /ˌrəʊlɪˈpəʊlɪ/ *n.* & *adj.* —*n.* (*pl.* **-ies**) (also **roly-poly pudding**) a pudding made of a strip of suet pastry covered with jam etc., formed into a roll, and boiled or baked. —*adj.* (usu. of a child) podgy, plump. [prob. formed on ROLL]

ROM /rɒm/ *n. Computing* read-only memory. [abbr.]

romaine /rəˈmeɪn/ *n. US* a cos lettuce. [F, fem. of *romain* (as ROMAN)]

Roman /ˈrəʊmən/ *adj.* & *n.* —*adj.* **1** of ancient Rome or its territory or people. **2** of medieval or modern Rome. **3** of papal Rome, esp. = ROMAN CATHOLIC. **4** (**roman**) (of type) of a plain upright kind used in ordinary print. **5** (of the alphabet etc.) based on the ancient Roman system with letters A–Z. —*n.* **1 a** a citizen of the ancient Roman Republic or Empire. **b** a soldier of the Roman Empire. **2** a citizen of modern Rome. **3** = ROMAN CATHOLIC. **4** (**roman**) roman type. □ **Roman candle** a firework discharging a series of flaming coloured balls and sparks. **Roman nose** one with a high bridge; an aquiline nose. **roman numeral** any of the Roman letters representing numbers: I = 1, V = 5, X = 10, L = 50, C = 100, D = 500, M = 1000. [ME f. OF *Romain* (n. & adj.) f. L *Romanus* f. *Roma* Rome]

Roman Catholic *adj.* & *n.* —*adj.* of the part of the Christian Church acknowledging the Pope as its head. —*n.* a member of this Church. □ **Roman Catholicism** *n.* [17th-c. transl. L (*Ecclesia*) *Romana Catholica* (*et Apostolica*), app. orig. as a conciliatory term: see ROMAN, CATHOLIC]

romance /rəʊˈmæns/ *n.*, *adj.*, & *v.* —*n.* / also *disp.* ˈrəʊ-/ **1** an atmosphere or tendency characterized by a sense of remoteness from or idealization of everyday life. **2 a** sentimental or idealized love. **b** a love affair. **3 a** a literary genre with romantic love or highly imaginative unrealistic episodes forming the central theme. **b** a work of this genre. **4** a medieval tale, usu. in verse, of some hero of chivalry, of the kind common in the Romance languages. **5 a** exaggeration or picturesque falsehood. **b** an instance of this. **6** (**Romance**) the languages descended from Latin regarded collectively. —*adj.* (**Romance**) of any of the languages descended from Latin (French, Italian, Spanish, etc.). —*v.* **1** *intr.* exaggerate or distort the truth, esp. fantastically. **2** *tr.* court, woo. [ME f. OF *romanz*, *-ans*, *-ance*, ult. f. L *Romanicus* ROMANIC]

■ **Usage** The alternative pronunciation given for the noun, with the stress on the first syllable, is considered incorrect by some people.

romancer /rəʊˈmænsə(r)/ *n.* **1** a writer of romances, esp. in the medieval period. **2** a liar who resorts to fantasy.

Romanesque /ˌrəʊməˈnesk/ *n.* & *adj.* —*n.* a style of architecture prevalent in Europe *c.*900–1200, with massive vaulting and round arches (cf. NORMAN). —*adj.* of the Romanesque style of architecture. [F f. *roman* ROMANCE]

Romanian /rəʊˈmeɪnɪən/ *n.* & *adj.* (also **Rumanian** /ruː-/) —*n.* **1 a** a native or national of Romania in E. Europe. **b** a person of Romanian descent. **2** the language of Romania. —*adj.* of or relating to Romania or its people or language.

Romanic /rəʊˈmænɪk/ *n.* & *adj.* —*n.* = ROMANCE *n.* 6. —*adj.* **1 a** of or relating to Romance. **b** Romance-speaking. **2** descended from the ancient Romans or inheriting aspects of their social or political life. [L *Romanicus* (as ROMAN)]

romanize /ˈrəʊmənaɪz/ *v.tr.* (also **-ise**) **1** make Roman or Roman Catholic in character. **2** put into the Roman alphabet or into roman type. □ **romanization** /-ˈzeɪʃ(ə)n/ *n.*

Romano- /rəʊˈmɑːnəʊ/ *comb. form* Roman; Roman and (*Romano-British*).

romantic /rəʊˈmæntɪk/ *adj.* & *n.* —*adj.* **1** of, characterized by, or suggestive of an idealized, sentimental, or fantastic view of reality; remote from experience (a *romantic picture*; a *romantic setting*). **2** inclined towards or suggestive of romance in love (a *romantic woman*; a *romantic evening*). **3** (of a person) imaginative, visionary, idealistic. **4** (of style in art, music, etc.) concerned more with feeling and emotion than with form and aesthetic qualities. **5** (of a project etc.) unpractical, fantastic. —*n.* **1** a romantic person. **2** a romanticist. □ **romantically** *adv.* [*romant* tale of chivalry etc. f. OF f. *romanz* ROMANCE]

romanticism /rəʊˈmæntɪˌsɪz(ə)m/ *n.* (also **Romanticism**) adherence to a romantic style in art, music, etc.

romanticist /rəʊˈmæntɪsɪst/ *n.* (also **Romanticist**) a writer or artist of the romantic school.

romanticize /rəʊˈmæntɪˌsaɪz/ *v.* (also **-ise**) **1** *tr.* **a** make or render romantic or unreal. **b** describe or portray in a romantic fashion. **2** *intr.* indulge in romantic thoughts or actions. □ **romanticization** /-ˈzeɪʃ(ə)n/ *n.*

Romany /ˈrɒmənɪ, ˈrəʊ-/ *n.* & *adj.* —*n.* (pl. **-ies**) **1** a Gypsy. **2** the Indo-European language of the Gypsies. —*adj.* **1** of or concerning Gypsies. **2** of the Romany language. [Romany *Romani* fem. and pl. of *Romano* (adj.) f. *Rom* man, husband]

romp *v.* & *n.* —*v.intr.* **1** play about roughly and energetically. **2** (foll. by *along*, *past*, etc.) *colloq.* proceed without effort. —*n.* a spell of romping or boisterous play. □ **romp in** (or **home**) *colloq.* finish as the easy winner. □ **rompingly** *adv.* **rompy** *adj.* (**rompier**, **rompiest**). [perh. var. of RAMP¹]

romper /ˈrɒmpə(r)/ *n.* (usu. in *pl.*) (also **romper suit**) a young child's one-piece garment covering legs and trunk.

rondeau /ˈrɒndəʊ/ *n.* (pl. **rondeaux** pronunc. same or /-əʊz/) a poem of ten or thirteen lines with only two rhymes throughout and with the opening words used twice as a refrain. [F, earlier *rondel*: see RONDEL]

rondel /ˈrɒnd(ə)l/ *n.* a rondeau, esp. one of special form. [ME f. OF f. *rond* ROUND: cf. ROUNDEL]

rondo /ˈrɒndəʊ/ *n.* (pl. **-os**) *Mus.* a form with a recurring leading theme. [It. f. F *rondeau*: see RONDEAU]

röntgen etc. var. of ROENTGEN etc.

roo /ruː/ *n.* (also **'roo**) *Austral. colloq.* a kangaroo. [abbr.]

rood /ruːd/ *n.* **1** a crucifix, esp. one raised on a screen or beam at the entrance to the chancel. **2** a quarter of an acre. □ **rood-screen** a wooden or stone carved screen separating nave and chancel. [OE *rōd*]

roof /ruːf/ *n.* & *v.* —*n.* (pl. **roofs** or *disp.* **rooves** /ruːvz/) **1 a** the upper covering of a building, usu. supported by its walls. **b** the top of a covered vehicle. **c** the top inner surface of an oven, refrigerator, etc. **2** the overhead rock in a cave or mine etc. **3** the branches or the sky etc. overhead. **4** (of prices etc.) the upper limit or ceiling. —*v.tr.* **1** (often foll. by *in*, *over*) cover with or as with a roof. **2** be the roof of. □ **go through the roof** *colloq.* (of prices etc.) reach extreme or unexpected heights. **hit** (or **go through** or **raise**) **the roof** *colloq.* become very angry. **roof-garden** a garden on the flat roof of a building. **roof of the mouth** the palate. **roof-rack** a framework for carrying luggage etc. on the roof of a vehicle. **roof-tree** the

ridge-piece of a roof. □ **roofed** *adj.* (also in *comb.*). **roofless** *adj.* [OE *hróf*]

roofer /ˈruːfə(r)/ *n.* a person who constructs or repairs roofs.

roofing /ˈruːfɪŋ/ *n.* **1** material for constructing a roof. **2** the process of constructing a roof or roofs.

rooftop /ˈruːftɒp/ *n.* **1** the outer surface of a roof. **2** (esp. in *pl.*) the level of a roof.

rook¹ /rʊk/ *n.* & *v.* —*n.* a black European and Asiatic bird, *Corvus frugilegus*, of the crow family, nesting in colonies in tree-tops. —*v.tr.* **1** charge (a customer) extortionately. **2** win money from (a person) at cards etc. esp. by swindling. [OE *hróc*]

rook² /rʊk/ *n.* a chess piece with its top in the shape of a battlement. [ME f. OF *roc(k)* ult. f. Arab. *rukk*, orig. sense uncert.]

rookery /ˈrʊkərɪ/ *n.* (pl. **-ies**) **1 a** a colony of rooks. **b** a clump of trees having rooks' nests. **2** a colony of sea birds (esp. penguins) or seals.

rookie /ˈrʊkɪ/ *n. sl.* **1** a new recruit, esp. in the army or police. **2** *US* a new member of a sports team. [corrupt. of *recruit*, after ROOK¹]

room /ruːm, rʊm/ *n.* & *v.* —*n.* **1 a** space that is or might be occupied by something; capaciousness or ability to accommodate contents (*it takes up too much room*; *there is plenty of room*; *we have no room here for idlers*). **b** space in or on (*houseroom*; *shelf-room*). **2 a** a part of a building enclosed by walls or partitions, floor and ceiling. **b** (in *pl.*) a set of these occupied by a person or family; apartments or lodgings. **c** persons present in a room (*the room fell silent*). **3** (in *comb.*) a room or area for a specified purpose (*auction-room*). **4** (foll. by *for*, or *to* + infin.) opportunity or scope (*room to improve things*; *no room for dispute*). —*v.intr.* *US* have a room or rooms; lodge, board. □ **rooming-house** a lodging house. **room-mate** a person occupying the same room as another. **room service** (in a hotel etc.) service of food or drink taken to a guest's room. □ **-roomed** *adj.* (in *comb.*). **roomful** *n.* (pl. **-fuls**) [OE *rūm* f. Gmc]

roomer /ˈruːmə(r), ˈrʊmə(r)/ *n.* *US* a lodger occupying a room or rooms without board.

roomy /ˈruːmɪ/ *adj.* (**roomier**, **roomiest**) having much room, spacious. □ **roomily** *adv.* **roominess** *n.*

roost /ruːst/ *n.* & *v.* —*n.* a branch or other support on which a bird perches, esp. a place where birds regularly settle to sleep. —*v. intr.* **1** (of a bird) settle for rest or sleep. **2** (of a person) stay for the night. □ **come home to roost** (of a scheme etc.) recoil unfavourably upon the originator. [OE *hróst*]

rooster /ˈruːstə(r)/ *n.* esp. *US* a domestic cock.

root¹ /ruːt/ *n.* & *v.* —*n.* **1 a** the part of a plant normally below the ground, attaching it to the earth and conveying nourishment to it from the soil. **b** (in *pl.*) such a part divided into branches or fibres. **c** any small plant with a root for transplanting. **2 a** any plant, e.g. a turnip or carrot, with an edible root. **b** such a root. **3** (in *pl.*) the sources or reasons for one's long-standing emotional attachment to a place, community, etc. **4 a** the embedded part of a bodily organ or structure, e.g. hair, tooth, nail, etc. **b** the part of a thing attaching it to a greater or more fundamental whole. **5 a** the basic cause, source, or origin (*love of money is the*

root of all evil). **b** (*attrib.*) (of an idea etc.) from which the rest originated. **6** the essential substance or nature of something (*get to the root of things*). **7** *Math.* **a** a number or quantity that when multiplied by itself a usu. specified number of times gives a specified number or quantity (*the cube root of eight is two*). **b** a square root. **c** a value of an unknown quantity satisfying a given equation. **8** *Philol.* any ultimate unanalysable element of language; a basis, not necessarily surviving as a word in itself, on which words are made by the addition of prefixes or suffixes or by other modification. —*v.* **1 a** *intr.* take root or grow roots. **b** *tr.* cause to do this (*take care to root them firmly*). **2** *tr.* **a** fix firmly; establish (*fear rooted him to the spot*). **b** (as **rooted** *adj.*) firmly established (*her affection was deeply rooted; rooted objection to*). **3** *tr.* (usu. foll. by *out, up*) drag or dig up by the roots. **4** *tr. Austral. coarse sl.* **a** have sexual intercourse with (a woman). **b** exhaust, frustrate. □ **pull up by the roots 1** uproot. **2** eradicate, destroy. **put down roots 1** begin to draw nourishment from the soil. **2** become settled or established. **root and branch** thorough(ly), radical(ly). **root beer** *US* an effervescent drink made from an extract of roots. **root out** find and get rid of. **strike (or take) root 1** begin to grow and draw nourishment from the soil. **2** become fixed or established. □ **rootage** *n.* **rootedness** *n.* **rootless** *adj.* **rootlet** *n.* **rootlike** *adj.* **rooty** *adj.* [OE rōt f. ON rót, rel. to -*wort* in plant names & L *radix*: see RADIX]

root² /ruːt/ *v.* **1** *intr.* (of an animal, esp. a pig) turn up the ground with the snout, beak, etc., in search of food. **b** *tr.* (foll. by *up*) turn up (the ground) by rooting. **2 a** *intr.* (foll. by *around, in,* etc.) rummage. **b** *tr.* (foll. by *out* or *up*) find or extract by rummaging. **3** *intr.* (foll. by *for*) *US sl.* encourage by applause or support. □ **rooter** *n.* (in sense 3). [earlier *wroot* f. OE *wrōtan* & ON *rōta*: rel. to OE *wrōt* snout]

rootle /ˈruːt(ə)l/ *v.intr.* & *tr. Brit.* = ROOT² 1, 2. [ROOT²]

rootstock /ˈruːtstɒk/ *n.* **1** a rhizome. **2** a plant into which a graft is inserted. **3** a primary form from which offshoots have arisen.

rooves see ROOF.

rope *n.* & *v.* —*n.* **1 a** a stout cord made by twisting together strands of hemp, sisal, flax, cotton, nylon, wire, or similar material. **b** a piece of this. **c** *US* a lasso. **2** (foll. by *of*) a quantity of onions, ova, or pearls strung together. **3** (in *pl.*, prec. by *the*) **a** the conditions in some sphere of action (*know the ropes; show a person the ropes*). **b** the ropes enclosing a boxing- or wrestling-ring or cricket ground. **4** (prec. by *the*) **a** a halter for hanging a person. **b** execution by hanging. —*v.* **1** *tr.* fasten, secure, or catch with rope. **2** *tr.* (usu. foll. by *off, in*) enclose (a space) with rope. **3** *Mountaineering* **a** *tr.* connect (a party) with a rope; attach (a person) to a rope. **b** (*absol.*) put on a rope. **c** *intr.* (foll. by *down, up*) climb down or up using a rope. □ **on the ropes 1** *Boxing* forced against the ropes by the opponent's attack. **2** near defeat. **rope in** persuade to take part. **rope into** persuade to take part in (*was roped into doing the washing-up*). **rope-ladder** two long ropes connected by short crosspieces, used as a ladder. [OE *rāp* f. Gmc]

roping /ˈrəʊpɪŋ/ *n.* a set or arrangement of ropes.

ropy /ˈrəʊpɪ/ *adj.* (also **ropey**) (**ropier**, **ropiest**) **1** *Brit. colloq.* poor in quality. **2** like a rope. □ **ropily** *adv.* **ropiness** *n.*

Roquefort /ˈrɒkfə(r)/ *n. propr.* a soft blue cheese made from ewes' milk. [*Roquefort* in S. France]

ro-ro /ˈrəʊrəʊ/ *adj.* roll-on roll-off. [abbr.]

rorqual /ˈrɔːkw(ə)l/ *n.* any of various whales of the family Balaenopteridae esp. *Balaenoptera musculus*, having a dorsal fin. [F f. Norw. *røyrkval* f. ON *reythr* + Norw. *kval* WHALE]

rosaceous /rəʊˈzeɪʃəs/ *adj. Bot.* of the large plant family Rosaceae, which includes the rose. [L *rosaceus* f. *rosa* rose]

rosarium /rəˈzeərɪəm/ *n.* a rose-garden. [L (as ROSARY)]

rosary /ˈrəʊzərɪ/ *n.* (*pl.* **-ies**) **1** *RC Ch.* **a** a form of devotion in which five (or fifteen) decades of Hail Marys are repeated. **b** a string of 55 (or 165) beads for keeping count in this. **2** a similar form of bead-string used in other religions. **3** a rose-garden or rose-bed. [ME f. L *rosarium* rose-garden, neut. of *rosarius* (as ROSE¹)]

rose¹ /rəʊz/ *n.* & *adj.*, —*n.* **1** any prickly bush or shrub of the genus *Rosa*, bearing usu. fragrant flowers generally of a red, pink, yellow, or white colour. **2** this flower. **3** any flowering plant resembling this (*Christmas rose; rock rose*). **4 a** a light crimson colour, pink. **b** (usu. in *pl.*) a rosy complexion (*roses in her cheeks*). **5 a** a representation of the flower in heraldry or decoration (esp. as the national emblem of England). **b** a rose-shaped design, e.g. on a compass card or on the sound-hole of a lute etc. **6** the sprinkling-nozzle of a watering-can or hose. **7** a circular mounting on a ceiling through which the wiring of an electric light passes. —*adj.* = *rose-coloured* 1. □ **rose-bush** a rose plant. **rose-colour** the colour of a pale red rose, warm pink. **rose-coloured 1** of rose-colour. **2** optimistic, sanguine, cheerful (*takes rose-coloured views*). **rose-hip** = HIP². **rose of Sharon 1** a species of hypericum, *Hypericum calycinum*, with dense foliage and golden-yellow flowers. **2** *Bibl.* a flowering plant of unknown identity. **rose-pink** = *rose-colour*, *rose-coloured*. **rose-tinted** = *rose-coloured*. **rose-tree** a rose plant, esp. a standard rose. **rose-water** perfume made from roses. **rose-window** a circular window, usu. with roselike or spokelike tracery. **see through rose-coloured** (or **-tinted**) **spectacles** regard (circumstances etc.) with unfounded favour or optimism. **Wars of the Roses** *hist.* the 15th-c. civil wars between Yorkists with a white rose as an emblem and Lancastrians with a red rose. □ **roseless** *adj.* **roselike** *adj.* [ME f. OE *rōse* f. L *rosa*]

rose² past of RISE.

rosé /ˈrəʊzeɪ/ *n.* any light pink wine, coloured by only brief contact with red grape-skins. [F, = pink]

roseate /ˈrəʊzɪət/ *adj.* **1** = *rose-coloured* (see ROSE¹). **2** having a partly pink plumage. [L *roseus* rosy (as ROSE¹)]

rosebay /ˈrəʊzbeɪ/ *n.* an oleander, rhododendron, or willow-herb.

rosebowl /ˈrəʊzbəʊl/ *n.* a bowl for displaying cut roses.

rosebud /ˈrəʊzbʌd/ *n.* **1** a bud of a rose. **2** a pretty young woman.

rosemary /ˈrəʊzmərɪ/ n. an evergreen fragrant shrub, *Rosmarinus officinalis*, with leaves used as a culinary herb, in perfumery, etc., and taken as an emblem of remembrance. [ME, earlier *rosmarine* ult. f. L *ros marinus* f. *ros* dew + *marinus* MARINE, with assim. to ROSE¹ and *Mary* name of the Virgin]

rosery /ˈrəʊzərɪ/ n. (pl. **-ies**) a rose-garden.

rosette /rəʊˈzet/ n. **1** a rose-shaped ornament made usu. of ribbon and worn esp. as a supporter's badge, or as an award or the symbol of an award in a competition, esp. by a prizewinning animal. **2** *Archit.* **a** a carved or moulded ornament resembling or representing a rose. **b** a rose-window. **3** an object or symbol or arrangement of parts resembling a rose. **4** *Biol.* **a** a roselike cluster of parts. **b** markings resembling a rose. □ **rosetted** adj. [F dimin. of *rose* ROSE¹]

rosewood /ˈrəʊzwʊd/ n. any of several fragrant close-grained woods used in making furniture.

Rosh Hashana /rɒʃ ˌhaːʃɑːˈnɑː, rəʊʃ həˈʃəʊnəʊ/ n. (also **Rosh Hashanah**) the Jewish New Year. [Heb., = beginning (lit. 'head') of the year]

rosin /ˈrɒzɪn/ n. & v. —n. resin, esp. the solid residue after distillation of oil of turpentine from crude turpentine. —v.tr. (**rosined, rosining**) **1** rub (esp. the bow of a violin etc.) with rosin. **2** smear or seal up with rosin. □ **rosiny** adj. [ME, alt. f. RESIN]

RoSPA /ˈrɒspə/ abbr. (in the UK) Royal Society for the Prevention of Accidents.

roster /ˈrɒstə(r), ˈrəʊstə(r)/ n. & v. —n. a list or plan showing turns of duty or leave for individuals or groups esp. of a military force. —v.tr. place on a roster. [Du. *rooster* list, orig. gridiron f. *roosten* ROAST, with ref. to its parallel lines]

rostra pl. of ROSTRUM.

rostrum /ˈrɒstrəm/ n. (pl. **rostra** /-strə/ or **rostrums**) **1 a** a platform for public speaking. **b** a conductor's platform facing the orchestra. **c** a similar platform for other purposes, e.g. for supporting a film or television camera. **2** *Zool.* & *Bot.* a beak, stiff snout, or beaklike part, esp. of an insect or arachnid. □ (all in sense 2) **rostrate** /-strət/ adj. **rostriferous** /-ˈstrɪfərəs/ adj. **rostriform** adj. [L, = beak f. *rodere ros-gnaw*: orig. *rostra* (pl., in sense 1a) in the Roman forum adorned with beaks of captured galleys]

rosy /ˈrəʊzɪ/ adj. (**rosier, rosiest**) **1** coloured like a pink or red rose (esp. of the complexion as indicating good health, of a blush, wine, the sky, light, etc.). **2** optimistic, hopeful, cheerful (*a rosy future; a rosy attitude to life*). □ **rosily** adv. **rosiness** n.

rot v., n., & int. —v. (**rotted, rotting**) **1** intr. **a** (of animal or vegetable matter) lose its original form by the chemical action of bacteria, fungi, etc.; decay. **b** (foll. by *off, away*) crumble or drop from a stem etc. through decomposition. **2** intr. **a** (of society, institutions, etc.) gradually perish from lack of vigour or use. **b** (of a prisoner etc.) waste away (*left to rot in prison*); (of a person) languish. **3** tr. cause to rot, make rotten. —n. **1** the process or state of rotting. **2** *sl.* nonsense; an absurd or foolish statement, argument, or proposal. **3** a sudden series of (usu. unaccountable) failures; a rapid decline in standards etc. (*a rot set in; we must try to stop the rot*). —int. expressing incredulity or ridicule. □ **rot-gut** *sl.*

cheap harmful alcoholic liquor. [OE *rotian* (v.): (n.) ME, perh. f. Scand.: cf. Icel., Norw. *rot*]

rota /ˈrəʊtə/ n. esp. *Brit.* a list of persons acting, or duties to be done, in rotation; a roster. [L, = wheel]

Rotarian /rəʊˈteərɪən/ n. & adj. —n. a member of Rotary. —adj. of Rotary. [ROTARY + -AN]

rotary /ˈrəʊtərɪ/ adj. & n. —adj. acting by rotation (*rotary drill; rotary pump*). —n. (pl. **-ies**) **1** a rotary machine. **2** *US* a traffic roundabout. **3** (**Rotary**) (in full **Rotary International**) a worldwide charitable society of businessmen, orig. named from members entertaining in rotation. □ **Rotary club** a local branch of Rotary. [med.L *rotarius* (as ROTA)]

rotate /rəʊˈteɪt/ v. **1** intr. & tr. move round an axis or centre, revolve. **2 a** tr. take or arrange in rotation. **b** intr. act or take place in rotation (*the chairmanship will rotate*). □ **rotatable** adj. [L *rotare* f. *rota* wheel]

rotative /ˈrəʊtətɪv/ adj. **rotatory** /ˈrəʊtətərɪ, -ˈteɪtərɪ/ adj. [L *rotare* f. *rota* wheel]

rotation /rəʊˈteɪʃ(ə)n/ n. **1** the act or an instance of rotating or being rotated. **2** a recurrence; a recurrent series or period; a regular succession of various members of a group in office etc. **3** a system of growing different crops in regular order to avoid exhausting the soil. □ **rotational** adj. **rotationally** adv. [L *rotatio*]

rotator /rəʊˈteɪtə(r)/ n. **1** a machine or device for causing something to rotate. **2** *Anat.* a muscle that rotates a limb etc. **3** a revolving apparatus or part. [L (as ROTATE)]

Rotavator /ˈrəʊtəˌveɪtə(r)/ n. (also **Rotovator**) *propr.* a machine with a rotating blade for breaking up or tilling the soil. □ **rotavate** v.tr. [ROTARY + CULTIVATOR]

rote n. (usu. prec. by *by*) mechanical or habitual repetition (with ref. to acquiring knowledge). [ME: orig. unkn.]

rotisserie /rəʊˈtɪsərɪ/ n. **1** a restaurant etc. where meat is roasted or barbecued. **2** a cooking appliance with a rotating spit for roasting and barbecuing meat. [F *rôtisserie* (as ROAST)]

rotor /ˈrəʊtə(r)/ n. **1** a rotary part of a machine, esp. in the distributor of an internal-combustion engine. **2** a set of radiating aerofoils round a hub on a helicopter, providing lift when rotated. [irreg. for ROTATOR]

rotten /ˈrɒt(ə)n/ adj. (**rottener, rottenest**) **1** rotting or rotted; falling to pieces or liable to break or tear from age or use. **2** morally, socially, or politically corrupt. **3** *sl.* **a** disagreeable, unpleasant (*had a rotten time*). **b** (of a plan etc.) ill-advised, unsatisfactory (*a rotten idea*). **c** disagreeably ill (*feel rotten today*). □ **rotten borough** *hist.* (before 1832) an English borough able to elect an MP though having very few voters. □ **rottenly** adv. **rottenness** n. [ME f. ON *rotinn*, rel. to ROT]

rotter /ˈrɒtə(r)/ n. esp. *Brit. sl.* an objectionable, unpleasant, or reprehensible person. [ROT]

Rottweiler /ˈrɒtˌvaɪlə(r), -ˌwaɪlə(r)/ n. **1** a dog of a tall black-and-tan breed. **2** this breed, noted for its ferocity. [G f. *Rottweil* in SW Germany]

rotund /rəʊˈtʌnd/ adj. **1 a** circular, round. **b** (of a person) large and plump, podgy. **2** (of speech, literary style, etc.) sonorous, grandiloquent. □ **rotundity** n. **rotundly** adv. [L *rotundus* f. *rotare* ROTATE]

rotunda /rəʊˈtʌndə/ n. **1** a building with a circular ground-plan, esp. one with a dome. **2** a circular hall or room. [earlier *rotonda* f. It. *rotonda (camera)* round (chamber), fem. of *rotondo* round (as ROTUND)]

rouble /ˈruːb(ə)l/ *n.* (also **ruble**) the chief monetary unit of Russia and the former USSR. [F f. Russ. *rubl'*]

roué /ˈruːeɪ/ *n.* a debauchee, esp. an elderly one; a rake. [F, past part. of *rouer* break on wheel, = one deserving this]

rouge /ruːʒ/ *n. & v. —n.* a red powder or cream used for colouring the cheeks. —*v.* **1** *tr.* colour with rouge. **2** *intr.* **a** apply rouge to one's cheeks. **b** become red, blush. [F, = red, f. L *rubeus*, rel. to RED]

rough /rʌf/ *adj., adv., n., & v. —adj.* **1** having an uneven or irregular surface, not smooth or level or polished. **2** (of ground, country, etc.) having many bumps, obstacles, etc. **3 a** hairy, shaggy. **b** (of cloth) coarse in texture. **4 a** (of a person or behaviour) not mild or quiet or gentle; boisterous, unrestrained (*rough manners; rough play*). **b** (of language etc.) coarse, indelicate. **c** (of wine etc.) sharp or harsh in taste. **5** (of the sea, weather, etc.) violent, stormy. **6** disorderly, riotous (*a rough part of town*). **7** harsh, insensitive, inconsiderate (*rough words; rough treatment*). **8 a** unpleasant, severe, demanding (*had a rough time*). **b** unfortunate, unreasonable, undeserved (*had rough luck*). **c** (foll. by *on*) hard or unfair towards. **9** lacking finish, elaboration, comfort, etc. (*rough lodgings; a rough welcome*). **10** incomplete, rudimentary (*a rough attempt; a rough makeshift*). **11 a** inexact, approximate, preliminary (*a rough estimate; a rough sketch*). **b** (of stationery etc.) for use in writing rough notes etc. **12** *colloq.* **a** ill, unwell (*am feeling rough*). **b** depressed, dejected. —*adv.* in a rough manner (*play rough*). —*n.* **1** (usu. prec. by *the*) a hard part or aspect of life; hardship (*take the rough with the smooth*). **2** rough ground (*over rough and smooth*). **3** a rough or violent person (*met a bunch of roughs*). **4** *Golf* rough ground off the fairway between tee and green. **5** an unfinished or provisional or natural state (*have written it in rough; shaped from the rough*). —*v.tr.* **1** (foll. by *up*) ruffle (feathers, hair, etc.) by rubbing against the grain. **2 a** (foll. by *out*) shape or plan roughly. **b** (foll. by *in*) sketch roughly. □ **rough-and-ready** rough or crude but effective; not elaborate or over-particular. **rough-and-tumble** *adj.* irregular, scrambling, disorderly. —*n.* a haphazard fight; a scuffle. **rough copy 1** a first or original draft. **2** a copy of a picture etc. showing only the essential features. **rough deal** hard or unfair treatment. **rough diamond 1** an uncut diamond. **2** a person of good nature but rough manners. **rough-dry** (**-dries, -dried**) dry (clothes) without ironing. **rough-hewn** uncouth, unrefined. **rough house** *sl.* a disturbance or row; boisterous play. **rough-house** *v. sl.* **1** *tr.* handle (a person) roughly. **2** *intr.* make a disturbance; act violently. **rough it** do without basic comforts. **rough justice 1** treatment that is approximately fair. **2** treatment that is not at all fair. **rough passage 1** a crossing over rough sea. **2** a difficult time or experience. **rough ride** a difficult time or experience. **rough stuff** *colloq.* boisterous or violent behaviour. **rough up** *sl.* treat (a person) with violence; attack violently. **sleep rough**

sleep outdoors, or not in a proper bed. □ **roughness** *n.* [OE *rūh* f. WG]

roughage /ˈrʌfɪdʒ/ *n.* coarse material with a high fibre content, the part of food which stimulates digestion. [ROUGH + -AGE 3]

roughcast /ˈrʌfkɑːst/ *n. & v. —n.* plaster of lime and gravel, used on outside walls. —*v.tr.* (*past* and *past part.* **-cast**) coat (a wall) with roughcast.

roughen /ˈrʌf(ə)n/ *v.tr. & intr.* make or become rough.

roughly /ˈrʌflɪ/ *adv.* **1** in a rough manner. **2** approximately (*roughly 20 people attended*). □ **roughly speaking** in an approximate sense (*it is, roughly speaking, a square*).

roughshod /ˈrʌfʃɒd/ *adj.* (of a horse) having shoes with nail-heads projecting to prevent slipping. □ **ride roughshod over** treat inconsiderately or arrogantly.

roulade /ruːˈlɑːd/ *n.* a dish cooked or served in the shape of a roll, esp. a rolled piece of meat or sponge with a filling. [F f. *rouler* to roll]

roulette /ruːˈlet/ *n.* a gambling game using a table in which a ball is dropped on to a revolving wheel with numbered compartments, players betting on the number at which the ball comes to rest. [F, dimin. of *rouelle* f. LL *rotella* dimin. of L *rota* wheel]

round /raʊnd/ *adj., n., adv., prep., & v. —adj.* **1** shaped like or approximately like a circle, sphere, or cylinder; having a convex or circular outline or surface; curved, not angular. **2** done with or involving circular motion. **3 a** entire, continuous, complete (*a round dozen*); fully expressed or developed; all together, not broken or defective or scanty. **b** (of a sum of money) considerable. **4** genuine, candid, outspoken; (of a statement etc.) categorical, unmistakable. **5** (usu. *attrib.*) (of a number) expressed for convenience or as an estimate in fewer significant numerals or with a fraction removed (*spent £297.32, or in round figures £300*). —*n.* **1** a round object or form. **2 a** a revolving motion, a circular or recurring course (*the earth in its yearly round*). **b** a regular recurring series of activities or functions (*one's daily round; a continuous round of pleasure*). **c** a recurring succession or series of meetings for discussion etc. (*a new round of talks on disarmament*). **3 a** a fixed route on which things are regularly delivered (*milk round*). **b** a route or sequence by which people or things are regularly supervised or inspected (*a watchman's round; a doctor's rounds*). **4** an allowance of something distributed or measured out, esp.: **a** a single provision of drinks etc. to each member of a group. **b** ammunition to fire one shot; the act of firing this. **5 a** a slice across a loaf of bread. **b** a sandwich made from whole slices of bread. **6** each of a set or series, a sequence of actions by each member of a group in turn, esp. **a** one spell of play in a game etc. **b** one stage in a competition. **7** *Golf* the playing of all the holes in a course once. **8** (**the round**) a form of sculpture in which the figure stands clear of any ground. **9** *Mus.* a canon for three or more unaccompanied voices singing at the same pitch or in octaves. **10** a rung of a ladder. —*adv.* **1** with circular motion (*wheels go round*). **2** with return to the starting-point or an earlier state (*summer soon comes round*). **3 a** with rotation, or change to an opposite position (*he turned round to look*). **b** with change to an opposite opinion etc. (*they were angry but I soon won them round*). **4** to, at, or affecting all or many points of a circumference or an area or the members of a company etc. (*tea was then handed round; may I look round?*). **5** in every direction from a centre or within a radius (*spread destruction round; everyone for a mile round*). **6** by a circuitous way (*will you jump over or go round?; go a long way round*). **7 a** to a person's house etc. (*ask him round; will be round soon*). **b** to a more prominent or convenient position (*brought the car round*). **8** measuring a (specified distance) in girth. —*prep.* **1** so as to encircle or enclose (*tour round the world; has a halter round him*). **2** at or to points on the circumference of (*sat round the table*). **3** with successive visits to (*hawks them round the cafés*). **4** in various directions from or with regard to (*towns round Birmingham; shells bursting round them*). **5** having as an axis of revolution or as a central point (*turns round its centre of gravity; write a book round an event*). **6 a** so as to double or pass in a curved course (*go round the corner*). **b** having passed in this way (*be round the corner*). **c** in the position that would result from this (*find them round the corner*). **7** so as to come close from various sides but not into contact. —*v.* **1 a** *tr.* give a round shape to. **b** *intr.* assume a round shape. **2** *tr.* double or pass round (a corner, cape, etc.). **3** *tr.* express (a number) in a less exact but more convenient form (also foll. by *down* when the number is decreased and *up* when it is increased). **4** *tr.* pronounce (a vowel) with rounded lips. □ **go the round** (or **rounds**) (of news etc.) be passed on from person to person. **in the round 1** with all features shown; all things considered. **2** *Theatr.* with the audience round at least three sides of the stage. **3** (of sculpture) with all sides shown; not in relief. **round about 1** in a ring (about); all round; on all sides (of). **2** with a change to an opposite position. **3** approximately (*cost round about £50*). **round and round** several times round. **round brackets** brackets of the form (). **round dance 1** a dance in which couples move in circles round the ballroom. **2** a dance in which the dancers form one large circle. **round down** see sense 3 of *v.* **round off** (or **out**) **1** bring to a complete or symmetrical or well-ordered state. **2** smooth out; blunt the corners or angles of. **round on a person** make a sudden verbal attack on or unexpected retort to a person. **round out** = **round off** 1. **round robin 1** a petition esp. with signatures written in a circle to conceal the order of writing. **2** *US* a tournament in which each competitor plays in turn against every other. **round-shouldered** with shoulders bent forward so that the back is rounded. **Round Table** (in allusion to that at which King Arthur and his knights sat so that none should have precedence) **1** an international charitable association which holds discussions, debates, etc., and undertakes community service. **2** (**round table**) an assembly for discussion, esp. at a conference (often *attrib.*: *round-table talks*). **round trip** a trip to one or more places and back again (esp. by a circular route). **round up** collect or bring together, esp. by going round (see also sense 3 of *v.*). **round-up** *n.* **1** a systematic rounding up of people or things. **2** a summary; a résumé of facts or events. □ **roundish** *adj.* **roundness** *n.* [ME f. OF *ro(u)nd-* stem of *ro(o)nt*, *reont* f. L *rotundus* ROTUND]

roundabout /ˈraʊndəˌbaʊt/ *n. & adj.* —*n.* **1** *Brit.* a road junction at which traffic moves in one direction round a central island. **2** *Brit.* **a** a large revolving device in a playground, for children to ride on. **b** = MERRY-GO-ROUND 1. —*adj.* circuitous, circumlocutory, indirect.

roundel /ˈraʊnd(ə)l/ *n.* **1** a small disc, esp. a decorative medallion. **2** a circular identifying mark painted on military aircraft, esp. the red, white, and blue of the RAF. [ME f. OF *rondel(le)* (as ROUND)]

roundelay /ˈraʊndɪˌleɪ/ *n.* a short simple song with a refrain. [F *rondelet* (as RONDEL), with assim. to LAY³ or *virelay*]

rounder /ˈraʊndə(r)/ *n.* **1** (in *pl.*; treated as *sing.*) a game with a bat and ball in which players after hitting the ball run through a round of bases. **2** a complete run of a player through all the bases as a unit of scoring in rounders.

Roundhead /ˈraʊndhed/ *n. hist.* a member of the Parliamentary party in the English Civil War. [f. their custom of wearing the hair cut short]

roundhouse /ˈraʊndhaʊs/ *n.* a circular repair-shed for railway locomotives, built round a turntable.

roundly /ˈraʊndlɪ/ *adv.* **1** bluntly, in plain language, severely (*was roundly criticized; told them roundly that he refused*). **2** in a thoroughgoing manner (*go roundly to work*). **3** in a circular way (*swells out roundly*).

roundsman /ˈraʊndzmən/ *n.* (*pl.* **-men**) **1** *Brit.* a tradesman's employee going round delivering and taking orders. **2** *US* a police officer in charge of a patrol. **3** *Austral.* a journalist covering a specified subject (*political roundsman*).

roundworm /ˈraʊndwɜːm/ *n.* a worm, esp. a nematode, with a rounded body.

rouse /raʊz/ *v.* **1 a** *tr.* (often foll. by *from, out of*) bring out of sleep, wake. **b** *intr.* (often foll. by *up*) cease to sleep, wake up. **2** (often foll. by *up*) **a** *tr.* stir up, make active or excited, startle out of inactivity or confidence or carelessness (*roused them from their complacency; was roused to protest*). **b** *intr.* become active. **3** *tr.* provoke to anger (*is terrible when roused*). **4** *tr.* evoke (feelings). □ **rouse oneself** overcome one's indolence. □ **rousable** *adj.* **rouser** *n.* [orig. as a hawking and hunting term, so prob. f. AF: orig. unkn.]

rouseabout /ˈraʊzəˌbaʊt/ *n. Austral. & NZ* an unskilled labourer or odd jobber, esp. on a farm.

rousing /ˈraʊzɪŋ/ *adj.* **1** exciting, stirring (*a rousing cheer; a rousing song*). **2** (of a fire) blazing strongly. □ **rousingly** *adv.*

roust /raʊst/ *v.tr.* **1** (often foll. by *up, out*) **a** rouse, stir up. **b** root out. **2** *US sl.* jostle, harass, rough up. □ **roust around** rummage. [perh. alt. of ROUSE]

roustabout /ˈraʊstəˌbaʊt/ *n.* **1** a labourer on an oil rig. **2** an unskilled or casual labourer. **3** *US* a dock labourer or deck hand. **4** *Austral.* = ROUSEABOUT.

rout¹ /raʊt/ *n. & v.* —*n.* a disorderly retreat of defeated troops. —*v.tr.* put to flight, defeat utterly. [ME f. AF *rute*, OF *route* ult. f. L *ruptus* broken]

rout² /raʊt/ *v. intr. & tr.* = ROOT². □ **rout out** force or fetch out of bed or from a house or hiding-place. [var. of ROOT²]

route /ruːt, *Mil.* also raʊt/ *n. & v.* —*n.* **1** a way or course taken (esp. regularly) in getting from a starting-point to a destination. **2** US a round travelled in delivering, selling, or collecting goods. —v.tr. (**routeing**) send or forward or direct to be sent by a particular route. □ **route march** a training-march for troops. [ME f. OF r(o)ute road ult. f. L ruptus broken]

routine /ruːˈtiːn/ n. & adj. —n. **1** a regular course or procedure, an unvarying performance of certain acts. **2** a set sequence in a performance, esp. a dance, comedy act, etc. **3** Computing a sequence of instructions for performing a task. —adj. **1** performed as part of a routine (routine duties). **2** of a customary or standard kind. □ **routinely** adv. [F (as ROUTE)]

roux /ruː/ n. (pl. same) a mixture of fat (esp. butter) and flour used in making sauces etc. [F, = browned (butter): see RUSSET]

rove[1] v. & n. —v. **1** intr. wander without a settled destination, roam, ramble. **2** intr. (of eyes) look in changing directions. **3** tr. wander over or through. —n. an act of roving (on the rove). □ **roving commission** authority given to a person or persons conducting an inquiry to travel as may be necessary. **roving eye** a tendency to ogle or towards infidelity. [ME, orig. a term in archery = shoot at a casual mark with the range not determined, perh. f. dial. rave stray, prob. of Scand. orig.]

rove[2] past of REEVE[2].

rover[1] /ˈrəʊvə(r)/ n. **1** a roving person; a wanderer. **2** (**Rover**) Brit. a senior Scout.

■ **Usage** Now called Venture Scout.

rover[2] /ˈrəʊvə(r)/ n. a sea robber, a pirate. [ME f. MLG, MDu. rōver, rōven rob, rel. to REAVE]

row[1] /rəʊ/ n. **1** a number of persons or things in a more or less straight line. **2** a line of seats across a theatre etc. (in the front row). **3** a street with a continuous line of houses along one or each side. **4** a line of plants in a field or garden. **5** a horizontal line of entries in a table etc. □ **in a row 1** forming a row. **2** colloq. in succession (two Sundays in a row). **row-house** US a terrace house. [ME raw, row, f. OE f. Gmc]

row[2] /rəʊ/ v. & n. —v. **1** tr. propel (a boat) with oars. **2** tr. convey (a passenger) in a boat in this way. **3** intr. propel a boat in this way. **4** tr. make (a stroke) or achieve (a rate of striking) in rowing. **5** tr. compete in (a race) by rowing. **6** tr. row a race with. —n. **1** a spell of rowing. **2** an excursion in a rowing-boat. □ **row-boat** US = rowing-boat. **rowing-boat** Brit. a small boat propelled by oars. **rowing-machine** a device for exercising the muscles used in rowing. □ **rower** n. [OE rōwan f. Gmc, rel. to RUDDER, L remus oar]

row[3] /raʊ/ n. & v. colloq. —n. **1** a loud noise or commotion. **2** a fierce quarrel or dispute. **3 a** a severe reprimand. **b** the condition of being reprimanded (shall get into a row). —v. **1** intr. make or engage in a row. **2** tr. reprimand. □ **make** (or **kick up**) **a row 1** raise a noise. **2** make a vigorous protest. [18th-c. sl.: orig. unkn.]

rowan /ˈrəʊən, ˈraʊ-/ n. (in full **rowan-tree**) **1** Sc. & N.Engl. the mountain ash. **2** (in full **rowan-berry**) the scarlet berry of either of these trees. [Scand., corresp. to Norw. rogn, raun, ON reynir]

rowdy /ˈraʊdɪ/ adj. & n. —adj. (**rowdier**, **rowdiest**) noisy and disorderly. —n. (pl. **-ies**) a rowdy person. □ **rowdily** adv. **rowdiness** n.

rowdyism n. [19th-c. US, orig. = lawless backwoodsman: orig. unkn.]

rowel /ˈraʊəl/ n. a spiked revolving disc at the end of a spur. [ME f. OF roel(e) f. LL rotella dimin. of L rota wheel]

rowlock /ˈrɒlək, ˈrʌlək/ n. a device on a boat's gunwale serving as a fulcrum for an oar and keeping it in place. [alt. of earlier OARLOCK, after ROW[2]]

royal /ˈrɔɪəl/ adj. & n. —adj. **1** of or suited to or worthy of a king or queen. **2** in the service or under the patronage of a king or queen. **3** belonging to the king or queen (the royal hands; the royal anger). **4** of the family of a king or queen. **5** kingly, majestic, stately, splendid. **6** on a great scale, of exceptional size or quality, first-rate (gave us royal entertainment). —n. colloq. a member of the royal family. □ **royal blue** Brit. a deep vivid blue. **Royal British Legion** a national association of ex-members of the armed forces, founded in 1921. **Royal Engineers** the engineering branch of the British army. **royal family** the family to which a sovereign belongs. **royal icing** a hard white icing made from icing sugar and egg-whites. **royal jelly** a substance secreted by honey-bee workers and fed by them to future queen bees. **Royal Society** (in full **Royal Society of London**) a society founded in 1662 to promote scientific discussion. **royal warrant** a warrant authorizing a tradesperson to supply goods to a specified royal person. □ **royally** adv. [ME f. OF roial f. L regalis REGAL]

royalist /ˈrɔɪəlɪst/ n. **1** a supporter of monarchy. **2** hist. a supporter of the royal side in the English Civil War. □ **royalism** n.

royalty /ˈrɔɪəltɪ/ n. (pl. **-ies**) **1** the office or dignity or power of a king or queen, sovereignty. **2 a** royal persons. **b** a member of a royal family. **3** a sum paid to a patentee for the use of a patent or to an author etc. for each copy of a book etc. sold or for each public performance of a work. **4 a** a royal right (now esp. over minerals) granted by the sovereign to an individual or corporation. **b** a payment made by a producer of minerals, oil, or natural gas to the owner of the site or of the mineral rights over it. [ME f. OF roialté (as ROYAL)]

RP abbr. received pronunciation.

RPI abbr. retail price index.

r.p.m. abbr. revolutions per minute.

RSM abbr. Regimental Sergeant-Major.

RSPB abbr. (in the UK) Royal Society for the Protection of Birds.

RSPCA abbr. (in the UK) Royal Society for the Prevention of Cruelty to Animals.

RSV abbr. Revised Standard Version (of the Bible).

RSVP abbr. (in an invitation etc.) please answer. [F répondez s'il vous plaît]

rt. abbr. right.

Rt. Hon. abbr. Brit. Right Honourable.

Rt. Revd. abbr. (also **Rt. Rev.**) Right Reverend.

Ru symb. Chem. the element ruthenium.

rub v. & n. —v. (**rubbed**, **rubbing**) **1** tr. move one's hand or another object with firm pressure over the surface of. **2** tr. (usu. foll. by against, in, on, over) apply (one's hand etc.) with firm pressure. **3** tr. clean or polish or make dry or bare by rubbing. **4** tr. (often foll. by over) apply (polish, ointment, etc.) by rubbing. **5** *tr.* (foll. by *in*, *into*, *through*) use rubbing to make (a substance) go into or through something. **6** *tr.* (often foll. by *together*) move or slide (objects) against each other. **7** *intr.* (foll. by *against*, *on*) move with contact or friction. **8** *tr.* chafe or make sore by rubbing. **9** *intr.* (of cloth, skin, etc.) become frayed or worn or sore or bare with friction. **10** *tr.* reproduce the design of (a sepulchral brass or a stone) by rubbing paper laid on it with heelball or coloured chalk etc. **11** *tr.* (foll. by *to*) reduce to powder etc. by rubbing. —*n.* **1** a spell or an instance of rubbing (*give it a rub*). **2 a** an impediment or difficulty (*there's the rub*). □ **rub along** *colloq.* cope or manage without undue difficulty. **rub down** dry or smooth or clean by rubbing. **rub elbows with** *US* = **rub shoulders with**. **rub one's hands** rub one's hands together usu. in sign of keen satisfaction, or for warmth. **rub it in** (or **rub a person's nose in it**) emphasize or repeat an embarrassing fact etc. **rub off** **1** (usu. foll. by *on*) be transferred by contact, be transmitted (*some of his attitudes have rubbed off on me*). **2** remove by rubbing. **rub out** **1** erase with a rubber. **2** esp. *US sl.* kill, eliminate. **rub shoulders with** associate or come into contact with (another person). **rub up** **1** polish (a tarnished object). **2** brush up (a subject or one's memory). **rub up the wrong way** irritate or repel as by stroking a cat against the lie of its fur. [ME *rubben*, perh. f. LG *rubben*, of unkn. orig.]

rubato /ruːˈbɑːtəʊ/ *adj. & n. Mus.* —*n.* (*pl.* **-os** or **rubati** /-tɪ/) the temporary disregarding of strict tempo. —*adj.* performed with a flexible tempo. [It., = robbed]

rubber[1] /ˈrʌbə(r)/ *n.* **1** a tough elastic polymeric substance made from the latex of plants or synthetically. **2** esp. *Brit.* a piece of this or another substance for erasing pencil or ink marks. **3** *colloq.* a condom. **4** (in *pl.*) *US* galoshes. □ **rubber band** a loop of rubber for holding papers etc. together. **rubber plant** **1** an evergreen plant, *Ficus elastica*, with dark-green shiny leaves, often cultivated as a house-plant. **2** (also **rubber tree**) any of various tropical trees yielding latex, esp. *Hevea brasiliensis*. **rubber solution** a liquid drying to a rubber-like material, used esp. as an adhesive in mending rubber articles. **rubber stamp** **1** a device for inking and imprinting on a surface. **2 a** a person who mechanically copies or agrees to others' actions. **b** an indication of such agreement. **rubber-stamp** *v.tr.* approve automatically without proper consideration. □ **rubbery** *adj.* **rubberiness** *n.* [RUB + -ER[1], from its early use to rub out pencil marks]

rubber[2] /ˈrʌbə(r)/ *n.* **1** a match of three or five successive games between the same sides or persons at whist, bridge, cricket, lawn tennis, etc. **2** (prec. by *the*) **a** the act of winning two games in a rubber. **b** a third game when each side has won one. [orig. unkn.: used as a term in bowls from *c.*1600]

rubberize /ˈrʌbəraɪz/ *v.tr.* (also **-ise**) treat or coat with rubber.

rubberneck /ˈrʌbənek/ *n. & v. colloq.* —*n.* a person who stares inquisitively or stupidly. —*v.intr.* act in this way.

rubbing /ˈrʌbɪŋ/ *n.* **1** in senses of RUB *v.* **2** an impression or copy made by rubbing (see RUB *v.* 10).

rubbish /ˈrʌbɪʃ/ *n. & v.* —*n.* esp. *Brit.* **1** waste material; debris, refuse, litter. **2** worthless material or articles; trash. **3** (often as *int.*) absurd ideas or suggestions; nonsense. —*v.tr. colloq.* **1** criticize severely. **2** reject as worthless. □ **rubbishy** *adj.* [ME f. AF *rubbous* etc., perh. f. RUBBLE]

rubble /ˈrʌb(ə)l/ *n.* waste or rough fragments of stone or brick etc. □ **rubbly** *adj.* [ME *robyl, rubel,* of uncert. orig.: cf. OF *robe* spoils]

rube /ruːb/ *n. US colloq.* a country bumpkin. [abbr. of the name *Reuben*]

rubella /ruːˈbelə/ *n. Med.* an acute infectious virus disease with a red rash; German measles. [mod.L, neut. pl. of L *rubellus* reddish]

Rubicon /ˈruːbɪkɒn/ *n.* a boundary which once crossed betokens irrevocable commitment; a point of no return. [the ancient name of a stream forming the boundary of Julius Caesar's province and crossed by him in 49 BC as the start of a war with Pompey]

rubicund /ˈruːbɪkʌnd/ *adj.* (of a face, complexion, or person in these respects) ruddy, high-coloured. □ **rubicundity** /-ˈkʌndɪtɪ/ *n.* [F *rubicond* or L *rubicundus* f. *rubēre* be red]

rubidium /ruːˈbɪdɪəm/ *n. Chem.* a soft silvery element occurring naturally in various minerals. [L *rubidus* red (with ref. to its spectral lines)]

Rubik's cube /ˈruːbɪks/ *n.* a puzzle in which the aim is to restore the faces of a composite cube to single colours by rotating layers of constituent smaller cubes. [E. *Rubík*, its Hung. inventor]

ruble var. of ROUBLE.

rubric /ˈruːbrɪk/ *n.* **1** a direction for the conduct of divine service inserted in a liturgical book. **2** a heading or passage in red or special lettering. **3** explanatory words. □ **rubrical** *adj.* [ME f. OF *rubrique, rubrice* or L *rubrica* (*terra*) red (earth or ochre) as writing-material, rel. to *rubeus* red]

ruby /ˈruːbɪ/ *n., adj., & v.* —*n.* (*pl.* **-ies**) **1** a rare precious stone consisting of corundum with a colour varying from deep crimson or purple to pale rose. **2** a glowing purple-tinged red colour. —*adj.* of this colour. —*v.tr.* (**-ies**, **-ied**) dye or tinge ruby-colour. □ **ruby wedding** the fortieth anniversary of a wedding. [ME f. OF *rubi* f. med.L *rubinus* (*lapis*) red (stone), rel. to L *rubeus* red]

RUC *abbr.* Royal Ulster Constabulary.

ruche /ruːʃ/ *n.* a frill or gathering of lace etc. as a trimming. □ **ruched** *adj.* **ruching** *n.* [F f. med.L *rusca* tree-bark, of Celt. orig.]

ruck[1] *n.* **1** (prec. by *the*) the main body of competitors not likely to overtake the leaders. **2** an undistinguished crowd of persons or things. **3** *Rugby Football* a loose scrum with the ball on the ground. **4** *Austral. Rules* a group of three mobile players. [ME, = stack of fuel, heap, rick: app. Scand., = Norw. *ruke* heap of hay]

ruck[2] *v. & n.* —*v.tr. & intr.* (often foll. by *up*) make or become creased or wrinkled. —*n.* a crease or wrinkle. [ON *hrukka*]

ruckle /ˈrʌk(ə)l/ *v. & n. Brit.* = RUCK[2].

rucksack /ˈrʌksæk, ˈrʊk-/ *n.* a bag slung by straps from both shoulders and resting on the back. [G f. *rucken* dial. var. of *Rücken* back + *Sack* SACK[1]]

ruckus /ˈrʌkəs/ *n.* esp. *US* a row or commotion. [cf. RUCTION, RUMPUS]

ruction /ˈrʌkʃ(ə)n/ *n. colloq.* **1** a disturbance or tumult. **2** (in *pl.*) unpleasant arguments or reactions. [19th c.: orig. unkn.]

rudder /ˈrʌdə(r)/ *n.* **1 a** a flat piece hinged vertically to the stern of a ship for steering. **b** a vertical aerofoil pivoted from the tailplane of an aircraft, for controlling its horizontal movement. **2** a guiding principle etc. □ **rudderless** *adj.* [OE *rōther* f. WG *rōthra-* f. the stem of ROW²]

ruddle /ˈrʌd(ə)l/ *n.* & *v.* —*n.* a red ochre, esp. of a kind used for marking sheep. —*v.tr.* mark or colour with or as with ruddle. [rel. to obs. *rud* red colour f. OE *rudu*, rel. to RED]

ruddy /ˈrʌdɪ/ *adj.* & *v.* —*adj.* (**ruddier, ruddiest**) **1 a** (of a person or complexion) freshly or healthily red. **b** (of health, youth, etc.) marked by this. **2** reddish. **3** *Brit. colloq.* bloody, damnable. —*v.tr.* & *intr.* (**-ies, -ied**) make or grow ruddy. □ **ruddily** *adv.* **ruddiness** *n.* [OE *rudig* (as RUDDLE)]

rude *adj.* **1** (of a person, remark, etc.) impolite or offensive. **2** roughly made or done; lacking subtlety or accuracy (*a rude plough*). **3** primitive or uneducated (*rude chaos; rude simplicity*). **4** abrupt, sudden, startling, violent (*a rude awakening; a rude reminder*). **5** *colloq.* indecent, lewd (*a rude joke*). **6** vigorous or hearty (*rude health*). □ **rudely** *adv.* **rudeness** *n.* **rudery** *n.* **rudish** *adj.* [ME f. OF f. L *rudis* unwrought]

rudiment /ˈruːdɪmənt/ *n.* **1** (in *pl.*) the elements or first principles of a subject. **2** (in *pl.*) an imperfect beginning of something undeveloped or yet to develop. **3** a part or organ imperfectly developed as being vestigial or having no function (e.g. the breast in males). [F *rudiment* or L *rudimentum* (as RUDE, after *elementum* ELEMENT)]

rudimentary /ˌruːdɪˈmentərɪ/ *adj.* **1** involving basic principles; fundamental. **2** incompletely developed; vestigial. □ **rudimentarily** /-ˈment ərɪlɪ/ *adv.* **rudimentariness** /-ˈment ərɪnɪs/ *n.*

rue¹ *v.tr.* (**rues, rued, rueing** or **ruing**) repent of; bitterly feel the consequences of; wish to be undone or non-existent (esp. *rue the day*). [OE *hrēow, hrēowan*]

rue² *n.* a perennial evergreen shrub, *Ruta graveolens*, with bitter leaves formerly used in medicine. [ME f. OF f. L *ruta* f. Gk *rhutē*]

rueful /ˈruːfʊl/ *adj.* expressing sorrow, genuine or humorously affected. □ **ruefully** *adv.* **ruefulness** *n.* [ME, f. RUE¹]

ruff¹ *n.* **1** a projecting starched frill worn round the neck esp. in the 16th c. **2** a projecting or conspicuously coloured ring of feathers or hair round a bird's or animal's neck. **3** (*fem.* **reeve** /riːv/) a wading bird, *Philomachus pugnax*, of which the male has a ruff and ear-tufts in the breeding season. □ **rufflike** *adj.* [perh. f. ruff = ROUGH]

ruff² /rʌf/ *v.* & *n.* —*v.intr.* & *tr.* trump at cards. —*n.* an act of ruffing. [orig. the name of a card-game: f. OF *roffle, rouffle,* = It. *ronfa* (perh. alt. of *trionfo* TRUMP¹)]

ruffian /ˈrʌfɪən/ *n.* a violent lawless person. □ **ruffianism** *n.* **ruffianly** *adv.* [F *ruf(f)ian* f. It. *ruffiano,* perh. f. dial. *rofia* scurf]

ruffle /ˈrʌf(ə)l/ *v.* & *n.* —*v.* **1** *tr.* disturb the smoothness or tranquillity of. **2** *tr.* upset the calmness of (a person). **3** *tr.* gather (lace etc.) into a ruffle. **4** *tr.* (often foll. by *up*) (of a bird) erect (its feathers) in anger, display, etc. **5** *intr.* undergo ruffling. —*n.* **1** an ornamental gathered or goffered frill of lace etc. worn at the opening of a garment esp. round the wrist, breast, or neck. **2** perturbation, bustle. **3** a rippling effect on water. [ME: orig. uncert.]

rufous /ˈruːfəs/ *adj.* (esp. of animals) reddish-brown. [L *rufus* red, reddish]

rug *n.* **1** a floor-mat of shaggy material or thick pile. **2** a thick woollen coverlet or wrap. □ **pull the rug from under** deprive of support; weaken, unsettle. [prob. f. Scand.: cf. Norw. dial. *rugga* coverlet, Sw. *rugg* ruffled hair: rel. to RAG¹]

Rugby /ˈrʌgbɪ/ *n.* (in full **Rugby football**) a team game played with an oval ball that may be kicked, carried, and passed from hand to hand. □ **Rugby League** partly professional Rugby football with teams of 13. **Rugby Union** amateur Rugby football with teams of 15. [*Rugby* School in S. England, where it was first played]

rugged /ˈrʌgɪd/ *adj.* **1** (of ground or terrain) having a rough uneven surface. **2** (of features) strongly marked; irregular in outline. **3 a** unpolished; lacking gentleness or refinement (*rugged grandeur*). **b** harsh in sound. **4** (esp. of a machine) robust, sturdy. □ **ruggedly** *adv.* **ruggedness** *n.* [ME, prob. f. Scand.: cf. RUG, Sw. *rugga,* roughen]

rugger /ˈrʌgə(r)/ *n. Brit. colloq.* Rugby football.

ruin /ˈruːɪn/ *n.* & *v.* —*n.* **1** a destroyed or wrecked state. **2** a person's or thing's downfall or elimination (*the ruin of my hopes*). **3 a** the complete loss of one's property or position (*bring to ruin*). **b** a person who has suffered ruin. **4** (in *sing.* or *pl.*) the remains of a building etc. that has suffered ruin. **5** a cause of ruin (*will be the ruin of us*). —*v.* **1** *tr.* **a** bring to ruin (*your extravagance has ruined me*). **b** utterly impair or wreck (*the rain ruined my hat*). **2** *tr.* (esp. as **ruined** *adj.*) reduce to ruins. □ **in ruins 1** in a state of ruin. **2** completely wrecked (*their hopes were in ruins*). [ME f. OF *ruine* f. L *ruina* f. *ruere* fall]

ruination /ˌruːɪˈneɪʃ(ə)n/ *n.* **1** the act of bringing to ruin. **2** the act of ruining or the state of being ruined. [obs. *ruinate* (as RUIN)]

ruinous /ˈruːɪnəs/ *adj.* **1** bringing ruin; disastrous (*at ruinous expense*). **2** in ruins; dilapidated. □ **ruinously** *adv.* **ruinousness** *n.* [ME f. L *ruinosus* (as RUIN)]

rule /ruːl/ *n.* & *v.* —*n.* **1** a principle to which an action conforms or is required to conform. **2** a prevailing custom or standard; the normal state of things. **3** government or dominion (*under British rule; the rule of law*). **4** a graduated straight measure used in carpentry etc.; a ruler. **5** *Printing* **a** a thin strip of metal for separating headings, columns, etc. **b** a thin line or dash. **6** a code of discipline of a religious order. **7** *Law* an order made by a judge or court with reference to a particular case only. **8** (**Rules**) *Austral.* = *Australian Rules.* —*v.* **1** *tr.* exercise decisive influence over; keep under control. **2** *tr.* & (foll. by *over*) *intr.* have sovereign control of (*rules over a vast kingdom*). **3** *tr.* (often foll. by *that* + clause) pronounce authoritatively (*was ruled out of order*). **4** *tr.* **a** make parallel lines across (paper). **b** make (a straight line) with a ruler etc. □ **as a rule** usually; more often than not. **rule of thumb** a rule for general guidance, based on experience or practice rather than theory. **rule out** exclude; pronounce irrelevant or ineligible. **rule the roost** (or **roast**) be in control. **run the rule over** examine cursorily for correctness or adequacy. □ **ruleless** adj. [ME f. OF reule, reuler f. LL regulare f. L regula straight stick]

ruler /ˈruːlə(r)/ n. **1** a person exercising government or dominion. **2** a straight usu. graduated strip or cylinder of wood, metal, etc., used to draw lines or measure distance. □ **rulership** n.

ruling /ˈruːlɪŋ/ n. & adj. —n. an authoritative decision or announcement. —adj. prevailing; currently in force (ruling prices). □ **ruling passion** a motive that habitually directs one's actions.

rum[1] n. **1** a spirit distilled from sugar-cane residues or molasses. **2** US intoxicating liquor. [17th c.: perh. abbr. of contemporary forms rumbullion, rumbustion, of unkn. orig.]

rum[2] adj. Brit. colloq. odd, strange, queer. □ **rumly** adv. **rumness** n. [16th-c. cant, orig. = fine, spirited, perh. var. of Romany Rom man]

Rumanian var. of ROMANIAN.

rumba /ˈrʌmbə/ n. & v. (also **rhumba**) —n. **1** a Cuban Negro dance. **2 a** a ballroom dance imitative of this. **b** the music for it. —v.intr. (**rumbas, rumbaed** /-bəd/ or **rumba'd, rumbaing** /-bəɪŋ/) dance the rumba. [Amer. Sp.]

rumble /ˈrʌmb(ə)l/ v. & n. —v. **1** intr. make a continuous deep resonant sound as of distant thunder. **2** intr. (foll. by along, by, past, etc.) (of a person or vehicle) move with a rumbling noise. **3** tr. (often foll. by out) utter or say with a rumbling sound. **4** tr. Brit. sl. find out about (esp. something illicit). —n. **1** a rumbling sound. **2** US sl. a street-fight between gangs. □ **rumbler** n. [ME romble, prob. f. MDu. rommelen, rummelen (imit.)]

rumbustious /rʌmˈbʌstʃəs/ adj. colloq. boisterous, noisy, uproarious. □ **rumbustiously** adv. **rumbustiousness** n. [prob. var. of robustious boisterous, ROBUST]

ruminant /ˈruːmɪnənt/ n. & adj. —n. an animal that chews the cud. —adj. **1** of or belonging to ruminants. **2** contemplative; given to or engaged in meditation. [L ruminari ruminant- f. rumen ruminis throat]

ruminate /ˈruːmɪˌneɪt/ v. **1** tr. & (foll. by over, on, etc.) intr. meditate, ponder. **2** intr. (of ruminants) chew the cud. □ **rumination** /-ˈneɪʃ(ə)n/ n. **ruminative** /-nətɪv/ adj. **ruminatively** /-nətɪvlɪ/ adv. **ruminator** n.

rummage /ˈrʌmɪdʒ/ v. & n. —v. **1** tr. & (foll. by in, through, among) intr. search, esp. untidily and unsystematically. **2** tr. (foll. by out, up) find among other things. **3** tr. (foll. by about) disarrange; make untidy in searching. —n. **1** an instance of rummaging. **2** things found by rummaging; a miscellaneous accumulation. □ **rummage sale** esp. US a jumble sale. □ **rummager** n. [earlier as noun in obs. sense 'arranging of casks etc. in a hold': OF arrumage f. arrumer stow (as AD-, run ship's hold f. MDu. ruim ROOM)]

rummy /ˈrʌmɪ/ n. a card-game in which the players try to form sets and sequences of cards. [20th c.: orig. unkn.]

rumour /ˈruːmə(r)/ n. & v. (US **rumor**) —n. **1** general talk or hearsay of doubtful accuracy. **2** (often foll. by of, or that + clause) a current but unverified statement or assertion (heard a rumour that you are leaving). —v.tr. (usu. in passive) report by way of rumour (it is rumoured that you are leaving; you are rumoured to be leaving). [ME f. OF rumur, rumor f. L rumor -oris noise]

rump n. **1** the hind part of a mammal, esp. the buttocks. **2** a small or contemptible remnant of a parliament or similar body. □ **rump steak** a cut of beef from the rump. □□ **rumpless** adj. [ME, prob. f. Scand.]

rumple /ˈrʌmp(ə)l/ v.tr. & intr. make or become creased or ruffled. □ **rumply** adj. [obs. rumple (n.) f. MDu. rompel f. rompe wrinkle]

rumpus /ˈrʌmpəs/ n. colloq. a disturbance, brawl, row, or uproar. □ **rumpus room** US a room in the basement of a house for games and play. [18th c.: prob. fanciful]

run v. & n. —v. (**running**; past **ran** /ræn/; past part. **run**) **1** intr. go with quick steps on alternate feet, never having both or all feet on the ground at the same time. **2** intr. flee, abscond. **3** intr. go or travel hurriedly, briefly, etc. **4** intr. **a** advance by or as by rolling or on wheels, or smoothly or easily. **b** be in action or operation (left the engine running). **5** intr. be current or operative; have duration (the lease runs for 99 years). **6** intr. (of a bus, train, etc.) travel or be travelling on its route (the train is running late). **7** intr. (of a play, exhibition, etc.) be staged or presented (is now running at the Apollo). **8** intr. extend; have a course or order or tendency (the road runs by the coast; prices are running high). **9 a** intr. compete in a race. **b** intr. finish a race in a specified position. **c** tr. compete in (a race). **10** intr. (often foll. by for) seek election (ran for president). **11 a** intr. (of a liquid etc. or its container) flow or be wet; drip. **b** tr. flow with. **12** tr. **a** cause (water etc.) to flow. **b** fill (a bath) with water. **13** intr. spread rapidly or beyond the proper place (ink ran over the table; a shiver ran down my spine). **14** intr. Cricket (of a batsman) run from one wicket to the other in scoring a run. **15** tr. traverse or make one's way through or over (a course, race, or distance). **16** tr. perform (an errand). **17** tr. publish (an article etc.) in a newspaper or magazine. **18 a** tr. cause (a machine or vehicle etc.) to operate. **b** intr. (of a mechanism or component etc.) move or work freely. **19** tr. direct or manage (a business etc.). **20** tr. own and use (a vehicle) regularly. **21** tr. take (a person) for a journey in a vehicle (shall I run you to the shops?). **22** tr. cause to run or go in a specified way (ran the car into a tree). **23** tr. enter (a horse etc.) for a race. **24** tr. smuggle (guns etc.). **25** tr. chase or hunt. **26** tr. allow (an account) to accumulate for a time before paying. **27** tr. (of a colour in a fabric) spread from the dyed parts. **28 a** intr. (of a thought, the eye, the memory, etc.) pass in a transitory or cursory way (ideas ran through my mind). **b** tr. cause (one's eye) to look cursorily (ran my eye down the page). **29** intr. (of hosiery) ladder. **30** intr. (of an orifice, esp. the eyes or nose) exude liquid matter. **31** tr. sew (fabric) loosely or hastily with running stitches. —n. **1** an act or spell of running. **2** a short trip or excursion, esp. for pleasure. **3** a distance travelled. **4** a general tendency of development or movement. **5** a rapid motion. **6** a regular route. **7** a continuous or long stretch or spell or course (had a run of bad luck). **8** (often foll. by on) **a** a high general demand (for a commodity, currency, etc.) (*a run on the dollar*). **b** a sudden demand for repayment by a large number of customers of (a bank). **9** a quantity produced in one period of production (*a print run*). **10** a general or average type or class (*not typical of the general run*). **11 a** *Cricket* a point scored by the batsmen each running to the other's wicket, or an equivalent point awarded for some other reason. **b** *Baseball* a point scored usu. by the batter returning to the plate after touching the other bases. **12** (foll. by *of*) free use of or access to (*had the run of the house*). **13 a** an animal's regular track. **b** an enclosure for fowls. **c** a range of pasture. **14 a** a ladder in hosiery. □ **at a** (or **the**) **run** running. **on the run 1** escaping, running away. **2** hurrying about from place to place. **run about 1** bustle; hurry from one person or place to another. **2** (esp. of children) play or wander without restraint. **run across 1** happen to meet. **2** (foll. by *to*) make a brief journey or a flying visit (to a place). **run after 1** pursue with attentions; seek the society of. **2** give much time to (a pursuit etc.). **3** pursue at a run. **run against** happen to meet. **run along** *colloq.* depart. **run around 1** *Brit.* take from place to place by car etc. **2** deceive or evade repeatedly. **3** (often foll. by *with*) *sl.* engage in sexual relations (esp. casually or illicitly). **run-around** *n.* (esp. in phr. **give a person the run-around**) deceit or evasion. **run at** attack by charging or rushing. **run away 1** get away by running; flee, abscond. **2** elope. **3** (of a horse) bolt. **run away with 1** carry off (a person, stolen property, etc.). **2** win (a prize) easily. **3** accept (a notion) hastily. **4** (of expense etc.) consume (money etc.). **5** (of a horse) bolt with (a rider, a carriage or its occupants. **run down 1** knock down or collide with. **2** reduce the strength or numbers of (resources). **3** (of an unwound clock etc.) stop. **4** (of a person or a person's health) become feeble from overwork or underfeeding. **5** discover after a search. **6** disparage. **run-down** *n.* **1** a reduction in numbers. **2** a detailed analysis. —*adj.* **1** decayed after prosperity. **2** enfeebled through overwork etc. **run dry** cease to flow, be exhausted. **run for it** flee. **a run** (or **a good run**) **for one's money 1** vigorous competition. **2** pleasure derived from an activity. **run a person hard** (or **close**) press a person severely in a race or competition, or in comparative merit. **run high 1** (of the sea) have a strong current with a high tide. **2** (of feelings) be strong. **run in 1** run (a new engine or vehicle) carefully in the early stages. **2** *colloq.* arrest. **3** (of a combatant) rush to close quarters. **4** incur (a debt). **run-in** *n.* **1** the approach to an action or event. **2** a quarrel. **run in the family** (of a trait) be common in the members of a family. **run into 1** collide with. **2** encounter. **3** reach as many as (a specified figure). **4** fall into (a practice, absurdity, etc.). **5** be continuous or coalesce with. **run into the ground** *colloq.* bring (a person) to exhaustion etc. **run its course** follow its natural progress; be left to itself. **run low** (or **short**) become depleted, have too little (*our tea ran short*; *we ran short of tea*). **run off 1** flee. **2** produce (copies etc.) on a machine. **3** decide (a race or other contest) after a series of heats or in the event of a tie. **4** flow or cause to flow away. **5** write or recite fluently. **run-off** *n.* **1** an additional competition, election,

race, etc., after a tie. **2** an amount of rainfall that is carried off an area by streams and rivers. **run off one's feet** very busy. **run-of-the-mill** ordinary, undistinguished. **run on 1** (of written characters) be joined together. **2** continue in operation. **3** elapse. **4** speak volubly. **5** talk incessantly. **6** *Printing* continue on the same line as the preceding matter. **run out 1** come to an end; become used up. **2** (foll. by *of*) exhaust one's stock of. **3** put down the wicket of (a batsman who is running). **4** escape from a containing vessel. **run-out** *n.* the dismissal of a batsman by being run out. **run out on** *colloq.* desert (a person). **run over 1** overflow. **2** study or repeat quickly. **3** (of a vehicle or its driver) pass over, knock down or crush. **run the show** *colloq.* dominate in an undertaking etc. **run a temperature** be feverish. **run through 1** examine or rehearse briefly. **2** peruse. **3** deal successively with. **4** consume (an estate etc.) by reckless or quick spending. **5** traverse. **6** pervade. **7** pierce with a sword etc. **8** draw a line through (written words). **run-through** *n.* **1** a rehearsal. **2** a brief survey. **run to 1** have the money or ability for. **2** reach (an amount or number). **3** (of a person) show a tendency to (*runs to fat*). **4 a** be enough for (some expense or undertaking). **b** have the resources or capacity for. **5** fall into (ruin). **run to earth 1** *Hunting* chase to its lair. **2** discover after a long search. **run to meet** anticipate (one's troubles etc.). **run up 1** accumulate (a debt etc.) quickly. **2** build or make hurriedly. **3** raise (a flag). **run-up** *n.* (often foll. by *to*) the period preceding an important event. **run up against** meet with (a difficulty or difficulties). **run upon** (of a person's thoughts etc.) be engrossed in; dwell upon. **run wild** grow or stray unchecked or undisciplined or untrained. □ **runnable** *adj.* [OE *rinnan*]

runabout /ˈrʌnəˌbaʊt/ *n.* a light car or aircraft.

runaway /ˈrʌnəˌweɪ/ *n.* **1** a fugitive. **2** an animal or vehicle that is running out of control. **3** (*attrib.*) **a** that is running away or out of control (*runaway inflation*; *had a runaway success*). **b** done or performed after running away (*a runaway wedding*).

runcible spoon /ˈrʌnsɪb(ə)l/ *n.* a fork curved like a spoon, with three broad prongs, one edged. [nonsense word used by E. Lear, Engl. humorist d. 1888, perh. after *rouncival* large pea]

rune *n.* **1** any of the letters of the earliest Germanic alphabet used by Scandinavians and Anglo-Saxons from about the 3rd c. **2** a similar mark of mysterious or magic significance. □ **runic** *adj.* [ON *rún* (only in pl. *rúnar*) magic sign, rel. to OE *rūn*]

rung[1] *n.* **1** each of the horizontal supports of a ladder. **2** a strengthening crosspiece in the structure of a chair etc. □ **runged** *adj.* **rungless** *adj.* [OE *hrung*]

rung[2] *past part.* of RING[2].

runnel /ˈrʌn(ə)l/ *n.* **1** a brook or rill. **2** a gutter. [later form (assim. to RUN) of *rinel* f. OE *rynel* (as RUN)]

runner /ˈrʌnə(r)/ *n.* **1** a person who runs, esp. in a race. **2 a** a creeping plant-stem that can take root. **b** a twining plant. **3** a rod or groove or blade on which a thing slides. **4** a sliding ring on a rod etc. **5** a messenger, scout, collector, or agent for a bank etc.; a tout. **6** (in full **runner bean**) *Brit.* a twining bean plant, *Phaseolus* *multiflorus*, with red flowers and long green seed pods. **7** each of the long pieces on the underside of a sledge etc. that forms the contact in sliding. **8** a long narrow ornamental cloth or rug. □ **do a runner** *sl.* leave hastily; flee. **runner-up** (*pl.* **runners-up** or **runner-ups**) the competitor or team taking second place.

running /ˈrʌnɪŋ/ *n. & adj.* —*n.* **1** the action of runners in a race etc. **2** the way a race etc. proceeds. —*adj.* **1** continuing on an essentially continuous basis though changing in detail (*a running battle*). **2** consecutive; one after another (*three days running*). **3** done with a run (*a running jump*). □ **in** (or **out of**) **the running** (of a competitor) with a good (or poor) chance of winning. **make** (or **take up**) **the running** take the lead; set the pace. **running-board** a footboard on either side of a vehicle. **running commentary** an oral description of events as they occur. **running head** (or **headline**) a heading printed at the top of a number of consecutive pages of a book etc. **running knot** a knot that slips along the rope etc. and changes the size of a noose. **running mate** *US* a candidate for a secondary position in an election. **running repairs** minor or temporary repairs etc. to machinery while in use. **running sore** a suppurating sore. **running stitch 1** a line of small non-overlapping stitches for gathering etc. **2** one of these stitches. **running water** water flowing in a stream or from a tap etc. **take a running jump** (esp. as *int.*) *sl.* go away.

runny /ˈrʌnɪ/ *adj.* (**runnier, runniest**) **1** tending to run or flow. **2** excessively fluid.

runt *n.* **1** a small pig, esp. the smallest in a litter. **2** a weakling; an undersized person. □ **runty** *adj.* [16th c.: orig. unkn.]

runway /ˈrʌnweɪ/ *n.* a specially prepared surface along which aircraft take off and land.

rupee /ruːˈpiː/ *n.* the chief monetary unit of India, Pakistan, Sri Lanka, Nepal, Mauritius, and the Seychelles. [Hind. *rūpiyah* f. Skr. *rūpya* wrought silver]

rupture /ˈrʌptʃə(r)/ *n. & v.* —*n.* **1** the act or an instance of breaking; a breach. **2** a breach of harmonious relations; a disagreement and parting. **3** *Med.* an abdominal hernia. —*v.* **1** *tr.* break or burst (a cell or membrane etc.). **2** *tr.* sever (a connection). **3** *intr.* undergo a rupture. **4** *tr. & intr.* affect with or suffer a hernia. □ **rupturable** *adj.* [ME f. OF *rupture* or L *ruptura* f. *rumpere rupt-* break]

rural /ˈrʊər(ə)l/ *adj.* in, of, or suggesting the country (opp. URBAN); pastoral or agricultural (*in rural seclusion; a rural constituency*). □ **ruralism** *n.* **ruralist** *n.* **rurality** /-ˈrælɪtɪ/ *n.* **ruralize** *v.* (also **-ise**). **ruralization** /-laɪˈzeɪʃ(ə)n/ *n.* **rurally** *adv.* [ME f. OF *rural* or LL *ruralis* f. *rus ruris* the country]

ruse /ruːz/ *n.* a stratagem or trick. [ME f. OF f. *ruser* drive back, perh. ult. f. L *rursus* backwards: cf. RUSH¹]

rush¹ /rʌʃ/ *v. & n.* —*v.* **1** *intr.* go, move, or act precipitately or with great speed. **2** *tr.* move or transport with great haste (*was rushed to hospital*). **3** *intr.* (foll. by *at*) **a** move suddenly and quickly towards. **b** begin impetuously. **4** *tr.* perform or deal with hurriedly (*don't rush your dinner; the bill was rushed through Parliament*). **5** *tr.* force (a person) to act hastily. **6** *tr.* attack or capture by

sudden assault. **7** *tr. sl.* overcharge (a customer). **8** *intr.* flow, fall, spread, or roll impetuously or fast (*felt the blood rush to my face; the river rushes past*). —*n.* **1** an act of rushing; a violent advance or attack. **2** a period of great activity. **3** (*attrib.*) done with great haste or speed (*a rush job*). **4** a sudden migration of large numbers. **5** (foll. by *on, for*) a sudden strong demand for a commodity. **6** (in *pl.*) *colloq.* the first prints of a film after a period of shooting. □ **rush one's fences** act with undue haste. **rush hour** a time each day when traffic is at its heaviest. □ **rusher** *n.* **rushingly** *adv.* [ME f. AF *russher*, = OF *ruser, russer*: see RUSE]

rush² *n.* **1** any marsh or waterside plant of the family Juncaceae, with slender tapering pith-filled stems (properly leaves) formerly used for strewing floors and still used for making chair-bottoms and plaiting baskets etc. **2** a stem of this. **3** (*collect.*) rushes as a material. □ **rushlike** *adv.* **rushy** *adj.* [OE *rysc, rysce*, corresp. to MLG, MHG *rusch*]

rushlight /ˈrʌʃlaɪt/ *n.* a candle made by dipping the pith of a rush in tallow.

rusk *n.* a slice of bread rebaked usu. as a light biscuit, esp. as food for babies. [Sp. or Port. *rosca* twist, coil, roll of bread]

russet /ˈrʌsɪt/ *adj. & n.* —*adj.* reddish-brown. —*n.* **1** a reddish-brown colour. **2** a kind of rough-skinned russet-coloured apple. □ **russety** *adj.* [ME f. AF f. OF *rosset, rousset*, dimin. of *roux* red f. Prov. *ros*, It. *rosso* f. L *russus* red]

Russian /ˈrʌʃ(ə)n/ *n. & adj.* —*n.* **1 a** a native or national of Russia or the former Soviet Union. **b** a person of Russian descent. **2** the language of Russia and the official language of the former Soviet Union. —*adj.* **1** of or relating to Russia. **2** of or in Russian. □ **Russian roulette 1** an act of daring in which one (usu. with others in turn) squeezes the trigger of a revolver held to one's head with one chamber loaded, having first spun the chamber. **2** a potentially dangerous enterprise. **Russian salad** a salad of mixed diced vegetables with mayonnaise. □ **Russianize** *v.tr.* (also **-ise**). **Russianization** /-naɪˈzeɪʃ(ə)n/ *n.* **Russianness** *n.* [med.L *Russianus*]

Russo- /ˈrʌsəʊ/ *comb. form* Russian; Russian and.

rust *n. & v.* —*n.* **1 a** a reddish or yellowish-brown coating formed on iron or steel by oxidation, esp. as a result of moisture. **b** a similar coating on other metals. **2 a** any of various plant-diseases with rust-coloured spots caused by fungi of the order Uredinales. **b** the fungus causing this. **3** an impaired state due to disuse or inactivity. —*v.* **1** *tr. & intr.* affect or be affected with rust; undergo oxidation. **2** *intr.* (of bracken etc.) become rust-coloured. **3** *intr.* (of a plant) be attacked by rust. **4** *intr.* lose quality or efficiency by disuse or inactivity. □ **rustless** *adj.* [OE *rūst* f. Gmc]

rustic /ˈrʌstɪk/ *adj. & n.* —*adj.* **1** having the characteristics of or associations with the country or country life. **2** unsophisticated, simple, unrefined. **3** of rude or country workmanship. **4** made of untrimmed branches or rough timber (*a rustic bench*). —*n.* a person from or living in the country, esp. a simple unsophisticated one. □ **rustically** *adv.* **rusticity** /-ˈtɪsɪtɪ/ *n.* [ME f. L *rusticus* f. *rus* the country]

rusticate /ˈrʌstɪˌkeɪt/ v. **1** tr. send down (a student) temporarily from university. **2** intr. retire to or live in the country. **3** tr. make rural. **4** tr. mark (masonry) with sunk joints or a roughened surface. □ **rustication** /-ˈkeɪʃ(ə)n/ n. [L rusticari live in the country (as RUSTIC)]

rustle /ˈrʌs(ə)l/ v. & n. —v. **1** intr. & tr. make or cause to make a gentle sound as of dry leaves blown in a breeze. **2** intr. (often foll. by along etc.) move with a rustling sound. **3** tr. (also absol.) steal (cattle or horses). **4** intr. US colloq. hustle. —n. a rustling sound or movement. □ **rustle up** colloq. produce quickly when needed. □ **rustler** n. (esp. in sense 3 of v.). [ME rustel etc. (imit.): cf. obs. Flem. ruysselen, Du. ritselen]

rustproof /ˈrʌstpruːf/ adj. & v. —adj. (of a metal) not susceptible to corrosion by rust. —v.tr. make rustproof.

rusty /ˈrʌstɪ/ adj. (**rustier**, **rustiest**) **1** rusted or affected by rust. **2** stiff with age or disuse. **3** (of knowledge etc.) faded or impaired by neglect (my French is a bit rusty). **4** rust-coloured. **5** (of black clothes) discoloured by age. □ **rustily** adv. **rustiness** n. [OE rūstig (as RUST)]

rut¹ n. & v. —n. **1** a deep track made by the passage of wheels. **2** an established (esp. tedious) mode of practice or procedure. —v.tr. (**rutted**, **rutting**) mark with ruts. □ **in a rut** following a fixed (esp. tedious or dreary) pattern of behaviour that is difficult to change. □ **rutty** adj. [prob. f. OF rote (as ROUTE)]

rut² n. & v. —n. the periodic sexual excitement of a male deer, goat, ram, etc. —v.intr. (**rutted**, **rutting**) be affected with rut. □ **ruttish** adj. [ME f. OF rut, ruit f. L rugitus f. rugire roar]

rutabaga /ˌruːtəˈbɑːɡə/ n. a swede. [Sw. dial. rotabagge]

ruthenium /ruːˈθiːnɪəm/ n. Chem. a rare hard white metallic transition element, used as a chemical catalyst and in certain alloys. [med.L Ruthenia Russia (from its discovery in ores from the Urals)]

rutherfordium /ˌrʌðəˈfɔːdɪəm/ n. Chem. an artificially made transuranic metallic element produced by bombarding an isotope of Californium. [E. Rutherford, Engl. physicist d. 1937]

ruthless /ˈruːθlɪs/ adj. having no pity or compassion. □ **ruthlessly** adv. **ruthlessness** n. [ME, f. ruth compassion f. RUE¹]

RV abbr. Revised Version (of the Bible).

-ry /rɪ/ suffix = -ERY (infantry; rivalry). [shortened f. -ERY, or by analogy]

rye /raɪ/ n. **1 a** a cereal plant, Secale cereale, with spikes bearing florets which yield wheatlike grains. **b** the grain of this used for bread and fodder. **2** (in full **rye whisky**) whisky distilled from fermented rye. [OE ryge f. Gmc]

ryegrass /ˈraɪɡrɑːs/ n. any forage or lawn grass of the genus Lolium, esp. L. perenne. [obs. ray-grass, of unkn. orig.]

Ss

S¹ /es/ *n.* (also **s**) (*pl.* **Ss** or **S's** /'esɪz/) **1** the nineteenth letter of the alphabet. **2** an S-shaped object or curve.

S² *abbr.* (also **S.**) **1** Society. **2** South, Southern.

S³ *symb. Chem.* the element sulphur.

s. *abbr.* **1** second(s). **2** shilling(s). **3** singular. **4** son. [sense 2 orig. f. L *solidus*: see SOLIDUS]

's¹ /s; z after a vowel sound or voiced consonant/ *abbr.* **1** is, has (*he's; it's; John's; Charles's*). **2** us (*let's*). **3** *colloq.* does (*what's he say?*).

-s¹ /s; z after a vowel sound or voiced consonant, e.g. *ways, bags*/ *suffix* denoting the plurals of nouns (cf. -ES¹). [OE *-as* pl. ending]

-s² /s; z after a vowel sound or voiced consonant, e.g. *ties, begs*/ *suffix* forming the 3rd person sing. present of verbs (cf. -ES²). [OE dial., prob. f. OE 2nd person sing. present ending *-es, -as*]

-s³ /s; z after a vowel sound or voiced consonant, e.g. *besides*/ *suffix* **1** forming adverbs (*afterwards; besides*). **2** forming possessive pronouns (*hers; ours*). [formed as -'s¹]

-s' /s; z after a vowel sound or voiced consonant/ *suffix* denoting the possessive case of plural nouns and sometimes of singular nouns ending in s (*the boys' shoes; Charles' book*). [as -'s¹]

-'s¹ /s; z after a vowel sound or voiced consonant/ *suffix* denoting the possessive case of singular nouns and of plural nouns not ending in *-s* (*John's book; the book's cover; the children's shoes*). [OE genit. sing. ending]

-'s² /s; z after a vowel sound or voiced consonant/ *suffix* denoting the plural of a letter or symbol (*S's; 8's*). [as -s¹]

SA *abbr.* **1** Salvation Army. **2** sex appeal. **3 a** South Africa. **b** South America. **c** South Australia.

Sabbatarian /ˌsæbə'teərɪən/ *n. & adj.* —*n.* **1** a strict sabbath-keeping Jew. **2** a Christian who favours observing Sunday strictly as the sabbath. **3** a Christian who observes Saturday as the sabbath. —*adj.* relating to or holding the tenets of Sabbatarians. □ **Sabbatarianism** *n.* [LL *sabbatarius* f. L *sabbatum*: see SABBATH]

sabbath /'sæbəθ/ *n.* (in full **sabbath day**) a day of rest and religious observance kept by Christians on Sunday, Jews on Saturday, and Muslims on Friday. [OE *sabat*, L *sabbatum*, & OF *sabbat*, f. Gk *sabbaton* f. Heb. *šabbāṯ* f. *šāḇaṯ* to rest]

sabbatical /sə'bætɪk(ə)l/ *adj. & n.* —*adj.* **1** of or appropriate to the sabbath. **2** (of leave) granted at intervals to a university teacher for study or travel, orig. every seventh year. —*n.* a period of sabbatical leave. □ **sabbatically** *adv.* [LL *sabbaticus* f. Gk *sabbatikos* of the sabbath]

sable¹ /'seɪb(ə)l/ *n.* **1 a** a small brown-furred flesh-eating mammal, *Martes zibellina*, of N. Europe and parts of N. Asia, related to the marten. **b** its skin or fur. **2** a fine paintbrush made of sable fur. [ME f. OF f. med.L *sabelum* f. Slav.]

sable² /'seɪb(ə)l/ *n. & adj.* —*n.* **1** esp. *poet.* black. **2** (in *pl.*) mourning garments. —*adj.* esp. *poet.* dark, gloomy. □ **sabled** *adj.* **sably** *adv.* [ME f. OF (in Heraldry): gen. taken to be identical with SABLE¹, although sable fur is dark brown]

sabot /'sæbəʊ, 'sæbəʊ/ *n.* **1** a kind of simple shoe hollowed out from a block of wood. **2** a wooden-soled shoe. □ **saboted** /'sæbəʊd/ *adj.* [F, blend of *savate* shoe + *botte* boot]

sabotage /'sæbəˌtɑːʒ/ *n. & v.* —*n.* deliberate damage to productive capacity, esp. as a political act. —*v.tr.* **1** commit sabotage on. **2** destroy; spoil; make useless (*sabotaged my plans*). [F f. *saboter* make a noise with sabots, bungle, wilfully destroy: see SABOT]

saboteur /ˌsæbə'tɜː(r)/ *n.* a person who commits sabotage. [F]

sabre /'seɪbə(r)/ *n.* (*US* **saber**) **1** a cavalry sword with a curved blade. **2** a cavalry soldier and horse. **3** a light fencing-sword with a tapering blade. □ **sabre-rattling** a display or threat of military force. **sabre-toothed** designating any of various extinct mammals having long sabre-shaped upper canines. [F, earlier *sable* f. G *Sabel, Säbel, Schabel* f. Pol. *szabla* or Magyar *szablya*]

SAC *abbr.* (in the UK) Senior Aircraftman.

sac *n.* a baglike cavity, enclosed by a membrane, in an animal or plant. [F *sac* or L *saccus* SACK¹]

saccharide /'sækəˌraɪd/ *n. Chem.* a type of sugar found esp. in plants. [mod.L *saccharum* sugar + -IDE]

saccharin /'sækərɪn/ *n.* a very sweet substance used as a non-fattening substitute for sugar. [G (as SACCHARIDE) + -IN]

saccharine /'sækəˌriːn/ *adj.* **1** sugary. **2** of, containing, or like sugar. **3** unpleasantly over-polite, sentimental, etc.

saccharo- /'sækərəʊ/ *comb. form* sugar; sugar and. [Gk *sakkharon* sugar]

sacerdotal /ˌsækə'dəʊt(ə)l/ *adj.* of priests or the priestly office; priestly. □ **sacerdotalism** *n.* **sacerdotalist** *n.* **sacerdotally** *adv.* [ME f. OF *sacerdotal* or L *sacerdotalis* f. *sacerdos -dotis* priest]

sachet /'sæʃeɪ/ *n.* **1** a small bag or packet containing a small portion of a substance, esp. shampoo. **2** a small perfumed bag. **3 a** dry perfume for laying among clothes etc. **b** a packet of this. [F, dimin. of *sac* f. L *saccus*]

sack¹ *n. & v.* —*n.* **1 a** a large strong bag, usu. made of hessian, paper, or plastic, for storing or conveying goods. **b** (usu. foll. by *of*) this with its contents (*a sack of potatoes*). **c** a quantity contained in a sack. **2** (prec. by *the*) *colloq.* dismissal from employment. **3** (prec. by *the*) *US sl.* bed. **4** a woman's short loose dress with a sacklike appearance. **5** a man's or woman's loose-hanging coat not shaped to the back. —*v.tr.* **1** put into a sack or sacks. **2** *colloq.* dismiss from employment. □ **sack race** a race between competitors in sacks up to the waist or neck. □ **sackful** *n.* (*pl.* **-fuls**). **sacklike** *adj.* [OE *sacc* f. L *saccus* f. Gk *sakkos*, of Semitic orig.]

sack² v. & n. —v.tr. **1** plunder and destroy (a captured town etc.). **2** steal valuables from (a place). —n. the sacking of a captured place. [orig. as noun, f. F *sac* in phr. *mettre à sac* put to sack, f. It. *sacco* SACK¹]

sack³ n. hist. a white wine formerly imported into Britain from Spain and the Canaries (*sherry sack*). [16th-c. *wyne seck*, f. F *vin sec* dry wine]

sackcloth /ˈsækklɒθ/ n. **1** a coarse fabric of flax or hemp. **2** clothing made of this, formerly worn as a penance or in mourning (esp. *sackcloth and ashes*).

sacking /ˈsækɪŋ/ n. material for making sacks; sackcloth.

sacra pl. of SACRUM.

sacral /ˈseɪkr(ə)l/ adj. **1** Anat. of or relating to the sacrum. **2** Anthropol. of or for sacred rites. [E or L *sacrum*: see SACRUM]

sacrament /ˈsækrəmənt/ n. **1** a religious ceremony or act of the Christian Churches regarded as an outward and visible sign of inward and spiritual grace, esp. baptism and the Eucharist. **2** a thing of mysterious and sacred significance; a sacred influence, symbol, etc. **3** (also **Blessed** or **Holy Sacrament**) (prec. by *the*) **a** the Eucharist. **b** the consecrated elements, esp. the bread or Host. **4** an oath or solemn engagement taken. [ME f. OF *sacrement* f. L *sacramentum* solemn oath etc. f. *sacrare* hallow f. *sacer* SACRED, used in Christian L as transl. of Gk *mustērion* MYSTERY]

sacramental /ˌsækrəˈment(ə)l/ adj. **1** of or of the nature of a sacrament or the sacrament. **2** (of a doctrine etc.) attaching great importance to the sacraments. □ **sacramentalism** n. **sacramentalist** n. **sacramentality** /-ˈtælɪtɪ/ n. **sacramentally** adv. [ME f. F *sacramental* or LL *sacramentalis* (as SACRAMENT)]

sacred /ˈseɪkrɪd/ adj. **1 a** (often foll. by *to*) exclusively dedicated or appropriated (to a god or to some religious purpose). **b** made holy by religious association. **c** connected with religion; used for a religious purpose (*sacred music*). **2 a** safeguarded or required by religion, reverence, or tradition. **b** sacrosanct. **3** (of writings etc.) embodying the laws or doctrines of a religion. □ **sacred cow** colloq. an idea or institution unreasonably held to be above criticism (with ref. to the Hindus' respect for the cow as a holy animal). □ **sacredly** adv. **sacredness** n. [ME, past part. of obs. *sacre* consecrate f. OF *sacrer* f. L *sacrare* f. *sacer sacri* holy]

sacrifice /ˈsækrɪˌfaɪs/ n. & v. —n. **1 a** the act of giving up something valued for the sake of something else more important or worthy. **b** a thing given up in this way. **c** the loss entailed in this. **2 a** the slaughter of an animal or person or the surrender of a possession as an offering to a deity. **b** an animal, person, or thing offered in this way. **3** an act of prayer, thanksgiving, or penitence as propitiation. **4** (in games) a loss incurred deliberately to avoid a greater loss or to obtain a compensating advantage. —v. **1** tr. give up (a thing) as a sacrifice. **2** tr. (foll. by *to*) devote or give over to. **3** tr. (also *absol.*) offer or kill as a sacrifice. □ **sacrificial** /-ˈfɪʃ(ə)l/ adj. **sacrificially** /-ˈfɪʃəlɪ/ adv. [ME f. OF f. L *sacrificium* f. *sacrificus* (as SACRED)]

sacrilege /ˈsækrɪlɪdʒ/ n. the violation or misuse of what is regarded as sacred. □ **sacrilegious** /-ˈlɪdʒəs/ adj. **sacrilegiously** /-ˈlɪdʒəslɪ/ adv. [ME

f. OF f. L *sacrilegium* f. *sacrilegus* stealer of sacred things, f. *sacer sacri* sacred + *legere* take possession of]

sacristan /ˈsækrɪst(ə)n/ n. **1** a person in charge of a sacristy and its contents. **2** archaic the sexton of a parish church. [ME f. med.L *sacristanus* (as SACRED)]

sacristy /ˈsækrɪstɪ/ n. (pl. **-ies**) a room in a church, where the vestments, sacred vessels, etc., are kept and the celebrant can prepare for a service. [F *sacristie* or It. *sacrestia* or med.L *sacristia* (as SACRED)]

sacro- /ˈseɪkrəʊ/ comb. form denoting the sacrum (*sacro-iliac*).

sacrosanct /ˈsækrəʊˌsæŋkt/ adj. (of a person, place, law, etc.) most sacred; inviolable. □ **sacrosanctity** /-ˈsæŋktɪtɪ/ n. [L *sacrosanctus* f. *sacro* ablat. of *sacrum* sacred rite (see SACRED) + *sanctus* (as SACRED)]

sacrum /ˈseɪkrəm/ n. (pl. **sacra** /-krə/ or **sacrums**) Anat. a triangular bone formed from fused vertebrae and situated between the two hip-bones of the pelvis. [L *os sacrum* transl. of Gk *hieron osteon* sacred bone (from its sacrificial use)]

SACW abbr. (in the UK) Senior Aircraftwoman.

SAD abbr. seasonal affective disorder.

sad adj. (**sadder, saddest**) **1** unhappy; feeling sorrow or regret. **2** causing or suggesting sorrow (*a sad story*). **3** regrettable. **4** shameful, deplorable (*is in a sad state*). □ **sad sack** US colloq. a very inept person. □ **saddish** adj. **sadly** adv. **sadness** n. [OE *sæd* f. Gmc, rel. to L *satis*]

sadden /ˈsæd(ə)n/ v.tr. & intr. make or become sad.

saddle /ˈsæd(ə)l/ n. & v. —n. **1** a seat of leather etc., usu. raised at the front and rear, fastened on a horse etc. for riding. **2** a seat for the rider of a bicycle etc. **3** a joint of meat consisting of the two loins. **4** a ridge rising to a summit at each end. **5** the part of a draught-horse's harness to which the shafts are attached. **6** a part of an animal's back resembling a saddle in shape or marking. —v.tr. **1** put a saddle on (a horse etc.). **2 a** (foll. by *with*) burden (a person) with a task, responsibility, etc. **b** (foll. by *on, upon*) impose (a burden) on a person. □ **in the saddle 1** mounted. **2** in office or control. **saddle-bag 1** each of a pair of bags laid across a horse etc. behind the saddle. **2** a bag attached behind the saddle of a bicycle or motor cycle. **saddle-sore** chafed by riding on a saddle. **saddle stitch** a stitch of thread or a wire staple passed through the centre of a magazine or booklet. □ **saddleless** adj. [OE *sadol, sadul* f. Gmc]

saddleback /ˈsæd(ə)lˌbæk/ n. **1** Archit. a tower-roof with two opposite gables. **2** a hill with a concave upper outline. **3** a black pig with a white stripe across the back. □ **saddlebacked** adj.

saddler /ˈsædlə(r)/ n. a maker of or dealer in saddles and other equipment for horses.

saddlery /ˈsædlərɪ/ n. (pl. **-ies**) **1** the saddles and other equipment of a saddler. **2** a saddler's business or premises.

Sadducee /ˈsædjʊˌsiː/ n. a member of a Jewish sect or party of the time of Christ that denied the resurrection of the dead, the existence of spirits, and the obligation of the traditional oral law. □ **Sadducean** /-ˈsiːən/ adj. [OE *sadducēas* f.

LL *Sadducaeus* f. Gk *Saddoukaios* f. Heb. ṣ̌ə̄dûk̠î, prob. = descendant of Zadok (2 Sam. 8:17)]

sadhu /ˈsɑːduː/ *n.* (in India) a holy man, sage, or ascetic. [Skr., = holy man]

sadism /ˈseɪdɪz(ə)m/ *n.* **1** a form of sexual perversion characterized by the enjoyment of inflicting pain or suffering on others. **2** *colloq.* the enjoyment of cruelty to others. □ **sadist** *n.* **sadistic** /səˈdɪstɪk/ *adj.* **sadistically** /səˈdɪstɪkəlɪ/ *adv.* [F *sadisme* f. Count or 'Marquis' de *Sade*, Fr. writer d. 1814]

sado-masochism /ˌseɪdəʊˈmæsəˌkɪz(ə)m/ *n.* the combination of sadism and masochism in one person. □ **sado-masochist** *n.* **sado-masochistic** /-ˈkɪstɪk/ *adj.*

s.a.e. *abbr.* stamped addressed envelope.

safari /səˈfɑːrɪ/ *n.* (*pl.* **safaris**) **1** a hunting or scientific expedition, esp. in E. Africa (*go on safari*). **2** a sightseeing trip to see African animals in their natural habitat. □ **safari park** an enclosed area where lions etc. are kept in relatively open spaces for public viewing from vehicles driven through. **safari suit** a lightweight suit usu. with short sleeves and four pleated pockets in the jacket. [Swahili f. Arab. *safara* to travel]

safe *adj. & n.* —*adj.* **1 a** free of danger or injury. **b** (often foll. by *from*) out of or not exposed to danger (*safe from their enemies*). **2** affording security or not involving danger or risk (*put it in a safe place*). **3** reliable, certain; that can be reckoned on (*a safe catch; a safe method; is safe to win*). **4** prevented from escaping or doing harm (*have got him safe*). **5** (also **safe and sound**) uninjured; with no harm done. **6** cautious and unenterprising; consistently moderate. —*n.* **1** a strong lockable cabinet etc. for valuables. **2** = *meat safe*. □ **on the safe side** with a margin of security against risks. **safe bet** a bet that is certain to succeed. **safe-breaker** (or **-blower** or **-cracker**) a person who breaks open and robs safes. **safe conduct 1** a privilege of immunity from arrest or harm, esp. on a particular occasion. **2** a document securing this. **safe deposit** a building containing strongrooms and safes let separately. **safe house** a place of refuge or rendezvous for spies etc. **safe keeping** preservation in a safe place. **safe sex** sexual activity in which precautions are taken to reduce the risk of spreading sexually transmitted diseases, esp. Aids. □ **safely** *adv.* **safeness** *n.* [ME f. AF *saf*, OF *sauf* f. L *salvus* uninjured: (n.) orig. *save* f. SAVE¹]

safeguard /ˈseɪfgɑːd/ *n. & v.* —*n.* **1** a proviso, stipulation, quality, or circumstance, that tends to prevent something undesirable. **2** a safe conduct. —*v.tr.* guard or protect (rights etc.) by a precaution or stipulation. [ME f. AF *salve garde*, OF *sauve garde* (as SAFE, GUARD)]

safety /ˈseɪftɪ/ *n.* (*pl.* **-ies**) **1** the condition of being safe; freedom from danger or risks. **2** (*attrib.*) **a** designating any of various devices for preventing injury from machinery (*safety bar; safety lock*). **b** designating items of protective clothing (*safety helmet*). □ **safety-belt 1** = *seat-belt*. **2** a belt or strap securing a person to prevent injury. **safety-catch** a contrivance for locking a gun-trigger or preventing the accidental operation of machinery. **safety curtain** a fireproof curtain that can be lowered to cut off the auditorium in a theatre from the stage.

safety first a motto advising caution. **safety glass** glass that will not splinter when broken. **safety harness** a system of belts or restraints to hold a person to prevent falling or injury. **safety lamp** a miner's lamp so protected as not to ignite firedamp. **safety match** a match igniting only on a specially prepared surface. **safety net** a net placed to catch an acrobat etc. in case of a fall. **safety pin** a pin with a point that is bent back to the head and is held in a guard when closed. **safety razor** a razor with a guard to reduce the risk of cutting the skin. **safety-valve 1** (in a steam boiler) a valve opening automatically to relieve excessive pressure. **2** a means of giving harmless vent to excitement etc. **safety zone** *US* an area of a road marked off for pedestrians etc. to wait safely. [ME *sauvete* f. OF *sauveté* f. med.L *salvitas -tatis* f. L *salvus* (as SAFE)]

safflower /ˈsæflaʊə(r)/ *n.* **1 a** a thistle-like plant, *Carthamus tinctorius*, yielding a red dye. **b** its dried petals. **2** a dye made from these, used in rouge etc. [Du. *saffloer* or G *Safflor* f. OF *saffleur* f. obs. It. *saffiore*, of unkn. orig.]

saffron /ˈsæfrən/ *n. & adj.* —*n.* **1** an orange flavouring and food colouring made from the dried stigmas of the crocus, *Crocus sativus*. **2** the colour of this. **3** = *meadow saffron.* —*adj.* saffron-coloured. □ **saffrony** *adj.* [ME f. OF *safran* f. Arab. *za'farān*]

sag *v. & n.* —*v.intr.* (**sagged**, **sagging**) **1** sink or subside under weight or pressure, esp. unevenly. **2** have a downward bulge or curve in the middle. **3** fall in price. —*n.* **1 a** the amount that a rope etc. sags. **b** the distance from the middle of its curve to a straight line between its supports. **2** a sinking condition; subsidence. **3** a fall in price. □ **saggy** *adj.* [ME f. MLG *sacken*, Du. *zakken* subside]

saga /ˈsɑːgə/ *n.* **1** a long story of heroic achievement, esp. a medieval Icelandic or Norwegian prose narrative. **2** a series of connected books giving the history of a family etc. **3** a long involved story. [ON, = narrative, rel. to SAW³]

sagacious /səˈgeɪʃ(ə)s/ *adj.* **1** mentally penetrating; gifted with discernment; having practical wisdom. **2** acute-minded, shrewd. **3** (of a saying, plan, etc.) showing wisdom. □ **sagaciously** *adv.* **sagacity** /səˈgæsɪtɪ/ *n.* [L *sagax sagacis*]

sage¹ *n.* **1** an aromatic herb, *Salvia officinalis*, with dull greyish-green leaves. **2** its leaves used in cookery. □ **sage Derby** (or **cheese**) a cheese made with an infusion of sage which flavours and mottles it. □ **sagy** *adj.* [ME f. OF *sauge* f. L *salvia* healing plant f. *salvus* safe]

sage² *n. & adj.* —*n.* **1** often *iron.* a profoundly wise man. **2** any of the ancients traditionally regarded as the wisest of their time. —*adj.* **1** profoundly wise, esp. from experience. **2** of or indicating profound wisdom. **3** often *iron.* wise-looking; solemn-faced. □ **sagely** *adv.* **sageness** *n.* **sageship** *n.* [ME f. OF ult. f. L *sapere* be wise]

sagebrush /ˈseɪdʒbrʌʃ/ *n.* **1** a growth of shrubby aromatic plants of the genus *Artemisia*, esp. *A. tridentata*, found in some semi-arid regions of western N. America. **2** this plant.

Sagittarius /ˌsædʒɪˈteərɪəs/ *n.* **1** a constellation, traditionally regarded as contained in the figure of an archer. **2 a** the ninth sign of the zodiac (the Archer). **b** a person born when the sun is in this sign. □ **Sagittarian** adj. & n. [ME f. L, = archer, f. sagitta arrow]

sago /ˈseɪgəʊ/ n. (pl. **-os**) **1** a kind of starch, made from the powdered pith of the sago palm and used in puddings etc. **2** (in full **sago palm**) any of several tropical palms and cycads, esp. Cycas circinalis and Metroxylon sagu, from which sago is made. [Malay sāgū (orig. through Port.)]

sahib /sɑːb, ˈsɑːhɪb/ n. **1** hist. (in India) a form of address, often placed after the name, to European men. **2** colloq. a gentleman (pukka sahib). [Urdu f. Arab. ṣāḥib friend, lord]

said past and past part. of SAY.

sail n. & v. —n. **1** a piece of material (orig. canvas, now usu. nylon etc.) extended on rigging to catch the wind and propel a boat or ship. **2** a ship's sails collectively. **3 a** a voyage or excursion in a sailing-ship. **b** a voyage of specified duration. **4** a ship, esp. as discerned from its sails. **5** a wind-catching apparatus, usu. a set of boards, attached to the arm of a windmill. —v. **1** intr. travel on water by the use of sails or engine-power. **2** tr. **a** navigate (a ship etc.). **b** travel on (a sea). **3** tr. set (a toy boat) afloat. **4** intr. glide or move smoothly or in a stately manner. **5** intr. (often foll. by through) colloq. succeed easily (sailed through the exams). □ **sail close to** (or **near**) **the wind 1** sail as nearly against the wind as possible. **2** come close to indecency or dishonesty; risk overstepping the mark. **sailing-boat** (or **-ship** or **-vessel**) a vessel driven by sails. **sail into** colloq. attack physically or verbally with force. **take in sail 1** furl the sail or sails of a vessel. **2** moderate one's ambitions. **under sail** with sails set. □ **sailable** adj. **sailed** adj. (also in comb.). **sailless** adj. [OE segel f. Gmc]

sailboard /ˈseɪlbɔːd/ n. a board with a mast and sail, used in windsurfing. □ **sailboarder** n. **sailboarding** n.

sailboat /ˈseɪlbəʊt/ n. US a boat driven by sails.

sailcloth /ˈseɪlklɒθ/ n. **1** canvas for sails. **2** a canvas-like dress material.

sailor /ˈseɪlə(r)/ n. **1** a seaman or mariner, esp. one below the rank of officer. **2** a person considered as liable or not liable to seasickness (a good sailor). □ **sailor hat 1** a straw hat with a straight narrow brim and flat top. **2** a hat with a turned-up brim in imitation of a sailor's, worn by women and children. □ **sailoring** n. **sailorless** adj. **sailorly** adj. [var. of earlier form sailer]

sailplane /ˈseɪlpleɪn/ n. a glider designed for sustained flight.

sainfoin /ˈseɪnfɔɪn, ˈsæn-/ n. a leguminous plant, Onobrychis viciifolia, grown for fodder and having pink flowers. [obs. F saintfoin f. mod.L sanum foenum wholesome hay (because of its medicinal properties)]

saint /seɪnt, before a name usu. sənt/ n. & v. —n. (abbr. **St** or **S**; pl. **Sts** or **SS**) **1** a holy or (in some Churches) a canonized person regarded as having a place in heaven. **2** (**Saint** or **St**) the title of a saint or archangel, hence the name of a church etc. (St Paul's) or (often with the loss of the apostrophe) the name of a town etc. (St Andrews; St Albans). **3** a very virtuous person; a person of great real or affected holiness (would try the patience of a saint). —v.tr. **1** canonize; admit to the calendar of saints. **2** call or regard as a saint. **3** (as **sainted** adj.) sacred; of a saintly life; worthy to be regarded as a saint. □ **saint's day** a Church festival in memory of a saint. □ **saintdom** n. **sainthood** n. **saintlike** adj. **saintling** n. **saintship** n. [ME f. OF seint, saint f. L sanctus holy, past part. of sancire consecrate]

St Bernard /ˈbɜːnəd/ n. (in full **St Bernard dog**) **1** a very large dog of a breed orig. kept to rescue travellers by the monks of the Hospice on the Great St Bernard pass in the Alps. **2** this breed.

St John's wort /dʒɒnz/ n. any yellow-flowered plant of the genus Hypericum, esp. H. androsaemum.

St Leger /ˈledʒə(r)/ n. a horse-race at Doncaster in England for three-year-olds. [f. the founder's name]

saintly /ˈseɪntlɪ/ adj. (**saintlier**, **saintliest**) very holy or virtuous. □ **saintliness** n.

saintpaulia /səntˈpɔːlɪə/ n. any plant of the genus Saintpaulia, esp. the African violet. [Baron W. von Saint Paul, Ger. soldier d. 1910, its discoverer]

St Vitus's dance /ˈvaɪtəsɪz/ n. chorea esp. in children as one of the manifestations of rheumatic fever.

saithe /seɪθ/ n. Sc. a codlike fish, Pollachius virens, with skin that soils fingers like wet coal. [ON seithr]

sake[1] n. (esp. **for the sake of** or **for one's sake**) **1** out of consideration for; in the interest of; because of; owing to (for my own sake as well as yours). **2** in order to please, honour, get, or keep (for the sake of uniformity). □ **for Christ's** (or **God's** or **goodness'** or **Heaven's** or **Pete's** etc.) **sake** an expression of urgency, impatience, supplication, anger, etc. **for old times' sake** in memory of former times. [OE sacu contention, charge, fault, sake f. Gmc]

sake[2] /ˈsɑːkɪ/ n. a Japanese alcoholic drink made from rice. [Jap.]

salaam /səˈlɑːm/ n. & v. —n. **1** the oriental salutation 'Peace'. **2** an Indian obeisance, with or without the salutation, consisting of a low bow of the head and body with the right palm on the forehead. **3** (in pl.) respectful compliments. —v. **1** tr. make a salaam to (a person). **2** intr. make a salaam. [Arab. salām]

salacious /səˈleɪʃəs/ adj. **1** lustful; lecherous. **2** (of writings, pictures, talk, etc.) tending to cause sexual desire. □ **salaciously** adv. **salaciousness** n. **salacity** /səˈlæsɪtɪ/ n. [L salax salacis f. salire leap]

salad /ˈsæləd/ n. **1** a cold dish of various mixtures of raw or cooked vegetables or herbs, usu. seasoned with oil, vinegar, etc. **2** a vegetable or herb suitable for eating raw. □ **salad cream** creamy salad-dressing. **salad days** a period of youthful inexperience. **salad-dressing** a mixture of oil, vinegar, etc., used with salad. [ME f. OF salade f. Prov. salada ult. f. L sal salt]

salamander /ˈsæləmændə(r)/ n. **1** Zool. any tailed newtlike amphibian of the order Urodela, esp. the genus Salamandra, once thought able to endure fire. **2** a mythical lizard-like creature credited with this property. **3** a metal plate heated and placed over food to brown it. □ **salamandrian** /-ˈmændrɪən/ adj. **salamandrine** /-ˈmændrɪn/ adj. **salamandroid** /-ˈmændrɔɪd/ adj. & n. (in sense 1). [ME f. OF salamandre f. L salamandra f. Gk salamandra]

salami /səˈlɑːmɪ/ n. (pl. **salamis**) a highly-seasoned orig. Italian sausage often flavoured with garlic. [It., pl. of *salame*, f. LL *salare* (unrecorded) to salt]

sal ammoniac /ˌsæl əˈməʊnɪˌæk/ n. ammonium chloride, a white crystalline salt. [L *sal ammoniacus* 'salt of Ammon', associated with the Roman temple of Ammon in N. Africa]

salariat /səˈleərɪət/ n. the salaried class. [F f. *salaire* (see SALARY), after *prolétariat*]

salary /ˈsælərɪ/ n. & v. —n. (pl. **-ies**) a fixed regular payment, usu. monthly or quarterly, made by an employer to an employee, esp. a professional or white-collar worker. —v.tr. (**-ies, -ied**) (usu. as **salaried** adj.) pay a salary to. [ME f. AF *salarie*, OF *salaire* f. L *salarium* orig. soldier's salt-money f. *sal* salt]

sale n. **1** the exchange of a commodity for money etc.; an act or instance of selling. **2** the amount sold (*the sales were enormous*). **3** the rapid disposal of goods at reduced prices for a period esp. at the end of a season etc. **4 a** an event at which goods are sold. **b** a public auction. □ **on** (or **for**) **sale** offered for purchase. **sale of work** an event where goods made by parishioners etc. are sold for charity. **sale or return** an arrangement by which a purchaser takes a quantity of goods with the right of returning surplus goods without payment. **sales clerk** US a salesman or saleswoman in a shop. **sales talk** persuasive talk to promote the sale of goods or the acceptance of an idea etc. **sales tax** a tax on sales or on the receipts from sales. [OE *sala* f. ON]

saleable /ˈseɪləb(ə)l/ adj. (also **salable**) fit to be sold; finding purchasers. □ **saleability** /-ˈbɪlɪtɪ/ n.

saleroom /ˈseɪlruːm, -rʊm/ n. esp. Brit. a room in which items are sold at auction.

salesgirl /ˈseɪlzɡɜːl/ n. a saleswoman.

saleslady /ˈseɪlzˌleɪdɪ/ n. (pl. **-ies**) a saleswoman.

salesman /ˈseɪlzmən/ n. (pl. **-men**; fem. **saleswoman**, pl. **-women**) **1** a person employed to sell goods in a shop, or as an agent between the producer and retailer. **2** US a commercial traveller.

salesmanship /ˈseɪlzmənʃɪp/ n. **1** skill in selling. **2** the techniques used in selling.

salesperson /ˈseɪlzˌpɜːs(ə)n/ n. a salesman or saleswoman (used as a neutral alternative).

salesroom /ˈseɪlzruːm, -rʊm/ n. US = SALEROOM.

Salic /ˈsælɪk, ˈseɪl-/ adj. □ **Salic law** hist. a law excluding females from dynastic succession. [F *Salique* or med.L *Salicus* f. *Salii*, a 4th-c. Frankish people]

salicylic acid /ˌsælɪˈsɪlɪk/ n. a bitter chemical used as a fungicide and in the manufacture of aspirin and dyestuffs. □ **salicylate** /səˈlɪsɪˌleɪt/ n. [*salicyl* its radical f. F *salicyle* f. L *salix -icis* willow]

salient /ˈseɪlɪənt/ adj. & n. —adj. **1** jutting out; prominent; conspicuous, most noticeable. **2** (of an angle, esp. in fortification) pointing outwards. —n. a salient angle or part of a work in fortification; an outward bulge in a line of military attack or defence. □ **salience** n. **saliency** n. **saliently** adv. [L *salire* leap]

saline /ˈseɪlaɪn/ adj. & n. —adj. **1** (of natural waters, springs, etc.) impregnated with or containing salt or salts. **2** (of food or drink etc.) tasting of salt. **3** of chemical salts. **4** of the nature of a salt. **5** (of medicine) containing a salt or salts of alkaline metals or magnesium. —n. **1** a salt lake, spring, marsh, etc. **2** a salt-pan or salt-works. **3** a saline substance, esp. a medicine. **4** a solution of salt in water. □ **salinity** /səˈlɪnɪtɪ/ n. **salinization** /ˌsælɪnaɪˈzeɪʃ(ə)n/ n. **salinometer** /ˌsælɪˈnɒmɪtə(r)/ n. [ME f. L *sal* salt]

saliva /səˈlaɪvə/ n. liquid secreted into the mouth by glands to provide moisture and facilitate chewing and swallowing. □ **salivary** /səˈlaɪ-, ˈsælɪ-/ adj. [ME f. L]

salivate /ˈsælɪˌveɪt/ v. intr. secrete or discharge saliva esp. in excess or in greedy anticipation. □ **salivation** /ˌsælɪˈveɪʃ(ə)n/ n. [L *salivare* (as SALIVA)]

Salk vaccine /sɔːlk/ n. a vaccine developed against polio. [J. E. *Salk*, Amer. scientist b. 1914]

sallow[1] /ˈsæləʊ/ adj. & v. —adj. (**sallower, sallowest**) (of the skin or complexion, or of a person) of a sickly yellow or pale brown. —v.tr. & intr. make or become sallow. □ **sallowish** adj. **sallowness** n. [OE *salo* dusky f. Gmc]

sallow[2] /ˈsæləʊ/ n. **1** a willow-tree, esp. one of a low-growing or shrubby kind. **2** the wood or a shoot of this. □ **sallowy** adj. [OE *salh* salg- f. Gmc, rel. to OHG *salaha*, ON *selja*, L *salix*]

Sally /ˈsælɪ/ n. (pl. **-ies**) colloq. **1** (usu. prec. by *the*) the Salvation Army. **2** a member of this. [abbr.]

sally[1] /ˈsælɪ/ n. & v. (pl. **-ies**) —n. **1** a sudden charge from a fortification upon its besiegers; a sortie. **2** a going forth; an excursion. **3** a witticism; a piece of banter; a lively remark esp. by way of attack upon a person or thing or of a diversion in argument. **4** a sudden start into activity; an outburst. —v.intr. (**-ies, -ied**) **1** (usu. foll. by *out*, *forth*) go for a walk, set out on a journey etc. **2** (usu. foll. by *out*) make a military sally. [F *saillie* fem. past part. of *saillir* issue f. OF *salir* f. L *salire* leap]

sally[2] /ˈsælɪ/ n. (pl. **-ies**) the part of a bell-rope prepared with inwoven wool for holding. [perh. f. SALLY[1] in sense 'leaping motion']

salmi /ˈsælmɪ/ n. (pl. **salmis**) a ragout or casserole esp. of partly roasted game-birds. [F *salmigondis* of unknown origin]

salmon /ˈsæmən/ n. & adj. —n. (pl. same or (esp. of types) **salmons**) **1** any fish of the family Salmonidae, esp. of the genus *Salmo*, much prized for its (often smoked) pink flesh. **2** *Austral.* & *NZ* the barramundi or a similar fish. —adj. salmon-pink. □ **salmon-pink** the colour of salmon flesh. **salmon trout** a large silver-coloured trout, *Salmo trutta*. □ **salmonoid** adj. & n. (in sense 1). **salmony** adj. [ME f. AF *sa(u)moun*, OF *saumon* f. L *salmo -onis*]

salmonella /ˌsælməˈnelə/ n. (pl. **salmonellae** /-liː/) **1** any bacterium of the genus *Salmonella*, esp. any of various types causing food poisoning. **2** food poisoning caused by infection with salmonellae. □ **salmonellosis** /-ˈləʊsɪs/ n. [mod.L f. D. E. *Salmon*, Amer. veterinary surgeon d. 1914]

salon /ˈsælɒn, -lɔ̃/ n. **1** the reception room of a large, esp. French or continental, house. **2** a room or establishment where a hairdresser, beautician, etc., conducts trade. [F: see SALOON]

saloon /səˈluːn/ n. **1 a** a large room or hall, esp. in a hotel or public building. **b** a public room or gallery for a specified purpose (*billiard-saloon*; *shooting-saloon*). **2** (in full **saloon car**) a motor car with a closed body and no partition behind the driver. **3** a public room on a ship. **4** *US* a drinking-bar. **5** (in full **saloon bar**) *Brit.* the more comfortable bar in a public house. [F *salon* f. It. *salone* augment. of *sala* hall]

Salopian /səˈləʊpɪən/ *n.* & *adj.* —*n.* a native or inhabitant of Shropshire. —*adj.* of or relating to Shropshire. [AF *Salopesberia* f. ME f. OE *Scrobbesbyrig* Shrewsbury]

salsa /ˈsælsə/ *n.* **1** a kind of dance music of Latin American origin, incorporating jazz and rock elements. **2** a dance performed to this music. [Sp. (as SAUCE)]

salsify /ˈsælsɪfɪ, -ˌfaɪ/ *n.* (*pl.* **-ies**) **1** a European plant, *Tragopogon porrifolius*, with long cylindrical fleshy roots. **2** this root used as a vegetable. □ **black salsify** scorzonera. [F *salsifis* f. obs. It. *salsefica*, of unkn. orig.]

SALT /sɔːlt, sɒlt/ *abbr.* Strategic Arms Limitation Talks (or Treaty).

salt /sɔːlt, sɒlt/ *n.*, *adj.*, & *v.* —*n.* **1** (also **common salt**) sodium chloride; the substance that gives sea water its characteristic taste, got in crystalline form by mining from strata consisting of it or by the evaporation of sea water, and used for seasoning or preserving food, or for other purposes. **2** a chemical compound formed from the reaction of an acid with a base, with all or part of the hydrogen of the acid replaced by a metal or metal-like radical. **3** sting; piquancy; pungency; wit (*added salt to the conversation*). **4** (in *sing.* or *pl.*) **a** a substance resembling salt in taste, form, etc. (*bath salts; Epsom salts; smelling-salts*). **b** (esp. in *pl.*) this type of substance used as a laxative. **5** a marsh, esp. one flooded by the tide, often used as a pasture or for collecting water for salt-making. **6** (also **old salt**) an experienced sailor. —*adj.* **1** impregnated with, containing, or tasting of salt; cured or preserved or seasoned with salt. **2** (of a plant) growing in the sea or in salt marshes. **3** (of tears etc.) bitter. **4** (of wit) pungent. —*v.tr.* **1** cure or preserve with salt or brine. **2** season with salt. **3** make (a narrative etc.) piquant. **4** sprinkle (the ground etc.) with salt esp. in order to melt snow etc. **5** treat with a solution of salt or mixture of salts. □ **salt-and-pepper** (of materials etc. and esp. of hair) with light and dark colours mixed together. **salt away** (or **down**) *sl.* put money etc. by. **salt lake** a lake of salt water. **salt-lick 1** a place where animals go to lick salt from the ground. **2** this salt. **salt-marsh** = sense 5 of *n.* **salt meadow** a meadow subject to flooding with salt water. **salt a mine** *sl.* introduce extraneous ore, material, etc., to make the source seem rich. **the salt of the earth** a person or people of great worthiness, reliability, honesty, etc.; those whose qualities are a model for the rest (Matt. 5:13). **salt-pan** a vessel, or a depression near the sea, used for getting salt by evaporation. **salt-shaker** *US* a container of salt for sprinkling on food. **salt-spoon** a small spoon usu. with a short handle and a roundish deep bowl for taking table salt. **salt water 1** sea water. **2** *sl.* tears. **salt-water** *adj.* of or living in the sea. **take with a pinch (or grain) of salt** regard as exaggerated; be incredulous about; believe only part of. **worth one's salt** efficient, capable. □ **saltish** *adj.* **saltless** *adj.* **saltly** *adv.* **saltness** *n.*

[OE *s(e)alt s(e)altan*, OS, ON, Goth. *salt*, OHG *salz* f. Gmc]

salt-cellar /ˈsɔːltˌselə(r), ˈsɒlt-/ *n.* a vessel holding salt for table use. [SALT + obs. *saler* f. AF f. OF *salier* salt-box f. L (as SALARY), assim. to CELLAR]

salter /ˈsɔːltə(r), ˈsɒl-/ *n.* **1** a manufacturer or dealer in salt. **2** a workman at a salt-works. **3** a person who salts fish etc. [OE *sealtere* (as SALT)]

salting /ˈsɔːltɪŋ, ˈsɒl-/ *n.* **1** in senses of SALT *v.* **2** (esp. in *pl.*) *Geol.* a salt marsh; a marsh overflowed by the sea.

saltire /ˈsɔːlˌtaɪə(r)/ *n.* An X-shaped cross. □ **saltirewise** *adv.* [ME f. OF *sau(l)toir* etc. stirrup-cord, stile, saltire, f. med.L *saltatorium* f. L *saltare* frequent. of *salire* salt- leap]

saltpetre /ˌsɒltˈpiːtə(r), ˌsɔːlt-/ *n.* (*US* **saltpeter**) potassium nitrate, a white crystalline salty substance used in preserving meat and as a constituent of gunpowder. [ME f. OF *salpetre* f. med.L *salpetra* prob. for *sal petrae* (unrecorded) salt of rock (i.e. found as an incrustation): assim. to SALT]

salty /ˈsɔːltɪ, ˈsɒl-/ *adj.* (**saltier**, **saltiest**) tasting of, containing, or preserved with salt. □ **saltiness** *n.*

salubrious /səˈluːbrɪəs, səˈljuː-/ *adj.* **1** health-giving; healthy. **2** (of surroundings etc.) pleasant; agreeable. □ **salubriously** *adv.* **salubriousness** *n.* **salubrity** *n.* [L *salubris* f. *salus* health]

saluki /səˈluːkɪ/ *n.* (*pl.* **salukis**) **1** a tall swift slender dog of a silky-coated breed with large ears and a fringed tail and feet. **2** this breed. [Arab. *salūḳī*]

salutary /ˈsæljʊtərɪ/ *adj.* **1** producing good effects; beneficial. **2** *archaic* health-giving. [ME f. F *salutaire* or L *salutaris* f. *salus -utis* health]

salutation /ˌsæljuːˈteɪʃ(ə)n/ *n.* **1** a sign or expression of greeting or recognition of another's arrival or departure. **2** words spoken or written to enquire about another's health or well-being. □ **salutational** *adj.* **salutatory** /səˈljuːtətərɪ/ *adj.* [ME f. OF *salutation* or L *salutatio* (as SALUTE)]

salute /səˈluːt, -ˈljuːt/ *n.* & *v.* —*n.* **1** a gesture of respect, homage, or courteous recognition, esp. made to or by a person when arriving or departing. **2 a** *Mil.* & *Naut.* a prescribed or specified movement of the hand or of weapons or flags as a sign of respect or recognition. **b** (prec. by *the*) the attitude taken by an individual soldier, sailor, policeman, etc., in saluting. **3** the discharge of a gun or guns as a formal or ceremonial sign of respect or celebration. —*v.* **1 a** *tr.* make a salute to. **b** *intr.* (often foll. by *to*) perform a salute. **2** *tr.* greet; make a salutation to. **3** *tr.* (foll. by *with*) receive or greet with (a smile etc.). □ **take the salute 1** (of the highest officer present) acknowledge it by gesture as is meant for him. **2** receive ceremonial salutes by members of a procession. □ **saluter** *n.* [ME f. L *salutare* f. *salus -utis* health]

salvage /ˈsælvɪdʒ/ *n.* & *v.* —*n.* **1** the rescue of a ship, its cargo, or other property, from loss at sea, destruction by fire, etc. **2** the property etc. saved in this way. **3 a** the saving and utilization of waste paper, scrap material, etc. **b** the materials salvaged. —*v.tr.* **1** save from a wreck, fire, etc. **2** retrieve or preserve (something favourable) in adverse circumstances (*tried to salvage some dignity*). □ **salvageable** *adj.* **salvager** *n.* [F f. med.L *salvagium* f. L *salvare* SAVE¹]

salvation /sælˈveɪʃ(ə)n/ n. **1** the act of saving or being saved; preservation from loss, calamity, etc. **2** deliverance from sin and its consequences and admission to heaven, brought about by Christ. **3** a religious conversion. **4** a person or thing that saves (*was the salvation of*). □ **Salvation Army** a worldwide evangelical organization on quasi-military lines for the revival of Christianity and helping the poor. □ **salvationism** n. **salvationist** n. (both nouns esp. with ref. to the Salvation Army). [ME f. OF *sauvacion, salvacion*, f. eccl.L *salvatio -onis* f. *salvare* SAVE¹, transl. Gk *sōtēria*]

salve¹ /sælv, sɑːv/ n. & v. —n. **1** a healing ointment. **2** (often foll. by *for*) a thing that is soothing or consoling for wounded feelings, an uneasy conscience, etc. —v.tr. soothe (pride, self-love, conscience, etc.). [OE *s(e)alf(e), s(e)alfian* f. Gmc; v. partly f. L *salvare* SAVE¹]

salve² /sælv/ v.tr. **1** save (a ship or its cargo) from loss at sea. **2** save (property) from fire. □ **salvable** adj. [back-form. f. SALVAGE]

salver /ˈsælvə(r)/ n. a tray usu. of gold, silver, brass, or electroplate, on which drinks, letters, etc., are offered. [F *salve* tray for presenting food to the king f. Sp. *salva* assaying of food f. *salvar* SAVE¹: assoc. with *platter*]

salvia /ˈsælvɪə/ n. any plant of the genus *Salvia*, esp. *S. splendens* with red or blue flowers. [L, = SAGE¹]

Salvo /ˈsælvəʊ/ n. (pl. **-os**) *Austral. sl.* a member of the Salvation Army. [abbr.]

salvo /ˈsælvəʊ/ n. (pl. **-oes** or **-os**) **1** the simultaneous firing of artillery or other guns esp. as a salute, or in a sea-fight. **2** a number of bombs released from aircraft at the same moment. **3** a round or volley of applause. [earlier *salve* f. F f. It. *salva* salutation (as SAVE¹)]

sal volatile /ˌsæl vɒˈlætɪlɪ/ n. ammonium carbonate, esp. in the form of a flavoured solution in alcohol used as smelling-salts. [mod.L, = volatile salt]

Samaritan /səˈmærɪt(ə)n/ n. & adj. —n. **1** (in full **good Samaritan**) a charitable or helpful person (with ref. to Luke 10:33 etc.). **2** a member of an organization which counsels people in distress by telephone or face to face. **3** a native of Samaria in West Jordan. **4** the language of this people. —adj. of Samaria or the Samaritans. □ **Samaritanism** n. [LL *Samaritanus* f. Gk *Samareitēs* f. *Samareia* Samaria]

samarium /səˈmeərɪəm/ n. *Chem.* a soft silvery metallic element of the lanthanide series, used in making ferromagnetic alloys. [*samarskite* the mineral in which its spectrum was first observed, f. *Samarski* name of a 19th-c. Russ. official]

samba /ˈsæmbə/ n. & v. —n. **1** a Brazilian dance of African origin. **2** a ballroom dance imitative of this. **3** the music for this. —v.intr. (**sambas, sambaed** /-bəd/ or **samba'd, sambaing** /-bəɪŋ/) dance the samba. [Port., of Afr. orig.]

Sam Browne /sæm ˈbraʊn/ n. (in full **Sam Browne belt**) an army officer's belt and the strap supporting it. [Sir *Samuel* J. *Browne*, Brit. military commander d. 1901]

same adj., pron., & adv. —adj. **1** (often prec. by *the*) identical; not different; unchanged (*everyone was looking in the same direction; the same car was used in another crime; saying the same thing over and over*). **2** unvarying, uniform, monotonous (*the same old story*). **3** (usu. prec. by *this, these, that, those*) (of a person or thing) previously alluded to; just mentioned; aforesaid (*this same man was later my husband*). —pron. (prec. by *the*) **1** the same person or thing (*the others asked for the same*). **2** *Law* or *archaic* the person or thing just mentioned (*detected the youth breaking in and apprehended the same*). —adv. (usu. prec. by *the*) similarly; in the same way (*we all feel the same; I want to go, the same as you do*). □ **all** (or **just**) **the same 1** emphatically the same. **2** in spite of changed conditions, adverse circumstances, etc. (*but you should offer, all the same*). **at the same time 1** simultaneously. **2** notwithstanding; in spite of circumstances etc. **be all** (or **just**) **the same to** an expression of indifference or impartiality (*it's all the same to me what we do*). **same here** *colloq.* the same applies to me. **the same to you!** may you do, have, find, etc., the same thing; likewise. **the very same** emphatically the same. □ **sameness** n. [ME f. ON *sami, sama*, with Gmc cognates]

samey /ˈseɪmɪ/ adj. (**samier, samiest**) *colloq.* lacking in variety; monotonous. □ **sameyness** n.

samizdat /ˈsæmɪzˌdæt, -ˈdæt/ n. *hist.* a system of clandestine publication of banned literature in the former USSR. [Russ., = self-publishing house]

samosa /səˈməʊsə/ n. a triangular pastry fried in ghee or oil, containing spiced vegetables or meat. [Hind.]

samovar /ˈsæməˌvɑː(r)/ n. a Russian urn for making tea, with an internal heating tube to keep water at boiling-point. [Russ., = self-boiler]

Samoyed /ˈsæməˌjed/ n. **1** a member of a people of northern Siberia. **2** the language of this people. **3** (also **samoyed**) **a** a dog of a white Arctic breed. **b** this breed. [Russ. *samoed*]

sampan /ˈsæmpæn/ n. a small boat usu. with a stern-oar or stern-oars, used in the Far East. [Chin. *san-ban* f. *san* three + *ban* board]

samphire /ˈsæmˌfaɪə(r)/ n. **1** an umbelliferous maritime rock plant, *Crithmum maritimum*, with aromatic fleshy leaves used in pickles. **2** the glasswort. [earlier *samp(i)ere* f. F (*herbe de*) *Saint Pierre* St Peter('s herb)]

sample /ˈsɑːmp(ə)l/ n. & v. —n. **1** a small part or quantity intended to show what the whole is like. **2** a small amount of fabric, food, or other commodity, esp. given to a prospective customer. **3** a specimen, esp. one taken for scientific testing or analysis. **4** an illustrative or typical example. —v.tr. **1** take or give samples of. **2** try the qualities of. **3** get a representative experience of. [ME f. AF *assample*, OF *essample* EXAMPLE]

sampler¹ /ˈsɑːmplə(r)/ n. a piece of embroidery worked in various stitches as a specimen of proficiency (often displayed on a wall etc.). [OF *essamplaire* (as EXEMPLAR)]

sampler² /ˈsɑːmplə(r)/ n. **1** a person who samples. **2** *US* a collection of representative items etc.

sampling /ˈsɑːmplɪŋ/ n. a technique in electronic music involving digitally encoding a piece of sound and re-using it as part of a composition or recording.

Samson /ˈsæms(ə)n/ n. a person of great strength or resembling Samson in some respect. [LL f. Gk Sampsōn f. Heb. šimšôn (Judg. 13–16)]

samurai /ˈsæmʊˌraɪ, -jʊˌraɪ/ n. (pl. same) 1 a Japanese army officer. 2 hist. a member of a military caste in Japan. [Jap.]

sanatorium /ˌsænəˈtɔːrɪəm/ n. (pl. **sanatoriums** or **sanatoria** /-rɪə/) 1 an establishment for the treatment of invalids, esp. of convalescents and the chronically sick. 2 Brit. a room or building for sick people in a school etc. [mod.L f. L sanare cure]

sanctify /ˈsæŋktɪˌfaɪ/ v.tr. (**-ies, -ied**) 1 consecrate; set apart or observe as holy. 2 purify or free from sin. 3 make legitimate or binding by religious sanction; justify; give the colour of morality or innocence to. 4 make productive of or conducive to holiness. □ **sanctification** /-fɪˈkeɪʃ(ə)n/ n. **sanctifier** n. [ME f. OF saintifier f. eccl.L sanctificare f. L sanctus holy]

sanctimonious /ˌsæŋktɪˈməʊnɪəs/ adj. making a show of sanctity or piety. □ **sanctimoniously** adv. **sanctimoniousness** n. **sanctimony** /ˈsæŋktɪmənɪ/ n. [L sanctimonia sanctity (as SAINT)]

sanction /ˈsæŋkʃ(ə)n/ n. & v. —n. 1 approval or encouragement given to an action etc. by custom or tradition; express permission. 2 confirmation or ratification of a law etc. 3 a a penalty for disobeying a law or rule, or a reward for obeying it. b a clause containing this. 4 Ethics a consideration operating to enforce obedience to any rule of conduct. 5 (esp. in pl.) military or esp. economic action by a State to coerce another to conform to an international agreement or norms of conduct. —v.tr. 1 authorize, countenance, or agree to (an action etc.). 2 ratify; attach a penalty or reward to; make binding. □ **sanctionable** adj. [F f. L sanctio -onis f. sancire sanct- make sacred]

sanctity /ˈsæŋktɪtɪ/ n. (pl. **-ies**) 1 holiness of life; saintliness. 2 sacredness; the state of being hallowed. 3 inviolability. 4 (in pl.) sacred obligations, feelings, etc. [ME f. OF sain(c)tité or L sanctitas (as SAINT)]

sanctuary /ˈsæŋktjʊərɪ/ n. (pl. **-ies**) 1 a holy place; a church, temple, etc. 2 a the inmost recess or holiest part of a temple etc. b the part of the chancel containing the high altar. 3 a place where birds, wild animals, etc., are bred and protected. 4 a place of refuge, esp. for political refugees. 5 a immunity from arrest. b the right to offer this. 6 hist. a sacred place where a fugitive from the law or a debtor was secured by medieval Church law against arrest or violence. □ **take sanctuary** resort to a place of refuge. [ME f. AF sanctuarie, OF sanctuaire f. L sanctuarium (as SAINT)]

sanctum /ˈsæŋktəm/ n. (pl. **sanctums**) 1 a holy place. 2 colloq. a person's private room, study, or den. [L, neut. of sanctus holy, past part. of sancire consecrate: sanctorum genit. pl. in transl. of Heb. ḳŏdeš haḳḳ°ḏāšîm holy of holies]

sand n. & v. —n. 1 a loose granular substance resulting from the wearing down of esp. siliceous rocks and found on the seashore, riverbeds, deserts, etc. 2 (in pl.) grains of sand. 3 (in pl.) an expanse or tracts of sand. 4 a light yellow-brown colour like that of sand. 5 (in pl.) a sandbank. —v.tr. 1 smooth or polish with sandpaper or sand. 2 sprinkle or overlay with,

or bury under, sand. □ **sand bar** a sandbank at the mouth of a river or US on the coast. **sand-dune** (or **-hill**) a mound or ridge of sand formed by the wind. **sand-hill** a dune. **sand-martin** a swallow-like bird, Riparia riparia, nesting in the side of a sandy bank etc. **the sands are running out** the allotted time is nearly at an end. **sand-shoe** a shoe with a canvas, rubber, hemp, etc., sole for use on sand. **sand-yacht** a boat on wheels propelled along a beach by wind. □ **sander** n. **sandlike** adj. [OE sand f. Gmc]

sandal[1] /ˈsænd(ə)l/ n. a light shoe with an openwork upper or no upper, attached to the foot usu. by straps. [ME f. L sandalium f. Gk sandalion dimin. of sandalon wooden shoe, prob. of Asiatic orig.]

sandal[2] /ˈsænd(ə)l/ n. = SANDALWOOD. □ **sandal-tree** any tree yielding sandalwood, esp. the white sandalwood, Santalum album, of India. [ME f. med.L sandalum, ult. f. Skr. candana]

sandalwood /ˈsænd(ə)lˌwʊd/ n. 1 the scented wood of a sandal-tree. 2 a perfume derived from this.

sandbag /ˈsændbæg/ n. & v. —n. a bag filled with sand for use: 1 (in fortification) for making temporary defences or for the protection of a building etc. against blast and splinters or floodwaters. 2 as ballast esp. for a boat or balloon. 3 as a weapon to inflict a heavy blow without leaving a mark. 4 to stop a draught from a window or door. —v.tr. (**-bagged, -bagging**) 1 barricade or defend. 2 place sandbags against (a window, chink, etc.). 3 fell with a blow from a sandbag. 4 US coerce by harsh means. □ **sandbagger** n.

sandbank /ˈsændbæŋk/ n. a deposit of sand forming a shallow place in the sea or a river.

sandblast /ˈsændblɑːst/ v. & n. —v.tr. roughen, treat, or clean with a jet of sand driven by compressed air or steam. —n. this jet. □ **sandblaster** n.

sandboy /ˈsændbɔɪ/ n. □ **happy as a sandboy** extremely happy or carefree. [prob. = a boy hawking sand for sale]

sandcastle /ˈsændˌkɑːs(ə)l/ n. a shape like a castle made in sand, usu. by a child on the seashore.

sandfly /ˈsændflaɪ/ n. (pl. **-ies**) any midge of the genus Simulium.

sandlot /ˈsændlɒt/ n. US a piece of unoccupied sandy land used for children's games.

sandman /ˈsændmæn/ n. the personification of tiredness causing children's eyes to smart towards bedtime.

sandpaper /ˈsændˌpeɪpə(r)/ n. paper with sand or another abrasive stuck to it for smoothing or polishing.

sandpiper /ˈsændˌpaɪpə(r)/ n. any of various wading birds of the family Scolopacidae, frequenting moorland and coastal areas.

sandpit /ˈsændpɪt/ n. a hollow partly filled with sand, usu. for children to play in.

sandstone /ˈsændstəʊn/ n. 1 a rock containing particles visible to the naked eye. 2 a sedimentary rock of consolidated sand commonly red, yellow, brown, grey, or white.

sandstorm /ˈsændstɔːm/ n. a desert storm of wind with clouds of sand.

sandwich /ˈsænwɪdʒ, -wɪtʃ/ n. & v. —n. 1 two or more slices of usu. buttered bread with a filling of meat, cheese, etc., between them. **2** a cake of two or more layers with jam or cream between (*bake a sponge sandwich*). —*v.tr.* **1** put (a thing, statement, etc.) between two of another character. **2** squeeze in between others (*sat sandwiched in the middle*). □ **sandwich-board** one of two advertisement boards carried by a sandwich-man. **sandwich course** a course of training with alternate periods of practical experience and theoretical instruction. **sandwich-man** (*pl.* **-men**) a man who walks the streets with sandwich-boards hanging before and behind. [4th Earl of *Sandwich*, Engl. nobleman d. 1792, said to have eaten food in this form so as not to leave the gaming-table]

sandy /ˈsændɪ/ *adj.* (**sandier**, **sandiest**) **1** having the texture of sand. **2** having much sand. **3 a** (of hair) yellowish-red. **b** (of a person) having sandy hair. □ **sandiness** *n.* **sandyish** *adj.* [OE *sandig* (as SAND)]

sane *adj.* **1** of sound mind; not mad. **2** (of views etc.) moderate; sensible. □ **sanely** *adv.* **saneness** *n.* [L *sanus* healthy]

sang *past of* SING.

sang-froid /sɑ̃ˈfrwɑː/ *n.* composure, coolness, etc., in danger or under agitating circumstances. [F, = cold blood]

sangria /sæŋˈɡriːə/ *n.* a Spanish drink of red wine with lemonade, fruit, etc. [Sp., = bleeding]

sanguinary /ˈsæŋɡwɪnərɪ/ *adj.* **1** accompanied by or delighting in bloodshed. **2** bloody; bloodthirsty. **3** (of laws) inflicting death freely. □ **sanguinarily** *adv.* **sanguinariness** *n.* [L *sanguinarius* f. *sanguis -inis* blood]

sanguine /ˈsæŋɡwɪn/ *adj.* **1** optimistic; confident. **2** (of the complexion) florid; bright; ruddy. □ **sanguinely** *adv.* **sanguineness** *n.* [ME f. OF *sanguin -ine* blood-red f. L *sanguineus* (as SANGUINARY)]

sanguineous /sæŋˈɡwɪnɪəs/ *adj.* **1** sanguinary. **2** *Med.* of or relating to blood. **3** blood-red. **4** full-blooded; plethoric. [L *sanguineus* (as SANGUINE)]

Sanhedrin /ˈsænɪdrɪn/ *n.* (also **Sanhedrim** /-rɪm/) the highest court of justice and the supreme council in ancient Jerusalem with 71 members. [late Heb. *sanhedrîn* f. Gk *sunedrion* (as SYN-, *hedra* seat)]

sanify /ˈsænɪˌfaɪ/ *v.tr.* (**-ies**, **-ied**) make healthy; improve the sanitary state of. [L *sanus* healthy]

sanitarium /ˌsænɪˈteərɪəm/ *n.* (*pl.* **sanitariums** or **sanitaria** /-rɪə/) *US* = SANATORIUM. [pseudo-L f. L *sanitas* health]

sanitary /ˈsænɪtərɪ/ *adj.* **1** of the conditions that affect health, esp. with regard to dirt and infection. **2** hygienic; free from or designed to kill germs, infection, etc. □ **sanitary engineer** a person dealing with systems needed to maintain public health. **sanitary towel** (*US* **napkin**) an absorbent pad used during menstruation. **sanitary ware** porcelain for lavatories etc. □ **sanitarian** /-ˈteərɪən/ *n.* & *adj.* **sanitarily** *adv.* **sanitariness** *n.* [F *sanitaire* f. L *sanitas*: see SANITY]

sanitation /ˌsænɪˈteɪʃ(ə)n/ *n.* **1** sanitary conditions. **2** the maintenance or improving of these. **3** the disposal of sewage and refuse from houses etc. □ **sanitate** /ˈsænɪˌteɪt/ *v.tr.* & *intr.* **sanitationist** *n.* [irreg. f. SANITARY]

sanitize /ˈsænɪˌtaɪz/ *v.tr.* (also **-ise**) **1** make sanitary; disinfect. **2** *US colloq.* render (information etc.) more acceptable by removing improper or disturbing material. □ **sanitizer** *n.*

sanity /ˈsænɪtɪ/ *n.* **1 a** the state of being sane. **b** mental health. **2** the tendency to avoid extreme views. [ME f. L *sanitas* (as SANE)]

sank *past of* SINK.

sans /sænz, sɑ̃/ *prep. archaic or joc.* without. [ME f. OF *san(z)*, *sen(s)* ult. f. L *sine*, infl. by L *absentia* in the absence of]

sanserif /sænˈserɪf/ *n.* & *adj.* (also **sans-serif**) *Printing* —*n.* a form of type without serifs. —*adj.* without serifs. [app. f. SANS + SERIF]

Sanskrit /ˈsænskrɪt/ *n.* & *adj.* —*n.* the ancient and sacred language of the Hindus in India. —*adj.* of or in this language. □ **Sanskritic** /-ˈskrɪtɪk/ *adj.* **Sanskritist** *n.* [Skr. *saṃskṛta* composed, elaborated, f. *saṃ* together, *kṛ* make, *-ta* past part. ending]

Santa Claus /ˈsæntə ˌklɔːz/ *n.* (also *colloq.* **Santa**) a person said to bring children presents on the night before Christmas. [orig. US f. Du. dial. *Sante Klaas* St Nicholas]

sap¹ *n.* & *v.* —*n.* **1** the vital juice circulating in plants. **2** vigour; vitality. **3** = SAPWOOD. **4** *US sl.* a bludgeon (orig. one made from a sapling). —*v.tr.* (**sapped**, **sapping**) **1** drain or dry (wood) of sap. **2** exhaust the vigour of (*my energy had been sapped by disappointment*). **3** *US sl.* hit with a sap. □ **sapful** *adj.* **sapless** *adj.* [OE *sæp* prob. f. Gmc]

sap² *n.* & *v.* —*n.* **1** a tunnel or trench to conceal assailants' approach to a fortified place; a covered siege-trench. **2** an insidious or slow undermining of a belief, resolution, etc. —*v.* (**sapped**, **sapping**) **1** *intr.* **a** dig a sap or saps. **b** approach by a sap. **2** *tr.* undermine; make insecure by removing the foundations. **3** *tr.* destroy insidiously. [ult. f. It. *zappa* spade, spadework, in part through F *sappe* sap(p)er, prob. of Arab. orig.]

sap³ *n. sl.* a foolish person. [abbr. of *sapskull* f. SAP¹ = sapwood + SKULL]

sapid /ˈsæpɪd/ *adj. literary* **1** having (esp. an agreeable) flavour; savoury; palatable; not insipid. **2** *literary* (of talk, writing, etc.) not vapid or uninteresting. □ **sapidity** /səˈpɪdɪtɪ/ *n.* [L *sapidus* f. *sapere* taste]

sapient /ˈseɪpɪənt/ *adj. literary* **1** wise. **2** aping wisdom; of fancied sagacity. □ **sapience** *n.* **sapiently** *adv.* [ME f. OF *sapient* or L part. stem of *sapere* be wise]

sapling /ˈsæplɪŋ/ *n.* **1** a young tree. **2** a youth. **3** a greyhound in its first year.

sapodilla /ˌsæpəˈdɪlə/ *n.* a large evergreen tropical American tree, *Manilkara zapota*, with sap from which chicle is obtained. [Sp. *zapotillo* dimin. of *zapote* f. Aztec *tzápotl*]

saponify /səˈpɒnɪˌfaɪ/ *v.* (**-ies**, **-ied**) **1** *tr.* turn (fat or oil) into soap by reaction with an alkali. **2** *tr.* convert (an ester) to an acid and alcohol. **3** *intr.* become saponified. □ **saponifiable** *adj.* **saponification** /-fɪˈkeɪʃ(ə)n/ *n.* [F *saponifier* f. mod. L *saponaceus* f. L *sapo -onis* soap]

sapper /ˈsæpə(r)/ *n.* **1** a person who digs saps. **2** *Brit.* a soldier of the Royal Engineers (esp. as the official term for a private).

Sapphic /ˈsæfɪk/ *adj.* & *n.* —*adj.* **1** of or relating to Sappho, poetess of Lesbos *c.*600 BC, or her poetry. **2** lesbian. —*n.* (in *pl.*) (**sapphics**) verse in a metre associated with Sappho. [F *sa(p)phique* f. L *Sapphicus* f. Gk *Sapphikos* f. *Sapphō*]

sapphire /'sæfaɪə(r)/ *n.* & *adj.* —*n.* **1** a transparent blue precious stone consisting of corundum. **2** precious transparent corundum of any colour. **3** the bright blue of a sapphire. —*adj.* of sapphire blue. □ **sapphire wedding** a 45th wedding anniversary. □ **sapphirine** /'sæfɪˌraɪn/ *adj.* [ME f. OF *safir* f. L *sapphirus* f. Gk *sappheiros* prob. = lapis lazuli]

sappy /'sæpɪ/ *adj.* (**sappier, sappiest**) **1** full of sap. **2** young and vigorous. □ **sappily** *adv.* **sappiness** *n.*

sapro- /'sæprəʊ/ *comb. form* Biol. rotten, putrefying. [Gk *sapros* putrid]

saprogenic /ˌsæprə'dʒenɪk/ *adj.* causing or produced by putrefaction.

saprophyte /'sæprəˌfaɪt/ *n.* any plant or microorganism living on dead or decayed organic matter. □ **saprophytic** /-'fɪtɪk/ *adj.*

sapwood /'sæpwʊd/ *n.* the soft outer layers of recently formed wood between the heartwood and the bark.

saraband /'særəˌbænd/ *n.* **1** a stately old Spanish dance. **2** music for this or in its rhythm, usu. in triple time. [F *sarabande* f. Sp. & It. *zarabanda*]

Saracen /'særəs(ə)n/ *n.* & *adj. hist.* —*n.* **1** an Arab or Muslim at the time of the Crusades. **2** a nomad of the Syrian and Arabian desert. —*adj.* of the Saracens. □ **Saracenic** /ˌsærə'senɪk/ *adj.* [ME f. OF *sar(r)azin, sar(r)acin* f. LL *Saracenus* f. late Gk *Sarakēnos* perh. f. Arab. *šarḳī* eastern]

sarcasm /'sɑːˌkæz(ə)m/ *n.* **1** a bitter or wounding remark. **2** a taunt, esp. one ironically worded. **3** language consisting of such remarks. **4** the faculty of using this. □ **sarcastic** /sɑː'kæstɪk/ *adj.* **sarcastically** /sɑː'kæstɪkəlɪ/ *adv.* [F *sarcasme* or f. LL *sarcasmus* f. late Gk *sarkasmos* f. Gk *sarkazō* tear flesh, in late Gk gnash the teeth, speak bitterly f. *sarx sarkos* flesh]

sarcoma /sɑː'kəʊmə/ *n.* (*pl.* **sarcomas** or **sarcomata** /-mətə/) a malignant tumour of connective or other non-epithelial tissue. □ **sarcomatosis** /-'təʊsɪs/ *n.* **sarcomatous** *adj.* [mod.L f. Gk *sarkōma* f. *sarkoō* become fleshy f. *sarx sarkos* flesh]

sarcophagus /sɑː'kɒfəgəs/ *n.* (*pl.* **sarcophagi** /-ˌgaɪ, -ˌdʒaɪ/) a stone coffin, esp. one adorned with a sculpture or inscription. [L f. Gk *sarkophagos* flesh-consuming (as SARCOMA, *-phagos* -eating)]

sard /sɑːd/ *n.* a yellow or orange-red cornelian. [ME f. F *sarde* or L *sarda* = LL *sardius* f. Gk *sardios* prob. f. *Sardō* Sardinia]

sardine[1] /sɑː'diːn/ *n.* a young pilchard or similar young or small herring-like marine fish. □ **like sardines** crowded close together (as sardines are in tins). [ME f. OF *sardine* = It. *sardina* f. L f. *sarda* f. Gk, perh. f. *Sardō* Sardinia]

sardine[2] /'sɑːdaɪn/ *n.* a precious stone mentioned in Rev. 4:3. [ME f. LL *sardinus* f. Gk *sardinos* var. of *sardios* SARD]

sardonic /sɑː'dɒnɪk/ *adj.* **1** grimly jocular. **2** (of laughter etc.) bitterly mocking or cynical. □ **sardonically** *adv.* **sardonicism** /-ˌsɪz(ə)m/ *n.* [F *sardonique*, earlier *sardonien* f. L *sardonius* f. Gk *sardonios* of Sardinia, alt. of *sardanios* Homeric epithet of bitter or scornful laughter]

sardonyx /'sɑːdənɪks/ *n.* onyx in which white layers alternate with sard. [ME f. L f. Gk *sardonux* (prob. as SARD, ONYX)]

sargasso /sɑː'gæsəʊ/ *n.* (also **sargassum**) (*pl.* **-os** or **-oes** or **sargassa**) any seaweed of the genus *Sargassum*, with berry-like air-vessels, found floating in island-like masses, esp. in the Sargasso Sea of the N. Atlantic. [Port. *sargaço*, of unkn. orig.]

sarge *n. sl.* sergeant. [abbr.]

sari /'sɑːrɪ/ *n.* (also **saree**) (*pl.* **saris** or **sarees**) a length of cotton or silk draped round the body, traditionally worn as a main garment by Indian women. [Hindi *sāṛ(h)ī*]

sarky /'sɑːkɪ/ *adj.* (**sarkier, sarkiest**) *Brit. sl.* sarcastic. □ **sarkily** *adv.* **sarkiness** *n.* [abbr.]

sarnie /'sɑːnɪ/ *n. Brit. colloq.* a sandwich. [abbr.]

sarong /sə'rɒŋ/ *n.* **1** a Malay and Javanese garment consisting of a long strip of (often striped) cloth worn by both sexes tucked round the waist or under the armpits. **2** a woman's garment resembling this. [Malay, lit. 'sheath']

sarsaparilla /ˌsɑːsəpə'rɪlə/ *n.* **1** a preparation of the dried roots of various plants, used to flavour some drinks and medicines and formerly as a tonic. **2** any of the plants yielding this. [Sp. *zarzaparilla* f. *zarza* bramble, prob. + dimin. of *parra* vine]

sarsen /'sɑːs(ə)n/ *n.* Geol. a sandstone boulder carried by ice during a glacial period. [prob. var. of SARACEN]

sarsenet /'sɑːsənɪt/ *n.* (also **sarcenet**) a fine soft silk material used esp. for linings. [ME f. AF *sarzinett* perh. dimin. of *sarzin* SARACEN after OF *drap sarrasinois* Saracen cloth]

sartorial /sɑː'tɔːrɪəl/ *adj.* **1** of a tailor or tailoring. **2** of men's clothes. □ **sartorially** *adv.* [L *sartor* tailor f. *sarcire sart-* patch]

SAS *abbr.* (in the UK) Special Air Service.

s.a.s.e. *abbr.* US self-addressed stamped envelope.

sash[1] *n.* a long strip or loop of cloth etc. worn over one shoulder usu. as part of a uniform or insignia, or worn round the waist, usu. by a woman or child. □ **sashed** *adj.* [earlier *shash* f. Arab. *šāš* muslin, turban]

sash[2] *n.* **1** a frame holding the glass in a sash-window and usu. made to slide up and down in the grooves of a window aperture. **2** the glazed sliding light of a glasshouse or garden frame. □ **sash-cord** a strong cord attaching the sash-weights to a sash. **sash-window** a window with one or two sashes of which one or each can be slid vertically over the other to make an opening. □ **sashed** *adj.* [*sashes* corrupt. of CHASSIS, mistaken for pl.]

sashay /'sæʃeɪ/ *v.intr.* esp. US colloq. walk or move ostentatiously, casually, or diagonally. [corrupt. of CHASSÉ]

sashimi /'sæʃɪmɪ/ *n.* a Japanese dish of garnished raw fish in thin slices. [Jap.]

sass *n.* & *v.* US colloq. —*n.* impudence, cheek. —*v.tr.* be impudent to, cheek. [var. of SAUCE]

sassafras /'sæsəˌfræs/ *n.* **1** a small tree, *Sassafras albidum*, native to N. America, with aromatic leaves and bark. **2** a preparation of oil extracted from the leaves, or from its bark, used medicinally or in perfumery. [Sp. *sasafrás* or Port. *sassafraz*, of unkn. orig.]

Sassenach /'sæsəˌnæx, -ˌnæk/ *n.* & *adj.* Sc. & Ir. usu. *derog.* —*n.* an English person. —*adj.* English. [Gael. *Sasunnoch*, Ir. *Sasanach* f. L *Saxones* Saxons]

sassy /ˈsæsɪ/ adj. (**sassier, sassiest**) esp. US colloq. = SAUCY. □ **sassily** adv. **sassiness** n. [var. of SAUCY]

Sat. abbr. Saturday.

sat past and past part. of SIT.

Satan /ˈseɪt(ə)n/ n. the Devil; Lucifer. [OE f. LL f. Gk f. Heb. *śāṭān* lit. 'adversary' f. *śaṭan* oppose, plot against]

satanic /səˈtænɪk/ adj. **1** of, like, or befitting Satan. **2** diabolical, hellish. □ **satanically** adv.

Satanism /ˈseɪtə‚nɪz(ə)m/ n. **1** the worship of Satan, with a travesty of Christian forms. **2** the pursuit of evil for its own sake. **3** deliberate wickedness. □ **Satanist** n. **Satanize** v.tr. (also **-ise**).

satay /ˈsæteɪ/ n. (also **satai, saté**) an Indonesian and Malaysian dish consisting of small pieces of meat grilled on a skewer and usu. served with spiced sauce. [Malayan *satai sate*, Indonesian *sate*]

satchel /ˈsætʃ(ə)l/ n. a small bag usu. of leather and hung from the shoulder with a strap, for carrying books etc. esp. to and from school. [ME f. OF *sachel* f. L *saccellus* (as SACK¹)]

sate v.tr. **1** gratify (desire, a desirous person) to the full. **2** cloy, surfeit, weary with overabundance (*sated with pleasure*). □ **sateless** adj. poet. [prob. f. dial. *sade*, OE *sadian* (as SAD), assim. to SATIATE]

sateen /sæˈtiːn/ n. cotton fabric woven like satin with a glossy surface. [*satin* after *velveteen*]

satellite /ˈsætə‚laɪt/ n. & adj. —n. **1** a celestial body orbiting the earth or another planet. **2** an artificial body placed in orbit round the earth or another planet. **3** a follower; a hanger-on. **4** an underling; a member of an important person's staff or retinue. **5** (in full **satellite State**) a small country etc. nominally independent but controlled by or dependent on another. —adj. **1** transmitted by satellite (*satellite communications; satellite television*). **2** esp. Computing secondary; dependent; minor (*networks of small satellite computers*). □ **satellite dish** a concave dish-shaped aerial for receiving broadcasting signals transmitted by satellite. **satellite town** a small town economically or otherwise dependent on a nearby larger town. □ **satellitic** /-ˈlɪtɪk/ adj. **satellitism** n. [F *satellite* or L *satelles satellitis* attendant]

sati var. of SUTTEE.

satiate /ˈseɪʃɪ‚eɪt/ adj. & v. —adj. archaic satiated. —v.tr. = SATE. □ **satiable** /-ʃəb(ə)l/ adj. archaic. **satiation** /-ˈeɪʃ(ə)n/ n. [L *satiatus* past part. of *satiare* f. *satis* enough]

satiety /səˈtaɪɪtɪ/ n. **1** the state of being glutted or satiated. **2** the feeling of having too much of something. **3** (foll. by *of*) a cloyed dislike of. □ **to satiety** to an extent beyond what is desired. [obs. F *sacieté* f. L *satietas -tatis* f. *satis* enough]

satin /ˈsætɪn/ n., adj., & v. —n. a fabric of silk or various man-made fibres, with a glossy surface on one side. —adj. smooth as satin. —v.tr. (**satined, satining**) give a glossy surface to (paper). □ **satin finish 1** a polish given to silver etc. with a metallic brush. **2** any effect resembling satin in texture produced on materials in various ways. **satin stitch** a long straight embroidery stitch, giving the appearance of satin. □ **satinized** adj. (also **-ised**). **satiny** adj. [ME f. OF f. Arab. *zaytūnī* of *Tseutung* in China]

satinette /‚sætɪˈnet/ n. (also **satinet**) a satin-like fabric made partly or wholly of cotton or synthetic fibre.

satinwood /ˈsætɪn‚wʊd/ n. **1 a** (in full **Ceylon satinwood**) a tree, *Chloroxylon swietenia*, native to central and southern India and Ceylon. **b** (in full **West Indian satinwood**) a tree, *Fagara flava*, native to the West Indies, Bermuda, the Bahamas, and southern Florida. **2** the yellow glossy timber of either of these trees.

satire /ˈsætaɪə(r)/ n. **1** the use of ridicule, irony, sarcasm, etc., to expose folly or vice or to lampoon an individual. **2** a work or composition in prose or verse using satire. **3** this branch of literature. **4** a thing that brings ridicule upon something else. [F *satire* or L *satira* later form of *satura* medley]

satiric /səˈtɪrɪk/ adj. **1** of satire or satires. **2** containing satire (*wrote a satiric review*). **3** writing satire (*a satiric poet*). [F *satirique* or LL *satiricus* (as SATIRE)]

satirical /səˈtɪrɪk(ə)l/ adj. **1** = SATIRIC. **2** given to the use of satire in speech or writing or to cynical observation of others; sarcastic; humorously critical. □ **satirically** adv.

satirist /ˈsætərɪst/ n. **1** a writer of satires. **2** a satirical person.

satirize /ˈsætɪ‚raɪz/ v.tr. (also **-ise**) **1** assail or ridicule with satire. **2** write a satire upon. **3** describe satirically. □ **satirization** /-ˈzeɪʃ(ə)n/ n. [F *satiriser* (as SATIRE)]

satisfaction /‚sætɪsˈfækʃ(ə)n/ n. **1** the act or an instance of satisfying; the state of being satisfied (*heard this with great satisfaction*). **2** a thing that satisfies desire or gratifies feeling (*is a great satisfaction to me*). **3** a thing that settles an obligation or pays a debt. **4** (foll. by *for*) atonement; compensation (*demanded satisfaction*). □ **to one's satisfaction** so that one is satisfied. [ME f. OF f. L *satisfactio -onis* (as SATISFY)]

satisfactory /‚sætɪsˈfæktərɪ/ adj. **1** adequate; causing or giving satisfaction (*was a satisfactory pupil*). **2** satisfying expectations or needs; leaving no room for complaint (*a satisfactory result*). □ **satisfactorily** adv. **satisfactoriness** n. [F *satisfactoire* or med.L *satisfactorius* (as SATISFY)]

satisfy /ˈsætɪs‚faɪ/ v. (**-ies, -ied**) **1** tr. **a** meet the expectations or desires of; comply with (a demand). **b** be accepted by (a person, his taste) as adequate; be equal to (a preconception etc.). **2** tr. put an end to (an appetite or want) by supplying what was required. **3** tr. rid (a person) of an appetite or want in a similar way. **4** intr. give satisfaction; leave nothing to be desired. **5** tr. pay (a debt or creditor). **6** tr. adequately meet, fulfil, or comply with (conditions, obligations, etc.) (*has satisfied all the legal conditions*). **7** tr. (often foll. by *of, that*) provide with adequate information or proof, convince (*satisfied the others that they were right; satisfy the court of their innocence*). **8** tr. Math. (of a quantity) make (an equation) true. **9** tr. (in passive) **a** (foll. by *with*) contented or pleased with. **b** (foll. by *to*) demand no more than or consider it enough to do. □ **satisfiable** adj. **satisfiability** /-ə‚bɪlɪtɪ/ n. **satisfiedly** adv. **satisfying** adj. **satisfyingly** adv. [ME f. OF *satisfier* f. L *satisfacere satisfact-* f. *satis* enough]

satori /səˈtɔːrɪ/ n. Buddhism sudden enlightenment. [Jap.]

satsuma /ˈsætsʊmə/ n. 1 /also sætˈsuːmə/ a variety of tangerine orig. grown in Japan. 2 (**Satsuma**) (in full **Satsuma ware**) cream-coloured Japanese pottery. [*Satsuma* a province in Japan]

saturate /ˈsætʃəˌreɪt, -tjʊˌreɪt/ v.tr. 1 fill with moisture; soak thoroughly. 2 (often foll. by *with*) fill to capacity. 3 cause (a substance, solution, vapour, metal, or air) to absorb, hold, or combine with the greatest possible amount of another substance, or of moisture, magnetism, electricity, etc. 4 cause (a substance) to combine with the maximum amount of another substance. 5 supply (a market) beyond the point at which the demand for a product is satisfied. 6 (foll. by *with, in*) imbue with or steep in (learning, tradition, prejudice, etc.). 7 overwhelm (enemy defences, a target area, etc.) by concentrated bombing. 8 (as **saturated** adj.) (of fat molecules) containing the greatest number of hydrogen atoms. □ **saturate** /-rət/ adj. *literary*. **saturable** /-rəb(ə)l/ adj. **saturant** /-rənt/ n. & adj. [L *saturare* f. *satur* full]

saturation /ˌsætʃəˈreɪʃ(ə)n, -tjʊˈreɪʃ(ə)n/ n. the act or an instance of saturating; the state of being saturated. □ **saturation point** the stage beyond which no more can be absorbed or accepted.

Saturday /ˈsætəˌdeɪ, -dɪ/ n. & adv. —n. the seventh day of the week, following Friday. —adv. *colloq*. 1 on Saturday. 2 (**Saturdays**) on Saturdays; each Saturday. [OE *Sætern(es) dæg* transl. of L *Saturni dies* day of Saturn]

saturnalia /ˌsætəˈneɪlɪə/ n. (pl. same or **saturnalias**) 1 (usu. **Saturnalia**) *Rom.Hist.* the festival of Saturn in December, characterized by unrestrained merrymaking for all, the predecessor of Christmas. 2 (as *sing.* or *pl.*) a scene of wild revelry or tumult; an orgy. □ **saturnalian** adj. [L, neut. pl. of *Saturnalis* f. *Saturnus*, Roman god of agriculture]

saturnine /ˈsætəˌnaɪn/ adj. 1 of a sluggish gloomy temperament. 2 (of looks etc.) dark and brooding. □ **saturninely** adv. [ME f. OF *saturnin* f. med.L *Saturninus* (as SATURNALIA)]

satyr /ˈsætə(r)/ n. 1 (in Greek mythology) one of a class of Greek woodland gods with a horse's ears and tail, or (in Roman representations) with a goat's ears, tail, legs, and budding horns. 2 a lustful or sensual man. [ME f. OF *satyre* or L *satyrus* f. Gk *saturos*]

satyriasis /ˌsætɪˈraɪəsɪs/ n. *Med.* excessive sexual desire in men. [LL f. Gk *saturiasis* (as SATYR)]

satyric /səˈtɪrɪk/ adj. (in Greek mythology) of or relating to satyrs. □ **satyric drama** a kind of ancient Greek comic play with a chorus of satyrs. [L *satyricus* f. Gk *saturikos* (as SATYR)]

sauce /sɔːs/ n. & v. —n. 1 any of various liquid or semi-solid preparations taken as a relish with food; the liquid constituent of a dish (*mint sauce; tomato sauce; chicken in a lemon sauce*). 2 something adding piquancy or excitement. 3 *colloq*. impudence, impertinence, cheek. 4 *US* stewed fruit etc. eaten as dessert or used as a garnish. —v.tr. 1 *colloq*. be impudent to; cheek. 2 *archaic* **a** season with sauce or condiments. **b** add excitement to. □ **sauce-boat** a kind of jug or dish used for serving sauces etc. □ **sauceless** adj. [ME f. OF ult. f. L *salsus* f. *salere sals-* to salt f. *sal* salt]

saucepan /ˈsɔːspən/ n. a usu. metal cooking pan, usu. round with a lid and a long handle at the side, used for boiling, stewing, etc., on top of a cooker. □ **saucepanful** n. (pl. **-fuls**).

saucer /ˈsɔːsə(r)/ n. 1 a shallow circular dish used for standing a cup on and to catch drips. 2 any similar dish used to stand a plant pot etc. on. □ **saucerful** n. (pl. **-fuls**). **saucerless** adj. [ME, = condiment-dish, f. OF *saussier(e)* sauce-boat, prob. f. LL *salsarium* (as SAUCE)]

saucy /ˈsɔːsɪ/ adj. (**saucier, sauciest**) 1 impudent, cheeky. 2 *colloq*. smart-looking (*a saucy hat*). 3 *colloq*. smutty, suggestive. □ **saucily** adv. **sauciness** n. [earlier sense 'savoury', f. SAUCE]

sauerkraut /ˈsaʊəˌkraʊt/ n. a German dish of chopped pickled cabbage. [G f. *sauer* SOUR + *Kraut* vegetable]

sauna /ˈsɔːnə/ n. 1 a Finnish-style steam bath. 2 a building used for this. [Finn.]

saunter /ˈsɔːntə(r)/ v. & n. —v.intr. 1 walk slowly; amble, stroll. 2 proceed without hurry or effort. —n. 1 a leisurely ramble. 2 a slow gait. □ **saunterer** n. [ME, = muse: orig. unkn.]

saurian /ˈsɔːrɪən/ adj. of or like a lizard. [mod.L *Sauria* f. Gk *saura* lizard]

sauropod /ˈsɔːrəʊˌpɒd/ n. any of a group of plant-eating dinosaurs with a long neck and tail, and four thick limbs. [Gk *saura* lizard + *pous pod-* foot]

sausage /ˈsɒsɪdʒ/ n. 1 **a** minced pork, beef, or other meat seasoned and often mixed with other ingredients, encased in cylindrical form in a skin, for cooking and eating hot or cold. **b** a length of this. 2 a sausage-shaped object. □ **not a sausage** *colloq*. nothing at all. **sausage dog** *Brit. colloq*. a dachshund. **sausage machine** 1 a sausage-making machine. 2 a relentlessly uniform process. **sausage meat** minced meat used in sausages or as a stuffing etc. **sausage roll** *Brit*. sausage meat enclosed in a pastry roll and baked. [ME f. ONF *saussiche* f. med.L *salsicia* f. L *salsus*: see SAUCE]

sauté /ˈsəʊteɪ/ adj., n., & v. —adj. (esp. of potatoes etc.) quickly fried in a little hot fat. —n. food cooked in this way. —v.tr. (**sautéd** or **sautéed**) cook in this way. [F, past part. of *sauter* jump]

Sauternes /səʊˈtɜːn/ n. a sweet white wine from Sauternes in the Bordeaux region of France.

savage /ˈsævɪdʒ/ adj., n., & v. —adj. 1 fierce; cruel (*a savage persecution; a savage blow*). 2 wild; primitive (*savage tribes; a savage animal*). 3 *colloq*. angry; bad-tempered (*in a savage mood*). —n. 1 *derog*. a member of a primitive tribe. 2 a cruel or barbarous person. —v.tr. 1 (esp. of a dog, wolf, etc.) attack and bite or trample. 2 (of a critic etc.) attack fiercely. □ **savagedom** n. **savagely** adv. **savageness** n. **savagery** n. (pl. **-ies**). [ME f. OF *sauvage* wild f. L *silvaticus* f. *silva* a wood]

savannah /səˈvænə/ n. (also **savanna**) a grassy plain in tropical and subtropical regions, with few or no trees. [Sp. *zavana* perh. of Carib orig.]

savant /ˈsæv(ə)nt, sæˈvɑ̃/ n. (*fem.* **savante** /ˈsæv(ə)nt or sæˈvɑ̃t/) a learned person, esp. a distinguished scientist etc. [F, part. of *savoir* know (as SAPIENT)]

save[1] v. & n. —v. 1 tr. (often foll. by *from*) rescue, preserve, protect, or deliver from danger, harm, discredit, etc. (*saved my life; saved me from drowning*). 2 tr. (often foll. by *up*) keep for future use; reserve; refrain from spending (*saved up £150 for a new bike; likes to save plastic bags*). 3 tr. (often *refl.*) **a** relieve (another person or oneself) from spending (money, time, trouble, etc.); prevent exposure to (annoyance etc.) (*saved myself £50; a word processor saves time*). **b** obviate the need or likelihood of (*soaking saves scrubbing*). **4** *tr.* preserve from damnation; convert (*saved her soul*). **5** *tr.* & *refl.* husband or preserve (one's strength, health, etc.) (*saving himself for the last lap; save your energy*). **6** *intr.* (often foll. by *up*) save money for future use. **7** *tr.* **a** avoid losing (a game, match, etc.). **b** prevent an opponent from scoring (a goal etc.). **c** stop (a ball etc.) from entering the goal. —*n.* Football etc. the act of preventing an opponent's scoring etc. □ **save appearances** present a prosperous, respectable, etc. appearance. **save-as-you-earn** *Brit.* a method of saving by regular deduction from earnings at source. **save one's breath** not waste time speaking to no effect. **save the situation** (or **day**) find or provide a solution to difficulty or disaster. **save one's skin** (or **neck** or **bacon**) avoid loss, injury, or death; escape from danger. □ **savable** *adj.* (also **saveable**). [ME f. AF sa(u)ver, OF salver, sauver f. LL salvare f. L salvus SAFE]

save² *prep.* & *conj.* archaic or poet. —*prep.* except; but (*all save him*). —*conj.* (often foll. by *for*) unless; but; except (*happy save for one want; is well save that he has a cold*). [ME f. OF sauf sauve f. L salvo, salva, ablat. sing. of salvus SAFE]

saveloy /ˈsævəˌlɔɪ/ *n.* a seasoned red pork sausage, dried and smoked, and sold ready to eat. [corrupt. of F cervelas, -at, f. It. cervellata (cervello brain)]

saver /ˈseɪvə(r)/ *n.* **1** a person who saves esp. money. **2** (often in *comb.*) a device for economical use (of time etc.) (*found the short cut a time-saver*).

saving /ˈseɪvɪŋ/ *adj.*, *n.*, & *prep.* —*adj.* (often in *comb.*) making economical use of (*labour-saving*). —*n.* **1** anything that is saved. **2** an economy (*a saving in expenses*). **3** (usu. in *pl.*) money saved. —*prep.* **1** with the exception of; except (*all saving that one*). **2** without offence to (*saving your presence*). □ **saving grace 1** the redeeming grace of God. **2** a redeeming quality or characteristic. **savings account** a deposit account. **savings bank** a bank receiving small deposits at interest and returning the profits to the depositors. **savings certificate** *Brit.* an interest-bearing document issued by the Government for the benefit of savers. [ME f. SAVE¹: prep. prob. f. SAVE² after *touching*]

saviour /ˈseɪvjə(r)/ *n.* (US **savior**) **1** a person who saves or delivers from danger, destruction, etc. (*the saviour of the nation*). **2** (**Saviour**) (prec. by *the, our*) Christ. [ME f. OF sauvëour f. eccl.L salvator -oris (transl. Gk sōtēr) f. LL salvare SAVE¹]

savoir faire /ˌsævwɑː ˈfeə(r)/ *n.* the ability to act suitably in any situation; tact. [F, = know how to do]

savory /ˈseɪvərɪ/ *n.* (*pl.* **-ies**) any herb of the genus Satureia, esp. S. hortensis and S. montana, used esp. in cookery. [ME saverey, perh. f. OE sætherie f. L satureia]

savour /ˈseɪvə(r)/ *n.* & *v.* (US **savor**) —*n.* **1** a characteristic taste, flavour, relish, etc. **2** a quality suggestive of or containing a small amount of another. **3** archaic a characteristic smell. —*v.* **1** *tr.* **a** appreciate and enjoy the taste of (food). **b** enjoy or appreciate (an experience etc.). **2** *intr.* (foll. by *of*) **a** suggest by taste, smell,

etc. (*savours of mushrooms*). **b** imply or suggest a specified quality (*savours of impertinence*). □ **savourless** *adj.* [ME f. OF f. L sapor -oris f. sapere to taste]

savoury /ˈseɪvərɪ/ *adj.* & *n.* (US **savory**) —*adj.* **1** having an appetizing taste or smell. **2** (of food) salty or piquant, not sweet (*a savoury omelette*). **3** pleasant; acceptable. —*n.* (*pl.* **-ies**) *Brit.* a savoury dish served as an appetizer or at the end of dinner. □ **savourily** *adv.* **savouriness** *n.* [ME f. OF savouré past part. (as SAVOUR)]

savoy /səˈvɔɪ/ *n.* a hardy variety of cabbage with wrinkled leaves. [*Savoy* in SE France]

savvy /ˈsævɪ/ *v.*, *n.*, & *adj.* sl. —*v.intr.* & *tr.* (**-ies**, **-ied**) know. —*n.* knowingness; shrewdness; understanding. —*adj.* (**savvier**, **savviest**) US knowing; wise. [orig. Black & Pidgin E after Sp. sabe usted you know]

saw¹ *n.* & *v.* —*n.* **1** a hand tool having a toothed blade used to cut esp. wood with a to-and-fro movement. **2** any of several mechanical power-driven devices with a toothed rotating disk or moving band, for cutting. —*v.* (*past part.* **sawn** or **sawed**) **1** *tr.* **a** cut (wood etc.) with a saw. **b** make (boards etc.) with a saw. **2** *intr.* use a saw. **3 a** *intr.* move to and fro with a motion as of a saw or person sawing (*sawing away on his violin*). **b** *tr.* divide (the air etc.) with gesticulations. □ **saw-edged** with a jagged edge like a saw. **saw-frame** a frame in which a saw-blade is held taut. **saw-gate** = *saw-frame.* **saw-horse** a rack supporting wood for sawing. **sawn-off** (US **sawed-off**) (of a gun) having part of the barrel sawn off to make it easier to handle and give a wider field of fire. □ **sawlike** *adj.* [OE saga f. Gmc]

saw² *past of* SEE¹.

saw³ /sɔː/ *n.* a proverb; a maxim (*that's just an old saw*). [OE sagu f. Gmc, rel. to SAY: cf. SAGA]

sawbuck /ˈsɔːbʌk/ *n.* US **1** a saw-horse. **2** *sl.* a $10 note.

sawdust /ˈsɔːdʌst/ *n.* powdery particles of wood produced in sawing.

sawfish /ˈsɔːfɪʃ/ *n.* any large marine fish of the family Pristidae, with a toothed flat snout used as a weapon.

sawfly /ˈsɔːflaɪ/ *n.* (*pl.* **-flies**) any insect of the superfamily Tenthredinidae, with a serrated ovipositor, the larvae of which are injurious to plants.

sawmill /ˈsɔːmɪl/ *n.* a factory in which wood is sawn mechanically into planks or boards.

sawn *past part.* of SAW¹.

sawtooth /ˈsɔːtuːθ/ *adj.* (also **sawtoothed** /-tuːθt/) (esp. of a roof, wave, etc.) shaped like the teeth of a saw with one steep and one slanting side.

sawyer /ˈsɔːjə(r)/ *n.* a person who saws timber professionally. [ME, earlier sawer, f. SAW¹]

sax *n.* colloq. **1** a saxophone. **2** a saxophone-player. □ **saxist** *n.* [abbr.]

saxe /sæks/ *n.* (in full **saxe blue**) (often *attrib.*) a lightish blue colour with a greyish tinge. [F, = Saxony, the source of a dye of this colour]

saxhorn /ˈsækshɔːn/ *n.* any of a series of different-sized brass wind instruments with valves and a funnel-shaped mouthpiece, used mainly in military and brass bands. [*Sax*, name of its Belgian inventors, + HORN]

saxifrage /ˈsæksɪˌfreɪdʒ/ *n.* any plant of the genus Saxifraga, growing on rocky or stony ground and usu. bearing small white, yellow, or red flowers. [ME f. OF *saxifrage* or LL *saxifraga* (*herba*) f. L *saxum* rock + *frangere* break]

Saxon /ˈsæks(ə)n/ n. & adj. —n. **1** hist. **a** a member of the Germanic people that conquered parts of England in 5th–6th c. **b** (usu. **Old Saxon**) the language of the Saxons. **2** = ANGLO-SAXON. —adj. **1** hist. of or concerning the Saxons. **2** belonging to or originating from the Saxon language or Old English. □ **Saxondom** n. **Saxonism** n. **Saxonist** n. **Saxonize** /-ˌnaɪz/ v.tr. & intr. (also **-ise**). [ME f. OF f. LL *Saxo* *-onis* f. Gk *Saxones* (pl.) f. WG: cf. OE *Seaxan*, *Seaxe* (pl.)]

saxophone /ˈsæksəˌfəʊn/ n. **1** a keyed brass reed instrument in several sizes and registers, used esp. in jazz and dance music. **2** a saxophone-player. □ **saxophonic** /-ˈfɒnɪk/ adj. **saxophonist** /-ˈsɒfənɪst, -səˌfəʊnɪst/ n. (*Sax* (as SAXHORN) + -PHONE)

say v. & n. —v. (3rd sing. present **says** /sez/; past and past part. **said** /sed/) **1** tr. (often foll. by *that* + clause) **a** utter (specified words) in a speaking voice; remark (*said 'Damn!'*; *said that he was satisfied*). **b** put into words; express (*that was well said*; *cannot say what I feel*). **2** tr. (often foll. by *that* + clause) **a** state; promise or prophesy (*says that there will be war*). **b** have specified wording; indicate (*says there that he was killed*; *the clock says ten to six*). **3** tr. (in passive; usu. foll. by *to* + infin.) be asserted or described (*is said to be 93 years old*). **4** tr. (foll. by *to* + infin.) colloq. tell a person to do something (*he said to bring the car*). **5** tr. convey (information) (*spoke for an hour but said little*). **6** tr. put forward as an argument or excuse (*much to be said in favour of it*; *what have you to say for yourself?*). **7** tr. (often absol.) form and give an opinion or decision as to (*who did it I cannot say*; *do say which you prefer*). **8** tr. select, assume, or take as an example or (a specified number etc.) as near enough (*shall we say this one?*; *paid, say, £20*). **9** tr. **a** speak the words of (prayers, Mass, a grace, etc.). **b** repeat (a lesson etc.); recite (*can't say his tables*). **10** tr. (**the said**) *Law* or *joc.* the previously mentioned (*the said witness*). **11** intr. (as int.) US an exclamation of surprise, to attract attention, etc. —n. **1** an opportunity for stating one's opinion etc. (*let him have his say*). **2** a stated opinion. **2** a share in a decision (*had no say in the matter*). □ **how say you?** *Law* how do you find? (addressed to the jury requesting its verdict). **I** etc. **cannot** (or **could not**) **say** I etc. do not know. **I'll say** colloq. yes indeed. **I say!** *Brit.* an exclamation expressing surprise, drawing attention, etc. **it is said** the rumour is that. **not to say** and indeed; or possibly even (*his language was rude not to say offensive*). **said he** (or **I** etc.) colloq. or poet. he etc. said. **say for oneself** say by way of conversation, oratory, etc. **say much** (or **something**) **for** indicate the high quality of. **say no** refuse or disagree. **says I** (or **he** etc.) colloq. I, he, etc., said (used in reporting conversation). **say-so 1** the power of decision. **2** mere assertion (*cannot proceed merely on his say-so*). **says you!** colloq. I disagree. **say when** colloq. indicate when enough drink or food has been given. **say the word 1** indicate that you agree or give permission. **2** give the order etc. **say yes** agree. **that is to say 1** in other words, more explicitly. **2** or at least. **they say** it is rumoured. **to say nothing of** = not to mention.

what do (or **would**) **you say to?** would you like? **when all is said and done** after all, in the long run. **you can say that again!** (or **you said it!**) colloq. I agree emphatically. **you don't say so** colloq. an expression of amazement or disbelief. □ **sayable** adj. **sayer** n. [OE *secgan* f. Gmc]

SAYE abbr. *Brit.* save-as-you-earn.

saying /ˈseɪɪŋ/ n. **1** the act or an instance of saying. **2** a maxim, proverb, adage, etc. □ **as the saying goes** (or **is**) an expression used in introducing a proverb, cliché, etc. **go without saying** be too well known or obvious to need mention. **there is no saying** it is impossible to know.

Sb symb. *Chem.* the element antimony. [L *stibium*]

Sc symb. *Chem.* the element scandium.

sc. abbr. scilicet.

scab n. & v. —n. **1** a dry rough crust formed over a cut, sore, etc. in healing. **2** (often attrib.) colloq. derog. a person who refuses to strike or join a trade union, or who tries to break a strike by working; a blackleg. **3** the mange or a similar skin disease esp. in animals. **4** a fungous plant-disease causing scablike roughness. **5** a dislikeable person. —v.intr. (**scabbed**, **scabbing**) **1** act as a scab. **2** (of a wound etc.) form a scab; heal over. □ **scabbed** adj. **scabby** adj. (**scabbier**, **scabbiest**). **scabbiness** n. **scablike** adj. [ME f. ON *skabbr* (unrecorded), corresp. to OE *sceabb*]

scabbard /ˈskæbəd/ n. **1** hist. a sheath for a sword, bayonet, etc. **2** US a sheath for a revolver etc. [ME *sca(u)berc* etc. f. AF prob. f. Frank.]

scabies /ˈskeɪbiːz/ n. a contagious skin disease causing severe itching. [ME f. L f. *scabere* scratch]

scabious /ˈskeɪbɪəs/ n. any plant of the genus *Scabiosa*, *Knautia*, etc., with pink, white, or esp. blue pincushion-shaped flowers. [ME f. med.L *scabiosa* (*herba*) formerly regarded as a cure for skin disease: see SCABIES]

scabrous /ˈskeɪbrəs/ adj. **1** having a rough surface; bearing short stiff hairs, scales, etc.; scurfy. **2** (of a subject, situation, etc.) requiring tactful treatment; hard to handle with decency. **3 a** indecent, salacious. **b** behaving licentiously. □ **scabrously** adv. **scabrousness** n. [F *scabreux* or LL *scabrosus* f. L *scaber* rough]

scads /skædz/ n.pl. US colloq. large quantities. [19th c.: orig. unkn.]

scaffold /ˈskæfəʊld, -f(ə)ld/ n. & v. —n. **1** hist. a raised wooden platform used for the execution of criminals. **2** = SCAFFOLDING. **3** (prec. by *the*) death by execution. —v.tr. attach scaffolding to (a building). □ **scaffolder** n. [ME f. AF f. OF (e)*schaffaut*, earlier *escadafaut*: cf. CATAFALQUE]

scaffolding /ˈskæfəʊldɪŋ, -fəldɪŋ/ n. **1** a temporary structure formed of poles, planks, etc., erected by workmen and used by them while building or repairing a house etc. **2** materials used for this.

scalable /ˈskeɪləb(ə)l/ adj. capable of being scaled or climbed. □ **scalability** /-ˈbɪlɪtɪ/ n.

scalar /ˈskeɪlə(r)/ adj. & n. *Math.* & *Physics* —adj. (of a quantity) having only magnitude, not direction. —n. a scalar quantity. [L *scalaris* f. *scala* ladder; see SCALE³]

scalawag var. of SCALLYWAG.

scald¹ /skɔːld, skɒld/ v. & n. —v.tr. **1** burn (the skin etc.) with hot liquid or steam. **2** heat (esp. milk) to near boiling-point. **3** (usu. foll. by *out*) clean (a pan etc.) by rinsing with boiling water. **4** treat (poultry etc.) with boiling water to remove feathers etc. —*n.* a burn etc. caused by scalding. □ **scalder** *n.* [ME f. AF, ONF *escalder*, OF *eschalder* f. LL *excaldare* (as EX-¹, L *calidus* hot)]

scald² var. of SKALD.

scale¹ *n.* & *v.* —*n.* **1** each of the small thin bony or horny overlapping plates protecting the skin of fish and reptiles. **2** something resembling a fish-scale, esp.: **a** a pod or husk. **b** a flake of skin; a scab. **c** a rudimentary leaf, feather, or bract. **d** each of the structures covering the wings of butterflies and moths. **e** *Bot.* a layer of a bulb. **3 a** a flake formed on the surface of rusty iron. **b** a thick white deposit formed in a kettle, boiler, etc. by the action of heat on water. **4** plaque formed on teeth. —*v.* **1** *tr.* remove scale or scales from (fish, nuts, iron, etc.). **2** *tr.* remove plaque from (teeth) by scraping. **3** *intr.* **a** (of skin, metal, etc.) form, come off in, or drop, scales. **b** (usu. foll. by *off*) (of scales) come off. □ **scale insect** any of various insects, esp. of the family Coccidae, clinging to plants and secreting a shieldlike scale as covering. **scales fall from a person's eyes** a person is no longer deceived (cf. Acts 9:18). □ **scaled** *adj.* (also in *comb.*). **scaleless** /ˈskeɪllɪs/ *adj.* **scaler** *n.* [ME f. OF *escale* f. Gmc, rel. to SCALE²]

scale² *n.* & *v.* —*n.* **1 a** (often in *pl.*) a weighing machine or device (*bathroom scales*). **b** (also **scale-pan**) each of the dishes on a simple scale balance. **2** (**the Scales**) the zodiacal sign or constellation Libra. —*v.tr.* (of something weighed) show (a specified weight) in the scales. □ **pair of scales** a simple balance. **throw into the scale** cause to be a factor in a contest, debate, etc. **tip** (or **turn**) **the scales 1** (usu. foll. by *at*) outweigh the opposite scale-pan (at a specified weight); weigh. **2** (of a motive, circumstance, etc.) be decisive. [ME f. ON *skál* bowl f. Gmc]

scale³ *n.* & *v.* —*n.* **1** a series of degrees; a graded classification system (*pay fees according to a prescribed scale*; *high on the social scale*; *seven points on the Richter scale*). **2 a** (often *attrib.*) *Geog.* & *Archit.* a ratio of size in a map, model, picture, etc. (*on a scale of one centimetre to the kilometre*; *a scale model*). **b** relative dimensions or degree (*generosity on a grand scale*). **3** *Mus.* an arrangement of all the notes in any system of music in ascending or descending order (*chromatic scale*; *major scale*). **4 a** a set of marks on a line used in measuring, reducing, enlarging, etc. **b** a rule determining the distances between these. **c** a piece of metal, apparatus, etc. on which these are marked. **5** (in full **scale of notation**) *Math.* the ratio between units in a numerical system (*decimal scale*). —*v.* **1** *tr.* **a** (also *absol.*) climb (a wall, height, etc.) esp. with a ladder. **b** climb (the social scale, heights of ambition, etc.). **2** *tr.* represent in proportional dimensions; reduce to a common scale. **3** *intr.* (of quantities etc.) have a common scale; be commensurable. □ **economies of scale** proportionate savings gained by using larger quantities. **in scale** (of drawing etc.) in proportion to the surroundings etc. **scale down** make smaller in proportion; reduce in size. **scale up** make larger in proportion; increase in size. **to scale** with a uniform reduction or enlargement. □ **scaler** *n.*

[(n.) ME (= ladder): (v.) ME f. OF *escaler* or med.L *scalare* f. L *scala* f. *scandere* climb]

scalene /ˈskeɪliːn/ *adj.* (esp. of a triangle) having sides unequal in length. [LL *scalenus* f. Gk *skalēnos* unequal, rel. to *skolios* bent]

scallion /ˈskæljən/ *n.* a shallot or spring onion; any long-necked onion with a small bulb. [ME f. AF *scal(o)un* = OF *escalo(i)gne* ult. f. L *Ascalonia* (*caepa*) (onion) of *Ascalon* in anc. Palestine]

scallop /ˈskæləp, ˈskɒl-/ *n.* & *v.* (also **scollop** /ˈskɒl-/) **1** any of various bivalve molluscs of the family Pectinidae, esp. of the genus *Chlamys* or *Pecten*, much prized as food. **2** (in full **scallop shell**) a single valve from the shell of a scallop, used for cooking or serving food. **3** (in *pl.*) an ornamental edging cut in material in imitation of a scallop-edge. **4** a small pan or dish shaped like a scallop shell and used for baking or serving food. —*v.tr.* (**scalloped**, **scalloping**) **1** cook in a scallop. **2** ornament (an edge or material) with scallops or scalloping. □ **scalloper** *n.* **scalloping** *n.* (in sense 3 of *n.*). [ME f. OF *escalope* prob. f. Gmc]

scallywag /ˈskælɪˌwæg/ *n.* (also **scalawag**, **scallawag** /ˈskæləɡ-/) a scamp; a rascal. [19th-c. US sl.: orig. unkn.]

scalp *n.* & *v.* —*n.* **1** the skin covering the top of the head, with the hair etc. attached. **2 a** *hist.* the scalp of an enemy cut or torn away as a trophy by an American Indian. **b** a trophy or symbol of triumph, conquest, etc. —*v.tr.* **1** *hist.* take the scalp of (an enemy). **2** criticize savagely. **3** *US* defeat; humiliate. **4** *US colloq.* resell (shares, tickets, etc.) at a high or quick profit. □ **scalper** *n.* **scalpless** *adj.* [ME, prob. of Scand. orig.]

scalpel /ˈskælp(ə)l/ *n.* a surgeon's small sharp knife shaped for holding like a pen. [F *scalpel* or L *scalpellum* dimin. of *scalprum* chisel f. *scalpere* scratch]

scaly /ˈskeɪlɪ/ *adj.* (**scalier**, **scaliest**) covered in or having many scales or flakes. □ **scaliness** *n.*

scam *n.* *US sl.* **1** a trick or swindle; a fraud. **2** a story or rumour. [20th c.: orig. unkn.]

scamp¹ *n.* *colloq.* a rascal; a rogue. □ **scampish** *adj.* [*scamp* rob on highway, prob. f. MDu. *schampen* decamp f. OF *esc(h)amper* (as EX-¹, L *campus* field)]

scamp² *v.tr.* do (work etc.) in a perfunctory or inadequate way. [perh. formed as SCAMP¹: cf. SKIMP]

scamper /ˈskæmpə(r)/ *v.* & *n.* —*v.intr.* (usu. foll. by *about*, *through*) run and skip impulsively or playfully. —*n.* the act or an instance of scampering. [prob. formed as SCAMP¹]

scampi /ˈskæmpɪ/ *n.pl.* **1** large prawns. **2** (often treated as *sing.*) a dish of these, usu. fried. [It.]

scan *v.* & *n.* —*v.* (**scanned**, **scanning**) **1** *tr.* look at intently or quickly (*scanned the horizon*; *rapidly scanned the speech for errors*). **2** *intr.* (of a verse etc.) be metrically correct; be capable of being recited etc. metrically (*this line doesn't scan*). **3** *tr.* **a** examine all parts of (a surface etc.) to detect radioactivity etc. **b** cause (a particular region) to be traversed by a radar etc. beam. **4** *tr.* resolve (a picture) into its elements of light and shade in a prearranged pattern for the purposes esp. of television transmission. **5** *tr.* test the metre of (a line of verse etc.) by reading with the emphasis on its rhythm, or by examining the number of feet etc. **6** *tr.* **a** make a scan of (the body or part of it). **b** examine (a patient etc.)

with a scanner. —*n.* **1** the act or an instance of scanning. **2** an image obtained by scanning or with a scanner. □ **scannable** *adj.* [ME f. L *scandere* climb: in LL = scan verses (from the raising of one's foot in marking rhythm)]

scandal /ˈskænd(ə)l/ *n.* **1** a thing or a person causing general public outrage or indignation. **2** the outrage etc. so caused, esp. as a subject of common talk. **c** malicious gossip or backbiting. □ **scandalous** *adj.* **scandalously** *adv.* **scandalousness** *n.* [ME f. OF *scandale* f. eccl.L *scandalum* f. Gk *skandalon* snare, stumbling-block]

scandalize /ˈskændəˌlaɪz/ *v.tr.* (also **-ise**) offend the moral feelings, sensibilities, etc. of; shock. [ME in sense 'make a scandal of' f. F *scandaliser* or eccl.L *scandaliso* f. Gk *skandalizō* (as SCANDAL)]

scandalmonger /ˈskænd(ə)lˌmʌŋgə(r)/ *n.* a person who spreads malicious scandal.

Scandinavian /ˌskændɪˈneɪvɪən/ *n.* & *adj.* —*n.* **1 a** a native or inhabitant of Scandinavia (Denmark, Norway, Sweden, and Iceland). **b** a person of Scandinavian descent. **2** the family of languages of Scandinavia. —*adj.* of or relating to Scandinavia or its people or languages. [L *Scandinavia*]

scandium /ˈskændɪəm/ *n. Chem.* a rare soft silver-white metallic element occurring naturally in lanthanide ores. [mod.L f. *Scandia* Scandinavia (source of the minerals containing it)]

scannable see SCAN.

scanner /ˈskænə(r)/ *n.* **1** a device for scanning or systematically examining all the parts of something. **2** a machine for measuring the intensity of radiation, ultrasound reflections, etc., from the body as a diagnostic aid. **3** a person who scans or examines critically. **4** a person who scans verse.

scansion /ˈskænʃ(ə)n/ *n.* **1** the metrical scanning of verse. **2** the way a verse etc. scans. [L *scansio* (LL of metre) f. *scandere scans-* climb]

scant *adj.* & *v.* —*adj.* barely sufficient; deficient (*with scant regard for the truth*; *scant of breath*). —*v.tr. archaic* provide (a supply, material, a person, etc.) grudgingly; skimp; stint. □ **scantly** *adv.* **scantness** *n.* [ME f. ON *skamt* neut. of *skammr* short]

scanty /ˈskæntɪ/ *adj.* (**scantier**, **scantiest**) **1** of small extent or amount. **2** barely sufficient. □ **scantily** *adv.* **scantiness** *n.* [obs. *scant* scanty supply f. ON *skamt* neut. adj.: see SCANT]

-scape /skeɪp/ *comb. form* forming nouns denoting a view or a representation of a view (*moonscape*; *seascape*). [after LANDSCAPE]

scapegoat /ˈskeɪpgəʊt/ *n.* & *v.* —*n.* a person bearing the blame for the sins, shortcomings, etc. of others, esp. as an expedient. —*v.tr.* make a scapegoat of. □ **scapegoater** *n.* [*scape* (archaic, = escape) + GOAT, = the goat that escapes (ref. to Lev. 16)]

scapegrace /ˈskeɪpgreɪs/ *n.* a rascal; a scamp, esp. a young person or child. [*scape* (as SCAPEGOAT) + GRACE = one who escapes the grace of God]

scapula /ˈskæpjʊlə/ *n.* (*pl.* **scapulae** /-ˌliː/ or **scapulas**) the shoulder-blade. [LL, sing. of L *scapulae*]

scapular /ˈskæpjʊlə(r)/ *adj.* & *n.* —*adj.* of or relating to the shoulder or shoulder-blade. —*n.*

a monastic short cloak covering the shoulders. [(adj.) f. SCAPULA: (n.) f. LL *scapulare* (as SCAPULA)]

scar[1] *n.* & *v.* —*n.* **1** a usu. permanent mark on the skin left after the healing of a wound, burn, or sore. **2** the lasting effect of grief etc. on a person's character or disposition. **3** a mark left by damage etc. (*the table bore many scars*). **4** a mark left on the stem etc. of a plant by the fall of a leaf etc. —*v.* (**scarred**, **scarring**) **1** *tr.* (esp. as **scarred** *adj.*) mark with a scar or scars (*was scarred for life*). **2** *intr.* heal over; form a scar. **3** *tr.* form a scar on. □ **scarless** *adj.* [ME f. OF *eschar(r)e* f. LL *eschara* f. Gk *eskhara* scab]

scar[2] *n.* (also **scaur** /skɔː(r)/) a steep craggy outcrop of a mountain or cliff. [ME f. ON *sker* low reef in the sea]

scarab /ˈskærəb/ *n.* **1** the sacred dung-beetle of ancient Egypt. **2** an ancient Egyptian gem cut in the form of a beetle and engraved with symbols on its flat side, used as a signet etc. [L *scarabaeus* f. Gk *skarabeios*]

scarce /skeəs/ *adj.* & *adv.* —*adj.* **1** (usu. *predic.*) (esp. of food, money, etc.) insufficient for the demand; scanty. **2** hard to find; rare. —*adv. archaic* or *literary* scarcely. □ **make oneself scarce** *colloq.* keep out of the way; surreptitiously disappear. □ **scarceness** *n.* [ME f. AF & ONF (*e*)*scars*, OF *eschars* f. L *excerpere*: see EXCERPT]

scarcely /ˈskeəslɪ/ *adv.* **1** hardly; barely; only just (*I scarcely know him*). **2** surely not (*he can scarcely have said so*). **3** a mild or apologetic or ironical substitute for 'not' (*I scarcely expected to be insulted*).

scarcity /ˈskeəsɪtɪ/ *n.* (*pl.* **-ies**) (often foll. by *of*) a lack or inadequacy, esp. of food.

scare /skeə(r)/ *v.* & *n.* —*v.* **1** *tr.* frighten, esp. suddenly (*his expression scared us*). **2** *tr.* (as **scared** *adj.*) (usu. foll. by *of*, or *to* + *infin.*) frightened; terrified (*scared of his own shadow*). **3** *tr.* (usu. foll. by *away*, *off*, *up*, etc.) drive away by frightening. **4** *intr.* become scared (*they don't scare easily*). —*n.* **1** a sudden attack of fright (*gave me a scare*). **2** a general, esp. baseless, fear of war, invasion, epidemic, etc. (*a measles scare*). **3** a financial panic causing share-selling etc. □ **scaredy-cat** /ˈskeədɪˌkæt/ *colloq.* a timid person. **scare up** (or **out**) esp. *US* **1** frighten (game etc.) out of cover. **2** *colloq.* manage to find; discover (*see if we can scare up a meal*). □ **scarer** *n.* [ME *skerre* f. ON *skirra* frighten f. *skjarr* timid]

scarecrow /ˈskeəˌkrəʊ/ *n.* **1** a human figure dressed in old clothes and set up in a field to scare birds away. **2** *colloq.* a badly-dressed, grotesque-looking, or very thin person.

scaremonger /ˈskeəˌmʌŋgə(r)/ *n.* a person who spreads frightening reports or rumours. □ **scaremongering** *n.*

scarf[1] *n.* (*pl.* **scarves** /skɑːvz/ or **scarfs**) a square, triangular, or esp. long narrow strip of material worn round the neck, over the shoulders, or tied round the head (of a woman), for warmth or ornament. □ **scarf-pin** (or **-ring**) *Brit.* an ornamental device for fastening a scarf. □ **scarfed** *adj.* [prob. alt. of *scarp* (infl. by SCARF[2]) f. ONF *escarpe* = OF *escherpe* sash]

scarf[2] /skɑːf/ *v.* & *n.* —*v.tr.* join the ends of (pieces of esp. timber, metal, or leather) by bevelling or notching them to fit and then bolting, brazing, or sewing them together. —*n.*

a joint made by scarfing. [ME (earlier as noun) prob. f. OF *escarf* (unrecorded) perh. f. ON]

scarifier /ˈskærɪˌfaɪə(r), ˈskeə-/ *n.* **1** a thing or person that scarifies. **2** a machine with prongs for loosening soil without turning it. **3** a spiked road-breaking machine.

scarify[1] /ˈskærɪˌfaɪ, ˈskeə-/ *v.tr.* (**-ies, -ied**) **1 a** make superficial incisions in. **b** cut off skin from. **2** hurt by severe criticism etc. **3** loosen (soil) with a scarifier. □ **scarification** /-fɪˈkeɪʃ(ə)n/ *n.* [ME f. F *scarifier* f. LL *scarificare* f. L *scarifare* f. Gk *skariphaomai* f. *skariphos* stylus]

scarify[2] /ˈskeərɪˌfaɪ/ *v.tr. & intr.* (**-ies, -ied**) *colloq.* scare; terrify.

scarlatina /ˌskɑːləˈtiːnə/ *n.* = *scarlet fever*. [mod.L f. It. *scarlattina* (*febbre* fever) dimin. of *scarlatto* SCARLET]

scarlet /ˈskɑːlɪt/ *n. & adj.* —*n.* **1** a brilliant red colour tinged with orange. **2** clothes or material of this colour (*dressed in scarlet*). —*adj.* of a scarlet colour. □ **scarlet fever** an infectious bacterial fever, affecting esp. children, with a scarlet rash. **scarlet hat** *RC Ch.* a cardinal's hat as a symbol of rank. **scarlet pimpernel** a small annual wild plant, *Anagallis arvensis*, with small esp. scarlet flowers closing in rainy or cloudy weather. **scarlet runner 1** a runner bean. **2** a scarlet-flowered climber bearing this bean. **scarlet woman** *derog.* a notoriously promiscuous woman, a prostitute. [ME f. OF *escarlate*: ult. orig. unkn.]

scarp *n. & v.* —*n.* **1** the inner wall or slope of a ditch in a fortification. **2** a steep slope. —*v.tr.* **1** make (a slope) perpendicular or steep. **2** provide (a ditch) with a steep scarp and counterscarp. **3** (as **scarped** *adj.*) (of a hillside etc.) steep; precipitous. [It. *scarpa*]

scarper /ˈskɑːpə(r)/ *v.intr. Brit. sl.* run away; escape. [prob. f. It. *scappare* escape, infl. by rhyming sl. *Scapa Flow* = go]

scarves *pl.* of SCARF[1].

scary /ˈskeərɪ/ *adj.* (**scarier, scariest**) *colloq.* scaring, frightening. □ **scarily** *adv.*

scat[1] *v. & int. colloq.* —*v.intr.* (**scatted, scatting**) depart quickly. —*int.* go! [perh. abbr. of SCATTER]

scat[2] *n. & v.* —*n.* improvised jazz singing using sounds imitating instruments, instead of words. —*v.intr.* (**scatted, scatting**) sing scat. [prob. imit.]

scathe /skeɪð/ *v. & n.* —*v.tr.* **1** *poet.* injure esp. by blasting or withering. **2** (as **scathing** *adj.*) witheringly scornful (*scathing sarcasm*). —*n.* (usu. with *neg.*) *archaic* harm; injury (*without scathe*). □ **scatheless** *predic.adj.* **scathingly** *adv.* [(v.) ME f. ON *skatha* = OE *sceathian*: (n.) OE f. ON *skathi* = OE *sceatha* malefactor, injury, f. Gmc]

scatology /skæˈtɒlədʒɪ/ *n.* **1 a** a morbid interest in excrement. **b** a preoccupation with obscene literature, esp. that concerned with the excretory functions. **c** such literature. **2** the study of fossilized dung. **3** the study of excrement for esp. diagnosis. □ **scatological** /-təˈlɒdʒɪk(ə)l/ *adj.* [Gk *skōr skatos* dung + -LOGY]

scatter /ˈskætə(r)/ *v. & n.* —*v.* **1** *tr.* **a** throw here and there; strew (*scattered gravel on the road*). **b** cover by scattering (*scattered the road with gravel*). **2** *tr. & intr.* **a** move or cause to move in flight etc.; disperse (*scattered to safety at the sound*). **b** disperse or cause (hopes, clouds, etc.) to disperse. **3** *tr.* (as **scattered** *adj.*) not clustered together; wide apart; sporadic (*scattered villages*). **4** *tr.*

Physics deflect or diffuse (light, particles, etc.). **5 a** *intr.* (of esp. a shotgun) fire a charge of shot diffusely. **b** *tr.* fire (a charge) in this way. —*n.* **1** the act or an instance of scattering. **2** a small amount scattered. **3** the extent of distribution of esp. shot. □ **scatter cushions** (or **rugs**, etc.) cushions, rugs, etc., placed here and there for effect. **scatter-shot** *n. & adj.* *US* firing at random. □ **scatterer** *n.* [ME, prob. var. of SHATTER]

scatterbrain /ˈskætəˌbreɪn/ *n.* a person given to silly or disorganized thought with lack of concentration. □ **scatterbrained** *adj.*

scatty /ˈskætɪ/ *adj.* (**scattier, scattiest**) *Brit. colloq.* scatterbrained; disorganized. □ **scattily** *adv.* **scattiness** *n.* [abbr.]

scaur var. of SCAR[2].

scavenge /ˈskævɪndʒ/ *v.* **1** *tr. & intr.* (usu. foll. by *for*) search for and collect (discarded items). **2** *tr.* remove unwanted products from (an internal-combustion engine cylinder etc.). [back-form. f. SCAVENGER]

scavenger /ˈskævɪndʒə(r)/ *n.* **1** a person who seeks and collects discarded items. **2** an animal, esp. a beetle, feeding on carrion, refuse, etc. □ **scavengery** *n.* [ME *scavager* f. AF *scawager* f. *scawage* f. ONF *escauwer* inspect f. Flem. *scauwen*, rel. to SHOW: for *-n-* cf. MESSENGER]

Sc.D. *abbr.* Doctor of Science. [L *scientiae doctor*]

SCE *abbr.* Scottish Certificate of Education.

scenario /sɪˈnɑːrɪəʊ, -ˈneərɪəʊ/ *n.* (*pl.* **-os**) **1** an outline of the plot of a play, film, opera, etc., with details of the scenes, situations, etc. **2** a postulated sequence of future events. □ **scenarist** *n.* (in sense 1). [It. f. L: see SCENE]

scene /siːn/ *n.* **1** a place in which events in real life, drama, or fiction occur; the locality of an event etc. (*the scene was set in India; the scene of the disaster*). **2 a** an incident in real life, fiction, etc. (*distressing scenes occurred*). **b** a description or representation of an incident etc. (*scenes of clerical life*). **3** a public incident displaying emotion, temper, etc., esp. when embarrassing to others (*made a scene in the restaurant*). **4 a** a continuous portion of a play in a fixed setting and usu. without a change of personnel; a subdivision of an act. **b** a similar section of a film, book, etc. **5 a** any of the pieces of scenery used in a play. **b** these collectively. **6** a landscape or a view (*a desolate scene*). **7** *colloq.* **a** an area of action or interest (*not my scene*). **b** a way of life; a milieu (*well-known on the jazz scene*). □ **behind the scenes 1** *Theatr.* among the actors, scenery, etc. offstage. **2** not known to the public; secret. **change of scene** a variety of surroundings esp. through travel. **come on the scene** arrive. **quit the scene** die; leave. **scene-shifter** a person who moves scenery in a theatre. **set the scene 1** describe the location of events. **2** give preliminary information. [L *scena* f. Gk *skēnē* tent, stage]

scenery /ˈsiːnərɪ/ *n.* **1** the general appearance of the natural features of a landscape, esp. when picturesque. **2** *Theatr.* the painted representations of landscape, rooms, etc., used as the background in a play etc. □ **change of scenery** = *change of scene*. [earlier *scenary* f. It. SCENARIO: assim. to -ERY]

scenic /ˈsiːnɪk/ *adj.* **1 a** picturesque; impressive or beautiful (*took the scenic route*). **b** of or concerning natural scenery (*flatness is the main* *scenic feature*). **2** (of a picture etc.) representing an incident. □ **scenic railway 1** a miniature railway running through artificial scenery at funfairs etc. **2** = *big dipper* 1. □ **scenically** *adv.* [L *scenicus* f. Gk *skēnikos* of the stage (as SCENE)]

scent /sent/ *n.* & *v.* —*n.* **1** a distinctive, esp. pleasant, smell (*the scent of hay*). **2 a** a scent trail left by an animal perceptible to hounds etc. **b** clues etc. that can be followed like a scent trail (*lost the scent in Paris*). **c** the power of detecting or distinguishing smells etc. or of discovering things (*some dogs have little scent*; *the scent for talent*). **3** *Brit.* = PERFUME 2. —*v.* **1** *tr.* **a** discern by scent (*the dog scented the game*). **b** sense the presence of (*scent treachery*). **2** *tr.* make fragrant or foul-smelling. **3** *tr.* (as **scented** *adj.*) having esp. a pleasant smell (*scented soap*). □ **on the scent** having a clue. **put** (or **throw**) **off the scent** deceive by false clues etc. **scent out** discover by smelling or searching. □ **scentless** *adj.* [ME *sent* f. OF *sentir* perceive, smell, f. L *sentire*; -c- (17th c.) unexpl.]

sceptic /'skeptɪk/ *n.* & *adj.* (US **skeptic**) —*n.* a person inclined to doubt all accepted opinions; a cynic. **2** a person who doubts the truth of Christianity and other religions. —*adj.* = SCEPTICAL. □ **scepticism** /-ˌsɪz(ə)m/ *n.* [F *sceptique* or L *scepticus* f. Gk *skeptikos* f. *skepsis* inquiry, doubt f. *skeptomai* consider]

sceptical /'skeptɪk(ə)l/ *adj.* (US **skeptical**) inclined to question the truth or soundness of accepted ideas, facts, etc.; critical; incredulous. □ **sceptically** *adv.*

sceptre /'septə(r)/ *n.* (US **scepter**) **1** a staff borne esp. at a coronation as a symbol of sovereignty. **2** royal or imperial authority. □ **sceptred** *adj.* [ME f. OF *(s)ceptre* f. L *sceptrum* f. Gk *skēptron* f. *skēptō* lean on]

schadenfreude /'ʃɑːdənˌfrɔɪdə/ *n.* the malicious enjoyment of another's misfortunes. [G f. *Schaden* harm + *Freude* joy]

schedule /'ʃedjuːl, 'skeː-/ *n.* & *v.* —*n.* **1 a** a list or plan of intended events, times, etc. **b** a plan of work (*not on my schedule for next week*). **2** a list of rates or prices. **3** *US* a timetable. **4** a tabulated inventory etc. esp. as an appendix to a document. —*v.tr.* **1** include in a schedule. **2** make a schedule of. **3** *Brit.* include (a building) in a list for preservation or protection. □ **according to schedule** (or **on schedule**) as planned; on time. **behind schedule** behind time. **scheduled flight** (or **service** etc.) a public flight, service, etc., according to a regular timetable. □ **scheduler** *n.* [ME f. OF *cedule* f. LL *schedula* slip of paper, dimin. of *scheda* f. Gk *skhedē* papyrus-leaf]

schema /'skiːmə/ *n.* (pl. **schemata** /-mətə/ or **schemas**) **1** a synopsis, outline, or diagram. **2** a proposed arrangement. [Gk *skhēma* -atos form, figure]

schematic /skɪ'mætɪk, skiː-/ *adj.* & *n.* —*adj.* **1** of or concerning a scheme or schema. **2** representing objects by symbols etc. —*n.* a schematic diagram, esp. of an electronic circuit. □ **schematically** *adv.*

schematize /'skiːməˌtaɪz/ *v.tr.* (also **-ise**) **1** put in a schematic form; arrange. **2** represent by a scheme or schema. □ **schematization** /-ˈzeɪʃ(ə)n/ *n.*

scheme /skiːm/ *n.* & *v.* —*n.* **1 a** a systematic plan or arrangement for work, action, etc. **b** a

proposed or operational systematic arrangement (*a colour scheme*). **2** an artful or deceitful plot. **3** a timetable, outline, syllabus, etc. —*v.* **1** *intr.* (often foll. by *for*, or *to* + infin.) plan esp. secretly or deceitfully; intrigue. **2** *tr.* plan to bring about, esp. artfully or deceitfully (*schemed their downfall*). □ **schemer** *n.* [L *schema* f. Gk (as SCHEMA)]

scheming /'skiːmɪŋ/ *adj.* & *n.* —*adj.* artful, cunning, or deceitful. —*n.* plots; intrigues. □ **schemingly** *adv.*

schemozzle var. of SHEMOZZLE.

scherzo /'skeəˌtsəʊ/ *n.* (pl. **-os**) *Mus.* a vigorous, light, or playful composition, usu. as a movement in a symphony, sonata, etc. [It., lit. 'jest']

schism /'sɪz(ə)m, 'skɪ-/ *n.* **1 a** the division of a group into opposing sections or parties. **b** any of the sections so formed. **2 a** the separation of a Church into two Churches or the secession of a group owing to doctrinal, disciplinary, etc., differences. **b** the offence of causing or promoting such a separation. [ME f. OF *s(c)isme* f. eccl.L *schisma* f. Gk *skhisma* -atos cleft f. *skhizō* to split]

schismatic /sɪz'mætɪk, skɪz-/ *adj.* & *n.* (also **schismatical**) —*adj.* inclining to, concerning, or guilty of, schism. —*n.* **1** a holder of schismatic opinions. **2** a member of a schismatic faction or a seceded branch of a Church. □ **schismatically** *adv.* [ME f. OF *scismatique* f. eccl.L *schismaticus* f. eccl.Gk *skhismatikos* (as SCHISM)]

schist /ʃɪst/ *n.* a foliated metamorphic rock composed of layers of different minerals and splitting into thin irregular plates. □ **schistose** *adj.* [F *schiste* f. L *schistos* f. Gk *skhistos* split (as SCHISM)]

schistosome /'ʃɪstəˌsəʊm/ *n.* = BILHARZIA 1. [Gk *skhistos* divided (as SCHISM) + *sōma* body]

schistosomiasis /ˌʃɪstəsəˈmaɪəsɪs/ *n.* = BILHARZIASIS. [mod.L *Schistosoma* (the genus-name, as SCHISTOSOME)]

schizo /'skɪtsəʊ/ *adj.* & *n.* colloq. —*adj.* schizophrenic. —*n.* (pl. **-os**) a schizophrenic. [abbr.]

schizoid /'skɪtsɔɪd/ *adj.* & *n.* —*adj.* (of a person or personality etc.) tending to or resembling schizophrenia or a schizophrenic, but usu. without delusions. —*n.* a schizoid person.

schizophrenia /ˌskɪtsəˈfriːnɪə/ *n.* a mental disease marked by a breakdown in the relation between thoughts, feelings, and actions, frequently accompanied by delusions and retreat from social life. □ **schizophrenic** /-ˈfrenɪk, -ˈfriːnɪk/ *adj.* & *n.* [mod.L f. Gk *skhizō* to split + *phrēn* mind]

schlemiel /ʃləˈmiːl/ *n.* *US colloq.* a foolish or unlucky person. [Yiddish *shlumiel*]

schlep /ʃlep/ *v.* & *n.* (also **schlepp**) colloq. —*v.* (**schlepped**, **schlepping**) **1** *tr.* carry, drag. **2** *intr.* go or work tediously or effortfully. —*n.* esp. *US* trouble or hard work. [Yiddish *shlepn* f. G *schleppen* drag]

schlock /ʃlɒk/ *n.* *US colloq.* inferior goods; trash. [Yiddish *shlak* a blow]

schmaltz /ʃmɔːlts, ʃmælts/ *n.* esp. *US colloq.* sentimentality, esp. in music, drama, etc. □ **schmaltzy** *adj.* (**schmaltzier**, **schmaltziest**). [Yiddish f. G *Schmalz* dripping, lard]

schmuck /ʃmʌk/ *n.* esp. *US sl.* a foolish or contemptible person. [Yiddish]

schnapps /ʃnæps/ n. any of various spirits drunk in N. Europe. [G. = dram of liquor f. LG & Du. *snaps* mouthful (as SNAP)]

schnitzel /ˈʃnɪtz(ə)l/ n. an escalope of veal. □ **Wiener** (or **Vienna**) **schnitzel** a breaded, fried, and garnished schnitzel. [G. = slice]

schnorkel var. of SNORKEL.

scholar /ˈskɒlə(r)/ n. **1 a** a learned person, esp. in language, literature, etc.; an academic. **2** the holder of a scholarship. **3 a** a person with specified academic ability (*is a poor scholar*). **b** a person who learns (*am a scholar of life*). □ **scholarly** adj. **scholarliness** n. [ME f. OE *scol(i)ere* & OF *escol(i)er* f. LL *scholaris* f. L *schola* SCHOOL[1]]

scholarship /ˈskɒləʃɪp/ n. **1 a** academic achievement; learning of a high level. **b** the methods and standards characteristic of a good scholar (*shows great scholarship*). **2** payment from the funds of a school, university, local government, etc., to maintain a student in full-time education.

scholastic /skəˈlæstɪk/ adj. & n. —adj. **1** of or concerning universities, schools, education, teachers, etc. **2** pedantic; formal (*shows scholastic precision*). □ **scholastically** adv. **scholasticism** /-ˌsɪz(ə)m/ n. [L *scholasticus* f. Gk *skholastikos* studious f. *skholazō* be at leisure, formed as SCHOOL]

school[1] /skuːl/ n. & v. —n. **1 a** an institution for educating or giving instruction, esp. *Brit.* for children under 19 years, or *US* for any level of instruction including college or university. **b** (*attrib.*) associated with or for use in school (*a school bag; school dinners*). **2 a** the buildings used by such an institution. **b** the pupils, staff, etc. of a school. **c** the time during which teaching is done, or the teaching itself (*no school today*). **3 a** branch of study with separate examinations at a university; a department or faculty (*the history school*). **4 a** the disciples, imitators, or followers of a philosopher, artist, etc. (*the school of Epicurus*). **b** a group of artists etc. whose works share distinctive characteristics. **c** a group of people sharing a cause, principle, method, etc. (*school of thought*). **5** *Brit.* a group of gamblers or of persons drinking together (*a poker school*). **6** *colloq.* instructive or disciplinary circumstances, occupation, etc. (*the school of adversity; learnt in a hard school*). **7** *hist.* a medieval lecture-room. —v.tr. **1** send to school; provide for the education of. **2** (often foll. by *to*) discipline; train; control. **3** (as **schooled** adj.) (foll. by *in*) educated or trained (*schooled in humility*). □ **at** (*US* **in**) **school** attending lessons etc. **go to school 1** begin one's education. **2** attend lessons. **leave school** finish one's education. **of the old school** according to former and esp. better tradition. **school board** *US* or *hist.* a board or authority for local education. **school-days** the time of being at school, esp. in retrospect. **school-inspector** a government official reporting on the efficiency, teaching standards, etc. of schools. **school-leaver** *Brit.* a child leaving school esp. at the minimum specified age. **school-ma'm** (or **-marm**) *US colloq.* a school-mistress. **school-marmish** *colloq.* prim and fussy. **school year** = *academic year.* [ME f. OE *scōl, scolu,* & f. OF *escole* ult. f. L *schola* school f. Gk *skholē* leisure, disputation, philosophy, lecture-place]

school[2] /skuːl/ n. & v. —n. (often foll. by *of*) a shoal of fish, porpoises, whales, etc. —v.intr. form schools. [ME f. MLG, MDu. *schōle* f. WG]

schoolable /ˈskuːləb(ə)l/ adj. liable by age etc. to compulsory education.

schoolboy /ˈskuːlbɔɪ/ n. a boy attending school.

schoolchild /ˈskuːltʃaɪld/ n. a child attending school.

schoolfellow /ˈskuːlˌfeləʊ/ n. a past or esp. present member of the same school.

schoolgirl /ˈskuːlgɜːl/ n. a girl attending school.

schoolhouse /ˈskuːlhaʊs/ n. *Brit.* **1** a building used as a school, esp. in a village. **2** a dwelling-house adjoining a school.

schoolie /ˈskuːlɪ/ n. *Austral. sl.* & *dial.* a schoolteacher.

schooling /ˈskuːlɪŋ/ n. **1** education, esp. at school. **2** training or discipline, esp. of an animal.

schoolmaster /ˈskuːlˌmɑːstə(r)/ n. a head or assistant male teacher. □ **schoolmasterly** adj.

schoolmastering /ˈskuːlˌmɑːstərɪŋ/ n. teaching as a profession.

schoolmate /ˈskuːlmeɪt/ n. = SCHOOLFELLOW.

schoolmistress /ˈskuːlˌmɪstrɪs/ n. a head or assistant female teacher.

schoolmistressy /ˈskuːlˌmɪstrɪsɪ/ adj. *colloq.* prim and fussy.

schoolroom /ˈskuːlruːm, -rʊm/ n. a room used for lessons in a school or esp. in a private house.

schoolteacher /ˈskuːlˌtiːtʃə(r)/ n. a person who teaches in a school. □ **schoolteaching** n.

schooner /ˈskuːnə(r)/ n. **1** a fore-and-aft rigged ship with two or more masts. **2 a** *Brit.* a measure or glass for esp. sherry. **b** *US* & *Austral.* a tall beer-glass. [18th c.: orig. uncert.]

schottische /ʃɒˈtiːʃ/ n. **1** a kind of slow polka. **2** the music for this. [G *der schottische Tanz* the Scottish dance]

schuss /ʃʊs/ n. & v. —n. a straight downhill run on skis. —v.intr. make a schuss. [G, lit. 'shot']

schwa /ʃwɑː, ʃvɑː/ n. (also **sheva** /ʃəˈvɑː/) *Phonet.* **1** the indistinct unstressed vowel sound as in *a moment ago*. **2** the symbol /ə/ representing this in the International Phonetic Alphabet. [G f. Heb. *šᵂwā*, app. f. Heb. *šaw* emptiness]

sciatic /saɪˈætɪk/ adj. **1** of the hip. **2** of or affecting the sciatic nerve. **3** suffering from or liable to sciatica. □ **sciatic nerve** the largest nerve in the human body, running from the pelvis to the thigh. □ **sciatically** adv. [F *sciatique* f. LL *sciaticus* f. L *ischiadicus* f. Gk *iskhiadikos* subject to sciatica f. *iskhion* hip-joint]

sciatica /saɪˈætɪkə/ n. neuralgia of the hip and thigh; a pain in the sciatic nerve. [ME f. LL *sciatica* (*passio*) fem. of *sciaticus*: see SCIATIC]

science /ˈsaɪəns/ n. **1** a branch of knowledge conducted on objective principles involving the systematized observation of and experiment with phenomena, esp. concerned with the material and functions of the physical universe (see also *natural science*). **2 a** systematic and formulated knowledge, esp. of a specified type or on a specified subject (*political science*). **b** the pursuit or principles of this. **3** an organized body of knowledge on a subject (*the science of philology*). **4** skilful technique rather than strength or natural ability. □ **science fiction** fiction based on imagined future scientific discoveries or environmental changes. **science park** an area devoted to scientific research or the development of science-based industries. [ME f. OF f. L *scientia* f. *scire* know]

scientific /ˌsaɪənˈtɪfɪk/ *adj.* **1 a** (of an investigation etc.) according to rules laid down in exact science for performing observations and testing the soundness of conclusions. **b** systematic, accurate. **2** used in, engaged in, or relating to (esp. natural) science (*scientific discoveries; scientific terminology*). **3** assisted by expert knowledge. □ **scientifically** *adv.* [F *scientifique* or LL *scientificus* (as SCIENCE)]

scientist /ˈsaɪəntɪst/ *n.* **1** a person with expert knowledge of a (usu. physical or natural) science. **2** a person using scientific methods.

Scientology /ˌsaɪənˈtɒlədʒɪ/ *n.* a religious system based on self-improvement and promotion through grades of esp. self-knowledge. □ **Scientologist** *n.* [L *scientia* knowledge + -LOGY]

sci-fi /ˈsaɪfaɪ, saɪˈfaɪ/ *n.* (often *attrib.*) *colloq.* science fiction. [abbr.: cf. HI-FI]

scilicet /ˈsaɪlɪˌset, ˈskiːliːˌket/ *adv.* to wit; that is to say; namely (introducing a word to be supplied or an explanation of an ambiguity). [ME f. L, = *scire licet* one is permitted to know]

Scillonian /sɪˈləʊnɪən/ *adj.* & *n.* —*adj.* of or relating to the Scilly Isles off the coast of Cornwall. —*n.* a native of the Scilly Isles. [*Scilly*, perh. after *Devonian*]

scimitar /ˈsɪmɪtə(r)/ *n.* an oriental curved sword usu. broadening towards the point. [F *cimeterre*, It. *scimitarra*, etc., of unkn. orig.]

scintilla /sɪnˈtɪlə/ *n.* **1** a trace. **2** a spark. [L]

scintillate /ˈsɪntɪˌleɪt/ *v.intr.* **1** (esp. as **scintillating** *adj.*) talk cleverly or wittily; be brilliant. **2** sparkle; twinkle; emit sparks. □ **scintillant** *adj.* **scintillatingly** *adv.* **scintillation** *n.* [L *scintillare* (as SCINTILLA)]

scion /ˈsaɪən/ *n.* **1** (*US* **cion**) a shoot of a plant etc., esp. one cut for grafting or planting. **2** a descendant; a younger member of (esp. a noble) family. [ME f. OF *ciun, cion, sion* shoot, twig, of unkn. orig.]

scirocco var. of SIROCCO.

scissor /ˈsɪzə(r)/ *v.tr.* **1** (usu. foll. by *off, up, into,* etc.) cut with scissors. **2** (usu. foll. by *out*) clip out (a newspaper cutting etc.).

scissors /ˈsɪzəz/ *n.pl.* **1** (also **pair of scissors** *sing.*) an instrument for cutting fabric, paper, hair, etc., having two pivoted blades with finger and thumb holes in the handles, operating by closing on the material to be cut. **2** (treated as *sing.*) **a** a method of high jump with a forward and backward movement of the legs. **b** a hold in wrestling in which the opponent's body or esp. head is gripped between the legs. □ **scissors and paste** a method of compiling a book, article, etc., from extracts from others or without independent research. □ **scissorwise** *adv.* [ME *sisoures* f. OF *cisoires* f. LL *cisoria* pl. of *cisorium* cutting instrument (as CHISEL): assoc. with L *scindere sciss-* cut]

sclera /ˈsklɪərə/ *n.* the white of the eye; a white membrane coating the eyeball. □ **scleral** *adj.* **scleritis** /sklɪˈraɪtɪs/ *n.* **sclerotomy** /-ˈrɒtəmɪ/ *n.* (pl. **-ies**). [mod.L f. fem. of Gk *sklēros* hard]

sclerosed /ˈsklɪəˌrəʊst, -ˌrəʊzd/ *adj.* affected by sclerosis.

sclerosis /sklɪəˈrəʊsɪs/ *n.* **1** an abnormal hardening of body tissue. **2** (in full **multiple** or **disseminated sclerosis**) a chronic and progressive disease of the nervous system resulting

in symptoms including paralysis and speech defects. [ME f. med.L f. Gk *sklērōsis* f. *sklēroō* harden]

sclerotic /sklɪəˈrɒtɪk/ *adj.* & *n.* —*adj.* **1** of or having sclerosis. **2** of or relating to the sclera. —*n.* = SCLERA. □ **sclerotitis** /-rəˈtaɪtɪs/ *n.* [med.L *sclerotica* (as SCLEROSIS)]

scoff[1] *v.* & *n.* —*v.intr.* (usu. foll. by *at*) speak derisively, esp. of serious subjects; mock; be scornful. —*n.* **1** mocking words; a taunt. **2** an object of ridicule. □ **scoffer** *n.* **scoffingly** *adv.* [perh. f. Scand.: cf. early mod. Da. *skuf, skof* jest, mockery]

scoff[2] *v.* & *n.* *colloq.* —*v.tr.* & *intr.* eat greedily. —*n.* food; a meal. [(n.) f. Afrik. *schoff* repr. Du. *schoft* quarter of a day (hence, meal): (v.) orig. var. of dial. *scaff,* assoc. with the noun]

scold /skəʊld/ *v.* & *n.* —*v.* **1** *tr.* rebuke (esp. a child, employee, or inferior). **2** *intr.* find fault noisily; complain; rail. —*n.* *archaic* a nagging or grumbling woman. □ **scolder** *n.* **scolding** *n.* [ME (earlier as noun), prob. f. ON *skáld* SKALD]

scollop var. of SCALLOP.

sconce[1] /skɒns/ *n.* **1** a flat candlestick with a handle. **2** a bracket candlestick to hang on a wall. [ME f. OF *esconse* lantern or med.L *sconsa* f. L *absconsa* fem. past part. of *abscondere* hide: see ABSCOND]

sconce[2] /skɒns/ *n.* **1** a small fort or earthwork usu. defending a ford, pass, etc. **2** *archaic* a shelter or screen. [Du. *schans* brushwood f. MHG *schanze*]

scone /skɒn, skəʊn/ *n.* a small sweet or savoury cake of flour, fat, and milk, baked quickly in an oven. [orig. Sc., perh. f. MDu. *schoon(broot),* MLG *schon(brot)* fine (bread)]

scoop /skuːp/ *n.* & *v.* —*n.* **1** any of various objects resembling a spoon, esp.: **a** a short-handled deep shovel used for transferring grain, sugar, coal, coins, etc. **b** a large long-handled ladle used for transferring liquids. **c** the excavating part of a digging-machine etc. **d** an instrument used for serving portions of mashed potato, ice-cream, etc. **2** a quantity taken up by a scoop. **3** a movement of or resembling scooping. **4** a piece of news published by a newspaper etc. in advance of its rivals. **5** a large profit made quickly or by anticipating one's competitors. **6** a scooped-out hollow etc. —*v.tr.* **1** (usu. foll. by *out*) hollow out with or as if with a scoop. **2** (usu. foll. by *up*) lift with or as if with a scoop. **3** forestall (a rival newspaper, reporter, etc.) with a scoop. **4** secure (a large profit etc.) esp. suddenly. □ **scoop-neck** the rounded low-cut neck of a garment. □ **scooper** *n.* **scoopful** *n.* (pl. **-fuls**). [ME f. MDu., MLG *schōpe* bucket etc., rel. to SHAPE]

scoot /skuːt/ *v.* & *n.* *colloq.* —*v.intr.* run or dart away, esp. quickly. —*n.* the act or an instance of scooting. [19th-c. US (earlier *scout*): orig. unkn.]

scooter /ˈskuːtə(r)/ *n.* & *v.* —*n.* **1** a child's toy consisting of a footboard mounted on two wheels and a long steering-handle, propelled by resting one foot on the footboard and pushing the other against the ground. **2** (in full **motor scooter**) a light two-wheeled open motor vehicle with a shieldlike protective front. **3** *US* a sailboat able to travel on both water and ice. —*v.intr.* travel or ride on a scooter. □ **scooterist** *n.* [f. SCOOT]

scope[1] *n.* **1** the extent to which it is possible to range; the opportunity for action etc. (*this is beyond the scope of our research*). **2** the sweep or reach of mental activity, observation, or outlook (*an intellect limited in its scope*). [It. *scopo* aim f. Gk *skopos* target f. *skeptomai* look at]

scope[2] /skəʊp/ *n. colloq.* a telescope, microscope, or other device ending in *-scope*. [abbr.]

-scope /skəʊp/ *comb. form* forming nouns denoting: **1** a device looked at or through (*kaleidoscope*; *telescope*). **2** an instrument for observing or showing (*gyroscope*; *oscilloscope*). □ **-scopic** /ˈskɒpɪk/ *comb. form* forming adjectives. [from or after mod. L *-scopium* f. Gk *skopeō* look at]

scopolamine /skəˈpɒləmɪn, -ˌmiːn/ *n.* = HYOSCINE. [*Scopolia* genus-name of the plants yielding it, f. G. A. *Scopoli*, It. naturalist d. 1788 + AMINE]

-scopy /skəpɪ/ *comb. form* indicating viewing or observation, usu. with an instrument ending in *-scope* (*microscopy*).

scorbutic /skɔːˈbjuːtɪk/ *adj. & n.* —*adj.* relating to, resembling, or affected with scurvy. —*n.* a person affected with scurvy. □ **scorbutically** *adv.* [mod.L *scorbuticus* f. med.L *scorbutus* scurvy, perh. f. MLG *schorbūk* f. *schoren* break + *būk* belly]

scorch *v. & n.* —*v.* **1** *tr.* **a** burn the surface of with flame or heat so as to discolour, parch, injure, or hurt. **b** affect with the sensation of burning. **2** *intr.* become discoloured etc. with heat. **3** *tr.* (as **scorching** *adj.*) *colloq.* **a** (of the weather) very hot. **b** (of criticism etc.) stringent; harsh. **4** *intr. colloq.* (of a motorist etc.) go at excessive speed. —*n.* **1** a mark made by scorching. **2** *colloq.* a spell of fast driving etc. □ **scorched earth policy** the burning of crops etc. and the removing or destroying of anything that might be of use to an enemy force occupying a country. □ **scorchingly** *adv.* [ME, perh. rel. to *skorkle* in the same sense]

scorcher /ˈskɔːtʃə(r)/ *n.* **1** a person or thing that scorches. **2** *colloq.* **a** a very hot day. **b** a fine specimen.

score *n. & v.* —*n.* **1 a** the number of points, goals, runs, etc., made by a player, side, etc., in some games. **b** the total number of points etc. at the end of a game (*the score was five—nil*). **c** the act of gaining esp. a goal (*a superb score there!*). **2** (*pl.* same or **scores**) twenty or a set of twenty. **3** (in *pl.*) a great many (*scores of people arrived*). **4 a** a reason or motive (*rejected on the score of absurdity*). **b** topic, subject (*no worries on that score*). **5** *Mus.* **a** a usu. printed copy of a composition showing all the vocal and instrumental parts arranged one below the other. **b** the music composed for a film or play, esp. for a musical. **6** *colloq.* **a** a piece of good fortune. **b** the act or an instance of scoring off another person. **7** *colloq.* the state of affairs; the present situation (*asked what the score was*). **8** a notch, line, etc. cut or scratched into a surface. **9** an amount due for payment. —*v.* **1** *tr.* **a** win or gain (a goal, run, points, etc., or success etc.) (*scored a century*). **b** count for a score of (points in a game etc.) (*a bull's-eye scores most points*). **c** allot a score to (a competitor etc.). **d** make a record of (a point etc.). **2** *intr.* **a** make a score in a game (*failed to score*). **b** keep the tally of points, runs, etc. in a game. **3** *tr.* mark with notches, incisions, lines, etc.; slash; furrow (*scored his name on the desk*). **4** *intr.* secure an advantage by luck, cunning, etc.

(*that is where he scores*). **5** *tr. Mus.* **a** orchestrate (a piece of music). **b** (usu. foll. by *for*) arrange for an instrument or instruments. **c** write the music for (a film, musical, etc.). **d** write out in a score. **6** *intr. sl.* **a** obtain drugs illegally. **b** (of a man) make a sexual conquest. **7** *tr.* (usu. foll. by *against, to*) mentally record (an offence etc.). □ **keep score** (or **the score**) register the score as it is made. **know the score** *colloq.* be aware of the essential facts. **on the score of** for the reason that; because of. **on that score** so far as that is concerned. **score-book** (or **-card** or **-sheet**) a book etc. prepared for entering esp. cricket scores in. **score draw** a draw in football in which goals are scored. **score off** (or **score points off**) *colloq.* humiliate, esp. verbally in repartee etc. **score out** draw a line through (words etc.). **score under** underline. □ **scorer** *n.* **scoring** *n. Mus.* [(n.) f. OE: sense 5 f. the line or bar drawn through all staves: (v.) partly f. ON *skora* f. ON *skor* notch, tally, twenty, f. Gmc: see SHEAR]

scoreboard /ˈskɔːbɔːd/ *n.* a large board for publicly displaying the score in a game or match.

scoria /ˈskɔːrɪə/ *n.* (*pl.* **scoriae** /-rɪˌiː/) **1** cellular lava, or fragments of it. **2** the slag or dross of metals. □ **scoriaceous** /-ˈeɪʃəs/ *adj.* [L f. Gk *skōria* refuse f. *skōr* dung]

scorn *n. & v.* —*n.* **1** disdain, contempt, derision. **2** an object of contempt etc. (*the scorn of all onlookers*). —*v.tr.* **1** hold in contempt or disdain. **2** (often foll. by *to* + infin.) abstain from or refuse to do as unworthy (*scorns lying; scorns to lie*). □ **scorner** *n.* [ME f. OF *esc(h)arn(ir)* ult. f. Gmc: cf. OS *skern* MOCKERY]

scornful /ˈskɔːnfʊl/ *adj.* (often foll. by *of*) full of scorn; contemptuous. □ **scornfully** *adv.* **scornfulness** *n.*

Scorpio /ˈskɔːpɪəʊ/ *n.* (*pl.* **-os**) **1** a constellation, traditionally regarded as contained in the figure of a scorpion. **2 a** the eighth sign of the zodiac (the Scorpion). **b** a person born when the sun is in this sign. □ **Scorpian** *adj. & n.* [ME f. L (as SCORPION)]

scorpion /ˈskɔːpɪən/ *n.* **1** an arachnid of the order Scorpionida, with lobster-like pincers and a jointed tail that can be bent over to inflict a poisoned sting on prey held in its pincers. **2** (**the Scorpion**) the zodiacal sign or constellation Scorpio. [ME f. OF f. L *scorpio -onis* f. *scorpius* f. Gk *skorpios*]

scorzonera /ˌskɔːzəˈnɪərə/ *n.* **1** a composite plant, *Scorzonera hispanica*, with long tapering purple-brown roots. **2** the root used as a vegetable. [It. f. *scorzone* venomous snake ult f. med.L *curtio*]

Scot *n.* **1 a** a native of Scotland. **b** a person of Scottish descent. **2** *hist.* a member of a Gaelic people that migrated from Ireland to Scotland around the 6th c. [OE *Scottas* (pl.) f. LL *Scottus*]

scot *n. hist.* a payment corresponding to a modern tax, rate, etc. □ **scot-free** unharmed; unpunished; safe. [ME f. ON *skot* & f. OF *escot*, of Gmc orig.: cf. SHOT[1]]

Scotch *adj. & n.* —*adj.* var. of SCOTTISH or SCOTS. —*n.* **1** var. of SCOTTISH or SCOTS. **2** Scotch whisky. □ **Scotch broth** a soup made from beef or mutton with pearl barley etc. **Scotch cap** = BONNET *n.* 1b. **Scotch egg** a hard-boiled egg enclosed in sausage meat and fried. **Scotch fir**

(or **pine**) a pine tree, *Pinus sylvestris*, native to Europe and Asia. **Scotch mist 1** a thick drizzly mist common in the Highlands. **2** a retort made to a person implying that he or she has imagined or failed to understand something. **Scotch pine** = *Scotch fir.* **Scotch terrier 1** a small terrier of a rough-haired short-legged breed. **2** this breed. **Scotch whisky** whisky distilled in Scotland, esp. from malted barley. [contr. of SCOTTISH]

■ **Usage** *Scots* or *Scottish* is preferred in Scotland, except in the compounds given above.

scotch *v.tr.* **1** put an end to; frustrate (*injury scotched his attempt*). **2** *archaic* **a** wound without killing; slightly disable. **b** make incisions in; score. [ME: orig. unkn.]

Scotchman /ˈskɒtʃmən/ *n.* (*pl.* **-men**; *fem.* **Scotchwoman**, *pl.* **-women**) = SCOTSMAN.

■ **Usage** *Scotsman* etc. are preferred in Scotland.

Scotland Yard /ˌskɒtlənd ˈjɑːd/ *n.* **1** the head-quarters of the London Metropolitan Police. **2** its Criminal Investigation Department. [*Great* and *New Scotland Yard*, streets where it was successively situated until 1967]

Scots *adj.* & *n.* esp. *Sc.* —*adj.* **1** = SCOTTISH *adj.* **2** in the dialect, accent, etc., of (esp. Lowlands) Scotland. —*n.* **1** = SCOTTISH *n.* **2** the form of English spoken in (esp. Lowlands) Scotland. [ME orig. *Scottis*, north. var. of SCOTTISH]

Scotsman /ˈskɒtsmən/ *n.* (*pl.* **-men**; *fem.* **Scotswoman**, *pl.* **-women**) **1** a native of Scotland. **2** a person of Scottish descent.

Scotticism /ˈskɒtɪˌsɪz(ə)m/ *n.* (also **Scoticism**) a Scottish phrase, word, or idiom. [LL *Scot*(*t*)*icus*]

Scotticize /ˈskɒtɪˌsaɪz/ *v.* (also **Scoticize, -ise**) **1** *tr.* imbue with or model on Scottish ways etc. **2** *intr.* imitate the Scottish in idiom or habits.

Scottie /ˈskɒtɪ/ *n. colloq.* **1** (also **Scottie dog**) a Scotch terrier. **2** a Scot.

Scottish /ˈskɒtɪʃ/ *adj.* & *n.* —*adj.* of or relating to Scotland or its inhabitants. —*n.* (prec. by *the*; treated as *pl.*) the people of Scotland (see also SCOTS). □ **Scottishness** *n.*

scoundrel /ˈskaʊndr(ə)l/ *n.* an unscrupulous villain; a rogue. □ **scoundreldom** *n.* **scoundrelism** *n.* **scoundrelly** *adj.* [16th c.: orig. unkn.]

scour[1] /ˈskaʊə(r)/ *v.* & *n.* —*v.tr.* **1 a** cleanse or brighten by rubbing, esp. with soap, chemicals, sand, etc. **b** (usu. foll. by *away, off,* etc.) clear (rust, stains, reputation, etc.) by rubbing, hard work, etc. (*scoured the slur from his name*). **2** (of water, or a person with water) clear out (a pipe, channel, etc.) by flushing through. —*n.* **1** the act or an instance of scouring; the state of being scoured, esp. by a swift water current (*the scour of the tide*). **2** *colloq.* □ **scourer** *n.* [ME f. MDu., MLG *schūren* f. F *escurer* f. LL *excurare* clean (off) (as EX-[1], CURE)]

scour[2] /ˈskaʊə(r)/ *v.* **1** *tr.* hasten over (an area etc.) searching thoroughly (*scoured the streets for him; scoured the pages of the newspaper*). **2** *intr.* range hastily esp. in search or pursuit. [ME: orig. unkn.]

scourge /skɜːdʒ/ *n.* & *v.* —*n.* **1** a whip used for punishment, esp. of people. **2** a person or thing seen as punishing, esp. on a large scale (*Genghis Khan, the scourge of Asia*). —*v.tr.* **1** whip. **2** punish; afflict; oppress. □ **scourger** *n.* [ME f. OF *escorge*

(n.), *escorgier* (v.) (ult. as EX-[1], L *corrigia* thong, whip)]

Scouse /skaʊs/ *n.* & *adj. colloq.* —*n.* **1** the dialect of Liverpool. **2** (also **Scouser** /ˈskaʊsə(r)/) a native of Liverpool. **3** (**scouse**) = LOBSCOUSE. —*adj.* of or relating to Liverpool. [abbr. of LOBSCOUSE]

scout[1] /skaʊt/ *n.* & *v.* —*n.* **1** a person, esp. a soldier, sent out to get information about the enemy's position, strength, etc. **2** the act of seeking (esp. military) information (*on the scout*). **3** = *talent-scout.* **4** (**Scout**) a member of the Scout Association, a boys' association intended to develop character esp. by open-air activities. **5** *colloq.* a person; a fellow. **6** a ship or aircraft designed for reconnoitring, esp. a small fast aircraft. —*v.* **1** *intr.* act as a scout. **2** *intr.* (foll. by *about, around*) make a search. **3** *tr.* (often foll. by *out*) *colloq.* explore to get information about (territory etc.). □ **Queen's** (or **King's**) **Scout** a Scout who has reached the highest standard of proficiency. □ **scouter** *n.* **scouting** *n.* [ME f. OF *escouter* listen, earlier *ascolter* ult. f. L *auscultare*]

scout[2] /skaʊt/ *v.tr.* reject (an idea etc.) with scorn. [Scand.: cf. ON *skúta, skúti* taunt]

Scouter /ˈskaʊtə(r)/ *n.* an adult member of the Scout Association.

Scoutmaster /ˈskaʊtˌmɑːstə(r)/ *n.* a person in charge of a group of Scouts.

scow /skaʊ/ *n.* esp. *US* a flat-bottomed boat used as a lighter etc. [Du. *schouw* ferry-boat]

scowl /skaʊl/ *n.* & *v.* —*n.* a severe frown producing a sullen, bad-tempered, or threatening look on a person's face. —*v.intr.* make a scowl. □ **scowler** *n.* [ME, prob. f. Scand.: cf. Da. *skule* look down or sidelong]

scrabble /ˈskræb(ə)l/ *v.* & *n.* —*v.intr.* (often foll. by *about, at*) scratch or grope to find or collect or hold on to something. —*n.* **1** an act of scrabbling. **2** (**Scrabble**) *propr.* a game in which players build up words from letter-blocks on a board. [MDu. *schrabbelen* frequent. of *schrabben* SCRAPE]

scrag *n.* & *v.* —*n.* **1** (also **scrag-end**) the inferior end of a neck of mutton. **2** a skinny person or animal. **3** *colloq.* a person's neck. —*v.tr.* (**scragged, scragging**) *sl.* **1** strangle, hang. **2** seize roughly by the neck. **3** handle roughly; beat up. [perh. alt. f. dial. *crag* neck, rel. to MDu. *crāghe*, MLG *krage*]

scraggly /ˈskræɡlɪ/ *adj.* sparse and irregular.

scraggy /ˈskræɡɪ/ *adj.* (**scraggier, scraggiest**) thin and bony. □ **scraggily** *adv.* **scragginess** *n.*

scram *v.intr.* (**scrammed, scramming**) (esp. in *imper.*) *colloq.* go away. [20th c.: perh. f. SCRAMBLE]

scramble /ˈskræmb(ə)l/ *v.* & *n.* —*v.* **1** *intr.* make one's way over rough ground, rocks, etc., by clambering, crawling, etc. **2** *intr.* (foll. by *for, at*) struggle with competitors (for a thing or share of it). **3** *intr.* move with difficulty, hastily, or anxiously. **4** *tr.* **a** mix together indiscriminately. **b** jumble or muddle. **5** *tr.* cook (eggs) by heating them when broken and well mixed with butter, milk, etc. **6** *tr.* change the speech frequency of (a broadcast transmission or telephone conversation) so as to make it unintelligible without a corresponding decoding device. **7** *intr.* move hastily. **8** *tr. colloq.* execute (an action etc.) awkwardly and inefficiently. **9** *intr.* (of fighter aircraft or their pilots) take off quickly in an emergency or for action. —*n.* **1** an act of scrambling. **2** a difficult climb or walk. **3** (foll. by *for*) an eager struggle or competition. **4** *Brit.* a motor-cycle race over rough ground. **5** an emergency take-off by fighter aircraft. [16th c. (imit.): cf. dial. synonyms *scamble, cramble*]

scrambler /ˈskræmblə(r)/ *n.* a device for scrambling telephone conversations.

scrap[1] *n.* & *v.* —*n.* **1** a small detached piece; a fragment or remnant. **2** rubbish or waste material. **3** an extract or cutting from something written or printed. **4** discarded metal for reprocessing (often *attrib.: scrap metal*). **5** (with *neg.*) the smallest piece or amount (*not a scrap of food left*). **6** (in *pl.*) **a** odds and ends. **b** bits of uneaten food. —*v.tr.* (**scrapped**, **scrapping**) discard as useless. □ **scrap heap 1** a pile of scrap materials. **2** a state of uselessness. **scrap merchant** a dealer in scrap. [ME f. ON *skrap*, rel. to *skrapa* SCRAPE]

scrap[2] *n.* & *v. colloq.* —*n.* a fight or rough quarrel, esp. a spontaneous one. —*v.tr.* (**scrapped**, **scrapping**) (often foll. by *with*) have a scrap. □ **scrapper** *n.* [perh. f. SCRAPE]

scrapbook /ˈskræpbʊk/ *n.* a book of blank pages for sticking cuttings, drawings, etc., in.

scrape *v.* & *n.* —*v.* **1** *tr.* **a** move a hard or sharp edge across (a surface), esp. to make something smooth. **b** apply (a hard or sharp edge) in this way. **2** *tr.* (foll. by *away, off,* etc.) remove (a stain, projection, etc.) by scraping. **3** *tr.* **a** rub (a surface) harshly against another. **b** scratch or damage by scraping. **4** *tr.* make (a hollow) by scraping. **5 a** *tr.* draw or move with a sound of, or resembling, scraping. **b** *intr.* emit or produce such a sound. **c** *tr.* produce such a sound from. **6** *intr.* (often foll. by *along, by, through*) move or pass along while almost touching close or surrounding features, obstacles, etc. (*the car scraped through the narrow lane*). **7** *tr.* just manage to achieve (a living, an examination pass, etc.). **8** *intr.* (often foll. by *by, through*) **a** barely manage. **b** pass an examination etc. with difficulty. **9** *tr.* (foll. by *together, up*) contrive to bring or provide; amass with difficulty. **10** *intr.* be economical. **11** *intr.* draw back a foot in making a clumsy bow. —*n.* **1** the act or sound of scraping. **2** a scraped place (on the skin etc.). **3** a thinly applied layer of butter etc. on bread. **4** the scraping of a foot in bowing. **5** *colloq.* an awkward predicament, esp. resulting from an escapade. □ **scrape acquaintance with** contrive to get to know (a person). **scrape the barrel** *colloq.* be reduced to one's last resources. [ME f. ON *skrapa* or MDu. *schrapen*]

scraper /ˈskreɪpə(r)/ *n.* a device used for scraping, esp. for removing dirt etc. from a surface.

scrapie /ˈskreɪpɪ/ *n.* a viral disease of sheep involving the central nervous system and characterized by lack of coordination causing affected animals to rub against trees etc. for support.

scraping /ˈskreɪpɪŋ/ *n.* **1** in senses of SCRAPE *v.* & *n.* **2** (esp. in *pl.*) a fragment produced by this.

scrappy /ˈskræpɪ/ *adj.* (**scrappier**, **scrappiest**) **1** consisting of scraps. **2** incomplete; carelessly arranged or put together. □ **scrappily** *adv.* **scrappiness** *n.*

scrapyard /ˈskræpjɑːd/ *n.* a place where (esp. metal) scrap is collected.

scratch *v., n.,* & *adj.* —*v.* **1** *tr.* score or mark the surface of with a sharp or pointed object. **2** *tr.* **a**

make a long narrow superficial wound in (the skin). **b** cause (a person or part of the body) to be scratched (*scratched himself on the table*). **3** *tr.* (also *absol.*) scrape without marking, esp. with the hand to relieve itching (*stood there scratching*). **4** *tr.* make or form by scratching. **5** *tr.* scribble; write hurriedly or awkwardly (*scratched a quick reply; scratched a large A*). **6** *tr.* (foll. by *together, up,* etc.) obtain (a thing) by scratching or with difficulty. **7** *tr.* (foll. by *out, off, through*) cancel or strike (out) with a pencil etc. **8** *tr.* (also *absol.*) withdraw (a competitor, candidate, etc.) from a race or competition. **9** *intr.* (often foll. by *about, around,* etc.) **a** scratch the ground etc. in search. **b** look around haphazardly (*they were scratching about for evidence*). —*n.* **1** a mark or wound made by scratching. **2** a sound of scratching. **3** a spell of scratching oneself. **4** *colloq.* a superficial wound. **5** a line from which competitors in a race (esp. those not receiving a handicap) start. —*attrib.adj.* **1** collected by chance. **2** collected or made from whatever is available; heterogeneous (*a scratch crew*). **3** with no handicap given (*a scratch race*). □ **from scratch 1** from the beginning. **2** without help or advantage. **scratch along** make a living etc. with difficulty. **scratch one's head** be perplexed. **scratch pad 1** esp. *US* a pad of paper for scribbling. **2** *Computing* a small fast memory for the temporary storage of data. **scratch the surface** deal with a matter only superficially. **up to scratch** up to the required standard. □ **scratcher** *n.* [ME, prob. f. synonymous ME *scrat* & *cratch*, both of uncert. orig.: cf. MLG *kratsen*, OHG *krazzōn*]

scratchy /ˈskrætʃɪ/ *adj.* (**scratchier**, **scratchiest**) **1** tending to make scratches or a scratching noise. **2** (esp. of a garment) tending to cause itchiness. **3** (of a drawing etc.) done in scratches or carelessly. □ **scratchily** *adv.* **scratchiness** *n.*

scrawl *v.* & *n.* —*v.* **1** *tr.* & *intr.* write in a hurried untidy way. **2** *tr.* (foll. by *out*) cross out by scrawling over. —*n.* **1** a piece of hurried writing. **2** a scrawled note. □ **scrawly** *adj.* [perh. f. obs. *scrawl* sprawl, alt. of CRAWL]

scrawny /ˈskrɔːnɪ/ *adj.* (**scrawnier**, **scrawniest**) lean, scraggy. □ **scrawniness** *n.* [var. of dial. *scranny*: cf. archaic *scrannel* (of sound) weak, feeble]

scream *n.* & *v.* —*n.* **1** a loud high-pitched piercing cry expressing fear, pain, extreme fright, etc. **2** the act of emitting a scream. **3** *colloq.* an irresistibly funny occurrence or person. —*v.* **1** *intr.* emit a scream. **2** *tr.* speak or sing (words etc.) in a screaming tone. **3** *intr.* make or move with a shrill sound like a scream. **4** *intr.* laugh uncontrollably. **5** *intr.* be blatantly obvious or conspicuous. [OE or MDu.]

screamer /ˈskriːmə(r)/ *n.* **1** a person or thing that screams. **2** *colloq.* a tale that raises screams of laughter. **3** *US colloq.* a sensational headline.

scree *n.* (in *sing.* or *pl.*) **1** small loose stones. **2** a mountain slope covered with these. [prob. back-form. f. *screes* (pl.) ult. f. ON *skritha* landslip, rel. to *skrítha* glide]

screech *n.* & *v.* —*n.* a harsh high-pitched scream. —*v.tr.* & *intr.* utter with or make a screech. □ **screech-owl** any owl that screeches instead of hooting, esp. a barn-owl. □ **screecher**

n. **screechy** *adj.* (**screechier**, **screechiest**). [16th-c. var. of ME *scritch* (imit.)]

screed *n.* **1** a long usu. tiresome piece of writing or speech. **2 a** a strip of plaster or other material placed on a surface as a guide to thickness. **b** a levelled layer of material (e.g. cement) applied to a floor or other surface. [ME, prob. var. of SHRED]

screen *n.* & *v.* —*n.* **1** a fixed or movable upright partition for separating, concealing, or sheltering from draughts or excessive heat or light. **2** a thing used as a shelter, esp. from observation. **3 a** a measure adopted for concealment. **b** the protection afforded by this (*under the screen of night*). **4 a** a blank usu. white or silver surface on which a photographic image is projected. **b** (prec. by *the*) the cinema industry. **5** the surface of a cathode-ray tube or similar electronic device, esp. of a television, VDU, etc., on which images appear. **6** = *sight-screen*. **7** = WINDSCREEN. **8** a frame with fine wire netting to keep out flies, mosquitoes, etc. **9** a large sieve or riddle, esp. for sorting grain, coal, etc., into sizes. **10** a system of checking for the presence or absence of a disease, ability, attribute, etc. **11** *Printing* a transparent finely-ruled plate or film used in half-tone reproduction. —*v.tr.* **1** (often foll. by *from*) **a** afford shelter to; hide partly or completely. **b** protect from detection, censure, etc. **2** (foll. by *off*) shut off or hide behind a screen. **3 a** show (a film etc.) on a screen. **b** broadcast (a television programme). **4** prevent from causing, or protect from, electrical interference. **5 a** test (a person or group) for the presence or absence of a disease. **b** check on (a person) for the presence or absence of a quality, esp. reliability or loyalty. **6** pass (grain, coal, etc.) through a screen. □ **screen printing** a process like stencilling with ink forced through a prepared sheet of fine material (orig. silk). **screen test** an audition for a part in a cinema film. □ **screenable** *adj.* **screener** *n.* [ME f. ONF *escren, escran*: cf. OHG *skrank* barrier]

screenplay /ˈskriːnpleɪ/ *n.* the script of a film, with acting instructions, scene directions, etc.

screenwriter /ˈskriːnˌraɪtə(r)/ *n.* a person who writes a screenplay.

screw *n.* & *v.* —*n.* **1** a thin cylinder or cone with a spiral ridge or thread running round the outside (**male screw**) or the inside (**female screw**). **2** (in full **wood-screw**) a metal male screw with a slotted head and a sharp point for fastening things, esp. in carpentry, by being rotated to form a thread in wood etc. **3** (in full **screw-bolt**) a metal male screw with a blunt end on which a nut is threaded to bolt things together. **4** a wooden or metal straight screw used to exert pressure. **5** (in *sing.* or *pl.*) an instrument of torture acting in this way. **6** (in full **screw-propeller**) a form of propeller with twisted blades acting like a screw on the water or air. **7** one turn of a screw. **8** (foll. by *of*) *Brit.* a small twisted-up paper (of tobacco etc.). **9** *Brit.* (in billiards etc.) an oblique curling motion of the ball. **10** *sl.* a prison warder. **11** *Brit. sl.* an amount of salary or wages. **12** *coarse sl.* **a** an act of sexual intercourse. **b** a partner in this. **13** *sl.* a mean or miserly person. **14** *sl.* a worn-out horse. —*v.* **1** *tr.* fasten or tighten with a screw or screws. **2** *tr.* turn (a screw). **3** *intr.* twist or turn round like a screw. **4** *intr.* (of a ball etc.)

swerve. **5** *tr.* **a** put psychological etc. pressure on to achieve an end. **b** oppress. **6** *tr.* (foll. by *out of*) extort (consent, money, etc.) from (a person). **7** *tr.* (also *absol.*) *coarse sl.* have sexual intercourse with. **8** *intr.* (of a rolling ball, or of a person etc.) take a curling course; swerve. **9** *intr.* (often foll. by *up*) make tenser or more efficient. □ **have one's head screwed on the right way** *colloq.* have common sense. **have a screw loose** *colloq.* be slightly crazy. **put the screws on** *colloq.* exert pressure, esp. to extort or intimidate. **screw cap** = *screw top*. **screw top** (also (with hyphen) *attrib.*) a cap or lid that can be screwed on to a bottle, jar, etc. **screw up 1** contract or contort (one's face etc.). **2** contract and crush into a tight mass (a piece of paper etc.). **3** summon up (one's courage etc.). **4** *sl.* **a** bungle or mismanage. **b** spoil or ruin (an event, opportunity, etc.). □ **screwable** *adj.* **screwer** *n.* [ME f. OF *escroue* female screw, nut, f. L *scrofa* sow]

screwball /ˈskruːbɔːl/ *n.* & *adj. US sl.* —*n.* a crazy or eccentric person. —*adj.* crazy.

screwdriver /ˈskruːˌdraɪvə(r)/ *n.* a tool with a shaped tip to fit into the head of a screw to turn it.

screwed /skruːd/ *adj.* **1** twisted. **2** *sl.* **a** ruined; rendered ineffective. **b** drunk.

screwy /ˈskruːɪ/ *adj.* (**screwier**, **screwiest**) *sl.* **1** crazy or eccentric. **2** absurd. □ **screwiness** *n.*

scribble /ˈskrɪb(ə)l/ *v.* & *n.* —*v.* **1** *tr.* & *intr.* write carelessly or hurriedly. **2** *intr.* often *derog.* be an author or writer. **3** *intr.* & *tr.* draw carelessly or meaninglessly. —*n.* **1** a scrawl. **2** a hasty note etc. **3** careless handwriting. □ **scribbler** *n.* **scribbly** *adj.* [ME f. med.L *scribillare* dimin. of L *scribere* write]

scribe *n.* & *v.* —*n.* **1** a person who writes out documents, esp. an ancient or medieval copyist of manuscripts. **2** *Bibl.* an ancient Jewish record-keeper or professional theologian and jurist. **3** (in full **scribe-awl**) a pointed instrument for making marks on wood, bricks, etc. **4** *US colloq.* a writer, esp. a journalist. —*v.tr.* mark (wood etc.) with a scribe (see sense 3 of *n.*). □ **scribal** *adj.* **scriber** *n.* [(n.) ME f. L *scriba* f. *scribere* write: (v.) perh. f. DESCRIBE]

scrim *n.* open-weave fabric for lining or upholstery etc. [18th c.: orig. unkn.]

scrimmage /ˈskrɪmɪdʒ/ *n.* & *v.* —*n.* **1** a rough or confused struggle; a brawl. **2** *Amer. Football* a sequence of play beginning with the placing of the ball on the ground with its longest axis at right angles to the goal-line. —*v.* **1** *intr.* engage in a scrimmage. **2** *tr. Amer. Football* put (the ball) into a scrimmage. □ **scrimmager** *n.* [var. of SKIRMISH]

scrimp *v.* **1** *intr.* be sparing or parsimonious. **2** *tr.* use sparingly. □ **scrimpy** *adj.* [18th c., orig. Sc.: perh. rel. to SHRIMP]

scrip *n.* **1** a provisional certificate of money subscribed to a bank or company etc. entitling the holder to a formal certificate and dividends. **2** (*collect.*) such certificates. **3** an extra share or shares instead of a dividend. [abbr. of *subscription receipt*]

script *n.* & *v.* —*n.* **1** handwriting as distinct from print; written characters. **2** type imitating handwriting. **3** an alphabet or system of writing (*the Russian script*). **4** the text of a play, film, or broadcast. **5** an examinee's set of written answers. —*v.tr.* write a script for (a film etc.).

[ME, = thing written, f. OF *escri(p)t* f. L *scriptum*, neut. past part. of *scribere* write]

scriptural /ˈskrɪptʃər(ə)l, -tʃʊər(ə)l/ *adj.* **1** of or relating to a scripture, esp. the Bible. **2** having the authority of a scripture. □ **scripturally** *adv.* [LL *scripturalis* f. L *scriptura*: see SCRIPTURE]

scripture /ˈskrɪptʃə(r)/ *n.* **1** sacred writings. **2** (**Scripture** or **the Scriptures**) **a** the Bible as a collection of sacred writings in Christianity. **b** the sacred writings of any other religion. [ME f. L *scriptura* (as SCRIPT)]

scriptwriter /ˈskrɪptˌraɪtə(r)/ *n.* a person who writes a script for a film, broadcast, etc. □ **scriptwriting** *n.*

scrivener /ˈskrɪvənə(r)/ *n. hist.* **1** a copyist or drafter of documents. **2** a notary. [ME f. obs. *scrivein* f. OF *escrivein* ult. f. L (as SCRIBE)]

scrofula /ˈskrɒfjʊlə/ *n. archaic* a disease with glandular swellings, prob. a form of tuberculosis. □ **scrofulous** *adj.* [ME f. med.L (sing.) f. LL *scrofulae* (pl.) scrofulous swelling, dimin. of L *scrofa* a sow]

scroll /skrəʊl/ *n. & v.* —*n.* **1** a roll of parchment or paper esp. with writing on it. **2** a book in the ancient roll form. **3** an ornamental design or carving imitating a roll of parchment. —*v.* **1** *tr.* (often foll. by *down, up*) move (a display on a VDU screen) in order to view new material. **2** *tr.* inscribe in or like a scroll. **3** *intr.* curl up like paper. [ME *scrowle* alt. f. *rowle* ROLL, perh. after *scrow* (in the same sense), formed as ESCROW]

scrolled /skrəʊld/ *adj.* having a scroll ornament.

scrollwork /ˈskrəʊlwɜːk/ *n.* decoration of spiral lines.

Scrooge /skruːdʒ/ *n.* a mean or miserly person. [a character in Dickens's *Christmas Carol*]

scrotum /ˈskrəʊtəm/ *n.* (pl. **scrota** /-tə/ or **scrotums**) a pouch of skin containing the testicles. □ **scrotal** *adj.* **scrotitis** /-ˈtaɪtɪs/ *n.* [L]

scrounge /skraʊndʒ/ *v. & n. colloq.* —*v.* **1** *tr.* (also *absol.*) obtain (things) illicitly or by cadging. **2** *intr.* search about to find something at no cost. —*n.* an act of scrounging. □ **on the scrounge** engaged in scrounging. □ **scrounger** *n.* [var. of dial. *scrunge* steal]

scrub[1] *v. & n.* —*v.* (**scrubbed, scrubbing**) **1** *tr.* rub hard so as to clean, esp. with a hard brush. **2** *intr.* use a brush in this way. **3** *intr.* (often foll. by *up*) (of a surgeon etc.) thoroughly clean the hands and arms by scrubbing, before operating. **4** *tr. colloq.* scrap or cancel (a plan, order, etc.). —*n.* the act or an instance of scrubbing; the process of being scrubbed. □ **scrubbing-brush** (US **scrub-brush**) a hard brush for scrubbing floors. **scrub round** *colloq.* circumvent, avoid. [ME prob. f. MLG, MDu. *schrobben, schrubben*]

scrub[2] *n.* **1 a** vegetation consisting mainly of brushwood or stunted forest growth. **b** an area of land covered with this. **2** (of livestock) of inferior breed or physique (often *attrib.*: *scrub horse*). **3** US *Sport colloq.* a team or player not of the first class. □ **scrubby** *adj.* [ME, var. of SHRUB[1]]

scrubber /ˈskrʌbə(r)/ *n.* **1** an apparatus using water or a solution for purifying gases etc. **2** *sl. derog.* a sexually promiscuous woman.

scruff[1] *n.* the back of the neck as used to grasp and lift or drag an animal or person by (esp. *scruff of the neck*). [alt. of *scuff*, perh. f. ON *skoft* hair]

scruff[2] *n. colloq.* an untidy or scruffy person. [orig. = SCURF, later 'worthless thing', or backform. f. SCRUFFY]

scruffy /ˈskrʌfɪ/ *adj.* (**scruffier, scruffiest**) *colloq.* shabby, slovenly, untidy. □ **scruffily** *adv.* **scruffiness** *n.* [*scruff* var. of SCURF + -Y[1]]

scrum *n.* **1** *Rugby Football* an arrangement of the forwards of each team in two opposing groups, each with arms interlocked and heads down, with the ball thrown in between them to restart play. **2** *colloq.* a milling crowd. □ **scrum-half** a half-back who puts the ball into the scrum. [abbr. of SCRUMMAGE]

scrummage /ˈskrʌmɪdʒ/ *n. Rugby Football* = SCRUM 1. [as SCRIMMAGE]

scrump /skrʌmp/ *v.tr. Brit. colloq.* steal (fruit) from an orchard or garden. [cf. SCRUMPY]

scrumptious /ˈskrʌmpʃəs/ *adj. colloq.* **1** delicious. **2** pleasing, delightful. □ **scrumptiously** *adv.* **scrumptiousness** *n.* [19th c.: orig. unkn.]

scrumpy /ˈskrʌmpɪ/ *n. Brit. colloq.* rough cider, esp. as made in the West Country of England. [dial. *scrump* small apple]

scrunch /skrʌntʃ/ *v. & n.* —*v.tr. & intr.* **1** (usu. foll. by *up*) make or become crushed or crumpled. **2** make or cause to make a crunching sound. —*n.* the act or an instance of scrunching. [var. of CRUNCH]

scruple /ˈskruːp(ə)l/ *n. & v.* —*n.* **1** (in *sing.* or *pl.*) **a** regard to the morality or propriety of an action. **b** a feeling of doubt or hesitation caused by this. **2** *Brit. hist.* an apothecaries' weight of 20 grains. —*v.intr.* **1** (foll. by *to* + infin.; usu. with *neg.*) be reluctant because of scruples (*did not scruple to stop their allowance*). **2** feel or be influenced by scruples. [F *scrupule* or L *scrupulus* f. *scrupus* rough pebble, anxiety]

scrupulous /ˈskruːpjʊləs/ *adj.* **1** conscientious or thorough even in small matters. **2** careful to avoid doing wrong. **3** punctilious; over-attentive to details. □ **scrupulosity** /-ˈlɒsɪtɪ/ *n.* **scrupulously** *adv.* **scrupulousness** *n.* [ME f. F *scrupuleux* or L *scrupulosus* (as SCRUPLE)]

scrutineer /ˌskruːtɪˈnɪə(r)/ *n.* a person who scrutinizes or examines something, esp. the conduct and result of a ballot.

scrutinize /ˈskruːtɪˌnaɪz/ *v.tr.* (also **-ise**) look closely at; examine with close scrutiny. □ **scrutinizer** *n.*

scrutiny /ˈskruːtɪnɪ/ *n.* (pl. **-ies**) **1** a critical gaze. **2** a close investigation or examination of details. **3** an official examination of ballot-papers to check their validity or accuracy of counting. [ME f. L *scrutinium* f. *scrutari* search f. *scruta* rubbish: orig. of rag-collectors]

scuba /ˈskuːbə, ˈskjuː-/ *n.* (pl. **scubas**) an aqualung. [acronym f. self-contained underwater breathing apparatus]

scuba-diving /ˈskuːbəˌdaɪvɪŋ, ˈskjuː-/ *n.* swimming underwater using a scuba, esp. as a sport. □ **scuba-dive** *v.intr.* **scuba-diver** *n.*

scud *v. & n.* —*v.intr.* (**scudded, scudding**) **1** fly or run straight, fast, and lightly; skim along. **2** *Naut.* run before the wind. —*n.* **1** a spell of scudding. **2** a scudding motion. **3** vapoury driving clouds. **4** a driving shower; a gust. **5** wind-blown spray. **6** (usu. with capital initial) a type of long-range surface-to-surface guided missile originally developed in the former Soviet Union. [perh. alt. of SCUT, as if to race like a hare]

scuff v. & n. —v. **1** tr. graze or brush against. **2** tr. mark or wear down (shoes) in this way. **3** intr. walk with dragging feet; shuffle. —n. a mark of scuffing. [imit.]

scuffle /ˈskʌf(ə)l/ n. & v. —n. a confused struggle or disorderly fight at close quarters. —v.intr. engage in a scuffle. [prob. f. Scand.: cf. Sw. *skuffa* to push, rel. to SHOVE]

sculduggery var. of SKULDUGGERY.

scull n. & v. —n. **1** either of a pair of small oars used by a single rower. **2** an oar placed over the stern of a boat to propel it, usu. by a twisting motion. **3** (in pl.) a race between boats with single pairs of oars. —v.tr. propel (a boat) with sculls. [ME: orig. unkn.]

sculler /ˈskʌlə(r)/ n. **1** a user of sculls. **2** a boat intended for sculling.

scullery /ˈskʌlərɪ/ n. (pl. **-ies**) a small kitchen or room at the back of a house for washing dishes etc. [ME f. AF *squillerie*, OF *escuelerie* f. *escuele* dish f. L *scutella* salver dimin. of *scutra* wooden platter]

scullion /ˈskʌljən/ n. archaic **1** a cook's boy. **2** a person who washes dishes etc. [ME: orig. unkn.]

sculpt v.tr. & intr. (also **sculp**) sculpture. [F *sculpter* f. *sculpteur* SCULPTOR: now regarded as an abbr.]

sculptor /ˈskʌlptə(r)/ n. (fem. **sculptress** /-trɪs/) an artist who makes sculptures. [L (as SCULPTURE)]

sculpture /ˈskʌlptʃə(r)/ n. & v. —n. **1** the art of making forms, often representational, in the round or in relief by chiselling stone, carving wood, modelling clay, casting metal, etc. **2** a work or works of sculpture. —v. **1** tr. represent in or adorn with sculpture. **2** intr. practise sculpture. □ **sculptural** adj. **sculpturally** adv. **sculpturesque** adj. [ME f. L *sculptura* f. *sculpere* sculpt- carve]

scum n. & v. —n. **1** a layer of dirt, froth, or impurities etc. forming at the top of liquid, esp. in boiling or fermentation. **2** (foll. by *of*) the most worthless part of something. **3** colloq. a worthless person or group. —v. (**scummed**, **scumming**) **1** tr. remove scum from; skim. **2** tr. be or form a scum on. **3** intr. (of a liquid) develop scum. □ **scummy** adj. (**scummier**, **scummiest**) adj. [ME f. MLG, MDu. *schūm*, OHG *scūm* f. Gmc]

scunge /skʌndʒ/ n. Austral. & NZ colloq. **1** dirt, scum. **2** a dirty or disagreeable person. □ **scungy** adj. (**scungier**, **scungiest**). [perh. f. E dial. *scrunge* steal: cf. SCROUNGE]

scupper[1] /ˈskʌpə(r)/ n. a hole in a ship's side to carry off water from the deck. [ME (perh. f. AF) f. OF *escopir* f. Rmc *skuppire* (unrecorded) to spit: orig. uncert.]

scupper[2] /ˈskʌpə(r)/ v.tr. Brit. sl. **1** sink (a ship or its crew). **2** defeat or ruin (a plan etc.). **3** kill. [19th c.: orig. unkn.]

scurf n. **1** flakes on the surface of the skin, cast off as fresh skin develops below, esp. those of the head; dandruff. **2** any scaly matter on a surface. □ **scurfy** adj. [OE, prob. f. ON & earlier OE *sceorf*, rel. to *sceorfan* gnaw, *sceorfian* cut to shreds]

scurrilous /ˈskʌrɪləs/ adj. **1** (of a person or language) grossly or indecently abusive. **2** given to or expressed with low humour. □ **scurrility** /-ˈrɪlɪtɪ/ n. (pl. **-ies**). **scurrilously** adv. **scurrilousness** n. [F *scurrile* or L *scurrilus* f. *scurra* buffoon]

scurry /ˈskʌrɪ/ v. & n. —v.intr. (**-ies**, **-ied**) run or move hurriedly, esp. with short quick steps; scamper. —n. (pl. **-ies**) **1** the act or sound of scurrying. **2** bustle, haste. **3** a flurry of rain or snow. [abbr. of *hurry-scurry* redupl. of HURRY]

scurvy /ˈskɜːvɪ/ n. & adj. —n. a disease caused by a deficiency of vitamin C. —adj. (**scurvier**, **scurviest**) paltry, low, mean, dishonourable, contemptible. □ **scurvied** adj. **scurvily** adv. [SCURF + -Y¹: noun sense by assoc. with F *scorbut* (cf. SCORBUTIC)]

scut n. a short tail, esp. of a hare, rabbit, or deer. [ME: orig. unkn.: cf. obs. *scut* short, shorten]

scutcheon /ˈskʌtʃ(ə)n/ n. **1** = ESCUTCHEON. **2** an ornamented brass etc. plate round or over a keyhole. **3** a plate for a name or inscription. [ME f. ESCUTCHEON]

scutter /ˈskʌtə(r)/ v. & n. —v.intr. colloq. scurry. —n. the act or an instance of scuttering. [perh. alt. of SCUTTLE²]

scuttle[1] /ˈskʌt(ə)l/ n. **1** a receptacle for carrying and holding a small supply of coal. **2** Brit. the part of a motor-car body between the windscreen and the bonnet. [ME f. ON *skutill*, OHG *scuzzila* f. L *scutella* dish]

scuttle[2] /ˈskʌt(ə)l/ v. & n. —v.intr. **1** scurry; hurry along. **2** run away; flee from danger or difficulty. —n. **1** a hurried gait. **2** a precipitate flight or departure. [cf. dial. *scuddle* frequent. of SCUD]

scuttle[3] /ˈskʌt(ə)l/ n. & v. —n. a hole with a lid in a ship's deck or side. —v.tr. let water into (a ship) to sink it, esp. by opening the seacocks. [ME, perh. f. obs. F *escoutille* f. Sp. *escotilla* hatchway dimin. of *escota* cutting out cloth]

scuttlebutt /ˈskʌt(ə)l₁bʌt/ n. **1** a water-butt on the deck of a ship, for drinking from. **2** colloq. rumour, gossip.

scuzzy /ˈskʌzɪ/ adj. sl. abhorrent or disgusting. [prob. f. DISGUSTING]

Scylla and Charybdis /₁sɪlə ənd kəˈrɪbdɪs/ n.pl. two dangers such that avoidance of one increases the risk from the other. [the names of a sea-monster and whirlpool in Gk mythology]

scythe /saɪð/ n. & v. —n. a mowing and reaping implement with a long curved blade swung over the ground by a long pole with two short handles projecting from it. —v.tr. cut with a scythe. [OE *sīthe* f. Gmc]

SDI abbr. strategic defence initiative.

SDLP abbr. (in N. Ireland) Social Democratic and Labour Party.

SDP abbr. (in the UK) Social Democratic Party.

SE abbr. **1** south-east. **2** south-eastern.

Se symb. Chem. the element selenium.

se- /sə, sɪ/ prefix apart, without (*seclude*; *secure*). [L f. OL *se* (prep. & adv.)]

sea n. **1** the expanse of salt water that covers most of the earth's surface and surrounds its land masses. **2** any part of this as opposed to land or fresh water. **3** a particular (usu. named) tract of salt water partly or wholly enclosed by land (*the North Sea*; *the Dead Sea*). **4** a large inland lake (*the Sea of Galilee*). **5** the waves of the sea, esp. with reference to their local motion or state (*a choppy sea*). **6** (foll. by *of*) a vast quantity or expanse (*a sea of troubles*; *a sea of faces*). **7** (attrib.) living or used in, on, or near the sea (often prefixed to the name of a marine animal, plant, etc., having a superficial resemblance to what it is named after) (*sea lettuce*). □ **at sea 1** in a ship on the sea. **2** (also **all at sea**) perplexed, confused. **by sea** in a ship or ships. **go to sea** become a sailor. **on the sea 1** in a ship at sea. **2** situated on the coast. **put** (or **put out**) **to sea** leave land or port. **sea anchor** a device such as a heavy bag dragged in the water to retard the drifting of a ship. **sea anemone** any of various coelenterates of the order Actiniaria bearing a ring of tentacles around the mouth. **sea bird** a bird frequenting the sea or the land near the sea. **sea breeze** a breeze blowing towards the land from the sea, esp. during the day. **sea change** a notable or unexpected transformation (with ref. to Shakesp. Tempest I. ii. 403). **sea-chest** a sailor's storage-chest. **sea cow 1** a sirenian. **2** a walrus. **sea cucumber** a holothurian. **sea dog** an old and experienced sailor. **sea-ear** = ORMER. **sea front** the part of a coastal town directly facing the sea. **sea-green** bluish-green (as of the sea). **sea holly** a spiny-leaved blue-flowered evergreen plant, *Eryngium maritimum*. **sea horse 1** any of various small upright marine fish of the family Syngnathidae, esp. *Hippocampus hippocampus*, having a body suggestive of the head and neck of a horse. **2** a mythical creature with a horse's head and fish's tail. **sea legs** the ability to keep one's balance and avoid seasickness when at sea. **sea level** the mean level of the sea's surface, used in reckoning the height of hills etc. and as a barometric standard. **sea lion** any large, eared seal of the Pacific, esp. of the genus *Zalophus* or *Otaria*. **sea loch** = LOCH 2. **Sea Lord** (in the UK) a naval member of the Admiralty Board. **sea mile** = *nautical mile*. **sea pink** a maritime plant, *Armeria maritima*, with bright pink flowers. **sea room** clear space at sea for a ship to turn or manoeuvre in. **sea salt** salt produced by evaporating sea water. **Sea Scout** a member of the maritime branch of the Scout Association. **sea serpent** (or **snake**) **1** a snake of the family Hydrophidae, living in the sea. **2** an enormous legendary serpent-like sea monster. **sea shell** the shell of a salt-water mollusc. **sea snail 1** a small slimy fish of the family Liparididae, with a ventral sucker. **2** any spiral-shelled mollusc, e.g. a whelk. **sea trout** = *salmon trout*. **sea urchin** a small marine echinoderm of the class Echinoidea, with a spherical or flattened spiny shell. **sea wall** a wall or embankment erected to prevent encroachment by the sea. **sea water** water in or taken from the sea. [OE sæ f. Gmc]

seabed /ˈsiːbed/ *n.* the ground under the sea; the ocean floor.

seaboard /ˈsiːbɔːd/ *n.* **1** the seashore or coastal region. **2** the line of a coast.

seaborne /ˈsiːbɔːn/ *adj.* transported by sea.

seacock /ˈsiːkɒk/ *n.* a valve below a ship's water-line for letting water in or out.

seafarer /ˈsiːˌfeərə(r)/ *n.* **1** a sailor. **2** a traveller by sea.

seafaring /ˈsiːˌfeərɪŋ/ *adj. & n.* travelling by sea, esp. regularly.

seafood /ˈsiːfuːd/ *n.* edible sea fish or shellfish.

seagoing /ˈsiːˌɡəʊɪŋ/ *adj.* **1** (of ships) fit for crossing the sea. **2** (of a person) seafaring.

seagull /ˈsiːɡʌl/ *n.* = GULL[1].

seakale /ˈsiːkeɪl/ *n.* a cruciferous maritime plant, *Crambe maritima*, having coarsely-toothed leaves and used as a vegetable. □ **seakale beet** = CHARD.

seal[1] *n. & v.* —*n.* **1** a piece of wax, lead, paper, etc., with a stamped design, attached to a document as a guarantee of authenticity. **2** a similar material attached to a receptacle, envelope, etc., affording security by having to be broken to allow access to the contents. **3** an engraved piece of metal, gemstone, etc., for stamping a design on a seal. **4 a** a substance or device used to close an aperture or act as a fastening. **b** an amount of water standing in the trap of a drain to prevent foul air from rising. **5** an act or gesture or event regarded as a confirmation or guarantee. **6** a significant or prophetic mark (*has the seal of death in his face*). **7** a decorative adhesive stamp. —*v.tr.* **1** close securely or hermetically. **2** stamp or fasten with a seal. **3** fix a seal to. **4** certify as correct with a seal or stamp. **5** (often foll. by *up*) confine or fasten securely. **6** settle or decide (*their fate is sealed*). **7** (foll. by *off*) put barriers round (an area) to prevent entry and exit, esp. as a security measure. **8** apply a non-porous coating to (a surface) to make it impervious. □ **one's lips are sealed** one is obliged to keep a secret. **sealed-beam** (*attrib.*) designating a vehicle headlamp with a sealed unit consisting of the light source, reflector, and lens. **sealed orders** orders for procedure not to be opened before a specified time. **sealing-wax** a mixture of shellac and rosin with turpentine and pigment, softened by heating and used to make seals. **seal ring** a finger ring with a seal. **seals of office** (in the UK) those held during tenure esp. by the Lord Chancellor or a Secretary of State. **set one's seal to** (or **on**) authorize or confirm. □ **sealable** *adj.* [ME f. AF seal, OF seel f. L sigillum dimin. of signum SIGN]

seal[2] *n. & v.* —*n.* any fish-eating amphibious sea mammal of the family Phocidae or Otariidae, with flippers and webbed feet. —*v.intr.* hunt for seals. [OE seolh seol- f. Gmc]

sealant /ˈsiːlənt/ *n.* material for sealing, esp. to make something airtight or watertight.

sealer /ˈsiːlə(r)/ *n.* a ship or person engaged in hunting seals.

sealskin /ˈsiːlskɪn/ *n.* **1** the skin or prepared fur of a seal. **2** (often *attrib.*) a garment made from this.

Sealyham /ˈsiːlɪəm/ *n.* (in full **Sealyham terrier**) **1** a terrier of a wire-haired short-legged breed. **2** this breed. [*Sealyham* in S. Wales]

seam *n. & v.* —*n.* **1** a line where two edges join, esp. of two pieces of cloth etc. turned back and stitched together, or of boards fitted edge to edge. **2** a fissure between parallel edges. **3** a wrinkle or scar. **4** a stratum of coal etc. —*v.tr.* **1** join with a seam. **2** (esp. as **seamed** *adj.*) mark or score with or as with a seam. □ **seam bowler** Cricket a bowler who makes the ball deviate by bouncing off its seam. □ **seamer** *n.* **seamless** *adj.* [OE sēam f. Gmc]

seaman /ˈsiːmən/ *n.* (pl. **-men**) **1** a sailor, esp. one below the rank of officer. **2** a person regarded in terms of skill in navigation (*a poor seaman*). □ **seamanlike** *adj.* **seamanly** *adj.* [OE sǣman (as SEA, MAN)]

seamanship /ˈsiːmənʃɪp/ *n.* skill in managing a ship or boat.

seamstress /ˈsemstrɪs/ *n.* (also **sempstress**) a woman who sews, esp. professionally; a needlewoman. [OE *sēamestre* fem. f. *sēamere* tailor, formed as SEAM + -STER + -ESS]

seamy /ˈsiːmɪ/ *adj.* (**seamier, seamiest**) **1** marked with or showing seams. **2** unpleasant, disreputable (esp. *the seamy side*). □ **seaminess** *n.*

seance /ˈseɪɑ̃s/ *n.* (also *séance*) a meeting at which spiritualists attempt to make contact with the dead. [F *séance* f. OF *seoir* f. L *sedēre* sit]

seaplane /ˈsiːpleɪn/ *n.* an aircraft designed to take off from and land and float on water.

seaport /ˈsiːpɔːt/ *n.* a town with a harbour for seagoing ships.

sear *v. & adj.* —*v.tr.* **1 a** scorch, esp. with a hot iron; cauterize, brand. **b** (as **searing** *adj.*) scorching, burning (*searing pain*). **2** cause pain or great anguish to. **3** brown (meat) quickly at a high temperature so that it will retain its juices in cooking. **4** make (one's conscience, feelings, etc.) callous. —*adj.* (also **sere**) *literary* (esp. of a plant etc.) withered, dried up. [OE *sēar* (adj.), *sēarian* (v.), f. Gmc]

search /sɜːtʃ/ *v. & n.* —*v.* **1** *tr.* look through or go over thoroughly to find something. **2** *tr.* examine or feel over (a person) to find anything concealed. **3** *tr.* **a** probe or penetrate into. **b** examine or question (one's mind, conscience, etc.) thoroughly. **4** *intr.* (often foll. by *for*) make a search or investigation. **5** *intr.* (as **searching** *adj.*) (of an examination) thorough; leaving no loopholes. **6** *tr.* (foll. by *out*) look probingly for; seek out. —*n.* **1** an act of searching. **2** an investigation. □ **in search of** trying to find. **search me!** *colloq.* I do not know. **search-party** a group of people organized to look for a lost person or thing. **search warrant** an official authorization to enter and search a building. □ **searchable** *adj.* **searcher** *n.* **searchingly** *adv.* [ME f. AF *sercher*, OF *cerchier* f. LL *circare* go round (as CIRCUS)]

searchlight /ˈsɜːtʃlaɪt/ *n.* **1** a powerful outdoor electric light with a concentrated beam that can be turned in any direction. **2** the light or beam from this.

seascape /ˈsiːskeɪp/ *n.* a picture or view of the sea.

seashore /ˈsiːʃɔː(r)/ *n.* land close to or bordering on the sea.

seasick /ˈsiːsɪk/ *adj.* suffering from sickness or nausea from the motion of a ship at sea. □ **seasickness** *n.*

seaside /ˈsiːsaɪd/ *n.* the sea-coast, esp. as a holiday resort.

season /ˈsiːz(ə)n/ *n. & v.* —*n.* **1** each of the four divisions of the year (spring, summer, autumn, and winter) associated with a type of weather and a stage of vegetation. **2** a time of year characterized by climatic or other features (*the dry season*). **3 a** the time of year when a plant is mature or flowering etc. **b** the time of year when an animal breeds or is hunted. **4** a proper or suitable time. **5** a time when something is plentiful or active or in vogue. **6** (usu. prec. by *the*) = high season. **7** the time of year regularly devoted to an activity (*the football season*). **8** the time of year dedicated to social life generally (*went up to London for the season*). **9** a period of indefinite or varying length. **10** *Brit. colloq.* = season ticket. —*v.* **1** *tr.* flavour (food) with salt, herbs, etc. **2** *tr.* enhance with wit, excitement, etc. **3** *tr.* temper or moderate. **4** *tr. & intr.* **a** make or become suitable or in the desired condition, esp. by exposure to the air or weather; mature. **b** make or become experienced or accustomed (*seasoned soldiers*). □ **in season 1** (of foodstuff) available in plenty and in good condition. **2** (of an animal) on heat. **3** timely. **season ticket** a ticket entitling the holder to any number of journeys, admittances, etc., in a given period. □ **seasoner** *n.* [ME f. OF *seson* f. L *satio -onis* (in Rmc sense 'seed-time') f. *serere* sat-sow]

seasonable /ˈsiːzənəb(ə)l/ *adj.* **1** suitable to or usual in the season. **2** opportune. **3** meeting the needs of the occasion. □ **seasonableness** *n.* **seasonably** *adv.*

seasonal /ˈsiːzən(ə)l/ *adj.* of, depending on, or varying with the season. □ **seasonal affective disorder** a depressive state associated with late autumn and winter and thought to be caused by a lack of light. □ **seasonality** /-ˈnælɪtɪ/ *n.* **seasonally** *adv.*

seasoning /ˈsiːzənɪŋ/ *n.* condiments added to food.

seat *n. & v.* —*n.* **1** a thing made or used for sitting on; a chair, stool, saddle, etc. **2** the buttocks. **3** the part of the trousers etc. covering the buttocks. **4** the part of a chair etc. on which the sitter's weight directly rests. **5** a place for one person in a theatre, vehicle, etc. **6** the occupation of a seat. **7** esp. *Brit.* **a** the right to occupy a seat, esp. as a Member of the House of Commons. **b** a member's constituency. **8** the part of a machine that supports or guides another part. **9** a site or location of something specified (*a seat of learning; the seat of the emotions*). **10** a country mansion, esp. with large grounds. **11** the manner of sitting on a horse etc. —*v.tr.* **1** cause to sit. **2 a** provide sitting accommodation for (*the cinema seats 500*). **b** provide with seats. **3** (as **seated** *adj.*) sitting. **4** put or fit in position. □ **be seated** sit down. **by the seat of one's pants** *colloq.* by instinct rather than logic or knowledge. **seat-belt** a belt securing a person in the seat of a car or aircraft. **take a** (or **one's**) **seat** sit down. □ **seatless** *adj.* [ME f. ON *sæti* (= OE *gesete* f. Gmc)]

seating /ˈsiːtɪŋ/ *n.* **1** seats collectively. **2** sitting accommodation.

seaward /ˈsiːwəd/ *adv., adj., & n.* —*adv.* (also **seawards**) towards the sea. —*adj.* going or facing towards the sea. —*n.* such a direction or position.

seaway /ˈsiːweɪ/ *n.* **1** an inland waterway open to seagoing ships. **2** a ship's progress. **3** a ship's path across the sea.

seaweed /ˈsiːwiːd/ *n.* any of various algae growing in the sea or on the rocks on a shore.

seaworthy /ˈsiːˌwɜːðɪ/ *adj.* (esp. of a ship) fit to put to sea. □ **seaworthiness** *n.*

sebaceous /sɪˈbeɪʃəs/ *adj.* fatty; of or relating to tallow or fat. □ **sebaceous gland** (or **follicle** or **duct**) a gland etc. secreting or conveying oily matter to lubricate the skin and hair. [L *sebaceus* f. *sebum* tallow]

sebum /ˈsiːbəm/ *n.* the oily secretion of the sebaceous glands. [mod.L f. L *sebum* grease]

Sec. *abbr.* secretary.

sec /sek/ *adj.* (of wine) dry. [F f. L *siccus*]

sec /sek/ *n. colloq.* (in phrases) a second (of time). [abbr.]

sec. *abbr.* second(s).

secateurs /ˌsekəˈtɜːz/ *n.pl.* esp. *Brit.* a pair of pruning clippers for use with one hand. [F *sécateur* cutter, irreg. f. L *secare* cut]

secede /sɪˈsiːd/ *v.intr.* (usu. foll. by *from*) withdraw formally from membership of a political federation or a religious body. □ **seceder** *n*. [L *secedere secess-* (as SE-, *cedere* go)]

secession /sɪˈseʃ(ə)n/ *n*. the act or an instance of seceding. □ **secessional** *adj.* **secessionism** *n*. **secessionist** *n*. [F *sécession* or L *secessio* (as SECEDE)]

seclude /sɪˈkluːd/ *v.tr.* (also *refl.*) **1** keep (a person or place) retired or away from company. **2** (esp. as **secluded** *adj.*) hide or screen from view. [ME f. L *secludere seclus-* (as SE-, *claudere* shut)]

seclusion /sɪˈkluːʒ(ə)n/ *n*. **1** a secluded state; retirement, privacy. **2** a secluded place. □ **seclusionist** *n*. **seclusive** /-sɪv/ *adj.* [med.L *seclusio* (as SECLUDE)]

second[1] /ˈsekənd/ *n., adj., & v.* —*n.* **1** the position in a sequence corresponding to that of the number 2 in the sequence 1–2. **2** something occupying this position. **3** the second person etc. in a race or competition. **4** = *second gear.* **5** another person or thing in addition to one previously mentioned or considered (*the policeman was then joined by a second*). **6** (in *pl.*) goods of a second or inferior quality. **7** (in *pl.*) *colloq.* **a** a second helping of food at a meal. **b** the second course of a meal. **8** an attendant assisting a combatant in a duel, boxing-match, etc. **9 a** a place in the second class of an examination. **b** a person having this. —*adj.* **1** that is the second; next after first. **2** additional, further; other besides one previously mentioned or considered (*ate a second cake*). **3** subordinate in position or importance etc.; inferior. **4** *Mus.* performing a lower or subordinate part (*second violins*). **5** such as to be comparable to; closely reminiscent of (*a second Callas*). —*v.tr.* **1** supplement, support; back up. **2** formally support or endorse (a nomination or resolution etc., or its proposer). □ **at second hand** by hearsay, not direct observation etc. **in the second place** as a second consideration etc. **second-best** *adj.* next after best. —*n*. a less adequate or desirable alternative. **second chamber** the upper house of a bicameral parliament. **second class** the second-best group or category, esp. of hotel or train accommodation or (in the UK) of postal services. **second-class** *adj.* **1** of or belonging to the second class. **2** inferior in quality, status, etc. (*second-class citizens*). —*adv.* by second-class post, train, etc. (*travelled second-class*). **second coming** the second advent of Christ on earth. **second-degree** *Med.* denoting burns that cause blistering but not permanent scars. **second floor 1** *Brit.* the floor two levels above the ground floor. **2** *US* the floor above the ground floor. **second gear** the second (and next to lowest) in a sequence of gears. **second-generation** denoting the offspring of a first generation, esp. of immigrants. **second-guess** *colloq.* **1** anticipate or predict by guesswork. **2** judge or criticize with hindsight. **second in command** the officer next in rank to the commanding or chief officer. **second lieutenant** an army officer next below lieutenant or *US* first lieutenant. **second name** a surname. **second nature** (often foll. by *to*) an acquired tendency that has become instinctive (*is second*

nature *to him*). **second officer** an assistant mate on a merchant ship. **second-rate** of mediocre quality; inferior. **second sight** the supposed power of being able to perceive future or distant events. **second string** an alternative course of action, means of livelihood, etc., invoked if the main one is unsuccessful. **second thoughts** a new opinion or resolution reached after further consideration. **second to none** surpassed by no other. **second wind 1** recovery of the power of normal breathing during exercise after initial breathlessness. **2** renewed energy to continue an effort. □ **seconder** *n*. (esp. in sense 2 of *v.*). [ME f. OF f. L *secundus* f. *sequi* follow]

second[2] /ˈsekənd/ *n*. **1** a sixtieth of a minute of time or angular distance. **2** the SI unit of time. **3** *colloq.* a very short time (*wait a second*). □ **second-hand** an extra hand in some watches and clocks, recording seconds. [F f. med.L *secunda* (*minuta*) secondary (minute)]

second[3] /sɪˈkɒnd/ *v.tr. Brit.* transfer (a military officer or other official or worker) temporarily to other employment or to another position. □ **secondment** *n*. [F *en second* in the second rank (of officers)]

secondary /ˈsekəndərɪ/ *adj. & n.* —*adj.* **1** coming after or next below what is primary. **2** derived from or depending on or supplementing what is primary. **3** (of education, a school, etc.) for those who have had primary education, usu. from 11 to 18 years. —*n.* (*pl.* **-ies**) a secondary thing. □ **secondary colour** the result of mixing two primary colours. **secondary picketing** the picketing of premises of a firm not otherwise involved in the dispute in question. **secondary sexual characteristics** those distinctive of one sex but not directly related to reproduction. □ **secondarily** *adv.* **secondariness** *n.* [ME f. L *secundarius* (as SECOND[1])]

second-hand /ˌsekəndˈhænd/ *adj. & adv.* —*adj.* /also ˈsek-/ **1 a** (of goods) having had a previous owner; not new. **b** (of a shop etc.) where such goods can be bought. **2** (of information etc.) accepted on another's authority and not from original investigation. —*adv.* **1** on a second-hand basis. **2** at second hand; not directly.

secondly /ˈsekəndlɪ/ *adv.* **1** furthermore; in the second place. **2** as a second item.

secrecy /ˈsiːkrɪsɪ/ *n*. **1** the keeping of secrets as a fact, habit, or faculty. **2** a state in which all information is withheld (*was done in great secrecy*). □ **sworn to secrecy** having promised to keep a secret. [ME f. *secretie* f. obs. *secre* (adj.) or SECRET *adj.*]

secret /ˈsiːkrɪt/ *adj. & n.* —*adj.* **1** kept or meant to be kept private, unknown, or hidden from all or all but a few. **2** acting or operating secretly. **3** fond of, prone to, or able to preserve secrecy. **4** (of a place) hidden, completely secluded. —*n.* **1** a thing kept or meant to be kept secret. **2** a thing known only to a few. **3** a mystery. **4** a valid but not commonly known or recognized method of achieving or maintaining something (*what's their secret?*; *correct breathing is the secret of good health*). □ **in secret** secretly. **in (or in on) the secret** among the number of those who know it. **keep a secret** not reveal it. **secret agent** a spy acting for a country. **secret ballot** a ballot in which votes are cast in secret. **secret police** a police force operating in secret for political purposes. **secret service** a government department concerned with espionage. **secret society** a society whose members are sworn to secrecy about it. □ **secretly** *adv*. [ME f. OF f. L *secretus* (adj.) separate, set apart f. *secernere secret-* (as SE-, *cernere* sift)]

secretaire /ˌsekrɪˈteə(r)/ *n*. an escritoire. [F (as SECRETARY)]

secretariat /ˌsekrəˈteərɪət/ *n*. **1** a permanent administrative office or department, esp. a governmental one. **2** its members or premises. [F *secrétariat* f. med.L *secretariatus* (as SECRETARY)]

secretary /ˈsekrɪtərɪ, ˈsekrətrɪ/ *n*. (*pl*. **-ies**) **1** a person employed by an individual or in an office etc. to assist with correspondence, keep records, make appointments, etc. **2** an official appointed by a society etc. to conduct its correspondence, keep its records, etc. **3** (in the UK) the principal assistant of a government minister, ambassador, etc. □ **secretary bird** a long-legged snake-eating African bird, *Sagittarius serpentarius*. **Secretary-General** the principal administrator of an organization. **Secretary of State 1** (in the UK) the head of a major government department. **2** (in the US) the chief government official responsible for foreign affairs. □ **secretarial** /-ˈteərɪəl/ *adj*. **secretaryship** *n*. [ME f. LL *secretarius* (as SECRET)]

secrete[1] /sɪˈkriːt/ *v.tr. Biol*. (of a cell, organ, etc.) produce by secretion. □ **secretor** *n*. **secretory** *adj*. [back-form. f. SECRETION]

secrete[2] /sɪˈkriːt/ *v.tr*. conceal; put into hiding. [obs. *secret* (v.) f. SECRET]

secretion /sɪˈkriːʃ(ə)n/ *n*. **1** *Biol*. **a** a process by which substances are produced and discharged from a cell for a function in the organism or for excretion. **b** the secreted substance. **2** the act or an instance of concealing (*the secretion of stolen goods*). [F *sécrétion* or L *secretio* separation (as SECRET)]

secretive /ˈsiːkrɪtɪv/ *adj*. inclined to make or keep secrets; uncommunicative. □ **secretively** *adv*. **secretiveness** *n*. [back-form. f. *secretiveness* after F *secrétivité* (as SECRET)]

sect *n*. **1 a** a body of people subscribing to religious doctrines usu. different from those of an established Church from which they have separated. **b** a religious denomination. **2** the followers of a particular philosopher or philosophy, or school of thought in politics etc. [ME f. OF *secte* or L *secta* f. the stem of *sequi secut-* follow]

sectarian /sekˈteərɪən/ *adj*. & *n*. —*adj*. **1** of or concerning a sect. **2** bigoted or narrow-minded in following the doctrines of one's sect. —*n*. **1** a member of a sect. **2** a bigot. □ **sectarianism** *n*. **sectarianize** *v.tr*. (also **-ise**). [med. L *sectarius* adherent (as SECT)]

section /ˈsekʃ(ə)n/ *n*. & *v*. —*n*. **1** a part cut off or separated from something. **2** each of the parts into which a thing is divided (actually or conceptually) or divisible or out of which a structure can be fitted together. **3** a distinct group or subdivision of a larger body of people (*the wind section of an orchestra*). **4** a subdivision of a book, document, statute, etc. **5** *US* **a** an area of land. **b** one square mile of land. **c** a particular district of a town (*residential section*). **6** a subdivision of an army platoon. **7** esp. *Surgery* a separation by cutting. **8** *Biol*. a thin slice of tissue etc., cut off for microscopic examination.

9 a the cutting of a solid by or along a plane. **b** the resulting figure or the area of this. **10** a representation of the internal structure of something as if cut across along a vertical or horizontal plane. —*v.tr*. **1** arrange in or divide into sections. **2** *Brit*. cause (a person) to be compulsorily committed to a psychiatric hospital in accordance with a section of a mental health act. **3** *Biol*. cut into thin slices for microscopic examination. □ **section-mark** the sign (§) used as a reference mark to indicate the start of a section of a book etc. [F *section* or L *sectio* f. *secare sect-* cut]

sectional /ˈsekʃən(ə)l/ *adj*. **1 a** relating to a section, esp. of a community. **b** partisan. **2** made in sections. **3** local rather than general. □ **sectionalism** *n*. **sectionalist** *n*. & *adj*. **sectionalize** *v.tr*. (also **-ise**). **sectionally** *adv*.

sector /ˈsektə(r)/ *n*. **1** a distinct part or branch of an enterprise, or of society, the economy, etc. **2** *Mil*. a subdivision of an area for military operations, controlled by one commander or headquarters. **3** the plane figure enclosed by two radii of a circle, ellipse, etc., and the arc between them. □ **sectoral** *adj*. [LL, techn. use of L *sector* cutter (as SECTION)]

secular /ˈsekjʊlə(r)/ *adj*. & *n*. —*adj*. **1** concerned with the affairs of this world; not spiritual or sacred. **2** (of education etc.) not concerned with religion or religious belief. **3 a** not ecclesiastical or monastic. **b** (of clergy) not bound by a religious rule. **4** occurring once in an age or century. □ **secularism** *n*. **secularist** *n*. **secularity** /-ˈlærɪtɪ/ *n*. **secularize** *v.tr*. (also **-ise**). **secularization** /-ˈzeɪʃ(ə)n/ *n*. **secularly** *adv*. [ME (in senses 1–3 f. OF *seculer*) f. L *saecularis* f. *saeculum* generation, age]

secure /sɪˈkjʊə(r)/ *adj*. & *v*. —*adj*. **1** untroubled by danger or fear. **2** safe against attack: impregnable. **3** reliable; certain not to fail (*the plan is secure*). **4** fixed or fastened so as not to give way or get loose or be lost (*made the door secure*). **5 a** (foll. by *of*) certain to achieve (*secure of victory*). **b** (foll. by *against*, *from*) safe, protected (*secure against attack*). —*v.tr*. **1** make secure or safe; fortify. **2** fasten, close, or confine securely. **3** succeed in obtaining or achieving (*have secured front seats*). **4** guarantee against loss (*a loan secured by property*). □ **securable** *adj*. **securely** *adv*. **securement** *n*. [L *securus* (as SE-, *cura* care)]

security /sɪˈkjʊərɪtɪ/ *n*. (*pl*. **-ies**) **1** a secure condition or feeling. **2** a thing that guards or guarantees. **3 a** the safety of a State, company, etc., against espionage, theft, or other danger. **b** an organization for ensuring this. **4** a thing deposited or pledged as a guarantee of the fulfilment of an undertaking or the payment of a loan, to be forfeited in case of default. **5** (often in *pl*.) a certificate attesting credit or the ownership of stock, bonds, etc. □ **on security of** using as a guarantee. **security blanket 1** an official sanction on information in the interest of security. **2** a blanket or other familiar object given as a comfort to a child. **Security Council** a permanent body of the United Nations seeking to maintain peace and security. **security guard** a person employed to protect the security of buildings, vehicles, etc. **security risk** a person whose presence may threaten security. [ME f. OF *securité* or L *securitas* (as SECURE)]

sedan /sɪˈdæn/ n. **1** (in full **sedan chair**) an enclosed chair for conveying one person, carried between horizontal poles by two porters, common in the 17th–18th c. **2** US an enclosed motor car for four or more people. [perh. alt. f. It. dial., ult. f. L *sella* saddle f. *sedēre* sit]

sedate[1] /sɪˈdeɪt/ adj. tranquil and dignified; equable, serious. □ **sedately** adv. **sedateness** n. [L *sedatus* past part. of *sedare* settle f. *sedēre* sit]

sedate[2] /sɪˈdeɪt/ v.tr. put under sedation. [back-form. f. SEDATION]

sedation /sɪˈdeɪʃ(ə)n/ n. a state of rest or sleep esp. produced by a sedative drug. [F *sédation* or L *sedatio* (as SEDATE[1])]

sedative /ˈsedətɪv/ n. & adj. —n. a drug, influence, etc., that tends to calm or soothe. —adj. calming, soothing; inducing sleep. [ME f. OF *sedatif* or med.L *sedativus* (as SEDATE[1])]

sedentary /ˈsedəntərɪ/ adj. **1** sitting (a *sedentary posture*). **2** (of work etc.) characterized by much sitting and little physical exercise. **3** (of a person) spending much time seated. □ **sedentarily** adv. **sedentariness** n. [F *sédentaire* or L *sedentarius* f. *sedēre* sit]

sedge n. **1** any grasslike plant of the genus *Carex* with triangular stems, usu. growing in wet areas. **2** an expanse of this plant. □ **sedgy** adj. [OE *secg* f. Gmc]

sediment /ˈsedɪmənt/ n. **1** matter that settles to the bottom of a liquid; dregs. **2** Geol. matter that is carried by water or wind and deposited on the surface of the land, and may in time become consolidated into rock. □ **sedimentary** /-ˈmentərɪ/ adj. **sedimentation** /-ˈteɪʃ(ə)n/ n. [F *sédiment* or L *sedimentum* f. *sedēre* sit]

sedition /sɪˈdɪʃ(ə)n/ n. **1** conduct or speech inciting to rebellion or a breach of public order. **2** agitation against the authority of a State. □ **seditious** adj. **seditiously** adv. [ME f. OF *sedition* or L *seditio* f. sed- = SE- + *ire* it- go]

seduce /sɪˈdjuːs/ v.tr. **1** tempt or entice into sexual activity or into wrongdoing. **2** coax or lead astray; tempt (*seduced by the smell of coffee*). □ **seducer** n. **seducible** adj. [L *seducere seduct-* (as SE-, *ducere* lead)]

seduction /sɪˈdʌkʃ(ə)n/ n. **1** the act or an instance of seducing; the process of being seduced. **2** something that tempts or allures. [F *séduction* or L *seductio* (as SEDUCE)]

seductive /sɪˈdʌktɪv/ adj. tending to seduce; alluring, enticing. □ **seductively** adv. **seductiveness** n. [SEDUCTION after *inductive* etc.]

seductress /sɪˈdʌktrɪs/ n. a female seducer. [obs. *seductor* male seducer (as SEDUCE)]

sedulous /ˈsedjʊləs/ adj. **1** persevering, diligent, assiduous. **2** (of an action etc.) deliberately and consciously continued; painstaking. □ **sedulity** /sɪˈdjuːlɪtɪ/ n. **sedulously** adv. **sedulousness** n. [L *sedulus* zealous]

see[1] v. (*past* **saw**; *past part.* **seen**) **1** tr. discern by use of the eyes; observe; look at (*can you see that spider?*; *saw him fall over*). **2** intr. have or use the power of discerning objects with the eyes (*sees best at night*). **3** tr. discern mentally; understand (*I see what you mean*; *could not see the joke*). **4** tr. watch; be a spectator of (a film, game, etc.). **5** tr. ascertain or establish by inquiry or research or reflection (*I will see if the door is open*). **6** tr. consider; deduce from observation (*I see that you are a brave man*). **7** tr. contemplate; foresee mentally (*we saw that no good would come of it*; *can*

see *myself doing this job indefinitely*). **8** tr. look at for information (usu. in *imper.* as a direction in or to a book: *see page 15*). **9** tr. meet or be near and recognize (*I saw your mother in town*). **10** tr. **a** meet socially (*sees her sister most weeks*). **b** meet regularly as a boyfriend or girlfriend; court (*is still seeing that tall man*). **11** tr. give an interview to (*the doctor will see you now*). **12** tr. visit to consult (*went to see the doctor*). **13** tr. find out or learn, esp. from a visual source (*I see the match has been cancelled*). **14** intr. reflect; consider further; wait until one knows more (*we shall have to see*). **15** tr. interpret or have an opinion of (*I see things differently now*). **16** tr. experience; have presented to one's attention (*I never thought I would see this day*). **17** tr. recognize as acceptable; foresee (*do you see your daughter marrying this man?*). **18** tr. observe without interfering (*stood by and saw them squander my money*). **19** tr. find attractive (*can't think what she sees in him*). **20** intr. (usu. foll. by *to*, or *that* + infin.) make provision for; ensure; attend to (*shall see to your request immediately*; *see that he gets home safely*) (cf. *see to it*). **21** tr. escort or conduct (to a place etc.) (*saw them home*). **22** tr. be a witness of (an event etc.) (*see the New Year in*). **23** tr. supervise (an action etc.) (*will stay and see the doors locked*). **24** tr. **a** (in gambling, esp. poker) equal (a bet). **b** equal the bet of (a player), esp. to see the player's cards. □ **as far as I can see** to the best of my understanding or belief. **as I see it** in my opinion. **do you see?** do you understand? **has seen better days** has declined from former prosperity, good condition, etc. **I see** I understand (referring to an explanation etc.). **let me see** an appeal for time to think before speaking etc. **see about** attend to. **see after 1** take care of. **2** = *see about*. **see the back of** colloq. be rid of (an unwanted person or thing). **see a person damned first** colloq. refuse categorically and with hostility to do what a person wants. **see into** investigate. **see life** gain experience of the world, often by enjoying oneself. **see the light 1** realize one's mistakes etc. **2** suddenly see the way to proceed. **3** undergo religious conversion. **see the light of day** (usu. with *neg.*) come into existence. **see off 1** be present at the departure of (a person) (*saw them off at Heathrow*). **2** colloq. ward off, get the better of (*managed to see off an investigation into their working methods*). **see out 1** accompany out of a building etc. **2** finish (a project etc.) completely. **3** remain awake, alive, etc., until the end of (a period). **4** last longer than; outlive. **see over** inspect; tour and examine. **see red** become suddenly enraged. **see a person right** make sure that a person is rewarded, safe, etc. **see stars** colloq. see lights before one's eyes as a result of a blow on the head. **see things** have hallucinations or false imaginings. **see through 1** not be deceived by; detect the true nature of. **2** penetrate visually. **see-through** adj. (esp. of clothing) translucent. **see a person through** support a person during a difficult time. **see a thing through** persist with it until it is completed. **see to it** (foll. by *that* + clause) ensure (*see to it that I am not disturbed*) (cf. sense 20 of v.). **see one's way clear to** feel able or entitled to. **see you** (or **see you later**) colloq. an expression on parting. **we shall see 1** let us await the outcome. **2** a formula for declining to act at once. **will see about it** a formula for declining to act at once. **you see 1** you understand. **2** you will understand when I explain. □ **seeable** adj. [OE *sēon* f. Gmc]

see[2] n. **1** the area under the authority of a bishop or archbishop, a diocese (*the see of Norwich*). **2** the office or jurisdiction of a bishop or archbishop. [ME f. AF *se(d)* ult. f. L *sedes* seat f. *sedēre* sit]

seed n. & v. —n. **1 a** a flowering plant's unit of reproduction (esp. in the form of grain) capable of developing into another such plant. **b** seeds collectively, esp. as collected for sowing (*is full of seed*; *to be kept for seed*). **2 a** semen. **b** milt. **3** (foll. by *of*) prime cause, beginning, germ (*seeds of doubt*). **4** archaic offspring, progeny, descendants (*the seed of Abraham*). **5** Sport a seeded player. —v. **1** tr. **a** place seeds in. **b** sprinkle with or as with seed. **2** intr. sow seeds. **3** intr. produce or drop seed. **4** tr. remove seeds from (fruit etc.). **5** tr. place a crystal or crystalline substance in (a solution etc.) to cause crystallization or condensation (esp. in a cloud to produce rain). **6** tr. Sport **a** assign to (a strong competitor in a knockout competition) a position in an ordered list so that strong competitors do not meet each other in early rounds (*is seeded seventh*). **b** arrange (the order of play) in this way. **7** intr. go to seed. □ **go** (or **run**) **to seed 1** cease flowering as seed develops. **2** become degenerate, unkempt, ineffective, etc. **seed-bed 1** a bed of fine soil in which to sow seeds. **2** a place of development. **seed-cake** cake containing whole seeds esp. of caraway as flavouring. **seed-corn 1** good quality corn kept for seed. **2** assets reused for future profit or benefit. **seed-pearl** a very small pearl. **seed-potato** a potato kept for seed. **seed-time** the sowing season. **seed-vessel** a pericarp. □ **seedless** adj. [OE *sǣd* f. Gmc, rel. to sow[1]]

seeder /ˈsiːdə(r)/ n. **1** a person or thing that seeds. **2** a machine for sowing seed, esp. a drill.

seedling /ˈsiːdlɪŋ/ n. a young plant, esp. one raised from seed and not from a cutting etc.

seedsman /ˈsiːdzmən/ n. (pl. **-men**) a dealer in seeds.

seedy /ˈsiːdɪ/ adj. (**seedier, seediest**) **1** full of seed. **2** going to seed. **3** shabby-looking, in worn clothes. **4** colloq. unwell. □ **seedily** adv. **seediness** n.

seeing /ˈsiːɪŋ/ conj. (usu. foll. by *that* + clause) considering that, inasmuch as, because (*seeing that you do not know it yourself*).

seek v. (past and past part. **sought** /sɔːt/) **1 a** tr. make a search or inquiry for. **b** intr. (foll. by *for*, *after*) make a search or inquiry. **2** tr. **a** try or want to find or get. **b** ask for; request (*sought help from him; seeks my aid*). **3** tr. (foll. by *to* + infin.) endeavour or try. **4** tr. make for or resort to (a place or person, for advice, health, etc.) (*sought his bed; sought a fortune-teller; sought the shore*). **5** tr. archaic aim at, attempt. □ **seek out 1** search for and find. **2** single out for companionship, etc. **sought-after** much in demand; generally desired or courted. **to seek** (or **much to seek** or **far to seek**) deficient, lacking, or not yet found (*the reason is not far to seek; an efficient leader is yet to seek*). □ **seeker** n. (also in comb.). [OE *sēcan* f. Gmc]

seem v.intr. **1** give the impression or sensation of being (*seems ridiculous; seems certain to win*). **2** (foll. by *to* + infin.) appear or be perceived or ascertained (*he seems to be breathing; they seem to* have left). □ **can't seem to** colloq. seem unable to. **do not seem to** colloq. somehow do not (*I do not seem to like him*). **it seems** (or **would seem**) (often foll. by *that* + clause) it appears to be true or the fact (in a hesitant, guarded, or ironical statement). [ME f. ON *sœma* honour f. *sœmr* fitting]

seeming[1] /ˈsiːmɪŋ/ adj. **1** apparent but perhaps not real (*with seeming sincerity*). **2** apparent only; ostensible (*the seeming and the real; seeming-virtuous*). □ **seemingly** adv.

seeming[2] /ˈsiːmɪŋ/ n. literary **1** appearance, aspect. **2** deceptive appearance.

seemly /ˈsiːmlɪ/ adj. (**seemlier, seemliest**) conforming to propriety or good taste; decorous, suitable. □ **seemliness** n. [ME f. ON *sœmiligr* (as SEEM)]

seen past part. of SEE[1].

seep v.intr. ooze out; percolate slowly. [perh. dial. form of OE *sipian* to soak]

seepage /ˈsiːpɪdʒ/ n. **1** the act of seeping. **2** the quantity that seeps out.

seer /ˈsiːə(r), sɪə(r)/ n. **1** a person who sees. **2** a prophet; a person who sees visions. [ME f. SEE[1]]

seersucker /ˈsɪəsʌkə(r)/ n. material of linen, cotton, etc., with a puckered surface. [Pers. *šir o šakar*, lit. 'milk and sugar']

see-saw /ˈsiːsɔː/ n., v., adj., & adv. —n. **1 a** a device consisting of a long plank balanced on a central support for children to sit on at each end and move up and down by pushing the ground with their feet. **b** a game played on this. **2** an up-and-down or to-and-fro motion. **3** a contest in which the advantage repeatedly changes from one side to the other. —v.intr. **1** play on a see-saw. **2** move up and down as on a see-saw. **3** vacillate in policy, emotion, etc. —adj. & adv. with up-and-down or backward-and-forward motion (*see-saw motion*). [redupl. of SAW[1]]

seethe /siːð/ v. **1** intr. boil, bubble over. **2** intr. be very agitated, esp. with anger (*seething with discontent; I was seething inwardly*). □ **seethingly** adv. [OE *sēothan* f. Gmc]

segment /ˈsɛgmənt/ n. & v. —n. **1** each of several parts into which a thing is or can be divided or marked off. **2** Geom. a part of a figure cut off by a line or plane intersecting it, esp.: **a** the part of a circle enclosed between an arc and a chord. **b** the part of a line included between two points. **c** the part of a sphere cut off by any plane not passing through the centre. **3** Zool. each of the longitudinal sections of the body of certain animals (e.g. worms). —v. /usu. -ˈment/ intr. & tr. divide into segments. □ **segmental** /-ˈment(ə)l/ adj. **segmentalize** /-ˈmentəˌlaɪz/ v.tr. (also **-ise**). **segmentalization** /-ˌmentəlaɪˈzeɪʃ(ə)n/ n. **segmentally** /-ˈmentəlɪ/ adv. **segmentary** adj. **segmentation** /-ˈteɪʃ(ə)n/ n. [L *segmentum* f. *secare* cut]

segregate /ˈsɛgrɪgeɪt/ v. **1** tr. put apart from the rest; isolate. **2** tr. enforce racial segregation on (persons) or in (a community etc.). **3** intr. separate from a mass and collect together. □ **segregable** /-gəb(ə)l/ adj. **segregative** adj. [L *segregare* (as SE-, *grex gregis* flock)]

segregation /ˌsɛgrɪˈgeɪʃ(ə)n/ n. **1** enforced separation of racial groups in a community etc. **2** the act or an instance of segregating; the state of being segregated. □ **segregational**

adj. **segregationist** *n.* & *adj.* [LL *segregatio* (as SEGREGATE)]

segue /ˈsegweɪ/ *v.* & *n.* esp. *Mus.* —*v.intr.* (**segues, segued, seguing**) (usu. foll. by *into*) go on without a pause. —*n.* an uninterrupted transition from one song or melody to another. [It., = follows]

seigneur /seɪˈnjɜː(r)/ *n.* (also **seignior** /ˈseɪnjə(r)/) a feudal lord; the lord of a manor. □ **seigneurial** *adj.* **seigniorial** /-ˈnjɔːrɪəl/ *adj.* [ME f. OF *seigneur, seignor* f. L SENIOR]

seine /seɪn/ *n.* & *v.* —*n.* (also **seine-net**) a fishing-net for encircling fish, with floats at the top and weights at the bottom edge, and usu. hauled ashore. —*v.intr.* & *tr.* fish or catch with a seine. [ME f. OF *saîne*, & OE *segne* f. WG f. L *sagena* f. Gk *sagēnē*]

seise var. of SEIZE 9.

seismic /ˈsaɪzmɪk/ *adj.* of or relating to an earthquake or earthquakes. □ **seismal** *adj.* **seismical** *adj.* **seismically** *adv.* [Gk *seismos* earthquake f. *seiō* shake]

seismo- /ˈsaɪzməʊ/ *comb. form* earthquake. [Gk *seismos*]

seismogram /ˈsaɪzməˌgræm/ *n.* a record given by a seismograph.

seismograph /ˈsaɪzməˌɡrɑːf/ *n.* an instrument that records the force, direction, etc., of earthquakes. □ **seismographic** /-ˈgræfɪk/ *adj.* **seismographical** /-ˈgræfɪk(ə)l/ *adj.*

seismology /saɪzˈmɒlədʒɪ/ *n.* the scientific study and recording of earthquakes and related phenomena. □ **seismological** /-məˈlɒdʒɪk(ə)l/ *adj.* **seismologically** /-məˈlɒdʒɪkəlɪ/ *adv.* **seismologist** *n.*

seize /siːz/ *v.* **1** *tr.* take hold of forcibly or suddenly. **2** *tr.* take possession of forcibly (*seized the fortress; seized power*). **3** *tr.* take possession of (contraband goods, documents, etc.) by warrant or legal right, confiscate, impound. **4** *tr.* affect suddenly (*panic seized us; was seized by apoplexy; was seized with remorse*). **5** *tr.* take advantage of (an opportunity). **6** *tr.* comprehend quickly or clearly. **7** *intr.* (usu. foll. by *on, upon*) **a** take hold forcibly or suddenly. **b** take advantage eagerly (*seized on a pretext*). **8** *intr.* (usu. foll. by *up*) (of a moving part in a machine) become stuck or jammed from undue heat, friction, etc. **9** *tr.* (also **seise**) (usu. foll. by *of*) *Law* put in possession of. **10** *tr. Naut.* fasten or attach by binding with turns of yarn etc. □ **seized** (or **seised**) **of 1** possessing legally. **2** aware or informed of. □ **seizable** *adj.* **seizer** *n.* [ME f. OF *seizir, saisir* give possession of land by freehold f. Frank. f. L *sacire* f. Gmc]

seizure /ˈsiːʒə(r)/ *n.* **1** the act or an instance of seizing; the state of being seized. **2** a sudden attack of apoplexy etc., a stroke.

seldom /ˈseldəm/ *adv.* & *adj.* —*adv.* rarely, not often. —*adj.* rare, uncommon. [OE *seldan* f. Gmc]

select /sɪˈlekt/ *v.* & *adj.* —*v.tr.* choose, esp. as the best or most suitable. —*adj.* **1** chosen for excellence or suitability; choice. **2** (of a society etc.) exclusive, cautious in admitting members. □ **selectable** *adj.* **selectness** *n.* [L *seligere select-* (as SE-, *legere* choose)]

selectee /sɪlekˈtiː/ *n. US* a conscript.

selection /sɪˈlekʃ(ə)n/ *n.* **1** the act or an instance of selecting; the state of being selected. **2** a selected person or thing. **3** things from which a choice may be made. **4** *Biol.* the process in which environmental and genetic influences determine which types of organism thrive better than others, regarded as a factor in evolution. □ **selectional** *adj.* **selectionally** *adv.* [L *selectio* (as SELECT)]

selective /sɪˈlektɪv/ *adj.* using or characterized by selection. □ **selectively** *adv.* **selectiveness** *n.* **selectivity** /ˌsɪlekˈtɪvɪtɪ, ˌsel-, ˌsiːl-/ *n.*

selector /sɪˈlektə(r)/ *n.* **1** a person who selects, esp. one who selects a representative team in a sport. **2** a device that selects, esp. a device in a vehicle that selects the required gear.

selenium /sɪˈliːnɪəm/ *n. Chem.* a non-metallic element characterized by the variation of its electrical resistivity with intensity of illumination. □ **selenium cell** a piece of this used as a photoelectric device. □ **selenate** /ˈselɪˌneɪt/ *n.* **selenic** /sɪˈliːnɪk/ *adj.* **selenious** *adj.* [mod.L f. Gk *selēnē* moon + -IUM]

seleno- /sɪˈliːnəʊ/ *comb. form* moon. [Gk *selēnē* moon]

self *n.* & *adj.* —*n.* (*pl.* **selves** /selvz/) **1** a person's or thing's own individuality or essence (*showed his true self*). **2** a person or thing as the object of introspection or reflexive action (*the consciousness of self*). **3 a** one's own interests or pleasure (*cares for nothing but self*). **b** concentration on these (*self is a bad guide to happiness*). **4** *Commerce* or *colloq.* myself, yourself, himself, etc. (*cheque drawn to self; ticket admitting self and friend*). **5** used in phrases equivalent to *myself, yourself, himself,* etc. (*his very self; your good selves*). —*adj.* **1** of the same colour as the rest or throughout. **2** (of a flower) of the natural wild colour. **3** (of colour) uniform, the same throughout. □ **one's better self** one's nobler impulses. **one's former** (or **old**) **self** oneself as one formerly was. [OE f. Gmc]

self- /self/ *comb. form* expressing reflexive action: **1** of or directed towards oneself or itself (*self-respect; self-cleaning*). **2** by oneself or itself, esp. without external agency (*self-evident*). **3** on, in, for, or relating to oneself or itself (*self-absorbed; self-confident*).

self-abasement /ˌselfəˈbeɪsmənt/ *n.* the abasement of oneself; self-humiliation; cringing.

self-abhorrence /ˌselfəbˈhɒrəns/ *n.* the abhorrence of oneself; self-hatred.

self-abnegation /ˌselfˌæbnɪˈɡeɪʃ(ə)n/ *n.* the abnegation of oneself, one's interests, needs, etc.; self-sacrifice.

self-absorption /ˌselfəbˈzɔːpʃ(ə)n/ *n.* absorption in oneself. □ **self-absorbed** /-ˈzɔːbd/ *adj.*

self-abuse /ˌselfəˈbjuːs/ *n.* **1** the reviling or abuse of oneself. **2** *archaic* masturbation.

self-accusation /ˌselfˌækjuːˈzeɪʃ(ə)n/ *n.* the accusing of oneself. □ **self-accusatory** /-əˈkjuːzətərɪ/ *adj.*

self-acting /selfˈæktɪŋ/ *adj.* acting without external influence or control; automatic. □ **self-action** /-ˈækʃ(ə)n/ *n.* **self-activity** /-ækˈtɪvɪtɪ/ *n.*

self-addressed /ˌselfəˈdrest/ *adj.* (of an envelope etc.) having one's own address on for return communication.

self-adhesive /ˌselfədˈhiːsɪv/ *adj.* (of an envelope, label, etc.) adhesive, esp. without being moistened.

self-adjusting /ˌselfəˈdʒʌstɪŋ/ *adj.* (of machinery etc.) adjusting itself. □ **self-adjustment** *n.*

self-advancement /ˌselfədˈvɑːnsmənt/ *n.* the advancement of oneself.

self-advertisement /ˌselfədˈvɜːtɪsmənt/ n. the advertising or promotion of oneself. □ **self-advertiser** /-ˈædvəˌtaɪzə(r)/ n.

self-aggrandizement /ˌselfəˈɡrændɪzmənt/ n. the act or process of enriching oneself or making oneself powerful. □ **self-aggrandizing** /-ˈɡrændaɪzɪŋ/ adj.

self-analysis /ˌselfəˈnæləsɪs/ n. Psychol. the analysis of oneself, one's motives, character, etc. □ **self-analysing** /-ˈænəˌlaɪzɪŋ/ adj.

self-appointed /ˌselfəˈpɔɪntɪd/ adj. designated so by oneself, not authorized by another (a self-appointed guardian).

self-assertion /ˌselfəˈsɜːʃ(ə)n/ n. the aggressive promotion of oneself, one's views, etc. □ **self-asserting** adj. **self-assertive** adj. **self-assertiveness** n.

self-assurance /ˌselfəˈʃʊərəns/ n. confidence in one's own abilities etc. □ **self-assured** adj. **self-assuredly** adv.

self-aware /ˌselfəˈweə(r)/ adj. conscious of one's character, feelings, motives, etc. □ **self-awareness** n.

self-betrayal /ˌselfbɪˈtreɪəl/ n. **1** the betrayal of oneself. **2** the inadvertent revelation of one's true thoughts etc.

self-catering /selfˈkeɪtərɪŋ/ adj. (esp. of a holiday or holiday premises) providing rented accommodation with cooking facilities but without food.

self-censorship /selfˈsensəʃɪp/ n. the censoring of oneself.

self-centred /selfˈsentəd/ adj. preoccupied with one's own personality or affairs. □ **self-centredly** adv. **self-centredness** n.

self-certification /self.sɜːtɪfɪˈkeɪʃ(ə)n/ n. the practice by which an employee declares in writing that an absence from work was due to illness.

self-cleaning /selfˈkliːnɪŋ/ adj. (esp. of an oven) cleaning itself when heated etc.

self-closing /selfˈkləʊzɪŋ/ adj. (of a door etc.) closing automatically.

self-cocking /selfˈkɒkɪŋ/ adj. (of a gun) with the hammer raised by the trigger, not by hand.

self-collected /ˌselfkəˈlektɪd/ adj. composed, serene, self-assured.

self-coloured /selfˈkʌləd/ adj. **1 a** having the same colour throughout (buttons and belt are self-coloured). **b** (of material) natural; undyed. **2 a** (of a flower) of uniform colour. **b** having its colour unchanged by cultivation or hybridization.

self-command /ˌselfkəˈmɑːnd/ n. = SELF-CONTROL.

self-conceit /ˌselfkənˈsiːt/ n. = SELF-SATISFACTION. □ **self-conceited** adj.

self-condemnation /self.kɒndemˈneɪʃ(ə)n/ n. **1** the blaming of oneself. **2** the inadvertent revelation of one's own sin, crime, etc. □ **self-condemned** /-kənˈdemd/ adj.

self-confessed /ˌselfkənˈfest/ adj. openly admitting oneself to be (a self-confessed thief).

self-confidence /selfˈkɒnfɪd(ə)ns/ n. = SELF-ASSURANCE. □ **self-confident** adj. **self-confidently** adv.

self-congratulation /ˌselfkənˌɡrætjʊˈleɪʃ(ə)n/ n. = SELF-SATISFACTION. □ **self-congratulatory** /-kənˈɡrætʊlətərɪ/ adj.

self-conscious /selfˈkɒnʃəs/ adj. **1** socially inept through embarrassment or shyness. **2** Philos. having knowledge of one's own existence; self-contemplating. □ **self-consciously** adv. **self-consciousness** n.

self-consistent /ˌselfkənˈsɪst(ə)nt/ adj. (of parts of the same whole etc.) consistent; not conflicting. □ **self-consistency** n.

self-constituted /selfˈkɒnstɪˌtjuːtɪd/ adj. (of a person, group, etc.) assuming a function without authorization or right; self-appointed.

self-contained /ˌselfkənˈteɪnd/ adj. **1** (of a person) uncommunicative; independent. **2** Brit. (esp. of living-accommodation) complete in itself. □ **self-containment** n.

self-contempt /ˌselfkənˈtempt/ n. contempt for oneself. □ **self-contemptuous** adj.

self-content /ˌselfkənˈtent/ n. satisfaction with oneself, one's life, achievements, etc. □ **self-contented** adj.

self-contradiction /self.kɒntrəˈdɪkʃ(ə)n/ n. internal inconsistency. □ **self-contradictory** adj.

self-control /ˌselfkənˈtrəʊl/ n. the power of controlling one's external reactions, emotions, etc. □ **self-controlled** adj.

self-correcting /ˌselfkəˈrektɪŋ/ adj. correcting itself without external help.

self-created /ˌselfkrɪˈeɪtɪd/ adj. created by oneself or itself. □ **self-creation** /-ˈeɪʃ(ə)n/ n.

self-critical /selfˈkrɪtɪk(ə)l/ adj. critical of oneself, one's abilities, etc. □ **self-criticism** /-ˌsɪz(ə)m/ n.

self-deception /ˌselfdɪˈsepʃ(ə)n/ n. deceiving oneself esp. concerning one's true feelings etc. □ **self-deceit** /-dɪˈsiːt/ n. **self-deceiver** /-dɪˈsiːvə(r)/ n. **self-deceiving** /-dɪˈsiːvɪŋ/ adj. **self-deceptive** adj.

self-defeating /ˌselfdɪˈfiːtɪŋ/ adj. (of an attempt, action, etc.) doomed to failure because of internal inconsistencies etc.

self-defence /ˌselfdɪˈfens/ n. **1** an aggressive act, speech, etc., intended as defence (had to hit him in self-defence). **2** (usu. **the noble art of self-defence**) boxing. □ **self-defensive** adj.

self-delusion /ˌselfdɪˈluːʒ(ə)n, -ˈljuːʒ(ə)n/ n. the act or an instance of deluding oneself.

self-denial /ˌselfdɪˈnaɪəl/ n. = SELF-ABNEGATION. □ **self-denying** adj.

self-deprecation /self.deprɪˈkeɪʃ(ə)n/ n. the act of disparaging or belittling oneself. □ **self-deprecating** /-ˈdeprɪˌkeɪtɪŋ/ adj. **self-deprecatingly** /-ˈdeprɪˌkeɪtɪŋlɪ/ adv.

self-despair /ˌselfdɪˈspeə(r)/ n. despair with oneself.

self-destroying /ˌselfdɪˈstrɔɪɪŋ/ adj. destroying oneself or itself.

self-destruct /ˌselfdɪˈstrʌkt/ v. & adj. esp. US —v.intr. (of a spacecraft, bomb, etc.) explode or disintegrate automatically, esp. when pre-set to do so. —attrib.adj. enabling a thing to self-destruct (a self-destruct device).

self-destruction /ˌselfdɪˈstrʌkʃ(ə)n/ n. **1** the process or an act of destroying oneself or itself. **2** esp. US the process or an act of self-destructing. □ **self-destructive** adj. **self-destructively** adv.

self-determination /ˌselfdɪˌtɜːmɪˈneɪʃ(ə)n/ n. **1** a nation's right to determine its own allegiance, government, etc. **2** the ability to act with free will, as opposed to fatalism etc. □ **self-determined** /-ˈtɜː.mɪnd/ *adj.* **self-determining** /-ˈtɜː.mɪnɪŋ/ *adj.*

self-development /ˌselfdɪˈveləpmənt/ *n.* the development of oneself, one's abilities, etc.

self-discipline /selfˈdɪsɪplɪn/ *n.* the act of or ability to apply oneself, control one's feelings, etc.; self-control. □ **self-disciplined** *adj.*

self-discovery /ˌselfdɪˈskʌvəri/ *n.* the process of acquiring insight into oneself, one's character, desires, etc.

self-disgust /ˌselfdɪsˈɡʌst/ *n.* disgust with oneself.

self-doubt /selfˈdaʊt/ *n.* lack of confidence in oneself, one's abilities, etc.

self-drive /selfˈdraɪv/ *adj.* (of a hired vehicle) driven by the hirer.

self-educated /selfˈedjuːˌkeɪtɪd/ *adj.* educated by oneself by reading etc., without formal instruction. □ **self-education** /-ˈkeɪʃ(ə)n/ *n.*

self-effacing /ˌselfɪˈfeɪsɪŋ/ *adj.* retiring; modest; timid. □ **self-effacement** *n.* **self-effacingly** *adv.*

self-employed /ˌselfɪmˈplɔɪd/ *adj.* working for oneself, as a freelance or owner of a business etc.; not employed by an employer. □ **self-employment** *n.*

self-esteem /ˌselfɪˈstiːm/ *n.* a good opinion of oneself.

self-evident /selfˈevɪd(ə)nt/ *adj.* obvious; without the need of evidence or further explanation. □ **self-evidence** *n.* **self-evidently** *adv.*

self-examination /ˌselfɪɡˌzæmɪˈneɪʃ(ə)n/ *n.* **1** the study of one's own conduct, reasons, etc. **2** the examining of one's body for signs of illness etc.

self-existent /ˌselfɪɡˈzɪst(ə)nt/ *adj.* existing without prior cause; independent.

self-explanatory /ˌselfɪkˈsplænətəri/ *adj.* easily understood; not needing explanation.

self-expression /ˌselfɪkˈspreʃ(ə)n/ *n.* the expression of one's feelings, thoughts, etc., esp. in writing, painting, music, etc. □ **self-expressive** *adj.*

self-feeder /selfˈfiːdə(r)/ *n.* **1** a furnace, machine, etc., that renews its own fuel or material automatically. **2** a device for supplying food to farm animals automatically. □ **self-feeding** *adj.*

self-fertile /selfˈfɜːtaɪl/ *adj.* (of a plant etc.) self-fertilizing. □ **self-fertility** /-ˈtɪlɪti/ *n.*

self-fertilization /selfˌfɜːtɪlaɪˈzeɪʃ(ə)n/ *n.* the fertilization of plants by their own pollen, not from others. □ **self-fertilized** /-ˈfɜːtɪˌlaɪzd/ *adj.* **self-fertilizing** /-ˈfɜːtɪˌlaɪzɪŋ/ *adj.*

self-financing /ˌselfˈfaɪnænsɪŋ/ *adj.* that finances itself, esp. (of a project or undertaking) that pays for its own implementation or continuation. □ **self-finance** *v.tr.*

self-forgetful /ˌselffəˈɡetfʊl/ *adj.* unselfish. □ **self-forgetfulness** *n.*

self-fulfilling /ˌselffʊlˈfɪlɪŋ/ *adj.* (of a prophecy, forecast, etc.) bound to come true as a result of actions brought about by its being made.

self-fulfilment /ˌselffʊlˈfɪlmənt/ *n.* (*US* **-fulfillment**) the fulfilment of one's own hopes and ambitions.

self-generating /selfˈdʒenəˌreɪtɪŋ/ *adj.* generated by itself or oneself, not externally.

self-glorification /selfˌɡlɔːrɪfɪˈkeɪʃ(ə)n/ *n.* the proclamation of oneself, one's abilities, etc.; self-satisfaction.

self-government /selfˈɡʌvənmənt/ *n.* **1** (esp. of a former colony etc.) government by its own people. **2** = SELF-CONTROL. □ **self-governed** *adj.* **self-governing** *adj.*

self-hate /selfˈheɪt/ *n.* = SELF-HATRED.

self-hatred /selfˈheɪtrɪd/ *n.* hatred of oneself, esp. of one's actual self when contrasted with one's imagined self.

self-help /selfˈhelp/ *n.* **1** the theory that individuals should provide for their own support and improvement in society. **2** the act or faculty of providing for or improving oneself.

selfhood /ˈselfhʊd/ *n.* personality, separate and conscious existence.

self-image /selfˈɪmɪdʒ/ *n.* one's own idea or picture of oneself, esp. in relation to others.

self-importance /ˌselfɪmˈpɔːt(ə)ns/ *n.* a high opinion of oneself; pompousness. □ **self-important** *adj.* **self-importantly** *adv.*

self-imposed /ˌselfɪmˈpəʊzd/ *adj.* (of a task or condition etc.) imposed on and by oneself, not externally (*self-imposed exile*).

self-improvement /ˌselfɪmˈpruːvmənt/ *n.* the improvement of one's own position or disposition by one's own efforts.

self-induced /ˌselfɪnˈdjuːst/ *adj.* induced by oneself or itself.

self-indulgent /ˌselfɪnˈdʌldʒ(ə)nt/ *adj.* indulging or tending to indulge oneself in pleasure, idleness, etc. □ **self-indulgence** *n.* **self-indulgently** *adv.*

self-inflicted /ˌselfɪnˈflɪktɪd/ *adj.* (esp. of a wound, damage, etc.) inflicted by and on oneself, not externally.

self-interest /selfˈɪntrəst, -trɪst/ *n.* one's personal interest or advantage. □ **self-interested** *adj.*

selfish /ˈselfɪʃ/ *adj.* **1** deficient in consideration for others; concerned chiefly with one's own personal profit or pleasure; actuated by self-interest. **2** (of a motive etc.) appealing to self-interest. □ **selfishly** *adv.* **selfishness** *n.*

self-justification /selfˌdʒʌstɪfɪˈkeɪʃ(ə)n/ *n.* the justification or excusing of oneself, one's actions, etc.

self-knowledge /selfˈnɒlɪdʒ/ *n.* the understanding of oneself, one's motives, etc.

selfless /ˈselflɪs/ *adj.* disregarding oneself or one's own interests; unselfish. □ **selflessly** *adv.* **selflessness** *n.*

self-loading /selfˈləʊdɪŋ/ *adj.* (esp. of a gun) loading itself. □ **self-loader** *n.*

self-locking /selfˈlɒkɪŋ/ *adj.* locking itself.

self-love /selfˈlʌv/ *n.* **1** selfishness; self-indulgence. **2** *Philos.* regard for one's own well-being and happiness.

self-made /ˈselfmeɪd/ *adj.* **1** successful or rich by one's own effort. **2** made by oneself.

self-mocking /selfˈmɒkɪŋ/ *adj.* mocking oneself or itself.

self-motivated /selfˈməʊtɪˌveɪtɪd/ *adj.* acting on one's own initiative without external pressure. □ **self-motivation** /-ˈveɪʃ(ə)n/ *n.*

self-murder /selfˈmɜːdə(r)/ *n.* = SUICIDE. □ **self-murderer** *n.*

self-neglect /ˌselfnɪˈɡlekt/ *n.* neglect of oneself.

self-opinionated /ˌselfəˈpɪnjəˌneɪtɪd/ *adj.* **1** stubbornly adhering to one's own opinions. **2** arrogant. □ **self-opinion** *n.*

self-perpetuating /ˌselfpəˈpetjuːˌeɪtɪŋ/ *adj.* perpetuating itself or oneself without external agency. □ **self-perpetuation** /-ˈeɪʃ(ə)n/ *n.*

self-pity /selfˈpɪtɪ/ *n.* extreme sorrow for one's own troubles etc. □ **self-pitying** *adj.* **self-pityingly** *adv.*

self-pollination /selfˌpɒlɪˈneɪʃ(ə)n/ *n.* the pollination of a flower by pollen from the same plant. □ **self-pollinated** *adj.* **self-pollinating** *adj.* **self-pollinator** *n.*

self-portrait /selfˈpɔːtrɪt/ *n.* a portrait or description of an artist, writer, etc., by himself or herself.

self-possessed /ˌselfpəˈzest/ *adj.* habitually exercising self-control; composed. □ **self-possession** /-ˈzeʃ(ə)n/ *n.*

self-preservation /selfˌprezəˈveɪʃ(ə)n/ *n.* **1** the preservation of one's own life, safety, etc. **2** this as a basic instinct of human beings and animals.

self-proclaimed /ˌselfprəˈkleɪmd/ *adj.* proclaimed by oneself or itself to be such.

self-propagating /selfˈprɒpəˌgeɪtɪŋ/ *adj.* (esp. of a plant) able to propagate itself.

self-propelled /ˌselfprəˈpeld/ *adj.* (esp. of a motor vehicle etc.) moving or able to move without external propulsion. □ **self-propelling** *adj.*

self-protection /ˌselfprəˈtekʃ(ə)n/ *n.* protecting oneself or itself. □ **self-protective** *adj.*

self-raising /selfˈreɪzɪŋ/ *adj.* *Brit.* (of flour) having a raising agent already added.

self-realization /selfˌrɪəlaɪˈzeɪʃ(ə)n/ *n.* **1** the development of one's faculties, abilities, etc. **2** this as an ethical principle.

self-regard /ˌselfrɪˈɡɑːd/ *n.* **1** a proper regard for oneself. **2 a** selfishness. **b** conceit.

self-regulating /selfˈreɡjʊˌleɪtɪŋ/ *adj.* regulating oneself or itself without intervention. □ **self-regulation** /-ˈleɪʃ(ə)n/ *n.* **self-regulatory** /-lətərɪ/ *adj.*

self-reliance /ˌselfrɪˈlaɪəns/ *n.* reliance on one's own resources etc.; independence. □ **self-reliant** *adj.* **self-reliantly** *adv.*

self-renewal /ˌselfrɪˈnjuːəl/ *n.* the act or process of renewing oneself or itself.

self-reproach /ˌselfrɪˈprəʊtʃ/ *n.* reproach or blame directed at oneself. □ **self-reproachful** *adj.*

self-respect /ˌselfrɪˈspekt/ *n.* respect for oneself, a feeling that one is behaving with honour, dignity, etc. □ **self-respecting** *adj.*

self-restraint /ˌselfrɪˈstreɪnt/ *n.* = SELF-CONTROL. □ **self-restrained** *adj.*

self-revealing /ˌselfrɪˈviːlɪŋ/ *adj.* revealing one's character, motives, etc., esp. inadvertently. □ **self-revelation** /-ˌrevəˈleɪʃ(ə)n/ *n.*

self-righteous /selfˈraɪtʃəs/ *adj.* excessively conscious of or insistent on one's rectitude, correctness, etc. □ **self-righteously** *adv.* **self-righteousness** *n.*

self-righting /selfˈraɪtɪŋ/ *adj.* (of a boat) righting itself when capsized.

self-rising /selfˈraɪzɪŋ/ *adj.* *US* = SELF-RAISING.

self-rule /selfˈruːl/ *n.* = SELF-GOVERNMENT 1.

self-sacrifice /selfˈsækrɪˌfaɪs/ *n.* the negation of one's own interests, wishes, etc., in favour of those of others. □ **self-sacrificing** *adj.*

selfsame /ˈselfseɪm/ *attrib.adj.* (prec. by *the*) the very same (*the selfsame village*).

self-satisfaction /selfˌsætɪsˈfækʃ(ə)n/ *n.* excessive and unwarranted satisfaction with oneself, one's achievements, etc.; complacency. □ **self-satisfied** /-ˈsætɪsˌfaɪd/ *adj.* **self-satisfiedly** /-ˈsætɪsˌfaɪdlɪ/ *adv.*

self-sealing /selfˈsiːlɪŋ/ *adj.* **1** (of a pneumatic tyre, fuel tank, etc.) automatically able to seal small punctures. **2** (of an envelope) self-adhesive.

self-seeking /ˈselfˌsiːkɪŋ/ *adj.* & *n.* seeking one's own welfare before that of others. □ **self-seeker** *n.*

self-selection /ˌselfsɪˈlekʃ(ə)n/ *n.* the act of selecting oneself or itself. □ **self-selecting** *adj.*

self-service /selfˈsɜːvɪs/ *adj.* & *n.* —*adj.* (often *attrib.*) **1** (of a shop, restaurant, garage, etc.) where customers serve themselves and pay at a checkout counter etc. **2** (of a machine) serving goods after the insertion of coins. —*n.* *colloq.* a self-service store, garage, etc.

self-serving /selfˈsɜːvɪŋ/ *adj.* = SELF-SEEKING.

self-slaughter /selfˈslɔːtə(r)/ *n.* = SUICIDE.

self-sown /selfˈsəʊn/ *adj.* grown from seed scattered naturally.

self-starter /selfˈstɑːtə(r)/ *n.* **1** an electric appliance for starting a motor vehicle engine without the use of a crank. **2** an ambitious person who needs no external motivation.

self-sterile /selfˈsteraɪl/ *adj.* *Biol.* not being self-fertile. □ **self-sterility** /-stəˈrɪlɪtɪ/ *n.*

self-styled /ˈselfstaɪld/ *adj.* called so by oneself; would-be; pretended (*a self-styled artist*).

self-sufficient /ˌselfsəˈfɪʃ(ə)nt/ *adj.* **1 a** needing nothing; independent. **b** (of a person, nation, etc.) able to supply one's needs for a commodity, esp. food, from one's own resources. **2** content with one's own opinion; arrogant. □ **self-sufficiency** *n.* **self-sufficiently** *adv.* **self-sufficing** /-səˈfaɪsɪŋ/ *adj.*

self-supporting /ˌselfsəˈpɔːtɪŋ/ *adj.* **1** capable of maintaining oneself or itself financially. **2** staying up or standing without external aid. □ **self-support** *n.*

self-sustaining /ˌselfsəˈsteɪnɪŋ/ *adj.* sustaining oneself or itself. □ **self-sustained** *adj.*

self-taught /selfˈtɔːt/ *adj.* educated or trained by oneself, not externally.

self-torture /selfˈtɔːtʃə(r)/ *n.* the inflicting of pain, esp. mental, on oneself.

self-willed /selfˈwɪld/ *adj.* obstinately pursuing one's own wishes. □ **self-will** *n.*

self-winding /selfˈwaɪndɪŋ/ *adj.* (of a watch etc.) having an automatic winding apparatus.

self-worth /selfˈwɜːθ/ *n.* = SELF-ESTEEM.

sell *v.* & *n.* —*v.* (*past* and *past part.* **sold** /səʊld/) **1** *tr.* make over or dispose of in exchange for money. **2** *tr.* keep a stock of for sale or be a dealer in (*do you sell candles?*). **3** *intr.* (of goods) be purchased (*will never sell*; *these are selling well*). **4** *intr.* (foll. by *at, for*) have a specified price (*sells at £5*). **5** *tr.* betray for money or other reward (*sell one's country*). **6** *tr.* offer dishonourably for money or other consideration; make a matter of corrupt bargaining (*sell justice*; *sell oneself*; *sell one's honour*). **7** *tr.* **a** advertise or publish the merits of. **b** give (a person) information on the value of something, inspire with a desire to buy or acquire or agree to something. **8** *tr.* cause to be sold (*the author's name alone will sell many copies*).

—*n. colloq.* **1** a manner of selling (*soft sell*). **2** a deception or disappointment. □ **sell-by date** the latest recommended date of sale marked on the packaging of esp. perishable food. **selling-point** an advantageous feature. **selling-race** a horse-race after which the winning horse must be auctioned. **sell one's life dear** (or **dearly**) do great injury before being killed. **sell off** sell the remainder of (goods) at reduced prices. **sell out 1 a** sell all one's stock-in-trade, one's shares in a company, etc. **b** sell (all or some of one's stock, shares, etc.). **2 a** betray. **b** be treacherous or disloyal. **sell-out** *n.* **1** a commercial success, esp. the selling of all tickets for a show. **2** a betrayal. **sell short** disparage, underestimate. **sell up** *Brit.* **1** sell one's business, house, etc. **2** sell the goods of (a debtor). **sold on** *colloq.* enthusiastic about. □ **sellable** *adj.* [OE *sellan* f. Gmc]

seller /'selə(r)/ *n.* **1** a person who sells. **2** a commodity that sells well or badly. □ **seller's** (or **sellers'**) **market** an economic position in which goods are scarce and expensive.

Sellotape /'seləˌteɪp/ *n. & v.* —*n. propr.* adhesive usu. transparent cellulose or plastic tape. —*v.tr.* (**sellotape**) fix with Sellotape. [CELLULOSE + TAPE]

selvage /'selvɪdʒ/ *n.* (also **selvedge**) **1** an edging that prevents cloth from unravelling (either an edge along the warp or a specially woven edging). **2** a border of different material or finish intended to be removed or hidden. [ME f. SELF + EDGE, after Du. *selfegghe*]

selves *pl.* of SELF.

semantic /sɪ'mæntɪk/ *adj.* relating to meaning in language; relating to the connotations of words. □ **semantically** *adv.* [F *sémantique* f. Gk *sēmantikos* significant f. *sēmainō* signify f. *sēma* sign]

semantics /sɪ'mæntɪks/ *n.pl.* (usu. treated as *sing.*) the branch of linguistics concerned with meaning. □ **semantician** /-'tɪʃ(ə)n/ *n.* **semanticist** /-tɪsɪst/ *n.*

semaphore /'seməˌfɔː(r)/ *n. & v.* —*n.* **1** *Mil.* etc. a system of sending messages by holding the arms or two flags in certain positions according to an alphabetic code. **2** a signalling apparatus consisting of a post with a movable arm or arms, lanterns, etc., for use (esp. on railways) by day or night. —*v.intr. & tr.* signal or send by semaphore. □ **semaphoric** /-'fɒrɪk/ *adj.* **semaphorically** /-'fɒrɪkəlɪ/ *adv.* [F *sémaphore*, irreg. f. Gk *sēma* sign + *-phoros* -PHORE]

semblance /'sembləns/ *n.* **1** the outward or superficial appearance of something (*put on a semblance of anger*). **2** resemblance. [ME f. OF f. *sembler* f. L *similare, simulare* SIMULATE]

semeiology var. of SEMIOLOGY.

semeiotics var. of SEMIOTICS.

semen /'siːmən/ *n.* the reproductive fluid of male animals, containing spermatozoa in suspension. [ME f. L *semen seminis* seed f. *serere* to sow]

semester /sɪ'mestə(r)/ *n.* a half-year course or term in (esp. German and US) universities. [G f. L *semestris* six-monthly f. *sex* six + *mensis* month]

semi /'semɪ/ *n.* (*pl.* **semis**) *colloq.* **1** *Brit.* a semi-detached house. **2** *US* a semi-trailer. [abbr.]

semi- /'semɪ/ *prefix* **1** half (*semicircle*). **2** partly; in some degree or particular (*semi-official; semi-detached*). **3** almost (*a semi-smile*). **4** occurring or

appearing twice in a specified period (*semi-annual*). [F, It., etc. or L corresp. to Gk HEMI-, Skr. *sāmi*]

semi-annual /ˌsemɪ'ænjʊəl/ *adj.* occurring, published, etc., twice a year. □ **semi-annually** *adv.*

semi-automatic /ˌsemɪˌɔːtə'mætɪk/ *adj.* **1** partially automatic. **2** (of a firearm) having a mechanism for continuous loading but not for continuous firing.

semi-basement /ˌsemɪ'beɪsmənt/ *n.* a storey partly below ground level.

semibreve /'semɪˌbriːv/ *n. Mus.* the longest note now in common use, having the time value of two minims or four crotchets, and represented by a ring with no stem.

semicircle /'semɪˌsɜːk(ə)l/ *n.* **1** half of a circle or of its circumference. **2** a set of objects ranged in, or an object forming, a semicircle. [L *semicirculus* (as SEMI-, CIRCLE)]

semicircular /ˌsemɪ'sɜːkjʊlə(r)/ *adj.* **1** forming or shaped like a semicircle. **2** arranged as or in a semicircle. [LL *semicircularis* (as SEMICIRCLE)]

semi-civilized /ˌsemɪ'sɪvɪˌlaɪzd/ *adj.* partially civilized.

semicolon /ˌsemɪ'kəʊlən, -lɒn/ *n.* a punctuation mark (;) of intermediate value between a comma and full stop.

semiconducting /ˌsemɪkən'dʌktɪŋ/ *adj.* having the properties of a semiconductor.

semiconductor /ˌsemɪkən'dʌktə(r)/ *n.* a solid substance that is a non-conductor when pure or at a low temperature but has a conductivity between that of insulators and that of most metals when containing a suitable impurity or at a higher temperature, and is used in integrated circuits, transistors, diodes, etc.

semi-conscious /ˌsemɪ'kɒnʃəs/ *adj.* partly or imperfectly conscious.

semicylinder /ˌsemɪ'sɪlɪndə(r)/ *n.* half of a cylinder cut longitudinally. □ **semicylindrical** /-'lɪndrɪk(ə)l/ *adj.*

semi-detached /ˌsemɪdɪ'tætʃt/ *adj. & n.* —*adj.* (of a house) joined to another by a party-wall on one side only. —*n.* a semi-detached house.

semifinal /ˌsemɪ'faɪn(ə)l/ *n.* a match or round immediately preceding the final.

semifinalist /ˌsemɪ'faɪnəlɪst/ *n.* a competitor in a semifinal.

semifluid /ˌsemɪ'fluːɪd/ *adj. & n.* —*adj.* of a consistency between solid and liquid. —*n.* a semifluid substance.

semi-invalid /ˌsemɪ'ɪnvəˌliːd, -lɪd/ *n.* a person somewhat enfeebled or partially disabled.

semi-liquid /ˌsemɪ'lɪkwɪd/ *adj. & n.* = SEMIFLUID.

semi-lunar /ˌsemɪ'luːnə(r)/ *adj.* shaped like a half moon or crescent. [mod.L *semilunaris* (as SEMI-, LUNAR)]

semi-monthly /ˌsemɪ'mʌnθlɪ/ *adj. & adv.* —*adj.* occurring, published, etc., twice a month. —*adv.* twice a month.

seminal /'semɪn(ə)l/ *adj.* **1** of or relating to seed, semen, or reproduction. **2** germinal. **3** rudimentary, undeveloped. **4** (of ideas etc.) providing the basis for future development. □ **seminal fluid** semen. □ **seminally** *adv.* [ME f. OF *seminal* or L *seminalis* (as SEMEN)]

seminar /'semɪˌnɑː(r)/ *n.* **1** a small class at a university etc. for discussion and research. **2** a short intensive course of study. **3** a conference of specialists. [G (as SEMINARY)]

seminary /ˈsemɪnərɪ/ n. (pl. **-ies**) **1** a training-college for priests, rabbis, etc. **2** a place of education or development. □ **seminarist** n. [ME f. L *seminarium* seed-plot, neut. of *seminarius* (adj.) (as SEMEN)]

semi-official /ˌsemɪəˈfɪʃ(ə)l/ adj. **1** partly official; rather less than official. **2** (of communications to newspapers etc.) made by an official with the stipulation that the source should not be revealed. □ **semi-officially** adv.

semiology /ˌsiːmɪˈɒlədʒɪ, ˌsem-/ n. (also **semeiology**) = SEMIOTICS. □ **semiological** /-əˈlɒdʒɪk(ə)l/ adj. **semiologist** n. [Gk *sēmeion* sign f. *sēma* mark]

semi-opaque /ˌsemɪəʊˈpeɪk/ adj. not fully transparent.

semiotics /ˌsiːmɪˈɒtɪks, ˌsem-/ n. (also **semeiotics**) the study of signs and symbols in various fields, esp. language. □ **semiotic** adj. **semiotical** adj. **semiotically** adv. **semiotician** /-ˈtɪʃ(ə)n/ n. [Gk *sēmeiōtikos* of signs (as SEMIOLOGY)]

semi-permanent /ˌsemɪˈpɜːmənənt/ adj. rather less than permanent.

semi-permeable /ˌsemɪˈpɜːmɪəb(ə)l/ adj. (of a membrane etc.) allowing small molecules, but not large ones, to pass through.

semiprecious /ˌsemɪˈpreʃəs/ adj. (of a gem) less valuable than a precious stone.

semi-professional /ˌsemɪprəˈfeʃən(ə)l/ adj. & n. —adj. **1** receiving payment for an activity but not relying on it for a living. **2** involving semi-professionals. —n. a semi-professional musician, sportsman, etc.

semiquaver /ˈsemɪˌkweɪvə(r)/ n. Mus. a note having the time value of half a quaver and represented by a large dot with a two-hooked stem.

semi-rigid /ˌsemɪˈrɪdʒɪd/ adj. (of an airship) having a stiffened keel attached to a flexible gas container.

semi-skilled /ˌsemɪˈskɪld/ adj. (of work or a worker) having or needing some training but less than for a skilled worker.

semi-solid /ˌsemɪˈsɒlɪd/ adj. viscous, semifluid.

semi-sweet /ˈsemɪˌswiːt/ adj. (of biscuits etc.) slightly sweetened.

Semite /ˈsiːmaɪt, ˈsem-/ n. a member of any of the peoples supposed to be descended from Shem, son of Noah (Gen. 10:21 ff.), including esp. the Jews, Arabs, Assyrians, and Phoenicians. □ **Semitism** /ˈsemɪˌtɪz(ə)m/ n. **Semitist** /ˈsemɪtɪst/ n. **Semitize** /ˈsemɪˌtaɪz/ v.tr. (also **-ise**). **Semitization** /ˌsemɪtaɪˈzeɪʃ(ə)n/ n. [mod.L *Semita* f. LL f. Gk *Sēm* Shem]

Semitic /sɪˈmɪtɪk/ adj. **1** of or relating to the Semites, esp. the Jews. **2** of or relating to the languages of the family including Hebrew and Arabic. [mod.L *Semiticus* (as SEMITE)]

semitone /ˈsemɪˌtəʊn/ n. Mus. the smallest interval used in classical European music; half a tone.

semi-trailer /ˌsemɪˈtreɪlə(r)/ n. a trailer having wheels at the back but supported at the front by a towing vehicle.

semi-transparent /ˌsemɪˌtrænsˈpærənt, -trɑːnz-, -ˈpeərənt/ adj. partially or imperfectly transparent.

semi-vowel /ˈsemɪˌvaʊəl/ n. **1** a sound intermediate between a vowel and a consonant (e.g. w, y). **2** a letter representing this. [after L *semivocalis*]

semi-weekly /ˌsemɪˈwiːklɪ/ adj. & adv. —adj. occurring, published, etc., twice a week. —adv. twice a week.

semolina /ˌseməˈliːnə/ n. **1** the hard grains left after the milling of flour, used in puddings etc. and in pasta. **2** a pudding etc. made of this. [It. *semolino* dimin. of *semola* bran f. L *simila* flour]

sempstress var. of SEAMSTRESS.

Semtex /ˈsemteks/ n. a malleable odourless plastic explosive. [f. *Semtín* in Czechoslovakia, where it was originally made]

SEN abbr. (in the UK) State Enrolled Nurse.

Sen. abbr. **1** Senior. **2** US **a** Senator. **b** Senate.

senate /ˈsenɪt/ n. **1** a legislative body, esp. the upper and smaller assembly in the US, France, and other countries, in the States of the US, etc. **2** the governing body of a university or (in the US) a college. **3** Rom.Hist. the State council of the republic and empire. [ME f. OF *senat* f. L *senatus* f. *senex* old man]

senator /ˈsenətə(r)/ n. a member of a senate. □ **senatorial** /-ˈtɔːrɪəl/ adj. **senatorship** n. [ME f. OF *senateur* f. L *senator -oris* (as SENATE)]

send v. (past and past part. **sent**) **1** tr. **a** order or cause to go or be conveyed (*send a message to headquarters*; *sent me a book*; *sends goods all over the world*). **b** propel; cause to move (*send a bullet*; *sent him flying*). **c** cause to go or become (*send into raptures*; *send to sleep*). **d** dismiss with or without force (*sent her away*; *sent him about his business*). **2** intr. send a message or letter (*he sent to warn me*). **3** tr. (of God, providence, etc.) grant or bestow or inflict; bring about; cause to be (*send rain*; *send her victorious!*). **4** tr. sl. affect emotionally, put into ecstasy. □ **send away for** send an order to a dealer for (goods). **send down** Brit. **1** rusticate or expel from a university. **2** sentence to imprisonment. **send for 1** summon. **2** order by post. **send in 1** cause to go in. **2** submit (an entry etc.) for a competition etc. **send off 1** get (a letter, parcel, etc.) dispatched. **2** attend the departure of (a person) as a sign of respect etc. **3** Sport (of a referee) order (a player) to leave the field and take no further part in the game. **send-off** n. a demonstration of goodwill etc. at the departure of a person, the start of a project, etc. **send off for** = *send away for*. **send on** transmit to a further destination or in advance of one's own arrival. **send up 1** cause to go up. **2** transmit to a higher authority. **3** Brit. colloq. satirize or ridicule, esp. by mimicking. **4** US sentence to imprisonment. **send-up** n. Brit. colloq. a satire or parody. **send word** send information. □ **sendable** adj. **sender** n. [OE *sendan* f. Gmc]

senesce /sɪˈnes/ v.intr. grow old. □ **senescence** n. **senescent** adj. [L *senescere* f. *senex* old]

seneschal /ˈsenɪʃ(ə)l/ n. **1** the steward or major-domo of a medieval great house. **2** a judge in Sark. [ME f. OF f. med.L *seniscalus* f. Gmc, = old servant]

senhor /seɪnˈjɔː(r)/ n. a title used of or to a Portuguese or Brazilian man. [Port. f. L *senior*: see SENIOR]

senhora /seɪnˈjɔːrə/ n. a title used of or to a Portuguese woman or a Brazilian married woman. [Port., fem. of SENHOR]

senhorita /ˌseɪnjəˈriːtə/ *n.* a title used of or to a Brazilian unmarried woman. [Port., dimin. of SENHORA]

senile /ˈsiːnaɪl/ *adj.* **1** of or characteristic of old age (*senile apathy*; *senile decay*). **2** having the weaknesses or diseases of old age. □ **senility** /sɪˈnɪlɪtɪ/ *n.* [F *sénile* or L *senilis* f. *senex* old man]

senior /ˈsiːnɪə(r)/ *adj. & n.* —*adj.* **1** (often foll. by *to*) more or most advanced in age or standing. **2** of high or highest position. **3** (placed after a person's name) senior to another of the same name. **4** (of a school) having pupils in an older age-range (esp. over 11). **5** *US* of the final year at a university, high school, etc. —*n.* **1** a person of advanced age or comparatively long service etc. **2** one's elder, or one's superior in length of service, membership, etc. (*is my senior*). **3** a senior student. □ **senior citizen** an elderly person, esp. an old-age pensioner. **senior nursing officer** the person in charge of nursing services in a hospital. **senior officer** an officer to whom a junior is responsible. **senior partner** the head of a firm. **senior service** *Brit.* the Royal Navy as opposed to the Army. □ **seniority** /ˌsiːnɪˈɒrɪtɪ/ *n.* [ME f. L, = older, older man, compar. of *senex senis* old man, old]

senna /ˈsenə/ *n.* **1** a cassia tree. **2** a laxative prepared from the dried pods of this. [med.L *sena* f. Arab. *sanā*]

señor /senˈjɔː(r)/ *n.* (pl. **señores** /-rez/) a title used of or to a Spanish-speaking man. [Sp. f. L *senior*: see SENIOR]

señora /senˈjɔːrə/ *n.* a title used of or to a Spanish-speaking married woman. [Sp., fem. of SEÑOR]

señorita /ˌsenjəˈriːtə/ *n.* a title used of or to a Spanish-speaking unmarried woman. [Sp., dimin. of SEÑORA]

sensation /senˈseɪʃ(ə)n/ *n.* **1** the consciousness of perceiving or seeming to perceive some state or condition of one's body or its parts or senses or of one's mind or its emotions; an instance of such consciousness (*lost all sensation in my left arm*; *had a sensation of giddiness*; *a sensation of pride*; *in search of a new sensation*). **2 a** a stirring of emotions or intense interest esp. among a large group of people (*the news caused a sensation*). **b** a person, event, etc., causing such interest. [med.L *sensatio* f. L *sensus* SENSE]

sensational /senˈseɪʃən(ə)l/ *adj.* **1** causing or intended to cause great public excitement etc. **2** causing sensation. □ **sensationally** *adv.*

sensationalism /senˈseɪʃənəˌlɪz(ə)m/ *n.* the use of or interest in the sensational in literature, political agitation, etc. □ **sensationalist** *n. & adj.* **sensationalistic** /-ˈlɪstɪk/ *adj.*

sense /sens/ *n. & v.* —*n.* **1 a** any of the special bodily faculties by which sensation is roused (*has keen senses*; *has a dull sense of smell*). **b** sensitiveness of all or any of these. **2** the ability to perceive or feel or to be conscious of the presence or properties of things. **3** (foll. by *of*) consciousness (*sense of having done well*; *sense of one's own importance*). **4** (often foll. by *of*) **a** quick or accurate appreciation, understanding, or instinct regarding a specified matter (*sense of the ridiculous*; *road sense*; *the moral sense*). **b** the habit of basing one's conduct on such instinct. **5** practical wisdom or judgement, common sense; conformity to these (*has plenty of sense*; *what is the sense of talking like that?*) **6 a** a meaning; the

way in which a word etc. is to be understood (*the sense of the word is clear*; *I mean that in the literal sense*). **b** intelligibility or coherence or possession of a meaning. **7** the prevailing opinion among a number of people. **8** (in *pl.*) a person's sanity or normal state of mind. —*v.tr.* **1** perceive by a sense or senses. **2** be vaguely aware of. **3** realize. **4** (of a machine etc.) detect. **5** *US* understand. □ **bring a person to his** or **her senses 1** cure a person of folly. **2** restore a person to consciousness. **come to one's senses 1** regain consciousness. **2** become sensible after acting foolishly. **the five senses** sight, hearing, smell, taste, and touch. **in a** (or **one**) **sense** if the statement is understood in a particular way (*what you say is true in a sense*). **in one's senses** sane. **make sense** be intelligible or practicable. **make sense of** show or find the meaning of. **man of sense** a sagacious man. **out of one's senses** in or into a state of madness (*is out of her senses*; *frightened him out of his senses*). **sense of direction** the ability to know without guidance the direction in which one is or should be moving. **sense-organ** a bodily organ conveying external stimuli to the sensory system. **take leave of one's senses** go mad. [ME f. L *sensus* faculty of feeling, thought, meaning, f. *sentire* *sens-* feel]

senseless /ˈsenslɪs/ *adj.* **1** unconscious. **2** wildly foolish. **3** without meaning or purpose. **4** incapable of sensation. □ **senselessly** *adv.* **senselessness** *n.*

sensibility /ˌsensɪˈbɪlɪtɪ/ *n.* (pl. **-ies**) **1** capacity to feel (*little finger lost its sensibility*). **2 a** openness to emotional impressions, susceptibility, sensitiveness (*sensibility to kindness*). **b** an exceptional or excessive degree of this (*sense and sensibility*). **3** (in *pl.*) a tendency to feel offended etc. [ME f. LL *sensibilitas* (as SENSIBLE)]

sensible /ˈsensɪb(ə)l/ *adj.* **1** having or showing wisdom or common sense; reasonable, judicious (*a sensible person*; *a sensible compromise*). **2 a** perceptible by the senses (*sensible phenomena*). **b** great enough to be perceived; appreciable (*a sensible difference*). **3** (of clothing etc.) practical and functional. **4** (foll. by *of*) aware; not unmindful (*was sensible of his peril*). □ **sensibleness** *n.* **sensibly** *adv.* [ME f. OF *sensible* or L *sensibilis* (as SENSE)]

sensitive /ˈsensɪtɪv/ *adj.* **1** (often foll. by *to*) very open to or acutely affected by external stimuli or mental impressions; having sensibility. **2** (of a person) easily offended or emotionally hurt. **3** (often foll. by *to*) (of an instrument etc.) responsive to or recording slight changes. **4** (often foll. by *to*) **a** (of photographic materials) prepared so as to respond (esp. rapidly) to the action of light. **b** (of any material) readily affected by or responsive to external action. **5** (of a topic etc.) subject to restriction of discussion to prevent embarrassment, ensure security, etc. □ **sensitive plant 1** a plant whose leaves curve downwards and leaflets fold together when touched, esp. mimosa. **2** a sensitive person. □ **sensitively** *adv.* **sensitiveness** *n.* [ME, = sensory, f. OF *sensitif* *-ive* or med.L *sensitivus*, irreg. f. L *sentire* *sens-* feel]

sensitivity /ˌsensɪˈtɪvɪtɪ/ *n.* the quality or degree of being sensitive.

sensitize /ˈsensɪˌtaɪz/ *v.tr.* (also **-ise**) **1** make sensitive. **2** *Photog.* make sensitive to light. **3**

make (an organism etc.) abnormally sensitive to a foreign substance. □ **sensitization** /-ˈzeɪʃ(ə)n/ n. **sensitizer** n.

sensor /ˈsensə(r)/ n. a device giving a signal for the detection or measurement of a physical property to which it responds. [SENSORY, after MOTOR]

sensory adj. of sensation or the senses. □ **sensorily** adv. [L sentire sens- feel]

sensual /ˈsensjʊəl, ˈsenʃʊəl/ adj. **1 a** of or depending on the senses only and not on the intellect or spirit; carnal, fleshly (sensual pleasures). **b** given to the pursuit of sensual pleasures or the gratification of the appetites; self-indulgent sexually or in regard to food and drink. **c** indicative of a sensual nature (sensual lips). **2** of sense or sensation, sensory. □ **sensualism** n. **sensualist** n. **sensualize** v.tr. (also -ise). **sensually** adv. [ME f. LL sensualis (as SENSE)]

sensuality /ˌsensjʊˈælɪtɪ, ˌsenʃʊ-/ n. gratification of the senses, self-indulgence. [ME f. F sensualité f. LL sensualitas (as SENSUAL)]

sensuous /ˈsensjʊəs/ adj. of or derived from or affecting the senses, esp. aesthetically rather than sensually. □ **sensuously** adv. **sensuousness** n. [L sensus sense]

sent past and past part. of SEND.

sentence /ˈsent(ə)ns/ n. & v. —n. **1 a** a set of words complete in itself as the expression of a thought, containing or implying a subject and predicate, and conveying a statement, question, exclamation, or command. **b** a piece of writing or speech between two full stops or equivalent pauses, often including several grammatical sentences (e.g. I went; he came). **2 a** a decision of a lawcourt, esp. the punishment allotted to a person convicted in a criminal trial. **b** the declaration of this. —v.tr. **1** declare the sentence of (a convicted criminal etc.). **2** (foll. by to) declare (such a person) to be condemned to a specified punishment. □ **under sentence of** having been condemned to (under sentence of death). [ME f. OF f. L sententia opinion f. sentire be of opinion]

sententious /senˈtenʃəs/ adj. **1** (of a person) fond of pompous moralizing. **2** (of a style) affectedly formal. **3** aphoristic, pithy, given to the use of maxims, affecting a concise impressive style. □ **sententiously** adv. **sententiousness** n. [L sententiosus (as SENTENCE)]

sentient /ˈsenʃ(ə)nt/ adj. having the power of perception by the senses. □ **sentience** n. **sentiency** n. **sentiently** adv. [L sentire feel]

sentiment /ˈsentɪmənt/ n. **1** a mental feeling (the sentiment of pity). **2 a** the sum of what one feels on some subject. **b** a verbal expression of this. **3** the expression of a view or desire esp. as formulated for a toast (concluded his speech with a sentiment). **4** an opinion as distinguished from the words meant to convey it (the sentiment is good though the words are injudicious). **5** a view or tendency based on or coloured with emotion (animated by noble sentiments). **6** such views collectively, esp. as an influence (sentiment unchecked by reason is a bad guide). **7** the tendency to be swayed by feeling rather than by reason. **8 a** mawkish tenderness. **b** the display of this. **9** an emotional feeling conveyed in literature or art. [ME f. OF sentement f. med.L sentimentum f. L sentire feel]

sentimental /ˌsentɪˈment(ə)l/ adj. **1** of or characterized by sentiment. **2** showing or affected by emotion rather than reason. **3** appealing to sentiment. □ **sentimental value** the value of a thing to a particular person because of its associations. □ **sentimentalism** n. **sentimentalist** n. **sentimentality** /-ˈtælɪtɪ/ n. **sentimentalize** v.intr. & tr. (also -ise). **sentimentalization** /-laɪˈzeɪʃ(ə)n/ n. **sentimentally** adv.

sentinel /ˈsentɪn(ə)l/ n. a sentry or lookout. [F sentinelle f. It. sentinella, of unkn. orig.]

sentry /ˈsentrɪ/ n. (pl. -ies) a soldier etc. stationed to keep guard. □ **sentry-box** a wooden cabin intended to shelter a standing sentry. **sentry-go** the duty of pacing up and down as a sentry. [perh. f. obs. centrinel, var. of SENTINEL]

sepal /ˈsep(ə)l, ˈsiː-/ n. Bot. each of the divisions or leaves of the calyx. [F sépale, mod.L sepalum, perh. formed as SEPARATE + PETAL]

separable /ˈsepərəb(ə)l/ adj. able to be separated. □ **separability** /-ˈbɪlɪtɪ/ n. **separableness** n. **separably** adv. [F séparable or L separabilis (as SEPARATE)]

separate adj., n., & v. —adj. /ˈsepərət/ (often foll. by from) forming a unit that is or may be regarded as apart or by itself; physically disconnected, distinct, or individual (living in separate rooms; the two questions are essentially separate). —n. /ˈsepərət/ **1** (in pl.) separate articles of clothing suitable for wearing separately in various combinations. **2** an offprint. —v. /ˈsepəˌreɪt/ **1** tr. make separate, sever, disunite. **2** tr. prevent union or contact of. **3** intr. go different ways, disperse. **4** intr. cease to live together as a married couple. **5** intr. (foll. by from) secede. **6** tr. **a** divide or sort into constituent parts or sizes. **b** (often foll. by out) extract or remove (an ingredient, waste product, etc.) by such a process for use or rejection. □ **separately** adv. **separateness** n. **separative** /-rətɪv/ adj. **separatory** /-rətərɪ/ adj. [L separare separat- (as SE-, parare make ready)]

separation /ˌsepəˈreɪʃ(ə)n/ n. **1** the act or an instance of separating; the state of being separated. **2** (in full **judicial separation** or **legal separation**) an arrangement by which a husband and wife remain married but live apart. [ME f. OF f. L separatio -onis (as SEPARATE)]

separatist /ˈsepərətɪst/ n. a person who favours separation, esp. for political or ecclesiastical independence. □ **separatism** n.

separator /ˈsepəˌreɪtə(r)/ n. a machine for separating, e.g. cream from milk.

Sephardi /sɪˈfɑːdɪ/ n. (pl. **Sephardim** /-dɪm/) a Jew of Spanish or Portuguese descent (cf. ASHKENAZI). □ **Sephardic** adj. [LHeb., f. sᵉp̄āraḏ, a country mentioned in Obad. 20 and taken to be Spain]

sepia /ˈsiːpɪə/ n. **1** a dark reddish-brown colour. **2 a** a brown pigment prepared from a black fluid secreted by cuttlefish, used in monochrome drawing and in water-colours. **b** a brown tint used in photography. **3** a drawing done in sepia. **4** the fluid secreted by cuttlefish. [L f. Gk sēpia cuttlefish]

sepoy /ˈsiːpɔɪ/ n. hist. a native Indian soldier under European, esp. British, discipline. [Urdu & Pers. sipāhī soldier f. sipāh army]

sepsis /ˈsepsɪs/ n. **1** the state of being septic. **2** blood-poisoning. [mod.L f. Gk *sēpsis* f. *sēpō* make rotten]

Sept. abbr. September.

sept- var. of SEPTI-.

septa pl. of SEPTUM.

September /sepˈtembə(r)/ n. the ninth month of the year. [ME f. L *September* f. *septem* seven: orig. the seventh month of the Roman year]

septennial /sepˈtenɪəl/ adj. **1** lasting for seven years. **2** recurring every seven years. [LL *septennis* f. L *septem* seven + *annus* year]

septet /sepˈtet/ n. (also **septette**) **1** *Mus.* **a** a composition for seven performers. **b** the performers of such a composition. **2** any group of seven. [G *Septett* f. L *septem* seven]

septi- /ˈseptɪ/ comb. form (also **sept-** before a vowel) seven. [L f. *septem* seven]

septic /ˈseptɪk/ adj. contaminated with bacteria from a festering wound etc., putrefying. □ **septic tank** a tank in which the organic matter in sewage is disintegrated through bacterial activity. □ **septically** adv. **septicity** /-ˈtɪsɪtɪ/ n. [L *septicus* f. Gk *sēptikos* f. *sēpō* make rotten]

septicaemia /ˌseptɪˈsiːmɪə/ n. (US **septicemia**) blood-poisoning. □ **septicaemic** adj. [mod.L f. Gk *sēptikos* + *haima* blood]

septuagenarian /ˌseptjʊədʒɪˈneərɪən/ n. & adj. —n. a person from 70 to 79 years old. —adj. of this age. [L *septuagenarius* f. *septuageni* distributive of *septuaginta* seventy]

Septuagesima /ˌseptjʊəˈdʒesɪmə/ n. (in full **Septuagesima Sunday**) the Sunday before Sexagesima. [ME f. L, = seventieth (day), formed as SEPTUAGINT, perh. after QUINQUAGESIMA or with ref. to the period of 70 days from Septuagesima to the Saturday after Easter]

Septuagint /ˈseptjʊəˌdʒɪnt/ n. a Greek version of the Old Testament including the Apocrypha, said to have been made about 270 BC by seventy-two translators. [L *septuaginta* seventy]

septum /ˈseptəm/ n. (pl. **septa** /-tə/) *Anat., Bot.*, & *Zool.* a partition such as that between the nostrils or the chambers of a poppy-fruit or of a shell. [L *s(a)eptum* f. *saepire saept-* enclose f. *saepes* hedge]

septuple /ˈseptjʊp(ə)l/ adj., n., & v. —adj. **1** sevenfold, having seven parts. **2** being seven times as many or as much. —n. a sevenfold number or amount. —v.tr. & intr. multiply by seven. [LL *septuplus* f. L *septem* seven]

sepulchral /sɪˈpʌlkr(ə)l/ adj. **1** of a tomb or interment (*sepulchral mound*; *sepulchral customs*). **2** suggestive of the tomb, funereal, gloomy, dismal (*sepulchral look*). □ **sepulchrally** adv. [F *sépulchral* or L *sepulchralis* (as SEPULCHRE)]

sepulchre /ˈsepəlkə(r)/ n. & v. (US **sepulcher**) —n. a tomb esp. cut in rock or built of stone or brick, a burial vault or cave. —v.tr. **1** lay in a sepulchre. **2** serve as a sepulchre for. [ME f. OF f. L *sepulc(h)rum* f. *sepelire sepult-* bury]

sequel /ˈsiːkw(ə)l/ n. **1** what follows (esp. as a result). **2** a novel, film, etc., that continues the story of an earlier one. [ME f. OF *sequelle* or L *sequel(l)a* f. *sequi* follow]

sequence /ˈsiːkwəns/ n. & v. —n. **1** succession, coming after or next. **2** order of succession (*shall follow the sequence of events*; *give the facts in historical sequence*). **3** a set of things belonging next to one another on some principle of order; a series

without gaps. **4** a part of a film dealing with one scene or topic. —v.tr. arrange in a definite order. [ME f. LL *sequentia* f. L *sequens* pres. part. of *sequi* follow]

sequencer /ˈsiːkwənsə(r)/ n. a programmable device for storing sequences of musical notes, chords, etc., and transmitting them when required to an electronic musical instrument.

sequential /sɪˈkwenʃ(ə)l/ adj. forming a sequence or consequence. □ **sequentiality** /-ʃɪˈælɪtɪ/ n. **sequentially** adv. [SEQUENCE, after CONSEQUENTIAL]

sequester /sɪˈkwestə(r)/ v.tr. **1** (esp. as **sequestered** adj.) seclude, isolate, set apart (*sequester oneself from the world*; *a sequestered life*; *a sequestered cottage*). **2** = SEQUESTRATE. [ME f. OF *sequestrer* or LL *sequestrare* commit for safe keeping f. L *sequester* trustee]

sequestrate /sɪˈkwestreɪt, ˈsiːkwɪ-/ v.tr. **1** confiscate, appropriate. **2** *Law* take temporary possession of (a debtor's estate etc.). □ **sequestrable** adj. **sequestration** /ˌsiːkwɪˈstreɪʃ(ə)n/ n. **sequestrator** /ˈsiːkwɪˌstreɪtə(r)/ n. [LL *sequestrare* (as SEQUESTER)]

sequin /ˈsiːkwɪn/ n. a circular spangle for attaching to clothing as an ornament. □ **sequinned** adj. (also **sequined**). [F f. It. *zecchino* a Venetian gold coin f. Arab. *sikka* a die]

sequoia /sɪˈkwɔɪə/ n. a Californian evergreen coniferous tree, *Sequoia sempervirens*, of very great height. [mod.L genus-name, f. *Sequoiah*, the name of a Cherokee]

sera pl. of SERUM.

seraglio /seˈrɑːlɪəʊ, sɪ-/ n. (pl. **-os**) **1** a harem. **2** *hist.* a Turkish palace, esp. that of the Sultan with government offices etc. at Constantinople. [It. *serraglio* f. Turk. f. Pers. *sarāy* palace: cf. SERAI]

serai /seˈraɪ, seˈrɑːɪ/ n. a caravanserai. [Turk. f. Pers. (as SERAGLIO)]

seraph /ˈserəf/ n. (pl. **seraphim** /-fɪm/ or **seraphs**) an angelic being, one of the highest order of the ninefold celestial hierarchy. [back-form. f. *seraphim* (cf. CHERUB) (pl.) f. LL f. Gk *seraphim* f. Heb. *śĕrāp̄īm*]

seraphic /səˈræfɪk/ adj. **1** of or like the seraphim. **2** ecstatically adoring, fervent, or serene. □ **seraphically** adv. [med.L *seraphicus* f. LL (as SERAPH)]

Serb n. & adj. —n. **1** a native of Serbia in Yugoslavia. **2** a person of Serbian descent. —adj. = SERBIAN. [Serbian *Srb*]

Serbian /ˈsɜːbɪən/ n. & adj. —n. **1** the dialect of the Serbs (cf. SERBO-CROAT). **2** = SERB. —adj. of or relating to the Serbs or their dialect.

Serbo- /ˈsɜːbəʊ/ comb. form Serbian.

Serbo-Croat /ˌsɜːbəʊˈkrəʊæt/ n. & adj. (also **Serbo-Croatian** /-krəʊˈeɪʃ(ə)n/) —n. the main official language of Yugoslavia, combining Serbian and Croatian dialects. —adj. of or relating to this language.

sere[1] var. of SEAR adj.

sere[2] /sɪə(r)/ n. *Ecol.* a sequence of animal or plant communities. [L *serere* join in a SERIES]

serenade /ˌserəˈneɪd/ n. & v. —n. a piece of music sung or played at night, esp. by a lover under his lady's window, or suitable for this. —v.tr. sing or play a serenade to. □ **serenader** n. [F *sérénade* f. It. *serenata* f. *sereno* SERENE]

serendipity /ˌserən'dɪpɪtɪ/ n. the faculty of making happy and unexpected discoveries by accident. □ **serendipitous** adj. **serendipitously** adv. [coined by Horace Walpole (1754) after *The Three Princes of Serendip* (Sri Lanka), a fairy-tale]

serene /sɪ'riːn, sə'riːn/ adj. (**serener**, **serenest**) **1 a** (of the sky, the air, etc.) clear and calm. **b** (of the sea etc.) unruffled. **2** placid, tranquil, unperturbed. □ **serenely** adv. **sereneness** n. [L *serenus*]

serenity /sɪ'renɪtɪ, sə'r-/ n. (pl. **-ies**) tranquillity, being serene. [F *sérénité* or L *serenitas* (as SERENE)]

serf n. **1** hist. a labourer not allowed to leave the land on which he worked, a villein. **2** an oppressed person, a drudge. □ **serfage** n. **serfdom** n. [OF f. L *servus* slave]

serge n. a durable twilled worsted etc. fabric. [ME f. OF *sarge*, *serge* ult. f. L *serica* (*lana*): see SILK]

sergeant /'sɑːdʒ(ə)nt/ n. **1** a non-commissioned Army or Air Force officer next below warrant officer. **2** a police officer ranking below (*Brit.*) inspector or (*US*) captain. □ **sergeant-major** Mil. **1** (in full **regimental sergeant-major**) Brit. a warrant-officer assisting the adjutant of a regiment or battalion. **2** US the highest-ranking non-commissioned officer. □ **sergeancy** n. (pl. **-ies**). **sergeantship** n. [ME f. OF *sergent* f. L *servens -entis* servant f. *servire* SERVE]

serial /'sɪərɪəl/ n. & adj. —n. **1** a story, play, or film which is published, broadcast, or shown in regular instalments. **2** a periodical. —adj. **1** of or in or forming a series. **2** (of a story etc.) in the form of a serial. **3** Mus. using transformations of a fixed series of notes (see SERIES). **4** (of a publication) appearing in successive parts published usu. at regular intervals, periodical. □ **serial killer** a person who murders continuously with no apparent motive. **serial number** a number showing the position of an item in a series. **serial rights** the right to publish a story or book as a serial. □ **seriality** /-ɪ'ælɪtɪ/ n. **serially** adv. [SERIES + -AL]

serialize /'sɪərɪəˌlaɪz/ v.tr. (also **-ise**) **1** publish or produce in instalments. **2** arrange in a series. **3** Mus. compose according to a serial technique. □ **serialization** /-'zeɪʃ(ə)n/ n.

sericulture /'serɪˌkʌltʃ(ə)r/ n. **1** silkworm-breeding. **2** the production of raw silk. □ **sericultural** /-'kʌltʃər(ə)l/ adj. **sericulturist** /-'kʌltʃərɪst/ n. [F *sériciculture* f. LL *sericum*: see SILK, CULTURE]

series /'sɪəriːz, -rɪz/ n. (pl. same) **1** a number of things of which each is similar to the preceding or in which each successive pair are similarly related; a sequence, succession, order, row, or set. **2** a set of successive games between the same teams. **3** a set of programmes with the same actors etc. or on related subjects but each complete in itself. **4** a set of lectures by the same speaker or on the same subject. **5 a** a set of successive issues of a periodical, of articles on one subject or by one writer, etc., esp. when numbered separately from a preceding or following set (*second series*). **b** a set of independent books in a common format or under a common title or supervised by a common general editor. **6** Geol. **a** a set of strata with a common characteristic. **b** the rocks deposited during a specific epoch. **7** Mus. an arrangement of the twelve notes of the chromatic scale as a basis for serial music. **8** Electr. **a** a set of circuits or components arranged so that the current passes through each successively. **b** a set of batteries etc. having the positive electrode of each connected with the negative electrode of the next. **9** Math. a set of quantities constituting a progression or having the several values determined by a common relation. □ **in series 1** in ordered succession. **2** Electr. (of a set of circuits or components) arranged so that the current passes through each successively. [L, = row, chain f. *serere* join, connect]

serif /'serɪf/ n. a slight projection finishing off a stroke of a letter as in T contrasted with T (cf. SANSERIF). □ **seriffed** adj. [perh. f. Du. *schreef* dash, line f. Gmc]

serio-comic /ˌsɪərɪəʊ'kɒmɪk/ adj. combining the serious and the comic, jocular in intention but simulating seriousness or vice versa. □ **serio-comically** adv.

serious /'sɪərɪəs/ adj. **1** thoughtful, earnest, sober, sedate, responsible, not reckless or given to trifling (*has a serious air; a serious young person*). **2** important, demanding consideration (*this is a serious matter*). **3** not slight or negligible (*a serious injury; a serious offence*). **4** sincere, in earnest, not ironical or joking (*are you serious?*). **5** (of music and literature) not merely for amusement. **6** not perfunctory (*serious thought*). **7** not to be trifled with (*a serious opponent*). **8** concerned with religion or ethics (*serious subjects*). □ **seriousness** n. [ME f. OF *serieux* or LL *seriosus* f. L *serius*]

seriously /'sɪərɪəslɪ/ adv. **1** in a serious manner (esp. introducing a sentence, implying that irony etc. is now to cease). **2** to a serious extent.

serjeant /'sɑːdʒ(ə)nt/ n. **1** (in full **serjeant-at-law**, pl. **serjeants-at-law**) hist. a barrister of the highest rank. **2** Brit. (in official lists) a sergeant in the Army. □ **Common Serjeant** Brit. a circuit judge of the Central Criminal Court with duties in the City of London. **serjeant-at-arms** (pl. **serjeants-at-arms**) an official of a court or city or parliament, with ceremonial duties. □ **serjeantship** n. [var. of SERGEANT]

sermon /'sɜːmən/ n. **1** a spoken or written discourse on a religious or moral subject, esp. a discourse based on a text or passage of Scripture and delivered in a service by way of religious instruction or exhortation. **2** a piece of admonition or reproof, a lecture. **3** a moral reflection suggested by natural objects etc. (*sermons in stones*). [ME f. AF *sermun*, OF *sermon* f. L *sermo -onis* discourse, talk]

sermonize /'sɜːməˌnaɪz/ v. (also **-ise**) **1** tr. deliver a moral lecture to. **2** intr. deliver a moral lecture. □ **sermonizer** n.

serous /'sɪərəs/ adj. of or like or producing serum; watery. □ **serous gland** (or **membrane**) a gland or membrane with a serous secretion. □ **serosity** /-'rɒsɪtɪ/ n. [F *séreux* or med.L *serosus* (as SERUM)]

serpent /'sɜːp(ə)nt/ n. **1** usu. literary. **a** a snake, esp. of a large kind. **b** a scaly limbless reptile. **2** a sly or treacherous person. **3** Mus. an old bass wind instrument made from leather-covered wood, roughly in the form of an S. **4** (**the Serpent**) Bibl. Satan (see Gen. 3, Rev. 20). [ME f. OF f. L *serpens -entis* part. of *serpere* creep]

serpentine /ˈsɜːpənˌtaɪn/ adj. & n. —adj. **1** of or like a serpent. **2** coiling, tortuous, sinuous, meandering, writhing (the serpentine windings of the stream). **3** cunning, subtle, treacherous. —n. a soft rock mainly of hydrated magnesium silicate, usu. dark green and sometimes mottled or spotted like a serpent's skin. □ **serpentine verse** a metrical line beginning and ending with the same word. [ME f. OF serpentin f. LL serpentinus (as SERPENT)]

serrate v. & adj. —v.tr. /seˈreɪt/ (usu. as **serrated** adj.) provide with a sawlike edge. —adj. /ˈsereɪt/ esp. Anat., Bot., & Zool. notched like a saw. □ **serration** n. [LL serrare serrat- f. L serra saw]

serried /ˈserɪd/ adj. (of ranks of soldiers, rows of trees, etc.) pressed together; without gaps; close. [past part. of serry press close prob. f. F serré past part. of serrer close ult. f. L sera lock, or past part. of obs. serr f. OF serrer]

serum /ˈsɪərəm/ n. (pl. **sera** /-rə/ or **serums**) **1 a** an amber-coloured liquid that separates from a clot when blood coagulates. **b** whey. **2** Med. blood serum (usu. from a non-human mammal) as an antitoxin or therapeutic agent, esp. in inoculation. **3** a watery fluid in animal bodies. [L, = whey]

servant /ˈsɜːv(ə)nt/ n. **1** a person who has undertaken (usu. in return for stipulated pay) to carry out the orders of an individual or corporate employer, esp. a person employed in a house on domestic duties or as a personal attendant. **2** a devoted follower, a person willing to serve another (a servant of Jesus Christ). □ **your humble servant** Brit. archaic a formula preceding a signature or expressing ironical courtesy. **your obedient servant** Brit. a formula preceding a signature, now used only in certain formal letters. [ME f. OF (as SERVE)]

serve v. & n. —v. **1** tr. do a service for (a person, community, etc.). **2** tr. (also absol.) be a servant to. **3** intr. carry out duties (served on six committees). **4** intr. **a** (foll. by in) be employed in (an organization, esp. the armed forces, or a place, esp. a foreign country) (served in the air force). **b** be a member of the armed forces. **5 a** tr. be useful to or serviceable for; meet the needs of; do what is required for (serve a purpose; one packet serves him for a week). **b** intr. meet requirements; perform a function (a sofa serving as a bed). **c** intr. (foll. by to + infin.) avail, suffice (his attempt served only to postpone the inevitable; it serves to show the folly of such action). **6** tr. go through a due period of (office, apprenticeship, a prison sentence, etc.). **7** tr. set out or present (food) for those about to eat it (asparagus served with butter; dinner was then served). **8** intr. (in full **serve at table**) act as a waiter. **9** tr. **a** attend to (a customer in a shop). **b** (foll. by with) supply with (goods) (was serving a customer with apples; served the town with gas). **10** tr. treat or act towards (a person) in a specified way (has served me shamefully; you may serve me as you will). **11** tr. **a** (often foll. by on) deliver (a writ etc.) to the person concerned in a legally formal manner (served a warrant on him). **b** (foll. by with) deliver a writ etc. to (a person) in this way (served her with a summons). **12** tr. Tennis etc. (also absol.) deliver (a ball etc.) to begin or resume play. **13** tr. Mil. keep (a gun, battery, etc.) firing. **14** tr. (of an animal, esp. a stallion etc. hired for the purpose) copulate with (a female). **15** tr. distribute (served the ammunition out; served the rations round). **16** tr. render obedience to (a deity etc.). —n. **1** Tennis etc. **a** the act or an instance of serving. **b** a manner of serving. **c** a person's turn to serve. **2** Austral. sl. a reprimand. □ **it will serve** it will be adequate. **serve one's needs** (or **need**) be adequate. **serve out** retaliate on. **serve the purpose of** take the place of, be used as. **serve a person right** be a person's deserved punishment or misfortune. **serve one's time 1** hold office for the normal period. **2** (also **serve time**) undergo imprisonment, apprenticeship, etc. **serve one's** (or **the**) **turn** be adequate. **serve up** offer for acceptance. [ME f. OF servir f. L servire f. servus slave]

server /ˈsɜːvə(r)/ n. **1** a person who serves. **2** Eccl. a person assisting the celebrant at a service.

servery /ˈsɜːvərɪ/ n. (pl. **-ies**) a room from which meals etc. are served and in which utensils are kept.

service[1] /ˈsɜːvɪs/ n. & v. —n. **1** the act of helping or doing work for another or for a community etc. **2** work done in this way. **3** assistance or benefit given to someone. **4** the provision or system of supplying a public need, e.g. transport, or (often in pl.) the supply of water, gas, electricity, telephone, etc. **5 a** the fact or status of being a servant. **b** employment or a position as a servant. **6** a state or period of employment doing work for an individual or organization (resigned after 15 years' service). **7 a** a public or Crown department or organization employing officials working for the State (civil service; secret service). **b** employment in this. **8** (in pl.) the armed forces. **9** (attrib.) of the kind issued to the armed forces (a service revolver). **10 a** a ceremony of worship according to prescribed forms. **b** a form of liturgy for this. **11** the provision of what is necessary for the installation and maintenance of a machine etc. or operation. **b** a periodic routine maintenance of a motor vehicle etc. **12** assistance or advice given to customers after the sale of goods. **13 a** the act or process of serving food, drinks, etc. **b** an extra charge nominally made for this. **14** a set of dishes, plates, etc., used for serving meals (a dinner service). **15** Tennis etc. **a** the act or an instance of serving. **b** (in full **service game**) a game in which a particular player serves. —v.tr. **1** provide service or services for, esp. maintain. **2** maintain or repair (a car, machine, etc.). **3** pay interest on (a debt). **4** supply with a service. □ **at a person's service** ready to serve or assist a person. **be of service** be available to assist. **in service 1** employed as a servant. **2** available for use. **on active service** serving in the armed forces in wartime. **out of service** not available for use. **see service 1** have experience of service, esp. in the armed forces. **2** (of a thing) be much used. **service area 1** an area beside a major road for the supply of petrol, refreshments, etc. **2** the area served by a broadcasting station. **service-book** a book of authorized forms of worship of a Church. **service bus** (or **car**) Austral. & NZ a motor coach. **service charge** an additional charge for service in a restaurant, hotel, etc. **service dress** ordinary military etc. uniform. **service flat** a flat in which domestic service and sometimes meals are provided by the management. **service industry** one providing services not goods. **service road** a road parallel to a main road, serving houses, shops, etc. **service station** an establishment beside a road selling petrol and oil etc. to motorists and often able to carry out maintenance. [ME f. OF *service* or L *servitium* f. *servus* slave]

service[2] /ˈsɜːvɪs/ n. (in full **service tree**) a European tree of the genus *Sorbus*, esp. *S. domestica*, with cream-coloured flowers and small round or pear-shaped fruit eaten when overripe. [earlier *serves*, pl. of obs. *serve* f. OE *syrfe* f. Gmc *surbhjōn* ult. f. L *sorbus*]

serviceable /ˈsɜːvɪsəb(ə)l/ adj. **1** useful or usable. **2** able to render service. **3** durable; capable of withstanding difficult conditions. **4** suited for ordinary use rather than ornament. □ **serviceability** /-ˈbɪlɪtɪ/ n. **serviceableness** n. **serviceably** adv. [ME f. OF *servisable* (as SERVICE[1])]

serviceman /ˈsɜːvɪsmən/ n. (pl. **-men**) **1** a man serving in the armed forces. **2** a man providing service or maintenance.

servicewoman /ˈsɜːvɪsˌwʊmən/ n. (pl. **-women**) a woman serving in the armed forces.

serviette /ˌsɜːvɪˈet/ n. esp. Brit. a napkin for use at table. [ME f. OF f. *servir* SERVE]

servile /ˈsɜːvaɪl/ adj. **1** of or being or like a slave or slaves. **2** slavish, fawning; completely dependent. □ **servilely** adv. **servility** /-ˈvɪlɪtɪ/ n. [ME f. L *servilis* f. *servus* slave]

serving /ˈsɜːvɪŋ/ n. a quantity of food served to one person.

servitor /ˈsɜːvɪt(ə)r/ n. archaic **1** a servant. **2** an attendant. □ **servitorship** n. [ME f. OF f. LL (as SERVE)]

servitude /ˈsɜːvɪtjuːd/ n. **1** slavery. **2** subjection (esp. involuntary); bondage. [ME f. OF f. L *servitudo -inis* f. *servus* slave]

servo /ˈsɜːvəʊ/ n. (pl. **-os**) **1** (in full **servo-mechanism**) a powered mechanism producing motion or forces at a higher level of energy than the input level, e.g. in the brakes and steering of large motor vehicles, esp. where feedback is employed to make the control automatic. **2** (in full **servo-motor**) the motive element in a servo-mechanism. **3** (in comb.) of or involving a servo-mechanism (*servo-assisted*). [L *servus* slave]

sesame /ˈsesəmɪ/ n. Bot. **1** an E. Indian herbaceous plant, *Sesamum indicum*, with seeds used as food and yielding an edible oil. **2** its seeds. □ **open sesame** a means of acquiring or achieving what is normally unattainable (from the magic words used in the *Arabian Nights' Entertainments*). [L *sesamum* f. Gk *sēsamon*, *sēsamē*]

sesqui- /ˈseskwɪ/ comb. form denoting one and a half. [L (as SEMI-, *-que* and)]

sesquicentenary /ˌseskwɪsenˈtiːnərɪ/ n. (pl. **-ies**) a one-hundred-and-fiftieth anniversary.

sesquicentennial /ˌseskwɪsenˈtenɪəl/ n. & adj. —n. = SESQUICENTENARY. —adj. of or relating to a sesquicentennial.

sessile /ˈsesaɪl/ adj. **1** Bot. & Zool. (of a flower, leaf, eye, etc.) attached directly by its base without a stalk or peduncle. **2** fixed in one position; immobile. [L *sessilis* f. *sedēre sess- sit*]

session /ˈseʃ(ə)n/ n. **1** the process of assembly of a deliberative or judicial body to conduct its business. **2** a single meeting for this purpose. **3** a period during which such meetings are regularly held. **4 a** an academic year. **b** the period during which a school etc. has classes. **5** a period devoted to an activity (*poker session*;

recording session). **6** the governing body of a Presbyterian Church. □ **in session** assembled for business; not on vacation. □ **sessional** adj. [ME f. OF *session* or L *sessio -onis* (as SESSILE)]

sestet /sesˈtet/ n. **1** the last six lines of a sonnet. **2** a sextet. [It. *sestetto* f. *sesto* f. L *sextus* a sixth]

set[1] v. (**setting**; past and past part. **set**) **1** tr. put, lay, or stand (a thing) in a certain position or location (*set it on the table*; *set it upright*). **2** tr. (foll. by *to*) apply (one thing) to (another) (*set pen to paper*). **3** tr. a fix ready or in position. **b** dispose suitably for use, action, or display. **4** tr. **a** adjust the hands of (a clock or watch) to show the right time. **b** adjust (an alarm clock) to sound at the required time. **5** tr. **a** fix, arrange, or mount. **b** insert (a jewel) in a ring, framework, etc. **6** tr. make (a device) ready to operate. **7** tr. lay (a table) for a meal. **8** tr. arrange (the hair) while damp so that it dries in the required style. **9** tr. (foll. by *with*) ornament or provide (a surface, esp. a precious item) (*gold set with gems*). **10** tr. bring by placing or arranging or other means into a specified state; cause to be (*set things in motion*; *set it on fire*). **11** intr. & tr. harden or solidify (*the jelly is set*; *the cement has set*). **12** intr. (of the sun, moon, etc.) appear to move towards and below the earth's horizon (as the earth rotates). **13** tr. represent (a story, play, scene, etc.) as happening in a certain time or place. **14** tr. **a** (foll. by *to* + infin.) cause or instruct (a person) to perform a specified activity (*set them to work*). **b** (foll. by pres. part.) start (a person or thing) doing something (*set him chatting*; *set the ball rolling*). **15** tr. present or impose as work to be done or a matter to be dealt with (*set them an essay*). **16** tr. exhibit as a type or model (*set a good example*). **17** tr. initiate; take the lead in (*set the fashion*; *set the pace*). **18** tr. establish (a record etc.). **19** tr. determine or decide (*the itinerary is set*). **20** tr. appoint or establish (*set them in authority*). **21** tr. join, attach, or fasten. **22** tr. **a** put parts of (a broken or dislocated bone, limb, etc.) into the correct position for healing. **b** deal with (a fracture or dislocation) in this way. **23** tr. (in full **set to music**) provide (words etc.) with music for singing. **24** tr. (often foll. by *up*) Printing **a** arrange or produce (type or film etc.) as required. **b** arrange the type or film etc. for (a book etc.). **25** intr. (of a tide, current, etc.) have a certain motion or direction. **26** intr. (of a face) assume a hard expression. **27** tr. **a** cause (a hen) to sit on eggs. **b** place (eggs) for a hen to sit on. **28** tr. put (a seed, plant, etc.) in the ground to grow. **29** tr. give the teeth of (a saw) an alternate outward inclination. **30** tr. esp. *US* start (a fire). **31** intr. (of eyes etc.) become motionless. **32** intr. feel or show a certain tendency (*opinion is setting against it*). **33** intr. **a** (of blossom) form into fruit. **b** (of fruit) develop from blossom. **c** (of a tree) develop fruit. **34** intr. (of a hunting dog) take a rigid attitude indicating the presence of game. □ **set about 1** begin or take steps towards. **2** colloq. attack. **set (a person or thing) against (another) 1** consider or reckon (a thing) as a counterpoise or compensation for. **2** cause to oppose. **set apart** separate, reserve, differentiate. **set back 1** place further back in place or time. **2** impede or reverse the progress of. **3** colloq. cost (a person) a specified amount. **set-back** n. **1** a reversal or arrest of progress. **2** a relapse. **set by** archaic save for future use. **set down 1** record in writing. **2** allow to alight from a vehicle. **3** (foll. by *to*) attribute to. **4** (foll. by *as*) explain or describe to oneself as. **set forth 1** begin a journey. **2** make known; expound. **set forward** begin to advance. **set free** release. **set one's heart** (or **hopes**) **on** want or hope for eagerly. **set in 1** (of weather, a condition, etc.) begin (and seem likely to continue), become established. **2** insert (esp. a sleeve etc. into a garment). **set much by** consider to be of much value. **set off 1** begin a journey. **2** detonate (a bomb etc.). **3** initiate, stimulate. **4** cause (a person) to start laughing, talking, etc. **5** serve as an adornment or foil to; enhance. **6** (foll. by *against*) use as a compensating item. **set on** (or **upon**) **1** attack violently. **2** cause or urge to attack. **set out 1** begin a journey. **2** (foll. by *to* + infin.) aim or intend. **3** demonstrate, arrange, or exhibit. **4** mark out. **5** declare. **set sail 1** hoist the sails. **2** begin a voyage. **set one's teeth 1** clench them. **2** summon one's resolve. **set to** begin doing something vigorously, esp. fighting, arguing, or eating. **set-to** *n.* (*pl.* **-tos**) *colloq.* a fight or argument. **set up 1** place in position or view. **2** organize or start (a business etc.). **3** establish in some capacity. **4** supply the needs of. **5** begin making (a loud sound). **6** cause or make arrangements for (a condition or situation). **7** prepare (a task etc. for another). **8** restore or enhance the health of (a person). **9** establish (a record). **10** propound (a theory). **11** *colloq.* put (a person) in a dangerous or vulnerable position. **set-up** *n.* **1** an arrangement or organization. **2** the manner or structure or position of this. **set oneself up as** make pretensions to being. [OE *settan* f. Gmc]

set² *n.* **1** a number of things or persons that belong together or resemble one another or are usually found together. **2** a collection or group. **3** a section of society consorting together or having similar interests etc. **4** a collection of implements, vessels, etc., regarded collectively and needed for a specified purpose (*cricket set*; *teaset*; *a set of teeth*). **5** a piece of electric or electronic apparatus, esp. a radio or television receiver. **6** (in tennis etc.) a group of games counting as a unit towards a match for the player or side that wins a defined number or proportion of the games. **7** *Math.* & *Logic* a collection of distinct entities, individually specified or satisfying specified conditions, forming a unit. **8** a group of pupils or students having the same average ability. **9 a** a slip, shoot, bulb, etc., for planting. **b** a young fruit just set. **10 a** a habitual posture or conformation; the way the head etc. is carried or a dress etc. flows. **b** (also **dead set**) a setter's pointing in the presence of game. **11** the way, drift, or tendency (of a current, public opinion, state of mind, etc.) (*the set of public feeling is against it*). **12** the way in which a machine, device, etc., is set or adjusted. **13** a setting, including stage furniture etc., for a play or film etc. **14** a sequence of songs or pieces performed in jazz or popular music. **15** the setting of the hair when damp. **16** (also **sett**) a badger's burrow. **17** (also **sett**) a granite paving-block. **18** a number of people making up a square dance. □ **make a dead set at 1** make a determined attack on. **2** seek to win the affections of. **set point** *Tennis* etc. **1** the state of a game when one side needs only one more point to win the set. **2** this point. **set theory** the branch of mathematics concerned with the manipulation of sets. [sense 1 (and related senses) f. OF *sette* f. L *secta* SECT: other senses f. SET¹]

set³ *adj.* **1** in senses of SET¹. **2** prescribed or determined in advance. **3** fixed, unchanging, unmoving. **4** (of a phrase or speech etc.) having invariable or predetermined wording; not extempore. **5** prepared for action. **6** (foll. by *on*, *upon*) determined to acquire or achieve etc. **7** (of a book etc.) specified for reading in preparation for an examination. **8** (of a meal) served according to a fixed menu. □ **set fair** (of the weather) fine without a sign of breaking. **set phrase** an invariable or usual arrangement of words. **set piece 1** a formal or elaborate arrangement, esp. in art or literature. **2** fireworks arranged on scaffolding etc. **set square** a right-angled triangular plate for drawing lines, esp. at 90°, 45°, 60°, or 30°. [past part. of SET¹]

sett var. of SET² 16, 17.

settee /se'ti:/ *n.* a seat (usu. upholstered), with a back and usu. arms, for more than one person. [18th c.: perh. a fanciful var. of SETTLE²]

setter /'setə(r)/ *n.* **1 a** a dog of a large long-haired breed trained to stand rigid when scenting game. **b** this breed. **2** a person or thing that sets.

setting /'setɪŋ/ *n.* **1** the position or manner in which a thing is set. **2** the immediate surroundings (of a house etc.). **3** the surroundings of any object regarded as its framework; the environment of a thing. **4** the place and time, scenery, etc., of a story, drama, etc. **5** a frame in which a jewel is set. **6** the music to which words of a poem, song, etc., are set. **7** a set of cutlery and other accessories for one person at a table. **8** the way in which or level at which a machine is set to operate.

settle¹ /'set(ə)l/ *v.* **1** *tr.* & *intr.* (often foll. by *down*) establish or become established in a more or less permanent abode or way of life. **2** *intr.* & *tr.* (often foll. by *down*) **a** cease or cause to cease from wandering, disturbance, movement, etc. **b** adopt a regular or secure style of life. **c** (foll. by *to*) apply oneself (to work, an activity, a way of life, etc.) (*settled down to writing letters*). **3 a** *intr.* sit or come down to stay for some time. **b** *tr.* cause to do this. **4** *tr.* & *intr.* bring to or attain fixity, certainty, composure, or quietness. **5** *tr.* determine or decide or agree upon (*shall we settle a date?*). **6** *tr.* **a** resolve (a dispute etc.). **b** deal with (a matter) finally. **7** *tr.* terminate (a lawsuit) by mutual agreement. **8** *intr.* **a** (foll. by *for*) accept or agree to (esp. an alternative not one's first choice). **b** (foll. by *on*) decide on. **9** *tr.* (also *absol.*) pay (a debt, an account, etc.). **10** *intr.* (as **settled** *adj.*) not likely to change for a time (*settled weather*). **11** *tr.* **a** aid the digestion of (food). **b** remedy the disordered state of (nerves, the stomach, etc.). **12** *tr.* **a** colonize. **b** establish colonists in. **13** *intr.* subside; fall to the bottom or on to a surface (*the foundations have settled*; *the dust will settle*). □ **settle one's affairs** make any necessary arrangements (e.g. write a will) when death is near. **settle in** become established in a place. **settle up 1** (also *absol.*) pay (an account, debt, etc.). **2** finally arrange (a matter). **settle with 1** pay all or part of an amount due to (a creditor). **2** get revenge on. □ **settleable** *adj.* [OE *setlan* (as SETTLE²) f. Gmc]

settle² /ˈset(ə)l/ *n.* a bench with a high back and arms and often with a box fitted below the seat. [OE *setl* place to sit f. Gmc]

settlement /ˈsetəlmənt/ *n.* **1** the act or an instance of settling; the process of being settled. **2 a** the colonization of a region. **b** a place or area occupied by settlers. **c** a small village. **3 a** a political or financial etc. agreement. **b** an arrangement ending a dispute. **4 a** the terms on which property is given to a person. **b** a deed stating these. **c** the amount of property given. **d** = *marriage settlement*. **5** the process of settling an account. **6** subsidence of a wall, house, soil, etc.

settler /ˈsetlə(r)/ *n.* a person who goes to settle in a new country or place; an early colonist.

seven /ˈsev(ə)n/ *n.* & *adj.* —*n.* **1** one more than six. **2** a symbol for this (7, vii, VII). **3** a size etc. denoted by seven. **4** a set or team of seven individuals. **5** the time of seven o'clock (*is it seven yet?*). **6** a card with seven pips. —*adj.* that amount to seven. □ **the seven deadly sins** the sins of pride, covetousness, lust, anger, gluttony, envy, and sloth. **the seven seas** the oceans of the world: the Arctic, Antarctic, N. Pacific, S. Pacific, N. Atlantic, S. Atlantic, and Indian Oceans. **seven year itch** a supposed tendency to infidelity after seven years of marriage. [OE *seofon* f. Gmc]

sevenfold /ˈsevənˌfəʊld/ *adj.* & *adv.* **1** seven times as much or as many. **2** consisting of seven parts.

seventeen /ˌsevənˈtiːn/ *n.* & *adj.* —*n.* **1** one more than sixteen. **2** a symbol for this (17, xvii, XVII). **3** a size etc. denoted by seventeen. —*adj.* that amount to seventeen. □ **seventeenth** *adj.* & *n.* [OE *seofontīene*]

seventh /ˈsev(ə)nθ/ *n.* & *adj.* —*n.* **1** the position in a sequence corresponding to the number 7 in the sequence 1–7. **2** something occupying this position. **3** one of seven equal parts of a thing. **4** *Mus.* **a** an interval or chord spanning seven consecutive notes in the diatonic scale (e.g. C to B). **b** a note separated from another by this interval. —*adj.* that is the seventh. □ **Seventh-Day Adventists** a staunchly protestant branch of the Adventists with beliefs based rigidly on faith and the Scriptures and the imminent return of Christ to earth, and observing the sabbath on Saturday. □ **seventhly** *adv.*

seventy /ˈsevəntɪ/ *n.* & *adj.* —*n.* (*pl.* **-ies**) **1** the product of seven and ten. **2** a symbol for this (70, lxx, LXX). **3** (in *pl.*) the numbers from 70 to 79, esp. the years of a century or of a person's life. —*adj.* that amount to seventy. □ **seventieth** *adj.* & *n.* **seventyfold** *adj.* & *adv.* [OE *-seofontig*]

sever /ˈsevə(r)/ *v.* **1** *tr.* & *intr.* (often foll. by *from*) divide, break, or make separate, esp. by cutting. **2** *tr.* & *intr.* break off or away; separate, part, divide (*severed our friendship*). **3** *tr.* end the employment contract of (a person). □ **severable** *adj.* [ME f. AF *severer*, OF *sevrer* ult. f. L *separare* SEPARATE *v.*]

several /ˈsevr(ə)l/ *adj.* & *n.* —*adj.* & *n.* more than two but not many. —*adj.* separate or respective; distinct (*all went their several ways*). □ **severally** *adv.* [ME f. AF f. AL *separalis* f. L *separ* SEPARATE *adj.*]

severance /ˈsevərəns/ *n.* **1** the act or an instance of severing. **2** a severed state. □ **severance pay** an amount paid to an employee on the early termination of a contract.

severe /sɪˈvɪə(r)/ *adj.* **1** rigorous, strict, and harsh in attitude or treatment (*a severe critic; severe discipline*). **2** serious, critical (*a severe shortage*). **3** vehement or forceful (*a severe storm*). **4** extreme (in an unpleasant quality) (*a severe winter; severe cold*). **5** arduous or exacting; making great demands on energy, skill, etc. (*severe competition*). **6** unadorned; plain in style (*severe dress*). □ **severely** *adv.* **severity** /-ˈverɪtɪ/ *n.* [F *sévère* or L *severus*]

Seville orange /ˈsevɪl/ *n.* a bitter orange used for marmalade. [*Seville* in Spain]

sew /səʊ/ *v.tr.* (*past part.* **sewn** /səʊn/ or **sewed**) **1** (also *absol.*) fasten, join, etc., by making stitches with a needle and thread or a sewing-machine. **2** make (a garment etc.) by sewing. **3** (often foll. by *on, in*, etc.) attach by sewing (*shall I sew on your buttons?*). □ **sew up 1** join or enclose by sewing. **2** *colloq.* (esp. in *passive*) satisfactorily arrange or finish dealing with (a project etc.). **3** esp. *US* obtain exclusive use of. □ **sewer** *n.* [OE *si(o)wan*]

sewage /ˈsuːɪdʒ, ˈsjuː-/ *n.* waste matter, esp. excremental, conveyed in sewers. □ **sewage farm** (or **works**) a place where sewage is treated, esp. to produce manure.

sewer /ˈsuːə(r), ˈsjuː-/ *n.* a conduit, usu. underground, for carrying off drainage water and sewage. □ **sewer rat** the common brown rat. [ME f. AF *sewere*, ONF *se(u)wiere* channel to carry off the overflow from a fishpond, ult. f. L *ex-* out of + *aqua* water]

sewerage /ˈsuːərɪdʒ, ˈsjuː-/ *n.* a system of or drainage by sewers.

sewing /ˈsəʊɪŋ/ *n.* a piece of material or work to be sewn.

sewing-machine /ˈsəʊɪŋməˌʃiːn/ *n.* a machine for sewing or stitching.

sewn *past part.* of SEW.

sex *n., adj.,* & *v.* —*n.* **1** either of the main divisions (male and female) into which living things are placed on the basis of their reproductive functions. **2** the fact of belonging to one of these. **3** males or females collectively. **4** sexual instincts, desires, etc., or their manifestation. **5** *colloq.* sexual intercourse. —*adj.* **1** of or relating to sex (*sex education*). **2** arising from a difference or consciousness of sex (*sex antagonism; sex urge*). —*v.tr.* **1** determine the sex of. **2** (as **sexed** *adj.*) **a** having a sexual appetite (*highly sexed*). **b** having sexual characteristics. □ **sex act** (usu. prec. by *the*) the (or an) act of sexual intercourse. **sex appeal** sexual attractiveness. **sex change** an apparent change of sex by surgical means and hormone treatment. **sex chromosome** a chromosome concerned in determining the sex of an organism, which in most animals are of two kinds, the X-chromosome and the Y-chromosome. **sex hormone** a hormone affecting sexual development or behaviour. **sex life** a person's activity related to sexual instincts. **sex-linked** *Genetics* carried on or by a sex chromosome. **sex maniac** *colloq.* a person needing or seeking excessive gratification of the sexual instincts. **sex object** a person regarded mainly in terms of sexual attractiveness. **sex-starved** lacking sexual gratification. **sex symbol** a person widely noted for sex appeal. □ **sexer** n. [ME f. OF *sexe* or L *sexus*]

sexagenarian /ˌseksədʒɪˈneərɪən/ n. & adj. —n. a person from 60 to 69 years old. —adj. of this age. [L *sexagenarius* f. *sexageni* distrib. of *sexaginta* sixty]

Sexagesima /ˌseksəˈdʒesɪmə/ n. the Sunday before Quinquagesima. [ME f. eccl.L, = sixtieth (day), prob. named loosely as preceding QUINQUAGESIMA]

sexennial /sekˈsenɪəl/ adj. **1** lasting six years. **2** recurring every six years. [SEXI- + L *annus* year]

sexi- /ˈseksɪ/ comb. form (also **sex-** before a vowel) six. [L *sex* six]

sexism /ˈseksɪz(ə)m/ n. prejudice or discrimination, esp. against women, on the grounds of sex. □ **sexist** adj. & n.

sexless /ˈsekslɪs/ adj. **1** Biol. neither male nor female. **2** lacking in sexual desire or attractiveness. □ **sexlessly** adv. **sexlessness** n.

sexology /sekˈsɒlədʒɪ/ n. the study of sexual life or relationships, esp. in human beings. □ **sexological** /-əˈlɒdʒɪk(ə)l/ adj. **sexologist** n.

sexploitation /ˌseksplɔɪˈteɪʃ(ə)n/ n. colloq. the exploitation of sex, esp. commercially.

sexpot /ˈsekspɒt/ n. colloq. a sexy person (esp. a woman).

sext n. Eccl. **1** the canonical hour of prayer appointed for the sixth daytime hour (i.e. noon). **2** the office of sext. [ME f. L *sexta hora* sixth hour f. *sextus* sixth]

sextant /ˈsekst(ə)nt/ n. an instrument with a graduated arc of 60° used in navigation and surveying for measuring the angular distance of objects by means of mirrors. [L *sextans -ntis* sixth part f. *sextus* sixth]

sextet /sekˈstet/ n. (also **sextette**) **1** Mus. a composition for six voices or instruments. **2** the performers of such a piece. **3** any group of six. [alt. of SESTET after L *sex* six]

sexton /ˈsekst(ə)n/ n. a person who looks after a church and churchyard, often acting as bell-ringer and gravedigger. [ME *segerstane* etc., f. AF, OF *segerstein*, *secrestein* f. med.L *sacristanus* SACRISTAN]

sextuple /ˈseksˌtjuːp(ə)l/ adj., n., & v. —adj. **1** sixfold. **2** having six parts. **3** being six times as many or much. —n. a sixfold number or amount. —v.tr. & intr. multiply by six; increase sixfold. □ **sextuply** adv. [med.L *sextuplus*, irreg. f. L *sex* six, after LL *quintuplus* QUINTUPLE]

sextuplet /ˈseksˌtjʊplɪt, -ˈtjuːplɪt/ n. each of six children born at one birth. [SEXTUPLE, after *triplet* etc.]

sexual /ˈseksjʊəl, -ʃʊəl/ adj. **1** of or relating to sex, or to the sexes or the relations between them. **2** Bot. (of classification) based on the distinction of sexes in plants. **3** Biol. having a sex. □ **sexual intercourse** the insertion of a man's erect penis into a woman's vagina, usu. followed by the ejaculation of semen. □ **sexuality** /-ˈælɪtɪ/ n. **sexually** adv. [LL *sexualis* (as SEX)]

sexy /ˈseksɪ/ adj. (**sexier**, **sexiest**) **1** sexually attractive or stimulating. **2** sexually aroused. **3** concerned with or engrossed in sex. □ **sexily** adv. **sexiness** n.

sez /sez/ sl. says (*sez you*). [phonetic repr.]

SF abbr. science fiction.

sf abbr. Mus. sforzando.

SFA abbr. Scottish Football Association.

sforzando /sfɔːˈtsændəʊ/ adj., adv., & n. (also **sforzato** /-ˈtsɑːtəʊ/) —adj. & adv. Mus. with sudden emphasis. —n. (pl. **-os** or **sforzandi** /-dɪ/) **1** a note or group of notes especially emphasized. **2** an increase in emphasis and loudness. [It., verbal noun and past part. of *sforzare* use force]

Sgt. abbr. Sergeant.

sh int. calling for silence. [var. of HUSH]

shabby /ˈʃæbɪ/ adj. (**shabbier**, **shabbiest**) **1** in bad repair or condition; faded and worn, dingy, dilapidated. **2** dressed in old or worn clothes. **3** of poor quality. **4** contemptible, dishonourable (*a shabby trick*). □ **shabbily** adv. **shabbiness** n. **shabbyish** adj. [*shab* scab f. OE *sceabb* f. ON, rel. to SCAB]

shack n. & v. —n. a roughly built hut or cabin. —v.intr. (foll. by *up*) sl. cohabit, esp. as lovers. [perh. f. Mex. *jacal*, Aztec *xacatli* wooden hut]

shackle /ˈʃæk(ə)l/ n. & v. —n. **1** a metal loop or link, closed by a bolt, to connect chains etc. **2** a fetter enclosing the ankle or wrist. **3** (usu. in pl.) a restraint or impediment. —v.tr. fetter, impede, restrain. [OE *sc(e)acul* fetter, corresp. to LG *shäkel* link, coupling, ON *skökull* wagon-pole f. Gmc]

shad n. (pl. same or **shads**) Zool. any deep-bodied edible marine fish of the genus *Alosa*, spawning in fresh water. [OE *sceadd*, of unkn. orig.]

shaddock /ˈʃædək/ n. Bot. **1** the largest citrus fruit, with a thick yellow skin and bitter pulp. **2** the tree, *Citrus grandis*, bearing these. [Capt. *Shaddock*, who introduced it to the W. Indies in the 17th c.]

shade n. & v. —n. **1** comparative darkness (and usu. coolness) caused by shelter from direct light and heat. **2** a place or area sheltered from the sun. **3** a darker part of a picture etc. **4** a colour, esp. with regard to its depth or as distinguished from one nearly like it. **5** comparative obscurity. **6** a slight amount (*am a shade better today*). **7** a translucent cover for a lamp etc. **8** a screen excluding or moderating light. **9** an eye-shield. **10** (in pl.) esp. US colloq. sunglasses. **11** a slightly differing variety (*all shades of opinion*). **12** literary **a** a ghost. **b** (in pl.) Hades. **13** (in pl.; foll. by *of*) suggesting reminiscence or unfavourable comparison (*shades of Dr Johnson!*). —v. **1** tr. screen from light. **2** tr. cover, moderate, or exclude the light of. **3** tr. darken, esp. with parallel pencil lines to represent shadow etc. **4** intr. & tr. (often foll. by *away*, *off*, *into*) pass or change by degrees. □ **in the shade** in comparative obscurity. □ **shadeless** adj. [OE *sc(e)adu* f. Gmc]

shading /ˈʃeɪdɪŋ/ n. **1** the representation of light and shade, e.g. by pencilled lines, on a map or drawing. **2** the graduation of tones from light to dark to create a sense of depth.

shadow /ˈʃædəʊ/ n. & v. —n. **1** shade or a patch of shade. **2** a dark figure projected by a body intercepting rays of light, often regarded as an appendage. **3** an inseparable attendant or companion. **4** a person secretly following another. **5** the slightest trace (*not the shadow of a doubt*). **6** a weak or insubstantial remnant or thing (*a shadow of his former self*). **7** (attrib.) Brit. denoting members of a political party in opposition holding responsibilities parallel to those of the government (*shadow Home Secretary*; *shadow cabinet*). **8** the shaded part of a picture. **9** a substance used to colour the eyelids. **10** gloom or sadness. —*v.tr.* **1** cast a shadow over. **2** secretly follow and watch the movements of. □ **shadow-boxing** boxing against an imaginary opponent as a form of training. □ **shadower** *n.* **shadowless** *adj.* [repr. OE *scead(u)we*, oblique case of *sceadu* SHADE]

shadowy /ˈʃædəʊɪ/ *adj.* **1** like a shadow. **2** full of shadows. **3** vague, indistinct. □ **shadowiness** *n.*

shady /ˈʃeɪdɪ/ *adj.* (**shadier, shadiest**) **1** giving shade. **2** situated in shade. **3** (of a person or behaviour) disreputable; of doubtful honesty. □ **shadily** *adv.* **shadiness** *n.*

shaft /ʃɑːft/ *n.* & *v.* —*n.* **1 a** an arrow or spear. **b** the long slender stem of these. **2** a remark intended to hurt or provoke (*a shaft of malice*; *shafts of wit*). **3** (foll. by *of*) **a** a ray (of light). **b** a bolt (of lightning). **4** the stem or handle of a tool, implement, etc. **5** a column, esp. between the base and capital. **6** a long narrow space, usu. vertical, for access to a mine, a lift in a building, for ventilation, etc. **7** a long and narrow part supporting or connecting or driving a part or parts of greater thickness etc. **8** each of the pair of poles between which a horse is harnessed to a vehicle. **9** *Mech.* a large axle or revolving bar transferring force by belts or cogs. **10** *US colloq.* harsh or unfair treatment. —*v.tr.* *US colloq.* treat unfairly. [OE *scæft, sceaft* f. Gmc]

shag[1] *n.* **1** a rough growth or mass of hair etc. **2** a coarse kind of cut tobacco. **3** a cormorant, esp. the crested cormorant, *Phalacrocorax aristotelis*. [OE *sceacga*, rel. to ON *skegg* beard, OE *sceaga* coppice]

shag[2] *v.tr.* (**shagged, shagging**) *coarse sl.* **1** have sexual intercourse with. **2** (usu. in *passive*; often foll. by *out*) exhaust; tire out. [18th c.: orig. unkn.]

shaggy /ˈʃægɪ/ *adj.* (**shaggier, shaggiest**) **1** hairy, rough-haired. **2** unkempt. **3** (of the hair) coarse and abundant. □ **shaggy-dog story** a long rambling story amusing only by its being inconsequential. □ **shaggily** *adv.* **shagginess** *n.*

shagreen /ʃæˈɡriːn/ *n.* **1** a kind of untanned leather with a rough granulated surface. **2** a sharkskin rough with natural papillae, used for rasping and polishing. [var. of CHAGRIN in the sense 'rough skin']

shah *n. hist.* a title of the former monarch of Iran. □ **shahdom** *n.* [Pers. *šāh* f. OPers. *kšāyṭiya* king]

shaikh var. of SHEIKH.

shake *v.* & *n.* —*v.* (*past* **shook** /ʃʊk/; *past part.* **shaken** /ˈʃeɪkən/) **1** *tr.* & *intr.* move forcefully or quickly up and down or to and fro. **2 a** *intr.* tremble or vibrate markedly. **b** *tr.* cause to do this. **3** *tr.* **a** agitate or shock. **b** *colloq.* upset the composure of. **4** *tr.* weaken or impair; make less convincing or firm or courageous (*shook his confidence*). **5** *intr.* (of a voice, note, etc.) make tremulous or rapidly alternating sounds; trill (*his voice shook with emotion*). **6** *tr.* brandish; make a threatening gesture with (one's fist, a stick, etc.). **7** *intr. colloq.* shake hands (*they shook on the deal*). **8** *tr.* esp. *US colloq.* = *shake off*. —*n.* **1** the act or an instance of shaking; the process of being shaken. **2** a jerk or shock. **3** (in *pl.*; prec. by *the*) a fit of or tendency to trembling or shivering. **4** = *milk shake*. □ **in two shakes (of a**

lamb's or dog's tail) very quickly. **no great shakes** *colloq.* not very good or significant. **shake a person by the hand** = *shake hands*. **shake down 1** settle or cause to fall by shaking. **2** settle down. **3** become established; get into harmony with circumstances, surroundings, etc. **4** *US sl.* extort money from. **shake the dust off one's feet** depart indignantly or disdainfully. **shake hands** (often foll. by *with*) clasp right hands at meeting or parting, in reconciliation or congratulation, or over a concluded bargain. **shake one's head** move one's head from side to side in refusal, denial, disapproval, or concern. **shake in one's shoes** tremble with apprehension. **shake a leg 1** begin dancing. **2** make a start. **shake off 1** get rid of (something unwanted). **2** manage to evade (a person who is following or pestering one). **shake out 1** empty by shaking. **2** spread or open (a sail, flag, etc.) by shaking. **shake-out** *n.* = *shake-up*. **shake up 1** mix (ingredients) by shaking. **2** restore to shape by shaking. **3** disturb or make uncomfortable. **4** rouse from lethargy, apathy, conventionality, etc. **shake-up** *n.* an upheaval or drastic reorganization. □ **shakeable** *adj.* (also **shakable**). [OE *sc(e)acan* f. Gmc]

shakedown /ˈʃeɪkdaʊn/ *n.* **1** a makeshift bed. **2** *US sl.* a swindle; a piece of extortion.

shaken *past part.* of SHAKE.

shaker /ˈʃeɪkə(r)/ *n.* **1** a person or thing that shakes. **2** a container for shaking together the ingredients of cocktails etc. **3** (**Shaker**) a member of an American religious sect living simply, in celibate mixed communities. □ **Shakeress** *n.* (in sense 3). **Shakerism** *n.* (in sense 3). [ME, f. SHAKE: sense 3 from religious dances]

Shakespearian /ʃeɪkˈspɪərɪən/ *adj.* & *n.* (also **Shakespearean**) —*adj.* **1** of or relating to William Shakespeare, English dramatist d. 1616. **2** in the style of Shakespeare. —*n.* a student of Shakespeare's works etc.

shako /ˈʃeɪkəʊ/ *n.* (*pl.* **-os**) a cylindrical peaked military hat with a plume. [F *schako* f. Magyar *csákó* (*süveg*) peaked (cap) f. *csák* peak f. G *Zacken* spike]

shaky /ˈʃeɪkɪ/ *adj.* (**shakier, shakiest**) **1** unsteady; apt to shake; trembling. **2** unsound, infirm (*a shaky hand*). **3** unreliable, wavering (*a shaky promise*; *got off to a shaky start*). □ **shakily** *adv.* **shakiness** *n.*

shale *n.* soft finely stratified rock that splits easily, consisting of consolidated mud or clay. □ **shaly** *adj.* [prob. f. G *Schale* f. OE *sc(e)alu* rel. to ON *skál* (see SCALE[2])]

shall /ʃæl, ʃ(ə)l/ *v.aux.* (*3rd sing. present* **shall**; *archaic 2nd sing. present* **shalt** as below; *past* **should** /ʃʊd, ʃəd/) (foll. by infin. without *to*, or *absol.*; present and past only in use) **1** (in the 1st person) expressing the future tense (*I shall return soon*) or (with *shall* stressed) emphatic intention (*I shall have a party*). **2** (in the 2nd and 3rd persons) expressing a strong assertion or command rather than a wish (cf. WILL[1]) (*you shall not catch me again*; *they shall go to the party*). **3** expressing a command or duty (*thou shalt not steal*; *they shall obey*). **4** (in 2nd-person questions) expressing an enquiry, esp. to avoid the form of a request (cf. WILL¹) (*shall you go to France?*). □ **shall I?** do you want me to? [OE *sceal* f. Gmc]

■ **Usage** For the other persons in senses 1, 2 see WILL¹.

shallot /ʃəˈlɒt/ *n.* an onion-like plant, *Allium ascalonicum*, with a cluster of small bulbs. [*eschalot* f. F *eschalotte* alt. of OF *eschaloigne*: see SCALLION]

shallow /ˈʃæləʊ/ *adj., n.,* & *v.* —*adj.* **1** of little depth. **2** superficial, trivial (*a shallow mind*). —*n.* (often in *pl.*) a shallow place. —*v.intr.* & *tr.* become or make shallow. □ **shallowly** *adv.* **shallowness** *n.* [ME, prob. rel. to *schald*, OE *sceald* SHOAL²]

shalom /ʃəˈlɒm/ *n.* & *int.* a Jewish salutation at meeting or parting. [Heb. *šālôm* peace]

sham *v., n.,* & *adj.* —*v.* (**shammed, shamming**) **1** *intr.* feign, pretend. **2** *tr.* **a** pretend to be. **b** simulate (*is shamming sleep*). —*n.* **1** imposture, pretence. **2** a person or thing pretending or pretended to be what he or she or it is not. —*adj.* pretended, counterfeit. □ **shammer** *n.* [perh. north. dial. var. of SHAME]

shaman /ˈʃæmən/ *n.* a witch-doctor or priest claiming to communicate with gods etc. □ **shamanism** *n.* **shamanist** *n.* & *adj.* **shamanistic** /-ˈnɪstɪk/ *adj.* [G *Schamane* & Russ. *shaman* f. Tungusian *samán*]

shamateur /ˈʃæməˌtɜː(r)/ *n. derog.* a sports player who makes money from sporting activities though classed as an amateur. □ **shamateurism** *n.* [SHAM + AMATEUR]

shamble /ˈʃæmb(ə)l/ *v.* & *n.* —*v.intr.* walk or run with a shuffling or awkward gait. —*n.* a shambling gait. [prob. f. dial. *shamble* (adj.) ungainly, perh. f. *shamble legs* with ref. to straddling trestles: see SHAMBLES]

shambles /ˈʃæmb(ə)lz/ *n.pl.* (usu. treated as *sing.*) **1** *colloq.* a mess or muddle (*the room was a shambles*). **2** a butcher's slaughterhouse. **3** a scene of carnage. [pl. of *shamble* stool, stall f. OE *sc(e)amul* f. WG f. L *scamellum* dimin. of *scamnum* bench]

shambolic /ʃæmˈbɒlɪk/ *adj. colloq.* chaotic, unorganized. [SHAMBLES, prob. after SYMBOLIC]

shame *n.* & *v.* —*n.* **1** a feeling of distress or humiliation caused by consciousness of the guilt or folly of oneself or an associate. **2** a capacity for experiencing this feeling, esp. as imposing a restraint on behaviour (*has no sense of shame*). **3** a state of disgrace, discredit, or intense regret. **4 a** a person or thing that brings disgrace etc. **b** a thing or action that is wrong or regrettable. —*v.tr.* **1** bring shame on; make ashamed; put to shame. **2** (foll. by *into, out of*) force by shame (*was shamed into confessing*). □ **for shame!** a reproof to a person for not showing shame. **put to shame** disgrace or humiliate by revealing superior qualities etc. **shame on you!** you should be ashamed. **what a shame!** how unfortunate! [OE *sc(e)amu*]

shamefaced /ˈʃeɪmˌfeɪst, ˈʃeɪm-/ *adj.* **1** showing shame. **2** bashful, diffident. □ **shamefacedly** /also -sɪdlɪ/ *adv.* **shamefacedness** *n.* [16th-c. alt. of *shamefast*, by assim. to FACE]

shameful /ˈʃeɪmfʊl/ *adj.* **1** that causes or is worthy of shame. **2** disgraceful, scandalous. □ **shamefully** *adv.* **shamefulness** *n.* [OE *sc(e)amful* (as SHAME, -FUL)]

shameless /ˈʃeɪmlɪs/ *adj.* **1** having or showing no sense of shame. **2** impudent. □ **shamelessly** *adv.* **shamelessness** *n.* [OE *sc(e)amlēas* (as SHAME, -LESS)]

shammy /ˈʃæmɪ/ *n.* (pl. **-ies**) (in full **shammy leather**) *colloq.* = CHAMOIS 2. [repr. corrupted pronunc.]

shampoo /ʃæmˈpuː/ *n.* & *v.* —*n.* **1** liquid or cream used to lather and wash the hair. **2** a similar substance for washing a car or carpet etc. **3** an act or instance of cleaning with shampoo. —*v.tr.* (**shampoos, shampooed**) wash with shampoo. [Hind. *chhāmpo*, imper. of *chhāmpnā* to press]

shamrock /ˈʃæmrɒk/ *n.* any of various plants with trifoliate leaves, esp. *Trifolium repens* or *Medicago lupulina*, used as the national emblem of Ireland. [Ir. *seamróg* trefoil, dimin. of *seamar* clover + *og* young]

shandy /ˈʃændɪ/ *n.* (pl. **-ies**) a mixture of beer with lemonade or ginger beer. [19th c.: orig. unkn.]

shanghai /ʃæŋˈhaɪ/ *v.* & *n.* —*v.tr.* (**shanghais, shanghaied, shanghaiing**) **1** force (a person) to be a sailor on a ship by using drugs or other trickery. **2** *colloq.* put into detention or an awkward situation by trickery. —*n.* (pl. **shanghais**) *Austral.* & *NZ* a catapult. [*Shanghai* in China]

shank *n.* **1 a** the leg. **b** the lower part of the leg; the leg from knee to ankle. **c** the shin-bone. **2** the lower part of an animal's foreleg, esp. as a cut of meat. **3** a shaft or stem. **4 a** the long narrow part of a tool etc. joining the handle to the working end. **b** the stem of a key, spoon, anchor, etc. □ **shanks's mare** (or **pony**) one's own legs as a means of conveyance. □ **shanked** *adj.* (also in *comb.*). [OE *sceanca* f. WG]

shan't /ʃɑːnt/ *contr.* shall not.

shantung /ʃænˈtʌŋ/ *n.* soft undressed Chinese silk, usu. undyed. [*Shantung*, Chinese province]

shanty¹ /ˈʃæntɪ/ *n.* (pl. **-ies**) **1** a hut or cabin. **2** a crudely built shack. □ **shanty town** a poor or depressed area of a town, consisting of shanties. [19th c., orig. N.Amer.: perh. f. Can.F *chantier*]

shanty² /ˈʃæntɪ/ *n.* (also **chanty**) (pl. **-ies**) (in full **sea shanty**) a song of a kind orig. sung by sailors while hauling ropes etc. [prob. F *chantez*, imper. pl. of *chanter* sing: see CHANT]

shape *n.* & *v.* —*n.* **1** the total effect produced by the outlines of a thing. **2** the external form or appearance of a person or thing. **3** a specific form or guise. **4** a definite or proper arrangement (*must get our ideas into shape*). **5 a** a condition, as qualified in some way (*in good shape; in poor shape*). **b** (when unqualified) good condition (*back in shape*). **6** a person or thing as seen, esp. indistinctly or in the imagination (*a shape emerged from the mist*). **7** a mould or pattern. **8** a piece of material, paper, etc., made or cut in a particular form. —*v.* **1** *tr.* give a certain shape or form to; fashion, create. **2** *tr.* (foll. by *to*) adapt or make conform. **3** *intr.* give signs of a future shape or development. **4** *tr.* frame mentally; imagine. **5** *intr.* assume or develop into a shape. **6** *tr.* direct (one's life, course, etc.). □ **lick** (or **knock**) **into shape** make presentable or efficient. **shape up 1** take a (specified) form. **2** show promise; make good progress. □ **shapable** *adj.* (also **shapeable**). **shaped** *adj.* (also in *comb.*). **shaper** *n.* [OE *gesceap* creation f. Gmc]

shapeless /ˈʃeɪplɪs/ adj. lacking definite or attractive shape. □ **shapelessly** adv. **shapelessness** n.

shapely /ˈʃeɪplɪ/ adj. (**shapelier, shapeliest**) 1 well formed or proportioned. 2 of elegant or pleasing shape or appearance. □ **shapeliness** n.

shard /ʃɑːd/ n. 1 a broken piece of pottery or glass etc. 2 = POTSHERD. [OE sceard]

share[1] /ʃeə(r)/ n. & v. —n. 1 a portion that a person receives from or gives to a common amount. 2 **a** a part contributed by an individual to an enterprise or commitment. **b** a part received by an individual from this (got a large share of the credit). 3 part-proprietorship of property held by joint owners, esp. any of the equal parts into which a company's capital is divided entitling its owner to a proportion of the profits. —v. 1 tr. get or have or give a share of. 2 tr. use or benefit from jointly with others. 3 intr. have a share; be a sharer (shall I share with you?). 4 intr. (foll. by in) participate. 5 tr. (often foll. by out) **a** divide and distribute. **b** give away part of. □ **share and share alike** make an equal division. **share-farmer** Austral. & NZ a tenant farmer who receives a share of the profits from the owner. □ **shareable** adj. (also **sharable**). **sharer** n. [ME f. OE scearu division, rel. to SHEAR]

share[2] /ʃeə(r)/ n. = PLOUGHSHARE. [OE scear, scær f. Gmc]

sharecropper /ˈʃeəˌkrɒpə(r)/ n. esp. US a tenant farmer who shares a part of each crop as rent. □ **sharecrop** v.tr. & intr. (**-cropped, -cropping**).

shareholder /ˈʃeəˌhəʊldə(r)/ n. an owner of shares in a company.

shareware /ˈʃeəweə(r)/ n. Computing software that is developed for sharing free of charge with other computer users rather than for sale.

shark[1] n. any of various large usu. voracious marine fish with a long body and prominent dorsal fin. [16th c.: orig. unkn.]

shark[2] n. colloq. a person who unscrupulously exploits or swindles others. [16th c.: orig. perh. f. G Schurke worthless rogue: infl. by SHARK[1]]

sharkskin /ˈʃɑːkskɪn/ n. 1 the skin of a shark. 2 a smooth dull-surfaced fabric.

sharp adj., n. & adv. —adj. 1 having an edge or point able to cut or pierce. 2 tapering to a point or edge. 3 abrupt, steep, angular (a sharp fall; a sharp turn). 4 well-defined, clean-cut. 5 **a** severe or intense (has a sharp temper). **b** (of food etc.) pungent, keen (a sharp appetite). **c** (of a frost) severe, hard. 6 (of a voice or sound) shrill and piercing. 7 (of sand etc.) composed of angular grains. 8 (of words or temper etc.) harsh or acrimonious (had a sharp tongue). 9 (of a person) acute; quick to perceive or comprehend. 10 quick to take advantage; artful, unscrupulous, dishonest. 11 vigorous or brisk. 12 Mus. above the normal pitch. **b** (of a key) having a sharp or sharps in the signature. **c** (C, F, etc., **sharp**) a semitone higher than C, F, etc. 13 colloq. stylish or flashy with regard to dress. —n. 1 Mus. **a** a note raised a semitone above natural pitch. **b** the sign (♯) indicating this. 2 colloq. a swindler or cheat. 3 a fine sewing-needle. 9 (of an edge) able to cut. —adv. 1 punctually (at nine o'clock sharp). 2 suddenly, abruptly, promptly (pulled up sharp). 3 at a sharp angle. 4 Mus. above the true pitch (sings sharp). □ **sharp end** colloq. 1 the bow of a ship. 2 the scene of direct action or decision. **sharp**

practice dishonest or barely honest dealings. □ **sharply** adv. **sharpness** n. [OE sc(e)arp f. Gmc]

sharpen /ˈʃɑːpən/ v.tr. & intr. make or become sharp. □ **sharpener** n.

sharper /ˈʃɑːpə(r)/ n. a swindler, esp. at cards.

sharpish /ˈʃɑːpɪʃ/ adj. & adv. colloq. —adj. fairly sharp. —adv. 1 fairly sharply. 2 quite quickly.

sharpshooter /ˈʃɑːpˌʃuːtə(r)/ n. a skilled marksman. □ **sharpshooting** n. & adj.

sharp-witted /ʃɑːpˈwɪtɪd/ adj. keenly perceptive or intelligent. □ **sharp-wittedly** adv. **sharp-wittedness** n.

shatter /ˈʃætə(r)/ v. 1 tr. & intr. break suddenly in pieces. 2 tr. severely damage or utterly destroy (shattered hopes). 3 tr. greatly upset or discompose. 4 tr. (usu. as **shattered** adj.) exhaust. □ **shatterer** n. **shattering** adj. **shatteringly** adv. **shatter-proof** adj. [ME, rel. to SCATTER]

shave v. & n. —v.tr. (past part. **shaved** or (as adj.) **shaven**) 1 remove (bristles or hair) from the face etc. with a razor. 2 (also absol.) remove bristles or hair with a razor from the face etc. of (a person) or (a part of the body). 3 **a** reduce by a small amount. **b** take (a small amount) away from. 4 cut thin slices from the surface of (wood etc.) to shape it. 5 pass close to without touching; miss narrowly. —n. 1 an act of shaving or the process of being shaved. 2 a close approach without contact. 3 a narrow miss or escape; = close shave. 4 a tool for shaving wood etc. [OE sc(e)afan (sense 4 of noun f. OE sceafa) f. Gmc]

shaven see SHAVE.

shaver /ˈʃeɪvə(r)/ n. 1 a person or thing that shaves. 2 an electric razor. 3 colloq. a young lad.

Shavian /ˈʃeɪvɪən/ adj. & n. —adj. of or in the manner of G. B. Shaw, Irish-born dramatist d. 1950, or his ideas. —n. an admirer of Shaw. [Shavius, Latinized form of Shaw]

shaving /ˈʃeɪvɪŋ/ n. 1 a thin strip cut off the surface of wood etc. 2 (attrib.) used in shaving the face (shaving-cream).

shawl n. a piece of fabric, usu. rectangular and often folded into a triangle, worn over the shoulders or head or wrapped round a baby. □ **shawled** adj. [Urdu etc. f. Pers. šāl, prob. f. Shālīāt in India]

she /ʃiː/ pron. & n. —pron. (obj. **her**; poss. **her**; pl. **they**) 1 the woman or girl or female animal previously named or in question. 2 a thing regarded as female, e.g. a vehicle or ship. 3 Austral. & NZ colloq. it; the state of affairs (she'll be right). —n. 1 a female; a woman. 2 (in comb.) female (she-goat). □ **she-devil** a malicious or spiteful woman. [ME scæ, sche, etc., f. OE fem. demonstr. pron. & adj. sīo, sēo, acc. sīe]

s/he pron. a written representation of 'he or she' used to indicate both sexes.

sheaf n. & v. —n. (pl. **sheaves** /ʃiːvz/) a group of things laid lengthways together and usu. tied, esp. a bundle of cornstalks tied after reaping, or a collection of papers. —v.tr. make into sheaves. [OE scēaf f. Gmc (as SHOVE)]

shear /ʃɪə(r)/ v. & n. —v. (past **sheared**, archaic except Austral. & NZ **shore** /ʃɔː(r)/; past part. **shorn** /ʃɔːn/ or **sheared**) 1 tr. cut with scissors or shears etc. 2 tr. remove or take off by cutting. 3 tr. clip the wool off (a sheep etc.). 4 tr. (foll. by of) **a** strip bare. **b** deprive. 5 tr. & intr. (often foll. by off) distort or be distorted, or break, from a structural strain. —n. 1 Mech. & Geol. a strain produced by pressure in the structure of a substance. **2** (in pl.) (also **pair of shears** sing.) a large clipping or cutting instrument shaped like scissors for use in gardens etc. □ **shearer** n. [OE sceran f. Gmc]

shearwater /ˈʃɪə¸wɔːtə(r)/ n. any long-winged sea bird of the genus Puffinus, usu. flying near the surface of the water.

sheath /ʃiːθ/ n. (pl. **sheaths** /ʃiːðz, ʃiːθs/) **1** a close-fitting cover, esp. for the blade of a knife or sword. **2** a condom. **3** Bot., Anat., & Zool. an enclosing case or tissue. **4** the protective covering round an electric cable. **5** a woman's close-fitting dress. □ **sheath knife** a dagger-like knife carried in a sheath. □ **sheathless** adj. [OE scǣth, scēath]

sheathe /ʃiːð/ v.tr. **1** put into a sheath. **2** encase; protect with a sheath. [ME f. SHEATH]

sheave /ʃiːv/ v.tr. make into sheaves.

sheaves pl. of SHEAF.

shebang /ʃɪˈbæŋ/ n. US sl. **1** a matter or affair (esp. the whole shebang). **2** a shed or hut. [19th c.: orig. unkn.]

shebeen /ʃɪˈbiːn/ n. esp. Ir. an unlicensed house selling alcoholic liquor. [Anglo-Ir. síbín f. séibe mugful]

shed[1] n. **1** a one-storeyed structure usu. of wood for storage or shelter for animals etc., or as a workshop. **2** a large roofed structure with one side open, for storing or maintaining machinery etc. **3** Austral. & NZ an open-sided building for shearing sheep or milking cattle. [app. var. of SHADE]

shed[2] v.tr. (**shedding**; past and past part. **shed**) **1** let or cause to fall off (trees shed their leaves). **2** take off (clothes). **3** reduce (an electrical power load) by disconnection etc. **4** cause to fall or flow (shed blood; shed tears). **5** disperse, diffuse, radiate (shed light). [OE sc(e)adan f. Gmc]

she'd /ʃiːd, ʃɪd/ contr. **1** she had. **2** she would.

sheen n. **1** a gloss or lustre on a surface. **2** radiance, brightness. □ **sheeny** adj. [obs. sheen beautiful, resplendent f. OE scēne: sense assim. to SHINE]

sheep n. (pl. same) **1** any ruminant mammal of the genus Ovis with a thick woolly coat, esp. kept in flocks for its wool or meat, and noted for its timidity. **2** a bashful, timid, or silly person. **3** (usu. in pl.) **a** a member of a minister's congregation. **b** a parishioner. □ **sheep-dip 1** a preparation for cleansing sheep of vermin or preserving their wool. **2** the place where sheep are dipped in this. **sheep-run** an extensive sheepwalk, esp. in Australia. □ **sheeplike** adj. [OE scēp, scæp, scēap]

sheepdog /ˈʃiːpdɒg/ n. **1** a dog trained to guard and herd sheep. **2** a dog of various breeds suitable for this. **b** any of these breeds.

sheepfold /ˈʃiːpfəʊld/ n. an enclosure for penning sheep.

sheepish /ˈʃiːpɪʃ/ adj. **1** bashful, shy, reticent. **2** embarrassed through shame. □ **sheepishly** adv. **sheepishness** n.

sheepshank /ˈʃiːpʃæŋk/ n. a knot used to shorten a rope temporarily.

sheepskin /ˈʃiːpskɪn/ n. **1** a garment or rug of sheep's skin with the wool on. **2** leather from a sheep's skin used in bookbinding.

sheepwalk /ˈʃiːpwɔːk/ n. Brit. a tract of land on which sheep are pastured.

sheer[1] adj. & adv. —adj. **1** no more or less than; mere, unqualified, absolute (sheer luck; sheer determination). **2** (of a cliff or ascent etc.) perpendicular; very steep. **3** (of a textile) very thin; diaphanous. —adv. **1** directly, outright. **2** perpendicularly. □ **sheerly** adv. **sheerness** n. [ME schere prob. f. dial. shire pure, clear f. OE scīr f. Gmc]

sheer[2] v.intr. **1** esp. Naut. swerve or change course. **2** (foll. by away, off) go away, esp. from a person or topic one dislikes or fears. [perh. f. MLG scheren = SHEAR v.]

sheet[1] n. & v. —n. **1** a large rectangular piece of cotton or other fabric, used esp. in pairs as inner bedclothes. **2 a** a broad usu. thin flat piece of material (e.g. paper or metal). **b** (attrib.) made in sheets (sheet iron). **3** a wide continuous surface or expanse of water, ice, flame, falling rain, etc. **4** a set of unseparated postage stamps. **5** derog. a newspaper, esp. a disreputable one. **6** a complete piece of paper of the size in which it was made, for printing and folding as part of a book. —v.tr. **1** provide or cover with sheets. **2** tr. form into sheets. **3** intr. (of rain etc.) fall in sheets. □ **sheet lightning** a lightning flash with its brightness diffused by reflection. **sheet metal** metal formed into thin sheets by rolling, hammering, etc. **sheet music** music published in cut or folded sheets, not bound. [OE scēte, scīete f. Gmc]

sheet[2] n. a rope or chain attached to the lower corner of a sail for securing or controlling it. □ **sheet anchor 1** a second anchor for use in emergencies. **2** a person or thing depended on in the last resort. **sheet bend** a method of temporarily fastening one rope through the loop of another. [ME f. OE scēata, ON skaut (as SHEET[1])]

sheeting /ˈʃiːtɪŋ/ n. material for making bed linen.

sheikh /ʃeɪk/ n. (also **shaikh**, **sheik**) **1** a chief or head of an Arab tribe, family, or village. **2** a Muslim leader. □ **sheikhdom** n. [ult. f. Arab. šayḳ old man, sheikh, f. šāḳa be or grow old]

sheila /ˈʃiːlə/ n. Austral. & NZ sl. a girl or young woman. [orig. shaler (of unkn. orig.): assim. to the name Sheila]

shekel /ˈʃek(ə)l/ n. **1** the chief monetary unit of modern Israel. **2** hist. a silver coin and unit of weight used in ancient Israel and the Middle East. **3** (in pl.) colloq. money; riches. [Heb. šeḳel f. šāḳal weigh]

shelduck /ˈʃeldʌk/ n. (pl. same or **shelducks**; masc. **sheldrake**, pl. same or **sheldrakes**) any bright-plumaged coastal wild duck of the genus Tadorna, esp. T. tadorna. [ME prob. f. dial. sheld pied, rel. to MDu. schillede variegated, + DRAKE]

shelf n. (pl. **shelves** /ʃelvz/) **1 a** a thin flat piece of wood or metal etc. projecting from a wall, or as part of a unit, used to support books etc. **b** a flat-topped recess in a wall etc. used for supporting objects. **2 a** a projecting horizontal ledge in a cliff face etc. **b** a reef or sandbank under water. □ **on the shelf 1** (of a woman) past the age when she might expect to be married. **2** (esp. of a retired person) no longer active or of use. **shelf-life** the amount of time for which a stored item of food etc. remains usable. **shelf-mark** a notation on a book showing its place in a library. **shelf-room** available space on a shelf. □ **shelved** /ʃelvd/ adj.

shelfful *n.* (*pl.* **-fuls**). **shelflike** *adj.* [ME f. (M)LG *schelf*, rel. to OE *scylfe* partition, *scylf* crag]

shell *n.* & *v.* —*n.* **1 a** the hard outer case of many marine molluscs (*cockle shell*). **b** the esp. hard but fragile outer covering of a bird's, reptile's, etc. egg. **c** the usu. hard outer case of a nut-kernel, seed, etc. **d** the carapace of a tortoise, turtle, etc. **e** the wing-case or pupa-case of many insects etc. **2 a** an explosive projectile or bomb for use in a big gun or mortar. **b** a hollow metal or paper case used as a container for fireworks, explosives, cartridges, etc. **c** US a cartridge. **3** a mere semblance or outer form without substance. **4** any of several things resembling a shell in being an outer case, esp.: **a** a light racing-boat. **b** a hollow pastry case. **c** the metal framework of a vehicle body etc. **d** the walls of an unfinished or gutted building, ship, etc. —*v.* **1** *tr.* remove the shell or pod from. **2** *tr.* bombard (a town, troops, etc.) with shells. □ **come out of one's shell** cease to be shy; become communicative. **shell out** (also *absol.*) *colloq.* **1** pay (money). **2** hand over (a required sum). **shell-pink** a delicate pale pink. **shell-shock** a nervous breakdown resulting from exposure to battle. **shell suit** a double-layered track suit with a soft lining and a showerproof outer nylon 'shell'. □ **shelled** *adj.* **shell-less** *adj.* **shell-like** *adj.* **shellproof** *adj.* (in sense 2a of *n.*). **shelly** *adj.* [OE *sc(i)ell* f. Gmc: cf. SCALE[1]]

she'll /ʃiːl, ʃɪl/ *contr.* she will; she shall.

shellac /ʃəˈlæk/ *n.* & *v.* —*n.* lac resin melted into thin flakes and used for making varnish (cf. LAC[1]). —*v.tr.* (**shellacked**, **shellacking**) **1** varnish with shellac. **2** US *sl.* defeat or thrash soundly. [SHELL + LAC, transl. F *laque en écailles* lac in thin plates]

shellfish /ˈʃelfɪʃ/ *n.* **1** an aquatic shelled mollusc, e.g. an oyster, winkle, etc. **2** a crustacean, e.g. a crab, shrimp, etc.

Shelta /ˈʃeltə/ *n.* an ancient hybrid secret language used by Irish tinkers, gypsies, etc. [19th c.: orig. unkn.]

shelter /ˈʃeltə(r)/ *n.* & *v.* —*n.* **1** anything serving as a shield or protection from danger, bad weather, etc. **2 a** a place of refuge provided esp. for the homeless etc. **b** US an animal sanctuary. **3** a metal condition; protection (*took shelter under a tree*). —*v.* **1** *tr.* act or serve as shelter to; protect; conceal; defend (*sheltered them from the storm*; *had a sheltered upbringing*). **2** *intr.* & *refl.* find refuge; take cover (*sheltered under a tree*; *sheltered themselves behind the wall*). □ **shelterer** *n.* **shelterless** *adj.* [16th c.: perh. f. obs. *sheltron* phalanx f. OE *scieldtruma* (as SHIELD, *truma* troop)]

shelve[1] *v.tr.* **1** put (books etc.) on a shelf. **2 a** abandon or defer (a plan etc.). **b** remove (a person) from active work etc. **3** fit (a cupboard etc.) with shelves. □ **shelver** *n.* **shelving** *n.* [*shelves* pl. of SHELF]

shelve[2] *v.intr.* (of ground etc.) slope in a specified direction (*land shelved away to the horizon*). [perh. f. *shelvy* (adj.) having underwater reefs f. *shelve* (n.) ledge, f. SHELVE[1]]

shelves *pl.* of SHELF.

shemozzle /ʃɪˈmɒz(ə)l/ *n.* (also **schemozzle**) *sl.* **1** a brawl or commotion. **2** a muddle. [Yiddish after LHeb. *šel-lō'-mazzāl* of no luck]

shenanigan /ʃɪˈnænɪgən/ *n.* (esp. in *pl.*) *colloq.* **1** high-spirited behaviour; nonsense. **2** trickery; dubious manoeuvres. [19th c.: orig. unkn.]

shepherd /ˈʃepəd/ *n.* & *v.* —*n.* **1** (*fem.* **shepherdess** /ˈʃepədɪs/) a person employed to tend sheep, esp. at pasture. **2** a member of the clergy etc. who cares for and guides a congregation. —*v.tr.* **1 a** tend (sheep etc.) as a shepherd. **b** guide (followers etc.). **2** marshal or drive (a crowd etc.) like sheep. □ **the Good Shepherd** Christ. **shepherd's pie** a dish of minced meat under a layer of mashed potato. [OE *scēaphierde* (as SHEEP, HERD)]

sherbet /ˈʃɜːbət/ *n.* **1 a** a flavoured sweet effervescent powder or drink. **b** US a water-ice. **2** a cooling drink of sweet diluted fruit-juices esp. in Arabic countries. [Turk. *şerbet*, Pers. *šerbet* f. Arab. *šarba* drink f. *šariba* to drink: cf. SHRUB[2], SYRUP]

sherd *n.* = POTSHERD. [var. of SHARD]

sheriff /ˈʃerɪf/ *n.* **1** Brit. **a** (also **High Sheriff**) the chief executive officer of the Crown in a county, administering justice etc. **b** an honorary officer elected annually in some towns. **2** US an elected officer in a county, responsible for keeping the peace. □ **sheriff court** Sc. a county court. □ **sheriffalty** *n.* (*pl.* **-ies**). **sheriffdom** *n.* **sheriffhood** *n.* **sheriffship** *n.* [OE *scīr-gerēfa* (as SHIRE, REEVE[1])]

Sherpa /ˈʃɜːpə/ *n.* (*pl.* same or **Sherpas**) **1** a Himalayan people living on the borders of Nepal and Tibet, and skilled in mountaineering. **2** a member of this people. [native name]

sherry /ˈʃerɪ/ *n.* (*pl.* **-ies**) **1** a fortified wine orig. from S. Spain. **2** a glass of this. [earlier *sherris* f. Sp. (*vino de*) *Xeres* (now Jerez de la Frontera) in Andalusia]

she's /ʃiːz, ʃɪz/ *contr.* **1** she is. **2** she has.

Shetlander /ˈʃetləndə(r)/ *n.* a native of the Shetland Islands, NNE of the mainland of Scotland.

Shetland pony /ˈʃetlənd/ *n.* **1** a pony of a small hardy rough-coated breed. **2** this breed.

Shetland wool /ˈʃetlənd/ *n.* a fine loosely twisted wool from Shetland sheep.

sheva var. of SCHWA.

shew *archaic* var. of SHOW.

Shiah /ˈʃiːə/ *n.* one of the two main branches of Islam, esp. in Iran, that rejects the first three Sunni Caliphs. [Arab. *šī'a* party (of Ali, Muhammad's cousin and son-in-law)]

shiatsu /ʃiˈætsuː/ *n.* a kind of therapy of Japanese origin, in which pressure is applied with the thumbs and palms to certain points of the body. [Jap., = finger pressure]

shibboleth /ˈʃɪbə‚leθ/ *n.* a long-standing formula, doctrine, or phrase, etc., held to be true by a party or sect (*must abandon outdated shibboleths*). [ME f. Heb. *šibbōleṭ* ear of corn, used as a test of nationality for its difficult pronunciation (Judg. 12:6)]

shicker /ˈʃɪkə(r)/ *adj.* (also **shickered** /ˈʃɪkəd/) *Austral.* & *NZ sl.* drunk. [Yiddish *shiker* f. Heb. *šikkōr* f. *šākar* be drunk]

shield /ʃiːld/ *n.* & *v.* —*n.* **1 a** esp. *hist.* a piece of armour of esp. metal, carried on the arm or in the hand to deflect blows from the head or body. **b** a thing serving to protect (*insurance is a shield against disaster*). **2** a thing resembling a shield, esp.: **a** a trophy in the form of a shield. **b** a protective plate or screen in machinery etc. **c**

a shieldlike part of an animal, esp. a shell. **d** a similar part of a plant. —*v.tr.* protect or screen, esp. from blame or lawful punishment. □ **shieldless** *adj.* [OE *sc(i)eld* f. Gmc: prob. orig. = board, rel. to SCALE¹]

shier *compar.* of SHY¹.

shiest *superl.* of SHY¹.

shift *v. & n.* —*v.* **1** *intr. & tr.* change or move or cause to change or move from one position to another. **2** *tr.* remove, esp. with effort (*washing won't shift the stains*). **3** *sl.* **a** *intr.* hurry (*we'll have to shift!*). **b** *tr.* consume (food or drink) hastily or in bulk. **c** *tr.* sell (esp. dubious goods). **4** *intr.* contrive or manage as best one can. **5** *US* **a** *tr.* change (gear) in a vehicle. **b** *intr.* change gear. **6** *intr.* (of cargo) get shaken out of place. —*n.* **1 a** the act or an instance of shifting. **b** the substitution of one thing for another; a rotation. **2 a** a relay of workers (*the night shift*). **b** the time for which they work (*an eight-hour shift*). **3 a** a device, stratagem, or expedient. **b** a dodge, trick, or evasion. **4 a** a woman's straight unwaisted dress. **b** *archaic* a loose-fitting undergarment. **5** a displacement of spectral lines. **6** a key on a keyboard used to switch between lower and upper case etc. **7** *US* **a** a gear lever in a motor vehicle. **b** a mechanism for this. □ **make shift** manage or contrive; get along somehow (*made shift without it*). **shift for oneself** rely on one's own efforts. **shift one's ground** take up a new position in an argument etc. **shift off** get rid of (responsibility etc.) to another. □ **shiftable** *adj.* **shifter** *n.* [OE *sciftan* arrange, divide, etc., f. Gmc]

shiftless /ˈʃɪftlɪs/ *adj.* lacking resourcefulness; lazy; inefficient. □ **shiftlessly** *adv.* **shiftlessness** *n.*

shifty /ˈʃɪftɪ/ *adj. colloq.* (**shiftier**, **shiftiest**) not straightforward; evasive; deceitful. □ **shiftily** *adv.* **shiftiness** *n.*

Shiite /ˈʃiːaɪt/ *n. & adj.* —*n.* an adherent of the Shiah branch of Islam. —*adj.* of or relating to Shiah. □ **Shiism** /ˈʃiːɪz(ə)m/ *n.*

shiksa /ˈʃɪksə/ *n.* often *offens.* (used by Jews) a gentile girl or woman. [Yiddish *shikse* f. Heb. *šiqṣâ* f. *sheqeṣ* detested thing + *-â fem. suffix*]

shillelagh /ʃɪˈleɪlə, -lɪ/ *n.* a thick stick of blackthorn or oak used in Ireland esp. as a weapon. [*Shillelagh* in Co. Wicklow, Ireland]

shilling /ˈʃɪlɪŋ/ *n.* **1** *hist.* a former British coin and monetary unit worth one-twentieth of a pound or twelve pence. **2** a monetary unit in Kenya, Tanzania, and Uganda. □ **take the King's** (or **Queen's**) **shilling** *hist.* enlist as a soldier (formerly a soldier was paid a shilling on enlisting). [OE *scilling*, f. Gmc]

shilly-shally /ˈʃɪlɪˌʃælɪ/ *v., adj., & n.* —*v.intr.* (**-ies**, **-ied**) hesitate to act or choose; be undecided; vacillate. —*adj.* vacillating. —*n.* indecision; vacillation. □ **shilly-shallyer** *n.* (also **-shallier**). [orig. *shill I, shall I*, redupl. of *shall I?*]

shily var. of SHYLY (see SHY¹).

shimmer /ˈʃɪmə(r)/ *v. & n.* —*v.intr.* shine with a tremulous or faint diffused light. —*n.* such a light. □ **shimmeringly** *adv.* **shimmery** *adj.* [OE *scymrian* f. Gmc: cf. SHINE]

shimmy /ˈʃɪmɪ/ *n. & v.* —*n.* (pl. **-ies**) *hist.* a kind of ragtime dance in which the whole body is shaken. —*v.intr.* (**-ies**, **-ied**) **1 a** *hist.* dance a shimmy. **b** move in a similar manner. **2** shake or vibrate abnormally. [20th c.: orig. uncert.]

shin *n. & v.* —*n.* **1** the front of the leg below the knee. **2** a cut of beef from the lower foreleg. —*v.tr. & (usu. foll. by up, down) intr.* (**shinned**, **shinning**) climb quickly by clinging with the arms and legs. □ **shin-bone** = TIBIA. **shin-pad** (or **-guard**) a protective pad for the shins, worn when playing football etc. [OE *sinu*]

shindig /ˈʃɪndɪg/ *n. colloq.* **1** a festive, esp. noisy, party. **2** = SHINDY 1. [prob. f. SHINDY]

shindy /ˈʃɪndɪ/ *n.* (pl. **-ies**) *colloq.* **1** a brawl, disturbance, or noise (*kicked up a shindy*). **2** = SHINDIG 1. [perh. alt. of SHINTY]

shine *v. & n.* —*v.* (*past and past part.* **shone** /ʃɒn/ or **shined**) **1** *intr.* emit or reflect light; be bright; glow (*the lamp was shining; his face shone with gratitude*). **2** *intr.* (of the sun, a star, etc.) not be obscured by clouds etc.; be visible. **3** *tr.* cause (a lamp etc.) to shine. **4** *tr.* (*past and past part.* **shined**) make bright; polish (*shined his shoes*). **5** *intr.* be brilliant in some respect; excel (*does not shine in conversation; is a shining example*). —*n.* **1** light; brightness, esp. reflected. **2** a high polish; lustre. **3** *US* the act or an instance of shining esp. shoes. □ **shine up to** *US* seek to ingratiate oneself with. **take the shine out of 1** spoil the brilliance or newness of. **2** throw into the shade by surpassing. **take a shine to** *colloq.* take a fancy to; like. □ **shiningly** *adv.* [OE *scīnan* f. Gmc]

shiner /ˈʃaɪnə(r)/ *n.* **1** a thing that shines. **2** *colloq.* a black eye.

shingle¹ /ˈʃɪŋg(ə)l/ *n.* (in *sing.* or *pl.*) small rounded pebbles, esp. on a sea-shore. □ **shingly** *adj.* [16th c.: orig. uncert.]

shingle² /ˈʃɪŋg(ə)l/ *n. & v.* —*n.* **1** a rectangular wooden tile used on roofs, spires, or esp. walls. **2** *archaic* **a** a shingled hair. **b** the act of shingling hair. **3** *US* a small signboard, esp. of a doctor, lawyer, etc. —*v.tr.* **1** roof or clad with shingles. **2** *archaic* **a** cut (a woman's hair) very short. **b** cut the hair of (a person or head) in this way. [ME app. f. L *scindula*, earlier *scandula*]

shingles /ˈʃɪŋg(ə)lz/ *n.pl.* (usu. treated as *sing.*) an acute painful viral inflammation of the nerve ganglia, with a skin eruption often forming a girdle around the middle of the body. [ME f. med.L *cingulus* f. L *cingulum* girdle f. *cingere* gird]

shinny /ˈʃɪnɪ/ *v.intr.* (**-ies**, **-ied**) (usu. foll. by *up, down*) *US colloq.* shin (up or down a tree etc.).

Shinto /ˈʃɪntəʊ/ *n.* the official religion of Japan incorporating the worship of ancestors and nature-spirits. □ **Shintoism** *n.* **Shintoist** *n.* [Jap. f. Chin. *shen dao* way of the gods]

shinty /ˈʃɪntɪ/ *n.* (pl. **-ies**) *Brit.* a game like hockey played with a ball and curved sticks. [earlier *shinny*, app. f. the cry used in the game *shin ye, shin you, shin t' ye*, of unkn. orig.]

shiny /ˈʃaɪnɪ/ *adj.* (**shinier**, **shiniest**) **1** having a shine; glistening; polished; bright. **2** (of clothing, esp. the seat of trousers etc.) having the nap worn off. □ **shinily** *adv.* **shininess** *n.* [SHINE]

ship *n. & v.* —*n.* **1 a** any large seagoing vessel (cf. BOAT). **b** a sailing-vessel with a bowsprit and three, four, or five square-rigged masts. **2** *US* an aircraft. **3** a spaceship. —*v.* (**shipped**, **shipping**) **1** *tr.* put, take, or send away (goods, passengers, sailors, etc.) on board ship. **2** *tr.* **a** take in (water) over the side of a ship, boat, etc. **b** take (oars) from the rowlocks and lay them inside a boat. **c** fix (a rudder etc.) in its place on a ship etc. **d** step (a mast). **3** *intr.* **a** take ship; embark. **b** (of a sailor) take service on a ship (*shipped for Africa*). **4** *tr.* deliver (goods) to a forwarding agent for conveyance. □ **ship-canal** a canal large enough for ships to pass inland. **ship of the desert** the camel. **ship off 1** send or transport by ship. **2** *colloq.* send (a person) away. **ship of the line** *hist.* a large battleship fighting in the front line of battle. **ship's boat** a small boat carried on board a ship. **ship's company** a ship's crew. **take ship** embark. **when a person's ship comes home** (or **in**) when a person's fortune is made. □ **shipless** *adj.* **shippable** *adj.* [OE *scip, scipian* f. Gmc]

-ship /ʃɪp/ *suffix* forming nouns denoting: **1** a quality or condition (*friendship; hardship*). **2** status, office, or honour (*authorship; lordship*). **3** a tenure of office (*chairmanship*). **4** a skill in a certain capacity (*workmanship*). **5** the collective individuals of a group (*membership*). [OE *-scipe* etc. f. Gmc]

shipboard /ˈʃɪpbɔːd/ *n.* (usu. *attrib.*) used or occurring on board a ship (*a shipboard romance*). □ **on shipboard** on board ship.

shipbuilder /ˈʃɪpˌbɪldə(r)/ *n.* a person, company, etc., that constructs ships. □ **shipbuilding** *n.*

shipload /ˈʃɪpləʊd/ *n.* a quantity of goods forming a cargo.

shipmate /ˈʃɪpmeɪt/ *n.* a fellow member of a ship's crew.

shipment /ˈʃɪpmənt/ *n.* **1** an amount of goods shipped; a consignment. **2** the act or an instance of shipping goods etc.

shipowner /ˈʃɪpˌəʊnə(r)/ *n.* a person owning a ship or ships or shares in ships.

shipper /ˈʃɪpə(r)/ *n.* a person or company that sends or receives goods by ship, or *US* by land or air. [OE *scipere* (as SHIP)]

shipping /ˈʃɪpɪŋ/ *n.* **1** the act or an instance of shipping goods etc. **2** ships, esp. the ships of a country, port, etc. □ **shipping-agent** a person acting for a ship or ships at a port etc. **shipping-office** the office of a shipping-agent.

shipshape /ˈʃɪpʃeɪp/ *adv.* & *predic.adj.* in good order; trim and neat.

shipway /ˈʃɪpweɪ/ *n.* a slope on which a ship is built and down which it slides to be launched.

shipwreck /ˈʃɪprek/ *n.* & *v.* —*n.* **1 a** the destruction of a ship by a storm, foundering, etc. **b** a ship so destroyed. **2** (often foll. by *of*) the destruction of hopes, dreams, etc. —*v.* **1** *tr.* inflict shipwreck on (a ship, a person's hopes, etc.). **2** *intr.* suffer shipwreck.

shipwright /ˈʃɪpraɪt/ *n.* **1** a shipbuilder. **2** a ship's carpenter.

shipyard /ˈʃɪpjɑːd/ *n.* a place where ships are built, repaired, etc.

shire *n.* *Brit.* **1** a county. **2** (**the Shires**) **a** a group of English counties with names ending or formerly ending in *-shire*, extending NE from Hampshire and Devon. **b** the midland counties of England. **3** *Austral.* a rural area with its own elected council. □ **shire-horse** a heavy powerful type of draught-horse. [OE *scīr*, OHG *scīra* care, official charge: orig. unkn.]

-shire /ʃə(r), ʃɪə(r)/ *suffix* forming the names of counties (*Derbyshire; Hampshire*).

shirk *v.* & *n.* —*v.tr.* (also *absol.*) shrink from; avoid; get out of (duty, work, responsibility, fighting, etc.). —*n.* a person who shirks. □ **shirker** *n.* [obs. *shirk* (n.) sponger, perh. f. G *Schurke* scoundrel]

shirr *n.* & *v.* —*n.* **1** two or more rows of esp. elastic gathered threads in a garment etc. forming smocking. **2** elastic webbing. —*v.tr.* **1** gather (material) with parallel threads. **2** *US* bake (eggs). □ **shirring** *n.* [19th c.: orig. unkn.]

shirt *n.* **1** a man's upper-body garment of cotton etc., having a collar, sleeves, and esp. buttons down the front, and often worn under a jacket or sweater. **2** a similar garment worn by a woman; a blouse. □ **keep one's shirt on** *colloq.* keep one's temper. **put one's shirt on** *colloq.* bet all one has on; be sure of. **shirt-dress** = SHIRTWAISTER. **shirt-front** the breast of a shirt, esp. of a stiffened evening shirt. **the shirt off one's back** *colloq.* one's last remaining possessions. **shirt-tail** the lower curved part of a shirt below the waist. □ **shirted** *adj.* **shirting** *n.* **shirtless** *adj.* [OE *scyrte*, corresp. to ON *skyrta* (cf. SKIRT) f. Gmc: cf. SHORT]

shirtsleeve /ˈʃɜːtsliːv/ *n.* (usu. in *pl.*) the sleeve of a shirt. □ **in shirtsleeves** wearing a shirt with no jacket etc. over it.

shirtwaist /ˈʃɜːtweɪst/ *n.* esp. *US* a woman's blouse resembling a shirt.

shirtwaister /ˈʃɜːtˌweɪstə(r)/ *n.* *US* a woman's dress with a bodice like a shirt. [SHIRT, WAIST]

shirty /ˈʃɜːtɪ/ *adj.* (**shirtier**, **shirtiest**) *colloq.* angry; annoyed. □ **shirtily** *adv.* **shirtiness** *n.*

shish kebab /ˌʃɪʃ kɪˈbæb/ *n.* a dish of pieces of marinated meat and vegetables cooked and served on skewers. [Turk. *şiş kebabı* f. *şiş* skewer, KEBAB roast meat]

shit *v., n., & int. coarse sl.* —*v.* (**shitting**; *past* and *past part.* **shitted** or **shit**) *intr.* & *tr.* expel faeces from the body or cause (faeces etc.) to be expelled. —*n.* **1** faeces. **2** an act of defecating. **3** a contemptible or worthless person or thing. **4** nonsense. —*int.* an exclamation of disgust, anger, etc. [OE *scītan* (unrecorded) f. Gmc]

shitty /ˈʃɪtɪ/ *adj.* (**shittier**, **shittiest**) *coarse sl.* **1** disgusting, contemptible. **2** covered with excrement.

shiver[1] /ˈʃɪvə(r)/ *v.* & *n.* —*v.intr.* **1** tremble with cold, fear, etc. **2** suffer a quick trembling movement of the body; shudder. —*n.* **1** a momentary shivering movement. **2** (in *pl.*) an attack of shivering, esp. from fear or horror (*got the shivers in the dark*). □ **shiverer** *n.* **shiveringly** *adv.* **shivery** *adj.* [ME *chivere*, perh. f. *chavele* chatter (as JOWL[1])]

shiver[2] /ˈʃɪvə(r)/ *n.* & *v.* —*n.* (esp. in *pl.*) each of the small pieces into which esp. glass is shattered when broken; a splinter. —*v.tr.* & *intr.* break into shivers. [ME *scifre*, rel. to OHG *scivaro* splinter f. Gmc]

shoal[1] /ʃəʊl/ *n.* & *v.* —*n.* **1** a great number of fish swimming together. **2** a multitude; a crowd (*shoals of letters*). —*v.intr.* (of fish) form shoals. [prob. re-adoption of MDu. *schōle* SCHOOL[2]]

shoal[2] /ʃəʊl/ *n.* & *v.* —*n.* **1 a** an area of shallow water. **b** a submerged sandbank visible at low water. **2** (esp. in *pl.*) hidden danger or difficulty. —*v.* *intr.* (of water) get shallower. □ **shoaly** *adj.* [OE *sceald* f. Gmc, rel. to SHALLOW]

shock[1] *n.* & *v.* —*n.* **1** a violent collision, impact, tremor, etc. **2** a sudden and disturbing effect on the emotions, physical reactions, etc. (*the news was a great shock*). **3** an acute state of prostration following a wound, pain, etc., esp. when much blood is lost (*died of shock*). **4** = *electric shock.* —*v.* **1** *tr.* **a** affect with shock; horrify; outrage;

disgust; sadden. **b** (*absol.*) cause shock. **2** *tr.* (esp. in *passive*) affect with an electric or pathological shock. **3** *intr.* experience shock (*I don't shock easily*). □ **shock absorber** a device on a vehicle etc. for absorbing shocks, vibrations, etc. **shock tactics 1** sudden and violent action. **2** *Mil.* a massed cavalry charge. **shock therapy** (or **treatment**) *Psychol.* a method of treating depressive patients by electric shock or drugs inducing coma and convulsions. **shock troops** troops specially trained for assault. **shock wave** a sharp change of pressure in a narrow region travelling through air etc. caused by explosion or by a body moving faster than sound. □ **shockable** *adj.* **shockability** /-'bɪlɪtɪ/ *n.* [F *choc*, *choquer*, of unkn. orig.]

shock² *n.* & *v.* —*n.* a group of usu. twelve corn-sheaves stood up with their heads together in a field. —*v.tr.* arrange (corn) in shocks. [ME, perh. repr. OE *sc(e)oc* (unrecorded)]

shock³ *n.* an unkempt or shaggy mass of hair. [cf. obs. *shock(-dog)*, earlier *shough*, shaggy-haired poodle]

shocker /'ʃɒkə(r)/ *n. colloq.* **1** a shocking, horrifying, unacceptable, etc. person or thing. **2** *hist.* a sordid or sensational novel etc. **3** a shock absorber.

shocking /'ʃɒkɪŋ/ *adj.* & *adv.* —*adj.* **1** causing indignation or disgust. **2** *colloq.* very bad (*shocking weather*). —*adv. colloq.* shockingly (*shocking bad manners*). □ **shocking pink** a vibrant shade of pink. □ **shockingly** *adv.* **shockingness** *n.*

shockproof /'ʃɒkpruːf/ *adj.* resistant to the effects of (esp. physical) shock.

shod *past* and *past part.* of SHOE.

shoddy /'ʃɒdɪ/ *adj.* & *n.* —*adj.* (**shoddier, shoddiest**) **1** trashy; shabby; poorly made. **2** counterfeit. —*n.* (*pl.* **-ies**) **1 a** an inferior cloth made partly from the shredded fibre of old woollen cloth. **b** such fibre. **2** any thing of shoddy quality. □ **shoddily** *adv.* **shoddiness** *n.* [19th c.: orig. dial.]

shoe /ʃuː/ *n.* & *v.* —*n.* **1** either of a pair of protective foot-coverings of leather, plastic, etc., having a sturdy sole and, in Britain, not reaching above the ankle. **2** a metal rim nailed to the hoof of a horse etc.; a horseshoe. **3** anything resembling a shoe in shape or use, esp.: **a** a drag for a wheel. **b** = *brake shoe*. —*v.tr.* (**shoes, shoeing**; *past* and *past part.* **shod** /ʃɒd/) **1** fit (esp. a horse etc.) with a shoe or shoes. **2** (as **shod** *adj.*) (in *comb.*) having shoes etc. of a specified kind (*dry-shod*; *roughshod*). □ **be in a person's shoes** be in his or her situation, difficulty, etc. **dead men's shoes** property or a position etc. coveted by a prospective successor. **if the shoe fits** *US* = *if the cap fits*. **shoe-leather** leather for shoes, esp. when worn through by walking. **shoe-tree** a shaped block for keeping a shoe in shape when not worn. □ **shoeless** *adj.* [OE *scōh, scōg(e)an* f. Gmc]

shoeblack /'ʃuːblæk/ *n.* a person who cleans the shoes of passers-by for payment.

shoebox /'ʃuːbɒks/ *n.* **1** a box for packing shoes. **2** a very small space or dwelling.

shoehorn /'ʃuːhɔːn/ *n.* a curved piece of horn, metal, etc., for easing the heel into a shoe.

shoelace /'ʃuːleɪs/ *n.* a cord for lacing up shoes.

shoemaker /'ʃuːˌmeɪkə(r)/ *n.* a maker of boots and shoes. □ **shoemaking** *n.*

shoeshine /'ʃuːʃaɪn/ *n.* esp. *US* a polish given to shoes.

shoestring /'ʃuːstrɪŋ/ *n.* **1** a shoelace. **2** *colloq.* a small esp. inadequate amount of money (*living on a shoestring*). **3** (*attrib.*) barely adequate; precarious (*a shoestring majority*).

shogun /'ʃəʊgʊn/ *n. hist.* any of a succession of Japanese hereditary Commanders-in-Chief and virtual rulers before 1868. □ **shogunate** /-nət/ *n.* [Jap., = general, f. Chin. *jiang jun*]

shone *past* and *past part.* of SHINE.

shoo *int.* & *v.* —*int.* an exclamation used to frighten away birds, children, etc. —*v.* (**shoos, shooed**) **1** *intr.* utter the word 'shoo!'. **2** *tr.* (usu. foll. by *away*) drive (birds etc.) away by shooing. [imit.]

shook /ʃʊk/ *past* of SHAKE. —*predic.adj. colloq.* **1** (foll. by *up*) emotionally or physically disturbed; upset. **2** (foll. by *on*) *Austral.* & *NZ* keen on; enthusiastic about.

shoot /ʃuːt/ *v., n.,* & *int.* —*v.* (*past* and *past part.* **shot** /ʃɒt/) **1** *tr.* **a** cause (a gun, bow, etc.) to fire. **b** discharge (a bullet, arrow, etc.) from a gun, bow, etc. **c** kill or wound (a person, animal, etc.) with a bullet, arrow, etc. from a gun, bow, etc. **2** *intr.* discharge a gun etc. esp. in a specified way (*shoots well*). **3** *tr.* send out, discharge, propel, etc., esp. violently or swiftly (*shot out the contents*; *shot a glance at his neighbour*). **4** *intr.* (often foll. by *out, along, forth,* etc.) come or go swiftly or vigorously. **5** *intr.* **a** (of a plant etc.) put forth buds etc. **b** (of a bud etc.) appear. **6** *intr.* **a** hunt game etc. with a gun. **b** (usu. foll. by *over*) shoot game over an estate etc. **7** *tr.* shoot game in or on (coverts, an estate, etc.). **8** *tr.* film or photograph (a scene, film, etc.). **9** *tr.* (also *absol.*) esp. *Football* **a** score (a goal). **b** take a shot at (the goal). **10** *tr.* (of a boat) sweep swiftly down or under (a bridge, rapids, falls, etc.). **11** *tr.* move (a door-bolt) to fasten or unfasten a door etc. —*n.* **1** the act or an instance of shooting. **2 a** a young branch or sucker. **b** the new growth of a plant. **3** *Brit.* **a** a hunting party, expedition, etc. **b** land shot over for game. **4** = CHUTE¹. **5** a rapid in a stream. —*int. colloq.* **1** a demand for a reply, information, etc. **2** *US euphem.* an exclamation of disgust, anger, etc. □ **shoot ahead** come quickly to the front of competitors etc. **shoot down 1** kill (a person) by shooting. **2** cause (an aircraft, its pilot, etc.) to crash by shooting. **3** argue effectively against (a person, argument, etc.). **shoot it out** *sl.* engage in a decisive gun-battle. **shoot a line** *sl.* talk pretentiously. **shoot one's mouth off** *sl.* talk too much or indiscreetly. **shoot-out** *colloq.* a decisive gun battle. **shoot through** *Austral.* & *NZ sl.* depart; escape; abscond. **shoot up 1** grow rapidly, esp. (of a person) grow taller. **2** rise suddenly. **3** terrorize (a district) by indiscriminate shooting. **4** *sl.* inject esp. oneself with (a drug). □ **shootable** *adj.* [OE *scēotan* f. Gmc: cf. SHEET¹, SHOT¹, SHUT]

shooter /'ʃuːtə(r)/ *n.* **1** a person or thing that shoots. **2 a** (in *comb.*) a gun or other device for shooting (*peashooter*; *six-shooter*). **b** *sl.* a pistol etc. **3** a player who shoots or is able to shoot a goal in football, netball, etc.

shooting /'ʃuːtɪŋ/ *n.* & *adj.* —*n.* **1** the act or an instance of shooting. **2 a** the right of shooting over an area of land. **b** an estate etc. rented to shoot over. —*adj.* moving, growing, etc. quickly (*a shooting pain in the arm*). □ **shooting-box** *Brit.* a lodge used by sportsmen in the shooting-season. **shooting-brake** (or **-break**) *Brit.* an estate car. **shooting-gallery** a place used for shooting at targets with rifles etc. **shooting-range** a ground with butts for rifle practice. **shooting star** a small meteor moving rapidly and burning up on entering the earth's atmosphere. **shooting-stick** a walking-stick with a foldable seat. **shooting war** a war in which there is shooting (opp. *cold war*). **the whole shooting match** *colloq.* everything.

shop *n. & v.* —*n.* **1** a building, room, etc., for the retail sale of goods or services (*chemist's shop; betting-shop*). **2** a place in which manufacture or repairing is done; a workshop (*engineering-shop*). **3** a profession, trade, business, etc., esp. as a subject of conversation (*talk shop*). **4** *colloq.* an institution, establishment, place of business, etc. —*v.* (**shopped, shopping**) **1** *intr.* **a** go to a shop or shops to buy goods. **b** *US* = window-shop. **2** *tr. esp. Brit. sl.* inform against (a criminal etc.). □ **all over the shop** *colloq.* **1** in disorder (*scattered all over the shop*). **2** in every place (*looked for it all over the shop*). **3** wildly (*hitting out all over the shop*). **set up shop** establish oneself in business etc. **shop around** look for the best bargain. **shop assistant** *Brit.* a person who serves customers in a shop. **shop-boy** (or **-girl**) an assistant in a shop. **shop-floor** workers in a factory etc. as distinct from management. **shop-soiled** (of an article) soiled or faded by display in a shop. **shop steward** a person elected by workers in a factory etc. to represent them in dealings with management. **shop-window 1** a display window in a shop. **2** an opportunity for displaying skills, talents, etc. **shop-worn** = shopsoiled. □ **shopless** *adj.* **shoppy** *adj.* [ME f. AF & OF *eschoppe* booth f. MLG *schoppe*, OHG *scopf* porch]

shopkeeper /ˈʃɒpˌkiːpə(r)/ *n.* the owner and manager of a shop. □ **shopkeeping** *n.*

shoplifter /ˈʃɒpˌlɪftə(r)/ *n.* a person who steals goods while appearing to shop. □ **shoplifting** *n.*

shopman /ˈʃɒpmən/ *n.* (*pl.* **-men**) **1** *Brit.* a shopkeeper or shop assistant. **2** a workman in a repair shop.

shopper /ˈʃɒpə(r)/ *n.* **1** a person who makes purchases in a shop. **2** a shopping bag or trolley.

shopping /ˈʃɒpɪŋ/ *n.* **1** (often *attrib.*) the purchase of goods etc. (*shopping expedition*). **2** goods purchased (*put the shopping on the table*). □ **shopping centre** an area or complex of shops, with associated facilities.

shopwalker /ˈʃɒpˌwɔːkə(r)/ *n. Brit.* an attendant in a large shop who directs customers, supervises assistants, etc.

shore¹ /ʃɔː(r)/ *n.* **1** the land that adjoins the sea or a large body of water. **2** (usu. in *pl.*) a country; a sea-coast (*often visits these shores; on a distant shore*). □ **in shore** on the water near or nearer to the shore. **on shore** ashore. □ **shoreless** *adj.* **shoreward** *adj. & adv.* **shorewards** *adv.* [ME f. MDu., MLG *schōre*, perh. rel. to SHEAR]

shore² /ʃɔː(r)/ *v. & n.* —*v.tr.* (often foll. by *up*) support with or as if with a shore or shores; hold up. —*n.* a prop or beam set obliquely against a ship, wall, tree, etc., as a support. □ **shoring** *n.* [ME f. MDu., MLG *schōre* prop, of unkn. orig.]

shore³ see SHEAR.

shorn *past part.* of SHEAR.

short *adj., adv., n., & v.* —*adj.* **1 a** measuring little; not long from end to end (*a short distance*). **b** not long in duration; brief (*a short time ago; had a short life*). **c** seeming less than the stated amount (*a few short years of happiness*). **2** of small height; not tall (*a short square tower; was shorter than average*). **3 a** (usu. foll. by *of, on*) having a partial or total lack; deficient; scanty (*short of spoons; is rather short on sense*). **b** not far-reaching; acting or being near at hand (*within short range*). **4 a** concise; brief (*kept his speech short*). **b** curt; uncivil (*was short with her*). **5** (of the memory) unable to remember distant events. **6** *Phonet.* & *Prosody* of a vowel or syllable: **a** having the lesser of the two recognized durations. **b** unstressed. **7** (of pastry) crumbling; not holding together. **8** esp. *Stock Exch.* (of stocks, a stockbroker, crops, etc.) sold or selling when the amount is not in hand, with reliance on getting the deficit in time for delivery. **9** (of a drink of spirits) undiluted. —*adv.* **1** before the natural or expected time or place; abruptly (*pulled up short; cut short the celebrations*). **2** rudely; uncivilly (*spoke to him short*). —*n.* **1** *colloq.* a short drink, esp. spirits. **2** a short circuit. **3** a short film. **4** *Stock Exch.* (in *pl.*) short-dated stocks. **5** *Phonet.* a short syllable or vowel. —*v.tr. & intr.* short-circuit. □ **be caught** (or **taken**) **short 1** be put at a disadvantage. **2** *colloq.* urgently need to urinate or defecate. **bring up** (or **pull up**) **short** check or pause abruptly. **come short of** fail to reach or amount to. **for short** as a short name (*Tom for short*). **get** (or **have**) **by the short hairs** *colloq.* be in complete control of (a person). **go short** (often foll. by *of*) not have enough. **in short** to use few words; briefly. **in short order** *US* immediately. **in the short run** over a short period of time. **in short supply** scarce. **in the short term** = in the short run. **make short work of** accomplish, dispose of, destroy, consume, etc. quickly. **short and sweet** esp. *iron.* brief and pleasant. **short change** insufficient money given as change. **short-change** *v.tr.* rob or cheat by giving short change. **short circuit** an electric circuit through small resistance, esp. instead of the resistance of a normal circuit. **short-circuit 1** cause a short circuit or a short circuit in. **2** shorten or avoid (a journey, work, etc.) by taking a more direct route etc. **short cut 1** a route shortening the distance travelled. **2** a quick way of accomplishing something. **short-dated** due for early payment or redemption. **short drink** a strong alcoholic drink served in small measures. **short for** an abbreviation for ('*Bob*' is short for '*Robert*'). **short fuse** a quick temper. **short-handed** undermanned or understaffed. **short haul 1** the transport of goods over a short distance. **2** a short-term effort. **short head** *Racing* a distance less than the length of a horse's head. **short list** *Brit.* a list of selected candidates from which a final choice is made. **short-list** *v.tr. Brit.* put on a short list. **short-lived** ephemeral; not long-lasting. **short measure** less than the professed amount. **short notice** an insufficient length of warning time. **short odds** nearly equal stakes or chances in betting. **short of 1** see sense 3a of *adj.* **2** less than (*nothing short of a miracle*). **3** distant from (*two miles short of home*). **4**

without going so far as; except (*did everything short of destroying it*). **short of breath** panting, short-winded. **short on** *colloq.* see sense 3a of *adj.* **short order** *US* an order in a restaurant for quickly cooked food. **short-range 1** having a short range. **2** relating to a fairly immediate future time (*short-range possibilities*). **short shrift** curt or dismissive treatment. **short sight** the inability to focus except on comparatively near objects. **short-sleeved** with sleeves not reaching below the elbow. **short-staffed** having insufficient staff. **short story** a story with a fully developed theme but shorter than a novel. **short temper** self-control soon or easily lost. **short-tempered** quick to lose one's temper; irascible. **short-term** occurring in or relating to a short period of time. **short time** the condition of working fewer than the regular hours per day or days per week. **short view** a consideration of the present only, not the future. **short waist 1** a high or shallow waist of a dress. **2** a short upper body. **short wave** a radio wave of frequency greater than 3 MHz. **short weight** weight less than it is alleged to be. **short wind** quickly exhausted breathing-power. **short-winded 1** having short wind. **2** incapable of sustained effort. □ **shortish** *adj.* **shortness** *n.* [OE *sceort* f. Gmc: cf. SHIRT, SKIRT]

shortage /ˈʃɔːtɪdʒ/ *n.* (often foll. by *of*) a deficiency; an amount lacking (*a shortage of 100 tons*).

shortbread /ˈʃɔːtbred/ *n.* a crisp rich crumbly type of biscuit made with butter, flour, and sugar.

shortcake /ˈʃɔːtkeɪk/ *n.* **1** = SHORTBREAD. **2** a cake made of short pastry and filled with fruit and cream.

shortcoming /ˈʃɔːtkʌmɪŋ/ *n.* failure to come up to a standard; a defect.

shortcrust /ˈʃɔːtkrʌst/ *n.* (in full **shortcrust pastry**) a type of crumbly pastry made with flour and fat.

shorten /ˈʃɔːt(ə)n/ *v.* **1** *intr.* & *tr.* become or make shorter or short; curtail. **2** *intr.* & *tr.* (with reference to gambling odds, prices, etc.) become or make shorter; decrease.

shortening /ˈʃɔːtənɪŋ/ *n.* fat used for making pastry, esp. for making short pastry.

shortfall /ˈʃɔːtfɔːl/ *n.* a deficit below what was expected.

shorthand /ˈʃɔːthænd/ *n.* **1** (often *attrib.*) a method of rapid writing in abbreviations and symbols esp. for taking dictation. **2** an abbreviated or symbolic mode of expression. □ **shorthand typist** *Brit.* a typist qualified to take and transcribe shorthand.

shorthorn /ˈʃɔːthɔːn/ *n.* **1** an animal of a breed of cattle with short horns. **2** this breed.

shortly /ˈʃɔːtlɪ/ *adv.* **1** (often foll. by *before, after*) before long; soon (*will arrive shortly; arrived shortly after him*). **2** in a few words; briefly. **3** curtly. [OE *scortlice* (as SHORT, -LY²)]

shorts *n.pl.* **1** trousers reaching only to the knees or higher. **2** *US* underpants.

short-sighted /ʃɔːtˈsaɪtɪd, ˈʃɔːt-/ *adj.* **1** having short sight. **2** lacking imagination or foresight. □ **short-sightedly** *adv.* **short-sightedness** *n.*

shortstop /ˈʃɔːtstɒp/ *n.* a baseball fielder between second and third base.

shorty /ˈʃɔːtɪ/ *n.* (also **shortie**) (*pl.* **-ies**) *colloq.* **1** a person shorter than average. **2** a short garment, esp. a nightdress or raincoat.

shot[1] *n.* **1** the act or an instance of firing a gun, cannon, etc. (*several shots were heard*). **2** an attempt to hit by shooting or throwing etc. (*took a shot at him*). **3 a** a single non-explosive missile for a cannon, gun, etc. **b** (*pl.* same or **shots**) a small lead pellet used in quantity in a single charge or cartridge in a shotgun. **c** (as *pl.*) these collectively. **4 a** a photograph. **b** a film sequence photographed continuously by one camera. **5 a** a stroke or a kick in a ball game. **b** *colloq.* an attempt to guess or do something (*let him have a shot at it*). **6** *colloq.* a person having a specified skill with a gun etc. (*is not a good shot*). **7** a heavy ball thrown by a shot-putter. **8** the launch of a space rocket (*a moonshot*). **9** the range, reach, or distance to or at which a thing will carry or act (*out of earshot*). **10** a remark aimed at a person. **11** *colloq.* **a** a drink of esp. spirits. **b** an injection of a drug, vaccine, etc. (*has had his shots*). □ **like a shot** *colloq.* without hesitation; willingly. **shot in the arm** *colloq.* **1** stimulus or encouragement. **2** an alcoholic drink. **shot in the dark** a mere guess. **shot-put** an athletic contest in which a shot is thrown a great distance. **shot-putter** an athlete who puts the shot. □ **shotproof** *adj.* [OE *sc(e)ot, gesc(e)ot* f. Gmc: cf. SHOOT]

shot[2] *past* and *past part.* of SHOOT. —*adj.* **1** (of coloured material) woven so as to show different colours at different angles. **2** *colloq.* **a** exhausted; finished. **b** drunk. □ **be** (or **get**) **shot of** *sl.* be (or get) rid of. **shot through** permeated or suffused. [past part. of SHOOT]

shot[3] *n.* *colloq.* a reckoning, a bill, esp. at an inn etc. (*paid his shot*). [ME, = SHOT¹: cf. OE *scēotan* shoot, pay, contribute, and SCOT]

shotgun /ˈʃɒtgʌn/ *n.* a smooth-bore gun for firing small shot at short range. □ **shotgun marriage** (or **wedding**) *colloq.* an enforced or hurried wedding, esp. because of the bride's pregnancy.

should /ʃʊd, ʃəd/ *v.aux.* (3rd sing. **should**) *past* of SHALL, used esp.: **1** in reported speech, esp. with the reported element in the 1st person (*I said I should be home by evening*). **2 a** to express a duty, obligation, or likelihood; = OUGHT¹ (*I should tell you; you should have been more careful; they should have arrived by now*). **b** (in the 1st person) to express a tentative suggestion (*I should like to say something*). **3 a** expressing the conditional mood in the 1st person (cf. WOULD) (*I should have been killed if I had gone*). **b** forming a conditional protasis or indefinite clause (*if you should see him; should they arrive, tell them where to go*). **4** expressing purpose = MAY, MIGHT¹ (*in order that we should not worry*).

■ **Usage** Cf. WILL¹, WOULD, now more common in this sense, esp. to avoid implications of sense 2.

shoulder /ˈʃəʊldə(r)/ *n.* & *v.* —*n.* **1 a** the part of the body at which the arm, foreleg, or wing is attached. **b** (in full **shoulder joint**) the end of the upper arm joining with the collar-bone and blade-bone. **c** either of the two projections below the neck from which the arms depend. **2** the upper foreleg and shoulder blade of a pig, lamb, etc. when butchered. **3** (often in *pl.*) **a** the upper part of the back and arms. **b** this part of the body regarded as capable of bearing a burden or blame, providing comfort, etc. (*needs a shoulder to cry on*). **4** a strip of land next to a

metalled road (*pulled over on to the shoulder*). **5 a**
part of a garment covering the shoulder. **6 a**
part of anything resembling a shoulder in form
or function, as in a bottle, mountain, tool, etc.
—*v.* **1 a** *tr.* push with the shoulder; jostle. **b** *intr.*
make one's way by jostling (*shouldered through
the crowd*). **2** *tr.* take (a burden etc.) on one's
shoulders (*shouldered the family's problems*). □ **put
(or set) one's shoulder to the wheel** make an
effort. **shoulder arms** hold a rifle with the
barrel against the shoulder and the butt in the
hand. **shoulder-bag** a woman's handbag that
can be hung from the shoulder. **shoulder-belt**
a bandolier or other strap passing over one
shoulder and under the opposite arm.
shoulder-blade *Anat.* either of the large flat
bones of the upper back; the scapula.
shoulder-pad a pad sewn into a garment to
bulk out the shoulder. **shoulder-strap** a strip
of fabric, leather, etc. suspending a bag or
garment from the shoulder. **shoulder to shoulder 1** side by side. **2** with closed ranks or united
effort. □ **shouldered** *adj.* (also in *comb.*). [OE
sculdor f. WG]

shouldn't /ˈʃʊd(ə)nt/ *contr.* should not.

shout /ʃaʊt/ *v. & n.* —*v.* **1** *intr.* make a loud
cry or vocal sound; speak loudly (*shouted for
attention*). **2** *tr.* say or express loudly; call out
(*shouted that the coast was clear*). **3** *tr.* (also *absol.*)
Austral. & NZ colloq. treat (another person) to
drinks etc. —*n.* **1** a loud cry expressing joy etc.
or calling attention. **2** *colloq.* one's turn to order
a round of drinks etc. □ **all over bar** (or **but**)
the shouting *colloq.* the contest is virtually
decided. **shout at** speak loudly to etc. **shout
down** reduce to silence by shouting. **shout for**
call for by shouting. □ **shouter** *n.* [ME, perh.
rel. to SHOOT: cf. ON *skúta* taunt]

shove /ʃʌv/ *v. & n.* —*v.* **1** *tr.* (also *absol.*) push
vigorously; move by hard or rough pushing
(*shoved him out of the way*). **2** *intr.* (usu. foll. by
along, past, through, etc.) make one's way by
pushing (*shoved through the crowd*). **3** *tr. colloq.*
put somewhere (*shoved it in the drawer*). —*n.* an
act of shoving or of prompting a person into
action. □ **shove-halfpenny** a form of shovelboard played with coins etc. on a table esp. in
licensed premises. **shove off 1** start from the
shore in a boat. **2** *sl.* depart; go away (*told him to
shove off*). [OE *scúfan* f. Gmc]

shovel /ˈʃʌv(ə)l/ *n. & v.* —*n.* **1 a** a spadelike tool
for shifting quantities of coal, earth, etc., esp.
having the sides curved upwards. **b** the amount
contained in a shovel; a shovelful. **2** a machine
or part of a machine having a similar form or
function. —*v.tr.* (**shovelled, shovelling;** *US*
shoveled, shoveling) **1** shift or clear (coal etc.)
with or as if with a shovel. **2** *colloq.* move (esp.
food) in large quantities or roughly (*shovelled
peas into his mouth*). □ **shovel hat** a broad-
brimmed hat esp. worn by some clergymen. □
shovelful *n.* (*pl.* **-fuls**). [OE *scofl* f. Gmc (see
SHOVE)]

shovelboard /ˈʃʌv(ə)l,bɔːd/ *n.* a game played esp.
on a ship's deck by pushing discs with the hand
or with a long-handled shovel over a marked
surface. [earlier *shoveboard* f. SHOVE + BOARD]

shoveller /ˈʃʌvələ(r)/ *n.* (also **shoveler**) **1** a person
or thing that shovels. **2** a duck, *Anas clypeata*,
with a broad shovel-like beak. [SHOVEL: sense 2
earlier *shovelard* f. -ARD, perh. after *mallard*]

show /ʃəʊ/ *v. & n.* —*v.* (*past part.* **shown** /ʃəʊn/
or **showed**) **1** *intr. & tr.* be, or allow or cause to be,
visible; manifest; appear (*the buds are beginning to
show; white shows the dirt*). **2** *tr.* (often foll. by *to*)
offer, exhibit, or produce (a thing) for scrutiny
etc. (*show your tickets please; showed him my poems*).
3 *tr.* **a** indicate (one's feelings) by one's behaviour
etc. (*showed mercy to him*). **b** indicate (one's
feelings to a person etc.) (*showed him particular
favour*). **4** *intr.* (of feelings etc.) be manifest (*his
dislike shows*). **5** *tr.* **a** demonstrate; point out;
prove (*has shown it to be false; showed that he knew
the answer*). **b** (usu. foll. by *how to* + infin.) cause
(a person) to understand or be capable of doing
(*showed them how to knit*). **6** *tr.* (*refl.*) exhibit
oneself as being (*showed herself to be fair*). **7** *tr. &
intr.* (with ref. to a film) be presented or cause
to be presented. **8** *tr.* exhibit (a picture, animal,
flower, etc.) in a show. **9** *tr.* (often foll. by *in, out,
up*, etc.) conduct or lead (*showed them to their
rooms*). **10** *intr.* = *show up* 3 (*waited but he didn't
show*). —*n.* **1** the act or an instance of showing;
the state of being shown. **2 a** a spectacle, display,
exhibition, etc. (*a fine show of blossom*). **b** a
collection of things etc. shown for public entertainment or in competition (*dog show; flower
show*). **3 a** a play etc., esp. a musical. **b** a light
entertainment programme on television etc. **c**
any public entertainment or performance. **4 a**
an outward appearance, semblance, or display
(*made a show of agreeing; a show of strength*). **b**
empty appearance; mere display (*did it for show;
that's all show*). **5** *Med.* a discharge of blood etc.
from the vagina at the onset of childbirth.
□ **give the show** (or **whole show**) **away**
demonstrate the inadequacies or reveal the
truth. **good** (or **bad** or **poor**) **show!** *colloq.* **1**
that was well (or badly) done. **2** that was lucky
(or unlucky). **nothing to show for** no visible
result of (effort etc.). **on show** being exhibited.
show business *colloq.* the theatrical profession.
show one's cards = *show one's hand.* **show a
clean pair of heels** *colloq.* retreat speedily; run
away. **show one's colours** make one's opinion
clear. **show a person the door** dismiss or eject
a person. **show one's face** make an appearance;
let oneself be seen. **show fight** be persistent or
belligerent. **show one's hand 1** disclose one's
plans. **2** reveal one's cards. **show house** (or **flat**
etc.) a furnished and decorated house (or flat
etc.) on a new estate shown to prospective
buyers. **show in** see sense 9 of *v.* **show a leg**
colloq. get out of bed. **show off 1** display to
advantage. **2** *colloq.* act pretentiously; display
one's wealth, knowledge, etc. **show-off** *n. colloq.*
a person who shows off. **show of force** proof
that one is prepared to use force. **show of
hands** raised hands indicating a vote for or
against, usu. without being counted. **show
oneself 1** be seen in public. **2** see sense 6 of *v.*
show out see sense 9 of *v.* **show-piece 1** an
item of work presented for exhibition or display.
2 an outstanding example or specimen. **show-
place** a house etc. that tourists go to see. **show
round** take (a person) to places of interest; act
as guide for (a person) in a building etc.
show-stopper *colloq.* a performance receiving
prolonged applause. **show one's teeth** reveal
one's strength; be aggressive. **show through 1**
be visible although supposedly concealed. **2** (of
real feelings etc.) be revealed inadvertently.
show trial esp. *hist.* a judicial trial designed by

the State to terrorize or impress the public.
show up 1 make or be conspicuous or clearly
visible. **2** expose (a fraud, impostor, inferiority,
etc.). **3** *colloq.* appear; be present; arrive. **4** *colloq.*
embarrass or humiliate (*don't show me up by
wearing jeans*). **show the way 1** indicate what
has to be done etc. by attempting it first. **2**
show others which way to go etc. **show willing**
display a willingness to help etc. **show-window**
a window for exhibiting goods etc. [ME f. OE
scēawian f. WG: cf. SHEEN]

showbiz /ˈʃəʊbɪz/ *n. colloq.* = show business.

showboat /ˈʃəʊbəʊt/ *n. US* a river steamer on
which theatrical performances are given.

showcase /ˈʃəʊkeɪs/ *n. & v.* —*n.* **1** a glass case
used for exhibiting goods etc. **2** a place or
medium for presenting (esp. attractively) to
general attention. —*v.tr.* display in or as if in a
showcase.

showdown /ˈʃəʊdaʊn/ *n.* **1** a final test or confrontation; a decisive situation. **2** the laying
down face up of the players' cards in poker.

shower /ˈʃaʊə(r)/ *n. & v.* —*n.* **1** a brief fall of esp.
rain, hail, sleet, or snow. **2 a** a brisk flurry of
arrows, bullets, dust, stones, sparks, etc. **b** a
similar flurry of gifts, letters, honours, praise,
etc. **3** (in full **shower-bath**) **a** a cubicle, bath,
etc. in which one stands under a spray of water.
b the apparatus etc. used for this. **c** the act of
bathing in a shower. **4** *US* a party for giving
presents to a prospective bride, etc. **5** *Brit. sl.* a
contemptible or unpleasant person or group of
people. —*v.* **1** *tr.* discharge (water, missiles, etc.)
in a shower. **2** *intr.* use a shower-bath. **3** *tr.* (usu.
foll. by *on*, *upon*) lavishly bestow (gifts etc.). **4**
intr. descend or come in a shower (*it showered on
and off all day*). □ **showery** *adj.* [OE *scūr* f. Gmc]

showerproof /ˈʃaʊəpruːf/ *adj. & v.* —*adj.* resistant to light rain. —*v.tr.* render showerproof.

showgirl /ˈʃəʊgɜːl/ *n.* an actress who sings and
dances in musicals, variety shows, etc.

showing /ˈʃəʊɪŋ/ *n.* **1** the act or an instance of
showing. **2** a usu. specified quality of performance (*made a poor showing*). **3** the presentation of a case; evidence (*on present showing
it must be true*). [OE *scēawung* (as SHOW)]

showjumping /ˈʃəʊdʒʌmpɪŋ/ *n.* the sport of
riding horses over a course of fences and other
obstacles, with penalty points for errors. □
showjump *v.intr.* **showjumper** *n.*

showman /ˈʃəʊmən/ *n.* (*pl.* **-men**) **1** the proprietor or manager of a circus etc. **2** a person
skilled in self-advertisement. □ **showmanship**
n.

shown *past part.* of SHOW.

showroom /ˈʃəʊruːm, -rʊm/ *n.* a room in a
factory, office building, etc. used to display
goods for sale.

showy /ˈʃəʊɪ/ *adj.* (**showier**, **showiest**) **1** brilliant; gaudy, esp. vulgarly so. **2** striking. □
showily *adv.* **showiness** *n.*

shrank *past* of SHRINK.

shrapnel /ˈʃræpn(ə)l/ *n.* **1** fragments of a bomb
etc. thrown out by an explosion. **2** a shell
containing bullets or pieces of metal timed to
burst short of impact. [Gen. H. *Shrapnel*, Brit.
soldier d. 1842, inventor of the shell]

shred *n. & v.* —*n.* **1** a scrap, fragment, or strip
of esp. cloth, paper, etc. **2** the least amount;
remnant (*not a shred of evidence*). —*v.tr.* (**shredded**, **shredding**) tear or cut into shreds. □ **tear**

to shreds completely refute (an argument etc.).
[OE *scrēad* (unrecorded) piece cut off, *scrēadian* f.
WG: see SHROUD]

shredder /ˈʃredə(r)/ *n.* **1** a machine used to
reduce documents to shreds. **2** any device used
for shredding.

shrew *n.* **1** any small usu. insect-eating mouselike mammal of the family Soricidae, with a
long pointed snout. **2** a bad-tempered or scolding
woman. □ **shrewish** *adj.* (in sense 2). **shrew-
ishly** *adv.* **shrewishness** *n.* [OE *scrēawa*, *scrēwa*
shrew-mouse: cf. OHG *scrawaz* dwarf, MHG
schrawaz etc. devil]

shrewd *adj.* **1** showing astute powers of judgement; clever and judicious (*a shrewd observer*;
made a shrewd guess). **2** (of a face etc.) shrewd-
looking. □ **shrewdly** *adv.* **shrewdness** *n.* [ME,
= malignant, f. SHREW in sense 'evil person or
thing', or past part. of obs. *shrew* to curse, f.
SHREW]

shriek /ʃriːk/ *v. & n.* —*v.* **1** *intr.* **a** utter a shrill
screeching sound or words esp. in pain or
terror. **b** (foll. by *of*) provide a clear or blatant
indication of. **2** *tr.* **a** utter (sounds or words) by
shrieking (*shrieked his name*). **b** indicate clearly
or blatantly. —*n.* a high- pitched piercing cry
or sound; a scream. □ **shriek out** say in shrill
tones. **shriek with laughter** laugh uncontrollably. □ **shrieker** *n.* [imit.: cf. dial. *screak*,
ON *skrækja*, and SCREECH]

shrift *n. archaic* **1** confession to a priest. **2**
confession and absolution. □ **short shrift** curt
treatment. [OE *scrift* (verbal noun) f. SHRIVE]

shrike *n.* any bird of the family Laniidae, that
impales its prey of small birds and insects on
thorns. [perh. rel. to OE *scric* thrush, MLG *schrīk*
corncrake (imit.): cf. SHRIEK]

shrill *adj. & v.* —*adj.* **1** piercing and high-pitched
in sound. **2** *derog.* (esp. of a protester) sharp,
unrestrained, unreasoning. —*v.* **1** *intr.* (of a cry
etc.) sound shrilly. **2** *tr.* (of a person etc.) utter
or send out (a song, complaint, etc.) shrilly. □
shrilly *adv.* **shrillness** *n.* [ME, rel. to LG *schrell*
sharp in tone or taste f. Gmc]

shrimp *n. & v.* —*n.* **1** (*pl.* same or **shrimps**) any
of various small (esp. marine) edible crusta-
ceans, with ten legs, pink when boiled. **2** *colloq.*
a very small slight person. —*v.intr.* go catching
shrimps. □ **shrimper** *n.* [ME, prob. rel. to MLG
schrempen wrinkle, MHG *schrimpfen* contract, and
SCRIMP]

shrine *n.* **1** esp. *RC Ch.* **a** a chapel, church, altar,
etc., sacred to a saint, holy person, relic, etc. **b**
the tomb of a saint etc. **c** a casket esp. containing
sacred relics; a reliquary. **d** a niche containing a
holy statue etc. **2** a place associated with or
containing memorabilia of a particular person,
event, etc. **3** a Shinto place of worship. [OE *scrīn*
f. Gmc f. L *scrinium* case for books etc.]

shrink *v. & n.* —*v.* (*past* **shrank**; *past part.*
shrunk or (esp. as *adj.*) **shrunken** /ˈʃrʌŋkən/) **1**
tr. & intr. make or become smaller; contract,
esp. by the action of moisture, heat, or cold. **2**
intr. (usu. foll. by *from*) **a** retire; recoil; flinch;
cower (*shrank from her touch*). **b** be averse from
doing (*shrinks from meeting them*). **3** (as **shrunken**
adj.) (esp. of a face, person, etc.) having grown
smaller esp. because of age, illness, etc. —*n.* **1**
the act or an instance of shrinking; shrinkage.
2 *sl.* a psychiatrist (from 'head-shrinker'). □
shrinking violet an exaggeratedly shy person.

shrink into oneself become withdrawn.
shrink-wrap (-wrapped, -wrapping) enclose (an article) in (esp. transparent) film that shrinks tightly on to it. □ **shrinkable** adj. **shrinker** n. **shrinkingly** adv. **shrink-proof** adj. [OE scrincan: cf. skrynka to wrinkle]

shrinkage /ˈʃrɪŋkɪdʒ/ n. **1 a** the process or fact of shrinking. **b** the degree or amount of shrinking. **2** an allowance made for the reduction in takings due to wastage, theft, etc.

shrive /ʃraɪv/ v.tr. (past **shrove** /ʃrəʊv/; past part. **shriven** /ˈʃrɪv(ə)n/) RC Ch. archaic **1** (of a priest) hear the confession of, assign penance to, and absolve. **2** (refl.) (of a penitent) submit oneself to a priest for confession etc. [OE scrīfan impose as penance, WG f. L scribere write]

shrivel /ˈʃrɪv(ə)l/ v.tr. & intr. (**shrivelled, shrivelling** or US **shriveled, shriveling**) contract or wither into a wrinkled, folded, rolled-up, contorted, or dried-up state. [perh. f. ON: cf. Sw. dial. skryvla to wrinkle]

shriven past part. of SHRIVE.

shroud /ʃraʊd/ n. & v. —n. **1** a sheetlike garment for wrapping a corpse for burial. **2** anything that conceals like a shroud (wrapped in a shroud of mystery). **3** (in pl.) Naut. a set of ropes forming part of the standing rigging and supporting the mast or topmast. —v.tr. **1** clothe (a body) for burial. **2** cover, conceal, or disguise (hills shrouded in mist). □ **shroudless** adj. [OE scrūd f. Gmc: see SHRED]

shrove past of SHRIVE.

Shrove Tuesday /ʃrəʊv/ n. the day before Ash Wednesday. [shrove past of SHRIVE]

shrub¹ n. a woody plant smaller than a tree and having a very short stem with branches near the ground. □ **shrubby** adj. [ME f. OE scrubb, scrybb shrubbery: cf. NFris. skrobb brushwood, WFlem. schrobbe vetch, Norw. skrubba dwarf cornel, and SCRUB²]

shrub² n. a cordial made of sweetened fruit-juice and spirits, esp. rum. [Arab. šurb, šarāb f. šariba to drink: cf. SHERBET, SYRUP]

shrubbery /ˈʃrʌbərɪ/ n. (pl. -ies) an area planted with shrubs.

shrug v. & n. —v. (**shrugged, shrugging**) **1** intr. slightly and momentarily raise the shoulders to express indifference, helplessness, contempt, etc. **2** tr. **a** raise (the shoulders) in this way. **b** shrug the shoulders to express (indifference etc.) (shrugged his consent). —n. the act or an instance of shrugging. □ **shrug off** dismiss as unimportant etc. by or as if by shrugging. [ME: orig. unkn.]

shrunk (also **shrunken**) past part. of SHRINK.

shuck n. & v. US —n. **1** a husk or pod. **2** the shell of an oyster or clam. **3** (in pl.) colloq. an expression of contempt or regret or self-deprecation in response to praise. —v.tr. remove the shucks of; shell. □ **shucker** n. [17th c.: orig. unkn.]

shudder /ˈʃʌdə(r)/ v. & n. —v.intr. **1** shiver esp. convulsively from fear, cold, repugnance, etc. **2** feel strong repugnance etc. (shudder to think what might happen). **3** (of a machine etc.) vibrate or quiver. —n. **1** the act or an instance of shuddering. **2** (in pl.; prec. by the) colloq. a state of shuddering. □ **shudderingly** adv. **shuddery** adj. [ME shod(d)er f. MDu. schūderen, MLG schōderen f. Gmc]

shuffle /ˈʃʌf(ə)l/ v. & n. —v. **1** tr. & intr. move with a scraping, sliding, or dragging motion (shuffles along; shuffling his feet). **2** tr. **a** (also absol.) rearrange (a pack of cards) by sliding them over each other quickly. **b** rearrange; intermingle; confuse (shuffled the documents). **3** tr. (usu. foll. by on, off, into) assume or remove (clothes, a burden, etc.) esp. clumsily or evasively (shuffled on his clothes; shuffled off responsibility). **4** intr. **a** equivocate; prevaricate. **b** continually shift one's position; fidget. —n. **1** a shuffling movement. **2** the act or an instance of shuffling cards. **3** a general change of relative positions. **4** a piece of equivocation; sharp practice. **5** a quick scraping movement of the feet in dancing. □ **shuffleboard** = SHOVELBOARD. □ **shuffler** n. [perh. f. LG schuffeln walk clumsily f. Gmc: cf. SHOVE]

shun v.tr. (**shunned, shunning**) avoid; keep clear of. [OE scunian, of unkn. orig.]

shunt v. & n. —v. **1** intr. & tr. diverge or cause (a train) to be diverted esp. on to a siding. **2** tr. divert (a decision etc.) on to another person etc. —n. **1** the act or an instance of shunting on to a siding. **2** Electr. a conductor joining two points of a circuit, through which more or less of a current may be diverted. **3** sl. a motor accident, esp. a collision of vehicles travelling one close behind another. □ **shunter** n. [ME, perh. f. SHUN]

shush /ʃʊʃ, ʃʌʃ/ int. & v. —int. = HUSH int. —v. **1** intr. **a** call for silence by saying shush. **b** be silent (they shushed at once). **2** tr. make or attempt to make silent. [imit.]

shut v. (**shutting**; past and past part. **shut**) **1** tr. **a** move (a door, window, lid, lips, etc.) into position so as to block an aperture (shut the lid). **b** close or seal (a room, window, box, eye, mouth, etc.) by moving a door etc. (shut the box). **2** intr. become or be capable of being closed or sealed (the door shut with a bang; the lid shuts automatically). **3** intr. & tr. become or make (a shop, business, etc.) closed for trade (the shops shut at five; shuts his shop at five). **4** tr. bring (a book, hand, telescope, etc.) into a folded-up or contracted state. **5** tr. (usu. foll. by in, out) keep (a person, sound, etc.) in or out of a room etc. by shutting a door etc. (shut out the noise; shut them in). **6** tr. (usu. foll. by in) catch (a finger, dress, etc.) by shutting something on it (shut her finger in the door). □ **be** (or **get**) **shut of** sl. be (or get) rid of (were glad to get shut of him). **shut down 1** stop (a factory, nuclear reactor, etc.) from operating. **2** (of a factory etc.) stop operating. **shut-eye** colloq. sleep. **shut one's eyes** (or **ears** or **heart** or **mind**) **to** pretend not to, or refuse, to see (or hear or feel sympathy for or think about). **shut in** (of hills, houses, etc.) encircle, prevent access etc. to or escape from (were shut in by the sea on three sides) (see also sense 5). **shut off 1** stop the flow of (water, gas, etc.) by shutting a valve. **2** separate from society etc. **shut-off** n. something used for stopping an operation. **shut out 1** exclude (a person, light, etc.) from a place, situation, etc. **2** screen (landscape etc.) from view. **3** prevent (a possibility etc.). **4** block (a painful memory etc.) from the mind. **shut up 1** close all doors and windows of (a house etc.); bolt and bar. **2** imprison (a person etc.). **3** close (a box etc.) securely. **4** colloq. reduce to silence by rebuke etc. **5** put (a thing) away in a box etc. **6**

(esp. in *imper.*) *colloq.* stop talking. **shut up shop 1** close a business, shop, etc. **2** cease business etc. permanently. [OE *scyttan* f. WG: cf. SHOOT]

shutter /ˈʃʌtə(r)/ *n. & v.* —*n.* **1** a person or thing that shuts. **2 a** each of a pair or set of panels fixed inside or outside a window for security or privacy or to keep the light in or out. **b** a structure of slats on rollers used for the same purpose. **3** a device that exposes the film in a photographic camera. —*v.tr.* **1** put up the shutters of. **2** provide with shutters. □ **put up the shutters 1** cease business for the day. **2** cease business etc. permanently. □ **shutterless** *adj.*

shuttle /ˈʃʌt(ə)l/ *n. & v.* —*n.* **1 a** a bobbin with two pointed ends used for carrying the weft-thread across between the warp-threads in weaving. **b** a bobbin carrying the lower thread in a sewing-machine. **2** a train, bus, etc., going to and fro over a short route continuously. **3** = SHUTTLECOCK. **4** = space shuttle. —*v.* **1** *intr. & tr.* move or cause to move to and fro like a shuttle. **2** *intr.* travel in a shuttle. □ **shuttle diplomacy** negotiations conducted by a mediator who travels successively to several countries. **shuttle service** a train or bus etc. service operating to and fro over a short route. [OE *scytel* dart f. Gmc: cf. SHOOT]

shuttlecock /ˈʃʌt(ə)lˌkɒk/ *n.* **1** a cork with a ring of feathers, or a similar device of plastic, used instead of a ball in badminton. **2** a thing passed repeatedly back and forth. [SHUTTLE + COCK¹, prob. f. the flying motion]

shy¹ *adj., v., & n.* —*adj.* (**shyer, shyest** or **shier, shiest**) **1 a** diffident or uneasy in company; timid. **b** (of an animal, bird, etc.) easily startled; timid. **2** (foll. by *of*) avoiding; chary of (*shy of his aunt*; *shy of going to meetings*). **3** (in *comb.*) showing fear of or distaste for (*gun-shy*; *work-shy*). —*v.intr.* (**shies, shied**) **1** (usu. foll. by *at*) (esp. of a horse) start suddenly aside (at an object, noise, etc.) in fright. **2** (usu. foll. by *away from*, *at*) avoid accepting or becoming involved in (a proposal etc.) in alarm. —*n.* a sudden startled movement. □ **shyer** *n.* **shyly** *adv.* (also **shily**). **shyness** *n.* [OE *sceoh* f. Gmc]

shy² *v. & n.* —*v.tr.* (**shies, shied**) (also *absol.*) fling or throw (a stone etc.). —*n.* (*pl.* **shies**) the act or an instance of shying. □ **shyer** *n.* [18th c.: orig. unkn.]

shyster /ˈʃaɪstə(r)/ *n.* esp. *US colloq.* a person, esp. a lawyer, who uses unscrupulous methods. [19th c.: orig. uncert.]

SI *abbr.* the international system of units of measurement (F *Système International*).

Si *symb. Chem.* the element silicon.

si /siː/ *n. Mus.* = TE. [F f. It., perh. f. the initials of *Sancte Iohannes*: see GAMUT]

Siamese /ˌsaɪəˈmiːz/ *n. & adj.* —*n.* (*pl.* same) **1 a** a native of Siam (now Thailand) in SE Asia. **b** the language of Siam. **2** (in full **Siamese cat**) **a** a cat of a cream-coloured short-haired breed with a brown face and ears and blue eyes. **b** this breed. —*adj.* of or concerning Siam, its people, or language. □ **Siamese twins** twins joined at any part of the body and sometimes sharing organs etc.

sib *n.* a brother or sister (cf. SIBLING). [OE *sib(b)*]

sibilant /ˈsɪbɪlənt/ *adj. & n.* —*adj.* **1** (of a letter or set of letters, as *s, sh*) sounded with a hiss. **2** hissing (*a sibilant whisper*). —*n.* a sibilant letter

or letters. □ **sibilance** *n.* **sibilancy** *n.* [L *sibilare sibilant-* hiss]

sibling /ˈsɪblɪŋ/ *n.* each of two or more children having one or both parents in common. [SIB + -LING¹]

sibyl /ˈsɪbɪl/ *n.* **1** any of the women in ancient times supposed to utter the oracles and prophecies of a god. **2** a prophetess, fortune-teller, or witch. [ME f. OF *Sibile* or med.L *Sibilla* f. L *Sibylla* f. Gk *Sibulla*]

sibylline /ˈsɪbɪˌlaɪn/ *adj.* **1** of or from a sibyl. **2** oracular; prophetic. [L *Sibyllinus* (as SIBYL)]

sic *adv.* (usu. in brackets) used, spelt, etc., as written (confirming, or calling attention to, the form of quoted or copied words). [L, = so, thus]

sick¹ *adj., n., & v.* —*adj.* **1** (often in *comb.*) esp. *Brit.* vomiting or tending to vomit (*feels sick*; *has been sick*; *seasick*). **2** esp. *US* ill; affected by illness (*has been sick for a week*; *a sick man*; *sick with measles*). **3 a** (often foll. by *at*) esp. mentally perturbed; disordered (*the product of a sick mind*; *sick at heart*). **b** (often foll. by *for*, or in *comb.*) pining; longing (*sick for a sight of home*; *lovesick*). **4** (often foll. by *of*) *colloq.* **a** disgusted; surfeited (*sick of chocolates*). **b** angry, esp. because of surfeit (*am sick of being teased*). **5** *colloq.* (of humour etc.) jeering at misfortune, illness, death, etc.; morbid (*sick joke*). —*n. Brit. colloq.* vomit. —*v.tr.* (usu. foll. by *up*) *Brit. colloq.* vomit (*sicked up his dinner*). □ **go sick** report oneself as ill. **sick at (or to) one's stomach** *US* vomiting or tending to vomit. **sick-benefit** *Brit.* an allowance made by the State to a person absent from work through sickness. **sick building syndrome** a high incidence of illness in office workers, attributed to the immediate working surroundings. **sick headache** a migraine headache with vomiting. **sick-leave** leave of absence granted because of illness. **sick-list** a list of the sick, esp. in a regiment, ship, etc. **sick-making** *colloq.* sickening. **sick-pay** pay given to an employee etc. on sick-leave. **take sick** *colloq.* be taken ill. □ **sickish** *adj.* [OE *sēoc* f. Gmc]

sick² *v.tr.* (usu. in *imper.*) (esp. to a dog) set upon (a rat etc.). [19th c., dial. var. of SEEK]

sickbay /ˈsɪkbeɪ/ *n.* **1** part of a ship used as a hospital. **2** any room etc. for sick people.

sickbed /ˈsɪkbed/ *n.* **1** an invalid's bed. **2** the state of being an invalid.

sicken /ˈsɪkən/ *v.* **1** *tr.* affect with loathing or disgust. **2** *intr.* **a** (often foll. by *for*) show symptoms of illness (*is sickening for measles*). **b** (often foll. by *at*, or *to* + infin.) feel nausea or disgust (*he sickened at the sight*). **3** (as **sickening** *adj.*) **a** a loathsome, disgusting. **b** *colloq.* very annoying. □ **sickeningly** *adv.*

sickie /ˈsɪkɪ/ *n. Austral. & NZ colloq.* a period of sick-leave, usu. taken with insufficient medical reason.

sickle /ˈsɪk(ə)l/ *n.* **1** a short-handled farming tool with a semicircular blade, used for cutting corn, lopping, or trimming. **2** anything sickle-shaped, esp. the crescent moon. □ **sickle-cell** a sickle-shaped blood-cell, esp. as found in a type of severe hereditary anaemia. [OE *sicol, sicel* f. L *secula* f. *secare* cut]

sickly /ˈsɪklɪ/ *adj.* (**sicklier, sickliest**) **1 a** of weak health; apt to be ill. **b** (of a person's complexion, look, etc.) languid, faint, or pale, suggesting sickness (*a sickly smile*). **c** (of light or colour) faint, pale, feeble. **2** causing ill health (*a* *sickly climate*). **3** (of a book etc.) sentimental or mawkish. **4** inducing or connected with nausea (*a sickly taste*). **5** (of a colour etc.) of an unpleasant shade inducing nausea (*a sickly green*). □ **sickliness** *n*. [ME, prob. after ON *sjúkligr* (as SICK¹)]

sickness /ˈsɪknɪs/ *n*. **1** the state of being ill; disease. **2** a specified disease (*sleeping sickness*). **3** vomiting or a tendency to vomit. □ **sickness benefit** (in the UK) benefit paid by the State for sickness interrupting paid employment. [OE *sēocnesse* (as SICK¹, -NESS)]

sickroom /ˈsɪkruːm, -rʊm/ *n*. **1** a room occupied by a sick person. **2** a room adapted for sick people.

side *n. & v. —n.* **1 a** each of the more or less flat surfaces bounding an object (*a cube has six sides*; *this side up*). **b** a more or less vertical inner or outer plane or surface (*the side of a house*; *a mountainside*). **c** such a vertical lateral surface or plane as distinct from the top or bottom, front or back, or ends (*at the side of the house*). **2 a** the half of a person or animal that is on the right or the left, esp. of the torso (*has a pain in his right side*). **b** the left or right half or a specified part of a thing, area, building, etc. (*put the box on that side*). **c** (often in *comb*.) a position next to a person or thing (*grave-side*; *seaside*; *stood at my side*). **d** a specified direction relating to a person or thing (*on the north side of*; *came from all sides*). **3 a** either surface of a thing regarded as having two surfaces. **b** the amount of writing needed to fill one side of a sheet of paper (*write three sides*). **4** any of several aspects of a question, character, etc. (*many sides to his character*; *look on the bright side*). **5 a** each of two sets of opponents in war, politics, games, etc. (*the side that bats first*; *much to be said on both sides*). **b** a cause or philosophical position etc. regarded as being in conflict with another (*on the side of right*). **6 a** a part or region near the edge and remote from the centre (*at the side of the room*). **b** (*attrib.*) a subordinate, peripheral, or detached part (*a side-road*; *a side-table*). **7 a** each of the bounding lines of a plane rectilinear figure (*a hexagon has six sides*). **b** each of two quantities stated to be equal in an equation. **8** a position nearer or farther than, or right or left of, a dividing line (*on this side of the Alps*; *on the other side of the road*). **9** a line of hereditary descent through the father or the mother. **10** *Brit. sl.* boastfulness; swagger (*has no side about him*). **11** *Brit. colloq.* a television channel (*shall we try another side?*). —*v.intr.* (usu. foll. by *with*) take part or be on the same side as a disputant etc. (*sided with his father*). □ **by the side of 1** close to. **2** compared with. **from side to side 1** right across. **2** alternately each way from a central line. **let the side down** fail one's colleagues, esp. by frustrating their efforts or embarrassing them. **on one side 1** not in the main or central position. **2** aside (*took him on one side to explain*). **on the . . . side** fairly, somewhat (qualifying an adjective: *on the high side*). **on the side 1** as a sideline; in addition to one's regular work etc. **2** secretly or illicitly. **3** *US* as a side dish. **side-bet** bet between opponents, esp. in card-games, over and above the ordinary stakes. **side by side** standing close together, esp. for mutual support. **side-car** a small car for a passenger or passengers attached to the side of a motor cycle. **side-chapel** a chapel in the aisle or at the side of a church. **side dish** an extra

dish subsidiary to the main course. **side-door 1** a door in or at the side of a building. **2** an indirect means of access. **side-drum** a small double-headed drum in a jazz or military band or in an orchestra (orig. hung at the drummer's side). **side-effect** a secondary, usu. undesirable, effect. **side-issue** a point that distracts attention from what is important. **side-on** *adv*. from the side. —*adj*. **1** from or towards one side. **2** (of a collision) involving the side of a vehicle. **side-road** a minor or subsidiary road, esp. joining or diverging from a main road. **side-saddle** *n*. a saddle for a woman rider with both feet on the same side of the horse. —*adv*. sitting in this position on a horse. **side salad** a salad served as a side dish. **side-splitting** causing violent laughter. **side-street** a minor or subsidiary street. **side-stroke 1** a stroke towards or from a side. **2** an incidental action. **3** a swimming stroke in which the swimmer lies on his or her side. **side-swipe** *n*. **1** a glancing blow along the side. **2** incidental criticism etc. —*v.tr.* hit with or as if with a side-swipe. **side-table** a table placed at the side of a room or apart from the main table. **side-view 1** a view obtained sideways. **2** a profile. **side-whiskers** whiskers growing on the cheeks. **side wind 1** wind from the side. **2** an indirect agency or influence. **take sides** support one or other cause etc. □ **sideless** *adj*. [OE *sīde* f. Gmc]

sideboard /ˈsaɪdbɔːd/ *n*. a table or esp. a flat-topped cupboard at the side of a dining-room for supporting and containing dishes, table linen, decanters, etc.

sideboards /ˈsaɪdbɔːdz/ *n.pl. Brit. colloq.* hair grown by a man down the sides of his face; side-whiskers.

sideburns /ˈsaɪdbɜːnz/ *n.pl.* = SIDEBOARDS. [*burnsides* pl. of *burnside* f. General Burnside d. 1881 who affected this style]

sided /ˈsaɪdɪd/ *adj.* **1** having sides. **2** (in *comb*.) having a specified side or sides (*one-sided*). □ **-sidedly** *adv*. **sidedness** *n*. (also in *comb*.).

sidekick /ˈsaɪdkɪk/ *n. colloq.* a close associate.

sidelight /ˈsaɪdlaɪt/ *n*. **1** a light from the side. **2** incidental information etc. **3** *Brit.* a light at the side of the front of a motor vehicle to warn of its presence. **4** *Naut.* the red port or green starboard light on a ship under way.

sideline /ˈsaɪdlaɪn/ *n. & v. —n.* **1** work etc. done in addition to one's main activity. **2** (usu. in *pl.*) **a** a line bounding the side of a hockey-pitch, tennis-court, etc. **b** the space next to these where spectators etc. sit. —*v.tr. US* remove (a player) from a team through injury, suspension, etc. □ **on** (or **from**) **the sidelines** in (or from) a position removed from the main action.

sidelong /ˈsaɪdlɒŋ/ *adj. & adv. —adj.* inclining to one side; oblique (*a sidelong glance*). —*adv.* obliquely (*moved sidelong*). [*sideling* (as SIDE, -LING²): see -LONG]

sidereal /saɪˈdɪərɪəl/ *adj.* of or concerning the constellations or fixed stars. □ **sidereal day** the time between successive meridional transits of a star, about four minutes shorter than the solar day. [L *sidereus* f. *sidus sideris* star]

sideshow /ˈsaɪdʃəʊ/ *n*. a minor show or attraction in an exhibition or entertainment.

sidesman /ˈsaɪdzmən/ *n.* (pl. **-men**) an assistant churchwarden, who shows worshippers to their seats, takes the collection, etc.

sidestep /ˈsaɪdstep/ n. & v. —n. a step taken sideways. —v.tr. (**-stepped**, **-stepping**) **1** esp. *Football* avoid (esp. a tackle) by stepping sideways. **2** evade. □ **sidestepper** n.

sidetrack /ˈsaɪdtræk/ n. & v. —n. a railway siding. —v.tr. **1** turn into a siding; shunt. **2 a** postpone, evade, or divert treatment or consideration. **b** divert (a person) from considering etc.

sidewalk /ˈsaɪdwɔːk/ n. US a pedestrian path at the side of a road; a pavement.

sideways /ˈsaɪdweɪz/ adv. & adj. —adv. **1** to or from a side (*moved sideways*). **2** with one side facing forward (*sat sideways on the bus*). —adj. to or from a side (*a sideways movement*). □ **sidewise** adv. & adj.

siding /ˈsaɪdɪŋ/ n. **1** a short track at the side of and opening on to a railway line, used for shunting trains. **2** US cladding material for the outside of a building.

sidle /ˈsaɪd(ə)l/ v. & n. —v.intr. (usu. foll. by *along*, *up*) walk in a timid, furtive, stealthy, or cringing manner. —n. the act or an instance of sidling. [back-form. f. *sideling*, SIDELONG]

SIDS abbr. sudden infant death syndrome; = *cot-death* (see COT[1]).

siege /siːdʒ/ n. **1 a** a military operation in which an attacking force seeks to compel the surrender of a fortified place by surrounding it and cutting off supplies etc. **b** a similar operation by police etc. to force the surrender of an armed person. **c** the period during which a siege lasts. **2** a persistent attack or campaign of persuasion. □ **lay siege to** esp. *Mil.* conduct the siege of. **raise the siege of** abandon or cause the abandonment of an attempt to take (a place) by siege. [ME f. OF *sege* seat f. *assegier* BESIEGE]

siemens /ˈsiːmənz/ n. *Electr.* the SI unit of conductance. [W. von *Siemens*, Ger. electrical engineer, d. 1892]

sienna /sɪˈenə/ n. **1** a kind of earth used as a pigment in paint. **2** its colour of yellowish-brown (**raw sienna**) or reddish-brown (**burnt sienna**). [It. (*terra di*) *Sienna* (earth of) Siena in Tuscany]

sierra /sɪˈerə/ n. a long jagged mountain chain, esp. in Spain or Spanish America. [Sp. f. L *serra* saw]

siesta /sɪˈestə/ n. an afternoon sleep or rest esp. in hot countries. [Sp. f. L *sexta* (*hora*) sixth hour]

sieve /sɪv/ n. & v. —n. a utensil having a perforated or meshed bottom for separating solids or coarse material from liquids or fine particles, or for reducing a soft solid to a fine pulp. —v.tr. **1** put through or sift with a sieve. **2** examine (evidence etc.) to select or separate. □ **sievelike** adj. [OE *sife* f. WG]

sift v. **1** tr. sieve (material) into finer and coarser parts. **2** tr. (usu. foll. by *from*, *out*) separate (finer or coarser parts) from material. **3** tr. sprinkle (esp. sugar) from a perforated container. **4** tr. examine (evidence, facts, etc.) in order to assess authenticity etc. □ **sift through** examine by sifting. □ **sifter** n. (also in *comb.*). [OE *siftan* f. WG]

sigh /saɪ/ v. & n. —v. intr. **1** emit a long deep audible breath expressive of sadness, weariness, longing, relief, etc. **2** intr. (foll. by *for*) yearn for (a lost person or thing). **3** intr. (of the wind etc.) make a sound like sighing. —n. **1** the act or an instance of sighing. **2** a sound made in sighing (*a sigh of relief*). [ME *sihen* etc., prob. back-form. f. *sihte* past of *sīhen* f. OE *sīcan*]

sight /saɪt/ n. & v. —n. **1 a** the faculty of seeing with the eyes (*lost his sight*). **b** the act or an instance of seeing; the state of being seen. **2** a thing seen; a display, show, or spectacle (*not a pretty sight*; *a beautiful sight*). **3** a way of looking at or considering a thing (*in my sight he can do no wrong*). **4** a range of space within which a person etc. can see or an object be seen (*he's out of sight*; *they are just coming into sight*). **5** (usu. in *pl.*) noteworthy features of a town, area, etc. (*went to see the sights*). **6 a** a device on a gun or optical instrument used for assisting the precise aim or observation. **b** the aim or observation so gained (*got a sight of him*). **7** *colloq.* a person or thing having a ridiculous, repulsive, or dishevelled appearance (*looked a perfect sight*). **8** *colloq.* a great quantity (*will cost a sight of money*; *is a sight better than he was*). —v.tr. **1** get sight of, esp. by approaching (*they sighted land*). **2** observe the presence of (esp. aircraft, animals, etc.) (*sighted buffalo*). **3** take observations of (a star etc.) with an instrument. **4** aim (a gun etc.) with sights. □ **at first sight** on first glimpse or impression. **at** (or **on**) **sight** as soon as a person or a thing has been seen (*plays music at sight*; *liked him on sight*). **catch** (or **lose**) **sight of** begin (or cease) to see or be aware of. **get a sight of** manage to see; glimpse. **have lost sight of** no longer know the whereabouts of. **in sight 1** visible. **2** near at hand (*salvation is in sight*). **in** (or **within**) **sight of** so as to see or be seen from. **lower one's sights** become less ambitious. **out of my sight!** go at once! **out of sight 1** not visible. **2** *colloq.* excellent; delightful. **set one's sights on** aim at (*set her sights on a directorship*). **sight-line** a hypothetical line from a person's eye to what is seen. **sight-read** (*past* and *past part.* **-read** /-red/) read and perform (music) at sight. **sight-screen** *Cricket* a large white screen on wheels placed near the boundary in line with the wicket to help the batsman see the ball. **sight unseen** without previous inspection. □ **sighter** n. [OE (*ge*)*sihth*]

sighted /ˈsaɪtɪd/ adj. **1** capable of seeing; not blind. **2** (in *comb.*) having a specified kind of sight (*long-sighted*).

sightless /ˈsaɪtlɪs/ adj. **1** blind. **2** *poet.* invisible. □ **sightlessly** adv. **sightlessness** n.

sightly /ˈsaɪtlɪ/ adj. attractive to the sight; not unsightly. □ **sightliness** n.

sightseer /ˈsaɪtˌsiːə(r)/ n. a person who visits places of interest; a tourist. □ **sightsee** v.intr. & tr. **sightseeing** n.

sigma /ˈsɪgmə/ n. the eighteenth letter of the Greek alphabet (Σ, σ, or, when final, ς). [L f. Gk]

sign /saɪn/ n. & v. —n. **1 a** a thing indicating or suggesting a quality or state etc.; a thing perceived as indicating a future state or occurrence (*violence is a sign of weakness*; *shows all the signs of decay*). **b** a miracle evidencing supernatural power; a portent (*did signs and wonders*). **2 a** a mark, symbol, or device used to represent something or to distinguish the thing on which it is put (*marked the jar with a sign*). **b** a technical symbol used in algebra, music, etc. (*a minus sign*; *a repeat sign*). **3** a gesture or action used to convey information, an order, request, etc. (*gave him a sign to leave*; *conversed by signs*). **4** a publicly displayed board etc. giving information; a sign-board or signpost. **5** a password (*advanced and gave the sign*). **6** any of the twelve divisions of the zodiac, named from the constellations formerly situated in them (*the sign of Cancer*). —*v*. **1** *tr*. **a** (also *absol*.) write (one's name, initials, etc.) on a document etc. indicating that one has authorized it. **b** write one's name etc. on (a document) as authorization. **2** *intr*. & *tr*. communicate by gesture (*signed to me to come*; *signed their assent*). **3** *tr*. & *intr*. engage or be engaged by signing a contract etc. (see also *sign on*, *sign up*). **4** *tr*. mark with a sign (esp. with the sign of the cross in baptism). □ **sign away** convey (one's right, property, etc.) by signing a deed etc. **sign for** acknowledge receipt of by signing. **sign language** a system of com-munication by visual gestures, used esp. by the deaf. **sign of the cross** a Christian sign made in blessing or prayer, by tracing a cross from the forehead to the chest and to each shoulder, or in the air. **sign off** **1** end work, broadcasting, a letter, etc., esp. by writing or speaking one's name. **2 a** end a period of employment, contract, etc. **b** end the period of employment or contract of (a person). **sign of the times** a portent etc. showing a likely trend. **sign on** **1** agree to a¹ contract, employment, etc. **2** begin work, broadcasting, etc., esp. by writing or announcing one's name. **3** employ (a person). **4** *Brit*. register as unemployed. **sign up** **1** engage or employ (a person). **2** enlist in the armed forces. **3 a** commit (another person or oneself) by signing etc. (*signed you up for dinner*). **b** enrol (*signed up for evening classes*). □ **signable** *adj*. **signer** *n*. [ME f. OF *signe, signer* f. L *signum, signare*]

signal¹ /ˈsɪɡn(ə)l/ *n*. & *v*. —*n*. **1 a** a usu. prearranged sign conveying information, guid-ance, etc. esp. at a distance (*waved as a signal to begin*). **b** a message made up of such signs (*signals made with flags*). **2** an immediate occasion or cause of movement, action, etc. (*the uprising was a signal for repression*). **3** *Electr*. **a** an electrical impulse or impulses or radio waves transmitted as a signal. **b** a sequence of these. **4** a light, semaphore, etc., on a railway giving instructions or warnings to train-drivers etc. —*v*. (**signalled**, **signalling**; US **signaled**, **signaling**) **1** *intr*. make signals. **2** *tr*. **a** (often foll. by *to* + infin.) make signals to; direct. **b** transmit (an order, information, etc.) by signal; announce (*signalled her agreement*; *signalled that the town had been taken*). □ **signal-box** *Brit*. a building beside a railway track from which signals are controlled. □ **signaller** *n*. [ME f. OF f. Rmc & med.L *signale* neut. of LL *signalis* f. L *signum* SIGN]

signal² /ˈsɪɡn(ə)l/ *adj*. remarkably good or bad; noteworthy (*a signal victory*). □ **signally** *adv*. [F *signalé* f. It. past part. *segnalato* distinguished f. *segnale* SIGNAL¹]

signalize /ˈsɪɡnəˌlaɪz/ *v.tr*. (also **-ise**) **1** make noteworthy or remarkable. **2** indicate.

signalman /ˈsɪɡn(ə)lmən/ *n*. (pl. **-men**) **1** a railway employee responsible for operating signals and points. **2** a person who displays or receives naval etc. signals.

signatory /ˈsɪɡnətərɪ/ *n*. & *adj*. —*n*. (pl. **-ies**) a party or esp. a State that has signed an agree-ment or esp. a treaty. —*adj*. having signed such an agreement etc. [L *signatorius* of sealing f. *signare signat-* mark]

signature /ˈsɪɡnətʃə(r)/ *n*. **1 a** a person's name, initials, or mark used in signing a letter, document, etc. **b** the act of signing a document etc. **2** *Mus*. **a** = *key signature*. **b** = *time signature*. □ **signature tune** esp. *Brit*. a distinctive tune used to introduce a particular programme or performer on television or radio. [med.L *signatura* (LL = marking of sheep), as SIGNATORY]

signboard /ˈsaɪnbɔːd/ *n*. a board with a name or symbol etc. displayed outside a shop or hotel etc.

signet /ˈsɪɡnɪt/ *n*. a seal used instead of or with a signature as authentication. □ **signet-ring** a ring with a seal set in it. [ME f. OF *signet* or med.L *signetum* (as SIGN)]

significance /sɪɡˈnɪfɪkəns/ *n*. **1** importance; noteworthiness (*his opinion is of no significance*). **2** a concealed or real meaning (*what is the sig-nificance of his statement?*). **3** the state of being significant. [OF *significance* or L *significantia* (as SIGNIFY)]

significant /sɪɡˈnɪfɪkənt/ *adj*. **1** having a mean-ing; indicative. **2** having an unstated or secret meaning; suggestive (*refused it with a significant gesture*). **3** noteworthy; important; consequential (*a significant figure in history*). □ **significant figure** *Math*. a digit conveying information about a number containing it, and not a zero used simply to fill vacant space at the beginning or end. □ **significantly** *adv*. [L *significare*: see SIGNIFY]

signification /ˌsɪɡnɪfɪˈkeɪʃ(ə)n/ *n*. **1** the act of signifying. **2** (usu. foll. by *of*) exact meaning or sense, esp. of a word or phrase. [ME f. OF f. L *significatio -onis* (as SIGNIFY)]

signify /ˈsɪɡnɪˌfaɪ/ *v*. (**-ies**, **-ied**) **1** *tr*. be a sign or indication of (*a yawn signifies boredom*). **2** *tr*. mean; have as its meaning ('*Dr*' *signifies* '*doctor*'). **3** *tr*. communicate; make known (*signified their agreement*). **4** *intr*. be of importance; matter (*it signifies little*). □ **signifier** *n*. [ME f. OF *signifier* f. L *significare* (as SIGN)]

signing /ˈsaɪnɪŋ/ *n*. a person who has signed a contract, esp. to join a professional sports team.

signor /ˈsiːnjɔː(r)/ *n*. (pl. **signori** /-ˈnjɔːriː/) **1** a title or form of address used of or to an Italian-speaking man, corresponding to Mr or sir. **2** an Italian man. [It. f. L *senior*: see SENIOR]

signora /siːnˈjɔːrə/ *n*. **1** a title or form of address used of or to an Italian-speaking married woman, corresponding to Mrs or madam. **2** a married Italian woman. [It., fem. of SIGNOR]

signorina /ˌsiːnjəˈriːnə/ *n*. **1** a title or form of address used of or to an Italian-speaking unmarried woman. **2** an Italian unmarried woman. [It., dimin. of SIGNORA]

signpost /ˈsaɪnpəʊst/ *n*. & *v*. —*n*. **1** a post erected at a crossroads with arms indicating the direction to and sometimes also the distance from various places. **2** a means of guidance; an indication. —*v.tr*. **1** provide with a signpost or signposts. **2** indicate (a course of action, direction, etc.).

Sikh /siːk, sɪk/ *n*. a member of an Indian monotheistic sect founded in the 16th c. [Hindi, = disciple, f. Skr. *sishya*]

Sikhism /ˈsiːkɪz(ə)m, ˈsɪk-/ *n*. the religious tenets of the Sikhs.

silage /ˈsaɪlɪdʒ/ *n*. & *v*. —*n*. **1** storage in a silo. **2** green fodder that has been stored in a silo. —*v.tr*. put into a silo. [alt. of ENSILAGE after *silo*]

sild /sɪld/ n. a small immature herring, esp. one caught in N. European seas. [Da. & Norw.]

silence /ˈsaɪləns/ n. & v. —n. **1** absence of sound. **2** abstinence from speech or noise. **3** the avoidance of mentioning a thing, betraying a secret, etc. **4** oblivion; the state of not being mentioned. —v.tr. make silent, esp. by coercion or superior argument. □ **in silence** without speech or other sound. [ME f. OF f. L *silentium* (as SILENT)]

silencer /ˈsaɪlənsə(r)/ n. any of various devices for reducing the noise emitted by the exhaust of a motor vehicle, a gun, etc.

silent /ˈsaɪlənt/ adj. **1** not speaking; not uttering or making or accompanied by any sound. **2** (of a letter) written but not pronounced, e.g. *b* in *doubt*. **3** (of a film) without a synchronized soundtrack. **4** (of a person) taciturn; speaking little. **5** saying or recording nothing on some subject (*the records are silent on the incident*). □ **silent majority** those of moderate opinions who rarely assert them. □ **silently** adv. [L *silēre silent-* be silent]

silhouette /ˌsɪluːˈet/ n. & v. —n. **1** a representation of a person or thing showing the outline only, usu. done in solid black on white or cut from paper. **2** the dark shadow or outline of a person or thing against a lighter background. —v.tr. represent or (usu. in *passive*) show in silhouette. [Étienne de *Silhouette*, Fr. author and politician d. 1767]

silica /ˈsɪlɪkə/ n. silicon dioxide, occurring as quartz etc. and as a principal constituent of sandstone and other rocks. □ **silica gel** hydrated silica in a hard granular form used as a desiccant. □ **siliceous** /-ˈlɪʃəs/ adj. (also **silicious**). **silicic** /-ˈlɪsɪk/ adj. **silicify** /-ˈlɪsɪˌfaɪ/ v.tr. & intr. (**-ies, -ied**) **silicification** /-sɪfɪˈkeɪʃ(ə)n/ n. [L *silex -icis* flint, after *alumina* etc.]

silicate /ˈsɪlɪˌkeɪt/ n. any of the many insoluble compounds of a metal combined with silicon and oxygen, occurring widely in the rocks of the earth's crust.

silicon /ˈsɪlɪkən/ n. *Chem.* a non-metallic element occurring widely in silica and silicates, and used in the manufacture of glass. □ **silicon chip** a silicon microchip. **silicon carbide** = CARBORUNDUM. **Silicon Valley** an area with a high concentration of electronics industries. [L *silex -icis* flint (after *carbon, boron*), alt. of earlier *silicium*]

silicone /ˈsɪlɪˌkəʊn/ n. any of the many polymeric organic compounds of silicon and oxygen with high resistance to cold, heat, water, and the passage of electricity.

silicosis /ˌsɪlɪˈkəʊsɪs/ n. lung fibrosis caused by the inhalation of dust containing silica. □ **silicotic** /-ˈkɒtɪk/ adj.

silk n. **1** a fine strong soft lustrous fibre produced by silkworms in making cocoons. **2** a similar fibre spun by some spiders etc. **3 a** a thread or cloth made from silk fibre. **b** a thread or fabric resembling silk. **4** (in *pl.*) kinds of silk cloth or garments made from it, esp. as worn by a jockey in a horse-owner's colours. **5** *Brit. colloq.* Queen's (or King's) Counsel, as having the right to wear a silk gown. **6** (*attrib.*) made of silk (*silk blouse*). □ **silk-screen printing** = *screen printing.* **take silk** *Brit.* become a Queen's (or King's) Counsel. □ **silklike** adj. [OE *sioloc, seolec* (cf. ON *silki*) f. LL

sericum neut. of L *sericus* f. *seres* f. Gk *Sēres* an oriental people]

silken /ˈsɪlkən/ adj. **1** made of silk. **2** wearing silk. **3** soft or lustrous as silk. **4** (of a person's manner etc.) suave or insinuating. [OE *seolcen* (as SILK)]

silkworm /ˈsɪlkwɜːm/ n. the caterpillar of the moth *Bombyx mori*, which spins its cocoon of silk.

silky /ˈsɪlkɪ/ adj. (**silkier, silkiest**) **1** like silk in smoothness, softness, fineness, or lustre. **2** (of a person's manner etc.) suave, insinuating. □ **silkily** adv. **silkiness** n.

sill n. (also **cill**) **1** a shelf or slab of stone, wood, or metal at the foot of a window or doorway. **2** a horizontal timber at the bottom of a dock or lock entrance, against which the gates close. [OE *syll, sylle*]

sillabub var. of SYLLABUB.

silly /ˈsɪlɪ/ adj. & n. —adj. (**sillier, silliest**) **1** lacking sense; foolish, imprudent, unwise. **2** weak-minded. **3** *Cricket* (of a fielder or position) very close to the batsman (*silly mid-off*). —n. (*pl.* **-ies**) *colloq.* a foolish person. □ **the silly season** high summer as the season when newspapers often publish trivial material for lack of important news. □ **sillily** adv. **silliness** n. [later form of ME *sely* (dial. *seely*) happy, repr. OE *sælig* (recorded in *unsælig* unhappy) f. Gmc]

silo /ˈsaɪləʊ/ n. & v. —n. (*pl.* **-os**) **1** a pit or airtight structure in which green crops are pressed and kept for fodder, undergoing fermentation. **2** a pit or tower for the storage of grain, cement, etc. **3** an underground chamber in which a guided missile is kept ready for firing. —v.tr. (**-oes, -oed**) make silage of. [Sp. f. L *sirus* f. Gk *siros* corn-pit]

silt n. & v. —n. sediment deposited by water in a channel, harbour, etc. —v.tr. & intr. (often foll. by *up*) choke or be choked with silt. □ **siltation** /-ˈteɪʃ(ə)n/ n. **silty** adj. [ME, perh. rel. to Da., Norw. *sylt*, OLG *sulta*, OHG *sulza* salt marsh, formed as SALT]

Silurian /saɪˈljʊərɪən/ adj. & n. *Geol.* —adj. of or relating to the third period of the Palaeozoic era. —n. this period or system. [L *Silures*, a people of ancient SE Wales]

silvan var. of SYLVAN.

silver /ˈsɪlvə(r)/ n., adj., & v. —n. *Chem.* **1** a greyish-white lustrous malleable ductile precious metallic element, used chiefly with an admixture of harder metals for coin, plate, and ornaments, as a subordinate monetary medium, and in compounds for photography etc. **2** the colour of silver. **3** silver or cupro-nickel coins. **4** silver vessels or implements, esp. cutlery. **5** = *silver medal.* —adj. **1** made wholly or chiefly of silver. **2** coloured like silver. —v. **1** tr. coat or plate with silver. **2** tr. provide (a mirror-glass) with a backing of tin amalgam etc. **3** tr. (of the moon or a white light) give a silvery appearance to. **4 a** tr. turn (the hair) grey or white. **b** intr. (of the hair) turn grey or white. □ **silver age** a period regarded as inferior to a golden age. **silver band** *Brit.* a band playing silver-plated instruments. **silver birch** a common birch, *Betula alba*, with silver-coloured bark. **silver jubilee 1** the 25th anniversary of a sovereign's accession. **2** any other 25th anniversary. **silver lining** a consolation or hopeful feature in misfortune. **silver medal** a medal of silver, usu. awarded as second prize. **silver paper** aluminium or tin foil. **silver plate** vessels, spoons, etc., of copper etc. plated with silver. **silver sand** a fine pure sand used in gardening. **silver screen** (usu. prec. by *the*) motion pictures collectively. **silver spoon** a sign of future prosperity. **silver tongue** eloquence. **silver wedding** the 25th anniversary of a wedding. [OE *seolfor* f. Gmc]

silverfish /ˈsɪlvəfɪʃ/ *n.* (*pl.* same or **-fishes**) any small silvery wingless insect of the order Thysanura, esp. *Lepisma saccharina* in houses and other buildings.

silverside /ˈsɪlvəˌsaɪd/ *n. Brit.* the upper side of a round of beef from the outside of the leg.

silversmith /ˈsɪlvəsmɪθ/ *n.* a worker in silver; a manufacturer of silver articles. □ **silversmithing** *n.*

silverware /ˈsɪlvəˌweə(r)/ *n.* articles made of or coated with silver.

silvery /ˈsɪlvərɪ/ *adj.* **1** like silver in colour or appearance. **2** having a clear gentle ringing sound. **3** (of the hair) white and lustrous. □ **silveriness** *n.*

silviculture /ˈsɪlvɪˌkʌltʃə(r)/ *n.* (also **sylviculture**) the growing and tending of trees as a branch of forestry. □ **silvicultural** /-ˈkʌltʃər(ə)l/ *adj.* **silviculturist** /-ˈkʌltʃərɪst/ *n.* [F f. L *silva* a wood + F *culture* CULTURE]

simian /ˈsɪmɪən/ *adj.* & *n.* —*adj.* **1** of or concerning the anthropoid apes. **2** like an ape or monkey (*a simian walk*). —*n.* an ape or monkey. [L *simia* ape, perh. f. L *simus* f. Gk *simos* flat-nosed]

similar /ˈsɪmɪlə(r)/ *adj.* **1** like, alike. **2** (often foll. by *to*) having a resemblance. **3** of the same kind, nature, or amount. □ **similarity** /-ˈlærɪtɪ/ *n.* (*pl.* **-ies**). **similarly** *adv.* [F *similaire* or med.L *similaris* f. L *similis* like]

simile /ˈsɪmɪlɪ/ *n.* **1** a figure of speech involving the comparison of one thing with another of a different kind, as an illustration or ornament (e.g. *as brave as a lion*). **2** the use of such comparison. [ME f. L, neut. of *similis* like]

similitude /sɪˈmɪlɪˌtjuːd/ *n.* **1** the likeness, guise, or outward appearance of a thing or person. **2** a comparison or the expression of a comparison. [ME f. OF *similitude* or L *similitudo* (as SIMILE)]

simmer /ˈsɪmə(r)/ *v.* & *n.* —*v.* **1** *intr.* & *tr.* be or keep bubbling or boiling gently. **2** *intr.* be in a state of suppressed anger or excitement. —*n.* a simmering condition. □ **simmer down** become calm or less agitated. [alt. of ME (now dial.) *simper*, perh. imit.]

simnel cake /ˈsɪmn(ə)l/ *n. Brit.* a rich fruit cake, usu. with a marzipan layer and decoration, eaten esp. at Easter or during Lent. [ME f. OF *simenel*, ult. f. L *simila* or Gk *semidalis* fine flour]

simony /ˈsaɪmənɪ, ˈsɪm-/ *n.* the buying or selling of ecclesiastical privileges, e.g. pardons or benefices. □ **simoniac** /-ˈməʊnɪˌæk/ *adj.* & *n.* **simoniacal** /-ˈnaɪək(ə)l/ *adj.* [ME f. OF *simonie* f. LL *simonia* f. *Simon Magus* (Acts 8:18)]

simoom /sɪˈmuːm/ *n.* (also **simoon** /-ˈmuːn/) a hot dry dust-laden wind blowing at intervals esp. in the Arabian desert. [Arab. *samūm* f. *samma* to poison]

simper /ˈsɪmpə(r)/ *v.* & *n.* —*v. intr.* smile in a silly or affected way. —*n.* such a smile. □ **simperingly** *adv.* [16th c.: cf. Du. and Scand. *semper*, *simper*, G *zimp(f)er* elegant, delicate]

simple /ˈsɪmp(ə)l/ *adj.* **1** easily understood or done; presenting no difficulty (*a simple explanation*; *a simple task*). **2** not complicated or elaborate; without luxury or sophistication. **3** not compound; consisting of or involving only one element or operation etc. **4** absolute, unqualified, straightforward (*the simple truth*; *a simple majority*). **5** foolish or ignorant; gullible, feeble-minded (*am not so simple as to agree to that*). **6** plain in appearance or manner; unsophisticated, ingenuous, artless. □ **simple fracture** a fracture of the bone only, without a skin wound. **simple interest** interest payable on a capital sum only. **simple sentence** a sentence with a single subject and predicate. □ **simpleness** *n.* [ME f. OF f. L *simplus*]

simple-minded /ˌsɪmp(ə)lˈmaɪndɪd/ *adj.* **1** natural, unsophisticated. **2** feeble-minded. □ **simple-mindedly** *adv.* **simple-mindedness** *n.*

simpleton /ˈsɪmp(ə)lt(ə)n/ *n.* a foolish, gullible, or halfwitted person. [SIMPLE after surnames f. place-names in *-ton*]

simplex /ˈsɪmpleks/ *adj.* simple; not compounded. [L, = single, var. of *simplus* simple]

simplicity /sɪmˈplɪsɪtɪ/ *n.* the fact or condition of being simple. □ **be simplicity itself** be extremely easy. [OF *simplicité* or L *simplicitas* (as SIMPLEX)]

simplify /ˈsɪmplɪˌfaɪ/ *v.tr.* (**-ies**, **-ied**) make simple; make easy or easier to do or understand. □ **simplification** /-fɪˈkeɪʃ(ə)n/ *n.* [F *simplifier* f. med.L *simplificare* (as SIMPLE)]

simplistic /sɪmˈplɪstɪk/ *adj.* **1** excessively or affectedly simple. **2** oversimplified so as to conceal or distort difficulties. □ **simplistically** *adv.*

simply /ˈsɪmplɪ/ *adv.* **1** in a simple manner. **2** absolutely; without doubt (*simply astonishing*). **3** merely (*was simply trying to please*).

simulacrum /ˌsɪmjʊˈleɪkrəm/ *n.* (*pl.* **simulacra** /-krə/) **1** an image of something. **2 a** a shadowy likeness; a deceptive substitute. **b** mere pretence. [L (as SIMULATE)]

simulate /ˈsɪmjʊˌleɪt/ *v.tr.* **1 a** pretend to have or feel (an attribute or feeling). **b** pretend to be. **2** imitate or counterfeit. **3 a** imitate the conditions of (a situation etc.), e.g. for training. **b** produce a computer model of (a process). **4** (as **simulated** *adj.*) made to resemble the real thing but not genuinely such (*simulated fur*). □ **simulation** /-ˈleɪʃ(ə)n/ *n.* **simulative** /-lətɪv/ *adj.* [L *simulare* f. *similis* like]

simulator /ˈsɪmjʊˌleɪtə(r)/ *n.* **1** a person or thing that simulates. **2** a device designed to simulate the operations of a complex system, used esp. in training.

simulcast /ˈsɪməlˌkɑːst/ *n.* simultaneous transmission of the same programme on radio and television. [SIMULTANEOUS + BROADCAST]

simultaneous /ˌsɪməlˈteɪnɪəs/ *adj.* (often foll. by *with*) occurring or operating at the same time. □ **simultaneity** /-təˈneɪɪtɪ/ *n.* **simultaneously** *adv.* **simultaneousness** *n.* [med.L *simultaneus* f. L *simul* at the same time, prob. after *instantaneus* etc.]

sin¹ *n.* & *v.* —*n.* **1 a** the breaking of divine or moral law, esp. by a conscious act. **b** such an act. **2** an offence against good taste or propriety etc. —*v.* (**sinned, sinning**) **1** *intr.* commit a sin. **2** *intr.* (foll. by *against*) offend. **3** *tr. archaic* commit (a sin). □ **live in sin** *colloq.* live together without being married. **sin bin** *colloq.* **1** *Ice Hockey* a penalty box. **2** a place set aside for offenders of various kinds. □ **sinless** *adj.* **sinlessly** *adv.* **sinlessness** *n.* [OE *syn(n)*]

sin² *abbr.* sine.

since *prep., conj., & adv.* —*prep.* throughout, or at a point in, the period between (a specified time, event, etc.) and the time present or being considered (*must have happened since yesterday; has been going on since June; the greatest composer since Beethoven*). —*conj.* **1** during or in the time after (*what have you been doing since we met?; has not spoken since the dog died*). **2** for the reason that, because; inasmuch as (*since you are drunk I will drive you home*). **3** (*ellipt.*) as being (*a more useful, since better designed, tool*). —*adv.* **1** from that time or event until now or the time being considered (*have not seen them since; had been healthy ever since; has since been cut down*). **2** ago (*happened many years since*). [ME, reduced form of obs. *sithence* or f. dial. *sin* (f. *sithen*) f. OE *siththon*]

sincere /sɪnˈsɪə(r)/ *adj.* (**sincerer, sincerest**) **1** free from pretence or deceit; the same in reality as in appearance. **2** genuine, honest, frank. □ **sincereness** *n.* **sincerity** /-ˈserɪtɪ/ *n.* [L *sincerus* clean, pure]

sincerely /sɪnˈsɪəlɪ/ *adv.* in a sincere manner. □ **yours sincerely** a formula for ending an informal letter.

sine /saɪn/ *n. Math.* the trigonometric function that is equal to the ratio of the side opposite a given angle (in a right-angled triangle) to the hypotenuse. [L *sinus* curve, fold of a toga, used in med.L as transl. of Arab. *jayb* bosom, sine]

sinecure /ˈsaɪnɪˌkjʊə(r), ˈsɪn-/ *n.* a position that requires little or no work but usu. yields profit or honour. □ **sinecurism** *n.* **sinecurist** *n.* [L *sine cura* without care]

sine die /ˌsaɪnɪ ˈdaɪiː, ˌsɪneɪ ˈdiːeɪ/ *adv.* (of business adjourned indefinitely) with no appointed date. [L, = without day]

sine qua non /ˌsaɪneɪ kwɑː ˈnəʊn/ *n.* an indispensable condition or qualification. [L, = without which not]

sinew /ˈsɪnjuː/ *n.* **1** tough fibrous tissue uniting muscle to bone; a tendon. **2** (in *pl.*) muscles; bodily strength; wiriness. **3** (in *pl.*) that which forms the strength or framework of a plan, city, organization, etc. □ **sinewless** *adj.* **sinewy** *adj.* [OE *sin(e)we* f. Gmc]

sinful /ˈsɪnfʊl/ *adj.* **1** (of a person) committing sin, esp. habitually. **2** (of an act) involving or characterized by sin. □ **sinfully** *adv.* **sinfulness** *n.* [OE *synfull* (as SIN¹, -FUL)]

sing *v. & n.* —*v.* (*past* **sang**; *past part.* **sung**) **1** *intr.* utter musical sounds with the voice, esp. words with a set tune. **2** *tr.* utter or produce by singing (*sing another song*). **3** *intr.* (of the wind, a kettle, etc.) make inarticulate melodious or humming, buzzing, or whistling sounds. **4** *intr.* (of the ears) be affected as with a buzzing sound. **5** *intr. sl.* turn informer; confess. —*n.* **1** an act or spell of singing. **2** *US* a meeting for amateur singing. □ **sing-along** a tune etc. to which one can sing in accompaniment. **sing out** call out loudly; shout. **sing up** sing more loudly. □ **singable** *adj.* **singer** *n.* **singingly** *adv.* [OE *singan* f. Gmc]

sing. *abbr.* singular.

singe /sɪndʒ/ *v. & n.* —*v.* (**singeing**) **1** *tr. & intr.* burn superficially or lightly. **2** *tr.* burn the bristles or down off (the carcass of a pig or fowl) to prepare it for cooking. —*n.* a superficial burn. [OE *sencgan* f. WG]

single /ˈsɪŋg(ə)l/ *adj., n., & v.* —*adj.* **1** one only, not double or multiple. **2** united or undivided. **3 a** designed or suitable for one person (*single room*). **b** used or done by one person etc. or one set or pair. **4** one by itself; not one of several (*a single tree*). **5** regarded separately (*every single thing*). **6** not married. **7** *Brit.* (of a ticket) valid for an outward journey only, not for the return. **8** (with *neg.* or *interrog.*) even one; not to speak of more (*did not see a single person*). **9** (of a flower) having only one circle of petals. —*n.* **1** a single thing, or item in a series. **2** *Brit.* a single ticket. **3** a short pop record with one piece of music etc. on each side. **4** *Cricket* a hit for one run. **5** (usu. in *pl.*) a game with one player on each side. **6** an unmarried person (*young singles*). **7** *sl. US* a one-dollar note. —*v.tr.* (foll. by *out*) choose as an example or as distinguishable or to serve some purpose. □ **single-breasted** (of a coat etc.) having only one set of buttons and buttonholes, not overlapping. **single combat** a duel. **single cream** thin cream with a relatively low fat-content. **single-decker** esp. *Brit.* a bus having only one deck. **single file** a line of people or things arranged one behind another. **single-handed** *adv.* **1** without help from another. **2** with one hand. —*adj.* **1** done etc. single-handed. **2** for one hand. **single market** *Commerce* a market which allows for free movement of goods between countries, a common currency, etc., e.g. in the EC. **single parent** a person bringing up a child or children without a partner. **singles bar** a bar for single people seeking company. □ **singleness** *n.* **singly** *adv.* [ME f. OF f. L *singulus*, rel. to *simplus* SIMPLE]

single-minded /ˌsɪŋg(ə)lˈmaɪndɪd/ *adj.* having or intent on only one purpose. □ **single-mindedly** *adv.* **single-mindedness** *n.*

singlet /ˈsɪŋglɪt/ *n. Brit.* a garment worn under or instead of a shirt; a vest. [SINGLE + -ET¹, after *doublet*, the garment being unlined]

singleton /ˈsɪŋg(ə)lt(ə)n/ *n.* **1** one card only of a suit, esp. as dealt to a player. **2 a** a single person or thing. **b** an only child. **3** a single child or animal born, not a twin etc. [SINGLE, after *simpleton*]

singsong /ˈsɪŋsɒŋ/ *adj., n., & v.* —*adj.* uttered with a monotonous rhythm or cadence. —*n.* **1** a singsong manner. **2** *Brit.* an informal gathering for singing. —*v.intr. & tr.* (*past* and *past part.* **singsonged**) speak or recite in a singsong manner.

singular /ˈsɪŋgjʊlə(r)/ *adj. & n.* —*adj.* **1** unique; much beyond the average; extraordinary. **2** eccentric or strange. **3** *Gram.* (of a word or form) denoting or referring to a single person or thing. **4** single, individual. —*n. Gram.* **1** a singular word or form. **2** the singular number. □ **singularly** *adv.* [ME f. OF *singuler* f. L *singularis* (as SINGLE)]

singularity /ˌsɪŋgjʊˈlærɪtɪ/ *n.* (*pl.* **-ies**) **1** the state or condition of being singular. **2** an odd trait or peculiarity. [ME f. OF *singularité* f. LL *singularitas* (as SINGULAR)]

singularize /ˈsɪŋɡjʊləˌraɪz/ v.tr. (also **-ise**) **1** distinguish, individualize. **2** make singular. □ **singularization** /-ˈzeɪʃ(ə)n/ n.

Sinhalese /ˌsɪnhəˈliːz, ˌsɪnəˈliːz/ n. & adj. (also **Singhalese** /ˌsɪŋg-/) —n. (pl. same) **1** a member of a people forming the majority of the population of Sri Lanka. **2** an Indic language spoken by this people. —adj. of or relating to this people or language. [Skr. siṅhalam Sri Lanka (Ceylon) + -ESE]

sinister /ˈsɪnɪstə(r)/ adj. **1** suggestive of evil; looking malignant or villainous. **2** wicked or criminal (a sinister motive). **3** of evil omen. **4** Heraldry of or on the left-hand side of a shield etc. (i.e. to the observer's right). **5** archaic left-hand. □ **sinisterly** adv. **sinisterness** n. [ME f. OF sinistre or L sinister left]

sink v. & n. —v. (past **sank** /sæŋk/ or **sunk** /sʌŋk/; past part. **sunk** or **sunken**) **1** intr. fall or come slowly downwards. **2** intr. disappear below the horizon (the sun is sinking). **3** intr. **a** go or penetrate below the surface esp. of a liquid. **b** (of a ship) go to the bottom of the sea etc. **4** intr. settle down comfortably (sank into a chair). **5** intr. **a** gradually lose strength or value or quality etc.; decline (my heart sank). **b** (of the voice) descend in pitch or volume. **6** tr. send (a ship) to the bottom of the sea etc. **7** tr. cause or allow to sink or penetrate (sank its teeth into my leg). **8** tr. cause the failure of (a plan etc.) or the discomfiture of (a person). **9** tr. dig (a well) or bore (a shaft). **10** tr. engrave (a die) or inlay (a design). **11** tr. **a** invest (money) (sunk a large sum into the business). **b** lose (money) by investment. **12** tr. cause (a ball) to enter a pocket in billiards, a hole at golf, etc. **13** intr. (of a price etc.) become lower. **14** intr. (of a storm or river) subside. **15** intr. (of ground) slope down, or reach a lower level by subsidence. **16** intr. (foll. by on, upon) (of darkness) descend on a place). **17** tr. lower the level of. **18** tr. (usu. in passive; foll. by in) absorb; hold the attention of (be sunk in thought). —n. **1** a fixed basin with a water-supply and outflow pipe. **2** a place where foul liquid collects. **3** a place of vice or corruption. □ **sink in 1** penetrate or make its way in. **2** become gradually comprehended (paused to let the words sink in). **sinking feeling** a bodily sensation caused by hunger or apprehension. **sinking fund** money set aside for the gradual repayment of a debt. **sunk fence** a fence formed by, or along the bottom of, a ditch. □ **sinkable** adj. **sinkage** n. [OE sincan f. Gmc]

sinker /ˈsɪŋkə(r)/ n. **1** a weight used to sink a fishing-line or sounding-line. **2** US a doughnut.

sinner /ˈsɪnə(r)/ n. a person who sins, esp. habitually.

Sinn Fein /ʃɪn ˈfeɪn/ n. a political movement and party seeking a united republican Ireland, now linked to the IRA. □ **Sinn Feiner** n. [Ir. sinn féin we ourselves]

Sino- /ˈsaɪnəʊ/ comb. form Chinese; Chinese and (Sino-American). [Gk Sinai the Chinese]

sinologue /ˈsaɪnəˌlɒg, ˈsɪ-/ n. an expert in sinology. [F, formed as SINO- + Gk -logos speaking]

sinology /saɪˈnɒlədʒɪ, sɪ-/ n. the study of Chinese language, history, customs, etc. □ **sinological** /-nəˈlɒdʒɪk(ə)l/ adj. **sinologist** n.

sinter /ˈsɪntə(r)/ n. & v. —n. **1** a siliceous or calcareous rock formed by deposition from springs. **2** a substance formed by sintering.

—v.intr. & tr. coalesce or cause to coalesce from powder into solid by heating. [G, = E sinder CINDER]

sinuous /ˈsɪnjʊəs/ adj. with many curves; tortuous, undulating. □ **sinuosity** /-ˈɒsɪtɪ/ n. **sinuously** adv. **sinuousness** n. [F sinueux or L sinuosus (as SINUS)]

sinus /ˈsaɪnəs/ n. a cavity of bone or tissue, esp. in the skull connecting with the nostrils. [L, = bosom, recess]

sinusitis /ˌsaɪnəˈsaɪtɪs/ n. inflammation of a nasal sinus.

-sion /ʃ(ə)n, ʒ(ə)n/ suffix forming nouns (see -ION) from Latin participial stems in -s- (mansion; mission; persuasion).

sip v. & n. —v.tr. & intr. (**sipped**, **sipping**) drink in one or more small amounts or by spoonfuls. —n. **1** a small mouthful of liquid (a sip of brandy). **2** the act of taking this. □ **sipper** n. [ME: perh. a modification of SUP¹]

siphon /ˈsaɪf(ə)n/ n. & v. (also **syphon**) —n. **1** a pipe or tube shaped like an inverted V or U with unequal legs to convey a liquid from a container to a lower level by atmospheric pressure. **2** (in full **siphon-bottle**) an aerated-water bottle from which liquid is forced out through a tube by the pressure of gas. —v.tr. & intr. (often foll. by off) **1** conduct or flow through a siphon. **2** divert or set aside (funds etc.). □ **siphonage** n. **siphonal** adj. **siphonic** /-ˈfɒnɪk/ adj. [F siphon or L sipho -onis f. Gk siphōn pipe]

sir n. **1** a polite or respectful form of address or mode of reference to a man. **2** (**Sir**) a titular prefix to the forename of a knight or baronet. [ME, reduced form of SIRE]

sire n. & v. —n. **1** the male parent of an animal, esp. a stallion kept for breeding. **2** archaic respectful form of address, now esp. to a king. **3** archaic poet. a father or male ancestor. —v.tr. (esp. of a stallion) beget. [ME f. OF ult. f. L senior: see SENIOR]

siren /ˈsaɪərən/ n. **1 a** a device for making a loud prolonged signal or warning sound, esp. by revolving a perforated disc over a jet of compressed air or steam. **b** the sound made by this. **2** (in Greek mythology) each of a number of women or winged creatures whose singing lured unwary sailors on to rocks. **3 a** a dangerously fascinating woman; a temptress. **b** a tempting pursuit etc. □ **siren suit** a one-piece garment for the whole body, easily put on or taken off, orig. for use in air-raid shelters. [ME f. OF sereine, sirene f. LL Sirena fem. f. L f. Gk Seirēn]

sirenian /saɪˈriːnɪən/ adj. & n. —adj. of the order Sirenia of large aquatic plant-eating mammals, e.g. the manatee and dugong. —n. any mammal of this order. [mod.L Sirenia (as SIREN)]

sirloin /ˈsɜːlɔɪn/ n. the upper and choicer part of a loin of beef. [OF (as SUR-, LOIN)]

sirocco /sɪˈrɒkəʊ/ n. (also **scirocco**) (pl. **-os**) **1** a Saharan simoom reaching the northern shores of the Mediterranean. **2** a warm sultry rainy wind in S. Europe. [F f. It. scirocco, ult. f. Arab. šarūḳ east wind]

sirree /sɪˈriː/ int. US colloq. as an emphatic, esp. after yes or no. [SIR + emphatic suffix]

sirup US var. of SYRUP.

sis /sɪs/ n. colloq. a sister. [abbr.]

sisal /ˈsaɪs(ə)l/ n. **1** a Mexican plant, Agave sisalana, with large fleshy leaves. **2** the fibre made from this plant, used for ropes etc. [*Sisal*, the port of Yucatan, Mexico]

siskin /ˈsɪskɪn/ *n.* a dark-streaked yellowish-green songbird, *Carduelis spinus*, allied to the goldfinch. [MDu. *siseken* dimin., rel. to MLG *sīsek*, MHG *zīse, zīsec*, of Slav. origin]

sissy /ˈsɪsɪ/ *n. & adj.* (also **cissy**) *colloq.* —*n.* (*pl.* -**ies**) an effeminate or cowardly person. —*adj.* (**sissier, sissiest**) effeminate; cowardly. □ **sissified** *adj.* **sissiness** *n.* **sissyish** *adj.* [SIS + -Y²]

sister /ˈsɪstə(r)/ *n.* 1 a woman or girl in relation to sons and other daughters of her parents. 2 a (often as a form of address) a close female friend or associate. b a female fellow member of a trade union, class, sect, or the human race. 3 a senior female nurse. 4 a member of a female religious order. 5 (*attrib.*) of the same type or design or origin etc. (*sister ship; prose, the younger sister of verse*). □ **sister-in-law** (*pl.* **sisters-in-law**) 1 the sister of one's wife or husband. 2 the wife of one's brother. 3 the wife of one's brother-in-law. □ **sisterless** *adj.* **sisterly** *adj.* **sisterliness** *n.* [ME *sister* (f. ON), *suster* etc. (repr. OE *sweoster* f. Gmc)]

sisterhood /ˈsɪstəˌhʊd/ *n.* 1 a the relationship between sisters. b sisterly friendliness; companionship; mutual support. 2 a a society or association of women, esp. when bound by monastic vows or devoting themselves to religious or charitable work or the feminist cause. b its members collectively.

Sisyphean /ˌsɪzɪˈfiːən/ *adj.* (of toil) endless and fruitless like that of Sisyphus in Greek mythology (whose task in Hades was to push uphill a stone that at once rolled down again).

sit *v.* (**sitting**; *past* and *past part.* **sat**) 1 *intr.* adopt or be in a position in which the body is supported more or less upright by the buttocks resting on the ground or a raised seat etc., with the thighs usu. horizontal. 2 *tr.* cause to sit; place in a sitting position. 3 *intr.* a (of a bird) perch. b (of an animal) rest with the hind legs bent and the body close to the ground. 4 *intr.* (of a bird) remain on its nest to hatch its eggs. 5 *intr.* a be engaged in an occupation in which the sitting position is usual. b (of a committee, legislative body, etc.) be engaged in business. c (of an individual) be entitled to hold some office or position (*sat as a magistrate*). 6 *intr.* (usu. foll. by *for*) pose in a sitting position (for a portrait). 7 *intr.* (foll. by *for*) be a Member of Parliament for (a constituency). 8 *tr.* & (foll. by *for*) *intr.* Brit. be a candidate for (an examination). 9 *intr.* be in a more or less permanent position or condition (esp. of inactivity or being out of use or out of place). 10 *intr.* (of clothes etc.) fit or hang in a certain way. 11 *tr.* keep or have one's seat on (a horse etc.). 12 *intr.* act as a babysitter. □ **make a person sit up** *colloq.* surprise or interest a person. **sit at a person's feet** be a person's pupil. **sit back** relax one's efforts. **sit by** look on without interfering. **sit down** 1 sit after standing. 2 cause to sit. 3 (foll. by *under*) submit tamely to (an insult etc.). **sit in** 1 occupy a place as a protest. 2 (foll. by *for*) take the place of. 3 (foll. by *on*) be present as a guest or observer at (a meeting etc.). **sit-in** *n.* a protest involving sitting in. **sit in judgement** assume the right of judging others; be censorious. **sit on 1** be a member of (a committee etc.). 2 hold a session

or inquiry concerning. 3 *colloq.* delay action about (*the government has been sitting on the report*). 4 *colloq.* repress or rebuke or snub (*felt rather sat on*). **sit on one's hands** 1 take no action. 2 refuse to applaud. **sit out** 1 take no part in (a dance etc.). 2 stay till the end of (esp. an ordeal). 3 sit outdoors. 4 outstay (other visitors). **sit tight** *colloq.* 1 remain firmly in one's place. 2 not be shaken off or move away or yield to distractions. **sit up 1** rise from a lying to a sitting position. 2 sit firmly upright. 3 go to bed later than the usual time. 4 *colloq.* become interested or aroused etc. **sit-up** *n.* a physical exercise in which a person sits up without raising the legs from the ground. **sit-upon** *colloq.* the buttocks. **sit well** have a good seat in riding. **sit well on** suit or fit. [OE *sittan* f. Gmc]

sitar /ˈsɪtɑː(r), sɪˈtɑː(r)/ *n.* a long-necked Indian lute with movable frets. □ **sitarist** /sɪˈtɑːrɪst/ *n.* [Hindi *sitār*]

sitcom /ˈsɪtkɒm/ *n.* *colloq.* a situation comedy. [abbr.]

site *n. & v.* —*n.* 1 the ground chosen or used for a town or building. 2 a place where some activity is or has been conducted (*camping site; launching site*). —*v.tr.* 1 locate or place. 2 provide with a site. [ME f. AF *site* or L *situs* local position]

sitter /ˈsɪtə(r)/ *n.* 1 a person who sits, esp. for a portrait. 2 = BABYSITTER (see BABYSIT). 3 *colloq.* a an easy catch or shot. b an easy task. 4 a sitting hen.

sitting /ˈsɪtɪŋ/ *n. & adj.* —*n.* 1 a continuous period of being seated, esp. engaged in an activity (*finished the book in one sitting*). 2 a time during which an assembly is engaged in business. 3 a session in which a meal is served (*dinner will be served in two sittings*). 4 a clutch of eggs. —*adj.* 1 having sat down. 2 (of an animal or bird) not running or flying. 3 (of a hen) engaged in hatching. □ **sitting duck** (or **target**) *colloq.* a vulnerable person or thing. **sitting-room** a room in a house for relaxed sitting in. **sitting tenant** a tenant already in occupation of premises.

situate *v. & adj.* —*v.tr.* /ˈsɪtjʊˌeɪt/ (usu. in *passive*) 1 put in a certain position or circumstances (*is situated at the top of a hill; how are you situated at the moment?*). 2 establish or indicate the place of; put in a context. —*adj.* /ˈsɪtjʊət/ *Law* or *archaic* situated. [med.L *situare situat-* f. L *situs* site]

situation /ˌsɪtjʊˈeɪʃ(ə)n/ *n.* 1 a place and its surroundings (*the house stands in a fine situation*). 2 a set of circumstances; a position in which one finds oneself; a state of affairs (*came out of a difficult situation with credit*). 3 an employee's position or job. □ **situation comedy** a comedy in which the humour derives from the situations the characters are placed in. □ **situational** *adj.* [ME f. F *situation* or med.L *situatio* (as SITUATE)]

six /sɪks/ *n. & adj.* —*n.* 1 one more than five. 2 a symbol for this (6, vi, VI). 3 a size etc. denoted by six. 4 a set or team of six individuals. 5 *Cricket* a hit scoring six runs by clearing the boundary without bouncing. 6 the time of six o'clock (*is it six yet?*). 7 a card etc. with six pips. —*adj.* that amount to six. □ **at sixes and sevens** in confusion or disagreement. **knock for six** *colloq.* utterly surprise or overcome (a person). **the Six Counties** the counties of N.

Ireland. **six-gun** = *six-shooter*. **six-shooter** a revolver with six chambers. [OE *siex* etc. f. Gmc]

sixer /ˈsɪksə(r)/ *n*. **1** the leader of a group of six Brownies or Cubs. **2** *Cricket* a hit for six runs.

sixfold /ˈsɪksfəʊld/ *adj*. & *adv*. **1** six times as much or as many. **2** consisting of six parts.

sixpence /ˈsɪkspəns/ *n*. *Brit*. **1** the sum of six pence, esp. before decimalization. **2** *hist*. a coin worth six old pence (2½p).

sixpenny /ˈsɪkspənɪ/ *adj*. *Brit*. costing or worth six pence, esp. before decimalization.

sixteen /ˌsɪksˈtiːn, ˈsɪks-/ *n*. & *adj*. —*n*. **1** one more than fifteen. **2** a symbol for this (16, xvi, XVI). **3** a size etc. denoted by sixteen. —*adj*. that amount to sixteen. □ **sixteenth** *adj*. & *n*. [OE *siextiene* (as SIX, -TEEN)]

sixth /sɪksθ/ *n*. & *adj*. —*n*. **1** the position in a sequence corresponding to that of the number 6 in the sequence 1–6. **2** something occupying this position. **3** any of six equal parts of a thing. **4** *Mus*. **a** an interval or chord spanning six consecutive notes in the diatonic scale (e.g. C to A). **b** a note separated from another by this interval. —*adj*. that is the sixth. □ **sixth form** *Brit*. a form in a secondary school for pupils over 16. **sixth-form college** *Brit*. a college for pupils over 16. **sixth sense 1** a supposed faculty giving intuitive or extrasensory knowledge. **2** such knowledge. □ **sixthly** *adv*. [SIX]

sixty /ˈsɪkstɪ/ *n*. & *adj*. —*n*. (*pl*. **-ies**) **1** the product of six and ten. **2** a symbol for this (60, lx, LX). **3** (in *pl*.) the numbers from 60 to 69, esp. the years of a century or of a person's life. **4** a set of sixty persons or things. —*adj*. that amount to sixty. □ **sixty-four thousand** (or **sixty-four**) **dollar question** a difficult and crucial question (from the top prize in a broadcast quiz show). □ **sixtieth** *adj*. & *n*. **sixtyfold** *adj*. & *adv*. [OE *siextig* (as SIX, -TY²)]

size¹ *n*. & *v*. —*n*. **1** the relative bigness or extent of a thing, dimensions, magnitude (*is of vast size*; *size matters less than quality*). **2** each of the classes, usu. numbered, into which things otherwise similar, esp. garments, are divided according to size (*is made in several sizes*; *takes size 7 in gloves*; *is three sizes too big*). —*v.tr.* sort or group in sizes or according to size. □ **of a size** having the same size. **of some size** fairly large. **the size of** as big as. **the size of it** *colloq*. a true account of the matter (*that is the size of it*). **size up 1** estimate the size of. **2** *colloq*. form a judgement of. **what size?** how big? □ **sized** *adj*. (also in *comb*.). **sizer** *n*. [ME f. OF *sise* f. *assise* ASSIZE, or f. ASSIZE]

size² *n*. & *v*. —*n*. a gelatinous solution used in glazing paper, stiffening textiles, preparing plastered walls for decoration, etc. —*v.tr.* glaze or stiffen or treat with size. [ME, perh. = SIZE¹]

sizeable /ˈsaɪzəb(ə)l/ *adj*. (also **sizable**) large or fairly large. □ **sizeably** *adv*.

sizzle /ˈsɪz(ə)l/ *v*. & *n*. —*v.intr.* **1** make a sputtering or hissing sound as of frying. **2** *colloq*. be in a state of great heat or excitement or marked effectiveness. —*n*. **1** a sizzling sound. **2** *colloq*. a state of great heat or excitement. □ **sizzler** *n*. **sizzling** *adj*. & *adv*. (*sizzling hot*). [imit.]

SJ *abbr*. Society of Jesus.

sjambok /ˈʃæmbɒk/ *n*. (in S. Africa) a rhinoceros-hide whip. [Afrik. f. Malay *samboq*, *chambok* f. Urdu *chābuk*]

skald /skɔːld, skɒld/ *n*. (also **scald**) (in ancient Scandinavia) a composer and reciter of poems honouring heroes and their deeds. □ **skaldic** *adj*. [ON *skáld*, of unkn. orig.]

skate¹ *n*. & *v*. —*n*. **1** each of a pair of steel blades (or of boots with blades attached) for gliding on ice. **2** (in full **roller skate**) each of a pair of metal frames with small wheels, fitted to shoes for riding on a hard surface. **3** a device on which a heavy object moves. —*v*. **1 a** *intr*. move on skates. **b** *tr*. perform (a specified figure) on skates. **2** *intr*. (foll. by *over*) refer fleetingly to, disregard. □ **get one's skates on** *Brit. sl*. make haste. **skate on thin ice** *colloq*. behave rashly, risk danger, esp. by dealing with a subject needing tactful treatment. **skating-rink** a piece of ice artificially made, or a floor used, for skating. □ **skater** *n*. [orig. *scates* (pl.) f. Du. *schaats* (sing.) f. ONF *escace*, OF *eschasse* stilt]

skate² *n*. (*pl*. same or **skates**) any cartilaginous marine fish of the family Rajidae, esp. *Raja batis*, a large flat rhomboidal fish used as food. [ME f. ON *skata*]

skate³ *n*. *sl*. a contemptible, mean, or dishonest person (esp. *cheap skate*). [19th c.: orig. uncert.]

skateboard /ˈskeɪtbɔːd/ *n*. & *v*. —*n*. a short narrow board on roller-skate wheels for riding on while standing. —*v.intr.* ride on a skateboard. □ **skateboarder** *n*.

skedaddle /skɪˈdæd(ə)l/ *v*. & *n*. *colloq*. —*v.intr.* run away, depart quickly, flee. —*n*. a hurried departure or flight. [19th c.: orig. unkn.]

skeeter¹ /ˈskiːtə(r)/ *n*. *US* & *Austral. sl*. a mosquito. [abbr.]

skeeter² var. of SKITTER.

skein /skeɪn/ *n*. **1** a loosely-coiled bundle of yarn or thread. **2** a flock of wild geese etc. in flight. **3** a tangle or confusion. [ME f. OF *escaigne*, of unkn. orig.]

skeleton /ˈskelɪt(ə)n/ *n*. **1 a** a hard internal or external framework of bones, cartilage, shell, woody fibre, etc., supporting or containing the body of an animal or plant. **b** the dried bones of a human being or other animal fastened together in the same relative positions as in life. **2** the supporting framework or structure or essential part of a thing. **3** a very thin or emaciated person or animal. **4** the remaining part of anything after its life or usefulness is gone. **5** an outline sketch, an epitome or abstract. **6** (*attrib*.) having only the essential or minimum number of persons, parts, etc. (*skeleton plan*; *skeleton staff*). □ **skeleton in the cupboard** (*US* **closet**) a discreditable or embarrassing fact kept secret. **skeleton key** a key designed to fit many locks by having the interior of the bit hollowed. □ **skeletal** *adj*. **skeletally** *adv*. **skeletonize** *v.tr.* (also **-ise**). [mod.L f. Gk, neut. of *skeletos* dried-up f. *skellō* dry up]

skep /skep/ *n*. **1 a** a wooden or wicker basket of any of various forms. **b** the quantity contained in this. **2** a straw or wicker beehive. [ME f. ON *skeppa*]

skeptic *US* var. of SCEPTIC.

skeptical *US* var. of SCEPTICAL.

skerry /ˈskerɪ/ *n*. (*pl*. **-ies**) *Sc*. a reef or rocky island. [Orkney dial. f. ON *sker*: cf. SCAR²]

sketch *n*. & *v*. —*n*. **1** a rough, slight, merely outlined, or unfinished drawing or painting, often made to assist in making a more finished picture. **2** a brief account without many details conveying a general idea of something, a rough draft or general outline. **3** a very short play, usu. humorous and limited to one scene. **4** a short descriptive piece of writing. —*v.* **1** *tr.* make or give a sketch of. **2** *intr.* draw sketches esp. of landscape (*went out sketching*). **3** *tr.* (often foll. by *in*, *out*) indicate briefly or in outline. □ **sketch-map** a roughly-drawn map with few details. □ **sketcher** *n.* [Du. *schets* or G *Skizze* f. It. *schizzo* f. *schizzare* make a sketch ult. f. Gk *skhēdios* extempore]

sketchy /ˈsketʃɪ/ *adj.* (**sketchier**, **sketchiest**) **1** giving only a slight or rough outline, like a sketch. **2** *colloq.* unsubstantial or imperfect esp. through haste. □ **sketchily** *adv.* **sketchiness** *n.*

skew *adj.*, *n.*, & *v.* —*adj.* oblique, slanting, set askew. —*v.* **1** *tr.* make skew. **2** *tr.* distort. **3** *intr.* move obliquely. **4** *intr.* twist. □ **on the skew** askew. **skew-whiff** /skjuːˈwɪf/ *Brit. colloq.* askew. □ **skewness** *n.* [ONF *eskiu(w)er* (v.) = OF *eschuer*: see ESCHEW]

skewbald /ˈskjuːbɔːld/ *adj.* & *n.* —*adj.* (of an animal) with irregular patches of white and another colour (properly not black). —*n.* a skewbald animal, esp. a horse. [ME *skued* (orig. uncert.), after PIEBALD]

skewer /ˈskjuːə(r)/ *n.* & *v.* —*n.* a long pin designed for holding meat compactly together while cooking. —*v.tr.* fasten together or pierce with or as with a skewer. [17th c., var. of dial. *skiver*: orig. unkn.]

ski /skiː/ *n.* & *v.* —*n.* (*pl.* **skis** or **ski**) **1** each of a pair of long narrow pieces of wood etc., usu. pointed and turned up at the front, fastened under the feet for travelling over snow. **2** a similar device under a vehicle or aircraft. **3** = WATER-SKI. **4** (*attrib.*) for wear when skiing (*ski boots*). —*v.* (**skis**, **ski'd** or **skied** /skiːd/; **skiing**) **1** *intr.* travel on skis. **2** *tr.* ski at (a place). □ **ski-bob** *n.* a machine like a bicycle with skis instead of wheels. **ski-jump 1** a steep slope levelling off before a sharp drop to allow a skier to leap through the air. **2** a jump made from this. **ski-jumping** the sport of leaping off a ski-jump with marks awarded for style and distance attained. **ski-lift** a device for carrying skiers up a slope, usu. on seats hung from an overhead cable. **ski-run** a slope prepared for skiing. □ **skiable** *adj.* [Norw. f. ON *skíth* billet, snow-shoe]

skid *v.* & *n.* —*v.* (**skidded**, **skidding**) **1** *intr.* (of a vehicle, a wheel, or a driver) slide on slippery ground, esp. sideways or obliquely. **2** *tr.* cause (a vehicle etc.) to skid. **3** *intr.* slip, slide. —*n.* **1** the act or an instance of skidding. **2** a piece of wood etc. serving as a support, ship's fender, inclined plane, etc. **3** a braking device, esp. a wooden or metal shoe preventing a wheel from revolving or used as a drag. **4** a runner beneath an aircraft for use when landing. □ **hit the skids** *colloq.* enter a rapid decline or deterioration. **on the skids** *colloq.* **1** about to be discarded or defeated. **2** ready for launching. **put the skids under** *colloq.* **1** hasten the downfall or failure of. **2** cause to hasten. **skid-lid** *sl.* a crash-helmet. **skid-pan** *Brit.* **1** a slippery surface prepared for vehicle-drivers to practise control of skidding. **2** a braking device. **skid row** *US* a part of a town frequented by vagrants, alcoholics, etc. [17th c.: orig. unkn.]

skier /ˈskiːə(r)/ *n.* a person who skis.

skiff *n.* a light rowing-boat or sculling-boat. [F *esquif* f. It. *schifo*, rel. to SHIP]

skiffle /ˈskɪf(ə)l/ *n.* a kind of folk music played by a small group, mainly with a rhythmic accompaniment to a singing guitarist etc. [perh. imit.]

skilful /ˈskɪlfʊl/ *adj.* (*US* **skillful**) (often foll. by *at*, *in*) having or showing skill; practised, expert, adroit, ingenious. □ **skilfully** *adv.* **skilfulness** *n.*

skill /skɪl/ *n.* (often foll. by *in*) expertness, practised ability, facility in an action; dexterity or tact. □ **skill-less** *adj.* [ME f. ON *skil* distinction]

skilled /skɪld/ *adj.* **1** (often foll. by *in*) having or showing skill; skilful. **2** (of a worker) highly trained or experienced. **3** (of work) requiring skill or special training.

skillet /ˈskɪlɪt/ *n.* **1** *Brit.* a small metal cooking-pot with a long handle and usu. legs. **2** *US* a frying-pan. [ME, perh. f. OF *escuelete* dimin. of *escuele* platter f. LL *scutella*]

skim *v.* & *n.* —*v.* (**skimmed**, **skimming**) **1** *tr.* **a** take scum or cream or a floating layer from the surface of (a liquid). **b** take (cream etc.) from the surface of a liquid. **2** *tr.* **a** keep touching lightly or nearly touching (a surface) in passing over. **b** deal with or treat (a subject) superficially. **3** *intr.* **a** (often foll. by *over*, *along*) go lightly over a surface, glide along in the air. **b** (foll. by *over*) = sense 2b of *v.* **4** *tr.* **a** read superficially, look over cursorily, gather the salient facts contained in. **b** *intr.* (usu. foll. by *through*) read or look over cursorily. —*n.* **1** the act or an instance of skimming. **2** a thin covering on a liquid (*skim of ice*). □ **skim** (or **skimmed**) **milk** milk from which the cream has been skimmed. [ME, back-form. f. SKIMMER]

skimmer /ˈskɪmə(r)/ *n.* **1** a device for skimming liquids. **2** a person who skims. **3** a flat hat, esp. a broad-brimmed straw hat. [ME f. OF *escumoir* f. *escumer* f. *escume* SCUM]

skimp *v.* **1** *tr.* (often foll. by *in*) supply (a person etc.) meagrely with food, money, etc. **2** *tr.* use a meagre or insufficient amount of, stint (material, expenses, etc.). **3** *intr.* be parsimonious. [18th c.: orig. unkn.: cf. SCRIMP]

skimpy /ˈskɪmpɪ/ *adj.* (**skimpier**, **skimpiest**) meagre; not ample or sufficient. □ **skimpily** *adv.* **skimpiness** *n.*

skin *n.* & *v.* —*n.* **1** the flexible continuous covering of a human or other animal body. **2 a** the skin of a flayed animal with or without the hair etc. **b** a material prepared from skins esp. of smaller animals (opp. HIDE²). **3** a person's skin with reference to its colour or complexion (*has a fair skin*). **4** an outer layer or covering, esp. the coating of a plant, fruit, or sausage. **5** a film like skin on the surface of a liquid etc. **6** a container for liquid, made of an animal's whole skin. **7 a** the planking or plating of a ship or boat, inside or outside the ribs. **b** the outer covering of any craft or vehicle, esp. an aircraft or spacecraft. —*v.* (**skinned**, **skinning**) **1** *tr.* remove the skin from. **2** (often foll. by *over*) **a** *tr.* cover (a sore etc.) with or as with skin. **b** *intr.* (of a wound etc.) become covered with new skin. **3** *tr.* *sl.* fleece or swindle. □ **by** (or **with**) **the skin of one's teeth** by a very narrow margin. **get under a person's skin** *colloq.* interest or annoy a person intensely. **have a thick** (or **thin**) **skin**

be insensitive (or sensitive) to criticism etc. **no skin off one's nose** *colloq.* a matter of indifference or even benefit to one. **skin-deep** (of a wound, or of an emotion, an impression, beauty, etc.) superficial, not deep or lasting. **skin-diver** a person who swims underwater without a diving-suit, usu. in deep water with an aqualung and flippers. **skin game** *US sl.* a swindling game. **skin-graft 1** the surgical transplanting of skin. **2** a piece of skin transferred in this way. **skin test** a test to determine whether an immune reaction is elicited when a substance is applied to or injected into the skin. **skin-tight** (of a garment) very close-fitting. **to the skin** through all one's clothing (*soaked to the skin*). □ **skinless** *adj.* **skin-like** *adj.* **skinned** *adj.* (also in *comb.*) **skinner** *n.* [OE *scin(n)* f. ON *skinn*]

skinflint /ˈskɪnflɪnt/ *n.* a miserly person.

skinful /ˈskɪnfʊl/ *n.* (pl. **-fuls**) *colloq.* enough alcoholic liquor to make one drunk.

skinhead /ˈskɪnhɛd/ *n.* **1** *Brit.* a youth with close-cropped hair, esp. one of an aggressive gang. **2** *US* a recruit in the Marines.

skinny /ˈskɪnɪ/ *adj.* (**skinnier**, **skinniest**) **1** thin or emaciated. **2** (of clothing) tight-fitting. □ **skinny-dipping** *US colloq.* bathing in the nude. □ **skinniness** *n.*

skint *adj. Brit. sl.* having no money left. [= *skinned*, past part. of SKIN]

skip[1] *v. & n.* —*v.* (**skipped**, **skipping**) **1** *intr.* **a** move along lightly, esp. by taking two steps with each foot in turn. **b** jump lightly from the ground, esp. so as to clear a skipping-rope. **c** jump about, gambol, caper, frisk. **2** *intr.* (often foll. by *from, off, to*) move quickly from one point, subject, or occupation to another; be desultory. **3** *tr.* (also *absol.*) omit in dealing with a series or in reading (*skip every tenth row*; *always skips the small print*). **4** *tr. colloq.* not participate in. **5** *tr. colloq.* depart quickly from; leave hurriedly. —*n.* **1** a skipping movement or action. **2** *Computing* the action of passing over part of a sequence of data or instructions. □ **skip it** *sl.* **1** abandon a topic etc. **2** make off, disappear. **skipping-rope** (*US* **skip-rope**) a length of rope revolved over the head and under the feet while jumping as a game or exercise. [ME, prob. f. Scand.]

skip[2] *n.* **1** a large container for builders' refuse etc. **2** a cage, bucket, etc., in which men or materials are lowered and raised in mines and quarries. **3** = SKEP. [var. of SKEP]

skipjack /ˈskɪpdʒæk/ *n.* (in full **skipjack tuna**) a small striped Pacific tuna, *Katsuwonus pelamus*, used as food. [SKIP[1] + JACK]

skipper /ˈskɪpə(r)/ *n. & v.* —*n.* **1** a sea captain, esp. the master of a small trading or fishing vessel. **2** the captain of an aircraft. **3** the captain of a side in games. —*v.tr.* act as captain of. [ME f. MDu., MLG *schipper* f. *schip* SHIP]

skirl *n. & v.* —*n.* the shrill sound characteristic of bagpipes. —*v.intr.* make a skirl. [prob. Scand.: ult. imit.]

skirmish /ˈskɜːmɪʃ/ *n. & v.* —*n.* **1** a piece of irregular or unpremeditated fighting esp. between small or outlying parts of armies or fleets, a slight engagement. **2** a short argument or contest of wit etc. —*v.intr.* engage in a skirmish. □ **skirmisher** *n.* [ME f. OF *eskirmir*, *escremir* f. Frank.]

skirt *n. & v.* —*n.* **1** a woman's outer garment hanging from the waist. **2** the part of a coat etc. that hangs below the waist. **3** a hanging part round the base of a hovercraft. **4** (in *sing.* or *pl.*) an edge, border, or extreme part. **5** (in full **skirt of beef** etc.) **a** the diaphragm and other membranes as food. **b** *Brit.* a cut of meat from the lower flank. —*v.* **1** *tr.* go along or round or past the edge of. **2** *tr.* be situated along. **3** *tr.* avoid dealing with (an issue etc.). **4** *intr.* (foll. by *along*) go along the coast, a wall, etc. □ **skirted** *adj.* (also in *comb.*). **skirtless** *adj.* [ME f. ON *skyrta* shirt, corresp. to OE *scyrte*: see SHIRT]

skirting /ˈskɜːtɪŋ/ *n.* (in full **skirting-board**) *Brit.* a narrow board etc. along the bottom of the wall of a room.

skit *n.* (often foll. by *on*) a light, usu. short, piece of satire or burlesque. [rel. to *skit* move lightly and rapidly, perh. f. ON (cf. *skjóta* SHOOT)]

skite *v. & n.. Austral. & NZ colloq.* —*v.intr* boast, brag. —*n.* **1** a boaster. **2** boasting; boastfulness. [Sc. & N.Engl. dial., = a person regarded with contempt]

skitter /ˈskɪtə(r)/ *v.intr.* (also **skeeter** /ˈskiːtə(r)/) **1** (usu. foll. by *along*, *across*) move lightly or hastily. **2** (usu. foll. by *about*, *off*) hurry about, dart off. [app. frequent. of dial. *skite*, perh. formed as SKIT]

skittery /ˈskɪtərɪ/ *adj.* skittish, restless.

skittish /ˈskɪtɪʃ/ *adj.* **1** lively, playful. **2** (of a horse etc.) nervous, inclined to shy, fidgety. □ **skittishly** *adv.* **skittishness** *n.* [ME, perh. formed as SKIT]

skittle /ˈskɪt(ə)l/ *n. & v.* —*n.* **1** a pin used in the game of skittles. **2** (in *pl.*; usu. treated as *sing.*) a game like ninepins played with usu. nine wooden pins set up at the end of an alley to be bowled down usu. with wooden balls. —*v.tr.* (often foll. by *out*) *Cricket* get (batsmen) out in rapid succession. [17th c. (also *kittle-pins*): orig. unkn.]

skive *v. & n.* —*v.* **1** *tr.* split or pare (hides, leather, etc.). **2** *intr. Brit. sl.* **a** evade a duty, shirk. **b** (often foll. by *off*) avoid work by absenting oneself, play truant. —*n. sl.* **1** an instance of shirking. **2** an easy option. □ **skiver** *n.* [ON *skífa*, rel. to ME *schíve* slice]

skivvy /ˈskɪvɪ/ *n.* (pl. **-ies**) *Brit. colloq. derog.* a female domestic servant. [20th c.: orig. unkn.]

skua /ˈskjuːə/ *n.* any large predatory sea bird of the family Stercorariidae. [mod.L f. Faroese *skúgvur*, ON *skúfr*]

skulduggery /skʌlˈdʌgərɪ/ *n.* (also **sculduggery**, **skullduggery**) trickery; unscrupulous behaviour. [earlier *sculduddery*, orig. Sc. = unchastity (18th c.: orig. unkn.)]

skulk *v.intr.* **1** move stealthily, lurk, or keep oneself concealed, esp. in a cowardly or sinister way. **2** stay or sneak away in time of danger. **3** shirk duty. □ **skulker** *n.* [ME f. Scand.: cf. Norw., Da. *skulke*, Sw. *skolka* shirk]

skull *n.* **1** the bony case of the brain of a vertebrate. **2 a** the part of the skeleton corresponding to the head. **b** this with the skin and soft internal parts removed. **c** a representation of this. **3** the head as the seat of intelligence. □ **skull and crossbones** a representation of a skull with two thigh-bones crossed below it as an emblem of piracy or death. □ **skulled** *adj.* (also in *comb.*). [ME *scolle*: orig. unkn.]

skullcap /ˈskʌlkæp/ n. **1** a small close-fitting peakless cap. **2** the top part of the skull.

skunk n. **1** any of various cat-sized flesh-eating mammals of the family Mustelidae, esp. *Mephitis mephitis* having a distinctive black and white striped fur and able to emit a powerful stench from a liquid secreted by its anal glands as a defence. **2** *colloq.* a thoroughly contemptible person. [Amer. Ind. *segankw, segongw*]

sky n. & v. —n. (pl. **skies**) (in *sing.* or *pl.*) **1** the region of the atmosphere and outer space seen from the earth. **2** the weather or climate evidenced by this. —*v.tr.* (**skies, skied**) **1** *Cricket* etc. hit (a ball) high into the air. **2** hang (a picture) high on a wall. □ **sky-high** adv. & adj. as if reaching the sky, very high. **sky pilot** sl. a clergyman. **sky-rocket** n. a rocket exploding high in the air. —*v.intr.* (**-rocketed, -rocketing**) (esp. of prices etc.) rise very steeply or rapidly. **to the skies** very highly; without reserve (*praised to the skies*). **under the open sky** out of doors. □ **skyey** adj. **skyless** adj. [ME *ski(es)* cloud(s) f. ON *ský*]

skydiving /ˈskaɪˌdaɪvɪŋ/ n. the sport of performing acrobatic manoeuvres under free fall with a parachute. □ **skydive** v.intr. **skydiver** n.

skyjack /ˈskaɪdʒæk/ v. & n. sl. —*v.tr.* hijack (an aircraft). —n. an act of skyjacking. □ **skyjacker** n. [SKY + HIJACK]

skylark /ˈskaɪlɑːk/ n. & v. —n. a lark, *Alauda arvensis* of Eurasia and N. Africa, that sings while hovering in flight. —*v.intr.* play tricks or practical jokes, indulge in horseplay, frolic. [SKY + LARK¹: (v.) with pun on LARK¹, LARK²]

skylight /ˈskaɪlaɪt/ n. a window set in the plane of a roof or ceiling.

skyline /ˈskaɪlaɪn/ n. the outline of hills, buildings, etc., defined against the sky; the visible horizon.

skyscraper /ˈskaɪˌskreɪpə(r)/ n. a very tall building of many storeys.

skyward /ˈskaɪwəd/ adv. & adj. —adv. (also **skywards**) towards the sky. —adj. moving skyward.

slab n. **1** a flat broad fairly thick usu. square or rectangular piece of solid material, esp. stone. **2** a large flat piece of cake, chocolate, etc. **3** (of timber) an outer piece sawn from a log. **4** *Brit.* a mortuary table. [ME: orig. unkn.]

slack¹ adj., n. & v. —adj. **1** (of rope etc.) not taut. **2** inactive or sluggish. **3** negligent or remiss. **4** (of tide etc.) neither ebbing nor flowing. **5** (of trade or business or a market) with little happening. **6** loose. —n. **1** the slack part of a rope (*haul in the slack*). **2** a slack time in trade etc. **3** *colloq.* a spell of inactivity or laziness. **4** (in *pl.*) full-length loosely-cut trousers for informal wear. —v. **1 a** *tr.* & *intr.* slacken. **b** *tr.* loosen (rope etc.). **2** *intr. colloq.* take a rest, be lazy. □ **slack off 1** loosen. **2** lose or cause to lose vigour. **slack suit** *US* casual clothes of slacks and a jacket or shirt. **slack up** reduce the speed of a train etc. before stopping. **take up the slack** use up a surplus or make up a deficiency; avoid an undesirable lull. □ **slackly** adv. **slackness** n. [OE *slæc* f. Gmc]

slack² n. coal-dust or small pieces of coal. [ME prob. f. LG or Du.]

slacken /ˈslækən/ v.tr. & intr. make or become slack. □ **slacken off** = *slack off* (see SLACK¹).

slacker /ˈslækə(r)/ n. a shirker; an indolent person.

slag n. & v. —n. **1** vitreous refuse left after ore has been smelted, dross separated in a fused state in the reduction of ore, clinkers. **2** sl. derog. a prostitute or promiscuous woman. —v. (**slagged, slagging**) **1** intr. **a** form slag. **b** cohere into a mass like slag. **2** tr. (often foll. by *off*) sl. criticize, insult. □ **slag-heap** a hill of refuse from a mine etc. □ **slaggy** adj. (**slaggier, slaggiest**). [MLG *slagge*, perh. f. *slagen* strike, with ref. to fragments formed by hammering]

slain past part. of SLAY.

slake v.tr. **1** assuage or satisfy (thirst, revenge, etc.). **2** disintegrate (quicklime) by chemical combination with water. [OE *slacian* f. *slæc* SLACK¹]

slalom /ˈslɑːləm/ n. **1** a ski-race down a zigzag course defined by artificial obstacles. **2** an obstacle race in canoes or cars or on skateboards or water-skis. [Norw. *slalåm*, lit. 'sloping track']

slam¹ v. & n. —v. (**slammed, slamming**) **1** tr. & intr. shut forcefully and loudly. **2** tr. put down (an object) with a similar sound. **3** intr. move violently (*he slammed out of the room*). **4** tr. & intr. put or come into sudden action (*slam the brakes on*). **5** tr. sl. criticize severely. **6** tr. sl. hit. **7** tr. sl. gain an easy victory over. —n. **1** a sound of or as of a slammed door. **2** the shutting of a door etc. with a loud bang. **3** (usu. prec. by *the*) *US* sl. prison. [prob. f. Scand.: cf. ON *slam(b)ra*]

slam² n. *Cards* the winning of every trick in a game. □ **grand slam 1** *Bridge* the winning of 13 tricks. **2** the winning of all of a group of championships or matches in a sport. [orig. name of a card-game: perh. f. obs. *slampant* trickery]

slammer /ˈslæmə(r)/ n. (usu. prec. by *the*) sl. prison.

slander /ˈslɑːndə(r)/ n. & v. —n. **1** a malicious, false, and injurious statement spoken about a person. **2** the uttering of such statements; calumny. **3** *Law* false oral defamation. —*v.tr.* utter slander about; defame falsely. □ **slanderer** n. **slanderous** adj. **slanderously** adv. [ME *sclaundre* f. AF *esclaundre*, OF *esclandre* alt. f. *escandle* f. LL *scandalum*: see SCANDAL]

slang n. & v. —n. words, phrases, and uses that are regarded as very informal and are often restricted to special contexts or are peculiar to a specified profession, class, etc. (*racing slang; schoolboy slang*). —v. **1** tr. use abusive language to. **2** intr. use such language. □ **slanging-match** a prolonged exchange of insults. [18th-c. cant: orig. unkn.]

slangy /ˈslæŋɪ/ adj. (**slangier, slangiest**) **1** of the character of slang. **2** fond of using slang. □ **slangily** adv. **slanginess** n.

slant /slɑːnt/ v., n., & adj. —v. **1** intr. slope; diverge from a line; lie or go obliquely to a vertical or horizontal line. **2** tr. cause to do this. **3** tr. (often as **slanted** adj.) present (information) from a particular angle esp. in a biased or unfair way. —n. **1** a slope; an oblique position. **2** a way of regarding a thing; a point of view, esp. a biased one. —adj. sloping, oblique. □ **on a** (or **the**) **slant** aslant. [aphetic form of ASLANT: (v.) rel. to ME *slent* f. ON *sletta* dash, throw]

slantwise /ˈslɑːntwaɪz/ adv. aslant.

slap v., n., & adv. —v. (**slapped, slapping**) **1** tr. & intr. strike with the palm of the hand or a flat object, or so as to make a similar noise. **2** *tr.* lay forcefully (*slapped the money on the table*; *slapped a writ on the offender*). **3** *tr.* put hastily or carelessly (*slap some paint on the walls*). **4** *tr.* (often foll. by *down*) *colloq.* reprimand or snub. —*n.* **1** a blow with the palm of the hand or a flat object. **2** a slapping sound. —*adv.* **1** with the suddenness or effectiveness or true aim of a blow, suddenly, fully, directly (*ran slap into him*; *hit me slap in the eye*). **2** = *slap-bang.* □ **slap and tickle** *Brit. colloq.* light-hearted amorous amusement. **slap-bang** violently, noisily, headlong. **slap-happy** *colloq.* **1** cheerfully casual or flippant. **2** punch-drunk. **slap in the face** a rebuff or affront. **slap on the back** *n.* congratulations. —*v.tr.* congratulate. **slap-up** esp. *Brit. colloq.* excellent, lavish; done regardless of expense (*slap-up meal*). [LG *slapp* (imit.)]

slapdash /ˈslæpdæʃ/ *adj.* & *adv.* —*adj.* hasty and careless. —*adv.* in a slapdash manner.

slapstick /ˈslæpstɪk/ *n.* boisterous knockabout comedy. [SLAP + STICK¹]

slash *v.* & *n.* —*v.* **1** *intr.* make a sweeping or random cut or cuts with a knife, whip, etc. **2** *tr.* make such a cut or cuts at. **3** *tr.* make a long narrow gash or gashes in. **4** *tr.* reduce (prices etc.) drastically. **5** *tr.* censure vigorously. **6** *tr.* make (one's way) by slashing. **7** *tr.* **a** lash (a person etc.) with a whip. **b** crack (a whip). —*n.* **1 a** a slashing cut or stroke. **b** a wound or slit made by this. **2** an oblique stroke; a solidus. **3** *Brit. sl.* an act of urinating. **4** *US* debris resulting from the felling or destruction of trees. □ **slasher** *n.* [ME perh. f. OF *esclachier* break in pieces]

slat *n.* a thin narrow piece of wood or plastic or metal, esp. used in an overlapping series as in a fence or Venetian blind. [ME *s(c)lat* f. OF *esclat* splinter etc. f. *esclater* split f. Rmc]

slate /sleɪt/ *n.*, *v.*, & *adj.* —*n.* **1** a fine-grained grey, green, or bluish-purple metamorphic rock easily split into flat smooth plates. **2** a piece of such a plate used as roofing-material. **3** a piece of such a plate used for writing on, usu. framed in wood. **4** the colour of slate. **5** *US* a list of nominees for office etc. —*v.tr.* **1** cover with slates esp. as roofing. **2** *Brit. colloq.* criticize severely; scold. **3** *US* make arrangements for (an event etc.). **4** *US* propose or nominate for office etc. —*adj.* made of slate. □ **on the slate** *Brit.* recorded as a debt to be paid. **slate-pencil** a small rod of soft slate used for writing on slate. **wipe the slate clean** forgive or cancel the record of past offences. □ **slating** *n.* **slaty** *adj.* [ME *s(c)late* f. OF *esclate,* fem. form of *esclat* SLAT]

slather /ˈslæðə(r)/ *n.* & *v.* —*n.* **1** (usu. in *pl.*) *US colloq.* a large amount. **2** (often **open slather**) *Austral.* & *NZ sl.* unrestricted scope for action. —*v.tr. US colloq.* **1** spread thickly. **2** squander. [19th c.: orig. unkn.]

slatted /ˈslætɪd/ *adj.* having slats.

slattern /ˈslæt(ə)n/ *n.* a slovenly woman. □ **slatternly** *adj.* **slatternliness** *n.* [17th c.: rel. to *slattering* slovenly, f. dial. *slatter* to spill, slop, waste, frequent. of *slat* strike]

slaughter /ˈslɔːtə(r)/ *n.* & *v.* —*n.* **1** the killing of an animal or animals for food. **2** the killing of many persons or animals at once or continuously; carnage, massacre. —*v.tr.* **1** kill (people) in a ruthless manner or on a great scale. **2** kill for food, butcher. **3** *colloq.* defeat

utterly. □ **slaughterer** *n.* **slaughterous** *adj.* [ME *slahter* ult. f. ON *slátr* butcher's meat, rel. to SLAY]

slaughterhouse /ˈslɔːtəˌhaʊs/ *n.* **1** a place for the slaughter of animals as food. **2** a place of carnage.

Slav /slɑːv/ *n.* & *adj.* —*n.* a member of a group of peoples in Central and Eastern Europe speaking Slavonic languages. —*adj.* **1** of or relating to the Slavs. **2** Slavonic. □ **Slavism** *n.* [ME *Sclave* f. med.L *Sclavus,* late Gk *Sklabos,* & f. med.L *Slavus*]

slave *n.* & *v.* —*n.* **1** a person who is the legal property of another or others and is bound to absolute obedience, a human chattel. **2** a drudge, a person working very hard. **3** (foll. by *of, to*) a helpless victim of some dominating influence (*slave of fashion*; *slave to duty*). **4** a machine, or part of one, directly controlled by another. —*v. intr.* (often foll. by *at, over*) work very hard. □ **slave-driver 1** an overseer of slaves at work. **2** a person who works others hard. **slave labour** forced labour. **slave-trade** *hist.* the procuring, transporting, and selling of human beings, esp. African Blacks, as slaves. [ME f. OF *esclave* = med.L *sclavus, sclava* Slav (captive): see SLAV]

slaver¹ /ˈsleɪvə(r)/ *n. hist.* a ship or person engaged in the slave-trade.

slaver² /ˈslævə(r)/ *n.* & *v.* —*n.* **1** saliva running from the mouth. **2** a fulsome or servile flattery. **b** drivel, nonsense. —*v.intr.* **1** let saliva run from the mouth, dribble. **2** (foll. by *over*) show excessive sentimentality over, or desire for. [ME prob. f. LG or Du.: cf. SLOBBER]

slavery /ˈsleɪvərɪ/ *n.* **1** the condition of a slave. **2** exhausting labour; drudgery. **3** the custom of having slaves.

Slavic /ˈslɑːvɪk/ *adj.* & *n.* = SLAVONIC.

slavish /ˈsleɪvɪʃ/ *adj.* **1** of, like, or as of slaves. **2** showing no attempt at originality or development. **3** abject, servile. □ **slavishly** *adv.* **slavishness** *n.*

Slavonic /sləˈvɒnɪk/ *adj.* & *n.* —*adj.* **1** of or relating to the group of Indo-European languages including Russian, Polish, and Czech. **2** of or relating to the Slavs. —*n.* the Slavonic language-group. [med.L *S(c)lavonicus* f. *S(c)lavonia* country of Slavs f. *Sclavus* SLAV]

slaw *n.* coleslaw. [Du. *sla,* shortened f. *salade* SALAD]

slay *v.tr.* (*past* **slew**; *past part.* **slain**) **1** *literary* or *joc.* kill. **2** *sl.* convulse with laughter. □ **slayer** *n.* [OE *slēan* f. Gmc]

sleaze *n.* & *v. colloq.* —*n.* **1** sleaziness. **2** a person of low moral standards. —*v.intr.* move in a sleazy fashion. [back-form. f. SLEAZY]

sleazy /ˈsliːzɪ/ *adj.* (**sleazier, sleaziest**) **1** squalid, tawdry. **2** slatternly. **3** (of textiles etc.) flimsy. □ **sleazily** *adv.* **sleaziness** *n.* [17th c.: orig. unkn.]

sled *n.* & *v. US* = a sledge. —*v.intr.* (**sledded, sledding**) ride on a sledge. [MLG *sledde,* rel. to SLIDE]

sledge¹ *n.* & *v.* —*n.* **1** a vehicle on runners for conveying loads or passengers esp. over snow, drawn by horses, dogs, or reindeer or pushed or pulled by one or more persons. **2** a toboggan. —*v.intr.* & *tr.* travel or convey by sledge. [MDu. *sleedse,* rel. to SLED]

sledge² *n.* = SLEDGEHAMMER.

sledgehammer /ˈsledʒˌhæmə(r)/ *n.* **1** a large heavy hammer used to break stone etc. **2** (*attrib.*)

heavy or powerful (*a sledgehammer blow*). [OE *slecg*, rel. to SLAY]

sleek *adj.* & *v.* —*adj.* **1** (of hair, fur, or skin, or an animal or person with such hair etc.) smooth and glossy. **2** looking well-fed and comfortable. **3** (of a thing) smooth and polished. —*v.tr.* make sleek, esp. by stroking or pressing down. □ **sleekly** *adv.* **sleekness** *n.* **sleeky** *adj.* [later var. of SLICK]

sleep *n.* & *v.* —*n.* **1** a condition of body and mind such as that which normally recurs for several hours every night, in which the nervous system is inactive, the eyes closed, the postural muscles relaxed, and consciousness practically suspended. **2** a period of sleep (*shall try to get a sleep*). **3** a state like sleep, such as rest, quiet, negligence, or death. **4** the prolonged inert condition of hibernating animals. **5** a substance found in the corners of the eyes after sleep. —*v.* (*past* and *past part.* **slept**) **1** *intr.* **a** be in a state of sleep. **b** fall asleep. **2** *intr.* (foll. by *at, in,* etc.) spend the night. **3** *tr.* provide sleeping accommodation for (*the house sleeps six*). **4** *intr.* (foll. by *with, together*) have sexual intercourse, esp. in bed. **5** *intr.* (foll. by *on, over*) not decide (a question) until the next day. **6** *intr.* (foll. by *through*) fail to be woken by. **7** *intr.* be inactive or dormant. **8** *intr.* be dead; lie in the grave. **go to sleep 1** enter a state of sleep. **2** (of a limb) become numbed by pressure. **in one's sleep** while asleep. **put to sleep 1** anaesthetize. **2** kill (an animal) painlessly. **sleep around** *colloq.* be sexually promiscuous. **sleep in 1** remain asleep later than usual in the morning. **2** sleep by night at one's place of work. **sleeping-bag** a lined or padded bag to sleep in esp. when camping etc. **sleeping-car** (or **-carriage**) a railway coach provided with beds or berths. **sleeping-draught** a drink to induce sleep. **sleeping partner** a partner not sharing in the actual work of a firm. **sleeping-pill** a pill to induce sleep. **sleeping policeman** a ramp etc. in the road intended to cause traffic to reduce speed. **sleeping sickness** any of several tropical diseases with extreme lethargy. **sleeping-suit** a child's one-piece night-garment. **sleep out** sleep by night out of doors, or not at one's place of work. **sleep-out** *n. Austral.* & *NZ* a veranda, porch, or outbuilding providing sleeping accommodation. [OE *slēp, slæp* (n.), *slēpan, slæpan* (v.) f. Gmc]

sleeper /ˈsliːpə(r)/ *n.* **1** a person or animal that sleeps. **2** *Brit.* a wooden or concrete beam laid horizontally as a support, esp. for railway track. **3 a** a sleeping-car. **b** a berth in this. **4** *Brit.* a ring worn in a pierced ear to keep the hole from closing. **5** a thing that is suddenly successful after being undistinguished.

sleepless /ˈsliːplɪs/ *adj.* **1** characterized by lack of sleep (*a sleepless night*). **2** unable to sleep. **3** continually active or moving. □ **sleeplessly** *adv.* **sleeplessness** *n.*

sleepwalk /ˈsliːpwɔːk/ *v.intr.* walk or perform other actions while asleep. □ **sleepwalker** *n.*

sleepy /ˈsliːpɪ/ *adj.* (**sleepier, sleepiest**) **1** drowsy; ready for sleep; about to fall asleep. **2** lacking activity or bustle (*a sleepy little town*). **3** habitually indolent, unobservant, etc. □ **sleepy sickness** an infection of the brain with drowsiness and sometimes a coma. □ **sleepily** *adv.* **sleepiness** *n.*

sleepyhead /ˈsliːpɪˌhed/ *n.* (esp. as a form of address) a sleepy or inattentive person.

sleet *n.* & *v.* —*n.* **1** a mixture of snow and rain falling together. **2** hail or snow melting as it falls. **3** *US* a thin coating of ice. —*v.intr.* (prec. by *it* as subject) sleet falls (*it is sleeting; if it sleets*). □ **sleety** *adj.* [ME prob. f. OE: rel. to MLG *slōten* (pl.) hail, MHG *slōz(e)* f. Gmc]

sleeve *n.* **1** the part of a garment that wholly or partly covers an arm. **2** the cover of a gramophone record. **3** a tube enclosing a rod or smaller tube. **4** a wind-sock. □ **roll up one's sleeves** prepare to fight or work. **up one's sleeve** concealed but ready for use, in reserve. □ **sleeved** *adj.* (also in *comb.*). **sleeveless** *adj.* [OE *slēfe, slīefe, slȳf*]

sleigh /sleɪ/ *n.* & *v.* —*n.* a sledge, esp. one for riding on. —*v.intr.* travel on a sleigh. □ **sleigh-bell** any of a number of tinkling bells attached to the harness of a sleigh-horse etc. [orig. US, f. Du. *slee*, rel. to SLED]

sleight /slaɪt/ *n. archaic* **1** a deceptive trick or device or movement. **2** dexterity. **3** cunning. □ **sleight of hand 1** dexterity esp. in conjuring or fencing. **2** a display of dexterity, esp. a conjuring trick. [ME *sleghth* f. ON *slœgth* f. *slœgr* SLY]

slender /ˈslendə(r)/ *adj.* (**slenderer, slenderest**) **1 a** of small girth or breadth (*a slender pillar*). **b** gracefully thin (*a slender waist*). **2** relatively small or scanty; slight, meagre, inadequate (*slender hopes; slender resources*). □ **slenderly** *adv.* **slenderness** *n.* [ME: orig. unkn.]

slenderize /ˈslendəˌraɪz/ *v.* (also **-ise**) **1** *tr.* **a** make (a thing) slender. **b** make (one's figure) appear slender. **2** *intr.* make oneself slender; slim.

slept *past* and *past part.* of SLEEP.

sleuth /sluːθ/ *n.* & *v. colloq.* —*n.* a detective. —*v.* **1** *intr.* act as a detective. **2** *tr.* investigate. □ **sleuth-hound 1** a bloodhound. **2** *colloq.* a detective, an investigator. [orig. in *sleuth-hound*: ME f. *sleuth* f. ON *slóth* track, trail]

slew[1] *v.* & *n.* (also **slue**) —*v.tr.* & *intr.* (often foll. by *round*) turn or swing forcibly or with effort out of the forward or ordinary position. —*n.* such a change of position. [18th-c. Naut.: orig. unkn.]

slew[2] *past* of SLAY.

slew[3] *n.* esp. *US colloq.* a large number or quantity. [Ir. *sluagh*]

slice *n.* & *v.* —*n.* **1** a thin broad piece or wedge cut off or out esp. from meat or bread or a cake, pie, or large fruit. **2** a share; a part taken or allotted or gained (*a slice of territory; a slice of the profits*). **3** an implement with a broad flat blade for serving fish etc. or for scraping or chipping. **4** *Golf* & *Lawn Tennis* a slicing stroke. —*v.* **1** *tr.* (often foll. by *up*) cut into slices. **2** *tr.* (foll. by *off*) cut (a piece) off. **3** *intr.* (foll. by *into, through*) cut with or like a knife. **4** *tr.* (also *absol.*) **a** *Golf* strike (the ball) so that it deviates away from the striker. **b** (in other sports) propel (the ball) forward at an angle. **5** *tr.* go through (air etc.) with a cutting motion. □ **sliceable** *adj.* **slicer** *n.* (also in *comb.*). [ME f. OF *esclice, esclicier* splinter f. Frank. *slītjan*, rel. to SLIT]

slick *adj., n.,* & *v.* —*adj. colloq.* **1 a** (of a person or action) skilful or efficient; dextrous (*gave a slick performance*). **b** superficially or pretentiously smooth and dextrous. **c** glib. **2 a** sleek, smooth.

b slippery. —*n.* a smooth patch of oil etc., esp. on the sea. —*v.tr. colloq.* **1** make sleek or smart. **2** (usu. foll. by *down*) flatten (one's hair etc.). □ **slickly** *adv.* **slickness** *n.* [ME *slike*(*n*), prob. f. OE: cf. SLEEK]

slicker /ˈslɪkə(r)/ *n. US* **1** *colloq.* **a** a plausible rogue. **b** a smart and sophisticated city-dweller (cf. *city slicker*). **2** a raincoat of smooth material.

slide *v. & n.* —*v.* (*past* and *past part.* **slid**) **1 a** *intr.* move along a smooth surface with continuous contact on the same part of the thing moving. **b** *tr.* cause to do this (*slide the drawer into place*). **2** *intr.* move quietly; glide; go smoothly along. **3** *intr.* pass gradually or imperceptibly. **4** *intr.* glide over ice on one or both feet without skates (under gravity or with momentum got by running). **5** *intr.* (foll. by *over*) barely touch upon (a delicate subject etc.). **6** *intr. & tr.* (often foll. by *into*) move or cause to move quietly or unobtrusively (*slid his hand into mine*). **7** *intr.* take its own course (*let it slide*). —*n.* **1 a** the act or an instance of sliding. **b** a rapid decline. **2** an inclined plane down which children, goods, etc., slide; a chute. **3 a** a track made by or for sliding, esp. on ice. **b** a slope prepared with snow or ice for tobogganing. **4** a part of a machine or instrument that slides, esp. a slide-valve. **5 a** a thing slid into place, esp. a piece of glass holding an object for a microscope. **b** a mounted transparency usu. placed in a projector for viewing on a screen. **6** *Brit.* = *hair-slide.* **7** a part or parts of a machine on or between which a sliding part works. □ **slide fastener** *US* a zip-fastener. **slide-rule** a ruler with a sliding central strip, graduated logarithmically for making rapid calculations, esp. multiplication and division. **sliding scale** a scale of fees, taxes, wages, etc., that varies as a whole in accordance with variation of some standard. □ **slidable** *adj.* **slidably** *adv.* **slider** *n.* [OE *slīdan*]

slight /slaɪt/ *adj., v., & n.* —*adj.* **1 a** inconsiderable; of little significance (*has a slight cold; the damage is very slight*). **b** barely perceptible (*a slight smell of gas*). **c** not much or great or thorough, inadequate, scanty (*a conclusion based on very slight observation; paid him slight attention*). **2** slender, frail-looking. **3** (in *superl.*, with *neg.* or *interrog.*) any whatever (*paid not the slightest attention*). —*v.tr.* treat or speak of (a person etc.) as not worth attention, fail in courtesy or respect towards, markedly neglect. —*n.* a marked piece of neglect, a failure to show due respect. □ **not in the slightest** not at all. □ **slightingly** *adv.* **slightish** *adj.* **slightly** *adv.* **slightness** *n.* [ME *slyght, sleght* f. ON *sléttr* level, smooth f. Gmc]

slily var. of SLYLY (see SLY).

slim *adj. & v.* —*adj.* (**slimmer, slimmest**) **1 a** of small girth or thickness, of long narrow shape. **b** gracefully thin, slenderly built. **c** not fat or overweight. **2** small, insufficient (*a slim chance of success*). —*v.* (**slimmed, slimming**) **1** *intr.* make oneself slimmer by dieting, exercise, etc. **2** *tr.* make slim or slimmer. □ **slimly** *adv.* **slimmer** *n.* **slimming** *n. & adj.* **slimmish** *adj.* **slimness** *n.* [LG or Du. f. Gmc]

slime *n. & v.* —*n.* thick slippery mud or a substance of similar consistency. —*v.tr.* cover with slime. [OE *slīm* f. Gmc, rel. to L *limus* mud, Gk *limnē* marsh]

slimline /ˈslɪmlaɪn/ *adj.* of slender design.

slimy /ˈslaɪmɪ/ *adj.* (**slimier, slimiest**) **1** of the consistency of slime. **2** covered, smeared with, or full of slime. **3** disgustingly dishonest, meek, or flattering. **4** slippery, hard to hold. □ **slimily** *adv.* **sliminess** *n.*

sling[1] *n. & v.* —*n.* **1** a strap, belt, etc., used to support or raise a hanging weight, e.g. a rifle, a ship's boat, or goods being transferred. **2** a bandage looped round the neck to support an injured arm. **3** a strap or string used with the hand to give impetus to a small missile, esp. a stone. —*v.tr.* (*past* and *past part.* **slung** /slʌŋ/) **1** (also *absol.*) hurl (a stone etc.) from a sling. **2** *colloq.* throw. **3** suspend with a sling, allow to swing suspended, arrange so as to be supported from above, hoist or transfer with a sling. □ **sling-back** a shoe held in place by a strap above the heel. **sling-bag** a bag with a long strap which may be hung from the shoulder. **sling off at** *Austral. & NZ sl.* disparage; mock; make fun of. [ME, prob. f. ON *slyngva* (v.)]

sling[2] *n.* a sweetened drink of spirits (esp. gin) and water. [18th c.: orig. unkn.]

slinger /ˈslɪŋə(r)/ *n.* a person who slings, esp. the user of a sling.

slingshot /ˈslɪŋʃɒt/ *n. US* a catapult.

slink *v.intr.* (*past* and *past part.* **slunk**) (often foll. by *off, away, by*) move in a stealthy or guilty or sneaking manner. [OE *slincan* crawl]

slinky /ˈslɪŋkɪ/ *adj.* (**slinkier, slinkiest**) **1** stealthy. **2** (of a garment) close-fitting and flowing, sinuous. **3** gracefully slender. □ **slinkily** *adv.* **slinkiness** *n.*

slip[1] *v. & n.* —*v.* (**slipped, slipping**) **1** *intr.* slide unintentionally esp. for a short distance; lose one's footing or balance or place by unintended sliding. **2** *intr.* go or move with a sliding motion (*as the door closes the catch slips into place; slipped into her nightdress*). **3** *intr.* escape restraint or capture by being slippery or hard to hold or by not being grasped (*the eel slipped through his fingers*). **4** *intr.* make one's or its way unobserved or quietly or quickly (*just slip across to the baker's; errors will slip in*). **5** *intr.* **a** make a careless or casual mistake. **b** fall below the normal standard, deteriorate, lapse. **6** *tr.* insert or transfer stealthily or casually or with a sliding motion (*slipped a coin into his hand; slipped the papers into his pocket*). **7** *tr.* a release from restraint (*slipped the greyhounds from the leash*). **b** release (the clutch of a motor vehicle) for a moment. **8** *tr.* move (a stitch) to the other needle without knitting it. **9** *tr.* (foll. by *on, off*) pull (a garment) hastily on or off. **10** *tr.* escape from; give the slip to (*the dog slipped its collar; point slipped my mind*). —*n.* **1** the act or an instance of slipping. **2** an accidental or slight error. **3** a loose covering or garment, esp. a petticoat or pillowcase. **4 a** a reduction in the movement of a pulley etc. due to slipping of the belt. **b** a reduction in the distance travelled by a ship or aircraft arising from the nature of the medium in which its propeller revolves. **5** (in *sing.* or *pl.*) **a** an artificial slope of stone etc. on which boats are landed. **b** an inclined structure on which ships are built or repaired. **6** *Cricket* **a** a fielder stationed for balls glancing off the bat to the off side. **b** (in *sing.* or *pl.*) the position of such a fielder (*caught in the slips; caught at slip*). □ **give a person the slip** escape from or evade him or her. **let slip 1** release accidentally or deliberately, esp. from a leash. **2** miss (an opportunity). **3** utter inadvertently. **slip away** depart without leavetaking etc. **slip-case** a close-fitting case for a book. **slip-cover 1 a** a calico etc. cover for furniture out of use. **b** *US* = *loose cover*. **2** a jacket or slip-case for a book. **slip-knot 1** a knot that can be undone by a pull. **2** a running knot. **slip off** depart without leave-taking etc. **slip of the pen** (or **tongue**) a small mistake in which something is written (or said) unintentionally. **slip-on** *adj.* (of shoes or clothes) that can be easily slipped on and off. —*n.* a slip-on shoe or garment. **slip-over** (of a garment) to be slipped on over the head. **slipped disc** a disc between vertebrae that has become displaced and causes lumbar pain. **slip-road** *Brit.* a road for entering or leaving a motorway etc. **slip-stitch** *n.* **1** a loose stitch joining layers of fabric and not visible externally. **2** a stitch moved to the other needle without being knitted. —*v.tr.* sew with slip-stitch. **slip up** *colloq.* make a mistake. **slip-up** *n. colloq.* a mistake, a blunder. [ME prob. f. MLG *slippen*: cf. SLIPPERY]

slip[2] *n.* **1** a small piece of paper esp. for writing on. **2** a cutting taken from a plant for grafting or planting, a scion. [ME, prob. f. MDu., MLG *slippe* cut, strip, etc.]

slip[3] *n.* clay in a creamy mixture with water, used mainly for decorating earthenware. [OE *slipa*, *slyppe* slime: cf. COWSLIP]

slipover /ˈslɪpˌəʊvə(r)/ *n.* a pullover, usu. without sleeves.

slippage /ˈslɪpɪdʒ/ *n.* **1** the act or an instance of slipping. **2 a** a decline, esp. in popularity or value. **b** failure to meet a deadline or fulfil a promise; delay.

slipper /ˈslɪpə(r)/ *n.* **1** a light loose comfortable indoor shoe. **2** a light slip-on shoe for dancing etc. □ **slippered** *adj.*

slippery /ˈslɪpərɪ/ *adj.* **1** difficult to hold firmly because of smoothness, wetness, sliminess, or elusive motion. **2** (of a surface) difficult to stand on, causing slips by its smoothness or muddiness. **3** unreliable, unscrupulous, shifty. **4** (of a subject) requiring tactful handling. □ **slippery slope** a course leading to disaster. □ **slipperily** *adv.* **slipperiness** *n.* [prob. coined by Coverdale (1535) after Luther's *schlipfferig*, MHG *slipferig* f. *slipfern*, *slipfen* f. Gmc: partly f. *slipper* slippery (now dial.) f. OE *slipor* f. Gmc]

slippy /ˈslɪpɪ/ *adj.* (**slippier**, **slippiest**) *colloq.* slippery. □ **look** (or **be**) **slippy** *Brit.* look sharp; make haste. □ **slippiness** *n.*

slipshod /ˈslɪpʃɒd/ *adj.* **1** (of speech or writing, a speaker or writer, a method of work, etc.) careless, unsystematic; loose in arrangement. **2** slovenly. **3** having shoes down at heel.

slipstream /ˈslɪpstriːm/ *n.* & *v.* —*n.* **1** a current of air or water driven back by a revolving propeller or a moving vehicle. **2** an assisting force regarded as drawing something along with or behind something else. —*v.tr.* **1** follow closely behind (another vehicle). **2** pass after travelling in another's slipstream.

slipway /ˈslɪpweɪ/ *n.* a slip for building ships or landing boats.

slit *n.* & *v.* —*n.* **1** a long straight narrow incision. **2** a long narrow opening comparable to a cut. —*v.tr.* (**slitting**; *past* and *past part.* **slit**) **1** make

a slit in; cut or tear lengthwise. **2** cut into strips. □ **slitter** *n.* [ME *slitte*, rel. to OE *slītan*, f. Gmc]

slither /ˈslɪðə(r)/ *v.* & *n.* —*v.intr.* slide unsteadily; go with an irregular slipping motion. —*n.* an instance of slithering. □ **slithery** *adj.* [ME var. of *slidder* (now dial.) f. OE *slid(e)rian* frequent. f. *slid-*, weak grade of *slīdan* SLIDE]

slitty /ˈslɪtɪ/ *adj.* (**slittier**, **slittiest**) (of the eyes) long and narrow.

sliver /ˈslɪvə(r), ˈslaɪvə(r)/ *n.* & *v.* —*n.* a long thin piece cut or split off. —*v.tr.* & *intr.* **1** break off as a sliver. **2** break up into slivers. **3** form into slivers. [ME, rel. to *slive* cleave (now dial.) f. OE]

Sloane /sləʊn/ *n.* (in full **Sloane Ranger**) *Brit. sl.* a fashionable and conventional upper-class young person, esp. living in London. □ **Sloaney** *adj.* [*Sloane Square*, London + *Lone Ranger*, a cowboy hero]

slob *n. colloq.* a stupid, careless, coarse, or fat person. □ **slobbish** *adj.* [Ir. *slab* mud f. E *slab* ooze, sludge, prob. f. Scand.]

slobber /ˈslɒbə(r)/ *v.* & *n.* —*v.intr.* **1** slaver. **2** (foll. by *over*) show excessive sentiment. —*n.* saliva running from the mouth; slaver. □ **slobbery** *adj.* [ME, = Du. *slobbern*, of imit. orig.]

sloe /sləʊ/ *n.* **1** = BLACKTHORN. **2** its small bluish-black fruit with a sharp sour taste. □ **sloe-gin** a liqueur of sloes steeped in gin. [OE *slā*(h) f. Gmc]

slog *v.* & *n.* —*v.* (**slogged**, **slogging**) **1** *intr.* & *tr.* hit hard and usu. wildly esp. in boxing or at cricket. **2** *intr.* (often foll. by *away*, *on*) walk or work doggedly. —*n.* **1** a hard random hit. **2 a** hard steady work. **b** a spell of this. □ **slogger** *n.* [19th c.: orig. unkn.: cf. SLUG[2]]

slogan /ˈsləʊgən/ *n.* **1** a short catchy phrase used in advertising etc. **2** a party cry; a watchword or motto. [Gael. *sluagh-ghairm* f. *sluagh* army + *gairm* shout]

sloop /sluːp/ *n.* a small one-masted fore-and-aft-rigged vessel. [Du. *sloep*(e), of unkn. orig.]

sloosh /sluːʃ/ *n.* & *v. colloq.* —*n.* a pouring or pouring sound of water. —*v.intr.* **1** flow with a rush. **2** make a heavy splashing or rushing noise. [imit.]

slop *v.* & *n.* —*v.* (**slopped**, **slopping**) **1** (often foll. by *over*) **a** *intr.* spill or flow over the edge of a vessel. **b** *tr.* allow to do this. **2** *tr.* make (the floor, clothes, etc.) wet or messy by slopping, spill or splash liquid on. **3** *intr.* (usu. foll. by *over*) gush; be effusive or maudlin. —*n.* **1** a quantity of liquid spilled or splashed. **2** sentimental language. **3** (in *pl.*) waste liquid, esp. dirty water or the waste contents of kitchen, bedroom, or prison vessels. **4** (in *sing.* or *pl.*) unappetizing weak liquid food. □ **slop about** move about in a slovenly manner. **slop-basin** *Brit.* a basin for the dregs of cups at table. **slop out** carry slops out (in prison etc.). [earlier sense 'slush', prob. rel. to *slyppe*: cf. COWSLIP]

slope *n.* & *v.* —*n.* **1** an inclined position or direction; a state in which one end or side is at a higher level than another; a position in a line neither parallel nor perpendicular to level ground or to a line serving as a standard. **2** a piece of rising or falling ground. **3 a** a difference in level between the two ends or sides of a thing (*a slope of 5 metres*). **b** the rate at which this increases with distance etc. **4** a place for skiing on the side of a hill or mountain. **5** (prec. by *the*) the position of a rifle when sloped. —*v.* **1**

sloppy | slug

intr. have or take a slope; slant esp. up or down; lie or tend obliquely, esp. to ground level. **2** *tr.* place or arrange or make in or at a slope. □ **slope arms** place one's rifle in a sloping position against one's shoulder. **slope off** *sl.* go away, esp. to evade work etc. [shortening of ME *aslope* sloping]

sloppy /ˈslɒpɪ/ *adj.* (**sloppier, sloppiest**) **1 a** (of the ground) wet with rain; full of puddles. **b** (of food etc.) watery and disagreeable. **c** (of a floor, table, etc.) wet with slops, having water etc. spilt on it. **2** unsystematic, careless, not thorough. **3** (of a garment) ill-fitting or untidy. **4** (of sentiment or talk) weakly emotional, maudlin. □ **sloppily** *adv.* **sloppiness** *n.*

slosh *v.* & *n.* —*v.* **1** *intr.* (often foll. by *about*) splash or flounder about, move with a splashing sound. **2** *tr. Brit. sl.* hit esp. heavily. **3** *tr. colloq.* **a** pour (liquid) clumsily. **b** pour liquid on. —*n.* **1** slush. **2 a** an instance of splashing. **b** the sound of this. **3** *Brit. sl.* a heavy blow. **4** a quantity of liquid. [var. of SLUSH]

sloshed /slɒʃt/ *adj. Brit. sl.* drunk.

sloshy /ˈslɒʃɪ/ *adj.* (**sloshier, sloshiest**) **1** slushy. **2** sloppy, sentimental.

slot *n.* & *v.* —*n.* **1** a slit or other aperture in a machine etc. for something (esp. a coin) to be inserted. **2** a slit, groove, channel, or long aperture into which something fits or in which something works. **3** an allotted place in an arrangement or scheme, esp. in a broadcasting schedule. —*v.* (**slotted, slotting**) **1** *tr.* & *intr.* place or be placed into or as if into a slot. **2** *tr.* provide with a slot or slots. □ **slot-machine** a machine worked by the insertion of a coin, esp.: **1** one for automatic retail of small articles. **2** one allowing a spell of play at a pin-table etc. **3** *US* = *fruit machine.* [ME, = hollow of the breast, f. OF *esclot,* of unkn. orig.]

sloth /sləʊθ/ *n.* **1** laziness or indolence; reluctance to make an effort. **2** any slow-moving nocturnal mammal of the family Bradypodidae or Megalonychidae of S. America, having long limbs and hooked claws for hanging upside down from branches of trees. [ME f. SLOW + -TH²]

slothful /ˈsləʊθfʊl/ *adj.* lazy; characterized by sloth. □ **slothfully** *adv.* **slothfulness** *n.*

slouch /slaʊtʃ/ *v.* & *n.* —*v.* **1** *intr.* stand or move or sit in a drooping ungainly fashion. **2** *tr.* bend one side of the brim of (a hat) downwards. **3** *intr.* droop, hang down loosely. —*n.* **1** a slouching posture or movement, a stoop. **2** a downward bend of a hat-brim. **3** *sl.* an incompetent or slovenly worker or operator or performance. □ **slouch hat** a hat with a wide flexible brim. □ **slouchy** *adj.* (**slouchier, slouchiest**). [16th c.: orig. unkn.]

slough¹ /slaʊ/ *n.* a swamp; a miry place; a quagmire. □ **Slough of Despond** a state of hopeless depression (with ref. to Bunyan's *Pilgrim's Progress*). □ **sloughy** *adj.* [OE *slōh, slō(g)*]

slough² /slʌf/ *n.* & *v.* —*n.* a part that an animal casts or moults, esp. a snake's cast skin. —*v.* **1** *tr.* cast off as a slough. **2** *intr.* (often foll. by *off*) drop off as a slough. **3** *intr.* cast off a slough. □ **sloughy** *adj.* [ME, perh. rel. to LG *slu(we)* husk]

Slovak /ˈsləʊvæk/ *n.* & *adj.* —*n.* **1** a member of a Slavonic people inhabiting Slovakia in Czechoslovakia. **2** the language of this people, one of the two official languages of Czechoslovakia.

—*adj.* of or relating to this people or language. [Slovak etc. *Slovák,* rel. to SLOVENE]

sloven /ˈslʌv(ə)n/ *n.* a person who is habitually untidy or careless. [ME perh. f. Flem. *sloef* dirty or Du. *slof* careless]

Slovene /ˈsləʊviːn, sləˈviːn/ (also **Slovenian** /-ˈviːnɪən/) *n.* & *adj.* —*n.* **1** a member of a Slavonic people in Slovenia, formerly in Yugoslavia. **2** the language of this people. —*adj.* of or relating to Slovenia or its people or language. [G *Slowene* f. Styrian etc. *Slovenec* f. OSlav. *Slov-,* perh. rel. to *slovo* word]

slovenly /ˈslʌvənlɪ/ *adj.* & *adv.* —*adj.* careless and untidy; unmethodical. —*adv.* in a slovenly manner. □ **slovenliness** *n.*

slow /sləʊ/ *adj., adv.,* & *v.* —*adj.* **1 a** taking a relatively long time to do a thing or cover a distance (also foll. by *of: slow of speech*). **b** not quick; acting or moving or done without speed. **2** gradual; obtained over a length of time (*slow growth*). **3** not producing, allowing, or conducive to speed (*in the slow lane*). **4** (of a clock etc.) showing a time earlier than is the case. **5** (of a person) not understanding readily; not learning easily. **6** dull; uninteresting; tedious. **7** slack or sluggish (*business is slow*). **8** (of a fire or oven) giving little heat. **9** *Photog.* **a** (of a film) needing long exposure. **b** (of a lens) having a small aperture. **10 a** reluctant; tardy (*not slow to defend himself*). **b** not hasty or easily moved (*slow to take offence*). —*adv.* **1** at a slow pace; slowly. **2** (in comb.) (*slow-moving traffic*). —*v.* (usu. foll. by *down, up*) **1** *intr.* & *tr.* reduce one's speed or the speed of (a vehicle etc.). **2** *intr.* reduce one's pace of life; live or work less intensely. □ **slow-down** the action of slowing down; a go-slow. **slow handclap** slow clapping by an audience as a sign of displeasure or boredom. **slow march** the marching time adopted by troops in a funeral procession etc. **slow motion 1** the operation or speed of a film using slower projection or more rapid exposure so that actions etc. appear much slower than usual. **2** the simulation of this in real action. □ **slowish** *adj.* **slowly** *adv.* **slowness** *n.* [OE *slāw* f. Gmc]

slowcoach /ˈsləʊkəʊtʃ/ *n. Brit.* **1** a slow or lazy person. **2** a dull-witted person. **3** a person behind the times in opinions etc.

slowpoke /ˈsləʊpəʊk/ *n. US* = SLOWCOACH.

slow-worm /ˈsləʊwɜːm/ *n.* a small European legless lizard, *Anguis fragilis.* [OE *slā-wyrm:* first element of uncert. orig., assim. to SLOW]

slub *n.* & *adj.* —*n.* **1** a lump or thick place in yarn or thread. **2** fabric woven from thread etc. with slubs. —*adj.* (of material etc.) with an irregular appearance caused by uneven thickness of the warp. [19th c.: orig. unkn.]

sludge *n.* **1** thick greasy mud. **2** muddy or slushy sediment. **3** sewage. **4** *Mech.* an accumulation of dirty oil, esp. in the sump of an internal-combustion engine. □ **sludgy** *adj.* [cf. SLUSH]

slue var. of SLEW¹.

slug¹ *n.* **1** a small shell-less mollusc of the class Gastropoda often destructive to plants. **2 a** a bullet esp. of irregular shape. **b** a missile for an airgun. **3** *Printing* **a** a metal bar used in spacing. **b** a line of type in Linotype printing. **4** esp. *US* a tot of liquor. [ME *slugg(e)* sluggard, prob. f. Scand.]

slug² *v.* & *n. US* —*v.tr.* (**slugged, slugging**) strike with a hard blow. —*n.* a hard blow. □ **slug it**

out 1 fight it out. **2** endure; stick it out. □ **slugger** n. [19th c.: orig. unkn.]

slugabed /ˈslʌɡəˌbed/ n. archaic a lazy person who lies late in bed. [slug (v.) (see SLUGGARD) + ABED]

sluggard /ˈslʌɡəd/ n. a lazy sluggish person. □ **sluggardly** adv. **sluggardliness** n. [ME f. slug (v.) be slothful (prob. f. Scand.: cf. SLUG¹) + -ARD]

sluggish /ˈslʌɡɪʃ/ adj. inert; inactive; slow-moving; torpid; indolent (a sluggish circulation; a sluggish stream). □ **sluggishly** adv. **sluggishness** n. [ME f. SLUG¹ or slug (v.): see SLUGGARD]

sluice /sluːs/ n. & v. —n. **1** (also **sluice-gate, sluice-valve**) a sliding gate or other contrivance for controlling the volume or flow of water. **2** (also **sluice-way**) an artificial water-channel esp. for washing ore. **3** a place for rinsing. **4** the act or an instance of rinsing. **5** the water above or below or issuing through a floodgate. —v. **1** tr. provide or wash with a sluice or sluices. **2** tr. rinse, pour or throw water freely upon. **3** (foll. by out, away) wash out or away with a flow of water. **4** tr. flood with water from a sluice. **5** intr. (of water) rush out from a sluice, or as if from a sluice. [ME f. OF escluse ult. f. L excludere EXCLUDE]

slum n. & v. —n. **1** an overcrowded and squalid back street, district, etc., usu. in a city and inhabited by very poor people. **2** a house or building unfit for human habitation. —v.intr. (**slummed, slumming**) **1** live in slumlike conditions. **2** go about the slums through curiosity, to examine the condition of the inhabitants, or for charitable purposes. □ **slum it** colloq. put up with conditions less comfortable than usual. □ **slummy** adj. (**slummier, slummiest**). **slumminess** n. [19th c.: orig. cant]

slumber /ˈslʌmbə(r)/ v. & n. poet. rhet. —v.intr. **1** sleep, esp. in a specified manner. **2** be idle, drowsy, or inactive. —n. a sleep, esp. of a specified kind (fell into a fitful slumber). □ **slumberer** n. **slumberous** adj. **slumbrous** adj. [ME slūmere etc. f. slūmen (v.) or slūme (n.) f. OE slūma: -b- as in number]

slump n. & v. —n. **1** a sudden severe or prolonged fall in prices or values of commodities or securities. **2** a sharp or sudden decline in trade or business usu. bringing widespread unemployment. **3** a lessening of interest or commitment in a subject or undertaking. —v.intr. **1** undergo a slump; fail; fall in price. **2** sit or fall heavily or limply (slumped into a chair). **3** lean or subside. [17th c., orig. 'sink in a bog': imit.]

slung past and past part. of SLING¹.

slunk past and past part. of SLINK.

slur v. & n. —v. (**slurred, slurring**) **1** tr. & intr. pronounce or write indistinctly so that the sounds or letters run into one another. **2** tr. Mus. **a** perform (a group of two or more notes) legato. **b** mark (notes) with a slur. **3** tr. archaic or US put a slur on (a person or a person's character); make insinuations against. **4** tr. (usu. foll. by over) pass over (a fact, fault, etc.) lightly; conceal or minimize. —n. **1** an imputation of wrongdoing; blame; stigma (a slur on my reputation). **2** the act or an instance of slurring in pronunciation, singing, or writing. **3** Mus. a curved line to show that two or more notes are to be sung to one syllable or played or sung legato. [17th c.: orig. unkn.]

slurp v. & n. —v.tr. eat or drink noisily. —n. the sound of this; a slurping gulp. [Du. slurpen, slorpen]

slurry /ˈslʌrɪ/ n. (pl. **-ies**) **1** a semi-liquid mixture of fine particles and water; thin mud. **2** thin liquid cement. **3** a fluid form of manure. [ME, rel. to dial. slur thin mud]

slush n. **1** watery mud or thawing snow. **2** silly sentiment. □ **slush fund** reserve funding esp. as used for political bribery. [17th c., also sludge and slutch: orig. unkn.]

slushy /ˈslʌʃɪ/ adj. (**slushier, slushiest**) like slush; watery. □ **slushiness** n.

slut n. derog. a slovenly woman; a slattern; a hussy. □ **sluttish** adj. **sluttishness** n. [ME: orig. unkn.]

sly adj. (**slyer, slyest**) **1** cunning; crafty; wily. **2 a** (of a person) practising secrecy or stealth. **b** (of an action etc.) done etc. in secret. **3** hypocritical; ironical. **4** knowing; arch; bantering; insinuating. **5** Austral. & NZ sl. (esp. of liquor) illicit. □ **on the sly** privately; covertly; without publicity. □ **slyly** adv. (also **slily**). **slyness** n. [ME sleh etc. f. ON slœgr cunning, orig. 'able to strike' f. slóg-past stem of slá strike: cf. SLEIGHT]

slyboots /ˈslaɪbuːts/ n. colloq. a sly person.

Sm symb. Chem. the element samarium.

smack¹ n., v., & adv. —n. **1** a sharp slap or blow esp. with the palm of the hand or a flat object. **2** a hard hit at cricket etc. **3** a loud kiss (gave her a hearty smack). **4** a loud sharp sound (heard the smack as it hit the floor). —v. **1** tr. strike with the open hand etc. **2** tr. part (one's lips) noisily in eager anticipation or enjoyment of food or another delight. **3** tr. crack (a whip). **4** tr. & intr. move, hit, etc., with a smack. —adv. colloq. **1** with a smack. **2** suddenly; directly; violently (landed smack on my desk). **3** exactly (hit it smack in the centre). □ **have a smack at** colloq. make an attempt, attack, etc., at. **a smack in the eye** (or **face**) colloq. a rebuff; a setback. [MDu. smack(en) of imit. orig.]

smack² v. & n. (foll. by of) —v.intr. **1** have a flavour of; taste of (smacked of garlic). **2** suggest the presence or effects of (it smacks of nepotism). —n. **1** a flavour; a taste that suggests the presence of something. **2** (in a person's character etc.) a barely discernible quality (just a smack of superciliousness). [OE smæc]

smack³ n. a single-masted sailing-boat for coasting or fishing. [Du. smak f. earlier smacke; orig. unkn.]

smack⁴ n. sl. a hard drug, esp. heroin, sold or used illegally. [prob. alt. of Yiddish schmeck sniff]

smacker /ˈsmækə(r)/ n. sl. **1** a loud kiss. **2** a resounding blow. **3 a** Brit. £1. **b** US $1.

small /smɔːl/ adj., n., & adv. —adj. **1** not large or big. **2** slender; thin. **3** not great in importance, amount, number, strength, or power. **4** not much; trifling (a small token; paid small attention). **5** insignificant; unimportant (a small matter; from small beginnings). **6** consisting of small particles (small gravel; small shot). **7** doing something on a small scale (a small farmer). **8** socially undistinguished; poor or humble. **9** petty; mean; ungenerous; paltry (a small spiteful nature). **10** young; not fully grown or developed (a small child). —n. **1** the slenderest part of something (esp. small of the back). **2** (in pl.) Brit. colloq. small items of laundry, esp. underwear. —adv. into small pieces (chop it small). □ **in a small way**

unambitiously; on a small scale. **no small** considerable; a good deal of (*no small excitement about it*). **small arms** portable firearms, esp. rifles, pistols, light machine-guns, sub-machine-guns, etc. **small beer 1** a trifling matter; something unimportant. **2** weak beer. **small change 1** money in the form of coins as opposed to notes. **2** trivial remarks. **small craft** a general term for small boats and fishing vessels. **small fry 1** young children or the young of various species. **2** small or insignificant things or people. **small hours** the early hours of the morning after midnight. **small letter** (in printed material) a lower-case letter. **small potatoes** an insignificant person or thing. **small print 1** printed matter in small type. **2** inconspicuous and usu. unfavourable limitations etc. in a contract. **small-scale** made or occurring in small amounts or to a lesser degree. **small talk** light social conversation. **small-time** *colloq.* unimportant or petty. **small-town** relating to or characteristic of a small town; unsophisticated; provincial. □ **smallish** *adj.* **smallness** *n.* [OE *smæl* f. Gmc]

smallgoods /ˈsmɔːlɡʊdz/ *n. Austral.* delicatessen meats.

smallholder /ˈsmɔːlˌhəʊldə(r)/ *n. Brit.* a person who farms a smallholding.

smallholding /ˈsmɔːlˌhəʊldɪŋ/ *n. Brit.* an agricultural holding smaller than a farm.

small-minded /smɔːlˈmaɪndɪd/ *adj.* petty; of rigid opinions or narrow outlook. □ **small-mindedly** *adv.* **small-mindedness** *n.*

smallpox /ˈsmɔːlpɒks/ *n. hist.* an acute contagious viral disease, with fever and pustules, usu. leaving permanent scars.

smarm *v.tr. colloq.* **1** (often foll. by *down*) smooth, plaster down (hair etc.) usu. with cream or oil. **2** flatter fulsomely. [orig. dial. (also *smalm*), of uncert. orig.]

smarmy /ˈsmɑːmɪ/ *adj.* (**smarmier**, **smarmiest**) *colloq.* ingratiating; flattering; obsequious. □ **smarmily** *adv.* **smarminess** *n.*

smart *adj., v., n., & adv.* —*adj.* **1 a** clever; ingenious; quickwitted (*a smart talker; gave a smart answer*). **b** keen in bargaining; quick to take advantage. **c** (of transactions etc.) unscrupulous to the point of dishonesty. **2** well-groomed; neat; fresh and bright in appearance (*a smart suit*). **3** in good repair; showing bright colours, new paint, etc. (*a smart red bicycle*). **4** stylish; fashionable; prominent in society (*in all the smart restaurants; the smart set*). **5** quick; brisk (*set a smart pace*). **6** painfully severe; sharp; vigorous (*a smart blow*). —*v.intr.* **1** (of a person or a part of the body) feel or give acute pain or distress (*my eye smarts; smarting from the insult*). **2** (of an insult, grievance, etc.) rankle. **3** (foll. by *for*) suffer the consequences of (*you will smart for this*). —*n.* a bodily or mental sharp pain; a stinging sensation. —*adv.* smartly; in a smart manner. □ **smart-arse** (or **-ass**) = SMART ALEC. **smart-money 1** money paid or exacted as a penalty or compensation. **2** money invested by persons with expert knowledge. □ **smartingly** *adv.* **smartish** *adj. & adv.* **smartly** *adv.* **smartness** *n.* [OE *smeart, smeortan*]

smart alec /ˈælɪk/ *n.* (also **aleck, alick**) *colloq.* a person displaying ostentatious or smug cleverness. □ **smart-alecky** *adj.* [SMART + *Alec*, dimin. of the name *Alexander*]

smarten /ˈsmɑːt(ə)n/ *v.tr. & intr.* (usu. foll. by *up*) make or become smart or smarter.

smarty /ˈsmɑːtɪ/ *n.* (pl. **-ies**) *colloq.* **1** a know-all; a smart alec. **2** a smartly-dressed person; a member of a smart set. □ **smarty-boots** (or **-pants**) = SMARTY 1. [SMART]

smash *v., n., & adv.* —*v.* **1** *tr. & intr.* (often foll. by *up*) **a** break into pieces; shatter. **b** bring or come to sudden or complete destruction, defeat, or disaster. **2** *tr.* (foll. by *into, through*) (of a vehicle etc.) move with great force and impact. **3** *tr. & intr.* (foll. by *in*) break in with a crushing blow (*smashed in the window*). **4** *tr.* (in tennis, squash, etc.) hit (a ball etc.) with great force, esp. downwards (*smashed it back over the net*). **5** *intr.* (of a business etc.) go bankrupt, come to grief. **6** *tr.* (as **smashed** *adj.*) *sl.* intoxicated. —*n.* **1** the act or an instance of smashing; a violent fall, collision, or disaster. **2** the sound of this. **3** (in full **smash hit**) a very successful play, song, performer, etc. **4** a stroke in tennis, squash, etc., in which the ball is hit esp. downwards with great force. **5** a violent blow with a fist etc. **6** bankruptcy; a series of commercial failures. —*adv.* with a smash (*fell smash on the floor*). □ **go to smash** be ruined etc. **smash-and-grab** (of a robbery etc.) in which the thief smashes a shop-window and seizes goods. **smash-up** a violent collision; a complete smash. [18th c., prob. imit. after *smack*, *smite* and *bash, mash*, etc.]

smasher /ˈsmæʃə(r)/ *n.* **1** *colloq.* a very beautiful or pleasing person or thing. **2** a person or thing that smashes.

smashing /ˈsmæʃɪŋ/ *adj. colloq.* superlative; excellent; wonderful; beautiful. □ **smashingly** *adv.*

smatter /ˈsmætə(r)/ *n.* (also **smattering**) a slight superficial knowledge of a language or subject. □ **smatterer** *n.* [ME *smatter* talk ignorantly, prate: orig. unkn.]

smear *v. & n.* —*v.tr.* **1** daub or mark with a greasy or sticky substance or with something that stains. **2** blot; smudge; obscure the outline of (writing, artwork, etc.). **3** defame the character of; slander; attempt to or succeed in discrediting (a person or his name) publicly. —*n.* **1** the act or an instance of smearing. **2** *Med.* a material smeared on a microscopic slide etc. for examination. **b** a specimen of this. □ **smear test** = *cervical smear.* □ **smearer** *n.* **smeary** *adj.* [OE *smierwan* f. Gmc]

smell *n. & v.* —*n.* **1** the faculty of perceiving odours or scents (*has a fine sense of smell*). **2** the quality in substances that is perceived by this (*the smell of thyme; this rose has no smell*). **3** an unpleasant odour. **4** the act of inhaling to ascertain smell. —*v.* (*past* and *past part.* **smelt** or **smelled**) **1** *tr.* perceive the smell of; examine by smell (*thought I could smell gas*). **2** *intr.* emit odour. **3** *intr.* seem by smell to be (*this milk smells sour*). **4** *intr.* (foll. by *of*) **a** be redolent of (*smells of fish*). **b** be suggestive of (*smells of dishonesty*). **5** *intr.* stink; be rank. **6** *tr.* perceive as if by smell; detect, discern, suspect (*smell a bargain; smell blood*). **7** *intr.* have or use a sense of smell. **8** *intr.* (foll. by *about*) sniff or search about. **9** *intr.* (foll. by *at*) inhale the smell of. □ **smelling-salts** ammonium carbonate mixed with scent to be sniffed as a restorative in faintness etc. **smell out 1** detect by smell; find out by investigation.

2 (of a dog etc.) hunt out by smell. □ **smell a rat** begin to suspect trickery etc. □ **smellable** *adj.* **smeller** *n.* **smell-less** *adj.* [ME *smel(le)*, prob. f. OE]

smelly /'smelɪ/ *adj.* (**smellier**, **smelliest**) having a strong or unpleasant smell. □ **smelliness** *n.*

smelt[1] *v.tr.* **1** extract metal from (ore) by melting. **2** extract (metal) from ore by melting. □ **smelter** *n.* **smeltery** *n.* (*pl.* **-ies**). [MDu., MLG *smelten*, rel. to MELT]

smelt[2] *past* and *past part.* of SMELL.

smelt[3] *n.* (*pl.* same or **smelts**) any small green and silver fish of the genus *Osmerus* etc. allied to salmon and used as food. [OE, of uncert. orig.]

smidgen /'smɪdʒ(ə)n/ *n.* (also **smidgin** /-dʒɪn/) *colloq.* a small bit or amount. [perh. f. *smitch* in the same sense: cf. dial. *smitch* wood-smoke]

smile *v.* & *n.* —*v.* **1** *intr.* relax the features into a pleased or kind or gently sceptical expression or a forced imitation of these, usu. with the lips parted and the corners of the mouth turned up. **2** *tr.* express by smiling (*smiled their consent*). **3** *tr.* give (a smile) of a specified kind (*smiled a sardonic smile*). **4** *intr.* (foll. by *on*, *upon*) adopt a favourable attitude towards; encourage (*fortune smiled on me*). **5** *intr.* have a bright or favourable aspect (*the smiling countryside*). **6** *intr.* (foll. by *at*) **a** ridicule or show indifference to (*smiled at my feeble attempts*). **b** favour; smile on. —*n.* **1** the act or an instance of smiling. **2** a smiling expression or aspect. □ **smileless** *adj.* **smiler** *n.* **smiley** *adj.* **smilingly** *adv.* [ME perh. f. Scand., rel. to SMIRK: cf. OHG *smīlenter*]

smirch *v.* & *n.* —*v.tr.* mark, soil, or smear (a thing, a person's reputation, etc.). —*n.* **1** a spot or stain. **2** a blot (on one's character etc.). [ME: orig. unkn.]

smirk *n.* & *v.* —*n.* an affected, conceited, or silly smile. —*v.intr.* put on or wear a smirk. □ **smirker** *n.* **smirkingly** *adv.* **smirky** *adj.* **smirkily** *adv.* [OE *sme(a)rcian*]

smite *v.* (*past* **smote**; *past part.* **smitten**) *archaic* or *literary* **1** *tr.* strike or hit. **2** *tr.* chastise; defeat. **3** *tr.* (in *passive*) **a** have a sudden strong effect on (*was smitten by his conscience*). **b** infatuate, fascinate (*was smitten by her beauty*). □ **smiter** *n.* [OE *smītan* smear f. Gmc]

smith /smɪθ/ *n.* & *v.* —*n.* **1** (esp. in *comb.*) a worker in metal (*goldsmith*; *tinsmith*). **2** a person who forges iron; a blacksmith. **3** a craftsman (*wordsmith*). —*v.tr.* make or treat by forging. [OE f. Gmc]

smithereens /ˌsmɪðə'riːnz/ *n.pl.* (also **smithers** /'smɪðəz/) small fragments (*smash into smithereens*). [19th c.: orig. unkn.]

smithy /'smɪðɪ/ *n.* (*pl.* **-ies**) a blacksmith's workshop; a forge. [ME f. ON *smithja*]

smitten *past part.* of SMITE.

smock *n.* & *v.* —*n.* **1** a loose shirtlike garment with the upper part closely gathered in smocking. **2** (also **smock-frock**) a loose overall, esp. *hist.* a field-labourer's outer linen garment. —*v.tr.* adorn with smocking. [OE *smoc*, prob. rel. to OE *smūgan* creep, ON *smjúga* put on a garment]

smocking /'smɒkɪŋ/ *n.* an ornamental effect on cloth made by gathering the material tightly into pleats, often with stitches in a honeycomb pattern.

smog *n.* fog intensified by smoke. □ **smoggy** *adj.* (**smoggier**, **smoggiest**). [portmanteau word]

smoke *n.* & *v.* —*n.* **1** a visible suspension of carbon etc. in air, emitted from a burning substance. **2** an act or period of smoking tobacco (*had a quiet smoke*). **3** *colloq.* a cigarette or cigar (*got a smoke?*). **4** (**the Smoke**) *Brit.* & *Austral. colloq.* a big city, esp. London. —*v.* **1** *intr.* **a** emit smoke or visible vapour (*smoking ruins*). **b** (of a lamp etc.) burn badly with the emission of smoke. **c** (of a chimney or fire) discharge smoke into the room. **2 a** *intr.* inhale and exhale the smoke of a cigarette or cigar or pipe. **b** *intr.* do this habitually. **c** *tr.* use (a cigarette etc.) in this way. **3** *tr.* darken or preserve by the action of smoke (*smoked salmon*). □ **go up in smoke** *colloq.* **1** be destroyed by fire. **2** (of a plan etc.) come to nothing. **smoke bomb** a bomb that emits dense smoke on exploding. **smoked glass** glass darkened with smoke. **smoke-ho** *Austral.* & *NZ colloq.* = SMOKO. **smoke out 1** drive out by means of smoke. **2** drive out of hiding or secrecy etc. **smoke-ring** smoke from a cigarette etc. exhaled in the shape of a ring. □ **smokable** *adj.* (also **smokeable**). [OE *smoca* f. weak grade of the stem of *smēocan* emit smoke]

smokeless /'sməʊklɪs/ *adj.* having or producing little or no smoke. □ **smokeless zone** a district in which it is illegal to create smoke and where only smokeless fuel may be used.

smoker /'sməʊkə(r)/ *n.* **1** a person or thing that smokes, esp. a person who habitually smokes tobacco. **2** a compartment on a train, in which smoking is allowed. **3** esp. *US* an informal social gathering of men.

smokescreen /'sməʊkskriːn/ *n.* **1** a cloud of smoke diffused to conceal (esp. military) operations. **2** a device or ruse for disguising one's activities.

smokestack /'sməʊkstæk/ *n.* **1** a chimney or funnel for discharging the smoke of a locomotive or steamer. **2** a tall chimney.

smoking-room /'sməʊkɪŋˌruːm, -ˌrʊm/ *n.* a room in a hotel or house, kept for smoking in.

smoko /'sməʊkəʊ/ *n.* (*pl.* **-os**) *Austral.* & *NZ colloq.* **1** a stoppage of work for a rest and a smoke. **2** a tea break.

smoky /'sməʊkɪ/ *adj.* (**smokier**, **smokiest**) **1** emitting, veiled or filled with, or obscured by, smoke (*smoky fire*; *smoky room*). **2** stained with or coloured like smoke (*smoky glass*). **3** having the taste or flavour of smoked food (*smoky bacon*). □ **smokily** *adv.* **smokiness** *n.*

smooch /smuːtʃ/ *n.* & *v. colloq.* —*n.* **1** *Brit.* a period of slow dancing close together. **2** a spell of kissing and caressing. —*v.intr.* engage in a smooch. □ **smoocher** *n.* **smoochy** *adj.* (**smoochier**, **smoochiest**). [dial. *smouch* imit.]

smoodge /smuːdʒ/ *v.intr.* (also **smooge**) *Austral.* & *NZ* **1** behave in a fawning or ingratiating manner. **2** behave amorously. [prob. var. of dial. *smudge* kiss, sidle up to, beg in a sneaking way]

smooth /smuːð/ *adj.*, *v.*, *n.*, & *adv.* —*adj.* **1** having a relatively even and regular surface; free from perceptible projections, lumps, indentations, and roughness. **2** not wrinkled, pitted, scored, or hairy (*smooth skin*). **3** that can be traversed without check. **4** (of liquids) of even consistency; without lumps (*mix to a smooth paste*). **5** (of the sea etc.) without waves or undulations. **6** (of a journey, passage, progress, etc.) untroubled by difficulties or adverse conditions. **7** having an easy flow or correct rhythm. **8 a** not harsh in sound or taste. **b** (of wine etc.) not astringent. **9** (of a person, his or her manner, etc.) suave, conciliatory, flattering, unruffled, or polite (*a smooth talker; he's very smooth*). **10** (of movement etc.) not suddenly varying; not jerky. —*v.* **1** *tr.* & *intr.* (often foll. by *out, down*) make or become smooth. **2** (often foll. by *out, down, over, away*) **a** *tr.* reduce or get rid of (differences, faults, difficulties, etc.) in fact or appearance. **b** *intr.* (of difficulties etc.) diminish, become less obtrusive (*it will all smooth over*). **3** *tr.* modify (a graph, curve, etc.) so as to lessen irregularities. **4** *tr.* free from impediments or discomfort (*smooth the way; smooth the declining years*). —*n.* **1** a smoothing touch or stroke (*gave his hair a smooth*). **2** the easy part of life (*take the rough with the smooth*). —*adv.* smoothly (*the course of true love never did run smooth*). □ **smooth-tongued** insincerely flattering. □ **smoothable** *adj.* **smoother** *n.* **smoothish** *adj.* **smoothly** *adv.* **smoothness** *n.* [OE *smōth*]

smoothie /ˈsmuːðɪ/ *n. colloq.* a person who is smooth (see SMOOTH *adj.* 9). [SMOOTH]

smorgasbord /ˈsmɔːɡəsˌbɔːd/ *n.* open sandwiches served with delicacies as hors d'œuvres or a buffet. [Sw. f. *smör* butter + *gås* goose, lump of butter + *bord* table]

smote *past of* SMITE.

smother /ˈsmʌðə(r)/ *v.* & *n.* —*v.* **1** *tr.* suffocate; stifle; kill by stopping the breath of or excluding air from. **2** *tr.* (often foll. by *with*) overwhelm with (kisses, gifts, kindness, etc.) (*smothered with affection*). **3** *tr.* (foll. by *in, with*) cover entirely in or with (*chicken smothered in mayonnaise*). **4** *tr.* extinguish or deaden (a fire or flame) by covering it or heaping it with ashes etc. **5** *intr.* **a** die of suffocation. **b** have difficulty breathing. **6** *tr.* (often foll. by *up*) suppress or conceal; keep from notice or publicity. **7** *tr.* US defeat rapidly or utterly. —*n.* **1** a cloud of dust or smoke. **2** obscurity caused by this. [ME *smorther* f. the stem of OE *smorian* suffocate]

smoulder /ˈsməʊldə(r)/ *v.* & *n.* (US **smolder**) —*v.intr.* **1** burn slowly with smoke but without a flame; slowly burn internally or invisibly. **2** (of emotions etc.) exist in a suppressed or concealed state. **3** (of a person) show silent or suppressed anger, hatred, etc. —*n.* a smouldering or slow-burning fire. [ME, rel. to LG *smöln*, MDu. *smölen*]

smudge *n.* & *v.* —*n.* **1** a blurred or smeared line or mark; a blot; a smear of dirt. **2** a stain or blot on a person's character etc. —*v.* **1** *tr.* make a smudge on. **2** *intr.* become smeared or blurred (*smudges easily*). **3** *tr.* smear or blur the lines of (writing, drawing, etc.) (*smudge the outline*). **4** *tr.* defile, sully, stain, or disgrace (a person's name, character, etc.). □ **smudgeless** *adj.* [ME: orig. unkn.]

smudgy /ˈsmʌdʒɪ/ *adj.* (**smudgier, smudgiest**) **1** smudged. **2** likely to produce smudges. □ **smudgily** *adv.* **smudginess** *n.*

smug *adj.* (**smugger, smuggest**) self-satisfied; complacent. □ **smugly** *adv.* **smugness** *n.* [16th c., orig. 'neat' f. LG *smuk* pretty]

smuggle /ˈsmʌɡ(ə)l/ *v.tr.* **1** (also *absol.*) import or export (goods) illegally esp. without payment of customs duties. **2** (foll. by *in, out*) convey secretly

3 (foll. by *away*) put into concealment. □ **smuggler** *n.* **smuggling** *n.* [17th c. (also *smuckle*) f. LG *smukkeln smuggelen*]

smut *n.* & *v.* —*n.* **1** a small flake of soot etc. **2** a spot or smudge made by this. **3** obscene or lascivious talk, pictures, or stories. **4** a fungous disease of cereals in which parts of the ear change to black powder. —*v.* (**smutted, smutting**) **1** *tr.* mark with smuts. **2** *tr.* infect (a plant) with smut. **3** *intr.* (of a plant) contract smut. □ **smutty** *adj.* (**smuttier, smuttiest**) (esp. in sense 3 of *n.*). **smuttily** *adv.* **smuttiness** *n.* [rel. to LG *smutt*, MHG *smutz(en)* etc.: cf. OE *smitt(ian)* smear, and SMUDGE]

Sn *symb. Chem.* the element tin.

snack *n.* & *v.* —*n.* **1** a light, casual, or hurried meal. **2** a small amount of food eaten between meals. **3** *Austral. sl.* something easy to accomplish. —*v.intr.* eat a snack. □ **snack bar** a place where snacks are sold. [ME, orig. a snap or bite, f. MDu. *snac(k)* f. *snacken* (v.), var. of *snappen*]

snaffle /ˈsnæf(ə)l/ *n.* & *v.* —*n.* (in full **snaffle-bit**) a simple bridle-bit without a curb and usu. with a single rein. —*v.tr.* **1** put a snaffle on. **2** *colloq.* steal; seize; appropriate. [prob. f. LG or Du.: cf. MLG, MDu. *snavel* beak, mouth]

snafu /snæˈfuː/ *adj.* & *n. sl.* —*adj.* in utter confusion or chaos. —*n.* this state. [acronym for 'situation normal: all fouled (or fucked) up']

snag *n.* & *v.* —*n.* **1** an unexpected or hidden obstacle or drawback. **2** a jagged or projecting point or broken stump. **3** a tear in material etc. —*v.tr.* (**snagged, snagging**) **1** catch or tear on a snag. **2** clear (land, a waterway, a tree-trunk, etc.) of snags. □ **snagged** *adj.* **snaggy** *adj.* [prob. f. Scand.: cf. Norw. *snag* sharp point]

snaggle-tooth /ˈsnæɡ(ə)l/ *n.* (*pl.* **snaggle-teeth**) an irregular or projecting tooth. □ **snaggle-toothed** *adj.* [SNAG + -LE²]

snail *n.* any slow-moving gastropod mollusc with a spiral shell able to enclose the whole body. □ **snail's pace** a very slow movement. □ **snail-like** *adj.* [OE *snæg(e)l* f. Gmc]

snake *n.* & *v.* —*n.* **1 a** any long limbless reptile of the suborder Ophidia, including boas, pythons, and poisonous forms such as cobras and vipers. **b** a limbless lizard or amphibian. **2** (also **snake in the grass**) a treacherous person or secret enemy. —*v.intr.* move or twist like a snake. □ **snake-charmer** a person appearing to make snakes move by music etc. **snakes and ladders** a game with counters moved along a board with advances up 'ladders' or returns down 'snakes' depicted on the board. □ **snake-like** *adj.* [OE *snaca*]

snaky /ˈsneɪkɪ/ *adj.* **1** of or like a snake. **2** winding; sinuous. **3** showing coldness, ingratitude, venom, or guile. **4** *Austral. sl.* angry; irritable. □ **snakily** *adv.* **snakiness** *n.*

snap *v., n., adv.,* & *adj.* —*v.* (**snapped, snapping**) **1** *intr.* & *tr.* break suddenly or with a snap. **2** *intr.* & *tr.* emit or cause to emit a sudden sharp sound or crack. **3** *intr.* & *tr.* open or close with a snapping sound (*the bag snapped shut*). **4 a** *intr.* (often foll. by *at*) speak irritably or spitefully (to a person) (*did not mean to snap at you*). **b** *tr.* say irritably or spitefully. **5** *intr.* (often foll. by *at*) (esp. of a dog etc.) make a sudden audible bite. **6** *tr.* & *intr.* move quickly (*snap into action*). **7** *tr.* take a snapshot of. —*n.* **1** an act or sound of snapping. **2** a crisp biscuit or cake (*brandy snap;*

ginger snap). **3** a snapshot. **4** (in full **cold snap**) a sudden brief spell of cold weather. **5** *Brit.* **a** a card-game in which players call 'snap' when two similar cards are exposed. **b** (as *int.*) on noticing the (often unexpected) similarity of two things. **6** crispness of style; fresh vigour or liveliness in action; zest; dash; spring. **7** *US sl.* an easy task (*it was a snap*). —*adv.* with the sound of a snap (*heard it go snap*). —*adj.* done or taken on the spur of the moment, unexpectedly, or without notice (*snap decision*). □ **snap bean** *US* a bean grown for its pods which are broken into pieces and eaten. **snap-brim** (of a hat) with a brim that can be turned up and down at opposite sides. **snap-fastener** = *press-stud* (see PRESS¹). **snap one's fingers 1** make an audible fillip, esp. in rhythm to music etc. **2** (often foll. by *at*) defy; show contempt for. **snap off** break off or bite off. **snap out** say irritably. **snap out of** *sl.* get rid of (a mood, habit, etc.) by a sudden effort. **snap up 1** accept (an offer, a bargain) quickly or eagerly. **2** pick up or catch hastily or smartly. **3** interrupt (another person) before he or she has finished speaking. □ **snappable** *adj.* **snappingly** *adv.* [prob. f. MDu. or MLG *snappen*, partly imit.]

snapdragon /ˈsnæpɪˌdrægən/ *n.* a plant, *Antirrhinum majus*, with a bag-shaped flower like a dragon's mouth.

snapper /ˈsnæpə(r)/ *n.* **1** a person or thing that snaps. **2** any of several fish of the family Lutjanidae, used as food.

snappish /ˈsnæpɪʃ/ *adj.* **1** (of a person's manner or a remark) curt; ill-tempered; sharp. **2** (of a dog etc.) inclined to snap. □ **snappishly** *adv.* **snappishness** *n.*

snappy /ˈsnæpɪ/ *adj.* (**snappier**, **snappiest**) *colloq.* **1** brisk, full of zest. **2** neat and elegant (*a snappy dresser*). **3** snappish. □ **make it snappy** be quick about it. □ **snappily** *adv.* **snappiness** *n.*

snapshot /ˈsnæpʃɒt/ *n.* a casual photograph taken quickly with a small hand-camera.

snare /sneə(r)/ *n. & v.* —*n.* **1** a trap for catching birds or animals, esp. with a noose of wire or cord. **2** a thing that acts as a temptation. **3** a device for tempting an enemy etc. to expose himself or herself to danger, failure, loss, capture, defeat, etc. **4** (in *sing.* or *pl.*) *Mus.* twisted strings of gut, hide, or wire stretched across the lower head of a side-drum to produce a rattling sound. **5** (in full **snare drum**) a drum fitted with snares. —*v.tr.* **1** catch (a bird etc.) in a snare. **2** ensnare; lure or trap (a person) with a snare. □ **snarer** *n.* (also in *comb.*). [OE *sneare* f. ON *snara*: senses 4 & 5 prob. f. MLG or MDu.]

snarl¹ /snɑːl/ *v. & n.* —*v.* **1** *intr.* (of a dog) make an angry growl with bared teeth. **2** *intr.* (of a person) speak cynically; make bad-tempered complaints or criticisms. **3** *tr.* (often foll. by *out*) **a** utter in a snarling tone. **b** express (discontent etc.) by snarling. —*n.* the act or sound of snarling. □ **snarler** *n.* **snarlingly** *adv.* **snarly** *adj.* (**snarlier**, **snarliest**). [earlier *snar* f. (M)LG, MHG *snarren*]

snarl² /snɑːl/ *v. & n.* —*v.* **1** *tr.* (often foll. by *up*) twist; entangle; confuse and hamper the movement of (traffic etc.). **2** *intr.* (often foll. by *up*) become entangled, congested, or confused. —*n.* a knot or tangle. □ **snarl-up** *colloq.* a traffic jam; a muddle; a mistake. [ME f. *snare* (n. & v.)]

snatch *v. & n.* —*v.tr.* **1** seize quickly, eagerly, or unexpectedly, esp. with outstretched hands. **2** steal (a wallet, handbag, etc.). **3** secure with difficulty (*snatched an hour's rest*). **4** (foll. by *away*, *from*) take away or from esp. suddenly (*snatched away my hand*). **5** (foll. by *from*) rescue narrowly (*snatched from the jaws of death*). **6** (foll. by *at*) **a** try to seize by stretching or grasping suddenly. **b** take (an offer etc.) eagerly. —*n.* **1** an act of snatching (*made a snatch at it*). **2** a fragment of a song or talk etc. (*caught a snatch of their conversation*). **3** *US sl.* a kidnapping. □ **in** (or **by**) **snatches** in fits and starts. □ **snatcher** *n.* (esp. in sense 3 of *n.*). **snatchy** *adj.* [ME *snecchen*, *sna(c)che*, perh. rel. to SNACK]

snazzy /ˈsnæzɪ/ *adj.* (**snazzier**, **snazziest**) *sl.* smart or attractive esp. in an ostentatious way. □ **snazzily** *adv.* **snazziness** *n.* [20th c.: orig. unkn.]

sneak *v., n., & adj.* —*v.* **1** *intr. & tr.* (foll. by *in*, *out*, *past*, *away*, etc.) go or convey furtively; slink. **2** *tr. sl.* steal unobserved; make off with. **3** *intr. Brit. school sl.* tell tales; turn informer. **4** *intr.* (as **sneaking** *adj.*) **a** furtive; undisclosed (*have a sneaking affection for him*). **b** persistent in one's mind; nagging (*a sneaking feeling that it is not right*). —*n.* **1** a mean-spirited cowardly underhand person. **2** *Brit. school sl.* a tell-tale. —*adj.* acting or done without warning; secret (*a sneak attack*). □ **sneak-thief** a thief who steals without breaking in; a pickpocket. □ **sneakingly** *adv.* [16th c., prob. dial.: perh. rel. to ME *snike*, OE *snīcan* creep]

sneaker /ˈsniːkə(r)/ *n. sl.* each of a pair of soft-soled canvas etc. shoes.

sneaky /ˈsniːkɪ/ *adj.* (**sneakier**, **sneakiest**) given to or characterized by sneaking; furtive, mean. □ **sneakily** *adv.* **sneakiness** *n.*

sneer *n. & v.* —*n.* a derisive smile or remark. —*v.* **1** *intr.* (often foll. by *at*) smile derisively. **2** *tr.* say sneeringly. **3** *intr.* (often foll. by *at*) speak derisively (*sneered at his attempts*). □ **sneerer** *n.* **sneeringly** *adv.* [16th c.: orig. unkn.]

sneeze *n. & v.* —*n.* **1** a sudden involuntary expulsion of air from the nose and mouth caused by irritation of the nostrils. **2** the sound of this. —*v.intr.* make a sneeze. □ **not to be sneezed at** *colloq.* not contemptible; considerable. □ **sneezer** *n.* **sneezy** *adj.* [ME *snese*, app. alt. of obs. *fnese* f. OE *-fnēsan*, ON *fnýsa* & replacing earlier and less expressive *nese*]

snick /snɪk/ *v. & n.* —*v.tr.* **1** cut a small notch in. **2** make a small incision in. **3** *Cricket* deflect (the ball) slightly with the bat. —*n.* **1** a small notch or cut. **2** *Cricket* a slight deflection of the ball by the bat. [18th c.: prob. f. *snick-a-snee* fight with knives]

snicker /ˈsnɪkə(r)/ *v. & n.* —*v.intr.* **1** = SNIGGER *v.* **2** whinny, neigh. —*n.* **1** = SNIGGER *n.* **2** a whinny, a neigh. □ **snickeringly** *adv.* [imit.]

snide *adj. & n.* —*adj.* **1** sneering; slyly derogatory; insinuating. **2** counterfeit; bogus. **3** *US* mean; underhand. —*n.* a snide person or remark. □ **snidely** *adv.* **snideness** *n.* [19th-c. colloq.: orig. unkn.]

sniff *v. & n.* —*v.* **1** *intr.* draw up air audibly through the nose to stop it running or to detect a smell or as an expression of contempt. **2** *tr.* (often foll. by *up*) draw in (a scent, drug, liquid, or air) through the nose. **3** *tr.* smell (something) by sniffing. —*n.* **1** an act or sound of sniffing. **2** the amount of air etc. sniffed up. □ **sniff at 1** try the smell of; show interest in. **2** show contempt for or discontent with. **sniff out** detect; discover by investigation. □ **sniffingly** *adv.* [ME, imit.]

sniffer /'snɪfə(r)/ *n.* **1** a person who sniffs, esp. one who sniffs a drug or toxic substances (often in *comb.*: *glue-sniffer*). **2** *sl.* the nose. **3** *colloq.* any device for detecting gas, radiation, etc. □ **sniffer-dog** *colloq.* a dog trained to sniff out drugs or explosives.

sniffle /'snɪf(ə)l/ *v. & n.* —*v.intr.* sniff slightly or repeatedly. —*n.* **1** the act of sniffling. **2** (in *sing.* or *pl.*) a cold in the head causing a running nose and sniffling. □ **sniffler** *n.* **sniffly** *adj.* [imit.: cf. SNIVEL]

sniffy /'snɪfɪ/ *adj.* *colloq.* (**sniffier**, **sniffiest**) **1** inclined to sniff. **2** disdainful; contemptuous. □ **sniffily** *adv.* **sniffiness** *n.*

snifter /'snɪftə(r)/ *n.* **1** *sl.* a small drink of alcohol. **2** *US* a balloon glass for brandy. [dial. *snift* sniff, perh. f. Scand.: imit.]

snigger /'snɪgə(r)/ *n. & v.* —*n.* a half-suppressed secretive laugh. —*v.intr.* utter such a laugh. □ **sniggerer** *n.* **sniggeringly** *adv.* [var. of SNICKER]

snip *v. & n.* —*v.tr.* (**snipped**, **snipping**) (also *absol.*) cut (cloth, a hole, etc.) with scissors or shears, esp. in small quick strokes. —*n.* **1** an act of snipping. **2** a piece of material etc. snipped off. **3** *sl.* **a** something easily achieved. **b** *Brit.* a bargain; something cheaply acquired. **4** (in *pl.*) hand-shears for metal cutting. □ **snipping** *n.* [LG & Du. *snippen* imit.]

snipe *n. & v.* —*n.* (*pl.* same or **snipes**) any of various wading birds, esp. of the genus *Gallinago*, with a long straight bill and frequenting marshes. —*v.intr.* **1** fire shots from hiding usu. at long range. **2** (foll. by *at*) make a sly critical attack. —*n.* [ME, prob. f. Scand.: cf. Icel. *mýrisnípa*, & MDu., MLG *snippe*, OHG *snepfa*]

snippet /'snɪpɪt/ *n.* **1** a small piece cut off. **2** (usu. in *pl.*; often foll. by *of*) **a** a scrap or fragment of information, knowledge, etc. **b** a short extract from a book, newspaper, etc. □ **snippety** *adj.*

snit *n.* *US* a rage; a sulk (esp. *in a snit*). [20th c.: orig. unkn.]

snitch *v. & n.* —*v.* *sl.* **1** *tr.* steal. **2** *intr.* (often foll. by *on*) inform on a person. —*n.* an informer. [17th c.: orig. unkn.]

snivel /'snɪv(ə)l/ *v. & n.* —*v.intr.* (**snivelled**, **snivelling**; *US* **sniveled**, **sniveling**) **1** weep with sniffling. **2** run at the nose; make a repeated sniffing sound. **3** show weak or tearful sentiment. —*n.* **1** running mucus. **2** hypocritical talk; cant. □ **sniveller** *n.* **snivelling** *adj.* **snivellingly** *adv.* [ME f. OE *snyflan* (unrecorded) f. *snofl* mucus: cf. SNUFFLE]

snob *n.* **1** a person with an exaggerated respect for social position or wealth and who despises socially inferior connections. **2** a person who behaves with servility to social superiors. **3** a person who despises others whose (usu. specified) tastes or attainments are considered inferior (*an intellectual snob; a wine snob*). □ **snobbery** *n.* (*pl.* **-ies**). **snobbish** *adj.* **snobbishly** *adv.* **snobbishness** *n.* **snobby** *adj.* (**snobbier**, **snobbiest**). [18th c. (now dial.) 'cobbler': orig. unkn.]

snog *v. & n.* *Brit. sl.* —*v.intr.* (**snogged**, **snogging**) engage in kissing and caressing. —*n.* a spell of snogging. [20th c.: orig. unkn.]

snood /snuːd/ *n.* **1** an ornamental hairnet usu. worn at the back of the head. **2** a ring of woollen etc. material worn as a hood. [OE *snōd*]

snook /snuːk/ *n. sl.* a contemptuous gesture with the thumb to the nose and the fingers spread out. □ **cock a snook** (often foll. by *at*) **1** make this gesture. **2** register one's contempt (for a person, establishment, etc.). [19th c.: orig. unkn.]

snooker /'snuːkə(r)/ *n. & v.* —*n.* **1** a game played with cues on a rectangular baize-covered table in which the players use a cue-ball (white) to pocket the other balls (15 red and 6 coloured) in a set order. **2** a position in this game in which a direct shot at a permitted ball is impossible. —*v.tr.* **1** (also *refl.*) subject (oneself or another player) to a snooker. **2** (esp. as **snookered** *adj.*) *sl.* defeat; thwart. [19th c.: orig. unkn.]

snoop /snuːp/ *v. & n.* *colloq.* —*v.intr.* **1** pry into matters one need not be concerned with. **2** (often foll. by *about*, *around*) investigate in order to find out transgressions of the law etc. —*n.* **1** an act of snooping. **2** a person who snoops; a detective. □ **snooper** *n.* **snoopy** *adj.* [Du. *snœpen* eat on the sly]

snooty /'snuːtɪ/ *adj.* (**snootier**, **snootiest**) *colloq.* supercilious; conceited. □ **snootily** *adv.* **snootiness** *n.* [20th c.: orig. unkn.]

snooze *n. & v.* *colloq.* —*n.* a short sleep, esp. in the daytime. —*v.intr.* take a snooze. □ **snoozer** *n.* **snoozy** *adj.* (**snoozier**, **snooziest**). [18th-c. *sl.*: orig. unkn.]

snore *n. & v.* —*n.* a snorting or grunting sound in breathing during sleep. —*v.intr.* make this sound. □ **snorer** *n.* **snoringly** *adv.* [ME, prob. imit.: cf. SNORT]

snorkel /'snɔːk(ə)l/ *n. & v.* (also **schnorkel** /'ʃnɔː-/) —*n.* **1** a breathing-tube for an underwater swimmer. **2** a device for supplying air to a submerged submarine. —*v.intr.* (**snorkelled**, **snorkelling**; *US* **snorkeled**, **snorkeling**) use a snorkel. □ **snorkeller** *n.* [G *Schnorchel*]

snort *n. & v.* —*n.* **1** an explosive sound made by the sudden forcing of breath through the nose, esp. expressing indignation or incredulity. **2** a similar sound made by an engine etc. **3** *colloq.* a small drink of liquor. **4** an inhaled dose of a (usu. illegal) powdered drug. —*v.* **1** *intr.* make a snort. **2** *intr.* (of an engine etc.) make a sound resembling this. **3** *tr.* (also *absol.*) *sl.* inhale (a usu. illegal narcotic drug, esp. cocaine or heroin). [ME, prob. imit.: cf. SNORE]

snorter /'snɔːtə(r)/ *n. colloq.* **1** something very impressive or difficult. **2** something vigorous or violent.

snot *n. sl.* **1** nasal mucus. **2** a term of contempt for a person. □ **snot-rag** a handkerchief. [prob. f. MDu., MLG *snotte*, MHG *snuz*, rel. to SNOUT]

snotty /'snɒtɪ/ *adj.* (**snottier**, **snottiest**) *sl.* **1** running or foul with nasal mucus. **2** contemptible. **3** supercilious. □ **snottily** *adv.* **snottiness** *n.*

snout /snaʊt/ *n.* **1** the projecting nose and mouth of an animal. **2** *derog.* a person's nose. **3** the pointed front of a thing; a nozzle. **4** *Brit. sl.* tobacco or a cigarette. □ **snouted** *adj.* (also in *comb.*). **snoutlike** *adj.* **snouty** *adj.* [ME f. MDu., MLG *snūt*]

snow /snaʊ/ *n. & v.* —*n.* **1** atmospheric vapour frozen into ice crystals and falling to earth in light white flakes. **2** a fall of this, or a layer of it on the ground. **3** a thing resembling snow in whiteness or texture etc. **4** a mass of flickering white spots on a television or radar screen, caused by interference or a poor signal. **5** *sl.* cocaine. —*v.* **1** *intr.* (prec. by *it* as subject) snow falls (*it is snowing*; *if it snows*). **2** *tr.* (foll. by *in*, *over*, *up*, etc.) confine or block with large quantities of snow. **3** *tr.* & *intr.* sprinkle or scatter or fall as or like snow. **4** *intr.* come in large numbers or quantities. □ **be snowed under** be overwhelmed, esp. with work. **snow-blind** temporarily blinded by the glare of light reflected by large expanses of snow. □ **snowless** *adj.* **snowlike** *adj.* [OE *snāw* f. Gmc]

snowball /ˈsnəʊbɔːl/ *n.* & *v.* —*n.* **1** snow pressed together into a ball, esp. for throwing in play. **2** anything that grows or increases rapidly like a snowball rolled on snow. —*v.* **1** *intr.* & *tr.* throw or pelt with snowballs. **2** *intr.* increase rapidly.

snowbound /ˈsnəʊbaʊnd/ *adj.* prevented by snow from going out or travelling.

snowdrift /ˈsnəʊdrɪft/ *n.* a bank of snow heaped up by the action of the wind.

snowdrop /ˈsnəʊdrɒp/ *n.* a bulbous plant, *Galanthus nivalis*, with white drooping flowers in the early spring.

snowfall /ˈsnəʊfɔːl/ *n.* **1** a fall of snow. **2** *Meteorol.* the amount of snow that falls on one occasion or on a given area within a given time.

snowflake /ˈsnəʊfleɪk/ *n.* each of the small collections of crystals in which snow falls.

snowline /ˈsnəʊlaɪn/ *n.* the level above which snow never melts entirely.

snowman /ˈsnəʊmæn/ *n.* (pl. **-men**) a figure resembling a man, made of compressed snow.

snowmobile /ˈsnəʊməˌbiːl/ *n.* a motor vehicle, esp. with runners or Caterpillar tracks, for travelling over snow.

snowplough /ˈsnəʊplaʊ/ *n.* (*US* **snowplow**) a device, or a vehicle equipped with one, for clearing roads of thick snow.

snowshoe /ˈsnəʊʃuː/ *n.* a flat device like a racket attached to a boot for walking on snow without sinking in.

snowstorm /ˈsnəʊstɔːm/ *n.* a heavy fall of snow, esp. with a high wind.

snowy /ˈsnəʊɪ/ *adj.* (**snowier, snowiest**) **1** of or like snow. **2** (of the weather etc.) with much snow. □ **snowily** *adv.* **snowiness** *n.*

SNP *abbr.* Scottish National Party.

Snr. *abbr.* Senior.

snub *v.*, *n.*, & *adj.* —*v.tr.* (**snubbed, snubbing**) rebuff or humiliate with sharp words or a marked lack of cordiality. —*n.* an act of snubbing; a rebuff. —*adj.* short and blunt in shape. □ **snub nose** a short turned-up nose. □ **snubber** *n.* **snubbingly** *adv.* [ME f. ON *snubba* chide, check the growth of]

snuff[1] *n.* & *v.* —*n.* the charred part of a candle-wick. —*v.tr.* trim the snuff from (a candle). □ **snuff it** *Brit. sl.* die. **snuff out 1** extinguish by snuffing. **2** kill; put an end to. [ME *snoffe*, *snuffe*: orig. unkn.]

snuff[2] *n.* & *v.* —*n.* powdered tobacco or medicine taken by sniffing it up the nostrils. —*v.intr.* take snuff. □ **up to snuff** *colloq.* **1** *Brit.* knowing; not easily deceived. **2** up to standard. □ **snuffy** *adj.* [Du. *snuf* (*tabak* tobacco) f. MDu. *snuffen* snuffle]

snuffbox /ˈsnʌfbɒks/ *n.* a small usu. ornamental box for holding snuff.

snuffer /ˈsnʌfə(r)/ *n.* **1** a small hollow cone with a handle used to extinguish a candle. **2** (in *pl.*) an implement like scissors used to extinguish a candle or trim its wick.

snuffle /ˈsnʌf(ə)l/ *v.* & *n.* —*v.* **1** *intr.* make sniffing sounds. **2 a** *intr.* speak nasally, whiningly, or like one with a cold. **b** *tr.* (often foll. by *out*) say in this way. **3** *intr.* breathe noisily as through a partially blocked nose. **4** *intr.* sniff. —*n.* **1** a snuffling sound or tone. **2** (in *pl.*) a partial blockage of the nose causing snuffling. **3** a sniff. □ **snuffler** *n.* **snuffly** *adj.* [prob. f. LG & Du. *snuffelen* (as SNUFF[2]); cf. SNIVEL]

snug *adj.* & *n.* —*adj.* (**snugger, snuggest**) **1 a** cosy, comfortable, sheltered; well enclosed or placed or arranged. **b** cosily protected from the weather or cold. **2** (of an income etc.) allowing comfort and comparative ease. —*n. Brit.* a small room in a pub or inn. □ **snugly** *adv.* **snugness** *n.* [16th c. (orig. Naut.): prob. of LG or Du. orig.]

snuggery /ˈsnʌgərɪ/ *n.* (pl. **-ies**) **1** a snug place, esp. a person's private room or den. **2** *Brit.* = SNUG *n.*

snuggle /ˈsnʌg(ə)l/ *v.intr.* & *tr.* (usu. foll. by *down*, *up*, *together*) settle or draw into a warm comfortable position [SNUG = -LE[4]]

so[1] *adv.* & *conj.* —*adv.* **1** (often foll. by *that* + clause) to such an extent, or to the extent implied (*why are you so angry?*; *do stop complaining so*; *they were so pleased that they gave us a bonus*). **2** (with *neg.*; often foll. by *as* + clause) to the extent to which . . . is or does etc., or to the extent implied (*was not so late as I expected*; *am not so eager as you*). **3** (foll. by *that* or *as* + clause) to the degree or in the manner implied (*so expensive that few can afford it*; *so small as to be invisible*; *am not so foolish as to agree to that*). **4** (adding emphasis) to that extent; in that or a similar manner (*I want to leave and so does she*; *you said it was good, and so it is*). **5** to a great or notable degree (*I am so glad*). **6** (with verbs of state) in the way described (*am not very fond of it but may become so*). **7** (with verb of saying or thinking etc.) as previously mentioned or described (*I think so*; *he said*; *so I should hope*). —*conj.* (often foll. by *that* + clause) **1** with the result that (*there was none left, so we had to go without*). **2** in order that (*came home early so that I could see you*). **3** and then; as the next step (*so then the car broke down*; *and so to bed*). **4 a** (introducing a question) then; after that (*so what did you tell them?*). **b** (absol.) = so what? □ **and so on** (or **forth**) **1** and others of the same kind. **2** and in other similar ways. **so as** (foll. by *to* + infin.) in order to (*did it so as to get it finished*). **so be it** an expression of acceptance or resignation. **so-called** commonly designated or known as, often incorrectly. **so long!** *colloq.* goodbye till we meet again. **so much 1** a certain amount (of). **2** a great deal of (*is so much nonsense*). **3** (with *neg.*) **a** less than; to a lesser extent (*not so much forgotten as ignored*). **b** not even (*didn't give me so much as a penny*). **so much for** that is all that need be done or said about. **so so** *adj.* (usu. *predic.*) indifferent; not very good. —*adv.* indifferently; only moderately well. **so to say** (or **speak**) an expression of reserve or apology for an exaggeration or neologism etc. **so what?**

colloq. why should that be considered significant? [OE *swā* etc.]

so² var. of SOH.

-so /səʊ/ *comb. form* = -SOEVER.

soak *v. & n.* —*v.* **1** *tr. & intr.* make or become thoroughly wet through saturation with or in liquid. **2** *tr.* (of rain etc.) drench. **3** *tr.* (foll. by *in*, *up*) **a** absorb (liquid). **b** acquire (knowledge etc.) copiously. **4** *refl.* (often foll. by *in*) steep (oneself) in a subject of study etc. **5** *intr.* (foll. by *in*, *into*, *through*) (of liquid) make its way or penetrate by saturation. **6** *tr. colloq.* extract money from by an extortionate charge, taxation, etc. (*soak the rich*). **7** *intr. colloq.* drink persistently, booze. **8** *tr.* (as **soaked** *adj.*) very drunk. —*n.* **1** the act of soaking or the state of being soaked. **2** a drinking-bout. **3** *colloq.* a hard drinker. □ **soakage** *n.* **soaker** *n.* **soaking** *n. & adj.* [OE *socian* rel. to *soc* sucking at the breast, *sūcan* SUCK]

soakaway /ˈsəʊkəˌweɪ/ *n.* an arrangement for disposing of waste water by letting it percolate through the soil.

so-and-so /ˈsəʊəndˌsəʊ/ *n.* (*pl.* **so-and-so's**) **1** a particular person or thing not needing to be specified (*told me to do so-and-so*). **2** *colloq.* a person disliked or regarded with disfavour (*the so-and-so left me behind*).

soap *n. & v.* —*n.* **1** a cleansing agent which when rubbed in water yields a lather used in washing. **2** *colloq.* = *soap opera*. —*v.tr.* **1** apply soap to. **2** scrub or rub with soap. □ **soap opera** a broadcast drama, usu. serialized in many episodes, dealing with sentimental domestic themes (so called because orig. sponsored in the US by soap manufacturers). **soap powder** powdered soap esp. with additives. □ **soapless** *adj.* **soaplike** *adj.* [OE *sāpe* f. WG]

soapbox /ˈsəʊpbɒks/ *n.* **1** a box for holding soap. **2** a makeshift stand for a public speaker.

soapstone /ˈsəʊpstəʊn/ *n.* steatite.

soapsuds /ˈsəʊpsʌdz/ *n.pl.* = SUDS 1.

soapy /ˈsəʊpɪ/ *adj.* (**soapier**, **soapiest**) **1** of or like soap. **2** containing or smeared with soap. **3** (of a person or manner) unctuous or flattering. □ **soapily** *adv.* **soapiness** *n.*

soar *v.intr.* **1** fly or rise high. **2** reach a high level or standard (*prices soared*). **3** maintain height in the air without flapping the wings or using power. □ **soarer** *n.* **soaringly** *adv.* [ME f. OF *essorer* ult. f. L (as EX-¹, *aura* breeze)]

sob *v. & n.* —*v.* (**sobbed**, **sobbing**) **1** *intr.* draw breath in convulsive gasps usu. with weeping under mental distress or physical exhaustion. **2** *tr.* (usu. foll. by *out*) utter with sobs. —*n.* a convulsive drawing of breath, esp. in weeping. □ **sob story** a story or explanation appealing mainly to the emotions. **sob-stuff** *colloq.* sentimental talk or writing. □ **sobber** *n.* **sobbingly** *adv.* [ME *sobbe* (prob. imit.)]

sober /ˈsəʊbə(r)/ *adj. & n.* —*adj.* (**soberer**, **soberest**) **1** not affected by alcohol. **2** not given to excessive drinking of alcohol. **3** moderate, well-balanced, tranquil, sedate. **4** not fanciful or exaggerated (*the sober truth*). **5** (of a colour etc.) quiet and inconspicuous. —*v.tr. & intr.* (often foll. by *down*, *up*) make or become sober or less wild, reckless, enthusiastic, visionary, etc. (*a sobering thought*). □ **soberingly** *adv.* **soberly** *adv.* [ME f. OF *sobre* f. L *sobrius*]

sobriety /səˈbraɪɪtɪ/ *n.* the state of being sober. [ME f. OF *sobrieté* or L *sobrietas* (as SOBER)]

sobriquet /ˈsəʊbrɪˌkeɪ/ *n.* (also **soubriquet** /ˈsuː-/) **1** a nickname. **2** an assumed name. [F, orig. = 'tap under the chin']

Soc. *abbr.* **1** Socialist. **2** Society.

soccer /ˈsɒkə(r)/ *n.* Association football. [Assoc. + -ER³]

sociable /ˈsəʊʃəb(ə)l/ *adj.* **1** fitted for or liking the society of other people; ready and willing to talk and act with others. **2** (of a person's manner or behaviour etc.) friendly. **3** (of a meeting etc.) marked by friendliness, not stiff or formal. □ **sociability** /-ˈbɪlɪtɪ/ *n.* **sociableness** *n.* **sociably** *adv.* [F *sociable* or L *sociabilis* f. *sociare* to unite f. *socius* companion]

social /ˈsəʊʃ(ə)l/ *adj. & n.* —*adj.* **1** of or relating to society or its organization. **2** concerned with the mutual relations of human beings or of classes of human beings. **3** living in organized communities; unfitted for a solitary life (*man is a social animal*). **4** needing companionship; gregarious, interdependent. **5 a** (of insects) living together in organized communities. **b** (of birds) nesting near each other in communities. —*n.* a social gathering, esp. one organized by a club, congregation, etc. □ **social anthropology** the comparative study of peoples through their culture and kinship systems. **social climber** *derog.* a person anxious to gain a higher social status. **social democracy** a socialist system achieved by democratic means. **social democrat** a person who advocates social democracy. **social order** the network of human relationships in society. **social realism** the expression of social or political views in art. **social science a** the scientific study of human society and social relationships. **b** a branch of this (e.g. politics or economics). **social scientist** a student of or expert in the social sciences. **social security** State assistance to those lacking in economic security and welfare, e.g. the aged and the unemployed. **social service** philanthropic activity. **social services** services provided by the State for the community, esp. education, health, and housing. **social work** work of benefit to those in need of help or welfare, esp. done by specially trained personnel. **social worker** a person trained to do social work. □ **sociality** /ˌsəʊʃɪˈælɪtɪ/ *n.* **socially** *adv.* [F *social* or L *socialis* allied f. *socius* friend]

socialism /ˈsəʊʃəˌlɪz(ə)m/ *n.* **1** a political and economic theory of social organization which advocates that the community as a whole should own and control the means of production, distribution, and exchange. **2** policy or practice based on this theory. □ **socialist** *n. & adj.* **socialistic** /-ˈlɪstɪk/ *adj.* **socialistically** /-ˈlɪstɪkəlɪ/ *adv.* [F *socialisme* (as SOCIAL)]

socialite /ˈsəʊʃəˌlaɪt/ *n.* a person prominent in fashionable society.

socialize /ˈsəʊʃəˌlaɪz/ *v.* (also **-ise**) **1** *intr.* act in a sociable manner. **2** *tr.* make social. **3** *tr.* organize on socialistic principles. □ **socialized medicine** *US* the provision of medical services for all from public funds. □ **socialization** /-ˈzeɪʃ(ə)n/ *n.*

society /səˈsaɪɪtɪ/ *n.* (*pl.* **-ies**) **1** the sum of human conditions and activity regarded as a whole functioning interdependently. **2** a social community (*all societies must have firm laws*). **3 a** a social mode of life. **b** the customs and organization of an ordered community. **4** *Ecol.* a plant community. **5 a** the socially advantaged or prominent members of a community (*society would not approve*). **b** this, or a part of it, qualified in some way (*is not done in polite society*). **6** participation in hospitality; other people's homes or company (*avoids society*). **7** companionship, company (*avoids the society of such people*). **8** an association of persons united by a common aim or interest or principle (*formed a music society*). □ **Society of Friends** see QUAKER. **Society of Jesus** see JESUIT. □ **societal** *adj.* (esp. in sense 1). **societally** *adv.* [F *société* f. L *societas -tatis* f. *socius* companion]

socio- /ˈsəʊsɪəʊ, -ʃɪəʊ/ *comb. form* **1** of society (and). **2** of or relating to sociology (and). [L *socius* companion]

sociobiology /ˌsəʊsɪəʊbaɪˈɒlədʒɪ, ˌsəʊʃɪəʊ-/ *n.* the scientific study of the biological aspects of social behaviour. □ **sociobiological** /-ˌbaɪəˈlɒdʒɪk(ə)l/ *adj.* **sociobiologically** /-ˌbaɪəˈlɒdʒɪkəlɪ/ *adv.* **sociobiologist** *n.*

socio-economic /ˌsəʊsɪəʊˌiːkəˈnɒmɪk, ˌsəʊʃɪəʊ-/ *adj.* relating to or concerned with the interaction of social and economic factors. □ **socio-economically** *adv.*

sociology /ˌsəʊsɪˈɒlədʒɪ, ˌsəʊʃɪ-/ *n.* **1** the study of the development, structure, and functioning of human society. **2** the study of social problems. □ **sociological** /-əˈlɒdʒɪk(ə)l/ *adj.* **sociologically** /-əˈlɒdʒɪkəlɪ/ *adv.* **sociologist** *n.* [F *sociologie* (as SOCIO-, -LOGY)]

sock[1] *n.* (*pl.* **socks** or *informal & Commerce* **sox**) **1** a short knitted covering for the foot, usu. not reaching the knee. **2** a removable inner sole put into a shoe for warmth etc. □ **pull one's socks up** *Brit. colloq.* make an effort to improve. **put a sock in it** *Brit. sl.* be quiet. [OE *socc* f. L *soccus* comic actor's shoe, light low-heeled slipper, f. Gk *sukkhos*]

sock[2] *v. & n. colloq.* —*v.tr.* hit (esp. a person) forcefully. —*n.* a hard blow. □ **sock it to** attack or address (a person) vigorously. [*c.*1700 (cant): orig. unkn.]

socket /ˈsɒkɪt/ *n.* **1** a natural or artificial hollow for something to fit into or stand firm or revolve in. **2** *Electr.* a device receiving a plug, light-bulb, etc., to make a connection. [ME f. AF, dimin. of OF *soc* ploughshare, prob. of Celt. orig.]

sockeye /ˈsɒkaɪ/ *n.* a blue-backed salmon of Alaska etc., *Oncorhynchus nerka.* [Salish *sukai* fish of fishes]

Socratic /səˈkrætɪk/ *adj.* of or relating to the Greek philosopher Socrates (d. 399 BC) or his philosophy, esp. the method associated with him of seeking the truth by a series of questions and answers. □ **Socratically** *adv.* [L *Socraticus* f. Gk *Sōkratikos* f. *Sōkratēs*]

sod[1] *n. & v.* —*n.* **1** turf or a piece of turf. **2** the surface of the ground. —*v.tr.* (**sodded, sodding**) cover (the ground) with sods. □ **under the sod** in the grave. [ME f. MDu., MLG *sode*, of unkn. orig.]

sod[2] *n. & v.* esp. *Brit. coarse sl.* —*n.* **1** an unpleasant or awkward person or thing. **2** a person of a specified kind; a fellow (*the lucky sod*). —*v.tr.* (**sodded, sodding**) **1** (often *absol.* or as *int.*) an exclamation of annoyance (*sod them, I don't care!*). **2** (as **sodding** *adj.*) a general term of contempt. □ **sod off** go away. **Sod's Law** any of various maxims about the perverseness of things. [abbr. of SODOMITE]

soda /ˈsəʊdə/ *n.* **1** any of various compounds of sodium in common use, e.g. washing soda,

caustic soda. **2** (in full **soda water**) water made effervescent by impregnation with carbon dioxide under pressure. **3** esp. *US* a sweet effervescent drink. □ **soda bread** bread leavened with baking-soda. **soda fountain 1** a device supplying soda water. **2** a shop or counter equipped with this. [med.L, perh. f. *sodanum* glasswort (used as a remedy for headaches) f. *soda* headache f. Arab. *ṣudāʿ* f. *ṣadaʿa* split]

sodden /ˈsɒd(ə)n/ *adj.* **1** saturated with liquid; soaked through. **2** rendered stupid or dull etc. with drunkenness. □ **soddenly** *adv.* **soddenness** *n.* [archaic past part. of SEETHE]

sodium /ˈsəʊdɪəm/ *n. Chem.* a soft silver-white reactive metallic element that is important in industry and is an essential element in living organisms. □ **sodium bicarbonate** a white soluble powder used in the manufacture of fire extinguishers and effervescent drinks. **sodium chloride** a colourless crystalline compound occurring naturally in sea water and halite; common salt. **sodium hydroxide** a deliquescent compound which is strongly alkaline. **sodium-vapour lamp** (or **sodium lamp**) a lamp using an electrical discharge in sodium vapour and giving a yellow light. □ **sodic** *adj.* [SODA + -IUM]

sodomite /ˈsɒdəˌmaɪt/ *n.* a person who practises sodomy. [ME f. OF f. LL *Sodomita* f. Gk *Sodomitēs* inhabitant of *Sodom* in ancient Palestine f. *Sodoma* Sodom]

sodomy /ˈsɒdəmɪ/ *n.* = BUGGERY. □ **sodomize** *v.tr.* (also **-ise**). [ME f. med.L *sodomia* f. LL *peccatum Sodomiticum* sin of Sodom (Gen. 18–19)]

-soever /səʊˈevə(r)/ *comb. form* (added to relative pronouns, adverbs, and adjectives) of any kind; to any extent (*whatsoever; howsoever*).

sofa /ˈsəʊfə/ *n.* a long upholstered seat with a back and arms, for two or more people. □ **sofa bed** a sofa that can be converted into a temporary bed. [F, ult. f. Arab. *ṣuffa*]

soffit /ˈsɒfɪt/ *n.* the under-surface of an architrave, arch, balcony, etc. [F *soffite* or It. *soffitta, -itto* ult. f. L *suffixus* (as SUFFIX)]

soft *adj. & adv.* —*adj.* **1** (of a substance, material, etc.) lacking hardness or firmness; yielding to pressure; easily cut. **2** (of cloth etc.) having a smooth surface or texture; not rough or coarse. **3** (of air etc.) mellow, mild, balmy; not noticeably cold or hot. **4** (of water) free from mineral salts and therefore good for lathering. **5** (of a light or colour etc.) not brilliant or glaring. **6** (of a voice or sounds) gentle and pleasing. **7** *Phonet.* **a** (of a consonant) sibilant or palatal (as *c* in *ice, g* in *age*). **b** voiced or unaspirated. **8** (of an outline etc.) not sharply defined. **9** (of an action or manner etc.) gentle, conciliatory, complimentary, amorous. **10** (of the heart or feelings etc.) compassionate, sympathetic. **11** (of a person's character or attitude etc.) feeble, lenient, silly, sentimental. **12** *colloq.* (of a job etc.) easy. **13** (of drugs) mild; not likely to cause addiction. **14** (also **soft-core**) (of pornography) suggestive or erotic but not explicit. **15** *Stock Exch.* (of currency, prices, etc.) likely to fall in value. **16** *Polit.* moderate; willing to compromise (*the soft left*). —*adv.* softly (*play soft*). —*n.* a silly weak person. □ **be soft on** *colloq.* **1** be lenient towards. **2** be infatuated with. **have a soft spot for** be fond of or affectionate towards (a person). **soft-boiled** (of an egg) lightly boiled with the yolk soft or liquid. **soft-centred** (of a person) soft-hearted, sentimental. **soft drink** a non-alcoholic drink. **soft focus** *Photog.* the slight deliberate blurring of a picture. **soft fruit** *Brit.* small stoneless fruit (strawberry, currant, etc.). **soft furnishings** *Brit.* curtains, rugs, etc. **soft-headed** feeble-minded. **soft-headedness** feeble-mindedness. **soft landing** a landing by a spacecraft without its suffering major damage. **soft option** the easier alternative. **soft palate** the rear part of the palate. **soft pedal** a pedal on a piano that makes the tone softer. **soft-pedal** *v.tr.* & (often foll. by *on*) *intr.* (**-pedalled**, **-pedalling**; *US* **-pedaled**, **-pedaling**) **1** refrain from emphasizing; be restrained (about). **2** play with the soft pedal down. **soft sell** restrained or subtly persuasive salesmanship. **soft soap 1** a semifluid soap made with potash. **2** *colloq.* persuasive flattery. **soft-spoken** speaking with a gentle voice. **soft tissues** tissues of the body that are not bony or cartilaginous. **soft touch** *colloq.* a gullible person, esp. over money. □ **softish** *adj.* **softness** *n.* [OE *sōfte* agreeable, earlier *sēfte* f. WG]

softball /ˈsɒftbɔːl/ *n.* **1** a ball like a baseball but softer and larger. **2** a modified form of baseball using this.

soften /ˈsɒf(ə)n/ *v.* **1** *tr.* & *intr.* make or become soft or softer. **2** *tr.* (often foll. by *up*) **a** reduce the strength of (defences) by bombing or some other preliminary attack. **b** reduce the resistance of (a person). □ **softener** *n.*

soft-hearted /sɒftˈhɑːtɪd/ *adj.* tender, compassionate; easily moved. □ **soft-heartedness** *n.*

softie /ˈsɒftɪ/ *n.* (also **softy**) *colloq.* a weak or silly or soft-hearted person.

softly /ˈsɒftlɪ/ *adv.* in a soft, gentle, or quiet manner. □ **softly softly** (of an approach or strategy) cautious; discreet and cunning.

software /ˈsɒftweə(r)/ *n.* the programs and other operating information used by a computer.

softwood /ˈsɒftwʊd/ *n.* the wood of pine, spruce, or other conifers, easily sawn.

soggy /ˈsɒgɪ/ *adj.* (**soggier**, **soggiest**) sodden, saturated, dank. □ **soggily** *adv.* **sogginess** *n.* [dial. *sog* a swamp]

soh /səʊ/ *n.* (also **so**, **sol** /sɒl/) *Mus.* **1** (in tonic sol-fa) the fifth note of a major scale. **2** the note G in the fixed-doh system. [*sol* f. ME *sol* f. L *solve*: see GAMUT]

soigné /ˈswɑːnjeɪ/ *adj.* (*fem.* **soignée** pronunc. same) carefully finished or arranged; well-groomed. [past part. of F *soigner* take care of f. *soin* care]

soil[1] *n.* **1** the upper layer of earth in which plants grow. **2** ground belonging to a nation; territory (*on British soil*). □ **soilless** *adj.* **soily** *adj.* [ME f. AF, perh. f. L *solium* seat, taken in sense of L *solum* ground]

soil[2] *v.* & *n.* —*v.tr.* **1** make dirty; smear or stain with dirt (*soiled linen*). **2** tarnish, defile; bring discredit to (*would not soil my hands with it*). —*n.* **1** a dirty mark; a stain, smear, or defilement. **2** filth; refuse matter. □ **soil pipe** the discharge-pipe of a lavatory. [ME f. OF *suiller*, *soiller*, etc., ult. f. L *sucula* dimin. of *sus* pig]

soirée /ˈswɑːreɪ/ *n.* an evening party, usu. in a private house, for conversation or music. [F f. *soir* evening]

sojourn /ˈsɒdʒ(ə)n, -dʒɜːn, ˈsʌ-/ *n.* & *v.* —*n.* a temporary stay. —*v.intr.* stay temporarily. □ **sojourner** *n.* [ME f. OF *sojorn* etc. f. LL SUB- + *diurnum* day]

sol[1] var. of SOH.

sol[2] /sɒl/ *n. Chem.* a liquid suspension of a colloid. [abbr. of SOLUTION]

sola /ˈsəʊlə/ *n.* a pithy-stemmed E. Indian swamp plant, *Aeschynomene indica.* □ **sola topi** an Indian sun-helmet made from its pith. [Urdu & Bengali *solā*, Hindi *sholā*]

solace /ˈsɒləs/ *n.* & *v.* —*n.* comfort in distress, disappointment, or tedium. —*v.tr.* give solace to. [ME f. OF *solas* f. L *solatium* f. *solari* CONSOLE[1]]

solan /ˈsəʊlən/ *n.* (in full **solan goose**) a gannet, *Sula bassana.* [prob. f. ON *súla* gannet + *önd*, *and*- duck]

solar /ˈsəʊlə(r)/ *adj.* of, relating to, or reckoned by the sun (*solar eclipse; solar time*). □ **solar battery** (or **cell**) a device converting solar radiation into electricity. **solar day** the interval between successive meridian transits of the sun at a place. **solar panel** a panel designed to absorb the sun's rays as a source of energy for operating electricity or heating. **solar plexus** a complex of radiating nerves at the pit of the stomach. **solar system** the sun and the celestial bodies whose motion it governs. **solar year** the time taken for the earth to travel once round the sun, equal to 365 days, 5 hours, 48 minutes, and 46 seconds. [ME f. L *solaris* f. *sol* sun]

solarium /səˈleərɪəm/ *n.* (*pl.* **solaria** /-rɪə/) a room equipped with sun-lamps or fitted with extensive areas of glass for exposure to the sun. [L, = sundial, sunning-place (as SOLAR)]

sold *past* and *past part.* of SELL.

solder /ˈsəʊldə(r)/, ˈsɒ-/ *n.* & *v.* —*n.* **1** a fusible alloy used to join less fusible metals or wires etc. **2** a cementing or joining agency. —*v.tr.* join with solder. □ **soldering iron** a tool used for applying solder. □ **solderable** *n.* **solderer** *n.* [ME f. OF *soudure* f. *souder* f. L *solidare* fasten f. *solidus* SOLID]

soldier /ˈsəʊldʒə(r)/ *n.* & *v.* —*n.* **1** a person serving in or having served in an army. **2** (in full **common soldier**) a private or NCO in an army. **3** a military commander of specified ability (*a great soldier*). —*v.intr.* serve as a soldier (*was off soldiering*). □ **soldier of fortune** an adventurous person ready to take service under any State or person; a mercenary. **soldier on** *colloq.* persevere doggedly. □ **soldierly** *adj.* **soldiership** *n.* [ME *souder* etc. f. OF *soudier*, *soldier* f. *soulde* (soldier's) pay f. L *solidus*: see SOLIDUS]

soldiery /ˈsəʊldʒərɪ/ *n.* (*pl.* **-ies**) **1** soldiers, esp. of a specified character. **2** a group of soldiers.

sole[1] *n.* & *v.* —*n.* **1** the under-surface of the foot. **2** the part of a shoe, sock, etc., corresponding to this (esp. excluding the heel). **3** the lower surface or base of an implement, e.g. a plough, golf-club head, etc. —*v.tr.* provide (a shoe etc.) with a sole. □ **-soled** *adj.* (in *comb.*). [OF ult. f. L *solea* sandal, sill: cf. OE unrecorded *solu* or *sola* f. *solum* bottom, pavement, sole]

sole[2] *n.* any flatfish of the family Soleidae, esp. *Solea solea* used as food. [ME f. OF f. Prov. *sola* ult. f. L *solea* (as SOLE[1], named from its shape)]

sole³ *adj.* (*attrib.*) one and only; single, exclusive (*the sole reason; has the sole right*). □ **solely** *adv.* [ME f. OF *soule* f. L *sola* fem. of *solus* alone]

solecism /ˈsɒlɪˌsɪz(ə)m/ *n.* **1** a mistake of grammar or idiom; a blunder in the manner of speaking or writing. **2** a piece of bad manners or incorrect behaviour. □ **solecist** *n.* **solecistic** /-ˈsɪstɪk/ *adj.* [F *solécisme* or L *soloecismus* f. Gk *soloikismos* f. *soloikos* speaking incorrectly]

solemn /ˈsɒləm/ *adj.* **1** serious and dignified (*a solemn occasion*). **2** formal; accompanied by ceremony (*a solemn oath*). **3** mysteriously impressive. **4** (of a person) serious or cheerless in manner (*looks rather solemn*). **5** full of importance; weighty (*a solemn warning*). **6** grave, sober, deliberate; slow in movement or action (*a solemn promise; solemn music*). □ **solemnly** *adv.* **solemnness** *n.* [ME f. OF *solemne* f. L *sol(l)emnis* customary, celebrated at a fixed date f. *sollus* entire]

solemnity /səˈlemnɪtɪ/ *n.* (*pl.* **-ies**) **1** the state of being solemn; a solemn character or feeling; solemn behaviour. **2** a rite or celebration; a piece of ceremony. [ME f. OF *solem(p)nité* f. L *sollemnitas -tatis* (as SOLEMN)]

solemnize /ˈsɒləmˌnaɪz/ *v.tr.* (also **-ise**) **1** duly perform (a ceremony esp. of marriage). **2** celebrate (a festival etc.). **3** make solemn. □ **solemnization** /-ˈzeɪʃ(ə)n/ *n.* [ME f. OF *solem(p)niser* f. med.L *solemnizare* (as SOLEMN)]

solenoid /ˈsəʊləˌnɔɪd, ˈsɒl-/ *n.* a cylindrical coil of wire acting as a magnet when carrying electric current. □ **solenoidal** /-ˈnɔɪd(ə)l/ *adj.* [F *solénoïde* f. Gk *sōlēn* tube]

sol-fa /ˈsɒlfɑː/ *n.* & *v.* —*n.* = SOLMIZATION; (cf. *tonic sol-fa*). —*v.tr.* (**-fas**, **-faed**) sing (a tune) with sol-fa syllables. [SOL¹ + FA]

soli *pl.* of SOLO.

solicit /səˈlɪsɪt/ *v.* (**solicited**, **soliciting**) **1** *tr.* & (foll. by *for*) *intr.* ask repeatedly or earnestly for or seek or invite (business etc.). **2** *tr.* (often foll. by *for*) make a request or petition to (a person). **3** *tr.* accost (a person) and offer one's services as a prostitute. □ **solicitation** /-ˈteɪʃ(ə)n/ *n.* [ME f. OF *solliciter* f. L *sollicitare* agitate f. *sollicitus* anxious f. *sollus* entire + *citus* past part., = set in motion]

solicitor /səˈlɪsɪtə(r)/ *n.* **1** Brit. a member of the legal profession qualified to deal with conveyancing, draw up wills, etc., and to advise clients and instruct barristers. **2** a person who solicits. **3** US a canvasser. [ME f. OF *solliciteur* (as SOLICIT)]

solicitous /səˈlɪsɪtəs/ *adj.* **1** (often foll. by *of*, *about*, etc.) showing interest or concern. **2** (foll. by *to* + infin.) eager, anxious. □ **solicitously** *adv.* **solicitousness** *n.* [L *sollicitus* (as SOLICIT)]

solicitude /səˈlɪsɪˌtjuːd/ *n.* **1** the state of being solicitous; solicitous behaviour. **2** anxiety or concern. [ME f. OF *sollicitude* f. L *sollicitudo* (as SOLICITOUS)]

solid /ˈsɒlɪd/ *adj.* & *n.* —*adj.* (**solider**, **solidest**) **1** firm and stable in shape; not liquid or fluid (*solid food; water becomes solid at 0°C*). **2** of such material throughout, not hollow or containing cavities (*a solid sphere*). **3** of the same substance throughout (*solid silver*). **4** of strong material or construction or build, not flimsy or slender etc. **5 a** having three dimensions. **b** concerned with solids (*solid geometry*). **6 a** sound and reliable; genuine (*solid arguments*). **b** staunch and dependable (*a solid Tory*). **7** sound but without any special flair etc. (*a solid piece of work*). **8** financially sound. **9** (of time) uninterrupted, continuous (*spend four solid hours on it*). **10 a** unanimous, undivided (*support has been pretty solid so far*). **b** (foll. by *for*) united in favour of. —*n.* **1** a solid substance or body. **2** (in *pl.*) solid food. **3** Geom. a body or magnitude having three dimensions. □ **solid-state** *adj.* using the electronic properties of solids (e.g. a semiconductor) to replace those of valves. □ **solidly** *adv.* **solidness** *n.* [ME f. OF *solide* f. L *solidus*, rel. to *salvus* safe, *sollus* entire]

solidarity /ˌsɒlɪˈdærɪtɪ/ *n.* **1** unity or agreement of feeling or action, esp. among individuals with a common interest. **2** mutual dependence. [F *solidarité* f. *solidaire* f. *solide* SOLID]

solidi *pl.* of SOLIDUS.

solidify /səˈlɪdɪˌfaɪ/ *v.tr.* & *intr.* (**-ies**, **-ied**) make or become solid. □ **solidification** /-fɪˈkeɪʃ(ə)n/ *n.* **solidifier** *n.*

solidity /səˈlɪdɪtɪ/ *n.* the state of being solid; firmness.

solidus /ˈsɒlɪdəs/ *n.* (*pl.* **solidi** /-ˌdaɪ/) an oblique stroke (/) used in writing fractions (3/4), to separate other figures and letters, or to denote alternatives (*and/or*) and ratios (*miles/day*). [ME f. L: see SOLID]

soliloquy /səˈlɪləkwɪ/ *n.* (*pl.* **-ies**) **1** the act of talking when alone or regardless of any hearers, esp. in drama. **2** part of a play involving this. □ **soliloquist** *n.* **soliloquize** *v.intr.* (also **-ise**). [LL *soliloquium* f. L *solus* alone + *loqui* speak]

solipsism /ˈsɒlɪpˌsɪz(ə)m/ *n.* Philos. the view that the self is all that exists or can be known. □ **solipsist** *n.* **solipsistic** /-ˈsɪstɪk/ *adj.* **solipsistically** /-ˈsɪstɪkəlɪ/ *adv.* [L *solus* alone + *ipse* self]

solitaire /ˈsɒlɪˌteə(r)/ *n.* **1** a diamond or other gem set by itself. **2** a ring having a single gem. **3** a game for one player played by removing pegs etc. one at a time from a board by jumping others over them until only one is left. **4** US = PATIENCE 4. [F f. L *solitarius* (as SOLITARY)]

solitary /ˈsɒlɪtərɪ/ *adj.* & *n.* —*adj.* **1** living alone; not gregarious; without companions; lonely (*a solitary existence*). **2** (of a place) secluded or unfrequented. **3** single or sole (*a solitary instance*). **4** (of an insect) not living in communities. **5** Bot. growing singly, not in a cluster. —*n.* (*pl.* **-ies**) **1** a recluse or anchorite. **2** colloq. = *solitary confinement*. □ **solitary confinement** isolation of a prisoner in a separate cell as a punishment. □ **solitarily** *adv.* **solitariness** *n.* [ME f. L *solitarius* f. *solus* alone]

solitude /ˈsɒlɪˌtjuːd/ *n.* **1** the state of being solitary. **2** a lonely place. [ME f. OF *solitude* or L *solitudo* f. *solus* alone]

solmization /ˌsɒlmɪˈzeɪʃ(ə)n/ *n.* Mus. a system of associating each note of a scale with a particular syllable, now usu. *doh ray me fah soh lah te*, with doh as C in the fixed-doh system and as the keynote in the movable-doh or tonic sol-fa system. □ **solmizate** /ˈsɒlmɪˌzeɪt/ *v.intr.* & *tr.* [F *solmisation* (as SOL¹, MI)]

solo /ˈsəʊləʊ/ *n.*, *v.*, & *adv.* —*n.* (*pl.* **-os**) **1** (*pl.* **-os** or **soli** /-lɪ/) **a** a vocal or instrumental piece or passage, or a dance, performed by one person with or without accompaniment. **b** (*attrib.*) performed or performing as a solo (*solo passage; solo violin*). **2 a** an unaccompanied flight by a pilot in an aircraft. **b** anything done by one person unaccompanied. **c** (*attrib.*) unaccompanied, alone. **3** (in full **solo whist**) a card-game like whist in which one player may oppose the others. —*v.* (**-oes, -oed**) **1** *intr.* perform a solo, esp. a solo flight. **2** *tr.* perform or achieve as a solo. —*adv.* unaccompanied, alone (*flew solo for the first time*). [It. f. L *solus* alone]

soloist /ˈsəʊləʊɪst/ *n.* a performer of a solo, esp. in music.

Solomon /ˈsɒləmən/ *n.* a very wise person. □ **Solomonic** /ˌsɒləˈmɒnɪk/ *adj.* [*Solomon*, king of Israel in the 10th c. BC, famed for his wisdom]

solstice /ˈsɒlstɪs/ *n.* either of the times when the sun is furthest from the equator. □ **summer solstice** the time at which the sun is furthest north from the equator, about 21 June in the northern hemisphere. **winter solstice** the time at which the sun is furthest south from the equator, about 22 Dec. in the northern hemisphere. □ **solstitial** /sɒlˈstɪʃ(ə)l/ *adj.* [ME f. OF f. L *solstitium* f. *sol* sun + *sistere* stit- make stand]

soluble /ˈsɒljʊb(ə)l/ *adj.* **1** that can be dissolved, esp. in water. **2** that can be solved. □ **solubility** /-ˈbɪlɪtɪ/ *n.* [ME f. OF f. LL *solubilis* (as SOLVE)]

solute /ˈsɒljuːt/ *n.* a dissolved substance. [L *solutum*, neut. of *solutus*: see SOLVE]

solution /səˈluːʃ(ə)n, -ˈljuːʃ(ə)n/ *n.* **1** the act or a means of solving a problem or difficulty. **2 a** the conversion of a solid or gas into a liquid by mixture with a liquid solvent. **b** the state resulting from this (*held in solution*). **3** the act of dissolving or the state of being dissolved. **4** the act of separating or breaking. [ME f. OF f. L *solutio -onis* (as SOLVE)]

solve /sɒlv/ *v.tr.* find an answer to, or an action or course that removes or effectively deals with (a problem or difficulty). □ **solvable** *adj.* **solver** *n.* [ME, = loosen, f. L *solvere solut-* unfasten, release]

solvent /ˈsɒlv(ə)nt/ *adj.* & *n.* —*adj.* **1** able to dissolve or form a solution with something. **2** having enough money to meet one's liabilities. —*n.* a solvent liquid etc. □ **solvency** *n.* (in sense 2).

somatic /səˈmætɪk/ *adj.* of or relating to the body, esp. as distinct from the mind. □ **somatically** *adv.* [Gk *sōmatikos* f. *sōma -atos* body]

somato- /ˈsəʊmətəʊ/ *comb. form* the human body. [Gk *sōma -atos* body]

sombre /ˈsɒmbə(r)/ *adj.* (also US **somber**) **1** dark, gloomy (*a sombre sky*). **2** oppressively solemn or sober. **3** dismal, foreboding (*a sombre prospect*). □ **sombrely** *adv.* **sombreness** *n.* [F *sombre* f. OF *sombre* (n.) ult. f. L SUB- + *umbra* shade]

sombrero /sɒmˈbreərəʊ/ *n.* (pl. **-os**) a broad-brimmed felt or straw hat worn esp. in Mexico and the south-west US. [Sp. f. *sombra* shade (as SOMBRE)]

some /sʌm/ *adj.*, *pron.*, & *adv.* —*adj.* **1** an unspecified amount or number of (*some water; some apples; some of them*). **2** that is unknown or unnamed (*will return some day; some fool has locked the door; to some extent*). **3** denoting an approximate number (*waited some twenty minutes*). **4** a considerable amount or number of (*went to some trouble*). **5** (usu. stressed) **a** at least a small amount of (*do have some consideration*). **b** such to a certain extent (*that is some help*). **c** *colloq.* notably such (*I call that some story*). —*pron.*

some people or things, some number or amount (*I have some already; would you like some more?*). —*adv. colloq.* to some extent (*we talked some; do it some more*). [OE *sum* f. Gmc]

-some[1] /səm/ *suffix* forming adjectives meaning: **1** adapted to; productive of (*cuddlesome; fearsome*). **2** characterized by being (*fulsome; lithesome*). **3** apt to (*tiresome; meddlesome*). [OE -*sum*]

-some[2] /səm/ *suffix* forming nouns from numerals, meaning 'a group of (so many)' (*foursome*). [OE *sum* SOME, used after numerals in genit. pl.]

-some[3] /səʊm/ *comb. form* denoting a portion of a body, esp. of a cell (*chromosome*). [Gk *sōma* body]

somebody /ˈsʌmbədɪ/ *pron.* & *n.* —*pron.* some person. —*n.* (pl. **-ies**) a person of importance (*is really somebody now*).

someday /ˈsʌmdeɪ/ *adv.* at some time in the future.

somehow /ˈsʌmhaʊ/ *adv.* **1** for some reason or other (*somehow I never liked them*). **2** in some unspecified or unknown way (*he somehow dropped behind*). **3** no matter how (*must get it finished somehow*).

someone /ˈsʌmwʌn/ *n.* & *pron.* = SOMEBODY.

someplace /ˈsʌmpleɪs/ *adv.* US *colloq.* = SOMEWHERE.

somersault /ˈsʌməsɒlt/ *n.* & *v.* (also **summersault**) —*n.* an acrobatic movement in which a person turns head over heels in the air or on the ground and lands on the feet. —*v.intr.* perform a somersault. [OF *sombresault* alt. f. *sobresault* ult. f. L *supra* above + *saltus* leap f. *salire* to leap]

something /ˈsʌmθɪŋ/ —*n.* & *pron.* **1 a** some unspecified or unknown thing (*have something to tell you; something has happened*). **b** (in full **something or other**) as a substitute for an unknown or forgotten description (*a student of something or other*). **2** a known or understood but unexpressed quantity, quality, or extent (*there is something about it I do not like; is something of a fool*). **3** *colloq.* an important or notable person or thing (*the party was quite something*). □ **or something** or some unspecified alternative possibility (*must have run away or something*). **see something of** encounter (a person) briefly or occasionally. **something else 1** something different. **2** *colloq.* something exceptional. **something like 1** an amount in the region of (*left something like a million pounds*). **2** somewhat like (*shaped something like a cigar*). **3** *colloq.* impressive; a fine specimen of. **something of** to some extent; in some sense (*is something of an expert*). [OE *sum thing* (as SOME, THING)]

sometime /ˈsʌmtaɪm/ *adv.* & *adj.* —*adv.* **1** at some unspecified time. **2** formerly. —*adj.* former (*the sometime mayor*).

sometimes /ˈsʌmtaɪmz/ *adv.* at some times; occasionally.

somewhat /ˈsʌmwɒt/ *adv.* to some extent (*behaviour that was somewhat strange; answered somewhat hastily*).

somewhen /ˈsʌmwen/ *adv. colloq.* at some time.

somewhere /ˈsʌmweə(r)/ *adv.* & *pron.* —*adv.* in or to some place. —*pron.* some unspecified place. □ **get somewhere** *colloq.* achieve success.

somnambulism /sɒmˈnæmbjʊˌlɪz(ə)m/ *n.* sleepwalking. □ **somnambulant** *adj.* **somnambulantly** *adv.* **somnambulist** *n.* **somnambulistic** /-ˈlɪstɪk/ *adj.* **somnambulistically**

/-'lɪstɪkəlɪ/ adv. [L somnus sleep + ambulare walk]

somnolent /'sɒmnələnt/ adj. **1** sleepy, drowsy. **2** inducing drowsiness. □ **somnolence** n. **somnolency** n. **somnolently** adv. [ME f. OF sompnolent or L somnolentus f. somnus sleep]

son /sʌn/ n. **1** a boy or man in relation to either or both of his parents. **2 a** a male descendant. **b** (foll. by of) a male member of a family, nation, etc. **3** a person regarded as inheriting an occupation, quality, etc., or associated with a particular attribute (sons of freedom; sons of the soil). **4** (in full **my son**) a form of address esp. to a boy. **5** (**the Son**) (in Christian belief) the second person of the Trinity. □ **son-in-law** (pl. **sons-in-law**) the husband of one's daughter. **son of a bitch** sl. a general term of contempt. **son of a gun** colloq. a jocular or affectionate form of address or reference. □ **sonless** adj. **sonship** n. [OE sunu f. Gmc]

sonar /'səʊnə(r)/ n. **1** a system for the underwater detection of objects by reflected or emitted sound. **2** an apparatus for this. [sound navigation and ranging, after radar]

sonata /sə'nɑːtə/ n. a composition for one instrument or two (one usu. being a piano accompaniment), usu. in several movements. [It., = sounded (orig. as distinct from sung): fem. past part. of sonare sound]

sonde /sɒnd/ n. a device sent up to obtain information about atmospheric conditions, esp. = RADIOSONDE. [F. = sounding(-line)]

son et lumière /ˌsɒneɪˈluːmjeə(r)/ n. an entertainment by night at a historic monument, building, etc., using lighting effects and recorded sound to give a dramatic narrative of its history. [F. = sound and light]

song n. **1** a short poem or other set of words set to music or meant to be sung. **2** singing or vocal music (burst into song). **3** a musical composition suggestive of a song. **4** the musical cry of some birds. □ **for a song** colloq. very cheaply. **on song** Brit. colloq. performing exceptionally well. **song and dance** colloq. a fuss or commotion. **song cycle** a set of musically linked songs on a romantic theme. **song thrush** a thrush, Turdus philomelos, of Europe and W. Asia, with a song partly mimicked from other birds. □ **songless** adj. [OE sang f. Gmc (as SING)]

songbird /'sɒŋbɜːd/ n. a bird with a musical call.

songbook /'sɒŋbʊk/ n. a collection of songs with music.

songster /'sɒŋstə(r)/ n. (fem. **songstress** /-strɪs/) **1** a singer, esp. a fluent and skilful one. **2** a songbird. **3** a poet. [OE sangestre (as SONG, -STER)]

songwriter /'sɒŋˌraɪtə(r)/ n. a writer of songs or the music for them.

sonic /'sɒnɪk/ adj. of or relating to or using sound or sound waves. □ **sonic bang** (or **boom**) a loud explosive noise caused by the shock wave from an aircraft when it passes the speed of sound. □ **sonically** adv. [L sonus sound]

sonnet /'sɒnɪt/ n. a poem of 14 lines using any of a number of formal rhyme schemes, in English usu. having ten syllables per line. [F sonnet or It. sonetto dimin. of suono SOUND[1]]

sonny /'sʌnɪ/ n. colloq. a familiar form of address to a young boy.

sonorous /'sɒnərəs, sə'nɔːrəs/ adj. **1** having a loud, full, or deep sound; resonant. **2** (of a speech, style, etc.) imposing, grand. □ **sonority**

/sə'nɒrɪtɪ/ n. **sonorously** adv. **sonorousness** n. [L sonorus f. sonor sound]

sool /suːl/ v.tr. Austral. & NZ sl. **1** (of a dog) attack or worry (an animal). **2** (often foll. by on) urge or goad. □ **sooler** n. [var. of 17th-c. (now dial.) sowl seize roughly, of unkn. orig.]

soon /suːn/ adv. **1** after no long interval of time (shall soon know the result). **2** relatively early (must you go so soon?). **3** (prec. by how) early (with relative rather than distinctive sense) (how soon will it be ready?). **4** readily or willingly (in expressing choice or preference: which would you sooner do?; would as soon stay behind). □ **as** (or **so**) **soon as** (implying a causal or temporal connection) at the moment that; not later than; as early as (came as soon as I heard about it; disappears as soon as it's time to pay). **no sooner ... than** at the very moment that (we no sooner arrived than the rain stopped). **sooner or later** at some future time; eventually. □ **soonish** adv. [OE sōna f. WG]

soot /sʊt/ n. & v. —n. a black carbonaceous substance rising in fine flakes in the smoke of wood, coal, oil, etc., and deposited on the sides of a chimney etc. —v.tr. cover with soot. [OE sōt f. Gmc]

sooth /suːθ/ n. archaic truth, fact. □ **in sooth** really, truly. [OE sōth (orig. adj., = true) f. Gmc]

soothe /suːð/ v.tr. **1** calm (a person or feelings). **2** soften or mitigate (pain). □ **soother** n. **soothing** adj. **soothingly** adv. [OE sōthian verify f. sōth true: see SOOTH]

soothsayer /'suːθˌseɪə(r)/ n. a diviner or seer. [ME, = one who says the truth: see SOOTH]

sooty /'sʊtɪ/ adj. (**sootier**, **sootiest**) **1** covered with or full of soot. **2** (esp. of an animal or bird) black or brownish-black. □ **sootily** adv. **sootiness** n.

sop n. & v. —n. **1** a piece of bread etc. dipped in gravy etc. **2** a thing given or done to pacify or bribe. —v. (**sopped**, **sopping**) **1** intr. be drenched (came home sopping; sopping wet clothes). **2** tr. (foll. by up) absorb (liquid) in a towel etc. **3** tr. wet thoroughly; soak. [OE sopp, corresp. to MLG soppe, OHG sopfa bread and milk, prob. f. a weak grade of the base of OE sūpan: see SUP[1]]

sophism /'sɒfɪz(ə)m/ n. a false argument, esp. one intended to deceive. [ME f. OF sophime f. L f. Gk sophisma clever device f. sophizomai become wise f. sophos wise]

sophist /'sɒfɪst/ n. one who reasons with clever but fallacious arguments. □ **sophistic** /-'fɪstɪk/ adj. **sophistical** /sə'fɪstɪk(ə)l/ adj. **sophistically** /sə'fɪstɪkəlɪ/ adv. [L sophistes f. Gk sophistēs f. sophizomai: see SOPHISM]

sophisticate v., adj., & n. —v. /sə'fɪstɪˌkeɪt/ **1** tr. make (a person etc.) educated, cultured, or refined. **2** tr. make (equipment or techniques etc.) highly developed or complex. **3** tr. deprive (a person or thing) of its natural simplicity, make artificial by worldly experience etc. —adj. /sə'fɪstɪkət/ sophisticated. —n. /sə'fɪstɪkət/ a sophisticated person. □ **sophistication** /-ˈkeɪʃ(ə)n/ n. [med.L sophisticare tamper with f. sophisticus (as SOPHISM)]

sophisticated /sə'fɪstɪˌkeɪtɪd/ adj. **1** (of a person) educated and refined; discriminating in taste and judgement. **2** (of a thing, idea, etc.) highly developed and complex. □ **sophisticatedly** adv.

sophistry /'sɒfɪstrɪ/ n. (pl. **-ies**) **1** the use of sophisms. **2** a sophism.

sophomore /ˈsɒfəˌmɔː(r)/ n. US a second-year university or high-school student. □ **sophomoric** /-ˈmɒrɪk/ adj. [earlier sophumer f. sophum, obs. var. of SOPHISM]

soporific /ˌsɒpəˈrɪfɪk/ adj. & n. —adj. tending to produce sleep. —n. a soporific drug or influence. □ **soporiferous** adj. **soporifically** adv. [L sopor sleep + -FIC]

sopping /ˈsɒpɪŋ/ adj. (also **sopping wet**) soaked with liquid; wet through. [pres. part. of SOP v.]

soppy /ˈsɒpɪ/ adj. (**soppier, soppiest**) **1** Brit. colloq. **a** silly or foolish in a feeble or self-indulgent way. **b** mawkishly sentimental. **2** Brit. colloq. (foll. by on) foolishly infatuated with. **3** soaked with water. □ **soppily** adv. **soppiness** n. [SOP + -Y¹]

soprano /səˈprɑːnəʊ/ n. (pl. **-os** or **soprani** /-nɪ/) **1 a** the highest singing-voice. **b** a female or boy singer with this voice. **c** a part written for it. **2 a** an instrument of a high or the highest pitch in its family. **b** its player. [It. f. sopra above f. L supra]

sorbet /ˈsɔːbeɪ, -bɪt/ n. **1** a water-ice. **2** sherbet. [F f. It. sorbetto f. Turk. şerbet f. Arab. šarba to drink: cf. SHERBET]

sorcerer /ˈsɔːsərə(r)/ n. (fem. **sorceress** /-rɪs/) a person who claims to use magic powers; a magician or wizard. □ **sorcerous** adj. **sorcery** n. (pl. **-ies**). [obs. sorcer f. OF sorcier ult. f. L sors sortis lot]

sordid /ˈsɔːdɪd/ adj. **1** dirty or squalid. **2** ignoble, mean, or mercenary. **3** mean or niggardly. **4** dull-coloured. □ **sordidly** adv. **sordidness** n. [F sordide or L sordidus f. sordēre be dirty]

sore /sɔː(r)/ adj., n., & adv. —adj. **1** (of a part of the body) painful from injury or disease (has a sore arm). **2** (of a person) suffering pain. **3** (often foll. by about, at) aggrieved or vexed. **4** archaic grievous or severe (in sore need). —n. **1** a sore place on the body. **2** a source of distress or annoyance (reopen old sores). —adv. archaic grievously, severely. □ **sore point** a subject causing distress or annoyance. **sore throat** an inflammation of the lining membrane at the back of the mouth etc. □ **soreness** n. [OE sār (n. & adj.), sāre (adv.), f. Gmc]

sorehead /ˈsɔːhed/ n. US a touchy or disgruntled person.

sorely /ˈsɔːlɪ/ adv. **1** extremely, badly (am sorely tempted; sorely in need of repair). **2** severely (am sorely vexed). [OE sārlīce (as SORE, -LY²)]

sorghum /ˈsɔːgəm/ n. any tropical cereal grass of the genus Sorghum, e.g. durra. [mod.L f. It. sorgo, perh. f. unrecorded Rmc syricum (gramen) Syrian (grass)]

soroptimist /səˈrɒptɪmɪst/ n. a member of an international association of clubs for professional and business women. [L soror sister + OPTIMIST (as OPTIMISM)]

sorority /səˈrɒrɪtɪ/ n. (pl. **-ies**) US a female students' society in a university or college. [med.L sororitas or L soror sister, after fraternity]

sorrel¹ /ˈsɒr(ə)l/ n. any acid-leaved herb of the genus Rumex, used in salads and for flavouring. [ME f. OF surele, sorele f. Gmc]

sorrel² /ˈsɒr(ə)l/ adj. & n. —adj. of a light reddish-brown colour. —n. **1** this colour. **2** a sorrel animal, esp. a horse. [ME f. OF sorel f. sor yellowish f. Frank.]

sorrow /ˈsɒrəʊ/ n. & v. —n. **1** mental distress caused by loss or disappointment etc. **2** a cause of sorrow. **3** lamentation. —v.intr. **1** feel sorrow. **2** mourn. □ **sorrower** n. **sorrowing** adj. [OE sorh, sorg]

sorrowful /ˈsɒrəʊfʊl/ adj. **1** feeling or showing sorrow. **2** distressing, lamentable. □ **sorrowfully** adv. **sorrowfulness** n. [OE sorhful (as SORROW, -FUL)]

sorry /ˈsɒrɪ/ adj. (**sorrier, sorriest**) **1** (predic.) pained or regretful or penitent (were sorry for what they had done; am sorry that you have to go). **2** (predic.; foll. by for) feeling pity or sympathy for (a person). **3** as an expression of apology. **4** wretched; in a poor state (a sorry sight). □ **sorry for oneself** dejected. □ **sorrily** adv. **sorriness** n. [OE sārig f. WG (as SORE, -Y²)]

sort /sɔːt/ n. & v. —n. **1** a group of things etc. with common attributes; a class or kind. **2** (foll. by of) roughly of the kind specified (is some sort of doctor). **3** colloq. a person of a specified character or kind (a good sort). **4** Printing a letter or piece in a fount of type. **5** Computing the arrangement of data in a prescribed sequence. —v.tr. (often foll. by out, over) arrange systematically or according to type, class, etc. □ **after a sort** after a fashion. **in some sort** to a certain extent. **of a sort** (or of sorts) colloq. not fully deserving the name (a holiday of sorts). **out of sorts 1** slightly unwell. **2** in low spirits; irritable. **sort of** colloq. as it were; to some extent (I sort of expected it). **sort out 1** separate into sorts. **2** select (things of one or more sorts) from a miscellaneous group. **3** disentangle or put into order. **4** resolve (a problem or difficulty). **5** colloq. deal with or reprimand (a person). □ **sortable** adj. **sorter** n. **sorting** n. [ME f. OF sorte ult. f. L sors sortis lot, condition]

sortie /ˈsɔːtɪ/ n. & v. —n. **1** a sally, esp. from a besieged garrison. **2** an operational flight by a single military aircraft. —v.intr. (**sorties, sortied, sortieing**) make a sortie; sally. [F, fem. past part. of sortir go out]

SOS /ˌesəʊˈes/ n. (pl. **SOSs**) **1** an international code-signal of extreme distress, used esp. by ships at sea. **2** an urgent appeal for help. **3** Brit. a message broadcast to an untraceable person in an emergency. [chosen as being easily transmitted and recognized in Morse code]

sostenuto /ˌsɒstəˈnuːtəʊ/ adv., adj., & n. Mus. —adv. & adj. in a sustained or prolonged manner. —n. (pl. **-os**) a passage to be played in this way. [It., past part. of sostenere SUSTAIN]

sot n. & v. —n. a habitual drunkard. —v.intr. (**sotted, sotting**) tipple. □ **sottish** adj. [OE sott & OF sot foolish, f. med.L sottus, of unkn. orig.]

sotto voce /ˌsɒtəʊ ˈvəʊtʃɪ/ adv. in an undertone or aside. [It. sotto under + voce voice]

sou /suː/ n. **1** hist. a former French coin of low value. **2** (usu. with neg.) colloq. a very small amount of money (hasn't a sou). [F, orig. pl. sous f. OF sout f. L SOLIDUS]

soubrette /suːˈbret/ n. **1** a pert maidservant or similar female character in a comedy. **2** an actress taking this part. [F f. Prov. soubreto fem. of soubret coy f. sobrar f. L superare be above]

soubriquet var. of SOBRIQUET.

souchong /ˈsuːʃɒŋ/ n. a fine black kind of China tea. [Chin. xiao small + zhong sort]

soufflé /ˈsuːfleɪ/ n. & adj. —n. **1** a light spongy dish usu. made with flavoured egg yolks added to stiffly beaten whites of eggs and baked (cheese soufflé). **2** any of various light sweet or savoury dishes made with beaten egg whites. —*adj.* light and frothy or spongy (*omelette soufflé*). [F past part. *souffler* blow f. L *sufflare*]

sough /sau, sʌf/ *v. & n.* —*v.intr.* make a moaning, whistling, or rushing sound as of the wind in trees etc. —*n.* this sound. [OE *swōgan* resound]

sought past and past part. of SEEK.

souk /suːk/ *n.* (also **suk, sukh, suq**) a market-place in Muslim countries. [Arab. *sūk*]

soul /səʊl/ *n.* **1** the spiritual or immaterial part of a human being, often regarded as immortal. **2** the moral or emotional or intellectual nature of a person or animal. **3** the personification or pattern of something (*the very soul of discretion*). **4** an individual (*not a soul in sight*). **5 a** a person regarded with familiarity or pity etc. (*the poor soul was utterly confused*). **b** a person regarded as embodying moral or intellectual qualities (*left that to meaner souls*). **6** a person regarded as the animating or essential part of something (*the life and soul of the party*). **7** emotional or intellectual energy or intensity, esp. as revealed in a work of art (*pictures that lack soul*). **8** Black American culture or music etc. □ **soul-destroying** (of an activity etc.) deadeningly monotonous. **soul food** the traditional food of American Blacks. **soul mate** a person ideally suited to another. **soul music** a kind of music incorporating elements of rhythm and blues and gospel music, popularized by American Blacks. □ **-souled** *adj.* (in *comb.*). [OE *sāwol, sāwel, sāwl,* f. Gmc]

soulful /ˈsəʊlfʊl/ *adj.* **1** having or expressing or evoking deep feeling. **2** *colloq.* over-emotional. □ **soulfully** *adv.* **soulfulness** *n.*

soulless /ˈsəʊllɪs/ *adj.* **1** lacking sensitivity or noble qualities. **2** having no soul. **3** undistinguished or uninteresting. □ **soullessly** *adv.* **soullessness** *n.*

sound[1] /saʊnd/ *n. & v.* —*n.* **1 a** a sensation caused in the ear by the vibration of the surrounding air or other medium. **2 a** vibrations causing this sensation. **b** similar vibrations whether audible or not. **3** what is or may be heard. An idea or impression conveyed by words (*don't like the sound of that*). **5** mere words (*sound and fury*). **6** (in full **musical sound**) sound produced by continuous and regular vibrations (opp. NOISE *n.* 3). **7** any of a series of articulate utterances (*vowel and consonant sounds*). **8** music, speech, etc., accompanying a film or other visual presentation. **9** (often *attrib.*) broadcasting by radio as distinct from television. —*v.* **1** *intr.* & *tr.* emit or cause to emit sound. **2** *tr.* utter or pronounce (*sound a note of alarm*). **3** *intr.* convey an impression when heard (*you sound worried*). **4** *tr.* give an audible signal for (an alarm etc.). **5** *tr.* test (the lungs etc.) by noting the sound produced. **6** *tr.* cause to resound; make known (*sound their praises*). □ **sound barrier** the high resistance of air to objects moving at speeds near that of sound. **sound bite** a short pithy extract from an interview, speech, etc. used as part of a media broadcast. **sound effect** a sound other than speech or music made artificially for use in a play, film, etc. **sound off** talk loudly or express one's opinions forcefully. **sound wave** a wave of compression and rarefaction, by which sound is propagated in an elastic medium, e.g. air. □ **soundless** *adj.* **soundlessly** *adv.* **soundlessness** *n.* [ME f. AF *soun,* OF *son* (n.), AF *suner,* OF *soner* (v.) f. L *sonus*]

sound[2] /saʊnd/ *adj. & adv.* —*adj.* **1** healthy; not diseased or injured. **2** (of an opinion or policy etc.) correct, orthodox, well-founded, judicious. **3** financially secure (*a sound investment*). **4** undisturbed (*a sound sleeper*). **5** severe, hard (*a sound blow*). —*adv.* soundly (*sound asleep*). □ **soundly** *adv.* **soundness** *n.* [ME *sund, isund* f. OE *gesund* f. WG]

sound[3] /saʊnd/ *v.tr. & intr.* **1** *tr.* test the depth or quality of the bottom of (the sea or a river etc.). **2** *tr.* (often foll. by *out*) inquire (esp. cautiously or discreetly) into the opinions or feelings of (a person). □ **sounder** *n.* [ME f. OF *sonder* ult. f. L SUB- + *unda* wave]

sound[4] /saʊnd/ *n.* **1** a narrow passage of water connecting two seas or a sea with a lake etc. **2** an arm of the sea. [OE *sund,* = ON *sund* swimming, strait, f. Gmc (as SWIM)]

sounding[1] /ˈsaʊndɪŋ/ *n.* **1 a** the action or process of measuring the depth of water, now usu. by means of echo. **b** an instance of this (*took a sounding*). **2** (in *pl.*) **a** a region close to the shore of the right depth for sounding. **b** cautious investigation (*made soundings as to his suitability*).

sounding[2] /ˈsaʊndɪŋ/ *adj.* **1** giving forth (esp. loud or resonant) sound (*sounding brass*). **2** emptily boastful, resonant, or imposing (*sounding promises*).

sounding-board /ˈsaʊndɪŋˌbɔːd/ *n.* **1** a canopy over a pulpit etc. to direct sound towards the congregation. **2** a means of causing opinions etc. to be more widely known (*used his students as a sounding-board*).

soundproof /ˈsaʊndpruːf/ *adj. & v.* —*adj.* impervious to sound. —*v.tr.* make soundproof.

soundtrack /ˈsaʊndtræk/ *n.* **1** the recorded sound element of a film. **2** this recorded on the edge of a film in optical or magnetic form.

soup /suːp/ *n. & v.* —*n.* a usu. savoury liquid dish made by boiling meat, fish, or vegetables etc. in stock or water. —*v.tr.* (usu. foll. by *up*) *colloq.* **1** increase the power and efficiency of (an engine). **2** increase the power or impact of (writing, music, etc.). □ **in the soup** *colloq.* in difficulties. **soup-kitchen** a place dispensing soup etc. to the poor. [F *soupe* sop, broth, f. LL *suppa* f. Gmc: cf. SOP, SUP[1]]

soupçon /ˈsuːpsɔ̃/ *n.* a very small quantity; a dash. [F f. OF *sou(s)peçon* f. med.L *suspectio -onis*: see SUSPICION]

soupy /ˈsuːpɪ/ *adj.* (**soupier, soupiest**) **1** of or resembling soup. **2** *colloq.* sentimental; mawkish. □ **soupily** *adv.* **soupiness** *n.*

sour /ˈsaʊə(r)/ *adj., n., & v.* —*adj.* **1** having an acid taste like lemon or vinegar, esp. because of unripeness (*sour apples*). **2 a** (of food, esp. milk or bread) bad because of fermentation. **b** smelling or tasting rancid or unpleasant. **3** (of a person, temper, etc.) harsh; morose; bitter. **4** (of a thing) unpleasant; distasteful. **5** (of the soil) deficient in lime and usually dank. —*n.* US a drink with lemon- or lime-juice (*whisky sour*). —*v.tr. & intr.* make or become sour (*soured the cream; soured by misfortune*). □ **go** (or **turn**) **sour 1** (of food etc.) become sour. **2** turn out badly (*the job went sour on him*). **3** lose one's keenness. **sour cream** cream deliberately fermented by adding bacteria. **sour grapes** resentful disparagement of something one cannot personally acquire. □ **sourish** *adj.* **sourly** *adv.* **sourness** *n.* [OE *sūr* f. Gmc]

source /sɔːs/ n. **1** a spring or fountain-head from which a stream issues (*the sources of the Nile*). **2** a place, person, or thing from which something originates (*the source of all our troubles*). **3** a person or document etc. providing evidence (*reliable sources of information; historical source material*). **4** a body emitting radiation etc. □ **at source** at the point of origin or issue. [ME f. OF *sors, sourse*, past part. of *sourdre* rise f. L *surgere*]

sourdough /ˈsaʊədəʊ/ n. *US* fermenting dough, esp. that left over from a previous baking, used as leaven. [dial., = leaven, in allusion to piece of sour dough for raising bread baked in winter]

sourpuss /ˈsaʊəˌpʊs/ n. *colloq.* a sour-tempered person. [SOUR + PUSS = face]

sous- /suː(z)/ *prefix* (in words adopted from French) subordinate, under (*sous-chef*). [F]

sousaphone /ˈsuːzəfəʊn/ n. a large brass bass wind instrument encircling the player's body. □ **sousaphonist** n. [J. P. *Sousa*, Amer. bandmaster d. 1932, after *saxophone*]

souse /saʊs/ v. & n. —v. **1** tr. put (gherkins, fish, etc.) in pickle. **2** tr. & intr. plunge into liquid. **3** tr. (as **soused** adj.) *colloq.* drunk. —n. **1 a** pickle made with salt. **b** *US* food in pickle. **2** a dip, plunge, or drenching in water. **3** *colloq.* **a** a drinking-bout. **b** a drunkard. [ME f. OF *sous, souz* pickle f. OS *sultia*, OHG *sulza* brine f. Gmc: cf. SALT]

soutane /suːˈtɑːn/ n. *RC Ch.* a cassock worn by a priest. [F f. It. *sottana* f. *sotto* under f. L *subtus*]

south /saʊθ/ n., adj., & adv. —n. **1** the point of the horizon 90° clockwise from east. **2** the compass point corresponding to this. **3** the direction in which this lies. **4** (usu. **the South**) **a** the part of the world or a country or a town lying to the south. **b** the Southern States of the US. —adj. **1** towards, at, near, or facing the south (*a south wall; south country*). **2** coming from the south (*south wind*). —adv. **1** towards, at, or near the south (*they travelled south*). **2** (foll. by *of*) further south than. □ **South African** adj. of or relating to the republic of South Africa. —n. **1** a native or national of South Africa. **2** a person of South African descent. **South American** adj. of or relating to South America. —n. a native or citizen of South America. **south-east** n. **1** the point of the horizon midway between south and east. **2** the compass point corresponding to this. **3** the direction in which this lies. —adj. of, towards, or coming from the south-east. —adv. towards, at, or near the south-east. **South-East** the part of a country or town lying to the south-east. **south-easterly** adj. & adv. = south-east. **south-eastern** lying on the south-east side. **South Sea** the southern Pacific Ocean. **south-south-east** the point or direction midway between south and south-east. **south-south-west** the point or direction midway between south and south-west. **south-west** n. **1** the point of the horizon midway between south and west. **2** the compass point corresponding to this. **3** the direction in which this lies. —adj. of, towards, or coming from the south-west. —adv. towards, at, or near the south-west. **South-West** the part of a country or town lying to the south-west. **south-westerly** adj. & adv. = south-west. **south-western** lying on the south-west side. **to the south** (often foll. by *of*) in a southerly direction. [OE *sūth*]

southbound /ˈsaʊθbaʊnd/ adj. travelling or leading southwards.

southeaster /saʊθˈiːstə(r)/ n. a south-east wind.

southerly /ˈsʌðəlɪ/ adj., adv., & n. —adj. & adv. **1** in a southern position or direction. **2** (of a wind) blowing from the south. —n. (pl. **-ies**) a southerly wind.

southern /ˈsʌð(ə)n/ adj. esp. *Geog.* **1** of or in the south; inhabiting the south. **2** lying or directed towards the south (*at the southern end*). □ **Southern Cross** a southern constellation in the shape of a cross. **Southern hemisphere** the half of the earth below the equator. **southern lights** the aurora australis. **Southern States** the States in the south, esp. the south-east, of the US. □ **southernmost** adj. [OE *sūtherne* (as SOUTH, -ERN)]

southerner /ˈsʌðənə(r)/ n. a native or inhabitant of the south.

southpaw /ˈsaʊθpɔː/ n. & adj. *colloq.* —n. a left-handed person, esp. in boxing. —adj. left-handed.

southward /ˈsaʊθwəd/ adj., adv., & n. —adj. & adv. (also **southwards**) towards the south. —n. a southward direction or region.

southwester /saʊθˈwestə(r)/ n. a south-west wind.

souvenir /ˌsuːvəˈnɪə(r)/ n. (often foll. by *of*) a memento of an occasion, place, etc. [F f. *souvenir* remember f. L *subvenire* occur to the mind (as SUB-, *venire* come)]

sou'wester /saʊˈwestə(r)/ n. **1** = SOUTHWESTER. **2** a waterproof hat with a broad flap covering the neck.

sovereign /ˈsɒvrɪn/ n. & adj. —n. **1** a supreme ruler, esp. a monarch. **2** *Brit. hist.* a gold coin nominally worth £1. —adj. **1 a** supreme (*sovereign power*). **b** unmitigated (*sovereign contempt*). **2** excellent; effective (*a sovereign remedy*). **3** possessing sovereign power (*a sovereign State*). **4** royal (*our sovereign lord*). □ **sovereignly** adv. **sovereignty** n. (pl. **-ies**). [ME f. OF *so(u)verain* f. L: -g- by assoc. with *reign*]

soviet /ˈsəʊvɪət, ˈsɒ-/ n. & adj. *hist.* —n. **1** an elected local, district, or national council in the former USSR. **2** (**Soviet**) a citizen of the former USSR. **3** a revolutionary council of workers, peasants, etc. before 1917. —adj. (usu. **Soviet**) of or concerning the former Soviet Union. □ **Sovietize** v.tr. (also **-ise**). **Sovietization** /-taɪˈzeɪʃ(ə)n/ n. [Russ. *sovet* council]

sow[1] /səʊ/ v.tr. (*past* **sowed** /səʊd/; *past part.* **sown** /səʊn/ or **sowed**) **1** (also *absol.*) **a** scatter (seed) on or in the earth. **b** (often foll. by *with*) plant (a field etc.) with seed. **2** initiate; arouse (*sowed doubt in her mind*). **3** (foll. by *with*) cover thickly with. □ **sow the seed** (or **seeds**) **of** first give rise to; implant (an idea etc.). □ **sower** n. **sowing** n. [OE *sāwan* f. Gmc]

sow[2] /saʊ/ n. **1** a female adult pig, esp. after farrowing. **2** a female guinea-pig. **3** the female of some other species. [OE *sugu*]

sown *past part.* of sow[1].

sox *informal or Commerce* pl. of SOCK[1].

soy n. (also **soya** /ˈsɔɪjə/) **1** (also **soy sauce**) a sauce made in Japan and China from pickled soya beans. **2** (in full **soy bean**) = *soya bean*. [Jap. *shō-yu* f. Chin. *shi-you* f. *shi* salted beans + *you* oil]

soya /ˈsɔɪə/ n. (in full **soya bean**) **1 a** a leguminous plant, *Glycine soja*, orig. of SE Asia, cultivated for the edible oil and flour it yields, and used as a replacement for animal protein in certain foods. **b** the seed of this. **2** (also **soya sauce**) = SOY 1. [Du. *soja* f. Malay *soi* (as SOY)]

sozzled /ˈsɒz(ə)ld/ *adj. colloq.* very drunk. [past part. of dial. *sozzle* mix sloppily (prob. imit.)]

spa *n.* **1** a curative mineral spring. **2** a place or resort with this. [*Spa* in Belgium]

space *n. & v.* —*n.* **1 a** a continuous unlimited area or expanse which may or may not contain objects etc. **b** an interval between one, two, or three-dimensional points or objects (*a space of 10 metres*). **c** an empty area; room (*clear a space in the corner; occupies too much space*). **2** a large unoccupied region (*the wide open spaces*). **3** = outer space. **4** an interval of time (*in the space of an hour*). **5** the amount of paper used in writing etc. (*hadn't the space to discuss it*). **6** a blank between printed, typed, or written words, etc. —*v.tr.* **1** set or arrange at intervals. **2** put spaces between (esp. words, letters, lines, etc. in printing, typing, or writing). **3** (as **spaced** *adj.*) (often foll. by *out*) *sl.* in a state of euphoria, esp. from taking drugs. □ **space age** the era when space travel has become possible. **space-bar** a long key in a typewriter for making a space between words etc. **space flight 1** a journey through space. **2** = *space travel*. **space out** put more or wider spaces or intervals between. **space rocket** a rocket used to launch a spacecraft. **space-saving** occupying little space. **space shuttle** a rocket for repeated use esp. between the earth and a space station. **space station** an artificial satellite used as a base for operations in space. **space-time** (or **space-time continuum**) the fusion of the concepts of space and time, esp. as a four-dimensional continuum. **space travel** travel through outer space. **space traveller** a traveller in outer space; an astronaut. □ **spacer** *n.* **spacing** *n.* (esp. in sense 2 of *v.*). [ME f. OF *espace* f. L *spatium*]

spacecraft /ˈspeɪskrɑːft/ *n.* a vehicle used for travelling in space.

spaceman /ˈspeɪsmæn/ *n.* (*pl.* **-men**; *fem.* **spacewoman**, *pl.* **-women**) = *space traveller*.

spaceship /ˈspeɪsʃɪp/ *n.* a spacecraft, esp. one controlled by its crew.

spacesuit /ˈspeɪssjuːt, -suːt/ *n.* a garment designed to allow an astronaut to survive in space.

spacial var. of SPATIAL.

spacious /ˈspeɪʃəs/ *adj.* having ample space; covering a large area; roomy. □ **spaciously** *adv.* **spaciousness** *n.* [ME f. OF *spacios* or L *spatiosus* (as SPACE)]

spade[1] *n. & v.* —*n.* **1** a tool used for digging or cutting the ground etc., with a sharp-edged metal blade and a long handle. **2** a tool of a similar shape for various purposes. —*v.tr.* dig over (ground) with a spade. □ **call a spade a spade** speak plainly or bluntly. **spade beard** an oblong-shaped beard. □ **spadeful** *n.* (*pl.* **-fuls**). [OE *spadu, spada*]

spade[2] *n.* **1 a** a playing-card of a suit denoted by black inverted heart-shaped figures with small stalks. **b** (in *pl.*) this suit. **2** *sl. offens.* a Black. □ **in spades** *sl.* to a high degree, with great force. [It. *spade* pl. of *spada* sword f. L *spatha* f. Gk *spathē*, rel. to SPADE[1]: assoc. with the shape of a pointed spade]

spadework /ˈspeɪdwɜːk/ *n.* hard or routine preparatory work.

spaghetti /spəˈɡetɪ/ *n.* pasta made in solid strings. □ **spaghetti Bolognese** /ˌbɒləˈneɪz/ spaghetti served with a sauce of minced beef, tomato, onion, etc. **spaghetti junction** a multi-level road junction, esp. on a motorway. **spaghetti western** a western film made cheaply in Italy. [It., pl. of dimin. of *spago* string: *Bolognese* It., = of Bologna]

Spam *n. propr.* a tinned meat product made mainly from ham. [*spiced ham*]

span[1] *n. & v.* —*n.* **1** the full extent from end to end in space or time (*the span of a bridge; the whole span of history*). **2** each arch or part of a bridge between piers or supports. **3** the maximum lateral extent of an aeroplane, its wing, a bird's wing, etc. **4 a** the maximum distance between the tips of the thumb and little finger. **b** this as a measurement, equal to 9 inches. **5** a short distance or time (*our life is but a span*). —*v.* (**spanned, spanning**) **1** *tr.* **a** (of a bridge, arch, etc.) stretch from side to side; extend across (*the bridge spanned the river*). **b** (of a builder etc.) bridge (a river etc.). **2** *tr.* extend across (space or a period of time etc.). **3** *tr.* measure or cover the extent of (a thing) with one's hand with the fingers stretched. [OE *span(n)* or OF *espan*]

span[2] see SPICK AND SPAN.

spangle /ˈspæŋɡ(ə)l/ *n. & v.* —*n.* **1** a small thin piece of glittering material esp. used in quantity to ornament a dress etc.; a sequin. **2** a small sparkling object. —*v.tr.* (esp. as **spangled** *adj.*) cover with or as with spangles (*star-spangled; spangled costume*). □ **spangly** /-ŋɡlɪ/ *adj.* [ME f. *spang* f. MDu. *spange*, OHG *spanga*, ON *spöng* brooch f. Gmc]

Spaniard /ˈspænjəd/ *n.* **1 a** a native or national of Spain in southern Europe. **b** a person of Spanish descent. **2** *NZ* a spear grass. [ME f. OF *Espaignart* f. *Espaigne* Spain]

spaniel /ˈspænj(ə)l/ *n.* **1 a** a dog of any of various breeds with a long silky coat and drooping ears. **b** any of these breeds. **2** an obsequious or fawning person. [ME f. OF *espaigneul* Spanish (dog) f. Rmc *Hispaniolus* (unrecorded) f. *Hispania* Spain]

Spanish /ˈspænɪʃ/ *adj. & n.* —*adj.* of or relating to Spain or its people or language. —*n.* **1** the language of Spain and Spanish America. **2** (prec. by *the*; treated as *pl.*) the people of Spain. □ **Spanish fly** a bright green beetle, *Lytta vesicatoria*, formerly dried and used for raising blisters, as a supposed aphrodisiac, etc. **Spanish guitar** the standard six-stringed acoustic guitar, used esp. for classical and folk music. **Spanish Main** *hist.* the NE coast of South America between the Orinoco river and Panama, and adjoining parts of the Caribbean Sea. **Spanish omelette** an omelette containing chopped vegetables and often not folded. **Spanish onion** a large mild-flavoured onion. [ME f. *Spain*, with shortening of the first element]

spank *v. & n.* —*v.* **1** *tr.* slap esp. on the buttocks with the open hand, a slipper, etc. **2** *intr.* (of a horse etc.) move briskly, esp. between a trot and a gallop. —*n.* a slap esp. with the open hand on the buttocks. [perh. imit.]

spanker /ˈspæŋkə(r)/ *n.* **1** a person or thing that spanks. **2** *Naut.* a fore-and-aft sail set on the after side of the mizen-mast.

spanking /ˈspæŋkɪŋ/ adj., adv., & n. —adj. **1** (esp. of a horse) moving quickly; lively; brisk (at a spanking trot). **2** colloq. striking; excellent. —adv. colloq. very, exceedingly (spanking clean). —n. the act or an instance of slapping, esp. on the buttocks as a punishment for children.

spanner /ˈspænə(r)/ n. Brit. an instrument for turning or gripping a nut on a screw etc. □ **a spanner in the works** Brit. colloq. a drawback or impediment. [G spannen draw tight, unite]

spar[1] n. **1** a stout pole esp. used for the mast, yard, etc. of a ship. **2** the main longitudinal beam of an aeroplane wing. [ME spar, sparre, sperre f. OF esparre or ON sperra or direct f. Gmc: cf. MDu., MLG sparre, OS, OHG sparro]

spar[2] /spɑː(r)/ v. & n. —v.intr. (**sparred**, **sparring**) **1** (often foll. by at) make the motions of boxing without landing heavy blows. **2** engage in argument (they are always sparring). —n. **1** a sparring motion. **2** a boxing-match. □ **sparring partner 1** a boxer employed to engage in sparring with another as training. **2** a person with whom one enjoys arguing. [ME f. OE sperran, spyrran, of unkn. orig.: cf. ON sperrask kick out]

spar[3] /spɑː(r)/ n. any crystalline, easily cleavable and non-lustrous mineral, e.g. calcite or fluorspar. □ **sparry** adj. [MLG, rel. to OE spæren of plaster, spærstān gypsum]

spare /speə(r)/ adj., n., & v. —adj. **1 a** not required for ordinary use; extra (have no spare cash; spare time). **b** reserved for emergency or occasional use (slept in the spare room). **2** lean; thin. **3** scanty; frugal; not copious (a spare diet; a spare prose style). **4** colloq. not wanted or used by others (a spare seat in the front row). —n. Brit. a spare part; a duplicate. —v. **1** tr. afford to give or do without; dispense with (cannot spare him just now; can spare you a couple). **2** tr. **a** abstain from killing, hurting, wounding, etc. (spared his feelings; spared her life). **b** abstain from inflicting or causing; relieve from (spare me this talk; spare my blushes). **3** tr. be frugal or grudging of (no expense spared). □ **go spare** colloq. **1** Brit. become extremely angry or distraught. **2** be unwanted by others. **not spare oneself** exert one's utmost efforts. **spare part** a duplicate part to replace a lost or damaged part of a machine etc. **spare tyre 1** an extra tyre carried in a motor vehicle for emergencies. **2** Brit. colloq. a roll of fat round the waist. **to spare** left over; additional (an hour to spare). □ **sparely** adv. **spareness** n. **sparer** n. [OE spær, sparian f. Gmc]

spare-rib /speəˈrɪb/ n. closely-trimmed ribs of esp. pork. [prob. f. MLG ribbesper, by transposition and assoc. with SPARE]

sparing /ˈspeərɪŋ/ adj. **1** inclined to save; economical. **2** restrained; limited. □ **sparingly** adv. **sparingness** n.

spark n. & v. —n. **1** a fiery particle thrown off from a fire, or alight in ashes, or produced by a flint, match, etc. **2** (often foll. by of) a particle of a quality etc. (not a spark of life; a spark of interest). **3** Electr. **a** a light produced by a sudden disruptive discharge through the air etc. **b** such a discharge serving to ignite the explosive mixture in an internal-combustion engine. **4 a** a flash of wit etc. **b** anything causing interest, excitement, etc. **c** (also **bright spark**) a witty or lively person. —v. **1** intr. emit sparks of fire or electricity. **2** tr. (often foll. by off) stir into activity;

initiate (a process) suddenly. □ **sparking-plug** Brit. = spark-plug. **spark-plug** a device for firing the explosive mixture in an internal-combustion engine. □ **sparkless** adj. **sparky** adj. [ME f. OE spærca, spearca]

sparkle /ˈspɑːk(ə)l/ v. & n. —v.intr. **1 a** emit or seem to emit sparks; glitter; glisten (her eyes sparkled). **b** be witty; scintillate (sparkling repartee). **2** (of wine etc.) effervesce (cf. STILL[1] adj. 4). —n. a gleam, spark. □ **sparkly** adj. [ME f. SPARK + -LE[4]]

sparkler /ˈspɑːklə(r)/ n. **1** a person or thing that sparkles. **2** a hand-held sparkling firework. **3** colloq. a diamond or other gem.

sparrow /ˈspærəʊ/ n. **1** any small brownish-grey bird of the genus Passer, esp. the house sparrow and tree sparrow. **2** any of various birds of similar appearance such as the hedge sparrow. [OE spearwa f. Gmc]

sparrowhawk /ˈspærəʊˌhɔːk/ n. a small hawk, Accipiter nisus, preying on small birds.

sparse /spɑːs/ adj. thinly dispersed or scattered; not dense (sparse population; sparse greying hair). □ **sparsely** adv. **sparseness** n. **sparsity** n. [L sparsus past part. of spargere scatter]

Spartan /ˈspɑːt(ə)n/ adj. & n. —adj. **1** of or relating to Sparta in ancient Greece. **2 a** possessing the qualities of courage, endurance, etc., associated with Sparta. **b** (of a regime, conditions, etc.) lacking comfort; austere. —n. a citizen of Sparta. [ME f. L Spartanus f. Sparta f. Gk Sparta, -tē]

spasm /ˈspæz(ə)m/ n. **1** a sudden involuntary muscular contraction. **2** a sudden convulsive movement or emotion etc. (a spasm of coughing). **3** (usu. foll. by of) colloq. a brief spell of an activity. [ME f. OF spasme or L spasmus f. Gk spasmos, spasma f. spaō pull]

spasmodic /spæzˈmɒdɪk/ adj. **1** of, caused by, or subject to, a spasm or spasms (a spasmodic jerk; spasmodic asthma). **2** occurring or done by fits and starts (spasmodic efforts). □ **spasmodically** adv. [mod.L spasmodicus f. Gk spasmōdēs (as SPASM)]

spastic /ˈspæstɪk/ adj. & n. —adj. **1** Med. suffering from cerebral palsy with spasm of the muscles. **2** offens. weak, feeble, incompetent. **3** spasmodic. —n. Med. a spastic person. □ **spastically** adv. **spasticity** /-ˈtɪsɪtɪ/ n. [L spasticus f. Gk spastikos pulling f. spaō pull]

spat[1] past and past part. of SPIT[1].

spat[2] n. (usu. in pl.) hist. a short cloth gaiter protecting the shoe from mud etc. [abbr. of spatterdash (SPATTER)]

spat[3] n. & v. US colloq. —n. **1** a petty quarrel. **2** a slight amount. —v.intr. (**spatted**, **spatting**) quarrel mildly. [prob. imit.]

spat[4] n. & v. —n. the spawn of shellfish, esp. the oyster. —v. (**spatted**, **spatting**) **1** intr. (of an oyster) spawn. **2** tr. shed (spawn). [AF, of unkn. orig.]

spatchcock /ˈspætʃkɒk/ n. & v. —n. a chicken or esp. game bird split open and grilled. —v.tr. treat (poultry) in this way. [orig. in Ir. use, expl. by Grose (1785) as f. dispatch-cock]

spate n. **1** a river-flood (the river is in spate). **2** a large or excessive amount (a spate of enquiries). [ME, Sc. & N.Engl.: orig. unkn.]

spathe /speɪð/ n. Bot. a large bract or pair of bracts enveloping a flower-cluster. □ **spathaceous** /spəˈðeɪʃəs/ adj. [L f. Gk spathē broad blade etc.]

spatial /ˈspeɪʃ(ə)l/ adj. (also **spacial**) of or concerning space (spatial extent). □ **spatiality** /-ʃɪˈælɪtɪ/ n. **spatialize** v.tr. (also **-ise**). **spatially** adv. [L spatium space]

spatio-temporal /ˌspeɪʃɪəʊˈtempər(ə)l/ adj. Physics & Philos. belonging to both space and time or to space-time. □ **spatio-temporally** adv. [formed as SPATIAL + TEMPORAL]

spatter /ˈspætə(r)/ v. & n. —v. 1 tr. **a** (often foll. by with) splash (a person etc.) (spattered him with mud). **b** scatter or splash (liquid, mud, etc.) here and there. 2 intr. (of rain etc.) fall here and there. —n. (usu. foll. by of) a splash (a spatter of mud). [frequent. f. base as in Du., LG spatten burst, spout]

spatula /ˈspætjʊlə/ n. 1 a broad-bladed knife-like implement used for spreading, stirring, mixing (paints), etc. 2 a doctor's instrument for pressing the tongue down or to one side. [L, var. of spathula, dimin. of spatha SPATHE]

spavin /ˈspævɪn/ n. Vet. a disease of a horse's hock with a hard bony tumour or excrescence. □ **spavined** adj. [ME f. OF espavin, var. of esparvain f. Gmc]

spawn v. & n. —v. 1 **a** tr. (also absol.) (of a fish, frog, mollusc, or crustacean) produce (eggs). **b** intr. be produced as eggs or young. 2 tr. derog. (of people) produce (offspring). 3 tr. produce or generate, esp. in large numbers. —n. 1 the eggs of fish, frogs, etc. 2 derog. human or other offspring. 3 a white fibrous matter from which fungi are produced; mycelium. □ **spawner** n. [ME f. AF espaundre shed roe, OF espandre EXPAND]

spay v.tr. sterilize (a female animal) by removing the ovaries. [ME f. AF espeier, OF espeer cut with a sword f. espee sword f. L spatha: see SPATHE]

speak v. (past **spoke**; past part. **spoken** /ˈspəʊkən/) 1 intr. make articulate verbal utterances in an ordinary (not singing) voice. 2 tr. **a** utter (words). **b** make known or communicate (one's opinion, the truth, etc.) in this way (never speaks sense). 3 intr. **a** (foll. by to, with) hold a conversation (spoke to him for an hour; spoke with them about their work). **b** (foll. by of) mention in writing etc. (speaks of it in his novel). **c** (foll. by for) articulate the feelings of (another person etc.) in speech or writing (speaks for our generation). 4 intr. (foll. by to) **a** address; converse with (a person etc.). **b** speak in confirmation of or with reference to (spoke to the resolution; can speak to his innocence). **c** colloq. reprove (spoke to them about their lateness). 5 intr. make a speech before an audience etc. (spoke for an hour on the topic; has a good speaking voice). 6 tr. use or be able to use (a specified language) (cannot speak French). □ **not** (or **nothing**) **to speak of** not (or nothing) worth mentioning; practically not (or nothing). **speak for itself** need no supporting evidence. **speak for oneself 1** give one's own opinions. **2** not presume to speak for others. **speak one's mind** speak bluntly or frankly. **speak out** speak loudly or freely, give one's opinion. **speak up** = speak out. **speak volumes** (of a fact etc.) be very significant. □ **speakable** adj. [OE sprecan, later specan]

speakeasy /ˈspiːkˌiːzɪ/ n. (pl. **-ies**) US hist. sl. an illicit liquor shop or drinking club during Prohibition.

speaker /ˈspiːkə(r)/ n. 1 a person who speaks, esp. in public. 2 a person who speaks a specified language (esp. in comb.: a French-speaker). 3 (**Speaker**) the presiding officer in a legislative assembly, esp. the House of Commons. 4 = LOUDSPEAKER. □ **speakership** n.

speaking /ˈspiːkɪŋ/ n. & adj. —n. the act or an instance of uttering words etc. —adj. 1 that speaks; capable of articulate speech. 2 (of a portrait) lifelike; true to its subject (a speaking likeness). 3 (in comb.) speaking or capable of speaking a specified foreign language (French-speaking). 4 with a reference to or from a point of view specified (roughly speaking; professionally speaking). □ **on speaking terms** (foll. by with) 1 slightly acquainted. 2 on friendly terms. **speaking acquaintance 1** a person one knows slightly. 2 this degree of familiarity. **speaking clock** Brit. a telephone service giving the correct time in words.

spear n. & v. —n. 1 a thrusting or throwing weapon with a pointed usu. steel tip and a long shaft. 2 a similar barbed instrument used for catching fish etc. 3 a pointed stem of asparagus etc. —v.tr. pierce or strike with or as if with a spear (speared an olive). □ **spear gun** a gun used to propel a spear in underwater fishing. [OE spere]

spearhead /ˈspɪəhed/ n. & v. —n. 1 the point of a spear. 2 an individual or group chosen to lead a thrust or attack. —v.tr. act as the spearhead of (an attack etc.).

spearmint /ˈspɪəmɪnt/ n. a common garden mint, Mentha spicata, used in cookery and to flavour chewing-gum.

spec[1] n. colloq. a commercial speculation or venture. □ **on spec** in the hope of success; as a gamble, on the off chance. [abbr. of SPECULATION]

spec[2] n. colloq. a detailed working description; a specification. [abbr. of SPECIFICATION]

special /ˈspeʃ(ə)l/ adj. & n. —adj. 1 **a** particularly good; exceptional; out of the ordinary (bought them a special present; took special trouble). **b** peculiar; specific; not general (lacks the special qualities required; the word has a special sense). 2 for a particular purpose (sent on a special assignment). 3 in which a person specializes (statistics is his special field). 4 denoting education for children with particular needs, e.g. the handicapped. —n. a special person or thing, e.g. a special constable, train, examination, edition of a newspaper, dish on a menu, etc. □ **Special Branch** (in the UK) a police department dealing with political security. **special case 1** a written statement of fact presented by litigants to a court. 2 an exceptional or unusual case. **special constable** Brit. a policeman sworn in to assist in times of emergency etc. **special correspondent** a journalist writing for a newspaper on special events or a special area of interest. **special delivery** a delivery of mail in advance of the regular delivery. **special edition** an extra edition of a newspaper including later news than the ordinary edition. **special effects** scenic illusions created by props and camerawork. **special licence** Brit. a marriage licence allowing immediate marriage without banns, or at an unusual time or place. **special pleading 1**

Law pleading with reference to new facts in a case. **2** a specious or unfair argument favouring the speaker's point of view. □ **specially** *adv.* **specialness** *n.* [ME f. OF *especial* ESPECIAL or L *specialis* (as SPECIES)]

specialist /ˈspeʃəlɪst/ *n.* (usu. foll. by *in*) **1** a person who is trained in a particular branch of a profession, esp. medicine (*a specialist in dermatology*). **2** a person who specially or exclusively studies a subject or a particular branch of a subject. □ **specialism** /-ˌlɪz(ə)m/ *n.* **specialistic** /-ˈlɪstɪk/ *adj.*

speciality /ˌspeʃɪˈælɪtɪ/ *n.* (*pl.* **-ies**) **1** a special pursuit, product, operation, etc., to which a company or a person gives special attention. **2** a special feature, characteristic, or skill. [ME f. OF *especialité* or LL *specialitas* (as SPECIAL)]

specialize /ˈspeʃəˌlaɪz/ *v.* (also **-ise**) **1** *intr.* (often foll. by *in*) a be or become a specialist (*specializes in optics*). **b** devote oneself to an area of interest, skill, etc. (*specializes in insulting people*). **2** *Biol.* **a** *tr.* (esp. in *passive*) adapt or set apart (an organ etc.) for a particular purpose. **b** *intr.* (of an organ etc.) become adapted etc. in this way. **3** *tr.* make specific or individual. □ **specialization** /-ˈzeɪʃ(ə)n/ *n.* [F *spécialiser* (as SPECIAL)]

specialty /ˈspeʃəltɪ/ *n.* (*pl.* **-ies**) esp. *US* = SPECIALITY. [ME f. OF (e)*specialté* (as SPECIAL)]

speciation /ˌspiːsɪˈeɪʃən, ˌspiːʃ-/ *n. Biol.* the formation of a new species in the course of evolution.

specie /ˈspiːʃiː, -ʃɪ/ *n.* coin money as opposed to paper money. [L, ablat. of SPECIES in phrase *in specie*]

species /ˈspiːʃiːz, -ʃiːz, ˈspiːs-/ *n.* (*pl.* same) **1** a class of things having some common characteristics. **2** *Biol.* a category in the system of classification of living organisms consisting of similar individuals capable of exchanging genes or interbreeding. **3** a kind or sort. [L, = appearance, kind, beauty, f. *specere* look]

specific /spɪˈsɪfɪk/ *adj.* & *n.* —*adj.* **1** clearly defined; definite (*has no specific name; told me so in specific terms*). **2** relating to a particular subject; peculiar (*a style specific to that*). **3** **a** of or concerning a species (*the specific name for a plant*). **b** possessing, or concerned with, the properties that characterize a species (*the specific forms of animals*). —*n.* a specific aspect or factor (*shall we discuss specifics?*). □ **specifically** *adv.* **specificity** /-ˈfɪsɪtɪ/ *n.* **specificness** *n.* [LL *specificus* (as SPECIES)]

specification /ˌspesɪfɪˈkeɪʃ(ə)n/ *n.* **1** the act or an instance of specifying; the state of being specified. **2** (esp. in *pl.*) a detailed description of the construction, workmanship, materials, etc., of work done or to be done, prepared by an architect, engineer, etc. **3** a description by an applicant for a patent of the construction and use of his invention. [med.L *specificatio* (as SPECIFY)]

specify /ˈspesɪfaɪ/ *v.tr.* (**-ies**, **-ied**) **1** (also *absol.*) name or mention expressly (*specified the type he needed*). **2** (usu. foll. by *that* + clause) name as a condition (*specified that he must be paid at once*). **3** include in specifications (*a French window was not specified*). □ **specifiable** *adj.* **specifier** *n.* [ME f. OF *specifier* or LL *specificare* (as SPECIFIC)]

specimen /ˈspesɪmən/ *n.* **1** an individual or part taken as an example of a class or whole, esp. when used for investigation or scientific examination (*specimens of copper ore; a specimen*

of your handwriting). **2** *Med.* a sample of urine for testing. **3** *colloq.* usu. *derog.* a person of a specified sort. [L f. *specere* look]

specious /ˈspiːʃəs/ *adj.* **1** superficially plausible but actually wrong (*a specious argument*). **2** misleadingly attractive in appearance. □ **speciosity** /-ʃɪˈɒsɪtɪ/ *n.* **speciously** *adv.* **speciousness** *n.* [ME, = beautiful, f. L *speciosus* (as SPECIES)]

speck *n.* & *v.* —*n.* **1** a small spot, dot, or stain. **2** (foll. by *of*) a particle (*speck of dirt*). **3** a rotten spot in fruit. —*v.tr.* (esp. as **specked** *adj.*) marked with specks. □ **speckless** *adj.* [OE *specca*: cf. SPECKLE]

speckle /ˈspek(ə)l/ *n.* & *v.* —*n.* a small spot, mark, or stain, esp. in quantity on the skin, a bird's egg, etc. —*v.tr.* (esp. as **speckled** *adj.*) mark with speckles or patches. [ME f. MDu. *spekkel*]

specs *n.pl. colloq.* a pair of spectacles. [abbr.]

spectacle /ˈspektək(ə)l/ *n.* **1** a public show, ceremony, etc. **2** anything attracting public attention (*a charming spectacle; a disgusting spectacle*). □ **make a spectacle of oneself** make oneself an object of ridicule. [ME f. OF f. L *spectaculum* f. *spectare* frequent. of *specere* look]

spectacled /ˈspektək(ə)ld/ *adj.* **1** wearing spectacles. **2** (of an animal) having facial markings resembling spectacles.

spectacles /ˈspektək(ə)lz/ *n.pl.* (also **pair of spectacles** *sing.*) a pair of lenses in a frame resting on the nose and ears, used to correct defective eyesight or protect the eyes.

spectacular /spekˈtækjʊlə(r)/ *adj.* & *n.* —*adj.* **1** of or like a public show; striking, amazing, lavish. **2** strikingly large or obvious (*a spectacular increase in output*). —*n.* an event intended to be spectacular, esp. a musical film or play. □ **spectacularly** *adv.* [SPECTACLE, after *oracular* etc.]

spectate /spekˈteɪt/ *v.intr.* be a spectator, esp. at a sporting event. [back-form. f. SPECTATOR]

spectator /spekˈteɪtə(r)/ *n.* a person who looks on at a show, game, incident, etc. □ **spectator sport** a sport attracting spectators rather than participants. □ **spectatorial** /-təˈtɔːrɪəl/ *adj.* [F *spectateur* or L *spectator* f. *spectare*: see SPECTACLE]

spectra *pl.* of SPECTRUM.

spectral /ˈspektr(ə)l/ *adj.* **1** **a** of or relating to spectres or ghosts. **b** ghostlike. **2** of or concerning spectra or the spectrum (*spectral colours; spectral analysis*). □ **spectrally** *adv.*

spectre /ˈspektə(r)/ *n.* (*US* **specter**) **1** a ghost. **2** a haunting presentiment or preoccupation (*the spectre of war*). [F *spectre* or L *spectrum*: see SPECTRUM]

spectro- /ˈspektrəʊ/ *comb. form* a spectrum.

spectrogram /ˈspektrəʊˌgræm/ *n.* a record obtained with a spectrograph.

spectrograph /ˈspektrəʊˌɡrɑːf/ *n.* an apparatus for photographing or otherwise recording spectra. □ **spectrographic** /-ˈɡræfɪk/ *adj.* **spectrographically** /-ˈɡræfɪkəlɪ/ *adv.* **spectrography** /spekˈtrɒɡrəfɪ/ *n.*

spectrometer /spekˈtrɒmɪtə(r)/ *n.* an instrument used for the measurement of observed spectra. □ **spectrometric** /ˌspektrəˈmetrɪk/ *adj.* **spectrometry** *n.* [G *Spektrometer* or F *spectromètre* (as SPECTRO-, -METER)]

spectroscope /'spektrə,skəʊp/ n. an instrument for producing and recording spectra for examination. □ **spectroscopic** /-'skɒpɪk/ adj. **spectroscopical** /-'skɒpɪk(ə)l/ adj. **spectroscopist** /-'trɒskəpɪst/ n. **spectroscopy** /-'trɒskəpɪ/ n. [G *Spektroskop* or F *spectroscope* (as SPECTRO-, -SCOPE)]

spectrum /'spektrəm/ n. (pl. **spectra** /-trə/) 1 the band of colours, as seen in a rainbow etc., arranged in a progressive series according to their refrangibility or wavelength. 2 the entire range of wavelengths of electromagnetic radiation. 3 **a** an image or distribution of parts of electromagnetic radiation arranged in a progressive series according to wavelength. **b** this as characteristic of a body or substance when emitting or absorbing radiation. 4 the entire range or a wide range of anything arranged by degree or quality etc. □ **spectrum** (or **spectral**) **analysis** chemical analysis by means of a spectroscope. [L, = image, apparition f. *specere* look]

specula pl. of SPECULUM.

speculate /'spekjʊ,leɪt/ v. 1 intr. (usu. foll. by *on*, *upon*, *about*) form a theory or conjecture, esp. without a firm factual basis; meditate (*speculated on their prospects*). 2 tr. (foll. by *that*, *how*, etc. + clause) conjecture, consider (*speculated how he might achieve it*). 3 intr. **a** invest in stocks etc. in the hope of gain but with the possibility of loss. **b** gamble recklessly. □ **speculator** n. [L *speculari* spy out, observe f. *specula* watch-tower f. *specere* look]

speculation /,spekjʊ'leɪʃ(ə)n/ n. 1 the act or an instance of speculating; a theory or conjecture (*made no speculation as to her age; is given to speculation*). 2 **a** a speculative investment or enterprise (*bought it as a speculation*). **b** the practice of business speculating. [ME f. OF *speculation* or LL *speculatio* (as SPECULATE)]

speculative /'spekjʊlətɪv/ adj. 1 of, based on, engaged in, or inclined to speculation. 2 (of a business investment) involving the risk of loss (*a speculative builder*). □ **speculatively** adv. **speculativeness** n. [ME f. OF *speculatif -ive* or LL *speculativus* (as SPECULATE)]

speculum /'spekjʊləm/ n. (pl. **specula** /-lə/) 1 *Surgery* an instrument for dilating the cavities of the human body for inspection. 2 a mirror, usu. of polished metal, esp. in a reflecting telescope. [L, = mirror, f. *specere* look]

sped past and past part. of SPEED.

speech n. 1 the faculty or act of speaking. 2 a formal public address. 3 a manner of speaking (*a man of blunt speech*). 4 a remark (*after this speech he was silent*). 5 the language of a nation, region, group, etc. 6 *Mus.* the act of sounding in an organ-pipe etc. □ **the Queen's** (or **King's**) **Speech** a statement including the Government's proposed measures read by the sovereign at the opening of Parliament. **speech day** *Brit.* an annual prize-giving day in many schools, usu. marked by speeches etc. **speech therapy** treatment to improve defective speech. □ **speechful** adj. [OE *sprǣc*, later *spēc* f. WG, rel. to SPEAK]

speechify /'spiːtʃɪ,faɪ/ v.intr. (-ies, -ied) joc. or derog. make esp. boring or long speeches. □ **speechification** /-fɪ'keɪʃ(ə)n/ n. **speechifier** n.

speechless /'spiːtʃlɪs/ adj. 1 temporarily unable to speak because of emotion etc. (*speechless with rage*). 2 dumb. □ **speechlessly** adv. **speechlessness** n. [OE *spǣclēas* (as SPEECH, -LESS)]

speed n. & v. —n. 1 rapidity of movement (*with all speed; at full speed*). 2 a rate of progress or motion over a distance in time (*attains a high speed*). 3 **a** a gear appropriate to a range of speeds of a bicycle. **b** *US* or *archaic* such a gear in a motor vehicle. 4 *Photog.* **a** the sensitivity of film to light. **b** the light-gathering power of a lens. **c** the duration of an exposure. 5 *sl.* an amphetamine drug, esp. methamphetamine. —v. (past and past part. **sped** /sped/) 1 intr. go fast (*sped down the street*). 2 (past and past part. **speeded**) **a** intr. (of a motorist etc.) travel at an illegal or dangerous speed. **b** tr. regulate the speed of (an engine etc.). **c** tr. cause (an engine etc.) to go at a fixed speed. 3 tr. send fast or on its way (*speed an arrow from the bow*). 4 intr. & tr. archaic make or become prosperous or successful (*how have you sped?; God speed you!*). □ **at speed** moving quickly. **speed bump** (or **hump**) a transverse ridge in the road to control the speed of vehicles. **speed limit** the maximum speed at which a road vehicle may legally be driven in a particular area etc. **speed up** move or work at greater speed. □ **speeder** n. [OE *spēd*, *spēdan* f. Gmc]

speedboat /'spiːdbəʊt/ n. a motor boat designed for high speed.

speedo /'spiːdəʊ/ n. (pl. **-os**) *colloq.* = SPEEDOMETER. [abbr.]

speedometer /spiː'dɒmɪtə(r)/ n. an instrument on a motor vehicle etc. indicating its speed to the driver. [SPEED + METER¹]

speedway /'spiːdweɪ/ n. 1 **a** motor-cycle racing. **b** a stadium or track used for this. 2 *US* a road or track used for fast motor traffic.

speedwell /'spiːdwel/ n. any small herb of the genus *Veronica*, with a creeping or ascending stem and tiny blue or pink flowers. [app. f. SPEED + WELL¹]

speedy /'spiːdɪ/ adj. (**speedier**, **speediest**) 1 moving quickly; rapid. 2 done without delay; prompt (*a speedy answer*). □ **speedily** adv. **speediness** n.

speleology /,spiːlɪ'ɒlədʒɪ, ,spe-/ n. 1 the scientific study of caves. 2 the exploration of caves. □ **speleological** /-ə'lɒdʒɪk(ə)l/ adj. **speleologist** n. [F *spéléologie* f. L *spelaeum* f. Gk *spēlaion* cave]

spell¹ v.tr. (past and past part. **spelt** or **spelled**) 1 (also *absol.*) write or name the letters that form (a word etc.) in correct sequence (*spell 'exaggerate'; cannot spell properly*). 2 **a** (of letters) make up or form (a word etc.). **b** (of circumstances, a scheme, etc.) result in; involve (*spell ruin*). □ **spell out** (or **over**) 1 make out (words, writing, etc.) letter by letter. 2 explain in detail (*spelled out what the change would mean*). □ **spellable** adj. [ME f. OF *espel(l)er*, f. Frank. (as SPELL²)]

spell² n. 1 a form of words used as a magical charm or incantation. 2 an attraction or fascination exercised by a person, activity, quality, etc. □ **under a spell** mastered by or as if by a spell. [OE *spel(l)* f. Gmc]

spell³ n. & v. 1 a short or fairly short period (*a cold spell in April*). 2 a turn of work (*did a spell of woodwork*). 3 *Austral.* a period of rest from work. —v. 1 tr. **a** relieve or take the place of (a person) in work etc. **b** allow to rest briefly. 2 intr. *Austral.* take a brief rest. [earlier as verb:

later form of dial. *spele* take place of f. OE *spelian*, of unkn. orig.]

spellbind /ˈspelbaɪnd/ *tr.* (*past* and *past part.* **spellbound**) **1** bind with or as if with a spell; entrance. **2** (as **spellbound** *adj.*) entranced, fascinated, esp. by a speaker, activity, quality, etc. □ **spellbinder** *n.* **spellbindingly** *adv.*

speller /ˈspelə(r)/ *n.* **1** a person who spells esp. in a specified way (*is a poor speller*). **2** a book on spelling.

spellican var. of SPILLIKIN.

spelling /ˈspelɪŋ/ *n.* **1** the process or activity of writing or naming the letters of a word etc. **2** the way a word is spelled. **3** the ability to spell (*his spelling is weak*). □ **spelling-bee** a spelling competition.

spelt[1] *past* and *past part.* of SPELL[1].

spelt[2] /spelt/ *n.* a species of wheat, *Triticum aestivum*. [OE f. OS *spelta* (OHG *spelza*), ME f. MLG, MDu. *spelte*]

spelunker /spɪˈlʌŋkə(r)/ *n. US* a person who explores caves, esp. as a hobby. □ **spelunking** *n.* [obs. *spelunk* cave f. L *spelunca*]

spencer /ˈspensə(r)/ *n.* **1** a short close-fitting jacket. **2** a woman's thin usu. woollen under-bodice worn for extra warmth in winter. [prob. f. the 2nd Earl *Spencer*, Engl. politician d. 1834]

spend *v.tr.* (*past* and *past part.* **spent**) **1** (usu. foll. by *on*) **a** (also *absol.*) pay out (money) in making a purchase etc. (*spent £5 on a new pen*). **b** pay out (money) for a particular person's benefit or for the improvement of a thing (*had to spend £200 on the car*). **2 a** use or consume (time or energy) (*shall spend no more effort; how do you spend your Sundays?*). **b** (also *refl.*) use up; exhaust; wear out (*their ammunition was all spent; his anger was soon spent*). **3** *tr.* (as **spent** *adj.*) having lost its original force or strength; exhausted (*the storm is spent; spent bullets*). □ **spending money** pocket money.

spend a penny *Brit. colloq.* urinate (from the coin-operated locks of public lavatories). □ **spendable** *adj.* **spender** *n.* [OE *spendan* f. L *expendere* (see EXPEND): in ME perh. also f. obs. *dispend* f. OF *despendre* expend f. L *dispendere*: see DISPENSE]

spendthrift /ˈspendθrɪft/ *n.* & *adj.* —*n.* an extravagant person; a prodigal. —*adj.* extravagant; prodigal.

spent *past* and *past part.* of SPEND.

sperm *n.* (*pl.* same or **sperms**) **1** = SPERMATOZOON. **2** the male reproductive fluid containing spermatozoa; semen. □ **sperm bank** a supply of semen stored for use in artificial insemination. **sperm count** the number of spermatozoa in one ejaculation or a measured amount of semen. **sperm oil** an oil obtained from the head of a sperm whale, and used as a lubricant. **sperm whale** a large whale, *Physeter macrocephalus*, hunted for spermaceti and sperm oil and ambergris. [ME f. LL *sperma* f. Gk *sperma -atos* seed f. *speirō* sow: in *sperm whale* an abbr. of SPERMACETI]

spermaceti /ˌspɜːməˈsetɪ/ *n.* a white waxy substance produced by the sperm whale to aid buoyancy, and used in the manufacture of candles, ointments, etc. □ **spermacetic** *adj.* [ME f. med.L f. LL *sperma* sperm + *ceti* genit. of *cetus* f. Gk *kētos* whale, from the belief that it was whale-spawn]

spermato- /ˈspɜːmətəʊ/ *comb. form Biol.* a sperm or seed.

spermatozoon /ˌspɜːmətəʊˈzəʊɒn/ *n.* (*pl.* **spermatozoa** /-ˈzəʊə/) the mature motile sex cell in animals. □ **spermatozoal** *adj.* **spermatozoan** *adj.* **spermatozoic** *adj.* [SPERM + Gk *zōion* animal]

spermicide /ˈspɜːmɪˌsaɪd/ *n.* a substance able to kill spermatozoa. □ **spermicidal** /-ˈsaɪd(ə)l/ *adj.*

spermo- /ˈspɜːməʊ/ *comb. form* = SPERMATO-.

spew *v.* (also **spue**) **1** *tr.* & *intr.* vomit. **2** (often foll. by *out*) **a** *tr.* expel (contents) rapidly and forcibly. **b** *intr.* (of contents) be expelled in this way. □ **spewer** *n.* [OE *spīwan*, *spēowan* f. Gmc]

sphagnum /ˈsfægnəm/ *n.* (*pl.* **sphagna** /-nə/) (in full **sphagnum moss**) any moss of the genus *Sphagnum*, growing in bogs and peat, and used as packing esp. for plants, as fertilizer, etc. [mod.L f. Gk *sphagnos* a moss]

sphere *n.* **1** a solid figure, or its surface, with every point on its surface equidistant from its centre. **2** an object having this shape; a ball or globe. **3 a** any celestial body. **b** a globe representing the earth. **c** *poet.* the heavens; the sky. **d** the sky perceived as a vault upon or in which celestial bodies are represented as lying. **e** *hist.* each of a series of revolving concentrically arranged spherical shells in which celestial bodies were formerly thought to be set in a fixed relationship. **4 a** a field of action, influence, or existence (*have much within their own sphere*). **b** a (usu. specified) stratum of society or social class (*moves in quite another sphere*). □ **music** (or **harmony**) **of the spheres** the natural harmonic tones supposedly produced by the movement of the celestial spheres (see sense 3e) or the bodies fixed in them. **sphere of influence** the claimed or recognized area of a State's interests, an individual's control, etc. □ **spheral** *adj.* [ME *sper(e)* f. OF *espere* f. LL *sphera*, L f. Gk *sphaira* ball]

-sphere /sfɪə(r)/ *comb. form* **1** having the form of a sphere (*bathysphere*). **2** a region round the earth (*atmosphere*).

spheric /ˈsfɪərɪk/ *adj.* = SPHERICAL. □ **sphericity** /-ˈrɪsɪtɪ/ *n.*

spherical /ˈsferɪk(ə)l/ *adj.* **1** shaped like a sphere; globular. **2** of or relating to the properties of spheres (*spherical geometry*). □ **spherically** *adv.* [LL *sphaericus* f. Gk *sphairikos* (as SPHERE)]

spheroid /ˈsfɪərɔɪd/ *n.* a spherelike but not perfectly spherical body. □ **spheroidal** /sfɪəˈrɔɪd(ə)l/ *adj.* **spheroidicity** /-ˈdɪsɪtɪ/ *n.*

sphincter /ˈsfɪŋktə(r)/ *n. Anat.* a ring of muscle surrounding and serving to guard or close an opening or tube, esp. the anus. □ **sphincteral** *adj.* **sphinctered** *adj.* **sphincterial** /-ˈtɪərɪəl/ *adj.* **sphincteric** /-ˈterɪk/ *adj.* [L f. Gk *sphigktēr* f. *sphiggō* bind tight]

sphinx /sfɪŋks/ *n.* **1** (**Sphinx**) (in Greek mythology) the winged monster of Thebes, having a woman's head and a lion's body. **2** *Antiq.* **a** any of several ancient Egyptian stone figures having a lion's body and a human or animal head. **b** (**the Sphinx**) the huge sphinx near the Pyramids at Giza. **3** an enigmatic or inscrutable person. [L f. Gk *Sphigx*, app. f. *sphiggō* draw tight]

sphygmo- /ˈsfɪgməʊ/ *comb. form Physiol.* a pulse or pulsation. [Gk *sphugmo-* f. *sphugmos* pulse f. *sphuzō* to throb]

sphygmomanometer /ˌsfɪgməʊməˈnɒmɪtə(r)/ *n.* an instrument for measuring blood pressure. □ **sphygmomanometric** /-nəˈmetrɪk/ *adj.*

spice *n. & v.* —*n.* **1** an aromatic or pungent vegetable substance used to flavour food, e.g. cloves, pepper, or mace. **2** spices collectively (*a dealer in spice*). **3 a** an interesting or piquant quality. **b** (foll. by *of*) a slight flavour or suggestion (*a spice of malice*). —*v.tr.* **1** flavour with spice. **2** add an interesting or piquant quality to (*a book spiced with humour*). [ME f. OF *espice*(r) f. L *species* specific kind: in LL pl. = merchandise]

spick and span /ˌspɪk ənd ˈspæn/ *adj.* **1** smart and new. **2** neat and clean. [16th-c. *spick and span new*, emphatic extension of ME *span new* f. ON *spán-nýr* f. *spánn* chip + *nýr* new]

spicy /ˈspaɪsɪ/ *adj.* (**spicier**, **spiciest**) **1** of, flavoured with, or fragrant with spice. **2** piquant, pungent; sensational or improper (*a spicy story*). □ **spicily** *adv.* **spiciness** *n.*

spider /ˈspaɪdə(r)/ *n. & v.* —*n.* **1 a** any eight-legged arthropod of the order Araneae with a round unsegmented body, many of which spin webs for the capture of insects as food. **b** any of various similar or related arachnids. **2** any object comparable to a spider, esp. as having numerous or prominent legs or radiating spokes. —*v.intr.* **1** move in a scuttling manner suggestive of a spider (*fingers spidered across the map*). **2** cause to move or appear in this way. **3** (as **spidering** *adj.*) spiderlike in form, manner, or movement (*spidering streets*). □ **spider crab** any of various crabs of the family Majidae with a pear-shaped body and long thin legs. **spider monkey** any S. American monkey of the genus *Ateles*, with long limbs and a prehensile tail. **spider plant** any of various house plants with long narrow striped leaves. □ **spiderish** *adj.* [OE *spīthra* (as SPIN)]

spiderman /ˈspaɪdəˌmæn/ *n.* (pl. **-men**) *Brit. colloq.* a person who works at great heights in building construction.

spidery /ˈspaɪdərɪ/ *adj.* elongated and thin (*spidery handwriting*).

spiel /ʃpiːl/ *n. & v. sl.* —*n.* a glib speech or story, esp. a salesman's patter. —*v.* **1** *intr.* speak glibly; hold forth. **2** *tr.* reel off (patter etc.). [G, = play, game]

spieler /ˈʃpiːlə(r)/ *n. sl.* **1** esp. *US* a person who spiels. **2** *Austral.* a gambler; a swindler. [G (as SPIEL)]

spigot /ˈspɪgət/ *n.* **1** a small peg or plug, esp. for insertion into the vent-hole of a cask. **2 a** *US* a tap. **b** a device for controlling the flow of liquid in a tap. [ME, perh. f. Prov. *espigou*(n) f. L *spiculum* dimin. of *spicum* SPIKE²]

spike¹ *n. & v.* —*n.* **1 a** a sharp point. **b** a pointed piece of metal, esp. the top of an iron railing etc. **2 a** any of several metal points set into the sole of a running-shoe to prevent slipping. **b** (in *pl.*) a pair of running-shoes with spikes. **3 a** a pointed metal rod standing on a base and used for filing news items etc. esp. when rejected for publication. **b** a similar spike used for bills etc. —*v.tr.* **1 a** fasten or provide with spikes. **b** fix on or pierce with spikes. **2** (of a newspaper editor etc.) reject (a story) by filing it on a spike. **3** *colloq.* **a** lace (a drink) with alcohol, a drug, etc. **b** contaminate (a substance) with something added. **4** make useless, put an end to, thwart (an idea etc.). **5** *hist.* plug up the vent of (a gun)

with a spike. □ **spike a person's guns** spoil his or her plans. **spike heel** a high tapering heel of a shoe. [ME perh. f. MLG, MDu. *spiker*, rel. to SPOKE¹]

spike² *n. Bot.* **1** a flower-cluster formed of many flower-heads attached closely on a long stem. **2** a separate sprig of any plant in which flowers form a spikelike cluster. □ **spikelet** *n.* [ME, = ear of corn, f. L *spica*, rel. to *spina* SPINE]

spikenard /ˈspaɪknɑːd/ *n.* **1** *Bot.* an Indian plant, *Nardostachys grandiflora.* **2** *hist.* a costly perfumed ointment made from this. [ME ult. f. med.L *spica nardi* (as SPIKE², NARD) after Gk *nardostakhus*]

spiky /ˈspaɪkɪ/ *adj.* (**spikier**, **spikiest**) **1** like a spike; having many spikes. **2** *colloq.* easily offended; prickly. □ **spikily** *adv.* **spikiness** *n.*

spill¹ *v. & n.* —*v.* (*past* and *past part.* **spilt** or **spilled**) **1** *intr. & tr.* fall or run or cause (a liquid, powder, etc.) to fall or run out of a vessel, esp. unintentionally. **2 a** *tr. & intr.* throw (a person etc.) from a vehicle, saddle, etc. **b** *intr.* (esp. of a crowd) tumble out quickly from a place etc. (*the fans spilled into the street*). **3** *tr. sl.* disclose (information etc.). —*n.* **1 a** the act or an instance of spilling or being spilt. **b** a quantity spilt. **2** a tumble or fall, esp. from a horse etc. (*had a nasty spill*). □ **spill the beans** *colloq.* divulge information etc., esp. unintentionally or indiscreetly. **spill blood** be guilty of bloodshed. **spill the blood of** kill or injure (a person). **spill over 1** overflow. **2** (of a surplus population) be forced to move (cf. OVERSPILL). □ **spillage** /-ɪdʒ/ *n.* **spiller** *n.* [OE *spillan* kill, rel. to OE *spildan* destroy: orig. unkn.]

spill² /spɪl/ *n.* a thin strip of wood, folded or twisted paper, etc., used for lighting a fire, candles, a pipe, etc. [ME, rel. to *spile* wooden peg]

spillikin /ˈspɪlɪkɪn/ *n.* (also **spellican** /ˈspelɪkən/) **1** a splinter of wood, bone, etc. **2** (in *pl.*) a game in which a heap of spillikins is to be removed one at a time without moving the others. [SPILL² + -KIN]

spillover /ˈspɪlˌəʊvə(r)/ *n.* **1 a** the process or an instance of spilling over. **b** a thing that spills over. **2** a consequence, repercussion, or by-product.

spillway /ˈspɪlweɪ/ *n.* a passage for surplus water from a dam.

spilt *past* and *past part.* of SPILL¹.

spin *v. & n.* —*v.* (**spinning**; *past* and *past part.* **spun**) **1** *intr. & tr.* turn or cause (a person or thing) to turn or whirl round quickly. **2** *tr.* (also *absol.*) **a** draw out and twist (wool, cotton, etc.) into threads. **b** make (yarn) in this way. **c** make a similar type of thread from (a synthetic substance etc.). **3** *tr.* (of a spider, silkworm, etc.) make (a web, gossamer, a cocoon, etc.) by extruding a fine viscous thread. **4** *tr.* tell or write (a story, essay, article, etc.) (*spins a good tale*). **5** *tr.* impart spin to (a ball). **6** *intr.* (of a person's head etc.) be dizzy through excitement, astonishment, etc. **7** *tr.* (as **spun** *adj.*) converted into threads (*spun glass; spun gold; spun sugar*). **8** *tr.* toss (a coin). **9** *tr.* = spin-dry. —*n.* **1 a** a spinning motion; a whirl. **2** an aircraft's diving descent combined with rotation. **3 a** a revolving motion through the air, esp. in a rifle bullet or in a billiard, tennis, or table tennis ball struck aslant. **b** *Cricket* a twisting motion given to the ball in bowling. **4** *colloq.* a brief drive in a motor vehicle, aeroplane, etc., esp. for pleasure. **5** *Austral.* & *NZ sl.* a piece of good or bad luck. □ **spin bowler** *Cricket* an expert at bowling with spin. **spin doctor** *US* a political pundit who is employed to promote a favourable interpretation of political developments to the media. **spin-drier** a machine for drying wet clothes etc. centrifugally in a revolving drum. **spin-dry (-dries, -dried)** dry (clothes etc.) in this way. **spin off** throw off by centrifugal force in spinning. **spin-off** *n.* an incidental result or results esp. as a side benefit from industrial technology. **spin out 1** prolong (a discussion etc.). **2** make (a story, money, etc.) last as long as possible. **3** spend or consume (time, one's life, etc., by discussion or in an occupation etc.). **spun silk** a cheap material made of short-fibred and waste silk. [OE *spinnan*]

spina bifida /ˌspaɪnə ˈbɪfɪdə/ *n.* a congenital defect of the spine, in which part of the spinal cord and its meninges are exposed through a gap in the backbone. [mod.L (as SPINE, BIFID)]

spinach /ˈspɪnɪdʒ, -ɪtʃ/ *n.* **1 a** a green garden vegetable, *Spinacia oleracea*, with succulent leaves. **2** the leaves of this plant used as food. □ **spinach beet** a variety of beetroot cultivated for its edible leaves. □ **spinaceous** /-ˈneɪʃəs/ *adj.* **spinachy** *adj.* [prob. MDu. *spinaetse*, *spinag(i)e*, f. OF *espinage*, *espinache* f. med.L *spinac(h)ia* etc. f. Arab. *'isfānāḵ* f. Pers. *ispānāḵ*: perh. assim. to L *spina* SPINE, with ref. to its prickly seeds]

spinal /ˈspaɪn(ə)l/ *adj.* of or relating to the spine (*spinal curvature*; *spinal disease*). □ **spinal column** the spine. **spinal cord** a cylindrical structure of the central nervous system enclosed in the spine, connecting all parts of the body with the brain. □ **spinally** *adv.* [LL *spinalis* (as SPINE)]

spindle /ˈspɪnd(ə)l/ *n.* **1 a** a pin in a spinning-wheel used for twisting and winding the thread. **b** a small bar with tapered ends used for the same purpose in hand-spinning. **c** a pin bearing the bobbin of a spinning-machine. **2** a pin or axis that revolves or on which something revolves. **3** a turned piece of wood used as a banister, chair leg, etc. □ **spindle-shanked** having long thin legs. **spindle-shanks** a person with such legs. **spindle-shaped** having a circular cross-section and tapering towards each end. [OE *spinel* (as SPIN)]

spindly /ˈspɪndlɪ/ *adj.* (**spindlier**, **spindliest**) long or tall and thin; thin and weak.

spindrift /ˈspɪndrɪft/ *n.* spray blown along the surface of the sea. [Sc. var. of *spoondrift* f. *spoon* run before wind or sea + DRIFT]

spine *n.* **1** a series of vertebrae extending from the skull to the small of the back, enclosing the spinal cord and providing support for the thorax and abdomen; the backbone. **2** *Zool.* & *Bot.* any hard pointed process or structure. **3** a sharp ridge or projection, esp. of a mountain range or slope. **4** a central feature, main support, or source of strength. **5** the part of a book's jacket or cover that encloses the page-fastening part and usu. faces outwards on a shelf. □ **spine-chilling** (esp. of a story etc.) frightening. □ **spined** *adj.* [ME f. OF *espine* f. L *spina* thorn, backbone]

spineless /ˈspaɪnlɪs/ *adj.* **1 a** having no spine; invertebrate. **b** (of a fish) having no fin-spines. **2** (of a person) lacking energy or resolution; weak and purposeless. □ **spinelessly** *adv.* **spinelessness** *n.*

spinet /spɪˈnet, ˈspɪnɪt/ *n.* *Mus. hist.* a small harpsichord with oblique strings. [obs. F *espinette* f. It. *spinetta* virginal, spinet, dimin. of *spina* thorn etc. (as SPINE), with ref. to the plucked strings]

spinnaker /ˈspɪnəkə(r)/ *n.* a large triangular sail carried opposite the mainsail of a racing-yacht running before the wind. [fanciful f. *Sphinx*, name of yacht first using it, perh. after *spanker*]

spinner /ˈspɪnə(r)/ *n.* **1** a person or thing that spins. **2** *Cricket* **a** a spin bowler. **b** a spun ball. **3** a spin-drier. **4 a** a real or artificial fly for esp. trout-fishing. **b** revolving bait. **5** a manufacturer or merchant engaged in (esp. cotton-) spinning.

spinneret /ˈspɪnəˌret/ *n.* **1** the spinning-organ in a spider, silkworm, etc. **2** a device for forming filaments of synthetic fibre.

spinney /ˈspɪnɪ/ *n.* (*pl.* **-eys**) *Brit.* a small wood; a thicket. [OF *espinei* f. L *spinetum* thicket f. *spina* thorn]

spinning /ˈspɪnɪŋ/ *n.* the act or an instance of spinning. □ **spinning-top** = TOP². **spinning-wheel** a household machine for spinning yarn or thread with a spindle driven by a wheel attached to a crank or treadle.

spinster /ˈspɪnstə(r)/ *n.* **1** an unmarried woman. **2** a woman, esp. elderly, thought unlikely to marry. □ **spinsterhood** *n.* **spinsterish** *adj.* **spinsterishness** *n.* [ME, orig. = woman who spins]

spiny /ˈspaɪnɪ/ *adj.* (**spinier**, **spiniest**) **1** full of spines; prickly. **2** perplexing, troublesome, thorny. □ **spiny anteater** = ECHIDNA. **spiny lobster** any of various large edible crustaceans of the family Palinuridae, esp. *Palinuris vulgaris*, with a spiny shell and no large anterior claws. □ **spininess** *n.*

spiraea /ˌspaɪəˈriːə/ *n.* (*US* **spirea**) any rosaceous shrub of the genus *Spiraea*, with clusters of small white or pink flowers. [L f. Gk *speiraia* f. *speira* coil]

spiral /ˈspaɪər(ə)l/ *adj.*, *n.*, & *v.* —*adj.* **1** winding about a centre in an enlarging or decreasing continuous circular motion, either on a flat plane or rising in a cone; coiled. **2** winding continuously along or as if along a cylinder, like the thread of a screw. —*n.* **1** a plane or three-dimensional spiral curve. **2** a spiral spring. **3** a spiral formation in a shell etc. **4** a spiral galaxy. **5** a progressive rise or fall of prices, wages, etc., each responding to an upward or downward stimulus provided by the other. —*v.* (**spiralled**, **spiralling**; *US* **spiraled**, **spiraling**) **1** *intr.* move in a spiral course, esp. upwards or downwards. **2** *tr.* make spiral. **3** *intr.* esp. *Econ.* (of prices, wages, etc.) rise or fall, esp. rapidly (cf. sense 5 of *n.*). □ **spiral galaxy** a galaxy in which the matter is concentrated mainly in one or more spiral arms. **spiral staircase** a staircase rising in a spiral round a central axis. □ **spirality** /-ˈrælɪtɪ/ *n.* **spirally** *adv.* [F *spiral* or med.L *spiralis* f. *spira* f. Gk *speira* coil]

spirant /ˈspaɪərənt/ *adj.* & *n.* *Phonet.* —*adj.* (of a consonant) uttered with a continuous expulsion of breath, esp. fricative. —*n.* such a consonant. [L *spirare spirant-* breathe]

spire *n.* & *v.* —*n.* **1** a tapering cone- or pyramid-shaped structure built esp. on a church tower. **2** any tapering thing, e.g. the spike of a flower. —*v.tr.* provide with a spire. □ **spiry** /ˈspaɪrɪ/ *adj.* [OE *spīr*]

spirit /ˈspɪrɪt/ n. & v. —n. **1 a** the vital animating essence of a person or animal (was sadly broken in spirit). **b** the intelligent non-physical part of a person; the soul. **2 a** a rational or intelligent being without a material body. **b** a supernatural being such as a ghost, fairy, etc. (haunted by spirits). **3** a prevailing mental or moral condition or attitude; a mood; a tendency (public spirit; took it in the wrong spirit). **4 a** (usu. in pl.) strong distilled liquor, e.g. brandy, whisky, gin, rum. **b** a distilled volatile liquid (wood spirit). **c** purified alcohol (methylated spirit). **d** a solution of a volatile principle in alcohol; a tincture (spirit of ammonia). **5 a** a person's mental or moral nature or qualities, usu. specified (has an unbending spirit). **b** a person viewed as possessing these (is an ardent spirit). **c** (in full **high spirit**) courage, energy, vivacity, dash (played with spirit; infused him with spirit). **6** the real meaning as opposed to lip service or verbal expression (the spirit of the law). —v.tr. (**spirited**, **spiriting**) (usu. foll. by away, off, etc.) convey rapidly and secretly by or as if by spirits. □ **in** (or **in the**) **spirit** inwardly (shall be with you in spirit). **spirit gum** a quick-drying solution of gum used esp. for attaching false hair. **spirit-lamp** a lamp burning methylated or other volatile spirits instead of oil. **spirit-level** a bent glass tube nearly filled with alcohol used to test horizontality by the position of an air-bubble. [ME f. AF (e)spirit, OF esp(e)rit, f. L spiritus breath, spirit f. spirare breathe]

spirited /ˈspɪrɪtɪd/ adj. **1** full of spirit; animated, lively, brisk, or courageous (a spirited attack; a spirited translation). **2** having a spirit or spirits of a specified kind (high-spirited; mean-spirited). □ **spiritedly** adv. **spiritedness** n.

spiritless /ˈspɪrɪtlɪs/ adj. lacking courage, vigour, or vivacity. □ **spiritlessly** adv. **spiritlessness** n.

spiritual /ˈspɪrɪtjʊəl/ adj. & n. —adj. **1** of or concerning the spirit as opposed to matter. **2** concerned with sacred or religious things; holy; divine; inspired (the spiritual life; spiritual songs). **3** (of the mind etc.) refined, sensitive; not concerned with the material. **4** (of a relationship etc.) concerned with the soul or spirit etc., not with external reality (his spiritual home). —n. = Negro spiritual. □ **spirituality** /-ˈælɪtɪ/ n. **spiritually** adv. **spiritualness** n. [ME f. OF spirituel f. L spiritualis (as SPIRIT)]

spiritualism /ˈspɪrɪtjʊəˌlɪz(ə)m/ n. **1** the belief that the spirits of the dead can communicate with the living, esp. through mediums. **2** the practice of this. □ **spiritualist** n. **spiritualistic** /-ˈlɪstɪk/ adj.

spiritualize /ˈspɪrɪtjʊəˌlaɪz/ v.tr. (also **-ise**) **1** make (a person or a person's character, thoughts, etc.) spiritual; elevate. **2** attach a spiritual as opposed to a literal meaning to. □ **spiritualization** /-ˈzeɪʃ(ə)n/ n.

spirituous /ˈspɪrɪtjʊəs/ adj. **1** containing much alcohol. **2** distilled, as whisky, rum, etc. (spirituous liquor). □ **spirituousness** n. [L spiritus spirit, or F spiritueux]

spiro-[1] /ˈspaɪərəʊ/ comb. form a coil. [L spira, Gk speira coil]

spiro-[2] /ˈspaɪərəʊ/ comb. form breath. [irreg. f. L spirare breathe]

spirochaete /ˈspaɪərəʊˌkiːt/ n. (US **spirochete**) any of various flexible spiral-shaped bacteria. [SPIRO-[1] + Gk khaitē long hair]

spirogyra /ˌspaɪərəʊˈdʒaɪərə/ n. any freshwater alga of the genus Spirogyra, with cells containing spiral bands of chlorophyll. [mod.L f. SPIRO-[1] + Gk guros gura round]

spirt var. of SPURT.

spit[1] v. & n. —v. (**spitting**; past and past part. **spat** or **spit**) **1** intr. **a** eject saliva from the mouth. **b** do this as a sign of hatred or contempt (spat at him). **2** tr. (usu. foll. by out) **a** eject (saliva, blood, food, etc.) from the mouth (spat the meat out). **b** utter (oaths, threats, etc.) vehemently. **3** intr. (of a fire, pen, pan, etc.) send out sparks, ink, hot fat, etc. **4** intr. (of rain) fall lightly (it's only spitting). **5** intr. (esp. of a cat) make a spitting or hissing noise in anger or hostility. —n. **1** spittle. **2** the act or an instance of spitting. **3** the foamy liquid secretion of some insects used to protect their young. □ **the spit** (or **very spit**) **of** colloq. the exact double of. **spit and polish 1** the cleaning and polishing duties of a soldier etc. **2** exaggerated neatness and smartness. **spit chips** Austral. sl. **1** feel extreme thirst. **2** be angry or frustrated. **spit it out** colloq. say what is on one's mind. **spitting distance** a very short distance. **spitting image** (foll. by of) colloq. the exact double of (another person or thing). □ **spitter** n. [OE spittan, of imit. orig.: cf. SPEW]

spit[2] n. & v. —n. **1** a slender rod on which meat is skewered before being roasted on a fire etc.; a skewer. **2 a** a small point of land projecting into the sea. **b** a long narrow underwater bank. —v.tr. (**spitted**, **spitting**) **1** thrust a spit through (meat etc.). **2** pierce or transfix with a sword etc. □ **spit-roast** cook on a spit. □ **spitty** adj. [OE spitu f. WG]

spit[3] n. (pl. same or **spits**) a spade-depth of earth (dig it two spit deep). [MDu. & MLG, = OE spittan dig with spade, prob. rel. to SPIT[2]]

spitball /ˈspɪtbɔːl/ n. & v. —n. US a ball of chewed paper etc. used as a missile. —v.intr. throw out suggestions for discussion. □ **spitballer** n.

spite n. & v. —n. **1** ill will, malice towards a person (did it from spite). **2** a grudge. —v.tr. thwart, mortify, annoy (does it to spite me). □ **in spite of** notwithstanding. **in spite of oneself** etc. though one would rather have done otherwise. [ME f. OF despit DESPITE]

spiteful /ˈspaɪtfʊl/ adj. motivated by spite; malevolent. □ **spitefully** adv. **spitefulness** n.

spitfire /ˈspɪtˌfaɪə(r)/ n. a person of fiery temper.

spittle /ˈspɪt(ə)l/ n. saliva, esp. as ejected from the mouth. □ **spittly** adj. [alt. of ME (now dial.) spattle = OE spātl f. spǣtan to spit, after SPIT[1]]

spittoon /spɪˈtuːn/ n. a metal or earthenware pot with esp. a funnel-shaped top, used for spitting into.

spiv n. Brit. colloq. a man, often characterized by flashy dress, who makes a living by illicit or unscrupulous dealings. □ **spivvish** adj. **spivvy** adj. [20th c.: orig. unkn.]

splash v. & n. —v. **1** intr. & tr. spatter or cause (liquid) to spatter in small drops. **2** tr. cause (a person) to be spattered with liquid etc. (splashed them with mud). **3** intr. **a** (of a person) cause liquid to spatter (was splashing about in the bath). **b** (usu. foll. by across, along, etc.) move while spattering liquid etc. (splashed across the carpet in *his boots).* **c** step, fall, or plunge etc. into a liquid etc. so as to cause a splash (*splashed into the sea*). **4** *tr.* display (news) prominently. **5** *tr.* decorate with scattered colour. **6** *tr.* spend (money) ostentatiously. —*n.* **1** the act or an instance of splashing. **2 a** a quantity of liquid splashed. **b** the resulting noise (*heard a splash*). **3** a spot of dirt etc. splashed on to a thing. **4** a prominent news feature etc. **5** a daub or patch of colour, esp. on an animal's coat. **6** *Brit. colloq.* a small quantity of liquid, esp. of soda water etc. to dilute spirits. □ **make a splash** attract much attention, esp. by extravagance. **splash out** *colloq.* spend money freely. □ **splashy** *adj.* (**splashier, splashiest**). [alt. of PLASH¹]

splashback /ˈsplæʃbæk/ *n.* a panel behind a sink etc. to protect the wall from splashes.

splashdown /ˈsplæʃdaʊn/ *n.* the alighting of a spacecraft on the sea.

splat¹ *n.* a flat piece of thin wood in the centre of a chair-back. [*splat* (v.) split up, rel. to SPLIT]

splat² *n.*, *adv.*, & *v. colloq.* —*n.* a sharp cracking or slapping sound (*hit the wall with a splat*). —*adv.* with a splat (*fell splat on his head*). —*v.intr.* & *tr.* (**splatted, splatting**) fall or hit with a splat. [abbr. of SPLATTER]

splatter /ˈsplætə(r)/ *v.* & *n.* —*v.tr.* & *intr.* **1** splash esp. with a continuous noisy action. **2** *US* spatter. —*n.* a noisy splashing sound. [imit.]

splay *v.*, *n.*, & *adj.* —*v.* **1** *tr.* (usu. foll. by *out*) spread (the elbows, feet, etc.) out. **2** *intr.* (of an aperture or its sides) diverge in shape or position. **3** *tr.* construct (a window, doorway, aperture, etc.) so that it diverges or is wider at one side of the wall than the other. —*n.* a surface making an oblique angle with another, e.g. the splayed side of a window or embrasure. —*adj.* **1** wide and flat. **2** turned outward. □ **splay-foot** a broad flat foot turned outward. [ME f. DISPLAY]

spleen *n.* **1** an abdominal organ involved in maintaining the proper condition of blood in most vertebrates. **2** lowness of spirits; moroseness, ill temper, spite (from the earlier belief that the spleen was the seat of such feelings) (*a fit of spleen; vented their spleen*). □ **spleenful** *adj.* **spleeny** *adj.* [ME f. OF *esplen* f. L *splen* f. Gk *splēn*]

splendid /ˈsplendɪd/ *adj.* **1** magnificent, gorgeous, brilliant, sumptuous (*a splendid palace; a splendid achievement*). **2** dignified; impressive (*splendid isolation*). **3** excellent; fine (*a splendid chance*). □ **splendidly** *adv.* **splendidness** *n.* [F *splendide* or L *splendidus* f. *splendēre* to shine]

splendiferous /splenˈdɪfərəs/ *adj. colloq.* or *joc.* splendid. □ **splendiferously** *adv.* **splendiferousness** *n.* [irreg. f. SPLENDOUR]

splendour /ˈsplendə(r)/ *n.* (*US* **splendor**) **1** great or dazzling brightness. **2** magnificence; grandeur. [ME f. AF *splendeur* or L *splendor* (as SPLENDID)]

splenetic /splɪˈnetɪk/ *adj.* & *n.* —*adj.* **1** ill-tempered; peevish. **2** of or concerning the spleen. —*n.* a splenetic person. □ **splenetically** *adv.* [LL *spleneticus* (as SPLEEN)]

splenic /ˈsplenɪk, ˈspliː-/ *adj.* of or in the spleen. □ **splenoid** /ˈspliːnɔɪd/ *adj.* [F *splénique* or L *splenicus* f. Gk *splēnikos* (as SPLEEN)]

splice *v.* & *n.* —*v.tr.* **1** join the ends of (ropes) by interweaving strands. **2** join (pieces of timber, magnetic tape, film, etc.) in an overlapping position. **3** (esp. as **spliced** *adj.*) *colloq.* join in marriage. —*n.* a joint consisting of two ropes, pieces of wood, film, etc., made by splicing, e.g. the handle and blade of a cricket bat. □ **splice the main brace** *Naut. hist.* issue an extra tot of rum. □ **splicer** *n.* [prob. f. MDu. *splissen*, of uncert. orig.]

spliff *n.* (also **splif**) *sl.* a cannabis cigarette. [20th c.: orig. unkn.]

splint *n.* & *v.* —*n.* **1 a** a strip of rigid material used for holding a broken bone etc. when set. **b** a rigid or flexible strip of esp. wood used in basketwork etc. **2** a thin strip of wood etc. used to light a fire, pipe, etc. —*v.tr.* secure (a broken limb etc.) with a splint or splints. [ME *splent(e)* f. MDu. *splinte* or MLG *splinte, splente* metal plate or pin, rel. to SPLINTER]

splinter /ˈsplɪntə(r)/ *v.* & *n.* —*v.tr.* & *intr.* break into fragments. —*n.* a small thin sharp-edged piece broken off from wood, stone, etc. □ **splinter group** (or **party**) a group or party that has broken away from a larger one. □ **splintery** *adj.* [ME f. MDu. (= LG) *splinter, splenter*, rel. to SPLINT]

split *v.* & *n.* —*v.* (**splitting**; *past* and *past part.* **split**) **1** *intr.* & *tr.* **a** break or cause to break forcibly into parts, esp. with the grain or into halves. **b** (often foll. by *up*) divide into parts (*split into groups; split up the money equally*). **2** *tr.* & *intr.* (often foll. by *off, away*) remove or be removed by breaking, separating, or dividing (*split the top off the bottle; split away from the main group*). **3** *intr.* & *tr.* **a** (usu. foll. by *up, on, over*, etc.) separate esp. through discord (*split up after ten years; they were split on the question of picketing*). **b** (foll. by *with*) quarrel or cease association with (another person etc.). **4** *tr.* cause the fission of (an atom). **5** *intr.* & *tr. sl.* leave, esp. suddenly. **6** *intr.* (usu. foll. by *on*) *colloq.* betray secrets; inform (*split on them to the police*). **7** *intr.* **a** (as **splitting** *adj.*) (esp. of a headache) very painful; acute. **b** (of the head) suffer great pain from a headache, noise, etc. —*n.* **1** the act or an instance of splitting; the state of being split. **2** a fissure, vent, crack, cleft, etc. **3** a separation into parties; a schism. **4** (in *pl.*) *Brit.* the athletic feat of leaping in the air or sitting down with the legs at right angles to the body in front and behind, or at the sides with the trunk facing forwards. **5 a** half a bottle of mineral water. **b** half a glass of liquor. **6** *colloq.* a division of money, esp. the proceeds of crime. □ **split the difference** take the average of two proposed amounts. **split hairs** make small and insignificant distinctions. **split infinitive** a phrase consisting of an infinitive with an adverb etc. inserted between *to* and the verb, e.g. *seems to really like it*. **split-level** (of a building) having a room or rooms a fraction of a storey higher than other parts. **split pea** a pea dried and split in half for cooking. **split personality** the alteration or dissociation of personality occurring in some mental illnesses, esp. schizophrenia and hysteria. **split pin** a metal cotter passed through a hole and held by the pressing back of the two ends. **split ring** a small steel ring with two spiral turns, such as a key-ring. **split-screen** a screen on which two or more separate images are displayed. **split second** a very brief moment of time. **split shift** a shift comprising two or more separate periods of duty. **split one's sides** convulsed with laughter. **split the ticket** (or **one's vote**) *US* vote for candidates of more than one party. **split the vote** *Brit.* (of a candidate or minority party) attract votes from another so that both are defeated by a third. □ **splitter** *n.* [orig. Naut. f. MDu. *splitten*, rel. to *spletten*, *splïten*, MHG *splïzen*]

splodge *n.* & *v.* *colloq.* —*n.* a daub, blot, or smear. —*v.tr.* make a large, esp. irregular, spot or patch on. □ **splodgy** *adj.* [imit., or alt. of SPLOTCH]

splosh *v.* & *n.* *colloq.* —*v.tr.* & *intr.* move with a splashing sound. —*n.* **1** a splashing sound. **2** a splash of water etc. **3** *sl.* money. [imit.]

splotch *n.* & *v.tr.* = SPLODGE. □ **splotchy** *adj.* [perh. f. SPOT + obs. *plotch* BLOTCH]

splurge *n.* & *v.* *colloq.* —*n.* **1** an ostentatious display or effort. **2** an instance of sudden great extravagance. —*v.intr.* **1** (usu. foll. by *on*) spend effort or esp. large sums of money (*splurged on new furniture*). **2** splash heavily. [19th-c. US: prob. imit.]

splutter /ˈsplʌtə(r)/ *v.* & *n.* —*v.* **1** *intr.* **a** speak in a hurried, vehement, or choking manner. **b** emit particles from the mouth, sparks, hot oil, etc., with spitting sounds. **2** *tr.* **a** speak or utter (words, threats, a language, etc.) rapidly or incoherently. **b** emit (food, sparks, hot oil, etc.) with a spitting sound. —*n.* spluttering speech. □ **splutterer** *n.* **splutteringly** *adv.* [SPUTTER by assoc. with *splash*]

spoil *v.* & *n.* —*v.* (*past* and *past part.* **spoilt** or **spoiled**) **1** *tr.* **a** damage; diminish the value of (*was spoilt by the rain; will spoil all the fun*). **b** reduce a person's enjoyment etc. of (*the news spoiled his dinner*). **2** *tr.* injure the character of (esp. a child, pet, etc.) by excessive indulgence. **3** *intr.* **a** (of food) go bad, decay; become unfit for eating. **b** (usu. in *neg.*) (of a joke, secret, etc.) become stale through long keeping. **4** *tr.* render (a ballot paper) invalid by improper marking. —*n.* **1** (usu. in *pl.*) **a** plunder taken from an enemy in war, or seized by force. **b** esp. *joc.* profit or advantages gained by succeeding to public office, high position, etc. **2** earth etc. thrown up in excavating, dredging, etc. □ **be spoiling for** aggressively seek (a fight etc.). **spoilt for choice** having so many choices that it is difficult to choose. [ME f. OF *espoillier*, *espoille* f. L *spoliare* f. *spolium* spoil, plunder, or f. DESPOIL]

spoilage /ˈspɔɪlɪdʒ/ *n.* **1** paper spoilt in printing. **2** the spoiling of food etc. by decay.

spoiler /ˈspɔɪlə(r)/ *n.* **1** a person or thing that spoils. **2 a** a device on an aircraft to retard its speed by interrupting the air flow. **b** a similar device on a vehicle to improve its road-holding at speed.

spoilsport /ˈspɔɪlspɔːt/ *n.* a person who spoils others' pleasure or enjoyment.

spoilt *past* and *past part.* of SPOIL.

spoke[1] *n.* & *v.* —*n.* **1** each of the bars running from the hub to the rim of a wheel. **2** a rung of a ladder. —*v.tr.* **1** provide with spokes. **2** obstruct (a wheel etc.) by thrusting a spoke in. □ **put a spoke in a person's wheel** *Brit.* thwart or hinder a person. □ **spokewise** *adv.* [OE *spāca* f. WG]

spoke[2] *past* of SPEAK.

spoken /ˈspəʊkən/ *past part.* of SPEAK. —*adj.* (in *comb.*) speaking in a specified way (*smooth-spoken*;

well-spoken). □ **spoken for** claimed, requisitioned (*this seat is spoken for*).

spokeshave /ˈspəʊkʃeɪv/ *n.* a blade set between two handles, used for shaping spokes and other esp. curved work where an ordinary plane is not suitable.

spokesman /ˈspəʊksmən/ *n.* (*pl.* **-men**; *fem.* **spokeswoman**, *pl.* **-women**) **1** a person who speaks on behalf of others, esp. in the course of public relations. **2** a person deputed to express the views of a group etc. [irreg. f. SPOKE[2] after *craftsman* etc.]

spokesperson /ˈspəʊksˌpɜːs(ə)n/ *n.* (*pl.* **-persons** or **-people**) a spokesman or spokeswoman.

spoliation /ˌspəʊlɪˈeɪʃ(ə)n/ *n.* plunder or pillage, esp. of neutral vessels in war. □ **spoliator** /ˈspəʊ-/ *n.* **spoliatory** /spəʊˈlɪətərɪ/ *adj.* [ME f. L *spoliatio* (as SPOIL)]

spondee /ˈspɒndiː/ *n.* *Prosody* a foot consisting of two long (or stressed) syllables. [ME f. OF *spondee* or L *spondeus* f. Gk *spondeios* (*pous* foot) f. *spondē* libation, as being characteristic of music accompanying libations]

spondulicks /spɒnˈdjuːlɪks/ *n.pl.* *sl.* money. [19th c.: orig. unkn.]

sponge /spʌndʒ/ *n.* & *v.* —*n.* **1** any aquatic animal of the phylum Porifera, with pores in its body wall and a rigid internal skeleton. **2 a** the skeleton of a sponge, esp. the soft light elastic absorbent kind used in bathing, cleansing surfaces, etc. **b** a piece of porous rubber or plastic etc. used similarly. **3** a thing of sponge-like absorbency or consistency, e.g. a sponge pudding, cake, porous metal, etc. (*lemon sponge*). **4** = SPONGER. **5** *colloq.* a person who drinks heavily. **6** cleansing with or as with a sponge (*had a quick sponge this morning*). —*v.* **1** *tr.* wipe or cleanse with a sponge. **2** *tr.* (also *absol.*; often foll. by *down*, *over*) sluice water over (the body, a car, etc.). **3** *tr.* (often foll. by *out*, *away*, etc.) wipe off or efface (writing, a memory, etc.) with or as with a sponge. **4** *tr.* (often foll. by *up*) absorb with or as with a sponge. **5** *intr.* (often foll. by *on*, *off*) live as a parasite; be meanly dependent upon (another person). **6** *tr.* obtain (drink etc.) by sponging. **7** *intr.* gather sponges. **8** *tr.* apply paint with a sponge to (walls, furniture, etc.). □ **sponge bag** a waterproof bag for toilet articles. **sponge cake** a very light cake with a spongelike consistency. **sponge cloth 1** soft, lightly-woven cloth with a slightly wrinkled surface. **2** a thin spongy material used for cleaning. **sponge pudding** *Brit.* a steamed or baked pudding of fat, flour, and eggs with a usu. specified flavour. **sponge rubber** liquid rubber latex processed into a spongelike substance. □ **spongeable** *adj.* **spongelike** *adj.* **spongiform** *adj.* (esp. in senses 1, 2). [OE f. L *spongia* f. Gk *spoggia*, *spoggos*]

sponger /ˈspʌndʒə(r)/ *n.* a person who contrives to live at another's expense.

spongy /ˈspʌndʒɪ/ *adj.* (**spongier**, **spongiest**) like a sponge, esp. in being porous, compressible, elastic, or absorbent. □ **spongily** *adv.* **sponginess** *n.*

sponsor /ˈspɒnsə(r)/ *n.* & *v.* —*n.* **1** a person who supports an activity done for charity by pledging money in advance. **2 a** a person or organization that promotes or supports an artistic or sporting activity etc. **b** esp. *US* a business organization that promotes a broadcast programme in return for advertising time. **3** an organization lending support to an election candidate. **4** a person who introduces a proposal for legislation. **5** a godparent at baptism or esp. *RC Ch.* a person who presents a candidate for confirmation. **6** a person who makes himself or herself responsible for another. —*v.tr.* be a sponsor for. □ **sponsorial** /spɒnˈsɔːrɪəl/ *adj.* **sponsorship** *n.* [L *spondēre* spons- promise solemnly]

spontaneous /spɒnˈteɪnɪəs/ *adj.* **1** acting or done or occurring without external cause. **2** voluntary, without external incitement (*made a spontaneous offer of his services*). **3** (of bodily movement, literary style, etc.) gracefully natural and unconstrained. **4** (of sudden movement etc.) involuntary, not due to conscious volition. **5** growing naturally without cultivation. □ **spontaneous combustion** the ignition of a mineral or vegetable substance (e.g. a heap of rags soaked with oil, a mass of wet coal) from heat engendered within itself. □ **spontaneity** /ˌspɒntəˈniːɪtɪ, -ˈneɪɪtɪ/ *n.* **spontaneously** *adv.* **spontaneousness** *n.* [LL *spontaneus* f. *sponte* of one's own accord]

spoof /spuːf/ *n.* & *v.* *colloq.* —*n.* **1** a parody. **2** a hoax or swindle. —*v.tr.* **1** parody. **2** hoax, swindle. □ **spoofer** *n.* **spoofery** *n.* [invented by A. Roberts, English comedian d. 1933]

spook /spuːk/ *n.* & *v.* —*n.* **1** *colloq.* a ghost. **2** *US sl.* a spy. —*v. US sl.* **1** *tr.* frighten, unnerve, alarm. **2** *intr.* take fright, become alarmed. [Du., = MLG *spōk*, of unkn. orig.]

spooky /ˈspuːkɪ/ *adj.* (**spookier**, **spookiest**) **1** *colloq.* ghostly, eerie. **2** *US sl.* nervous; easily frightened. **3** *US sl.* of spies or espionage. □ **spookily** *adv.* **spookiness** *n.*

spool /spuːl/ *n.* & *v.* —*n.* **1** **a** a reel for winding magnetic tape, photographic film, etc., on. **b** a reel for winding yarn or *US* thread on. **c** a quantity of tape, yarn, etc., wound on a spool. **2** the revolving cylinder of an angler's reel. —*v.tr.* wind on a spool. [ME f. OF *espole* or f. MLG *spôle*, MDu. *spoele*, OHG *spuolo*, of unkn. orig.]

spoon /spuːn/ *n.* & *v.* —*n.* **1** **a** a utensil consisting of an oval or round bowl and a handle for conveying food (esp. liquid) to the mouth, for stirring, etc. **b** a spoonful, esp. of sugar. **c** (in *pl.*) *Mus.* a pair of spoons held in the hand and beaten together rhythmically. **2** a spoon-shaped thing, esp.: **a** (in full **spoon-bait**) a bright revolving piece of metal used as a lure in fishing. **b** an oar with a broad curved blade. **c** a wooden-headed golf club. —*v.* **1** *tr.* (often foll. by *up*, *out*) take (liquid etc.) with a spoon. **2** *tr.* hit (a ball) feebly upwards. **3** *intr. colloq.* behave in an amorous way, esp. foolishly. **4** *intr.* fish with a spoon-bait. □ **born with a silver spoon in one's mouth** born in affluence. **spoon-bread** *US* soft maize bread. □ **spooner** *n.* **spoonful** *n.* (*pl.* **-fuls**). [OE *spōn* chip of wood f. Gmc]

spoonbill /ˈspuːnbɪl/ *n.* **1** any large wading bird of the subfamily Plataleidae, having a bill with a very broad flat tip. **2** a shoveller duck.

spoonerism /ˈspuːnəˌrɪz(ə)m/ *n.* a transposition, usu. accidental, of the initial letters etc. of two or more words, e.g. *you have hissed the mystery lectures.* [Revd W. A. Spooner, English scholar d. 1930, reputed to make such errors in speaking]

spoonfeed /ˈspuːnfiːd/ *v.tr.* (*past* and *past part.* **-fed**) **1** feed (a baby etc.) with a spoon. **2** provide

help, information, etc., to (a person) without requiring any effort on the recipient's part.

spoor /spʊə(r)/ *n.* & *v.* —*n.* the track or scent of an animal. —*v.tr.* & *intr.* follow by the spoor. □ **spoorer** *n.* [Afrik. f. MDu. *spo(o)r* f. Gmc]

sporadic /spəˈrædɪk/ *adj.* occurring only here and there or occasionally, separate, scattered. □ **sporadically** *adv.* [med.L *sporadicus* f. Gk *sporadikos* f. *sporas -ados* scattered: cf. *speirō* to sow]

spore /spɔː(r)/ *n.* **1** a specialized reproductive cell of many plants and micro-organisms. **2** these collectively. [mod.L *spora* f. Gk *spora* sowing, seed f. *speirō* sow]

sporran /ˈspɒrən/ *n.* a pouch, worn by a Highlander in front of the kilt. [Gael. *sporan* f. med.L *bursa* PURSE]

sport *n.* & *v.* —*n.* **1** **a** a game or competitive activity, esp. an outdoor one involving physical exertion, e.g. cricket, football, racing, hunting. **b** such activities collectively (*the world of sport*). **2** (in *pl.*) *Brit.* **a** a meeting for competing in sports, esp. athletics (*school sports*). **b** athletics. **3** amusement, diversion, fun. **4** *colloq.* **a** a fair or generous person. **b** a person behaving in a specified way, esp. regarding games, rules, etc. (*a bad sport at tennis*). **c** *Austral.* a form of address, esp. between males. **5** *Biol.* an animal or plant deviating suddenly or strikingly from the normal type. **6** a plaything or butt (*was the sport of Fortune*). —*v.* **1** *intr.* divert oneself, take part in a pastime. **2** *tr.* wear, exhibit, or produce, esp. ostentatiously (*sported a gold tie-pin*). **3** *intr. Biol.* become or produce a sport. □ **in sport** jestingly. **make sport of** make fun of, ridicule. **the sport of kings** horse-racing. **sports car** an open, low-built fast car. **sports coat** (or **jacket**) a man's jacket for informal wear. **sports writer** a person who writes (esp. as a journalist) on sports. □ **sporter** *n.* [ME f. DISPORT]

sporting /ˈspɔːtɪŋ/ *adj.* **1** interested in sport (*a sporting man*). **2** sportsmanlike, generous (*a sporting offer*). **3** concerned in sport (*a sporting dog*; *sporting news*). □ **a sporting chance** some possibility of success. □ **sportingly** *adv.*

sportive /ˈspɔːtɪv/ *adj.* playful. □ **sportively** *adv.* **sportiveness** *n.*

sportscast /ˈspɔːtskɑːst/ *n. US* a broadcast of a sports event or information about sport. □ **sportscaster** *n.*

sportsman /ˈspɔːtsmən/ *n.* (*pl.* **-men**; *fem.* **sportswoman**, *pl.* **-women**) **1** a person who takes part in much sport, esp. professionally. **2** a person who behaves fairly and generously. □ **sportsmanlike** *adj.* **sportsmanly** *adj.* **sportsmanship** *n.*

sporty /ˈspɔːtɪ/ *adj.* (**sportier**, **sportiest**) *colloq.* **1** fond of sport. **2** rakish, showy. □ **sportily** *adv.* **sportiness** *n.*

spot *n.* & *v.* —*n.* **1** **a** a small part of the surface of a thing distinguished by colour, texture, etc., usu. round or less elongated than a streak or stripe (*a blue tie with pink spots*). **b** a small mark or stain. **c** a pimple. **d** a small circle or other shape used in various numbers to distinguish faces of dice, playing-cards in a suit, etc. **e** a moral blemish or stain (*without a spot on his reputation*). **2** **a** a particular place; a definite locality (*dropped it on this precise spot*; *the spot where William III landed*). **b** a place used for a particular activity (often in *comb.*: *nightspot*). **c**

(prec. by *the*) *Football* the place from which a penalty kick is taken. **3** a particular part of one's body or aspect of one's character. **4** a *colloq.* one's esp. regular position in an organization, programme of events, etc. **b** a place or position in a performance or show (*did the spot before the interval*). **5** *Brit.* **a** *colloq.* a small quantity of anything (*a spot of lunch; a spot of trouble*). **b** a drop (*a spot of rain*). **c** *colloq.* a drink. **6** = SPOTLIGHT. **7** (usu. *attrib.*) money paid or goods delivered immediately after a sale (*spot cash; spot silver*). —*v.* (**spotted, spotting**) **1** *tr.* a *colloq.* single out beforehand (the winner of a race etc.). **b** *colloq.* recognize the identity, nationality, etc., of (*spotted him at once as the murderer*). **c** watch for and take note of (trains, talent, etc.). **d** *colloq.* catch sight of. **e** *Mil.* locate (an enemy's position), esp. from the air. **2** a *intr.* & *intr.* mark or become marked with spots. **b** *tr.* stain, soil (a person's character etc.). **3** *intr.* make spots, rain slightly (*it was spotting with rain*). □ **in a spot** (or **in a tight** etc. **spot**) *colloq.* in difficulty. **on the spot 1** at the scene of an action or event. **2** *colloq.* in a position such that response or action is required. **3** without delay or change of place, then and there. **4** (of a person) wide awake, equal to the situation, in good form at a game etc. **running on the spot** raising the feet alternately as in running but without moving forwards or backwards. **spot check** a test made on the spot or on a randomly-selected subject. **spot on** *Brit. colloq. adj.* precise; on target. —*adv.* precisely. **spot-weld** *v.tr.* join by spot welding. **spot welding** welding two surfaces together in a series of discrete points. [ME, perh. f. MDu. *spotte*, LG *spot*, ON *spotti* small piece]

spotless /ˈspɒtlɪs/ *adj.* immaculate; absolutely clean or pure. □ **spotlessly** *adv.* **spotlessness** *n.*

spotlight /ˈspɒtlaɪt/ *n.* & *v.* —*n.* **1** a beam of light directed on a small area, esp. on a particular part of a theatre stage or of the road in front of a vehicle. **2** a lamp directing this. **3** full attention or publicity. —*v.tr.* (*past* and *past part.* **-lighted** or **-lit**) **1** direct a spotlight on. **2** make conspicuous, draw attention to.

spotted /ˈspɒtɪd/ *adj.* marked or decorated with spots. □ **spotted dick** (or **dog**) **1** *Brit.* a suet pudding containing currants. **2** a Dalmatian dog. □ **spottedness** *n.*

spotter /ˈspɒtə(r)/ *n.* **1** (often in *comb.*) a person who spots people or things (*train-spotter*). **2** an aviator or aircraft employed in locating enemy positions etc.

spotty /ˈspɒtɪ/ *adj.* (**spottier, spottiest**) **1** marked with spots. **2** patchy, irregular. □ **spottily** *adv.* **spottiness** *n.*

spouse /spaʊz, spaʊs/ *n.* a husband or wife. [ME *spūs(e)* f. OF *sp(o)us* (masc.), *sp(o)use* (fem.), vars. of *espous(e)* f. L *sponsus sponsa* past part. of *spondēre* betroth]

spout /spaʊt/ *n.* & *v.* —*n.* **1 a** a projecting tube or lip through which a liquid etc. is poured from a teapot, kettle, jug, etc., or issues from a fountain, pump, etc. **b** a sloping trough down which a thing may be shot into a receptacle. **2** a jet or column of liquid, grain, etc. **3** (in full **spout-hole**) a whale's blow-hole. —*v.tr.* & *intr.* **1** discharge or issue forcibly in a jet. **2** utter (verses etc.) or speak in a declamatory manner,

speechify. □ **up the spout** *sl.* **1** useless, ruined, hopeless. **2** pawned. **3** pregnant. □ **spouter** *n.*

spoutless *adj.* [ME f. MDu. *spouten*, orig. imit.]

sprain *v.* & *n.* —*v.tr.* wrench (an ankle, wrist, etc.) violently so as to cause pain and swelling but not dislocation. —*n.* **1** such a wrench. **2** the resulting inflammation and swelling. [17th c.: orig. unkn.]

sprang *past* of SPRING.

sprat *n.* **1** a small European herring-like fish, *Sprattus sprattus*, much used as food. **2** a similar fish, e.g. a young herring. □ **a sprat to catch a mackerel** a small risk to gain much. □ **spratter** *n.* **spratting** *n.* [OE *sprot*]

sprawl *v.* & *n.* —*v.* **1 a** *intr.* sit or lie or fall with limbs flung out or in an ungainly way. **b** *tr.* spread (one's limbs) in this way. **2** *intr.* (of handwriting, a plant, a town, etc.) be of irregular or straggling form. —*n.* **1** a sprawling movement or attitude. **2** a straggling group or mass. **3** the straggling expansion of an urban or industrial area. □ **sprawlingly** *adv.* [OE *spreawlian*]

spray[1] *n.* & *v.* —*n.* **1** water or other liquid flying in small drops from the force of the wind, the dashing of waves, or the action of an atomizer etc. **2** a liquid preparation to be applied in this form with an atomizer etc., esp. for medical purposes. **3** an instrument or apparatus for such application. —*v.tr.* (also *absol.*) **1** throw (liquid) in the form of spray. **2** sprinkle (an object) with small drops or particles, esp. (a plant) with an insecticide. **3** (*absol.*) (of a tom-cat) mark its environment with the smell of its urine, as an attraction to females. □ **spray-dry** (**-dries, -dried**) dry (milk etc.) by spraying into hot air etc. **spray-gun** a gunlike device for spraying paint etc. **spray-paint** paint (a surface) by means of a spray. □ **sprayable** *adj.* **sprayer** *n.* [earlier *spry*, perh. rel. to MDu. *spra(e)yen*, MHG *spræjen* sprinkle]

spray[2] *n.* **1** a sprig of flowers or leaves, or a branch of a tree with branchlets or flowers, esp. a slender or graceful one. **2** an ornament in a similar form (*a spray of diamonds*). □ **sprayey** /ˈspreɪɪ/ *adj.* [ME f. OE *spræg* (unrecorded)]

spread /spred/ *v.* & *n.* —*v.* (*past* and *past part.* **spread**) **1** *tr.* (often foll. by *out*) **a** open or extend the surface of. **b** cause to cover a larger surface (*spread butter on bread*). **c** display to the eye or the mind (*the view was spread out before us*). **2** *intr.* (often foll. by *out*) have a wide or specified or increasing extent (*on every side spread a vast desert; spreading trees*). **3** *intr.* & *tr.* become or make widely known, felt, etc. (*rumours are spreading; spread a little happiness*). **4** *tr.* **a** cover the surface of (*spread the wall with paint; a meadow spread with daisies*). **b** lay (a table). —*n.* **1** the act or an instance of spreading. **2** capability of expanding (*has a large spread*). **3** diffusion (*spread of learning*). **4** breadth, compass (*arches of equal spread*). **5** an aircraft's wing-span. **6** increased bodily girth (*middle-aged spread*). **7** the difference between two rates, prices, etc. **8** *colloq.* an elaborate meal. **9** a sweet or savoury paste for spreading on bread etc. **10** a bedspread. **11** printed matter spread across two facing pages or across more than one column. **12** *US* a ranch with extensive land. □ **spread eagle 1** a representation of an eagle with legs and wings extended as an emblem. **2** *hist.* a person secured

with arms and legs spread out, esp. to be flogged.
spread-eagle *v.tr.* (usu. as **spread-eagled** *adj.*)
1 place (a person) in this position. **2** defeat
utterly. **3** spread out. **spread oneself** be lavish
or discursive. □ **spreadable** *adj.* **spreader** *n.*
[OE *-sprǣdan* f. WG]

spreadsheet /ˈspredʃiːt/ *n.* a computer program
allowing manipulation and flexible retrieval of
esp. tabulated numerical data.

spree *n.* & *v. colloq.* —*n.* **1** a lively extravagant
outing (*shopping spree*). **2** a bout of fun or
drinking etc. —*v.intr.* (**sprees**, **spreed**) have a
spree. □ **on the spree** engaged in a spree. [19th
c.: orig. unkn.]

sprig[1] *n.* & *v.* —*n.* **1** a small branch or shoot. **2**
an ornament resembling this, esp. on fabric. **3**
usu. *derog.* a youth or young man (*a sprig of the
nobility*). —*v.tr.* (**sprigged**, **sprigging**) ornament
with sprigs (*a dress of sprigged muslin*). □ **spriggy**
adj. [ME f. or rel. to LG *sprick*]

sprig[2] *n.* a small tapering headless tack. [ME:
orig. unkn.]

sprightly /ˈspraɪtlɪ/ *adj.* (**sprightlier**, **spright-
liest**) vivacious, lively, brisk. □ **sprightliness** *n.*
[*spright* var. of SPRITE + -LY[1]]

spring *v.* & *n.* —*v.* (*past* **sprang** or *US* **sprung**;
past part. **sprung**) **1** *intr.* jump; move rapidly or
suddenly (*sprang from his seat*; *sprang through the
gap*; *sprang to their assistance*). **2** *intr.* move rapidly
as from a constrained position or by the action
of a spring (*the branch sprang back*; *the door sprang
to*). **3** *intr.* (usu. foll. by *from*) originate or arise
(*springs from an old family*; *their actions spring from
a false conviction*). **4** *intr.* (usu. foll. by *up*) come
into being; appear, esp. suddenly (*a breeze sprang
up*; *the belief has sprung up*). **5** *tr.* cause to act
suddenly, esp. by means of a spring (*spring a
trap*). **6** *tr.* (often foll. by *on*) produce or develop
or make known suddenly or unexpectedly (*loves
to spring surprises*). **7** *tr. sl.* contrive the escape or
release of. **8** *tr.* rouse (game) from earth or
covert. **9** *tr.* (usu. as **sprung** *adj.*) provide (a
motor vehicle etc.) with springs. —*n.* **1** a jump
(*took a spring*; *rose with a spring*). **2** a backward
movement from a constrained position; a recoil,
e.g. of a bow. **3** elasticity; ability to spring back
strongly (*a mattress with plenty of spring*). **4** a
resilient device usu. of bent or coiled metal
used esp. to drive clockwork or for cushioning
in furniture or vehicles. **5 a** the season in which
vegetation begins to appear, the first season of
the year, in the N. hemisphere from March to
May and in the S. hemisphere from September
to November. **b** *Astron.* the period from the
vernal equinox to the summer solstice. **c** (often
foll. by *of*) the early stage of life etc. **d** = *spring
tide*. **6** a place where water, oil, etc., wells up
from the earth; the basin or flow so formed (*hot
springs*; *mineral springs*). **7** the motive for or
origin of an action, custom, etc. (*the springs of
human action*). □ **spring balance** a balance that
measures weight by the tension of a spring.
spring chicken 1 a young fowl for eating (orig.
available only in spring). **2** (esp. with *neg.*) a
young person (*she's no spring chicken*). **spring-
clean** *n.* a thorough cleaning of a house or
room, esp. in spring. —*v.tr.* clean (a house or
room) in this way. **spring fever** a restless or
lethargic feeling sometimes associated with
spring. **spring greens** the leaves of young
cabbage plants. **spring a leak** develop a leak

(orig. *Naut.*, from timbers springing out of
position). **spring-loaded** containing a compressed or stretched spring pressing one part
against another. **spring mattress** a mattress
containing or consisting of springs. **spring
onion** an onion taken from the ground before
the bulb has formed, and eaten raw in salad.
spring roll a Chinese snack consisting of a
pancake filled with vegetables etc. and fried.
spring tide a tide just after new and full moon
when there is the greatest difference between
high and low water. **spring water** water from
a spring, as opposed to river or rain water. □
springless *adj.* **springlet** *n.* **springlike** *adj.*
[OE *springan* f. Gmc]

springboard /ˈsprɪŋbɔːd/ *n.* **1** a springy board
giving impetus in leaping, diving, etc. **2** a source
of impetus in any activity.

springbok /ˈsprɪŋbɒk/ *n.* **1** a southern African
gazelle, *Antidorcas marsupialis*, with the ability to
run with high springing jumps. **2** (**Springbok**) a
South African, esp. one who has played for South
Africa in international sporting competitions.
[Afrik. f. Du. *springen* SPRING + *bok* antelope]

springer /ˈsprɪŋə(r)/ *n.* **1** a person or thing that
springs. **2 a** a small spaniel of a breed used to
spring game. **b** this breed.

springtide /ˈsprɪŋtaɪd/ *n. poet.* = SPRINGTIME.

springtime /ˈsprɪŋtaɪm/ *n.* **1** the season of
spring. **2** a time compared to this.

springy /ˈsprɪŋɪ/ *adj.* (**springier**, **springiest**)
1 springing back quickly when squeezed or
stretched, elastic. **2** (of movements) as of a
springy substance. □ **springily** *adv.* **springi-
ness** *n.*

sprinkle /ˈsprɪŋk(ə)l/ *v.* & *n.* —*v.tr.* **1** scatter
(liquid, ashes, crumbs, etc.) in small drops or
particles. **2** (often foll. by *with*) subject (the
ground or an object) to sprinkling with liquid
etc. **3** (of liquid etc.) fall on in this way. **4**
distribute in small amounts. —*n.* (usu. foll. by
of) **1** a light shower. **2** = SPRINKLING. [ME, perh.
f. MDu. *sprenkelen*]

sprinkler /ˈsprɪŋklə(r)/ *n.* a person or thing that
sprinkles, esp. a device for sprinkling water on
a lawn or to extinguish fires.

sprinkling /ˈsprɪŋklɪŋ/ *n.* (usu. foll. by *of*) a small
thinly distributed number or amount.

sprint *v.* & *n.* —*v.* **1** *intr.* run a short distance at
full speed. **2** *tr.* run (a specified distance) in this
way. —*n.* **1** such a run. **2** a similar short spell of
maximum effort in cycling, swimming, motor
racing, etc. □ **sprinter** *n.* [ON *sprinta* (unrecorded), of unkn. orig.]

sprit *n.* a small spar reaching diagonally from
the mast to the upper outer corner of the sail.
[OE *sprēot* pole, rel. to SPROUT]

sprite *n.* an elf, fairy, or goblin. [ME f. *sprit* var.
of SPIRIT]

spritzer /ˈsprɪtsə(r)/ *n.* a mixture of wine and
soda water. [G *Spritzer* a splash]

sprocket /ˈsprɒkɪt/ *n.* **1** each of several teeth
on a wheel engaging with links of a chain, e.g. on
a bicycle, or with holes in film or tape or paper.
2 (also **sprocket-wheel**) a wheel with sprockets.
[16th c.: orig. unkn.]

sprog /sprɒg/ *n. sl.* a child; a baby. [orig. services'
sl., = new recruit: perh. f. obs. *sprag* lively
young man]

sprout /spraʊt/ v. & n. —v. **1** tr. put forth, produce (shoots, hair, etc.) (has sprouted a moustache). **2** intr. begin to grow, put forth shoots. **3** intr. spring up, grow to a height. —n. **1** a shoot of a plant. **2** = BRUSSELS SPROUT. [OE sprūtan (unrecorded) f. WG]

spruce¹ /spruːs/ adj. & v. —adj. neat in dress and appearance; trim, smart. —v.tr. & intr. (also refl.; usu. foll. by up) make or become smart. □ **sprucely** adv. **spruceness** n. [perh. f. SPRUCE² in obs. sense 'Prussian', in the collocation spruce (leather) jerkin]

spruce² /spruːs/ n. **1** any coniferous tree of the genus Picea, with dense foliage growing in a distinctive conical shape. **2** the wood of this tree used as timber. [alt. of obs. Pruce Prussia: cf. PRUSSIAN]

sprung see SPRING.

spry /spraɪ/ adj. (**spryer, spryest**) active, lively. □ **spryly** adv. **spryness** n. [18th c., dial. & US: orig. unkn.]

spud n. & v. —n. **1** sl. a potato. **2** a small narrow spade for cutting the roots of weeds etc. —v.tr. (**spudded, spudding**) **1** (foll. by up, out) remove (weeds) with a spud. **2** (also absol.; often foll. by in) make the initial drilling for (an oil well). [ME: orig. unkn.]

spue var. of SPEW.

spumante /spuːˈmæntɪ/ n. an Italian sparkling white wine. [It., = 'sparkling']

spume /spjuːm/ n. & v.intr. froth, foam. □ **spumous** adj. **spumy** adj. (**spumier, spumiest**). [ME f. OF (e)spume or L spuma]

spun past and past part. of SPIN.

spunk n. **1** touchwood. **2** colloq. courage, mettle, spirit. **3** coarse sl. semen. [16th c.: orig. unkn.: cf. PUNK]

spunky /ˈspʌŋkɪ/ adj. (**spunkier, spunkiest**) colloq. brave, spirited. □ **spunkily** adv.

spur n. & v. —n. **1** a device with a small spike or a spiked wheel worn on a rider's heel for urging a horse forward. **2** a stimulus or incentive. **3** a spur-shaped thing, esp.: **a** a projection from a mountain or mountain range. **b** a branch road or railway. **c** a hard projection on a cock's leg. —v. (**spurred, spurring**) **1** tr. prick (a horse) with spurs. **2** tr. **a** (often foll. by on) incite (a person) (spurred him on to greater efforts; spurred her to try again). **b** stimulate (interest etc.). **3** intr. (often foll. by on, forward) ride a horse hard. **4** tr. (esp. as **spurred** adj.) provide (a person, boots, a gamecock) with spurs. □ **on the spur of the moment** on a momentary impulse; impromptu. **put** (or **set**) **spurs to 1** spur (a horse). **2** stimulate (resolution etc.). □ **spurless** adj. [OE spora, spura f. Gmc, rel. to SPURN]

spurge n. any plant of the genus Euphorbia, exuding an acrid milky juice once used medicinally as a purgative. [ME f. OF espurge f. espurgier f. L expurgare (as EX-¹, PURGE)]

spurious /ˈspjʊərɪəs/ adj. **1** not genuine, not being what it purports to be, not proceeding from the pretended source (a spurious excuse). **2** having an outward similarity of form or function only. **3** (of offspring) illegitimate. □ **spuriously** adv. **spuriousness** n. [L spurius false]

spurn v.tr. **1** reject with disdain; treat with contempt. **2** repel or thrust back with one's foot. □ **spurner** n. [OE spurnan, spornan, rel. to SPUR]

spurt v. & n. —v. **1** (also **spirt**) **a** intr. gush out in a jet or stream. **b** tr. cause (liquid etc.) to do this. **2** intr. make a sudden effort. —n. **1** (also **spirt**) a sudden gushing out, a jet. **2** a short sudden effort or increase of pace esp. in racing. [16th c.: orig. unkn.]

sputnik /ˈspʊtnɪk, ˈspʌt-/ n. each of a series of Russian artificial satellites launched from 1957. [Russ., = fellow-traveller]

sputter /ˈspʌtə(r)/ v. & n. —v. **1** intr. emit spitting sounds, esp. when being heated. **2** intr. (often foll. by at) speak in a hurried or vehement fashion. **3** tr. emit with a spitting sound. **4** tr. speak or utter (words, threats, a language, etc.) rapidly or incoherently. —n. a sputtering sound. □ **sputterer** n. [Du. sputteren (imit.)]

sputum /ˈspjuːtəm/ n. (pl. **sputa** /-tə/) **1** saliva, spittle. **2** a mixture of saliva and mucus expectorated from the respiratory tract, usu. a sign of disease. [L, neut. past part. of spuere spit]

spy n. & v. —n. (pl. **spies**) **1** a person who secretly collects and reports information on the activities, movements, etc., of an enemy, competitor, etc. **2** a person who keeps watch on others, esp. furtively. —v. (**spies, spied**) **1** tr. discern or make out, esp. by careful observation (spied a house in the distance). **2** intr. (often foll. by on) act as a spy, keep a close and secret watch. **3** intr. (often foll. by into) pry. □ **I spy** a children's game of guessing a visible object from the initial letter of its name. **spy-master** colloq. the head of an organization of spies. **spy out** explore or discover, esp. secretly. [ME f. OF espie espying, espier espy f. Gmc]

spyglass /ˈspaɪglɑːs/ n. a small telescope.

spyhole /ˈspaɪhəʊl/ n. a peep-hole.

sq. abbr. square.

Sqn. Ldr. abbr. Squadron Leader.

squab /skwɒb/ n. & adj. —n. **1** a short fat person. **2** a young esp. unfledged pigeon or other bird. **3 a** a stuffed cushion. **b** Brit. the padded back or side of a car-seat. **4** a sofa or ottoman. —adj. short and fat, squat. [17th c.: orig. unkn.: cf. obs. quab shapeless thing, Sw. dial. sqvabba fat woman]

squabble /ˈskwɒb(ə)l/ n. & v. —n. a petty or noisy quarrel. —v.intr. engage in a squabble. □ **squabbler** n. [prob. imit.: cf. Sw. dial. sqvabbel a dispute]

squabby /ˈskwɒbɪ/ adj. (**squabbier, squabbiest**) short and fat; squat.

squad /skwɒd/ n. **1** a small group of people sharing a task etc. **2** Mil. a small number of men assembled for drill etc. **3** Sport a group of players forming a team. **4 a** (often in comb.) a specialized unit within a police force (drug squad). **b** = flying squad. **5** a group or class of people of a specified kind (the awkward squad). □ **squad car** a police car having a radio link with headquarters. [F escouade var. of escadre f. It. squadra SQUARE]

squaddie /ˈskwɒdɪ/ n. (also **squaddy**) (pl. **-ies**) Brit. Mil. sl. **1** a recruit. **2** a private.

squadron /ˈskwɒdrən/ n. **1** an organized body of persons. **2** a principal division of a cavalry regiment or armoured formation, consisting of two troops. **3** a detachment of warships employed on a particular duty. **4** a unit of the Royal Air Force with 10 to 18 aircraft. □

Squadron Leader the commander of a squadron of the Royal Air Force, the officer next below Wing Commander. [It. *squadrone* (as SQUAD)]

squalid /ˈskwɒlɪd/ *adj.* **1** filthy, repulsively dirty. **2** mean or poor in appearance. **3** wretched, sordid. □ **squalidly** /-ˈlɪdɪtɪ/ **squalidly** *adv.* **squalidness** *n.* [L *squalidus* f. *squalēre* be rough or dirty]

squall /skwɔːl/ *n. & v.* —*n.* **1** a sudden or violent gust or storm of wind, esp. with rain or snow or sleet. **2** a discordant cry; a scream (esp. of a baby). **3** (esp. in *pl.*) trouble, difficulty. —*v.* **1** *intr.* utter a squall; scream, cry out violently as in fear or pain. **2** *tr.* utter in a screaming or discordant voice. □ **squally** *adj.* [prob. f. SQUEAL after BAWL]

squalor /ˈskwɒlə(r)/ *n.* the state of being filthy or squalid. [L, as SQUALID]

squander /ˈskwɒndə(r)/ *v.tr.* **1** spend (money, time, etc.) wastefully. **2** dissipate (a fortune etc.) wastefully. □ **squanderer** *n.* [16th c.: orig. unkn.]

square /skweə(r)/ *n., adj., adv., & v.* —*n.* **1** an equilateral rectangle. **2 a** an object of this shape or approximately this shape. **b** a small square area on a game-board. **c** a square scarf. **3 a** an open (usu. four-sided) area surrounded by buildings, esp. one planted with trees etc. and surrounded by houses. **b** an open area at the meeting of streets. **c** *Cricket* a closer-cut area at the centre of a ground, any strip of which may be prepared as a wicket. **d** an area within barracks etc. for drill. **e** *US* a block of buildings bounded by four streets. **4** the product of a number multiplied by itself (*81 is the square of 9*). **5** an L-shaped or T-shaped instrument for obtaining or testing right angles. **6** *sl.* a conventional or old-fashioned person, one ignorant of or opposed to current trends. **7** a square arrangement of letters, figures, etc. **8** a body of infantry drawn up in rectangular form. —*adj.* **1** having the shape of a square. **2** having or in the form of a right angle (*table with square corners*). **3** angular and not round; of square section (*has a square jaw*). **4** designating a unit of measure equal to the area of a square whose side is one of the unit specified (*square metre*). **5** (often foll. by *with*) **a** level, parallel. **b** on a proper footing; even, quits. **6** (usu. foll. by *to*) at right angles. **7** having the breadth more nearly equal to the length or height than is usual (*a man of square frame*). **8** properly arranged; in good order, settled (*get things square*). **9** (also **all square**) **a** not in debt, with no money owed. **b** having equal scores. **c** (of scores) equal. **10** fair and honest (*his dealings are not always quite square*). **11** uncompromising, direct, thorough (*was met with a square refusal*). **12** *sl.* conventional or old-fashioned, unsophisticated, conservative. —*adv.* **1** squarely (*sat square on his seat*). **2** fairly, honestly (*play square*). —*v.* **1** *tr.* make square or rectangular, give a rectangular cross-section to (timber etc.). **2** *tr.* multiply (a number) by itself (*3 squared is 9*). **3** *tr. & intr.* (usu. foll. by *to, with*) adjust; make or be suitable or consistent; reconcile (*the results do not square with your conclusions*). **4** *tr.* mark out in squares. **5** *tr.* settle or pay (a bill etc.). **6** *tr.* place (one's shoulders etc.) squarely facing forwards. **7** *tr. colloq.* **a** pay or bribe. **b** secure the acquiescence etc. of (a person) in this way. **8** *tr.* (also *absol.*) make the scores of (a match etc.) all square. □ **back to square one** *colloq.* back to the starting-point with no progress made. **get square with** pay or compound with (a creditor). **on the square** *adj.* **1** *colloq.* honest, fair. **2** having membership of the Freemasons. —*adv. colloq.* honestly, fairly (*can be trusted to act on the square*). **out of square** not at right angles. **square-bashing** *Brit. Mil. sl.* drill on a barrack-square. **square brackets** brackets of the form []. **square-built** of comparatively broad shape. **square the circle 1** construct a square equal in area to a given circle (a problem incapable of a purely geometrical solution). **2** do what is impossible. **square dance** a dance with usu. four couples facing inwards from four sides. **square deal** a fair bargain, fair treatment. **square-eyed** *joc.* affected by or given to excessive viewing of television. **square leg** *Cricket* the fielding position at some distance on the batsman's leg side and nearly opposite the stumps. **square meal** a substantial and satisfying meal. **square measure** measure expressed in square units. **square number** the square of an integer e.g. 1, 4, 9, 16. **square off 1** *US* assume the attitude of a boxer. **2** *Austral.* placate or conciliate. **3** mark out in squares. **square-rigged** with the principal sails at right angles to the length of the ship. **square root** the number that multiplied by itself gives a specified number (3 is the square root of 9). **square up** settle an account etc. **square up to 1** move towards (a person) in a fighting attitude. **2** face and tackle (a difficulty etc.) resolutely. □ **squarely** *adv.* **squareness** *n.* **squarer** *n.* **squarish** *adj.* [ME f. OF *esquare*, *esquarré*, *esquarrer*, ult. f. EX-¹ + L *quadra* square]

Squarial /ˈskweərɪəl/ *n. propr.* a diamond-shaped satellite dish. [SQUARE + AERIAL]

squash¹ /skwɒʃ/ *v. & n.* —*v.* **1** *tr.* crush or squeeze flat or into pulp. **2** *intr.* (often foll. by *into*) make one's way by squeezing. **3** *tr.* pack tight, crowd. **4** *tr.* **a** silence (a person) with a crushing retort etc. **b** dismiss (a proposal etc.). **c** quash (a rebellion). —*n.* **1** a crowd; a crowded assembly. **2** a sound of or as of something being squashed, or of a soft body falling. **3** *Brit.* a concentrated drink made of crushed fruit etc., diluted with water. **4** (in full **squash rackets**) a game played with rackets and a small fairly soft ball against the walls of a closed court. **5** a squashed thing or mass. □ **squashy** *adj.* (**squashier**, **squashiest**). **squashily** *adv.* **squashiness** *n.* [alt. of QUASH]

squash² /skwɒʃ/ *n.* (pl. same or **squashes**) **1** any of various trailing plants of the genus *Cucurbita*, esp. *C. maxima*, *C. moschata*, and *C. pepo*, having pumpkin-like fruits. **2** the fruit of these cooked and eaten as a vegetable. [obs. (*i*)*squoutersquash* f. Narraganset *asquutasquash* f. *asq* uncooked + *squash* green]

squat /skwɒt/ *v., adj., & n.* —*v.* (**squatted**, **squatting**) **1** *intr.* **a** crouch with the hams resting on the backs of the heels. **b** sit on the ground etc. with the knees drawn up and the heels close to or touching the hams. **2** *tr.* put (a person) into a squatting position. **3** *intr. colloq.* sit down. **4 a** *intr.* act as a squatter. **b** *tr.* occupy (a building) as a squatter. **5** *intr.* (of an animal) crouch close to the ground. —*adj.* (**squatter**, **squattest**) **1** (of a person etc.) short and thick, dumpy. **2** in a squatting posture. —*n.* **1** a squatting posture. **2 a** a place occupied by a squatter or squatters. **b** being a squatter. □ **squatly** *adv.* **squatness** *n.* [ME f. OF *esquatir* flatten f. *es-* EX-¹ + *quatir* press down, crouch ult. f. L *coactus* past part. of *cogere* compel: see COGENT]

squatter /ˈskwɒtə(r)/ *n.* **1** a person who takes unauthorized possession of unoccupied premises. **2** *Austral.* a sheep-farmer esp. on a large scale. **3** a person who squats.

squaw *n.* a N. American Indian woman or wife. [Narraganset *squaws*, Massachusetts *squaw* woman]

squawk *n. & v.* —*n.* **1** a loud harsh cry esp. of a bird. **2** a complaint. —*v.intr.* utter a squawk. □ **squawk-box** *colloq.* a loudspeaker or intercom. □ **squawker** *n.* [imit.]

squeak *n. & v.* —*n.* **1 a** a short shrill cry as of a mouse. **b** a slight high-pitched sound as of an unoiled hinge. **2** (also **narrow squeak**) a narrow escape, a success barely attained. —*v.* **1** *intr.* make a squeak. **2** *tr.* utter (words) shrilly. **3** *intr.* (foll. by *by*, *through*) *colloq.* pass narrowly. **4** *intr. sl.* turn informer. □ **squeaker** *n.* [ME, imit.: cf. SQUEAL, SHRIEK, and Sw. *skväka* croak]

squeaky /ˈskwiːkɪ/ *adj.* (**squeakier**, **squeakiest**) making a squeaking sound. □ **squeaky clean 1** completely clean. **2** above criticism; beyond reproach. □ **squeakily** *adv.* **squeakiness** *n.*

squeal *n. & v.* —*n.* a prolonged shrill sound, esp. a cry of a child or a pig. —*v.* **1** *intr.* make a squeal. **2** *tr.* utter (words) with a squeal. **3** *intr. sl.* turn informer. **4** *intr. sl.* protest loudly or excitedly. □ **squealer** *n.* [ME, imit.]

squeamish /ˈskwiːmɪʃ/ *adj.* **1** easily nauseated or disgusted. **2** fastidious or overscrupulous in questions of propriety, honesty, etc. □ **squeamishly** *adv.* **squeamishness** *n.* [ME var. of *squeamous* (now dial.), f. AF *escoymous*, of unkn. orig.]

squeegee /ˈskwiːdʒiː/ *n. & v.* —*n.* a rubber-edged implement set on a long handle and used for cleaning windows, etc. —*v.tr.* (**squeegees**, **squeegeed**) treat with a squeegee. [*squeege*, strengthened form of SQUEEZE]

squeeze *v. & n.* —*v.* **1** *tr.* **a** exert pressure on from opposite or all sides, esp. in order to extract moisture or reduce size. **b** compress with one's hand or between two bodies. **c** reduce the size of or alter the shape of by squeezing. **2** *tr.* (often foll. by *out*) extract (moisture) by squeezing. **3 a** *tr.* force (a person or thing) into or through a small or narrow space. **b** *intr.* make one's way by squeezing. **c** *tr.* make (one's way) by squeezing. **4** *tr.* **a** harass by exactions; extort money etc. from. **b** constrain; bring pressure to bear on. **c** (usu. foll. by *out of*) obtain (money etc.) by extortion, entreaty, etc. **5** *tr.* press (a person's hand) with one's own as a sign of sympathy, affection, etc. **6** *tr.* (often foll. by *out*) produce with effort (*squeezed out a tear*). —*n.* **1** an instance of squeezing; the state of being squeezed. **2** *Brit.* a close embrace. **3** a crowd or crowded state; a crush. **4** a small quantity produced by squeezing (*a squeeze of lemon*). **5** a sum of money extorted or exacted, esp. an illicit commission. **6** *Econ.* a restriction on borrowing, investment, etc., in a financial crisis. □ **put the squeeze on** *colloq.* coerce or pressure (a person). **squeeze bottle** a flexible container whose contents are extracted by squeezing it. **squeeze-box** *sl.* an accordion or concertina. □

squeezable *adj.* **squeezer** *n.* [earlier *squise*, intensive of obs. *queise*, of unkn. orig.]

squelch *v. & n.* —*v.* **1** *intr.* **a** make a sucking sound as of treading in thick mud. **b** move with a squelching sound. **2** *tr.* **a** disconcert, silence. **b** stamp on, crush flat, put an end to. —*n.* an instance of squelching. □ **squelcher** *n.* **squelchy** *adj.* [imit.]

squib *n.* **1** a small firework burning with a hissing sound and usu. with a final explosion. **2** a short satirical composition, a lampoon. [16th c.: orig. unkn.: perh. imit.]

squid *n.* any of various ten-armed cephalopods, esp. of the genus *Loligo*, used as bait or food. [17th c.: orig. unkn.]

squidgy /ˈskwɪdʒɪ/ *adj.* (**squidgier**, **squidgiest**) *colloq.* squashy, soggy. [imit.]

squiffed /skwɪft/ *adj. sl.* = SQUIFFY.

squiffy /ˈskwɪfɪ/ *adj.* (**squiffier**, **squiffiest**) esp. *Brit. sl.* slightly drunk. [19th c.: orig. unkn.]

squiggle /ˈskwɪg(ə)l/ *n. & v.* —*n.* a short curly line, esp. in handwriting or doodling. —*v.* **1** *tr.* write in a squiggly manner; scrawl. **2** *intr.* wriggle, squirm. □ **squiggly** *adj.* [imit.]

squill /skwɪl/ *n.* **1** any bulbous plant of the genus *Scilla*, esp. *S. autumnalis*. **2** a seashore plant, *Urginea maritima*, having bulbs used in diuretic and purgative preparations. [ME f. L *squilla*, *scilla* f. Gk *skilla*]

squint *v., n., & adj.* —*v.* **1** *intr.* have the eyes turned in different directions, have a squint. **2** *intr.* (often foll. by *at*) look obliquely or with half-closed eyes. **3** *tr.* close (one's eyes) quickly, hold (one's eyes) half-shut. —*n.* **1** = STRABISMUS. **2** a stealthy or sidelong glance. **3** *colloq.* a glance or look (*had a squint at it*). **4** an oblique opening through the wall of a church affording a view of the altar. —*adj.* **1** squinting. **2** looking different ways. □ **squint-eyed 1** squinting. **2** malignant, ill-willed. □ **squinter** *n.* **squinty** *adj.* [ME perh. f. Du. *schuinte* slant]

squire *n. & v.* —*n.* **1** a country gentleman, esp. the chief landowner in a country district. **2** *hist.* a knight's attendant. **3** *Brit. colloq.* a jocular form of address to a man. —*v.tr.* (of a man) attend upon or escort (a woman). □ **squiredom** *n.* **squirehood** *n.* **squirelet** *n.* **squireling** *n.* **squirely** *adj.* **squireship** *n.* [ME f. OF *esquier* ESQUIRE]

squirearch /ˈskwaɪəˌrɑːk/ *n.* a member of the squirearchy. □ **squirearchical** /-ˈrɑːkɪk(ə)l/ *adj.* (also **squirarchical**). [back-form. f. SQUIRE-ARCHY, after MONARCH]

squirearchy /ˈskwaɪəˌrɑːkɪ/ *n.* (also **squirarchy**) (*pl.* **-ies**) landowners collectively, esp. as a class having political or social influence; a class or body of squires. [SQUIRE, after HIERARCHY etc.]

squirl *n. colloq.* a flourish or twirl, esp. in handwriting. [perh. f. SQUIGGLE + TWIRL or WHIRL]

squirm *v. & n.* —*v.intr.* **1** wriggle, writhe. **2** show or feel embarrassment or discomfiture. —*n.* a squirming movement. □ **squirmer** *n.* **squirmy** *adj.* (**squirmier**, **squirmiest**). [imit., prob. assoc. with WORM]

squirrel /ˈskwɪr(ə)l/ *n. & v.* —*n.* **1** any rodent of the family Sciuridae, e.g. the red squirrel, grey squirrel, etc., often of arboreal habits, with a bushy tail arching over its back. **2** the fur of this animal. **3** a person who hoards objects, food, etc. —*v.* (**squirrelled**, **squirrelling**; *US* **squirreled**, **squirreling**) **1** *tr.* (often foll. by *away*) hoard (objects, food, time, etc.) (*squirrelled it away in the cupboard*). **2** *intr.* (often foll. by *around*) bustle about. [ME f. AF *esquirel*, OF *esquireul*, ult. f. L *sciurus* f. Gk *skiouros* f. *skia* shade + *oura* tail]

squirrelly /ˈskwɪrəlɪ/ *adj.* **1** like a squirrel. **2 a** inclined to bustle about. **b** (of a person) unpredictable, nervous, demented.

squirt *v. & n.* —*v.* **1** *tr.* eject (liquid or powder) in a jet as from a syringe. **2** *intr.* (of liquid or powder) be discharged in this way. **3** *tr.* splash with liquid or powder ejected by squirting. —*n.* **1 a** a jet of water etc. **b** a small quantity produced by squirting. **2** a syringe. **3** *colloq.* an insignificant but presumptuous person. □ **squirter** *n.* [ME, imit.]

squish *n. & v.* —*n.* a slight squelching sound. —*v.* **1** *intr.* move with a squish. **2** *tr. colloq.* squash, squeeze. □ **squishy** *adj.* (**squishier**, **squishiest**). [imit.]

squit *n. Brit.* **1** *sl.* a small or insignificant person. **2** *dial.* nonsense. [cf. dial. *squirt* insignificant person, and *squit* to squirt]

Sr *symb. Chem.* the element strontium.

Sr. *abbr.* **1** Senior. **2** Señor. **3** Signor. **4** *Eccl.* Sister.

SRN *abbr.* (in the UK) State Registered Nurse.

SS *abbr.* **1** Saints. **2** steamship. **3** *hist.* Nazi special police force. [sense 3 f. G *Schutz-Staffel*]

SSE *abbr.* south-south-east.

SSSI *abbr.* (in the UK) Site of Special Scientific Interest.

SSW *abbr.* south-south-west.

St *abbr.* **1** Saint. **2** stokes.

St. *abbr.* Street.

st. *abbr.* **1** stone (in weight). **2** *Cricket* stumped by.

stab *v. & n.* —*v.* (**stabbed**, **stabbing**) **1** *tr.* pierce or wound with a (usu. short) pointed tool or weapon e.g. a knife or dagger. **2** *intr.* (often foll. by *at*) aim a blow with such a weapon. **3** *intr.* cause a sensation like being stabbed (*stabbing pain*). **4** *tr.* hurt or distress (a person, feelings, conscience, etc.). **5** *intr.* (foll. by *at*) aim a blow at a person's reputation, etc. —*n.* **1 a** an instance of stabbing. **b** a blow or thrust with a knife etc. **2** a wound made in this way. **3** a blow or pain inflicted on a person's feelings. **4** *colloq.* an attempt, a try. □ **stab in the back** *n.* a treacherous or slanderous attack. —*v.tr.* slander or betray. □ **stabber** *n.* [ME: cf. dial. *stob* in sense 1 of *v.*]

stability /stəˈbɪlɪtɪ/ *n.* the quality or state of being stable. [ME f. OF *stableté* f. L *stabilitas* f. *stabilis* STABLE¹]

stabilize /ˈsteɪbɪˌlaɪz/ *v.tr. & intr.* (also **-ise**) make or become stable. □ **stabilization** /-ˈzeɪʃ(ə)n/ *n.*

stabilizer /ˈsteɪbɪˌlaɪzə(r)/ *n.* (also **-iser**) a device or substance used to keep something stable, esp.: **1** a gyroscope device to prevent rolling of a ship. **2** *US* the horizontal tailplane of an aircraft. **3** (in *pl.*) a pair of small wheels fitted to the rear wheel of a child's bicycle.

stable¹ /ˈsteɪb(ə)l/ *adj.* (**stabler**, **stablest**) **1** firmly fixed or established; not easily adjusted, destroyed, or altered (*a stable structure*; *a stable government*). **2** firm, resolute; not wavering or fickle (*a stable and steadfast friend*). **3** *Chem.* (of a

compound) not readily decomposing. **4** *Physics* (of an isotope) not subject to radioactive decay. □ **stableness** *n.* **stably** *adv.* [ME f. AF *stable*, OF *estable* f. L *stabilis* f. *stare* stand]

stable² /ˈsteɪb(ə)l/ *n. & v.* —*n.* **1** a building set apart and adapted for keeping horses. **2** an establishment where racehorses are kept and trained. **3** the racehorses of a particular stable. **4** persons, products, etc., having a common origin or affiliation. **5** such an origin or affiliation. —*v.tr.* put or keep (a horse) in a stable. □ **stable-boy** a boy employed in a stable. **stable-companion** (or **-mate**) **1** a horse of the same stable. **2** a member of the same organization. **stable-girl** a girl employed in a stable. **stable-lad** a person employed in a stable. □ **stableful** *n.* (*pl.* **-fuls**). [ME f. OF *estable* f. L *stabulum* f. *stare* stand]

stabling /ˈsteɪblɪŋ/ *n.* accommodation for horses.

staccato /stəˈkɑːtəʊ/ *adv., adj., & n. esp. Mus.* —*adv. & adj.* with each sound or note sharply detached or separated from the others. —*n.* (*pl.* **-os**) **1** a staccato passage in music etc. **2** staccato delivery or presentation. [It., past part. of *staccare* = *distaccare* DETACH]

stack *n. & v.* —*n.* **1** a pile or heap, esp. in orderly arrangement. **2** a circular or rectangular pile of hay, straw, etc., or of grain in sheaf, often with a sloping thatched top, a rick. **3** *colloq.* a large quantity (*a stack of work*; *has stacks of money*). **4 a** = *chimney-stack*. **b** = SMOKESTACK. **c** a tall factory chimney. **5** a stacked group of aircraft. **6** (also **stack-room**) a part of a library where books are compactly stored, esp. one to which the public does not have direct access. **7** *Brit.* a high detached rock esp. off the coast of Scotland and the Orkneys. **8** *Computing* a set of storage locations which store data in such a way that the most recently stored item is the first to be retrieved. —*v.tr.* **1** pile in a stack or stacks. **2 a** arrange (cards) secretly for cheating. **b** manipulate (circumstances etc.) to one's advantage. **3** cause (aircraft) to fly round the same point at different levels while waiting to land at an airport. □ **stack up** *US* *colloq.* present oneself, measure up. **stack-yard** an enclosure for stacks of hay, straw, etc. □ **stackable** *adj.* **stacker** *n.* [ME f. ON *stakkr* haystack f. Gmc]

staddle /ˈstæd(ə)l/ *n.* a platform or framework supporting a rick etc. □ **staddle-stone** a stone supporting a staddle or rick etc. [OE *stathol* base f. Gmc, rel. to STAND]

stadium /ˈsteɪdɪəm/ *n.* (*pl.* **stadiums**) an athletic or sports ground with tiers of seats for spectators. [ME f. L f. Gk *stadion*]

staff /stɑːf/ *n. & v.* —*n.* **1 a** a stick or pole for use in walking or climbing or as a weapon. **b** a stick or pole as a sign of office or authority. **c** a person or thing that supports or sustains. **d** a flagstaff. **2 a** a body of persons employed in a business etc. (*editorial staff of a newspaper*). **b** those in authority within an organization, esp. the teachers in a school. **c** *Mil.* etc. a body of officers assisting an officer in high command and concerned with an army, regiment, fleet, or air force as a whole (*general staff*). **d** (usu. **Staff**) *Mil.* = *staff sergeant*. **3** (*pl.* **staffs** or **staves** /steɪvz/) *Mus.* a set of usu. five parallel lines on any one or between any adjacent two of which a note is placed to indicate its pitch. —*v.tr.* provide (an institution etc.) with staff. □ **staff**

college *Brit. Mil.* etc. a college at which officers are trained for staff duties. **staff nurse** *Brit.* a nurse ranking just below a sister. **staff officer** *Mil.* an officer serving on the staff of an army etc. **staff sergeant 1** *Brit.* the senior sergeant of a non-infantry company. **2** *US* a non-commissioned officer ranking just above sergeant. □ **staffed** *adj.* (also in *comb.*). [OE *stæf* f. Gmc]

staffer /ˈstɑːfə(r)/ *n. US* a member of a staff, esp. of a newspaper.

stag *n.* & *v.* —*n.* **1** an adult male deer, esp. one with a set of antlers. **2** *Brit. Stock Exch.* a person who applies for shares of a new issue with a view to selling at once for a profit. **3** a man who attends a social gathering unaccompanied by a woman. —*v.tr.* (**stagged, stagging**) *Brit. Stock Exch.* deal in (shares) as a stag. □ **stag beetle** any beetle of the family Lucanidae, the male of which has large branched mandibles resembling a stag's antlers. **stag-night** (or **-party**) an all-male celebration, esp. in honour of a man about to marry. [ME f. OF *stacga, stagga* (unrecorded): cf. *docga* dog, *frogga* frog, etc., and ON *staggr, staggi* male bird]

stage *n.* & *v.* —*n.* **1** a point or period in a process or development (*reached a critical stage*; *is in the larval stage*). **2 a** a raised floor or platform, esp. one on which plays etc. are performed before an audience. **b** (prec. by *the*) the acting or theatrical profession, dramatic art or literature, the drama. **c** the scene of action (*the stage of politics*). **d** = *landing-stage*. **3 a** a regular stopping-place on a route. **b** the distance between two stopping-places. **c** *Brit.* = *fare-stage*. **4** *Astronaut.* a section of a rocket with a separate engine, jettisoned when its propellant is exhausted. —*v.tr.* **1** present (a play etc.) on stage. **2** arrange the occurrence of (*staged a demonstration*; *staged a comeback*). □ **go on the stage** become an actor. **hold the stage** dominate a conversation etc. **stage direction** an instruction in the text of a play as to the movement, position, tone, etc., of an actor, or sound effects etc. **stage door** an actors' and workmen's entrance from the street to a theatre behind the stage. **stage effect 1** an effect produced in acting or on the stage. **2** an artificial or theatrical effect produced in real life. **stage fright** nervousness on facing an audience esp. for the first time. **stage-hand** a person handling scenery etc. during a performance on stage. **stage left** (or **right**) on the left (or right) side of the stage, facing the audience. **stage-manage 1** be the stage-manager of. **2** arrange and control for effect. **stage-manager** the person responsible for lighting and other mechanical arrangements for a play etc. **stage name** a name assumed for professional purposes by an actor. **stage play** a play performed on stage rather than broadcast etc. **stage-struck** filled with an inordinate desire to go on the stage. **stage whisper 1** an aside. **2** a loud whisper meant to be heard by others than the person addressed. □ **stageable** *adj.* **stageability** /-dʒəˈbɪlɪtɪ/ *n.* **stager** *n.* [ME f. OF *estage* dwelling ult. f. L *stare* stand]

stagecoach /ˈsteɪdʒkəʊtʃ/ *n. hist.* a large closed horse-drawn coach running regularly by stages between two places.

stagecraft /ˈsteɪdʒkrɑːft/ *n.* skill or experience in writing or staging plays.

stagflation /stægˈfleɪʃ(ə)n/ *n. Econ.* a state of inflation without a corresponding increase of demand and employment. [STAGNATION (as STAGNATE) + INFLATION]

stagger /ˈstægə(r)/ *v.* & *n.* —*v.* **1 a** *intr.* walk unsteadily, totter. **b** *tr.* cause to totter (*was staggered by the blow*). **2 a** *tr.* shock, confuse; cause to hesitate or waver (*the question staggered them*; *they were staggered at the suggestion*). **b** *intr.* hesitate; waver in purpose. **3** *tr.* arrange (events, hours of work, etc.) so that they do not coincide. **4** *tr.* arrange (objects) so that they are not in line. —*n.* **1** a tottering movement. **2** (in *pl.*) a disease of the brain and spinal cord esp. in horses and cattle, causing staggering. **3** an overhanging or slantwise or zigzag arrangement of like parts in a structure etc. □ **staggerer** *n.* [alt. of ME *stacker* (now dial.) f. ON *stakra* frequent. of *staka* push, stagger]

staggering /ˈstægərɪŋ/ *adj.* **1** astonishing, bewildering. **2** that staggers. □ **staggeringly** *adv.*

staghound /ˈstæghaʊnd/ *n.* **1** any large dog of a breed used for hunting deer by sight or scent. **2** this breed.

staging /ˈsteɪdʒɪŋ/ *n.* **1** the presentation of a play etc. **2 a** a platform or support or scaffolding, esp. temporary. **b** shelves for plants in a greenhouse. □ **staging post** a regular stopping-place, esp. on an air route.

stagnant /ˈstægnənt/ *adj.* **1** (of liquid) motionless, having no current. **2** (of life, action, the mind, business, a person) showing no activity, dull, sluggish. □ **stagnancy** *n.* **stagnantly** *adv.* [L *stagnare stagnant-* f. *stagnum* pool]

stagnate /stægˈneɪt/ *v.intr.* be or become stagnant. □ **stagnation** *n.*

stagy /ˈsteɪdʒɪ/ *adj.* (also **stagey**) (**stagier, stagiest**) theatrical, artificial, exaggerated. □ **stagily** *adv.* **staginess** *n.*

staid *adj.* of quiet and steady character; sedate. □ **staidly** *adv.* **staidness** *n.* [= *stayed*, past part. of STAY¹]

stain *v.* & *n.* —*v.* **1** *tr.* & *intr.* discolour or be discoloured by the action of liquid sinking in. **2** *tr.* sully, blemish, spoil, damage (a reputation, character, etc.). **3** *tr.* colour (wood, glass, etc.) by a process other than painting or covering the surface. **4** *tr.* impregnate (a specimen) for microscopic examination with colouring matter that makes the structure visible by being deposited in some parts more than in others. —*n.* **1** a discoloration, a spot or mark caused esp. by contact with foreign matter and not easily removed (*a cloth covered with tea-stains*). **2 a** a blot or blemish. **b** damage to a reputation etc. (*a stain on one's character*). **3** a substance used in staining. □ **stained glass** dyed or coloured glass, esp. in a lead framework in a window (also (with hyphen) *attrib.*: *stained-glass window*). □ **stainable** *adj.* **stainer** *n.* [ME f. *distain* f. OF *desteindre desteign-* (as DIS-, TINGE)]

stainless /ˈsteɪnlɪs/ *adj.* **1** (esp. of a reputation) without stains. **2** not liable to stain. □ **stainless steel** chrome steel not liable to rust or tarnish under ordinary conditions.

stair *n.* **1** each of a set of fixed indoor steps (*on the top stair but one*). **2** (usu. in *pl.*) a set of indoor steps (*passed him on the stairs*; *down a winding stair*). □ **stair-rod** a rod for securing a carpet in the angle between two steps. [OE *stæger* f. Gmc]

staircase /ˈsteəkeɪs/ n. **1** a flight of stairs and the supporting structure. **2** a part of a building containing a staircase.

stairhead /ˈsteəhed/ n. a level space at the top of stairs.

stairway /ˈsteəweɪ/ n. **1** a flight of stairs, a staircase. **2** the way up this.

stairwell /ˈsteəwel/ n. the shaft in which a staircase is built.

stake[1] n. & v. —n. **1** a stout stick or post sharpened at one end and driven into the ground as a support, boundary mark, etc. **2** *hist.* **a** the post to which a person was tied to be burnt alive. **b** (prec. by *the*) death by burning as a punishment (*was condemned to the stake*). —v.tr. **1** fasten, secure, or support with a stake or stakes. **2** (foll. by *off*, *out*) mark off (an area) with stakes. **3** state or establish (a claim). □ **stake out** *colloq.* **1** place under surveillance. **2** place (a person) to maintain surveillance. **stake-out** n. esp. *US colloq.* a period of surveillance. [OE *staca* f. WG, rel. to STICK[2]]

stake[2] n. & v. —n. **1** a sum of money etc. wagered on an event, esp. deposited with a stakeholder. **2** (often foll. by *in*) an interest or concern, esp. financial. **3** (in *pl.*) **a** money offered as a prize esp. in a horse-race. **b** such a race (*maiden stakes*; *trial stakes*). —v.tr. **1 a** wager (*staked £5 on the next race*). **b** risk (*staked everything on convincing him*). **2** *US colloq.* give financial or other support to. □ **at stake 1** risked, to be won or lost (*life itself is at stake*). **2** at issue, in question. □ **staker** n. [16th c.: perh. f. STAKE[1]]

stakeholder /ˈsteɪkˌhəʊldə(r)/ n. an independent party with whom each of those who make a wager deposits the money etc. wagered.

Stakhanovite /stəˈkɑːnəˌvaɪt/ n. *hist.* a worker (esp. in the former USSR) who increased his output to an exceptional extent, and so gained special awards. □ **Stakhanovism** /-ˌvɪz(ə)m/ n. **Stakhanovist** /-vɪst/ n. [A. G. *Stakhanov*, Russian coal-miner d. 1977]

stalactite /ˈstæləktaɪt, stəˈlæk-/ n. a deposit of calcium carbonate having the shape of a large icicle, formed by the trickling of water from the roof of a cave, cliff overhang, etc. □ **stalactic** /-ˈlæktɪk/ adj. **stalactiform** /-ˈlæktɪˌfɔːm/ adj. **stalactitic** /-ˈtɪtɪk/ adj. [mod.L *stalactites* f. Gk *stalaktos* dripping f. *stalassō* drip]

stalagmite /ˈstæləɡˌmaɪt/ n. a deposit of calcium carbonate formed by the dripping of water into the shape of a large inverted icicle rising from the floor of a cave etc. □ **stalagmitic** /-ˈmɪtɪk/ adj. [mod.L *stalagmites* f. Gk *stalagma* a drop f. *stalassō* (as STALACTITE)]

stale[1] adj. & v. —adj. (**staler**, **stalest**) **1 a** not fresh, not quite new (*stale bread is best for toast*). **b** musty, insipid, or otherwise the worse for age or use. **2** trite or unoriginal (*a stale joke*; *stale news*). **3** (of an athlete or other performer) having ability impaired by excessive exertion or practice. —v.tr. & intr. make or become stale. □ **stalely** adv. **staleness** n. [ME, prob. f. AF & OF f. *estaler* halt: cf. STALL[1]]

stale[2] n. & v. —n. the urine of horses and cattle. —v.intr. (esp. of horses and cattle) urinate. [ME, perh. f. OF *estaler* adopt a position (cf. STALE[1])]

stalemate /ˈsteɪlmeɪt/ n. & v. —n. **1** *Chess* a position counting as a draw, in which a player is not in check but cannot move except into check. **2** a deadlock or drawn contest. —v.tr. **1** *Chess* bring (a player) to a stalemate. **2** bring to a standstill. [obs. *stale* (f. AF *estale* f. *estaler* be placed: cf. STALE[1]) + MATE[2]]

stalk[1] /stɔːk/ n. **1** the main stem of a herbaceous plant. **2** the slender attachment or support of a leaf, flower, fruit, etc. **3** a similar support for an organ etc. in an animal. **4** a slender support or linking shaft in a machine, object, etc., e.g. the stem of a wineglass. □ **stalked** adj. (also in comb.). **stalkless** adj. **stalklet** n. **stalklike** adj. **stalky** adj. [ME *stalke*, prob. dimin. of (now dial.) *stale* rung of a ladder, long handle, f. OE *stalu*]

stalk[2] /stɔːk/ v. & n. —v. **1 a** tr. pursue or approach (game or an enemy) stealthily. **b** intr. steal up to game under cover. **2** intr. stride, walk in a stately or haughty manner. —n. **1** the stalking of game. **2** an imposing gait. □ **stalking-horse 1** a horse behind which a hunter is concealed. **2** a pretext concealing one's real intentions or actions. □ **stalker** n. (also in comb.). [OE f. Gmc, rel. to STEAL]

stall[1] /stɔːl/ n. & v. —n. **1 a** a trader's stand or booth in a market etc., or out of doors. **b** a compartment in a building for the sale of goods. **c** a table in this on which goods are exposed. **2 a** a stable or cowhouse. **b** a compartment for one animal in this. **3** a fixed seat in the choir or chancel of a church, more or less enclosed at the back and sides and often canopied, esp. one appropriated to a clergyman (*canon's stall*; *dean's stall*). **4** (usu. in *pl.*) *Brit.* each of a set of seats in a theatre, usu. on the ground floor. **5 a** a compartment for one person in a shower-bath, lavatory, etc. **b** a compartment for one horse at the start of a race. **6 a** the stalling of an engine or aircraft. **b** the condition resulting from this. **7** a receptacle for one object (*finger-stall*). —v. **1 a** intr. (of a motor vehicle or its engine) stop because of an overload on the engine or an inadequate supply of fuel to it. **b** intr. (of an aircraft or its pilot) reach a condition where the speed is too low to allow effective operation of the controls. **c** tr. cause (an engine or vehicle or aircraft) to stall. **2** tr. put or keep (cattle etc.) in a stall or stalls esp. for fattening (*a stalled ox*). [OE *steall* f. Gmc, rel. to STAND: partly f. OF *estal* f. Frank.]

stall[2] /stɔːl/ v. **1** intr. play for time when being questioned etc. **2** tr. delay, obstruct, block. [*stall* pickpocket's confederate, orig. 'decoy' f. AF *estal*(e), prob. rel. to STALL[1]]

stallholder /ˈstɔːlˌhəʊldə(r)/ n. a person in charge of a stall at a market etc.

stallion /ˈstæljən/ n. an uncastrated adult male horse, esp. one kept for breeding. [ME f. OF *estalon* ult. f. a Gmc root rel. to STALL[1]]

stalwart /ˈstɔːlwət/ adj. & n. —adj. **1** strongly built, sturdy. **2** courageous, resolute, determined (*stalwart supporters*). —n. a stalwart person, esp. a loyal uncompromising partisan. □ **stalwartly** adv. **stalwartness** n. [Sc. var. of obs. *stalworth* f. OE *stælwierthe* f. *stæl* place, WORTH]

stamen /ˈsteɪmən/ n. the male fertilizing organ of a flowering plant, including the anther containing pollen. □ **staminiferous** /ˌstæmɪˈnɪfərəs/ adj. [L *stamen staminis* warp in an upright loom, thread]

stamina /ˈstæmɪnə/ n. the ability to endure prolonged physical or mental strain; staying power, power of endurance. [L, pl. of STAMEN in sense 'warp, threads spun by the Fates']

stammer /ˈstæmə(r)/ v. & n. —v. **1** intr. speak (habitually, or on occasion from embarrassment etc.) with halting articulation, esp. with pauses or rapid repetitions of the same syllable. **2** tr. (often foll. by out) utter (words) in this way (stammered out an excuse). —n. **1** a tendency to stammer. **2** an instance of stammering. □ **stammerer** n. **stammeringly** adv. [OE stamerian f. WG]

stamp v. & n. —v. **1 a** tr. bring down (one's foot) heavily on the ground etc. **b** tr. crush, flatten, or bring into a specified state in this way (stamped down the earth round the plant). **c** intr. bring down one's foot heavily; walk with heavy steps. **2** tr. **a** impress (a pattern, mark, etc.) on metal, paper, butter, etc., with a die or similar instrument of metal, wood, rubber, etc. **b** impress (a surface) with a pattern etc. in this way. **3** tr. affix a postage or other stamp to (an envelope or document). **4** tr. assign a specific character to; characterize; mark out (stamps the story an invention). —n. **1** an instrument for stamping a pattern or mark. **2 a** a mark or pattern made by this. **b** the impression of an official mark required to be made for revenue purposes on deeds, bills of exchange, etc., as evidence of payment of tax. **3** a small adhesive piece of paper indicating that a price, fee, or tax has been paid, esp. a postage stamp. **4** a mark impressed on or label etc. affixed to a commodity as evidence of quality etc. **5 a** a heavy downward blow with the foot. **b** the sound of this. **6 a** a characteristic mark or impress (bears the stamp of genius). **b** character, kind (avoid people of that stamp). □ **stamp-collecting** the collecting of postage stamps as objects of interest or value. **stamp-duty** a duty imposed on certain kinds of legal document. **stamping-ground** a favourite haunt or place of action. **stamp on 1** impress (an idea etc.) on (the memory etc.). **2** suppress. **stamp out 1** produce by cutting out with a die etc. **2** put an end to, crush, destroy. □ **stamper** n. [prob. f. OE stampian (v.) (unrecorded) f. Gmc: infl. by OF estamper (v.) and F estampe (n.) also f. Gmc]

stampede /stæmˈpiːd/ n. & v. —n. **1** a sudden flight and scattering of a number of horses, cattle, etc. **2** a sudden flight or hurried movement of people due to interest or panic. **3** US the spontaneous response of many persons to a common impulse. —v. **1** intr. take part in a stampede. **2** tr. cause to do this. **3** tr. cause to act hurriedly or unreasonably. □ **stampeder** n. [Sp. estampida crash, uproar, ult. f. Gmc, rel. to STAMP]

stance /stɑːns, stæns/ n. **1** an attitude or position of the body esp. when hitting a ball etc. **2** a standpoint; an attitude of mind. [F f. It. stanza: see STANZA]

stanch[1] /stɑːntʃ, stɔːntʃ/ v.tr. (also **staunch**) **1** restrain the flow of (esp. blood). **2** restrain the flow from (esp. a wound). [ME f. OF estanchier f. Rmc]

stanch[2] var. of STAUNCH[1].

stanchion /ˈstɑːnʃ(ə)n/ n. & v. —n. **1** a post or pillar, an upright support, a vertical strut. **2** an upright bar, pair of bars, or frame, for confining cattle in a stall. —v.tr. **1** supply with a stanchion. **2** fasten (cattle) to a stanchion. [ME f. AF stanchon, OF estanchon f. estance prob. ult. f. L stare stand]

stand v. & n. —v. (past and past part. **stood** /stʊd/) **1** intr. have or take or maintain an upright position, esp. on the feet or a base. **2** intr. be situated or located (here once stood a village). **3** intr. be of a specified height (stands six foot three). **4** intr. be in a specified condition (stands accused; the thermometer stood at 90°; stood in awe of them). **5** tr. place or set in an upright or specified position (stood it against the wall). **6** intr. **a** move to and remain in a specified position (stand aside). **b** take a specified attitude (stand aloof). **7** intr. maintain a position; avoid falling or moving or being moved (the house will stand for another century; stood for hours arguing). **8** intr. assume a stationary position; cease to move (now stand still). **9** intr. remain valid or unaltered; hold good (the former conditions must stand). **10** intr. Naut. hold a specified course (stand in for the shore; you are standing into danger). **11** tr. endure without yielding or complaining; tolerate (cannot stand the pain; how can you stand him?). **12** tr. provide for another or others at one's own expense (stood him a drink). **13** intr. (often foll. by for) Brit. be a candidate (for an office, legislature, or constituency) (stood for Parliament; stood for Finchley). **14** intr. act in a specified capacity (stood proxy). **15** tr. undergo (trial). —n. **1** a cessation from motion or progress, a stoppage (was brought to a stand). **2 a** a halt made, or a stationary condition assumed, for the purpose of resistance. **b** resistance to attack or compulsion (esp. make a stand). **c** Cricket a prolonged period at the wicket by two batsmen. **3 a** a position taken up (took his stand near the door). **b** an attitude adopted. **4** a rack, set of shelves, table, etc., on or in which things may be placed (music stand; hatstand). **5 a** a small open-fronted structure for a trader outdoors or in a market etc. **b** a structure occupied by a participating organization at an exhibition. **6** a standing-place for vehicles (cab-stand). **7 a** a raised structure for persons to sit or stand on. **b** US a witness-box (take the stand). **8** Theatr. etc. each halt made on a tour to give one or more performances. **9** a group of growing plants (stand of trees; stand of clover). □ **as it stands 1** in its present condition, unaltered. **2** in the present circumstances. **stand alone** be unequalled. **stand and deliver!** hist. a highwayman's order to hand over valuables etc. **stand back 1** withdraw; take up a position further from the front. **2** withdraw psychologically in order to take an objective view. **stand by 1** stand nearby; look on without interfering (will not stand by and see him ill-treated). **2** uphold, support, side with (a person). **3** adhere to, abide by (terms or promises). **4** Naut. stand ready to take hold of or operate (an anchor etc.). **stand-by** n. (pl. **-bys**) **1** a person or thing ready if needed in an emergency etc. **2** readiness for duty (on stand-by). —adj. **1** ready for immediate use. **2** (of air travel) not booked in advance but allocated on the basis of earliest availability. **stand corrected** accept correction. **stand down 1** withdraw (a person) or retire from a team, witness-box, or similar position. **2** Brit. cease to be a candidate etc. **3** Brit. Mil. go off duty. **stand for 1** represent, signify, imply ('US' stands for 'United States'; democracy stands for a great deal more than that). **2** (often with neg.) colloq. endure, tolerate, acquiesce in. **3** espouse the cause of. **stand one's ground** maintain one's position, not yield. **stand in** (usu. foll. by

for) deputize; act in place of another. **stand-in**
n. a deputy or substitute, esp. for an actor when
the latter's acting ability is not needed. **stand
off 1** move or keep away, keep one's distance. **2**
Brit. temporarily dispense with the services of
(an employee). **stand-off** *n.* **1** *US* a deadlock. **2**
= *stand-off half.* **stand-off half** *Rugby Football*
a half-back who forms a link between the
scrum-half and the three-quarters. **stand on**
insist on, observe scrupulously (*stand on ceremony; stand on one's dignity*). **stand on one's
own feet** (or **legs**) be self-reliant or independent.
stand out 1 be prominent or conspicuous or
outstanding. **2** (usu. foll. by *against, for*) hold out;
persist in opposition or support or endurance.
stand over 1 stand close to (a person) to watch,
control, threaten, etc. **2** be postponed, be left
for later settlement etc. **stand to 1** *Mil.* stand
ready for an attack (esp. before dawn or after
dark). **2** abide by, adhere to (terms or promises).
3 be likely or certain to (*stands to lose everything*).
4 uphold, support, or side with (a person). **stand
up 1** rise to one's feet from a sitting or other
position. **b** come to or remain in or place in a
standing position. **2** (of an argument etc.) be
valid. **3** *colloq.* fail to keep an appointment with.
stand-up *attrib. adj.* **1** (of a meal) eaten standing.
2 (of a fight) violent, thorough, or fair and
square. **3** (of a collar) upright, not turned down.
4 (of a comedian) performing by standing before
an audience and telling jokes. **stand up for**
support, side with, maintain (a person or cause).
stand upon = *stand on.* **stand up to 1** meet or
face (an opponent) courageously. **2** be resistant
to the harmful effects of (wear, use, etc.). **stand
well** (usu. foll. by *with*) be on good terms or in
good repute. **take one's stand on** base one's
argument etc. on, rely on. □ **stander** *n.* [OE
standan f. Gmc]

standalone /ˌstændəˈləʊn/ *adj.* (of a computer)
operating independently of a network or other
system.

standard /ˈstændəd/ *n. & adj.* —*n.* **1** an object
or quality or measure serving as a basis or
example or principle to which others conform
or should conform or by which the accuracy
or quality of others is judged (*by present-day
standards*). **2 a** the degree of excellence etc.
required for a particular purpose (*not up to
standard*). **b** average quality (*of a low standard*). **3**
the ordinary procedure, or quality or design of
a product, without added or novel features. **4** a
distinctive flag. **5 a** an upright support. **b** an
upright water or gas pipe. **6 a** a tree or shrub
that stands alone without support. **b** a shrub
grafted on an upright stem and trained in tree
form (*standard rose*). **7** a document specifying
nationally or internationally agreed properties
for manufactured goods etc. (*British Standard*). **8**
a thing recognized as a model for imitation etc.
9 a tune or song of established popularity.
—*adj.* **1** serving or used as a standard (*a standard
size*). **2** of a normal or prescribed quality or size
etc. **3** having recognized and permanent value;
authoritative (*the standard book on the subject*). **4** (of
language) conforming to established educated
usage (*Standard English*). □ **raise a standard**
take up arms; rally support (*raised the standard
of revolt*). **standard-bearer 1** a soldier who
carries a standard. **2** a prominent leader in a
cause. **standard lamp** *Brit.* a lamp set on a tall

upright with its base standing on the floor.
standard of living the degree of material
comfort available to a person or class or community. [ME f. AF *estaundart,* OF *estendart* f.
estendre, as EXTEND: in senses 5 and 6 of *n.*
affected by association with STAND]

standardize /ˈstændəˌdaɪz/ *v.tr.* (also **-ise**) **1**
cause to conform to a standard. **2** determine
the properties of by comparison with a standard.
□ **standardizable** *adj.* **standardization**
/-ˈzeɪʃ(ə)n/ *n.* **standardizer** *n.*

standee /stænˈdiː/ *n. colloq.* a person who stands,
esp. when all seats are occupied.

standing /ˈstændɪŋ/ *n. & adj.* —*n.* **1** esteem or
repute, esp. high; status, position (*people of high
standing; is of no standing*). **2** duration (*a dispute of
long standing*). —*adj.* **1** that stands, upright. **2 a**
established, permanent (*a standing rule*). **b** not
made, raised, etc., for the occasion (*a standing
army*). **3** (of a jump, start, race, etc.) performed
from rest or from a standing position. **4** (of
water) stagnant. **5** (of corn) unreaped. □ **leave a
person standing** make far more rapid progress
than he or she. **standing joke** an object of
permanent ridicule. **standing order** an
instruction to a banker to make regular payments, or to a newsagent etc. for a regular
supply of a periodical etc. **standing orders**
the rules governing the manner in which all
business shall be conducted in a parliament,
council, society, etc. **standing ovation** a rousing ovation conferred by an audience risen from
their seats. **standing-room** space to stand in.

standoffish /stændˈɒfɪʃ/ *adj.* cold or distant in
manner. □ **standoffishly** *adv.* **standoffishness**
n.

standpipe /ˈstændpaɪp/ *n.* a vertical pipe extending from a water supply, esp. one connecting a
temporary tap to the mains.

standpoint /ˈstændpɔɪnt/ *n.* **1** the position from
which a thing is viewed. **2** a mental attitude.

standstill /ˈstændstɪl/ *n.* a stoppage; an inability
to proceed.

stank *past of* STINK.

stannary /ˈstænərɪ/ *n.* (*pl.* **-ies**) *Brit.* a tin-mine.
[med.L *stannaria* (pl.) f. LL *stannum* tin]

stanza /ˈstænzə/ *n.* the basic metrical unit in a
poem or verse consisting of a recurring group
of lines (often four lines and usu. not more
than twelve) which may or may not rhyme. □
stanza'd *adj.* (also **stanzaed**) (also in *comb.*).
stanzaic /-ˈzeɪɪk/ *adj.* [It., = standing-place,
chamber, stanza, ult. f. L *stare* stand]

staphylococcus /ˌstæfɪləˈkɒkəs/ *n.* (*pl.* **sta-
phylococci** /-kaɪ/) any bacterium of the genus
Staphylococcus, sometimes causing pus formation usu. in the skin and mucous membranes
of animals. □ **staphylococcal** *adj.* [mod.L f. Gk
staphulē bunch of grapes + *kokkos* berry]

staple[1] /ˈsteɪp(ə)l/ *n. & v.* —*n.* a U-shaped metal
bar or piece of wire with pointed ends for
driving into, securing, or fastening together
various materials or for driving through and
clenching papers, netting, electric wire, etc.
—*v.tr.* provide or fasten with a staple. □ **staple
gun** a hand-held device for driving in staples. □
stapler *n.* [OE *stapol* f. Gmc]

staple[2] /ˈsteɪp(ə)l/ *n. & adj.* —*n.* **1** the principal
or an important article of commerce (*the staples
of British Industry*). **2** the chief element or a main
component, e.g. of a diet. **3** a raw material. **4**

the fibre of cotton or wool etc. as determining its quality (*cotton of fine staple*). —*adj.* **1** main or principal (*staple commodities*). **2** important as a product or an export. [ME f. OF *estaple* market f. MLG, MDu. *stapel* market (as STAPLE¹)]

star *n. & v.* —*n.* **1** a celestial body appearing as a luminous point in the night sky. **2** (in full **fixed star**) such a body so far from the earth as to appear motionless (cf. PLANET, COMET). **3** a large naturally luminous gaseous body such as the sun is. **4** a celestial body regarded as influencing a person's fortunes etc. (*born under a lucky star*). **5** a thing resembling a star in shape or appearance. **6** a figure or object with radiating points esp. as the insignia of an order, as a decoration or mark of rank, or showing a category of excellence (*a five-star hotel*; *was awarded a gold star*). **7 a** a famous or brilliant person; the principal or most prominent performer in a play, film, etc. (*the star of the show*). **b** (*attrib.*) outstanding; particularly brilliant (*star pupil*). —*v.* (**starred, starring**) **1 a** *tr.* (of a film etc.) feature as a principal performer. **b** *intr.* (of a performer) be featured in a film etc. **2** (esp. as **starred** *adj.*) **a** mark, set, or adorn with a star or stars. **b** put an asterisk or star beside (a name, an item in a list, etc.). □ **star-crossed** *archaic* ill-fated. **star fruit** = CARAMBOLA. **stargazer** *colloq.* usu. *derog.* or *joc.* an astronomer or astrologer. **Star of David** a figure consisting of two interlaced equilateral triangles used as a Jewish and Israeli symbol. **Stars and Stripes** the national flag of the US. **star shell** an explosive projectile designed to burst in the air and light up the enemy's position. **star-spangled** (esp. of the US national flag) covered or glittering with stars. **star-studded** containing or covered with many stars, esp. featuring many famous performers. **star turn** the principal item in an entertainment or performance. **Star Wars** *colloq.* the strategic defence initiative. □ **stardom** *n.* **starless** *adj.* **starlike** *adj.* [OE *steorra* f. Gmc]

starboard /ˈstɑːbəd/ *n. & v. Naut. & Aeron.* —*n.* the right-hand side (looking forward) of a ship, boat, or aircraft. —*v.tr.* (also *absol.*) turn (the helm) to starboard. [OE *stēorbord* = rudder side (see STEER¹, BOARD), early Teutonic ships being steered with a paddle over the right side]

starch *n. & v.* **1** an odourless tasteless polysaccharide occurring widely in plants and obtained chiefly from cereals and potatoes, forming an important constituent of the human diet. **2** a preparation of this for stiffening fabric before ironing. **3** stiffness of manner; formality. —*v.tr.* stiffen (clothing) with starch. □ **starcher** *n.* [earlier as verb: ME *sterche* f. OE *stercan* (unrecorded) stiffen f. Gmc: cf. STARK]

starchy /ˈstɑːtʃɪ/ *adj.* (**starchier, starchiest**) **1 a** of or like starch. **b** containing much starch. **2** (of a person) precise, prim. □ **starchily** *adv.* **starchiness** *n.*

stardust /ˈstɑːdʌst/ *n.* **1** a twinkling mass. **2** a romantic mystical look or sensation. **3** a multitude of stars looking like dust.

stare /steə(r)/ *v. & n.* —*v.* **1** *intr.* (usu. foll. by *at*) look fixedly with eyes open, esp. as the result of curiosity, surprise, bewilderment, admiration, horror, etc. (*sat staring at the door*; *stared in amazement*). **2** *intr.* (of eyes) be wide open and fixed. **3** *intr.* be unpleasantly prominent or

striking. **4** *tr.* (foll. by *into*) reduce (a person) to a specified condition by staring (*stared me into silence*). —*n.* a staring gaze. □ **stare down** (or **out**) outstare. **stare a person in the face** be evident or imminent. □ **starer** *n.* [OE *starian* f. Gmc]

starfish /ˈstɑːfɪʃ/ *n.* an echinoderm of the class Asteroidea with five or more radiating arms.

stark *adj. & adv.* —*adj.* **1** desolate, bare (*a stark landscape*). **2** sharply evident (*in stark contrast*). **3** downright, sheer (*stark madness*). **4** completely naked. —*adv.* completely, wholly (*stark mad*; *stark naked*). □ **starkly** *adv.* **starkness** *n.* [OE *stearc* f. Gmc: stark naked f. earlier *start-naked* f. obs. *start* tail: cf. REDSTART]

starkers /ˈstɑːkəz/ *adj. Brit. sl.* stark naked.

starlet /ˈstɑːlɪt/ *n.* **1** a promising young performer, esp. a woman. **2** a little star.

starlight /ˈstɑːlaɪt/ *n.* **1** the light of the stars (*walked home by starlight*). **2** (*attrib.*) = STARLIT (*a starlight night*).

starling /ˈstɑːlɪŋ/ *n.* **1** a small gregarious partly migratory bird, *Sturnus vulgaris*, with blackish-brown speckled lustrous plumage, chiefly inhabiting cultivated areas. **2** any similar bird of the family Sturnidae. [OE *stærlinc* f. *stær* starling f. Gmc: cf. -LING¹]

starlit /ˈstɑːlɪt/ *adj.* **1** lighted by stars. **2** with stars visible.

starry /ˈstɑːrɪ/ *adj.* (**starrier, starriest**) **1** covered with stars. **2** resembling a star. □ **starry-eyed** *colloq.* **1** visionary; enthusiastic but impractical. **2** euphoric. □ **starrily** *adv.* **starriness** *n.*

START /stɑːt/ *abbr.* Strategic Arms Reduction Treaty (or Talks).

start *v. & n.* —*v.* **1** *tr. & intr.* begin; commence (*started work*; *started crying*; *started to shout*; *the play starts at eight*). **2** *tr.* set (proceedings, an event, etc.) in motion (*start the meeting*; *started a fire*). **3** *intr.* (often foll. by *on*) make a beginning (*started on a new project*). **4** *intr.* (often foll. by *after, for*) set oneself in motion or action ('*wait!*' *he shouted, and started after her*). **5** *intr.* set out; begin a journey etc. (*we start at 6 a.m.*). **6** (often foll. by *up*) **a** *intr.* (of a machine) begin operating (*the car wouldn't start*). **b** *tr.* cause (a machine etc.) to begin operating (*tried to start the engine*). **7** *tr.* **a** cause or enable (a person) to make a beginning (with something) (*started me in business with £10,000*). **b** (foll. by *pres. part.*) cause (a person) to begin (doing something) (*the smoke started me coughing*). **c** *Brit. colloq.* complain or be critical (*don't you start*). **8** *tr.* (often foll. by *up*) found or establish; originate. **9** *intr.* (foll. by *at, with*) have as the first of a series of items, e.g. in a meal (*we started with soup*). **10** *tr.* give a signal to (competitors) to start in a race. **11** *intr.* (often foll. by *up, from,* etc.) make a sudden movement from surprise, pain, etc. (*started at the sound of my voice*). **12** *intr.* (foll. by *out, up, from,* etc.) spring out, up, etc. (*started up from the chair*). **13** *tr.* conceive (a baby). **14** *tr.* rouse (game etc.) from its lair. **15 a** *intr.* (of timbers etc.) spring from their proper position; give way. **b** *tr.* cause or experience (timbers etc.) to do this. **16** *intr.* (foll. by *out, to,* etc.) (of a thing) move or appear suddenly (*tears started to his eyes*). **17** *intr.* (foll. by *from*) (of eyes, usu. with exaggeration) burst forward (*from their sockets etc.*). —*n.* **1** a beginning of an event, action, journey, etc.

(*missed the start; made a fresh start*). **2** the place from which a race etc. begins. **3** an advantage given at the beginning of a race etc. (*a 15-second start*). **4** an advantageous initial position in life, business, etc. (*a good start in life*). **5** a sudden movement of surprise, pain, etc. (*you gave me a start*). **6** an intermittent or spasmodic effort or movement (esp. *in* or *by fits and starts*). □ **for a start** *colloq.* as a beginning; in the first place. **start in** *colloq.* **1** begin. **2** (foll. by *on*) US make a beginning on. **start off 1** begin; commence (*started off on a lengthy monologue*). **2** begin to move (*it's time we started off*). **start out 1** begin a journey. **2** *colloq.* (foll. by *to* + infin.) proceed as intending (to do something). **start over** US begin again. **start school** attend school for the first time. **start up** arise; occur. **to start with 1** in the first place; before anything else is considered (*should never have been there to start with*). **2** at the beginning (*had six members to start with*). [OE (orig. in sense 11) f. Gmc]

starter /ˈstɑːtə(r)/ *n.* **1** a person or thing that starts. **2** an esp. automatic device for starting the engine of a motor vehicle etc. **3** a person giving the signal for the start of a race. **4** a horse or competitor starting in a race (*a list of probable starters*). **5** the first course of a meal. **6** the initial action etc. □ **for starters** *sl.* to start with. **under starter's orders** (of racehorses etc.) in a position to start a race and awaiting the starting-signal.

starting /ˈstɑːtɪŋ/ *n.* in senses of START *v.* □ **starting-block** a shaped rigid block for bracing the feet of a runner at the start of a race. **starting-gate** a movable barrier for securing a fair start in horse-races. **starting pistol** a pistol used to give the signal for the start of a race. **starting-point** the point from which a journey, process, argument, etc. begins. **starting post** the post from which competitors start in a race. **starting price** the odds ruling at the start of a horse-race.

startle /ˈstɑːt(ə)l/ *v.tr.* give a shock or surprise to; cause (a person etc.) to start with surprise or sudden alarm. □ **startler** *n.* [OE *steartlian* (as START, -LE⁴)]

startling /ˈstɑːtlɪŋ/ *adj.* **1** surprising. **2** alarming (*startling news*). □ **startlingly** *adv.*

starve *v.* **1** *intr.* die of hunger; suffer from malnourishment. **2** *tr.* cause to die of hunger or suffer from lack of food. **3** *intr.* suffer from extreme poverty. **4** *intr. colloq.* feel very hungry (*I'm starving*). **5** *intr.* **a** suffer from mental or spiritual want. **b** (foll. by *for*) feel a strong craving for (sympathy, amusement, knowledge, etc.). **6** *tr.* **a** (foll. by *of*) deprive of; keep scantily supplied with (*starved of affection*). **b** cause to suffer from mental or spiritual want. **7** *tr.* **a** (foll. by *into*) compel by starving (*starved into submission*). **b** (foll. by *out*) compel to surrender etc. by starving (*starved them out*). □ **starvation** /-ˈveɪʃ(ə)n/ *n.* [OE *steorfan* die]

starveling /ˈstɑːvlɪŋ/ *n. & adj. archaic* —*n.* a starving or ill-fed person or animal. —*adj.* **1** starving. **2** meagre.

stash *v. & n. colloq.* —*v.tr.* (often foll. by *away*) **1** conceal; put in a safe or hidden place. **2** hoard, stow, store. —*n.* **1** a hiding-place or hide-out. **2** a thing hidden; a cache. [18th c.: orig. unkn.]

stasis /ˈsteɪsɪs, ˈstæsɪs/ *n.* (pl. **stases** /-siːz/) **1** inactivity; stagnation; a state of equilibrium. **2**

a stoppage of circulation of any of the body fluids. [mod.L f. Gk f. *sta-* STAND]

-stat *comb. form* forming nouns with ref. to keeping fixed or stationary (*rheostat*). [Gk *statos* stationary]

state *n. & v.* —*n.* **1** the existing condition or position of a person or thing (*in a bad state of repair; in a precarious state of health*). **2** *colloq.* **a** excited, anxious, or agitated mental condition (esp. *in a state*). **b** an untidy condition. **3** (usu. **State**) **a** an organized political community under one government; a commonwealth; a nation. **b** such a community forming part of a federal republic, esp. the United States of America. **4** (usu. **State**) (*attrib.*) **a** of, for, or concerned with the State (*State documents*). **b** reserved for or done on occasions of ceremony (*State apartments; State visit*). **c** involving ceremony (*State opening of Parliament*). **5** (usu. **State**) civil government (*Church and State; Secretary of State*). **6** pomp, rank, dignity (*as befits their state*). —*v.tr.* **1** express, esp. fully or clearly, in speech or writing (*have stated my opinion; must state full particulars*). **2** fix, specify (*at stated intervals*). □ **in state** with all due ceremony. **of State** concerning politics or government. **State Department** (in the US) the department of foreign affairs. **State-house** US the building where the legislature of a State meets. **State house** NZ a private house built at the government's expense. **state of the art 1** the current stage of development of a practical or technological subject. **2** (usu. **state-of-the-art**) (*attrib.*) using the latest techniques or equipment (*state-of-the-art weaponry*). **state of grace** the condition of being free from grave sin. **state of things** (or **affairs** or **play**) the circumstances; the current situation. **state of war** the situation when war has been declared or is in progress. **State school** a school managed and funded by the public authorities. □ **statable** *adj.* **statedly** *adv.* **statehood** *n.* [ME: partly f. ESTATE, partly f. L STATUS]

statecraft /ˈsteɪtkrɑːft/ *n.* the art of conducting affairs of state.

stateless /ˈsteɪtlɪs/ *adj.* **1** (of a person) having no nationality or citizenship. **2** without a State. □ **statelessness** *n.*

stately /ˈsteɪtlɪ/ *adj.* (**statelier**, **stateliest**) dignified; imposing; grand. □ **stately home** *Brit.* a large magnificent house, esp. one open to the public. □ **stateliness** *n.*

statement /ˈsteɪtmənt/ *n.* **1** the act or an instance of stating or being stated; expression in words. **2** a thing stated; a declaration (*that statement is unfounded*). **3** a formal account of facts, esp. to the police or in a court of law (*make a statement*). **4** a record of transactions in a bank account etc. **5** a formal notification of the amount due to a tradesman etc.

stateroom /ˈsteɪtruːm, -rʊm/ *n.* **1** a state apartment in a palace, hotel, etc. **2** a private compartment in a passenger ship or US train.

Stateside /ˈsteɪtsaɪd/ *adj.* US *colloq.* of, in, or towards the United States.

statesman /ˈsteɪtsmən/ *n.* (pl. **-men**; *fem.* **stateswoman**, pl. **-women**) **1** a person skilled in affairs of State, esp. one taking an active part in politics. **2** a distinguished and capable politician. □ **statesmanlike** *adj.* **statesmanly** *adj.* **statesmanship** *n.* [= *state's man* after F *homme d'état*]

static /ˈstætɪk/ *adj. & n.* —*adj.* **1** stationary; not acting or changing; passive. **2** *Physics* concerned with bodies at rest or forces in equilibrium. —*n.* **1** static electricity. **2** atmospherics. □ **static electricity** electricity not flowing as a current. [mod.L *staticus* f. Gk *statikos* f. *sta*- stand]

statics /ˈstætɪks/ *n.pl.* (usu. treated as *sing.*) **1** the science of bodies at rest or of forces in equilibrium. **2** = STATIC. [STATIC *n.* in the same senses + -ICS]

station /ˈsteɪʃ(ə)n/ *n. & v.* —*n.* **1 a** a regular stopping place on a railway line, with a platform and usu. administrative buildings. **b** these buildings (see also *bus station, coach station*). **2** a place or building etc. where a person or thing stands or is placed, esp. habitually or for a definite purpose. **3** a designated point or establishment where a particular service or activity is based or organized (*police station; polling station*). **4** an establishment involved in radio or television broadcasting. **5** a military or naval base esp. *hist.* in India. **6** position in life; rank or status (*ideas above your station*). **7** *Austral. & NZ* a large sheep or cattle farm. —*v.tr.* **1** assign a station to. **2** put in position. □ **station of the cross** *RC Ch.* each of a series of usu. 14 images or pictures representing the events in Christ's passion before which devotions are performed in some churches. **station sergeant** *Brit.* the sergeant in charge of a police station. **station-wagon** an estate car. [ME, = standing, f. OF f. L *statio -onis* f. *stare* stand]

stationary /ˈsteɪʃ(ə)nərɪ/ *adj.* **1** remaining in one place, not moving (*hit a stationary car*). **2** not meant to be moved; not portable (*stationary troops*). **3** not changing in magnitude, number, quality, efficiency, etc. (*stationary temperature*). □ **stationary bicycle** a fixed exercise-machine resembling a bicycle. □ **stationariness** *n.* [ME f. L *stationarius* (as STATION)]

stationer /ˈsteɪʃ(ə)nə(r)/ *n.* a person who sells writing materials etc. [ME, = bookseller (as STATIONARY in med.L sense 'shopkeeper', esp. bookseller, as opposed to pedlar)]

stationery /ˈsteɪʃ(ə)nərɪ/ *n.* writing materials etc. sold by a stationer. □ **Stationery Office** (in the UK) the Government's publishing house which also provides stationery for Government offices.

stationmaster /ˈsteɪʃ(ə)nˌmɑːstə(r)/ *n.* the official in charge of a railway station.

statism /ˈsteɪtɪz(ə)m/ *n.* centralized State administration and control of social and economic affairs. □ **statist** *n.*

statistic /stəˈtɪstɪk/ *n. & adj.* —*n.* a statistical fact or item. —*adj.* = STATISTICAL. [G *statistisch, Statistik* f. *Statist* politician f. It. *statista* (as STATE)]

statistical /stəˈtɪstɪk(ə)l/ *adj.* of or relating to statistics. □ **statistically** *adv.*

statistics /stəˈtɪstɪks/ *n.pl.* **1** (usu. treated as *sing.*) the science of collecting and analysing numerical data, esp. in or for large quantities, and usu. inferring proportions in a whole from proportions in a representative sample. **2** any systematic collection or presentation of such facts. □ **statistician** /ˌstætɪˈstɪʃ(ə)n/ *n.*

statuary /ˈstætjʊərɪ/ *adj. & n.* —*adj.* of or for statues (*statuary art*). —*n.* (*pl.* -**ies**) **1** statues collectively. **2** the art of making statues. **3** a sculptor. [L *statuarius* (as STATUE)]

statue /ˈstætjuː, ˈstætʃuː/ *n.* a sculptured, cast, carved, or moulded figure of a person or animal, esp. life-size or larger. □ **statued** *adj.* [ME f. OF f. L *statua* f. *stare* stand]

statuesque /ˌstætjʊˈesk, ˌstætʃʊˈesk/ *adj.* like, or having the dignity or beauty of a statue. □ **statuesquely** *adv.* **statuesqueness** *n.* [STATUE + -ESQUE, after *picturesque*]

statuette /ˌstætjʊˈet, ˌstætʃʊˈet/ *n.* a small statue; a statue less than life-size. [F, dimin. of *statue*]

stature /ˈstætʃə(r)/ *n.* **1** the height of a (esp. human) body. **2** a degree of eminence, social standing, or advancement (*recruit someone of his stature*). □ **statured** *adj.* (also in *comb.*). [ME f. OF f. L *statura* f. *stare* stat- stand]

status /ˈsteɪtəs/ *n.* **1** rank, social position, relation to others, relative importance (*not sure of their status in the hierarchy*). **2** a superior social etc. position (*considering your status in the business*). □ **status symbol** a possession etc. taken to indicate a person's high status. [L, = standing f. *stare* stand]

status quo /ˌsteɪtəs ˈkwəʊ/ *n.* the existing state of affairs. [L, = the state in which]

statute /ˈstætjuːt/ *n.* **1** a written law passed by a legislative body, e.g. an Act of Parliament. **2** a rule of a corporation, founder, etc., intended to be permanent (*against the University Statutes*). □ **statute-book 1** a book or books containing the statute law. **2** the body of a country's statutes. **statute law 1** (*collect.*) the body of principles and rules of law laid down in statutes as distinct from rules formulated in practical application. **2** a statute. [ME f. OF *statut* f. LL *statutum* neut. past part. of L *statuere* set up f. *status*: see STATUS]

statutory /ˈstatjʊtərɪ/ *adj.* required, permitted, or enacted by statute (*statutory minimum; statutory provisions*). □ **statutory rape** *US* the act of sexual intercourse with a minor. □ **statutorily** *adv.*

staunch[1] /stɔːntʃ, stɑːntʃ/ *adj.* (also **stanch**) **1** trustworthy, loyal (*my staunch friend and supporter*). **2** (of a ship, joint, etc.) strong, watertight, airtight, etc. □ **staunchly** *adv.* **staunchness** *n.* [ME f. OF *estanche* fem. of *estanc* f. Rmc: see STANCH[1]]

staunch[2] var. of STANCH[1].

stave *n. & v.* —*n.* **1** each of the curved pieces of wood forming the sides of a cask, pail, etc. **2** = STAFF *n.* 3. **3** a stanza or verse. —*v.tr.* (*past and past part.* **stove** or **staved**) **1** break a hole in. **2** crush or knock out of shape. □ **stave in** crush by forcing inwards. **stave off** avert or defer (danger or misfortune). [ME, back-form. f. *staves*, pl. of STAFF]

staves *pl.* of STAFF *n.* 3.

stay[1] *v. & n.* —*v.* **1** *intr.* continue to be in the same place or condition; not depart or change (*stay here until I come back*). **2** *intr.* **a** (often foll. by *at, in, with*) have temporary residence as a visitor etc. (*stayed with them for Christmas*). **b** *Sc. & S.Afr.* dwell permanently. **3** *tr. archaic* or *literary* stop or check (*progress, the inroads of a disease,* etc.). **4** *tr.* postpone (*judgement, decision,* etc.). **5** *tr.* assuage (hunger etc.) esp. for a short time. **6 a** *intr.* show endurance. **b** *tr.* show endurance to the end of (a race etc.). **7** *intr.* (foll. by *for, to*) wait long enough to share or join in an activity etc. (*stay to supper; stay for the film*). —*n.* **1 a** the act or an instance of staying or dwelling in one place. **b** the duration of this (*just a ten-minute* *stay; a long stay in London*). **2** a suspension or postponement of a sentence, judgement, etc. (*was granted a stay of execution*). **3** a prop or support. **4** (in *pl.*) *hist.* a corset esp. with whalebone etc. stiffening, and laced. □ **has come** (or **is here**) **to stay** *colloq.* must be regarded as permanent. **stay-at-home** *adj.* remaining habitually at home. —*n.* a person who does this. **stay the course** pursue a course of action or endure a struggle etc. to the end. **stay in** remain indoors or at home, esp. in school after hours as a punishment. **staying power** endurance, stamina. **stay the night** remain until the next day. **stay put** *colloq.* remain where it is placed or where one is. **stay up** not go to bed (until late at night). □ **stayer** *n.* [AF *estai-* stem of OF *ester* f. L *stare* stand: *n.* sense 3 f. OF *estaye(r)* prop, formed as STAY²]

stay² *n.* **1** *Naut.* a rope or guy supporting a mast, spar, flagstaff, etc. **2** a tie-piece in an aircraft etc. [OE *stæg* be firm, f. Gmc]

staysail /ˈsteɪseɪl, ˈsteɪs(ə)l/ *n.* a triangular fore-and-aft sail extended on a stay.

STD *abbr.* subscriber trunk dialling.

stead /sted/ *n.* □ **in a person's** or **thing's stead** as a substitute; instead of him or her or it. **stand a person in good stead** be advantageous or serviceable to him or her. [OE *stede* f. Gmc]

steadfast /ˈstedfɑːst, ˈstedfəst/ *adj.* constant, firm, unwavering. □ **steadfastly** *adv.* **steadfastness** *n.* [OE *stedefæst* (as STEAD, FAST¹)]

steading /ˈstediŋ/ *n.* Brit. a farmstead.

steady /ˈstedi/ *adj., v., adv., int.,* & *n.* —*adj.* (**steadier, steadiest**) **1** firmly fixed or supported or standing or balanced; not tottering, rocking, or wavering. **2** done or operating or happening in a uniform and regular manner (*a steady pace; a steady increase*). **3 a** constant in mind or conduct; not changeable. **b** persistent. **4** (of a person) serious and dependable in behaviour; of industrious and temperate habits; safe; cautious. **5** regular, established (*a steady girlfriend*). **6** accurately directed; not faltering (*a steady hand; a steady eye*). —*v.tr.* & *intr.* (**-ies, -ied**) make or become steady (*steady the boat*). —*adv.* steadily (*hold it steady*). —*int.* as a command or warning to take care. —*n.* (*pl.* **-ies**) *colloq.* a regular boyfriend or girlfriend. □ **go steady** (often foll. by *with*) *colloq.* have as a regular boyfriend or girlfriend. **steady on!** a call to take care. **steady state** an unvarying condition, esp. in a physical process, e.g. of the universe having no beginning and no end. □ **steadier** *n.* **steadily** *adv.* **steadiness** *n.* [STEAD = place, + -Y¹]

steak /steɪk/ *n.* **1** a thick slice of meat (esp. beef) or fish, often cut for grilling, frying, etc. **2** beef cut for stewing or braising. □ **steak-house** a restaurant specializing in serving beefsteaks. **steak-knife** a knife with a serrated steel blade for eating steak. [ME f. ON *steik* rel. to *steikja* roast on spit, *stikna* be roasted]

steal *v.* & *n.* —*v.* (*past* **stole** /stəʊl/; *past part.* **stolen** /ˈstəʊlən/) **1** *tr.* (also *absol.*) **a** take (another person's property) illegally. **b** take (property etc.) without right or permission, esp. in secret with the intention of not returning it. **2** *tr.* obtain surreptitiously or by surprise (*stole a kiss*). **3** *tr.* **a** gain insidiously or artfully. **b** (often foll. by *away*) win or get possession of (a person's affections etc.), esp. insidiously (*stole her heart*

away). **4** *intr.* (foll. by *in, out, away, up,* etc.) move, esp. silently or stealthily (*stole out of the room*). **5** *tr.* **a** (in various sports) gain (a run, the ball, etc.) surreptitiously or by luck. **b** *Baseball* reach (a base) by deceiving the fielders. —*n.* **1** *US colloq.* the act or an instance of stealing or theft. **2** *colloq.* an unexpectedly easy task or good bargain. □ **steal a march on** get an advantage over by surreptitious means; anticipate. **steal the show** outshine other performers, esp. unexpectedly. **steal a person's thunder** use another person's words, ideas, etc., without permission and without giving credit. □ **stealer** *n.* (also in *comb.*). [OE *stelan* f. Gmc]

stealth /stelθ/ *n.* secrecy, a secret procedure. □ **by stealth** surreptitiously. [ME f. OE (as STEAL, -TH²)]

stealthy /ˈstelθi/ *adj.* (**stealthier, stealthiest**) **1** (of an action) done with stealth; proceeding imperceptibly. **2** (of a person or thing) moving with stealth. □ **stealthily** *adv.* **stealthiness** *n.*

steam *n.* & *v.* —*n.* **1 a** the gas into which water is changed by boiling, used as a source of power by virtue of its expansion of volume. **b** a mist of liquid particles of water produced by the condensation of this gas. **2** any similar vapour. **3 a** energy or power provided by a steam engine or other machine. **b** *colloq.* power or energy generally. —*v.* **1** *tr.* **a** cook (food) in steam. **b** soften or make pliable (timber etc.) or otherwise treat with steam. **2** *intr.* give off steam or other vapour, esp. visibly. **3** *intr.* move under steam power (*the ship steamed down the river*). **b** (foll. by *ahead, away,* etc.) *colloq.* proceed or travel fast or with vigour. **4** *tr.* & *intr.* (usu. foll. by *up*) **a** cover or become covered with condensed steam. **b** (as **steamed up** *adj.*) *colloq.* angry or excited. **5** *tr.* (foll. by *open* etc.) apply steam to the gum of (a sealed envelope) to get it open. □ **get up steam 1** generate enough power to work a steam engine. **2** work oneself into an energetic or angry state. **let off steam** relieve one's pent up feelings or energy. **run out of steam** lose one's impetus or energy. **steam bath** a room etc. filled with steam for bathing in. **steam engine 1** an engine which uses the expansion or rapid condensation of steam to generate power. **2** a locomotive powered by this. **steam hammer** a forging-hammer powered by steam. **steam iron** an electric iron that emits steam from its flat surface, to improve its pressing ability. **steam organ** a fairground pipe-organ driven by a steam engine and played by means of a keyboard or a system of punched cards. **steam power** the force of steam applied to machinery etc. **steam train** a train driven by a steam engine. **steam turbine** a turbine in which a high-velocity jet of steam rotates a bladed disc or drum. **under one's own steam** without assistance; unaided. [OE *stēam* f. Gmc]

steamboat /ˈstiːmbəʊt/ *n.* a boat propelled by a steam engine.

steamer /ˈstiːmə(r)/ *n.* **1** a person or thing that steams. **2** a vessel propelled by steam, esp. a ship. **3** a vessel in which things are steamed, esp. cooked by steam.

steamroller /ˈstiːmˌrəʊlə(r)/ *n.* & *v.* —*n.* **1** a heavy slow-moving vehicle with a roller, used to flatten new-made roads. **2** a crushing power or force. —*v.tr.* **1** crush forcibly or indiscriminately. **2** (foll. by *through*) force (a measure etc.) through a legislature by overriding opposition.

steamship /ˈstiːmʃɪp/ n. a ship propelled by a steam engine.

steamy /ˈstiːmɪ/ adj. (**steamier, steamiest**) 1 like or full of steam. 2 colloq. erotic, salacious. □ **steamily** adv. **steaminess** n.

stearic /ˈstɪərɪk/ adj. derived from stearin. □ **stearic acid** a solid saturated fatty acid obtained from animal or vegetable fats. □ **stearate** /-ˌreɪt/ n. [F stéarique f. Gk stear steatos tallow]

stearin /ˈstɪərɪn/ n. 1 an ester of stearic acid, esp. in the form of a white crystalline constituent of tallow etc. 2 a mixture of fatty acids used in candle-making. [F stéarine f. Gk stear steatos tallow]

steatite /ˈstɪətaɪt/ n. a soapstone or other impure form of talc. □ **steatitic** /-ˈtɪtɪk/ adj. [L steatitis f. Gk steatītēs f. stear steatos tallow]

steed n. archaic or poet. a horse, esp. a fast powerful one. [OE stēda stallion, rel. to STUD²]

steel n., adj., & v. —n. 1 any of various alloys of iron and carbon with other elements increasing strength and malleability, much used for making tools, weapons, etc., and capable of being tempered to many different degrees of hardness. 2 hardness of character; strength, firmness (nerves of steel). 3 a rod of steel, usu. roughened and tapering, on which knives are sharpened. 4 (not in pl.) literary a sword, lance, etc. (foemen worthy of their steel). —adj. 1 made of steel. 2 like or having the characteristics of steel. —v.tr. & refl. harden or make resolute (steeled myself for a shock). □ **steel band** a group of usu. W. Indian musicians with percussion instruments made from oil drums. **steel wool** an abrasive substance consisting of a mass of fine steel shavings. [OE stýle, stéli f. Gmc, rel. to STAY²]

steelworks /ˈstiːlwɜːks/ n.pl. (usu. treated as sing.) a place where steel is manufactured. □ **steelworker** n.

steely /ˈstiːlɪ/ adj. (**steelier, steeliest**) 1 of, or hard as, steel. 2 inflexibly severe; cold; ruthless (steely composure; steely-eyed glance). □ **steeliness** n.

steelyard /ˈstiːljɑːd/ n. a kind of balance with a short arm to take the item to be weighed and a long graduated arm along which a weight is moved until it balances.

steep¹ adj. & n. —adj. 1 sloping sharply; almost perpendicular (a steep hill; steep stairs). 2 (of a rise or fall) rapid (a steep drop in share prices). 3 (predic.) colloq. a (of a price etc.) exorbitant; unreasonable (esp. a bit steep). b (of a story etc.) exaggerated; incredible. —n. a steep slope; a precipice. □ **steepen** v.intr. & tr. **steepish** adj. **steeply** adv. **steepness** n. [OE stēap f. WG, rel. to STOOP¹]

steep² v. & n. —v.tr. soak or bathe in liquid. —n. 1 the act or process of steeping. 2 the liquid for steeping. □ **steep in 1** pervade or imbue with (steeped in misery). 2 make deeply acquainted with (a subject etc.) (steeped in the classics). [ME f. OE f. Gmc (as STOUP)]

steeple /ˈstiːp(ə)l/ n. a tall tower, esp. one surmounted by a spire, above the roof of a church. □ **steepled** adj. [OE stēpel stýpel f. Gmc (as STEEP¹)]

steeplechase /ˈstiːp(ə)ltʃeɪs/ n. 1 a horse-race (orig. with a steeple as the goal) across the

countryside or on a racecourse with ditches, hedges, etc., to jump. 2 a cross-country foot-race. □ **steeplechaser** n. **steeplechasing** n.

steeplejack /ˈstiːp(ə)ldʒæk/ n. a person who climbs tall chimneys, steeples, etc., to do repairs etc.

steer¹ v. 1 tr. a guide (a vehicle, aircraft, etc.) by a wheel etc. b guide (a vessel) by a rudder or helm. 2 intr. guide a vessel or vehicle in a specified direction (tried to steer left). 3 tr. direct (one's course). 4 intr. direct one's course in a specified direction (steered for the railway station). 5 tr. guide the movement or trend of (steered them into the garden; steered the conversation away from that subject). □ **steer clear of** take care to avoid. **steering-column** the shaft or column which connects the steering-wheel, handlebars, etc. of a vehicle to the rest of the steering-gear. **steering committee** a committee deciding the order of dealing with business, or priorities and the general course of operations. **steering-wheel** a wheel by which a vehicle etc. is steered. □ **steerable** adj. **steerer** n. **steering** n. (esp. in senses 1, 2). [OE stieran f. Gmc]

steer² /stɪə(r)/ n. a young male bovine animal, esp. one castrated and raised for beef. [OE stēor f. Gmc]

steerage /ˈstɪərɪdʒ/ n. 1 the act of steering. 2 archaic the part of a ship allotted to passengers travelling at the cheapest rate.

steersman /ˈstɪəzmən/ n. (pl. **-men**) a person who steers a vessel.

stegosaurus /ˌstegəˈsɔːrəs/ n. any of a group of plant-eating dinosaurs with a double row of large bony plates along the spine. [mod. L f. Gk stegē covering + sauros lizard]

stein /staɪn/ n. a large earthenware mug, esp. for beer. [G, lit. 'stone']

stellar /ˈstelə(r)/ adj. of or relating to a star or stars. □ **stelliform** adj. [LL stellaris f. L stella star]

stellate /ˈsteleɪt/ adj. (also **stellated** /steˈleɪtɪd/) arranged like a star; radiating. [L stellatus f. stella star]

stellular /ˈsteljʊlə(r)/ adj. shaped like, or set with, small stars. [LL stellula dimin. of L stella star]

stem¹ n. & v. —n. 1 the main body or stalk of a plant or shrub, usu. rising into light, but occasionally subterranean. 2 the stalk supporting a fruit, flower, or leaf, and attaching it to a larger branch, twig, or stalk. 3 a stem-shaped part of an object: a the slender part of a wineglass between the body and the foot. b the tube of a tobacco-pipe. c a vertical stroke in a letter or musical note. 4 Gram. the root or main part of a noun, verb, etc., to which inflections are added; the part that appears unchanged throughout the cases and derivatives of a noun, persons of a tense, etc. 5 Naut. the main upright timber or metal piece at the bow of a ship (from stem to stern). —v. (**stemmed, stemming**) 1 intr. (foll. by from) spring or originate from (stems from a desire to win). 2 tr. remove the stem or stems from (fruit, tobacco, etc.). 3 tr. (of a vessel etc.) hold its own or make headway against (the tide etc.). □ **stem stitch** an embroidery stitch used for narrow stems etc. □ **stemless** adj. **stemlet** n. **stemlike** adj. **stemmed** adj. (also in comb.). [OE stemn, stefn f. Gmc, rel. to STAND]

stem² v. (**stemmed**, **stemming**) **1** tr. check or stop. **2** tr. dam up (a stream etc.). [ON *stemma* f. Gmc: cf. STAMMER]

stemware /ˈstemweə(r)/ n. US glasses with stems.

stench n. an offensive or foul smell. [OE *stenc* smell f. Gmc, rel. to STINK]

stencil /ˈstensɪl/ n. & v. —n. **1** (in full **stencil-plate**) a thin sheet of plastic, metal, card, etc., in which a pattern or lettering is cut, used to produce a corresponding pattern on the surface beneath it by applying ink, paint, etc. **2** the pattern, lettering, etc., produced by a stencil-plate. —v.tr. (**stencilled**, **stencilling**; US **stenciled**, **stenciling**) **1** (often foll. by *on*) produce (a pattern) with a stencil. **2** decorate or mark (a surface) in this way. [ME f. OF *estanceler* sparkle, cover with stars, f. *estencele* spark ult. f. L *scintilla*]

Sten gun /sten/ n. a type of lightweight sub-machine-gun. [*S* and *T* (the initials of the inventors' surnames, Shepherd and Turpin) + -*en* after BREN]

stenography /steˈnɒɡrəfɪ/ n. shorthand or the art of writing this. □ **stenographer** n. **stenographic** /-nəˈɡræfɪk/ adj. [Gk *stenos* narrow + -GRAPHY]

Stentor /ˈstentə(r)/ n. (also **stentor**) a person with a powerful voice. □ **stentorian** /-ˈtɔːrɪən/ adj. [Gk *Stentōr*, herald in the Trojan War (Homer, *Iliad* v. 785)]

step n. & v. —n. **1 a** the complete movement of one leg in walking or running (*took a step forward*). **b** the distance covered by this. **2** a unit of movement in dancing. **3** a measure taken, esp. one of several in a course of action (*took steps to prevent it*; *considered it a wise step*). **4 a** a surface on which a foot is placed on ascending or descending a stair or tread. **b** a block of stone or other platform before a door, altar, etc. **c** the rung of a ladder. **d** a platform etc. in a vehicle provided for stepping up or down. **5** a short distance (*only a step from my door*). **6** the sound or mark made by a foot in walking etc. (*heard a step on the stairs*). **7** the manner of walking etc. as seen or heard (*know her by her step*). **8 a** a degree in the scale of promotion, advancement, or precedence. **b** one of a series of fixed points on a payscale etc. **9 a** stepping (or not stepping) in time with others or music (esp. *in* or *out of step*). **b** the state of conforming to what others are doing (*refuses to keep step with the team*). **10** (in pl.) (also **pair of steps** *sing.*) = STEPLADDER. —v. (**stepped**, **stepping**) **1** intr. lift and set down one's foot or alternate feet in walking. **2** intr. come or go in a specified direction by stepping. **3** intr. make progress in a specified way (*stepped into a new job*). **4** tr. (foll. by *off*, *out*) measure (distance) by stepping. **5** tr. perform (a dance). □ **in a person's steps** following a person's example. **mind** (or **watch**) **one's step** be careful. **step by step** gradually; cautiously; by stages or degrees. **step down 1** resign from a position etc. **2** Electr. decrease (voltage) by using a transformer. **step in 1** enter a room, house, etc. **2 a** intervene to help or hinder. **b** act as a substitute for an indisposed colleague etc. **step on it** (or **on the gas** etc.) colloq. **1** accelerate a motor vehicle. **2** hurry up. **step out 1** leave a room, house, etc. **2** be active socially. **3** take large steps. **stepping-stone 1** a raised stone,

usu. one of a set in a stream, muddy place, etc., to help in crossing. **2** a means or stage of progress to an end. **step up 1** increase, intensify (*must step up production*). **2** Electr. increase (voltage) using a transformer. **turn one's steps** go in a specified direction. □ **steplike** adj. **stepped** adj. **stepwise** adv. & adj. [OE *stæpe*, *stepe* (n.), *stæppan*, *steppan* (v.), f. Gmc]

step- /step/ comb. form denoting a relationship like the one specified but resulting from a parent's remarriage. [OE *stēop-* orphan-]

stepbrother /ˈstepˌbrʌðə(r)/ n. a son of a step-parent by a marriage other than with one's father or mother.

stepchild /ˈsteptʃaɪld/ n. a child of one's husband or wife by a previous marriage. [OE *stēopcīld* (as STEP-, CHILD)]

stepdaughter /ˈstepˌdɔːtə(r)/ n. a female step-child. [OE *stēopdohtor* (as STEP-, DAUGHTER)]

stepfather /ˈstepˌfɑːðə(r)/ n. a male step-parent. [OE *stēopfæder* (as STEP-, FATHER)]

stephanotis /ˌstefəˈnəʊtɪs/ n. any climbing tropical plant of the genus *Stephanotis*, cultivated for its fragrant waxy usu. white flowers. [mod.L f. Gk, = fit for a wreath f. *stephanos* wreath]

stepladder /ˈstepˌlædə(r)/ n. a short ladder with flat steps and a folding prop, used without being leant against a surface.

stepmother /ˈstepˌmʌðə(r)/ n. a female step-parent. [OE *stēopmōdor* (as STEP-, MOTHER)]

step-parent /ˈstepˌpeərənt/ n. a mother's or father's later husband or wife.

steppe /step/ n. a level grassy unforested plain, esp. in SE Europe and Siberia. [Russ *step'*]

stepsister /ˈstepˌsɪstə(r)/ n. a daughter of a step-parent by a marriage other than with one's father or mother.

stepson /ˈstepsʌn/ n. a male stepchild. [OE *stēopsunu* (as STEP-, SON)]

-ster /stə(r)/ suffix denoting a person engaged in or associated with a particular activity or thing (*brewster*; *gangster*; *youngster*). [OE -*estre* etc. f. Gmc]

stereo /ˈsterɪəʊ, ˈstɪə-/ n. & adj. —n. (pl. **-os**) **1 a** a stereophonic record-player, tape recorder, etc. **b** = STEREOPHONY (see STEREOPHONIC). **2** = STEREOSCOPE. —adj. **1** = STEREOPHONIC. **2** = STEREOSCOPIC (see STEREOSCOPE). [abbr.]

stereo- /ˈsterɪəʊ, ˈstɪə-/ comb. form solid; having three dimensions. [Gk *stereos* solid]

stereophonic /ˌsterɪəʊˈfɒnɪk, ˌstɪə-/ adj. (of sound reproduction) using two or more channels so that the sound has the effect of being distributed and of coming from more than one source. □ **stereophonically** adv. **stereophony** /-ˈɒfənɪ/ n.

stereoscope /ˈsterɪəˌskəʊp, ˈstɪə-/ n. a device by which two photographs of the same object taken at slightly different angles are viewed together, giving an impression of depth and solidity as in ordinary human vision. □ **stereoscopic** /-ˈskɒpɪk/ adj. **stereoscopically** /-ˈskɒpɪkəlɪ/ adv. **stereoscopy** /-ˈɒskəpɪ/ n.

stereotype /ˈsterɪəˌtaɪp, ˈstɪə-/ n. & v. —n. **1 a** a person or thing that conforms to an unjustifiably fixed, usu. standardized, mental picture. **b** such an impression or attitude. **2** a printing-plate cast from a mould of composed type. —v.tr. **1** (esp. as **stereotyped** adj.) formalize, standardize; cause to conform to a type. **2**

a print from a stereotype. **b** make a stereotype of. □ **stereotypic** /-'tɪpɪk/ *adj.* **stereotypical** /-'tɪpɪk(ə)l/ *adj.* **stereotypically** /-'tɪpɪkəlɪ/ *adv.* **stereotypy** *n.* [F *stéréotype* (adj.) (as STEREO-, TYPE)]

sterile /'sterail/ *adj.* **1** not able to produce crop or fruit or (of an animal) young; barren. **2** unfruitful, unproductive (*sterile discussions*). **3** free from living micro-organisms etc. **4** lacking originality or emotive force; mentally barren. □ **sterilely** *adv.* **sterility** /stə'rɪlɪtɪ/ *n.* [F *stérile* or L *sterilis*]

sterilize /'sterɪˌlaɪz/ *v.tr.* (also **-ise**) **1** make sterile. **2** deprive of the power of reproduction. □ **sterilizable** *adj.* **sterilization** /-'zeɪʃ(ə)n/ *n.* **sterilizer** *n.*

sterling /'stɜːlɪŋ/ *adj.* & *n.* —*adj.* **1** of or in British money (*pound sterling*). **2** (of a coin or precious metal) genuine; of standard value or purity. **3** (of a person or qualities etc.) of solid worth; genuine, reliable (*sterling work*). —*n.* British money (*paid in sterling*). □ **sterling area** a group of countries with currencies tied to British sterling and holding reserves mainly in sterling. **sterling silver** silver of 92½% purity. □ **sterlingness** *n.* [prob. f. late OE *steorling* (unrecorded) f. *steorra* star + -LING¹ (because some early Norman pennies bore a small star): recorded earlier in OF *esterlin*]

stern¹ *adj.* severe, grim, strict; enforcing discipline or submission (*a stern expression; stern treatment*). □ **sternly** *adv.* **sternness** *n.* [OE *styrne*, prob. f. a Gmc root = be rigid]

stern² *n.* **1** the rear part of a ship or boat. **2** any rear part. □ **stern-post** the central upright support at the stern, usu. bearing the rudder. □ **sterned** *adj.* (also in *comb.*). **sternmost** *adj.* **sternward** *adj.* & *adv.* **sternwards** *adv.* [ME prob. f. ON *stjórn* steering f. *stýra* STEER¹]

sternal /'stɜːn(ə)l/ *adj.* of or relating to the sternum. □ **sternal rib** = *true rib*.

sternum /'stɜːnəm/ *n.* (*pl.* **sternums** or **sterna** /-nə/) the breastbone. [mod.L f. Gk *sternon* chest]

steroid /'stɪərɔɪd, 'ste-/ *n. Biochem.* any of a group of organic compounds with a characteristic structure, including many hormones, alkaloids, and vitamins. □ **steroidal** /-'rɔɪd(ə)l/ *adj.* [STEROL + -OID]

sterol /'sterɒl/ *n. Chem.* any of a group of naturally occurring steroid alcohols. [CHO-LESTEROL etc.]

stertorous /'stɜːtərəs/ *adj.* (of breathing etc.) heavy; sounding like snoring. □ **stertorously** *adv.* **stertorousness** *n.* [stertor, mod.L f. L *stertere* snore]

stet *v.* (**stetted, stetting**) **1** *intr.* (usu. as an instruction written on a proof-sheet etc.) ignore or cancel the correction or alteration; let the original form stand. **2** *tr.* write 'stet' against; cancel the correction of. [L, = let it stand, f. *stare* stand]

stethoscope /'steθəˌskəʊp/ *n.* an instrument used in listening to the action of the heart, lungs, etc., usu. consisting of a circular piece placed against the chest, with tubes leading to earpieces. □ **stethoscopic** /-'skɒpɪk/ *adj.* **stethoscopically** /-'skɒpɪkəlɪ/ *adv.* **stethoscopist** /-'θɒskəpɪst/ *n.* **stethoscopy** /-'θɒskəpɪ/ *n.* [F *stéthoscope* f. Gk *stēthos* breast: see -SCOPE]

stetson /'stets(ə)n/ *n.* a slouch hat with a very wide brim and a high crown. [J. B. *Stetson*, Amer. hat-maker d. 1906]

stevedore /'stiːvəˌdɔː(r)/ *n.* a person employed in loading and unloading ships. [Sp. *estivador* f. *estivar* stow a cargo f. L *stipare* pack tight]

stew *v.* & *n.* —*v.* **1** *tr.* & *intr.* cook by long simmering in a closed vessel with liquid. **2** *intr. colloq.* be oppressed by heat or humidity, esp. in a confined space. **3** *intr. colloq.* **a** suffer prolonged embarrassment, anxiety, etc. **b** (foll. by *over*) fret or be anxious. **4** *tr.* make (tea) bitter or strong with prolonged brewing. **5** *tr.* (as **stewed** *adj.*) *colloq.* drunk. —*n.* **1** a dish of stewed meat etc. **2** *colloq.* an agitated or angry state (*be in a stew*). □ **stew in one's own juice** be left to suffer the consequences of one's own actions. [ME f. OF *estuve, estuver* prob. ult. f. EX-¹ + Gk *tuphos* smoke, steam]

steward /'stjuːəd/ *n.* & *v.* **1 a** passengers' attendant on a ship or aircraft or train. **2** an official appointed to keep order or supervise arrangements at a meeting or show or demonstration etc. **3** = *shop steward.* **4** a person responsible for supplies of food etc. for a college or club etc. **5** a person employed to manage another's property. **6** *Brit.* the title of several officers of State or the royal household (*Lord High Steward*). —*v.tr.* act as a steward of (*will steward the meeting*). □ **stewardship** *n.* [OE *stīweard* f. *stig* prob. = house, hall + *weard* WARD]

stewardess /ˌstjuː'ɔ'des, 'stjuːədɪs/ *n.* a female steward, esp. on a ship or aircraft.

stick¹ *n.* **1 a** a short slender branch or length of wood broken or cut from a tree. **b** this trimmed for use as a support or weapon. **2** a thin rod or spike of wood etc. for a particular purpose (*cocktail stick*). **3** an implement used to propel the ball in hockey or polo etc. **4** a gear lever. **5** a conductor's baton. **6 a** a slender piece of a thing, e.g. celery, dynamite, deodorant, etc. **b** a number of bombs or paratroops released rapidly from aircraft. **7** (often prec. by *the*) punishment, esp. by beating. **8** *colloq.* adverse criticism; censure, reproof (*took a lot of stick*). **9** *colloq.* a piece of wood as part of a house or furniture (*a few sticks of furniture*). **10** *colloq.* a person, esp. one who is dull or unsociable (*a funny old stick*). **11** (in *pl.*; prec. by *the*) *colloq.* remote rural areas. **12** (in *pl.*) *Austral. sl.* goal-posts. □ **stick insect** any usu. wingless female insect of the family Phasmidae with a twiglike body. **up sticks** *colloq.* go to live elsewhere. □ **stickless** *adj.* **sticklike** *adj.* [OE *sticca* f. WG]

stick² *v.* (*past* and *past part.* **stuck**) **1** *tr.* (foll. by *in, into, through*) insert or thrust (a thing or its point) (*stick a finger in my eye; stick a pin through it*). **2** *tr.* insert a pointed thing into; stab. **3** *tr.* & *intr.* (foll. by *in, into, on,* etc.) **a** fix or be fixed on a pointed thing. **b** fix or be fixed by or as by a pointed end. **4** *tr.* & *intr.* fix or become or remain fixed by or as by adhesive etc. (*stick a label on it; the label won't stick*). **5** *intr.* endure; make a continued impression (*the scene stuck in my mind; the name stuck*). **6** *intr.* lose or be deprived of the power of motion or action through adhesion or jamming or other impediment. **7** *colloq.* **a** *tr.* put in a specified position or place, esp. quickly or haphazardly (*stick them down anywhere*). **b** *intr.* remain in a place (*stuck indoors*). **8** *colloq.* **a** *intr.* (of an accusation etc.) be convincing or regarded as valid (*could not make the charges stick*). **b** *tr.* (foll. by *on*) place the blame for (a thing) on (a person). **9** *tr. colloq.* endure, tolerate (*could not stick it any longer*). **10** *tr.* (foll. by *at*) *colloq.* persevere with. □ **be stuck for** be at a loss for or in need of. **be stuck on** *colloq.* be infatuated with. **be stuck with** *colloq.* be unable to get rid of or escape from; be permanently involved with. **get stuck in** (or **into**) *sl.* begin in earnest. **stick around** *colloq.* linger; remain at the same place. **stick at it** *colloq.* persevere. **stick at nothing** allow nothing, esp. no scruples, to deter one. **stick by** (or **with** or **to**) stay loyal or close to. **stick 'em up!** *colloq.* hands up! **stick fast** adhere or become firmly fixed or trapped in a position or place. **sticking-plaster** an adhesive plaster for wounds etc. **sticking-point** the limit of progress, agreement, etc. **stick-in-the-mud** *colloq.* an unprogressive or old-fashioned person. **stick in one's throat** be against one's principles. **stick it on** *sl.* **1** make high charges. **2** tell an exaggerated story. **stick it out** *colloq.* put up with or persevere with a burden etc. to the end. **stick one's neck** (or **chin**) **out** expose oneself to censure etc. by acting or speaking boldly. **stick out** protrude or cause to protrude or project (*stuck his tongue out; stick out your chest*). **stick out for** persist in demanding. **stick out a mile** (or **like a sore thumb**) *colloq.* be very obvious or incongruous. **stick to 1** remain close to or fixed on or to. **2** remain faithful to. **3** keep to (a subject etc.) (*stick to the point*). **stick to a person's fingers** *colloq.* (of money) be embezzled by a person. **stick together** *colloq.* remain united or mutually loyal. **stick to it** persevere. **stick up 1** be or make erect or protruding upwards. **2** fasten to an upright surface. **3** *colloq.* rob or threaten with a gun. **stick-up** *n. colloq.* an armed robbery. **stick up for** support or defend or champion (a person or cause). **stick up to** be assertive in the face of; offer resistance to. **stick with** *colloq.* remain in touch with or faithful to. **stuck-up** *colloq.* affectedly superior and aloof, snobbish. □ **stickability** /-kə'bılıtı/ *n.* [OE *stician* f. Gmc]

sticker /'stıkə(r)/ *n.* **1** an adhesive label or notice etc. **2** a person or thing that sticks. **3** a persistent person.

stickleback /'stık(ə)lˌbæk/ *n.* any small fish of the family Gasterosteidae, esp. *Gasterosteus aculeatus*, with sharp spines along the back. [ME f. OE *sticel* thorn, sting + *bæc* BACK]

stickler /'stıklə(r)/ *n.* (foll. by *for*) a person who insists on something (*a stickler for accuracy*). [obs. *stickle* be umpire, ME *stightle* control, frequent. of *stight* f. OE *stiht(i)an* set in order]

stickpin /'stıkpın/ *n.* US an ornamental tie-pin.

sticky /'stıkı/ *adj.* (**stickier, stickiest**) **1** tending or intended to stick or adhere. **2** glutinous, viscous. **3** (of the weather) humid. **4** *colloq.* awkward or uncooperative; intransigent (*was very sticky about giving me leave*). **5** *colloq.* difficult, awkward (*a sticky problem*). **6** *colloq.* very unpleasant or painful (*came to a sticky end*). □ **sticky wicket** *colloq.* difficult or awkward circumstances. □ **stickily** *adv.* **stickiness** *n.*

stickybeak /'stıkıˌbiːk/ *n. & v. Austral. & NZ sl.* —*n.* an inquisitive person. —*v.intr.* pry.

stiff *adj. & n.* —*adj.* **1** rigid; not flexible. **2** hard to bend or move or turn etc.; not working freely. **3** hard to cope with; needing strength or effort

(*a stiff test; a stiff climb*). **4** severe or strong (*a stiff breeze; a stiff penalty*). **5** (of a person or manner) formal, constrained; lacking spontaneity. **6** (of a muscle or limb etc., or a person affected by these) aching when used, owing to previous exertion, injury, etc. **7** (of an alcoholic or medicinal drink) strong. **8** (*predic.*) *colloq.* to an extreme degree (*bored stiff; scared stiff*). **9** (foll. by *with*) *colloq.* abounding in (*a place stiff with tourists*). —*n. sl.* a corpse. □ **stiff neck** a rheumatic condition in which the head cannot be turned without pain. **stiff-necked** obstinate or haughty. **stiff upper lip** firmness, fortitude. □ **stiffish** *adj.* **stiffly** *adv.* **stiffness** *n.* [OE *stif* f. Gmc]

stiffen /'stıf(ə)n/ *v.tr. & intr.* make or become stiff. □ **stiffener** *n.* **stiffening** *n.*

stifle /'staıf(ə)l/ *v.* **1** *tr.* smother, suppress (*stifled a yawn*). **2** *intr. & tr.* experience or cause to experience constraint of breathing (*stifling heat*). **3** *tr.* kill by suffocating. □ **stifler** /-flə(r)/ *n.* **stiflingly** *adv.* [perh. alt. of ME *stuffe, stuffle* f. OF *estouffer*]

stigma /'stıgmə/ *n.* (*pl.* **stigmas** or esp. in sense 4 **stigmata** /-mətə, -'mɑːtə/) **1** a mark or sign of disgrace or discredit. **2** (foll. by *of*) a distinguishing mark or characteristic. **3** the part of a pistil that receives the pollen in pollination. **4** (in *pl.*) *Eccl.* (in Christian belief) marks corresponding to those left on Christ's body by the Crucifixion, said to have been impressed on the bodies of St Francis of Assisi and others. [L f. Gk *stigma -atos* a mark made by a pointed instrument, a brand, a dot: rel. to STICK¹]

stigmatize /'stıgməˌtaız/ *v.tr.* (also **-ise**) (often foll. by *as*) describe as unworthy or disgraceful. □ **stigmatization** /-'zeıʃ(ə)n/ *n.* [F *stigmatiser* or med.L *stigmatizo* f. Gk *stigmatizō* (as STIGMA)]

stile *n.* an arrangement of steps allowing people but not animals to climb over a fence or wall. [OE *stigel* f. a Gmc root *stig-* (unrecorded) climb]

stiletto /stı'letəʊ/ *n.* (*pl.* **-os**) **1** a short dagger with a thick blade. **2** a pointed instrument for making eyelets etc. **3** (in full **stiletto heel**) **a** a long tapering heel of a shoe. **b** a shoe with such a heel. [It., dimin. of *stilo* dagger (as STYLUS)]

still¹ *adj., n., adv., & v.* —*adj.* **1** not or hardly moving. **2** with little or no sound; calm and tranquil (*a still evening*). **3** (of sounds) hushed, stilled. **4** (of a drink) not effervescing. —*n.* **1** deep silence (*in the still of the night*). **2** an ordinary static photograph (as opposed to a motion picture), esp. a single shot from a cinema film. —*adv.* **1** without moving (*stand still*). **2** even now or at a particular time (*they still did not understand; why are you still here?*). **3** nevertheless; all the same. **4** (with *compar.* etc.) even, yet, increasingly (*still greater efforts; still another explanation*). —*v.tr. & intr.* make or become still; quieten. □ **still life** (*pl.* **still lifes**) a painting or drawing of inanimate objects such as fruit or flowers. □ **stillness** *n.* [OE *stille* (adj. & adv.), *stillan* (v.), f. WG]

still² *n.* an apparatus for distilling spirituous liquors etc. [obs. *still* (v.), ME f. DISTILL]

stillbirth /'stılbɜːθ/ *n.* the birth of a dead child.

stillborn /'stılbɔːn/ *adj.* **1** (of a child) born dead. **2** (of an idea, plan, etc.) abortive; not able to succeed.

Stillson /'stıls(ə)n/ *n.* (in full **Stillson wrench**) a large wrench with jaws that tighten as pressure is increased. [D. C. *Stillson*, its inventor d. 1899]

stilt *n.* **1** either of a pair of poles with supports for the feet enabling the user to walk at a distance above the ground. **2** each of a set of piles or posts supporting a building etc. **3** any wading bird of the genus *Himantopus* with long legs. □ **stiltless** *adj.* [ME & LG *stilte* f. Gmc]

stilted /ˈstɪltɪd/ *adj.* **1** (of a literary style etc.) stiff and unnatural; bombastic. **2** standing on stilts. □ **stiltedly** *adv.* **stiltedness** *n.*

Stilton /ˈstɪlt(ə)n/ *n. propr.* a kind of strong rich cheese, often with blue veins, orig. made in Stilton in S. England.

stimulant /ˈstɪmjʊlənt/ *adj.* & *n.* —*adj.* that stimulates, esp. bodily or mental activity. —*n.* **1** a stimulant substance, esp. a drug or alcoholic drink. **2** a stimulating influence. [L *stimulare stimulant-* urge, goad]

stimulate /ˈstɪmjʊˌleɪt/ *v.tr.* **1** apply or act as a stimulus to. **2** animate, excite, arouse. **3** be a stimulant to. □ **stimulating** *adj.* **stimulatingly** *adv.* **stimulation** /-ˈleɪʃ(ə)n/ *n.* **stimulative** /-lətɪv/ *adj.* **stimulator** *n.*

stimulus /ˈstɪmjʊləs/ *n.* (*pl.* **stimuli** /-ˌlaɪ/) **1** a thing that rouses to activity or energy. **2** a stimulating or rousing effect. [L, = goad, spur, incentive]

stimy var. of STYMIE.

sting *n.* & *v.* —*n.* **1** a sharp often poisonous wounding organ of an insect, snake, nettle, etc. **2 a** the act of inflicting a wound with this. **b** the wound itself or the pain caused by it. **3** a wounding or painful quality or effect (*the sting of hunger*; *stings of remorse*). **4** pungency, sharpness, vigour (*a sting in the voice*). **5** *sl.* a swindle or robbery. —*v.* (*past* and *past part.* **stung**) **1 a** *tr.* wound or pierce with a sting. **b** *intr.* be able to sting; have a sting. **2** *intr.* & *tr.* feel or cause to feel a tingling physical or sharp mental pain. **3** *tr.* (foll. by *into*) incite by a strong or painful mental effect (*was stung into replying*). **4** *tr. sl.* swindle or charge exorbitantly. □ **stinging-nettle** a nettle, *Urtica dioica*, having stinging hairs. **sting in the tail** unexpected pain or difficulty at the end. □ **stingingly** *adv.* **stingless** *adj.* **stinglike** *adj.* [OE *sting* (n.), *stingan* (v.), f. Gmc]

stinger /ˈstɪŋə(r)/ *n.* **1** a stinging insect, snake, nettle, etc. **2** a sharp painful blow.

stingray /ˈstɪŋreɪ/ *n.* any of various broad flat-fish esp. of the family Dasyatidae, having a long poisonous serrated spine at the base of its tail.

stingy /ˈstɪndʒɪ/ *adj.* (**stingier**, **stingiest**) niggardly, mean. □ **stingily** *adv.* **stinginess** *n.* [perh. f. dial. *stinge* STING]

stink *v.* & *n.* —*v.* (*past* **stank** or **stunk**; *past part.* **stunk**) **1** *intr.* emit a strong offensive smell. **2** *tr.* (often foll. by *out*) fill (a place) with a stink. **3** *tr.* (foll. by *out* etc.) drive (a person) out etc. by a stink. **4** *intr. colloq.* be or seem very unpleasant, contemptible, or scandalous. —*n.* **1** a strong or offensive smell; a stench. **2** *colloq.* a row or fuss (*the affair caused quite a stink*). □ **like stink** *colloq.* intensely; extremely hard or fast etc. (*working like stink*). **stink bomb** a device emitting a stink when exploded. [OE *stincan* ult. f. WG: cf. STENCH]

stinker /ˈstɪŋkə(r)/ *n.* **1** a person or thing that stinks. **2** *sl.* an objectionable person or thing.

stinkhorn /ˈstɪŋkhɔːn/ *n.* any foul-smelling fungus of the order Phallales.

stinking /ˈstɪŋkɪŋ/ *adj.* & *adv.* —*adj.* **1** that stinks. **2** *sl.* very objectionable. —*adv. sl.* extremely and usu. objectionably (*stinking rich*). □ **stinkingly** *adv.*

stint *v.* & *n.* —*v.tr.* **1** supply (food or aid etc.) in a niggardly amount or grudgingly. **2** (often *refl.*) supply (a person etc.) in this way. —*n.* **1** a limitation of supply or effort (*without stint*). **2** a fixed or allotted amount of work (*do one's stint*). **3** a small sandpiper, esp. a dunlin. □ **stinter** *n.* **stintless** *adj.* [OE *styntan* to blunt, dull, f. Gmc, rel. to STUNT¹]

stipend /ˈstaɪpend/ *n.* a fixed regular allowance or salary, esp. paid to a clergyman. [ME f. OF *stipend(i)e* or L *stipendium* f. *stips* wages + *pendere* to pay]

stipendiary /staɪˈpendjərɪ, stɪ-/ *adj.* & *n.* —*adj.* **1** receiving a stipend. **2** working for pay, not voluntarily. —*n.* (*pl.* **-ies**) a person receiving a stipend. □ **stipendiary magistrate** a paid professional magistrate. [L *stipendiarius* (as STIPEND)]

stipple /ˈstɪp(ə)l/ *v.* & *n.* —*v.* **1** *tr.* & *intr.* draw or paint or engrave etc. with dots instead of lines. **2** *tr.* roughen the surface of (paint, cement, etc.). —*n.* **1** the process or technique of stippling. **2** the effect of stippling. □ **stippler** *n.* **stippling** *n.* [Du. *stippelen* frequent. of *stippen* to prick f. *stip* point]

stipulate /ˈstɪpjʊˌleɪt/ *v.tr.* **1** demand or specify as part of a bargain or agreement. **2** (foll. by *for*) mention or insist upon as an essential condition. **3** (as **stipulated** *adj.*) laid down in the terms of an agreement. □ **stipulation** /-ˈleɪʃ(ə)n/ *n.* **stipulator** *n.* [L *stipulari*]

stir¹ *v.* & *n.* —*v.* (**stirred**, **stirring**) **1** *tr.* move a spoon or other implement round and round in (a liquid etc.) to mix the ingredients or constituents. **2 a** *tr.* cause to move or be disturbed, esp. slightly (*a breeze stirred the lake*). **b** *intr.* be or begin to be in motion (*not a creature was stirring*). **c** *refl.* rouse (oneself), esp. from a lethargic state. **3** *intr.* rise from sleep (*is still not stirring*). **4** *intr.* (foll. by *out of*) leave; go out of (esp. one's house). **5** *tr.* arouse or inspire or excite (the emotions etc., or a person as regards these) (*was stirred to anger*; *it stirred the imagination*). —*n.* **1** an act of stirring (*give it a good stir*). **2** commotion or excitement; public attention (*caused quite a stir*). **3** the slightest movement (*not a stir*). □ **stir the blood** inspire enthusiasm etc. **stir in** mix (an added ingredient) with a substance by stirring. **stir one's stumps** *colloq.* **1** begin to move. **2** become active. **stir up 1** mix thoroughly by stirring. **2** incite (trouble etc.) (*loved stirring things up*). **3** stimulate, excite, arouse (*stirred up their curiosity*). □ **stirless** *adj.* **stirrer** *n.* [OE *styrian* f. Gmc]

stir² *n. sl.* a prison (esp. *in stir*). □ **stir-crazy** deranged from long imprisonment. [19th c.: orig. unkn.]

stir-fry /ˈstɜːfraɪ/ *v.tr.* (**-ies**, **-ied**) fry rapidly while stirring and tossing.

stirrer /ˈstɜːrə(r)/ *n.* **1** a thing or a person that stirs. **2** *colloq.* a troublemaker; an agitator.

stirring /ˈstɜːrɪŋ/ *adj.* **1** stimulating, exciting, rousing. **2** actively occupied (*lead a stirring life*). □ **stirringly** *adv.* [OE *styrende* (as STIR¹)]

stirrup /ˈstɪrəp/ *n.* **1** each of a pair of devices attached to each side of a horse's saddle, in the form of a loop with a flat base to support the rider's foot. □ **stirrup-cup** a cup of wine etc. offered to a person about to depart, orig. on horseback. **stirrup-pump** a hand-operated water-pump with a foot-rest, used to extinguish small fires. [OE *stigrāp* f. *stigan* climb (as STILE) + ROPE]

stitch *n.* & *v.* —*n.* **1 a** (in sewing or knitting or crocheting etc.) a single pass of a needle or the thread or loop etc. resulting from this. **b** a particular method of sewing or knitting etc. (*am learning a new stitch*). **2** (usu. in *pl.*) *Surgery* each of the loops of material used in sewing up a wound. **3** the least bit of clothing (*hadn't a stitch on*). **4** an acute pain in the side of the body induced by running etc. —*v.tr.* **1** sew; make stitches (in). **2** join or close with stitches. **in stitches** *colloq.* laughing uncontrollably. **a stitch in time** a timely remedy. **stitch up 1** join or mend by sewing or stitching. **2** *sl.* betray or cheat. □ **stitcher** *n.* **stitchery** *n.* **stitchless** *adj.* [OE *stice* f. Gmc, rel. to STICK²]

stoat *n.* a flesh-eating mammal, *Mustela erminea*, of the weasel family, having brown fur in the summer turning mainly white in the winter. [ME: orig. unkn.]

stock *n.*, *adj.*, & *v.* —*n.* **1** a store of goods etc. ready for sale or distribution etc. **2** a supply or quantity of anything for use (*lay in winter stocks of fuel*; *a great stock of information*). **3** equipment or raw material for manufacture or trade etc. (*rolling-stock*; *paper stock*). **4 a** farm animals or equipment. **b** = FATSTOCK. **5 a** the capital of a business company. **b** shares in this. **6** one's reputation or popularity (*his stock is rising*). **7 a** money lent to a government at fixed interest. **b** the right to receive such interest. **8** a line of ancestry; family origins (*comes of Cornish stock*). **9** liquid made by stewing bones, vegetables, fish, etc., as a basis for soup, gravy, sauce, etc. **10** any of various fragrant-flowered cruciferous plants of the genus *Matthiola* or *Malcolmia*. **11** a plant into which a graft is inserted. **12** the main trunk of a tree etc. **13** (in *pl.*) *hist.* a timber frame with holes for the feet and occas. the hands and head, in which offenders were locked as a public punishment. **14** *US* **a** = *stock company*. **b** the repertory of this. **15** (in *pl.*) the supports for a ship during building. **16** a band of material worn round the neck. **17** hard solid brick pressed in a mould. —*adj.* **1** kept in stock and so regularly available (*stock sizes*). **2** perpetually repeated; hackneyed, conventional (*a stock answer*). —*v.tr.* **1** have or keep (goods) in stock. **2 a** provide (a shop or a farm etc.) with goods, equipment, or livestock. **b** fill with items needed (*shelves well-stocked with books*). □ **in stock** available immediately for sale etc. **on the stocks** in construction or preparation. **out of stock** not immediately available for sale. **stock-car 1** a specially strengthened production car for use in racing in which collision occurs. **2** *US* a railway truck for transporting livestock. **stock company** *US* a repertory company performing mainly at a particular theatre. **Stock Exchange 1** a place where stocks and shares are bought and sold. **2** the dealers working there. **stock-in-trade 1** all the requisites of a trade or profession. **2** a ready supply of characteristic phrases, attitudes, etc. **stock market 1** = *Stock Exchange*. **2** transactions on this. **stock-still** motionless. **stock up 1** provide with or get

stocks or supplies. **2** (foll. by *with*) get in or gather a stock of (food, fuel, etc.). **take stock 1** make an inventory of one's stock. **2** (often foll. by *of*) make a review or estimate of (a situation etc.). **3** (foll. by *in*) concern oneself with. □ **stocker** *n.* **stockless** *adj.* [OE *stoc*, *stocc* f. Gmc]

stockade /stɒˈkeɪd/ *n.* & *v.* —*n.* a line or enclosure of upright stakes. —*v.tr.* fortify with a stockade. [obs. F *estocade*, alt. of *estacade* f. Sp. *estacada*: rel. to STAKE¹]

stockbreeder /ˈstɒkˌbriːdə(r)/ *n.* a farmer who raises livestock. □ **stockbreeding** *n.*

stockbroker /ˈstɒkˌbrəʊkə(r)/ *n.* = BROKER 2. □ **stockbroker belt** *Brit.* an affluent residential area, esp. near a business centre such as London. □ **stockbrokerage** *n.* **stockbroking** *n.*

stockholder /ˈstɒkˌhəʊldə(r)/ *n.* an owner of stocks or shares. □ **stockholding** *n.*

stockinet /ˌstɒkɪˈnet/ *n.* (also **stockinette**) an elastic knitted material. [prob. f. *stocking-net*]

stocking /ˈstɒkɪŋ/ *n.* **1 a** either of a pair of long separate coverings for the legs and feet, usu. close-woven in wool or nylon and worn esp. by women and girls. **b** esp. *US* = SOCK¹. **2** any close-fitting garment resembling a stocking (*bodystocking*). □ **in one's stocking** (or **stocking-inged**) **feet** without shoes (esp. while being measured). **stocking-stitch** *Knitting* a stitch of alternate rows of plain and purl, making an even pattern. □ **stockinged** *adj.* (also in *comb.*). **stockingless** *adj.* [STOCK in (now dial.) sense 'stocking' + -ING¹]

stockist /ˈstɒkɪst/ *n.* *Brit.* a dealer who stocks goods of a particular type for sale.

stockjobber /ˈstɒkˌdʒɒbə(r)/ *n.* **1** *Brit.* = JOBBER 1. **2** *US* = JOBBER 2b. □ **stockjobbing** *n.*

stocklist /ˈstɒklɪst/ *n.* *Brit.* a regular publication stating a dealer's stock of goods with current prices etc.

stockman /ˈstɒkmən/ *n.* (*pl.* **-men**) **1 a** *Austral.* a man in charge of livestock. **b** *US* an owner of livestock. **2** *US* a person in charge of a stock of goods in a warehouse etc.

stockpile /ˈstɒkpaɪl/ *n.* & *v.* —*n.* an accumulated stock of goods, materials, weapons, etc., held in reserve. —*v.tr.* accumulate a stockpile of. □ **stockpiler** *n.*

stockpot /ˈstɒkpɒt/ *n.* a pot for cooking stock for soup etc.

stockroom /ˈstɒkruːm, -rʊm/ *n.* a room for storing goods in stock.

stocktaking /ˈstɒkˌteɪkɪŋ/ *n.* **1** the process of making an inventory of stock in a shop etc. **2** a review of one's position and resources.

stocky /ˈstɒkɪ/ *adj.* (**stockier**, **stockiest**) (of a person, plant, or animal) short and strongly built; thickset. □ **stockily** *adv.* **stockiness** *n.*

stockyard /ˈstɒkjɑːd/ *n.* an enclosure with pens etc. for sorting or temporary keeping of cattle.

stodge *n.* *colloq.* **1** food esp. of a thick heavy kind. **2** an unimaginative person or idea. [earlier as verb: imit., after *stuff* and *podge*]

stodgy /ˈstɒdʒɪ/ *adj.* (**stodgier**, **stodgiest**) **1** (of food) heavy and indigestible. **2** dull and uninteresting. **3** (of a literary style etc.) turgid and dull. □ **stodgily** *adv.* **stodginess** *n.*

stoep /stuːp/ *n.* *S.Afr.* a terraced veranda in front of a house. [Du., rel. to STEP]

Stoic /ˈstəʊɪk/ *n.* & *adj.* —*n.* **1** a member of the ancient Greek school of philosophy founded at

Athens by Zeno *c.*308 BC, which sought virtue as the greatest good and taught control of one's feelings and passions. **2** (**stoic**) a stoical person. —*adj.* **1** of or like the Stoics. **2** (**stoic**) = STOICAL. [ME f. L *stoicus* f. Gk *stōikos* f. *stoa* porch (with ref. to Zeno's teaching in the *Stoa Poikilē* or Painted Porch at Athens)]

stoical /ˈstəʊɪk(ə)l/ *adj.* having or showing great self-control in adversity. □ **stoically** *adv.*

Stoicism /ˈstəʊɪˌsɪz(ə)m/ *n.* **1** the philosophy of the Stoics. **2** (**stoicism**) a stoical attitude.

stoke *v.* (often foll. by *up*) **1 a** *tr.* feed and tend (a fire or furnace etc.). **b** *intr.* act as a stoker. **2** *intr. colloq.* consume food, esp. steadily and in large quantities. [back-form. f. STOKER]

stokehold /ˈstəʊkhəʊld/ *n.* a compartment in a steamship, containing its boilers and furnace.

stokehole /ˈstəʊkhəʊl/ *n.* a space for stokers in front of a furnace.

stoker /ˈstəʊkə(r)/ *n.* a person who tends to the furnace on a steamship. [Du. f. *stoken* stoke f. MDu. *stoken* push, rel. to STICK¹]

STOL *abbr. Aeron.* short take-off and landing.

stole¹ *n.* **1** a woman's long garment like a scarf, worn over the shoulders. **2** a strip of silk etc. worn similarly as a vestment by a priest. [OE *stol, stole* (orig. a long robe) f. L *stola* f. Gk *stolē* equipment, clothing]

stole² *past* of STEAL.

stolen *past part.* of STEAL.

stolid /ˈstɒlɪd/ *adj.* **1** lacking or concealing emotion or animation. **2** not easily excited or moved. □ **stolidity** /-ˈlɪdɪtɪ/ *n.* **stolidly** *adv.* **stolidness** *n.* [obs. F *stolide* or L *stolidus*]

stomach /ˈstʌmək/ *n.* & *v.* —*n.* **1 a** the internal organ in which the first part of digestion occurs. **b** any of several such organs in animals, esp. ruminants, in which there are four. **2 a** the belly, abdomen, or lower front of the body (*pit of the stomach*). **b** a protuberant belly (*what a stomach he has got!*). **3** (usu. foll. by *for*) **a** an appetite (for food). **b** liking, readiness, or inclination (for controversy, conflict, danger, or an undertaking) (*had no stomach for the fight*). —*v.tr.* **1** find sufficiently palatable to swallow or keep down. **2** submit to or endure (an affront etc.) (usu. with *neg.*: *cannot stomach it*). □ **stomach-ache** a pain in the belly or bowels. **stomach-pump** a syringe for forcing liquid etc. into or out of the stomach. **stomach upset** (or **upset stomach**) a temporary slight disorder of the digestive system. □ **stomachful** *n.* (*pl.* **-fuls**). **stomachless** *adj.* [ME *stomak* f. OF *stomaque, estomac* f. L *stomachus* f. Gk *stomakhos* gullet f. *stoma* mouth]

stomp *v.* & *n.* —*v.intr.* tread or stamp heavily. —*n.* a lively jazz dance with heavy stamping. □ **stomper** *n.* [US dial. var. of STAMP]

stone *n.* & *v.* —*n.* **1 a** a solid non-metallic mineral matter, of which rock is made. **b** a piece of this, esp. a small piece. **2** *Building* **a** = LIMESTONE (*Portland stone*). **b** = SANDSTONE (*Bath stone*). **3** *Mineral.* = *precious stone.* **4** (often in *comb.*) a piece of stone of a definite shape or for a particular purpose (*tombstone; stepping-stone*). **5 a** a thing resembling stone in hardness or form, e.g. the hard case of the kernel in some fruits. **b** *Med.* (often in *pl.*) a hard morbid concretion in the body esp. in the kidney or gall-bladder (*gallstones*). **6** (*pl.* same) *Brit.* a unit of weight equal to 14 lb. (6.35 kg). **7** (*attrib.*) **a** made of

stone. **b** of the colour of stone. —*v.tr.* **1** pelt with stones. **2** remove the stones from (fruit). □ **cast** (or **throw**) **stones** (or **the first stone**) make aspersions on a person's character etc. **leave no stone unturned** try all possible means. **Stone Age** a prehistoric period when weapons and tools were made of stone. **stone-cold** completely cold. **stone-cold sober** completely sober. **stone-dead** completely dead. **stone-deaf** completely deaf. **stone-fruit** a fruit with flesh or pulp enclosing a stone. **a stone's throw** a short distance. □ **stoned** *adj.* (also in *comb.*). **stoneless** *adj.* **stoner** *n.* [OE *stān* f. Gmc]

stonechat /ˈstəʊntʃæt/ *n.* any small brown bird of the thrush family with black and white markings, esp. *Saxicola torquata* with a call like stones being knocked together.

stonecrop /ˈstəʊnkrɒp/ *n.* any succulent plant of the genus *Sedum*, usu. having yellow or white flowers and growing amongst rocks or in walls.

stonecutter /ˈstəʊnˌkʌtə(r)/ *n.* a person or machine that cuts or carves stone.

stoned /stəʊnd/ *adj. sl.* under the influence of alcohol or drugs.

stoneground /ˈstəʊngraʊnd/ *adj.* (of flour) ground with millstones.

stonemason /ˈstəʊnˌmeɪs(ə)n/ *n.* a person who cuts, prepares, and builds with stone. □ **stonemasonry** *n.*

stonewall /ˈstəʊnwɔːl/ *v.* **1** *tr.* & *intr.* obstruct (discussion or investigation) or be obstructive with evasive answers or denials etc. **2** *intr. Cricket* bat with excessive caution. □ **stonewaller** *n.* **stonewalling** *n.*

stoneware /ˈstəʊnweə(r)/ *n.* ceramic ware which is impermeable and partly vitrified but opaque.

stonewashed /ˈstəʊnwɒʃd/ *adj.* (of a garment or fabric, esp. denim) washed with abrasives to produce a worn or faded appearance.

stonework /ˈstəʊnwɜːk/ *n.* **1** masonry. **2** the parts of a building made of stone. □ **stoneworker** *n.*

stonkered /ˈstɒŋkəd/ *adj. Austral.* & *NZ sl.* utterly defeated or exhausted. [20th c.: orig. unkn.]

stony /ˈstəʊnɪ/ *adj.* (**stonier, stoniest**) **1** full of or covered with stones (*stony soil*; *a stony road*). **2 a** hard, rigid. **b** cold, unfeeling, uncompromising (*a stony stare*; *a stony silence*). □ **stony-broke** *Brit. sl.* entirely without money. **stony-hearted** unfeeling, obdurate. □ **stonily** *adv.* **stoniness** *n.* [OE *stānig* (as STONE)]

stood *past* and *past part.* of STAND.

stooge /stuːdʒ/ *n.* & *v. colloq.* —*n.* **1** a butt or foil, esp. for a comedian. **2** an assistant or subordinate, esp. for routine or unpleasant work. **3** a compliant person; a puppet. —*v.intr.* **1** (foll. by *for*) act as a stooge for. **2** (foll. by *about, around,* etc.) move about aimlessly. [20th c.: orig. unkn.]

stook /stuːk, stʊk/ *n.* & *v.* —*n.* a group of sheaves of grain stood on end in a field. —*v.tr.* arrange in stooks. [ME *stouk,* from or rel. to MLG *stūke*]

stool /stuːl/ *n.* **1** a seat without a back or arms, usu. for one person and consisting of a wooden slab on three or four short legs. **2** = FOOTSTOOL. **3** (usu. in *pl.*) = FAECES. **4** the root or stump of a tree or plant from which the shoots spring. □ **fall between two stools** fail from vacillation between two courses etc. **stool-pigeon 1** a person acting as a decoy (orig. a decoy of a pigeon fixed to a stool). **2** a police informer. [OE *stōl* f. Gmc, rel. to STAND]

stoolball /ˈstuːlbɔːl/ n. a team-game played in the UK, with a bat and ball and pairs of batters scoring runs between bases.

stoolie /ˈstuːlɪ/ n. US sl. a person acting as a stool-pigeon.

stoop[1] /stuːp/ v. & n. —v. 1 tr. bend (one's head or body) forwards and downwards. 2 intr. carry one's head and shoulders bowed forward. 3 intr. (foll. by to + infin.) deign or condescend. 4 intr. (foll. by to) descend or lower oneself to (some conduct) (has stooped to crime). —n. a stooping posture. [OE stūpian f. Gmc, rel. to STEEP[1]]

stoop[2] /stuːp/ n. US a porch or small veranda or set of steps in front of a house. [Du. stoep: see STOEP]

stoop[3] var. of STOUP.

stop v. & n. —v. (**stopped, stopping**) 1 tr. **a** put an end to (motion etc.); completely check the progress or motion or operation of. **b** effectively hinder or prevent (stopped them playing so loudly). **c** discontinue (an action or sequence of actions) (stopped playing; stopped my visits). 2 intr. come to an end; cease (supplies suddenly stopped). 3 intr. cease from motion or speaking or action; make a halt or pause (the car stopped at the lights; he stopped in the middle of a sentence; my watch has stopped). 4 tr. cause to cease action; defeat. 5 tr. sl. receive (a blow etc.). 6 intr. remain; stay for a short time. 7 tr. (often foll. by up) block or close up (a hole or leak etc.). 8 tr. not permit or supply as usual; discontinue or withhold (shall stop their wages). 9 tr. (in full **stop payment** of or on) instruct a bank to withhold payment on (a cheque). 10 tr. Brit. put a filling in (a tooth). 11 tr. obtain the required pitch from (the string of a violin etc.) by pressing at the appropriate point with the finger. 12 tr. Boxing **a** parry (a blow). **b** knock out (an opponent). 13 tr. Hort. pinch back (a plant). —n. 1 the act or an instance of stopping; the state of being stopped (put a stop to; the vehicle was brought to a stop). 2 a place designated for a bus or train etc. to stop. 3 a punctuation mark, esp. = full stop. 4 a device for stopping motion at a particular point. 5 a change of pitch effected by stopping a string. 6 **a** (in an organ) a row of pipes of one character. **b** a knob etc. operating these. 7 **a** the effective diameter of a lens. **b** a device for reducing this. **c** a unit of change of relative aperture or exposure. 8 (of sound) = PLOSIVE. □ **put a stop to** cause to end, esp. abruptly. **stop at nothing** be ruthless. **stop by** (also absol.) call at (a place). **stop dead** (or **short**) cease abruptly. **stop down** Photog. reduce the aperture of (a lens) with a diaphragm. **stop one's ears 1** put one's fingers in one's ears to avoid hearing. **2** refuse to listen. **stop lamp** a light on the rear of a vehicle showing when the brakes are applied. **stop light 1** a red traffic-light. **2** = stop lamp. **stop a person's mouth** induce a person by bribery or other means to keep silence about something. **stop off** (or **over**) break one's journey. **stop out** stay out. **stop press** Brit. **1** (often attrib.) late news inserted in a newspaper after printing has begun. **2** a column in a newspaper reserved for this. **with all the stops out** exerting extreme effort. □ **stopless** adj. **stoppable** adj. [ME f. OE -stoppian f. LL stuppare STUFF f. L stuppa tow]

stopcock /ˈstɒpkɒk/ n. an externally operated valve regulating the flow of a liquid or gas through a pipe etc.

stopgap /ˈstɒpgæp/ n. (often attrib.) a temporary substitute.

stopoff /ˈstɒpɒf/ n. a break in one's journey.

stopover /ˈstɒpˌəʊvə(r)/ n. = STOPOFF.

stoppage /ˈstɒpɪdʒ/ n. **1** the condition of being blocked or stopped. **2** a stopping (of pay). **3** a stopping or interruption of work in a factory etc.

stopper /ˈstɒpə(r)/ n. & v. —n. **1** a plug for closing a bottle etc. **2** a person or thing that stops something. —v.tr. close or secure with a stopper. □ **put a stopper on 1** put an end to (a thing). **2** keep (a person) quiet.

stopping /ˈstɒpɪŋ/ n. Brit. a filling for a tooth.

stopwatch /ˈstɒpwɒtʃ/ n. a watch with a mechanism for recording elapsed time, used to time races etc.

storage /ˈstɔːrɪdʒ/ n. **1 a** the storing of goods etc. **b** a particular method of storing or the space available for it. **2** the cost of storing. **3** the electronic retention of data in a computer etc. □ **storage battery** (or **cell**) a battery (or cell) for storing electricity. **storage heater** Brit. an electric heater accumulating heat outside peak hours for later release.

store n. & v. —n. **1** a quantity of something kept available for use (a store of wine; a store of wit). **2** (in pl.) **a** articles for a particular purpose accumulated for use (naval stores). **b** a supply of these or the place where they are kept. **3 a** = department store. **b** esp. US any retail outlet or shop. **c** (often in pl.) a shop selling basic necessities (general stores). **4** a warehouse for the temporary keeping of furniture etc. **5** a device in a computer for storing retrievable data; a memory. —v.tr. **1** put (furniture etc.) in store. **2** (often foll. by up, away) accumulate (stores, energy, electricity, etc.) for future use. **3** stock or provide with something useful (a mind stored with facts). **4** (of a receptacle) have storage capacity for. **5** enter or retain (data) for retrieval. □ **in store 1** kept in readiness. **2** coming in the future. **3** (foll. by for) destined or intended. **set** (or **lay** or **put**) **store by** (or **on**) consider important or valuable. □ **storable** adj. **storer** n. [ME f. obs. astore (n. & v.) f. OF estore, estorer f. L instaurare renew: cf. RESTORE]

storefront /ˈstɔːfrʌnt/ n. esp. US **1** the side of a shop facing the street. **2** a room at the front of a shop.

storehouse /ˈstɔːhaʊs/ n. a place where things are stored.

storekeeper /ˈstɔːˌkiːpə(r)/ n. **1** a storeman. **2** US a shopkeeper.

storeman /ˈstɔːmən/ n. (pl. **-men**) a person responsible for stored goods.

storeroom /ˈstɔːruːm, -rʊm/ n. a room in which items are stored.

storey /ˈstɔːrɪ/ n. (also **story**) (pl. **-eys** or **-ies**) **1** any of the parts into which a building is divided horizontally; the whole of the rooms etc. having a continuous floor (a third-storey window; a house of five storeys). **2** a thing forming a horizontal division. □ **-storeyed** (in comb.) (also **-storied**). [ME f. AL historia HISTORY (perh. orig. meaning a tier of painted windows or sculpture)]

storied /ˈstɔːrɪd/ adj. literary celebrated in or associated with stories or legends.

stork *n.* **1** any long-legged large wading bird of the family Ciconiidae, esp. *Ciconia ciconia* with white plumage, black wing-tips, a long reddish beak, and red feet, nesting esp. on tall buildings. **2** this bird as the pretended bringer of babies. [OE *storc,* prob. rel. to STARK (from its rigid posture)]

storm *n.* & *v.* —*n.* **1** a violent disturbance of the atmosphere with strong winds and usu. with thunder and rain or snow etc. **2** a violent disturbance of the established order in human affairs. **3** (foll. by *of*) **a** a violent shower of missiles or blows. **b** an outbreak of applause, indignation, hisses, etc. (*they were greeted by a storm of abuse*). **4 a** a direct assault by troops on a fortified place. **b** the capture of a place by such an assault. —*v.* **1** *intr.* (often foll. by *at, away*) talk violently, rage, bluster. **2** *intr.* (usu. foll. by *in, out of,* etc.) move violently or angrily (*stormed out of the meeting*). **3** *tr.* attack or capture by storm. **4** *intr.* (of wind, rain, etc.) rage; be violent. □ **storm centre 1** the point to which the wind blows spirally inward in a cyclonic storm. **2** a subject etc. upon which agitation or disturbance is concentrated. **storm cloud 1** a heavy rain-cloud. **2** a threatening state of affairs. **storm-door** an additional outer door for protection in bad weather or winter. **storm in a teacup** *Brit.* great excitement over a trivial matter. **storm-lantern** *Brit.* a hurricane lamp. **storm petrel 1** a small petrel, *Hydrobates pelagicus,* of the North Atlantic, with black and white plumage. **2** a person causing unrest. **storm trooper 1** *hist.* a member of the Nazi political militia. **2** a member of the shock troops. **storm troops 1** = *shock troops.* **2** *hist.* the Nazi political militia. **storm window** an additional outer sash-window used like a storm-door. **take by storm 1** capture by direct assault. **2** rapidly captivate (a person, audience, etc.). □ **stormless** *adj.* **stormproof** *adj.* [OE f. Gmc]

stormbound /ˈstɔːmbaʊnd/ *adj.* prevented by storms from leaving port or continuing a voyage.

stormy /ˈstɔːmɪ/ *adj.* (**stormier, stormiest**) **1** of or affected by storms. **2** (of a wind etc.) violent, raging, vehement. **3** full of feeling or outbursts; lively, boisterous (*a stormy meeting*). □ **stormy petrel** = *storm petrel.* □ **stormily** *adv.* **storminess** *n.*

story[1] /ˈstɔːrɪ/ *n.* (*pl.* **-ies**) **1** an account of imaginary or past events; a narrative, tale, or anecdote. **2** the past course of the life of a person or institution etc. (*my story is a strange one*). **3** (in full **story-line**) the narrative or plot of a novel or play etc. **4** facts or experiences that deserve narration. **5** *colloq.* a fib or lie. **6** a narrative or descriptive item of news. [ME *storie* f. AF *estorie* (OF *estoire*) f. L *historia* (as HISTORY)]

story[2] var. of STOREY.

storyboard /ˈstɔːrɪˌbɔːd/ *n.* a displayed sequence of pictures etc. outlining the plan of a film, television advertisement, etc.

storyteller /ˈstɔːrɪˌtelə(r)/ *n.* **1** a person who tells stories. **2** *colloq.* a liar. □ **storytelling** *n.* & *adj.*

stoup /stuːp/ *n.* (also **stoop**) **1** a holy-water basin. **2** *archaic* a flagon, beaker, or drinking-vessel. [ME f. ON *staup* (= OE *stēap*) f. Gmc, rel. to STEEP[2]]

stout /staʊt/ *adj.* & *n.* —*adj.* **1** rather fat; corpulent; bulky. **2** of considerable thickness or strength (*a stout stick*). **3** brave, resolute, vigorous (*a stout fellow; put up stout resistance*). —*n.* a strong dark beer brewed with roasted malt or barley. □ **a stout heart** courage, resolve. **stout-hearted** courageous. □ **stoutish** *adj.* **stoutly** *adv.* **stoutness** *n.* [ME f. AF & dial. OF *stout* f. WG, perh. rel. to STILT]

stove[1] *n.* a closed apparatus burning fuel or electricity for heating or cooking. □ **stove-enamel** a heatproof enamel. **stove-pipe** a pipe conducting smoke and gases from a stove to a chimney. [ME = sweating-room, f. MDu., MLG *stove,* OHG *stuba* f. Gmc, perh. rel. to STEW]

stove[2] *past* and *past part.* of STAVE *v.*

stow /stəʊ/ *v.tr.* **1** pack (goods etc.) tidily and compactly. **2** *Naut.* place (a cargo or provisions) in its proper place and order. **3** fill (a receptacle) with articles compactly arranged. **4** (usu. in *imper.*) *sl.* abstain or cease from (*stow the noise!*). □ **stow away 1** place (a thing) where it will not cause an obstruction. **2** be a stowaway on a ship etc. [ME, f. BESTOW: in Naut. use perh. infl. by Du. *stouwen*]

stowage /ˈstəʊɪdʒ/ *n.* **1** the act or an instance of stowing. **2** a place for this.

stowaway /ˈstəʊəˌweɪ/ *n.* a person who hides on board a ship or aircraft etc. to get free passage.

strabismus /strəˈbɪzməs/ *n. Med.* the abnormal condition of one or both eyes not correctly aligned in direction; a squint. □ **strabismal** *adj.* **strabismic** *adj.* [mod.L f. Gk *strabismos* f. *strabizō* squint f. *strabos* squinting]

straddle /ˈstræd(ə)l/ *v.* & *n.* —*v.* **1** *tr.* **a** sit or stand across (a thing) with the legs wide apart. **b** be situated across or on both sides of (*the town straddles the border*). **2** *intr.* **a** sit or stand in this way. **b** (of the legs) be wide apart. **3** *tr.* part (one's legs) widely. **4** *tr.* drop shots or bombs short of and beyond (a target). —*n.* the act or an instance of straddling. □ **straddler** *n.* [alt. of *striddle,* back-form. f. *striddlings* astride f. *strid-* = STRIDE]

strafe /strɑːf, streɪf/ *v.* & *n.* —*v.tr.* **1** bombard; harass with gunfire. **2** abuse. —*n.* an act of strafing. [joc. adaptation of G catchword (1914) *Gott strafe England* may God punish England]

straggle /ˈstræg(ə)l/ *v.* & *n.* —*v.intr.* **1** lack or lose compactness or tidiness. **2** be or become dispersed or sporadic. **3** trail behind others in a march or race etc. **4** (of a plant, beard, etc.) grow long and loose. —*n.* a body or group of straggling or scattered persons or things. □ **straggler** *n.* **straggly** *adj.* (**stragglier, straggliest**). [ME, perh. rel. to dial. *strake* go, rel. to STRETCH]

straight /streɪt/ *adj., n.,* & *adv.* —*adj.* **1** extending uniformly in the same direction; without a curve or bend etc. **2** successive, uninterrupted (*three straight wins*). **3** in proper order or place or condition; duly arranged; level, symmetrical (*is the picture straight?; put things straight*). **4** honest, candid; not evasive (*a straight answer*). **5** (of thinking etc.) logical, unemotional. **6** (of drama etc.) serious as opposed to popular or comic; employing the conventional techniques of its art form. **7 a** unmodified. **b** (of a drink) undiluted. **8** *colloq.* (of music) classical. **9** *colloq.* **a** (of a person etc.) conventional or respectable. **b** heterosexual. **10** (of a person's back) not bowed. **11** (of the hair) not curly or wavy. **12** (of a knee) not bent. **13** (of a garment) not flared. **14** coming direct from its source. **15** (of an aim, look, blow, or course) going direct to the mark. —n. **1** the straight part of something, esp. the concluding stretch of a racecourse. **2** a straight condition. **3** a sequence of five cards in poker. **4** colloq. a conventional person; a heterosexual. —adv. **1** in a straight line; direct; without deviation or hesitation or circumlocution (came straight from Paris; I told them straight). **2** in the right direction, with a good aim (shoot straight). **3** correctly (can't see straight). □ **go straight** live an honest life after being a criminal. **the straight and narrow** morally correct behaviour. **straight away** at once; immediately. **straight face** an intentionally expressionless face, esp. avoiding a smile though amused. **straight fight** Brit. Polit. a direct contest between two candidates. **straight from the shoulder 1** (of a blow) well delivered. **2** (of a verbal attack) frank or direct. **straight man** a comedian's stooge. **straight off** colloq. without hesitation, deliberation, etc. (cannot tell you straight off). **straight-out** US **1** uncompromising. **2** straightforward, genuine. □ **straightly** adv. **straightness** n. [ME, past part. of STRETCH]

straighten /ˈstreɪt(ə)n/ v.tr. & intr. **1** (often foll. by out) make or become straight. **2** (foll. by up) stand erect after bending. □ **straightener** n.

straightforward /streɪtˈfɔːwəd/ adj. **1** honest or frank. **2** (of a task etc.) uncomplicated. □ **straightforwardly** adv. **straightforwardness** n.

strain[1] v. & n. —v. **1** tr. & intr. stretch tightly; make or become taut or tense. **2** tr. exercise (oneself, one's senses, a thing, etc.) intensely or excessively, press to extremes. **3** a intr. make an intensive effort. **b** intr. (foll. by after) strive intensely for (straining after perfection). **4** intr. (foll. by at) tug, pull (the dog strained at the leash). **5** intr. hold out with difficulty under pressure (straining under the load). **6** tr. **a** distort from the true intention or meaning. **b** apply (authority, laws, etc.) beyond their province or in violation of their true intention. **7** tr. overtask or injure by overuse or excessive demands (strain a muscle; strained their loyalty). **8 a** tr. clear (a liquid) of solid matter by passing it through a sieve etc. **b** tr. (foll. by out) filter (solids) out from a liquid. **c** intr. (of a liquid) percolate. **9** tr. use (one's ears, eyes, voice, etc.) to the best of one's power. —n. **1 a** the act or an instance of straining. **b** the force exerted in this. **2** an injury caused by straining a muscle etc. **3 a** a severe demand on physical strength or resources. **b** the exertion needed to meet this (is suffering from strain). **4** (in sing. or pl.) a snatch or spell of music or poetry. **5** a tone or tendency in speech or writing (more in the same strain). □ **strain oneself 1** injure oneself by effort. **2** make undue efforts. □ **strainable** adj. [ME f. OF estreindre estreign- f. L stringere strict- draw tight]

strain[2] n. **1** a breed or stock of animals, plants, etc. **2** a moral tendency as part of a person's character (a strain of aggression). [ME, = progeny, f. OE strēon (recorded in ġestrēonan beget), rel. to L struere build]

strained /streɪnd/ adj. **1** constrained, forced, artificial. **2** (of a relationship) mutually distrustful or tense. **3** (of an interpretation) involving an unreasonable assumption; far-fetched, laboured.

strainer /ˈstreɪnə(r)/ n. a device for straining liquids, vegetables, etc.

strait n. & adj. —n. **1** (in sing. or pl.) a narrow passage of water connecting two seas or large bodies of water. **2** (usu. in pl.) difficulty, trouble, or distress (usu. in dire or desperate straits). —adj. archaic **1** narrow, limited; confined or confining. **2** strict or rigorous. □ **strait-laced** severely virtuous; morally scrupulous; puritanical. □ **straitly** adv. **straitness** n. [ME streit f. OF estreit tight, narrow f. L strictus STRICT]

straiten /ˈstreɪt(ə)n/ v. **1** tr. restrict in range or scope. **2** tr. (as **straitened** adj.) of or marked by poverty. **3** tr. & intr. archaic make or become narrow.

strait-jacket /ˈstreɪtˌdʒækɪt/ n. & v. —n. **1** a strong garment with long arms for confining the arms of a violent prisoner, mental patient, etc. **2** restrictive measures. —v.tr. (**-jacketed, -jacketing**) **1** restrain with a strait-jacket. **2** severely restrict.

strand[1] v. & n. —v. **1** tr. & intr. run aground. **2** tr. (as **stranded** adj.) in difficulties, esp. without money or means of transport. —n. rhet. or poet. the margin of a sea, lake, or river, esp. the foreshore. [OE]

strand[2] n. **1** each of the threads or wires twisted round each other to make a rope or cable. **2 a** a single thread or strip of fibre. **b** a constituent filament. **3** a lock of hair. **4** an element or strain in any composite whole. [ME: orig. unkn.]

strange /streɪndʒ/ adj. **1** unusual, peculiar, surprising, eccentric, novel. **2 a** (often foll. by to) unfamiliar, alien, foreign (lost in a strange land). **b** not one's own (strange gods). **3** (foll. by to) unaccustomed. **4** not at ease; out of one's element (felt strange in such company). □ **feel strange** be unwell. □ **strangely** adv. [ME f. OF estrange f. L extraneus EXTRANEOUS]

strangeness /ˈstreɪndʒnɪs/ n. **1** the state or fact of being strange or unfamiliar etc. **2** Physics a property of certain elementary particles that is conserved in strong interactions.

stranger /ˈstreɪndʒə(r)/ n. **1** a person who does not know or is not known in a particular place or company. **2** (often foll. by to) a person one does not know (was a complete stranger to me). **3** (foll. by to) a person entirely unaccustomed to (a feeling, experience, etc.) (no stranger to controversy). [ME f. OF estrangier ult. f. L (as STRANGE)]

strangle /ˈstræŋg(ə)l/ v.tr. **1** squeeze the windpipe or neck of, esp. so as to kill. **2** hamper or suppress (a movement, impulse, cry, etc.). □ **strangler** n. [ME f. OF estrangler f. L strangulare f. Gk straggalaō f. straggalē halter: cf. straggos twisted]

stranglehold /ˈstræŋg(ə)lˌhəʊld/ n. **1** a wrestling hold that throttles an opponent. **2** a deadly grip. **3** complete and exclusive control.

strangulate /ˈstræŋgjʊˌleɪt/ v.tr. Surgery prevent circulation through (a vein, intestine, etc.) by compression. □ **strangulated hernia** Med. a hernia in which the protruding part is constricted, preventing circulation. [L strangulare strangulat- (as STRANGLE)]

strangulation /ˌstræŋgjʊˈleɪʃ(ə)n/ n. **1** the act of strangling or the state of being strangled. **2** the act of strangulating. [L strangulatio (as STRANGULATE)]

strap *n.* & *v.* —*n.* **1** a strip of leather or other flexible material, often with a buckle or other fastening for holding things together etc. **2** a thing like this for keeping a garment in place. **3** a loop for grasping to steady oneself in a moving vehicle. —*v.tr.* (**strapped**, **strapping**) **1** (often foll. by *down*, *up*, etc.) secure or bind with a strap. **2** beat with a strap. **3** (esp. as **strapped** *adj.*) *colloq.* subject to a shortage. **4** (often foll. by *up*) close (a wound) or bind (a part) with adhesive plaster. □ **strapper** *n.* **strappy** *adj.* [dial. form of STROP]

straphanger /ˈstræpˌhæŋgə(r)/ *n.* *sl.* a standing passenger in a bus or train. □ **straphang** *v.intr.*

strapless /ˈstræplɪs/ *adj.* (of a garment) without straps, esp. shoulder-straps.

strapping /ˈstræpɪŋ/ *adj.* (esp. of a person) large and sturdy.

strata *pl.* of STRATUM.

stratagem /ˈstrætədʒəm/ *n.* **1** a cunning plan or scheme, esp. for deceiving an enemy. **2** trickery. [ME f. F *stratagème* f. L *stratagema* f. Gk *stratēgēma* f. *stratēgeō* be a general (*stratēgos*) f. *stratos* army + *agō* lead]

stratal see STRATUM.

strategic /strəˈtiːdʒɪk/ *adj.* **1** of or serving the ends of strategy (*strategic considerations*). **2** (of materials) essential in fighting a war. **3** (of bombing or weapons) done or for use against an enemy's home territory as a longer-term military objective (opp. TACTICAL). □ **strategic defence initiative** a projected US system of defence against nuclear weapons using satellites. □ **strategical** *adj.* **strategically** *adv.* **strategics** *n.pl.* (usu. treated as *sing.*). [F *stratégique* f. Gk *stratēgikos* (as STRATAGEM)]

strategy /ˈstrætɪdʒɪ/ *n.* (*pl.* **-ies**) **1** the art of war. **2 a** the management of an army or armies in a campaign. **b** the art of moving troops, ships, aircraft, etc. into favourable positions. **c** an instance of this or a plan formed according to it. **3** a plan of action or policy in business or politics etc. (*economic strategy*). □ **strategist** *n.* [F *stratégie* f. Gk *stratēgia* generalship f. *stratēgos*: see STRATAGEM]

strath /stræθ/ *n.* *Sc.* a broad mountain valley. [Gael. *srath*]

strathspey /stræθˈspeɪ/ *n.* **1** a slow Scottish dance. **2** the music for this. [*Strathspey*, valley of the river Spey]

strati *pl.* of STRATUS.

stratify /ˈstrætɪˌfaɪ/ *v.tr.* (**-ies**, **-ied**) **1** (esp. as **stratified** *adj.*) arrange in strata. **2** construct in layers, social grades, etc. □ **stratification** /-fɪˈkeɪʃ(ə)n/ *n.* [F *stratifier* (as STRATUM)]

stratigraphy /strəˈtɪgrəfɪ/ *n.* *Geol.* & *Archaeol.* **1** the order and relative position of strata. **2** the study of this as a means of historical interpretation. □ **stratigraphic** /ˌstrætɪˈgræfɪk/ *adj.* **stratigraphical** /ˌstrætɪˈgræfɪk(ə)l/ *adj.* [STRATUM + -GRAPHY]

strato- /ˈstrætəʊ/ *comb. form* stratus.

stratosphere /ˈstrætəˌsfɪə(r)/ *n.* a layer of atmospheric air above the troposphere. □ **stratospheric** /-ˈsferɪk/ *adj.* [STRATUM + SPHERE after *atmosphere*]

stratum /ˈstrɑːtəm, ˈstreɪ-/ *n.* (*pl.* **strata** /-tə/) **1** esp. *Geol.* a layer or set of successive layers of any deposited substance. **2** an atmospheric layer. **3** a layer of tissue etc. **4** a social grade, class, etc. (*the various strata of society*). □ **stratal**

adj. [L, = something spread or laid down, neut. past part. of *sternere* strew]

stratus /ˈstreɪtəs, ˈstrɑː-/ *n.* (*pl.* **strati** /-taɪ/) a continuous horizontal sheet of cloud. [L, past part. of *sternere*: see STRATUM]

straw *n.* **1** dry cut stalks of grain for use as fodder or as material for thatching, packing, making hats, etc. **2** a single stalk or piece of straw. **3** a thin hollow paper or plastic tube for sucking drink from a glass etc. **4** an insignificant thing (*not worth a straw*). **5** the pale yellow colour of straw. □ **catch** (or **grasp**) **at a straw** resort to an utterly inadequate expedient in desperation, like a person drowning. **straw in the wind** a slight hint of future developments. **straw vote** (or **poll**) an unofficial ballot as a test of opinion. □ **strawy** *adj.* [OE *strēaw* f. Gmc, rel. to STREW]

strawberry /ˈstrɔːbərɪ/ *n.* (*pl.* **-ies**) **1 a** any plant of the genus *Fragaria*, esp. any of various cultivated varieties, with white flowers, trifoliate leaves, and runners. **b** the pulpy red edible fruit of this, having a seed-studded surface. **2** a deep pinkish-red colour. □ **strawberry blonde** **1** pinkish-blonde hair. **2** a woman with such hair. **strawberry mark** a soft reddish birthmark. [OE *strēa(w)berige*, *strēowberige* (as STRAW, BERRY): reason for the name unkn.]

stray *v.*, *n.*, & *adj.* —*v.intr.* **1** wander from the right place; become separated from one's companions etc.; go astray. **2** deviate morally. **3** (as **strayed** *adj.*) that has gone astray. —*n.* a person or thing that has strayed, esp. a domestic animal. —*adj.* **1** strayed or lost. **2** isolated; found or occurring occasionally (*a stray customer or two; hit by a stray bullet*). □ **strayer** *n.* [ME f. AF & OF *estrayer* (v.), AF *strey* (n. & adj.) f. OF *estraié* (as ASTRAY)]

streak *n.* & *v.* —*n.* **1** a long thin usu. irregular line or band, esp. distinguished by colour (*black with red streaks; a streak of light above the horizon*). **2** a strain or element in a person's character (*has a streak of mischief*). **3** a spell or series (*a winning streak*). —*v.* **1** *tr.* mark with streaks. **2** *intr.* move very rapidly. **3** *intr.* *colloq.* run naked in a public place as a stunt. □ **streak of lightning** a sudden prominent flash of lightning. □ **streaker** *n.* **streaking** *n.* [OE *strica* pen-stroke f. Gmc: rel. to STRIKE]

streaky /ˈstriːkɪ/ *adj.* (**streakier**, **streakiest**) **1** full of streaks. **2** (of bacon) with alternate streaks of fat and lean. □ **streakily** *adv.* **streakiness** *n.*

stream *n.* & *v.* —*n.* **1** a flowing body of water, esp. a small river. **2 a** the flow of a fluid or of a mass of people (*a stream of lava*). **b** (in *sing.* or *pl.*) a large quantity of something that flows or moves along. **3** a current or direction in which things are moving or tending (*against the stream*). **4** *Brit.* a group of schoolchildren taught together as being of similar ability for a given age. —*v.* **1** *intr.* flow or move as a stream. **2** *intr.* run with liquid (*my eyes were streaming*). **3** *intr.* (of a banner or hair etc.) float or wave in the wind. **4** *tr.* emit a stream of (blood etc.). **5** *tr.* *Brit.* arrange (schoolchildren) in streams. □ **on stream** (of a factory etc.) in operation. **stream of consciousness 1** *Psychol.* a person's thoughts and conscious reactions to events perceived as a continuous flow. **2** a literary style depicting events in such a flow in the mind of a character.

▫ **streamless** adj. **streamlet** n. [OE *strēam* f. Gmc]

streamer /ˈstriːmə(r)/ n. **1** a long narrow flag. **2** a long narrow strip of ribbon or paper, esp. in a coil that unrolls when thrown. **3** a banner headline.

streamline /ˈstriːmlaɪn/ v.tr. **1** give (a vehicle etc.) the form which presents the least resistance to motion. **2** make (an organization, process, etc.) simple or more efficient or better organized.

street n. **1 a** a public road in a city, town, or village. **b** this with the houses or other buildings on each side. **2** the persons who live or work on a particular street. ▫ **on the streets 1** living by prostitution. **2** homeless. **street credibility** familiarity with a fashionable urban subculture. **street door** a main outer house-door opening on the street. **streets ahead** (often foll. by *of*) *colloq.* much superior (to). **street value** the value of drugs sold illicitly. **up** (or **right up**) **one's street** *colloq.* **1** within one's range of interest or knowledge. **2** to one's liking. ▫ **streeted** adj. (also in *comb.*). **streetward** adj. & adv. [OE *strǣt* f. LL *strāta* (*via*) paved (way), fem. past part. of *sternere* lay down]

streetcar /ˈstriːtkɑː(r)/ n. *US* a tram.

streetwalker /ˈstriːtˌwɔːkə(r)/ n. a prostitute seeking customers in the street. ▫ **streetwalking** n. & adj.

streetwise /ˈstriːtwaɪz/ n. esp. *US* familiar with the ways of modern urban life.

strength /streŋθ, streŋkθ/ n. **1** the state of being strong; the degree or respect in which a person or thing is strong. **2 a** a person or thing affording strength or support. **b** an attribute making for strength of character (*patience is your great strength*). **3** the number of persons present or available. **4** a full complement (*below strength*). ▫ **from strength** from a strong position. **from strength to strength** with ever-increasing success. **in strength** in large numbers. **on the strength of** relying on; on the basis of. **the strength of** the essence or main features of. ▫ **strengthless** adj. [OE *strengthu* f. Gmc (as STRONG)]

strengthen /ˈstreŋθ(ə)n, -ŋkθ(ə)n/ v.tr. & intr. make or become stronger. ▫ **strengthen a person's hand** (or **hands**) encourage a person to vigorous action. ▫ **strengthener** n.

strenuous /ˈstrenjʊəs/ adj. **1** requiring or using great effort. **2** energetic or unrelaxing. ▫ **strenuously** adv. **strenuousness** n. [L *strenuus* brisk]

streptococcus /ˌstreptəˈkɒkəs/ n. (pl. **streptococci** /-ˈkɒkaɪ/) any bacterium of the genus *Streptococcus*, some of which cause infectious diseases. ▫ **streptococcal** adj. [Gk *streptos* twisted f. *strephō* turn + COCCUS]

streptomycin /ˌstreptəʊˈmaɪsɪn/ n. an antibiotic produced by the bacterium *Streptomyces griseus*, effective against many disease-producing bacteria. [Gk *streptos* (as STREPTOCOCCUS) + *mukēs* fungus]

stress n. & v. —n. **1 a** a pressure or tension exerted on a material object. **b** a quantity measuring this. **2 a** a demand on physical or mental energy. **b** distress caused by this (*suffering from stress*). **3 a** emphasis (*the stress was on the need for success*). **b** accentuation; emphasis laid on a syllable or word. **c** an accent, esp. the principal one in a word (*the stress is on the first syllable*). —v.tr. **1** lay stress on; emphasize. **2** subject to mechanical or physical or mental stress. ▫ **lay stress on** indicate as important. **stress disease** a disease resulting from continuous mental stress. ▫ **stressless** adj. [ME f. DISTRESS, or partly f. OF *estresse* narrowness, oppression, ult. f. L *strictus* STRICT]

stressful /ˈstresfʊl/ adj. causing stress; mentally tiring (*had a stressful day*). ▫ **stressfully** adv. **stressfulness** n.

stretch v. & n. —v. **1** tr. & intr. draw or be drawn or admit of being drawn out into greater length or size. **2** tr. & intr. make or become taut. **3** tr. & intr. place or lie at full length or spread out (*with a canopy stretched over them*). **4** tr. (also *absol.*) **a** extend (an arm, leg, etc.). **b** (often *refl.*) thrust out one's limbs and tighten one's muscles after being relaxed. **5** intr. have a specified length or extension; extend (*farmland stretches for many miles*). **6** tr. strain or exert extremely or excessively; exaggerate (*stretch the truth*). **7** intr. (as **stretched** adj.) lying at full length. —n. **1** a continuous extent or expanse or period (*a stretch of open road*). **2** the act or an instance of stretching; the state of being stretched. **3** (*attrib.*) able to stretch; elastic (*stretch fabric*). **4** a *colloq.* period of imprisonment. **b** a period of service. ▫ **at full stretch** working to capacity. **at a stretch 1** in one continuous period (*slept for two hours at a stretch*). **2** with much effort. **stretch one's legs** exercise oneself by walking. **stretch out 1** tr. extend (a hand or foot etc.). **2** intr. & tr. last for a longer period; prolong. **3** tr. make (money etc.) last for a sufficient time. **stretch a point** agree to something not normally allowed. ▫ **stretchable** adj. **stretchability** /-əˈbɪlɪtɪ/ n. **stretchy** adj. **stretchiness** n. [OE *streccan* f. WG: cf. STRAIGHT]

stretcher /ˈstretʃə(r)/ n. & v. —n. **1** a framework of two poles with canvas etc. between, for carrying sick, injured, or dead persons in a lying position. **2** a brick or stone laid with its long side along the face of a wall. **3** a wooden frame over which a canvas is stretched ready for painting. —v.tr. (often foll. by *off*) convey (a sick or injured person) on a stretcher.

strew v.tr. (past part. **strewn** or **strewed**) **1** scatter or spread about over a surface. **2** (usu. foll. by *with*) spread (a surface) with scattered things. ▫ **strewer** n. [OE *stre(o)wian*]

'strewth var. of **'STRUTH**.

stria /ˈstraɪə/ n. (pl. **-ae** /-iː/) *Anat.*, *Zool.*, *Bot.*, *Geol.* **1** a linear mark on a surface. **2** a slight ridge, furrow, or score. [L]

striate adj. & v. —adj. /ˈstraɪɪt/ (also **striated** /-eɪtɪd/) *Anat.*, *Zool.*, *Bot.*, & *Geol.* marked with striae. —v.tr. /ˈstraɪeɪt/ mark with striae. ▫ **striation** /straɪˈeɪʃ(ə)n/ n.

stricken /ˈstrɪkən/ adj. **1** affected or overcome with illness or misfortune etc. (*stricken with measles*; *grief-stricken*). **2** (often foll. by *from* etc.) *US Law* deleted. ▫ **stricken in years** *archaic* enfeebled by age. [archaic past part. of STRIKE]

strict adj. **1** precisely limited or defined; without exception or deviation (*lives in strict seclusion*). **2** requiring complete compliance or exact performance; enforced rigidly (*gave strict orders*). ▫ **strictness** n. [L *strictus* past part. of *stringere* tighten]

strictly /ˈstrɪktlɪ/ adv. **1** in a strict manner. **2** (also **strictly speaking**) applying words in their strict sense (*he is, strictly, an absconder*). **3** esp. *US colloq.* definitely.

stricture /ˈstrɪktʃə(r)/ *n.* (usu. in *pl.*; often foll. by *on, upon*) a critical or censorious remark. □ **strictured** *adj.* [ME f. L *strictura* (as STRICT)]

stride *v.* & *n.* —*v.* (*past* **strode**; *past part.* **stridden**) **1** *intr.* & *tr.* walk with long firm steps. **2** *tr.* cross with one step. **3** *tr.* bestride; straddle. —*n.* **1 a** a single long step. **b** the length of this. **2** a person's gait as determined by the length of stride. **3** (usu. in *pl.*) progress (*has made great strides*). **4** a settled rate of progress (*get into one's stride; be thrown out of one's stride*). **5** (in *pl.*) *sl.* trousers. □ **take in one's stride 1** clear (an obstacle) without changing one's gait to jump. **2** manage without difficulty. □ **strider** *n.* [OE *strīdan*]

strident /ˈstraɪd(ə)nt/ *adj.* loud and harsh. □ **stridency** *n.* **stridently** *adv.* [L *stridere strident-* creak]

stridulate /ˈstrɪdjʊˌleɪt/ *v.intr.* (of insects, esp. the cicada and grasshopper) make a shrill sound by rubbing esp. the legs or wing-cases together. □ **stridulant** *adj.* **stridulation** /-ˈleɪʃ(ə)n/ *n.* [F *striduler* f. L *stridulus* creaking (as STRIDENT)]

strife *n.* **1** conflict; struggle between opposed persons or things. **2** *Austral. colloq.* trouble of any kind. [ME f. OF *estrif*; cf. OF *estriver* STRIVE]

strike *v.* & *n.* —*v.* (*past* **struck**; *past part.* **struck** or *archaic* **stricken**) **1 a** *tr.* subject to an impact. **b** *tr.* deliver (a blow) or inflict a blow on. **2** *tr.* come or bring sharply into contact with (*the ship struck a rock*). **3** *tr.* propel or divert with a blow (*struck the ball into the pond*). **4** *intr.* (foll. by *at*) try to hit. **5** *tr.* penetrate or cause to penetrate (*struck terror into him*). **6** *tr.* ignite (a match) or produce (sparks etc.) by rubbing. **7** *tr.* make (a coin) by stamping. **8** *tr.* produce (a musical note) by striking. **9 a** *tr.* (also *absol.*) (of a clock) indicate (the time) by the sounding of a chime etc. **b** *intr.* (of time) be indicated in this way. **10** *tr.* **a** attack suddenly (*was struck with sudden terror*). **b** (of a disease) afflict. **11** *tr.* cause to become suddenly (*was struck dumb*). **12** *tr.* reach or achieve (*strike a balance*). **13** *tr.* agree on (a bargain). **14** *tr.* assume (an attitude) suddenly and dramatically. **15** *tr.* **a** discover or come across. **b** find (oil etc.) by drilling. **c** encounter (an unusual thing etc.). **16** come to the attention of or appear to (*it strikes me as silly; an idea suddenly struck me*). **17** *intr.* (of employees) engage in a strike; cease work as a protest. **18** *tr.* lower or take down (a flag or tent etc.). **19** *intr.* take a specified direction (*struck east*). **20 a** *tr.* insert (the cutting of a plant) in soil to take root. **b** *tr.* (also *absol.*) (of a plant or cutting etc.) put forth (roots). **21** *tr.* **a** ascertain (a balance) by deducting credit or debit from the other. **b** arrive at (an average, state of balance) by equalizing all items. —*n.* **1** the act or an instance of striking. **2 a** the organized refusal by employees to work until some grievance is remedied. **b** a similar refusal to participate in some other expected activity. **3** a sudden find or success (*a lucky strike*). **4** an attack, esp. from the air. **5** *Baseball* a batter's unsuccessful attempt to hit a pitched ball, or another event counting equivalently against a batter. □ **on strike** taking part in an industrial etc. strike. **strike back** strike or attack in return. **strike down 1** knock down. **2** bring low; afflict (*struck down by a virus*). **strike home**

1 deal an effective blow. **2** have an intended effect (*my words struck home*). **strike it rich** *colloq.* find a source of abundance or success. **strike a light 1** produce a light by striking a match. **2** *Brit. sl.* an expression of surprise, disgust, etc. **strike lucky** have a lucky success. **strike off 1** remove with a stroke. **2** delete (a name etc.) from a list. **3** produce (copies of a document). **strike oil 1** find petroleum by sinking a shaft. **2** attain prosperity or success. **strike out 1** hit out. **2** act vigorously. **3** delete (an item or name etc.). **4** set off or begin (*struck out eastwards*). **5** use the arms and legs in swimming. **6** forge or devise (a plan etc.). **7** *Baseball* **a** dismiss (a batter) by means of three strikes. **b** be dismissed in this way. **strike pay** an allowance paid to strikers by their trade union. **strike through** delete (a word etc.) with a stroke of one's pen. **strike up 1** start (an acquaintance, conversation, etc.) esp. casually. **2** (also *absol.*) begin playing (a tune etc.). **strike upon 1** have (an idea etc.) luckily occur to one. **2** (of light) illuminate. **strike while the iron is hot** act promptly at a good opportunity. **struck on** *colloq.* infatuated with. □ **strikable** *adj.* [OE *strīcan* go, stroke f. WG]

strikebound /ˈstraɪkbaʊnd/ *adj.* immobilized or closed by a strike.

strikebreaker /ˈstraɪkˌbreɪkə(r)/ *n.* a person working or employed in place of others who are on strike. □ **strikebreak** *v.intr.*

striker /ˈstraɪkə(r)/ *n.* **1** a person or thing that strikes. **2** an employee on strike. **3** *Sport* the player who is to strike, or who is to be the next to strike, the ball. **4** *Football* an attacking player positioned well forward in order to score goals.

striking /ˈstraɪkɪŋ/ *adj.* impressive; attracting attention. □ **within striking distance** near enough to hit or achieve. □ **strikingly** *adv.* **strikingness** *n.*

Strine *n.* **1** a comic transliteration of Australian speech, e.g. *Emma Chissitt* = 'How much is it?' **2** (esp. uneducated) Australian English. [= *Australian* in Strine]

string *n.* & *v.* —*n.* **1** twine or narrow cord. **2** a piece of this or of similar material used for tying or holding together, pulling, etc. **3** a length of catgut or wire etc. on a musical instrument, producing a note by vibration. **4 a** (in *pl.*) the stringed instruments in an orchestra etc. **b** (*attrib.*) relating to or consisting of stringed instruments (*string quartet*). **5** (in *pl.*) an awkward condition or complication (*the offer has no strings*). **6** a set of things strung together; a series or line of persons or things (*a string of beads; a string of oaths*). **7** a group of racehorses trained at one stable. **8** a tough piece connecting the two halves of a bean-pod etc. **9** a piece of catgut etc. interwoven with others to form the head of a tennis etc. racket. —*v.* (*past* and *past part.* **strung** /strʌŋ/) **1** *tr.* supply with a string or strings. **2** *tr.* tie with string. **3** *tr.* thread (beads etc.) on a string. **4** *tr.* arrange in or as a string. **5** *tr.* remove the strings from (a bean). **6** *tr.* place a string ready for use on (a bow). □ **on a string** under one's control or influence. **string along** *colloq.* **1** deceive, esp. by appearing to comply with (a person). **2** (often foll. by *with*) keep company (with). **string bass** *Mus.* a double-bass. **string bean 1** any of various beans eaten in their fibrous pods, esp. runner beans or French beans. **2** *colloq.* a tall thin person. **string-course** a raised horizontal band or course of bricks etc. on a building. **string out** extend; prolong (esp. unduly). **string up 1** hang up on strings etc. **2** kill by hanging. **3** make tense. **string vest** a vest with large meshes. □ **stringless** *adj.* **stringlike** *adj.* [OE *streng* f. Gmc: cf. STRONG]

stringed /striŋd/ *adj.* (of musical instruments) having strings (also in *comb.*: *twelve-stringed guitar*).

stringent /ˈstrɪndʒ(ə)nt/ *adj.* **1** (of rules etc.) strict, precise; requiring exact performance; leaving no loophole or discretion. **2** (of a money market etc.) tight; hampered by scarcity; unaccommodating; hard to operate in. □ **stringency** *n.* **stringently** *adv.* [L *stringere* draw tight]

stringer /ˈstrɪŋə(r)/ *n.* **1** a longitudinal structural member in a framework, esp. of a ship or aircraft. **2** *colloq.* a newspaper correspondent not on the regular staff.

stringy /ˈstrɪŋɪ/ *adj.* (**stringier**, **stringiest**) **1** (of food etc.) fibrous, tough. **2** of or like string. **3** (of a person) tall, wiry, and thin. □ **stringily** *adv.* **stringiness** *n.*

strip[1] *v. & n.* —*v.* (**stripped**, **stripping**) **1** *tr.* (often foll. by *of*) remove the clothes or covering from (a person or thing). **2** *intr.* (often foll. by *off*) undress oneself. **3** *tr.* (often foll. by *of*) deprive (a person) of property or titles. **4** *tr.* leave bare of accessories or fittings. **5** *tr.* remove bark and branches from (a tree). **6** *tr.* (often foll. by *down*) remove the accessory fittings of or take apart (a machine etc.) to inspect or adjust it. **7** *tr.* tear the thread from (a screw). **8** *tr.* remove (paint) or remove paint from (a surface) with solvent. **9** *tr.* (often foll. by *from*) pull or tear (a covering or property etc.) off (*stripped the masks from their faces*). —*n.* **1** an act of stripping, esp. of undressing in striptease. **2** *colloq.* the identifying outfit worn by the members of a sports team while playing. □ **strip club** a club at which striptease performances are given. **strip-search** *n.* a search of a person involving the removal of all clothes. —*v.tr.* search in this way. [ME f. OE *bestrīepan* plunder f. Gmc]

strip[2] *n.* **1** a long narrow piece (*a strip of land*). **2** (in full **strip cartoon**) = *comic strip.* □ **strip light** a tubular fluorescent lamp. **tear a person off a strip** *colloq.* angrily rebuke a person. [ME, from or rel. to MLG *strippe* strap, thong, prob. rel. to STRIPE]

stripe *n.* **1** a long narrow band or strip differing in colour or texture from the surface on either side of it (*black with a red stripe*). **2** *Mil.* a chevron etc. denoting military rank. **3** *US* a category of character, opinion, etc. (*a man of that stripe*). [perh. back-form. f. *striped*: cf. MDu., MLG *stripe*, MHG *strife*]

striped /straɪpt/ *adj.* marked with stripes (also in *comb.*: *red-striped*).

stripling /ˈstrɪplɪŋ/ *n.* a youth not yet fully grown. [ME, prob. f. STRIP[2] + -LING[1], in the sense of having a figure not yet filled out]

stripper /ˈstrɪpə(r)/ *n.* **1** a person or thing that strips something. **2** a device or solvent for removing paint etc. **3** a striptease performer.

striptease /ˈstrɪptiːz/ *n. & v.* —*n.* an entertainment in which the performer gradually undresses before the audience. —*v.intr.* perform a striptease. □ **stripteaser** *n.*

stripy /ˈstraɪpɪ/ *adj.* (**stripier**, **stripiest**) striped; having many stripes.

strive *v.intr.* (past **strove**; past part. **striven** /ˈstrɪv(ə)n/) **1** (often foll. by *for*, or to + infin.) try hard, make efforts (*strive to succeed*). **2** (often foll. by *with*, *against*) struggle or contend. □ **striver** *n.* [ME f. OF *estriver*, rel. to *estrif* STRIFE]

strobe *n. colloq.* **1** a stroboscope. **2** a stroboscopic lamp. [abbr.]

stroboscope /ˈstrəʊbəˌskəʊp/ *n.* **1** *Physics* an instrument for determining speeds of rotation etc. by shining a bright light at intervals so that a rotating object appears stationary. **2** a lamp made to flash intermittently, esp. for this purpose. □ **stroboscopic** /-ˈskɒpɪk/ *adj.* **stroboscopical** /-ˈskɒpɪk(ə)l/ *adj.* **stroboscopically** /-ˈskɒpɪkəlɪ/ *adv.* [Gk *strobos* whirling + -SCOPE]

strode past of STRIDE.

Stroganoff /ˈstrɒɡəˌnɒf/ *adj.* (of meat) cut into strips and cooked in sour-cream sauce (*beef Stroganoff*). [P. *Stroganoff*, 19th-c. Russ. diplomat]

stroke *n. & v.* —*n.* **1** the act or an instance of striking; a blow or hit (*with a single stroke*; *a stroke of lightning*). **2** a sudden disabling attack or loss of consciousness caused by an interruption in the flow of blood to the brain, esp. through thrombosis; apoplexy. **3 a** an action or movement esp. as one of a series. **b** the time or way in which such movements are done. **c** the slightest such action (*has not done a stroke of work*). **4** the whole of the motion (of a wing, oar, etc.) until the starting-position is regained. **5** (in rowing) the mode or action of moving the oar (*row a fast stroke*). **6** the whole motion (of a piston) in either direction. **7** *Golf* the action of hitting (or hitting at) a ball with a club, as a unit of scoring. **8** a mode of moving the arms and legs in swimming. **9** a method of striking with the bat etc. in games etc. (*played some unorthodox strokes*). **10** a specially successful or skilful effort (*a stroke of diplomacy*). **11 a** a mark made by the movement in one direction of a pen or pencil or paintbrush. **b** a similar mark printed. **12** a detail contributing to the general effect in a description. **13** the sound made by a striking clock. **14** (in full **stroke oar**) the oar or oarsman nearest the stern, setting the time of the stroke. **15** the act or a spell of stroking. —*v.tr.* **1** pass one's hand gently along the surface of (hair or fur etc.); caress lightly. **2** act as the stroke of (a boat or crew). □ **at a stroke** by a single action. **finishing stroke** a *coup de grâce*; a final and fatal stroke. **off one's stroke** not performing as well as usual. **on the stroke of nine** etc. with the clock about to strike nine etc. **stroke of business** a profitable transaction. **stroke of genius** an original or strikingly successful idea. **stroke of luck** (or **good luck**) an unforeseen opportune occurrence. **stroke play** *Golf* play in which the score is reckoned by counting the number of strokes taken for the round. [OE *strācian* f. Gmc, rel. to STRIKE]

stroll /strəʊl/ *v. & n.* —*v.intr.* saunter or walk in a leisurely way. —*n.* a short leisurely walk (*go for a stroll*). □ **strolling players** actors etc. going from place to place to give performances. [orig. of a vagrant, prob. f. G *strollen*, *strolchen* f. *Strolch* vagabond, of unkn. orig.]

stroller /ˈstrəʊlə(r)/ *n.* **1** a person who strolls. **2** *US* a pushchair.

strong *adj. & adv.* —*adj.* (**stronger** /ˈstrɒŋgə(r)/; **strongest** /ˈstrɒŋgɪst/) **1** having the power of resistance; able to withstand great force or opposition; not easily damaged or overcome (*strong material; strong faith; a strong character*). **2** (of a person's constitution) able to overcome, or not liable to, disease. **3** (of a person's nerves) proof against fright, irritation, etc. **4** (of a patient) restored to health. **5** (of a market) having steadily high or rising prices. **6** capable of exerting great force or of doing much; muscular, powerful. **7** forceful or powerful in effect (*a strong wind; a strong protest*). **8** decided or firmly held (*a strong suspicion; strong views*). **9** (of an argument etc.) convincing or striking. **10** powerfully affecting the senses or emotions (*a strong light; strong acting*). **11** powerful in terms of size or numbers or quality (*a strong army*). **12** capable of doing much when united (*a strong combination*). **13** formidable; likely to succeed (*a strong candidate*). **14** (of a solution or drink etc.) containing a large proportion of a substance in water or another solvent (*strong tea*). **15** (of a group) having a specified number (*200 strong*). **16** (of a voice) loud or penetrating. **17** (of food or its flavour) pungent. **18** (of a measure) drastic. **19** *Gram.* in Germanic languages: **a** (of a verb) forming inflections by change of vowel within the stem rather than by the addition of a suffix (e.g. *swim, swam*). **b** (of a noun or adjective) belonging to a declension in which the stem originally ended otherwise than in *-n*. —*adv.* strongly (*the tide is running strong*). □ **come it strong** *colloq.* go to great lengths; use exaggeration. **going strong** *colloq.* continuing action vigorously; in good health or trim. **strong-arm** using force (*strong-arm tactics*). **strong language** forceful language; swearing. **strong meat** a doctrine or action acceptable only to vigorous or instructed minds. **strong-minded** having determination. **strong point 1** a thing at which one excels. **2** a specially fortified defensive position. **strong stomach** a stomach not easily affected by nausea. **strong suit 1** a suit at cards in which one can take tricks. **2** a thing at which one excels. □ **strongish** *adj.* **strongly** *adv.* [OE f. Gmc: cf. STRING]

strongbox /ˈstrɒŋbɒks/ *n.* a strongly made small chest for valuables.

stronghold /ˈstrɒŋhəʊld/ *n.* **1** a fortified place. **2** a secure refuge. **3** a centre of support for a cause etc.

strongroom /ˈstrɒŋruːm, -rʊm/ *n.* a room designed to protect valuables against fire and theft.

strontia /ˈstrɒnʃə/ *n. Chem.* strontium oxide. [*strontian* native strontium carbonate f. Strontian in the Highland Region of Scotland, where it was discovered]

strontium /ˈstrɒntɪəm/ *n. Chem.* a soft silver-white metallic element occurring naturally in various minerals. □ **strontium-90** a radioactive isotope of strontium concentrated selectively in bones and teeth when taken into the body. **strontium oxide** a white compound used in the manufacture of fireworks. [STRONTIA + -IUM]

strop *n. & v.* —*n.* a device, esp. a strip of leather, for sharpening razors. —*v.tr.* (**stropped, stropping**) sharpen on or with a strop. [ME f. MDu., MLG *strop*, OHG *strupf*, WG f. L *stroppus*]

stroppy /ˈstrɒpɪ/ *adj.* (**stroppier, stroppiest**) *Brit. colloq.* bad-tempered; awkward to deal with. □ **stroppily** *adv.* **stroppiness** *n.* [20th c.: perh. abbr. of OBSTREPEROUS]

strove *past* of STRIVE.

strow /strəʊ/ *v.tr.* (*past part.* **strown** /strəʊn/ or **strowed**) *archaic* = STREW. [var. of STREW]

struck *past* and *past part.* of STRIKE.

structural /ˈstrʌktʃər(ə)l/ *adj.* of, concerning, or having a structure. □ **structural linguistics** the study of language as a system of interrelated elements. **structural psychology** the study of the arrangement and composition of mental states and conscious experiences. □ **structurally** *adv.*

structuralism /ˈstrʌktʃərəˌlɪz(ə)m/ *n.* **1** the doctrine that structure rather than function is important. **2** structural linguistics. **3** structural psychology. □ **structuralist** *n.*

structure /ˈstrʌktʃə(r)/ *n. & v.* —*n.* **1 a** a whole constructed unit, esp. a building. **b** the way in which a building etc. is constructed (*has a flimsy structure*). **2** a set of interconnecting parts of any complex thing; a framework (*the structure of a sentence; a new wages structure*). —*v.tr.* give structure to; organize; frame. □ **structured** *adj.* (also in *comb.*). **structureless** *adj.* [ME f. OF *structure* or L *structura* f. *struere struct-* build]

strudel /ˈstruːd(ə)l/ *n.* a confection of thin pastry rolled up round a filling and baked (*apple strudel*). [G]

struggle /ˈstrʌg(ə)l/ *v. & n.* —*v.intr.* **1** make forceful or violent efforts to get free of restraint or constriction. **2** (often foll. by *for*, or *to* + *infin.*) make violent or determined efforts under difficulties; strive hard (*struggled for supremacy; struggled to get the words out*). **3** (foll. by *with, against*) contend; fight strenuously (*struggled with the disease; struggled against superior numbers*). **4** (foll. by *along, up*, etc.) make one's way with difficulty (*struggled to my feet*). **5** (esp. as **struggling** *adj.*) have difficulty in gaining recognition or a living (*a struggling artist*). —*n.* **1** the act or a spell of struggling. **2** a hard or confused contest. **3** a determined effort under difficulties. **struggler** *n.* [ME *strugle* frequent. of uncert. orig. (perh. imit.)]

strum *v. & n.* —*v.tr.* (**strummed, strumming**) **1** play on (a stringed or keyboard instrument) esp. carelessly or unskilfully. **2** play (a tune etc.) in this way. —*n.* the sound made by strumming. □ **strummer** *n.* [imit.: cf. THRUM¹]

strumpet /ˈstrʌmpɪt/ *n. archaic* or *rhet.* a prostitute. [ME: orig. unkn.]

strung *past* and *past part.* of STRING.

strut *n. & v.* —*n.* **1** a bar forming part of a framework and designed to resist compression. **2** a strutting gait. —*v.* (**strutted, strutting**) **1** *intr.* walk with a pompous or affected stiff erect gait. **2** *tr.* brace with a strut or struts. □ **strutter** *n.* **struttingly** *adv.* [ME 'bulge, swell, strive', earlier *stroute* f. OE *strūtian* be rigid (?)]

'struth /struːθ/ *int.* (also **'strewth**) *colloq.* a mild oath. [*God's truth*]

strychnine /ˈstrɪkniːn/ *n.* a vegetable alkaloid obtained from plants of the genus *Strychnos* (esp. *nux vomica*), bitter and highly poisonous, used as a stimulant and (in small amounts) a tonic. □ **strychnic** *adj.* [F f. L *strychnos* f. Gk *strukhnos* a kind of nightshade]

stub n. & v. —n. **1** the remnant of a pencil or cigarette etc. after use. **2** the counterfoil of a cheque or receipt etc. **3** a stunted tail etc. **4** the stump of a tree, tooth, etc. —v.tr. (**stubbed, stubbing**) **1** strike (one's toe) against something. **2** (usu. foll. by *out*) extinguish (a lighted cigarette) by pressing the lighted end against something. **3** (foll. by *up*) grub up by the roots. **4** clear (land) of stubs. [OE *stub, stubb* f. Gmc]

stubble /ˈstʌb(ə)l/ n. **1** the cut stalks of cereal plants left sticking up after the harvest. **2 a** cropped hair or a cropped beard. **b** a short growth of unshaven hair. □ **stubbled** adj. **stubbly** adj. [ME f. AF *stuble*, OF *estuble* f. L *stupla, stupula* var. of *stipula* straw]

stubborn /ˈstʌbən/ adj. **1** unreasonably obstinate. **2** unyielding, obdurate, inflexible. **3** refractory, intractable. □ **stubbornly** adv. **stubbornness** n. [ME *stiborn, stoburn*, etc., of unkn. orig.]

stubby /ˈstʌbɪ/ adj. & n. —adj. (**stubbier, stubbiest**) short and thick. —n. (pl. **-ies**) Austral. colloq. a small squat bottle of beer. □ **stubbily** adv. **stubbiness** n.

stucco /ˈstʌkəʊ/ n. & v. —n. (pl. **-oes**) plaster or cement used for coating wall surfaces or moulding into architectural decorations. —v.tr. (**-oes, -oed**) coat with stucco. [It., of Gmc orig.]

stuck past and past part. of STICK².

stuck-up see STICK².

stud¹ n. & v. —n. **1** a large-headed nail, boss, or knob, projecting from a surface esp. for ornament. **2** a double button esp. for use with two buttonholes in a shirt-front. **3** a small object projecting slightly from a road-surface as a marker etc. —v.tr. (**studded, studding**) **1** set with or as with studs. **2** (as **studded** adj.) (foll. by *with*) thickly set or strewn (*studded with diamonds*). **3** be scattered over or about (a surface). [OE *studu, stuthu* post, prop, rel. to G *stützen* to prop]

stud² n. **1 a** a number of horses kept for breeding etc. **b** a place where these are kept. **2** (in full **stud-horse**) a stallion. **3** colloq. a young man (esp. one noted for sexual prowess). **4** (in full **stud poker**) a form of poker with betting after the dealing of successive rounds of cards face up. □ **at stud** (of a male horse) publicly available for breeding on payment of a fee. **stud-book** a book containing the pedigrees of horses. **stud-farm** a place where horses are bred. [OE *stōd* f. Gmc: rel. to STAND]

student /ˈstjuːd(ə)nt/ n. **1** a person who is studying, esp. at university or another place of higher education. **2** (*attrib.*) studying in order to become (*a student nurse*). **3** a person of studious habits. [ME f. L *studēre* f. *studium* STUDY]

studio /ˈstjuːdɪəʊ/ n. (pl. **-os**) **1** the workroom of a painter or photographer etc. **2** a place where cinema films or recordings are made or where television or radio programmes are made or produced. □ **studio couch** a couch that can be converted into a bed. **studio flat** a flat containing a room suitable as an artist's studio, or only one main room. [It. f. L (as STUDY)]

studious /ˈstjuːdɪəs/ adj. **1** devoted to or assiduous in study or reading. **2** studied, deliberate, painstaking (*with studious care*). **3** (foll. by *to* + infin. or *in* + verbal noun) showing care or

attention. □ **studiously** adv. **studiousness** n. [ME f. L *studiosus* (as STUDY)]

study /ˈstʌdɪ/ n. & v. —n. (pl. **-ies**) **1** the devotion of time and attention to acquiring information or knowledge, esp. from books. **2** (in *pl.*) the pursuit of academic knowledge (*continued their studies abroad*). **3** a room used for reading, writing, etc. **4** a piece of work, esp. a drawing, done for practice or as an experiment (*a study of a head*). **5** the portrayal in literature or another art form of an aspect of behaviour or character etc. **6** a musical composition designed to develop a player's skill. **7** a thing worth observing closely (*your face was a study*). **8** a thing that is or deserves to be investigated. —v. (**-ies, -ied**) **1** tr. make a study of; investigate or examine (a subject) (*study law*). **2** intr. (often foll. by *for*) apply oneself to study. **3** tr. scrutinize or earnestly contemplate (a visible object) (*studied their faces*). **4** tr. (as **studied** adj.) deliberate, intentional, affected (*with studied politeness*). **5** tr. read (a book) attentively. □ **make a study of** investigate carefully. **study group** a group of people meeting from time to time to study a particular subject or topic. □ **studiedly** adv. **studiedness** n. [ME f. OF *estudie* f. L *studium* zeal, study]

stuff n. & v. —n. **1** the material that a thing is made of; material that may be used for some purpose. **2** a substance or things or belongings of an indeterminate kind or a quality not needing to be specified (*there's a lot of stuff about it in the newspapers*). **3** a particular knowledge or activity (*know one's stuff*). **4** woollen fabric (esp. as distinct from silk, cotton, and linen). **5** valueless matter, trash, refuse, nonsense (*take that stuff away*). **6** (prec. by *the*) **a** colloq. use an available supply of something, esp. drink or drugs. **b** sl. money. —v. **1** tr. pack (a receptacle) tightly (*stuff a cushion with feathers*; *a head stuffed with weird notions*). **2** tr. (foll. by *in, into*) force or cram (a thing) (*stuffed the socks in the drawer*). **3** tr. fill out the skin of (an animal or bird etc.) with material to restore the original shape (*a stuffed owl*). **4** tr. fill (poultry etc.) with a savoury or sweet mixture, esp. before cooking. **5 a** tr. & refl. fill (a person or oneself) with food. **b** tr. & intr. eat greedily. **6** tr. push, esp. hastily or clumsily (*stuffed the note behind the cushion*). **7** tr. (usu. in *passive*; foll. by *up*) block up (a person's nose etc.). **8** tr. sl. (esp. as an expression of contemptuous dismissal) dispose of as unwanted (*you can stuff the job*). □ **do one's stuff** colloq. do what one has to. **get stuffed** sl. an exclamation of dismissal, contempt, etc. **stuff and nonsense** an exclamation of incredulity or ridicule. **stuffed shirt** colloq. a pompous person. **stuff it** sl. an expression of rejection or disdain. **that's the stuff** colloq. that is what is wanted. □ **stuffer** n. (also in *comb.*). [ME *stoffe* f. OF *estoffe* (n.), *estoffer* (v.) equip, furnish f. Gk *stuphō* draw together]

stuffing /ˈstʌfɪŋ/ n. **1** padding used to stuff cushions etc. **2** a mixture used to stuff poultry etc., esp. before cooking. □ **knock** (or **take**) **the stuffing out of** colloq. make feeble or weak; defeat.

stuffy /ˈstʌfɪ/ adj. (**stuffier, stuffiest**) **1** (of a room or the atmosphere in it) lacking fresh air or ventilation; close. **2** dull or uninteresting. **3** (of a person's nose etc.) stuffed up. **4** (of a person) dull and conventional. □ **stuffily** adv. **stuffiness** n.

stultify /ˈstʌltɪˌfaɪ/ v.tr. (**-ies, -ied**) **1** make ineffective, useless, or futile, esp. as a result of tedious routine (*stultifying boredom*). **2** cause to appear foolish or absurd. **3** negate or neutralize. □ **stultification** /-fɪˈkeɪʃ(ə)n/ n. **stultifier** n. [LL *stultificare* f. L *stultus* foolish]

stumble /ˈstʌmb(ə)l/ v. & n. —v. **1** intr. lurch forward or have a partial fall from catching or striking or misplacing one's foot. **2** intr. (often foll. by *along*) walk with repeated stumbles. **3** intr. make a mistake or repeated mistakes in speaking etc. **4** intr. (foll. by *on, upon, across*) find or encounter by chance (*stumbled on a disused well*). —n. an act of stumbling. □ **stumbling-block** an obstacle or circumstance causing difficulty or hesitation. □ **stumbler** n. **stumblingly** adv. [ME *stumble* (with intrusive *b*) corresp. to Norw. *stumla*: rel. to STAMMER]

stumblebum /ˈstʌmb(ə)l,bʌm/ n. US colloq. a clumsy or inept person.

stump n. & v. —n. **1** the projecting remnant of a cut or fallen tree. **2** the similar remnant of anything else (e.g. a branch or limb) cut off or worn down. **3** *Cricket* each of the three uprights of a wicket. **4** (in pl.) *joc.* the legs. **5** the stump of a tree, or other place, used by an orator to address a meeting. —v. **1** tr. (of a question etc.) be too hard for; puzzle. **2** tr. (as **stumped** adj.) at a loss; baffled. **3** tr. *Cricket* (esp. of a wicket-keeper) put (a batsman) out by touching the stumps with the ball while the batsman is out of the crease. **4** intr. walk stiffly or noisily as on a wooden leg. **5** tr. (also absol.) US traverse (a district) making political speeches. □ **on the stump** colloq. engaged in political speech-making or agitation. **stump up** Brit. colloq. pay or produce (the money required). **up a stump** US in difficulties. □ **stumper** n. [ME *stompe* f. MDu. *stomp*, OHG *stumpf*]

stumpy /ˈstʌmpɪ/ adj. (**stumpier, stumpiest**) short and thick. □ **stumpily** adv. **stumpiness** n.

stun v.tr. (**stunned, stunning**) **1** knock senseless; stupefy. **2** bewilder or shock. **3** (of a sound) deafen temporarily. [ME f. OF *estoner* ASTONISH]

stung past and past part. of STING.

stunk past and past part. of STINK.

stunner /ˈstʌnə(r)/ n. colloq. a stunning person or thing.

stunning /ˈstʌnɪŋ/ adj. colloq. extremely impressive or attractive. □ **stunningly** adv.

stunt[1] v.tr. **1** retard the growth or development of. **2** dwarf, cramp. □ **stuntedness** n. [*stunt* foolish (now dial.), MHG *stunz*, ON *stuttr* short f. Gmc, perh. rel. to STUMP]

stunt[2] n. & v. —n. **1** something unusual done to attract attention. **2** a trick or daring manoeuvre. **3** a display of concentrated energy. —v.intr. perform stunts, esp. aerobatics. □ **stunt man** a man employed to take an actor's place in performing dangerous stunts. [orig. unkn.: first used in 19th-c. US college athletics]

stupefy /ˈstjuːpɪˌfaɪ/ v.tr. (**-ies, -ied**) **1** make stupid or insensible (*stupefied with drink*). **2** stun with astonishment (*the news was stupefying*). □ **stupefacient** /-ˈfeɪʃ(ə)nt/ adj. & n. **stupefaction** /-ˈfækʃ(ə)n/ n. **stupefactive** adj. **stupefier** n. **stupefying** adj. **stupefyingly** adv. [F *stupéfier* f. L *stupefacere* f. *stupēre* be amazed]

stupendous /stjuːˈpendəs/ adj. amazing or prodigious, esp. in terms of size or degree (a *stupendous achievement*). □ **stupendously** adv. **stupendousness** n. [L *stupendus* gerundive of *stupēre* be amazed at]

stupid /ˈstjuːpɪd/ adj. (**stupider, stupidest**) adj. & n. —adj. **1** unintelligent, slow-witted, foolish (a *stupid fellow*). **2** typical of stupid persons (*put it in a stupid place*). **3** uninteresting or boring. **4** in a state of stupor or lethargy. **5** obtuse; lacking in sensibility. —n. colloq. a stupid person. □ **stupidity** /-ˈpɪdɪtɪ/ n. (pl. **-ies**). **stupidly** adv. [F *stupide* or L *stupidus* (as STUPENDOUS)]

stupor /ˈstjuːpə(r)/ n. a dazed, torpid, or helplessly amazed state. □ **stuporous** adj. [ME f. L (as STUPENDOUS)]

sturdy /ˈstɜːdɪ/ adj. (**sturdier, sturdiest**) **1** robust; strongly built. **2** vigorous and determined (*sturdy resistance*). □ **sturdily** adv. **sturdiness** n. [ME 'reckless, violent', f. OF *esturdi, estourdi* past part. of *estourdir* stun, daze ult. f. L *ex* EX-¹ + *turdus* thrush (taken as a type of drunkenness)]

sturgeon /ˈstɜːdʒ(ə)n/ n. any large mailed shark-like fish of the family Acipenseridae etc., used as food and a source of caviare and isinglass. [ME f. AF *sturgeon*, OF *esturgeon* ult. f. Gmc]

stutter /ˈstʌtə(r)/ v. & n. —v. **1** intr. stammer, esp. by involuntarily repeating the first consonants of words. **2** tr. (often foll. by *out*) utter (words) in this way. —n. **1** the act or habit of stuttering. **2** an instance of stuttering. □ **stutterer** n. **stutteringly** adv. [frequent. of ME (now dial.) *stut* f. Gmc]

sty[1] n. (pl. **sties**) **1** a pen or enclosure for pigs. **2** a filthy room or dwelling. **3** a place of debauchery. [OE *stī*, prob. = *stig* hall (cf. STEWARD), f. Gmc]

sty[2] n. (also **stye**) (pl. **sties** or **styes**) an inflamed swelling on the edge of an eyelid. [*styany* (now dial.) = *styan* eye f. OE *stīgend* sty, lit. 'riser' f. *stīgan* rise + EYE, shortened as if = *sty on eye*]

Stygian /ˈstɪdʒɪən/ adj. **1** (in Greek mythology) of or relating to the Styx, a river in Hades. **2** literary dark, gloomy, indistinct. [L *stugius* f. Gk *stugios* f. *Stux -ugos* Styx f. *stugnos* hateful, gloomy]

style n. & v. —n. **1** a kind or sort, esp. in regard to appearance and form (*an elegant style of house*). **2** a manner of writing or speaking or performing (*written in a florid style*; *started off in fine style*). **3** the distinctive manner of a person or school or period, esp. in relation to painting, architecture, furniture, dress, etc. **4** the correct way of designating a person or thing. **5** a superior quality or manner (*do it in style*). **6** a particular make, shape, or pattern (*in all sizes and styles*). **7** *Bot.* the narrow extension of the ovary supporting the stigma. **8** (in comb.) = -WISE. —v.tr. **1** design or make etc. in a particular (esp. fashionable) style. **2** designate in a specified way. □ **styleless** adj. **stylelessness** n. **styler** n. [ME f. OF *stile, style* f. L *stilus*: spelling *style* due to assoc. with Gk *stulos* column]

styli pl. of STYLUS.

stylish /ˈstaɪlɪʃ/ adj. **1** fashionable; elegant. **2** having a superior quality, manner, etc. □ **stylishly** adv. **stylishness** n.

stylist /ˈstaɪlɪst/ n. **1 a** a designer of fashionable styles etc. **b** a hairdresser. **2 a** a writer noted for or aspiring to good literary style. **b** (in sport or music) a person who performs with style.

stylistic /staɪˈlɪstɪk/ *adj.* of or concerning esp. literary style. □ **stylistically** *adv.* [STYLIST + -IC, after G *stilistisch*]

stylistics /staɪˈlɪstɪks/ *n.* the study of literary style.

stylize /ˈstaɪlaɪz/ *v.tr.* (also **-ise**) (esp. as **stylized** *adj.*) paint, draw, etc. (a subject) in a conventional non-realistic style. □ **stylization** /-ˈzeɪʃ(ə)n/ *n.* [STYLE + -IZE, after G *stilisieren*]

stylus /ˈstaɪləs/ *n.* (*pl.* **-li** /-laɪ/ or **-luses**) **1** a hard, esp. diamond or sapphire, point following a groove in a gramophone record and transmitting the recorded sound for reproduction. **2** a similar point producing such a groove when recording sound. [erron. spelling of L *stilus*: cf. STYLE]

stymie /ˈstaɪmɪ/ *n.* & *v.* (also **stimy**) —*n.* (*pl.* **-ies**) **1** *Golf* a situation where an opponent's ball lies between the player and the hole, forming a possible obstruction to play (*lay a stymie*). **2** a difficult situation. —*v.tr.* (**stymies, stymied, stymying** or **stymieing**) **1** obstruct; thwart. **2** *Golf* block (an opponent, his ball, or oneself) with a stymie. [19th c.: orig. unkn.]

styptic /ˈstɪptɪk/ *adj.* & *n.* —*adj.* (of a drug etc.) that checks bleeding. —*n.* a styptic drug or substance. [ME f. L *stypticus* f. Gk *stuptikos* f. *stuphō* contract]

styrene /ˈstaɪriːn/ *n. Chem.* a liquid hydrocarbon easily polymerized and used in making plastics etc. [Gk *sturax* a resin-yielding tree + -ENE]

suable /ˈsuːəb(ə)l, ˈsjuː-/ *adj.* capable of being sued. □ **suability** /-ˈbɪlɪtɪ/ *n.*

suasion /ˈsweɪʒ(ə)n/ *n. formal* persuasion as opposed to force (*moral suasion*). □ **suasive** /ˈsweɪsɪv/ *adj.* [ME f. OF *suasion* or L *suasio* f. *suadēre suas-* urge]

suave /swɑːv/ *adj.* (of a person, esp. a man) smooth; polite; sophisticated. □ **suavely** *adv.* **suaveness** *n.* **suavity** /-vɪtɪ/ *n.* (*pl.* **-ies**) [F *suave* or L *suavis* agreeable: cf. SWEET]

sub *n.* & *v. colloq.* —*n.* **1** a submarine. **2** a subscription. **3** a substitute. **4** a sub-editor. **5** *Brit.* an advance or loan against expected income. —*v.* (**subbed, subbing**) **1** *intr.* (usu. foll. by *for*) act as a substitute for a person. **2** *tr. Brit.* lend or advance (a sum) to (a person) against expected income. **3** *tr.* sub-edit. [abbr.]

sub- /sʌb, səb/ *prefix* (also **suc-** before *c*, **suf-** before *f*, **sug-** before *g*, **sup-** before *p*, **sur-** before *c, p, t*) **1** at or to or from a lower position (*subordinate; submerge; subtract; subsoil*). **2** secondary or inferior in rank or position (*subclass; subcommittee; sub-lieutenant; subtotal*). **3** somewhat, nearly; more or less (*subacid; subarctic; subaquatic*). **4** (forming verbs) denoting secondary action (*subdivide; sublet*). **5** denoting support (*subvention*). **6** *Chem.* (of a salt) basic (*subacetate*). [from or after L *sub-* f. *sub* under, close to, towards]

subacid /sʌbˈæsɪd/ *adj.* moderately acid or tart (*subacid fruit; a subacid remark*). □ **subacidity** /ˌsʌbəˈsɪdɪtɪ/ *n.* [L *subacidus* (as SUB-, ACID)]

subacute /ˌsʌbəˈkjuːt/ *adj. Med.* (of a condition) between acute and chronic.

subalpine /sʌbˈælpaɪn/ *adj.* of or situated in the higher slopes of mountains just below the timberline.

subaltern /ˈsʌbəlt(ə)n/ *n. Brit. Mil.* an officer below the rank of captain, esp. a second lieutenant. [LL *subalternus* f. *alternus* ALTERNATE *adj.*]

subantarctic /ˌsʌbæntˈɑːktɪk/ *adj.* of or like regions immediately north of the Antarctic Circle.

sub-aqua /sʌbˈækwə/ *adj.* of or concerning underwater swimming or diving.

subaquatic /ˌsʌbəˈkwætɪk/ *adj.* **1** of more or less aquatic habits or kind. **2** underwater.

subaqueous /sʌbˈeɪkwɪəs/ *adj.* existing, formed, or taking place under water.

subarctic /sʌbˈɑːktɪk/ *adj.* of or like regions immediately south of the Arctic Circle.

subatomic /ˌsʌbəˈtɒmɪk/ *adj.* occurring in or smaller than an atom.

sub-basement /ˈsʌbˌbeɪsmənt/ *n.* a storey below a basement.

sub-branch /ˈsʌbbrɑːntʃ/ *n.* a secondary or subordinate branch.

subcategory /ˈsʌbˌkætɪɡərɪ/ *n.* (*pl.* **-ies**) a secondary or subordinate category. □ **subcategorize** *v.tr.* (also **-ise**). **subcategorization** /-ˈzeɪʃ(ə)n/ *n.*

subclass /ˈsʌbklɑːs/ *n.* **1** a secondary or subordinate class. **2** *Biol.* a taxonomic category below a class.

sub-clause /ˈsʌbklɔːz/ *n.* **1** esp. *Law* a subsidiary section of a clause. **2** *Gram.* a subordinate clause.

subcommissioner /ˈsʌbkəˌmɪʃənə(r)/ *n.* a deputy commissioner.

subcommittee /ˈsʌbkəˌmɪtɪ/ *n.* a secondary committee.

subconscious /sʌbˈkɒnʃəs/ *adj.* & *n.* —*adj.* of or concerning the part of the mind which is not fully conscious but influences actions etc. —*n.* this part of the mind. □ **subconsciously** *adv.* **subconsciousness** *n.*

subcontinent /ˈsʌbˌkɒntɪnənt/ *n.* **1** a large land mass, smaller than a continent. **2** a large geographically or politically independent part of a continent. □ **subcontinental** /-ˈnent(ə)l/ *adj.*

subcontract *v.* & *suavis.* —*v.* /ˌsʌbkənˈtrækt/ **1** *tr.* employ a firm etc. to do (work) as part of a larger project. **2** *intr.* make or carry out a subcontract. —*n.* /sʌbˈkɒntrækt/ a secondary contract, esp. to supply materials, labour, etc. □ **subcontractor** /-ˈtræktə(r)/ *n.*

subculture /ˈsʌbˌkʌltʃə(r)/ *n.* a cultural group within a larger culture, often having beliefs or interests at variance with those of the larger culture. □ **subcultural** /-ˈkʌltʃər(ə)l/ *adj.*

subcutaneous /ˌsʌbkjuːˈteɪnɪəs/ *adj.* under the skin. □ **subcutaneously** *adv.*

subdean /sʌbˈdiːn/ *n.* an official ranking next below, or acting as a deputy for, a dean. □ **subdeanery** *n.* (*pl.* **-ies**). **subdecanal** /-dɪˈkeɪn(ə)l/ *adj.*

subdivide /ˈsʌbdɪˌvaɪd, -ˈvaɪd/ *v.tr.* & *intr.* divide again after a first division. [ME f. L *subdividere* (as SUB-, DIVIDE)]

subdivision /ˈsʌbdɪˌvɪʒ(ə)n, -ˈvɪʒ(ə)n/ *n.* **1** the act or an instance of subdividing. **2** a secondary or subordinate division. **3** *US & Austral.* an area of land divided into plots for sale.

subdue /səbˈdjuː/ *v.tr.* (**subdues, subdued, subduing**) **1** conquer, subjugate, or tame (an enemy, nature, one's emotions, etc.). **2** (as **subdued** *adj.*) softened; lacking in intensity; toned down (*subdued light; in a subdued mood*). □ **subduable**

adj. **subdual** *n.* [ME *sodewe* f. OF *so(u)duire* f. L *subducere* (as SUB-, *ducere* lead, bring) used with the sense of *subdere* conquer (as SUB-, *-dere* put)]

sub-editor /sʌbˈedɪtə(r)/ *n.* **1** an assistant editor. **2** *Brit.* a person who edits material for printing in a book, newspaper, etc. □ **sub-edit** *v.tr.* (**-edited, -editing**). **sub-editorial** /-ˈtɔːrɪəl/ *adj.*

subfamily /ˈsʌbˌfæmɪlɪ/ *n.* (*pl.* **-ies**) **1** *Biol.* a taxonomic category below a family. **2** any subdivision of a group.

subform /ˈsʌbfɔːm/ *n.* a subordinate or secondary form.

subgenus /sʌbˈdʒiːnəs/ *n.* (*pl.* **subgenera** /-ˈdʒenərə/) *Biol.* a taxonomic category below a genus. □ **subgeneric** /-dʒɪˈnerɪk/ *adj.*

subgroup /ˈsʌbgruːp/ *n. Math.* etc. a subset of a group.

subhead /ˈsʌbhed/ *n.* (also **subheading**) **1** a subordinate heading or title in a chapter, article, etc. **2** a subordinate division in a classification.

subhuman /sʌbˈhjuːmən/ *adj.* **1** (of an animal) closely related to man. **2** (of behaviour, intelligence, etc.) less than human.

subject *n., adj., adv.,* & *v.* —*n.* /ˈsʌbdʒɪkt/ **1 a** a matter, theme, etc. to be discussed, described, represented, dealt with, etc. **b** (foll. by *for*) a person, circumstance, etc., giving rise to specified feeling, action, etc. (*a subject for congratulation*). **2** a department or field of study (*his best subject is geography*). **3** *Gram.* a noun or its equivalent about which a sentence is predicated and with which the verb agrees. **4 a** any person except a monarch living under a monarchy or any other form of government (*the ruler and his subjects*). **b** any person owing obedience to another. **5** a person of specified mental or physical tendencies (*a hysterical subject*). —*adj.* /ˈsʌbdʒɪkt/ **1** (often foll. by *to*) owing obedience to a government, colonizing power, force, etc.; in subjection. **2** (foll. by *to*) liable, exposed, or prone to (*is subject to infection*). **3** (foll. by *to*) conditional upon; on the assumption of (*the arrangement is subject to your approval*). —*adv.* /ˈsʌbdʒɪkt/ (foll. by *to*) conditionally upon (*subject to your consent, I propose to try again*). —*v.tr.* /səbˈdʒekt/ **1** (foll. by *to*) make liable; expose; treat (*subjected us to hours of waiting*). **2** (usu. foll. by *to*) subdue (a nation, person, etc.) to one's sway etc. □ **on the subject of** concerning, about. **subject-matter** the matter treated of in a book, lawsuit, etc. □ **subjection** /səbˈdʒekʃ(ə)n/ *n.* **subjectless** /ˈsʌbdʒɪktlɪs/ *adj.* [ME *soget* etc. f. OF *suget* etc. f. L *subjectus* past part. of *subjicere* (as SUB-, *jacere* throw)]

subjective /səbˈdʒektɪv/ *adj.* **1** (of art, literature, written history, a person's views, etc.) proceeding from personal idiosyncrasy or individuality; not impartial or literal. **2** *Gram.* of or concerning the subject. □ **subjectively** *adv.* **subjectiveness** *n.* **subjectivity** /ˌsʌbdʒekˈtɪvɪtɪ/ *n.* [ME f. L *subjectivus* (as SUBJECT)]

subjoin /sʌbˈdʒɔɪn/ *v.tr.* add or append (an illustration, anecdote, etc.) at the end. [obs. F *subjoindre* f. L *subjungere* (as SUB-, *jungere junct-* join)]

sub judice /sʌb ˈdʒuːdɪsɪ, sʊb ˈjuːdɪˌkeɪ/ *Law* under judicial consideration and therefore prohibited from public discussion elsewhere. [L, = under a judge]

subjugate /ˈsʌbdʒʊˌgeɪt/ *v.tr.* bring into subjection; subdue; vanquish. □ **subjugable**

/-gəb(ə)l/ *adj.* **subjugation** /-ˈgeɪʃ(ə)n/ *n.* **subjugator** *n.* [ME f. LL *subjugare* bring under the yoke (as SUB-, *jugum* yoke)]

subjunctive /səbˈdʒʌŋktɪv/ *adj.* & *n. Gram.* —*adj.* (of a mood) denoting what is imagined or wished or possible (e.g. *if I were you, God help you, be that as it may*). —*n.* **1** the subjunctive mood. **2** a verb in this mood. □ **subjunctively** *adv.* [F *subjonctif -ive* or LL *subjunctivus* f. L (as SUBJOIN), transl. Gk *hupotaktikos*, as being used in subjoined clauses]

subkingdom /sʌbˈkɪŋdəm/ *n. Biol.* a taxonomic category below a kingdom.

sublease *n.* & *v.* —*n.* /ˈsʌbliːs/ a lease of a property by a tenant to a subtenant. —*v.tr.* /sʌbˈliːs/ lease (a property) to a subtenant.

sublessee /ˌsʌbleˈsiː/ *n.* a person who holds a sublease.

sublessor /ˌsʌbleˈsɔː(r)/ *n.* a person who grants a sublease.

sublet *n.* & *v.* —*n.* /ˈsʌblet/ = SUBLEASE *n.* —*v.tr.* /sʌbˈlet/ (**-letting;** past and past part. **-let**) = SUBLEASE *v.*

sub-lieutenant /ˌsʌblefˈtenənt/ *n. Brit.* an officer ranking next below lieutenant.

sublimate *v., adj.,* & *n.* —*v.tr.* /ˈsʌblɪˌmeɪt/ **1** divert the energy of (a primitive impulse, esp. sexual) into a culturally higher activity. **2** *Chem.* convert (a substance) from the solid state directly to its vapour by heat, and usu. allow it to solidify again. **3** refine; purify; idealize. —*adj.* /ˈsʌblɪmət/ **1** *Chem.* (of a substance) sublimated. **2** purified, refined. —*n.* /ˈsʌblɪmət/ *Chem.* a sublimated substance. □ **sublimation** /-ˈmeɪʃ(ə)n/ *n.* [L *sublimare sublimat-* SUBLIME *v.*]

sublime /səˈblaɪm/ *adj.* & *v.* —*adj.* (**sublimer, sublimest**) **1** of the most exalted, grand, or noble kind; awe-inspiring (*sublime genius*). **2** (of indifference, ignorance, etc.) arrogantly unruffled. —*v.* **1** *tr.* & *intr. Chem.* = SUBLIMATE *v.* **2. 2** *tr.* purify or elevate by or as if by sublimation; make sublime. **3** *intr.* become pure by or as if by sublimation. □ **sublimely** *adv.* **sublimity** /-ˈlɪmɪtɪ/ *n.* [L *sublimis* (as SUB-, second element perh. rel. to *limen* threshold, *limus* oblique)]

subliminal /səbˈlɪmɪn(ə)l/ *adj. Psychol.* (of a stimulus etc.) below the threshold of consciousness. □ **subliminal advertising** the use of subliminal images in advertising on television etc. to influence the viewer at an unconscious level. □ **subliminally** *adv.* [SUB- + L *limen -inis* threshold]

Sub-Lt. *abbr. Brit.* Sub-Lieutenant.

sublunary /sʌbˈluːnərɪ, -ˈljuːnərɪ/ *adj.* **1** beneath the moon. **2** *Astron.* **a** within the moon's orbit. **b** subject to the moon's influence. **3** of this world; earthly. [LL *sublunaris* (as SUB-, LUNAR)]

sub-machine-gun /ˌsʌbməˈʃiːnˌgʌn/ *n.* a hand-held lightweight machine-gun.

submarine /ˌsʌbməˈriːn, ˈsʌb-/ *n.* & *adj.* —*n.* a vessel, esp. a warship, capable of operating under water and usu. equipped with torpedoes, missiles, and a periscope. —*adj.* existing, occurring, done, or used under the surface of the sea (*submarine cable*). □ **submariner** /-ˈmærɪnə(r)/ *n.*

submerge /səbˈmɜːdʒ/ *v.* **1** *tr.* **a** place under water; flood; inundate. **b** flood or inundate with work, problems, etc. **2** *intr.* (of a submarine, its crew, a diver, etc.) dive below the surface of water. □ **submergence** *n.* **submergible** *adj.*

submersion /-ˈmɜːʃ(ə)n/ *n.* [L *submergere* (as SUB-, *mergere mers-* dip)]

submersible /səbˈmɜːsɪb(ə)l/ *n.* & *adj.* —*n.* a submarine operating under water for short periods. —*adj.* capable of being submerged. [*submerse* (v.) = SUBMERGE]

submicroscopic /sʌbˌmaɪkrəˈskɒpɪk/ *adj.* too small to be seen by an ordinary microscope.

subminiature /sʌbˈmɪnɪtʃə(r)/ *adj.* **1** of greatly reduced size. **2** (of a camera) very small and using 16-mm film.

submission /səbˈmɪʃ(ə)n/ *n.* **1 a** the act or an instance of submitting; the state of being submitted. **b** anything that is submitted. **2** humility, meekness, obedience, submissiveness (*showed great submission of spirit*). **3** *Law* a theory etc. submitted by counsel to a judge or jury. **4** (in wrestling) the surrender of a participant yielding to the pain of a hold. [ME f. OF *submission* or L *submissio* (as SUBMIT)]

submissive /səbˈmɪsɪv/ *adj.* **1** humble; obedient. **2** yielding to power or authority; willing to submit. □ **submissively** *adv.* **submissiveness** *n.* [SUBMISSION after *remissive* etc.]

submit /səbˈmɪt/ *v.* (**submitted**, **submitting**) **1** (usu. foll. by *to*) **a** *intr.* cease resistance; give way; yield (*had to submit to defeat; will never submit*). **b** *refl.* surrender (oneself) to the control of another etc. **2** *tr.* present for consideration or decision. **3** *tr.* (usu. foll. by *to*) subject (a person or thing) to an operation, process, treatment, etc. (*submitted it to the flames*). **4** *tr.* esp. *Law* urge or represent esp. deferentially (*that, I submit, is a misrepresentation*). □ **submitter** *n.* [ME f. L *submittere* (as SUB-, *mittere miss-* send)]

subnormal /sʌbˈnɔːm(ə)l/ *adj.* **1** (esp. as regards intelligence) below normal. **2** less than normal. □ **subnormality** /-ˈmælɪtɪ/ *n.*

suborder /ˈsʌbˌɔːdə(r)/ *n.* a taxonomic category between an order and a family. □ **subordinal** /-ˈɔːdɪn(ə)l/ *adj.*

subordinate *adj., n.,* & *v.* —*adj.* /səˈbɔːdɪnət/ (usu. foll. by *to*) of inferior importance or rank; secondary, subservient. —*n.* /səˈbɔːdɪnət/ a person working under another's control or orders. —*v.tr.* /səˈbɔːdɪˌneɪt/ (usu. foll. by *to*) **1** make subordinate; treat or regard as of minor importance. **2** make subservient. □ **subordinate clause** a clause serving as an adjective, adverb, or noun in a main sentence because of its position or a preceding conjunction. □ **subordinately** /səˈbɔːdɪnətlɪ/ *adv.* **subordination** /-ˈneɪʃ(ə)n/ *n.* **subordinative** /səˈbɔːdɪnətɪv/ *adj.* [med.L *subordinare, subordinat-* (as SUB-, L *ordinare* ordain)]

suborn /səˈbɔːn/ *v.tr.* induce by bribery etc. to commit perjury or any other unlawful act. □ **subornation** /ˌsʌbɔːˈneɪʃ(ə)n/ *n.* **suborner** *n.* [L *subornare* incite secretly (as SUB-, *ornare* equip)]

subphylum /ˈsʌbˈfaɪləm/ *n.* (*pl.* **subphyla** /-lə/) *Biol.* a taxonomic category below a phylum.

sub-plot /ˈsʌbplɒt/ *n.* a subordinate plot in a play etc.

subpoena /səbˈpiːnə, səˈpiːnə/ *n.* & *v.* —*n.* a writ ordering a person to attend a lawcourt. —*v.tr.* (*past* and *past part.* **subpoenaed** or **subpoena'd**) serve a subpoena on. [ME f. L *sub poena* under penalty (the first words of the writ)]

sub rosa /sʌb ˈrəʊzə/ *adj.* & *adv.* (of communication, consultation, etc.) in secrecy or

confidence. [L, lit. 'under the rose', as emblem of secrecy]

subroutine /ˈsʌbruːˌtiːn/ *n.* *Computing* a routine designed to perform a frequently used operation within a program.

subscribe /səbˈskraɪb/ *v.* **1** (usu. foll. by *to, for*) *tr.* & *intr.* contribute (a specified sum) or make or promise a contribution to a fund, project, charity, etc. esp. regularly. **2** *intr.* (usu. foll. by *to*) express one's agreement with an opinion, resolution, etc. (*cannot subscribe to that*). **3** *tr.* write (esp. one's name) at the foot of a document etc. (*subscribed a motto*). □ **subscribe to** arrange to receive (a periodical etc.) regularly. [ME f. L *subscribere* (as SUB-, *scribere script-* write)]

subscriber /səbˈskraɪbə(r)/ *n.* **1** a person who subscribes. **2** a person paying for the hire of a telephone line. □ **subscriber trunk dialling** *Brit.* the automatic connection of trunk calls by dialling without the assistance of an operator.

subscript /ˈsʌbskrɪpt/ *adj.* & *n.* —*adj.* written or printed below the line, esp. *Math.* (of a symbol) written below and to the right of another symbol. —*n.* a subscript number or symbol. [L *subscriptus* (as SUBSCRIBE)]

subscription /səbˈskrɪpʃ(ə)n/ *n.* **1 a** the act or an instance of subscribing. **b** money subscribed. **2** *Brit.* a fee for the membership of a society etc., esp. paid regularly. **3 a** an agreement to take and pay for usu. a specified number of issues of a newspaper, magazine, etc. **b** the money paid by this. **4** a signature on a document etc. □ **subscription concert** etc. each of a series of concerts etc. for which tickets are sold in advance. [ME f. L *subscriptio* (as SUBSCRIBE)]

subsection /ˈsʌbˌsekʃ(ə)n/ *n.* a division of a section.

subsequent /ˈsʌbsɪkwənt/ *adj.* (usu. foll. by *to*) following a specified event etc. in time, esp. as a consequence. □ **subsequently** *adv.* [ME f. OF *subsequent* or L *subsequi* (as SUB-, *sequi* follow)]

subserve /səbˈsɜːv/ *v.tr.* serve as a means in furthering (a purpose, action, etc.). [L *subservire* (as SUB-, SERVE)]

subservient /səbˈsɜːvɪənt/ *adj.* **1** cringing; obsequious. **2** (usu. foll. by *to*) serving as a means; instrumental. **3** (usu. foll. by *to*) subordinate. □ **subservience** *n.* **subserviency** *n.* **subserviently** *adv.* [L *subserviens subservient-* (as SUBSERVE)]

subset /ˈsʌbset/ *n.* **1** a secondary part of a set. **2** *Math.* a set all the elements of which are contained in another set.

subshrub /ˈsʌbʃrʌb/ *n.* a low-growing or small shrub.

subside /səbˈsaɪd/ *v.intr.* **1** cease from agitation; become tranquil; abate (*excitement subsided*). **2** (of water, suspended matter, etc.) sink. **3** (of the ground) cave in; sink. **4** (of a building, ship, etc.) sink lower in the ground or water. **5** (of a swelling etc.) become less. **6** usu. *joc.* (of a person) sink into a sitting, kneeling, or lying posture. □ **subsidence** /-ˈsaɪd(ə)ns, ˈsʌbsɪd(ə)ns/ *n.* [L *subsidere* (as SUB-, *sidere* settle rel. to *sedēre* sit)]

subsidiary /səbˈsɪdɪərɪ/ *adj.* & *n.* —*adj.* **1** serving to assist or supplement; auxiliary. **2** (of a company) controlled by another. —*n.* (*pl.* **-ies**) **1** a subsidiary thing or person; an accessory. **2** a subsidiary company. □ **subsidiarily** *adv.*

subsidiarity /-ˈærɪtɪ/ n. [L subsidiarius (as SUBSIDY)]

subsidize /ˈsʌbsɪˌdaɪz/ v.tr. (also **-ise**) **1** pay a subsidy to. **2** reduce the cost of by subsidy (subsidized lunches). □ **subsidization** /-ˈzeɪʃ(ə)n/ n. **subsidizer** n.

subsidy /ˈsʌbsɪdɪ/ n. (pl. **-ies**) **1** money granted by the State or a public body etc. to keep down the price of commodities etc. (housing subsidy). **2** money granted to a charity or other undertaking held to be in the public interest. **3** any grant or contribution of money. [ME f. AF subsidie, OF subside f. L subsidium assistance]

subsist /səbˈsɪst/ v. intr. **1** (often foll. by on) keep oneself alive; be kept alive (subsists on vegetables). **2** intr. remain in being; exist. **3** (foll. by in) be attributable to (its excellence subsists in its freshness). □ **subsistent** adj. [L subsistere stand firm (as SUB-, sistere set, stand)]

subsistence /səbˈsɪst(ə)ns/ n. **1** the state or an instance of subsisting. **2 a** the means of supporting life; a livelihood. **b** a minimal level of existence or the income providing this (a bare subsistence). □ **subsistence allowance** (or **money**) esp. Brit. an allowance or advance on pay granted esp. as travelling expenses. **subsistence farming** farming which directly supports the farmer's household without producing a significant surplus for trade. **subsistence level** (or **wage**) a standard of living (or wage) providing only the bare necessities of life.

subsoil /ˈsʌbsɔɪl/ n. soil lying immediately under the surface soil (opp. TOPSOIL).

subsonic /sʌbˈsɒnɪk/ adj. relating to speeds less than that of sound. □ **subsonically** adv.

subspecies /ˈsʌbˌspiːʃiːz, -ʃɪz/ n. (pl. same) Biol. a taxonomic category below a species, usu. a fairly permanent geographically isolated variety. □ **subspecific** /-spəˈsɪfɪk/ adj.

substance /ˈsʌbst(ə)ns/ n. **1 a** the essential material, esp. solid, forming a thing (the substance was transparent). **b** a particular kind of material having uniform properties (this substance is salt). **2 a** reality; solidity (ghosts have no substance). **b** seriousness or steadiness of character (there is no substance in him). **3** the theme or subject of esp. a work of art, argument, etc. (prefer the substance to the style). **4** the real meaning or essence of a thing. **5** wealth and possessions (a woman of substance). □ **in substance** generally; apart from details. [ME f. OF f. L substantia (as SUB-, stare stand)]

substandard /sʌbˈstændəd/ adj. **1** of less than the required or normal quality or size; inferior. **2** (of language) not conforming to standard usage.

substantial /səbˈstænʃ(ə)l/ adj. **1 a** of real importance or value (made a substantial contribution). **b** of large size or amount (awarded substantial damages). **2** of solid material or structure; stout (a man of substantial build; a substantial house). **3** commercially successful; wealthy. **4** essential; true in large part (substantial truth). **5** having substance; real. □ **substantiality** /-ʃɪˈælɪtɪ/ n. **substantially** adv. [ME f. OF substantiel or LL substantialis (as SUBSTANCE)]

substantiate /səbˈstænʃɪˌeɪt/ v.tr. prove the truth of (a charge, statement, claim, etc.); give good grounds for. □ **substantiation** /-ˈeɪʃ(ə)n/ n. [med.L substantiare give substance to (as SUBSTANCE)]

substantive /ˈsʌbstəntɪv/ adj. & n. —adj. /also səbˈstæntɪv/ **1** having separate and independent existence. **2** Gram. expressing existence. **3** Mil. (of a rank etc.) permanent, not acting or temporary. —n. Gram. = NOUN. □ **substantival** /-ˈtaɪv(ə)l/ adj. **substantively** adv. esp. Gram. [ME f. OF substantif -ive, or LL substantivus (as SUBSTANCE)]

substation /ˈsʌbˌsteɪʃ(ə)n/ n. a subordinate station, esp. one reducing the high voltage of electric power transmission to that suitable for supply to consumers.

substitute /ˈsʌbstɪˌtjuːt/ n. & v. —n. **1** (also attrib.) a person or thing acting or serving in place of another. **2** an artificial alternative to a natural substance (butter substitute). —v. **1** intr. & tr. (often foll. by for) act or cause to act as a substitute; put or serve in exchange (substituted for her mother; substituted it for the broken one). **2** tr. (usu. foll. by by, with) colloq. replace (a person or thing) with another. □ **substitutable** adj. **substitutability** /-ˈbɪlɪtɪ/ n. **substitution** /-ˈtjuːʃ(ə)n/ n. **substitutional** /-ˈtjuːʃən(ə)l/ adj. **substitutionary** /-ˈtjuːʃənərɪ/ adj. **substitutive** adj. [ME f. L substitutus past part. of substituere (as SUB-, statuere set up)]

substratum /ˈsʌbˌstrɑːtəm, -ˌstreɪtəm/ n. (pl. **substrata** /-tə/) **1** an underlying layer or substance. **2** a layer of rock or soil beneath the surface. **3** a foundation or basis (there is a substratum of truth in it). [mod.L, past part. of L substernere (as SUB-, sternere strew): cf. STRATUM]

substructure /ˈsʌbˌstrʌktʃə(r)/ n. an underlying or supporting structure. □ **substructural** adj.

subsume /səbˈsjuːm/ v.tr. (usu. foll. by under) include (an instance, idea, category, etc.) in a rule, class, category, etc. □ **subsumable** adj. **subsumption** /-ˈsʌmpʃ(ə)n/ n. [med.L subsumere (as SUB-, sumere sumpt- take)]

subtenant /ˈsʌbˌtenənt/ n. a person who leases a property from a tenant. □ **subtenancy** n.

subtend /sʌbˈtend/ v.tr. **1** (usu. foll. by at) (of a line, arc, figure, etc.) form (an angle) at a particular point when its extremities are joined at that point. **2** (of an angle or chord) have bounding lines or points that meet or coincide with those of (a line or arc). [L subtendere (as SUB-, tendere stretch)]

subterfuge /ˈsʌbtəˌfjuːdʒ/ n. **1 a** an attempt to avoid blame or defeat esp. by lying or deceit. **b** a statement etc. resorted to for such a purpose. **2** this as a practice or policy. [F subterfuge or LL subterfugium f. L subterfugere escape secretly f. subter beneath + fugere flee]

subterranean /ˌsʌbtəˈreɪnɪən/ adj. **1** existing, occurring, or done under the earth's surface. **2** secret, underground, concealed. □ **subterraneously** adv. [L subterraneus (as SUB-, terra earth)]

subtext /ˈsʌbtekst/ n. an underlying often distinct theme in a piece of writing.

subtitle /ˈsʌbˌtaɪt(ə)l/ n. & v. —n. **1** a secondary or additional title of a book etc. **2** a printed caption at the bottom of a film etc., esp. translating dialogue. —v.tr. provide with a subtitle or subtitles.

subtle /ˈsʌt(ə)l/ adj. (**subtler**, **subtlest**) **1** evasive or mysterious; hard to grasp (subtle charm; a subtle distinction). **2** (of scent, colour, etc.) faint, delicate, elusive (*subtle perfume*). **3 a** capable of making fine distinctions; perceptive; acute (*subtle intellect; subtle senses*). **b** ingenious; elaborate; clever (*a subtle device*). □ **subtleness** *n.* **subtly** *adv.* [ME f. OF *sotil* f. L *subtilis*]

subtlety /ˈsʌtəltɪ/ *n.* (*pl.* **-ies**) **1** something subtle. **2** a fine distinction; an instance of hairsplitting. [ME f. OF *s(o)utilté* f. L *subtilitas -tatis* (as SUBTLE)]

subtopia /sʌbˈtəʊpɪə/ *n. Brit. derog.* unsightly and sprawling suburban development. □ **subtopian** *adj.* [SUBURB, UTOPIA]

subtotal /ˈsʌbˌtəʊt(ə)l/ *n.* the total of one part of a group of figures to be added.

subtract /səbˈtrækt/ *v.tr.* (often foll. by *from*) deduct (a part, quantity, or number) from another. □ **subtraction** /-ˈtrækʃ(ə)n/ *n.* **subtractive** *adj.* [L *subtrahere subtract-* (as SUB-, *trahere* draw)]

subtropics /sʌbˈtrɒpɪks/ *n.pl.* the regions adjacent to or bordering on the tropics. □ **subtropical** *adj.*

suburb /ˈsʌbɜːb/ *n.* an outlying district of a city, esp. residential. [ME f. OF *suburbe* or L *suburbium* (as SUB-, *urbs urbis* city)]

suburban /səˈbɜːbən/ *adj.* **1** of or characteristic of suburbs. **2** *derog.* provincial, uncultured, or naïve. □ **suburbanite** *n.* **suburbanize** *v.tr.* (also **-ise**). **suburbanization** /-ˌzeɪʃ(ə)n/ *n.* [L *suburbanus* (as SUBURB)]

suburbia /səˈbɜːbɪə/ *n.* often *derog.* the suburbs, their inhabitants, and their way of life.

subvention /səbˈvenʃ(ə)n/ *n.* a grant of money from a government etc.; a subsidy. [ME f. OF f. LL *subventio -onis* f. L *subvenire subvent-* assist (as SUB-, *venire* come)]

subversive /səbˈvɜːsɪv/ *adj. & n.* —*adj.* (of a person, organization, activity, etc.) seeking to subvert (esp. a government). —*n.* a subversive person; a revolutionary. □ **subversion** /-ˈvɜːʃ(ə)n/ *n.* **subversively** *adv.* **subversiveness** *n.* [med.L *subversivus* (as SUBVERT)]

subvert /səbˈvɜːt/ *v.tr.* esp. *Polit.* overturn, overthrow, or upset (religion, government, the monarchy, morality, etc.). □ **subverter** *n.* [ME f. OF *subvertir* or L *subvertere* (as SUB-, *vertere vers-* turn)]

subway /ˈsʌbweɪ/ *n.* **1 a** a tunnel beneath a road etc. for pedestrians. **b** an underground passage for pipes, cables, etc. **2** esp. *US* an underground railway.

subzero /sʌbˈzɪərəʊ/ *adj.* (esp. of temperature) lower than zero.

succeed /səkˈsiːd/ *v.* **1** *intr.* **a** (often foll. by *in*) accomplish one's purpose; have success; prosper (*succeeded in his ambition*). **b** (of a plan etc.) be successful. **2 a** *tr.* follow in order; come next after (*night succeeded day*). **b** *intr.* (foll. by *to*) come next, be subsequent. **3** *intr.* (often foll. by *to*) come by an inheritance, office, title, or property (*succeeded to the throne*). **4** *tr.* take over an office, property, inheritance, etc. from (*succeeded his father; succeeded the manager*). □ **succeeder** *n.* [ME f. OF *succeder* or L *succedere* (as SUB-, *cedere cess-* go)]

success /səkˈses/ *n.* **1** the accomplishment of an aim; a favourable outcome (*their efforts met with success*). **2** the attainment of wealth, fame, or position (*spoilt by success*). **3** a thing or person that turns out well. [L *successus* (as SUCCEED)]

successful /səkˈsesfʊl/ *adj.* having success; prosperous. □ **successfully** *adv.* **successfulness** *n.*

succession /səkˈseʃ(ə)n/ *n.* **1 a** the process of following in order; succeeding. **b** a series of things or people in succession. **2 a** the right of succeeding to the throne, an office, inheritance, etc. **b** the act or process of so succeeding. **c** those having such a right. **3** *Biol.* the order of development of a species or community. □ **in succession** one after another, without intervention. **in succession to** as the successor of. □ **successional** *adj.* [ME f. OF *succession* or L *successio* (as SUCCEED)]

successive /səkˈsesɪv/ *adj.* following one after another; running, consecutive. □ **successively** *adv.* **successiveness** *n.* [ME f. med.L *successivus* (as SUCCEED)]

successor /səkˈsesə(r)/ *n.* (often foll. by *to*) a person or thing that succeeds to another. [ME f. OF *successour* f. L *successor* (as SUCCEED)]

succinct /səkˈsɪŋkt/ *adj.* briefly expressed; terse, concise. □ **succinctly** *adv.* **succinctness** *n.* [ME f. L *succinctus* past part. of *succingere* tuck up (as SUB-, *cingere* gird)]

succotash /ˈsʌkəˌtæʃ/ *n. US* a dish of green maize and beans boiled together. [Narraganset *msiquatash*]

succour /ˈsʌkə(r)/ *n. & v.* (*US* **succor**) —*n.* aid; assistance, esp. in time of need. —*v.tr.* assist or aid (esp. a person in danger or distress). □ **succourless** *adj.* [ME f. OF *socours* f. med.L *succursus* f. L *succurrere* (as SUB-, *currere curs-* run)]

succulent /ˈsʌkjʊlənt/ *adj. & n.* —*adj.* **1** juicy; palatable. **2** *colloq.* desirable. **3** *Bot.* (of a plant, its leaves, or stems) thick and fleshy. —*n. Bot.* a succulent plant, esp. a cactus. □ **succulence** *n.* **succulently** *adv.* [L *succulentus* f. *succus* juice]

succumb /səˈkʌm/ *v.intr.* (usu. foll. by *to*) **1** be forced to give way; be overcome (*succumbed to temptation*). **2** be overcome by death (*succumbed to his injuries*). [ME f. OF *succomber* or L *succumbere* (as SUB-, *cumbere* lie)]

such /sʌtʃ/ *adj. & pron.* —*adj.* **1** (often foll. by *as*) of the kind or degree in question or under consideration (*such a person; such people; people such as these*). **2** (usu. foll. by *as to* + infin. or *that* + clause) so great; in such high degree (*not such a fool as to believe them; had such a fright that he fainted*). **3** of a more than normal kind or degree (*we had such an enjoyable evening; such horrid language*). **4** of the kind or degree already indicated, or implied by the context (*there are no such things; such is life*). —*pron.* **1** the thing or action in question or referred to (*such were his words; such was not my intention*). **2 a** *Commerce* or *colloq.* the aforesaid thing or things; it, they, or them (*those without tickets should purchase such*). **b** similar things; suchlike (*brought sandwiches and such*). □ **as such** as being what has been indicated or named (*a stranger is welcomed as such; there is no theatre as such*). **such-and-such** —*adj.* of a particular kind but not needing to be specified. —*n.* a person or thing of this kind. **such-and-such a person** someone; so-and-so. **such as 1** of a kind that; like (*a person such as we all admire*). **2** for example (*insects, such as moths and bees*). **3** those who (*such as don't need help*). **such as it is** despite its shortcomings (*you are welcome to it, such as it is*). **such a one** (usu. foll. by *as*) such a person or such a thing. [OE *swilc, swylc* f. Gmc: cf. LIKE¹]

suchlike /ˈsʌtʃlaɪk/ *adj. & n. colloq.* —*adj.* of such a kind. —*n.* things, people, etc. of such a kind.

suck *v.* & *n.* —*v.* **1** *tr.* draw (a fluid) into the mouth by making a partial vacuum. **2** *tr.* (also *absol.*) **a** draw milk or other fluid from or through (the breast etc. or a container). **b** extract juice from (a fruit) by sucking. **3** *tr.* **a** draw sustenance, knowledge, or advantage from (a book etc.). **b** imbibe or gain (knowledge, advantage, etc.) as if by sucking. **4** *tr.* roll the tongue round (a sweet, teeth, one's thumb, etc.). **5** *intr.* make a sucking action or sound (*sucking at his pipe*). —*n.* **1** the act or an instance of sucking, esp. the breast. **2** (in *pl.*; esp. as *int.*) *colloq.* **a** an expression of disappointment. **b** an expression of derision or amusement at another's discomfiture. □ **give suck** *archaic* (of a mother, dam, etc.). suckle. **suck dry 1** exhaust the contents of (a bottle, the breast, etc.) by sucking. **2** exhaust (a person's sympathy, resources, etc.) as if by sucking. **suck in 1** absorb. **2** involve (a person) in an activity etc. esp. against his or her will. **suck up 1** (often foll. by *to*) *colloq.* behave obsequiously esp. for one's own advantage. **2** absorb. [OE *sūcan*, = L *sugere*]

sucker /ˈsʌkə(r)/ *n.* & *v.* —*n.* **1 a** a person or thing that sucks. **b** a sucking-pig, newborn whale, etc. **2** *sl.* **a** a gullible or easily deceived person. **b** (foll. by *for*) a person especially susceptible to. **3 a** a rubber cup etc. that adheres to a surface by suction. **b** an organ enabling an organism to cling to a surface by suction. **4** *Bot.* a shoot springing from the rooted part of a stem, from the root at a distance from the main stem, from an axil, or occasionally from a branch. **5** *US colloq.* a lollipop. —*v.* *Bot.* **1** *tr.* remove suckers from. **2** *intr.* produce suckers.

sucking /ˈsʌkɪŋ/ *adj.* (of a child, animal, etc.) not yet weaned.

suckle /ˈsʌk(ə)l/ *v.* **1** *tr.* **a** feed (young) from the breast or udder. **b** nourish (*suckled his talent*). **2** *intr.* feed by sucking the breast etc. □ **suckler** *n.* [ME, prob. back-form. f. SUCKLING]

suckling /ˈsʌklɪŋ/ *n.* an unweaned child or animal.

sucrose /ˈsuːkrəʊz, ˈsjuː-/ *n.* *Chem.* sugar, a disaccharide obtained from sugar cane, sugar beet, etc. [F *sucre* SUGAR]

suction /ˈsʌkʃ(ə)n/ *n.* **1** the act or an instance of sucking. **2 a** the production of a partial vacuum by the removal of air etc. in order to force in liquid etc. or procure adhesion. **b** the force produced by this process (*suction keeps the lid on*). □ **suction-pump** a pump for drawing liquid through a pipe into a chamber emptied by a piston. [LL *suctio* f. L *sugere suct-* SUCK]

sudden /ˈsʌd(ə)n/ *adj.* occurring or done unexpectedly or without warning; abrupt, hurried, hasty (*a sudden storm; a sudden departure*). □ **all of a sudden** unexpectedly; hurriedly; suddenly. **sudden death** *colloq.* a decision in a tied game etc. dependent on one move, card, toss of a coin, etc. **sudden infant death syndrome** *Med.* = *cot-death.* □ **suddenly** *adv.* **suddenness** /-dənnɪs/ *n.* [ME f. AF *sodein, sudein,* OF *soudain* f. LL *subitanus* f. L *subitaneus* f. *subitus* sudden]

sudorific /ˌsjuːdəˈrɪfɪk/ *adj.* & *n.* —*adj.* (of a drug) causing sweating. —*n.* a sudorific drug. [mod.L *sudorificus* f. L *sudor* sweat]

suds *n.* & *v.* —*n.pl.* **1** froth of soap and water. **2** *US colloq.* beer. —*v.* **1** *intr.* form suds. **2** *tr.* lather, cover, or wash in soapy water. □ **sudsy** *adj.* [orig. = fen waters etc., of uncert. orig.: cf.

MDu., MLG *sudde*, MDu. *sudse* marsh, bog, prob. rel. to SEETHE]

sue /suː, sjuː/ *v.* (**sues, sued, suing**) **1** *tr.* (also *absol.*) *Law* institute legal proceedings against (a person). **2** *intr.* (often foll. by *to, for*) *Law* make application to a lawcourt for redress. **3** *intr.* (often foll. by *to, for*) make entreaty to a person for a favour. □ **suer** *n.* [ME f. AF *suer, siwer,* etc. f. OF *siu-* etc. stem of *sivre* f. L *sequi* follow]

suede /sweɪd/ *n.* (often *attrib.*) **1** leather, esp. kidskin, with the flesh side rubbed to make a velvety nap. **2** (also **suede-cloth**) a woven fabric resembling suede. [F (*gants de*) *Suède* (gloves of) Sweden]

suet /ˈsuːɪt, ˈsjuːɪt/ *n.* the hard white fat on the kidneys or loins of oxen, sheep, etc., used to make dough etc. □ **suet pudding** a pudding of suet etc., usu. boiled or steamed. □ **suety** *adj.* [ME f. AF f. OF *seu* f. L *sebum* tallow]

suffer /ˈsʌfə(r)/ *v.* **1** *intr.* undergo pain, grief, damage, etc. (*suffers acutely; your reputation will suffer; suffers from neglect*). **2** *tr.* undergo, experience, or be subjected to (pain, loss, defeat, change, etc.) (*suffered banishment*). **3** *tr.* put up with; tolerate (*does not suffer fools gladly*). **4** *intr.* undergo martyrdom. **5** *intr.* (usu. foll. by *to* + infin.) *archaic* allow. □ **sufferable** *adj.* **sufferer** *n.* **suffering** *n.* [ME f. AF *suffrir, soeffrir,* OF *sof(f)rir* f. L *sufferre* (as SUB-, *ferre* bear)]

sufferance /ˈsʌfərəns/ *n.* tacit consent, abstinence from objection. □ **on sufferance** with toleration implied by lack of consent or objection. [ME f. AF, OF *suffraunce* f. LL *sufferentia* (as SUFFER)]

suffice /səˈfaɪs/ *v.* **1** *intr.* (often foll. by *for,* or *to* + infin.) be enough or adequate (*that will suffice for our purpose; suffices to prove it*). **2** *tr.* meet the needs of; satisfy (*six sufficed him*). □ **suffice it to say** I shall content myself with saying. [ME f. OF *suffire* (*suffis-*) f. L *sufficere* (as SUB-, *facere* make)]

sufficiency /səˈfɪʃənsɪ/ *n.* (*pl.* **-ies**) (often foll. by *of*) an adequate amount or adequate resources. [LL *sufficientia* (as SUFFICIENT)]

sufficient /səˈfɪʃ(ə)nt/ *adj.* **1** sufficing, adequate, enough (*is sufficient for a family; didn't have sufficient funds*). **2** = SELF-SUFFICIENT. □ **sufficiently** *adv.* [ME f. OF *sufficient* or L *sufficiens* (as SUFFICE)]

suffix /ˈsʌfɪks/ *n.* & *v.* —*n.* **1** a verbal element added at the end of a word to form a derivative (e.g. *-ation, -fy, -ing, -itis*). **2** *Math.* = SUBSCRIPT. —*v.tr.* /also səˈfɪks/ append, esp. as a suffix. □ **suffixation** /-ˈseɪʃ(ə)n/ *n.* [*suffixum, suffixus* past part. of L *suffigere* (as SUB-, *figere fix-* fasten)]

suffocate /ˈsʌfəˌkeɪt/ *v.* **1** *tr.* choke or kill by stopping breathing, esp. by pressure, fumes, etc. **2** *tr.* (often foll. by *by, with*) produce a choking or breathless sensation in, esp. by excitement, terror, etc. **3** *intr.* be or feel suffocated or breathless. □ **suffocating** *adj.* **suffocatingly** *adv.* **suffocation** /-ˈkeɪʃ(ə)n/ *n.* [L *suffocare* (as SUB-, *fauces* throat)]

suffragan /ˈsʌfrəgən/ *n.* (in full **suffragan bishop** or **bishop suffragan**) **1** a bishop appointed to help a diocesan bishop in the administration of a diocese. **2** a bishop in relation to his archbishop or metropolitan. □ **suffraganship** *n.* [ME f. AF & OF, repr. med.L *suffraganeus* assistant (bishop) f. L *suffragium* (see

SUFFRAGE): orig. of a bishop summoned to vote in synod]

suffrage /ˈsʌfrɪdʒ/ *n.* the right of voting in political elections (*full adult suffrage*). [ME f. L *suffragium*, partly through F *suffrage*]

suffragette /ˌsʌfrəˈdʒet/ *n. hist.* a woman seeking the right to vote through organized protest. [SUFFRAGE + -ETTE]

suffragist /ˈsʌfrədʒɪst/ *n.* esp. *hist.* a person who advocates the extension of the suffrage, esp. to women. □ **suffragism** *n.*

suffuse /səˈfjuːz/ *v.tr.* **1** (of colour, moisture, etc.) spread from within to colour or moisten (*a blush suffused her cheeks*). **2** cover with colour etc. □ **suffusion** /-ˈfjuːʒ(ə)n/ *n.* [L *suffundere suffus-* (as SUB-, *fundere* pour)]

Sufi /ˈsuːfɪ/ *n.* (*pl.* **Sufis**) a Muslim ascetic and mystic. □ **Sufic** *adj.* **Sufism** *n.* [Arab. *ṣūfī*, perh. f. *ṣūf* wool (from the woollen garment worn)]

sugar /ˈʃʊɡə(r)/ *n. & v.* —*n.* **1** a sweet crystalline substance obtained from various plants, esp. the sugar cane and sugar beet, used in cookery, confectionery, brewing, etc.; sucrose. **2** *Chem.* any of a group of soluble usu. sweet-tasting crystalline carbohydrates found esp. in plants, e.g. glucose. **3** esp. *US colloq.* darling, dear (used as a term of address). **4** sweet words; flattery. **5** anything comparable to sugar encasing a pill in reconciling a person to what is unpalatable. —*v.tr.* **1** sweeten with sugar. **2** make (one's words, meaning, etc.) more pleasant or welcome. **3** coat with sugar (*sugared almond*). □ **sugar beet** a beet, *Beta vulgaris*, from which sugar is extracted. **sugar cane** *Bot.* any perennial tropical grass of the genus *Saccharum*, esp. *S. officinarum*, with tall stout jointed stems from which sugar is made. **sugar-coated 1** (of food) enclosed in sugar. **2** made superficially attractive. **sugar-daddy** (*pl.* **-ies**) *sl.* an elderly man who lavishes gifts on a young woman. **sugar-pea** a variety of pea eaten whole including the pod. **sugar soap** an alkaline compound for cleaning or removing paint. □ **sugarless** *adj.* [ME f. OF *çukre*, *sukere* f. It. *zucchero* prob. f. med.L *succarum* f. Arab. *sukkar*]

sugary /ˈʃʊɡərɪ/ *adj.* **1** containing or resembling sugar. **2** excessively sweet or esp. sentimental. **3** falsely sweet or pleasant (*sugary compliments*). □ **sugariness** *n.*

suggest /səˈdʒest/ *v.tr.* **1** (often foll. by *that* + clause) propose (a theory, plan, or hypothesis) (*suggested to them that they should wait*; *suggested a different plan*). **2 a** cause (an idea, memory, association, etc.) to present itself; evoke (*poem suggests peace*). **b** hint at (*his behaviour suggests guilt*). □ **suggest itself** (of an idea etc.) come into the mind. □ **suggester** *n.* [L *suggerere suggest-* (as SUB-, *gerere* bring)]

suggestible /səˈdʒestɪb(ə)l/ *adj.* **1** capable of being suggested. **2** open to suggestion; easily swayed. □ **suggestibility** /-ˈbɪlɪtɪ/ *n.*

suggestion /səˈdʒestʃ(ə)n/ *n.* **1** the act or an instance of suggesting; the state of being suggested. **2** a theory, plan, etc., suggested (*made a helpful suggestion*). **3** a slight trace; a hint (*a suggestion of garlic*). **4** *Psychol.* **a** the insinuation of a belief etc. into the mind. **b** such a belief etc. [ME f. OF f. L *suggestio -onis* (as SUGGEST)]

suggestive /səˈdʒestɪv/ *adj.* **1** (usu. foll. by *of*) conveying a suggestion; evocative. **2** (esp. of a remark, joke, etc.) indecent; improper. □ **suggestively** *adv.* **suggestiveness** *n.*

suicidal /ˌsuːɪˈsaɪd(ə)l, ˌsjuː-/ *adj.* **1** inclined to commit suicide. **2** of or concerning suicide. **3** self-destructive; fatally or disastrously rash. □ **suicidally** *adv.*

suicide /ˈsuːɪˌsaɪd, ˈsjuː-/ *n. & v.* —*n.* **1 a** the intentional killing of oneself. **b** a person who commits suicide. **2** a self-destructive action or course (*political suicide*). —*v.intr.* commit suicide. □ **suicide pact** an agreement between two or more people to commit suicide together. [mod.L *suicida*, *suicidium* f. L *sui* of oneself]

sui generis /ˌsjuːaɪ ˈdʒenərɪs, ˌsuːɪ ˈgen-/ *adj.* of its own kind; unique. [L: of one's own]

suit /suːt, sjuːt/ *n. & v.* —*n.* **1 a** a set of outer clothes of matching material for men, consisting usu. of a jacket, trousers, and sometimes a waistcoat. **b** a similar set of clothes for women usu. having a skirt instead of trousers. **c** (esp. in *comb.*) a set of clothes for a special occasion, occupation, etc. (*play-suit; swimsuit*). **2** any of the four sets (spades, hearts, diamonds, clubs) into which a pack of cards is divided. **3** (in full **suit at law**) a lawsuit (*criminal suit*). **4 a** a petition esp. to a person in authority. **b** the process of courting a woman (*paid suit to her*). **5** (usu. foll. by *of*) a set of sails, armour, etc. —*v.* **1** *tr.* go well with (a person's figure, features, character, etc.); become. **2** *tr.* (also *absol.*) meet the demands or requirements of; satisfy; agree with (*does not suit all tastes; that date will suit*). **3** *tr.* make fitting or appropriate; accommodate; adapt (*suited his style to his audience*). **4** *tr.* (as **suited** *adj.*) appropriate; well-fitted (*not suited to be an engineer*). **5** *intr.* (usu. foll. by *with*) go well with the appearance etc. of a person. □ **suit oneself 1** do as one chooses. **2** find something that satisfies one. [ME f. AF *siute*, OF *si(e)ute* f. fem. past part. of Rmc *sequere* (unrecorded) follow: see SUE]

suitable /ˈsuːtəb(ə)l, ˈsjuː-/ *adj.* (usu. foll. by *to, for*) well fitted for the purpose; appropriate. □ **suitability** /-ˈbɪlɪtɪ/ *n.* **suitableness** *n.* **suitably** *adv.* [SUIT + -ABLE, after *agreeable*]

suitcase /ˈsuːtkeɪs, ˈsjuː-/ *n.* a usu. oblong case for carrying clothes etc., having a handle and a flat hinged lid. □ **suitcaseful** *n.* (*pl.* **-fuls**).

suite /swiːt/ *n.* **1** a set of things belonging together, esp.: **a** a set of rooms in a hotel etc. **b** a sofa, armchairs, etc., of the same design. **2** *Mus.* **a** a set of instrumental compositions, orig. in dance style, to be played in succession. **b** a set of selected pieces from an opera, musical, etc., arranged to be played as one instrumental work. **3** a set of people in attendance; a retinue. [F (as SUIT)]

suiting /ˈsuːtɪŋ, ˈsjuː-/ *n.* cloth used for making suits.

suitor /ˈsuːtə(r), ˈsjuː-/ *n.* **1** a man seeking to marry a specified woman; a wooer. **2** a plaintiff or petitioner in a lawsuit. [ME f. AF *seutor*, *suitour*, etc., f. L *secutor -oris* f. *sequi secut-* follow]

suk (also **sukh**) var. of SOUK.

sukiyaki /ˌsʊkɪˈjɑːkɪ/ *n.* a Japanese dish of sliced meat simmered with vegetables and sauce. [Jap.]

sulk *v. & n.* —*v.intr.* indulge in a sulk, be sulky. —*n.* (also in *pl.*, prec. by *the*) a period of sullen esp. resentful silence (*having a sulk; got the sulks*). □ **sulker** *n.* [perh. back-form. f. SULKY]

sulky /ˈsʌlkɪ/ adj. & n. —adj. (**sulkier, sulkiest**) 1 sullen, morose, or silent, esp. from resentment or ill temper. 2 sluggish. —n. (pl. **-ies**) a light two-wheeled horse-drawn vehicle for one, esp. used in trotting-races. □ **sulkily** adv. **sulkiness** n. [perh. f. obs. *sulke* hard to dispose of]

sullen /ˈsʌlən/ adj. 1 morose, resentful, sulky, unforgiving, unsociable. 2 a (of a thing) slow-moving. b dismal, melancholy (*a sullen sky*). □ **sullenly** adv. **sullenness** /-ənnɪs/ n. [16th-c. alt. of ME *solein* f. AF f. *sol* SOLE³]

sully /ˈsʌlɪ/ v.tr. (**-ies, -ied**) 1 disgrace or tarnish (a person's reputation or character, a victory, etc.). 2 poet. dirty; soil. [perh. f. F *souiller* (as SOIL²)]

sulpha /ˈsʌlfə/ n. (US **sulfa**) any drug derived from sulphanilamide (often attrib.: *sulpha drug*). [abbr.]

sulphamic acid /sʌlˈfæmɪk/ n. (US **sulfamic**) a strong acid used in weed-killer, an amide of sulphuric acid. □ **sulphamate** /ˈsʌlfəˌmeɪt/ n. [SULPHUR + AMIDE]

sulphanilamide /ˌsʌlfəˈnɪləˌmaɪd/ n. (US **sulfanilamide**) a colourless sulphonamide drug with anti-bacterial properties. [*sulphanilic* (SULPHUR, ANILINE) + AMIDE]

sulphate /ˈsʌlfeɪt/ n. (US **sulfate**) a salt or ester of sulphuric acid. [F *sulfate* f. L *sulphur*]

sulphide /ˈsʌlfaɪd/ n. (US **sulfide**) Chem. a binary compound of sulphur.

sulphite /ˈsʌlfaɪt/ n. (US **sulfite**) Chem. a salt or ester of sulphurous acid. [F *sulfite* alt. of *sulfate* SULPHATE]

sulphonamide /sʌlˈfɒnəˌmaɪd/ n. (US **sulfonamide**) an organic substance able to prevent the multiplication of some pathogenic bacteria. [G *Sulfon* (as SULPHUR) + AMIDE]

sulphur /ˈsʌlfə(r)/ n. & v. (US **sulfur**) —n. 1 a a pale-yellow non-metallic element burning with a blue flame and a suffocating smell, used in making gunpowder, matches, and sulphuric acid. b (attrib.) like or containing sulphur. 2 the material of which hell-fire and lightning were believed to consist. 3 any yellow butterfly of the family Pieridae. 4 a pale greenish yellow colour. —v.tr. 1 treat with sulphur. 2 fumigate with sulphur. □ **sulphur dioxide** a colourless pungent gas formed by burning sulphur in air and used as a food preservative. **sulphur spring** a spring impregnated with sulphur or its compounds. □ **sulphury** adj. [ME f. AF *sulf(e)re*, OF *soufre* f. L *sulfur*, *sulp(h)ur*]

sulphureous /sʌlˈfjʊərɪəs/ adj. (US **sulfureous**) 1 of, like, or suggesting sulphur. 2 sulphur-coloured; yellow. [L *sulphureus* f. SULPHUR]

sulphuric /sʌlˈfjʊərɪk/ adj. (US **sulfuric**) Chem. containing sulphur. □ **sulphuric acid** a dense oily colourless highly acid and corrosive fluid much used in the chemical industry. [F *sulfurique* (as SULPHUR)]

sulphurous /ˈsʌlfərəs/ adj. (US **sulfurous**) 1 relating to or suggestive of sulphur, esp. in colour. 2 Chem. containing sulphur. □ **sulphurous acid** an unstable weak acid used as a reducing and bleaching acid. [L *sulphurosus* f. SULPHUR]

sultan /ˈsʌlt(ə)n/ n. a Muslim sovereign. □ **sultanate** /-ˌneɪt/ n. [F *sultan* or med.L *sultanus* f. Arab. *sulṭān* power, ruler f. *saluṭa* rule]

sultana /sʌlˈtɑːnə/ n. 1 a a seedless raisin used in puddings, cakes, etc. b the small pale yellow

grape producing this. 2 the mother, wife, concubine, or daughter of a sultan. [It., fem. of *sultano* = SULTAN]

sultry /ˈsʌltrɪ/ adj. (**sultrier, sultriest**) 1 (of the atmosphere or the weather) hot or oppressive; close. 2 (of a person, character, etc.) passionate; sensual. □ **sultrily** adv. **sultriness** n. [obs. *sulter* SWELTER]

sum n. & v. —n. 1 the total amount resulting from the addition of two or more items, facts, ideas, feelings, etc. (*the sum of two and three is five*; *the sum of my objections is this*). 2 a particular amount of money (*paid a large sum for it*). 3 a an arithmetical problem (*could not work out the sum*). b (esp. pl.) colloq. arithmetic work, esp. at an elementary level (*was good at sums*). —v.tr. (**summed, summing**) find the sum of. □ **in sum** in brief. **summing-up** 1 a review of evidence and a direction given by a judge to a jury. 2 a recapitulation of the main points of an argument, case, etc. **sum total** = sense 1 of n. **sum up** 1 (esp. of a judge) recapitulate or review the evidence in a case etc. 2 form or express an idea of the character of (a person, situation, etc.). 3 collect into or express as a total or whole. [ME f. OF *summe*, *somme* f. L *summa* main part, fem. of *summus* highest]

sumac /ˈsuːmæk, ˈʃuː-, ˈʃjuː-/ n. (also **sumach**) 1 any shrub or tree of the genus *Rhus*. 2 the dried and ground leaves of this used in tanning and dyeing. [ME f. OF *sumac* or med.L *sumac(h)* f. Arab. *summāk*]

summarize /ˈsʌməˌraɪz/ v.tr. (also **-ise**) make or be a summary of; sum up. □ **summarist** n. **summarizable** adj. **summarization** /-ˈzeɪʃ(ə)n/ n. **summarizer** n.

summary /ˈsʌmərɪ/ n. & adj. —n. (pl. **-ies**) a brief account; an abridgement. —adj. 1 dispensing with needless details or formalities; brief (*a summary account*). 2 Law (of a trial etc.) without the customary legal formalities (*summary justice*). □ **summarily** adv. **summariness** n. [ME f. L *summarium* f. L *summa* SUM]

summation /səˈmeɪʃ(ə)n/ n. 1 the finding of a total or sum; an addition. 2 a summing-up. □ **summational** adj.

summer /ˈsʌmə(r)/ n. & v. —n. 1 the warmest season of the year, in the N. hemisphere from June to August and in the S. hemisphere from December to February. 2 Astron. the period from the summer solstice to the autumnal equinox. 3 the hot weather typical of summer. 4 (often foll. by *of*) the mature stage of life; the height of achievement, powers, etc. 5 (esp. in pl.) poet. a year (esp. of a person's age) (*a child of ten summers*). 6 (attrib.) characteristic of or suitable for summer (*summer clothes*). —v. intr. (usu. foll. by *at*, *in*) pass the summer. □ **summer-house** a light building in a garden etc. used for sitting in in fine weather. **summer pudding** Brit. a pudding of soft summer fruit encased in bread or sponge. **summer school** a course of lectures etc. held during the summer vacation, esp. at a university. **summer time** Brit. the period between March and October during which the clocks are advanced an hour (cf. SUMMERTIME). □ **summerless** adj. **summerly** adv. **summery** adj. [OE *sumor*]

summersault var. of SOMERSAULT.

summertime /ˈsʌməˌtaɪm/ n. the season or period of summer (cf. *summer time*).

summit /ˈsʌmɪt/ n. **1** the highest point, esp. of a mountain; the apex. **2** the highest degree of power, ambition, etc. **3** (in full **summit meeting, talks,** etc.) a discussion, esp. on disarmament etc., between heads of government. □ **summitless** adj. [ME f. OF *somet, som(m)ete* f. *som* top f. L *summum* neut. of *summus*]

summon /ˈsʌmən/ v.tr. **1** call upon to appear, esp. as a defendant or witness in a lawcourt. **2** (usu. foll. by *to* + infin.) call upon (*summoned her to assist*). **3** call together for a meeting or some other purpose (*summoned the members to attend*). □ **summon up** (often foll. by *to, for*) gather (courage, spirits, resources, etc.) (*summoned up her strength for the task*). □ **summonable** adj. **summoner** n. [ME f. OF *somondre* f. L *summonēre* (as SUB-, *monēre* warn)]

summons /ˈsʌmənz/ n. & v. —n. (pl. **summonses**) **1** an authoritative or urgent call to attend on some occasion or do something. **2 a** a call to appear before a judge or magistrate. **b** the writ containing such a summons. —v.tr. esp. *Law* serve with a summons. [ME f. OF *somonce, sumunse* f. L *summonita* fem. past part. of *summonēre*: see SUMMON]

sumo /ˈsuːməʊ/ n. (pl. **-os**) **1** a style of Japanese wrestling, in which a participant is defeated by touching the ground with any part of the body except the soles of the feet or by moving outside the marked area. **2** a sumo wrestler. [Jap.]

sump n. **1** a pit, well, hole, etc. in which superfluous liquid collects in mines, machines, etc. **2** a cesspool. [ME, = marsh f. MDu., MLG *sump*, or (mining) G *Sumpf*, rel. to SWAMP]

sumptuary /ˈsʌmptjʊərɪ/ adj. **1** regulating expenditure. **2** (of a law or edict etc.) limiting private expenditure in the interests of the State. [L *sumptuarius* f. *sumptus* cost f. *sumere* sumpt-take]

sumptuous /ˈsʌmptjʊəs/ adj. rich, lavish, costly (*a sumptuous setting*). □ **sumptuosity** /-ˈɒsɪtɪ/ n. **sumptuously** adv. **sumptuousness** n. [ME f. OF *somptueux* f. L *sumptuosus* (as SUMPTUARY)]

Sun. abbr. Sunday.

sun n. & v. —n. **1 a** the star round which the earth orbits and from which it receives light and warmth. **b** any similar star in the universe with or without planets. **2** the light or warmth received from the sun (*pull down the blinds and keep out the sun*). —v. (**sunned, sunning**) **1** refl. bask in the sun. **2** tr. expose to the sun. **3** intr. sun oneself. □ **beneath** (or **under**) **the sun** anywhere in the world. **in the sun** exposed to the sun's rays. **sun-blind** *Brit.* a window awning. **sun-bonnet** a bonnet of cotton etc. covering the neck and shading the face, esp. for children. **sun-dress** a dress without sleeves and with a low neck. **sun-glasses** glasses tinted to protect the eyes from sunlight or glare. **sun-god** the sun worshipped as a deity. **sun-hat** a hat designed to protect the head from the sun. **sun-helmet** a helmet of cork etc. formerly worn by White people in the tropics. **sun-lamp** a lamp giving ultraviolet rays for an artificial suntan, therapy, etc. **sun lounge** a room with large windows, designed to receive sunlight. **sun parlor** *US* = *sun lounge*. **sun-roof** a sliding roof on a car. **sun-up** esp. *US* sunrise. □ **sunless** adj. **sunlessness** n. **sunlike** adj.

sunproof adj. **sunward** adj. & adv. **sunwards** adv. [OE *sunne, sunna*]

sunbathe /ˈsʌnbeɪð/ v.intr. bask in the sun, esp. to tan the body. □ **sunbather** n.

sunbeam /ˈsʌnbiːm/ n. a ray of sunlight.

sunbed /ˈsʌnbed/ n. **1** a lightweight, usu. folding, chair with a seat long enough to support the legs, used for sunbathing. **2** a bed for lying on under a sun-lamp.

sunbelt /ˈsʌnbelt/ n. a strip of territory receiving a high amount of sunshine, esp. the region in the southern US stretching from California to Florida.

sunblock /ˈsʌnblɒk/ n. a cream or lotion for protecting the skin from the sun.

sunburn /ˈsʌnbɜːn/ n. & v. —n. tanning and inflammation of the skin caused by overexposure to the sun. —v.intr. **1** suffer from sunburn. **2** (as **sunburnt** or **sunburned** adj.) suffering from sunburn; brown or tanned.

sunburst /ˈsʌnbɜːst/ n. **1** something resembling the sun and its rays, esp.: **a** an ornament, brooch, etc. **b** a firework. **2** the sun shining suddenly from behind clouds.

sundae /ˈsʌndeɪ, -dɪ/ n. a dish of ice-cream with fruit, nuts, syrup, etc. [perh. f. SUNDAY]

Sunday /ˈsʌndeɪ, -dɪ/ n. & adv. —n. **1** the first day of the week, a Christian holiday and day of worship. **2** a newspaper published on a Sunday. —adv. colloq. **1** on Sunday. **2** (**Sundays**) on Sundays; each Sunday. □ **Sunday best** joc. a person's best clothes, kept for Sunday use. **Sunday school** a school for the religious instruction of children on Sundays. [OE *sunnandæg*, transl. of L *dies solis*, Gk *hēmera hēliou* day of the sun]

sunder /ˈsʌndə(r)/ v.tr. & intr. archaic or literary separate, sever □ **in sunder** apart. [OE *sundrian*, f. *āsundrian* etc.: *in sunder* f. ME f. *o(n)sunder* ASUNDER]

sundew /ˈsʌndjuː/ n. any small insect-consuming bog-plant of the family Droseraceae, esp. of the genus *Drosera* with hairs secreting drops of moisture.

sundial /ˈsʌndaɪəl/ n. an instrument showing the time by the shadow of a pointer cast by the sun on to a graduated disc.

sundown /ˈsʌndaʊn/ n. sunset.

sundowner /ˈsʌnˌdaʊnə(r)/ n. **1** *Austral.* a tramp who arrives at a sheep station etc. in the evening for food and shelter. **2** *Brit. colloq.* an alcoholic drink taken at sunset.

sundry /ˈsʌndrɪ/ adj. & n. —adj. various; several (*sundry items*). —n. (pl. **-ies**) **1** (in pl.) items or oddments not mentioned individually. **2** *Austral. Cricket* = EXTRA n. 5. [OE *syndrig* separate, rel. to SUNDER]

sunflower /ˈsʌnˌflaʊə(r)/ n. any very tall plant of the genus *Helianthus*, esp. *H. annus* with very large showy golden-rayed flowers, grown also for its seeds which yield an edible oil.

sung past part. of SING.

sunk past and past part. of SINK.

sunken /ˈsʌŋkən/ adj. **1** that has been sunk. **2** beneath the surface; submerged. **3** (of the eyes, cheeks, etc.) hollow, depressed. [past part. of SINK]

sunlight /ˈsʌnlaɪt/ n. light from the sun.

sunlit /ˈsʌnlɪt/ adj. illuminated by sunlight.

Sunna /ˈsʌnə/ n. a traditional portion of Muslim law based on Muhammad's words or acts, accepted as authoritative by many Muslims but rejected by the Shiites. [Arab., = form, way, course, rule]

Sunni /ˈsʌnɪ/ n. & adj. —n. (pl. same or **Sunnis**) **1** one of the two main branches of Islam, regarding the Sunna as equal in authority to the Koran. **2** an adherent of this branch of Islam. —adj. (also **Sunnite**) of or relating to Sunni.

sunny /ˈsʌnɪ/ adj. (**sunnier, sunniest**) **1 a** bright with sunlight. **b** exposed to or warmed by the sun. **2** cheery and bright in temperament. □ **sunnily** adv. **sunniness** n.

sunrise /ˈsʌnraɪz/ n. **1** the sun's rising at dawn. **2** the coloured sky associated with this. **3** the time at which sunrise occurs. □ **sunrise industry** any newly established industry, esp. in electronics and telecommunications, regarded as signalling prosperity.

sunset /ˈsʌnset/ n. **1** the sun's setting in the evening. **2** the coloured sky associated with this. **3** the time at which sunset occurs. **4** the declining period of life.

sunshade /ˈsʌnʃeɪd/ n. **1** a parasol. **2** an awning.

sunshine /ˈsʌnʃaɪn/ n. **1 a** the light of the sun. **b** an area lit by the sun. **2** fine weather. **3** cheerfulness; joy (brought sunshine into her life). □ **sunshine roof** = sun-roof. □ **sunshiny** adj.

sunspot /ˈsʌnspɒt/ n. one of the dark patches, changing in shape and size and lasting for varying periods, observed on the sun's surface.

sunstroke /ˈsʌnstrəʊk/ n. acute prostration or collapse from the excessive heat of the sun.

suntan /ˈsʌntæn/ n. & v. —n. the brownish colouring of skin caused by exposure to the sun. —v.intr. (**-tanned, -tanning**) colour the skin with a suntan.

suntrap /ˈsʌntræp/ n. a place sheltered from the wind and suitable for catching the sunshine.

sup¹ v. & n. —v.tr. (**supped, supping**) **1** take (soup, tea, etc.) by sips or spoonfuls. **2** esp. N.Engl. colloq. drink (alcohol). —n. a sip of liquid. [OE sūpan]

sup² v.intr. (**supped, supping**) (usu. foll. by off, on) archaic take supper. [OF super, soper]

super /ˈsuːpə(r), ˈsjuː-/ adj. & n. (also **super-duper** /-ˈduːpə(r)/) colloq. (also as int.) exceptional; splendid. —n. colloq. **1** Theatr. a supernumerary actor. **2** a superintendent. [abbr.]

super- /ˈsuːpə(r), ˈsjuː-/ comb. form forming nouns, adjectives, and verbs, meaning: **1** above, beyond, or over in place or time or conceptually (superstructure; supernormal; superimpose). **2** to a great or extreme degree (superabundant; superhuman). **3** extra good or large of its kind (supertanker). **4** of a higher kind, esp. in names of classificatory divisions (superclass). [from or after L super- f. super above, beyond]

superable /ˈsuːpərəb(ə)l, ˈsjuː-/ adj. able to be overcome. [L superabilis f. superare overcome]

superabundant /ˌsuːpərəˈbʌnd(ə)nt, ˌsjuː-/ adj. abounding beyond what is normal or right. □ **superabundance** n. **superabundantly** adv. [ME f. LL superabundare (as SUPER-, ABOUND)]

superannuate /ˌsuːpərˈænjʊˌeɪt, ˌsjuː-/ v.tr. **1** retire (a person) with a pension. **2** dismiss or discard as too old for use, work, etc. **3** (as **superannuated** adj.) too old for work or use;

obsolete. □ **superannuable** adj. [back-form. f. superannuated f. med.L superannuatus f. L SUPER- + annus year]

superannuation /ˌsuːpərˌænjʊˈeɪʃ(ə)n, ˌsjuː-/ n. **1** a pension paid to a retired person. **2** a regular payment made towards this by an employed person. **3** the process or an instance of superannuating.

superb /suːˈpɜːb, sjuː-/ adj. **1** of the most impressive, splendid, grand, or majestic kind (superb courage; a superb specimen). **2** colloq. excellent; fine. □ **superbly** adv. **superbness** n. [F superbe or L superbus proud]

supercargo /ˈsuːpəˌkɑːgəʊ, ˈsjuː-/ n. (pl. **-oes**) an officer in a merchant ship managing sales etc. of cargo. [earlier supracargo f. Sp. sobrecargo f. sobre over + cargo CARGO]

supercharge /ˈsuːpəˌtʃɑːdʒ, ˈsjuː-/ v.tr. **1** (usu. foll. by with) charge (the atmosphere etc.) with energy, emotion, etc. **2** use a supercharger on (an internal-combustion engine).

supercharger /ˈsuːpəˌtʃɑːdʒə(r), ˈsjuː-/ n. a device supplying air or fuel to an internal-combustion engine at above normal pressure to increase efficiency.

supercilious /ˌsuːpəˈsɪlɪəs, ˌsjuː-/ adj. assuming an air of contemptuous indifference or superiority. □ **superciliously** adv. **superciliousness** n. [L superciliosus f. supercilium eyebrow (as SUPER-, cilium eyelid)]

superclass /ˈsuːpəˌklɑːs, ˈsjuː-/ n. a taxonomic category between class and phylum.

supercomputer /ˌsuːpəkəmˈpjuːtə(r)/ n. a powerful computer capable of dealing with complex problems. □ **supercomputing** n.

superconductivity /ˌsuːpəˌkɒndʌkˈtɪvɪtɪ, ˌsjuː-/ n. Physics the property of zero electrical resistance in some substances at very low absolute temperatures. □ **superconducting** /-kənˈdʌktɪŋ/ adj. **superconductive** /-kənˈdʌktɪv/ adj.

superconductor /ˌsuːpəkənˈdʌktə(r), ˌsjuː-/ n. Physics a substance having superconductivity.

supercool /ˈsuːpəˌkuːl, -ˈkuːl, ˈsjuː-/ v. & adj. —v. Chem. **1** tr. cool (a liquid) below its freezing-point without solidification or crystallization. **2** intr. (of a liquid) be cooled in this way. —adj. sl. very cool, relaxed, fine, etc.

super-duper var. of SUPER adj.

superego /ˌsuːpərˈiːgəʊ, -ˈegəʊ, ˌsjuː-/ n. (pl. **-os**) Psychol. the part of the mind that acts as a conscience and responds to social rules.

supererogation /ˌsuːpərˌerəˈgeɪʃ(ə)n, ˌsjuː-/ n. the performance of more than duty requires. □ **supererogatory** /-ɪˈrɒgətərɪ/ adj. [LL supererogatio f. supererogare pay in addition (as SUPER-, erogare pay out)]

superfamily /ˈsuːpəˌfæmɪlɪ, ˈsjuː-/ n. (pl. **-ies**) a taxonomic category between family and order.

superficial /ˌsuːpəˈfɪʃ(ə)l, ˌsjuː-/ adj. **1** of or on the surface; lacking depth (a superficial knowledge; superficial wounds). **2** swift or cursory (a superficial examination). **3** apparent but not real (a superficial resemblance). **4** (esp. of a person) having no depth of character or knowledge; trivial; shallow. □ **superficiality** /-ʃɪˈælɪtɪ/ n. (pl. **-ies**). **superficially** adv. **superficialness** n. [LL superficialis f. L (as SUPERFICIES)]

superficies /ˌsuːpəˈfɪʃɪˌiːz, ˌsjuː-/ n. (pl. same) Geom. a surface. [L (as SUPER-, facies face)]

superfine /ˈsuːˌfaɪn, ˈsjuː-/ adj. **1** Commerce of extra quality. **2** pretending great refinement. [med.L superfinus (as SUPER-, FINE[1])]

superfluity /ˌsuːpəˈfluːɪtɪ, ˌsjuː-/ n. (pl. **-ies**) **1** the state of being superfluous. **2** a superfluous amount or thing. [ME f. OF superfluité f. LL superfluitas -tatis f. L superfluus: see SUPERFLUOUS]

superfluous /suːˈpɜːfluəs, sjuː-/ adj. more than enough, redundant, needless. □ **superfluously** adv. **superfluousness** n. [ME f. L superfluus (as SUPER-, fluere to flow)]

supergiant /ˈsuːpəˌdʒaɪənt, ˈsjuː-/ n. a star of very great luminosity and size.

superglue /ˈsuːpəˌgluː/ n. any of various adhesives with an exceptional bonding capability.

supergrass /ˈsuːpəˌgrɑːs, ˈsjuː-/ n. colloq. a police informer who implicates a large number of people.

superheat /ˌsuːpəˈhiːt, ˌsjuː-/ v.tr. Physics **1** heat (a liquid) above its boiling-point without vaporization. **2** heat (a vapour) above its boiling-point (superheated steam). □ **superheater** n.

superhighway /ˈsuːpəˌhaɪweɪ, ˈsjuː-/ n. US a broad main road for fast traffic.

superhuman /ˌsuːpəˈhjuːmən, ˌsjuː-/ adj. **1** beyond normal human capability. **2** higher than man. □ **superhumanly** adv. [LL superhumanus (as SUPER-, HUMAN)]

superimpose /ˌsuːpərɪmˈpəʊz, ˌsjuː-/ v.tr. (usu. foll. by on) lay (a thing) on something else. □ **superimposition** /-pəˈzɪʃ(ə)n/ n.

superintend /ˌsuːpərɪnˈtend, ˌsjuː-/ v.tr. & intr. be responsible for the management or arrangement of (an activity etc.); supervise and inspect. □ **superintendence** n. **superintendency** n. [eccl.L superintendere (as SUPER-, INTEND), transl. Gk episkopō]

superintendent /ˌsuːpərɪnˈtend(ə)nt, ˌsjuː-/ n. & adj. —n. **1 a** a person who superintends. **b** a director of an institution etc. **2 a** Brit. a police officer above the rank of inspector. **b** US the head of a police department. **3** US the caretaker of a building. —adj. superintending. [eccl.L superintendent- part. stem of superintendere: see SUPERINTEND]

superior /suːˈpɪərɪə(r), sjuː-, sʊ-/ adj. & n. —adj. **1** in a higher position; of higher rank (a superior officer; a superior court). **2 a** above the average in quality etc. (made of superior leather). **b** having or showing a high opinion of oneself; supercilious (had a superior air). **3** (often foll. by to) better or greater in some respect (superior to its rivals in speed). **b** above yielding, making concessions, paying attention, etc. (is superior to bribery; superior to temptation). **4** Printing (of figures or letters) placed above the line. —n. **1** a person superior to another in rank, character, etc. (is deferential to his superiors; is his superior in courage). **2** (fem. **superioress** /-rɪs/) Eccl. the head of a monastery or other religious institution (Mother Superior; Father Superior). **3** Printing a superior letter or figure. □ **superior numbers** esp. Mil. more men etc. or their strength (overcome by superior numbers). □ **superiorly** adv. [ME f. OF superiour f. L superior -oris, compar. of superus that is above f. super above]

superiority /suːˌpɪərɪˈbrɪtɪ, sjuː-, sʊ-/ n. the state of being superior. □ **superiority complex** Psychol. an undue conviction of one's own superiority to others.

superlative /suːˈpɜːlətɪv, sjuː-/ adj. & n. —adj. **1** of the highest quality or degree (superlative wisdom). **2** Gram. (of an adjective or adverb) expressing the highest or a very high degree of a quality (e.g. bravest, most fiercely). —n. **1** Gram. **a** the superlative expression or form of an adjective or adverb. **b** a word in the superlative. **2** something embodying excellence; the highest form of a thing. □ **superlatively** adv. **superlativeness** n. [ME f. OF superlatif -ive f. LL superlativus f. L superlatus (as SUPER-, latus past part. of ferre take)]

superlunary /ˌsuːpəˈluːnərɪ, ˌsjuː-, -ˈljuːnərɪ/ adj. **1** situated beyond the moon. **2** belonging to a higher world, celestial. [med.L superlunaris (as SUPER-, LUNAR)]

superman /ˈsuːpəˌmæn, ˈsjuː-/ n. (pl. **-men**) colloq. a man of exceptional strength or ability. [SUPER-, MAN]

supermarket /ˈsuːpəˌmɑːkɪt, ˈsjuː-/ n. a large self-service store selling foods, household goods, etc.

supernatural /ˌsuːpəˈnætʃər(ə)l, ˌsjuː-/ adj. & n. —adj. attributed to or thought to reveal some force above the laws of nature; magical; mystical. —n. (prec. by the) supernatural, occult, or magical forces, effects, etc. □ **supernaturalism** n. **supernaturalist** n. **supernaturalize** v.tr. (also **-ise**) **supernaturally** adv. **supernaturalness** n.

supernormal /ˌsuːpəˈnɔːm(ə)l, ˌsjuː-/ adj. beyond what is normal or natural. □ **supernormality** /-ˈmælɪtɪ/ n.

supernova /ˌsuːpəˈnəʊvə, ˌsjuː-/ n. (pl. **-novae** /-viː/ or **-novas**) Astron. a star that suddenly increases very greatly in brightness because of an explosion ejecting most of its mass.

supernumerary /ˌsuːpəˈnjuːmərərɪ, ˌsjuː-/ adj. & n. —adj. **1** in excess of the normal number; extra. **2** (of a person) engaged for extra work. **3** (of an actor) appearing on stage but not speaking. —n. (pl. **-ies**) **1** an extra or unwanted person or thing. **2** a supernumerary actor. **3** a person engaged for extra work. [LL supernumerarius (soldier) added to a legion already complete, f. L super numerum beyond the number]

superorder /ˈsuːpərˌɔːdə(r), ˈsjuː-/ n. Biol. a taxonomic category between order and class. □ **superordinal** /-ˈɔːdɪn(ə)l/ adj.

superphosphate /ˌsuːpəˈfɒsfeɪt, ˌsjuː-/ n. a fertilizer made by treating phosphate rock with sulphuric or phosphoric acid.

superpower /ˈsuːpəˌpaʊə(r), ˈsjuː-/ n. a State of supreme power and influence, esp. the US and the former USSR.

superscribe /ˈsuːpəˌskraɪb, ˈsjuː-, -ˈskraɪb/ v.tr. **1** write (an inscription) at the top of or on the outside of a document etc. **2** write an inscription over or on (a thing). □ **superscription** /-ˈskrɪpʃ(ə)n/ n. [L superscribere (as SUPER-, scribere script- write)]

superscript /ˈsuːpəˌskrɪpt, ˈsjuː-/ adj. & n. —adj. written or printed above the line, esp. Math. (of a symbol) written above and to the right of another. —n. a superscript number or symbol. [L superscriptus past part. of superscribere: see SUPERSCRIBE]

supersede /ˌsuːpəˈsiːd, ˌsjuː-/ v.tr. **1 a** adopt or appoint another person or thing in place of. **b** set aside; cease to employ. **2** (of a person or thing) take the place of. □ **supersedence** n.

supersedure /-ˈdʒə(r)/ n. **supersession** /-ˈseʃ(ə)n/ n. [OF *superseder* f. L *supersedēre* be superior to (as SUPER-, *sedēre sess-* sit)]

supersonic /ˌsuːpəˈsɒnɪk, ˌsjuː-/ adj. designating or having a speed greater than that of sound. □ **supersonically** adv.

supersonics /ˌsuːpəˈsɒnɪks, ˌsjuː-/ n.pl. (treated as *sing.*) = ULTRASONICS.

superstar /ˈsuːpəstɑː(r), ˈsjuː-/ n. an extremely famous or renowned actor, film star, musician, etc. □ **superstardom** n.

superstition /ˌsuːpəˈstɪʃ(ə)n, ˌsjuː-/ n. 1 credulity regarding the supernatural. 2 an irrational fear of the unknown or mysterious. 3 misdirected reverence. 4 a practice, opinion, or religion based on these tendencies. 5 a widely held but unjustified idea of the effects or nature of a thing. □ **superstitious** adj. **superstitiously** adv. **superstitiousness** n. [ME f. OF *superstition* or L *superstitio* (as SUPER-, *stare stat-* stand)]

superstore /ˈsuːpəstɔː(r), ˈsjuː-/ n. a large supermarket selling a wide range of goods.

superstructure /ˈsuːpəstrʌktʃə(r), ˈsjuː-/ n. 1 the part of a building above its foundations. 2 a structure built on top of something else. 3 a concept or idea based on others. □ **superstructural** adj.

supertanker /ˈsuːpətæŋkə(r), ˈsjuː-/ n. a very large tanker ship.

supertax /ˈsuːpətæks, ˈsjuː-/ n. a tax on incomes above a certain level, esp. a surtax.

supervene /ˌsuːpəˈviːn, ˌsjuː-/ v.intr. occur as an interruption in or a change from some state. □ **supervenient** adj. **supervention** /-ˈvenʃ(ə)n/ n. [L *supervenire supervent-* (as SUPER-, *venire* come)]

supervise /ˈsuːpəvaɪz, ˈsjuː-/ v.tr. 1 superintend, oversee the execution of (a task etc.). 2 oversee the actions or work of (a person). □ **supervision** /-ˈvɪʒ(ə)n/ n. **supervisor** n. **supervisory** adj. [med.L *supervidēre supervis-* (as SUPER-, *vidēre* see)]

superwoman /ˈsuːpəwʊmən, ˈsjuː-/ n. (pl. **-women**) colloq. a woman of exceptional strength or ability.

supine /ˈsuːpaɪn, ˈsjuː-/ adj. 1 lying face upwards. 2 having the front or ventral part upwards; (of the hand) with the palm upwards. 3 inert, indolent; morally or mentally inactive. □ **supinely** adv. **supineness** n. [L *supinus*, rel. to *super:* (n.) f. LL *supinum* neut. (reason unkn.)]

supper /ˈsʌpə(r)/ n. a light evening meal. □ **sing for one's supper** do something in return for a benefit. □ **supperless** adj. [ME f. OF *soper, super*]

supplant /səˈplɑːnt/ v.tr. dispossess and take the place of, esp. by underhand means. □ **supplanter** n. [ME f. OF *supplanter* or L *supplantare* trip up (as SUB-, *planta* sole)]

supple /ˈsʌp(ə)l/ adj. (**suppler, supplest**) flexible, pliant; easily bent. □ **suppleness** n. [ME f. OF *souple* ult. f. L *supplex supplicis* submissive]

supplely var. of SUPPLY[2].

supplement n. & v. —n. /ˈsʌplɪmənt/ 1 a thing or part added to remedy deficiencies (*dietary supplement*). 2 a part added to a book etc. to provide further information. 3 a separate section, esp. a colour magazine, added to a newspaper or periodical. —v.tr. /ˈsʌplɪmənt, ˌsʌplɪˈment/ provide a supplement for. □ **supplemental** /-ˈment(ə)l/ adj. **supplementally** /-ˈmentəlɪ/ adv. **supplementation** /-ˈteɪʃ(ə)n/ n. [ME f. L *supplementum* (as SUB-, *plēre* fill)]

supplementary /ˌsʌplɪˈmentərɪ/ adj. forming or serving as a supplement; additional. □ **supplementary benefit** (in the UK) a weekly allowance paid by the State to those not in full-time employment and with an income below a certain level. □ **supplementarily** adv.

suppliant /ˈsʌplɪənt/ adj. & n. —adj. 1 supplicating. 2 expressing supplication. —n. a supplicating person. □ **suppliantly** adv. [ME f. F *supplier* beseech f. L (as SUPPLICATE)]

supplicate /ˈsʌplɪˌkeɪt/ v. 1 tr. petition humbly to (a person) or for (a thing). 2 intr. (foll. by *to, for*) make a petition. □ **supplicant** adj. & n. **supplication** /-ˈkeɪʃ(ə)n/ n. **supplicatory** adj. [ME f. L *supplicare* (as SUB-, *plicare* bend)]

supply[1] /səˈplaɪ/ v. & n. —v.tr. (**-ies, -ied**) 1 provide or furnish (a thing needed). 2 (often foll. by *with*) provide (a person etc. with a thing needed). 3 meet or make up for (a deficiency or need etc.). 4 fill (a vacancy, place, etc.) as a substitute. —n. (pl. **-ies**) 1 the act or an instance of providing what is needed. 2 a stock, store, amount, etc., of something provided or obtainable (*a large supply of water; the gas-supply*). 3 (in pl.) the collected provisions and equipment for an army, expedition, etc. 4 (often *attrib.*) a person, esp. a schoolteacher or clergyman, acting as a temporary substitute for another. □ **in short supply** available in limited quantity. **supply and demand** *Econ.* quantities available and required as factors regulating the price of commodities. **supply-side** *Econ.* denoting a policy of low taxation and other incentives to produce goods and invest. □ **supplier** n. [ME f. OF *so(u)pleer* etc. f. L *supplēre* (as SUB-, *plēre* fill)]

supply[2] /ˈsʌplɪ/ adv. (also **supplely** /ˈsʌpəlɪ/) in a supple manner.

support /səˈpɔːt/ v. & n. —v.tr. 1 carry all or part of the weight of. 2 keep from falling or sinking or failing. 3 provide with a home and the necessities of life (*has a family to support*). 4 enable to last out; give strength to; encourage. 5 bear out; tend to substantiate or corroborate (a statement, charge, theory, etc.). 6 give help or countenance to, back up; second, further. 7 speak in favour of (a resolution etc.). 8 be actively interested in (a particular team or sport). 9 take a part that is secondary to (a principal actor etc.). 10 endure, tolerate (*can no longer support the noise*). —n. 1 the act or an instance of supporting; the process of being supported. 2 a person or thing that supports. □ **in support of** in order to support. **supporting film** (or **picture** etc.) a less important film in a cinema programme. **support price** a minimum price guaranteed to a farmer for agricultural produce and maintained by subsidy etc. □ **supportable** adj. **supportability** /-təˈbɪlɪtɪ/ n. **supportably** adv. **supportingly** adv. **supportless** adj. [ME f. OF *supporter* f. L *supportare* (as SUB-, *portare* carry)]

supporter /səˈpɔːtə(r)/ n. a person or thing that supports, esp. a person supporting a team or sport.

supportive /səˈpɔːtɪv/ adj. providing support or encouragement. □ **supportively** adv. **supportiveness** n.

suppose /səˈpəʊz/ v.tr. (often foll. by *that* + clause) 1 assume, esp. in default of knowledge; be inclined to think (*I suppose they will return; what do you suppose he meant?*). 2 take as a possibility or hypothesis (*let us suppose you are right*). **3** (in *imper.*) as a formula of proposal (*suppose we go to the party*). **4** (of a theory or result etc.) require as a condition (*design in creation supposes a creator*). **5** (in *imper.* or *pres. part.* forming a question) in the circumstances that; if (*suppose he won't let you; supposing we stay*). **6** (as **supposed** *adj.*) generally accepted as being so; believed (*his supposed brother; generally supposed to be wealthy*). **7** (in *passive*; foll. by *to* + infin.) **a** be expected or required (*was supposed to write to you*). **b** (with *neg.*) not have to; not be allowed to (*you are not supposed to go in there*). □ **I suppose** so an expression of hesitant agreement. □ **supposable** *adj.* [ME f. OF *supposer* (as SUB-, POSE¹)]

supposedly /sə'pəʊzɪdlɪ/ *adv.* as is generally supposed.

supposition /ˌsʌpə'zɪʃ(ə)n/ *n.* **1** a fact or idea etc. supposed. **2** the act or an instance of supposing. □ **suppositional** *adj.*

supposititious /ˌsʌpə'zɪʃəs/ *adj.* hypothetical, assumed. □ **suppositiously** *adv.* **suppositiousness** *n.* [partly f. SUPPOSITITIOUS, partly f. SUPPOSITION + -OUS]

supposititious /səˌpɒzɪ'tɪʃəs/ *adj.* spurious; substituted for the real. □ **suppositiiously** *adv.* **suppositiiousness** *n.* [L *supposititius, -icius* f. *supponere supposit-* substitute (as SUB- *ponere* place)]

suppository /sə'pɒzɪtərɪ/ *n.* (*pl.* -ies) a medical preparation to be inserted into the rectum or vagina to melt. [ME f. med.L *suppositorium*, neut. of LL *suppositorius* placed underneath (as SUPPOSITITIOUS)]

suppress /sə'pres/ *v.tr.* **1** end the activity or existence of, esp. forcibly. **2** prevent (information, feelings, a reaction, etc.) from being seen, heard, or known (*tried to suppress the report; suppressed a yawn*). **3 a** partly or wholly eliminate (electrical interference etc.). **b** equip (a device) to reduce such interference due to it. □ **suppressible** *adj.* **suppression** *n.* **suppressive** *adj.* **suppressor** *n.* [ME f. L *supprimere suppress-* (as SUB-, *premere* press)]

suppurate /'sʌpjəreɪt/ *v.intr.* **1** form pus. **2** fester. □ **suppuration** /-'reɪʃ(ə)n/ *n.* **suppurative** /-rətɪv/ *adj.* [L *suppurare* (as SUB-, *purare* as PUS)]

supra /'suːprə, 'sjuː-/ *adv.* above or earlier on (in a book etc.). [L, = above]

supra- /'suːprə, 'sjuː-/ *prefix* **1** above. **2** beyond, transcending (*supranational*). [from or after L *supra-* f. *supra* above, beyond, before in time]

supranational /ˌsuːprə'næʃ(ə)l, ˌsjuː-/ *adj.* transcending national limits. □ **supranationalism** *n.* **supranationality** /-'nælɪtɪ/ *n.*

supremacist /suː'preməsɪst, sjuː-/ *n.* & *adj.* —*n.* an advocate of the supremacy of a particular group, esp. determined by race or sex. —*adj.* relating to or advocating such supremacy. □ **supremacism** *n.*

supremacy /suː'preməsɪ, sjuː-/ *n.* (*pl.* -ies) **1** the state of being supreme. **2** the highest authority.

supreme /suː'priːm, sjuː-/ *adj.* & *n.* —*adj.* **1** highest in authority or rank. **2** greatest; most important. **3** (of a penalty or sacrifice etc.) involving death. □ **the Supreme Being** a name for God. **Supreme Court** the highest judicial court in a State etc. □ **supremely** *adv.*

supremeness *n.* [L *supremus*, superl. of *superus* that is above f. *super* above]

supremo /suː'priːməʊ, sjuː-/ *n.* (*pl.* -os) **1** a supreme leader or ruler. **2** a person in overall charge. [Sp., = SUPREME]

sur- /sɜː(r), sə(r)/ *prefix* = SUPER- (*surcharge; surrealism*). [OF]

surcease /sɜː'siːs/ *n.* & *v. literary* —*n.* a cessation. —*v.intr.* & *tr.* cease. [ME f. OF *sursis, -ise* (cf. AF *sursise* omission), past part. of OF *surseoir* refrain, delay f. L (as SUPERSEDE), with assim. to CEASE]

surcharge *n.* & *v.* —*n.* /'sɜːtʃɑːdʒ/ **1** an additional charge or payment. **2** a mark printed on a postage stamp changing its value. **3** an additional or excessive load. —*v.tr.* /'sɜːtʃɑːdʒ, -'tʃɑːdʒ/ **1** exact a surcharge from. **2** exact (a sum) as a surcharge. **3** mark (a postage stamp) with a surcharge. **4** overload. **5** fill or saturate to excess. [ME f. OF *surcharger* (as SUR-, CHARGE)]

surculose /'sɜːkjʊˌləʊs/ *adj. Bot.* producing suckers. [L *surculosus* f. *surculus* twig]

surd *adj.* & *n.* —*adj.* **1** *Math.* (of a number) irrational. **2** *Phonet.* (of a sound) uttered with the breath and not the voice (e.g. *f, k, p, s, t*). —*n.* **1** *Math.* a surd number, esp. the root of an integer. **2** *Phonet.* a surd sound. [L *surdus* deaf, mute: sense 1 by mistransl. into L of Gk *alogos* irrational, speechless, through Arab. *jaḏr aṣamm* deaf root]

sure /ʃʊə(r), ʃɔː(r)/ *adj.* & *adv.* —*adj.* **1** having or seeming to have adequate reason for a belief or assertion. **2** (often foll. by *of*, or *that* + clause) convinced. **3** (foll. by *of*) having a certain prospect or confident anticipation or satisfactory knowledge of. **4** reliable or unfailing (*there is one sure way to find out*). **5** (foll. by *to* + infin.) certain. **6** undoubtedly true or truthful. —*adv. colloq.* certainly. □ **be sure** (in *imper.* or *infin.*; foll. by *that* + clause or *to* + infin.) take care to; not fail to (*be sure to turn the lights out*). **for sure** *colloq.* without doubt. **make sure 1** make or become certain; ensure. **2** (foll. by *of*) establish the truth or ensure the existence or happening of. **sure enough** *colloq.* **1** in fact; certainly. **2** with near certainty (*they will come sure enough*). **sure-fire** *colloq.* certain to succeed. **sure-footed** never stumbling or making a mistake. **sure thing** *int.* esp. *US colloq.* certainly. **to be sure 1** it is undeniable or admitted. **2** it must be admitted. □ **sureness** *n.* [ME f. OF *sur sure* (earlier *seür*) f. L *securus* SECURE]

surely /'ʃʊəlɪ/ *adv.* **1** with certainty (*the time approaches slowly but surely*). **2** as an appeal to likelihood or reason (*surely that can't be right*). **3** with safety; securely (*the goat plants its feet surely*).

surety /'ʃʊərɪtɪ, 'ʃʊətɪ/ *n.* (*pl.* -ies) a person who takes responsibility for another's performance of an undertaking, e.g. to appear in court, or payment of a debt. □ **stand surety** become a surety, go bail. □ **suretyship** *n.* [ME f. OF *surté, seürté* f. L *securitas -tatis* SECURITY]

surf *n.* & *v.* —*n.* **1** the swell of the sea breaking on the shore or reefs. **2** the foam produced by this. —*v.intr.* go surf-riding. □ **surf-riding** the sport of being carried over the surf to the shore on a surfboard. □ **surfer** *n.* **surfy** *adj.* [app. f. obs. *suff*, perh. assim. to *surge*: orig. applied to the Indian coast]

surface /'sɜːfɪs/ *n.* & *v.* —*n.* **1 a** the outside of a material body. **b** the area of this. **2** any of the limits terminating a solid. **3** the upper boundary of a liquid or of the ground etc. **4** the outward aspect of anything; what is apparent on a casual view or consideration (*presents a large surface to view; all is quiet on the surface*). **5** *Geom.* a set of points that has length and breadth but no thickness. **6** (*attrib.*) **a** of or on the surface (*surface area*). **b** superficial (*surface politeness*). —*v.* **1** *tr.* give the required surface to (a road, paper, etc.). **2** *intr.* & *tr.* rise or bring to the surface. **3** *intr.* become visible or known. **4** *intr. colloq.* become conscious; wake up. □ **come to the surface** become perceptible after being hidden. **surface mail** mail carried over land and by sea, and not by air. **surface tension** the tension of the surface-film of a liquid, tending to minimize its surface area. □ **surfaced** *adj.* (usu. in *comb.*). **surfacer** *n.* [F (as SUR-, FACE)]

surfactant /sɜːˈfækt(ə)nt/ *n.* a substance which reduces surface tension. [*surface-active*]

surfboard /ˈsɜːfbɔːd/ *n.* a long narrow board used in surf-riding.

surfeit /ˈsɜːfɪt/ *n.* & *v.* —*n.* **1** an excess esp. in eating or drinking. **2** a feeling of satiety or disgust resulting from this. —*v.* (**surfeited**, **surfeiting**) **1** *tr.* overfeed. **2** *intr.* overeat. **3** *intr.* & *tr.* (foll. by *with*) be or cause to be wearied through excess. [ME f. OF *sorfe(i)t*, *surfe(i)t* (as SUPER-, L *facere fact*- do)]

surge /sɜːdʒ/ *n.* & *v.* —*n.* **1** a sudden or impetuous onset (*a surge of anger*). **2** the swell of the waves at sea. **3** a heavy forward or upward motion. **4** a rapid increase in price, activity, etc. over a short period. **5** a sudden marked increase in voltage of an electric current. —*v.intr.* **1** (of waves, the sea, etc.) rise and fall or move heavily forward. **2** (of a crowd etc.) move suddenly and powerfully forwards in large numbers. **3** (of an electric current etc.) increase suddenly. [OF *sourdre sourge-*, or *sorgir* f. Cat., f. L *surgere* rise]

surgeon /ˈsɜːdʒ(ə)n/ *n.* **1** a medical practitioner qualified to practise surgery. **2** a medical officer in a navy or army or military hospital. □ **surgeon general** (*pl.* **surgeons general**) *US* the head of a public health service or of an army etc. medical service. [ME f. AF *surgien* f. OF *serurgien* (as SURGERY)]

surgery /ˈsɜːdʒərɪ/ *n.* (*pl.* **-ies**) **1** the branch of medicine concerned with treatment of injuries or disorders of the body by incision, manipulation or alteration of organs etc., with the hands or with instruments. **2** *Brit.* **a** a place where a doctor, dentist, etc., treats patients. **b** the occasion of this (*the doctor will see you after surgery*). **3** *Brit.* **a** a place where an MP, lawyer, or other professional person gives advice. **b** the occasion of this. [ME f. OF *surgerie* f. L *chirurgia* f. Gk *kheirourgia* handiwork, surgery f. *kheir* hand + *erg-* work]

surgical /ˈsɜːdʒɪk(ə)l/ *adj.* **1** of or relating to or done by surgeons or surgery. **2** resulting from surgery (*surgical fever*). **3 a** used in surgery. **b** (of a special garment etc.) worn to correct a deformity etc. □ **surgical spirit** methylated spirit used in surgery for cleansing etc. □ **surgically** *adv.* [earlier *chirurgical* f. *chirurgy* f. OF *sirurgie*: see SURGEON]

suricate /ˈsʊərɪˌkeɪt/ *n.* a South African burrowing mongoose, *Suricata suricatta*, with grey and black stripes. [F f. S.Afr. native name]

surly /ˈsɜːlɪ/ *adj.* (**surlier**, **surliest**) bad-tempered and unfriendly; churlish. □ **surlily** *adv.* **surliness** *n.* [alt. spelling of obs. *sirly* haughty f. SIR + -LY[1]]

surmise /səˈmaɪz/ *n.* & *v.* —*n.* a conjecture or suspicion about the existence or truth of something. —*v.* **1** *tr.* (often foll. by *that* + clause) infer doubtfully; make a surmise about. **2** *tr.* suspect the existence of. **3** *intr.* make a guess. [ME f. AF & OF fem. past part. of *surmettre* accuse f. LL *supermittere supermiss-* (as SUPER-, *mittere* send)]

surmount /səˈmaʊnt/ *v.tr.* **1** overcome or get over (a difficulty or obstacle). **2** (usu. in *passive*) cap or crown (*peaks surmounted with snow*). □ **surmountable** *adj.* [ME f. OF *surmonter* (as SUR-, MOUNT[1])]

surname /ˈsɜːneɪm/ *n.* & *v.* —*n.* a hereditary name common to all members of a family, as distinct from a Christian or first name. —*v.tr.* **1** give a surname to. **2** give (a person) a surname). **3** (as **surnamed** *adj.*) having as a family name. [ME, alt. of *surnoun* f. AF (as SUR-, NOUN name)]

surpass /səˈpɑːs/ *v.tr.* **1** outdo, be greater or better than. **2** (as **surpassing** *adj.*) pre-eminent, matchless (*of surpassing intelligence*). □ **surpassingly** *adv.* [F *surpasser* (as SUR-, PASS[1])]

surplice /ˈsɜːplɪs/ *n.* a loose white linen vestment reaching the knees, worn over a cassock by clergy and choristers at services. □ **surpliced** *adj.* [ME f. AF *surplis*, OF *sourpelis*, f. med.L *superpellicium* (as SUPER-, *pellicia* PELISSE)]

surplus /ˈsɜːpləs/ *n.* & *adj.* —*n.* **1** an amount left over when requirements have been met. **2 a** an excess of revenue over expenditure in a given period, esp. a financial year. **b** the excess value of a company's assets over the face value of its stock. —*adj.* exceeding what is needed or used. [ME f. AF *surplus*, OF *s(o)urplus* f. med.L *superplus* (as SUPER-, + *plus* more)]

surprise /səˈpraɪz/ *n.* & *v.* —*n.* **1** an unexpected or astonishing event or circumstance. **2** the emotion caused by this. **3** the act of catching a person etc. unawares, or the process of being caught unawares. **4** (*attrib.*) unexpected; made or done etc. without warning (*a surprise visit*). —*v.tr.* **1** affect with surprise; turn out contrary to the expectations of (*your answer surprised me; I surprised her by arriving early*). **2** (usu. in *passive*; foll. by *at*) shock, scandalize (*I am surprised at you*). **3** capture or attack by surprise. **4** come upon (a person) unawares (*surprised him taking a biscuit*). **5** (foll. by *into*) startle (a person) by surprise into an action etc. (*surprised them into consenting*). □ **take by surprise** affect with surprise, esp. by an unexpected encounter or statement. □ **surprisedly** /-zɪdlɪ/ *adv.* **surprising** *adj.* **surprisingly** *adv.* **surprisingness** *n.* [OF, fem. past part. of *surprendre* (as SUR-, *prendre* f. L *praehendere* seize)]

surreal /səˈrɪəl/ *adj.* **1** having the qualities of surrealism. **2** strange, bizarre. □ **surreality** /-ˈælɪtɪ/ *n.* **surreally** *adv.* [back-form. f. SURREALISM etc.]

surrealism /səˈrɪəˌlɪz(ə)m/ *n.* a 20th-c. movement in art and literature aiming at expressing the subconscious mind, e.g. by the irrational juxtaposition of images. □ **surrealist** *n.* & *adj.* **surrealistic** /-ˈlɪstɪk/ *adj.* **surrealistically** /-ˈlɪstɪkəlɪ/ *adv.* [F *surréalisme* (as SUR-, REALISM)]

surrender /səˈrendə(r)/ v. & n. —v. 1 tr. hand over; relinquish possession of, esp. on compulsion or demand; give into another's power or control. 2 intr. **a** accept an enemy's demand for submission. **b** give oneself up; cease from resistance; submit. 3 intr. & refl. (foll. by to) give oneself over to a habit, emotion, influence, etc. 4 tr. give up rights under (a life-insurance policy) in return for a smaller sum received immediately. —n. the act or an instance of surrendering. □ **surrender value** the amount payable to one who surrenders a life-insurance policy. [ME f. AF f. OF surrendre (as SUR-, RENDER)]

surreptitious /ˌsʌrəpˈtɪʃəs/ adj. 1 covert; kept secret. 2 done by stealth; clandestine. □ **surreptitiously** adv. **surreptitiousness** n. [ME f. L surrepticius -itius f. surripere surrept- (as SUR-, rapere seize)]

surrey /ˈsʌrɪ/ n. (pl. **surreys**) US a light four-wheeled carriage with two seats facing forwards. [orig. of an adaptation of the Surrey cart, orig. made in Surrey in England]

surrogate /ˈsʌrəgət/ n. 1 a substitute, esp. for a person in a specific role or office. 2 Brit. a deputy, esp. of a bishop. □ **surrogate mother** 1 a person acting the role of mother. 2 a woman who bears a child on behalf of another woman, from her own egg fertilized by the other woman's partner. □ **surrogacy** n. **surrogateship** n. [L surrogatus past part. of surrogare elect as a substitute (as SUR-, rogare ask)]

surround /səˈraʊnd/ v. & n. —v.tr. 1 come or be all round; encircle, enclose. 2 (in passive; foll. by by, with) have on all sides (the house is surrounded by trees). —n. 1 Brit. **a** a border or edging, esp. an area between the walls and carpet of a room. **b** a floor-covering for this. 2 an area or substance surrounding something. □ **surrounding** adj. [ME = overflow, f. AF sur(o)under, OF s(o)uronder f. LL superundare (as SUPER-, undare flow f. unda wave)]

surroundings /səˈraʊndɪŋz/ n.pl. the things in the neighbourhood of, or the conditions affecting, a person or thing.

surtax /ˈsɜːtæks/ n. & v. —n. an additional tax, esp. levied on incomes above a certain level. —v.tr. impose a surtax on. [F surtaxe (as SUR-, TAX)]

surtitle /ˈsɜːˌtaɪt(ə)l/ n. (esp. in opera) each of a sequence of captions projected above the stage, translating the text being sung.

surveillance /sɜːˈveɪləns/ n. close observation, esp. of a suspected person. [F f. surveiller (as SUR-, veiller f. L vigilare keep watch)]

survey v. & n. —v.tr. /səˈveɪ/ 1 take or present a general view of. 2 examine the condition of (a building etc.). 3 determine the boundaries, extent, ownership, etc., of (a district etc.). —n. /ˈsɜːveɪ/ 1 a general view or consideration of something. 2 **a** the act of surveying property. **b** the result or findings of this, esp. in a written report. 3 an inspection or investigation. 4 a map or plan made by surveying an area. 5 a department carrying out the surveying of land. [ME f. AF survei(e)r, OF so(u)rveeir (pres. stem survey-) f. med.L supervidēre (as SUPER-, vidēre see)]

surveyor /səˈveɪə(r)/ n. 1 a person who surveys land and buildings, esp. professionally. 2 a person who carries out surveys. [ME f. AF & OF surve(i)our (as SURVEY)]

survival /səˈvaɪv(ə)l/ n. 1 the process or an instance of surviving. 2 a person, thing, or practice that has remained from a former time. □ **survival of the fittest** the process or result of natural selection.

survivalism /səˈvaɪvəlɪz(ə)m/ n. the practising of outdoor survival skills as a sport or hobby. □ **survivalist** adj. & n.

survive /səˈvaɪv/ v. 1 intr. continue to live or exist; be still alive or existent. 2 tr. live or exist longer than. 3 tr. remain alive after going through, or continue to exist in spite of (a danger, accident, etc.). [ME f. AF survivre, OF sourvivre f. L supervivere (as SUPER-, vivere live)]

survivor /səˈvaɪvə(r)/ n. a person who survives or has survived.

sus var. of SUSS.

susceptibility /səˌseptɪˈbɪlɪtɪ/ n. (pl. **-ies**) 1 the state of being susceptible. 2 (in pl.) a person's sensitive feelings.

susceptible /səˈseptɪb(ə)l/ adj. 1 impressionable, sensitive; easily moved by emotion. 2 (predic.) **a** (foll. by to) likely to be affected by; liable or vulnerable to (susceptible to pain). **b** (foll. by of) allowing; admitting of (facts not susceptible of proof). □ **susceptibly** adv. [LL susceptibilis f. L suscipere suscept- (as SUB-, capere take)]

sushi /ˈsuːʃɪ/ n. a Japanese dish of balls of cold rice flavoured and garnished. [Jap.]

suspect v., n., & adj. —v.tr. /səˈspekt/ 1 have an impression of the existence or presence of (suspects poisoning). 2 (foll. by to be) believe tentatively, without clear ground. 3 (foll. by that + clause) be inclined to think. 4 (often foll. by of) be inclined to mentally accuse; doubt the innocence of (suspect him of complicity). 5 doubt the genuineness or truth of. —n. /ˈsʌspekt/ a suspected person. —adj. /ˈsʌspekt/ subject to or deserving suspicion or distrust; not sound or trustworthy. [ME f. L suspicere suspect- (as SUB-, specere look)]

suspend /səˈspend/ v.tr. 1 hang up. 2 keep inoperative or undecided for a time; defer. 3 debar temporarily from a function, office, privilege, etc. 4 (as **suspended** adj.) (of solid particles or a body in a fluid medium) sustained somewhere between top and bottom. □ **suspended animation** a temporary cessation of the vital functions without death. **suspended sentence** a judicial sentence left unenforced subject to good behaviour during a specified period. □ **suspensible** adj. [ME f. OF suspendre or L suspendere suspens- (as SUB-, pendere hang)]

suspender /səˈspendə(r)/ n. 1 an attachment to hold up a stocking or sock by its top. 2 (in pl.) US a pair of braces. □ **suspender belt** a woman's undergarment with suspenders.

suspense /səˈspens/ n. a state of anxious uncertainty or expectation. □ **keep in suspense** delay informing (a person) of urgent information. □ **suspenseful** adj. [ME f. AF & OF suspens f. past part. of L suspendere SUSPEND]

suspension /səˈspenʃ(ə)n/ n. 1 the act of suspending or the condition of being suspended. 2 the means by which a vehicle is supported on its axles. 3 a substance consisting of particles suspended in a medium. □ **suspension bridge** a bridge with a roadway suspended from cables supported by structures at each end. [F suspension or L suspensio (as SUSPEND)]

suspicion /səˈspɪʃ(ə)n/ n. **1** the feeling or thought of a person who suspects. **2** the act or an instance of suspecting; the state of being suspected. **3** (foll. by *of*) a slight trace of. □ **above suspicion** too obviously good etc. to be suspected. **under suspicion** suspected. [ME f. AF *suspeciun* (OF *sospeçon*) f. med.L *suspectio -onis* f. L *suspicere* (as SUSPECT): assim. to F *suspicion* & L *suspicio*]

suspicious /səˈspɪʃəs/ adj. **1** prone to or feeling suspicion. **2** indicating suspicion (*a suspicious glance*). **3** inviting or justifying suspicion (*a suspicious lack of surprise*). □ **suspiciously** adv. **suspiciousness** n. [ME f. AF & OF f. L *suspiciosus* (as SUSPICION)]

suss /sʌs/ v. & n. (also **sus**) Brit. sl. —v.tr. (**sussed**, **sussing**) **1** suspect of a crime. **2** (usu. foll. by *out*) **a** investigate, inspect (*go and suss out the restaurants*). **b** work out; grasp, understand, realize (*he had the market sussed*). —n. **1** a suspect. **2** a suspicion; suspicious behaviour. □ **on suss** on suspicion (of having committed a crime). [abbr. of SUSPECT, SUSPICION]

sustain /səˈsteɪn/ v.tr. **1** support, bear the weight of, esp. for a long period. **2** give strength to; encourage, support. **3** (of food) give nourishment to. **4** endure, stand; bear up against. **5** undergo or suffer (defeat or injury etc.). **6** (of a court etc.) uphold or decide in favour of (an objection etc.). **7** substantiate or corroborate (a statement or charge). **8** maintain or keep (a sound, effort, etc.) going continuously. □ **sustainable** adj. **sustainedly** /-nɪdlɪ/ adv. **sustainer** n. **sustainment** n. [ME f. AF *sustein-*, OF *so(u)stein-* stressed stem of *so(u)stenir* f. L *sustinēre sustent-* (as SUB-, *tenēre* hold)]

sustenance /ˈsʌstɪnəns/ n. **1 a** nourishment, food. **b** the process of nourishing. **2** a means of support. [ME f. AF *sustenaunce*, OF *so(u)stenance* (as SUSTAIN)]

sutler /ˈsʌtlə(r)/ n. hist. a person following an army and selling provisions etc. to the soldiers. [obs. Du. *soeteler* f. *soetelen* befoul, perform mean duties, f. Gmc]

Sutra /ˈsuːtrə/ n. **1** an aphorism or set of aphorisms in Hindu literature. **2** a narrative part of Buddhist literature. **3** Jainist scripture. [Skr. *sūtra* thread, rule, f. *siv* SEW]

suttee /sʌˈtiː, ˈsʌtɪ/ n. (also **sati**) (pl. **suttees** or **satis**) esp. hist. **1** the Hindu practice of a widow immolating herself on her husband's funeral pyre. **2** a widow who undergoes or has undergone this. [Hindi & Urdu f. Skr. *satī* faithful wife f. *sat* good]

suture /ˈsuːtʃə(r)/ n. & v. —n. **1** Surgery **a** the joining of the edges of a wound or incision by stitching. **b** the thread or wire used for this. **2** the seamlike junction of two bones, esp. in the skull. —v.tr. Surgery stitch up (a wound or incision) with a suture. □ **sutural** adj. **sutured** adj. [F *suture* or L *sutura* f. *suere sut-* sew]

suzerain /ˈsuːzərən/ n. **1** a feudal overlord. **2** a sovereign or State having some control over another State that is internally autonomous. □ **suzerainty** n. [F, app. f. *sus* above f. L *su(r)sum* upward, after *souverain* SOVEREIGN]

s.v. abbr. (in a reference) under the word or heading given. [L *sub voce* (or *verbo*)]

svelte /svelt/ adj. slender, lissom, graceful. [F f. It. *svelto*]

SW abbr. **1** south-west. **2** south-western.

swab /swɒb/ n. & v. (also **swob**) —n. **1** a mop or other absorbent device for cleaning or mopping up. **2 a** an absorbent pad used in surgery. **b** a specimen of a possibly morbid secretion taken with a swab for examination. —v.tr. (**swabbed**, **swabbing**) **1** clean with a swab. **2** (foll. by *up*) absorb (moisture) with a swab. [back-form. f. *swabber* f. early mod.Du. *zwabber* f. a Gmc base = 'splash, sway']

swaddle /ˈswɒd(ə)l/ v.tr. swathe (esp. an infant) in garments or bandages etc. □ **swaddling-clothes** narrow bandages formerly wrapped round a newborn child to restrain its movements and quieten it. [ME f. SWATHE + -LE⁴]

swag n. & v. —n. **1** sl. **a** the booty carried off by burglars etc. **b** illicit gains. **2 a** an ornamental festoon of flowers etc. **b** a carved etc. representation of this. **c** drapery of similar appearance. **3** Austral. & NZ a traveller's or miner's bundle of personal belongings. —v. (**swagged**, **swagging**) **1** tr. arrange (a curtain etc.) in swags. **2** intr. **a** hang heavily. **b** sway from side to side. **3** tr. cause to sway or sag. [16th c.: prob. f. Scand.]

swagger /ˈswægə(r)/ v. & n. —v.intr. **1** walk arrogantly or self-importantly. **2** behave arrogantly; be domineering. —n. **1** a swaggering gait or manner. **2** swaggering behaviour. **3** a dashing or confident air or way of doing something. **4** smartness. □ **swagger stick** a short cane carried by a military officer. □ **swaggerer** n. **swaggeringly** adv. [app. f. SWAG v. + -ER⁴]

swagman /ˈswægmæn/ n. (pl. **-men**) Austral. & NZ a tramp carrying a swag (see SWAG n. 3).

Swahili /swəˈhiːlɪ, swɑːˈhiːlɪ/ n. (pl. same) **1** a member of a Bantu people of Zanzibar and adjacent coasts. **2** their language, used widely as a lingua franca in E. Africa. [Arab. *sawāḥil* pl. of *sāḥil* coast]

swain n. **1** archaic a country youth. **2** poet. a young lover or suitor. [ME *swein* f. ON *sveinn* lad = OE *swān* swineherd, f. Gmc]

swallow¹ /ˈswɒləʊ/ v. & n. —v. **1** tr. cause or allow (food etc.) to pass down the throat. **2** intr. perform the muscular movement of the oesophagus required to do this. **3** tr. **a** accept meekly; put up with (an affront etc.). **b** accept credulously (an unlikely assertion etc.). **4** tr. repress; resist the expression of (a feeling etc.) (*swallow one's pride*). **5** tr. articulate (words etc.) indistinctly. **6** tr. (often foll. by *up*) engulf or absorb; exhaust; cause to disappear. —n. **1** the act of swallowing. **2** an amount swallowed in one action. □ **swallowable** adj. **swallower** n. [OE *swelg* (n.), *swelgan* (v.) f. Gmc]

swallow² /ˈswɒləʊ/ n. any of various migratory swift-flying insect-eating birds of the family Hirundinidae, esp. *Hirundo rustica*, with a forked tail and long pointed wings. □ **swallow-dive** a dive with the arms outspread until close to the water. **swallow-tail 1** a deeply forked tail. **2** anything resembling this shape. **3** any butterfly of the family Papilionidae with wings extended at the back to this shape. [OE *swealwe* f. Gmc]

swam past of SWIM.

swami /ˈswɑːmɪ/ n. (pl. **swamis**) a Hindu male religious teacher. [Hindi *swāmī* master, prince, f. Skr. *svāmin*]

swamp /swɒmp/ n. & v. —n. a piece of water-logged ground; a bog or marsh. —v. **1 a** tr. overwhelm, flood, or soak with water. **b** intr.

become swamped. **2** *tr.* overwhelm or make invisible etc. with an excess or large amount of something. □ **swampy** *adj.* (**swampier**, **swampiest**). [17th c., = dial. *swamp* sunk (14th c.), prob. of Gmc orig.]

swan /swɒn/ *n. & v.* —*n.* a large water-bird of the genus *Cygnus* etc., having a long flexible neck, webbed feet, and in most species snow-white plumage. —*v.intr.* (**swanned**, **swanning**) (usu. foll. by *about*, *off*, etc.) *colloq.* move or go aimlessly or casually or with a superior air. □ **Swan of Avon** *literary* Shakespeare. **swan-upping** *Brit.* the annual taking up and marking of Thames swans. □ **swanlike** *adj. & adv.* [OE f. Gmc]

swank *n., v., & adj. colloq.* —*n.* ostentation, swagger, bluff. —*v.intr.* behave with swank; show off. —*adj. esp. US* = SWANKY. [19th c.: orig. uncert.]

swanky /ˈswæŋkɪ/ *adj.* (**swankier**, **swankiest**) **1** marked by swank; ostentatiously smart or showy. **2** (of a person) inclined to swank; boastful. □ **swankily** *adv.* **swankiness** *n.*

swannery /ˈswɒnərɪ/ *n.* (pl. **-ies**) a place where swans are bred.

swansdown /ˈswɒnzdaʊn/ *n.* **1** the fine down of a swan, used in trimmings and esp. in powder-puffs. **2** a kind of thick cotton cloth with a soft nap on one side.

swansong /ˈswɒnsɒŋ/ *n.* a person's last work or act before death or retirement etc.

swap /swɒp/ *v. & n.* (also **swop**) —*v.tr. & intr.* (**swapped**, **swapping**) exchange or barter (one thing for another). —*n.* **1** an act of swapping. **2** a thing suitable for swapping. **3** a thing swapped. □ **swapper** *n.* [ME, orig. = 'hit': prob. imit.]

sward /swɔːd/ *n. literary* **1** an expanse of short grass. **2** turf. □ **swarded** *adj.* [OE *sweard* skin]

swarf /swɔːf/ *n.* **1** fine chips or filings of stone, metal, etc. **2** wax etc. removed in cutting a gramophone record. [ON *svarf* file-dust]

swarm[1] /swɔːm/ *n. & v.* —*n.* **1** a cluster of bees leaving the hive with the queen to establish a new colony. **2** a large number of insects or birds moving in a cluster. **3** a large group of people, esp. moving over or filling a large area. **4** (in *pl.*; foll. by *of*) great numbers. —*v.intr.* **1** move in or form a swarm. **2** gather or move in large numbers. **3** (foll. by *with*) (of a place) be overrun, crowded, or infested (*was swarming with tourists*). [OE *swearm* f. Gmc]

swarm[2] /swɔːm/ *v.intr.* (foll. by *up*) & *tr.* climb (a rope or tree etc.) by clasping or clinging with the hands and knees etc. [16th c.: orig. unkn.]

swarthy /ˈswɔːðɪ/ *adj.* (**swarthier**, **swarthiest**) dark, dark-complexioned. □ **swarthily** *adv.* **swarthiness** *n.* [var. of obs. *swarty* f. OE *sweart* f. Gmc]

swash /swɒʃ/ *v. & n.* —*v.* **1** *intr.* (of water etc.) wash about; make the sound of washing or rising and falling. **2** *tr. archaic* strike violently. **3** *intr. archaic* swagger. —*n.* the motion or sound of swashing water. [imit.]

swashbuckler /ˈswɒʃˌbʌklə(r)/ *n.* a swaggering bully or ruffian. □ **swashbuckling** *adj. & n.* [SWASH + BUCKLER]

swastika /ˈswɒstɪkə/ *n.* **1** an ancient symbol formed by an equal-armed cross with each arm continued at a right angle. **2** this with clockwise continuations as the symbol of Nazi Germany.

[Skr. *svastika* f. *svastí* well-being f. *sú* good + *astí* being]

swat /swɒt/ *v. & n.* —*v.tr.* (**swatted**, **swatting**) **1** crush (a fly etc.) with a sharp blow. **2** hit hard and abruptly. —*n.* a swatting blow. [17th c. in the sense 'sit down': N.Engl. dial. & US var. of SQUAT]

swatch /swɒtʃ/ *n.* **1** a sample, esp. of cloth or fabric. **2** a collection of samples. [17th c.: orig. unkn.]

swath /swɔːθ/ *n.* (also **swathe** /sweɪð/) (pl. **swaths** /swɔːθs, swɔːðs/ or **swathes**) **1** a ridge of grass or corn etc. lying after being cut. **2** a space left clear after the passage of a mower etc. **3** a broad strip. □ **cut a wide swath** be effective in destruction. [OE *swæth, swathu*]

swathe /sweɪð/ *v. & n.* —*v.tr.* bind or enclose in bandages or garments etc. —*n.* a bandage or wrapping. [OE *swathian*]

swatter /ˈswɒtə(r)/ *n.* an implement for swatting flies.

sway /sweɪ/ *v. & n.* —*v.* **1** *intr. & tr.* lean or cause to lean unsteadily in different directions alternately. **2** *intr.* oscillate irregularly; waver. **3** *tr.* **a** control the motion or direction of. **b** have influence or rule over. —*n.* **1** rule, influence, or government (*hold sway*). **2** a swaying motion or position. [ME: cf. LG *swājen* be blown to and fro, Du. *zwaaien* swing, wave]

swear /sweə(r)/ *v.* (*past* **swore**; *past part.* **sworn**) **1** *tr.* **a** (often foll. by *to* + infin. or *that* + clause) state or promise solemnly or on oath. **b** take (an oath). **2** *tr. colloq.* say emphatically; insist (*swore he had not seen it*). **3** *tr.* cause to take an oath (*swore them to secrecy*). **4** *intr.* (often foll. by *at*) use profane or indecent language, esp. as an expletive or from anger. **5** *tr.* (often foll. by *against*) make a sworn affirmation of (an offence) (*swear treason against*). **6** *intr.* (foll. by *by*) **a** appeal to as a witness in taking an oath (*swear by Almighty God*). **b** *colloq.* have or express great confidence in (*swears by yoga*). **7** *intr.* (foll. by *to*; usu. in *neg.*) admit the certainty of (*could not swear to it*). □ **swear blind** *colloq.* affirm emphatically. **swear in** induct into office etc. by administering an oath. **swear off** *colloq.* promise to abstain from (drink etc.). **swear-word** a profane or indecent word, esp. uttered as an expletive. □ **swearer** *n.* [OE *swerian* f. Gmc, rel. to ANSWER]

sweat /swet/ *n. & v.* —*n.* **1** moisture exuded through the pores of the skin, esp. from heat or nervousness. **2** a state or period of sweating. **3** *colloq.* a state of anxiety (*was in a sweat about it*). **4** *colloq.* **a** drudgery, effort. **b** a laborious task or undertaking. **5** condensed moisture on a surface. —*v.* (*past* and *past part.* **sweated** or *US* **sweat**) **1** *intr.* exude sweat; perspire. **2** *intr.* be terrified, suffering, etc. **3** *intr.* (of a wall etc.) exhibit surface moisture. **4** *intr.* drudge, toil. **5** *tr.* heat (meat or vegetables) slowly in fat or water to extract the juices. **6** *tr.* emit (blood, gum, etc.) like sweat. **7** *tr.* make (a horse, athlete, etc.) sweat by exercise. **8** *tr.* a cause to drudge or toil. **b** (as **sweated** *adj.*) (of goods, workers, or labour) produced by or subjected to long hours under poor conditions. □ **no sweat** *colloq.* there is no need to worry. **sweat-band** a band of absorbent material inside a hat or round a wrist etc. to soak up sweat. **sweat blood** *colloq.* **1** work strenuously. **2** be extremely anxious. **sweat it**

out *colloq.* endure a difficult experience to the end. [ME *swet(e)*, alt. (after *swete* v. f. OE *swǣtan* OHG *sweizzen* roast) of *swote* f. OE *swāt* f. Gmc]

sweater /ˈswetə(r)/ n. a jersey or pullover of a kind worn before, during, or after exercise, or as an informal garment.

sweatshirt /ˈswetʃɜːt/ n. a sleeved cotton sweater of a kind worn by athletes before and after exercise.

sweatshop /ˈswetʃɒp/ n. a workshop where sweated labour is used.

sweatsuit /ˈswetsuːt, -sjuːt/ n. a suit of a sweatshirt and loose trousers, as worn by athletes etc.

sweaty /ˈsweti/ adj. (**sweatier**, **sweatiest**) **1** sweating; covered with sweat. **2** causing sweat. □ **sweatily** adv. **sweatiness** n.

Swede /swiːd/ n. **1 a** a native or national of Sweden. **b** a person of Swedish descent. **2** (**swede**) (in full **swede turnip**) a large yellow-fleshed turnip, *Brassica napus*, orig. from Sweden. [MLG & MDu. *Swēde*, prob. f. ON *Svíthjóth* f. *Svíar* Swedes + *thjóth* people]

Swedish /ˈswiːdɪʃ/ adj. & n. —adj. of or relating to Sweden or its people or language. —n. the language of Sweden.

Sweeney /ˈswiːnɪ/ n. (prec. by *the*) *Brit. sl.* the members of a flying squad. [rhyming sl. f. *Sweeney* Todd, a barber who murdered his customers]

sweep v. & n. —v. (past and past part. **swept**) **1** *tr.* clean or clear (a room or area etc.) with or as with a broom. **2** *intr.* (often foll. by *up*) clean a room etc. in this way. **3** *tr.* (often foll. by *up*) collect or remove (dirt or litter etc.) by sweeping. **4** *tr.* (foll. by *aside*, *away*, etc.) **a** push with or as with a broom. **b** dismiss or reject abruptly (*their objections were swept aside*). **5** *tr.* (foll. by *along*, *down*, etc.) carry or drive along with force. **6** *tr.* (foll. by *off*, *away*, etc.) remove or clear forcefully. **7** *tr.* traverse swiftly or lightly (*the wind swept the hillside*). **8** *tr.* impart a sweeping motion to (*swept his hand across*). **9** *tr.* swiftly cover or affect (*a new fashion swept the country*). **10** *intr.* **a** glide swiftly; speed along with unchecked motion. **b** go majestically. —n. **1** the act or motion or an instance of sweeping. **2** a curve in the road, a sweeping line of a hill, etc. **3** range or scope (*beyond the sweep of the human mind*). **4** = *chimney-sweep*. **5** a sortie by aircraft. **6** *colloq.* = SWEEPSTAKE. □ **make a clean sweep of 1** completely abolish or expel. **2** win all the prizes etc. in (a competition etc.). **sweep away 1** abolish swiftly. **2** (usu. in *passive*) powerfully affect, esp. emotionally. **sweep the board 1** win all the money in a gambling-game. **2** win all possible prizes etc. **swept-back** (of an aircraft wing) fixed at an acute angle to the fuselage, inclining outwards towards the rear. **swept-wing** (of an aircraft) having swept-back wings. [ME *swepe* (earlier *swōpe*) f. OE *swāpan*]

sweeper /ˈswiːpə(r)/ n. **1** a person who cleans by sweeping. **2** a device for sweeping carpets etc. **3** *Football* a defensive player positioned close to the goalkeeper.

sweeping /ˈswiːpɪŋ/ adj. & n. —adj. **1** wide in range or effect (*sweeping changes*). **2** taking no account of particular cases or exceptions (*a sweeping statement*). —n. (in pl.) dirt etc. collected by sweeping. □ **sweepingly** adv. **sweepingness** n.

sweepstake /ˈswiːpsteɪk/ n. **1** a form of gambling on horse-races etc. in which all competitors' stakes are paid to the winners. **2** a race with betting of this kind. **3** a prize or prizes won in a sweepstake.

sweet adj. & n. —adj. **1** having the pleasant taste characteristic of sugar. **2** smelling pleasant like roses or perfume etc.; fragrant. **3** (of sound etc.) melodious or harmonious. **4 a** not salt, sour, or bitter. **b** fresh, with flavour unimpaired by rottenness. **c** (of water) fresh and readily drinkable. **5** highly gratifying or attractive. **6** amiable, pleasant (*has a sweet nature*). **7** *colloq.* (of a person or thing) pretty, charming, endearing. **8** (foll. by *on*) *colloq.* fond of; in love with. —n. **1** *Brit.* a small shaped piece of confectionery usu. made with sugar or sweet chocolate. **2** *Brit.* a sweet dish forming a course of a meal. **3** a sweet part of something; sweetness. **4** (in pl.) delights, gratification. □ **sweet-and-sour** cooked in a sauce containing sugar and vinegar or lemon etc. **sweet cicely** a white-flowered aromatic plant, *Myrrhis odorata*. **sweet corn 1** a kind of maize with kernels having a high sugar content. **2** these kernels, eaten as a vegetable when young. **sweet pea** any climbing plant of the genus *Lathyrus*, esp. *L. odoratus* with fragrant flowers in many colours. **sweet potato 1** a tropical climbing plant, *Ipomoea batatas*, with sweet tuberous roots used for food. **2** the root of this. **sweet talk** flattery, blandishment. **sweet-talk** v.tr. *colloq.* flatter in order to persuade. **sweet-tempered** amiable. **sweet tooth** a liking for sweet-tasting things. **sweet william** a plant, *Dianthus barbatus*, with clusters of vivid fragrant flowers. □ **sweetish** adj. **sweetly** adv. **sweetness** n. [OE *swēte* f. Gmc]

sweetbread /ˈswiːtbred/ n. the pancreas or thymus of an animal, esp. as food.

sweeten /ˈswiːt(ə)n/ v.tr. & intr. **1** make or become sweet or sweeter. **2** make agreeable or less painful. □ **sweetening** n.

sweetener /ˈswiːtənə(r)/ n. **1** a substance used to sweeten food or drink. **2** *colloq.* a bribe or inducement.

sweetheart /ˈswiːthɑːt/ n. **1** a lover or darling. **2** a term of endearment (esp. as a form of address). □ **sweetheart agreement** (or **deal**) *colloq.* an industrial agreement reached privately by employers and trade unions in their own interests.

sweetie /ˈswiːtɪ/ n. *colloq.* **1** *Brit.* a sweet. **2** (also **sweetie-pie**) a term of endearment (esp. as a form of address).

sweetmeal /ˈswiːtmiːl/ n. **1** sweetened wholemeal. **2** a sweetmeal biscuit.

sweetmeat /ˈswiːtmiːt/ n. **1** a sweet (see SWEET n. 1). **2** a small fancy cake.

sweetshop /ˈswiːtʃɒp/ n. *Brit.* a shop selling sweets as its main item.

swell v., n., & adj. —v. (past part. **swollen** /ˈswəʊlən/ or **swelled**) **1** intr. & tr. grow bigger or louder or more intense; expand; increase in force or intensity. **2** intr. (often foll. by *up*) & tr. rise up from the surrounding surface. **3** intr. (foll. by *out*) bulge. **4** intr. (of the heart as the seat of emotion) feel full of joy, pride, relief, etc. **5** intr. (foll. by *with*) be hardly able to restrain (pride etc.). —n. **1** an act or the state of swelling. **2** the heaving of the sea with waves that do not break, e.g. after a storm. **3 a** a crescendo. **b** a mechanism in an organ etc. for obtaining a crescendo or diminuendo. **4** *colloq.* a person of distinction or of dashing or fashionable appearance. —*adj.* **1** esp. *US colloq.* fine, splendid, excellent. **2** *colloq.* smart, fashionable. □ **swelled** (or **swollen**) **head** *colloq.* conceit. □ **swellish** *adj.* [OE *swellan* f. Gmc]

swelling /'swelɪŋ/ *n.* an abnormal protuberance on or in the body.

swelter /'sweltə(r)/ *v. & n.* —*v.intr.* (of the atmosphere, or a person etc. suffering from it) be uncomfortably hot. —*n.* a sweltering atmosphere or condition. □ **swelteringly** *adv.* [base of (now dial.) *swelt* f. OE *sweltan* perish f. Gmc]

swept *past* and *past part.* of SWEEP.

swerve *v. & n.* —*v.intr. & tr.* change or cause to change direction, esp. abruptly. —*n.* **1** a swerving movement. **2** divergence from a course. □ **swerveless** *adj.* **swerver** *n.* [ME, repr. OE *sweorfan* SCOUR¹]

swift *adj., adv., & n.* —*adj.* **1** quick, rapid; soon coming or passing. **2** speedy, prompt (*a swift response; was swift to act*). —*adv.* (*archaic* except in comb.) swiftly (*swift-moving*). —*n.* any swift-flying insect-eating bird of the family Apodidae, with long wings and a superficial resemblance to a swallow. □ **swiftly** *adv.* **swiftness** *n.* [OE, rel. to *swīfan* move in a course]

swig *v. & n.* —*v.tr. & intr.* (**swigged, swigging**) *colloq.* drink in large draughts. —*n.* a swallow of drink, esp. a large amount. □ **swigger** *n.* [16th c., orig. as noun in obs. sense 'liquor': orig. unkn.]

swill *v. & n.* —*v.* **1** *tr.* (often foll. by *out*) rinse or flush; pour water over or through. **2** *tr. & intr.* drink greedily. —*n.* **1** an act of rinsing. **2** mainly liquid refuse as pig-food. **3** inferior liquor. □ **swiller** *n.* [OE *swillan, swilian,* of unkn. orig.]

swim *v. & n.* —*v.* (**swimming;** *past* **swam;** *past part.* **swum**) **1** *intr.* propel the body through water by working the arms and legs, or (of a fish) the fins and tail. **2** *tr.* **a** traverse (a stretch of water or its distance) by swimming. **b** compete in (a race) by swimming. **c** use (a particular stroke) in swimming. **3** *intr.* float on or at the surface of a liquid (*bubbles swimming on the surface*). **4** *intr.* appear to undulate or reel or whirl. **5** *intr.* have a dizzy effect or sensation (*my head swam*). **6** *intr.* (foll. by *in, with*) be flooded. —*n.* **1** a spell or the act of swimming. **2** a deep pool frequented by fish in a river. □ **in the swim** involved in or acquainted with what is going on. **swim-bladder** a gas-filled sac in fishes used to maintain buoyancy. **swimming-bath** (or **-pool**) an artificial indoor or outdoor pool for swimming. **swimming-costume** *Brit.* a garment worn for swimming. □ **swimmable** *adj.* **swimmer** *n.* [OE *swimman* f. Gmc]

swimmingly /'swɪmɪŋlɪ/ *adv.* with easy and unobstructed progress.

swimsuit /'swɪmsuːt, -sjuːt/ *n.* a one-piece swimming-costume worn by women. □ **swimsuited** *adj.*

swimwear /'swɪmweə(r)/ *n.* clothing worn for swimming.

swindle /'swɪnd(ə)l/ *v. & n.* —*v.tr.* (often foll. by *out of*) **1** cheat (a person) of money, possessions, etc. (*was swindled out of all his savings*). **2** cheat a person of (money etc.) (*swindled all his savings out of him*). —*n.* **1** an act of swindling. **2** a person or thing represented as what it is not. **3** a fraudulent scheme. □ **swindler** *n.* [back-form. f. *swindler* f. G *Schwindler* extravagant maker of schemes, swindler, f. *schwindeln* be dizzy]

swine *n.* (pl. same) **1** *formal* or *US* a pig. **2** *colloq.* (pl. **swine** or **swines**) **a** a term of contempt or disgust for a person. **b** a very unpleasant or difficult thing. □ **swine fever** an intestinal virus disease of pigs. □ **swinish** *adj.* (esp. in sense 2). **swinishly** *adv.* **swinishness** *n.* [OE *swīn* f. Gmc]

swing *v. & n.* —*v.* (*past* and *past part.* **swung**) **1** *intr. & tr.* move or cause to move with a to-and-fro or curving motion, as of an object attached at one end and hanging free at the other. **2** *intr. & tr.* **a** sway. **b** hang so as to be free to sway. **c** oscillate or cause to oscillate. **3** *intr. & tr.* revolve or cause to revolve. **4** *intr.* move by gripping something and leaping etc. (*swung from tree to tree*). **5** *intr.* go with a swinging gait (*swung out of the room*). **6** *intr.* (foll. by *round*) move round to the opposite direction. **7** *intr.* change from one opinion or mood to another. **8** *intr.* (foll. by *at*) attempt to hit or punch. **9 a** *intr.* (also **swing it**) play music with a swing rhythm. **b** *tr.* play (a tune) with swing. **10** *intr. colloq.* **a** be lively or up to date; enjoy oneself. **b** be promiscuous. **11** *intr. colloq.* (of a party etc.) be lively, successful, etc. **12** *tr.* have a decisive influence on (esp. voting etc.). **13** *tr. colloq.* deal with or achieve; manage. **14** *intr. colloq.* be executed by hanging. —*n.* **1** the act or instance of swinging. **2** the motion of swinging. **3** the extent of swinging. **4** a swinging or smooth gait or rhythm or action. **5 a** a seat slung by ropes or chains etc. for swinging on or in. **b** a spell of swinging on this. **6** an easy but vigorous continued action. **7 a** jazz or dance music with an easy flowing rhythm. **b** the rhythmic feeling or drive of this music. **8** a discernible change in opinion, esp. the amount by which votes or points scored etc. change from one side to another. □ **swing-boat** a boat-shaped swing at fairs. **swing-bridge** a bridge that can be swung to one side to allow the passage of ships. **swing-door** a door able to open in either direction and close itself when released. **swings and roundabouts** a situation affording no eventual gain or loss (from the phr. *lose on the swings what you make on the roundabouts*). **swing-wing** an aircraft wing that can move from a right-angled to a swept-back position. □ **swinger** *n.* (esp. in sense 10 of *v.*). [OE *swingan* to beat f. Gmc]

swingeing /'swɪndʒɪŋ/ *adj.* esp. *Brit.* **1** (of a blow) forcible. **2** far-reaching, esp. in severity (*swingeing economies*). □ **swingeingly** *adv.* [swinge, alt. f. ME *swenge* f. OE *swengan* shake, shatter, f. Gmc]

swinging /'swɪŋɪŋ/ *adj.* **1** (of gait, melody, etc.) vigorously rhythmical. **2** *colloq.* **a** lively; up to date; excellent. **b** promiscuous. □ **swingingly** *adv.*

swipe *v. & n. colloq.* —*v.* **1** *tr. & (*often foll. by *at*) *intr.* hit hard and recklessly. **2** *tr.* steal. —*n.* a reckless hard hit or attempted hit. □ **swiper** *n.* [perh. var. of SWEEP]

swirl *v. & n.* —*v.intr. & tr.* move or flow or carry along with a whirling motion. —*n.* **1** a swirling motion of or in water, air, etc. **2** the act of swirling. **3** a twist or curl, esp. as part of a pattern or design. □ **swirly** *adj.* [ME (orig. as noun): orig. Sc., perh. of LG or Du. orig.]

swish *v.*, *n.*, & *adj.* —*v.* **1** *tr.* swing (a scythe or stick etc.) audibly through the air, grass, etc. **2** *intr.* move with or make a swishing sound. **3** *tr.* (foll. by *off*) cut (a flower etc.) in this way. —*n.* a swishing action or sound. —*adj. colloq.* smart, fashionable. □ **swishy** *adj.* [imit.]

Swiss *adj.* & *n.* —*adj.* of or relating to Switzerland in Western Europe or its people. —*n.* (*pl.* same) **1** a native or national of Switzerland. **2** a person of Swiss descent. □ **Swiss cheese plant** a climbing house-plant, *Monstera deliciosa*, with aerial roots and holes in the leaves (as in some Swiss cheeses). **Swiss roll** a cylindrical cake with a spiral cross-section, made from a flat piece of sponge cake spread with jam etc. and rolled up. [F *Suisse* f. MHG *Swīz*]

switch *n.* & *v.* —*n.* **1** a device for making and breaking the connection in an electric circuit. **2 a** a transfer, change-over, or deviation. **b** an exchange. **3** a slender flexible shoot cut from a tree. **4** a light tapering rod. **5** *US* a device at the junction of railway tracks for transferring a train from one track to another; = POINT *n.* 17. **6** a tress of false or detached hair tied at one end used in hairdressing. —*v.* **1** *tr.* (foll. by *on*, *off*) turn (an electrical device) on or off. **2** *intr.* change or transfer position, subject, etc. **3** *tr.* change or transfer. **4** *tr.* reverse the positions of; exchange (*switched chairs*). **5** *tr.* swing or snatch (a thing) suddenly (*switched it out of my hand*). **6** *tr.* beat or flick with a switch. □ **switch-blade** a pocket knife with the blade released by a spring. **switched-on** *colloq.* **1** up to date; aware of what is going on. **2** excited; under the influence of drugs. **switch off** *colloq.* cease to pay attention. **switch over** change or exchange. □ **switcher** *n.* [earlier *swits, switz*, prob. f. LG]

switchback /ˈswɪtʃbæk/ *n.* **1** *Brit.* a railway at a fair etc., in which the train's ascents are effected by the momentum of its previous descents. **2** a railway or road with alternate sharp ascents and descents.

switchboard /ˈswɪtʃbɔːd/ *n.* an apparatus for varying connections between electric circuits, esp. in telephony.

swivel /ˈswɪv(ə)l/ *n.* & *v.* —*n.* a coupling between two parts enabling one to revolve without turning the other. —*v.tr.* & *intr.* (**swivelled, swivelling**; *US* **swiveled, swiveling**) turn on or as on a swivel. □ **swivel chair** a chair with a seat able to be turned horizontally. [ME f. weak grade *swif-* of OE *swīfan* sweep + -LE¹: cf. SWIFT]

swizz *n.* (also **swiz**) (*pl.* **swizzes**) *Brit. colloq.* **1** something unfair or disappointing. **2** a swindle. [abbr. of SWIZZLE²]

swizzle¹ /ˈswɪz(ə)l/ *n.* & *v. colloq.* —*n.* a mixed alcoholic drink esp. of rum or gin and bitters made frothy. —*v.tr.* stir with a swizzle-stick. □ **swizzle-stick** a stick used for frothing or flattening drinks. [19th c.: orig. unkn.]

swizzle² /ˈswɪz(ə)l/ *n. Brit. colloq.* = SWIZZ. [20th c.: prob. alt. of SWINDLE]

swob var. of SWAB.

swollen *past part.* of SWELL.

swoon /swuːn/ *v.* & *n. literary* —*v.intr.* faint; fall into a fainting-fit. —*n.* an occurrence of fainting. [ME *swoune* perh. back-form. f. *swogning* (n.) f. *iswogen* f. OE *geswogen* overcome]

swoop /swuːp/ *v.* & *n.* —*v.* **1** *intr.* (often foll. by *down*) descend rapidly like a bird of prey. **2** *intr.* (often foll. by *on*) make a sudden attack from a distance. **3** *tr.* (often foll. by *up*) snatch the whole of at one swoop. —*n.* a swooping or snatching movement or action. [perh. dial. var. of obs. *swōpe* f. OE *swāpan*: see SWEEP]

swoosh /swʊʃ/ *n.* & *v.* —*n.* the noise of a sudden rush of liquid, air, etc. —*v.intr.* move with this noise. [imit.]

swop var. of SWAP.

sword /sɔːd/ *n.* **1** a weapon usu. of metal with a long blade and hilt with a handguard, used esp. for thrusting or striking, and often worn as part of ceremonial dress. **2** (prec. by *the*) **a** war. **b** military power. □ **put to the sword** kill, esp. in war. **sword dance** a dance in which the performers brandish swords or step about swords laid on the ground. **sword of Damocles** /ˈdæməˌkliːz/ an imminent danger (from *Damokles*, flatterer of Dionysius of Syracuse (4th c. BC) made to feast while a sword hung by a hair over him). □ **swordlike** *adj.* [OE *sw(e)ord* f. Gmc]

swordfish /ˈsɔːdfɪʃ/ *n.* a large marine fish, *Xiphias gladius*, with an extended swordlike upper jaw.

swordplay /ˈsɔːdpleɪ/ *n.* **1** fencing. **2** repartee; cut-and-thrust argument.

swordsman /ˈsɔːdzmən/ *n.* (*pl.* **-men**) a person of (usu. specified) skill with a sword. □ **swordsmanship** *n.*

swordstick /ˈsɔːdstɪk/ *n.* a hollow walking-stick containing a blade that can be used as a sword.

swore *past* of SWEAR.

sworn 1 *past part.* of SWEAR. **2** *adj.* bound by or as by an oath (*sworn enemies*).

swot *v.* & *n. Brit. colloq.* —*v.* (**swotted, swotting**) **1** *intr.* study assiduously. **2** *tr.* (often foll. by *up*) study (a subject) hard or hurriedly. —*n.* **1** a person who swots. **2 a** hard study. **b** a thing that requires this. [dial. var. of SWEAT]

swum *past part.* of SWIM.

swung *past* and *past part.* of SWING.

sybarite /ˈsɪbəˌraɪt/ *n.* & *adj.* —*n.* a person who is self-indulgent or devoted to sensuous luxury. —*adj.* fond of luxury or sensuousness. □ **sybaritic** /-ˈrɪtɪk/ *adj.* **sybaritical** /-ˈrɪtɪk(ə)l/ *adj.* **sybaritically** /-ˈrɪtɪkəlɪ/ *adv.* **sybaritism** *n.* [orig. an inhabitant of Sybaris in S. Italy, noted for luxury, f. L *sybarita* f. Gk *subarītēs*]

sycamore /ˈsɪkəˌmɔː(r)/ *n.* **1** (in full **sycamore maple**) **a** a large maple, *Acer pseudoplatanus*, with winged seeds, grown for its shade and timber. **b** its wood. **2** *US* the plane-tree or its wood. [ME f. OF *sic(h)amor* f. L *sycomorus* f. Gk *sukomoros* f. *sukon* fig + *moron* mulberry]

sycophant /ˈsɪkəˌfænt/ *n.* a servile flatterer; a toady. □ **sycophancy** *n.* **sycophantic** /-ˈfæntɪk/ *adj.* **sycophantically** /-ˈfæntɪkəlɪ/ *adv.* [F *sycophante* or L *sycophanta* f. Gk *sukophantēs* informer f. *sukon* fig + *phainō* show: the reason for the name is uncert., association with informing against the illegal exportation of figs from ancient Athens (recorded by Plutarch) cannot be substantiated]

syllabary /ˈsɪləbərɪ/ *n.* (*pl.* **-ies**) a list of characters representing syllables. [mod.L *syllabarium* (as SYLLABLE)]

syllabi *pl.* of SYLLABUS.

syllabic /sɪˈlæbɪk/ *adj.* of, relating to, or based on syllables. □ **syllabically** *adv.* **syllabicity**

/-'bɪsɪtɪ/ n. [F syllabique or LL syllabicus f. Gk sullabikos (as SYLLABLE)]

syllabication /ˌsɪlæbɪˈkeɪʃ(ə)n/ n. (also **syllabification**) (/-fɪˈkeɪʃ(ə)n/) division into or articulation by syllables. □ **syllabify** v.tr. (**-ies**, **-ied**). [med.L syllabicatio f. syllabicare f. L syllaba: see SYLLABLE]

syllable /ˈsɪləb(ə)l/ n. **1** a unit of pronunciation uttered without interruption, forming the whole or a part of a word and usu. having one vowel sound often with a consonant or consonants before or after. **2** a character or characters representing a syllable. **3** (usu. with neg.) the least amount of speech or writing (did not utter a syllable). □ **syllabled** adj. (also in comb.). [ME f. AF sillable f. OF sillabe f. L syllaba f. Gk sullabē (as SYN-, lambanō take)]

syllabub /ˈsɪləˌbʌb/ n. (also **sillabub**) a dessert made of cream or milk flavoured, sweetened, and whipped to thicken it. [16th c.: orig. unkn.]

syllabus /ˈsɪləbəs/ n. (pl. **syllabuses** or **syllabi** /-ˌbaɪ/) **1 a** the programme or outline of a course of study, teaching, etc. **b** a statement of the requirements for a particular examination. [mod.L, orig. a misreading of L sittybas accus. pl. of sittyba f. Gk sittuba title-slip or label]

syllepsis /sɪˈlepsɪs/ n. (pl. **syllepses** /-siːz/) a figure of speech in which a word is applied to two others in different senses (e.g. caught the train and a bad cold) or to two others of which it grammatically suits one only (e.g. neither they nor it is working). □ **sylleptic** adj. **sylleptically** adv. [LL f. Gk sullēpsis taking together f. sullambanō: see SYLLABLE]

syllogism /ˈsɪləˌdʒɪz(ə)m/ n. a form of reasoning in which a conclusion is drawn from two given or assumed propositions (premisses). □ **syllogistic** /-ˈdʒɪstɪk/ adj. **syllogistically** /-ˈdʒɪstɪkəlɪ/ adv. [ME f. OF silogisme or L syllogismus f. Gk sullogismos f. sullogizomai (as SYN-, logizomai to reason f. logos reason)]

sylph /sɪlf/ n. **1** an elemental spirit of the air. **2** a slender graceful woman or girl. □ **sylphlike** adj. [mod.L sylphes, G Sylphen (pl.), perh. based on L sylvestris of the woods + nympha nymph]

sylvan /ˈsɪlv(ə)n/ adj. (also **silvan**) **1 a** of the woods. **b** having woods; wooded. **2** rural. [F sylvain (obs. silvain) or L Silvanus woodland deity f. silva a wood]

sylviculture var. of SILVICULTURE.

symbiont /ˈsɪmbɪənt/ n. an organism living in symbiosis. [Gk sumbiōn -ountos part. of sumbioō live together (as SYMBIOSIS)]

symbiosis /ˌsɪmbaɪˈəʊsɪs, ˌsɪmbɪ-/ n. (pl. **symbioses** /-siːz/) **1 a** an interaction between two different organisms living in close physical association, usu. to the advantage of both. **b** an instance of this. **2 a** a mutually advantageous association or relationship between persons. **b** an instance of this. □ **symbiotic** /-ˈɒtɪk/ adj. **symbiotically** /-ˈɒtɪkəlɪ/ adv. [mod.L f. Gk sumbiōsis a living together f. sumbioō live together, sumbios companion (as SYN-, bios life)]

symbol /ˈsɪmb(ə)l/ n. **1** a thing conventionally regarded as typifying, representing, or recalling something, esp. an idea or quality (white is a symbol of purity). **2** a mark or character taken as the conventional sign of some object, idea, function, or process, e.g. the letters standing for the chemical elements or the characters in musical notation. □ **symbology** /-ˈbɒlədʒɪ/ n.

[ME f. L symbolum f. Gk sumbolon mark, token (as SYN-, ballō throw)]

symbolic /sɪmˈbɒlɪk/ adj. (also **symbolical** /-ˈbɒlɪk(ə)l/) **1** of or serving as a symbol. **2** involving the use of symbols or symbolism. □ **symbolically** adv. [F symbolique or LL symbolicus f. Gk sumbolikos]

symbolism /ˈsɪmbəˌlɪz(ə)m/ n. **1 a** the use of symbols to represent ideas. **b** symbols collectively. **2** an artistic and poetic movement or style using symbols and indirect suggestion to express ideas, emotions, etc. □ **symbolist** n. **symbolistic** /-ˈlɪstɪk/ adj.

symbolize /ˈsɪmbəˌlaɪz/ v.tr. (also **-ise**) **1** be a symbol of. **2** represent by means of symbols. □ **symbolization** /-ˈzeɪʃ(ə)n/ n. [F symboliser f. symbole SYMBOL]

symmetry /ˈsɪmɪtrɪ/ n. (pl. **-ies**) **1 a** correct proportion of the parts of a thing; balance, harmony. **b** beauty resulting from this. **2 a** a structure that allows an object to be divided into parts of an equal shape and size and similar position to the point or line or plane of division. **b** the possession of such a structure. **3** the repetition of exactly similar parts facing each other or a centre. □ **symmetric** /sɪˈmetrɪk/ adj. **symmetrical** /-ˈmetrɪk(ə)l/ adj. **symmetrically** /-ˈmetrɪkəlɪ/ adv. **symmetrize** v.tr. (also **-ise**). [obs. F symmétrie or L summetria f. Gk (as SYN-, metron measure)]

sympathetic /ˌsɪmpəˈθetɪk/ adj. **1** of, showing, or expressing sympathy. **2** due to sympathy. **3** likeable or capable of evoking sympathy. **4** (of a person) friendly and cooperative. **5** (foll. by to) inclined to favour (a proposal etc.) (was most sympathetic to the idea). **6** designating the part of the nervous system consisting of nerves leaving the thoracic and lumbar regions of the spinal cord and connecting with the nerve cells in or near the viscera □ **sympathetic magic** a type of magic that seeks to achieve an effect by performing an associated action or using an associated thing. □ **sympathetically** adv. [SYMPATHY, after pathetic]

sympathize /ˈsɪmpəˌθaɪz/ v.intr. (also **-ise**) (often foll. by with) **1** feel or express sympathy; share a feeling or opinion. **2** agree with a sentiment or opinion. □ **sympathizer** n. [F sympathiser (as SYMPATHY)]

sympathy /ˈsɪmpəθɪ/ n. (pl. **-ies**) **1 a** the state of being simultaneously affected with the same feeling as another. **b** the capacity for this. **2** (often foll. by with) the act of sharing or tendency to share (with a person etc.) in an emotion or sensation or condition of another person or thing. **b** (in sing. or pl.) compassion or commiseration; condolences. **3** (often foll. by for) a favourable attitude; approval. **4** (in sing. or pl.; often foll. by with) agreement (with a person etc.) in opinion or desire. **5** (attrib.) in support of another cause (sympathy strike). □ **in sympathy** (often foll. by with) **1** having or showing or resulting from sympathy (with another). **2** by way of sympathetic action. [L sympathia f. Gk sumpatheia (as SYN-, pathēs f. pathos feeling)]

symphonic /sɪmˈfɒnɪk/ adj. (of music) relating to or having the form or character of a symphony. □ **symphonic poem** an extended orchestral piece, usu. in one movement, on a descriptive or rhapsodic theme. □ **symphonically** adv.

symphony /'sɪmfənɪ/ n. (pl. **-ies**) **1** an elaborate composition usu. for full orchestra, and in several movements with one or more in sonata form. **2** = *symphony orchestra*. □ **symphony orchestra** a large orchestra suitable for playing symphonies etc. [ME, = harmony of sound, f. OF *symphonie* f. L *symphonia* f. Gk *sumphōnia* (as SYN-, *-phōnos* f. *phōnē* sound)]

symposium /sɪm'pəʊzɪəm/ n. (pl. **symposia** /-zɪə/) **1 a** a conference or meeting to discuss a particular subject. **b** a collection of essays or papers for this purpose. **2** a philosophical or other friendly discussion. [L f. Gk *sumposion* drinking-party (as SYN-, *-potēs* drinker)]

symptom /'sɪmptəm/ n. **1** *Med.* a change in the physical or mental condition of a person, regarded as evidence of a disease. **2** a sign of the existence of something. [ME *synthoma* f. med.L *sinthoma*, & f. LL *symptoma* f. Gk *sumptōma -atos* chance, symptom, f. *sumpiptō* happen (as SYN-, *piptō* fall)]

symptomatic /ˌsɪmptə'mætɪk/ adj. serving as a symptom. □ **symptomatically** adv.

syn- /sɪn/ prefix (also **syl-** before *l*, **sym-** before *b, m, f*) with, together, alike. [from or after Gk *sun-* f. *sun* with]

synaesthesia /ˌsɪniːs'θiːzɪə/ n. (*US* **synesthesia**) **1** *Psychol.* the production of a mental sense-impression relating to one sense by the stimulation of another sense. **2** a sensation produced in a part of the body by stimulation of another part. □ **synaesthetic** /-'θetɪk/ adj. [mod.L f. SYN- after *anaesthesia*]

synagogue /'sɪnəˌgɒg/ n. **1** the building where a Jewish assembly or congregation meets for religious observance and instruction. **2** the assembly itself. □ **synagogal** /-'gɒg(ə)l/ adj. **synagogical** /-'gɒdʒɪk(ə)l/ adj. [ME f. OF *sinagoge* f. LL *synagoga* f. Gk *sunagōgē* meeting (as SYN-, *agō* bring)]

synapse /'saɪnæps, 'sɪn-/ n. *Anat.* a junction of two nerve-cells. □ **synaptic** /-'næptɪk/ **synaptically** /-'næptɪkəlt/ adv. [Gk *synapsis* (as SYN-, *hapsis* f. *haptō* join)]

sync /sɪŋk/ n. & v. (also **synch**) *colloq.* —n. synchronization. —v.tr. & intr. synchronize. □ **in** (or **out of**) **sync** (often foll. by *with*) according or agreeing well (or badly). [abbr.]

synchro- /'sɪŋkrəʊ/ comb. form synchronized, synchronous.

synchromesh /'sɪŋkrəʊˌmeʃ/ n. & adj. —n. a system of gear-changing, esp. in motor vehicles, in which the driving and driven gearwheels are made to revolve at the same speed during engagement by means of a set of friction clutches, thereby easing the change. —adj. relating to or using this system. [abbr. of *synchronized mesh*]

synchronic /sɪŋ'krɒnɪk, sɪn-/ adj. describing a subject (esp. a language) as it exists at one point in time. □ **synchronically** adv. [LL *synchronus*: see SYNCHRONOUS]

synchronism /'sɪŋkrəˌnɪz(ə)m/ n. **1** = SYNCHRONY. **2** the process of synchronizing sound and picture in cinematography, television, etc. □ **synchronistic** /-'nɪstɪk/ adj. **synchronistically** /-'nɪstɪkəlɪ/ adv. [Gk *sugkhronismos* (as SYNCHRONOUS)]

synchronize /'sɪŋkrəˌnaɪz/ v. (also **-ise**) **1** *intr.* (often foll. by *with*) occur at the same time; be simultaneous. **2** *tr.* cause to occur at the same time. **3** *tr.* carry out the synchronism of (a film). **4** *tr.* ascertain or set forth the correspondence in the date of (events). **5 a** *tr.* cause (clocks etc.) to show a standard or uniform time. **b** *intr.* (of clocks etc.) be synchronized. □ **synchronized swimming** a form of swimming in which participants make coordinated leg and arm movements in time to music. □ **synchronization** /-'zeɪʃ(ə)n/ n. **synchronizer** n.

synchronous /'sɪŋkrənəs/ adj. (often foll. by *with*) existing or occurring at the same time. □ **synchronously** adv. [LL *synchronus* f. Gk *sugkhronos* (as SYN-, *khronos* time)]

synchrony /'sɪŋkrənɪ/ n. **1** the state of being synchronic or synchronous. **2** the treatment of events etc. as being synchronous. [Gk *sugkhronos*: see SYNCHRONOUS]

syncopate /'sɪŋkəˌpeɪt/ v.tr. **1** *Mus.* displace the beats or accents in (a passage) so that strong beats become weak and vice versa. **2** shorten (a word) by dropping interior sounds or letters, as *symbology* for *symbolology*, *Gloster* for *Gloucester*. □ **syncopation** /-'peɪʃ(ə)n/ n. **syncopator** n. [LL *syncopare* swoon (as SYNCOPE)]

syncope /'sɪŋkəpɪ/ n. **1** *Gram.* the omission of interior sounds or letters in a word (see SYNCOPATE 2). **2** *Med.* a temporary loss of consciousness caused by a fall in blood pressure. □ **syncopal** adj. [ME f. LL *syncopē* f. Gk *sugkopē* (as SYN-, *koptō* strike, cut off)]

syncretism /'sɪŋkrəˌtɪz(ə)m/ n. **1** *Philos.* & *Theol.* the process or an instance of syncretizing. □ **syncretic** /-'kretɪk/ adj. **syncretist** n. **syncretistic** /-'tɪstɪk/ adj. [mod.L *syncretismus* f. Gk *sugkrētismos* f. *sugkrētizō* (of two parties) combine against a third f. *krēs* Cretan (orig. of ancient Cretan communities)]

syncretize /'sɪŋkrəˌtaɪz/ v.tr. (also **-ise**) *Philos.* & *Theol.* attempt, esp. inconsistently, to unify or reconcile differing schools of thought.

syndic /'sɪndɪk/ n. **1** a government official in various countries. **2** *Brit.* a business agent of certain universities and corporations. □ **syndical** adj. [F f. LL *syndicus* f. Gk *sundikos* (as SYN-, *-dikos* f. *dikē* justice)]

syndicalism /'sɪndɪkəˌlɪz(ə)m/ n. *hist.* a movement for transferring the ownership and control of the means of production and distribution to workers' unions. □ **syndicalist** n. [F *syndicalisme* f. *syndical* (as SYNDIC)]

syndicate n. & v. —n. /'sɪndɪkət/ **1** a combination of individuals or commercial firms to promote some common interest. **2** an association or agency supplying material simultaneously to a number of newspapers or periodicals. **3** a group of people who combine to buy or rent property, gamble, organize crime, etc. **4** a committee of syndics. —v.tr. /'sɪndɪˌkeɪt/ **1** form into a syndicate. **2** publish (material) through a syndicate. □ **syndication** /-'keɪʃ(ə)n/ n. [F *syndicat* f. med.L *syndicatus* f. LL *syndicus*: see SYNDIC]

syndrome /'sɪndrəʊm/ n. **1** a group of concurrent symptoms of a disease. **2** a characteristic combination of opinions, emotions, behaviour, etc. □ **syndromic** /-'drɒmɪk/ adj. [mod.L f. Gk *sundromē* (as SYN-, *dromē* f. *dramein* to run)]

syne /saɪn/ adv., conj., & prep. *Sc.* since. [contr. f. ME *sithen* SINCE]

synecdoche /sɪ'nekdəkɪ/ n. a figure of speech in which a part is made to represent the whole or vice versa (e.g. *new faces at the meeting*; *England* lost by six wickets). □ **synecdochic** /-'dɒkɪk/ adj. [ME f. L f. Gk sunekdokhē (as SYN-, ekdokhē f. ekdekhomai take up)]

synecology /ˌsɪnɪ'kɒlədʒɪ/ n. the ecological study of plant or animal communities. □ **synecological** /-ˌiːkə'lɒdʒɪk(ə)l/ adj. **synecologist** n.

synergism /'sɪnəˌdʒɪz(ə)m/ n. (also **synergy** /'sɪnədʒɪ/) the combined effect of drugs, organs, etc., that exceeds the sum of their individual effects. □ **synergist** /-'dʒetɪk/ adj. **synergic** /-'nɜːdʒɪk/ adj. **synergistic** /-'dʒɪstɪk/ adj. **synergistically** /-'dʒɪstɪkəlɪ/ adv. [Gk sunergos working together (as SYN-, ergon work)]

synesthesia US var. of SYNAESTHESIA.

synod /'sɪnəd/ n. **1** a Church council attended by delegated clergy and sometimes laity. **2** a Presbyterian ecclesiastical court above the presbyteries and subject to the General Assembly. □ **synodal** adj. **synodical** /-'nɒdɪk(ə)l/ adj. [ME f. LL synodus f. Gk sunodos meeting (as SYN-, hodos way)]

synonym /'sɪnənɪm/ n. a word or phrase that means exactly or nearly the same as another in the same language (e.g. shut and close). □ **synonymic** /-'nɪmɪk/ adj. **synonymity** /-'nɪmɪtɪ/ n. [ME f. L synonymum f. Gk sunōnumon neut. of sunōnumos (as SYN-, onoma name): cf. ANONYMOUS]

synonymous /sɪ'nɒnɪməs/ adj. (often foll. by with) **1** having the same meaning; being a synonym (of). **2** (of a name, idea, etc.) suggestive of or associated with another (excessive drinking regarded as synonymous with violence). □ **synonymously** adv. **synonymousness** n.

synonymy /sɪ'nɒnɪmɪ/ n. (pl. **-ies**) **1** the state of being synonymous. **2** the collocation of synonyms for emphasis (e.g. in any shape or form). [LL synonymia f. Gk sunōnumia (as SYNONYM)]

synopsis /sɪ'nɒpsɪs/ n. (pl. **synopses** /-siːz/) **1** a summary or outline. **2** a brief general survey. □ **synopsize** v.tr. (also **-ise**). [LL f. Gk (as SYN-, opsis seeing)]

synoptic /sɪ'nɒptɪk/ adj. & n. —adj. **1** of, forming, or giving a synopsis. **2** taking or affording a comprehensive mental view. **3** of the Synoptic Gospels. —n. **1** a Synoptic Gospel. **2** the writer of a Synoptic Gospel. □ **Synoptic Gospels** the Gospels of Matthew, Mark, and Luke, describing events from a similar point of view. □ **synoptical** adj. **synoptically** adv. [Gk sunoptikos (as SYNOPSIS)]

synovia /saɪ'nəʊvɪə, sɪn-/ n. Physiol. a viscous fluid lubricating joints and tendon sheaths. □ **synovial membrane** a dense membrane of connective tissue secreting synovia. □ **synovial** adj. [mod.L, formed prob. arbitrarily by Paracelsus]

synovitis /ˌsaɪnəʊ'vaɪtɪs, sɪn-/ n. inflammation of the synovial membrane.

syntactic /sɪn'tæktɪk/ adj. of or according to syntax. □ **syntactical** adj. **syntactically** adv. [Gk suntaktikos (as SYNTAX)]

syntax /'sɪntæks/ n. **1** the grammatical arrangement of words, showing their connection and relation. **2** a set of rules for or an analysis of this. [F syntaxe or LL syntaxis f. Gk suntaxis (as SYN-, taxis f. tassō arrange)]

synth /sɪnθ/ n. colloq. = SYNTHESIZER.

synthesis /'sɪnθɪsɪs/ n. (pl. **syntheses** /-ˌsiːz/) **1** the process or result of building up separate elements, esp. ideas, into a connected whole, esp. into a theory or system. **2** a combination or composition. **3** Chem. the artificial production of compounds from their constituents as distinct from extraction from plants etc. □ **synthesist** n. [L f. Gk sunthesis (as SYN-, THESIS)]

synthesize /'sɪnθɪˌsaɪz/ v.tr. (also **synthetize** /-ˌtaɪz/, **-ise**) **1** make a synthesis of. **2** combine into a coherent whole.

synthesizer /'sɪnθɪˌsaɪzə(r)/ n. an electronic musical instrument, esp. operated by a keyboard, producing a wide variety of sounds by generating and combining signals of different frequencies.

synthetic /sɪn'θetɪk/ adj. & n. —adj. **1** made by chemical synthesis, esp. to imitate a natural product (synthetic rubber). **2** (of emotions etc.) affected, insincere. —n. Chem. a synthetic substance. □ **synthetical** adj. **synthetically** adv. [F synthétique or mod.L syntheticus f. Gk sunthetikos f. sunthetos f. suntithēmi (as SYN-, tithēmi put)]

syphilis /'sɪfɪlɪs/ n. a contagious venereal disease progressing from infection of the genitals via the skin and mucous membrane to the bones, muscles, and brain. □ **syphilitic** /-'lɪtɪk/ adj. **syphilize** /-ˌlaɪz/ v.tr. (also **-ise**). **syphiloid** /-ˌlɔɪd/ adj. [mod.L f. title (Syphilis, sive Morbus Gallicus) of a Latin poem (1530), f. Syphilus, a character in it, the supposed first sufferer from the disease]

syphon var. of SIPHON.

syringa /sɪ'rɪŋgə/ n. Bot. **1** = mock orange. **2** any plant of the genus Syringa, esp. the lilac. [mod.L, formed as SYRINX (with ref. to the use of its stems as pipe-stems)]

syringe /sɪ'rɪndʒ, 'sɪr-/ n. & v. —n. **1** Med. **a** a tube with a nozzle and piston or bulb for sucking in and ejecting liquid in a fine stream, used in surgery. **b** (in full **hypodermic syringe**) a similar device with a hollow needle for insertion under the skin. **2** any similar device used in gardening, cooking, etc. —v.tr. sluice or spray (the ear, a plant, etc.) with a syringe. [ME f. med.L syringa (as SYRINX)]

syrinx /'sɪrɪŋks/ n. (pl. **syrinxes** or **syringes** /sɪ'rɪndʒiːz/) a set of pan-pipes. □ **syringeal** /sɪ'rɪndʒɪəl/ adj. [L syrinx -ngis f. Gk surigx suriggos pipe, channel]

syrup /'sɪrəp/ n. (US **sirup**) **1 a** a sweet sauce made by dissolving sugar in boiling water, often used for preserving fruit etc. **b** a similar sauce of a specified flavour as a drink, medicine, etc. (rose-hip syrup). **2** condensed sugar-cane juice; part of this remaining uncrystallized at various stages of refining; molasses, treacle. **3** excessive sweetness of style or manner. □ **syrupy** adj. [ME f. OF sirop or med.L siropus f. Arab. šarāb beverage: cf. SHERBET, SHRUB[2]]

systaltic /sɪ'stæltɪk/ adj. (esp. of the heart) contracting and dilating rhythmically; pulsatory. [LL systalticus f. Gk sustaltikos (as SYN-, staltos f. stellō put)]

system /'sɪstəm/ n. **1** a complex whole; a set of connected things or parts; an organized body of material or immaterial things. **2** a set of devices (e.g. pulleys) functioning together. **3** Physiol. **a** a set of organs in the body with a common structure or function (the digestive system). **b** the human or animal body as a whole. **4** a method; considered principles of procedure or classification. **b** classification. **5** orderliness. **6 a** a body of theory or practice relating to or prescribing a particular form of government, religion, etc. **b** (prec. by *the*) the prevailing political or social order, esp. regarded as oppressive and intransigent. **7** a method of choosing one's procedure in gambling etc. **8** *Computing* a group of related hardware units or programs or both, esp. when dedicated to a single application. **9** a major group of geological strata (*the Devonian system*). □ **get a thing out of one's system** *colloq.* be rid of a preoccupation or anxiety. **systems analysis** the analysis of a complex process or operation in order to improve its efficiency, esp. by applying a computer system. □ **systemless** *adj.* [F *système* or LL *systema* f. Gk *sustēma -atos* (as SYN-, *histēmi* set up)]

systematic /ˌsɪstəˈmætɪk/ *adj.* **1** methodical; done or conceived according to a plan or system. **2** regular, deliberate (*a systematic liar*).

□ **systematically** *adv.* **systematism** /ˈsɪstəməˌtɪz(ə)m/ *n.* **systematist** /ˈsɪstəmətɪst/ *n.* [F *systématique* f. LL *systematicus* f. late Gk *sustēmatikos* (as SYSTEM)]

systematize /ˈsɪstəməˌtaɪz/ *v.tr.* (also **-ise**) **1** make systematic. **2** devise a system for. □ **systematization** /-ˈzeɪʃ(ə)n/ *n.* **systematizer** *n.*

systemic /sɪˈstemɪk/ *adj.* **1** *Physiol.* of or concerning the whole body, not confined to a particular part (*systemic infection*). **2** *Hort.* (of an insecticide, fungicide, etc.) entering the plant via the roots or shoots and passing through the tissues. □ **systemically** *adv.* [irreg. f. SYSTEM]

systemize /ˈsɪstəˌmaɪz/ *v.tr.* = SYSTEMATIZE. □ **systemization** /-ˈzeɪʃ(ə)n/ *n.* **systemizer** *n.*

systole /ˈsɪstəlɪ/ *n. Physiol.* the contraction of the heart, when blood is pumped into the arteries (cf. DIASTOLE). □ **systolic** /-ˈstɒlɪk/ *adj.* [LL f. Gk *sustolē* f. *sustellō* contract (as SYSTALTIC)]

Tt

T¹ /tiː/ n. (also **t**) (pl. **Ts** or **T's**) **1** the twentieth letter of the alphabet. **2** a T-shaped thing (esp. *attrib.*: *T-joint*). □ **to a T** exactly; to a nicety.

T² *abbr.* tesla.

T³ *symb. Chem.* the isotope tritium.

t. *abbr.* **1** ton(s). **2** tonne(s).

't *pron. contr.* of IT¹ (*'tis*).

-t /t/ *suffix* = -ED¹ (*crept*; *sent*).

TA *abbr.* (in the UK) Territorial Army.

Ta *symb. Chem.* the element tantalum.

ta /tɑː/ *int. Brit. colloq.* thank you. [infantile form]

TAB *abbr.* **1** typhoid-paratyphoid A and B vaccine. **2** *Austral.* Totalizator Agency Board.

tab¹ n. & v. —n. **1 a** a small flap or strip of material attached for grasping, fastening, or hanging up, or for identification. **b** a similar object as part of a garment etc. **2** *US colloq.* a bill or price (*picked up the tab*). **3 a** a stage-curtain. **b** a loop for suspending this. —v.tr. (**tabbed**, **tabbing**) provide with a tab or tabs. □ **keep tabs** (or **a tab**) **on** *colloq.* **1** keep account of. **2** have under observation or in check. [prob. f. dial.: cf. TAG¹]

tab² n. = TABULATOR 2. [abbr.]

tabard /ˈtæbəd/ n. **1** a herald's official coat emblazoned with the arms of the sovereign. **2** a woman's or girl's sleeveless jerkin. **3** *hist.* a knight's short emblazoned garment worn over armour. [ME f. OF *tabart*, of unkn. orig.]

tabasco /təˈbæskəʊ/ n. **1** a pungent pepper made from the fruit of *Capsicum frutescens*. **2** (**Tabasco**) *propr.* a sauce made from this used to flavour food. [*Tabasco* in Mexico]

tabbouleh /təˈbuːleɪ/ n. an Arabic vegetable salad made with cracked wheat. [Arab. *tabbūla*]

tabby /ˈtæbɪ/ n. (pl. **-ies**) **1** (in full **tabby cat**) **a** a grey or brownish cat mottled or streaked with dark stripes. **b** any domestic cat, esp. female. **2** a kind of watered silk. **3** a plain weave. [F *tabis* (in sense 2) f. Arab. *al-'attabiya* the quarter of Baghdad where tabby was manufactured: connection of other senses uncert.]

tabernacle /ˈtæbəˌnæk(ə)l/ n. **1** *hist.* a tent used as a sanctuary for the Ark of the Covenant by the Israelites during the Exodus. **2** *Eccl.* a canopied niche or receptacle esp. for the Eucharistic elements. **3** a place of worship in nonconformist creeds. □ **tabernacled** adj. [ME f. OF *tabernacle* or L *tabernaculum* tent, dimin. of *taberna* hut]

tabla /ˈtæblə, ˈtɑ-/ n. *Ind. Mus.* a pair of small drums played with the hands. [Hind. f. Arab. *ṭabla* drum]

table /ˈteɪb(ə)l/ n. & v. —n. **1** a piece of furniture with a flat top and one or more legs, providing a level surface for eating, writing, or working at, playing games on, etc. **2** a flat surface serving a specified purpose (*altar table*; *bird table*). **3 a** food provided in a household (*keeps a good table*).

b a group seated at table for dinner etc. **4 a** a set of facts or figures systematically displayed, esp. in columns (*a table of contents*). **b** matter contained in this. **c** = *multiplication table*. **5** a flat surface for working on or for machinery to operate on. **6 a** a slab of wood or stone etc. for bearing an inscription. **b** matter inscribed on this. —v.tr. **1** bring forward for discussion or consideration at a meeting. **2** postpone consideration of (a matter). □ **at table** taking a meal at a table. **on the table** offered for discussion. **table licence** a licence to serve alcoholic drinks only with meals. **table linen** tablecloths, napkins, etc. **table-mat** a mat for protecting a tabletop from hot dishes, etc. **table tennis** an indoor game based on lawn tennis, played with small bats and a ball bounced on a table divided by a net. **table wine** ordinary wine for drinking with a meal. **turn the tables** (often foll. by *on*) reverse one's relations (with), esp. by turning an inferior into a superior position. **under the table** *colloq.* drunken after a meal. □ **tableful** n. (pl. **-fuls**). **tabling** n. [ME f. OF f. L *tabula* plank, tablet, list]

tableau /ˈtæbləʊ/ n. (pl. **tableaux** /-ləʊz/) **1** a picturesque presentation. **2** = TABLEAU VIVANT. **3** a dramatic or effective situation suddenly brought about. [F, = picture, dimin. of *table*: see TABLE]

tableau vivant /ˌtæbləʊ ˈviːvɑ̃/ n. (pl. **tableaux vivants** pronunc. same) *Theatr.* a silent and motionless group of people arranged to represent a scene. [F, lit. 'living picture']

tablecloth /ˈteɪb(ə)lˌklɒθ/ n. a cloth spread over the top of a table, esp. for meals.

table d'hôte /ˌtɑːb(ə)l ˈdəʊt/ n. a meal consisting of a set menu at a fixed price, esp. in a hotel (cf. À LA CARTE). [F, = host's table]

tableland /ˈteɪb(ə)lˌlænd/ n. an extensive elevated region with a level surface; a plateau.

tablespoon /ˈteɪb(ə)lˌspuːn/ n. **1** a large spoon for serving food. **2** an amount held by this. □ **tablespoonful** n. (pl. **-fuls**).

tablet /ˈtæblɪt/ n. **1** a small measured and compressed amount of a substance, esp. of a medicine or drug. **2** a small flat piece of soap etc. **3** a flat slab of stone or wood, esp. for display or an inscription. **4** *US* a writing-pad. [ME f. OF *tablete* f. Rmc. dimin. of L *tabula* TABLE]

tabletop /ˈteɪb(ə)lˌtɒp/ n. **1** the top or surface of a table. **2** (*attrib.*) that can be placed or used on a tabletop.

tableware /ˈteɪb(ə)lˌweə(r)/ n. dishes, plates, implements, etc., for use at meals.

tabloid /ˈtæblɔɪd/ n. **1** a newspaper, usu. popular in style with bold headlines and large photographs, having pages of half size. **2** anything in a compressed or concentrated form. [orig. the propr. name of a medicine sold in tablets]

taboo /təˈbuː/ n., adj., & v. (also **tabu**) —n. (pl. **taboos** or **tabus**) **1** a system or the act of setting a person or thing apart as sacred or accursed. **2** a prohibition or restriction imposed by social custom. —*adj.* **1** avoided or prohibited, esp. by social custom (*taboo words*). **2** designated as sacred and prohibited. —*v.tr.* (**taboos, tabooed** or **tabus, tabued**) **1** put (a thing, practice, etc.) under taboo. **2** exclude or prohibit by authority or social influence. [Tongan *tabu*]

tabor /ˈteɪbə(r)/ *n. hist.* a small drum, esp. one used to accompany a pipe. [ME f. OF *tabour, tabur*: cf. TABLA, Pers. *tabīra* drum]

tabouret /ˈtæbərɪt/ *n.* (*US* **taboret**) a low seat usu. without arms or a back. [F, = stool, dimin. as TABOR]

tabu var. of TABOO.

tabular /ˈtæbjʊlə(r)/ *adj.* **1** of or arranged in tables or lists. **2** broad and flat like a table. □ **tabularly** *adv.* [L *tabularis* (as TABLE)]

tabulate /ˈtæbjʊˌleɪt/ *v.tr.* arrange (figures or facts) in tabular form. □ **tabulation** /-ˈleɪʃ(ə)n/ *n.* [LL *tabulare tabulat-* f. *tabula* table]

tabulator /ˈtæbjʊˌleɪtə(r)/ *n.* **1** a person or thing that tabulates. **2** a device on a typewriter for advancing to a sequence of set positions in tabular work.

tacet /ˈtæsɪt, ˈteɪ-/ *v.intr. Mus.* an instruction for a particular voice or instrument to be silent. [L, = is silent]

tachism /ˈtæʃɪz(ə)m/ *n.* (also **tachisme**) a form of action painting with dabs of colour arranged randomly to evoke a subconscious feeling. [F *tachisme* f. *tache* stain]

tacho /ˈtækəʊ/ *n.* (*pl.* **-os**) *colloq.* = TACHOMETER. [abbr.]

tacho- /ˈtækəʊ/ *comb. form* speed. [Gk *takhos* speed]

tachograph /ˈtækəˌɡrɑːf/ *n.* a device used esp. in heavy goods vehicles and coaches etc. for automatically recording speed and travel time.

tachometer /təˈkɒmɪtə(r)/ *n.* an instrument for measuring the rate of rotation of a shaft and hence the speed or velocity of a vehicle.

tachy- /ˈtækɪ/ *comb. form* swift. [Gk *takhus* swift]

tachycardia /ˌtækɪˈkɑːdɪə/ *n. Med.* an abnormally rapid heart rate. [TACHY- + Gk *kardia* heart]

tacit /ˈtæsɪt/ *adj.* understood or implied without being stated (*tacit consent*). □ **tacitly** *adv.* [L *tacitus* silent f. *tacēre* be silent]

taciturn /ˈtæsɪˌtɜːn/ *adj.* reserved in speech; saying little; uncommunicative. □ **taciturnity** /-ˈtɜːnɪtɪ/ *n.* **taciturnly** *adv.* [F *taciturne* or L *taciturnus* (as TACIT)]

tack[1] *n. & v.* —*n.* **1** a small sharp broad-headed nail. **2** *US* a drawing-pin. **3** a long stitch used in fastening fabrics etc. lightly or temporarily together. **4 a** the direction in which a ship moves as determined by the position of its sails and regarded in terms of the direction of the wind (*starboard tack*). **b** a temporary change of direction in sailing to take advantage of a side wind etc. **5** a course of action or policy (*try another tack*). **6** a sticky condition of varnish etc. —*v.* **1** *tr.* (often foll. by *down* etc.) fasten with tacks. **2** *tr.* (stitches pieces of cloth etc.) lightly together. **3** *tr.* (foll. by *to, on*) annex (a thing). **4** *intr.* (often foll. by *about*) **a** change a ship's course by turning its head to the wind (cf. WEAR[2]). **b** make a series of tacks. **5** *intr.* change one's conduct or policy etc. □ **tacker** *n.* [ME *tak*

etc., of uncert. orig.: cf. Bibl. *tache* clasp, link f. OF *tache*]

tack[2] *n.* the saddle, bridle, etc., of a horse. [shortened f. TACKLE]

tack[3] /tæk/ *n. colloq.* cheap or shoddy material; tat, kitsch. [back-form. f. TACKY[2]]

tackle /ˈtæk(ə)l/ *n. & v.* —*n.* **1** equipment for a task or sport (*fishing-tackle*). **2** a mechanism, esp. of ropes, pulley-blocks, hooks, etc., for lifting weights, managing sails, etc. (*block and tackle*). **3** a windlass with its ropes and hooks. **4** an act of tackling in football etc. **5** *Amer. Football* **a** the position next to the end of the forward line. **b** the player in this position. —*v.tr.* **1** try to deal with (a problem or difficulty). **2** grapple with or try to overcome (an opponent). **3** enter into discussion with. **4** obstruct, intercept, or seize and stop (a player running with the ball). **5** secure by means of tackle. □ **tackle-block** a pulley over which a rope runs. □ **tackler** *n.* **tackling** *n.* [ME, prob. f. MLG *takel* f. *taken* lay hold of]

tacky[1] /ˈtækɪ/ *adj.* (**tackier, tackiest**) (of glue or paint etc.) still slightly sticky after application. □ **tackiness** *n.* [TACK[1] + -Y[1]]

tacky[2] /ˈtækɪ/ *adj.* (**tackier, tackiest**) esp. *US colloq.* **1** showing poor taste or style. **2** tatty or seedy. □ **tackily** *adv.* **tackiness** *n.* [19th c.: orig. unkn.]

taco /ˈtɑːkəʊ/ *n.* (*pl.* **-os**) a Mexican dish of meat etc. in a folded or rolled tortilla. [Mex. Sp.]

tact /tækt/ *n.* **1** adroitness in dealing with others or with difficulties arising from personal feeling. **2** intuitive perception of the right thing to do or say. [F f. L *tactus* touch, sense of touch f. *tangere tact-* touch]

tactful /ˈtæktfʊl/ *adj.* having or showing tact. □ **tactfully** *adv.* **tactfulness** *n.*

tactic /ˈtæktɪk/ *n.* **1** a tactical manoeuvre. **2** = TACTICS. [mod.L *tactica* f. Gk *taktikē* (*tekhnē* art): see TACTICS]

tactical /ˈtæktɪk(ə)l/ *adj.* **1** of, relating to, or constituting tactics (*a tactical retreat*). **2** (of bombing or weapons) done or for use in immediate support of military or naval operations (opp. STRATEGIC). **3** adroitly planning or planned. **4** (of voting) aimed at preventing the strongest candidate from winning by supporting the next strongest. □ **tactically** *adv.* [Gk *taktikos* (as TACTICS)]

tactics /ˈtæktɪks/ *n.pl.* **1** (also treated as *sing.*) the art of disposing armed forces esp. in contact with an enemy. **2 a** the plans and means adopted in carrying out a scheme or achieving some end. **b** a skilful device or devices. □ **tactician** /tækˈtɪʃ(ə)n/ *n.* [mod.L *tactica* f. Gk *taktika* neut.pl. f. *taktos* ordered f. *tassō* arrange]

tactile /ˈtæktaɪl/ *adj.* **1** of or connected with the sense of touch. **2** perceived by touch. **3** tangible. □ **tactual** /ˈtæktjʊəl/ *adj.* (in senses 1, 2). **tactility** /-ˈtɪlɪtɪ/ *n.* [L *tactilis* f. *tangere tact-* touch]

tactless /ˈtæktlɪs/ *adj.* having or showing no tact. □ **tactlessly** *adv.* **tactlessness** *n.*

tad *n.* *US colloq.* a small amount (often used adverbially: *a tad too salty*). [19th c.: orig. unkn.]

tadpole /ˈtædpəʊl/ *n.* a larva of an amphibian, esp. a frog, toad, or newt in its aquatic stage and breathing through gills. [ME *taddepolle* (as TOAD, POLL from the size of its head)]

taffeta /ˈtæfɪtə/ n. a fine lustrous silk or silklike fabric. [ME f. OF *taffetas* or med.L *taffata*, ult. f. Pers. *tāfta* past part. of *tāftan* twist]

taffrail /ˈtæfreɪl/ n. Naut. a rail round a ship's stern. [earlier *tafferel* f. Du. *tafereel* panel, dimin. of *tafel* (as TABLE): assim. to RAIL¹]

Taffy /ˈtæfɪ/ n. (pl. **-ies**) colloq. often offens. a Welshman. [supposed Welsh pronunc. of *Davy* = *David* (Welsh *Dafydd*)]

taffy /ˈtæfɪ/ n. (pl. **-ies**) US **1** a confection like toffee. **2** insincere flattery. [19th c.: orig. unkn.]

tafia /ˈtæfɪə/ n. W.Ind. rum distilled from molasses etc. [18th c.: orig. uncert.]

tag¹ n. & v. —n. **1** a label, esp. one for tying on an object to show its address, price, etc. **2** a metal or plastic point at the end of a lace etc. to assist insertion. **3** a loop at the back of a boot used in pulling it on. **4** US a licence plate of a motor vehicle. **5** a loose or ragged end of anything. **6** a trite quotation or stock phrase. —v.tr. (**tagged**, **tagging**) **1** provide with a tag or tags. **2** (often foll. by *on*, *on to*) join or attach. **3** colloq. follow closely or trail behind. **4** Computing identify (an item of data) by its type for later retrieval. **5** label radioactively. □ **tag along** (often foll. by *with*) go along or accompany passively. **tag end** esp. US the last remnant of something. [ME: orig. unkn.]

tag² n. & v. —n. **1** a children's game in which one chases the rest, and anyone who is caught then becomes the pursuer. **2** Baseball the act of tagging a runner. —v.tr. (**tagged**, **tagging**) **1** touch in a game of tag. **2** (often foll. by *out*) put (a runner) out by touching with the ball or with the hand holding the ball. [18th c.: orig. unkn.]

tagliatelle /ˌtæljəˈtelɪ/ n. a form of pasta in narrow ribbons. [It.]

t'ai chi ch'uan /ˌtaɪ tʃiː ˈtʃwɑːn/ n. (also **t'ai chi** /taɪ ˈtʃiː/) a Chinese martial art and system of callisthenics consisting of sequences of very slow controlled movements. [Chin., = great ultimate boxing]

taiga /ˈtaɪgə/ n. coniferous forest lying between tundra and steppe, esp. in Siberia. [Russ.]

tail¹ n. & v. **1** the hindmost part of an animal, esp. when prolonged beyond the rest of the body. **2 a** a thing like a tail in form or position, esp. something extending downwards or outwards at an extremity. **b** the rear end of anything, e.g. of a procession. **c** a long train or line of people, vehicles, etc. **3 a** the rear part of an aeroplane, with the tailplane and rudder, or of a rocket. **b** the rear part of a motor vehicle. **4** the luminous trail of particles following a comet. **5 a** the inferior or weaker part of anything, esp. in a sequence. **b** Cricket the end of the batting order, with the weakest batsmen. **6 a** the part of a shirt below the waist. **b** the hanging part of the back of a coat. **7** (in pl.) colloq. **a** a tailcoat. **b** evening dress including this. **8** (in pl.) the reverse of a coin as a choice when tossing. **9** colloq. a person following or shadowing another. **10** an extra strip attached to the lower end of a kite. **11** the stem of a note in music. **12** the part of a letter (e.g. y) below the line. —v. **1** tr. remove the stalks of (fruit). **2** tr. & (foll. by *after*) intr. colloq. shadow or follow closely. **3** tr. provide with a tail. **4** tr. dock the tail of (a lamb etc.). **5** tr. (often foll. by *on to*) join (one thing to another). □ **on a person's tail** closely following a person. **tail back** (of traffic)

form a tailback. **tail-end 1** the hindmost or lowest or last part. **2** (sense 5 of the *n*.). **tail-ender** a person at the tail-end of something, esp. in cricket and athletic races. **tail-light** (or **-lamp**) US a light at the rear of a train, motor vehicle, or bicycle. **tail off** (or **away**) **1** become fewer, smaller, or slighter. **2** fall behind or away in a scattered line. **tail-off** n. a decline or gradual reduction, esp. in demand. **tail wind** a wind blowing in the direction of travel of a vehicle or aircraft etc. **with one's tail between one's legs** in a state of dejection or humiliation. **with one's tail up** in good spirits; cheerful. □ **tailed** adj. (also in comb.). **tailless** adj. [OE *tægl*, *tægel* f. Gmc]

tail² n. & adj. Law —n. limitation of ownership, esp. of an estate limited to a person and that person's heirs. —adj. so limited (*estate tail*; *fee tail*). □ **in tail** under such a limitation. **tail off** [ME f. OF *taille* notch, cut, tax, f. *taillier* cut ult. f. L *talea* twig]

tailback /ˈteɪlbæk/ n. a long line of traffic extending back from an obstruction.

tailboard /ˈteɪlbɔːd/ n. a hinged or removable flap at the rear of a lorry etc.

tailcoat /ˈteɪlkəʊt/ n. a man's morning or evening coat with a long skirt divided at the back into tails and cut away in front, worn as part of formal dress.

tailgate /ˈteɪlɡeɪt/ n. & v. —n. **1** esp. US **a** = TAILBOARD. **b** the tail door of an estate car or hatchback. **2** the lower end of a canal lock. —v. US colloq. **1** intr. drive too closely behind another vehicle. **2** tr. follow (a vehicle) too closely. □ **tailgater** n.

tailor /ˈteɪlə(r)/ n. & v. —n. a maker of clothes, esp. one who makes men's outer garments to measure. —v. **1** tr. make (clothes) as a tailor. **2** tr. make or adapt for a special purpose. **3** intr. work as or be a tailor. **4** tr. (esp. as **tailored** adj.) make clothes for (*he was immaculately tailored*). **5** tr. (as **tailored** adj.) = tailor-made. □ **tailor-made** adj. **1** (of clothing) made to order by a tailor. **2** made or suited for a particular purpose (*a job tailor-made for me*). —n. a tailor-made garment. □ **tailoring** n. [ME & AF *taillour*, OF *tailleur* cutter, formed as TAIL²]

tailored /ˈteɪləd/ adj. (of clothing) well or closely fitted.

tailpiece /ˈteɪlpiːs/ n. **1** an appendage at the rear of anything. **2** the final part of a thing. **3** a decoration in a blank space at the end of a chapter etc. in a book.

tailpipe /ˈteɪlpaɪp/ n. the rear section of the exhaust pipe of a motor vehicle.

tailplane /ˈteɪlpleɪn/ n. a horizontal aerofoil at the tail of an aircraft.

tailspin /ˈteɪlspɪn/ n. & v. —n. **1** a spin by an aircraft with the tail spiralling. **2** a state of chaos or panic. —v.intr. (**-spinning**; past and past part. **-spun**) perform a tailspin.

taint n. & v. —n. **1** a spot or trace of decay, infection, or some bad quality. **2** a corrupt condition or infection. —v. **1** tr. affect with a taint. **2** tr. (foll. by *with*) affect slightly. **3** intr. become tainted. □ **taintless** adj. [ME, partly f. OF *teint(e)* f. L *tinctus* f. *tingere* dye, partly as ATTAIN]

taipan /ˈtaɪpæn/ n. the head of a foreign business in China. [Chin.]

take v. & n. —v. (**took** /tʊk/; **taken** /ˈteɪkən/) **1** tr. lay hold of; get into one's hands. **2** tr. acquire, get possession of, capture, earn, or win. **3** tr. get the use of by purchase or formal agreement (*take lodgings*). **4** tr. (in a recipe) avail oneself of; use. **5** tr. use as a means of transport (*took a taxi*). **6** tr. regularly buy or subscribe to (a particular newspaper or periodical etc.). **7** tr. obtain after fulfilling the required conditions (*take a degree*). **8** tr. occupy (*take a chair*). **9** tr. make use of (*take the next turning on the left*). **10** tr. consume as food or medicine (*took tea; took the pills*). **11** tr. **a** be successful or effective (*the inoculation did not take*). **b** (of a plant, seed, etc.) begin to grow. **12** tr. require or use up (*will only take a minute; these things take time*). **13** tr. cause to come or go with one; convey (*take the book home; the bus will take you all the way*). **14** tr. remove; dispossess a person of (*someone has taken my pen*). **15** tr. catch or be infected with (fire or fever etc.). **16** tr. **a** experience or be affected by (*take fright; take pleasure*). **b** give play to (*take comfort*). **c** exert (*take courage; take no notice*). **17** tr. find out and note (a name and address; a person's temperature etc.) by enquiry or measurement. **18** tr. grasp mentally; understand (*I take your point; I took you to mean yes*). **19** tr. treat or regard in a specified way (*took the news calmly; took it badly*). **20** tr. (foll. by *for*) regard as being (*do you take me for an idiot?*). **21** tr. **a** accept (*take the offer*). **b** submit to (*take a joke; take no nonsense; took a risk*). **22** tr. choose or assume (*took a different view; took a job; took the initiative*). **23** tr. derive (*takes its name from the inventor*). **24** tr. (foll. by *from*) subtract (*take 3 from 9*). **25** tr. execute, make, or undertake; perform or effect (*take notes; take an oath; take a decision; take a look*). **26** tr. occupy or engage oneself in; indulge in; enjoy (*take a rest; take exercise; take a holiday*). **27** tr. conduct (*took the school assembly*). **28** tr. deal with in a certain way (*took the corner too fast*). **29** tr. **a** teach or be taught (a subject). **b** be examined in (a subject). **30** tr. make a photograph) with a camera; photograph (a person or thing). **31** tr. use as an instance (*let us take Napoleon*). **32** tr. *Gram.* have or require as part of the appropriate construction (*this verb takes an object*). **33** tr. have sexual intercourse with (a woman). **34** tr. (in *passive*; foll. by *by*, *with*) be attracted or charmed by. —n. **1** an amount taken or caught in one session or attempt etc. **2** a scene or sequence of film photographed continuously at one time. **3** esp. *US* takings, esp. money received at a theatre for seats. □ **be taken ill** become ill, esp. suddenly. **have what it takes** *colloq.* have the necessary qualities etc. for success. **take after** resemble (esp. a parent or ancestor). **take against** begin to dislike, esp. impulsively. **take apart 1** dismantle. **2** *colloq.* beat or defeat. **take as read** accept without reading or discussing. **take away 1** remove or carry elsewhere. **2** subtract. **3** *Brit.* buy (food etc.) at a shop or restaurant for eating elsewhere. **take-away** *Brit. attrib.adj.* (of food) bought at a shop or restaurant for eating elsewhere. —n. **1** an establishment selling this. **2** the food itself (*let's get a take-away*). **take back 1** retract (a statement). **2** convey (a person or thing) to his or her or its original position. **3** carry (a person) in thought to a past time. **4** *Printing* transfer to the previous line. **take the biscuit** (or **bun** or **cake**) *colloq.* be the most remarkable. **take down**

1 write down (spoken words). **2** remove (a structure) by separating it into pieces. **3** humiliate. **take from** diminish; weaken; detract from. **take heart** be encouraged. **take-home pay** the pay received by an employee after the deduction of tax etc. **take ill** (*US* **sick**) *colloq.* be taken ill. **take in 1** receive as a lodger etc. **2** undertake (work) at home. **3** make (a garment etc.) smaller. **4** understand (*did you take that in?*). **5** cheat (*managed to take them all in*). **6** include or comprise. **7** *colloq.* visit (a place) on the way to another (*shall we take in Avebury?*). **8** furl (a sail). **9** *Brit.* regularly buy (a newspaper etc.). **take-in** n. a deception. **take in hand 1** undertake; start doing or dealing with. **2** undertake the control or reform of (a person). **take it 1** (often foll. by *that* + clause) assume (*I take it that you have finished*). **2** *colloq.* endure a difficulty or hardship in a specified way (*took it badly*). **take it from me** (or **take my word for it**) I can assure you. **take it ill** resent it. **take it on one** (or **oneself**) (foll. by *to* + infin.) venture or presume. **take it or leave it** (esp. in *imper.*) an expression of indifference or impatience about another's decision after making an offer. **take it out of 1** exhaust the strength of. **2** have revenge on. **take it out on** relieve one's frustration by attacking or treating harshly. **take a lot of** (or **some**) **doing** be hard to do. **take off 1 a** remove (clothing) from one's or another's body. **b** remove or lead away. **2** deduct (part of an amount). **3** depart, esp. hastily (*took off in a fast car*). **4** *colloq.* mimic humorously. **5** jump from the ground. **6** become airborne. **7** (of a scheme, enterprise, etc.) become successful or popular. **8** have (a period) away from work. **take-off 1** the act of becoming airborne. **2** an act of mimicking. **3** a place from which one jumps. **take oneself off** go away. **take on 1** undertake (work etc.). **2** engage (an employee). **3** be willing or ready to meet (an adversary in sport, argument, etc., esp. a stronger one). **4** acquire (a new meaning etc.). **5** *colloq.* show strong emotion. **take out 1** remove from within a place; extract. **2** escort on an outing. **3** get (a licence or summons etc.) issued. **4** *US* = **take away** 3. **5** murder or destroy. **take a person out of himself** or **herself** make a person forget his or her worries. **take over 1** succeed to the management or ownership of. **2** take control. **3** *Printing* transfer to the next line. **take-over** n. the assumption of control (esp. of a business); the buying-out of one company by another. **take shape** assume a distinct form; develop into something definite. **take that!** an exclamation accompanying a blow etc. **take one's time** not hurry. **take to 1** begin or fall into the habit of (*took to smoking*). **2** have recourse to. **3** adapt oneself to. **4** form a liking for. **take up 1** become interested or engaged in (a pursuit). **2** adopt as a protégé. **3** occupy (time or space). **4** begin (residence etc.). **5** resume after an interruption. **6** interrupt or question (a speaker). **7** accept (an offer etc.). **8** shorten (a garment). **9** lift up. **10** absorb (*sponges take up water*). **11** take (a person) into a vehicle. **12** pursue (a matter etc.) further. **take a person up on** accept (a person's offer etc.). **take up with** begin to associate with. □ **takable** *adj.* (also **takeable**). [OE *tacan* f. ON *taka*]

taker /ˈteɪkə(r)/ n. **1** a person who takes a bet. **2** a person who accepts an offer.

taking /ˈteɪkɪŋ/ adj. & n. —adj. **1** attractive or captivating. **2** catching or infectious. —n. (in pl.) an amount of money taken in business. □ **takingly** adv. **takingness** n.

talc n. & v. —n. **1** talcum powder. **2** any crystalline form of magnesium silicate that occurs in soft flat plates, used as a lubricator etc. —v.tr. (**talcked**, **talcking**) treat (a surface) with talc to lubricate or dry it. □ **talcose** adj. **talcous** adj. **talcy** adj. (in sense 1). [F talc or med.L talcum, f. Arab. ṭalk f. Pers. ṭalk]

talcum /ˈtælkəm/ n. **1** = TALC. **2** (in full **talcum powder**) powdered talc for toilet and cosmetic use, usu. perfumed. [med.L: see TALC]

tale n. **1** a narrative or story, esp. fictitious and imaginatively treated. **2** a report of an alleged fact, often malicious or in breach of confidence (all sorts of tales will get about). [OE talu f. Gmc: cf. TELL]

talebearer /ˈteɪlˌbeərə(r)/ n. a person who maliciously gossips or reveals secrets. □ **talebearing** n. & adj.

talent /ˈtælənt/ n. **1** a special aptitude or faculty (a talent for music; has real talent). **2** high mental ability. **3 a** a person or persons of talent (is a real talent; plenty of local talent). **b** colloq. members of the opposite sex regarded in terms of sexual promise. **4** an ancient weight and unit of currency, esp. among the Greeks. □ **talentscout** (or **-spotter**) a person looking for talented performers, esp. in sport and entertainment. □ **talented** adj. **talentless** adj. [OE talente & OF talent f. L talentum inclination of mind f. Gk talanton balance, weight, sum of money]

taleteller /ˈteɪlˌtelə(r)/ n. a person who tells stories. **2** a person who spreads malicious reports.

talisman /ˈtælɪzmən/ n. (pl. **talismans**) **1** an object, esp. an inscribed ring or stone, supposed to be endowed with magic powers esp. of averting evil from or bringing good luck to its holder. **2** a charm or amulet; a thing supposed capable of working wonders. □ **talismanic** /-ˈmænɪk/ adj. [F & Sp., = It. talismano, f. med.Gk telesmon, Gk telesma completion, religious rite f. teleō complete f. telos end]

talk /tɔːk/ v. & n. —v. **1** intr. (often foll. by to, with) converse or communicate ideas by spoken words. **2** intr. have the power of speech. **3** intr. (foll. by about) **a** have as the subject of discussion. **b** (in imper.) colloq. as an emphatic statement (talk about expense! It cost me £50). **4** tr. express or utter in words (you are talking nonsense; talked cricket all day). **5** tr. use (a language) in speech (is talking Spanish). **6** intr. (foll. by at) address pompously. **7** tr. (usu. foll. by into, out of) bring into a specified condition etc. by talking (talked himself hoarse; how did you talk them into it?; talked them out of the difficulty). **8** intr. reveal (esp. secret) information; betray secrets. **9** intr. gossip (people are beginning to talk). **10** intr. have influence (money talks). **11** intr. communicate by radio. —n. **1** conversation or talking. **2** a particular mode of speech (baby-talk). **3** an informal address or lecture. **4 a** a rumour or gossip (there is talk of a merger). **b** its theme (their success was the talk of the town). **5** (often in pl.) extended discussions or negotiations. □ **know**

what one is talking about be expert or authoritative. **now you're talking** colloq. I like what you say, suggest, etc. **talk back 1** reply defiantly. **2** respond on a two-way radio system. **talk big** colloq. talk boastfully. **talk down to** speak patronizingly or condescendingly to. **talk a person down 1** silence a person by greater loudness or persistence. **2** bring (a pilot or aircraft) to landing by radio instructions from the ground. **talk the hind leg off a donkey** talk incessantly. **talk of 1** discuss or mention. **2** (often foll. by verbal noun) express some intention of (talked of moving to London). **talk out** Brit. block the course of (a bill in Parliament) by prolonging discussion to the time of adjournment. **talk over** discuss at length. **talk a person over** (or **round**) gain agreement or compliance from a person by talking. **talk shop** talk, esp. tediously or inopportunely, about one's occupation, business, etc. **talk show** = chat show. **talk through one's hat** (or **neck**) colloq. **1** exaggerate. **2** bluff. **3** talk wildly or nonsensically. **talk to** reprove or scold (a person). **talk to oneself** soliloquize. **talk up** discuss (a subject) in order to arouse interest in it. **you can't** (or **can**) **talk** colloq. a reproof that the person addressed is just as culpable etc. in the matter at issue. □ **talker** n. [ME talken frequent. verb f. TALE or TELL]

talkathon /ˈtɔːkəθɒn/ n. colloq. a prolonged session of talking or discussion. [TALK + MARATHON]

talkative /ˈtɔːkətɪv/ adj. fond of or given to talking. □ **talkatively** adv. **talkativeness** n.

talkback /ˈtɔːkbæk/ n. **1** (often attrib.) a system of two-way communication by loudspeaker. **2** Austral. & NZ = phone-in.

talkie /ˈtɔːkɪ/ n. esp. US colloq. a film with a soundtrack, as distinct from a silent film. [TALK + -IE, after movie]

talking /ˈtɔːkɪŋ/ adj. & n. —adj. **1** that talks. **2** having the power of speech (a talking parrot). **3** expressive (talking eyes). —n. in senses of TALK v. □ **talking book** a recorded reading of a book, esp. for the blind. **talking film** (or **picture**) a film with a soundtrack. **talking head** colloq. a presenter etc. on television, speaking to the camera and viewed in close-up. **talking of** while we are discussing (talking of food, what time is lunch?). **talking-point** a topic for discussion or argument. **talking-shop** derog. an institution regarded as a place of argument rather than action. **talking-to** colloq. a reproof or reprimand (gave them a good talking-to).

tall /tɔːl/ adj. & adv. —adj. **1** of more than average height. **2** of a specified height (looks about six feet tall). **3** higher than the surrounding objects (a tall building). **4** colloq. extravagant or excessive (a tall story; tall talk). —adv. as if tall; proudly; in a tall or extravagant way (sit tall). □ **tall hat** = top hat. **tall order** an exorbitant or unreasonable demand. **tall ship** a sailing ship with a high mast. □ **tallish** adj. **tallness** n. [ME, repr. OE getæl swift, prompt]

tallboy /ˈtɔːlbɔɪ/ n. a tall chest of drawers sometimes in lower and upper sections or mounted on legs.

tallow /ˈtæləʊ/ n. & v. —n. the harder kinds of (esp. animal) fat melted down for use in making candles, soap, etc. —v.tr. grease with tallow. □ **vegetable tallow** a vegetable fat used as tallow.

□ **tallowish** adj. **tallowy** adj. [ME *talg, talug,* f. MLG *talg, talch,* of unkn. orig.]

tally /'tælɪ/ n. & v. —n. (pl. **-ies**) **1** the reckoning of a debt or score. **2** a total score or amount. **3 a** a mark registering a fixed number of objects delivered or received. **b** such a number as a unit. **4** *hist.* **a** a piece of wood scored across with notches for the items of an account and then split into halves, each party keeping one. **b** an account kept in this way. **5** a ticket or label for identification. **6** a corresponding thing, counterpart, or duplicate. —v. (**-ies, -ied**) (often foll. by *with*) **1** *intr.* agree or correspond. **2** *tr.* record or reckon by tally. □ **tally system** a system of sale on short credit or instalments with an account kept by tally. □ **tallier** n. [ME f. AF *tallie,* AL *tallia, talia* f. L *talea:* cf. TAIL²]

tally-ho /ˌtælɪ'həʊ/ int., n., & v. —int. a huntsman's cry to the hounds on sighting a fox. —n. (pl. **-hos**) an utterance of this. —v. (**-hoes, -hoed**) **1** *intr.* utter a cry of 'tally-ho'. **2** *tr.* indicate (a fox) or urge (hounds) with this cry. [cf. F *taïaut*]

tallyman /'tælɪmən/ n. (pl. **-men**) **1** a person who keeps a tally. **2** a person who sells goods on credit, esp. from door to door.

Talmud /'tælmʊd, -məd/ n. the body of Jewish civil and ceremonial law and legend. □ **Talmudic** /-'mʊdɪk/ adj. **Talmudical** /-'mʊdɪk(ə)l/ adj. **Talmudist** n. [late Heb. *talmûd* instruction f. Heb. *lāmaḏ* learn]

talon /'tælən/ n. a claw, esp. of a bird of prey. □ **taloned** adj. (also in comb.). [ME f. OF, = heel, ult. f. L *talus* ankle, heel]

tam n. a tam-o'-shanter. [abbr.]

tamarillo /ˌtæmə'rɪləʊ/ n. (pl. **-os**) esp. *Austral.* & *NZ* = tree tomato. [arbitrary marketing name: cf. Sp. *tomatillo* dimin. of *tomate* TOMATO]

tamarind /'tæmərɪnd/ n. **1** a tropical evergreen tree, *Tamarindus indica.* **2** the fruit of this, containing an acid pulp used as food and in making drinks. [med.L *tamarindus* f. Arab. *tamr-hindī* Indian date]

tamarisk /'tæmərɪsk/ n. any shrub of the genus *Tamarix,* usu. with long slender branches and small pink or white flowers, that thrives by the sea. [ME f. LL *tamariscus,* L *tamarix*]

tambour /'tæmbʊə(r)/ n. & v. —n. **1** a drum. **2 a** a circular frame for holding fabric taut while it is being embroidered. **b** material embroidered in this way. —v.tr. (also *absol.*) decorate or embroider on a tambour. [F f. *tabour* TABOR]

tambourine /ˌtæmbə'riːn/ n. a percussion instrument consisting of a hoop with a parchment stretched over one side and jingling discs in slots round the hoop. □ **tambourinist** n. [F, dimin. of TAMBOUR]

tame adj. & v. —adj. **1** (of an animal) domesticated; not wild or shy. **2** insipid; lacking spirit or interest; dull (*tame acquiescence*). **3** (of a person) amenable and available. **4** *US* **a** (of land) cultivated. **b** (of a plant) produced by cultivation. —v.tr. **1** make tame; domesticate; break in. **2** subdue, curb, humble; break the spirit of. □ **tamely** adv. **tameness** n. **tamer** n. (also in comb.). [OE *tam* f. Gmc]

tameable /'teɪməb(ə)l/ adj. (also **tamable**) capable of being tamed. □ **tameability** /-'bɪlɪtɪ/ n. **tameableness** n.

tammy /'tæmɪ/ n. (pl. **-ies**) = TAM-O'-SHANTER.

tam-o'-shanter /ˌtæmə'ʃæntə(r)/ n. a round woollen or cloth cap of Scottish origin fitting closely round the brows but large and full above. [the hero of Burns's *Tam o' Shanter*]

tamp v.tr. **1** pack (a blast-hole) full of clay etc. to get the full force of an explosion. **2** ram down (road material etc.). □ **tamper** n. **tamping** n. (in sense 1). [perh. back-form. f. f *tampin* (var. of *tampion* TAMPON, taken as = *tamping*)]

tamper /'tæmpə(r)/ v.intr. (foll. by *with*) **1** meddle with or make unauthorized changes in. **2** exert a secret or corrupt influence upon; bribe. □ **tamperer** n. **tamper-proof** adj. [var. of TEMPER]

tampon /'tæmpɒn/ n. & v. —n. a plug of soft material used to stop a wound or absorb secretions, esp. one inserted into the vagina. —v.tr. (**tamponed, tamponing**) plug with a tampon. [F, nasalized var. of *tapon,* rel. to TAP¹]

tam-tam /'tæmtæm/ n. a large metal gong. [Hindi: see TOM-TOM]

tan¹ n., adj. & v. —n. **1** a brown skin colour resulting from exposure to ultraviolet light. **2** a yellowish-brown colour. **3** bark, esp. of oak, bruised and used to tan hides. —adj. yellowish-brown. —v. (**tanned, tanning**) **1** *tr.* & *intr.* make or become brown by exposure to ultraviolet light. **2** *tr.* convert (raw hide) into leather by soaking in a liquid containing tannic acid or by the use of mineral salts etc. **3** *tr. sl.* beat, thrash. □ **tannable** adj. **tanning** n. **tannish** adj. [OE *tannian,* prob. f. med.L *tanare, tannare,* perh. f. Celtic]

tan² abbr. tangent.

tandem /'tændəm/ n. & adv. —n. **1** a bicycle or tricycle with two or more seats one behind another. **2** a group of two persons or machines etc. with one behind or following the other. **3** a carriage driven tandem. —adv. with two or more horses harnessed one behind another (*drive tandem*). □ **in tandem** one behind another. [L, = at length (of time), used punningly]

tandoor /'tænduə(r)/ n. a clay oven. [Hind.]

tandoori /tæn'duərɪ/ n. food cooked over charcoal in a tandoor (often *attrib.*: *tandoori chicken*). [Hind.]

tang¹ n. **1** a strong taste or flavour or smell. **2** a characteristic quality. **3** the projection on the blade of a tool, esp. a knife, by which the blade is held firm in the handle. [ME f. ON *tange* point, tang of a knife]

tang² v. & n. —v.tr. & intr. ring, clang; sound loudly. —n. a tanging sound. [imit.]

tangelo /'tændʒəˌləʊ/ n. (pl. **-os**) a hybrid of the tangerine and grapefruit. [TANGERINE + POMELO]

tangent /'tændʒ(ə)nt/ n. **1** a straight line, curve, or surface that meets another curve or curved surface at a point, but if extended does not intersect it at that point. **2** the ratio of the sides opposite and adjacent to an angle in a right-angled triangle. □ **at a tangent** diverging from a previous course of action or thought etc. (*go off at a tangent*). □ **tangency** n. [L *tangere tangent-* touch]

tangential /tæn'dʒenʃ(ə)l/ adj. **1** of or along a tangent. **2** divergent. **3** peripheral. □ **tangentially** adv.

tangerine /'tændʒəˌriːn/ n. **1** a small sweet orange-coloured citrus fruit with a thin skin; a mandarin. **2** a deep orange-yellow colour. [*Tangier* in Morocco]

tangible /ˈtændʒɪb(ə)l/ *adj.* **1** perceptible by touch. **2** definite; clearly intelligible; not elusive or visionary (*tangible proof*). □ **tangibility** /-ˈbɪlɪtɪ/ *n.* **tangibleness** *n.* **tangibly** /-blɪ/ *adv.* [F *tangible* or LL *tangibilis* f. *tangere* touch]

tangle /ˈtæŋg(ə)l/ *v. & n.* —*v.* **1 a** *tr.* intertwine (threads or hairs etc.) in a confused mass; entangle. **b** *intr.* become tangled. **2** *intr.* (foll. by *with*) *colloq.* become involved (esp. in conflict or argument) with (*don't tangle with me*). **3** *tr.* complicate (*a tangled affair*). —*n.* **1** a confused mass of intertwined threads etc. **2** a confused or complicated state (*be in a tangle*; *a love tangle*). [ME var. of obs. *tagle*, of uncert. orig.]

tangly /ˈtæŋglɪ/ *adj.* (**tanglier, tangliest**) tangled.

tango /ˈtæŋgəʊ/ *n. & v.* —*n.* (*pl.* **-os**) **1** a slow S. American ballroom dance. **2** the music for this. —*v.intr.* (**-oes, -oed**) dance the tango. [Amer. Sp.]

tangram /ˈtæŋgræm/ *n.* a Chinese puzzle square cut into seven pieces to be combined into various figures. [19th c.: orig. unkn.]

tangy /ˈtæŋɪ/ *adj.* (**tangier, tangiest**) having a strong tang. spicy tang. □ **tanginess** *n.*

tank *n. & v.* —*n.* **1** a large receptacle or storage chamber usu. for liquid or gas. **2** a heavy armoured fighting vehicle carrying guns and moving on a tracked carriage. **3** a container for the fuel supply in a motor vehicle. **4** the part of a locomotive tender containing water for the boiler. **5** *Ind. & Austral.* a reservoir. —*v.* (usu. foll. by *up*) esp. *Brit.* **1** *tr.* fill the tank of (a vehicle etc.) with fuel. **2** *intr. & colloq. tr.* (in *passive*) drink heavily; become drunk. □ **tank engine** a railway engine carrying fuel and water receptacles in its own frame, not in a tender. **tank top** a sleeveless, close-fitting upper garment with a scoop-neck. □ **tankful** *n.* (*pl.* **-fuls**) **tankless** *adj.* [Gujarati *tānkh* etc., perh. f. Skr. *tadāga* pond]

tankard /ˈtæŋkəd/ *n.* **1** a tall mug with a handle and sometimes a hinged lid, esp. of silver or pewter for beer. **2** the contents of or an amount held by a tankard (*drank a tankard of ale*). [ME: orig. unkn.: cf. MDu. *tanckaert*]

tanker /ˈtæŋkə(r)/ *n.* a ship, aircraft, or road vehicle for carrying liquids, esp. mineral oils, in bulk.

tanner /ˈtænə(r)/ *n.* a person who tans hides.

tannery /ˈtænərɪ/ *n.* (*pl.* **-ies**) a place where hides are tanned.

tannic /ˈtænɪk/ *adj.* of or produced from tan. □ **tannic acid** a complex natural organic compound of a yellowish colour used as a mordant and astringent. □ **tannate** /-neɪt/ *n.* [F *tannique* (as TANNIN)]

tannin /ˈtænɪn/ *n.* any of a group of complex organic compounds found in certain tree-barks and oak-galls, used in leather production and ink manufacture. [F *tanin* (as TAN¹, -IN)]

tannish see TAN¹.

Tannoy /ˈtænɔɪ/ *n. propr.* a type of public-address system. [20th c.: orig. uncert.]

tansy /ˈtænzɪ/ *n.* (*pl.* **-ies**) any plant of the genus *Tanacetum*, esp. *T. vulgare* with yellow button-like flowers and aromatic leaves, formerly used in medicines and cookery. [ME f. OF *tanesie* f. med.L *athanasia* immortality f. Gk]

tantalize /ˈtæntəˌlaɪz/ *v.tr.* (also **-ise**) **1** torment or tease by the sight or promise of what is unobtainable. **2** raise and then dash the hopes of; torment with disappointment. □ **tantalization** /-ˈzeɪʃ(ə)n/ *n.* **tantalizer** *n.* **tantalizingly** *adv.* [Gk *Tantalos* mythical king of Phrygia condemned to stand in water that receded when he tried to drink it and under branches that drew back when he tried to pick the fruit]

tantalum /ˈtæntələm/ *n. Chem.* a rare hard white metallic element used in surgery and for electronic components. □ **tantalic** *adj.* [formed as TANTALUS with ref. to its non-absorbent quality]

tantalus /ˈtæntələs/ *n.* a stand in which spirit-decanters may be locked up but visible. [see TANTALIZE]

tantamount /ˈtæntəˌmaʊnt/ *predic.adj.* (foll. by *to*) equivalent to (*was tantamount to a denial*). [f. obs. verb f. It. *tanto montare* amount to so much]

tantra /ˈtæntrə/ *n.* any of a class of Hindu or Buddhist mystical and magical writings. □ **tantric** *adj.* **tantrism** *n.* **tantrist** *n.* [Skr., = loom, groundwork, doctrine f. *tan* stretch]

tantrum /ˈtæntrəm/ *n.* an outburst of bad temper or petulance (*threw a tantrum*). [18th c.: orig. unkn.]

Taoiseach /ˈtiːʃəx/ *n.* the Prime Minister of the Irish Republic. [Ir., = chief, leader]

Taoism /ˈtaʊɪz(ə)m, ˈtaːʊ-/ *n.* a Chinese philosophy based on the writings of Laoze (*c.*500 BC), advocating humility and religious piety. □ **Taoist** /-ɪst/ *n.* **Taoistic** /-ˈɪstɪk/ *adj.* [Chin. *dao* (right) way]

tap¹ *n. & v.* —*n.* **1** a device by which a flow of liquid or gas from a pipe or vessel can be controlled. **2** an act of tapping a telephone etc. **3** *Brit.* a taproom. —*v.tr.* (**tapped, tapping**) **1 a** provide (a cask) with a tap. **b** let out (a liquid) by means of, or as if by means of, a tap. **2** draw sap from (a tree) by cutting into it. **3 a** obtain information or supplies or resources from. **b** establish communication or trade with. **4** connect a listening device to (a telephone or telegraph line etc.) to listen to a call or transmission. **5** cut a female screw-thread in. □ **on tap 1** ready to be drawn off by tap. **2** *colloq.* ready for immediate use; freely available. **tap root** a tapering root growing vertically downwards. **tap water** water from a piped supply. □ **tapless** *adj.* **tappable** *adj.* [OE *tæppian* (v.), *tæppa* (n.) f. Gmc]

tap² *v. & n.* —*v.* (**tapped, tapping**) **1** *intr.* (foll. by *at, on*) strike a gentle but audible blow. **2** *tr.* strike lightly (*tapped me on the shoulder*). **3** *tr.* (foll. by *against* etc.) cause (a thing) to strike lightly (*tapped a stick against the window*). —*n.* **1 a** a light blow; a rap. **b** the sound of this (*heard a tap at the door*). **2 a** = TAP-DANCE *n.* (*goes to tap classes*). **b** a piece of metal attached to the toe and heel of a tap-dancer's shoe to make the tapping sound. **3** (in *pl.*, usu. treated as *sing.*) *US* **a** a bugle call for lights to be put out in army quarters. **b** a similar signal at a military funeral. □ **tapper** *n.* [ME *tappe* (imit.), perh. through F *taper*]

tap-dance /ˈtæpdɑːns/ *n. & v.* —*n.* a form of display dance performed wearing shoes fitted with metal taps, with rhythmical tapping of the toes and heels. —*v.intr.* perform a tap-dance. □ **tap-dancer** *n.* **tap-dancing** *n.*

tape *n. & v.* —*n.* **1** a narrow strip of woven material for tying up, fastening, etc. **2 a** a strip of material stretched across the finishing line of a race. **b** a similar strip for marking off an area or forming a notional barrier. **3** (in full **adhesive tape**) a strip of opaque or transparent paper or plastic etc., esp. coated with adhesive for fastening, sticking, masking, insulating, etc. **4 a** = *magnetic tape.* **b** a tape recording or tape cassette. **5** = *tape-measure.* —*v.tr.* **1 a** tie up or join etc. with tape. **b** apply tape to. **2** (foll. by *off*) seal or mark off an area or thing with tape. **3** record on magnetic tape. □ **breast the tape** win a race. **have** (or **get**) **a person** or **thing taped** *Brit. colloq.* understand a person or thing fully. **on tape** recorded on magnetic tape. **tape deck** a platform with capstans for using magnetic tape. **tape machine** a machine for receiving and recording telegraph messages. **tape-measure** a strip of tape or thin flexible metal marked for measuring lengths. **tape-record** record (sounds) on magnetic tape. **tape recorder** apparatus for recording sounds on magnetic tape and afterwards reproducing them. **tape recording** a recording on magnetic tape. □ **tapeable** *adj.* (esp. in sense 3 of *v.*). **tapeless** *adj.* **tapelike** *adj.* [OE *tæppa, tæppe,* of unkn. orig.]

taper /ˈteɪpə(r)/ *n. & v.* —*n.* **1** a wick coated with wax etc. for conveying a flame. **2** a slender candle. —*v.* (often foll. by *off*) **1** *intr. & tr.* diminish or reduce in thickness towards one end. **2** *tr. & intr.* make or become gradually less. [OE *tapur, -or, -er* wax candle, f. L PAPYRUS, whose pith was used for candle-wicks]

tapestry /ˈtæpɪstrɪ/ *n.* (*pl.* **-ies**) **1 a** a thick textile fabric in which coloured weft threads are woven to form pictures or designs. **b** embroidery imitating this, usu. in wools on canvas. **c** a piece of such embroidery. **2** events or circumstances etc. compared with a tapestry in being intricate, interwoven, etc. (*life's rich tapestry*). □ **tapestried** *adj.* [ME, alt. f. *tapissery* f. OF *tapisserie* f. *tapissier* tapestry-worker or *tapisser* to carpet, f. *tapis* f. OF *tapiz* f. LL *tapetium* f. Gk *tapētion* dimin. of *tapēs tapētos* tapestry]

tapeworm /ˈteɪpwɜːm/ *n.* any flatworm of the class Cestoda, living as a parasite in the intestines.

tapioca /ˌtæpɪˈəʊkə/ *n.* a starchy substance in hard white grains obtained from cassava and used for puddings etc. [Tupi-Guarani *tipioca* f. *tipi* dregs + *og, ok* squeeze out]

tapir /ˈteɪpə(r), -pɪə(r)/ *n.* any nocturnal hoofed mammal of the genus *Tapirus*, native to Central and S. America and Malaysia, having a short flexible protruding snout used for feeding on vegetation. □ **tapiroid** *adj. & n.* [Tupi *tapira*]

tapper see TAP².

tappet /ˈtæpɪt/ *n.* a lever or projecting part used in machinery to give intermittent motion, often in conjunction with a cam. [app. f. TAP² + -ET¹]

taproom /ˈtæpruːm, -rʊm/ *n.* a room in which alcoholic drinks are available on tap.

tapster /ˈtæpstə(r)/ *n.* a person who draws and serves alcoholic drinks at a bar. [OE *tæppestre* orig. fem. (as TAP¹, -STER)]

tapu /ˈtɑːpuː/ *n. & adj.* NZ = TABOO. [Maori]

tar¹ *n. & v.* —*n.* **1** a dark thick inflammable liquid distilled from wood or coal etc. and used as a preservative of wood and iron, in making roads, as an antiseptic, etc. **2** a similar substance formed in the combustion of tobacco etc. —*v.tr.* (**tarred, tarring**) cover with tar. □ **tar and feather** smear with tar and then cover with feathers as a punishment. **tar-brush** a brush for applying tar. **tarred with the same brush** having the same faults. [OE *te(o)ru* f. Gmc, rel. to TREE]

tar² *n. colloq.* a sailor. [abbr. of TARPAULIN]

taradiddle /ˈtærəˌdɪd(ə)l/ *n.* (also **tarradiddle**) *colloq.* **1** a petty lie. **2** pretentious nonsense. [18th c.: cf. DIDDLE]

taramasalata /ˌtærəməsəˈlɑːtə/ *n.* (also **tarama** /ˈtærəmə/) a pinkish pâté made from the roe of mullet or other fish with olive oil, seasoning, etc. [mod.Gk *taramas* roe (f. Turk. *tarama*) + *salata* SALAD]

tarantella /ˌtærənˈtelə/ *n.* (also **tarantelle** /-ˈtel/) **1** a rapid whirling S. Italian dance. **2** the music for this. [It., f. *Taranto* in Italy (because the dance was once thought to be a cure for a tarantula bite)]

tarantula /təˈræntjʊlə/ *n.* **1** any large hairy tropical spider of the family Theraphosidae. **2** a large black S. European spider, *Lycosa tarentula*. [med.L f. It. *tarantola*, rel. to TARANTELLA]

tarboosh /tɑːˈbuːʃ/ *n.* a cap like a fez, sometimes worn as part of a turban. [Egypt. Arab. *ṭarbūš*, ult. f. Pers. *sar-būš* head-cover]

tardy /ˈtɑːdɪ/ *adj.* (**tardier, tardiest**) **1** slow to act or come or happen. **2** delaying or delayed beyond the right or expected time. □ **tardily** *adv.* **tardiness** *n.* [F *tardif, tardive* ult. f. L *tardus* slow]

tare¹ /teə(r)/ *n.* **1** vetch, esp. as corn-weed or fodder. **2** (in *pl.*) *Bibl.* an injurious corn-weed (Matt. 13:24–30). [ME: orig. unkn.]

tare² /teə(r)/ *n.* **1** an allowance made for the weight of the packing or wrapping around goods. **2** the weight of a motor vehicle without its fuel or load. [ME f. F, = deficiency, tare, f. med.L *tara* f. Arab. *ṭarḥa* what is rejected f. *ṭaraḥa* reject]

target /ˈtɑːgɪt/ *n. & v.* —*n.* **1** a mark or point fired or aimed at, esp. a round or rectangular object marked with concentric circles. **2** a person or thing aimed at, or exposed to gunfire etc. (*they were an easy target*). **3** (also *attrib.*) an objective or result aimed at (*our export targets; target date*). **4** a person or thing against whom criticism, abuse, etc., is or may be directed. **5** *archaic* a shield or buckler, esp. a small round one. —*v.tr.* (**targeted, targeting**) **1** identify or single out (a person or thing) as an object of attention or attack. **2** aim or direct (*missiles targeted on major cities; should target our efforts where needed*). □ **targetable** *adj.* [ME, dimin. of ME and OF *targe* shield]

tariff /ˈtærɪf/ *n.* **1** a table of fixed charges (a *hotel tariff*). **2 a** a duty on a particular class of imports or exports. **b** a list of duties or customs to be paid. [F *tarif* f. It. *tariffa* f. Turk. *tarife* f. Arab. *ta'rifa* f. *'arrafa* notify]

tarlatan /ˈtɑːlət(ə)n/ *n.* a thin stiff open-weave muslin. [F *tarlatane*, prob. f. Ind. orig.]

Tarmac /ˈtɑːmæk/ *n. & v.* —*n. propr.* **1** = TARMACADAM. **2** a surface made of this, e.g. a runway. —*v.tr.* (**tarmac**) (**tarmacked, tarmacking**) apply tarmacadam to. [abbr.]

tarmacadam /ˌtɑːməˈkædəm/ n. a material of stone or slag bound with tar, used in paving roads etc. [TAR¹ + MACADAM]

tarn n. a small mountain lake. [ME *terne, tarne* f. ON]

tarnish /ˈtɑːnɪʃ/ v. & n. —v. **1** tr. lessen or destroy the lustre of (metal etc.). **2** tr. impair (one's reputation etc.). **3** intr. (of metal etc.) lose lustre. —n. **1 a** a loss of lustre. **b** a film of colour formed on an exposed surface of a mineral or metal. **2** a blemish; a stain. □ **tarnishable** adj. [F *ternir* f. *terne* dark]

taro /ˈtɑːrəʊ/ n. (pl. **-os**) a tropical plant, *Colocasia esculenta*, with tuberous roots used as food. [Polynesian]

tarot /ˈtærəʊ/ n. **1** (in sing. or pl.) **a** any of several games played with a pack of cards having five suits, the last of which is a set of permanent trumps. **b** a similar pack used in fortune-telling. **2 a** any of the trump cards. **b** any of the cards from a fortune-telling pack. [F *tarot*, It. *tarocchi*, of unkn. orig.]

tarp n. US & Austral. colloq. tarpaulin. [abbr.]

tarpaulin /tɑːˈpɔːlɪn/ n. **1** heavy-duty waterproof cloth esp. of tarred canvas. **2** a sheet or covering of this. [prob. f. TAR¹ + PALL¹ + -ING¹]

tarragon /ˈtærəgən/ n. a bushy herb, *Artemisia dracunculus*, with leaves used to flavour salads, stuffings, vinegar, etc. [= med.L *tarchon* f. med. Gk *tarkhōn*, perh. through Arab. f. Gk *drakōn* dragon]

tarry¹ /ˈtɑːrɪ/ adj. (**tarrier, tarriest**) of or like tar. □ **tarriness** n.

tarry² /ˈtærɪ/ v.intr. (**-ies, -ied**) archaic or literary **1** defer coming or going. **2** linger, stay, wait. **3** be tardy. □ **tarrier** n. [ME: orig. uncert.]

tarsal /ˈtɑːs(ə)l/ adj. & n. —adj. of or relating to the bones in the ankle. —n. a tarsal bone. [TARSUS + -AL]

tarsi pl. of TARSUS.

tarsus /ˈtɑːsəs/ n. (pl. **tarsi** /-saɪ/) **1** the group of bones forming the ankle and upper foot. **2** the shank of a bird's leg. [mod.L f. Gk *tarsos* flat of the foot]

tart¹ n. **1** an open pastry case containing jam etc. **2** esp. Brit. a pie with a fruit or sweet filling. □ **tartlet** n. [ME f. OF *tarte* = med.L *tarta*, of unkn. orig.]

tart² n. & v. —n. sl. **1** a prostitute; a promiscuous woman. **2** sl. offens. a girl or woman. —v. (foll. by up) esp. Brit. colloq. **1** tr. (usu. refl.) smarten (oneself or a thing) up, esp. flashily or gaudily. **2** intr. dress up gaudily. [prob. abbr. of SWEETHEART]

tart³ adj. **1** sharp or acid in taste. **2** (of a remark etc.) cutting, bitter. □ **tartly** adv. **tartness** n. [OE *teart*, of unkn. orig.]

tartan /ˈtɑːt(ə)n/ n. **1** a pattern of coloured stripes crossing at right angles, esp. the distinctive plaid worn by the Scottish Highlanders to denote their clan. **2** woollen cloth woven in this pattern (often attrib.: *a tartan scarf*). [perh. f. OF *tertaine, tiretaine*]

Tartar /ˈtɑːtə(r)/ n. & adj. (also **Tatar** except in sense 2 of n.) —n. **1 a** a member of a group of Central Asian peoples including Mongols and Turks. **b** the Turkic language of these peoples. **2** (**tartar**) a violent-tempered or intractable person. —adj. of or relating to the Tartars. □ **tartar sauce** a sauce of mayonnaise and chopped gherkins, capers, etc. □ **Tartarian** /-ˈteərɪən/ adj. [ME *tartre* f. OF *Tartare* or med.L *Tartarus*]

tartar /ˈtɑːtə(r)/ n. **1** a hard deposit of saliva, calcium phosphate, etc., that forms on the teeth. **2** a deposit of acid potassium tartrate that forms a hard crust on the inside of a cask during the fermentation of wine. □ **tartarize** v.tr. (also **-ise**). [ME f. med.L f. med.Gk *tartaron*]

tartare /tɑːˈtɑː(r)/ adj. (in full **sauce tartare**) = *tartar sauce*. [F, = tartar]

tartaric /tɑːˈtærɪk/ adj. Chem. of or produced from tartar. □ **tartaric acid** a natural carboxylic acid found esp. in unripe grapes, used in baking powders and as a food additive. [F *tartarique* f. med.L *tartarum*: see TARTAR]

tartrate /ˈtɑːtreɪt/ n. Chem. any salt or ester of tartaric acid. [F (as TARTAR, -ATE¹)]

tartrazine /ˈtɑːtrəˌziːn/ n. Chem. a brilliant yellow dye derived from tartaric acid and used to colour food, drugs, and cosmetics. [as TARTAR + F *azote* nitrogen + -INE⁴]

tarty /ˈtɑːtɪ/ adj. colloq. (**tartier, tartiest**) (esp. of a woman) vulgar, gaudy; promiscuous. □ **tartily** adv. **tartiness** n. [TART² + -Y¹]

Tarzan /ˈtɑːz(ə)n/ n. a man of great agility and powerful physique. [name of the hero of stories by E. R. Burroughs, Amer. writer d. 1950]

task /tɑːsk/ n. & v. —n. a piece of work to be done or undertaken. —v.tr. make great demands on (a person's powers etc.). □ **take to task** rebuke, scold. **task force** (or **group**) **1** Mil. an armed force organized for a special operation. **2** a unit specially organized for a task. [ME f. ONF *tasque* = OF *tasche* f. med.L *tasca*, perh. f. *taxa* f. L *taxare* TAX]

taskmaster /ˈtɑːskˌmɑːstə(r)/ n. (fem. **taskmistress** /-ˌmɪstrɪs/) a person who imposes a task or burden, esp. regularly or severely.

Tass /tæs/ n. the official news agency of the former Soviet Union. [the initials of Russ. *Telegrafnoe agentstvo Sovetskogo Soyuza* Telegraphic Agency of the Soviet Union]

tassel /ˈtæs(ə)l/ n. **1** a tuft of loosely hanging threads or cords etc. attached for decoration to a cushion, scarf, cap, etc. **2** a tassel-like head of some plants. [ME f. OF *tas(s)el* clasp, of unkn. orig.]

taste /teɪst/ n. & v. —n. **1 a** the sensation characteristic of a soluble substance caused in the mouth and throat by contact with that substance (*disliked the taste of garlic*). **b** the faculty of perceiving this sensation (*was bitter to the taste*). **2** a small portion of food or drink taken as a sample. **3** a slight experience (*a taste of success*). **4** (often foll. by for) a liking or predilection (*has expensive tastes; is not to my taste*). **5** aesthetic discernment in art, literature, conduct, etc., esp. of a specified kind (*a person of taste; dresses in poor taste*). —v. **1** tr. sample or test the flavour of (food etc.) by taking it into the mouth. **2** tr. (also absol.) perceive the flavour of (*could taste the lemon; cannot taste with a cold*). **3** tr. (esp. with neg.) eat or drink a small portion of (*had not tasted food for days*). **4** tr. have experience of (*had never tasted failure*). **5** intr. (often foll. by of) have a specified flavour (*tastes bitter; tastes of onions*). □ **a bad** (or **bitter** etc.) **taste** colloq. a strong feeling of regret or unease. **taste bud** any of the cells or nerve-endings on the surface of the tongue by which things are tasted. **to taste** in the amount needed for a

pleasing result (*add salt and pepper to taste*). □
tasteable *adj.* [ME, = touch, taste, f. OF *tast*, *taster* touch, try, taste, ult. perh. f. L *tangere* touch + *gustare* taste]

tasteful /ˈteɪstfʊl/ *adj.* having, or done in, good taste. □ **tastefully** *adv.* **tastefulness** *n.*

tasteless /ˈteɪstlɪs/ *adj.* **1** lacking flavour. **2** having, or done in, bad taste. □ **tastelessly** *adv.* **tastelessness** *n.*

taster /ˈteɪstə(r)/ *n.* **1** a person employed to test food or drink by tasting it, esp. for quality or *hist.* to detect poisoning. **2** a small cup used by a wine-taster. **3** an instrument for extracting a small sample from within a cheese. [ME f. AF *tastour*, OF *tasteur* f. *taster*: see TASTE]

tasting /ˈteɪstɪŋ/ *n.* a gathering at which food or drink (esp. wine) is tasted and evaluated.

tasty /ˈteɪstɪ/ *adj.* (**tastier**, **tastiest**) (of food) pleasing in flavour; appetizing. □ **tastily** *adv.* **tastiness** *n.*

tat[1] *n. colloq.* **1** tatty or tasteless clothes; worthless goods. **2** rubbish, junk. [back-form. f. TATTY]

tat[2] *v.* (**tatted**, **tatting**) **1** *intr.* do tatting. **2** *tr.* make by tatting. [19th c.: orig. unkn.]

tat[3] see TIT[2].

ta-ta /tæˈtɑː/ *int. Brit. colloq.* goodbye (said esp. to or by a child). [19th c.: orig. unkn.]

tatter /ˈtætə(r)/ *n.* (usu. in *pl.*) a rag; an irregularly torn piece of cloth or paper etc. □ **in tatters** *colloq.* (of a negotiation, argument, etc.) ruined, demolished. □ **tattery** *adj.* [ME f. ON *tötrar* rags: cf. Icel. *töturr*]

tattered /ˈtætəd/ *adj.* in tatters.

tatting /ˈtætɪŋ/ *n.* **1** a kind of knotted lace made by hand with a small shuttle and used for trimming etc. **2** the process of making this. [19th c.: orig. unkn.]

tattle /ˈtæt(ə)l/ *v. & n.* —*v.* **1** *intr.* prattle, chatter; gossip idly. **2** *tr.* utter (words) idly. —*n.* gossip; idle or trivial talk. □ **tattle-tale** *US* a tell-tale, esp. a child. [ME f. MFlem. *tatelen*, *tateren* (imit.)]

tattoo[1] /təˈtuː/ *n.* **1** an evening drum or bugle signal recalling soldiers to their quarters. **2** an elaboration of this with music and marching, presented as an entertainment. **3** a rhythmic tapping or drumming. [17th-c. *tap-too* f. Du. *taptoe*, lit. 'close the tap' (of the cask)]

tattoo[2] /təˈtuː, tæ-/ *v. & n.* —*v.tr.* (**tattoos**, **tattooed**) **1** mark (the skin) with an indelible design by puncturing it and inserting pigment. **2** make (a design) in this way. —*n.* a design made by tattooing. □ **tattooer** *n.* **tattooist** *n.* [Polynesian]

tatty /ˈtætɪ/ *adj.* (**tattier**, **tattiest**) *colloq.* **1** tattered; worn and shabby. **2** inferior. **3** tawdry. □ **tattily** *adv.* **tattiness** *n.* [orig. Sc., = shaggy, app. rel. to OE *tættec* rag, TATTER]

tau /taʊ, tɔː/ *n.* the nineteenth letter of the Greek alphabet (*T*, *τ*). □ **tau cross** a T-shaped cross. **tau particle** *Physics* an unstable, heavy, and charged elementary particle of the lepton class. [ME f. Gk]

taught *past* and *past part.* of TEACH.

taunt *n. & v.* —*n.* a thing said in order to anger or wound a person. —*v.tr.* **1** assail with taunts. **2** reproach (a person) contemptuously. □ **taunter** *n.* **tauntingly** *adv.* [16th c., in phr. *taunt for taunt* f. F *tant pour tant* tit for tat, hence a smart rejoinder]

taupe /təʊp/ *n.* a grey with a tinge of another colour, usu. brown. [F, = MOLE[1]]

taurine /ˈtɔːriːn, -raɪn/ *adj.* of or like a bull; bullish. [L *taurinus* f. *taurus* bull]

Taurus /ˈtɔːrəs/ *n.* **1** a constellation. **2 a** the second sign of the zodiac (the Bull). **b** a person born when the sun is in this sign. □ **Taurean** *adj. & n.* [ME f. L, = bull]

taut *adj.* **1** (of a rope, muscles, etc.) tight; not slack. **2** (of nerves) tense. **3** (of a ship etc.) in good order or condition. □ **tauten** *v.tr. & intr.* **tautly** *adv.* **tautness** *n.* [ME *touht*, *togt*, perh. = TOUGH, infl. by *tog-* past part. stem of obs. *tee* (OE *tēon*) pull]

tauto- /ˈtɔːtəʊ/ *comb. form* the same. [Gk, f. *tauto*, *to auto* the same]

tautology /tɔːˈtɒlədʒɪ/ *n.* (*pl.* **-ies**) **1** the saying of the same thing twice over in different words, esp. as a fault of style (e.g. *arrived one after the other in succession*). **2** a statement that is necessarily true. □ **tautologic** /-təˈlɒdʒɪk/ *adj.* **tautological** /-təˈlɒdʒɪk(ə)l/ *adj.* **tautologically** /-təˈlɒdʒɪkəlɪ/ *adv.* **tautologist** *n.* **tautologize** /-ˌdʒaɪz/ *v.intr.* (also **-ise**). **tautologous** /-ləgəs/ *adj.* [LL *tautologia* f. Gk (as TAUTO-, -LOGY)]

tavern /ˈtæv(ə)n/ *n. literary* an inn or public house. [ME f. OF *taverne* f. L *taberna* hut, tavern]

taverna /təˈvɜːnə/ *n.* a Greek eating house. [mod. Gk (as TAVERN)]

tawdry /ˈtɔːdrɪ/ *adj.* (**tawdrier**, **tawdriest**) **1** showy but worthless. **2** over-ornamented, gaudy, vulgar. □ **tawdrily** *adv.* **tawdriness** *n.* [earlier as noun: short for *tawdry lace*, orig. *St Audrey's lace* f. *Audrey* = Etheldrida, patron saint of Ely]

tawny /ˈtɔːnɪ/ *adj.* (**tawnier**, **tawniest**) of an orange- or yellow-brown colour. □ **tawny owl** a reddish-brown European owl, *Strix aluco*. □ **tawniness** *n.* [ME f. AF *tauné*, OF *tané* f. *tan* TAN[1]]

tax *n. & v.* —*n.* **1** a contribution to State revenue compulsorily levied on individuals, property, or businesses (often foll. by *on*: *a tax on luxury goods*). **2** (usu. foll. by *on*, *upon*) a strain or heavy demand; an oppressive or burdensome obligation. —*v.tr.* **1** impose a tax on (persons or goods etc.). **2** deduct tax from (income etc.). **3** make heavy demands on (a person's powers or resources etc.) (*you really tax my patience*). **4** (foll. by *with*) confront (a person) with a wrongdoing etc. **5** call to account. □ **tax avoidance** the arrangement of financial affairs to minimize payment of tax. **tax-deductible** (of expenditure) that may be paid out of income before the deduction of income tax. **tax disc** *Brit.* a paper disc displayed on the windscreen of a motor vehicle, certifying payment of excise duty. **tax evasion** the illegal non-payment or underpayment of income tax. **tax-free** exempt from taxes. **tax haven** a country etc. where income tax is low. **tax return** a declaration of income for taxation purposes. **tax shelter** a means of organizing business affairs to minimize payment of tax. **tax year** see *financial year*. □ **taxable** *adj.* **taxless** *adj.* [ME f. OF *taxer* f. L *taxare* censure, charge, compute, perh. f. Gk *tassō* fix]

taxa *pl.* of TAXON.

taxation /tækˈseɪʃ(ə)n/ *n.* the imposition or payment of tax. [ME f. AF *taxacioun*, OF *taxation* f. L *taxatio -onis* f. *taxare*: see TAX]

taxi /ˈtæksɪ/ *n. & v.* —*n.* (*pl.* **taxis**) **1** (in full **taxi-cab**) a motor car licensed to ply for hire and usu. fitted with a taximeter. **2** a boat etc. similarly used. —*v.* (**taxis, taxied, taxiing** or **taxying**) **1 a** *intr.* (of an aircraft or pilot) move along the ground under the machine's own power before take-off or after landing. **b** *tr.* cause (an aircraft) to taxi. **2** *intr.* & *tr.* go or convey in a taxi. □ **taxi-driver** a driver of a taxi. **taxi rank** (*US* **stand**) a place where taxis wait to be hired. [abbr. of *taximeter cab*]

taxidermy /ˈtæksɪˌdɜːmɪ/ *n.* the art of preparing, stuffing, and mounting the skins of animals with lifelike effect. □ **taxidermal** /-ˈdɜːm(ə)l/ *adj.* **taxidermic** /-ˈdɜːmɪk/ *adj.* **taxidermist** *n.* [Gk *taxis* arrangement + *derma* skin]

taximeter /ˈtæksɪˌmiːtə(r)/ *n.* an automatic device fitted to a taxi, recording the distance travelled and the fare payable. [F *taximètre* f. *taxe* tariff, TAX + -METER]

taxman /ˈtæksmæn/ *n. colloq.* (*pl.* **-men**) an inspector or collector of taxes.

taxon /ˈtæks(ə)n/ *n.* (*pl.* **taxa** /ˈtæksə/) any taxonomic group. [back-form. f. TAXONOMY]

taxonomy /tækˈsɒnəmɪ/ *n.* **1** the science of the classification of living and extinct organisms. **2** the practice of this. □ **taxonomic** /-səˈnɒmɪk/ *adj.* **taxonomical** /-səˈnɒmɪk(ə)l/ *adj.* **taxonomically** /-səˈnɒmɪkəlɪ/ *adv.* **taxonomist** *n.* [F *taxonomie* f. Gk *taxis* f. *tassō* arrange + *-nomia* distribution]

taxpayer /ˈtæksˌpeɪə(r)/ *n.* a person who pays taxes.

tayberry /ˈteɪbərɪ/ *n.* (*pl.* **-ies**) a dark red soft fruit produced by crossing the blackberry and raspberry. [*Tay* in Scotland (where introduced in 1977)]

TB *abbr.* **1** tuberculosis. **2** torpedo boat.

Tb *symb. Chem.* the element terbium.

T-bone /ˈtiːbəʊn/ *n.* a T-shaped bone, esp. in steak from the thin end of a loin.

tbsp. *abbr.* tablespoonful.

Tc *symb. Chem.* the element technetium.

TCP *abbr. propr.* a disinfectant and germicide. [trichlorophenylmethyliodasalicyl]

TD *abbr. Ir.* Teachta Dála, Member of the Dáil.

Te *symb. Chem.* the element tellurium.

te /tiː/ *n.* (also **ti**) **1** (in tonic sol-fa) the seventh note of a major scale. **2** the note B in the fixed-doh system. [earlier *si*: F f. It., perh. f. Sancte Iohannes: see GAMUT]

tea *n.* **1 a** (in full **tea plant**) an evergreen shrub or small tree, *Camellia sinensis*, of India, China, etc. **b** its dried leaves. **2** a drink made by infusing tea-leaves in boiling water. **3** a similar drink made from the leaves of other plants or from another substance (*camomile tea; beef tea*). **4 a** a light afternoon meal consisting of tea, bread, cakes, etc. **b** *Brit.* a cooked evening meal. □ **tea bag** a small perforated bag of tea for infusion. **tea break** *Brit.* a pause in work etc. to drink tea. **tea caddy** a container for tea. **tea chest** a light metal-lined wooden box in which tea is transported. **tea cloth** = *tea towel.* **tea cosy** a cover to keep a teapot warm. **tea dance** an afternoon tea with dancing. **tea-leaf 1** a dried leaf of tea, used to make a drink of tea. **2** (esp. in *pl.*) these after infusion or as dregs. **3** *rhyming sl.* a thief. **tea party** a party at teatime. **tea rose** a hybrid shrub, *Rosa odorata*, with a scent resembling that of tea. **tea towel** a towel for drying washed crockery etc. **tea-tree** *Austral.* & *NZ* an aromatic evergreen flowering shrub,

Leptospermum scoparium. [17th-c. *tay, tey*, prob. f. Du. *tee* f. Chin. (Amoy dial.) *te*, = Mandarin dial. *cha*]

teacake /ˈtiːkeɪk/ *n. Brit.* a light yeast-based usu. sweet bun eaten at tea, often toasted.

teach *v.tr.* (*past* and *past part.* **taught** /tɔːt/) **1 a** give systematic information to (a person) or about (a subject or skill). **b** (*absol.*) practise this professionally. **c** enable (a person) to do something by instruction and training (*taught me to swim; taught me how to dance*). **2** advocate as a moral etc. principle (*my parents taught me tolerance*). **3** (foll. by *to* + infin.) **a** induce (a person) by example or punishment to do or not to do a thing (*that will teach you to sit still*). **b** *colloq.* make (a person) disinclined to do a thing (*I will teach you to interfere*). □ **teach-in 1** an informal lecture and discussion on a subject of public interest. **2** a series of these. **teach school** *US* be a teacher in a school. [OE *tǣcan* f. a Gmc root = 'show']

teachable /ˈtiːtʃəb(ə)l/ *adj.* **1** apt at learning. **2** (of a subject) that can be taught. □ **teachability** /-ˈbɪlɪtɪ/ *n.* **teachableness** *n.*

teacher /ˈtiːtʃə(r)/ *n.* a person who teaches, esp. in a school. □ **teacherly** *adj.*

teaching /ˈtiːtʃɪŋ/ *n.* **1** the profession of a teacher. **2** (often in *pl.*) what is taught; a doctrine. □ **teaching hospital** a hospital where medical students are taught.

teacup /ˈtiːkʌp/ *n.* **1** a cup from which tea is drunk. **2** an amount held by this, about 150 ml. □ **teacupful** *n.* (*pl.* **-fuls**).

teak *n.* **1** a large deciduous tree, *Tectona grandis*, native to India and SE Asia. **2** its hard durable timber, much used in shipbuilding and furniture. [Port. *teca* f. Malayalam *tēkka*]

teal *n.* (*pl.* same) **1** any of various small freshwater ducks of the genus *Anas*, esp. *A. crecca*. **2** a dark greenish-blue colour. [rel. to MDu. *tēling*, of unkn. orig.]

team *n.* & *v.* —*n.* **1** a set of players forming one side in a game (*a cricket team*). **2** two or more persons working together. **3 a** a set of draught animals. **b** one animal or more in harness with a vehicle. —*v.* **1** *intr.* & *tr.* (usu. foll. by *up*) join in a team or in common action (*decided to team up with them*). **2** *tr.* harness (horses etc.) in a team. **3** *tr.* (foll. by *with*) match or coordinate (clothes). □ **team-mate** a fellow-member of a team or group. **team spirit** willingness to act as a member of a group rather than as an individual. **team-teaching** teaching by a team of teachers working together. [OE *tēam* offspring f. a Gmc root = 'pull', rel. to TOW¹]

teamster /ˈtiːmstə(r)/ *n.* **1** *US* a lorry-driver. **2** a driver of a team of animals.

teamwork /ˈtiːmwɜːk/ *n.* the combined action of a team, group, etc., esp. when effective and efficient.

teapot /ˈtiːpɒt/ *n.* a pot with a handle, spout, and lid, in which tea is brewed and from which it is poured.

tear¹ /teə(r)/ *v.* & *n.* —*v.* (*past* **tore**; *past part.* **torn**) **1** *tr.* (often foll. by *up*) pull apart or to pieces with some force (*tear it in half; tore up the letter*). **2** *tr.* **a** make a hole or rent in by tearing (*have torn my coat*). **b** make (a hole or rent). **3** *tr.* (foll. by *away, off*, etc.) pull violently or with some force (*tore the book away from me; tore off the cover; tore a page out; tore down the notice*). **4** *tr.*

violently disrupt or divide (*the country was torn by civil war; torn by conflicting emotions*). **5** *intr. colloq.* go or travel hurriedly or impetuously (*tore across the road*). **6** *intr.* undergo tearing (*the curtain tore down the middle*). **7** *intr.* (foll. by *at* etc.) pull violently or with some force. —*n.* **1** a hole or other damage caused by tearing. **2** a torn part of cloth etc. □ **be torn between** have difficulty in choosing between. **tear apart 1** search (a place) exhaustively. **2** criticize forcefully. **tear one's hair out** behave with extreme desperation or anger. **tear into 1** attack verbally; reprimand. **2** make a vigorous start on (an activity). **tear oneself away** leave despite a strong desire to stay. **tear to shreds** *colloq.* refute or criticize thoroughly. **that's torn it** *Brit. colloq.* that has spoiled things, caused a problem, etc. □ **tearable** *adj.* **tearer** *n.* [OE *teran* f. Gmc]

tear[2] /tɪə(r)/ *n.* **1** a drop of clear salty liquid secreted by glands, that serves to moisten and wash the eye and is shed from it in grief or other strong emotions. **2** a tearlike thing; a drop. □ **in tears** crying; shedding tears. **tear-drop** a single tear. **tear-duct** a drain for carrying tears to the eye or from the eye to the nose. **tear-gas** gas that disables by causing severe irritation to the eyes. **tear-jerker** *colloq.* a story, film, etc., calculated to evoke sadness or sympathy. □ **tearlike** *adj.* [OE *tēar*]

tearaway /ˈteərəˌweɪ/ *n. Brit.* **1** an impetuous or reckless young person. **2** a hooligan.

tearful /ˈtɪəfʊl/ *adj.* **1** crying or inclined to cry. **2** causing or accompanied with tears; sad (*a tearful event*). □ **tearfully** *adv.* **tearfulness** *n.*

tearing /ˈteərɪŋ/ *adj.* extreme, overwhelming, violent (*in a tearing hurry*).

tearoom /ˈtiːruːm, -rʊm/ *n.* a small restaurant or café where tea is served.

tease /tiːz/ *v. & n.* —*v.tr.* (also *absol.*) **1 a** make fun of (a person or animal) playfully or unkindly or annoyingly. **b** tempt or allure, esp. sexually, while refusing to satisfy the desire aroused. **2** pick (wool, hair, etc.) into separate fibres. **3** dress (cloth) esp. with teasels. —*n.* **1** *colloq.* a person fond of teasing. **2** an instance of teasing (*it was only a tease*). □ **tease out** separate by disentangling. □ **teasingly** *adv.* [OE *tǣsan* f. WG]

teasel /ˈtiːz(ə)l/ *n. & v.* (also **teazel, teazle**) —*n.* **1** any plant of the genus *Dipsacus*, with large prickly heads that are dried and used to raise the nap on woven cloth. **2** a device used as a substitute for teasels. —*v.tr.* dress (cloth) with teasels. □ **teaseler** *n.* [OE *tǣs(e)l*, = OHG *zeisala* (as TEASE)]

teaser /ˈtiːzə(r)/ *n.* **1** *colloq.* a hard question or task. **2** a teasing person. **3** esp. *US* a short introductory advertisement etc.

teaset /ˈtiːset/ *n.* a set of crockery for serving tea.

teashop /ˈtiːʃɒp/ *n.* esp. *Brit.* = TEAROOM.

teaspoon /ˈtiːspuːn/ *n.* **1** a small spoon for stirring tea. **2** an amount held by this. □ **teaspoonful** *n.* (*pl.* **-fuls**).

teat /tiːt/ *n.* **1** a mammary nipple, esp. of an animal. **2** a thing resembling this, esp. a device of rubber etc. for sucking milk from a bottle. [ME f. OF *tete*, prob. of Gmc orig., replacing TIT[3]]

teatime /ˈtiːtaɪm/ *n.* the time in the afternoon when tea is served.

tec *n. colloq.* a detective. [abbr.]

tech /tek/ *n.* (also **tec**) *colloq.* a technical college. [abbr.]

technetium /tekˈniːʃ(ə)m/ *n. Chem.* an artificially produced radioactive metallic element occurring in the fission products of uranium. [mod.L f. Gk *tekhnētos* artificial f. *tekhnē* art]

technical /ˈteknɪk(ə)l/ *adj.* **1** of or involving or concerned with the mechanical arts and applied sciences (*technical college; a technical education*). **2** of or relating to a particular subject or craft etc. or its techniques (*technical terms; technical merit*). **3** (of a book or discourse etc.) using technical language; requiring special knowledge to be understood. **4** due to mechanical failure (*a technical hitch*). **5** legally such; such in strict interpretation (*technical assault; lost on a technical point*). □ **technical hitch** a temporary breakdown or problem in machinery etc. **technical knockout** *Boxing* a termination of a fight by the referee on the grounds of a contestant's inability to continue, the opponent being declared the winner. □ **technically** *adv.* **technicalness** *n.* [L *technicus* f. Gk *tekhnikos* f. *tekhnē* art]

technicality /ˌteknɪˈkælɪtɪ/ *n.* (*pl.* **-ies**) **1** the state of being technical. **2** a technical expression. **3** a technical point or detail (*was acquitted on a technicality*).

technician /tekˈnɪʃ(ə)n/ *n.* **1** an expert in the practical application of a science. **2** a person skilled in the technique of an art or craft. **3** a person employed to look after technical equipment and do practical work in a laboratory etc.

Technicolor /ˈteknɪˌkʌlə(r)/ *n.* (often *attrib.*) **1** *propr.* a process of colour cinematography. **2** (usu. **technicolor**) *colloq.* **a** a vivid colour. **b** artificial brilliance. □ **technicolored** *adj.* [TECHNICAL + COLOR]

technique /tekˈniːk/ *n.* **1** mechanical skill in an art. **2** a means of achieving one's purpose, esp. skilfully. **3** a manner of artistic execution in music, painting, etc. [F (as TECHNICAL)]

technobabble /ˈteknəʊˌbæb(ə)l/ *n. colloq.* incomprehensible technical jargon.

technocracy /tekˈnɒkrəsɪ/ *n.* (*pl.* **-ies**) **1** the government or control of society or industry by technical experts. **2** an instance or application of this. [Gk *tekhnē* art + -CRACY]

technocrat /ˈteknəˌkræt/ *n.* an exponent or advocate of technocracy. □ **technocratic** /-ˈkrætɪk/ *adj.* **technocratically** /-ˈkrætɪkəlɪ/ *adv.*

technological /ˌteknəˈlɒdʒɪk(ə)l/ *adj.* of or using technology. □ **technologically** *adv.*

technology /tekˈnɒlədʒɪ/ *n.* (*pl.* **-ies**) **1** the study or use of the mechanical arts and applied sciences. **2** these subjects collectively. □ **technologist** *n.* [Gk *tekhnologia* systematic treatment f. *tekhnē* art]

techy var. of TETCHY.

tectonic /tekˈtɒnɪk/ *adj.* **1** of or relating to building or construction. **2** *Geol.* relating to the deformation of the earth's crust or to the structural changes caused by this (see *plate tectonics*). □ **tectonically** *adv.* [LL *tectonicus* f. Gk *tektonikos* f. *tektōn -onos* carpenter]

tectonics /tekˈtɒnɪks/ *n.pl.* (usu. treated as *sing.*) *Geol.* the study of large-scale structural features (cf. *plate tectonics*).

Ted *n.* (also **ted**) *Brit. colloq.* a Teddy boy. [abbr.]

teddy /'tedɪ/ n. (also **Teddy**) (pl. **-ies**) (in full **teddy bear**) a soft toy bear. [*Teddy*, pet-name of *Theodore* Roosevelt, US president d. 1919, famous as a bear-hunter]

Teddy boy /'tedɪ/ n. *Brit. colloq.* **1** a youth, esp. of the 1950s, affecting an Edwardian style of dress and appearance. **2** a young rowdy male. [*Teddy*, pet-form of *Edward*]

tedious /'tiːdɪəs/ *adj.* tiresomely long; wearisome. □ **tediously** *adv.* **tediousness** n. [ME f. OF *tedieus* or LL *taediosus* (as TEDIUM)]

tedium /'tiːdɪəm/ n. the state of being tedious; boredom. [L *taedium* f. *taedēre* to weary]

tee[1] n. = T[1]. [phonet. spelling]

tee[2] n. & v. —n. *Golf* **1** a cleared space from which a golf ball is struck at the beginning of play for each hole. **2** a small support of wood or plastic from which a ball is struck at a tee. —v.tr. (**tees, teed**) (often foll. by *up*) *Golf* place (a ball) on a tee ready to strike it. □ **tee off 1** *Golf* play a ball from a tee. **2** *colloq.* start, begin. [earlier (17th-c.) *teaz*, of unkn. orig.]

tee-hee /tiː'hiː/ n. & v. (also **te-hee**) —n. **1** a titter. **2** a restrained or contemptuous laugh. —v.intr. (**tee-hees, tee-heed**) titter or laugh in this way. [imit.]

teem[1] v.intr. **1** be abundant (*fish teem in these waters*). **2** (foll. by *with*) be full of or swarming with (*teeming with fish; teeming with ideas*). [OE *tēman* etc. give birth to f. Gmc, rel. to TEAM]

teem[2] v.intr. (often foll. by *down*) (of water etc.) flow copiously; pour (*it was teeming with rain*). [ME *tēmen* f. ON *tœma* f. *tómr* (adj.) empty]

teen adj. & n. —adj. = TEENAGE. —n. = TEENAGER. [abbr. of TEENAGE, TEENAGER]

-teen suffix forming the names of numerals from 13 to 19. [OE inflected form of TEN]

teenage /'tiːneɪdʒ/ adj. relating to or characteristic of teenagers. □ **teenaged** adj.

teenager /'tiːˌneɪdʒə(r)/ n. a person from 13 to 19 years of age.

teens n.pl. the years of one's age from 13 to 19 (*in one's teens*).

teensy /'tiːnzɪ/ adj. (**teensier, teensiest**) *colloq.* = TEENY. □ **teensy–weensy** = *teeny-weeny*.

teeny /'tiːnɪ/ adj. (**teenier, teeniest**) *colloq.* tiny. □ **teeny–weeny** very tiny. [var. of TINY]

teeny-bopper /'tiːnɪˌbɒpə(r)/ n. *colloq.* a young teenager, usu. a girl, who keenly follows the latest fashions in clothes, pop music, etc.

teepee var. of TEPEE.

teeshirt var. of T-SHIRT.

teeter /'tiːtə(r)/ v.intr. **1** totter; stand or move unsteadily. **2** hesitate; be indecisive. [var. of dial. *titter*]

teeth pl. of TOOTH.

teethe /tiːð/ v.intr. grow or cut teeth, esp. milk teeth. □ **teething-ring** a small ring for an infant to bite on while teething. **teething troubles** initial difficulties in an enterprise etc., regarded as temporary. □ **teething** n.

teetotal /tiː'təʊt(ə)l/ adj. advocating or characterized by total abstinence from alcoholic drink. □ **teetotalism** n. [redupl. of TOTAL]

teetotaller /tiː'təʊtələ(r)/ n. (US **teetotaler**) a person advocating or practising abstinence from alcoholic drink.

Teflon /'teflɒn/ n. *propr.* polytetrafluoroethylene, esp. used as a non-stick coating for kitchen utensils. [*tetra-* + *fluor-* + *-on*]

tele- /'telɪ/ comb. form **1** at or to a distance (*telekinesis*). **2** forming names of instruments for operating over long distances (*telescope*). **3** television (*telecast*). **4** done by means of the telephone (*telesales*). [Gk *tēle-* f. *tēle* far off: sense 3 f. TELEVISION: sense 4 f. TELEPHONE]

tele-ad /'telɪˌæd/ n. an advertisement placed in a newspaper etc. by telephone.

telecamera /'telɪˌkæmrə, -mərə/ n. **1** a television camera. **2** a telephotographic camera.

telecast /'telɪˌkɑːst/ n. & v. —n. a television broadcast. —v.tr. transmit by television. □ **telecaster** n. [TELE- + BROADCAST]

telecommunication /ˌtelɪkəˌmjuːnɪ'keɪʃ(ə)n/ n. **1** communication over a distance by cable, telegraph, telephone, or broadcasting. **2** (usu. in pl.) the branch of technology concerned with this. [F *télécommunication* (as TELE-, COMMUNICATION)]

teleconference /ˌtelɪ'kɒnfərəns/ n. a conference with participants in different locations linked by telecommunication devices. □ **teleconferencing** n.

telefacsimile /ˌtelɪfæk'sɪmɪlɪ/ n. facsimile transmission (see FACSIMILE n. 2).

telefax /'telɪˌfæks/ n. = TELEFACSIMILE. [abbr.]

telegenic /ˌtelɪ'dʒenɪk/ adj. having an appearance or manner that looks pleasing on television. [TELEVISION + *-genic* in PHOTOGENIC]

telegram /'telɪˌgræm/ n. a message sent by telegraph and usu. delivered in written form. [TELE- + -GRAM, after TELEGRAPH]

■ **Usage** Since 1981 the term has not been in UK official use, except for international messages.

telegraph /'telɪˌgrɑːf, -ˌgræf/ n. & v. —n. **1** a system of or device for transmitting messages or signals to a distance esp. by making and breaking an electrical connection. **2** (*attrib.*) used in this system (*telegraph pole; telegraph wire*). —v. **1** tr. send a message by telegraph to. **2** tr. send by telegraph. **3** tr. give an advance indication of. **4** intr. make signals (*telegraphed to me to come up*). □ **telegrapher** /'telɪˌgrɑːfə(r), tɪ'legrəfə(r)/ n. [F *télégraphe* (as TELE-, -GRAPH)]

telegraphese /ˌtelɪgrə'fiːz/ n. *colloq.* or *joc.* an abbreviated style usual in telegrams.

telegraphic /ˌtelɪ'græfɪk/ adj. **1** of or by telegraphs or telegrams. **2** economically worded. □ **telegraphic address** an abbreviated or other registered address for use in telegrams. □ **telegraphically** adv.

telegraphist /tɪ'legrəfɪst/ n. a person skilled or employed in telegraphy.

telegraphy /tɪ'legrəfɪ/ n. the science or practice of using or constructing communication systems for the reproduction of information.

telemarketing /'telɪˌmɑːkɪtɪŋ/ n. the marketing of goods etc. by means of usu. unsolicited telephone calls. □ **telemarketer** n.

telemessage /'telɪˌmesɪdʒ/ n. a message sent by telephone or telex and delivered in written form.

telemeter /'telɪˌmiːtə(r), tɪ'lemɪtə(r)/ n. & v. —n. an apparatus for recording the readings of an instrument and transmitting them by radio. —v. **1** intr. record readings in this way. **2** tr. transmit (readings etc.) to a distant receiving set or station. □ **telemetric** /-'metrɪk/ adj. **telemetry** /tɪ'lemətrɪ/ n.

teleology /ˌtelɪˈɒlədʒɪ, ˌtiː-/ n. (pl. **-ies**) Philos. **1** the explanation of phenomena by the purpose they serve rather than by postulated causes. **2** Theol. the doctrine of design and purpose in the material world. □ **teleologic** /-əˈlɒdʒɪk/ adj. **teleological** /-əˈlɒdʒɪk(ə)l/ adj. **teleologically** /-əˈlɒdʒɪkəlɪ/ adv. **teleologism** n. **teleologist** n. [mod.L teleologia f. Gk telos teleos end + -LOGY]

telepath /ˈtelɪˌpæθ/ n. a telepathic person. [back-form. f. TELEPATHY]

telepathy /tɪˈlepəθɪ/ n. the supposed communication of thoughts or ideas otherwise than by the known senses. □ **telepathic** /ˌtelɪˈpæθɪk/ adj. **telepathically** /ˌtelɪˈpæθɪkəlɪ/ adv. **telepathist** n. **telepathize** v.tr. & intr. (also **-ise**).

telephone /ˈtelɪˌfəʊn/ n. & v. —n. **1** an apparatus for transmitting sound (esp. speech) to a distance by wire or cord or radio, esp. by converting acoustic vibrations to electrical signals. **2** a transmitting and receiving instrument used in this. **3** a system of communication using a network of telephones. —v. **1** tr. speak to (a person) by telephone. **2** tr. send (a message) by telephone. **3** intr. make a telephone call. □ **on the telephone 1** having a telephone. **2** by use of or using the telephone. **over the telephone** by use of or using the telephone. **telephone book** = telephone directory. **telephone booth** (or **kiosk**) a public booth or enclosure from which telephone calls can be made. **telephone box** Brit. = telephone booth. **telephone call** = CALL n. **4**. **telephone directory** a book listing telephone subscribers and numbers in a particular area. **telephone exchange** = EXCHANGE n. **3**. **telephone number** a number assigned to a particular telephone and used in making connections to it. **telephone operator** esp. US an operator in a telephone exchange. □ **telephoner** n. **telephonic** /-ˈfɒnɪk/ adj. **telephonically** /-ˈfɒnɪkəlɪ/ adv.

telephonist /tɪˈlefənɪst/ n. Brit. an operator in a telephone exchange or at a switchboard.

telephony /tɪˈlefənɪ/ n. the use or a system of telephones.

telephoto /ˌtelɪˈfəʊtəʊ/ n. (pl. **-os**) (in full **telephoto lens**) a lens used in telephotography.

telephotographic /ˌtelɪˌfəʊtəˈɡræfɪk/ adj. of or for or using telephotography. □ **telephotographically** adv.

telephotography /ˌtelɪfəˈtɒɡrəfɪ/ n. the photographing of distant objects with a system of lenses giving a large image.

teleprinter /ˈtelɪˌprɪntə(r)/ n. a device for transmitting telegraph messages as they are keyed, and for printing messages received.

teleprompter /ˈtelɪˌprɒmptə(r)/ n. a device beside a television or cinema camera that slowly unrolls a speaker's script out of sight of the audience.

telesales /ˈtelɪˌseɪlz/ n.pl. selling by means of the telephone.

telescope /ˈtelɪˌskəʊp/ n. & v. —n. **1** an optical instrument using lenses or mirrors or both to make distant objects appear nearer and larger. **2** = radio telescope. —v. **1** tr. press or drive (sections of a tube, colliding vehicles, etc.) together so that one slides into another like the sections of a folding telescope. **2** intr. close or be driven or be capable of closing in this way. **3** tr. compress so as to occupy less space or time. [It. telescopio or mod.L telescopium (as TELE-, -SCOPE)]

telescopic /ˌtelɪˈskɒpɪk/ adj. **1 a** of, relating to, or made with a telescope (telescopic observations). **b** visible only through a telescope (telescopic stars). **2** (esp. of a lens) able to focus on and magnify distant objects. **3** consisting of sections that telescope. □ **telescopic sight** a telescope used for sighting on a rifle etc. □ **telescopically** adv.

teletext /ˈtelɪˌtekst/ n. a news and information service, in the form of text and graphics, from a computer source transmitted to televisions with appropriate receivers.

telethon /ˈtelɪˌθɒn/ n. esp. US an exceptionally long television programme, esp. to raise money for a charity. [TELE- + -thon in MARATHON]

Teletype /ˈtelɪˌtaɪp/ n. & v. —n. propr. a kind of teleprinter. —v. (**teletype**) **1** intr. operate a teleprinter. **2** tr. send by means of a teleprinter.

televangelist /ˌtelɪˈvændʒəlɪst/ n. US a preacher who uses television as a medium for evangelism.

televise /ˈtelɪˌvaɪz/ v.tr. transmit by television. □ **televisable** adj. [back-form. f. TELEVISION]

television /ˈtelɪˌvɪʒ(ə)n, -ˈvɪʒ(ə)n/ n. **1** a system for reproducing on a screen visual images transmitted (usu. with sound) by radio signals. **2** (in full **television set**) a device with a screen for receiving these signals. **3** television broadcasting generally.

televisual /ˌtelɪˈvɪʒʊəl, -ˈvɪzjʊəl/ adj. relating to or suitable for television. □ **televisually** adv.

telex /ˈteleks/ n. & v. (also **Telex**) —n. an international system of telegraphy with printed messages transmitted and received by teleprinters using the public telecommunications network. —v.tr. send or communicate with by telex. [TELEPRINTER + EXCHANGE]

tell /tel/ v. (past and past part. **told** /təʊld/) **1** tr. relate or narrate in speech or writing; give an account of (tell me a story). **2** tr. make known; express in words; divulge (tell me your name; tell me what you want). **3** tr. reveal or signify to (a person) (your face tells me everything). **4** tr. **a** utter (don't tell lies). **b** warn (I told you so). **5** intr. **a** (often foll. by of, about) divulge information or a description; reveal a secret (I told of the plan; promise you won't tell). **b** (foll. by on) colloq. inform against (a person). **6** tr. (foll. by to + infin.) give (a person) a direction or order (tell them to wait; do as you are told). **7** tr. assure (it's true, I tell you). **8** tr. explain in writing; instruct (this book tells you how to cook). **9** tr. decide, determine, distinguish (cannot tell which button to press; how do you tell one from the other?). **10** intr. **a** (often foll. by on) produce a noticeable effect (every disappointment tells; the strain was beginning to tell on me). **b** reveal the truth (time will tell). **c** have an influence (the evidence tells against you). **11** tr. (often absol.) count (votes) at a meeting, election, etc. □ **tell apart** distinguish between (usu. with neg. or interrog.: could not tell them apart). **tell off 1** colloq. reprimand, scold. **2** count off or detach for duty. **tell tales** report a discreditable fact about another. **tell the time** determine the time from the face of a clock or watch. **there is no telling** it is impossible to know (there's no telling what may happen). **you're telling me** colloq. I agree wholeheartedly. □ **tellable** adj. [OE tellan f. Gmc, rel. to TALE]

teller /ˈtelə(r)/ n. **1** a person employed to receive and pay out money in a bank etc. **2** a person who counts (votes). **3** a person who tells esp. stories (*a teller of tales*). □ **tellership** n.

telling /ˈtelɪŋ/ adj. **1** having a marked effect; striking. **2** significant. □ **tellingly** adv.

telling-off /ˌtelɪŋˈɒf/ n. (pl. **tellings-off**) colloq. a reproof or reprimand.

tell-tale /ˈtelteɪl/ n. **1** a person who reveals (esp. discreditable) information about another's private affairs or behaviour. **2** (*attrib.*) that reveals or betrays (*a tell-tale smile*).

tellurium /teˈljʊərɪəm/ n. Chem. a rare brittle lustrous silver-white element used in semi-conductors. □ **telluride** /ˈteljʊəˌraɪd/ n. **tellurite** /ˈteljʊəˌraɪt/ n. **tellurous** adj. [L *tellus -uris* earth, prob. named in contrast to *uranium*]

telly /ˈtelɪ/ n. (pl. **-ies**) esp. Brit. colloq. **1** television. **2** a television set. [abbr.]

temerity /tɪˈmerɪtɪ/ n. **1** rashness. **2** audacity, impudence. [L *temeritas* f. *temere* rashly]

temp n. & v. colloq. —n. a temporary employee, esp. a secretary. —v.intr. work as a temp. [abbr.]

temper /ˈtempə(r)/ n. & v. —n. **1** habitual or temporary disposition of mind esp. as regards composure (*a person of a placid temper*). **2** irritation or anger (*in a fit of temper*). **3** a tendency to have fits of anger (*have a temper*). **4** composure or calmness (*keep one's temper; lose one's temper*). **5** the condition of metal as regards hardness and elasticity. —v.tr. **1** bring (metal or clay) to a proper hardness or consistency. **2** (foll. by *with*) moderate or mitigate (*temper justice with mercy*). □ **in a bad temper** angry, peevish. **in a good temper** in an amiable mood. **out of temper** angry, peevish. □ **temperable** adj. **temperative** /-ətɪv/ adj. **tempered** adj. **temperedly** adv. **temperer** n. [OE *temprian* (v.) f. L *temperare* mingle: infl. by OF *temprer, tremper*]

tempera /ˈtempərə/ n. a method of painting using an emulsion e.g. of pigment with egg, esp. in fine art on canvas. [It.: cf. DISTEMPER¹]

temperament /ˈtempərəmənt/ n. **1** a person's distinct nature and character, esp. as determined by physical constitution and permanently affecting behaviour (*a nervous temperament; the artistic temperament*). **2** a creative or spirited personality (*was full of temperament*). [ME f. L *temperamentum* (as TEMPER)]

temperamental /ˌtempərəˈment(ə)l/ adj. **1** of or having temperament. **2 a** (of a person) liable to erratic or moody behaviour. **b** (of a thing, e.g. a machine) working unpredictably; unreliable. □ **temperamentally** adv.

temperance /ˈtempərəns/ n. **1** moderation or self-restraint esp. in eating and drinking. **2 a** total or partial abstinence from alcoholic drink. **b** (*attrib.*) advocating or concerned with abstinence. [ME f. AF *temperaunce* f. L *temperantia* (as TEMPER)]

temperate /ˈtempərət/ adj. **1** avoiding excess; self-restrained. **2** moderate. **3** (of a region or climate) characterized by mild temperatures. □ **temperately** adv. **temperateness** n. [ME f. L *temperatus* past part. of *temperare*: see TEMPER]

temperature /ˈtemprɪtʃə(r)/ n. **1** the degree or intensity of heat of a body in relation to others, esp. as shown by a thermometer or perceived by touch etc. **2** Med. the degree of internal heat of the body. **3** colloq. a body temperature above the normal (*have a temperature*). **4** the degree of excitement in a discussion etc. [F *température* or L *temperatura* (as TEMPER)]

-tempered /ˈtempəd/ comb. form having a specified temper or disposition (*bad-tempered; hot-tempered*). □ **-temperedly** adv. **-temperedness** n.

tempest /ˈtempɪst/ n. **1** a violent windy storm. **2** violent agitation or tumult. [ME f. OF *tempest(e)* ult. f. L *tempestas* season, storm, f. *tempus* time]

tempestuous /temˈpestjʊəs/ adj. **1** stormy. **2** (of a person, emotion, etc.) turbulent, violent, passionate. □ **tempestuously** adv. **tempestuousness** n. [LL *tempestuosus* (as TEMPEST)]

tempi pl. of TEMPO.

template /ˈtemplɪt, -pleɪt/ n. (also **templet**) **1** a pattern or gauge, usu. a piece of thin board or metal plate, used as a guide in cutting or drilling metal, stone, wood, etc. **2** a flat card or plastic pattern esp. for cutting cloth for patchwork etc. [orig. *templet*: prob. f. *temple* device in a loom + -ET¹, alt. after *plate*]

temple¹ /ˈtemp(ə)l/ n. a building devoted to the worship, or regarded as the dwelling-place, of a god or gods or other objects of religious reverence. [OE *temp(e)l*, reinforced in ME by OF *temple*, f. L *templum* open or consecrated space]

temple² /ˈtemp(ə)l/ n. the flat part of either side of the head between the forehead and the ear. [ME f. OF ult. f. L *tempora* pl. of *tempus*]

tempo /ˈtempəʊ/ n. (pl. **-os** or **tempi** /-piː/) **1** Mus. the speed at which music is or should be played, esp. as characteristic (*waltz tempo*). **2** the rate of motion or activity (*the tempo of the war is quickening*). [It. f. L *tempus* time]

temporal /ˈtempər(ə)l/ adj. **1** of worldly as opposed to spiritual affairs; of this life; secular. **2** of or relating to time. **3** Gram. relating to or denoting time or tense (*temporal conjunction*). **4** of the temples of the head (*temporal artery; temporal bone*). □ **temporally** adv. [ME f. OF *temporel* or f. L *temporalis* f. *tempus -oris* time]

temporary /ˈtempərərɪ/ adj. & n. —adj. lasting or meant to last only for a limited time (*temporary buildings; temporary relief*). —n. (pl. **-ies**) a person employed temporarily. □ **temporarily** adv. **temporariness** n. [L *temporarius* f. *tempus -oris* time]

temporize /ˈtempəˌraɪz/ v.intr. (also **-ise**) **1** avoid committing oneself so as to gain time; employ delaying tactics. **2** comply temporarily with the requirements of the occasion, adopt a time-serving policy. □ **temporization** /-ˈzeɪʃ(ə)n/ n. **temporizer** n. [F *temporiser* bide one's time f. med.L *temporizare* delay f. *tempus -oris* time]

tempt v.tr. **1** entice or incite (a person) to do a wrong or forbidden thing (*tempted him to steal it*). **2** allure, attract. **3** risk provoking (esp. an abstract force or power) (*would be tempting fate to try it*). □ **be tempted to** be strongly disposed to (*I am tempted to question this*). □ **temptable** adj. **temptability** /-ˈbɪlɪtɪ/ n. **tempter** n. **temptress** n. [ME f. OF *tenter, tempter* test f. L *temptare* handle, test, try]

temptation /tempˈteɪʃ(ə)n/ n. **1** the act or an instance of tempting; the state of being tempted; incitement esp. to wrongdoing. **2** an attractive thing or course of action. [ME f. OF *tentacion, temptacion* f. L *temptatio -onis* (as TEMPT)]

tempting /ˈtemptɪŋ/ adj. **1** attractive, inviting. **2** enticing to evil. □ **temptingly** adv.

tempura /ˈtempʊərə/ n. a Japanese dish of fish, shellfish, or vegetables, fried in batter. [Jap.]

ten n. & adj. —n. **1** one more than nine. **2** a symbol for this (10, x, X). **3** a size etc. denoted by ten. **4** the time of ten o'clock (*is it ten yet?*). **5** a card with ten pips. **6** a set of ten. —adj. **1** that amount to ten. **2** (as a round number) several (*ten times as easy*). □ **ten-gallon hat** a cowboy's large broad-brimmed hat. [OE *tīen*, *tēn* f. Gmc]

tenable /ˈtenəb(ə)l/ adj. **1** that can be maintained or defended against attack or objection (*a tenable position*; *a tenable theory*). **2** (foll. by *for*, *by*) (of an office etc.) that can be held for (a specified period) or by (a specified class of person). □ **tenability** /-ˈbɪlɪtɪ/ n. **tenableness** n. [F f. *tenir* hold f. L *tenēre*]

tenacious /tɪˈneɪʃəs/ adj. **1** (often foll. by *of*) keeping a firm hold of property, principles, life, etc.; not readily relinquishing. **2** (of memory) retentive. **3** holding fast. **4** strongly cohesive. **5** persistent, resolute. **6** adhesive, sticky. □ **tenaciously** adv. **tenaciousness** n. **tenacity** /tɪˈnæsɪtɪ/ n. [L *tenax* -*acis* f. *tenēre* hold]

tenancy /ˈtenənsɪ/ n. (pl. **-ies**) **1** the status of a tenant; possession as a tenant. **2** the duration or period of this.

tenant /ˈtenənt/ n. & v. —n. **1** a person who rents land or property from a landlord. **2** (often foll. by *of*) the occupant of a place. —v.tr. occupy as a tenant. □ **tenant farmer** a person who farms rented land. □ **tenantable** adj. **tenantless** adj. [ME f. OF, pres. part. of *tenir* hold f. L *tenēre*]

tenantry /ˈtenəntrɪ/ n. the tenants of an estate etc.

tench n. (pl. same) a European freshwater fish, *Tinca tinca*, of the carp family. [ME f. OF *tenche* f. LL *tinca*]

tend¹ v.intr. **1** (usu. foll. by *to*) be apt or inclined (*tends to lose his temper*). **2** serve, conduce. **3** be moving; be directed; hold a course (*tends in our direction*; *tends to the same conclusion*). [ME f. OF *tendre* stretch f. L *tendere* *tens-* or *tent-*]

tend² v. **1** tr. take care of, look after (a person esp. an invalid, animals esp. sheep, a machine). **2** intr. (foll. by *on*, *upon*) wait on. **3** intr. (foll. by *to*) esp. US give attention to. [ME f. ATTEND]

tendency /ˈtendənsɪ/ n. (pl. **-ies**) **1** (often foll. by *to*, *towards*) a leaning or inclination, a way of tending. **2** a group within a larger political party or movement. [med.L *tendentia* (as TEND¹)]

tendentious /tenˈdenʃəs/ adj. derog. (of writing etc.) calculated to promote a particular cause or viewpoint; having an underlying purpose. □ **tendentiously** adv. **tendentiousness** n. [as TENDENCY + -OUS]

tender¹ /ˈtendə(r)/ adj. (**tenderer**, **tenderest**) **1** easily cut or chewed, not tough (*tender steak*). **2** easily touched or wounded, susceptible to pain or grief (*a tender heart*; *a tender conscience*). **3** easily hurt, sensitive (*tender skin*; *a tender place*). **4** delicate, fragile (*a tender reputation*). **5** loving, affectionate, fond (*tender parents*; *wrote tender verses*). **6** requiring tact or careful handling, ticklish (*a tender subject*). **7** (of age) early, immature (*of tender years*). **8** (usu. foll. by *of*) solicitous, concerned (*tender of his honour*). □ **tender-hearted** having a tender heart, easily moved by pity etc. **tender mercies** iron. attention or treatment which is not in the best interests of its recipient. **tender spot** a subject on which a person is touchy. □ **tenderly** adv. **tenderness** n. [ME f. OF *tendre* f. L *tener*]

tender² /ˈtendə(r)/ v. & n. —v. **1** tr. **a** offer, present (one's services, apologies, resignation, etc.). **b** offer (money etc.) as payment. **2** intr. (often foll. by *for*) make a tender for the supply of a thing or the execution of work. —n. an offer, esp. an offer in writing to execute work or supply goods at a fixed price. □ **put out to tender** seek tenders in respect of (work etc.). □ **tenderer** n. [OF *tendre*: see TEND¹]

tender³ /ˈtendə(r)/ n. **1** a person who looks after people or things. **2** a vessel attending a larger one to supply stores, convey passengers or orders, etc. **3** a special truck closely coupled to a steam locomotive to carry fuel, water, etc. [ME f. TEND² or f. ATTENDER (as ATTEND)]

tenderfoot /ˈtendəfʊt/ n. a newcomer or novice, esp. in the bush or in the Scouts or Guides.

tenderize /ˈtendəraɪz/ v.tr. (also **-ise**) make tender, esp. make (meat) tender by beating etc. □ **tenderizer** n.

tenderloin /ˈtendəlɔɪn/ n. **1** Brit. the middle part of a pork loin. **2** US the undercut of a sirloin.

tendon /ˈtend(ə)n/ n. **1** a cord or strand of strong tissue attaching a muscle to a bone etc. **2** (in a quadruped) = HAMSTRING. □ **tendinitis** /ˌtendɪˈnaɪtɪs/ n. **tendinous** /-dɪnəs/ adj. [F *tendon* or med.L *tendo* -*dinis* f. Gk *tenōn* sinew f. *teinō* stretch]

tendril /ˈtendrɪl/ n. **1** each of the slender leafless shoots by which some climbing plants cling for support. **2** a slender curl of hair etc. [prob. f. obs. F *tendrillon* dimin. of obs. *tendron* young shoot ult. f. L *tener* TENDER¹]

tenement /ˈtenɪmənt/ n. **1** a room or a set of rooms forming a separate residence within a house or block of flats. **2** US & Sc. a house divided into and let in tenements. □ **tenemental** /-ˈment(ə)l/ adj. **tenementary** /-ˈmentərɪ/ adj. [ME f. OF f. med.L *tenementum* f. *tenēre* hold]

tenet /ˈtenɪt, ˈtiːnɛt/ n. a doctrine, dogma, or principle held by a group or person. [L, = he etc. holds f. *tenēre* hold]

tenfold /ˈtenfəʊld/ adj. & adv. **1** ten times as much or as many. **2** consisting of ten parts.

tenner /ˈtenə(r)/ n. colloq. a ten-pound or ten-dollar note. [TEN]

tennis /ˈtenɪs/ n. either of two games (lawn tennis and real tennis) in which two or four players strike a ball with rackets over a net stretched across a court. [ME *tenetz*, *tenes*, etc., app. f. OF *tenez* 'take, receive', called by the server to an opponent, imper. of *tenir* take]

tenon /ˈtenən/ n. a projecting piece of wood made for insertion into a corresponding cavity (esp. a mortise) in another piece. [ME f. F f. *tenir* hold f. L *tenēre*]

tenor /ˈtenə(r)/ n. **1 a** a singing-voice between baritone and alto or counter-tenor, the highest of the ordinary adult male range. **b** a singer with this voice. **c** a part written for it. **2** an instrument, esp. a viola, recorder, or saxophone, of which the range is roughly that of a tenor voice. **3** (usu. foll. by *of*) the general purport or drift of a document or speech. **4** (usu. foll. by *of*) a settled or prevailing course or direction, esp. the course of a person's life or habits. □ **tenor clef** Mus. a clef placing middle C on the second highest line of the staff. [ME f. AF *tenur*, OF *tenour* f. L *tenor* -*oris* f. *tenēre* hold]

tenosynovitis /ˌtenəʊˌsaɪnəʊˈvaɪtɪs/ *n.* inflammation and swelling of a tendon, usu. in the wrist, often caused by repetitive movements such as typing. [Gk *tenōn* tendon + SYNOVITIS]

tenpin /ˈtenpɪn/ *n.* **1** a pin used in tenpin bowling. **2** (in *pl.*) *US* = *tenpin bowling*. □ **tenpin bowling** a game developed from ninepins in which ten pins are set up at the end of an alley and bowled down with hard rubber balls.

tense[1] /tens/ *adj. & v.* —*adj.* **1** stretched tight, strained (*tense cord*; *tense muscle*; *tense nerves*; *tense emotion*). **2** causing tenseness (*a tense moment*). —*v.tr. & intr.* make or become tense. □ **tense up** become tense. □ **tensely** *adv.* **tenseness** *n.* **tensity** *n.* [L *tensus* past part. of *tendere* stretch]

tense[2] /tens/ *n. Gram.* **1** a form taken by a verb to indicate the time (also the continuance or completeness) of the action etc. (*present tense*; *imperfect tense*). **2** a set of such forms for the various persons and numbers. □ **tenseless** *adj.* [ME f. OF *tens* f. L *tempus* time]

tensile /ˈtensaɪl/ *adj.* **1** of or relating to tension. **2** capable of being drawn out or stretched. □ **tensile strength** resistance to breaking under tension. □ **tensility** /tenˈsɪlɪtɪ/ *n.* [med.L *tensilis* (as TENSE[1])]

tension /ˈtenʃ(ə)n/ *n. & v.* —*n.* **1** the act or an instance of stretching; the state of being stretched; tenseness. **2** mental strain or excitement. **3** a strained (political, social, etc.) state or relationship. **4** electromagnetic force (*high tension*; *low tension*). —*v.tr.* subject to tension. □ **tensional** *adj.* **tensionally** *adv.* **tensionless** *adj.* [F *tension* or L *tensio* (as TEND[1])]

tent *n.* **1** a portable shelter or dwelling of canvas, cloth, etc., supported by a pole or poles and stretched by cords attached to pegs driven into the ground. **2** *Med.* a tentlike enclosure for control of the air supply to a patient. [ME f. OF *tente* ult. f. L *tendere* stretch]

tentacle /ˈtentək(ə)l/ *n.* **1** a long slender flexible appendage of an (esp. invertebrate) animal, used for feeling, grasping, or moving. **2** a thing used like a tentacle as a feeler etc. □ **tentacled** *adj.* (also in *comb.*). **tentacular** /-ˈtækjʊlə(r)/ *adj.* **tentaculate** /-ˈtækjʊlət/ *adj.* [mod.L *tentaculum* f. L *tentare* = *temptare* (see TEMPT) + *-culum* -CULE]

tentative /ˈtentətɪv/ *adj.* **1** done by way of trial, experimental. **2** hesitant, not definite (*tentative suggestion*; *tentative acceptance*). □ **tentatively** *adv.* **tentativeness** *n.* [med.L *tentativus* (as TENTACLE)]

tenter /ˈtentə(r)/ *n.* **1** a machine for stretching cloth to dry in shape. **2** = TENTERHOOK. [ME ult. f. med.L *tentorium* (as TEND[1])]

tenterhook /ˈtentəˌhʊk/ *n.* any of the hooks to which cloth is fastened on a tenter. □ **on tenterhooks** in a state of suspense or mental agitation due to uncertainty.

tenth *n. & adj.* —*n.* **1** the position in a sequence corresponding to the number 10 in the sequence 1–10. **2** something occupying this position. **3** one of ten equal parts of a thing. —*adj.* that is the tenth. □ **tenth-rate** of extremely poor quality. □ **tenthly** *adv.* [ME *tenthe*, alt. of OE *teogotha*]

tenuity /tɪˈnjuːɪtɪ/ *n.* **1** slenderness. **2** (of a fluid, esp. air) rarity, thinness. [L *tenuitas* f. L *tenuis* thin, transl. Gk *psilos* smooth]

tenuous /ˈtenjʊəs/ *adj.* **1** slight, of little substance (*tenuous connection*). **2** (of a distinction etc.)

oversubtle. **3** thin, slender, small. **4** rarefied. □ **tenuously** *adv.* **tenuousness** *n.* [L *tenuis*]

tenure /ˈtenjə(r)/ *n.* **1** a condition, or form of right or title, under which (esp. real) property is held. **2** (often foll. by *of*) **a** a holding or possession of an office or property. **b** the period of this (*during his tenure of office*). **3** guaranteed permanent employment, esp. as a teacher or lecturer after a probationary period. [ME f. OF f. *tenir* hold f. L *tenēre*]

tenured /ˈtenjəd/ *adj.* **1** (of an official position) carrying a guarantee of permanent employment. **2** (of a teacher, lecturer, etc.) having guaranteed tenure of office.

tepee /ˈtiːpiː/ *n.* (also **teepee**) a N. American Indian's conical tent, made of skins, cloth, or canvas on a frame of poles. [Sioux or Dakota Indian *tīpī*]

tepid /ˈtepɪd/ *adj.* **1** slightly warm. **2** unenthusiastic. □ **tepidity** /tɪˈpɪdɪtɪ/ *n.* **tepidly** *adv.* **tepidness** *n.* [L *tepidus* f. *tepēre* be lukewarm]

tequila /teˈkiːlə/ *n.* a Mexican liquor made from an agave. [*Tequila* in Mexico]

ter- /tɜː(r)/ *comb. form* three; threefold (*tercentenary*). [L *ter* thrice]

terato- /ˈterətəʊ/ *comb. form* monster. [Gk *teras -atos* monster]

teratogen /təˈrætədʒ(ə)n/ *n. Med.* an agent or factor causing malformation of an embryo. **teratogenic** /ˌterətəˈdʒenɪk/ *adj.* **teratogeny** /ˌterəˈtɒdʒənɪ/ *n.*

terbium /ˈtɜːbɪəm/ *n. Chem.* a silvery metallic element of the lanthanide series. [mod.L f. *Ytterby* in Sweden]

terce /tɜːs/ *n. Eccl.* **1** the office of the canonical hour of prayer appointed for the third daytime hour (i.e. 9 a.m.). **2** this hour. [var. of TIERCE]

tercel /ˈtɜːs(ə)l/ *n.* (also **tiercel** /ˈtɪəs(ə)l/) *Falconry* the male of the hawk. [ME f. OF *tercel*, ult. a dimin. of L *tertius* third, perh. from a belief that the third egg of a clutch produced a male bird, or that the male was one-third smaller than the female]

tercentenary /ˌtɜːsenˈtiːnərɪ, -ˈtenərɪ, tɜːˈsen tɪnərɪ/ *n. & adj.* —*n.* (*pl.* **-ies**) **1** a three-hundredth anniversary. **2** a celebration of this. —*adj.* of this anniversary.

tercentennial /ˌtɜːsenˈtenɪəl/ *adj. & n.* —*adj.* **1** occurring every three hundred years. **2** lasting three hundred years. —*n.* a tercentenary.

terebinth /ˈterɪbɪnθ/ *n.* a small Southern European tree, *Pistacia terebinthus*, yielding turpentine. [ME f. OF *terebinte* or L *terebinthus* f. Gk *terebinthos*]

teredo /təˈriːdəʊ/ *n.* (*pl.* **-os**) any bivalve mollusc of the genus *Teredo*, esp. *T. navalis*, that bores into wooden ships etc. [L f. Gk *terēdōn* f. *teirō* rub hard, wear away, bore]

tergal /ˈtɜːɡ(ə)l/ *adj.* of or relating to the back; dorsal. [L *tergum* back]

tergiversate /ˈtɜːdʒɪvɜːseɪt/ *v.intr.* **1** be apostate; change one's party or principles. **2** equivocate; make conflicting or evasive statements. **3** turn one's back on something. □ **tergiversation** /-ˈseɪʃ(ə)n/ *n.* **tergiversator** *n.* [L *tergiversari* turn one's back f. *tergum* back + *vertere vers-* turn]

-teria /ˈtɪərɪə/ *suffix* denoting self-service establishments (*washeteria*). [after CAFETERIA]

term *n. & v.* —*n.* **1** a word used to express a definite concept, esp. in a particular branch of study etc. (*a technical term*). **2** (in *pl.*) language used; mode of expression (*answered in no uncertain terms*). **3** (in *pl.*) a relation or footing (*we are on familiar terms*). **4** (in *pl.*) **a** conditions or stipulations (*cannot accept your terms; do it on your own terms*). **b** charge or price (*his terms are £20 a lesson*). **5 a** a limited period of some state or activity (*for a term of five years*). **b** a period over which operations are conducted or results contemplated (*in the short term*). **c** a period of some weeks, alternating with holiday or vacation, during which instruction is given in a school, college, or university, or *Brit.* during which a lawcourt holds sessions. **d** a period of imprisonment. **e** a period of tenure. **6** *Logic* a word or words that may be the subject or predicate of a proposition. **7** *Math.* **a** each of the two quantities in a ratio. **b** each quantity in a series. **c** a part of an expression joined to the rest by + or − (e.g. *a*, *b*, *c* in *a* + *b* − *c*). **8** the completion of a normal length of pregnancy. —*v.tr.* denominate, call; assign a term to (*the music termed classical*). □ **bring to terms** cause to accept conditions. **come to terms** yield, give way. **come to terms with** 1 reconcile oneself to (a difficulty etc.). 2 conclude an agreement with. **in set terms** in definite terms. **in terms** explicitly. **in terms of** in the language peculiar to, using as a basis of expression or thought. **make terms** conclude an agreement. **on terms** on terms of friendship or equality. **terms of reference** *Brit.* points referred to an individual or body of persons for decision or report; the scope of an inquiry etc.; a definition of this. **terms of trade** *Brit.* the ratio between prices paid for imports and those received for exports. □ **termless** *adj.* **termly** *adj.* & *adv.* [ME f. OF *terme* f. L TERMINUS]

termagant /ˈtɜːməgənt/ *n.* an overbearing or brawling woman; a virago or shrew. [ME *Tervagant* f. OF *Tervagan* f. It. *Trivigante*]

terminable /ˈtɜːmɪnəb(ə)l/ *adj.* **1** that may be terminated. **2** coming to an end after a certain time (*terminable annuity*). □ **terminableness** *n.*

terminal /ˈtɜːmɪn(ə)l/ *adj.* & *n.* —*adj.* **1 a** (of a disease) ending in death, fatal. **b** (of a patient) in the last stage of a fatal disease. **c** (of a morbid condition) forming the last stage of a fatal disease. **d** *colloq.* ruinous, disastrous, very great (*terminal laziness*). **2** of or forming a limit or terminus (*terminal station*). **3** of or done etc. each term (*terminal accounts; terminal examinations*). —*n.* **1** a terminating thing; an extremity. **2** a terminus for trains or long-distance buses. **3** a departure and arrival building for air passengers. **4** a point of connection for closing an electric circuit. **5** an apparatus for transmission of messages between a user and a computer, communications system, etc. **6** an installation where oil is stored at the end of a pipeline or at a port. □ **terminally** *adv.* [L *terminalis* (as TERMINUS)]

terminate /ˈtɜːmɪˌneɪt/ *v.* **1** *tr.* & *intr.* bring or come to an end. **2** *intr.* (foll. by *in*) (of a word) end in (a specified letter or syllable etc.). **3** *tr.* end (a pregnancy) before term by artificial means. **4** *tr.* bound, limit. □ **terminator** *n.* [L *terminare* (as TERMINUS)]

termination /ˌtɜːmɪˈneɪʃ(ə)n/ *n.* **1** the act or an instance of terminating; the state of being terminated. **2** *Med.* an induced abortion. **3** an ending or result of a specified kind (*a happy termination*). **4** a word's final syllable or letters or letter esp. as an element in inflection or derivation. □ **put a termination to** (or **bring to a termination**) make an end of. □ **terminational** *adj.* [ME f. OF *termination* or L *terminatio* (as TERMINATE)]

termini *pl.* of TERMINUS.

terminological /ˌtɜːmɪnəˈlɒdʒɪk(ə)l/ *adj.* of terminology. □ **terminological inexactitude** *joc.* a lie. □ **terminologically** *adv.*

terminology /ˌtɜːmɪˈnɒlədʒɪ/ *n.* (*pl.* **-ies**) **1** the system of terms used in a particular subject. **2** the science of the proper use of terms. □ **terminologist** *n.* [G *Terminologie* f. med.L TERMINUS term]

terminus /ˈtɜːmɪnəs/ *n.* (*pl.* **termini** /-ˌnaɪ/ or **terminuses**) **1** a station at the end of a railway or bus route. **2** a point at the end of a pipeline etc. **3** a final point, a goal. **4** a starting-point. [L, = end, limit, boundary]

termitary /ˈtɜːmɪtərɪ/ *n.* (*pl.* **-ies**) a nest of termites, usu. a large mound of earth.

termite /ˈtɜːmaɪt/ *n.* a small antlike social insect of the order Isoptera, chiefly tropical and destructive to timber. [LL *termes -mitis*, alt. of L *tarmes* after *terere* rub]

tern *n.* any marine bird of the subfamily Sterninae, like a gull but usu. smaller and with a long forked tail. [of Scand. orig.: cf. Da. *terne*, Sw. *tärna* f. ON *therna*]

ternary /ˈtɜːnərɪ/ *adj.* **1** composed of three parts. **2** *Math.* using three as a base (*ternary scale*). [ME f. L *ternarius* f. *terni* three each]

terrace /ˈterəs, -rɪs/ *n.* & *v.* —*n.* **1** each of a series of flat areas formed on a slope and used for cultivation. **2** a level paved area next to a house. **3 a** a row of houses on a raised level or along the top or face of a slope. **b** a row of houses built in one block of uniform style. **4** a flight of wide shallow steps as for spectators at a sports ground. —*v.tr.* form into or provide with a terrace or terraces. □ **terraced house** *Brit.* = terrace house. **terrace house** *Brit.* any of a row of houses joined by party-walls. [OF ult. f. L *terra* earth]

terracotta /ˌterəˈkɒtə/ *n.* **1 a** unglazed usu. brownish-red earthenware used chiefly as an ornamental building-material and in modelling. **b** a statuette of this. **2** its colour. [It. *terra cotta* baked earth]

terra firma /ˌterə ˈfɜːmə/ *n.* dry land, firm ground. [L, = firm land]

terrain /teˈreɪn, təˈ-/ *n.* a tract of land as regarded by the physical geographer or the military tactician. [F, ult. f. L *terrenum* neut. of *terrenus* TERRENE]

terrapin /ˈterəpɪn/ *n.* **1** any of various N. American edible freshwater turtles of the family Emydidae. **2** (**Terrapin**) *propr.* a type of prefabricated one-storey building. [Algonquian]

terrarium /teˈreərɪəm/ *n.* (*pl.* **terrariums** or **terraria** /-rɪə/) **1** a vivarium for small land animals. **2** a sealed transparent globe etc. containing growing plants. [mod.L f. L *terra* earth, after AQUARIUM]

terrazzo /teˈrætsəʊ/ *n.* (*pl.* **-os**) a flooring-material of stone chips set in concrete and given a smooth surface. [It., = terrace]

terrene /teˈriːn/ adj. **1** of the earth; earthly, worldly. **2** of earth, earthy. **3** of dry land; terrestrial. [ME f. AF f. L terrenus f. terra earth]

terrestrial /təˈrestrɪəl, tɪ-/ adj. & n. —adj. **1** of or on or relating to the earth; earthly. **2 a** of or on dry land. **b** Zool. living on or in the ground. **c** Bot. growing in the soil. **3** of this world, worldly (terrestrial sins; terrestrial interests). —n. an inhabitant of the earth. □ **a terrestrial globe** a globe representing the earth. **the terrestrial globe** the earth. □ **terrestrially** adv. [ME f. L terrestris f. terra earth]

terrible /ˈterɪb(ə)l/ adj. **1** colloq. very great or bad (a terrible bore). **2** colloq. very incompetent (terrible at tennis). **3** causing terror; fit to cause terror; awful, dreadful, formidable. □ **terribleness** n. [ME f. F f. L terribilis f. terrēre frighten]

terribly /ˈterɪblɪ/ adv. **1** colloq. very, extremely (he was terribly nice about it). **2** in a terrible manner.

terrier /ˈterɪə(r)/ n. **1 a** a small dog of various breeds originally used for turning out foxes etc. from their earths. **b** any of these breeds. **2** an eager or tenacious person or animal. **3 (Terrier)** Brit. colloq. a member of the Territorial Army etc. [ME f. OF (chien) terrier f. med.L terrarius f. L terra earth]

terrific /təˈrɪfɪk/ adj. **1** colloq. **a** of great size or intensity. **b** excellent (did a terrific job). **c** excessive (making a terrific noise). **2** causing terror. □ **terrifically** adv. [L terrificus f. terrēre frighten]

terrify /ˈterɪˌfaɪ/ v.tr. (-ies, -ied) fill with terror; frighten severely (terrified them into submission; is terrified of dogs). □ **terrifier** n. **terrifyingly** adv. [L terrificare (as TERRIFIC)]

terrine /təˈriːn/ n. **1** pâté or similar food. **2** an earthenware vessel, esp. one in which such food is cooked or sold. [orig. form of TUREEN]

territorial /ˌterɪˈtɔːrɪəl/ adj. & n. —adj. **1** of territory (territorial possessions). **2** limited to a district (the right was strictly territorial). **3** (of a person or animal etc.) tending to defend an area of territory. **4** (usu. **Territorial**) of any of the Territories of the US or Canada. —n. **(Territorial)** (in the UK) a member of the Territorial Army. □ **Territorial Army** (in the UK) a volunteer force locally organized to provide a reserve of trained and disciplined manpower for use in an emergency. **territorial waters** the waters under the jurisdiction of a State, esp. the part of the sea within a stated distance of the shore (traditionally three miles from low-water mark). □ **territoriality** /-ˈælɪtɪ/ n. **territorialize** v.tr. (also **-ise**). **territorialization** /-laɪˈzeɪʃ(ə)n/ n. **territorially** adv. [LL territorialis (as TERRITORY)]

territory /ˈterɪtərɪ, -trɪ/ n. (pl. **-ies**) **1** the extent of the land under the jurisdiction of a ruler, State, city, etc. **2 (Territory)** an organized division of a country, esp. one not yet admitted to the full rights of a State. **3** a sphere of action or thought; a province. **4** the area over which a commercial traveller or goods-distributor operates. **5** Zool. an area defended by an animal or animals against others of the same species. **6** an area defended by a team or player in a game. [ME f. L territorium f. terra land]

terror /ˈterə(r)/ n. **1** extreme fear. **2 a** a person or thing that causes terror. **b** (also **holy terror**) colloq. a formidable person; a troublesome person or thing (the twins are little terrors). **3** the use of organized intimidation; terrorism. □ **terror-stricken** (or **-struck**) affected with terror. [ME f. OF terrour f. L terror -oris f. terrēre frighten]

terrorist /ˈterərɪst/ n. a person who uses or favours violent and intimidating methods of coercing a government or community. □ **terrorism** n. **terroristic** /-ˈrɪstɪk/ adj. **terroristically** /-ˈrɪstɪkəlɪ/ adv. [F terroriste (as TERROR)]

terrorize /ˈterəˌraɪz/ v.tr. (also **-ise**) **1** fill with terror. **2** use terrorism against. □ **terrorization** /-ˈzeɪʃ(ə)n/ n. **terrorizer** n.

terry /ˈterɪ/ n. & adj. —n. (pl. **-ies**) a pile fabric with the loops uncut, used esp. for towels. —adj. of this fabric. [18th c.: orig. unkn.]

terse /tɜːs/ adj. (**terser**, **tersest**) **1** (of language) brief, concise, to the point. **2** curt, abrupt. □ **tersely** adv. **terseness** n. [L tersus past part. of tergēre wipe, polish]

tertiary /ˈtɜːʃərɪ/ adj. & n. —adj. **1** third in order or rank etc. **2 (Tertiary)** Geol. of or relating to the first period in the Cenozoic era. —n. Geol. this period or system. □ **tertiary education** education, esp. in a college or university, that follows secondary education. [L tertiarius f. tertius third]

tervalent /tɜːˈveɪlənt, -ˈveɪlənt/ adj. Chem. having a valency of three. [TER- + L valent- part. stem of valēre be strong]

Terylene /ˈterɪˌliːn/ n. propr. a synthetic polyester used as a textile fibre. [terephthalic acid + ETHYLENE]

tesla /ˈteslə/ n. the SI unit of magnetic flux density. [N. Tesla, Croatian-born Amer. scientist d. 1943]

TESSA /ˈtesə/ n. (also **Tessa**) (in the UK) tax exempt special savings account.

tessellate /ˈtesəˌleɪt/ v.tr. **1** make from tesserae. **2** Math. cover (a plane surface) by repeated use of a single shape. [L tessellare f. tessella dimin. of TESSERA]

tessellated /ˈtesəˌleɪtɪd/ adj. **1** of or resembling mosaic. **2** Bot. & Zool. regularly chequered. [L tessellatus or It. tessellato (as TESSELLATE)]

tessellation /ˌtesəˈleɪʃ(ə)n/ n. **1** the act or an instance of tessellating; the state of being tessellated. **2** an arrangement of polygons without gaps or overlapping, esp. in a repeated pattern.

tessera /ˈtesərə/ n. (pl. **tesserae** /-ˌriː/) a small square block used in mosaic. □ **tesseral** adj. [L f. Gk, neut. of tesseres, tessares four]

test[1] n. & v. —n. **1** a critical examination or trial of a person's or thing's qualities. **2** the means of so examining; a standard for comparison or trial; circumstances suitable for this (success is not a fair test). **3** a minor examination, esp. in school (spelling test). **4** colloq. a test match. **5** a ground of admission or rejection (is excluded by our test). **6** Chem. a reagent or a procedure employed to reveal the presence of another in a compound. —v.tr. **1** put to the test; make trial of (a person or thing or quality). **2** try severely; tax a person's powers of endurance etc. **3** Chem. examine by means of a reagent. □ **put to the test** cause to undergo a test. **test bed** equipment for testing aircraft engines before acceptance for general use. **test card** a still television picture transmitted outside normal programme hours and designed for use in judging the quality and position of the image. **test case** *Law* a case setting a precedent for other cases involving the same question of law. **test drive** a drive taken to determine the qualities of a motor vehicle with a view to its regular use. **test-drive** *v.tr.* (*past* **-drove**; *past part.* **-driven**) drive (a vehicle) for this purpose. **test flight** a flight during which the performance of an aircraft is tested. **test-fly** *v.tr.* (**-flies**; *past* **-flew**; *past part.* **-flown**) fly (an aircraft) for this purpose. **test match** a cricket or Rugby match between teams of certain countries, usu. each of a series in a tour. **test out** put (a theory etc.) to a practical test. **test paper 1** a minor examination paper. **2** *Chem.* a paper impregnated with a substance changing colour under known conditions. **test pilot** a pilot who test-flies aircraft. **test-tube** a thin glass tube closed at one end used for chemical tests etc. **test-tube baby** *colloq.* a baby conceived by *in vitro* fertilization. □ **testable** *adj.* **testability** /-ə'bɪlɪtɪ/ *n.* **testee** /tesˈtiː/ *n.* [ME f. OF f. L *testu(m)* earthen pot, collateral form of *testa* TEST²]

test² /test/ *n.* the shell of some invertebrates, esp. foraminiferars and tunicates. [L *testa* tile, jug, shell, etc.: cf. TEST¹]

testa /'testə/ *n.* (*pl.* **testae** /-tiː/) *Bot.* a seed-coat. [L (as TEST²)]

testaceous /te'steɪʃəs/ *adj.* **1** *Biol.* having a hard continuous outer covering. **2** *Bot.* & *Zool.* of a brick-red colour. [L *testaceus* (as TEST²)]

testament /'testəmənt/ *n.* **1** a will (esp. *last will and testament*). **2** (usu. foll. by *to*) evidence, proof (*is testament to his loyalty*). **3** *Bibl.* **a** a covenant or dispensation. **b** (**Testament**) a division of the Christian Bible (see *Old Testament, New Testament*). **c** (**Testament**) a copy of the New Testament. [ME f. L *testamentum* will (as TESTATE): in early Christian L rendering Gk *diathēkē* covenant]

testamentary /ˌtestə'mentərɪ/ *adj.* of or by or in a will. [L *testamentarius* (as TESTAMENT)]

testate /'testeɪt/ *adj.* & *n.* —*adj.* having left a valid will at death. —*n.* a testate person. □ **testacy** *n.* (*pl.* **-ies**). [L *testatus* past part. of *testari* testify, make a will, f. *testis* witness]

testator /te'steɪtə(r)/ *n.* (*fem.* **testatrix** /te'steɪtrɪks/) a person who has made a will, esp. one who dies testate. [ME f. AF *testatour* f. L *testator* (as TESTATE)]

tester¹ /'testə(r)/ *n.* **1** a person or thing that tests. **2** a sample of a cosmetic etc., allowing customers to try it before purchase.

tester² /'testə(r)/ *n.* a canopy, esp. over a four-poster bed. [ME f. med.L *testerium, testrum, testura,* ult. f. L *testa* tile]

testes *pl.* of TESTIS.

testicle /'testɪk(ə)l/ *n.* a male organ that produces spermatozoa etc., esp. one of a pair enclosed in the scrotum behind the penis of a man and most mammals. □ **testicular** /-'stɪkjʊlə(r)/ *adj.* [ME f. L *testiculus* dimin. of *testis* witness (of virility)]

testify /'testɪfaɪ/ *v.* (**-ies, -ied**) **1** *intr.* (of a person or thing) bear witness (*testified to the facts*). **2** *intr. Law* give evidence. **3** *tr.* affirm or declare (*testified his regret; testified that she had been present*). **4** *tr.* (of a thing) be evidence of, evince. □ **testifier** *n.* [ME f. L *testificari* f. *testis* witness]

testimonial /ˌtestɪ'məʊnɪəl/ *n.* **1** a certificate of character, conduct, or qualifications. **2** a gift presented to a person (esp. in public) as a mark of esteem, in acknowledgement of services, etc. [ME f. OF *testimoignal* (adj.) f. *tesmoin* or LL *testimonialis* (as TESTIMONY)]

testimony /'testɪmənɪ/ *n.* (*pl.* **-ies**) **1** *Law* an oral or written statement under oath or affirmation. **2** declaration or statement of fact. **3** evidence, demonstration (*called him in testimony; produce testimony*). [ME f. L *testimonium* f. *testis* witness]

testis /'testɪs/ *n.* (*pl.* **testes** /-tiːz/) *Anat.* & *Zool.* a testicle. [L. = witness: cf. TESTICLE]

testosterone /te'stɒstərəʊn/ *n.* a steroid androgen formed in the testicles. [TESTIS + STEROL + -ONE]

testy /'testɪ/ *adj.* (**testier, testiest**) irritable, touchy. □ **testily** *adv.* **testiness** *n.* [ME f. AF *testif* f. OF *teste* head (as TEST²)]

tetanic /tɪ'tænɪk/ *adj.* of or such as occurs in tetanus. □ **tetanically** *adv.* [L *tetanicus* f. Gk *tetanikos* (as TETANUS)]

tetanus /'tetənəs/ *n.* a bacterial disease affecting the nervous system and marked by tonic spasm of the voluntary muscles. □ **tetanize** *v.tr.* (also **-ise**). **tetanoid** *adj.* [ME f. L f. Gk *tetanos* muscular spasm f. *teinō* stretch]

tetany /'tetənɪ/ *n.* a disease with intermittent muscular spasms caused by malfunction of the parathyroid glands and a consequent deficiency of calcium. [F *tétanie* (as TETANUS)]

tetchy /'tetʃɪ/ *adj.* (also **techy**) (**-ier, -iest**) peevish, irritable. □ **tetchily** *adv.* **tetchiness** *n.* [prob. f. *tecche, tache* blemish, fault f. OF *teche, tache*]

tête-à-tête /ˌteɪtɑː'teɪt/ *n., adv.,* & *adj.* —*n.* a private conversation or interview usu. between two persons. —*adv.* together in private (*dined tête-à-tête*). —*adj.* **1** private, confidential. **2** concerning only two persons. [F, lit. 'head-to-head']

tether /'teðə(r)/ *n.* & *v.* —*n.* **1** a rope etc. by which an animal is tied to confine it to the spot. **2** the extent of one's knowledge, authority, etc.; scope, limit. —*v.tr.* tie (an animal) with a tether. □ **at the end of one's tether** having reached the limit of one's patience, resources, abilities, etc. [ME f. ON *tjóthr* f. Gmc]

tetra- /'tetrə/ *comb. form* (also **tetr-** before a vowel) **1** four (*tetrapod*). **2** *Chem.* (forming names of compounds) containing four atoms or groups of a specified kind (*tetroxide*). [Gk f. *tettares* four]

tetrad /'tetræd/ *n.* **1** a group of four. **2** the number four. [Gk *tetras -ados* (as TETRA-)]

tetraethyl lead /ˌtetrə'iː θaɪl/ *n.* a liquid added to petrol as an antiknock agent.

tetragon /'tetrəˌɡɒn/ *n.* a plane figure with four angles and four sides. [Gk *tetragōnon* quadrangle (as TETRA-, -GON)]

tetragonal /tɪ'træɡən(ə)l/ *adj.* of or like a tetragon. □ **tetragonally** *adv.*

tetrahedron /ˌtetrə'hiːdrən, -'hedrən/ *n.* (*pl.* **tetrahedra** /-drə/ or **tetrahedrons**) a four-sided solid; a triangular pyramid. □ **tetrahedral** *adj.* [late Gk *tetraedron* neut. of *tetraedros* four-sided (as TETRA-, -HEDRON)]

tetralogy /tɪ'trælədʒɪ/ *n.* (*pl.* **-ies**) a group of four related literary or operatic works.

tetrameter /tɪ'træmɪtə(r)/ *n.* *Prosody* a verse of four measures. [LL *tetrametrus* f. Gk *tetrametros* (as TETRA-, *metron* measure)]

tetraplegia /ˌtetrə'pliːdʒɪə, -dʒə/ *n.* *Med.* = QUADRIPLEGIA. □ **tetraplegic** *adj.* & *n.* [mod.L (as TETRA-, Gk *plēgē* blow, strike)]

tetraploid /ˈtetrəˌplɔɪd/ adj. & n. Biol. —adj. (of an organism or cell) having four times the haploid set of chromosomes. —n. a tetraploid organism or cell.

tetrapod /ˈtetrəˌpɒd/ n. 1 Zool. an animal with four feet. 2 a structure supported by four feet radiating from a centre. □ **tetrapodous** /tɪˈtræpədəs/ adj. [mod.L tetrapodus f. Gk tetrapous (as TETRA-, pous podos foot)]

tetrasyllable /ˈtetrəˌsɪləb(ə)l/ n. a word of four syllables. □ **tetrasyllabic** /-ˈlæbɪk/ adj.

tetrathlon /teˈtræθlən/ n. a contest comprising four events, esp. riding, shooting, swimming, and running. [TETRA- + Gk athlon contest, after PENTATHLON]

tetratomic /ˌtetrəˈtɒmɪk/ adj. Chem. having four atoms (of a specified kind) in the molecule.

tetrode /ˈtetrəʊd/ n. a thermionic valve having four electrodes. [TETRA- + Gk hodos way]

Teuton /ˈtjuːt(ə)n/ n. a member of a Teutonic nation, esp. a German. [L Teutones, Teutoni, f. an IE base meaning 'people' or 'country']

Teutonic /tjuːˈtɒnɪk/ adj. & n. —adj. 1 relating to or characteristic of the Germanic peoples or their languages. 2 German. —n. the early language usu. called Germanic. □ **Teutonicism** /-ˌsɪz(ə)m/ n. [F teutonique f. L Teutonicus (as TEUTON)]

text n. 1 the main body of a book as distinct from notes, appendices, pictures, etc. 2 the original words of an author or document, esp. as distinct from a paraphrase of or commentary on them. 3 a passage quoted from Scripture, esp. as the subject of a sermon. 4 a subject or theme. 5 (in pl.) books prescribed for study. 6 US a textbook. □ **text editor** Computing a system or program allowing the user to enter and edit text. **text processing** Computing the manipulation of text, esp. transforming it from one format to another. □ **textless** adj. [ME f. ONF tixte, texte f. L textus tissue, literary style (in med.L = Gospel) f. L texere text- weave]

textbook /ˈtekstbʊk/ n. & adj. —n. a book for use in studying, esp. a standard account of a subject. —attrib.adj. 1 exemplary, accurate. 2 instructively typical. □ **textbookish** adj.

textile /ˈtekstaɪl/ n. & adj. —n. 1 any woven material. 2 any cloth. —adj. 1 of weaving or cloth (textile industry). 2 woven (textile fabrics). 3 suitable for weaving (textile materials). [L textilis (as TEXT)]

textual /ˈtekstjʊəl/ adj. of, in, or concerning a text (textual errors). □ **textual criticism** the process of attempting to ascertain the correct reading of a text. □ **textually** adv. [ME f. med.L textualis (as TEXT)]

textualist /ˈtekstjʊəlɪst/ n. a person who adheres strictly to the letter of the text. □ **textualism** n.

texture /ˈtekstʃə(r)/ n. & v. —n. 1 the feel or appearance of a surface or substance. 2 the arrangement of threads etc. in textile fabric. 3 the arrangement of small constituent parts. —v.tr. (usu. as **textured** adj.) provide with a texture. □ **textural** adj. **texturally** adv. **textureless** adj. [ME f. L textura weaving (as TEXT)]

texturize /ˈtekstʃəˌraɪz/ v.tr. (also -ise) (usu. as **texturized** adj.) impart a particular texture to (fabrics or food).

Th symb. Chem. the element thorium.

-th¹ /θ/ suffix (also **-eth** /ɪθ/) forming ordinal and fractional numbers from four onwards (fourth; thirtieth). [OE -tha, -the, -otha, -othe]

-th² /θ/ suffix forming nouns denoting an action or process: 1 from verbs (birth; growth). 2 from adjectives (breadth; filth; length). [OE -thu, -tho, -th]

thalamus /ˈθæləməs/ n. (pl. **thalami** /-ˌmaɪ/) Anat. either of two masses of grey matter in the forebrain, serving as relay stations for sensory tracts. □ **thalamic** /θəˈlæmɪk, ˈθæləmɪk/ adj. (in senses 1 and 2). [L f. Gk thalamos]

thalassic /θəˈlæsɪk/ adj. of the sea or seas, esp. small or inland seas. [F thalassique f. Gk thalassa sea]

thalidomide /θəˈlɪdəˌmaɪd/ n. a drug formerly used as a sedative but found in 1961 to cause foetal malformation when taken by a mother early in pregnancy. □ **thalidomide baby** (or **child**) a baby or child born deformed from the effects of thalidomide. [phthalimidoglutarimide]

thalli pl. of THALLUS.

thallium /ˈθælɪəm/ n. Chem. a rare soft white metallic element. □ **thallic** adj. **thallous** adj. [formed as THALLUS, from the green line in its spectrum]

thallus /ˈθæləs/ n. (pl. **thalli** /-laɪ/) a plant-body without vascular tissue and not differentiated into root, stem, and leaves. □ **thalloid** adj. [L f. Gk thallos green shoot f. thallō bloom]

than /ðən, ðæn/ conj. 1 introducing the second element in a comparison (you are older than he is; you are older than he). 2 introducing the second element in a statement of difference (anyone other than me). [OE thanne etc., orig. the same word as THEN]

■ **Usage** With reference to the examples in sense 1, it is also legitimate to say you are older than him, with than treated as a preposition, esp. in less formal contexts.

thanatology /ˌθænəˈtɒlədʒɪ/ n. the scientific study of death and its associated phenomena and practices. [Gk thanatos death + -LOGY]

thane /θeɪn/ n. hist. 1 a man who held land from an English king or other superior by military service, ranking between ordinary freemen and hereditary nobles. 2 a man who held land from a Scottish king and ranked with an earl's son; the chief of a clan. □ **thanedom** n. [OE theg(e)n servant, soldier f. Gmc]

thank /θæŋk/ v. & n. —v.tr. 1 express gratitude to (thanked him for the present). 2 hold responsible (you can thank yourself for that). —n. (in pl.) 1 gratitude (expressed his heartfelt thanks). 2 an expression of gratitude (give thanks to Heaven). 3 (as a formula) thank you (thanks for your help; thanks very much). □ **give thanks** say grace at a meal. **no** (or **small**) **thanks to** despite. **thank goodness** (or **God** or **heavens** etc.) 1 colloq. an expression of relief or pleasure. 2 an expression of pious gratitude. **thank-offering** an offering made as an act of thanksgiving. **thanks to** as the (good or bad) result of (thanks to my foresight; thanks to your obstinacy). **thank you** a polite formula acknowledging a gift or service or an offer accepted or refused. [OE thancian, thanc f. Gmc, rel. to THINK]

thankful /ˈθæŋkfʊl/ adj. 1 grateful, pleased. 2 (of words or acts) expressive of thanks. □ **thankfulness** n. [OE thancful (as THANK, -FUL)]

thankfully /ˈθæŋkfʊlɪ/ adv. **1** in a thankful manner. **2** disp. let us be thankful; fortunately (thankfully, nobody was hurt). [OE thancfullice (as THANKFUL, -LY²)]

thankless /ˈθæŋklɪs/ adj. **1** not expressing or feeling gratitude. **2** (of a task etc.) giving no pleasure or profit. **3** not deserving thanks. □ **thanklessly** adv. **thanklessness** n.

thanksgiving /ˈθæŋks͵ɡɪvɪŋ, -ˈɡɪvɪŋ/ n. **1 a** the expression of gratitude, esp. to God. **b** a form of words for this. **2** (**Thanksgiving** or **Thanksgiving Day**) a national holiday for giving thanks to God, the fourth Thursday in November in the US, usu. the second Monday in October in Canada.

that /ðæt/ pron., adj., adv., & conj. —demons.pron. (pl. **those** /ðəʊz/) **1** the person or thing indicated, named, or understood, esp. when observed by the speaker or when familiar to the person addressed (I heard that; who is that in the garden?; I knew all that before; that is not fair). **2** (contrasted with this) the further or less immediate or obvious etc. of two (this bag is much heavier than that). **3** the action, behaviour, or circumstances just observed or mentioned (don't do that again). **4** Brit. (on the telephone etc.) the person spoken to (who is that?). **5** colloq. referring to a strong feeling just mentioned ('Are you glad?' 'I am that'). **6** (esp. in relative constructions) the one, the person, etc., described or specified in some way (those who have cars can take the luggage; those unfit for use; a table like that described above). **7** /ðət/ (pl. **that**) used instead of which or whom to introduce a defining clause, esp. one essential to identification (the book that you sent me; there is nothing here that matters). —demons.adj. (pl. **those** /ðəʊz/) **1** designating the person or thing indicated, named, understood, etc. (cf. sense 1 of pron.) (look at that dog; what was that noise?; things were easier in those days). **2** contrasted with this (cf. sense 2 of pron.) (this bag is heavier than that one). **3** expressing strong feeling (shall not easily forget that day). —adv. **1** to such a degree; so (have done that much; will go that far). **2** Brit. colloq. very (not that good). **3** /ðət/ at which, on which, etc. (at the speed that he was going he could not stop; the day that I first met her). —conj. /ðət/ except when stressed/ introducing a subordinate clause indicating: **1** a statement or hypothesis (they say that he is better; there is no doubt that he meant it; the result was that the handle fell off). **2** a purpose (we live that we may eat). **3** a result (am so sleepy that I cannot keep my eyes open). **4** a reason or clause (it is rather that he lacks the time). **5** a wish (Oh, that summer were here!). □ **all that** very (not all that good). **and all that** (or **and that** colloq.) and all or various things associated with or similar to what has been mentioned; and so forth. **like that 1** of that kind (is fond of books like that). **2** in that manner, as you are doing, as he has been doing, etc. (wish they would not talk like that). **3** colloq. without effort (did the job like that). **4** of that character (he would not accept any payment—he is like that). **that is** (or **that is to say**) a formula introducing or following an explanation of a preceding word or words. **that's** colloq. you are (by virtue of present or future obedience etc.) (that's a good boy). **that's more like it** an acknowledgement of improvement. **that's right** an expression of approval or colloq. assent. **that's that** a formula concluding a

narrative or discussion or indicating completion of a task. **that will do** no more is needed or desirable. [OE thæt, nom. & acc. sing. neut. of demons. pron. & adj. se, sēo, thæt f. Gmc; those f. OE thās pl. of thes THIS]

───────────

■ **Usage** In sense 7 of the pronoun, that usually specifies or identifies something referred to, whereas who or which need not: compare the book that you sent me is lost with the book, which I gave you, is lost. The conjunction that is often omitted in senses 1 and 3: they say he is better.

───────────

thatch /θætʃ/ n. & v. —n. **1** a roof-covering of straw, reeds, palm-leaves, or similar material. **2** colloq. the hair of the head. —v.tr. (also absol.) cover (a roof or a building) with thatch. □ **thatcher** n. [n. late collateral form of thack (now dial.) f. OE thæc, after v. f. OE theccan f. Gmc, assim. to thack]

thaw /θɔː/ v. & n. —v. **1** intr. (often foll. by out) (of ice or snow or a frozen thing) pass into a liquid or unfrozen state. **2** intr. (usu. prec. by it as subject) (of the weather) become warm enough to melt ice etc. (it began to thaw). **3** intr. become warm enough to lose numbness etc. **4** intr. become less cold or stiff in manner; become genial. **5** tr. (often foll. by out) cause to thaw. **6** tr. make cordial or animated. —n. **1** the act or an instance of thawing. **2** the warmth of weather that thaws (a thaw has set in). **3** Polit. a relaxation of control or restriction. □ **thawless** adj. [OE thawian f. WG; orig. unkn.]

the /before a vowel ðɪ, before a consonant ðə, when stressed ðiː/ adj. & adv. —adj. (called the definite article) **1** denoting one or more persons or things already mentioned, under discussion, implied, or familiar (gave the man a wave; shall let the matter drop; hurt myself in the arm; went to the theatre). **2** serving to describe as unique (the Queen; the Thames). **3 a** (foll. by defining adj.) which is, who are, etc. (ignored the embarrassed Mr Smith; Edward the Seventh). **b** (foll. by adj. used absol.) denoting a class described (from the sublime to the ridiculous). **4** best known or best entitled to the name (with the stressed: no relation to the Kipling; this is the book on this subject). **5** used to indicate a following defining clause or phrase (the book that you borrowed; the best I can do for you; the bottom of a well). **6 a** used to indicate that a singular noun represents a species, class, etc. (the cat loves comfort; has the novel a future?). **b** used with a noun which figuratively represents an occupation, pursuit, etc. (went on the stage; too fond of the bottle). **c** (foll. by the name of a unit) a, per (5p in the pound; £5 the square metre; allow 8 minutes to the mile). **d** colloq. or archaic designating a disease, affliction, etc. (the measles; the toothache; the blues). **7** (foll. by a unit of time) the present, the current (man of the moment; questions of the day; book of the month). **8** Brit. colloq. my, our (the dog; the fridge). —adv. (preceding comparatives in expressions of proportional variation) in or by that (or such a) degree; on that account (the more the merrier; the more he gets the more he wants). □ **all the** in the full degree to be expected (that makes it all the worse). **so much the** (tautologically) so much, in that degree (so much the worse for him). [(adj.) OE, replacing se, sēo, thæt (= THAT), f. Gmc: (adv.) f. OE thȳ, thē, instrumental case]

thearchy /ˈθiːɑːkɪ/ n. (pl. **-ies**) **1** government by a god or gods. **2** a system or order of gods (the

Olympian *thearchy*). [eccl.Gk *thearkhia* godhead f. *theos* god + *-arkhia* f. *arkhō* rule]

theatre /ˈθɪətə(r)/ n. (US **theater**) **1 a** a building or outdoor area for dramatic performances. **b** a cinema. **2 a** the writing and production of plays. **b** effective material for the stage (*makes good theatre*). **3** a room or hall for lectures etc. with seats in tiers. **4** Brit. an operating theatre. **5 a** a scene or field of action (*the theatre of war*). **b** (*attrib.*) designating weapons intermediate between tactical and strategic (*theatre nuclear missiles*). **6** a natural land-formation in a gradually rising part-circle like ancient Greek and Roman theatres. □ **theatre-goer** a frequenter of theatres. **theatre-going** frequenting theatres. **theatre-in-the-round** a dramatic performance on a stage surrounded by spectators. **theatre sister** a nurse supervising the nursing team in an operating theatre. [ME f. OF *t(h)eatre* or f. L *theatrum* f. Gk *theatron* f. *theaomai* behold]

theatric /θɪˈætrɪk/ adj. & n. —adj. = THEATRICAL. —n. (in pl.) theatrical actions.

theatrical /θɪˈætrɪk(ə)l/ adj. & n. —adj. **1** of or for the theatre; of acting or actors. **2** (of a manner, speech, gesture, or person) calculated for effect; showy, artificial, affected. —n. (in pl.) **1** dramatic performances (*amateur theatricals*). **2** theatrical actions. □ **theatricalism** n. **theatricality** /-ˈkælɪtɪ/ n. **theatricalize** v.tr. (also **-ise**). **theatricalization** /-laɪˈzeɪʃ(ə)n/ n. **theatrically** adv. [LL *theatricus* f. Gk *theatrikos* f. *theatron* THEATRE]

thee /ðiː/ pron. objective case of THOU[1]. [OE]

theft /θeft/ n. the act or an instance of stealing. [OE *thiefth*, *theofth*, later *theoft*, f. Gmc (as THIEF)]

their /ðeə(r)/ poss.pron. (attrib.) **1** of or belonging to them or themselves (*their house; their own business*). **2 (Their)** (in titles) that they are (*Their Majesties*). **3** disp. as a third person sing. indefinite meaning 'his or her' (*has anyone lost their purse?*). [ME f. ON *their(r)a* of them, genit. pl. of *sá* THE, THAT]

theirs /ðeəz/ poss.pron. the one or ones belonging to or associated with them (*it is theirs; theirs are over here*). □ **of theirs** of or belonging to them (*a friend of theirs*). [ME f. THEIR]

theism /ˈθiːɪz(ə)m/ n. belief in the existence of gods or a god, esp. a God supernaturally revealed to man and sustaining a personal relation to his creatures. □ **theist** n. **theistic** /-ˈɪstɪk/ adj. **theistical** /-ˈɪstɪk(ə)l/ adj. **theistically** /-ˈɪstɪkəlɪ/ adv. [Gk *theos* god + -ISM]

them /ð(ə)m, or, when stressed, ðem/ pron. & adj. —pron. **1** objective case of THEY (*I saw them*). **2** colloq. they (*it's them again; is older than them*). —adj. sl. or dial. those (*them bones*). [ME *theim* f. ON: see THEY]

thematic /θɪˈmætɪk/ adj. of or relating to subjects or topics (*thematic philately; the arrangement of the anthology is thematic*). □ **thematically** adv. [Gk *thematikos* (as THEME)]

theme /θiːm/ n. **1** a subject or topic on which a person speaks, writes, or thinks. **2** Mus. a prominent or frequently recurring melody or group of notes in a composition. **3** US a school exercise, esp. an essay, on a given subject. □ **theme park** an amusement park organized round a unifying idea. **theme song** (or **tune**) **1** a recurrent melody in a musical play or film. **2** a signature tune. [ME *teme* ult. f. Gk *thema -matos* f. *tithēmi* set, place]

themselves /ðəmˈselvz/ pron. **1 a** emphat. form of THEY or THEM. **b** refl. form of THEM; (cf. HERSELF). **2** in their normal state of body or mind (*are quite themselves again*). □ **be themselves** act in their normal, unconstrained manner.

then /ðen/ adv., adj., & n. —adv. **1** at that time; at the time in question (*was then too busy; then comes the trouble; the then existing laws*). **2 a** next, afterwards; after that (*then he told me to come in*). **b** and also (*then, there are the children to consider*). **c** after all (*it is a problem, but then that is what we are here for*). **3 a** in that case; therefore; it follows that (*then you should have said so*). **b** if what you say is true (*but then why did you take it?*). **c** (implying grudging or impatient concession) if you must have it so (*all right then, have it your own way*). **d** used parenthetically to resume a narrative etc. (*the policeman, then, knocked on the door*). —adj. that or who was such at the time in question (*the then Duke*). —n. that time (*until then*). □ **then and there** immediately and on the spot. [OE *thanne, thonne*, etc., f. Gmc, rel. to THAT, THE]

thence /ðens/ adv. (also **from thence**) archaic or literary **1** from that place or source. **2** for that reason. [ME *thannes, thennes* f. *thanne, thenne* f. OE *thanon(e)* etc. f. WG]

thenceforth /ðensˈfɔːθ/ adv. (also **from thenceforth**) archaic or literary from that time onward.

thenceforward /ðensˈfɔːwəd/ adv. archaic or literary thenceforward.

theo- /ˈθiːəʊ/ comb. form God or gods. [Gk f. *theos* god]

theobromine /θɪəˈbrəʊmɪn, -miːn/ n. a bitter white alkaloid obtained from cacao seeds, related to caffeine. [*Theobroma* cacao genus: mod.L f. Gk *theos* god + *brōma* food, + -INE[4]]

theocentric /θɪəˈsentrɪk/ adj. having God as its centre.

theocracy /θɪˈɒkrəsɪ/ n. (pl. **-ies**) a form of government by God or a god directly or through a priestly order etc. □ **theocrat** /ˈθɪəˌkræt/ n. **theocratic** /θɪəˈkrætɪk/ adj. **theocratically** /θɪəˈkrætɪkəlɪ/ adv.

theodolite /θɪˈɒdəˌlaɪt/ n. a surveying-instrument for measuring horizontal and vertical angles with a rotating telescope. □ **theodolitic** /-ˈlɪtɪk/ adj. [16th c. *theodelitus*, of unkn. orig.]

theologian /θɪəˈləʊdʒɪən, -dʒ(ə)n/ n. a person trained in theology. [ME f. OF *theologien* (as THEOLOGY)]

theological /θɪəˈlɒdʒɪk(ə)l/ adj. of theology. □ **theologically** adv. [med.L *theologicalis* f. L *theologicus* f. Gk *theologikos* (as THEOLOGY)]

theology /θɪˈɒlədʒɪ/ n. (pl. **-ies**) **1** the study of theistic (esp. Christian) religion. **2** a system of theistic (esp. Christian) religion. □ **theologist** n. **theologize** v.tr. & intr. (also **-ise**). [ME f. OF *theologie* f. L *theologia* f. Gk (as THEO-, -LOGY)]

theorem /ˈθɪərəm/ n. esp. Math. **1** a general proposition not self-evident but proved by a chain of reasoning; a truth established by means of accepted truths. **2** a rule in algebra etc. esp. one expressed by symbols or formulae (*binomial theorem*). □ **theorematic** /-ˈmætɪk/ adj. [F *théorème* or LL *theorema* f. Gk *theōrēma* speculation, proposition f. *theōreō* look at]

theoretic /θɪəˈretɪk/ adj. & n. —adj. = THEORETICAL. —n. (in sing. or pl.) the theoretical part of a science etc. [LL *theoreticus* f. Gk *theōrētikos* (as THEORY)]

theoretical /θɪəˈretɪk(ə)l/ *adj.* **1** concerned with knowledge but not with its practical application. **2** based on theory rather than experience or practice. □ **theoretically** *adv.*

theoretician /ˌθɪərɪˈtɪʃ(ə)n/ *n.* a person concerned with the theoretical aspects of a subject.

theorist /ˈθɪərɪst/ *n.* a holder or inventor of a theory or theories.

theorize /ˈθɪəraɪz/ *v.intr.* (also **-ise**) evolve or indulge in theories. □ **theorizer** *n.*

theory /ˈθɪərɪ/ *n.* (*pl.* **-ies**) **1** a supposition or system of ideas explaining something, esp. one based on general principles independent of the particular things to be explained (*atomic theory*; *theory of evolution*). **2** a speculative (esp. fanciful) view (*one of my pet theories*). **3** the sphere of abstract knowledge or speculative thought (*this is all very well in theory, but how will it work in practice?*). **4** the exposition of the principles of a science etc. (*the theory of music*). [LL *theoria* f. Gk *theōria* f. *theōros* spectator f. *theōreō* look at]

theosophy /θɪˈɒsəfɪ/ *n.* (*pl.* **-ies**) any of various philosophies professing to achieve a knowledge of God by spiritual ecstasy, direct intuition, or special individual relations, esp. a modern movement following Hindu and Buddhist teachings and seeking universal brotherhood. □ **theosopher** *n.* **theosophic** /θɪəˈsɒfɪk/ *adj.* **theosophical** /θɪəˈsɒfɪk(ə)l/ *adj.* **theosophically** /θɪəˈsɒfɪkəlɪ/ *adv.* **theosophist** *n.* [med.L *theosophia* f. late Gk *theosophia* f. *theosophos* wise concerning God (as THEO-, *sophos* wise)]

therapeutic /ˌθerəˈpjuːtɪk/ *adj.* **1** of, for, or contributing to the cure of disease. **2** contributing to general, esp. mental, well-being (*finds walking therapeutic*). □ **therapeutical** *adj.* **therapeutically** *adv.* **therapeutist** *n.* [attrib. use of *therapeutic*, orig. form of THERAPEUTICS]

therapeutics /ˌθerəˈpjuːtɪks/ *n.pl.* (usu. treated as *sing.*) the branch of medicine concerned with the treatment of disease and the action of remedial agents. [F *thérapeutique* or LL *therapeutica* (pl.) f. Gk *therapeutika* neut. pl. of *therapeutikos* f. *therapeuō* wait on, cure]

therapy /ˈθerəpɪ/ *n.* (*pl.* **-ies**) **1** the treatment of physical or mental disorders, other than by surgery. **2** a particular type of such treatment. □ **therapist** *n.* [mod.L *therapia* f. Gk *therapeia* healing]

there /ðeə(r)/ *adv., n., & int.* —*adv.* **1** in, at, or to that place or position (*lived there for some years*; *goes there every day*). **2** at that point (in speech, performance, writing, etc.) (*there he stopped*). **3** in that respect (*I agree with you there*). **4** used for emphasis in calling attention (*you there!*; *there goes the bell*). **5** used to indicate the fact or existence of something (*there is a house on the corner*). —*n.* that place (*lives somewhere near there*). —*int.* **1** expressing confirmation, triumph, dismay, etc. (*there! what did I tell you?*). **2** used to soothe a child etc. (*there, there, never mind*). □ **have been there before** *sl.* know all about it. **so there** *colloq.* that is my final decision (whether you like it or not). **there and then** immediately and on the spot. **there it is 1** that is the trouble. **2** nothing can be done about it. **there's** *colloq.* you are (by virtue of present or future obedience etc.) (*there's a dear*). **there you are** (or **go**) *colloq.* **1** this is what you wanted etc. **2** expressing

confirmation, triumph, resignation, etc. [OE *thǣr, thēr* f. Gmc, rel. to THAT, THE]

thereabouts /ˈðeərəˌbaʊts, -ˈbaʊts/ *adv.* (also **thereabout**) **1** near that place (*ought to be somewhere thereabouts*). **2** near that number, quantity, etc. (*two litres or thereabouts*).

thereafter /ðeərˈɑːftə(r)/ *adv. formal* after that.

thereat /ðeərˈæt/ *adv. archaic* **1** at that place. **2** on that account. **3** after that.

thereby /ðeəˈbaɪ, ˈðeə-/ *adv.* by that means, as a result of that. □ **thereby hangs a tale** much could be said about that.

therefore /ˈðeəfɔː(r)/ *adv.* for that reason; accordingly, consequently.

therefrom /ðeəˈfrɒm/ *adv. archaic* from that or it.

therein /ðeərˈɪn/ *adv. formal* **1** in that place etc. **2** in that respect.

thereinafter /ˌðeərɪnˈɑːftə(r)/ *adv. formal* later in the same document etc.

thereinto /ðeərˈɪntʊ/ *adv. archaic* into that place.

thereof /ðeərˈɒv/ *adv. formal* of that or it.

thereon /ðeərˈɒn/ *adv. archaic* on that or it (of motion or position).

thereto /ðeəˈtuː/ *adv. formal* **1** to that or it. **2** in addition, to boot.

thereupon /ˌðeərəˈpɒn/ *adv.* **1** in consequence of that. **2** soon or immediately after that. **3** *archaic* upon that (of motion or position).

therewith /ðeəˈwɪð/ *adv. archaic* **1** with that. **2** soon or immediately after that.

therm /θɜːm/ *n.* a unit of heat, esp. as the statutory unit of gas supplied in the UK equivalent to 100,000 British thermal units or 1.055 × 10⁸ joules. [Gk *thermē* heat]

thermal /ˈθɜːm(ə)l/ *adj. & n.* —*adj.* **1** of, for, or producing heat. **2** promoting the retention of heat (*thermal underwear*). —*n.* a rising current of heated air (used by gliders, balloons, and birds to gain height). □ **British thermal unit** the amount of heat needed to raise 1 lb. of water at maximum density through one degree Fahrenheit, equivalent to 1.055 × 10³ joules. **thermal capacity** the number of heat units needed to raise the temperature of a body by one degree. **thermal springs** springs of naturally hot water. **thermal unit** a unit for measuring heat. □ **thermalize** *v.tr. & intr.* (also **-ise**). **thermalization** /-laɪˈzeɪʃ(ə)n/ *n.* **thermally** *adv.* [F (as THERM)]

thermic /ˈθɜːmɪk/ *adj.* of or relating to heat.

thermion /ˈθɜːmɪˌɒn/ *n.* an ion or electron emitted by a substance at high temperature. [THERMO- + ION]

thermionic /ˌθɜːmɪˈɒnɪk/ *adj.* of or relating to electrons emitted from a substance at very high temperature. □ **thermionic emission** the emission of electrons from a heated source. **thermionic valve** (US **tube**) a device giving a flow of thermionic electrons in one direction, used esp. in the rectification of a current and in radio reception.

thermionics /ˌθɜːmɪˈɒnɪks/ *n.pl.* (treated as *sing.*) the branch of science and technology concerned with thermionic emission.

thermistor /θɜːˈmɪstə(r)/ *n. Electr.* a resistor whose resistance is greatly reduced by heating, used for measurement and control. [*thermal resistor*]

thermo- /ˈθɜːməʊ/ *comb. form* denoting heat. [Gk f. *thermos* hot, *thermē* heat]

thermocouple /ˈθɜːməʊˌkʌp(ə)l/ *n.* a pair of different metals in contact at a point, generating a thermoelectric voltage that can serve as a measure of temperature at this point relative to their other parts.

thermodynamics /ˌθɜːməʊdaɪˈnæmɪks/ *n.pl.* (usu. treated as *sing.*) the science of the relations between heat and other (mechanical, electrical, etc.) forms of energy. □ **thermodynamic** *adj.* **thermodynamical** *adj.* **thermodynamically** *adv.* **thermodynamicist** /-sɪst/ *n.*

thermoelectric /ˌθɜːməʊɪˈlektrɪk/ *adj.* producing electricity by a difference of temperatures. □ **thermoelectrically** *adv.* **thermoelectricity** /-ˌɪlek ˈtrɪsɪtɪ/ *n.*

thermogram /ˈθɜːməˌgræm/ *n.* a record made by a thermograph.

thermograph /ˈθɜːməˌgrɑːf/ *n.* **1** an instrument that gives a continuous record of temperature. **2** an apparatus used to obtain an image produced by infrared radiation from a human or animal body. □ **thermographic** /-ˈgræfɪk/ *adj.*

thermography /θɜːˈmɒgrəfɪ/ *n.* Med. the taking or use of infrared thermograms, esp. to detect tumours.

thermoluminescence /ˌθɜːməʊˌluːmɪˈnes(ə)ns/ *n.* the property of becoming luminescent when pretreated and subjected to high temperatures, used as a means of dating ancient artefacts. □ **thermoluminescent** *adj.*

thermometer /θəˈmɒmɪtə(r)/ *n.* an instrument for measuring temperature, esp. a graduated glass tube with a small bore containing mercury or alcohol which expands when heated. □ **thermometric** /ˌθɜːməˈmetrɪk/ *adj.* **thermometrical** /ˌθɜːmə ˈmetrɪk(ə)l/ *adj.* **thermometry** *n.* [F *thermomètre* or mod. L *thermometrum* (as THERMO-, -METER)]

thermonuclear /ˌθɜːməʊˈnjuːklɪə(r)/ *adj.* **1** relating to or using nuclear reactions that occur only at very high temperatures. **2** relating to or characterized by weapons using thermonuclear reactions.

thermopile /ˈθɜːməʊˌpaɪl/ *n.* a set of thermocouples esp. arranged for measuring small quantities of radiant heat.

thermoplastic /ˌθɜːməʊˈplæstɪk/ *adj.* & *n.* —*adj.* (of a substance) that becomes plastic on heating and hardens on cooling, and is able to repeat these processes. —*n.* a thermoplastic substance.

Thermos /ˈθɜːməs/ *n.* (in full **Thermos flask**) *propr.* a vacuum flask. [Gk (as THERMO-)]

thermosetting /ˌθɜːməʊˈsetɪŋ/ *adj.* (of plastics) setting permanently when heated. □ **thermoset** /ˈθɜː-/ *adj.*

thermosphere /ˈθɜːməˌsfɪə(r)/ *n.* the region of the atmosphere beyond the mesosphere.

thermostat /ˈθɜːməˌstæt/ *n.* a device that automatically regulates temperature, or that activates a device when the temperature reaches a certain point. □ **thermostatic** /-ˈstætɪk/ *adj.* **thermostatically** /-ˈstætɪkəlɪ/ *adv.* [THERMO- + Gk *statos* standing]

thesaurus /θɪˈsɔːrəs/ *n.* (*pl.* **thesauri** /-raɪ/ or **thesauruses**) **1 a** a collection of concepts or words arranged according to sense. **b** *US* a book of synonyms and antonyms. **2** a dictionary or encyclopedia. [L f. Gk *thēsauros* treasure]

these *pl.* of THIS.

thesis /ˈθiːsɪs/ *n.* (*pl.* **theses** /-siːz/) **1** a proposition to be maintained or proved. **2** a dissertation, esp. by a candidate for a degree. [ME f. LL f. Gk, = putting, placing, a proposition etc. f. the- root of *tithēmi* place]

Thespian /ˈθespɪən/ *adj.* & *n.* —*adj.* of or relating to tragedy or drama. —*n.* an actor or actress. [Gk *Thespis* the traditional originator of Greek tragedy]

theta /ˈθiːtə/ *n.* the eighth letter of the Greek alphabet (Θ, θ). [Gk]

thew /θjuː/ *n.* (often in *pl.*) *literary* **1** muscular strength. **2** mental or moral vigour. [OE *thēaw* usage, conduct, of unkn. orig.]

they /ðeɪ/ *pron.* (*obj.* **them**; *poss.* **their, theirs**) **1** the people, animals, or things previously named or in question (*pl.* of HE, SHE, IT). **2** people in general (*they say we are wrong*). **3** those in authority (*they have raised the fees*). **4** *disp.* as a third person sing. indefinite pronoun meaning 'he or she' (*anyone can come if they want to*). [ME *thei*, obj. *theim*, f. ON *their* nom. pl. masc., *theim* dat. pl. of *sá* that]

they'd /ðeɪd/ *contr.* **1** they had. **2** they would.

they'll /ðeɪl, ðel/ *contr.* **1** they will. **2** they shall.

they're /ðe(r), ˈðeɪə(r)/ *contr.* they are.

they've /ðeɪv/ *contr.* they have.

thiamine /ˈθaɪəmɪn, -ˌmiːn/ *n.* (also **thiamin**) a vitamin of the B complex, found in unrefined cereals, beans, and liver. [THIO- + *amin* from VITAMIN]

thick /θɪk/ *adj.*, *n.*, & *adv.* —*adj.* **1 a** of great or specified extent between opposite surfaces (*a thick wall; a wall two metres thick*). **b** of large diameter (*a thick rope*). **2 a** (of a line etc.) broad; not fine. **b** (of script or type, etc.) consisting of thick lines. **3** arranged closely; crowded together; dense. **4** (usu. foll. by *with*) densely covered or filled (*air thick with snow*). **5 a** firm in consistency; containing much solid matter; viscous (*a thick paste; thick soup*). **b** made of thick material (*a thick coat*). **6** muddy; cloudy; impenetrable by sight (*thick darkness*). **7** *colloq.* (of a person) stupid, dull. **8** (of a voice) indistinct. **9** *colloq.* intimate or very friendly (esp. *thick as thieves*). —*n.* a thick part of anything. —*adv.* thickly (*snow was falling thick; blows rained down thick and fast*). □ **a bit thick** *Brit. colloq.* unreasonable or intolerable. **in the thick of 1** at the busiest part of. **2** heavily occupied with. **thick ear** *Brit. sl.* the external ear swollen as a result of a blow (esp. *give a person a thick ear*). **thick-skinned** not sensitive to reproach or criticism. **through thick and thin** under all conditions; in spite of all difficulties. □ **thickish** *adj.* **thickly** *adv.* [OE *thicce* (adj. & adv.) f. Gmc]

thicken /ˈθɪkən/ *v.* **1** tr. & intr. make or become thick or thicker. **2** intr. become more complicated (*the plot thickens*). □ **thickener** *n.*

thickening /ˈθɪkənɪŋ/ *n.* **1** the process of becoming thick or thicker. **2** a substance used to thicken liquid. **3** a thickened part.

thicket /ˈθɪkɪt/ *n.* a tangle of shrubs or trees. [OE *thiccet* (as THICK, -ET[1])]

thickhead /ˈθɪkhed/ *n. colloq.* a stupid person; a blockhead. □ **thickheaded** /-ˈhedɪd/ *adj.* **thickheadedness** /-ˈhedɪdnɪs/ *n.*

thickness /ˈθɪknɪs/ *n.* **1** the state of being thick. **2** the extent to which a thing is thick. **3** a layer of material of a certain thickness (*three thicknesses* *of cardboard*). **4** a part that is thick or lies between opposite surfaces (*steps cut in the thickness of the wall*). [OE *thicnes* (as THICK, -NESS)]

thickset /ˈθɪkˈsɛt/ *adj. & n.* —*adj.* **1** heavily or solidly built. **2** set or growing close together. —*n.* a thicket.

thief /θiːf/ *n.* (*pl.* **thieves** /θiːvz/) a person who steals esp. secretly and without violence. [OE *thēof* f. Gmc]

thieve /θiːv/ *v.* **1** *intr.* be a thief. **2** *tr.* steal (a thing). [OE *thēofian* (as THIEF)]

thievery /ˈθiːvərɪ/ *n.* the act or practice of stealing.

thieves *pl.* of THIEF.

thievish /ˈθiːvɪʃ/ *adj.* given to stealing. □ **thievishly** *adv.* **thievishness** *n.*

thigh /θaɪ/ *n.* **1** the part of the human leg between the hip and the knee. **2** a corresponding part in other animals. □ **thigh-bone** = FEMUR. □ **-thighed** *adj.* (in *comb.*). [OE *thēh, thēoh, thīoh,* OHG *dioh,* ON *thjó* f. Gmc]

thimble /ˈθɪmb(ə)l/ *n.* a metal or plastic cap, usu. with a closed end, worn to protect the finger and push the needle in sewing. [OE *thȳmel* (as THUMB, -LE¹)]

thimbleful /ˈθɪmb(ə)lˌfʊl/ *n.* (*pl.* **-fuls**) a small quantity, esp. of liquid to drink.

thin /θɪn/ *adj., adv., & v.* —*adj.* (**thinner, thinnest**) **1** having the opposite surfaces close together; of small thickness or diameter. **2 a** (of a line) narrow or fine. **b** (of a script or type etc.) consisting of thin lines. **3** made of thin material (*a thin dress*). **4** lean; not plump. **5 a** not dense or copious (*thin hair; a thin haze*). **b** not full or closely packed (*a thin audience*). **6** of slight consistency (*a thin paste*). **7** weak; lacking an important ingredient (*thin blood; a thin voice*). **8** (of an excuse, argument, disguise, etc.) flimsy or transparent. —*adv.* thinly (*cut the bread very thin*). —*v.* (**thinned, thinning**) **1** *tr. & intr.* make or become thin or thinner. **2** *tr. & intr.* (often foll. by *out*) reduce; make or become less dense or crowded or numerous. **3** *tr.* (often foll. by *out*) remove some of a crop of (seedlings, saplings, etc.) or some young fruit from (a vine or tree) to improve the growth of the rest. □ **have a thin time** *colloq.* have a wretched or uncomfortable time. **thin air** a state of invisibility or non-existence (*vanished into thin air*). **thin on top** balding. **thin-skinned** sensitive to reproach or criticism; easily upset. □ **thinly** *adv.* **thinness** *n.* **thinnish** *adj.* [OE *thynne* f. Gmc]

thine /ðaɪn/ *poss.pron. archaic* or *dial.* **1** (*predic.* or *absol.*) of or belonging to thee. **2** (*attrib.* before a vowel) = THY. [OE *thīn* f. Gmc]

thing /θɪŋ/ *n.* **1** a material or non-material entity, idea, action, etc., that is or may be thought about or perceived. **2** an inanimate material object (*take that thing away*). **3** an unspecified object or item (*have a few things to buy*). **4** an act, idea, or utterance (*a silly thing to do*). **5** an event (*an unfortunate thing to happen*). **6** a quality (*patience is a useful thing*). **7** (with ref. to a person) expressing pity, contempt, or affection (*poor thing!; a dear old thing*). **8** a specimen or type of something (*the latest thing in hats*). **9** *colloq.* one's special interest or concern (*not my thing at all*). **10** *colloq.* something remarkable (*now there's a thing!*). **11** (*prec.* by *the*) *colloq.* **a** what is conventionally proper or fashionable. **b** what is needed or required (*your suggestion was just the thing*). **c** what is to be considered (*the thing is, shall we go or not?*). **d** what is important (*the thing about them is their reliability*). **12** (in *pl.*) personal belongings or clothing (*where have I left my things?*). **13** (in *pl.*) equipment (*painting things*). **14** (in *pl.*) affairs in general (*not in the nature of things*). **15** (in *pl.*) circumstances or conditions (*things look good*). **16** (in *pl.* with a following adjective) all that is so describable (*all things Greek*). **17** (in *pl.*) *Law* property. □ **do one's own thing** *colloq.* pursue one's own interests or inclinations. **do things to** *colloq.* affect remarkably. **have a thing about** *colloq.* be obsessed or prejudiced about. **make a thing of** *colloq.* **1** regard as essential. **2** cause a fuss about. **one** (or **just one**) **of those things** *colloq.* something unavoidable or to be accepted. [OE f. Gmc]

thingummy /ˈθɪŋəmɪ/ *n.* (*pl.* **-ies**) (also **thingamy, thingumabob** /-məˌbɒb/, **thingumajig** /-məˌdʒɪg/) *colloq.* a person or thing whose name one has forgotten or does not know or does not wish to mention. [THING + meaningless suffix]

thingy /ˈθɪŋɪ/ *n.* (*pl.* **-ies**) = THINGUMMY.

think /θɪŋk/ *v. & n.* —*v.* (*past* and *past part.* **thought** /θɔːt/) **1** *tr.* (foll. by *that* + clause) be of the opinion (*we think that they will come*). **2** *tr.* (foll. by *that* + clause or *to* + *infin.*) judge or consider (*is thought to be a fraud*). **3** *intr.* exercise the mind positively with one's ideas etc. (*let me think for a moment*). **4** *tr.* (foll. by *of* or *about*) **a** consider; be or become mentally aware of (*think of you constantly*). **b** form or entertain the idea of; imagine to oneself (*couldn't think of such a thing*). **c** choose mentally; hit upon (*think of a number*). **5** *tr.* have a half-formed intention (*I think I'll stay*). **6** *tr.* form a conception of (*cannot think how you do it*). **7** *tr.* reduce to a specified condition by thinking (*cannot think away a toothache*). **8** *tr.* (foll. by *to* + *infin.*) intend or expect (*thinks to deceive us*). **9** *tr.* (foll. by *to* + *infin.*) remember (*did not think to lock the door*). —*n. colloq.* an act of thinking (*must have a think about that*). □ **think again** revise one's plans or opinions. **think aloud** utter one's thoughts as soon as they occur. **think back to** recall (a past event or time). **think better of** change one's mind about (an intention) after reconsideration. **think for oneself** have an independent mind or attitude. **think little** (or **nothing**) **of** consider to be insignificant or unremarkable. **think much** (or **highly**) **of** have a high opinion of. **think on** (or **upon**) *archaic* think of or about. **think out 1** consider carefully. **2** produce (an idea etc.) by thinking. **think over** reflect upon in order to reach a decision. **think through** reflect fully upon (a problem etc.). **think twice** use careful consideration, avoid hasty action, etc. **think up** *colloq.* devise; produce by thought. □ **thinkable** *adj.* [OE *thencan thōhte gethōht* f. Gmc]

thinker /ˈθɪŋkə(r)/ *n.* **1** a person who thinks, esp. in a specified way (*an original thinker*). **2** a person with a skilled or powerful mind.

thinking /ˈθɪŋkɪŋ/ *adj. & n.* —*adj.* using thought or rational judgement. —*n.* **1** opinion or judgement. **2** (in *pl.*) thoughts; courses of thought.

think-tank /ˈθɪŋktæŋk/ *n.* a body of experts providing advice and ideas on specific national and commercial problems.

thinner /ˈθɪnə(r)/ *n.* a volatile liquid used to dilute paint etc.

thio- /ˈθaɪəʊ/ *comb. form* sulphur, esp. replacing oxygen in compounds (*thio-acid*). [Gk *theion* sulphur]

thiosulphate /ˌθaɪəʊˈsʌlfeɪt/ *n.* a sulphate in which one oxygen atom is replaced by sulphur.

third /θɜːd/ *n.* & *adj.* —*n.* **1** the position in a sequence corresponding to that of the number 3 in the sequence 1–3. **2** something occupying this position. **3** each of three equal parts of a thing. **4** = *third gear.* **5** *Mus.* **a** an interval of or chord spanning three consecutive notes in the diatonic scale (e.g. C to E). **b** a note separated from another by this interval. **6 a** a place in the third class in an examination. **b** a person having this. —*adj.* that is the third. □ **third-best** *adj.* of third quality. —*n.* a thing in this category. **third class** the third- best group or category, esp. of hotel and train accommodation. **third-class** *adj.* **1** belonging to or travelling by the third class. **2** of lower quality; inferior. —*adv.* by the third class (*travels third-class*). **third degree** long and severe questioning esp. by police to obtain information or a confession. **third-degree** *Med.* denoting burns of the most severe kind, affecting lower layers of tissue. **third force** a political group or party acting as a check on conflict between two opposing parties. **third gear** the third (and often next to highest) in a sequence of gears. **third man** *Cricket.* **1** a fielder positioned near the boundary behind the slips. **2** this position. **third part** each of three equal parts into which a thing is or might be divided. **third party 1** another party besides the two principals. **2** a bystander etc. **third-party** *adj.* (of insurance) covering damage or injury suffered by a person other than the insured. **third person 1** = *third party.* **2** *Gram.* see PERSON. **third-rate** inferior; very poor in quality. **Third World** (usu. prec. by *the*) the developing countries of Asia, Africa, and Latin America. □ **thirdly** *adv.* [OE *third(d)a, thridda* f. Gmc]

thirst /θɜːst/ *n.* & *v.* —*n.* **1** a physical need to drink liquid, or the feeling of discomfort caused by this. **2** a strong desire or craving (*a thirst for power*). —*v.intr.* (often foll. by *for* or *after*) **1** feel thirst. **2** have a strong desire. [OE *thurst, thyrstan* f. WG]

thirsty /ˈθɜːstɪ/ *adj.* (**thirstier, thirstiest**) **1** feeling thirst. **2** (of land, a season, etc.) dry or parched. **3** (often foll. by *for* or *after*) eager. **4** *colloq.* causing thirst (*thirsty work*). □ **thirstily** *adv.* **thirstiness** *n.* [OE *thurstig, thyrstig* (as THIRST, -Y¹)]

thirteen /θɜːˈtiːn, ˈθɜː-/ *n.* & *adj.* —*n.* **1** one more than twelve. **2** a symbol for this (13, xiii, XIII). **3** a size etc. denoted by thirteen. —*adj.* that amount to thirteen. □ **thirteenth** *adj.* & *n.* [OE *thrēotīene* (as THREE, -TEEN)]

thirty /ˈθɜːtɪ/ *n.* & *adj.* —*n.* (*pl.* **-ies**) **1** the product of three and ten. **2** a symbol for this (30, xxx, XXX). **3** (in *pl.*) the numbers from 30 to 39, esp. the years of a century or of a person's life. —*adj.* that amount to thirty. □ **Thirty-nine Articles** the points of doctrine assented to by those taking orders in the Church of England. □ **thirtieth** *adj.* & *n.* **thirtyfold** *adj.* & *adv.* [OE *thrītig* (as THREE, -TY²)]

this /ðɪs/ *pron., adj.,* & *adv.* —*demons.pron.* (*pl.* **these** /ðiːz/) **1** the person or thing close at hand or indicated or already named or understood (*can you see this?; this is my cousin*). **2** (contrasted with *that*) the person or thing nearer to hand or more immediately in mind. **3** the action, behaviour, or circumstances under consideration (*this won't do at all; what do you think of this?*). **4** (on the telephone): **a** *Brit.* the person speaking. **b** *US* the person spoken to. —*demons.adj.* (*pl.* **these** /ðiːz/) **1** designating the person or thing close at hand etc. (cf. senses 1, 2 of *pron.*). **2** (of time): **a** the present or current (*am busy all this week*). **b** relating to today (*this morning*). **c** just past or to come (*have been asking for it these three weeks*). **3** *colloq.* (in narrative) designating a person or thing previously unspecified (*then up came this policeman*). —*adv.* to this degree or extent (*knew him when he was this high; did not reach this far*). □ **this and that** *colloq.* various unspecified examples of things (esp. trivial). **this here** *sl.* this particular (person or thing). **this much** the amount or extent about to be stated (*I know this much, that he was not there*). **this world** mortal life. [OE, neut. of *thes*]

thistle /ˈθɪs(ə)l/ *n.* **1** any of various prickly composite herbaceous plants of the genus *Cirsium, Carlina,* or *Carduus* etc., usu. with globular heads of purple flowers. **2** this as the Scottish national emblem. [OE *thistel* f. Gmc]

thistledown /ˈθɪs(ə)l,daʊn/ *n.* a light fluffy stuff attached to thistle-seeds and blown about in the wind.

thistly /ˈθɪslɪ/ *adj.* overgrown with thistles.

thither /ˈðɪðə(r)/ *adv. archaic* or *formal* to or towards that place. [OE *thider,* alt. (after HITHER) of *thæder*]

thole /θəʊl/ *n.* (in full **thole-pin**) **1** a pin in the gunwale of a boat as the fulcrum for an oar. **2** each of two such pins forming a rowlock. [OE *thol* fir-tree, peg]

thong /θɒŋ/ *n.* **1** a narrow strip of hide or leather used as the lash of a whip, as a halter or rein, etc. **2** *Austral., NZ,* & *US* = FLIP-FLOP. [OE *thwang, thwong* f. Gmc]

thorax /ˈθɔːræks/ *n.* (*pl.* **thoraces** /ˈθɔːrə,siːz/ or **thoraxes**) *Anat.* & *Zool.* the part of the trunk between the neck and the abdomen. □ **thoracal** /ˈθɔːrək(ə)l/ *adj.* **thoracic** /θɔːˈræsɪk/ *adj.* [L f. Gk *thōrax -akos*]

thorium /ˈθɔːrɪəm/ *n. Chem.* a radioactive metallic element, the oxide of which is used in gas-mantles. [*Thor,* Scand. god of thunder]

thorn /θɔːn/ *n.* **1** a stiff sharp-pointed projection on a plant. **2** a thorn-bearing shrub or tree. □ **on thorns** continuously uneasy esp. in fear of being detected. **a thorn in one's flesh** (or **side**) a constant annoyance. □ **thornless** *adj.* **thornproof** *adj.* [OE f. Gmc]

thorny /ˈθɔːnɪ/ *adj.* (**thornier, thorniest**) **1** having many thorns. **2** (of a subject) hard to handle without offence; problematic. □ **thornily** *adv.* **thorniness** *n.*

thorough /ˈθʌrə/ *adj.* **1** complete and unqualified; not superficial (*needs a thorough change*). **2** acting or done with great care and completeness (*the report is most thorough*). **3** absolute (*a thorough nuisance*). □ **thorough-paced 1** (of a horse) trained to all paces. **2** complete or unqualified. □ **thoroughly** *adv.* **thoroughness** *n.* [orig. as adv. and prep. in the senses of *through,* f. OE *thuruh* var. of *thurh* THROUGH]

thoroughbred /ˈθʌrəˌbred/ adj. & n. —adj. **1** of pure breed. **2** high-spirited. —n. a thoroughbred animal, esp. a horse.

thoroughfare /ˈθʌrəˌfeə(r)/ n. a road or path open at both ends, esp. for traffic.

thoroughgoing /ˈθʌrəˌgəʊɪŋ, -ˈgəʊɪŋ/ adj. **1** uncompromising; not superficial. **2** (usu. attrib.) extreme; out and out.

thorp /θɔːp/ n. (also **thorpe**) archaic a village or hamlet. [OE thorp, throp, f. Gmc]

■ Usage Now usually only in place-names.

those pl. of THAT.

thou¹ /ðaʊ/ pron. (obj. **thee** /ðiː/; poss. **thy** or **thine**; pl. **ye** or **you**) second person singular pronoun, now replaced by you except in some formal, liturgical, dialect, and poetic uses. [OE thu f. Gmc]

thou² /θaʊ/ n. (pl. same or **thous**) colloq. **1** a thousand. **2** one thousandth. [abbr.]

though /ðəʊ/ conj. & adv. (also **tho'**) —conj. **1** despite the fact that (though it was early we went to bed; though annoyed, I agreed). **2** (introducing a possibility) even if (ask him though he may refuse; would not attend though the Queen herself were there). **3** and yet; nevertheless (she read on, though not to the very end). **4** in spite of being (ready though unwilling). —adv. colloq. however; all the same (I wish you had told me, though). [ME thoh etc. f. ON thó etc., corresp. to OE thēah, f. Gmc]

thought¹ /θɔːt/ n. **1** the process or power of thinking; the faculty of reason. **2** a way of thinking characteristic of or associated with a particular time, people, group, etc. (medieval European thought). **3** sober reflection or consideration (gave it much thought). **4** an idea or piece of reasoning produced by thinking (many good thoughts came out of the discussion). **5** (foll. by of + verbal noun or to + infin.) a partly formed intention or hope (gave up all thoughts of winning; had no thought to go). **6** (usu. in pl.) what one is thinking; one's opinion (have you any thoughts on this?). **7** the subject of one's thinking (my one thought was to get away). **8** (prec. by a) somewhat (seems to me a thought arrogant). □ **give thought to** consider; think about. **in thought** thinking, meditating. **take thought** consider matters. **thought-provoking** stimulating serious thought. **thought-reader** a person supposedly able to perceive another's thoughts. **thought-reading** the supposed perception of what another is thinking. **thought transference** telepathy. □ **-thoughted** adj. (in comb.). [OE thōht (as THINK)]

thought² past and past part. of THINK.

thoughtful /ˈθɔːtfʊl/ adj. **1** engaged in or given to meditation. **2** (of a book, writer, remark, etc.) giving signs of serious thought. **3** (often foll. by of) (of a person or conduct) considerate; not haphazard or unfeeling. □ **thoughtfully** adv. **thoughtfulness** n.

thoughtless /ˈθɔːtlɪs/ adj. **1** careless of consequences or of others' feelings. **2** due to lack of thought. □ **thoughtlessly** adv. **thoughtlessness** n.

thousand /ˈθaʊz(ə)nd/ n. & adj. —n. (pl. **thousands** or (in sense 1) **thousand**) (in sing. prec. by a or one) **1** the product of a hundred and ten. **2** a symbol for this (1,000, m, M). **3** a set of a thousand things. **4** (in sing. or pl.) colloq. a large number. —adj. that amount to a thousand. □

thousandfold adj. & adv. **thousandth** adj. & n. [OE thūsend f. Gmc]

thrall /θrɔːl/ n. literary **1** (often foll. by of, to) a slave (of a person, or a power or influence). **2** bondage; a state of slavery or servitude (in thrall). □ **thraldom** n. (also **thralldom**) [OE thrǣl f. ON thrǽll, perh. f. a Gmc root = run]

thrash /θræʃ/ v. & n. —v. **1** tr. beat severely, esp. with a stick or whip. **2** tr. defeat thoroughly in a contest. **3** intr. (of a paddle wheel, branch, etc.) act like a flail; deliver repeated blows. **4** intr. (foll. by about, around) move or fling the limbs about violently or in panic. —n. **1** an act of thrashing. **2** colloq. a party, esp. a lavish one. □ **thrash out** discuss to a conclusion. □ **thrasher** n. **thrashing** n. [OE therscan, later threscan, f. Gmc]

thread /θred/ n. & v. —n. **1 a** a spun-out filament of cotton, silk, or glass etc.; yarn. **b** a length of this. **2** a thin cord of twisted yarns used esp. in sewing and weaving. **3** anything regarded as threadlike with reference to its continuity or connectedness (the thread of life; lost the thread of his argument). **4** the spiral ridge of a screw. **5** (in pl.) sl. clothes. —v.tr. **1** pass a thread through the eye of (a needle). **2** put (beads) on a thread. **3** arrange (material in a strip form, e.g. film or magnetic tape) in the proper position on equipment. **4** make (one's way) carefully through a crowded place, over a difficult route, etc. **5** form a screw-thread on. □ **hang by a thread** be in a precarious state, position, etc. □ **threader** n. **threadlike** adj. [OE thrǣd f. Gmc]

threadbare /ˈθredbeə(r)/ adj. **1** (of cloth) so worn that the nap is lost and the thread visible. **2** (of a person) wearing such clothes. **3 a** hackneyed. **b** feeble or insubstantial (a threadbare excuse).

threadworm /ˈθredwɜːm/ n. any of various esp. parasitic threadlike nematode worms, e.g. the pinworm.

thready /ˈθredɪ/ adj. (**threadier**, **threadiest**) **1** of or like a thread. **2** (of a person's pulse) scarcely perceptible.

threat /θret/ n. **1** a declaration of an intention to punish or hurt. **2** an indication of something undesirable coming (the threat of war). **3** a person or thing as a likely cause of harm etc. [OE thrēat affliction etc. f. Gmc]

threaten /ˈθret(ə)n/ v.tr. **1** make a threat or threats against. **2** be a sign or indication of (something undesirable). **3** (foll. by to + infin.) announce one's intention to do an undesirable or unexpected thing (threatened to resign). **4** (also absol.) give warning of the infliction of (harm etc.) (the clouds were threatening rain). □ **threatener** n. **threateningly** adv. [OE thrēatnian (as THREAT)]

three /θriː/ n. & adj. —n. **1 a** one more than two. **b** a symbol for this (3, iii, III). **2** a size etc. denoted by three. **3** the time of three o'clock. **4** a set of three. **5** a card with three pips. —adj. that amount to three. □ **three-cornered 1** triangular. **2** (of a contest etc.) between three parties as individuals. **three-decker 1** a warship with three gun-decks. **2** a novel in three volumes. **3** a sandwich with three slices of bread. **three-dimensional** having or appearing to have length, breadth, and depth. **three-handed 1** having or using three hands. **2** involving three players. **three-legged race** a running-race between pairs, one member of each pair having the left leg tied to the right leg of the other. **three-line whip** a written notice, underlined three times to denote urgency, to members of a political party to attend a parliamentary vote. **three parts** three quarters. **three-piece** consisting of three items (esp. of a suit of clothes or a suite of furniture). **three-ply** adj. of three strands, webs, or thicknesses. —n. **1** three-ply wool. **2** three-ply wood made by gluing together three layers with the grain in different directions. **three-point turn** a method of turning a vehicle round in a narrow space by moving forwards, backwards, and forwards again in a sequence of arcs. **three-quarter** n. (also **three-quarter back**) *Rugby Football* any of three or four players just behind the half-backs. —adj. **1** consisting of three-fourths of something. **2** (of a portrait) going down to the hips or showing three-fourths of the face (between full face and profile). **three-quarters** three parts out of four. **the three Rs** reading, writing, and arithmetic, regarded as the fundamentals of learning. [OE *thrī* f. Gmc]

threefold /ˈθriːfəʊld/ adj. & adv. **1** three times as much or as many. **2** consisting of three parts.

threepence /ˈθrepəns, ˈθrʊpəns/ n. *Brit.* the sum of three pence, esp. before decimalization.

threepenny /ˈθrepənɪ, ˈθrʊpənɪ/ adj. *Brit.* costing three pence, esp. before decimalization. □ **threepenny bit** *hist.* a former coin worth three old pence.

threescore /ˈθriːskɔː(r)/ n. *archaic* sixty.

threesome /ˈθriːsəm/ n. **1** a group of three persons. **2** a game etc. for three, esp. *Golf* of one against three.

threnody /ˈθrenədɪ/ n. (also **threnode** /ˈθrenəʊd/) (pl. **-ies** or **threnodes**) **1** a lamentation, esp. on a person's death. **2** a song of lamentation. □ **threnodial** /-ˈnəʊdɪəl/ adj. **threnodic** /-ˈnɒdɪk/ adj. **threnodist** /ˈθrenədɪst/ n. [Gk *thrēnōidia* f. *thrēnos* wailing + *ōidē* ODE]

threonine /ˈθriːəˌniːn, -nɪn/ n. *Biochem.* an amino acid, considered essential for growth. [*threose* (name of a tetrose sugar) ult. f. Gk *eruthros* red + -INE⁴]

thresh /θreʃ/ v. **1** tr. beat out or separate grain from (corn etc.). **2** intr. = THRASH v. 4. **3** tr. (foll. by *over*) analyse (a problem etc.) in search of a solution. □ **threshing-floor** a hard level floor for threshing esp. with flails. **thresh out** = *thrash out*. [var. of THRASH]

thresher /ˈθreʃə(r)/ n. **1** a person or machine that threshes. **2** a shark, *Alopias vulpinus*, with a long upper lobe to its tail, that it can lash about.

threshold /ˈθreʃəʊld, -həʊld/ n. **1** a strip of wood or stone forming the bottom of a doorway and crossed in entering a house or room etc. **2** a point of entry or beginning (*on the threshold of a new century*). **3** *Physiol.* & *Psychol.* a limit below which a stimulus causes no reaction (*pain threshold*). **4** (often *attrib.*) a step in a scale of wages or taxation, usu. operative in specified conditions. [OE *therscold*, *threscold*, etc., rel. to THRASH in the sense 'tread']

threw *past* of THROW.

thrice /θraɪs/ adv. *archaic* or *literary* **1** three times. **2** (esp. in *comb.*) highly (*thrice-blessed*). [ME *thries* f. *thrie* (adv.) f. OE *thrīwa*, *thrīga* (as THREE)]

thrift /θrɪft/ n. **1** frugality; economical management. **2** a plant of the genus *Armeria*, esp.

the sea pink. □ **thrift shop** (or **store**) a shop selling second-hand items usu. for charity. [ME f. ON (as THRIVE)]

thriftless /ˈθrɪftlɪs/ adj. wasteful, improvident. □ **thriftlessly** adv. **thriftlessness** n.

thrifty /ˈθrɪftɪ/ adj. (**thriftier**, **thriftiest**) **1** economical, frugal. **2** thriving, prosperous. □ **thriftily** adv. **thriftiness** n.

thrill /θrɪl/ n. & v. —n. **1** a wave or nervous tremor of emotion or sensation (*a thrill of joy*; *a thrill of recognition*). **2** a throb or pulsation. —v. **1** intr. & tr. feel or cause to feel a thrill (*thrilled to the sound*; *a voice that thrilled millions*). **2** intr. quiver or throb with or as with emotion. **3** intr. (foll. by *through*, *over*, *along*) (of an emotion etc.) pass with a thrill through etc. (*fear thrilled through my veins*). □ **thrilling** adj. **thrillingly** adv. [*thirl* (now dial.) f. OE *thyrlian* pierce f. *thȳrel* hole f. *thurh* THROUGH]

thriller /ˈθrɪlə(r)/ n. an exciting or sensational story or play etc., esp. one involving crime or espionage.

thrips /θrɪps/ n. (pl. same) any insect of the order Thysanoptera, esp. a pest injurious to plants. [L f. Gk, = woodworm]

thrive /θraɪv/ v.intr. (past **throve** /θrəʊv/ or **thrived**; past part. **thriven** /ˈθrɪv(ə)n/ or **thrived**) **1** prosper or flourish. **2** grow rich. **3** (of a child, animal, or plant) grow vigorously. [ME f. ON *thrífask* refl. of *thrífa* grasp]

throat /θrəʊt/ n. **1 a** the windpipe or gullet. **b** the front part of the neck containing this. **2** *literary* **a** a voice, esp. of a songbird. **b** a thing compared to a throat, esp. a narrow passage, entrance, or exit. □ **cut one's own throat** bring about one's own downfall. **ram** (or **thrust**) **down a person's throat** force (a thing) on a person's attention. □ **-throated** adj. (in *comb.*). [OE *throte*, *throtu* f. Gmc]

throaty /ˈθrəʊtɪ/ adj. (**throatier**, **throatiest**) **1** (of a voice) deficient in clarity; hoarsely resonant. **2** guttural; uttered in the throat. **3** having a prominent or capacious throat. □ **throatily** adv. **throatiness** n.

throb /θrɒb/ v. & n. —v.intr. (**throbbed**, **throbbing**) **1** palpitate or pulsate, esp. with more than the usual force or rapidity. **2** vibrate or quiver with a persistent rhythm or with emotion. —n. **1** a throbbing. **2** a palpitation or (esp. violent) pulsation. [ME, app. imit.]

throe /θrəʊ/ n. (usu. in *pl.*) **1** a violent pang, esp. of childbirth or death. **2** anguish. □ **in the throes of** struggling with the task of. [ME *throwe* perh. f. OE *thrēa*, *thrawu* calamity, alt. perh. by assoc. with *woe*]

thrombose /θrɒmˈbəʊz/ v.tr. & intr. affect with or undergo thrombosis. [back-form. f. THROMBOSIS]

thrombosis /θrɒmˈbəʊsɪs/ n. (pl. **thromboses** /-siːz/) the coagulation of the blood in a blood-vessel or organ. □ **thrombotic** /-ˈbɒtɪk/ adj. [mod.L f. Gk *thrombōsis* curdling f. *thrombos* lump, blood-clot]

throne /θrəʊn/ n. & v. —n. **1** a chair of State for a sovereign or bishop etc. **2** sovereign power (*came to the throne*). —v.tr. place on a throne. □ **throneless** adj. [ME f. OF *trone* f. L *thronus* f. Gk *thronos* high seat]

throng /θrɒŋ/ n. & v. —n. **1** a crowd of people. **2** (often foll. by *of*) a multitude, esp. in a small space. —v. **1** intr. come in great numbers (*crowds thronged to the stadium*). **2** tr. flock into or crowd round; fill with or as with a crowd (*crowds thronged the streets*). [ME *thrang*, *throng*, OE *gethrang*, f. verbal stem *thring- thrang-*]

throstle /'θrɒs(ə)l/ *n.* a song thrush. [OE f. Gmc: rel. to THRUSH¹]

throttle /'θrɒt(ə)l/ *n.* & *v.* —*n.* **1 a** (in full **throttle-valve**) a valve controlling the flow of fuel or steam etc. in an engine. **b** (in full **throttle-lever**) a lever or pedal operating this valve. **2** the throat, gullet, or windpipe. —*v.tr.* **1** choke or strangle. **2** prevent the utterance etc. of. **3** control (an engine or steam etc.) with a throttle. □ **throttle back** (or **down**) reduce the speed of (an engine or vehicle) by throttling. □ **throttler** *n.* [ME *throtel* (v.), perh. f. THROAT + -LE⁴: (n.) perh. a dimin. of THROAT]

through /θru:/ *prep.*, *adv.*, & *adj.* (also **thro'**, *US* **thru**) —*prep.* **1 a** from end to end or from side to side of. **b** going in one side or end and out the other of. **2** between or among (*swam through the waves*). **3** from beginning to end (*read through the letter*; *went through many difficulties*). **4** because of; by the agency, means, or fault of (*lost it through carelessness*). **5** *US* up to and including (*Monday through Friday*). —*adv.* **1** through a thing; from side to side, end to end, or beginning to end (*went through to the garden*; *would not let us through*). **2** having completed (esp. successfully) (*are through their exams*). **3** so as to be connected by telephone (*will put you through*). —*attrib.adj.* **1** (of a journey, route, etc.) done without a change of line or vehicle etc. or with one ticket. **2** (of traffic) going through a place to its destination. □ **be through** *colloq.* **1** (often foll. by *with*) have finished. **2** (often foll. by *with*) cease to have dealings. **3** have no further prospects (*is through as a politician*). **no through road** = *no thorough-fare*. **through and through 1** thoroughly, completely. **2** through again and again. [OE *thurh* f. WG]

throughout /θru:'aʊt/ *prep.* & *adv.* —*prep.* right through; from end to end of (*throughout the town*; *throughout the 18th century*). —*adv.* in every part or respect (*the timber was rotten throughout*).

throughput /'θru:pʊt/ *n.* the amount of material put through a process, esp. in manufacturing or computing.

throughway /'θru:weɪ/ *n.* (also **thruway**) *US* a thoroughfare, esp. a motorway.

throve *past* of THRIVE.

throw /θrəʊ/ *v.* & *n.* —*v.tr.* (*past* **threw** /θru:/; *past part.* **thrown** /θrəʊn/) **1** propel with some force through the air or in a particular direction. **2** force violently into a specified position or state (*the ship was thrown on the rocks*; *threw themselves down*). **3** compel suddenly to be in a specified condition (*was thrown out of work*). **4** turn or move (part of the body) quickly or suddenly (*threw an arm out*). **5** project or cast (light, a shadow, a spell, etc.). **6 a** bring to the ground in wrestling. **b** (of a horse) unseat (its rider). **7** *colloq.* disconcert (*the question threw me for a moment*). **8** (foll. by *on*, *off*, etc.) put (clothes etc.) hastily on or off etc. **9 a** cause (dice) to fall on a table. **b** obtain (a specified number) by throwing dice. **10** cause to pass or extend suddenly to another state or position (*threw in the army*; *threw a bridge across the river*). **11** move (a switch or lever) so as to operate it. **12** form (ceramic ware) on a potter's wheel. **13** have (a fit or tantrum etc.). **14** give (a party). **15** *colloq.*

lose (a contest or race etc.) intentionally. —*n.* **1** an act of throwing. **2** the distance a thing is or may be thrown (*a record throw with the hammer*). **3** the act of being thrown in wrestling. **4** (in full **throw rug**) *US* **a** a light cover for furniture. **b** a light rug. **5** (prec. by *a*) *sl.* each; per item (*sold at £10 a throw*). □ **throw about** (or **around**) **1** throw in various directions. **2** spend (one's money) ostentatiously. **throw away 1** discard as useless or unwanted. **2** waste or fail to make use of (an opportunity etc.). **3** discard (a card). **4** *Theatr.* speak (lines) with deliberate under-emphasis. **5** (in *passive*; often foll. by *on*) be wasted (*the advice was thrown away on him*). **throw-away** *adj.* **1** meant to be thrown away after (one) use. **2** (of lines etc.) deliberately underemphasized. —*n.* a thing to be thrown away after (one) use. **throw back 1** revert to ancestral character. **2** (usu. in *passive*; foll. by *on*) compel to rely on (*was thrown back on his savings*). **throw-back** *n.* **1** reversion to ancestral character. **2** an instance of this. **throw down** cause to fall. **throw down the gauntlet** (or **glove**) issue a challenge. **throw one's hand in 1** abandon one's chances in a card game, esp. poker. **2** give up; withdraw from a contest. **throw in 1** interpose (a word or remark). **2** include at no extra cost. **3** throw (a football) from the edge of the pitch where it has gone out of play. **4** *Cricket* return (the ball) from the outfield. **throw-in** *n.* the throwing in of a football during play. **throw in the towel** admit defeat. **throw off 1** discard; contrive to get rid of. **2** write or utter in an offhand manner. **throw oneself at** seek blatantly as a spouse or sexual partner. **throw oneself into** engage vigorously in. **throw oneself on** (or **upon**) **1** rely completely on. **2** attack. **throw open** (often foll. by *to*) **1** cause to be suddenly or widely open. **2** make accessible. **throw out 1** put out forcibly or suddenly. **2** discard as unwanted. **3** expel (a troublemaker etc.). **4** build (a wing of a house, a pier, or a projecting or prominent thing). **5** put forward tentatively. **6** reject (a proposal or bill in Parliament). **7** confuse or distract (a person speaking, thinking, or acting) from the matter in hand. **throw over** desert or abandon. **throw stones** cast aspersions. **throw together 1** assemble hastily. **2** bring into casual contact. **throw up 1** abandon. **2** resign from. **3** *colloq.* vomit. **4** erect hastily. **5** bring to notice. **throw up** (or **in**) **the sponge 1** (of a boxer or his attendant) throw the sponge used between rounds into the air as a token of defeat. **2** abandon a contest; admit defeat. **throw one's weight about** (or **around**) *colloq.* act with unpleasant self-assertiveness. □ **throwable** *adj.* **thrower** *n.* (also in *comb.*). [OE *thrā- wan* twist, turn f. WG]

thrum¹ /θrʌm/ *v.* & *n.* —*v.* (**thrummed**, **thrumming**) **1** *tr.* play (a stringed instrument) monotonously or unskilfully. **2** *intr.* (often foll. by *on*) drum idly. —*n.* **1** such playing. **2** the resulting sound. [imit.]

thrum² /θrʌm/ *n.* & *v.* —*n.* **1** the unwoven end of a warp-thread, or the whole of such ends, left when the finished web is cut away. **2** any short loose thread. —*v.tr.* (**thrummed**, **thrumming**) make of or cover with thrums. □ **thrummer** *n.* **thrummy** *adj.* [OE f. Gmc]

thrush[1] /θrʌʃ/ n. any small or medium-sized songbird of the family Turdidae, esp. a song thrush or mistle thrush. [OE *thrysce* f. Gmc: cf. THROSTLE]

thrush[2] /θrʌʃ/ n. 1 a disease, esp. of children, marked by whitish fungous vesicles in the mouth and throat. 2 a similar disease of the vagina. [17th c.: orig. unkn.]

thrust /θrʌst/ v. & n. —v. (past and past part. **thrust**) 1 tr. push with a sudden impulse or with force (*thrust the letter into my pocket*). 2 tr. (foll. by *on*) impose (a thing) forcibly; enforce acceptance of (a thing) (*had it thrust on me*). 3 intr. (foll. by *at, through*) pierce or stab; make a sudden lunge. 4 tr. make (one's way) forcibly. 5 intr. (foll. by *through, past,* etc.) force oneself (*thrust past me abruptly*). —n. 1 a sudden or forcible push or lunge. 2 the propulsive force developed by a jet or rocket engine. 3 a strong attempt to penetrate an enemy's line or territory. 4 a remark aimed at a person. 5 the stress between the parts of an arch etc. 6 (often foll. by *of*) the chief theme or gist of remarks etc. 7 an attack with the point of a weapon. □ **thrust oneself** (or **one's nose**) **in** obtrude, interfere. [ME *thruste* etc. f. ON *thrýsta*]

thruster /ˈθrʌstə(r)/ n. 1 a person or thing that thrusts. 2 a small rocket engine used to provide extra or correcting thrust on a spacecraft.

thud /θʌd/ n. & v. —n. a low dull sound as of a blow on a non-resonant surface. —v.intr. (**thudded, thudding**) make or fall with a thud. □ **thuddingly** adv. [prob. f. OE *thyddan* thrust]

thug /θʌg/ n. 1 a vicious or brutal ruffian. 2 (**Thug**) hist. a member of a religious organization of robbers and assassins in India. □ **thuggery** n. **thuggish** adj. **thuggishly** adv. **thuggishness** n. [Hindi & Marathi *ṭhag* swindler]

thulium /ˈθjuːlɪəm/ n. Chem. a soft metallic element of the lanthanide series. [mod.L f. L *Thule* name of a region in the remote north]

thumb /θʌm/ n. & v. —n. 1 a a short thick terminal projection on the human hand, set lower and apart from the other four and opposable to them. b a digit of other animals corresponding to this. 2 part of a glove etc. for a thumb. —v. 1 tr. wear or soil (pages etc.) with a thumb (*a well-thumbed book*). 2 intr. turn over pages with or as with a thumb (*thumbed through the directory*). 3 tr. request or obtain (a lift in a passing vehicle) by signalling with a raised thumb. 4 tr. use the thumb in a gesture. □ **be all thumbs** be clumsy with one's hands. **thumb index** n. a set of lettered grooves cut down the side of a diary, dictionary, etc. for easy reference. —v.tr. provide (a book etc.) with these. **thumb one's nose** = *cock a snook* (SNOOK). **thumbs down** an indication of rejection or failure. **thumbs up** an indication of satisfaction or approval. **under a person's thumb** completely dominated by a person. □ **thumbed** adj. (also in *comb.*). **thumbless** adj. [OE *thūma* f. a WG root = swell]

thumbnail /ˈθʌmneɪl/ n. 1 the nail of a thumb. 2 (*attrib.*) denoting conciseness (*a thumbnail sketch*).

thumbprint /ˈθʌmprɪnt/ n. an impression of a thumb esp. as used for identification.

thumbscrew /ˈθʌmskruː/ n. 1 an instrument of torture for crushing the thumbs. 2 a screw with

a flattened head for turning with the thumb and forefinger.

thumbtack /ˈθʌmtæk/ n. esp. US a drawing-pin.

thump /θʌmp/ v. & n. —v. 1 tr. beat or strike heavily esp. with the fist (*threatened to thump me*). 2 intr. throb or pulsate strongly (*my heart was thumping*). 3 intr. (foll. by *at, on,* etc.) deliver blows, esp. to attract attention (*thumped on the door*). 4 tr. (often foll. by *out*) play (a tune on a piano etc.) with a heavy touch. 5 intr. tread heavily. —n. 1 a heavy blow. 2 the sound of this. □ **thumper** n. [imit.]

thumping /ˈθʌmpɪŋ/ adj. colloq. big, prominent (*a thumping majority; a thumping lie*).

thunder /ˈθʌndə(r)/ n. & v. —n. 1 a loud rumbling or crashing noise heard after a lightning flash and due to the expansion of rapidly heated air. 2 a resounding loud deep noise (*thunders of applause*). 3 strong censure or denunciation. —v. 1 intr. (prec. by *it* as subject) thunder sounds (*it is thundering; if it thunders*). 2 intr. make or proceed with a noise suggestive of thunder (*the applause thundered in my ears; the traffic thundered past*). 3 tr. utter or communicate (approval, disapproval, etc.) loudly or impressively. 4 intr. (foll. by *against* etc.) a make violent threats etc. against. b criticize violently. □ **steal a person's thunder** spoil the effect of another's idea, action, etc. by expressing or doing it first. □ **thunderer** n. **thunderless** adj. **thundery** adj. [OE *thunor* f. Gmc]

thunderbolt /ˈθʌndəˌbəʊlt/ n. 1 a flash of lightning with a simultaneous crash of thunder. 2 a sudden or unexpected occurrence or item of news. 3 a supposed bolt or shaft as a destructive agent, esp. as an attribute of a god.

thunderclap /ˈθʌndəˌklæp/ n. 1 a crash of thunder. 2 something startling or unexpected.

thundercloud /ˈθʌndəˌklaʊd/ n. a cumulus cloud with a tall diffuse top, charged with electricity and producing thunder and lightning.

thunderhead /ˈθʌndəˌhed/ n. esp. US a rounded cumulus cloud projecting upwards and heralding thunder.

thundering /ˈθʌndərɪŋ/ adj. colloq. very big or great (*a thundering nuisance*). □ **thunderingly** adv.

thunderous /ˈθʌndərəs/ adj. 1 like thunder. 2 very loud. □ **thunderously** adv. **thunderousness** n.

thunderstorm /ˈθʌndəˌstɔːm/ n. a storm with thunder and lightning and usu. heavy rain or hail.

thunderstruck /ˈθʌndəˌstrʌk/ adj. amazed; overwhelmingly surprised or startled.

Thur. abbr. Thursday.

thurible /ˈθjʊərɪb(ə)l/ n. a censer. [ME f. OF *thurible* or L t(h)*uribulum* f. *thus thur-* incense (as THURIFER)]

thurifer /ˈθjʊərɪfə(r)/ n. an acolyte carrying a censer. [LL f. *thus thuris* incense f. Gk *thuos* sacrifice + -*fer* -bearing]

Thurs. abbr. Thursday.

Thursday /ˈθɜːzdeɪ, -dɪ/ n. & adv. —n. the fifth day of the week, following Wednesday. —adv. colloq. 1 on Thursday. 2 (**Thursdays**) on Thursdays; each Thursday. [OE *thunresdæg, thur(e)sdæg*, day of thunder, representing LL *Jovis dies* day of Jupiter]

thus /ðʌs/ *adv. formal* **1 a** in this way. **b** as indicated. **2 a** accordingly. **b** as a result or inference. **3** to this extent; so (*thus far*; *thus much*). [OE (= OS *thus*), of unkn. orig.]

thwack /θwæk/ *v. & n.* —*v.tr.* hit with a heavy blow; whack. —*n.* a heavy blow. [imit.]

thwart /θwɔːt/ *v. & n.* —*v.tr.* frustrate or foil (a person or purpose etc.). —*n.* a rower's seat placed across a boat. [ME *thwert* (adv.) f. ON *thvert* neut. of *thverr* transverse = OE *thwe(o)rh* f. Gmc]

thy /ðaɪ/ *poss.pron.* (*attrib.*) (also **thine** /ðaɪn/ before a vowel) of or belonging to thee: now replaced by *your* except in some formal, liturgical, dialect, and poetic uses. [ME *thī*, reduced f. *thīn* THINE]

thyme /taɪm/ *n.* any herb or shrub of the genus *Thymus* with aromatic leaves, esp. *T. vulgare* grown for culinary use. □ **thymy** *adj.* [ME f. OF *thym* f. *thymum* f. Gk *thumon* f. *thuō* burn a sacrifice]

thymi *pl.* of THYMUS.

thymol /ˈθaɪmɒl/ *n. Chem.* a white crystalline phenol obtained from oil of thyme and used as an antiseptic. [as THYME + -OL¹]

thymus /ˈθaɪməs/ *n.* (*pl.* **thymi** /-maɪ/) (in full **thymus gland**) *Anat.* a lymphoid organ situated in the neck of vertebrates producing lymphocytes for the immune response. [mod.L f. Gk *thumos*]

thyristor /θaɪˈrɪstə(r)/ *n. Electronics* a semiconductor rectifier in which the current between two electrodes is controlled by a signal applied to a third electrode. [Gk *thura* gate + TRANSISTOR]

thyro- /ˈθaɪrəʊ/ *comb. form* (also **thyreo-** /-rɪəʊ/) thyroid.

thyroid /ˈθaɪrɔɪd/ *n.* (in full **thyroid gland**) a large ductless gland in the neck of vertebrates secreting a hormone which regulates growth and development through the rate of metabolism. [obs.F *thyroide* or mod.L *thyroides*, irreg. f. Gk *thureoeidēs* f. *thureos* oblong shield]

thyroxine /θaɪˈrɒksɪn/ *n.* the main hormone produced by the thyroid gland, involved in controlling the rate of metabolic processes. [THYROID + OXYGEN + -INE⁴]

thyself /ðaɪˈself/ *pron. archaic emphat. & refl.* form of THOU¹, THEE.

Ti *symb. Chem.* the element titanium.

ti var. of TE.

tiara /tɪˈɑːrə/ *n.* **1** a jewelled ornamental band worn on the front of a woman's hair. **2** a three-crowned diadem worn by a pope. □ **tiaraed** *adj.* (also **tiara'd**) [L f. Gk, of unkn. orig.]

tibia /ˈtɪbɪə/ *n.* (*pl.* **tibiae** /-bɪˌiː/) *Anat.* the inner and usu. larger of two bones extending from the knee to the ankle. □ **tibial** *adj.* [L, = shin-bone]

tic *n.* a habitual spasmodic contraction of the muscles esp. of the face. [F f. It. *ticchio*]

tick¹ *n. & v.* —*n.* **1** a slight recurring click esp. that of a watch or clock. **2** esp. *Brit. colloq.* a moment; an instant. **3** a mark (√) to denote correctness, check items in a list, etc. —*v.* **1** *intr.* **a** (of a clock etc.) make ticks. **b** (foll. by *away*) (of time etc.) pass. **2** *intr.* (of a mechanism) work, function (*take it apart to see how it ticks*). **3** *tr.* **a** mark (a written answer etc.) with a tick. **b**

(often foll. by *off*) mark (an item in a list etc.) with a tick in checking. □ **in two ticks** *Brit. colloq.* in a very short time. **tick off** *colloq.* reprimand. **tick over 1** (of an engine etc.) idle. **2** (of a person, project, etc.) be working or functioning at a basic or minimum level. **ticktack** (or **tic-tac**) *Brit.* a kind of manual semaphore signalling used by racecourse bookmakers to exchange information. **tick-tack-toe** *US* noughts and crosses. **tick-tock** the ticking of a large clock etc. **what makes a person tick** *colloq.* a person's motivation. □ **tickless** *adj.* [ME: cf. Du. *tik*, LG *tikk* touch, tick]

tick² *n.* **1** any of various arachnids of the order Acarina, parasitic on the skin of dogs and cattle etc. **2** any of various insects of the family Hippoboscidae, parasitic on sheep and birds etc. **3** *colloq.* an unpleasant or despicable person. [OE *ticca* (recorded as *ticia*); ME *teke, tyke*: cf. MDu., MLG *tēke*, OHG *zēcho*]

tick³ *n. colloq.* credit (*buy goods on tick*). [app. an abbr. of TICKET in phr. *on the ticket*]

tick⁴ *n.* **1** the cover of a mattress or pillow. **2** = TICKING. [ME *tikke, tēke* f. WG f. L *theca* f. Gk *thēkē* case]

ticker /ˈtɪkə(r)/ *n. colloq.* **1** the heart. **2** a watch. **3** *US* a tape machine. □ **ticker-tape 1** a paper strip from a tape machine. **2** this or similar material thrown from windows etc. to greet a celebrity.

ticket /ˈtɪkɪt/ *n. & v.* —*n.* **1** a written or printed piece of paper or card entitling the holder to enter a place, participate in an event, travel by public transport, use a public amenity, etc. **2** an official notification of a traffic offence etc. (*parking ticket*). **3** *Brit.* a certificate of discharge from the army. **4** a certificate of qualification as a ship's master, pilot, etc. **5** a label attached to a thing and giving its price or other details. **6** esp. *US* **a** a list of candidates put forward by one group esp. a political party. **b** the principles of a party. **7** (prec. by *the*) *colloq.* what is correct or needed. —*v.tr.* (**ticketed, ticketing**) attach a ticket to. □ **ticket office** an office or kiosk where tickets are sold for transport, entertainment, etc. □ **ticketed** *adj.* **ticketless** *adj.* [obs.F *étiquet* f. OF *estiquet(te)* f. *estiquier, estechier* fix f. MDu. *steken*]

ticking /ˈtɪkɪŋ/ *n.* a stout usu. striped material used to cover mattresses etc. [TICK⁴ + -ING¹]

tickle /ˈtɪk(ə)l/ *v. & n.* —*v.* **1 a** *tr.* apply light touches or strokes to (a person or part of a person's body) so as to excite the nerves and usu. produce laughter and spasmodic movement. **b** *intr.* feel this sensation (*my foot tickles*). **2** *tr.* excite agreeably; amuse or divert (a person, a sense of humour, vanity, etc.) (*was highly tickled at the idea*; *this will tickle your fancy*). **3** *tr.* catch (a trout etc.) by rubbing it so that it moves backwards into the hand. —*n.* **1** an act of tickling. **2** a tickling sensation. □ **tickled pink** (or **to death**) *colloq.* extremely amused or pleased. □ **tickler** *n.* **tickly** *adj.* [ME, prob. frequent. of TICK¹]

ticklish /ˈtɪklɪʃ/ *adj.* **1** sensitive to tickling. **2** (of a matter or person to be dealt with) difficult; requiring careful handling. □ **ticklishly** *adv.* **ticklishness** *n.*

tic-tac var. of *tick-tack* (see TICK¹).

tidal /ˈtaɪd(ə)l/ *adj.* relating to, like, or affected by tides (*tidal basin*; *tidal river*). □ **tidal bore** a large wave or bore caused by constriction of the spring tide as it enters a long narrow shallow inlet. **tidal flow** the regulated movement of traffic in opposite directions on the same stretch of road at different times of the day. **tidal wave** 1 *Geog.* an exceptionally large ocean wave esp. one caused by an underwater earthquake or volcanic eruption. 2 a widespread manifestation of feeling etc. □ **tidally** *adv.*

tidbit US var. of TITBIT.

tiddledy-wink US var. of TIDDLY-WINK.

tiddler /ˈtɪdlə(r)/ *n. Brit. colloq.* 1 a small fish, esp. a stickleback or minnow. 2 an unusually small thing or person. [perh. rel. to TIDDLY² and *tittlebat*, a childish form of *stickleback*]

tiddly¹ /ˈtɪdlɪ/ *adj.* (**tiddlier, tiddliest**) esp. *Brit. colloq.* slightly drunk. [19th c., earlier = a drink: orig. unkn.]

tiddly² /ˈtɪdlɪ/ *adj.* (**tiddlier, tiddliest**) *Brit. colloq.* little.

tiddly-wink /ˈtɪdlɪwɪŋk/ *n.* (US **tiddledy-** /ˈtɪdəldɪ-/) 1 a counter flicked with another into a cup etc. 2 (in *pl.*) this game. [19th c.: perh. rel. to TIDDLY¹]

tide *n. & v.* —*n.* 1 **a** the periodic rise and fall of the sea due to the attraction of the moon and sun (see EBB *n.* 1, FLOOD *n.* 3). **b** the water as affected by this. 2 a time or season (usu. in *comb.: Whitsuntide*). 3 a marked trend of opinion, fortune, or events. —*v.intr.* drift with the tide, esp. work in or out of harbour with the help of the tide. □ **tide over** enable or help (a person) to deal with an awkward situation, difficult period, etc. (*the money will tide me over until Friday*). □ **tideless** *adj.* [OE *tīd* f. Gmc, rel. to TIME]

tidemark /ˈtaɪdmɑːk/ *n.* 1 a mark made by the tide at high water. 2 esp. *Brit.* **a** a mark left round a bath at the level of the water in it. **b** a line on a person's body marking the extent to which it has been washed.

tidetable /ˈtaɪdˌteɪb(ə)l/ *n.* a table indicating the times of high and low tides at a place.

tidewater /ˈtaɪdˌwɔːtə(r)/ *n.* 1 water brought by or affected by tides. 2 (*attrib.*) US affected by tides (*tidewater region*).

tideway /ˈtaɪdweɪ/ *n.* 1 a channel in which a tide runs, esp. the tidal part of a river. 2 the ebb or flow in a tidal channel.

tidings /ˈtaɪdɪŋz/ *n.* (as *sing.* or *pl.*) *literary* news, information. [OE *tīdung*, prob. f. ON *títhindi* events f. *tīthr* occurring]

tidy /ˈtaɪdɪ/ *adj., n., & v.* —*adj.* (**tidier, tidiest**) 1 neat, orderly; methodically arranged. 2 (of a person) methodically inclined. 3 *colloq.* considerable (*it cost a tidy sum*). —*n.* (*pl.* **-ies**) 1 a receptacle for holding small objects or waste scraps, esp. in a kitchen sink. 2 an act or spell of tidying. 3 esp. US a detachable ornamental cover for a chair-back etc. —*v.tr.* (**-ies, -ied**) (also *absol.*; often foll. by *up*) put in good order; make (oneself, a room, etc.) tidy. □ **tidily** *adv.* **tidiness** *n.* [ME, = timely etc., f. TIDE + -Y¹]

tie *v. & n.* —*v.* (**tying**) 1 *tr.* attach or fasten with string or cord etc. (*tie the dog to the gate; tie his hands together; tied on a label*). 2 *tr.* **a** form (a string, ribbon, shoelace, necktie, etc.) into a knot or bow. **b** form (a knot or bow) in this way. 3 *tr.* restrict or limit (a person) as to conditions, occupation, place, etc. (*is tied to his family*). 4 *intr.* (often foll. by *with*) achieve the same score or

place as another competitor (*they tied at ten games each; tied with her for first place*). 5 *tr.* hold (rafters etc.) together by a crosspiece etc. 6 *tr. Mus.* **a** unite (written notes) by a tie. **b** perform (two notes) as one unbroken note. —*n.* 1 a cord or chain etc. used for fastening. 2 a strip of material worn round the collar and tied in a knot at the front with the ends hanging down. 3 a thing that unites or restricts persons; a bond or obligation (*family ties; ties of friendship; children are a real tie*). 4 a draw, dead heat, or equality of score among competitors. 5 *Brit.* a match between any pair from a group of competing players or teams. 6 (also **tie-beam** etc.) a rod or beam holding parts of a structure together. 7 *Mus.* a curved line above or below two notes of the same pitch indicating that they are to be played for the combined duration of their time values. □ **fit to be tied** *colloq.* very angry. **tie-break** (or **-breaker**) a means of deciding a winner from competitors who have tied. **tie-dye** (or **tie and dye**) a method of producing dyed patterns by tying string etc. to protect parts of the fabric from the dye. **tie in** (foll. by *with*) bring into or have a close association or agreement. **tie-in** *n.* 1 a connection or association. 2 (often *attrib.*) esp. US a form of sale or advertising that offers or requires more than a single purchase. 3 the joint promotion of related commodities etc. (e.g. a book and a film). **tie-pin** (or **-clip**) an ornamental pin or clip for holding a tie in place. **tie up** 1 bind or fasten securely with cord etc. 2 invest or reserve (capital etc.) so that it is not immediately available for use. 3 moor (a boat). 4 secure (an animal). 5 obstruct; prevent from acting freely. 6 secure or complete (an undertaking etc.). 7 (often foll. by *with*) = **tie in.** 8 (usu. in *passive*) fully occupy (a person). □ **tieless** *adj.* [OE *tīgan*, *tēgan* (v.), *tēah*, *tēg* (n.) f. Gmc]

tied *adj. Brit.* 1 (of a house) occupied subject to the tenant's working for its owner. 2 (of a public house etc.) bound to supply the products of a particular brewery only.

tier /tɪə(r)/ *n.* a row or rank or unit of a structure, as one of several placed one above another (*tiers of seats.* □ **tiered** *adj.* (also in *comb.*). [earlier *tire* f. F f. *tirer* draw, elongate f. Rmc]

tierce /tɪəs/ *n. Eccl.* = TERCE. [ME f. OF *t(i)erce* f. L *tertia* fem. of *tertius* third]

tiercel var. of TERCEL.

tiff *n.* 1 a slight or petty quarrel. 2 a fit of peevishness. [18th c.: orig. unkn.]

tiffin /ˈtɪfɪn/ *n. & v. Ind.* —*n.* a light meal, esp. lunch. —*v.intr.* (**tiffined, tiffining**) take lunch etc. [app. f. *tiffing* sipping]

tig *n.* = TAG². [var. of TICK¹]

tiger /ˈtaɪgə(r)/ *n.* 1 a large Asian flesh-eating feline, *Panthera tigris*, having a yellow-brown coat with black stripes. 2 a fierce, energetic, or formidable person. □ **tiger-cat** 1 any moderate-sized feline resembling the tiger, e.g. the ocelot. **tiger lily** a tall garden lily, *Lilium tigrinum*, with flowers of dull orange spotted with black or purple. **tiger moth** any moth of the family Arctiidae, esp. *Arctia caja*, having richly spotted and streaked wings suggesting a tiger's skin. □ **tigerish** *adj.* **tigerishly** *adv.* [ME f. OF *tigre* f. L *tigris* f. Gk *tigris*]

tight /taɪt/ *adj., n., & adv.* —*adj.* 1 closely held, drawn, fastened, fitting, etc. (*a tight hold; a tight* skirt). **2** closely and firmly put together (*a tight joint*). **3** (of clothes etc.) too closely fitting (*my shoes are rather tight*). **4** impermeable, impervious, esp. (in *comb.*) to a specified thing (*watertight*). **5** tense; stretched so as to leave no slack (*a tight bowstring*). **6** *colloq.* drunk. **7** *colloq.* (of a person) mean, stingy. **8 a** (of money or materials) not easily obtainable. **b** (of a money market) in which money is tight. **9 a** (of precautions, a programme, etc.) stringent, demanding. **b** presenting difficulties (*a tight situation*). **10** produced by or requiring great exertion or pressure (*a tight squeeze*). **11** (of control etc.) strictly imposed. —*adv.* tightly (*hold tight!*). □ **tight corner** (or **place** or **spot**) a difficult situation. **tight-fisted** stingy. **tight-fitting** (of a garment) fitting (often too) close to the body. **tight-lipped** with or as with the lips compressed to restrain emotion or speech. □ **tightly** *adv.* **tightness** *n.* [prob. alt. of *thight* f. ON *théttr* watertight, of close texture]

tighten /ˈtaɪt(ə)n/ *v.tr.* & *intr.* make or become tight or tighter. □ **tighten one's belt** see BELT.

tightrope /ˈtaɪtrəʊp/ *n.* a rope stretched tightly high above the ground, on which acrobats perform.

tights /taɪts/ *n.pl.* **1** a thin close-fitting wool or nylon etc. garment covering the legs and the lower part of the torso, worn by women in place of stockings. **2** a similar garment worn by a dancer, acrobat, etc.

tigress /ˈtaɪgrɪs/ *n.* **1** a female tiger. **2** a fierce or passionate woman.

tike var. of TYKE.

tiki /ˈtɪkɪ/ *n.* (pl. **tikis**) NZ a large wooden or small ornamental greenstone image representing a human figure. [Maori]

tilde /ˈtɪldə/ *n.* a mark (˜), put over a letter, e.g. over a Spanish *n* when pronounced *ny* (as in *señor*) or a Portuguese *a* or *o* when nasalized (as in *São Paulo*). [Sp., ult. f. L *titulus* TITLE]

tile *n.* & *v.* —*n.* **1** a thin slab of concrete or baked clay etc. used in series for covering a roof or pavement etc. **2** a similar slab of glazed pottery, cork, linoleum, etc., for covering a floor, wall, etc. **3** a thin flat piece used in a game (esp. mah-jong). —*v.tr.* cover with tiles. □ **on the tiles** *colloq.* having a spree. [OE *tigule, -ele,* f. L *tegula*]

tiling /ˈtaɪlɪŋ/ *n.* **1** the process of fixing tiles. **2** an area of tiles.

till[1] *prep.* & *conj.* —*prep.* **1** up to or as late as (*wait till six o'clock; did not return till night*). **2** up to the time of (*faithful till death; waited till the end*). —*conj.* **1** up to the time when (*wait till I return*). **2** so long that (*laughed till I cried*). [OE & ON *til* to, rel. to TILL[3]]

till[2] *n.* a drawer for money in a shop or bank etc., esp. with a device recording the amount of each purchase. [ME: orig. unkn.]

till[3] *v.tr.* prepare and cultivate (land) for crops. □ **tillable** *adj.* **tiller** *n.* [OE *tilian* strive for, cultivate, f. Gmc]

tillage /ˈtɪlɪdʒ/ *n.* **1** the preparation of land for crop-bearing. **2** tilled land.

tiller /ˈtɪlə(r)/ *n.* a horizontal bar fitted to the head of a boat's rudder to turn it in steering. [ME f. AF *telier* weaver's beam f. med.L *telarium* f. L *tela* web]

tilt *v.* & *n.* —*v.* **1** *intr.* & *tr.* assume or cause to assume a sloping position; heel over. **2** *intr.* (foll.

by *at*) strike, thrust, or run at, with a weapon, esp. in jousting. **3** *intr.* (foll. by *with*) engage in a contest. —*n.* **1** the act or an instance of tilting. **2** a sloping position. **3** (of medieval knights etc.) the act of charging with a lance against an opponent or at a mark, done for exercise or as a sport. **4** an encounter between opponents; an attack esp. with argument or satire (*have a tilt at*). □ **full** (or **at full**) **tilt 1** at full speed. **2** with full force. □ **tilter** *n.* [ME *tilte* perh. f. an OE form rel. to *tealt* unsteady f. Gmc: weapon senses of unkn. orig.]

tilth /tɪlθ/ *n.* **1** tillage, cultivation. **2** the condition of tilled soil (*in good tilth*). [OE *tilth(e)* (as TILL[3])]

timbale /tãˈbɑːl/ *n.* a drum-shaped dish of minced meat or fish in a pastry shell. [F, earlier *tamballe* f. Sp. *atabal* f. Arab. *aṭ-ṭabl* the drum]

timber /ˈtɪmbə(r)/ *n.* **1** wood prepared for building, carpentry, etc. **2** a piece of wood or beam, esp. as the rib of a vessel. **3** large standing trees suitable for timber; woods or forest. **4** (esp. as *int.*) a warning cry that a tree is about to fall. □ **timber wolf** a type of large N. American grey wolf. □ **timbering** *n.* [OE, = building, f. Gmc]

timbered /ˈtɪmbəd/ *adj.* **1** (esp. of a building) made wholly or partly of timber. **2** (of country) wooded.

timberland /ˈtɪmbəˌlænd/ *n.* US land covered with forest yielding timber.

timberline /ˈtɪmbəˌlaɪn/ *n.* (on a mountain) the line or level above which no trees grow.

timbre /ˈtæmbə(r), ˈtæbrə/ *n.* the distinctive character of a musical sound or voice apart from its pitch and intensity. [F f. Rmc f. med.Gk *timbanon* f. Gk *tumpanon* drum]

time *n.* & *v.* —*n.* **1** the indefinite continued progress of existence, events, etc., in past, present, and future regarded as a whole. **2** the progress of this as affecting persons or things (*stood the test of time*). **3** a more or less definite portion of time belonging to particular events or circumstances (*the time of the Plague; the scientists of the time*). **4** an allotted, available, or measurable portion of time; the period of time at one's disposal (*am wasting my time; how much time do you need?*). **5** a point of time esp. in hours and minutes (*the time is 7.30; what time is it?*). **6** (prec. by *a*) an indefinite period (*waited for a time*). **7** time or an amount of time as reckoned by a conventional standard (*the time allowed is one hour; ran the mile in record time; eight o'clock New York time*). **8 a** an occasion (*last time I saw you*). **b** an event or occasion qualified in some way (*had a good time*). **9** a moment or definite portion of time destined or suitable for a purpose etc. (*now is the time to act; shall we fix a time?*). **10** (in *pl.*) expressing multiplication (*is four times as old; five times six is thirty*). **11** a lifetime (*will last my time*). **12** (in *sing.* or *pl.*) **a** the conditions of life or of a period (*hard times; times have changed*). **b** (prec. by *the*) the present age, or that being considered. **13** *colloq.* a prison sentence (*is doing time*). **14** an apprenticeship (*served his time*). **15** a period of gestation. **16** the date or expected date of childbirth (*is near her time*) or of death (*my time is drawing near*). **17** measured time spent in work (*put them on short time*). **18 a** any of several rhythmic patterns of music (*in waltz time*). **b** the duration of a note as indicated by a crotchet, minim, etc. **19** *Brit.* the moment at which the opening hours of a public house end. —*v.tr.* **1** choose the time or occasion for (*time your remarks carefully*). **2** do at a chosen or correct time. **3** arrange the time of arrival of. **4** ascertain the time taken by (a process or activity, or a person doing it). **5** regulate the duration or interval of; set times for (*trains are timed to arrive every hour*). □ **against time** with utmost speed, so as to finish by a specified time (*working against time*). **ahead of time** earlier than expected. **ahead of one's time** having ideas too enlightened or advanced to be accepted by one's contemporaries. **all the time 1** during the whole of the time referred to (often despite some contrary expectation etc.) (*we never noticed, but he was there all the time*). **2** constantly (*nags all the time*). **3** at all times (*leaves a light on all the time*). **at one time 1** in or during a known but un- specified past period. **2** simultaneously (*ran three businesses at one time*). **at the same time 1** simultaneously; at a time that is the same for all. **2** nevertheless (*at the same time, I do not want to offend you*). **at a time** separately in the specified groups or numbers (*came three at a time*). **at times** occasionally, intermittently. **before time** (usu. prec. by *not*) before the due or expected time. **before one's time** prematurely (*old before his time*). **for the time being** for the present; until some other arrangement is made. **have no time for 1** be unable or unwilling to spend time on. **2** dislike. **have the time 1** be able to spend the time needed. **2** know from a watch etc. what time it is. **have a time of it** undergo trouble or difficulty. **in no** (or **less than no**) **time 1** very soon. **2** very quickly. **in one's own good time** at a time and a rate decided by oneself. **in one's own time** outside working hours. **in time 1** not late, punctual (*was in time to catch the bus*). **2** eventually (*in time you may agree*). **3** in accordance with a given rhythm or tempo, esp. of music. **in one's time** at or during some previous period of one's life (*in his time he was a great hurdler*). **keep good** (or **bad**) **time 1** (of a clock etc.) record time accurately (or inaccurately). **2** be habitually punctual (or not punctual). **keep time** move or sing etc. in time. **know the time of day** be well informed. **lose no time** (often foll. by *in* + verbal noun) act immediately (*lost no time in cashing the cheque*). **not before time** not too soon; timely. **no time** *colloq.* a very short interval (*it was no time before they came*). **out of time** unseasonable; unseasonably. **pass the time of day** *colloq.* exchange a greeting or casual remarks. **time after time 1** repeatedly, on many occasions. **2** in many instances. **time and** (or **time and time**) **again** on many occasions. **time and a half** a rate of payment for work at one and a half times the normal rate. **time-and-motion** (usu. *attrib.*) concerned with measuring the efficiency of industrial and other operations. **time bomb** a bomb designed to explode at a pre-set time. **time capsule** a box etc. containing objects typical of the present time, buried for discovery in the future. **time clock 1** a clock with a device for recording workers' hours of work. **2** a switch mechanism activated at pre-set times by a built-in clock. **time-consuming** using much or too much time. **time exposure** the exposure of photographic film for longer than the maximum normal shutter setting. **time-fuse** a fuse calculated to burn for or explode at a given

time. **time-honoured** esteemed by tradition or through custom. **time immemorial** (or **out of mind**) a longer time than anyone can remember or trace. **time-lag** an interval of time between an event, a cause, etc. and its effect. **time-lapse** (of photography) using frames taken at long intervals to photograph a slow process, and shown continuously as if at normal speed. **time-limit** the limit of time within which a task must be done. **the time of day** the hour by the clock. **time off** time for rest or recreation etc. **the time of one's life** a period or occasion of exceptional enjoyment. **time out** esp. *US* **1** a brief intermission in a game etc. **2** = *time off*. **time-scale** the time allowed for or taken by a sequence of events in relation to a broader period of time. **time-server** a person who changes his or her views to suit the prevailing circumstances, fashion, etc. **time-share** a share in a property under a time-sharing scheme. **time-sharing 1** the operation of a computer system by several users for different operations at one time. **2** the use of a holiday home at agreed different times by several joint owners. **time sheet** a sheet of paper for recording hours of work etc. **time signal** an audible (esp. broadcast) signal or announcement of the exact time of day. **time signature** *Mus.* an indication of tempo following a clef, expressed as a fraction with the numerator giving the number of beats in each bar and the denominator giving the duration of each beat. **time switch** a switch acting automatically at a pre-set time. **time warp** an imaginary distortion of space in relation to time, whereby persons or objects of one age can be moved to another. **time was** there was a time (*time was when I could do that*). **time-worn** impaired by age. **time zone** a range of longitudes where a common standard time is used. [OE *tīma* f. Gmc]

timekeeper /ˈtaɪmˌkiːpə(r)/ *n.* **1** a person who records time, esp. of workers or in a game. **2 a** a watch or clock as regards accuracy (*a good timekeeper*). **b** a person as regards punctuality. □ **timekeeping** *n.*

timeless /ˈtaɪmlɪs/ *adj.* not affected by the passage of time; eternal. □ **timelessly** *adv.* **timelessness** *n.*

timely /ˈtaɪmlɪ/ *adj.* (**timelier, timeliest**) opportune; coming at the right time. □ **timeliness** *n.*

timepiece /ˈtaɪmpiːs/ *n.* an instrument, such as a clock or watch, for measuring time.

timer /ˈtaɪmə(r)/ *n.* **1** a person or device that measures or records time taken. **2** an automatic mechanism for activating a device etc. at a pre-set time.

timetable /ˈtaɪmˌteɪb(ə)l/ *n.* & *v.* —*n.* a list of times at which events are scheduled to take place, esp. the arrival and departure of buses or trains etc., or a sequence of lessons in a school or college. —*v.tr.* include in or arrange to a timetable; schedule.

timid /ˈtɪmɪd/ *adj.* (**timider, timidest**) easily frightened; apprehensive, shy. □ **timidity** /-ˈmɪdɪtɪ/ *n.* **timidly** *adv.* **timidness** *n.* [F *timide* or L *timidus* f. *timēre* fear]

timing /ˈtaɪmɪŋ/ *n.* the way an action or process is timed, esp. in relation to others.

timorous /ˈtɪmərəs/ *adj.* **1** timid; easily alarmed. **2** frightened. □ **timorously** *adv.* **timorousness**

n. [ME f. OF *temoreus* f. med.L *timorosus* f. L *timor* f. *timēre* fear]

timpani /ˈtɪmpənɪ/ *n.pl.* (also **tympani**) kettle-drums. □ **timpanist** *n.* [It., pl. of *timpano* = TYMPANUM]

tin *n.* & *v.* —*n.* **1** *Chem.* a silvery-white malleable metallic element resisting corrosion, used esp. in alloys and for plating thin iron or steel sheets to form tin plate. **2 a** a vessel or container made of tin or tinned iron. **b** *Brit.* an airtight sealed container made of tin plate or aluminium for preserving food. **3** = *tin plate.* —*v.tr.* (**tinned**, **tinning**) **1** seal (food) in an airtight tin for preservation. **2** cover or coat with tin. □ **tin can** a tin container (see sense 2 of *n.*), esp. an empty one. **tin foil** foil made of tin, aluminium, or tin alloy, used for wrapping food for cooking or storing. **tin god 1** an object of unjustified veneration. **2** a self-important person. **tin hat** *colloq.* a military steel helmet. **tin-opener** a tool for opening tins. **tin-pan alley** the world of composers and publishers of popular music. **tin plate** sheet iron or sheet steel coated with tin. **tin-plate** *v.tr.* coat with tin. **tin-tack** an iron tack. [OE f. Gmc]

tincture /ˈtɪŋktʃə(r), -tʃə(r)/ *n.* & *v.* —*n.* (often foll. by *of*) **1** a slight flavour or trace. **2** a tinge (of a colour). **3** a medicinal solution (of a drug) in alcohol (*tincture of quinine*). **4** *colloq.* an alcoholic drink. —*v.tr.* **1** colour slightly; tinge, flavour. **2** (often foll. by *with*) affect slightly (with a quality). [ME f. L *tinctura* dyeing (as TINGE)]

tinder /ˈtɪndə(r)/ *n.* a dry substance such as wood that readily catches fire from a spark. □ **tinder-box** *hist.* a box containing tinder, flint, and steel, formerly used for kindling fires. □ **tindery** *adj.* [OE *tynder*, *tyndre* f. Gmc]

tine *n.* a prong or tooth or point of a fork, comb, antler, etc. □ **tined** *adj.* [OE *tind*]

ting *n.* & *v.* —*n.* a tinkling sound as of a bell. —*v.intr.* & *tr.* emit or cause to emit this sound. [imit.]

tinge /tɪndʒ/ *v.* & *n.* —*v.tr.* (also **tingeing**) (often foll. by *with*; often in *passive*) **1** colour slightly (*is tinged with red*). **2** affect slightly (*regret tinged with satisfaction*). —*n.* **1** a tendency towards or trace of some colour. **2** a slight admixture of a feeling or quality. [ME f. L *tingere tinct-* dye, stain]

tingle /ˈtɪŋɡ(ə)l/ *v.* & *n.* —*v.* **1** *intr.* feel a slight prickling, stinging, or throbbing sensation. **b** cause this (*the reply tingled in my ears*). **2** *tr.* make (the ear etc.) tingle. —*n.* a tingling sensation. [ME, perh. var. of TINKLE]

tingly /ˈtɪŋɡlɪ/ *adj.* (**tinglier**, **tingliest**) causing or characterized by tingling.

tinker /ˈtɪŋkə(r)/ *n.* & *v.* —*n.* **1** an itinerant mender of kettles and pans etc. **2** *Sc.* & *Ir.* a gypsy. **3** *colloq.* a mischievous person or animal. **4** a spell of tinkering. —*v.* **1** *intr.* (foll. by *at*, *with*) work in an amateurish or desultory way, esp. to adjust or mend machinery etc. **2 a** *intr.* work as a tinker. **b** *tr.* repair (pots and pans). □ **tinkerer** *n.* [ME: orig. unkn.]

tinkle /ˈtɪŋk(ə)l/ *v.* & *n.* —*v.intr.* & *tr.* make or cause to make a succession of short light ringing sounds. —*n.* **1** a tinkling sound. **2** *Brit. colloq.* a telephone call (*will give you a tinkle on Monday*). **3** *colloq.* an act of urinating. [ME f. obs. *tink* to chink (imit.)]

tinnitus /tɪˈnaɪtəs/ *n. Med.* a ringing in the ears. [L f. *tinnire tinnit-* ring, tinkle, of imit. orig.]

tinny /ˈtɪnɪ/ *adj.* & *n.* —*adj.* (**tinnier**, **tinniest**) **1** of or like tin. **2** (of a metal object) flimsy, insubstantial. **3 a** sounding like struck tin. **b** (of reproduced sound) thin and metallic, lacking low frequencies. **4** *Austral. sl.* lucky. —*n.* (also **tinnie**) (*pl.* **-ies**) *Austral. sl.* a can of beer. □ **tinnily** *adv.* **tinniness** *n.*

tinpot /ˈtɪnpɒt/ *adj. Brit.* cheap, inferior.

tinsel /ˈtɪns(ə)l/ *n.* & *v.* —*n.* **1** glittering metallic strips, threads, etc., used as decoration to give a sparkling effect. **2** a fabric adorned with tinsel. **3** superficial brilliance or splendour. **4** (*attrib.*) showy, gaudy, flashy. —*v.tr.* (**tinselled**, **tinselling**) adorn with or as with tinsel. □ **tinselled** *adj.* **tinselly** *adj.* [OF *estincele* spark f. L *scintilla*]

tinsmith /ˈtɪnsmɪθ/ *n.* a worker in tin and tin plate.

tinsnips /ˈtɪnsnɪps/ *n.* a pair of clippers for cutting sheet metal.

tint *n.* & *v.* —*n.* **1** a variety of a colour, esp. one made lighter by adding white. **2** a tendency towards or admixture of a different colour (*red with a blue tint*). **3** a faint colour spread over a surface, esp. as a background for printing on. —*v.tr.* apply a tint to; colour. □ **tinter** *n.* [alt. of earlier *tinct* f. L *tinctus* dyeing (as TINGE), perh. infl. by It. *tinto*]

tintinnabulation /ˌtɪntɪˌnæbjʊˈleɪʃ(ə)n/ *n.* a ringing or tinkling of bells. [as L *tintinnabulum* tinkling bell f. *tintinnare* redupl. form of *tinnire* ring]

tiny /ˈtaɪnɪ/ *adj.* (**tinier**, **tiniest**) very small or slight. □ **tinily** *adv.* **tininess** *n.* [obs. *tine*, *tyne* (adj. & n.) small, a little: ME, of unkn. orig.]

-tion /ʃ(ə)n/ *suffix* forming nouns of action, condition, etc. (see -ION, -ATION, -ITION, -UTION). [from or after F -*tion* f. L -*tio -tionis*]

tip¹ *n.* & *v.* —*n.* **1** an extremity or end, esp. of a small or tapering thing (*tips of the fingers*). **2** a small piece or part attached to the end of a thing, e.g. a ferrule on a stick. **3** a leaf-bud of tea. —*v.tr.* (**tipped**, **tipping**) provide with a tip. □ **on the tip of one's tongue** about to be said, esp. after difficulty in recalling to mind. **the tip of the iceberg** a small evident part of something much larger or more significant. □ **tipless** *adj.* **tippy** *adj.* (in sense 3). [ME f. ON *typpi* (n.), *typpa* (v.), *typptr* tipped f. Gmc (rel. to TOP¹): prob. reinforced by MDu. & MLG *tip*]

tip² *v.* & *n.* —*v.* (**tipped**, **tipping**) **1 a** *intr.* lean or slant. **b** *tr.* cause to do this. **2** *tr.* (foll. by *into* etc.) **a** overturn or cause to overbalance (*was tipped into the pond*). **b** discharge the contents of (a container etc.) in this way. —*n.* **1** a slight push or tilt. **2** *Brit.* a place where material (esp. refuse) is tipped. □ **tip the balance** make the critical difference. **tip-up** able to be tipped, e.g. of a seat in a theatre to allow passage past. [17th c.: orig. uncert.]

tip³ *v.* & *n.* —*v.* (**tipped**, **tipping**) (often foll. by *over*, *up*) **1** *tr.* make a small present of money to, esp. for a service given (*have you tipped the porter?*). **2** *tr.* name as the likely winner of a race or contest etc. **3** *tr.* strike or touch lightly. —*n.* **1** a small money present, esp. for a service given. **2** a piece of private or special information, esp. regarding betting or investment. **3** a small or casual piece of advice. □ **tip off** give (a person) a hint or piece of special information or warning, esp. discreetly or confidentially. **tip-off** a hint or warning etc. given discreetly or confidentially. **tip a person the wink** give a person private information. □ **tipper** n. [ME: orig. uncert.]

tipper /ˈtɪpə(r)/ n. (often *attrib*.) a road haulage vehicle that tips at the back to discharge its load.

tippet /ˈtɪpɪt/ n. **1** a covering of fur etc. for the shoulders formerly worn by women. **2** a similar garment worn as part of some official costumes, esp. by the clergy. [ME, prob. f. TIP¹]

tipple /ˈtɪp(ə)l/ v. & n. —v. **1** intr. drink intoxicating liquor habitually. **2** tr. drink (liquor) repeatedly in small amounts. —n. colloq. a drink, esp. a strong one. □ **tippler** n. [ME, back-form. f. *tippler*, of unkn. orig.]

tipstaff /ˈtɪpstɑːf/ n. **1** a sheriff's officer. **2** a metal-tipped staff carried as a symbol of office. [contr. of *tipped staff*, i.e. tipped with metal]

tipster /ˈtɪpstə(r)/ n. a person who gives tips, esp. about betting at horse-races.

tipsy /ˈtɪpsɪ/ adj. (**tipsier, tipsiest**) **1** slightly intoxicated. **2** caused by or showing intoxication (*a tipsy leer*). □ **tipsily** adv. **tipsiness** n. [prob. f. TIP² = inclined to lean, unsteady: for -*sy* cf. FLIMSY, TRICKSY]

tiptoe /ˈtɪptəʊ/ n., v., & adv. —n. the tips of the toes. —v.intr. (**tiptoes, tiptoed, tiptoeing**) walk on tiptoe, or very stealthily. —adv. (also **on tiptoe**) with the heels off the ground and the weight on the balls of the feet.

tiptop /ˈtɪptɒp/ adj., adv., & n. colloq. —adj. & adv. highest in excellence; very best. —n. the highest point of excellence.

TIR abbr. international road transport (esp. with ref. to EC regulations). [F, = *transport international routier*]

tirade /taɪˈreɪd, tɪ-/ n. a long vehement denunciation or declamation. [F, = long speech, f. It. *tirata* volley f. *tirare* pull f. Rmc]

tire¹ v. **1** tr. & intr. make or grow weary. **2** tr. exhaust the patience or interest of; bore. **3** tr. (in passive; foll. by *of*) have had enough of; be fed up with (*was tired of arguing*). [OE *tēorian*, of unkn. orig.]

tire² n. **1** a band of metal placed round the rim of a wheel to strengthen it. **2** US var. of TYRE. [ME, perh. = archaic *tire* head-dress]

tired /ˈtaɪəd/ adj. **1** weary, exhausted; ready for sleep. **2** (of an idea etc.) hackneyed. □ **tiredly** adv. **tiredness** n.

tireless /ˈtaɪəlɪs/ adj. having inexhaustible energy. □ **tirelessly** adv. **tirelessness** n.

tiresome /ˈtaɪəsəm/ adj. **1** wearisome, tedious. **2** colloq. annoying (*how tiresome of you!*). □ **tiresomely** adv. **tiresomeness** n.

tiro /ˈtaɪərəʊ/ n. (also **tyro**) (pl. -**os**) a beginner or novice. [L *tiro*, med.L *tyro*, recruit]

'tis /tɪz/ archaic it is. [contr.]

tisane /tɪˈzæn/ n. an infusion of dried herbs etc. [ME & OF *tizzane* etc. f. L *ptisana* f. Gk *ptisanē* peeled barley]

tissue /ˈtɪʃuː, ˈtɪsjuː/ n. **1** any of the coherent collections of specialized cells of which animals or plants are made (*muscular tissue; nervous tissue*). **2** = *tissue-paper*. **3** a disposable piece of thin soft absorbent paper for wiping, drying, etc. **4** fine woven esp. gauzy fabric. **5** (foll. by *of*) a connected series (*a tissue of lies*). □ **tissue-paper** thin soft unsized paper for wrapping or protecting fragile or delicate articles. [ME f. OF *tissu*

rich material, past part. of *tistre* f. L *texere* weave]

tit¹ n. any of various small birds esp. of the family Paridae. [prob. f. Scand.]

tit² n. □ **tit for tat** blow for blow; retaliation. [= earlier *tip* (TIP²) *for tap*]

tit³ n. **1** colloq. a nipple. **2** coarse sl. a woman's breast. [OE: cf. MLG *titte*]

Titan /ˈtaɪt(ə)n/ n. **1** (often **titan**) a person of very great strength, intellect, or importance. **2** (in Greek mythology) a member of a family of early gigantic gods, the offspring of Heaven and Earth. [ME f. L f. Gk]

titanic /taɪˈtænɪk/ adj. **1** of or like the Titans. **2** gigantic, colossal. □ **titanically** adv. [Gk *titanikos* (as TITAN)]

titanium /taɪˈteɪnɪəm, tɪ-/ n. Chem. a grey metallic element used to make strong light alloys that are resistant to corrosion. [Gk (as TITAN) + -IUM, after *uranium*]

titbit /ˈtɪtbɪt/ n. (US **tidbit** /ˈtɪd-/) **1** a dainty morsel. **2** a piquant item of news etc. [perh. f. dial. *tid* tender + BIT¹]

titch n. (also **tich**) colloq. a small person. [*Tich*, stage name of Harry Relph (d. 1928), Engl. music-hall comedian]

titchy /ˈtɪtʃɪ/ adj. (**titchier, titchiest**) colloq. very small.

titfer /ˈtɪtfə(r)/ n. Brit. sl. a hat. [abbr. of *tit for tat*, rhyming sl.]

tithe /taɪð/ n. & v. —n. **1** one tenth of the annual produce of land or labour, formerly taken as a tax for the support of the Church and clergy. **2** a tenth part. —v. **1** tr. subject to tithes. **2** intr. pay tithes. □ **tithe barn** a barn built to hold tithes paid in kind. □ **tithable** adj. [OE *teogotha* tenth]

Titian /ˈtɪʃ(ə)n/ adj. (in full **Titian red**) (of hair) bright golden auburn. [name of *Tiziano Vecelli*, It. painter d. 1576]

titillate /ˈtɪtɪˌleɪt/ v.tr. **1** excite pleasantly. **2** tickle. □ **titillatingly** adv. **titillation** /-ˈleɪʃ(ə)n/ n. [L *titillare titillat*-]

titivate /ˈtɪtɪˌveɪt/ v.tr. (also **tittivate**) colloq. **1** adorn, smarten. **2** (often *refl*.) put the finishing touches to. □ **titivation** /-ˈveɪʃ(ə)n/ n. [earlier *tidivate*, perh. f. TIDY after *cultivate*]

title /ˈtaɪt(ə)l/ n. & v. —n. **1** the name of a book, work of art, piece of music, etc. **2** the heading of a chapter, poem, document, etc. **3 a** the contents of the title-page of a book. **b** a book regarded in terms of its title (*published 20 new titles*). **4** a caption or credit in a film, broadcast, etc. **5** a form of nomenclature indicating a person's status (e.g. *professor, queen*) or used as a form of address or reference (e.g. *Lord, Mr, Your Grace*). **6** a championship in sport. **7** Law **a** the right to ownership of property with or without possession. **b** the facts constituting this. **c** (foll. by *to*) a just or recognized claim. —v.tr. give a title to. □ **title-deed** a legal instrument as evidence of a right, esp. to property. **title-page** a page at the beginning of a book giving the title and particulars of authorship etc. **title role** the part in a play etc. that gives it its name (e.g. *Othello*). [ME f. OF f. L *titulus* placard, title]

titled /ˈtaɪt(ə)ld/ adj. having a title of nobility or rank.

titmouse /ˈtɪtmaʊs/ n. (pl. **titmice** /-maɪs/) any of various small tits, esp. of the genus *Parus*. [ME *titmōse* f. TIT¹ + OE *māse* titmouse, assim. to MOUSE]

titrate /ˈtaɪtreɪt, ˈtɪ-/ v.tr. *Chem.* ascertain the amount of a constituent in (a solution) by measuring the volume of a known concentration of reagent required to complete the reaction. □ **titratable** adj. **titration** /-ˈtreɪʃ(ə)n/ n. [F *titre* TITLE]

titter /ˈtɪtə(r)/ v. & n. —v.intr. laugh in a furtive or restrained way; giggle. —n. a furtive or restrained laugh. □ **titterer** n. **titteringly** adv. [imit.]

tittle /ˈtɪt(ə)l/ n. 1 a small written or printed stroke or dot. 2 a particle; a whit (esp. in *not one jot or tittle*). [ME f. L (as TITLE)]

tittle-tattle /ˈtɪt(ə)lˌtæt(ə)l/ n. & v. —n. petty gossip. —v.intr. gossip, chatter. [redupl. of TATTLE]

tittup /ˈtɪtəp/ v. & n. —v.intr. (**tittuped, tittuping** or **tittupped, tittupping**) go about friskily or jerkily; bob up and down; canter. —n. such a gait or movement. [perh. imit. of hoof-beats]

titty /ˈtɪtɪ/ n. (pl. **-ies**) sl. = TIT³ (esp. as a child's term).

titular /ˈtɪtjʊlə(r)/ adj. 1 of or relating to a title (*the book's titular hero*). 2 existing, or being what is specified, in name or title only (*titular ruler; titular sovereignty*). □ **titularly** adv. [F *titulaire* or mod.L *titularis* f. *titulus* TITLE]

tizzy /ˈtɪzɪ/ n. (pl. **-ies**) (also **tizz, tiz**) colloq. a state of nervous agitation (*in a tizzy*). [20th c.: orig. unkn.]

T-junction /ˈtiːˌdʒʌŋkʃ(ə)n/ n. a road junction at which one road joins another at right angles without crossing it.

Tl symb. *Chem.* the element thallium.

Tm symb. *Chem.* the element thulium.

TNT abbr. trinitrotoluene, a high explosive formed from toluene.

to /tə, *before a vowel* tʊ, *emphat.* tuː/ prep. & adv. —prep. 1 introducing a noun: **a** expressing what is reached, approached, or touched (*fell to the ground; went to Paris; put her face to the window; five minutes to six*). **b** expressing what is aimed at: often introducing the indirect object of a verb (*throw it to me; explained the problem to them*). **c** as far as; up to (*went on to the end; have to stay from Tuesday to Friday; am sorry to hear that*). **d** to the extent of (*were all drunk to a man; was starved to death*). **e** expressing what is followed (*according to instructions; made to order*). **f** expressing what is considered or affected (*am used to that; that is nothing to me*). **g** expressing what is caused or produced (*turn to stone; tear to shreds*). **h** expressing what is compared (*nothing to what it once was; comparable to any other; equal to the occasion; won by three goals to two*). **i** expressing what is increased (*add it to mine*). **j** expressing what is involved or composed as specified (*there is nothing to it; more to him than meets the eye*). **k** expressing the substance of a debit entry in accounting (*to four chairs, sixty pounds*). 2 introducing the infinitive: **a** as a verbal noun (*to get there is the priority*). **b** expressing purpose, consequence, or cause (*we eat to live; left him to starve; am sorry to hear that*). **c** as a substitute for *to* + infinitive (*wanted to come but was unable to*). —adv. 1 in the normal or required position or condition (*come to; heave to*). 2 (of a door) in a nearly closed position. □ **to and fro 1** backwards and forwards. 2 repeatedly between the same points. [OE *tō* (adv. & prep.) f. WG]

toad n. 1 any froglike amphibian of the family Bufonidae, esp. of the genus *Bufo*, breeding in water but living chiefly on land. 2 any of various similar amphibians. 3 a repulsive or detestable person. □ **toad-in-the-hole** *Brit.* sausages or other meat baked in batter. □ **toadish** adj. [OE *tādige, tādde, tāda*, of unkn. orig.]

toadflax /ˈtəʊdflæks/ n. 1 any plant of the genus *Linaria* or *Chaenorrhinum*, with flaxlike leaves and spurred yellow or purple flowers. 2 a related plant, *Cymbalaria muralis*, with lilac flowers and ivy-shaped leaves.

toadstool /ˈtəʊdstuːl/ n. the spore-bearing structure of various fungi, usu. poisonous, with a round top and slender stalk.

toady /ˈtəʊdɪ/ n. & v. —n. (pl. **-ies**) a sycophant; an obsequious hanger-on. —v.tr. & (foll. by *to*) intr. (**-ies, -ied**) behave servilely to; fawn upon. □ **toadyish** adj. **toadyism** n. [contr. of *toad-eater*, a charlatan's attendant who ate toads (regarded as poisonous)]

toast n. & v. —n. 1 bread in slices browned on both sides by radiant heat. 2 **a** a person (orig. esp. a woman) or thing in whose honour a company is requested to drink. **b** a call to drink or an instance of drinking in this way. —v. 1 tr. cook or brown (bread, a teacake, cheese, etc.) by radiant heat. 2 intr. (of bread etc.) become brown in this way. 3 tr. warm (one's feet, oneself, etc.) at a fire etc. 4 tr. drink to the health or in honour of (a person or thing). □ **toasting-fork** a long-handled fork for making toast before a fire. **toast rack** a rack for holding slices of toast at table. [ME (orig. as verb) f. OF *toster* roast, ult. f. L *torrēre tost-* parch: sense 2 of the noun reflects the notion that a woman's name flavours the drink as spiced toast would]

toaster /ˈtəʊstə(r)/ n. an electrical device for making toast.

toastmaster /ˈtəʊstˌmɑːstə(r)/ n. (fem. **toastmistress** /-ˌmɪstrɪs/) an official responsible for announcing toasts at a public occasion.

tobacco /təˈbækəʊ/ n. (pl. **-os**) 1 (in full **tobacco-plant**) any plant of the genus *Nicotiana*, of American origin, with narcotic leaves used for smoking, chewing, or snuff. 2 its leaves, esp. as prepared for smoking. [Sp. *tabaco*, of Amer. Ind. orig.]

tobacconist /təˈbækənɪst/ n. a retail dealer in tobacco and cigarettes etc.

toboggan /təˈbɒgən/ n. & v. —n. a long light narrow sledge for sliding downhill esp. over compacted snow or ice. —v.intr. ride on a toboggan. □ **tobogganer** n. **tobogganing** n. **tobogganist** n. [Can. F *tabaganne* f. Algonquian]

toby jug /ˈtəʊbɪ/ n. a jug or mug for ale etc., usu. in the form of a stout old man wearing a three-cornered hat. [familiar form of the name *Tobias*]

toccata /təˈkɑːtə/ n. a musical composition for a keyboard instrument designed to exhibit the performer's touch and technique. [It., fem. past part. of *toccare* touch]

tocopherol /ˌtəʊkəʊˈfiərɒl/ n. any of several closely related vitamins, found in wheat-germ oil, egg yolk, and leafy vegetables, and important in the stabilization of cell membranes etc. [Gk *tokos* offspring + *pherō* bear + -OL¹]

tocsin /ˈtɒksɪn/ n. an alarm bell or signal. [F f. OF *touquesain, toquassen* f. Prov. *tocasenh* f. *tocar* TOUCH + *senh* signal-bell]

tod *n. Brit. sl.* □ **on one's tod** alone; on one's own. [20th c.: perh. f. rhyming sl. *on one's Tod Sloan* (name of a jockey)]

today /təˈdeɪ/ *adv. & n.* —*adv.* **1** on or in the course of this present day (*shall we go today?*). **2** nowadays, in modern times. —*n.* **1** this present day (*today is my birthday*). **2** modern times. □ **today week** (or **fortnight** etc.) a week (or fortnight etc.) from today. [OE *tō dæg* on (this) day (as TO, DAY)]

toddle /ˈtɒd(ə)l/ *v. & n.* —*v.intr.* **1** walk with short unsteady steps like those of a small child. **2** *colloq.* **a** (often foll. by *round, to,* etc.) take a casual or leisurely walk. **b** (usu. foll. by *off*) depart. —*n.* **1** a toddling walk. **2** *colloq.* a stroll or short walk. [16th-c. *todle* (Sc. & N.Engl.), of unkn. orig.]

toddler /ˈtɒdlə(r)/ *n.* a child who is just beginning to walk. □ **toddlerhood** *n.*

toddy /ˈtɒdɪ/ *n.* (*pl.* **-ies**) **1** a drink of spirits with hot water and sugar or spices. **2** the sap of some kinds of palm, fermented to produce arrack. [Hind. *tāṛī* f. *tāṛ* palm f. Skr. *tāla*]

to-do /təˈduː/ *n.* a commotion or fuss. [*to do* as in *what's to do* (= to be done)]

toe *n. & v.* —*n.* **1** any of the five terminal projections of the foot. **2** the corresponding part of an animal. **3** the part of an item of footwear that covers the toes. **4** the lower end or tip of an implement etc. —*v.* (**toes, toed, toeing**) *tr.* touch (a starting-line etc.) with the toes before starting a race. □ **on one's toes** alert, eager. **toe-clip** a clip on a bicycle-pedal to prevent the foot from slipping. **toe-hold 1** a small foothold. **2** a small beginning or advantage. **toe the line** conform to a general policy or principle, esp. unwillingly or under pressure. **turn up one's toes** *colloq.* die. □ **toed** *adj.* (also in *comb.*). **toeless** *adj.* [OE *tā* f. Gmc]

toecap /ˈtəʊkæp/ *n.* the (usu. strengthened) outer covering of the toe of a boot or shoe.

toenail /ˈtəʊneɪl/ *n.* **1** the nail at the tip of each toe. **2** a nail driven obliquely through the end of a board etc.

toerag /ˈtəʊræg/ *n. Brit. sl.* a term of contempt for a person. [earlier = tramp, vagrant, f. the rag wrapped round the foot in place of a sock]

toff *n. Brit. sl.* a distinguished or well-dressed person; a dandy. [perh. a perversion of *tuft* = titled undergraduate (from the gold tassel formerly worn on the cap)]

toffee /ˈtɒfɪ/ *n.* (also **toffy**) (*pl.* **toffees** or **toffies**) **1** a kind of firm or hard sweet softening when sucked or chewed, made by boiling sugar, butter, etc. **2** *Brit.* a small piece of this. □ **for toffee** *sl.* (prec. by *can't* etc.) (denoting incompetence) at all (*they couldn't sing for toffee*). **toffee-apple** an apple with a thin coating of toffee. **toffee-nosed** esp. *Brit. sl.* snobbish, pretentious. [earlier TAFFY]

tofu /ˈtəʊfuː/ *n.* (esp. in China and Japan) a curd made from mashed soya beans. [Jap. *tōfu* f. Chin., = rotten beans]

tog[1] *n. & v. colloq.* —*n.* (usu. in *pl.*) an item of clothing. —*v.tr. & intr.* (**togged, togging**) (foll. by *out, up*) dress, esp. elaborately. [app. abbr. of 16th-c. cant *togeman(s)*, *togman*, f. F *toge* or L *toga*: see TOGA]

tog[2] *n.* a unit of thermal resistance used to express the insulating properties of clothes and quilts. [arbitrary, prob. f. TOG[1]]

toga /ˈtəʊgə/ *n. hist.* an ancient Roman citizen's loose flowing outer garment. □ **togaed** *adj.* (also **toga'd**). [L, rel. to *tegere* cover]

together /təˈgeðə(r)/ *adv. & adj.* —*adv.* **1** in company or conjunction (*walking together; built it together; were at school together*). **2** simultaneously; at the same time (*both shouted together*). **3** one with another (*were talking together*). **4** into conjunction; so as to unite (*tied them together; put two and two together*). **5** into company or companionship (*came together in friendship*). **6** uninterruptedly (*could talk for hours together*). —*adj. colloq.* well organized or controlled. □ **together with** as well as; and also. [OE *tōgædere* f. TO + *gædre* together: cf. GATHER]

togetherness /təˈgeðənɪs/ *n.* **1** the condition of being together. **2** a feeling of comfort from being together.

toggle /ˈtɒg(ə)l/ *n. & v.* —*n.* **1** a device for fastening (esp. a garment), consisting of a crosspiece which can pass through a hole or loop in one position but not in another. **2** *Computing* a switch action that is operated the same way but with opposite effect on successive occasions. —*v.tr.* provide or fasten with a toggle. [18th-c. Naut.: orig. unkn.]

toil *v. & n.* —*v.intr.* **1** work laboriously or incessantly. **2** make slow painful progress (*toiled along the path*). —*n.* prolonged or intensive labour; drudgery. □ **toiler** *n.* [ME f. AF *toiler* (v.), *toil* (n.), dispute, OF *tooilier, tooil,* f. L *tudiculare* stir about f. *tudicula* machine for bruising olives, rel. to *tundere* beat]

toilet /ˈtɔɪlɪt/ *n.* **1** = LAVATORY. **2** the process of washing oneself, dressing, etc. (*make one's toilet*). □ **toilet paper** (or **tissue**) paper for cleaning oneself after excreting. **toilet roll** a roll of toilet paper. **toilet soap** soap for washing oneself. **toilet-training** the training of a young child to use the lavatory. **toilet water** a dilute form of perfume used after washing. [F *toilette* cloth, wrapper, dimin. f. *toile* cloth f. L *tela* web]

toiletry /ˈtɔɪlɪtrɪ/ *n.* (*pl.* **-ies**) (usu. in *pl.*) any of various articles or cosmetics used in washing, dressing, etc.

toilette /twɑːˈlet/ *n.* = TOILET 2. [F: see TOILET]

toils *n.pl.* a net or snare. [pl. of *toil* f. OF *toile* cloth f. L *tela* web]

toilsome /ˈtɔɪlsəm/ *adj.* involving toil; laborious. □ **toilsomely** *adv.* **toilsomeness** *n.*

toing and froing /ˌtuːɪŋ ənd ˈfrəʊɪŋ/ *n.* constant movement to and fro; bustle; dispersed activity. [TO *adv.* + FRO + -ING[1]]

token /ˈtəʊkən/ *n. & adj.* —*n.* **1** a thing serving as a symbol, reminder, or distinctive mark of something (*as a token of affection; in token of my esteem*). **2** a thing serving as evidence of authenticity or as a guarantee. **3** a voucher exchangeable for goods (often of a specified kind), given as a gift. **4** anything used to represent something else, esp. a metal disc etc. used instead of money in coin-operated machines etc. **5** (*attrib.*) **a** nominal or perfunctory (*token effort*). **b** conducted briefly to demonstrate strength of feeling (*token resistance; token strike*). **c** serving to acknowledge a principle only (*token payment*). **d** chosen by way of tokenism to represent a particular group (*the token woman on the committee*). □ **by this** (or **the same**) **token 1**

similarly. **2** moreover. [OE *tāc(e)n* f. Gmc, rel. to TEACH]

tokenism /ˈtəʊkəˌnɪz(ə)m/ *n.* **1** esp. *Polit.* the principle or practice of granting minimum concessions, esp. to appease radical demands etc. **2** making only a token effort.

told *past* and *past part.* of TELL.

tolerable /ˈtɒlərəb(ə)l/ *adj.* **1** able to be endured. **2** fairly good; mediocre. □ **tolerability** /-ˈbɪlɪtɪ/ *n.* **tolerableness** *n.* **tolerably** *adv.* [ME f. OF f. L *tolerabilis* (as TOLERATE)]

tolerance /ˈtɒlərəns/ *n.* **1** a willingness or ability to tolerate; forbearance. **2** the capacity to tolerate. **3** an allowable variation in any measurable property. **4** the ability to tolerate the effects of a drug etc. after continued use. [ME f. OF f. L *tolerantia* (as TOLERATE)]

tolerant /ˈtɒlərənt/ *adj.* **1** disposed or accustomed to tolerate others or their acts or opinions. **2** (foll. by *of*) enduring or patient. □ **tolerantly** *adv.* [F *tolérant* f. L *tolerare* (as TOLERATE)]

tolerate /ˈtɒləˌreɪt/ *v.tr.* **1** allow the existence or occurrence of without authoritative interference. **2** leave unmolested. **3** endure or permit, esp. with forbearance. **4** sustain or endure (suffering etc.). **5** be capable of continued subjection to (a drug, radiation, etc.) without harm. **6** find or treat as endurable. □ **tolerator** *n.* [L *tolerare tolerat-* endure]

toleration /ˌtɒləˈreɪʃ(ə)n/ *n.* the process or practice of tolerating, esp. the allowing of differences in religious opinion without discrimination. [F *tolération* f. L *toleratio* (as TOLERATE)]

toll¹ /təʊl/ *n.* **1** a charge payable for permission to pass a barrier or use a bridge or road etc. **2** the cost or damage caused by a disaster, battle, etc., or incurred in an achievement (*death toll*). □ **take its toll** be accompanied by loss or injury etc. **toll-bridge** a bridge at which a toll is charged. **toll-gate** a gate preventing passage until a toll is paid. **toll-road** a road maintained by the tolls collected on it. [OE f. med.L *toloneum* f. LL *teloneum* f. Gk *telōnion* toll-house f. *telos* tax]

toll² /təʊl/ *v.* & *n.* —*v.* **1 a** *intr.* (of a bell) sound with a slow uniform succession of strokes. **b** *tr.* ring (a bell) in this way. **c** *tr.* (of a bell) announce or mark (a death etc.) in this way. **2** *tr.* strike (the hour). —*n.* **1** the act of tolling. **2** a stroke of a bell. [ME, special use of (now dial.) *toll* entice, pull, f. an OE root *-tyllan* (recorded in *fortyllan* seduce)]

tolu /təˈluː, ˈtɒluː/ *n.* a fragrant brown balsam obtained from either of two South American trees, *Myroxylon balsamum* or *M. toluifera*, and used in perfumery and medicine. [Santiago de *Tolu* in Colombia]

toluene /ˈtɒljʊˌiːn/ *n.* a colourless aromatic liquid hydrocarbon derivative of benzene, orig. obtained from tolu, used in the manufacture of explosives etc. □ **toluic** *adj.* **toluol** *n.* [TOLU + -ENE]

tom *n.* a male of various animals, esp. (in full **tom-cat**) a male cat. [abbr. of the name *Thomas*]

tomahawk /ˈtɒməˌhɔːk/ *n.* & *v.* —*n.* **1** a N. American Indian war-axe with a stone or iron head. **2** *Austral.* a hatchet. —*v.tr.* strike, cut, or kill with a tomahawk. [Renape *tämähāk* f. *tämäham* he hit etc. cuts]

tomato /təˈmɑːtəʊ/ *n.* (*pl.* **-oes**) **1** a glossy red or yellow pulpy edible fruit. **2** a plant, *Lycopersicon*

esculentum, bearing this. □ **tomatoey** *adj.* [17th-c. *tomate*, = F or Sp. & Port., f. Mex. *tomatl*]

tomb /tuːm/ *n.* **1** a large esp. underground vault for the burial of the dead. **2** an enclosure cut in the earth or in rock to receive a dead body. **3** a sepulchral monument. **4** (prec. by *the*) the state of death. [ME t(o)*umbe* f. AF *tumbe*, OF *tombe* f. LL *tumba* f. Gk *tumbos*]

tombola /tɒmˈbəʊlə/ *n. Brit.* a kind of lottery with tickets usu. drawn from a turning drum-shaped container, esp. at a fête or fair. [F *tombola* or It. f. *tombolare* tumble]

tomboy /ˈtɒmbɔɪ/ *n.* a girl who behaves in a rough boyish way. □ **tomboyish** *adj.* **tomboyishness** *n.*

tombstone /ˈtuːmstəʊn/ *n.* a stone standing or laid over a grave, usu. with an epitaph.

Tom, Dick, and Harry /ˌtɒm dɪk ənd ˈhærɪ/ *n.* (usu. prec. by *any*, *every*) usu. *derog.* ordinary people taken at random.

tome *n.* a large heavy book or volume. [F f. L *tomus* f. Gk *tomos* section, volume f. *temnō* cut]

tomfool /tɒmˈfuːl/ *n.* **1** a foolish person. **2** (*attrib.*) silly, foolish (*a tomfool idea*).

tomfoolery /tɒmˈfuːlərɪ/ *n.* (*pl.* **-ies**) **1** foolish behaviour; nonsense. **2** an instance of this.

Tommy /ˈtɒmɪ/ *n.* (*pl.* **-ies**) *colloq.* a British private soldier. [*Tommy (Thomas) Atkins*, a name used in specimens of completed official forms]

tommy-gun /ˈtɒmɪˌgʌn/ *n.* a type of sub-machine-gun. [J. T. *Thompson*, US Army officer d. 1940, its co-inventor]

tommy-rot /ˈtɒmɪˌrɒt/ *n. sl.* nonsense.

tomogram /ˈtɒməˌgræm/ *n.* a record obtained by tomography.

tomography /təˈmɒgrəfɪ/ *n.* a method of radiography displaying details in a selected plane within the body. [Gk *tomē* a cutting + -GRAPHY]

tomorrow /təˈmɒrəʊ/ *adv.* & *n.* —*adv.* **1** on the day after today. **2** at some future time. —*n.* **1** the day after today. **2** the near future. □ **tomorrow morning** (or **afternoon** etc.) in the morning (or afternoon etc.) of tomorrow. **tomorrow week** a week from tomorrow. [TO + MORROW: cf. TODAY]

Tom Thumb /tɒm ˈθʌm/ *n.* **1** a dwarf or midget. **2** a dwarf variety of various plants. [the name of a tiny person in fairy stories]

tomtit /ˈtɒmtɪt/ *n.* a tit, esp. a blue tit.

tom-tom /ˈtɒmtɒm/ *n.* **1** a primitive drum beaten with the hands. **2** a tall drum beaten with the hands and used in jazz bands etc. [Hindi *tamtam*, imit.]

-tomy /təmɪ/ *comb. form* forming nouns denoting cutting, esp. in surgery (*laparotomy*). [Gk *-tomia* cutting f. *temnō* cut]

ton /tʌn/ *n.* **1** (in full **long ton**) a unit of weight equal to 2,240 lb. avoirdupois (1016.05 kg). **2** (in full **short ton**) a unit of weight equal to 2,000 lb. avoirdupois (907.19 kg). **3** (in full **metric ton**) = TONNE. **4 a** (in full **displacement ton**) a unit of measurement of a ship's weight or volume in terms of its displacement of water with the loadline just immersed, equal to 2,240 lb. or 35 cu. ft. (0.99 cubic metres). **b** (in full **freight ton**) a unit of weight or volume of cargo, equal to a metric ton (1,000 kg) or 40 cu. ft. **5** (usu. in *pl.*) *colloq.* a large number or amount (*tons of money*). **6** esp. *Brit. sl.* **a** a speed of 100 m.p.h. **b** a sum of £100. **c** a score of 100. □

ton-up *Brit. sl. n.* a speed of 100 m.p.h. —*attrib.adj.* **1** (of a motor cyclist) achieving this, esp. habitually and recklessly (*ton-up kid*). **2** fond or capable of travelling at high speed. **weigh a ton** *colloq.* be very heavy. [orig. the same word as TUN: differentiated in the 17th c.]

tonal /ˈtəʊn(ə)l/ *adj.* **1** of or relating to tone or tonality. **2** (of a fugue etc.) having repetitions of the subject at different pitches in the same key. □ **tonally** *adv.* [med.L *tonalis* (as TONE)]

tonality /təˈnælɪtɪ/ *n. (pl. -ies)* **1** *Mus.* **a** the relationship between the tones of a musical scale. **b** the observance of a single tonic key as the basis of a composition. **2** the tone or colour scheme of a picture.

tone *n. & v.* —*n.* **1** a musical or vocal sound, esp. with reference to its pitch, quality, and strength. **2** (often in *pl.*) modulation of the voice expressing a particular feeling or mood (*a cheerful tone*; *suspicious tones*). **3** a manner of expression in writing. **4** *Mus.* **a** a musical sound, esp. of a definite pitch and character. **b** an interval of a major second, e.g. C–D. **5 a** the general effect of colour or of light and shade in a picture. **b** the tint or shade of a colour. **6 a** the prevailing character of the morals and sentiments etc. in a group. **b** an attitude or sentiment expressed esp. in a letter etc. **7** the proper firmness of bodily organs. **8** a state of good or specified health or quality. **9** *Phonet.* **a** an accent on one syllable of a word. **b** a way of pronouncing a word to distinguish it from others of a similar sound (*Mandarin Chinese has four tones*). —*v.* **1** *tr.* give the desired tone to. **2** *tr.* modify the tone of. **3** *intr.* (often foll. by *to*) attune. **4** *intr.* (foll. by *with*) be in harmony (esp. of colour) (*does not tone with the wallpaper*). □ **tone-arm** the movable arm supporting the pick-up of a record-player. **tone control** a switch for varying the proportion of high and low frequencies in reproduced sound. **tone-deaf** unable to perceive differences of musical pitch accurately. **tone down 1** make or become softer in tone of sound or colour. **2** make (a statement etc.) less harsh or emphatic. **tone poem** = *symphonic poem*. **tone up 1** make or become stronger in tone of sound or colour. **2** make (a statement etc.) more emphatic. □ **toneless** *adj.* **tonelessly** *adv.* **toner** *n.* [ME f. OF *ton* or L *tonus* f. Gk *tonos* tension, tone f. *teinō* stretch]

tongs *n.pl.* (also **pair of tongs** *sing.*) an instrument with two hinged or sprung arms for grasping and holding. [pl. of *tong* f. OE *tang(e)* f. Gmc]

tongue /tʌŋ/ *n.* **1** the fleshy muscular organ in the mouth used in tasting, licking, and swallowing, and (in man) for speech. **2** the tongue of an ox etc. as food. **3** the faculty of or a tendency in speech (*a sharp tongue*). **4** a particular language (*the German tongue*). **5** a thing like a tongue in shape or position, esp.: **a** a long low promontory. **b** a strip of leather etc., attached at one end only, under the laces in a shoe. **c** the clapper of a bell. **d** the pin of a buckle. **e** the projecting strip on a wooden etc. board fitting into the groove of another. **f** a jet of flame. □ **find (or lose) one's tongue** be able (or unable) to express oneself after a shock etc. **the gift of tongues** the power of speaking in unknown languages, regarded as one of the gifts of the Holy Spirit (Acts 2). **keep a civil**

tongue in one's head avoid rudeness. **tongue-and-groove** applied to boards in which a tongue along one edge fits into a groove along the edge of the next, each board having a tongue on one edge and a groove on the other. **tongue-in-cheek** *adj.* ironic; slyly humorous. —*adv.* insincerely or ironically. **tongue-lashing** a severe scolding or reprimand. **tongue-tied** too shy or embarrassed to speak. **tongue-twister** a sequence of words difficult to pronounce quickly and correctly. **with one's tongue hanging out** eagerly or expectantly. **with one's tongue in one's cheek** insincerely or ironically. □ **tongued** *adj.* (also in *comb.*). **tongueless** *adj.* [OE *tunge* f. Gmc, rel. to L *lingua*]

tonguing /ˈtʌŋɪŋ/ *n. Mus.* the technique of playing a wind instrument using the tongue to articulate certain notes.

tonic /ˈtɒnɪk/ *n. & adj.* —*n.* **1** an invigorating medicine. **2** anything serving to invigorate. **3** = *tonic water*. **4** *Mus.* the first degree of a scale, forming the keynote of a piece. —*adj.* **1** serving as a tonic; invigorating. **2** *Mus.* denoting the first degree of a scale. □ **tonic sol-fa** *Mus.* a system of notation used esp. in teaching singing, with doh as the keynote of all major keys and lah as the keynote of all minor keys. **tonic water** a carbonated mineral water containing quinine. □ **tonically** *adv.* [F *tonique* f. Gk *tonikos* (as TONE)]

tonicity /təˈnɪsɪtɪ/ *n.* **1** the state of being tonic. **2** a healthy elasticity of muscles etc.

tonight /təˈnaɪt/ *adv. & n.* —*adv.* on the present or approaching evening or night. —*n.* the evening or night of the present day. [TO + NIGHT: cf. TODAY]

tonnage /ˈtʌnɪdʒ/ *n.* **1** a ship's internal cubic capacity or freight-carrying capacity measured in tons. **2** the total carrying capacity esp. of a country's mercantile marine. **3** a charge per ton on freight or cargo. [orig. in sense 'duty on a tun of wine': OF *tonnage* f. *tonne* TUN: later f. TON]

tonne /tʌn/ *n.* a metric ton equal to 1,000 kg. [F: see TUN]

tonsil /ˈtɒns(ə)l, -sɪl/ *n.* either of two small masses of lymphoid tissue on each side of the root of the tongue. □ **tonsillar** *adj.* [F *tonsilles* or L *tonsillae* (pl.)]

tonsillectomy /ˌtɒnsɪˈlektəmɪ/ *n. (pl. -ies)* the surgical removal of the tonsils.

tonsillitis /ˌtɒnsɪˈlaɪtɪs/ *n.* inflammation of the tonsils.

tonsorial /tɒnˈsɔːrɪəl/ *adj. usu. joc.* of or relating to a hairdresser or hairdressing. [L *tonsorius* f. *tonsor* barber f. *tondēre tons-* shave]

tonsure /ˈtɒnsjə(r), ˈtɒnʃə(r)/ *n. & v.* —*n.* **1** the shaving of the crown of the head or the entire head, esp. of a person entering a priesthood or monastic order. **2** a bare patch made in this way. —*v.tr.* give a tonsure to. [ME f. OF *tonsure* or L *tonsura* (as TONSORIAL)]

too /tuː/ *adv.* **1** to a greater extent than is desirable, permissible, or possible for a specified or understood purpose (*too colourful for my taste*; *too large to fit*). **2** *colloq.* extremely (*you're too kind*). **3** in addition (*are they coming too?*). **4** moreover (*we must consider, too, the time of year*). □ **none too 1** rather less than (*feeling none too good*). **2** barely. [stressed form of TO, f. 16th-c. spelling *too*]

took *past* of TAKE.

tool /tuːl/ n. & v. —n. **1** any device or implement used to carry out mechanical functions whether manually or by a machine. **2** a thing used in an occupation or pursuit (*the tools of one's trade*; *literary tools*). **3** a person used as a mere instrument by another. —v.tr. **1** dress (stone) with a chisel. **2** impress a design on (a leather book-cover). **3** (foll. by *along*, *around*, etc.) *sl.* drive or ride, esp. in a casual or leisurely manner. **4** (often foll. by *up*) equip with tools. □ **tool-pusher** a worker directing the drilling on an oil rig. **tool up 1** *sl.* arm oneself. **2** equip oneself. □ **tooler** n. [OE *tōl* f. Gmc]

tooling /ˈtuːlɪŋ/ n. **1** the process of dressing stone with a chisel. **2** the ornamentation of a book-cover with designs impressed by heated tools.

toot /tuːt/ n. & v. —n. **1** a short sharp sound as made by a horn, trumpet, or whistle. **2** *US sl.* cocaine or a snort of cocaine. —v. **1** *tr.* sound (a horn etc.) with a short sharp sound. **2** *intr.* give out such a sound. □ **tooter** n. [prob. f. MLG *tūten*, or imit.]

tooth /tuːθ/ n. (pl. **teeth** /tiːθ/) **1** each of a set of hard bony enamel-coated structures in the jaws of most vertebrates, used for biting and chewing. **2** a toothlike part or projection, e.g. the cog of a gearwheel, the point of a saw or comb, etc. **3** (often foll. by *for*) one's sense of taste; an appetite or liking. **4** (in *pl.*) force or effectiveness (*the penalties give the contract teeth*). □ **armed to the teeth** completely and elaborately armed or equipped. **fight tooth and nail** fight very fiercely. **get one's teeth into** devote oneself seriously to. **in the teeth of 1** in spite of (opposition or difficulty etc.). **2** contrary to (instructions etc.). **3** directly against (the wind etc.). **tooth-comb** = *fine-tooth comb*. **tooth powder** powder for cleaning the teeth. □ **toothed** adj. (also in *comb.*). **toothless** adj. **toothlike** adj. [OE *tōth* (pl. *tēth*) f. Gmc]

toothache /ˈtuːθeɪk/ n. a (usu. prolonged) pain in a tooth or teeth.

toothbrush /ˈtuːθbrʌʃ/ n. a brush for cleaning the teeth.

toothpaste /ˈtuːθpeɪst/ n. a paste for cleaning the teeth.

toothpick /ˈtuːθpɪk/ n. a small sharp instrument for removing small pieces of food lodged between the teeth.

toothsome /ˈtuːθsəm/ adj. (of food) delicious, appetizing. □ **toothsomely** adv. **toothsomeness** n.

toothy /ˈtuːθɪ/ adj. (**toothier**, **toothiest**) having or showing large, numerous, or prominent teeth (*a toothy grin*). □ **toothily** adv.

tootle /ˈtuːt(ə)l/ v.intr. **1** toot gently or repeatedly. **2** (usu. foll. by *along*, *around*, etc.) *colloq.* move casually or aimlessly. □ **tootler** n.

tootsy /ˈtʊtsɪ/ n. (also **tootsie**) (pl. **-ies**) *sl.* usu. *joc.* a foot. [E *joc.* dimin.]

top[1] n., adj., & v. —n. **1** the highest point or part (*the top of the house*). **2 a** the highest rank or place (*at the top of the school*). **b** a person occupying this (*was top in maths*). **c** the upper end or head (*the top of the table*). **3** the upper surface of a thing, esp. of the ground, a table, etc. **4** the upper part of a thing, esp.: **a** a blouse, jumper, etc. for wearing with a skirt or trousers. **b** the upper part of a shoe or boot. **c** the stopper of a bottle. **d** the lid of a jar, saucepan, etc. **e** the creamy part of milk. **f** the folding roof of a car, pram, or carriage. **g** the upper edge or edges of a page or pages in a book (*gilt top*). **5** the utmost degree; height (*called at the top of his voice*). **6** (in *pl.*) *colloq.* a person or thing of the best quality (*he's tops at cricket*). **7** (esp. in *pl.*) the leaves etc. of a plant grown esp. for its root (*turnip-tops*). **8** *Brit.* = *top gear* (*climbed the hill in top*). **9** = TOPSPIN. —adj. **1** highest in position (*the top shelf*). **2** highest in degree or importance (*at top speed*; *the top job*). —v.tr. (**topped**, **topping**) **1** provide with a top, cap, etc. (*cake topped with icing*). **2** remove the top of (a plant, fruit, etc.), esp. to improve growth, prepare for cooking, etc. **3** be higher or better than; surpass; be at the top of (*topped the list*). **4** *sl.* **a** execute esp. by hanging, kill. **b** (*refl.*) commit suicide. **5** reach the top of (a hill etc.). **6** *Golf* **a** hit (a ball) above the centre. **b** make (a stroke) in this way. □ **at the top** (or **at the top of the tree**) in the highest rank of a profession etc. **come to the top** win distinction. **from top to toe** from head to foot; completely. **on top 1** in a superior position; above. **2** on the upper part of the head (*bald on top*). **on top of 1** fully in command of. **2** in close proximity to. **3** in addition to. **on top of the world** *colloq.* exuberant. **over the top 1** over the parapet of a trench (and into battle). **2** into a final or decisive state. **3** to excess, beyond reasonable limits (*that joke was over the top*). **top brass** esp. *Mil. colloq.* the highest-ranking officers, heads of industries, etc. **top dog** *colloq.* a victor or master. **top drawer 1** the uppermost drawer in a chest etc. **2** *colloq.* high social position or origin. **top-dress** apply manure or fertilizer on the top of (earth) instead of ploughing it in. **top-dressing 1** this process. **2** manure so applied. **3** a superficial show. **top-flight** in the highest rank of achievement. **top fruit** *Brit.* fruit grown on trees, not bushes. **top gear** *Brit.* the highest gear in a motor vehicle or bicycle. **top hat** a man's tall silk hat. **top-level** of the highest level of importance, prestige, etc. **top-notch** *colloq.* first-rate. **top off** (or **up**) put an end or the finishing touch to (a thing). **top out** put the highest stone on (a building). **top secret** of the highest secrecy. **top ten** (or **twenty** etc.) the first ten (or twenty etc.) gramophone records in the charts. **top up** esp. *Brit.* **1 a** complete (an amount or number). **b** fill up (a glass or other partly full container). **2** top up something for (a person) (*may I top you up with sherry?*). **top-up** n. an addition; something that serves to top up (esp. a partly full glass). □ **topmost** adj. [OE *topp*]

top[2] n. a wooden or metal toy, usu. conical or pear-shaped, spinning on a point when set in motion by hand, string, etc. [OE, of uncert. orig.]

topaz /ˈtəʊpæz/ n. a transparent or translucent aluminium silicate mineral, usu. yellow, used as a gem. [ME f. OF *topace*, *topaze* f. L *topazus* f. Gk *topazos*]

topcoat /ˈtɒpkəʊt/ n. **1** an overcoat. **2** an outer coat of paint etc.

tope[1] v.intr. *archaic* or *literary* drink alcohol to excess, esp. habitually. □ **toper** n. [perh. f. obs. *top* quaff]

tope[2] /təʊp/ n. a small shark, *Galeorhinus galeus*. [perh. f. Corn.]

topgallant /tɒpˈgælənt, təˈgælənt/ n. Naut. the mast, sail, yard, or rigging immediately above the topmast and topsail.

top-heavy /tɒpˈhevɪ/ adj. 1 disproportionately heavy at the top so as to be in danger of toppling. 2 (of an organization, business, etc.) having a disproportionately large number of people in senior administrative positions. □ **top-heavily** adv. **top-heaviness** n.

topi /ˈtəʊpɪ/ n. (also **topee**) (pl. **topis** or **topees**) Anglo-Ind. a hat, esp. a sola topi. [Hindi ṭopī]

topiary /ˈtəʊpɪərɪ/ adj. & n. —adj. concerned with or formed by clipping shrubs, trees, etc. into ornamental shapes. —n. (pl. **-ies**) 1 topiary art. 2 an example of this. □ **topiarian** /-pɪˈeərɪən/ adj. **topiarist** n. [F topiaire f. L topiarius landscape-gardener f. topia opera fancy gardening f. Gk topia pl. dimin. of topos place]

topic /ˈtɒpɪk/ n. 1 a theme for a book, discourse, essay, sermon, etc. 2 the subject of a conversation or argument. [L topica f. Gk (ta) topika topics, as title of a treatise by Aristotle f. topos a place, a commonplace]

topical /ˈtɒpɪk(ə)l/ adj. 1 dealing with the news, current affairs, etc. (a topical song). 2 dealing with a place; local. □ **topicality** /-ˈkælɪtɪ/ n. **topically** adv.

topknot /ˈtɒpnɒt/ n. a knot, tuft, crest, or bow of ribbon, worn or growing on the head.

topless /ˈtɒplɪs/ adj. 1 without or seeming to be without a top. 2 **a** (of clothes) having no upper part. **b** (of a person) wearing such clothes; bare-breasted. **c** (of a place, esp. a beach) where women go topless. □ **toplessness** n.

topmast /ˈtɒpmɑːst/ n. Naut. the mast next above the lower mast.

topography /təˈpɒgrəfɪ/ n. 1 a detailed description, representation on a map, etc., of the natural and artificial features of a town, district, etc. 2 such features. □ **topographer** n. **topographic** /-ˈgræfɪk/ adj. **topographical** /-ˈgræfɪk(ə)l/ adj. **topographically** /-ˈgræfɪkəlɪ/ adv. [ME f. LL topographia f. Gk f. topos place]

topology /təˈpɒlədʒɪ/ n. Math. the study of geometrical properties and spatial relations unaffected by the continuous change of shape or size of figures. □ **topological** /ˌtɒpəˈlɒdʒɪk(ə)l/ adj. **topologically** /ˌtɒpəˈlɒdʒɪkəlɪ/ adv. **topologist** n. [G Topologie f. Gk topos place]

toponymy /təˈpɒnɪmɪ/ n. the study of the place-names of a region. □ **toponymic** /-ˈnɪmɪk/ adj. [Gk topos place + onoma name]

topper /ˈtɒpə(r)/ n. 1 a thing that tops. 2 colloq. = top hat. 3 colloq. a good fellow; a good sort.

topping /ˈtɒpɪŋ/ n. anything that tops something else, esp. icing etc. on a cake.

topple /ˈtɒp(ə)l/ v.intr. & tr. (usu. foll. by over, down) 1 fall or cause to fall as if top-heavy. 2 totter or cause to totter and fall. [TOP¹ + -LE⁴]

topsail /ˈtɒpseɪl, -s(ə)l/ n. a square sail next above the lowest fore-and-aft sail on a gaff.

topside /ˈtɒpsaɪd/ n. 1 Brit. the outer side of a round of beef. 2 the side of a ship above the water-line.

topsoil /ˈtɒpsɔɪl/ n. the top layer of soil (opp. SUBSOIL).

topspin /ˈtɒpspɪn/ n. a fast forward spinning motion imparted to a ball in tennis etc. by hitting it forward and upward.

topsy-turvy /ˌtɒpsɪˈtɜːvɪ/ adv., adj., & n. —adv. & adj. 1 upside down. 2 in utter confusion. —n. utter confusion. □ **topsy-turvily** adv. **topsy-turviness** n. [app. f. TOP¹ + obs. terve overturn]

toque /təʊk/ n. a woman's small brimless hat. [F, app. = It. tocca, Sp. toca, of unkn. orig.]

tor n. a hill or rocky peak, esp. in Devon or Cornwall. [OE torr: cf. Gael. tòrr bulging hill]

Torah /ˈtɔːrə/ n. 1 (usu. prec. by the) **a** the Pentateuch. **b** a scroll containing this. 2 the will of God as revealed in Mosaic law. [Heb. tōrāh instruction]

torc var. of TORQUE 1.

torch n. & v. —n. 1 (also **electric torch**) Brit. a portable battery-powered electric lamp. 2 **a** a piece of wood, cloth, etc., soaked in tallow and lighted for illumination. **b** any similar lamp, e.g. an oil-lamp on a pole. 3 a source of heat, illumination, or enlightenment (bore aloft the torch of freedom). 4 esp. US a blowlamp. 5 US sl. an arsonist. —v.tr. esp. US sl. set alight with a torch. □ **carry a torch for** suffer from unrequited love for. **torch singer** a woman who sings torch songs. **torch song** a popular song of unrequited love. [ME f. OF torche f. L torqua f. torquēre twist]

torchlight /ˈtɔːtʃlaɪt/ n. the light of a torch or torches.

tore past of TEAR¹.

toreador /ˈtɒrɪəˌdɔː(r)/ n. a bullfighter, esp. on horseback. □ **toreador pants** close-fitting calf-length women's trousers. [Sp. f. torear fight bulls f. toro bull f. L taurus]

tori pl. of TORUS.

toric /ˈtɒrɪk/ adj. Geom. having the form of a torus or part of a torus.

torment n. & v. —n. /ˈtɔːment/ 1 severe physical or mental suffering (was in torment). 2 a cause of this. —v.tr. /tɔːˈment/ 1 subject to torment (tormented with worry). 2 tease or worry excessively (enjoyed tormenting the teacher). □ **tormentedly** adv. **tormentingly** adv. **tormentor** /-ˈmentə(r)/ n. [ME f. OF torment, tormenter f. L tormentum missile-engine f. torquēre to twist]

torn past part. of TEAR¹.

tornado /tɔːˈneɪdəʊ/ n. (pl. **-oes**) 1 a violent storm of small extent with whirling winds, esp.: **a** in West Africa at the beginning and end of the rainy season. **b** in the US etc. over a narrow path often accompanied by a funnel-shaped cloud. 2 an outburst or volley of cheers, hisses, missiles, etc. □ **tornadic** /-ˈnædɪk/ adj. [app. assim. of Sp. tronada thunderstorm (f. tronar to thunder) to Sp. tornar to turn]

toroid /ˈtɔːrɔɪd/ n. a figure of toroidal shape.

toroidal /tɔːˈrɔɪd(ə)l/ adj. Geom. of or resembling a torus. □ **toroidally** adv.

torpedo /tɔːˈpiːdəʊ/ n. & v. —n. (pl. **-oes**) 1 a cigar-shaped self-propelled underwater missile that explodes on impact with a ship. 2 (in full **aerial torpedo**) a similar device dropped from an aircraft. —v.tr. (**-oes**, **-oed**) 1 destroy or attack with a torpedo. 2 make (a policy, institution, plan, etc.) ineffective or inoperative; destroy. □ **torpedo-boat** a small fast lightly armed warship for carrying or discharging torpedoes. □ **torpedo-like** adj. [L, = numbness, electric ray f. torpēre be numb]

torpid /ˈtɔːpɪd/ adj. 1 sluggish, inactive, dull, apathetic. 2 numb. 3 (of a hibernating animal) dormant. □ **torpidity** /-'pɪdɪtɪ/ n. **torpidly** adv. **torpidness** n. [L torpidus (as TORPOR)]

torpor /'tɔːpə(r)/ n. torpidity. □ **torporific** /-'rɪfɪk/ adj. [L f. torpēre be sluggish]

torque /tɔːk/ n. **1** (also **torc**) hist. a necklace of twisted metal, esp. of the ancient Gauls and Britons. **2** Mech. the moment of a system of forces tending to cause rotation. □ **torque converter** a device to transmit the correct torque from the engine to the axle in a motor vehicle. [(sense 1 F f. L torques) f. L torquēre to twist]

torrent /'tɒrənt/ n. **1** a rushing stream of water, lava, etc. **2** (in pl.) a great downpour of rain (came down in torrents). **3** (usu. foll. by of) a violent or copious flow (uttered a torrent of abuse). □ **torrential** /tə'renʃ(ə)l/ adj. **torrentially** /tə'renʃəlɪ/ adv. [F f. It. torrente f. L torrens -entis scorching, boiling, roaring f. torrēre scorch]

torrid /'tɒrɪd/ adj. **1 a** (of the weather) very hot and dry. **b** (of land etc.) parched by such weather. **2** (of language or actions) emotionally charged; passionate, intense. □ **torridity** /-'rɪdɪtɪ/ n. **torridly** adv. **torridness** n. [F torride or L torridus f. torrēre parch]

torsion /'tɔːʃ(ə)n/ n. twisting, esp. of one end of a body while the other is held fixed. □ **torsion bar** a bar forming part of a vehicle suspension, twisting in response to the motion of the wheels, and absorbing their vertical movement. □ **torsional** adj. **torsionally** adv. **torsionless** adj. [ME f. OF f. LL torsio -onis f. L tortio (as TORT)]

torso /'tɔːsəʊ/ n. (pl. **-os**) **1** the trunk of the human body. **2** a statue of a human consisting of the trunk alone, without head or limbs. [It., = stalk, stump, torso, f. L thyrsus]

tort n. Law a breach of duty (other than under contract) leading to liability for damages. [ME f. OF f. med.L tortum wrong, neut. past part. of L torquēre tort- twist]

tortilla /tɔː'tiːjə, -'tiːljə/ n. a thin flat orig. Mexican maize cake eaten hot or cold with or without a filling. [Sp. dimin. of torta cake f. LL]

tortoise /'tɔːtəs/ n. any slow-moving land or freshwater reptile of the family Testudinidae, encased in a scaly or leathery domed shell, and having a retractile head and elephantine legs. □ **tortoise-like** adj. & adv. [ME tortuce, OF tortue, f. med.L tortuca, of uncert. orig.]

tortoiseshell /'tɔːtəsˌʃel/ n. & adj. —n. the yellowish-brown mottled or clouded outer shell of some turtles, used for decorative hair-combs, jewellery, etc. —adj. having the colouring or appearance of tortoiseshell. □ **tortoiseshell butterfly** any of various butterflies, esp. of the genus Aglais or Nymphalis, with wings mottled like tortoiseshell. **tortoiseshell cat** a domestic cat with markings resembling tortoiseshell.

tortuous /'tɔːtjʊəs/ adj. **1** full of twists and turns (followed a tortuous route). **2** devious, circuitous, crooked (has a tortuous mind). □ **tortuosity** /-'ɒsɪtɪ/ n. (pl. **-ies**). **tortuously** adv. **tortuousness** n. [ME f. OF f. L tortuosus f. tortus a twist (as TORT)]

torture /'tɔːtʃə(r)/ n. & v. —n. **1** the infliction of severe bodily pain esp. as a punishment or a means of persuasion. **2** severe physical or mental suffering (the torture of defeat). —v.tr. **1** subject to torture. **2** force out of a natural position or state; deform; pervert. □ **torturable**

adj. **torturer** n. **torturous** adj. **torturously** adv. [F f. LL tortura twisting (as TORT)]

torus /'tɔːrəs/ n. (pl. **tori** /-raɪ/) Geom. a surface or solid formed by rotating a closed curve, esp. a circle, about a line in its plane but not intersecting it. [L, = swelling, bulge, cushion, etc.]

Tory /'tɔːrɪ/ n. & adj. —n. (pl. **-ies**) **1** colloq. = CONSERVATIVE n. 2. **2** hist. a member of the party that opposed the exclusion of James II and gave rise to the Conservative party. —adj. colloq. = CONSERVATIVE adj. 3. □ **Toryism** n. [orig. = Irish outlaw, prob. f. Ir. f. tóir pursue]

tosh n. colloq. rubbish, nonsense. [19th c.: orig. unkn.]

toss v. & n. —v. **1** tr. throw up (a ball etc.) esp. with the hand. **2** tr. & intr. roll about, throw, or be thrown, restlessly or from side to side (the ship tossed on the ocean; was tossing and turning all night; tossed her head angrily). **3** tr. (usu. foll. by to, away, aside, out, etc.) throw (a thing) lightly or carelessly (tossed the letter away). **4** tr. **a** throw (a coin) into the air to decide a choice etc. by the side on which it lands. **b** (also absol.; often foll. by for) settle a question or dispute with (a person) in this way (tossed him for the armchair; tossed for it). **5** tr. **a** (of a bull etc.) throw (a person etc.) up with the horns. **b** (of a horse etc.) throw (a rider) off its back. **6** tr. coat (food) with dressing etc. by shaking. **7** tr. bandy about in debate; discuss (tossed the question back and forth). —n. **1** the act or an instance of tossing (a coin, the head, etc.). **2** Brit. a fall, esp. from a horse. □ **toss one's head** throw it back esp. in anger, impatience, etc. **tossing the caber** the Scottish sport of throwing a tree-trunk. **toss off 1** drink off at a draught. **2** dispatch (work) rapidly or without effort (tossed off an omelette). **toss a pancake** throw it up so that it flips on to the other side in the frying-pan. **toss up** toss a coin to decide a choice etc. **toss-up** n. **1** a doubtful matter; a close thing (it's a toss-up whether he wins). **2** the tossing of a coin. [16th c.: orig. unkn.]

tosser /'tɒsə(r)/ n. **1** Brit. coarse sl. an unpleasant or contemptible person. **2** a person or thing that tosses.

tot¹ n. **1** a small child (a tiny tot). **2** a dram of liquor. [18th c., of dial. orig.]

tot² v. (**totted**, **totting**) **1** tr. (usu. foll. by up) add (figures etc.). **2** intr. (foll. by up) (of items) mount up. □ **totting-up 1** the adding of separate items. **2** Brit. the adding of convictions for driving offences to cause disqualification. **tot up to** amount to. [abbr. of TOTAL or of L totum the whole]

total /'təʊt(ə)l/ adj., n., & v. —adj. **1** complete, comprising the whole (the total number of people). **2** absolute, unqualified (in total ignorance; total abstinence). —n. a total number or amount. —v. (**totalled**, **totalling**; US **totaled**, **totaling**) **1** tr. **a** amount in number to (they totalled 131). **b** find the total of (things, a set of figures, etc.). **2** intr. (foll. by to, up to) amount to, mount up to. **3** tr. US sl. wreck completely. □ **total abstinence** abstaining completely from alcohol. **total eclipse** an eclipse in which the whole disc (of the sun, moon, etc.) is obscured. **total recall** the ability to remember every detail of one's experience clearly. **total war** a war in which all available weapons and resources are employed. □ **totally** adv. [ME f. OF f. med.L totalis f. totus entire]

totalitarian /təʊˌtælɪˈteərɪən/ adj. & n. —adj. of or relating to a centralized dictatorial form of government requiring complete subservience to the State. —n. a person advocating such a system. □ **totalitarianism** n.

totality /təʊˈtælɪtɪ/ n. 1 the complete amount or sum. 2 Astron. the time during which an eclipse is total.

totalizator /ˈtəʊtəlaɪˌzeɪtə(r)/ n. (also **totalisator**) 1 a device showing the number and amount of bets staked on a race, to facilitate the division of the total among those backing the winner. 2 a system of betting based on this.

totalize /ˈtəʊtəˌlaɪz/ v.tr. (also **-ise**) collect into a total; find the total of. □ **totalization** /-ˈzeɪʃ(ə)n/ n.

totalizer /ˈtəʊtəˌlaɪzə(r)/ n. = TOTALIZATOR.

tote[1] /təʊt/ n. sl. 1 a totalizator. 2 a lottery. [abbr.]

tote[2] /təʊt/ v.tr. esp. US colloq. carry, convey, esp. a heavy load (toting a gun). □ **toter** n. (also in comb.). [17th-c. US, prob. of dial. orig.]

totem /ˈtəʊtəm/ n. 1 a natural object, esp. an animal, adopted by North American Indians as an emblem of a clan or an individual. 2 an image of this. □ **totem-pole** a pole on which totems are carved or hung. □ **totemic** /-ˈtemɪk/ adj. **totemism** n. **totemist** n. **totemistic** /-ˈmɪstɪk/ adj. [Algonquian]

totter /ˈtɒtə(r)/ v. & n. —v.intr. 1 stand or walk unsteadily or feebly (tottered out of the pub). 2 a (of a building etc.) shake or rock as if about to collapse. b (of a system of government etc.) be about to fall. —n. an unsteady or shaky movement or gait. □ **totterer** n. **tottery** adj. [ME f. MDu. touteren to swing].

toucan /ˈtuːkən/ n. any tropical American fruit-eating bird of the family Ramphastidae, with an immense beak and brightly coloured plumage. [Tupi tucana, Guarani tucã]

touch /tʌtʃ/ v. & n. —v. 1 tr. come into or be in physical contact with (another thing) at one or more points. 2 tr. (often foll. by with) bring the hand etc. into contact with (touched her arm). 3 a intr. (of two things etc.) be in or come into contact with one another (the balls were touching). b tr. bring (two things) into mutual contact (they touched hands). 4 tr. rouse tender or painful feelings in (was touched by his appeal). 5 tr. strike lightly (just touched the wall with the back bumper). 6 tr. (usu. with neg.) a disturb or harm (don't touch my things). b have any dealings with (won't touch bricklaying). c consume; use up; make use of (has not touched her breakfast; need not touch your savings). d cope with; affect; manage (soap won't touch this dirt). 7 tr. a deal with (a subject) lightly or in passing (touched the matter of their expenses). b concern (it touches you closely). 8 tr. a reach or rise as far as, esp. momentarily (the thermometer touched 90°). b (usu. with neg.) approach in excellence etc. (can't touch him for style). 9 tr. affect slightly; modify (pity touched with fear). 10 tr. (as **touched** adj.) slightly mad. 11 tr. a strike (the keys, strings, etc. of a musical instrument). b strike the keys or strings of (a piano etc.). 12 tr. (usu. foll. by for) sl. ask for and get money etc. from (a person) as a loan or gift (touched him for £5). 13 tr. injure slightly (blossom touched by frost). —n. 1 the act or an instance of touching, esp. with the body or hand (felt a touch

on my arm). 2 a the faculty of perception through physical contact, esp. with the fingers (has no sense of touch in her right arm). b the qualities of an object etc. as perceived in this way (the soft touch of silk). 3 a small amount; a slight trace (a touch of salt; a touch of irony). 4 a a musician's manner of playing keys or strings. b the manner in which the keys or strings respond to touch. c an artist's or writer's style of workmanship, writing, etc. (has a delicate touch). 5 a distinguishing quality or trait (a professional touch). 6 (esp. in pl.) a a light stroke with a pen, pencil, etc. b a slight alteration or improvement (speech needs a few touches). 7 (prec. by a) slightly (is a touch too arrogant). 8 sl. a the act of asking for and getting money etc. from a person. b a person from whom money etc. is so obtained. 9 Football the part of the field outside the side limits. □ **at a touch** if touched, however lightly (opened at a touch). **easy touch** sl. a person who readily parts with money. **finishing touch** (or **touches**) the final details completing and enhancing a piece of work etc. **in touch** (often foll. by with) 1 in communication (we're still in touch after all these years). 2 up to date, esp. regarding news etc. (keeps in touch with events). 3 aware, conscious, empathetic (not in touch with her own feelings). **lose touch** (often foll. by with) 1 cease to be informed. 2 cease to correspond with or be in contact with another person. **lose one's touch** not show one's customary skill. **out of touch** (often foll. by with) 1 not in correspondence. 2 not up to date or modern. 3 lacking in awareness or sympathy (out of touch with his son's beliefs). **personal touch** a characteristic or individual approach to a situation. **soft touch** = easy touch. **to the touch** when touched (was cold to the touch). **touch-and-go** uncertain regarding a result; risky (it was touch-and-go whether we'd catch the train). **touch at** (of a ship) call at (a port etc.). **touch bottom** 1 reach the bottom of water with one's feet. 2 be at the lowest or worst point. 3 be in possession of the full facts. **touch down** 1 Rugby Football & Amer. Football touch the ground with the ball behind one's own or the opponent's goal. 2 (of an aircraft) make contact with the ground in landing. **touch football** US football with touching in place of tackling. **touch-judge** Rugby Football a linesman. **touch-line** (in various sports) either of the lines marking the side boundaries of the pitch. **touch off** 1 represent exactly (in a portrait etc.). 2 explode by touching with a match etc. 3 initiate (a process) suddenly (touched off a run on the pound). **touch on** (or **upon**) 1 treat (a subject) briefly, refer to or mention casually. 2 verge on (that touches on impudence). **touch-paper** paper impregnated with nitre, for firing gunpowder, fireworks, etc. **touch the spot** colloq. find out or do exactly what was needed. **touch-type** type without looking at the keys. **touch-typist** a person who touch-types. **touch up** 1 give finishing touches to or retouch (a picture, writing, etc.). 2 Brit. sl. a caress so as to excite sexually. b sexually molest. **touch wood** touch something wooden with the hand to avert ill luck. □ **touchable** adj. **toucher** n. [ME f. OF tochier, tuchier (v.), touche (n.): prob. imit., imitating a knock]

touchdown /ˈtʌtʃdaʊn/ n. 1 the act or an instance of an aircraft making contact with the ground during landing. **2** *Rugby Football* & *Amer. Football* the act or an instance of touching down.

touché /tuːˈʃeɪ/ *int.* **1** the acknowledgement of a hit by a fencing-opponent. **2** the acknowledgement of a justified accusation, a witticism, or a point made in reply to one's own. [F, past part. of *toucher* TOUCH]

touching /ˈtʌtʃɪŋ/ *adj.* & *prep.* —*adj.* moving; pathetic (*a touching incident*; *touching confidence*). —*prep.* literary concerning; about. □ **touchingly** *adv.* **touchingness** *n.* [ME f. TOUCH: (prep.) f. OF *touchant* pres. part. (as TOUCH)]

touchstone /ˈtʌtʃstəʊn/ *n.* **1** a fine-grained dark schist or jasper used for testing alloys of gold etc. by marking it with them and observing the colour of the mark. **2** a standard or criterion.

touchwood /ˈtʌtʃwʊd/ *n.* readily inflammable wood, esp. when made soft by fungi, used as tinder.

touchy /ˈtʌtʃɪ/ *adj.* (**touchier, touchiest**) apt to take offence; over-sensitive. □ **touchily** *adv.* **touchiness** *n.* [perh. alt. of TETCHY after TOUCH]

tough /tʌf/ *adj.* & *n.* —*adj.* **1** hard to break, cut, tear, or chew; durable; strong. **2** (of a person) able to endure hardship; hardy. **3** unyielding, stubborn, difficult (*it was a tough job*; *a tough customer*). **4** *colloq.* **a** acting sternly; hard (*get tough with*). **b** (of circumstances, luck, etc.) severe, unpleasant, hard, unjust. **5** *colloq.* criminal or violent (*tough guys*). —*n.* a tough person, esp. a ruffian or criminal. □ **tough guy** *colloq.* **1** a hard unyielding person. **2** a violent aggressive person. **tough it** (or **tough it out**) *colloq.* endure or withstand difficult conditions. **tough-minded** realistic, not sentimental. □ **toughen** *v.tr.* & *intr.* **toughener** *n.* **toughish** *adj.* **toughly** *adv.* **toughness** *n.* [OE *tōh*]

toupee /ˈtuːpeɪ/ *n.* (also *toupet* /tuːˈpeɪ/) a wig or artificial hairpiece to cover a bald spot. [F *toupet* hair-tuft dimin. of OF *toup* tuft (as TOP¹)]

tour /tʊə(r)/ *n.* & *v.* —*n.* **1 a** a journey from place to place as a holiday. **b** an excursion, ramble, or walk (*made a tour of the garden*). **2 a** a spell of duty on military or diplomatic service. **b** the time to be spent at a particular post. **3** a series of performances, matches, etc., at different places on a route through a country etc. —*v.* **1** *intr.* (usu. foll. by *through*) make a tour (*toured through India*). **2** *tr.* make a tour of (a country etc.). □ **on tour** (esp. of a team, theatre company, etc.) touring. **tour operator** a travel agent specializing in package holidays. [ME f. OF *to(u)r* f. L *tornus* f. Gk *tornos* lathe]

tour de force /ˌtʊə də ˈfɔːs/ *n.* a feat of strength or skill. [F]

tourer /ˈtʊərə(r)/ *n.* a vehicle, esp. a car, for touring. [TOUR]

tourism /ˈtʊərɪz(ə)m/ *n.* the organization and operation of (esp. foreign) holidays, esp. as a commercial enterprise.

tourist /ˈtʊərɪst/ *n.* a person making a visit or tour as a holiday; a traveller, esp. abroad (often *attrib.*: *tourist accommodation*). □ **touristic** /-ˈrɪstɪk/ *adj.* **touristically** /-ˈrɪstɪkəlɪ/ *adv.*

touristy /ˈtʊərɪstɪ/ *adj.* usu. *derog.* appealing to or visited by many tourists.

tourmaline /ˈtʊəməlɪn, -məˌliːn/ *n.* a boron aluminium silicate mineral of various colours, used in electrical and optical instruments and as a gemstone. [F f. Sinh. *toramalli* porcelain]

tournament /ˈtʊənəmənt/ *n.* **1** any contest of skill between a number of competitors, esp. played in heats (*chess tournament*; *tennis tournament*). **2** a display of military exercises etc. (*Royal Tournament*). **3** *hist.* **a** a pageant in which jousting with blunted weapons took place. **b** a meeting for jousting between single knights for a prize etc. [ME f. OF *torneiement* f. *torneier* TOURNEY]

tournedos /ˈtʊənəˌdəʊ/ *n.* (*pl.* same /-ˌdəʊz/) a small round thick cut from a fillet of beef. [F]

tourney /ˈtʊənɪ/ *n.* & *v.* —*n.* (*pl.* **-eys**) a tournament. —*v.intr.* (**-eys, -eyed**) take part in a tournament. [ME f. OF *tornei* (n.), *torneier* (v.), ult. f. L *tornus* a turn]

tourniquet /ˈtʊənɪˌkeɪ/ *n.* a device for stopping the flow of blood through an artery by twisting a bar etc. in a ligature or bandage. [F prob. f. OF *tournicle* coat of mail (as TUNIC), infl. by *tourner* TURN]

tousle /ˈtaʊz(ə)l/ *v.tr.* **1** make (esp. the hair) untidy; rumple. **2** handle roughly or rudely. [frequent. of (now dial.) *touse*, ME f. OE rel. to OHG *-zuson*]

tout /taʊt/ *v.* & *n.* —*v.* **1** *intr.* (usu. foll. by *for*) solicit custom persistently; pester customers (*touting for business*). **2** *tr.* solicit the custom of (a person) or for (a thing). **3** *intr.* **a** *Brit.* spy out the movements and condition of racehorses in training. **b** *US* offer racing tips for a share of the resulting profit. —*n.* a person employed in touting. □ **touter** *n.* [ME *tūte* look out = ME (now dial.) *toot* (OE *tōtian*) f. Gmc]

tow¹ /təʊ/ *v.* & *n.* —*v.tr.* **1** (of a motor vehicle, horse, or person controlling it) pull (a boat, another motor vehicle, a caravan, etc.) along by a rope, tow-bar, etc. **2** pull (a person or thing) along behind one. —*n.* the act or an instance of towing; the state of being towed. □ **have in** (or **on**) **tow 1** be towing. **2** be accompanied by and often in charge of (a person). **tow-bar** a bar for towing esp. a trailer or caravan. **tow-** (or **towing-**) **line** (or **rope**) a line etc. used in towing. **tow-** (or **towing-**) **path** a path beside a river or canal used for towing a boat by horse. □ **towable** *adj.* **towage** /-ɪdʒ/ *n.* [OE *togian* f. Gmc, rel. to TUG]

tow² /təʊ/ *n.* the coarse and broken part of flax or hemp prepared for spinning. □ **tow-coloured** (of hair) very light. **tow-headed** having very light or unkempt hair. □ **towy** /ˈtəʊɪ/ *adj.* [ME f. MLG *touw* f. OS *tou*, rel. to ON *tó* wool: cf. TOOL]

towards /təˈwɔːdz, twɔːdz, tɔːdz/ *prep.* (also **toward**) **1** in the direction of (*set out towards town*). **2** as regards; in relation to (*his attitude towards death*). **3** as a contribution to; for (*put this towards your expenses*). **4** near (*towards the end of our journey*). [OE *tōweard* (adj.) future (as TO, -WARD)]

towel /ˈtaʊəl/ *n.* & *v.* —*n.* **1 a** a piece of rough-surfaced absorbent cloth used for drying oneself or a thing after washing. **b** absorbent paper used for this. **c** a cloth used for drying plates, dishes, etc.; a tea towel. **2** *Brit.* = *sanitary towel.* —*v.* (**towelled, towelling**; *US* **toweled, toweling**) **1** *tr.* (often *refl.*) wipe or dry with a towel. **2** *intr.* wipe or dry oneself with a towel. □ **towel-horse** (or **-rail**) a frame for hanging towels on. □ **towelling** *n.* [ME f. OF *toail(l)e* f. Gmc]

tower /ˈtaʊə(r)/ n. & v. —n. **1 a** a tall esp. square or circular structure, often part of a church, castle, etc. **b** a fortress etc. comprising or including a tower. **c** a tall structure housing machinery, apparatus, operators, etc. (*cooling tower; control tower*). **2** a place of defence; a protection. —v.intr. **1** (usu. foll. by *above, high*) reach or be high or above; be superior. **2** (of a bird) soar or hover. **3** (as **towering** adj.) **a** high, lofty (*towering intellect*). **b** violent (*towering rage*). □ **tower block** a tall building containing offices or flats. **tower of strength** a person who gives strong and reliable support. □ **towered** /ˈtaʊəd/ adj. **towery** adj. [OE *torr*, & ME *tūr*, AF & OF *tur* etc., f. L *turris* f. Gk]

town /taʊn/ n. **1 a** a large urban area with a name, defined boundaries, and local government, being larger than a village and usu. not created a city. **b** any densely populated area, esp. as opposed to the country or suburbs. **c** the people of a town (*the whole town knows of it*). **2 a** Brit. London or the chief city or town in one's neighbourhood (*went up to town*). **b** the central business or shopping area in a neighbourhood (*just going into town*). **3** US = TOWNSHIP 2. □ **go to town** colloq. act or work with energy or enthusiasm. **on the town** colloq. enjoying the entertainments, esp. the night-life, of a town; celebrating. **town clerk** US & hist. the officer of the corporation of a town in charge of records etc. **town council** the elective governing body in a municipality. **town councillor** an elected member of this. **town gas** manufactured gas for domestic and commercial use. **town hall** a building for the administration of local government, having public meeting rooms etc. **town house 1** a town residence, esp. of a person with a house in the country. **2** a terrace house. **town meeting** US a meeting of the voters of a town for the transaction of public business. **town planning** the planning of the construction and growth of towns. □ **townish** adj. **townless** adj. **townlet** n. **townward** adj. & adv. **townwards** adv. [OE *tūn* enclosure f. Gmc]

townee /taʊˈniː/ n. (also **townie** /ˈtaʊnɪ/) derog. a person living in a town, esp. as opposed to a countryman.

townscape /ˈtaʊnskeɪp/ n. **1** the visual appearance of a town or towns. **2** a picture of a town.

townsfolk /ˈtaʊnzfəʊk/ n. the inhabitants of a particular town or towns.

township /ˈtaʊnʃɪp/ n. **1** S.Afr. **a** an urban area set aside for Black (usu. African) occupation. **b** a White urban area (esp. if new or about to be developed). **2** US & Can. **a** a division of a county with some corporate powers. **b** a district six miles square. **3** Austral. & NZ a small town; a town-site. [OE *tūnscipe* (as TOWN, -SHIP)]

townsman /ˈtaʊnzmən/ n. (pl. **-men**; fem. **townswoman**, pl. **-women**) an inhabitant of a town; a fellow citizen.

townspeople /ˈtaʊnzˌpiːp(ə)l/ n.pl. the people of a town.

towy see TOW².

toxaemia /tɒkˈsiːmɪə/ n. (US **toxemia**) **1** blood-poisoning. **2** a condition in pregnancy characterized by increased blood pressure. □ **toxaemic** adj. [as TOXI- + Gk *haima* blood]

toxi- /ˈtɒksɪ/ comb. form (also **toxico-** /ˈtɒksɪˌkəʊ/, **toxo-** /ˈtɒksəʊ/) poison; poisonous, toxic.

toxic /ˈtɒksɪk/ adj. **1** of or relating to poison (*toxic symptoms*). **2** poisonous (*toxic gas*). **3** caused by poison (*toxic anaemia*). □ **toxically** adv. **toxicity** /-ˈsɪsɪtɪ/ n. [med.L *toxicus* poisoned f. L *toxicum* f. Gk *toxikon* (*pharmakon*) (poison for) arrows f. *toxon* bow, *toxa* arrows]

toxicology /ˌtɒksɪˈkɒlədʒɪ/ n. the scientific study of poisons. □ **toxicological** /-kəˈlɒdʒɪk(ə)l/ adj. **toxicologist** n.

toxin /ˈtɒksɪn/ n. a poison produced by a living organism. [TOXIC + -IN]

toxocara /ˌtɒksəˈkaːrə/ n. any nematode worm of the genus *Toxocara*, parasitic in the alimentary canal of dogs and cats. □ **toxocariasis** /-kəˈraɪəsɪs/ n. [TOXO- (see TOXI-) + Gk *kara* head]

toy n. & v. —n. **1 a** a plaything, esp. for a child. **b** (often attrib.) a model or miniature replica of a thing, esp. as a plaything (*toy gun*). **2 a** a thing, esp. a gadget or instrument, regarded as providing amusement or pleasure. **b** a task or undertaking regarded in an unserious way. **3** (usu. attrib.) a diminutive breed or variety of dog etc. —v.intr. (usu. foll. by *with*) **1** trifle, amuse oneself, esp. with a person's affections; flirt (*toyed with the idea of going to Africa*). **2 a** move a material object idly (*toyed with her necklace*). **b** nibble at food etc. unenthusiastically (*toyed with a peach*). □ **toy boy** colloq. a woman's much younger male lover. **toy soldier 1** a miniature figure of a soldier. **2** sl. a soldier in a peacetime army. [16th c.: earlier = dallying, fun, jest, whim, trifle: orig. unkn.]

trace¹ v. & n. —v.tr. **1 a** observe, discover, or find vestiges or signs of by investigation. **b** (often foll. by *along, through, to*, etc.) follow or mark the track or position of (*traced their footprints in the mud; traced the outlines of a wall*). **c** (often foll. by *back*) follow to its origins (*can trace my family to the 12th century; the report has been traced back to you*). **2** (often foll. by *over*) copy (a drawing etc.) by drawing over its lines on a superimposed piece of translucent paper, or by using carbon paper. **3** (often foll. by *out*) mark out, delineate, sketch, or write esp. laboriously (*traced out a plan of the district; traced out his vision of the future*). **4** pursue one's way along (a path etc.). —n. **1 a** a sign or mark or other indication of something having existed; a vestige (*no trace remains of the castle; has the traces of a vanished beauty*). **b** a very small quantity. **2** a track or footprint left by a person or animal. **3** a track left by the moving pen of an instrument etc. **4** a line on the screen of a cathode-ray tube showing the path of a moving spot. □ **trace element 1** a chemical element occurring in minute amounts. **2** a chemical element required only in minute amounts by living organisms for normal growth. □ **traceable** adj. **traceability** /-ˈbɪlɪtɪ/ n. **traceless** adj. [ME f. OF *trace* (n.), *tracier* (v.) f. L *tractus* drawing: see TRACT¹]

trace² n. each of the two side-straps, chains, or ropes by which a horse draws a vehicle. □ **kick over the traces** become insubordinate or reckless. [ME f. OF *trais*, pl. of TRAIT]

tracer /ˈtreɪsə(r)/ n. **1** a person or thing that traces. **2** Mil. a bullet etc. that is visible in flight because of flames etc. emitted. **3** an artificially produced radioactive isotope capable of being followed through the body by the radiation it produces.

tracery /ˈtreɪsərɪ/ n. (pl. **-ies**) **1** ornamental stone openwork esp. in the upper part of a Gothic window. **2** a fine decorative pattern. □ **traceried** adj.

trachea /trəˈkiːə, ˈtreɪkɪə/ n. (pl. **tracheae** /-ˈkiːiː/) the passage through which air reaches the bronchial tubes from the larynx; the windpipe. □ **tracheal** /ˈtreɪkɪəl/ adj. **tracheate** /ˈtreɪkɪˌeɪt/ adj. [ME f. med.L, = LL trachia f. Gk trakheia (artēria) rough (artery), f. trakhus rough]

tracheo- /ˈtreɪkɪəʊ/ comb. form.

tracheotomy /ˌtreɪkɪˈɒtəmɪ/ n. (also **tracheostomy** /-ˈɒstəmɪ/) (pl. **-ies**) an incision made in the trachea to relieve an obstruction to breathing. □ **tracheotomy tube** a breathing-tube inserted into this incision.

tracing /ˈtreɪsɪŋ/ n. **1** a copy of a drawing etc. made by tracing. **2** = TRACE¹ n. 3. **3** the act or an instance of tracing. □ **tracing-paper** translucent paper used for making tracings.

track n. & v. —n. **1 a** a mark or marks left by a person, animal, or thing in passing. **b** (in pl.) such marks esp. footprints. **2** a rough path, esp. one beaten by use. **3** a continuous railway line (laid three miles of track). **4 a** a racecourse for horses, dogs, etc. **b** a prepared course for runners etc. **5 a** a groove on a gramophone record. **b** a section of a gramophone record containing one song etc. (this side has six tracks). **c** a lengthwise strip of magnetic tape containing one sequence of signals. **6 a** a line of travel, passage, or motion (followed the track of the hurricane; America followed in the same track). **b** the path travelled by a ship, aircraft, etc. **7** a continuous band round the wheels of a tank, tractor, etc. **8** = SOUNDTRACK. **9** a line of reasoning or thought (this track proved fruitless). —v. **1** tr. follow the track of (an animal, person, spacecraft, etc.). **2** tr. make out (a course, development, etc.); trace by vestiges. **3** intr. (often foll. by back, in, etc.) (of a film or television camera) move in relation to the subject being filmed. **4** intr. (of a gramophone stylus) follow a groove. **5** tr. US **a** make a track with (dirt etc.) from the feet. **b** leave such a track on (a floor etc.). □ **in one's tracks** colloq. where one stands, there and then (stopped him in his tracks). **keep** (or **lose**) **track of** follow (or fail to follow) the course or development of. **make tracks** colloq. go or run away. **make tracks for** colloq. go in pursuit of or towards. **off the track** away from the subject. **on a person's track 1** in pursuit of him or her. **2** in possession of a clue to a person's conduct, plans, etc. **on the wrong side of** (or **across**) **the tracks** colloq. in an inferior or dubious part of town. **on the wrong** (or **right**) **track** following the wrong (or right) line of inquiry. **track down** reach or capture by tracking. **track events** running-races as opposed to jumping etc. **tracking station** an establishment set up to track objects in the sky. **track-laying** (of a vehicle) having a caterpillar tread. **track record** a person's past performance or achievements. **track shoe** a spiked shoe worn by a runner. **track suit** a loose warm suit worn by an athlete etc. for exercising or jogging. □ **trackage** US n. [ME f. OF trac, perh. f. LG or Du. tre(c)k draught etc.]

tracker /ˈtrækə(r)/ n. **1** a person or thing that tracks. **2** a police dog tracking by scent.

tracklement /ˈtrækəlmənt/ n. an item of food, esp. a jelly, served with meat. [20th c.: orig. unkn.]

trackless /ˈtræklɪs/ adj. **1** without a track or tracks; untrodden. **2** leaving no track or trace. **3** not running on a track.

trackway /ˈtrækweɪ/ n. a beaten path; an ancient roadway.

tract¹ n. **1** a region or area of indefinite, esp. large, extent (pathless desert tracts). **2** Anat. an area of an organ or system (respiratory tract). [L tractus drawing f. trahere tract- draw, pull]

tract² n. a short treatise in pamphlet form esp. on a religious subject. [app. abbr. of L tractatus TRACTATE]

tractable /ˈtræktəb(ə)l/ adj. **1** (of a person) easily handled; manageable; docile. **2** (of material etc.) pliant, malleable. □ **tractability** /-ˈbɪlɪtɪ/ n. **tractableness** n. **tractably** adv. [L tractabilis f. tractare handle, frequent. of trahere tract- draw]

tractate /ˈtrækteɪt/ n. a treatise. [L tractatus f. tractare: see TRACTABLE]

traction /ˈtrækʃ(ə)n/ n. **1** the act of drawing or pulling a thing over a surface, esp. a road or track (steam traction). **2 a** a sustained pulling on a limb, muscle, etc., by means of pulleys, weights, etc. **b** contraction, e.g. of a muscle. **3** the grip of a tyre on a road, a wheel on a rail, etc. **4** US the public transport service. □ **traction-engine** a steam or diesel engine for drawing heavy loads on roads, fields, etc. **traction-wheel** the driving-wheel of a locomotive etc. □ **tractional** adj. **tractive** /ˈtræktɪv/ adj. [F traction or med.L tractio f. L trahere tract- draw]

tractor /ˈtræktə(r)/ n. **1** a motor vehicle used for hauling esp. farm machinery, heavy loads, etc. **2** a traction-engine. [LL tractor (as TRACTION)]

trad /træd/ n. & adj. esp. Brit. colloq. —n. traditional jazz. —adj. traditional. [abbr.]

trade /treɪd/ n. & v. —n. **1 a** buying and selling. **b** buying and selling conducted between nations etc. **c** business conducted for profit (esp. as distinct from a profession) (a butcher by trade). **d** business of a specified nature or time (Christmas trade; tourist trade). **2** a skilled handicraft esp. requiring an apprenticeship (learnt a trade; his trade is plumbing). **3** (usu. prec. by the) the people engaged in a specific trade (the trade will never agree to it; trade enquiries only). **4** US a transaction, esp. a swap. **5** (usu. in pl.) a trade wind. —v. **1** intr. (often foll. by in, with) engage in trade; buy and sell (trades in plastic novelties; we trade with Japan). **2** tr. **a** exchange in commerce; barter (goods). **b** exchange (insults, blows, etc.). **3** intr. (usu. foll. by with, for) have a transaction with a person for a thing. **4** intr. (usu. foll. by to) carry goods to a place. □ **trade cycle** Brit. recurring periods of boom and recession. **trade gap** the extent by which a country's imports exceed its exports. **trade in** (often foll. by for) exchange (esp. a used car etc.) in esp. part payment for another. **trade-in** n. a thing, esp. a car, exchanged in this way. **trade journal** a periodical containing news etc. concerning a particular trade. **trade mark 1** a device, word, or words, secured by legal registration or established by use as representing a company, product, etc. **2** a distinctive characteristic etc. **trade name 1** a name by which a thing is called in a trade. **2** a name given to a product. **3** a name under which a business trades. **trade off** exchange, esp. as a compromise. **trade-off** n. such an exchange. **trade on** take advantage of (a person's credulity, one's reputation, etc.). **trade paper** = *trade journal*. **trade plates** number-plates used by a car-dealer etc. on unlicensed cars. **trade price** a wholesale price charged to the dealer before goods are retailed. **trade secret 1** a secret device or technique used esp. in a trade. **2** *joc.* any secret. **Trades Union Congress** *Brit.* the official representative body of British trade unions, meeting annually. **trade** (or **trades**) **union** an organized association of workers in a trade, group of trades, or a profession, formed to protect and further their rights and interests. **trade-** (or **trades-**) **unionist** a member of a trade union. **trade wind** a wind blowing continually towards the equator and deflected westward, f. obs. *blow trade* = blow regularly. □ **tradable** adj. **tradeable** adj. [ME f. MLG *trade* track f. OS *trada*, OHG *trata*: cf. TREAD]

trader /ˈtreɪdə(r)/ n. **1** a person engaged in trade. **2** a merchant ship.

tradescantia /ˌtrædɪˈskæntɪə/ n. any usu. trailing plant of the genus *Tradescantia*, with large blue, white, or pink flowers. [mod.L f. J. *Tradescant*, Engl. naturalist d. 1638]

tradesman /ˈtreɪdzmən/ n. (pl. **-men**; *fem.* **tradeswoman**, pl. **-women**) a person engaged in trading or a trade, esp. a shopkeeper or skilled craftsman.

tradespeople /ˈtreɪdzˌpiːp(ə)l/ n.pl. people engaged in trade and their families.

trading /ˈtreɪdɪŋ/ n. the act of engaging in trade. □ **trading estate** esp. *Brit.* a specially-designed industrial and commercial area. **trading post** a store etc. established in a remote or unsettled region. **trading-stamp** a stamp given to customers by some stores which is exchangeable in large numbers for various articles.

tradition /trəˈdɪʃ(ə)n/ n. **1 a** a custom, opinion, or belief handed down to posterity esp. orally or by practice. **b** this process of handing down. **2** esp. *joc.* an established practice or custom (*it's a tradition to complain about the weather*). **3** artistic, literary, etc. principles based on experience and practice; any one of these (*stage tradition; traditions of the Dutch School*). □ **traditionary** adj. **traditionist** n. **traditionless** adj. [ME f. OF *tradicion* or L *traditio* f. *tradere* hand on, betray (as TRANS-, *dare* give)]

traditional /trəˈdɪʃ(ə)n(ə)l/ adj. **1** of, based on, or obtained by tradition. **2** (of jazz) in the style of the early 20th c. □ **traditionally** adv.

traditionalism /trəˈdɪʃ(ə)nəˌlɪz(ə)m/ n. respect, esp. excessive, for tradition, esp. in religion. □ **traditionalist** n. **traditionalistic** /-ˈlɪstɪk/ adj.

traduce /trəˈdjuːs/ v.tr. speak ill of; misrepresent. □ **traducement** n. **traducer** n. [L *traducere* disgrace (as TRANS-, *ducere* duct- lead)]

traffic /ˈtræfɪk/ n. & v. —n. **1** (often *attrib.*) **a** vehicles moving in a public highway, esp. of a specified kind, density, etc. (*heavy traffic on the M1; traffic warden*). **b** such movement in the air or at sea. **2** (usu. foll. by *in*) trade, esp. illegal (*the traffic in drugs*). **3 a** the transportation of goods, the coming and going of people or goods by road, rail, air, sea, etc. **b** the persons or goods so transported. **4** dealings or communication between people etc. (*had no traffic with them*). **5**

the messages, signals, etc., transmitted through a communications system; the flow or volume of such business. —v. (**trafficked**, **trafficking**) **1** *intr.* (usu. foll. by *in*) deal in something, esp. illegally (*trafficked in narcotics; traffics in innuendo*). **2** *tr.* deal in; barter. □ **traffic circle** *US* a roundabout. **traffic island** a paved or grassed area in a road to divert traffic and provide a refuge for pedestrians. **traffic jam** traffic at a standstill because of roadworks, an accident, etc. **traffic-light** (or **-lights** or **-signal**) a usu. automatic signal controlling road traffic esp. at junctions by coloured lights. **traffic warden** *Brit.* a uniformed official employed to help control road traffic and esp. parking. □ **trafficker** n. **trafficless** adj. [F *traf(f)ique*, Sp. *tráfico*, It. *traffico*, of unkn. orig.]

tragacanth /ˈtræɡəˌkænθ/ n. a white or reddish gum from a plant, *Astragalus gummifer*, used as a vehicle for drugs, dye, etc. [F *tragacante* f. L *tragacantha* f. Gk *tragakantha*, name of a shrub, f. *tragos* goat + *akantha* thorn]

tragedian /trəˈdʒiːdɪən/ n. **1** a writer of tragedies. **2** an actor in tragedy. [ME f. OF *tragediane* (as TRAGEDY)]

tragedienne /trəˌdʒiːdɪˈen/ n. an actress in tragedy. [F fem. (as TRAGEDIAN)]

tragedy /ˈtrædʒɪdɪ/ n. (pl. **-ies**) **1** a serious accident, crime, or natural catastrophe. **2** a sad event; a calamity (*the team's defeat is a tragedy*). **3 a** a play dealing with tragic events and with an unhappy ending. **b** tragic plays as a genre (cf. COMEDY). [ME f. OF *tragedie* f. L *tragoedia* f. Gk *tragōidia* app. goat-song f. *tragos* goat + *ōidē* song]

tragic /ˈtrædʒɪk/ adj. **1** (also **tragical** /-k(ə)l/) sad; calamitous; greatly distressing (*a tragic tale*). **2** of, or in the style of, tragedy (*tragic drama; a tragic actor*). □ **tragic irony** a device by which words carry a tragic, esp. prophetic, meaning to the audience, unknown to the character speaking. □ **tragically** adv. [F *tragique* f. L *tragicus* f. Gk *tragikos* f. *tragos* goat: see TRAGEDY]

tragicomedy /ˌtrædʒɪˈkɒmɪdɪ/ n. (pl. **-ies**) **1 a** a play having a mixture of comedy and tragedy. **b** plays of this kind as a genre. **2** an event etc. having tragic and comic elements. □ **tragicomic** adj. **tragicomically** adv. [F *tragicomédie* or It. *tragicomedia* f. LL *tragicomoedia* f. L *tragico-comoedia* (as TRAGIC, COMEDY)]

trail n. & v. —n. **1 a** a track left by a thing, person, etc., moving over a surface (*left a trail of wreckage; a slug's slimy trail*). **b** a track or scent followed in hunting, seeking, etc. (*he's on the trail*). **2** a beaten path or track, esp. through a wild region. **3** a part dragging behind a thing or person; an appendage (*a trail of smoke; a condensation trail*). —v. **1** *tr.* & *intr.* draw or be drawn along behind, esp. on the ground. **2** *intr.* (often foll. by *behind*) walk wearily; lag; straggle. **3** *tr.* follow the trail of; pursue (*trailed him to his home*). **4** *intr.* be losing in a game or other contest (*trailing by three points*). **5** *intr.* (usu. foll. by *away, off*) peter out; tail off. **6** *intr.* **a** (of a plant etc.) grow or hang over a wall, along the ground etc. **b** (of a garment etc.) hang loosely. **7** *tr.* (often *refl.*) drag (oneself, one's limbs, etc.) along wearily etc. **8** *tr.* advertise (a film, a radio or television programme, etc.) in advance by showing extracts etc. □ **trail arms** *Mil.* let a rifle etc. hang balanced in one hand and, *Brit.*, parallel to the ground. **trail bike** a light motor cycle for use in rough terrain. **trail-blazer 1** a person who marks a new track through wild country. **2** a pioneer; an innovator. **trail-blazing** *n.* the act or process of blazing a trail. —*attrib.adj.* that blazes a trail; pioneering. **trailing edge** the rear edge of an aircraft's wing etc. [ME (earlier as verb) f. OF *traillier* to tow, or f. MLG *treilen* haul f. L *tragula* drag-net]

trailer /ˈtreɪlə(r)/ *n.* **1** a person or thing that trails. **2** a series of brief extracts from a film etc., used to advertise it in advance. **3** a vehicle towed by another, esp.: **a** the rear section of an articulated lorry. **b** an open cart. **c** a platform for transporting a boat etc. **d** *US* a caravan. **4** a trailing plant.

train *v. & n.* —*v.* **1** *a tr.* (often foll. by *to* + infin.) teach (a person, animal, oneself, etc.) a specified skill esp. by practice (*trained the dog to beg*; *was trained in midwifery*). **b** *intr.* undergo this process (*trained as a teacher*). **2** *tr. & intr.* bring or come into a state of physical efficiency by exercise, diet, etc.; undergo physical exercise, esp. for a specific purpose. **3** *tr.* cause (a plant) to grow in a required shape (*trained the peach tree up the wall*). **4** (usu. as **trained** *adj.*) make (the mind, eye, etc.) sharp or discerning as a result of instruction, practice, etc. **5** *tr.* (often foll. by *on*) point or aim (a gun, camera, etc.) at an object etc. **6** *colloq.* **a** *intr.* go by train. **b** *tr.* (foll. by *it* as object) make a journey by train (*trained it to Aberdeen*). —*n.* **1** a series of railway carriages or trucks drawn by an engine. **2** something dragged along behind or forming the back part of a dress, robe, etc. (*wore a dress with a long train*; *the train of the peacock*). **3** a succession or series of people, things, events, etc. (*a long train of camels*; *interrupted by train of thought*). **4** a body of followers; a retinue (*a train of admirers*). **5** a succession of military vehicles etc., including artillery, supplies, etc. (*baggage train*). □ **in train** properly arranged or directed. **in a person's train** following behind a person. **in the train of** as a sequel of. **train-spotter** a person who collects locomotive numbers as a hobby. **train-spotting** this hobby. □ **trainable** *adj.* **trainability** /-ˈbɪlɪtɪ/ *n.* **trainee** /-ˈniː/ *n.* **trainless** *adj.* [ME f. OF *trainer, trahiner*, ult. f. L *trahere* draw]

trainer /ˈtreɪnə(r)/ *n.* **1** a person who trains. **2** a person who trains horses, athletes, footballers, etc., as a profession. **3** *Brit.* a soft running shoe of leather, canvas, etc.

training /ˈtreɪnɪŋ/ *n.* the act or process of teaching or learning a skill, discipline, etc. (*physical training*). □ **in training 1** undergoing physical training. **2** physically fit as a result of this. **out of training 1** no longer training. **2** physically unfit. **training-college** a college or school for training esp. prospective teachers. **training-ship** a ship on which young people are taught seamanship etc.

trainman /ˈtreɪnmæn/ *n.* (*pl.* **-men**) a railway employee working on trains.

traipse /treɪps/ *v. & n.* (also **trapes**) *colloq.* or *dial.* —*v.intr.* **1** tramp or trudge wearily. **2** (often foll. by *about*) go on errands. —*n.* a tedious journey on foot. [16th-c. *trapes* (v.), of unkn. orig.]

trait /treɪ, treɪt/ *n.* a distinguishing feature or characteristic esp. of a person. [F f. L *tractus* (as TRACT¹)]

traitor /ˈtreɪtə(r)/ *n.* (*fem.* **traitress** /-trɪs/) (often foll. by *to*) a person who is treacherous or disloyal, esp. to his country. □ **traitorous** *adj.* **traitorously** *adv.* [ME f. OF *traīt(o)ur* f. L *traditor -oris* f. *tradere*: see TRADITION]

trajectory /trəˈdʒektərɪ, ˈtrædʒɪk-/ *n.* (*pl.* **-ies**) the path described by a projectile flying or an object moving under the action of given forces. [(orig. adj.) f. med.L *trajectorius* f. L *traicere traject-* (as TRANS-, *jacere* throw)]

tram *n. Brit.* an electrically-powered passenger vehicle running on rails laid in a public road. [MLG & MDu. *trame* balk, beam, barrow-shaft]

tramcar /ˈtræmkɑː(r)/ *n. Brit.* = TRAM.

tramlines /ˈtræmlaɪnz/ *n.pl.* **1** rails for a tramcar. **2** *colloq.* **a** either pair of two sets of long parallel lines at the sides of a lawn-tennis court. **b** similar lines at the side or back of a badminton court. **3** inflexible principles or courses of action etc.

trammel /ˈtræm(ə)l/ *n. & v.* —*n.* **1** (usu. in *pl.*) an impediment to free movement; a hindrance (*the trammels of domesticity*). **2** a triple drag-net for fish. —*v.tr.* (**trammelled, trammelling**; *US* **trammeled, trammeling**) confine or hamper with or as if with trammels. [in sense 'net' ME f. OF *tramail* f. med.L *tramaculum, tremaculum*, perh. formed as TRI- + *macula* (MAIL²): later history uncert.]

tramp *v. & n.* —*v.* **1** *intr.* **a** walk heavily and firmly (*tramping about upstairs*). **b** go on foot, esp. a distance. **2** *tr.* **a** cross on foot, esp. wearily or reluctantly. **b** cover (a distance) in this way (*tramped forty miles*). **3** *tr.* (often foll. by *down*) tread on; trample; stamp on. —*n.* **1** an itinerant vagrant or beggar. **2** the sound of a person, esp. people, walking, marching, etc., or of horses' hooves. **3** a journey on foot, esp. protracted. **4** esp. *US sl. derog.* a promiscuous woman. **tramper** *n.* **trampish** *adj.* [ME *trampe* f. Gmc]

trample /ˈtræmp(ə)l/ *v. & n.* —*v.tr.* **1** tread under foot. **2** press down or crush in this way. —*n.* the sound or act of trampling. □ **trample on 1** tread heavily on. **2** treat roughly or with contempt; disregard (a person's feelings etc.). □ **trampler** *n.* [ME f. TRAMP + -LE⁴]

trampoline /ˈtræmpəˌliːn/ *n. & v.* —*n.* a strong fabric sheet connected by springs to a horizontal frame, used by gymnasts etc. for somersaults, as a springboard, etc. —*v.intr.* use a trampoline. □ **trampolinist** *n.* [It. *trampolino* f. *trampoli* stilts]

tramway /ˈtræmweɪ/ *n.* **1** rails for a tramcar. **2** a tramcar system.

trance /trɑːns/ *n. & v.* —*n.* **1 a** a sleeplike or half-conscious state without response to stimuli. **b** a hypnotic or cataleptic state. **2** such a state as entered into by a medium. **3** a state of extreme exaltation or rapture; ecstasy. —*v.tr. poet.* = ENTRANCE². □ **trancelike** *adj.* [ME f. OF *transe* f. *transir* depart, fall into trance f. L *transire*: see TRANSIT]

tranche /trɑːnʃ/ *n.* a portion, esp. of income, or of a block of shares. [F, = slice (as TRENCH)]

tranny /ˈtrænɪ/ *n.* (*pl.* **-ies**) esp. *Brit. colloq.* a transistor radio. [abbr.]

tranquil /ˈtræŋkwɪl/ *adj.* calm, serene, unruffled. □ **tranquillity** /-ˈkwɪlɪtɪ/ *n.* **tranquilly** *adv.* [F *tranquille* or L *tranquillus*]

tranquillize /ˈtræŋkwɪˌlaɪz/ *v.tr.* (US **tranquilize, -ise**) make tranquil, esp. by a drug etc.

tranquillizer /ˈtræŋkwɪˌlaɪzə(r)/ *n.* (US **tranquilizer, -iser**) a drug used to diminish anxiety.

trans- /træns, trɑːns, -nz/ *prefix* **1** across, beyond (*transcontinental*; *transgress*). **2** on or to the other side of (*transatlantic*). **3** through (*transonic*). **4** into another state or place (*transform*; *transcribe*). **5** surpassing, transcending (*transfinite*). [from or after L *trans* across]

transact /trænˈzækt, trɑːn-, -ˈsækt/ *v.tr.* perform or carry through (business). □ **transactor** *n.* [L *transigere transact-* (as TRANS-, *agere* do)]

transaction /trænˈzækʃ(ə)n, trɑːn-, -ˈsækʃ(ə)n/ *n.* **1** a piece of esp. commercial business done; a deal (*a profitable transaction*). **2** (in *pl.*) published reports of discussions, papers read, etc., at the meetings of a learned society. □ **transactional** *adj.* **transactionally** *adv.* [ME f. LL *transactio* (as TRANSACT)]

transalpine /trænzˈælpaɪn, trɑːn-, -sˈælpaɪn/ *adj.* beyond the Alps, esp. from the Italian point of view. [L *transalpinus* (as TRANS-, *alpinus* ALPINE)]

transatlantic /ˌtrænzətˈlæntɪk, ˌtrɑːn-, -sətˈlæntɪk/ *adj.* **1** beyond the Atlantic, esp.: **a** *Brit.* American. **b** *US* European. **2** crossing the Atlantic (*a transatlantic flight*).

transceiver /trænˈsiːvə(r), trɑːn-/ *n.* a combined radio transmitter and receiver.

transcend /trænˈsend, trɑːn-/ *v.tr.* **1** be beyond the range or grasp of (human experience, reason, belief, etc.). **2** excel; surpass. [ME f. OF *transcendre* or L *transcendere* (as TRANS-, *scandere* climb)]

transcendent /trænˈsend(ə)nt, trɑːn-/ *adj.* **1** excelling, surpassing (*transcendent merit*). **2** transcending human experience. **3** (esp. of the supreme being) existing apart from, not subject to the limitations of, the material universe. □ **transcendence** *n.* **transcendency** *n.* **transcendently** *adv.*

transcendental /ˌtrænsenˈdent(ə)l, ˌtrɑːn-/ *adj.* **1** = TRANSCENDENT. **2** *Philos.* **a** a priori. **b** explaining matter and objective things as products of the subjective mind. **3 a** visionary, abstract. **b** vague, obscure. □ **Transcendental Meditation** a method of detaching oneself from problems, anxiety, etc., by silent meditation and repetition of a mantra. □ **transcendentally** *adv.* [med.L *transcendentalis* (as TRANSCENDENT)]

transcendentalism /ˌtrænsenˈdentəˌlɪz(ə)m, ˌtrɑːn-/ *n.* **1** transcendental philosophy. **2** exalted or visionary language. □ **transcendentalist** *n.* **transcendentalize** *v.tr.* (also **-ise**).

transcontinental /ˌtrænzˌkɒntɪˈnent(ə)l, trɑːnz-, træns-, trɑːns-/ *adj. & n.* —*adj.* (of a railway etc.) extending across a continent. —*n.* a transcontinental railway or train. □ **transcontinentally** *adv.*

transcribe /trænˈskraɪb, trɑːn-/ *v.tr.* **1** make a copy of, esp. in writing. **2** transliterate. **3** write out (shorthand, notes, etc.) in ordinary characters or continuous prose. **4** arrange (music) for a different instrument etc. □ **transcriber** *n.* **transcription** /-ˈskrɪpʃ(ə)n/ *n.* **transcriptional** /-ˈskrɪpʃən(ə)l/ *adj.* **transcriptive** /-ˈskrɪptɪv/ *adj.* [L *transcribere transcript-* (as TRANS-, *scribere* write)]

transcript /ˈtrænskrɪpt, ˈtrɑːn-/ *n.* **1** a written or recorded copy. **2** any copy. [ME f. OF *transcrit* f. L *transcriptum* neut. past part.: see TRANSCRIBE]

transducer /trænsˈdjuːsə(r), trɑːns-, -zˈdjuːsə(r)/ *n.* any device for converting a non-electrical signal into an electrical one e.g. pressure into voltage. [L *transducere* lead across (as TRANS-, *ducere* lead)]

transept /ˈtrænsept, ˈtrɑːn-/ *n.* **1** either arm of the part of a cross-shaped church at right angles to the nave (*north transept*; *south transept*). **2** this part as a whole. □ **transeptal** /-ˈsept(ə)l/ *adj.* [mod.L *transeptum* (as TRANS-, SEPTUM)]

transexual var. of TRANSSEXUAL.

transfer *v. & n.* —*v.* /trænsˈfɜː(r), trɑːns-/ (**transferred, transferring**) **1** *tr.* (often foll. by *to*) **a** convey, remove, or hand over (a thing etc.) (*transferred the bag from the car to the station*). **b** make over the possession of (property, a ticket, rights, etc.) to a person (*transferred his membership to his son*). **2** *tr. & intr.* change or move to another group, club, department, etc. **3** *intr.* change from one station, route, etc., to another on a journey. **4** *tr.* convey (a drawing etc.) from one surface to another. **5** *tr.* change (the sense of a word etc.) by extension or metaphor. —*n.* /ˈtrænsfɜː(r), ˈtrɑːns-/ **1** the act or an instance of transferring or being transferred. **2 a** a design etc. conveyed or to be conveyed from one surface to another. **b** a small usu. coloured picture or design on paper, which is transferable to another surface. **3** a football player etc. who is or is to be transferred. **4 a** the conveyance of property, a right, etc. **b** a document effecting this. **5** *US* a ticket allowing a journey to be continued on another route etc. □ **transfer fee** a fee paid for the transfer of esp. a professional footballer. **transfer list** a list of footballers available for transfer. □ **transferee** /-ˈriː/ *n.* **transferor** /-ˈfɜːrə(r)/ esp. *Law n.* **transferrer** /-ˈfɜːrə(r)/ *n.* [ME f. F *transférer* or L *transferre* (as TRANS-, *ferre lat-* bear)]

transferable /trænsˈfɜːrəb(ə)l, trɑːns-, ˈtr-/ *adj.* capable of being transferred. □ **transferable vote** a vote that can be transferred to another candidate if the first choice is eliminated. □ **transferability** /-ˈbɪlɪtɪ/ *n.*

transference /ˈtrænsfərəns, ˈtrɑː-/ *n.* the act or an instance of transferring; the state of being transferred.

transferral /trænsˈfɜːr(ə)l, trɑːns-/ *n.* = TRANSFER *n.* 1.

transfiguration /ˌtrænsˌfɪɡjʊˈreɪʃ(ə)n, trɑː-/ *n.* **1** a change of form or appearance. **2 a** Christ's appearance in radiant glory to three of his disciples (Matt. 17:2, Mark 9:2–3). **b** (**Transfiguration**) the festival of Christ's transfiguration, 6 Aug. [ME f. OF *transfiguration* or L *transfiguratio* (as TRANSFIGURE)]

transfigure /trænsˈfɪɡə(r), trɑː-/ *v.tr.* change in form or appearance, esp. so as to elevate or idealize. [ME f. OF *transfigurer* or L *transfigurare* (as TRANS-, FIGURE)]

transfix /trænsˈfɪks, trɑː-/ *v.tr.* **1** pierce with a sharp implement or weapon. **2** root (a person) to the spot with horror or astonishment; paralyse the faculties of. □ **transfixion** /-ˈfɪkʃ(ə)n/ *n.* [L *transfigere transfix-* (as TRANS-, FIX)]

transform /trænsˈfɔːm, trɑː-/ v. **1 a** tr. make a thorough or dramatic change in the form, outward appearance, character, etc., of. **b** intr. (often foll. by *into*, *to*) undergo such a change. **2** tr. Electr. change the voltage etc. of (a current). □ **transformable** adj. **transformation** /-ˈmeɪʃ(ə)n/ n. **transformative** adj. [ME f. OF transformer or L transformare (as TRANS-, FORM)]

transformer /trænsˈfɔːmə(r), trɑː-, -zˈfɔːmə(r)/ n. **1** an apparatus for reducing or increasing the voltage of an alternating current. **2** a person or thing that transforms.

transfuse /trænsˈfjuːz, trɑː-/ v.tr. **1** permeate (*purple dye transfused the water*). **2 a** transfer (blood) from one person or animal to another. **b** inject (liquid) into a blood-vessel to replace lost fluid. □ **transfusion** /-ˈfjuːʒ(ə)n/ n. [ME f. L transfundere transfus- (as TRANS-, fundere pour)]

transgress /trænzˈgres, trɑː-, -sˈgres/ v.tr. (also absol.) go beyond the bounds or limits set by (a commandment, law, etc.); violate; infringe. □ **transgression** /-ˈgreʃ(ə)n/ n. **transgressive** adj. **transgressor** n. [F transgresser or L transgredi transgress- (as TRANS-, gradi go)]

tranship var. of TRANSSHIP.

transient /ˈtrænzɪənt, ˈtrɑː-, -sɪənt/ adj. & n. —adj. of short duration; momentary; passing; impermanent (*life is transient; of transient interest*). —n. a temporary visitor, worker, etc. □ **transience** n. **transiency** n. **transiently** adv. [L transire (as TRANS-, ire go)]

transistor /trænˈzɪstə(r), trɑː-, -ˈsɪstə(r)/ n. **1** a semiconductor device with three connections, capable of amplification in addition to rectification. **2** (in full **transistor radio**) a portable radio with transistors. [portmanteau word, f. TRANSFER + RESISTOR]

transistorize /trænˈzɪstəˌraɪz, trɑː-, -ˈsɪstəˌraɪz/ v.tr. (also **-ise**) design or equip with, or convert to, transistors rather than valves. □ **transistorization** /-ˈzeɪʃ(ə)n/ n.

transit /ˈtrænzɪt, ˈtrɑː-, -sɪt/ n. & v. —n. **1** the act or process of going, conveying, or being conveyed, esp. over a distance (*transit by rail; made a transit of the lake*). **2** a passage or route (*the overland transit*). **3 a** the apparent passage of a celestial body across the meridian of a place. **b** such an apparent passage across the sun or a planet. **4** US the local conveyance of passengers on public routes. —v. (**transited, transiting**) **1** tr. make a transit across. **2** intr. make a transit. □ **in transit** while going or being conveyed. **transit camp** a camp for the temporary accommodation of soldiers, refugees, etc. **transit lounge** a lounge at an airport for passengers waiting between flights. **transit visa** a visa allowing only passage through a country. [ME f. L transitus f. transire (as TRANSIENT)]

transition /trænˈzɪʃ(ə)n, trɑː-, -ˈsɪʃ(ə)n/ n. **1** a passing or change from one place, state, condition, etc., to another (*an age of transition; a transition from plain to hills*). **2** Art a change from one style to another, esp. Archit. from Norman to Early English. □ **transitional** adj. **transitionally** adv. **transitionary** adj. [F transition or L transitio (as TRANSIT)]

transitive /ˈtrænsɪtɪv, ˈtrɑː-, -zɪtɪv/ adj. Gram. (of a verb or sense of a verb) that takes a direct object (whether expressed or implied), e.g. saw in *saw the donkey, saw that she was ill.* □ **transitively** adv. **transitiveness** n. **transitivity** /-ˈtɪvɪtɪ/ n. [LL transitivus (as TRANSIT)]

transitory /ˈtrænsɪtərɪ, ˈtrɑː-, -zɪtərɪ/ adj. not permanent, brief, transient. □ **transitorily** adv. **transitoriness** n. [ME f. AF transitorie, OF transitoire f. L transitorius (as TRANSIT)]

translate /trænsˈleɪt, trɑː-, -ˈzleɪt/ v. **1** tr. (also absol.) **a** (often foll. by *into*) express the sense of (a word, sentence, speech, book, etc.) in another language. **b** do this as a profession etc. (*translates for the UN*). **2** intr. (of a literary work etc.) be translatable, bear translation (*does not translate well*). **3** tr. express (an idea, book, etc.) in another, esp. simpler, form. **4** tr. interpret the significance of; infer as (*translated his silence as dissent*). **5** tr. move or change, esp. from one person, place, or condition, to another (*was translated by joy*). **6** intr. (foll. by *into*) result in; be converted into; manifest itself as. **7** tr. Eccl. **a** remove (a bishop) to another see. **b** remove (a saint's relics etc.) to another place. □ **translatable** adj. **translatability** /-ˈbɪlɪtɪ/ n. [ME f. L translatus, past part. of transferre: see TRANSFER]

translation /trænsˈleɪʃ(ə)n, trɑː-, -zˈleɪʃ(ə)n/ n. **1** the act or an instance of translating. **2** a written or spoken expression of the meaning of a word, speech, book, etc. in another language. □ **translational** adj. **translationally** adv.

translator /trænsˈleɪtə(r), trɑː-, -zˈleɪtə(r)/ n. **1** a person who translates from one language into another. **2** a television relay transmitter. **3** a program that translates from one (esp. programming) language into another.

transliterate /trænzˈlɪtəˌreɪt, trɑː-, -sˈlɪtəˌreɪt/ v.tr. represent (a word etc.) in the closest corresponding letters of a different alphabet or language. □ **transliteration** /-ˈreɪʃ(ə)n/ n. **transliterator** n. [TRANS- + L littera letter]

translocate /ˌtrænzləʊˈkeɪt, ˌtrɑː-, -sləʊˈkeɪt/ v.tr. move from one place to another. □ **translocation** n.

translucent /trænzˈluːs(ə)nt, trɑː-, -ˈljuːs(ə)nt, -sˈl-/ adj. **1** allowing light to pass through diffusely; semi-transparent. **2** transparent. □ **translucence** n. **translucency** n. **translucently** adv. [L translucēre (as TRANS-, lucēre shine)]

transmigrate /ˌtrænzmaɪˈgreɪt, ˌtrɑː-, -smaɪˈgreɪt/ v.intr. **1** (of the soul) pass into a different body; undergo metempsychosis. **2** migrate. □ **transmigration** /-ˈgreɪʃ(ə)n/ n. **transmigrator** n. **transmigratory** /-ˈmaɪgrətərɪ/ adj. [ME f. L transmigrare (as TRANS-, MIGRATE)]

transmission /trænzˈmɪʃ(ə)n, trɑː-, -sˈmɪʃ(ə)n/ n. **1** the act or an instance of transmitting; the state of being transmitted. **2** a broadcast radio or television programme. **3** the mechanism by which power is transmitted from an engine to the axle in a motor vehicle. [L transmissio (as TRANS-, MISSION)]

transmit /trænzˈmɪt, trɑː-, -sˈmɪt/ v.tr. (**transmitted, transmitting**) **1 a** pass or hand on; transfer (*transmitted the message; how diseases are transmitted*). **b** communicate (ideas, emotions, etc.). **2 a** allow (heat, light, sound, electricity, etc.) to pass through; be a medium for. **b** be a medium for (ideas, emotions, etc.) (*his message transmits hope*). **3** broadcast (a radio or television programme). □ **transmissible** /-ˈmɪsəb(ə)l/ adj.

transmissive /-ˈmɪsɪv/ adj. **transmittable** adj. **transmittal** n. [ME f. L transmittere (as TRANS-, mittere miss- send)]

transmitter /trænsˈmɪtə(r), trɑː-, -zˈmɪtə(r)/ n. **1** a person or thing that transmits. **2** a set of equipment used to generate and transmit electromagnetic waves carrying messages, signals, etc., esp. those of radio or television.

transmogrify /trænzˈmɒgrɪˌfaɪ, trɑː-, -sˈmɒgrɪˌfaɪ/ v.tr. (**-ies, -ied**) joc. transform, esp. in a magical or surprising manner. □ **transmogrification** /-fɪˈkeɪʃ(ə)n/ n. [17th c.: orig. unkn.]

transmutation /ˌtrænzmjuːˈteɪʃ(ə)n, ˌtrɑː-, -smjuːˈteɪʃ(ə)n/ n. **1** the act or an instance of transmuting or changing into another form etc. **2** Alchemy hist. the supposed process of changing base metals into gold. **3** Physics the changing of one element into another by nuclear bombardment etc. □ **transmutational** adj. **transmutationist** n. [ME f. OF transmutation or LL transmutatio (as TRANS- MUTE)]

transmute /trænzˈmjuːt, trɑː-, -sˈmjuːt/ v.tr. **1** change the form, nature, or substance of. **2** Alchemy hist. subject (base metals) to transmutation. □ **transmutable** adj. **transmutability** /-ˈbɪlɪtɪ/ n. **transmutative** /-tətɪv/ adj. **transmuter** n. [ME f. L transmutare (as TRANS-, mutare change)]

transnational /trænzˈnæʃən(ə)l, trɑː-, -sˈnæʃən(ə)l/ adj. extending beyond national boundaries.

transoceanic /ˌtrænzˌəʊʃɪˈænɪk, trɑː-, -sˌəʊʃɪˈænɪk/ adj. **1** situated beyond the ocean. **2** concerned with crossing the ocean (transoceanic flight).

transom /ˈtrænsəm/ n. **1** a horizontal bar of wood or stone across a window or the top of a door. **2** a strengthening crossbar. **3** US = transom window. □ **transom window 1** a window divided by a transom. **2** a window placed above the transom of a door or larger window; a fanlight. □ **transomed** adj. [ME traversayn, transyn, -ing, f. OF traversin f. traverse TRAVERSE]

transonic /trænˈsɒnɪk, trɑː-/ adj. (also **transsonic**) relating to speeds close to that of sound. [TRANS- + SONIC, after supersonic etc.]

transpacific /ˌtrænzpəˈsɪfɪk, ˌtrɑː-, -spəˈsɪfɪk/ adj. **1** beyond the Pacific. **2** crossing the Pacific.

transparence /trænsˈpærəns, trɑː-, -ˈpeərəns/ n. = TRANSPARENCY 1.

transparency /trænsˈpærənsɪ, trɑː-, -ˈpeərənsɪ/ n. (pl. **-ies**) **1** the condition of being transparent. **2** Photog. a positive transparent photograph on glass or in a frame to be viewed using a slide projector etc. **3** a picture, inscription, etc., made visible by a light behind it. [med.L transparentia (as TRANSPARENT)]

transparent /trænsˈpærənt, trɑː-, -ˈpeərənt/ adj. **1** allowing light to pass through so that bodies can be distinctly seen. **2 a** (of a disguise, pretext, etc.) easily seen through. **b** (of a motive, quality, etc.) easily discerned; obvious. **3** (of a person etc.) easily understood; frank; open. □ **transparently** adv. **transparentness** n. [ME f. OF f. med.L transparens f. L transparēre shine through (as TRANS-, parēre appear)]

transpire /trænˈspaɪə(r), trɑː-/ v. **1** intr. (of a secret or something unknown) leak out; come to be known. **2** intr. disp. **a** (prec. by it as subject) turn out; prove to be the case (it transpired he knew nothing about it). **b** occur; happen. **3** tr. & intr. emit (vapour, sweat, etc.), or be emitted, through the skin or lungs; perspire. **4** intr. (of a plant or leaf) release water vapour. □ **transpirable** adj. **transpiration** /-spɪˈreɪʃ(ə)n/ n. **transpiratory** /-rətərɪ/ adj. [F transpirer or med.L transpirare (as TRANS-, L spirare breathe)]

transplant v. & n. —v.tr. /trænsˈplɑːnt, trɑː-/ **1 a** plant in another place (transplanted the daffodils). **b** move to another place (whole nations were transplanted). **2** Surgery transfer (living tissue or an organ) and implant in another part of the body or in another body. —n. /ˈtrænsplɑːnt, ˈtrɑː-/ **1** Surgery **a** the transplanting of an organ or tissue. **b** such an organ etc. **2** a thing, esp. a plant, transplanted. □ **transplantable** /-ˈplɑːntəb(ə)l/ adj. **transplantation** /-ˈteɪʃ(ə)n/ n. **transplanter** /-ˈplɑːntə(r)/ n. [ME f. LL transplantare (as TRANS-, PLANT)]

transponder /trænˈspɒndə(r), trɑː-/ n. a device for receiving a radio signal and automatically transmitting a different signal. [TRANSMIT + RESPOND]

transpontine /trænsˈpɒntaɪn, trɑː-, -zˈpɒntaɪn/ adj. on the other side of a bridge, esp. on the south side of the Thames. [TRANS- + L pons pontis bridge]

transport v. & n. —v.tr. /trænsˈpɔːt, trɑː-/ **1** take or carry (a person, goods, troops, baggage, etc.) from one place to another. **2** hist. take (a criminal) to a penal colony; deport. **3** (as **transported** adj.) (usu. foll. by with) affected with strong emotion. —n. /ˈtrænspɔːt, ˈtrɑː-/ **1 a** a system of conveying people, goods, etc., from place to place. **b** the means of this (our transport has arrived). **2** a ship, aircraft, etc. used to carry soldiers, stores, etc. **3** (esp. in pl.) vehement emotion (transports of joy). □ **transport café** Brit. a roadside café for (esp. commercial) drivers. [ME f. OF transporter or L transportare (as TRANS-, portare carry)]

transportable /trænsˈpɔːtəb(ə)l, trɑː-/ adj. **1** capable of being transported. **2** hist. (of an offender or an offence) punishable by transportation. □ **transportability** /-ˈbɪlɪtɪ/ n.

transportation /ˌtrænspɔːˈteɪʃ(ə)n, ˌtrɑː-/ n. **1** the act of conveying or the process of being conveyed. **2 a** a system of conveying. **b** esp. US the means of this. **3** hist. removal to a penal colony.

transporter /trænsˈpɔːtə(r), trɑː-/ n. **1** a person or device that transports. **2** a vehicle used to transport other vehicles or large pieces of machinery etc. by road. □ **transporter bridge** a bridge carrying vehicles etc. across water on a suspended moving platform.

transpose /trænsˈpəʊz, trɑː-, -zˈpəʊz/ v.tr. **1 a** cause (two or more things) to change places. **b** change the position of (a thing) in a series. **c** change the order or position of (words or a word) in a sentence. **2** Mus. write or play in a different key. □ **transposable** adj. **transposal** n. **transposer** n. [ME, = transform f. OF transposer (as TRANS-, L ponere put)]

transposition /ˌtrænspəˈzɪʃ(ə)n, ˌtrɑː-, -zpəˈzɪʃ(ə)n/ n. the act or an instance of transposing; the state of being transposed. □ **transpositional** adj. **transpositive** /-ˈpɒzɪtɪv/ adj. [F transposition or LL transpositio (as TRANS-, POSITION)]

transputer /trænsˈpjuːtə(r), trɑː-, -zˈpjuːtə(r)/ *n.* a microprocessor with integral memory designed for parallel processing. [TRANSISTOR + COMPUTER]

transsexual /trænzˈseksjʊəl, trɑː-, -ʃʊəl/ *adj.* & *n.* (also **transexual**) —*adj.* having the physical characteristics of one sex and the supposed psychological characteristics of the other. —*n.* **1** a transsexual person. **2** a person whose sex has been changed by surgery. □ **transsexualism** *n.*

transship /trænˈʃɪp, trɑː-, trænz-/ *v.tr.* (also **tranship**) *intr.* (**-shipped**, **-shipping**) transfer from one ship or form of transport to another. □ **transshipment** *n.*

transubstantiation /ˌtrænsəbˌstænʃɪˈeɪʃ(ə)n, ˌtrɑː-/ *n. Theol.* & *RC Ch.* the conversion of the Eucharistic elements wholly into the body and blood of Christ, only the appearance of bread and wine still remaining. [med.L (as TRANS-, SUBSTANCE)]

transuranic /ˌtrænsjʊəˈrænɪk, ˌtrɑː-/ *adj. Chem.* (of an element) having a higher atomic number than uranium.

transverse /ˈtrænzvɜːs, ˈtrɑː-, -ˈvɜːs, -ns-/ *adj.* situated, arranged, or acting in a crosswise direction. □ **transversely** *adv.* [L *transvertere transvers-* turn across (as TRANS-, *vertere* turn)]

transvestism /trænzˈvestɪz(ə)m, trɑː-, -sˈvestɪz(ə)m/ *n.* the practice of wearing the clothes of the opposite sex, esp. as a sexual stimulus. □ **transvestist** *n.* [G *Transvestismus* f. TRANS- + L *vestire* clothe]

transvestite /trænzˈvestaɪt, trɑː-, -sˈvestaɪt/ *n.* a person given to transvestism.

trap[1] *n.* & *v.* —*n.* **1 a** an enclosure or device, often baited, for catching animals. **b** a device with bait for killing vermin, esp. = MOUSETRAP. **2** a trick betraying a person into speech or an act (*is this question a trap?*). **3** an arrangement to catch an unsuspecting person, e.g. a speeding motorist. **4** a device for hurling an object such as a clay pigeon into the air to be shot at. **5** a compartment from which a greyhound is released at the start of a race. **6 a** a curve in a downpipe etc. that fills with liquid and forms a seal against the upward passage of gases. **b** a device for preventing the passage of steam etc. **7** a two-wheeled carriage (*a pony and trap*). **8** = TRAPDOOR. **9** *sl.* the mouth (esp. *shut one's trap*). **10** (esp. in *pl.*) *colloq.* a percussion instrument esp. in a jazz band. —*v.tr.* (**trapped**, **trapping**) **1** catch (an animal) in a trap. **2** catch or catch out (a person) by means of a trick, plan, etc. **3** stop and retain in or as in a trap. □ **trap-shooting** the sport of shooting at objects released from a trap. □ **traplike** *adj.* [OE *treppe*, *træppe*, rel. to MDu. *trappe*, med.L *trappa*, of uncert. orig.]

trap[2] *v.tr.* (**trapped**, **trapping**) (often foll. by *out*) **1** provide with trappings. **2** adorn. [obs. *trap* (n.): ME f. OF *drap*: see DRAPE]

trap[3] *n.* (in full **trap-rock**) any dark-coloured igneous rock, fine-grained and columnar in structure, esp. basalt. [Sw. *trapp* f. *trappa* stair, f. the often stairlike appearance of its outcroppings]

trapdoor /ˈtræpdɔː(r)/ *n.* a door or hatch in a floor, ceiling, or roof, usu. made flush with the surface.

trapes var. of TRAIPSE.

trapeze /trəˈpiːz/ *n.* a crossbar or set of crossbars suspended by ropes used as a swing for acrobatics etc. [F *trapèze* f. LL *trapezium*: see TRAPEZIUM]

trapezium /trəˈpiːzɪəm/ *n.* (*pl.* **trapezia** /-zɪə/ or **trapeziums**) **1** *Brit.* a quadrilateral with only one pair of sides parallel. **2** *US* = TRAPEZOID 1. [LL f. Gk *trapezion* f. *trapeza* table]

trapezoid /ˈtræpɪzɔɪd/ *n.* **1** *Brit.* a quadrilateral with no two sides parallel. **2** *US* = TRAPEZIUM 1. □ **trapezoidal** *adj.* [mod.L *trapezoides* f. Gk *trapezoeidēs* (as TRAPEZIUM)]

trapper /ˈtræpə(r)/ *n.* a person who traps wild animals esp. to obtain furs.

trappings /ˈtræpɪŋz/ *n.pl.* **1** ornamental accessories, esp. as an indication of status (*the trappings of office*). **2** the harness of a horse esp. when ornamental. [ME (as TRAP[2])]

Trappist /ˈtræpɪst/ *n.* & *adj.* —*n.* a member of a branch of the Cistercian order founded in 1664 at La Trappe in Normandy and noted for an austere rule including a vow of silence. —*adj.* of or relating to this order. [F *trappiste* f. *La Trappe*]

traps *n.pl. colloq.* personal belongings; baggage. [perh. contr. f. TRAPPINGS]

trash *n.* & *v.* —*n.* **1** esp. *US* worthless or waste stuff; rubbish, refuse. **2** a worthless person or persons. **3** a thing of poor workmanship or material. —*v.tr.* **1** esp. *US colloq.* wreck. **2** esp. *US colloq.* expose the worthless nature of; disparage. □ **trash can** *US* a dustbin. [16th c.: orig. unkn.]

trashy /ˈtræʃɪ/ *adj.* (**trashier**, **trashiest**) worthless; poorly made. □ **trashily** *adv.* **trashiness** *n.*

trattoria /ˌtrætəˈriːə/ *n.* an Italian restaurant. [It.]

trauma /ˈtrɔːmə, ˈtraʊ-/ *n.* (*pl.* **traumata** /-mətə/ or **traumas**) **1** any physical wound or injury. **2** physical shock following this, characterized by a drop in body temperature, mental confusion, etc. **3** *Psychol.* emotional shock following a stressful event, sometimes leading to long-term neurosis. □ **traumatize** *v.tr.* (also **-ise**). **traumatization** /-taɪˈzeɪʃ(ə)n/ *n.* [Gk *trauma traumatos* wound]

traumatic /trɔːˈmætɪk, traʊ-/ *adj.* **1** of or causing trauma. **2** *colloq.* (in general use) distressing; emotionally disturbing (*a traumatic experience*). **3** of or for wounds. □ **traumatically** *adv.* [LL *traumaticus* f. Gk *traumatikos* (as TRAUMA)]

travail /ˈtræveɪl/ *n.* & *v. literary* —*n.* **1** painful or laborious effort. **2** the pangs of childbirth. —*v.intr.* undergo a painful effort, esp. in childbirth. [ME f. OF *travail*, *travaillier* ult. f. med.L *trepalium* instrument of torture f. L *tres* three + *palus* stake]

travel /ˈtræv(ə)l/ *v.* & *n.* —*v.intr.* & *tr.* (**travelled**, **travelling**; *US* **traveled**, **traveling**) **1** *intr.* go from one place to another; make a journey esp. of some length or abroad. **2** *tr.* **a** a journey along or through (a country). **b** cover (a distance) in travelling. **3** *intr. colloq.* withstand a long journey (*wines that do not travel*). **4** *intr.* go from place to place as a salesman. **5** *intr.* move or proceed in a specified manner or at a specified rate (*light travels faster than sound*). **6** *intr. colloq.* move quickly. **7** *intr.* pass esp. in a deliberate or systematic manner from point to point (*the photographer's eye travelled over the scene*). —*n.* **1** the act of travelling, esp. in foreign countries. **2**

(often in *pl.*) a spell of this (*have returned from their travels*). □ **travel agency** (or **bureau**) an agency that makes the necessary arrangements for travellers. **travel agent** a person or firm acting as a travel agency. **travelling crane** a crane able to move on rails, esp. along an overhead support. **travel-sick** suffering from nausea caused by motion in travelling. **travel-sickness** the condition of being travel-sick. [ME, orig. = TRAVAIL]

travelled /ˈtræv(ə)ld/ *adj.* experienced in travelling (also in *comb.*: *much-travelled*).

traveller /ˈtrævələ(r)/ *n.* (*US* **traveler**) **1** a person who travels or is travelling. **2** a travelling salesman. **3** a Gypsy. **4** *Austral.* an itinerant workman; a swagman. □ **traveller's cheque** (*US* **check**) a cheque for a fixed amount that may be cashed on signature, usu. internationally. **traveller's joy** a wild clematis, *Clematis vitalba*.

travelogue /ˈtrævəlɒg/ *n.* a film or illustrated lecture about travel. [TRAVEL after *monologue* etc.]

traverse /ˈtrævəs, trəˈvɜːs/ *v.* & *n.* —*v.* **1** *tr.* travel or lie across (*traversed the country; a pit traversed by a beam*). **2** *tr.* consider or discuss the whole extent of (a subject). **3** *tr.* turn (a large gun) horizontally. —*n.* **1** a sideways movement. **2** an act of traversing. **3** a thing, esp. part of a structure, that crosses another. **4** the sideways movement of a part in a machine. **5 a** a sideways motion across a rock-face from one practicable line of ascent or descent to another. **b** a place where this is necessary. **6** the act of turning a large gun horizontally to the required direction. □ **traversable** *adj.* **traversal** *n.* **traverser** *n.* [OF *traverser* f. LL *traversare, transversare* (as TRANSVERSE)]

travesty /ˈtrævɪstɪ/ *n.* & *v.* —*n.* (*pl.* **-ies**) a grotesque misrepresentation or imitation (*a travesty of justice*). —*v.tr.* (**-ies, -ied**) make or be a travesty of. [(orig. *adj.*) f. F *travesti* past part. of *travestir* disguise, change the clothes of, f. It. *travestire* (as TRANS-, *vestire* clothe)]

trawl *v.* & *n.* —*v.* **1** *intr.* **a** fish with a trawl or seine. **b** seek a suitable candidate etc. by sifting through a large number. **2** *tr.* **a** catch by trawling. **b** seek a suitable candidate etc. from (a certain area or group etc.) (*trawled the schools for new trainees*). —*n.* **1** an act of trawling. **2** (in full **trawl-net**) a large wide-mouthed fishing-net dragged by a boat along the bottom. **3** (in full **trawl-line**) *US* a long sea-fishing line buoyed and supporting short lines with baited hooks. [prob. f. MDu. *traghelen* to drag (cf. *traghel* drag-net), perh. f. L *tragula*]

trawler /ˈtrɔːlə(r)/ *n.* **1** a boat used for trawling. **2** a person who trawls.

tray *n.* **1** a flat shallow vessel usu. with a raised rim for carrying dishes etc. or containing small articles, papers, etc. **2** a shallow lidless box forming a compartment of a trunk. □ **trayful** *n.* (*pl.* **-fuls**). [OE *trīg* f. Gmc, rel. to TREE]

treacherous /ˈtretʃərəs/ *adj.* **1** guilty of or involving treachery. **2** (of the weather, ice, the memory, etc.) not to be relied on; likely to fail or give way. □ **treacherously** *adv.* **treacherousness** *n.* [ME f. OF *trecherous* f. *trecheor* a cheat f. *trechier, trichier*: see TRICK]

treachery /ˈtretʃərɪ/ *n.* (*pl.* **-ies**) **1** violation of faith or trust; betrayal. **2** an instance of this.

treacle /ˈtriːk(ə)l/ *n.* **1** esp. *Brit.* **a** a syrup produced in refining sugar. **b** molasses. **2** cloying sentimentality or flattery. □ **treacly** *adj.* [ME *triacle* f. OF f. L *theriaca* f. Gk *thēriakē* antidote against venom, fem. of *thēriakos* (adj.) f. *thērion* wild beast]

tread /tred/ *v.* & *n.* —*v.* (**trod; trodden** or **trod**) **1** *intr.* (often foll. by *on*) **a** set down one's foot; walk or step (*do not tread on the grass; trod on a snail*). **b** (of the foot) be set down. **2** *tr.* walk on. **b** (often foll. by *down*) press or crush with the feet. **3** *tr.* perform (steps etc.) by walking (*trod a few paces*). **4** *tr.* make (a hole etc.) by treading. **5** *intr.* (foll. by *on*) suppress; subdue mercilessly. **6** *tr.* make a track with (dirt etc.) from the feet. **7** *tr.* (often foll. by *in, into*) press down into the ground with the feet (*trod dirt into the carpet*). **8** *tr.* (also *absol.*) (of a male bird) copulate with (a hen). —*n.* **1** a manner or sound of walking (*recognized the heavy tread*). **2** (in full **tread-board**) the top surface of a step or stair. **3** the thick moulded part of a vehicle tyre for gripping the road. **4** the part of a wheel that touches the ground or rail. **5** the part of the sole of a shoe that rests on the ground. **6** (of a male bird) copulation. □ **tread the boards** (or **stage**) be an actor; appear on the stage. **tread on a person's toes** offend a person or encroach on a person's privileges etc. **tread out 1** stamp out (a fire etc.). **2** press out (wine or grain) with the feet. **tread water** maintain an upright position in the water by moving the feet with a walking movement and the hands with a downward circular motion. **tread-wheel** a treadmill or similar appliance. □ **treader** *n.* [OE *tredan* f. WG]

treadle /ˈtred(ə)l/ *n.* & *v.* —*n.* a lever worked by the foot and imparting motion to a machine. —*v.intr.* work a treadle. [OE *tredel* stair (as TREAD)]

treadmill /ˈtredmɪl/ *n.* **1** a device for producing motion by the weight of persons or animals stepping on movable steps on the inner surface of a revolving upright wheel. **2** monotonous routine work.

treason /ˈtriːz(ə)n/ *n.* **1** (in full **high treason**: see note below) violation by a subject of allegiance to the sovereign or to the State, esp. by attempting to kill or overthrow the sovereign or to overthrow the government. **2** (in full **petty treason**) *hist.* murder of one's master or husband, regarded as a form of treason. □ **treasonous** *adj.* [ME f. AF *treisoun* etc., OF *traison*, f. L *traditio* handing over (as TRADITION)]

■ **Usage** The crime of *petty treason* was abolished in 1828; the term *high treason*, originally distinguished from *petty treason*, now has the same meaning as *treason*.

treasonable /ˈtriːzənəb(ə)l/ *adj.* involving or guilty of treason. □ **treasonably** *adv.*

treasure /ˈtreʒə(r)/ *n.* & *v.* —*n.* **1 a** precious metals or gems. **b** a hoard of these. **2** accumulated wealth. **2** a thing valued for its rarity, workmanship, associations, etc. (*art treasures*). **3** *colloq.* a much loved or highly valued person. —*v.tr.* **1** (often foll. by *up*) store up as valuable. **2** value (esp. a long-kept possession) highly. □ **treasure hunt 1** a search for treasure. **2** a game in which players seek a hidden object from a series of clues. **treasure trove** *Law* treasure of unknown ownership found hidden. [ME f. OF *tresor*, ult. f. Gk *thēsauros*: see THESAURUS]

treasurer /ˈtreʒərə(r)/ *n.* **1** a person appointed to administer the funds of a society or municipality etc. **2** an officer authorized to receive and disburse public revenues. □ **treasurership** *n.* [ME f. AF *tresorer*, OF *tresorier* f. *tresor* (see TREASURE) after LL *thesaurarius*]

treasury /ˈtreʒərɪ/ *n.* (*pl.* **-ies**) **1** a place or building where treasure is stored. **2** the funds or revenue of a State, institution, or society. **3** (**Treasury**) **a** the department managing the public revenue of a country. **b** the offices and officers of this. **c** the place where the public revenues are kept. □ **Treasury bench** (in the UK) the front bench in the House of Commons occupied by the Prime Minister, Chancellor of the Exchequer, etc. **treasury bill** a bill of exchange issued by the government to raise money for temporary needs. **treasury note** *US & hist.* a note issued by the Treasury for use as currency. [ME f. OF *tresorie* (as TREASURE)]

treat /triːt/ *v. & n.* —*v.* **1** *tr.* act or behave towards or deal with (a person or thing) in a certain way (*treated me kindly; treat it as a joke*). **2** *tr.* deal with or apply a process to; act upon to obtain a particular result (*treat it with acid*). **3** *tr.* apply medical care or attention to. **4** *tr.* present or deal with (a subject) in literature or art. **5** *tr.* (often foll. by *to*) provide with food or drink or entertainment at one's own expense (*treated us to dinner*). **6** *intr.* (often foll. by *with*) negotiate terms (with a person). **7** *intr.* (often foll. by *of*) give a spoken or written exposition. —*n.* **1** an event or circumstance (esp. when unexpected or unusual) that gives great pleasure. **2** a meal, entertainment, etc., provided by one person for the enjoyment of another or others. **3** (prec. by *a*) extremely good or well (*they looked a treat; has come on a treat*). □ **treatable** *adj.* **treater** *n.* **treating** *n.* [ME f. AF *treter*, OF *traitier* f. L *tractare* handle, frequent. of *trahere tract-* draw, pull]

treatise /ˈtriːtɪs, -ɪz/ *n.* a written work dealing formally and systematically with a subject. [ME f. AF *tretis* f. OF *traitier* TREAT]

treatment /ˈtriːtmənt/ *n.* **1** a process or manner of behaving towards or dealing with a person or thing (*received rough treatment*). **2** the application of medical care or attention to a patient. **3** a manner of treating a subject in literature or art. **4** (prec. by *the*) *colloq.* the customary way of dealing with a person, situation, etc. (*got the full treatment*).

treaty /ˈtriːtɪ/ *n.* (*pl.* **-ies**) **1** a formally concluded and ratified agreement between States. **2** an agreement between individuals or parties, esp. for the purchase of property. [ME f. AF *treté* f. L *tractatus* TRACTATE]

treble /ˈtreb(ə)l/ *adj., n., & v.* —*adj.* **1 a** threefold. **b** triple. **c** three times as much or many (*treble the amount*). **2** (of a voice) high-pitched. **3** *Mus.* = SOPRANO (esp. of an instrument or with ref. to a boy's voice). —*n.* **1** a treble quantity or thing. **2** *Darts* a hit on the narrow ring enclosed by the two middle circles of a dartboard, scoring treble. **3 a** *Mus.* = SOPRANO (esp. a boy's voice or part, or an instrument). **b** a high-pitched voice. **4** the high-frequency output of a radio, record-player, etc., corresponding to the treble in music. **5** a system of betting in which the winnings and stake from the first bet are transferred to a second and then (if successful) to a third. **6** *Sport* three victories or championships in the same game, sport, etc. —*v.* **1** *tr. & intr.* make or become three times as much or many; increase threefold; multiply by three. **2** *tr.* amount to three times as much as. □ **treble chance** a method of competing in a football pool in which the chances of winning depend on the number of draws and home and away wins predicted by the competitors. **treble clef** a clef placing G above middle C on the second lowest line of the staff. □ **trebly** *adv.* (in sense 1 of *adj.*). [ME f. OF f. L *triplus* TRIPLE]

tree /triː/ *n. & v.* **1 a** a perennial plant with a woody self-supporting main stem or trunk when mature and usu. unbranched for some distance above the ground. **b** any similar plant having a tall erect usu. single stem, e.g. palm tree. **2** a piece or frame of wood etc. for various purposes (*shoe-tree*). **3** (in full **tree diagram**) *Math.* a diagram with a structure of branching connecting lines. **4** = *family tree.* —*v.tr.* **1** force to take refuge in a tree. **2** esp. *US* put into a difficult position. **3** stretch on a shoe-tree. □ **grow on trees** (usu. with *neg.*) be plentiful. **tree house** a structure in a tree for children to play in. **tree line** = TIMBERLINE. **tree of knowledge** the branches of knowledge as a whole. **tree ring** a ring in a cross section of a tree, from one year's growth. **tree surgeon** a person who treats decayed trees in order to preserve them. **tree surgery** the art or practice of such treatment. **tree tomato** a South American shrub, *Cyphomandra betacea*, with egg-shaped red fruit. **tree-trunk** the trunk of a tree. **up a tree** esp. *US* cornered; nonplussed. □ **treeless** *adj.* **treelessness** *n.* **tree-like** *adj.* [OE *trēow* f. Gmc]

treecreeper /ˈtriːˌkriːpə(r)/ *n.* any small creeping bird, of the family Certhiidae, feeding on insects in the bark of trees.

treetop /ˈtriːtɒp/ *n.* the topmost part of a tree.

trefoil /ˈtrefɔɪl, ˈtriː-/ *n. & adj.* —*n.* **1** any leguminous plant of the genus *Trifolium*, with leaves of three leaflets and flowers of various colours, esp. clover. **2** any plant with similar leaves. **3** a three-lobed ornamentation, esp. in tracery windows. **4** a thing arranged in or with three lobes. —*adj.* of or concerning a three-lobed plant, window tracery, etc. □ **trefoiled** *adj.* (also in *comb.*). [ME f. AF *trifoil* f. L *trifolium* (as TRI-, *folium* leaf)]

trek *v. & n. orig. S.Afr.* —*v.intr.* (**trekked, trekking**) **1** travel or make one's way arduously (*trekking through the forest*). **2** esp. *hist.* migrate or journey with one's belongings by ox-wagon. **3** (of an ox) draw a vehicle or pull a load. —*n.* **1 a** a journey or walk made by trekking (*it was a trek to the nearest launderette*). **b** each stage of such a journey. **2** an organized migration of a body of persons. □ **trekker** *n.* [S.Afr. Du. *trek* (n.), *trekken* (v.) draw, travel]

trellis /ˈtrelɪs/ *n. & v.* —*n.* (in full **trellis-work**) a lattice or grating of light wooden or metal bars used esp. as a support for fruit-trees or creepers and often fastened against a wall. —*v.tr.* (**trellised, trellising**) **1** provide with a trellis. **2** support (a vine etc.) with a trellis. [ME f. OF *trelis, trelice* ult. f. L *trilix* three-ply (as TRI-, *licium* warp-thread)]

trematode /ˈtrɛməˌtəʊd/ n. any parasitic flatworm of the class Trematoda, esp. a fluke, equipped with hooks or suckers, e.g. a liver fluke. [mod.L *Trematoda* f. Gk *trēmatōdēs* perforated f. *trēma* hole]

tremble /ˈtrɛmb(ə)l/ v. & n. —v.intr. **1** shake involuntarily from fear, excitement, weakness, etc. **2** be in a state of extreme apprehension (*trembled at the very thought of it*). **3** move in a quivering manner (*leaves trembled in the breeze*). —n. a trembling state or movement; a quiver (*couldn't speak without a tremble*). □ **all of a tremble** *colloq.* **1** trembling all over. **2** extremely agitated. □ **tremblingly** *adv.* [ME f. OF *trembler* f. med.L *tremulare* f. L *tremulus* TREMULOUS]

trembler /ˈtrɛmblə(r)/ n. an automatic vibrator for making and breaking an electrical circuit.

trembly /ˈtrɛmblɪ/ adj. (**tremblier**, **trembliest**) *colloq.* trembling; agitated.

tremendous /trɪˈmɛndəs/ adj. **1** awe-inspiring, fearful, overpowering. **2** *colloq.* remarkable, considerable, excellent (*a tremendous explosion; gave a tremendous performance*). □ **tremendously** *adv.* **tremendousness** n. [L *tremendus*, gerundive of *tremere* tremble]

tremolo /ˈtrɛmələʊ/ n. *Mus.* **1** a tremulous effect in playing stringed and keyboard instruments or singing, esp. by rapid reiteration of a note; in other instruments, by rapid alternation between two notes. **2** a device in an organ producing a tremulous effect. [It. (as TREMULOUS)]

tremor /ˈtrɛmə(r)/ n. & v. —n. **1** a shaking or quivering. **2** a thrill (of fear or exultation etc.). **3** (in full **earth tremor**) a slight earthquake. —v.intr. undergo a tremor or tremors. [ME f. OF *tremour* & L *tremor* f. *tremere* tremble]

tremulous /ˈtrɛmjʊləs/ adj. **1** trembling or quivering (*in a tremulous voice*). **2** (of a line etc.) drawn by a tremulous hand. **3** timid or vacillating. □ **tremulously** *adv.* **tremulousness** n. [L *tremulus* f. *tremere* tremble]

trench /trɛntʃ/ n. & v. —n. **1** a long narrow usu. deep depression or ditch. **2** *Mil.* **a** this dug by troops to stand in and be sheltered from enemy fire. **b** (in *pl.*) a defensive system of these. —v. **1** *tr.* dig a trench or trenches in (the ground). **2** *tr.* turn over the earth of (a field, garden, etc.) by digging a succession of adjoining ditches. □ **trench coat 1** a soldier's lined or padded waterproof coat. **2** a loose belted raincoat. **trench warfare** hostilities carried on from more or less permanent trenches. [ME f. OF *trenche* (n.) *trenchier* (v.), ult. f. L *truncare* TRUNCATE]

trenchant /ˈtrɛntʃ(ə)nt/ adj. (of a style or language etc.) incisive, terse, vigorous. □ **trenchancy** n. **trenchantly** *adv.* [ME f. OF, part. of *trenchier*: see TRENCH]

trencher /ˈtrɛntʃə(r)/ n. *hist.* a wooden or earthenware platter for serving food. [ME f. AF *trenchour*, OF *trencheoir* f. *trenchier*: see TRENCH]

trencherman /ˈtrɛntʃəmən/ n. (pl. **-men**) a person who eats well, or in a specified manner (*a good trencherman*).

trend n. & v. —n. a general direction and tendency (esp. of events, fashion, or opinion etc.). —v.intr. **1** bend or turn away in a specified direction. **2** be chiefly directed; have a general and continued tendency. □ **trend-setter** a person who leads the way in fashion etc. [ME 'revolve' etc. f. OE *trendan* f. Gmc: cf. TRUNDLE]

trendy /ˈtrɛndɪ/ adj. & n. *colloq.* —adj. (**trendier**, **trendiest**) often *derog.* fashionable; following fashionable trends. —n. (pl. **-ies**) a fashionable person. □ **trendily** *adv.* **trendiness** n.

trepan /trɪˈpæn/ n. & v. —n. **1** a cylindrical saw formerly used by surgeons for removing part of the bone of the skull. **2** a borer for sinking shafts. —v.tr. (**trepanned**, **trepanning**) perforate (the skull) with a trepan. □ **trepanation** /ˌtrɛpəˈneɪʃ(ə)n/ n. **trepanning** n. [ME f. med.L *trepanum* f. Gk *trupanon* f. *trupaō* bore f. *trupē* hole]

trepidation /ˌtrɛpɪˈdeɪʃ(ə)n/ n. **1** a feeling of fear or alarm; perturbation of the mind. **2** tremulous agitation. [L *trepidatio* f. *trepidare* be agitated, tremble, f. *trepidus* alarmed]

trespass /ˈtrɛspəs/ v. & n. —v.intr. **1** (usu. foll. by *on, upon*) make an unlawful or unwarrantable intrusion (esp. on land or property). **2** (foll. by *on*) make unwarrantable claims (*shall not trespass on your hospitality*). **3** (foll. by *against*) *literary* or *archaic* offend. —n. **1** unlawful entry to a person's land or property. **2** *archaic* a sin or offence. □ **trespasser** n. [ME f. OF *trespasser* pass over, trespass, *trespas* (n.), f. med.L *transpassare* (as TRANS-, PASS¹)]

tress n. **1** a long lock of human (esp. female) hair. **2** (in *pl.*) a woman's or girl's head of hair. □ **tressed** adj. (also in *comb.*). **tressy** adj. [ME f. OF *tresse*, perh. ult. f. Gk *trikha* threefold]

trestle /ˈtrɛs(ə)l/ n. **1** a supporting structure for a table etc., consisting of two frames fixed at an angle or hinged or of a bar supported by two divergent pairs of legs. **2** (in full **trestle-table**) a table consisting of a board or boards laid on trestles or other supports. **3** (in full **trestlework**) an open braced framework to support a bridge etc. [ME f. OF *trestel* ult. f. L *transtrum*]

trevally /trɪˈvælɪ/ n. (pl. **-ies**) any Australian fish of the genus *Caranx*, used as food. [prob. alt. f. *cavally*, a kind of fish, f. Sp. *caballo* horse f. L (as CAVALRY)]

trews /truːz/ n.pl. esp. *Brit.* trousers, esp. close-fitting tartan trousers worn by women. [Ir. *trius*, Gael. *triubhas* (sing.): cf. TROUSERS]

TRH *abbr.* Their Royal Highnesses.

tri- /traɪ/ *comb. form* forming nouns and adjectives meaning: **1** three or three times. **2** *Chem.* (forming the names of compounds) containing three atoms or groups of a specified kind (*triacetate*). [L & Gk f. L *tres*, Gk *treis* three]

triacetate /traɪˈæsɪˌteɪt/ n. a cellulose derivative containing three acetate groups, esp. as a base for man-made fibres.

triad /ˈtraɪæd/ n. **1** a group of three (esp. notes in a chord). **2** the number three. **3** a Chinese secret society, usu. criminal. □ **triadic** /-ˈædɪk/ adj. **triadically** /-ˈædɪkəlɪ/ adv. [F *triade* or LL *trias triad-* f. Gk *trias -ados* f. *treis* three]

trial /ˈtraɪəl/ n. **1** a judicial examination and determination of issues between parties by a judge with or without a jury (*stood trial for murder*). **2 a** a process or mode of testing qualities. **b** experimental treatment. **c** a test (*will give you a trial*). **3** a trying thing or experience or person, esp. hardship or trouble (*the trials of old age*). **4** a sports match to test the ability of players eligible for selection to a team. **5** a test of individual ability on a motor cycle over rough ground or on a road. **6** any of various contests involving performance by horses, dogs, or other animals. □ **on trial 1** being tried in a court of law. **2** being tested; to be chosen or retained only if suitable. **trial and error** repeated (usu. varied and unsystematic) attempts or experiments continued until successful. **trial run** a preliminary test of a vehicle, vessel, machine, etc. [AF *trial*, *triel* f. *trier* TRY]

trialist /ˈtraɪəlɪst/ *n.* **1** a person who takes part in a sports trial, motor-cycle trial, etc. **2** a person involved in a judicial trial.

triangle /ˈtraɪˌæŋg(ə)l/ *n.* **1** a plane figure with three sides and angles. **2** any three things not in a straight line, with imaginary lines joining them. **3** an implement of this shape. **4** a musical instrument consisting of a steel rod bent into a triangle and sounded by striking it with a small steel rod. **5** a situation, esp. an emotional relationship, involving three people. **6** a right-angled triangle of wood etc. as a drawing-implement. [ME f. OF *triangle* or L *triangulum* neut. of *triangulus* three-cornered (as TRI-, ANGLE¹)]

triangular /traɪˈæŋgjʊlə(r)/ *adj.* **1** triangle-shaped, three-cornered. **2** (of a contest or treaty etc.) between three persons or parties. **3** (of a pyramid) having a three-sided base. □ **triangularity** /-ˈlærɪtɪ/ *n.* **triangularly** *adv.* [LL *triangularis* (as TRIANGLE)]

triangulate /traɪˈæŋgjʊˌleɪt/ *v.tr.* **1** divide (an area) into triangles for surveying purposes. **2 a** measure and map (an area) by the use of triangles with a known base length and base angles. **b** determine (a height, distance, etc.) in this way. □ **triangulation** /-ˈleɪʃ(ə)n/ *n.* [L *triangulatus* triangular (as TRIANGLE)]

Triassic /traɪˈæsɪk/ *adj. & n. Geol.* —*adj.* of or relating to the earliest period of the Mesozoic era. —*n.* this period or system. [LL *trias* (as TRIAD), because the strata are divisible into three groups]

triathlon /traɪˈæθlɒn/ *n.* an athletic contest consisting of three different events. □ **triathlete** *n.* [TRI- after DECATHLON]

triatomic /ˌtraɪəˈtɒmɪk/ *adj. Chem.* **1** having three atoms (of a specified kind) in the molecule. **2** having three replacement atoms or radicals.

tribal /ˈtraɪb(ə)l/ *adj.* of, relating to, or characteristic of a tribe or tribes. □ **tribally** *adv.*

tribalism /ˈtraɪbəˌlɪz(ə)m/ *n.* tribal organization. □ **tribalist** *n.* **tribalistic** /-ˈlɪstɪk/ *adj.*

tribe *n.* **1** a group of (esp. primitive) families or communities, linked by social, economic, religious, or blood ties, and usu. having a common culture and dialect, and a recognized leader. **2** any similar natural or political division. **3** usu. *derog.* a set or number of persons esp. of one profession etc. or family (*the whole tribe of actors*). [ME, orig. in pl. form *tribuz*, *tribus* f. OF or L *tribus* (sing. & pl.)]

tribesman /ˈtraɪbzmən/ *n.* (*pl.* **-men**) a member of a tribe or of one's own tribe.

tribo- /ˈtrɪbəʊ-, ˈtraɪ-/ *comb. form* rubbing, friction. [Gk *tribos* rubbing]

tribology /traɪˈbɒlədʒɪ/ *n.* the study of friction, wear, lubrication, and the design of bearings; the science of interacting surfaces in relative motion. □ **tribologist** *n.*

tribulation /ˌtrɪbjʊˈleɪʃ(ə)n/ *n.* **1** great affliction or oppression. **2** a cause of this (*was a real tribulation to me*). [ME f. OF f. eccl.L *tribulatio -onis*

f. L *tribulare* press, oppress, f. *tribulum* sledge for threshing, f. *terere* trit- rub]

tribunal /traɪˈbjuːn(ə)l, trɪ-/ *n.* **1** *Brit.* a board appointed to adjudicate in some matter, esp. one appointed by the government to investigate a matter of public concern. **2** a court of justice. **3** a seat or bench for a judge or judges. **4 a** a place of judgement. **b** judicial authority (*the tribunal of public opinion*). [F *tribunal* or L *tribunus* (as TRIBUNE²)]

tribune¹ /ˈtrɪbjuːn/ *n.* **1** a popular leader or demagogue. **2** (in full **tribune of the people**) an official in ancient Rome chosen by the people to protect their interests. **3** (in full **military tribune**) a Roman legionary officer. □ **tribunate** /-nət/ *n.* **tribuneship** *n.* [ME f. L *tribunus*, prob. f. *tribus* tribe]

tribune² /ˈtrɪbjuːn/ *n.* **1 a** a bishop's throne in a basilica. **b** an apse containing this. **2** a dais or rostrum. **3** a raised area with seats. [F f. It. f. med.L *tribuna* TRIBUNAL]

tributary /ˈtrɪbjʊtərɪ/ *n. & adj.* —*n.* (*pl.* **-ies**) **1** a river or stream flowing into a larger river or lake. **2** *hist.* a person or State paying or subject to tribute. —*adj.* **1** (of a river etc.) that is a tributary. **2** *hist.* **a** paying tribute. **b** serving as tribute. □ **tributarily** *adv.* **tributariness** *n.* [ME f. L *tributarius* (as TRIBUTE)]

tribute /ˈtrɪbjuːt/ *n.* **1** a thing said or done or given as a mark of respect or affection etc. (*paid tribute to their achievements; floral tributes*). **2** *hist.* a payment made periodically by one State or ruler to another, esp. as a sign of dependence. **3** (foll. by *to*) an indication of (some praiseworthy quality) (*their success is a tribute to their perseverance*). [ME f. L *tributum* neut. past part. of *tribuere tribut-* assign, orig. divide between tribes (*tribus*)]

trice *n.* □ **in a trice** in a moment; instantly. [ME *trice* (v.) pull, haul f. MDu. *trisen*, MLG *trîssen*, rel. to MDu. *trîse* windlass, pulley]

tricentenary /ˌtraɪsenˈtiːnərɪ/ *n.* (*pl.* **-ies**) = TERCENTENARY.

triceps /ˈtraɪseps/ *adj. & n.* —*adj.* (of a muscle) having three heads or points of attachment. —*n.* any triceps muscle, esp. the large muscle at the back of the upper arm. [L, = three-headed (as TRI-, -*ceps* f. *caput* head)]

triceratops /ˌtraɪˈserəˌtɒps/ *n.* a plant-eating dinosaur with three sharp horns on the forehead and a wavy-edged collar round the neck. [mod.L f. Gk *trikeratos* three-horned + *ōps* face]

trichina /trɪˈkaɪnə/ *n.* (*pl.* **trichinae** /-niː/) any hairlike parasitic nematode worm of the genus *Trichinella*, esp. *T. spiralis*, whose larvae live in the muscle tissue of humans and flesh-eating animals. □ **trichinous** *adj.* [mod.L f. Gk *trikhinos* of hair: see TRICHO-]

trichinosis /ˌtrɪkɪˈnəʊsɪs/ *n.* a disease caused by trichinae, usu. ingested in meat, and characterized by digestive disturbance, fever, and muscular rigidity.

tricho- /ˈtrɪkəʊ/ *comb. form* hair. [Gk *thrix trikhos* hair]

trichology /trɪˈkɒlədʒɪ, traɪ-/ *n.* the study of the structure, functions, and diseases of the hair. □ **trichologist** *n.*

trichromatic /ˌtraɪkrəˈmætɪk/ *adj.* **1** having or using three colours. **2** (of vision) having the normal three colour-sensations, i.e. red, green, and purple. □ **trichromatism** /-ˈkrəʊməˌtɪz(ə)m/ n.

trick n. & v. —n. **1** an action or scheme undertaken to fool, outwit, or deceive. **2** an optical or other illusion (*a trick of the light*). **3** a special technique; a knack or special way of doing something. **4 a** a feat of skill or dexterity. **b** an unusual action (e.g. begging) learned by an animal. **5** a mischievous, foolish, or discreditable act; a practical joke (*a mean trick to play*). **6** a peculiar or characteristic habit or mannerism (*has a trick of repeating himself*). **7 a** the cards played in a single round of a card-game, usu. one from each player. **b** such a round. **c** a point gained as a result of this. **8** (*attrib.*) done to deceive or mystify or to create an illusion (*trick photography; trick question*). —v.tr. **1** deceive by a trick; outwit. **2** (often foll. by *out of* or *into* + verbal noun) cheat; treat deceitfully so as to deprive (*were tricked into agreeing; were tricked out of their savings*). □ **do the trick** *colloq.* accomplish one's purpose; achieve the required result. **how's tricks?** *colloq.* how are you? **trick cyclist 1** a cyclist who performs tricks, esp. in a circus. **2** *sl.* a psychiatrist. **trick of the trade** a special usu. ingenious technique or method of achieving a result in an industry or profession etc. **trick or treat** esp. *US* a children's custom of calling at houses at Hallowe'en with the threat of pranks if they are not given a small gift. **trick out** (or **up**) dress, decorate, or deck out esp. showily. **up to one's tricks** *colloq.* misbehaving. **up to a person's tricks** aware of what a person is likely to do by way of mischief. □ **tricker** n. **trickish** adj. **trickless** adj. [ME f. OF dial. *trique*, OF *triche* f. *trichier* deceive, of unkn. orig.]

trickery /ˈtrɪkərɪ/ n. (*pl.* -**ies**) **1** the practice or an instance of deception. **2** the use of tricks.

trickle /ˈtrɪk(ə)l/ v. & n. —v. **1** intr. & tr. flow or cause to flow in drops or a small stream (*water trickled through the crack*). **2** tr. come or go slowly or gradually (*information trickles out*). —n. a trickling flow. □ **trickle charger** an electrical charger for batteries that works at a steady slow rate from the mains. [ME *trekel, trikle*, prob. imit.]

trickster /ˈtrɪkstə(r)/ n. a deceiver or rogue.

tricksy /ˈtrɪksɪ/ adj. (**tricksier, tricksiest**) full of tricks; playful. □ **tricksily** adv. **tricksiness** n. [TRICK: for -*sy* cf. FLIMSY, TIPSY]

tricky /ˈtrɪkɪ/ adj. (**trickier, trickiest**) **1** difficult or intricate; requiring care and adroitness (*a tricky job*). **2** crafty or deceitful. **3** resourceful or adroit. □ **trickily** adv. **trickiness** n.

tricolour /ˈtrɪkələ(r), ˈtraɪˌkʌlə(r)/ n. & adj. (*US* **tricolor**) —n. a flag of three colours, esp. the French national flag of blue, white, and red. —adj. (also **tricoloured**) having three colours. [F *tricolore* f. LL *tricolor* (as TRI-, COLOUR)]

tricorn /ˈtraɪkɔːn/ adj. (also **tricorne**) (of a hat) having a brim turned up on three sides. [F *tricorne* or L *tricornis* (as TRI-, *cornu* horn)]

tricot /ˈtrɪkəʊ, ˈtriː-/ n. **1 a** a hand-knitted woollen fabric. **b** an imitation of this. **2** a ribbed woollen cloth. [F, = knitting f. *tricoter* knit, of unkn. orig.]

tricycle /ˈtraɪsɪk(ə)l/ n. & v. —n. **1** a vehicle having three wheels, two on an axle at the back and one at the front, driven by pedals in the same way as a bicycle. **2** a three-wheeled motor vehicle for a disabled driver. —v.intr. ride on a tricycle. □ **tricyclist** n.

trident /ˈtraɪd(ə)nt/ n. **1** a three-pronged spear, esp. as an attribute of Poseidon (Neptune) or Britannia. **2** (**Trident**) a US type of submarine-launched ballistic missile. [L *tridens trident-* (as TRI-, *dens* tooth)]

Tridentine /traɪˈdentaɪn, trɪ-/ adj. & n. —adj. of or relating to the Council of Trent, held at Trento in Italy 1545–63, esp. as the basis of Roman Catholic doctrine. —n. a Roman Catholic adhering to this traditional doctrine. □ **Tridentine mass** the eucharistic liturgy used by the Roman Catholic Church from 1570 to 1964. [med.L *Tridentinus* f. *Tridentum* Trent]

tried past and past part. of TRY.

triennial /traɪˈenɪəl/ adj. **1** lasting three years. **2** recurring every three years. □ **triennially** adv. [LL *triennis* (as TRI-, L *annus* year)]

triennium /traɪˈenɪəm/ n. (*pl.* **trienniums** or **triennia** /-nɪə/) a period of three years. [L TRIENNIAL)]

trier /ˈtraɪə(r)/ n. **1** a person who perseveres (*is a real trier*). **2** a tester, esp. of foodstuffs.

trifid /ˈtraɪfɪd/ adj. esp. *Biol.* partly or wholly split into three divisions or lobes. [L *trifidus* (as TRI-, *findere fid-* split)]

trifle /ˈtraɪf(ə)l/ n. & v. —n. **1** a thing of slight value or importance. **2 a** a small amount esp. of money (*was sold for a trifle*). **b** (prec. by *a*) somewhat (*seems a trifle annoyed*). **3** *Brit.* a confection of sponge cake with custard, jelly, fruit, cream, etc. —v. **1** intr. talk or act frivolously. **2** intr. (foll. by *with*) **a** treat or deal with frivolously or derisively; flirt heartlessly with. **b** refuse to take seriously. **3** tr. (foll. by *away*) waste (time, energies, money, etc.) frivolously. □ **trifler** n. [ME f. OF *truf(f)le* by-form of *trufe* deceit, of unkn. orig.]

trifling /ˈtraɪflɪŋ/ adj. **1** unimportant, petty. **2** frivolous. □ **triflingly** adv.

triforium /traɪˈfɔːrɪəm/ n. (*pl.* **triforia** /-rɪə/) a gallery or arcade above the arches of the nave, choir, and transepts of a church. [AL, of unkn. orig.]

trigger /ˈtrɪgə(r)/ n. & v. —n. **1** a movable device for releasing a spring or catch and so setting off a mechanism (esp. that of a gun). **2** an event, occurrence, etc., that sets off a chain reaction. —v.tr. **1** (often foll. by *off*) set (an action or process) in motion; initiate, precipitate. **2** fire (a gun) by the use of a trigger. □ **quick on the trigger** quick to respond. **trigger-happy** apt to shoot with little or no provocation. □ **triggered** adj. [17th-c. *tricker* f. Du. *trekker* f. *trekken* pull: cf. TREK]

trigonometry /ˌtrɪgəˈnɒmɪtrɪ/ n. the branch of mathematics dealing with the relations of the sides and angles of triangles and with the relevant functions of any angles. □ **trigonometric** /-nəˈmetrɪk/ adj. **trigonometrical** /-nəˈmetrɪk(ə)l/ adj. [mod.L *trigonometria* f. L *trigonum* f. Gk *trigōnon* neut. of *trigōnos* three-cornered (as TRI-, -GON) + -METRY]

trigraph /ˈtraɪgrɑːf/ n. (also **trigram** /-græm/) **1** a group of three letters representing one sound. **2** a figure of three lines.

trike /traɪk/ n. & v.intr. *colloq.* tricycle. [abbr.]

trilateral /traɪˈlætər(ə)l/ adj. & n. —adj. **1** of, on, or with three sides. **2** shared by or involving three parties, countries, etc. (*trilateral negotiations*). —*n.* a figure having three sides.

trilby /ˈtrɪlbɪ/ *n.* (*pl.* **-ies**) *Brit.* a soft felt hat with a narrow brim and indented crown. □ **trilbied** *adj.* [name of the heroine in G. du Maurier's novel *Trilby* (1894), in the stage version of which such a hat was worn]

trilingual /traɪˈlɪŋgw(ə)l/ *adj.* **1** able to speak three languages, esp. fluently. **2** spoken or written in three languages. □ **trilingualism** *n.*

trill *n.* & *v.* —*n.* **1** a quavering or vibratory sound, esp. a rapid alternation of sung or played notes. **2** a bird's warbling sound. **3** the pronunciation of *r* with a vibration of the tongue. —*v.* **1** *intr.* produce a trill. **2** *tr.* warble (a song) or pronounce (*r* etc.) with a trill. [It. *trillo* (n.), *trillare* (v.)]

trillion /ˈtrɪljən/ *n.* (*pl.* same or (in sense 3) **trillions**) **1** a million million (1,000,000,000,000 or 10¹²). **2** (formerly, esp. *Brit.*) a million million million (1,000,000,000,000,000,000 or 10¹⁸). **3** (in *pl.*) *colloq.* a very large number (*trillions of times*). □ **trillionth** *adj.* & *n.* [F *trillion* or It. *trilione* (as TRI-, MILLION), after *billion*]

trilobite /ˈtraɪləˌbaɪt/ *n.* any fossil marine arthropod of the class Trilobita of Palaeozoic times, characterized by a three-lobed body. [mod.L *Trilobites* (as TRI-, Gk *lobos* lobe)]

trilogy /ˈtrɪlədʒɪ/ *n.* (*pl.* **-ies**) a group of three related literary or operatic works. [Gk *trilogia* (as TRI-, -LOGY)]

trim *v.*, *n.*, & *adj.* —*v.* (**trimmed, trimming**) **1** *tr.* a set in good order. **b** make neat or of the required size or form, esp. by cutting away irregular or unwanted parts. **2** *tr.* (foll. by *off*, *away*) remove by cutting off (such parts). **3** *tr.* **a** (often foll. by *up*) make (a person) neat in dress and appearance. **b** ornament or decorate (esp. clothing, a hat, etc. by adding ribbons, lace, etc.). **4** *tr.* adjust the balance of (a ship or aircraft) by the arrangement of its cargo etc. **5** *tr.* arrange (sails) to suit the wind. **6** *intr.* **a** associate oneself with currently prevailing views, esp. to advance oneself. **b** hold a middle course in politics or opinion. **7** *tr.* *colloq.* **a** rebuke sharply. **b** thrash. **c** get the better of in a bargain etc. —*n.* **1** the state or degree of readiness or fitness (*found everything in perfect trim*). **2** ornament or decorative material. **3** dress or equipment. **4** the act of trimming a person's hair. —*adj.* **1** neat or spruce. **2** in good order; well arranged or equipped. □ **in trim** looking smart, healthy, etc. □ **trimly** *adv.* **trimmer** *n.* **trimness** *n.* [perh. f. OE *trymman, trymian* make firm, arrange: but there is no connecting evidence between OE and 1500]

trimaran /ˈtraɪməˌræn/ *n.* a vessel like a catamaran, with three hulls side by side. [TRI- + CATAMARAN]

trimer /ˈtraɪmə(r)/ *n.* *Chem.* a polymer comprising three monomer units. □ **trimeric** /-ˈmerɪk/ *adj.* [TRI- + -MER]

trimester /traɪˈmestə(r)/ *n.* a period of three months, esp. of human gestation or *US* as a university term. □ **trimestral** *adj.* **trimestrial** *adj.* [F *trimestre* f. L *trimestris* (as TRI-, -*mestris* f. *mensis* month)]

trimeter /ˈtrɪmɪtə(r)/ *n.* *Prosody* a verse of three measures. □ **trimetric** /traɪˈmetrɪk/ *adj.* **trimetrical** /traɪˈmetrɪk(ə)l/ *adj.* [L *trimetrus* f. Gk *trimetros* (as TRI-, *metron* measure)]

trimming /ˈtrɪmɪŋ/ *n.* **1** ornamentation or decoration, esp. for clothing. **2** (in *pl.*) *colloq.* the usual accompaniments, esp. of the main course of a meal. **3** (in *pl.*) pieces cut off in trimming.

trimorphism /traɪˈmɔːfɪz(ə)m/ *n.* *Bot.*, *Zool.*, & *Crystallog.* existence in three distinct forms. □ **trimorphic** *adj.* **trimorphous** *adj.*

Trinitarian /ˌtrɪnɪˈteərɪən/ *n.* & *adj.* —*n.* a person who believes in the doctrine of the Trinity. —*adj.* of or relating to this belief. □ **Trinitarianism** *n.*

trinitrotoluene /traɪˌnaɪtrəˈtɒljuˌiːn/ *n.* (also **trinitrotoluol** /-ˈtɒljuˌɒl/) = TNT.

trinity /ˈtrɪnɪtɪ/ *n.* (*pl.* **-ies**) **1** the state of being three. **2** a group of three. **3** (**the Trinity** or **Holy Trinity**) *Theol.* the three persons of the Christian Godhead (Father, Son, and Holy Spirit). □ **Trinity House** *Brit.* an association concerned with the licensing of pilots, the erection and maintenance of buoys, lighthouses, etc., in England, Wales, etc. **Trinity Sunday** the next Sunday after Whit Sunday. **Trinity term** *Brit.* the university and law term beginning after Easter. [ME f. OF *trinité* f. L *trinitas* -*tatis* triad f. L *trinus* threefold f. *tres* three]

trinket /ˈtrɪŋkɪt/ *n.* a trifling ornament, jewel, etc., esp. one worn on the person. □ **trinketry** *n.* [16th c.: orig. unkn.]

trinomial /traɪˈnəʊmɪəl/ *adj.* & *n.* —*adj.* consisting of three terms. —*n.* a scientific name or algebraic expression of three terms. [TRI- after BINOMIAL]

trio /ˈtriːəʊ/ *n.* (*pl.* **-os**) **1** a set or group of three. **2** *Mus.* **a** a composition for three performers. **b** a group of three performers. [F & It. f. L *tres* three, after *duo*]

triode /ˈtraɪəʊd/ *n.* **1** a thermionic valve having three electrodes. **2** a semiconductor rectifier having three connections. [TRI- + ELECTRODE]

trioxide /traɪˈɒksaɪd/ *n.* *Chem.* an oxide containing three oxygen atoms.

trip *v.* & *n.* —*v.intr.* & *tr.* (**tripped, tripping**) **1** *intr.* **a** walk or dance with quick light steps. **b** (of a rhythm etc.) run lightly. **2 a** *intr.* & *tr.* (often foll. by *up*) stumble or cause to stumble, esp. by catching or entangling the feet. **b** *intr.* & *tr.* (foll. by *up*) make or cause to make a slip or blunder. **3** *tr.* detect (a person) in a blunder. **4** *intr.* make an excursion to a place. **5** *tr.* release (part of a machine) suddenly by knocking aside a catch etc. **6** *intr.* *colloq.* have a hallucinatory experience caused by a drug. —*n.* **1** a journey or excursion, esp. for pleasure. **2 a** a stumble or blunder. **b** the act of tripping or the state of being tripped up. **3** a nimble step. **4** *colloq.* a hallucinatory experience caused by a drug. **5** a contrivance for a tripping mechanism etc. □ **trip-wire** a wire stretched close to the ground, operating an alarm etc. when disturbed. [ME f. OF *triper, tripper,* f. MDu. *trippen* skip, hop]

tripartite /traɪˈpɑːtaɪt/ *adj.* **1** consisting of three parts. **2** shared by or involving three parties. **3** *Bot.* (of a leaf) divided into three segments almost to the base. □ **tripartitely** *adv.* **tripartition** /-ˈtɪʃ(ə)n/ *n.* [ME f. L *tripartitus* (as TRI-, *partitus* past part. of *partiri* divide)]

tripe *n.* **1** the first or second stomach of a ruminant, esp. an ox, as food. **2** *colloq.* nonsense, rubbish (*don't talk such tripe*). [ME f. OF, of unkn. orig.]

triple /ˈtrɪp(ə)l/ adj., n., & v. —adj. **1** consisting of three usu. equal parts or things; threefold. **2** involving three parties. **3** three times as much or many (triple the amount; triple thickness). —n. **1** a threefold number or amount. **2** a set of three. —v.tr. & intr. multiply or increase by three. □ **triple crown 1** RC Ch. the pope's tiara. **2** the act of winning all three of a group of important events in horse-racing, rugby football, etc. **triple jump** an athletic exercise or contest comprising a hop, a step, and a jump. **triple play** Baseball the act of putting out three runners in a row. **triple time** Mus. that with three beats to the bar; waltz time. □ **triply** adv. [OF triple or L triplus f. Gk triplous]

triplet /ˈtrɪplɪt/ n. **1** each of three children or animals born at one birth. **2** a set of three things, esp. of equal notes played in the time of two or of verses rhyming together. [TRIPLE + -ET¹, after doublet]

triplex /ˈtrɪpleks/ adj. & n. —adj. triple or threefold. —n. (**Triplex**) Brit. propr. toughened or laminated safety glass for car windows etc. [L triplex -plicis (as TRI-, plic- fold)]

triplicate adj., n., & v. —adj. /ˈtrɪplɪkət/ **1** existing in three examples or copies. **2** having three corresponding parts. **3** tripled. —n. /ˈtrɪplɪkət/ each of a set of three copies or corresponding parts. —v.tr. /ˈtrɪplɪˌkeɪt/ **1** make in three copies. **2** multiply by three. □ **in triplicate** consisting of three exact copies. □ **triplication** /-ˈkeɪʃ(ə)n/ n. [ME f. L triplicatus past part. of triplicare (as TRIPLEX)]

triploid /ˈtrɪplɔɪd/ n. & adj. Biol. —n. an organism or cell having three times the haploid set of chromosomes. —adj. of or being a triploid. [mod.L triploides f. Gk (as TRIPLE)]

triploidy /ˈtrɪplɔɪdɪ/ n. the condition of being triploid.

tripmeter /ˈtrɪpˌmiːtə(r)/ n. a vehicle instrument that can be set to record the distance of individual journeys.

tripod /ˈtraɪpɒd/ n. **1** a three-legged stand for supporting a camera etc. **2** a stool, table, or utensil resting on three feet or legs. □ **tripodal** /ˈtrɪpəd(ə)l/ adj. [L tripus tripodis f. Gk tripous (as TRI-, pous podos foot)]

tripos /ˈtraɪpɒs/ n. Brit. (at Cambridge University) the honours examination for the BA degree. [as TRIPOD, with ref. to the stool on which graduates sat to deliver a satirical speech at the degree ceremony]

tripper /ˈtrɪpə(r)/ n. **1** Brit. a person who goes on a pleasure trip or excursion. **2** colloq. a person experiencing hallucinatory effects of a drug.

triptych /ˈtrɪptɪk/ n. **1** a picture or relief carving on three panels, usu. hinged vertically together and often used as an altarpiece. **2** a set of three artistic works. [TRI-, after DIPTYCH]

trireme /ˈtraɪriːm/ n. an ancient Greek warship, with three files of oarsmen on each side. [F trirème or L triremis (as TRI-, remus oar)]

trisaccharide /traɪˈsækəˌraɪd/ n. Chem. a sugar consisting of three linked monosaccharides.

trisect /traɪˈsekt/ v.tr. cut or divide into three (usu. equal) parts. □ **trisection** n. **trisector** n. [TRI- + L secare sect- cut]

trishaw /ˈtraɪʃɔː/ n. a light three-wheeled ped-alled vehicle used in the Far East. [TRI- + RICKSHAW]

trismus /ˈtrɪzməs/ n. Med. a variety of tetanus with tonic spasm of the jaw muscles causing the mouth to remain tightly closed. [mod.L f. Gk trismos = trigmos a scream, grinding]

trisyllable /traɪˈsɪləb(ə)l, trɪ-/ n. a word or metrical foot of three syllables. □ **trisyllabic** /-ˈlæbɪk/ adj.

trite adj. (of a phrase, opinion, etc.) hackneyed, worn out by constant repetition. □ **tritely** adv. **triteness** n. [L tritus past part. of terere rub]

tritium /ˈtrɪtɪəm/ n. Chem. a radioactive isotope of hydrogen with a mass about three times that of ordinary hydrogen. [mod.L f. Gk tritos third]

trito- /ˈtraɪtəʊ, ˈtrɪtəʊ/ comb. form third. [Gk tritos third]

triumph /ˈtraɪəmf, -ʌmf/ n. & v. —n. **1 a** the state of being victorious or successful (returned home in triumph). **b** a great success or achievement. **2** a supreme example (a triumph of engineering). **3** joy at success; exultation (could see triumph in her face). —v.intr. **1** (often foll. by over) gain a victory; be successful; prevail. **2** ride in triumph. **3** (often foll. by over) exult. [ME f. OF triumphe (n.), triumpher (v.), f. L triump(h)us prob. f. Gk thriambos hymn to Bacchus]

triumphal /traɪˈʌmf(ə)l/ adj. of or used in or celebrating a triumph. [ME f. OF triumphal or L triumphalis (as TRIUMPH)]

triumphant /traɪˈʌmf(ə)nt/ adj. **1** victorious or successful. **2** exultant. □ **triumphantly** adv. [ME f. OF triumphant or L triumphare (as TRIUMPH)]

triumvir /ˈtraɪəmvɪə(r), -ˈʌmvə(r)/ n. (pl. **triumvirs** or **triumviri** /-raɪ/) **1** each of three men holding a joint office. **2** a member of a triumvirate. □ **triumviral** adj. [L, orig. in pl. triumviri, back-form. f. trium virorum genit. of tres viri three men]

triumvirate /traɪˈʌmvɪrət/ n. **1** a board or ruling group of three men, esp. in ancient Rome. **2** the office of triumvir.

triune /ˈtraɪjuːn/ adj. three in one, esp. with ref. to the Trinity. □ **triunity** /-ˈjuːnɪtɪ/ n. (pl. **-ies**). [TRI- + L unus one]

trivalent /traɪˈveɪlənt/ adj. Chem. having a valency of three; tervalent. □ **trivalency** n.

trivet /ˈtrɪvɪt/ n. **1** an iron tripod or bracket for a cooking pot or kettle to stand on. **2** an iron bracket designed to hook on to bars of a grate for a similar purpose. □ **as right as a trivet** colloq. in a perfectly good state, esp. healthy. [ME trevet, app. f. L tripes (as TRI-, pes pedis foot)]

trivia /ˈtrɪvɪə/ n.pl. trifles or trivialities. [mod.L, pl. of trivium place where three roads meet, infl. by TRIVIAL]

trivial /ˈtrɪvɪəl/ adj. **1** of small value or importance; trifling (raised trivial objections). **2** (of a person) concerned only with trivial things. □ **triviality** /-ˈælɪtɪ/ n. (pl. **-ies**). **trivially** adv. **trivialness** n. [L trivialis commonplace f. trivium place where three roads meet (as TRI-, via road)]

trivialize /ˈtrɪvɪəˌlaɪz/ v.tr. (also **-ise**) make trivial or apparently trivial; minimize. □ **trivialization** /-ˈzeɪʃ(ə)n/ n.

tri-weekly /traɪˈwiːklɪ/ adj. produced or occurring three times a week or every three weeks.

-trix suffix (pl. **-trices** /trɪsiːz, ˈtraɪsiːz/ or **-trixes**) forming feminine agent nouns corresponding to masculine nouns in -tor, esp. in Law (executrix). [L -trix -tricis]

trochaic /trəˈkeɪɪk/ adj. & n. Prosody —adj. of or using trochees. —n. (usu. in pl.) trochaic verse. [L trochaicus f. Gk trokhaikos (as TROCHEE)]

trochee /ˈtrəʊkiː, -kɪ/ n. Prosody a foot consisting of one long or stressed syllable followed by one short or unstressed syllable. [L trochaeus f. Gk trokhaios (pous) running (foot) f. trekhō run]

trod past and past part. of TREAD.

trodden past part. of TREAD.

troglodyte /ˈtrɒɡlə,daɪt/ n. 1 a cave-dweller, esp. of prehistoric times. 2 a hermit. 3 derog. a wilfully obscurantist or old-fashioned person. □ **troglodytic** /-ˈdɪtɪk/ adj. **troglodytical** /-ˈdɪtɪk(ə)l/ adj. **troglodytism** n. [L troglodyta f. Gk trōglodutēs f. the name of an Ethiopian people, after trōglē hole]

troika /ˈtrɔɪkə/ n. 1 **a** a Russian vehicle with a team of three horses abreast. **b** this team. 2 a group of three people, esp. as an administrative council. [Russ. f. troe three]

troilism /ˈtrɔɪlɪz(ə)m/ n. sexual activity involving three participants. [perh. f. F trois three]

Trojan /ˈtrəʊdʒ(ə)n/ adj. & n. —adj. of or relating to ancient Troy in Asia Minor. —n. 1 a native or inhabitant of Troy. 2 a person who works, fights, etc. courageously (works like a Trojan). □ **Trojan Horse** 1 a hollow wooden horse said to have been used by the Greeks to enter Troy. 2 a person or device planted to bring about an enemy's downfall. [ME f. L Troianus f. Troia Troy]

troll¹ /trəʊl/ n. (in Scandinavian folklore) a fabulous being, esp. a giant or dwarf dwelling in a cave. [ON & Sw. troll, Da. trold]

troll² /trəʊl/ v. & n. —v. 1 intr. sing out in a carefree jovial manner. 2 tr. & intr. fish by drawing bait along in the water. 3 intr. esp. Brit. walk, stroll. —n. 1 the act of trolling for fish. 2 a line or bait used in this. □ **troller** n. [ME 'stroll, roll': cf. OF troller quest, MHG trollen stroll]

trolley /ˈtrɒlɪ/ n. (pl. -eys) 1 esp. Brit. a table, stand, or basket on wheels or castors for serving food, transporting luggage or shopping, gathering purchases in a supermarket, etc. 2 esp. Brit. a low truck running on rails. 3 (in full **trolley-wheel**) a wheel attached to a pole etc. used for collecting current from an overhead electric wire to drive a vehicle. 4 **a** US = trolley-car. **b** Brit. = trolley bus. □ **trolley bus** Brit. an electric bus running on the road and using a trolley-wheel. **trolley-car** US an electric tram using a trolley-wheel. [of dial. orig., perh. f. TROLL²]

trollop /ˈtrɒləp/ n. 1 a disreputable girl or woman. 2 a prostitute. □ **trollopish** adj. **trollopy** adj. [17th c.: perh. rel. to G Trulle]

trombone /trɒmˈbəʊn/ n. 1 **a** a large brass wind instrument with a sliding tube. **b** its player. 2 an organ stop with the quality of a trombone. □ **trombonist** n. [F or It. f. It. tromba TRUMPET]

trompe-l'œil /trɒpˈlɜːɪ/ n. a still-life painting etc. designed to give an illusion of reality. [F, lit. 'deceives the eye']

-tron suffix Physics forming nouns denoting: 1 an elementary particle (positron). 2 a particle accelerator. 3 a thermionic valve. [after ELECTRON]

troop /truːp/ n. & v. —n. 1 an assembled company; an assemblage of people or animals. 2 (in pl.) soldiers or armed forces. 3 a cavalry unit commanded by a captain. 4 a unit of artillery and armoured formation. 5 a grouping of three or more Scout patrols. —v. 1 intr. (foll. by in, out, off, etc.) come together or move in large numbers. 2 tr. form (a regiment) into troops. □ **troop the colour** esp. Brit. transfer a flag ceremonially at a public mounting of garrison guards. **troop-ship** a ship used for transporting troops. [F troupe, back-form. f. troupeau dimin. of med.L troppus flock, prob. of Gmc orig.]

trooper /ˈtruːpə(r)/ n. 1 a private soldier in a cavalry or armoured unit. 2 Austral. & US a mounted or motor-borne policeman. 3 a cavalry horse. 4 esp. Brit. a troop-ship.

trope n. a figurative (e.g. metaphorical or ironical) use of a word. [L tropus f. Gk tropos turn, way, trope f. trepō turn]

-trophic /ˈtrɒfɪk/ comb. form relating to nutrition. [Gk trophikos f. trophē nourishment f. trephō nourish]

trophy /ˈtrəʊfɪ/ n. (pl. -ies) 1 a cup or other decorative object awarded as a prize or memento of victory or success in a contest etc. 2 Gk & Rom. Antiq. the weapons etc. of a defeated army set up as a memorial of victory. 3 an ornamental group of symbolic or typical objects arranged for display. □ **trophied** adj. (also in comb.). [F trophée f. L trophaeum f. Gk tropaion f. tropē rout f. trepō turn]

tropic /ˈtrɒpɪk/ n. & adj. —n. 1 the parallel of latitude 23° 27′ north (**tropic of Cancer**) or south (**tropic of Capricorn**) of the Equator. 2 each of two corresponding circles on the celestial sphere where the sun appears to turn after reaching its greatest declination. 3 (**the Tropics**) the region between the tropics of Cancer and Capricorn. —adj. 1 = TROPICAL 1. 2 of tropism. [ME f. L tropicus f. Gk tropikos f. tropē turning f. trepō turn]

-tropic /ˈtrɒpɪk/ comb. form 1 = -TROPHIC. 2 turning towards (heliotropic).

tropical /ˈtrɒpɪk(ə)l/ adj. 1 of, peculiar to, or suggesting the Tropics (tropical fish; tropical diseases). 2 very hot; passionate, luxuriant. □ **tropically** adv.

tropism /ˈtrəʊpɪz(ə)m/ n. Biol. the turning of all or part of an organism in a particular direction in response to an external stimulus. [Gk tropos turning f. trepō turn]

troposphere /ˈtrɒpə,sfɪə(r), ˈtrəʊ-/ n. a layer of atmospheric air extending from about 6–10 km upwards from the earth's surface. □ **tropospheric** /-ˈsferɪk/ adj. [Gk tropos turning + SPHERE]

trot v. & n. —v. (**trotted, trotting**) 1 intr. (of a person) run at a moderate pace esp. with short strides. 2 intr. (of a horse) proceed at a steady pace faster than a walk lifting each diagonal pair of legs alternately. 3 intr. colloq. walk or go. 4 tr. cause (a horse or person) to trot. 5 tr. traverse (a distance) at a trot. —n. 1 the action or exercise of trotting (proceed at a trot; went for a trot). 2 (**the trots**) sl. an attack of diarrhoea. 3 a brisk steady movement or occupation. □ **on the trot** colloq. 1 continually busy (kept them on the trot). 2 in succession (five weeks on the trot). **trot out** 1 cause (a horse) to trot to show its paces. 2 produce or introduce (as if) for inspection and approval, esp. tediously or repeatedly. [ME f. OF troter f. Rmc & med.L trottare, of Gmc orig.]

troth /trəʊθ/ *n. archaic* **1** faith, loyalty. **2** truth. □ **pledge** (or **plight**) **one's troth** pledge one's word esp. in marriage or betrothal. [ME *trowthe*, for OE *trēowth* TRUTH]

trotter /ˈtrɒtə(r)/ *n.* **1** a horse bred or trained for trotting. **2** (usu. in *pl.*) **a** an animal's foot as food (*pig's trotters*). **b** *joc.* a human foot.

trotting /ˈtrɒtɪŋ/ *n.* racing for trotting horses pulling a two-wheeled vehicle and driver.

troubadour /ˈtruːbəˌdɔː(r)/ *n.* **1** any of a number of French medieval lyric poets composing and singing in Provençal in the 11th–13th c. on the theme of courtly love. **2** a singer or poet. [F f. Prov. *trobador* f. *trobar* find, invent, compose in verse]

trouble /ˈtrʌb(ə)l/ *n. & v.* —*n.* **1** difficulty or distress; vexation, affliction (*am having trouble with my car*). **2 a** inconvenience; unpleasant exertion; bother (*went to a lot of trouble*). **b** a cause of this (*the child was no trouble*). **3** a cause of annoyance or concern (*the trouble with you is that you can't say no*). **4** a faulty condition or operation (*kidney trouble; engine trouble*). **5 a** fighting, disturbance (*crowd trouble; don't want any trouble*). **b** (in *pl.*) political or social unrest, public disturbances. **6** disagreement, strife (*is having trouble at home*). —*v.* **1** *tr.* cause distress or anxiety to; disturb (*were much troubled by their debts*). **2** *intr.* be disturbed or worried (*don't trouble about it*). **3** *tr.* afflict; cause pain etc. to (*am troubled with arthritis*). **4** *tr. & intr.* (often *refl.*) subject or be subjected to inconvenience or unpleasant exertion (*sorry to trouble you; don't trouble yourself; don't trouble to explain*). □ **ask** (or **look**) **for trouble** *colloq.* invite trouble or difficulty by one's actions, behaviour, etc.; behave rashly or indiscreetly. **be no trouble** cause no inconvenience etc. **go to the trouble** (or **some trouble** etc.) exert oneself to do something. **in trouble 1** involved in a matter likely to bring censure or punishment. **2** *colloq.* pregnant while unmarried. **take trouble** (or **the trouble**) exert oneself to do something. **trouble spot** a place where difficulties regularly occur. □ **troubler** *n.* [ME f. OF *truble* (n.), *trubler*, *turbler* (v.) ult. f. L *turbidus* TURBID]

troubled /ˈtrʌb(ə)ld/ *adj.* showing, experiencing, or reflecting trouble, anxiety, etc. (*a troubled mind; a troubled childhood*).

troublemaker /ˈtrʌb(ə)lˌmeɪkə(r)/ *n.* a person who habitually causes trouble. □ **troublemaking** *n.*

troubleshooter /ˈtrʌb(ə)lˌʃuːtə(r)/ *n.* **1** a mediator in industrial or diplomatic etc. disputes. **2** a person who traces and corrects faults in machinery etc. □ **troubleshooting** *n.*

troublesome /ˈtrʌb(ə)lsəm/ *adj.* **1** causing trouble. **2** vexing, annoying. □ **troublesomely** *adv.* **troublesomeness** *n.*

troublous /ˈtrʌbləs/ *adj. archaic* or *literary* full of troubles; agitated, disturbed (*troublous times*). [ME f. OF *troubleus* (as TROUBLE)]

trough /trɒf/ *n.* **1** a long narrow open receptacle for water, animal feed, etc. **2** a channel for conveying a liquid. **3** an elongated region of low barometric pressure. **4** a hollow between two wave crests. **5** the time of lowest economic performance etc. [OE *trog* f. Gmc]

trounce /traʊns/ *v.tr.* **1** defeat heavily. **2** beat, thrash. **3** punish severely. □ **trouncer** *n.* **trouncing** *n.* [16th c., = afflict: orig. unkn.]

troupe /truːp/ *n.* a company of actors or acrobats etc. [F, = TROOP]

trouper /ˈtruːpə(r)/ *n.* **1** a member of a theatrical troupe. **2** a staunch colleague.

trousers /ˈtraʊzəz/ *n.pl.* **1** an outer garment reaching from the waist usu. to the ankles, divided into two parts to cover the legs. **2** (**trouser**) (*attrib.*) designating parts of this (*trouser leg*). □ **trouser suit** a woman's suit of trousers and jacket. **wear the trousers** be the dominant partner in a marriage. □ **trousered** *adj.* **trouserless** *adj.* [archaic *trouse* (sing.) f. Ir. & Gael. *triubhas* TREWS: pl. form after *drawers*]

trousseau /ˈtruːsəʊ/ *n.* (*pl.* **trousseaus** or **trousseaux** /-səʊz/) the clothes collected by a bride for her marriage. [F, lit. bundle, dimin. of *trousse* TRUSS]

trout /traʊt/ *n.* (*pl.* same or **trouts**) **1** any of various freshwater fish of the genus *Salmo* of the northern hemisphere, valued as food. **2** a similar fish of the family Salmonidae. **3** *sl. derog.* a woman, esp. an old or ill-tempered one (usu. *old trout*). □ **troutlet** *n.* **troutling** *n.* **trouty** *adj.* [OE *truht* f. LL *tructa*]

trove *n.* = treasure trove. [AF *trové* f. *trover* find]

trow /traʊ, trəʊ/ *v.tr. archaic* think, believe. [OE *trūwian*, *trēowian*, rel. to TRUCE]

trowel /ˈtraʊəl/ *n. & v.* —*n.* **1** a small hand-held tool with a flat pointed blade, used to apply and spread mortar etc. **2** a similar tool with a curved scoop for lifting plants or earth. —*v.tr.* (**trowelled**, **trowelling**; *US* **troweled**, **troweling**) apply (plaster etc.). [ME f. OF *truele* f. med.L *truella* f. L *trulla* scoop, dimin. of *trua* ladle etc.]

troy *n.* (in full **troy weight**) a system of weights used for precious metals and gems, with a pound of 12 ounces or 5,760 grains. [ME, prob. f. *Troyes* in France]

truant /ˈtruːənt/ *n., adj., & v.* —*n.* **1** a child who stays away from school without leave or explanation. **2** a person missing from work etc. —*adj.* (of a person, conduct, thoughts, etc.) shirking, idle, wandering. —*v.intr.* (also **play truant**) stay away as a truant. □ **truancy** *n.* [ME f. OF, prob. ult. f. Celt.: cf. Welsh *truan*, Gael. *truaghan* wretched]

truce *n.* **1** a temporary agreement to cease hostilities. **2** a suspension of private feuding or bickering. □ **truceless** *adj.* [ME *trew(e)s* (pl.) f. OE *trēow*, rel. to TRUE]

truck[1] *n. & v.* —*n.* **1** *Brit.* an open railway wagon for carrying freight. **2** esp. *US* a vehicle for carrying heavy goods; a lorry. **3** a vehicle for transporting troops, supplies, etc. **4** a railway bogie. —*v.* **1** *tr.* convey on or in a truck. **2** *intr. US* drive a truck. **3** *intr. US sl.* proceed; go, stroll. □ **truckage** *n.* [perh. short for TRUCKLE in sense 'wheel, pulley']

truck[2] *n.* dealings; exchange, barter. □ **have no truck with** avoid dealing with. [ME f. OF *troquer* (unrecorded) = *trocare*, of unkn. orig.]

trucker /ˈtrʌkə(r)/ *n.* esp. *US* **1** a long-distance lorry-driver. **2** a firm dealing in long-distance carriage of goods.

truckie /ˈtrʌkɪ/ *n. Austral. colloq.* a lorry-driver; a trucker.

trucking /ˈtrʌkɪŋ/ *n. US* conveyance of goods by lorry.

truckle /'trʌk(ə)l/ n. & v. —n. 1 (in full **truckle-bed**) a low bed on wheels that can be stored under a larger bed. 2 orig. dial. a small barrel-shaped cheese. —v.intr. (foll. by to) submit obsequiously. □ **truckler** n. [orig. = wheel, pulley, f. AF trocle f. L trochlea pulley]

truculent /'trʌkjʊlənt/ adj. 1 aggressively defiant. 2 aggressive, pugnacious. 3 fierce, savage. □ **truculence** n. **truculency** n. **truculently** adv. [L truculentus f. trux trucis fierce]

trudge v. & n. —v. 1 intr. go on foot esp. laboriously. 2 tr. traverse (a distance) in this way. —n. a trudging walk. □ **trudger** n. [16th c.: orig. unkn.]

true adj., adv., & v. —adj. 1 in accordance with fact or reality (a true story). 2 genuine; rightly or strictly so called; not spurious or counterfeit (a true friend; the true heir to the throne). 3 (often foll. by to) loyal or faithful (true to one's word). 4 (foll. by to) accurately conforming (to a standard or expectation etc.) (true to form). 5 correctly positioned or balanced; upright, level. 6 exact, accurate (a true aim; a true copy). 7 (absol.) (also **it is true**) certainly, admittedly (true, it would cost more). 8 (of a note) exactly in tune. 9 archaic honest, upright (twelve good men and true). —adv. 1 truly (tell me true). 2 accurately (aim true). 3 without variation (breed true). —v.tr. (**trues, trued, truing** or **trueing**) bring (a tool, wheel, frame, etc.) into the exact position or form required. □ **come true** actually happen or be the case. **out of true** (or **the true**) not in the correct or exact position. **true-blue** adj. extremely loyal or orthodox. —n. such a person, esp. a Conservative. **true-love** a sweetheart. **true north** etc. north etc. according to the earth's axis, not magnetic north. **true to form** (or **type**) being or behaving etc. as expected. **true to life** accurately representing life. □ **trueish** adj. **trueness** n. [OE trēowe, trȳwe, f. the Gmc noun repr. by TRUCE]

truffle /'trʌf(ə)l/ n. 1 any strong-smelling underground fungus of the order Tuberales, used as a culinary delicacy and found esp. in France by trained dogs or pigs. 2 a usu. round sweet made of chocolate mixture covered with cocoa etc. [prob. f. Du. truffel f. obs. F truffle ult. f. L tubera pl. of TUBER]

trug n. Brit. a shallow oblong garden-basket usu. of wood strips. [perh. a dial. var. of TROUGH]

truism /'truːɪz(ə)m/ n. 1 an obviously true or hackneyed statement. 2 a proposition that states nothing beyond what is implied in any of its terms. □ **truistic** /-'ɪstɪk/ adj.

truly /'truːlɪ/ adv. 1 sincerely, genuinely (am truly grateful). 2 really, indeed (truly, I do not know). 3 faithfully, loyally (served them truly). 4 accurately, truthfully (is not truly depicted; has been truly stated). 5 rightly, properly (well and truly). [OE trēowlice (as TRUE, -LY²)]

trump¹ n. & v. —n. 1 a playing-card of a suit ranking above the others. 2 an advantage esp. involving surprise. 3 colloq. a helpful or admired person. b Austral. & NZ a person in authority. —v. 1 a tr. defeat (a card or its player) with a trump. b intr. play a trump card when another suit has been led. 2 tr. colloq. gain a surprising advantage over (a person, proposal, etc.). □ **trump card 1** a card belonging to, or turned up to determine, a trump suit. 2 colloq. a a valuable resource. b a surprise move to gain

an advantage. **trump up** fabricate or invent (an accusation, excuse, etc.) (on a trumped-up charge). **turn up trumps** Brit. colloq. 1 turn out better than expected. 2 be greatly successful or helpful. [corrupt. of TRIUMPH in the same (now obs.) sense]

trump² n. archaic a trumpet-blast. □ **the last trump** the trumpet-blast to wake the dead on Judgement Day. [ME f. OF trompe f. Frank.: prob. imit.]

trumpery /'trʌmpərɪ/ n. & adj. —n. (pl. **-ies**) 1 a worthless finery. b a worthless article. 2 rubbish. —adj. 1 showy but worthless (trumpery jewels). 2 delusive, shallow (trumpery arguments). [ME f. OF tromperie f. tromper deceive]

trumpet /'trʌmpɪt/ n. & v. —n. 1 a a tubular or conical brass instrument with a flared bell and a bright penetrating tone. b its player. 2 a the tubular corona of a daffodil etc. b a trumpet-shaped thing (ear-trumpet). 3 a sound of or like a trumpet. —v. (**trumpeted, trumpeting**) 1 intr. a blow a trumpet. b (of an elephant etc.) make a loud sound as of a trumpet. 2 tr. proclaim loudly (a person's or thing's merit). □ **trumpet-call** an urgent summons to action. **trumpet major** the chief trumpeter of a cavalry regiment. □ **trumpetless** adj. [ME f. OF trompette dimin. (as TRUMP²)]

trumpeter /'trʌmpɪtə(r)/ n. a person who plays or sounds a trumpet, esp. a cavalry soldier giving signals.

truncate /trʌŋ'keɪt, 'trʌŋ-/ v.tr. cut the top or the end from (a tree, a body, a piece of writing, etc.). □ **truncation** /-'keɪʃ(ə)n/ n. [L truncare truncat- maim]

truncheon /'trʌntʃ(ə)n/ n. 1 esp. Brit. a short club or cudgel, esp. carried by a policeman. 2 a staff or baton as a symbol of authority. [ME f. OF tronchon stump ult. f. L truncus trunk]

trundle /'trʌnd(ə)l/ v.tr. & intr. roll or move heavily or noisily esp. on or as on wheels. □ **trundle-bed** = TRUCKLE 1. [var. of obs. or dial. trendle, trindle, f. OE trendel circle (as TREND)]

trunk n. 1 the main stem of a tree as distinct from its branches and roots. 2 a person's or animal's body apart from the limbs and head. 3 the main part of any structure. 4 a large box with a hinged lid for transporting luggage, clothes, etc. 5 US the luggage compartment of a motor car. 6 an elephant's elongated prehensile nose. 7 (in pl.) men's close-fitting shorts worn for swimming, boxing, etc. □ **trunk call** esp. Brit. a telephone call on a trunk line with charges made according to distance. **trunk line** a main line of a railway, telephone system, etc. **trunk road** esp. Brit. an important main road. □ **trunkful** n. (pl. **-fuls**). **trunkless** adj. [ME f. OF tronc f. L truncus]

trunking /'trʌŋkɪŋ/ n. 1 a system of shafts or conduits for cables, ventilation, etc. 2 the use or arrangement of trunk lines.

truss n. & v. —n. 1 a framework, e.g. of rafters and struts, supporting a roof or bridge etc. 2 a surgical appliance worn to support a hernia. 3 Brit. a bundle of hay or straw. 4 a compact terminal cluster of flowers or fruit. —v.tr. 1 tie up (a fowl) compactly for cooking. 2 (often foll. by up) tie (a person) up with the arms to the sides. 3 support (a roof or bridge etc.) with a truss or trusses. □ **trusser** n. [ME f. OF trusser (v.), trusse (n.), of unkn. orig.]

trust *n.* & *v.* —*n.* **1 a** a firm belief in the reliability or truth or strength etc. of a person or thing. **b** the state of being relied on. **2 a** a confident expectation. **3 a** a thing or person committed to one's care. **b** the resulting obligation or responsibility (*am in a position of trust; have fulfilled my trust*). **4** a person or thing confided in (*is our sole trust*). **5** reliance on the truth of a statement etc. without examination. **6** commercial credit (*obtained goods on trust*). **7** *Law* confidence placed in a person by making that person the nominal owner of property to be used for another's benefit. **8 a** a body of trustees. **b** an organization managed by trustees. **c** an organized association of several companies for the purpose of reducing or defeating competition etc. —*v.* **1** *tr.* place trust in; believe in; rely on the character or behaviour of. **2** *tr.* (foll. by *with*) allow (a person) to have or use (a thing) from confidence in its proper use (*was reluctant to trust them with my books*). **3** *tr.* (often foll. by *that* + clause) have faith or confidence or hope that a thing will take place (*I trust you will not be late; I trust that she is recovering*). **4** *tr.* (foll. by *to*) consign (a thing) to (a person) with trust. **5** *tr.* (foll. by *for*) allow credit to (a customer) for (goods). **6** *intr.* (foll. by *in*) place reliance in (*we trust in you*). **7** *intr.* (foll. by *to*) place (esp. undue) reliance on (*shall have to trust to luck*). □ **in trust** *Law* held on the basis of trust (see sense 7 of *n.*). **on trust 1** on credit. **2** on the basis of trust or confidence. **take on trust** accept (an assertion, claim, etc.) without evidence or investigation. **trust company** a company formed to act as a trustee or to deal with trusts. **trust fund** a fund of money etc. held in trust. □ **trustable** *adj.* **truster** *n.* [ME *troste, truste* (n.) f. ON *traust* f. *traustr* strong: (v.) f. ON *treysta,* assim. to the noun]

trustee /trʌsˈtiː/ *n.* **1** *Law* a person or member of a board given control or powers of administration of property in trust with a legal obligation to administer it solely for the purposes specified. **2** a State made responsible for the government of an area. □ **trusteeship** *n.*

trustful /ˈtrʌstfʊl/ *adj.* **1** full of trust or confidence. **2** not feeling or showing suspicion. □ **trustfully** *adv.* **trustfulness** *n.*

trusting /ˈtrʌstɪŋ/ *adj.* having trust (esp. characteristically); trustful. □ **trustingly** *adv.* **trustingness** *n.*

trustworthy /ˈtrʌstˌwɜːðɪ/ *adj.* deserving of trust; reliable. □ **trustworthily** *adv.* **trustworthiness** *n.*

trusty /ˈtrʌstɪ/ *adj.* & *n.* —*adj.* (**trustier, trustiest**) *archaic* or *joc.* trustworthy (*a trusty steed*). —*n.* (*pl.* **-ies**) a prisoner who is given special privileges for good behaviour. □ **trustily** *adv.* **trustiness** *n.*

truth /truːθ/ *n.* (*pl.* **truths** /truːðz, truːθs/) **1** the quality or a state of being true or truthful (*doubted the truth of the statement; there may be some truth in it*). **2 a** what is true (*tell us the whole truth; the truth is that I forgot*). **b** what is accepted as true (*one of the fundamental truths*). □ **in truth** *literary* truly, really. **to tell the truth** (or **truth to tell**) to be frank. □ **truthless** *adj.* [OE *trīewth, trēowth* (as TRUE)]

truthful /ˈtruːθfʊl/ *adj.* **1** habitually speaking the truth. **2** (of a story etc.) true. **3** (of a likeness etc.) corresponding to reality. □ **truthfully** *adv.* **truthfulness** *n.*

try *v.* & *n.* —*v.* (**-ies, -ied**) **1** *intr.* make an effort with a view to success (often foll. by *to* + infin.; *colloq.* foll. by *and* + infin.: *tried to be on time; try and be early; I shall try hard*). **2** *tr.* make an effort to achieve (*tried my best; had better try something easier*). **3** *tr.* **a** test (the quality of a thing) by use or experiment. **b** test the qualities of (a person or thing) (*try it before you buy*). **4** *tr.* make severe demands on (a person, quality, etc.) (*my patience has been sorely tried*). **5** *tr.* examine the effectiveness or usefulness of for a purpose (*try cold water; have you tried kicking it?*). **6** *tr.* **a** investigate and decide (a case or issue) judicially. **b** subject (a person) to trial (*will be tried for murder*). **7** *tr.* make an experiment in order to find out (*let us try which takes longest*). **8** *intr.* (foll. by *for*) **a** apply or compete for. **b** seek to reach or attain (*am going to try for a gold medal*). —*n.* (*pl.* **-ies**) **1** an effort to accomplish something; an attempt (*give it a try*). **2** *Rugby Football* the act of touching the ball down behind the opposing goal-line, scoring points and entitling the scoring side to a kick at goal. **3** *Amer. Football* an attempt to score an extra point in various ways after a touchdown. □ **try for size** try out or test for suitability. **try one's hand** see how skilful one is, esp. at the first attempt. **try it on** *colloq.* **1** test another's patience. **2** attempt to outwit or deceive another person. **try on** put on (clothes etc.) to see if they fit or suit the wearer. **try-on** *n.* *Brit. colloq.* **1** an act of trying it on. **2** an attempt to fool or deceive. **try out 1** put to the test. **2** test thoroughly. **try-out** *n.* an experimental test of efficiency, popularity, etc. [ME = separate, distinguish, etc., f. OF *trier* sift, of unkn. orig.]

■ **Usage** Use of the verb with *and* (see sense 1) is uncommon in negative contexts (except in the imperative, e.g. *don't try and get the better of me*) and in the past tense.

trying /ˈtraɪɪŋ/ *adj.* annoying, vexatious; hard to endure. □ **tryingly** *adv.*

tryst /trɪst/ *n.* & *v.* *archaic* —*n.* **1** a time and place for a meeting, esp. of lovers. **2** such a meeting (*keep a tryst; break one's tryst*). —*v.intr.* (foll. by *with*) make a tryst. □ **tryster** *n.* [ME, = obs. *trist* (= TRUST) f. OF *triste* an appointed station in hunting]

tsar /zɑː(r)/ *n.* (also **czar**) **1** *hist.* the title of the former emperor of Russia. **2** a person with great authority. □ **tsardom** *n.* **tsarism** *n.* **tsarist** *n.* [Russ. *tsar',* ult. f. L *Caesar*]

tsarevich /ˈzɑːrɪvɪtʃ/ *n.* (also **czarevich**) *hist.* the eldest son of an emperor of Russia. [Russ. *tsarevich* son of a tsar]

tsarina /zɑːˈriːnə/ *n.* (also **czarina**) *hist.* the title of the former empress of Russia. [It. & Sp. (c)*zarina* f. G *Czarin, Zarin,* fem. of *Czar, Zar*]

tsetse /ˈtsetsɪ, ˈtetsɪ/ *n.* any fly of the genus *Glossina* native to Africa, that feeds on human and animal blood. [Tswana]

T-shirt /ˈtiːʃɜːt/ *n.* (also **teeshirt**) a short-sleeved casual top, usu. of knitted cotton and having the form of a T when spread out.

tsp. *abbr.* (*pl.* **tsps.**) teaspoonful.

T-square /ˈtiːskweə(r)/ *n.* a T-shaped instrument for drawing or testing right angles.

tsunami /tsuːˈnɑːmɪ/ n. (pl. **tsunamis**) a long high sea wave caused by underwater earthquakes or other disturbances. [Jap. f. *tsu* harbour + *nami* wave]

TT abbr. **1** Tourist Trophy. **2** tuberculin-tested. **3 a** teetotal. **b** teetotaller.

tub n. & v. —n. **1** an open flat-bottomed usu. round container for various purposes. **2** a tub-shaped (usu. plastic) carton. **3** the amount a tub will hold. **4** colloq. a bath. **5** colloq. a clumsy slow boat. —v. (**tubbed**, **tubbing**) tr. & intr. plant, bathe, or wash in a tub. □ **tub-thumping** colloq. ranting oratory. □ **tubbable** adj. **tubbish** adj. **tubful** n. (pl. **-fuls**). [ME, prob. of LG or Du. orig.: cf. MLG, MDu. *tubbe*]

tuba /ˈtjuːbə/ n. (pl. **tubas**) **1** a low-pitched brass wind instrument. **2** its player. [It. f. L, = trumpet]

tubal /ˈtjuːb(ə)l/ adj. Anat. of or relating to a tube, esp. the bronchial or Fallopian tubes.

tubby /ˈtʌbɪ/ adj. (**tubbier**, **tubbiest**) (of a person) short and fat; tub-shaped. □ **tubbiness** n.

tube n. & v. —n. **1** a long hollow rigid or flexible cylinder, esp. for holding or carrying air, liquids, etc. **2** a soft metal or plastic cylinder sealed at one end and having a screw cap at the other, for holding a semi-liquid substance ready for use (*a tube of toothpaste*). **3** Anat. & Zool. a hollow cylindrical organ in the body (*bronchial tubes*; *Fallopian tubes*). **4** (often prec. by *the*) colloq. the London underground railway system (*went by tube*). **5 a** a cathode-ray tube esp. in a television set. **b** (prec. by *the*) esp. US colloq. television. **6** US a thermionic valve. **7** = *inner tube*. **8** Austral. sl. a can of beer. —v.tr. **1** equip with tubes. **2** enclose in a tube. □ **tubeless** adj. (esp. in sense 7 of n.). **tubelike** adj. [F *tube* or L *tubus*]

tubectomy /tjuːˈbektəmɪ/ n. (pl. **-ies**) Surgery removal of a Fallopian tube.

tuber /ˈtjuːbə(r)/ n. **1** the short thick rounded part of a stem or rhizome, usu. found underground and covered with modified buds, e.g. in a potato. **2** the similar root of a dahlia etc. [L, = hump, swelling]

tubercle /ˈtjuːbək(ə)l/ n. **1** a small rounded protuberance esp. on a bone. **2** a small rounded swelling on the body or in an organ, esp. a nodular lesion characteristic of tuberculosis in the lungs etc. □ **tubercle bacillus** a bacterium causing tuberculosis. □ **tuberculate** /-ˈbɜːkjʊlət/ adj. **tuberculous** /-ˈbɜːkjʊləs/ adj. [L *tuberculum*, dimin. of *tuber*: see TUBER]

tubercular /tjʊˈbɜːkjʊlə(r)/ adj. & n. —adj. of or having tubercles or tuberculosis. —n. a person with tuberculosis. [f. L *tuberculum* (as TUBERCLE)]

tuberculin /tjʊˈbɜːkjʊlɪn/ n. a sterile liquid from cultures of tubercle bacillus, used in the diagnosis and treatment of tuberculosis. □ **tuberculin test** a hypodermic injection of tuberculin to detect a tubercular infection. **tuberculin-tested** (of milk) from cows giving a negative response to a tuberculin test. [f. L *tuberculum* (as TUBERCLE)]

tuberculosis /tjʊˌbɜːkjʊˈləʊsɪs/ n. an infectious disease caused by the bacillus *Mycobacterium tuberculosis*, characterized by tubercles, esp. in the lungs.

tuberose¹ /ˈtjuːbərəʊs/ adj. **1** covered with tubers; knobby. **2** of or resembling a tuber. **3** bearing tubers. □ **tuberosity** /-ˈrɒsɪtɪ/ n. [L *tuberosus* f. TUBER]

tuberose² /ˈtjuːbəˌrəʊz/ n. a plant, *Polianthes tuberosa*, native to Mexico, having heavily scented white funnel-like flowers and strap-shaped leaves. [L *tuberosa* fem. (as TUBEROSE¹)]

tuberous /ˈtjuːbərəs/ adj. = TUBEROSE¹. □ **tuberous root** a thick and fleshy root like a tuber but without buds. [F *tubéreux* or L *tuberosus* f. TUBER]

tubifex /ˈtjuːbɪˌfeks/ n. any red annelid worm of the genus *Tubifex*, found in mud at the bottom of rivers and lakes and used as food for aquarium fish. [mod.L f. L *tubus* tube + *-fex* f. *facere* make]

tubiform /ˈtjuːbɪˌfɔːm/ adj. tube-shaped.

tubing /ˈtjuːbɪŋ/ n. **1** a length of tube. **2** a quantity of tubes.

tubular /ˈtjuːbjʊlə(r)/ adj. **1** tube-shaped. **2** having or consisting of tubes. **3** (of furniture etc.) made of tubular pieces. □ **tubular bells** an orchestral instrument consisting of a row of vertically suspended brass tubes that are struck with a hammer.

tubule /ˈtjuːbjuːl/ n. a small tube in a plant or an animal body. [L *tubulus*, dimin. of *tubus* tube]

TUC abbr. (in the UK) Trades Union Congress.

tuck v. & n. —v. **1** tr. (often foll. by *in*, *up*) **a** draw, fold, or turn the outer or end parts of (cloth or clothes etc.) close together so as to be held; thrust in the edge of (a thing) so as to confine it (*tucked his shirt into his trousers*; *tucked the sheet under the mattress*). **b** thrust in the edges of bedclothes around (a person) (*came to tuck me in*). **2** tr. draw together into a small space (*tucked her legs under her*; *the bird tucked its head under its wing*). **3** tr. stow (a thing) away in a specified place or way (*tucked it in a corner*; *tucked it out of sight*). **4** tr. **a** make a stitched fold in (material, a garment, etc.). **b** shorten, tighten, or ornament with stitched folds. —n. **1** a flattened usu. stitched fold in material, a garment, etc., often one of several parallel folds for shortening, tightening, or ornament. **2** Brit. colloq. food, esp. cakes and sweets eaten by children (also attrib.: *tuck box*). **3** (in full **tuck position**) (in diving, gymnastics, etc.) a position with the knees bent upwards into the chest and the hands clasped round the shins. □ **tuck in** colloq. eat food heartily. **tuck into** (or **away**) colloq. eat (food) heartily (*tucked into their dinner*; *could really tuck it away*). **tuck shop** Brit. a small shop, esp. near or in a school, selling food to children. [ME *tukke*, *tokke*, f. MDu., MLG *tucken*, = OHG *zucchen* pull, rel. to TUG]

tucker /ˈtʌkə(r)/ n. & v. —n. **1** a person or thing that tucks. **2** hist. a piece of lace or linen etc. in or on a woman's bodice. **3** Austral. colloq. food. —v.tr. (esp. in passive; often foll. by *out*) US colloq. tire, exhaust. □ **tucker-bag** (or **-box**) Austral. colloq. a container for food.

tucking /ˈtʌkɪŋ/ n. a series of usu. stitched tucks in material or a garment.

-tude /tjuːd/ suffix forming abstract nouns (*altitude*; *attitude*; *solitude*). [from or after F *-tude* f. L *-tudo -tudinis*]

Tudor /ˈtjuːdə(r)/ adj. & n. hist. —adj. **1** of, characteristic of, or associated with the royal family of England ruling 1485–1603 or this period. **2** of or relating to the architectural style of this period, esp. with half-timbering and elaborately decorated houses. —*n.* a member of the Tudor royal family. □ **Tudor rose** a conventional five-lobed figure of a rose esp. a red rose encircling a white one. [Owen *Tudor* of Wales, grandfather of Henry VII]

Tues. *abbr.* (also **Tue.**) Tuesday.

Tuesday /ˈtjuːzdeɪ, -dɪ/ *n. & adv.* —*n.* the third day of the week, following Monday. —*adv.* **1** *colloq.* on Tuesday. **2** (**Tuesdays**) on Tuesdays; each Tuesday. [OE *Tīwesdæg* f. *Tīw* the Gmc god of war, identified with Roman Mars]

tufa /ˈtjuːfə/ *n.* **1** a porous rock composed of calcium carbonate and formed round mineral springs. **2** = TUFF. □ **tufaceous** /-ˈfeɪʃəs/ *adj.* [It., var. of *tufo*: see TUFF]

tuff *n.* rock formed by the consolidation of volcanic ash. □ **tuffaceous** /-ˈfeɪʃəs/ *adj.* [F *tuf, tuffe* f. It. *tufo* f. LL *tofus*, L *tophus*, = loose porous stones]

tuffet /ˈtʌfɪt/ *n.* **1** = TUFT 1. **2** a low seat. [var. of TUFT]

tuft *n. & v.* —*n.* a bunch or collection of threads, grass, feathers, hair, etc., held or growing together at the base. —*v.* **1** *tr.* provide with a tuft or tufts. **2** *tr.* make depressions at regular intervals in (a mattress etc.) by passing a thread through. **3** *intr.* grow in tufts. □ **tufty** *adj.* [ME, prob. f. OF *tofe, toffe*, of unkn. orig.: for *-t* cf. GRAFT¹]

tufted /ˈtʌftɪd/ *adj.* having or growing in a tuft or tufts.

tug *v. & n.* —*v.* (**tugged, tugging**) **1** *tr. &* (foll. by *at*) *intr.* pull hard or violently; jerk (*tugged it from my gown*) *intr.* pull hard or violently; jerk (*tugged it from my gown*). **2** *tr.* tow (a ship etc.) by means of a tugboat. —*n.* **1** a hard, violent, or jerky pull (*gave a tug on the rope*). **2** a sudden strong emotional feeling (*felt a tug as I watched them go*). **3** a small powerful boat for towing larger boats and ships. □ **tug of love** *colloq.* a dispute over the custody of a child. **tug of war 1** a trial of strength between two sides pulling against each other on a rope. **2** a decisive or severe contest. □ **tugger** *n.* [ME *togge, tugge*, intensive f. Gmc: see TOW¹]

tugboat /ˈtʌgbəʊt/ *n.* = TUG *n.* 3.

tuition /tjuːˈɪʃ(ə)n/ *n.* **1** teaching or instruction, esp. if paid for (*driving tuition; music tuition*). **2** a fee for this. □ **tuitional** *adj.* [ME f. OF f. L *tuitio -onis* f. *tuēri tuit-* watch, guard]

tulip /ˈtjuːlɪp/ *n.* **1** any bulbous spring-flowering plant of the genus *Tulipa*, esp. one of the many cultivated forms with showy cup-shaped flowers of various colours and markings. **2** a flower of this plant. □ **tulip-tree** any of various trees esp. of the genus *Liriodendron*, producing tulip-like flowers. [orig. *tulipa*(*n*) f. mod.L *tulipa* f. Turk. *tul(i)band* f. Pers. *dulband* TURBAN (from the shape of the expanded flower)]

tulle /tjuːl/ *n.* a soft fine silk etc. net for veils and dresses. [*Tulle* in SW France, where it was first made]

tum *n. colloq.* stomach. [abbr. of TUMMY]

tumble /ˈtʌmb(ə)l/ *v. & n.* —*v.* **1** *intr. & tr.* fall or cause to fall suddenly, clumsily, or headlong. **2** *intr.* fall rapidly in amount etc. (*prices tumbled*). **3** *intr.* (often foll. by *about, around*) roll or toss erratically or helplessly to and fro. **4** *intr.* move or rush in a headlong or blundering manner (*the children tumbled out of the car*). **5** *intr.* (often foll. by *to*) *colloq.* grasp the meaning or hidden implication of an idea, circumstance, etc. (*they

quickly tumbled to our intentions*). **6** *tr.* overturn; fling or push roughly or carelessly. **7** *intr.* perform acrobatic feats, esp. somersaults. **8** *tr.* rumple or disarrange; pull about; disorder. **9** *tr.* dry (washing) in a tumble-drier. —*n.* **1** a sudden or headlong fall. **2** a somersault or other acrobatic feat. **3** an untidy or confused state. □ **tumble-drier** *n.* a machine for drying washing in a heated rotating drum. **tumble-dry** *v.tr. & intr.* (**-dries, -dried**) dry in a tumble-drier. [ME *tumbel* f. MLG *tummelen*, OHG *tumalōn* frequent. of *tūmōn*: cf. OE *tumbian* dance]

tumbledown /ˈtʌmb(ə)lˌdaʊn/ *adj.* falling or fallen into ruin; dilapidated.

tumbler /ˈtʌmblə(r)/ *n.* **1** a drinking-glass with no handle or foot (formerly with a rounded bottom so as not to stand upright). **2** an acrobat, esp. one performing somersaults. **3** (in full **tumbler-drier**) = tumble-drier. **4** a pivoted piece in a lock that holds the bolt until lifted by a key. **5** a toy figure that rocks when touched. □ **tumblerful** *n.* (*pl.* **-fuls**).

tumbleweed /ˈtʌmb(ə)lˌwiːd/ *n.* US & Austral. a plant, *Amaranthus albus*, that forms a globular bush that breaks off in late summer and is tumbled about by the wind.

tumbrel /ˈtʌmbr(ə)l/ *n.* (also **tumbril** /-rɪl/) *hist.* **1** an open cart in which condemned persons were conveyed to their execution, esp. to the guillotine during the French Revolution. **2** a two-wheeled covered cart for carrying tools, ammunition, etc. **3** a cart that tips to empty its load, esp. one carrying dung. [ME f. OF *tumberel, tomberel* f. *tomber* fall]

tumescent /tjuːˈmes(ə)nt/ *adj.* **1** becoming tumid; swelling. **2** swelling as a response to sexual stimulation. □ **tumescence** *n.* **tumescently** *adv.* [L *tumescere* f. *tumefacere* f. *tumēre* swell]

tumid /ˈtjuːmɪd/ *adj.* **1** (of parts of the body etc.) swollen, inflated. **2** (of a style etc.) inflated, bombastic. □ **tumidity** /-ˈmɪdɪtɪ/ *n.* **tumidly** *adv.* **tumidness** *n.* [L *tumidus* f. *tumēre* swell]

tummy /ˈtʌmɪ/ *n.* (*pl.* **-ies**) *colloq.* the stomach. □ **tummy-button** the navel. [childish pronunc. of STOMACH]

tumour /ˈtjuːmə(r)/ *n.* (US **tumor**) a swelling, esp. from an abnormal growth of tissue. □ **tumorous** *adj.* [L *tumor* f. *tumēre* swell]

tumult /ˈtjuːmʌlt/ *n.* **1** an uproar or din, esp. of a disorderly crowd. **2** an angry demonstration by a mob; a riot; a public disturbance. **3** a conflict of emotions in the mind. [ME f. OF *tumulte* or L *tumultus*]

tumultuous /tjuːˈmʌltjʊəs/ *adj.* **1** noisily vehement; uproarious; making a tumult (*a tumultuous welcome*). **2** disorderly. **3** agitated. □ **tumultuously** *adv.* **tumultuousness** *n.* [OF *tumultuous* or L *tumultuosus* (as TUMULT)]

tumulus /ˈtjuːmjʊləs/ *n.* (*pl.* **tumuli** /-ˌlaɪ/) an ancient burial mound or barrow. □ **tumular** *adj.* [L f. *tumēre* swell]

tun *n. & v.* —*n.* **1** a large beer or wine cask. **2** a brewer's fermenting-vat. [OE *tunne* f. med.L *tunna*, prob. of Gaulish orig.]

tuna /ˈtjuːnə/ *n.* (*pl.* same or **tunas**) **1** any marine fish of the family Scombridae native to tropical and warm waters, having a round body and pointed snout, and used for food. **2** (in full **tuna-fish**) the flesh of the tuna or tunny, usu. tinned in oil or brine. [Amer. Sp., perh. f. Sp. *atún* tunny]

tundra /ˈtʌndrə/ n. a vast level treeless Arctic region usu. with a marshy surface and underlying permafrost. [Lappish]

tune n. & v. —n. a melody with or without harmony. —v. **1** tr. put (a musical instrument) in tune. **2 a** tr. adjust (a radio receiver etc.) to the particular frequency of the required signals. **b** intr. (foll. by in) adjust a radio receiver to the required signal (tuned in to Radio 2). **3** tr. adjust (an engine etc.) to run smoothly and efficiently. **4** tr. (foll. by to) adjust or adapt to a required or different purpose, situation, etc. **5** intr. (foll. by with) be in harmony with. □ **in tune 1** having the correct pitch or intonation (sings in tune). **2** (usu. foll. by with) harmonizing with one's company, surroundings, etc. **out of tune 1** not having the correct pitch or intonation (always plays out of tune). **2** (usu. foll. by with) clashing with one's company etc. **to the tune of** colloq. to the considerable sum or amount of. **tune up 1** (of an orchestra) bring the instruments to the proper or uniform pitch. **2** begin to play or sing. **3** bring to the most efficient condition. □ **tunable** adj. (also **tuneable**). [ME: unexpl. var. of TONE]

tuneful /ˈtjuːnfʊl/ adj. melodious, musical. □ **tunefully** adv. **tunefulness** n.

tuneless /ˈtjuːnlɪs/ adj. **1** unmelodious, unmusical. **2** out of tune. □ **tunelessly** adv. **tunelessness** n.

tuner /ˈtjuːnə(r)/ n. **1** a person who tunes musical instruments, esp. pianos. **2** a device for tuning a radio receiver.

tungsten /ˈtʌŋst(ə)n/ n. Chem. a steel-grey dense metallic element with a very high melting-point, used for the filaments of electric lamps and for alloying steel etc. □ **tungsten carbide** a very hard black substance used in making dies and cutting tools. □ **tungstate** /-steɪt/ n. **tungstic** adj. **tungstous** adj. [Sw. f. tung heavy + sten stone]

tunic /ˈtjuːnɪk/ n. **1** a close-fitting short coat of police or military etc. uniform. **2** a loose, often sleeveless garment usu. reaching to about the knees, as worn in ancient Greece and Rome. **3** any of various loose, pleated dresses gathered at the waist with a belt or cord. [F tunique or L tunica]

tuning /ˈtjuːnɪŋ/ n. the process or a system of putting a musical instrument in tune. □ **tuning-fork** a two-pronged steel fork that gives a particular note when struck, used in tuning.

tunnel /ˈtʌn(ə)l/ n. & v. —n. **1** an artificial underground passage through a hill or under a road or river etc., esp. for a railway or road to pass through, or in a mine. **2** an underground passage dug by a burrowing animal. **3** a prolonged period of difficulty or suffering (esp. in metaphors, e.g. the end of the tunnel). —v. (**tunnelled, tunnelling**; US **tunneled, tunneling**) **1** intr. (foll. by through, into, etc.) make a tunnel through (a hill etc.). **2** tr. make (one's way) by tunnelling. □ **tunnel vision 1** vision that is defective in not adequately including objects away from the centre of the field of view. **2** colloq. inability to grasp the wider implications of a situation. □ **tunneller** n. [ME f. OF tonel dimin. of tonne TUN]

tunny /ˈtʌnɪ/ n. (pl. same or **-ies**) = TUNA. [F thon f. Prov. ton, f. L thunnus f. Gk thunnos]

tup n. & v. —n. esp. Brit. a male sheep; a ram. —v.tr. (**tupped, tupping**) esp. Brit. (of a ram) copulate with (a ewe). [ME toje, tupe, of unkn. orig.]

tuppence /ˈtʌpəns/ n. Brit. = TWOPENCE. [phonet. spelling]

tuppenny /ˈtʌpənɪ/ adj. Brit. = TWOPENNY. [phonet. spelling]

Tupperware /ˈtʌpəˌweə(r)/ n. propr. a range of plastic containers for storing food. [Tupper, name of the US manufacturer, + WARE¹]

tuque /tuːk/ n. a Canadian stocking cap. [Can. F form of TOQUE]

turban /ˈtɜːbən/ n. **1** a man's headdress of cotton or silk wound round a cap or the head, worn esp. by Muslims and Sikhs. **2** a woman's headdress or hat resembling this. □ **turbaned** adj. [16th c. (also tulbant etc.), ult. f. Turk. tülbent f. Pers. dulband: cf. TULIP]

turbid /ˈtɜːbɪd/ adj. **1** (of a liquid or colour) muddy, thick; not clear. **2** (of a style etc.) confused, disordered. □ **turbidity** /-ˈbɪdɪtɪ/ n. **turbidly** adv. **turbidness** n. [L turbidus f. turba a crowd, a disturbance]

turbine /ˈtɜːbaɪn/ n. a rotary motor or engine driven by a flow of water, steam, gas, wind, etc., esp. to produce electrical power. [F f. L turbo -binis spinning-top, whirlwind]

turbo /ˈtɜːbəʊ/ n. (pl. **-os**) = TURBOCHARGER.

turbo- /ˈtɜːbəʊ/ comb. form turbine.

turbocharger /ˈtɜːbəʊˌtʃɑːdʒə(r)/ n. a supercharger driven by a turbine powered by the engine's exhaust gases.

turbofan /ˈtɜːbəʊˌfæn/ n. **1** a jet engine in which a turbine-driven fan provides additional thrust. **2** an aircraft powered by this.

turbojet /ˈtɜːbəʊˌdʒet/ n. Aeron. **1** a jet engine in which the jet also operates a turbine-driven compressor for the air drawn into the engine. **2** an aircraft powered by this.

turboprop /ˈtɜːbəʊˌprɒp/ n. Aeron. **1** a jet engine in which a turbine is used as in a turbojet and also to drive a propeller. **2** an aircraft powered by this.

turboshaft /ˈtɜːbəʊˌʃɑːft/ n. a gas turbine that powers a shaft for driving heavy vehicles, generators, pumps, etc.

turbosupercharger /ˌtɜːbəʊˈsuːpəˌtʃɑːdʒə(r)/ n. = TURBOCHARGER.

turbot /ˈtɜːbət/ n. **1** a flatfish, Scophthalmus maximus, prized as food. **2** any of various similar fishes including halibut. [ME f. OF f. OSw. törnbut f. törn thorn + but BUTT³]

turbulence /ˈtɜːbjʊləns/ n. **1** an irregularly fluctuating flow of air or fluid. **2** Meteorol. stormy conditions as a result of atmospheric disturbance. **3** a disturbance, commotion, or tumult.

turbulent /ˈtɜːbjʊlənt/ adj. **1** disturbed; in commotion. **2** (of a flow of air etc.) varying irregularly; causing disturbance. **3** tumultuous. **4** insubordinate, riotous. □ **turbulently** adv. [L turbulentus f. turba crowd]

Turco- /ˈtɜːkəʊ/ comb. form (also **Turko-**) Turkish; Turkish and. [med.L (as TURK)]

turd n. coarse sl. **1** a lump of excrement. **2** a term of contempt for a person. [OE tord f. Gmc]

tureen /tjʊəˈriːn, tə-/ n. a deep covered dish for serving soup etc. [earlier terrine, -ene f. F terrine large circular earthenware dish, fem. of OF *terrin* earthen ult. f. L *terra* earth]

turf *n. & v.* —*n.* (pl. **turfs** or **turves**) **1 a** a layer of grass etc. with earth and matted roots as the surface of grassland. **b** a piece of this cut from the ground. **2** a slab of peat for fuel. **3** (prec. by *the*) **a** horse-racing generally. **b** a general term for racecourses. —*v.tr.* **1** cover (ground) with turf. **2** (foll. by *out*) esp. *Brit. colloq.* expel or eject (a person or thing). □ **turf accountant** *Brit.* a bookmaker. [OE f. Gmc]

turfman /ˈtɜːfmən/ *n.* (pl. **-men**) esp. *US* a devotee of horse-racing.

turfy /ˈtɜːfɪ/ *adj.* (**turfier, turfiest**) like turf; grassy.

turgescent /tɜːˈdʒes(ə)nt/ *adj.* becoming turgid; swelling. □ **turgescence** *n.*

turgid /ˈtɜːdʒɪd/ *adj.* **1** swollen, inflated, enlarged. **2** (of language) pompous, bombastic. □ **turgidity** /-ˈdʒɪdɪtɪ/ *n.* **turgidly** *adv.* **turgidness** *n.* [L *turgidus* f. *turgēre* swell]

Turk *n.* **1 a** a native or national of Turkey in SE Europe and Asia Minor. **b** a person of Turkish descent. **2** a member of a Central Asian people from whom the Ottomans derived. **3** *offens.* a ferocious, wild, or unmanageable person. [ME, = F *Turc*, It. etc. *Turco*, med.L *Turcus*, Pers. & Arab. *Turk*, of unkn. orig.]

turkey /ˈtɜːkɪ/ *n.* (pl. **-eys**) **1** a large mainly domesticated game-bird, *Meleagris gallopavo*, orig. of N. America, having dark plumage with a green or bronze sheen, prized as food esp. on festive occasions including Christmas and, in the US, Thanksgiving. **2** the flesh of the turkey as food. **3** *US sl.* **a** a theatrical failure; a flop. **b** a stupid or inept person. □ **talk turkey** *US colloq.* talk frankly and straightforwardly; get down to business. [16th c.: short for *turkeycock* or *turkeyhen*, orig. applied to the guinea-fowl which was imported through Turkey, and then erron. to the Amer. bird]

Turkey carpet /ˈtɜːkɪ/ *n.* = *Turkish carpet.*

turkeycock /ˈtɜːkɪkɒk/ *n.* **1** a male turkey. **2** a pompous or self-important person.

Turkish /ˈtɜːkɪʃ/ *adj. & n.* —*adj.* of or relating to Turkey in SE Europe and Asia Minor, or to the Turks or their language. —*n.* this language. □ **Turkish bath 1** a hot-air or steam bath followed by washing, massage, etc. **2** (in *sing.* or *pl.*) a building for this. **Turkish carpet** a wool carpet with a thick pile and traditional bold design. **Turkish coffee** a strong black coffee. **Turkish delight** a sweet of lumps of flavoured gelatine coated in powdered sugar. **Turkish towel** a towel made of cotton terry.

turmeric /ˈtɜːmərɪk/ *n.* **1** an E. Indian plant, *Curcuma longa*, of the ginger family, yielding aromatic rhizomes used as a spice and for yellow dye. **2** this powdered rhizome used as a spice esp. in curry-powder. [16th-c. forms *tarmaret* etc. perh. f. F *terre mérite* and mod.L *terra merita*, of unkn. orig.]

turmoil /ˈtɜːmɔɪl/ *n.* **1** violent confusion; agitation. **2** din and bustle. [16th c.: orig. unkn.]

turn *v. & n.* —*v.* **1** *tr. & intr.* move around a point or axis so that the point or axis remains in a central position; give a rotary motion to or receive a rotary motion (*turned the wheel; the wheel turns; the key turns in the lock*). **2** *tr. & intr.* change in position so that a different side, end, or part becomes outermost or uppermost etc.; invert or reverse or cause to be inverted or reversed (*turned inside out; turned it upside down*). **3 a** *tr.* give a new direction to (*turn your face this way*). **b** *intr.* take a new direction (*turn left here; my thoughts have often turned to you*). **4** *tr.* aim in a certain way (*turned the hose on them*). **5** *intr. & tr.* (foll. by *into*) change in nature, form, or condition to (*turned into a dragon; then turned him into a frog; turned the book into a play*). **6** *intr.* (foll. by *to*) **a** apply oneself to; set about (*turned to doing the ironing*). **b** have recourse to; begin to indulge in habitually (*turned to drink; turned to me for help*). **c** go on to consider next (*let us now turn to your report*). **7** *intr. & tr.* become or cause to become (*turned hostile; has turned informer; your comment turned them angry*). **8 a** *tr. & intr.* (foll. by *against*) make or become hostile to (*has turned them against us*). **b** *intr.* (foll. by *on, upon*) become hostile to; attack (*suddenly turned on them*). **9** *intr.* (of hair or leaves) change colour. **10** *intr.* (of milk) become sour. **11** *intr.* (of the stomach) be nauseated. **12** *intr.* (of the head) become giddy. **13** *tr.* cause (milk) to become sour, (the stomach) to be nauseated, or (the head) to become giddy. **14** *tr.* translate (*turn it into French*). **15** *tr.* move to the other side of; go round (*turned the corner*). **16** *tr.* pass the age or time of (*he has turned 40; it has now turned 4 o'clock*). **17** *intr.* (foll. by *on*) depend on; be determined by (*it all turns on the weather tomorrow*). **18** *tr.* send or put into a specified place or condition; cause to go (*was turned loose; turned the water out into a basin*). **19** *tr.* perform (a somersault etc.) with rotary motion. **20** *tr.* make (a profit). **21** *tr.* divert (a bullet). **22** *tr.* blunt (the edge of a knife, slot of a screw-head, etc.). **23** *tr.* shape (an object) on a lathe. **24** *tr.* give an (esp. elegant) form to (*turn a compliment*). **25** *intr.* (of the tide) change from flood to ebb or vice versa. —*n.* **1** the act or process or an instance of turning; rotary motion (*a single turn of the handle*). **2 a** a changed or a change of direction or tendency (*took a sudden turn to the left*). **b** a deflection or deflected part (*full of twists and turns*). **3** a point at which a turning or change occurs. **4** a turning of a road. **5** a change of the tide from ebb to flow or from flow to ebb. **6** a change in the course of events. **7** a tendency or disposition (*is of a mechanical turn of mind*). **8** an opportunity or obligation etc. that comes successively to each of several persons etc. (*your turn will come; my turn to read*). **9** a short walk or ride (*shall take a turn in the garden*). **10** a short performance on stage or in a circus etc. **11** service of a specified kind (*did me a good turn*). **12** purpose (*served my turn*). **13** *colloq.* a momentary nervous shock or ill feeling (*gave me quite a turn*). **14** *Mus.* an ornament consisting of the principal note with those above and below it. □ **at every turn** continually; at each new stage etc. **by turns** in rotation of individuals or groups; alternately. **in turn** in succession; one by one. **in one's turn** when one's turn or opportunity comes. **not know which way** (or **where**) **to turn** be completely at a loss, unsure how to act, etc. **on the turn 1** changing. **2** (of milk) becoming sour. **3** at the turning-point. **out of turn 1** at a time when it is not one's turn. **2** inappropriately; inadvisedly or tactlessly (*did I speak out of turn?*). **take turns** (or **take it in turns**) act or work alternately or in succession. **to a turn** (esp. cooked) to exactly the right degree etc. **turn about** move so as to face in a new direction. **turn–about** *n.* **1** an act of turning about. **2** an abrupt change of policy etc. **turn and turn about** alternately. **turn around** esp. *US* = turn round. **turn away 1** turn to face in another direction. **2** refuse to accept; reject. **3** send away. **turn back 1** begin or cause to retrace one's steps. **2** fold back. **turn the corner 1** pass round it into another street. **2** pass the critical point in an illness, difficulty, etc. **turn down 1** reject (a proposal, application, etc.). **2** reduce the volume or strength of (sound, heat, etc.) by turning a knob etc. **3** fold down. **4** place downwards. **turn–down** (of a collar) turned down. **turn in 1** hand in or return. **2** achieve or register (a performance, score, etc.). **3** *colloq.* go to bed in the evening. **4** fold inwards. **5** incline inwards (*his toes turn in*). **6** *colloq.* abandon (a plan etc.). **turn off 1 a** stop the flow or operation of (water, electricity, etc.) by means of a tap, switch, etc. **b** operate (a tap, switch, etc.) to achieve this. **2 a** enter a side-road. **b** (of a side-road) lead off from another road. **3** *colloq.* repel; cause to lose interest (*turned me right off with their complaining*). **4** dismiss from employment. **turn–off** *n.* **1** a turning off a main road. **2** *colloq.* something that repels or causes a loss of interest. **turn of speed** the ability to go fast when necessary. **turn on 1 a** start the flow or operation of (water, electricity, etc.) by means of a tap, switch, etc. **b** operate (a tap, switch, etc.) to achieve this. **2** *colloq.* excite; stimulate the interest of, esp. sexually. **3** *tr.* & *intr.* intoxicate or become intoxicated with drugs. **turn–on** *n. colloq.* a person or thing that causes (esp. sexual) arousal. **turn out 1** expel. **2** extinguish (an electric light etc.). **3** dress or equip (*well turned out*). **4** produce (manufactured goods etc.). **5** empty or clean out (a room etc.). **6** empty (a pocket) to see the contents. **7** *colloq.* **a** get out of bed. **b** go out of doors. **8** *colloq.* assemble; attend a meeting etc. **9** (often foll. by *to* + infin. or *that* + clause) prove to be the case; result (*turned out to be true; we shall see how things turn out*). **10** *Mil.* call (a guard) from the guardroom. **turn over 1** reverse or cause to reverse vertical position; bring the under or reverse side into view (*turn over the page*). **2** upset; fall or cause to fall over. **3** cause (an engine) to run. **b** (of an engine) start running. **4** consider thoroughly. **5** (foll. by *to*) transfer the care or conduct of (a person or thing) to (a person) (*shall turn it all over to my deputy; turned him over to the authorities*). **6** do business to the amount of (*turns over £5000 a week*). **turn over a new leaf** improve one's conduct or performance. **turn round 1** turn so as to face in a new direction. **2 a** *Commerce* unload and reload (a ship, vehicle, etc.). **b** receive, process, and send out again; cause to progress through a system. **3** adopt new opinions or policy. **turn–round** *n.* **1 a** the process of loading and unloading. **b** the process of receiving, processing, and sending out again; progress through a system. **2** the reversal of an opinion or tendency. **turn tail** turn one's back; run away. **turn the tide** reverse the trend of events. **turn to** set about one's work (*came home and immediately turned to*). **turn up 1** increase the volume or strength of (sound, heat, etc.) by turning a knob etc. **2** place upwards. **3** discover or reveal. **4** be found, esp. by chance (*it turned up on a rubbish dump*). **5** happen or present itself; (of a person) put in an

appearance (*a few people turned up late*). **6** *colloq.* cause to vomit (*the sight turned me up*). **7** shorten (a garment) by increasing the size of the hem. [OE *tyrnan, turnian* f. L *tornare* f. *tornus* lathe f. Gk *tornos* lathe, circular movement: prob. reinforced in ME f. OF *turner, torner*]

turn-up *n.* **1** *Brit.* the lower turned up end of a trouser leg. **2** *colloq.* an unexpected (esp. welcome) happening; a surprise. [OE *tyrnan, turnian* f. L *tornare* f. *tornus* lathe f. Gk *tornos* lathe, circular movement: prob. reinforced in ME f. OF *turner, torner*]

turncoat /ˈtɜːnkəʊt/ *n.* a person who changes sides in a conflict, dispute, etc.

turner /ˈtɜːnə(r)/ *n.* **1** a person or thing that turns. **2** a person who works with a lathe. [ME f. OF *tornere -eor* f. LL *tornator* (as TURN)]

turnery /ˈtɜːnərɪ/ *n.* **1** objects made on a lathe. **2** work with a lathe.

turning /ˈtɜːnɪŋ/ *n.* **1 a** a road that branches off another. **b** a place where this occurs. **2 a** use of the lathe. **b** (in *pl.*) chips or shavings from a lathe. □ **turning-circle** the smallest circle in which a vehicle can turn without reversing. **turning-point** a point at which a decisive change occurs.

turnip /ˈtɜːnɪp/ *n.* **1** a cruciferous plant, *Brassica rapa*, with a large white globular root and sprouting leaves. **2** this root used as a vegetable. □ **turnip-top** the leaves of the turnip eaten as a vegetable. □ **turnipy** *adj.* [earlier *turnep(e)* f. *neep* f. L *napus*: first element of uncert. orig.]

turnkey /ˈtɜːnkiː/ *n.* & *adj.* —*n.* (*pl.* **-eys**) *archaic* a gaoler. —*adj.* (of a contract etc.) providing for a supply of equipment in a state ready for operation.

turnout /ˈtɜːnaʊt/ *n.* **1** the number of people attending a meeting, voting at an election, etc. (*rain reduced the turnout*). **2** the quantity of goods produced in a given time. **3** a set or display of equipment, clothes, etc.

turnover /ˈtɜːnˌəʊvə(r)/ *n.* **1** the act or an instance of turning over. **2** the amount of money taken in a business. **3** the number of people entering and leaving employment etc. **4** a small pie or tart made by folding a piece of pastry over a filling.

turnpike /ˈtɜːnpaɪk/ *n.* **1** *hist.* **a** a toll-gate. **b** a road on which a toll was collected at a toll-gate. **2** *US* a motorway on which a toll is charged.

turnstile /ˈtɜːnstaɪl/ *n.* a gate for admission or exit, with revolving arms allowing people through singly.

turntable /ˈtɜːnˌteɪb(ə)l/ *n.* **1** a circular revolving plate supporting a gramophone record that is being played. **2** a circular revolving platform for turning a railway locomotive or other vehicle.

turpentine /ˈtɜːpəntaɪn/ *n.* & *v.* —*n.* an oleoresin secreted by several trees esp. of the genus *Pinus, Pistacia, Syncarpia,* or *Copaifera,* and used in various commercial preparations. —*v.tr.* apply turpentine to. □ **oil of turpentine** a volatile pungent oil distilled from turpentine, used in mixing paints and varnishes, and in medicine. [ME f. OF *ter(e)bentine* f. L *ter(e)binthina* (resina resin) (as TEREBINTH)]

turpitude /ˈtɜːpɪˌtjuːd/ *n.* *formal* baseness, depravity, wickedness. [F *turpitude* or L *turpitudo* f. *turpis* disgraceful, base]

turps *n.* *colloq.* oil of turpentine. [abbr.]

turquoise /ˈtɜːkwɔɪz, -kwɑːz/ *n.* **1** a semiprecious stone, usu. opaque and greenish- or sky-blue,

turret | tweezers

consisting of hydrated copper aluminium phosphate. **2** a greenish-blue colour. [ME *turkeis* etc. f. OF *turqueise* (later *-oise*) Turkish (stone)]

turret /ˈtʌrɪt/ *n.* **1** a small tower, usu. projecting from the wall of a building as a decorative addition. **2** a low flat usu. revolving armoured tower for a gun and gunners in a ship, aircraft, fort, or tank. **3** a rotating holder for tools in a lathe etc. □ **turret lathe** = *capstan lathe.* □ **turreted** *adj.* [ME f. OF *to(u)rete* dimin. of *to(u)r* TOWER]

turtle /ˈtɜːt(ə)l/ *n.* **1** any of various marine or freshwater reptiles of the order Chelonia, encased in a shell of bony plates, and having flippers or webbed toes used in swimming. **2** the flesh of the turtle, esp. used for soup. **3** *Computing* a directional cursor in a computer graphics system which can be instructed to move around a screen. □ **turn turtle** capsize. **turtle-neck 1** a high close-fitting neck on a knitted garment. **2** *US* = *polo-neck.* [app. alt. of *tortue*: see TORTOISE]

turtle-dove /ˈtɜːt(ə)ldʌv/ *n.* any wild dove of the genus *Streptopelia*, esp. *S. turtur*, noted for its soft cooing and its affection for its mate and young. [archaic *turtle* (in the same sense) f. OE *turtla*, *turtle* f. L *turtur*, of imit. orig.]

turves *pl.* of TURF.

Tuscan /ˈtʌskən/ *n. & adj.* —*n.* **1** an inhabitant of Tuscany in central Italy. **2** the classical Italian language of Tuscany. —*adj.* **1** of or relating to Tuscany or the Tuscans. **2** *Archit.* denoting the least ornamented of the classical orders. □ **Tuscan straw** fine yellow wheat-straw used for hats etc. [ME f. F f. L *Tuscanus* f. *Tuscus* Etruscan]

tush *int. archaic* expressing strong disapproval or scorn. [ME: imit.]

tusk *n.* **1** a long pointed tooth, esp. protruding from a closed mouth, as in the elephant, walrus, etc. **2** a tusklike tooth or other object. □ **tusked** *adj.* (also in *comb.*). **tusky** *adj.* [ME alt. of OE *tux* var. of *tusc*]

tusker /ˈtʌskə(r)/ *n.* an elephant or wild boar with well-developed tusks.

tussle /ˈtʌs(ə)l/ *n. & v.* —*n.* a struggle or scuffle. —*v.intr.* engage in a tussle. [orig. Sc. & N.Engl., perh. dimin. of *touse*: see TOUSLE]

tussock /ˈtʌsək/ *n.* a clump of grass etc. □ **tussock grass** grass growing in tussocks, esp. *Poa flabellata* from Patagonia etc. □ **tussocky** *adj.* [16th c.: perh. alt. f. dial. *tusk* tuft]

tussore /ˈtʌsɔː(r), ˈtʌsə(r)/ *n.* (also **tusser**, *US* **tussah** /ˈtʌsə(r)/) **1** an Indian or Chinese silkworm, *Antheraea mylitta*, yielding strong but coarse brown silk. **2** (in full **tussore-silk**) silk from this and some other silkworms. [Urdu f. Hindi *tasar* f. Skr. *tasara* shuttle]

tutelage /ˈtjuːtɪlɪdʒ/ *n.* **1** guardianship. **2** the state or duration of being under this. **3** instruction, tuition. [L *tutela* f. *tuēri* *tuit-* or *tut-* watch]

tutelary /ˈtjuːtɪlərɪ/ *adj.* (also **tutelar** /-tɪlə(r)/) **1 a** serving as guardian. **b** relating to a guardian (*tutelary authority*). **2** giving protection (*tutelary saint*). [LL *tutelaris*, L *-arius* f. *tutela*: see TUTELAGE]

tutor /ˈtjuːtə(r)/ *n. & v.* —*n.* **1** a private teacher, esp. in general charge of a person's education. **2** a university teacher supervising the studies or welfare of assigned undergraduates. **3** *Brit.* a book of instruction in a subject. —*v.* **1** *tr.* act as a tutor to. **2** *intr.* work as a tutor. **3** *tr.* restrain,

discipline. **4** *intr. US* receive tuition. □ **tutorage** *n.* **tutorship** *n.* [ME f. AF, OF *tutour* or L *tutor* f. *tuēri tut-* watch]

tutorial /tjuːˈtɔːrɪəl/ *adj. & n.* —*adj.* of or relating to a tutor or tuition. —*n.* a period of individual tuition given by a tutor. □ **tutorially** *adv.* [L *tutorius* (as TUTOR)]

tutti /ˈtʊtɪ/ *adv. & n. Mus.* —*adv.* with all voices or instruments together. —*n.* (*pl.* **tuttis**) a passage to be performed in this way. [It., pl. of *tutto* all]

tutti-frutti /ˌtuːtɪˈfruːtɪ/ *n.* (*pl.* **-fruttis**) a confection, esp. ice-cream, of or flavoured with mixed fruits. [It., = all fruits]

tut-tut /tʌtˈtʌt/ *int., n., & v.* (also **tut** /tʌt/) —*int.* expressing rebuke, impatience, or contempt. —*n.* such an exclamation. —*v.intr.* (**-tutted**, **-tutting**) exclaim this. [imit. of a click of the tongue against the teeth]

tutu /ˈtuːtuː/ *n.* a ballet dancer's short skirt of stiffened projecting frills. [F]

tu-whit, tu-whoo /tʊˌwɪt tʊˈwuː/ *n.* a representation of the cry of an owl. [imit.]

tux *n. US colloq.* = TUXEDO.

tuxedo /tʌkˈsiːdəʊ/ *n.* (*pl.* **-os** or **-oes**) *US* **1** a dinner-jacket. **2** a suit of clothes including this. [after a country club at *Tuxedo* Park, New York]

TV *abbr.* television.

TVP *abbr. propr.* textured vegetable protein (in foods made from vegetable but given a meatlike texture).

twaddle /ˈtwɒd(ə)l/ *n. & v.* —*n.* useless, senseless, or dull writing or talk. —*v.intr.* indulge in this. □ **twaddler** *n.* [alt. of earlier *twattle*, alt. of TATTLE]

twain *adj. & n. archaic* two (usu. *in twain*). [OE *twegen*, masc. form of *twā* TWO]

twang *n. & v.* —*n.* **1** a strong ringing sound made by the plucked string of a musical instrument or bow. **2** the nasal quality of a voice compared to this. —*v.* **1** *intr. & tr.* emit or cause to emit this sound. **2** *tr.* usu. *derog.* play (a tune or instrument) in this way. **3** *tr.* utter with a nasal twang. □ **twangy** *adj.* [imit.]

'twas /twɒz, twəz/ *archaic* it was. [contr.]

twat /twɒt/ *n. coarse sl.* **1** the female genitals. **2** *Brit.* a term of contempt for a person. [17th c.: orig. unkn.]

tweak *v. & n.* —*v.tr.* **1** pinch and twist sharply; pull with a sharp jerk; twitch. **2** make fine adjustments to (a mechanism). —*n.* an instance of tweaking. [prob. alt. of dial. *twick* & TWITCH]

twee *adj.* (**tweer** /ˈtwiːə(r)/; **tweest** /ˈtwiːɪst/) *Brit.* usu. *derog.* affectedly dainty or quaint. □ **tweely** *adv.* **tweeness** *n.* [childish pronunc. of SWEET]

tweed *n.* **1** a rough-surfaced woollen cloth, usu. of mixed flecked colours, orig. produced in Scotland. **2** (in *pl.*) clothes made of tweed. [orig. a misreading of *tweel*, Sc. form of TWILL, infl. by assoc. with the river *Tweed*]

tweedy /ˈtwiːdɪ/ *adj.* (**tweedier**, **tweediest**) **1** of or relating to tweed cloth. **2** characteristic of the country gentry, heartily informal. □ **tweedily** *adv.* **tweediness** *n.*

tweet *n. & v.* —*n.* the chirp of a small bird. —*v.intr.* make a chirping noise. [imit.]

tweeter /ˈtwiːtə(r)/ *n.* a loudspeaker designed to reproduce high frequencies.

tweezers /ˈtwiːzəz/ *n.pl.* a small pair of pincers for taking up small objects, plucking out hairs, etc. [extended form of *tweezes* (cf. *pincers* etc.) pl. of obs. *tweeze* case for small instruments. f. *etweese* = *étuis*, pl. of ÉTUI]

twelfth /twelfθ/ *n. & adj.* —*n.* **1** the position in a sequence corresponding to the number 12 in the sequence 1–12. **2** something occupying this position. **3** each of twelve equal parts of a thing. —*adj.* that is the twelfth. □ **Twelfth Day** 6 Jan., the twelfth day after Christmas, the festival of the Epiphany. **twelfth man** a reserve member of a cricket team. **Twelfth Night** the evening of 5 Jan., the eve of the Epiphany. □ **twelfthly** *adv.* [OE *twelfta* (as TWELVE)]

twelve /twelv/ *n. & adj.* —*n.* **1** one more than eleven. **2** a symbol for this (12, xii, XII). **3** a size etc. denoted by twelve. **4** the time denoted by twelve o'clock (*is it twelve yet?*). **5** (**the Twelve**) the twelve apostles. **6** (**12**) *Brit.* (of films) classified as suitable for persons of 12 years and over. —*adj.* that amount to twelve. □ **twelve-note** (or **-tone**) *Mus.* using the twelve chromatic notes of the octave on an equal basis without dependence on a key system. [OE *twelf(e)* f. Gmc, prob. rel. to TWO]

twelvefold /'twelvfəʊld/ *adj. & adv.* **1** twelve times as much or as many. **2** consisting of twelve parts.

twelvemonth /'twelvmʌnθ/ *n. archaic* a year; a period of twelve months.

twenty /'twentɪ/ *n. & adj.* —*n.* (pl. **-ies**) **1** the product of two and ten. **2** a symbol for this (20, xx, XX). **3** (in *pl.*) the numbers from 20 to 29, esp. the years of a century or of a person's life. **4** *colloq.* a large indefinite number (*have told you twenty times*). —*adj.* that amount to twenty. □ **twenty-twenty** (or **20/20**) **1** denoting vision of normal acuity. **2** *colloq.* denoting clear perception or hindsight. □ **twentieth** *adj. & n.* **twentyfold** *adj. & adv.* [OE *twentig* (perh. as TWO, -TY²)]

twerp *n.* (also **twirp**) *sl.* a stupid or objectionable person. [20th c.: orig. unkn.]

twice *adv.* **1** two times (esp. of multiplication); on two occasions. **2** in double degree or quantity (*twice as good*). [ME *twiges* f. OE *twige* (as TWO, -S³)]

twiddle /'twɪd(ə)l/ *v. & n.* —*v.* **1** *tr.* & (foll. by *with* etc.) *intr.* twirl, adjust, or play randomly or idly. **2** *intr.* move twirlingly. —*n.* **1** an act of twiddling. **2** a twirled mark or sign. □ **twiddle one's thumbs 1** make them rotate round each other. **2** have nothing to do. □ **twiddler** *n.* **twiddly** *adj.* [app. imit., after *twirl*, *twist*, and *fiddle*, *piddle*]

twig¹ *n.* a small branch or shoot of a tree or shrub. □ **twigged** *adj.* (also in *comb.*). **twiggy** *adj.* [OE *twigge* f. a Gmc root *twi-* (unrecorded) as in TWICE, TWO]

twig² *v.tr.* (**twigged**, **twigging**) *colloq.* **1** (also *absol.*) understand; grasp the meaning or nature of. **2** perceive, observe. [18th c.: orig. unkn.]

twilight /'twaɪlaɪt/ *n.* **1** the soft glowing light from the sky when the sun is below the horizon, esp. in the evening. **2** the period of this. **3** a faint light. **4** a state of imperfect knowledge or understanding. **5** a period of decline or destruction. □ **twilight zone 1** an urban area that is becoming dilapidated. **2** any physical or conceptual area which is undefined or intermediate. [ME f. OE *twi-* two (in uncert. sense) + LIGHT¹]

twilit /'twaɪlɪt/ *adj.* (also **twilighted** /-ˌlaɪtɪd/) dimly illuminated by or as by twilight. [past part. of *twilight* (v.) f. TWILIGHT]

twill *n. & v.* —*n.* a fabric so woven as to have a surface of diagonal parallel ridges. —*v.tr.* (esp. as **twilled** *adj.*) weave (fabric) in this way. □ **twilled** *adj.* [N.Engl. var. of obs. *twilly*, OE *twili*, f. *twi-* double, after L *bilix* (as BI-, *licium* thread)]

twin *n., adj., & v.* —*n.* **1** each of a closely related or associated pair, esp. of children or animals born at a birth. **2** the exact counterpart of a person or thing. **3** (**the Twins**) the zodiacal sign or constellation Gemini. —*adj.* **1** forming, or being one of, such a pair (*twin brothers*). **2** consisting of two closely connected and similar parts. —*v.* (**twinned**, **twinning**) **1** *tr.* & *intr.* join intimately together. **b** (foll. by *with*) pair. **2** *intr.* bear twins. **3** *intr.* & *tr. Brit.* link or cause (a town) to link with one in a different country, for the purposes of friendship and cultural exchange. □ **twin bed** each of a pair of single beds. **twin-engined** having two engines. **twin-screw** (of a ship) having two propellers on separate shafts with opposite twists. **twin set** esp. *Brit.* a woman's matching cardigan and jumper. **twin town** *Brit.* a town which is twinned with another. □ **twinning** *n.* [OE *twinn* double, f. *twi-* two: cf. ON *tvinnr*]

twine *n. & v.* —*n.* **1** a strong thread or string of two or more strands of hemp or cotton etc. twisted together. **2** a coil or twist. **3** a tangle; an interlacing. —*v.* **1** *tr.* form (a string or thread etc.) by twisting strands together. **2** *tr.* form (a garland etc.) of interwoven material. **3** *intr.* (often foll. by *round*, *about*) coil or wind. **4** *intr.* & *refl.* (of a plant) grow in this way. □ **twiner** *n.* [OE *twīn*, *twigin* linen, ult. f. the stem of *twi-* two]

twinge /twɪndʒ/ *n. & v.* —*n.* a sharp momentary local pain or pang (*a twinge of toothache; a twinge of conscience*). —*v.intr.* & *tr.* experience or cause to experience a twinge. [*twinge* (v.) pinch, wring f. OE *twengan* f. Gmc]

twinkle /'twɪŋk(ə)l/ *v. & n.* —*v.* **1** *intr.* (of a star or light etc.) shine with rapidly intermittent gleams. **2** *intr.* (of the eyes) sparkle. **3** *intr.* (of the feet in dancing) move lightly and rapidly. **4** *tr.* emit (a light or signal) in quick gleams. **5** *tr.* blink or wink (one's eyes). —*n.* **1** **a** a sparkle or gleam of the eyes. **b** a blink or wink. **2** a slight flash of light; a glimmer. **3** a short rapid movement. □ **in a twinkle** (or **a twinkling** or **the twinkling of an eye**) in an instant. □ **twinkler** *n.* **twinkly** *adj.* [OE *twinclian*]

twirl *v. & n.* —*v.tr.* & *intr.* spin or swing or twist quickly and lightly round. —*n.* **1** a twirling motion. **2** a form made by twirling, esp. a flourish made with a pen. □ **twirler** *n.* **twirly** *adj.* [16th c.: prob. alt. (after *whirl*) of obs. *tirl* TRILL]

twist *v. & n.* —*v.* **1** **a** *tr.* change the form of by rotating one end and not the other or the two ends in opposite directions. **b** *intr.* undergo such a change; take a twisted position (*twisted round in his seat*). **c** *tr.* wrench or pull out of shape with a twisting action (*twisted my ankle*). **2** *tr.* **a** wind (strands etc.) about each other. **b** form (a rope etc.) by winding the strands. **c** (foll. by *with*, *in with*) interweave. **d** form by interweaving or twining. **3** **a** *tr.* give a spiral form to (a rod, column, cord, etc.) as by rotating the ends in opposite directions. **b** *intr.* take a spiral form. **4** *tr.* (foll. by *off*) break off or separate by twisting. **5** *tr.* distort or misrepresent the meaning of (words). **6 a** *tr.* take a curved course. **b** *tr.* make (one's way) in a winding manner. **7** *tr. Brit. colloq.* cheat (*twisted me out of £20*). **8** *tr.* (as **twisted** *adj.*) (of a person or mind) emotionally unbalanced. **9** *intr.* dance the twist. —*n.* **1** the act or an instance of twisting. **2 a** a twisted state. **b** the manner or degree in which a thing is twisted. **3** a thing formed by or as by twisting, esp. a thread or rope etc. made by winding strands together. **4** the point at which a thing twists or bends. **5** usu. *derog.* a peculiar tendency of mind or character etc. **6** an unexpected development of events, esp. in a story etc. **7** a fine strong silk thread used by tailors etc. **8** a roll of bread, tobacco, etc., in the form of a twist. **9** *Brit.* a paper packet with screwed-up ends. **10** a curled piece of lemon etc. peel to flavour a drink. **11** (prec. by *the*) a dance with a twisting movement of the body, popular in the 1960s. □ **round the twist** *Brit. sl.* crazy. **twist a person's arm** *colloq.* apply coercion, esp. by moral pressure. □ **twistable** *adj.* **twisty** *adj.* (**twistier, twistiest**). [ME, rel. to TWIN, TWINE]

twister /ˈtwɪstə(r)/ *n.* **1** *Brit. colloq.* a swindler; a dishonest person. **2** *US* a tornado, waterspout, etc.

twit[1] *n.* esp. *Brit. sl.* a silly or foolish person. [orig. dial.: perh. f. TWIT[2]]

twit[2] *v.tr.* (**twitted, twitting**) reproach or taunt, usu. good-humouredly. [16th-c. *twite* f. *atwite* f. OE *ætwītan* reproach with f. *æt* at + *wītan* blame]

twitch *v.* & *n.* —*v.* **1** *intr.* (of the features, muscles, limbs, etc.) move or contract spasmodically. **2** *tr.* give a short sharp pull at. —*n.* **1** a sudden involuntary contraction or movement. **2** a sudden pull or jerk. **3** *colloq.* a state of nervousness. □ **twitchy** *adj.* (**twitchier, twitchiest**) (in sense 3 of *n.*). [ME f. Gmc: cf. OE *twiccian*, dial. *twick*]

twitcher /ˈtwɪtʃə(r)/ *n.* **1** *colloq.* a bird-watcher who tries to get sightings of rare birds. **2** a person or thing that twitches.

twitter /ˈtwɪtə(r)/ *v.* & *n.* —*v.* **1** *intr.* (of or like a bird) emit a succession of light tremulous sounds. **2** *tr.* utter or express in this way. —*n.* **1** the act or an instance of twittering. **2** *colloq.* a tremulously excited state. □ **twitterer** *n.* **twittery** *adj.* [ME, imit.: cf. -ER[4]]

two /tuː/ *n.* & *adj.* —*n.* **1** one more than one. **2** a symbol for this (2, ii, II). **3** a size etc. denoted by two. **4** the time of two o'clock (*is it two yet?*). **5** a set of two. **6** a card with two pips. —*adj.* that amount to two. □ **in two** in or into two pieces. **or two** denoting several (*a thing or two* = several things). **put two and two together** make (esp. an obvious) inference from what is known or evident. **that makes two of us** *colloq.* that is true of me also. **two-bit** *US colloq.* cheap, petty. **two-by-four** a length of timber with a rectangular cross-section 2 in. by 4 in. **two by two** (or **two and two**) in pairs. **two-dimensional 1** having or appearing to have length and breadth but no depth. **2** lacking depth or substance; superficial. **two-edged** double-edged. **two-faced 1** having two faces. **2** insincere; deceitful. **two-handed 1** having, using, or requiring the use of two hands. **2** (of a card-game) for two players. **two-piece** *adj.* (of a

suit etc.) consisting of two matching items. —*n.* a two-piece suit etc. **two-ply** *adj.* of two strands, webs, or thicknesses. —*n.* **1** two-ply wool. **2** two-ply wood made by gluing together two layers with the grain in different directions. **two-seater 1** a vehicle or aircraft with two seats. **2** a sofa etc. for two people. **two-sided 1** having two sides. **2** having two aspects; controversial. **two-step** a round dance with a sliding step in march or polka time. **two-stroke** esp. *Brit.* (of an internal-combustion engine) having its power cycle completed in one up-and-down movement of the piston. **two-time** *colloq.* **1** deceive or be unfaithful to (esp. a partner or lover). **2** swindle, double-cross. **two-tone** having two colours or sounds. **two-up** *Austral.* & *NZ* a gambling game with bets placed on a showing of two heads or two tails. **two-way 1** involving two ways or participants. **2** (of a switch) permitting a current to be switched on or off from either of two points. **3** (of a radio) capable of transmitting and receiving signals. **4** (of a tap etc.) permitting fluid etc. to flow in either of two channels or directions. **5** (of traffic etc.) moving in two esp. opposite directions. **two-way mirror** a panel of glass that can be seen through from one side and is a mirror on the other. [OE *twā* (fem. & neut.), *tū* (neut.), with Gmc cognates and rel. to Skr. *dwau, dwe*, Gk & L *duo*]

twofold /ˈtuːfəʊld/ *adj.* & *adv.* **1** twice as much or as many. **2** consisting of two parts.

twopence /ˈtʌpəns/ *n. Brit.* **1** the sum of two pence, esp. before decimalization. **2** *colloq.* (esp. with *neg.*) a thing of little value (*don't care twopence*).

twopenny /ˈtʌpənɪ/ *adj. Brit.* **1** costing two pence, esp. before decimalization. **2** *colloq.* cheap, worthless. □ **twopenny-halfpenny** /ˌtʌpnɪˈheɪpnɪ/ cheap, insignificant.

twosome /ˈtuːsəm/ *n.* **1** two persons together. **2** a game, dance, etc., for two persons.

-ty[1] /tɪ/ *suffix* forming nouns denoting quality or condition (*cruelty*; *plenty*). [ME *-tie, -tee, -te* f. OF *-té, -tet* f. L *-tas -tatis*: cf. -ITY]

-ty[2] /tɪ/ *suffix* denoting tens (*twenty*; *thirty*; *ninety*). [OE *-tig*]

tycoon /taɪˈkuːn/ *n.* **1** a business magnate. **2** *hist.* a title applied by foreigners to the shogun of Japan 1854–68. [Jap. *taikun* great lord]

tying *pres. part.* of TIE.

tyke /taɪk/ *n.* (also **tike**) **1** esp. *Brit.* an unpleasant or coarse man. **2** a mongrel. **3** a small child. **4** *Brit. sl.* a Yorkshireman. [ME f. ON *tík* bitch]

tympana *pl.* of TYMPANUM.

tympani *var.* of TIMPANI.

tympanum /ˈtɪmpənəm/ *n.* (*pl.* **tympanums** or **tympana** /-nə/) **1** *Anat.* the middle ear. **2** *Archit.* **a** a vertical triangular space forming the centre of a pediment. **b** a similar space over a door between the lintel and the arch; a carving on this space. [L f. Gk *tumpanon* drum f. *tuptō* strike]

Tynwald /ˈtɪnwɒld/ *n.* the parliament of the Isle of Man. [ON *thing-völlr* place of assembly f. *thing* assembly + *völlr* field]

type *n.* & *v.* —*n.* **1 a** a class of things or persons having common characteristics. **b** a kind or sort (*would like a different type of car*). **2** a person, thing, or event serving as an illustration, symbol, or characteristic specimen of another, or of a class. **3** (in *comb.*) made of, resembling, or functioning as (*ceramic-type material*; *Cheddar-type cheese*). **4** *colloq.* a person, esp. of a specified character (*is rather a quiet type*; *is not really my type*). **5** an object, conception, or work of art serving as a model for subsequent artists. **6** *Printing* **a** a piece of metal etc. with a raised letter or character on its upper surface for use in printing. **b** a kind or size of such pieces (*printed in large type*). **c** a set or supply of these (*ran short of type*). —*v.* **1** *tr.* be a type or example of. **2** *tr.* & *intr.* write with a typewriter. **3** *tr.* esp. *Biol.* & *Med.* assign to a type; classify. **4** *tr.* = TYPECAST. □ **in type** *Printing* composed and ready for printing. □ **typal** *adj.* [ME f. F *type* or L *typus* f. Gk *tupos* impression, figure, type, f. *tuptō* strike]

typecast /ˈtaɪpkɑːst/ *v.tr.* (*past* and *past part.* **-cast**) assign (an actor or actress) repeatedly to the same type of role, esp. one in character.

typeface /ˈtaɪpfeɪs/ *n. Printing* **1** a set of types or characters in a particular design. **2** the inked part of type, or the impression made by this.

typescript /ˈtaɪpskrɪpt/ *n.* a typewritten document.

typesetter /ˈtaɪpˌsetə(r)/ *n. Printing* **1** a person who composes type. **2** a composing-machine. □ **typesetting** *n.*

typewrite /ˈtaɪpraɪt/ *v.tr.* & *intr.* (*past* **-wrote**; *past part.* **-written**) *formal* = TYPE *v.* 2.

typewriter /ˈtaɪpˌraɪtə(r)/ *n.* a machine with keys for producing printlike characters one at a time on paper inserted round a roller.

typewritten /ˈtaɪpˌrɪt(ə)n/ *adj.* produced with a typewriter.

typhoid /ˈtaɪfɔɪd/ *n.* & *adj.* —*n.* **1** (in full **typhoid fever**) an infectious bacterial fever with an eruption of red spots on the chest and abdomen and severe intestinal irritation. **2** a similar disease of animals. —*adj.* like typhus. □ **typhoidal** *adj.* [TYPHUS + -OID]

typhoon /taɪˈfuːn/ *n.* a violent hurricane in E. Asian seas. □ **typhonic** /-ˈfɒnɪk/ *adj.* [partly f. Port. *tufão* f. Arab. *ṭūfān* perh. f. Gk *tuphōn* whirlwind; partly f. Chin. dial. *tai fung* big wind]

typhus /ˈtaɪfəs/ *n.* an infectious fever characterized by a purple rash, headaches, fever, and usu. delirium. □ **typhous** *adj.* [mod.L f. Gk *tuphos* smoke, stupor f. *tuphō* to smoke]

typical /ˈtɪpɪk(ə)l/ *adj.* **1** serving as a characteristic example; representative. **2** characteristic of or serving to distinguish a type. **3** (often foll. by *of*) conforming to expected behaviour, attitudes, etc. (*is typical of them to forget*). □ **typicality** /-ˈkælɪtɪ/ *n.* **typically** *adv.* [med.L *typicalis* f. L *typicus* f. Gk *tupikos* (as TYPE)]

typify /ˈtɪpɪˌfaɪ/ *v.tr.* (**-ies**, **-ied**) **1** be a representative example of; embody the characteristics of. **2** represent by a type or symbol; serve as a type, figure, or emblem of; symbolize.

□ **typification** /-fɪˈkeɪʃ(ə)n/ *n.* **typifier** *n.* [L *typus* TYPE + -FY]

typist /ˈtaɪpɪst/ *n.* a person who uses a typewriter, esp. professionally.

typo /ˈtaɪpəʊ/ *n.* (*pl.* **-os**) *colloq.* **1** a typographical error. **2** a typographer. [abbr.]

typographer /taɪˈpɒɡrəfə(r)/ *n.* a person skilled in typography.

typography /taɪˈpɒɡrəfɪ/ *n.* **1** printing as an art. **2** the style and appearance of printed matter. □ **typographic** /-pəˈɡræfɪk/ *adj.* **typographical** /-pəˈɡræfɪk(ə)l/ *adj.* **typographically** /-pəˈɡræfɪkəlɪ/ *adv.* [F *typographie* or mod.L *typographia* (as TYPE, -GRAPHY)]

tyrannical /tɪˈrænɪk(ə)l/ *adj.* **1** acting like a tyrant; imperious, arbitrary. **2** given to or characteristic of tyranny. □ **tyrannically** *adv.* [OF *tyrannique* f. L *tyrannicus* f. Gk *turannikos* (as TYRANT)]

tyrannicide /tɪˈrænɪˌsaɪd/ *n.* **1** the act or an instance of killing a tyrant. **2** the killer of a tyrant. □ **tyrannicidal** /-ˈsaɪd(ə)l/ *adj.* [F f. L *tyrannicida*, *-cidium* (as TYRANT, -CIDE)]

tyrannize /ˈtɪrəˌnaɪz/ *v.tr.* & (foll. by *over*) *intr.* (also **-ise**) behave like a tyrant towards; rule or treat despotically or cruelly. [F *tyranniser* (as TYRANT)]

tyrannosaurus /tɪˌrænəˈsɔːrəs/ *n.* (also **tyrannosaur**) any bipedal flesh-eating dinosaur of the genus *Tyrannosaurus*, esp. *T. rex* having powerful hind legs, small clawlike front legs, and a long well-developed tail. [Gk *turannos* TYRANT, after *dinosaur*]

tyranny /ˈtɪrənɪ/ *n.* (*pl.* **-ies**) **1** the cruel and arbitrary use of authority. **2** a tyrannical act; tyrannical behaviour. **3 a** rule by a tyrant. **b** a period of this. **c** a State ruled by a tyrant. □ **tyrannous** *adj.* **tyrannously** *adv.* [ME f. OF *tyrannie* f. med.L *tyrannia* f. Gk *turannia* (as TYRANT)]

tyrant /ˈtaɪərənt/ *n.* **1** an oppressive or cruel ruler. **2** a person exercising power arbitrarily or cruelly. [ME *tyran*, *-ant*, f. OF *tiran*, *tyrant* f. L *tyrannus* f. Gk *turannos*]

tyre /ˈtaɪə(r)/ *n.* (US **tire**) a rubber covering, usu. inflated, placed round a wheel to form a soft contact with the road. □ **tyre-gauge** a portable device for measuring the air-pressure in a tyre. [var. of TIRE²]

tyro var. of TIRO.

Tyrolean /ˌtɪrəˈliːən/ *adj.* of or characteristic of the Tyrol, an Alpine province of Austria. □ **Tyrolese** *adj.* & *n.*

tzatziki /tsætˈsiːkɪ/ *n.* a Greek side dish of yoghurt with cucumber. [mod. Gk]

tzigane /tsɪˈɡɑːn/ *n.* **1** a Hungarian gypsy. **2** (*attrib.*) characteristic of the tziganes or (esp.) their music. [F f. Magyar *c(z)igány*]

Uu

U¹ /juː/ *n.* (also **u**) (*pl.* **Us** or **U's**) **1** the twenty-first letter of the alphabet. **2** a U-shaped object or curve (esp. in *comb.*: U-bolt).

U² /juː/ *adj.* esp. *Brit. colloq.* **1** upper class. **2** supposedly characteristic of the upper class. [abbr.]

U³ *abbr.* (also **U.**) *Brit.* universal (of films classified as suitable without restriction).

U⁴ *symb. Chem.* the element uranium.

-ubility /juˈbɪlɪtɪ/ *suffix* forming nouns from, or corresponding to, adjectives in *-uble* (*solubility*; *volubility*). [L *-ubilitas*: cf. *-ITY*]

ubiquitous /juːˈbɪkwɪtəs/ *adj.* **1** present everywhere or in several places simultaneously. **2** often encountered. □ **ubiquitously** *adv.* **ubiquitousness** *n.* **ubiquity** *n.* [mod.L *ubiquitas* f. L *ubique* everywhere f. *ubi* where]

-uble /jʊb(ə)l/ *suffix* forming adjectives meaning 'that may or must be' (see *-ABLE*) (*soluble*; *voluble*). [F f. L *-ubilis*]

-ubly /jʊblɪ/ *suffix* forming adverbs corresponding to adjectives in *-uble*.

U-boat /ˈjuːbəʊt/ *n. hist.* a German submarine. [G *U-boot* = *Unterseeboot* under-sea boat]

UCCA /ˈʌkə/ *abbr.* (in the UK) Universities Central Council on Admissions.

UDA *abbr.* Ulster Defence Association (a loyalist paramilitary organization).

udder /ˈʌdə(r)/ *n.* the mammary gland of cattle, sheep, etc., hanging as a baglike organ with several teats. □ **uddered** *adj.* (also in *comb.*). [OE *ūder* f. WG]

UDI *abbr.* unilateral declaration of independence.

UFO /ˈjuːfəʊ/ *n.* (also **ufo**) (*pl.* **UFOs** or **ufos**) unidentified flying object. [abbr.]

ufology /juːˈfɒlədʒɪ/ *n.* the study of UFOs. □ **ufologist** *n.*

ugh /əx, ʌɡ, ʌx/ *int.* **1** expressing disgust or horror. **2** the sound of a cough or grunt. [imit.]

Ugli /ˈʌɡlɪ/ *n.* (*pl.* **Uglis** or **Uglies**) *propr.* a mottled green and yellow citrus fruit, a hybrid of a grapefruit and tangerine. [UGLY]

uglify /ˈʌɡlɪˌfaɪ/ *v.tr.* (**-ies**, **-ied**) make ugly. □ **uglification** /-fɪˈkeɪʃ(ə)n/ *n.*

ugly /ˈʌɡlɪ/ *adj.* (**uglier**, **ugliest**) **1** unpleasing or repulsive to see or hear (*an ugly scar*; *spoke with an ugly snarl*). **2** unpleasantly suggestive; discreditable (*ugly rumours are about*). **3** threatening, dangerous (*the sky has an ugly look*). **4** morally repulsive; vile (*ugly vices*). □ **ugly customer** an unpleasantly formidable person. **ugly duckling** a person who turns out to be beautiful or talented etc. against all expectations (with ref. to a cygnet in a brood of ducks in a tale by Andersen). □ **uglily** *adv.* **ugliness** *n.* [ME f. ON *uggligr* frightful f. *ugga* to dread]

UHF *abbr.* ultra-high frequency.

UHT *abbr.* ultra heat treated (esp. of milk, for long keeping).

UK *abbr.* United Kingdom.

ukase /juːˈkeɪz/ *n.* **1** an arbitrary command. **2** *hist.* an edict of the Tsarist Russian government. [Russ. *ukaz* ordinance, edict f. *ukazat'* show, decree]

ukulele /ˌjuːkəˈleɪlɪ/ *n.* a small four-stringed Hawaiian (orig. Portuguese) guitar. [Hawaiian, = jumping flea]

-ular /jʊlə(r)/ *suffix* forming adjectives, sometimes corresp. to nouns in *-ule* (*pustular*) but often without diminutive force (*angular*; *granular*). □ **-ularity** /-ˈlærɪtɪ/ *suffix* forming nouns. [from or after L *-ularis* (as *-ULE*, *-AR*)]

ulcer /ˈʌlsə(r)/ *n.* **1** an open sore on an external or internal surface of the body, often forming pus. **2 a** a moral blemish. **b** a corroding or corrupting influence etc. □ **ulcered** *adj.* **ulcerous** *adj.* [ME f. L *ulcus -eris*, rel. to Gk *helkos*]

ulcerate /ˈʌlsəˌreɪt/ *v.tr. & intr.* form into or affect with an ulcer. □ **ulcerable** *adj.* **ulceration** /-ˈreɪʃ(ə)n/ *n.* **ulcerative** /-rətɪv/ *adj.* [ME f. L *ulcerare ulcerat-* (as ULCER)]

-ule /juːl/ *suffix* forming diminutive nouns (*capsule*; *globule*). [from or after L *-ulus*, *-ula*, *-ulum*]

-ulent /jʊlənt/ *suffix* forming adjectives meaning 'abounding in, full of' (*fraudulent*; *turbulent*). □ **-ulence** *suffix* forming nouns. [L *-ulentus*]

ulna /ˈʌlnə/ *n.* (*pl.* **ulnae** /-niː/) **1** the thinner and longer bone in the forearm, on the side opposite to the thumb. **2** *Zool.* a corresponding bone in an animal's foreleg or a bird's wing. □ **ulnar** *adj.* [L, rel. to Gk *ōlenē* and ELL]

-ulous /jʊləs/ *suffix* forming adjectives (*fabulous*; *populous*). [L *-ulosus*, *-ulus*]

ulster /ˈʌlstə(r)/ *n.* a man's long loose overcoat of rough cloth. [*Ulster* in Ireland, where it was orig. sold]

Ulsterman /ˈʌlstəmən/ *n.* (*pl.* **-men**; *fem.* **Ulsterwoman**; *pl.* **-women**) a native of Ulster.

ult. *abbr.* ultimo.

ulterior /ʌlˈtɪərɪə(r)/ *adj.* existing in the background, or beyond what is evident or admitted; hidden, secret (esp. *ulterior motive*). □ **ulteriorly** *adv.* [L, = further, more distant]

ultimata *pl.* of ULTIMATUM.

ultimate /ˈʌltɪmət/ *adj. & n.* —*adj.* **1** last, final. **2** beyond which no other exists or is possible (*the ultimate analysis*). **3** fundamental, primary, unanalysable (*ultimate truths*). **4** maximum (*ultimate tensile strength*). —*n.* **1** (prec. by *the*) the best achievable or imaginable. **2** a final or fundamental fact or principle. □ **ultimately** *adv.* **ultimateness** *n.* [LL *ultimatus* past part. of *ultimare* come to an end]

ultimatum /ˌʌltɪˈmeɪtəm/ *n.* (*pl.* **ultimatums** or **ultimata** /-tə/) a final demand or statement of terms by one party, the rejection of which by another could cause a breakdown in relations, war, or an end of cooperation etc. [L neut. past part.: see ULTIMATE]

ultimo /ˈʌltɪˌməʊ/ *adj. Commerce* of last month (*the 28th ultimo*). [L *ultimo mense* in the last month]

ultra /ˈʌltrə/ *adj. & n.* —*adj.* favouring extreme views or measures, esp. in religion or politics. —*n.* an extremist. [orig. as abbr. of F *ultra-royaliste*: see ULTRA-]

ultra- /ˈʌltrə/ *comb. form* **1** beyond; on the other side of (opp. CIS-). **2** extreme(ly), excessive(ly) (*ultra-modern*; *ultra-modern*). [L *ultra* beyond]

ultra-high /ˌʌltrəˈhaɪ/ *adj.* (of a frequency) in the range 300 to 3000 megahertz.

ultramarine /ˌʌltrəməˈriːn/ *n. & adj.* —*n.* **1** a brilliant blue pigment orig. obtained from lapis lazuli. **2** the colour of this. —*adj.* of this colour. [obs. It. *oltramarino* & med.L *ultramarinus* beyond the sea (as ULTRA-, MARINE), because lapis lazuli was brought from beyond the sea]

ultramontane /ˌʌltrəˈmɒnteɪn/ *adj. & n.* —*adj.* **1** situated on the other side of the Alps from the point of view of the speaker. **2** advocating supreme papal authority in matters of faith and discipline. —*n.* **1** a person living on the other side of the Alps. **2** a person advocating supreme papal authority. [med.L *ultramontanus* (as ULTRA-, L *mons montis* mountain)]

ultrasonic /ˌʌltrəˈsɒnɪk/ *adj.* of or involving sound waves with a frequency above the upper limit of human hearing. □ **ultrasonically** *adv.*

ultrasonics /ˌʌltrəˈsɒnɪks/ *n.pl.* (usu. treated as *sing.*) the science and application of ultrasonic waves.

ultrasound /ˈʌltrəˌsaʊnd/ *n.* **1** sound having an ultrasonic frequency. **2** ultrasonic waves.

ultraviolet /ˌʌltrəˈvaɪələt/ *adj. Physics* **1** having a wavelength (just) beyond the violet end of the visible spectrum. **2** of or using such radiation.

ululate /ˈjuːljʊˌleɪt/ *v.intr.* howl, wail; make a hooting cry. □ **ululant** *adj.* **ululation** /-ˈleɪʃ(ə)n/ *n.* [L *ululare ululat-* (imit.)]

um /ʌm, əm/ *int.* expressing hesitation or a pause in speech. [imit.]

-um var. of -IUM 1.

umbel /ˈʌmb(ə)l/ *n. Bot.* a flower-cluster in which stalks nearly equal in length spring from a common centre and form a flat or curved surface, as in parsley. □ **umbellar** *adj.* **umbellate** /-bəˌleɪt/ *adj.* **umbellule** /-ˈbeljuːl/ *adj.* [obs. F *umbelle* or L *umbella* sunshade, dimin. of UMBRA]

umbellifer /ʌmˈbelɪfə(r)/ *n.* any plant of the family Umbelliferae bearing umbels, including parsley and parsnip. □ **umbelliferous** /-bəˈlɪfərəs/ *adj.* [obs. F *umbellifère* f. L (as UMBEL, *-fer* bearing)]

umber /ˈʌmbə(r)/ *n. & adj.* —*n.* **1** a natural pigment like ochre but darker and browner. **2** the colour of this. —*adj.* **1** of this colour. **2** dark, dusky. [F (*terre d'*)*ombre* or It. (*terra di*) *ombra* = shadow (earth), f. L UMBRA or *Umbra* fem. of *Umber* Umbrian]

umbilical /ʌmˈbɪlɪk(ə)l, ˌʌmbɪˈlaɪk(ə)l/ *adj.* **1** of, situated near, or affecting the navel. **2** centrally placed. □ **umbilical cord 1** a flexible cordlike structure attaching a foetus to the placenta. **2** *Astronaut.* a supply cable linking a missile to its launcher, or an astronaut in space to a spacecraft. [obs. F *umbilical* or f. UMBILICUS]

umbilicus /ʌmˈbɪlɪkəs, ˌʌmbɪˈlaɪkəs/ *n.* (pl. **umbilici** /-ˌsaɪ/ or **umbilicuses**) **1** *Anat.* the navel. **2** *Bot. & Zool.* a navel-like formation. [L, rel. to Gk *omphalos* and to NAVEL]

umbles /ˈʌmb(ə)lz/ *n.pl.* the edible offal of deer etc. (cf. *eat humble pie*: see HUMBLE). [ME var. of *numbles* f. L *lumbulus* dimin. of *lumbus* loin]

umbra /ˈʌmbrə/ *n.* (pl. **umbras** or **umbrae** /-briː/) *Astron.* **1** a total shadow usu. cast on the earth by the moon during a solar eclipse. **2** the dark central part of a sunspot. □ **umbral** *adj.* [L, = shade]

umbrage /ˈʌmbrɪdʒ/ *n.* offence; a sense of slight or injury (esp. *give* or *take umbrage at*). [ME f. OF ult. f. L *umbraticus* f. *umbra*: see UMBRA]

umbrella /ʌmˈbrelə/ *n.* **1** a light portable device for protection against rain, strong sun, etc., consisting of a usu. circular canopy of cloth mounted by means of a collapsible metal frame on a central stick. **2** protection or patronage. **3** (often *attrib.*) a coordinating or unifying agency (*umbrella organization*). □ **umbrellaed** /-ləd/ *adj.* **umbrella-like** *adj.* [It. *ombrella*, dimin. of *ombra* shade f. L *umbra*: see UMBRA]

umlaut /ˈʊmlaʊt/ *n.* **1** a mark (¨) used over a vowel, esp. in Germanic languages, to indicate a vowel change. **2** such a vowel change, e.g. German *Mann*, *Männer*, English *man*, *men*. [G f. *um* about + *Laut* sound]

umpire /ˈʌmpaɪə(r)/ *n. & v.* —*n.* **1** a person chosen to enforce the rules and settle disputes in various sports. **2** a person chosen to arbitrate between disputants, or to see fair play. —*v.* **1** *intr.* (usu. foll. by *for*, in, etc.) act as umpire. **2** *tr.* act as umpire in (a game etc.). □ **umpirage** /-rɪdʒ/ *n.* **umpireship** *n.* [ME, later form of *noumpere* f. OF *nonper* not equal (as NON-, PEER²): for loss of *n*- cf. ADDER]

umpteen /ʌmpˈtiːn/ *adj. & pron. sl.* —*adj.* indefinitely many; a lot of. —*pron.* indefinitely many. □ **umpteenth** *adj.* **umpty** /ˈʌmptɪ/ *adj.* [joc. form. on -TEEN]

UN *abbr.* United Nations.

un-¹ /ʌn/ *prefix* **1** added to adjectives and participles and their derivative nouns and adverbs, meaning: **a** not: denoting the absence of a quality or state (*unusable*; *uncalled-for*; *uneducated*; *unfailing*; *unofficially*; *unhappiness*). **b** the reverse of, usu. with an implication of approval or disapproval, or with some other special connotation (*unselfish*; *unsociable*; *unscientific*). **2** (less often) added to nouns, meaning 'a lack of' (*unrest*; *untruth*). [OE f. Gmc, rel. to L *in-*]

■ **Usage** The number of words that can be formed with this prefix (and with *un-*²) is virtually unlimited; consequently only a selection can be given here.

un-² /ʌn/ *prefix* added to verbs and (less often) nouns, forming verbs denoting: **1** the reversal or cancellation of an action or state (*undress*; *unlock*; *unsettle*). **2** deprivation or separation (*unmask*). **3** release from (*unburden*; *uncage*). **4** causing to be no longer (*unman*). [OE *un-*, *on-* f. Gmc]

■ **Usage** See the note at *un-*¹.

'un /ən/ *pron. colloq.* one (*that's a good 'un*). [dial. var.]

unabashed /ˌʌnəˈbæʃt/ *adj.* not abashed. □ **unabashedly** /-ʃɪdlɪ/ *adv.*

unabated /ˌʌnəˈbeɪtɪd/ *adj.* not abated; undiminished. □ **unabatedly** *adv.*

unable /ʌnˈeɪb(ə)l/ *adj.* (usu. foll. by *to* + infin.) not able; lacking ability.

unabridged /ˌʌnəˈbrɪdʒd/ *adj.* (of a text etc.) complete; not abridged.

unabsorbed /ˌʌnəbˈzɔːbd, -ˈsɔːbd/ *adj.* not absorbed.

unacademic /ˌʌnækəˈdemɪk/ *adj.* 1 not academic (esp. not scholarly or theoretical). 2 (of a person) not suited to academic study.

unaccented /ˌʌnækˈsentɪd/ *adj.* not accented; not emphasized.

unacceptable /ˌʌnəkˈseptəb(ə)l/ *adj.* not acceptable. □ **unacceptableness** *n.* **unacceptably** *adv.*

unacclaimed /ˌʌnəˈkleɪmd/ *adj.* not acclaimed.

unaccommodating /ˌʌnəˈkɒmədeɪtɪŋ/ *adj.* not accommodating; disobliging.

unaccompanied /ˌʌnəˈkʌmpənɪd/ *adj.* 1 not accompanied. 2 *Mus.* without accompaniment.

unaccomplished /ˌʌnəˈkʌmplɪʃt, -ˈkɒmplɪʃt/ *adj.* 1 not accomplished; uncompleted. 2 lacking accomplishments.

unaccountable /ˌʌnəˈkaʊntəb(ə)l/ *adj.* 1 unable to be explained. 2 unpredictable or strange in behaviour. 3 not responsible. □ **unaccountability** /-ˈbɪlɪtɪ/ *n.* **unaccountableness** *n.* **unaccountably** *adv.*

unaccounted /ˌʌnəˈkaʊntɪd/ *adj.* of which no account is given. □ **unaccounted for** unexplained; not included in an account.

unaccustomed /ˌʌnəˈkʌstəmd/ *adj.* 1 (usu. foll. by *to*) not accustomed. 2 not customary; unusual (*his unaccustomed silence*). □ **unaccustomedly** *adv.*

unacknowledged /ˌʌnəkˈnɒlɪdʒd/ *adj.* not acknowledged.

unacquainted /ˌʌnəˈkweɪntɪd/ *adj.* (usu. foll. by *with*) not acquainted.

unadopted /ˌʌnəˈdɒptɪd/ *adj.* 1 not adopted. 2 *Brit.* (of a road) not taken over for maintenance by a local authority.

unadorned /ˌʌnəˈdɔːnd/ *adj.* not adorned; plain.

unadulterated /ˌʌnəˈdʌltəˌreɪtɪd/ *adj.* 1 not adulterated; pure; concentrated. 2 sheer, complete, utter (*unadulterated nonsense*).

unadventurous /ˌʌnədˈventʃərəs/ *adj.* not adventurous. □ **unadventurously** *adv.*

unadvised /ˌʌnədˈvaɪzd/ *adj.* 1 indiscreet; rash. 2 not having had advice. □ **unadvisedly** /-zɪdlɪ/ *adv.* **unadvisedness** *n.*

unaffected /ˌʌnəˈfektɪd/ *adj.* 1 (usu. foll. by *by*) not affected. 2 free from affectation; genuine; sincere. □ **unaffectedly** *adv.* **unaffectedness** *n.*

unaffiliated /ˌʌnəˈfɪlɪˌeɪtɪd/ *adj.* not affiliated.

unafraid /ˌʌnəˈfreɪd/ *adj.* not afraid.

unaided /ʌnˈeɪdɪd/ *adj.* not aided; without help.

unalike /ˌʌnəˈlaɪk/ *adj.* not alike; different.

unalleviated /ˌʌnəˈliːvɪˌeɪtɪd/ *adj.* not alleviated; relentless.

unalloyed /ˌʌnəˈlɔɪd, ʌnˈæl-/ *adj.* 1 not alloyed; pure. 2 complete; utter (*unalloyed joy*).

unalterable /ʌnˈɔːltərəb(ə)l, ʌnˈɒl-/ *adj.* not alterable. □ **unalterableness** *n.* **unalterably** *adv.*

unaltered /ʌnˈɔːltəd, ʌnˈɒl-/ *adj.* not altered; remaining the same.

unambiguous /ˌʌnæmˈbɪɡjuəs/ *adj.* not ambiguous; clear or definite in meaning. □ **unambiguity** /-ˈɡjuːɪtɪ/ *n.* **unambiguously** *adv.*

unambitious /ˌʌnæmˈbɪʃəs/ *adj.* not ambitious; without ambition. □ **unambitiously** *adv.* **unambitiousness** *n.*

unambivalent /ˌʌnæmˈbɪvələnt/ *adj.* (of feelings etc.) not ambivalent; straightforward. □ **unambivalently** *adv.*

un-American /ˌʌnəˈmerɪkən/ *adj.* 1 not in accordance with American characteristics etc. 2 contrary to the interests of the US; (in the US) treasonable. □ **un-Americanism** *n.*

unamiable /ʌnˈeɪmɪəb(ə)l/ *adj.* not amiable.

unamused /ˌʌnəˈmjuːzd/ *adj.* not amused.

unanimous /juːˈnænɪməs/ *adj.* 1 all in agreement (*the committee was unanimous*). 2 (of an opinion, vote, etc.) held or given by general consent (*the unanimous choice*). □ **unanimity** /-nəˈnɪmɪtɪ/ *n.* **unanimously** *adv.* **unanimousness** *n.* [LL *unanimis*, L *unanimus* f. *unus* one + *animus* mind]

unannounced /ˌʌnəˈnaʊnst/ *adj.* not announced; without warning (of arrival etc.).

unanswerable /ʌnˈɑːnsərəb(ə)l/ *adj.* 1 unable to be refuted (*has an unanswerable case*). 2 unable to be answered (*an unanswerable question*). □ **unanswerableness** *n.* **unanswerably** *adv.*

unanswered /ʌnˈɑːnsəd/ *adj.* not answered.

unanticipated /ˌʌnænˈtɪsɪˌpeɪtɪd/ *adj.* not anticipated.

unapparent /ˌʌnəˈpærənt/ *adj.* not apparent.

unappealing /ˌʌnəˈpiːlɪŋ/ *adj.* not appealing; unattractive. □ **unappealingly** *adv.*

unappeased /ˌʌnəˈpiːzd/ *adj.* not appeased.

unappetizing /ʌnˈæpɪˌtaɪzɪŋ/ *adj.* not appetizing. □ **unappetizingly** *adv.*

unappreciated /ˌʌnəˈpriːʃɪˌeɪtɪd/ *adj.* not appreciated.

unappreciative /ˌʌnəˈpriːʃətɪv/ *adj.* not appreciative.

unapproachable /ˌʌnəˈprəʊtʃəb(ə)l/ *adj.* 1 not approachable; remote, inaccessible. 2 (of a person) unfriendly. □ **unapproachability** /-ˈbɪlɪtɪ/ *n.* **unapproachableness** *n.* **unapproachably** *adv.*

unapproved /ˌʌnəˈpruːvd/ *adj.* not approved or sanctioned.

unapt /ʌnˈæpt/ *adj.* 1 (usu. foll. by *for*) not suitable. 2 (usu. foll. by *to* + infin.) not apt. □ **unaptly** *adv.* **unaptness** *n.*

unarguable /ʌnˈɑːɡjʊəb(ə)l/ *adj.* not arguable; certain.

unarmed /ʌnˈɑːmd/ *adj.* not armed; without weapons.

unarresting /ˌʌnəˈrestɪŋ/ *adj.* uninteresting; dull. □ **unarrestingly** *adv.*

unartistic /ˌʌnɑːˈtɪstɪk/ *adj.* not artistic, esp. not concerned with art. □ **unartistically** *adv.*

unashamed /ˌʌnəˈʃeɪmd/ *adj.* 1 feeling no guilt, shameless. 2 blatant; bold. □ **unashamedly** /-mɪdlɪ/ *adv.* **unashamedness** /-mɪdnɪs/ *n.*

unasked /ʌnˈɑːskt/ *adj.* (often foll. by *for*) not asked, requested, or invited.

unassailable /ˌʌnəˈseɪləb(ə)l/ *adj.* unable to be attacked or questioned; impregnable. □ **unassailability** /-ˈbɪlɪtɪ/ *n.* **unassailableness** *n.* **unassailably** *adv.*

unassertive /ˌʌnəˈsɜːtɪv/ *adj.* (of a person) not assertive or forthcoming; reticent. □ **unassertively** *adv.* **unassertiveness** *n.*

unassigned /ˌʌnəˈsaɪnd/ *adj.* not assigned.

unassimilated /ˌʌnəˈsɪmɪˌleɪtɪd/ *adj.* not assimilated. □ **unassimilable** *adj.*

unassisted /ˌʌnəˈsɪstɪd/ *adj.* not assisted.

unassuaged /ˌʌnəˈsweɪdʒd/ adj. not assuaged. □ **unassuageable** adj.

unassuming /ˌʌnəˈsjuːmɪŋ/ adj. not pretentious or arrogant; modest. **unassumingly** adv. **unassumingness** n.

unattached /ˌʌnəˈtætʃt/ adj. **1** (often foll. by to) not attached, esp. to a particular body, organization, etc. **2** not engaged or married.

unattainable /ˌʌnəˈteɪnəb(ə)l/ adj. not attainable. □ **unattainableness** n. **unattainably** adv.

unattempted /ˌʌnəˈtemptɪd/ adj. not attempted.

unattended /ˌʌnəˈtendɪd/ adj. **1** (usu. foll. by to) not attended. **2** (of a person, vehicle, etc.) not accompanied; alone; uncared for.

unattractive /ˌʌnəˈtræktɪv/ adj. not attractive. □ **unattractively** adv. **unattractiveness** n.

unattributable /ˌʌnəˈtrɪbjʊtəb(ə)l/ adj. (esp. of information) that cannot or may not be attributed to a source etc. □ **unattributably** adv.

unauthenticated /ˌʌnɔːˈθentɪˌkeɪtɪd/ adj. not authenticated.

unauthorized /ʌnˈɔːθəˌraɪzd/ adj. (also **unauthorised**) not authorized.

unavailable /ˌʌnəˈveɪləb(ə)l/ adj. not available. □ **unavailability** /-ˈbɪlɪtɪ/ n. **unavailableness** n.

unavailing /ˌʌnəˈveɪlɪŋ/ adj. not availing; achieving nothing; ineffectual. □ **unavailingly** adv.

unavoidable /ˌʌnəˈvɔɪdəb(ə)l/ adj. not avoidable; inevitable. □ **unavoidability** /-ˈbɪlɪtɪ/ n. **unavoidableness** n. **unavoidably** adv.

unaware /ˌʌnəˈweə(r)/ adj. & adv. —adj. **1** (usu. foll. by of, or that + clause) not aware; ignorant (unaware of her presence). **2** (of a person) insensitive; unperceptive. —adv. = UNAWARES. □ **unawareness** n.

unawares /ˌʌnəˈweəz/ adv. **1** unexpectedly (met them unawares). **2** inadvertently (dropped it unawares). [earlier unware(s) f. OE unwær(es): see WARE²]

unbacked /ʌnˈbækt/ adj. **1** not supported. **2** (of a horse etc.) having no backers. **3** (of a chair, picture, etc.) having no back or backing.

unbalance /ʌnˈbæləns/ v. & n. —v.tr. **1** upset the physical or mental balance of (unbalanced by the blow; the shock unbalanced him). **2** (as **unbalanced** adj.) **a** not balanced. **b** (of a mind or a person) unstable or deranged. —n. lack of balance; instability, esp. mental.

unban /ʌnˈbæn/ v.tr. (**unbanned, unbanning**) cease to ban; remove a ban from.

unbar /ʌnˈbɑː(r)/ v.tr. (**unbarred, unbarring**) **1** remove a bar or bars from (a gate etc.). **2** unlock.

unbearable /ʌnˈbeərəb(ə)l/ adj. not bearable. □ **unbearableness** n. **unbearably** adv.

unbeatable /ʌnˈbiːtəb(ə)l/ adj. not beatable; excelling.

unbeaten /ʌnˈbiːt(ə)n/ adj. **1** not beaten. **2** (of a record etc.) not surpassed.

unbecoming /ˌʌnbɪˈkʌmɪŋ/ adj. **1** (esp. of clothing) not flattering or suiting a person. **2** (usu. foll. by to, for) not fitting; indecorous or unsuitable. □ **unbecomingly** adv. **unbecomingness** n.

unbeknown /ˌʌnbɪˈnəʊn/ adj. (also **unbeknownst** /-ˈnəʊnst/) (foll. by to) without the knowledge of (was there all the time unbeknown to us). [UN-¹ + beknown (archaic) = KNOWN]

unbelief /ˌʌnbɪˈliːf/ n. lack of belief, esp. in religious matters. □ **unbeliever** n. **unbelieving** adj. **unbelievingly** adv. **unbelievingness** n.

unbelievable /ˌʌnbɪˈliːvəb(ə)l/ adj. not believable; incredible. □ **unbelievability** /-ˈbɪlɪtɪ/ n. **unbelievableness** n. **unbelievably** adv.

unbend /ʌnˈbend/ v. (past and past part. **unbent**) **1** tr. & intr. change from a bent position; straighten. **2** intr. relax from strain or severity; become affable (likes to unbend with a glass of beer).

unbending /ʌnˈbendɪŋ/ adj. **1** not bending; inflexible. **2** firm; austere (unbending rectitude). **3** relaxing from strain, activity, or formality. □ **unbendingly** adv. **unbendingness** n.

unbiased /ʌnˈbaɪəst/ adj. (also **unbiassed**) not biased; impartial.

unbidden /ʌnˈbɪd(ə)n/ adj. not commanded or invited (arrived unbidden).

unbind /ʌnˈbaɪnd/ v.tr. (past and past part. **unbound**) release from bonds or binding.

unbirthday /ʌnˈbɜːθdeɪ/ n. (often attrib.) joc. any day but one's birthday (an unbirthday party).

unbleached /ʌnˈbliːtʃt/ adj. not bleached.

unblemished /ʌnˈblemɪʃt/ adj. not blemished.

unblinking /ʌnˈblɪŋkɪŋ/ adj. **1** not blinking. **2** steadfast; not hesitating. **3** stolid; cool. □ **unblinkingly** adv.

unblock /ʌnˈblɒk/ v.tr. remove an obstruction from (esp. a pipe, drain, etc.).

unblushing /ʌnˈblʌʃɪŋ/ adj. **1** not blushing. **2** unashamed; frank. □ **unblushingly** adv.

unbolt /ʌnˈbəʊlt/ v.tr. release (a door etc.) by drawing back the bolt.

unbolted /ʌnˈbəʊltɪd/ adj. **1** not bolted. **2** (of flour etc.) not sifted.

unborn /ʌnˈbɔːn/ adj. **1** not yet born (an unborn child). **2** never to be brought into being (unborn hopes).

unbosom /ʌnˈbʊz(ə)m/ v.tr. **1** disclose (thoughts, secrets, etc.). **2** (refl.) unburden (oneself) of one's thoughts, secrets, etc.

unbothered /ʌnˈbɒðəd/ adj. not bothered; unconcerned.

unbound¹ /ʌnˈbaʊnd/ adj. **1** not bound or tied up. **2** unconstrained. **3 a** (of a book) not having a binding. **b** having paper covers. **4** (of a substance or particle) in a loose or free state.

unbound² past and past part. of UNBIND.

unbounded /ʌnˈbaʊndɪd/ adj. not bounded; infinite (unbounded optimism). □ **unboundedly** adv. **unboundedness** n.

unbreakable /ʌnˈbreɪkəb(ə)l/ adj. not breakable.

unbreathable /ʌnˈbriːðəb(ə)l/ adj. not able to be breathed.

unbribable /ʌnˈbraɪbəb(ə)l/ adj. not bribable.

unbridgeable /ʌnˈbrɪdʒəb(ə)l/ adj. unable to be bridged.

unbridle /ʌnˈbraɪd(ə)l/ v.tr. **1** remove a bridle from (a horse). **2** remove constraints from (one's tongue, a person, etc.). **3** (as **unbridled** adj.) unconstrained (unbridled insolence).

unbroken /ʌnˈbrəʊkən/ adj. **1** not broken. **2** not tamed (an unbroken horse). **3** not interrupted (unbroken sleep). **4** not surpassed (an unbroken record). □ **unbrokenly** adv. **unbrokenness** /-ənnɪs/ n.

unbruised /ʌnˈbruːzd/ adj. not bruised.

unbuckle /ʌnˈbʌk(ə)l/ v.tr. release the buckle of (a strap, shoe, etc.).

unbuild /ʌnˈbɪld/ v.tr. (past and past part. **unbuilt**) **1** demolish or destroy (a building, theory, system, etc.). **2** (as **unbuilt** *adj.*) not yet built or (of land etc.) not yet built on.

unburden /ʌnˈbɜːd(ə)n/ *v.tr.* **1** relieve of a burden. **2** (esp. *refl.*; often foll. by *to*) relieve (oneself, one's conscience, etc.) by confession etc. □ **unburdened** *adj.*

unburied /ʌnˈberɪd/ *adj.* not buried.

unbusinesslike /ʌnˈbɪznɪsˌlaɪk/ *adj.* not businesslike.

unbutton /ʌnˈbʌt(ə)n/ *v.tr.* **1 a** unfasten (a coat etc.) by taking the buttons out of the button-holes. **b** unbutton the clothes of (a person). **2** (*absol.*) *colloq.* relax from tension or formality, become communicative. **3** (as **unbuttoned** *adj.*) **a** not buttoned. **b** *colloq.* communicative; informal.

uncalled /ʌnˈkɔːld/ *adj.* not summoned or invited. □ **uncalled-for** (of an opinion, action, etc.) impertinent or unnecessary (*an uncalled-for remark*).

uncanny /ʌnˈkænɪ/ *adj.* (**uncannier**, **uncanniest**) seemingly supernatural; mysterious. □ **uncannily** *adv.* **uncanniness** *n.* [(orig. Sc. & N.Engl.) f. UN-¹ + CANNY]

uncanonical /ˌʌnkəˈnɒnɪk(ə)l/ *adj.* not canonical. □ **uncanonically** *adv.*

uncap /ʌnˈkæp/ *v.tr.* (**uncapped**, **uncapping**) remove the cap from (a jar, bottle, etc.).

uncared-for /ʌnˈkeədfɔː(r)/ *adj.* disregarded; neglected.

uncashed /ʌnˈkæʃt/ *adj.* not cashed.

uncaught /ʌnˈkɔːt/ *adj.* not caught.

unceasing /ʌnˈsiːsɪŋ/ *adj.* not ceasing; continuous (*unceasing effort*). □ **unceasingly** *adv.*

uncensored /ʌnˈsensəd/ *adj.* not censored.

uncensured /ʌnˈsensjəd/ *adj.* not censured.

unceremonious /ˌʌnserɪˈməʊnɪəs/ *adj.* **1** lacking ceremony or formality. **2** abrupt; discourteous. □ **unceremoniously** *adv.* **unceremoniousness** *n.*

uncertain /ʌnˈsɜːt(ə)n/ *adj.* **1** not certainly knowing or known (*uncertain what it means; the result is uncertain*). **2** unreliable (*his aim is uncertain*). **3** changeable, erratic (*uncertain weather*). □ **in no uncertain terms** clearly and forcefully. □ **uncertainly** *adv.*

uncertainty /ʌnˈsɜːtəntɪ/ *n.* (*pl.* **-ies**) **1** the fact or condition of being uncertain. **2** an uncertain matter or circumstance.

uncertified /ʌnˈsɜːtɪˌfaɪd/ *adj.* **1** not attested as certain. **2** not guaranteed by a certificate of competence etc. **3** not certified as insane.

unchain /ʌnˈtʃeɪn/ *v.tr.* **1** remove the chains from. **2** release; liberate.

unchallengeable /ʌnˈtʃælɪndʒəb(ə)l/ *adj.* not challengeable; unassailable. □ **unchallengeably** *adv.*

unchallenged /ʌnˈtʃælɪndʒd/ *adj.* not challenged.

unchangeable /ʌnˈtʃeɪndʒəb(ə)l/ *adj.* not changeable; immutable, invariable. □ **unchangeability** /-ˈbɪlɪtɪ/ *n.* **unchangeableness** *n.* **unchangeably** *adv.*

unchanged /ʌnˈtʃeɪndʒd/ *adj.* not changed; unaltered.

unchanging /ʌnˈtʃeɪndʒɪŋ/ *adj.* not changing; remaining the same. □ **unchangingly** *adv.* **unchangingness** *n.*

unchaperoned /ʌnˈʃæpəˌrəʊnd/ *adj.* without a chaperone.

uncharacteristic /ˌʌnkærɪktəˈrɪstɪk/ *adj.* not characteristic. □ **uncharacteristically** *adv.*

uncharitable /ʌnˈtʃærɪtəb(ə)l/ *adj.* censorious, severe in judgement. □ **uncharitableness** *n.* **uncharitably** *adv.*

uncharted /ʌnˈtʃɑːtɪd/ *adj.* not charted, mapped, or surveyed.

unchartered /ʌnˈtʃɑːtəd/ *adj.* **1** not furnished with a charter; not formally privileged or constituted. **2** unauthorized; illegal.

unchaste /ʌnˈtʃeɪst/ *adj.* not chaste. □ **unchastely** *adv.* **unchasteness** *n.* **unchastity** /-ˈtʃæstɪtɪ/ *n.*

unchecked /ʌnˈtʃekt/ *adj.* **1** not checked. **2** freely allowed; unrestrained (*unchecked violence*).

unchivalrous /ʌnˈʃɪvəlrəs/ *adj.* not chivalrous; rude. □ **unchivalrously** *adv.*

unchosen /ʌnˈtʃəʊz(ə)n/ *adj.* not chosen.

unchristian /ʌnˈkrɪstjən/ *adj.* **1** contrary to Christian principles, esp. uncaring or selfish. **2** not Christian. □ **unchristianly** *adv.*

uncial /ˈʌnsɪəl, -ʃ(ə)l/ *adj.* & *n.* —*adj.* of or written in majuscule writing with rounded unjoined letters found in manuscripts of the 4th–8th c., from which modern capitals are derived. —*n.* **1** an uncial letter. **2** an uncial style or MS. [LL *unciales litterae*, the orig. application of which is unclear, f. L *uncialis* f. *uncia* inch]

uncircumcised /ʌnˈsɜːkəmˌsaɪzd/ *adj.* **1** not circumcised. **2** spiritually impure; heathen. □ **uncircumcision** /-ˈsɪʒ(ə)n/ *n.*

uncivil /ʌnˈsɪvɪl/ *adj.* **1** ill-mannered; impolite. **2** not public-spirited. □ **uncivilly** *adv.*

uncivilized /ʌnˈsɪvɪˌlaɪzd/ *adj.* (also **uncivilised**) **1** not civilized. **2** rough; uncultured.

unclad /ʌnˈklæd/ *adj.* not clad; naked.

unclaimed /ʌnˈkleɪmd/ *adj.* not claimed.

unclasp /ʌnˈklɑːsp/ *v.tr.* **1** loosen the clasp or clasps of. **2** release the grip of (a hand etc.).

unclassifiable /ʌnˈklæsɪˌfaɪəb(ə)l/ *adj.* not classifiable.

unclassified /ʌnˈklæsɪˌfaɪd/ *adj.* **1** not classified. **2** (of State information) not secret.

uncle /ˈʌŋk(ə)l/ *n.* **1 a** the brother of one's father or mother. **b** an aunt's husband. **2** *colloq.* a name given by children to a male family friend. **3** *sl.* esp. *hist.* a pawnbroker. □ **Uncle Sam** *colloq.* the federal government or citizens of the US (*will fight for Uncle Sam*). **Uncle Tom** *derog.* a Black man considered to be servile, cringing, etc. (from the hero of H. B. Stowe's *Uncle Tom's Cabin*, 1852). [ME f. AF *uncle*, OF *oncle* f. LL *aunculus* f. L *avunculus* maternal uncle: see AVUNCULAR]

-uncle /ˈʌŋk(ə)l/ *suffix* forming nouns, usu. diminutives (*carbuncle*). [OF *-uncle*, *-oncle* or L *-unculus*, *-la*, a special form of *-ulus* -ULE]

unclean /ʌnˈkliːn/ *adj.* **1** not clean. **2** unchaste. **3** unfit to be eaten; ceremonially impure. **4** *Bibl.* (of a spirit) wicked. □ **uncleanly** *adv.* **uncleanly** /-ˈklenlɪ/ *adj.* **uncleanliness** /-ˈklenlɪnɪs/ *n.* **uncleanness** *n.* [OE *unclæne* (as UN-¹, CLEAN)]

unclear /ʌnˈklɪə(r)/ *adj.* **1** not clear or easy to understand; obscure, uncertain. **2** (of a person) doubtful, uncertain (*I'm unclear as to what you mean*). □ **unclearly** *adv.* **unclearness** *n.*

unclench /ʌnˈklentʃ/ *v.* **1** *tr.* release (clenched hands, features, teeth, etc.). **2** *intr.* (of clenched hands etc.) become relaxed or open.

unclog /ʌnˈklɒg/ v.tr. (**unclogged, unclogging**) unblock (a drain, pipe, etc.).

unclose /ʌnˈkləʊz/ v. **1** tr. & intr. open. **2** tr. reveal; disclose.

unclothe /ʌnˈkləʊð/ v.tr. **1** remove the clothes from. **2** strip of leaves or vegetation (*trees unclothed by the wind*). **3** expose, reveal. □ **unclothed** adj.

unclouded /ʌnˈklaʊdɪd/ adj. **1** not clouded; clear; bright. **2** untroubled (*unclouded serenity*).

uncluttered /ʌnˈklʌtəd/ adj. not cluttered; austere, simple.

uncoil /ʌnˈkɔɪl/ v.tr. & intr. unwind.

uncoloured /ʌnˈkʌləd/ adj. (US **uncolored**) **1** having no colour. **2** not influenced; impartial. **3** not exaggerated.

uncombed /ʌnˈkəʊmd/ adj. (of hair or a person) not combed.

uncome-at-able /ˌʌnkʌmˈætəb(ə)l/ adj. colloq. inaccessible; unattainable. [UN-¹ + *come-at-able*: see COME]

uncomfortable /ʌnˈkʌmftəb(ə)l/ adj. **1** not comfortable. **2** uneasy; causing or feeling disquiet (*an uncomfortable silence*). □ **uncomfortableness** n. **uncomfortably** adv.

uncommercial /ˌʌnkəˈmɜː.ʃ(ə)l/ adj. **1** not commercial. **2** contrary to commercial principles.

uncommitted /ˌʌnkəˈmɪtɪd/ adj. **1** not committed. **2** unattached to any specific political cause or group.

uncommon /ʌnˈkɒmən/ adj. **1** not common; unusual; remarkable. **2** remarkably great etc. (*an uncommon fear of spiders*). □ **uncommonly** adv. **uncommonness** /-mənnɪs/ n.

uncommunicative /ˌʌnkəˈmjuːnɪkətɪv/ adj. not wanting to communicate; taciturn. □ **uncommunicatively** adv. **uncommunicativeness** n.

uncompetitive /ˌʌnkəmˈpetɪtɪv/ adj. not competitive.

uncomplaining /ˌʌnkəmˈpleɪnɪŋ/ adj. not complaining; resigned. □ **uncomplainingly** adv.

uncompleted /ˌʌnkəmˈpliːtɪd/ adj. not completed; incomplete.

uncomplicated /ʌnˈkɒmplɪˌkeɪtɪd/ adj. not complicated; simple; straightforward.

uncomplimentary /ˌʌnkɒmplɪˈmentərɪ/ adj. not complimentary; insulting.

uncomprehending /ˌʌnkɒmprɪˈhendɪŋ/ adj. not comprehending. □ **uncomprehendingly** adv. **uncomprehension** /-ˈʃ(ə)n/ n.

uncompromising /ʌnˈkɒmprəˌmaɪzɪŋ/ adj. unwilling to compromise; stubborn; unyielding. □ **uncompromisingly** adv. **uncompromisingness** n.

unconcealed /ˌʌnkənˈsiːld/ adj. not concealed; obvious.

unconcern /ˌʌnkənˈsɜːn/ n. lack of concern; indifference; apathy. □ **unconcerned** adj. **unconcernedly** /-nɪdlɪ/ adv.

unconditional /ˌʌnkənˈdɪʃ(ə)n(ə)l/ adj. not subject to conditions; complete (*unconditional surrender*). □ **unconditionality** /-ˈnælɪtɪ/ n. **unconditionally** adv.

unconditioned /ˌʌnkənˈdɪʃ(ə)nd/ adj. **1** not subject to conditions or to an antecedent condition. **2** (of behaviour etc.) not determined by conditioning; natural. □ **unconditioned reflex** an instinctive response to a stimulus.

unconfined /ˌʌnkənˈfaɪnd/ adj. not confined; boundless.

unconfirmed /ˌʌnkənˈfɜːmd/ adj. not confirmed.

uncongenial /ˌʌnkənˈdʒiːnɪəl/ adj. not congenial.

unconnected /ˌʌnkəˈnektɪd/ adj. **1** not physically joined. **2** not connected or associated. **3** (of speech etc.) disconnected; not joined in order or sequence (*unconnected ideas*). **4** not related by family ties. □ **unconnectedly** adv. **unconnectedness** n.

unconquerable /ʌnˈkɒŋkərəb(ə)l/ adj. not conquerable. □ **unconquerableness** n. **unconquerably** adv.

unconquered /ʌnˈkɒŋkəd/ adj. not conquered or defeated.

unconscionable /ʌnˈkɒnʃənəb(ə)l/ adj. **1 a** having no conscience. **b** contrary to conscience. **2 a** unreasonably excessive (*an unconscionable length of time*). **b** not right or reasonable. □ **unconscionableness** n. **unconscionably** adv. [UN-¹ + obs. *conscionable* f. *conscions* obs. var. of CONSCIENCE]

unconscious /ʌnˈkɒnʃəs/ adj. & n. —adj. not conscious (*unconscious of any change; fell unconscious on the floor; an unconscious prejudice*). —n. that part of the mind which is inaccessible to the conscious mind but which affects behaviour, emotions, etc. □ **unconsciously** adv. **unconsciousness** n.

unconsecrated /ʌnˈkɒnsɪˌkreɪtɪd/ adj. not consecrated.

unconsidered /ˌʌnkənˈsɪdəd/ adj. **1** not considered; disregarded. **2** (of a response etc.) immediate; not premeditated.

unconstitutional /ˌʌnkɒnstɪˈtjuːʃ(ə)n(ə)l/ adj. not in accordance with the political constitution or with procedural rules. □ **unconstitutionality** /-ˈnælɪtɪ/ n. **unconstitutionally** adv.

unconstrained /ˌʌnkənˈstreɪnd/ adj. not constrained or compelled. □ **unconstrainedly** /-nɪdlɪ/ adv.

unconstricted /ˌʌnkənˈstrɪktɪd/ adj. not constricted.

unconsumed /ˌʌnkənˈsjuːmd/ adj. not consumed.

unconsummated /ʌnˈkɒnsjʊˌmeɪtɪd/ adj. not consummated.

uncontaminated /ˌʌnkənˈtæmɪˌneɪtɪd/ adj. not contaminated.

uncontested /ˌʌnkənˈtestɪd/ adj. not contested. □ **uncontestedly** adv.

uncontradicted /ˌʌnkɒntrəˈdɪktɪd/ adj. not contradicted.

uncontrollable /ˌʌnkənˈtrəʊləb(ə)l/ adj. not controllable. □ **uncontrollableness** n. **uncontrollably** adv.

uncontrolled /ˌʌnkənˈtrəʊld/ adj. not controlled; unrestrained, unchecked.

uncontroversial /ˌʌnkɒntrəˈvɜːʃ(ə)l/ adj. not controversial. □ **uncontroversially** adv.

unconventional /ˌʌnkənˈvenʃən(ə)l/ adj. not bound by convention or custom; unusual; unorthodox. □ **unconventionalism** n. **unconventionality** /-ˈnælɪtɪ/ n. **unconventionally** adv.

unconverted /ˌʌnkənˈvɜːtɪd/ adj. not converted.

unconvinced /ˌʌnkənˈvɪnst/ adj. not convinced.

unconvincing /ˌʌnkənˈvɪnsɪŋ/ adj. not convincing. □ **unconvincingly** adv.

uncooked /ʌnˈkʊkt/ adj. not cooked; raw.

uncool /ʌnˈkuːl/ adj. sl. **1** unrelaxed; unpleasant. **2** (of jazz) not cool.

uncooperative /ˌʌnkəʊˈɒpərətɪv/ *adj.* not cooperative. □ **uncooperatively** *adv.*

uncoordinated /ˌʌnkəʊˈɔːdɪˌneɪtɪd/ *adj.* 1 not coordinated. 2 (of a person's movements etc.) clumsy.

uncork /ʌnˈkɔːk/ *v.tr.* 1 draw the cork from (a bottle). 2 allow (feelings etc.) to be vented.

uncorroborated /ˌʌnkəˈrɒbəˌreɪtɪd/ *adj.* (esp. of evidence etc.) not corroborated.

uncorrupted /ˌʌnkəˈrʌptɪd/ *adj.* not corrupted.

uncountable /ʌnˈkaʊntəb(ə)l/ *adj.* 1 inestimable, immense (*uncountable wealth*). 2 *Gram.* (of a noun) that cannot form a plural or be used with the indefinite article (e.g. *happiness*). □ **uncountability** /-ˈbɪlɪtɪ/ *n.* **uncountably** *adv.*

uncounted /ʌnˈkaʊntɪd/ *adj.* 1 not counted. 2 very many; innumerable.

uncouple /ʌnˈkʌp(ə)l/ *v.tr.* release (wagons) from couplings. □ **uncoupled** *adj.*

uncouth /ʌnˈkuːθ/ *adj.* (of a person, manners, appearance, etc.) lacking in ease and polish; uncultured, rough (*uncouth voices; behaviour was uncouth*). □ **uncouthly** *adv.* **uncouthness** *n.* [OE *uncūth* unknown (as UN-[1] + *cūth* past part. of *cunnan* know, CAN[1])]

uncover /ʌnˈkʌvə(r)/ *v.* 1 *tr.* **a** remove a cover or covering from. **b** make known; disclose (*uncovered the truth at last*). 2 *intr. archaic* remove one's hat, cap, etc. 3 *tr.* (as **uncovered** *adj.*) **a** not covered by a roof, clothing, etc. **b** not wearing a hat.

uncreative /ˌʌnkrɪˈeɪtɪv/ *adj.* not creative.

uncritical /ʌnˈkrɪtɪk(ə)l/ *adj.* 1 not critical; complacently accepting. 2 not in accordance with the principles of criticism. □ **uncritically** *adv.*

uncross /ʌnˈkrɒs/ *v.tr.* 1 remove (the limbs, knives, etc.) from a crossed position. 2 (as **uncrossed** *adj.*) **a** *Brit.* (of a cheque) not crossed. **b** not thwarted or challenged.

uncrown /ʌnˈkraʊn/ *v.tr.* 1 deprive (a monarch etc.) of a crown. 2 deprive (a person) of a position. 3 (as **uncrowned** *adj.*) **a** not crowned. **b** having the status but not the name of (*the uncrowned king of boxing*).

unction /ˈʌŋkʃ(ə)n/ *n.* 1 **a** the act of anointing with oil etc. as a religious rite. **b** the oil etc. so used. 2 **a** soothing words or thought. **b** excessive or insincere flattery. 3 **a** the act of anointing for medical purposes. **b** an ointment so used. 4 **a** a fervent or sympathetic quality in words or tone caused by or causing deep emotion. **b** a pretence of this. [ME f. L *unctio* f. *ung(u)ere unct-* anoint]

unctuous /ˈʌŋktjʊəs/ *adj.* 1 (of behaviour, speech, etc.) unpleasantly flattering; oily. 2 (esp. of minerals) having a greasy or soapy feel; oily. □ **unctuously** *adv.* **unctuousness** *n.* [ME f. med.L *unctuosus* f. L *unctus* anointing (as UNCTION)]

uncultivated /ʌnˈkʌltɪˌveɪtɪd/ *adj.* (esp. of land) not cultivated.

uncultured /ʌnˈkʌltʃəd/ *adj.* 1 not cultured, unrefined. 2 (of soil or plants) not cultivated.

uncured /ʌnˈkjʊəd/ *adj.* 1 not cured. 2 (of pork etc.) not salted or smoked.

uncurl /ʌnˈkɜːl/ *v.intr.* & *tr.* relax from a curled position, untwist.

uncurtained /ʌnˈkɜːt(ə)nd/ *adj.* not curtained.

uncut /ʌnˈkʌt/ *adj.* 1 not cut. 2 (of a book) with the pages not cut open or with untrimmed margins. 3 (of a book, film, etc.) complete; uncensored. 4 (of a stone, esp. a diamond) not

shaped by cutting. 5 (of fabric) having its pile-loops intact (*uncut moquette*).

undamaged /ʌnˈdæmɪdʒd/ *adj.* not damaged; intact.

undated /ʌnˈdeɪtɪd/ *adj.* not provided or marked with a date.

undaunted /ʌnˈdɔːntɪd/ *adj.* not daunted. □ **undauntedly** *adv.* **undauntedness** *n.*

undeceive /ˌʌndɪˈsiːv/ *v.tr.* (often foll. by *of*) free (a person) from a misconception, deception, or error.

undecided /ˌʌndɪˈsaɪdɪd/ *adj.* 1 not settled or certain (*the question is undecided*). 2 hesitating; irresolute (*undecided about their relative merits*). □ **undecidedly** *adv.*

undecipherable /ˌʌndɪˈsaɪfərəb(ə)l/ *adj.* not decipherable.

undeclared /ˌʌndɪˈkleəd/ *adj.* not declared.

undefeated /ˌʌndɪˈfiːtɪd/ *adj.* not defeated.

undefended /ˌʌndɪˈfendɪd/ *adj.* (esp. of a lawsuit) not defended.

undefiled /ˌʌndɪˈfaɪld/ *adj.* not defiled; pure.

undefined /ˌʌndɪˈfaɪnd/ *adj.* 1 not defined. 2 not clearly marked; vague, indefinite. □ **undefinable** *adj.* **undefinably** *adv.*

undelivered /ˌʌndɪˈlɪvəd/ *adj.* 1 not delivered or handed over. 2 not set free or released. 3 **a** (of a pregnant woman) not yet having given birth. **b** (of a child) not yet born.

undemanding /ˌʌndɪˈmɑːndɪŋ/ *adj.* not demanding; easily satisfied. □ **undemandingness** *n.*

undemocratic /ˌʌndeməˈkrætɪk/ *adj.* not democratic. □ **undemocratically** *adv.*

undemonstrative /ˌʌndɪˈmɒnstrətɪv/ *adj.* not expressing feelings etc. outwardly; reserved. □ **undemonstratively** *adv.* **undemonstrativeness** *n.*

undeniable /ˌʌndɪˈnaɪəb(ə)l/ *adj.* 1 unable to be denied or disputed; certain. 2 excellent (*was of undeniable character*). □ **undeniableness** *n.* **undeniably** *adv.*

undenied /ˌʌndɪˈnaɪd/ *adj.* not denied.

undependable /ˌʌndɪˈpendəb(ə)l/ *adj.* not to be depended upon; unreliable.

under /ˈʌndə(r)/ *prep., adv.,* & *adj.* —*prep.* 1 **a** in or to a position lower than; below; beneath (*fell under the table; under the left eye*). **b** within, on the inside of (a surface etc.) (*wore a vest under his shirt*). 2 **a** inferior to; less than (*a captain is under a major; is under 18*). **b** at or for a lower cost than (*was under £20*). 3 **a** subject or liable to; controlled or bound by (*lives under oppression; under pain of death; born under Saturn; the country prospered under him*). **b** undergoing (*is under repair*). **c** classified or subsumed in (*that book goes under biology; goes under many names*). 4 at the foot of or sheltered by (*hid under the wall; under the cliff*). 5 planted with (a crop). 6 powered by (sail, steam, etc.). —*adv.* 1 in or to a lower position or condition (*kept him under*). 2 *colloq.* in or into a state of unconsciousness (*put him under for the operation*). —*adj.* lower (*the under jaw*). □ **under separate cover** in another envelope. **under the sun** anywhere in the world. **under water** in and covered by water. **under way** in motion; in progress. □ **undermost** *adj.* [OE f. Gmc]

under- /ˈʌndə(r)/ *prefix* in senses of UNDER: 1 below, beneath (*undercarriage; underground*). 2 lower in status; subordinate (*under-secretary*). 3

insufficiently, incompletely (*undercook*; *under-developed*). [OE (as UNDER)]

underachieve /ˌʌndərəˈtʃiːv/ *v.intr.* do less well than might be expected (esp. scholastically). □ **underachievement** *n.* **underachiever** *n.*

underarm /ˈʌndərˌɑːm/ *adj.* & *adv.* **1** *Sport*, esp. *Cricket* with the arm below shoulder-level. **2** under the arm. **3** in the armpit.

underbelly /ˈʌndəˌbelɪ/ *n.* (*pl.* **-ies**) the under surface of an animal, vehicle, etc., esp. as an area vulnerable to attack.

underbid *v.* & *n.* —*v.tr.* /ˌʌndəˈbɪd/ (**-bidding**; *past* and *past part.* **-bid**) **1** make a lower bid than (a person). **2** (also *absol.*) *Bridge* etc. bid less on (one's hand) than its strength warrants. —*n.* /ˈʌndəˌbɪd/ **1** such a bid. **2** the act or an instance of underbidding.

underbrush /ˈʌndəˌbrʌʃ/ *n.* US undergrowth in a forest.

undercarriage /ˈʌndəˌkærɪdʒ/ *n.* **1** a wheeled structure beneath an aircraft, usu. retracted when not in use, to receive the impact on landing and support the frame of a vehicle. **2** the supporting frame of a vehicle.

undercharge /ˌʌndəˈtʃɑːdʒ/ *v.tr.* **1** charge too little for (a thing) or to (a person). **2** give less than the proper charge to (a gun, an electric battery, etc.).

underclass /ˈʌndəˌklɑːs/ *n.* a subordinate social class.

undercliff /ˈʌndəklɪf/ *n.* a terrace or lower cliff formed by a landslip.

underclothes /ˈʌndəˌkləʊðz, -ˌkləʊz/ *n.pl.* clothes worn under others, esp. next to the skin.

underclothing /ˈʌndəˌkləʊðɪŋ/ *n.* underclothes collectively.

undercoat /ˈʌndəˌkəʊt/ *n.* **1 a** a preliminary layer of paint under the finishing coat. **b** the paint used for this. **2** an animal's under layer of hair or down. □ **undercoating** *n.*

undercover /ˌʌndəˈkʌvə(r), ˈʌn-/ *adj.* (usu. *attrib.*) **1** surreptitious. **2** engaged in spying, esp. by working with or among those to be observed (*undercover agent*).

undercroft /ˈʌndəˌkrɒft/ *n.* a crypt. [ME f. UNDER- + *croft* crypt f. MDu. *crofte* cave f. med.L *crupta* for L *crypta*: see CRYPT]

undercurrent /ˈʌndəˌkʌrənt/ *n.* **1** a current below the surface. **2** an underlying often contrary feeling, activity, or influence (*an undercurrent of protest*).

undercut *v.* & *n.* —*v.tr.* /ˌʌndəˈkʌt/ (**-cutting**; *past* and *past part.* **-cut**) **1** sell or work at a lower price or lower wages than. **2** *Golf* strike (a ball) so as to make it rise high. **3** cut away the part below or under (a thing). **4** render unstable or less firm, undermine. —*n.* /ˈʌndəˌkʌt/ *Brit.* the underside of a sirloin.

underdeveloped /ˌʌndədɪˈveləpt/ *adj.* **1** not fully developed; immature. **2** (of a country etc.) below its potential economic level. **3** *Photog.* not developed sufficiently to give a normal image. □ **underdevelopment** *n.*

underdog /ˈʌndəˌdɒg/ *n.* **1** a dog, or usu. a person, losing a fight. **2** a person who is in a state of inferiority or subjection.

underdone /ˌʌndəˈdʌn, ˈʌn-/ *adj.* **1** not thoroughly done. **2** (of food) lightly or insufficiently cooked.

underdress /ˌʌndəˈdres/ *v.tr.* & *intr.* dress too plainly or too lightly.

underemphasis /ˌʌndərˈemfəsɪs/ *n.* (*pl.* **-emphases** /-ˌsiːz/) an insufficient degree of emphasis. □ **underemphasize** *v.tr.* (also **-ise**).

underemployed /ˌʌndərɪmˈplɔɪd/ *adj.* not fully employed. □ **underemployment** *n.*

underestimate *v.* & *n.* —*v.tr.* /ˌʌndərˈestɪˌmeɪt/ form too low an estimate of. —*n.* /ˌʌndərˈestɪmət/ an estimate that is too low. □ **underestimation** /-ˈmeɪʃ(ə)n/ *n.*

underexpose /ˌʌndərɪkˈspəʊz/ *v.tr. Photog.* expose (film) for too short a time or with insufficient light. □ **underexposure** *n.*

underfed /ˌʌndəˈfed/ *adj.* insufficiently fed.

underfelt /ˈʌndəˌfelt/ *n.* felt for laying under a carpet.

underfloor /ˈʌndəˌflɔː(r)/ *attrib.adj.* situated or operating beneath the floor (*underfloor heating*).

underfoot /ˌʌndəˈfʊt/ *adv.* **1** under one's feet. **2** on the ground. **3** in a state of subjection. **4** so as to obstruct or inconvenience.

undergarment /ˈʌndəˌgɑːmənt/ *n.* a piece of underclothing.

undergo /ˌʌndəˈgəʊ/ *v.tr.* (*3rd sing. present* **-goes**; *past* **-went**; *past part.* **-gone**) be subjected to; suffer; endure. [OE *undergān* (as UNDER-, GO[1])]

undergraduate /ˌʌndəˈgrædjʊət/ *n.* a student at a university who has not yet taken a first degree.

underground *adv.*, *adj.*, & *n.* —*adv.* /ˌʌndəˈgraʊnd/ **1** beneath the surface of the ground. **2** in or into secrecy or hiding. —*adj.* /ˈʌndəˌgraʊnd/ **1** situated underground. **2** secret, hidden, esp. working secretly to subvert a ruling power. **3** unconventional, experimental (*underground press*). —*n.* /ˈʌndə ˌgraʊnd/ **1** an underground railway. **2** a secret group or activity, esp. aiming to subvert the established order.

undergrowth /ˈʌndəˌgrəʊθ/ *n.* a dense growth of shrubs etc., esp. under large trees.

underhand *adj.* & *adv.* —*adj.* /ˈʌndəˌhænd/ **1** secret, clandestine, not above-board. **2** deceptive, crafty. **3** *Sport*, esp. *Cricket* underarm. —*adv.* /ˌʌndəˈhænd/ in an underhand manner. [OE (as UNDER-, HAND)]

underhanded /ˌʌndəˈhændɪd/ *adj.* & *adv.* = UNDERHAND.

underlay[1] *v.* & *n.* —*v.tr.* /ˌʌndəˈleɪ/ (*past* and *past part.* **-laid**) lay something under (a thing) to support or raise it. —*n.* /ˈʌndəˌleɪ/ a thing laid under another, esp. material laid under a carpet or mattress as protection or support. [OE *underlecgan* (as UNDER-, LAY[1])]

underlay[2] *past* of UNDERLIE.

underlie /ˌʌndəˈleɪ/ *v.tr.* (**-lying**; *past* **-lay**; *past part.* **-lain**) **1** (also *absol.*) lie or be situated under (a stratum etc.). **2** (also *absol.*) (esp. as **underlying** *adj.*) (of a principle, reason, etc.) be the basis of (a doctrine, law, conduct, etc.). **3** exist beneath the superficial aspect of. [OE *underlicgan* (as UNDER-, LIE[1])]

underline *v.* & *n.* —*v.tr.* /ˌʌndəˈlaɪn/ **1** draw a line under (a word etc.) to give emphasis or draw attention to or indicate italic or other special type. **2** emphasize, stress. —*n.* /ˈʌndəˌlaɪn/ **1** a line drawn under a word etc. **2** a caption below an illustration.

underling /ˈʌndəlɪŋ/ *n.* usu. *derog.* a subordinate.

underlying *pres. part.* of UNDERLIE.

undermanned /ˌʌndəˈmænd/ adj. having too few people as crew or staff.

undermentioned /ˌʌndəˈmenʃ(ə)nd, ˈʌn-/ adj. Brit. mentioned at a later place in a book etc.

undermine /ˌʌndəˈmaɪn/ v.tr. **1** injure (a person, reputation, influence, etc.) by secret or insidious means. **2** weaken, injure, or wear out (health etc.) imperceptibly or insidiously. **3** wear away the base or foundation of (*rivers undermine their banks*). **4** make a mine or excavation under. □ **underminer** n. **underminingly** adv. [ME f. UNDER- + MINE²]

underneath /ˌʌndəˈniːθ/ prep., adv., n., & adj. —prep. **1** at or to a lower place than, below. **2** on the inside of, within. —adv. **1** at or to a lower place. **2** inside. —n. the lower surface or part. —adj. lower. [OE *underneothan* (as UNDER + *neothan*: cf. BENEATH)]

undernourished /ˌʌndəˈnʌrɪʃt/ adj. insufficiently nourished. □ **undernourishment** n.

underpaid past and past part. of UNDERPAY.

underpants /ˈʌndəˌpænts/ n.pl. an undergarment, esp. men's, covering the lower part of the body and part of the legs.

under-part /ˈʌndəˌpɑːt/ n. **1** a lower part, esp. of an animal. **2** a subordinate part in a play etc.

underpass /ˈʌndəˌpɑːs/ n. **1** a road etc. passing under another. **2** a crossing of this form.

underpay /ˌʌndəˈpeɪ/ v.tr. (past and past part. **-paid**) pay too little to (a person) or for (a thing). □ **underpayment** n.

underpin /ˌʌndəˈpɪn/ v.tr. (**-pinned**, **-pinning**) **1** support from below with masonry etc. **2** support, strengthen.

underplay /ˌʌndəˈpleɪ/ v. **1** tr. play down the importance of. **2** intr. & tr. Theatr. **a** perform with deliberate restraint. **b** underact.

underpopulated /ˌʌndəˈpɒpjʊˈleɪtɪd/ adj. having an insufficient or very small population.

underprice /ˌʌndəˈpraɪs/ v.tr. price lower than what is usual or appropriate.

underprivileged /ˌʌndəˈprɪvɪlɪdʒd/ adj. **1** less privileged than others. **2** not enjoying the normal standard of living or rights in a society.

underproduction /ˌʌndəprəˈdʌkʃ(ə)n/ n. production of less than is usual or required.

underrate /ˌʌndəˈreɪt/ v.tr. have too low an opinion of.

underscore v. & n. —v.tr. /ˌʌndəˈskɔː(r)/ = UNDERLINE v. —n. /ˈʌndəˌskɔː(r)/ = UNDERLINE n. **1**.

undersea /ˈʌndəˌsiː/ adj. below the sea or the surface of the sea, submarine.

underseal /ˈʌndəˌsiːl/ v. & n. —v.tr. seal the under-part of (esp. a motor vehicle against rust etc.). —n. a protective coating for this.

under-secretary /ˌʌndəˈsekrətərɪ/ n. (pl. **-ies**) a subordinate official, esp. a junior minister or senior civil servant.

undersell /ˌʌndəˈsel/ v.tr. (past and past part. **-sold**) **1** sell at a lower price than (another seller). **2** sell at less than the true value.

undersexed /ˌʌndəˈsekst/ adj. having unusually weak sexual desires.

undershirt /ˈʌndəˌʃɜːt/ n. esp. US an undergarment worn under a shirt; a vest.

undershoot v. & n. —v.tr. /ˌʌndəˈʃuːt/ (past and past part. **-shot**) **1** (of an aircraft) land short of (a runway etc.). —n. /ˈʌndəˌʃuːt/ the act or an instance of undershooting.

undershorts /ˈʌndəˌʃɔːts/ n. US short underpants; trunks.

underside /ˈʌndəˌsaɪd/ n. the lower or under side or surface.

undersigned /ˈʌndəˌsaɪnd, -ˈsaɪnd/ adj. whose signature is appended (*we, the undersigned, wish to state . . .*).

undersized /ˈʌndəˌsaɪzd, -ˈsaɪzd/ adj. of less than the usual size.

underskirt /ˈʌndəˌskɜːt/ n. a skirt worn under another; a petticoat.

underslung /ˈʌndəˌslʌŋ/ adj. **1** supported from above. **2** (of a vehicle chassis) hanging lower than the axles.

undersold past and past part. of UNDERSELL.

underspend /ˌʌndəˈspend/ v. (past and past part. **-spent**) **1** tr. spend less than (a specified amount). **2** intr. & refl. spend too little.

understaffed /ˌʌndəˈstɑːft/ adj. having too few staff.

understand /ˌʌndəˈstænd/ v. (past and past part. **-stood** /-ˈstʊd/) **1** tr. perceive the meaning of (words, a person, a language, etc.) (*does not understand what you say; understood you perfectly; cannot understand French*). **2** tr. perceive the significance or explanation or cause of (*do not understand why he came; do not understand the point of his remark*). **3** tr. be sympathetically aware of the character or nature of, know how to deal with (*quite understand your difficulty; cannot understand him at all; could never understand algebra*). **4** tr. **a** (often foll. by *that* + clause) infer esp. from information received, take as implied, take for granted (*I understand that it begins at noon; I understand him to be a distant relation*). **b** (absol.) believe or assume from knowledge or inference (*he is coming tomorrow, I understand*). **5** tr. supply (a word) mentally (*the verb may be either expressed or understood*). **6** intr. have understanding (in general or in particular). □ **understand each other 1** know each other's views or feelings. **2** be in agreement or collusion. □ **understandable** adj. **understandably** adv. **understander** n. [OE *understandan* (as UNDER-, STAND)]

understanding /ˌʌndəˈstændɪŋ/ n. & adj. —n. **1 a** the ability to understand or think; intelligence. **b** the power of apprehension; the power of abstract thought. **2** an individual's perception or judgement of a situation etc. **3** an agreement; a thing agreed upon, esp. informally (*had an understanding with the rival company; consented only on this understanding*). **4** harmony in opinion or feeling (*disturbed the good understanding between them*). **5** sympathetic awareness or tolerance. —adj. **1** having understanding or insight or good judgement. **2** sympathetic to others' feelings. □ **understandingly** adv. [OE (as UNDERSTAND)]

understate /ˌʌndəˈsteɪt/ v.tr. **1** express in greatly or unduly restrained terms. **2** represent as being less than it actually is. □ **understatement** /ˌʌndəˈsteɪtmənt, ˈʌndə-/ n. **understater** n.

understeer /ˈʌndəˌstɪə(r)/ n. & v. —n. a tendency of a motor vehicle to turn less sharply than was intended. —v.intr. have such a tendency.

understood past and past part. of UNDERSTAND.

understorey /ˈʌndəˌstɔːrɪ/ n. (pl. **-eys**) **1** a layer of vegetation beneath the main canopy of a forest. **2** the plants forming this.

understudy /ˈʌndəˌstʌdɪ/ n. & v. esp. *Theatr.* —n. (pl. **-ies**) a person who studies another's role or duties in order to act at short notice in the absence of the other. —v.tr. (**-ies**, **-ied**) **1** study (a role etc.) as an understudy. **2** act as an understudy to (a person).

undersubscribed /ˌʌndəsəbˈskraɪbd/ adj. without sufficient subscribers, participants, etc.

undersurface /ˈʌndəˌsɜːfɪs/ n. the lower or under surface.

undertake /ˌʌndəˈteɪk/ v.tr. (*past* **-took**; *past part.* **-taken**) **1** bind oneself to perform, make oneself responsible for, engage in, enter upon (work, an enterprise, a responsibility). **2** (usu. foll. by *to* + infin.) accept an obligation, promise. **3** guarantee, affirm (*I will undertake that he has not heard a word*).

undertaker /ˈʌndəˌteɪkə(r)/ n. **1** a person whose business is to make arrangements for funerals. **2** /also -ˈteɪkə(r)/ a person who undertakes to do something.

undertaking /ˌʌndəˈteɪkɪŋ/ n. **1** work etc. undertaken, an enterprise (*a serious undertaking*). **2** a pledge or promise. **3** /ˈʌn-/ the management of funerals as a profession.

underthings /ˈʌndəθɪŋz/ n.pl. *colloq.* underclothes.

undertone /ˈʌndəˌtəʊn/ n. **1** a subdued tone of sound or colour. **2** an underlying quality. **3** an undercurrent of feeling.

undertook *past* of UNDERTAKE.

undertow /ˈʌndəˌtəʊ/ n. a current below the surface of the sea moving in the opposite direction to the surface current.

undervalue /ˌʌndəˈvæljuː/ v.tr. (**-values**, **-valued**, **-valuing**) **1** value insufficiently. **2** underestimate. □ **undervaluation** /-juːˈeɪʃ(ə)n/ n.

undervest /ˈʌndəˌvest/ n. *Brit.* an undergarment worn on the upper part of the body; a vest.

underwater /ˌʌndəˈwɔːtə(r)/ adj. & adv. —adj. situated or done under water. —adv. under water.

underwear /ˈʌndəˌweə(r)/ n. underclothes.

underweight adj. & n. —adj. /ˌʌndəˈweɪt/ weighing less than is normal or desirable. —n. /ˈʌndəˌweɪt/ insufficient weight.

underwent *past* of UNDERGO.

underwhelm /ˌʌndəˈwelm/ v.tr. *joc.* fail to impress. [after OVERWHELM]

underwood /ˈʌndəˌwʊd/ n. undergrowth.

underwork /ˌʌndəˈwɜːk/ v. **1** tr. impose too little work on. **2** intr. do too little work.

underworld /ˈʌndəˌwɜːld/ n. **1** the part of society comprising those who live by organized crime and immorality. **2** the mythical abode of the dead under the earth.

underwrite /ˌʌndəˈraɪt, ˈʌn-/ v. (*past* **-wrote**; *past part.* **-written**) **1 a** tr. sign, and accept liability under (an insurance policy, esp. on shipping etc.). **b** tr. accept (liability) in this way. **c** intr. practice (marine) insurance. **2** tr. undertake to finance or support. **3** tr. engage to buy all the stock in (a company etc.) not bought by the public. **4** tr. write below (*the underwritten names*). □ **underwriter** /ˈʌn-/ n.

undeserved /ˌʌndɪˈzɜːvd/ adj. not deserved (as reward or punishment).**undeservedly** /-vɪdlɪ/ adv.

undeserving /ˌʌndɪˈzɜːvɪŋ/ adj. not deserving. □ **undeservingly** adv.

undesigned /ˌʌndɪˈzaɪnd/ adj. unintentional. □ **undesignedly** /-nɪdlɪ/ adv.

undesirable /ˌʌndɪˈzaɪərəb(ə)l/ adj. & n. —adj. not desirable, objectionable, unpleasant. —n. an undesirable person. □ **undesirability** /-ˈbɪlɪtɪ/ n. **undesirableness** n. **undesirably** adv.

undesired /ˌʌndɪˈzaɪəd/ adj. not desired.

undesirous /ˌʌndɪˈzaɪərəs/ adj. not desirous.

undetectable /ˌʌndɪˈtektəb(ə)l/ adj. not detectable. □ **undetectability** /-ˈbɪlɪtɪ/ n. **undetectably** adv.

undetected /ˌʌndɪˈtektɪd/ adj. not detected.

undeterred /ˌʌndɪˈtɜːd/ adj. not deterred.

undeveloped /ˌʌndɪˈveləpt/ adj. not developed.

undiagnosed /ʌnˈdaɪəɡˌnəʊzd, ˌʌndaɪəɡˈnəʊzd/ adj. not diagnosed.

undid *past* of UNDO.

undies /ˈʌndɪz/ n.pl. *colloq.* (esp. women's) underclothes. [abbr.]

undifferentiated /ˌʌndɪfəˈrenʃɪˌeɪtɪd/ adj. not differentiated; amorphous.

undigested /ˌʌndɪˈdʒestɪd, ˌʌndaɪ-/ adj. **1** not digested. **2** (esp. of information, facts, etc.) not properly arranged or considered.

undignified /ʌnˈdɪɡnɪˌfaɪd/ adj. lacking dignity.

undiluted /ˌʌndaɪˈljuːtɪd/ adj. not diluted.

undiminished /ˌʌndɪˈmɪnɪʃt/ adj. not diminished or lessened.

undine /ˈʌndiːn/ n. a female water-spirit. [mod.L *undina* f. L *unda* wave]

undiplomatic /ˌʌndɪpləˈmætɪk/ adj. tactless. □ **undiplomatically** adv.

undischarged /ˌʌndɪsˈtʃɑːdʒd/ adj. (esp. of a bankrupt or a debt) not discharged.

undisciplined /ʌnˈdɪsɪplɪnd/ adj. lacking discipline; not disciplined.

undisclosed /ˌʌndɪsˈkləʊzd/ adj. not revealed or made known.

undiscoverable /ˌʌndɪsˈkʌvərəb(ə)l/ adj. that cannot be discovered.

undiscovered /ˌʌndɪsˈkʌvəd/ adj. not discovered.

undiscriminating /ˌʌndɪsˈkrɪmɪˌneɪtɪŋ/ adj. not showing good judgement.

undisguised /ˌʌndɪsˈɡaɪzd/ adj. not disguised. □ **undisguisedly** /-zɪdlɪ/ adv.

undisputed /ˌʌndɪˈspjuːtɪd/ adj. not disputed or called in question.

undissolved /ˌʌndɪˈzɒlvd/ adj. not dissolved.

undistinguished /ˌʌndɪˈstɪŋɡwɪʃt/ adj. not distinguished; mediocre.

undisturbed /ˌʌndɪˈstɜːbd/ adj. not disturbed or interfered with.

undivided /ˌʌndɪˈvaɪdɪd/ adj. not divided or shared; whole, entire (*gave him my undivided attention*).

undo /ʌnˈduː/ v.tr. (*3rd sing. present* **-does**; *past* **-did**; *past part.* **-done**) **1 a** unfasten or untie (a coat, button, parcel, etc.). **b** unfasten the clothing of (a person). **2** annul, cancel (*cannot undo the past*). **3** ruin the prospects, reputation, or morals of. [OE *undōn* (as UN-², DO¹)]

undocumented /ʌnˈdɒkjʊˌmentɪd/ adj. **1** *US* not having the appropriate document. **2** not proved by or recorded in documents.

undoing /ʌnˈduːɪŋ/ n. **1** ruin or a cause of ruin. **2** the process of reversing what has been done. **3** the action of opening or unfastening.

undomesticated /ˌʌndə'mestɪˌkeɪtɪd/ adj. not domesticated.

undone /ʌn'dʌn/ adj. **1** not done; incomplete (left the job undone). **2** not fastened (left the buttons undone). **3** archaic ruined.

undoubted /ʌn'daʊtɪd/ adj. certain, not questioned, not regarded as doubtful. □ **undoubtedly** adv.

undraped /ʌn'dreɪpt/ adj. **1** not covered with drapery. **2** naked.

undreamed /ʌn'driːmd, ʌn'dremt/ adj. (also **undreamt** /ʌn'dremt/) (often foll. by of) not dreamed or thought of or imagined.

undress /ʌn'dres/ v. & n. —v. **1** intr. take off one's clothes. **2** tr. take the clothes off (a person). —n. **1** ordinary dress as opposed to full dress or uniform. **2** casual or informal dress.

undressed /ʌn'drest/ adj. **1** not or no longer dressed; partly or wholly naked. **2** (of leather etc.) not treated. **3** (of food) not having a dressing.

undrinkable /ʌn'drɪŋkəb(ə)l/ adj. unfit for drinking.

undue /ʌn'djuː/ adj. **1** excessive, disproportionate. **2** not suitable. □ **unduly** adv.

undulate /'ʌndjʊˌleɪt/ v.intr. & tr. have or cause to have a wavy motion or look. [LL undulatus f. L unda wave]

undulation /ˌʌndjʊ'leɪʃ(ə)n/ n. **1** a wavy motion or form, a gentle rise and fall. **2** each wave of this. **3** a set of wavy lines.

undulatory /'ʌndjʊlətərɪ/ adj. **1** undulating, wavy. **2** of or due to undulation.

undutiful /ʌn'djuːtɪˌfʊl/ adj. not dutiful. □ **undutifully** adv. **undutifulness** n.

undyed /ʌn'daɪd/ adj. not dyed.

undying /ʌn'daɪɪŋ/ adj. **1** immortal. **2** never-ending (undying love). □ **undyingly** adv.

unearned /ʌn'ɜːnd/ adj. not earned. □ **unearned income** income from interest payments etc. as opposed to salary, wages, or fees.

unearth /ʌn'ɜːθ/ v.tr. **1 a** discover by searching or in the course of digging or rummaging. **b** dig out of the earth. **2** drive (a fox etc.) from its earth.

unearthly /ʌn'ɜːθlɪ/ adj. **1** supernatural, mysterious. **2** colloq. absurdly early or inconvenient (an unearthly hour). **3** not earthly. □ **unearthliness** n.

unease /ʌn'iːz/ n. lack of ease, discomfort, distress.

uneasy /ʌn'iːzɪ/ adj. (**uneasier**, **uneasiest**) **1** disturbed or uncomfortable in mind or body (passed an uneasy night). **2** disturbing (had an uneasy suspicion). □ **uneasily** adv. **uneasiness** n.

uneatable /ʌn'iːtəb(ə)l/ adj. not able to be eaten, esp. because of its condition.

uneaten /ʌn'iːt(ə)n/ adj. not eaten; left undevoured.

uneconomic /ˌʌniːkə'nɒmɪk, ˌʌnek-/ adj. not economic; incapable of being profitably operated etc. □ **uneconomically** adv.

uneconomical /ˌʌniːkə'nɒmɪk(ə)l, ˌʌnek-/ adj. not economical; wasteful.

unedifying /ʌn'edɪˌfaɪɪŋ/ adj. not edifying, esp. uninstructive or degrading. □ **unedifyingly** adv.

unedited /ʌn'edɪtɪd/ adj. not edited.

uneducated /ʌn'edjʊˌkeɪtɪd/ adj. not educated. □ **uneducable** /-kəb(ə)l/ adj.

unelectable /ˌʌnɪ'lektəb(ə)l/ adj. (of a candidate, party, etc.) holding views likely to bring defeat at an election.

unemotional /ˌʌnɪ'məʊʃ(ə)l/ adj. not emotional; lacking emotion. □ **unemotionally** adv.

unemphatic /ˌʌnɪm'fætɪk/ adj. not emphatic. □ **unemphatically** adv.

unemployable /ˌʌnɪm'plɔɪəb(ə)l/ adj. & n. —adj. unfitted for paid employment. —n. an unemployable person. □ **unemployability** /-'bɪlɪtɪ/ n.

unemployed /ˌʌnɪm'plɔɪd/ adj. **1** not having paid employment; out of work. **2** not in use.

unemployment /ˌʌnɪm'plɔɪmənt/ n. **1** the state of being unemployed. **2** the condition or extent of this in a country or region etc. (the North has higher unemployment). □ **unemployment benefit** a payment made by the State or (in the US) a trade union to an unemployed person.

unencumbered /ˌʌnɪn'kʌmbəd/ adj. **1** (of an estate) not having any liabilities (e.g. a mortgage) on it. **2** having no encumbrance; free.

unending /ʌn'endɪŋ/ adj. having or apparently having no end. □ **unendingly** adv. **unendingness** n.

unendurable /ˌʌnɪn'djʊərəb(ə)l/ adj. that cannot be endured. □ **unendurably** adv.

unengaged /ˌʌnɪn'geɪdʒd/ adj. not engaged; uncommitted.

un-English /ʌn'ɪŋglɪʃ/ adj. **1** not characteristic of the English. **2** not English.

unenlightened /ˌʌnɪn'laɪt(ə)nd/ adj. not enlightened.

unenterprising /ʌn'entəˌpraɪzɪŋ/ adj. not enterprising.

unenthusiastic /ˌʌnɪnˌθjuːzɪ'æstɪk, ˌʌnɪnˌθuː-/ adj. not enthusiastic. □ **unenthusiastically** adv.

unenviable /ʌn'envɪəb(ə)l/ adj. not enviable. □ **unenviably** adv.

unenvied /ʌn'envɪd/ adj. not envied.

unequal /ʌn'iːkw(ə)l/ adj. **1** (often foll. by to) not equal. **2** of varying quality. **3** lacking equal advantage to both sides (an unequal bargain). □ **unequally** adv.

unequalled /ʌn'iːkw(ə)ld/ adj. superior to all others.

unequipped /ˌʌnɪ'kwɪpt/ adj. not equipped.

unequivocal /ˌʌnɪ'kwɪvək(ə)l/ adj. not ambiguous, plain, unmistakable. □ **unequivocally** adv. **unequivocalness** n.

unerring /ʌn'ɜːrɪŋ/ adj. not erring, failing, or missing the mark; true, certain. □ **unerringly** adv. **unerringness** n.

UNESCO /juː'neskəʊ/ abbr. (also **Unesco**) United Nations Educational, Scientific, and Cultural Organization.

unessential /ˌʌnɪ'senʃ(ə)l/ adj. & n. —adj. **1** not essential (cf. INESSENTIAL). **2** not of the first importance. —n. an unessential part or thing.

unestablished /ˌʌnɪ'stæblɪʃt/ adj. not established.

unethical /ʌn'eθɪk(ə)l/ adj. not ethical, esp. unscrupulous in business or professional conduct. □ **unethically** adv.

uneven /ʌn'iːv(ə)n/ adj. **1** not level or smooth. **2** not uniform or equable. **3** (of a contest) unequal. □ **unevenly** adv. **unevenness** n. [OE unefen (as UN-[1], EVEN[1])]

uneventful /ˌʌnɪ'ventfʊl/ adj. not eventful. □ **uneventfully** adv. **uneventfulness** n.

unexamined /ˌʌnɪgˈzæmɪnd/ adj. not examined.

unexceptionable /ˌʌnɪkˈsepʃənəb(ə)l/ adj. with which no fault can be found; entirely satisfactory. □ **unexceptionableness** n. **unexceptionably** adv.

unexceptional /ˌʌnɪkˈsepʃən(ə)l/ adj. not out of the ordinary; usual, normal. □ **unexceptionally** adv.

unexcitable /ˌʌnɪkˈsaɪtəb(ə)l/ adj. not easily excited. □ **unexcitability** /-ˈbɪlɪtɪ/ n.

unexciting /ˌʌnɪkˈsaɪtɪŋ/ adj. not exciting; dull.

unexpected /ˌʌnɪkˈspektɪd/ adj. not expected; surprising. □ **unexpectedly** adv. **unexpectedness** n.

unexpired /ˌʌnɪkˈspaɪəd/ adj. that has not yet expired.

unexplained /ˌʌnɪkˈspleɪnd/ adj. not explained.

unexplored /ˌʌnɪkˈsplɔːd/ adj. not explored.

unexposed /ˌʌnɪkˈspəʊzd/ adj. not exposed.

unexpressed /ˌʌnɪkˈsprest/ adj. not expressed or made known (*unexpressed fears*).

unexpurgated /ʌnˈekspəˌgeɪtɪd/ adj. (esp. of a text etc.) not expurgated; complete.

unfading /ʌnˈfeɪdɪŋ/ adj. that never fades. □ **unfadingly** adv.

unfailing /ʌnˈfeɪlɪŋ/ adj. **1** not failing. **2** not running short. **3** constant. **4** reliable. □ **unfailingly** adv. **unfailingness** n.

unfair /ʌnˈfeə(r)/ adj. **1** not equitable or honest (*obtained by unfair means*). **2** not impartial or according to the rules (*unfair play*). □ **unfairly** adv. **unfairness** n. [OE *unfæger* (as UN-¹, FAIR¹)]

unfaithful /ʌnˈfeɪθfʊl/ adj. **1** not faithful, esp. adulterous. **2** not loyal. **3** treacherous. □ **unfaithfully** adv. **unfaithfulness** n.

unfamiliar /ˌʌnfəˈmɪljə(r)/ adj. not familiar. □ **unfamiliarity** /-lɪˈærɪtɪ/ n.

unfashionable /ʌnˈfæʃənəb(ə)l/ adj. not fashionable. □ **unfashionableness** n. **unfashionably** adv.

unfasten /ʌnˈfɑːs(ə)n/ v. **1** tr. & intr. make or become loose. **2** tr. open the fastening(s) of. **3** tr. detach.

unfastened /ʌnˈfɑːs(ə)nd/ adj. **1** that has not been fastened. **2** that has been loosened, opened, or detached.

unfatherly /ʌnˈfɑːðəlɪ/ adj. not befitting a father. □ **unfatherliness** n.

unfathomable /ʌnˈfæðəməb(ə)l/ adj. incapable of being fathomed. □ **unfathomableness** n. **unfathomably** adv.

unfavourable /ʌnˈfeɪvərəb(ə)l/ adj. (US **unfavorable**) not favourable; adverse, hostile. □ **unfavourableness** n. **unfavourably** adv.

unfavourite /ʌnˈfeɪvərɪt/ adj. (US **unfavorite**) colloq. least favourite; most disliked.

unfazed /ʌnˈfeɪzd/ adj. colloq. untroubled; not disconcerted.

unfed /ʌnˈfed/ adj. not fed.

unfeeling /ʌnˈfiːlɪŋ/ adj. **1** unsympathetic, harsh, not caring about others' feelings. **2** lacking sensation or sensitivity. □ **unfeelingly** adv. **unfeelingness** n. [OE *unfelende* (as UN-¹, FEELING)]

unfeigned /ʌnˈfeɪnd/ adj. genuine, sincere. □ **unfeignedly** adv.

unfeminine /ʌnˈfemɪnɪn/ adj. not in accordance with, or appropriate to, female character. □ **unfemininity** /-ˈnɪnɪtɪ/ n.

unfenced /ʌnˈfenst/ adj. **1** not provided with fences. **2** unprotected.

unfertilized /ʌnˈfɜːtɪˌlaɪzd/ adj. (also **unfertilised**) not fertilized.

unfettered /ʌnˈfetəd/ adj. unrestrained, unrestricted.

unfilled /ʌnˈfɪld/ adj. not filled.

unfinished /ʌnˈfɪnɪʃt/ adj. not finished; incomplete.

unfit /ʌnˈfɪt/ adj. & v. —adj. (often foll. by for, or to + infin.) not fit. —v.tr. (**unfitted, unfitting**) (usu. foll. by for) make unsuitable. □ **unfitly** adv. **unfitness** n.

unfitted /ʌnˈfɪtɪd/ adj. **1** not fit. **2** not fitted or suited. **3** not provided with fittings.

unfitting /ʌnˈfɪtɪŋ/ adj. not fitting or suitable, unbecoming. □ **unfittingly** adv.

unfix /ʌnˈfɪks/ v.tr. **1** release or loosen from a fixed state. **2** detach.

unfixed /ʌnˈfɪkst/ adj. not fixed.

unflagging /ʌnˈflægɪŋ/ adj. tireless, persistent. □ **unflaggingly** adv.

unflappable /ʌnˈflæpəb(ə)l/ adj. colloq. imperturbable; remaining calm in a crisis. □ **unflappability** /-ˈbɪlɪtɪ/ n. **unflappably** adv.

unflattering /ʌnˈflætərɪŋ/ adj. not flattering. □ **unflatteringly** adv.

unfledged /ʌnˈfledʒd/ adj. **1** (of a person) inexperienced. **2** (of a bird) not yet fledged.

unflinching /ʌnˈflɪntʃɪŋ/ adj. not flinching. □ **unflinchingly** adv.

unfocused /ʌnˈfəʊkəst/ adj. (also **unfocussed**) not focused.

unfold /ʌnˈfəʊld/ v. **1** tr. open the fold or folds of, spread out. **2** tr. reveal (thoughts etc.). **3** intr. become opened out. **4** intr. develop. □ **unfoldment** n. US. [OE *unfealdan* (as UN-², FOLD³)]

unforced /ʌnˈfɔːst/ adj. **1** not produced by effort; easy, natural. **2** not compelled or constrained. □ **unforcedly** adv.

unforeseeable /ˌʌnfɔːˈsiːəb(ə)l/ adj. not foreseeable.

unforeseen /ˌʌnfɔːˈsiːn/ adj. not foreseen.

unforgettable /ˌʌnfəˈgetəb(ə)l/ adj. that cannot be forgotten; memorable, wonderful (*an unforgettable experience*). □ **unforgettably** adv.

unforgivable /ˌʌnfəˈgɪvəb(ə)l/ adj. that cannot be forgiven. □ **unforgivably** adv.

unforgiving /ˌʌnfəˈgɪvɪŋ/ adj. not forgiving. □ **unforgivingly** adv. **unforgivingness** n.

unforgotten /ˌʌnfəˈgɒt(ə)n/ adj. not forgotten.

unformed /ʌnˈfɔːmd/ adj. **1** not formed. **2** shapeless. **3** not developed.

unforthcoming /ˌʌnfɔːθˈkʌmɪŋ/ adj. not forthcoming.

unfortified /ʌnˈfɔːtɪˌfaɪd/ adj. not fortified.

unfortunate /ʌnˈfɔːtjʊnət, -tʃənət/ adj. & n. —adj. **1** having bad fortune; unlucky. **2** unhappy. **3** regrettable. **4** disastrous. —n. an unfortunate person.

unfortunately /ʌnˈfɔːtjʊnətlɪ, -tʃənətlɪ/ adv. **1** (qualifying a whole sentence) it is unfortunate that. **2** in an unfortunate manner.

unfounded /ʌnˈfaʊndɪd/ adj. having no foundation (*unfounded hopes; unfounded rumour*). □ **unfoundedly** adv. **unfoundedness** n.

unfreeze /ʌnˈfriːz/ v. (*past* **unfroze**; *past part.* **unfrozen**) **1** tr. cause to thaw. **2** intr. thaw. **3** tr. remove restrictions from, make (assets, credits, etc.) realizable.

unfriendly /ʌnˈfrendlɪ/ adj. (**unfriendlier, unfriendliest**) not friendly. □ **unfriendliness** n.

unfrock /ʌnˈfrɒk/ v.tr. = DEFROCK.

unfroze past of UNFREEZE.

unfrozen past part. of UNFREEZE.

unfruitful /ʌnˈfruːtfʊl/ adj. **1** not producing good results, unprofitable. **2** not producing fruit or crops. □ **unfruitfully** adv. **unfruitfulness** n.

unfulfilled /ˌʌnfʊlˈfɪld/ adj. not fulfilled. □ **unfulfillable** adj.

unfunny /ʌnˈfʌnɪ/ adj. (**unfunnier, unfunniest**) not amusing (though meant to be). □ **unfunnily** adv. **unfunniness** n.

unfurl /ʌnˈfɜːl/ v. **1** tr. spread out (a sail, umbrella, etc.). **2** intr. become spread out.

unfurnished /ʌnˈfɜːnɪʃt/ adj. **1** (usu. foll. by with) not supplied. **2** without furniture.

ungainly /ʌnˈɡeɪnlɪ/ adj. (of a person, animal, or movement) awkward, clumsy. □ **ungainliness** n. [UN-¹ + obs. gainly graceful ult. f. ON gegn straight]

ungallant /ʌnˈɡælənt/ adj. not gallant. □ **ungallantly** adv.

ungenerous /ʌnˈdʒenərəs/ adj. not generous; mean. □ **ungenerously** adv. **ungenerousness** n.

ungentlemanly /ʌnˈdʒentəlmənlɪ/ adj. not gentlemanly. □ **ungentlemanliness** n.

unget-at-able /ˌʌnɡetˈætəb(ə)l/ adj. colloq. inaccessible.

ungird /ʌnˈɡɜːd/ v.tr. **1** release the girdle, belt, or girth of. **2** release or take off by undoing a belt or girth.

unglazed /ʌnˈɡleɪzd/ adj. not glazed.

ungloved /ʌnˈɡlʌvd/ adj. not wearing a glove or gloves.

ungodly /ʌnˈɡɒdlɪ/ adj. **1** impious, wicked. **2** colloq. outrageous (an ungodly hour to arrive). □ **ungodliness** n.

ungovernable /ʌnˈɡʌvənəb(ə)l/ adj. uncontrollable, violent. □ **ungovernability** /-ˈbɪlɪtɪ/ n. **ungovernably** adv.

ungraceful /ʌnˈɡreɪsfʊl/ adj. not graceful. □ **ungracefully** adv. **ungracefulness** n.

ungracious /ʌnˈɡreɪʃəs/ adj. **1** not kindly or courteous; unkind. **2** unattractive. □ **ungraciously** adv. **ungraciousness** n.

ungrammatical /ˌʌnɡrəˈmætɪk(ə)l/ adj. contrary to the rules of grammar. □ **ungrammaticality** /-ˈkælɪtɪ/ n. **ungrammatically** adv. **ungrammaticalness** n.

ungrateful /ʌnˈɡreɪtfʊl/ adj. **1** not feeling or showing gratitude. **2** not pleasant or acceptable. □ **ungratefully** adv. **ungratefulness** n.

ungrounded /ʌnˈɡraʊndɪd/ adj. **1** having no basis or justification; unfounded. **2** (foll. by in a subject) not properly instructed.

ungrudging /ʌnˈɡrʌdʒɪŋ/ adj. not grudging. □ **ungrudgingly** adv.

unguarded /ʌnˈɡɑːdɪd/ adj. **1** incautious, thoughtless (an unguarded remark). **2** not guarded; without a guard. □ **unguardedly** adv. **unguardedness** n.

unguent /ˈʌnɡwənt/ n. a soft substance used as ointment or for lubrication. [L unguentum f. unguere anoint]

ungulate /ˈʌnɡjʊlət, -ˌleɪt/ adj. & n. —adj. hoofed. —n. a hoofed mammal. [LL ungulatus f. ungula hoof, dimin. of unguis nail, claw]

unhallowed /ʌnˈhæləʊd/ adj. **1** not consecrated. **2** not sacred; unholy, wicked.

unhampered /ʌnˈhæmpəd/ adj. not hampered.

unhand /ʌnˈhænd/ v.tr. rhet. or joc. **1** take one's hands off (a person). **2** release from one's grasp.

unhandy /ʌnˈhændɪ/ adj. **1** not easy to handle or manage; awkward. **2** not skilful in using the hands. □ **unhandily** adv. **unhandiness** n.

unhappy /ʌnˈhæpɪ/ adj. (**unhappier, unhappiest**) **1** not happy, miserable. **2** unsuccessful, unfortunate. **3** causing misfortune. **4** disastrous. **5** inauspicious. □ **unhappily** adv. **unhappiness** n.

unharmed /ʌnˈhɑːmd/ adj. not harmed.

unharness /ʌnˈhɑːnɪs/ v.tr. remove a harness from.

unhatched /ʌnˈhætʃt/ adj. (of an egg etc.) not hatched.

unhealthy /ʌnˈhelθɪ/ adj. (**unhealthier, unhealthiest**) **1** not in good health. **2 a** (of a place etc.) harmful to health. **b** unwholesome. **c** sl. dangerous to life. □ **unhealthily** adv. **unhealthiness** n.

unheard /ʌnˈhɜːd/ adj. **1** not heard. **2** (usu. **unheard-of**) unprecedented, unknown.

unheated /ʌnˈhiːtɪd/ adj. not heated.

unheeded /ʌnˈhiːdɪd/ adj. not heeded; disregarded.

unheeding /ʌnˈhiːdɪŋ/ adj. not giving heed; heedless. □ **unheedingly** adv.

unhelpful /ʌnˈhelpfʊl/ adj. not helpful. □ **unhelpfully** adv. **unhelpfulness** n.

unheralded /ʌnˈherəldɪd/ adj. not heralded; unannounced.

unheroic /ʌnhɪˈrəʊɪk/ adj. not heroic. □ **unheroically** adv.

unhesitating /ʌnˈhezɪˌteɪtɪŋ/ adj. without hesitation. □ **unhesitatingly** adv. **unhesitatingness** n.

unhindered /ʌnˈhɪndəd/ adj. not hindered.

unhinge /ʌnˈhɪndʒ/ v.tr. **1** take (a door etc.) off its hinges. **2** (esp. as **unhinged** adj.) unsettle or disorder (a person's mind etc.), make (a person) crazy.

unhistorical /ˌʌnhɪˈstɒrɪk(ə)l/ adj. not historical. □ **unhistorically** adv.

unhitch /ʌnˈhɪtʃ/ v.tr. **1** release from a hitched state. **2** unhook, unfasten.

unholy /ʌnˈhəʊlɪ/ adj. (**unholier, unholiest**) **1** impious, profane, wicked. **2** colloq. dreadful, outrageous (made an unholy row about it). **3** not holy. □ **unholiness** n. [OE unhālig (as UN-¹, HOLY)]

unhook /ʌnˈhʊk/ v.tr. **1** remove from a hook or hooks. **2** unfasten by releasing a hook or hooks.

unhoped /ʌnˈhəʊpt/ adj. (foll. by for) not hoped for or expected.

unhorse /ʌnˈhɔːs/ v.tr. **1** throw or drag from a horse. **2** (of a horse) throw (a rider). **3** dislodge, overthrow.

unhouse /ʌnˈhaʊz/ v.tr. deprive of shelter; turn out of a house.

unhuman /ʌnˈhjuːmən/ adj. **1** not human. **2** superhuman. **3** inhuman, brutal.

unhung /ʌnˈhʌŋ/ adj. **1** not (yet) executed by hanging. **2** not hung up (for exhibition).

unhurried /ʌnˈhʌrɪd/ adj. not hurried. □ **unhurriedly** adv.

unhurt /ʌnˈhɜːt/ *adj.* not hurt.

unhygienic /ˌʌnhaɪˈdʒiːnɪk/ *adj.* not hygienic. □ **unhygienically** *adv.*

unhyphenated /ʌnˈhaɪfəˌneɪtɪd/ *adj.* not hyphenated.

uni /ˈjuːnɪ/ *n.* (pl. **unis**) esp. *Austral.* & *NZ colloq.* a university. [abbr.]

uni- /ˈjuːnɪ/ *comb. form* one; having or consisting of one. [L f. *unus* one]

Uniat /ˈjuːnɪˌæt, -ɪət/ *adj.* & *n.* (also **Uniate** /-ˌeɪt/) —*adj.* of or relating to any community of Christians in E. Europe or the Near East that acknowledges papal supremacy but retains its own liturgy etc. —*n.* a member of such a community. [Russ. *uniyat* f. *uniya* f. L *unio* UNION]

unicameral /ˌjuːnɪˈkæmər(ə)l/ *adj.* with a single legislative chamber.

UNICEF /ˈjuːnɪˌsef/ *abbr.* United Nations Children's (orig. International Children's Emergency) Fund.

unicellular /ˌjuːnɪˈseljʊlə(r)/ *adj.* (of an organism, organ, tissue, etc.) consisting of a single cell.

unicorn /ˈjuːnɪˌkɔːn/ *n.* a fabulous animal with a horse's body and a single straight horn. [ME f. OF *unicorne* f. L *unicornis* f. UNI- + *cornu* horn, transl. Gk *monocerōs*]

unicycle /ˈjuːnɪˌsaɪk(ə)l/ *n.* a single-wheeled cycle, esp. as used by acrobats. □ **unicyclist** *n.*

unideal /ˌʌnaɪˈdɪəl/ *adj.* not ideal.

unidentifiable /ˌʌnaɪˈdentɪˌfaɪəb(ə)l/ *adj.* unable to be identified.

unidentified /ˌʌnaɪˈdentɪˌfaɪd/ *adj.* not identified.

unidirectional /ˌjuːnɪdɪˈrekʃən(ə)l, ˌjuːnɪdaɪ-/ *adj.* having only one direction of motion, operation, etc. □ **unidirectionality** /-ˈnælɪtɪ/ *n.* **unidirectionally** *adv.*

unification /ˌjuːnɪfɪˈkeɪʃ(ə)n/ *n.* the act or an instance of unifying; the state of being unified. □ **Unification Church** a religious organization founded in 1954 in Korea by Sun Myung Moon (cf. MOONIE). □ **unificatory** *adj.*

uniform /ˈjuːnɪˌfɔːm/ *adj.*, *n.*, & *v.* —*adj.* **1** not changing in form or character; the same, unvarying (*present a uniform appearance*; *all of uniform size and shape*). **2** conforming to the same standard, rules, or pattern. —*n.* uniform distinctive clothing worn by members of the same body, e.g. by soldiers, police, and schoolchildren. —*v.tr.* clothe in uniform (*a uniformed officer*). □ **uniformly** *adv.* [F *uniforme* or L *uniformis* (as UNI-, FORM)]

uniformity /ˌjuːnɪˈfɔːmɪtɪ/ *n.* (pl. **-ies**) **1** being uniform; sameness, consistency. **2** an instance of this. □ [ME f. OF *uniformité* or LL *uniformitas* (as UNIFORM)]

unify /ˈjuːnɪˌfaɪ/ *v.tr.* (also *absol.*) (**-ies**, **-ied**) reduce to unity or uniformity. □ **unifier** *n.* [F *unifier* or LL *unificare* (as UNI-, -FY)]

unilateral /ˌjuːnɪˈlætər(ə)l/ *adj.* **1** performed by or affecting only one person or party (*unilateral disarmament*; *unilateral declaration of independence*). **2** one-sided. □ **unilaterally** *adv.*

unilateralism /ˌjuːnɪˈlætərəˌlɪz(ə)m/ *n.* **1** unilateral disarmament. **2** US the pursuit of a foreign policy without allies. □ **unilateralist** *n.* & *adj.*

unilluminated /ˌʌnɪˈluːmɪˌneɪtɪd, ˌʌnɪˈljuː-/ *adj.* not illuminated.

unillustrated /ʌnˈɪləˌstreɪtɪd/ *adj.* (esp. of a book) without illustrations.

unimaginable /ˌʌnɪˈmædʒɪnəb(ə)l/ *adj.* impossible to imagine. □ **unimaginably** *adv.*

unimaginative /ˌʌnɪˈmædʒɪnətɪv/ *adj.* lacking imagination; stolid, dull. □ **unimaginatively** *adv.* **unimaginativeness** *n.*

unimpaired /ˌʌnɪmˈpeəd/ *adj.* not impaired.

unimpeachable /ˌʌnɪmˈpiːtʃəb(ə)l/ *adj.* giving no opportunity for censure; beyond reproach or question. □ **unimpeachably** *adv.*

unimpeded /ˌʌnɪmˈpiːdɪd/ *adj.* not impeded. □ **unimpededly** *adv.*

unimportance /ˌʌnɪmˈpɔːt(ə)ns/ *n.* lack of importance.

unimportant /ˌʌnɪmˈpɔːt(ə)nt/ *adj.* not important.

unimposing /ˌʌnɪmˈpəʊzɪŋ/ *adj.* unimpressive. □ **unimposingly** *adv.*

unimpressed /ˌʌnɪmˈprest/ *adj.* not impressed.

unimpressionable /ˌʌnɪmˈpreʃənəb(ə)l/ *adj.* not impressionable.

unimpressive /ˌʌnɪmˈpresɪv/ *adj.* not impressive. □ **unimpressively** *adv.* **unimpressiveness** *n.*

uninflammable /ˌʌnɪnˈflæməb(ə)l/ *adj.* not inflammable.

uninflected /ˌʌnɪnˈflektɪd/ *adj. Gram.* (of a language) not having inflections.

uninfluenced /ʌnˈɪnflʊənst/ *adj.* (often foll. by *by*) not influenced.

uninfluential /ˌʌnɪnflʊˈenʃ(ə)l/ *adj.* having little or no influence.

uninformative /ˌʌnɪnˈfɔːmətɪv/ *adj.* not informative; giving little information.

uninformed /ˌʌnɪnˈfɔːmd/ *adj.* **1** not informed or instructed. **2** ignorant, uneducated.

uninhabitable /ˌʌnɪnˈhæbɪtəb(ə)l/ *adj.* that cannot be inhabited. □ **uninhabitableness** *n.*

uninhabited /ˌʌnɪnˈhæbɪtɪd/ *adj.* not inhabited.

uninhibited /ˌʌnɪnˈhɪbɪtɪd/ *adj.* not inhibited. □ **uninhibitedly** *adv.* **uninhibitedness** *n.*

uninitiated /ˌʌnɪˈnɪʃɪˌeɪtɪd/ *adj.* not initiated; not admitted or instructed.

uninjured /ʌnˈɪndʒəd/ *adj.* not injured.

uninspired /ˌʌnɪnˈspaɪəd/ *adj.* **1** not inspired. **2** (of oratory etc.) commonplace.

uninspiring /ˌʌnɪnˈspaɪərɪŋ/ *adj.* not inspiring. □ **uninspiringly** *adv.*

uninsurable /ˌʌnɪnˈʃʊərəb(ə)l/ *adj.* that cannot be insured.

uninsured /ˌʌnɪnˈʃʊəd/ *adj.* not insured.

unintelligent /ˌʌnɪnˈtelɪdʒ(ə)nt/ *adj.* not intelligent. □ **unintelligently** *adv.*

unintelligible /ˌʌnɪnˈtelɪdʒɪb(ə)l/ *adj.* not intelligible. □ **unintelligibility** /-ˈbɪlɪtɪ/ *n.* **unintelligibleness** *n.* **unintelligibly** *adv.*

unintended /ˌʌnɪnˈtendɪd/ *adj.* not intended.

unintentional /ˌʌnɪnˈtenʃən(ə)l/ *adj.* not intentional. □ **unintentionally** *adv.*

uninterested /ʌnˈɪntrəstɪd, -trɪstɪd/ *adj.* **1** not interested. **2** unconcerned, indifferent. □ **uninterestedly** *adv.* **uninterestedness** *n.*

uninteresting /ʌnˈɪntrəstɪŋ, -trɪstɪŋ/ *adj.* not interesting. □ **uninterestingly** *adv.* **uninterestingness** *n.*

uninterrupted /ˌʌnɪntəˈrʌptɪd/ *adj.* not interrupted. □ **uninterruptedly** *adv.* **uninterruptedness** *n.*

uninvited /ˌʌnɪnˈvaɪtɪd/ *adj.* not invited. □ **uninvitedly** *adv.*

uninviting /ˌʌnɪnˈvaɪtɪŋ/ *adj.* not inviting, unattractive, repellent. □ **uninvitingly** *adv.*

uninvolved /ˌʌnɪnˈvɒlvd/ *adj.* not involved.

union /ˈjuːnjən, -nɪən/ *n.* **1 a** the act or an instance of uniting; the state of being united. **b** (**the Union**) *hist.* the uniting of the English and Scottish crowns in 1603, of the English and Scottish parliaments in 1707, or of Great Britain and Ireland in 1801. **2 a** a whole resulting from the combination of parts or members. **b** a political unit formed in this way, esp. the US, the UK, or South Africa. **3** = *trade union.* **4** marriage, matrimony. **5** concord, agreement (*lived together in perfect union*). **6** (**Union**) **a** a general social club and debating society at some universities and colleges. **b** the buildings or accommodation of such a society. **7** *Math.* the totality of the members of two or more sets. **8** a fabric of mixed materials, e.g. cotton with linen or silk. □ **Union Jack** (or **flag**) the national ensign of the United Kingdom formed by the union of the crosses of St George, St Andrew, and St Patrick. **union suit** *US* a single undergarment for the body and legs; combinations. [ME f. OF *union* or eccl.L *unio* unity f. L *unus* one]

unionist /ˈjuːnjənɪst, ˈjuːnɪən-/ *n.* **1 a** a member of a trade union. **b** an advocate of trade unions. **2** (usu. **Unionist**) an advocate of union, esp. a person opposed to the rupture of the parliamentary union between Great Britain and Northern Ireland. □ **unionism** *n.* **unionistic** /-ˈnɪstɪk/ *adj.*

unionize /ˈjuːnjənaɪz, ˈjuːnɪən-/ *v.tr.* & *intr.* (also **-ise**) bring or come under trade-union organization or rules. □ **unionization** /-ˈzeɪʃ(ə)n/ *n.*

unique /juˈniːk, juːˈniːk/ *adj.* **1** of which there is only one; unequalled; having no like, equal, or parallel (*his position was unique*; *this vase is considered unique*). **2** *disp.* unusual, remarkable (*the most unique man I ever met*). □ **uniquely** *adv.* **uniqueness** *n.* [F f. L *unicus* f. *unus* one]

unironed /ʌnˈaɪənd/ *adj.* (esp. of clothing, linen, etc.) not ironed.

unisex /ˈjuːnɪˌseks/ *adj.* (of clothing, hairstyles, etc.) designed to be suitable for both sexes.

unison /ˈjuːnɪs(ə)n/ *n.* **1** *Mus.* **a** coincidence in pitch of sounds or notes. **b** this regarded as an interval. **2** *Mus.* a combination of voices or instruments at the same pitch or at pitches differing by one or more octaves (*sang in unison*). **3** agreement, concord (*acted in perfect unison*). **unisonant** /juˈnɪsənənt/ *adj.* **unisonous** /juˈnɪsənəs/ *adj.* [OF *unison* or LL *unisonus* (as UNI-, *sonus* SOUND¹)]

unit /ˈjuːnɪt/ *n.* **1 a** an individual thing, person, or group regarded as single and complete, esp. for purposes of calculation. **b** each of the (smallest) separate individuals or groups into which a complex whole may be analysed (*the family as the unit of society*). **2** a quantity chosen as a standard in terms of which other quantities may be expressed (*unit of heat*; *SI unit*). **3** *Brit.* the smallest share in a unit trust. **4** a device with a specified function forming part of a complex mechanism. **5** a piece of furniture for fitting with others like it or made of complementary parts. **6** a group with a special function in an organization. **7** a group of buildings, wards, etc.,

the cost of producing one item of manufacture. **unit trust** *Brit.* an investment company investing combined contributions from many persons in various securities and paying them dividends in proportion to their holdings. [L *unus*, prob. after DIGIT]

Unitarian /ˌjuːnɪˈteərɪən/ *n.* & *adj.* —*n.* **1** a person who believes that God is not a Trinity but one person. **2** a member of a religious body maintaining this and advocating freedom from formal dogma or doctrine. —*adj.* of or relating to the Unitarians. □ **Unitarianism** *n.* [mod.L *unitarius* f. L *unitas* UNITY]

unitary /ˈjuːnɪtəri/ *adj.* **1** of a unit or units. **2** marked by unity or uniformity. □ **unitarily** *adv.* **unitarity** /-ˈtærɪti/ *n.*

unite /juˈnaɪt, juː-/ *v.* **1** *tr.* & *intr.* join together; make or become one; combine. **2** *tr.* & *intr.* join together for a common purpose or action (*united in their struggle against injustice*). **3** *tr.* & *intr.* join in marriage. **4** *tr.* possess (qualities, features, etc.) in combination (*united anger with mercy*). □ **United Kingdom** Great Britain and Northern Ireland (until 1922, Great Britain and Ireland). **United Nations** a supranational peace-seeking organization of many States. **United Reformed Church** a Church formed in 1972 from the English Presbyterian and Congregational Churches. **United States** (in full **United States of America**) a federal republic of 50 States, mostly in N. America and including Alaska and Hawaii. □ **unitedly** *adv.* **unitive** /ˈjuːnɪtɪv/ *adj.* **unitively** /ˈjuːnɪtɪvli/ *adv.* [ME f. L *unire* *unit-* f. *unus* one]

unity /ˈjuːnɪti/ *n.* (*pl.* **-ies**) **1** oneness; being one, single, or individual; being formed of parts that constitute a whole; due interconnection and coherence of parts (*disturbs the unity of the idea*; *the pictures lack unity*; *national unity*). **2** harmony or concord between persons etc. (*lived together in unity*). **3** a thing forming a complex whole (*a person regarded as a unity*). **4** *Math.* the number 'one', the factor that leaves unchanged the quantity on which it operates. [ME f. OF *unité* f. L *unitas -tatis* f. *unus* one]

universal /ˌjuːnɪˈvɜːs(ə)l/ *adj.* & *n.* —*adj.* of, belonging to, or done etc. by all persons or things in the world or in the class concerned; applicable to all cases (*the feeling was universal*; *met with universal approval*). —*n.* a term or concept of general application. □ **universal coupling** (or **joint**) a coupling or joint which can transmit rotary power by a shaft at any selected angle. **universal language** an artificial language intended for use by all nations. **universal suffrage** a suffrage extending to all adults with minor exceptions. □ **universality** /-ˈsælɪti/ *n.* **universalize** *v.tr.* (also **-ise**). **universalization** /-ˈzeɪʃ(ə)n/ *n.* **universally** *adv.* [ME f. OF *universal* or L *universalis* (as UNIVERSE)]

universe /ˈjuːnɪˌvɜːs/ *n.* **1** all existing things; the whole creation; the cosmos. **2** all mankind. [F *univers* f. L *universum* neut. of *universus* combined into one, whole f. UNI- + *versus* past part. of *vertere* turn]

university /ˌjuːnɪˈvɜːsɪti/ *n.* (*pl.* **-ies**) **1** an educational institution designed for instruction, examination, or both, of students in many branches of advanced learning, conferring degrees in various faculties, and often embody-

members of this collectively. □ **at university** studying at a university. [ME f. OF *université* f. L *universitas -tatis* the whole (world), in LL college, guild (as UNIVERSE)]

unjust /ʌnˈdʒʌst/ *adj.* not just, contrary to justice or fairness. □ **unjustly** *adv.* **unjustness** *n.*

unjustifiable /ʌnˈdʒʌstɪˌfaɪəb(ə)l/ *adj.* not justifiable. □ **unjustifiably** *adv.*

unjustified /ʌnˈdʒʌstɪˌfaɪd/ *adj.* not justified.

unkempt /ʌnˈkempt/ *adj.* **1** untidy, of neglected appearance. **2** uncombed, dishevelled. □ **unkemptly** *adv.* **unkemptness** *n.* [UN-¹ + archaic *kempt* past part. of *kemb* comb f. OE *cemban*]

unkept /ʌnˈkept/ *adj.* **1** (of a promise, law, etc.) not observed; disregarded. **2** not tended; neglected.

unkind /ʌnˈkaɪnd/ *adj.* **1** not kind. **2** harsh, cruel. **3** unpleasant. □ **unkindly** *adv.* **unkindness** *n.*

unknot /ʌnˈnɒt/ *v.tr.* (**unknotted, unknotting**) release the knot or knots of, untie.

unknowable /ʌnˈnəʊəb(ə)l/ *adj.* & *n.* —*adj.* that cannot be known. —*n.* an unknowable thing.

unknowing /ʌnˈnəʊɪŋ/ *adj.* & *n.* —*adj.* (often foll. by *of*) not knowing; ignorant, unconscious. —*n.* ignorance (*cloud of unknowing*). □ **unknowingly** *adv.* **unknowingness** *n.*

unknown /ʌnˈnəʊn/ *adj.* & *n.* —*adj.* (often foll. by *to*) not known, unfamiliar (*his purpose was unknown to me*). —*n.* **1** an unknown thing or person. **2** an unknown quantity (*equation in two unknowns*). □ **unknown quantity** a person or thing whose nature, significance, etc., cannot be determined. **Unknown Soldier** an unidentified representative member of a country's armed forces killed in war, given burial with special honours in a national memorial. **unknown to** without the knowledge of (*did it unknown to me*). **Unknown Warrior** = *Unknown Soldier*. □ **unknownness** *n.*

unlabelled /ʌnˈleɪb(ə)ld/ *adj.* (US **unlabeled**) not labelled; without a label.

unlace /ʌnˈleɪs/ *v.tr.* **1** undo the lace or laces of. **2** unfasten or loosen in this way.

unladen /ʌnˈleɪd(ə)n/ *adj.* not laden. □ **unladen weight** the weight of a vehicle etc. when not loaded with goods etc.

unladylike /ʌnˈleɪdɪˌlaɪk/ *adj.* not ladylike.

unlamented /ˌʌnləˈmentɪd/ *adj.* not lamented.

unlatch /ʌnˈlætʃ/ *v.* **1** *tr.* release the latch of. **2** *tr.* & *intr.* open or be opened in this way.

unlawful /ʌnˈlɔːfʊl/ *adj.* not lawful; illegal, not permissible. □ **unlawfully** *adv.* **unlawfulness** *n.*

unleaded /ʌnˈledɪd/ *adj.* **1** (of petrol etc.) without added lead. **2** not covered, weighted, or framed with lead. **3** *Printing* not spaced with leads.

unlearn /ʌnˈlɜːn/ *v.tr.* (*past* and *past part.* **unlearned** or **unlearnt**) **1** discard from one's memory. **2** rid oneself of (a habit, false information, etc.).

unlearned¹ /ʌnˈlɜːnɪd/ *adj.* not well educated; untaught, ignorant. □ **unlearnedly** *adv.*

unlearned² /ʌnˈlɜːnd/ *adj.* (also **unlearnt** /-ˈlɜːnt/) that has not been learnt.

unleash /ʌnˈliːʃ/ *v.tr.* **1** release from a leash or restraint. **2** set free to engage in pursuit or attack.

unleavened /ʌnˈlev(ə)nd/ *adj.* not leavened; made without yeast or other raising agent.

unless /ʌnˈles, ənˈles/ *conj.* if not; except when (*shall go unless I hear from you; always walked unless I had a bicycle*). [ON or IN + LESS, assim. to UN-¹]

unlettered /ʌnˈletəd/ *adj.* **1** illiterate. **2** not well educated.

unliberated /ʌnˈlɪbəˌreɪtɪd/ *adj.* not liberated.

unlicensed /ʌnˈlaɪs(ə)nst/ *adj.* not licensed, esp. without a licence to sell alcoholic drink.

unlighted /ʌnˈlaɪtɪd/ *adj.* **1** not provided with light. **2** not set burning.

unlike /ʌnˈlaɪk/ *adj.* & *prep.* —*adj.* **1** not like; different from (*is unlike both his parents*). **2** uncharacteristic of (*such behaviour is unlike him*). **3** dissimilar, different. —*prep.* differently from (*acts quite unlike anyone else*). □ **unlikeness** *n.* [perh. f. ON * úlíkr*, OE *ungelic*: see LIKE¹]

unlikeable /ʌnˈlaɪkəb(ə)l/ *adj.* (also **unlikable**) not easy to like; unpleasant.

unlikely /ʌnˈlaɪklɪ/ *adj.* (**unlikelier, unlikeliest**) **1** improbable (*unlikely tale*). **2** (foll. by to + infin.) not to be expected to do something (*he's unlikely to be available*). **3** unpromising (*an unlikely candidate*). □ **unlikelihood** *n.* **unlikeliness** *n.*

unlimited /ʌnˈlɪmɪtɪd/ *adj.* without limit; unrestricted; very great in number or quantity (*has unlimited possibilities; an unlimited expanse of sea*). □ **unlimitedly** *adv.* **unlimitedness** *n.*

unlined¹ /ʌnˈlaɪnd/ *adj.* **1** (of paper etc.) without lines. **2** (of a face etc.) without wrinkles.

unlined² /ʌnˈlaɪnd/ *adj.* (of a garment etc.) without lining.

unlisted /ʌnˈlɪstɪd/ *adj.* not included in a published list, esp. of Stock Exchange prices or of telephone numbers.

unlit /ʌnˈlɪt/ *adj.* not lit.

unlivable /ʌnˈlɪvəb(ə)l/ *adj.* that cannot be lived or lived in.

unlived-in /ʌnˈlɪvdɪn/ *adj.* **1** appearing to be uninhabited. **2** unused by the inhabitants.

unload /ʌnˈləʊd/ *v.tr.* **1** (also *absol.*) remove a load from (a vehicle etc.). **2** remove (a load) from a vehicle etc. **3** remove the charge from (a firearm etc.). **4** *colloq.* get rid of. **5** (often foll. by *on*) *colloq.* **a** divulge (information). **b** (also *absol.*) give vent to (feelings). □ **unloader** *n.*

unlock /ʌnˈlɒk/ *v.tr.* **1 a** release the lock of (a door, box, etc.). **b** release or disclose by unlocking. **2** release thoughts, feelings, etc., from (one's mind etc.).

unlocked /ʌnˈlɒkt/ *adj.* not locked.

unlooked-for /ʌnˈlʊktfɔː(r)/ *adj.* unexpected, unforeseen.

unloose /ʌnˈluːs/ *v.tr.* (also **unloosen**) loose; set free.

unlovable /ʌnˈlʌvəb(ə)l/ *adj.* not lovable.

unloved /ʌnˈlʌvd/ *adj.* not loved.

unlovely /ʌnˈlʌvlɪ/ *adj.* not attractive; unpleasant, ugly. □ **unloveliness** *n.*

unloving /ʌnˈlʌvɪŋ/ *adj.* not loving. □ **unlovingly** *adv.* **unlovingness** *n.*

unlucky /ʌnˈlʌkɪ/ *adj.* (**unluckier, unluckiest**) **1** not fortunate or successful. **2** wretched. **3** bringing bad luck. **4** ill-judged. □ **unluckily** *adv.* **unluckiness** *n.*

unmade /ʌnˈmeɪd/ *adj.* **1** not made. **2** destroyed, annulled.

unmake /ʌnˈmeɪk/ *v.tr.* (*past* and *past part.* **unmade**) undo the making of; destroy, depose, annul.

unman /ʌnˈmæn/ v.tr. (**unmanned, unmanning**) deprive of supposed manly qualities (e.g. self-control, courage); cause to weep etc., discourage.

unmanageable /ʌnˈmænɪdʒəb(ə)l/ adj. not (easily) managed, manipulated, or controlled. □ **unmanageableness** n. **unmanageably** adv.

unmanly /ʌnˈmænlɪ/ adj. not manly □ **unmanliness** n.

unmanned /ʌnˈmænd/ adj. 1 not manned. 2 overcome by emotion etc.

unmannerly /ʌnˈmænəlɪ/ adj. 1 without good manners. 2 (of actions, speech, etc.) showing a lack of good manners. □ **unmannerliness** n.

unmarked /ʌnˈmɑːkt/ adj. 1 not marked. 2 not noticed.

unmarried /ʌnˈmærɪd/ adj. not married; single.

unmask /ʌnˈmɑːsk/ v. 1 tr. **a** remove the mask from. **b** expose the true character of. 2 intr. remove one's mask. □ **unmasker** n.

unmatched /ʌnˈmætʃt/ adj. not matched or equalled.

unmeaning /ʌnˈmiːnɪŋ/ adj. having no meaning or significance; meaningless. □ **unmeaningly** adv. **unmeaningness** n.

unmeant /ʌnˈment/ adj. not meant or intended.

unmemorable /ʌnˈmem(ə)rəb(ə)l/ adj. not memorable. □ **unmemorably** adv.

unmentionable /ʌnˈmenʃ(ə)nəb(ə)l/ adj. & n. —adj. that cannot (properly) be mentioned. —n. 1 (in pl.) joc. undergarments. 2 a person or thing not to be mentioned. □ **unmentionability** /-ˈbɪlɪtɪ/ n. **unmentionableness** n. **unmentionably** adv.

unmerciful /ʌnˈmɜːsɪˌfʊl/ adj. merciless. □ **unmercifully** adv. **unmercifulness** n.

unmerited /ʌnˈmerɪtɪd/ adj. not merited.

unmet /ʌnˈmet/ adj. (of a quota, demand, goal, etc.) not achieved or fulfilled.

unmetalled /ʌnˈmet(ə)ld/ adj. Brit. (of a road etc.) not made with road-metal.

unmethodical /ˌʌnmɪˈθɒdɪk(ə)l/ adj. not methodical. □ **unmethodically** adv.

unmindful /ʌnˈmaɪndfʊl/ adj. (often foll. by of) not mindful. □ **unmindfully** adv. **unmindfulness** n.

unmissable /ʌnˈmɪsəb(ə)l/ adj. that cannot or should not be missed.

unmistakable /ˌʌnmɪˈsteɪkəb(ə)l/ adj. that cannot be mistaken or doubted, clear. □ **unmistakability** /-ˈbɪlɪtɪ/ n. **unmistakableness** n. **unmistakably** adv.

unmitigated /ʌnˈmɪtɪˌɡeɪtɪd/ adj. 1 not mitigated or modified. 2 absolute, unqualified (an unmitigated disaster). □ **unmitigatedly** adv.

unmixed /ʌnˈmɪkst/ adj. not mixed. □ **unmixed blessing** a thing having advantages and no disadvantages.

unmodified /ʌnˈmɒdɪˌfaɪd/ adj. not modified.

unmolested /ˌʌnməˈlestɪd/ adj. not molested.

unmoral /ʌnˈmɒr(ə)l/ adj. not concerned with morality (cf. IMMORAL). □ **unmorality** /ˌʌnməˈrælɪtɪ/ n. **unmorally** adv.

unmotherly /ʌnˈmʌðəlɪ/ adj. not motherly.

unmotivated /ʌnˈməʊtɪˌveɪtɪd/ adj. without motivation; without a motive.

unmounted /ʌnˈmaʊntɪd/ adj. not mounted.

unmourned /ʌnˈmɔːnd/ adj. not mourned.

unmoved /ʌnˈmuːvd/ adj. 1 not moved. 2 not changed in one's purpose. 3 not affected by

emotion. □ **unmovable** adj. (also **unmoveable**).

unmusical /ʌnˈmjuːzɪk(ə)l/ adj. 1 not pleasing to the ear. 2 unskilled in or indifferent to music. □ **unmusicality** /-ˈkælɪtɪ/ n. **unmusically** adv. **unmusicalness** n.

unmuzzle /ʌnˈmʌz(ə)l/ v.tr. 1 remove a muzzle from. 2 relieve of an obligation to remain silent.

unnameable /ʌnˈneɪməb(ə)l/ adj. that cannot be named, esp. too bad to be named.

unnamed /ʌnˈneɪmd/ adj. not named.

unnatural /ʌnˈnætʃər(ə)l/ adj. 1 contrary to nature or the usual course of nature; not normal. 2 **a** lacking natural feelings. **b** extremely cruel or wicked. 3 artificial. 4 affected. □ **unnaturally** adv. **unnaturalness** n.

unnecessary /ʌnˈnesəsərɪ/ adj. & n. —adj. 1 not necessary. 2 more than is necessary (with unnecessary care). —n. (pl. **-ies**) (usu. in pl.) an unnecessary thing. □ **unnecessarily** adv. **unnecessariness** n.

unneeded /ʌnˈniːdɪd/ adj. not needed.

unneighbourly /ʌnˈneɪbəlɪ/ adj. not neighbourly. □ **unneighbourliness** n.

unnerve /ʌnˈnɜːv/ v.tr. deprive of strength or resolution. □ **unnervingly** adv.

unnoticeable /ʌnˈnəʊtɪsəb(ə)l/ adj. not easily seen or noticed. □ **unnoticeably** adv.

unnoticed /ʌnˈnəʊtɪst/ adj. not noticed.

unnumbered /ʌnˈnʌmbəd/ adj. 1 not marked with a number. 2 not counted. 3 countless.

UNO /ˈjuːnəʊ/ abbr. United Nations Organization.

unobjectionable /ˌʌnəbˈdʒekʃənəb(ə)l/ adj. not objectionable; acceptable. □ **unobjectionableness** n. **unobjectionably** adv.

unobservant /ˌʌnəbˈzɜːv(ə)nt/ adj. not observant. □ **unobservantly** adv.

unobserved /ˌʌnəbˈzɜːvd/ adj. not observed. □ **unobservedly** /-vɪdlɪ/ adv.

unobstructed /ˌʌnəbˈstrʌktɪd/ adj. not obstructed.

unobtainable /ˌʌnəbˈteɪnəb(ə)l/ adj. that cannot be obtained.

unobtrusive /ˌʌnəbˈtruːsɪv/ adj. not making oneself or itself noticed. □ **unobtrusively** adv. **unobtrusiveness** n.

unoccupied /ʌnˈɒkjʊˌpaɪd/ adj. not occupied.

unoffending /ˌʌnəˈfendɪŋ/ adj. not offending; harmless, innocent. □ **unoffended** adj.

unofficial /ˌʌnəˈfɪʃ(ə)l/ adj. 1 not officially authorized or confirmed. 2 not characteristic of officials. □ **unofficial strike** a strike not formally approved by the strikers' trade union. □ **unofficially** adv.

unopened /ʌnˈəʊpənd/ adj. not opened.

unopposed /ˌʌnəˈpəʊzd/ adj. not opposed.

unorganized /ʌnˈɔːɡəˌnaɪzd/ adj. (also **-ised**) not organized (cf. DISORGANIZE).

unoriginal /ˌʌnəˈrɪdʒɪn(ə)l/ adj. lacking originality; derivative. □ **unoriginality** /-ˈnælɪtɪ/ n. **unoriginally** adv.

unorthodox /ʌnˈɔːθəˌdɒks/ adj. not orthodox. □ **unorthodoxly** adv. **unorthodoxy** n.

unostentatious /ˌʌnɒstenˈteɪʃəs/ adj. not ostentatious. □ **unostentatiously** adv. **unostentatiousness** n.

unpack /ʌnˈpæk/ v.tr. 1 (also absol.) open and remove the contents of (a package, luggage, etc.). 2 take (a thing) out from a package etc. □ **unpacker** n.

unpaged /ʌnˈpeɪdʒd/ *adj.* with pages not numbered.

unpaid /ʌnˈpeɪd/ *adj.* (of a debt or a person) not paid.

unpainted /ʌnˈpeɪntɪd/ *adj.* not painted.

unpaired /ʌnˈpeəd/ *adj.* **1** not arranged in pairs. **2** not forming one of a pair.

unpalatable /ʌnˈpælətəb(ə)l/ *adj.* **1** not pleasant to taste. **2** (of an idea, suggestion, etc.) disagreeable, distasteful. □ **unpalatability** /-ˈbɪlɪtɪ/ *n.* **unpalatableness** *n.*

unparalleled /ʌnˈpærəˌleld/ *adj.* having no parallel or equal.

unpardonable /ʌnˈpɑːdənəb(ə)l/ *adj.* that cannot be pardoned. □ **unpardonableness** *n.* **unpardonably** *adv.*

unparliamentary /ˌʌnpɑːləˈmentərɪ/ *adj.* contrary to proper parliamentary usage. □ **unparliamentary language** oaths or abuse.

unpasteurized /ʌnˈpɑːstjəˌraɪzd, -tʃəˌraɪzd, ʌnˈpæs-/ *adj.* not pasteurized.

unpatriotic /ˌʌnpætrɪˈɒtɪk, ˌʌnpeɪt-/ *adj.* not patriotic. □ **unpatriotically** *adv.*

unpaved /ʌnˈpeɪvd/ *adj.* not paved.

unpeeled /ʌnˈpiːld/ *adj.* not peeled.

unperceived /ˌʌnpəˈsiːvd/ *adj.* not perceived; unobserved.

unperceptive /ˌʌnpəˈseptɪv/ *adj.* not perceptive. □ **unperceptively** *adv.* **unperceptiveness** *n.*

unperforated /ʌnˈpɜːfəˌreɪtɪd/ *adj.* not perforated.

unperformed /ˌʌnpəˈfɔːmd/ *adj.* not performed.

unperfumed /ʌnˈpɜːfjuːmd/ *adj.* not perfumed.

unperson /ˈʌnˌpɜːs(ə)n/ *n.* a person whose name or existence is denied or ignored.

unpersuaded /ˌʌnpəˈsweɪdɪd/ *adj.* not persuaded.

unpersuasive /ˌʌnpəˈsweɪsɪv/ *adj.* not persuasive. □ **unpersuasively** *adv.*

unperturbed /ˌʌnpəˈtɜːbd/ *adj.* not perturbed. □ **unperturbedly** /-bɪdlɪ/ *adv.*

unpick /ʌnˈpɪk/ *v.tr.* undo the sewing of (stitches, a garment, etc.).

unpicked /ʌnˈpɪkt/ *adj.* **1** not selected. **2** (of a flower) not plucked.

unpin /ʌnˈpɪn/ *v.tr.* (**unpinned**, **unpinning**) unfasten or detach by removing a pin or pins.

unpitied /ʌnˈpɪtɪd/ *adj.* not pitied.

unplaceable /ʌnˈpleɪsəb(ə)l/ *adj.* that cannot be placed or classified (*his accent was unplaceable*).

unplaced /ʌnˈpleɪst/ *adj.* not placed, esp. not placed as one of the first three finishing in a race etc.

unplanned /ʌnˈplænd/ *adj.* not planned.

unplayable /ʌnˈpleɪəb(ə)l/ *adj.* **1** *Sport* (of a ball) that cannot be struck or returned. **2** that cannot be played. □ **unplayably** *adv.*

unpleasant /ʌnˈplez(ə)nt/ *adj.* not pleasant; displeasing; disagreeable. □ **unpleasantly** *adv.* **unpleasantness** *n.*

unpleasing /ʌnˈpliːzɪŋ/ *adj.* not pleasing. □ **unpleasingly** *adv.*

unplug /ʌnˈplʌɡ/ *v.tr.* (**unplugged**, **unplugging**) **1** disconnect (an electrical device) by removing its plug from the socket. **2** unstop.

unplumbed /ʌnˈplʌmd/ *adj.* **1** not plumbed. **2** not fully explored or understood. □ **unplumbable** *adj.*

unpointed /ʌnˈpɔɪntɪd/ *adj.* **1** having no point or points. **2 a** not punctuated. **b** (of written

Hebrew etc.) without vowel points. **3** (of masonry or brickwork) not pointed.

unpolished /ʌnˈpɒlɪʃt/ *adj.* **1** not polished; rough. **2** without refinement; crude.

unpolitical /ˌʌnpəˈlɪtɪk(ə)l/ *adj.* not concerned with politics. □ **unpolitically** *adv.*

unpolluted /ˌʌnpəˈluːtɪd/ *adj.* not polluted.

unpopular /ʌnˈpɒpjʊlə(r)/ *adj.* not popular; not liked by the public or by people in general. □ **unpopularity** /-ˈlærɪtɪ/ *n.* **unpopularly** *adv.*

unpopulated /ʌnˈpɒpjʊˌleɪtɪd/ *adj.* not populated.

unpractical /ʌnˈpræktɪk(ə)l/ *adj.* **1** not practical. **2** (of a person) not having practical skill. □ **unpracticality** /-ˈkælɪtɪ/ *n.* **unpractically** *adv.*

unpractised /ʌnˈpræktɪst/ *adj.* (US **unpracticed**) **1** not experienced or skilled. **2** not put into practice.

unprecedented /ʌnˈpresɪˌdentɪd/ *adj.* **1** having no precedent; unparalleled. **2** novel. □ **unprecedentedly** *adv.*

unpredictable /ˌʌnprɪˈdɪktəb(ə)l/ *adj.* that cannot be predicted. □ **unpredictability** /-ˈbɪlɪtɪ/ *n.* **unpredictableness** *n.* **unpredictably** *adv.*

unprejudiced /ʌnˈpredʒʊdɪst/ *adj.* not prejudiced.

unpremeditated /ˌʌnprɪˈmedɪˌteɪtɪd/ *adj.* not previously thought over, not deliberately planned, unintentional. □ **unpremeditatedly** *adv.*

unprepared /ˌʌnprɪˈpeəd/ *adj.* not prepared (in advance); not ready. □ **unpreparedly** *adv.* **unpreparedness** *n.*

unprepossessing /ˌʌnpriːpəˈzesɪŋ/ *adj.* not prepossessing; unattractive.

unpresentable /ˌʌnprɪˈzentəb(ə)l/ *adj.* not presentable.

unpressed /ʌnˈprest/ *adj.* not pressed, esp. (of clothing) unironed.

unpresuming /ˌʌnprɪˈzjuːmɪŋ/ *adj.* not presuming; modest.

unpretending /ˌʌnprɪˈtendɪŋ/ *adj.* unpretentious. □ **unpretendingly** *adv.* **unpretendingness** *n.*

unpretentious /ˌʌnprɪˈtenʃəs/ *adj.* not making a great display; simple, modest. □ **unpretentiously** *adv.* **unpretentiousness** *n.*

unpriced /ʌnˈpraɪst/ *adj.* not having a price or prices fixed, marked, or stated.

unprincipled /ʌnˈprɪnsɪp(ə)ld/ *adj.* lacking or not based on good moral principles. □ **unprincipledness** *n.*

unprintable /ʌnˈprɪntəb(ə)l/ *adj.* that cannot be printed, esp. because too indecent or libellous or blasphemous. □ **unprintably** *adv.*

unprinted /ʌnˈprɪntɪd/ *adj.* not printed.

unprivileged /ʌnˈprɪvɪlɪdʒd/ *adj.* not privileged.

unproblematic /ˌʌnprɒbləˈmætɪk/ *adj.* causing no difficulty. □ **unproblematically** *adv.*

unproductive /ˌʌnprəˈdʌktɪv/ *adj.* not productive. □ **unproductively** *adv.* **unproductiveness** *n.*

unprofessional /ˌʌnprəˈfeʃ(ə)n(ə)l/ *adj.* **1** contrary to professional standards of behaviour etc. **2** not belonging to a profession; amateur. □ **unprofessionally** *adv.*

unprofitable /ʌnˈprɒfɪtəb(ə)l/ *adj.* not profitable. □ **unprofitableness** *n.* **unprofitably** *adv.*

unprogressive /ˌʌnprəˈɡresɪv/ *adj.* not progressive.

unpromising /ʌnˈprɒmɪsɪŋ/ *adj.* not likely to turn out well. □ **unpromisingly** *adv.*

unprompted /ʌnˈprɒmptɪd/ *adj.* spontaneous.

unpronounceable /ˌʌnprəˈnaʊnsəb(ə)l/ *adj.* that cannot be pronounced. □ **unpronounceably** *adv.*

unpropitious /ˌʌnprəˈpɪʃəs/ *adj.* not propitious. □ **unpropitiously** *adv.*

unprotected /ˌʌnprəˈtektɪd/ *adj.* not protected. □ **unprotectedness** *n.*

unprotesting /ˌʌnprəˈtestɪŋ/ *adj.* not protesting. □ **unprotestingly** *adv.*

unprovable /ʌnˈpruːvəb(ə)l/ *adj.* that cannot be proved. □ **unprovability** /-ˈbɪlɪtɪ/ *n.* **unprovableness** *n.*

unproved /ʌnˈpruːvd/ *adj.* (also **unproven** /-v(ə)n/) not proved.

unprovided /ˌʌnprəˈvaɪdɪd/ *adj.* (usu. foll. by *with*) not furnished, supplied, or equipped.

unprovoked /ˌʌnprəˈvəʊkt/ *adj.* (of a person or act) without provocation.

unpublished /ʌnˈpʌblɪʃt/ *adj.* not published. □ **unpublishable** *adj.*

unpunctual /ʌnˈpʌŋktjʊəl/ *adj.* not punctual. □ **unpunctuality** /-tjʊˈælɪtɪ/ *n.*

unpunctuated /ʌnˈpʌŋktjʊˌeɪtɪd/ *adj.* not punctuated.

unpunished /ʌnˈpʌnɪʃt/ *adj.* not punished.

unpurified /ʌnˈpjʊərɪˌfaɪd/ *adj.* not purified.

unputdownable /ˌʌnpʊtˈdaʊnəb(ə)l/ *adj.* *colloq.* (of a book) so engrossing that one has to go on reading it.

unqualified /ʌnˈkwɒlɪˌfaɪd/ *adj.* **1** not competent (*unqualified to give an answer*). **2** not legally or officially qualified (*an unqualified practitioner*). **3** not modified or restricted; complete (*unqualified assent; unqualified success*).

unquenchable /ʌnˈkwentʃəb(ə)l/ *adj.* that cannot be quenched. □ **unquenchably** *adv.*

unquestionable /ʌnˈkwestʃənəb(ə)l/ *adj.* that cannot be disputed or doubted. □ **unquestionability** /-ˈbɪlɪtɪ/ *n.* **unquestionableness** *n.* **unquestionably** *adv.*

unquestioned /ʌnˈkwestʃ(ə)nd/ *adj.* **1** not disputed or doubted; definite, certain. **2** not interrogated.

unquestioning /ʌnˈkwestʃənɪŋ/ *adj.* **1** asking no questions. **2** done etc. without asking questions. □ **unquestioningly** *adv.*

unquiet /ʌnˈkwaɪət/ *adj.* **1** restless, agitated, stirring. **2** perturbed, anxious. □ **unquietly** *adv.* **unquietness** *n.*

unquotable /ʌnˈkwəʊtəb(ə)l/ *adj.* that cannot be quoted.

unquote /ʌnˈkwəʊt/ *v.tr.* (as *int.*) (in dictation, reading aloud, etc.) indicate the presence of closing quotation marks.

unravel /ʌnˈræv(ə)l/ *v.* (**unravelled**, **unravelling**; *US* **unraveled**, **unraveling**) **1** *tr.* cause to be no longer ravelled, tangled, or intertwined. **2** *tr.* probe and solve (a mystery etc.). **3** *tr.* undo (a fabric, esp. a knitted one). **4** *intr.* become disentangled or unknitted.

unreachable /ʌnˈriːtʃəb(ə)l/ *adj.* that cannot be reached. □ **unreachableness** *n.* **unreachably** *adv.*

unread /ʌnˈred/ *adj.* **1** (of a book etc.) not read. **2** (of a person) not well-read.

unreadable /ʌnˈriːdəb(ə)l/ *adj.* **1** too dull or too difficult to be worth reading. **2** illegible. □ **unreadability** /-ˈbɪlɪtɪ/ *n.* **unreadably** *adv.*

unready /ʌnˈredɪ/ *adj.* **1** not ready. **2** not prompt in action. □ **unreadily** *adv.* **unreadiness** *n.*

unreal /ʌnˈrɪəl/ *adj.* **1** not real. **2** imaginary, illusory. **3** *US & Austral. sl.* incredible, amazing. □ **unreality** /-ɪˈælɪtɪ/ *n.* **unreally** *adv.*

unrealistic /ˌʌnrɪəˈlɪstɪk/ *adj.* not realistic. □ **unrealistically** *adv.*

unrealizable /ʌnˈrɪəlaɪzəb(ə)l/ *adj.* that cannot be realized.

unrealized /ʌnˈrɪəlaɪzd/ *adj.* not realized.

unreason /ʌnˈriːz(ə)n/ *n.* lack of reasonable thought or action. [ME, = injustice, f. UN-¹ + REASON]

unreasonable /ʌnˈriːzənəb(ə)l/ *adj.* **1** going beyond the limits of what is reasonable or equitable (*unreasonable demands*). **2** not guided by or listening to reason. □ **unreasonableness** *n.* **unreasonably** *adv.*

unreasoned /ʌnˈriːz(ə)nd/ *adj.* not reasoned.

unreasoning /ʌnˈriːzənɪŋ/ *adj.* not reasoning. □ **unreasoningly** *adv.*

unreceptive /ˌʌnrɪˈseptɪv/ *adj.* not receptive.

unreciprocated /ˌʌnrɪˈsɪprəˌkeɪtɪd/ *adj.* not reciprocated.

unrecognizable /ʌnˈrekəgˌnaɪzəb(ə)l/ *adj.* (also **-isable**) that cannot be recognized. □ **unrecognizableness** *n.* **unrecognizably** *adv.*

unrecognized /ʌnˈrekəgˌnaɪzd/ *adj.* (also **-ised**) not recognized.

unreconciled /ʌnˈrekənˌsaɪld/ *adj.* not reconciled.

unreconstructed /ˌʌnriːkənˈstrʌktɪd/ *adj.* **1** not reconciled or converted to the current political orthodoxy. **2** not rebuilt.

unrecorded /ˌʌnrɪˈkɔːdɪd/ *adj.* not recorded. □ **unrecordable** *adj.*

unredeemable /ˌʌnrɪˈdiːməb(ə)l/ *adj.* that cannot be redeemed. □ **unredeemably** *adv.*

unredeemed /ˌʌnrɪˈdiːmd/ *adj.* not redeemed.

unreel /ʌnˈriːl/ *v.tr. & intr.* unwind from a reel.

unrefined /ˌʌnrɪˈfaɪnd/ *adj.* not refined.

unreflecting /ˌʌnrɪˈflektɪŋ/ *adj.* not thoughtful. □ **unreflectingly** *adv.* **unreflectingness** *n.*

unreformed /ˌʌnrɪˈfɔːmd/ *adj.* not reformed.

unregarded /ˌʌnrɪˈɡɑːdɪd/ *adj.* not regarded.

unregenerate /ˌʌnrɪˈdʒenərət/ *adj.* not regenerate; obstinately wrong or bad. □ **unregeneracy** *n.* **unregenerately** *adv.*

unregistered /ʌnˈredʒɪstəd/ *adj.* not registered.

unregulated /ʌnˈreɡjʊˌleɪtɪd/ *adj.* not regulated.

unrehearsed /ˌʌnrɪˈhɜːst/ *adj.* not rehearsed.

unrelated /ˌʌnrɪˈleɪtɪd/ *adj.* not related. □ **unrelatedness** *n.*

unrelaxed /ˌʌnrɪˈlækst/ *adj.* not relaxed.

unrelenting /ˌʌnrɪˈlentɪŋ/ *adj.* **1** not relenting or yielding. **2** unmerciful. **3** not abating or relaxing. □ **unrelentingly** *adv.* **unrelentingness** *n.*

unreliable /ˌʌnrɪˈlaɪəb(ə)l/ *adj.* not reliable; erratic. □ **unreliability** /-ˈbɪlɪtɪ/ *n.* **unreliableness** *n.* **unreliably** *adv.*

unrelieved /ˌʌnrɪˈliːvd/ *adj.* **1** lacking the relief given by contrast or variation. **2** not aided or assisted. □ **unrelievedly** *adv.*

unremarkable /ˌʌnrɪˈmɑːkəb(ə)l/ *adj.* not remarkable; uninteresting. □ **unremarkably** *adv.*

unremembered /ˌʌnrɪˈmembəd/ *adj.* not remembered; forgotten.

unremitting /ˌʌnrɪˈmɪtɪŋ/ *adj.* never relaxing or slackening, incessant. □ **unremittingly** *adv.* **unremittingness** *n.*

unremunerative /ˌʌnrɪˈmjuːnərətɪv/ *adj.* bringing no, or not enough, profit or income. □ **unremuneratively** *adv.* **unremunerativeness** *n.*

unrenewable /ˌʌnrɪˈnjuːəb(ə)l/ *adj.* that cannot be renewed. □ **unrenewed** *adj.*

unrepeatable /ˌʌnrɪˈpiːtəb(ə)l/ *adj.* **1** that cannot be done, made, or said again. **2** too indecent to be said again. □ **unrepeatability** /-ˈbɪlɪtɪ/ *n.*

unrepentant /ˌʌnrɪˈpent(ə)nt/ *adj.* not repentant, impenitent. □ **unrepentantly** *adv.*

unreported /ˌʌnrɪˈpɔːtɪd/ *adj.* not reported.

unrepresentative /ˌʌnreprɪˈzentətɪv/ *adj.* not representative. □ **unrepresentativeness** *n.*

unrepresented /ˌʌnreprɪˈzentɪd/ *adj.* not represented.

unrequited /ˌʌnrɪˈkwaɪtɪd/ *adj.* (of love etc.) not returned. □ **unrequitedly** *adv.* **unrequitedness** *n.*

unreserve /ˌʌnrɪˈzɜːv/ *n.* lack of reserve; frankness.

unreserved /ˌʌnrɪˈzɜːvd/ *adj.* **1** not reserved (*unreserved seats*). **2** without reservations; absolute (*unreserved confidence*). **3** free from reserve (*an unreserved nature*). □ **unreservedly** /-vɪdlɪ/ *adv.* **unreservedness** *n.*

unresisting /ˌʌnrɪˈzɪstɪŋ/ *adj.* not resisting. □ **unresistingly** *adv.* **unresistingness** *n.*

unresolved /ˌʌnrɪˈzɒlvd/ *adj.* **1 a** uncertain how to act, irresolute. **b** uncertain in opinion, undecided. **2** (of questions etc.) undetermined, undecided, unsolved. **3** not broken up or dissolved. □ **unresolvedly** /-vɪdlɪ/ *adv.* **unresolvedness** *n.*

unresponsive /ˌʌnrɪˈspɒnsɪv/ *adj.* not responsive. □ **unresponsively** *adv.* **unresponsiveness** *n.*

unrest /ʌnˈrest/ *n.* **1** lack of rest. **2** restlessness, disturbance, agitation.

unrestful /ʌnˈrestfʊl/ *adj.* not restful. □ **unrestfully** *adv.*

unrestored /ˌʌnrɪˈstɔːd/ *adj.* not restored.

unrestrained /ˌʌnrɪˈstreɪnd/ *adj.* not restrained. □ **unrestrainedly** /-nɪdlɪ/ *adv.* **unrestrainedness** *n.*

unrestricted /ˌʌnrɪˈstrɪktɪd/ *adj.* not restricted. □ **unrestrictedly** *adv.* **unrestrictedness** *n.*

unreturned /ˌʌnrɪˈtɜːnd/ *adj.* **1** not reciprocated or responded to. **2** not having returned or been returned.

unrevealed /ˌʌnrɪˈviːld/ *adj.* not revealed; secret.

unrevised /ˌʌnrɪˈvaɪzd/ *adj.* not revised; in an original form.

unrevoked /ˌʌnrɪˈvəʊkt/ *adj.* not revoked or annulled; still in force.

unrewarded /ˌʌnrɪˈwɔːdɪd/ *adj.* not rewarded.

unrewarding /ˌʌnrɪˈwɔːdɪŋ/ *adj.* not rewarding or satisfying.

unridable /ʌnˈraɪdəb(ə)l/ *adj.* that cannot be ridden.

unrighteous /ʌnˈraɪtʃəs/ *adj.* not righteous; unjust, wicked, dishonest. □ **unrighteously** *adv.* **unrighteousness** *n.* [OE *unrihtwīs* (as UN-¹, RIGHTEOUS)]

unrip /ʌnˈrɪp/ *v.tr.* (**unripped, unripping**) open by ripping.

unripe /ʌnˈraɪp/ *adj.* not ripe. □ **unripeness** *n.*

unrivalled /ʌnˈraɪv(ə)ld/ *adj.* (US **unrivaled**) having no equal; peerless.

unroll /ʌnˈrəʊl/ *v.tr.* & *intr.* **1** open out from a rolled-up state. **2** display or be displayed in this form.

unromantic /ˌʌnrəˈmæntɪk/ *adj.* not romantic. □ **unromantically** *adv.*

unroofed /ʌnˈruːft/ *adj.* not provided with a roof.

unruffled /ʌnˈrʌf(ə)ld/ *adj.* **1** not agitated or disturbed; calm. **2** not physically ruffled.

unruled /ʌnˈruːld/ *adj.* **1** not ruled or governed. **2** not having ruled lines.

unruly /ʌnˈruːlɪ/ *adj.* (**unrulier, unruliest**) not easily controlled or disciplined, disorderly. □ **unruliness** *n.* [ME f. UN-¹ + *ruly* f. RULE]

unsaddle /ʌnˈsæd(ə)l/ *v.tr.* **1** remove the saddle from (a horse etc.). **2** dislodge from a saddle.

unsafe /ʌnˈseɪf/ *adj.* not safe. □ **unsafely** *adv.* **unsafeness** *n.*

unsaid¹ /ʌnˈsed/ *adj.* not said or uttered.

unsaid² *past* and *past part.* of UNSAY.

unsaleable /ʌnˈseɪləb(ə)l/ *adj.* not saleable. □ **unsaleability** /-ˈbɪlɪtɪ/ *n.*

unsalted /ʌnˈsɔːltɪd, ʌnˈsɒl-/ *adj.* not salted.

unsanctified /ʌnˈsæŋktɪˌfaɪd/ *adj.* not sanctified.

unsanctioned /ʌnˈsæŋkʃ(ə)nd/ *adj.* not sanctioned.

unsatisfactory /ˌʌnsætɪsˈfæktərɪ/ *adj.* not satisfactory; poor, unacceptable. □ **unsatisfactorily** *adv.* **unsatisfactoriness** *n.*

unsatisfied /ʌnˈsætɪsˌfaɪd/ *adj.* not satisfied. □ **unsatisfiedness** *n.*

unsatisfying /ʌnˈsætɪsˌfaɪɪŋ/ *adj.* not satisfying. □ **unsatisfyingly** *adv.*

unsaturated /ʌnˈsætʃəˌreɪtɪd, -tjʊˌreɪtɪd/ *adj.* **1** *Chem.* (of a compound, esp. a fat or oil) having double or triple bonds in its molecule and therefore capable of further reaction. **2** not saturated. □ **unsaturation** /-ˈreɪʃ(ə)n/ *n.*

unsavoury /ʌnˈseɪvərɪ/ *adj.* (US **unsavory**) **1** disagreeable to the taste, smell, or feelings; disgusting. **2** disagreeable, unpleasant (*an unsavoury character*). **3** morally offensive. □ **unsavourily** *adv.* **unsavouriness** *n.*

unsay /ʌnˈseɪ/ *v.tr.* (*past* and *past part.* **unsaid**) retract (a statement).

unsayable /ʌnˈseɪəb(ə)l/ *adj.* that cannot be said.

unscalable /ʌnˈskeɪləb(ə)l/ *adj.* that cannot be scaled.

unscarred /ʌnˈskɑːd/ *adj.* not scarred or damaged.

unscathed /ʌnˈskeɪðd/ *adj.* without suffering any injury.

unscented /ʌnˈsentɪd/ *adj.* not scented.

unscheduled /ʌnˈʃedjuːld/ *adj.* not scheduled.

unscholarly /ʌnˈskɒləlɪ/ *adj.* not scholarly. □ **unscholarliness** *n.*

unschooled /ʌnˈskuːld/ *adj.* **1** uneducated, untaught. **2** not sent to school. **3** untrained, undisciplined. **4** not made artificial by education.

unscientific /ˌʌnsaɪən'tɪfɪk/ *adj.* **1** not in accordance with scientific principles. **2** not familiar with science. □ **unscientifically** *adv.*

unscramble /ʌnˈskræmb(ə)l/ v.tr. restore from a scrambled state, esp. interpret (a scrambled transmission etc.). □ **unscrambler** n.

unscrew /ʌnˈskruː/ v. **1** tr. & intr. unfasten or be unfastened by turning or removing a screw or screws or by twisting like a screw. **2** tr. loosen (a screw).

unscripted /ʌnˈskrɪptɪd/ adj. (of a speech etc.) delivered without a prepared script.

unscrupulous /ʌnˈskruːpjʊləs/ adj. having no scruples, unprincipled. □ **unscrupulously** adv. **unscrupulousness** n.

unseal /ʌnˈsiːl/ v.tr. break the seal of; open (a letter, receptacle, etc.).

unsealed /ʌnˈsiːld/ adj. not sealed.

unseasonable /ʌnˈsiːzənəb(ə)l/ adj. **1** not appropriate to the season. **2** untimely, inopportune. □ **unseasonableness** n. **unseasonably** adv.

unseasoned /ʌnˈsiːz(ə)nd/ adj. **1** not flavoured with salt, herbs, etc. **2** (esp. of timber) not matured. **3** not habituated.

unseat /ʌnˈsiːt/ v.tr. **1** remove from a seat, esp. in an election. **2** dislodge from a seat, esp. on horseback.

unseaworthy /ʌnˈsiːˌwɜːðɪ/ adj. not seaworthy.

unsecured /ˌʌnsɪˈkjʊəd/ adj. not secured.

unseeded /ʌnˈsiːdɪd/ adj. Sport (of a player) not seeded.

unseeing /ʌnˈsiːɪŋ/ adj. **1** unobservant. **2** blind. □ **unseeingly** adv.

unseemly /ʌnˈsiːmlɪ/ adj. (**unseemlier, unseemliest**) **1** indecent. **2** unbecoming. □ **unseemliness** n.

unseen /ʌnˈsiːn/ adj. & n. —adj. **1** not seen. **2** invisible. **3** (of a translation) to be done without preparation. —n. Brit. an unseen translation.

unsegregated /ʌnˈsegrɪˌgeɪtɪd/ adj. not segregated.

unselective /ˌʌnsɪˈlektɪv/ adj. not selective.

unselfconscious /ˌʌnselfˈkɒnʃəs/ adj. not self-conscious. □ **unselfconsciously** adv. **unselfconsciousness** n.

unselfish /ʌnˈselfɪʃ/ adj. mindful of others' interests. □ **unselfishly** adv. **unselfishness** n.

unsentimental /ˌʌnsentɪˈment(ə)l/ adj. not sentimental. □ **unsentimentality** /-ˈtælɪtɪ/ n. **unsentimentally** adv.

unserviceable /ʌnˈsɜːvɪsəb(ə)l/ adj. not serviceable; unfit for use. □ **unserviceability** /-ˈbɪlɪtɪ/ n.

unsettle /ʌnˈset(ə)l/ v. **1** tr. disturb the settled state or arrangement of; discompose. **2** tr. derange. **3** intr. become unsettled. □ **unsettlement** n.

unsettled /ʌnˈset(ə)ld/ adj. **1** not (yet) settled. **2** liable or open to change or further discussion. **3** (of a bill etc.) unpaid. □ **unsettledness** n.

unsex /ʌnˈseks/ v.tr. deprive (a person, esp. a woman) of the qualities of her or his sex.

unsexed /ʌnˈsekst/ adj. having no sexual characteristics.

unshackle /ʌnˈʃæk(ə)l/ v.tr. **1** release from shackles. **2** set free.

unshakeable /ʌnˈʃeɪkəb(ə)l/ adj. that cannot be shaken; firm, obstinate. □ **unshakeability** /-ˈbɪlɪtɪ/ **unshakeably** adv.

unshaken /ʌnˈʃeɪkən/ adj. not shaken. □ **unshakenly** adv.

unshaven /ʌnˈʃeɪv(ə)n/ adj. not shaved.

unsheathe /ʌnˈʃiːð/ v.tr. remove (a knife etc.) from a sheath.

unsheltered /ʌnˈʃeltəd/ adj. not sheltered.

unshockable /ʌnˈʃɒkəb(ə)l/ adj. that cannot be shocked. □ **unshockability** /-ˈbɪlɪtɪ/ n. **unshockably** adv.

unshrinkable /ʌnˈʃrɪŋkəb(ə)l/ adj. (of fabric etc.) not liable to shrink. □ **unshrinkability** /-ˈbɪlɪtɪ/ n.

unshrinking /ʌnˈʃrɪŋkɪŋ/ adj. unhesitating, fearless. □ **unshrinkingly** adv.

unsighted /ʌnˈsaɪtɪd/ adj. **1** not sighted or seen. **2** prevented from seeing, esp. by an obstruction.

unsightly /ʌnˈsaɪtlɪ/ adj. unpleasant to look at, ugly. □ **unsightliness** n.

unsigned /ʌnˈsaɪnd/ adj. not signed.

unsinkable /ʌnˈsɪŋkəb(ə)l/ adj. unable to be sunk. □ **unsinkability** /-ˈbɪlɪtɪ/ n.

unsized[1] /ʌnˈsaɪzd/ adj. **1** not made to a size. **2** not sorted by size.

unsized[2] /ʌnˈsaɪzd/ adj. not treated with size.

unskilful /ʌnˈskɪlfʊl/ adj. (US **unskillful**) not skilful. □ **unskilfully** adv. **unskilfulness** n.

unskilled /ʌnˈskɪld/ adj. lacking or not needing special skill or training.

unsleeping /ʌnˈsliːpɪŋ/ adj. not or never sleeping. □ **unsleepingly** adv.

unsliced /ʌnˈslaɪst/ adj. (esp. of a loaf of bread when it is bought) not having been cut into slices.

unsmiling /ʌnˈsmaɪlɪŋ/ adj. not smiling. □ **unsmilingly** adv. **unsmilingness** n.

unsmoked /ʌnˈsməʊkt/ adj. **1** not cured by smoking (unsmoked bacon). **2** not consumed by smoking (an unsmoked cigar).

unsociable /ʌnˈsəʊʃəb(ə)l/ adj. not sociable, disliking the company of others. □ **unsociability** /-ˈbɪlɪtɪ/ n. **unsociableness** n. **unsociably** adv.

unsocial /ʌnˈsəʊʃ(ə)l/ adj. **1** not social; not suitable for, seeking, or conforming to society. **2** outside the normal working day (unsocial hours). **3** antisocial. □ **unsocially** adv.

unsoiled /ʌnˈsɔɪld/ adj. not soiled or dirtied.

unsold /ʌnˈsəʊld/ adj. not sold.

unsolicited /ˌʌnsəˈlɪsɪtɪd/ adj. not asked for; given or done voluntarily. □ **unsolicitedly** adv.

unsolvable /ʌnˈsɒlvəb(ə)l/ adj. that cannot be solved, insoluble. □ **unsolvability** /-ˈbɪlɪtɪ/ n. **unsolvableness** n.

unsolved /ʌnˈsɒlvd/ adj. not solved.

unsophisticated /ˌʌnsəˈfɪstɪˌkeɪtɪd/ adj. **1** artless, simple, natural, ingenuous. **2** not adulterated or artificial. □ **unsophisticatedly** adv. **unsophisticatedness** n. **unsophistication** /-ˈkeɪʃ(ə)n/ n.

unsorted /ʌnˈsɔːtɪd/ adj. not sorted.

unsought /ʌnˈsɔːt/ adj. **1** not searched out or sought for. **2** unasked; without being requested.

unsound /ʌnˈsaʊnd/ adj. **1** unhealthy, diseased. **2** rotten, weak. **3 a** ill-founded, fallacious. **b** unorthodox, heretical. **4** unreliable. **5** wicked. □ **of unsound mind** insane. □ **unsoundly** adv. **unsoundness** n.

unsparing /ʌnˈspeərɪŋ/ adj. **1** lavish, profuse. **2** merciless. □ **unsparingly** adv. **unsparingness** n.

unspeakable /ʌnˈspiːkəb(ə)l/ adj. **1** that cannot be expressed in words. **2** indescribably bad or objectionable. □ **unspeakableness** n. **unspeakably** adv.

unspecialized /ʌnˈspeʃəˌlaɪzd/ *adj.* not specialized.

unspecified /ʌnˈspesɪˌfaɪd/ *adj.* not specified.

unspectacular /ˌʌnspekˈtækjʊlə(r)/ *adj.* not spectacular; dull. □ **unspectacularly** *adv.*

unspilled /ʌnˈspɪld/ *adj.* not spilt.

unspilt /ʌnˈspɪlt/ *adj.* not spilt.

unspoiled /ʌnˈspɔɪld/ *adj.* **1** unspoilt. **2** not plundered.

unspoilt /ʌnˈspɔɪlt/ *adj.* not spoilt.

unspoken /ʌnˈspəʊkən/ *adj.* **1** not expressed in speech. **2** not uttered as speech.

unsporting /ʌnˈspɔːtɪŋ/ *adj.* not sportsmanlike; not fair or generous. □ **unsportingly** *adv.* **unsportingness** *n.*

unsportsmanlike /ʌnˈspɔːtsmənˌlaɪk/ *adj.* unsporting.

unspotted /ʌnˈspɒtɪd/ *adj.* **1 a** not marked with a spot or spots. **b** morally pure. **2** unnoticed.

unstable /ʌnˈsteɪb(ə)l/ *adj.* (**unstabler**, **unstablest**) **1** not stable. **2** changeable. **3** showing a tendency to sudden mental or emotional changes. □ **unstableness** *n.* **unstably** *adv.*

unstained /ʌnˈsteɪnd/ *adj.* not stained.

unstamped /ʌnˈstæmpt/ *adj.* **1** not marked by stamping. **2** not having a stamp affixed.

unstarched /ʌnˈstɑːtʃt/ *adj.* not starched.

unstated /ʌnˈsteɪtɪd/ *adj.* not stated or declared.

unstatesmanlike /ʌnˈsteɪtsmənˌlaɪk/ *adj.* not statesmanlike.

unsteady /ʌnˈstedɪ/ *adj.* (**unsteadier**, **unsteadiest**) **1** not steady or firm. **2** changeable, fluctuating. **3** not uniform or regular. □ **unsteadily** *adv.* **unsteadiness** *n.*

unstick *v.* /ʌnˈstɪk/ (*past* and *past part.* **unstuck**) *tr.* separate (a thing stuck to another). □ **come unstuck** *colloq.* come to grief, fail.

unstinted /ʌnˈstɪntɪd/ *adj.* not stinted. □ **unstintedly** *adv.*

unstinting /ʌnˈstɪntɪŋ/ *adj.* ungrudging, lavish. □ **unstintingly** *adv.*

unstitch /ʌnˈstɪtʃ/ *v.tr.* undo the stitches of.

unstop /ʌnˈstɒp/ *v.tr.* (**unstopped, unstopping**) **1** free from obstruction. **2** remove the stopper from.

unstoppable /ʌnˈstɒpəb(ə)l/ *adj.* that cannot be stopped or prevented. □ **unstoppability** /-ˈbɪlɪtɪ/ *n.* **unstoppably** *adv.*

unstopper /ʌnˈstɒpə(r)/ *v.tr.* remove the stopper from.

unstrained /ʌnˈstreɪnd/ *adj.* **1** not subjected to straining or stretching. **2** not injured by overuse or excessive demands. **3** not forced or produced by effort. **4** not passed through a strainer.

unstreamed /ʌnˈstriːmd/ *adj. Brit.* (of schoolchildren) not arranged in streams.

unstressed /ʌnˈstrest/ *adj.* **1** (of a word, syllable, etc.) not pronounced with stress. **2** not subjected to stress.

unstring /ʌnˈstrɪŋ/ *v.tr.* (*past* and *past part.* **unstrung**) **1** remove or relax the string or strings of (a bow, harp, etc.). **2** remove from a string. **3** (esp. as **unstrung** *adj.*) unnerve.

unstructured /ʌnˈstrʌktʃəd/ *adj.* **1** not structured. **2** informal.

unstuck *past* and *past part.* of UNSTICK.

unstudied /ʌnˈstʌdɪd/ *adj.* easy, natural, spontaneous. □ **unstudiedly** *adv.*

unstuffy /ʌnˈstʌfɪ/ *adj.* **1** informal, casual. **2** not stuffy.

unsubstantial /ˌʌnsəbˈstænʃ(ə)l/ *adj.* having little or no solidity, reality, or factual basis. □ **unsubstantiality** /-ʃɪˈælɪtɪ/ *n.* **unsubstantially** *adv.*

unsubstantiated /ˌʌnsəbˈstænʃɪˌeɪtɪd/ *adj.* not substantiated.

unsuccessful /ˌʌnsəkˈsesfʊl/ *adj.* not successful. □ **unsuccessfully** *adv.* **unsuccessfulness** *n.*

unsuitable /ʌnˈsuːtəb(ə)l, ʌnˈsjuː-/ *adj.* not suitable. □ **unsuitability** /-ˈbɪlɪtɪ/ *n.* **unsuitableness** *n.* **unsuitably** *adv.*

unsuited /ʌnˈsuːtɪd, ʌnˈsjuː-/ *adj.* **1** (usu. foll. by *for*) not fit for a purpose. **2** (usu. foll. by *to*) not adapted.

unsullied /ʌnˈsʌlɪd/ *adj.* not sullied.

unsung /ʌnˈsʌŋ/ *adj.* **1** not celebrated in song; unknown. **2** not sung.

unsupervised /ʌnˈsuːpəˌvaɪzd, ʌnˈsjuː-/ *adj.* not supervised.

unsupportable /ˌʌnsəˈpɔːtəb(ə)l/ *adj.* **1** that cannot be endured. **2** indefensible. □ **unsupportably** *adv.*

unsupported /ˌʌnsəˈpɔːtɪd/ *adj.* not supported. □ **unsupportedly** *adv.*

unsure /ʌnˈʃʊə(r), ʌnˈʃɔː(r)/ *adj.* not sure. □ **unsurely** *adv.* **unsureness** *n.*

unsurpassable /ˌʌnsəˈpɑːsəb(ə)l/ *adj.* that cannot be surpassed. □ **unsurpassably** *adv.*

unsurpassed /ˌʌnsəˈpɑːst/ *adj.* not surpassed.

unsurprising /ˌʌnsəˈpraɪzɪŋ/ *adj.* not surprising. □ **unsurprisingly** *adv.*

unsusceptible /ˌʌnsəˈseptɪb(ə)l/ *adj.* not susceptible. □ **unsusceptibility** /-ˈbɪlɪtɪ/ *n.*

unsuspected /ˌʌnsəˈspektɪd/ *adj.* not suspected. □ **unsuspectedly** *adv.*

unsuspecting /ˌʌnsəˈspektɪŋ/ *adj.* not suspecting. □ **unsuspectingly** *adv.* **unsuspectingness** *n.*

unsuspicious /ˌʌnsəˈspɪʃəs/ *adj.* not suspicious. □ **unsuspiciously** *adv.* **unsuspiciousness** *n.*

unsustained /ˌʌnsəˈsteɪnd/ *adj.* not sustained.

unswayed /ʌnˈsweɪd/ *adj.* uninfluenced, unaffected.

unsweetened /ʌnˈswiːt(ə)nd/ *adj.* not sweetened.

unswept /ʌnˈswept/ *adj.* not swept.

unswerving /ʌnˈswɜːvɪŋ/ *adj.* **1** steady, constant. **2** not turning aside. □ **unswervingly** *adv.*

unsymmetrical /ˌʌnsɪˈmetrɪk(ə)l/ *adj.* not symmetrical. □ **unsymmetrically** *adv.*

unsympathetic /ˌʌnsɪmpəˈθetɪk/ *adj.* not sympathetic. □ **unsympathetically** *adv.*

unsystematic /ˌʌnsɪstəˈmætɪk/ *adj.* not systematic. □ **unsystematically** *adv.*

untainted /ʌnˈteɪntɪd/ *adj.* not tainted.

untalented /ʌnˈtæləntɪd/ *adj.* not talented.

untameable /ʌnˈteɪməb(ə)l/ *adj.* that cannot be tamed.

untamed /ʌnˈteɪmd/ *adj.* not tamed, wild.

untangle /ʌnˈtæŋg(ə)l/ *v.tr.* **1** free from a tangled state. **2** free from entanglement.

untanned /ʌnˈtænd/ *adj.* not tanned.

untapped /ʌnˈtæpt/ *adj.* not (yet) tapped or wired (*untapped resources*).

untarnished /ʌnˈtɑːnɪʃt/ *adj.* not tarnished.

untasted /ʌnˈteɪstɪd/ *adj.* not tasted.

untaught /ʌnˈtɔːt/ *adj.* **1** not instructed by teaching; ignorant. **2** not acquired by teaching; natural, spontaneous.

untaxed /ʌnˈtækst/ *adj.* not required to pay or not attracting taxes.

unteachable /ʌnˈtiːtʃəb(ə)l/ adj. **1** incapable of being instructed. **2** that cannot be imparted by teaching.

untechnical /ʌnˈteknɪk(ə)l/ adj. not technical. □ **untechnically** adv.

untenable /ʌnˈtenəb(ə)l/ adj. not tenable; that cannot be defended. □ **untenability** /-ˈbɪlɪtɪ/ n. **untenableness** n. **untenably** adv.

untended /ʌnˈtendɪd/ adj. not tended; neglected.

untested /ʌnˈtestɪd/ adj. not tested or proved.

untether /ʌnˈteðə(r)/ v.tr. release (an animal) from a tether.

untethered /ʌnˈteðəd/ adj. not tethered.

unthankful /ʌnˈθæŋkfʊl/ adj. not thankful. □ **unthankfully** adv. **unthankfulness** n.

unthinkable /ʌnˈθɪŋkəb(ə)l/ adj. **1** that cannot be imagined or grasped by the mind. **2** colloq. highly unlikely or undesirable. □ **unthinkability** /-ˈbɪlɪtɪ/ n. **unthinkableness** n. **unthinkably** adv.

unthinking /ʌnˈθɪŋkɪŋ/ adj. **1** thoughtless. **2** unintentional, inadvertent. □ **unthinkingly** adv. **unthinkingness** n.

unthread /ʌnˈθred/ v.tr. **1** take the thread out of (a needle etc.). **2** find one's way out of (a maze).

unthrone /ʌnˈθrəʊn/ v.tr. dethrone.

untidy /ʌnˈtaɪdɪ/ adj. (**untidier**, **untidiest**) not neat or orderly. □ **untidily** adv. **untidiness** n.

untie /ʌnˈtaɪ/ v.tr. (pres. part. **untying**) **1** undo (a knot etc.). **2** unfasten the cords etc. of (a package etc.). **3** release from bonds or attachment. [OE *untīgan* (as UN-², TIE)]

untied /ʌnˈtaɪd/ adj. not tied.

until /ənˈtɪl, ʌn-/ prep. & conj. = TILL¹. [orig. northern ME *untill* f. ON *und* as far as + TILL¹]

■ **Usage** Used esp. at the beginning of a sentence and in formal style, e.g. *until you told me, I had no idea*; *he resided there until his decease.*

untilled /ʌnˈtɪld/ adj. not tilled.

untimely /ʌnˈtaɪmlɪ/ adj. & adv. —adj. **1** inopportune. **2** (of death) premature. —adv. archaic **1** inopportunely. **2** prematurely. □ **untimeliness** n.

untiring /ʌnˈtaɪərɪŋ/ adj. tireless. □ **untiringly** adv.

untitled /ʌnˈtaɪt(ə)ld/ adj. having no title.

unto /ˈʌntʊ, ˈʌntə/ prep. archaic = TO prep. (in all uses except as the sign of the infinitive); (*do unto others*; *faithful unto death*; *take unto oneself*). [ME f. UNTIL, with TO replacing northern TILL¹]

untold /ʌnˈtəʊld/ adj. **1** not told. **2** not (able to be) counted or measured (*untold misery*). [OE *untēald* (as UN-¹, TOLD)]

untouchable /ʌnˈtʌtʃəb(ə)l/ adj. & n. —adj. that may not or cannot be touched. —n. a member of a hereditary Hindu group held to defile members of higher castes on contact. □ **untouchability** /-ˈbɪlɪtɪ/ n. **untouchableness** n.

■ **Usage** The use of this term, and social restrictions accompanying it, were declared illegal under the Indian constitution in 1949.

untouched /ʌnˈtʌtʃt/ adj. **1** not touched. **2** not affected physically, not harmed, modified, used, or tasted. **3** not affected by emotion. **4** not discussed.

untoward /ˌʌntəˈwɔːd, ʌnˈtəʊəd/ adj. **1** inconvenient, unlucky. **2** awkward. **3** perverse, refractory. **4** unseemly. □ **untowardly** adv. **untowardness** n.

untraceable /ʌnˈtreɪsəb(ə)l/ adj. that cannot be traced. □ **untraceably** adv.

untraced /ʌnˈtreɪst/ adj. not traced.

untrained /ʌnˈtreɪnd/ adj. not trained.

untrammelled /ʌnˈtræm(ə)ld/ adj. not trammelled, unhampered.

untransferable /ˌʌntrænsˈfɜːrəb(ə)l, ˌʌntrɑːns-, ʌnˈt-/ adj. not transferable.

untranslatable /ˌʌntrænsˈleɪtəb(ə)l, ˌʌntrɑːn-, -zˈleɪtəb(ə)l/ adj. that cannot be translated satisfactorily. □ **untranslatability** /-ˈbɪlɪtɪ/ n. **untranslatably** adv.

untravelled /ʌnˈtræv(ə)ld/ adj. (US **untraveled**) **1** that has not travelled. **2** that has not been travelled over or through.

untreatable /ʌnˈtriːtəb(ə)l/ adj. (of a disease etc.) that cannot be treated.

untreated /ʌnˈtriːtɪd/ adj. not treated.

untried /ʌnˈtraɪd/ adj. **1** not tried or tested. **2** inexperienced. **3** not yet tried by a judge.

untrodden /ʌnˈtrɒd(ə)n/ adj. not trodden, stepped on, or traversed.

untroubled /ʌnˈtrʌb(ə)ld/ adj. not troubled; calm, tranquil.

untrue /ʌnˈtruː/ adj. **1** not true, contrary to what is the fact. **2** (often foll. by *to*) not faithful or loyal. **3** deviating from an accepted standard. □ **untruly** adv. [OE *untrēowe* etc. (as UN-¹, TRUE)]

untrustworthy /ʌnˈtrʌstˌwɜːðɪ/ adj. not trustworthy. □ **untrustworthiness** n.

untruth /ʌnˈtruːθ/ n. (pl. /-ˈtruːðz, -ˈtruːθs/) **1** the state of being untrue, falsehood. **2** a false statement (*told me an untruth*). [OE *untrēowth* etc. (as UN-¹, TRUTH)]

untruthful /ʌnˈtruːθfʊl/ adj. not truthful. □ **untruthfully** adv. **untruthfulness** n.

untuck /ʌnˈtʌk/ v.tr. free (bedclothes etc.) from being tucked in or up.

untuned /ʌnˈtjuːnd/ adj. **1** not in tune, not made tuneful. **2** (of a radio receiver etc.) not tuned to any one frequency. **3** not in harmony or concord, disordered.

unturned /ʌnˈtɜːnd/ adj. **1** not turned over, round, away, etc. **2** not shaped by turning.

untutored /ʌnˈtjuːtəd/ adj. uneducated, untaught.

untwine /ʌnˈtwaɪn/ v.tr. & intr. untwist, unwind.

untwist /ʌnˈtwɪst/ v.tr. & intr. open from a twisted or spiralled state.

untying pres. part. of UNTIE.

unusable /ʌnˈjuːzəb(ə)l/ adj. not usable.

unused adj. **1** /ʌnˈjuːzd/ **a** not in use. **b** never having been used. **2** /ʌnˈjuːst/ (foll. by *to*) not accustomed.

unusual /ʌnˈjuːʒʊəl/ adj. **1** not usual. **2** exceptional, remarkable. □ **unusually** adv. **unusualness** n.

unutterable /ʌnˈʌtərəb(ə)l/ adj. inexpressible; beyond description (*unutterable torment*; *an unutterable fool*). □ **unutterableness** n. **unutterably** adv.

unvaccinated /ʌnˈvæksɪˌneɪtɪd/ adj. not vaccinated.

unvalued /ʌnˈvæljuːd/ adj. **1** not regarded as valuable. **2** not having been valued.

unvanquished /ʌnˈvæŋkwɪʃt/ *adj.* not vanquished.

unvaried /ʌnˈveərɪd/ *adj.* not varied.

unvarnished /ʌnˈvaːnɪʃt/ *adj.* 1 not varnished. 2 (of a statement or person) plain and straightforward (*the unvarnished truth*).

unvarying /ʌnˈveərɪɪŋ/ *adj.* not varying. □ **unvaryingly** *adv.* **unvaryingness** *n.*

unveil /ʌnˈveɪl/ *v.* 1 *tr.* remove a veil from. 2 *tr.* remove a covering from (a statue, plaque, etc.) as part of the ceremony of the first public display. 3 *tr.* disclose, reveal, make publicly known. 4 *intr.* remove one's veil.

unventilated /ʌnˈventɪˌleɪtɪd/ *adj.* 1 not provided with a means of ventilation. 2 not discussed.

unverifiable /ʌnˈverɪˌfaɪəb(ə)l/ *adj.* that cannot be verified.

unverified /ʌnˈverɪfaɪd/ *adj.* not verified.

unversed /ʌnˈvɜːst/ *adj.* (usu. foll. by *in*) not experienced or skilled.

unviable /ʌnˈvaɪəb(ə)l/ *adj.* not viable. □ **unviability** /-ˈbɪlɪtɪ/ *n.*

unvoiced /ʌnˈvɔɪst/ *adj.* 1 not spoken. 2 *Phonet.* not voiced.

unwaged /ʌnˈweɪdʒd/ *adj.* not receiving a wage; out of work.

unwanted /ʌnˈwɒntɪd/ *adj.* not wanted.

unwarlike /ʌnˈwɔːlaɪk/ *adj.* not warlike.

unwarrantable /ʌnˈwɒrəntəb(ə)l/ *adj.* indefensible, unjustifiable. □ **unwarrantableness** *n.* **unwarrantably** *adv.*

unwarranted /ʌnˈwɒrəntɪd/ *adj.* 1 unauthorized. 2 unjustified.

unwary /ʌnˈweərɪ/ *adj.* 1 not cautious. 2 (often foll. by *of*) not aware of possible danger etc. □ **unwarily** *adv.* **unwariness** *n.*

unwashed /ʌnˈwɒʃt/ *adj.* 1 not washed. 2 not usually washed or clean. □ **the great unwashed** *colloq.* the rabble.

unwatered /ʌnˈwɔːtəd/ *adj.* not watered.

unwavering /ʌnˈweɪvərɪŋ/ *adj.* not wavering. □ **unwaveringly** *adv.*

unweaned /ʌnˈwiːnd/ *adj.* not weaned.

unwearable /ʌnˈweərəb(ə)l/ *adj.* that cannot be worn.

unwearied /ʌnˈwɪərɪd/ *adj.* 1 not wearied or tired. 2 never becoming weary, indefatigable. 3 unremitting. □ **unweariedly** *adv.* **unweariedness** *n.*

unwearying /ʌnˈwɪərɪɪŋ/ *adj.* 1 persistent. 2 not causing or producing weariness. □ **unwearyingly** *adv.*

unwed /ʌnˈwed/ *adj.* unmarried.

unwedded /ʌnˈwedɪd/ *adj.* unmarried. □ **unweddedness** *n.*

unwelcome /ʌnˈwelkəm/ *adj.* not welcome or acceptable. □ **unwelcomely** *adv.* **unwelcomeness** *n.*

unwell /ʌnˈwel/ *adj.* 1 not in good health; (somewhat) ill. 2 indisposed.

unwept /ʌnˈwept/ *adj.* 1 not wept for. 2 (of tears) not wept.

unwholesome /ʌnˈhəʊlsəm/ *adj.* 1 not promoting, or detrimental to, physical or moral health. 2 unhealthy, insalubrious. 3 unhealthy-looking. □ **unwholesomely** *adv.* **unwholesomeness** *n.*

unwieldy /ʌnˈwiːldɪ/ *adj.* (**unwieldier**, **unwieldiest**) cumbersome, clumsy, or hard to manage, owing to size, shape, or weight. □ **unwieldily** *adv.* **unwieldiness** *n.* [ME f. UN-¹ + *wieldy* active (now dial.) f. WIELD]

unwilling /ʌnˈwɪlɪŋ/ *adj.* not willing or inclined; reluctant. □ **unwillingly** *adv.* **unwillingness** *n.* [OE *unwillende* (as UN-¹, WILLING)]

unwind /ʌnˈwaɪnd/ *v.* (*past* and *past part.* **unwound**) 1 **a** *tr.* draw out (a thing that has been wound). **b** *intr.* become drawn out after having been wound. 2 *intr.* & *tr.* *colloq.* relax.

unwinking /ʌnˈwɪŋkɪŋ/ *adj.* 1 not winking. 2 watchful, vigilant. □ **unwinkingly** *adv.*

unwinnable /ʌnˈwɪnəb(ə)l/ *adj.* that cannot be won.

unwisdom /ʌnˈwɪzdəm/ *n.* lack of wisdom, folly, imprudence. [OE *unwīsdōm* (as UN-¹, WISDOM)]

unwise /ʌnˈwaɪz/ *adj.* 1 foolish, imprudent. 2 injudicious. □ **unwisely** *adv.* [OE *unwīs* (as UN-¹, WISE¹)]

unwished /ʌnˈwɪʃt/ *adj.* (usu. foll. by *for*) not wished for.

unwithered /ʌnˈwɪðəd/ *adj.* not withered; still vigorous or fresh.

unwitting /ʌnˈwɪtɪŋ/ *adj.* 1 unaware of the state of the case (*an unwitting offender*). 2 unintentional. □ **unwittingly** *adv.* **unwittingness** *n.* [OE *unwitende* (as UN-¹, WIT²)]

unwomanly /ʌnˈwʊmənlɪ/ *adj.* not womanly; not befitting a woman. □ **unwomanliness** *n.*

unwonted /ʌnˈwəʊntɪd/ *adj.* not customary or usual. □ **unwontedly** *adv.* **unwontedness** *n.*

unworkable /ʌnˈwɜːkəb(ə)l/ *adj.* not workable; impracticable. □ **unworkability** /-ˈbɪlɪtɪ/ *n.* **unworkableness** *n.* **unworkably** *adv.*

unworkmanlike /ʌnˈwɜːkmənˌlaɪk/ *adj.* badly done or made.

unworldly /ʌnˈwɜːldlɪ/ *adj.* 1 spiritually-minded. 2 spiritual. □ **unworldliness** *n.*

unworn /ʌnˈwɔːn/ *adj.* not worn or impaired by wear.

unworried /ʌnˈwʌrɪd/ *adj.* not worried; calm.

unworthy /ʌnˈwɜːðɪ/ *adj.* (**unworthier**, **unworthiest**) 1 (often foll. by *of*) not worthy or befitting the character of a person etc. 2 discreditable, unseemly. 3 contemptible, base. □ **unworthily** *adv.* **unworthiness** *n.*

unwound¹ /ʌnˈwaʊnd/ *adj.* not wound or wound up.

unwound² *past* and *past part.* of UNWIND.

unwounded /ʌnˈwuːndɪd/ *adj.* not wounded, unhurt.

unwrap /ʌnˈræp/ *v.* (**unwrapped**, **unwrapping**) 1 *tr.* remove the wrapping from. 2 *tr.* open or unfold. 3 *intr.* become unwrapped.

unwritten /ʌnˈrɪt(ə)n/ *adj.* 1 not written. 2 (of a law etc.) resting originally on custom or judicial decision, not on statute.

unwrought /ʌnˈrɔːt/ *adj.* (of metals) not hammered into shape or worked into a finished condition.

unyielding /ʌnˈjiːldɪŋ/ *adj.* 1 not yielding to pressure etc. 2 firm, obstinate. □ **unyieldingly** *adv.* **unyieldingness** *n.*

unyoke /ʌnˈjəʊk/ *v.* 1 *tr.* release from a yoke. 2 *intr.* cease work.

unzip /ʌnˈzɪp/ *v.tr.* (**unzipped**, **unzipping**) unfasten the zip of.

up *adv.*, *prep.*, *adj.*, *n.*, & *v.* —*adv.* 1 at, in, or towards a higher place or position (*jumped up in the air*; *what are they doing up there?*). 2 to or in a place regarded as higher, esp.: **a** northwards (*up* *in Scotland*). **b** *Brit.* towards a major city or a university (*went up to London*). **3** *colloq.* ahead etc. as indicated (*went up front*). **4 a** to or in an erect position or condition (*stood it up*). **b** to or in a prepared or required position (*wound up the watch*). **c** in or into a condition of efficiency, activity, or progress (*stirred up trouble; the house is up for sale; the hunt is up*). **5** *Brit.* in a stronger or winning position or condition (*our team was three goals up; am £10 up on the transaction*). **6** (of a computer) running and available for use. **7** to the place or time in question or where the speaker etc. is (*a child came up to me; went straight up to the door; has been fine up till now*). **8** at or to a higher price or value (*our costs are up; shares are up*). **9 a** completely or effectually (*burn up; eat up; tear up; use up*). **b** more loudly or clearly (*speak up*). **10** in a state of completion; denoting the end of availability, supply, etc. (*time is up*). **11** into a compact, accumulated, or secure state (*pack up; save up; tie up*). **12** out of bed (*are you up yet?*). **13** (of the sun etc.) having risen. **14** happening, esp. unusually or unexpectedly (*something is up*). **15** taught or informed (*is well up in French*). **16** (usu. foll. by *before*) appearing for trial etc. (*was up before the magistrate*). **17** (of a road etc.) being repaired. **18** (of a jockey) in the saddle. **19** towards the source of a river. **20** inland. **21** upstairs, esp. to bed (*are you going up yet?*). **22** (of a theatre-curtain) raised etc. to reveal the stage. —*prep.* **1** upwards along, through, or into (*climbed up the ladder*). **2** from the bottom to the top of. **3** along (*walked up the road*). **4 a** at or in a higher part of (*is situated up the street*). **b** towards the source of (a river). —*adj.* **1** directed upwards (*up stroke*). **2** *Brit.* of travel towards a capital or centre (*the up train*). —*n.* a spell of good fortune. —*v.* (**upped**, **upping**) **1** *intr. colloq.* start up; begin abruptly to say or do something (*upped and hit him*). **2** *intr.* (foll. by *with*) raise; pick up (*upped with his stick*). **3** *tr.* increase or raise, esp. abruptly (*upped all their prices*). □ **be all up with** be disastrous or hopeless for (a person). **on the up and up** *colloq.* **1** *Brit.* steadily improving. **2** esp. *US* honest(ly); on the level. **something is up** *colloq.* something unusual or undesirable is afoot or happening. **up against 1** close to. **2** in or into contact with. **3** *colloq.* confronted with (*up against a problem*). **up against it** *colloq.* in great difficulties. **up and about** (or **doing**) having risen from bed; active. **up-and-coming** *colloq.* (of a person) making good progress and likely to succeed. **up and down 1** to and fro (along). **2** in every direction. **3** *colloq.* in varying health or spirits. **up-and-over** (of a door) opened by being raised and pushed back into a horizontal position. **up for** available for or being considered for (office etc.). **up-market** *adj.* & *adv.* towards or relating to the dearer or more affluent sector of the market. **ups and downs 1** rises and falls. **2** alternate good and bad fortune. **up stage** at or to the back of a theatre stage. **up-stroke** a stroke made or written upwards. **up to 1** until (*up to the present*). **2** not more than (*you can have up to five*). **3** less than or equal to (*sums up to £10*). **4** incumbent on (*it is up to you to say*). **5** capable of or fit for (*am not up to a long walk*). **6** occupied or busy with (*what have you been up to?*). **up with** *int.* expressing support for a stated person or thing. **what's up?** *colloq.*

1 what is going on? **2** what is the matter? [OE *up(p)*, *uppe*, rel. to OHG *ūf*]

up- /ʌp/ *prefix* in senses of UP, added: **1** as an adverb to verbs and verbal derivations, = 'upwards' (*upcurved*; *update*). **2** as a preposition to nouns forming adverbs and adjectives (*up-country*; *uphill*). **3** as an adjective to nouns (*upland*; *up-stroke*). [OE *up(p)-*, = UP]

upbeat /ˈʌpbiːt/ *n.* & *v.* —*n.* an unaccented beat in music. —*adj. colloq.* optimistic or cheerful.

upbraid /ʌpˈbreɪd/ *v.tr.* (often foll. by *with*, *for*) chide or reproach (a person). □ **upbraiding** *n.* [OE *upbrēdan* (as UP-, *brēdan* = *bregdan* BRAID in obs. sense 'brandish')]

upbringing /ˈʌpˌbrɪŋɪŋ/ *n.* the bringing up of a child; education. [obs. *upbring* to rear (as UP-, BRING)]

upcoming /ʌpˈkʌmɪŋ/ *adj.* esp. *US* forthcoming; about to happen.

up-country /ʌpˈkʌntrɪ, ˈʌp-/ *adv.* & *adj.* inland; towards the interior of a country.

update *v.* & *n.* —*v.tr.* /ʌpˈdeɪt/ bring up to date. —*n.* /ˈʌpdeɪt/ **1** the act or an instance of updating. **2** an updated version; a set of updated information. □ **updater** *n.*

up-end /ʌpˈend/ *v.tr.* & *intr.* set or rise up on end.

upfield /ˈʌpfiːld/ *adv.* in or to a position nearer to the opponents' end of a football etc. field.

upfront /ʌpˈfrʌnt, ˈʌp-/ *adv.* & *adj. colloq.* —*adv.* (usu. **up front**) **1** at the front; in front. **2** (of payments) in advance. —*adj.* **1** honest, open, frank. **2** (of payments) made in advance. **3** at the front or most prominent.

upgrade *v.* & *n.* /ʌpˈgreɪd/ **1** raise in rank etc. **2** improve (equipment, machinery, etc.) esp. by replacing components. —*n.* /ˈʌpgreɪd/ **1** the act or an instance of upgrading. **2** an upgraded piece of equipment etc. □ **on the upgrade 1** improving in health etc. **2** advancing, progressing. □ **upgrader** *n.*

upheaval /ʌpˈhiːv(ə)l/ *n.* a violent or sudden change or disruption.

uphill *adv.*, *adj.*, & *n.* —*adv.* /ʌpˈhɪl/ in an ascending direction up a hill, slope, etc. —*adj.* /ˈʌphɪl/ **1** sloping up; ascending. **2** arduous, difficult (*an uphill task*). —*n.* /ˈʌphɪl/ an upward slope.

uphold /ʌpˈhəʊld/ *v.tr.* (*past* and *past part.* **upheld**) **1** confirm or maintain (a decision etc., esp. of another). **2** give support or countenance to (a person, practice, etc.). □ **upholder** *n.*

upholster /ʌpˈhəʊlstə(r)/ *v.tr.* **1** provide (furniture) with upholstery. **2** furnish (a room etc.) with furniture, carpets, etc. □ **well-upholstered** *joc.* (of a person) fat. [back-form. f. UPHOLSTERER]

upholsterer /ʌpˈhəʊlstərə(r)/ *n.* a person who upholsters furniture, esp. professionally. [obs. *upholster* (n.) f. UPHOLD (in obs. sense 'keep in repair') + -STER]

upholstery /ʌpˈhəʊlstərɪ/ *n.* **1** textile covering, padding, springs, etc., for furniture. **2** an upholsterer's work.

upkeep /ˈʌpkiːp/ *n.* **1** maintenance in good condition. **2** the cost or means of this.

upland /ˈʌplənd/ *n.* & *adj.* —*n.* the higher or inland parts of a country. —*adj.* of or relating to these parts.

uplift v. & n. —v.tr. /ʌpˈlɪft/ **1** raise; lift up. **2** elevate or stimulate morally or spiritually. —n. /ˈʌplɪft/ **1** the act or an instance of being raised. **2** colloq. a morally or spiritually elevating influence. **3** support for the bust etc. from a garment. □ **uplifter** /-ˈlɪftə(r)/ n. **uplifting** /-ˈlɪftɪŋ/ adj. (esp. in sense 2 of v.).

upon /əˈpɒn/ prep. = ON. [ME f. UP + ON prep., after ON upp á]

■ **Usage** Upon is sometimes more formal than on, but is standard in once upon a time and upon my word.

upper[1] /ˈʌpə(r)/ adj. & n. —adj. **1** higher in place; situated above another part (the upper atmosphere; the upper lip). **2** higher in rank or dignity etc. (the upper class). **3** situated on higher ground (Upper Egypt). —n. the part of a boot or shoe above the sole. □ **on one's uppers** colloq. extremely short of money. **upper class** the highest class of society, esp. the aristocracy. **upper-class** adj. of the upper class. **the upper crust** colloq. the aristocracy. **upper-cut** n. an upwards blow delivered with the arm bent. —v.tr. hit with an upper-cut. **the upper hand** dominance or control. **Upper House** the higher house in a legislature, esp. the House of Lords. [ME f. UP + -ER[2]]

upper[2] /ˈʌpə(r)/ n. sl. a stimulant drug, esp. an amphetamine. [UP v. + -ER[1]]

uppermost /ˈʌpəˌməʊst/ adj. & adv. —adj. (also **upmost** /ˈʌpməʊst/) **1** highest in place or rank. **2** predominant. —adv. at or to the highest or most prominent position.

uppish /ˈʌpɪʃ/ adj. esp. Brit. colloq. self-assertive or arrogant. □ **uppishly** adv. **uppishness** n.

uppity /ˈʌpɪtɪ/ adj. colloq. uppish, snobbish. [fanciful f. UP]

upright /ˈʌpraɪt/ adj. & n. —adj. **1** erect, vertical (an upright posture; stood upright). **2** (of a piano) with vertical strings. **3** (of a person or behaviour) righteous; strictly honourable or honest. **4** (of a picture, book, etc.) greater in height than breadth. —n. **1** a post or rod fixed upright esp. as a structural support. **2** an upright piano. □ **uprightly** adv. **uprightness** n. [OE upriht (as UP, RIGHT)]

uprising /ˈʌpˌraɪzɪŋ/ n. a rebellion or revolt.

uproar /ˈʌprɔː(r)/ n. a tumult; a violent disturbance. [Du. oproer f. op up + roer confusion, assoc. with ROAR]

uproarious /ʌpˈrɔːrɪəs/ adj. **1** very noisy. **2** provoking loud laughter. □ **uproariously** adv. **uproariousness** n.

uproot /ʌpˈruːt/ v.tr. **1** pull (a plant etc.) up from the ground. **2** displace (a person) from an accustomed location. **3** eradicate, destroy. □ **uprooter** n.

uprush /ˈʌprʌʃ/ n. an upward rush, esp. Psychol. from the subconscious.

upset v., n., & adj. —v. /ʌpˈset/ (**upsetting**; past and past part. **upset**) **1** tr. & intr. overturn or be overturned. **2** tr. disturb the composure or digestion of (was very upset by the news; ate something that upset me). **3** tr. disrupt. —n. /ˈʌpset/ **1** a condition of upsetting or being upset (a stomach upset). **2** a surprising result in a game etc. —adj. /ˈʌpset/ disturbed (an upset stomach). □ **upsetter** /-ˈsetə(r)/ n. **upsettingly** /-ˈsetɪŋlɪ/ adv.

upshot /ˈʌpʃɒt/ n. the final or eventual outcome or conclusion.

upside down /ˌʌpsaɪd ˈdaʊn/ adv. & adj. —adv. **1** with the upper part where the lower part should be; in an inverted position. **2** in or into total disorder (everything was turned upside down). —adj. (also **upside-down** attrib.) that is positioned upside down; inverted. [ME, orig. up so down, perh. = 'up as if down']

upsilon /ˈjuːˌpsɪˌlɒn, ʌpˈsaɪlən/ n. the twentieth letter of the Greek alphabet (Υ, υ). [Gk, = slender U f. psilos slender, with ref. to its later coincidence in sound with Gk oi]

upstage /ʌpˈsteɪdʒ/ adj., adv., & v. —adj. & adv. **1** nearer the back of a theatre stage. **2** snobbish(ly). —v.tr. **1** (of an actor) move upstage to make (another actor) face away from the audience. **2** divert attention from (a person) to oneself; outshine.

upstairs adv., adj., & n. —adv. /ʌpˈsteəz/ to or on an upper floor. —adj. /ˈʌpsteəz/ (also **upstair**) situated upstairs. —n. /ˈʌpsteəz/ an upper floor.

upstanding /ʌpˈstændɪŋ/ adj. **1** standing up. **2** strong and healthy. **3** honest or straightforward.

upstart /ˈʌpstɑːt/ n. & adj. —n. a person who has risen suddenly to prominence, esp. one who behaves arrogantly. —adj. **1** that is an upstart. **2** of or characteristic of an upstart.

upstate /ʌpˈsteɪt/ n., adj., & adv. US —n. part of a State remote from its large cities, esp. the northern part. —adj. of or relating to this part. —adv. in or to this part. □ **upstater** n.

upstream /ˈʌpstriːm/ adv. & adj. —adv. against the flow of a stream etc. —adj. moving upstream.

upsurge /ˈʌpsɜːdʒ/ n. an upward surge; a rise (esp. in feelings etc.).

upswept /ˈʌpswept/ adj. **1** (of the hair) combed to the top of the head. **2** curved or sloped upwards.

upswing /ˈʌpswɪŋ/ n. an upward movement or trend.

upsy-daisy /ˈʌpsɪˌdeɪzɪ/ int. (also **ups-a-daisy**) expressing encouragement to a child who is being lifted or has fallen. [earlier up-a-daisy: cf. LACKADAISICAL]

uptake /ˈʌpteɪk/ n. **1** colloq. understanding; comprehension (esp. quick or slow on the uptake). **2** the act or an instance of taking up.

upthrust /ˈʌpθrʌst/ n. upward thrust, e.g. of a fluid on an immersed body.

uptight /ʌpˈtaɪt, ˈʌptaɪt/ adj. colloq. **1** nervously tense or angry. **2** US rigidly conventional.

uptown /ʌpˈtaʊn/ adj., adv., & n. US —adj. of or in the residential part of a town or city. —adv. in or into this part. —n. this part. □ **uptowner** n.

upturn n. & v. —n. /ˈʌptɜːn/ **1** an upward trend; an improvement. **2** an upheaval. —v.tr. /ʌpˈtɜːn/ turn up or upside down.

upward /ˈʌpwəd/ adv. & adj. —adv. (also **upwards**) towards what is higher, superior, larger in amount, more important, or earlier. —adj. moving, extending, pointing, or leading upward. □ **upwards of** more than (found upwards of forty specimens). [OE upweard(es) (as UP, -WARD)]

upwardly /ˈʌpwədlɪ/ adv. in an upward direction. □ **upwardly mobile** able or aspiring to advance socially or professionally.

upwind /ˈʌpwɪnd/ adj. & adv. against the direction of the wind.

ur- /ʊə(r)/ comb. form primitive, original, earliest. [G]

uranium /jʊˈreɪnɪəm/ *n. Chem.* a radioactive grey dense metallic element capable of nuclear fission and therefore used as a source of nuclear energy. □ **uranic** /-ˈrænɪk/ *adj.* [mod.L, f. *Uranus* f. Gk *Ouranos* heaven, Uranus, in Gk mythol. the son of Gaea (Earth): cf. *tellurium*]

urban /ˈɜːbən/ *adj.* of, living in, or situated in a town or city (*an urban population*). □ **urban guerrilla** a terrorist operating in an urban area. [L *urbanus* f. *urbs urbis* city]

urbane /ɜːˈbeɪn/ *adj.* courteous; suave; elegant and refined in manner. □ **urbanely** *adv.* **urbaneness** *n.* [F *urbain* or L *urbanus*: see URBAN]

urbanism /ˈɜːbəˌnɪz(ə)m/ *n.* 1 urban character or way of life. 2 a study of urban life. □ **urbanist** *n.*

urbanite /ˈɜːbəˌnaɪt/ *n.* a dweller in a city or town.

urbanity /ɜːˈbænɪtɪ/ *n.* 1 an urbane quality; refinement of manner. 2 urban life. [F *urbanité* or L *urbanitas* (as URBAN)]

urbanize /ˈɜːbəˌnaɪz/ *v.tr.* (also **-ise**) 1 make urban. 2 destroy the rural quality of (a district). □ **urbanization** /-ˈzeɪʃ(ə)n/ *n.* [F *urbaniser* (as URBAN)]

urchin /ˈɜːtʃɪn/ *n.* 1 a mischievous child, esp. young and raggedly dressed. 2 = *sea urchin*. [ME *hirchon, urcheon* f. ONF *herichon*, OF *heriçon* ult. f. L *(h)ericius* hedgehog]

Urdu /ˈʊədu:, ˈɜː-/ *n.* a language related to Hindi but with many Persian words, an official language of Pakistan and also used in India. [Hind. (*zabān i*) *urdū* (language of the) camp, f. Pers. *urdū* f. Turki *ordū*: see HORDE]

-ure /jə(r)/ *suffix* forming: 1 nouns of action or process (*censure; closure; seizure*). 2 nouns of result (*creature; scripture*). 3 collective nouns (*legislature; nature*). 4 nouns of function (*judicature; ligature*). [from or after OF *-ure* f. L *-ura*]

urea /ˈjʊərɪə, -ˈriːə/ *n. Biochem.* a soluble colourless crystalline nitrogenous compound contained esp. in the urine of mammals. □ **ureal** *adj.* [mod.L f. F *urée* f. Gk *ouron* urine]

ureter /jʊəˈriːtə(r)/ *n.* the duct by which urine passes from the kidney to the bladder or cloaca. □ **ureteral** *adj.* **ureteric** /ˌjʊərɪˈterɪk/ *adj.* **ureteritis** /-ˈraɪtɪs/ *n.* [F *uretère* or mod.L *ureter* f. Gk *ourēthr* f. *oureō* urinate]

urethane /jʊˈriːθeɪn, ˈjʊərɪˌθeɪn/ *n. Chem.* a crystalline amide, used in plastics and paints. [F *uréthane* (as UREA, ETHANE)]

urethra /jʊəˈriːθrə/ *n.* (pl. **urethrae** /-riː/ or **urethras**) the duct by which urine is discharged from the bladder. □ **urethral** *adj.* **urethritis** /-rɪˈθraɪtɪs/ *n.* [LL f. Gk *ourēthra* (as URETER)]

urge *v. & n.* —*v.tr.* 1 (often foll. by *on*) drive forcibly; impel; hasten (*urged them on; urged the horses forward*). 2 (often foll. by *to* + infin. or *that* + clause) encourage or entreat earnestly or persistently (*urged them to go; urged them to action; urged that they should go*). 3 (often foll. by *on, upon*) advocate (an action or argument etc.) pressingly or emphatically (to a person). 4 adduce forcefully as a reason or justification (*urged the seriousness of the problem*). 5 ply (a person etc.) hard with argument or entreaty. —*n.* 1 an urging impulse or tendency. 2 a strong desire. □ **urger** *n.* [L *urgēre* press, drive]

urgent /ˈɜːdʒ(ə)nt/ *adj.* 1 requiring immediate action or attention (*an urgent need for help*). 2 importunate; earnest and persistent in demand. □ **urgency** *n.* **urgently** *adv.* [ME f. F (as URGE)]

uric /ˈjʊərɪk/ *adj.* of or relating to urine. □ **uric acid** a crystalline acid forming a constituent of urine. [F *urique* (as URINE)]

urinal /jʊəˈraɪn(ə)l, ˈjʊərɪn(ə)l/ *n.* 1 a sanitary fitting, usu. against a wall, for men to urinate into. 2 a place or receptacle for urination. [ME f. OF f. LL *urinal* neut. of *urinalis* (as URINE)]

urinary /ˈjʊərɪnərɪ/ *adj.* 1 of or relating to urine. 2 affecting or occurring in the urinary system (*urinary diseases*).

urinate /ˈjʊərɪˌneɪt/ *v.intr.* discharge urine. □ **urination** /-ˈneɪʃ(ə)n/ *n.* [med.L *urinare* (as URINE)]

urine /ˈjʊərɪn/ *n.* a pale-yellow fluid secreted as waste from the blood by the kidneys, stored in the bladder, and discharged through the urethra. □ **urinous** *adj.* [ME f. OF f. L *urina*]

urn *n.* 1 a vase with a foot and usu. a rounded body, esp. for storing the ashes of the cremated dead or as a vessel or measure. 2 a large vessel with a tap, in which tea or coffee etc. is made or kept hot. □ **urnful** *n.* (pl. **-fuls**). [ME f. L *urna*, rel. to *urceus* pitcher]

uro- /ˈjʊərəʊ/ *comb. form* urine. [Gk *ouron* urine]

urogenital /ˌjʊərəˈdʒenɪt(ə)l/ *adj.* of or relating to urinary and genital products or organs.

urology /jʊəˈrɒlədʒɪ/ *n.* the scientific study of the urinary system. □ **urologic** /-rəˈlɒdʒɪk/ *adj.* **urologist** *n.*

Ursa Major /ˌɜːsə ˈmeɪdʒə(r)/ *n.* = *the Great Bear* (see BEAR²). [L, = greater bear]

Ursa Minor /ˌɜːsə ˈmaɪnə(r)/ *n.* = *the Little Bear* (see BEAR²). [L, = lesser bear]

ursine /ˈɜːsaɪn/ *adj.* of or like a bear. [L *ursinus* f. *ursus* bear]

urticaria /ˌɜːtɪˈkeərɪə/ *n. Med.* nettle-rash. [mod.L f. L *urtica* nettle f. *urere* burn]

US *abbr.* United States (of America).

us /ʌs, əs/ *pron.* 1 objective case of WE (*they saw us*). 2 *colloq.* = WE (*it's us again*). 3 *colloq.* = ME¹ (*give us a kiss*). [OE *ūs* f. Gmc]

USA *abbr.* 1 United States of America. 2 US United States Army.

usable /ˈjuːzəb(ə)l/ *adj.* that can be used. □ **usability** /-ˈbɪlɪtɪ/ *n.* **usableness** *n.*

USAF *abbr.* United States Air Force.

usage /ˈjuːsɪdʒ/ *n.* 1 a manner of using or treating; treatment (*damaged by rough usage*). 2 habitual or customary practice, esp. as creating a right, obligation, or standard. [ME f. OF f. *us* USE *n.*]

use *v. & n.* —*v.tr.* /juːz/ 1 cause to act or serve for a purpose; bring into service; avail oneself of (*rarely uses the car; use your discretion*). 2 treat (a person) in a specified manner (*they used him shamefully*). 3 exploit for one's own ends (*they are just using you*). 4 (in *past* /juːst/; foll. by *to* + infin.) did or had in the past (but no longer) as a customary practice or state (*I used to be an archaeologist; it used not (or did not use) to rain so often*). 5 (as **used** *adj.*) second-hand. 6 (as **used** /juːst/ *predic. adj.*) (foll. by *to*) familiar by habit; accustomed (*not used to hard work*). 7 apply (a name or title etc.) to oneself. —*n.* /juːs/ 1 the act of using or the state of being used; application to a purpose (*put it to good use; is in daily use; worn and polished with use*). 2 the right or power of using (*lost the use of my right arm*). 3 **a** the ability to be used (*a torch would be of use*). **b** the purpose for which a thing can be used (*it's no use talking*). 4 custom or usage (*long use has reconciled me to it*). □ **could use** *colloq.* would be glad to have; would be improved by having.

have no use for 1 be unable to find a use for. **2** dislike or be impatient with. **make use of 1** employ, apply. **2** benefit from. **use up 1** consume completely, use the whole of. **2** find a use for (something remaining). **3** exhaust or wear out e.g. with overwork. [ME f. OF *us*, *user*, ult. f. L *uti us-* use]

useful /'juːsfʊl/ *adj.* **1 a** of use; serviceable. **b** producing or able to produce good results (*gave me some useful hints*). **2** *colloq.* highly creditable or efficient (*a useful performance*). □ **make oneself useful** perform useful services. □ **usefully** *adv.* **usefulness** *n.*

useless /'juːslɪs/ *adj.* **1** serving no purpose; unavailing (*protest is useless*). **2** *colloq.* feeble or ineffectual (*am useless at swimming*). □ **uselessly** *adv.* **uselessness** *n.*

user /'juːze(r)/ *n.* **1** a person who uses (esp. a particular commodity or service, or a computer). **2** *colloq.* a drug addict. □ **user-friendly** esp. *Computing* (of a machine or system) designed to be easy to use.

usher /'ʌʃə(r)/ *n.* & *v.* —*n.* **1** a person who shows people to their seats in a hall or theatre etc. **2** a doorkeeper at a court etc. **3** *Brit.* an officer walking before a person of rank. —*v.tr.* **1** act as usher to. **2** (usu. foll. by *in*) announce or show in etc. (*ushered us into the room; ushered in a new era*). □ **ushership** *n.* [ME f. AF *usser*, OF *uissier*, var. of *huissier* f. med.L *ustiarius* for L *ostiarius* f. *ostium* door]

usherette /ˌʌʃə'ret/ *n.* a female usher esp. in a cinema.

USN *abbr.* United States Navy.

USSR *abbr. hist.* Union of Soviet Socialist Republics.

usual /'juːʒʊəl/ *adj.* **1** such as commonly occurs, or is observed or done; customary, habitual (*the usual formalities; it is usual to tip them; forgot my keys as usual*). **2** (prec. by *the*, *my*, etc.) *colloq.* a person's usual drink etc. □ **usually** *adv.* **usualness** *n.* [ME f. OF *usual*, *usuel* or LL *usualis* (as USE)]

usurer /'juːʒərə(r)/ *n.* a person who practises usury. [ME f. AF *usurer*, OF *usureor* f. *usure* f. L *usura*: see USURY]

usurious /juˈʒʊərɪəs/ *adj.* of, involving, or prac- tising usury. □ **usuriously** *adv.*

usurp /juˈzɜːp/ *v.* **1** *tr.* seize or assume (a throne or power etc.) wrongfully. **2** *intr.* (foll. by *on*, *upon*) encroach. □ **usurpation** /ˌjuːzəˈpeɪʃ(ə)n/ *n.* **usurper** *n.* [ME f. OF *usurper* f. L *usurpare* seize for use]

usury /'juːʒərɪ/ *n.* **1** the act or practice of lending money at interest, esp. *Law* at an exorbitant rate. **2** interest at this rate. □ **with usury** *rhet.* or *poet.* with increased force etc. [ME f. med.L *usuria* f. L *usura* (as USE)]

utensil /juːˈtens(ə)l/ *n.* an implement or vessel, esp. for domestic use (*cooking utensils*). [ME f. OF *utensile* f. med.L, neut. of L *utensilis* usable (as USE)]

uterine /'juːtəˌraɪn, -rɪn/ *adj.* **1** of or relating to the uterus. **2** born of the same mother but not

the same father (*sister uterine*). [ME f. LL *uterinus* (as UTERUS)]

uterus /'juːtərəs/ *n.* (*pl.* **uteri** /-ˌraɪ/) the womb. □ **uteritis** /-'raɪtɪs/ *n.* [L]

utilitarian /ˌjuːtɪlɪˈteərɪən/ *adj.* & *n.* —*adj.* **1** designed to be useful for a purpose rather than attractive; severely practical. **2** of utilitarianism. —*n.* an adherent of utilitarianism.

utilitarianism /ˌjuːtɪlɪˈteərɪəˌnɪz(ə)m/ *n.* **1** the doctrine that actions are right if they are useful or for the benefit of a majority. **2** the doctrine that the greatest happiness of the greatest number should be the guiding principle of conduct.

utility /juːˈtɪlɪtɪ/ *n.* (*pl.* **-ies**) **1** the condition of being useful or profitable. **2** a useful thing. **3** = *public utility*. **4** (*attrib.*) **a** severely practical and standardized (*utility furniture*). **b** made or serving for utility. □ **utility room** a room equipped with appliances for washing, ironing, and other domestic work. **utility vehicle** (or **truck** etc.) a vehicle capable of serving various functions. [ME f. OF *utilité* f. L *utilitas -tatis* f *utilis* f *uti* use]

utilize /'juːtɪˌlaɪz/ *v.tr.* (also **-ise**) make practical use of; turn to account; use effectively. □ **utilizable** *adj.* **utilization** /-ˈzeɪʃ(ə)n/ *n.* **utilizer** *n.* [F *utiliser* f. It. *utilizzare* (as UTILITY)]

-ution /'juːʃ(ə)n, 'uːʃ(ə)n/ *suffix* forming nouns, = -ATION (*solution*). [F f. L *-utio*]

utmost /'ʌtməʊst/ *adj.* & *n.* furthest, extreme, or greatest (*the utmost limits; showed the utmost reluctance*). —*n.* (prec. by *the*) the utmost point or degree etc. □ **do one's utmost** do all that one can. [OE *ūt(e)mest* (as OUT, -MOST)]

Utopia /juːˈtəʊpɪə/ *n.* an imagined perfect place or state of things. [title of a book (1516) by Thomas More: mod.L f. Gk *ou* not + *topos* place]

Utopian /juːˈtəʊpɪən/ *adj.* & *n.* (also **utopian**) —*adj.* characteristic of Utopia; idealistic. —*n.* an idealistic reformer. □ **Utopianism** *n.*

utter[1] /'ʌtə(r)/ *attrib.adj.* complete, total, absolute (*utter misery; saw the utter absurdity of it*). □ **utterly** *adv.* **utterness** *n.* [OE *ūtera*, *ūttra*, compar. adj. f. *ūt* OUT: cf. OUTER]

utter[2] /'ʌtə(r)/ *v.tr.* **1** emit audibly (*uttered a startled cry*). **2** express in spoken or written words. **3** *Law* put (esp. forged money) into circulation. □ **utterable** *adj.* **utterer** *n.* [ME f. MDu. *ūteren* make known, assim. to UTTER[1]]

utterance /'ʌtərəns/ *n.* **1** the act or an instance of uttering. **2** a thing spoken. **3 a** the power of speaking. **b** a manner of speaking.

uttermost /'ʌtəˌməʊst/ *adj.* furthest, extreme.

U-turn /'juːtɜːn/ *n.* **1** the turning of a vehicle in a U-shaped course so as to face in the opposite direction. **2** a reversal of policy.

UV *abbr.* ultraviolet.

uvula /'juːvjʊlə/ *n.* (*pl.* **uvulae** /-ˌliː/) a fleshy extension of the soft palate hanging above the throat. □ **uvular** *adj.* [ME f. LL, dimin. of L *uva* grape]

uxorious /ʌkˈsɔːrɪəs/ *adj.* **1** greatly or excessively fond of one's wife. **2** (of behaviour etc.) showing such fondness. □ **uxoriously** *adv.* **uxori- ousness** *n.* [L *uxoriosus* f. *uxor* wife]

Vv

V¹ /viː/ n. (also **v**) (pl. **Vs** or **V's**) **1** the twenty-second letter of the alphabet. **2** a V-shaped thing. **3** (as a Roman numeral) five.

V² abbr. (also **V.**) volt(s).

V³ symb. Chem. the element vanadium.

v. abbr. **1** verse. **2** verso. **3** versus. **4** vide.

vacancy /ˈveɪkənsɪ/ n. (pl. **-ies**) **1** the state of being vacant or empty. **2** an unoccupied post or job (there are three vacancies for typists). **3** an available room in a hotel etc.

vacant /ˈveɪkənt/ adj. **1** not filled or occupied; empty. **2** not mentally active; showing no interest (had a vacant stare). □ **vacant possession** Brit. ownership of a house etc. with no current occupant. □ **vacantly** adv. [ME f. OF vacant or L vacare (as VACATE)]

vacate /vəˈkeɪt, veɪ-/ v.tr. **1** leave vacant or cease to occupy (a house, room, etc.). **2** give up tenure of (a post etc.). □ **vacatable** adj. [L vacare vacat-be empty]

vacation /vəˈkeɪʃ(ə)n/ n. & v. —n. **1** a fixed period of cessation from work, esp. in universities and lawcourts. **2** US a holiday. **3** the act of vacating (a house or post etc.). —v. intr. US take a holiday. [ME f. OF vacation or L vacatio (as VACATE)]

vaccinate /ˈvæksɪˌneɪt/ v.tr. inoculate with a vaccine to procure immunity from a disease. □ **vaccination** /-ˈneɪʃ(ə)n/ n. **vaccinator** n.

vaccine /ˈvæksiːn/ n. & adj. —n. a preparation used to stimulate the production of antibodies and procure immunity from one or several diseases. □ **vaccinal** /-sɪn(ə)l/ adj. [L vaccinus f. vacca cow]

vacillate /ˈvæsɪˌleɪt/ v.intr. **1** fluctuate in opinion or resolution. **2** oscillate, waver. □ **vacillation** /-ˈleɪʃ(ə)n/ n. **vacillator** n. [L vacillare vacillat-sway]

vacuole /ˈvækjʊˌəʊl/ n. Biol. a tiny space within a cell containing air, fluid, food particles, etc. □ **vacuolar** /ˈvækjʊələ(r)/ adj. **vacuolation** /-ˈleɪʃ(ə)n/ n. [F, dimin. of L vacuus empty]

vacuous /ˈvækjʊəs/ adj. **1** lacking expression (a vacuous stare). **2** unintelligent (a vacuous remark). □ **vacuity** /vəˈkjuːɪtɪ/ n. **vacuously** adv. **vacuousness** n. [L vacuus empty (as VACATE)]

vacuum /ˈvækjʊəm/ n. & v. —n. (pl. **vacuums** or **vacua** /-jʊə/) **1** a space entirely devoid of matter. **2** a space or vessel from which the air has been completely or partly removed by a pump etc. **3 a** the absence of the normal or previous content of a place, environment, etc. **b** the absence of former circumstances, activities, etc. **4** (pl. **vacuums**) colloq. a vacuum cleaner. —v. colloq. **1** tr. clean with a vacuum cleaner. **2** intr. use a vacuum cleaner. □ **vacuum brake** a brake in which pressure is caused by the exhaustion of air. **vacuum-clean** clean with a vacuum cleaner. **vacuum cleaner** an apparatus for removing dust etc. by suction. **vacuum flask** Brit. a vessel with a double wall enclosing a vacuum so that the liquid in the inner receptacle retains its temperature. **vacuum-packed** sealed after the partial removal of air. **vacuum pump** a pump for producing a vacuum. **vacuum tube** a tube with a near-vacuum for the free passage of electric current. [mod.L, neut. of L vacuus empty]

vagabond /ˈvægəˌbɒnd/ n. & adj. —n. **1** a wanderer or vagrant, esp. an idle one. **2** colloq. a scamp or rascal. —adj. having no fixed habitation; wandering. □ **vagabondage** n. [ME f. OF vagabond or L vagabundus f. vagari wander]

vagary /ˈveɪgərɪ/ n. (pl. **-ies**) a caprice; an eccentric idea or act. [L vagari wander]

vagina /vəˈdʒaɪnə/ n. (pl. **vaginas** or **vaginae** /-niː/) the canal between the uterus and vulva of a female mammal. □ **vaginal** adj. **vaginitis** /ˌvædʒɪˈnaɪtɪs/ n. [L, = sheath, scabbard]

vaginismus /ˌvædʒɪˈnɪzməs/ n. a painful spasmodic contraction of the vagina, usu. in response to pressure. [mod.L (as VAGINA)]

vagrant /ˈveɪgrənt/ n. & adj. —n. **1** a person without a settled home or regular work. **2** a wanderer or vagabond. —adj. **1** wandering or roving (a vagrant musician). **2** being a vagrant. □ **vagrancy** n. **vagrantly** adv. [ME f. AF vag(a)raunt, perh. alt. f. AF wakerant etc. by assoc. with L vagari wander]

vague /veɪg/ adj. **1** of uncertain or ill-defined meaning or character. **2** (of a person or mind) inexact in thought, expression, or understanding. □ **vaguely** adv. **vagueness** n. **vaguish** adj. [F vague or L vagus wandering, uncertain]

vagus /ˈveɪgəs/ n. (pl. **vagi** /-gaɪ/) Anat. either of the tenth pair of cranial nerves with branches to the heart, lungs, and viscera. □ **vagal** adj. [L: see VAGUE]

vain /veɪn/ adj. **1** excessively proud or conceited. **2** empty, unsubstantial (vain boasts; vain triumphs). **3** useless; followed by no good result (in the vain hope of dissuading them). □ **in vain** without result or success. **take a person's name in vain** use it lightly or profanely. □ **vainly** adv. **vainness** n. [ME f. OF f. L vanus empty, without substance]

valance /ˈvæləns/ n. (also **valence**) a short curtain round the frame or canopy of a bedstead, above a window, or under a shelf. □ **valanced** adj. [ME ult. f. OF avaler descend]

vale n. archaic or poet. (except in place-names) a valley. [ME f. OF val f. L vallis, valles]

valediction /ˌvælɪˈdɪkʃ(ə)n/ n. **1** the act or an instance of bidding farewell. **2** the words used in this. [L valedicere valedict-, f vale, imper. of valēre be well or strong. dicere say), after benediction]

valedictory /ˌvælɪˈdɪktərɪ/ adj. & n. —adj. serving as a farewell. —n. (pl. **-ies**) a farewell address.

valency /ˈveɪlənsɪ/ n. (pl. **-ies**) Brit. Chem. the combining power of an atom measured by the number of hydrogen atoms it can displace or combine with. [LL *valentia* power, competence f. *valēre* be well or strong]

valentine /ˈvælənˌtaɪn/ n. **1** a card or gift sent, often anonymously, as a mark of love or affection on St Valentine's Day (14 Feb.). **2** a sweetheart chosen on this day. [ME f. OF *Valentin* f. L *Valentinus*, name of two saints]

valerian /vəˈlɪərɪən/ n. **1** any of various flowering plants of the family Valerianaceae. **2** the root of any of these used as a medicinal sedative. □ **common valerian 1** a valerian, *Valeriana officinalis*, with pink or white flowers and a strong smell liked by cats: also called SETWALL. **2** the root of this used as a medicinal sedative. [ME f. OF *valeriane* f. med.L *valeriana (herba)*, app. fem. of *Valerianus* of Valerius]

valet /ˈvælɪt, -leɪ/ n. & v. —n. **1** a gentleman's personal attendant who looks after his clothes etc. **2** a hotel etc. employee with similar duties. —v. (**valeted, valeting**) **1** intr. work as a valet. **2** tr. act as a valet to. **3** tr. clean or clean out (a car). [F, = OF *valet, vaslet*, VARLET: rel. to VASSAL]

valetudinarian /ˌvælɪˌtjuːdɪˈneərɪən/ n. & adj. —n. a person of poor health or unduly anxious about health. —adj. **1** of or being a valetudinarian. **2** of poor health. **3** seeking to recover one's health. □ **valetudinarianism** n. [L *valetudinarius* in ill health f. *valetudo -dinis* health f. *valēre* be well]

Valhalla /vælˈhælə/ n. (in Norse mythology) a palace in which the souls of slain heroes feasted for eternity. [mod.L f. ON *Valhöll* f. *valr* the slain + *höll* HALL]

valiant /ˈvæljənt/ adj. (of a person or conduct) brave, courageous. □ **valiantly** adv. [ME f. AF *valiaunt*, OF *vailant* ult. f. L *valēre* be strong]

valid /ˈvælɪd/ adj. **1** (of a reason, objection, etc.) sound or defensible; well-grounded. **2 a** executed with the proper formalities (*a valid contract*). **b** still legally acceptable (*a valid passport*). □ **validity** /vəˈlɪdɪtɪ/ n. **validly** adv. [F *valide* or L *validus* strong (as VALIANT)]

validate /ˈvælɪdeɪt/ v.tr. make valid; ratify. □ **validation** /-ˈdeɪʃ(ə)n/ n. [med.L *validare* f. L (as VALID)]

valise /vəˈliːz/ n. **1** a kitbag. **2** US a small portmanteau. [F f. It. *valigia* corresp. to med.L *valisia*, of unkn. orig.]

Valium /ˈvælɪəm/ n. propr. the drug diazepam used as a tranquillizer and relaxant. [20th c.: orig. uncert.]

Valkyrie /vælˈkɪərɪ, ˈvælkɪrɪ/ n. (in Norse mythology) each of Odin's twelve handmaidens who selected heroes destined to be slain in battle. [ON *Valkyrja*, lit. 'chooser of the slain' f. *valr* the slain + (unrecorded) *kur-, kuz-* rel. to CHOOSE]

valley /ˈvælɪ/ n. (pl. **-eys**) **1** a low area more or less enclosed by hills and usu. with a stream flowing through it. **2** any depression compared to this. **3** *Archit.* an internal angle formed by the intersecting planes of a roof. [ME f. AF *valey*, OF *valee* ult. f. L *vallis, valles*: cf. VALE]

valour /ˈvælə(r)/ n. (US **valor**) personal courage, esp. in battle. □ **valorous** adj. [ME f. OF f. LL *valor -oris* f. *valēre* be strong]

valse /vɑːls, vɔːls/ n. a waltz. [F f. G (as WALTZ)]

valuable /ˈvæljʊəb(ə)l/ adj. & n. —adj. of considerable value, price, or worth. —n. (usu. in pl.) a valuable thing, esp. a small article of personal property. □ **valuably** adv.

valuation /ˌvæljʊˈeɪʃ(ə)n/ n. **1** an estimation (esp. by a professional valuer) of a thing's worth. **2** the price set on a thing.

valuator /ˈvæljʊˌeɪtə(r)/ n. a person who makes valuations; a valuer.

value /ˈvæljuː/ n. & v. —n. **1** the worth, desirability, or utility of a thing (*the value of regular exercise*). **2** worth as estimated (*set a high value on my time*). **3** the amount of money or goods for which a thing can be exchanged in the open market; purchasing power. **4** the equivalent of a thing; what represents or is represented by or may be substituted for a thing (*paid them the value of their lost property*). **5** the ability of a thing to cause an effect (*news value; nuisance value*). **6** (in pl.) one's standards; one's judgement of what is valuable or important in life. **7** *Mus.* the duration of the sound signified by a note. **8** *Math.* the amount denoted by an algebraic term or expression. **9** the relative rank or importance of a playing-card, chess-piece, etc., according to the rules of the game. **10** *Physics & Chem.* the numerical measure of a quantity or a number denoting magnitude on some conventional scale (*the value of gravity at the equator*). —v.tr. (**values, valued, valuing**) **1** estimate the value of; appraise (esp. professionally (*valued the property at £200,000*). **2** have a high or specified opinion of. □ **value added tax** a tax on the amount by which the value of an article has been increased at each stage of its production. **value judgement** a subjective estimate of quality etc. [ME f. OF, fem. past part. of *valoir* be worth f. L *valēre*]

valve n. **1** a device for controlling the passage of fluid through a pipe etc., esp. an automatic device allowing movement in one direction only. **2** *Anat. & Zool.* a membranous part of an organ etc. allowing a flow of blood etc. in one direction only. **3** *Brit.* = thermionic valve. **4** a device to vary the effective length of the tube in a brass musical instrument. □ **valvate** /-veɪt/ adj. **valved** adj. (also in comb.). **valvule** n. [ME f. L *valva* leaf of a folding door]

valvular /ˈvælvjʊlə(r)/ adj. **1** having a valve or valves. **2** having the form or function of a valve. [mod.L *valvula*, dimin. of L *valva*]

vamoose /vəˈmuːs/ v.intr. US (esp. as int.) sl. depart hurriedly. [Sp. *vamos* let us go]

vamp[1] n. & v. —n. **1** the upper front part of a boot or shoe. **2** an improvised musical accompaniment. —v. **1** (often foll. by *up*) repair or furbish. **2 a** tr. & intr. improvise a musical accompaniment (to). **b** tr. improvise (a musical accompaniment). [ME f. OF *avantpié* f. *avant* before (ult. f. L *ab* from + *ante* before) + *pied* foot]

vamp[2] /væmp/ n. & v. colloq. —n. a woman who uses sexual attraction to exploit men. —v. act as a vamp. [abbr. of VAMPIRE]

vampire /ˈvæmpaɪə(r)/ n. **1** a reanimated corpse supposed to leave its grave at night to suck the blood of persons sleeping. **2** a person who preys ruthlessly on others. **3** (in full **vampire bat**) any tropical (esp. South American) bat of the family Desmodontidae, with incisors for piercing flesh and feeding on blood. □ **vampiric** /-ˈpɪrɪk/ adj. [F *vampire* or G *Vampir* f. Magyar *vampir* perh. f. Turk. *uber* witch]

vampirism /ˈvæmpaɪəˌrɪz(ə)m/ n. the practices of a vampire.

van[1] *n.* **1** a covered vehicle for conveying goods etc. **2** *Brit.* a railway carriage for luggage or for the use of the guard. [abbr. of CARAVAN]

van[2] *n.* **1** a vanguard. **2** the forefront (*in the van of progress*). [abbr. of VANGUARD]

van[3] *n. Brit. Tennis colloq.* = ADVANTAGE. [abbr.]

vanadium /vəˈneɪdɪəm/ *n. Chem.* a hard grey metallic transition element occurring naturally in several ores and used in small quantities for strengthening some steels. □ **vanadate** /ˈvænəˌdeɪt/ *n.* **vanadic** /-ˈnædɪk/ *adj.* **vanadous** /ˈvænədəs/ *adj.* [mod.L f. ON *Vanadís* name of the Scand. goddess Freyja + -IUM]

vandal /ˈvænd(ə)l/ *n. & adj.* —*n.* **1** a person who wilfully or maliciously destroys or damages property. **2** (**Vandal**) a member of a Germanic people that ravaged Gaul, Spain, N. Africa, and Rome in the 4th–5th c. —*adj.* of or relating to the Vandals. [L *Vandalus* f. Gmc]

vandalism /ˈvændəˌlɪz(ə)m/ *n.* wilful or malicious destruction or damage to works of art or other property. □ **vandalistic** /-ˈlɪstɪk/ *adj.* **vandalistically** /-ˈlɪstɪkəlɪ/ *adv.*

vandalize /ˈvændəˌlaɪz/ *v.tr.* (also **-ise**) destroy or damage wilfully or maliciously.

vandyke /vænˈdaɪk/ *n. & adj.* —*n.* **1** each of a series of large points forming a border to lace or cloth etc. **2** a cape or collar etc. with these. —*adj.* (**Vandyke**) in the style of dress, esp. with pointed beards, common in portraits by Van Dyck. □ **Vandyke beard** a neat pointed beard. **Vandyke brown** a deep rich brown. [Sir A. *Van Dyck*, Anglicized *Vandyke*, Flem. painter d. 1641]

vane /veɪn/ *n.* **1** (in full **weather-vane**) a revolving pointer mounted on a church spire or other high place to show the direction of the wind (cf. WEATHERCOCK). **2** a blade of a screw propeller or a windmill etc. □ **vaned** *adj.* **vaneless** *adj.* [ME, southern & western var. of obs. *fane* f. OE *fana* banner f. Gmc]

vanguard /ˈvænɡɑːd/ *n.* **1** the foremost part of an army or fleet advancing or ready to advance. **2** the leaders of a movement or of opinion etc. [earlier *vandgard*, (*a*)*vantgard*, f. OF *avan*(t)*garde* f. *avant* before (see VAMP[1]) + *garde* GUARD]

vanilla /vəˈnɪlə/ *n.* **1 a** any tropical climbing orchid of the genus *Vanilla*, with fragrant flowers. **b** (in full **vanilla-pod**) the fruit of these. **2** a substance obtained from the vanilla-pod or synthesized and used to flavour ice-cream, chocolate, etc. [Sp. *vainilla* pod, dimin. of *vaina* sheath, pod, f. L VAGINA]

vanillin /vəˈnɪlɪn/ *n.* the fragrant principle of vanilla.

vanish /ˈvænɪʃ/ *v.* **1** *intr.* **a** disappear suddenly. **b** disappear gradually; fade away. **2** *intr.* cease to exist. □ **vanishing-point** the point at which receding parallel lines viewed in perspective appear to meet. [ME f. OF *e*(*s*)*vaniss*- stem of *e*(*s*)*vanir* ult. f. L *evanescere* (as EX-[1], *vanus* empty)]

Vanitory /ˈvænɪtərɪ/ *n.* (*pl.* **-ies**) *propr.* = *vanity unit.*

vanity /ˈvænɪtɪ/ *n.* (*pl.* **-ies**) **1** conceit and desire for admiration of one's personal attainments or attractions. **2** futility or unsubstantiality (*the vanity of human achievement*). □ **vanity bag** (or **case**) a bag or case carried by a woman and containing a small mirror, make-up, etc. **vanity unit** a unit consisting of a wash-basin set into a flat top with cupboards beneath. [ME f. OF *vanité* f. L *vanitas -tatis* (as VAIN)]

vanquish /ˈvæŋkwɪʃ/ *v.tr. literary* conquer or overcome. □ **vanquishable** *adj.* **vanquisher** *n.* [ME *venkus, -quis*, etc., f. OF *vencus* past part. and *venquis* past tenses of *veintre* f. L *vincere*: assim. to -ISH[2]]

vantage /ˈvɑːntɪdʒ/ *n.* (also **vantage point** or **ground**) a place affording a good view or prospect. [ME f. AF f. OF *avantage* ADVANTAGE]

vapid /ˈvæpɪd/ *adj.* insipid; lacking interest; flat, dull. □ **vapidity** /vəˈpɪdɪtɪ/ *n.* **vapidly** *adv.* **vapidness** *n.* [L *vapidus*]

vaporific /ˌveɪpəˈrɪfɪk/ *adj.* concerned with or causing vapour or vaporization.

vaporimeter /ˌveɪpəˈrɪmɪtə(r)/ *n.* an instrument for measuring the amount of vapour.

vaporize /ˈveɪpəˌraɪz/ *v.tr. & intr.* (also **-ise**) convert or be converted into vapour. □ **vaporizable** *adj.* (also **vaporable**). **vaporization** /-ˈzeɪʃ(ə)n/ *n.*

vaporizer /ˈveɪpəˌraɪz(ə)r/ *n.* a device that vaporizes substances, esp. for medicinal inhalation.

vapour /ˈveɪpə(r)/ *n.* (*US* **vapor**) —*n.* **1** moisture or another substance diffused or suspended in air, e.g. mist or smoke. **2** *Physics* a gaseous form of a normally liquid or solid substance (cf. GAS). **3** a medicinal agent for inhaling. □ **vapour trail** a trail of condensed water from an aircraft or rocket at high altitude, seen as a white streak against the sky. □ **vaporous** *adj.* **vaporously** *adv.* **vaporousness** *n.* **vapourer** *n.* **vapouring** *n.* **vapourish** *adj.* **vapoury** *adj.* [ME f. OF *vapour* or L *vapor* steam, heat]

var. *abbr.* **1** variant. **2** variety.

variable /ˈveərɪəb(ə)l/ *adj. & n.* —*adj.* **1 a** that can be varied or adapted **b** (of a gear) designed to give varying speeds. **2** apt to vary; not constant; unsteady. **3** *Math.* (of a quantity) indeterminate; able to assume different numerical values. **4** (of wind or currents) tending to change direction. **5** *Astron.* (of a star) periodically varying in brightness. **6** *Bot. & Zool.* (of a species) including individuals or groups that depart from the type. —*n.* **1** a variable thing or quantity. **2** *Math.* a variable quantity. **3** *Naut.* **a** a shifting wind. **b** (in *pl.*) the region between the NE and SE trade winds. □ **variability** /-ˈbɪlɪtɪ/ *n.* **variableness** *n.* **variably** *adv.* [ME f. OF f. L *variabilis* (as VARY)]

variance /ˈveərɪəns/ *n.* **1** difference of opinion; dispute, disagreement; lack of harmony (*at variance among ourselves; a theory at variance with all known facts*). **2** *Law* a discrepancy between statements or documents. **3** *Statistics* a quantity equal to the square of the standard deviation. [ME f. OF f. L *variantia* difference (as VARY)]

variant /ˈveərɪənt/ *adj. & n.* —*adj.* **1** differing in form or details from the main one (*a variant spelling*). **2** having different forms. **3** variable or changing. —*n.* a variant form, spelling, type, reading, etc. [ME f. OF (as VARY)]

variation /ˌveərɪˈeɪʃ(ə)n/ *n.* **1** the act or an instance of varying. **2** departure from a former or normal condition, action, or amount, or from a standard or type (*prices are subject to variation*). **3** the extent of this. **4** a thing that varies from a type. **5** *Mus.* a repetition (usu. one of several) of a theme in a changed or elaborated form. □ **variational** *adj.* [ME f. OF *variation* or L *variatio* (as VARY)]

varicella /ˌværɪˈselə/ *n. Med.* = CHICKENPOX. [mod.L, irreg. dimin. of VARIOLA]

varicoloured /ˈveərɪˌkʌləd/ adj. (US **varicolored**) **1** variegated in colour. **2** of various or different colours. [L *varius* VARIOUS + COLOURED]

varicose /ˈværɪˌkəʊs/ adj. (esp. of the veins of the legs) affected by a condition causing them to become dilated and swollen. □ **varicosity** /-ˈkɒsɪtɪ/ n. [L *varicosus* f. *varix -icis* varicose vein]

varied /ˈveərɪd/ adj. showing variety; diverse. □ **variedly** adv.

variegate /ˈveərɪˌɡeɪt, -rɪəˌɡeɪt/ v.tr. **1** mark with irregular patches of different colours. **2** diversify in appearance, esp. in colour. **3** (as **variegated** adj.) Bot. (of plants) having leaves containing two or more colours. □ **variegation** /-ˈɡeɪʃ(ə)n/ n. [L *variegare variegat-* f. *varius* various]

varietal /vəˈraɪət(ə)l/ adj. **1** esp. Bot. & Zool. of, forming, or designating a variety. **2** (of wine) made from a single designated variety of grape. □ **varietally** adv.

variety /vəˈraɪətɪ/ n. (pl. **-ies**) **1** diversity; absence of uniformity; many-sidedness; the condition of being various (*not enough variety in our lives*). **2** a quantity or collection of different things (*for a variety of reasons*). **3** a class of things different in some common qualities from the rest of a larger class to which they belong. **4** (foll. by *of*) a different form of a thing, quality, etc. **5** Biol. **a** a subspecies. **b** a cultivar. **c** an individual or group usually fertile within the species to which it belongs but differing from the species type in some qualities capable of perpetuation. **6** a mixed sequence of dances, songs, comedy acts, etc. (usu. attrib.: *a variety show*). [F *variété* or L *varietas* (as VARIOUS)]

variform /ˈveərɪˌfɔːm/ adj. having various forms. [L *varius* + -FORM]

variola /vəˈraɪələ/ n. Med. smallpox. □ **variolar** adj. **varioloid** /ˈveərɪəˌlɔɪd/ adj. **variolous** adj. [med.L, = pustule, pock (as VARIOUS)]

variole /ˈveərɪˌəʊl/ n. a shallow pit like a smallpox mark. [med.L *variola*: see VARIOLA]

variometer /ˌveərɪˈɒmɪtə(r)/ n. **1** a device for varying the inductance in an electric circuit. **2** a device for indicating an aircraft's rate of change of altitude. [as VARIOUS + -METER]

variorum /ˌveərɪˈɔːrəm/ adj. & n. —adj. **1** (of an edition of a text) having notes by various editors or commentators. **2** (of an edition of an author's works) including variant readings. —n. a variorum edition. [L f. *editio cum notis variorum* edition with notes by various (commentators): genit. pl. of *varius* VARIOUS]

various /ˈveərɪəs/ adj. **1** different, diverse (*too various to form a group*). **2** more than one, several (*for various reasons*). □ **variously** adv. **variousness** n. [L *varius* changing, diverse]

varlet /ˈvɑːlɪt/ n. archaic or joc. **1** a menial or rascal. **2** hist. a knight's attendant. □ **varletry** n. [ME f. OF, var. of *vaslet*: see VALET]

varmint /ˈvɑːmɪnt/ n. US or dial. a mischievous or discreditable person or animal. [var. of *varmin*, VERMIN]

varnish /ˈvɑːnɪʃ/ n. & v. —n. **1** a resinous solution used to give a hard shiny transparent coating to wood, metal, paintings, etc. **2** any other preparation for a similar purpose (*nail varnish*). —v.tr. **1** apply varnish to. **2** gloss over (a fact). □ **varnisher** n. [ME f. OF *vernis* f. med.L *veronix* fragrant resin, sandarac or med.Gk *berenikē* prob. f. *Berenice* in Cyrenaica]

varsity /ˈvɑːsɪtɪ/ n. (pl. **-ies**) **1** Brit. colloq. (esp. with ref. to sports) university. **2** US a university etc. first team in a sport. [abbr.]

vary /ˈveərɪ/ v. (**-ies, -ied**) **1** tr. make different; modify, diversify (*seldom varies the routine; the style is not sufficiently varied*). **2** intr. **a** undergo change; become or be different (*the temperature varies from 30° to 70°*). **b** be of different kinds (*his mood varies*). **3** intr. (foll. by *as*) be in proportion to. □ **varyingly** adv. [ME f. OF *varier* or L *variare* (as VARIOUS)]

vas n. (pl. **vasa** /ˈveɪsə/) Anat. a vessel or duct. □ **vas deferens** /ˈdefəˌrenz/ (pl. **vasa deferentia** /ˌdefəˈrenʃɪə/) Anat. the spermatic duct from the testicle to the urethra. □ **vasal** /ˈveɪs(ə)l/ adj. [L, = vessel]

vascular /ˈvæskjʊlə(r)/ adj. of, made up of, or containing vessels for conveying blood or sap etc. (*vascular functions; vascular tissue*). □ **vascularity** /-ˈlærɪtɪ/ n. **vascularize** v.tr. (also **-ise**). **vascularly** adv. [mod.L *vascularis* f. L VAS]

vase /vɑːz/ n. a vessel, usu. tall and circular, used as an ornament or container, esp. for flowers. □ **vaseful** n. (pl. **-fuls**). [F f. L VAS]

vasectomy /vəˈsektəmɪ/ n. (pl. **-ies**) the surgical removal of part of each vas deferens esp. as a means of sterilization. □ **vasectomize** v.tr. (also **-ise**).

Vaseline /ˈvæsɪˌliːn/ n. & v. —n. propr. a type of petroleum jelly used as an ointment, lubricant, etc. —v.tr. (**vaseline**) treat with Vaseline. [irreg. f. G *Wasser* + Gk *elaion* oil]

vasiform /ˈveɪzɪˌfɔːm/ adj. **1** duct-shaped. **2** vase-shaped. [L *vasi-* f. VAS + -FORM]

vaso- /ˈveɪzəʊ/ comb. form a vessel, esp. a blood-vessel (*vasoconstrictive*). [L *vas*: see VAS]

vasoactive /ˌveɪzəʊˈæktɪv/ adj. = VASOMOTOR.

vasoconstrictive /ˌveɪzəʊkənˈstrɪktɪv/ adj. causing constriction of blood-vessels.

vasodilating /ˌveɪzəʊdaɪˈleɪtɪŋ/ adj. causing dilatation of blood-vessels. □ **vasodilation** n.

vasomotor /ˈveɪzəʊˌməʊtə(r)/ adj. causing constriction or dilatation of blood-vessels.

vassal /ˈvæs(ə)l/ n. hist. a holder of land by feudal tenure on conditions of homage and allegiance. □ **vassalage** n. [ME f. OF f. med.L *vassallus* retainer, of Celt. orig.: the root *vassus* corresp. to OBret. *uuas*, Welsh *gwas*, Ir. *foss*]

vast /vɑːst/ adj. immense, huge; very great. □ **vastly** adv. **vastness** n. [L *vastus* void, immense]

VAT /ˌviːeɪˈtiː, væt/ abbr. (in the UK) value added tax.

vat n. a large tank or other vessel, esp. for holding liquids or something in liquid in the process of brewing, tanning, dyeing, etc. [ME, southern & western var. of *fat*, OE *fæt* f. Gmc]

vatic /ˈvætɪk/ adj. formal prophetic or inspired. [L *vates* prophet]

Vatican /ˈvætɪkən/ n. **1** the palace and official residence of the Pope in Rome. **2** papal government. □ **Vatican City** an independent Papal State in Rome, instituted in 1929. **Vatican Council** an ecumenical council of the Roman Catholic Church, esp. that held in 1869–70 or that held in 1962–5. □ **Vaticanism** n. **Vaticanist** n. [F *Vatican* or L *Vaticanus* name of a hill in Rome]

vaticinate /væˈtɪsɪˌneɪt/ v.tr. & intr. formal prophesy. □ **vaticinal** adj. **vaticination** /-ˈneɪʃ(ə)n/ n. **vaticinator** n. [L *vaticinari* f. *vates* prophet]

VATman /ˈvætmæn/ n. (pl. **-men**) colloq. a customs and excise officer who administers VAT.

vaudeville /ˈvɔːdəvɪl, ˈvəʊ-/ n. **1** esp. US variety entertainment. **2** a stage play on a trivial theme with interspersed songs. □ **vaudevillian** /-ˈvɪlɪən/ adj. & n. [F, orig. of convivial song esp. any of those composed by O. Basselin, 15th-c. poet born at Vau de Vire in Normandy]

Vaudois[1] /ˈvəʊdwɑː/ n. & adj. —n. (pl. same) **1** a native of Vaud in W. Switzerland. **2** the French dialect spoken in Vaud. —adj. of or relating to Vaud or its dialect. [F]

Vaudois[2] /ˈvəʊdwɑː/ n. & adj. —n. (pl. same) a member of the Waldenses. —adj. of or relating to the Waldenses. [F, repr. med.L Valdensis: see WALDENSES]

vault /vɔːlt, vɒlt/ n. & v. —n. **1 a** an arched roof. **b** a continuous arch. **c** a set or series of arches whose joints radiate from a central point or line. **2** a vaultlike covering (the vault of heaven). **3** an underground chamber: **a** as a place of storage (bank vaults). **b** as a place of interment beneath a church or in a cemetery etc. (family vault). **4** an act of vaulting. **5** Anat. the arched roof of a cavity. —v. **1** intr. leap or spring, esp. while resting on one or both hands or with the help of a pole. **2** tr. spring over (a gate etc.) in this way. **3** tr. (esp. as **vaulted**) **a** make in the form of a vault. **b** provide with a vault or vaults. □ **vaulter** n. [OF voute, vaute, ult. f. L volvere roll]

vaulting /ˈvɔːltɪŋ, ˈvɒltɪŋ/ n. **1** arched work in a vaulted roof or ceiling. **2** a gymnastic or athletic exercise in which participants vault over obstacles. □ **vaulting-horse** a wooden block to be vaulted over by gymnasts.

vaunt /vɔːnt/ v. literary **1** intr. boast, brag. **2** tr. boast of; extol boastfully. □ **vauntingly** adv. [ME f. AF vaunter, OF vanter f. LL vantare f. L vanus VAIN: partly obs. avaunt (v.) f. avanter f. a-intensive + vanter]

VCR abbr. video cassette recorder.

VD abbr. venereal disease.

VDU abbr. visual display unit.

VE abbr. Victory in Europe (in 1945). □ **VE day** 8 May, the day marking this.

've abbr. (chiefly after pronouns) = HAVE (I've; they've).

veal n. calf's flesh as food. [ME f. AF ve(e)l, OF veiaus veel f. L vitellus dimin. of vitulus calf]

vector /ˈvektə(r)/ n. **1** Math. & Physics a quantity having direction as well as magnitude, esp. as determining the position of one point in space relative to another (radius vector). **2** a course to be taken by an aircraft. □ **vectorial** /-ˈtɔːrɪəl/ adj. **vectorize** v.tr. (also **-ise**) (in sense 1 of n.). **vectorization** /-təraɪˈzeɪʃ(ə)n/ n. [L, = carrier, f. vehere vect- convey]

Veda /ˈveɪdə, ˈviː-/ n. (in sing. or pl.) the most ancient Hindu scriptures. [Skr. véda, lit. (sacred) knowledge]

Vedanta /vɪˈdæntə, veˈdɑː-/ n. **1** the Upanishads. **2** the Hindu philosophy based on these, esp. in its monistic form. □ **Vedantic** adj. **Vedantist** n. [Skr. vedānta (as VEDA, anta end)]

Vedic /ˈveɪdɪk, ˈviː-/ adj. —adj. of or relating to the Veda or Vedas. —n. the language of the Vedas, an older form of Sanskrit. [F Védique or G Vedisch (as VEDA)]

vee n. **1** the letter V. **2** a thing shaped like a V. [name of the letter]

veer /vɪə(r)/ v.intr. **1** change direction, esp. (of the wind) clockwise (cf. BACK v. 5). **2** Naut. = WEAR[2]. [F virer f. Rmc, perh. alt. f. L gyrare GYRATE]

veg /vedʒ/ n. colloq. a vegetable or vegetables. [abbr.]

Vega /ˈviːgə/ n. Astron. a star in the constellation of the Lyre. [Sp. or med.L Vega f. Arab., = the falling vulture]

vegan /ˈviːgən/ n. & adj. —n. a person who does not eat or use animal products. —adj. using or containing no animal products. [contr. of VEGET-ARIAN]

vegetable /ˈvedʒɪtəb(ə)l, ˈvedʒtəb(ə)l/ n. & adj. —n. **1** Bot. any of various plants, esp. a herbaceous plant used wholly or partly for food, e.g. a cabbage, potato, or bean. **2** colloq. a person who is incapable of normal intellectual activity, esp. through brain injury etc. —adj. **1** of, derived from, relating to, or comprising plants or plant life, esp. as distinct from animal life or mineral substances. **2** of or relating to vegetables as food. □ **vegetable spaghetti** a variety of marrow with flesh resembling spaghetti. [ME f. OF vegetable or LL vegetabilis animating (as VEGETATE)]

vegetal /ˈvedʒɪt(ə)l/ adj. **1** of or having the nature of plants (vegetal growth). **2** vegetative. [med.L vegetalis f. L vegetare animate]

vegetarian /ˌvedʒɪˈteərɪən/ n. & adj. —n. a person who abstains from animal food, esp. that from slaughtered animals, though often not eggs and dairy products. —adj. excluding animal food, esp. meat (a vegetarian diet). □ **vegetarianism** n. [irreg. f. VEGETABLE + -ARIAN]

vegetate /ˈvedʒɪˌteɪt/ v.intr. **1** live an uneventful or monotonous life. **2** grow as plants do; fulfil vegetal functions. [L vegetare animate f. vegetus f. vegére be active]

vegetation /ˌvedʒɪˈteɪʃ(ə)n/ n. **1** plants collectively; plant life. **2** the process of vegetating. □ **vegetational** adj. [med.L vegetatio growth (as VEGETATE)]

vegetative /ˈvedʒɪtətɪv/ adj. **1** concerned with growth and development as distinct from sexual reproduction. **2** of or relating to vegetation or plant life. □ **vegetatively** adv. **vegetativeness** n. [ME f. OF vegetatif -ive or med.L vegetativus (as VEGETATE)]

vehement /ˈviːəmənt/ adj. showing or caused by strong feeling; forceful, ardent. □ **vehemence** n. **vehemently** adv. [ME f. F véhément or L vehemens -entis, perh. f. vemens (unrecorded) deprived of mind, assoc. with vehere carry]

vehicle /ˈviːɪk(ə)l, ˈvɪək(ə)l/ n. **1** any conveyance for transporting people, goods, etc., esp. on land. **2** a medium for thought, feeling, or action (the stage is the best vehicle for their talents). **3** a liquid etc. as a medium for suspending pigments, drugs, etc. □ **vehicular** /vɪˈhɪkjʊlə(r)/ adj. [F véhicule or L vehiculum f. vehere carry]

veil /veɪl/ n. & v. —n. **1** a piece of usu. more or less transparent fabric attached to a woman's hat etc., esp. to conceal the face or protect against the sun, dust, etc. **2** a piece of linen etc. as part of a nun's head-dress, resting on the head and shoulders. **3** a curtain, esp. that separating the sanctuary in the Jewish Temple. —v.tr. **1** cover with a veil. **2** (esp. as **veiled** adj.) partly conceal (veiled threats). □ **beyond the veil** in the unknown state of life after death. **take**

the veil become a nun. □ **veilless** adj. [ME f. AF veil(e), OF voil(e) f. L vela pl. of VELUM]

vein /veɪn/ n. & v. —n. **1 a** any of the tubes by which blood is conveyed to the heart (cf. ARTERY). **b** (in general use) any blood-vessel (has royal blood in his veins). **2** a nervure of an insect's wing. **3** a slender bundle of tissue forming a rib in the framework of a leaf. **4** a streak or stripe of a different colour in wood, marble, cheese, etc. **5** a fissure in rock filled with ore or other deposited material. **6** a source of a particular characteristic (a rich vein of humour). **7** a distinctive character or tendency. —v.tr. fill or cover with or as with veins. □ **veinlet** n. **veiny** adj. (**veinier**, **veiniest**). [ME f. OF veine f. L vena]

veining /ˈveɪnɪŋ/ n. a pattern of streaks or veins.

velar /ˈviːlə(r)/ adj. **1** of a veil or velum. **2** Phonet. (of a sound) pronounced with the back of the tongue near the soft palate. [L velaris f. velum: see VELUM]

Velcro /ˈvelkrəʊ/ n. propr. a fastener for clothes etc. consisting of two strips of nylon fabric, one looped and one burred, which adhere when pressed together. □ **Velcroed** adj. [F velours croché hooked velvet]

veld /velt/ n. (also **veldt**) S.Afr. open country; grassland. [Afrik. f. Du., = FIELD]

vellum /ˈveləm/ n. **1 a** fine parchment orig. from the skin of a calf. **b** a manuscript written on this. **2** smooth writing-paper imitating vellum. [ME f. OF velin (as VEAL)]

velocimeter /ˌveləˈsɪmɪtə(r)/ n. an instrument for measuring velocity.

velocipede /vɪˈlɒsɪpiːd/ n. **1** hist. an early form of bicycle propelled by pressure from the rider's feet on the ground. **2** US a child's tricycle. □ **velocipedist** n. [F vélocipède f. L velox -ocis swift + pes pedis foot]

velocity /vɪˈlɒsɪtɪ/ n. (pl. **-ies**) **1** the measure of the rate of movement of a usu. inanimate object in a given direction. **2** speed in a given direction. **3** (in general use) speed. [F vélocité or L velocitas f. velox -ocis swift]

velour /vəˈlʊə(r)/ n. (also **velours**) plushlike woven fabric or felt. [F velours velvet f. OF velour, velous f. L villosus hairy f. villus: see VELVET]

velouté /vəˈluːteɪ/ n. a sauce made from a roux of butter and flour with white stock. [F, = velvety]

velum /ˈviːləm/ n. (pl. **vela** /-lə/) a membrane, membranous covering, or flap. [L, = sail, curtain, covering, veil]

velvet /ˈvelvɪt/ n. & adj. —n. **1** a closely woven fabric of silk, cotton, etc., with a thick short pile on one side. **2** the furry skin on a deer's growing antler. —adj. of, like, or soft as velvet. □ **velveted** adj. **velvety** adj. [ME f. OF veluotte f. velu velvety f. med.L villutus f. L villus tuft, down]

velveteen /ˌvelvɪˈtiːn/ n. a cotton fabric with a pile like velvet.

Ven. abbr. Venerable (as the title of an archdeacon).

vena cava /ˌviːnə ˈkeɪvə/ n. (pl. **venae cavae** /-niː -viː/) each of usu. two veins carrying blood into the heart. [L, = hollow vein]

venal /ˈviːn(ə)l/ adj. **1** (of a person) able to be bribed or corrupted. **2** (of conduct etc.) characteristic of a venal person. □ **venality** /-ˈnælɪtɪ/ n. **venally** adv. [L venalis f. venum thing for sale]

vend /vend/ v.tr. **1** offer (small wares) for sale. **2** Law sell. □ **vending-machine** a machine that dispenses small articles for sale when a coin or token is inserted. □ **vender** n. (usu. in comb.). [F vendre or L vendere sell (as VENAL, dare give)]

vendetta /venˈdetə/ n. **1** a blood feud in which the family of a murdered person seeks vengeance on the murderer or the murderer's family **2** a prolonged bitter quarrel. [It. f. L vindicta: see VINDICTIVE]

vendor /ˈvendə(r), -dɔː(r)/ n. **1** Law the seller in a sale, esp. of property. **2** = vending-machine (see VEND). [AF vendour (as VEND)]

veneer /vɪˈnɪə(r)/ n. & v.tr. —n. **1** a thin covering of fine wood or other surface material applied to a coarser wood. **2** (often foll. by of) a deceptive outward appearance of a good quality etc. —v.tr. apply a veneer to (wood, furniture, etc.). [earlier fineer f. G furni(e)ren f. OF fournir FURNISH]

venerable /ˈvenərəb(ə)l/ adj. **1** entitled to veneration on account of character, age, associations, etc. (a venerable priest; venerable relics). **2** as the title of an archdeacon in the Church of England. **3** RC Ch. as the title of a deceased person who has attained a certain degree of sanctity but has not been fully beatified or canonized. □ **venerability** /-ˈbɪlɪtɪ/ n. **venerableness** n. **venerably** adv. [ME f. OF venerable or L venerabilis (as VENERATE)]

venerate /ˈvenəreɪt/ v.tr. **1** regard with deep respect. **2** revere on account of sanctity etc. □ **veneration** /-ˈreɪʃ(ə)n/ n. **venerator** n. [L venerari adore, revere]

venereal /vɪˈnɪərɪəl/ adj. **1** of or relating to sexual desire or intercourse. **2** relating to venereal disease. □ **venereal disease** any of various diseases contracted chiefly by sexual intercourse with a person already infected. □ **venereally** adv. [ME f. L venereus f. venus veneris sexual love]

venereology /vɪˌnɪərɪˈɒlədʒɪ/ n. the scientific study of venereal diseases. □ **venereological** /-ə'lɒdʒ ɪk(ə)l/ adj. **venereologist** n.

Venetian /vɪˈniːʃ(ə)n/ n. & adj. —n. **1** a native or citizen of Venice in NE Italy. **2** the Italian dialect of Venice. —adj. of Venice. □ **venetian blind** a window-blind of adjustable horizontal slats to control the light. [ME f. OF Venicien, assim. to med.L Venetianus f. Venetia Venice]

vengeance /ˈvendʒ(ə)ns/ n. punishment inflicted or retribution exacted for wrong to oneself or to a person etc. whose cause one supports. □ **with a vengeance** in a higher degree than was expected or desired; in the fullest sense (punctuality with a vengeance). [ME f. OF f. venger avenge f. L (as VINDICATE)]

vengeful /ˈvendʒfʊl/ adj. vindictive; seeking vengeance. □ **vengefully** adv. **vengefulness** n. [obs. venge avenge (as VENGEANCE)]

venial /ˈviːnɪəl/ adj. (of a sin or fault) pardonable, excusable; not mortal. □ **veniality** /-ˈælɪtɪ/ n. **venially** adv. **venialness** n. [ME f. OF f. LL venialis f. venia forgiveness]

venison /ˈvenɪs(ə)n, -z(ə)n/ n. a deer's flesh as food. [ME f. OF veneso(u)n f. L venatio -onis hunting f. venari to hunt]

venom /ˈvenəm/ n. **1** a poisonous fluid secreted by snakes, scorpions, etc., usu. transmitted by a bite or sting. **2** malignity. □ **venomed** adj. [ME f. OF venim, var. of venin ult. f. L venenum poison]

venomous /ˈvenəməs/ adj. **1 a** containing, secreting, or injecting venom. **b** (of a snake etc.) inflicting poisonous wounds by this means. **2** (of a person etc.) virulent, malignant. □ **venomously** adv. **venomousness** n. [ME f. OF venimeux f. venim: see VENOM]

venose /ˈviːnəʊz/ adj. having many or very marked veins. [L venosus f. vena vein]

venous /ˈviːnəs/ adj. of, full of, or contained in veins. □ **venosity** /vɪˈnɒsɪtɪ/ n. **venously** adv. [L venosus VENOSE or L vena vein + -OUS]

vent[1] n. & v. —n. **1** (also **vent-hole**) a hole or opening allowing motion of air etc. out of or into a confined space. **2** an outlet; free passage or play (gave vent to their indignation). **3** the anus esp. of a lower animal, serving for both excretion and reproduction. —v. **1** tr. **a** make a vent in (a cask etc.). **b** provide (a machine) with a vent. **2** tr. give vent or free expression to (vented my anger on the cat). □ **vent one's spleen on** scold or ill-treat without cause. [partly F vent f. L ventus wind, partly F évent f. éventer expose to air f. OF esventer ult. f. L ventus wind]

vent[2] n. a slit in a garment, esp. in the lower edge of the back of a coat. [ME, var. of fent f. OF fente slip ult. f. L findere cleave]

ventilate /ˈventɪleɪt/ v.tr. **1** cause air to circulate freely in (a room etc.). **2** submit (a question, grievance, etc.) to public consideration and discussion. **3** Med. **a** oxygenate (the blood). **b** admit or force air into (the lungs). □ **ventilation** /-ˈleɪʃ(ə)n/ n. [L ventilare ventilat- blow, winnow, f. ventus wind]

ventilator /ˈventɪleɪtə(r)/ n. **1** an appliance or aperture for ventilating a room etc. **2** Med. = RESPIRATOR 2.

ventral /ˈventr(ə)l/ adj. **1** Anat. & Zool. of or on the abdomen (cf. DORSAL). **2** Bot. of the front or lower surface. □ **ventral fin** either of the ventrally placed fins on a fish. □ **ventrally** adv. [obs. venter abdomen f. L venter ventr-]

ventricle /ˈventrɪk(ə)l/ n. Anat. **1** a cavity in the body. **2** a hollow part of an organ, esp. in the brain or heart. □ **ventricular** /-ˈtrɪkjʊlə(r)/ adj. [ME f. L ventriculus dimin. of venter belly]

ventriloquism /venˈtrɪləˌkwɪz(ə)m/ n. the skill of speaking or uttering sounds so that they seem to come from a source other than the speaker. □ **ventriloquial** /ˌventrɪˈləʊkwɪəl/ adj. **ventriloquist** n. **ventriloquize** v.intr. (also **-ise**). [ult. f. L ventriloquus ventriloquist f. venter belly + loqui speak]

ventriloquy /venˈtrɪləkwɪ/ n. = VENTRILOQUISM.

venture /ˈventʃə(r)/ n. & v. —n. **1 a** an undertaking of a risk. **b** a risky undertaking. **2** a commercial speculation. —v. **1** intr. dare; **2** intr. (usu. foll. by out etc.) dare to go (out), esp. outdoors. **3** tr. dare to put forward (an opinion, suggestion, etc.). **4** tr. expose to risk; stake (a bet etc.). **5** intr. (foll. by on, upon) dare to engage in etc. (ventured on a longer journey). [aventure = ADVENTURE]

venturesome /ˈventʃəsəm/ adj. **1** disposed to take risks. **2** risky. □ **venturesomely** adv. **venturesomeness** n.

venue /ˈvenjuː/ n. **1** an appointed meeting-place esp. for a sports event, meeting, concert, etc. [F, = a coming, fem. past part. of venir come f. L venire]

venule /ˈvenjuːl/ n. Anat. a small vein adjoining the capillaries. [L venula dimin. of vena vein]

Venus /ˈviːnəs/ n. (pl. **Venuses**) the planet second from the sun in the solar system. □ **Venus (or Venus's) fly-trap** a flesh-consuming plant, Dionaea muscipula, with leaves that close on insects etc. □ **Venusian** /vɪˈnjuːzɪən/ adj. & n. [OE f. L Venus Veneris, the goddess of love]

veracious /vəˈreɪʃəs/ adj. formal **1** speaking or disposed to speak the truth. **2** (of a statement etc.) true or meant to be true. □ **veraciously** adv. **veraciousness** n. [L verax veracis f. verus true]

veracity /vəˈræsɪtɪ/ n. **1** truthfulness, honesty. **2** accuracy (of a statement etc.). [F veracité or med.L veracitas (as VERACIOUS)]

veranda /vəˈrændə/ n. (also **verandah**) **1** a portico or external gallery, usu. with a roof, along the side of a house. **2** Austral. & NZ a roof over a pavement in front of a shop. [Hindi varandā f. Port. varanda]

verb n. Gram. a word used to indicate an action, state, or occurrence, and forming the main part of the predicate of a sentence (e.g. hear, become, happen). [ME f. OF verbe or L verbum word, verb]

verbal /ˈvɜːb(ə)l/ adj., n., & v. —adj. **1** of or concerned with words (made a verbal distinction). **2** Gram. of or in the nature of a verb (verbal inflections). —n. **1** sl. a verbal statement, esp. one made to the police. **2** sl. an insult; abuse (gave them the verbal). □ **verbal noun** Gram. a noun formed as an inflection of a verb and partly sharing its constructions (e.g. smoking in smoking is forbidden: see -ING[1]). □ **verbally** adv. [ME f. OF verbal or LL verbalis (as VERB)]

verbalism /ˈvɜːbəlɪz(ə)m/ n. **1** minute attention to words. **2** merely verbal expression. □ **verbalist** n. **verbalistic** /-ˈlɪstɪk/ adj.

verbalize /ˈvɜːbəlaɪz/ v. (also **-ise**) **1** tr. express in words. **2** tr. make (a noun etc.) into a verb. □ **verbalizable** adj. **verbalization** /-ˈzeɪʃ(ə)n/ n. **verbalizer** n.

verbatim /vɜːˈbeɪtɪm/ adv. & adj. in exactly the same words; word for word (copied it verbatim; a verbatim report). [ME f. med.L (adv.), f. L verbum word]

verbena /vɜːˈbiːnə/ n. any plant of the genus Verbena, bearing clusters of fragrant flowers. [L, = sacred bough of olive etc., in med.L vervain]

verbiage /ˈvɜːbɪɪdʒ/ n. needless accumulation of words; verbosity. [F f. obs. verbeier chatter f. verbe word: see VERB]

verbose /vɜːˈbəʊs/ adj. using or expressed in more words than are needed. □ **verbosely** adv. **verboseness** n. **verbosity** /-ˈbɒsɪtɪ/ n. [L verbosus f. verbum word]

verboten /fɜːˈbəʊt(ə)n/ adj. forbidden, esp. by an authority. [G]

verdant /ˈvɜːd(ə)nt/ adj. **1** (of grass etc.) green, fresh-coloured. **2** (of a field etc.) covered with green grass etc. □ **verdancy** n. **verdantly** adv. [perh. f. OF verdeant part. of verdoier be green ult. f. L viridis green]

verdict /ˈvɜːdɪkt/ n. **1** a decision on an issue of fact in a civil or criminal cause or an inquest. **2** a decision; a judgement. [ME f. AF verdit, OF voirdit f. voir, veir true f. L verus + dit f. L DICTUM saying]

verdigris /ˈvɜːdɪgrɪs, -ˌgriːs/ n. **1** a green crystallized substance formed on copper by the action of acetic acid. **2** green rust on copper or brass. [ME f. OF verte-gres, vert de Grece green of Greece]

verdure /ˈvɜːdjə(r)/ n. **1** green vegetation. **2** the greenness of this. □ **verdured** adj. **verdurous** adj. [ME f. OF f. verd green f. L viridis]

verge¹ n. **1** an edge or border. **2** a grass edging of a road, flower-bed, etc. [ME f. OF f. L virga rod]

verge² v.intr. **1** incline downwards or in a specified direction (the now verging sun; verge to a close). **2** (foll. by on) border on; approach closely (verging on the ridiculous). [L vergere bend, incline]

verger /ˈvɜːdʒə(r)/ n. (also **virger**) **1** an official in a church who acts as caretaker and attendant. **2** an officer who bears the staff before a bishop etc. □ **vergership** n. [ME f. AF (as VERGE¹)]

veridical /vɪˈrɪdɪk(ə)l/ adj. **1** formal truthful. **2** Psychol. (of visions etc.) coinciding with reality. □ **veridicality** n. **veridically** adv. [L veridicus f. verus true + dicere say]

verification /ˌverɪfɪˈkeɪʃ(ə)n/ n. **1** the process or an instance of establishing the truth or validity of something. **2** Philos. the establishment of the validity of a proposition empirically. **3** the process of verifying procedures laid down in weapons agreements.

verify /ˈverɪfaɪ/ v.tr. (-ies, -ied) establish the truth or correctness of by examination or demonstration (must verify the statement; verified my figures). □ **verifiable** adj. **verifiably** adv. **verifier** n. [ME f. OF verifier f. med.L verificare f. verus true]

verisimilitude /ˌverɪsɪˈmɪlɪˌtjuːd/ n. **1** the appearance or semblance of being true or real. **2** a statement etc. that seems true. □ **verisimilar** /-ˈsɪmɪlə(r)/ adj. [L verisimilitudo f. verisimilis probable f. veri genit. of verus true + similis like]

veritable /ˈverɪtəb(ə)l/ adj. real; rightly so called (a veritable feast). □ **veritably** adv. [OF (as VERITY)]

verity /ˈverɪtɪ/ n. (pl. -ies) **1** a true statement, esp. one of fundamental import. **2** truth. **3** a really existent thing. [ME f. OF verité, verté f. L veritas -tatis f. verus true]

vermi- /ˈvɜːmɪ/ comb. form worm. [L vermis worm]

vermicelli /ˌvɜːmɪˈselɪ, -ˈtʃelɪ/ n. **1** pasta made in long slender threads. **2** shreds of chocolate used as cake decoration etc. [It., pl. of vermicello dimin. of verme f. L vermis worm]

vermicide /ˈvɜːmɪˌsaɪd/ n. a substance that kills worms.

vermicular /vəˈmɪkjʊlə(r)/ adj. **1** like a worm in form or movement; vermiform. **2** Med. of or caused by intestinal worms. **3** marked with close wavy lines. [med.L vermicularis f. L vermiculus dimin. of vermis worm]

vermiculate /vəˈmɪkjʊlət/ adj. **1** = VERMICULAR. **2** wormeaten. [L vermiculatus past part. of vermiculari be full of worms (as VERMICULAR)]

vermiculation /vəˌmɪkjʊˈleɪʃ(ə)n/ n. **1** the state or process of being eaten or infested by or converted into worms. **2** a vermicular marking. [L vermiculatio (as VERMICULATE)]

vermiculite /vəˈmɪkjʊˌlaɪt/ n. a hydrous silicate mineral expandable into sponge by heating, used as an insulation material. [as VERMICULATE + -ITE¹]

vermifuge /ˈvɜːmɪˌfjuːdʒ/ adj. & n. —adj. that expels intestinal worms. —n. a drug that does this.

vermilion /vəˈmɪljən/ n. & adj. —n. **1** cinnabar. **2 a** a brilliant red pigment made by grinding this or artificially. **b** the colour of this. —adj. of this colour. [ME f. OF vermeillon f. vermeil f. L vermiculus dimin. of vermis worm]

vermin /ˈvɜːmɪn/ n. (usu. treated as pl.) **1** mammals and birds injurious to game, crops, etc., e.g. foxes, rodents, and noxious insects. **2** parasitic worms or insects. **3** vile persons. □ **verminous** adj. [ME f. OF vermin, -ine ult. f. L vermis worm]

vermouth /ˈvɜːməθ, vəˈmuːθ/ n. a wine flavoured with aromatic herbs. [F vermout f. G Wermut WORMWOOD]

vernacular /vəˈnækjʊlə(r)/ n. & adj. —n. **1** the language or dialect of a particular country (Latin gave place to the vernacular). **2** the language of a particular clan or group. **3** homely speech. —adj. **1** (of language) of one's native country; not of foreign origin or of learned formation. **2** (of architecture) concerned with ordinary rather than monumental buildings. □ **vernacularism** n. **vernacularity** /-ˈlærɪtɪ/ n. **vernacularize** v.tr. (also **-ise**). **vernacularly** adv. [L vernaculus domestic, native f. verna home-born slave]

vernal /ˈvɜːn(ə)l/ adj. of, in, or appropriate to spring (vernal equinox; vernal breezes). □ **vernal grass** a sweet-scented European grass, Anthoxanthum odoratum, grown for hay. □ **vernally** adv. [L vernalis f. vernus f. ver spring]

vernalization /ˌvɜːnəlaɪˈzeɪʃ(ə)n/ n. (also **-isation**) the cooling of seed before planting, in order to accelerate flowering. □ **vernalize** /ˈvɜːnəˌlaɪz/ v.tr. (also **-ise**). [(transl. of Russ. yarovizatsiya) f. VERNAL]

veronal /ˈverən(ə)l/ n. propr. a sedative drug, a derivative of barbituric acid. [G, f. Verona in Italy]

veronica /vəˈrɒnɪkə/ n. **1** any plant of the genus Veronica or Hebe. **2** a cloth supposedly impressed with an image of Christ's face. **3** Bullfighting the movement of a matador's cape away from a charging bull. [med.L f. the name Veronica: in sense 2 from the association with St Veronica]

verruca /vəˈruːkə/ n. (pl. **verrucae** /-siː/ or **verrucas**) a wart or similar growth. □ **verrucose** /ˈveruˌkəʊz/ adj. **verrucous** /ˈverukəs/ adj. [L]

versatile /ˈvɜːsəˌtaɪl/ adj. **1** turning easily or readily from one subject or occupation to another; capable of dealing with many subjects (a versatile mind). **2** (of a device etc.) having many uses. □ **versatilely** adv. **versatility** /-ˈtɪlɪtɪ/ n. [F versatile or L versatilis f. versare turn]

verse /vɜːs/ n. & v. —n. **1 a** a metrical composition in general (wrote pages of verse). **b** a particular type of this (English verse). **2 a** a metrical line in accordance with the rules of prosody. **b** a group of a definite number of such lines. **c** a stanza of a poem or song with or without refrain. **3** each of the short numbered divisions of a chapter in the Bible or other scripture. —v.tr. (usu. refl. or pass.; foll. by in) instruct; make knowledgeable. [OE fers f. L versus a turn of the plough, a furrow, a line of writing f. vertere vers- turn: in ME reinforced by OF vers f. L versus]

versed /vɜːst/ adj. (foll. by in) experienced or skilled in; knowledgeable about. [F versé or L versatus past part. of versari be engaged in]

versicle /ˈvɜːsɪk(ə)l/ n. each of the short sentences in a liturgy said or sung by a priest etc. and alternating with responses. □ **versicular**

/-'sɪkjʊlə(r)/ adj. [ME f. OF versicule or L versiculus dimin. of versus: see VERSE]

versify /'vɜːsɪˌfaɪ/ v. (**-ies, -ied**) **1** tr. turn into or express in verse. **2** intr. compose verses. □ **versification** /-fɪ'keɪʃ(ə)n/ n. **versifier** n. [ME f. OF versifier f. L versificare (as VERSE)]

version /'vɜːʃ(ə)n/ n. **1** an account of a matter from a particular person's point of view (told them my version of the incident). **2** a book or work etc. in a particular edition or translation (Authorized Version). **3** a form or variant of a thing as performed, adapted, etc. [F version or med.L versio f. L vertere vers- turn]

vers libre /veə 'liːbrə/ n. irregular or unrhymed verse in which the traditional rules of prosody are disregarded. [F, = free verse]

verso /'vɜːsəʊ/ n. (pl. **-os**) **1** the left-hand page of an open book. **2** the back of a printed leaf of paper or manuscript (opp. RECTO). [L verso (folio) on the turned (leaf)]

verst /vɜːst/ n. a Russian measure of length, about 1.1 km (0.66 mile). [Russ. versta]

versus /'vɜːsəs/ prep. against (esp. in legal and sports use). [L, = towards, in med.L against]

vertebra /'vɜːtɪbrə/ n. (pl. **vertebrae** /-briː/) each segment of the backbone. □ **vertebral** adj. [L f. vertere turn]

vertebrate /'vɜːtɪbrət, -ˌbreɪt/ n. & adj. —n. any animal with a spinal column, including mammals, birds, reptiles, amphibians, and fishes. —adj. of or relating to the vertebrates. [L vertebratus jointed (as VERTEBRA)]

vertex /'vɜːteks/ n. (pl. **vertices** /-tɪˌsiːz/ or **vertexes**) **1** the highest point; the top or apex. **2** Geom. **a** each angular point of a polygon, polyhedron, etc. **b** a meeting-point of two lines that form an angle. **c** the point at which an axis meets a curve or surface. **3** Anat. the crown of the head. [L vertex -ticis whirlpool, crown of a head, vertex, f. vertere turn]

vertical /'vɜːtɪk(ə)l/ adj. & n. —adj. **1** at right angles to a horizontal plane, perpendicular. **2** in a direction from top to bottom of a picture etc. **3** at, or passing through, the zenith. **4** involving all the levels in an organizational hierarchy or stages in the production of a class of goods (vertical integration). —n. a vertical line or plane. □ **vertical take-off** the take-off of an aircraft directly upwards. □ **verticality** /-'kælɪtɪ/ n. **verticalize** v.tr. (also **-ise**). **vertically** adv. [F vertical or LL verticalis (as VERTEX)]

vertiginous /vɜː'tɪdʒɪnəs/ adj. of or causing vertigo. □ **vertiginously** adv. [L vertiginosus (as VERTIGO)]

vertigo /'vɜːtɪˌgəʊ/ n. a condition with a sensation of whirling and a tendency to lose balance; dizziness, giddiness. [L vertigo -ginis whirling f. vertere turn]

vervain /'vɜːveɪn/ n. Bot. any of various herbaceous plants of the genus Verbena. [ME f. OF verveine f. L VERBENA]

verve /vɜːv/ n. enthusiasm, vigour, spirit, esp. in artistic or literary work. [F, earlier = a form of expression, f. L verba words]

vervet /'vɜːvɪt/ n. a small grey African monkey, Cercopithecus aethiops. [F]

very /'verɪ/ adv. & adj. —adv. **1** in a high degree (did it very easily; had a very bad cough; am very much better). **2** in the fullest sense (foll. by own or superl. adj.: at the very latest; do your very best; my very own room). —adj. **1** real, true, actual; truly such (usu. prec. by the, this, his, etc. emphasizing identity, significance, or extreme degree: the very thing we need; those were his very words). **2** archaic real, genuine (very God). □ **not very** **1** in a low degree. **2** far from being. **very good** (or **well**) a formula of consent or approval. **very high frequency** (of radio frequency) in the range 30–300 megahertz. **Very Reverend** the title of a dean. **the very same** see SAME. [ME f. OF verai ult. f. L verus true]

Very light /'verɪ, 'vɪərɪ/ n. a flare projected from a pistol for signalling or temporarily illuminating the surroundings. [E. W. Very, Amer. inventor d. 1910]

Very pistol /'verɪ, 'vɪərɪ/ n. a gun for firing a Very light.

vesica /'vesɪkə/ n. **1** Anat. & Zool. a bladder, esp. the urinary bladder. **2** (in full **vesica piscis** or **piscium**) Art a pointed oval used as an aureole in medieval sculpture and painting. □ **vesical** adj. [L]

vesicle /'vesɪk(ə)l/ n. **1** Anat., Zool., & Bot. a small bladder, bubble, or hollow structure. **2** Geol. a small cavity in volcanic rock produced by gas bubbles. **3** Med. a blister. □ **vesicular** /vɪ'sɪkjʊlə(r)/ adj. **vesiculate** /vɪ'sɪkjʊlət/ adj. **vesiculation** /vɪˌsɪkjʊ'leɪʃ(ə)n/ n. [F vésicule or L vesicula dimin. of VESICA]

vesper /'vespə(r)/ n. **1** Venus as the evening star. **2** poet. evening. **3** (in pl.) **a** the sixth of the canonical hours of prayer. **b** evensong. [L vesper evening (star): sense 3 partly f. OF vespres f. eccl.L vesperas f. L vespera evening]

vessel /'ves(ə)l/ n. **1** a hollow receptacle esp. for liquid, e.g. a cask, cup, pot, bottle, or dish. **2** a ship or boat, esp. a large one. **3** Anat. a duct or canal etc. holding or conveying blood or other fluid, esp. = blood-vessel. [ME f. AF vessel(e) f. LL vascellum dimin. of vas vessel]

vest n. & v. —n. **1** an undergarment worn on the upper part of the body. **2** US & Austral. a waistcoat. —v. **1** tr. (esp. in passive; foll. by with) bestow or confer (powers, authority, etc.) on (a person). **2** tr. (foll. by in) confer (property or power) on (a person) with an immediate fixed right of immediate or future possession. □ **vested interest 1** Law an interest (usu. in land or money held in trust) recognized as belonging to a person. **2** a personal esp. covert interest in a state of affairs, usu. with an expectation of gain. [(n.) F veste f. It. veste f. L vestis garment: (v.) ME, orig. past part. f. OF vestu f. vestir f. L vestire vestit- clothe]

vesta /'vestə/ n. hist. a short wooden or wax match. [Vesta, Roman goddess of the hearth and household]

vestal /'vest(ə)l/ adj. & n. —adj. **1** chaste, pure. **2** of or relating to the Roman goddess Vesta. —n. **1** a chaste woman, esp. a nun. **2** Rom. Antiq. a vestal virgin. □ **vestal virgin** Rom. Antiq. a virgin consecrated to Vesta and vowed to chastity, who shared the charge of maintaining the sacred fire burning on the goddess's altar. [ME f. L vestalis (adj. & n.) (as VESTA)]

vestibule /'vestɪˌbjuːl/ n. **1 a** an antechamber, hall, or lobby next to the outer door of a building. **b** a porch of a church etc. **2** US an enclosed entrance to a railway-carriage. **3** Anat. a chamber or channel communicating with others. □ **vestibular** /-'stɪbjʊlə(r)/ adj. [F vestibule or L vestibulum entrance-court]

vestige /ˈvestɪdʒ/ n. **1** a trace or piece of evidence; a sign. **2** a slight amount; a particle (*showed not a vestige of decency*). [F f. L *vestigium* footprint]

vestigial /veˈstɪdʒɪəl, -dʒ(ə)l/ adj. **1** being a vestige or trace. **2** *Biol.* (of an organ) atrophied or functionless from the process of evolution (*a vestigial wing*). □ **vestigially** adv.

vestment /ˈvestmənt/ n. **1** any of the official robes of clergy, choristers, etc., worn during divine service, esp. a chasuble. **2** a garment, esp. an official or state robe. [ME f. OF *vestiment*, *vestement* f. L *vestimentum* (as VEST)]

vestry /ˈvestrɪ/ n. (pl. **-ies**) a room or building attached to a church for keeping vestments in. [ME f. OF *vestiaire*, *vestiarie*, f. L *vestiarium*]

vet[1] n. & v. —n. *colloq.* a veterinary surgeon. —v.tr. (**vetted**, **vetting**) make a careful and critical examination of a scheme, work, candidate, etc.). [abbr.]

vet[2] n. *US colloq.* a veteran. [abbr.]

vetch n. any plant of the genus *Vicia*, largely used for silage or fodder. [ME f. AF & ONF *veche* f. L *vicia*]

veteran /ˈvetərən/ n. **1** a person who has grown old in or had long experience of esp. military service or an occupation (*a war veteran*; *a veteran of the theatre*; *a veteran marksman*). **2** *US* an ex-serviceman or servicewoman. **3** (*attrib.*) of or for veterans. □ **veteran car** *Brit.* a car made before 1916, or (strictly) before 1905. [F *vétéran* or L *veteranus* (adj. & n.) f. *vetus* -*eris* old]

veterinarian /ˌvetərɪˈneərɪən/ n. *US* a veterinary surgeon. [L *veterinarius* (as VETERINARY)]

veterinary /ˈvetəˌrɪnərɪ/ adj. & n. —adj. of or for diseases and injuries of farm and domestic animals, or their treatment. —n. (pl. **-ies**) a veterinary surgeon. □ **veterinary surgeon** *Brit.* a person qualified to treat diseased or injured animals. [L *veterinarius* f. *veterinae* cattle]

vetiver /ˈvetɪvə(r)/ n. the fibrous root of an Indian grass, *Vetiver zizanoides*, used for making fans etc. [F *vétiver* f. Tamil *veṭṭivēru* f. *vēr* root]

veto /ˈviːtəʊ/ n. & v. —n. (pl. **-oes**) **1 a** a constitutional right to reject a legislative enactment. **b** the right of a permanent member of the UN Security Council to reject a resolution. **c** such a rejection. **2** a prohibition (*put one's veto on a proposal*). —v.tr. (**-oes**, **-oed**) **1** exercise a veto against (a measure etc.). **2** forbid authoritatively. [L, = I forbid, with ref. to its use by Roman tribunes of the people in opposing measures of the Senate]

vex v.tr. anger by a slight or a petty annoyance; irritate. □ **vexer** n. **vexing** adj. **vexingly** adv. [ME f. OF *vexer* f. L *vexare* shake, disturb]

vexation /vekˈseɪʃ(ə)n/ n. **1** the act or an instance of vexing; the state of being vexed. **2** an annoying or distressing thing. [ME f. OF *vexation* or L *vexatio* -*onis* (as VEX)]

vexatious /vekˈseɪʃ(ə)s/ adj. **1** such as to cause vexation. **2** *Law* not having sufficient grounds for action and seeking only to annoy the defendant. □ **vexatiously** adv. **vexatiousness** n.

vexed /vekst/ adj. **1** irritated, angered. **2** (of a problem, issue, etc.) difficult and much discussed; problematic. □ **vexedly** /ˈveksɪdlɪ/ adv.

VG abbr. **1** very good. **2** Vicar-General.

VHF abbr. very high frequency.

VI abbr. Virgin Islands.

via /ˈvaɪə/ prep. by way of; through (*London to Rome via Paris*; *send it via your secretary*). [L, ablat. of *via* way, road]

viable /ˈvaɪəb(ə)l/ adj. **1** (of a plan etc.) feasible; practicable esp. from an economic standpoint. **2 a** (of a plant, animal, etc.) capable of living or existing in a particular climate etc. **b** (of a foetus or newborn child) capable of maintaining life. **3** (of a seed or spore) able to germinate. □ **viability** /-ˈbɪlɪtɪ/ n. **viably** adv. [F f. L *vie* life f. L *vita*]

viaduct /ˈvaɪəˌdʌkt/ n. **1** a long bridgelike structure, esp. a series of arches, carrying a road or railway across a valley or dip in the ground. **2** such a road or railway. [L *via* way, after AQUEDUCT]

vial /ˈvaɪəl/ n. a small (usu. cylindrical glass) vessel esp. for holding liquid medicines. [ME, var. of *fiole* etc.: see PHIAL]

viaticum /vaɪˈætɪkəm/ n. (pl. **viatica** /-kə/) the Eucharist as given to a person near or in danger of death. [L, neut. of *viaticus* f. *via* road]

vibes /vaɪbz/ n.pl. *colloq.* **1** vibrations, esp. in the sense of feelings or atmosphere communicated (*the house had bad vibes*). **2** = VIBRAPHONE. [abbr.]

vibrant /ˈvaɪbrənt/ adj. **1** vibrating. **2** (often foll. by *with*) (of a person or thing) thrilling, quivering (*vibrant with emotion*). **3** (of sound) resonant. □ **vibrancy** n. **vibrantly** adv. [L *vibrare*: see VIBRATE]

vibraphone /ˈvaɪbrəˌfəʊn/ n. a percussion instrument of tuned metal bars with motor-driven resonators and metal tubes giving a vibrato effect. □ **vibraphonist** n. [VIBRATO + -PHONE]

vibrate /vaɪˈbreɪt/ v. **1** intr. & tr. move or cause to move continuously and rapidly to and fro; oscillate. **2** intr. *Physics* move unceasingly to and fro, esp. rapidly. **3** intr. (of a sound) throb; continue to be heard. □ **vibrative** /-rətɪv/ adj. [L *vibrare vibrat-* shake, swing]

vibration /vaɪˈbreɪʃ(ə)n/ n. **1** the act or an instance of vibrating; oscillation. **2** *Physics* (esp. rapid) motion to and fro. **3** (in pl.) **a** a mental (esp. occult) influence. **b** a characteristic atmosphere or feeling in a place, regarded as communicable to people present in it. □ **vibrational** adj. [L *vibratio* (as VIBRATE)]

vibrato /vɪˈbrɑːtəʊ/ n. *Mus.* a rapid slight variation in pitch in singing or playing a stringed or wind instrument, producing a tremulous effect (cf. TREMOLO). [It., past part. of *vibrare* VIBRATE]

vibrator /vaɪˈbreɪtə(r)/ n. a device that vibrates or causes vibration, esp. an electric or other instrument used in massage or for sexual stimulation.

vibratory /ˈvaɪbrətərɪ, -ˈbreɪtərɪ/ adj. causing vibration.

viburnum /vaɪˈbɜːnəm, vɪ-/ n. *Bot.* any shrub of the genus *Viburnum*, e.g. the guelder rose and wayfaring-tree. [L, = wayfaring-tree]

vicar /ˈvɪkə(r)/ n. **1 a** (in the Church of England) an incumbent of a parish where tithes formerly passed to a chapter or religious house or layman (cf. RECTOR). **b** (in an Episcopal Church) a member of the clergy deputizing for another. **2** *RC Ch.* a representative or deputy of a bishop. □ **vicar-general** (pl. **vicars-general**) **1** an Anglican official assisting or representing a bishop esp. in administrative matters. **2** *RC Ch.*

a bishop's assistant in matters of jurisdiction etc. □ **vicariate** /-ˈkeərɪət/ n. **vicarship** n. [ME f. AF viker(e), OF vicaire f. L vicarius substitute f. vicis: see VICE-]

vicarage /ˈvɪkərɪdʒ/ n. the residence or benefice of a vicar.

vicarious /vɪˈkeərɪəs/ adj. **1** experienced in the imagination through another person (vicarious pleasure). **2** acting or done for another (vicarious suffering). **3** deputed, delegated (vicarious authority). □ **vicariously** adv. **vicariousness** n. [L vicarius: see VICAR]

vice[1] n. **1 a** evil or grossly immoral conduct. **b** a particular form of this, esp. involving prostitution, drugs, etc. **2 a** depravity. **b** a particular form of depravity (has the vice of gluttony). □ **vice ring** a group of criminals involved in organizing illegal prostitution. **vice squad** a police department enforcing laws against prostitution, drug abuse, etc. [ME f. OF f. L vitium]

vice[2] n. & v. —n. (US **vise**) an instrument, esp. attached to a workbench, with two movable jaws between which an object may be clamped so as to leave the hands free to work on it. —v.tr. secure in a vice. □ **vicelike** adj. [ME, = winding stair, screw, f. OF vis f. L vitis vine]

vice[3] n. colloq. a person whose role is that of deputy or second-in-command: see VICE-. [abbr.]

vice- comb. form forming nouns meaning: **1** acting as a substitute or deputy for (vice-president). **2** next in rank to (vice admiral). [L, ablat. of vix vic- change]

vicegerent /vaɪsˈdʒerənt/ adj. & n. —adj. exercising delegated power. —n. a vicegerent person; a deputy. □ **vicegerency** n. (pl. **-ies**). [med.L vicegerens (as VICE-, L gerere carry on)]

vicennial /vaɪˈsenɪəl/ adj. lasting for or occurring every twenty years. [LL vicennium period of 20 years f. vicies 20 times f. viginti 20 + annus year]

viceregal /vaɪsˈriːg(ə)l/ adj. of or relating to a viceroy. □ **viceregally** adv.

viceroy /ˈvaɪsrɔɪ/ n. a ruler exercising authority on behalf of a sovereign in a colony, province, etc. □ **viceroyal** /-ˈrɔɪəl/ adj. **viceroyalty** /-ˈrɔɪəltɪ/ n. **viceroyship** n. [F (as VICE-, roy king)]

vice versa /ˌvaɪsɪ ˈvɜːsə/ adv. with the order of the terms or conditions changed; the other way round (could go from left to right or vice versa). [L, = the position being reversed (as VICE-, versa ablat. fem. past part. of vertere turn)]

vichyssoise /ˌviːʃiːˈswɑːz/ n. a creamy soup of leeks and potatoes, usu. served chilled. [F vichyssois -oise of Vichy (in France)]

Vichy water /ˈviːʃiː/ n. an effervescent mineral water from Vichy in France.

vicinal /ˈvɪsɪn(ə)l/, -ˈsaɪn(ə)l/ adj. **1** neighbouring, adjacent. **2** of a neighbourhood; local. [F vicinal or L vicinalis f. vicinus neighbour]

vicinity /vɪˈsɪnɪtɪ/ n. (pl. **-ies**) **1** a surrounding district. **2** (foll. by to) nearness or closeness of place or relationship. □ **in the vicinity** (often foll. by of) near (to). [L vicinitas (as VICINAL)]

vicious /ˈvɪʃəs/ adj. **1** bad-tempered, spiteful (a vicious dog; vicious remarks). **2** violent, severe (a vicious attack). **3** of the nature of or addicted to vice. □ **viciously** adv. **viciousness** n. [ME f. OF vicious or L vitiosus f. vitium VICE[1]]

vicissitude /vɪˈsɪsɪˌtjuːd, vaɪ-/ n. a change of circumstances, esp. variation of fortune. □

vicissitudinous /-ˈtjuːdɪnəs/ adj. [F vicissitude or L vicissitudo -dinis f. vicissim by turns (as VICE-)]

victim /ˈvɪktɪm/ n. **1** a person injured or killed as a result of an event or circumstance (a road victim; the victims of war). **2** a prey; a dupe (fell victim to a confidence trick). **3** a living creature sacrificed to a deity or in a religious rite. [L victima]

victimize /ˈvɪktɪˌmaɪz/ v.tr. (also **-ise**) single out (a person) for punishment or unfair treatment. □ **victimization** /-ˈzeɪʃ(ə)n/ n. **victimizer** n.

victor /ˈvɪktə(r)/ n. a winner in battle or in a contest. [ME f. AF victo(u)r or L victor f. vincere vict- conquer]

victoria /vɪkˈtɔːrɪə/ n. (also **victoria plum**) Brit. a large red luscious variety of plum. [Queen Victoria, d. 1901]

Victoria Cross /vɪkˈtɔːrɪə/ n. a decoration awarded for conspicuous bravery in the armed services, instituted by Queen Victoria in 1856.

Victorian /vɪkˈtɔːrɪən/ adj. & n. —adj. **1** of or characteristic of the time of Queen Victoria. **2** associated with attitudes attributed to this time, esp. of prudery and moral strictness. —n. a person, esp. a writer, of this time. □ **Victorianism** n.

Victoriana /vɪkˌtɔːrɪˈɑːnə/ n.pl. articles, esp. collectors' items, of the Victorian period.

Victoria sandwich /vɪkˈtɔːrɪə/ n. (also **Victoria sponge**) a sponge cake consisting of two layers of sponge with a jam filling.

victorious /vɪkˈtɔːrɪəs/ adj. **1** having won a victory; conquering, triumphant. **2** marked by victory (victorious day). □ **victoriously** adv. **victoriousness** n. [ME f. AF victorious, OF victorieux, f. L victoriosus (as VICTORY)]

victor ludorum /ˌvɪktə luːˈdɔːrəm/ n. the overall champion in a sports competition. [L, = victor of the games]

victory /ˈvɪktərɪ/ n. (pl. **-ies**) **1** the process of defeating an enemy in battle or war or an opponent in a contest. **2** an instance of this; a triumph. [ME f. AF victorie, OF victoire, f. L victoria (as VICTOR)]

victual /ˈvɪt(ə)l/ n. & v. —n. (usu. in pl.) food, provisions, esp. as prepared for use. —v. (**victualled, victualling**; US **victualed, victualing**) **1** tr. supply with victuals. **2** intr. obtain stores. **3** intr. eat victuals. □ **victualless** adj. [ME f. OF vitaille f. LL victualia, neut. pl. of L victualis f. victus food, rel. to vivere live]

victualler /ˈvɪtlə(r)/ n. (US **victualer**) **1** a person etc. who supplies victuals. **2** (in full **licensed victualler**) Brit. a publican etc. licensed to sell alcoholic liquor. [ME f. OF vitaill(i)er, vitaillour (as VICTUAL)]

vicuña /vɪˈkjuːnə/ n. **1** a S. American mammal, related to the llama [Sp. f. Quechua]

vide /ˈvɪdeɪ, ˈviː-, ˈvaɪdɪ/ v.tr. (as an instruction in a reference to a passage in a book etc.) see, consult. [L, imper. of vidēre see]

video /ˈvɪdɪəʊ/ adj., n., & v. —adj. relating to the recording, reproducing, or broadcasting of visual images on magnetic tape. —n. (pl. **-os**) **1** the process of recording, reproducing, or broadcasting visual images on magnetic tape. **2** colloq. = video recorder. **3** a film etc. recorded on a videotape. —v.tr. (**-oes, -oed**) make a video recording of. □ **video cassette** a cassette of videotape. **video game** a game played by electronically manipulating images produced by a computer program on a television screen. **video nasty** *colloq.* an explicitly horrific or pornographic video film. **video** (or **video cassette**) **recorder** an apparatus for recording and playing videotapes. [L *vidēre* see, after AUDIO]

videotape /ˈvɪdɪəʊˌteɪp/ *n. & v.* —*n.* magnetic tape for recording television pictures and sound. —*v.tr.* make a recording of (broadcast material etc.) with this.

vie /vaɪ/ *v.intr.* (**vying**) (often foll. by *with*) compete; strive for superiority (*vied with each other for recognition*). [prob. f. ME (as ENVY)]

Viennese /vɪəˈniːz/ *adj. & n.* —*adj.* of, relating to, or associated with Vienna in Austria. —*n.* (*pl.* same) a native or citizen of Vienna.

Vietnamese /ˌvjetnəˈmiːz/ *adj. & n.* —*adj.* of or relating to Vietnam in SE Asia. —*n.* (*pl.* same) **1** a native or national of Vietnam. **2** the language of Vietnam.

view /vjuː/ *n. & v.* —*n.* **1** range of vision; extent of visibility (*came into view; in full view of the crowd*). **2 a** what is seen from a particular point; a scene or prospect. **b** a picture etc. representing this. **3** a visual or mental survey. **4** an opportunity for visual inspection; a viewing (*a private view of the exhibition*). **5 a** an opinion. **b** a mental attitude (*took a favourable view of the matter*). **c** a manner of considering a thing (*took a long-term view of it*). —*v.* **1** *tr.* survey visually; inspect. **2** *tr.* survey mentally (*different ways of viewing a subject*). **3** *tr.* form a mental impression or opinion of; consider (*does not view the matter in the same light*). **4** *intr.* watch television. □ **have in view 1** have as one's object. **2** bear (a circumstance) in mind in forming a judgement etc. **in view of** having regard to; considering. **on view** being shown (for observation or inspection); being exhibited. **with a view to 1** with the hope or intention of. **2** with the aim of attaining (*with a view to marriage*). □ **viewable** *adj.* [ME f. AF v(i)ewe, OF *vëue* fem. past part. f. *vëoir* see f. L *vidēre*]

viewer /ˈvjuːə(r)/ *n.* **1** a person who views. **2** a person watching television. **3** a device for looking at film transparencies etc.

viewfinder /ˈvjuːˌfaɪndə(r)/ *n.* a device on a camera showing the area covered by the lens in taking a photograph.

viewing /ˈvjuːɪŋ/ *n.* **1** an opportunity or occasion to view; an exhibition. **2** the act or practice of watching television.

viewpoint /ˈvjuːpɔɪnt/ *n.* a point of view, a standpoint.

vigesimal /vɪˈdʒesɪm(ə)l, vaɪ-/ *adj.* **1** of twentieths or twenty. **2** reckoning or reckoned by twenties. □ **vigesimally** *adv.* [L *vigesimus* f. *viginti* twenty]

vigil /ˈvɪdʒɪl/ *n.* **1** keeping awake during the time usually given to sleep, esp. to keep watch or pray (*keep vigil*). **2** a period of this. [ME f. OF *vigile* f. L *vigilia* f. *vigil* awake]

vigilance /ˈvɪdʒɪləns/ *n.* watchfulness, caution, circumspection. □ **vigilance committee** *US* a self-appointed body for the maintenance of order etc. [F *vigilance* or L *vigilantia* f. *vigilare* keep awake (as VIGIL)]

vigilant /ˈvɪdʒɪlənt/ *adj.* watchful against danger, difficulty, etc. □ **vigilantly** *adv.* [L *vigilans -antis* (as VIGILANCE)]

vigilante /ˌvɪdʒɪˈlæntɪ/ *n.* a member of a vigilance committee or similar body. [Sp., = vigilant]

vigneron /ˈviːnjəˌrɔ̃/ *n.* a vine-grower. [F f. *vigne* VINE]

vignette /viːˈnjet/ *n. & v.* —*n.* **1** a short descriptive essay or character sketch. **2** an illustration or decorative design, esp. on the title-page of a book, not enclosed in a definite border. **3** a photograph or portrait showing only the head and shoulders with the background gradually shaded off. —*v.tr.* **1** make a portrait of (a person) in vignette style. **2** shade off (a photograph or portrait). □ **vignettist** *n.* [F, dimin. of *vigne* VINE]

vigorous /ˈvɪgərəs/ *adj.* **1** strong and active; robust. **2** (of a plant) growing strongly. **3** forceful; acting or done with physical or mental vigour; energetic. **4** full of vigour; showing or requiring physical strength or activity. □ **vigorously** *adv.* **vigorousness** *n.* [ME f. OF f. med.L *vigorosus* f. L *vigor* (as VIGOUR)]

vigour /ˈvɪgə(r)/ *n.* (*US* **vigor**) **1** active physical strength or energy. **2** a flourishing physical condition. **3** healthy growth; vitality; vital force. **4 a** mental strength or activity shown in thought or speech or in literary style. **b** forcefulness; trenchancy, animation. □ **vigourless** *adj.* [ME f. OF *vigour* f. L *vigor -oris* f. *vigēre* be lively]

Viking /ˈvaɪkɪŋ/ *n. & adj.* —*n.* any of the Scandinavian seafaring pirates and traders who raided and settled in parts of NW Europe in the 8th–11th c. —*adj.* of or relating to the Vikings or their time. [ON *víkingr*, perh. f. OE *wīcing* f. *wīc* camp]

vile *adj.* **1** disgusting. **2** morally base; depraved, shameful. **3** *colloq.* abominably bad (*vile weather*). **4** *archaic* worthless. □ **vilely** *adv.* **vileness** *n.* [ME f. OF *vil vile* f. L *vilis* cheap, base]

vilify /ˈvɪlɪˌfaɪ/ *v.tr.* (**-ies, -ied**) defame; speak evil of. □ **vilification** /-fɪˈkeɪʃ(ə)n/ *n.* **vilifier** *n.* [ME in sense 'lower in value', f. LL *vilificare* (as VILE)]

villa /ˈvɪlə/ *n.* **1** *Rom. Antiq.* a large country house with an estate. **2** a country residence. **3** a rented holiday home, esp. abroad. [It. & L]

village /ˈvɪlɪdʒ/ *n.* **1 a** a group of houses and associated buildings, larger than a hamlet and smaller than a town, esp. in a rural area. **b** the inhabitants of a village regarded as a community. **2** *Brit.* a self-contained district or community within a town or city, regarded as having features characteristic of village life. **3** *US* a small municipality with limited corporate powers. **4** *Austral.* a select suburban shopping centre. □ **villager** *n.* **villagey** *adj.* [ME f. OF f. L *villa*]

villain /ˈvɪlən/ *n.* **1** a person guilty or capable of great wickedness. **2** *colloq.* usu. *joc.* a rascal or rogue. **3** (also **villain of the piece**) (in a play etc.) a character whose evil actions or motives are important in the plot. [ME f. OF *vilein, vilain* ult. f. L *villa*: see VILLA]

villainous /ˈvɪlənəs/ *adj.* **1** characteristic of a villain; wicked. **2** *colloq.* abominably bad; vile. □ **villainously** *adv.* **villainousness** *n.*

villainy /ˈvɪlənɪ/ *n.* (*pl.* **-ies**) **1** villainous behaviour. **2** a wicked act. [OF *vilenie* (as VILLAIN)]

-ville /vɪl/ *comb. form colloq.* forming the names of fictitious places with ref. to a particular quality etc. (*dragsville; squaresville*). [F *ville* town, as in many US town-names]

villus /ˈvɪləs/ *n.* (*pl.* **villi** /-laɪ/) *Anat.* each of the short finger-like processes on some membranes, esp. on the mucous membrane of the small

intestine. □ **villiform** adj. **villose** adj. **villosity**
/-'lɒsɪtɪ/ n. **villous** adj. [L, = shaggy hair]

vim n. colloq. vigour. [perh. f. L, accus. of vis
energy]

vinaigrette /ˌvɪnɪ'gret/ n. (in full **vinaigrette
sauce**) a salad dressing of oil, wine vinegar, and
seasoning. [F, dimin. of vinaigre VINEGAR]

vindicate /'vɪndɪˌkeɪt/ v.tr. **1** clear of blame or
suspicion. **2** establish the existence, merits, or
justice of (one's courage, conduct, assertion,
etc.). **3** justify (a person, oneself, etc.) by evidence
or argument. □ **vindicable** /-kəb(ə)l/ adj. **vindication** /-'keɪʃ(ə)n/ n. **vindicative** /-kətɪv/ adj.
vindicator n. [L vindicare claim, avenge f. vindex
-dicis claimant, avenger]

vindicatory /'vɪndɪˌkeɪtərɪ/ adj. **1** tending to
vindicate. **2** (of laws) punitive.

vindictive /vɪn'dɪktɪv/ adj. **1** tending to seek
revenge. **2** spiteful. □ **vindictive damages** Law
damages exceeding simple compensation and
awarded to punish the defendant. □ **vindictively** adv. **vindictiveness** n. [L vindicta
vengeance (as VINDI- CATE)]

vine n. **1** any climbing or trailing woody-
stemmed plant, esp. of the genus Vitis, bearing
grapes. **2** a slender trailing or climbing stem. □
vine-dresser n. a person who prunes, trains, and
cultivates vines. □ **viny** adj. [ME f. OF vi(g)ne f. L
vinea vineyard f. vinum wine]

vinegar /'vɪnɪgə(r)/ n. a sour liquid obtained
from wine, cider, etc., by fermentation and used
as a condiment or for pickling. □ **vinegarish**
adj. **vinegary** adj. [ME f. OF vyn egre ult. f. L
vinum wine + acer, acre sour]

vinery /'vaɪnərɪ/ n. (pl. **-ies**) **1** a greenhouse for
grapevines. **2** a vineyard.

vineyard /'vɪnjɑːd, -jəd/ n. a plantation of grapevines, esp. for wine-making. [ME f. VINE +
YARD²]

vingt-et-un /ˌvæ̃teɪ'ɜː/ n. = PONTOON¹. [F, =
twenty-one]

vini- /'vɪnɪ/ comb. form wine. [L vinum]

viniculture /'vɪnɪˌkʌltʃə(r)/ n. the cultivation of
grapevines. □ **vinicultural** /-'kʌltʃər(ə)l/ adj.
viniculturist /-'kʌltʃərɪst/ n.

vinification /ˌvɪnɪfɪ'keɪʃ(ə)n/ n. the conversion
of grape-juice etc. into wine.

vino /'viːnəʊ/ n. sl. wine, esp. of an inferior kind.
[Sp. & It., = wine]

vin ordinaire /ˌvæ̃ ɔːdɪ'neə(r)/ n. cheap (usu.
red) wine as drunk in France mixed with water.
[F, = ordinary wine]

vinous /'vaɪnəs/ adj. **1** of, like, or associated with
wine. **2** addicted to wine. □ **vinosity** /-'nɒsɪtɪ/ n.
[L vinum wine]

vin rosé /ˌvæ̃ rəʊ'zeɪ/ n. = ROSÉ. [F]

vint v.tr. make (wine). [back-form. f. VINTAGE]

vintage /'vɪntɪdʒ/ n. & adj. —n. **1 a** a season's
produce of grapes. **b** the wine made from this.
2 a the gathering of grapes for wine-making. **b**
the season of this. **3** a wine of high quality from
a single identified year and district. **4** the year
etc. when a thing was made etc. —adj. **1** of high
quality, esp. from the past or characteristic of
the best period of a person's work. □ **vintage
car** Brit. a car made between 1917 and 1930.
[alt. (after VINTNER) of ME vendage, vindage f. OF
vendange f. L vindemia f. vinum wine + demere
remove]

vintner /'vɪntnə(r)/ n. a wine-merchant. [ME f.
AL vintenarius, vinetarius f. AF vineter, OF vinetier
f. med.L vinetarius f. L vinetum vineyard f. vinum
wine]

viny see VINE.

vinyl /'vaɪnɪl/ n. plastic made by polymerization.
[L vinum wine + -YL]

viol /'vaɪəl/ n. a medieval stringed musical
instrument, played with a bow and held vertically on the knees or between the legs. [ME
viel etc. f. OF viel(l)e, alt. of viole f. Prov. viola,
viula, prob. ult. f. L vitulari be joyful: cf. FIDDLE]

viola¹ /vɪ'əʊlə/ n. **1 a** an instrument of the violin
family, larger than the violin and of lower pitch.
b a viola-player. **2** a viol. □ **viola da gamba** /də
'gæmbə/ a viol held between the player's legs,
esp. one corresponding to the modern cello.
viola d'amore /dæ'mɔːreɪ/ a sweet-toned tenor
viol. [It. & Sp., prob. f. Prov.: see VIOL]

viola² /'vaɪələ/ n. **1** any plant of the genus Viola,
including the pansy and violet. **2** a cultivated
hybrid of this genus. [L, = violet]

violate /'vaɪəˌleɪt/ v.tr. **1** disregard; fail to comply
with (an oath, treaty, law, etc.). **2** treat (a
sanctuary etc.) profanely or with disrespect. **3**
break in upon, disturb (a person's privacy
etc.). **4** assault sexually; rape. □ **violable** adj.
violation /-'leɪʃ(ə)n/ n. **violator** n. [ME f. L violare
treat violently]

violence /'vaɪələns/ n. **1** the quality of being
violent. **2** violent conduct or treatment, outrage,
injury. **3** Law **a** the unlawful exercise of physical
force. **b** intimidation by the exhibition of this.
□ **do violence to** act contrary to; outrage. [ME
f. OF f. L violentia (as VIOLENT)]

violent /'vaɪələnt/ adj. **1** involving or using
great physical force. **2 a** intense, vehement,
passionate, furious (a violent contrast; violent
dislike). **b** vivid (violent colours). **3** (of death)
resulting from external force or from poison
(cf. NATURAL adj. 2). □ **violently** adv. [ME f. OF f.
L violentus]

violet /'vaɪələt/ n. & adj. —n. **1** any plant of the
genus Viola, with usu. purple, blue, or white
flowers. **2** the bluish-purple colour seen at the
end of the spectrum opposite red. **3** pigment of
this colour. —adj. of this colour. [ME f. OF
violet(te) dimin. of viole f. L VIOLA²]

violin /vaɪə'lɪn/ n. **1** a musical instrument with
four strings of treble pitch played with a bow. **2**
a violin-player. □ **violinist** n. [It. violino dimin.
of VIOLA¹]

violist /'vaɪəlɪst/ n. a viol- or viola-player.

violoncello /ˌvaɪələn'tʃeləʊ, ˌviːə-/ n. (pl. **-os**)
formal = CELLO. □ **violoncellist** n. [It., dimin. of
violone double-bass viol]

VIP abbr. very important person.

viper /'vaɪpə(r)/ n. **1** any venomous snake of the
family Viperidae (see ADDER). **2** a malignant or
treacherous person. □ **viper's bugloss** a stiff
bristly blue-flowered plant. □ **viperine** /-ˌraɪn/
adj. **viperish** adj. **viper-like** adj. **viperous** adj.
[F vipère or L vipera f. vivus alive + parere bring
forth]

virago /vɪ'rɑːgəʊ, -'reɪgəʊ/ n. (pl. **-os**) a fierce or
abusive woman. [OE f. L, = female warrior, f.
vir man]

viral /'vaɪər(ə)l/ adj. of or caused by a virus. □
virally adv.

virescence /vɪ'res(ə)ns/ n. **1** greenness. **2** Bot.
abnormal greenness in petals etc. normally of

some bright colour. □ **virescent** *adj.* [L *virescere*, incept. of *virēre* be green]

Virgilian /vɜːˈdʒɪlɪən/ *adj.* of, or in the style of, the Roman poet Virgil (d. 19 BC). [L *Vergilianus* f. P. *Vergilius* Maro, Virgil]

virgin /ˈvɜːdʒɪn/ *n.* & *adj.* —*n.* **1** a person (woman) who has never had sexual intercourse. **2 (the Virgin)** Christ's mother the Blessed Virgin Mary. **3 (the Virgin)** the zodiacal sign or constellation Virgo. —*adj.* **1** that is a virgin. **2** of or befitting a virgin (*virgin modesty*). **3** not yet used, penetrated, or tried (*virgin soil*). **4** (of clay) not fired. **5** (of metal) made from ore by smelting. **6** (of wool) not yet, or only once, spun or woven. □ **virgin birth 1** the doctrine of Christ's birth without a human father. **2** parthenogenesis. **virgin forest** a forest in its untouched natural state. **the Virgin Queen** Queen Elizabeth I of England. □ **virginhood** *n.* **virginity** *n.* [ME f. AF & OF *virgine* f. L *virgo -ginis*]

virginal /ˈvɜːdʒɪn(ə)l/ *adj.* & *n.* —*adj.* that is or befits or belongs to a virgin. —*n.* (usu. in *pl.*) (in full **pair of virginals**) an early form of spinet in a box, used in the sixteenth and seventeenth centuries. □ **virginalist** *n.* **virginally** *adv.* [ME f. OF *virginal* or L *virginalis* (as VIRGIN): name of the instrument perh. from its use by young women]

Virginia /vəˈdʒɪnɪə/ *n.* **1** tobacco from Virginia. **2** a cigarette made of this. □ **Virginia creeper** a N. American vine cultivated for ornament. **Virginia** (or **Virginian**) **stock** a cruciferous plant with white or pink flowers. □ **Virginian** *n.* & *adj.* [*Virginia* in US, orig. the first English settlement (1607), f. *Virgin Queen*]

Virgo /ˈvɜːgəʊ/ *n.* (*pl.* **-os**) **1** a constellation, traditionally regarded as contained in the figure of a woman. **2 a** the sixth sign of the zodiac (the Virgin). **b** a person born when the sun is in this sign. □ **Virgoan** *n.* & *adj.* [OE f. L, = virgin]

viridescent /ˌvɪrɪˈdes(ə)nt/ *adj.* greenish, tending to become green. □ **viridescence** *n.* [LL *viridescere* f. L *viridis*: see VIRIDIAN]

viridian /vɪˈrɪdɪən/ *n.* & *adj.* —*n.* **1** a bluish-green chromium oxide pigment. **2** the colour of this. —*adj.* bluish-green. [L *viridis* green f. *virēre* be green]

viridity /vɪˈrɪdɪtɪ/ *n. literary* greenness, verdancy. [ME f. OF *viridité* or L *viriditas* f. *viridis*: see VIRIDIAN]

virile /ˈvɪraɪl/ *adj.* **1** of or characteristic of a man; having masculine (esp. sexual) vigour or strength. **2** of or having procreative power. **3** of a man as distinct from a woman or child. □ **virility** /vɪˈrɪlɪtɪ/ *n.* [ME f. F *viril* or L *virilis* f. *vir* man]

virilism /ˈvɪrɪˌlɪz(ə)m/ *n. Med.* the development of secondary male characteristics in a female or precociously in a male.

virology /vaɪˈrɒlədʒɪ/ *n.* the scientific study of viruses. □ **virological** /-rəˈlɒdʒɪk(ə)l/ *adj.* **virologically** /-rəˈlɒdʒɪkəlɪ/ *adv.* **virologist** *n.*

virtual /ˈvɜːtjʊəl/ *adj.* **1** that is such for practical purposes though not in name or according to strict definition. **2** *Optics* relating to the points at which rays would meet if produced backwards (*virtual focus*; *virtual image*). **3** *Mech.* relating to an infinitesimal displacement of a point in a system. **4** *Computing* not physically existing as such but made by software to appear to do so.

virtuality /-jʊˈælɪtɪ/ *n.* **virtually** *adv.* [ME f. med.L *virtualis* f. L *virtus* after LL *virtuosus*]

virtue /ˈvɜːtjuː, -tʃuː/ *n.* **1** moral excellence; uprightness, goodness. **2** a particular form of this (*patience is a virtue*). **3** chastity, esp. of a woman. **4** a good quality (*has the virtue of being adjustable*). **5** efficacy; inherent power (*no virtue in such drugs*). □ **by** (or **in**) **virtue of** on the strength or ground of (*got the job by virtue of his experience*). **make a virtue of necessity** derive some credit or benefit from an unwelcome obligation. □ **virtueless** *adj.* [ME f. OF *vertu* f. L *virtus -tutis* f. *vir* man]

virtuoso /ˌvɜːtjʊˈəʊsəʊ, -zəʊ/ *n.* (*pl.* **virtuosi** /-iː/ or **-os**) **1** a person highly skilled in the technique of a fine art, esp. music. **2** (*attrib.*) displaying the skills of a virtuoso. □ **virtuosic** /-ˈɒsɪk/ *adj.* **virtuosity** /-ˈɒsɪtɪ/ *n.* **virtuosoship** *n.* [It., = learned, skilful, f. LL (as VIRTUOUS)]

virtuous /ˈvɜːtjʊəs, -tʃʊəs/ *adj.* **1** possessing or showing moral rectitude. **2** chaste. □ **virtuously** *adv.* **virtuousness** *n.* [ME f. OF *vertuous* f. LL *virtuosus* f. *virtus* VIRTUE]

virulent /ˈvɪrʊlənt, ˈvɪrjʊ-/ *adj.* **1** strongly poisonous. **2** (of a disease) violent or malignant. **3** bitterly hostile □ **virulence** *n.* **virulently** *adv.* [ME, orig. of a poisoned wound, f. L *virulentus* (as VIRUS)]

virus /ˈvaɪərəs/ *n.* **1** a microscopic organism multiplying only in living cells and often causing diseases. **2** *Computing* = *computer virus*. [L, = slimy liquid, poison]

Vis. *abbr.* Viscount.

visa /ˈviːzə/ *n.* an endorsement on a passport etc. showing that it has been found correct, esp. as allowing the holder to enter or leave a country. [F f. L *visa* neut. pl. past part. of *vidēre* see]

visage /ˈvɪzɪdʒ/ *n. literary* a face, a countenance. □ **visaged** *adj.* (also in *comb.*). [ME f. OF f. L *visus* sight (as VISA)]

vis-à-vis /ˌviːzɑːˈviː/ *prep.*, *adv.*, & *n.* —*prep.* in relation to. —*adv.* facing one another. —*n.* (*pl.* same) **1** a person or thing facing another, esp. in some dances. **2** a person occupying a corresponding position in another group. [F, = face to face, f. *vis* face f. L (as VISAGE)]

Visc. *abbr.* Viscount.

viscera /ˈvɪsərə/ *n.pl.* the interior organs in the great cavities of the body (e.g. brain, heart, liver), esp. in the abdomen (e.g. the intestines). [L, pl. of *viscus*]

visceral /ˈvɪsər(ə)l/ *adj.* **1** of the viscera. **2** relating to inward feelings rather than conscious reasoning. □ **viscerally** *adv.*

viscid /ˈvɪsɪd/ *adj.* **1** glutinous, sticky. **2** semifluid. □ **viscidity** /vɪˈsɪdɪtɪ/ *n.* [LL *viscidus* f. L *viscum* birdlime]

viscose /ˈvɪskəʊz, -kəʊs/ *n.* **1** a form of cellulose in a highly viscous state suitable for drawing into yarn. **2** rayon made from this. [LL *viscosus* (as VISCOUS)]

viscosity /vɪˈskɒsɪtɪ/ *n.* (*pl.* **-ies**) **1** the quality or degree of being viscous. **2** *Physics* (of a fluid) internal friction, the resistance to flow. [ME f. OF *viscosité* or med.L *viscositas* (as VISCOUS)]

viscount /ˈvaɪkaʊnt/ *n.* a British nobleman ranking between an earl and a baron. □ **viscountcy** *n.* (*pl.* **-ies**). **viscountship** *n.* **viscounty** *n.* (*pl.* **-ies**). [ME f. AF *viscounte*, OF *vi(s)conte* f. med.L *vicecomes -mitis* (as VICE-, COUNT²)]

viscountess /ˈvaɪkaʊntɪs/ n. 1 a viscount's wife or widow. 2 a woman holding the rank of viscount in her own right.

viscous /ˈvɪskəs/ adj. 1 glutinous. 2 semifluid. 3 Physics having a high viscosity; not flowing freely. □ **viscously** adv. **viscousness** n. [ME f. AF viscous or LL viscosus (as VISCID)]

vise US var. of VICE².

Vishnu /ˈvɪʃnuː/ n. a Hindu god regarded by his worshippers as the supreme deity and saviour, by others as the second member of a triad with Brahma and Siva. □ **Vishnuism** n. **Vishnuite** n. & adj. [Skr. Vishṇu]

visibility /ˌvɪzɪˈbɪlɪtɪ/ n. 1 the state of being visible. 2 the range or possibility of vision as determined by the conditions of light and atmosphere. [F visibilité or LL visibilitas f. L visibilis: see VISIBLE]

visible /ˈvɪzɪb(ə)l/ adj. 1 a that can be seen by the eye. b (of light) within the range of wavelengths to which the eye is sensitive. 2 that can be perceived or ascertained (has no visible means of support; spoke with visible impatience). 3 (of exports etc.) consisting of actual goods (cf. invisible exports). □ **visibleness** n. **visibly** adv. [ME f. OF visible or L visibilis f. vidēre vis- see]

vision /ˈvɪʒ(ə)n/ n. & v. —n. 1 the act or faculty of seeing, sight. 2 a a thing or person seen in a dream or trance. b a supernatural apparition. 3 a thing or idea perceived vividly in the imagination. 4 imaginative insight. 5 foresight; sagacity in planning. □ **field of vision** all that comes into view when the eyes are turned in some direction. **vision-mixer** a person whose job is to switch from one image to another in television broadcasting or recording. □ **visional** adj. **visionless** adj. [ME f. OF f. L visio -onis (as VISIBLE)]

visionary /ˈvɪʒənərɪ/ adj. & n. —adj. 1 informed or inspired by vision(s). 2 existing in or characteristic of a vision or the imagination. —n. (pl. **-ies**) a visionary person. □ **visionariness** n.

visit /ˈvɪzɪt/ v. & n. —v. (**visited, visiting**) 1 tr. (also absol.) go or come to see (a person, place, etc.) 2 tr. reside temporarily with (a person) or at (a place). 3 intr. be a visitor. 4 tr. (of a disease, calamity, etc.) come upon, attack. 5 tr. Bibl. a (foll. by with) punish (a person). b (often foll. by upon) inflict punishment for (a sin). 6 intr. US a (foll. by with) go to see (a person) esp. socially. b (usu. foll. by with) converse, chat. —n. 1 a an act of visiting, a call on a person or at a place (was on a visit to some friends; paid him a long visit). b temporary residence with a person or at a place. 2 (foll. by to) an occasion of going to a doctor, dentist, etc. 3 a formal or official call for the purpose of inspection etc. 4 US a chat. □ **visitable** adj. [ME f. OF visiter or L visitare go to see, frequent. of visare view f. vidēre vis- see: (n.) perh. f. F visite]

visitant /ˈvɪzɪt(ə)nt/ n. a visitor, esp. a supposedly supernatural one. [F visitant or L visitare (as VISIT)]

visitation /ˌvɪzɪˈteɪʃ(ə)n/ n. 1 an official visit of inspection, esp. a bishop's examination of a church in his diocese. 2 trouble or difficulty regarded as a divine punishment. [ME f. OF visitation or LL visitatio (as VISIT)]

visiting /ˈvɪzɪtɪŋ/ n. & adj. —n. paying a visit or visits. —attrib.adj. (of an academic) spending some time at another institution (a visiting professor). □ **visiting-card** a card with a person's name etc., sent or left in lieu of a formal visit.

visitor /ˈvɪzɪtə(r)/ n. 1 a person who visits a person or place. 2 a migratory bird present in a locality for part of the year (winter visitor). □ **visitors' book** a book in which visitors to a hotel, church, embassy, etc., write their names and addresses and sometimes remarks. [ME f. AF visitour, OF visiteur (as VISIT)]

visor /ˈvaɪzə(r)/ n. (also **vizor**) 1 a a movable part of a helmet covering the face. b the projecting front part of a cap. 2 a shield (fixed or movable) to protect the eyes from unwanted light. □ **visored** adj. **visorless** adj. [ME f. AF viser, OF visiere f. vis face f. L visus: see VISAGE]

vista /ˈvɪstə/ n. 1 a long narrow view as between rows of trees. 2 a mental view of a long succession of remembered or anticipated events □ **vistaed** adj. [It., = view, f. visto seen, past part. of vedere see f. L vidēre]

visual /ˈvɪzjʊəl, ˈvɪʒ-/ adj. & n. —adj. of, concerned with, or used in seeing. —n. (usu. in pl.) a visual image or display, a picture. □ **visual aid** a film, model, etc., as an aid to learning. **visual display unit** Computing a device displaying data as characters on a screen and usu. incorporating a keyboard. **visual field** field of vision. □ **visuality** /-ʊˈælɪtɪ/ n. **visually** adv. [ME f. LL visualis f. L visus sight f. vidēre see]

visualize /ˈvɪzjʊəˌlaɪz, ˈvɪʒ-/ v.tr. (also **-ise**) make visible esp. to one's mind (a thing not visible to the eye). □ **visualizable** adj. **visualization** /-ˈzeɪʃ(ə)n/ n.

vital /ˈvaɪt(ə)l/ adj. & n. —adj. 1 of, concerned with, or essential to organic life (vital functions). 2 essential to the existence of a thing or to the matter in hand (a vital question; secrecy is vital). 3 full of life or activity. 4 affecting life. —n. (in pl.) the body's vital organs, e.g. the heart and brain. □ **vital force** 1 (in Bergson's philosophy) life-force. 2 any mysterious vital principle. **vital statistics** 1 the number of births, marriages, deaths, etc. 2 colloq. the measurements of a woman's bust, waist, and hips. □ **vitally** adv. [ME f. OF f. L vitalis f. vita life]

vitalism /ˈvaɪtəˌlɪz(ə)m/ n. Biol. the doctrine that life originates in a vital principle distinct from chemical and other physical forces. □ **vitalist** n. **vitalistic** /-ˈlɪstɪk/ adj. [F vitalisme or f. VITAL]

vitality /vaɪˈtælɪtɪ/ n. 1 liveliness, animation. 2 the ability to sustain life, vital power. [L vitalitas (as VITAL)]

vitalize /ˈvaɪtəˌlaɪz/ v.tr. (also **-ise**) 1 endow with life. 2 infuse with vigour. □ **vitalization** /-ˈzeɪʃ(ə)n/ n.

vitally /ˈvaɪtəlɪ/ adv. essentially, indispensably.

vitamin /ˈvɪtəmɪn, ˈvaɪt-/ n. any of a group of organic compounds essential in small amounts for many living organisms to maintain normal health and development. □ **vitamin A** = RETINOL. **vitamin B complex** (or **B vitamins**) any of a group of vitamins which, although not chemically related, are often found together in the same foods. **vitamin B_1** = THIAMINE. **vitamin B_2** = RIBOFLAVIN. **vitamin B_6** = PYRIDOXINE. **vitamin B_{12}** = CYANOCOBALAMIN. **vitamin C** = ASCORBIC ACID. **vitamin D** any of a group of vitamins found in liver and fish oils, essential for the absorption of calcium and the prevention of rickets in children and osteomalacia in adults. **vitamin D₂** = CALCIFEROL. **vitamin D₃** = CHOLECALCIFEROL. **vitamin E** = TOCOPHEROL. **vitamin K** any of a group of vitamins found mainly in green leaves and essential for the blood-clotting process. **vitamin K₁** = PHYLLOQUINONE. **vitamin K₂** = MENAQUINONE. **vitamin M** esp. US = FOLIC ACID. [orig. *vitamine* f. L *vita* life + AMINE, because orig. thought to contain an amino acid]

vitaminize /ˈvɪtəmɪˌnaɪz/ v.tr. (also **-ise**) add vitamins to.

vitiate /ˈvɪʃɪˌeɪt/ v.tr. **1** impair the quality or efficiency of; corrupt, debase, contaminate. **2** make invalid or ineffectual. □ **vitiation** /-ˈeɪʃ(ə)n/ n. **vitiator** n. [L *vitiare* f. *vitium* VICE¹]

viticulture /ˈvɪtɪˌkʌltʃə(r)/ n. the cultivation of grapevines; the science or study of this. □ **viticultural** /-ˈkʌltʃər(ə)l/ adj. **viticulturist** /-ˈkʌltʃərɪst/ n. [L *vitis* vine + CULTURE]

vitreous /ˈvɪtrɪəs/ adj. **1** of, or of the nature of, glass. **2** like glass in hardness, brittleness, transparency, structure, etc. (*vitreous enamel*). □ **vitreous humour** (or **body**) Anat. a transparent jelly-like tissue filling the eyeball. □ **vitreousness** n. [L *vitreus* f. *vitrum* glass]

vitrescent /vɪˈtres(ə)nt/ adj. tending to become glass. □ **vitrescence** n.

vitriform /ˈvɪtrɪˌfɔːm/ adj. having the form or appearance of glass.

vitrify /ˈvɪtrɪˌfaɪ/ v.tr. & intr. (**-ies, -ied**) convert or be converted into glass or a glasslike substance esp. by heat. □ **vitrifaction** /-ˈfækʃ(ə)n/ n. **vitrifiable** adj. **vitrification** /-fɪˈkeɪʃ(ə)n/ n. [F *vitrifier* or med.L *vitrificare* (as VITREOUS)]

vitriol /ˈvɪtrɪəl/ n. **1** sulphuric acid or a sulphate, orig. one of glassy appearance. **2** caustic or hostile speech, criticism, or feeling. □ **copper vitriol** copper sulphate. **oil of vitriol** concentrated sulphuric acid. [ME f. OF *vitriol* or med.L *vitriolum* f. L *vitrum* glass]

vitriolic /ˌvɪtrɪˈɒlɪk/ adj. (of speech or criticism) caustic or hostile.

vituperate /vɪˈtjuːpəˌreɪt, vaɪ-/ v.tr. & intr. revile, abuse. □ **vituperation** /-ˈreɪʃ(ə)n/ n. **vituperative** /-rətɪv/ adj. **vituperator** n. [L *vituperare* f. *vitium* VICE¹]

viva¹ /ˈvaɪvə/ n. & v. Brit. colloq. —n. = VIVA VOCE n. —v.tr. (**vivas, vivaed** /-vəd/ or **viva'd, vivaing**) = VIVA VOCE v. [abbr.]

viva² /ˈviːvə/ int. & n. —int. long live. —n. a cry of this as a salute etc. [It., 3rd sing. pres. subj. of *vivere* live f. L]

vivace /vɪˈvɑːtʃɪ/ adv. Mus. in a lively brisk manner. [It. f. L (as VIVACIOUS)]

vivacious /vɪˈveɪʃəs/ adj. lively, sprightly, animated. □ **vivaciously** adv. **vivaciousness** n. **vivacity** /vɪˈvæsɪtɪ/ n. [L *vivax -acis* f. *vivere* live]

vivarium /vaɪˈveərɪəm, vɪ-/ n. (pl. **vivaria** /-rɪə/) a place artificially prepared for keeping animals in (nearly) their natural state. [L, = warren, fishpond, f. *vivus* living f. *vivere* live]

viva voce /ˌvaɪvə ˈvəʊtʃɪ, ˈvəʊsɪ/ adj., adv., n., & v. —adj. oral. —adv. orally. —n. an oral examination for an academic qualification. —v.tr. (**viva-voce**) (**-vocees, -voceed, -voceing**) examine orally. [med.L, = with the living voice]

vivid /ˈvɪvɪd/ adj. **1** (of light or colour) strong, intense, glaring (*a vivid flash of lightning; of a*

vivid green). **2** (of a mental faculty, impression, or description) clear, lively, graphic. □ **vividly** adv. **vividness** n. [L *vividus* f. *vivere* live]

vivify /ˈvɪvɪˌfaɪ/ v.tr. (**-ies, -ied**) enliven, animate, make lively or living. □ **vivification** n. [F *vivifier* f. LL *vivificare* f. L *vivus* living f. *vivere* live]

viviparous /vɪˈvɪpərəs, vaɪ-/ adj. Zool. bringing forth young alive, not hatching them by means of eggs (cf. OVIPAROUS). □ **viviparity** /ˌvɪvɪˈpærɪtɪ/ n. **viviparously** adv. **viviparousness** n. [L *viviparus* f. *vivus*: see VIVIFY]

vivisect /ˈvɪvɪˌsekt/ v.tr. perform vivisection on. [back-form. f. VIVISECTION]

vivisection /ˌvɪvɪˈsekʃ(ə)n/ n. dissection or other painful treatment of living animals for purposes of scientific research. □ **vivisectional** adj. **vivisectionist** n. **vivisector** /ˈvɪvɪˌsektə(r)/ n. [L *vivus* living (as VIVIFY), after DISSECTION (as DISSECT)]

vixen /ˈvɪks(ə)n/ n. **1** a female fox. **2** a spiteful or quarrelsome woman. □ **vixenish** adj. **vixenly** adj. [ME *fixen* f. OE, fem. of FOX]

viz. /vɪz, or by substitution ˈneɪmlɪ/ adv. (usu. introducing a gloss or explanation) namely; that is to say; in other words [abbr. of L *videlicet* (f. *vidēre* see + *licet* it is permissible), z being med.L symbol for abbr. of *-et*]

vizier /vɪˈzɪə(r), ˈvɪzɪə(r)/ n. hist. a high official in some Muslim countries, esp. in Turkey under Ottoman rule. □ **vizierate** /-rət/ n. **vizierial** /vɪˈzɪərɪəl/ adj. **viziership** n. [ult. f. Arab. *wazīr* caliph's chief counsellor]

vizor var. of VISOR.

V-neck /viːˈnek, ˈviː-/ n. (often attrib.) a neck of a pullover etc. with straight sides meeting at an angle in the front to form a V.

VO abbr. (in the UK) Royal Victorian Order.

vocabulary /vəˈkæbjʊlərɪ/ n. (pl. **-ies**) **1** the (principal) words used in a language or a particular book or branch of science etc. or by a particular author (*scientific vocabulary; the vocabulary of Shakespeare*). **2** the range of words known to an individual (*his vocabulary is limited*). [med.L *vocabularius, -um* f. *vocare* call]

vocal /ˈvəʊk(ə)l/ adj. & n. —adj. **1** of or concerned with or uttered by the voice (*a vocal communication*). **2** expressing one's feelings freely in speech (*was very vocal about his rights*). **3** Phonet. voiced. **4** (of music) written for or produced by the voice with or without accompaniment (cf. INSTRUMENTAL). —n. (in sing. or pl.) the sung part of a musical composition. □ **vocal cords** folds of the lining membrane of the larynx near the opening of the glottis, with edges vibrating in the air-stream to produce the voice. **vocal score** a musical score showing the voice parts in full. □ **vocality** /vəˈkælɪtɪ/ n. **vocally** adv. [ME f. L *vocalis* (as VOICE)]

vocalist /ˈvəʊkəlɪst/ n. a singer, esp. of jazz or popular songs.

vocalize /ˈvəʊkəˌlaɪz/ v. (also **-ise**) **1** tr. form (a sound) or utter (a word) with the voice. **2** make sonant (*f is vocalized into v*). □ **vocalization** /-ˈzeɪʃ(ə)n/ n. **vocalizer** n.

vocation /vəˈkeɪʃ(ə)n/ n. **1** a strong feeling of fitness for a particular career or occupation (in religious contexts regarded as a divine call). **2** a person's employment, esp. regarded as requiring dedication. [ME f. OF *vocation* or L *vocatio* f. *vocare* call]

vocational /vəˈkeɪʃən(ə)l/ adj. **1** of or relating to an occupation or employment. **2** (of education or training) directed at a particular occupation and its skills. □ **vocationalism** n. **vocationalize** v.tr. (also **-ise**). **vocationally** adv.

vocative /ˈvɒkətɪv/ n. & adj. Gram. —n. the case of nouns, pronouns, and adjectives used in addressing or invoking a person or thing. —adj. of or in this case. [ME f. OF vocatif -ive or L vocativus f. vocare call]

vociferate /vəˈsɪfəˌreɪt/ v. 1 tr. utter (words etc.) noisily. 2 intr. shout, bawl. □ **vociferance** n. **vociferant** adj. & n. **vociferation** /-ˈreɪʃ(ə)n/ n. **vociferator** n. [L vociferari f. vox voice + ferre bear]

vociferous /vəˈsɪfərəs/ adj. 1 (of a person, speech, etc.) noisy, clamorous. 2 insistently and forcibly expressing one's views. □ **vociferously** adv. **vociferousness** n.

vodka /ˈvɒdkə/ n. an alcoholic spirit made esp. in Russia by distillation of rye etc. [Russ., dimin. of voda water]

vogue /vəʊɡ/ n. 1 (prec. by the) the prevailing fashion. 2 popular use or currency (has had a great vogue). □ **in vogue** in fashion, generally current. **vogue-word** a word currently fashionable. □ **voguish** adj. [F f. It. voga rowing, fashion f. vogare row, go well]

voice n. & v. —n. 1 **a** sound formed in the larynx etc. and uttered by the mouth, esp. human utterance in speaking, shouting, singing, etc. (heard a voice; spoke in a low voice). **b** the ability to produce this (has lost her voice). 2 **a** the use of the voice; utterance (esp. give voice). **b** an opinion so expressed. **c** the right to express an opinion (I have no voice in the matter). 3 Gram. a form or set of forms of a verb showing the relation of the subject to the action (active voice; passive voice). —v.tr. 1 give utterance to; express (the letter voices our opinion). 2 (esp. as voiced adj.) Phonet. utter with vibration of the vocal cords (e.g. b, d, g, v, z). □ **in voice** (or **good voice**) in proper vocal condition for singing or speaking. **voice-box** the larynx. **voice-over** narration in a film etc. not accompanied by a picture of the speaker. **voice-print** a visual record of speech, analysed with respect to frequency, duration, and amplitude. **with one voice** unanimously. □ **-voiced** adj. **voicer** n. (in sense 3 of v.). [ME f. AF voiz, OF vois f. L vox vocis]

voiceless /ˈvɔɪslɪs/ adj. 1 dumb, mute, speechless. 2 Phonet. uttered without vibration of the vocal cords (e.g. f, k, p, s, t). □ **voicelessly** adv. **voicelessness** n.

void adj., n., & v. —adj. 1 **a** empty, vacant. **b** (foll. by of) free from (a style void of affectation). 2 esp. Law (of a contract, deed, promise, etc.) invalid, not binding (null and void). 3 (often foll. by in) Cards (of a hand) having no cards in a given suit. —n. 1 an empty space, a vacuum (vanished into the void; cannot fill the void made by death). 2 an unfilled space in a wall or building. 3 (often foll. by in) Cards the absence of cards in a particular suit. —v.tr. 1 render invalid. 2 (also absol.) excrete. □ **voidable** adj. **voidness** n. [ME f. OF dial. voide, OF vuide, vuit, rel. to L vacare VACATE: v. partly f. AVOID, partly f. OF voider]

voidance /ˈvɔɪd(ə)ns/ n. 1 Eccl. a vacancy in a benefice. 2 the act or an instance of voiding; the state of being voided. [ME f. OF (as VOID)]

voile /vɔɪl, vwɑːl/ n. a thin semi-transparent dress-material. [F, = VEIL]

vol. abbr. volume.

volatile /ˈvɒləˌtaɪl/ adj. & n. —adj. 1 evaporating rapidly (volatile salts). 2 changeable, fickle. 3 lively, light-hearted. 4 apt to break out into violence. 5 transient. —n. a volatile substance. □ **volatileness** n. **volatility** /-ˈtɪlɪtɪ/ n. [OF volatil or L volatilis f. volare volat- fly]

vol-au-vent /ˈvɒləʊˌvɑ̃/ n. a (usu. small) round case of puff pastry filled with meat, fish, etc., and sauce. [F, lit. 'flight in the wind']

volcanic /vɒlˈkænɪk/ adj. (also **vulcanic** /vʌl-/) of, like, or produced by a volcano. □ **volcanic glass** obsidian. □ **volcanically** adv. **volcanicity** /ˌvɒlkəˈnɪsɪtɪ/ n. [F volcanique f. volcan VOLCANO]

volcano /vɒlˈkeɪnəʊ/ n. (pl. **-oes**) a mountain or hill having an opening or openings in the earth's crust through which lava, cinders, steam, gases, etc., are or have been expelled continuously or at intervals. [It. f. L Volcanus Vulcan, Roman god of fire]

volcanology var. of VULCANOLOGY.

vole n. any small ratlike or mouselike plant-eating rodent. [orig. vole-mouse f. Norw. voll field + mus mouse]

volition /vəˈlɪʃ(ə)n/ n. 1 the exercise of the will. 2 the power of willing. □ **of** (or **by**) **one's own volition** voluntarily. □ **volitional** adj. **volitionally** adv. [F volition or med.L volitio f. volo I wish]

volley /ˈvɒlɪ/ n. & v. —n. (pl. **-eys**) 1 the simultaneous discharge of a number of weapons. 2 (usu. foll. by of) a noisy emission of oaths etc. in quick succession. 3 Tennis the return of a ball in play before it touches the ground. 4 Football the kicking of a ball in play before it touches the ground. 5 Cricket a ball pitched right up to the batsman or the stumps without bouncing. —v. (**-eys**, **-eyed**) 1 tr. (also absol.) Tennis & Football return or send (a ball) by a volley. 2 tr. & absol. discharge (bullets, abuse, etc.) in a volley. 3 intr. (of bullets etc.) fly in a volley. 4 intr. (of guns etc.) sound together. [F volée ult. f. L volare fly]

volleyball /ˈvɒlɪˌbɔːl/ n. a game for two teams of six hitting a large ball by hand over a net.

volt /vəʊlt/ n. the SI unit of electromotive force, the difference of potential that would carry one ampere of current against one ohm resistance. [A. Volta, It. physicist d. 1827]

voltage /ˈvəʊltɪdʒ/ n. electromotive force or potential difference expressed in volts.

voltameter /vɒlˈtæmɪtə(r)/ n. an instrument for measuring an electric charge.

volte-face /vɒltˈfɑːs/ n. 1 a complete reversal of position in argument or opinion. 2 the act or an instance of turning round. [F f. It. voltafaccia, ult. f. L volvere roll + facies appearance, face]

voltmeter /ˈvəʊltˌmiːtə(r)/ n. an instrument for measuring electric potential in volts.

voluble /ˈvɒljʊb(ə)l/ adj. speaking or spoken vehemently, incessantly, or fluently (voluble spokesman; voluble excuses). □ **volubility** /-ˈbɪlɪtɪ/ n. **volubleness** n. **volubly** adv. [F voluble or L volubilis f. volvere roll]

volume /ˈvɒljuːm/ n. 1 a set of sheets of paper, usu. printed, bound together and forming part or the whole of a work or comprising several works. 2 **a** solid content, bulk. **b** the space occupied by a gas or liquid. **c** (foll. by of) an amount or quantity (large volume of business). 3 **a** quantity or power of sound. **b** fullness of tone.

[ME f. OF *volum(e)* f. L *volumen -minis* roll f. *volvere* to roll]

volumetric /ˌvɒljʊˈmetrɪk/ *adj.* of or relating to measurement by volume. □ **volumetrically** *adv.* [VOLUME + METRIC]

voluminous /vəˈljuːmɪnəs, vəˈluː-/ *adj.* **1** large in volume; bulky. **2** (of drapery etc.) loose and ample. □ **voluminosity** /-ˈɪnɒsɪtɪ/ *n.* **voluminously** *adv.* **voluminousness** *n.* [LL *voluminosus* (as VOLUME)]

voluntarism /ˈvɒləntəˌrɪz(ə)m/ *n.* **1** the principle of relying on voluntary action rather than compulsion. **2** *Philos.* the doctrine that the will is a fundamental or dominant factor in the individual or the universe. □ **voluntarist** *n.* [irreg. f. VOLUNTARY]

voluntary /ˈvɒləntərɪ/ *adj. & n.* —*adj.* **1** done, acting, or able to act of one's own free will; not constrained or compulsory, intentional (*a voluntary gift*). **2** unpaid (*voluntary work*). **3** (of an institution) supported by voluntary contributions. **4** (of a movement, muscle, or limb) controlled by the will. **5** (of a confession by a criminal) not prompted by a promise or threat. —*n.* (*pl.* **-ies**) **1** an organ solo played before, during, or after a church service. **2** the music for this. □ **Voluntary Service Overseas** a British organization promoting voluntary work in underdeveloped countries. □ **voluntarily** *adv.* [ME f. OF *volontaire* or L *voluntarius* f. *voluntas* will]

volunteer /ˌvɒlənˈtɪə(r)/ *n. & v.* —*n.* a person who voluntarily undertakes a task or enters military or other service, esp. *Mil. hist.* a member of any of the corps of voluntary soldiers formerly organized in the UK and provided with instructors, arms, etc., by the State. —*v.* **1** *tr.* (often foll. by *to* + infin.) undertake or offer (one's services, a remark or explanation, etc.) voluntarily. **2** *intr.* (often foll. by *for*) make a voluntary offer of one's services; be a volunteer. [F *volontaire* (as VOLUNTARY), assim. to -EER]

voluptuary /vəˈlʌptjʊərɪ/ *n. & adj.* —*n.* (*pl.* **-ies**) a person given up to luxury and sensual pleasure. —*adj.* concerned with luxury and sensual pleasure. [L *volupt(u)arius* (as VOLUPTUOUS)]

voluptuous /vəˈlʌptjʊəs/ *adj.* of, tending to, occupied with, or derived from, sensuous or sensual pleasure. □ **voluptuously** *adv.* **voluptuousness** *n.* [ME f. OF *voluptueux* or L *voluptuosus* f. *voluptas* pleasure]

volute /vəˈljuːt/ *n. & adj.* —*n.* **1** *Archit.* a spiral scroll characteristic of Ionic capitals and also used in Corinthian and composite capitals. **2 a** any marine gastropod mollusc of the genus *Voluta.* **b** the spiral shell of this. —*adj.* esp. *Bot.* rolled up. □ **voluted** *adj.* [F *volute* or L *voluta* fem. past part. of *volvere* roll]

volution /vəˈluːʃ(ə)n, vəˈljuː-/ *n.* **1** a rolling motion. **2** a spiral turn. **3** a whorl of a spiral shell. **4** *Anat.* a convolution. [as VOLUTE, after REVOLUTION etc.]

vomer /ˈvəʊmə(r)/ *n. Anat.* the small thin bone separating the nostrils in man and most vertebrates. [L, = ploughshare]

vomit /ˈvɒmɪt/ *v. & n.* —*v.tr.* (**vomited, vomiting**) **1** (also *absol.*) eject (matter) from the stomach through the mouth. **2** (of a volcano, chimney, etc.) eject violently, belch forth. —*n.*

matter vomited from the stomach. [ME ult. f. L *vomere* vomit- or frequent. L *vomitare*]

vomitorium /ˌvɒmɪˈtɔːrɪəm/ *n.* (*pl.* **vomitoria** /-rɪə/) *Rom. Antiq.* a vomitory. [L; see VOMITORY]

vomitory /ˈvɒmɪtərɪ/ *adj. & n.* —*adj.* emetic. —*n.* (*pl.* **-ies**) *Rom. Antiq.* each of a series of passages for entrance and exit in an amphitheatre or theatre. [L *vomitorius* (adj.), *-um* (n.) (as VOMIT)]

voodoo /ˈvuːduː/ *n. & v.* —*n.* **1** use of or belief in witchcraft as practised among Blacks esp. in the W. Indies. **2** a person skilled in this. **3** a voodoo spell. —*v.tr.* (**voodoos, voodooed**) affect by voodoo; bewitch. □ **voodooism** *n.* **voodooist** *n.* [Dahomey *vodu*]

voracious /vəˈreɪʃəs/ *adj.* **1** greedy in eating, ravenous. **2** very eager in some activity (*a voracious reader*). □ **voraciously** *adv.* **voraciousness** *n.* **voracity** /vəˈræsɪtɪ/ *n.* [L *vorax* f. *vorare* devour]

-vorous /vərəs/ *comb. form* forming adjectives meaning 'feeding on' (*carnivorous*). □ **-vora** /vərə/ *comb. form* forming names of groups. **-vore** /vɔː(r)/ *comb. form* forming names of individuals. [L *-vorus* f. *vorare* devour]

vortex /ˈvɔːteks/ *n.* (*pl.* **vortexes** or **vortices** /-tɪˌsiːz/) **1** a mass of whirling fluid, esp. a whirlpool or whirlwind. **2** any whirling motion or mass. **3** a system, occupation, pursuit, etc., viewed as swallowing up or engrossing those who approach it (*the vortex of society*). **4** *Physics* a portion of fluid whose particles have rotatory motion. □ **vortical** *adj.* **vortically** *adv.* **vorticity** /vɔːˈtɪsɪtɪ/ *n.* **vorticular** /vɔːˈtɪkjʊlə(r)/ *adj.* [L *vortex -icis* eddy, var. of VERTEX]

vorticist /ˈvɔːtɪsɪst/ *n.* **1** *Art* a painter, writer, etc., of a school influenced by futurism and using the 'vortices' of modern civilization as a basis. **2** *Metaphysics* a person regarding the universe, with Descartes, as a plenum in which motion propagates itself in circles. □ **vorticism** *n.*

votary /ˈvəʊtərɪ/ *n.* (*pl.* **-ies**; *fem.* **votaress**) (usu. foll. by *of*) **1** a person vowed to the service of God or a god or cult. **2** a devoted follower, adherent, or advocate of a person, system, occupation, etc. □ **votarist** *n.* [L *vot-*: see VOTE]

vote *n. & v.* —*n.* **1** a formal expression of choice or opinion by means of a ballot, show of hands, etc., concerning a choice of candidate, approval of a motion or resolution, etc. (*let us take a vote on it; gave my vote to the independent candidate*). **2** (usu. prec. by *the*) the right to vote, esp. in a State election. **3** an opinion expressed by a majority of votes. **4** the collective votes that are or may be given by or for a particular group (*will lose the Welsh vote; the Conservative vote increased*). —*v.* **1** *intr.* (often foll. by *for, against,* or *to* + infin.) give a vote. **2** *tr.* **a** (often foll. by *that* + clause) enact or resolve by a majority of votes. **b** grant (a sum of money) by a majority of votes. **c** cause to be in a specified position by a majority of votes (*was voted off the committee*). **3** *tr. colloq.* pronounce or declare by general consent (*was voted a failure*). **4** *tr.* (often foll. by *that* + clause) *colloq.* announce one's proposal (*I vote that we all go home*). □ **put to a** (or **the**) **vote** submit to a decision by voting. **vote in** elect by votes. **vote of censure** = *vote of no confidence.* **vote of confidence** (or **no confidence**) a vote showing that the majority support (or do not support) the policy of the governing body etc.

voting-paper a paper used in voting by ballot. □ **votable** *adj.* **voteless** *adj.* [ME f. past part. stem *vot-* of L *vovēre* vow]

voter *n.* **1** a person with the right to vote at an election. **2** a person voting.

votive /ˈvəʊtɪv/ *adj.* offered or consecrated in fulfilment of a vow (*votive offering; votive picture*). [L *votivus* (as VOTE)]

vouch /vaʊtʃ/ *v. intr.* (foll. by *for*) answer for, be surety for (*will vouch for the truth of this; can vouch for him; could not vouch for his honesty*). [ME f. OF *vo(u)cher* summon etc., ult. f. L *vocare* call]

voucher /ˈvaʊtʃə(r)/ *n.* a document which can be exchanged for goods or services as a token of payment made or promised by the holder or another. [AF *voucher* (as VOUCH) or f. VOUCH]

vouchsafe /vaʊtʃˈseɪf/ *v.tr. formal* **1** condescend to give or grant (*vouchsafed me no answer*). **2** (foll. by *to* + infin.) condescend. [ME f. VOUCH in sense 'warrant' + SAFE]

vow /vaʊ/ *n.* & *v.* —*n.* **1** *Relig.* a solemn promise esp. in the form of an oath to God or another deity or to a saint. **2** (in *pl.*) the promises by which a monk or nun is bound to poverty, chastity, and obedience. **3** a promise of fidelity (*lovers' vows; marriage vows*). **4** (usu. as **baptismal vows**) the promises given at baptism by the baptized person or by sponsors. —*v.tr.* **1** promise solemnly (*vowed obedience*). **2** dedicate to a deity. [ME f. AF *v(o)u*, OF *vo(u)*, f. L (as VOTE): (v.) f. OF *vouer*, in sense 2 partly f. AVOW]

vowel /ˈvaʊəl/ *n.* **1** a speech-sound made with vibration of the vocal cords but without audible friction, more open than a consonant and capable of forming a syllable. **2** a letter or letters representing this, as *a, e, i, o, u, aw, ah*. □ **vowelled** *adj.* (also in *comb.*). **vowelless** *adj.* **vowelly** *adj.* [ME f. OF *vouel, voiel* f. L *vocalis* (*littera*) VOCAL (letter)]

vox pop /vɒks ˈpɒp/ *n. Broadcasting colloq.* popular opinion as represented by informal comments from members of the public [abbr. of vox POPULI]

vox populi /ˌvɒks ˈpɒpjʊˌliː, -ˌlaɪ/ *n.* public opinion, the general verdict. [L, = the people's voice]

voyage /ˈvɔɪɪdʒ/ *n.* & *v.* —*n.* a journey, esp. a long one by water, air, or in space. —*v.* **1** *intr.* make a voyage. **2** *tr.* traverse, esp. by water or air. □ **voyageable** *adj.* **voyager** *n.* [ME f. AF & OF *veiage, voiage* f. L *viaticum*]

voyeur /vwɑːˈjɜː(r)/ *n.* a person who obtains sexual gratification from observing others' sexual actions or organs. □ **voyeurism** *n.* **voyeuristic** /-ˈrɪstɪk/ *adj.* **voyeuristically** /-ˈrɪstɪkəlɪ/ *adj.* [F f. *voir* see]

VP *abbr.* Vice-President.

vs. *abbr.* versus.

V-sign /ˈviːsaɪn/ *n.* **1** *Brit.* a sign of the letter V made with the first two fingers pointing up and the back of the hand facing outwards, as a gesture of abuse, contempt, etc. **2** a similar sign made with the palm of the hand facing outwards, as a symbol of victory.

VSO *abbr.* Voluntary Service Overseas.

VSOP *abbr.* Very Special Old Pale (brandy).

Vt. *abbr.* Vermont.

VTO *abbr.* vertical take-off.

VTOL /ˈviːtɒl/ *abbr.* vertical take-off and landing.

V-2 /viːˈtuː/ *n.* a type of German rocket-powered missile used in the war of 1939–45. [abbr. of G *Vergeltungswaffe* reprisal weapon]

vulcanic var. of VOLCANIC.

vulcanite /ˈvʌlkəˌnaɪt/ *n.* a hard black vulcanized rubber, ebonite. [as VULCANIZE]

vulcanize /ˈvʌlkəˌnaɪz/ *v.tr.* (also **-ise**) treat (rubber etc.) with sulphur etc. esp. at a high temperature to increase its strength. □ **vulcanizable** *adj.* **vulcanization** /-ˈzeɪʃ(ə)n/ *n.* **vulcanizer** *n.* [*Vulcan*, Roman god of fire and metal-working]

vulcanology /ˌvʌlkəˈnɒlədʒɪ/ *n.* (also **volcanology** /ˌvɒl-/) the scientific study of volcanoes. □ **vulcanological** /-nəˈlɒdʒɪk(ə)l/ *adj.* **vulcanologist** *n.*

vulgar /ˈvʌlɡə(r)/ *adj.* **1 a** of or characteristic of the common people, plebeian. **b** coarse in manners; low (*vulgar expressions; vulgar tastes*). **2** in common use; generally prevalent (*vulgar errors*). □ **vulgar fraction** a fraction expressed by numerator and denominator, not decimally. [ME f. L *vulgaris* f. *vulgus* common people]

vulgarism /ˈvʌlɡəˌrɪz(ə)m/ *n.* **1** a word or expression in coarse or uneducated use. **2** an instance of coarse or uneducated behaviour.

vulgarity /vʌlˈɡærɪtɪ/ *n.* (*pl.* **-ies**) **1** the quality of being vulgar. **2** an instance of this.

vulgarize /ˈvʌlɡəˌraɪz/ *v.tr.* (also **-ise**) **1** make (a person, manners, etc.) vulgar, infect with vulgarity. **2** spoil (a scene, sentiment, etc.) by making it too common, frequented, or well known. **3** popularize. □ **vulgarization** /-ˈzeɪʃ(ə)n/ *n.*

Vulgate /ˈvʌlɡeɪt, -ɡət/ *n.* **1** the Latin version of the Bible prepared mainly by St Jerome in the late fourth century. **2** the official Roman Catholic Latin text as revised in 1592. [L *vulgata* (*editio* edition), fem. past part. of *vulgare* make public f. *vulgus*: see VULGAR]

vulnerable /ˈvʌlnərəb(ə)l/ *adj.* **1** that may be wounded or harmed. **2** (foll. by *to*) exposed to damage by a weapon, criticism, etc. **3** *Bridge* having won one game towards rubber and therefore liable to higher penalties. □ **vulnerability** /-ˈbɪlɪtɪ/ *n.* **vulnerableness** *n.* **vulnerably** *adv.* [LL *vulnerabilis* f. L *vulnerare* to wound f. *vulnus -eris* wound]

vulnerary /ˈvʌlnərərɪ/ *adj.* & *n.* —*adj.* useful or used for the healing of wounds. —*n.* (*pl.* **-ies**) a vulnerary drug, plant, etc. [L *vulnerarius* f. *vulnus*: see VULNERABLE]

vulpine /ˈvʌlpaɪn/ *adj.* of or like a fox. [L *vulpinus* f. *vulpes* fox]

vulture /ˈvʌltʃə(r)/ *n.* **1** any of various large birds of prey of the family Cathartidae or Accipitridae, with the head and neck more or less bare of feathers, feeding chiefly on carrion. **2** a rapacious person. □ **vulturine** /-ˌraɪn/ *adj.* **vulturish** *adj.* **vulturous** *adj.* [ME f. AF *vultur*, OF *voltour* etc., f. L *vulturius*]

vulva /ˈvʌlvə/ *n.* (*pl.* **vulvas**) *Anat.* the external female genitals, esp. the external opening of the vagina. □ **vulvar** *adj.* **vulvitis** /-ˈvaɪtɪs/ *n.* [L, = womb]

vv. *abbr.* **1** verses. **2** volumes.

vying *pres. part.* of VIE.

Ww

W¹ /'dʌb(ə)lju:/ *n.* (also **w**) (*pl.* **Ws** or **W's**) the twenty-third letter of the alphabet.

W² *abbr.* (also **W.**) **1** watt(s). **2** West; Western.

W³ *symb. Chem.* the element tungsten.

w. *abbr.* **1** wicket(s). **2** wide.

Waac /wæk/ *n. hist.* a member of the Women's Army Auxiliary Corps (*Brit.* 1917–19 or *US* 1942–8). [initials *WAAC*]

Waaf /wæf/ *n. Brit. hist.* a member of the Women's Auxiliary Air Force (1939–48). [initials *WAAF*]

WAC *abbr.* (in the US) Women's Army Corps.

wacko /'wækəʊ/ *adj.* & *n. US sl.* —*adj.* crazy. —*n.* (*pl.* **-os** or **-oes**) a crazy person. [WACKY + -o]

wacky *adj.* & *n.* (also **whacky**) *sl.* —*adj.* (**-ier, -iest**) crazy. —*n.* (*pl.* **-ies**) a crazy person. □ **wackily** *adv.* **wackiness** *n.* [orig. dial., = left-handed, f. WHACK]

wad /wɒd/ *n.* & *v.* —*n.* **1** a lump or bundle of soft material used esp. to keep things apart or in place or to stuff up an opening. **2** a disc of felt etc. keeping powder or shot in place in a gun. **3** a number of banknotes or documents placed together. **4** (in *sing.* or *pl.*) a large quantity esp. of money. —*v.tr.* (**wadded, wadding**) **1** stop up (an aperture or a gun-barrel) with a wad. **2** keep (powder etc.) in place with a wad. **3** line or stuff (a garment or coverlet) with wadding. **4** protect (a person, walls, etc.) with wadding. **5** press (cotton etc.) into a wad or wadding. [perh. rel. to Du. *watten*, F *ouate* padding, cotton wool]

wadding /'wɒdɪŋ/ *n.* **1** soft pliable material of cotton or wool etc. used to line or stuff garments, quilts, etc., or to pack fragile articles. **2** any material from which gun-wads are made.

waddle /'wɒd(ə)l/ *v.* & *n.* —*v.intr.* walk with short steps and a swaying motion, like a stout short-legged person or a bird with short legs set far apart (a duck or goose). —*n.* a waddling gait. □ **waddler** *n.* [perh. frequent. of WADE]

wade *v.* & *n.* —*v.* **1** *intr.* walk through water or some impeding medium e.g. snow, mud, or sand. **2** *intr.* make one's way with difficulty or by force. **3** *intr.* (foll. by *through*) read (a book etc.) in spite of its dullness etc. **4** *intr.* (foll. by *into*) *colloq.* attack (a person or task) vigorously. **5** *tr.* ford (a stream etc.) on foot. —*n.* a spell of wading. □ **wade in** *colloq.* make a vigorous attack or intervention. **wading bird** any long-legged water-bird that wades. □ **wadable** *adj.* (also **wadeable**). [OE *wadan* f. Gmc, = go (through)]

wader *n.* **1 a** a person who wades. **b** a wading bird. **2** (in *pl.*) high waterproof boots, or a waterproof garment for the legs and body, worn in fishing etc.

WAF *abbr.* (in the US) Women in the Air Force.

wafer /'weɪfə(r)/ *n.* **1** a very thin light crisp sweet biscuit, esp. of a kind eaten with ice-cream. **2** a thin disc of unleavened bread used in the Eucharist. **3** a disc of red paper stuck on a legal document instead of a seal. **4** *Electronics* a very thin slice of a semiconductor crystal used as the substrate for solid-state circuitry. □ **wafer-thin** very thin. □ **wafery** *adj.* [ME f. AF *wafre*, ONF *waufre*, OF *gaufre* (cf. GOFFER) f. MLG *wāfel* waffle: cf. WAFFLE²]

waffle¹ /'wɒf(ə)l/ *n.* & *v.* esp. *Brit. colloq.* —*n.* verbose but aimless or ignorant talk or writing. —*v.intr.* indulge in waffle. □ **waffler** *n.* **waffly** *adj.* [orig. dial., frequent. of *waff* = yelp, yap (imit.)]

waffle² /'wɒf(ə)l/ *n.* esp. *US* a small crisp batter cake. [Du. *wafel*, *waefel* f. MLG *wāfel*: cf. WAFER]

waft /wɒft, wɑːft/ *v.* & *n.* —*v.tr.* & *intr.* convey or travel easily as through air or over water; sweep smoothly and lightly along. —*n.* **1** (usu. foll. by *of*) a whiff or scent. **2** a transient sensation of peace, joy, etc. [orig. 'convoy (ship etc.)', back-form. f. obs. *waughter*, *wafter* armed convoy-ship, f. Du. or LG *wachter* f. *wachten* to guard]

wag¹ *v.* & *n.* —*v.* (**wagged, wagging**) *tr.* & *intr.* shake or wave rapidly or energetically to and fro. —*n.* a single wagging motion (*with a wag of his tail*). [ME *waggen* f. root of OE *wagian* sway]

wag² *n.* a facetious person, a joker. [prob. f. obs. *waghalter* one likely to be hanged (as WAG¹, HALTER)]

wage *n.* & *v.* —*n.* **1** (in *sing.* or *pl.*) a fixed regular payment, usu. daily or weekly, made by an employer to an employee, esp. to a manual or unskilled worker (cf. SALARY). **2** (in *sing.* or *pl.*) requital. —*v.tr.* carry on (a war, conflict, or contest). □ **living wage** a wage that affords the means of normal subsistence. **wages council** a board of workers' and employers' representatives determining wages where there is no collective bargaining. [ME f. AF & ONF *wage*, OF *g(u)age*, f. Gmc, rel. to GAGE¹, WED]

wager /'weɪdʒə(r)/ *n.* & *v.tr.* & *intr.* = BET. [ME f. AF *wageure* f. *wager* (as WAGE)]

waggish /'wægɪʃ/ *adj.* playful, facetious. □ **waggishly** *adv.* **waggishness** *n.*

waggle /'wæg(ə)l/ *v.* & *n. colloq.* —*v. intr.* & *tr.* wag. —*n.* a waggling motion. [WAG¹ + -LE⁴]

waggly /'wæglɪ/ *adj.* unsteady.

Wagnerian /vɑːg'nɪərɪən/ *adj.* & *n.* —*adj.* of, relating to, or characteristic of the music dramas of Richard Wagner, German composer d. 1883, esp. with reference to their large scale. —*n.* an admirer of Wagner or his music.

wagon /'wægən/ *n.* (also *Brit.* **waggon**) **1** a four-wheeled vehicle for heavy loads, often with a removable tilt or cover. **2** *Brit.* a railway vehicle for goods, esp. an open truck. **3** *colloq.* a motor car, esp. an estate car. □ **on the wagon** *sl.* teetotal. [earlier *wagon*, *wag(h)en*, f. Du. *wag(h)en*, rel. to OE *wægn*]

wagoner /'wægənə(r)/ *n.* (also *Brit.* **waggoner**) the driver of a wagon. [Du. *wagenaar* (as WAGON)]

wagon-lit /ˌvægɔ̃ˈliː/ n. (pl. **wagons-lits** pronunc. same) a sleeping-car on a Continental railway. [F]

wagtail /ˈwægteɪl/ n. any small bird of the genus *Motacilla* with a long tail in frequent motion.

waif /weɪf/ n. a homeless and helpless person, esp. an abandoned child. □ **waifs and strays** homeless or neglected children. □ **waifish** adj. [ME f. AF *waif, weif*, ONF *gaif*, prob. of Scand. orig.]

wail /weɪl/ n. & v. —n. **1** a prolonged plaintive inarticulate loud high-pitched cry of pain, grief, etc. **2** a sound like or suggestive of this. —v. **1** intr. utter a wail. **2** intr. lament or complain persistently or bitterly. **3** intr. (of the wind etc.) make a sound like a person wailing. □ **wailer** n. **wailful** adj. poet. **wailingly** adv. [ME f. ON, rel. to WOE]

wainscot /ˈweɪnskət/ n. & v. —n. boarding or wooden panelling on the lower part of a room-wall. —v.tr. (**wainscoted, wainscoting**) line with wainscot. [ME f. MLG *wagenschot*, app. f. *wagen* WAGON + *schot* of uncert. meaning]

wainscoting /ˈweɪnskətɪŋ/ n. **1** a wainscot. **2** material for this.

waist /weɪst/ n. **1 a** the part of the human body below the ribs and above the hips, usu. of smaller circumference than these; the narrower middle part of the normal human figure. **b** the circumference of this. **2** a similar narrow part in the middle of a violin, hourglass, wasp, etc. **3 a** the part of a garment encircling or covering the waist. **b** the narrow middle part of a woman's dress etc. □ **waisted** adj. (also in comb.). **waistless** adj. [ME *wast*, perh. f. OE f. the root of WAX²]

waistband /ˈweɪstbænd/ n. a strip of cloth forming the waist of a garment.

waistcoat /ˈweɪskəʊt, ˈweɪstkəʊt, ˈweskət/ n. Brit. a close-fitting open-fronted waist-length garment without sleeves or collar.

waistline /ˈweɪstlaɪn/ n. the outline of a person's body at the waist.

wait /weɪt/ v. & n. —v. **1** intr. **a** defer action or departure for a specified time or until some expected event occurs (*wait a minute; wait till I come; wait for a fine day*). **b** be expectant or on the watch (*waited to see what would happen*). **2** tr. await (an opportunity, one's turn, etc.). **3** intr. (usu. as **waiting** n.) park a vehicle for a short time at the side of a road etc. (*no waiting*). **4** intr. (in full **wait at** or US **on table**) act as a waiter or as a servant with similar functions. **5** intr. (foll. by *on, upon*) **a** await the convenience of. **b** serve as an attendant to. —n. **1** a period of waiting (*had a long wait for the train*). **2** (usu. foll. by *for*) watching for an enemy; ambush (*lie in wait; lay wait*). **3** (in pl.) Brit. archaic street singers of Christmas carols. □ **cannot wait 1** is impatient. **2** needs to be dealt with immediately. **can wait** need not be dealt with immediately. **wait and see** await the progress of events. **wait for it!** colloq. used to create an interval of suspense before saying something unexpected or amusing. **wait up** (often foll. by *for*) not go to bed until a person arrives or an event happens. **you wait!** used to imply a threat, warning, or promise. [ME f. ONF *waitier* f. Gmc, rel. to WAKE¹]

waiter /ˈweɪtə(r)/ n. a man who serves at table in a hotel or restaurant etc.

waiting /ˈweɪtɪŋ/ n. **1** in senses of WAIT v. **2 a** official attendance at court. **b** one's period of this. □ **waiting-list** a list of people waiting for a thing not immediately available.

waitress /ˈweɪtrɪs/ n. a woman who serves at table in a hotel or restaurant etc.

waive /weɪv/ v.tr. refrain from insisting on or using (a right, claim, opportunity, legitimate plea, etc.). [ME f. AF *weyver*, OF *gaiver* allow to become a waif, abandon]

waiver /ˈweɪvə(r)/ n. Law the act or an instance of waiving. [as WAIVE]

wake¹ /weɪk/ v. & n. —v. (past **woke** /wəʊk/ or **waked**; past part. **woken** /ˈwəʊkən/ or **waked**) **1** intr. & tr. (often foll. by *up*) cease or cause to cease to sleep. **2** intr. & tr. (often foll. by *up*) become or cause to become alert, attentive, or active (*needs something to wake him up*). —n. a watch beside a corpse before burial; lamentation and (less often) merrymaking in connection with this. □ **waker** n. [OE *wacan* (recorded only in past *woc*), *wacian* (weak form), rel. to WATCH: sense 'vigil' perh. f. ON]

wake² n. **1** the track left on the water's surface by a moving ship. **2** turbulent air left behind a moving aircraft etc. □ **in the wake of** behind, following, as a result of. [prob. f. MLG f. ON *vök* hole or opening in ice]

wakeful adj. **1** unable to sleep. **2** (of a night etc.) passed with little or no sleep. **3** vigilant. □ **wakefully** adv. **wakefulness** n.

waken /ˈweɪkən/ v.tr. & intr. make or become awake. [ON *vakna* f. Gmc, rel. to WAKE¹]

Waldenses /wɒlˈdensiːz/ n.pl. a puritan religious sect orig. in S. France, now chiefly in Italy and America, founded c.1170 and much persecuted. □ **Waldensian** adj. & n. [med.L f. Peter *Waldo* of Lyons, founder]

wale /weɪl/ n. **1** = WEAL². **2** a ridge on a woven fabric, e.g. corduroy. **3** Naut. a broad thick timber along a ship's side. [OE *walu* stripe, ridge]

walk /wɔːk/ v. & n. —v. **1** intr. **a** (of a person or other biped) progress by lifting and setting down each foot in turn, never having both feet off the ground at once. **b** progress with similar movements (*walked on his hands*). **c** (of a quadruped) go with the slowest gait, always having at least two feet on the ground at once. **2** intr. **a** travel or go on foot. **b** take exercise in this way (*walks for two hours each day*). **3** tr. perambulate, traverse on foot at walking speed; tread the floor or surface of. **4** tr. **a** cause to walk with one. **b** accompany in walking. **c** ride or lead (a horse, dog, etc.) at walking pace. **5** intr. US sl. be released from suspicion or from a charge. —n. **1 a** an act of walking, the ordinary human gait (*go at a walk*). **b** the slowest gait of an animal. **2 a** a person's manner of walking (*know him by his walk*). **2 a** a taking of a (usu. specified) time to walk a distance (*is only ten minutes' walk from here; it's quite a walk to the bus-stop*). **b** an excursion on foot, a stroll or constitutional (*go for a walk*). **3 a** a place, track, or route intended or suitable for walking; a promenade, colonnade, or footpath. **b** a person's favourite place or route for walking. □ **walk all over** colloq. **1** defeat easily. **2** take advantage of. **walk away from 1** easily outdistance. **2** refuse to become involved with; fail to deal with. **3** survive (an accident etc.) without serious injury. **walk away with** colloq.

= *walk off with*. **walk off 1** depart (esp. abruptly). **2** get rid of the effects of (a meal, ailment, etc.) by walking (*walked off his anger*). **walk off with** *colloq.* **1** steal. **2** win easily. **walk of life** an occupation, profession, or calling. **walk-on 1** (in full **walk-on part**) a non-speaking dramatic role. **2** the player of this. **walk out 1** depart suddenly or angrily. **2** (usu. foll. by *with*) *Brit.* *archaic* go for walks in courtship. **walk-out** *n.* a sudden angry departure, esp. as a protest or strike. **walk over** *colloq.* = *walk all over*. **walk-over** *n.* an easy victory or achievement. **walk the streets 1** be a prostitute. **2** traverse the streets esp. in search of work etc. **walk tall** *colloq.* feel justifiable pride. □ **walkable** *adj.* [OE *wealcan* roll, toss, wander, f. Gmc]

walkabout /ˈwɔːkəˌbaʊt/ *n.* **1** an informal stroll among a crowd by a visiting dignitary. **2** a period of wandering in the bush by an Australian Aboriginal.

walkathon /ˈwɔːkəˌθɒn/ *n.* an organized fund-raising walk. [WALK, after MARATHON]

walker /ˈwɔːkə(r)/ *n.* **1** a person or animal that walks. **2** a wheeled or footed framework in which a baby can learn to walk.

walkie-talkie /ˌwɔːkiˈtɔːkɪ/ *n.* a two-way radio carried on the person, esp. by policemen etc.

walking /ˈwɔːkɪŋ/ *n.* & *adj.* in senses of WALK *v.* □ **walking dictionary** (or **encyclopedia**) *colloq.* a person having a wide general knowledge. **walking frame** a usu. tubular metal frame with rubberized ferrules, used by disabled or old people to help them walk. **walking-stick 1** a stick carried when walking, esp. for extra support. **2** *US* = *stick insect* (see STICK¹). **walking-tour** a holiday journey on foot, esp. of several days. **walking wounded 1** (of soldiers etc.) able to walk despite injuries; not bedridden. **2** *colloq.* a person or people having esp. mental or emotional difficulties.

Walkman /ˈwɔːkmən/ *n.* (pl. **-mans**) *propr.* a type of personal stereo equipment.

walkway /ˈwɔːkweɪ/ *n.* a passage or path for walking along, esp.: **1** a raised passageway connecting different sections of a building. **2** a wide path in a garden etc.

wall /wɔːl/ *n.* & *v.* —*n.* **1 a** a continuous and usu. vertical structure of usu. brick or stone, having little width in proportion to its length and height and esp. enclosing, protecting, or dividing a space or supporting a roof. **b** the surface of a wall, esp. inside a room (*hung the picture on the wall*). **2** anything like a wall in appearance or effect, esp.: **a** the steep side of a mountain. **b** a protection or obstacle (*a wall of steel bayonets*; *a wall of indifference*). **c** *Anat.* the outermost layer or enclosing membrane etc. of an organ, structure, etc. **d** the outermost part of a hollow structure (*stomach wall*). **e** *Mining* rock enclosing a lode or seam. —*v.tr.* **1** (esp. as **walled** *adj.*) surround or protect with a wall (*walled garden*). **2 a** (usu. foll. by *up*, *off*) block or seal (a space etc.) with a wall. **b** (foll. by *up*) enclose (a person) within a sealed space (*walled them up in the dungeon*). □ **go to the wall** be defeated or pushed aside. **off the wall** *US sl.* unorthodox, unconventional. **up the wall** *colloq.* crazy or furious (*went up the wall when he heard*). **wall bar** one of a set of parallel bars, attached to the wall of a gymnasium, on which exercises are performed. **walls have ears** it is unsafe to speak openly, as there may be eavesdroppers. **wall-to-wall 1** (of a carpet) fitted to cover a whole room etc. **2** *colloq.* profuse, ubiquitous (*wall-to-wall pop music*). □ **walling** *n.* **wall-less** *adj.* [OE f. L *vallum* rampart f. *vallus* stake]

wallaby /ˈwɒləbɪ/ *n.* (pl. **-ies**) **1** any of various marsupials of the family Macropodidae, smaller than kangaroos, and having large hind feet and long tails. **2** (**Wallabies**) *colloq.* the Australian international Rugby Union team. [Aboriginal *wolabā*]

wallah /ˈwɒlə/ *n.* orig. *Anglo-Ind.*, now *sl.* **1** a person concerned with or in charge of a usu. specified thing, business, etc. (*asked the ticket wallah*). **2** a person doing a routine administrative job; a bureaucrat. [Hindi *-wālā* suffix = -ER¹]

wallet /ˈwɒlɪt/ *n.* **1** a small flat esp. leather case for holding banknotes etc. **2** *archaic* a bag for carrying food etc. on a journey, esp. as used by a pilgrim or beggar. [ME *walet*, prob. f. AF *walet* (unrecorded), perh. f. Gmc]

wall-eye /ˈwɔːlaɪ/ *n.* **1** an eye with a streaked or opaque white iris. **2** an eye squinting outwards. □ **wall-eyed** *adj.* [back-form. f. *wall-eyed*: ME f. ON *vagleygr* f. *vagl* (unrecorded: cf. Icel. *vagl* film over the eye) + *auga* EYE]

wallflower /ˈwɔːlˌflaʊə(r)/ *n.* **1** a fragrant spring garden-plant with esp. brown, yellow, or dark-red clustered flowers. **2** *colloq.* a neglected or socially awkward person, esp. a woman sitting out at a dance for lack of partners.

Walloon /wɒˈluːn/ *n.* & *adj.* —*n.* **1** a member of a French-speaking people inhabiting S. and E. Belgium and neighbouring France (see also FLEMING). **2** the French dialect spoken by this people. —*adj.* of or concerning the Walloons or their language. [F *Wallon* f. med.L *Wallo -onis* f. Gmc: cf. WELSH]

wallop /ˈwɒləp/ *v.* & *n.* *sl.* —*v.tr.* (**walloped**, **walloping**) **1 a** thrash; beat. **b** hit hard. **2** (as **walloping** *adj.*) big; strapping; thumping (*a walloping profit*). —*n.* **1** a heavy blow; a thump. **2** *Brit.* beer or any alcoholic drink. □ **walloping** *n.* [earlier senses 'gallop', 'boil', f. ONF (*walop* n. f.) *waloper*, OF *galoper*: cf. GALLOP]

wallow /ˈwɒləʊ/ *v.* & *n.* —*v.intr.* **1** (esp. of an animal) roll about in mud, sand, water, etc. **2** (usu. foll. by *in*) indulge in unrestrained sensuality, pleasure, misery, etc. (*wallows in nostalgia*). —*n.* **1** the act or an instance of wallowing. **2** a place used by buffalo etc. for wallowing. □ **wallower** *n.* [OE *walwian* roll f. Gmc]

wallpaper /ˈwɔːlˌpeɪpə(r)/ *n.* & *v.* —*n.* **1** paper sold in rolls for pasting on to interior walls as decoration. **2** an unobtrusive background, esp. (usu. *derog.*) with ref. to sound, music, etc. —*v.tr.* (often *absol.*) decorate with wallpaper.

Wall Street /ˈwɔːl striːt/ *n.* the American financial world or money market. [street in New York City where banks, the Stock Exchange, etc. are situated]

wally /ˈwɒlɪ/ *n.* (pl. **-ies**) *Brit. sl.* a foolish or inept person. [orig. uncert., perh. shortened form of *Walter*]

walnut /ˈwɔːlnʌt/ *n.* **1** any tree of the genus *Juglans*, having aromatic leaves and drooping catkins. **2** the nut of this tree containing an edible kernel in two hemispherical half shells.

3 the timber of the walnut-tree used in cabinet-making. [OE *walh-hnutu* f. Gmc NUT]

walrus /ˈwɔːlrəs, ˈwɒl-/ *n.* a large amphibious long-tusked arctic mammal, related to the seal and sea lion. □ **walrus moustache** a long thick drooping moustache. [prob. f. Du. *walrus, -ros*, perh. by metath. after *walvisch* 'whale-fish' f. word repr. by OE *horshwæl* 'horse-whale']

waltz /wɔːls, wɔːlts, wɒ-/ *n. & v.* —*n.* **1** a dance in triple time performed by couples who rotate and progress round the floor. **2** the usu. flowing and melodious music for this. —*v.* **1** *intr.* dance a waltz. **2** *intr.* (often foll. by *in, out, round*, etc.) *colloq.* move lightly, casually, with deceptive ease, etc. (*waltzed in and took first prize*). **3** *tr.* move (a person) in or as if in a waltz, with ease (*was waltzed off to Paris*). □ **waltzer** *n.* [G *Walzer* f. *walzen* revolve]

wampum /ˈwɒmpəm/ *n.* beads made from shells and strung together for use as money, decoration, or as aids to memory by N. American Indians. [Algonquin *wampumpeag* f. *wap* white + *umpe* string + *-ag* pl. suffix]

wan /wɒn/ *adj.* **1** (of a person's complexion or appearance) pale; exhausted; worn. **2** (of a star etc. or its light) faint. □ **wanly** *adv.* **wanness** *n.* [OE *wann* dark, black, of unkn. orig.]

wand /wɒnd/ *n.* **1 a** a supposedly magic stick used in casting spells by a fairy, magician, etc. **b** a stick used by a conjuror for effect. **2** a slender rod carried or used as a marker in the ground. **3** a staff symbolizing some officials' authority. [ME prob. f. Gmc: cf. WEND, WIND²]

wander /ˈwɒndə(r)/ *v. & n.* **1** *intr.* (often foll. by *in, off*, etc.) go about from place to place aimlessly. **2** *intr.* **a** (of a person, river, road, etc.) wind about; diverge; meander. **b** (of esp. a person) get lost; leave home; stray from a path etc. **3** *intr.* talk or think incoherently; be inattentive or delirious. **4** *tr.* cover while wandering (*wanders the world*). —*n.* the act or an instance of wandering (*went for a wander round the garden*). □ **wandering Jew 1 a** a legendary person said to have been condemned by Christ to wander the earth until the second advent. **b** a person who never settles down. **2 a** a climbing plant, with stemless variegated leaves. **b** a trailing plant with pink flowers. □ **wanderer** *n.* **wandering** *n.* (esp. in *pl.*). [OE *wandrian* (as WEND)]

wanderlust /ˈwɒndəˌlʌst, ˈvændəˌlʊst/ *n.* an eagerness for travelling or wandering. [G]

wane *v. & n.* —*v.intr.* **1** (of the moon) decrease in apparent size after the full moon (cf. WAX²). **2** decrease in power, vigour, importance, brilliance, size, etc.; decline. —*n.* the process of waning. □ **on the wane** waning; declining. [OE *wanian* lessen f. Gmc]

wangle /ˈwæŋg(ə)l/ *v. & n.* *colloq.* —*v.tr.* (often *refl.*) to obtain (a favour etc.) by scheming etc. (*wangled himself a free trip*). —*n.* the act or an instance of wangling. □ **wangler** *n.* [19th-c. printers' sl.: orig. unkn.]

wank *v. & n. coarse sl.* —*v.intr. & tr.* masturbate. —*n.* an act of masturbating. [20th c.: orig. unkn.]

■ **Usage** This is usually considered a taboo word.

wanker *n. coarse sl.* **1** a contemptible or ineffectual person. **2** a person who masturbates.

■ **Usage** This is usually considered a taboo word.

wannabe /ˈwɒnəbɪ/ *n. sl.* an avid fan who tries to emulate the person he or she admires; also, anyone who would like to be someone else.

want /wɒnt/ *v. & n.* —*v.* **1** *tr.* **a** (often foll. by *to* + infin.) desire; wish for possession of; need (*wants a toy train; wants it done immediately; wanted to leave; wanted him to leave*). **b** need or desire (a person, esp. sexually). **c** esp. *Brit.* require to be attended to in esp. a specified way (*the garden wants weeding*). **d** (foll. by *to* + infin.) *colloq.* ought; should; need. **2** *intr.* (usu. foll. by *for*) lack; be deficient (*wants for nothing*). **3** *intr.* (foll. by *in, out*) esp. *US colloq.* desire to be in, out, etc. (*wants in on the deal*). **4** *tr.* (as **wanted** *adj.*) (of a suspected criminal etc.) sought by the police. —*n.* **1** (often foll. by *of*) **a** a lack, absence, or deficiency (*could not go for want of time; shows great want of judgement*). **b** poverty; need (*living in great want; in want of necessities*). **2 a** a desire for a thing etc. (*meets a long-felt want*). **b** a thing so desired (*can supply your wants*). □ **do not want to** am unwilling to. [ME f. ON *vant* neut. of *vanr* lacking = OE *wana*, formed as WANE]

wanting /ˈwɒntɪŋ/ *adj.* **1** lacking (in quality or quantity); deficient, not equal to requirements (*wanting in judgement; the standard is sadly wanting*). **2** absent, not supplied or provided. □ **be found wanting** fail to meet requirements.

wanton /ˈwɒnt(ə)n/ *adj., n., & v.* —*adj.* **1** licentious; lewd; sexually promiscuous. **2** capricious; random; arbitrary; motiveless (*wanton destruction; wanton wind*). **3** luxuriant; unrestrained (*wanton profusion*). —*n.* literary an immoral or licentious person, esp. a woman. —*v.intr. literary* **1** gambol; sport; move capriciously. **2** (foll. by *with*) behave licentiously. □ **wantonly** *adv.* **wantonness** *n.* [ME *wantowen* (wan- UN-¹ + *towen* f. OE *togen* past part. of *tēon* discipline, rel. to TEAM)]

wapiti /ˈwɒpɪtɪ/ *n.* (*pl.* **wapitis**) a N. American deer. [Cree *wapitik* white deer]

war /wɔː(r)/ *n. & v.* —*n.* **1 a** armed hostilities between esp. nations; conflict (*war broke out; war zone*). **b** a specific conflict or the period of time during which such conflict exists (*was before the war*). **c** the suspension of international law etc. during such a conflict. **2** (as **the War**) a war in progress or recently ended; the most recent major war. **3 a** hostility or contention between people, groups, etc. (*war of words*). **b** (often foll. by *on*) a sustained campaign against crime, disease, poverty, etc. —*v.intr.* (**warred, warring**) **1** (as **warring** *adj.*) **a** rival; fighting (*warring factions*). **b** conflicting (*warring principles*). **2** make war. □ **at war** (often foll. by *with*) engaged in a war. **go to war** declare or begin a war. **war crime** a crime violating the international laws of war. **war cry** a phrase or name shouted to rally one's troops. **war dance** a dance performed by primitive peoples etc. before a battle or to celebrate victory. **war department** the State office in charge of the army etc. **war-game 1** a military exercise testing or improving tactical knowledge etc. **2** a battle etc. conducted with toy soldiers. **war loan** stock issued by the British Government to raise funds in wartime.

war memorial a monument etc. commemorating those killed in a war. **war of attrition** a war in which each side seeks to wear out the other over a long period. **war widow** a woman whose husband has been killed in war. **war zone** an area in which a war takes place. [ME *werre* f. AF, ONF var. of OF *guerre*: cf. WORSE]

warble /ˈwɔːb(ə)l/ v. & n. —v. 1 intr. & tr. sing in a gentle trilling manner. 2 tr. speak or utter in a warbling manner. —n. a warbled song or utterance. [ME f. ONF *werble(r)* f. Frank. *hwirbilōn* whirl, trill]

warbler /ˈwɔːblə(r)/ n. 1 a person, bird, etc. that warbles. 2 any small insect-eating bird of the family Sylviidae or, in N. America, Parulidae.

ward /wɔːd/ n. & v. —n. 1 a separate room or division of a hospital, prison, etc. (*men's surgical ward*). 2 a Brit. an administrative division of a constituency, usu. electing a councillor or councillors etc. b esp. US a similar administrative division. 3 a a minor under the care of a guardian appointed by the parents or a court. b (in full **ward of court**) a minor or mentally deficient person placed under the protection of a court. —v.intr. (foll. by *off*) 1 parry (a blow). 2 avert (danger, poverty, etc.). [OE *weard*, *weardian* f. Gmc: cf. GUARD]

-ward /wəd/ suffix (also **-wards**) added to nouns of place or destination and to adverbs of direction and forming: 1 adverbs (usu. **-wards**) meaning 'towards the place etc.' (*moving backwards*; *set off homewards*). 2 adjectives (usu. **-ward**) meaning 'turned or tending towards' (*a downward look*; *an onward rush*). 3 (less commonly) nouns meaning 'the region towards or about' (*look to the eastward*). [from or after OE *-weard* f. a Gmc root meaning 'turn']

warden /ˈwɔːd(ə)n/ n. 1 (usu. in *comb.*) a supervising official (*churchwarden*; *traffic warden*). 2 a Brit. a president or governor of a college, school, hospital, youth hostel, etc. b esp. US a prison governor. □ **wardenship** n. [ME f. AF & ONF *wardein* var. of OF *g(u)arden* GUARDIAN]

warder /ˈwɔːdə(r)/ n. 1 Brit. (*fem.* **wardress**) a prison officer. 2 a guard. [ME f. AF *wardere*, *-our* f. ONF *warder*, OF *garder* to GUARD]

wardrobe /ˈwɔːdrəʊb/ n. 1 a large movable or built-in cupboard with rails, shelves, hooks, etc., for storing clothes. 2 a person's entire stock of clothes. 3 the costume department or costumes of a theatre, a film company, etc. 4 a department of a royal household in charge of clothing. □ **wardrobe mistress** (or **master**) a person in charge of a theatrical or film wardrobe. [ME f. ONF *warderobe*, OF *garderobe* (as GUARD, ROBE)]

wardroom /ˈwɔːdruːm, -rʊm/ n. a room in a warship for the use of commissioned officers.

-wards var. of -WARD.

wardship /ˈwɔːdʃɪp/ n. 1 a guardian's care or tutelage (*under his wardship*). 2 the condition of being a ward.

ware[1] /weə(r)/ n. 1 (esp. in *comb.*) things of the same kind, esp. ceramics, made usu. for sale (*chinaware*; *hardware*). 2 (usu. in *pl.*) articles for sale (*displayed his wares*). 3 ceramics etc. of a specified material, factory, or kind (*Wedgwood ware*; *Delft ware*). [OE *waru* f. Gmc, perh. orig. = 'object of care', rel. to WARD]

ware[2] /weə(r)/ v.tr. (also **'ware**) (esp. in hunting) look out for; avoid (usu. in *imper.*: *ware hounds!*). [OE *warian* f. Gmc (cf. WARD), & f. ONF *warer*]

warehouse /ˈweəhaʊs/ n. & v. —n. 1 a building in which esp. retail goods are stored; a repository. 2 esp. Brit. a wholesale or large retail store. —v.tr. /also -haʊz/ store (esp. furniture or bonded goods) temporarily in a repository. □ **warehouseman** n. (pl. **-men**).

warfare /ˈwɔːfeə(r)/ n. a state of war; campaigning, engaging in war (*chemical warfare*).

warfarin /ˈwɔːfərɪn/ n. a water-soluble anticoagulant used esp. as a rat poison. [Wisconsin Alumni Research Foundation + *-arin*, after F suffix *-arine*]

warhead /ˈwɔːhed/ n. the explosive head of a missile, torpedo, or similar weapon.

warhorse /ˈwɔːhɔːs/ n. 1 hist. a knight's or trooper's powerful horse. 2 colloq. a veteran soldier, politician, etc.; a reliable hack.

warlike /ˈwɔːlaɪk/ adj. 1 threatening war; hostile. 2 martial; soldierly. 3 of or for war; military (*warlike preparations*).

warlock /ˈwɔːlɒk/ n. archaic a sorcerer or wizard. [OE *wǣr-loga* traitor f. *wǣr* covenant: *loga* rel. to LIE[2]]

warlord /ˈwɔːlɔːd/ n. a military commander or commander-in-chief.

warm /wɔːm/ adj., v., & n. —adj. 1 of or at a fairly or comfortably high temperature. 2 (of clothes etc.) affording warmth. 3 a (of a person, action, feelings, etc.) sympathetic; cordial; friendly; loving. b enthusiastic; hearty (*was warm in her praise*). 4 animated, heated, excited; indignant (*the dispute grew warm*). 5 colloq. a (of a participant in esp. a children's game of seeking) close to the object etc. sought. b near to guessing or finding out a secret. 6 (of a colour, light, etc.) reddish, pink, or yellowish, etc., suggestive of warmth. —v. 1 tr. a make warm (*fire warms the room*). b excite; make cheerful (*warms the heart*). 2 a tr. (often foll. by *up*) warm oneself at a fire etc. b intr. (often foll. by *to*) become animated, enthusiastic, or sympathetic (*warmed to his subject*). —n. the act of warming; the state of being warmed (*gave it a warm*; *had a nice warm by the fire*). □ **warmed-up** (US **-over**) 1 (of food etc.) reheated or stale. 2 stale; second-hand. **warm front** an advancing mass of warm air. **warming-pan** hist. a usu. brass container for live coals with a flat body and a long handle, used for warming a bed. **warm up** 1 (of an athlete, performer, etc.) prepare for a contest, performance, etc. by practising. 2 (of a room etc.) become warmer. 3 (of a person) become enthusiastic etc. 4 (of a radio, engine, etc.) reach a temperature for efficient working. 5 reheat (food). **warm-up** n. a period of preparatory exercise for a contest or performance. □ **warmer** n. (also in *comb.*). **warmish** adj. **warmly** adv. **warmness** n. **warmth** n. [OE *wearm* f. Gmc]

warm-blooded /wɔːmˈblʌdɪd/ adj. 1 having warm blood; mammalian. 2 ardent, passionate. □ **warm-bloodedness** n.

warm-hearted /wɔːmˈhɑːtɪd/ adj. kind, friendly. □ **warm-heartedly** adv. **warm-heartedness** n.

warmonger /ˈwɔːˌmʌŋgə(r)/ n. a person who seeks to bring about or promote war. □ **warmongering** n. & adj.

warn /wɔːn/ v.tr. **1** (also absol.) **a** (often foll. by of, or that + clause, or to + infin.) inform of danger, unknown circumstances, etc. (warned them of the danger; warned her that she was being watched; warned him to expect a visit). **b** (often foll. by against) inform (a person etc.) about a specific danger, hostile person, etc. (warned her against trusting him). **2** (usu. with neg.) admonish; tell forcefully (has been warned not to go). **3** give (a person) cautionary notice regarding conduct etc. (shall not warn you again). □ **warn off** tell (a person) to keep away (from). □ **warner** n. [OE war(e)nian, wearnian ult. f. Gmc: cf. WARD]

warning /ˈwɔːnɪŋ/ n. **1** in senses of WARN v. **2** anything that serves to warn; a hint or indication of difficulty, danger, etc. [OE war(e)nung etc. (as WARN, -ING¹)]

warp /wɔːp/ v. & n. —v. **1** tr. & intr. **a** make or become bent or twisted out of shape, esp. by the action of heat, damp, etc. **b** make or become perverted, bitter, or strange (a warped sense of humour). **2** tr. haul (a ship) by a rope attached to a fixed point. —n. **1 a** a state of being warped, esp. of shrunken or expanded timber. **b** perversion, bitterness, etc. of the mind or character. **2** the threads stretched lengthwise in a loom to be crossed by the weft. **3** a rope used in towing or warping, or attached to a trawl-net. □ **warpage** n. (esp. in sense 1a of v.). **warper** n. (in sense 5 of v.). [OE weorpan throw, wearp f. Gmc]

warpaint /ˈwɔːpeɪnt/ n. **1** paint used to adorn the body before battle, esp. by N. American Indians. **2** colloq. elaborate make-up.

warpath /ˈwɔːpɑːθ/ n. a warlike expedition of N. American Indians (on the warpath).

warrant /ˈwɒrənt/ n. & v. —n. **1** anything or anyone that authorizes a person or an action. **2 a** a written authorization, money voucher, travel document, etc. (a dividend warrant). **b** a written authorization allowing police to search premises, arrest a suspect, etc. **3** a document authorizing counsel to represent the principal in a lawsuit (warrant of attorney). —v.tr. **1** serve as a warrant for; justify (nothing can warrant his behaviour). **2** guarantee or attest to the genuineness of an article, the worth of a person, etc. □ **I** (or **I'll**) **warrant** I am certain; no doubt (he'll be sorry, I'll warrant). **warrant-officer** an officer ranking between commissioned officers and NCOs. □ **warranter** n. **warrantor** n. [ME f. ONF warant, var. of OF guarant, -and f. Frank. werênd (unrecorded) f. giwerên be surety for]

warrantable /ˈwɒrəntəb(ə)l/ adj. able to be warranted. □ **warrantableness** n. **warrantably** adv.

warrantee /ˌwɒrənˈtiː/ n. a person to whom a warranty is given.

warranty /ˈwɒrəntɪ/ n. (pl. -ies) **1** an undertaking as to the ownership or quality of a thing sold, hired, etc., often accepting responsibility for defects or liability for repairs needed over a specified period. **2** (usu. foll. by for + verbal noun) an authority or justification. **3** an undertaking by an insured person of the truth of a statement or fulfilment of a condition. [ME f. AF warantie, var. of garantie (as WARRANT)]

warren /ˈwɒrən/ n. **1 a** a network of interconnecting rabbit burrows. **b** a piece of ground occupied by this. **2** a densely populated or labyrinthine building or district. [ME f. AF & ONF warenne, OF garenne game-park f. Gmc]

warrior /ˈwɒrɪə(r)/ n. **1** a person, nation etc., experienced or distinguished in fighting (also attrib.). **2** a fighting man, esp. of primitive peoples. [ME f. ONF werreior etc., OF guerreior etc. f. werreier, guerreier make WAR]

warship /ˈwɔːʃɪp/ n. an armoured ship used in war.

wart /wɔːt/ n. **1** a small hardish roundish growth on the skin caused by a virus-induced abnormal growth of papillae and thickening of the epidermis. **2** a protuberance on the skin of an animal, surface of a plant, etc. □ **wart-hog** an African wild pig with a large head and warty lumps on its face, and large curved tusks. **warts and all** colloq. with no attempt to conceal blemishes or inadequacies. □ **warty** adj. [OE wearte f. Gmc]

wartime /ˈwɔːtaɪm/ n. the period during which a war is waged.

wary /ˈweərɪ/ adj. (**warier, wariest**) **1** on one's guard; given to caution; circumspect. **2** (foll. by of) cautious, suspicious (am wary of using lifts). **3** showing or done with caution or suspicion (a wary expression). □ **warily** adv. **wariness** n. [WARE² + -Y¹]

was 1st & 3rd sing. past of BE.

wash /wɒʃ/ v. & n. —v. **1** tr. cleanse (oneself or a part of oneself, clothes, etc.) with liquid, esp. water. **2** tr. (foll. by out, off, away, etc.) remove a stain or dirt in this way. **3** intr. wash oneself or esp. one's hands and face. **4** intr. wash clothes etc. **5** intr. (of fabric or dye) bear washing without damage. **6** intr. (foll. by off, out) (of a stain etc.) be removed by washing. **7** tr. (of moving liquid) carry along in a specified direction. **8** tr. brush a thin coat of watery paint or ink over (paper in water-colour painting etc., or a wall). —n. **1 a** the act or an instance of washing; the process of being washed (give them a good wash; only needed one wash). **b** (prec. by the) treatment at a laundry etc. (sent them to the wash). **2** a quantity of clothes for washing or just washed. **3** the visible or audible motion of agitated water or air, esp. due to the passage of a ship etc. or aircraft. **4** soil swept off by water; alluvium. **5** kitchen slops and scraps given to pigs. **6** liquid food for animals. **7** a liquid to spread over a surface to cleanse, heal, or colour. **8** a thin coating of water-colour, wall-colouring, or metal. □ **come out in the wash** colloq. be clarified, or (of contingent difficulties) be resolved or removed, in the course of events. **wash-and-wear** adj. (of a fabric or garment) easily and quickly laundered. **wash-basin** a basin for washing one's hands, face, etc. **wash down 1** wash completely (esp. a large surface or object). **2** (usu. foll. by with) accompany or follow (food) with a drink. **washed out 1** faded by washing. **2** pale. **3** colloq. limp, enfeebled. **washed up** esp. US sl. defeated, having failed. **wash one's hands** euphem. go to the lavatory. **wash one's hands of** renounce responsibility for. **wash-leather** chamois or similar leather for washing windows etc. **wash out 1** clean the inside of (a thing) by washing. **2** clean (a garment etc.) by brief washing. **3 a** rain off (an event etc.). **b** colloq. cancel. **4** (of a flood, downpour, etc.) make a breach in (a road etc.). **wash-out** n. **1** colloq. a fiasco; a complete failure. **2** a breach in a road, railway track, etc., caused by flooding. **wash up 1** *tr.* (also *absol.*) esp. *Brit.* wash (crockery and cutlery) after use. **2** *US* wash one's face and hands. **won't wash** esp. *Brit. colloq.* (of an argument etc.) will not be believed or accepted. [OE *wæscan* etc. f. Gmc, rel. to WATER]

washable /ˈwɒʃəb(ə)l/ *adj.* that can be washed, esp. without damage. □ **washability** /-ˈbɪlɪtɪ/ *n.*

washboard /ˈwɒʃbɔːd/ *n.* **1** a board of ribbed wood or a sheet of corrugated zinc on which clothes are scrubbed in washing. **2** this used as a percussion instrument, played with the fingers.

washday /ˈwɒʃdeɪ/ *n.* a day on which clothes etc. are washed.

washer /ˈwɒʃə(r)/ *n.* **1 a** a person or thing that washes. **b** a washing-machine. **2** a flat ring of rubber etc. inserted at a joint to tighten it and prevent leakage. **3** a similar ring placed under the head of a screw, bolt, etc., or under a nut, to disperse its pressure.

washerwoman /ˈwɒʃəˌwʊmən/ *n.* (*pl.* **-women**) a woman whose occupation is washing clothes; a laundress.

washeteria /ˌwɒʃəˈtɪərɪə/ *n.* = LAUNDERETTE.

washing /ˈwɒʃɪŋ/ *n.* a quantity of clothes for washing or just washed. □ **washing-machine** a machine for washing clothes and linen etc. **washing-powder** powder of soap or detergent for washing clothes. **washing-soda** sodium carbonate, used dissolved in water for washing and cleaning. **washing-up** *Brit.* **1** the process of washing dishes etc. after use. **2** used dishes etc. for washing.

washroom /ˈwɒʃruːm, -rʊm/ *n.* *US* a room with washing and toilet facilities.

washstand /ˈwɒʃstænd/ *n.* a piece of furniture to hold a basin, jug, soap, etc.

washtub /ˈwɒʃtʌb/ *n.* a tub or vessel for washing clothes etc.

washy /ˈwɒʃɪ/ *adj.* (**washier, washiest**) **1** (of liquid food) too watery; insipid. **2** (of colour) faded-looking. □ **washily** *adv.* **washiness** *n.*

wasn't /ˈwɒz(ə)nt/ *contr.* was not.

Wasp /wɒsp/ *n.* (also **WASP**) *US* usu. *derog.* a middle-class American White Protestant descended from early European settlers. □ **Waspy** *adj.* (also **WASPy**). [White Anglo-Saxon Protestant]

wasp /wɒsp/ *n.* **1** a stinging often flesh-eating insect with black and yellow stripes and a very thin waist. **2** (in *comb.*) any of various insects resembling a wasp in some way (*wasp-beetle*). □ **wasp-waist** a very slender waist. **wasp-waisted** having a very slender waist. □ **wasp-like** *adj.* [OE *wæfs, wæps, wæsp,* f. WG: perh. rel. to WEAVE¹ (from the weblike form of its nest)]

waspish /ˈwɒspɪʃ/ *adj.* irritable, petulant; sharp in retort. □ **waspishly** *adv.* **waspishness** *n.*

wassail /ˈwɒseɪl, ˈwɒs(ə)l/ *n.* & *v. archaic* —*n.* **1** a festive occasion; a drinking-bout. **2** a kind of liquor drunk on such an occasion. —*v.intr.* make merry; celebrate with drinking etc. □ **wassail-bowl** (or **-cup**) a bowl or cup from which healths were drunk, esp. on Christmas Eve and Twelfth Night. □ **wassailer** *n.* [ME *wæs hæil* etc. f. ON *ves heill,* corresp. to OE *wes hāl* 'be in health', a form of salutation: cf. HALE¹]

wastage /ˈweɪstɪdʒ/ *n.* **1** an amount wasted. **2** loss by use, wear, or leakage. **3** *Commerce* loss of employees other than by redundancy.

waste /weɪst/ *v., adj.,* & *n.* —*v.* **1** *tr.* use to no purpose or for inadequate result (*waste time*). **2** *tr.* fail to use (esp. an opportunity). **3** *tr.* & *intr.* wear gradually away; make or become weak; wither. **4** *tr.* ravage, devastate. **5** *intr.* be expended without useful effect. —*adj.* **1** superfluous; no longer serving a purpose. **2** (of a district etc.) not inhabited or cultivated; desolate. —*n.* **1** the act or an instance of wasting; extravagant or ineffectual use of an asset, of time, etc. **2** waste material or food; refuse; useless remains or by-products. **3** a waste region; a desert etc. **4** the state of being used up; diminution by wear and tear. □ **go** (or **run**) **to waste** be wasted. **lay waste** ravage, devastate. **waste-basket** esp. *US* = *waste-paper basket*. **waste paper** spoiled or valueless paper. **waste-paper basket** esp. *Brit.* a receptacle for waste paper. **waste pipe** a pipe to carry off waste material, e.g. from a sink. □ **wastable** *adj.* **wasteless** *adj.* [ME f. ONF *wast(e),* var. of OF *g(u)ast(e),* f. L *vastus*]

wasteful /ˈweɪstfʊl/ *adj.* **1** extravagant. **2** causing or showing waste. □ **wastefully** *adv.* **wastefulness** *n.*

wasteland /ˈweɪstlænd/ *n.* an unproductive or useless area of land.

wastrel /ˈweɪstr(ə)l/ *n.* a wasteful or good-for-nothing person.

watch /wɒtʃ/ *v.* & *n.* —*v.* **1** *tr.* keep the eyes fixed on; look at attentively. **2** *tr.* **a** keep under observation; follow observantly. **b** monitor or consider carefully; pay attention to (*have to watch my weight; watched their progress with interest*). **3** *intr.* (often foll. by *for*) be in an alert state; be vigilant; take heed (*watch for the holes in the road; watch for an opportunity*). **4** *intr.* (foll. by *over*) look after; take care of. —*n.* **1** a small portable timepiece for carrying on one's person. **2** a state of alert or constant observation or attention. **3** *Naut.* **a** a four-hour spell of duty. **b** (in full **starboard** or **port watch**) each of the halves, divided according to the position of the bunks, into which a ship's crew is divided to take alternate watches. □ **on the watch** waiting for an expected or feared occurrence. **watch-case** the outer metal case enclosing the works of a watch. **watch-chain** a metal chain for securing a pocket-watch. **watch-glass** a glass disc covering the dial of a watch. **watch it** (or **oneself**) *colloq.* be careful. **watch out** (often foll. by *for*) be on one's guard. **1** as a warning of immediate danger. **2** as a warning of immediate danger. **watch-spring** the mainspring of a watch. **watch one's step** proceed cautiously. □ **watchable** *adj.* **watcher** *n.* (also in *comb.*). [OE *wæcce* (n.), rel. to WAKE¹]

watchdog /ˈwɒtʃdɒg/ *n.* & *v.* —*n.* **1** a dog kept to guard property etc. **2** a person or body monitoring others' rights, behaviour, etc. —*v.tr.* (**-dogged, -dogging**) maintain surveillance over.

watchful /ˈwɒtʃfʊl/ *adj.* **1** accustomed to watching. **2** on the watch. **3** showing vigilance. **4** *archaic* wakeful. □ **watchfully** *adv.* **watchfulness** *n.*

watchmaker /ˈwɒtʃˌmeɪkə(r)/ *n.* a person who makes and repairs watches and clocks. □ **watchmaking** *n.*

watchman /ˈwɒtʃmən/ *n.* (*pl.* **-men**) **1** a man employed to look after an empty building etc.

at night. **2** *archaic* or *hist.* a member of a night-watch.

watchword /ˈwɒtʃwɜːd/ *n.* **1** a phrase summarizing a guiding principle; a slogan. **2** *hist.* a military password.

water /ˈwɔːtə(r)/ *n.* & *v.* —*n.* **1** a colourless transparent odourless tasteless liquid compound of oxygen and hydrogen. **2** a liquid consisting chiefly of this and found in seas, lakes, and rivers, rain, etc. **3** (in *pl.*) part of a sea or river (*in Icelandic waters*). **4** (often as **the waters**) mineral water at a spa etc. **5** the state of a tide (*high water*). **6** a solution of a specified substance in water (*lavender-water*). **7** the quality of the transparency and brilliance of a gem, esp. a diamond. **8** (*attrib.*) **a** found in or near water. **b** of, for, or worked by water. **c** involving, using, or yielding water. —*v.* **1** *tr.* sprinkle or soak with water. **2** *tr.* supply (a plant) with water. **3** *tr.* give water to (an animal) to drink. **4** *intr.* (of the mouth or eyes) secrete water as saliva or tears. **5** *tr.* (as **watered** *adj.*) (of silk etc.) having irregular wavy glossy markings. **6** *tr.* adulterate (milk, beer, etc.) with water. □ **like water** lavishly, profusely. **make one's mouth water** stimulate one's appetite or anticipation. **of the first water 1** (of a diamond) of the greatest brilliance and transparency. **2** of the finest quality or extreme degree. **water-bed** a mattress of rubber or plastic etc. filled with water. **water-biscuit** a thin crisp unsweetened biscuit made from flour and water. **water-boatman** an aquatic bug which swims with oarlike hind legs. **water-borne 1** (of goods etc.) conveyed by or travelling on water. **2** (of a disease) communicated or propagated by contaminated water. **water-buffalo** the common domestic Indian buffalo. **water-butt** a barrel used to catch rainwater. **water-cannon** a device giving a powerful jet of water to disperse a crowd etc. **the Water-carrier** (or **-bearer**) the zodiacal sign or constellation Aquarius. **water chestnut 1** an aquatic plant bearing an edible seed. **2 a** a sedge with rushlike leaves arising from a corm. **b** this corm used as food. **water-closet 1** a lavatory with the means for flushing the pan with water. **2** a room containing this. **water-colour** (*US* **-color**) **1** artists' paint made of pigment to be diluted with water and not oil. **2** a picture painted with this. **3** the art of painting with water-colours. **water-colourist** (*US* **-colorist**) a painter in water-colours. **water-cooled** cooled by the circulation of water. **water-cooler** a tank of cooled drinking-water. **water-diviner** *Brit.* a person who dowses (see DOWSE¹) for water. **water down 1** dilute with water. **2** make less vivid, forceful, or horrifying. **water-hole** a shallow depression in which water collects (esp. in the bed of a river otherwise dry). **water-ice** a confection of flavoured and frozen water and sugar etc.; a sorbet. **water jump** a place where a horse in a steeplechase etc. must jump over water. **water lily** an aquatic plant with broad flat floating leaves and large usu. cup-shaped floating flowers. **water-line 1** the line along which the surface of water touches a ship's side (marked on a ship for use in loading). **2** a linear watermark. **water main** the main pipe in a water-supply system. **water-meadow** a meadow periodically flooded by a stream. **water**

melon a large smooth green melon with red pulp and watery juice. **water meter** a device for measuring and recording the amount of water supplied to a house etc. **water-mill** a mill worked by a water-wheel. **water-nymph** a nymph regarded as inhabiting or presiding over water. **water-pipe 1** a pipe for conveying water. **2** a hookah. **water-pistol** a toy pistol shooting a jet of water. **water plantain** a ditch-plant with plantain-like leaves. **water polo** a game played by swimmers, with a ball like a football. **water-power** mechanical force derived from the weight or motion of water. **water-rat** = *water-vole*. **water-repellent** not easily penetrated by water. **water-softener** an apparatus or substance for softening hard water. **water-soluble** soluble in water. **water-table** the level below which the ground is saturated with water. **water torture** a form of torture in which the victim is exposed to the incessant dripping of water on the head, or the sound of dripping. **water-tower** a tower with an elevated tank to give pressure for distributing water. **water under the bridge** past events accepted as past and irrevocable. **water-vole** an aquatic vole. **water-weed** any of various aquatic plants. **water-wheel** a wheel driven by water to work machinery, or to raise water. **water-wings** inflated floats fixed on the arms of a person learning to swim. □ **waterer** *n.* **waterless** *adj.* [OE *wæter* f. Gmc, rel. to WET]

watercourse /ˈwɔːtəˌkɔːs/ *n.* **1** a brook, stream, or artificial water-channel. **2** the bed along which this flows.

watercress /ˈwɔːtəˌkres/ *n.* a hardy perennial cress, which grows in running water, with pungent leaves used in salad.

waterfall /ˈwɔːtəˌfɔːl/ *n.* a stream or river flowing over a precipice or down a steep hillside.

Waterford glass /ˈwɔːtəfəd/ *n.* a clear colourless flint glass. [*Waterford* in Ireland]

waterfowl /ˈwɔːtəˌfaʊl/ *n.* (usu. collect. as *pl.*) birds frequenting water, esp. swimming game-birds.

waterfront /ˈwɔːtəˌfrʌnt/ *n.* the part of a town adjoining a river, lake, harbour, etc.

watergate /ˈwɔːtəˌgeɪt/ *n.* **1** a floodgate. **2** a gate giving access to a river etc.

watering /ˈwɔːtərɪŋ/ *n.* the act or an instance of supplying water or (of an animal) obtaining water. □ **watering-can** a portable container with a long spout for watering plants. **watering-hole 1** a pool of water from which animals regularly drink; = *water-hole*. **2** *sl.* a bar. **watering-place 1** = *watering-hole*. **2** a spa or seaside resort. **3** a place where water is obtained. [OE *wæterung* (as WATER, -ING¹)]

waterlogged /ˈwɔːtəˌlɒgd/ *adj.* **1** saturated with water. **2** (of a boat etc.) hardly able to float from being saturated or filled with water. **3** (of ground) made useless by being saturated with water. [*waterlog* (v.), f. WATER + LOG¹, prob. orig. = 'reduce (a ship) to the condition of a log']

Waterloo /ˌwɔːtəˈluː/ *n.* a decisive defeat or contest (*meet one's Waterloo*). [*Waterloo* in Belgium, where Napoleon was finally defeated in 1815]

waterman /ˈwɔːtəmən/ *n.* (*pl.* **-men**) **1** a boatman plying for hire. **2** an oarsman as regards skill in keeping the boat balanced.

watermark /ˈwɔːtəˌmɑːk/ n. & v. —n. a faint design made in some paper during manufacture, visible when held against the light, identifying the maker etc. —v.tr. mark with this.

waterproof /ˈwɔːtəˌpruːf/ adj., n., & v. —adj. impervious to water. —n. a waterproof garment or material. —v.tr. make waterproof.

watershed /ˈwɔːtəˌʃed/ n. 1 a line of separation between waters flowing to different rivers, basins, or seas. 2 a turning-point in affairs. [WATER + shed ridge of high ground (rel. to SHED²), after G Wasserscheide]

waterside /ˈwɔːtəˌsaɪd/ n. the margin of a sea, lake, or river.

water-ski /ˈwɔːtəˌskiː/ n. & v. —n. (pl. -skis) each of a pair of skis for skimming the surface of the water when towed by a motor boat. —v.intr. (-skis, -ski'd or -skied /-skiːd/; -skiing) travel on water-skis. □ **water-skier** n.

waterspout /ˈwɔːtəˌspaʊt/ n. a gyrating column of water and spray formed by a whirlwind between sea and cloud.

watertight /ˈwɔːtəˌtaɪt/ adj. 1 (of a joint, container, vessel, etc.) closely fastened or fitted or made so as to prevent the passage of water. 2 (of an argument etc.) unassailable.

waterway /ˈwɔːtəˌweɪ/ n. 1 a navigable channel. 2 a route for travel by water.

waterworks /ˈwɔːtəˌwɜːks/ n. 1 an establishment for managing a ..ater-supply. 2 colloq. the shedding of tears. 3 Brit. colloq. the urinary system.

watery /ˈwɔːtərɪ/ adj. 1 containing too much water. 2 too thin in consistency. 3 of or consisting of water. 4 (of the eyes) suffused or running with water. 5 (of colour) pale. □ **wateriness** n. [OE wæterig (as WATER, -Y¹)]

watt /wɒt/ n. the SI unit of power, equivalent to one joule per second, corresponding to the rate of energy in an electric circuit where the potential difference is one volt and the current one ampere. □ **watt-hour** the energy used when one watt is applied for one hour. [J. Watt, Sc. engineer d. 1819]

wattage /ˈwɒtɪdʒ/ n. an amount of electrical power expressed in watts.

wattle¹ /ˈwɒt(ə)l/ n. 1 a interlaced rods and split rods as a material for making fences, walls, etc. b (in sing. or pl.) rods and twigs for this use. 2 an Australian acacia with long pliant branches, with bark used in tanning and golden flowers used as the national emblem. □ **wattle and daub** a network of rods and twigs plastered with mud or clay as a building material. [OE watul, of unkn. orig.]

wattle² /ˈwɒt(ə)l/ n. 1 a loose fleshy appendage on the head or throat of a turkey or other birds. 2 = BARB n. 3. □ **wattled** adj. [16th c.: orig. unkn.]

wave v. & n. —v. 1 a intr. (often foll. by to) move a hand etc. to and fro in greeting or as a signal. b tr. move (a hand etc.) in this way. 2 a intr. show a sinuous or sweeping motion as of a flag or a cornfield in the wind; flutter, undulate. b tr. impart a waving motion to. 3 tr. direct by waving (waved them away; waved them to follow). 4 tr. express (a greeting etc.) by waving (waved goodbye to them). 5 tr. give an undulating form to; make wavy. 6 intr. (of hair etc.) have such a form; be wavy. —n. 1 a ridge of water between two depressions. 2 a long body of water curling

into an arched form and breaking on the shore. 3 a thing compared to this, e.g. a body of persons in one of successive advancing groups. 4 a gesture of waving. 5 a the process of waving the hair. b an undulating form produced in the hair by waving. 6 a a temporary occurrence or increase of a condition, emotion, or influence (a wave of enthusiasm). b a specified period of widespread weather (heat wave). 7 Physics a the disturbance of the particles of a fluid medium to form ridges and troughs for the propagation or direction of motion, heat, light, sound, etc., without the advance of the particles. b a single curve in the course of this motion. 8 Electr. a similar variation of an electromagnetic field in the propagation of radiation through a medium or vacuum. □ **make waves** colloq. cause a disturbance. **wave aside** dismiss as intrusive or irrelevant. **wave-form** Physics a curve showing the shape of a wave at a given time. **wave mechanics** a method of analysis of the behaviour esp. of atomic phenomena with particles represented by wave equations (see quantum mechanics). **wave theory** hist. the theory that light is propagated through the ether by a wave-motion imparted to the ether by the molecular vibrations of the radiant body. □ **waveless** adj. **wavelike** adj. & adv. [OE wafian (v.) f. Gmc: (n.) also alt. of ME wawe, wage]

waveband n. a range of (esp. radio) wavelengths between certain limits.

wavelength /ˈweɪvlɛŋθ, -leŋkθ/ n. 1 the distance between successive crests of a wave. 2 this as a distinctive feature of radio waves from a transmitter. 3 colloq. a particular range of sensibility (we don't seem to be on the same wavelength).

wavelet n. a small wave on water.

waver v.intr. 1 be or become unsteady; falter; begin to give way. 2 be irresolute or undecided between different courses or opinions; be shaken in resolution or belief. 3 (of a light) flicker. □ **waverer** n. **waveringly** adv. [ME f. ON vafra flicker f. Gmc, rel. to WAVE]

wavy adj. (**wavier, waviest**) (of a line or surface) having waves or alternate contrary curves (wavy hair). □ **wavily** adv. **waviness** n.

wax¹ n. & v. —n. 1 a sticky plastic yellowish substance secreted by bees as the material of honey-comb cells; beeswax. 2 a white translucent material obtained from this by bleaching and purifying and used for candles, in modelling, as a basis of polishes, and for other purposes. 3 any similar substance. 4 (attrib.) made of wax. —v.tr. cover or treat with wax. □ **be wax in a person's hands** be entirely subservient to a person. **wax paper** paper waterproofed with a layer of wax. □ **waxer** n. [OE wæx, weax f. Gmc]

wax² v.intr. 1 (of the moon between new and full) have a progressively larger part of its visible surface illuminated, increasing in apparent size. 2 become larger or stronger. 3 pass into a specified state or mood (wax lyrical). □ **wax and wane** undergo alternate increases and decreases. [OE weaxan f. Gmc]

waxen adj. 1 having a smooth pale translucent surface as of wax. 2 able to receive impressions like wax; plastic. 3 archaic made of wax.

waxwing n. any bird of the genus Bombycilla.

waxwork /ˈwækswɜːk/ n. an object, esp. a lifelike dummy, modelled in wax.

waxy adj. (**waxier**, **waxiest**) resembling wax in consistency or in its surface. □ **waxily** adv. **waxiness** n. [WAX¹ + -Y¹]

way n. & adv. —n. 1 a road, track, path, etc., for passing along. 2 a course or route for reaching a place, esp. the best one (asked the way to London). 3 a place of passage into a building, through a door, etc. (could not find the way out). 4 **a** a method or plan for attaining an object (that is not the way to do it). **b** the ability to obtain one's object (has a way with him). 5 **a** a person's desired or chosen course of action. **b** a custom or manner of behaving; a personal peculiarity (has a way of forgetting things; things had a way of going badly). 6 a specific manner of life or procedure (soon got into the way of it). 7 the normal course of events (that is always the way). 8 a travelling distance; a length traversed or to be traversed (is a long way away). 9 impetus, progress (pushed my way through). 10 movement of a ship etc. (gather way; lose way). 11 the state of being engaged in movement from place to place; time spent in this (met them on the way home; with songs to cheer the way). 12 a specified direction. 13 (in pl.) parts into which a thing is divided (split it three ways). 14 a specified condition or state (things are in a bad way). 15 a respect. —adv. colloq. to a considerable extent; far (you're way off the mark). □ **across** (or **over**) **the way** opposite. **any way** = ANYWAY. **be on one's way** set off; depart. **by the way** incidentally. **by way of 1** through; by means of. **2** as a substitute for or as a form of (did it by way of apology). **come one's way** become available to one. **find a way** discover a means of obtaining one's object. **get** (or **have**) **one's way** (or **have it one's own way** etc.) get what one wants; ensure one's wishes are met. **give way 1 a** make concessions. **b** fail to resist; yield. **2** (often foll. by to) concede precedence (to). **3** (of a structure etc.) be dislodged or broken under a load; collapse. **4** (foll. by to) be superseded by. **5** (foll. by to) be overcome by (an emotion etc.). **go out of one's way** (often foll. by to + infin.) make a special effort; act gratuitously or without compulsion (went out of their way to help). **go one's own way** act independently, esp. against contrary advice. **go one's way 1** leave, depart. **2** (of events, circumstances, etc.) be favourable to one. **in its way** if regarded from a particular standpoint appropriate to it. **in no way** not at all; by no means. **in a way** in a certain respect but not altogether or completely. **in the** (or **one's**) **way** forming an obstacle or hindrance. **lead the way 1** act as guide or leader. **2** show how to do something. **one way and another** taking various considerations into account. **one way or another** by some means. **on the** (or **one's**) **way 1** in the course of a journey etc. **2** having progressed (is well on the way to completion). **3** colloq. (of a child) conceived but not yet born. **on the way out** colloq. going down in status, estimation, popularity, or favour. **the other way about** (or **round**) in an inverted or reversed position or direction. **out of the way 1** no longer an obstacle or hindrance. **2** disposed of; settled. **3** (of a person) imprisoned or killed. **4** (with neg.) common or unremarkable (nothing out of the way). **5** (of a place) remote, inaccessible.

out of one's way not on one's intended route. **way back** colloq. long ago. **ways and means 1** methods of achieving something. **2** methods of raising government revenue. [OE weg f. Gmc: (adv.) f. AWAY]

wayfarer /ˈweɪˌfeərə(r)/ n. a traveller, esp. on foot.

wayfaring /ˈweɪˌfeərɪŋ/ n. travelling, esp. on foot. □ **wayfaring-tree** a white-flowered European and Asian shrub commonly found along roadsides.

waylay /weɪˈleɪ/ v.tr. (past and past part. **waylaid**) **1** lie in wait for. **2** stop to rob or interview. □ **waylayer** n.

-ways /weɪz/ suffix forming adjectives and adverbs of direction or manner (sideways) (cf. -WISE). [WAY + -'s]

wayside n. **1** the side or margin of a road. **2** the land at the side of a road. □ **fall by the wayside** fail to continue in an undertaking (after Luke 8: 5).

wayward /ˈweɪwəd/ adj. **1** childishly self-willed or perverse; capricious. **2** unaccountable or freakish. □ **waywardly** adv. **waywardness** n. [ME f. obs. awayward turned away f. AWAY + -WARD: cf. FROWARD]

WC abbr. **1** water-closet. **2** West Central.

WCC abbr. World Council of Churches.

W/Cdr. abbr. Wing Commander.

WD abbr. **1** War Department. **2** Works Department.

we /wiː, wɪ/ pron. (obj. **us**; poss. **our**, **ours**) **1** (pl. of I²) used by and with reference to more than one person speaking or writing, or one such person and one or more associated persons. **2** used for or by a royal person in a proclamation etc. and by a writer or editor in a formal context. **3** people in general (cf. ONE pron. 2). **4** colloq. = I² (give us a chance). **5** colloq. (often implying condescension) you (how are we feeling today?). [OE f. Gmc]

WEA abbr. (in the UK) Workers' Educational Association.

weak adj. **1** deficient in strength, power, or number; fragile; easily broken or bent or defeated. **2** deficient in vigour; sickly, feeble (weak health; a weak imagination). **3 a** deficient in resolution; easily led (a weak character). **b** indicating a lack of resolution (a weak chin). **4 a** unconvincing or logically deficient (weak evidence; a weak argument). **b** ineffectual (a weak move). **5** (of a mixed liquid or solution) watery, thin, dilute (weak tea). **6** slipshod. **7** (of a crew) short-handed. **8** (of a syllable etc.) unstressed. **9** Gram. in Germanic languages: **a** (of a verb) forming inflections by the addition of a suffix to the stem. **b** (of a noun or adjective) belonging to a declension in which the stem originally ended in -n (opp. STRONG adj. 19). □ **the weaker sex** derog. women. **weak-kneed** colloq. lacking resolution. **weak-minded 1** mentally deficient. **2** lacking in resolution. **weak moment** a time when one is unusually compliant or temptable. **weak point** (or **spot**) **1** a place where defences are assailable. **2** a flaw in an argument or character or in resistance to temptation. □ **weakish** adj. [ME f. ON veikr f. Gmc]

weaken v.tr. & intr. make or become weak or weaker. □ **weakener** n.

weakling n. a feeble person or animal.

weakly /ˈwiːklɪ/ adv. & adj. —adv. in a weak manner. —adj. (**weaklier, weakliest**) sickly, not robust. □ **weakliness** n.

weakness n. **1** the state or condition of being weak. **2** a weak point; a defect. **3** the inability to resist a particular temptation. **4** (foll. by *for*) a self-indulgent liking (*have a weakness for chocolate*).

weal /wiːl/ n. & v. —n. a ridge raised on the flesh by a stroke of a rod or whip. —v.tr. mark with a weal. [var. of WALE, infl. by obs. *wheal* suppurate]

wealth /welθ/ n. **1** riches; abundant possessions; opulence. **2** the state of being rich. **3** (foll. by *of*) an abundance or profusion (*a wealth of new material*). [ME *welthe*, f. WELL¹ + -TH², after *health*]

wealthy /ˈwelθɪ/ adj. (**wealthier, wealthiest**) having an abundance esp. of money. □ **wealthily** adv. **wealthiness** n.

wean¹ /wiːn/ v.tr. **1** accustom (an infant or other young mammal) to food other than (esp. its mother's) milk. **2** (often foll. by *from, away from*) disengage (from a habit etc.) by enforced discontinuance. [OE *wenian* accustom f. Gmc: cf. WONT]

wean² /wiːn/ n. Sc. a young child. [contr. of *wee ane* little one]

weapon /ˈwepən/ n. **1** a thing designed or used or usable for inflicting bodily harm. **2** a means employed for trying to gain the advantage in a conflict. □ **weaponed** adj. (also in *comb.*). [OE *wǣp(e)n* f. Gmc]

weaponry /ˈwepənrɪ/ n. weapons collectively.

wear¹ /weə(r)/ v. & n. —v. (*past* **wore** /wɔː(r)/; *past part.* **worn** /wɔːn/) **1** tr. have on one's person as clothing or an ornament etc. (*is wearing shorts*; *wears earrings*). **2** tr. exhibit or present (a facial expression or appearance). **3** tr. Brit. colloq. (usu. with *neg.*) tolerate, accept (*they won't wear that excuse*). **4** (often foll. by *away*) **a** tr. injure the surface of, or partly obliterate or alter, by rubbing, stress, or use. **b** intr. undergo such injury or change. **5** tr. & intr. (foll. by *off, away*) rub or be rubbed off. **6** tr. make (a hole etc.) by constant rubbing or dripping etc. **7** tr. & intr. (often foll. by *out*) exhaust, tire or be tired. **8** tr. (foll. by *down*) overcome by persistence. **9** intr. (often foll. by *well, badly,* etc.) endure continued use or life. **10** intr. (often foll. by *on, away* etc.) (of time) pass, esp. tediously. —n. **1** the act of wearing or the state of being worn (*suitable for informal wear*). **2** things worn; fashionable or suitable clothing (*sportswear*; *footwear*). **3** (in full **wear and tear**) damage sustained from continuous use. **4** the capacity for resisting wear and tear (*still a great deal of wear left in it*). **in wear** being regularly worn. **wear off** lose effectiveness or intensity. **wear out 1** use or be used until no longer usable. **2** tire or be tired out. **wear thin** (of patience, excuses, etc.) begin to fail. □ **wearable** adj. **wearability** /-ˈbɪlɪtɪ/ n. **wearer** n. **wearingly** adv. [OE *werian* f. Gmc]

wear² /weə(r)/ v. (*past* and *past part.* **wore** /wɔː(r)/) **1** tr. bring (a ship) about by turning its head away from the wind. **2** intr. (of a ship) come about in this way (cf. TACK¹ v. 4). [17th c.: orig. unkn.]

wearisome /ˈwɪərɪsəm/ adj. tedious; tiring by monotony or length. □ **wearisomely** adv. **wearisomeness** n.

weary /ˈwɪərɪ/ adj. & v. —adj. (**wearier, weariest**) **1** unequal to or disinclined for further exertion or endurance; tired. **2** (foll. by *of*) dismayed at the continuing of; impatient of. **3** tiring or tedious. —v. (**-ies, -ied**) **1** tr. & intr. make or grow weary. **2** intr. esp. Sc. long. □ **weariless** adj. **wearily** adv. **weariness** n. **wearyingly** adv. [OE *wērig, wǣrig* f. WG]

weasel /ˈwiːz(ə)l/ n. & v. —n. a small reddish-brown flesh-eating mammal related to the stoat and ferret. —v.intr. (**weaselled, weaselling**; US **weaseled, weaseling**) **1** esp. US equivocate or quibble. **2** (foll. by *on, out*) default on an obligation. □ **weaselly** adj. [OE *wesle, wesule* f. WG]

weather /ˈweðə(r)/ n. & v. —n. **1** the state of the atmosphere at a place and time as regards heat, cloudiness, dryness, sunshine, wind, and rain etc. **2** (*attrib.*) Naut. windward (*on the weather side*). —v. **1** tr. expose to or affect by atmospheric changes, esp. deliberately to dry, season, etc. (*weathered timber*). **2 a** tr. (usu. in *passive*) discolour or partly disintegrate (rock or stones) by exposure to air. **b** intr. be discoloured or worn in this way. **3** tr. come safely through (a storm). □ **keep a** (or **one's**) **weather eye open** be watchful. **make heavy weather of** colloq. exaggerate a difficulty or burden. **under the weather** colloq. indisposed or out of sorts. **weather-beaten** affected by exposure to the weather. **weather side** the side from which the wind is blowing (opp. *lee side*). **weather station** an observation post for recording meteorological data. **weather-strip** a piece of material used to make a door or window proof against rain or wind. [OE *weder* f. Gmc]

weatherboard /ˈweðəˌbɔːd/ n. **1** a sloping board attached to the bottom of an outside door to keep out the rain etc. **2** each of a series of horizontal boards with edges overlapping to keep out the rain etc. □ **weatherboarding** n. (in sense 2).

weathercock /ˈweðəˌkɒk/ n. a weather-vane (see VANE) in the form of a cock.

weathering /ˈweðərɪŋ/ n. **1** the action of the weather on materials etc. exposed to it. **2** exposure to adverse weather conditions (see WEATHER v. 1).

weatherman /ˈweðəˌmæn/ n. (pl. **-men**) a meteorologist.

weatherproof /ˈweðəˌpruːf/ adj. & v. —adj. resistant to the effects of bad weather, esp. rain. —v.tr. make weatherproof. □ **weatherproofed** adj.

weave¹ /wiːv/ v. & n. —v. (*past* **wove** /wəʊv/; *past part.* **woven** /ˈwəʊv(ə)n/ or **wove**) **1** tr. **a** form (fabric) by interlacing long threads in two directions. **b** form (thread) into fabric in this way. **2** intr. make fabric in this way. **3** tr. **a** (foll. by *into*) make (facts etc.) into a story or connected whole. **b** make (a story) in this way. —n. a style of weaving. [OE *wefan* f. Gmc]

weave² v.intr. move repeatedly from side to side; take an intricate course to avoid obstructions. □ **get weaving** sl. begin action; hurry. [prob. f. ME *weve*, var. of *waive* f. ON *veifa* WAVE]

weaver n. **1** a person whose occupation is weaving. **2** (in full **weaver-bird**) any tropical bird of the family Ploceidae, building elaborately woven nests.

web n. & v. —n. **1** a woven fabric. **2** a complete structure or connected series (*a web of lies*). **3** a cobweb, gossamer, or a similar product of a spinning creature. **4** a membrane between the toes of a swimming animal or bird. **5** a thin flat part connecting thicker or more solid parts in machinery etc. —*v.* (**webbed, webbing**) **1** *tr.* weave a web on. **2** *intr.* weave a web. □ **web-footed** having the toes connected by webs. □ **webbed** *adj.* [OE *web, webb* f. Gmc]

webbing *n.* strong narrow closely-woven fabric used for supporting upholstery, for belts, etc.

wed *v.tr.* & *intr.* (**wedding**; *past* and *past part.* **wedded** or **wed**) **1** usu. *formal* or *literary* **a** *tr.* & *intr.* marry. **b** *tr.* join in marriage. **2** *tr.* unite (*wed efficiency to economy*). **3** *tr.* (as **wedded** *adj.*) of or in marriage (*wedded bliss*). **4** *tr.* (as **wedded** *adj.*) (foll. by *to*) obstinately attached or devoted (to a pursuit etc.). [OE *weddian* to pledge f. Gmc]

we'd /wiːd, wɪd/ *contr.* **1** we had. **2** we should; we would.

wedding /ˈwedɪŋ/ *n.* a marriage ceremony (considered by itself or with the associated celebrations). □ **wedding breakfast** a meal etc. usually served between a wedding and the departure for the honeymoon. **wedding ring** a ring worn by a married person. [OE *weddung* (as WED, -ING[1])]

wedge[1] *n.* & *v.* —*n.* **1** a piece of wood or metal etc. tapering to a sharp edge, that is driven between two objects or parts of an object to secure or separate them. **2** anything resembling a wedge (*a wedge of cheese; troops formed a wedge*). **3** a golf club with a wedge-shaped head. **4 a** a wedge-shaped heel. **b** a shoe with this. —*v.tr.* **1** tighten, secure, or fasten by means of a wedge (*wedged the door open*). **2** (foll. by *in, into*) pack or thrust (a thing or oneself) tightly in or into. □ **thin end of the wedge** *colloq.* an action or procedure of little importance in itself, but likely to lead to more serious developments. **wedge-shaped** shaped like a solid wedge. □ **wedgelike** *adj.* **wedgewise** *adv.* [OE *wecg* f. Gmc]

wedge[2] *v.tr. Pottery* prepare (clay) for use by cutting, kneading, and throwing down. [17th c.: orig. uncert.]

Wedgwood /ˈwedʒwʊd/ *n. propr.* ceramic ware made by J. Wedgwood, Engl. potter d. 1795, and his successors.

wedlock /ˈwedlɒk/ *n.* the married state. □ **born in** (or **out of**) **wedlock** born of married (or unmarried) parents. [OE *wedlāc* marriage vow f. *wed* pledge (rel. to WED) + -*lāc* suffix denoting action]

Wednesday /ˈwenzdeɪ, -dɪ/ *n.* & *adv.* —*n.* the fourth day of the week, following Tuesday. —*adv. colloq.* **1** on Wednesday. **2** (**Wednesdays**) on Wednesdays; each Wednesday. [ME *wednesdei*, OE *wōdnesdæg* day of (the god) Odin]

wee[1] *adj.* (**weer** /ˈwiːə(r)/; **weest** /ˈwiːɪst/) **1** esp. *Sc.* little; very small. **2** *colloq.* tiny; extremely small (*a wee bit*). [orig. *Sc.* noun, f. north.ME *wei* (small) quantity f. Anglian *wēg*: cf. WEY]

wee[2] /wiː/ *n.* esp. *Brit. sl.* = WEE-WEE.

weed *n.* & *v.* —*n.* **1** a wild plant growing where it is not wanted. **2** a thin weak-looking person or horse. **3** (often prec. by *the*) *sl.* **a** marijuana. **b** tobacco. —*v.* **1** *tr.* **a** clear (an area) of weeds. **b** remove unwanted parts from. **2** *tr.* (foll. by *out*) sort out (inferior or unwanted parts, members etc.) for removal. **3** *intr.* cut off or uproot weeds. □ **weed-killer** a substance used to destroy weeds. □ **weeder** *n.* [OE *wēod*, of unkn. orig.]

weedy *adj.* (**weedier, weediest**) **1** having many weeds. **2** (esp. of a person) weak, feeble; of poor stature. □ **weediness** *n.*

week *n.* **1** a period of seven days reckoned usu. from and to midnight on Saturday–Sunday. **2** a period of seven days reckoned from any point (*would like to stay for a week*). **3** the six days between Sundays. **4 a** the five days Monday to Friday. **b** a normal amount of work done in this period (*a 35-hour week*). **5** (prec. by a specified day) a week after (that day) (*Tuesday week; tomorrow week*). [OE *wice* f. Gmc, prob. orig. = sequence]

weekday *n.* a day other than Sunday or other than at a weekend (often *attrib.: a weekday afternoon*).

weekend /wiːkˈend, ˈwiːk-/ *n.* & *v.* —*n.* **1** Sunday and Saturday or part of Saturday. **2** this period extended slightly esp. for a holiday or visit etc. (*going away for the weekend; a weekend cottage*). —*v.intr.* spend a weekend (*decided to weekend in the country*).

weeklong *adj.* lasting for a week.

weekly *adj., adv.,* & *n.* —*adj.* done, produced, or occurring once a week. —*adv.* once a week; from week to week. —*n.* (*pl.* **-ies**) a weekly newspaper or periodical.

weep *v.* & *n.* —*v.* (*past* and *past part.* **wept** /wept/) **1** *intr.* shed tears. **2 a** *tr.* & (foll. by *for*) *intr.* shed tears for; bewail, lament over. **b** *tr.* utter or express with tears ('*Don't go*,' *he wept; wept her thanks*). **3** *intr.* & *tr.* come or send forth in drops; exude liquid (*weeping sore*). **4** *intr.* (as **weeping** *adj.*) (of a tree) having drooping branches (*weeping willow*). —*n.* a fit or spell of weeping. [OE *wēpan* f. Gmc (prob. imit.)]

weepie /ˈwiːpɪ/ *n.* (also **weepy**) (*pl.* **-ies**) *colloq.* a sentimental or emotional film, play, etc.

weevil /ˈwiːvɪl/ *n.* **1** any destructive beetle of the family Curculionidae. **2** any insect damaging stored grain. □ **weevily** *adj.* [ME f. MLG *wevel* f. Gmc]

wee-wee /ˈwiːwiː/ *n.* & *v.* esp. *Brit. sl.* —*n.* **1** the act or an instance of urinating. **2** urine. —*v.intr.* (**-wees, -weed**) urinate. [20th c.: orig. unkn.]

weft *n.* **1 a** the threads woven across a warp to make fabric. **b** yarn for these. **c** a thing woven. **2** filling-strips in basket-weaving. [OE *weft(a)* f. Gmc: rel. to WEAVE[1]]

weigh /weɪ/ *v.* **1** *tr.* find the weight of. **2** *tr.* balance in the hands to guess or as if to guess the weight of. **3** *tr.* (often foll. by *out*) **a** take a definite weight of; take a specified weight from a larger quantity. **b** distribute in exact amounts by weight. **4** *tr.* **a** estimate the relative value, importance, or desirability of; consider with a view to choice, rejection, or preference (*weighed the consequences; weighed the merits of the candidates*). **b** (foll. by *with, against*) compare (one consideration with another). **5** *tr.* be equal to (a specified weight) (*weighs three kilos; weighs very little*). **6** *intr.* **a** have (esp. a specified) importance; exert an influence. **b** (foll. by *with*) be regarded as important by (*the point that weighs with me*). **7** *intr.* (often foll. by *on*) be heavy or burdensome (to); be depressing (to). □ **weigh down** **1** bring or keep down by exerting weight. **2** be oppressive or burdensome to (*weighed down with worries*). **weigh in** (of a boxer before a contest, or a jockey after a race) be weighed. **weigh-in** *n.* the weighing of a boxer before a fight. **weighing-machine** a machine for weighing persons or large weights. **weigh into** *colloq.* attack (physically or verbally). **weigh up** *colloq.* form an estimate of; consider carefully. **weigh one's words** carefully choose the way one expresses something. □ **weighable** *adj.* **weigher** *n.* [OE *wegan* f. Gmc, rel. to WAY]

weighbridge /ˈweɪbrɪdʒ/ *n.* a weighing-machine for vehicles, usu. having a plate set into the road for vehicles to drive on to.

weight /weɪt/ *n.* & *v.* —*n.* **1** *Physics* **a** the force experienced by a body as a result of the earth's gravitation (cf. MASS¹ *n.* 8). **b** any similar force with which a body tends to a centre of attraction. **2** the heaviness of a body regarded as a property of it; its relative mass or the quantity of matter contained in it giving rise to a downward force (*is twice your weight*; *kept in position by its weight*). **3** the quantitative expression of a body's weight (*has a weight of three pounds*). **4** a body of a known weight for use in weighing. **5** a heavy body esp. used in a mechanism etc. (*a clock worked by weights*). **6** a load or burden (*a weight off my mind*). **7 a** influence, importance (*carried weight with the public*). **b** preponderance (*the weight of evidence was against them*). **8 a** a heavy object lifted as an athletic exercise. **b** = SHOT¹ 7. **9** the surface density of cloth etc. —*v.tr.* **1 a** attach a weight to. **b** hold down with a weight or weights. **2** (foll. by *with*) impede or burden. **3** *Statistics* multiply the components of (an average) by factors to take account of their importance. **4** assign a handicap weight to (a horse). □ **put on weight 1** increase one's weight. **2** get fat. **throw one's weight about** (or **around**) *colloq.* be unpleasantly self-assertive. [OE (*ge)wiht* f. Gmc: cf. WEIGH]

weighting /ˈweɪtɪŋ/ *n.* an extra allowance paid in special cases, esp. to allow for a higher cost of living (*London weighting*).

weightless /ˈweɪtlɪs/ *adj.* (of a body, esp. in an orbiting spacecraft etc.) not apparently acted on by gravity. □ **weightlessly** *adv.* **weightlessness** *n.*

weightlifting /ˈweɪtˌlɪftɪŋ/ *n.* the sport or exercise of lifting a heavy weight. □ **weightlifter** *n.*

weighty /ˈweɪtɪ/ *adj.* (**weightier**, **weightiest**) **1** weighing much; heavy. **2** momentous, important. **3** deserving consideration; careful and serious. □ **weightily** *adv.* **weightiness** *n.*

weir /wɪə(r)/ *n.* **1** a dam built across a river to raise the level of water upstream or regulate its flow. **2** an enclosure of stakes etc. set in a stream as a trap for fish. [OE *wer* f. *werian* dam up]

weird /wɪəd/ *adj.* **1** uncanny, supernatural. **2** *colloq.* strange, queer, incomprehensible. □ **weirdly** *adv.* **weirdness** *n.* [(earlier as noun) f. OE *wyrd* destiny f. Gmc]

weirdo /ˈwɪədəʊ/ *n.* (*pl.* **-os**) *colloq.* an odd or eccentric person.

welcome /ˈwelkəm/ *n.*, *int.*, *v.*, & *adj.* —*n.* the act or an instance of greeting or receiving (a person, idea, etc.) gladly; a kind or glad reception. —*int.* expressing such a greeting. —*v.tr.* receive with a welcome. —*adj.* **1** that one receives with pleasure (*a welcome guest*; *welcome news*). **2** (foll. by *to*, or *to* + infin.) **a** cordially allowed or invited; released of obligation (*you are welcome to use my car*). **b** *iron.* gladly given (an unwelcome

task, thing, etc.) (*here's my work and you are welcome to it*). □ **make welcome** receive hospitably. **you are welcome** there is no need for thanks. □ **welcomer** *n.* **welcoming** *adj.* **welcomingly** *adv.* [orig. OE *wilcuma* one whose coming is pleasing f. *wil-* desire, pleasure + *cuma* comer, with later change to *wel-* WELL¹ after OF *bien venu* or ON *velkominn*]

weld *v.* & *n.* —*v.tr.* **1** hammer or press (pieces of iron or other metal usu. heated but not melted) into one piece. **2** join by fusion with an electric arc etc. **3** form by welding into some article. —*n.* a welded joint. □ **weldable** *adj.* **weldability** /-ˈbɪlɪtɪ/ *n.* **welder** *n.* [alt. of WELL² *v.* in obs. sense 'melt or weld (heated metal)', prob. infl. by past part.]

welfare /ˈwelfeə(r)/ *n.* **1** well-being, happiness; health and prosperity (of a person or a community etc.). **2** (**Welfare**) **a** the maintenance of persons in such a condition esp. by statutory procedure or social effort. **b** financial support given for this purpose. □ **welfare state 1** a system whereby the State undertakes to protect the health and well-being of its citizens, esp. those in financial or social need, by means of grants, pensions, etc. **2** a country practising this system. [ME f. WELL¹ + FARE]

well¹ /wel/ *adv.*, *adj.*, & *int.* —*adv.* (**better**, **best**) **1** in a satisfactory way. **2** in the right way. **3** with some talent or distinction (*plays the piano well*). **4** in a kind way. **5** thoroughly, carefully (*polish it well*). **6** with heartiness or approval; favourably (*speak well of*; *the book was well reviewed*). **7** probably, reasonably, advisably (*you may well be right*; *you may well ask*; *we might well take the risk*). **8** to a considerable extent (*is well over forty*). **9** successfully, fortunately (*it turned out well*). **10** luckily, opportunely (*well met!*). **11** comfortably, abundantly, liberally (*we live well here*; *the job pays well*). —*adj.* (**better**, **best**) **1** (usu. *predic.*) in good health (*are you well?*; *was not a well person*). **2** (*predic.*) **a** in a satisfactory state or position (*all is well*). **b** advisable (*it would be well to enquire*). —*int.* expressing surprise, resignation, insistence, etc., or resumption or continuation of talk, used esp. after a pause in speaking (*well I never!*; *well, I suppose so*; *well, who was it?*). □ **as well 1** in addition; to an equal extent. **2** (also **just as well**) with equal reason; with no loss of advantage or need for regret (*may as well give up*; *it would be just as well to stop now*). **as well as** in addition to. **leave** (or **let**) **well alone** avoid needless change or disturbance. **well-acquainted** (usu. foll. by *with*) familiar. **well-adjusted 1** in a good state of adjustment. **2** *Psychol.* mentally and emotionally stable. **well-advised** (usu. foll. by *to* + infin.) (of a person) prudent (*would be well-advised to wait*). **well and truly** decisively, completely. **well-appointed** having all the necessary equipment. **well aware** certainly aware (*well aware of the danger*). **well-balanced 1** sane, sensible. **2** equally matched. **well-being** a state of being well, healthy, contented, etc. **well-beloved** *adj.* dearly loved. —*n.* (*pl.* same) a dearly loved person. **well-born** of noble family. **well-bred** having or showing good breeding or manners. **well-built 1** of good construction. **2** (of a person) big and strong and well-proportioned. **well-chosen** (of words etc.) carefully selected for effect. **well-defined** clearly indicated or determined. **well-deserved** rightfully merited or earned. **well-disposed** (often foll. by *towards*) having a good disposition or friendly feeling (for). **well done 1** (of meat etc.) thoroughly cooked. **2** (of a task etc.) performed well (also as *int.*). **well-dressed** fashionably smart. **well-earned** fully deserved. **well-endowed 1** well provided with talent etc. **2** *colloq.* sexually potent or attractive. **well-favoured** good-looking. **well-fed** having or having had plenty to eat. **well-founded** (of suspicions etc.) based on good evidence; having a foundation in fact or reason. **well-groomed** (of a person) with carefully tended hair, clothes, etc. **well-grounded 1** = *well-founded*. **2** having a good training in or knowledge of the groundwork of a subject. **well-heeled** *colloq.* wealthy. **well-hung** *colloq.* (of a man or male mammal) having large genitals. **well-informed** having much knowledge or information about a subject. **well-intentioned** having or showing good intentions. **well-judged** opportunely, skilfully, or discreetly done. **well-kept** kept in good order or condition. **well-knit** (esp. of a person) compact; not loose-jointed or sprawling. **well-known 1** known to many. **2** known thoroughly. **well-made 1** strongly or skilfully manufactured. **2** (of a person or animal) having a good build. **well-mannered** having good manners. **well-meaning** (or **-meant**) well-intentioned (but ineffective or unwise). **well off 1** having plenty of money. **2** in a fortunate situation or circumstances. **well-oiled** *colloq.* **1** drunk. **2** (of a compliment etc.) easily expressed through habitual use. **well-ordered** arranged in an orderly manner. **well-paid 1** (of a job) that pays well. **2** (of a person) amply rewarded for a job. **well-read** knowledgeable through much reading. **well-received** welcomed; favourably received. **well-rounded 1** complete and symmetrical. **2** (of a phrase etc.) complete and well expressed. **3** (of a person) having or showing a fully developed personality, ability, etc. **well-spent** (esp. of money or time) used profitably. **well-spoken** articulate or refined in speech. **well-thought-of** having a good reputation; esteemed, respected. **well-thought-out** carefully devised. **well-thumbed** bearing marks of frequent handling. **well-timed** opportune, timely. **well-to-do** prosperous. **well-tried** often tested with good results. **well-trodden** much frequented. **well-turned 1** (of a compliment, phrase, or verse) elegantly expressed. **2** (of a leg, ankle, etc.) elegantly shaped or displayed. **well-wisher** a person who wishes one well. **well-worn 1** much worn by use. **2** (of a phrase etc.) trite, hackneyed. **well worth** certainly worth (*well worth a visit*; *well worth visiting*). □ **wellness** *n.* [OE *wel*, *well* prob. f. the same stem as WILL¹]

■ **Usage** A hyphen is normally used in combinations of *well-* when used attributively, but not when used predicatively, e.g. *a well-made coat* but *the coat is well made*.

well² *n. & v. —n.* **1** a shaft sunk into the ground to obtain water, oil, etc. **2** an enclosed space like a well-shaft, e.g. in the middle of a building for stairs or a lift, or for light or ventilation. **3** (foll. by *of*) a source, esp. a copious one (*a well of information*). **4 a** a mineral spring. **b** (in *pl.*) a spa. *—v.intr.* (foll. by *out*, *up*) spring as from

a fountain; flow copiously. □ **well-head** (or **-spring**) a source. [OE *wella* (= OHG *wella* wave, ON *vella* boiling heat), *wellan* boil, melt f. Gmc]

we'll /wiːl, wɪl/ *contr.* we shall; we will.

wellies /ˈwelɪz/ *n.pl. Brit. colloq.* wellingtons. [abbr.]

wellington /ˈwelɪŋt(ə)n/ *n.* (in full **wellington boot**) *Brit.* a waterproof rubber or plastic boot usu. reaching the knee. [after the 1st Duke of *Wellington*, Brit. general and statesman d. 1852]

Welsh *adj. & n. —adj.* of or relating to Wales or its people or language. *—n.* **1** the Celtic language of Wales. **2** (prec. by *the*; treated as *pl.*) the people of Wales. □ **Welsh dresser** a type of dresser with open shelves above a cupboard. **Welsh rabbit** (or **rarebit** by folk etymology) a dish of melted cheese etc. on toast. [OE *Welisc*, *Wælisc*, etc., f. Gmc f. L *Volcae*, the name of a Celtic people]

welsh *v.intr.* (also **welch** /weltʃ/) **1** (of a loser of a bet, esp. a bookmaker) decamp without paying. **2** evade an obligation. **3** (foll. by *on*) **a** fail to carry out a promise to (a person). **b** fail to honour (an obligation). □ **welsher** *n.* [19th c.: orig. unkn.]

Welshman *n.* (*pl.* **-men**) a man who is Welsh by birth or descent.

Welshwoman *n.* (*pl.* **-women**) a woman who is Welsh by birth or descent.

welt *n.* **1** a leather rim sewn round the edge of a shoe-upper for the sole to be attached to. **2** = WEAL. **3** a ribbed or reinforced border of a garment; a trimming. **4** a heavy blow. [ME *welte*, *walt*, of unkn. orig.]

Weltanschauung /ˌveltaːnˈʃaʊʊŋ/ *n.* a particular philosophy or view of life; a conception of the world. [G f. *Welt* world + *Anschauung* perception]

welter /ˈweltə(r)/ *v. & n. —v.intr.* **1** roll, wallow; be washed about. **2** (foll. by *in*) lie prostrate or be soaked or steeped in blood etc. *—n.* **1** a state of general confusion. **2** (foll. by *of*) a disorderly mixture or contrast of beliefs, policies, etc. [ME f. MDu., MLG *welteren*]

welterweight /ˈweltəˌweɪt/ *n.* **1** a weight in certain sports intermediate between lightweight and middleweight. **2** a sportsman of this weight.

wen *n.* a benign tumour on the skin esp. of the scalp. □ **the great wen** London. [OE *wen*, *wenn*, of unkn. orig.: cf. Du. *wen*, MLG *wene*, LG *wehne* tumour, wart]

wench *n. & v. —n. joc.* a girl or young woman. *—v.intr. archaic* (of a man) consort with prostitutes. □ **wencher** *n.* [ME *wenche*, *wenchel* f. OE *wencel* child: cf. OE *wancol* weak, tottering]

wend /wend/ *v.tr. & intr. literary* or *archaic* go. □ **wend one's way** make one's way. [OE *wendan* turn f. Gmc, rel. to WIND²]

Wendy house /ˈwendɪ/ *n.* a children's small houselike tent or structure for playing in. [after the house built around *Wendy* in Barrie's *Peter Pan*]

Wensleydale /ˈwenzlɪˌdeɪl/ *n.* **1** a variety of white or blue cheese. **2 a** a sheep of a breed with long wool. **b** this breed. [*Wensleydale* in Yorkshire]

went *past of* GO¹.

wept *past of* WEEP.

were *2nd sing. past, pl. past, and past subj. of* BE.

we're /wɪə(r)/ *contr.* we are.

weren't /wɜːnt/ *contr.* were not.

werewolf /ˈwɪəwʊlf, ˈweə-/ *n.* (also **werwolf** /ˈwɜː-/) (*pl.* **-wolves**) a mythical being who at times changes from a person to a wolf. [OE *werewulf*: first element perh. f. OE *wer* man = L *vir*]

Wesleyan /ˈwezlɪən/ *adj.* & *n.* —*adj.* of or relating to a Protestant denomination founded by the English evangelist John Wesley (cf. METHODIST). —*n.* a member of this denomination. □ **Wesleyanism** *n.*

west *n.*, *adj.*, & *adv.* —*n.* **1 a** the point of the horizon where the sun sets at the equinoxes (cardinal point 90° to the left of north). **b** the compass point corresponding to this. **c** the direction in which this lies. **2** (usu. **the West**) **a** European in contrast to Oriental civilization. **b** the non-Communist States of Europe and N. America. **c** the western part of a country, town, etc. **3** *Bridge* a player occupying the position designated 'west'. —*adj.* **1** towards, at, near, or facing west. **2** coming from the west (*west wind*). —*adv.* **1** towards, at, or near the west. **2** (foll. by *of*) further west than. □ **go west** *sl.* be killed or destroyed etc. **West Bank** a region west of the River Jordan assigned to Jordan in 1948 and occupied by Israel since 1967. **West Country** the south-western counties of England. **West End** the entertainment and shopping area of London to the west of the City. **West Indian 1** a native or national of any island of the West Indies. **2** a person of West Indian descent. **West Indies** the islands of Central America, including Cuba and the Bahamas. **west-north-** (or **south-**) **west** the direction or compass-point midway between west and north-west (or south-west). **West Side** *US* the western part of Manhattan. [OE f. Gmc]

westbound /ˈwestbaʊnd/ *adj.* travelling or leading westwards.

westering /ˈwestərɪŋ/ *adj.* (of the sun) nearing the west. [*wester* (v.) ME f. WEST]

westerly /ˈwestəlɪ/ *adj.*, *adv.*, & *n.* —*adj.* & *adv.* **1** in a western position or direction. **2** (of a wind) blowing from the west. —*n.* (*pl.* **-ies**) a wind blowing from the west. [*wester* (adj.) f. OE *westra* f. WEST]

western /ˈwest(ə)n/ *adj.* & *n.* —*adj.* **1** of or in the west; inhabiting the west. **2** lying or directed towards the west. **3** (**Western**) of or relating to the West (see WEST *n.* 2). —*n.* a film or novel about cowboys in western North America. □ **Western hemisphere** the half of the earth containing the Americas. [OE *westerne* (as WEST, -ERN)]

westerner /ˈwestənə(r)/ *n.* a native or inhabitant of the west.

westernize /ˈwestənaɪz/ *v.tr.* (also **Westernize**, **-ise**) influence with or convert to the ideas and customs etc. of the West. □ **westernization** /-ˈzeɪʃ(ə)n/ *n.* **westernizer** *n.*

westward /ˈwestwəd/ *adj.*, *adv.*, & *n.* —*adj.* & *adv.* (also **westwards**) towards the west. —*n.* a westward direction or region.

wet *adj.*, *v.*, & *n.* —*adj.* (**wetter, wettest**) **1** soaked, covered, or dampened with water or other liquid (*a wet sponge*; *a wet surface*; *got my feet wet*). **2** (of the weather etc.) rainy (*a wet day*). **3** (of paint, ink, etc.) not yet dried. **4** *Brit. colloq.* feeble, inept. **5** *Brit. Polit. colloq.* Conservative with liberal tendencies, esp. as regarded by right-wing Conservatives. **6** (of a baby or young child) incontinent (*is still wet at night*). —*v.tr.* (**wetting**; *past* and *past part.* **wet** or **wetted**) **1** make wet. **2 a** urinate in or on (*wet the bed*). **b** *refl.* urinate involuntarily. —*n.* **1** moisture. **2** *Brit. colloq.* a feeble or inept person. **3** *Brit. Polit. colloq.* a Conservative with liberal tendencies (see sense 5 of *adj.*). □ **wet behind the ears** immature, inexperienced. **wet dream** an erotic dream with involuntary ejaculation of semen. **wet-nurse** *n.* a woman employed to suckle another's child. —*v.tr.* **1** act as a wet-nurse to. **2** *colloq.* treat as if helpless. **wet suit** a close-fitting rubber garment worn by skin-divers etc. to keep warm. **wet through** (or **to the skin**) with one's clothes soaked. **wetting agent** a substance that helps water etc. to spread or penetrate. **wet one's whistle** *colloq.* drink. □ **wetly** *adv.* **wetness** *n.* **wettable** *adj.* **wetting** *n.* **wettish** *adj.* [OE *wǣt* (adj. & n.), *wǣtan* (v.), rel. to WATER: in ME replaced by past part. of the verb]

wether /ˈweðə(r)/ *n.* a castrated ram. [OE f. Gmc]

wetlands *n.pl.* swamps and other damp areas of land.

we've /wiːv/ *contr.* we have.

WFTU *abbr.* World Federation of Trade Unions.

Wg. Cdr. *abbr.* Wing Commander.

whack /wæk/ *v.* & *n. colloq.* —*v.tr.* **1** strike or beat forcefully with a sharp blow. **2** (as **whacked** *adj.*) esp. *Brit.* tired out; exhausted. —*n.* **1** a sharp or resounding blow. **2** *sl.* a share. □ **have a whack at** *sl.* attempt. **out of whack** esp. *US sl.* out of order; malfunctioning. [imit., or alt. of THWACK]

whacking /ˈwækɪŋ/ *adj.* & *adv. colloq.* —*adj.* very large. —*adv.* very (*a whacking great skyscraper*).

whacko /ˈwækəʊ/ *int. sl.* expressing delight or enjoyment.

whacky var. of WACKY.

whale /weɪl/ *n.* (*pl.* same or **whales**) any of the larger marine mammals of the order Cetacea, having a streamlined body and horizontal tail, and breathing through a blowhole on the head. □ **a whale of a** *colloq.* an exceedingly good or fine etc.

whalebone /ˈweɪlbəʊn/ *n.* an elastic horny substance growing in thin parallel plates in the upper jaw of some whales, used as stiffening etc.

whaler /ˈweɪlə(r)/ *n.* a whaling ship or a seaman engaged in whaling.

whaling /ˈweɪlɪŋ/ *n.* the practice or industry of hunting and killing whales.

wham /wæm/ *int.*, *n.*, & *v. colloq.* —*int.* expressing the sound of a forcible impact. —*n.* such a sound. —*v.* (**whammed, whamming**) **1** *intr.* make such a sound or impact. **2** *tr.* strike forcibly. [imit.]

wharf /wɔːf/ *n.* (*pl.* **wharves** /wɔːvz/ or **wharfs**) a level quayside area to which a ship may be moved to load and unload. [OE *hwearf*]

wharfage /ˈwɔːfɪdʒ/ *n.* **1** accommodation at a wharf. **2** a fee for this.

wharfinger /ˈwɔːfɪndʒə(r)/ *n.* an owner or keeper of a wharf. [prob. ult. f. WHARFAGE]

wharves pl. of WHARF.

what /wɒt/ *adj.*, *pron.*, & *adv.* —*interrog.adj.* **1** asking for a choice from an indefinite number or for a statement of amount, number, or kind (*what books have you read?*; *what news have you?*). **2** *colloq.* = WHICH *interrog.adj.* (*what book have you chosen?*). —*adj.* (usu. in exclam.) how great or remarkable (*what luck!*). —*rel.adj.* the or any . . . that (*will give you what help I can*). —*pron.* (corresp. to the functions of the *adj.*) **1** what thing or things? (*what is your name?*; *I don't know what you mean*). **2** (asking for a remark to be repeated) = what did you say? **3** asking for confirmation or agreement of something not completely understood (*you did what?*; *what, you really mean it?*). **4** how much (*what you must have suffered!*). **5** (as *rel.pron.*) that or those which; a or the or any thing which (*what followed was worse*; *tell me what you think*). —*adv.* to what extent (*what does it matter?*). □ **what about** what is the news or position or your opinion of (*what about me?*; *what about a game of tennis?*). **what-d'you-call-it** (or **what's-its-name**) a substitute for a name not recalled. **what ever** what at all or in any way (*what ever do you mean?*) (see also WHATEVER). **what for** *colloq.* **1** for what reason? **2** a severe reprimand (esp. *give a person what for*). **what have you** *colloq.* (prec. by *or*) anything else similar. **what if?** 1 what would result etc. if. **2** what would it matter if. **what is more** and as an additional point; moreover. **what next?** *colloq.* what more absurd, shocking, or surprising thing is possible? **what not** (prec. by *and*) other similar things. **what of?** what is the news concerning? **what of it?** why should that be considered significant? **what's-his** (or **-its**) **-name** = what-d'you-call-it. **what's what** *colloq.* what is useful or important etc. **what with** *colloq.* because of (usu. several things). [OE *hwæt* f. Gmc]

whate'er /wɒtˈeər/ *poet.* var. of WHATEVER.

whatever /wɒtˈevə(r)/ *adj.* & *pron.* **1** = WHAT (in relative uses) with the emphasis on indefiniteness (*lend me whatever you can*; *whatever money you have*). **2** though anything (*we are safe whatever happens*). **3** (with *neg.* or *interrog.*) at all; of any kind (*there is no doubt whatever*). **4** *colloq.* = what ever. □ **or whatever** *colloq.* or anything similar.

whatnot /ˈwɒtnɒt/ *n.* **1** an indefinite or trivial thing. **2** a stand with shelves for small objects.

whatsoever /ˌwɒtsəʊˈevə(r)/ *adj.* & *pron.* = WHATEVER 1, 2, 3.

wheat /wiːt/ *n.* **1** any cereal plant of the genus *Triticum.* **2** its grain, used in making flour etc. □ **wheat germ** the embryo of the wheat grain, extracted as a source of vitamins. **wheat-grass** = couch grass (see COUCH²). [OE *hwǣte* f. Gmc, rel. to WHITE]

wheatear /ˈwiːtɪə(r)/ *n.* any small migratory bird of the genus *Oenanthe.* [app. f. *wheatears* (as WHITE, ARSE)]

wheaten /ˈwiːt(ə)n/ *adj.* made of wheat.

wheatmeal /ˈwiːtmiːl/ *n.* flour made from wheat with some of the bran and germ removed.

whee /wiː/ *int.* expressing delight or excitement. [imit.]

wheedle /ˈwiːd(ə)l/ *v.tr.* **1** coax by flattery or endearments. **2** (foll. by *out*) **a** get (a thing) out of a person by wheedling. **b** cheat (a person) out of a thing by wheedling. □ **wheedler** *n.* **wheedling** *adj.* **wheedlingly** *adv.* [perh. f. G *wedeln* fawn, cringe f. *Wedel* tail]

wheel /wiːl/ *n.* & *v.* —*n.* **1** a circular frame or disc arranged to revolve on an axle and used to facilitate the motion of a vehicle or for various mechanical purposes. **2** a wheel-like thing (*Catherine wheel*; *potter's wheel*; *steering wheel*). **3** motion as of a wheel, esp. the movement of a line of people with one end as a pivot. **4** a machine etc. of which a wheel is an essential part. **5** (in *pl.*) *sl.* a car. **6** *US sl.* = big wheel 2. **7** a set of short lines concluding a stanza. —*v.* **1** *intr.* & *tr.* **a** turn on an axis or pivot. **b** swing round in line with one end as a pivot. **2 a** *intr.* (often foll. by *about, round*) change direction or face another way. **b** *tr.* cause to do this. **3** *tr.* push or pull (a wheeled thing esp. a barrow, bicycle, or pram, or its load or occupant). **4** *intr.* go in circles or curves (*seagulls wheeling overhead*). □ **at the wheel** **1** driving a vehicle. **2** directing a ship. **3** in control of affairs. **wheel and deal** engage in political or commercial scheming. **wheel clamp** a clamp for locking to the wheel of an illegally parked motor vehicle, in order to immobilize it temporarily. **wheel-house** a steersman's shelter. **wheel-spin** rotation of a vehicle's wheels without traction. **wheels within wheels** **1** intricate machinery. **2** *colloq.* indirect or secret agencies. □ **wheeled** *adj.* (also in *comb.*). **wheelless** *adj.* [OE *hwēol, hwēogol* f. Gmc]

wheelbarrow /ˈwiːlˌbærəʊ/ *n.* a small cart with one wheel and two shafts for carrying garden loads etc.

wheelbase /ˈwiːlbeɪs/ *n.* the distance between the front and rear axles of a vehicle.

wheelchair /ˈwiːltʃeə(r)/ *n.* a chair on wheels for an invalid or disabled person.

wheeler-dealer a person who wheels and deals.

wheelie /ˈwiːlɪ/ *n. sl.* the stunt of riding a bicycle or motor cycle for a short distance with the front wheel off the ground.

wheelwright /ˈwiːlraɪt/ *n.* a person who makes or repairs esp. wooden wheels.

wheeze /wiːz/ *v.* & *n.* —*v.* **1** *intr.* breathe with an audible chesty whistling sound. **2** *tr.* (often foll. by *out*) utter in this way. —*n.* **1** a sound of wheezing. **2** *colloq. Brit.* a clever scheme. □ **wheezer** *n.* **wheezingly** *adv.* **wheezy** *adj.* (**wheezier, wheeziest**). **wheezily** *adv.* **wheeziness** *n.* [prob. f. ON *hvæsa* to hiss]

whelk /welk/ *n.* any predatory marine gastropod mollusc of the family Buccinidae. [OE *wioloc, weoloc,* of unkn. orig.]

whelm /welm/ *v.tr. poet.* **1** engulf, submerge. **2** crush with weight, overwhelm. [OE *hwelman* (unrecorded) = *hwylfan* overturn]

whelp /welp/ *n.* & *v.* —*n.* **1** a young dog; a puppy. **2** an ill-mannered child or youth. —*v.tr.* (also *absol.*) bring forth (a whelp or whelps). [OE *hwelp*]

when /wen/ *adv., conj., pron.,* & *n.* —*interrog.adv.* **1** at what time? **2** on what occasion? **3** how soon? **4** how long ago? —*rel.adv.* (prec. by *time* etc.) at or on which (*there are times when I could cry*). —*conj.* **1** at the or any time that; as soon as (*come when you like*; *come when ready*; *when I was your age*). **2** although; considering that (*why stand up when you could sit down?*). **3** after which; and then; but just then (*was nearly asleep when the bell rang*). —*pron.* what time? (*till when can you stay?*; *since when it has been better*). —*n.* time, occasion, date (*fixed the where and when*). [OE *hwanne, hwenne*]

whence /wens/ *adv. & conj. formal* —*adv.* from what place? (*where did they come?*). —*conj.* **1** to the place from which (*return whence you came*). **2** (often prec. by *place* etc.) from which (*the source whence these errors arise*). **3** and thence (*whence it follows that*). [ME *whannes, whennes* f. *whanne, whenne* f. OE *hwanon(e)* whence, formed as WHEN + -S³: cf. THENCE]

■ **Usage** The use of *from whence* (as in *the place from whence they came*), though common, is generally considered incorrect.

whenever /wen'evə(r)/ *conj. & adv.* **1** at whatever time; on whatever occasion. **2** every time that. □ **or whenever** *colloq.* or at any similar time.

where /weə(r)/ *adv., conj., pron., & n.* —*interrog.adv.* **1** in or to what place or position? (*where is the milk?; where are you going?*). **2** in what direction or respect? (*where does the argument lead?; where does it concern us?*). **3** in what book etc.?; from whom? (*where did you read that?; where did you hear that?*). **4** in what situation or condition? (*where does that leave us?*). —*rel.adv.* (prec. by *place* etc.) in or to which (*places where they meet*). —*conj.* **1** in or to the or any place, direction, or respect in which (*go where you like; that is where you are wrong; delete where applicable*). **2** and there (*reached Crewe, where the car broke down*). —*pron.* what place? (*where do you come from?; where are you going to?*). —*n.* place; scene of something (see WHEN *n.*). [OE *hwær, hwār*]

whereabouts *adv. & n.* —*adv.* /ˌweərə'baʊts/ where or approximately where? (*whereabouts are they?; show me whereabouts to look*). —*n.* /'weərəˌbaʊts/ (as *sing.* or *pl.*) a person's or thing's location roughly defined.

whereafter /weər'ɑːftə(r)/ *conj. formal* after which.

whereas /weər'æz/ *conj.* **1** in contrast or comparison with the fact that. **2** (esp. in legal preambles) taking into consideration the fact that.

whereby /weə'baɪ/ *conj.* by what or which means.

wherefore /'weəfɔː(r), -'fɔː(r)/ *adv. & n.* —*adv.* *archaic* **1** for what reason? **2** for which reason. —*n.* a reason (*the whys and wherefores*).

wherein /weər'ɪn/ *conj. & adv. formal* —*conj.* in what or which place or respect. —*adv.* in what place or respect?

whereof /weər'ɒv/ *conj. & adv. formal* —*conj.* of what or which (*the means whereof*). —*adv.* of what?

wheresoever /ˌweəsəʊ'evə(r)/ *conj. & adv. formal* or *literary* = WHEREVER.

whereto /weə'tuː/ *conj. & adv. formal* —*conj.* to what or which. —*adv.* to what?

whereupon /ˌweərə'pɒn, 'weər-/ *conj.* immediately after which.

wherever /weər'evə(r)/ *adv. & conj.* —*adv.* in or to whatever place. —*conj.* in every place that. □ **or wherever** *colloq.* or in any similar place.

wherewithal /'weəwɪˌðɔːl/ *n. colloq.* money etc. needed for a purpose (*has not the wherewithal to do it*).

whet /wet/ *v. & n.* —*v.tr.* (**whetted, whetting**) **1** sharpen (a scythe or other tool) by grinding. **2** stimulate (the appetite or a desire, interest, etc.). —*n.* **1** the act or an instance of whetting. **2** a small quantity stimulating one's appetite for more. □ **whetter** *n.* (also in *comb.*). [OE *hwettan* f. Gmc]

whether /'weðə(r)/ *conj.* introducing the first or both of alternative possibilities (*I doubt whether it matters; I do not know whether they have arrived or not*). [OE *hwæther, hwether* f. Gmc]

whetstone /'wetstəʊn/ *n.* a tapered stone used with water to sharpen curved tools, e.g. sickles, hooks (cf. OILSTONE).

whew /hwjuː/ *int.* expressing surprise, consternation, or relief. [imit.: cf. PHEW]

whey /weɪ/ *n.* the watery liquid left when milk forms curds. □ **whey-faced** pale esp. with fear. [OE *hwæg, hweg* f. LG]

which /wɪtʃ/ *adj. & pron.* —*interrog.adj.* asking for choice from a definite set of alternatives (*which John do you mean?; say which book you prefer; which way shall we go?*). —*rel.adj.* being the one just referred to; and this or these (*ten years, during which time they admitted nothing; a word of advice, which action is within your power, will set things straight*). —*interrog.pron.* **1** which person or persons (*which of you is responsible?*). **2** which thing or things (*say which you prefer*). —*rel.pron.* (*poss.* **of which, whose** /huːz/) **1** which thing or things, usu. introducing a clause not essential for identification (cf. THAT *pron.* 7) (*the house, which is empty, has been damaged*). **2** used in place of *that* after *in* or *that* (*there is the house in which I was born; that which you have just seen*). □ **which is which** a phrase used when two or more persons or things are difficult to distinguish from each other. [OE *hwilc* f. Gmc]

whichever /wɪtʃ'evə(r)/ *adj. & pron.* **1** any which (*take whichever you like; whichever one you like*). **2** no matter which (*whichever one wins, they both get a prize*).

whiff /wɪf/ *n. & v.* —*n.* **1** a puff or breath of air, smoke, etc. (*went outside for a whiff of fresh air*). **2** a smell (*caught the whiff of a cigar*). **3** (foll. by *of*) a trace or suggestion of scandal etc. **4** a small cigar. —*v.* **1** *tr. & intr.* blow or puff lightly. **2** *intr. Brit.* smell (esp. unpleasant). **3** *tr.* get a slight smell of. [imit.]

whiffle /'wɪf(ə)l/ *v. & n.* —*v.* **1** *intr. & tr.* (of the wind) blow lightly, shift about. **2** *intr.* be variable or evasive. **3** *intr.* (of a flame, leaves, etc.) flicker, flutter. **4** *intr.* make the sound of a light wind in breathing etc. —*n.* a slight movement of air. □ **whiffler** *n.* [WHIFF + -LE⁴]

whiffy /'wɪfɪ/ *adj. colloq.* (**whiffier, whiffiest**) having an unpleasant smell.

Whig /wɪg/ *n. hist.* **1** *Polit.* a member of the British reforming and constitutional party that after 1688 sought the supremacy of Parliament and was eventually succeeded in the 19th c. by the Liberal Party (opp. TORY 2). **2** a 17th-c. Scottish Presbyterian. **3** *US* **a** a supporter of the American Revolution. **b** a member of an American political party in the 19th c., succeeded by the Republicans. □ **Whiggery** *n.* **Whiggish** *adj.* **Whiggism** *n.* [prob. a shortening of Sc. *whiggamer, -more*, nickname of 17th-c. Sc. rebels, f. *whig* to drive + MARE¹]

while /waɪl/ *n., conj., & v.* —*n.* **1** a space of time, time spent in some action (*a long while ago; waited a while; all this while*). **2** (prec. by *the*) during some other process. **3** (prec. by *a*) for some time (*have not seen you a while*). —*conj.* **1** during the time that; for as long as; at the same time as (*while I was away, the house was burgled; fell asleep while reading*). **2** in spite of the fact that; although, whereas (*while I want to believe it,*

I cannot. **3** *N.Engl.* until (*wait while Monday*). —*v.tr.* (foll. by *away*) pass (time etc.) in a leisurely or interesting manner. □ **all the while** during the whole time (that). **for a long while** for a long time past. **for a while** for some time. **a good** (or **great**) **while** a considerable time. **in a while** (or **little while**) soon, shortly. **worth while** (or **one's while**) worth the time or effort spent. [OE *hwīl* f. Gmc: (conj.) abbr. of OE *thā hwīle the*, ME *the while that*]

whilst /waɪlst/ *adv. & conj.* esp. *Brit.* while. [ME f. archaic *whiles*: cf. AGAINST]

whim /wɪm/ *n.* **1** a sudden fancy; a caprice. **2** capriciousness. [17th c.: orig. unkn.]

whimbrel /ˈwɪmbrɪl/ *n.* a small curlew. [WHIM-PER (imit.): cf. *dotterel*]

whimper /ˈwɪmpə(r)/ *v. & n.* —*v.* **1** *intr.* make feeble, querulous, or frightened sounds; cry and whine softly. **2** *tr.* utter whimperingly. —*n.* a whimpering sound. □ **whimperer** *n.* **whimperingly** *adv.* [imit., f. dial. *whimp*]

whimsical /ˈwɪmzɪk(ə)l/ *adj.* **1** capricious. **2** fantastic; odd or quaint; fanciful, humorous. □ **whimsicality** /-ˈkælɪti/ *n.* **whimsically** *adv.* **whimsicalness** *n.*

whimsy /ˈwɪmzɪ/ *n.* (also **whimsey**) (*pl.* **-ies** or **-eys**) **1** a whim; a capricious notion or fancy. **2** capricious or quaint humour. [rel. to WHIM: cf. *flimsy*]

whin /wɪn/ *n.* (in *sing.* or *pl.*) furze, gorse. [prob. Scand.: cf. Sw. *ven*, Norw. *kvein*, Da. *hvene*]

whinchat /ˈwɪntʃæt/ *n.* a small brownish songbird. [WHIN + *chat*, prob. imit.]

whine /waɪn/ *n. & v.* —*n.* **1** a complaining long-drawn wail as of a dog. **2** a similar shrill prolonged sound. **3 a** a querulous tone. **b** an instance of feeble or undignified complaining. —*v.* **1** *intr.* emit or utter a whine. **2** *intr.* complain in a querulous tone or in a feeble or undignified way. **3** *tr.* utter in a whining tone. □ **whiner** *n.* **whiningly** *adv.* **whiny** *adj.* (**whinier, whiniest**). [OE *hwīnan*]

whinge /wɪndʒ/ *v. & n. colloq.* —*v.intr.* whine; grumble peevishly. —*n.* a whining complaint; a peevish grumbling. □ **whinger** *n.* **whingingly** *adv.* **whingy** *adj.* [OE *hwinsian* f. Gmc]

whinny /ˈwɪnɪ/ *n. & v.* —*n.* (*pl.* **-ies**) a gentle or joyful neigh. —*v.intr.* (**-ies, -ied**) give a whinny. [imit.: cf. WHINE]

whip /wɪp/ *n. & v.* —*n.* **1** a lash attached to a stick for urging on animals or punishing etc. **2 a** a member of a political party in Parliament appointed to control its parliamentary discipline and tactics, esp. ensuring attendance and voting in debates. **b** *Brit.* the whips' written notice requesting or requiring attendance for voting at a division etc., variously underlined according to the degree of urgency (*three-line whip*). **c** (prec. by *the*) party discipline and instructions (*asked for the Labour whip*). —*v.* (**whipped, whipping**) **1** *tr.* beat or urge on with a whip. **2** *tr.* beat (cream or eggs etc.) into a froth. **3** *tr. & intr.* take or move suddenly, unexpectedly, or rapidly. **4** *tr. Brit. sl.* steal (*who's whipped my pen?*). **5** *tr. sl.* **a** excel. **b** defeat. **6** *tr.* bind with spirally wound twine. **7** *tr.* sew with overcast stitches. □ **whip hand 1** a hand that holds the whip (in riding etc.). **2** (usu. prec. by *the*) the advantage or control in any situation. **whip in** bring (hounds) together. **whip on** urge into action. **whip-round** esp. *Brit. colloq.* an

informal collection of money from a group of people. **whip-stitch** a stitch made by whipping. **whip up 1** excite or stir up (feeling etc.). **2** summon (attendance). □ **whipless** *adj.* **whiplike** *adj.* **whipper** *n.* [ME (h)wippen (v.), prob. f. MLG & MDu. wippen swing, leap, dance]

whipcord /ˈwɪpkɔːd/ *n.* **1** a tightly twisted cord such as is used for making whiplashes. **2** a close-woven worsted fabric.

whiplash /ˈwɪplæʃ/ *n.* **1** the flexible end of a whip. **2** a blow with a whip. □ **whiplash injury** an injury to the neck caused by a jerk of the head, esp. as in a motor accident.

whipper-in /ˌwɪpəˈrɪn/ *n.* a huntsman's assistant who manages the hounds.

whippersnapper /ˈwɪpəˌsnæpə(r)/ *n.* **1** a small child. **2** an insignificant but presumptuous or intrusive (esp. young) person. [perh. for *whipsnapper*, implying noise and unimportance]

whippet /ˈwɪpɪt/ *n.* a dog of the greyhound type used for racing. [prob. f. obs. *whippet* move briskly, f. *whip it*]

whipping /ˈwɪpɪŋ/ *n.* **1** a beating, esp. with a whip. **2** cord wound round in binding. □ **whipping-top** a top kept spinning by blows of a lash.

whippoorwill /ˈwɪpʊəˌwɪl/ *n.* an American nightjar. [imit. of its cry]

whippy /ˈwɪpɪ/ *adj.* (**whippier, whippiest**) flexible, springy. □ **whippiness** *n.*

whirl /wɜːl/ *v. & n.* —*v.* **1** *tr. & intr.* swing round and round; revolve rapidly. **2** *tr. & intr.* (foll. by *away*) convey or go rapidly in a vehicle etc. **3** *tr. & intr.* send or travel swiftly in an orbit or a curve. **4** *intr.* **a** (of the brain, senses, etc.) seem to spin round. **b** (of thoughts etc.) be confused. —*n.* **1** a whirling movement (*vanished in a whirl of dust*). **2** a state of intense activity (*the social whirl*). **3** a state of confusion (*my mind is in a whirl*). **4** *colloq.* an attempt (*give it a whirl*). □ **whirler** *n.* **whirlingly** *adv.* [ME: (v.) f. ON *hvirfla*: (n.) f. MLG & MDu. *wervel* spindle & ON *hvirfill* circle f. Gmc]

whirligig /ˈwɜːlɪgɪg/ *n.* **1** a spinning or whirling toy. **2** a merry-go-round. **3** a revolving motion. **4** anything regarded as hectic or constantly changing (*the whirligig of time*). **5** any freshwater beetle of the family Gyrinidae that circles about on the surface. [ME f. WHIRL + obs. *gig* whipping-top]

whirlpool /ˈwɜːlpuːl/ *n.* a powerful circular eddy in the sea etc. often causing suction to its centre.

whirlwind /ˈwɜːlwɪnd/ *n.* **1** a mass or column of air whirling rapidly round and round in a cylindrical or funnel shape over land or water. **2** a confused tumultuous process. **3** (*attrib.*) very rapid (*a whirlwind romance*).

whirlybird /ˈwɜːlɪˌbɜːd/ *n. colloq.* a helicopter.

whirr /wɜː(r)/ *n. & v.* (also **whir**) —*n.* a continuous rapid buzzing or softly clicking sound as of a bird's wings or of cog-wheels in constant motion. —*v.intr.* (**whirred, whirring**) make this sound. [ME, prob. Scand.: cf. Da. *hvirre*, Norw. *kvirre*, perh. rel. to WHIRL]

whisht /hwɪʃt/ *v.* (also **whist** /hwɪst/) esp. *Sc. & Ir. dial.* **1** *intr.* (esp. as *int.*) be quiet; hush. **2** *tr.* quieten. [imit.]

whisk /wɪsk/ *v. & n.* —*v.* **1** *tr.* (foll. by *away, off*) **a** brush with a sweeping movement. **b** take with a sudden motion (*whisked the plate away*). **2** *tr.*

whip (cream, eggs, etc.). **3** *tr.* & *intr.* convey or go (esp. out of sight) lightly or quickly (*whisked me off to the doctor; the mouse whisked into its hole*). —*n.* **1** a whisking action or motion. **2** a utensil for whisking eggs or cream etc. **3** a bunch of grass, twigs, bristles, etc., for removing dust or flies. [ME *wisk*, prob. Scand.: cf. ON *visk* wisp]

whisker /ˈwɪskə(r)/ *n.* **1** (usu. in *pl.*) the hair growing on a man's face, esp. on the cheek. **2** each of the bristles on the face of a cat etc. **3** *colloq.* a small distance (*within a whisker of; won by a whisker*). **4** a strong hairlike crystal of metal etc. □ **have** (or **have grown**) **whiskers** *colloq.* (esp. of a story etc.) be very old. □ **whiskered** *adj.* **whiskery** *adj.* [WHISK + -ER¹]

whisky /ˈwɪskɪ/ *n.* (*Ir.*, *US* **whiskey**) (*pl.* **-ies** or **-eys**) **1** a spirit distilled esp. from malted barley. **2** a drink of this. [abbr. of obs. *whiskybae*, ult. f. Ir. & Sc. Gael. *uisge beatha* water of life]

whisper /ˈwɪspə(r)/ *v.* & *n.* —*v.* **1** a *intr.* speak without vibration of the vocal cords. **b** *intr.* & *tr.* talk or say in a barely audible tone. **2** *intr.* speak privately or conspiratorially. —*n.* **1** whispering speech (*talking in whispers*). **2** a whispering sound. □ **whispering-gallery** a gallery esp. under a dome with acoustic properties such that a whisper may be heard round its entire circumference. □ **whisperer** *n.* **whispering** *n.* [OE *hwisprian* f. Gmc]

whist¹ /wɪst/ *n.* a card-game usu. for four players, with the winning of tricks. □ **whist drive** a social occasion with the playing of progressive whist. [earlier *whisk*, perh. f. WHISK (with ref. to whisking away the tricks): perh. assoc. with WHIST²]

whist² var. of WHISHT.

whistle /ˈwɪs(ə)l/ *n.* & *v.* —*n.* **1** a clear shrill sound made by forcing breath through a small hole between nearly closed lips. **2** a similar sound made by a bird, the wind, a missile, etc. **3** an instrument used to produce such a sound. —*v.* **1** *intr.* emit a whistle. **2** a *intr.* give a signal or express surprise or derision by whistling. **b** *tr.* (often foll. by *up*) summon or give a signal to (a dog etc.) by whistling. **3** *tr.* (also *absol.*) produce (a tune) by whistling. **4** *intr.* (foll. by *for*) vainly seek or desire. □ **as clean** (or **clear** or **dry**) **as a whistle** very clean or clear or dry. **blow the whistle on** *colloq.* bring (an activity) to an end; inform on (those responsible). **whistle-stop 1** *US* a small unimportant town on a railway. **2** a politician's brief pause for an electioneering speech on tour. **3** (*attrib.*) with brief pauses (*a whistle-stop tour*). [OE (h)*wistlian* (v.), (h)*wistle* (n.) of imit. orig.: cf. ON *hvísla* whisper, MSw. *hvisla* whistle]

Whit /wɪt/ *adj.* connected with, belonging to, or following Whit Sunday (*Whit Monday; Whit weekend*). □ **Whit Sunday** the seventh Sunday after Easter, commemorating the descent of the Holy Spirit at Pentecost (Acts 2). [OE *Hwita Sunnandæg*, lit. white Sunday, prob. f. the white robes of the newly-baptized at Pentecost]

whit /wɪt/ *n.* a particle; a least possible amount (*not a whit better*). [earlier *w*(*h*)*yt* app. alt. f. OE *wiht* thing, in phr. *no wight* etc.]

white /waɪt/ *adj.* & *n.* —*adj.* **1** resembling a surface reflecting sunlight without absorbing any of the visible rays; of the colour of milk or fresh snow. **2** approaching such a colour; pale esp. in the face. **3** (**White**) **a** of the human group having light-coloured skin. **b** of or relating to White people. **4** (of a person) white-haired. **5 a** (of a plant) having white flowers or pale-coloured fruit etc. **b** (of a tree) having light-coloured bark etc. (*white poplar*). **6** (of wine) made from white grapes or dark grapes with the skins removed. **7** (of coffee) with milk or cream added. **8** colourless (*white glass*). —*n.* **1** a white colour or pigment. **2 a** white clothes or material (*dressed in white*). **b** (in *pl.*) white garments as worn in cricket, tennis, etc. **3 a** (in a game or sport) a white piece, ball, etc. **b** the player using such pieces. **4** the white part or albumen round the yolk of an egg. **5** the visible part of the eyeball round the iris. **6** (**White**) a member of a light-skinned race. **7** a white butterfly. □ **bleed white** drain (a person, country, etc.) of wealth etc. **white ant** a termite. **white cell** (or **corpuscle**) a leucocyte. **white Christmas** Christmas with snow on the ground. **white-collar** (of a worker) engaged in clerical or administrative rather than manual work. **white dwarf** a small very dense star. **white elephant** a useless and troublesome possession or thing. **white fish** fish with pale flesh, e.g. plaice, cod, etc. **white flag** a symbol of surrender or a period of truce. **White Friar** a Carmelite. **white goods 1** domestic linen. **2** large domestic electrical equipment. **white heat 1** the temperature at which metal emits white light. **2** a state of intense passion or activity. **white horses** white-crested waves at sea. **white-hot** at white heat. **White House** the official residence of the US President in Washington. **white lie** a harmless or trivial untruth. **white light** colourless light, e.g. ordinary daylight. **white magic** magic used only for beneficent purposes. **white meat** poultry, veal, rabbit, and pork. **white metal** a white or silvery alloy. **white noise** noise containing many frequencies with equal intensities. **white-out** a dense blizzard esp. in polar regions. **White Paper** (in the UK) a Government report giving information or proposals on an issue. **white poplar** = ABELE. **white rose** the emblem of Yorkshire or the House of York. **white sauce** a sauce of flour, melted butter, and milk or cream. **White slave** a woman tricked or forced into prostitution, usu. abroad. **white spirit** light petroleum as a solvent. **white sugar** purified sugar. **white tie** a man's white bow-tie as part of full evening dress. **white water** a shallow or foamy stretch of water. **white wedding** a wedding at which the bride wears a formal white wedding dress. **white whale** a northern cetacean, *Delphinapterus leucas*, white when adult. □ **whitely** *adv.* **whiteness** *n.* **whitish** *adj.* [OE *hwit* f. Gmc]

whitebait /ˈwaɪtbeɪt/ *n.* (*pl.* same) (usu. *pl.*) the small silvery-white young of herrings and sprats esp. as food.

whitebeam /ˈwaɪtbiːm/ *n.* a rosaceous tree, *Sorbus aria*, having red berries and leaves with a white downy under-side.

whiteface /ˈwaɪtfeɪs/ *n.* the white make-up of an actor etc.

whitefish /ˈwaɪtfɪʃ/ *n.* (*pl.* same or **-fishes**) any freshwater fish of the genus *Coregonus* etc., of the trout family, and used esp. for food.

whitefly /ˈwaɪtflaɪ/ *n.* (*pl.* **-flies**) any small insect of the family Aleyrodidae, having wings covered with white powder and feeding on the sap of shrubs, crops, etc.

Whitehall /ˈwaɪthɔːl/ n. **1** the British Government. **2** its offices or policy. [a street in London in which Government offices are situated]

whitehead /ˈwaɪthed/ n. colloq. a white or white-topped skin-pustule.

whiten /ˈwaɪt(ə)n/ v.tr. & intr. make or become white. □ **whitener** n. **whitening** n.

whitesmith /ˈwaɪtsmɪθ/ n. **1** a worker in tin. **2** a polisher or finisher of metal goods.

whitethorn /ˈwaɪtθɔːn/ n. the hawthorn.

whitethroat /ˈwaɪtθrəʊt/ n. a warbler, Sylvia communis, with a white patch on the throat.

whitewash /ˈwaɪtwɒʃ/ n. & v. —n. **1** a solution of quicklime or of whiting and size for whitening walls etc. **2** a means employed to conceal mistakes or faults in order to clear a person or institution of imputations. —v.tr. **1** cover with whitewash. **2** attempt by concealment to clear the reputation of. **3** US defeat (an opponent) without allowing any opposing score.

whither /ˈwɪðə(r)/ adv. & conj. archaic —adv. **1** to what place, position, or state? **2** (prec. by place etc.) to which (the house whither we were walking). —conj. **1** to or any place to which (go whither you will). **2** and thither (we saw a house, whither we walked). [OE hwider f. Gmc: cf. WHICH, HITHER, THITHER]

whiting[1] /ˈwaɪtɪŋ/ n. a small white-fleshed fish. [ME f. MDu. wijting, app. formed as WHITE + -ING[3]]

whiting[2] /ˈwaɪtɪŋ/ n. ground chalk used in whitewashing, plate-cleaning, etc.

whitlow /ˈwɪtləʊ/ n. an inflammation near a fingernail or toenail. [ME whitflaw, -flow, app. = WHITE + FLAW[1] in the sense 'crack', but perh. of LG orig.: cf. Du. fijt, LG fīt whitlow]

Whitsun /ˈwɪts(ə)n/ n. & adj. —n. = WHIT-SUNTIDE. —adj. = WHIT. [ME, f. Whitsun Day = Whit Sunday]

Whitsuntide /ˈwɪts(ə)n͵taɪd/ n. the weekend or week including Whit Sunday.

whittle /ˈwɪt(ə)l/ v. **1** tr. & (foll. by at) intr. pare (wood etc.) with repeated slicing with a knife. **2** tr. (often foll. by away, down) reduce by repeated subtractions. [var. of ME thwitel long knife f. OE thwītan to cut off]

whity /ˈwaɪtɪ/ adj. whitish; rather white (usu. in comb.: whity-brown) (cf. WHITEY).

whiz /wɪz/ n. & v. (also **whizz**) colloq. —n. **1** the sound made by the friction of a body moving through the air at great speed. **2** (also **wiz**) colloq. a person who is remarkable or skilful in some respect (is a whiz at chess). —v.intr. (**whizzed**, **whizzing**) move with or make a whiz. □ **whiz-bang** colloq. **1** a high-velocity shell from a small-calibre gun, whose passage is heard before the gun's report. **2** a jumping kind of firework. **whiz-kid** colloq. a brilliant or highly successful young person. [imit.: in sense 2 infl. by WIZARD]

WHO abbr. World Health Organization.

who /huː/ pron. (obj. **whom** /huːm/ or colloq. **who**; poss. **whose** /huːz/) **1 a** what or which person or persons? (who called?; you know who it was; whom or who did you see?). **b** what sort of person or persons? (who am I to object?). **2** (a person) that (anyone who wishes can come; the woman whom you met; the man who you saw). **3** and or but he, she,

they, etc. (gave it to Tom, who sold it to Jim). □ **who's who 1** who or what each person is (know who's who). **2** a list or directory with facts about notable persons. [OE hwā f. Gmc: whom f. OE dative hwām, hwæm: whose f. genit. hwæs]

■ **Usage** In the last example at sense 1a and the last two examples at sense 2, whom is correct but who is common in less formal contexts.

whoa /wəʊ/ int. used as a command to stop or slow a horse etc. [var. of HO]

who'd /huːd/ contr. **1** who had. **2** who would.

whodunit /huːˈdʌnɪt/ n. (also **whodunnit**) colloq. a story or play about the detection of a crime etc., esp. murder. [= who done (illiterate for did) it?]

whoever /huːˈevə(r)/ pron. (obj. **whomever** /huːm-/ or colloq. **whoever**; poss. **whosever** /huːz-/) **1** the or any person or persons who (whoever comes is welcome). **2** though anyone (whoever else objects, I do not; whosever it is, I want it). **3** colloq. (as an intensive) who ever; who at all (whoever heard of such a thing?).

whole /həʊl/ adj. & n. —adj. **1** in an uninjured, unbroken, intact, or undiminished state (swallowed it whole; there is not a plate left whole). **2** not less than; all there is of; entire, complete. —n. **1** a thing complete in itself. **2** all there is of a thing (spent the whole of the summer by the sea). **3** (foll. by of) all members, inhabitants, etc., of (the whole of London knows it). □ **as a whole** as a unity; not as separate parts. **on the whole** taking everything relevant into account; in general. **whole number** a number without fractions; an integer. **whole-tone scale** Mus. a scale consisting entirely of tones, with no semitones. □ **wholeness** n. [OE hāl f. Gmc]

wholefood /ˈhəʊlfuːd/ n. food which has not been unnecessarily processed or refined.

wholegrain /ˈhəʊlɡreɪn/ adj. made with or containing whole grains (wholegrain bread).

wholehearted /həʊlˈhɑːtɪd/ adj. **1** (of a person) completely devoted or committed. **2** (of an action etc.) done with all possible effort, attention, or sincerity; thorough. □ **wholeheartedly** adv. **wholeheartedness** n.

wholemeal /ˈhəʊlmiːl/ n. (usu. attrib.) Brit. meal of wheat or other cereals with none of the bran or germ removed.

wholesale /ˈhəʊlseɪl/ n., adj., adv., & v. —n. the selling of things in large quantities to be retailed by others (cf. RETAIL). —adj. & adv. **1** by wholesale; at a wholesale price (can get it for you wholesale). **2** on a large scale (wholesale destruction occurred; was handing out samples wholesale). —v.tr. sell wholesale. □ **wholesaler** n. [ME: orig. by whole sale]

wholesome /ˈhəʊlsəm/ adj. **1** promoting or indicating physical, mental, or moral health (wholesome pursuits; a wholesome appearance). **2** prudent (wholesome respect). □ **wholesomely** adv. **wholesomeness** n. [ME, prob. f. OE (unrecorded) hālsum as WHOLE, -SOME[1]]

wholewheat /ˈhəʊlwiːt/ n. (usu. attrib.) wheat with none of the bran or germ removed.

wholism var. of HOLISM.

wholly /ˈhəʊllɪ/ adv. entirely; without limitation or diminution. [ME, f. OE (unrecorded) hāllīce (as WHOLE, -LY[2])]

whom objective case of WHO.

whomever objective case of WHOEVER.

whomsoever *objective case* of WHOSOEVER.

whoop /huːp, wuːp/ *n.* & *v.* (also **hoop**) —*n.* **1** a loud cry of or as of excitement etc. **2** a long rasping indrawn breath in whooping cough. —*v.intr.* utter a whoop. □ **whooping cough** an infectious bacterial disease, esp. of children, with a series of short violent coughs followed by a whoop. **whoop it up** *colloq.* **1** engage in revelry. **2** *US* make a stir. [ME: imit.]

whoopee *int.* & *n. colloq.* —*int.* /wʊˈpiː/ expressing exuberant joy. —*n.* /ˈwʊpɪ/ exuberant enjoyment or revelry. □ **make whoopee** *colloq.* rejoice noisily or hilariously.

whoops /wʊps/ *int. colloq.* expressing surprise or apology, esp. on making an obvious mistake. [var. of OOPS]

whoosh /wʊʃ/ *v.*, *n.*, & *int.* (also **woosh**) —*v.intr.* & *tr.* move or cause to move with a rushing sound. —*n.* a sudden movement accompanied by a rushing sound. —*int.* an exclamation imitating this. [imit.]

whopper /ˈwɒpə(r)/ *n. sl.* **1** something big of its kind. **2** a great lie.

whopping /ˈwɒpɪŋ/ *adj. sl.* very big (*a whopping lie*; *a whopping fish*).

whore /hɔː(r)/ *n.* & *v.* —*n.* a prostitute. —*v.intr.* (of a man) pursue sexual activity with whores or promiscuous women. □ **whore-house** a brothel. □ **whoredom** *n.* **whorer** *n.* [OE *hōre* f. Gmc]

whorish /ˈhɔːrɪʃ/ *adj.* of or like a whore. □ **whorishly** *adv.* **whorishness** *n.*

whorl /wɔːl, wɜːl/ *n.* **1** a ring of leaves or other organs round a stem of a plant. **2** one turn of a spiral, esp. on a shell. **3** a complete circle in a fingerprint. □ **whorled** *adj.* [ME *wharwyl*, *whorwil*, app. var. of WHIRL: infl. by *wharve* (n.) = whorl of a spindle]

whose /huːz/ *pron.* & *adj.* —*pron.* of or belonging to which person (*whose is this book?*). —*adj.* of whom or which (*whose book is this?*; *the man, whose name was Tim*; *the house whose roof was damaged*).

whosever /huːzˈevə(r)/ *poss.* of WHOEVER.

whosoever /ˌhuːsəʊˈevə(r)/ *pron.* (*obj.* **whomsoever** /ˌhuːm-/; *poss.* **whosesoever** /ˌhuːz-/) *archaic* = WHOEVER.

why /waɪ/ *adv.*, *int.*, & *n.* —*adv.* **1 a** for what reason or purpose (*why did you do it?*; *I do not know why you came*). **b** on what grounds (*why do you say that?*). **2** (prec. by *reason* etc.) for which (*the reasons why I did it*). —*int.* expressing: **1** surprised discovery or recognition (*why, it's you!*). **2** impatience (*why, of course I do!*). **3** reflection (*why, yes, I think so*). **4** objection (*why, what is wrong with it?*). —*n.* (pl. **whys**) a reason or explanation (esp. *whys and wherefores*). [OE *hwī*, *hwȳ* instr. of *hwæt* WHAT f. Gmc]

WI *abbr.* **1** West Indies. **2** *Brit.* Women's Institute.

wick *n.* a strip or thread of fibrous or spongy material feeding a flame with fuel in a candle, lamp, etc. [OE *wēoce*, *-wēoc* (cf. MDu. *wiecke*, MLG *wēke*), of unkn. orig.]

wicked /ˈwɪkɪd/ *adj.* (**wickeder**, **wickedest**) **1** sinful, iniquitous, given to or involving immorality. **2** spiteful, ill-tempered; intending or intended to give pain. **3** playfully malicious. **4** *colloq.* foul; very bad; formidable (*wicked weather*; *a wicked cough*). **5** *sl.* excellent, remarkable. □ **wickedly** *adv.* **wickedness** *n.* [ME f. obs. *wick*

(perh. adj. use of OE *wicca* wizard) + -ED[1] as in *wretched*]

wicker *n.* plaited twigs or osiers etc. as material for chairs, baskets, mats, etc. [ME, f. E.Scand.: cf. Sw. *viker* willow, rel. to *vika* bend]

wickerwork /ˈwɪkəˌwɜːk/ *n.* **1** wicker. **2** things made of wicker.

wicket /ˈwɪkɪt/ *n.* **1** *Cricket* **a** a set of three stumps with the bails in position defended by a batsman. **b** the ground between two wickets. **2** (in full **wicket-door** or **-gate**) a small door or gate esp. beside or in a larger one or closing the lower part only of a doorway. **3** *US* an aperture in a door or wall usu. closed with a sliding panel. □ **at the wicket** *Cricket* **1** batting. **2** by the wicket-keeper (*caught at the wicket*). **keep wicket** *Cricket* be a wicket-keeper. **on a good** (or **sticky**) **wicket** *colloq.* in a favourable (or unfavourable) position. **take a wicket** (of a bowler and his team) get a batsman out. **wicket-keeper** *Cricket* the fieldsman stationed close behind a batsman's wicket. [ME f. AF & ONF *wiket*, OF *guichet*, of uncert. orig.]

widdershins var. of WITHERSHINS.

wide *adj.*, *adv.*, & *n.* —*adj.* **1** measuring much or more than other things of the same kind across or from side to side. **2** (following a measurement) in width (*a metre wide*). **3** extending far; embracing much; of great extent. **4** not tight or close or restricted; loose. **5** open to the full extent (*staring with wide eyes*). **6** at a considerable distance from a point or mark. **7** (in *comb.*) extending over the whole of (*nationwide*). —*adv.* **1** widely. **2** to the full extent (*wide awake*). **3** far from the target etc. (*is shooting wide*). —*n.* **1** *Cricket* a ball judged to pass the wicket beyond the batsman's reach and so scoring a run. **2** (prec. by *the*) the wide world. □ **wide-angle** (of a lens) having a short focal length and hence a field covering a wide angle. **wide awake 1** fully awake. **2** *colloq.* wary, knowing. **wide-eyed** surprised or naïve. **wide open** (often foll. by *to*) exposed or vulnerable (to attack etc.). **wide-ranging** covering an extensive range. □ **wideness** *n.* **widish** *adj.* [OE *wīd* (adj.), *wīde* (adv.) f. Gmc]

widely /ˈwaɪdlɪ/ *adv.* **1** to a wide extent; far apart. **2** extensively (*widely read*; *widely distributed*). **3** by many people (*it is widely thought that*). **4** considerably; to a large degree (*holds a widely different view*).

widen /ˈwaɪd(ə)n/ *v.tr.* & *intr.* make or become wider. □ **widener** *n.*

widespread /ˈwaɪdsprɛd, -ˈsprɛd/ *adj.* widely distributed or disseminated.

widow /ˈwɪdəʊ/ *n.* & *v.* —*n.* **1** a woman who has lost her husband by death and has not married again. **2** a woman whose husband is often away on a specified activity (*golf widow*). **3** extra cards dealt separately and taken by the highest bidder. **4** *Printing* the short last line of a paragraph at the top of a page or column. —*v.tr.* **1** make into a widow or widower. **2** (as **widowed** *adj.*) bereft by the death of a spouse (*my widowed mother*). **widow's mite** a small money contribution (see Mark 12:42). **widow's peak** a V-shaped growth of hair towards the centre of the forehead. [OE *widewe*, rel. to OHG *wituwa*, Skr. *vidhávā*, L *viduus* bereft, widowed, Gk *ēitheos* unmarried man]

widower /ˈwɪdəʊə(r)/ *n.* a man who has lost his wife by death and has not married again.

widowhood /ˈwɪdəʊˌhʊd/ n. the state or period of being a widow.

width /wɪtθ, wɪdθ/ n. **1** measurement or distance from side to side. **2** a large extent. **3** breadth or liberality of thought, views, etc. **4** a strip of material of full width as woven. □ **widthways** adv. **widthwise** adv. [17th c. (as WIDE, -TH²) replacing wideness]

wield /wiːld/ v.tr. **1** hold and use (a weapon or tool). **2** exert or command (power or authority etc.). □ **wielder** n. [OE wealdan, wieldan f. Gmc]

Wiener schnitzel /ˈviːnə ˌʃnɪts(ə)l/ n. a veal escalope breaded, fried, and garnished. [G, = Viennese slice]

wife n. (pl. **wives** /waɪvz/) a married woman esp. in relation to her husband. □ **have** (or **take**) **to wife** archaic marry (a woman). **wife-swapping** colloq. exchanging wives for sexual relations. □ **wifehood** n. **wifely** adj. **wifeliness** n. **wifish** adj. [OE wif woman: ult. orig. unkn.]

wig n. an artificial head of hair esp. to conceal baldness or as a disguise, or worn by a judge or barrister or as period dress. □ **wigged** adj. (also in comb.). **wigless** adj. [abbr. of PERIWIG: cf. WINKLE]

wigging /ˈwɪgɪŋ/ n. colloq. a reprimand.

wiggle /ˈwɪg(ə)l/ v. & n. colloq. —v.intr. & tr. move or cause to move quickly from side to side etc. —n. an act of wiggling. □ **wiggler** n. [ME f. MLG & MDu. wiggelen: cf. WAG¹, WAGGLE]

wiggly /ˈwɪglɪ/ adj. (**wigglier**, **wiggliest**) colloq. **1** showing wiggles. **2** having small irregular undulations.

wigwam /ˈwɪgwæm/ n. a N. American Indian's hut or tent of skins, mats, or bark on poles. [Ojibwa wigwaum, Algonquin wikiwam their house]

wild /waɪld/ adj., adv., & n. —adj. **1** (of an animal or plant) in its original natural state (esp. of species or varieties allied to others that are not wild). **2** not civilized; barbarous. **3** (of scenery etc.) having a conspicuously desolate appearance. **4** unrestrained, disorderly, uncontrolled (a wild youth; wild hair). **5** tempestuous, violent (a wild night). **6 a** excited, frantic (wild with excitement; wild delight). **b** (foll. by about) colloq. enthusiastically devoted to (a person or subject). **7** colloq. infuriated, angry (makes me wild). **8** haphazard, ill-aimed, rash (a wild guess; a wild shot; a wild venture). **9** (of a horse, game-bird, etc.) shy; easily startled. **10** colloq. exciting, delightful. **11** (of a card) having any rank chosen by the player holding it (the joker is wild). —adv. in a wild manner (shooting wild). —n. a wild tract. □ **in the wild** in an uncultivated etc. state. **in** (or **out in**) **the wilds** colloq. far from normal habitation. **run wild** grow or stray unchecked or undisciplined. **wild card 1** see sense 11 of adj. **2** Computing a character that will match any character or sequence of characters in a file name etc. **3** Sport an extra player or team chosen to enter a competition at the selectors' discretion. **wild cat** any of various smallish cats, esp. the European Felis sylvestris (cf. WILDCAT). **wild-goose chase** a foolish or hopeless and unproductive quest. **wild hyacinth** = BLUEBELL. **wild rice** any tall grass of the genus Zizania, yielding edible grains. **wild silk 1** silk from wild silkworms. **2** an imitation of this from short silk fibres. **Wild West** the western US in a time of lawlessness in its early

history. □ **wildish** adj. **wildly** adv. **wildness** n. [OE wilde f. Gmc]

wildcat /ˈwaɪldkæt/ n. & adj. —n. **1** a hot-tempered or violent person. **2** US a bobcat (cf. wild cat). **3** an exploratory oil well. —adj. (attrib.) **1** esp. US reckless; financially unsound. **2** (of a strike) sudden and unofficial.

wildebeest /ˈwɪldəˌbiːst, ˈvɪl-/ n. = GNU. [Afrik. (as WILD, BEAST)]

wilderness /ˈwɪldənɪs/ n. **1** a desert; an uncultivated and uninhabited region. **2** part of a garden left with an uncultivated appearance. [OE wildēornes f. wild dēor wild deer]

wildfire /ˈwaɪldˌfaɪə(r)/ n. hist. **1** a combustible liquid, esp. Greek fire, formerly used in warfare. **2** = WILL-O'-THE-WISP. □ **spread like wildfire** spread with great speed.

wildfowl /ˈwaɪldfaʊl/ n. (pl. same) a game-bird, esp. an aquatic one.

wildlife /ˈwaɪldlaɪf/ n. wild animals collectively.

wildwood /ˈwaɪldwʊd/ n. poet. uncultivated or unfrequented woodland.

wile n. & v. —n. (usu. in pl.) a stratagem; a trick or cunning procedure. —v.tr. (foll. by away, into, etc.) lure or entice. [ME wīl, perh. f. Scand. (ON vél craft)]

wilful /ˈwɪlfʊl/ adj. (US **willful**) **1** (of an action or state) intentional, deliberate (wilful murder; wilful neglect; wilful disobedience). **2** (of a person) obstinate, headstrong. □ **wilfully** adv. **wilfulness** n. [ME f. WILL² + -FUL]

wiliness see WILY.

will¹ v.aux. & tr. (3rd sing. present **will**; past **would** /wʊd/) (foll. by infin. without to, or absol.; present and past only in use) **1** (in the 2nd and 3rd persons, and often in the 1st: see SHALL) expressing the future tense in statements, commands, or questions (you will regret this; they will leave at once; will you go to the party?). **2** (in the 1st person) expressing a wish or intention (I will return soon). **3** expressing desire, consent, or inclination (will you have a sandwich?; come when you will; the door will not open). **4** expressing ability or capacity (the jar will hold a kilo). **5** expressing habitual or intended tendency (accidents will happen; will sit there for hours). **6** expressing probability or expectation (that will be my wife). □ **will do** colloq. expressing willingness to carry out a request. [OE wyllan, (unrecorded) willan f. Gmc: rel. to L volo]

■ **Usage** For the other persons in senses 1 & 2, see SHALL.

will² n. & v. —n. **1** the faculty by which a person decides or is regarded as deciding on and initiating action (the mind consists of the understanding and the will). **2** (also **will-power**) control exercised by deliberate purpose over impulse; self-control (has a strong will; overcame his shyness by will-power). **3** a deliberate or fixed desire or intention (a will to live). **4** energy of intention; the power of effecting one's intentions or dominating others. **5** directions (usu. written) in legal form for the disposition of one's property after death (make one's will). **6** disposition towards others (good will). **7** archaic one's intentions (thy will be done). —v.tr. **1** have as the object of one's will; intend unconditionally (what God wills; willed that we should succeed). **2** instigate or impel or compel by the exercise of will-power (you can will yourself into contentment).

4 bequeath by the terms of a will (*shall will my money to charity*). □ **at will 1** whenever one pleases. **2** *Law* able to be evicted without notice (*tenant at will*). **have one's will** obtain what one wants. **where there's a will there's a way** determination will overcome any obstacle. **a will of one's own** obstinacy; wilfulness of character. **with the best will in the world** however good one's intentions. **with a will** energetically or resolutely. □ **willed** adj. (also in comb.). **willer** n. **will-less** adj. [OE *willa* f. Gmc]

willies /ˈwɪlɪz/ n.pl. colloq. nervous discomfort (esp. *give* or *get the willies*). [19th c.: orig. unkn.]

willing /ˈwɪlɪŋ/ adj. & n. —adj. **1** ready to consent or undertake (*a willing ally*; *am willing to do it*). **2** given or done etc. by a willing person (*willing hands*; *willing help*). —n. cheerful intention (*show willing*). □ **willingly** adv. **willingness** n.

will-o'-the-wisp /ˌwɪləðəˈwɪsp/ n. **1** a phosphorescent light seen on marshy ground, perhaps resulting from the combustion of gases. **2** an elusive person. **3** a delusive hope or plan. [orig. *Will with the wisp*: *wisp* = handful of (lighted) hay etc.]

willow /ˈwɪləʊ/ n. **1** a tree or shrub growing usu. near water in temperate climates, with small flowers borne on catkins, and pliant branches. **2** a cricket-bat. □ **willow-herb** any plant of the genus *Epilobium* etc. **willow-pattern** a conventional design representing a Chinese scene, often with a willow tree, of blue on white porcelain, stoneware, or earthenware. **willow-warbler** (or **-wren**) a small woodland bird with a tuneful song. [OE *welig*]

willowy /ˈwɪləʊɪ/ adj. **1** having or bordered by willows. **2** lithe and slender.

willy /ˈwɪlɪ/ n. (also **willie**) (pl. **-ies**) *Brit. sl.* the penis.

willy-nilly /ˌwɪlɪˈnɪlɪ/ adv. & adj. —adv. whether one likes it or not. —adj. existing or occurring willy-nilly. [later spelling of *will I*, *nill I* I am willing, I am unwilling]

wilt v. & n. —v. **1** intr. (of a plant, leaf, or flower) wither, droop. **2** intr. (of a person) lose one's energy, flag, tire, droop. —n. a plant-disease causing wilting. [orig. dial.: perh. alt. f. *wilk*, *welk*, of LG or Du. orig.]

Wilton /ˈwɪlt(ə)n/ n. a kind of woven carpet with a thick pile. [*Wilton* in S. England]

wily /ˈwaɪlɪ/ adj. (**wilier**, **wiliest**) full of wiles; crafty, cunning. □ **wilily** adv. **wiliness** n.

wimp n. colloq. a feeble or ineffectual person. □ **wimpish** adj. **wimpishly** adv. **wimpishness** n. **wimpy** adj. [20th c.: orig. uncert.]

Wimpy /ˈwɪmpɪ/ n. (pl. **-ies**) propr. a hamburger served in a plain bun.

win v. & n. —v. (**winning**; past and past part. **won** /wʌn/) **1** tr. acquire or secure as a result of a fight, contest, bet, litigation, or some other effort (*won some money*; *won my admiration*). **2** tr. be victorious in (a fight, game, race, etc.). **3** intr. **a** be the victor. (*who won?*; *persevere, and you will win*). **b** (foll. by *through*, *free*, etc.) make one's way or become by successful effort. **4** tr. reach by effort (*win the summit*; *win the shore*). **5** tr. obtain (ore) from a mine. —n. victory in a game or bet etc. □ **win over** persuade, gain the support of. **win through** (or **out**) overcome obstacles. **you can't win** colloq. there is no way to succeed. **you can't win them all** colloq. a resigned

expression of consolation on failure. □ **winnable** adj. [OE *winnan* toil, endure: cf. OHG *winnan*, ON *vinna*]

wince n. & v. —n. a start or involuntary shrinking movement showing pain or distress. —v.intr. give a wince. □ **wincingly** adv. [ME f. OF *guenchir* turn aside: cf. WINCH, WINK]

winceyette /ˌwɪnsɪˈet/ n. *Brit.* a lightweight napped flannelette used esp. for nightclothes.

winch n. & v. —n. **1** the crank of a wheel or axle. **2** a windlass. —v.tr. lift with a winch. □ **wincher** n. [OE *wince* f. Gmc: cf. WINCE]

Winchester /ˈwɪntʃɪstə(r)/ n. propr. a breech-loading repeating rifle. [O. F. *Winchester* d. 1880, US manufacturer of the rifle]

wind[1] n. & v. —n. **1 a** air in more or less rapid natural motion, esp. from an area of high pressure to one of low pressure. **b** a current of wind blowing from a specified direction or otherwise defined (*north wind*; *contrary wind*). **2 a** breath as needed in physical exertion or in speech. **b** the power of breathing without difficulty while running or making a similar continuous effort (*let me recover my wind*). **3** mere empty words; meaningless rhetoric. **4** gas generated in the bowels etc. by indigestion; flatulence. **5** the wind instruments of an orchestra collectively (*poor balance between wind and strings*). —v.tr. **1** exhaust or paralyse the wind of by exertion or a blow. **2** renew the wind of by rest (*stopped to wind the horses*). **3** make (a baby) bring up wind after feeding. **4** detect the presence of by a scent. **5** /waɪnd/ (past and past part. **winded** or **wound** /waʊnd/) *poet.* sound (a bugle or call) by blowing. □ **close to** (or **near**) **the wind 1** sailing as nearly against the wind as is consistent with using its force. **2** colloq. verging on indecency or dishonesty. **get wind of 1** smell out. **2** begin to suspect; hear a rumour of. **get** (or **have**) **the wind up** colloq. be alarmed or frightened. **how** (or **which way**) **the wind blows** (or **lies**) **1** what is the state of opinion. **2** what developments are likely. **in the wind** happening or about to happen. **like the wind** swiftly. **put the wind up** colloq. alarm or frighten. **take the wind out of a person's sails** frustrate a person by anticipating an action or remark etc. **to the winds** (or **four winds**) **1** in all directions. **2** into a state of abandonment or neglect. **wind-break** a row of trees or a fence or wall etc. serving to break the force of the wind. **wind-gauge 1** an anemometer. **2** an apparatus attached to the sights of a gun enabling allowance to be made for the wind in shooting. **3** a device showing the amount of wind in an organ. **wind instrument** a musical instrument in which sound is produced by a current of air, esp. the breath. **wind machine** a device for producing a blast of air or the sound of wind. **wind** (or **winds**) **of change** a force or influence for reform. **wind-sleeve** = wind-sock. **wind-sock** a canvas cylinder or cone on a mast to show the direction of the wind at an airfield etc. **wind-tunnel** a tunnel-like device to produce an air-stream past models of aircraft etc. for the study of wind effects on them. □ **windless** adj. [OE f. Gmc]

wind[2] /waɪnd/ v. & n. —v. (past and past part. **wound** /waʊnd/) **1** intr. go in a circular, spiral, curved, or crooked course. **2** tr. make (one's way) by such a course (*wind your way up to bed*). **3** tr.

wrap closely; surround with or as with a coil (*wound the blanket round me*; *wound my arms round the child*; *wound the child in my arms*). **4 a** *tr.* coil; provide with a coiled thread etc. (*wind the ribbon on to the card*; *wound cotton on a reel*; *winding wool into a ball*). **b** *intr.* coil (*the creeper winds round the pole*; *the wool wound into a ball*). **5** *tr.* wind up (a clock etc.). **6** *tr.* hoist or draw with a windlass etc. (*wound the cable-car up the mountain*). —*n.* **1** a bend or turn in a course. **2** a single turn when winding. □ **wind down 1** lower by winding. **2** (of a mechanism) unwind. **3** (of a person) relax. **4** draw gradually to a close. **wind up 1** coil the whole of (a piece of string etc.). **2** tighten the coiling or coiled spring of (esp. a clock etc.). **3 a** *colloq.* increase the tension or intensity of (*wound myself up to fever pitch*). **b** irritate or provoke (a person) to the point of anger. **4** bring to a conclusion; end (*wound up his speech*). **5** *Commerce* **a** arrange the affairs of and dissolve (a company). **b** (of a company) cease business and go into liquidation. **6** *colloq.* arrive finally; end in a specified state or circumstance (*you'll wind up in prison*; *wound up owing £100*). **wind-up** *n.* **1** a conclusion; a finish. **2** a state of anxiety; the provocation of this. **wound up** *adj.* (of a person) excited or tense or angry. [OE *windan* f. Gmc, rel. to WANDER, WEND]

windbag /ˈwɪndbæg/ *n. colloq.* a person who talks a lot but says little of any value.

windbound /ˈwɪndbaʊnd/ *adj.* unable to sail because of contrary winds.

windbreaker /ˈwɪndˌbreɪkə(r)/ *n. US* = WIND-CHEATER.

windburn /ˈwɪndbɜːn/ *n.* inflammation of the skin caused by exposure to the wind.

windcheater /ˈwɪndˌtʃiːtə(r)/ *n.* a kind of wind-resistant outer jacket with close-fitting neck, cuffs, and lower edge.

winder /ˈwaɪndə(r)/ *n.* a winding mechanism esp. of a clock or watch.

windfall /ˈwɪndfɔːl/ *n.* **1** an apple or other fruit blown to the ground by the wind. **2** a piece of unexpected good fortune, esp. a legacy.

windflower /ˈwɪndˌflaʊə(r)/ *n.* an anemone.

windhover /ˈwɪndˌhɒvə(r)/ *n. Brit.* a kestrel.

winding-sheet a sheet in which a corpse is wrapped for burial.

windlass /ˈwɪndləs/ *n. & v.* —*n.* a machine with a horizontal axle for hauling or hoisting. —*v.tr.* hoist or haul with a windlass. [alt. (perh. by assoc. with dial. *windle* to wind) of obs. *windas* f. OF *guindas* f. ON *vindáss* f. *vinda* WIND² + *áss* pole]

windmill *n.* **1** a mill worked by the action of the wind on its sails. **2** esp. *Brit.* a toy consisting of a stick with curved vanes attached that revolve in a wind.

window /ˈwɪndəʊ/ *n.* **1** an opening in a wall, roof, or vehicle etc., usu. with glass in fixed, sliding, or hinged frames, to admit light or air etc. and allow the occupants to see out. **2** a space for display behind the front window of a shop. **3** an aperture in a wall etc. through which customers are served in a bank, ticket office, etc. **4** an opening or transparent part in an envelope to show an address. **5** a part of a VDU display selected to show a particular category or part of the data. □ **window-box** a box placed on an outside window-sill for growing flowers. **window-cleaner** a person who is employed to clean windows. **window-dressing 1** the art of

arranging a display in a shop-window etc. **2** an adroit presentation of facts etc. to give a deceptively favourable impression. **window-ledge** = *window-sill*. **window-pane** a pane of glass in a window. **window-seat 1** a seat below a window, esp. in a bay or alcove. **2** a seat next to a window in an aircraft, train, etc. **window-shop** (**-shopped**, **-shopping**) look at goods displayed in shop-windows, usu. without buying anything. **window-shopper** a person who window-shops. **window-sill** a sill below a window. □ **windowed** *adj.* (also in *comb.*). **windowless** *adj.* [ME f. ON *vindauga* (as WIND¹, EYE)]

windowing /ˈwɪndəʊɪŋ/ *n. Computing* the selection of part of a stored image for display or enlargement.

windpipe *n.* the air-passage from the throat to the lungs.

windscreen /ˈwɪndskriːn/ *n. Brit.* a screen of glass at the front of a motor vehicle. □ **windscreen wiper** a device consisting of a rubber blade on an arm, moving in an arc, for keeping a windscreen clear of rain etc.

windshield /ˈwɪndʃiːld/ *n. US* = WINDSCREEN.

Windsor /ˈwɪnzə(r)/ *n.* (usu. *attrib.*) denoting or relating to the British Royal Family since 1917. [*Windsor* in S. England, site of the royal residence at Windsor Castle]

Windsor chair /ˈwɪnzə(r)/ *n.* a wooden dining chair with a semicircular back supported by upright rods.

windsurfing /ˈwɪndˌsɜːfɪŋ/ *n.* the sport of riding on water on a sailboard. □ **windsurf** *v.intr.* **windsurfer** *n.*

windswept *adj.* exposed to or swept back by the wind.

windward /ˈwɪndwəd/ *adj., adv., & n.* —*adj. & adv.* on the side from which the wind is blowing (opp. LEEWARD). —*n.* the windward region, side, or direction (*to windward*; *on the windward of*).

windy /ˈwɪndɪ/ *adj.* (**windier, windiest**) **1** stormy with wind (*a windy night*). **2** exposed to the wind; windswept (*a windy plain*). **3** generating or suffering from flatulence. **4** *colloq.* nervous, frightened. □ **windily** *adv.* **windiness** *n.* [OE *windig* (as WIND¹, -Y¹)]

wine *n. & v.* —*n.* **1** fermented grape-juice as an alcoholic drink. **2** a fermented drink resembling this made from other fruits etc. as specified (*elderberry wine*; *ginger wine*). **3** the dark-red colour of red wine. —*v.* **1** *intr.* drink wine. **2** *tr.* entertain to wine. □ **wine box** a square carton of wine with a dispensing tap. **wine cellar 1** a cellar for storing wine. **2** the contents of this. **wine-grower** a cultivator of grapes for wine. **wine list** a list of wines available in a restaurant etc. **wine-tasting 1** judging the quality of wine by tasting it. **2** an occasion for this. **wine vinegar** vinegar made from wine as distinct from malt. **wine waiter** a waiter responsible for serving wine. □ **wineless** *adj.* [OE *wīn* f. Gmc f. L *vinum*]

wineglass /ˈwaɪnɡlɑːs/ *n.* **1** a glass for wine, usu. with a stem and foot. **2** the contents of this, a wineglassful.

wineglassful /ˈwaɪnɡlɑːsˌfʊl/ *n.* (*pl.* **-fuls**) **1** the capacity of a wineglass, esp. of the size used for sherry, as a measure of liquid, about four tablespoons. **2** the contents of a wineglass.

winepress /ˈwaɪnpres/ *n.* a press in which grapes are squeezed in making wine.

winery /ˈwaɪnərɪ/ n. (pl. **-ies**) esp. US an establishment where wine is made.

wing n. & v. —n. **1** each of the limbs or organs by which a bird, bat, or insect is able to fly. **2** a rigid horizontal winglike structure forming a supporting part of an aircraft. **3** part of a building etc. which projects or is extended in a certain direction (*lived in the north wing*). **4 a** a forward player at either end of a line in football, hockey, etc. **b** the side part of a playing-area. **5** (in pl.) the sides of a theatre stage out of view of the audience. **6** a section of a political party in terms of the extremity of its views. **7** a flank of a battle array (*the cavalry were massed on the left wing*). **8** Brit. the part of a motor vehicle covering a wheel. **9 a** an air-force unit of several squadrons or groups. **b** (in pl.) a pilot's badge in the RAF etc. (*get one's wings*). —v. **1** intr. & tr. travel or traverse on wings or in an aircraft (*winging through the air; am winging my way home*). **2** tr. wound in a wing or an arm. **3** tr. enable to fly; send in flight (*fear winged my steps; winged an arrow towards them*). □ **on the wing** flying or in flight. **spread** (or **stretch**) **one's wings** develop one's powers fully. **take under one's wing** treat as a protégé. **take wing** fly away; soar. **wing-case** the horny cover of an insect's wing. **wing-collar** a man's high stiff collar with turned-down corners. **wing commander** an RAF officer next below group captain. **wing-nut** a nut with projections for the fingers to turn it on a screw. **wing-span** (or **-spread**) measurement right across the wings of a bird or aircraft. □ **winged** adj. (also in comb.). **wingless** adj. **winglet** n. **winglike** adj. [ME pl. wenge, -en, -es f. ON vængir, pl. of vængr]

winger /ˈwɪŋə(r)/ n. **1** a player on a wing in football, hockey, etc. **2** (in comb.) a member of a specified political wing (*left-winger*).

wink v. & n. —v. **1 a** tr. close and open (one eye or both eyes) quickly. **b** intr. close and open an eye. **2** intr. (often foll. by at) wink one eye as a signal of friendship or greeting or to convey a message to a person. **3** intr. (of a light etc.) twinkle; shine or flash intermittently. —n. **1** the act or an instance of winking, esp. as a signal etc. **2** colloq. a brief moment of sleep (*didn't sleep a wink*). □ **as easy as winking** colloq. very easy. **wink at** purposely avoid seeing; pretend not to notice. [OE wincian f. Gmc: cf. WINCE, WINCH]

winker /ˈwɪŋkə(r)/ n. a flashing indicator light on a motor vehicle.

winkle /ˈwɪŋk(ə)l/ n. & v. —n. any edible marine gastropod mollusc of the genus *Littorina*; a periwinkle. —v.tr. (foll. by out) esp. Brit. extract or eject (*winkled the information out of them*). □ **winkle-picker** sl. a shoe with a long pointed toe. □ **winkler** n. [abbr. of PERIWINKLE²: cf. WIG]

winner /ˈwɪnə(r)/ n. **1** a person, racehorse, etc. that wins. **2** colloq. a successful or highly promising idea, enterprise, etc. (*the new scheme seemed a winner*).

winning /ˈwɪnɪŋ/ adj. & n. —adj. **1** having or bringing victory or an advantage (*the winning entry; a winning stroke*). **2** attractive, persuasive (*a winning smile; winning ways*). —n. (in pl.) money won esp. in betting etc. □ **winning-post** a post marking the end of a race. □ **winningly** adv. **winningness** n.

winnow /ˈwɪnəʊ/ v.tr. **1** blow (grain) free of chaff etc. by an air-current. **2** (foll. by out, away, from, etc.) get rid of (chaff etc.) from grain. **3** sift, separate. □ **winnower** n. (in senses 1, 2). [OE windwian (as WIND¹)]

wino /ˈwaɪnəʊ/ n. (pl. **-os**) sl. a habitual excessive drinker of cheap wine.

winsome /ˈwɪnsəm/ adj. (of a person, looks, or manner) winning, attractive, engaging. □ **winsomely** adv. **winsomeness** n. [OE wynsum f. wyn JOY + -SOME¹]

winter /ˈwɪntə(r)/ n. & v. —n. **1** the coldest season of the year. **2** Astron. the period from the winter solstice to the vernal equinox. **3** (attrib.) **a** characteristic of or suitable for winter (*winter light; winter clothes*). **b** (of fruit) ripening late or keeping until or during winter. **c** (of wheat or other crops) sown in autumn for harvesting the following year. —v. **1** intr. (usu. foll. by at, in) pass the winter (*likes to winter in the Canaries*). **2** tr. keep or feed (plants, cattle) during winter. □ **winter jasmine** a jasmine with yellow flowers. **winter quarters** a place where soldiers spend the winter. **winter sports** sports performed on snow or ice esp. in winter (e.g. skiing and ice-skating). □ **winterer** n. **winterless** adj. **winterly** adj. [OE f. Gmc, prob. rel. to WET]

wintergreen /ˈwɪntəˌɡriːn/ n. any of several plants remaining green through the winter.

winterize /ˈwɪntəˌraɪz/ v.tr. (also **-ise**) esp. US adapt for operation or use in cold weather. □ **winterization** /-ˈzeɪʃ(ə)n/ n.

wintry /ˈwɪntrɪ/ adj. (also **wintery**) (/-tərɪ/; **wintrier**, **wintriest**) **1** characteristic of winter. **2** (of a smile, greeting, etc.) lacking warmth or enthusiasm. □ **wintrily** adv. **wintriness** n. [OE wintrig, or f. WINTER]

winy adj. (**winier**, **winiest**) resembling wine in taste or appearance. □ **wininess** n.

wipe v. & n. —v.tr. **1** clean or dry the surface of by rubbing with the hands or a cloth etc. **2** rub (a cloth) over a surface. **3** (often foll. by away, off, etc.) clear or remove by wiping (*wiped the mess off the table; wipe away your tears*). **4 a** erase (data, a recording, etc., from a magnetic medium). **b** erase data from (the medium). **5** Austral. & NZ sl. reject or dismiss (a person or idea). —n. **1** an act of wiping (*give the floor a wipe*). **2** a piece of disposable absorbent cloth, usu. treated with a cleansing agent, for wiping something clean (*antiseptic wipes*). □ **wipe down** clean (esp. a vertical surface) by wiping. **wipe the floor with** colloq. inflict a humiliating defeat on. **wipe off** annul (a debt etc.). **wipe out 1** destroy, annihilate (*the whole population was wiped out*). **b** obliterate (*wiped it out of my memory*). **2** sl. murder. **3** clean the inside of. **4** avenge (an insult etc.). **wipe-out** n. **1** the obliteration of one radio signal by another. **2** an instance of destruction or annihilation. **3** sl. a fall from a surfboard. **wipe up 1** Brit. dry (dishes etc.). **2** take up (a liquid etc.) by wiping. □ **wipeable** adj. [OE wipian: cf. OHG wīfan wind round, Goth. weipan crown: rel. to WHIP]

wiper n. = windscreen wiper.

wire /ˈwaɪə(r)/ n. & v. —n. **1 a** metal drawn out into the form of a thread or thin flexible rod. **b** a piece of this. **c** (attrib.) made of wire. **2** a length or quantity of wire used for fencing or to carry an electric current etc. **3** esp. US colloq. a telegram or cablegram. —v.tr. **1** provide, fasten, strengthen, etc., with wire. **2** (often foll. by *up*) *Electr.* install electrical circuits in (a building, piece of equipment, etc.). **3** esp. *US colloq.* telegraph (*wired me that they were coming*). □ **by wire** by telegraph. **get one's wires crossed** become confused and misunderstood. **wire brush 1** a brush with tough wire bristles. **2** a brush with wire strands brushed against cymbals to produce a soft metallic sound. **wire gauge 1** a gauge for measuring the diameter of wire etc. **2** a standard series of sizes in which wire etc. is made. **wire-haired** (esp. of a dog) having stiff or wiry hair. **wire netting** netting of wire twisted into meshes. **wire-tapper** a person who indulges in wire-tapping. **wire-tapping** the practice of tapping (see TAP[1] *v.* 4) a telephone or telegraph line to eavesdrop. **wire-walker** an acrobat performing feats on a wire rope. **wire wool** a mass of fine wire for cleaning. □ **wirer** *n.* [OE *wir*]

wireless /ˈwaɪəlɪs/ *n.* & *adj.* —*n.* **1** esp. *Brit.* **a** (in full **wireless set**) a radio receiving set. **b** the transmission and reception of radio signals. **2** = RADIO-TELEGRAPHY. —*adj.* lacking or not requiring wires.

■ **Usage** Now old-fashioned, esp. with ref. to broadcasting, and superseded by *radio*.

wireworm /ˈwaɪəˌwɜːm/ *n.* the larva of the click beetle causing damage to crop plants.

wiring /ˈwaɪərɪŋ/ *n.* **1** a system of wires providing electrical circuits. **2** the installation of this (*came to do the wiring*).

wiry /ˈwaɪərɪ/ *adj.* (**wirier**, **wiriest**) **1** tough and flexible as wire. **2** (of a person) thin and sinewy; untiring. **3** made of wire. □ **wirily** *adv.* **wiriness** *n.*

wisdom /ˈwɪzdəm/ *n.* **1** the state of being wise. **2** experience and knowledge together with the power of applying them critically or practically. **3** sagacity, prudence; common sense. **4** wise sayings, thoughts, etc., regarded collectively. □ **wisdom tooth** each of four hindmost molars not usu. cut before 20 years of age. [OE *wisdom* (as WISE[1], -DOM)]

wise[1] *adj.* & *v.* —*adj.* **1 a** having experience and knowledge and judiciously applying them. **b** (of an action, behaviour, etc.) determined by or showing or in harmony with such experience and knowledge. **2** sagacious, prudent, sensible, discreet. **3** having knowledge. **4** suggestive of wisdom (*with a wise nod of the head*). **5** *US colloq.* **a** alert, crafty. **b** (often foll. by *to*) having (usu. confidential) information (about). —*v.tr.* & *intr.* (foll. by *up*) esp. *US colloq.* put or get wise. □ **be** (or **get**) **wise to** *colloq.* become aware of. **no** (or **none the** or **not much**) **wiser** knowing no more than before. **wise after the event** able to understand and assess an event or circumstance after its implications have become obvious. **wise guy** *colloq.* a know-all. **wise man** a wizard, esp. one of the Magi. □ **wisely** *adv.* [OE *wis* f. Gmc: see WIT[2]]

wise[2] /waɪz/ *n. archaic* way, manner, or degree (*in solemn wise*; *on this wise*). □ **in no wise** not at all. [OE *wise* f. Gmc f. WIT[2]]

-wise *suffix* forming adjectives and adverbs of manner (*crosswise*; *clockwise*; *lengthwise*) or respect (*moneywise*) (cf. -WAYS). [as WISE[2]]

■ **Usage** More fanciful phrase-based combinations, such as *employment-wise* (= as regards employment), are *colloq.* and restricted to informal contexts.

wisecrack /ˈwaɪzkræk/ *n.* & *v. colloq.* —*n.* a smart pithy remark. —*v.intr.* make a wisecrack. □ **wisecracker** *n.*

wish *v.* & *n.* —*v.* **1** *intr.* (often foll. by *for*) have or express a desire or aspiration for. **2** *tr.* (often foll. by *that* + clause, usu. with *that* omitted) have as a desire or aspiration. **3** *tr.* want or demand, usu. so as to bring about what is wanted. **4** *tr.* express one's hopes for (*we wish you well*; *wish them no harm*; *wished us a pleasant journey*). **5** *tr.* (foll. by *on*, *upon*) *colloq.* foist on a person. —*n.* **1 a** a desire, request, or aspiration. **b** an expression of this. **2** a thing desired (*got my wish*). □ **best** (or **good**) **wishes** hopes felt or expressed for another's happiness etc. **wish-fulfilment** a tendency for subconscious desire to be satisfied in fantasy. **wishing-well** a well into which coins are dropped and a wish is made. □ **wisher** *n.* (in sense 4 of *v.*); (also in *comb.*). [OE *wȳscan*, OHG *wunsken* f. Gmc, ult. rel. to WONT]

wishbone *n.* a forked bone between the neck and breast of a cooked bird: when broken between two people the longer portion entitles the holder to make a wish.

wishful /ˈwɪʃfʊl/ *adj.* **1** (often foll. by *to* + infin.) desiring, wishing. **2** having or expressing a wish. □ **wishful thinking** belief founded on wishes rather than facts. □ **wishfully** *adv.* **wishfulness** *n.*

wishy-washy /ˈwɪʃɪˌwɒʃɪ/ *adj.* **1** feeble, insipid, or indecisive in quality or character. **2** (of tea, soup, etc.) weak, watery, sloppy. [redupl. of WASHY]

wisp *n.* **1** a small bundle or twist of straw etc. **a** small fine separate quantity of smoke, hair, etc. **3** a flock (of snipe). □ **wispy** *adj.* (**wispier**, **wispiest**). **wispily** *adv.* **wispiness** *n.* [ME: orig. uncert.: cf. WFris. *wisp*, and WHISK]

wisteria /wɪˈstɪərɪə/ *n.* (also **wistaria** /-ˈsteərɪə/) any climbing plant of the genus *Wisteria*. [C. *Wistar* (or *Wister*), Amer. anatomist d. 1818]

wistful *adj.* (of a person, looks, etc.) yearningly or mournfully expectant or wishful. □ **wistfully** *adv.* **wistfulness** *n.* [app. assim. of obs. *wistly* (adv.) intently (cf. WHISHT) to *wishful*, with corresp. change of sense]

wit[1] *n.* **1** (in *sing.* or *pl.*) intelligence; quick understanding (*has quick wits*; *a nimble wit*). **2 a** the unexpected, quick, and humorous combining or contrasting of ideas or expressions (*conversation sparkling with wit*). **b** the power of giving intellectual pleasure by this. **3** a person possessing such a power, esp. a cleverly humorous person. □ **at one's wit's** (or **wits'**) **end** utterly at a loss or in despair. **have** (or **keep**) **one's wits about one** be alert or vigilant or of lively intelligence. **live by one's wits** live by ingenious or crafty expedients, without a settled occupation. **out of one's wits** mad, distracted. □ **witted** *adj.* (in sense 1); (also in *comb.*). [OE *wit(t)*, *gewit(t)* f. Gmc]

wit[2] only in □ **to wit** that is to say; namely. [OE *witan* f. Gmc]

witch *n.* & *v.* —*n.* **1** a sorceress, esp. a woman supposed to have dealings with the devil or evil spirits. **2** an ugly old woman; a hag. **3** a fascinating girl or woman. —*v.tr. archaic* **1**

bewitch. **2** fascinate, charm, lure. □ **witch-doctor** a tribal magician of primitive people. **witch-hunt 1** *hist.* a search for and persecution of supposed witches. **2** a campaign directed against a particular group of those holding unpopular or unorthodox views. □ **witching** *adj.* **witchlike** *adj.* [OE *wicca* (masc.), *wicce* (fem.), rel. to *wiccian* (v.) practise magic arts]

witchcraft /ˈwɪtʃkrɑːft/ *n.* the use of magic; sorcery.

witchery /ˈwɪtʃərɪ/ *n.* witchcraft.

witch-hazel /ˈwɪtʃheɪz(ə)l/ *n.* (also **wych-hazel**) **1** any American shrub of the genus *Hamamelis*, with bark yielding an astringent lotion. **2** this lotion.

with /wɪð/ *prep.* expressing: **1** an instrument or means used (*cut with a knife; can walk with assistance*). **2** association or company (*lives with his mother; works with Shell; lamb with mint sauce*). **3** cause or origin (*shiver with fear; in bed with measles*). **4** possession, attribution (*the man with dark hair; a vase with handles*). **5** circumstances; accompanying conditions (*sleep with the window open; a holiday with all expenses paid*). **6** manner adopted or displayed (*behaved with dignity; spoke with vehemence; handle with care; won with ease*). **7** agreement or harmony (*sympathize with; I believe with you that it can be done*). **8** disagreement, antagonism, competition (*clashing with; stop arguing with me*). **9** responsibility or care for (*the decision rests with you; leave the child with me*). **10** material (*made with gold*). **11** addition or supply; possession of as a material, attribute, circumstance, etc. (*fill it with water; threaten with dismissal; decorate with holly*). **12** reference or regard (*be patient with them; how are things with you?; what do you want with me?; there's nothing wrong with expressing one's opinion*). **13** relation or causative association (*changes with the weather; keeps pace with the cost of living*). **14** an accepted circumstance or consideration (*with all your faults, we like you*). □ **away** (or **in** or **out** etc.) **with** (as *int.*) take, send, or put (a person or thing) away, in, out, etc. **be with a person 1** agree with and support a person. **2** *colloq.* follow a person's meaning (*are you with me?*). **with child** (or **young**) *literary* pregnant. **with it** *colloq.* **1** up to date; conversant with modern ideas etc. **2** alert and comprehending. **with that** thereupon. [OE, prob. shortened f. a Gmc prep. corresp. to OE *wither*, OHG *widar* against]

withdraw /wɪðˈdrɔː/ *v.* (*past* **withdrew** /-ˈdruː/; *past part.* **withdrawn** /-ˈdrɔːn/) **1** *tr.* pull or take aside or back (*withdrew my hand*). **2** *tr.* discontinue, cancel, retract (*withdrew my support; the promise was later withdrawn*). **3** *tr.* remove; take away (*withdrew the child from school; withdrew their troops*). **4** *tr.* take (money) out of an account. **5** *intr.* retire or go away; move away or back. **6** *intr.* (as **withdrawn** *adj.*) abnormally shy and unsociable; mentally detached. [ME f. *with-* away (as WITH) + DRAW]

withdrawal /wɪðˈdrɔːəl/ *n.* **1** the act or an instance of withdrawing or being withdrawn. **2** a process of ceasing to take addictive drugs, often with an unpleasant physical reaction (*withdrawal symptoms*). **3** = *coitus interruptus*.

wither /ˈwɪðə(r)/ *v.* **1** *tr.* & *intr.* (often foll. by *up*) make or become dry and shrivelled (*withered flowers*). **2** *tr.* & *intr.* (often foll. by *away*) deprive of or lose vigour or importance. **3** *intr.* decay,

decline. **4** *tr.* **a** blight with scorn etc. **b** (as **withering** *adj.*) scornful (*a withering look*). □ **witheringly** *adv.* [ME, app. var. of WEATHER differentiated for certain senses]

withers /ˈwɪðəz/ *n.pl.* the ridge between a horse's shoulder-blades. [shortening of (16th-c.) *wider-some* (or *-sone*) f. *wider-*, *wither-* against (cf. WITH), as the part that resists the strain of the collar; second element obscure]

withershins /ˈwɪðəʃɪnz/ *adv.* (also **widdershins** /ˈwɪd-/) esp. *Sc.* **1** in a direction contrary to the sun's course (*considered as unlucky*). **2** anticlockwise. [MLG *weddersins* f. MHG *widersinnes* f. *wider* against + *sin* direction]

withhold /wɪðˈhəʊld/ *v.tr.* (*past* and *past part.* **-held** /-ˈheld/) **1** (often foll. by *from*) hold back; restrain. **2** refuse to give, grant, or allow (*withhold one's consent; withhold the truth*). □ **withholder** *n.* [ME f. *with-* away (as WITH) + HOLD¹]

within /wɪˈðɪn/ *adv.* & *prep.* —*adv.* archaic or literary **1** inside; to, at, or on the inside; internally. **2** indoors (*is anyone within?*). **3** in spirit (*make me pure within*). —*prep.* **1** inside; enclosed or contained by. **2 a** not beyond or exceeding (*within one's means*). **b** not transgressing (*within the law*). **3** not further off than (*within three miles of a station; within shouting distance; within ten days*). □ **within reach** (or **sight**) **of** near enough to be reached or seen. [OE *withinnan* on the inside (as WITH, *innan* (adv. & prep.) within, formed as IN)]

without /wɪˈðaʊt/ *prep.* & *adv.* —*prep.* **1** not having, feeling, or showing (*came without any money; without hesitation; without any emotion*). **2** with freedom from (*without fear; without embarrassment*). **3** in the absence of (*cannot live without you; the train left without us*). **4** with neglect or avoidance of (*do not leave without telling me*). **5** archaic outside (*without the city wall*). —*adv.* archaic or literary outside. □ **without end** infinite, eternal. [OE *withūtan* (as WITH, *ūtan* from outside, formed as OUT)]

■ **Usage** Use as a *conj.*, as in *do not leave without you tell me*, is non-standard.

withstand /wɪðˈstænd/ *v.* (*past* and *past part.* **-stood** /-ˈstʊd/) **1** *tr.* oppose, resist, hold out against (a person, force, etc.). **2** *intr.* make opposition; offer resistance. □ **withstander** *n.* [OE *withstandan* f. *with-* against (as WITH) + STAND]

witless /ˈwɪtlɪs/ *adj.* **1** lacking wits; foolish, stupid. **2** crazy. □ **witlessly** *adv.* **witlessness** *n.* [OE *witlēas* (as WIT¹, -LESS)]

witness /ˈwɪtnɪs/ *n.* & *v.* —*n.* **1** a person present at some event and able to give information about it (cf. EYEWITNESS). **2 a** a person giving sworn testimony. **b** a person attesting another's signature to a document. **3** (foll. by *to*, *of*) a person or thing whose existence, condition, etc., attests or proves something (*is a living witness to their generosity*). **4** testimony, evidence, confirmation. —*v.* **1** be a witness of (an event etc.) (*did you witness the accident?*). **2** *tr.* be witness to the authenticity of (a document or signature). **3** *tr.* serve as evidence or an indication of. **4** *intr.* (foll. by *against*, *for*, *to*) give or serve as evidence. □ **bear witness to** (or **of**) **1** attest the truth of. **2** state one's belief in. **call to witness** appeal to for confirmation etc. **witness-box** (*US* **-stand**) an enclosure in a lawcourt from which witnesses give evidence. [OE *witnes* (as WIT[1], -NESS)]

witter *v.intr.* (often foll. by *on*) *colloq.* speak tediously on trivial matters. [20th c.: prob. imit.]

witticism /ˈwɪtɪˌsɪz(ə)m/ *n.* a witty remark. [coined by Dryden (1677) f. WITTY, after *criticism*]

witty *adj.* (**wittier, wittiest**) **1** showing verbal wit. **2** characterized by wit or humour. □ **wittily** *adv.* **wittiness** *n.* [OE *witig, wittig* (as WIT[1], -Y[1])]

wives *pl.* of WIFE.

wiz var. of WHIZ *n.* 2.

wizard /ˈwɪzəd/ *n.* & *adj.* —*n.* **1** a sorcerer; a magician. **2** a person of remarkable powers, a genius. **3** a conjuror. —*adj. sl. esp. Brit.* wonderful, excellent. □ **wizardly** *adj.* **wizardry** *n.* [ME f. WISE[1] + -ARD]

wizened /ˈwɪz(ə)nd/ *adj.* (also **wizen**) (of a person or face etc.) shrivelled-looking. [past part. of *wizen* shrivel f. OE *wisnian* f. Gmc]

wk. *abbr.* week.

wks. *abbr.* weeks.

WNW *abbr.* west-north-west.

WO *abbr.* Warrant Officer.

wo /wəʊ/ *int.* = WHOA. [var. of *who* (int.), HO]

woad *n. hist.* **1** a plant yielding a blue dye now superseded by indigo. **2** the dye obtained from this. [OE *wād* f. Gmc]

wobble /ˈwɒb(ə)l/ *v.* & *n.* —*v.* **1 a** *intr.* sway or vibrate unsteadily from side to side. **b** *tr.* cause to do this. **2** *intr.* stand or go unsteadily; stagger. **3** *intr.* waver, vacillate. **4** *intr.* (of the voice or sound) quaver, pulsate. —*n.* **1** a wobbling movement. **2** an instance of vacillation or pulsation. □ **wobbler** *n.* [earlier *wabble*, corresp. to LG *wabbeln*, ON *vafla* waver f. Gmc: cf. WAVE, WAVER, -LE[4]]

wobbly /ˈwɒblɪ/ *adj.* (**wobblier, wobbliest**) **1** wobbling or tending to wobble. **2** wavy, undulating (*a wobbly line*). **3** unsteady; weak after illness (*feeling wobbly*). **4** wavering, insecure (*the economy was wobbly*). □ **throw a wobbly** *sl.* have a fit of nerves or temper. □ **wobbliness** *n.*

woe /wəʊ/ *n. archaic* or *literary* **1** affliction; distress. **2** (in *pl.*) calamities, troubles. **3** *joc.* problems (*told me a tale of woe*). □ **woe betide** there will be unfortunate consequences for (*woe betide you if you are late*). **woe is me** an exclamation of distress. [OE *wā, wǣ* f. Gmc, a natural exclam. of lament]

woebegone /ˈwəʊbɪˌɡɒn/ *adj.* dismal-looking. [WOE + *begone* = surrounded f. OE *begān* (as BE-, GO[1])]

woeful /ˈwəʊfʊl/ *adj.* **1** sorrowful. **2** causing sorrow or affliction. **3** very bad; wretched (*woeful ignorance*). □ **woefully** *adv.* **woefulness** *n.*

wog *n. sl. offens.* a foreigner, esp. a non-White one. [20th c.: orig. unkn.]

wok /wɒk/ *n.* a bowl-shaped frying-pan used in esp. Chinese cookery. [Cantonese]

woke *past* of WAKE[1].

woken *past part.* of WAKE[1].

wolf /wʊlf/ *n.* & *v.* —*n.* (*pl.* **wolves** /wʊlvz/) **1** a wild flesh-eating tawny-grey mammal related to the dog. **2** *sl.* a man given to seducing women. **3** a rapacious or greedy person. —*v.tr.* (often foll. by *down*) devour (food) greedily. □ **cry wolf** raise repeated false alarms (so that a genuine one is disregarded). **keep the wolf from the door** avert hunger or starvation. **lone wolf** a person who prefers to act alone. **throw to**

the **wolves** sacrifice without compunction. **wolf-whistle** *n.* a sexually admiring whistle, usually by a man to a woman. —*v.intr.* make a wolf-whistle. □ **wolfish** *adj.* **wolfishly** *adv.* **wolflike** *adj.* & *adv.* [OE *wulf* f. Gmc]

wolfhound /ˈwʊlfhaʊnd/ *n.* a borzoi or other dog of a kind used orig. to hunt wolves.

wolfram /ˈwʊlfrəm/ *n.* **1** tungsten. **2** tungsten ore. [G: perh. f. *Wolf* WOLF + *Rahm* cream, or MHG *rām* dirt, soot]

woman /ˈwʊmən/ *n.* (*pl.* **women** /ˈwɪmɪn/) **1** an adult human female. **2** the female sex; any or an average woman (*how does woman differ from man?*). **3** a wife or female sexual partner. **4** (prec. by *the*) emotions or characteristics traditionally associated with women (*brought out the woman in him*). **5** (*attrib.*) female (*woman driver; women friends*). **6** (as second element in *comb.*) a woman of a specified nationality, profession, skill, etc. (*Englishwoman; horsewoman*). □ **Women's Institute** an organization of women in rural areas to meet regularly and participate in crafts, cultural activities, etc. **women's lib** *colloq.* = *women's liberation*. **women's libber** *colloq.* a supporter of women's liberation. **women's liberation** the liberation of women from inequalities and subservient status in relation to men, and from attitudes causing these. **Women's Liberation** (or **Movement**) a movement campaigning for women's liberation. **women's rights** rights that promote a position of legal and social equality of women with men. [OE *wīfmon, -man* (as WIFE, MAN), a formation peculiar to English, the ancient word being WIFE]

womanhood /ˈwʊmənˌhʊd/ *n.* **1** female maturity. **2** womanly instinct. **3** womankind.

womanish /ˈwʊmənɪʃ/ *adj. usu. derog.* **1** (of a man) effeminate, unmanly. **2** suitable to or characteristic of a woman. □ **womanishly** *adv.* **womanishness** *n.*

womanist /ˈwʊmənɪst/ *n.* esp. *US* A Black feminist.

womanize /ˈwʊməˌnaɪz/ *v.* (also **-ise**) *intr.* chase after women; philander. □ **womanizer** *n.*

womankind /ˈwʊmənˌkaɪnd/ *n.* (also **womenkind** /ˈwɪmɪn-/) women in general.

womanly /ˈwʊmənlɪ/ *adj.* (of a woman) having or showing qualities traditionally associated with women; not masculine or girlish. □ **womanliness** *n.*

womb /wuːm/ *n.* **1** the organ of conception and gestation in a woman and other female mammals; the uterus. **2** a place of origination and development. □ **womblike** *adj.* [OE *wamb, womb*]

wombat /ˈwɒmbæt/ *n.* any burrowing plant-eating Australian marsupial of the family Vombatidae. [Aboriginal]

women *pl.* of WOMAN.

womenfolk /ˈwɪmɪnˌfəʊk/ *n.* **1** women in general. **2** the women in a family.

womenkind var. of WOMANKIND.

won *past* and *past part.* of WIN.

wonder /ˈwʌndə(r)/ *n.* & *v.* —*n.* **1** an emotion excited by what is unexpected, unfamiliar, or inexplicable, esp. surprise mingled with admiration or curiosity etc. **2** a strange or remarkable person or thing, specimen, event, etc. **3** (*attrib.*) having marvellous or amazing properties etc. (*a wonder drug*). **4** a surprising thing (*it is a wonder you were not hurt*). —v. **1** intr. (often foll. by *at*, or *to* + infin.) be filled with wonder or great surprise. **2** tr. (foll. by *that* + clause) be surprised to find. **3** tr. desire or be curious to know (*I wonder what the time is*). **4** tr. expressing a tentative enquiry (*I wonder whether you would mind?*). □ **I wonder** I very much doubt it. **no** (or **small**) **wonder** (often foll. by *that* + clause) one cannot be surprised; one might have guessed; it is natural. **wonder-struck** (or **-stricken**) reduced to silence by wonder. **wonders will never cease** an exclamation of extreme (usu. agreeable) surprise. **work** (or **do**) **wonders 1** do miracles. **2** succeed remarkably. □ **wonderer** n. [OE *wundor*, *wundrian*, of unkn. orig.]

wonderful /ˈwʌndəˌfʊl/ adj. **1** very remarkable or admirable. **2** arousing wonder. □ **wonderfully** adv. **wonderfulness** n. [OE *wunderfull* (as WONDER, -FUL)]

wondering /ˈwʌndərɪŋ/ adj. filled with wonder; marvelling (*their wondering gaze*). □ **wonderingly** adv.

wonderland /ˈwʌndəˌlænd/ n. **1** a fairyland. **2** a land of surprises or marvels.

wonderment /ˈwʌndəmənt/ n. surprise, awe.

wondrous /ˈwʌndrəs/ adj. & adv. poet. —adj. wonderful. —adv. wonderfully (*wondrous kind*). □ **wondrously** adv. **wondrousness** n. [alt. of obs. **wonders** (adj. & adv.), = genit. of WONDER (cf. -S³) after *marvellous*]

wonky /ˈwɒŋkɪ/ adj. (**wonkier**, **wonkiest**) Brit. sl. **1** crooked. **2** loose, unsteady. **3** unreliable. □ **wonkily** adv. **wonkiness** n. [fanciful formation]

wont /wəʊnt/ adj., n., & v. —predic.adj. archaic or literary (foll. by *to* + infin.) accustomed (*as we were wont to say*). —n. formal or joc. what is customary, one's habit (*as is my wont*). —v.tr. & intr. (3rd sing. present **wonts** or **wont**; past **wont** or **wonted**) archaic make or become accustomed. [OE *gewunod* past part. of *gewunian* f. *wunian* dwell]

won't /wəʊnt/ contr. will not.

wonted /ˈwəʊntɪd/ attrib.adj. habitual, accustomed, usual.

woo v.tr. (**woos**, **wooed**) **1** court; seek the hand or love of (a woman). **2** try to win (fame, fortune, etc.). **3** seek the favour or support of. **4** coax or importune. □ **wooable** adj. **wooer** n. [OE *wōgian* (intr.), *āwōgian* (tr.), of unkn. orig.]

wood /wʊd/ n. **1 a** a hard fibrous material that forms the main substance of the trunk or branches of a tree or shrub. **b** this cut for timber or for fuel, or for use in crafts, manufacture, etc. **2** (in sing. or pl.) growing trees densely occupying a tract of land. **3** (prec. by *the*) wooden storage, esp. a cask, for wine etc. (*poured straight from the wood*). **4** a wooden-headed golf club. **5** = BOWL² n. 1. □ **not see the wood for the trees** fail to grasp the main issue from over-attention to details. **out of the wood** (or **woods**) out of danger or difficulty. **wood alcohol** methanol. **wood anemone** a wild spring-flowering anemone. **wood-engraving 1** a relief cut on a block of wood sawn across the grain. **2** a print made from this. **3** the technique of making such reliefs and prints. **wood hyacinth** = BLUEBELL 1. **wood nymph** a dryad or hamadryad. **wood pulp** fibre obtained from wood and reduced chemically or mechanically to pulp as raw material for paper. **wood-screw**

a metal male screw with a slotted head and sharp point. **wood sorrel** a small plant with trifoliate leaves and white flowers streaked with purple. **wood warbler 1** a European woodland bird. **2** any American warbler of the family Parulidae. **wood wool** fine pine etc. shavings used as a surgical dressing or for packing. [OE *wudu*, *w(o)du* f. Gmc]

woodbine /ˈwʊdbaɪn/ n. **1** wild honeysuckle. **2** US Virginia creeper.

woodblock /ˈwʊdblɒk/ n. a block from which woodcuts are made.

woodchuck /ˈwʊdtʃʌk/ n. a reddish-brown and grey N. American marmot. [Amer.Ind. name: cf. Cree *wuchak*, *otchock*]

woodcock /ˈwʊdkɒk/ n. (pl. same) any game-bird of the genus *Scolopax*.

woodcraft /ˈwʊdkrɑːft/ n. esp. US **1** skill in woodwork. **2** knowledge of woodland esp. in camping, scouting, etc.

woodcut /ˈwʊdkʌt/ n. **1** a relief cut on a block of wood sawn along the grain. **2** a print made from this, esp. as an illustration in a book.

woodcutter /ˈwʊdˌkʌtə(r)/ n. **1** a person who cuts wood. **2** a maker of woodcuts.

wooded /ˈwʊdɪd/ adj. having woods or many trees.

wooden /ˈwʊd(ə)n/ adj. **1** made of wood. **2** like wood. **3 a** stiff, clumsy, or stilted; without animation or flexibility. **b** expressionless (*a wooden stare*). □ **woodenly** adv. **woodenness** n.

woodgrouse /ˈwʊdgraʊs/ n. = CAPERCAILLIE.

woodland /ˈwʊdlənd/ n. wooded country, woods (often attrib.: *woodland scenery*). □ **woodlander** n.

woodlouse /ˈwʊdlaʊs/ n. (pl. **-lice** /-laɪs/) any small terrestrial crustacean of the genus *Oniscus* etc. feeding on rotten wood etc.

woodman /ˈwʊdmən/ n. (pl. **-men**) **1** a forester. **2** a woodcutter.

woodpecker /ˈwʊdˌpekə(r)/ n. any bird of the family Picidae that climbs and taps tree-trunks in search of insects.

woodpigeon /ˈwʊdˌpɪdʒ(ə)n/ n. a dove which has white patches like a ring round its neck.

woodruff /ˈwʊdrʌf/ n. a white-flowered plant of the genus *Galium*.

woodshed /ˈwʊdʃed/ n. a shed where wood for fuel is stored.

woodsman /ˈwʊdzmən/ n. (pl. **-men**) **1** a person who lives in or is familiar with woodland. **2** a person skilled in woodcraft.

woodwind /ˈwʊdwɪnd/ n. (often attrib.) **1** (collect.) the wind instruments of the orchestra that were (mostly) orig. made of wood, e.g. the flute and clarinet. **2** (usu. in pl.) an individual instrument of this kind or its player (*the woodwinds are out of tune*).

woodwork /ˈwʊdwɜːk/ n. **1** the making of things in wood. **2** things made of wood, esp. the wooden parts of a building. □ **crawl** (or **come**) **out of the woodwork** colloq. (of something unwelcome) appear; become known. □ **woodworker** n. **woodworking** n.

woodworm /ˈwʊdwɜːm/ n. the wood-boring larva of the furniture beetle.

woody /ˈwʊdɪ/ adj. (**woodier**, **woodiest**) **1** (of a region) wooded; abounding in woods. **2** like or of wood (*woody tissue*). □ **woody nightshade** see NIGHTSHADE. □ **woodiness** n.

woodyard | work

woodyard /ˈwʊdjɑːd/ n. a yard where wood is used or stored.

woof[1] /wʊf/ n. & v. —n. the gruff bark of a dog. —v.intr. give a woof. [imit.]

woof[2] /wuːf/ n. = WEFT. [OE ōwef, alt. of ōwebb (after wefan WEAVE[1]), formed as A-[2], WEB: infl. by warp]

woofer /ˈwuːfə(r)/ n. a loudspeaker designed to reproduce low frequencies (cf. TWEETER). [WOOF[1] + -ER[1]]

wool /wʊl/ n. 1 fine soft wavy hair from the fleece of sheep, goats, etc. 2 a yarn produced from this hair. b cloth or clothing made from it. 3 any of various wool-like substances (steel wool). 4 soft short under-fur or down. □ **pull the wool over a person's eyes** deceive a person. **wool-gathering** absent-mindedness; dreamy inattention. □ **wool-like** adj. [OE wull f. Gmc]

woollen /ˈwʊlən/ adj. & n. (US **woolen**) —adj. made wholly or partly of wool, esp. from short fibres. —n. 1 a fabric produced from wool. 2 (in pl.) woollen garments. [OE wullen (as WOOL, -EN[2])]

woolly /ˈwʊlɪ/ adj. & n. —adj. (**woollier, woolliest**) 1 bearing or naturally covered with wool or wool-like hair. 2 resembling or suggesting wool (woolly clouds). 3 (of a sound) indistinct. 4 (of thought) vague or confused. —n. (pl. -ies) colloq. a woollen garment, esp. a knitted pullover. □ **woolly-bear** a large hairy caterpillar, esp. of the tiger moth. □ **woolliness** n.

woosh var. of WHOOSH.

woozy /ˈwuːzɪ/ adj. (**woozier, wooziest**) colloq. 1 dizzy or unsteady. 2 dazed or slightly drunk. □ **woozily** adv. **wooziness** n. [19th c.: orig. unkn.]

wop /wɒp/ n. sl. offens. an Italian or other S. European. [20th c.: orig. uncert.: perh. f. It. guappo bold, showy, f. Sp. guapo dandy]

word /wɜːd/ n. & v. —n. 1 a sound or combination of sounds forming a meaningful element of speech, usu. shown with a space on either side of it when written or printed, used as part (or occas. as the whole) of a sentence. 2 speech, esp. as distinct from action (bold in word only). 3 one's promise or assurance (gave us their word). 4 (in sing. or pl.) a thing said, a remark or conversation. 5 (in pl.) the text of a song or an actor's part. 6 (in pl.) angry talk (they had words). 7 news, intelligence. 8 a command or password (gave the word to begin). —v.tr. put into words; select words to express (how shall we word that?). □ **be as good as** (or **better than**) **one's word** fulfil (or exceed) what one has promised. **break one's word** fail to do what one has promised. **have no words for** be unable to express. **have a word** (often foll. by with) speak briefly (to). **in other words** expressing the same thing differently. **in so many words** explicitly or bluntly. **in a** (or **one**) **word** briefly. **keep one's word** do what one has promised. **my** (or **upon my**) **word** an exclamation of surprise or consternation. **not the word for it** not an adequate or appropriate description. **of few words** taciturn. **of one's word** reliable in keeping promises (a woman of her word). **on** (or **upon**) **my word** a form of asseveration. **put into words** express in speech or writing. **take a person at his** or **her word** interpret a person's words literally or exactly. **take a person's word for it** believe a person's statement without investigation etc. **too ... for**

words too ... to be adequately described (was too funny for words). **waste words** talk in vain. **the Word** (or **Word of God**) the Bible. **word for word** in exactly the same or (of translation) corresponding words. **word-game** a game involving the making or selection etc. of words. **word of honour** an assurance given upon one's honour. **word of mouth** speech (only). **word-perfect** knowing one's part etc. by heart. **word processor** a purpose-built computer system for electronically storing text entered from a keyboard, incorporating corrections, and providing a printout. **words fail me** an expression of disbelief, dismay, etc. □ **wordage** n. **wordless** adj. **wordlessly** adv. **wordlessness** n. [OE f. Gmc]

wordbook /ˈwɜːdbʊk/ n. a book with lists of words; a vocabulary or dictionary.

wording /ˈwɜːdɪŋ/ n. 1 a form of words used. 2 the way in which something is expressed.

wordplay /ˈwɜːdpleɪ/ n. use of words to witty effect, esp. by punning.

wordy /ˈwɜːdɪ/ adj. (**wordier, wordiest**) 1 using or expressed in many or too many words; verbose. 2 consisting of words. □ **wordily** adv. **wordiness** n. [OE wordig (as WORD, -Y[1])]

wore[1] past of WEAR[1].

wore[2] past and past part. of WEAR[2].

work /wɜːk/ n. & v. —n. 1 the application of mental or physical effort to a purpose; the use of energy. 2 a a task to be undertaken. b (prec. by the; foll. by of) a task occupying (no more than) a specified time (the work of a moment). 3 a thing done or made by work; the result of an action; an achievement; a thing made. 4 a person's employment or occupation etc., esp. as a means of earning income (looked for work; is out of work). 5 a a literary or musical composition. b (in pl.) all such by an author or composer etc. 6 actions or experiences of a specified kind (good work!; this is thirsty work). 7 (in comb.) things or parts made of a specified material or with specified tools etc. (ironwork; needlework). 8 (in pl.) the operative part of a clock or machine. 9 Physics the exertion of force overcoming resistance or producing molecular change (convert heat into work). 10 (in pl.) colloq. all that is available; everything needed. 11 (in pl.) operations of building or repair (road works). 12 (in pl.; often treated as sing.) a place where manufacture is carried on. 13 (in comb.) a ornamentation of a specified kind (poker-work). b articles having this. —v. (past and past part. **worked** or (esp. as adj.) **wrought**) 1 intr. (often foll. by at, on) do work; be engaged in bodily or mental activity. 2 intr. be employed in certain work (works in industry; works as a secretary). 3 intr. (often foll. by for) make efforts; conduct a campaign (works for peace). 4 intr. (foll. by in) be a craftsman (in a material). 5 intr. operate or function, esp. effectively (how does this machine work?; your idea will not work). 6 intr. (of a part of a machine) run, revolve; go through regular motions. 7 tr. carry on, manage, or control (cannot work the machine). 8 tr. a put or keep in operation or at work; cause to toil (this mine is no longer worked; works the staff very hard). b cultivate (land). 9 tr. bring about; produce as a result (worked miracles). 10 tr. knead, hammer; bring to a desired shape or consistency. 11 tr. do, or make by, needlework etc. 12 tr. & intr.

(cause to) progress or penetrate, or make (one's way), gradually or with difficulty in a specified way (*worked our way through the crowd*; *worked the peg into the hole*). **13** *intr.* (foll. by *loose* etc.) gradually become (loose etc.) by constant movement. **14** *tr.* artificially excite (*worked themselves into a rage*). **15** *tr.* **a** purchase with one's labour instead of money (*work one's passage*). **b** obtain by labour the money for (one's way through university etc.). **16** *intr.* (foll. by *on*, *upon*) have influence. **17** *intr.* be in motion or agitated; cause agitation, ferment (*his features worked violently*; *the yeast began to work*). □ **at work** in action or engaged in work. **have one's work cut out** be faced with a hard task. **set to work** begin or cause to begin operations. **work away** (or **on**) continue to work. **work-basket** (or **-bag** etc.) a basket or bag etc. containing sewing materials. **work in** find a place for. **work it** *colloq.* bring it about; achieve a desired result. **work of art** a fine picture, poem, or building etc. **work off** get rid of by work or activity. **work out 1** solve (a sum) or find out (an amount) by calculation. **2** (foll. by *at*) be calculated (*the total works out at 230*). **3** give a definite result (*this sum will not work out*). **4** have a specified result (*the plan worked out well*). **5** provide for the details of (*has worked out a scheme*). **6** accomplish or attain with difficulty (*work out one's salvation*). **7** exhaust with work (*the mine is worked out*). **8** engage in physical exercise or training. **work over 1** examine thoroughly. **2** *colloq.* treat with violence. **work table** a table for working at, esp. with a sewing-machine. **work to rule** (esp. as a form of industrial action) follow official working rules exactly in order to reduce output and efficiency. **work-to-rule** the act or an instance of working to rule. **work up 1** bring gradually to an efficient state. **2** (foll. by *to*) advance gradually to a climax. **3** elaborate or excite by degrees. **4** learn (a subject) by study. **work one's will** (foll. by *on*, *upon*) *archaic* accomplish one's purpose on (a person or thing). **work wonders** see WONDER. □ **workless** *adj.* [OE *weorc* etc. f. Gmc]

workable /ˈwɜːkəb(ə)l/ *adj.* **1** that can be worked or will work. **2** that is worth working; practicable, feasible (*a workable quarry*; *a workable scheme*). □ **workability** (/-ˈbɪlɪtɪ/) *n.* **workableness** *n.* **workably** *adv.*

workaday /ˈwɜːkədeɪ/ *adj.* ordinary, everyday, practical.

workaholic /ˌwɜːkəˈhɒlɪk/ *n. colloq.* a person addicted to working.

workbench /ˈwɜːkbentʃ/ *n.* a bench for doing mechanical or practical work, esp. carpentry.

workbox /ˈwɜːkbɒks/ *n.* a box for holding tools, materials for sewing, etc.

worker /ˈwɜːkə(r)/ *n.* **1** a person who works, esp. a manual or industrial employee. **2** a neuter or undeveloped female of various social insects, esp. a bee or ant, that does the basic work of its colony.

workforce /ˈwɜːkfɔːs/ *n.* **1** the workers engaged or available in an industry etc. **2** the number of such workers.

workhorse /ˈwɜːkhɔːs/ *n.* a horse, person, or machine that performs hard work.

workhouse /ˈwɜːkhaʊs/ *n.* **1** *Brit. hist.* a public institution in which the destitute of a parish received board and lodging in return for work done. **2** *US* a house of correction for petty offenders.

working /ˈwɜːkɪŋ/ *adj. & n.* —*adj.* **1** engaged in work, esp. in manual or industrial labour. **2** functioning or able to function. —*n.* **1** the activity of work. **2** the act or manner of functioning of a thing. **3 a** a mine or quarry. **b** the part of this in which work is being or has been done (*a disused working*). □ **working capital** the capital actually used in a business. **working class** the class of people who are employed for wages, esp. in manual or industrial work. **working-class** *adj.* of the working class. **working day** esp. *Brit.* **1** a day on which work is done. **2** the part of the day devoted to work. **working drawing** a drawing to scale, serving as a guide for construction or manufacture. **working hours** hours normally devoted to work. **working hypothesis** a hypothesis used as a basis for action. **working knowledge** knowledge adequate to work with. **working lunch** etc. a meal at which business is conducted. **working order** the condition in which a machine works (satisfactorily or as specified). **working-out 1** the calculation of results. **2** the elaboration of details. **working party** a group of people appointed to study a particular problem or advise on some question.

workload /ˈwɜːkləʊd/ *n.* the amount of work to be done by an individual etc.

workman /ˈwɜːkmən/ *n.* (*pl.* **-men**) **1** a man employed to do manual labour. **2** a person considered with regard to skill in a job (*a good workman*).

workmanlike /ˈwɜːkmənˌlaɪk/ *adj.* characteristic of a good workman; showing practised skill.

workmanship /ˈwɜːkmənʃɪp/ *n.* the degree of skill in doing a task or of finish in the product made.

workmate /ˈwɜːkmeɪt/ *n.* a person engaged in the same place and type of work as another.

workout /ˈwɜːkaʊt/ *n.* a session of physical exercise.

workplace /ˈwɜːkpleɪs/ *n.* a place at which a person works; an office, factory, etc.

workshop /ˈwɜːkʃɒp/ *n.* **1** a room or building in which goods are manufactured. **2** a meeting for concerted study (*a dance workshop*).

workstation /ˈwɜːkˌsteɪʃ(ə)n/ *n.* **1** the location of a stage in a manufacturing process. **2** a computer terminal or the desk etc. where this is located.

worktop /ˈwɜːktɒp/ *n.* a flat surface for working on.

world /wɜːld/ *n.* **1 a** the earth, or a planetary body like it. **b** its countries and their inhabitants. **c** all people. **2 a** the universe or all that exists; everything. **b** everything that exists outside oneself (*dead to the world*). **3 a** the time, state, or scene of human existence. **b** (prec. by *the*, *this*) mortal life. **4** secular interests and affairs. **5** human affairs; active life (*how goes the world with you?*). **6** average, respectable, or fashionable people or their customs or opinions. **7** all that concerns or all who belong to a specified class, time, domain, or sphere of activity (*the medieval world*; *the world of sport*). **8** (foll. by *of*) a vast amount (*that makes a world of difference*). **9** (*attrib.*) affecting many nations, of all nations (*world politics*; *a world champion*). □ **bring into the**

world give birth to or attend at the birth of. **come into the world** be born. **for all the world** (foll. by *like*, *as if*) precisely (*looked for all the world as if they were real*). **get the best of both worlds** benefit from two incompatible sets of ideas, circumstances, etc. **in the world** of all; at all (used as an intensifier in questions) (*what in the world is it?*). **man** (or **woman**) **of the world** a person experienced and practical in human affairs. **the next** (or **other**) **world** a supposed life after death. **out of this world** *colloq.* extremely good etc. (*the food was out of this world*). **see the world** travel widely; gain wide experience. **think the world of** have a very high regard for. **World Cup** a competition between football or other sporting teams from various countries. **world-famous** known throughout the world. **the** (or **all the**) **world over** throughout the world. **world power** a nation having power and influence in world affairs. **World Series** the US championship for baseball teams. **world war** a war involving many important nations (*First World War* of 1914–18; *Second World War* of 1939–45). **world-weariness** being world-weary. **world-weary** weary of the world and life in it. **world without end** for ever. [OE *w(e)orold*, *world* f. a Gmc root meaning 'age': rel. to OLD]

worldling /ˈwɜːldlɪŋ/ n. a worldly person.

worldly /ˈwɜːldlɪ/ adj. (**worldlier**, **worldliest**) **1** temporal or earthly (*worldly goods*). **2** engrossed in temporal affairs, esp. the pursuit of wealth and pleasure. □ **worldly wisdom** prudence as regards one's own interests. **worldly-wise** having worldly wisdom. □ **worldliness** n. [OE *woruldlic* (as WORLD, -LY¹)]

worldwide /ˈwɜːldwaɪd, -ˈwaɪd/ adj. & adv. —adj. affecting, occurring in, or known in all parts of the world. —adv. throughout the world.

worm /wɜːm/ n. & v. —n. **1** any of various types of creeping or burrowing invertebrate animals with long slender bodies and no limbs. **2** the long slender larva of an insect. **3** (in *pl.*) intestinal or other internal parasites. **4** a blindworm or slow-worm. **5** a maggot supposed to eat dead bodies in the grave. **6** an insignificant or contemptible person. —v. **1** *intr.* & *tr.* (often *refl.*) move with a crawling motion. **2** *intr.* & *refl.* (foll. by *into*) insinuate oneself into a person's favour, confidence, etc. **3** *tr.* (foll. by *out*) obtain (a secret etc.) by cunning persistence (*managed to worm the truth out of them*). **4** *tr.* rid (a plant or dog etc.) of worms. □ **worm-cast** a convoluted mass of earth left on the surface by a burrowing earthworm. **worm-hole** a hole left by the passage of a worm. **worm's-eye view** a view as seen from below or from a humble position. **a** (or **even a**) **worm will turn** the meekest will resist or retaliate if pushed too far. □ **wormer** n. **wormlike** adj. [OE *wyrm* f. Gmc]

wormeaten /ˈwɜːmˌiːt(ə)n/ adj. **1** eaten into by worms. **2** rotten, decayed.

wormwood /ˈwɜːmwʊd/ n. any woody shrub of the genus *Artemisia*, with a bitter aromatic taste. [ME, alt. f. obs. *wormod* f. OE *wormōd*, *wermōd*, after *worm*, *wood*: cf. VERMOUTH]

wormy /ˈwɜːmɪ/ adj. (**wormier**, **wormiest**) **1** full of worms. **2** wormeaten. □ **worminess** n.

worn /wɔːn/ *past part.* of WEAR¹. —adj. **1** damaged by use or wear. **2** looking tired and exhausted. **3** (in full **well-worn**) (of a joke etc.) stale; often heard.

worriment /ˈwʌrɪmənt/ n. esp. *US* **1** the act of worrying or state of being worried. **2** a cause of worry.

worrisome /ˈwʌrɪsəm/ adj. causing or apt to cause worry or distress. □ **worrisomely** adv.

worry /ˈwʌrɪ/ v. & n. —v. (**-ies**, **-ied**) **1** *intr.* give way to anxiety or unease; allow one's mind to dwell on difficulty or troubles. **2** *tr.* harass, importune; be a trouble or anxiety to. **3** *tr.* (of a dog etc.) shake or pull about with the teeth. **4** (as **worried** adj.) **a** uneasy, troubled in the mind. **b** suggesting worry (*a worried look*). —n. (pl. **-ies**) **1** a thing that causes anxiety or disturbs a person's tranquillity. **2** a disturbed state of mind. □ **not to worry** *colloq.* there is no need to worry. **worry beads** a string of beads manipulated with the fingers to occupy or calm oneself. **worry oneself** (usu. in *neg.*) take needless trouble. □ **worriedly** adv. **worrier** n. **worryingly** adv. [OE *wyrgan* strangle f. WG]

worse /wɜːs/ adj., adv., & n. —adj. **1** more bad. **2** (*predic.*) in or into worse health or a worse condition (*is getting worse*; *is none the worse for it*). —adv. more badly or more ill. —n. **1** a worse thing or things (*you might do worse than accept*). **2** (*prec.* by *the*) a worse condition (*a change for the worse*). □ **none the worse** (often foll. by *for*) not adversely affected (by). **or worse** or as an even worse alternative. **the worse for drink** fairly drunk. **the worse for wear 1** damaged by use. **2** injured. **worse off** in a worse (esp. financial) position. [OE *wyrsa*, *wiersa* f. Gmc]

worsen /ˈwɜːs(ə)n/ v.tr. & intr. make or become worse.

worship /ˈwɜːʃɪp/ n. & v. —n. **1 a** homage or reverence paid to a deity, esp. in a formal service. **b** the acts, rites, or ceremonies of worship. **2** adoration or devotion shown towards a person or principle (*the worship of wealth*; *regarded them with worship in their eyes*). —v. (**worshipped**, **worshipping**; *US* **worshiped**, **worshiping**) **1** *tr.* adore as divine; honour with religious rites. **2** *tr.* idolize or regard with adoration (*worships the ground she walks on*). **3** *intr.* attend public worship. **4** *intr.* be full of adoration. □ **Your** (or **His** or **Her**) **Worship** esp. *Brit.* a title of respect used to or of a mayor, certain magistrates, etc. □ **worshipper** n. (*US* **worshiper**). [OE *weorthscipe* (as WORTH, -SHIP)]

worshipful /ˈwɜːʃɪpfʊl/ adj. (usu. **Worshipful**) *Brit.* a title given to justices of the peace and to certain old companies or their officers etc. □ **worshipfully** adv. **worshipfulness** n.

worst /wɜːst/ adj., adv., n., & v. —adj. most bad. —adv. most badly. —n. the worst part, event, circumstance, or possibility (*the worst of the storm is over*; *prepare for the worst*). —v.tr. get the better of; defeat, outdo. □ **at its** etc. **worst** in the worst state. **at worst** (or **the worst**) in the worst possible case. **do your worst** an expression of defiance. **get** (or **have**) **the worst of it** be defeated. **if the worst comes to the worst** if the worst happens. [OE *wierresta*, *wyrresta* (adj.), *wyrst*, *wyrrest* (adv.), f. Gmc]

worsted /ˈwʊstɪd/ n. **1** a fine smooth yarn spun from combed long staple wool. **2** fabric made from this. [*Worste(a)d* in S. England]

worth /wɜːθ/ adj. & n. —*predic.adj.* (governing a noun like a preposition) **1** of a value equivalent to (*is worth £50; is worth very little*). **2** such as to justify or repay; deserving; bringing compensation for (*worth doing; not worth the trouble*). **3** possessing or having property amounting to (*is worth a million pounds*). —*n.* **1** what a person or thing is worth; the (usu. specified) merit of (*of great worth; persons of worth*). **2** the equivalent of money in a commodity (*ten pounds' worth of petrol*). □ **for all one is worth** *colloq.* with one's utmost efforts; without reserve. **for what it is worth** without a guarantee of its truth or value. **worth it** *colloq.* worth the time or effort spent. [OE *w(e)orth*]

worthless /ˈwɜːθlɪs/ *adj.* without value or merit. □ **worthlessly** *adv.* **worthlessness** *n.*

worthwhile /ˈwɜːθˈwaɪl, -ˈwaɪl/ *adj.* that is worth the time or effort spent; of value or importance. □ **worthwhileness** *n.*

worthy /ˈwɜːðɪ/ *adj.* & *n.* —*adj.* (**worthier, worthiest**) **1** estimable; having some moral worth; deserving respect (*lived a worthy life*). **2** (of a person) entitled to (esp. condescending) recognition (*a worthy old couple*). **3 a** (foll. by *of* or *to* + infin.) deserving (*worthy of a mention; worthy to be remembered*). **b** (foll. by *of*) adequate or suitable to the dignity etc. of (*in words worthy of the occasion*). —*n.* (*pl.* **-ies**) **1** a worthy person. **2** a person of some distinction. □ **worthily** *adv.* **worthiness** *n.* [ME *wurthi* etc. f. WORTH]

-worthy /ˈwɜːðɪ/ *comb. form* forming adjectives meaning: **1** deserving of (*blameworthy; noteworthy*). **2** suitable or fit for (*newsworthy; roadworthy*).

would /wʊd, wəd/ *v.aux.* (3rd sing. **would**) past of WILL¹, used esp.: **1** (in the 2nd and 3rd persons, and often in the 1st: see SHOULD). **a** in reported speech (*he said he would be home by evening*). **b** to express the conditional mood (*they would have been killed if they had gone*). **2** to express habitual action (*would wait for her every evening*). **3** to express a question or polite request (*would they like it?; would you come in, please?*). **4** to express probability (*I guess she would be over fifty by now*). **5** (foll. by *that* + clause) *literary* to express a wish (*would that you were here*). **6** to express consent (*they would not help*). □ **would-be** often *derog.* desiring or aspiring to be (*a would-be politician*). [OE *wolde*, past of *wyllan*: see WILL¹]

wouldn't /ˈwʊd(ə)nt/ *contr.* would not. □ **I wouldn't know** *colloq.* (as is to be expected) I do not know.

wound¹ /wuːnd/ *n.* & *v.* —*n.* **1** an injury done to living tissue by a cut or blow etc., esp. beyond the cutting or piercing of the skin. **2** an injury to a person's reputation or a pain inflicted on a person's feelings. —*v.tr.* inflict a wound on (*wounded soldiers; wounded feelings*). □ **woundingly** *adv.* **woundless** *adj.* [OE *wund* (n.), *wundian* (v.)]

wound² *past* and *past part.* of WIND² (cf. WIND¹ v. 5).

wove¹ *past* of WEAVE¹.

wove² *adj.* (of paper) made on a wire-gauze mesh and so having a uniform unlined surface. [var. of *woven*, past part. of WEAVE¹.]

woven *past part.* of WEAVE¹.

wow *int., n.,* & *v.* —*int.* expressing astonishment or admiration. —*n. sl.* a sensational success. —*v.tr. sl.* impress or excite greatly. [orig. Sc.: imit.]

WP *abbr.* word processor or processing.

WPC *abbr.* (in the UK) woman police constable.

w.p.m. *abbr.* words per minute.

WRAC *abbr.* (in the UK) Women's Royal Army Corps.

wrack /ræk/ *n.* **1** seaweed cast up or growing on the shore. **2** destruction. **3** a wreck or wreckage. [ME f. MDu. *wrak* or MLG *wra(c)k*, a parallel formation to OE *wræc*, rel. to *wrecan* WREAK: cf. WRECK]

WRAF *abbr.* (in the UK) Women's Royal Air Force.

wrangle /ˈræŋg(ə)l/ *n.* & *v.* —*n.* a noisy argument, altercation, or dispute. —*v. intr.* engage in a wrangle. [ME, prob. f. LG or Du.: cf. LG *wrangelen*, frequent. of *wrangen* to struggle, rel. to WRING]

wrangler /ˈræŋglə(r)/ *n.* **1** a person who wrangles. **2** *US* a cowboy. **3** (at Cambridge University) a person placed in the first class of the mathematical tripos.

wrap /ræp/ *v.* & *n.* —*v.tr.* (**wrapped, wrapping**) **1** (often foll. by *up*) envelop in folded or soft encircling material (*wrap it up in paper; wrap up a parcel*). **2** (foll. by *round, about*) arrange or draw (a pliant covering) round (a person) (*wrapped the scarf closer around me*). —*n.* **1** a shawl or scarf or other such addition to clothing; a wrapper. **2** esp. *US* material used for wrapping. □ **take the wraps off** disclose. **under wraps** in secrecy.

wrap-over *adj.* (*attrib.*) (of a garment) having no seam at one side but wrapped around the body and fastened. **wrapped up in** engrossed or absorbed in. **wrap up 1** finish off, bring to completion (*wrapped up the deal in two days*). **2** put on warm clothes (*mind you wrap up well*). **3** (in *imper.*) *sl.* be quiet. [ME: orig. unkn.]

wraparound /ˈræpəˌraʊnd/ *adj.* & *n.* (also **wrapround** /ˈræpraʊnd/) —*adj.* (esp. of clothing) designed to wrap round. —*n.* anything that wraps round.

wrapper /ˈræpə(r)/ *n.* **1** a cover for a sweet, chocolate, etc. **2** a cover enclosing a newspaper or similar packet for posting.

wrapping /ˈræpɪŋ/ *n.* (esp. in *pl.*) material used to wrap; wraps, wrappers. □ **wrapping paper** strong or decorative paper for wrapping parcels.

wrasse /ræs/ *n.* any bright-coloured marine fish of the family Labridae. [Corn. *wrach*, var. of *gwrach*, = Welsh *gwrach*, lit. 'old woman']

wrath /rɒθ, rɔːθ/ *n. literary* extreme anger. [OE *wræththu* f. *wrāth* angry]

wrathful /ˈrɒθfʊl/ *adj. literary* extremely angry. □ **wrathfully** *adv.* **wrathfulness** *n.*

wreak /riːk/ *v.tr.* **1** (usu. foll. by *upon*) give play or satisfaction to; put in operation (*vengeance or one's anger etc.*). **2** cause (damage etc.) (*the hurricane wreaked havoc on the crops*). □ **wreaker** *n.* [OE *wrecan* drive, avenge, etc., f. Gmc: cf. WRACK, WRECK, WRETCH]

wreath /riːθ/ *n.* (*pl.* **wreaths** /riːðz, riːθs/) **1** flowers or leaves fastened in a ring esp. as an ornament for a person's head or a building or for laying on a grave etc. as a mark of honour or respect. **2** a carved representation of a wreath. **3** (foll. by *of*) a curl or ring of smoke or cloud. [OE *writha* f. weak grade of *writhan* WRITHE]

wreathe /riːð/ *v.* **1** *tr.* encircle as, with, or like a wreath. **2** *tr.* (foll. by *round*) put (one's arms etc.) round (a person etc.). **3** *intr.* (of smoke etc.) move in the shape of wreaths. [partly back-form. f. archaic *wrethen* past part. of WRITHE; partly f. WREATH]

wreck /rek/ *n. & v.* —*n.* **1** the destruction or disablement esp. of a ship. **2** a ship that has suffered a wreck (*the shores are strewn with wrecks*). **3** a greatly damaged or disabled building, thing, or person. **4** *Law* goods etc. cast up by the sea. —*v.* **1** *tr.* cause the wreck of (a ship etc.). **2** *tr.* completely ruin (hopes, chances, etc.). **3** *tr.* (as **wrecked** *adj.*) involved in a shipwreck (*wrecked sailors*). [ME f. AF *wrec* etc. f. a Gmc root meaning 'to drive': cf. WREAK]

wreckage /'rekɪdʒ/ *n.* **1** wrecked material. **2** the remnants of a wreck. **3** the action or process of wrecking.

Wren /ren/ *n.* (in the UK) a member of the Women's Royal Naval Service. [orig. in pl., f. abbr. WRNS]

wren /ren/ *n.* any small short-winged songbird of the family Troglodytidae, esp. *Troglodytes troglodytes* of Europe. [OE *wrenna*, rel. to OHG *wrendo*, *wrendilo*, Icel. *rindill*]

wrench /rentʃ/ *n. & v.* —*n.* **1** a violent twist or oblique pull or act of tearing off. **2** an adjustable tool like a spanner for gripping and turning nuts etc. **3** an instance of painful uprooting or parting (*leaving home was a great wrench*). —*v.tr.* **1** twist or pull violently round or sideways. **2** (often foll. by *off*, *away*, etc.) pull off with a wrench. **3** distort (facts) to suit a theory etc. [(earlier as verb:) OE *wrencan* twist]

wrest /rest/ *v.tr.* **1** force or wrench away from a person's grasp. **2** (foll. by *from*) obtain by effort or with difficulty. [OE *wrǣstan* f. Gmc, rel. to WRIST]

wrestle /'res(ə)l/ *n. & v.* —*n.* a contest in which two opponents grapple and try to throw each other to the ground. —*v.* **1** *intr.* (often foll. by *with*) take part in a wrestle. **2** *tr.* fight (a person) in a wrestle (*wrestled his opponent to the ground*). **3** *intr.* (foll. by *with*, *against*) struggle, contend. □ **wrestler** *n.* **wrestling** *n.* [OE (unrecorded) *wrǣstlian*: cf. MLG *wrostelen*, OE *wraxlian*]

wretch /retʃ/ *n.* **1** an unfortunate or pitiable person. **2** (often as a playful term of depreciation) a reprehensible or contemptible person. [OE *wrecca* f. Gmc]

wretched /'retʃɪd/ *adj.* (**wretcheder**, **wretchedest**) **1** unhappy or miserable. **2** of bad quality or no merit; contemptible. □ **feel wretched 1** be unwell. **2** be much embarrassed. □ **wretchedly** *adv.* **wretchedness** *n.* [ME, irreg. f. WRETCH + -ED¹: cf. WICKED]

wriggle /'rɪg(ə)l/ *v. & n.* —*v.* **1** *intr.* (of a worm etc.) twist or turn its body with short writhing movements. **2** *intr.* (of a person or animal) make wriggling motions. **3** *tr. & intr.* (foll. by *along* etc.) move or go in this way (*wriggled into the corner*; *wriggled his hand into the hole*). **4** *intr.* practise evasion. —*n.* an act of wriggling. □ **wriggle out of** *colloq.* avoid on a pretext. □ **wriggler** *n.* **wriggly** *adj.* [ME f. MLG *wriggelen* frequent. of *wriggen*]

wring /rɪŋ/ *v. & n.* —*v.tr.* (*past* and *past part.* **wrung** /rʌŋ/) **1 a** squeeze tightly. **b** (often foll. by *out*) squeeze and twist esp. to remove liquid. **2** twist forcibly; break by twisting. **3** distress or torture. **4** extract by squeezing. **5** (foll. by *out*, *from*) obtain by pressure or importunity; extort. —*n.* an act of wringing; a squeeze. □ **wring a person's hand** clasp it forcibly or press it with emotion. **wring one's hands** clasp them as a gesture of great distress. [OE *wringan*, rel. to WRONG]

wringer /'rɪŋə(r)/ *n.* a device for wringing water from washed clothes etc.

wringing /'rɪŋɪŋ/ *adj.* (in full **wringing wet**) so wet that water can be wrung out.

wrinkle /'rɪŋk(ə)l/ *n. & v.* —*n.* **1** a slight crease or depression in the skin such as is produced by age. **2** a similar mark in another flexible surface. —*v.* **1** *tr.* make wrinkles in. **2** *intr.* form wrinkles; become marked with wrinkles. [orig. repr. OE *gewrinclod* sinuous]

wrinkly /'rɪŋklɪ/ *adj.* & *n.* —*adj.* (**wrinklier**, **wrinkliest**) having many wrinkles. —*n.* (also **wrinklie**) (*pl.* -**ies**) *sl. offens.* an old or middle-aged person.

wrist /rɪst/ *n.* **1** the part connecting the hand with the forearm. **2** the part of a garment covering the wrist. □ **wrist-watch** a small watch worn on a strap round the wrist. [OE f. Gmc, prob. f. a root rel. to WRITHE]

wristband /'rɪstbænd/ *n.* a band forming or concealing the end of a shirt-sleeve.

wristlet /'rɪstlɪt/ *n.* a band or ring worn on the wrist to strengthen or guard it or as an ornament, bracelet, handcuff, etc.

writ¹ /rɪt/ *n.* a form of written command in the name of a sovereign, court, State, etc., to act or abstain from acting in some way. □ **serve a writ on** deliver a writ to (a person). [OE (as WRITE)]

writ² /rɪt/ *archaic past part.* of WRITE. □ **writ large** in magnified or emphasized form.

write /raɪt/ *v.* (*past* **wrote** /rəʊt/; *past part.* **written** /'rɪt(ə)n/) **1** *intr.* mark paper or some other surface by means of a pen, pencil, etc., with symbols, letters, or words. **2** *tr.* form or mark (such symbols etc.). **3** *tr.* form or mark the symbols that represent or constitute (a word or sentence, or a document etc.). **4** *tr.* fill or complete (a sheet, cheque, etc.) with writing. **5** *tr.* put (data) into a computer store. **6** *tr.* (esp. in *passive*) indicate (a quality or condition) by one's or its appearance (*guilt was written on his face*). **7** *tr.* compose (a text, article, novel, etc.) for written or printed reproduction or publication; put into literary etc. form and set down in writing. **8** *intr.* be engaged in composing a text, article, etc. (*writes for the local newspaper*). **9** *intr.* (foll. by *to*) write and send a letter (to a recipient). **10** *tr.* *US* or *colloq.* write and send a letter to (a person) (*wrote him last week*). **11** *tr.* convey (news, information, etc.) by letter (*wrote that they would arrive next Friday*). □ **nothing to write home about** *colloq.* of little interest or value. **write down 1** record or take note of in writing. **2** write and send a letter. **3** disparage in writing. **4** reduce the nominal value of (stock, goods, etc.). **write in** send a suggestion, query, etc., in writing to an organization, esp. a broadcasting station. **write off 1** write and send a letter. **2** cancel the record of (a bad debt etc.); acknowledge the loss of or failure to recover (an asset). **3** damage (a vehicle etc.) so badly that it cannot be repaired. **write-off** *n.* a thing written off, esp. a vehicle too badly damaged to be repaired. **write out** write in full or in finished form. **write up 1** write a full account of. **2** make entries to bring (a diary etc.) up to date. **write-up** *n.* *colloq.* a written or published account, a review. □

writable *adj.* [OE *wrītan* scratch, score, write, f. Gmc: orig. used of symbols inscribed with sharp tools on stone or wood]

writer /ˈraɪtə(r)/ *n.* **1** a person who writes or has written something. **2** a person who writes books; an author. □ **writer's cramp** a muscular spasm due to excessive writing. [OE *wrītere* (as WRITE)]

writhe /raɪð/ *v. & n.* —*v.* **1** *intr.* twist or roll oneself about in or as if in acute pain. **2** *intr.* suffer severe mental discomfort or embarrassment. —*n.* an act of writhing. [OE *wrīthan*, rel. to WREATHE]

writing /ˈraɪtɪŋ/ *n.* **1** a group or sequence of letters or symbols. **2** = HANDWRITING. **3** (usu. in *pl.*) a piece of literary work done; a book, article, etc. □ **in writing** in written form. **writing-pad** a pad (see PAD¹ *n.* 2) of paper for writing on. **writing-paper** paper for writing (esp. letters) on.

written *past part.* of WRITE.

WRNS *abbr.* (in the UK) Women's Royal Naval Service.

wrong /rɒŋ/ *adj., adv., n., & v.* —*adj.* **1** mistaken; not true; in error (*gave a wrong answer; we were wrong to think that*). **2** unsuitable; less or least desirable (*the wrong road; a wrong decision*). **3** contrary to law or morality (*it is wrong to steal*). **4** amiss; out of order (*something wrong with my heart; my watch has gone wrong*). —*adv.* (usually placed last) in a wrong manner or direction; with an incorrect result (*guessed wrong; told them wrong*). —*n.* **1** what is morally wrong; a wrong action. **2** injustice; unjust action or treatment (*suffer wrong*). —*v.tr.* treat unjustly; do wrong to. □ **get on the wrong side of** fall into disfavour with. **get wrong** misunderstand (a person, statement, etc.). **get** (or **get hold of**) **the wrong end of the stick** misunderstand completely. **go wrong 1** take the wrong path. **2** stop functioning properly. **3** depart from virtuous or suitable behaviour. **in the wrong** responsible for a quarrel, mistake, or offence. **on the wrong side of 1** out of favour with (a person). **2** somewhat more than (a stated age). **wrong-foot** *colloq.* **1** (in tennis, football, etc.) play so as to catch (an opponent) off balance. **2** disconcert; catch unprepared. **wrong-headed** perverse and obstinate. **wrong-headedly** in a wrong-headed manner. **wrong-headedness** the state of being wrong-headed. **wrong side** the worse or undesired or unusable side of something, esp. fabric. **wrong way round** in the opposite or reverse of the normal or desirable orientation or sequence etc. □ **wronger** *n.* **wrongly** *adv.* **wrongness** *n.* [OE *wrang* f. ON *rangr* awry, unjust, rel. to WRING]

wrongdoer /ˈrɒŋˌduːə(r)/ *n.* a person who behaves immorally or illegally. □ **wrongdoing** *n.*

wrongful /ˈrɒŋfʊl/ *adj.* **1** characterized by unfairness or injustice. **2** contrary to law. **3** (of a person) not entitled to the position etc. occupied. □ **wrongfully** *adv.* **wrongfulness** *n.*

wrote *past* of WRITE.

wrought /rɔːt/ *archaic past* and *past part.* of WORK. —*adj.* (of metals) beaten out or shaped by hammering. □ **wrought iron** a tough malleable form of iron suitable for forging or rolling, not cast.

wrung *past* and *past part.* of WRING.

WRVS *abbr.* (in the UK) Women's Royal Voluntary Service.

wry /raɪ/ *adj.* (**wryer, wryest** or **wrier, wriest**) **1** distorted or turned to one side. **2** (of a face or smile etc.) contorted in disgust, disappointment, or mockery. **3** (of humour) dry and mocking. □ **wryly** *adv.* **wryness** *n.* [wry (v.) f. OE *wrīgian* tend, incline, in ME deviate, swerve, contort]

WSW *abbr.* west-south-west.

wt. *abbr.* weight.

wych-elm /ˈwɪtʃelm/ *n.* a species of elm, *Ulmus glabra.*

WYSIWYG /ˈwɪzɪwɪg/ *adj.* (also **wysiwyg**) *Computing* denoting the representation of text on-screen in a form exactly corresponding to its appearance on a printout. [acronym of *what you see is what you get*]

Xx

X[1] /eks/ *n.* (also **x**) (*pl.* **Xs** or **X's**) **1** the twenty-fourth letter of the alphabet. **2** (as a Roman numeral) ten. **3** (usu. **x**) *Algebra* the first unknown quantity. **4** *Geom.* the first coordinate. **5** an unknown or unspecified number or person etc. **6** a cross-shaped symbol esp. used to indicate position (*X marks the spot*) or incorrectness or to symbolize a kiss or a vote, or as the signature of a person who cannot write.

X[2] *symb.* (of films) classified as suitable for adults only.

■ **Usage** This symbol was superseded in the UK in 1983 by **18**, but it is still used in the US.

-x /z/ *suffix* forming the plural of many nouns in *-u* taken from French (*beaux*; *tableaux*). [F]

X-chromosome /ˈeksˌkrəʊməˌsəʊm/ *n.* a sex chromosome of which the number in female cells is twice that in male cells. [X as an arbitrary label + CHROMOSOME]

Xe *symb. Chem.* the element xenon.

xeno- /ˈzenəʊ/ *comb. form* **1 a** foreign. **b** a foreigner. **2** other. [Gk *xenos* strange, foreign, stranger]

xenolith /ˈzenəlɪθ/ *n. Geol.* an inclusion within an igneous rock mass, usu. derived from the immediately surrounding rock.

xenon /ˈzenɒn/ *n. Chem.* a heavy colourless odourless inert gaseous element occurring in traces in the atmosphere and used in fluorescent lamps. [Gk, neut. of *xenos* strange]

xenophobe /ˈzenəˌfəʊb/ *n.* a person given to xenophobia.

xenophobia /ˌzenəˈfəʊbɪə/ *n.* a deep dislike of foreigners. □ **xenophobic** *adj.*

xeranthemum /zɪəˈrænθɪməm/ *n.* a composite plant of the genus *Xeranthemum*, with dry everlasting composite flowers. [mod.L f. Gk *xēros* dry + *anthemon* flower]

xero- /ˈzɪərəʊ, ˈzerəʊ/ *comb. form* dry. [Gk *xēros* dry]

xeroderma /ˌzɪərəˈdɜːmə/ *n.* any of various diseases characterized by extreme dryness of the skin, esp. ichthyosis. [mod.L (as XERO-, Gk *derma* skin)]

xerograph /ˈzɪərəˌɡrɑːf, ˈze-/ *n.* a copy produced by xerography.

xerography /zɪəˈrɒɡrəfɪ, ze-/ *n.* a dry copying process in which black or coloured powder adheres to parts of a surface remaining electrically charged after exposure of the surface to light from an image of the document to be copied. □ **xerographic** /-rəˈɡræfɪk/ *adj.* **xerographically** /-rəˈɡræfɪkəlɪ/ *adv.*

xerophilous /zɪəˈrɒfɪləs, ze-/ *adj.* (of a plant) adapted to extremely dry conditions.

xerophyte /ˈzɪərəˌfaɪt, ˈze-/ *n.* (also **xerophile** /-ˌfaɪl/) a plant able to grow in very dry conditions, e.g. in a desert.

Xerox /ˈzɪərɒks, ˈze-/ *n. & v. —n. propr.* **1** a machine for copying by xerography. **2** a copy made using this machine. *—v.tr.* (**xerox**) reproduce by this process. [invented f. XEROGRAPHY]

xi /saɪ, ɡzaɪ, zaɪ/ *n.* the fourteenth letter of the Greek alphabet (Ξ, ξ). [Gk]

xiphoid /ˈzɪfɔɪd/ *adj. Biol.* sword-shaped. [Gk *xiphoeidēs* f. *xiphos* sword]

Xmas /ˈkrɪsməs, ˈeksməs/ *n. colloq.* = CHRISTMAS. [abbr., with X for the initial chi of Gk *Khristos* Christ]

X-ray /ˈeksreɪ/ *n. & v.* (also **x-ray**) *—n.* **1** (in *pl.*) electromagnetic radiation of short wavelength, able to pass through opaque bodies. **2** an image made by the effect of X-rays on a photographic plate, esp. showing the position of bones etc. by their greater absorption of the rays. *—v.tr.* photograph, examine, or treat with X-rays. □ **X-ray astronomy** the branch of astronomy concerned with the X-ray emissions of celestial bodies. **X-ray crystallography** the study of crystals and their structure by means of the diffraction of X-rays by the regularly spaced atoms of a crystalline material. **X-ray tube** a device for generating X-rays by accelerating electrons to high energies and causing them to strike a metal target from which the X-rays are emitted. [transl. of G *x-Strahlen* (pl.) f. *Strahl* ray, so called because when discovered in 1895 the nature of the rays was unknown]

xylene /ˈzaɪliːn/ *n. Chem.* one of three isomeric hydrocarbons formed from benzene by the substitution of two methyl groups, obtained from wood etc. [Gk *xulon* wood + -ENE]

xylo- /ˈzaɪləʊ/ *comb. form* wood. [Gk *xulon* wood]

xylophone /ˈzaɪləˌfəʊn/ *n.* a musical instrument of wooden or metal bars graduated in length and struck with a small wooden hammer or hammers. □ **xylophonic** /-ˈfɒnɪk/ *adj.* **xylophonist** *n.* [Gk *xulon* wood + -PHONE]

Yy

Y¹ /waɪ/ n. (also **y**) (pl. **Ys** or **Y's**) **1** the twenty-fifth letter of the alphabet. **2** (usu. **y**) *Algebra* the second unknown quantity. **3** *Geom.* the second coordinate. **4** a Y-shaped thing, esp. an arrangement of lines, piping, roads, etc.

Y² *symb. Chem.* the element yttrium.

y. *abbr.* year(s).

-y¹ /ɪ/ *suffix* forming adjectives: **1** from nouns and adjectives, meaning: **a** full of; having the quality of (*messy*; *icy*; *horsy*). **b** addicted to (*boozy*). **2** from verbs, meaning 'inclined to', 'apt to' (*runny*; *sticky*). [from or after OE *-ig* f. Gmc]

-y² /ɪ/ *suffix* (also **-ey**, **-ie**) forming diminutive nouns, pet names, etc. (*granny*; *Sally*; *nightie*; *Mickey*). [ME (orig. Sc.)]

-y³ /ɪ/ *suffix* forming nouns denoting: **1** state, condition, or quality (*courtesy*; *orthodoxy*; *modesty*). **2** an action or its result (*colloquy*; *remedy*; *subsidy*). [from or after F *-ie* f. L *-ia*, *-ium*, Gk *-eia*, *-ia*: cf. -ACY, -ERY, -GRAPHY, and others]

yacht /jɒt/ n. & v. **1** a light sailing-vessel, esp. equipped for racing. **2** a larger usu. power-driven vessel equipped for cruising. **3** a light vessel for travel on sand or ice. —*v.intr.* race or cruise in a yacht. □ **yacht-club** a club esp. for yacht-racing. □ **yachting** n. [early mod.Du. *jaghte* = *jaghtschip* fast pirate-ship f. *jag(h)t* chase f. *jagen* to hunt + *schip* SHIP]

yachtsman /ˈjɒtsmən/ n. (pl. **-men**; *fem.* **yachtswoman**, pl. **-women**) a person who sails yachts.

yack n. & v. (also **yackety-yack** /ˌjækətɪˈjæk/) sl. *derog.* —n. trivial or unduly persistent conversation. —*v.intr.* engage in this. [imit.]

yaffle /ˈjæf(ə)l/ n. *dial.* a green woodpecker. [imit. of its laughing cry]

yah /jɑ:/ *int.* expressing derision or defiance. [imit.]

yahoo /jəˈhu:, jɑ:-/ n. a coarse bestial person. [name of an imaginary race of brutish creatures in Swift's *Gulliver's Travels* (1726)]

Yahweh /ˈjɑːweɪ/ n. (also **Yahveh** /-veɪ/) the Hebrew name of God in the Old Testament. [Heb. *YHVH* with added vowels: see JEHOVAH]

yak /jæk/ n. a long-haired humped Tibetan ox. [Tibetan *gyag*]

Yale lock /jeɪl/ n. *propr.* a type of lock for doors etc. with a cylindrical barrel turned by a flat key with a serrated edge. [L. *Yale*, Amer. inventor d. 1868]

yam /jæm/ n. **1 a** any tropical or subtropical climbing plant of the genus *Dioscorea*. **b** the edible starchy tuber of this. **2** *US* a sweet potato. [Port. *inhame* or Sp. *iñame*, of unkn. orig.]

yammer /ˈjæmə(r)/ n. & v. *colloq.* or *dial.* —n. **1** a lament, wail, or grumble. **2** voluble talk. —*v.intr.* **1** utter a yammer. **2** talk volubly. □ **yammerer** n. [OE *geōmrian* f. *geōmor* sorrowful]

yang n. (in Chinese philosophy) the active male principle of the universe (cf. YIN). [Chin.]

Yank n. *colloq.* often *derog.* an inhabitant of the US; an American. [abbr.]

yank v. & n. *colloq.* —*v.tr.* pull with a jerk. —n. a sudden hard pull. [19th c.: orig. unkn.]

Yankee /ˈjæŋkɪ/ n. *colloq.* **1** often *derog.* = YANK. **2** *US* an inhabitant of New England or one of the northern States. **3** *hist.* a Federal soldier in the Civil War. **4** a type of bet on four or more horses to win (or be placed) in different races. **5** (*attrib.*) of or as of the Yankees. □ **Yankee Doodle 1** an American tune and song regarded as a national air. **2** = YANKEE. [18th c.: orig. uncert.: perh. f. Du. *Janke* dimin. of *Jan* John attested (17th c.) as a nickname]

yap v. & n. —*v.intr.* (**yapped**, **yapping**) **1** bark shrilly or fussily. **2** *colloq.* talk noisily, foolishly, or complainingly. —n. a sound of yapping. □ **yapper** n. [imit.]

yarborough /ˈjɑːbərə/ n. a whist or bridge hand with no card above a 9. [Earl of *Yarborough* (d. 1897), said to have betted against its occurrence]

yard¹ n. **1** a unit of linear measure equal to 3 feet (0.9144 metre). **2** this length of material (*a yard and a half of cloth*). **3** a square or cubic yard esp. (in building) of sand etc. **4** a cylindrical spar, tapering to each end, slung across a mast for a sail to hang from. **5** (in *pl.*; foll. by *of*) *colloq.* a great length (*yards of spare wallpaper*). □ **by the yard** at great length. **yard-arm** the outer extremity of a ship's yard. **yard of ale** *Brit.* **1** a deep slender beer glass, about a yard long and holding two to three pints. **2** the contents of this. [OE *gerd* f. WG]

yard² n. **1** a piece of enclosed ground esp. attached to a building or used for a particular purpose. **2** *US* the garden of a house. □ **the Yard** *Brit. colloq.* = SCOTLAND YARD. **yard-man 1** a person working in a railway-yard or timber-yard. **2** *US* a gardener or a person who does various outdoor jobs. [OE *geard* enclosure, region, f. Gmc: cf. GARDEN]

yardage /ˈjɑːdɪdʒ/ n. **1** a number of yards of material etc. **2 a** the use of a stockyard etc. **b** payment for this.

yardstick /ˈjɑːdstɪk/ n. **1** a standard used for comparison. **2** a measuring rod a yard long, usu. divided into inches etc.

yarmulke /ˈjɑːmʊlkə/ n. (also **yarmulka**) a skullcap worn by Jewish men. [Yiddish]

yarn n. & v. —n. **1** any spun thread. **2** *colloq.* a long or rambling story or discourse. —*v.intr. colloq.* tell yarns. [OE *gearn*]

yarrow /ˈjærəʊ/ n. any perennial herb of the genus *Achillea*, esp. milfoil. [OE *gearwe*, of unkn. orig.]

yashmak /ˈjæʃmæk/ n. a veil concealing the face except the eyes, worn by some Muslim women when in public. [Arab. *yašmaḳ*, Turk. *yaşmak*]

yaw v. & n. —*v.intr.* (of a ship or aircraft etc.) fail to hold a straight course; fall off; go unsteadily (esp. turning from side to side). —n. the yawing of a ship etc. from its course. [16th c.: orig. unkn.]

yawl n. **1** a two-masted fore-and-aft sailing-boat with the mizen-mast stepped far aft. **2** a small kind of fishing-boat. [MLG *jolle* or Du. *jol*, of unkn. orig.: cf. JOLLY²]

yawn v. & n. —v. **1** *intr.* (as a reflex) open the mouth wide and inhale esp. when sleepy or bored. **2** *intr.* (of a chasm etc.) gape, be wide open. **3** *tr.* utter or say with a yawn. —n. **1** an act of yawning. **2** *colloq.* a boring or tedious idea, activity, etc. □ **yawner** n. **yawningly** adv. [OE *ginian*, *geonian*]

yaws n.pl. (usu. treated as *sing.*) a contagious tropical skin-disease with large red swellings. [17th c.: orig. unkn.]

Yb symb. Chem. the element ytterbium.

Y-chromosome /ˈwaɪˌkrəʊməˌsəʊm/ n. a sex chromosome occurring only in male cells. [Y as an arbitrary label + CHROMOSOME]

yd. abbr. yard (measure).

yds. abbr. yards (measure).

ye¹ /jiː/ pron. archaic pl. of THOU¹. □ **ye gods!** joc. an exclamation of astonishment. [OE *ge* f. Gmc]

ye² /jiː/ adj. pseudo-archaic = THE (*ye olde tea-shoppe*). [var. spelling f. the *y*-shaped letter THORN (representing *th*) in the 14th c.]

yea /jeɪ/ adv. & n. archaic —adv. **1** yes. **2** indeed, nay (*ready, yea eager*). —n. the word 'yea'. □ **yeas and nays** affirmative and negative votes. [OE *gea*, *ge* f. Gmc]

yeah /jeə/ adv. colloq. yes. □ **oh yeah?** expressing incredulity. [casual pronunc. of YES]

year /jɪə(r), jɜː(r)/ n. **1** (also **astronomical year**, **equinoctial year**, **natural year**, **solar year**, **tropical year**) the time occupied by the earth in one revolution round the sun, 365 days, 5 hours, 48 minutes, and 46 seconds in length. **2** (also **calendar year**, **civil year**) the period of 365 days (**common year**) or 366 days (see *leap year*) from 1 Jan. to 31 Dec., used for reckoning time in ordinary affairs. **3 a** a period of the same length as this starting at any point (*four years ago*). **b** such a period in terms of a particular activity etc. occupying its duration (*school year; tax year*). **4** (in pl.) age or time of life (*young for his years*). **5** (usu. in pl.) colloq. a very long time (*it took years to get served*). **6** a group of students entering college etc. in the same academic year. □ **in the year of Our Lord** (foll. by the year) in a specified year AD. **of the year** chosen as outstanding in a particular year (*sportsman of the year*). **year in, year out** continually over a period of years. **year-long** lasting a year or the whole year. **year-round** existing etc. throughout the year. [OE *gē(a)r* f. Gmc]

yearbook /ˈjɪəbʊk, ˈjɜː-/ n. an annual publication dealing with events or aspects of the (usu. preceding) year.

yearling /ˈjɪəlɪŋ, ˈjɜː-/ n. & adj. —n. **1** an animal between one and two years old. **2** a racehorse in the calendar year after the year of foaling. —adj. a year old; having existed or been such for a year (*a yearling heifer*).

yearly /ˈjɪəlɪ, ˈjɜː-/ adj. & adv. —adj. done, produced, or occurring once a year. —adv. once a year; from year to year. [OE *gēarlic*, *-lice* (as YEAR)]

yearn /jɜːn/ v.intr. **1** (usu. foll. by for, after, or to + infin.) have a strong emotional longing. **2** (usu. foll. by to, towards) be filled with compassion or tenderness. □ **yearner** n. **yearning** n. & adj. **yearningly** adv. [OE *giernan* f. a Gmc root meaning 'eager']

yeast n. **1** a greyish-yellow fungous substance obtained esp. from fermenting malt liquors and used as a fermenting agent, to raise bread, etc. **2** any of various unicellular fungi in which vegetative reproduction takes place by budding or fission. □ **yeastless** adj. **yeastlike** adj. [OE *gist*, *giest* (unrecorded): cf. MDu. *ghist*, MHG *jist*, ON *jöstr*]

yeasty /ˈjiːstɪ/ adj. (**yeastier**, **yeastiest**) **1** frothy or tasting like yeast. **2** in a ferment. **3** working like yeast. □ **yeastily** adv. **yeastiness** n.

yell n. & v. —n. **1** a loud sharp cry of pain, anger, fright, encouragement, delight, etc. **2** a shout. **3** US an organized cry, used esp. to support a sports team. —v.intr. & tr. make or utter with a yell. [OE *g(i)ellan* f. Gmc]

yellow /ˈjeləʊ/ adj., n., & v. —adj. **1** of the colour between green and orange in the spectrum, of buttercups, lemons, egg-yolks, or gold. **2** of the colour of faded leaves, ripe wheat, etc. **3** having a yellow skin or complexion. **4** colloq. cowardly. —n. **1** a yellow colour or pigment. **2** yellow clothes or material (*dressed in yellow*). **3 a** a yellow ball, piece, etc., in a game or sport. **b** the player using such pieces. **4** (usu. in comb.) a yellow moth or butterfly. —v.tr. & intr. make or become yellow. □ **yellow-belly 1** colloq. a coward. **2** any of various fish with yellow underparts. **yellow card** Football a card shown by the referee to a player being cautioned. **yellow fever** a tropical virus disease with fever and jaundice. **yellow line** (in the UK) a line painted along the side of the road in yellow, either singly or in pairs, to denote parking restrictions. **Yellow Pages** propr. a section of a telephone directory on yellow paper and listing business subscribers according to the goods or services they offer. □ **yellowish** adj. **yellowly** adv. **yellowness** n. **yellowy** adj. [OE *geolu*, *geolo* f. WG, rel. to GOLD]

yellowhammer /ˈjeləʊˌhæmə(r)/ n. a bunting, of which the male has a yellow head, neck, and breast. [16th c.: orig. of *hammer* uncert.]

yelp n. & v. —n. a sharp shrill cry of or as of a dog in pain or excitement. —v.intr. utter a yelp. □ **yelper** n. [OE *gielp(an)* boast (imit.)]

yen¹ n. (pl. same) the chief monetary unit of Japan. [Jap. f. Chin. *yuan* round, dollar]

yen² n. & v. colloq. —n. a longing or yearning. —v.intr. (**yenned**, **yenning**) feel a longing. [Chin. dial.]

yeoman /ˈjəʊmən/ n. (pl. **-men**) **1** esp. hist. a man holding and cultivating a small landed estate. **2** hist. a person qualified by possessing free land of an annual value of 40 shillings to serve on juries, vote for the knight of the shire, etc. **3** Brit. a member of the yeomanry force. **4** hist. a servant in a royal or noble household. **5** (in full **yeoman of signals**) a petty officer in the Navy, concerned with visual signalling. **6** US a petty officer performing clerical duties on board ship. □ **Yeoman of the Guard 1** a member of the British sovereign's bodyguard. **2** (in general use) a warder in the Tower of London. □ **yeomanly** adj. [ME *yoman*, *yeman*, etc., prob. f. YOUNG + MAN]

yeomanry /ˈjəʊmənrɪ/ n. (pl. **-ies**) a body of yeomen.

yep *adv. & n.* (also **yup** /jʌp/) *US colloq.* = YES. [corrupt.]

yes *adv. & n.* —*adv.* **1** equivalent to an affirmative sentence: the answer to your question is affirmative, it is as you say or as I have said, the statement etc. made is correct, the request or command will be complied with, the negative statement etc. made is not correct. **2** (in answer to a summons or address) an acknowledgement of one's presence. —*n.* an utterance of the word *yes*. □ **say yes** grant a request or confirm a statement. **yes?** **1** indeed? is that so? **2** what do you want? **yes and no** that is partly true and partly untrue. **yes-man** (*pl.* **-men**) *colloq.* a weakly acquiescent person. [OE *gēse*, *gīse*, prob. f. *gīa sīe* may it be (*gīa* is unrecorded)]

yester- /ˈjestə(r)/ *comb. form poet.* or *archaic* of yesterday; that is the last past (*yester-eve*). [OE *geostran*]

yesterday /ˈjestəˌdeɪ/ *adv. & n.* —*adv.* **1** on the day before today. **2** in the recent past. —*n.* **1** the day before today. **2** the recent past. □ **yesterday morning** (or **afternoon** etc.) in the morning (or afternoon etc.) of yesterday. [OE *giestran dæg* (as YESTER-, DAY)]

yesteryear /ˈjestəˌjɪə(r)/ *n. literary* **1** last year. **2** the recent past.

yet *adv. & conj.* —*adv.* **1** as late as, or until, now or then (*there is yet time*; *your best work yet*). **2** (with *neg.* or *interrog.*) so soon as, or by, now or then (*it is not time yet*; *have you finished yet?*). **3** again; in addition (*more and yet more*). **4** in the remaining time available; before all is over (*I will do it yet*). **5** (foll. by *compar.*) even (*a yet more difficult task*). **6** nevertheless; and in spite of that; but for all that (*it is strange, and yet it is true*). —*conj.* but at the same time; but nevertheless (*I won, yet what good has it done?*). □ **nor yet** and also not (*won't listen to me nor yet to you*). [OE *gīet(a)*, = OFris. *iēta*, of unkn. orig.]

yeti /ˈjetɪ/ *n.* = Abominable Snowman. [Tibetan]

yew /juː/ *n.* **1** any dark-leaved evergreen coniferous tree of the genus *Taxus*, having seeds enclosed in a fleshy red aril, and often planted in churchyards. **2** its wood. [OE *īw*, *ēow* f. Gmc]

Y-fronts /ˈwaɪfrʌnts/ *n. propr.* men's or boys' briefs with a Y-shaped seam at the front.

Yggdrasil /ˈɪgdrəsɪl/ *n.* (in Scandinavian mythology) an ash-tree whose roots and branches join heaven, earth, and hell. [ON *yg(g)drasill* f. *Yggr* Odin + *drasill* horse]

YHA *abbr.* (in the UK) Youth Hostels Association.

Yid *n. sl. offens.* a Jew. [back-form. f. YIDDISH]

Yiddish /ˈjɪdɪʃ/ *n. & adj.* —*n.* a vernacular used by Jews in or from central and eastern Europe, orig. a German dialect with words from Hebrew and several modern languages. —*adj.* of or relating to this language. [G *jüdisch* Jewish]

yield /jiːld/ *v. & n.* —*v.* **1** *tr.* (also *absol.*) produce or return as a fruit, profit, or result (*the land yields crops*; *the land yields poorly*; *the investment yields 15%*). **2** *tr.* give up; surrender, concede; comply with a demand for (*yielded the fortress*; *yielded themselves prisoners*). **3** *intr.* (often foll. by *to*) **a** surrender; make submission. **b** give consent or change one's course of action in deference to; respond as required to (*yielded to persuasion*). **4** *intr.* (foll. by *to*) be inferior or confess inferiority to (*I yield to none in understanding the problem*). **5** *intr.* (foll. by *to*) give right of way to other traffic. **6** *intr. US* allow another the right to speak in a

debate etc. —*n.* an amount yielded or produced; an output or return. □ **yielder** *n.* [OE *g(i)eldan* pay f. Gmc]

yielding /ˈjiːldɪŋ/ *adj.* **1** compliant, submissive. **2** (of a substance) able to bend; not stiff or rigid. □ **yieldingly** *adv.* **yieldingness** *n.*

yin *n.* (in Chinese philosophy) the passive female principle of the universe (cf. YANG). [Chin.]

yippee /ˈjɪpiː, -ˈpiː/ *int.* expressing delight or excitement. [natural excl.]

-yl /ɪl/ *suffix Chem.* forming nouns denoting a radical (*ethyl*; *hydroxyl*; *phenyl*).

ylang-ylang /ˈiːlæŋˌiːlæŋ/ *n.* (also **ilang-ilang**) **1** a Malayan tree, from the fragrant yellow flowers of which a perfume is distilled. **2** the perfume itself. [Tagalog *álang-ilang*]

YMCA *abbr.* Young Men's Christian Association.

yob *n. Brit. sl.* a lout or hooligan. □ **yobbish** *adj.* **yobbishly** *adv.* **yobbishness** *n.* [back sl. for BOY]

yobbo /ˈjɒbəʊ/ *n.* (*pl.* **-os**) *Brit. sl.* = YOB.

yod *n.* **1** the tenth and smallest letter of the Hebrew alphabet. **2** its semivowel sound /j/. [Heb. *yōd* f. *yad* hand]

yodel /ˈjəʊd(ə)l/ *v. & n.* —*v.tr. & intr.* (**yodelled**, **yodelling**; *US* **yodeled**, **yodeling**) sing with melodious inarticulate sounds and oscilla between falsetto and the normal voice in the manner of the Swiss mountain-dwellers. —*n.* a yodelling cry. □ **yodeller** *n.* [G *jodeln*]

yoga /ˈjəʊgə/ *n.* **1** a Hindu system of philosophic meditation and asceticism designed to effect reunion with the universal spirit. **2** a system of physical exercises and breathing control used in yoga. □ **yogic** /ˈjəʊgɪk/ *adj.* [Hind. f. Skr., = union]

yoghurt /ˈjɒgət/ *n.* (also **yogurt**) a semi-solid sourish food prepared from milk fermented by added bacteria. [Turk. *yoğurt*]

yogi /ˈjəʊgɪ/ *n.* a person proficient in yoga. □ **yogism** *n.* [Hind. f. YOGA]

yo-ho /jəʊˈhəʊ/ *int.* (also **yo-heave-ho** /ˈjəʊhiːˌvhəʊ/ or **yo-ho-ho** /ˌjəʊhəʊˈhəʊ/) **1** used to attract attention. **2** a sailor's cry, esp. on raising the anchor.

yoke /jəʊk/ *n. & v.* —*n.* **1** a wooden crosspiece fastened over the necks of two oxen etc. and attached to the plough or wagon to be drawn. **2** (*pl.* same or **yokes**) a pair (of oxen etc.). **3** an object like a yoke in form or function, e.g. a wooden shoulder-piece for carrying a pair of pails, the top section of a dress or skirt etc. from which the rest hangs. **4** sway, dominion, or servitude, esp. when oppressive. —*v.* **1** *tr.* put a yoke on. **2** *tr.* couple or unite (a pair). **3** *tr.* (foll. by *to*) link (one thing) to (another). [OE *geoc* f. Gmc]

yokel /ˈjəʊk(ə)l/ *n.* a rustic; a country bumpkin. [perh. f. dial. *yokel* green woodpecker]

yolk /jəʊk/ *n.* **1** the yellow internal part of an egg that nourishes the young before it hatches. **2** *Biol.* the corresponding part of any animal ovum. □ **yolked** *adj.* (also in *comb.*). **yolkless** *adj.* **yolky** *adj.* [OE *geol(o)ca* f. *geolu* YELLOW]

yomp /jɒmp/ *v.intr. Brit. sl.* march with heavy equipment over difficult terrain. [20th c.: orig. unkn.]

yon *adj., adv., & pron. literary & dial.* —*adj. & adv.* yonder. —*pron.* yonder person or thing. [OE *geon*]

yonder /ˈjɒndə(r)/ *adv. & adj.* —*adv.* over there; at some distance in that direction; in the place indicated by pointing etc. —*adj.* situated yonder. [ME: cf. OS *gendra*, Goth. *jaindrē*]

yonks /jɒŋks/ *n.pl. sl.* a long time (*haven't seen them for yonks*). [20th c.: orig. unkn.]

yoo-hoo /ˈjuːhuː/ *int.* used to attract a person's attention. [natural excl.]

Yorkshireman /ˈjɔːkʃəmən/ *n.* (*pl.* **-men**; *fem.* **Yorkshirewoman**, *pl.* **-women**) a native of Yorkshire in N. England.

Yorkshire pudding /ˈjɔːkʃə/ *n.* a baked batter pudding usu. eaten with roast beef. [*Yorkshire* in N. England]

Yorkshire terrier /ˈjɔːkʃə/ *n.* a small long-haired blue-grey and tan kind of terrier.

Yoruba /ˈjɒrʊbə/ *n.* **1** a member of a Black African people inhabiting the west coast, esp. Nigeria. **2** the language of this people. [native name]

you /juː/ *pron.* (*obj.* **you**; *poss.* **your**, **yours**) **1** used with reference to the person or persons addressed or one such person and one or more associated persons. **2** (as *int.* with a noun) in an exclamatory statement (*you fools!*). **3** (in general statements) one, a person, anyone, or everyone (*it's bad at first, but you get used to it*). □ **you-all** *US colloq.* you (usu. more than one person). **you and yours** you together with your family, property, etc. **you-know-what** (or **-who**) something or someone unspecified but understood. [OE *ēow* accus. & dative of *gē* YE¹ f. WG: supplanting *ye* because of the more frequent use of the obj. case, and *thou* and *thee* as the more courteous form]

you'd /juːd, jʊd/ *contr.* **1** you had. **2** you would.

you'll /juːl, jʊl, jəl/ *contr.* you will; you shall.

young /jʌŋ/ *adj.* & *n.* —*adj.* (**younger** /ˈjʌŋɡə(r)/; **youngest** /ˈjʌŋɡɪst/) **1** not far advanced in life, development, or existence; not yet old. **2** immature or inexperienced. **3** felt in or characteristic of youth (*young love*; *young ambition*). **4** representing young people (*Young Conservatives*; *Young England*). **5** (**younger**) distinguishing one person from another of the same name (*the younger Pitt*). —*n.* (collect.) offspring, esp. of animals before or soon after birth. □ **young lady** *colloq.* a girlfriend or sweetheart. **young man** a boyfriend or sweetheart. **young person** *Law* (in the UK) a person generally between 14 and 17 years of age. **young thing** *archaic* or *colloq.* an indulgent term for a young person. **young woman** *colloq.* a girlfriend or sweetheart. □ **youngish** *adj.* [OE *g(e)ong* f. Gmc]

youngster /ˈjʌŋstə(r)/ *n.* a child or young person.

your /jɔː(r), jʊə(r)/ *poss.pron.* (*attrib.*) **1** of or belonging to you or yourself or yourselves (*your house*; *your own business*). **2** *colloq.* usu. *derog.* much talked of; well known (*none so fallible as your self-styled expert*). [OE *ēower* genit. of *gē* YE¹]

you're /jʊə(r), jə(r), jɔː(r)/ *contr.* you are.

yours /jɔːz, jʊəz/ *poss.pron.* **1** the one or ones belonging to or associated with you (*it is yours*; *yours are over there*). **2** your letter (*yours of the 10th*). **3** introducing a formula ending a letter (*yours ever*; *yours truly*). □ **of yours** of or belonging to you (*a friend of yours*).

yourself /jɔːˈself, jʊə-/ *pron.* (*pl.* **yourselves** /-ˈselvz/) **1 a** *emphat. form* of YOU. **b** *refl. form* of YOU. **2** in your normal state of body or mind (*are*

quite yourself again). □ **be yourself** act in your normal, unconstrained manner.

youth /juːθ/ *n.* (*pl.* **youths** /juːðz/) **1** the state of being young; the period between childhood and adult age. **2** the vigour or enthusiasm, inexperience, or other characteristic of this period. **3** an early stage of development etc. **4** a young person (esp. male). **5** (*pl.*) young people collectively (*the youth of the country*). □ **youth club** (or **centre**) a place or organization provided for young people's leisure activities. **youth hostel** a place where (esp. young) holiday-makers can put up cheaply for the night. **youth hosteller** a user of a youth hostel. [OE *geoguth* f. Gmc, rel. to YOUNG]

youthful /ˈjuːθfʊl/ *adj.* **1** young, esp. in appearance or manner. **2** having the characteristics of youth (*youthful impatience*). **3** having the freshness or vigour of youth (*a youthful complexion*). □ **youthfully** *adv.* **youthfulness** *n.*

you've /juːv, jʊv/ *contr.* you have.

yowl *n.* & *v.* —*n.* a loud wailing cry of or as of a cat or dog in pain or distress. —*v.intr.* utter a yowl. [imit.]

yo-yo /ˈjəʊjəʊ/ *n.* & *v.* —*n.* (*pl.* **yo-yos**) **1** a toy consisting of a pair of discs with a deep groove between them in which string is attached and wound, and which can be spun alternately downward and upward by its weight and momentum as the string unwinds and rewinds. **2** a thing that repeatedly falls and rises again. —*v.intr.* (**yo-yoes**, **yo-yoed**) **1** play with a yo-yo. **2** move up and down; fluctuate. [20th c.: orig. unkn.]

yr. *abbr.* **1** year(s). **2** younger. **3** your.

yrs. *abbr.* **1** years. **2** yours.

ytterbium /ɪˈtɜːbɪəm/ *n. Chem.* a silvery metallic element of the lanthanide series occurring naturally as various isotopes. [mod.L f. *Ytterby* in Sweden]

yttrium /ˈɪtrɪəm/ *n. Chem.* a greyish metallic element resembling the lanthanides, occurring naturally in uranium ores and used in making superconductors. [formed as YTTERBIUM]

yucca /ˈjʌkə/ *n.* any plant of the genus *Yucca*, with swordlike leaves. [Carib]

yuck *int.* & *n.* (also **yuk**) *sl.* —*int.* an expression of strong distaste or disgust. —*n.* something messy or repellent. [imit.]

yucky *adj.* (also **yukky**) (**-ier**, **-iest**) *sl.* **1** messy, repellent. **2** sickly, sentimental.

Yugoslav /ˈjuːɡəˌslɑːv/ *n.* & *adj.* (also **Jugoslav**) —*n.* **1** a native or national of Yugoslavia. **2** a person of Yugoslav descent. —*adj.* of or relating to Yugoslavia or its people. □ **Yugoslavian** *adj.* & *n.* [Austrian G *Jugoslav* f. Serb. *jugo-* f. *jug* south + SLAV]

yule *n.* (in full **yule-tide**) *archaic* the Christmas festival. □ **yule-log 1** a large log burnt in the hearth on Christmas Eve. **2** a log-shaped chocolate cake eaten at Christmas. [OE *gēol(a)*: cf. ON *jól*]

yummy /ˈjʌmɪ/ *adj.* (**yummier**, **yummiest**) *colloq.* tasty, delicious. [YUM-YUM + -Y¹]

yum-yum /jʌmˈjʌm/ *int.* expressing pleasure from eating or the prospect of eating. [natural excl.]

yup var. of YEP.

yuppy /ˈjʌpɪ/ *n.* (*pl.* **-ies**) *colloq.*, usu. *derog.* a young middle-class professional person working in a city. [young urban professional]

YWCA *abbr.* Young Women's Christian Association.

Zz

Z /zed/ n. (also **z**) (pl. **Zs** or **Z's**) **1** the twenty-sixth letter of the alphabet. **2** (usu. **z**) *Algebra* the third unknown quantity. **3** *Geom.* the third coordinate.

zabaglione /ˌzɑːbəˈljəʊneɪ/ n. an Italian sweet of whipped and heated egg yolks, sugar, and wine. [It.]

zag n. a sharp change of direction in a zigzag course. [ZIGZAG]

ZANU /ˈzɑːnuː/ abbr. Zimbabwe African National Union.

zany /ˈzeɪnɪ/ adj. & n. —adj. (**zanier**, **zaniest**) comically idiotic; crazily ridiculous. —n. a buffoon or jester. □ **zanily** adv. **zaniness** n. [F *zani* or It. *zan(n)i*, Venetian form of *Gianni*, *Giovanni* John]

zap v., n., & int. sl. —v. (**zapped**, **zapping**) **1** tr. **a** kill or destroy; deal a sudden blow to. **b** hit forcibly (*zapped the ball over the net*). **2** intr. & tr. move quickly and vigorously. **3** tr. overwhelm emotionally. **4** tr. *Computing* erase or change (an item in a program). **5** intr. (foll. by *through*) fast-wind a videotape to skip a section. —n. **1** energy, vigour. **2** a strong emotional effect. —int. expressing the sound or impact of a bullet, ray gun, etc., or any sudden event. [imit.]

zappy adj. (**zappier**, **zappiest**) *colloq.* **1** lively, energetic. **2** striking.

ZAPU /ˈzɑːpuː/ abbr. Zimbabwe African People's Union.

Zarathustrian var. of ZOROASTRIAN.

zarzuela /θɑːˈθweɪlə/ n. a Spanish traditional form of musical comedy. [Sp.: app. f. a place-name]

zeal n. **1** earnestness or fervour in advancing a cause or rendering service. [ME *zele* f. eccl.L *zelus* f. Gk *zēlos*]

zealot /ˈzelət/ n. **1** an uncompromising or extreme partisan; a fanatic. **2** (**Zealot**) *hist.* a member of an ancient Jewish sect aiming at a world Jewish theocracy and resisting the Romans until AD 70. □ **zealotry** n. [eccl.L *zelotes* f. Gk *zēlōtēs* (as ZEAL)]

zealous /ˈzeləs/ adj. full of zeal; enthusiastic. □ **zealously** adv. **zealousness** n.

zebra /ˈzebrə, ˈziː-/ n. **1** any of various African quadrupeds related to the ass and horse, with black and white stripes. **2** (attrib.) with alternate dark and pale stripes. □ **zebra crossing** Brit. a striped street-crossing where pedestrians have precedence over vehicles. □ **zebrine** /-braɪn/ adj. [It. or Port. f. Congolese]

zebu /ˈziːbuː/ n. a humped ox, *Bos indicus*, of India, E. Asia, and Africa. [F *zébu*, of unkn. orig.]

zed /zed/ n. Brit. the letter Z. [F *zède* f. LL *zeta* f. Gk ZETA]

zee n. US the letter Z. [17th c.: var. of ZED]

Zeitgeist /ˈtsaɪtgaɪst/ n. **1** the spirit of the times. **2** the trend of thought and feeling in a period. [G f. *Zeit* time + *Geist* spirit]

Zen n. a form of Mahayana Buddhism emphasizing the value of meditation and intuition. □ **Zenist** n. (also **Zennist**). [Jap., = meditation]

zenith /ˈzenɪθ, ˈziː-/ n. **1** the part of the celestial sphere directly above an observer (opp. NADIR). **2** the highest point in one's fortunes; a time of great prosperity etc. [ME f. OF *cenit* or med.L *cenit* ult. f. Arab. *samt* (*ar-ra's*) path (over the head)]

zeolite /ˈziːəˌlaɪt/ n. each of a number of minerals consisting mainly of hydrous silicates of calcium, sodium, and aluminium, able to act as cation exchangers. □ **zeolitic** /-ˈlɪtɪk/ adj. [Sw. & G *zeolit* f. Gk *zeō* boil + -LITE (from their characteristic swelling and fusing under the blowpipe)]

zephyr /ˈzefə(r)/ n. *literary* a mild gentle wind or breeze. [F *zéphyr* or L *zephyrus* f. Gk *zephuros* (god of the) west wind]

Zeppelin /ˈzepəlɪn/ n. hist. a German large dirigible airship of the early 20th c., orig. for military use. [Count F. von *Zeppelin*, Ger. airman d. 1917, its first constructor]

zero /ˈzɪərəʊ/ n. & v. —n. (pl. **-os**) **1 a** the figure 0; nought. **b** no quantity or number; nil. **2** a point on the scale of an instrument from which a positive or negative quantity is reckoned. **3** (attrib.) having a value of zero; no, not any (*zero population growth*). **4** (in full **zero-hour**) **a** the hour at which a planned, esp. military, operation is timed to begin. **b** a crucial moment. **5** the lowest point; a nullity or nonentity. —v.tr. (**-oes**, **-oed**) **1** adjust (an instrument etc.) to zero point. **2** set the sights of (a gun) for firing. □ **zero in on 1** take aim at. **2** focus one's attention on. **zero option** a disarmament proposal for the total removal of certain types of weapons on both sides. **zero-rated** on which no value added tax is charged. [F *zéro* or It. *zero* f. OSp. f. Arab. *ṣifr* CIPHER]

zest n. **1** piquancy; a stimulating flavour or quality. **2 a** keen enjoyment or interest. **b** (often foll. by *for*) relish. **c** gusto (*entered into it with zest*). **3** a scraping of orange or lemon peel as flavouring. □ **zestful** adj. **zestfully** adv. **zestfulness** n. **zesty** adj. (**zestier**, **zestiest**). [F *zeste* orange or lemon peel, of unkn. orig.]

zeta /ˈziːtə/ n. the sixth letter of the Greek alphabet (Z, ζ). [Gk *zēta*]

zeugma /ˈzjuːgmə/ n. a figure of speech using a verb or adjective with two nouns, to one of which it is strictly applicable while the word appropriate to the other is not used (e.g. *with weeping eyes and* [sc. *grieving*] *hearts*) (cf. SYLLEPSIS). □ **zeugmatic** /-ˈmætɪk/ adj. [L f. Gk *zeugma -atos* f. *zeugnumi* to yoke, *zugon* yoke]

ziggurat /ˈzɪgəˌræt/ n. a rectangular stepped tower in ancient Mesopotamia, surmounted by a temple. [Assyr. *ziqquratu* pinnacle]

zigzag /ˈzɪgzæg/ n., adj., adv., & v. —n. **1** a line or course having abrupt alternate right and left turns. **2** (often in *pl.*) each of these turns. —*adj.* having the form of a zigzag; alternating right and left. —*adv.* with a zigzag course. —*v.intr.* (**zigzagged**, **zigzagging**) move in a zigzag course. □ **zigzaggedly** *adv.* [F f. G *zickzack*]

zilch /zɪltʃ/ *n.* esp. *US sl.* nothing. [20th c.: orig. uncert.]

zillion /ˈzɪljən/ *n. colloq.* an indefinite large number. □ **zillionth** *adj. & n.* [Z (perh. = unknown quantity) + MILLION]

zinc /zɪŋk/ *n. Chem.* a white metallic element occurring naturally as zinc blende, and used as a component of brass, in galvanizing sheet iron, in electric batteries, and in printing-plates. □ **flowers of zinc** = *zinc oxide*. **zinc oxide** a powder used as a white pigment and in medicinal ointments. □ **zinced** /zɪŋkd/ *adj.* [G *Zink*, of unkn. orig.]

zing /zɪŋ/ *n. & v. colloq.* —*n.* vigour, energy. —*v.intr.* move swiftly or with a shrill sound. □ **zingy** *adj.* (**zingier**, **zingiest**). [imit.]

zinger /ˈzɪŋə(r)/ *n. US sl.* an outstanding person or thing.

zinnia /ˈzɪnɪə/ *n.* a composite plant with showy rayed flowers of deep red and other colours. [J. G. *Zinn*, Ger. physician and botanist d. 1759]

Zion /ˈzaɪən/ *n.* (also **Sion** /ˈsaɪən/) **1** the hill of Jerusalem on which the city of David was built. **2 a** the Jewish people or religion. **b** the Christian Church. **3** (in Christian thought) the Kingdom of God in Heaven. [OE f. eccl.L *Sion* f. Heb. *ṣīyôn*]

Zionism /ˈzaɪəˌnɪz(ə)m/ *n.* a movement (orig.) for the reestablishment and (now) the development of a Jewish nation in what is now Israel. □ **Zionist** *n.*

zip *n. & v.* —*n.* **1** a light fast sound, as of a bullet passing through air. **2** energy, vigour. **3** esp. *Brit.* **a** (in full **zip-fastener**) a fastening device of two flexible strips with interlocking projections closed or opened by pulling a slide along them. **b** (*attrib.*) having a zip-fastener (*zip bag*). —*v.* (**zipped**, **zipping**) **1** *tr. & intr.* (often foll. by *up*) fasten with a zip-fastener. **2** *intr.* move with zip or at high speed. [imit.]

Zip code *n. US* a system of postal codes consisting of five-digit numbers. [*zone improvement plan*]

zipper *n. & v.* esp. *US* —*n.* a zip-fastener. —*v.tr.* (often foll. by *up*) fasten with a zipper. □ **zippered** *adj.*

zippy *adj.* (**zippier**, **zippiest**) *colloq.* **1** bright, fresh, lively. **2** fast, speedy. □ **zippily** *adv.* **zippiness** *n.*

zircon /ˈzɜːkən/ *n.* a zirconium silicate of which some translucent varieties are cut into gems. [G *Zirkon*]

zirconium /zɜːˈkəʊnɪəm/ *n. Chem.* a grey metallic element occurring naturally in zircon and used in various industrial applications. [mod.L f. ZIRCON + -IUM]

zit *n.* esp. *US sl.* a pimple. [20th c.: orig. unkn.]

zither /ˈzɪðə(r)/ *n.* a musical instrument consisting of a flat wooden soundbox with numerous strings stretched across it, placed horizontally and played with the fingers and a plectrum. □ **zitherist** *n.* [G f. Gk *kithara* harp]

zizz *n. & v. colloq.* —*n.* **1** a whizzing or buzzing sound. **2** a short sleep. —*v.intr.* **1** make a whizzing sound. **2** doze or sleep. [imit.]

zloty /ˈzlɒtɪ/ *n.* (*pl.* same or **zlotys**) the chief monetary unit of Poland. [Pol., lit. 'golden']

Zn *symb. Chem.* the element zinc.

zodiac /ˈzəʊdɪˌæk/ *n.* **1** a belt of the heavens limited by lines about 8° from the ecliptic on each side, including all apparent positions of the sun, moon, and planets as known to ancient astronomers, and divided into twelve equal parts (**signs of the zodiac**). **2** a diagram of these signs. [ME f. OF *zodiaque* f. L *zodiacus* f. Gk *zōidiakos* f. *zōidion* sculptured animal-figure, dimin. of *zōion* animal]

zodiacal /zəˈdaɪək(ə)l/ *adj.* of or in the zodiac. [(as ZODIAC)]

zoetrope /ˈzəʊɪˌtrəʊp/ *n. hist.* an optical toy in the form of a cylinder with a series of pictures on the inner surface which give an impression of continuous motion when viewed through slits with the cylinder rotating. [irreg. f. Gk *zōē* life + *-tropos* turning]

zoic /ˈzəʊɪk/ *adj.* **1** of or relating to animals. **2** *Geol.* (of rock etc.) containing fossils; with traces of animal or plant life. [prob. back-form. f. *azoic*, ult. f. Gk *zoē* life]

zombie /ˈzɒmbɪ/ *n.* **1** *colloq.* a dull or apathetic person. **2** a corpse said to be revived by witchcraft. [W.Afr. *zumbi* fetish]

zonation /zəʊˈneɪʃ(ə)n/ *n.* distribution in zones, esp. (*Ecol.*) of plants into zones characterized by the dominant species.

zone *n. & v.* —*n.* **1** an area having particular features, properties, purpose, or use (*danger zone*; *erogenous zone*; *smokeless zone*). **2** any well-defined region of more or less beltlike form. **3 a** an area between two exact or approximate concentric circles. **b** a part of the surface of a sphere enclosed between two parallel planes, or of a cone or cylinder etc., between such planes cutting it perpendicularly to the axis. **4** (in full **time zone**) a range of longitudes where a common standard time is used. **5** *Geol.* etc. a range between specified limits of depth, height, etc., esp. a section of strata distinguished by characteristic fossils. **6** *Geog.* any of five divisions of the earth bounded by circles parallel to the equator (see FRIGID, TEMPERATE, TORRID). —*v.tr.* **1** encircle as or with a zone. **2** arrange or distribute by zones. **3** assign as or to a particular area. □ **zonal** *adj.* **zoning** *n.* (in sense 3 of *v.*). [F *zone* or L *zona* girdle f. Gk *zōnē*]

zonk *v. & n. sl.* —*v.* **1** *tr.* hit or strike. **2** (foll. by *out*) **a** *tr.* overcome with sleep; intoxicate. **b** *intr.* fall heavily asleep. —*n.* (often as *int.*) the sound of a blow or heavy impact. [imit.]

zoo *n.* a zoological garden. [abbr.]

zoo- /ˈzəʊə/ *comb. form* of animals or animal life. [Gk *zōio-* f. *zōion* animal]

zooid /ˈzəʊɔɪd/ *n.* **1** a more or less independent invertebrate organism arising by budding or fission. **2** a distinct member of an invertebrate colony. □ **zooidal** /-ˈɔɪd(ə)l/ *adj.* [formed as zoo- + -OID]

zoological /ˌzəʊəˈlɒdʒɪk(ə)l/, *disp.* ˌzuːə-/ *adj.* of or relating to zoology. □ **zoological garden** (or **gardens**) a public garden or park with a collection of animals for exhibition and study. □ **zoologically** *adv.*

zoology /zəʊˈɒlədʒɪ, ˌzuː-/ *n.* the scientific study of animals, esp. with reference to their structure, physiology, classification, and distribution. □ **zoologist** n. [mod.L zoologia (as ZOO-, -LOGY)]

■ **Usage** The pronunciation of zoology, zoological, and zoologist as /zu:-/, although extremely common, is considered incorrect by some people.

---

zoom v. & n. —v. **1** intr. move quickly, esp. with a buzzing sound. **2 a** intr. cause an aeroplane to mount at high speed and a steep angle. **b** tr. cause (an aeroplane) to do this. **3 a** intr. (of a camera) close up rapidly from a long shot to a close-up. **b** tr. cause (a lens or camera) to do this. —n. **1** an aeroplane's steep climb. **2** a zooming camera shot. □ **zoom lens** a lens allowing a camera to zoom by varying the focal length. [imit.]

zoomorphic /ˌzəʊəˈmɔːfɪk/ adj. **1** dealing with or represented in animal forms. **2** having gods of animal form. □ **zoomorphism** n.

zoonosis /ˌzəʊəˈnəʊsɪs/ n. (pl. **zoonoses**) any of various diseases which can be transmitted to humans from animals. [ZOO- + Gk nosos disease]

zoophyte /ˈzəʊəfaɪt/ n. a plantlike animal, esp. a coral, sea anemone, or sponge. □ **zoophytic** /-ˈfɪtɪk/ adj. [Gk zōophuton (as ZOO-, -PHYTE)]

zootomy /zəʊˈɒtəmɪ/ n. the dissection or anatomy of animals.

Zoroastrian /ˌzɒrəʊˈæstrɪən/ adj. & n. (also **Zarathustrian** /ˌzærəˈθʊstrɪən/) —adj. of or relating to Zoroaster (or Zarathustra) or the dualistic religious system taught by him or his followers in the Zend-Avesta. —n. a follower of Zoroaster. □ **Zoroastrianism** n. [L Zoroastres f. Gk Zōroastrēs f. Avestan Zarathustra, Persian founder of the religion in the 6th c. BC]

Zouave /zuːˈɑːv, zwɑːv/ n. a member of a French light-infantry corps originally formed of Algerians and retaining their oriental uniform. [F f. Zouaoua, name of a tribe]

zouk /zuːk/ n. an exuberant style of popular music from the French Antilles which combines local features with Western rock styles. [Guadeloupean creole = to party]

ZPG abbr. zero population growth.

Zr symb. Chem. the element zirconium.

zucchetto /tsʊˈketəʊ/ n. (pl. **-os**) a Roman Catholic ecclesiastic's skullcap, black for a priest, purple for a bishop, red for a cardinal, and white for a pope. [It. zucchetta dimin. of zucca gourd, head]

zucchini /zuːˈkiːnɪ/ n. (pl. same or **zucchinis**) esp. US & Austral. a courgette. [It., pl. of zucchino dimin. of zucca gourd]

Zulu /ˈzuːluː/ n. & adj. —n. **1** a member of a Black South African people orig. inhabiting Zululand and Natal. **2** the language of this people. —adj. of or relating to this people or language. [native name]

zwieback /ˈzwiːbæk, ˈtsviːbɑːk/ n. a kind of biscuit rusk or sweet cake toasted in slices. [G, = twice baked]

zygo- /ˈzaɪgəʊ/ comb. form joining, pairing. [Gk zugo- f. zugon yoke]

zygoma /zaɪˈgəʊmə, zɪ/ n. (pl. **zygomata** /-tə/) the bony arch of the cheek formed by connection of the zygomatic and temporal bones. [Gk zugōma -atos f. zugon yoke]

zygomatic /ˌzaɪgəˈmætɪk, ˌzɪ-/ adj. of or relating to the zygoma. □ **zygomatic arch** = ZYGOMA. **zygomatic bone** the bone that forms the prominent part of the cheek.

zygospore /ˈzaɪgəˌspɔː(r)/ n. a thick-walled spore formed by certain fungi.

zygote /ˈzaɪgəʊt/ n. Biol. a cell formed by the union of two gametes. □ **zygotic** /-ˈgɒtɪk/ adj. **zygotically** /-ˈgɒtɪkəlɪ/ adv. [Gk zugōtos yoked f. zugoō to yoke]

APPENDIX I

Weights and Measures

1. British and American, with Approximate Metric Equivalents

Linear Measure

1 inch	= 25.4 millimetres exactly
1 foot = 12 inches	= 0.3048 metre exactly
1 yard = 3 feet	= 0.9144 metre exactly
1 (statute) mile = 1,760 yards	= 1.609 kilometres

Square Measure

1 square inch	= 6.45 sq. centimetres
1 square foot = 144 sq. in.	= 9.29 sq. decimetres
1 square yard = 9 sq. ft.	= 0.836 sq. metre
1 acre = 4,840 sq. yd.	= 0.405 hectare
1 square mile = 640 acres	= 259 hectares

Cubic Measure

1 cubic inch	= 16.4 cu. centimetres
1 cubic foot = 1,728 cu. in.	= 0.0283 cu. metre
1 cubic yard = 27 cu. ft.	= 0.765 cu. metre

Capacity Measure

BRITISH

1 pint = 20 fluid oz.	
= 34.68 cu. in.	= 0.568 litre
1 quart = 2 pints	= 1.136 litres
1 gallon = 4 quarts	= 4.546 litres
1 peck = 2 gallons	= 9.092 litres
1 bushel = 4 pecks	= 36.4 litres
1 quarter = 8 bushels	= 2.91 hectolitres

AMERICAN DRY

1 pint = 33.60 cu. in.	= 0.550 litre
1 quart = 2 pints	= 1.101 litres
1 peck = 8 quarts	= 8.81 litres
1 bushel = 4 pecks	= 35.3 litres

AMERICAN LIQUID

1 pint = 16 fluid oz.	
= 28.88 cu. in.	= 0.473 litre
1 quart = 2 pints	= 0.946 litre
1 gallon = 4 quarts	= 3.785 litres

Avoirdupois Weight

1 grain	= 0.065 gram
1 dram	= 1.772 grams
1 ounce = 16 drams	= 28.35 grams
1 pound = 16 ounces	
= 7,000 grains	= 0.4536 kilogram
1 stone = 14 pounds	= 6.35 kilograms
1 quarter = 2 stones	= 12.70 kilograms
1 hundredweight = 4 quarters	= 50.80 kilograms

1 short ton = 2,000 pounds   = 0.907 tonne
1 (long) ton = 20 hundredweight   = 1.016 tonnes

2. Metric, with Approximate British Equivalents

Linear Measure

1 millimetre   = 0.039 inch
1 centimetre = 10 mm   = 0.394 inch
1 decimetre = 10 cm   = 3.94 inches
1 metre = 10 dm   = 1.094 yards
1 decametre = 10 m   = 10.94 yards
1 hectometre = 100 m   = 109.4 yards
1 kilometre = 1,000 m   = 0.6214 mile

Square Measure

1 square centimetre   = 0.155 sq. inch
1 square metre   = 1.196 sq. yards
1 are = 100 square metres   = 119.6 sq. yards
1 hectare = 100 ares   = 2.471 acres
1 square kilometre   = 0.386 sq. mile

Cubic Measure

1 cubic centimetre   = 0.061 cu. inch
1 cubic metre   = 1.308 cu. yards

Capacity Measure

1 millilitre   = 0.002 pint (British)
1 centilitre = 10 ml   = 0.018 pint
1 decilitre = 10 cl   = 0.176 pint
1 litre = 10 dl   = 1.76 pints
1 decalitre = 10 l   = 2.20 gallons
1 hectolitre = 100 l   = 2.75 bushels
1 kilolitre = 1,000 l   = 3.44 quarters

Weight

1 milligram   = 0.015 grain
1 centigram = 10 mg   = 0.154 grain
1 decigram = 10 cg   = 1.543 grains
1 gram = 10 dg   = 15.43 grains
1 decagram = 10 g   = 5.64 drams
1 hectogram = 100 g   = 3.527 ounces
1 kilogram = 1,000 g   = 2.205 pounds
1 tonne (metric ton) = 1,000 kg   = 0.984 (long) ton

3. Temperature

Fahrenheit: water boils (under standard conditions) at 212° and freezes at 32°.
Celsius or Centigrade: water boils at 100° and freezes at 0°.
Kelvin: water boils at 373.15 K and freezes at 273.15 K.
To convert Centigrade into Fahrenheit: multiply by 9, divide by 5, and add 32.
To convert Fahrenheit into Centigrade: subtract 32, multiply by 5, and divide by 9.
To convert Centigrade into Kelvin: add 273.15.

4. The Power Notation

This expresses concisely any power of 10 (any number that is composed of factors 10), and is sometimes used in the dictionary.

$$10^2 \text{ or ten squared} = 10 \times 10 = 100$$
$$10^3 \text{ or ten cubed} = 10 \times 10 \times 10 = 1{,}000$$
$$10^4 = 10 \times 10 \times 10 \times 10 = 10{,}000$$
$$10^{10} = 1 \text{ followed by ten noughts} = 10{,}000{,}000{,}000$$
$$10^{-2} = 1/10^2 = 1/100$$
$$10^{-10} = 1/10^{10} = 1/10{,}000{,}000{,}000$$

5. The Metric Prefixes

	Abbreviations	Factors
deca	da	10
hecto	h	10^2
kilo	k	10^3
mega	M	10^6
giga	G	10^9
tera	T	10^{12}
peta	P	10^{15}
exa	E	10^{18}
deci	d	10^{-1}
centi	c	10^{-2}
milli	m	10^{-3}
micro	μ	10^{-6}
nano	n	10^{-9}
pico	p	10^{-12}
femto	f	10^{-15}
atto	a	10^{-18}

Pronunciations and derivations of these are given at their alphabetical places in the dictionary. They may be applied to any units of the metric system: hectogram (abbr. hg) = 100 grams; kilowatt (abbr. kW) = 1,000 watts; megahertz (MHz) = 1 million hertz; centimetre (cm) = $\frac{1}{100}$ metre; microvolt (μV) = one millionth of a volt; picofarad (pF) = 10^{-12} farad, and are sometimes applied to other units (megabit, microinch).

6. Chemical Notation

The symbol for a molecule shows the symbols for the elements contained in it (C = carbon, H = hydrogen, etc.), each followed by a subscript numeral denoting the number of atoms of the element in the molecule where this number is more than one. For example, the water molecule (H_2O) contains two atoms of hydrogen and one of oxygen.

APPENDIX II

Punctuation Marks

Punctuation is a complicated subject, and only the main principles can be discussed here. The explanations are based on practice in British English; usage in American English differs in some instances. The main headings are as follows:

1. General remarks
2. Capital letter
3. Full stop
4. Semicolon
5. Comma
6. Colon
7. Question mark
8. Exclamation mark
9. Apostrophe
10. Quotation marks
11. Brackets
12. Dash
13. Hyphen

1. General remarks

The purpose of punctuation is to mark out strings of words into manageable groups and help clarify their meaning (or in some cases to prevent a wrong meaning being deduced). The marks most commonly used to divide a piece of prose or other writing are the full stop, the semicolon, and the comma, with the strength of the dividing or separating role diminishing from the full stop to the comma. The full stop therefore marks the main division into sentences; the semicolon joins sentences (as in this sentence); and the comma (which is the most flexible in use and causes most problems) separates smaller elements with the least loss of continuity. Brackets and dashes also serve as separators—often more strikingly than commas, as in this sentence.

2. Capital letter

2.1.1 This is used for the first letter of the word beginning a sentence in most cases:

He decided not to come. Later he changed his mind.

2.1.2 A sentence or clause contained in a subordinate or parenthetic role within a larger one does not normally begin with a capital letter:

I have written several letters (there are many to be written) and hope to finish them tomorrow.

2.1.3 In the following, however, the sentence is a separate one and therefore does begin with a capital letter:

There is more than one possibility. (I have said this often before.) So we should think carefully before acting.

2.1.4 A capital letter also begins sentences that form quoted speech:

The assistant turned and replied, 'There are no more left.'

2.2 It is used in proper names (*Paris, John Smith*), names of people and languages and related adjectives (*Englishman, Austrian, French*), names of institutions and institutional groups (*the British Museum, Protestants, Conservatives*), and names of days and months

(*Tuesday*, *March*) and related words (*Easter Sunday*). It is also used by convention in names that are trade marks (*Biro*, *Jacuzzi*).

2.3 It is used in titles of books, newspapers, plays, films, television programmes, etc., and in headings and captions.

2.4 It is used in designations of rank or relationship when used as titles (*King John*, *Aunt Mabel*, *Pope Gregory*), and to designate divinity (*God*, *the Almighty*, etc.).

2.5 Lines of verse often begin with a capital letter.

2.6 Many abbreviations consist partly or entirely of the initial letters of words in capital letters (with or without a full stop): *BBC*, *DoE*, *M.Litt*.

3. Full stop   •

3.1 This is used to mark the end of a sentence when it is a statement (and not a question or exclamation). In prose, sentences marked by full stops normally represent a discrete or distinct statement; more closely connected or complementary statements are joined by a semicolon (as here).

3.2.1 Full stops are used to mark many abbreviations (*Weds.*, *Gen.*, *p.m.*). They are often omitted in abbreviations that are familiar or very common (*Dr*, *Mr*, *Mrs*, etc.), in abbreviations that consist entirely of capital letters (*BBC*, *GMT*, etc.), and in acronyms that are pronounced as a word rather than a sequence of letters (*Nato*, *Ernie*, etc.).

3.2.2 If an abbreviation with a full stop comes at the end of a sentence, another full stop is not added when the full stop of the abbreviation is the last character:

> *They have a collection of many animals, including dogs, cats, tortoises, snakes, etc.*

but

> *They have a collection of many animals (dogs, cats, tortoises, snakes, etc.).*

3.3 A sequence of three full stops is used to mark an ellipsis or omission in a sequence of words, especially when forming an incomplete quotation. When the omission occurs at the end of a sentence, a fourth point is added as the full stop of the whole sentence:

> *He left the room, banged the door, ... and went out.*
> *The report said: 'There are many issues to be considered, of which the chief are money, time, and personnel. . . . Let us consider personnel first.'*

3.4 A full stop is used as a decimal point (*10.5 per cent*; *£1.65*), and to divide hours and minutes in giving time (*6.15 p.m.*), although a colon is usual in American use (*6:15 p.m.*).

4. Semicolon   ;

4.1.1 The main role of the semicolon is to unite sentences that are closely associated or that complement or parallel each other in some way, as in the following:

> *In the north of the city there is a large industrial area with little private housing; further east is the university.*
> *To err is human; to forgive, divine.*

4.1.2 It is often used as a stronger division in a sentence that already includes divisions by means of commas:

> *He came out of the house, which lay back from the road, and saw her at the end of the path; but instead of continuing towards her, he hid until she had gone.*

4.2 It is used in a similar way in lists of names or other items, to indicate a stronger division:

> *I should like to thank the managing director, Stephen Jones; my secretary, Mary Cartwright; and my assistant, Kenneth Sloane.*

5. Comma   ,

5.1 Use of the comma is more difficult to describe than other punctuation marks, and there is much variation in practice. Essentially, its role is to give detail to the structure of sentences, especially longer ones, and make their meaning clear. Too many commas can be distracting; too few can make a piece of writing difficult to read or, worse, difficult to understand.

5.2.1 The comma is widely used to separate the main clauses of a compound sentence when they are not sufficiently close in meaning or content to form a continuous unpunctuated sentence, and are not distinct enough to warrant a semicolon. A conjunction such as *and*, *but*, *yet*, etc., is normally used:

> *The road runs through a beautiful wooded valley, and the railway line follows it closely.*

5.2.2 It is considered incorrect to join the clauses of a compound sentence without a conjunction. In the following sentence, the comma should either be replaced by a semicolon, or be retained and followed by *and*:

> *I like swimming very much, I go to the pool every week.*

5.2.3 It is also considered incorrect to separate a subject from its verb with a comma:

> *Those with the smallest incomes and no other means, should get most support.*

5.3.1 Commas are usually inserted between adjectives coming before a noun:

> *An enterprising, ambitious person.*
> *A cold, damp, badly heated room.*

5.3.2 But the comma is omitted when the last adjective has a closer relation to the noun than the others:

> *A distinguished foreign politician.*
> *A little old lady.*

5.4 An important role of the comma is to prevent ambiguity or (momentary) mis-understanding, especially after a verb used intransitively where it might otherwise be taken to be transitive:

> *With the police pursuing, the people shouted loudly.*

Other examples follow:

> *He did not want to leave, from a feeling of loyalty.*
> *In the valley below, the houses appeared very small.*

However, much as I should like to I cannot agree.
(compare *However much I should like to I cannot agree.*)

5.5.1 The comma is used in pairs to separate elements in a sentence that are not part of the main statement:

I should like you all, ladies and gentlemen, to raise your glasses.
There is no sense, as far as I can see, in this suggestion.
It appears, however, that we were wrong.

5.5.2 It is also used to separate a relative clause from its antecedent when the clause is not serving an identifying function:

The book, which was on the table, was a present.

In the above sentence, the information in the *which* clause is incidental to the main statement; without the comma, it would form an essential part of it in identifying which book is being referred to (and could be replaced by *that*):

The book which/that was on the table was a present.

5.6.1 Commas are used to separate items in a list or sequence. Usage varies as to the inclusion of a comma before *and* in the last item; the practice in this dictionary is to include it:

The following will report at 9.30 sharp: Jones, Smith, Thompson, and Williams.

5.6.2 A final comma before *and*, when used regularly and consistently, has the advantage of clarifying the grouping at a composite name occurring at the end of a list:

We shall go to Smiths, Boots, Woolworths, and Marks and Spencer.

5.7 A comma is used in numbers of four or more figures, to separate each group of three consecutive figures starting from the right (e.g. *10,135,793*).

6. Colon   :

6.1 The main role of the colon is to separate main clauses when there is a step forward from the first to the second, especially from introduction to main point, from general statement to example, from cause to effect, and from premiss to conclusion:

There is something I want to say: I should like you all to know how grateful I am to you.
It was not easy: to begin with I had to find the right house.
The weather was bad: so we decided to stay at home.
(In this example, a comma could be used, but the emphasis on cause and effect would be much reduced.)

6.2 It also introduces a list of items. In this use a dash should not be added:

The following will be needed: a pen, pencil, rubber, piece of paper, and ruler.

6.3 It is used to introduce, more formally and emphatically than a comma would, speech or quoted material:

I told them last week: 'Do not in any circumstances open this door.'

7. Question mark

?

7.1.1 This is used in place of the full stop to show that the preceding sentence is a question:

Do you want another piece of cake?
He really is her husband?

7.1.2 It is not used when the question is implied by indirect speech:

I asked you whether you wanted another piece of cake.

7.2 It is used (often in brackets) to express doubt or uncertainty about a word or phrase immediately following or preceding it:

Julius Caesar, born (?) 100 BC.
They were then seen boarding a bus (to London?).

8. Exclamation mark

!

This is used after an exclamatory word, phrase, or sentence expressing any of the following:

8.1 Absurdity:	*What an idea!*
8.2 Command or warning:	*Go to your room!* *Be careful!*
8.3 Contempt or disgust:	*They are revolting!*
8.4 Emotion or pain:	*I hate you!* *That really hurts!* *Ouch!*
8.5 Enthusiasm:	*I'd love to come!*
8.6 Wish or regret:	*Let me come!* *If only I could swim!*
8.7 Wonder, admiration, or surprise:	*What a good idea!* *Aren't they beautiful!*

9. Apostrophe

'

9.1.1 The main use is to indicate the possessive case, as in *John's book*, *the girls' mother*, etc. It comes before the *s* in singular and plural nouns not ending in *s*, as in *the boy's games* and *the women's games*. It comes after the *s* in plural nouns ending in *s*, as in *the boys' games*.

9.1.2 In singular nouns ending in *s* practice differs between (for example) *Charles'* and *Charles's*; in some cases the shorter form is preferable for reasons of sound, as in *Xerxes' fleet*.

9.1.3 It is also used to indicate a place or business, e.g. *the butcher's*. In this use it is often omitted in some names, e.g. *Smiths*, *Lloyds Bank*.

9.2 It is used to indicate a contraction, e.g. *he's, wouldn't, Bo's'un, o'clock.*

9.3 It is sometimes used to form a plural of individual letters or numbers, although this use is diminishing. It is helpful in *cross your t's* but unnecessary in *MPs* and *1940s*.

9.4 For its use as a quotation mark, see section 10.

10. Quotation marks

99

10.1 The main use is to indicate direct speech and quotations. A single turned comma (')
is normally used at the beginning, and a single apostrophe (') at the end of the quoted matter:

> *She said, 'I have something to ask you.'*

10.2 The closing quotation mark should come after any punctuation mark which is part of the quoted matter, but before any mark which is not:

> *They shouted, 'Watch out!'.*
> *They were described as 'an unruly bunch'.*
> *Did I hear you say 'go away!'?*

10.3 Punctuation dividing a sentence of reported speech is put inside the quotation marks:

> *'Go away,' he said, 'and don't ever come back.'*

10.4 Quotation marks are also used of cited words and phrases:

> *What does 'integrated circuit' mean?*

10.5 A quotation within a quotation is put in double quotation marks:

> *'Have you any idea,' he said, 'what "integrated circuit" means?'*

11. Brackets

([ ])

11.1 The types of brackets used in normal punctuation are round brackets ( ) and square brackets [ ].

11.2 The main use of round brackets is to enclose explanations and extra information or comment:

> *He is (as he always was) a rebel.*
> *Zimbabwe (formerly Rhodesia).*
> *They talked about Machtpolitik (power politics).*

11.3 They are used to give references and citations:

> *Thomas Carlyle (1795–1881).*
> *A discussion of integrated circuits (see p. 38).*

11.4 They are used to enclose reference letters or figures, e.g. *(1) (a).*

11.5 They are used to enclose optional words:

> *There are many (apparent) difficulties.*

(In this example, the difficulties may or may not be only apparent.)

11.6.1 Square brackets are used less often. The main use is to enclose extra information attributable to someone (normally an editor) other than the writer of the surrounding text:

> *The man walked in, and his sister [Sarah] greeted him.*

11.6.2 They are used in some contexts to convey special kinds of information, especially when round brackets are also used for other purposes: for example, in this dictionary they are used to give the etymologies at the end of entries.

12. Dash

12.1 A single dash is used to indicate a pause, whether a hesitation in speech or to introduce an explanation or expansion of what comes before it:

> *'I think you should have—told me,' he replied.*
> *We then saw the reptiles—snakes, crocodiles, that sort of thing.*

12.2 A pair of dashes is used to indicate asides and parentheses, like the use of commas as explained at 5.5.1 above, but forming a more distinct break:

> *People in the north are more friendly—and helpful—than those in the south.*
> *There is nothing to be gained—unless you want a more active social life—in moving to the city.*

12.3 It is sometimes used to indicate an omitted word, for example a coarse word in reported speech:

> *'— you all,' he said.*

13. Hyphen

13.1 The hyphen has two main functions: to link words or elements of words into longer words and compounds, and to mark the division of a word at the end of a line in print or writing.

13.2.1 The use of the hyphen to connect words to form compound words is diminishing in English, especially when the elements are of one syllable as in *birdsong*, *eardrum*, and *playgroup*, and also in some longer formations such as *figurehead* and *nationwide*. The hyphen is used more often in routine and occasional couplings, especially when reference to the senses of the separate elements is considered important or unavoidable, as in *boiler-room*. It is often retained to avoid awkward collisions of letters, as in *breast-stroke*.

13.2.2 The hyphen serves to connect words that have a syntactic link, as in *hard-covered books* and *French-speaking people*, where the reference is to books with hard covers and people who speak French, rather than hard books with covers and French people who can speak (which would be the senses conveyed if the hyphens were omitted). It is also used to avoid more extreme kinds of ambiguity, as in *twenty-odd people*.

13.2.3 A particularly important use of the hyphen is to link compounds and phrases used attributively, as in *a well-known man* (but *the man is well known*), and *Christmas-tree lights* (but *the lights on the Christmas tree*).

13.2.4 It is also used to connect elements to form words in cases such as *re-enact* (where the collision of two *es* would be awkward), *re-form* (= to form again, to distinguish it from *reform*), and some other prefixed words such as those in *anti-*, *non-*, *over-*, and *post-*. Usage varies in this regard, and much depends on how well established and clearly recognizable the resulting formation is. When the second element is a name, a hyphen is usual (as in *anti-Darwinian*).

13.2.5 It is used to indicate a common second element in all but the last of a list, e.g. *two-*, *three-*, or *fourfold*.

13.3 The hyphen used to divide a word at the end of a line is a different matter, because it is not a permanent feature of the spelling. It is more common in print, where the text has to be accurately spaced and the margin justified; in handwritten and typed or word-processed material it can be avoided altogether. In print, words need to be divided carefully and consistently, taking account of the appearance and structure of the word. Detailed guidance on word-division may be found in the *Oxford Spelling Dictionary* (1986).